# Human Resource Management

## GAINING A COMPETITIVE ADVANTAGE 6e

RAYMOND A. NOE
The Ohio State University

JOHN R. HOLLENBECK
Michigan State University

BARRY GERHART
University of Wisconsin–Madison

PATRICK M. WRIGHT
Cornell University

McGraw-Hill Irwin

Boston Burr Ridge, IL Dubuque, IA New York San Francisco St. Louis
Bangkok Bogotá Caracas Kuala Lumpur Lisbon London Madrid Mexico City
Milan Montreal New Delhi Santiago Seoul Singapore Sydney Taipei Toronto

McGraw-Hill Irwin

HUMAN RESOURCE MANAGEMENT: GAINING A COMPETITIVE ADVANTAGE
Published by McGraw-Hill/Irwin, a business unit of The McGraw-Hill Companies, Inc., 1221 Avenue of the Americas, New York, NY, 10020. 

This book is printed on acid-free paper.

1 2 3 4 5 6 7 8 9 0 QPD/QPD 0 9 8 7

ISBN 978-0-07-353020-8
MHID 0-07-353020-4

Editorial director: *Brent Gordon*
Publisher: *Paul Ducham*
Executive editor: *John Weimeister*
Developmental editor: *Donielle Xu*
Editorial assistant: *Heather Darr*
Managing editor: *Lori Koetters*
Production supervisor: *Gina Hangos*
Design coordinator: *Jillian Lindner*
Senior photo research coordinator: *Jeremy Cheshareck*
Photo researcher: *Jennifer Blankenship*
Senior media project manager: *Matthew Perry*
Cover and interior design: *Jillian Lindner*
Typeface: *10.5/12 Goudy*
Compositor: *Aptara, Inc.*
Printer: *Quebecor World Dubuque Inc.*

**Library of Congress Cataloging-in-Publication Data**

Human resource management : gaining a competitive advantage / Raymond A. Noe ... [et al.]—6th ed.
p. cm.
Includes bibliographical references and index.
ISBN-13: 978-0-07-353020-8 (alk. paper)
ISBN-10: 0-07-353020-4 (alk. paper)
1. Personnel management—United States. I. Noe, Raymond A.
HF5549.2.U5H8 2008
658.3—dc22

2007032737

www.mhhe.com

In tribute to the life and ways of my dad
Raymond J. Noe
— R. A. N.

To my parents, Harold and Elizabeth, my wife, Patty, and my children, Jennifer, Marie, Timothy, and Jeffrey
— J. R. H.

To my parents, Robert and Shirley, my wife, Heather, and my children, Chris and Annie
— B. G.

To my parents, Patricia and Paul, my wife, Mary, and my sons, Michael and Matthew
— P. M. W.

# About the Authors

**Raymond A. Noe** is the Robert and Anne Hoyt Professor of Management at The Ohio State University. He was previously a professor in the Department of Management at Michigan State University and the Industrial Relations Center of the Carlson School of Management, University of Minnesota. He received his BS in psychology from The Ohio State University and his MA and PhD in psychology from Michigan State University. Professor Noe conducts research and teaches undergraduate as well as MBA and PhD students in human resource management, managerial skills, quantitative methods, human resource information systems, training, employee development, and organizational behavior. He has published articles in the *Academy of Management Journal, Academy of Management Review, Journal of Applied Psychology, Journal of Vocational Behavior*, and *Personnel Psychology*. Professor Noe is currently on the editorial boards of several journals including *Personnel Psychology, Journal of Applied Psychology*, and *Journal of Organizational Behavior*. Professor Noe has received awards for his teaching and research excellence, including the Herbert G. Heneman Distinguished Teaching Award in 1991 and the Ernest J. McCormick Award for Distinguished Early Career Contribution from the Society for Industrial and Organizational Psychology in 1993. He is also a fellow of the Society for Industrial and Organizational Psychology.

**John R. Hollenbeck** received his PhD in Management from New York University in 1984, and is currently the Eli Broad Professor of Management at the Eli Broad Graduate School of Business Administration at Michigan State University. Dr. Hollenbeck was the first recipient of the Ernest J. McCormick Award for Early Contributions to the field of Industrial and Organizational Psychology in 1992, and is currently a Fellow of the Academy of Management, the American Psychological Association, and the Society of Industrial and Organizational Psychology. He has published over 70 articles and book chapters on the topics of work motivation and group behavior with more than 40 of these appearing in the most highly cited refereed outlets. According to the Institute for Scientific Research, this body of work has been cited over 1,300 times by other researchers. Dr. Hollenbeck was the acting editor at *Organizational Behavior and Human Decision Processes* in 1995, the associate editor at *Decision Sciences* between 1998 and 2004, and the editor of *Personnel Psychology* from 1996 to 2002. He currently serves on the editorial board of the *Academy of Management Journal*, the *Journal of Applied Psychology, Personnel Psychology*, and *Organizational Behavior and Human Decision Processes*. Dr. Hollenbeck's teaching has been recognized with several awards, including the Michigan State University Teacher-Scholar Award in 1987 and the Michigan State University Distinguished Faculty Award in 2006. Within the Broad School of Business, he was awarded the Dorothy Withrow Teaching Award in 2002, the Lewis Quality of Excellence Award in both 2001 and 2004, and Most Outstanding MBA Faculty Award in 2007.

**Barry Gerhart** is the Bruce R. Ellig Distinguished Chair in Pay and Organizational Effectiveness and Director of the Strategic Human Resources Program at the University of Wisconsin–Madison. He was previously the Frances Hampton Currey Chair in Organizational Studies at the Owen School of Management at Vanderbilt University and Associate Professor and Chairman of the Department of Human Resource Studies, School of Industrial and Labor Relations at Cornell University. He received his BS in psychology from Bowling Green State University in 1979 and his PhD in industrial relations from the University of Wisconsin–Madison in 1985. His research is in the areas of compensation/rewards, staffing, and employee attitudes. Professor Gerhart has worked with a variety of organizations, including TRW, Corning, and Bausch & Lomb. His work has appeared in the *Academy of Management Journal*, *Industrial Relations*, *Industrial and Labor Relations Review*, *Journal of Applied Psychology*, *Personnel Psychology*, and *Handbook of Industrial and Organizational Psychology*, and he has served on the editorial boards of the *Academy of Management Journal*, *Industrial and Labor Relations Review*, and the *Journal of Applied Psychology*. He was a corecipient of the 1991 Scholarly Achievement Award, Human Resources Division, Academy of Management.

**Patrick M. Wright** is Professor of Human Resource Studies and Director of the Center for Advanced Human Resource Studies in the School of Industrial and Labor Relations at Cornell University. He was formerly Associate Professor of Management and Coordinator of the Master of Science in Human Resource Management program in the College of Business Administration and Graduate School of Business at Texas A&M University. He holds a BA in psychology from Wheaton College and an MBA and a PhD in organizational behavior/human resource management from Michigan State University. He teaches, conducts research, and consults in the areas of personnel selection, employee motivation, and strategic human resource management. His research articles have appeared in journals such as the *Academy of Management Journal*, *Journal of Applied Psychology*, *Organizational Behavior and Human Decision Processes*, *Journal of Management*, and *Human Resource Management Review*. He has served on the editorial boards of *Journal of Applied Psychology* and *Journal of Management* and also serves as an ad hoc reviewer for *Organizational Behavior and Human Decision Processes*, *Academy of Management Journal*, and *Academy of Management Review*. In addition, he has consulted for a number of organizations, including Whirlpool Corporation, Amoco Oil Company, and the North Carolina State government.

# PREFACE

If you have watched television or read any newspapers or magazines, you have undoubtedly come across reports dealing with ethical and legal challenges to business practices (such as the discrimination lawsuits against Wal-Mart), immigration reform, and changes in benefits and pension plans (consider Scott Miracle-Gro Company's complete ban on smoking to reduce health insurance costs, which involves regularly screening new hires and current employees for nicotine). Also, companies such as Google (Web search services company), the Container Store (the storage and organization store), and S.C. Johnson & Son (the household-products company) give employees a chance to make a difference at work and as a result have received positive media attention for being included on *Fortune* magazine's list of "The 100 Best Companies to Work For." These media reports highlight how choices that companies have made about human resource management practices influence employees, managers, shareholders, the community, and ultimately, the success of the company.

Companies are continuing to reexamine their business priorities and find ways to provide more value to customers, shareholders, employees, and the community where they are located. Traditionally, the concept of value has been considered to be the primary concern of finance and accounting. However, we believe that how human resources are managed is crucial to the long-term value of a company and ultimately to its survival. Our definition of value includes not only profits but also employee growth and satisfaction, additional employment opportunities, protection of the environment, and contributions to community programs. Managers must make decisions about how to allocate resources across the different organization functions, including marketing, production, finance, accounting, information systems, and human resources, and how to ensure that they contribute to achievement of the company's goals and strategies. All company functions are being scrutinized for the value they add.

We believe that all aspects of human resource management—including how companies interact with the environment; acquire, prepare, develop, and compensate employees; and design and evaluate work—can help companies meet their competitive challenges and create value. Meeting challenges is necessary to create value and to gain a competitive advantage.

## The Competitive Challenges

The challenges that organizations face today can be grouped into three categories:

- **The sustainability challenge.** Sustainability refers to the ability of a company to survive and exceed in a dynamic competitive environment. Sustainability depends on how well a company meets the needs of those who have an interest in seeing that the company succeeds. Challenges to sustainability include the ability to deal with economic and social changes, engage in responsible and ethical business practices, provide high-quality products and services, and develop methods and measures (also known as metrics) to determine if the company is meeting stakeholder needs. Companies in today's economy use mergers and acquisitions, growth, and downsizing to successfully compete. Companies rely on skilled workers to be productive, creative, and innovative and to provide high-quality customer service; their work is demanding and companies cannot guarantee job security. One issue is how to attract and retain a committed, productive workforce in turbulent economic conditions that offer opportunity for financial success, but can also turn sour, making every employee expendable. Forward-looking businesses are capitalizing on the strengths of a diverse workforce. The examples of Enron and WorldCom provide a vivid example of how sustainability depends on ethical and responsible business practices, including the management of human resources. Another important issue is how to meet financial objectives through meeting both customer and employee needs. To meet the sustainability challenge companies must engage in human resource management practices that address short-term needs but help to ensure the long-term success of the firm. The development and choice of human resource management practices should support business goals and strategy.

- **The global challenge.** Companies must be prepared to compete with companies from around the world either in the United States or abroad. Companies must both defend their domestic markets from foreign competitors and broaden their scope to encompass global markets. Recent threats to and successes of U.S. businesses (consider the semiconductor and steel industries) have proven that globalization is a continuing challenge
- **The technology challenge.** Using new technologies such as computer-aided manufacturing, virtual reality, expert systems, and the Internet can give companies an edge. New technologies can result in employees "working smarter" as well as providing higher-quality products and more efficient services to customers. Companies that have realized the greatest gains from new technology have human resource management practices that support the use of technology to create what is known as high-performance work systems. Work, training programs, and reward systems often need to be reconfigured to support employees' use of new technology. The three important aspects of high-performance work systems are (1) human resources and their capabilities, (2) new technology and its opportunities, and (3) efficient work structures and policies that allow employees and technology to interact. Companies are also using e-HRM (electronic HRM) applications to give employees more ownership of the employment relationship through the ability to enroll in and participate in training programs, change benefits, communicate with co-workers and customers online, and work "virtually" with peers in geographically different locations.

We believe that organizations must successfully deal with these challenges to create and maintain value, and the key to facing these challenges is a motivated, well-trained, and committed workforce.

## The Changing Role of the Human Resource Management Function

The human resource management (HRM) profession and practices have undergone substantial change and redefinition. Many articles written in both the academic and practitioner literature have been critical of the traditional HRM function. Unfortunately, in many organizations HRM services are not providing value but instead are mired down in managing trivial administrative tasks. Where this is true, HRM departments can be replaced with new technology or outsourced to a vendor who can provide higher-quality services at a lower cost. Although this recommendation is indeed somewhat extreme (and threatening to both HRM practitioners and those who teach human resource management!), it does demonstrate that companies need to ensure that their HRM functions are creating value for the firm.

Technology should be used where appropriate to automate routine activities, and managers should concentrate on HRM activities that can add substantial value to the company. Consider employee benefits: Technology is available to automate the process by which employees enroll in benefits programs and to keep detailed records of benefits usage. This use of technology frees up time for the manager to focus on activities that can create value for the firm (such as how to control health care costs and reduce workers' compensation claims).

Although the importance of some HRM departments is being debated, everyone agrees on the need to successfully manage human resources for a company to maximize its competitiveness. Several themes emerge from our conversations with managers and our review of research on HRM practices. First, in today's organizations, managers themselves are becoming more responsible for HRM practices and most believe that people issues are critical to business success. Second, most managers believe that their HRM departments are not well respected because of a perceived lack of competence, business sense, and contact with operations. A recent study by Deloitte consulting and *The Economist* Intelligence Unit found that only 23 percent of business executives believe that HR currently plays a significant role in strategy and operational results. Third, many managers believe that for HRM practices to be effective they need to be related to the strategic direction of the business. This text emphasizes how HRM practices can and should contribute to business goals and help to improve product and service quality and effectiveness.

Our intent is to provide students with the background to be successful HRM professionals, to manage human resources effectively, and to be knowledgeable consumers of HRM products. Managers must be able to identify effective HRM practices to purchase these services from a consultant, to work with the HRM department, or to design and implement them personally. The text emphasizes how a manager can more effectively manage human resources and highlights important issues in current HRM practice.

We think this book represents a valuable approach to teaching human resource management for several reasons:

- The text draws from the diverse research, teaching, and consulting experiences of four authors who have taught human resource management to undergraduates, traditional day MBA students as a required and elective course, and more experienced managers and professional employees in weekend and evening MBA programs. The teamwork approach gives a depth and breadth to the coverage that is not found in other texts.
- Human resource management is viewed as critical to the success of a business. The text emphasizes how the HRM function, as well as the management of human resources, can help companies gain a competitive advantage.
- The book discusses current issues such as e-HRM, finding and keeping talented employees, diversity, and employee engagement, all of which have a major impact on business and HRM practice.
- Strategic human resource management is introduced early in the book and integrated throughout the text.
- Examples of how new technologies are being used to improve the efficiency and effectiveness of HRM practices are provided throughout the text.

# Organization

*Human Resource Management: Gaining a Competitive Advantage* includes an introductory chapter (Chapter 1) and five parts.

Chapter 1 provides a detailed discussion of the global, new economy, stakeholder, and work system challenges that influence companies' abilities to successfully meet the needs of shareholders, customers, employees, and other stakeholders. We discuss how the management of human resources can help companies meet the competitive challenges.

Part 1 includes a discussion of the environmental forces that companies face in attempting to capitalize on their human resources as a means to gain competitive advantage. The environmental forces include the strategic direction of the business, the legal environment, and the type of work performed, and physical arrangement of the work.

A key focus of the strategic human resource management chapter is highlighting the role that staffing, performance management, training and development, and compensation play in different types of business strategies. A key focus of the legal chapter is enhancing managers' understanding of laws related to sexual harassment, affirmative action, and accommodations for disabled employees. The various types of discrimination and ways they have been interpreted by the courts are discussed. The chapter on analysis and design of work emphasizes how work systems can improve company competitiveness by alleviating job stress and by improving employees' motivation and satisfaction with their jobs.

Part 2 deals with the acquisition and preparation of human resources, including human resource planning and recruitment, selection, and training. The human resource planning chapter illustrates the process of developing a human resource plan. Also, the strengths and weaknesses of staffing options such as outsourcing, use of contingent workers, and downsizing are discussed. Strategies for recruiting talented employees are emphasized. The selection chapter emphasizes ways to minimize errors in employee selection and placement to improve the company's competitive position. Selection method standards such as validity and reliability are discussed in easily understandable terms without compromising the technical complexity of these issues. The chapter discusses selection methods such as interviews and various types of tests (including personality, honesty, and drug tests) and compares them on measures of validity, reliability, utility, and legality.

We discuss the components of effective training systems and the manager's role in determining employees' readiness for training, creating a positive learning environment, and ensuring that training is used on the job. The advantages and disadvantages of different training methods are described, such as e-learning.

Part 3 explores how companies can determine the value of employees and capitalize on their talents through retention and development strategies. The performance management chapter examines the strengths and weaknesses of performance management methods that use ratings, objectives, or behaviors. The employee development chapter introduces the student to how assessment, job experiences, formal courses, and mentoring relationships are used to develop employees. The chapter on retention and separation discusses how managers can maximize employee productivity and satisfaction to avoid absenteeism and turnover. The use of employee surveys to monitor job and organizational characteristics that affect satisfaction and subsequently retention is emphasized.

Part 4 covers rewarding and compensating human resources, including designing pay structures, recognizing individual contributions, and providing benefits. Here we explore how managers should decide the pay rate for different jobs, given the company's compensation strategy and the worth of jobs. The advantages and disadvantages of merit pay, gainsharing, and skill-based pay are discussed. The benefits chapter highlights the different types of employer-provided benefits and discusses how benefit costs can be contained. International comparisons of compensation and benefit practices are provided.

Part 5 covers special topics in human resource management, including labor–management relations, international HRM, and managing the HRM function. The collective bargaining and labor relations chapter focuses on traditional issues in labor–management relations, such as union structure and membership, the organizing process, and contract negotiations; it also discusses new union agendas and less adversarial approaches to labor–management relations. Social and political changes, such as introduction of the euro currency in the European Community, are discussed in the chapter on global human resource management. Selecting, preparing, and rewarding employees for foreign assignments are also discussed. The text concludes with a chapter that emphasizes how HRM practices should be aligned to help the company meet its business objectives. The chapter emphasizes that the HRM function needs to have a customer focus to be effective.

## Acknowledgments

As this book enters its sixth edition, it is important to acknowledge those who started it all. The first edition of this book would not have been possible if not for the entrepreneurial spirit of two individuals. Bill Schoof, president of Austen Press, gave us the resources and had the confidence that four unproven textbook writers could provide a new perspective for teaching human resource management. John Weimeister, our editor, provided us with valuable marketing information, helped us in making major decisions regarding the book, and made writing this book an enjoyable process. We continue to enjoy John's friendship and hospitality at national meetings. We were fortunate to have the opportunity in the sixth edition to work with John again. Donielle Xu joined the team as developmental editor. Donielle's suggestions, patience, gentle prodding, and organizational ability kept the author team focused and allowed us to meet publication deadlines. We thank Heather Darr for her work as Editorial Coordinator on this edition as well. Many thanks to Lori Koetters, project manager, for her careful review of the revised manuscript. Amit Shah of Frostburg State University wrote a first-class Instructor's Manual, PowerPoint presentation, and Test Bank, and he developed important content and study material for the OLC. Also, many thanks go to Interactive Learning LLC for their help with content for the OLC.

We would also like to thank the professors who gave of their time to review the text to help craft this sixth edition. Their helpful comments and suggestions during manuscript reviews have greatly helped to enhance this edition:

Steve Ash
*University of Akron*

Carlson Austin
*South Carolina State University*

James E. Bartlett, II
*University of South Carolina–Columbia*

Philip Benson
*New Mexico State University*

Wendy Boswell
*Texas A&M University*

Mary Connerley
*Virginia Tech University*

Berrin Erdogan
*Portland State University*

Dyanne Ferk
*University of Illinois–Springfield*

Lou Firenze
*Northwood University*

Barry Friedman
*State University of New York at Oswego*

Daniel J. Gallagher
*University of Illinois–Springfield*

Elias Konwufine
*Keiser University*

Renee Lerche
*University of Michigan*

Nancy Boyd Lillie
*University of North Texas*

Liz Malatestinic
*Indiana University*

Gwen Rivkin
*Cardinal Stritch University*

Howard Stanger
*Canisius College*

Peg Thomas
*Pennsylvania State University–Behrend*

Steven L. Thomas
*Missouri State University*

Renee Warning
*University of Central Oklahoma*

George Whaley
*San Jose State University*

Ryan D. Zimmerman
*Texas A&M University*

We would also like to thank the reviewers and focus group participants who made important suggestions for previous editions of this text. Their comments have helped to develop the book from edition to edition:

Richard Arvey
*National University of Singapore*

Alison Barber
*Michigan State University*

Kathleen Barnes
*University of Wisconsin, Superior*

Ron Beaulieu
*Central Michigan University*

Nancy Bereman
*Wichita State University*

Chris Berger
*Purdue University*

Carol Bibly
*Triton College*

Sarah Bowman
*Idaho State University*

Charles Braun
*University of Kentucky*

James Browne
*University of Southern Colorado*

Gerald Calvasina
*Southern Utah University*

Martin Carrigan
*University of Findlay*

Georgia Chao
*Michigan State University*

Walter Coleman
*Florida Southern College*

Donna Cooke
*Florida Atlantic University, Davis*

Craig Cowles
*Bridgewater State College*

Michael Crant
*University of Notre Dame*

Shannon Davis
*North Carolina State University*

Roger Dean
*Washington & Lee University*

John Delery
*University of Arkansas*

Jennifer Dose
*Messiah College*

Tom Dougherty
*University of Missouri*

Angela Farrar
*University of Nevada, Las Vegas*

Robert Figler
*University of Akron*

Art Fischer
*Pittsburgh State University*

Cynthia Fukami
*University of Denver*

Donald G. Gardner
*University of Colorado at Colorado Springs*

Bonnie Fox Garrity
*D'Youville College*

Sonia Goltz
*Michigan Technological University*

Bob Graham
*Sacred Heart University*

Terri Griffith
*Washington University*

Ken Gross
*University of Oklahoma, Norman*

John Hannon
*SUNY—Buffalo*

Bob Hatfield
*Indiana University*

Alan Heffner
*James Monroe Center*

Fred Heidrich
*Black Hills State University*

Rob Heneman
*Ohio State University*

Gary Hensel
*McHenry County College*

Kim Hester
*Arkansas State University*

Nancy Higgins
*Montgomery College, Rockville*

Wayne Hockwater
*Florida State University*

Denise Tanguay Hoyer
*Eastern Michigan University*

Fred Hughes
*Faulkner University*

Natalie J. Hunter
*Portland State University*

Sanford Jacoby
*University of California, Los Angeles*

Frank Jeffries
*University of Alaska, Anchorage*

Gwen Jones
*Fairleigh Dickinson University*

Marianne Koch
*University of Oregon*

Tom Kolenko
*Kennesaw State College*

Ken Kovach
*George Mason University*

Vonda Laughlin
*Carson-Newman College*

Helen LaVan
*DePaul University*

Larry Mainstone
*Valparaiso University*

Nicholas Mathys
*DePaul University*

Patricia Martina
*University of Texas, San Antonio*

Lisa McConnell
*Oklahoma State University*

Stuart Milne
*Georgia Institute of Technology*

Jim Morgan
*California State University, Chico*

Gary Murray
*Rose State College*

Cheri Ostroff
*Teachers College Columbia*

Teresa Palmer
*Illinois State University*

Robert Paul
*Kansas State University*

Sam Rabinowitz
*Rutgers University*

Katherine Ready
*University of Wisconsin*

Mike Ritchie
*University of South Carolina*

Mark Roehling
*Michigan State University*

Mary Ellen Rosetti
*Hudson Valley Community College*

Miyako Schanely
*Jefferson Community College*

Robert Schappe
*University of Michigan, Dearborn*

Josh Schwarz
*Miami University, Ohio*

Christina Shalley
*Georgia Tech*

Richard Simpson
*University of Utah*

Mark Smith
*Mississippi Gulf Coast Community College, Gulfport*

Scott Snell
*University of Virginia*

Cynthia Sutton
*Indiana University, South Bend*

Tom Timmerman
*Tennessee Technology University*

George Tompson
*University of Tampa*

K. J. Tullis
*University of Central Oklahoma*

Dan Turban
*University of Missouri, Columbia*

Charles Vance
*Loyola Marymount University*

Kim Wade
*Washington State University*

Daniel Yazak
*Montana State University, Billings*

**Raymond A. Noe**
**John R. Hollenbeck**
**Barry Gerhart**
**Patrick M. Wright**
*June 2007*

# A Guided Tour

*The Sixth Edition of Human Resource Management: Gaining a Competitive Advantage* was developed to teach students how to face and meet a variety of challenges within their organizations and how to gain a competitive advantage for their companies.

Throughout this text, the pedagogy focuses on HRM practices and strategies companies can employ to be competitive. These boxes, cases, and applications are found in every chapter and provide excellent real-business examples to underscore key concepts throughout the text.

Please take a moment to learn about this new edition and its exciting enhancements by paging through this visual guide outlining the text's new features.

The popular boxes **"Competing through Sustainability," "Competing through Globalization,"** and **"Competing through Technology"** have been updated with all new references to recent companies and examples. Their practical relevance and timeliness to HR issues are essential for student learning in the classroom.

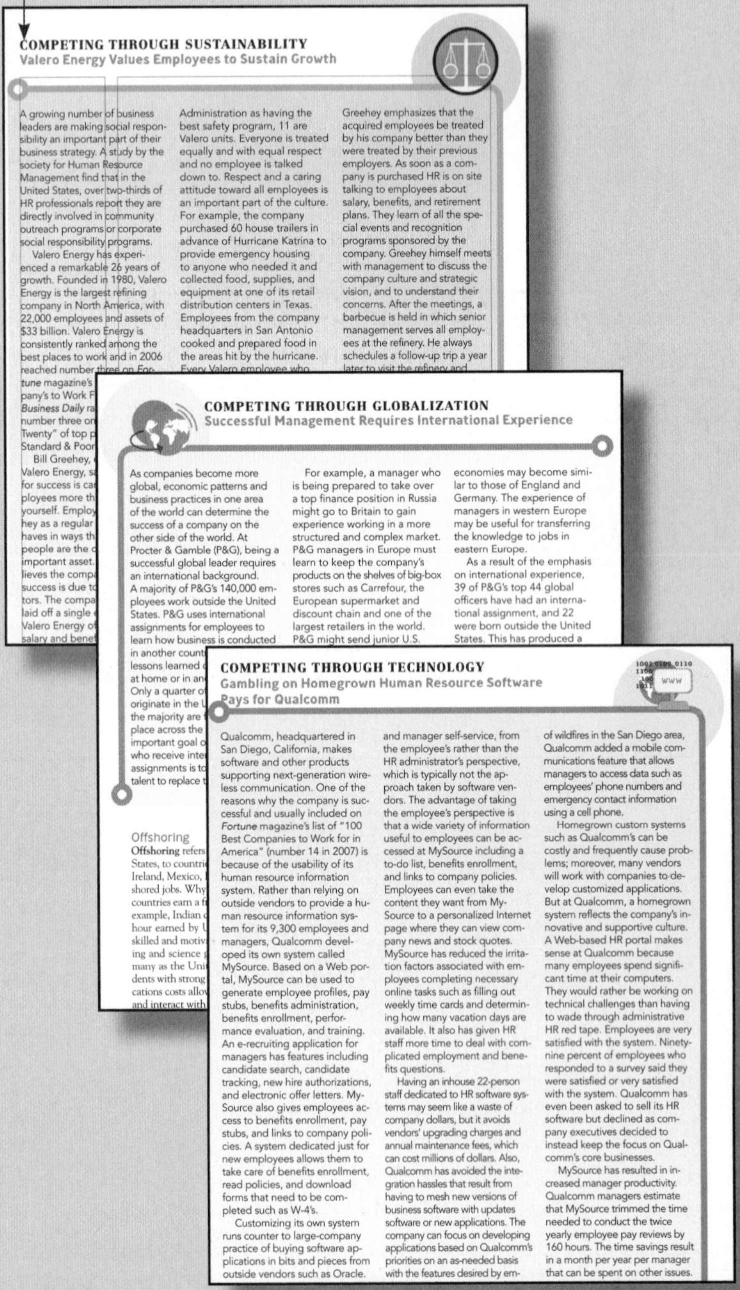

**COMPETING THROUGH SUSTAINABILITY**

**Valero Energy Values Employees to Sustain Growth**

A growing number of business leaders are making social responsibility an important part of their business strategy. A study by the Society for Human Resource Management find that in the United States, over two-thirds of HR professionals report they are directly involved in community outreach programs or corporate social responsibility programs.

Valero Energy has experienced a remarkable 26 years of growth. Founded in 1980, Valero Energy is the largest refining company in North America, with 22,000 employees and assets of $33 billion. Valero Energy is consistently ranked among the best places to work and in 2006 reached number three on *Fortune* magazine's ...

Administration as having the best safety program, 11 are Valero units. Everyone is treated equally and with equal respect and no employee is talked down to. Respect and a caring attitude toward all employees is an important part of the culture. For example, the company purchased 60 house trailers in advance of Hurricane Katrina to provide emergency housing to anyone who needed it and collected food, supplies, and equipment at one of its retail distribution centers in Texas. Employees from the company headquarters in San Antonio cooked and prepared food in the areas hit by the hurricane. ...

Greehey emphasizes that the acquired employees be treated by his company better than they were treated by their previous employers. As soon as a company is purchased HR is on site talking to employees about salary, benefits, and retirement plans. They learn of all the special events and recognition programs sponsored by the company. Greehey himself meets with management to discuss the company culture and strategic vision, and to understand their concerns. After the meetings, a barbecue is held in which senior management serves all employees at the refinery. He always schedules a follow-up trip a year ...

**COMPETING THROUGH GLOBALIZATION**

**Successful Management Requires International Experience**

As companies become more global, economic patterns and business practices in one area of the world can determine the success of a company on the other side of the world. At Procter & Gamble (P&G), being a successful global leader requires an international background. A majority of P&G's 140,000 employees work outside the United States. P&G uses international assignments for employees to learn how business is conducted ...

For example, a manager who is being prepared to take over a top finance position in Russia might go to Britain to gain experience working in a more structured and complex market. P&G managers in Europe must learn to keep the company's products on the shelves of big-box stores such as Carrefour, the European supermarket and discount chain and one of the largest retailers in the world. P&G might send junior U.S. ...

economies may become similar to those of England and Germany. The experience of managers in western Europe may be useful for transferring the knowledge to jobs in eastern Europe.

As a result of the emphasis on international experience, 39 of P&G's top 44 global officers have had an international assignment, and 22 were born outside the United States. This has produced a ...

**COMPETING THROUGH TECHNOLOGY**

**Gambling on Homegrown Human Resource Software Pays for Qualcomm**

Qualcomm, headquartered in San Diego, California, makes software and other products supporting next-generation wireless communication. One of the reasons why the company is successful and usually included on *Fortune* magazine's list of "100 Best Companies to Work for in America" (number 14 in 2007) is because of the usability of its human resource information system. Rather than relying on outside vendors to provide a human resource information system for its 9,300 employees and managers, Qualcomm developed its own system called MySource. Based on a Web portal, MySource can be used to generate employee profiles, pay stubs, benefits administration, benefits enrollment, performance evaluation, and training. An e-recruiting application for managers has features including candidate search, candidate tracking, new hire authorizations, and electronic offer letters. MySource also gives employees access to benefits enrollment, pay stubs, and links to company policies. A system dedicated just for new employees allows them to take care of benefits enrollment, read policies, and download forms that need to be completed such as W-4's.

Customizing its own system runs counter to large-company practice of buying software applications in bits and pieces from outside vendors such as Oracle. and manager self-service, from the employee's rather than the HR administrator's perspective, which is typically not the approach taken by software vendors. The advantage of taking the employee's perspective is that a wide variety of information useful to employees can be accessed at MySource including a to-do list, benefits enrollment, and links to company policies. Employees can even take the content they want from MySource to a personalized Internet page where they can view company news and stock quotes. MySource has reduced the irritation factors associated with employees completing necessary online tasks such as filling out weekly time cards and determining how many vacation days are available. It also has given HR staff more time to deal with complicated employment and benefits questions.

Having an inhouse 22-person staff dedicated to HR software systems may seem like a waste of company dollars, but it avoids vendors' upgrading charges and annual maintenance fees, which can cost millions of dollars. Also, Qualcomm has avoided the integration hassles that result from having to mesh new versions of business software with updates software or new applications. The company can focus on developing applications based on Qualcomm's priorities on an as-needed basis with the features desired by em- of wildfires in the San Diego area, Qualcomm added a mobile communications feature that allows managers to access data such as employees' phone numbers and emergency contact information using a cell phone.

Homegrown custom systems such as Qualcomm's can be costly and frequently cause problems; moreover, many vendors will work with companies to develop customized applications. But at Qualcomm, a homegrown system reflects the company's innovative and supportive culture. A Web-based HR portal makes sense at Qualcomm because many employees spend significant time at their computers. They would rather be working on technical challenges than having to wade through administrative HR red tape. Employees are very satisfied with the system. Ninety-nine percent of employees who responded to a survey said they were satisfied or very satisfied with the system. Qualcomm has even been asked to sell its HR software but declined as company executives decided to instead keep the focus on Qualcomm's core businesses.

MySource has resulted in increased manager productivity. Qualcomm managers estimate that MySource trimmed the time needed to conduct the twice yearly employee pay reviews by 160 hours. The time savings result in a month per year per manager that can be spent on other issues.

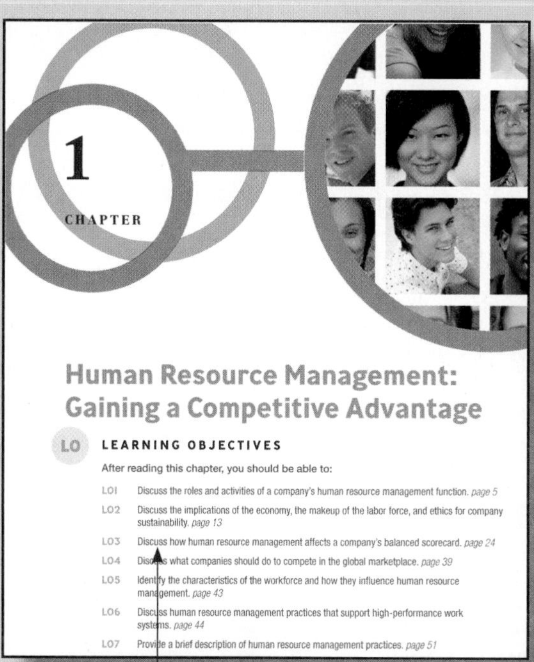
1

CHAPTER

# Human Resource Management: Gaining a Competitive Advantage

LO **LEARNING OBJECTIVES**

After reading this chapter, you should be able to:

- LO1 Discuss the roles and activities of a company's human resource management function. *page 5*
- LO2 Discuss the implications of the economy, the makeup of the labor force, and ethics for company sustainability. *page 13*
- LO3 Discuss how human resource management affects a company's balanced scorecard. *page 24*
- LO4 Discuss what companies should do to compete in the global marketplace. *page 39*
- LO5 Identify the characteristics of the workforce and how they influence human resource management. *page 43*
- LO6 Discuss human resource management practices that support high-performance work systems. *page 44*
- LO7 Provide a brief description of human resource management practices. *page 51*

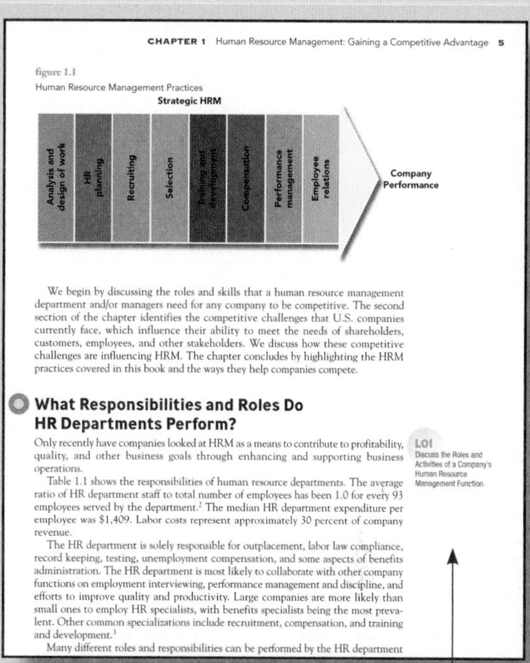
**CHAPTER 1** Human Resource Management: Gaining a Competitive Advantage **5**

figure 1.1

Human Resource Management Practices



We begin by discussing the roles and skills that a human resource management department and/or managers need for any company to be competitive. The second section of the chapter identifies the competitive challenges that U.S. companies currently face, which influence their ability to meet the needs of shareholders, customers, employees, and other stakeholders. We discuss how these competitive challenges are influencing HRM. The chapter concludes by highlighting the HRM practices covered in this book and the ways they help companies compete.

## What Responsibilities and Roles Do HR Departments Perform?

Only recently have companies looked at HRM as a means to contribute to profitability, quality, and other business goals through enhancing and supporting business operations.

LO1 Discuss the Roles and Activities of a Company's Human Resource Management Function.

Table 1.1 shows the responsibilities of human resource departments. The average ratio of HR department staff to total number of employees has been 1.0 for every 93 employees served by the department.[2] The median HR department expenditure per employee was $1,409. Labor costs represent approximately 30 percent of company revenue.

The HR department is solely responsible for outplacement, labor law compliance, record keeping, testing, unemployment compensation, and some aspects of benefits administration. The HR department is most likely to collaborate with other company functions on employment interviewing, performance management and discipline, and efforts to improve quality and productivity. Large companies are more likely than small ones to employ HR specialists, with benefits specialists being the most prevalent. Other common specializations include recruitment, compensation, and training and development.[3]

Many different roles and responsibilities can be performed by the HR department

**Learning objectives** at the beginning of each chapter inform students about the key concepts they should understand after reading through the chapter.

**NEW**

Throughout each chapter, a new design element calls out where the learning for each learning objective begins in the text. This element will guide students in their comprehension of the chapter topics and provide a reminder of the learning objectives throughout the chapter.

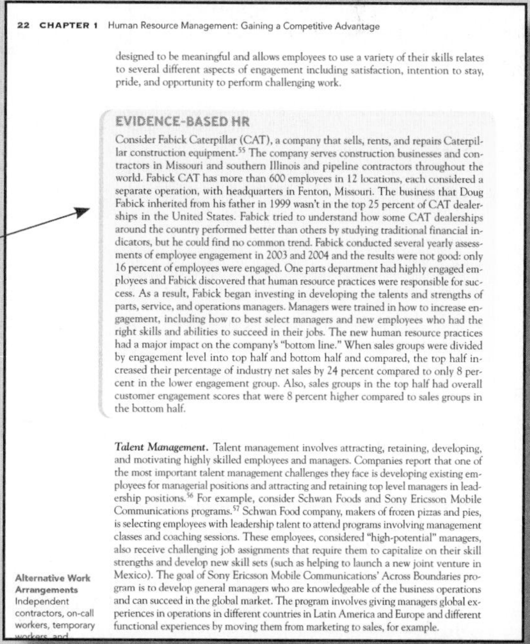
**22 CHAPTER 1** Human Resource Management: Gaining a Competitive Advantage

designed to be meaningful and allows employees to use a variety of their skills relates to several different aspects of engagement including satisfaction, intention to stay, pride, and opportunity to perform challenging work.

**EVIDENCE-BASED HR**

Consider Fabick Caterpillar (CAT), a company that sells, rents, and repairs Caterpillar construction equipment.[55] The company serves construction businesses and contractors in Missouri and southern Illinois and pipeline contractors throughout the world. Fabick CAT has more than 600 employees in 12 locations, each considered a separate operation, with headquarters in Fenton, Missouri. The business that Doug Fabick inherited from his father in 1999 wasn't in the top 25 percent of CAT dealerships in the United States. Fabick tried to understand how some CAT dealerships around the country performed better than others by studying traditional financial indicators, but he could find no common trend. Fabick conducted several yearly assessments of employee engagement in 2003 and 2004 and the results were not good: only 16 percent of employees were engaged. One parts department had highly engaged employees and Fabick discovered that human resource practices were responsible for success. As a result, Fabick began investing in developing the talents and strengths of parts, service, and operations managers. Managers were trained in how to increase engagement, including how to best select managers and new employees who had the right skills and abilities to succeed in their jobs. The new human resource practices had a major impact on the company's "bottom line." When sales groups were divided by engagement level into top half and bottom half and compared, the top half increased their percentage of industry net sales by 24 percent compared to only 8 percent in the lower engagement group. Also, sales groups in the top half had overall customer engagement scores that were 8 percent higher compared to sales groups in the bottom half.

***Talent Management.*** Talent management involves attracting, retaining, developing, and motivating highly skilled employees and managers. Companies report that one of the most important talent management challenges they face is developing existing employees for managerial positions and attracting and retaining top level managers in leadership positions.[56] For example, consider Schwan Foods and Sony Ericsson Mobile Communications programs.[57] Schwan Food company, makers of frozen pizzas and pies, is selecting employees with leadership talent to attend programs involving management classes and coaching sessions. These employees, considered "high-potential" managers, also receive challenging job assignments that require them to capitalize on their skill strengths and develop new skill sets (such as helping to launch a new joint venture in Mexico). The goal of Sony Ericsson Mobile Communications' Across Boundaries program is to develop general managers who are knowledgeable of the business operations and can succeed in the global market. The program involves giving managers global experiences in operations in different countries in Latin America and Europe and different functional experiences by moving them from marketing to sales, for example.

**Alternative Work Arrangements** Independent contractors, on-call workers, temporary workers, and

**NEW**

**"Evidence-Based HR"** sections within the chapters highlight the growing trend to demonstrate how HR contributes to a company's competitive advantage. Two of the six new HR competencies of high-performing HR professionals (credible activist and strategic architect) emphasize the need to influence managers, share information, and develop people strategies that contribute to the business. Evidence-based HR shows how HR decisions are based on data and not just intuition. The company examples used show how HR practices influence the company's bottom line or key stakeholders including shareholders, employees, customers, or the community.

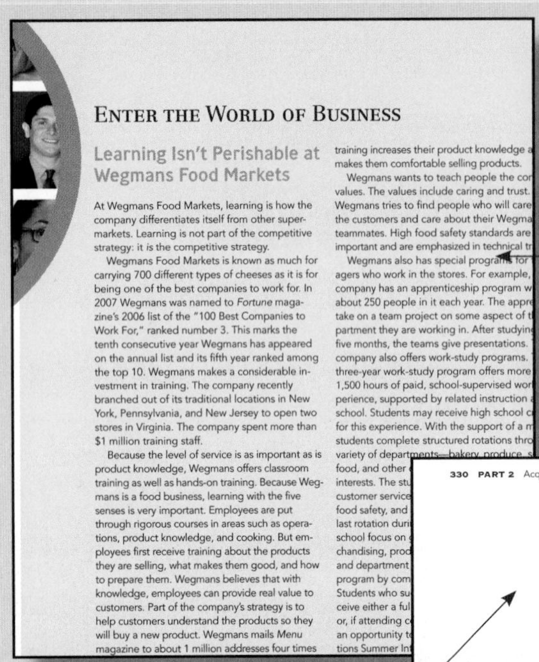

# Enter the World of Business

## Learning Isn't Perishable at Wegmans Food Markets

At Wegmans Food Markets, learning is how the company differentiates itself from other supermarkets. Learning is not part of the competitive strategy: it is the competitive strategy.

Wegmans Food Markets is known as much for carrying 700 different types of cheeses as it is for being one of the best companies to work for. In 2007 Wegmans was named to *Fortune* magazine's 2006 list of the "100 Best Companies to Work For," ranked number 3. This marks the tenth consecutive year Wegmans has appeared on the annual list and its fifth year ranked among the top 10. Wegmans makes a considerable investment in training. The company recently branched out of its traditional locations in New York, Pennsylvania, and New Jersey to open two stores in Virginia. The company spent more than $1 million training staff.

Because the level of service is as important as is product knowledge, Wegmans offers classroom training as well as hands-on training. Because Wegmans is a food business, learning with the five senses is very important. Employees are put through rigorous courses in areas such as operations, product knowledge, and cooking. But employees first receive training about the products they are selling, what makes them good, and how to prepare them. Wegmans believes that with knowledge, employees can provide real value to customers. Part of the company's strategy is to help customers understand the products so they will buy a new product. Wegmans mails Menu magazine to about 1 million addresses four times

The **chapter opening stories** are updated with new, relevant examples of real business problems or issues that provide background for the issues discussed in the chapter.

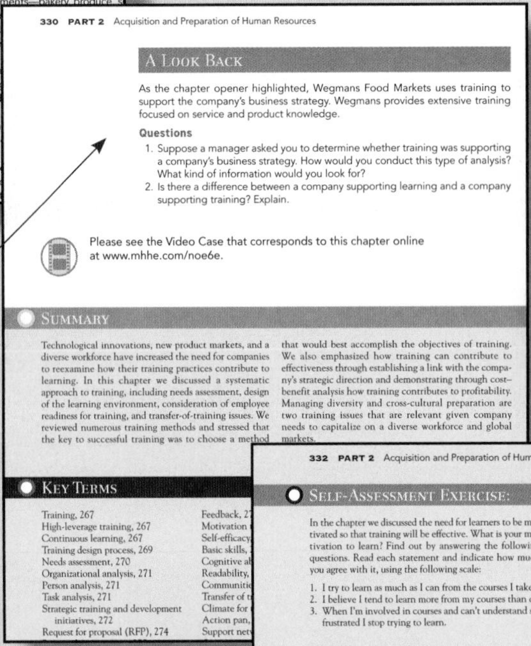

330 PART 2 Acquisition and Preparation of Human Resources

## A Look Back

As the chapter opener highlighted, Wegmans Food Markets uses training to support the company's business strategy. Wegmans provides extensive training focused on service and product knowledge.

**Questions**

1. Suppose a manager asked you to determine whether training was supporting a company's business strategy. How would you conduct this type of analysis? What kind of information would you look for?
2. Is there a difference between a company supporting learning and a company supporting training? Explain.

Please see the Video Case that corresponds to this chapter online at www.mhhe.com/noe6e.

## Summary

Technological innovations, new product markets, and a diverse workforce have increased the need for companies to reexamine how their training practices contribute to learning. In this chapter we discussed a systematic approach to training, including needs assessment, design of the learning environment, consideration of employee readiness for training, and transfer-of-training issues. We reviewed numerous training methods and stressed that the key to successful training was to choose a method that would best accomplish the objectives of training. We also emphasized how training can contribute to effectiveness through establishing a link with the company's strategic direction and demonstrating through cost–benefit analysis how training contributes to profitability. Managing diversity and cross-cultural preparation are two training issues that are relevant given company needs to capitalize on a diverse workforce and global markets.

## Key Terms

Training, 267
High-leverage training, 267
Continuous learning, 267
Training design process, 269
Needs assessment, 270
Organizational analysis, 271
Person analysis, 271
Task analysis, 271
Strategic training and development initiatives, 272
Request for proposal (RFP), 274

The end-of-chapter segment, **"A Look Back,"** encourages students to recall the chapter's opening story and apply it to what they have just learned.

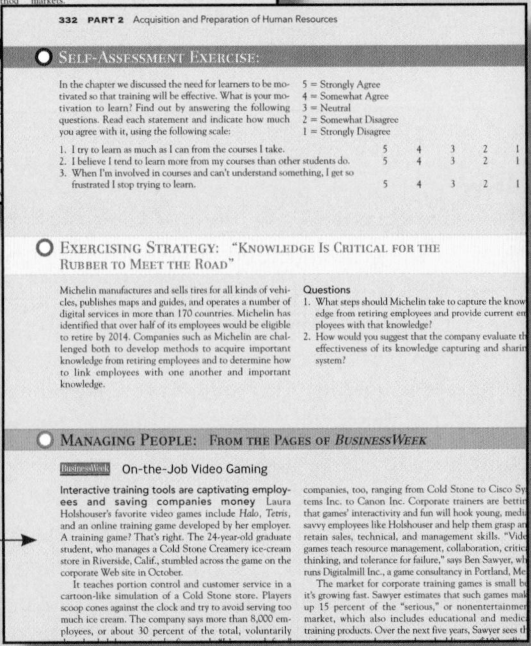

332 PART 2 Acquisition and Preparation of Human Resources

## Self-Assessment Exercise:

In the chapter we discussed the need for learners to be motivated so that training will be effective. What is your motivation to learn? Find out by answering the following questions. Read each statement and indicate how much you agree with it, using the following scale:

5 = Strongly Agree
4 = Somewhat Agree
3 = Neutral
2 = Somewhat Disagree
1 = Strongly Disagree

| | | | | | |
|---|---|---|---|---|---|
| 1. I try to learn as much as I can from the courses I take. | 5 | 4 | 3 | 2 | 1 |
| 2. I believe I tend to learn more from my courses than other students do. | 5 | 4 | 3 | 2 | 1 |
| 3. When I'm involved in courses and can't understand something, I get so frustrated I stop trying to learn. | 5 | 4 | 3 | 2 | 1 |

## Exercising Strategy: "Knowledge Is Critical for the Rubber to Meet the Road"

Michelin manufactures and sells tires for all kinds of vehicles, publishes maps and guides, and operates a number of digital services in more than 170 countries. Michelin has identified that over half of its employees would be eligible to retire by 2014. Companies such as Michelin are challenged both to develop methods to acquire important knowledge from retiring employees and to determine how to link employees with one another and important knowledge.

**Questions**

1. What steps should Michelin take to capture the knowledge from retiring employees and provide current employees with that knowledge?
2. How would you suggest that the company evaluate the effectiveness of its knowledge capturing and sharing system?

## Managing People: From the Pages of *BusinessWeek*

BusinessWeek On-the-Job Video Gaming

**Interactive training tools are captivating employees and saving companies money** Laura Holshouser's favorite video games include *Halo*, *Tetris*, and an online training game developed by her employer. A training game? That's right. The 24-year-old graduate student, who manages a Cold Stone Creamery ice-cream store in Riverside, Calif., stumbled across the game on the corporate Web site in October.

It teaches portion control and customer service in a cartoon-like simulation of a Cold Stone store. Players scoop cones against the clock and try to avoid serving too much ice cream. The company says more than 8,000 employees, or about 30 percent of the total, voluntarily

companies, too, ranging from Cold Stone to Cisco Systems Inc. to Canon Inc. Corporate trainers are betting that games' interactivity and fun will hook young, media-savvy employees like Holshouser and help them grasp and retain sales, technical, and management skills. "Video games teach resource management, collaboration, critical thinking, and tolerance for failure," says Ben Sawyer, who runs Digitalmill Inc., a game consultancy in Portland, Me.

The market for corporate training games is small but it's growing fast. Sawyer estimates that such games make up 15 percent of the "serious," or nonentertainment market, which also includes educational and medical training products. Over the next five years, Sawyer sees the

***BusinessWeek* cases** look at incidents and real companies as reported by the nation's number one business weekly and encourage students to critically evaluate each problem and apply the chapter contents.

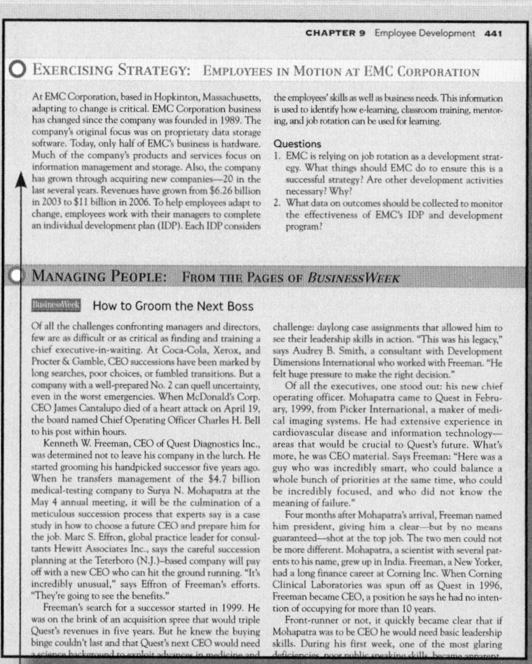



## Exercising Strategy: Employees in Motion at EMC Corporation

At EMC Corporation, based in Hopkinton, Massachusetts, adapting to change is critical. EMC Corporation business has changed since the company was founded in 1989. The company's original focus was on proprietary data storage software. Today, only half of EMC's business is hardware. Much of the company's products and services focus on information management and storage. Also, the company has grown through acquiring new companies—20 in the last several years. Revenues have grown from $6.26 billion in 2003 to $11 billion in 2006. To help employees adapt to change, employees work with their managers to complete an individual development plan (IDP). Each IDP considers the employees' skills as well as business needs. This information is used to identify how e-learning, classroom training, mentoring, and job rotation can be used for learning.

**Questions**

1. EMC is relying on job rotation as a development strategy. What things should EMC do to ensure this is a successful strategy? Are other development activities necessary? Why?
2. What data on outcomes should be collected to monitor the effectiveness of EMC's IDP and development program?

## Managing People: From the Pages of *BusinessWeek*

BusinessWeek **How to Groom the Next Boss**

Of all the challenges confronting managers and directors, few are as difficult or as critical as finding and training a chief executive-in-waiting. At Coca-Cola, Xerox, and Procter & Gamble, CEO successions have been marked by long searches, poor choices, or fumbled transitions. But a company with a well-prepared No. 2 can quell uncertainty, even in the worst emergencies. When McDonald's Corp. CEO James Cantalupo died of a heart attack on April 19, the board named Chief Operating Officer Charles H. Bell to his post within hours.

Kenneth W. Freeman, CEO of Quest Diagnostics Inc., was determined not to leave his company in the lurch. He started grooming his handpicked successor five years ago. When he transfers management of the $4.7 billion medical-testing company to Surya N. Mohapatra at the May 4 annual meeting, it will be the culmination of a meticulous succession process that experts say is a case study in how to choose a future CEO and prepare him for the job. Marc S. Effron, global practice leader for consultants Hewitt Associates Inc., says the careful succession planning at the Teterboro (N.J.)-based company will pay off with a new CEO who can hit the ground running. "It's incredibly unusual," says Effron of Freeman's efforts. "They're going to see the benefits."

Freeman's search for a successor started in 1999. He was on the brink of an acquisition spree that would triple Quest's revenues in five years. But he knew the buying binge couldn't last and that Quest's next CEO would need a science background to exploit advances in medicine and challenge: daylong case assignments that allowed him to see their leadership skills in action. "This was his legacy," says Audrey B. Smith, a consultant with Development Dimensions International who worked with Freeman. "He felt huge pressure to make the right decision."

Of all the executives, one stood out: his new chief operating officer. Mohapatra came to Quest in February, 1999, from Picker International, a maker of medical imaging systems. He had extensive experience in cardiovascular disease and information technology—areas that would be crucial to Quest's future. What's more, he was CEO material. Says Freeman: "Here was a guy who was incredibly smart, who could balance a whole bunch of priorities at the same time, who could be incredibly focused, and who did not know the meaning of failure."

Four months after Mohapatra's arrival, Freeman named him president, giving him a clear—but by no means guaranteed—shot at the top job. The two men could not be more different. Mohapatra, a scientist with several patents to his name, grew up in India. Freeman, a New Yorker, had a long finance career at Corning Inc. When Corning Clinical Laboratories was spun off as Quest in 1996, Freeman became CEO, a position he says he had no intention of occupying for more than 10 years.

Front-runner or not, it quickly became clear that if Mohapatra was to be CEO he would need basic leadership skills. During his first week, one of the most glaring deficiencies, poor public speaking skills, became apparent.

**Exercising Strategy** cases at the end of each chapter provide additional cases with discussion questions. These examples pose strategic questions based on real-life practices.

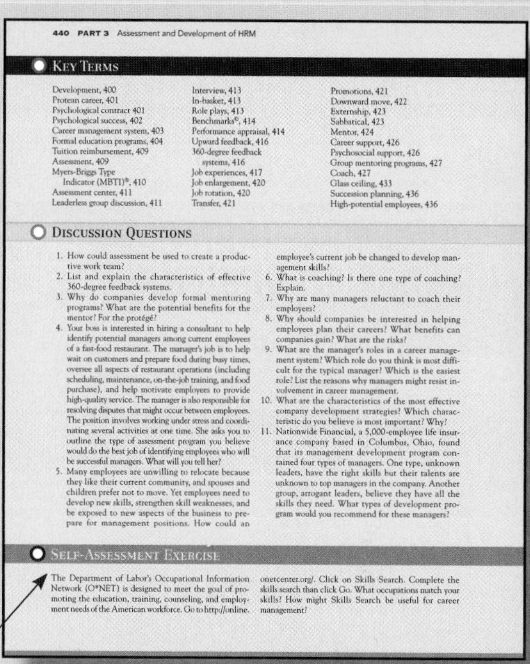



## Key Terms



## Discussion Questions

1. How could assessment be used to create a productive work team?
2. List and explain the characteristics of effective 360-degree feedback systems.
3. Why do companies develop formal mentoring programs? What are the potential benefits for the mentor? For the protégé?
4. Your boss is interested in hiring a consultant to help identify potential managers among current employees of a fast-food restaurant. The manager's job is to help wait on customers and prepare food during busy times, oversee all aspects of restaurant operations (including scheduling, maintenance, on-the-job training, and food purchase), and help motivate employees to provide high-quality service. The manager is also responsible for resolving disputes that might occur between employees. The position involves working under stress and coordinating several activities at one time. She asks you to outline the type of assessment program you believe would do the best job of identifying employees who will be successful managers. What will you tell her?
5. Many employees are unwilling to relocate because they like their current community, and spouses and children prefer not to move. Yet employees need to develop new skills, strengthen skill weaknesses, and be exposed to new aspects of the business to prepare for management positions. How could an employee's current job be changed to develop management skills?
6. What is coaching? Is there one type of coaching? Explain.
7. Why are many managers reluctant to coach their employees?
8. Why should companies be interested in helping employees plan their careers? What benefits can companies gain? What are the risks?
9. What are the manager's roles in a career management system? Which role do you think is most difficult for the typical manager? Which is the easiest role? List the reasons why managers might resist involvement in career management.
10. What are the characteristics of the most effective company development strategies? Which characteristic do you believe is most important? Why?
11. Nationwide Financial, a 5,000-employee life insurance company based in Columbus, Ohio, found that its management development program contained four types of managers. One type, unknown leaders, have the right skills but their talents are unknown to top managers in the company. Another group, arrogant leaders, believe they have all the skills they need. What types of development program would you recommend for these managers?

## Self-Assessment Exercise

The Department of Labor's Occupational Information Network (O*NET) is designed to meet the goal of promoting the education, training, counseling, and employment needs of the American workforce. Go to http://online.onetcenter.org/. Click on Skills Search. Complete the skills search than click Go. What occupations match your skills? How might Skills Search be useful for career management?

**Self-Assessment Exercises** at the end of chapters provide a brief exercise for students to complete and evaluate their own skills.

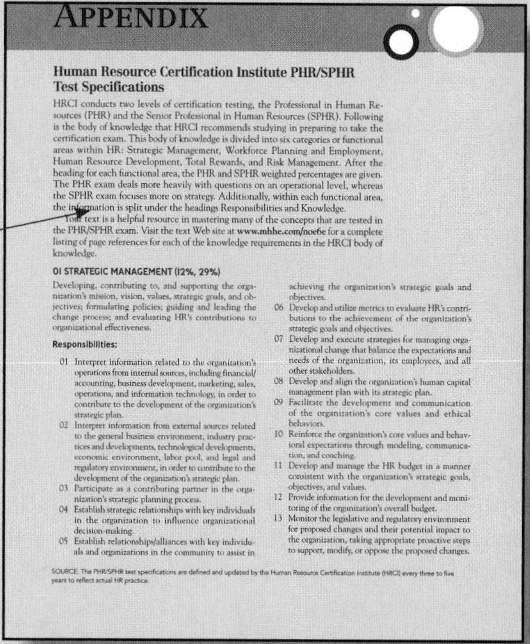

# Appendix

**Human Resource Certification Institute PHR/SPHR Test Specifications**

HRCI conducts two levels of certification testing, the Professional in Human Resources (PHR) and the Senior Professional in Human Resources (SPHR). Following is the body of knowledge that HRCI recommends studying in preparing to take the certification exam. This body of knowledge is divided into six categories or functional areas within HR: Strategic Management, Workforce Planning and Employment, Human Resource Development, Total Rewards, and Risk Management. After the heading for each functional area, the PHR and SPHR weighted percentages are given. The PHR exam deals more heavily with questions on an operational level, whereas the SPHR exam focuses more on strategy. Additionally, within each functional area, the information is split under the headings Responsibilities and Knowledge.

This text is a helpful resource in mastering many of the concepts that are tested in the PHR/SPHR exam. Visit the text Web site at **www.mhhe.com/noe6e** for a complete listing of page references for each of the knowledge requirements in the HRCI body of knowledge.

**01 STRATEGIC MANAGEMENT (12%, 29%)**

Developing, contributing to, and supporting the organization's mission, vision, values, strategic goals, and objectives; formulating policies; guiding and leading the change process; and evaluating HR's contributions to organizational effectiveness.

**Responsibilities:**

01 Interpret information related to the organization's operations from internal sources, including financial/accounting, business development, marketing, sales, operations, and information technology, in order to contribute to the development of the organization's strategic plan.
02 Interpret information from external sources related to the general business environment, industry practices and developments, technological developments, economic environment, labor pool, and legal and regulatory environment, in order to contribute to the development of the organization's strategic plan.
03 Participate as a contributing partner in the organization's strategic planning process.
04 Establish strategic relationships with key individuals in the organization to influence organizational decision-making.
05 Establish relationships/alliances with key individuals and organizations in the community to assist in achieving the organization's strategic goals and objectives.
06 Develop and utilize metrics to evaluate HR's contributions to the achievement of the organization's strategic goals and objectives.
07 Develop and execute strategies for managing organizational change that balance the expectations and needs of the organization, its employees, and all other stakeholders.
08 Develop and align the organization's human capital management plan with its strategic plan.
09 Facilitate the development and communication of the organization's core values and ethical behaviors.
10 Reinforce the organization's core values and behavioral expectations through modeling, communication, and coaching.
11 Develop and manage the HR budget in a manner consistent with the organization's strategic goals, objectives, and values.
12 Provide information for the development and monitoring of the organization's overall budget.
13 Monitor the legislative and regulatory environment for proposed changes and their potential impact to the organization, taking appropriate proactive steps to support, modify, or oppose the proposed changes.

SOURCE: The PHR/SPHR test specifications are defined and updated by the Human Resource Certification Institute (HRCI) every three to five years to reflect actual HR practice.

**NEW**

An **appendix** has been included to provide students with the information they need to study for the PHR or SPHR exam at their fingertips. Page references to the topics found in this text can be found on the text Web site at www.mhhe.com/noe6e.

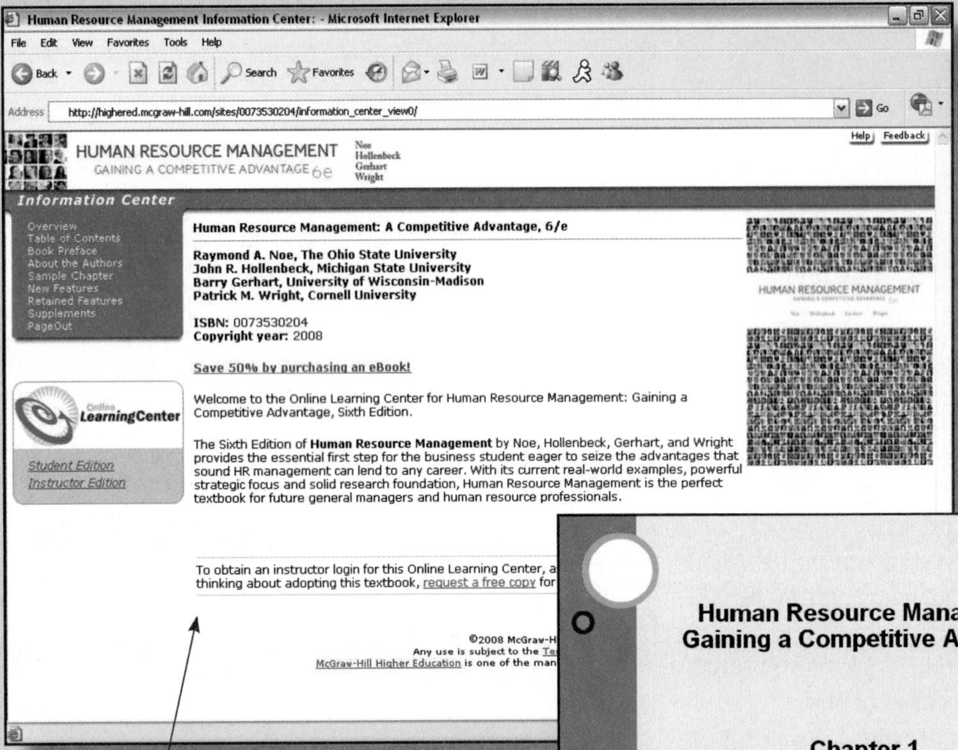


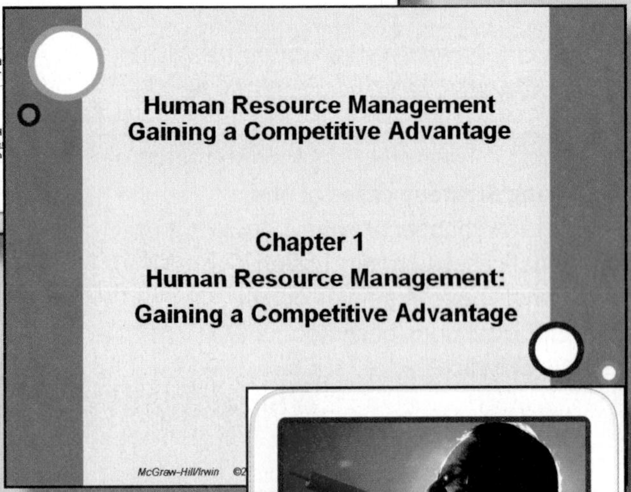


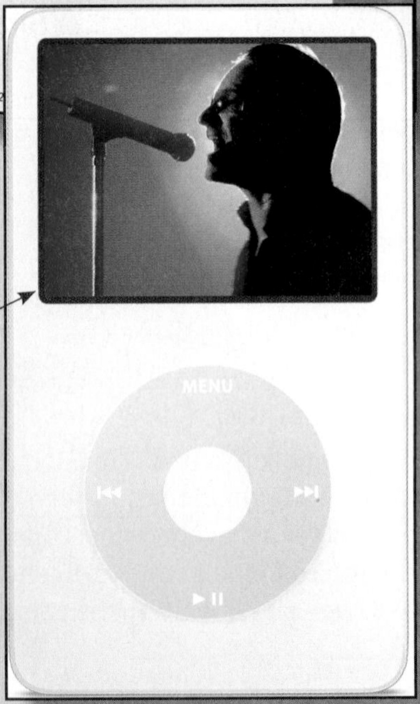

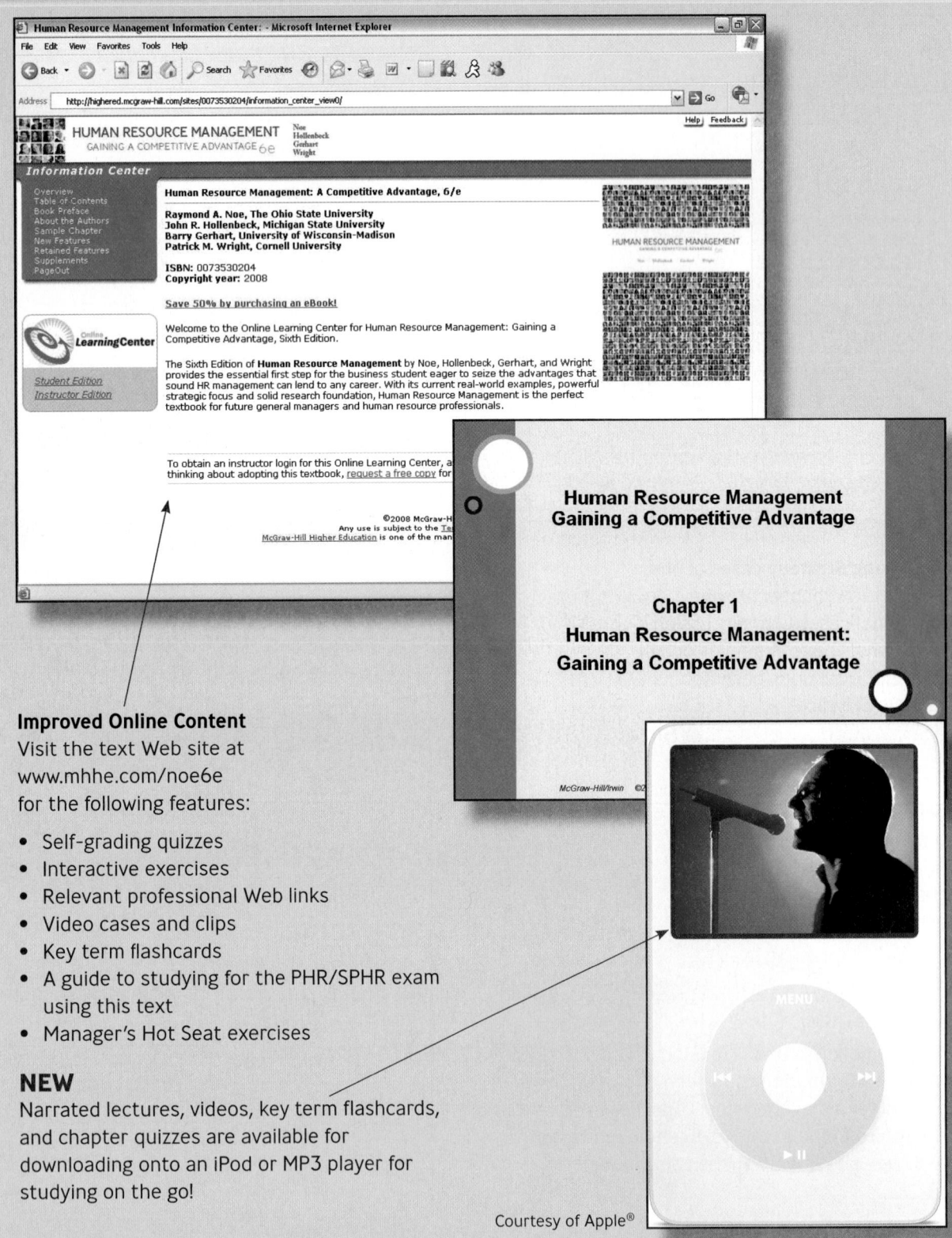

**Improved Online Content**
Visit the text Web site at
www.mhhe.com/noe6e
for the following features:

- Self-grading quizzes
- Interactive exercises
- Relevant professional Web links
- Video cases and clips
- Key term flashcards
- A guide to studying for the PHR/SPHR exam using this text
- Manager's Hot Seat exercises

**NEW**
Narrated lectures, videos, key term flashcards, and chapter quizzes are available for downloading onto an iPod or MP3 player for studying on the go!

Courtesy of Apple®

# Supplements for Students and Instructors

**INSTRUCTOR'S RESOURCE CD**
This multimedia CD-Rom includes the instructor's manual, test bank, computerized test bank, and PowerPoint. These individual supplements are available in print-on-demand only.

**INSTRUCTOR'S MANUAL**
The Instructor's Manual contains a lecture outline and notes, answers to the discussion questions, additional questions and exercises, teaching suggestions, video case notes and answers, and answers to the end-of-chapter case questions.

**TEST BANK**
The test bank has been revised and updated to reflect the content of the 6th edition of the book. Each chapter includes multiple choice, true/false, and essay questions.

**EZ TEST**
McGraw-Hill's EZ Test is a flexible and easy-to-use electronic testing program. The program allows instructors to create tests from book-specific items. It accommodates a wide range of question types and instructors may add their own questions. Multiple versions of the test can be created and any test can be exported for use with course management systems such as WebCT, BlackBoard or PageOut. The program is available for Windows and Macintosh environments.

**VIDEOS**
Videos for each chapter on HRM issues are available with this edition. On the HRM video DVD, you'll find two new videos produced by the SHRM Foundations "HR in Alignment: The Link to Business Results at Sysco Food Services" and "Ethics: The Fabric of Business." Other notable new videos available for this edition include "Johnson & Johnson eUniversity" for the chapter on training and "Hollywood Labor Unions" for the chapter on collective bargaining and labor relations.

**POWERPOINT**
This presentation program features detailed slides for each chapter, which are also found on the OLC.

**ONLINE LEARNING CENTER (www.mhhe.com/noe6e)**
This text-specific Web site follows the text chapter by chapter. As students read the book, they can go online to take self-grading quizzes, review material, or work through interactive exercises. Also available on the OLC are video clips with discussion questions, relevant professional Web links, additional Internet activities, and current news with daily updates. Professors can also download the supplements here (these are password protected). OLCs can be delivered multiple ways—professors and students can access them directly through the textbook Web site, through PageOut, or within a course management system (i.e., WebCT, Blackboard, TopClass).

**NEW! ENHANCED CARTRIDGE WITH IPOD CONTENT**
The Enhanced Cartridge is developed to help you get your course up and running in WebCT, BlackBoard, and other course management systems. The content is *prepopulated* into appropriate chapters and content categories. Simply choose to hide content we provide and add your own—just as you have before in WebCT and Blackboard. Every Enhanced Cartridge contains iPod/MP3 content, chapter pre- and post-tests, discussion boards, additional assignments, and grade book functionality. The enhanced cartridge with iPod content will either be sold with a password card included in the book, or students can purchase the content via the book's Web site at www.mhhe.com/noe6e.

**MANAGER'S HOT SEAT**
This interactive video software is an optional package with the text. It includes 15 interactive segments with actors in situations with real-life managers—and the managers have to react live and

unscripted. Segments include topics like interviewing, office romance, personal disclosure, and diversity.

**NEW! MANAGEMENT IN THE MOVIES (ISBN: 0073317713)**

McGraw-Hill is now offering a *Management in the Movies* DVD loaded with scenes from major Hollywood movies and TV shows. Each movie has been clipped to highlight a specific scene (each is less than two and a half minutes) and linked to specific topics including groups, ethics, diversity, global management, and more. Along with the DVD, McGraw-Hill provides an instructor's manual with suggestions for use of the clip, clip summaries, and discussion questions to accompany each segment.

**NEW! GUIDE TO USING NBC'S *THE OFFICE***

The *Instructor's Guide for Using Clips from NBC's The Office in Your HRM Classroom* is a new supplement with this 6th edition and includes teaching notes and discussion questions that tie specific chapter content into scenes from the popular NBC sitcom *The Office*. Instructors will need to obtain copies of the television show episodes.

# Brief Contents

# CONTENTS

# Human Resource Management

## GAINING A COMPETITIVE ADVANTAGE

1

CHAPTER

# Human Resource Management: Gaining a Competitive Advantage

LO

## LEARNING OBJECTIVES

After reading this chapter, you should be able to:

LO1 Discuss the roles and activities of a company's human resource management function. *page 5*

LO2 Discuss the implications of the economy, the makeup of the labor force, and ethics for company sustainability. *page 13*

LO3 Discuss how human resource management affects a company's balanced scorecard. *page 24*

LO4 Discuss what companies should do to compete in the global marketplace. *page 39*

LO5 Identify the characteristics of the workforce and how they influence human resource management. *page 43*

LO6 Discuss human resource management practices that support high-performance work systems. *page 44*

LO7 Provide a brief description of human resource management practices. *page 51*

# ENTER THE WORLD OF BUSINESS

## Starbucks' HR Practices Ensure Its Brew Is a Winner

Starbucks, the Seattle-based coffee store, is growing globally by more than four stores and 200 employees each day. But Starbucks wants to maintain the company's atmosphere and culture despite its growth. There are 8,900 stores in 35 countries, but Starbucks would like to increase the total number of stores to 30,000 worldwide including 15,000 stores in the United States. In 2006, Starbucks added 28,000 jobs globally!

Starbucks believes that the key to company success is its employees, called partners. The attitudes and abilities of the partners who greet and serve customers is key to creating a positive customer service and repeat business. Starbucks' progressive employment practices help its reputation. At Starbucks the value-and-treat-employees-right approach is part of the company culture. Dave Pace, the executive vice president for human resources, says, "We don't overanalyze this philosophy. You either believe in it or you don't and we believe in it." One of the company's six guiding principles is to "provide a great work environment and treat each other with respect and dignity." Starbucks believes its financial success results from its HR practices, not the other way around.

As a result of the important role of Starbucks' partners, the company emphasizes selecting the right new employees, training them, and rewarding and retaining employees with above-minimum salaries. Job fairs, in-store advertisements, a company Web site, and employee referrals are used to recruit new employees. The Web site also helps potential job candidates determine if they will fit in at Starbucks. Starbucks wants employees who are dependable, adaptable, and team players. Managers are provided with interview guidelines that are used to question job candidates to determine whether they have the skills and behaviors necessary for the position.

Although 85 percent of its employees are part-time, they are still eligible for full-time benefits if they work 240 hours a quarter. Less than 30 percent of part-time workers in the United States receive health care, paid sick leave, or eligibility for bonuses and stock options. Starbucks provides all employees and their same-sex or opposite-sex partners comprehensive health benefits that include medical, dental, and vision care as well as tuition reimbursement, stock options, vacation, and a 401(k) retirement plan. Partners also receive a free pound of coffee each week.

Starbucks also has an intensive training program. All new U.S. employees start their jobs in paid training called "First Impressions." Store managers serve as trainers. The training focuses on coffee knowledge and how to create a positive experience for customers. Training specialists from headquarters work with store managers to ensure training is consistent across all stores. The training courses are also frequently updated. Managers and assistant store managers take a 10-week retail management training course. Computer, leadership, and diversity training are available. Most corporate employees begin their careers with Starbucks in immersion training. Immersion training involves working in a Starbucks store and learning the business by making beverages and interacting with customers. When Starbucks enters a new international market, partners are brought to Seattle for 6 to 12 weeks of training and to other locations to get store experience.

Starbucks not only values employees and uses human resource practices to support the business strategy but it also seeks out evidence that human resource practices have a positive impact on the business and support the company's mission and values. That is, Starbucks engages in evidence-based HR. Pace watches all of the traditional HR success indicators such as turnover and employee engagement and satisfaction scores. Starbucks' approximately 70 percent turnover rate may seem high, but it is low for the industry. Employee engagement and satisfaction scores put the company in the top world-class category. Starbucks also has a group that is responsible for "mission review," reviewing hundreds of employee comments and questions monthly to be sure the corporate mission statement is being followed. There are other indicators of the success of Starbucks' HR practices. Starbucks is in the top one-third of other Fortune 500 companies in earnings per share as well as total return to shareholders. Starbucks has been recognized as one of the best companies to work for several years and was ranked 16th on *Fortune* magazine's list of the 100 best companies to work for in 2007.

Sources: Based on "Tops of the Trade," *Human Resource Executive*, December 2005, pp. 1, 16–25; G. Weber, "Preserving the Counter Culture," *Workforce Management*, February 2005, pp. 28–34. Starbucks corporate Web site at www.starbucks.com.

## Introduction

Starbucks illustrates the key role that human resource management (HRM) plays in determining the survival, effectiveness, and competitiveness of U.S. businesses. **Competitiveness** refers to a company's ability to maintain and gain market share in its industry. Starbucks' human resource management practices have helped support the company's business strategy and provide services the customer values. The value of a product or service is determined by its quality and how closely the product fits customer needs.

**Competitiveness**
A company's ability to maintain and gain market share in its industry.

Competitiveness is related to company effectiveness, which is determined by whether the company satisfies the needs of stakeholders (groups affected by business practices). Important stakeholders include stockholders, who want a return on their investment; customers, who want a high-quality product or service; and employees, who desire interesting work and reasonable compensation for their services. The community, which wants the company to contribute to activities and projects and minimize pollution of the environment, is also an important stakeholder. Companies that do not meet stakeholders' needs are unlikely to have a competitive advantage over other firms in their industry.

**Human resource management (HRM)** refers to the policies, practices, and systems that influence employees' behavior, attitudes, and performance. Many companies refer to HRM as involving "people practices." Figure 1.1 emphasizes that there are several important HRM practices. The strategy underlying these practices needs to be considered to maximize their influence on company performance. As the figure shows, HRM practices include analyzing and designing work, determining human resource needs (HR planning), attracting potential employees (recruiting), choosing employees (selection), teaching employees how to perform their jobs and preparing them for the future (training and development), rewarding employees (compensation), evaluating their performance (performance management), and creating a positive work environment (employee relations). The HRM practices discussed in this chapter's opening highlighted how effective HRM practices support business goals and objectives. That is, effective HRM practices are strategic! Effective HRM has been shown to enhance company performance by contributing to employee and customer satisfaction, innovation, productivity, and development of a favorable reputation in the firm's community.[1] The potential role of HRM in company performance has only recently been recognized.

**Human Resource Management (HRM)**
Policies, practices, and systems that influence employees' behavior, attitudes, and performance.

figure 1.1

Human Resource Management Practices

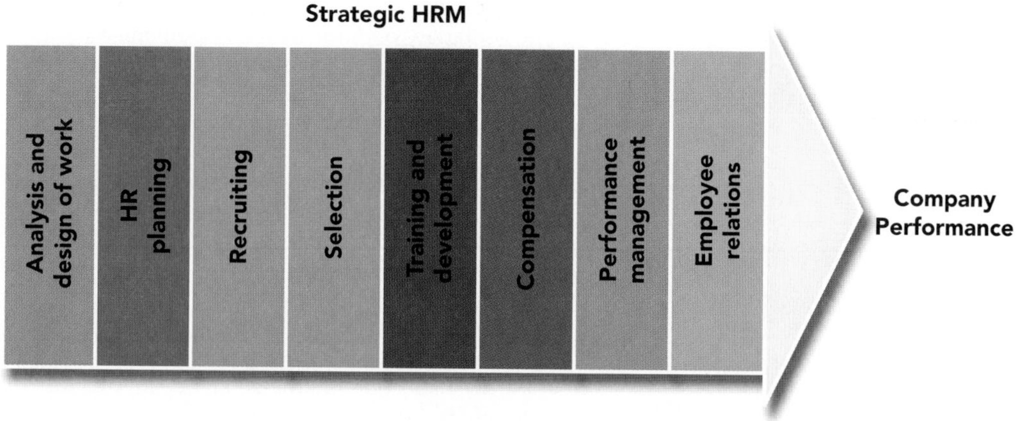


We begin by discussing the roles and skills that a human resource management department and/or managers need for any company to be competitive. The second section of the chapter identifies the competitive challenges that U.S. companies currently face, which influence their ability to meet the needs of shareholders, customers, employees, and other stakeholders. We discuss how these competitive challenges are influencing HRM. The chapter concludes by highlighting the HRM practices covered in this book and the ways they help companies compete.

## What Responsibilities and Roles Do HR Departments Perform?

**LO1** Discuss the Roles and Activities of a Company's Human Resource Management Function.

Only recently have companies looked at HRM as a means to contribute to profitability, quality, and other business goals through enhancing and supporting business operations.

Table 1.1 shows the responsibilities of human resource departments. The average ratio of HR department staff to total number of employees has been 1.0 for every 93 employees served by the department.[2] The median HR department expenditure per employee was $1,409. Labor costs represent approximately 30 percent of company revenue.

The HR department is solely responsible for outplacement, labor law compliance, record keeping, testing, unemployment compensation, and some aspects of benefits administration. The HR department is most likely to collaborate with other company functions on employment interviewing, performance management and discipline, and efforts to improve quality and productivity. Large companies are more likely than small ones to employ HR specialists, with benefits specialists being the most prevalent. Other common specializations include recruitment, compensation, and training and development.[3]

Many different roles and responsibilities can be performed by the HR department depending on the size of the company, the characteristics of the workforce, the industry, and the value system of company management. The HR department may take full responsibility for human resource activities in some companies, whereas in others it may share the roles and responsibilities with managers of other departments

**table 1.1**

Responsibilities of HR Departments

| | |
|---|---|
| Employment and recruiting | Interviewing, recruiting, testing, temporary labor coordination |
| Training and development | Orientation, performance management skills training, productivity enhancement |
| Compensation | Wage and salary administration, job descriptions, executive compensation, incentive pay, job evaluation |
| Benefits | Insurance, vacation leave administration, retirement plans, profit sharing, stock plans |
| Employee services | Employee assistance programs, relocation services, outplacement services |
| Employee and community relations | Attitude surveys, labor relations, publications, labor law compliance, discipline |
| Personnel records | Information systems, records |
| Health and safety | Safety inspection, drug testing, health, wellness |
| Strategic planning | International human resources, forecasting, planning, mergers and acquisitions |

SOURCE: Based on SHRM-BNA Survey No. 66, "Policy and Practice Forum: Human Resource Activities, Budgets, and Staffs, 2000–2001," Bulletin to Management, Bureau of National Affairs Policy and Practice Series, June 28, 2001. Washington, DC: Bureau of National Affairs.

such as finance, operations, or information technology. In some companies the HR department advises top-level management; in others the HR department may make decisions regarding staffing, training, and compensation after top managers have decided relevant business issues.

One way to think about the roles and responsibilities of HR departments is to consider HR as a business within the company with three product lines. Figure 1.2 shows the three product lines of HR. The first product line, administrative services and transactions, is the traditional product that HR has historically provided. The newer

**figure 1.2**

HR as a Business with Three Product Lines

**Administrative Services and Transactions:** Compensation, hiring and staffing
- Emphasis: Resource efficiency and service quality

**Business Partner Services:** Developing effective HR systems and helping implement business plans, talent management
- Emphasis: Knowing the business and exercising influence—problem solving, designing effective systems to ensure needed competencies

**Strategic Partner:** Contributing to business strategy based on considerations of human capital, business capabilities, readiness, and developing HR practices as strategic differentiators
- Emphasis: Knowledge of HR and of the business, competition, the market, and business strategies

SOURCE: Adapted from Figure 1, "HR Product Lines," in E. E. Lawler, "From Human Resource Management to Organizational Effectiveness," *Human Resource Management* 44 (2005), pp. 165–69.

HR products—business partner services and the strategic partner role—are the HR functions that are being challenged by top managers to deliver. For example, consider the expectations and perceptions the CEOs of Hyperion, Revlon, and Air Products and Chemicals Inc. have for HR.[4] The Hyperion CEO wants his HR leaders to be able to question the CEO and executive team members and ensure the success of basic administrative functions, thus the HR team can elevate itself to a higher level of performance within the company culture and ensure that employees are able to perform at the highest level. At Revlon, the expectation is that HR can think strategically and innovatively, plan and execute, and have a very strong connection to the business. The CEO of Air Products and Chemicals believes the HR function is critical for the long-term success of the company because it can help get people excited about change, when most are by nature resistant to change.

HR at SYSCO Corporation, the number one food service marketer and distributor in North America, is successfully delivering business partner services and serving as a strategic partner.[5] The senior vice president and chief administrative officer is responsible for ensuring that HR strategy is aligned with the business strategy. SYSCO tries to differentiate itself from competitors in the marketplace by providing value in its products and customer service to the customer. HR at SYSCO focuses on ensuring that five processes are in place. These processes stress a common understanding of the company's mission values and goals, establishment of clear expectations between employees and managers using the performance management process, operating within laws, ensuring that employees are inspired to come to work, and giving every employee the skills and technology needed to contribute to the company. HR, a strategic partner in all of the processes, works together with senior management to develop programs and guidelines to support the processes. It then markets them to line managers, who execute and customize the programs for their specific business. To determine if these processes are working three key dimensions are measured: employee satisfaction, number of employees the company uses per 100,000 cases it sells, and employee retention data for each function in the company. Top executives meet four times each year to review the metrics to see if they are consistent with operating expenses and pretax earnings. For example, since the late 1990s SYSCO has moved the retention rate for its 10,000 marketing associates from 70 to 82 percent, resulting in more than $70 million dollars saved per year.

## What Competencies Do HR Professionals Need?

HR professionals need to have the six competencies shown in Figure 1.3. These are the most recent competencies identified by the Human Resource Competency Study which has identified HR competencies for over fifteen years. The competencies are shown as a three-tier pyramid with the Credible Activist Competency the most important for high performance as an HR professional and effective HR leader. Demonstrating these competencies can help HR professionals show managers that they are capable of helping the HR function create value, contribute to the business strategy, and shape the company culture. They also help the HR department effectively and efficiently provide the three HR products discussed above and shown in Figure 1.2. Although great emphasis is placed on the strategic role of HR, effective execution of the operational executor competency—necessary administrative services filling open jobs, paying employees, benefits enrollment, keeping employee records, and completing legally required paperwork (such as W-2 forms and EEO reports)—is still important! As we

figure 1.3
Six Competencies for the HR Profession

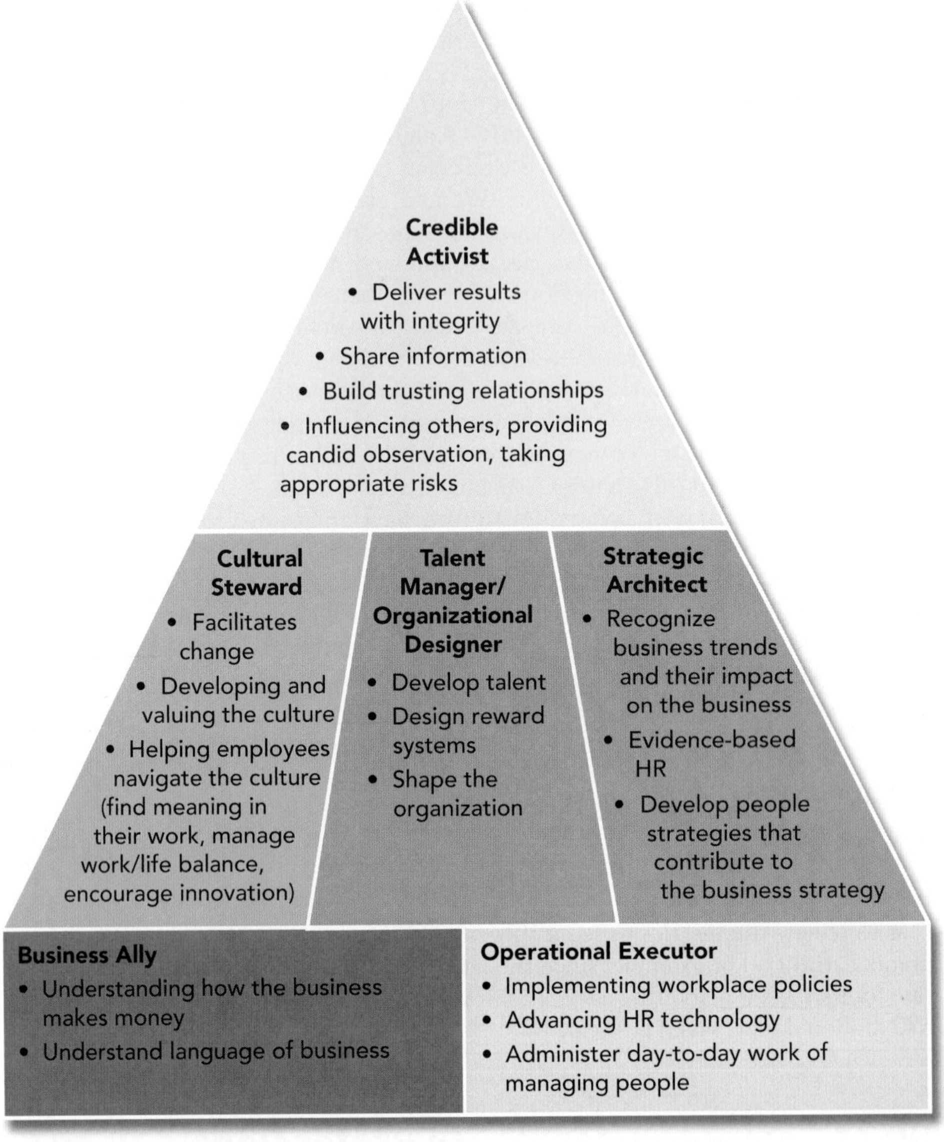

Credible Activist
• Deliver results with integrity
• Share information
• Build trusting relationships
• Influencing others, providing candid observation, taking appropriate risks
Cultural Steward
• Facilitates change
• Developing and valuing the culture
• Helping employees navigate the culture (find meaning in their work, manage work/life balance, encourage innovation)
Talent Manager/ Organizational Designer
• Develop talent
• Design reward systems
• Shape the organization
Strategic Architect
• Recognize business trends and their impact on the business
• Evidence-based HR
• Develop people strategies that contribute to the business strategy
Business Ally
• Understanding how the business makes money
• Understand language of business
Operational Executor
• Implementing workplace policies
• Advancing HR technology
• Administer day-to-day work of managing people


SOURCE: Based on R. Grossman, "New Competencies for HR," *HR Magazine* (June 2007): pp. 58–62; HR Competency Assessment Tools at www.shrm.org/competencies/benefits.asp

will discuss later in the chapter, technological advances have made available e-HRM and human resource information systems, which make administration of services more efficient and effective and free up time for HR to focus on strategic issues. Successful HR professionals must be able to share information, build relationships, and influence persons both inside and outside the company, including managers, employees, community members, schools, customers, vendors, and suppliers.

Sometimes helping employees can also involve crisis management activities such as those HR professionals had to perform during and following Hurricane Katrina. The Avis executive vice president of human resources was responsible for making sure that employees in Katrina's path got to safety.[6] Employees were given 1-800 phone numbers to call if they got into trouble. Employees were given release time to evacuate their families as the storm approached. When employees called in following the storm, they were asked if they needed housing, food, or medical care or if they had missing relatives. HR called emergency shelters to find missing employees and sent trucks with Avis signs throughout the stricken area trying to locate missing employees who had evacuated. Employees were paid their salaries even if they were unable to work, and copayments for medical care were waived.

## How Is the HRM Function Changing?

The amount of time that the HRM function devotes to administrative tasks is decreasing, and its roles as a strategic business partner, change agent, and employee advocate are increasing.[7] HR managers face two important challenges: shifting their focus from current operations to strategies for the future[8] and preparing non-HR managers to develop and implement human resource practices (recall the role of HR in Starbucks' success from the chapter opening story).

The role of HRM in administration is decreasing as technology is used for many administrative purposes, such as managing employee records and allowing employees to get information about and enroll in training, benefits, and other programs. Advances in technology such as the Internet have decreased the HRM role in maintaining records and providing self-service to employees.[9] **Self-service** refers to giving employees online access to information about HR issues such as training, benefits, compensation, and contracts; enrolling online in programs and services; and completing online attitude surveys. For example, General Motors' (GM) goal for its e-HR investment was to create an employee-friendly one-stop shop for employees to enroll in benefits, review their HR data, and get certificates for employee car discounts.[10] The portal, known as "mySocrates," is the place employees go for information about GM. Managers use the system for performance reviews. HR uses it for communications of benefits, training programs, and other programs, which saves time as well as printing and distribution costs. Annual benefits enrollment used to take several days. Now it takes a few minutes.

**Self-Service**
Giving employees online access to HR information.

Outsourcing of the administrative role has also occurred. **Outsourcing** refers to the practice of having another company (a vendor, third-party provider, or consultant) provide services. One study suggests that 80 percent of companies now outsource at least one HR activity.[11] Outsource providers such as Exult, Accenture HR Services, Convergys, and Hewitt provide payroll services as well as recruiting, training, record managements, and expatriation. The primary reasons for outsourcing are to save money and spend more time on strategic business issues. One study suggests that 91 percent of U.S. companies have taken steps to standardize their HR processes to prepare for outsourcing.[12]

**Outsourcing**
The practice of having another company provide services.

Examples of strategic business issues that HR might help address include identifying new business opportunities, assessing possible merger, acquisition, or divestiture strategies, or working on recruiting and developing talent.[13] As a result, HR functions related to these areas such as employee development, performance management, and organizational development are outsourced least frequently. For example, outsourcing payroll and benefits administration is saving the American Stock Exchange in New York $2.8 million per year. When the Canadian Imperial Bank of Commerce contracted with Electronic Data Systems (EDS) Corporation to take over payroll, benefits administration, and other HR processing for the Toronto-based bank, the bank had 30 incompatible HR systems and had not invested in e-HRM (use of the Web for HR operations).[14] EDS revised the bank's payroll, benefits, executive compensation, and human resources information technology systems, and it created my.HR, a Web portal used by managers and employees. Use of EDS has not required any additional costs over the bank's yearly HR budget. When the bank outsourced payroll it cut 200 jobs from its centralized HR staff, leaving the remaining HR staff to focus on strategic issues such as recruiting, training, and union contract negotiations. The centralized staff members moved over to EDS.

Cardinal Health, a provider of health care products, services, and technology, headquartered in Dublin, Ohio, signed a contract with ExcellerateHRO to provide administrative functions.[15] The goal of the outsourcing is to increase the contribution of human resources to strategy and increase the company's global human resource capabilities. Human resource professionals remaining at Cardinal will work in strategic areas such as talent management, organizational effectiveness, and total rewards. In addition, human resource "business partners" placed across the company will focus on strategic activities while establishing new HR operations in the field. Although the outsourcing of HR is expected to grow, many contracts have ended because of lack of understanding of the outsourcing provider's capabilities, failure to reach goals such as anticipated cost reductions, and poor delivery of services.[16] A key aspect of any outsourcing decision is an understanding of the company's vision for HR and an assessment of the costs of performing HR functions within the company compared to the potential savings through outsourcing.

Traditionally, the HRM department (also known as "Personnel" or "Employee Relations") was primarily an administrative expert and employee advocate. The department took care of employee problems, made sure employees were paid correctly, administered labor contracts, and avoided legal problems. The HRM department ensured that employee-related issues did not interfere with the manufacturing or sales of products or services. Human resource management was primarily reactive; that is, human resource issues were a concern only if they directly affected the business. Although that still remains the case in many companies that have yet to recognize the competitive value of human resource management, other companies believe that HRM is important for business success and therefore have expanded the role of HRM as a change agent and strategic partner.

Other roles such as practice development and strategic business partnering have increased. One of the most comprehensive studies ever conducted regarding HRM concluded that "human resources is being transformed from a specialized, stand-alone function to a broad corporate competency in which human resources and line managers build partnerships to gain competitive advantage and achieve overall business goals."[17] HR managers are increasingly included on high-level committees that are shaping the strategic direction of the company. These managers report directly to the CEO, president, or board of directors and propose solutions to business problems.

Consider the role of HR at retail closeout chain Big Lots, which sells clothes, computers, and even cookies at 70 percent off retail prices.[18] At Big Lots the vice president of human resources and the chief financial officer sit on the operating review committee. The HR VP provides information regarding labor costs, theft, and employee and customer attitudes. HR is responsible for risk management and loss prevention, which are traditionally handled by finance. This was an opportunity for HR to tie more strategically to the business because it helps make business units more profitable. The reduction of theft and dishonesty can save the company millions of dollars. At Big Lots, the executive team includes the chief executive officer, chief financial officer, chief administrative officer, vice president of human resources, and the executive vice president of store

**table 1.2**

Questions Used to Determine If Human Resources Are Playing a Strategic Role in the Business

1. What is HR doing to provide value-added services to internal clients?
2. What can the HR department add to the bottom line?
3. How are you measuring the effectiveness of HR?
4. How can we reinvest in employees?
5. What HR strategy will we use to get the business from point A to point B?
6. What makes an employee want to stay at our company?
7. How are we going to invest in HR so that we have a better HR department than our competitors?
8. From an HR perspective, what should we be doing to improve our marketplace position?
9. What's the best change we can make to prepare for the future?

SOURCE: Data from A. Halcrow, "Survey Shows HR in Transition," *Workforce*, June 1988, p. 74.

operations. All members of the team contribute to sales, operations, or human resource issues. When the executive team determined that the company had to become more customer centered, the vice president of human resources proposed a project to measure the relationship between employee and customer attitudes and business outcomes including sales, profitability, inventory shrinkage, and customer satisfaction at every store.

As part of its strategic role, one of the key contributions that HR can make is to engage in evidence-based HR. **Evidence-based HR** refers to demonstrating that human resources practices have a positive influence on the company's bottom line or key stakeholders (employees, customers, community, shareholders). This helps show that the money invested in HR programs is justified and that HR is contributing to the company's goals and objectives. Evidence-based HR requires collecting data on such metrics as productivity, turnover, accidents, employee attitudes and medical costs and showing their relationship with HR practices. This provides evidence that HR is as important to the business as finance, accounting, and marketing! HR decisions should be made on the basis of data and not just intuition. The chapter opener showed how Starbucks is using turnover and employee satisfaction data as metrics or indicators of the success of its HR programs. Throughout each chapter of the book we provide examples of evidence-based HR.

**Evidence-Based HR**
Demonstrating that human resource practices have a positive influence on the company's bottom line or key stakeholders (employees, customers, community, shareholders).

Table 1.2 provides several questions that managers can use to determine if HRM is playing a strategic role in the business. If these questions have not been considered, it is highly unlikely that (1) the company is prepared to deal with competitive challenges or (2) human resources are being used to help a company gain a competitive advantage. We will discuss strategic human resource management in more detail in Chapter 2.

Why have HRM roles changed? Managers see HRM as the most important lever for companies to gain a competitive advantage over both domestic and foreign competitors. We believe this is because HRM practices are directly related to companies' success in meeting competitive challenges. These challenges and their implications for HRM are discussed later in the chapter.

## The HRM Profession

There are many different types of jobs in the HRM profession. Table 1.3 shows various HRM positions and their salaries. A survey conducted by the Society of Human Resource Management to better understand what HR professionals do found that the

**table 1.3**
Median Salaries for HRM Positions

| POSITION | SALARY |
|---|---|
| Top corporate HR executive | $245,392 |
| HR director | 141,119 |
| HR manager | 97, 996 |
| Benefits manager | 92,598 |
| Training manager | 82,700 |
| General recruiter | 51,869 |

SOURCE: Based on the 2006 Mercer Benchmark Database—Human Resource Module as reported in J. Vocino, "Rewards Rise for Rewards Specialists," *HR Magazine* 51 (2006), pp. 70–78.

primary activities of HR professionals are performing the HR generalist role (providing a wide range of HR services), with fewer involved in other activities such as the HR function at the executive level of the company, training and development, HR consulting, and administrative activities.[19]

HR salaries vary depending on education and experience as well as the type of industry. As you can see from Table 1.3, some positions involve work in specialized areas of HRM like recruiting, training, or labor and industrial relations. HR generalists usually make between $60,000 and $80,000 depending on their experience and education level. Generalists usually perform the full range of HRM activities including recruiting, training, compensation, and employee relations. Most HR professionals chose HR as a career because they found HR appealing as a career, they wanted to work with people, or they were asked by chance to perform HR tasks and responsibilities.[20]

A college degree is held by the vast majority of HRM professionals, many of whom also have completed postgraduate work. Business typically is the field of study (human resources or industrial relations), although some HRM professionals have degrees in the social sciences (economics or psychology), the humanities, or law. Those who have completed graduate work have master's degrees in HR management, business management, or a similar field. Professional certification in HRM is less common than membership in professional associations. A well-rounded educational background will likely serve a person well in an HRM position. As one HR professional noted, "One of the biggest misconceptions is that it is all warm and fuzzy communications with the workers. Or that it is creative and involved in making a more congenial atmosphere for people at work. Actually it is both of those some of the time, but most of the time it is a big mountain of paperwork which calls on a myriad of skills besides the 'people' type. It is law, accounting, philosophy, and logic as well as psychology, spirituality, tolerance, and humility."[21]

Many top-level managers and HR professionals believe that the best way to develop the future effective professionals needed in HR is to take employees with a business point of view and train them. At companies like General Electric, Citigroup, and Baxter Health Care training programs are used to develop HR professionals' skills. Also, HR professionals often rotate through job assignments in non-HR functions to help them learn about the business and become more strategic business partners.[22] For example, just several years ago for the first time in company history at General Motors, an HR person reported directly to the company CEO.[23] Many of the transactional activities are being outsourced or performed with the use of technology. GM is trying to develop HR people so that they can take on the role of internal consultants. The company has a global HR curriculum that helps HR employees understand what the goals of HR are, what the changes in HR at GM mean to them, and what the plans are for the HR function. The courses focus on helping HR employees gain business knowledge such as finance, change management skills, and the ability to develop relationships across the company. GM hopes that in the near future HR employees will be able to work with business units to diagnose problems. At the same time HR employees are being trained, top HR managers are working with line managers to help them understand that HR is available to help them with strategy, not transactional work. Line managers are now taking responsibility for some HR activities. For example, GM recently introduced a new compensation plan for employees that was implemented by line managers without any help from HR.

The primary professional organization for HRM is the Society for Human Resource Management (SHRM). SHRM is the world's largest human resource management association with more than 210,000 professional and student members throughout the world. SHRM provides education and information services, conferences and seminars, government and media representation, and online services and publications (such as *HR Magazine*). You can visit SHRM's Web site to see their services at www.shrm.org.

**Sustainability**
The ability of a company to survive in a dynamic competitive environment. Based on an approach to organizational decision making that considers the long-term impact of strategies on stakeholders (e.g., employees, shareholders, suppliers, community).

## Competitive Challenges Influencing Human Resource Management

Three competitive challenges that companies now face will increase the importance of human resource management practices: the challenge of sustainability, the global challenge, the technology challenge. These challenges are shown in Figure 1.4.

### The Sustainability Challenge

**LO2**
Discuss the Implications of the Economy, the Makeup of the Labor Force, and Ethics for Company Sustainability.

Traditionally, sustainability has been viewed as one aspect of corporate social responsibility related to the impact of the business on the environment.[24] However, we take a broader view of sustainability. For our purposes, **sustainability** refers to the ability of a company to survive and succeed in a dynamic competitive environment. Company success is based on how well the company meets the needs of its stakeholders. **Stakeholders** refers to shareholders, the community, customers, employees, and all of the other parties that have an interest in seeing that the company succeeds. Sustainability includes the ability to deal with economic and social changes, engage in responsible and ethical business practices, provide high-quality products and services, and put in place methods to determine if the company is meeting stakeholders' needs.

**Stakeholders**
The various interest groups who have relationships with, and consequently, whose interests are tied to the organization (e.g., employees, suppliers, customers, shareholders, community).

Several changes in the economy have important implications for human resource management. Some key statistics about the economy and the workforce are shown in Table 1.4. These include the changing structure of the economy, the development of e-business, and more growth in professional and service occupations. Growth in these occupations means that skill demands for jobs have changed, with knowledge becoming more valuable. Not only have skill demands changed, but remaining competitive in a global economy requires demanding work hours and changes in traditional employment patterns. The creation of new jobs, aging employees leaving the workforce, slow population growth, and a lack of employees who have the skills needed to perform the jobs in greatest demand means that demand for employees will exceed supply. This has created a "war for talent" that has increased the attention companies pay to attracting and retaining human resources.

figure 1.4
Competitive Challenges Influencing U.S. Companies

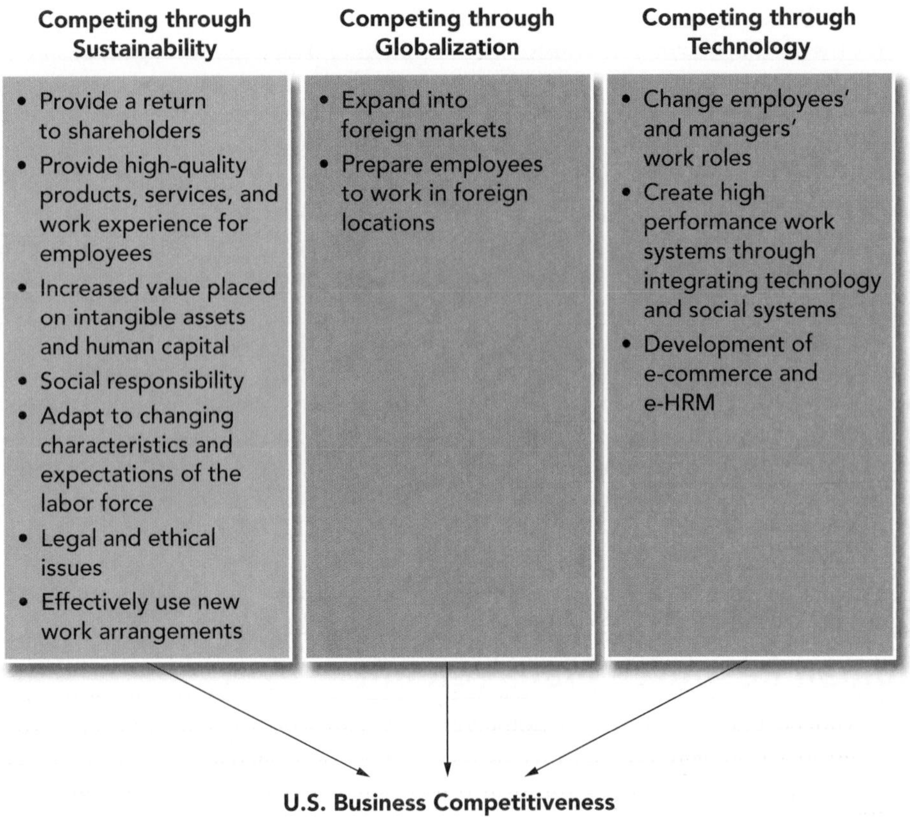

Competing through Sustainability
• Provide a return to shareholders
• Provide high-quality products, services, and work experience for employees
• Increased value placed on intangible assets and human capital
• Social responsibility
• Adapt to changing characteristics and expectations of the labor force
• Legal and ethical issues
• Effectively use new work arrangements
Competing through Globalization
• Expand into foreign markets
• Prepare employees to work in foreign locations
Competing through Technology
• Change employees' and managers' work roles
• Create high performance work systems through integrating technology and social systems
• Development of e-commerce and e-HRM
U.S. Business Competitiveness


## Economic Changes

A number of factors have put companies and employees into a more uncertain economic future as companies continue to recover from the events of September 11, 2001, and the dot-com bust in the early 2000s that triggered an economic recession.[25] Continued concerns with the war in Iraq, global competition, changes from a manufacturing to service economy, increased merger and acquisition activity, and company

**table 1.4**
Summary of Key Labor Statistics Influencing HRM

| |
|---|
| • The economy is expected to add 19 million new jobs. |
| • Professional specialty and service occupations will grow the fastest and add the most jobs from 2002 to 2012. |
| • More job openings are expected from the need to replace workers (35 million) than from employment growth in the economy. |
| • More than 25% of the workers will reach retirement age by 2010, resulting in a potential worker shortage of 10 million. |
| • The projected median age of the labor force by 2012 is 41, the highest ever recorded. |
| • Rising trends in immigration levels will add approximately 1 million persons through 2012. |

SOURCES: Based on U.S. Bureau of Labor Statistics Web site http://stats.bls.gov; D. Hecker, "Occupational Projections to 2014," *Monthly Labor Review,* November 2005, pp. 70–101; M. Harrigan, "Employment Projections to 2012: Concepts and Context," *Monthly Labor Review* 127 (2004), pp. 3–22; M. Toossi, "Labor Force Projections to 2014: Retiring Boomers," *Monthly Labor Review,* November 2005, pp. 25–44.

downsizing means that many employees who were able to earn high wages in low-skilled factory jobs may have to turn to service jobs with less security and fewer benefits. As political unrest and instability across the globe increase, the global economy becomes more uncertain affecting investment decisions in physical and human capital. Companies are investing more in global and domestic security. For example, consider the steps that General Motors is taking to compete more successfully against global competitors in the auto industry. General Motors is cutting costs, restructuring, and introducing new products.[26] General Motors restructured its pension and other benefits for salaried employees and offered a combination of early retirement incentives and other financial incentives to reduce the number of employees. General Motors is also developing and introducing new products such as the extended-length luxury SUV Escalade model.

According to the SHRM Workplace survey of human resource professionals, the two most important economic trends in the United States are rising health care costs affecting the country's ability to compete globally and the economic implications of increasing retiree benefit costs.[27] Companies are under pressure to increase employee productivity to alleviate higher costs such as health care. To control costs, companies have cut employee and retiree health care benefits and pension contributions, increased the employee contribution to pay for these benefits, and even hired and fired employees based on their smoking habits! For example as discussed in Chapter 10 and in the *BusinessWeek* case in Chapter 13, you will see that Scott's Miracle-Gro Company, the lawn care company, banned smoking and encourages employees to complete a health-risk assessment designed to identify employees who are at risk for heart, cancer, and other diseases.[28] Employees at risk are assigned a health coach, who draws up an action plan that may include recommendations such as exercise or change of diet. Employees who refuse the health assessment pay $40 per month more in health care premiums; at-risk employees who refuse to work with a health coach pay an additional $67 per month. We will discuss what companies are doing to offset health care and pension costs in Chapter 13, Employee Benefits.

The implications of this economic period for human resource management are far-reaching. For example, HR programs and the HR function have increased pressure to relate to the business strategy and show a return on investment. Customer focus needs to be included in all HRM practices. New technology combined with economic uncertainty will mean that administrative and transactional HR activities will be delivered via technology, creating less need for HR professionals to provide these activities. The aging workforce combined with reduced immigration because of security concerns may lead employers to focus more on retraining employees or encouraging older, skilled workers to delay retirement or work part-time. Some suggest that the weak economy and the effects of 9/11 may change the ways employees view work. Employees may not want to travel as much, may spend more time with friends and family, and may be more interested in training and development activities related to personal growth.[29]

***Employment and Occupational Growth Projections and Skill Requirements.*** The competition for labor is affected by the growth and decline of industries, jobs, and occupations. Competition for labor is also influenced by the number and skills of persons available for full-time work. Between 2004 and 2014, employment is expected to increase by 18.9 million, or 13 percent. New workers will be needed to fill job openings due to death, disability, retirement, or people leaving the workforce to stay home.[30] The U.S. population is expected to increase by 24 million from 2000 to 2010. The growth will mean more consumers of goods and services and more demand for employees.[31]

Table 1.5 shows examples of the projected fastest growing occupations between 2004 and 2014. For 23 of the 30 fastest growing occupations, the most significant source of postsecondary education or training is an associate degree or higher.[32] Computer- and health-related occupations account for over 70 percent of the top 30 fastest growing occupations. Among the major occupational groups, professional and related occupations and service occupations are expected to increase fastest and add the most jobs from 2004 to 2014.[33] These occupational groups have distinctly different educational requirements, with the professional and related occupations (including health care practitioners, computer and mathematical science, architecture and engineering) typically requiring more than high-school-level education while service occupations (e.g., food preparation and serving, personal care and service, building maintenance) do not. The continued dominance of professional and service occupations has important implications for HRM. Research shows that employee perceptions of HRM practices are positively related to customers' evaluations of service quality. To maximize customer service, companies need to provide a positive experience for the customer and progressive HR practices.

Table 1.6 shows the top 10 content and skill areas that corporate leaders surveyed considered most critical over the next five years. However, new entrants to the workplace lack these and other skills needed for companies to compete in the global economy. A study of American manufacturers conducted by the National Association of Manufacturing found that 36 percent indicated that employees had insufficient reading, writing, and communications skills.[34] Eighty percent of the manufacturers reported that they are facing a shortage of experienced workers, especially production workers, machinists, and craft workers. An online poll of members of the American Society for Training and Development found that 97 percent of respondents indicated a current skill gap in their companies.[35] Also, business leaders

**table 1.5**

Examples of the Fastest Growing Occupations

| | EMPLOYMENT CHANGE 2004–14 | | |
|---|---|---|---|
| OCCUPATION | NUMBER (IN THOUSANDS) | PERCENT | MOST SIGNIFICANT EDUCATION OR TRAINING |
| Home health aides | 350 | 56 | Short-term on-the-job training |
| Network systems and data communications analysts | 126 | 55 | Bachelor's degree |
| Medical assistants | 202 | 52 | Moderate-term on-the-job training |
| Physical assistants | 31 | 50 | Bachelor's degree |
| Computer software engineering applications | 222 | 48 | Bachelor's degree |
| Physical therapist assistants | 26 | 44 | Associate degree |
| Dental hygienists | 68 | 43 | Associate degree |
| Postsecondary teachers | 524 | 32 | Doctoral degree |
| Occupational therapists | 31 | 34 | Master's degree |

SOURCE: Based on Bureau of Labor Statistics, "2006–07 Editions of the Occupational Outlook Handbook and the Career Guide to Industries Available on the Internet," news release, December 21, 2005, Table 1. Available at www.bls.gov/news.release/ooh.t01.htm.

**table 1.6**

Top 10 Knowledge and Skills Expected to Increase in Importance over the Next Five Years

| RANK | BASIC KNOWLEDGE AND APPLIED SKILLS | PERCENTAGE |
|---|---|---|
| 1 | Critical thinking/problem solving | 77.8% |
| 2 | Information technology application | 77.4 |
| 3 | Teamwork/collaboration | 74.2 |
| 4 | Creativity/innovation | 73.6 |
| 5 | Diversity | 67.1 |
| 6 | Leadership | 66.9 |
| 7 | Oral communications | 65.9 |
| 8 | Professionalism/work ethic | 64.4 |
| 9 | Ethics/social responsibility | 64.3 |
| 10 | Written communications | 64.0 |

SOURCE: J. Casner-Lotto and L. Barrington, "*Are They Really Ready to Work?*" Research Report, The Conference Board, Corporate Voices for Working Families, Partnership for 21st Century Skills, and Society for Human Resource Management, October 2006.

such as Bill Gates have expressed their concern at the comparatively low numbers of U.S. students in the science and engineering fields. One estimate shows that 70,000 engineers graduated in the United States in 2005 compared to 350,000 in India and 600,000 in China. This has resulted in a shortage of engineering and other technical professionals.

Companies are involved in training current employees as well as establishing partnerships with schools to help improve the skills of the current and future U.S. workforce. For example, at Whirlpool, building a dishwasher requires that the sheet of steel used on the sides of the machine be the correct width.[36] Employees must be able to ensure that the steel meets specifications by calibrating equipment, which requires algebra-level math knowledge. Whirpool is finding that employees lack the math problem-solving skills needed to perform the job. As a result, Whirpool has developed training programs to improve workforce skills. About 25 percent of the programs focus on remedial skills. IBM, Hewlett-Packard, and Advanced Micro Devices are making efforts to increase the skills of the workforce by investing in local secondary schools.[37] IBM's Transition to Teaching program allows employees to take leaves of absence to student teach for three months. Eligible employees must meet certain requirements such as 10 years of service with IBM, a bachelor's degree in math or science or a higher degree in a related field, and some experience teaching, tutoring, or volunteering in schools. IBM hopes that many of its experienced employees with math and engineering backgrounds will take advantage of the program providing high-quality math and science teachers for public schools. Hewlett-Packard (HP) supports about 70 U.S. school districts with plans to enhance math and science programs. HP also helps equip schools with the technologies required for state-of-the-art technical education. Advanced Micro Devices, a company in the semiconductor industry, devotes half of its corporate contributions to education programs including a summer math and science academy.

Another way to look at occupational growth is to consider the pay related to the occupation. That is, occupations that are fastest growing provide high pay (average earnings are in the top half of distribution of earnings of all occupations). Examples of these occupations include network systems and data communications analysts, database administrators, physician assistants, software engineers, graphic designers, and structural iron and steel workers.[38] It is important to notice that the fastest growing and highest paid occupations are not exclusively limited to health or computer-related occupations or occupations which require a college degree. However, employers have a preference for hiring individuals with skills associated with higher levels of education. This also translates into higher earnings for employees.

***Increased Value Placed on Intangible Assets and Human Capital.*** Today more and more companies are interested in using intangible assets and human capital as a way to gain an advantage over competitors. A company's value includes three types of assets that are critical for the company to provide goods and services: financial assets (cash and securities), physical assets (property, plant, equipment), and intangible assets. Table 1.7 provides examples of intangible assets. **Intangible assets** include human capital, customer capital, social capital, and intellectual capital. Intangible assets are equally or even more valuable than financial and physical assets but they are difficult to duplicate or imitate.[39] By one estimate, up to 75 percent of the source of value in a company is in intangible assets.[40]

**Intangible Assets**
A type of company asset including human capital, customer capital, social capital, and intellectual capital.

Intangible assets have been shown to be responsible for a company's competitive advantage. Human resource management practices such as training, selection, performance management, and compensation have a direct influence on human and social capital through influencing customer service, work-related know-how and competence, and work relationships. For example, consider companies in the airline industry. Southwest Airlines consistently is profitable and highly ranked in on-time arrivals and other indicators of airline success.[41] One of the distinctions between Southwest

**table 1.7**
Examples of Intangible Assets

| |
|---|
| Human capital<br>• Tacit knowledge<br>• Education<br>• Work-related knowhow<br>• Work-related competence |
| Customer capital<br>• Customer relationships<br>• Brands<br>• Customer loyalty<br>• Distribution channels |
| Social capital<br>• Corporate culture<br>• Management philosophy<br>• Management practices<br>• Informal networking systems<br>• Coaching/mentoring relationships |
| Intellectual capital<br>• Patents<br>• Copyrights<br>• Trade secrets<br>• Intellectual property |

SOURCE: Based on L. Weatherly, *Human Capital: The Elusive Asset* (Alexandria, VA: 2003 SHRM Research Quarterly); E. Holton and S. Naquin, "New Metrics for Employee Development," *Performance Improvement Quarterly* 17 (2004), pp. 56–80; M. Huselid, B. Becker, and R. Beatty, *The Workforce Scorecard* (Boston: Harvard University Press, 2005).

Airlines and its competitors is how it treats its employees. For example, Southwest has a policy of no layoffs and was able to maintain this record even during the difficult time for airlines following 9/11. Southwest also emphasizes training and development to provide its employees with skills to perform multiple jobs. This allows Southwest airplanes to be quickly cleaned and serviced at airports because employees have multiple skill sets that can be applied to various aspects of getting an aircraft ready for departure. As a result of these human resource policies Southwest employees are loyal, productive, and flexible (which contributes to the success of the airline). Other airlines may have similar or greater levels of financial assets and have physical assets that are comparable to Southwest's (e.g., same type of airplanes, similar gates), but what contributes to Southwest's success and gives the company a competitive advantage are its intangible assets in the form of human capital. American and United Airlines have similar (or greater!) financial and physical assets but have not been successful trying to compete with Southwest by offering flights on the same routes.

Intangible assets have been shown to be related to a company's bottom line. A study by the American Society for Training and Development of more than 500 publicly traded U.S.-based companies found that companies that invested the most in training and development had a shareholder return 86 percent higher than companies in the bottom half and 46 percent higher than the market average.[42]

One way companies try to increase intangible assets is through attracting, developing, and retaining knowledge workers. **Knowledge workers** are employees who contribute to the company not through manual labor, but through what they know about customers or a specialized body of knowledge. Employees cannot simply be ordered to perform tasks; they must share knowledge and collaborate on solutions. Knowledge workers contribute specialized knowledge that their managers may not have, such as information about customers. Managers depend on them to share information. Knowledge workers have many job opportunities. If they choose, they can leave a company and take their knowledge to a competitor. Knowledge workers are in demand because companies need their skills and jobs requiring them are growing (see Tables 1.5 and 1.6).

**Knowledge Workers**
Employees who own the intellectual means of producing a product or service.

To completely benefit from employees' knowledge requires a management style that focuses on developing and empowering employees. **Empowering** means giving employees responsibility and authority to make decisions regarding all aspects of product development or customer service.[43] Employees are then held accountable for products and services; in return, they share the rewards and losses of the results. For empowerment to be successful, managers must be trained to link employees to resources within and outside the company (people, Web sites, etc.), help employees interact with their fellow employees and managers throughout the company, and ensure that employees are updated on important issues and cooperate with each other. Employees must also be trained to understand how to use the Web, e-mail, and other tools for communicating, collecting, and sharing information.

**Empowering**
Giving employees responsibility and authority to make decisions.

As more companies become knowledge-based, it's important that they promote and capture learning at the employee, team, and company levels. At Nissan Motor's U.S. operations, 16 teams, each with 8 to 16 salaried employees from different departments, meet weekly to discuss issues such as quality, diversity, or supply chain management.[44] The team members, chosen by management, are considered to be high performers who have demonstrated that they are receptive to new ideas. The teams are used to challenge the organization and propose new initiatives to make the company more creative and innovative. For example, as a result of one team's discussion of how to save money, a proposal for working at home was developed. The team conducted an experiment to determine the benefits of working at home. A pilot study of working at home with 41 employees found that it resulted in reduced operating costs and improved morale, as well as productivity increases for employees who worked at home. As a result, a virtual office initiative is in place at Nissan's headquarters in Nashville, Tennessee. The company's employees who analyze market trends and identify concepts for Nissan will work from home in Los Angeles.

In addition to acquiring and retaining knowledge workers, companies need to be able to adapt to change. *Change* refers to the adoption of a new idea or behavior by a company. Technological advances, changes in the workforce or government regulations, globalization, and new competitors are among the many factors that require companies to change. Change is inevitable in companies as products, companies, and entire industries experience shorter life cycles.[45] For example, Chrysler announced a restructuring plan that will eliminate 11,000 production jobs and 2,000 white-collar jobs as the company sells businesses that do not fit with its car building mission and productivity improvements.[46]

**Learning Organization**
Employees are continually trying to learn new things.

A changing environment means that all employees must embrace a philosophy of learning. A **learning organization** embraces a culture of lifelong learning, enabling all employees to continually acquire and share knowledge. Improvements in product or service quality do not stop when formal training is completed.[47] Employees need to have the financial, time, and content resources (courses, experiences, development opportunities) available to increase their knowledge. Managers take an active role in identifying training needs and helping to ensure that employees use training in their work. Also, employees should be actively encouraged to share knowledge with colleagues and other work groups across the company using e-mail and the Internet.[48] For a learning organization to be successful requires that teams of employees collaborate to meet customer needs. Managers need to empower employees to share knowledge, identify problems, and make decisions. This allows the company to continuously experiment and improve.

***Changes in Employment Expectations.*** The need for companies to make rapid changes as a result of new technologies, competitors, and customer demands has played a major role in reshaping the employment relationship.[49] New or emergent business strategies that result from these changes cause companies to merge, acquire new companies, grow, and in some cases downsize and restructure. This has resulted in changes in the employment relationship. The **psychological contract** describes what an employee expects to contribute and what the company will provide to the employee for these contributions.[50] Unlike a sales contract, a psychological contract is not written. Traditionally, companies expected employees to contribute time, effort, skills, abilities, and loyalty. In return, companies would provide job security and opportunities for promotion. However, in the new economy a new type of psychological contract is emerging.[51] The competitive business environment demands frequent changes in the quality, innovation, creativeness, and timeliness of employee contributions and the skills needed to provide them. This has led to company restructuring, mergers and acquisitions, layoffs, and longer hours for many employees. Companies demand excellent customer service and high productivity levels. Employees are expected to take more responsibility for their own careers, from seeking training to balancing work and family. In exchange for top performance and working longer hours without job security, employees want companies to provide flexible work schedules, comfortable working conditions, more autonomy in accomplishing work, training and development opportunities, and financial incentives based on how the company performs. Employees realize that companies cannot provide employment security, so they want employability—

**Psychological Contract**
Expectations of employee contributions and what the company will provide in return.

that is, they want their company to provide training and job experiences to help ensure that employees can find other employment opportunities. The human resource management challenge is how to build a committed, productive workforce in turbulent economic conditions that offer opportunity for financial success but can also quickly turn sour, making every employee expendable.

***Concerns with Employee Engagement.*** **Employee engagement** refers to the degree to which employees are fully involved in their work and the strength of their commitment to their job and the company.[52] Employees who are engaged in their work and committed to the company they work for give companies competitive advantage including higher productivity, better customer service, and lower turnover.[53] What is the state of employee engagement in U.S. companies? One survey of 50,000 employees across different companies showed that about 13 percent of employees are disengaged, poor performers who put in minimal effort on the job and are likely to leave the organization. Some 76 percent of employees exhibit moderate engagement, that is, they are marginally committed to the company and perform their jobs to the level expected by their manager. Only 11 percent of employees had high levels of engagement: they exhibited strong commitment to the company and were high performers who helped other employees with their work, volunteered for new responsibilities, and were constantly looking for ways to perform their jobs better.[54]

**Employee Engagement**
The degree to which employees are fully involved in their work and the strength of their job and company commitment.

Perhaps the best way to understand engagement is to consider how companies measure employee engagement. Companies measure employees' engagement levels with attitude or opinion surveys (we discuss these in detail in Chapter 10). Although the types of questions asked on these surveys vary from company to company, research suggests the questions generally measure 10 common themes shown in Table 1.8. As you probably realize after reviewing the themes shown in Table 1.8, employees' engagement is influenced by how managers treat employees as well as human resource practices such as recruiting, selection, training and development, performance management, work design, and compensation. For example, companies should recruit and select employees who are able to perform the job, are willing to work toward achieving the company strategy, and will react favorably to the work environment. Performance management systems need to provide employees with opportunities to receive performance feedback and recognition for their accomplishments. Compensation including incentives, benefits, and nonfinancial perks such as on-site day care or travel discounts contribute to employee engagement. Training and development gives employees the opportunity for personal growth within the company. Work that is

**table 1.8**

Common Themes of Employee Engagement

| |
|---|
| Pride in employer |
| Satisfaction with employer |
| Satisfaction with the job |
| Opportunity to perform challenging work |
| Recognition and positive feedback from contributions |
| Personal support from manager |
| Effort above and beyond the minimum |
| Understanding the link between one's job and the company's mission |
| Prospects for future growth with the company |
| Intention to stay with the company |

SOURCE: Based on R. Vance, *Employee Engagement and Commitment* (Alexandria, VA: Society for Human Resource Management, 2006).

designed to be meaningful and allows employees to use a variety of their skills relates to several different aspects of engagement including satisfaction, intention to stay, pride, and opportunity to perform challenging work.

## EVIDENCE-BASED HR

Consider Fabick Caterpillar (CAT), a company that sells, rents, and repairs Caterpillar construction equipment.[55] The company serves construction businesses and contractors in Missouri and southern Illinois and pipeline contractors throughout the world. Fabick CAT has more than 600 employees in 12 locations, each considered a separate operation, with headquarters in Fenton, Missouri. The business that Doug Fabick inherited from his father in 1999 wasn't in the top 25 percent of CAT dealerships in the United States. Fabick tried to understand how some CAT dealerships around the country performed better than others by studying traditional financial indicators, but he could find no common trend. Fabick conducted several yearly assessments of employee engagement in 2003 and 2004 and the results were not good: only 16 percent of employees were engaged. One parts department had highly engaged employees and Fabick discovered that human resource practices were responsible for success. As a result, Fabick began investing in developing the talents and strengths of parts, service, and operations managers. Managers were trained in how to increase engagement, including how to best select managers and new employees who had the right skills and abilities to succeed in their jobs. The new human resource practices had a major impact on the company's "bottom line." When sales groups were divided by engagement level into top half and bottom half and compared, the top half increased their percentage of industry net sales by 24 percent compared to only 8 percent in the lower engagement group. Also, sales groups in the top half had overall customer engagement scores that were 8 percent higher compared to sales groups in the bottom half.

***Talent Management.*** Talent management involves attracting, retaining, developing, and motivating highly skilled employees and managers. Companies report that one of the most important talent management challenges they face is developing existing employees for managerial positions and attracting and retaining top level managers in leadership positions.[56] For example, consider Schwan Foods and Sony Ericsson Mobile Communications programs.[57] Schwan Food company, makers of frozen pizzas and pies, is selecting employees with leadership talent to attend programs involving management classes and coaching sessions. These employees, considered "high-potential" managers, also receive challenging job assignments that require them to capitalize on their skill strengths and develop new skill sets (such as helping to launch a new joint venture in Mexico). The goal of Sony Ericsson Mobile Communications' Across Boundaries program is to develop general managers who are knowledgeable of the business operations and can succeed in the global market. The program involves giving managers global experiences in operations in different countries in Latin America and Europe and different functional experiences by moving them from marketing to sales, for example.

**Alternative Work Arrangements**
Independent contractors, on-call workers, temporary workers, and contract company workers who are not employed full-time by the company.

***Use of Alternative Work Arrangements.*** **Alternative work arrangements** include use of independent contractors, on-call workers, temporary workers, and contract company workers. The Bureau of Labor Statistics estimates that alternative work arrangements make up 11 percent of total employment.[58] There are 10.3 million independent contractors, 2.5 million on-call workers, 1.2 million temporary help agency workers, and approximately 813, 000 workers provided by contract firms. Since 2001 the proportion of total employed workers who were independent contractors has increased approximately 6 percent but the proportion is similar for the other alternative arrangements. Contingent workers, or workers who do not expect their jobs to last or who believe their jobs are temporary, account for approximately 2 to 4 percent of total employment.

More workers in alternative employment relationships are choosing these arrangements. Alternative work arrangements can benefit both individuals and employers. More and more individuals don't want to be attached to any one company. They want the flexibility to work when and where they choose. They may want to work fewer hours to effectively balance work and family responsibilities. Also, individuals who have been downsized may choose alternative work arrangements while they are seeking full-time employment. From the company perspective, it is easier to add temporary employees when they are needed and easier to terminate their employment when they are not needed. Part-time workers can be a valuable source of skills that current employees may not have and are needed for a specific project that has a set completion date. Nike uses 3,700 temporary employees each year as part of its global workforce of 28,000.[59] The temporary employees help Nike deal with cyclical labor needs during the business cycle and ongoing needs for specialized talent to meet strategic initiatives such as new-product development or retail store concepts. Companies like BMW are using contingent workers to help staff new production lines and also to take over old production lines while permanent employees train for and move to a new production process. Employees who may elect alternative work arrangements include those with a wide range and level of skills such as teachers, engineers, managers, administrative assistants, nurses, and bank tellers.

***Demanding Work, but with More Flexibility.*** The globalization of the world economy and the development of e-commerce have made the notion of a 40-hour work week obsolete. As a result, companies need to be staffed 24 hours a day, seven days a week. Employees in manufacturing environments and service call centers are being asked to move from 8- to 12-hour days or to work afternoon or midnight shifts. Similarly, professional employees face long hours and and work demands that spill over into their personal lives. Personal data assistants (PDAs), pagers, and cell phones bombard employees with information and work demands. In the car, on vacation, on planes, and even in the bathroom, employees can be interrupted by work demands. More demanding work results in greater employee stress, less satisfied employees, loss of productivity, and higher turnover—all of which are costly for companies.

Many companies are taking steps to provide more flexible work schedules, protect employees' free time, and more productively use employees' work time. Employees consider flexible schedules a valuable way to ease the pressures and conflicts of trying to balance work and nonwork activities. Employers are using flexible schedules to recruit and retain employees and to increase satisfaction and productivity.

Best Buy, the largest consumer electronics outlet in the United States, created a radical new workplace in response to concerns of headquarters' employees that their managers lacked trust that they would do their work without close supervision and that employee evaluations were being influenced by whether they looked busy and filled up their schedule with meetings that created the appearance of work.[60] The Results-Only Work Environment (ROWE) allows employees to decide how, when, and where they get the job done. Whether they choose to work in the office or somewhere else, salaried

The Results-Only Work Environment (ROWE) at Best Buy has dramatically changed the way employees at the company work. This alternative work arrangement allows them flexibility to get their work done when and where they wish, as long as they continue to meet productivity goals.

employees are required to put in as much time as it takes to do the work. The goal of the experiment is to reshape the workplace, achieve a greater degree of work/life balance, and redefine the nature of work. Physical attendance at meetings is optional. The only requirement is that employees meet productivity goals. When employee relations manager Steve Hance participates in a morning teleconference with co-workers or corporate clients he may be calling in using a cell phone from his fishing boat on a lake or from the woods where he hunts wild turkeys. He says, "No one at Best Buy really knows where I am. Nor do they really care." Surveys of employees who work in divisions that have converted to ROWE suggest they have improved relationships with family and friends and are more engaged at work. They feel more focused and energized about their work and are more committed to the company. The ROWE and its implications for employee retention are discussed in Chapter 10.

Dow Corning has a no-meetings week once a quarter which allows employees to reduce travel and work without interruptions.[61] The no-meeting weeks allow employees such as Laura Asiala, a global manager, a break from her normal workday, which starts as early as 5 AM and lasts as late as midnight. The no-meetings weeks give her the opportunity to spend evenings with her two sons, free from overseas calls. IBM has "ThinkFridays," free time on Friday afternoons, which IBM programmers spread across three continents can use to research new technologies or work on papers or patents, free from phone calls, e-mails, and instant messaging.

## Meeting the Needs of Stakeholders, Shareholders, Customers, Employees, and Community

As we mentioned earlier, company effectiveness and competitiveness are determined by whether the company satisfies the needs of stakeholders. Stakeholders include stockholders (who want a return on their investment), customers (who want a high-quality product or service), and employees (who desire interesting work and reasonable compensation for their services). The community, which wants the company to contribute to activities and projects and minimize pollution of the environment, is also an important stakeholder.

**Balanced Scorecard**
A means of performance measurement that gives managers a chance to look at their company from the perspectives of internal and external customers, employees, and shareholders.

***Measuring Performance to Stakeholders: The Balanced Scorecard.*** The **balanced scorecard** gives managers an indication of the performance of a company based on the degree to which stakeholder needs are satisfied; it depicts the company from the perspective of internal and external customers, employees, and shareholders.[62] The balanced scorecard is important because it brings together most of the features that a company needs to focus on to be competitive. These include being customer-focused, improving quality, emphasizing teamwork, reducing new product and service development times, and managing for the long term.

The balanced scorecard differs from traditional measures of company performance by emphasizing that the critical indicators chosen are based on the company's business strategy and competitive demands. Companies need to customize their balanced scorecards based on different market situations, products, and competitive environments.

**LO3**
Discuss How Human Resource Management Affects a Company's Balanced Scorecard.

The balanced scorecard can be useful in managing human resources. Communicating the scorecard to employees gives them a framework that helps them see the goals and strategies of the company, how these goals and strategies are measured, and how

**table 1.9**

The Balanced Scorecard

| PERSPECTIVE | QUESTIONS ANSWERED | EXAMPLES OF CRITICAL BUSINESS INDICATORS | EXAMPLES OF CRITICAL HR INDICATORS |
|---|---|---|---|
| Customer | How do customers see us? | Time, quality, performance, service, cost | Employee satisfaction with HR department services Employee perceptions of the company as an employer |
| Internal | What must we excel at? | Processes that influence customer satisfaction, availability of information on service and/or manufacturing processes | Training costs per employee, turnover rates, time to fill open positions |
| Innovation and learning | Can we continue to improve and create value? | Improve operating efficiency, launch new products, continuous improvement, empowering of workforce, employee satisfaction | Employee/skills competency levels, engagement survey results, change management capability |
| Financial | How do we look to shareholders? | Profitability, growth, shareholder value | Compensation and benefits per employee, turnover costs, profits per employee, revenues per employee |

SOURCE: Based on B. Becker, M. Huselid, and D. Ulrich, "*The HR Scorecard: Linking People, Strategy, and Performance* (Boston: Harvard Business School Press, 2001).

they influence the critical indicators. For example, Chase Manhattan Bank used the balanced scorecard to change the behavior of customer service representatives.[63] Before the company implemented the scorecard, if a customer requested a change in a banking service, the representative would have simply met the customer's need. Based on knowledge of the scorecard, the customer service representative might now ask if the customer is interested in the bank's other services such as financial planning, mortgages, loans, or insurance.

The balanced scorecard should be used to (1) link human resource management activities to the company's business strategy and (2) evaluate the extent to which the HRM function is helping the company meet its strategic objectives. Measures of HRM practices primarily relate to productivity, people, and process.[64] Productivity measures involve determining output per employee (such as revenue per employee). Measuring people includes assessing employees' behavior, attitudes, or knowledge. Process measures focus on assessing employees' satisfaction with people systems within the company. People systems can include the performance management system, the compensation and benefits system, and the development system. To show that HRM activities contribute to a company's competitive advantage, managers need to consider the questions shown in Table 1.9 and be able to identify critical indicators or metrics related to human resources. As shown in the last column of Table 1.9, critical indicators of HR practices primarily relate to people, productivity, and processes.

For example, at Tellabs, a company that provides communication service products (such as optical networking) around the world, key results tracked on the balanced scorecard include revenue growth, customer satisfaction, time to market for new

## COMPETING THROUGH SUSTAINABILITY

### Valero Energy Values Employees to Sustain Growth

A growing number of business leaders are making social responsibility an important part of their business strategy. A study by the society for Human Resource Management found that in the United States, over two-thirds of HR professionals report they are directly involved in community outreach programs or corporate social responsibility programs.

Valero Energy has experienced a remarkable 26 years of growth. Founded in 1980, Valero Energy is the largest refining company in North America, with 22,000 employees and assets of $33 billion. Valero Energy is consistently ranked among the best places to work and in 2006 reached number three on *Fortune* magazine's "100 Best Company's to Work For." *Investors Business Daily* ranked Valero number three on its "Big Cap Twenty" of top performers in the Standard & Poor's 500 Index.

Bill Greehey, chairman of Valero Energy, says his formula for success is care for your employees more than you care for yourself. Employees see Greehey as a regular guy who behaves in ways that show that people are the company's most important asset. Greehey believes the company's current success is due to several factors. The company has never laid off a single employee. Valero Energy offers the best salary and benefits and gives all employees stock options. Every employee has received at least one month's bonus pay in each of the past several years. Safety is emphasized. Of the 23 refineries designated by the Occupational Health and Safety Administration as having the best safety program, 11 are Valero units. Everyone is treated equally and with equal respect and no employee is talked down to. Respect and a caring attitude toward all employees is an important part of the culture. For example, the company purchased 60 house trailers in advance of Hurricane Katrina to provide emergency housing to anyone who needed it and collected food, supplies, and equipment at one of its retail distribution centers in Texas. Employees from the company headquarters in San Antonio cooked and prepared food in the areas hit by the hurricane. Every Valero employee who showed up at the refinery was given $1,500 in cash because all the banks were closed—and the money did not have to be paid back. Valero employees bought and distributed new clothes to anyone who needed them.

Valero Energy encourages employees to get involved and give back to the community. Besides benefiting the communities, the volunteer work helps build strong feelings of camaraderie and teamwork. The caring attitude and culture has not only resulted in the company being one of the best companies for shareholder returns but also one of the best companies for giving back to the community. Valero has twice won the United Way of America's Spirit of America Award, which honors the best companies for giving back to their communities.

Valero has grown rapidly in recent years through acquisitions and mergers. Not surprisingly, Greehey emphasizes that the acquired employees be treated by his company better than they were treated by their previous employers. As soon as a company is purchased HR is on site talking to employees about salary, benefits, and retirement plans. They learn of all the special events and recognition programs sponsored by the company. Greehey himself meets with management to discuss the company culture and strategic vision, and to understand their concerns. After the meetings, a barbecue is held in which senior management serves all employees at the refinery. He always schedules a follow-up trip a year later to visit the refinery and make sure that his company has lived up to his word.

For Greehey the key to sustaining success is to be a growth company and continue to offer more opportunities for employees. Employees have to feel that they are an important part of the company's success and they have the opportunity to develop their job skills. He doesn't emphasize expenses. Rather, he believes that employees and managers have to spend more time on how to improve operations, how to increase yields, how to increase refinery capacity, and how to make the company run better.

SOURCES: Based on B. Leonard, "Taking Care of Their Own," *HR Magazine*, June 2006, pp. 112–15; R. Levering and M. Moskowitz, "The 100 Best Companies to Work For: In Good Company," *Fortune*, January 22, 2007, pp. 94–116; J. Schramm, "Social Responsibility and HR Strategy" *Workplace Visions*, 2 (2007, Alexandria, VA: Society for Human Resource Management).

products, and employee satisfaction.[65] Every employee has a bonus plan; bonuses are tied to performance as measured by the scorecard. The performance appraisal process measures employee performance according to departmental objectives that support the scorecard. At quarterly meetings, how employee performance is evaluated according to the scorecard is shared with every employee, and the information is also available on the company intranet Web site.

***Social Responsibility.*** Increasingly, companies are recognizing that social responsibility can help boost a company's image with customers, gain access to new markets, and help attract and retain talented employees. Companies thus try to meet shareholder and general public demands that they be more socially, ethically, and environmentally responsible. For example, Bill Gates, former chief executive officer and Microsoft Corporation founder, through personal involvement in a charitable foundation dedicated to bringing science and technology to improve lives around the world, has improved Microsoft's corporate reputation. Whole Foods has been praised as environmentally and socially responsible for its focus on high-quality organic products.[66] Other companies such as Halliburton and BP are viewed less positively due to perceptions that they are responsible for environmental damage or are using political connections to profit from the Iraq war.

Cell phone manufacturers such as Nokia, Motorola, and Palm are introducing phones that have fewer toxic materials and are easily recyclable. This helps these companies improve their image in the marketplace and helps them get better access to global markets in which new rules and laws restrict the amount of toxic substances (such as lead and mercury) in electronics. [67] Virgin Group's Chairman Richard Branson has pledged to use $3 billion of Virgin's profit in fighting climate change.

Danone, a company that makes yogurts (Danon) and mineral waters (Evian), recently invested in a factory in Bangladesh to make a yogurt fortified to help stop malnutrition and priced at seven cents to be affordable. [68] This investment gives Danone access to a large market for its products, demonstrates the company is socially responsible, and at the same time helps alleviate local malnutrition as well as creating jobs.

The "Competing through Sustainability" box shows how Valero Energy has sustained growth through creating a positive work environment for employees while practicing social responsibility.

## Customer Service and Quality Emphasis

Companies' customers judge quality and performance. As a result, customer excellence requires attention to product and service features as well as to interactions with customers. Customer-driven excellence includes understanding what the customer wants and anticipating future needs. Customer-driven excellence includes reducing defects and errors, meeting specifications, and reducing complaints. How the company recovers from defects and errors is also important for retaining and attracting customers.

Due to increased availability of knowledge and competition, consumers are very knowledgeable and expect excellent service. This presents a challenge for employees who interact with customers. The way in which clerks, sales staff, front-desk personnel, and service providers interact with customers influences a company's reputation and financial performance. Employees need product knowledge and service skills, and they need to be clear about the types of decisions they can make when dealing with customers.

To compete in today's economy, whether on a local or global level, companies need to provide a quality product or service. If companies do not adhere to quality standards, their ability to sell their product or service to vendors, suppliers, or customers will be restricted. Some countries even have quality standards that companies must meet to conduct business there. **Total Quality Management (TQM)** is a companywide effort to continuously improve the ways people, machines, and systems accomplish work.[69] Core values of TQM include the following:[70]

**Total Quality Management (TQM)**
A cooperative form of doing business that relies on the talents and capabilities of both labor and management to continually improve quality and productivity.

- Methods and processes are designed to meet the needs of internal and external customers.
- Every employee in the company receives training in quality.
- Quality is designed into a product or service so that errors are prevented from occurring rather than being detected and corrected.
- The company promotes cooperation with vendors, suppliers, and customers to improve quality and hold down costs.
- Managers measure progress with feedback based on data.

There is no universal definition of quality. The major differences in its various definitions relate to whether customer, product, or manufacturing process is emphasized. For example, quality expert W. Edwards Deming emphasized how well a product or service meets customer needs. Phillip Crosby's approach emphasizes how well the service or manufacturing process meets engineering standards.

**Malcolm Baldrige National Quality Award**
An award established in 1987 to promote quality awareness, to recognize quality achievements of U.S. companies, and to publicize successful quality strategies.

**ISO 9000:2000**
Quality standards adopted worldwide.

The emphasis on quality is seen in the establishment of the **Malcolm Baldrige National Quality Award** and the **ISO 9000:2000** quality standards. The Baldrige award, created by public law, is the highest level of national recognition for quality that a U.S. company can receive. To become eligible for the Baldrige, a company must complete a detailed application that consists of basic information about the firm as well as an in-depth presentation of how it addresses specific criteria related to quality improvement. The categories and point values for the Baldrige award are found in Table 1.10. The award is not given for specific products or services. Three awards may be given annually in each of these categories: manufacturing, service, small business, education, and health care. All applicants for the Baldrige Award undergo a rigorous examination process that takes from 300 to 1,000 hours. Applications are reviewed by an independent board of about 400 examiners who come primarily from the private sector. One of the major benefits of applying for the Baldrige Award is the feedback report from the examining team noting the company's strengths and areas for improvement.[71]

Park Place Lexus (PPL) is a winner of the 2005 Malcolm Baldrige National Quality Award in the small business category.[72] PPL is the first automobile dealership ever to receive the award. With 420 employees in two locations in the Dallas, Texas, area, PPL sells new and preowned Lexuses and other luxury vehicles, services luxury vehicles, and sells parts to the wholesale and retail markets. On a number of different quality and service measures, PPL was successful. For example, the company's gross profit had increased by 51 percent from 2000 to 2004 and it had the highest customer satisfaction index of any Lexus dealership in the United States. To support its quality and customer satisfaction goals, PPL uses a difficult hiring process that includes aptitude and personality tests to ensure that the company hires the right person for the right job. All positions at PPL have been analyzed and training requirements identified. Once hired, each employee has a training plan that includes classroom training, on-the-job training, coaching and mentoring, observation, and assessments. Employees also have the opportunity to work with their manager to develop a plan for how to reach a specific position at PPL. The learning focus helps motivate employees to achieve, which in

**table 1.10**

Categories and Point Values for the Malcolm Baldrige National Quality Award Examination

| | |
|---|---|
| **Leadership**<br>The way senior executives create and sustain corporate citizenship, customer focus, clear values, and expectations and promote quality and performance excellence | **120** |
| **Measurement, Analysis, and Knowledge Management**<br>The way the company selects, gathers, analyzes, manages, and improves its data, information, and knowledge assets | **90** |
| **Strategic Planning**<br>The way the company sets strategic direction, how it determines plan requirements, and how plan requirements relate to performance management | **85** |
| **Workforce Focus**<br>Company's efforts to develop and utilize the workforce and to maintain an environment conducive to full participation, continuous improvement, and personal and organizational growth | **85** |
| **Process Management**<br>Process design and control, including customer-focused design, product and service delivery, support services, and supply management | **85** |
| **Business Results**<br>Company's performance and improvement in key business areas (product, service, and supply quality; productivity; and operational effectiveness and related financial indicators) | **450** |
| **Customer and Market Focus**<br>Company's knowledge of the customer, customer service systems, responsiveness to customer, customer satisfaction | **85** |
| **Total Points** | **1,000** |

SOURCE: Based on 2007 Baldrige National Quality Program Criteria for Performance Excellence from the Web site for the National Institute of Standards and Technology, www.quality.nist.gov.

turn results in understanding of customer needs and the ability to deliver top quality customer service. To encourage employee engagement, employees hold monthly 50/50 meetings. Half of the meeting focuses on listening to employee ideas and concerns and the other half on solutions. PPL has also established performance standards for every activity that requires client contact including requiring phones to be answered within three rings and e-mail to be responded to within 24 hours. It has determined the key performance requirements for both service and sales departments such as fixing the car right the first time and providing an accurate estimate for repairs and service.

The ISO 9000:2000 standards were developed by the International Organization for Standardization (ISO) in Geneva, Switzerland.[73] ISO 9000 is the name of a family of standards (ISO 9000, 9001, 9004 and 10011) that include requirements for dealing with issues such as how to establish quality standards and document work processes to help companies understand quality system requirements. ISO 9000:2000 has been adopted as a quality standard in nearly 100 countries including Austria, Switzerland, Norway, Australia, and Japan. The ISO 9000:2000 standards apply to companies in many different industries—for example, manufacturing, processing, servicing, printing, forestry, electronics, steel, computing, legal services, and financial services. ISO 9001 is the most comprehensive standard because it covers product or service design and development, manufacturing, installation, and customer service. It includes the actual specification for a quality management system. ISO 9004 provides a guide for companies that want to improve.

Why are standards useful? Customers may want to check that the product they ordered from a supplier meets the purpose for which it is required. One of the most efficient ways to do this is when the specifications of the product have been defined in an International Standard. That way, both supplier and customer are on the same wavelength, even if they are based in different countries, because they are both using the same references. Today many products require testing for conformance with specifications or compliance with safety or other regulations before they can be put on many markets. Even simpler products may require supporting technical documentation that includes test data. With so much trade taking place across borders, it may just not be practical for these activities to be carried out by suppliers and customers, but rather by specialized third parties. In addition, national legislation may require such testing to be carried out by independent bodies, particularly when the products concerned have health or environmental implications. One example of an ISO standard is on the back cover of this book and nearly every other book. On the back cover is something called an ISBN number. ISBN stands for International Standard Book Number. Publishers and booksellers are very familiar with ISBN numbers, since they are the method through which books are ordered and bought. Try buying a book on the Internet, and you will soon learn the value of the ISBN number—there is a unique number for the book you want! And it is based on an ISO standard.

**Six Sigma Process**
System of measuring, analyzing, improving, and controlling processes once they meet quality standards.

In addition to competing for quality awards and seeking ISO certification, many companies are using the Six Sigma process. The **Six Sigma process** refers to a process of measuring, analyzing, improving, and then controlling processes once they have been brought within the narrow Six Sigma quality tolerances or standards. The objective of Six Sigma is to create a total business focus on serving the customer, that is, to deliver what customers really want when they want it. For example, at General Electric introducing the Six Sigma quality initiative meant going from approximately 35,000 defects per million operations—which is average for most companies, including GE—to fewer than 4 defects per million in every element of every process GE businesses perform—from manufacturing a locomotive part to servicing a credit card account to processing a mortgage application to answering a phone.[74] Training is an important component of the process. Six Sigma involves highly trained employees known as Champions, Master Black Belts, Black Belts, and Green Belts who lead and teach teams that are focusing on an ever-growing number of quality projects. The quality projects focus on improving efficiency and reducing errors in products and services. Today GE has over 100,000 employees trained in Six Sigma. Employees are working on more than 6,000 quality projects. Since 1996, when the Six Sigma quality initiative was started, it has produced more than $2 billion in benefits for GE.

In addition to developing products or providing services that meet customer needs, one of the most important ways to improve customer satisfaction is to improve the quality of employees' work experiences. Research shows that satisfied employees are more likely to provide high-quality customer service. Customers who receive high-quality service are more likely to be repeat customers. As Table 1.11 shows, companies that are recognized as providing elite customer service emphasize state-of the art human resource practices including rigorous employee selection, employee loyalty, training, and keeping employees satisfied by offering generous benefits.

**Internal Labor Force**
Labor force of current employees.

**External Labor Market**
Persons outside the firm who are actively seeking employment.

## Changing Demographics and Diversity of the Workforce

Company performance on the balanced scorecard is influenced by the characteristics of its labor force. The labor force of current employees is often referred to as the **internal labor force.** Employers identify and select new employees from the external labor market through recruiting and selection. The **external labor market** includes persons actively seeking employment. As a result, the skills and motivation of a company's internal labor force are influenced by the composition of the available labor

**table 1.11**

Examples of HR Practices That Enhance Customer Service

| |
|---|
| **Wegmans**<br>Gives away $59 million in scholarships to 19,000 employees. Senior managers sit side-by-side with employees listening in on phones in the company's call center. |
| **Ritz Carlton**<br>Despite having 20 service standards, front-line employees have flexibility to make customers' experiences more personal, unusual, and memorable. |
| **Four Seasons Hotels**<br>No employee gets a job before passing four interviews. Each employee receives a free nights' stay for himself or herself and a guest, along with free dinner at employee orientation. The free stay helps employees, most of whom otherwise could not afford to stay at the hotel, understand what being a customer feels like. They grade the hotel services such as time for room service to arrive and number of times a phone rings when calling the front desk. |
| **Cadillac**<br>Performance of repair technicians is carefully monitored to ensure they are not repeating mistakes in repairs. Dealers who maintain good customer service ratings based on customer surveys receive cash rewards. |
| **Starbucks**<br>Entry-level baristas get 24 hours of training that prepares them to stay calm and courteous in busy times |
| **Publix Super Markets**<br>Employees receive bonuses based on their unit's performance and share grants as part of their incentive plans |
| **Cabela**<br>Job candidates must pass a difficult 150-question test that measures their outdoor sports expertise |

SOURCE: Based on J. McGregor, "Customer Service Champs," *BusinessWeek,* March 5, 2007, pp. 52–64.

market (the external labor market). The skills and motivation of a company's internal labor force determine the need for training and development practices and the effectiveness of the company's compensation and reward systems.

Three important changes in the demographics and diversity of the workforce are projected. First, the average age of the workforce will increase. Second, the workforce will become more diverse in terms of gender and racial composition, and immigration will continue to affect the size and diversity of the workforce.

***Aging of the Workforce.*** Figure 1.5 compares the projected distribution of the age of the workforce in 2004 and 2014. In 2014, baby boomers will be 50–68 years old, and this age group will grow significantly from 2004 to 2014. The total size of the 2014 labor force is projected to be 162 million workers, with 34 million workers 55 years of age or older. The estimated 34 million workers 55 years of age or older is a 49 percent increase in the size of this age group from 2004–2014, suggesting that the labor force will continue to age.[75] This increase represents five times the 10 percent growth projected for the overall labor force! The aging population means companies are likely to employ a growing share of older workers—many in their second or third career. Older people want to work and many say they plan a working retirement. Despite myths to the contrary, worker performance and learning are not adversely affected by aging.[76] Older employees are willing and able to learn new technology. An emerging trend is for qualified older workers to ask to work part-time or for only a few months at a time as a means to transition to retirement. Employees and companies are redefining the meaning

figure 1.5
Comparison of the Age Distribution of the 2004 and 2014 Labor Force

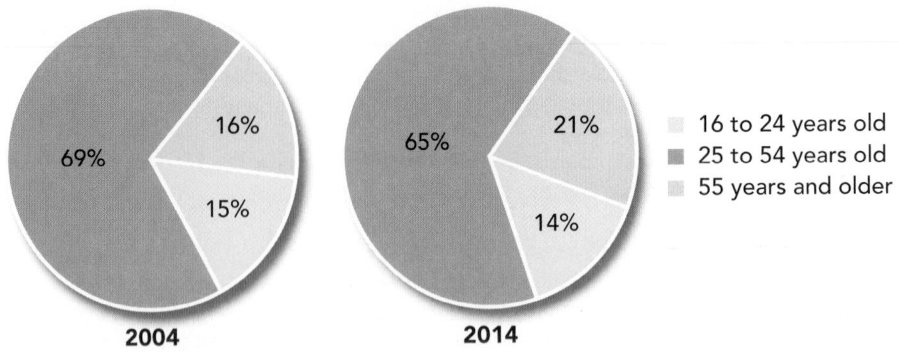


SOURCE: Based on M. Toossi, "Labor Force Projections to 2014: Retiring Boomers," *Monthly Labor Review,* November 2005, pp. 25–44.

of retirement to include second careers as well as part-time and temporary work assignments. An aging workforce means that employers will increasingly face HRM issues such as career plateauing, retirement planning, and retraining older workers to avoid skill obsolescence. Companies will struggle with how to control the rising costs of benefits and health care. Companies face competing challenges with older workers. Companies will have to ensure that older workers are not discriminated against in hiring, training, and workforce reduction decisions. At the same time companies will want to encourage retirement and make it financially and psychologically acceptable.

Consider how Borders Group, the book store, is capitalizing on older workers through hiring and retention.[77] Because 50 percent of book purchases in the United States are made by customers over 45, Borders believes that older workers can relate better to its customers. To attract and retain older workers, Borders added medical and dental benefits for part-time workers. The company is planning to add a "passport" program enabling employees to work half time in one part of the country and half time at a different store in another part of the country. This accommodates the needs of older employees who may live in warmer climates such as Florida during winter months but in other areas the rest of the year. Some 16 percent of Borders' employees are over the age of 50, over 75 percent more than when the program started. Borders' investment is having a positive impact on retention. The turnover rate for workers over 50 is 10 times less than for those under 30 years old, and turnover has dropped 30 percent since the start of the program.

As many older workers leave the workforce permanently or decide to work part-time, another challenge companies face is how to capture their unique knowledge and expertise so it can be used and shared with remaining employees. To ensure that the expertise of retiring engineers isn't lost, NASA is using phone interviews to capture their experiences.[78] The engineers have been designated as NASA Discipline Experts because each has been identified by NASA as an expert in a specific field of study such as propulsion or shuttle life support. The experiences captured on audiotape are turned into courses held at universities that offer graduate programs in aeronautics such as the University of Maryland. A similar approach is used at the federal Department of Housing and Urban Development, where many employees are now retirement-eligible.[79] Subject matter experts are identified and trained to conduct workshops or make presentations. The agency uses its own studios to videotape the presentations and broadcast the information to Housing and Urban Development sites across the United States. The video is made available on the company's internal Web site. When interviewers are used to "capture knowledge," it is important that they know what questions to ask and how to get the employee to talk about the

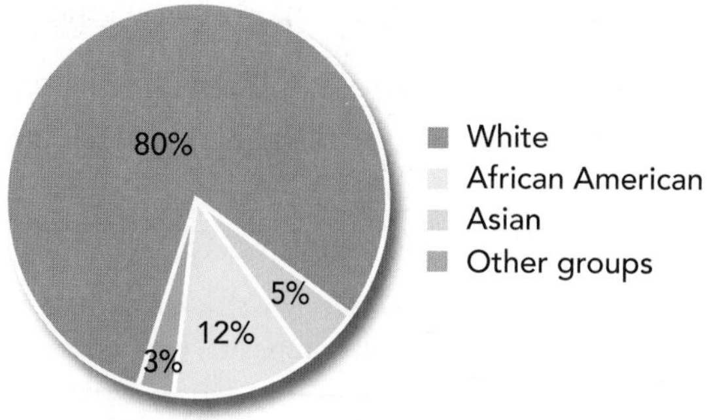


figure 1.6
The U.S. Workforce, 2014

SOURCES: Based on M. Toossi, "Labor Force Projections to 2014: Retiring Boomers," *Monthly Labor Review,* November 2005, pp. 25–44; "BLS Releases 2004–14 Employment Projections," U.S. Bureau of Labor Statistics Web site, www.stats.bls.gov.

knowledge. Many experienced employees may not recognize what is special about their personal knowledge and, as a result, have a difficult time speaking about it.

***Increased Diversity of Workforce.*** As Figure 1.6 shows, by 2014 the workforce is expected to be 80 percent white, 12 percent African America, 5 percent Asian, and 3 percent other groups, which includes individuals of multiple racial origin, American Indian, Alaskan Native or Native Hawaiian, and other Pacific Islanders.[80] Labor force participation of women in all age groups is expected to increase, while men's participation rates are expected to continue to decline for all age groups. Due to immigration contributing to population growth and with the high labor force participation rates of Hispanic and Asian groups, the diversity of the workforce is expected to increase from 2004–2014. Asians are expected to be the fastest growing segment of the workforce. By 2012 the size of the Hispanic labor force is expected to exceed that of the African-American labor force because of higher birth rates, immigration, and more Hispanic women in the workforce.

***Influence of Immigration.*** Many U.S. industries, including meatpacking, construction, farming, and service, rely on immigrants from Mexico and other countries to perform short-term or labor-intensive jobs. Although determining exactly the number of illegal workers in the United States is difficult, estimates are that of the hotel industry's 1.5 million employees, 150,000 are illegal immigrants, in the roofing industry one in three workers are thought to be illegal immigrants, and one-third of restaurant workers are Hispanic. While the U.S. government is debating how to deal with illegal immigration, many companies would face a labor crisis if they were forced to terminate employment of illegal immigrants, many of whom have lived and worked in the United States for years but lack the work authorizations and visas needed to work legally in this country. For example, one landscape company owner employs 60 people, including 40 immigrants. Without their labor, he would be out of business.[81] Even if employers do check immigrants' documentation, they have no way of knowing if the documents are real and may not even have a legal obligation to validate work documents. For example, in the California agriculture industry, farmers are required to check only that workers have the necessary papers and then forward the information to the government before putting a worker on the job.[82]

Many employers argue that most of the immigrants are hard-working and loyal and deserve to be granted legal status and citizenship. Others argue that illegal immigrants should be jailed or immediately extradited to their home country. While the national debate over this issue continues it is important to note that many midsized to small companies in the hotel, building cleaning, roofing, poultry, and construction industries could face a severe labor shortage crippling their businesses if immigration reform requires illegal immigrants to quit their jobs or return to their home countries before applying for work permits.[83] U.S. immigration and customs officials are increasing efforts to stop illegal immigration. Three top executives of a national cleaning service were arrested for allegedly employing illegal immigrants as well as nearly 200 employees believed to be illegal immigrants.[84]

Besides women and minorities another source of diversity in the workforce is disabled workers. Disabled workers can also be a source of competitive advantage. Wiscraft Inc., a Milwaukee company, contracts with companies such as Briggs & Stratton Corporation and Harley-Davidson to do assembly, packaging, and machining work.[85] At least 75 percent of Wiscraft's employees are legally blind. But the company is not a charity. It competes with other companies for contracts. It receives no subsidies from local, state, or federal governments. Employees have to rely on public transportation or friends or relatives to get to work. Kathy Walters said she could have worked at another company but chose Wiscraft because of its supportive culture. Walters, who is legally blind, believes she would have had trouble finding a job that offered health benefits and paid as well as her job at Wiscraft. The company has received ISO 9001:2000 certification, evidence that it provides high-quality work and can compete internationally.

The heterogeneous composition of the workforce challenges companies to create HRM practices that ensure that the talents, skills, and values of all employees are fully utilized to help deliver high-quality products and services.

Because the workforce is predicted to become more diverse in terms of age, ethnicity, and racial background, it is unlikely that one set of values will characterize all employees. For example, the "Silent Generation," born between 1925 and 1945, tend to be uncomfortable challenging the status quo and authority. They value income and employment security. "Baby boomers," born between 1946 and 1964, value unexpected rewards for work accomplishments, opportunities to learn new things, praise, recognition, and time with the manager. "Millennials," born between 1978 and 1999, love the latest technology, are ambitious and goal-oriented, and seek meaningful work. They want to be noticed, respected, and involved. Millennials work to live while boomers live to work. Companies are being proactive to help employees and managers understand generational differences. For example, both Georgia Power and CSX Corporation, a rail transportation company, provide training seminars that focus on identifying and understanding generational differences to get a better understanding of how people work.[86]

Most employees, however, value several aspects of work regardless of their background. Employees view work as a means to self-fulfillment—that is, a means to more fully use their skills and abilities, meet their interests, and allow them to live a desirable life-style.[87] One report indicated that employees who are given opportunities to fully use and develop their skills receive greater job responsibilities, believe the promotion system is fair, and have a trustworthy manager who represents the employees' best interests are more committed to their companies.[88] Fostering these values requires companies to develop HRM practices that provide more opportunity for individual contribution and entrepreneurship.[89] Because many employees place more value on the quality of nonwork activities and family life than on pay and production, employees will demand more flexible work policies that allow them to choose work hours and locations where work is performed.

The implications of the changing labor market for managing human resources are far-reaching. Because labor market growth will be primarily in female and minority populations, U.S. companies will have to ensure that employees and human resource

**table 1.12**

How Managing Cultural Diversity Can Provide Competitive Advantage

| | |
|---|---|
| 1. Cost argument | As organizations become more diverse, the cost of a poor job in integrating workers will increase. Those who handle this well will thus create cost advantages over those who don't. |
| 2. Employee attraction and retention argument | Companies develop reputations on favorability as prospective employers for women and ethnic minorities. Those with the best reputations for managing diversity will win the competition for the best personnel. As the labor pool shrinks and changes composition, this edge will become increasingly important. |
| 3. Marketing argument | For multinational organizations, the insight and cultural sensitivity that members with roots in other countries bring to the marketing effort should improve these efforts in important ways. The same rationale applies to marketing to subpopulations within domestic operations. |
| 4. Creativity argument | Diversity of perspectives and less emphasis on conformity to norms of the past (which characterize the modern approach to management of diversity) should improve the level of creativity. |
| 5. Problem-solving argument | Heterogeneity in decisions and problem-solving groups potentially produces better decisions through a wider range of perspectives and more thorough critical analysis of issues. |
| 6. System flexibility argument | An implication of the multicultural model for managing diversity is that the system will become less determinate, less standardized, and therefore more fluid. The increased fluidity should create greater flexibility to react to environmental changes (i.e., reactions should be faster and cost less). |

SOURCES: *Academy of Management Executive,* by T. H. Cox and S. Blake. Copyright © 1991 by Academy of Management. Reproduced with permission of Academy of Management via Copyright Clearance Center; N. Lockwood, *Workplace Diversity: Leveraging the Power of Difference for Competitive Advantage* (Alexandria, VA: Society for Human Resource Management, 2005).

management systems are free of bias to capitalize on the perspectives and values that women and minorities can contribute to improving product quality, customer service, product development, and market share. Managing cultural diversity involves many different activities, including creating an organizational culture that values diversity, ensuring that HRM systems are bias-free, facilitating higher career involvement of women, promoting knowledge and acceptance of cultural differences, ensuring involvement in education both within and outside the company, and dealing with employees' resistance to diversity.[90] Table 1.12 presents ways that managing cultural diversity can provide a competitive advantage. Traditionally, in many U.S. companies the costs of poorly managing cultural diversity were viewed mainly as increased legal fees associated with discrimination cases. However, as Table 1.12 illustrates, the implications of successfully managing a diverse workforce go beyond legal concerns. How diversity issues are managed has implications for creativity, problem solving, retaining good employees, and developing markets for the firm's products and services. To successfully manage a diverse workforce, managers must develop a new set of skills, including

1. Communicating effectively with employees from a wide variety of cultural backgrounds.
2. Coaching and developing employees of different ages, educational backgrounds, ethnicity, physical ability, and race.

3. Providing performance feedback that is based on objective outcomes rather than values and stereotypes that work against women, minorities, and handicapped persons by prejudging these persons' abilities and talents.
4. Creating a work environment that makes it comfortable for employees of all backgrounds to be creative and innovative.[91]
5. Recognizing and responding to generational issues.

Diversity is important for tapping all employees' creative, cultural, and communication skills and using those skills to provide competitive advantage as shown in Table 1.12. For example, the Latino Employee Network at Frito-Lay played a key role during the development of Doritos Guacamole Flavored Tortilla Chips.[92] The chips generated more than $500 million in sales during their first year, making this one of the most successful product launches in the company's history. Network members provided feedback on the taste and packaging to ensure that the product would be seen as authentic in the Latino community. Texas Instruments (TI) was interested in hiring a talented engineer but she was reluctant to accept employment because she feared the Dallas location would not welcome an Indian woman.[93] Representatives of TI's Indian Diversity Initiative spoke with her and shared their experiences. The Indian-American employee network was key in making her decision to join the company.

The retail grocer Safeway's market share is being challenged by specialty grocers and big-box stores such as Wal-Mart and Target.[94] To beat the competition Safeway invested in programs to attract, develop, and retain its best talent and to position the company as an employer of choice. Since 70 percent of its customers are women, Safeway wanted to broaden the diversity of its workforce to better reflect its customers. Male leaders had been the norm in the retail grocery industry, but Safeway took initiatives to help women and women of color advance into management. The initiatives included the CEO speaking regularly with employees about diversity issues in live discussions, and taped satellite broadcasts sent weekly to store managers. Employees have access to DVDs featuring interviews with successful employees who are women and people of color. The company ensures that all employees who qualify for its Retail Leadership Program (RLP) , including women who work part-time and used flextime to coordinate work schedules with family responsibilities, have the same opportunities for coaching, development, and advancement as employees who work traditional hours. A women's leadership network sponsors development meetings between high-potential women and executives who suggest new job opportunities that can help them advance to the next level. Every Safeway manager is expected to mentor his or her own employees. The women's programs have been very successful. Since 2000, the number of women store managers has increased by 42 percent, including an increase of 31 percent of white women and 92 percent of women of color. The number of women who completed the RLP program increased by 37 percent. Safeway has won national recognition as a company that promotes the career advancement of women and minorities. Independent financial analysts have concluded that the advancement of women and minorities has increased the company's sales and earnings.

The bottom line is that to gain a competitive advantage, companies must harness the power of the diverse workforce. These practices are needed not only to meet employee needs but to reduce turnover costs and ensure that customers receive the best service possible. The implication of diversity for HRM practices will be highlighted throughout this book. For example, from a staffing perspective, it is important to ensure that tests used to select employees are not biased against minority groups. From a work design perspective, employees need flexible schedules that allow them to meet nonwork needs. From a training perspective, it is clear that all employees need to be made aware of the potential damaging effects of stereotypes. From a compensation perspective, new benefits such as elder care and day care need to be included in reward systems to accommodate the needs of a diverse workforce.

## Legal and Ethical Issues

Five main areas of the legal environment have influenced human resource management over the past 25 years.[95] These areas are equal employment opportunity legislation, employee safety and health, employee pay and benefits, employee privacy, and job security. Attention is likely to continue to be paid to age, race, and religious discrimination, and discrimination against physically challenged employees.

There is also likely to be continued discussion about legislation to prohibit discrimination by employers and health insurers against employees based on their genetic makeup. Advances in medicine and genetics allow scientists to predict from DNA samples a person's likelihood of contracting certain diseases. To reduce health care costs, companies may want to use this information to screen out job candidates or reassign current employees who have a genetic predisposition to a disease that is triggered by exposure to certain working conditions. Legislation is being debated that permits genetic testing only to monitor the adverse effects of exposure to hazardous workplace contaminants (such as chemicals) and prohibits the requirement to provide or request predictive genetic information.

The number of court battles over company policies to reduce health care and other benefits costs is likely to increase. Many companies (such as IBM, Microsoft, and Harrah's Entertainment) are calculating the health care premiums that employees pay on the basis of their health and habits and participation in wellness programs (e.g., counseling, weight loss, smoking cessation, physical fitness). For example, Scott's Miracle-Gro has an antismoking policy designed to improve employee health and cut medical costs.[96] A two-week employee of Scott's Miracle-Grow who was fired when his drug test detected nicotine in his blood is suing the company, claiming that Scott's antismoking policy is discriminatory because the company fired him before he was eligible for health benefits and had the opportunity to take advantage of the company's wellness program (see the *BusinessWeek* case in Chapter 13).

Congress is considering a bill barring discrimination by employers and insurers based on genetic information.[97] The legislation would be the first federal law prohibiting health insurers from denying coverage or charging higher premiums based on genetic information. It would also prohibit companies from using genetic information to make hiring, firing, and other job placement decisions.

Although women and minorities are advancing into top management ranks, "glass ceilings" are still keeping women and minorities from getting the experiences necessary to move to top management positions.[98] A survey showed that women held only 10 percent of all of the corporate officer positions in the *Fortune* top 50 companies.[99] We are likely to see more challenges to sex and race discrimination focusing on lack of access to training and development opportunities that are needed to be considered for top management positions.

An area of litigation that will continue to have a major influence on HRM practices involves job security. As companies are forced to close plants and lay off employees because of restructuring, technology changes, or financial crisis, cases dealing with the illegal discharge of employees have increased. The issue of what constitutes employment at will—that is, employment that can be terminated at any time without notice—will be debated. As the age of the workforce increases, the number of cases dealing with age discrimination in layoffs, promotions, and benefits will likely rise. Employers' work rules, recruitment practices, and performance evaluation systems will need to be revised to ensure that these systems do not falsely communicate employment agreements the company does not intend to honor (such as lifetime employment) or discriminate on the basis of age.

Recent court rulings in discrimination and privacy cases suggest that companies need to pay more attention to extant electronic records and voice mails, where they might be found, and what the information contained in the records is used for.[100] Courts are likely to react negatively to informal nonstandardized communications of performance evaluations, pay raises, and other decisions from managers to employees using e-mail and voice mails.

Many decisions related to managing human resources are characterized by uncertainty. Ethics can be considered the fundamental principles by which employees and companies interact.[101] These principles should be considered in making business decisions and interacting with clients and customers. As a result of corporate scandals at Enron, Arthur Andersen, Tyco International, and WorldCom Inc., current interests in ethics focus on transparency and honesty in accounting systems as well as criminal behavior.

Ethical, successful companies can be characterized by four principles.[102] First, in their relationships with customers, vendors, and clients, these companies emphasize mutual benefits. Second, employees assume responsibility for the actions of the company. Third, such companies have a sense of purpose or vision the employees value and use in their day-to-day work. Finally, they emphasize fairness; that is, another person's interests count as much as their own.

**Sarbanes-Oxley Act of 2002**
A congressional act passed in response to illegal and unethical behavior by managers and executives. The Act sets stricter rules for business especially accounting practices including requiring more open and consistent disclosure of financial data, CEOs' assurance that the data is completely accurate, and provisions that affect the employee–employer relationship (e.g., development of a code of conduct for senior financial officers).

Corporate scandals such as those at Enron and WorldCom have increased attention on preventing illegal and unethical behavior by managers and executives. The **Sarbanes-Oxley Act of 2002** sets strict rules for corporate behavior and sets heavy fines and prison terms for noncompliance: Organizations are spending millions of dollars each year to comply with regulations under the Sarbanes-Oxley Act, which imposes criminal penalties for corporate governing and accounting lapses, including retaliation against whistle-blowers reporting violations of Security and Exchange Commission rules.[103] Due to Sarbanes-Oxley and new Security and Exchange Commission regulations that impose stricter standards for disclosing executive pay, corporate boards are paying more attention to executive pay as well as issues like leadership development and succession planning.[104] This has resulted in an increase in the number of HR executives and individuals with HR expertise who are being asked to serve on corporate boards to provide data and analysis. For example, a CEO or CFO who falsely represents company finances may be fined up to $1 million and/or imprisoned for up to 10 years. The penalty for willful violations is up to $5 million and/or 20 years imprisonment. The law requires CEOs and CFOs to certify corporate financial reports, prohibits personal loans to officers and directors, and prohibits insider trading during pension fund blackout periods.[105] A "blackout" is any period of more than three consecutive business days during which the company temporarily stops 50 percent or more of company plan participants or beneficiaries from acquiring, selling, or transferring an interest in any of the company's equity securities in the pension plan. The law also requires retention of all documents relevant to a government investigation.

The law also has a number of provisions that directly affect the employer–employee relationship.[106] For example, the act prohibits retaliation against whistle-blowers (individuals who have turned in the company or one of its officers for an illegal act) and government informants. To comply with the act, every employer will need to issue new policies. For example, the act requires all public companies to develop a code of ethics for senior financial officers. HR professionals will need to document the fact that employees have received these policies and have attended training to ensure their compliance with the act. Because of the potential liability for retaliation in the context of discrimination and harassment, policies should include assurances that an employee will not be retaliated against for making a complaint or for serving as a witness. Executive compensation programs will need to be reviewed and modified to ensure that the program is in compliance with the no personal loans and no sales of pension funds during blackout periods provisions.

One way for companies to cope with the responsibilities under Sarbanes-Oxley when a whistle-blowing complaint is made is through use of a ombudsman. British Petroleum America created an ombudsman position to make sure that concerns and complaints from employees, especially regarding safety, are heard.[107] The ombudsman is a former U.S. district court judge who is recognized for independence and integrity, so employees can be comfortable expressing their concerns. The ombudsman's job is to find the facts and resolve problems in as considerate, fair, thoughtful a way as possible. The position was developed in response to the lack of attention that managers paid to employees' complaints about pipeline corrosion and other problems at an oil field in Alaska that caused BP to shut down production, leading to a rise in oil prices.

Nationwide Insurance has a confidential employee "helpline."[108] Many of the calls require interaction between the company's three-person ethics staff and much larger HR staff. As is typical for most such help lines, about two-thirds of the calls concern issues squarely in HR's bailiwick—conflicts with co-workers, for example, or treatment by supervisors or sexual harassment. The reason, says Pat Hendey, director of associate relations, is that "a lot of times employees don't know who to call, but they always seem to be able to find the ethics hotline. What they like is that they can do it anonymously."

HR investigates many concerns, including employee allegations of internal conflicts of interest. The rest of the help-line cases are delegated to internal security, legal, and other departments for investigation. The ethics staff itself handles the legwork for only about 5 percent of the cases that come in via the help line. HR relies on ethics officers to look into issues such as potential conflicts of interest. For example, the ethics officers have checked out employees who would like to run a business or who want to go out and teach a particular course with a competitor. What brings HR and ethics into even closer quarters at Nationwide than at other companies is that Nationwide has moved beyond a compliance-based stance on ethics toward a "value-based" approach where expectations and transmission of ethical behavior become integral to the company culture. To promote an ethical culture, HR and the ethics office collaborate on activities such as the ethics office's periodic communications blitzes.

Human resource managers must satisfy three basic standards for their practices to be considered ethical.[109] First, HRM practices must result in the greatest good for the largest number of people. Second, employment practices must respect basic human rights of privacy, due process, consent, and free speech. Third, managers must treat employees and customers equitably and fairly. Throughout the book we will highlight ethical dilemmas in human resource management practices.

HRM ethics standards

## The Global Challenge

Companies are finding that to survive they must compete in international markets as well as fend off foreign corporations' attempts to gain ground in the United States. To meet these challenges, U.S. businesses must develop global markets, use their practices to improve global competitiveness, and better prepare employees for global

**LO4**
Discuss What Companies Should Do to Compete in the Global Marketplace.

assignments. The "Competing through Globalization" box shows how Procter & Gamble prepares its managers to be successful global business leaders.

Every business must be prepared to deal with the global economy. Global business expansion has been made easier by technology. The Internet allows data and information to be instantly accessible and sent around the world. The Internet, e-mail, and video conferencing enable business deals to be completed between companies thousands of miles apart.

Globalization has affected not just businesses with international operations. Companies without international operations may buy or use goods that have been produced overseas, hire employees with diverse backgrounds, or compete with foreign-owned companies operating within the United States. To succeed in the global marketplace the challenge for all businesses is to understand cultural differences and invest in human resources.

## Entering International Markets

Many companies are entering international markets by exporting their products overseas, building manufacturing facilities in other countries, entering into alliances with foreign companies, and engaging in e-commerce. Developing nations such as Taiwan, Indonesia, and China may account for over 60 percent of the world economy by 2020.[110] Globalization is not limited to a particular sector of the economy or product market. For example, Procter & Gamble is targeting feminine hygiene products to new markets such as Brazil. The demand for steel in China, India, and Brazil is expected to grow at three times the U.S. rate. Starbucks Coffee expanded into Beijing, China.[111] Competition for local managers exceeds the available supply. As a result, companies have to take steps to attract and retain managers. Starbucks researched the motivation and needs of the potential local management workforce. The company found that managers were moving from one local Western company to another for several reasons. In the traditional Chinese-owned companies, rules and regulations allow little creativity and autonomy. Also, in many joint U.S.–China ventures, local managers were not trusted. To avoid local management turnover, in its recruiting efforts Starbucks emphasized its casual culture and opportunities for development. Starbucks also spent considerable time in training. New managers were sent to Tacoma, Washington, to learn the corporate culture as well as the secrets of brewing flavorful coffee.

Besides training and developing local employees and managers, many companies are sending U.S. employees and managers to work in international locations. Cross-cultural training is important to prepare employees and their families for overseas assignments. Cross-cultural training prepares employees and their families (1) to understand the culture and norms of the country they are being relocated to and (2) to return to the United States after their assignment.

Cross-cultural training has become even more important since 9/11. Since 9/11 U.S. companies doing business overseas have recognized that many parts of the world have the potential to become dangerous.[112] Before 9/11 many U.S. employees working abroad had lived normal lives without any security concerns. But recent attacks and threats on American interests have shattered that sense of security. Overseas assignments are now considered more risky by many employees. Also, companies with a global workforce must manage across boundaries that are more nationalistic. Whereas most U.S. citizens have felt united in actions such as the invasion of Afghanistan, which they believe are justified as a valid response to hostile intentions, citizens of some countries consider the U.S. military response an act of aggression.

## COMPETING THROUGH GLOBALIZATION

### Successful Management Requires International Experience

As companies become more global, economic patterns and business practices in one area of the world can determine the success of a company on the other side of the world. At Procter & Gamble (P&G), being a successful global leader requires an international background. A majority of P&G's 140,000 employees work outside the United States. P&G uses international assignments for employees to learn how business is conducted in another country so that lessons learned can be applied at home or in another region. Only a quarter of relocations originate in the United States; the majority are from place to place across the world. An important goal of employees who receive international assignments is to develop local talent to replace themselves.

For example, a manager who is being prepared to take over a top finance position in Russia might go to Britain to gain experience working in a more structured and complex market. P&G managers in Europe must learn to keep the company's products on the shelves of big-box stores such as Carrefour, the European supermarket and discount chain and one of the largest retailers in the world. P&G might send junior U.S. managers to work with European managers who are responsible for products at Carrefour, expecting them to transfer skills learned in the United States when dealing with product placement in big-box retailers such as Wal-Mart and Costco. As Poland, Hungary, and the Czech Republic integrate into the European Union, their economies may become similar to those of England and Germany. The experience of managers in western Europe may be useful for transferring the knowledge to jobs in eastern Europe.

As a result of the emphasis on international experience, 39 of P&G's top 44 global officers have had an international assignment, and 22 were born outside the United States. This has produced a deep pool of internationally savvy managers who have produced results such as increasing P&G's business in China from less than $90 million to nearly $1 billion!

SOURCE: Based on M. Schoeff, "P&G Places a Premium on International Experience," *Workforce Management*, April 10, 2006, p. 28.

## Offshoring

**Offshoring**
Exporting jobs from developed to less developed countries.

**Offshoring** refers to the exporting of jobs from developed countries, such as the United States, to countries where labor and other costs are lower. India, Canada, China, Russia, Ireland, Mexico, Brazil, and the Philippines are some of the destination countries for offshored jobs. Why are jobs offshored?[113] The main reason is labor costs. Workers in other countries earn a fraction of the wages of American workers performing the same job. For example, Indian computer programmers receive about $10 an hour compared to $60 per hour earned by U.S. programmers. Other reasons include the availability of a highly skilled and motivated workforce. Both India and China have high numbers of engineering and science graduates. China graduated 325,000 engineers in 2004, five times as many as the United States. Each year, India graduates 2 million English-speaking students with strong technical and quantitative skills.[114] Finally, cheap global telecommunications costs allow companies with engineers 6,000 miles away to complete design work and interact with other engineers as if they were located in the office down the hall.

Initially, offshoring involved low-skilled manufacturing jobs with repeatable tasks and specific guidelines for how the work was to be completed. Offshoring now includes high-skilled manufacturing jobs and is also prevalent in the service and information technology sectors, for example, telephone call center, accounting bookkeeping and payroll, legal research, software engineers, architecture, and design.

For example, in contrast to computer and printer manufacturer Hewlett-Packard, which hired its first foreign workers 20 years after its founding in 1939, search engine Google employed people outside the United States just three years after its 1998 start.[115] OfficeTiger, which provides business services to banks, insurance companies, and other clients, has 200 employees in the United States and 2,000 in southern India. Whether its clients need typesetting or marketing research, Indian employees can submit their work over the Internet. Because Indian workers are generally paid only one-fifth U.S. earnings for comparable jobs, OfficeTiger offers attractive prices. The company is growing and expects that two-thirds of its future hires will be in India, Sri Lanka, and countries other than the United States.[116] Regardless of company size, talent comparable to that in the United States is available at lower costs overseas.[117] Gen3Partners, a Boston-based product innovation company, has a research and development lab in St. Petersburg, Russia, with 90 scientists and engineers, all with advanced degrees. Russia has a tradition of scientific excellence and comparable talent costs less than in the United States. For small companies such as Cobalt Group, a Seattle, Washington, automotive online services company, labor costs for its 50 research and development engineers who work in a technology center in India are about one-third of the U.S. costs.

However, as a result of 9/11 and concerns that American employees should get the first chance at U.S. jobs, immigration rules have made it difficult for immigrants to seek employment. Also, visa limits have restricted the number of highly skilled professionals and technical employees who can work in the United States. A maximum of 65,000 H1B visas, which allow a U.S. company to employ a foreign worker for up to six years, are made available each year, and all are taken on the first day they are available.[118] The US Senate is considering legislation which would impact immigrant employment.

Although companies may be attracted to offshoring because of potential lower labor costs, several other issues have emerged that are also important. First, can employees in the offshored locations provide a level of customer service the same as or higher than customers receive from U.S. operations? Second, would offshoring demoralize U.S. employees such that the gains from offshoring would be negated by lower motivation, lower satisfaction, and higher turnover? Third, are local managers adequately trained to motivate and retain offshore employees? Fourth, what is the potential effect, if any, of political unrest in the countries in which operations are offshored? Fifth, what effect would offshoring have on the public image of the company? Would customers or potential customers avoid purchasing products or services because they believe offshoring costs U.S. employees their jobs? Would offshoring have an adverse effect on recruiting new employees?

**Onshoring**
Exporting jobs to rural parts of the United States

Because of the disadvantages of offshoring discussed above and the total costs of working with different languages, cultures, and time zones, many companies are **onshoring,** or moving jobs to rural America.[119] Onshoring may be most attractive to companies that have brands tied to the United States because they fear the political fallout related to offshoring. Dell recently opened a call center in Twins Falls, Idaho, after closing one in India because of customer complaints. US Bank considered opening a call center in India but decided against it because of the bad publicity that would have resulted. US Bank chose instead to put the call center in Coeur d'Alene, Idaho, where the 500 new jobs would reduce the area's unemployment rate and make a difference in the quality of life in the community.[120]

There is considerable debate whether offshoring results in loss of jobs for Americans or actually creates new jobs. Smaller entrepreneurial companies are finding that offshoring helps them expand their business. For example, Xpitax, a 50-employee company in Braintree, Massachusetts, helps small accounting firms transfer the work of preparing clients' tax forms to a team of accountants in India. Trained in U.S. tax law, the accountants are paid the same wages per day as an American accountant can earn in one hour. The returns are prepared in 12 to 24 hours.[121] Companies such as GE Medical Systems are hiring highly skilled Indian engineers at lower wages than U.S. engineers receive (a top engineering graduate from India earns about one-eighth of U.S. starting pay) enabling the company to create better research and development teams to speed up product launches and prototype development and to upgrade quality.[122] This will allow GE Medical Systems and other companies to cut research and development costs, introduce new products, and save or create new jobs in the United States.

## The Technology Challenge

Technology has reshaped the way we play (e.g., games on the Internet), communicate (e.g., cell phones), plan our lives (e.g., electronic calendars that include Internet access), and where we work (e.g., small, powerful personal computers allow us to work at home, while we travel, and even while we lie on the beach!). The Internet has created a new business model—e-commerce, in which business transactions and relationships can be conducted electronically. The Internet is a global collection of computer networks that allows users to exchange data and information. More than two-thirds of all Americans age 12 or older have used the Internet; half of these users report they go online every day.[123] Nearly 70 percent access the Internet most often from home, while 17 percent do so from work. A full 86 percent are communicating with others via e-mail, and 50 percent are purchasing products or services.[124] For example, customers can now read *The Wall Street Journal* and many local newspapers online. They can send online greeting cards from Blue Mountain Arts. Through the Web you can purchase clothes, flowers, and airline tickets and even have someone pick up groceries for you. Companies can connect with job candidates across the world on www.monster.com.

### How and Where People Work

**LO5**
Identify the Characteristics of the Workforce and How They Influence Human Resource Management.

Advances in sophisticated technology along with reduced costs for the technology are changing many aspects of human resource management. Technological advances in electronics and communications software have made possible mobile technology such as personal digital assistants (PDAs) and iPods as well as improving the Internet. The Internet and the Web allow employees to send and receive information as well as to locate and gather resources, including software, reports, photos, and videos. The Internet gives employees instant access to experts whom they can communicate with and to newsgroups, which are bulletin boards dedicated to specific areas of interest, where employees can read, post, and respond to messages and articles. Internet sites also have home pages—mailboxes that identify the person or company and contain text, images, sounds, and video.

For example, Willow CSN is a provider of home-based call center agents (CyberAgents).[125] Willow contracts with businesses such as Office Depot, whose call centers need more employees at certain hours. The CyberAgents choose the shifts they want to work on a Web site. They work a variable number of hours ranging from 10 to

32 hours per week and are paid based on the number of calls they answer. They take calls at home using the same software and equipment as the agents at the client's call center. The agents are monitored and calls recorded just as though they were working in a traditional call center. They can get help from supervisors or co-workers in an online chat room.

Technology is pushing the boundaries of artificial intelligence, speech synthesis, wireless communications, and networked virtual reality.[126] Realistic graphics, dialogue, and sensory cues can now be stored onto tiny, inexpensive computer chips. These advances have the potential for freeing workers from going to a specific location to work and from traditional work schedules. For example, a recent survey found that 37 percent of employers offer telecommuting on a part-time basis and 23 percent on a full-time basis.[127] Telecommuting has the potential to increase employee productivity, encourage family-friendly work arrangements, and help reduce traffic and air pollution. But at the same time technologies may result in employees being on call 24 hours a day, seven days a week. Many companies are taking steps to provide more flexible work schedules to protect employees' free time and to more productively use employees' work time. For example, employees at Sun Microsystems can work almost anywhere and anytime because their work and information are available online.[128] Under Sun's iWork program, which uses both flexible hours and flexible workspaces, employees can work in several different locations. They may use Sun's flexible offices located in 12 drop-in centers, as well as 115 other locations around the world. The locations of the drop-in centers help employees reduce the amount of time they spend commuting to a central location. This also helps employees set up flexible arrangements where they can go to and from work to pick up and drop off family members, perhaps finishing work at home. They may also receive approval to work at home. Most employees are happy with the flexibility the program gives them including the convenience of choosing a location and the greater personal control over how to balance work and personal time. Sun is saving money by reducing office space and the expenses related to a traditional office arrangement.

## High-Performance Work Systems

**High-Performance-Work Systems**
Work systems that maximize the fit between the company's social system and technical system.

New technology causes changes in skill requirements and work roles and often results in redesigning work structures (e.g., using work teams).[129] **High-performance work systems** maximize the fit between the company's social system (employees) and its technical system.[130] For example, computer-integrated manufacturing uses robots and computers to automate the manufacturing process. The computer allows the production of different products simply by reprogramming the computer. As a result, laborer, material handler, operator/assembler, and maintenance jobs may be merged into one position. Computer-integrated manufacturing requires employees to monitor equipment and troubleshoot problems with sophisticated equipment, share information with other employees, and understand the relationships between all components of the manufacturing process.[131] Consider the changes Canon Inc., known for office imaging, computer peripherals, and cameras, has made to speed up the development and production process.[132] Canon is using a procedure called concurrent engineering, where production engineers work together with designers. This allows them to more easily exchange ideas to improve a product or make it easier to manufacture. Canon also now has production employees work in "cells," where they perform multiple tasks and can more easily improve the production process. Previously, employees worked in an assembly line controlled by a conveyor belt. The new cell system requires lower parts inventory and less space, cutting factory operating and

**LO6**
Discuss Human Resource Management Practices That Support High-Performance Work Systems.

real estate costs. Also, employees are more satisfied working in cells because they feel more responsibility for their work.

***Working in Teams.*** Through technology, the information needed to improve customer service and product quality becomes more accessible to employees. This means that employees are expected to take more responsibility for satisfying the customer and determining how they perform their jobs. One of the most popular methods for increasing employee responsibility and control is work teams. *Work teams* involve employees with various skills who interact to assemble a product or provide a service. Work teams may assume many of the activities usually reserved for managers, including selecting new team members, scheduling work, and coordinating activities with customers and other units in the company. To give teams maximum flexibility, cross training of team members occurs. *Cross training* refers to training employees in a wide range of skills so they can fill any of the roles needed to be performed on the team.

Use of new technology and work designs such as work teams needs to be supported by specific human resource management practices. These practices include the following actions:

- Employees choose or select new employees or team members.
- Employees receive formal performance feedback and are involved in the performance improvement process.
- Ongoing training is emphasized and rewarded.
- Rewards and compensation are linked to company performance.
- Equipment and work processes encourage maximum flexibility and interaction between employees.
- Employees participate in planning changes in equipment, layout, and work methods.
- Employees understand how their jobs contribute to the finished product or service.

***Changes in Skill Requirements.*** High-performance work systems have implications for employee selection and training. Employees need job-specific knowledge and basic skills to work with the equipment created with the new technology. Because technology is often used as a means to achieve product diversification and customization, employees must have the ability to listen and communicate with customers. Interpersonal skills, such as negotiation and conflict management, and problem-solving skills are more important than physical strength, coordination, and fine-motor skills—previous job requirements for many manufacturing and service jobs. Although technological advances have made it possible for employees to improve products and services, managers must empower employees to make changes.

***Working in Partnerships.*** Besides changing the way that products are built or services are provided within companies, technology has allowed companies to form partnerships with one or more other companies. **Virtual teams** refer to teams that are separated by time, geographic distance, culture, and/or organizational boundaries and that rely almost exclusively on technology (e-mail, Internet, video conferencing) to interact and complete their projects. Virtual teams can be formed within one company whose facilities are scattered throughout the country or the world. A company may also use virtual teams in partnerships with suppliers or competitors to pull together the necessary talent to complete a project or speed the delivery of a product to the marketplace. PriceWaterhouseCoopers's learning and education department has 190 employees who are located in 70 offices in different cities.[133] These employees work together on virtual teams that range in size from 5 to 50 people. Shared databases are

**Virtual Teams**
Teams that are separated by time, geographic distance, culture and/or organizational boundaries and rely exclusively on technology for interaction between team members.

used for background information and developing work, each office has videoconferencing, software is used to track calendars and connect employees via their personal computers to their virtual teams.

Employees must be trained in principles of employee selection, quality, and customer service. They need to understand financial data so they can see the link between their performance and company performance.

***Changes in Company Structure and Reporting Relationships.*** The traditional design of U.S. companies emphasizes efficiency, decision making by managers, and dissemination of information from the top of the company to lower levels. However, this structure will not be effective in the current work environment, in which personal computers give employees immediate access to information needed to complete customer orders or modify product lines. In the adaptive organizational structure, employees are in a constant state of learning and performance improvement. Employees are free to move wherever they are needed in the company. The adaptive organization is characterized by a core set of values or a vital vision that drives all organizational efforts.[134] Previously established boundaries between managers and employees, employees and customers, employees and vendors, and the various functions within the company are abandoned. Employees, managers, vendors, customers, and suppliers work together to improve service and product quality and to create new products and services. Line employees are trained in multiple jobs, communicate directly with suppliers and customers, and interact frequently with engineers, quality experts, and employees from other functions.

Consider the case of Putnam Investments, where the company culture and organizational structure may have contributed to unethical behavior.[135] Putnam has taken several steps in response to a corporate scandal in which portfolio managers were violating company policies by rapidly trading funds and allowing certain clients to do the same. The company believed that the unethical and illegal behavior was a result of a rigid hierarchical organizational structure and a hypercompetitive business environment. To create a more relaxed culture better for collaboration and reduced focus on short-term gains the CEO prepared guiding principles for the company including personal integrity, mutual respect, and the highest professional standards. Putnam reduced its staff to flatten the organization and give employees more autonomy and independence in their jobs. The flatter structure has provided more opportunities for retail and institutional portfolio managers to cross-sell investment products. To create a more collegial environment, dress is now business casual. Also, to increase employee involvement when developing human resource policies and practices Putnam now has an employee advisory council, which meets four time a year with the CEO.

**Electronic Human Resource Management (e-HRM)**
The processing and transmission of digitized information used in HRM.

***Increased Use and Availability of e-HRM and Human Resource Information Systems.*** **Electronic human resource management (e-HRM)** refers to the processing and transmission of digitized information used in HRM, including text, sound, and visual images from one computer or electronic device to another. New technologies and advances in software, including avatars, collaborative social networks, and mobile technologies such as personal digital assistants and iPods, are influencing training, development, work design, recruiting, and other aspects of HR. Table 1.13 shows the implications of e-HRM. For example, Capital One, a financial service company, uses an audio learning program that allows employees to learn through their iPods at their own convenience.[136] The company has also developed a mobile audio learning channel. The channel supplements competency-

**table 1.13**
Implications of e-HRM for HRM Practices

| HRM PRACTICE | IMPLICATIONS OF e-HRM |
|---|---|
| Analysis and design of work | Employees in geographically dispersed locations can work together in virtual teams using video, e-mail, and the Internet. |
| Recruiting | Post job openings online; candidates can apply for jobs online. |
| Training | Online learning can bring training to employees anywhere, anytime. |
| Selection | Online simulations, including tests, videos, and e-mail, can measure job candidates' ability to deal with real-life business challenges. |
| Compensation and benefits | Employees can review salary and bonus information and seek information about and enroll in benefit plans. |

based and leadership and management programs and other existing company training courses. It is also used to ensure that employees receive information when they need it. The Federal Aviation Administration (FAA) has 50,000 employees spread throughout the country.[137] Proposals that required input from employees spread throughout the country took years to complete. New software allows the FAA to create virtual shared workspaces for employees. FAA employees and industry experts can now interact in virtual "rooms" to debate ideas and work on shared documents. The virtual rooms have saved the FAA more than $3 million in travel costs and $2 million in employee time, and they have reduced the time needed for most proposals to become rules to one year. United Parcel Service (UPS) implemented a new software system that each evening maps out the next day's schedule for its drivers.[138] The software designs each route to minimize the number of left turns, reducing the time and gas that drivers waste at traffic lights. Customers get their packages on time and drivers can make it home in the evening for dinner.

Companies continue to use human resource information systems to store large quantities of employee data including personal information, training records, skills, compensation rates, absence records, and benefits usages and costs. A **human resource information system (HRIS)** is a computer system used to acquire, store, retrieve, and distribute information related to a company's human resources.[139] An HRIS can support strategic decision making, help the company avoid lawsuits, provide data for evaluating policies and programs, and support day-to-day HR decisions. Florida Power & Light Company, based in Juno Beach, Florida, uses HRIS applications to provide information to employees and to support decision making by managers. More than 10,000 employees in 20 states can use the information system to learn about their benefits. Managers use the system to track employees' vacation and sick days and to make changes in staffing and pay. Using the HRIS, managers can request the HRIS system to automatically prepare a personnel report; they no longer have to contact the HR department to request one.[140]

**Human Resource Information System (HRIS)**
A system used to acquire, store, manipulate, analyze, retrieve, and distribute HR information.

The use of company intranets, a network that uses Internet tools but limits access to authorized users in the company, and Web portals designed to serve as gateways to the Internet that highlight links to relevant information are becoming common practice. As we mentioned earlier in the chapter (in the discussion of how HR's role in administration is decreasing), company intranets and Web portals allow employees and managers online access to information about HR issues, offer self-enrollment programs, and provide feedback through surveys (self-service). Employees can look up workplace policies and information about training programs and enroll online, choose benefits and change salary deductions, and review employment contracts. Self-service at Mapics, a software developer based in Atlanta, allows managers and employees to keep track of vacation time.[141] This helps with scheduling and enables managers to encourage employees to use their remaining vacation time. Mapics changed its vacation policy to require that employees take their vacation time or lose it at the end of the year. Before self-service, Mapics lacked reliable information on company vacation time, resulting in a liability of a million dollars worth of accrued, unused vacation time. Self-service improved management and employee satisfaction with HR services at the same time it cut costs. The "Competing through Technology" box shows how Qualcomm has used its HRIS system and software to improve HR services.

More sophisticated systems extend management applications to decision making in areas such as compensation and performance management. Managers can schedule job interviews or performance appraisals, guided by the system to provide the necessary information and follow every step called for by the procedure.[142] One of the most creative uses of Internet technology is the development of HR dashboards. An **HR dashboard** is a series of indicators or metrics that managers and employees have access to on the company intranet or human resource information system. For example, Cisco Systems views building talent as a priority so it has added to its dashboard of people measures a metric to track how many people move and the reasons why.[143] This allows Cisco to identify divisions that are developing new talent.

**HR Dashboard**
HR metrics such as productivity, absenteeism that are accessible by employees and managers through the company intranet or human resource information system.

***Competitiveness in High-Performance Work Systems.*** Unfortunately, many managers have tended to consider technological and structural innovations independent of each other. That is, because of immediate demands for productivity, service, and short-term profitability, many managers implement a new technology (such as a networked computer system) or a new work design (like service teams organized by product) without considering how a new technology might influence the efficiency or effectiveness of the way work is organized.[144] Without integrating technology and structure, a company cannot maximize production and service.

Human resource management practices that support high-performance work systems are shown in Table 1.14. The HRM practices involved include employee selection, performance management, training, work design, and compensation. These practices are designed to give employees skills, incentives, knowledge, and autonomy. Research studies suggest that high-performance work practices are usually associated with increases in productivity and long-term financial performance.[145] Research also suggests that it is more effective to improve HRM practices as a whole, rather than focus on one or two isolated practices (such as the pay system or selection system).[146] There may be a best HRM system, but whatever the company does, the practices must be aligned with each other and be consistent with the system if they are to positively affect company performance.[147] We will discuss this alignment in more detail in Chapters 2 and 16.

Consider how human resource management practices support the high-performance work system at the Global Engineering Manufacturing Alliance (GEMA) plant in Dundee, Michigan.[148] The plant is more automated and employs fewer workers than most engine plants, 275 compared to 600–2,000 employees at other engine plants.

**table 1.14**
How HRM Practices Support High-Performance Work Systems

| | |
|---|---|
| Staffing | • Employees participate in selecting new employees, e.g., peer interviews. |
| Work Design | • Employees understand how their jobs contribute to the finished product or service.<br>• Employees participate in planning changes in equipment, layout, and work methods.<br>• Work may be organized in teams.<br>• Job rotation used to develop skills.<br>• Equipment and work processes are structured and technology is used to encourage flexibility and interaction between employees.<br>• Work design allows employees to use a variety of skills.<br>• Decentralized decision making, reduced status distinctions, information sharing.<br>• Increased safety. |
| Training | • Ongoing training emphasized and rewarded.<br>• Training in finance and quality control methods. |
| Compensation | • Team-based performance pay.<br>• Part of compensation may be based on company or division financial performance. |
| Performance Management | • Employees receive performance feedback and are actively involved in the performance improvement process. |

SOURCES: Based on A. Zacharatos, J. Barling, and R. Iverson, "High Performance Work Systems and Occupational Safety," *Journal of Applied Psychology* 90 (2005), pp. 77–93; S. Way, "High Performance Work Systems and Intermediate Indicators of Performance within the U.S. Small Business Sector," *Journal of Management* 28 (2002), pp. 765–85; J. A. Neal and C. L. Tromley, "From Incremental Change to Retrofit: Creating High-Performance Work Systems," *Academy of Management Executive* 9 (1995), pp. 42–54; M. A. Huselid, "The Impact of Human Resource Management Practices on Turnover, Productivity, and Corporate Financial Performance," *Academy of Management Journal* 38 (1995), pp. 635–72.

The goal of the plant is to be the most productive engine plant in the world. The UAW endorsed the high-performance workplace because it recognized that the company needs to be competitive to avoid losing jobs. The implications of this work system for labor relations is discussed in Chapter 14.

The plant's hourly employees rotate jobs and shifts, increasing the company's flexibility. The plant's culture emphasizes problem solving and that anyone can do anything, anytime, anywhere. Everyone has the same title: team member or team leader. By rotating jobs the plant wants to keep workers motivated in their work and avoid injuries. Team leaders and engineers don't stay in their offices; they are expected to work on the shop floor as part of six-person teams. Contractors are also seen as part of the team, working alongside assembly workers and engineers and wearing the same uniforms. Most auto plants have a day and night shift with senior workers usually choosing to work the day shift. At GEMA, employees rotate shifts in crews of three, working 10 hours per day, four days per week, alternating between days and nights. Every third week of their rotation they get five days off in addition to any vacation time. Counseling is available to help employees adjust to the rotating work schedule. The work schedule allows the plant to be in operation 21 hours per day, 6 days per week, 294 days a year. But employees

## COMPETING THROUGH TECHNOLOGY

### Gambling on Homegrown Human Resource Software Pays for Qualcomm

Qualcomm, headquartered in San Diego, California, makes software and other products supporting next-generation wireless communication. One of the reasons why the company is successful and usually included on *Fortune* magazine's list of "100 Best Companies to Work for in America" (number 14 in 2007) is because of the usability of its human resource information system. Rather than relying on outside vendors to provide a human resource information system for its 9,300 employees and managers, Qualcomm developed its own system called MySource. Based on a Web portal, MySource can be used to generate employee profiles, pay stubs, benefits administration, benefits enrollment, performance evaluation, and training. An e-recruiting application for managers has features including candidate search, candidate tracking, new hire authorizations, and electronic offer letters. MySource also gives employees access to benefits enrollment, pay stubs, and links to company policies. A system dedicated just for new employees allows them to take care of benefits enrollment, read policies, and download forms that need to be completed such as W-4's.

Customizing its own system runs counter to large-company practice of buying software applications in bits and pieces from outside vendors such as Oracle. However, homegrown systems such as Qualcomm's do have significant advantages. Qualcomm built its Web portal for employee and manager self-service, from the employee's rather than the HR administrator's perspective, which is typically not the approach taken by software vendors. The advantage of taking the employee's perspective is that a wide variety of information useful to employees can be accessed at MySource including a to-do list, benefits enrollment, and links to company policies. Employees can even take the content they want from MySource to a personalized Internet page where they can view company news and stock quotes. MySource has reduced the irritation factors associated with employees completing necessary online tasks such as filling out weekly time cards and determining how many vacation days are available. It also has given HR staff more time to deal with complicated employment and benefits questions.

Having an inhouse 22-person staff dedicated to HR software systems may seem like a waste of company dollars, but it avoids vendors' upgrading charges and annual maintenance fees, which can cost millions of dollars. Also, Qualcomm has avoided the integration hassles that result from having to mesh new versions of business software with updates software or new applications. The company can focus on developing applications based on Qualcomm's priorities on an as-needed basis with the features desired by employees and managers. Qualcomm is able to enhance its system quickly in response to user requests. For example, as a result of wildfires in the San Diego area, Qualcomm added a mobile communications feature that allows managers to access data such as employees' phone numbers and emergency contact information using a cell phone.

Homegrown custom systems such as Qualcomm's can be costly and frequently cause problems; moreover, many vendors will work with companies to develop customized applications. But at Qualcomm, a homegrown system reflects the company's innovative and supportive culture. A Web-based HR portal makes sense at Qualcomm because many employees spend significant time at their computers. They would rather be working on technical challenges than having to wade through administrative HR red tape. Employees are very satisfied with the system. Ninety-nine percent of employees who responded to a survey said they were satisfied or very satisfied with the system. Qualcomm has even been asked to sell its HR software but declined as company executives decided to instead keep the focus on Qualcomm's core businesses.

MySource has resulted in increased manager productivity. Qualcomm managers estimate that MySource trimmed the time needed to conduct the twice yearly employee pay reviews by 160 hours. The time savings result in a month per year per manager that can be spent on other issues.

SOURCE: Based on E. Frauenheim, "Homegrown HR Technology," *Workforce Management*, July 17, 2006, pp. 32–38; "About Qualcomm" at www.qualcomm.com.

work only 196 days a year. The alternating shifts also help employees to know and work with each other and salaried employees, who work only during daytime.

To hire employees who could work in a team environment emphasizing problem solving and flexibility, GEMA recruited using local newspapers within 70 miles of Dundee. GEMA worked with local civil rights organizations to find diverse candidates. Nonexempt employees whose wages start at $21 and increase to $30 within five years must have a two-year technical degree, a skilled journeyman's card, or five years experience in advanced machining.

Job candidates have to make it through a difficult screening process that takes 12 hours. The process requires candidates to take tests, participate in team activities in which they confront challenges facing the plant (e.g., process in the plant is inefficient), and interviews with operations managers and team leaders. When the plant is ahead of its production schedule employees receive training in class and on the shop floor in topics such as how to assemble an engine to math skills.

GEMA gives employees access to technology that helps them monitor productivity. Large electronic screens hanging from the plant ceiling provide alerts of any machinery parts that are ending their lifespan and need to be replaced before they malfunction. A performance management system available on personal computers, as well as a display board, alerts employees to delays or breakdowns in productivity. This is different from most engine plants where only managers have access to this information. The technology empowers all employees to fix problems, not just managers or engineers. GEMA provides rewards and bonuses for employees who develop innovative problem solutions.

## Meeting Competitive Challenges through HRM Practices

**LO7**
Provide a Brief Description of Human Resource Management Practices.

We have discussed the global, stakeholder, new economy, and high-performance work system challenges U.S. companies are facing. We have emphasized that management of human resources plays a critical role in determining companies' success in meeting these challenges. HRM practices have not traditionally been seen as providing economic value to the company. Economic value is usually associated with equipment, technology, and facilities. However, HRM practices have been shown to be valuable. Compensation, staffing, training and development, performance management, and other HRM practices are investments that directly affect employees' motivation and ability to provide products and services that are valued by customers. Research has shown that companies that attempt to increase their competitiveness by investing in new technology and becoming involved in the quality movement also invest in state-of-the-art staffing, training, and compensation practices.[149] Figure 1.7 shows examples of human resource management practices that help companies deal with the three challenges. For example, to meet the sustainability challenge, companies need to identify through their selection processes whether prospective employees value customer relations and have the levels of interpersonal skills necessary to work with fellow employees in teams. To meet all three challenges, companies need to capitalize on the diversity of values, abilities, and perspectives that employees bring to the workplace.

HRM practices that help companies deal with the competitive challenges can be grouped into the four dimensions shown in Figure 1.8. These dimensions include the

figure 1.7
Examples of How HRM Practices Can Help Companies Meet Competitive Challenges

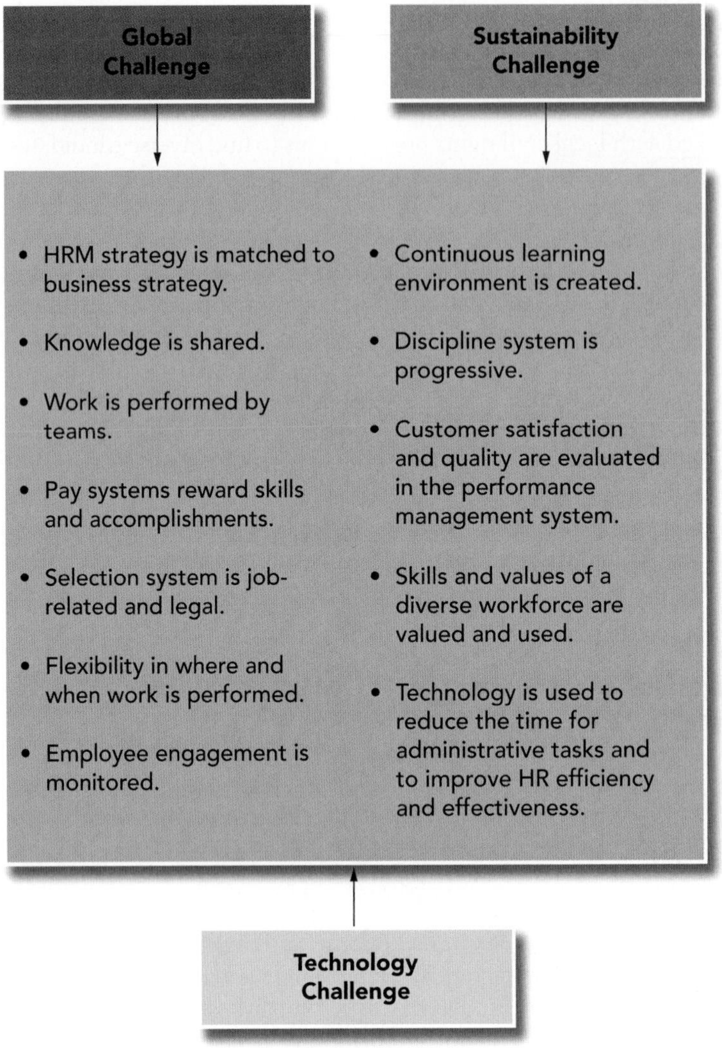


figure 1.8
Major Dimensions of HRM Practices Contributing to Company Competitiveness

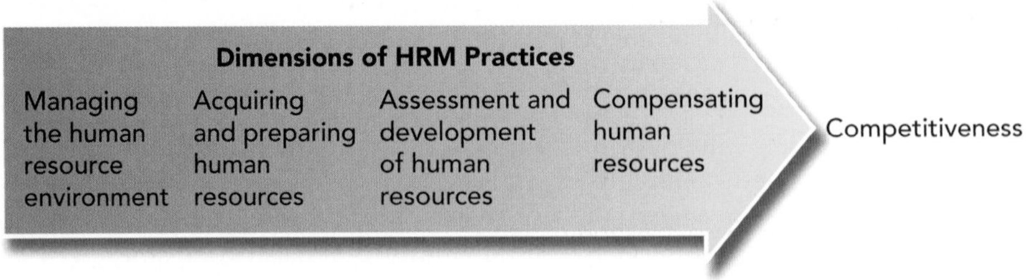


human resource environment, acquiring and preparing human resources, assessment and development of human resources, and compensating human resources. In addition, some companies have special issues related to labor–management relations, international human resource management, and managing the human resource function.

## Managing the Human Resource Environment

Managing internal and external environmental factors allows employees to make the greatest possible contribution to company productivity and competitiveness. Creating a positive environment for human resources involves

- Linking HRM practices to the company's business objectives—that is, strategic human resource management.
- Ensuring that HRM practices comply with federal, state, and local laws.
- Designing work that motivates and satisfies the employee as well as maximizes customer service, quality, and productivity.

## Acquiring and Preparing Human Resources

Customer needs for new products or services influence the number and type of employees businesses need to be successful. Terminations, promotions, and retirements also influence human resource requirements. Managers need to predict the number and type of employees who are needed to meet customer demands for products and services. Managers must also identify current or potential employees who can successfully deliver products and services. This area of human resource management deals with

- Identifying human resource requirements—that is, human resource planning, recruiting employees, and selecting employees.
- Training employees to have the skills needed to perform their jobs.

## Assessment and Development of Human Resources

Managers need to ensure that employees have the necessary skills to perform current and future jobs. As we discussed earlier, because of new technology and the quality movement, many companies are redesigning work so that it is performed by teams. As a result, managers and employees may need to develop new skills to succeed in a team environment. Companies need to create a work environment that supports employees' work and nonwork activities. This area of human resource management addresses

- Measuring employees' performance.
- Preparing employees for future work roles and identifying employees' work interests, goals, values, and other career issues.
- Creating an employment relationship and work environment that benefits both the company and the employee.

## Compensating Human Resources

Besides interesting work, pay and benefits are the most important incentives that companies can offer employees in exchange for contributing to productivity, quality, and customer service. Also, pay and benefits are used to reward employees' membership in the company and attract new employees. The positive influence of new work designs, new technology, and the quality movement on productivity can be damaged if employees are not satisfied with the level of pay and benefits or believe pay and benefits are unfairly distributed. This area of human resource management includes

- Creating pay systems.
- Rewarding employee contributions.
- Providing employees with benefits.

### Special Issues

In some companies, employees are represented by a labor union. Managing human resources in a union environment requires knowledge of specific laws, contract administration, and the collective bargaining process.

Many companies are globally expanding their business through joint ventures, mergers, acquisitions, and establishing new operations. Successful global expansion depends on the extent to which HRM practices are aligned with cultural factors as well as management of employees sent to work in another country. Human resource management practices must contribute to organizational effectiveness.

Human resource management practices of both managers and the human resource function must be aligned and contribute to the company's strategic goals. The final chapter of the book explains how to effectively integrate human resource management practices.

## Organization of This Book

The topics in this book are organized according to the four areas of human resource management and special issues. Table 1.15 lists the chapters covered in the book.

The content of each chapter is based on academic research and examples of effective company practices. Each chapter includes examples of how the human resource management practice covered in the chapter helps a company gain a competitive advantage by addressing sustainability, global, and technological challenges. Also, each chapter includes an example of a company that demonstrates how HR practices add value (evidence-based HR).

**table 1.15**

Topics Covered in This Book

| | |
|---|---|
| I | The Human Resource Environment |
| 2 | Strategic Human Resource Management |
| 3 | The Legal Environment: Equal Employment Opportunity and Safety |
| 4 | The Analysis and Design of Work |
| II | Acquisition and Preparation of Human Resources |
| 5 | Human Resource Planning and Recruitment |
| 6 | Selection and Placement |
| 7 | Training |
| III | Assessment and Development of HRM |
| 8 | Performance Management |
| 9 | Employee Development |
| 10 | Employee Separation and Retention |
| IV | Compensation of Human Resources |
| 11 | Pay Structure Decisions |
| 12 | Recognizing Employee Contributions with Pay |
| 13 | Employee Benefits |
| V | Special Topics in Human Resource Management |
| 14 | Collective Bargaining and Labor Relations |
| 15 | Managing Human Resources Globally |
| 16 | Strategically Managing the HRM Function |

## A Look Back

Starbucks is in the midst of an incredible expansion, growing 20 percent a year.

**Questions**

1. What HR practices do you believe are most critical for Starbucks to maintain the coffee experience and customer service it's known for as the company expands in the United States and abroad?
2. Do you think the culture and HR practices that appear to be effective at Starbucks would also help the bottom line at companies in other industries such as health care, manufacturing, or research and development? Explain why or why not.
3. Could Starbucks be as successful without its current HR practices? Explain.

Please see the Video Case that corresponds to this chapter online at www.mhhe.com/noe6e.

## Summary

This chapter introduced the roles and activities of a company's human resource management function and emphasized that effective management of human resources can contribute to a company's business strategy and competitive advantage. HR can be viewed as having three product lines: administrative services, business partner services, and strategic services. To successfully manage human resources, individuals need personal credibility, business knowledge, understanding of the business strategy, technology knowledge, and the ability to deliver HR services. Human resource management practices should be evidence-based, that is, based on data showing the relationship between the practice and business outcomes related to key company stakeholders (customers, shareholders, employees, community). In addition to contributing to a company's business strategy, human resource practices are important for helping companies deal with sustainability, globalization, and technology challenges. The sustainability challenges are related to the economy, the characteristics and expectations of the labor force, how and where work is done, the value placed on intangible assets and human capital, and meeting stakeholder needs (ethical practices, high-quality products and services, return to shareholders, and social responsibility). Global challenges include entering international markets, immigration, and offshoring. Technology challenges include using new technologies to support flexible and virtual work arrangements, high-performance work systems, and developing effective e-HRM practices and human resource information systems.

The chapter concludes by showing how the book is organized. The book includes four topical areas: the human resource environment (strategic HRM, legal, analysis and design of work), acquisition and preparation of human resources (HR planning and recruitment, selection, training), assessment and development of human resources (performance management, development, training), compensation of human resources (pay structures, recognizing employee contributions with pay, benefits), and special topics (collective bargaining and labor relations, managing human resources globally, and strategically managing the HR function). All of the topical areas are important for companies to deal with the competitive challenges and contribute to business strategy.

## Key Terms

Competitiveness, 4
Human resource management (HRM), 4
Outsourcing, 9
Self-service, 9
Evidence-based HR, 11
Stakeholders, 13
Sustainability, 13
Intangible assets, 18
Empowering, 19
Knowledge workers, 19
Learning organization, 20
Psychological contract, 20
Employee engagement, 21
Alternative work arrangements 22

Balanced scorecard, 24
ISO 9000:2000, 28
Malcolm Baldrige National Quality Award, 28
Total quality management (TQM), 28
External labor market, 30
Internal labor force, 30
Six Sigma process, 30
Sarbanes-Oxley Act of 2002, 38
Offshoring, 41
Onshoring, 42
High-performance work systems, 44
Virtual teams, 45
Electronic human resource management (e-HRM), 46
Human resource information system (HRIS), 47
HR dashboard, 48

## Discussion Questions

1. Traditionally, human resource management practices were developed and administered by the company's human resource department. Line managers are now playing a major role in developing and implementing HRM practices. Why do you think non-HR managers are becoming more involved in developing and implementing HRM practices?
2. Staffing, training, compensation, and performance management are important HRM functions. How can each of these functions help companies succeed in meeting the global challenge, the challenge of using new technology, and the sustainability challenge?
3. What are intangible assets? How are they influenced by human resource management practices?
4. What is "evidence-based HR"? Why might an HR department resist becoming evidence-based?
5. Do you agree with the statement "Employee engagement is something companies should be concerned about only if they are making money"? Explain.
6. This book covers four human resource management practice areas: managing the human resource environment, acquiring and preparing human resources, assessment and development of human resources, and compensating human resources. Which area do you believe contributes most to helping a company gain a competitive advantage? Which area do you believe contributes the least? Why?
7. What is the balanced scorecard? Identify the four perspectives included in the balanced scorecard. How can HRM practices influence the four perspectives?
8. Is HRM becoming more strategic? Explain your answer.
9. Explain the implications of each of the following labor force trends for HRM: (1) aging workforce, (2) diverse workforce, (3) skill deficiencies.
10. What role do HRM practices play in a business decision to expand internationally?
11. What might a quality goal and high-performance work systems have in common in terms of HRM practices?
12. What disadvantages might result from outsourcing HRM practices? From employee self-service? From increased line manager involvement in designing and using HR practices?
13. What factors should a company consider before offshoring? What are the advantages and disadvantages of offshoring?

## Self-Assessment Exercise: Do You Have What It Takes to Work in HR?

***Instructions:*** Read each statement and circle *yes* or *no*.

Yes No 1. I have leadership and management skills I have developed through prior job experiences, extracurricular activities, community service, or other noncourse activities.

Yes No 2. I have excellent communications, dispute resolution, and interpersonal skills.

Yes No 3. I can demonstrate an understanding of the fundamentals of running a business and making a profit.

Yes No 4. I can use spreadsheets and the World Wide Web, and I am familiar with information systems technology.

Yes No 5. I can work effectively with people of different cultural backgrounds.

Yes No 6. I have expertise in more than one area of human resource management.

***Scoring:*** The greater the number of yes answers, the better prepared you are to work in an HR department. For questions you answered *no*, you should seek courses and experiences to change your answer to *yes*—and better prepare yourself for a career in HR!

SOURCE: Based on B. E. Kaufman, "What Companies Want from HR Graduates," *HR Magazine*, September 1994.

## Exercising Strategy: Container Store Does Great HRM

The Container Store, a retailer of boxes, bags, racks, and shelves that organize everything from spices to shoes, is respected for its commitment to employees. The Dallas-based company has 2,000 employees in 11 states. The company has been ranked as one of the best companies to work for by *Fortune* magazine and has received awards for its people management strategies. The company's success is attributed to its low turnover rate (15–20 percent in an industry where 100 percent is common) and a strong customer service philosophy that allows employees to take ownership and make decisions they believe will benefit the customer. Company founders Kip Tindell and Garrett Boone attribute the financial success of the company to their belief that if employees are treated well, financial success will follow and their policies that prepare employees to offer exemplary customer service and recognize employee accomplishment and adherence to company values. The company invests more than 235 hours of training in first-year employees, far above the industry average of 7 hours per year. Employees are paid 50–100 percent above the industry average and benefits are offered to both full- and part-time employees. They communicate financial data and expansion plans to all employees to help build their sense of ownership in the company. Formal recognition plans include honoring employees on 10 years of service to the company by flying them and their spouses to Dallas for a staff meeting. Also, each year the Container Store treats 11 employees who best exemplify the values of the founders to a week-long vacation in Colorado (at one of the founder's cabin).

Until recently managers were responsible for many traditional human resource management functions such as attracting, motivating, and retaining employees. This is based on the philosophy that because managers are closest to employees they best understand what human resource management practices are necessary. The company now has a semiformal human resource management structure with recruiting, training, payroll, and benefits departments. HR managers are given responsibilities for other areas such as store operations and are required to take store-level positions so they can better understand the company's purpose. Most HRM employees begin with the company as salespeople. Despite the new HRM structure, managers take the lead in recruiting and evaluating potential employees as well as in employee training.

SOURCES: Based on R. Laglow, "Container Store Does Great HRM: Even without an HR Department," *HR Executive*, August 2001, p. 23; J. Labbs, "Thinking Outside the Box at the Container Store," *Workforce*, March 2001, pp. 34–38; S. Gale, "Hiking with the Honchos at the Container Store," *Workforce Management*, August 2003, pp. 80–82; P. Babcock, "Ensuring Lasting Foundations," *HR Magazine*, January 2004, pp. 48–52. Visit The Container Store's Web site at www.containerstore.com.

### Questions

1. As the Container Store continues to expand and grow (the company has grown at an annual rate of 20–25 percent), do you think the manager's role in human resource management should grow, shrink, or remain the same? Explain. Indicate what HRM practices managers should be responsible for and what practices should be the responsibility of human resource management staff?
2. Consider our discussion in this chapter of HR roles and competencies. What are the advantages and disadvantages for successfully performing these roles by having human resource management staff come from store-level positions?
3. Should the Container Store consider outsourcing any HRM practices? Which ones? How might they determine which ones?

## Managing People: From the Pages of *BusinessWeek*

BusinessWeek **An Extraordinary Stumble at JetBlue**

You've got to give the guy some credit. It's not every day that the CEO of a public company—especially a CEO who's just emerging from a crisis like the one JetBlue Airways CEO David Neeleman weathered recently—shows up on the *Late Show with David Letterman*. But there he was on national TV just after midnight on Feb. 21, suffering through guffaws at his expense ("We'll make him wait for a change," Letterman told Barbara Walters, who preceded Neeleman as a guest) and somberly promising that his airline would do better. "What will you do now," Letterman asked as the crowd roared, "to keep JetBlue from being the punchline to a joke—which is my contribution?"

Good question. Since Feb. 14, when a devastating ice storm struck JetBlue's home base, New York's John F. Kennedy International Airport, the airline has been digging itself out of an operational and public-relations quagmire. Suddenly the carrier that was going to "bring humanity back to air travel" was trapping passengers on planes for hours, canceling more than 1,000 flights over six days, and admitting to near-chaos in its operations. "We should have acted quicker," says Neeleman. "We should have had contingency plans that were better baked to be able to [unload] customers. We should have called the Port Authority quicker. These were all lessons learned from that experience."

Sharpen your pencils, business school profs. JetBlue's service recovery has all the makings of a Tylenol-caliber case study, starring a repentant CEO, a host of grand gestures to customers, and a few daring publicity coups (like *Letterman*). Still, the road to recovery isn't paved with TV appearances. What matters most is execution—doing the deep, hard, organizational work to ensure the crisis never happens again. While JetBlue recognizes that fact, it still has plenty to prove, especially to those passengers fuming over their ruined vacation or time forever lost to the inside of an airplane.

That's why we decided, despite its initial No. 4 spot on our ranking, which was based on consumer responses from the first half of 2006, to yank JetBlue from our list of Customer Service Champs. It was a tough call. JetBlue has piled up service accolades faster than most airlines collect complaints, winning the University of Nebraska's national Airline Quality Rating study each year since 2003, a Readers' Choice Award from discerning *Condé Nast Traveler* for five years running, and ranking high in every measured category in the airline satisfaction ratings by J.D. Power & Associates.

All that, plus JetBlue's own trumpeting of its customer-friendly approach, means its passengers' expectations are inevitably higher. Other airlines, after all, had long waits at JFK, too: JetBlue's average delay between Feb. 13 and 15 was 230 minutes, according to FlightStats, a travel data company, while Delta Air Lines' was 205 minutes and American Airlines' 202. But interminable delays, cancellations, and service snafus, says UNC Kenan-Flagler Business School marketing professor Valarie Zeithaml, can be "more detrimental [to JetBlue] than to a larger airline. It runs totally counter to who they are coming out and saying they are and what they live."

That means JetBlue has to respond differently. Its first step toward apologizing was to offer immediate refunds and travel vouchers to customers stuck on Valentine's Day planes for more than three hours—far more than Northwest Airlines handed over following its infamous plane delays in 1999, and quicker than American's response to its December flights full of customers stranded on the runway for as long as eight hours. But the centerpiece of Neeleman's strategy is a new Customer Bill of Rights, a written policy unique among U.S. carriers that JetBlue announced on Feb. 20. It requires the airline to dole out vouchers or refunds in certain situations, such as $100 for passengers on arriving flights unable to reach their gates in one to two hours or $50 for any two- to four-hour delays caused by events under JetBlue's control.

Creating a "service guarantee" is a smart move, says Leonard L. Berry, a Texas A&M University marketing professor and author of books on customer service. His research shows that the two biggest ways a company can destroy a service reputation are when its service proves unreliable—as JetBlue's did recently—and when the company doesn't seem to be fairly resolving its problems. Berry warns, however, "that a well-executed service guarantee is very clear on what is guaranteed and what is not." Currently, JetBlue's policy doesn't outline what is under its control and this could cause confusion. It says it will be adding more details.

Neeleman is doing far more than just apologizing and outlining refunds and guarantees. He's making a host of changes he believes will help JetBlue keep future weather-related operational snafus from spiraling out of control. On *Letterman*, he vowed that "we are going to rebound from this." If he can make good on that, JetBlue will indeed be a Customer Service Champ—and Neeleman need never again ask for forgiveness on late-night TV.

SOURCE: Jena McGregor, *BusinessWeek*, March 5, 2007, pp. 58–59.

## Questions

1. David Barger, who had been President of JetBlue, is now CEO of JetBlue, replacing David Neelman who will focus on more strategic long-term initiatives for JetBlue as chairman of the board. What advice would you give Mr. Barger about HR practices that should be implemented to help improve JetBlue and avoid future situations such as those that occurred in February 2007. Identify the HR practices and support your recommendations. Explain.
2. Search the Internet for magazine articles and stories about JetBlue prior to February 14, 2007. Based on your research (1) identify JetBlue's business strategy, and (2) discuss whether its HR practices support its business strategy. Identify specific practices that you believe support its business strategy.

# NOTES


1. A. S. Tsui and L. R. Gomez-Mejia, "Evaluating Human Resource Effectiveness," in *Human Resource Management: Evolving Rules and Responsibilities*, ed. L. Dyer (Washington, DC: BNA Books, 1988), pp. 1187–227; M. A. Hitt, B. W. Keats, and S. M. DeMarie, "Navigating in the New Competitive Landscape: Building Strategic Flexibility and Competitive Advantage in the 21st Century," *Academy of Management Executive* 12, no. 4 (1998), pp. 22–42; J. T. Delaney and M. A. Huselid, "The Impact of Human Resource Management Practices on Perceptions of Organizational Performance," *Academy of Management Journal* 39 (1996), pp. 949–69.
2. F. Hansen, "2006 Data Bank Annual," *Workforce Management*, December 11, 2006, p. 48.
3. SHRM-BNA Survey No. 66, "Policy and Practice Forum: Human Resources Activities, Budgets, and Staffs: 2000–2001," Bulletin to Management, Bureau of National Affairs Policy and Practice Series, June 28, 2001 (Washington, DC: Bureau of National Affairs).
4. R. Stolz, "CEOs Who Get It," *Human Resource Executive*, March 16, 2006, pp. 1, 18–25.
5. W. Cascio, "From Business Partner to Driving Business Success: The Next Step in the Evolution of HR Management," *Human Resource Management* 44 (2005), pp. 159–63.
6. C. Cornell, "Riding Out the Storm," *Human Resource Executive*, April 2006, pp. 44, 46.
7. A. Halcrow, "Survey Shows HRM in Transition," *Workforce*, June 1998, pp. 73–80: J. Laabs, "Why HR Can't Win Today," *Workforce*, May 1998, pp. 62–74; C. Cole. "Kodak Snapshots," *Workforce*, June 2000, pp. 65–72; W. Ruona and S. Gibson, "The Making of Twenty-First Century HR: An Analysis of the Convergence of HRM, HRD, and OD," *Human Resource Management* 43 (2004), pp. 49–66.
8. Towers Perrin, *Priorities for Competitive Advantage: An IBM Study Conducted by Towers Perrin*, 1992.
9. S. Greengard, "Building a Self-Service Culture That Works," *Workforce*, July 1998, pp. 60–64.
10. G. Yohe, "Building Your Case," *Human Resource Executive*, March 2, 2003, pp. 22–26.
11. S. Caudron, "HR Is Dead Long Live HR," *Workforce*, January 2003, pp. 26–29.
12. P. Ketter, "HR Outsourcing Accelerates," *T+D*, February 2007, pp. 12–13.
13. P. Babcock, "A Crowded Space," *HR Magazine*, March 2006, pp. 68–74.
14. M. Rafter, "Promise Fulfilled," *Workforce Management*, September 2005, pp. 51–54.
15. M. Schoeff Jr., "Cardinal Health HR to Take More Strategic Role," *Workforce Management*, April 24, 2006, p. 7.
16. T. Starner, "Managing the Handoff," *Human Resource Executive*, March 2, 2005, pp. 1, 18–25; S. Westcott, "Should It Stay or Go?" *Human Resource Executive*, May 16, 2005, pp. 30–33.
17. Towers Perrin, *Priorities for Competitive Advantage*.
18. F. Hansen, "The CFO Connection," *Workforce Management*, July 2003, pp. 50–54.
19. L. Claus and J. Collison, *The Maturing Profession of Human Resources: Worldwide and Regional View* (Alexandria, VA: Society for Human Resource Management, 2005).
20. Ibid.
21. J. Wiscombe, "Your Wonderful, Terrible HR Life," *Workforce*, June 2001, pp. 32–38.
22. R. Grossman, "Putting HR in Rotation," *HR Magazine*, March 2003, pp. 50–57.
23. Caudron, "HR Is Dead Long Live HR"; S. Bates, "Business Partners," *HR Magazine*, September 2003, pp. 45–49.
24. A. Jones, "Evolutionary Science, Work/Life Integration, and Corporate Responsibility," *Organizational Dynamics* 32 (2002), pp. 17–31.
25. J. Schramm and M. Burke, *SHRM 2004-2005 Workplace Forecast* (Alexandria, VA: Society for Human Resource Management, 2004).
26. GM Media online, "GM, the UAW and Delphi Reach Agreement on Accelerated Attrition Program" (March 22, 2006); "2007 Escalade: Cadillac Prepares Complete Model Lineup" (March 21, 2006); "GM Announces Restructuring of Its U.S. Salaried Retirement Benefits" (March 7, 2006) at www.gm.com/company/news_events/press_releases/.
27. *SHRM Workplace Forecast 2006-2007 Executive Summary* (Alexandria, VA: Society for Human Resource Management, 2006).
28. M. Conlin, "Get Healthy or Else," *BusinessWeek*, February 26, 2007, pp. 58–69.
29. "Workplace Visions," *Society for Human Resource Management* 4 (2002).
30. D. Hecker, "Occupational Employment Projections to 2014," *Monthly Labor Review*, November 2005, pp. 70–101.
31. Ibid.
32. News release from Bureau of Labor Statistics, "BLS Releases 2004–14 Employment Projections," at www.bls.gov/news release/ecopro.nr0.htm.
33. Ibid.; D. Hecker, "Occupational Employment Projections to 2014," *Monthly Labor Review*, November 2005, pp. 70–101.
34. J. Rossi, "The 'Future' of U.S. Manufacturing," *TD*, March 2006, pp. 12–13.
35. R. Davenport, "Eliminate the Skills Gap," *TD*, February 2006, pp. 26–34.
36. M. Schoeff, "Amid Calls to Bolster U.S. Innovation, Experts Lament Paucity of Basic Math Skills," *Workforce Management*, March 2006, pp. 46–49.
37. J. Barbian, "Get'em while They're Young," *Training*, January 2004, pp. 44–46; E. Frauenheim, "IBM Urged to Take Tech Skills to Classrooms," *Workforce Management*, October 24, 2005, pp. 8–9; K. Maher, "Skills Shortage Gives Training Programs New Life," *The Wall Street Journal*, June 3, 2005, p. A2.
38. M. Horrigan, "Employment Projections to 2012: Concepts and Context," *Monthly Labor Review* 127 (2004), pp. 3–22.
39. J. Barney, *Gaining and Sustaining a Competitive Advantage* (Upper Saddle River, NJ: Prentice Hall, 2002).
40. L. Weatherly, *Human Capital: The Elusive Asset* (Alexandria, VA: 2003 SHRM Research Quarterly).
41. W. Zeller, "Southwest: After Kelleher, More Blue Skies," *BusinessWeek*, April 2, 2001, p. 45; S. McCartney, "Southwest Sets Standards on Costs," *The Wall Street Journal*, October 10, 2002, p. A2; S. Warren and M. Trottman, "Southwest's Dallas Duel," *The Wall Street Journal*, May 10, 2005, pp. B1, B4.
42. L. Bassi, J. Ludwig, D. McMurrer, and M. Van Buren, *Profiting from Learning: Do Firms' Investments in Education and Training Pay Off?* (Alexandria, VA: American Society for Training and Development, September 2000).

43. T. J. Atchison, "The Employment Relationship: Untied or Re-Tied," *Academy of Management Executive* 5 (1991), pp. 52–62.
44. J. Marquez, "Driving Ideas Forward at Nissan," *Workforce Management*, July 17, 2006, p. 28.
45. P. Drucker, *Management Challenges for the 21st Century* (New York: Harper Business, 1999); Howard N. Fullerton Jr., "Labor Force Projections to 2008: Steady Growth and Changing Composition," *Monthly Labor Review*, November 1999, pp. 19–32.
46. J. Stoll, "Chrysler Details Program to Cut White-Collar Jobs," *The Wall Street Journal*, February 24–25, 2007, p. A3.
47. D. Senge, "The Learning Organization Made Plain and Simple," *Training and Development Journal*, October 1991, pp. 37–44.
48. L. Thornburg, "Accounting for Knowledge," *HR Magazine*, October 1994, pp. 51–56.
49. J. O'Toole and E. Lawler III, *The New American Workplace* (New York: Palgrave McMillan, 2006).
50. D. M. Rousseau, "Psychological and Implied Contracts in Organizations," *Employee Rights and Responsibilities Journal* 2 (1989), pp. 121–29.
51. D. Rousseau, "Changing the Deal While Keeping the People," *Academy of Management Executive* 11 (1996), pp. 50–61; M. A. Cavanaugh and R. Noe, "Antecedents and Consequences of the New Psychological Contract," *Journal of Organizational Behavior* 20 (1999), pp. 323–40.
52. R. Vance, *Employee Engagement and Commitment* (Alexandria, VA: Society for Human Resource Management, 2006).
53. For examples see M. Huselid, "The Impact of Human Resource Management Practices on Turnover, Productivity, and Corporate Financial Performance," *Academy of Management Journal* 38 (1995), pp. 635–72; S. Payne and S. Webber, "Effects of Service Provider Attitudes and Employment Status on Citizenship Behaviors and Customers' Attitudes and Loyalty Behavior," *Journal of Applied Psychology* 91 (2006), pp. 365–68; J. Hartner, F. Schmidt, and T. Hayes, "Business-Unit Level Relationship between Employee Satisfaction, Employee Engagement, and Business Outcomes: A Meta-analysis," *Journal of Applied Psychology* 87 (2002), pp. 268–79; I. Fulmer, B. Gerhart, and K. Scott, "Are the 100 Best Better? An Empirical Investigation of the Relationship between Being a 'Great Place to Work' and Firm Performance," *Personnel Psychology* 56 (2003), pp. 965–93; "Working Today: Understanding What Drives Employee Engagement," *Towers Perrin Talent Report* (2003).
54. Corporate Leadership Council, *Driving Performance and Retention through Employee Engagement* (Washington, DC: Corporate Executive Board, 2004).
55. J. Robinson, "A Caterpillar Dealer Unearths Employee Engagement" (October 12, 2006), at http://gmj.gallup.com/content/24874/1/A-Caterpillar-Dealer-Unearths-Employee-Engagement.aspx.
56. Towers Perrin, *Talent Management: The State of the Art*, 2005.
57. E. White, "Manager Shortage Spurs Small Firms to Grow Their Own," *The Wall Street Journal*, February 5, 2007, pp. B1, B4; M. McGraw, "Going Mobile," *Human Resource Executive*, Sept. 1, 2006, pp. 44–48.
58. "Contingent and Alternative Employment Arrangements, February 2005," U.S. Department of Labor news release, July 27, 2005 from Bureau of Labor Statistics Web site at www.bls.gov/news.release/conemp.nr0.htm.
59. F. Hansen, "A Permanent Strategy for Temporary Hires," *Workforce Management*, February 26, 2007, pp. 25–30.
60. P. Kiger, "Flexibility to the Fullest," *Workforce Management*, September 25, 2006, pp. 1, 16–23.
61. S. Shellenbarger, "Time-Zoned: Working around the Round-the-Clock Workday," *The Wall Street Journal*, February 15, 2007, p. D1.
62. R. S. Kaplan and D. P. Norton, "The Balanced Scorecard—Measures That Drive Performance," *Harvard Business Review*, January–February 1992, pp. 71–79; R. S. Kaplan and D. P. Norton, "Putting the Balanced Scorecard to Work," *Harvard Business Review*, September–October 1993, pp. 134–47.
63. M. Gendron, "Using the Balanced Scorecard," *Harvard Business Review*, October 1997, pp. 3–5.
64. S. Bates, "The Metrics Maze," *HR Magazine*, December 2003, pp. 50–55; D. Ulrich, "Measuring Human Resources: An Overview of Practice and a Prescription for Results," *Human Resource Management* 36 (1997), pp. 303–20.
65. E. Raimy, "A Plan for All Seasons," *Human Resource Executive*, April 2001, pp. 34–38.
66. R. Alsop, "How Boss's Deeds Buff a Firm's Reputation," *The Wall Street Journal*, January 31, 2007, pp. B1, B2; S. Zadek, "Separating Smart from Great," *Fortune*, October 23, 2006. From CNNMoney.com.
67. M. Lev-Ram, "Cell-Phone Makers See Green by Going Green," *Business 2.0 Magazine*, August 11, 2006. From CNNMONEY.com.
68. S. Prasso, "Saving the World One Cup of Yogurt at a Time," *Fortune*, February 19, 2007, pp. 96–102.
69. J. R. Jablonski, *Implementing Total Quality Management: An Overview* (San Diego: Pfeiffer, 1991).
70. R. Hodgetts, F. Luthans, and S. Lee, "New Paradigm Organizations: From Total Quality to Learning World-Class," *Organizational Dynamics*, Winter 1994, pp. 5–19.
71. A. Pomeroy, "Winners and Learners," *HR Magazine*, April 2006, pp. 62–67.
72. Malcolm Baldrige National Quality Award 2005 Award Recipient, Small Business, Park Place Lexus. From Baldrige Award Recipient profiles at www.nist.gov, the Web site for the National Institute of Standards and Technology.
73. S. L. Jackson, "What You Should Know about ISO 9000," *Training*, May 1992, pp. 48–52; Bureau of Best Practices, *Profile of ISO 9000* (Boston: Allyn and Bacon, 1992); "ISO 9000 International Standards for Quality Assurance," *Design Matters*, July 1995, http://www.best.com/ISO 9000/att/ISONet.html/. See www.iso9000y2k.com, a Web site containing ISO 9000:2000 documentation.
74. General Electric 1999 Annual Report, www.ge.com/annual99.
75. Bureau of Labor Statistics, "BLS Releases 2004–14 employment projections"; M. Toossi, "Labor Force Projections to 2014: Retiring Boomers," *Monthly Labor Review*, November 2005, pp. 25–44.
76. N. Lockwood, *The Aging Workforce* (Alexandria, VA: Society for Human Resource Management, 2003).
77. J. Marquez, "Novel Ideas at Borders Lure Older Workers," *Workforce Management*, May 2005, pp. 28, 30.
78. M. Weinstein, "NASA Training Program Blasts Off," *Training*, December 2005, pp. 8–9; J. Salopek, "The New Brain Drain," *TD*, June 2005, pp. 23–25; P. Harris, "Beware of the Boomer Brain Drain!" *TD*, January 2006, pp. 30–33; M. McGraw, "Bye-Bye Boomers," *Human Resource Executive*, March 2, 2006, pp. 34–37.
79. P. Harden, "The Federal Exodus," *Human Resource Executive*, November 2005, pp. 70–73.
80. Bureau of Labor Statistics, "BLS Releases 2004–14 Employment Projections"; Toossi, "Labor Force Projections to 2014."
81. B. Newman, "Employers Have a Lot to Lose," *The Wall Street Journal*, April 11, 2006, pp. B1, B4.
82. M. Jordan, J. Kronholz, and B. Newman, "Off the Job, onto the Streets," *The Wall Street Journal*, April 11, 2006, pp. B1, B4;

I. Speizer, "Roots of the Immigration Debate," *Workforce Management*, August 14, 2006, pp. 1, 18–26.
83. Ibid.
84. R. Block, "Homeland Security Strategy Hits Executives, Illegal Workers," *The Wall Street Journal*, February 23, 2007, p. A5.
85. M. Johnson, "Blind Workers Find Fulfillment at Wiscraft Inc.," *Columbus Dispatch*, February 18, 2006, p. F2.
86. C. Hirshman, "Here They Come," *HR Executive*, July 2006, pp. 1, 22–26; P. Harris, "The Work War?" *TD*, May 2005, pp. 45–48.
87. B. Wooldridge and J. Wester, "The Turbulent Environment of Public Personnel Administration: Responding to the Challenge of the Changing Workplace of the Twenty-First Century," *Public Personnel Management* 20 (1991), pp. 207–24; J. Laabs, "The New Loyalty: Grasp It. Earn It. Keep It," *Workforce*, November 1998, pp. 34–39.
88. "Employee Dissatisfaction on Rise in Last 10 Years, New Report Says," *Employee Relations Weekly* (Washington, DC: Bureau of National Affairs, 1986).
89. D. T. Hall and J. Richter, "Career Gridlock: Baby Boomers Hit the Wall," *The Executive* 4 (1990), pp. 7–22.
90. T. H. Cox and S. Blake, "Managing Cultural Diversity: Implications for Organizational Competitiveness," *The Executive* 5 (1991), pp. 45–56.
91. M. Loden and J. B. Rosener, *Workforce America!* (Homewood, IL: Business One Irwin, 1991); N. Lockwood, *Workplace Diversity: Leveraging the Power of Difference for Competitive Advantage* (Alexandria: VA: Society for Human Resource Management, 2005).
92. R. Rodriguez, "Diversity Finds Its Place," *HR Magazine*, August 2006, pp. 56–61.
93. J. Taylor Arnold, "Employee Networks," *HR Magazine*, June 2006, pp. 145–52.
94. A. Pomeroy, "Cultivating Female Leaders," *HR Magazine*, February 2007, pp. 44–50.
95. J. Ledvinka and V. G. Scarpello, *Federal Regulation of Personnel and Human Resource Management*, 2nd ed. (Boston: PWS-Kent, 1991).
96. D. White, "The New Frontier," *Human Resource Executive*, October 16, 2005, pp. 32–34.
97. M. Conlin, "Get Healthy—Or Else," *BusinessWeek*, February 26, 2007, pp. 58–64, 69.
98. N. Lockwood, *The Glass Ceiling: Domestic and International Perspectives* (Alexandria, VA: Society for Human Resource Management, 2004).
99. *Women in U.S. Corporate Leadership: 2003* (New York: Catalyst, 2003).
100. J. Zhang, "Genetic-Discrimination Ban Nears Congressional Approval," *The Wall Street Journal*, February 15, 2007, p. A11.
101. M. Pastin, *The Hard Problems of Management: Gaining the Ethics Edge* (San Francisco: Jossey-Bass, 1986). T. Thomas, J. Schermerhorn, Jr., and J. Dienhart, "Strategic Leadership of Ethical Behavior in Business," *Academy of Management Executive* 18 (2004), pp. 56–66.
102. Ibid.
103. K. Gurchiek, "Sarbanes-Oxley Compliance Costs Rising," *HR Magazine*, January 2005, pp. 29, 33.
104. R. Grossman, "HR and the Board," *HR Magazine*, January 2007, pp. 52–58.
105. J. Segal, "The 'Joy' of Uncooking," *HR Magazine* 47 (11) (2002).
106. D. Buss, "Corporate Compasses," *HR Magazine* 49 (6) (2004), pp. 126–32.
107. C. Cornell, "Someone Who Will Listen," *Human Resource Executive*, February 2007, p. 16.
108. D. Buss, "Working It Out," *HRMagazine online*, www.shrm.org/hrmagazine/04June.
109. G. F. Cavanaugh, D. Moberg, and M. Velasquez, "The Ethics of Organizational Politics," *Academy of Management Review* 6 (1981), pp. 363–74.
110. C. Hill, *International Business* (Burr Ridge, IL: Irwin/ McGraw-Hill, 1997).
111. J. Lee Young, "Starbucks Expansion into China Is Slated," *The Wall Street Journal*, October 5, 1998, p. B13C.
112. E. Tahmincioglu, "Opportunities Mingle with Fear Overseas," *The New York Times*, October 24, 2001, p. G1.
113. J. Schramm, "Offshoring," *Workplace Visions* 2 (Alexandria, VA: Society for Human Resource Management, 2004); P. Babcock, "America's Newest Export: White Collar Jobs," *HR Magazine* 49 (4) (2004), pp. 50–57.
114. F. Hansen, "U.S. Firms Going Wherever the Knowledge Workers Are," *Workforce Management*, October 2005, pp. 43–44.
115. Jim Hopkins, "To Start Up Here, Companies Hire Over There," *USA Today*, February 10, 2005, downloaded at www.usatoday.com.
116. Ibid.
117. Hansen, "U.S. Firms Going Where the Knowledge Workers Are."
118. R. Grossman, "The Truth about the Coming Labor Shortage," *HR Magazine*, March 2005, pp. 47–53; S. Ladika, "The Brain Race," *HR Magazine*, April 2006, pp. 69–74.
119. J. Marquez, "Going Rural: A U.S. Alternative to Offshoring," *Workforce Management*, September 2005, pp. 16–17.
120. R. Chittum, "Call Centers Phone Home," *The Wall Street Journal*, June 9, 2004, pp. B1, B8.
121. J. Kahn, "Small Firms Find That Outsourcing Cuts Both Ways," *Fortune*, April 28, 2004, at www.fortune.com.
122. M. Kripalani and P. Engardio, "The Rise of India," *BusinessWeek*, December 8, 2003, pp. 66–76.
123. "Two-Thirds of Americans Online," *CyberAtlas* (May 10, 2000), http://cyberatlas.internet.com.
124. Ibid.
125. H. Dolezalek, "Virtual Agent Nation," *Training*, June 2004, p. 12.
126. A. Weintraub, "High Tech's Future Is in the Toy Chest," *BusinessWeek*, August 26, 2002, pp. 124–26.
127. *2002 Benefits Survey* (Alexandria, VA: Society of Human Resource Management Foundation, 2002).
128. S. Greengard, "Sun's Shining Example," *Workforce Management*, March 2005, pp. 48–49.
129. P. Choate and P. Linger, *The High-Flex Society* (New York: Knopf, 1986); P. B. Doeringer, *Turbulence in the American Workplace* (New York: Oxford University Press, 1991).
130. J. A. Neal and C. L. Tromley, "From Incremental Change to Retrofit: Creating High-Performance Work Systems," *Academy of Management Executive* 9 (1995), pp. 42–54.
131. K. A. Miller, *Retraining the American Workforce* (Reading, MA: Addison-Wesley, 1989).
132. S. Moffett, "Separation Anxiety," *The Wall Street Journal*, September 27, 2004, p. R11.
133. J. Gordon, "Do Your Virtual Teams Deliver Only Virtual Performance?" *Training*, June 2005, pp. 20–25.
134. T. Peters, "Restoring American Competitiveness: Looking for New Models of Organizations," *The Executive* 2 (1988), pp. 103–10.
135. J. Marquez, "Taking a Longer View," *Workforce Management*, May 22, 2006, pp. 18–22.
136. "Outstanding Training Initiatives: Capital One: Audio Learning in Stereo," *Training*, March 2006, p. 64.
137. J. Marquez, "Firms Tap Virtual Work Spaces to Ease Collaboration, Debate among Scattered Employees," *Workforce Management*, May 22, 2006, pp. 38–39.

138. D. Foust, "How Technology Delivers for UPS," *BusinessWeek*, March 5, 2007, p. 60.
139. M. J. Kavanaugh, H. G. Guetal, and S. I. Tannenbaum, *Human Resource Information Systems: Development and Application* (Boston: PWS-Kent, 1990).
140. Bill Roberts, "Empowerment or Imposition?" *HR Magazine*, June 2004, downloaded from Infotrac at http://web7.infotrac.galegroup.com.
141. Ibid.
142. L. Weatherly, "HR Technology: Leveraging the Shift to Self-Service," *HR Magazine*, March 2005.
143. N. Lockwood, *Maximizing Human Capital: Demonstrating HR Value with Key Performance Indicators* (Alexandria, VA: SHRM Research Quarterly 2006).
144. R. N. Ashkenas, "Beyond the Fads: How Leaders Drive Change with Results," *Human Resource Planning* 17 (1994), pp. 25–44.
145. M. A. Huselid, "The Impact of Human Resource Management Practices on Turnover, Productivity, and Corporate Financial Performance," *Academy of Management Journal* 38 (1995), pp. 635–72; U.S. Dept. of Labor, *High-Performance Work Practices and Firm Performance* (Washington, DC: U.S. Government Printing Office, 1993); J. Combs, Y. Liu, A. Hall, and D. Ketchen, "How Much Do High-Performance Work Practices Matter? A Meta-analysis of Their Effects on Organizational Performance," *Personnel Psychology* 59 (2006), pp. 501–28.
146. B. Becker and M. A. Huselid, "High-Performance Work Systems and Firm Performance: A Synthesis of Research and Managerial Implications," in *Research in Personnel and Human Resource Management* 16, ed. G. R. Ferris (Stamford, CT: JAI Press, 1998), pp. 53–101; A. Zacharatos, J. Barling, and R. Iverson, "High Performance Work Systems and Occupational Safety," *Journal of Applied Psychology* 90 (2005), pp. 77–93.
147. B. Becker and B. Gerhart, "The Impact of Human Resource Management on Organizational Performance: Progress and Prospects," *Academy of Management Journal* 39 (1996), pp. 779–801.
148. J. Marquez, "Engine of Change," *Workforce Management*, July 17, 2006, pp. 20–30.
149. S. A. Snell and J. W. Dean, "Integrated Manufacturing and Human Resource Management: A Human Capital Perspective," *Academy of Management Journal* 35 (1992), pp. 467–504; M. A. Youndt, S. Snell, J. W. Dean Jr., and D. P. Lepak, "Human Resource Management, Manufacturing Strategy, and Firm Performance," *Academy of Management Journal* 39 (1996), pp. 836–66.

# PART 1

# The Human Resource Environment

# 2
CHAPTER

# Strategic Human Resource Management

## LO LEARNING OBJECTIVES

After reading this chapter, you should be able to:

LO1 Describe the differences between strategy formulation and strategy implementation. *page 68*

LO2 List the components of the strategic management process. *page 69*

LO3 Discuss the role of the HRM function in strategy formulation. *page 72*

LO4 Describe the linkages between HRM and strategy formulation. *page 73*

LO5 Discuss the more popular typologies of generic strategies and the various HRM practices associated with each. *page 77*

LO6 Describe the different HRM issues and practices associated with various directional strategies. *page 86*

# Enter the World of Business

## Chrysler's Recovery and Transformation Plan

Having hoped to grow its way out of problems, Chrysler has finally succumbed to imitating the other two of the Big Three Detroit automakers, by announcing a massive restructuring of the U.S. operations.

Chrysler, which merged with Daimler-Benz in 1998 to form DaimlerChrysler AG, had faced financial difficulties before. Early after the merger in 2000, Chrysler reported a $1.3 million loss, largely due to the flop of a newly designed minivan. Dieter Zetsche was sent from Germany to take over the North American operations, and he found mass inefficiencies, runaway expenses, drab products, and nothing in the product pipeline. His strategy was to first shrink the division, cutting 26,000 jobs and closing six plants, and then launch an exciting set of new vehicles to increase sales. Over two years he cut back on the development budget, asking engineers to use one set of basic components across three or four different vehicles. The designers were also tasked with creating bold, eye-catching vehicles, an approach he called "disciplined pizzazz."

Another aspect of the strategy was to emphasize sport utility vehicles (SUVs) and pickup trucks through Chrysler expanding Jeep's three-model lineup and adding variants to its Dodge Ram pickup line. The result was that trucks, SUVs, and minivans accounted for 75 percent of its sales by 2005, which is not a good position in a world of $3 per gallon gasoline. Most problematic, as the vehicles failed to sell, Chrysler kept its plants running, resulting in huge inventories of unsold cars and trucks. To move the inventory, Chrysler offered deep employee-pricing discounts and embarked on an advertising campaign highlighting Mr. Zetsche as "Dr. Z." The campaign didn't work, and by July 2006, Chrysler fell 40,000 units short of its sales goal. By September, Chrysler announced it would suffer a $1.5 billion operating loss in the third quarter. Chrysler CEO Tom LaSorda described it as "We lost money building inventory and then we lost money trying to get rid of it. It was a tough lesson."

Dr. Z's strategy was then completely overhauled. His projections that Chrysler would see sales increase to 3.2 million vehicles by 2012 from 2.2 million in 2002 were revised. In fact, sales were only 2.1 million in 2006 and the plan called for a reduced capacity of 400,000 units. The result is Chrysler's "Recovery and Transformation Plan." Of Chrysler's 83,000 workers (61,000 of whom are hourly), it expected to cut 2,000 managerial professional and 11,000 hourly workers over the following two years. In addition, it planned to close one of its 12 North American assembly plants while cutting entire shifts at 3 of the plants. It also planned to close one of its parts distribution centers and cut back operations at its 17 component and stamping plants to reflect the reduction in capacity of 400,000 units.

According to the company's press release, this reflects a "redesigned business model for long-term competitiveness, including greater

**Losing Traction** Chrysler Group operating profit/loss since Daimler-Benz AG and Chrysler Corp. merged:

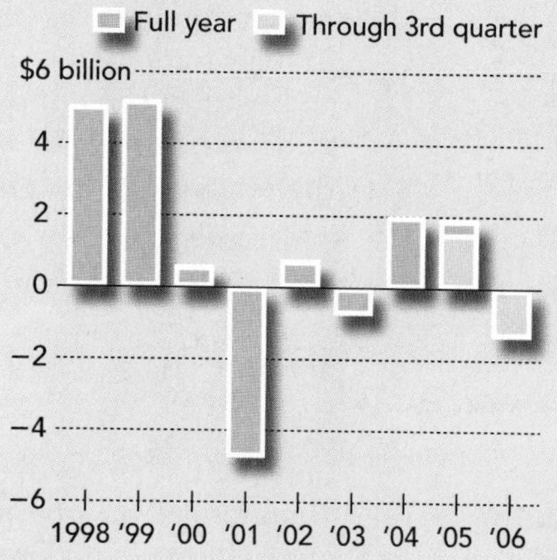


SOURCE: the company

emphasis on fuel-efficient products, global growth and partnerships." LaSorda describes the plan as having two integrated parts. "First, the Chrysler Group needs to solidify its position in the North American marketplace. In addition, the key to our long-term success will be our ability to transform the organization into a different company to achieve and sustain long-term profitability.

Source: S. Power, G. Chon, and N. Boudette, "In Humbling Overhaul, Chrysler Faces Big Cuts," *The Wall Street Journal*, February 14, 2007, p. A1.

## Introduction

As the Chrysler example just illustrated, business organizations exist in an environment of competition. They can use a number of resources to compete with other companies. These resources are physical (such as plant, equipment, technology, and geographic location), organizational (the structure, planning, controlling, and coordinating systems, and group relations), and human (the experience, skill, and intelligence of employees). It is these resources under the control of the company that provide competitive advantage.[1]

The goal of strategic management in an organization is to deploy and allocate resources in a way that gives it a competitive advantage. As you can see, two of the three classes of resources (organizational and human) are directly tied to the human resource management function. As Chapter 1 pointed out, the role of human resource management is to ensure that a company's human resources provide a competitive advantage. Chapter 1 also pointed out some of the major competitive challenges that companies face today. These challenges require companies to take a proactive, strategic approach in the marketplace.

To be maximally effective, the HRM function must be integrally involved in the company's strategic management process.[2] This means that human resource managers should (1) have input into the strategic plan, both in terms of people-related issues and in terms of the ability of the human resource pool to implement particular strategic alternatives; (2) have specific knowledge of the organization's strategic goals; (3) know what types of employee skills, behaviors, and attitudes are needed to support the strategic plan; and (4) develop programs to ensure that employees have those skills, behaviors, and attitudes.

We begin this chapter by discussing the concepts of business models and strategy and by depicting the strategic management process. Then we discuss the levels of integration between the HRM function and the strategic management process in strategy formulation. Next we review some of the more common strategic models and, within the context of these models, discuss the various types of employee skills, behaviors, and attitudes, and the ways HRM practices aid in implementing the strategic plan. Finally, we discuss the role of HR in creating competitive advantage.

## What Is a Business Model?

A business model is a story of how the firm will create value for customers and, more important, how it will do so profitably. We often hear or read of companies that have "transformed their business model" in one way or another, but what that means is not always clear. To understand this, we need to grasp a few basic accounting concepts.

First, fixed costs are generally considered the costs that are incurred regardless of the number of units produced. For instance, if you are producing widgets in a factory, you have the rent you pay for the factory, depreciation of the machines, the utilities, the property taxes, and so on. In addition, you generally have a set number of employees who work a set number of hours with a specified level of benefits, and while you might be able to vary these over time, on a regular basis you pay the same total labor costs whether your factory runs at 70 percent capacity or 95 percent capacity.

Second, you have a number of variable costs, which are those costs that vary directly with the units produced. For instance, all of the materials that go into the widget might cost a total of $10, which means that you have to charge at least $10 per widget, or you cannot even cover the variable costs of production.

Third is the concept of "contribution margins," or margins. Margins are the difference between what you charge for your product and the variable costs of that product. They are called contribution margins because they are what contributes to your ability to cover your fixed costs. So, for instance, if you charged $15 for each widget, your contribution margin would be $5 ($15 price − $10 variable cost).

Fourth, the gross margin is the total amount of margin you made and is calculated as the number of units sold times the contribution margin. If you sold 1,000,000 units, your gross margin would then be $5,000,000. Did you make a profit? That depends. Profit refers to what is left after you have paid your variable costs and your fixed costs. If your gross margin was $5,000,000, and your fixed costs were $6,000,000, then you lost $1,000,000.

So, returning to the Chrysler case that began this chapter, what does the company press release mean when it says "Redesigned business model for long-term competitiveness"? If you look at Figure 2.1, you'll see that the solid lines represent the old Chrysler business model, which was based on projections that Chrysler would be able to sell 2.5 million units at a reasonably high margin, and thus completely cover its fixed costs to make a strong profit. However, the reality was that its products didn't sell at the higher prices, so to try to sell 2.5 million vehicles, Chrysler offered discounts which cut into its margins. When Chrysler ended up selling only 2.1 million vehicles, and those were sold at a lower margin, the company could not cover its fixed costs, resulting in a projected $1.6 billion loss (this is illustrated by the dotted blue line in the figure). So, when Chrysler refers to the "redesigned business model," what it is referring to is a significant reduction in fixed costs (through closing plants and cutting

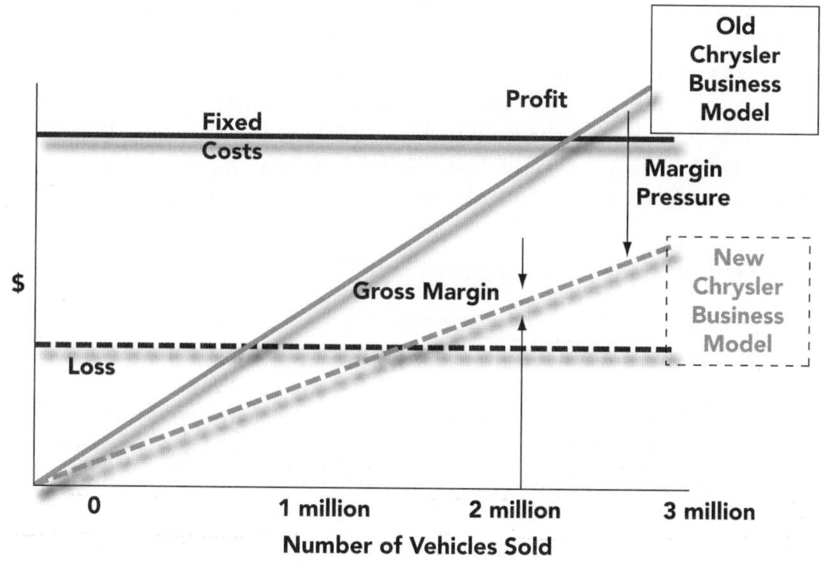


**figure 2.1**
An Illustration of a Business Model for Chrysler

Solid = old
dashed = new

## COMPETING THROUGH TECHNOLOGY

### Wal-Mart Leverages Technology to Lower Labor Costs

Wal-Mart, the global retailing giant that built its success in large part by using information technology to hold down inventory costs, is now using that technology to lower its labor costs. The technology will enable the firm to move its 1.3 million employees from normal eight-hour shifts to a variety of more flexible shifts that better match customer buying patterns.

The change is made possible by a computerized management tool, a so-called scheduling-optimization system, which integrates data such as the number of customers at different hours of the day, the time needed to sell certain products, and/or the time needed to unload a truck to help predict how many workers a store needs at any given hour. This enables the stores to cut costs by having fewer unnecessary paid employees being paid during slow times, as well as cutting litigation by enabling the company to better comply with federal wage-and-hour laws. In addition, some retailers say that it lets them better serve customers because it minimizes long checkout lines. Nikki Baird of Forrester Research Inc. says, "There's been a new push for labor optimization. You want to have the flexibility to more closely match . . . shifts to when the demand is there."

According to Wal-Mart, in a test of 39 stores, 70 percent of customers said the checkout experience had improved. Wal-Mart spokeswoman Sarah Clark states, "The advantages are simple. We will benefit by improving the shopping experience by having the right number of associates to meet our customers' needs when they shop our stores."

While Wal-Mart seems to be leading the way, it is not alone in this effort. Payless ShoeSource Inc., RadioShack Corp., and Mervyn's LLC all have all rolled out similar systems.

SOURCE: K. Maher, "Wal-Mart Seeks New Flexibility in Worker Shifts," *The Wall Street Journal*, January 3, 2007, at http://online.wsj.com/article/SB116779472314165646.html.

workers) to get the fixed-cost base low enough (the dotted red line) to be able to still be profitable selling fewer cars at lower margins (again, the dotted blue line).

One can easily see how, given the large component that labor costs are to most companies, reference to business models almost inevitably leads to discussions of labor costs. These can be the high cost associated with current unionized employees in developed countries within North America or Europe or, in some cases, the high costs associated with a legacy workforce. For instance, the Big Three automakers have huge numbers of retired or laid-off workers for whom they still have the liability of paying pensions and health care benefits. This is a significant component of their fixed-cost base, which makes it difficult for them to compete with other automakers that either have fewer retirees to cover or have no comparable costs because their home governments provide pensions and health care. The "Competing through Technology" box describes how Wal-Mart (along with other retailers) is using technology to effectively match employee schedules to customer traffic in order to effectively serve their customers in an efficient manner.

## What Is Strategic Management?

**LO1**
Describe the Differences between Strategy Formulation and Strategy Implementation.

Many authors have noted that in today's competitive market, organizations must engage in strategic planning to survive and prosper. Strategy comes from the Greek word *strategos*, which has its roots in military language. It refers to a general's grand design behind a war or battle. In fact, *Webster's New American Dictionary* defines strategy as the "skillful employment and coordination of tactics" and as "artful planning and management."

Strategic management is a process, an approach to addressing the competitive challenges an organization faces. It can be thought of as managing the "pattern or plan that integrates an organization's major goals, policies, and action sequences into a cohesive whole."[3] These strategies can be either the generic approach to competing or the specific adjustments and actions taken to deal with a particular situation.

First, business organizations engage in generic strategies that often fit into some strategic type. One example is "cost, differentiation, or focus."[4] Another is "defender, analyzer, prospector, or reactor."[5] Different organizations within the same industry often have different generic strategies. These generic strategy types describe the consistent way the company attempts to position itself relative to competitors.

However, a generic strategy is only a small part of strategic management. The second aspect of strategic management is the process of developing strategies for achieving the company's goals in light of its current environment. Thus, business organizations engage in generic strategies, but they also make choices about such things as how to scare off competitors, how to keep competitors weaker, how to react to and influence pending legislation, how to deal with various stakeholders and special interest groups, how to lower production costs, how to raise revenues, what technology to implement, and how many and what types of people to employ. Each of these decisions may present competitive challenges that have to be considered.

Strategic management is more than a collection of strategic types. It is a process for analyzing a company's competitive situation, developing the company's strategic goals, and devising a plan of action and allocation of resources (human, organizational, and physical) that will increase the likelihood of achieving those goals. This kind of strategic approach should be emphasized in human resource management. HR managers should be trained to identify the competitive issues the company faces with regard to human resources and think strategically about how to respond.

**Strategic human resource management (SHRM)** can be thought of as "the pattern of planned human resource deployments and activities intended to enable an organization to achieve its goals."[6] For example, many firms have developed integrated manufacturing systems such as advanced manufacturing technology, just-in-time inventory control, and total quality management in an effort to increase their competitive position. However, these systems must be run by people. SHRM in these cases entails assessing the employee skills required to run these systems and engaging in HRM practices, such as selection and training, that develop these skills in employees.[7] To take a strategic approach to HRM, we must first understand the role of HRM in the strategic management process.

**Strategic Human Resource Management (SHRM)**
A pattern of planned human resource deployments and activities intended to enable an organization to achieve its goals.

**Strategy Formulation**
The process of deciding on a strategic direction by defining a company's mission and goals, its external opportunities and threats, and its internal strengths and weaknesses.

## Components of the Strategic Management Process

The strategic management process has two distinct yet interdependent phases: strategy formulation and strategy implementation. During **strategy formulation** the strategic planning groups decide on a strategic direction by defining the company's mission and goals, its external opportunities and threats, and its internal strengths and weaknesses. They then generate various strategic alternatives and compare those alternatives' ability to achieve the company's mission and goals. During **strategy implementation,** the organization follows through on the chosen strategy. This consists of structuring the organization, allocating resources, ensuring that the firm has skilled employees in place, and developing reward systems that align employee behavior with the organization's strategic goals. Both of these strategic management phases must be performed effectively. It is important to note that this process does not happen sequentially. As we will discuss later with regard to emergent strategies, this process entails a constant cycling of information and decision making. Figure 2.2 presents the strategic management process.

**LO2**
List the Components of the Strategic Management Process.

— SWOT

**Strategy Implementation**
The process of devising structures and allocating resources to enact the strategy a company has chosen.

figure 2.2

A Model of the Strategic Management Process

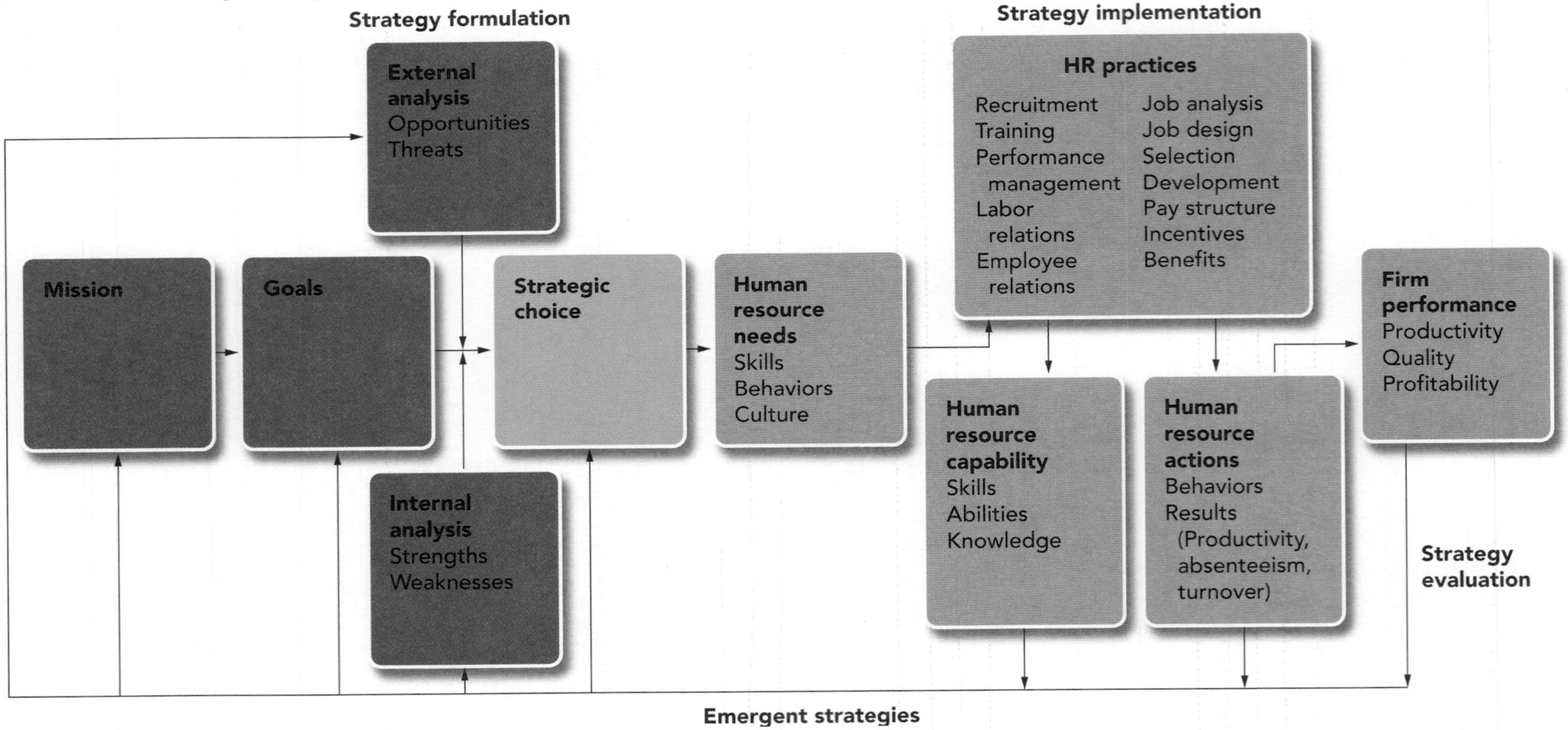

Strategy formulation
External analysis
Opportunities
Threats
Mission
Goals
Strategic choice
Internal analysis
Strengths
Weaknesses
Human resource needs
Skills
Behaviors
Culture
Strategy implementation
HR practices
Recruitment
Training
Performance management
Labor relations
Employee relations
Job analysis
Job design
Selection
Development
Pay structure
Incentives
Benefits
Human resource capability
Skills
Abilities
Knowledge
Human resource actions
Behaviors
Results (Productivity, absenteeism, turnover)
Firm performance
Productivity
Quality
Profitability
Strategy evaluation
Emergent strategies

In recent years organizations have recognized that the success of the strategic management process depends largely on the extent to which the HRM function is involved.[8]

## Linkage between HRM and the Strategic Management Process

The strategic choice really consists of answering questions about competition—that is, how the firm will compete to achieve its missions and goals. These decisions consist of addressing the issues of where to compete, how to compete, and with what to compete, which are described in Figure 2.3. With this in mind, consider the situation at Chrysler discussed in the opening case. Remember that the Recovery and Transformation Plan suggested a new focus on fuel-efficient products and global growth. The shift from gas-guzzling trucks and SUVs to fuel-efficient products suggests a different answer to the "how to compete" question. The emphasis on global growth indicates a different answer to the "where to compete" question.

Although these decisions are all important, strategic decision makers often pay less attention to the "with what will we compete" issue, resulting in poor strategic decisions. For example, PepsiCo in the 1980s acquired the fast-food chains of Kentucky Fried Chicken, Taco Bell, and Pizza Hut ("where to compete" decisions) in an effort to increase its customer base. However, it failed to adequately recognize the differences between its existing workforce (mostly professionals) and that of the fast-food industry (lower skilled people and high schoolers) as well as its ability to manage such a workforce. This was one reason that PepsiCo, in 1998, spun off the fast-food chains. In essence, it had made a decision about where to compete without fully understanding what resources would be needed to compete in that market.

Boeing illustrates how failing to address the "with what" issue resulted in problems in its "how to compete" decisions. When the aerospace firm's consumer products division entered into a price war with Airbus Industrie, it was forced to move away from its traditional customer service strategy toward emphasizing cost reduction.[9] The strategy was a success on the sales end as Boeing received large numbers of orders for aircraft from firms such as Delta, Continental, Southwest, and Singapore Airlines. However, it had recently gone through a large workforce reduction (thus, it didn't have enough people to fill the orders) and did not have the production technology to enable the necessary increase in productivity. The result of this failure to address "with what will we compete" in making a decision about how to compete resulted in the firm's inability to meet delivery deadlines and the ensuing penalties it had to pay to its customers. The end result is that after all the travails, for the first time in the history of the industry, Airbus sold more planes than Boeing in 2003. Luckily, Boeing was

**figure 2.3**
Strategy—Decisions about Competition

1. Where to compete?
   In what market or markets (industries, products, etc.) will we compete?
2. How to compete?
   On what criterion or differentiating characteristic(s) will we compete? Cost? Quality? Reliability? Delivery?
3. With what will we compete?
   What resources will allow us to beat our competition?
   How will we acquire, develop, and deploy those resources to compete?

## COMPETING THROUGH GLOBALIZATION

### Creating a "Buzz" in China

In most major U.S. cities it's almost impossible to walk down the street for five minutes without coming across a Starbucks coffee outlet. While the stores and the brand have become ubiquitous in the United States, Starbucks' global expansion has faced some difficulties, and overcoming the obstacles actually requires having the right people in the right place at the right time doing the right things.

For instance, Starbucks began its expansion into China in 1999. During the early years it had to partner with local firms in order to open stores, which resulted in an inability to control the quality to the desired extent. As regulations were relaxed, and Starbucks was able to buy out its partners, the challenge was to get a tea-drinking culture to switch to coffee.

The first key was to get the right leader in China. That leader turned out to be Wang Jinlong. Mr. Wang began his career with Starbucks in the legal department and worked for the company for a number of years before leaving to set up convenience stores in China. However, he stayed in touch with founder Howard Schultz and on one occasion told Mr. Schultz that Starbucks' expansion was taking too long. "In China there is only one speed: faster," he said. Mr. Schultz says, "I knew he was right but we didn't have the right people." Consequently, he hired Mr. Wang back. As the new leader, Mr. Wang overhauled the strategy to focus on opening more stores in major metropolises rather than expanding to new cities.

Having the right leader, now Starbucks focuses on leveraging the many workers to make it successful. For instance, on certain mornings, at the Starbucks headquarters in Shanghai, workers go through coffee-tasting competitions. They sample two cups of coffee and have to guess from which country each came as well as guessing its acidity. They are then able to hold formal tastings for customers in the stores to introduce Chinese customers to coffee.

However, the success of Starbucks in China is not dependent upon coffee. The stores also have a broad assortment of teas and fruit frapaccinos, which are more to the liking of the Chinese palate. In addition, just as in the United States it's not so much the coffee as the atmosphere that Chinese customers find appealing. For example, Guo Shi Yuan, a 48-year-old Buddhist monk, traveled from a nearby mountain village to meet with another monk. "I come here because I prefer the environment more than the coffee," he said. "It makes people feel comfortable."

SOURCE: J. Adamy, "Eyeing a Billion Tea Drinkers, Starbucks Puts It on in China," *The Wall Street Journal*, November 29, 2006, at http://online.wsj.com/article/SB116476973580035391.html.

able to overcome this stumble, in large part because of a number of stumbles on the part of its chief rival, Airbus. Boeing's 787 Dreamliner has generated a number of orders, while Airbus's behemoth A380 has been beset by a number of production delays, enabling Boeing to regain its market lead. The "Competing through Globalization" box describes Starbucks' entrance into China and illustrates how the "how to compete" and "with what to compete" questions are all tied up with the "where to compete" question.

## Role of HRM in Strategy Formulation

**LO3** Discuss the Role of the HRM Function in Strategy Formulation.

As the preceding examples illustrate, often the "with what will we compete" questions present ideal avenues for HRM to influence the strategic management process. This might be through either limiting strategic options or forcing thoughtfulness among the executive team regarding how and at what cost the firm might gain or develop the human resources (people) necessary for such a strategy to be successful. For example, HRM executives at PepsiCo could have noted that the firm had no expertise in managing the workforce of fast-food restaurants. The limiting role would have been for these executives to argue against the acquisition because of this lack of resources. On the other hand, they might have influenced the decision by educating top executives as to the costs (of hiring, training, and so on) associated with gaining people who had the right skills to manage such a workforce.

A firm's strategic management decision-making process usually takes place at its top levels, with a strategic planning group consisting of the chief executive officer, the chief financial officer, the president, and various vice presidents. However, each component of the process involves people-related business issues. Therefore, the HRM function needs to be involved in each of those components. One recent study of 115 strategic business units within Fortune 500 corporations found that between 49 and 69 percent of the companies had some link between HRM and the strategic planning process.[10] However, the level of linkage varied, and it is important to understand these different levels.

Four levels of integration seem to exist between the HRM function and the strategic management function: administrative linkage, one-way linkage, two-way linkage, and integrative linkage.[11] These levels of linkage will be discussed in relation to the different components of strategic management. The linkages are illustrated in Figure 2.4.

## Administrative Linkage

**LO4**
Describe the Linkages between HRM and Strategy Formulation.

In administrative linkage (the lowest level of integration), the HRM function's attention is focused on day-to-day activities. The HRM executive has no time or opportunity to take a strategic outlook toward HRM issues. The company's strategic business planning function exists without any input from the HRM department. Thus, in this level of integration, the HRM department is completely divorced from any component of the strategic management process in both strategy formulation and strategy implementation. The department simply engages in administrative work unrelated to the company's core business needs.

figure 2.4
Linkages of Strategic Planning and HRM

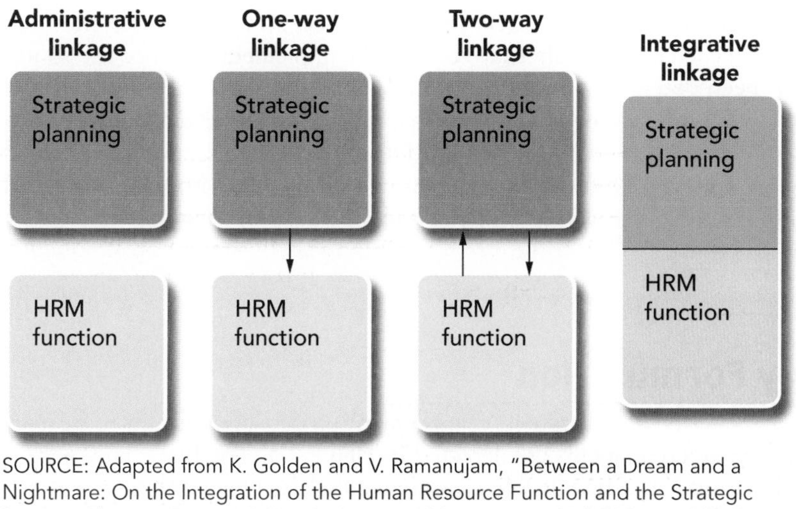


SOURCE: Adapted from K. Golden and V. Ramanujam, "Between a Dream and a Nightmare: On the Integration of the Human Resource Function and the Strategic Business Planning Process," *Human Resource Management* 24 (1985), pp. 429–51.

### One-Way Linkage

In one-way linkage, the firm's strategic business planning function develops the strategic plan and then informs the HRM function of the plan. Many believe this level of integration constitutes strategic HRM—that is, the role of the HRM function is to design systems and/or programs that implement the strategic plan. Although one-way linkage does recognize the importance of human resources in implementing the strategic plan, it precludes the company from considering human resource issues while formulating the strategic plan. This level of integration often leads to strategic plans that the company cannot successfully implement.

### Two-Way Linkage

Two-way linkage allows for consideration of human resource issues during the strategy formulation process. This integration occurs in three sequential steps. First, the strategic planning team informs the HRM function of the various strategies the company is considering. Then HRM executives analyze the human resource implications of the various strategies, presenting the results of this analysis to the strategic planning team. Finally, after the strategic decision has been made, the strategic plan is passed on to the HRM executive, who develops programs to implement it. The strategic planning function and the HRM function are interdependent in two-way linkage.

### Integrative Linkage

Integrative linkage is dynamic and multifaceted, based on continuing rather than sequential interaction. In most cases the HRM executive is an integral member of the senior management team. Rather than an iterative process of information exchange, companies with integrative linkage have their HRM functions built right into the strategy formulation and implementation processes. It is this role that we will discuss throughout the rest of this chapter.

Thus, in strategic HRM, the HRM function is involved in both strategy formulation and strategy implementation. The HRM executive gives strategic planners information about the company's human resource capabilities, and these capabilities are usually a direct function of the HRM practices.[12] This information about human resource capabilities helps top managers choose the best strategy because they can consider how well each strategic alternative would be implemented. Once the strategic choice has been determined, the role of HRM changes to the development and alignment of HRM practices that will give the company employees having the necessary skills to implement the strategy.[13] In addition, HRM practices must be designed to elicit actions from employees in the company.[14] In the next two sections of this chapter we show how HRM can provide a competitive advantage in the strategic management process.

## Strategy Formulation

Five major components of the strategic management process are relevant to strategy formulation.[15] These components are depicted in Figure 2.5. The first component is the organization's mission. The mission is a statement of the organization's reason for being; it usually specifies the customers served, the needs satisfied and/or the values

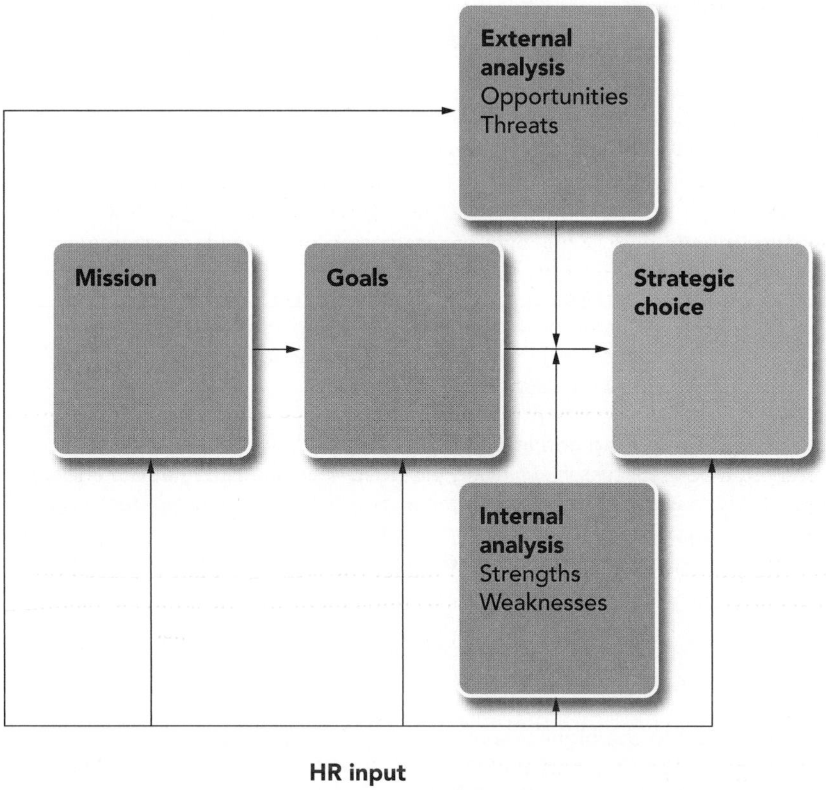


figure 2.5
Strategy Formulation

SOURCE: Adapted from K. Golden and V. Ramanujam, "Between a Dream and a Nightmare," *Human Resource Management* 24 (1985), pp. 429–51.

received by the customers, and the technology used. The mission statement is often accompanied by a statement of a company's vision and/or values. For example, Table 2.1 illustrates the mission and values of Merck & Co., Inc.

An organization's **goals** are what it hopes to achieve in the medium- to long-term future; they reflect how the mission will be operationalized. The overarching goal of most profit-making companies in the United States is to maximize stockholder wealth. But companies have to set other long-term goals in order to maximize stockholder wealth.

**Goals**
What an organization hopes to achieve in the medium- to long-term future.

**External analysis** consists of examining the organization's operating environment to identify the strategic opportunities and threats. Examples of opportunities are customer markets that are not being served, technological advances that can aid the company, and labor pools that have not been tapped. Threats include potential labor shortages, new competitors entering the market, pending legislation that might adversely affect the company, and competitors' technological innovations.

**External Analysis**
Examining the organization's operating environment to identify strategic opportunities and threats.

**Internal analysis** attempts to identify the organization's strengths and weaknesses. It focuses on the quantity and quality of resources available to the organization— financial, capital, technological, and human resources. Organizations have to honestly and accurately assess each resource to decide whether it is a strength or a weakness.

**Internal Analysis**
The process of examining an organization's strengths and weaknesses.

External analysis and internal analysis combined constitute what has come to be called the SWOT (strengths, weaknesses, opportunities, threats) analysis. After going through the SWOT analysis, the strategic planning team has all the information it needs to generate a number of strategic alternatives. The strategic managers compare these alternatives' ability to attain the organization's strategic goals; then they make

**table 2.1**
Merck & Co.'s Mission and Values

| MISSION STATEMENT |
|---|
| Merck & Co., Inc. is a leading research-driven pharmaceutical products and services company. Merck discovers, develops, manufactures and markets a broad range of innovative products to improve human and animal health. The Merck-Medco Managed Care Division manages pharmacy benefits for more than 40 million Americans, encouraging the appropriate use of medicines and providing disease management programs. |
| **Our Mission** |
| The mission of Merck is to provide society with superior products and services—innovations and solutions that improve the quality of life and satisfy customer needs—to provide employees with meaningful work and advancement opportunities and investors with a superior rate of return. |
| **Our Values** |
| 1. **Our business is preserving and improving human life.** All of our actions must be measured by our success in achieving this goal. We value above all our ability to serve everyone who can benefit from the appropriate use of our products and services, thereby providing lasting consumer satisfaction. |
| 2. **We are committed to the highest standards of ethics and integrity.** We are responsible to our customers, to Merck employees and their families, to the environments we inhabit, and to the societies we serve worldwide. In discharging our responsibilities, we do not take professional or ethical shortcuts. Our interactions with all segments of society must reflect the high standards we profess. |
| 3. **We are dedicated to the highest level of scientific excellence and commit our research to improving human and animal health and the quality of life.** We strive to identify the most critical needs of consumers and customers; we devote our resources to meeting those needs. |
| 4. **We expect profits, but only from work that satisfies customer needs and benefits humanity.** Our ability to meet our responsibilities depends on maintaining a financial position that invites investment in leading-edge research and that makes possible effective delivery of research results. |
| 5. **We recognize that the ability to excel—to most competitively meet society's and customers' needs—depends on the integrity, knowledge, imagination, skill, diversity, and teamwork of employees, and we value these qualities most highly.** To this end, we strive to create an environment of mutual respect, encouragement, and teamwork—a working environment that rewards commitment and performance and is responsive to the needs of employees and their families. |

SOURCE: www.merck.com/about/mission.html.

**Strategic Choice**
The organization's strategy; the ways an organization will attempt to fulfill its mission and achieve its long-term goals.

their **strategic choice.** The strategic choice is the organization's strategy; it describes the ways the organization will attempt to fulfill its mission and achieve its long-term goals.

Many of the opportunities and threats in the external environment are people-related. With fewer and fewer highly qualified individuals entering the labor market, organizations compete not just for customers but for employees. It is HRM's role to keep close tabs on the external environment for human resource–related opportunities and threats, especially those directly related to the HRM function: potential labor shortages, competitor wage rates, government regulations affecting employment, and so on. For example, as discussed in Chapter 1, U.S. companies are finding that more and more high school graduates lack the basic skills needed to work, which is one source of the "human capital shortage."[16] However, not recognizing this environmental threat, many companies have encouraged the exit of older, more skilled workers while hiring less skilled younger workers who require basic skills training.[17]

An analysis of a company's internal strengths and weaknesses also requires input from the HRM function. Today companies are increasingly realizing that their human resources are one of their most important assets. In fact, one estimate is that over one-third of the total growth in U.S. GNP between 1943 and 1990 was the result of increases in human capital. A company's failure to consider the strengths and weaknesses of its workforce may result in its choosing strategies it is not capable of pursuing.[18] However, some research has demonstrated that few companies have achieved this level of linkage.[19] For example, one company chose a strategy of cost reduction through technological improvements. It built a plant designed around a computer-integrated manufacturing system with statistical process controls. Though this choice may seem like a good one, the company soon learned otherwise. It discovered that its employees could not operate the new equipment because 25 percent of the workforce was functionally illiterate.[20]

Thus, with an integrative linkage, strategic planners consider all the people-related business issues before making a strategic choice. These issues are identified with regard to the mission, goals, opportunities, threats, strengths, and weaknesses, leading the strategic planning team to make a more intelligent strategic choice. Although this process does not guarantee success, companies that address these issues are more likely to make choices that will ultimately succeed.

Recent research has supported the need to have HRM executives integrally involved in strategy formulation. One study of U.S. petrochemical refineries found that the level of HRM involvement was positively related to the refinery manager's evaluation of the effectiveness of the HRM function.[21] A second study of manufacturing firms found that HRM involvement was highest when top managers viewed employees as a strategic asset and associated with reduced turnover.[22] However, both studies found that HRM involvement was unrelated to operating unit financial performance.

Research has indicated that few companies have fully integrated HRM into the strategy formulation process.[23] As we've mentioned before, companies are beginning to recognize that in an intensely competitive environment, managing human resources strategically can provide a competitive advantage. Thus companies at the administrative linkage level will either become more integrated or face extinction. In addition, companies will move toward becoming integratively linked in an effort to manage human resources strategically.

It is of utmost importance that all people-related business issues be considered during strategy formulation. These issues are identified in the HRM function. Mechanisms or structures for integrating the HRM function into strategy formulation may help the strategic planning team make the most effective strategic choice. Once that strategic choice is determined, HRM must take an active role in implementing it. This role will be discussed in the next section.

## Strategy Implementation

**LO5**
Discuss the More Popular Typologies of Generic Strategies and the Various HRM Practices Associated with Each.

After an organization has chosen its strategy, it has to execute that strategy—make it come to life in its day-to-day workings. The strategy a company pursues dictates certain HR needs. For a company to have a good strategy foundation, certain tasks must be accomplished in pursuit of the company's goals, individuals must possess certain skills to perform those tasks, and these individuals must be motivated to perform their skills effectively.

figure 2.6
Variables to Be Considered in Strategy Implementation

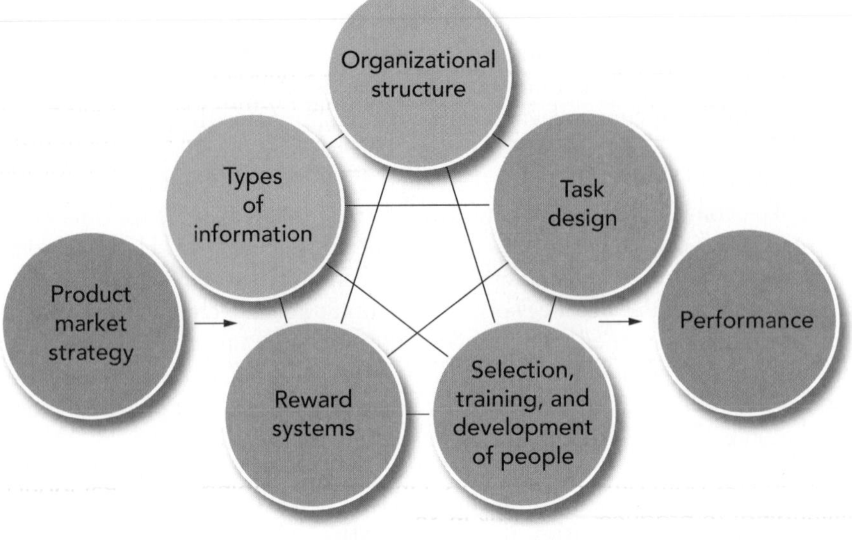


The basic premise behind strategy implementation is that "an organization has a variety of structural forms and organizational processes to choose from when implementing a given strategy," and these choices make an economic difference.[24] Five important variables determine success in strategy implementation: organizational structure; task design; the selection, training, and development of people; reward systems; and types of information and information systems.

As we see in Figure 2.6, HRM has primary responsibility for three of these five implementation variables: task, people, and reward systems. In addition, HRM can directly affect the two remaining variables: structure and information and decision processes. First, for the strategy to be successfully implemented, the tasks must be designed and grouped into jobs in a way that is efficient and effective.[25] In Chapter 4 we will examine how this can be done through the processes of job analysis and job design. Second, the HRM function must ensure that the organization is staffed with people who have the necessary knowledge, skill, and ability to perform their part in implementing the strategy. This goal is achieved primarily through recruitment, selection and placement, training, development, and career management—topics covered in Chapters 5, 6, 7, and 9. In addition, the HRM function must develop performance management and reward systems that lead employees to work for and support the strategic plan. The specific types of performance management systems are covered in Chapter 8, and the many issues involved in developing reward systems are discussed in Chapters 11 through 13. In other words, the role of the HRM function becomes one of (1) ensuring that the company has the proper number of employees with the levels and types of skills required by the strategic plan[26] and (2) developing "control" systems that ensure that those employees are acting in ways that promote the achievement of the goals specified in the strategic plan.[27]

In essence, this is what has been referred to as the "vertical alignment" of HR with strategy. Vertical alignment means that the HR practices and processes are aimed at addressing the strategic needs of the business. But the link between strategy and HR practices is primarily through people. For instance, as IBM moved from being a manufacturer of personal computers to being a fully integrated service provider, the types of people it needed changed significantly. Instead of employing thousands of workers in

## COMPETING THROUGH SUSTAINABILITY

### Patagonia's Passion for the Planet Attracts Talent

In a world that is constantly focused on the "War for Talent," firms have gone to great lengths to find compensation and benefits packages that attract and retain high performers. However, outdoor clothing and equipment seller Patagonia, Inc., uses its sustainability philosophy to capture and enrapture top-notch talent. Founder and chairman Yvon Chouinard articulates the company's goal as both simple and challenging: to produce the highest quality products while doing the least possible harm to the planet. And it is this mission that inspires the over 1,200 employees at Patagonia.

It was this philosophy that brought Southern Californian Scott Robinson to Patagonia. Having an undergraduate degree from Bucknell, two MBAs, and internships at two global companies, he begged for a job as a stock handler at Patagonia's Cardiff-by-the-Sea, California, store. On a trip back from France, he had read Chouinard's book *Let My People Go Surfing*, and was attracted to the employee and environmental philosophy described.

The company encourages employees to enjoy the outdoors as a way to devise new product ideas. For instance, during a mountain-climbing trek in Yosemite National Park, Dean Potter cut the legs off his climbing pants at midcalf in order to see his feet while he climbed. The next year Patagonia came out with a successful line of climbing pants based on his ideas.

Overall, Patagonia pays at or slightly above market, but the overall number is misleading. All employees get a bonus based on profits, without which the salaries would be below market. However, most work there not just for the money, but for the other rewards. For instance, one perk is a "green sabbatical," which allows employees two months off at full pay to work for environmental groups.

The Patagonia culture makes it a talent magnet. It receives approximately 900 résumés for every job opening, which allows Patagonia to be very selective in whom it hires. Even though the company is relatively small, it has been able to attract executives from larger competitors such as North Face. Patagonia exemplifies that fact that a corporate philosophy that appeals to the values of talented individuals is better able to attract talented employees than money alone.

SOURCE: S. Hamm, "A Passion for the Planet," *BusinessWeek*. August 21/28, 2006, pp. 92–94.

manufacturing or assembly plants, IBM increasingly needed software engineers to help write new "middleware" programs, and an army of consultants who could help their corporate customers to implement these systems. In addition, as IBM increasingly differentiated itself as being the "integrated solutions" provider (meaning it could sell the hardware, software, consulting, and service for a company's entire information technology needs), employees needed a new mindset which emphasized cooperating across different business divisions rather than running independently. Thus, the change in strategy required different kinds of skills, different kinds of employees, and different kinds of behaviors. The "Competing through Sustainability" box illustrates how Patagonia is using its corporate social responsibility philosophy and HR practices to attract talent to the firm.

How does the HRM function implement strategy? As Figure 2.7 shows, it is through administering HRM practices: job analysis/design, recruitment, selection systems, training and development programs, performance management systems, reward systems, and labor relations programs. The details of each of these HRM practices are the focus of the rest of this book. However, at this point it is important to present a general overview of the HRM practices and their role in strategy implementation. We will then discuss the

figure 2.7
Strategy Implementation

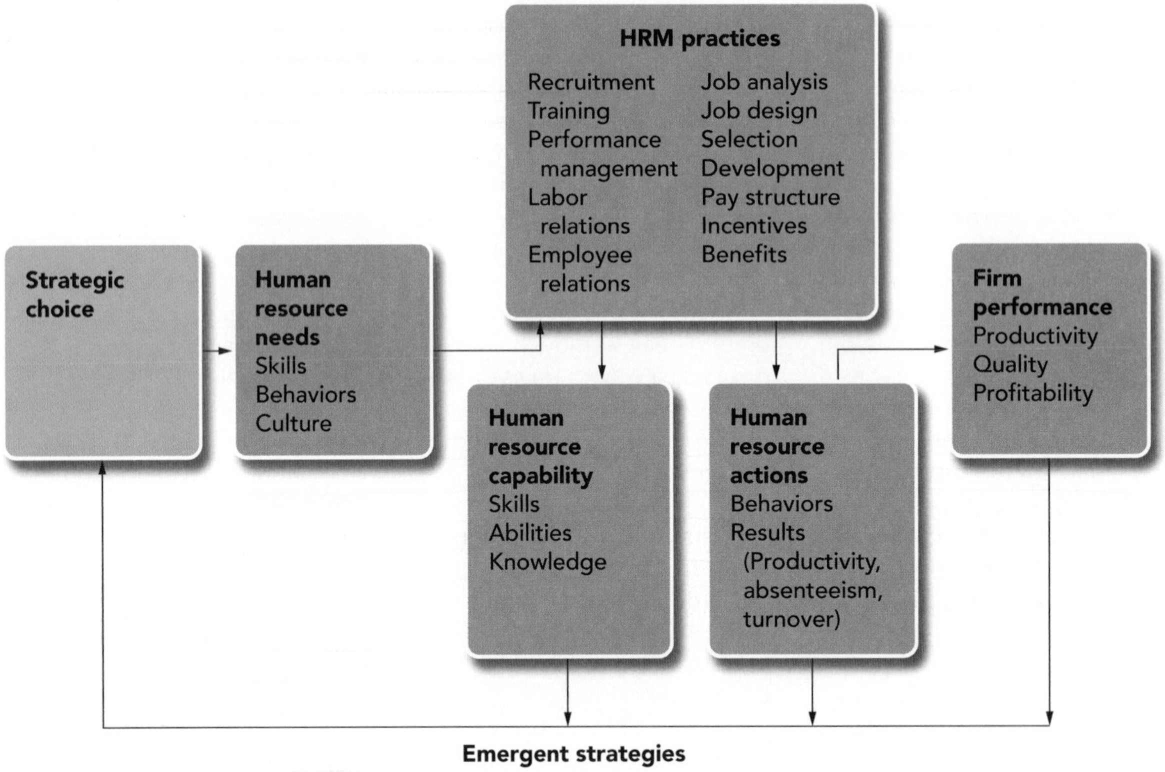


various strategies companies pursue and the types of HRM systems congruent with those strategies. First we focus on how the strategic types are implemented; then we discuss the HRM practices associated with various directional strategies.

## HRM Practices

The HRM function can be thought of as having six menus of HRM practices, from which companies can choose the ones most appropriate for implementing their strategy. Each of these menus refers to a particular functional area of HRM: job analysis/ design, recruitment/ selection, training and development, performance management, pay structure/incentives/ benefits, and labor–employee relations.[28] These menus are presented in Table 2.2.

**Job Analysis**
The process of getting detailed information about jobs.

**Job Design**
The process of defining the way work will be performed and the tasks that will be required in a given job.

### Job Analysis and Design

Companies produce a given product or service (or set of products or services), and the manufacture of these products requires that a number of tasks be performed. These tasks are grouped together to form jobs. **Job analysis** is the process of getting detailed information about jobs. **Job design** addresses what tasks should be grouped into a particular job. The way that jobs are designed should have an important tie to the strategy of an organization because the strategy requires either new and different tasks or different ways of performing the same tasks. In addition, because many strategies entail the introduction of new technologies, this impacts the way that work is performed.[29]

**table 2.2**

Menu of HRM Practice Options

| | | |
|---|---|---|
| **Job Analysis and Design** | | |
| Few tasks | ⟷ | Many tasks |
| Simple tasks | ⟷ | Complex tasks |
| Few skills required | ⟷ | Many skills required |
| Specific job descriptions | ⟷ | General job descriptions |
| **Recruitment and Selection** | | |
| External sources | ⟷ | Internal sources |
| Limited socialization | ⟷ | Extensive socialization |
| Assessment of specific skills | ⟷ | Assessment of general skills |
| Narrow career paths | ⟷ | Broad career paths |
| **Training and Development** | | |
| Focus on current job skills | ⟷ | Focus on future job skills |
| Individual orientation | ⟷ | Group orientation |
| Train few employees | ⟷ | Train all employees |
| Spontaneous, unplanned | ⟷ | Planned, systematic |
| **Performance Management** | | |
| Behavioral criteria | ⟷ | Results criteria |
| Developmental orientation | ⟷ | Administrative orientation |
| Short-term criteria | ⟷ | Long-term criteria |
| Individual orientation | ⟷ | Group orientation |
| **Pay Structure, Incentives, and Benefits** | | |
| Pay weighted toward salary and benefits | ⟷ | Pay weighted toward incentives |
| Short-term incentives | ⟷ | Long-term incentives |
| Emphasis on internal equity | ⟷ | Emphasis on external equity |
| Individual incentives | ⟷ | Group incentives |
| **Labor and Employee Relations** | | |
| Collective bargaining | ⟷ | Individual bargaining |
| Top-down decision making | ⟷ | Participation in decision making |
| Formal due process | ⟷ | No due process |
| View employees as expense | ⟷ | View employees as assets |

SOURCE: Adapted from R. S. Schuler and S. F. Jackson, "Linking Competitive Strategies with Human Resource Management Practices," *Academy of Management Executive* 1 (1987), pp. 207–19; and C. Fisher, L. Schoenfeldt, and B. Shaw, *Human Resource Management*, 2nd ed. (Boston: Houghton Mifflin, 1992).

In general, jobs can vary from having a narrow range of tasks (most of which are simplified and require a limited range of skills) to having a broad array of complex tasks requiring multiple skills. In the past, the narrow design of jobs has been used to increase efficiency, while the broad design of jobs has been associated with efforts to increase innovation. However, with the advent of total quality management methods and a variety of employee involvement programs such as quality circles, many jobs are moving toward the broader end of the spectrum.[30]

## Employee Recruitment and Selection

**Recruitment** is the process through which the organization seeks applicants for potential employment. **Selection** refers to the process by which it attempts to identify applicants with the necessary knowledge, skills, abilities, and other characteristics that will help the company achieve its goals. Companies engaging in different strategies need different types and numbers of employees. Thus the strategy a company is pursuing will have a direct impact on the types of employees that it seeks to recruit and select.[31]

**Recruitment**
The process of seeking applicants for potential employment.

**Selection**
The process by which an organization attempts to identify applicants with the necessary knowledge, skills, abilities, and other characteristics that will help it achieve its goals.

## Employee Training and Development

A number of skills are instilled in employees through training and development. **Training** refers to a planned effort to facilitate the learning of job-related knowledge, skills, and behavior by employees. **Development** involves acquiring knowledge, skills, and behavior that improve employees' ability to meet the challenges of a variety of existing jobs or jobs that do not yet exist. Changes in strategies often require changes in the types, levels, and mixes of skills. Thus the acquisition of strategy-related skills is an essential element of the implementation of strategy. For example, many companies have recently emphasized quality in their products, engaging in total quality management programs. These programs require extensive training of all employees in the TQM philosophy, methods, and often other skills that ensure quality.[32]

Through recruitment, selection, training, and development, companies can obtain a pool of human resources capable of implementing a given strategy.[33]

**Training**
A planned effort to facilitate the learning of job-related knowledge, skills, and behavior by employees.

**Development**
The acquisition of knowledge, skills, and behaviors that improve an employee's ability to meet changes in job requirements and in client and customer demands.

**Performance Management**
The means through which managers ensure that employees' activities and outputs are congruent with the organization's goals.

## Performance Management

**Performance management** is used to ensure that employees' activities and outcomes are congruent with the organization's objectives. It entails specifying those activities and outcomes that will result in the firm's successfully implementing the strategy. For example, companies that are "steady state" (not diversified) tend to have evaluation systems that call for subjective performance assessments of managers. This stems from the fact that those above the first-level managers in the hierarchy have extensive knowledge about how the work should be performed. On the other hand, diversified companies are more likely to use quantitative measures of performance to evaluate managers because top managers have less knowledge about how work should be performed by those below them in the hierarchy.[34]

Similarly, executives who have extensive knowledge of the behaviors that lead to effective performance use performance management systems that focus on the behaviors of their subordinate managers. However, when executives are unclear about the specific behaviors that lead to effective performance, they tend to focus on evaluating the objective performance results of their subordinate managers.[35]

An example of how performance management can be aligned with strategy is provided in Figure 2.8. This comes from a firm in the health care industry whose strategy consisted of five "strategic imperatives," or things that the company was trying to accomplish. In this company all individuals set performance objectives each year, and each of their objectives have to be tied to at least one of the strategic imperatives. The senior VP of HR used the firm's technology system to examine the extent to which each business unit or function was focused on each of the imperatives. The figure illustrates the percentage of objectives that were tied to each imperative across the different units. It allows the company to determine if the mix of objectives is right enterprisewide as well as within each business unit or function.

## Pay Structure, Incentives, and Benefits

The pay system has an important role in implementing strategies. First, a high level of pay and/or benefits relative to that of competitors can ensure that the company attracts and retains high-quality employees, but this might have a negative impact on the company's overall labor costs.[36] Second, by tying pay to performance, the company can elicit specific activities and levels of performance from employees.

In a study of how compensation practices are tied to strategies, researchers examined 33 high-tech and 72 traditional companies. They classified them by whether they were in a growth stage (greater than 20 percent inflation-adjusted increases in

figure 2.8

Percentage of Objectives Identified in Individual Performance Plans that Are Tied to Each Strategic Imperative

| Strategic Imperative | Business A | Business B | International | Investment | Finance | Legal | IT | HR&S | Enterprise |
|---|---|---|---|---|---|---|---|---|---|
| Achieve superior medical performance | 10.5% | 12.5% | 2.7% | 7.6% | 3.1% | 2.7% | 11.4% | 2.1% | 10.0% |
| Effectively serve our customers | 24.7% | 27.2% | 36.7% | 12.2% | 10.3% | 27.2% | 18.9% | 19.5% | 23.7% |
| Create great products and services | 5.6% | 6.1% | 10.1% | 9.8% | 5.0% | 10.1% | 15.3% | 8.9% | 6.9% |
| Create a winning environment | 27.7% | 29.7% | 30.1% | 29.9% | 30.3% | 33.7% | 22.4% | 39.4% | 27.7% |
| Establish a cost advantage | 31.5% | 24.5% | 20.5% | 40.5% | 51.3% | 26.3% | 32% | 30.0% | 31.7% |
| Total | 100% | 100% | 100% | 100% | 100% | 100% | 100% | 100% | 100% |

annual sales) or a maturity stage. They found that high-tech companies in the growth stage used compensation systems that were highly geared toward incentive pay, with a lower percentage of total pay devoted to salary and benefits. On the other hand, compensation systems among mature companies (both high-tech and traditional) devoted a lower percentage of total pay to incentives and a high percentage to benefits.[37]

## Labor and Employee Relations

Whether companies are unionized or not, the general approach to relations with employees can strongly affect their potential for gaining competitive advantage. In the late 1970s Chrysler Corporation was faced with bankruptcy. Lee Iacocca, the new president of Chrysler, asked the union for wage and work-rule concessions in an effort to turn the company around. The union agreed to the concessions, in return receiving profit sharing and a representative on the board. Within only a few years, the relationship with and support from the union allowed Chrysler to pull itself out of bankruptcy and into record profitability.[38]

The relationship between management and employees can strongly affect the company's potential for competitive advantage. How do you think the manager here is building strong relationships with his employee?

However, as the opening case illustrates, Chrysler has not been quite so lucky this time around. Ford and General Motors already have gone to their unions to ask for givebacks that would help them reduce their costs. While this was a tough sell, the unions finally gave some ground. However, Chrysler did not capitalize on this, and has failed to negotiate any reductions.

Companies can choose to treat employees as an asset that requires investment of resources or as an expense to be minimized.[39] They have to make choices about how much employees can and should participate in decision making, what rights employees have, and what the company's responsibility is to them. The approach a company takes in making these decisions can result in it either successfully achieving its short- and long-term goals or ceasing to exist.

Recent research has begun to examine how companies develop sets of HRM practices that maximize performance and productivity. For example, one study of automobile assembly plants around the world found that plants that exhibited both high productivity and high quality used "HRM best practices," such as heavy emphasis on recruitment and hiring, compensation tied to performance, low levels of status differentiation, high levels of training for both new and experienced employees, and employee participation through structures such as work teams and problem-solving groups.[40] Another study found that HRM systems composed of selection testing, training, contingent pay, performance appraisal, attitude surveys, employee participation, and information sharing resulted in higher levels of productivity and corporate financial performance, as well as lower employee turnover.[41] Finally, a recent study found that companies identified as some of the "best places to work" had higher financial performances than a set of matched companies that did not make the list.[42] Similar results have also been observed in a number of other studies.[43]

HRM Best Practices

In addition to the relationship between HR practices and performance in general, in today's fast-changing environment, businesses have to change quickly, requiring changes in employees' skills and behaviors. In one study the researchers found that the flexibility of HR practices, employee skills, and employee behaviors were all positively related to firm financial performance, but only the skill flexibility was related to cost efficiency.[44] While these relationships are promising, the causal direction has not yet been proven. For instance, while effective HR practices should help firms perform better, it is also true that highly profitable firms can invest more in HR practices.[45] The research seems to indicate that while the relationship between practices and performance is consistently positive, we should not go too far out on a limb arguing that increasing the use of HRM practices will automatically result in increased profitability.[46]

## Strategic Types

As we previously discussed, companies can be classified by the generic strategies they pursue. It is important to note that these generic "strategies" are not what we mean by a strategic plan. They are merely similarities in the ways companies seek to compete in their industries. Various typologies have been offered, but we will focus on the two generic strategies proposed by Porter: cost and differentiation.[47]

According to Michael Porter of Harvard, competitive advantage stems from a company's being able to create value in its production process. Value can be created in one of two ways. First, value can be created by reducing costs. Second, value can be created by differentiating a product or service in such a way that it allows the company to charge a premium price relative to its competitors. This leads to two basic strategies. According to Porter, the "overall cost leadership" strategy focuses on becoming the lowest cost producer in an industry. This strategy is achieved by constructing efficient large-scale facilities, by reducing costs through capitalizing on the experience curve, and by controlling overhead costs and costs in such areas as research and development, service, sales force, and advertising. This strategy provides above-average returns within an industry, and it tends to bar other firms' entry into the industry because the firm can lower its prices below competitors' costs. For example, IBM-clone computer manufacturers like Dell and Compaq have captured an increased share of the personal computer market by offering personal computers at lower cost than IBM and Apple.

The "differentiation" strategy, according to Porter, attempts to create the impression that the company's product or service is different from that of others in the industry. The perceived differentiation can come from creating a brand image, from technology, from offering unique features, or from unique customer service. If a company succeeds in differentiating its product, it will achieve above-average returns, and the differentiation may protect it from price sensitivity. For example, IBM has consistently emphasized its brand image and its reputation for superior service while charging a higher price for its computers.

## HRM Needs in Strategic Types

While all of the strategic types require competent people in a generic sense, each of the strategies also requires different types of employees with different types of behaviors and attitudes. As we noted earlier, different strategies require employees with specific skills and also require these employees to exhibit different "role behaviors."[48] **Role behaviors** are the behaviors required of an individual in his or her role as a job holder in a social work environment. These role behaviors vary on a number of dimensions. Additionally, different role behaviors are required by the different strategies. For example, companies engaged in a cost strategy require employees to have a high concern for quantity and a short-term focus, to be comfortable with stability, and to be risk averse. These employees are expected to exhibit role behaviors that are relatively repetitive and performed independently or autonomously.

**Role Behaviors**
Behaviors that are required of an individual in his or her role as a jobholder in a social work environment.

Thus companies engaged in cost strategies, because of the focus on efficient production, tend to specifically define the skills they require and invest in training employees in these skill areas. They also rely on behavioral performance management systems with a large performance-based compensation component. These companies promote internally and develop internally consistent pay systems with high pay differentials between superiors and subordinates. They seek efficiency through worker participation, soliciting employees' ideas on how to achieve more efficient production.

On the other hand, employees in companies with a differentiation strategy need to be highly creative and cooperative; to have only a moderate concern for quantity, a long-term focus, and a tolerance for ambiguity; and to be risk takers. Employees in these companies are expected to exhibit role behaviors that include cooperating with others, developing new ideas, and taking a balanced approach to process and results.

Thus differentiation companies will seek to generate more creativity through broadly defined jobs with general job descriptions. They may recruit more from outside, engage in limited socialization of newcomers, and provide broader career paths. Training and development activities focus on cooperation. The compensation system is geared toward external equity, as it is heavily driven by recruiting needs. These companies develop results-based performance management system and divisional–corporate performance evaluations to encourage risk taking on the part of managers.[49]

### EVIDENCE-BASED HR

A recent study of HRM among steel minimills in the United States found that mills pursuing different strategies used different systems of HRM. Mills seeking cost leadership tended to use control-oriented HRM systems that were characterized by high centralization, low participation, low training, low wages, low benefits, and highly contingent pay, whereas differentiator mills used "commitment" HRM systems, characterized as the opposite on each of those dimensions. A later study from the same sample revealed that the mills with the commitment systems had higher productivity, lower scrap rates, and lower employee turnover than those with the control systems.

SOURCE: J. Arthur, "The Link between Business Strategy and Industrial Relations Systems in American Steel Mini-Mills," *Industrial and Labor Relations Review* 45 (1992), pp. 488–506.

## Directional Strategies

LO6
Describe the Different HRM Issues and Practices Associated with Various Directional Strategies.

As discussed earlier in this chapter, strategic typologies are useful for classifying the ways different organizations seek to compete within an industry. However, it is also necessary to understand how increasing size (growth) or decreasing it (downsizing) affects the HRM function. For example, the top management team might decide that they need to invest more in product development or to diversify as a means for growth. With these types of strategies, it is more useful for the HRM function to aid in evaluating the feasibility of the various alternatives and to develop programs that support the strategic choice.

Companies have used five possible categories of directional strategies to meet objectives.[50] Strategies emphasizing market share or operating costs are considered "concentration" strategies. With this type of strategy, a company attempts to focus on what it does best within its established markets and can be thought of as "sticking to its knitting." Strategies focusing on market development, product development, innovation, or joint ventures make up the "internal growth" strategy. Companies with an internal growth strategy channel their resources toward building on existing strengths. Those attempting to integrate vertically or horizontally or to diversify are exhibiting an **"external growth" strategy,** usually through mergers or acquisitions. This strategy attempts to expand a company's resources or to strengthen its market position through acquiring or creating new businesses. Finally, a "divestment," or downsizing, strategy is one made up of retrenchment, divestitures, or liquidation. These strategies are observed among companies facing serious economic difficulties and seeking to pare down their operations. The human resource implications of each of these strategies are quite different.

**External Growth Strategy**
An emphasis on acquiring vendors and suppliers or buying businesses that allow a company to expand into new markets.

### Concentration Strategies

**Concentration strategies** require that the company maintain the current skills that exist in the organization. This requires that training programs provide a means of keeping those skills sharp among people in the organization and that compensation programs focus on retaining people who have those skills. Appraisals in this strategy tend to be more behavioral because the environment is more certain, and the behaviors necessary for effective performance tend to be established through extensive experience.

**Concentration Strategy**
A strategy focusing on increasing market share, reducing costs, or creating and maintaining a market niche for products and services.

### Internal Growth Strategies

**Internal growth strategies** present unique staffing problems. Growth requires that a company constantly hire, transfer, and promote individuals, and expansion into different markets may change the necessary skills that prospective employees must have. In addition, appraisals often consist of a combination of behaviors and results. The behavioral appraisal emphasis stems from the knowledge of effective behaviors in a particular product market, and the results appraisals focus on achieving growth goals. Compensation packages are heavily weighted toward incentives for achieving growth goals. Training needs differ depending on the way the company attempts to grow internally. For example, if the organization seeks to expand its markets, training will focus on knowledge of each market, particularly when the company is expanding into international markets. On the other hand, when the company is seeking innovation or product development, training will be of a more technical nature, as well

**Internal Growth Strategy**
A focus on new market and product development, innovation, and joint ventures.

as focusing on interpersonal skills such as team building. Joint ventures require extensive training in conflict resolution techniques because of the problems associated with combining people from two distinct organizational cultures.

## Mergers and Acquisitions (External Growth)

Increasingly we see both consolidation within industries and mergers across industries. For example, British Petroleum's recent agreement to acquire Amoco Oil represents a consolidation, or reduction in number of firms within the industry. On the other hand, Citicorp's merger with Traveller's Group to form Citigroup represents firms from different industries (pure financial services and insurance) combining to change the dynamics within both. Whatever the type, one thing is for sure—mergers and acquisitions are on the increase, and HRM needs to be involved.[51] In addition, these mergers more frequently consist of global megamergers, in spite of some warnings that these might not be effective

According to a report by the Conference Board, "people issues" may be one of the major reasons that mergers do not always live up to expectations. Some companies now heavily weigh firm cultures before embarking on a merger or acquisition. For example, prior to acquiring ValueRx, executives at Express Scripts, Inc., interviewed senior executives and middle managers at the potential target firm in order to get a sense of its culture.[52] In spite of this, fewer than one-third of the HRM executives surveyed said that they had a major influence in how mergers are planned, yet 80 percent of them said that people issues have a significant impact after the deals are finalized.[53]

In addition to the desirability of HRM playing a role in evaluating a merger opportunity, HRM certainly has a role in the actual implementation of a merger or acquisition. Training in conflict resolution is also necessary when companies engage in an external growth strategy. All the options for external growth consist of acquiring or developing new businesses, and these businesses often have distinct cultures. Thus many HRM programs face problems in integrating and standardizing practices across the company's businesses. The relative value of standardizing practices across businesses must be weighed against the unique environmental requirements of each business and the extent of desired integration of the two firms. For example, with regard to pay practices, a company may desire a consistent internal wage structure to maintain employee perceptions of equity in the larger organization. In a recent new business developed by IBM, the employees pressured the company to maintain the same wage structure as IBM's main operation. However, some businesses may function in environments where pay practices are driven heavily by market forces. Requiring these businesses to adhere to pay practices in other environments may result in an ineffective wage structure.

## Downsizing

Of increasing importance to organizations in today's competitive environment is HRM's role in **downsizing** or "rightsizing." The number of organizations undergoing downsizing has increased significantly. In fact, from 1988 to 1993, some 1.4 million executives, managers, and administrators were laid off during downsizing, compared with only 782,000 from 1976 to 1981.[54]

**Downsizing**
The planned elimination of large numbers of personnel, designed to enhance organizational effectiveness.

One would have great difficulty ignoring the massive "war for talent" that went on during the late 1990s, particularly with the notable dot-com craze. Firms during this time sought to become "employers of choice," to establish "employment brands," and to develop "employee value propositions" as ways to ensure that they would be able to attract and retain talented employees. However, what few probably noticed was that in spite of the hiring craze, this was also a time of massive layoffs. In fact, 1998, the height of the war for talent, also saw the largest number of layoffs in the decade.

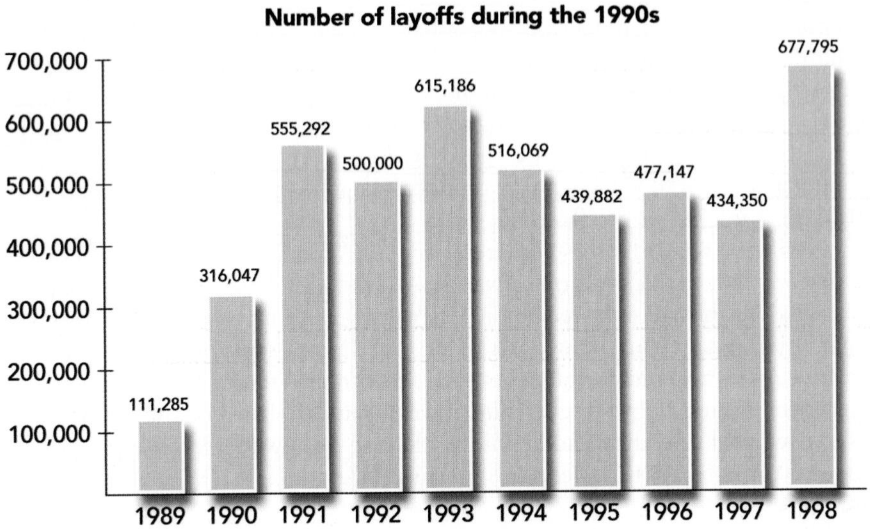


SOURCE: Challenger, Gray, and Christmas, 1998.

This new trend seems to represent a "churn" of employees, in which firms lay off those with outdated skills or cut whole businesses that are in declining markets while simultaneously building businesses and employee bases in newer, high-growth markets. For example, IBM cut 69,256 people and increased its workforce by 16,000 in 1996. Today IBM's Senior Vice President for Human Resources Randy MacDonald estimates that 15% of their workforce's skills become obsolete each year.

The important question facing firms is, How can we develop a reputation as an employer of choice, and engage employees to the goals of the firm, while constantly laying off a significant portion of our workforce? How firms answer this question will determine how they can compete by meeting the stakeholder needs of their employees.

In spite of the increasing frequency of downsizing, research reveals that it is far from universally successful for achieving the goals of increased productivity and increased profitability. For example, Table 2.3 illustrates the results of a survey conducted by the American Management Association indicating that only about one-third of the companies that went through downsizings actually achieved their goal of increased productivity. Another survey by the AMA found that over two-thirds of the companies that downsize repeat the effort a year later.[55] Also, research by the consulting firm Mitchell & Company found that companies that downsized during the 1980s lagged the industry average stock price in 1991.[56] Thus it is important to understand the best ways of managing downsizings, particularly from the standpoint of HRM.

Downsizing presents a number of challenges and opportunities for HRM.[57] In terms of challenges, the HRM function must "surgically" reduce the workforce by cutting

**table 2.3**

Effects of Downsizing on Desired Outcomes

| DESIRED OUTCOME | PERCENTAGE THAT ACHIEVED DESIRED RESULT |
|---|---|
| Reduced expenses | 46% |
| Increased profits | 32 |
| Improved cash flow | 24 |
| Increased productivity | 22 |
| Increased return on investment | 21 |
| Increased competitive advantage | 19 |
| Reduced bureaucracy | 17 |
| Improved decision making | 14 |
| Increased customer satisfaction | 14 |
| Increased sales | 13 |
| Increased market share | 12 |
| Improved product quality | 9 |
| Technological advances | 9 |
| Increased innovation | 7 |
| Avoidance of a takeover | 6 |

SOURCE: From *The Wall Street Journal,* Eastern Edition June 6, 1991. Copyright © 1991 by Dow Jones & Co. Inc. Reproduced with permission of Dow Jones & Co., Inc. via Copyright Clearance Center.

only the workers who are less valuable in their performance. Achieving this is difficult because the best workers are most able (and often willing) to find alternative employment and may leave voluntarily prior to any layoff. For example, in 1992 General Motors and the United Auto Workers agreed to an early retirement program for individuals between the ages of 51 and 65 who have been employed for 10 or more years. The program provided those who agreed to retire their full pension benefits, even if they obtained employment elsewhere, and as much as $13,000 toward the purchase of a GM car.[58]

Early retirement programs, although humane, essentially reduce the workforce with a "grenade" approach. This type of reduction does not distinguish between good and poor performers but rather eliminates an entire group of employees. In fact, recent research indicates that when companies downsize by offering early retirement programs, they usually end up rehiring to replace essential talent within a year. Often the company does not achieve its cost-cutting goals because it spends 50 to 150 percent of the departing employee's salary in hiring and retraining new workers.[59]

Another HRM challenge is to boost the morale of employees who remain after the reduction; this is discussed in greater detail in Chapter 5. Survivors may feel guilt over keeping their jobs when their friends have been laid off, or they may envy their friends who have retired with attractive severance and pension benefits. Their reduced satisfaction with and commitment to the organization may interfere with work performance. Thus the HRM function must maintain open communication with remaining employees to build their trust and commitment rather than withholding information.[60] All employees should be informed of the purpose of the downsizing, the costs to be cut, the duration of the downsizing, and the strategies to be pursued. In addition, companies going through downsizing often develop compensation programs that tie the individual's compensation to the company's success. Employee ownership programs often result from downsizing, and gainsharing plans such as the Scanlon plan (discussed in Chapter 12) originated in companies facing economic difficulties.

In spite of these challenges, downsizing provides opportunities for HRM. First, it often allows the company to "get rid of dead wood" and make way for fresh ideas. In addition, downsizing is often a unique opportunity to change an organization's culture. In firms characterized by antagonistic labor–management relations, downsizing can force the parties to cooperate and to develop new, positive relationships.[61] Finally, downsizing can demonstrate to top-management decision makers the value of the company's human resources to its ultimate success. The role of HRM is to effectively manage the process in a way that makes this value undeniable. We discuss the implications of downsizing as a labor force management strategy in Chapter 5.

### Strategy Evaluation and Control

A final component to the strategic management process is that of strategy evaluation and control. Thus far we have focused on the planning and implementation of strategy. However, it is extremely important for the firm to constantly monitor the effectiveness of both the strategy and the implementation process. This monitoring makes it possible for the company to identify problem areas and either revise existing structures and strategies or devise new ones. In this process we see emergent strategies appear as well as the critical nature of human resources in competitive advantage.

## The Role of Human Resources in Providing Strategic Competitive Advantage

Thus far we have presented the strategic management process as including a step-by-step procedure by which HRM issues are raised prior to deciding on a strategy and then HRM practices are developed to implement that strategy. However, we must note that human resources can provide a strategic competitive advantage in two additional ways: through emergent strategies and through enhancing competitiveness.

### Emergent Strategies

Having discussed the process of strategic management, we also must distinguish between intended strategies and emergent strategies. Most people think of strategies as being proactive, rational decisions aimed toward some predetermined goal. The view of strategy we have presented thus far in the chapter focuses on intended strategies. Intended strategies are the result of the rational decision-making process used by top managers as they develop a strategic plan. This is consistent with the definition of strategy as "the pattern or plan that integrates an organization's major goals, policies, and action sequences into a cohesive whole."[62] The idea of emergent strategies is evidenced by the feedback loop in Figure 2.2.

Most strategies that companies espouse are intended strategies. For example, when Compaq was founded, the company had its strategy summarized in its name, an amalgam of the words computer, compact, and quality. Thus the intended strategy was to build compact portable computers that were completely free of any defect, and all of the company's efforts were directed toward implementing that strategy. Following that strategy allowed Compaq to become one of the fastest growing companies in the world, commanding 20 percent of the world market in 1991. In 1992 Compaq's performance began to falter again, sparking new CEO Eckhard Pfieffer to change Compaq's strategy to one focused on being a low-cost producer. This strategic change resulted in Compaq becoming the leading PC maker in the world in 1994.[63] More recently, Compaq merged with Hewlett-Packard to create an integrated information technology company that could compete with IBM.

Emergent strategies, on the other hand, consist of the strategies that evolve from the grassroots of the organization and can be thought of as what organizations actually do, as opposed to what they intend to do. Strategy can also be thought of as "a pattern in a stream of decisions or actions."[64] For example, when Honda Motor Company first entered the U.S. market with its 250-cc and 350-cc motorcycles in 1959, it believed that no market existed for its smaller 50-cc bike. However, the sales on the larger motorcycles were sluggish, and Japanese executives running errands around Los Angeles on Honda 50's attracted a lot of attention, including that of a buyer with Sears, Roebuck. Honda found a previously undiscovered market as well as a new distribution outlet (general retailers) that it had not planned on. This emergent strategy gave Honda a 50 percent market share by 1964.[65]

The distinction between intended and emergent strategies has important implications for human resource management.[66] The new focus on strategic HRM has tended to focus primarily on intended strategies. Thus HRM's role has been seen as identifying for top management the people-related business issues relevant to strategy formulation and then developing HRM systems that aid in the implementation of the strategic plan.

However, most emergent strategies are identified by those lower in the organizational hierarchy. It is often the rank-and-file employees who provide ideas for new markets, new products, and new strategies. HRM plays an important role in facilitating communication throughout the organization, and it is this communication that allows for effective emergent strategies to make their way up to top management. This fact led Philip Caldwell, Ford's chairman in the early 1980s, to state, "It's stupid to deny yourself the intellectual capability and constructive attitude of tens of thousands of workers."[67]

## Enhancing Firm Competitiveness

A related way in which human resources can be a source of competitive advantage is through developing a human capital pool that gives the company the unique ability to adapt to an ever-changing environment. Recently managers have become interested in the idea of a "learning organization," in which people continually expand their capacity to achieve the results they desire.[68] This requires the company to be in a constant state of learning through monitoring the environment, assimilating information, making decisions, and flexibly restructuring to compete in that environment. Companies that develop such learning capability have a competitive advantage. Although certain organizational information-processing systems can be an aid, ultimately the people (human capital) who make up the company provide the raw materials in a learning organization.[69]

Thus the role of human resources in competitive advantage should continue to increase because of the fast-paced change characterizing today's business environment. It is becoming increasingly clear that even as U.S. automakers have improved the quality of their cars to compete with the Japanese, these competitors have developed such flexible and adaptable manufacturing systems that they can respond to customer needs more quickly.[70] This flexibility of the manufacturing process allows the emergent strategy to come directly from the marketplace by determining and responding to the exact mix of customer desires. It requires, however, that the company have people in place who have the skills to similarly adapt quickly.[71] As Howard Schultz, the founder and chairman of Starbucks, says, "If people relate to the company they work for, if they form an emotional tie to it and buy into its dreams, they will pour their heart into making it better. When employees have self-esteem and self-respect they can contribute so much more; to their company, to their family, to the world."[72] This statement exemplifies the increasing importance of human resources in developing and maintaining competitive advantage.[73]

## A Look Back

### HANDLING THE TRANSFORMATION AT CHRYSLER

Chrysler's Recovery and Transformation Plan, while creating tremendous economic and social upheaval, provides a thorough example of strategic HRM. First, it illustrates how changing business models almost universally reflect changing labor cost structures. This means fewer employees at high wages and benefits, and over time may reflect new employees being brought in at considerably lower cost. Second, it exemplifies a change in strategy, as the product mix moves from large gas-guzzling SUVs, trucks, and luxury cars to smaller, more fuel-efficient vehicles. Third, it shows the need to transform the capabilities of the firm to meet the new strategic needs, with the attendant change in the types of employees brought into the firm.

It is too early to tell if the plan will meet its objectives and even to know how much of the plan itself might be changed over the course of time. With DaimlerChrysler now having sold off the Chrysler unit, and other automakers such as Nissan exploring partnerships, the future is uncertain. What is certain, though, is that the pressures that are driving Chrysler to change its business model and strategy are neither new nor temporary. The increased globalization of the marketplace will continue to change the nature of every business across every industry for as far as the eye can see.

SOURCE: S. Power, G. Chon, and N. Boudette, "In Humbling Overhaul, Chrysler Faces Big Cuts," *The Wall Street Journal*, February 14, 2007, p. A1.

#### Questions

1. What do you think will be the major people issues that will emerge as Chrysler attempts to transform its business model and strategy?
2. How might HRM practices potentially solve some of the issues that you identified in the question above?

Please see the Video Case that corresponds to this chapter online at www.mhhe.com/noe6e.

## Summary

A strategic approach to human resource management seeks to proactively provide a competitive advantage through the company's most important asset: its human resources. While human resources are the most important asset, they are also usually the single largest controllable cost within the firm's business model. The HRM function needs to be integrally involved in the formulation of strategy to identify the people-related business issues the company faces. Once the strategy has been determined, HRM has a profound impact on the implementation of the plan by developing and aligning HRM practices that ensure that the company has motivated employees with the necessary skills. Finally, the emerging strategic role of the HRM function requires that HR professionals in the future develop business, professional–technical, change management, and integration competencies. As you will see more clearly in later chapters, this strategic approach requires more than simply developing a valid selection procedure or state-of-the-art performance management systems. Only through these competencies can the HR professional take a strategic approach to human resource management.

## Key Terms

Strategic human resource management (SHRM), 69
Strategy formulation, 69
Strategy implementation, 69
Goals, 75
External analysis, 75
Internal analysis, 75
Strategic choice, 76
Job analysis, 80
Job design, 80
Recruitment, 81
Selection, 81
Training, 82
Development, 82
Performance management, 82
Role behaviors, 85
External growth strategy, 86
Concentration strategy, 86
Internal growth strategy, 86
Downsizing, 87

## Discussion Questions

1. Pick one of your university's major sports teams (like football or basketball). How would you characterize that team's generic strategy? How does the composition of the team members (in terms of size, speed, ability, and so on) relate to that strategy? What are the strengths and weaknesses of the team? How do they dictate the team's generic strategy and its approach to a particular game?
2. Do you think that it is easier to tie human resources to the strategic management process in large or in small organizations? Why?
3. Consider one of the organizations you have been affiliated with. What are some examples of human resource practices that were consistent with that organization's strategy? What are examples of practices that were inconsistent with its strategy?
4. How can strategic management within the HRM department ensure that HRM plays an effective role in the company's strategic management process?
5. What types of specific skills (such as knowledge of financial accounting methods) do you think HR professionals will need to have the business, professional-technical, change management, and integrative competencies necessary in the future? Where can you develop each of these skills?
6. What are some of the key environmental variables that you see changing in the business world today? What impact will those changes have on the HRM function in organizations?

## Self-Assessment Exercise

Think of a company you have worked for, or find an annual report for a company you are interested in working for. (Many companies post their annual reports online at their Web site.) Then answer the following questions.

### Questions

1. How has the company been affected by the trends discussed in this chapter?
2. Does the company use the HR practices recommended in this chapter?
3. What else should the company do to deal with the challenges posed by the trends discussed in this chapter?

## Exercising Strategy: Strategy and HRM at Delta Airlines

In 1994 top executives at Delta Air Lines faced a crucial strategic decision. Delta, which had established an unrivaled reputation within the industry for having highly committed employees who delivered the highest quality customer service, had lost over $10 per share for two straight years. A large portion of its financial trouble was due to the $491 million acquisition of Pan Am in 1991, which was followed by the Gulf War (driving up fuel costs) and the early 1990s recession (causing people to fly less). Its cost per available seat mile (the cost to fly one passenger one mile) was 9.26 cents, among the highest in the industry. In addition, it was threatened by new discount competitors with significantly lower costs—in particular, Valujet, which flew out of Delta's Atlanta hub. How could Delta survive and thrive in such an environment? Determining the strategy for doing so was the top executives' challenge.

Chairman and chief executive officer Ron Allen embarked upon the "Leadership 7.5" strategy, whose goal was to reduce the cost per available seat mile to 7.5 cents, comparable with Southwest Airlines. Implementing this strategy required a significant downsizing over the following three years, trimming 11,458 people from its 69,555-employee workforce (the latter number representing an 8 percent reduction from two years earlier). Many experienced customer service representatives were laid off and replaced with lower paid, inexperienced, part-time workers. Cleaning service of planes as well as baggage handling were outsourced, resulting in layoffs of long-term Delta employees. The numbers of maintenance workers and flight attendants were reduced substantially.

The results of the strategy were mixed as financial performance improved but operational performance plummeted. Since it began its cost cutting, its stock price more than doubled in just over two years and its debt was upgraded. On the other hand, customer complaints about dirty airplanes rose from 219 in 1993 to 358 in 1994 and 634 in 1995. On-time performance was so bad that passengers joked that Delta stands for "Doesn't Ever Leave The Airport." Delta slipped from fourth to seventh among the top 10 carriers in baggage handling. Employee morale hit an all-time low, and unions were beginning to make headway toward organizing some of Delta's employee groups. In 1996 CEO Allen was quoted as saying, "This has tested our people. There have been some morale problems. But so be it. You go back to the question of survival, and it makes the decision very easy."

Shortly after, employees began donning cynical "so be it" buttons. Delta's board saw union organizers stirring blue-collar discontent, employee morale destroyed, the customer service reputation in near shambles, and senior managers exiting the company in droves. Less than one year later, Allen was fired despite Delta's financial turnaround. His firing was "not because the company was going broke, but because its spirit was broken."

Delta's Leadership 7.5 strategy destroyed the firm's core competence of a highly experienced, highly skilled, and highly committed workforce that delivered the highest quality customer service in the industry. HRM might have affected the strategy by pointing out the negative impact that this strategy would have on the firm. Given the strategy and competitive environment, Delta might have sought to implement the cost cutting differently to reduce the cost structure but preserve its source of differentiation.

The present state of Delta provides further support to these conclusions. With the family atmosphere dissolved and the bond between management and rank-and-file employees broken, employees have begun to seek other ways to gain voice and security. By Fall 2001 Delta had two union organizing drives under way with both the flight attendants and the mechanics. In addition, labor costs have been driven up as a result of the union activity. The pilots signed a lucrative five-year contract that will place them at the highest pay in the industry. In an effort to head off the organizing drive, the mechanics were recently given raises to similarly put them at the industry top. Now the flight attendants are seeking industry-leading pay regardless of but certainly encouraged by the union drive.[74]

The Delta Air Lines story provides a perfect example of the perils that can await firms that fail to adequately address human resource issues in the formulation and implementation of strategy.

SOURCE: M. Brannigan and E. De Lisser, "Cost Cutting at Delta Raises the Stock Price but Lowers the Service," *The Wall Street Journal*, June 20, 1996, pp. A1, A8; M. Brannigan and J. White, "So Be It: Why Delta Air Lines Decided It Was Time for CEO to Take Off," *The Wall Street Journal*, May 30, 1997, p. A1.

### Questions

1. How does the experience of Delta Air Lines illustrate the interdependence between strategic decisions of "how to compete" and "with what to compete"? Consider this with regard to both strategy formulation and strategy implementation.
2. If you were in charge of HRM for Delta Air Lines now, what would be your major priorities?

## MANAGING PEOPLE: FROM THE PAGES OF *BUSINESSWEEK*

BusinessWeek

### Is Dell Too Big for Michael Dell?

#### He's back in charge—and he may have the toughest job in the computer business

Welcome back, Michael. Don't get too comfortable.

By returning to the top job at Dell Inc., replacing departing chief executive Kevin Rollins, founder Michael S. Dell takes on perhaps the toughest job in the computer industry. Since mid-2005 the PC maker has battled problems with customer service, quality, and the effectiveness of its direct-sales model. Lately, rivals Hewlett-Packard Co. and Apple Inc. have been gaining in sales and market share. On January 31, the day Rollins's departure was announced, the Round Rock (Texas) company disclosed that its fourth-quarter earnings and sales would fall short of analyst estimates. It's also under scrutiny by the Securities & Exchange Commission and a U.S. attorney for accounting irregularities.

As recently as last November, Dell insisted to *BusinessWeek* that Rollins's job was safe. Now, in an interview, he insists the decision to push Rollins out started with him. "I recommended to our board that I become the CEO," Dell says. For years, Dell and Rollins were held up as a prime example of the company's "two-in-a-box" management structure, in which two leaders worked together in lockstep. When Rollins was president, Michael Dell was CEO; when Rollins was promoted to CEO in 2004, Michael remained chairman. But financial performance has been deteriorating for a while now, and Michael Dell apparently ran out of patience in light of the latest disappointment. "People are looking forward to a change," said an analyst at one of Dell's largest institutional shareholders. Indeed, the company's share price jumped 3.6 percent in the couple of hours after the shift was announced.

But does Michael Dell have what it takes to turn the company around? It's been years since he shouldered day-to-day operational responsibility on his own. Since the early 1990s, Dell has always had a strong No. 2; back then, the company had less than $3 billion in yearly sales. Today it is a $60 billion company. But Dell says he has a clear plan. He believes the company's supply chain and manufacturing can be improved. "I think you're going to see a more streamlined organization, with a much clearer strategy."

But none of the paths to improve performance will be easy. Dell doesn't have the innovation DNA of an Apple or even an HP, should it want to overhaul its utilitarian products and services. Any effort to crank up R&D would crimp margins. Trying to win over more consumers, the fastest-growing part of the market, may well require a move away from its direct-sales model into retail. That could prove costly as well. Dell himself says he doesn't anticipate leaving the direct-sales model behind: "It's a significant strength of the company." Nor does a big acquisition seem to be an option, given that Dell has never done one in the past.

#### Slots to Fill

But standing in place also looks hazardous, since Dell may now be slipping in its core corporate business, too. According to a January 30 study done by Goldman, Sachs & Co., Dell is losing share in business spending for PCs. (Hewlett-Packard is also losing share of spending, while Lenovo and Apple are gaining.) "Dell's troubles seem to be bleeding into its corporate business, which, up until now, had been a stronghold," the report said. Dell has also lost the top spot in the worldwide PC market-share rankings. In the fourth quarter, Hewlett-Packard's worldwide market share grew to 18.1 percent, while Dell's share dropped to 14.7 percent, according to market researcher IDC.

Dell also has several slots to fill in the executive suite; Rollins is only the latest departure among key managers. But for the first time in years, the tough choices will be solely in the lap of the man who started the company in his University of Texas dorm room back in 1984. "I'm not hiring a COO or a CEO," Dell says, "I'm going to be the CEO for the next several years." He adds: "We're going to fix this business."

SOURCE: L. Lee and P. Burrows, "Is Dell Too Big for Michael Dell?" Reprinted from the April 4, 2007, issue of *BusinessWeek* by special permission. 

### Questions

1. How does the case describe Dell's transformed strategy over the years in terms of where to compete, how to compete, and with what to compete?
2. What are the major people issues that exist as Michael Dell retakes the reins at Dell?
3. How would HR help in addressing the issues that Dell faces?

## NOTES


1. J. Barney, "Firm Resources and Sustained Competitive Advantage," *Journal of Management* 17 (1991), pp. 99–120.
2. L. Dyer, "Strategic Human Resource Management and Planning," in *Research in Personnel and Human Resources Management*, ed. K. Rowland and G. Ferris (Greenwich, CT: JAI Press, 1985), pp. 1–30.
3. J. Quinn, *Strategies for Change: Logical Incrementalism* (Homewood, IL: Richard D. Irwin, 1980).
4. M. Porter, *Competitive Strategy: Techniques for Analyzing Industries and Competitors* (New York: Free Press, 1980).
5. R. Miles and C. Snow, *Organizational Strategy, Structure, and Process* (New York: McGraw-Hill, 1978).
6. P. Wright and G. McMahan, "Theoretical Perspectives for Strategic Human Resource Management," *Journal of Management* 18 (1992), pp. 295–320.
7. D. Guest, "Human Resource Management, Corporate Performance and Employee Well-Being: Building the Worker into HRM," *Journal of Industrial Relations* 44 (2002), pp. 335–58; B. Becker, M. Huselid, P. Pinckus, and M. Spratt, "HR as a Source of Shareholder Value: Research and Recommendations, *Human Resource Management* 36 (1997), pp. 39–47.
8. P. Boxall and J. Purcell, *Strategy and Human Resource Management* (Basingstoke, Hants, U.K.: Palgrave MacMillan, 2003).
9. F. Biddle and J. Helyar, "Behind Boeing's Woes: Chunky Assembly Line, Price War with Airbus," *The Wall Street Journal*, April 24, 1998, pp. A1, A16.
10. K. Martell and S. Carroll, "How Strategic Is HRM?" *Human Resource Management* 34 (1995), pp. 253–67.
11. K. Golden and V. Ramanujam, "Between a Dream and a Nightmare: On the Integration of the Human Resource Function and the Strategic Business Planning Process," *Human Resource Management* 24 (1985), pp. 429–51.
12. P. Wright, B. Dunford, and S. Snell, "Contributions of the Resource-Based View of the Firm to the Field of Strategic HRM: Convergence of Two Fields," *Journal of Management* 27 (2001), pp. 701–21.
13. J. Purcell, N. Kinnie, S. Hutchinson, B. Rayton, and J. Swart, *Understanding the People and Performance Link: Unlocking the Black Box* (London: CIPD, 2003).
14. P. M. Wright, T. Gardner, and L. Moynihan, "The Impact of Human Resource Practices on Business Unit Operating and Financial Performance," *Human Resource Management Journal* 13 no. 3, (2003), pp. 21–36.
15. C. Hill and G. Jones, *Strategic Management Theory: An Integrated Approach* (Boston: Houghton Mifflin, 1989).
16. W. Johnston and A. Packer, *Workforce 2000: Work and Workers for the Twenty-First Century* (Indianapolis, IN: Hudson Institute, 1987).
17. "Labor Letter," *The Wall Street Journal*, December 15, 1992, p. A1.
18. P. Wright, G. McMahan, and A. McWilliams, "Human Resources and Sustained Competitive Advantage: A Resource-Based Perspective," *International Journal of Human Resource Management* 5 (1994), pp. 301–26.
19. P. Buller, "Successful Partnerships: HR and Strategic Planning at Eight Top Firms," *Organizational Dynamics* 17 (1988), pp. 27–42.
20. M. Hitt, R. Hoskisson, and J. Harrison, "Strategic Competitiveness in the 1990s: Challenges and Opportunities for U.S. Executives," *The Executive* 5 (May 1991), pp. 7–22.
21. P. Wright, G. McMahan, B. McCormick, and S. Sherman, "Strategy, Core Competence, and HR Involvement as Determinants of HR Effectiveness and Refinery Performance." Paper presented at the 1996 International Federation of Scholarly Associations in Management, Paris, France.
22. N. Bennett, D. Ketchen, and E. Schultz, "Antecedents and Consequences of Human Resource Integration with Strategic Decision Making." Paper presented at the 1995 Academy of Management Meeting, Vancouver, BC, Canada.
23. Golden and Ramanujam, "Between a Dream and a Nightmare."
24. J. Galbraith and R. Kazanjian, *Strategy Implementation: Structure, Systems, and Process* (St. Paul, MN: West, 1986).
25. B. Schneider and A. Konz, "Strategic Job Analysis," *Human Resource Management* 27 (1989), pp. 51–64.
26. P. Wright and S. Snell, "Toward an Integrative View of Strategic Human Resource Management," *Human Resource Management Review* 1 (1991), pp. 203–25.
27. S. Snell, "Control Theory in Strategic Human Resource Management: The Mediating Effect of Administrative Information," *Academy of Management Journal* 35 (1992), pp. 292–327.
28. R. Schuler, "Personnel and Human Resource Management Choices and Organizational Strategy," in *Readings in Personnel and Human Resource Management*, 3rd ed., ed. R. Schuler, S. Youngblood, and V. Huber (St. Paul, MN: West, 1988).
29. J. Dean and S. Snell, "Integrated Manufacturing and Job Design: Moderating Effects of Organizational Inertia," *Academy of Management Journal* 34 (1991), pp. 776–804.
30. E. Lawler, *The Ultimate Advantage: Creating the High Involvement Organization* (San Francisco: Jossey-Bass, 1992).
31. J. Olian and S. Rynes, "Organizational Staffing: Integrating Practice with Strategy," *Industrial Relations* 23 (1984), pp. 170–83.
32. G. Smith, "Quality: Small and Midsize Companies Seize the Challenge—Not a Moment Too Soon," *BusinessWeek*, November 30, 1992, pp. 66–75.
33. J. Kerr and E. Jackofsky, "Aligning Managers with Strategies: Management Development versus Selection," *Strategic Management Journal* 10 (1989), pp. 157–70.

34. J. Kerr, "Strategic Control through Performance Appraisal and Rewards," *Human Resource Planning* 11 (1988), pp. 215–23.
35. Snell, "Control Theory in Strategic Human Resource Management."
36. B. Gerhart and G. Milkovich, "Employee Compensation: Research and Practice," in *Handbook of Industrial and Organizational Psychology*, 2nd ed., ed. M. Dunnette and L. Hough (Palo Alto, CA: Consulting Psychologists Press, 1992), pp. 481–569.
37. D. Balkin and L. Gomez-Mejia, "Toward a Contingency Theory of Compensation Strategy," *Strategic Management Journal* 8 (1987), pp. 169–82.
38. A. Taylor, "U.S. Cars Come Back," *Fortune*, November 16, 1992, pp. 52, 85.
39. S. Cronshaw and R. Alexander, "One Answer to the Demand for Accountability: Selection Utility as an Investment Decision," *Organizational Behavior and Human Decision Processes* 35 (1986), pp. 102–18.
40. P. MacDuffie, "Human Resource Bundles and Manufacturing Performance: Organizational Logic and Flexible Production Systems in the World Auto Industry," *Industrial and Labor Relations Review* 48 (1995), pp. 197–221; P. McGraw, "A Hard Drive to the Top," *U.S. News & World Report* 118 (1995), pp. 43–44.
41. M. Huselid, "The Impact of Human Resource Management Practices on Turnover, Productivity, and Corporate Financial Performance," *Academy of Management Journal* 38 (1995), pp. 635–72.
42. B. Fulmer, B. Gerhart, and K. Scott, "Are the 100 Best Better? An Empirical Investigation of the Relationship between Being a 'Great Place to Work' and Firm Performance," *Personnel Psychology* 56 (2003), pp. 965–93.
43. J. E. Delery and D. H. Doty, "Modes of Theorizing in Strategic Human Resource Management: Tests of Universalistic, Contingency and Configurational Performance Predictions," *Academy of Management Journal* 39 (1996), pp. 802–83; D. Guest, J. Michie, N. Conway, and M. Sheehan, "Human Resource Management and Corporate Performance in the UK," *British Journal of Industrial Relations* 41 (2003), pp. 291–314; J. Guthrie, "High Involvement Work Practices, Turnover, and Productivity: Evidence from New Zealand," *Academy of Management Journal* 44 (2001), pp. 180–192; J. Harter, F. Schmidt, and T. Hayes, "Business-Unit-Level Relationship between Employee Satisfaction, Employee Engagement, and Business Outcomes: A Meta-analysis," *Journal of Applied Psychology* 87 (2002), pp. 268–79; Watson Wyatt, Worldwide, "Human Capital Index®: Human Capital as a Lead Indicator of Shareholder Value" (2002).
44. M. Bhattacharya, D. Gibson, and H. Doty, "The Effects of Flexibility in Employee Skills, Employee Behaviors, and Human Resource Practices on Firm Performance," *Journal of Management* 31 (2005), pp. 622–40.
45. D. Guest, J. Michie, N. Conway, and M. Sheehan, "Human Resource Management and Corporate Performance in the UK," *British Journal of Industrial Relations* 41 (2003), pp. 291–314.
46. P. Wright, T. Gardner, L. Moynihan, and M. Allen, "The HR–Performance Relationship: Examining Causal Direction," *Personnel Psychology* 58 (2005), pp. 409–76.
47. M. Porter, *Competitive Advantage* (New York: Free Press, 1985).
48. R. Schuler and S. Jackson, "Linking Competitive Strategies with Human Resource Management Practices," *Academy of Management Executive* 1 (1987), pp. 207–19.
49. R. Miles and C. Snow, "Designing Strategic Human Resource Management Systems," *Organizational Dynamics* 13, no. 1 (1984), pp. 36–52.
50. A. Thompson and A. Strickland, *Strategy Formulation and Implementation: Tasks of the General Manager*, 3rd ed. (Plano, TX: BPI, 1986).
51. J. Schmidt, *Making Mergers Work: The Strategic Importance of People* (Arlington, VA: SHRM Foundation, 2003).
52. G. Fairclough, "Business Bulletin," *The Wall Street Journal*, March 5, 1998, p. A1.
53. P. Sebastian, "Business Bulletin," *The Wall Street Journal*, October 2, 1997, p. A1.
54. J. S. Champy, *Reengineering Management: The Mandate for New Leadership* (New York: Harper Business, 1995).
55. S. Pearlstein, "Corporate Cutback Yet to Pay Off," *Washington Post*, January 4, 1994, p. B6.
56. K. Cameron, "Guest Editor's Note: Investigating Organizational Downsizing—Fundamental Issues," *Human Resource Management* 33 (1994), pp. 183–88.
57. W. Cascio, *Responsible Restructuring: Creative and Profitable Alternatives to Layoffs* (San Francisco: Berrett-Koehler, 2002).
58. N. Templin, "UAW to Unveil Pact on Slashing GM's Payroll," *The Wall Street Journal*, December 15, 1992, p. A3.
59. J. Lopez, "Managing: Early-Retirement Offers Lead to Renewed Hiring," *The Wall Street Journal*, January 26, 1993, p. B1.
60. A. Church, "Organizational Downsizing: What Is the Role of the Practitioner?" *Industrial–Organizational Psychologist* 33, no. 1 (1995), pp. 63–74.
61. N. Templin, "A Decisive Response to Crisis Brought Ford Enhanced Productivity," *The Wall Street Journal*, December 15, 1992, p. A1.
62. Quinn, *Strategies for Change*.
63. H. Mintzberg, "Patterns in Strategy Formulation," *Management Science* 24 (1978), pp. 934–48.
64. R. Pascale, "Perspectives on Strategy: The Real Story behind Honda's Success," *California Management Review* 26 (1984), pp. 47–72.
65. Templin, "A Decisive Response to Crisis."
66. P. Wright and S. Snell, "Toward a Unifying Framework for Exploring Fit and Flexibility in Strategic Human Resource Management," *Academy of Management Review* 23, no. 4 (1998), pp. 756–72.
67. P. Senge, *The Fifth Discipline* (New York: Doubleday, 1990).
68. T. Stewart, "Brace for Japan's Hot New Strategy," *Fortune*, September 21, 1992, pp. 62–76.
69. B. Dunford, P. Wright, and S. Snell, "Contributions of the Resource-Based View of the Firm to the Field of Strategic HRM: Convergence of Two Fields," *Journal of Management* 27 (2001), pp. 701–21.
70. C. Snow and S. Snell, *Staffing as Strategy*, vol. 4 of *Personnel Selection* (San Francisco: Jossey-Bass, 1992).
71. T. Batten, "Education Key to Prosperity—Report," *Houston Chronicle*, September 7, 1992, p. 1B.
72. H. Schultz and D. Yang, *Pour Your Heart Into It* (New York: Hyperion, 1997).
73. G. McMahan, University of Texas at Arlington, personal communications.
74. M. Brannigan, "Delta Lifts Mechanics' Pay to Top of Industry Amid Push by Union," *The Wall Street Journal Interactive*, August 16, 2001; M. Adams, "Delta May See Second Big Union," *USA Today*, August 27, 2001, p. 1B.

3

CHAPTER

# The Legal Environment: Equal Employment Opportunity and Safety

LO

## LEARNING OBJECTIVES

**After reading this chapter, you should be able to:**

LO1 Identify the three branches of government and the role each plays in influencing the legal environment of human resource management. *page 100*

LO2 List the major federal laws that require equal employment opportunity and the protections provided by each of these laws. *page 103*

LO3 Discuss the roles, responsibilities, and requirements of the federal agencies responsible for enforcing equal employment opportunity laws. *page 109*

LO4 Identify the four theories of discrimination under Title VII of the Civil Rights Act and apply these theories to different discrimination situations. *page 112*

LO5 Discuss the legal issues involved with preferential treatment programs. *page 122*

LO6 Identify behavior that constitutes sexual harassment and list things that an organization can do to eliminate or minimize it. *page 123*

LO7 Identify the major provisions of the Occupational Safety and Health Act (1970) and the rights of employees that are guaranteed by this act. *page 129*

# Enter the World of Business

## Problems at Boeing

Boeing, the global aerospace company best known for its 737 and 747 aircraft, has faced a number of problems over the past few years. As discussed in Chapter 2, competition with Airbus placed the company in a difficult position in the marketplace. However, a number of its problems have been internal as well.

In addition to being embroiled in several ethics scandals on its defense contracting side of the business, Boeing has faced a number of discrimination complaints as well. For example, 38 female manufacturing engineers filed a sex-discrimination case against the company in 2000. While the company denied the charges, some internal documents obtained by *BusinessWeek* may tell a completely different story. In 1997 Boeing created an internal Diversity Salary Assessment team tasked with examining its compensation and promotion practices. One presentation concluded that "females . . . are paid less" and "gender differences in starting salaries generally continue and often increase as a result of salary planning decisions." According to *BusinessWeek* these documents "seem to tell the story of a company that underpaid women, knew it, and yet bitterly contested both the sex-discrimination case and a 1998 Labor Dept. audit into the same issues."

The documents suggest that Boeing knew of the pay disparities as far back as 1994. A salary analysis project from 1999 showed that Boeing needed to allocate $30 million to eliminate the gender-based pay differences, but allocated only $10 million. Boeing HR executive Erika Lochow testified that she and her colleagues were shocked at just how big the pay disparity was. The company treated the studies with utmost confidentiality, keeping them in a "secured office location" not even janitors had access to, using special e-mail encryption software so that outside counsel and executives could exchange data in a "secure and safe" manner, and forbidding executives from taking any notes at meetings where the salary data were discussed.

The class action lawsuit facing Boeing includes 28,000 potential plaintiffs, and a potential liability exceeding $1 billion including compensatory damages, punitive damages, and attorneys' fees. As part of its settlement with the Office of Federal Contract Compliance Procedures (OFCCP) in 1999, Boeing agreed to settle for $4.5 million, but its potential liability could have been over $120 million. In addition, Marcella Fleming, then Boeing's director of employee relations and one of Boeing's key dealmakers as part of the settlement, stated at a meeting following the settlement, "The fact that our compensation comes up . . . negative, negative, negative would suggest that there's something generally not right about the way we're doing it."

Boeing spokesman Kenneth B. Mercer stated that the company is committed to equal rights and argued that the statistical studies were intended to help identify and eliminate pay disparities. In fact, Frank Marshall, the former senior compensation manager at Boeing, testified that he created a "stealth" compensation program to minimize the legal risks. The plan entailed embedding the fixes in the salary planning process so that even senior managers were not aware of them. Mercer says, "When the jury has the full story, they will find that the company did not practice discrimination of any kind."

Source: S. Holmes, "A New Black Eye for Boeing?" *BusinessWeek*, April 26, 2004, pp. 90–91.

## Introduction

In the opening chapter we discussed the environment of the HRM function, and we noted that several environmental factors affect an organization's HRM function. One is the legal environment, particularly the laws affecting the management of people. As the troubles at Boeing indicate, legal issues can cause serious problems for a company's success and survival. In this chapter we first present an overview of the U.S. legal system, noting the different legislative bodies, regulatory agencies, and judicial bodies that determine the legality of certain HRM practices. We then discuss the major laws and executive orders that govern these practices.

One point to make clear at the outset is that managers often want a list of "dos and don'ts" that will keep them out of legal trouble. They rely on rules such as "Don't ever ask a female applicant if she is married" without understanding the "why" behind these rules. Clearly, certain practices are illegal or inadvisable, and this chapter will provide some valuable tips for avoiding discrimination lawsuits. However, such lists are not compatible with a strategic approach to HRM and are certainly not the route to developing a competitive advantage. They are simply mechanical reactions to the situations. Our goal is to provide an understanding of how the legislative, regulatory, and judicial systems work to define equal employment opportunity law. Armed with this understanding, a manager is better prepared to manage people within the limits imposed by the legal system. Doing so effectively is a source of competitive advantage. Doing so ineffectively results in competitive disadvantage. Rather than viewing the legal system as a constraint, firms that embrace the concept of diversity can often find that they are able to leverage the differences among people as a tremendous competitive tool. The nearby "Competing through Globalization" box illustrates how one company used blind employees as the basis of their business model.

## The Legal System in the United States

**LO1**
Identify the Three Branches of Government and the Role Each Plays in Influencing the Legal Environment of Human Resource Management.

The foundation for the U.S. legal system is set forth in the U.S. Constitution, which affects HRM in two ways. First, it delineates a citizen's constitutional rights, on which the government cannot impinge.[1] Most individuals are aware of the Bill of Rights, the first 10 amendments to the Constitution; but other amendments, such as the Fourteenth Amendment, also influence HRM practices. The Fourteenth Amendment, called the equal protection clause, states that all individuals are entitled to equal protection under the law.

Second, the Constitution established three major governing bodies: the legislative, executive, and judicial branches. The Constitution explicitly defines the roles and responsibilities of each of these branches. Each branch has its own areas of authority, but these areas have often overlapped, and the borders between the branches are often blurred.

### Legislative Branch

The legislative branch of the federal government consists of the House of Representatives and the Senate. These bodies develop laws that govern many HRM activities. Most of the laws stem from a perceived societal need. For example, during the civil rights movement of the early 1960s, the legislative branch moved to ensure that various minority groups received equal opportunities in many areas of life. One of

## COMPETING THROUGH GLOBALIZATION

### Blind Feeding the Blind

Many teachers use an exercise where students must walk around blindfolded for a few hours to help appreciate the situation of those who truly are blind. However, until recently, nobody actually made a business out of this.

At the Blind Cow restaurant in Zurich, Switzerland, nothing looks good to eat. The reason is not that the food is bad, but because patrons dine in total darkness. Rev. Jorge Spielman, a 37-year-old blind pastor, came up with the idea while tending bar at a public exhibit in Zurich. The exhibit required sighted people to grope their way through various dark rooms to experience what it is like to be blind. He and four blind colleagues decided to create a restaurant that would help sighted people appreciate the situation of the blind while providing jobs for the blind and visually impaired.

A blind waitress leads diners to their tables, asking one guest to place both hands on her shoulders, and other guests to do likewise to the guest in front of them. She explains the rules: no flashlights, no iridescent watches, and no wandering. Waitresses and waiters should be called by shouting, and guests who need to use the restrooms must be led by a waitress. The staff all wear bells to allow them to avoid colliding with one another while carrying hot plates of food.

The restaurant has been an unarguable success. Although Rev. Spielman worried that the novelty would wear off after a few months, a year after its opening the restaurant was still booked solid for the following three months. In addition, the breakage of dishes and glasses is no different from other restaurants because guests are extremely careful. In fact, the business has been such a success that the owners are now considering expanding into big U.S. cities like New York and Los Angeles.

Such expansion could succeed because the atmosphere provides for a variety of novel experiences. For instance, a group of three couples dined there, and when the ladies went to the restroom, the men changed places. When they returned, the men planted kisses on their "new" dates; not all the women noticed that the lips kissing them were unfamiliar ones. In addition, the restaurant was the site for a "blind date." The lady arrived early and sipped a drink until the man was led to her table. Unfortunately, according to the staff, they departed separately. Finally, Rev. Spielman has some ideas to keep the restaurant fresh. He plans to make Monday night "date night," bringing in guest speakers to discuss sex and relationships. He explains, "People can ask all kinds of questions in the dark."

SOURCE: J. Costello, "Swiss Eatery Operated by the Blind Keeps Diners Completely in the Dark," *The Wall Street Journal*, November 28, 2001, p. 1.

these areas was employment, and thus Congress enacted Title VII of the Civil Rights Act. Similar perceived societal needs have brought about labor laws such as the Occupational Safety and Health Act, the Employee Retirement Income Security Act, the Age Discrimination in Employment Act, and, more recently, the Americans with Disabilities Act of 1990 and the Civil Rights Act of 1991.

### Executive Branch

The executive branch consists of the president of the United States and the many regulatory agencies the president oversees. Although the legislative branch passes the laws, the executive branch affects these laws in many ways. First, the president can propose bills to Congress that, if passed, would become laws. Second, the president has the power to veto any law passed by Congress, thus ensuring that few laws are passed without presidential approval—which allows the president to influence how laws are written.

Third, the regulatory agencies, under the authority of the president, have responsibility for enforcing the laws. Thus a president can influence what types of violations are pursued. For example, many laws affecting employment discrimination are enforced by the Equal Employment Opportunity Commission under the Department of Justice. During President Jimmy Carter's administration, the Department of Justice brought a lawsuit against Birmingham, Alabama's, fire department for not having enough black firefighters. This suit resulted in a consent decree that required blacks to receive preferential treatment in hiring and promotion decisions. Two years later, during Ronald Reagan's administration, the Department of Justice sided with white firefighters in a lawsuit against the city of Birmingham, alleging that the preferential treatment required by the consent decree discriminated against white firefighters.[2]

Fourth, the president can issue executive orders, which sometimes regulate the activities of organizations that have contracts with the federal government. For example, Executive Order 11246, signed by President Lyndon Johnson, required all federal contractors and subcontractors to engage in affirmative action programs designed to hire and promote women and minorities within their organizations. Fifth, the president can influence the Supreme Court to interpret laws in certain ways. When particularly sensitive cases come before the Court, the attorney general, representing the executive branch, argues for certain preferred outcomes. For example, one court case involved a white female schoolteacher who was laid off from her job in favor of retaining a black schoolteacher with equal seniority and performance with the reason given as "diversity." The white woman filed a lawsuit in federal court and the (first) Bush administration filed a brief on her behalf, arguing that diversity was not a legitimate reason to use race in decision making. She won in federal court, and the school district appealed. The Clinton administration, having been elected in the meantime, filed a brief on behalf of the school district, arguing that diversity was a legitimate defense.

Finally, the president appoints all the judges in the federal judicial system, subject to approval from the legislative branch. This affects the interpretation of many laws.

## Judicial Branch

The judicial branch consists of the federal court system, which is made up of three levels. The first level consists of the U.S. District Courts and quasi-judicial administrative agencies. The district courts hear cases involving alleged violations of federal laws. The quasi-judicial agencies, such as the National Labor Relations Board (or NLRB, which is actually an arm of the executive branch, but serves a judicial function), hear cases regarding their particular jurisdictions (in the NLRB's case, disputes between unions and management). If neither party to a suit is satisfied with the decision of the court at this level, the parties can appeal the decision to the U.S. Courts of Appeals. These courts were originally set up to ease the Supreme Court's caseload, so appeals generally go from the federal trial level to one of the 13 appellate courts before they can be heard by the highest level, the Supreme Court. The Supreme Court must grant certiorari before hearing an appealed case. However, this is not usually granted unless two appellate courts have come to differing decisions on the same point of law or if the case deals with an important interpretation of constitutional law.

The Supreme Court serves as the court of final appeal. Decisions made by the Supreme Court are binding; they can be overturned only through legislation. For example, Congress, dissatisfied with the Supreme Court's decisions in certain cases such as *Wards Cove Packing v. Atonio*, overturned those decisions through the Civil Rights Act of 1991.[3]

Having described the legal system that affects the management of HR, we now explore some laws that regulate HRM activities, particularly equal employment opportunity laws. We first discuss the major laws that mandate equal employment opportunity in the United States. Then we examine the agencies involved in enforcing these laws. This leads us into an examination of the four theories of discrimination, with a discussion of some relevant court cases. Finally, we explore some equal employment opportunity issues facing today's managers.

# Equal Employment Opportunity

**Equal employment opportunity (EEO)** refers to the government's attempt to ensure that all individuals have an equal chance for employment, regardless of race, color, religion, sex, age, disability, or national origin. To accomplish this, the federal government has used constitutional amendments, legislation, and executive orders, as well as the court decisions that interpret these laws. (However, equal employment laws are not the same in all countries.) The major EEO laws we discuss are summarized in Table 3.1.

**LO2**
List the Major Federal Laws that Require Equal Employment Opportunity and the Protections Provided by Each of These Laws.

**Equal Employment Opportunity (EEO)**
The government's attempt to ensure that all individuals have an equal opportunity for employment, regardless of race, color, religion, sex, age, disability, or national origin.

## Constitutional Amendments

### Thirteenth Amendment

The Thirteenth Amendment of the Constitution abolished slavery in the United States. Though one might be hard-pressed to cite an example of race-based slavery in the United States today, the Thirteenth Amendment has been applied in cases where the discrimination involved the "badges" (symbols) and "incidents" of slavery.

### Fourteenth Amendment

The Fourteenth Amendment forbids the states from taking life, liberty, or property without due process of law and prevents the states from denying equal protection of the laws. Passed immediately after the Civil War, this amendment originally applied only to discrimination against blacks. It was soon broadened to protect other groups such as aliens and Asian-Americans, and more recently it has been applied to the protection of whites in allegations of reverse discrimination. In *Bakke v. California Board of Regents*, Alan Bakke alleged that he had been discriminated against in the selection of entrants to the University of California at Davis medical school.[4] The university had set aside 16 of the available 100 places for "disadvantaged" applicants who were members of racial minority groups. Under this quota system, Bakke was able to compete for only 84 positions, whereas a minority applicant was able to compete for all 100. The court ruled in favor of Bakke, noting that this quota system had violated white individuals' right to equal protection under the law.

One important point regarding the Fourteenth Amendment is that it is applicable only to "state actions." This means that only the decisions or actions of the government or of private groups whose activities are deemed state actions can be construed as violations of the Fourteenth Amendment. Thus, one could file a claim under the Fourteenth Amendment if one were fired from a state university (a government organization) but not if one were fired by a private employer.

**table 3.1**

Summary of Major EEO Laws and Regulations

| ACT | REQUIREMENTS | COVERS | ENFORCEMENT AGENCY |
|---|---|---|---|
| Thirteenth Amendment | Abolished slavery | All individuals | Court system |
| Fourteenth Amendment | Provides equal protection for all citizens and requires due process in state action | State actions (e.g., decisions of government organizations) | Court system |
| Civil Rights Acts (CRAs) of 1866 and 1871 (as amended) | Grants all citizens the right to make, perform, modify, and terminate contracts and enjoy all benefits, terms, and conditions of the contractual relationship | All individuals | Court system |
| Equal Pay Act of 1963 | Requires that men and women performing equal jobs receive equal pay | Employers engaged in interstate commerce | EEOC |
| Title VII of CRA | Forbids discrimination based on race, color, religion, sex, or national origin | Employers with 15 or more employees working 20 or more weeks per year; labor unions; and employment agencies | EEOC |
| Age Discrimination in Employment Act of 1967 | Prohibits discrimination in employment against individuals 40 years of age and older | Employers with 15 or more employees working 20 or more weeks per year; labor unions; employment agencies; federal government | EEOC |
| Rehabilitation Act of 1973 | Requires affirmative action in the employment of individuals with disabilities | Government agencies; federal contractors and subcontractors with contracts greater than $2,500 | OFCCP |
| Americans with Disabilities Act of 1990 | Prohibits discrimination against individuals with disabilities | Employers with more than 15 employees | EEOC |
| Pregnancy Discrimination Act | Prohibits discrimination on the basis of pregnancy, childbirth, or related medical conditions | Employers with more than 15 employees | EEOC |
| Executive Order 11246 | Requires affirmative action in hiring women and minorities | Federal contractors and subcontractors with contracts greater than $10,000 | OFCCP |
| Civil Rights Act of 1991 | Prohibits discrimination (same as Title VII) | Same as Title VII, plus applies Section 1981 to employment discrimination cases | EEOC |

## Congressional Legislation

### The Reconstruction Civil Rights Acts (1866 and 1871)

The Thirteenth Amendment eradicated slavery in the United States, and the Reconstruction Civil Rights Acts were attempts to further this goal. The Civil Rights Act passed in 1866 was later broken into two statutes. Section 1982 granted all persons the same property rights as white citizens. Section 1981 granted other rights, including the right to enter into and enforce contracts. Courts have interpreted Section 1981 as granting individuals the right to make and enforce employment contracts. The Civil Rights Act of 1871 granted all citizens the right to sue in federal court if they felt they had been deprived of some civil right. Although these laws might seem outdated, they are still used because they allow the plaintiff to recover both compensatory and punitive damages.

In fact, these laws came to the forefront in a Supreme Court case: *Patterson v. McClean Credit Union*.[5] The plaintiff had filed a discrimination complaint under Section 1981 for racial harassment. After being hired by McClean Credit Union, Patterson failed to receive any promotions or pay raises while she was employed there. She was also told that "blacks work slower than whites." Thus she had grounds to prove discrimination and filed suit under Section 1981, arguing that she had been discriminated against in the making and enforcement of an employment contract. The Supreme Court ruled that this situation did not fall under Section 1981 because it did not involve the making and enforcement of contracts. However, the Civil Rights Act of 1991 amended this act to include the making, performance, modification, and termination of contracts, as well as all benefits, privileges, terms, and conditions of the contractual relationship.

### The Equal Pay Act of 1963

The Equal Pay Act, an amendment to the Fair Labor Standards Act, requires that men and women in the same organization who are doing equal work must be paid equally. The act defines equal in terms of skill, effort, responsibility, and working conditions. However, the act allows for reasons why men and women performing the same job might be paid differently. If the pay differences are the result of differences in seniority, merit, quantity or quality of production, or any factor other than sex (such as shift differentials or training programs), then differences are legally allowable.

### Title VII of the Civil Rights Act of 1964

This is the major legislation regulating equal employment opportunity in the United States. It was a direct result of the civil rights movement of the early 1960s, led by such individuals as Dr. Martin Luther King Jr. It was Dr. King's philosophy that people should "not be judged by the color of their skin but by the content of their character." To ensure that employment opportunities would be based on character or ability rather than on race, Congress wrote and passed Title VII, which President Lyndon Johnson signed into law.

Title VII states that it is illegal for an employer to "(1) fail or refuse to hire or discharge any individual, or otherwise discriminate against any individual with respect to his compensation, terms, conditions, or privileges of employment because of such individual's race, color, religion, sex, or national origin, or (2) to limit, segregate, or classify his employees or applicants for employment in any way that would deprive or tend to deprive any individual of employment opportunities or otherwise adversely affect his status as an employee because of such individual's race, color, religion, sex, or national origin." The act applies to organizations with 15 or more employees working 20 or more weeks a year that are involved in interstate commerce, as well as state and local governments, employment agencies, and labor organizations.

## Age Discrimination in Employment Act (ADEA)

Passed in 1967 and amended in 1986, this act prohibits discrimination against employees over the age of 40. The act almost exactly mirrors Title VII in terms of its substantive provisions and the procedures to be followed in pursuing a case.[6] As with Title VII, the EEOC is responsible for enforcing this act.

No upper

The ADEA was designed to protect older employees when a firm reduces its workforce through layoffs. By targeting older employees, who tend to have higher pay, a firm can substantially cut labor costs. Recently, firms have often offered early retirement incentives, a possible violation of the act because of the focus on older employees. Early retirement incentives require employees to sign an agreement waiving their rights to sue under the ADEA. Courts have tended to uphold the use of early retirement incentives and waivers as long as the individuals were not coerced into signing the agreements, the agreements were presented in a way that the employees could understand, and the employees were given enough time to make a decision.[7]

However, age discrimination complaints make up a large percentage of the complaints filed with the Equal Employment Opportunity Commission, and the number of complaints continues to grow whenever the economy is slow. For example, as we see in Figure 3.1, the cases increased during the early 1990s when many firms were downsizing, but the number of cases decreased as the economy expanded. The number of charges increased again as the economy began slowing again in 2000. This often stems from firms seeking to lay off older (and thus higher paid) employees when they are downsizing. These cases can be costly; most cases are settled out of court, but such settlements run from \$50,000 to \$400,000 per employee.[8] In one recent case Schering-Plough fired 35-year employee Fred Maiorino after he twice failed to accept an early retirement offer made to all sales representatives. After hearing testimony that Maiorino's boss had plastered his file with negative paperwork aimed at firing him, rather than trying to help him improve his performance, the jurors unanimously

**figure 3.1**

Age Discrimination Complaints, 1991–2006

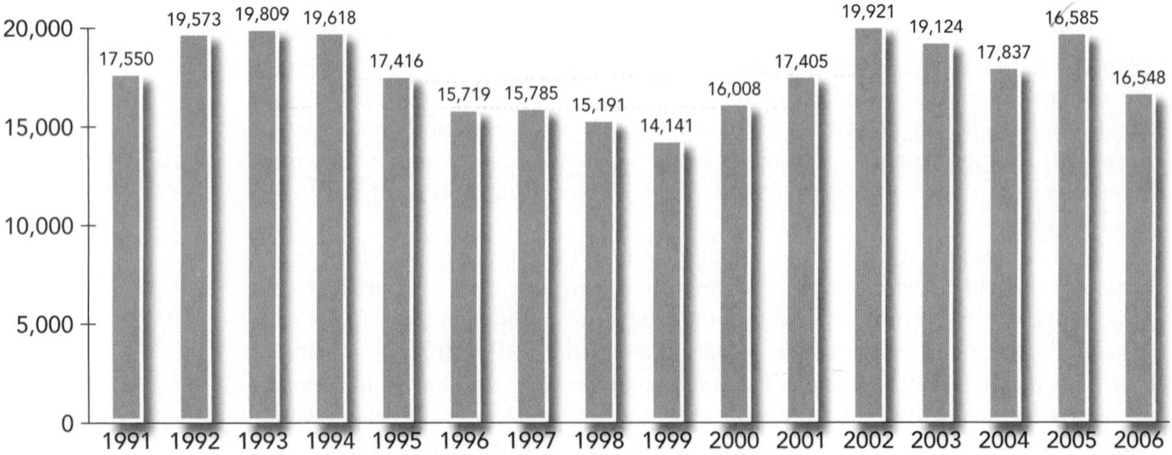


SOURCE: Equal Employment Opportunity Commission, at http://eeoc.gov/stats/adea.html.

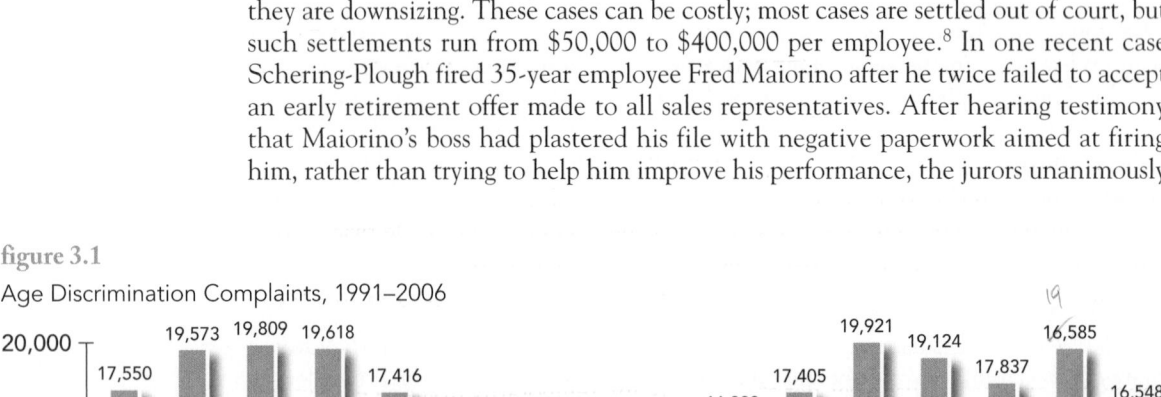

decided he had been discriminated against because of his age. They awarded him $435,000 in compensatory damages and $8 million in punitive damages.[9]

### The Vocational Rehabilitation Act of 1973

This act covers executive agencies and contractors and subcontractors that receive more than $2,500 annually from the federal government. It requires them to engage in affirmative action for individuals with disabilities. Congress designed this act to encourage employers to actively recruit qualified individuals with disabilities and to make reasonable accommodations to allow them to become active members of the labor market. The Employment Standards Administration of the Department of Labor enforces this act.

### Vietnam Era Veteran's Readjustment Act of 1974

Similar to the Rehabilitation Act, this act requires federal contractors and subcontractors to take affirmative action toward employing Vietnam veterans (those serving between August 5, 1964, and May 7, 1975). The Office of Federal Contract Compliance Procedures, discussed later in this chapter, has authority to enforce this act.

### Pregnancy Discrimination Act (1978)

The Pregnancy Discrimination Act is an amendment to Title VII of the Civil Rights Act. It makes illegal discrimination on the basis of pregnancy, childbirth, or related medical conditions as a form of unlawful sex discrimination. An employer cannot refuse to hire a pregnant woman because of her pregnancy, a pregnancy-related condition, or the prejudices of co-workers, clients, or customers. For instance, in a recent court case, the retail store Motherhood Maternity, a Philadelphia-based maternity clothes retailer, settled a pregnancy discrimination and retaliation lawsuit brought by the Equal Opportunity Employment Commission (EEOC). The EEOC had charged that the company refused to hire qualified female applicants because they were pregnant. As a result of the settlement, Motherhood Maternity agreed to a three-year consent decree requiring them to pay plaintiffs $375,000, adopt and distribute an antidiscrimination policy specifically prohibiting discrimination on the basis of pregnancy, train its Florida employees on the new policy, post a notice of resolution of the lawsuit, and provide twice a year reports to the EEOC on any pregnancy discrimination complaints.[10]

In addition, regarding pregnancy and maternity leave, employers may not single out pregnancy-related conditions for special procedures to determine an employee's ability to work, and if an employee is temporarily unable to perform during her pregnancy, the employer must treat her the same as any temporarily disabled employees. The act also requires that any health insurance must cover expenses for pregnancy-related conditions on the same basis as costs for other medical conditions. Finally, pregnancy-related benefits cannot be limited to married employees, and if an employer provides any benefits to workers on leave, they must also provide the same benefits for those on leave for pregnancy-related conditions.

### Civil Rights Act of 1991

The Civil Rights Act of 1991 (CRA 1991) amends Title VII of the Civil Rights Act of 1964, Section 1981 of the Civil Rights Act of 1866, the Americans with Disabilities Act, and the Age Discrimination in Employment Act of 1967. One major change in EEO law under CRA 1991 has been the addition of compensatory and punitive damages in cases of discrimination under Title VII and the Americans with Disabilities

**table 3.2**
Maximum Punitive Damages Allowed under the Civil Rights Act of 1991

| EMPLOYER SIZE | DAMAGE LIMIT |
|---|---|
| 14 to 100 employees | $ 50,000 |
| 101 to 200 employees | 100,000 |
| 201 to 500 employees | 200,000 |
| More than 500 employees | 300,000 |

Act. Before CRA 1991, Title VII limited damage claims to equitable relief such as back pay, lost benefits, front pay in some cases, and attorneys' fees and costs. CRA 1991 allows compensatory and punitive damages when intentional or reckless discrimination is proven. Compensatory damages include such things as future pecuniary loss, emotional pain, suffering, and loss of enjoyment of life. Punitive damages are meant to discourage employers from discriminating by providing for payments to the plaintiff beyond the actual damages suffered.

Recognizing that one or a few discrimination cases could put an organization out of business, thus adversely affecting many innocent employees, Congress has put limits on the amount of punitive damages. Table 3.2 depicts these limits. As can be seen, damages range from $50,000 to $300,000 per violation, depending on the size of the organization. Punitive damages are available only if the employer intentionally discriminated against the plaintiff(s) or if the employer discriminated with malice or reckless indifference to the employee's federally protected rights. These damages are excluded for an employment practice held to be unlawful because of its disparate impact.[11]

The addition of damages to CRA 1991 has had two immediate effects. First, by increasing the potential payoff for a successful discrimination suit, it has increased the number of suits filed against businesses. Second, organizations are now more likely to grant all employees an equal opportunity for employment, regardless of their race, sex, religion, or national origin. Many organizations have felt the need to make the composition of their workforce mirror the general population to avoid costly lawsuits. This act adds a financial incentive for doing so.

## Americans with Disabilities Act (ADA) of 1990

**Americans with Disabilities Act (ADA) of 1990**
A 1990 act prohibiting individuals with disabilities from being discriminated against in the workplace.

One of the most far-reaching acts concerning the management of human resources is the **Americans with Disabilities Act.** This act protects individuals with disabilities from being discriminated against in the workplace. It prohibits discrimination based on disability in all employment practices such as job application procedures, hiring, firing, promotions, compensation, and training—in addition to other employment activities such as advertising, recruitment, tenure, layoff, leave, and fringe benefits. Because this act is so new, we will cover its various stipulations individually.

The ADA defines a disability as a physical or mental impairment that substantially limits one or more major life activities, a record of having such an impairment, or being regarded as having such an impairment. The first part of the definition refers to individuals who have serious disabilities—such as epilepsy, blindness, deafness, or paralysis—that affect their ability to perform major life activities such as walking, seeing, performing manual tasks, learning, caring for oneself, and working. The second part refers to individuals who have a history of disability, such as someone who has had cancer but is currently in remission, someone with a history of mental illness, and someone with a history of heart disease. The third part of the definition, "being regarded as having a disability," refers, for example, to an individual who is severely disfigured and is denied employment because an employer fears negative reactions from others.[12]

Thus the ADA covers specific physiological disabilities such as cosmetic disfigurement and anatomical loss affecting the neurological, musculoskeletal, sensory, respiratory, cardiovascular, reproductive, digestive, genitourinary, hemic, or lymphatic systems. In addition, it covers mental and psychological disorders such as mental retardation, organic brain syndrome, emotional or mental illness, and learning disabilities. However, conditions such as obesity, substance abuse, eye and hair color, and lefthandedness are not covered.[13]

### Executive Orders

Executive orders are directives issued and amended unilaterally by the president. These orders do not require congressional approval, yet they have the force of law. Two executive orders directly affect HRM.

#### Executive Order 11246

President Johnson issued this executive order, which prohibits discrimination based on race, color, religion, sex, and national origin. Unlike Title VII, this order applies only to federal contractors and subcontractors. Employers receiving more than $10,000 from the federal government must take affirmative action to ensure against discrimination, and those with contracts greater than $50,000 must develop a written affirmative action plan for each of their establishments within 120 days of the beginning of the contract. The Office of Federal Contract Compliance Procedures enforces this executive order.

#### Executive Order 11478

President Richard M. Nixon issued this order, which requires the federal government to base all its employment policies on merit and fitness, and specifies that race, color, sex, religion, and national origin should not be considered. (The U.S. Office of Personnel Management is in charge of this.) The order also extends to all contractors and subcontractors doing $10,000 worth of business with the federal government. (The relevant government agencies have the responsibility to ensure that the contractors and subcontractors comply with the order.)

## Enforcement of Equal Employment Opportunity

**LO3**
Discuss the Roles, Responsibilities, and Requirements of the Federal Agencies Responsible for Enforcing Equal Employment Opportunity Laws.

As discussed previously, the executive branch of the federal government bears most of the responsibility for enforcing all EEO laws passed by the legislative branch. In addition, the executive branch must enforce the executive orders issued by the president. The two agencies responsible for the enforcement of these laws and executive orders are the Equal Employment Opportunity Commission and the Office of Federal Contract Compliance Programs, respectively.

EEOC

**Equal Employment Opportunity Commission (EEOC)** The government commission to ensure that all individuals have an equal opportunity for employment, regardless of race, color, religion, sex, age, disability, or national origin.

## Equal Employment Opportunity Commission (EEOC)

An independent federal agency, the EEOC is responsible for enforcing most of the EEO laws, such as Title VII, the Equal Pay Act, and the Americans with Disabilities Act. The EEOC has three major responsibilities: investigating and resolving discrimination complaints, gathering information, and issuing guidelines.

### Investigation and Resolution

Individuals who feel they have been discriminated against must file a complaint with the EEOC or a similar state agency within 180 days of the incident. Failure to file a complaint within the 180 days results in the case's being dismissed immediately, with certain exceptions, such as the enactment of a seniority system that has an intentionally discriminatory purpose.

Once the complaint is filed, the EEOC takes responsibility for investigating the claim of discrimination. The complainant must give the EEOC 60 days to investigate the complaint. If the EEOC either does not believe the complaint to be valid or fails to complete the investigation, the complainant may sue in federal court. If the EEOC determines that discrimination has taken place, its representatives will attempt to provide a reconciliation between the two parties without burdening the court system with a lawsuit. Sometimes the EEOC enters into a consent decree with the discriminating organization. This decree is an agreement between the agency and the organization that the organization will cease certain discriminatory practices and possibly institute additional affirmative action practices to rectify its history of discrimination.

If the EEOC cannot come to an agreement with the organization, it has two options. First, it can issue a "right to sue" letter to the alleged victim, which certifies that the agency has investigated and found validity in the victim's allegations. Second, although less likely, the agency may aid the alleged victim in bringing suit in federal court.

### Information Gathering

The EEOC also plays a role in monitoring the hiring practices of organizations. Each year organizations with 100 or more employees must file a report (EEO-1) with the EEOC that provides the number of women and minorities employed in nine different job categories. The EEOC computer analyzes these reports to identify patterns of discrimination that can then be attacked through class-action suits.

### Issuance of Guidelines

A third responsibility of the EEOC is to issue guidelines that help employers determine when their decisions are violations of the laws enforced by the EEOC. These guidelines are not laws themselves, but the courts give great deference to them when hearing employment discrimination cases.

For example, the *Uniform Guidelines on Employee Selection Procedures* is a set of guidelines issued by the EEOC, the Department of Labor, the Department of Justice, and the U.S. Civil Service Commission.[14] This document provides guidance on the ways an organization should develop and administer selection systems so as not to violate Title VII. The courts often refer to the *Uniform Guidelines* to determine whether a company has engaged in discriminatory conduct or to determine the validity of the procedures it used to validate a selection system. Another example: Since the passage of the ADA, employers have been somewhat confused about the act's implications for their hiring procedures. Therefore, the EEOC issued guidelines in the *Federal Register* that provided more detailed information regarding what the agency will consider legal and illegal employment practices concerning disabled individuals. Although companies are well advised to follow these guidelines, it is possible that courts will interpret the ADA differently from the EEOC. Thus, through the issuance of guidelines the EEOC gives employers directions for making employment decisions that do not conflict with existing laws.

## Office of Federal Contract Compliance Programs (OFCCP)

The OFCCP is the agency responsible for enforcing the executive orders that cover companies doing business with the federal government. Businesses with contracts for more than $50,000 cannot discriminate in employment based on race, color, religion, national origin, or sex, and they must have a written affirmative action plan on file.

These plans have three basic components.[15] First, the **utilization analysis** compares the race, sex, and ethnic composition of the employer's workforce with that of the available labor supply. For each job group, the employer must identify the percentage of its workforce with that characteristic (female, for example) and identify the percentage of workers in the relevant labor market with that characteristic. If the percentage in the employer's workforce is much less than the percentage in the comparison group, then that minority group is considered to be "underutilized."

**Utilization Analysis**
A comparison of the race, sex, and ethnic composition of an employer's workforce with that of the available labor supply.

Second, the employer must develop specific **goals and timetables** for achieving balance in the workforce concerning these characteristics (particularly where underutilization exists). Goals and timetables specify the percentage of women and minorities that the employer seeks to have in each job group and the date by which that percentage is to be attained. These are not to be viewed as quotas, which entail setting aside a specific number of positions to be filled only by members of the protected class. Goals and timetables are much more flexible, requiring only that the employer have specific goals and take steps to achieve those goals. In fact, one study that examined companies with the goal of increasing black employment found that only 10 percent of them actually achieved their goals. Although this may sound discouragingly low, it is important to note that these companies increased their black employment more than companies that set no such goals.[16]

**Goals and Timetables**
The part of a written affirmative action plan that specifies the percentage of women and minorities that an employer seeks to have in each job group and the date by which that percentage is to be attained.

Third, employers with federal contracts must develop a list of **action steps** they will take toward attaining their goals to reduce underutilization. The company's CEO must make it clear to the entire organization that the company is committed to reducing underutilization, and all management levels must be involved in the planning process. For example, organizations can communicate job openings to women and minorities through publishing the company's affirmative action policy, recruiting at predominantly female or minority schools, participating in programs designed to increase employment opportunities for underemployed groups, and removing unnecessary barriers to employment. Organizations must also take affirmative steps toward hiring Vietnam veterans and individuals with disabilities.

**Action Steps**
The written affirmative plan that specifies what an employer plans to do to reduce underutilization of protected groups.

The OFCCP annually audits government contractors to ensure that they actively pursue the goals in their plans. These audits consist of (1) examining the company's affirmative action plan and (2) conducting on-site visits to examine how individual employees perceive the company's affirmative action policies. If the OFCCP finds that the contractors or subcontractors are not complying with the executive order, then its representatives may notify the EEOC (if there is evidence that Title VII has been violated), advise the Department of Justice to institute criminal proceedings, request that the Secretary of

Labor cancel or suspend any current contracts, and forbid the firm from bidding on future contracts. This last penalty, called debarment, is the OFCCP's most potent weapon.

Having discussed the major laws defining equal employment opportunity and the agencies that enforce these laws, we now address the various types of discrimination and the ways these forms of discrimination have been interpreted by the courts in a number of cases.

## Types of Discrimination

**LO4**
Identify the Four Theories of Discrimination under Title VII of the Civil Rights Act and Apply These Theories to Different Discrimination Situations.

How would you know if you had been discriminated against? Assume that you have applied for a job and were not hired. How do you know if the organization decided not to hire you because you are unqualified, because you are less qualified than the individual ultimately hired, or simply because the person in charge of the hiring decision "didn't like your type"? Discrimination is a multifaceted issue. It is often not easy to determine the extent to which unfair discrimination affects an employer's decisions.

Legal scholars have identified three theories of discrimination: disparate treatment, disparate impact, and reasonable accommodation. In addition, there is protection for those participating in discrimination cases or opposing discriminatory actions. In the act, these theories are stated in very general terms. However, the court system has defined and delineated these theories through the cases brought before it. A comparison of the theories of discrimination is given in Table 3.3.

**table 3.3**
Comparison of Discrimination Theories

| TYPES OF DISCRIMINATION | DISPARATE TREATMENT | DISPARATE IMPACT | REASONABLE ACCOMMODATION |
|---|---|---|---|
| Show intent? | Yes | No | Yes |
| Prima facie case | Individual is member of a protected group, was qualified for the job, and was turned down for the job, and the job remained open | Statistical disparity in the effects of a facially neutral employment practice | Individual has a belief or disability, provided the employer with notice (request to accommodate), and was adversely affected by a failure to be accommodated |
| Employer's defense | Produce a legitimate, nondiscriminatory reason for the employment decision or show bona fide occupational qualification (BFOQ) | Prove that the employment practice bears a manifest relationship with job performance | Job-relatedness and business necessity, undue hardship, or direct threat to health or safety |
| Plaintiff's rebuttal | Reason offered was merely a "pretext" for discrimination | Alternative procedures exist that meet the employer's goal without having disparate impact | |
| Monetary damages | Compensatory and punitive damages | Equitable relief (e.g., back pay) | Compensatory and punitive damages (if discrimination was intentional or employer failed to show good faith efforts to accommodate) |

## Disparate Treatment

**Disparate treatment** exists when individuals in similar situations are treated differently and the different treatment is based on the individual's race, color, religion, sex, national origin, age, or disability status. If two people with the same qualifications apply for a job and the employer decides whom to hire based on one individual's race, the individual not hired is a victim of disparate treatment. In the disparate treatment case the plaintiff must prove that there was a discriminatory motive—that is, that the employer intended to discriminate.

**Disparate Treatment**
A theory of discrimination based on different treatments given to individuals because of their race, color, religion, sex, national origin, age, or disability status.

Whenever individuals are treated differently because of their race, sex, or the like, there is disparate treatment. For example, if a company fails to hire women with school-age children (claiming the women will be frequently absent) but hires men with school-age children, the applicants are being treated differently based on sex. Another example would be an employer who checks the references and investigates the conviction records of minority applicants but does not do so for white applicants. Why are managers advised not to ask about marital status? Because in most cases, a manager will either ask only the female applicants or, if the manager asks both males and females, he or she will make different assumptions about females (such as "She will have to move if her husband gets a job elsewhere") and males (such as "He's very stable"). In all these examples, notice that (1) people are being treated differently and (2) there is an actual intent to treat them differently.[17]

The nearby "Competing through Globalization" box illustrates how people can be subtly treated differently in France.

To understand how disparate treatment is applied in the law, let's look at how an actual court case, filed under disparate treatment, would proceed.

### The Plaintiff's Burden

As in any legal case, the plaintiff has the burden of proving that the defendant has committed an illegal act. This is the idea of a "prima facie" case. In a disparate treatment case, the plaintiff meets the prima facie burden by showing four things:

1. The plaintiff belongs to a protected group.
2. The plaintiff applied for and was qualified for the job.
3. Despite possessing the qualifications, the plaintiff was rejected.
4. After the plaintiff was rejected, the position remained open and the employer continued to seek applicants with similar qualifications, or the position was filled by someone with similar qualifications.

Although these four elements may seem easy to prove, it is important to note that what the court is trying to do is rule out the most obvious reasons for rejecting the plaintiff's claim (for example, the plaintiff did not apply or was not qualified, or the position was already filled or had been eliminated). If these alternative explanations are ruled out, the court assumes that the hiring decision was based on a discriminatory motive.

### The Defendant's Rebuttal

Once the plaintiff has made the prima facie case for discrimination, the burden shifts to the defendant. The burden is different depending on whether the prima facie case presents only circumstantial evidence (there is no direct evidence of discrimination such as a formal policy to discriminate, but rather discriminatory intent must be

## COMPETING THROUGH GLOBALIZATION

### Seeking Diversity in France

The year 2006 saw a string of violent protests and riots in and around Paris as poor ethnic (mostly North African) residents sought to express their dissatisfaction with their current state. Now a number of companies and the government are working together to try to effectively manage the diverse workforce and potentially reduce the economic disparities that exist in this "egalitarian" society.

The basic problem stems from what appears to be widespread discrimination in employment among French companies. According to research conducted by Jean-Francois Amadieu, a professor of sociology at the University of Paris, job candidates with North African–sounding names have one-third the chance of getting an interview compared to those with French-sounding names. He concludes that a significant number of French firms could be rightfully sued for discrimination.

As an example, Manuella Arulnayagam graduated from engineering school in 2003 and spent a year sending out her résumé. The daughter of Sri Lankan immigrants, she did not receive a single interview. In fact, at one job fair, a recruiter took one glance at her résumé and dropped it in the garbage can. She states, "Throughout my whole life and studies I never wanted to believe that my name or my address could be a problem."

One of the potential obstacles to better managing diversity in France actually stems from the legal system. In the interest of ensuring equality, French law precludes collecting information on race, ethnicity, religion, and other characteristics. However, this makes it difficult for French employers to proactively recruit or target particular minority groups.

One solution has been to go straight to the so-called *banlieues,* or poor immigrant neighborhoods, to attempt to recruit minority workers. Firms such as the cosmetic maker L'Oreal send managers to poor-area high schools to coach students in writing résumés and proper behavior in job interviews.

In addition, more progressive HR departments in companies like insurer AXA or carmaker Peugeot automatically strip personal data that might imply racial or ethnic status from résumés before forwarding them to recruiters. If those making the decisions to offer interviews do not know the ethnicity of the applicant, they cannot discriminate on that basis.

SOURCE: M. Valla, "France Seeks Path to Workplace Diversity," *The Wall Street Journal,* January 3, 2007, p. A2

inferred) or direct evidence (a formal policy of discrimination for some perceived legitimate reason). In cases of circumstantial evidence, the defendant simply must produce a legitimate, nondiscriminatory reason, such as that, although the plaintiff was qualified, the individual hired was more qualified.

However, in cases where direct evidence exists, such as a formal policy of hiring only women for waitress jobs because the business is aimed at catering to male customers, then the defendant is more likely to offer a different defense. This defense argues that for this job, a factor such as race, sex, or religion was a **bona fide occupational qualification (BFOQ).** For example, if one were hiring an individual to hand out towels in a women's locker room, being a woman might be a BFOQ. However, there are very few cases in which race or sex qualifies as a BFOQ, and in these cases it must be a necessary, rather than simply a preferred characteristic of the job.

**Bona Fide Occupational Qualification (BFOQ)**
A job qualification based on race, sex, religion, and so on, that an employer asserts is a necessary qualification for the job.

*UAW v. Johnson Controls, Inc.*, illustrates the difficulty in using a BFOQ as a defense.[18] Johnson Controls, a manufacturer of car batteries, had instituted a "fetal protection" policy that excluded women of childbearing age from a number of jobs in which they would be exposed to lead, which can cause birth defects in children. The company argued that sex was a BFOQ essential to maintaining a safe workplace. The

Supreme Court did not uphold the company's policy, arguing that BFOQs are limited to policies that are directly related to a worker's ability to do the job.

## The Plaintiff's Rebuttal

If the defendant provides a legitimate, nondiscriminatory reason for its employment decision, the burden shifts back to the plaintiff. The plaintiff must now show that the reason offered by the defendant was not in fact the reason for its decision but merely a "pretext" or excuse for its actual discriminatory decision. This could entail providing evidence that white applicants with very similar qualifications to the plaintiff have often been hired while black applicants with very similar qualifications were all rejected. To illustrate disparate treatment, let's look at the first major case dealing with disparate treatment, *McDonnell Douglas Corp. v. Green.*

***McDonnell Douglas Corp. v. Green.*** This Supreme Court case was the first to delineate the four criteria for a prima facie case of discrimination. From 1956 to 1964, Green had been an employee at McDonnell Douglas, a manufacturing plant in St. Louis, Missouri, that employed about 30,000 people. In 1964 he was laid off during a general workforce reduction. While unemployed, he participated in some activities that the company undoubtedly frowned upon: a "lock-in," where he and others placed a chain and padlock on the front door of a building to prevent the employees from leaving; and a "stall-in," where a group of employees stalled their cars at the gates of the plant so that no one could enter or leave the parking lot. About three weeks after the lock-in, McDonnell Douglas advertised for qualified mechanics, Green's trade, and he reapplied. When the company rejected his application, he sued, arguing that the company didn't hire him because of his race and because of his persistent involvement in the civil rights movement.

In making his prima facie case, Green had no problem showing that he was a member of a protected group, that he had applied for and was qualified for the job (having already worked in the job), that he was rejected, and that the company continued to advertise the position. The company's defense was that the plaintiff was not hired because he participated in the lock-in and the stall-in. In other words, the company was merely refusing to hire a troublemaker.

The plaintiff responded that the company's stated reason for not hiring him was a pretext for discrimination. He pointed out that white employees who had participated in the same activities (the lock-in and stall-in) were rehired, whereas he was not. The court found in favor of the plaintiff.

This case illustrates how similarly situated individuals (white and black) can be treated differently (whites were hired back whereas blacks were not) with the differences in treatment based on race. As we discuss later, most plaintiffs bring cases of sexual harassment under this theory of discrimination, sexual harassment being a situation where individuals are treated differently because of their sex.

## Mixed-Motive Cases

In a mixed-motive case, the defendant acknowledges that some discriminatory motive existed but argues that the same hiring decision would have been reached even without the discriminatory motive. In *Hopkins v. Price Waterhouse,* Elizabeth Hopkins was an accountant who had applied for partnership in her firm. Although she had brought in a large amount of business and had received high praise from her clients, she was turned down for a partnership on two separate occasions. In her performance reviews, she had been told to adopt more feminine dress and speech and received many other comments that suggested gender-based stereotypes. In court, the company admitted that a sex-based stereotype existed but argued that it would have come to the same decision (not promoted Hopkins) even if the stereotype had not existed.

One of the main questions that came out of this case was, Who has the burden of proof? Does the plaintiff have to prove that a different decision would have been made (that Hopkins would have been promoted) in the absence of the discriminatory motive? Or does the defendant have to prove that the same decision would have been made?

According to CRA 1991, if the plaintiff demonstrates that race, sex, color, religion, or national origin was a motivating factor for any employment practice, the prima facie burden has been met, and the burden of proof is on the employer to demonstrate that the same decision would have been made even if the discriminatory motive had not been present. If the employer can do this, the plaintiff cannot collect compensatory or punitive damages. However, the court may order the employer to quit using the discriminatory motive in its future employment decisions.

## Disparate Impact

**Disparate Impact**
A theory of discrimination based on facially neutral employment practices that disproportionately exclude a protected group from employment opportunities.

The second type of discrimination is called **disparate impact.** It occurs when a facially neutral employment practice disproportionately excludes a protected group from employment opportunities. A facially neutral employment practice is one that lacks obvious discriminatory content yet affects one group to a greater extent than other groups, such as an employment test. Although the Supreme Court inferred disparate impact from Title VII in the *Griggs v. Duke Power* case, it has since been codified into the Civil Rights Act of 1991.

There is an important distinction between disparate impact and disparate treatment discrimination. For there to be discrimination under disparate treatment, there has to be intentional discrimination. Under disparate impact, intent is irrelevant. The important criterion is that the consequences of the employment practice are discriminatory.

For example, if, for some practical reason, you hired individuals based on their height, you may not have intended to discriminate against anyone, and yet using height would have a disproportionate impact on certain protected groups. Women tend to be shorter than men, so fewer women will be hired. Certain ethnic groups, such as those of Asian ancestry, also tend to be shorter than those of European ancestry. Thus, your facially neutral employment practice will have a disparate impact on certain protected groups.

This is not to imply that simply because a selection practice has disparate impact, it is necessarily illegal. Some characteristics (such as height) are not equally distributed across race and gender groups; however, the important question is whether the characteristic is related to successful performance on the job. To help you understand how disparate impact works, let's look at a court proceeding involving a disparate impact claim.

### The Plaintiff's Burden

In a disparate impact case, the plaintiff must make the prima facie case by showing that the employment practice in question disproportionately affects a protected group relative to the majority group. To illustrate this theory, let's assume that you are a manager who has 60 positions to fill. Your applicant pool has 80 white and 40 black applicants. You use a test that selects 48 of the white and 12 of the black applicants. Is this a disparate impact? Two alternative quantitative analyses are often used to determine whether a test has adverse impact.

The **four-fifths rule** states that a test has disparate impact if the hiring rate for the minority group is less than four-fifths (or 80 percent) of the hiring rate for the majority group. Applying this analysis to the preceding example, we would first calculate the hiring rates for each group:

**Four-Fifths Rule**
A rule that states that an employment test has disparate impact if the hiring rate for a minority group is less than four-fifths, or 80 percent, of the hiring rate for the majority group.

$$\text{Whites} = 48/80 = 60\%$$
$$\text{Blacks} = 12/40 = 30\%$$

Then we would compare the hiring rate of the minority group (30%) with that of the majority group (60%). Using the four-fifths rule, we would determine that the test has adverse impact if the hiring rate of the minority group is less than 80 percent of the hiring rate of the majority group. Because it is less (that is, 30%/60% = 50%, which is less than 80%), we would conclude that the test has adverse impact. The four-fifths rule is used as a rule of thumb by the EEOC in determining adverse impact.

The **standard deviation rule** uses actual probability distributions to determine adverse impact. This analysis uses the difference between the expected representation (or hiring rates) for minority groups and the actual representation (or hiring rate) to determine whether the difference between these two values is greater than would occur by chance. Thus, in our example, 33 percent (40 of 120) of the applicants were blacks, so one would expect 33 percent (20 of 60) of those hired to be black. However, only 12 black applicants were hired. To determine if the difference between the expected representation and the actual representation is greater than we would expect by chance, we calculate the standard deviation (which, you might remember from your statistics class, is the standard deviation in a binomial distribution):

**Standard Deviation Rule**
A rule used to analyze employment tests to determine disparate impact; it uses the difference between the expected representation for minority groups and the actual representation to determine whether the difference between the two is greater than would occur by chance.

$$\sqrt{\text{Number hired} \times \frac{\text{Number of minority applicants}}{\text{Number of total applicants}} \times \frac{\text{Number of nonminority applicants}}{\text{Number of total applicants}}}$$

or in this case:

$$\sqrt{60 \times \frac{40}{120} \times \frac{80}{120}} = 3.6$$

If the difference between the actual representation and the expected representation (20 − 12 = 8 in this case) of blacks is greater than 2 standard deviations (2 × 3.6, = 7.2 in this case), we would conclude that the test had adverse impact against blacks, because we would expect this result less than 1 time in 20 if the test were equally difficult for both whites and blacks.

The *Wards Cove Packing Co. v. Atonio* case involved an interesting use of statistics. The plaintiffs showed that the jobs in the cannery (lower paying jobs) were filled primarily with minority applicants (in this case, American Eskimos). However, only a small percentage of the noncannery jobs (those with higher pay) were filled by nonminorities. The plaintiffs argued that this statistical disparity in the racial makeup of the cannery and noncannery jobs was proof of discrimination. The federal district, appellate, and Supreme Courts all found for the defendant, stating that this disparity was not proof of discrimination.

Once the plaintiff has demonstrated adverse impact, he or she has met the burden of a prima facie case of discrimination.[19]

### Defendant's Rebuttal

According to CRA 1991, once the plaintiff has made a prima facie case, the burden of proof shifts to the defendant, who must show that the employment practice is a "business necessity." This is accomplished by showing that the practice bears a relationship with some legitimate employer goal. With respect to job selection, this relationship is demonstrated by showing the job relatedness of the test, usually by reporting a validity study of some type, to be discussed in Chapter 6. For now, suffice it to say that the employer shows that the test scores are significantly correlated with measures of job performance.

Measures of job performance used in validation studies can include such things as objective measures of output, supervisor ratings of job performance, and success in training.[20] Normally, performance appraisal ratings are used, but these ratings must be valid for the court to accept the validation results. For example, in *Albermarle Paper v. Moody*, the employer demonstrated that the selection battery predicted performance (measured with supervisors' overall rankings of employees) in only some of the 13 occupational groups in which it was used. In this case, the court was especially critical of the supervisory ratings used as the measure of job performance. The court stated, "There is no way of knowing precisely what criteria of job performance the supervisors were considering."[21]

### Plaintiff's Rebuttal

If the employer shows that the employment practice is the result of some business necessity, the plaintiff's last resort is to argue that other employment practices could sufficiently meet the employer's goal without adverse impact. Thus, if a plaintiff can demonstrate that selection tests other than the one used by the employer exist, do not have adverse impact, and correlate with job performance as highly as the employer's test, then the defendant can be found guilty of discrimination. Many cases deal with standardized tests of cognitive ability, so it is important to examine alternatives to these tests that have less adverse impact while still meeting the employer's goal. At least two separate studies reviewing alternative selection devices such as interviews, biographical data, assessment centers, and work sample tests have concluded that none of them met both criteria.[22] It seems that when the employment practice in question is a standardized test of cognitive ability, plaintiffs will have a difficult time rebutting the defendant's rebuttal.

***Griggs v. Duke Power.*** To illustrate how this process works, let's look at the *Griggs v. Duke Power* case.[23] Following the passage of Title VII, Duke Power instituted a new system for making selection and promotion decisions. The system required either a high school diploma or a passing score on two professionally developed tests (the Wonderlic Personnel Test and the Bennett Mechanical Comprehension Test). A passing score was set so that it would be equal to the national median for high school graduates who had taken the tests.

The plaintiffs met their prima facie burden showing that both the high school diploma requirement and the test battery had adverse impacts on blacks. According to the 1960 census, 34 percent of white males had high school diplomas, compared with only 12 percent of black males. Similarly, 58 percent of white males passed the test battery, whereas only 6 percent of blacks passed.

Duke Power was unable to defend its use of these employment practices. A company vice president testified that the company had not studied the relationship between these employment practices and the employees' ability to perform the job. In addition, employees already on the job who did not have high school diplomas and had never taken the tests were performing satisfactorily. Thus Duke Power lost the case.

It is interesting to note that the court recognized that the company had not intended to discriminate, mentioning that the company was making special efforts to help undereducated employees through financing two-thirds of the cost of tuition for high school training. This illustrates the importance of the consequences, as opposed to the motivation, in determining discrimination under the disparate impact theory.

## Reasonable Accommodation

**Reasonable accommodation** presents a relatively new theory of discrimination. It began with regard to religious discrimination, but has recently been both expanded and popularized with the passage of the ADA. Reasonable accommodation differs from these two theories in that rather than simply requiring an employer to refrain from some action, reasonable accommodation places a special obligation on an employer to affirmatively do something to accommodate an individual's disability or religion. This theory is violated when an employer fails to make reasonable accommodation, where that is required, to a qualified person with a disability or to a person's religious observation and/or practices.

**Reasonable Accommodation**
Making facilities readily accessible to and usable by individuals with disabilities.

### Religion and Accommodation

Often individuals with strong religious beliefs find that some observations and practices of their religion come into direct conflict with their work duties. For example, some religions forbid individuals from working on the sabbath day when the employer schedules them for work. Others might have beliefs that preclude them from shaving, which might conflict with a company's dress code. Although Title VII forbids discrimination on the basis of religion just like race or sex, religion also receives special treatment requiring employers to exercise an affirmative duty to accommodate individuals' religious beliefs and practices. As Figure 3.2 shows, the number of religious discrimination charges has consistently increased over the past few years, jumping significantly in 2002.

In cases of religious discrimination, an employee's burden is to demonstrate that he or she has a legitimate religious belief and provided the employer with notice of the need to accommodate the religious practice, and that adverse consequences occurred due to the employer's failure to accommodate. In such cases, the employer's major defense is to assert that to accommodate the employee would require an undue hardship.

Examples of reasonably accommodating a person's religious obligations might include redesigning work schedules (most often accommodating those who cannot work on their sabbath), providing alternative testing dates for applicants, not requiring union membership and/or allowing payment of "charitable contributions" in lieu of union dues, or altering certain dress or grooming requirements. Note that although an employer is required to make a reasonable accommodation, it need not be the one that is offered by the employee.[24]

In one case, Wal-Mart agreed to settle with a former employee who alleged that he was forced to quit in 1993 after refusing to work on Sunday. Wal-Mart agreed to pay the former employee unspecified damages, to instruct managers on employees' rights to have their religious beliefs accommodated, and to prepare a computer-based manual describing employees' rights and religious harassment.[25]

Following the attack of 9/11, a number of cases sprang up with regard to discrimination against Muslims, partly accounting for the significant increase in religious discrimination complaints in 2002. In one case, the EEOC and Electrolux Group settled a religious accommodation case brought by Muslim workers from Somalia. The Islamic

figure 3.2

Religious Discrimination Complaints, 1991–2006

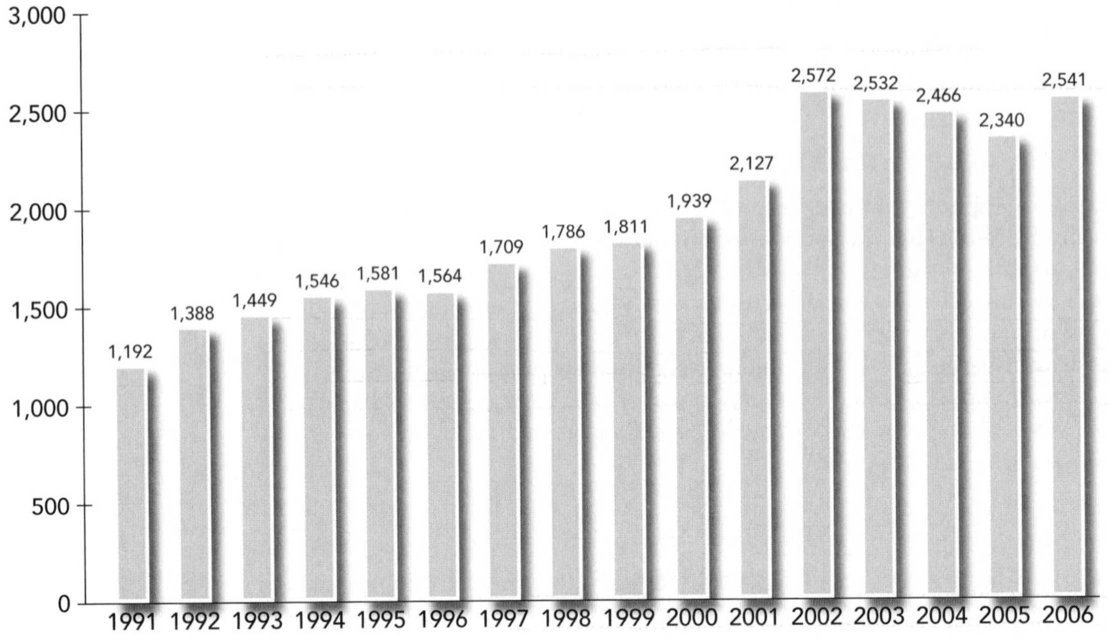


SOURCE: www.eeoc.gov/stats/religion.html.

faith requires Muslims to offer five prayers a day, with two of these prayers offered within restricted time periods (early morning and sunset). Muslim employees alleged that they were disciplined for using an unscheduled break traditionally offered to line employees on an as-needed basis to observe their sunset prayer. Electrolux worked with the EEOC to respect the needs of its Muslim workers without creating a business hardship by affording them with an opportunity to observe their sunset prayer.[26]

Religion and accommodation also bring up the question as to what to do when different rights collide. For instance, John Nemecek had been a respected business professor at Spring Arbor University for 15 years. Spring Arbor is an evangelical college in Michigan which began to take issue with some of his behavior. After he began wearing earrings and makeup and asking friends to call him "Julie" he found himself demoted and fired because his womanly appearance violated "Christian behavior." In 2004 a doctor diagnosed Prof. Nemecek with a "gender-identify disorder," in which one's sexual identity differs from one's body. Soon after, the school began taking away some of his responsibilities, and then issued him a contract revoking his dean's post, reassigning him to a non-tenure-track role in which he would work from home, teaching online. It also required him to not wear any makeup or female clothing or to display any outward signs of femininity when visiting campus. Gayle Beebe, the university's president, said "We felt through a job reassignment we could give him the space to work on this issue." Prof. Nemecek signed the contract but then violated it by showing up on campus with earrings and makeup on four separate occasions. The professor filed his complaint with the EEOC and the university then declined to renew his contract. Prof. Nemecek, whose Baptist church also asked him to leave the congregation, says of the university, "Essentially, they're saying they can define who is a Christian. I don't agree that our biology determines our gender."[27]

## COMPETING THROUGH TECHNOLOGY
### Nontraditional Solutions to a Traditional Employment Problem

Schukra Manufacturing of Toronto is an award-winning designer and manufacturer that has seen its production soar and workforce double over the past decade due to the popularity of its nontraditional seat installations. Its Schukra Lumbar Systems, which provide lower back support and encourage correct seating posture, have been adopted by a range of firms in the furniture manufacturing, health care, automotive, and aviation fields, including such household names as Air Canada, VIA Rail, Sears Manufacturing, Chrysler, and Ferrari.

To meet the demand for its products, Schukra has sought out employees with disabilities. For example, Schukra employs two hearing-impaired press operators, while a mechanical engineer who has postpolio syndrome works for Sherwood Industries, its associated company. One of the hearing-impaired employees was initially hired to work on a small press, but he now operates presses in the 400- to 600-ton range. Other than having an interpreter present for his annual review, no ongoing accommodations have been required for this employee, he adds. The second hearing-impaired employee was so comfortable with lip reading that an interpreter's services were never needed.

No major accommodations were made for the employee with postpolio syndrome, although the company did work with the person and the employment services coordinator to determine job duties that matched his current physical ability. For example, the majority of the work performed by the employee can be done sitting down and he is not assigned tasks that require heavy lifting. Also, once a week the person is allowed to leave work at 1 P.M. to attend physiotherapy appointments.

"Accommodations for these employees haven't been significant or costly," states Jim Carroll, the former head of human resources. "However, if their needs do change, we'll make accommodations to assist them to do their jobs or to improve the processes that affect their work, particularly where safety is concerned."

SOURCE: Canadian Ministry of Citizenship, "Qualified Workers with Disabilities, Found through TCG LINK-Up Employment Services, Allow Schukra Manufacturing to Save Money while Recruiting Staff," October 23, 2001, at http://www.equalopportunity.on.ca.

### Disability and Accommodation

As previously discussed, the ADA made discrimination against individuals with disabilities illegal. However, the act itself states that the employer is obligated not just to refrain from discriminating, but to take affirmative steps to accommodate individuals who are protected under the act.

Under disability claims, the plaintiff must show that she or he is a qualified applicant with a disability and that adverse action was taken by a covered entity. The employer's defense then depends on whether the decision was made without regard to the disability or in light of the disability. For example, if the employer argues that the plaintiff is not qualified, then it has met the burden, and the question of reasonable accommodation becomes irrelevant.

If, however, the decision was made "in light of" the disability, then the question becomes one of whether the person could perform adequately with a reasonable accommodation. This leads to three potential defenses. First, the employer could allege job-relatedness or business necessity through demonstrating, for example, that it is using a test that assesses ability to perform essential job functions. However, then the question arises of whether the applicant could perform the essential job functions with a reasonable accommodation. Second, the employer could claim an undue hardship to accommodate the individual. In essence, this argues that the accommodation necessary is an action requiring significant difficulty or expense. Finally, the employer could argue that the individual with the disability might pose a direct threat to his own or others' health or safety in the workplace. This requires examining the duration of the risk, the nature and severity of potential harm, the probability of the harm occurring, and the imminence of the potential harm.

What are some examples of reasonable accommodation with regard to disabilities? First is providing readily accessible facilities such as ramps and/or elevators for disabled individuals to enter the workplace. Second, job restructuring might include eliminating marginal tasks, shifting these tasks to other employees, redesigning job procedures, or altering work schedules. Third, an employer might reassign a disabled employee to a job with essential job functions he or she could perform. Fourth, an employer might accommodate applicants for employment who must take tests through providing alternative testing formats, providing readers, or providing additional time for taking the test. Fifth, readers, interpreters, or technology to offer reading assistance might be given to a disabled employee. Sixth, an employer could allow employees to provide their own accommodation such as bringing a guide dog to work.[28] Note that most accommodations are inexpensive. A study by Sears Roebuck & Co. found that 69 percent of all accommodations cost nothing, 29 percent cost less than $1,000, and only 3 percent cost more than $1,000.[29] In addition, the "Competing through Technology" box illustrates how accommodating disabled individuals can actually provide competitive advantage.

## EVIDENCE-BASED HR

As information technology becomes more and more ubiquitous in the workplace, some have begun to explore the implications for people with disabilities. Researchers at the Employment and Disability Institute at Cornell University recently reviewed the accessibility of 10 job boards and 31 corporate e-recruiting Web sites using Bobby 3.2, a software program designed to check for errors that cause accessibility concerns. They found that none of the job boards and only a small minority of the e-recruiting sites met the Bobby standards.

In phase 2 of the study, they surveyed 813 HR professionals who were members of the Society for Human Resource Management (SHRM). Between 16 and 46 percent of the HR professionals were familiar with six of the most common assistive technologies to adapt computers for disabled individuals (screen magnifiers, speech recognitions software, video captioning, Braille readers/displays, screen readers, guidelines for Web design). In addition, only 1 in 10 said they knew that their firm had evaluated the Web sites for accessibility to people with disabilities.

This study indicates that while firms may not have any intention of discriminating against people with disabilities, the rapid expansion of information technology combined with an inattention to and/or lack of education regarding accessibility issues may accidentally lead them to do so.

SOURCE: S. Bruyere, S. Erickson, and S. VanLooy. "Information Technology and the Workplace: Implications for Persons with Disabilities," *Disability Studies Quarterly* 25, no. 2 (Spring 2005), at www.dsq-sds.org.

## Retaliation for Participation and Opposition

**LO5**
Discuss the Legal Issues Involved with Preferential Treatment Programs.

Suppose you overhear a supervisor in your workplace telling someone that he refuses to hire women because he knows they are just not cut out for the job. Believing this to be illegal discrimination, you face a dilemma. Should you come forward and report this statement? Or if someone else files a lawsuit for gender discrimination, should you testify on behalf of the plaintiff? What happens if your employer threatens to fire you if you do anything?

Title VII of the Civil Rights Act of 1964 protects you. It states that employers cannot retaliate against employees for either "opposing" a perceived illegal employment practice or "participating in a proceeding" related to an alleged illegal employment practice. Opposition refers to expressing to someone through proper channels that you believe that an illegal employment act has taken place or is taking place. Participation refers to actually testifying in an investigation, hearing, or court proceeding regarding an illegal employment act. Clearly, the purpose of this provision is to protect employees from employers' threats and other forms of intimidation aimed at discouraging the employees from bringing to light acts they believe to be illegal.

These cases can be extremely costly for companies because they are alleging acts of intentional discrimination, and therefore plaintiffs are entitled to punitive damages. For example, a 41-year-old former Allstate employee who claimed that a company official told her that the company wanted a "younger and cuter" image was awarded $2.8 million in damages by an Oregon jury. The jury concluded that the employee was forced out of the company for opposing age discrimination against other employees.[30]

In a recent case, Target Corporation agreed to pay $775,000 to a group of black workers who charged that at one store, the company condoned a racially hostile work environment exemplified by inappropriate comments and verbal berating based on race. When one of the black employees objected to this treatment, he was allegedly retaliated against, forcing him to resign.[31]

This does not mean that employees have an unlimited right to talk about how racist or sexist their employers are. The courts tend to frown on employees whose activities result in a poor public image for the company unless those employees had attempted to use the organization's internal channels—approaching one's manager, raising the issue with the HRM department, and so on—before going public.

## Current Issues Regarding Diversity and Equal Employment Opportunity

Because of recent changes in the labor market, most organizations' demographic compositions are becoming increasingly diverse. A study by the Hudson Institute projected that 85 percent of the new entrants into the U.S. labor force over the next decade will be females and minorities.[32] Integrating these groups into organizations made up predominantly of able-bodied white males will bring attention to important issues like sexual harassment, affirmative action, and the "reasonable accommodation" of employees with disabilities.

### Sexual Harassment

**LO6**
Identify Behavior that Constitutes Sexual Harassment and List Things that an Organization can do to Eliminate or Minimize it.

Clarence Thomas's Supreme Court confirmation hearings in 1991 brought the issue of sexual harassment into increased prominence. Anita Hill, one of Thomas's former employees, alleged that he had sexually harassed her while she was working under his supervision at the Department of Education and the Equal Employment Opportunity Commission. Although the allegations were never substantiated, the hearing made many people more aware of how often employees are sexually harassed in the workplace and, combined with other events, resulted in a tremendous increase in the number of sexual harassment complaints being filed with the EEOC, as we see in Figure 3.3.

**figure 3.3**

Sexual Harassment Charges, 1991–2006

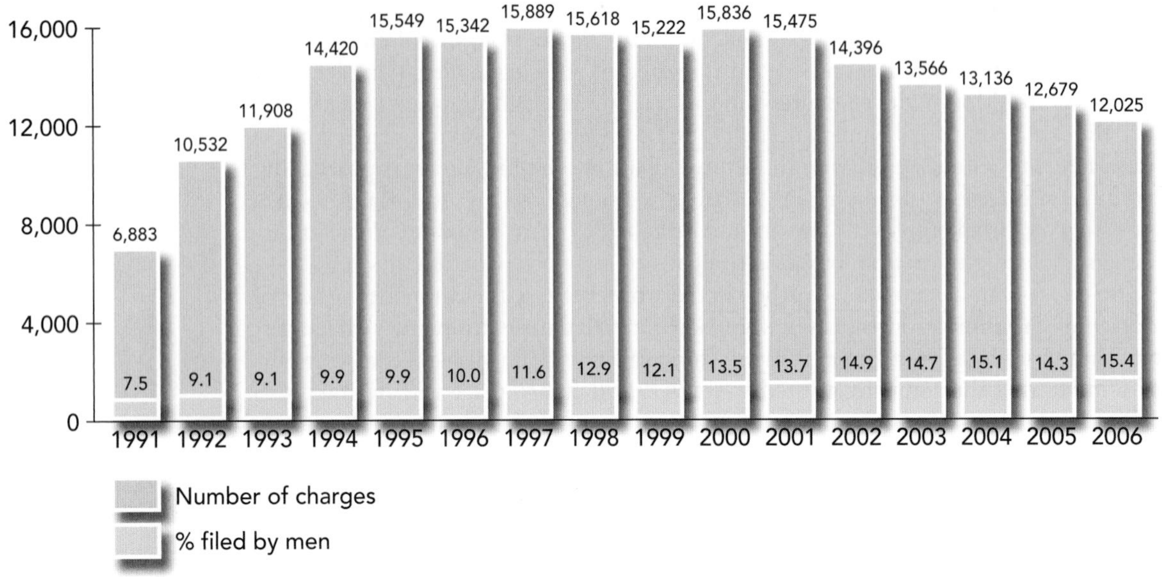


SOURCE: www.eeoc.gov/stats/harass.html.

In addition, after President Clinton took office and faced a sexual harassment lawsuit by Paula Corbin Jones for his alleged proposition to her in a Little Rock hotel room, the number of sexual harassment complaints took another jump from 1993 to 1994—again, potentially due to the tremendous amount of publicity regarding sexual harassment. However, the number of cases filed has actually decreased substantially since 2000.

Sexual harassment refers to unwelcome sexual advances. (See Table 3.4.) It can take place in two basic ways. "Quid pro quo" harassment occurs when some kind of benefit (or punishment) is made contingent on the employee's submitting (or not submitting) to sexual advances. For example, a male manager tells his female secretary that if she has sex with him, he will help her get promoted, or he threatens to fire her if she fails to do so; these are clearly cases of quid pro quo sexual harassment.

The *Bundy v. Jackson* case illustrates quid pro quo sexual harassment.[33] Sandra Bundy was a personnel clerk with the District of Columbia Department of

**table 3.4**

EEOC Definition of Sexual Harassment

| |
|---|
| Unwelcome sexual advances, requests for sexual favors, and other verbal or physical contact of a sexual nature constitute sexual harassment when |
| 1. Submission to such conduct is made either explicitly or implicitly a term or condition of an individual's employment, |
| 2. Submission to or rejection of such conduct by an individual is used as the basis for employment decisions affecting such individual, or |
| 3. Such conduct has the purpose or effect of unreasonably interfering with an individual's work performance or creating an intimidating, hostile, or offensive working environment. |

SOURCE: EEOC guideline based on the Civil Rights Act of 1964, Title VII.

Corrections. She received repeated sexual propositions from Delbert Jackson, who was at the time a fellow employee (although he later became the director of the agency). She later began to receive propositions from two of her supervisors: Arthur Burton and James Gainey. When she raised the issue to their supervisor, Lawrence Swain, he dismissed her complaints, telling her that "any man in his right mind would want to rape you," and asked her to begin a sexual relationship with him. When Bundy became eligible for a promotion, she was passed over because of her "inadequate work performance," although she had never been told that her work performance was unsatisfactory. The U.S. Court of Appeals found that Bundy had been discriminated against because of her sex, thereby extending the idea of discrimination to sexual harassment.

A more subtle, and possibly more pervasive, form of sexual harassment is "hostile working environment." This occurs when someone's behavior in the workplace creates an environment that makes it difficult for someone of a particular sex to work. Many plaintiffs in sexual harassment lawsuits have alleged that men ran their fingers through the plaintiffs' hair, made suggestive remarks, and physically assaulted them by touching their intimate body parts. Other examples include having pictures of naked women posted in the workplace, using offensive sexually explicit language, or using sex-related jokes or innuendoes in conversations.[34]

Note that these types of behaviors are actionable under Title VII because they treat individuals differently based on their sex. In addition, although most harassment cases involve male-on-female harassment, any individual can be harassed. For example, male employees at Jenny Craig alleged that they were sexually harassed, and a federal jury found that a male employee had been sexually harassed by his male boss.[35]

In addition, Ron Clark Ford of Amarillo, Texas, recently agreed to pay $140,000 to six male plaintiffs who alleged that they and others were subjected to a sexually hostile work environment and different treatment because of their gender by male managers. Evidence gathered showed that the men were subjected to lewd, inappropriate comments of a sexual nature, and had their genitals and buttocks grabbed against their will by their male managers. The defendants argued that the conduct was "harmless horseplay."[36]

Finally, Babies 'R' Us agreed to pay $205,000 to resolve a same-sex suit. The lawsuit alleged that Andres Vasquez was subjected to a sexually hostile working environment and was the target of unwelcome and derogatory comments as well as behavior that mocked him because he did not conform to societal stereotypes of how a male should appear or behave.

Sexual harassment charge filings with the EEOC by men have increased to 15 percent of all filings in 2002 from 10 percent of filings in 1994. While the commission does not track same-sex, male-on-male charges, anecdotal evidence shows that most harassment allegations by men are against other men.[37]

There are three critical issues in these cases. First, the plaintiff cannot have "invited or incited" the advances. Often the plaintiff's sexual history, whether she or he wears provocative clothing, and whether she or he engages in sexually explicit conversations are used to prove or disprove that the advance was unwelcome. However, in the absence of substantial evidence that the plaintiff invited the behavior, courts usually lean toward assuming that sexual advances do not belong in the workplace and thus are unwelcome. In *Meritor Savings Bank v. Vinson*, Michelle Vinson claimed that during the four years she worked at a bank she was continually harassed by the bank's vice president, who repeatedly asked her to have sex with him (she eventually agreed) and sexually assaulted her.[38] The Supreme Court ruled that the victim's voluntary participation in sexual relations was not the major issue, saying that the focus of the case was on whether the vice president's advances were unwelcome.

A second critical issue is that the harassment must have been severe enough to alter the terms, conditions, and privileges of employment. Although it has not yet been consistently applied, many courts have used the "reasonable woman" standard in determining the severity or pervasiveness of the harassment. This consists of assessing whether a reasonable woman, faced with the same situation, would have reacted similarly. The reasonable woman standard recognizes that behavior that might be considered appropriate by a man (like off-color jokes) might not be considered appropriate by a woman.

The third issue is that the courts must determine whether the organization is liable for the actions of its employees. In doing so, the court usually examines two things. First, did the employer know about, or should he or she have known about, the harassment? Second, did the employer act to stop the behavior? If the employer knew about it and the behavior did not stop, the court usually decides that the employer did not act appropriately to stop it.

To ensure a workplace free from sexual harassment, organizations can follow some important steps. First, the organization can develop a policy statement that makes it very clear that sexual harassment will not be tolerated in the workplace. Second, all employees, new and old, can be trained to identify inappropriate workplace behavior. Third, the organization can develop a mechanism for reporting sexual harassment that encourages people to speak out. Fourth, management can prepare to take prompt disciplinary action against those who commit sexual harassment as well as appropriate action to protect the victims of sexual harassment.[39]

## Affirmative Action and Reverse Discrimination

Few would disagree that having a diverse workforce in terms of race and gender is a desirable goal, if all individuals have the necessary qualifications. In fact, many organizations today are concerned with developing and managing diversity. To eliminate discrimination in the workplace, many organizations have affirmative action programs to increase minority representation. Affirmative action was originally conceived as a way of taking extra effort to attract and retain minority employees. This was normally done by extensively recruiting minorities on college campuses, advertising in minority-oriented publications, and providing educational and training opportunities to minorities.[40] However, over the years, many organizations have resorted to quotalike hiring to ensure that their workforce composition mirrors that of the labor market. Sometimes these organizations act voluntarily; in other cases, the quotas are imposed by the courts or by the EEOC. Whatever the impetus for these hiring practices, many white and/or male individuals have fought against them, alleging what is called reverse discrimination.

An example of an imposed quota program is found at the fire department in Birmingham, Alabama. Having admitted a history of discriminating against blacks, the department entered into a consent decree with the EEOC to hold 50 percent of positions at all levels in the fire department open for minorities even though minorities made up only 28 percent of the relevant labor market. The result was that some white applicants were denied employment or promotion in favor of black applicants who scored lower on a selection battery. The federal court found that the city's use of the inflexible hiring formula violated federal civil rights law and the constitutional guarantee of equal protection. The appellate court agreed, and the Supreme Court refused to hear the case, thus making the decision final.

The entire issue of affirmative action should evoke considerable attention and debate over the next few years. Although most individuals support the idea of diversity, few argue for the kinds of quotas that have to some extent resulted from the present legal climate. In fact, one recent survey revealed that only 16 percent of the respondents favored affirmative action with quotas, 46 percent favored it without quotas, and 28 percent opposed all affirmative action programs. One study found that people favor affirmative action when it is operationalized as recruitment, training, and attention to applicant qualifications but oppose it when it consists of discrimination, quotas, and preferential treatment.[41] Affirmative action and quotas constituted an important topic of debate for the 2004 presidential candidates, and there is reason to believe that some changes in the legal system will be observed over the next few years.

## Outcomes of the Americans with Disabilities Act

The ADA was passed with the laudable goals of providing employment opportunities for the truly disabled who, in the absence of legislation, were unable to find employment. Certainly, some individuals with disabilities have found employment as a result of its passage. However, as often occurs with legislation, the impact is not necessarily what was intended. First, there has been increased litigation. The EEOC reports that over 200,000 complaints have been filed since passage of the act. Approximately 50 percent of the complaints filed have been found to be without reasonable cause. For example, in July 1992 GTE Data Services fired an employee for stealing from other employees and bringing a loaded gun to work. The fired employee sued for reinstatement under the ADA, claiming that he was the victim of a mental illness and thus should be considered disabled.[42]

A second problem is that the kinds of cases being filed are not what Congress intended to protect. Although the act was passed because of the belief that discrimination against individuals with disabilities occurred in the failure to hire them, 52.2 percent of the claims deal with firings, 28.9 percent with failure to make reasonable accommodation, and 12.5 percent with harassment. Only 9.4 percent of the complaints allege a failure to hire or rehire.[43] In addition, although the act was passed to protect people with major disabilities such as blindness, deafness, lost limbs, or paralysis, these disabilities combined account for a small minority of the disabilities claimed. As we see in Table 3.5, the biggest disability category is "other," meaning that the plaintiff claims a disability that is not one of the 35 types of impairment listed in the EEOC charge data system. The second largest category is "being regarded as disabled" accounting for 17.2 percent of all charges, followed by "back impairment" claims at 8.1 percent. As an example, recently a fired employee sued IBM asking for $5 million in damages for violation of the Americans with Disabilities Act. The employee had been fired for spending hours at work visiting adult chat rooms on his computer. He alleged that his addiction to sex and the Internet stemmed from trauma experienced by seeing a friend killed in 1969 during an Army patrol in Vietnam.[44]

Finally, the act does not appear to have had its anticipated impact on the employment of Americans with disabilities. According to the National Organization on Disability, 22 million of the 54 million disabled Americans are unemployed.[45]

For these reasons, Congress has explored the possibility of amending the act to more narrowly define the term disability.[46] The debate continues regarding the effectiveness of the ADA.

**table 3.5**

Sample of Complaints Filed under the ADA

| | 1997 | 1998 | 1999 | 2000 | 2001 | 2002 | 2003 | 2004 | 2005 | 2006 |
|---|---|---|---|---|---|---|---|---|---|---|
| Number of complaints | 18,108 | 17,806 | 17,007 | 15,864 | 16,470 | 15,964 | 15,377 | 15,576 | 14,893 | 15,625 |
| **% dealing with*** | | | | | | | | | | |
| Asthma | 1.5% | 1.9% | 1.8% | 2.0% | 1.6% | 1.6% | 1.6% | 1.5% | 1.6% | 1.7% |
| Back impairment | 14.9 | 12.9 | 12.2 | 10.2 | 9.3 | 9.5 | 8.6 | 8.0 | 8.4 | 8.1 |
| Cancer | 2.5 | 2.6 | 2.3 | 2.7 | 2.8 | 2.9 | 2.9 | 2.8 | 2.7 | 3.2 |
| Diabetes | 3.7 | 3.7 | 4.0 | 4.1 | 4.3 | 4.7 | 4.8 | 4.7 | 4.5 | 4.8 |
| Hearing | 2.8 | 2.9 | 2.9 | 3.1 | 2.9 | 3.2 | 3.1 | 3.4 | 3.2 | 3.3 |
| Vision | 2.4 | 2.4 | 2.5 | 2.3 | 2.3 | 2.6 | 2.6 | 2.5 | 2.3 | 2.3 |
| Heart | 3.7 | 3.8 | 3.8 | 3.3 | 3.6 | 4.0 | 3.7 | 3.5 | 3.3 | 3.0 |
| Regarded as disabled | 11.4 | 11.1 | 11.6 | 13.7 | 12.8 | 13.7 | 16.8 | 18.2 | 17.4 | 17.2 |
| Drug addiction | 0.8 | 0.7 | 0.5 | 0.6 | 0.5 | 0.6 | 0.6 | 0.5 | 0.3 | 0.5 |
| Other | 27.7 | 27.8 | 28.7 | 30.0 | 31.7 | 30.1 | 26.3 | 19.0 | 21.4 | 21.8 |

*Not all complaints are listed.

SOURCE: EEOC, http://www.eeoc.gov/stats/ada-receipts.html.

# Employee Safety

In March 2005, officials at the BP refinery in Texas City, Texas, were aware of the fact that some repairs needed to be done on some of the equipment in an octane-boosting processing unit. On March 23, knowing that some of the key alarms were not working, managers authorized a start-up of the unit. The start-up resulted in the deadliest petrochemical accident in 15 years, killing 15 people and injuring an additional 170.[47]

Like equal employment opportunity, employee safety is regulated by both the federal and state governments. However, to fully maximize the safety and health of workers, employers need to go well beyond the letter of the law and embrace its spirit. With this in mind, we first spell out the specific protections guaranteed by federal legislation and then discuss various kinds of safety awareness programs that attempt to reinforce these standards.

**LO7**
Identify the Major Provisions of the Occupational Safety and Health Act (1970) and the Rights of Employees that are Guaranteed by This Act.

## The Occupational Safety and Health Act (OSHA)

**Occupational Safety and Health Act (OSHA)**
The law that authorizes the federal government to establish and enforce occupational safety and health standards for all places of employment engaging in interstate commerce.

Although concern for worker safety would seem to be a universal societal goal, the **Occupational Safety and Health Act of 1970 (OSHA)**—the most comprehensive legislation regarding worker safety—did not emerge in this country until the early 1970s. At that time, there were roughly 15,000 work-related fatalities every year.

OSHA authorized the federal government to establish and enforce occupational safety and health standards for all places of employment engaging in interstate commerce. The responsibility for inspecting employers, applying the standards, and levying fines was assigned to the Department of Labor. The Department of Health was assigned responsibility for conducting research to determine the criteria for specific operations or occupations and for training employers to comply with the act. Much of this research is conducted by the National Institute for Occupational Safety and Health (NIOSH).

### Employee Rights under OSHA

**General Duty Clause**
The provision of the Occupational Health and Safety Act that states that an employer has an overall obligation to furnish employees with a place of employment free from recognized hazards.

The main provision of OSHA states that each employer has a general duty to furnish each employee a place of employment free from recognized hazards that cause or are likely to cause death or serious physical harm. This is referred to as the **general duty clause.** Some specific rights granted to workers under this act are listed in Table 3.6. The Department of Labor recognizes many specific types of hazards, and employers are required to comply with all the occupational safety and health standards published by NIOSH.

**table 3.6**
Rights Granted to Workers under the Occupational Safety and Health Act

Employees have the right to
1. Request an inspection.
2. Have a representative present at an inspection.
3. Have dangerous substances identified.
4. Be promptly informed about exposure to hazards and be given access to accurate records regarding exposures.
5. Have employer violations posted at the work site.

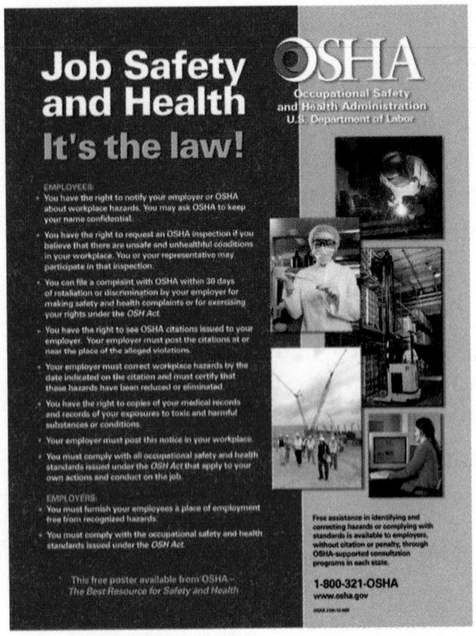


● OSHA is responsible for inspecting businesses, applying safety and health standards, and levying fines for violations. OSHA regulations prohibit notifying employers of inspections in advance.

A recent example is the development of OSHA standards for occupational exposure to blood-borne pathogens such as the AIDS virus. These standards identify 24 affected industrial sectors, encompassing 500,000 establishments and 5.6 million workers. Among other features, these standards require employers to develop an exposure control plan (ECP). An ECP must include a list of jobs whose incumbents might be exposed to blood, methods for implementing precautions in these jobs, postexposure follow-up plans, and procedures for evaluating incidents in which workers are accidentally infected.

Although NIOSH publishes numerous standards, regulators clearly cannot anticipate all possible hazards that could occur in the workplace. Thus, the general duty clause requires employers to be constantly alert for potential sources of harm in the workplace (as defined by the standards of a reasonably prudent person) and to correct them. For example, managers at Amoco's Joliet, Illinois, plant realized that over the years some employees had created undocumented shortcuts and built them into their process for handling flammable materials. These changes appeared to be labor saving but created a problem: workers did not have uniform procedures for dealing with flammable products. This became an urgent issue because many of the experienced workers were reaching retirement age, and the plant was in danger of losing critical technical expertise. To solve this problem, the plant adopted a training program that met all the standards required by OSHA. That is, it conducted a needs analysis highlighting each task new employees had to learn and then documented these processes in written guidelines. New employees were given hands-on training with the new procedures and were then certified in writing by their supervisor. A computer tracking system was installed to monitor who was handling flammable materials, and this system immediately identified anyone who was not certified. The plant met requirements for both ISO 9000 standards and OSHA regulations and continues to use the same model for safety training in other areas of the plant.[48]

## OSHA Inspections

OSHA inspections are conducted by specially trained agents of the Department of Labor called compliance officers. These inspections usually follow a tight "script." Typically, the compliance officer shows up unannounced. For obvious reasons, OSHA's regulations prohibit advance notice of inspections. The officer, after presenting credentials, tells the employer the reasons for the inspection and describes, in a general way, the procedures necessary to conduct the investigation.

An OSHA inspection has four major components. First, the compliance officer reviews the employer's records of deaths, injuries, and illnesses. OSHA requires this kind of record keeping from all firms with 11 or more full- or part-time employees. Second, the officer, typically accompanied by a representative of the employer (and perhaps by a representative of the employees), conducts a "walkaround" tour of the employer's premises. On this tour, the officer notes any conditions that may violate specific published standards or the less specific general duty clause. The third component of the inspection, employee interviews, may take place during the tour. At this time, any person who is aware of a violation can bring it to the attention of the officer. Finally, in a closing conference the compliance officer discusses the findings with the employer, noting any violations. The employer is given a reasonable time frame in which to correct these violations. If any violation represents imminent danger (that is, could cause serious injury or death before being eliminated through the normal enforcement procedures), the officer may, through the Department of Labor, seek a restraining order from a U.S. district court. Such an order compels the employer to correct the problem immediately.

## Citations and Penalties

If a compliance officer believes that a violation has occurred, he or she issues a citation to the employer that specifies the exact practice or situation that violates the act. The employer is required to post this citation in a prominent place near the location of the violation—even if the employer intends to contest it. Nonserious violations may be assessed up to $1,000 for each incident, but this may be adjusted downward if the employer has no prior history of violations or if the employer has made a good-faith effort to comply with the act. Serious violations of the act or willful, repeated violations may be fined up to $10,000 per incident. Fines for safety violations are never levied against the employees themselves. The assumption is that safety is primarily the responsibility of the employer, who needs to work with employees to ensure that they use safe working procedures.

In addition to these civil penalties, criminal penalties may also be assessed for willful violations that kill an employee. Fines can go as high as $20,000, and the employer or agents of the employer can be imprisoned. Criminal charges can also be brought against anyone who falsifies records that are subject to OSHA inspection or anyone who gives advance notice of an OSHA inspection without permission from the Department of Labor.

## The Effect of OSHA

OSHA has been unquestionably successful in raising the level of awareness of occupational safety. Table 3.7 presents recent data on occupational injuries and illnesses. Yet legislation alone cannot solve all the problems of work site safety.[49] Many industrial accidents are a product of unsafe behaviors, not unsafe working conditions. Because the

**table 3.7**

Some of the Most Recent Statistics Provided by the Bureau of Labor Statistics Regarding Workplace Illnesses and Injuries.

| NONFATAL INJURIES AND ILLNESSES, PRIVATE INDUSTRY | FATAL WORK-RELATED INJURIES |
|---|---|
| Total recordable cases:<br>4,214,200 in 2005 | Total fatalities (all sectors):<br>5,734 in 2005 |
| Cases involving days away from work:<br>1,234,700 in 2005 | Total fatalities (private industry):<br>5,214 in 2005 |
| Cases involving sprains, strains, tears:<br>503,530 in 2005 | Highway incidents (private industry):<br>1,265 in 2005 |
| Cases involving injuries to the back:<br>270,890 in 2005 | Falls (private industry):<br>735 in 2005 |
| Cases involving falls:<br>255,750 in 2005 | Homicides (private industry):<br>481 in 2005 |

SOURCE: www.bls.gov

act does not directly regulate employee behavior, little behavior change can be expected unless employees are convinced of the standards' importance.[50] This has been recognized by labor leaders. For example, Lynn Williams, president of the United Steelworkers of America, noted, "We can't count on government. We can't count on employers. We must rely on ourselves to bring about the safety and health of our workers."[51]

Because conforming to the statute alone does not necessarily guarantee safety, many employers go beyond the letter of the law. In the next section we examine various kinds of employer-initiated safety awareness programs that comply with OSHA requirements and, in some cases, exceed them.

## Safety Awareness Programs

**Safety Awareness Programs**
Employer programs that attempt to instill symbolic and substantive changes in the organization's emphasis on safety.

**Safety awareness programs** go beyond compliance with OSHA and attempt to instill symbolic and substantive changes in the organization's emphasis on safety. These programs typically focus either on specific jobs and job elements or on specific types of injuries or disabilities. A safety awareness program has three primary components: identifying and communicating hazards, reinforcing safe practices, and promoting safety internationally.

### Identifying and Communicating Job Hazards

**Job Hazard Analysis Technique**
A breakdown of each job into basic elements, each of which is rated for its potential for harm or injury.

**Technic of Operations Review (TOR)**
Method of determining safety problems via an analysis of past accidents.

Employees, supervisors, and other knowledgeable sources need to sit down and discuss potential problems related to safety. The **job hazard analysis technique** is one means of accomplishing this.[52] With this technique, each job is broken down into basic elements, and each of these is rated for its potential for harm or injury. If there is consensus that some job element has high hazard potential, this element is isolated and potential technological or behavioral changes are considered.

Another means of isolating unsafe job elements is to study past accidents. The **technic of operations review (TOR)** is an analysis methodology that helps managers determine which specific element of a job led to a past accident.[53] The first step in a TOR analysis is to establish the facts surrounding the incident. To accomplish this, all members of the work group involved in the accident give their initial impressions of what happened. The group must then, through group discussion, reach a consensus on the single, systematic failure that most contributed to the incident as well as two or three major secondary factors that contributed to it.

An analysis of jobs at Burger King, for example, revealed that certain jobs required employees to walk across wet or slippery surfaces, which led to many falls. Specific corrective action was taken based on analysis of where people were falling and what conditions led to these falls. Now Burger King provides mats at critical locations and has generally upgraded its floor maintenance. The company also makes slip-resistant shoes available to employees in certain job categories.[54]

Communication of an employee's risk should take advantage of several media. Direct verbal supervisory contact is important for its saliency and immediacy. Written memos are important because they help establish a "paper trail" that can later document a history of concern regarding the job hazard. Posters, especially those placed near the hazard, serve as a constant reminder, reinforcing other messages.

In communicating risk, it is important to recognize two distinct audiences. Sometimes relatively young or inexperienced workers need special attention. Research by the National Safety Council indicates that 40 percent of all accidents happen to individuals in the 20-to-29 age group and that 48 percent of all accidents happen to workers during their first year on the job.[55] The employer's primary concern with respect to this group is to inform them. However, the employer must not overlook experienced workers. Here the key concern is to remind them. Research indicates that long-term exposure to and familiarity with a specific threat lead to complacency.[56] Experienced employees need retraining to jar them from complacency about the real dangers associated with their work. This is especially the case if the hazard in question poses a greater threat to older employees. For example, falling off a ladder is a greater threat to older workers than to younger ones. Over 20 percent of such falls lead to a fatality for workers in the 55-to-65 age group, compared with just 10 percent for all other workers.[57]

## Reinforcing Safe Practices

One common technique for reinforcing safe practices is implementing a safety incentive program to reward workers for their support and commitment to safety goals. Initially, programs are set up to focus on improving short-term monthly or quarterly goals or to encourage safety suggestions. These short-term goals are later expanded to include more wide-ranging, long-term goals. Prizes are typically distributed in highly public forums (like annual meetings or events). These prizes usually consist of merchandise rather than cash because merchandise represents a lasting symbol of achievement. A good deal of evidence suggests that such programs are effective in reducing injuries and their cost.[58]

Whereas the safety awareness programs just described focus primarily on the job, other programs focus on specific injuries or disabilities. Lower back disability (LBD), for example, is a major problem that afflicts many employees. LBD accounts for approximately 25 percent of all workdays lost, costing firms nearly $30 billion a year.[59] Human resource managers can take many steps to prevent LBD and rehabilitate those who are already afflicted. Eye injuries are another target of safety awareness programs. The National Society to Prevent Blindness estimates that 1,000 eye injuries occur every day in occupational settings.[60] A 10-step program to reduce eye injuries is outlined in Table 3.8. Similar guidelines can be found for everything from chemical burns to electrocution to injuries caused by boiler explosions.[61]

## Promoting Safety Internationally

Given the increasing focus on international management, organizations also need to consider how to best ensure the safety of people regardless of the nation in which they

**table 3.8**

A 10-Step Program for Reducing Eye-Related Injuries

1. Conduct an eye hazard job analysis.
2. Test all employees' vision to establish a baseline.
3. Select protective eyewear designed for specific operations.
4. Establish a 100 percent behavioral compliance program for eyewear.
5. Ensure that eyewear is properly fitted.
6. Train employees in emergency procedures.
7. Conduct ongoing education programs regarding eye care.
8. Continually review accident prevention strategies.
9. Provide management support.
10. Establish written policies detailing sanctions and rewards for specific results.

SOURCE: T. W. Turrif, "NSPB Suggests 10-Step Program to Prevent Eye Injury," *Occupational Health and Safety* 60 (1991), pp. 62–66.

## COMPETING THROUGH SUSTAINABILITY

### The Gap Hopes Honesty Pays Off

The Gap, Inc., is one of the world's largest specialty retailers, with more than 3,000 stores and fiscal 2005 revenues of $16 billion. It operates four of the most recognized apparel brands in the world—The Gap, Banana Republic, Old Navy, and Forth & Towne.

In 2003 The Gap was the first retailer to release a social responsibility report, offering a comprehensive overview of its approach to social responsibility. The report was broadly lauded for its openness and honesty about both the successes and failures in this arena. In fact, this report won *Business Ethics* magazine's Social Reporting Award for "unprecedented honesty in reporting on factory conditions."

The Gap's 2004 Social Responsibility Report continued that discussion and provided new information on the company's progress, challenges, and new initiatives. Eva Sage-Gavin is the executive vice president of Human Resources and Corporate Communications at Gap, and here's how she describes its CSR efforts.

"There are really four key areas, and we think of corporate social responsibility across Gap, Inc., in these four strategic ways. The first one is this whole idea of sustainable solutions in our supply chain. This consists of working on a four-part strategy to improve working conditions, monitor factories, integrate labor standards into our business practices, and the whole idea of collaborating with outside partners to drive industry-wide change. So that's the first big centerpiece of how we think about CSR. The second is with our employees and making Gap, Inc., a place where people can really flourish and build their careers in a positive work environment. The third is community involvement, including everything from our foundation to our volunteerism. And the fourth key area in corporate social responsibility for us is environment, health, and safety. This is everything from the average store energy consumption to the safety of our stores for customers and employees to a high-level environmental impact assessment for all of our business operations.

"We think that this is critical to our long-term growth and the sustainability of our business. We see there are three elements to the benefits. First is the idea of our employee attraction and retention. Our employees tell us they want to work for a company that's socially responsible and they tell us through a variety of channels that they love working for a company that they believe is doing what's right. The second piece for us is a better supply chain. We know that better factory working conditions lead to better factories, and better factories make better products. The sourcing team can also select and make better buying decisions. We also introduced an integrated scorecard into the retail industry that gives factories feedback and scores on criteria such as quality, innovation, speed to market, and cost, and it considers the manufacturers' compliance history. Finally, our focus on sustainability creates win-win scenarios for everyone involved in our environmental impact. When we reduce our energy usage we also reduce cost. Obviously that's a win-win all the way around.

"I can say confidently that it's a critical part of our long-term growth and sustainability of our business. We know that our success depends on our employees and it depends on creating value for our shareholders, but ultimately it's about the customer experience and their desire to purchase great products. We know that we won't do that without employees who are engaged, satisfied, proud to work here—employees that want to exceed our customers' expectations. It's a very competitive global environment. We also know that improved factory working conditions lead to better factories, and that leads to a better supply chain. That's why some of these tools we've talked about provide a simple, clear, transparent way to make really good decisions for partners that are like-minded about CSR. The thing I'm probably most proud of, though—and I think other forward-looking global retailers and global brands will have to think about this—is this must be sustainable in good times and bad. If you look at the last two years since we've published this report in May of '04, our CSR efforts have continued, even though our financial performance has not been as high as we would like. So whether it is looking back at the last two years or any prediction of the next eight, at Gap, Inc., this is a long-term commitment. So I think it's easy for Gap, Inc. CSR is just critical to who we are, what our brand stands for, and it is absolutely essential to sustain."

SOURCE: E. Sage-Gavin, and P. Wright, "Corporate Social Responsibility at Gap, Inc.: An Interview with Eva Sage-Gavin," *Human Resource Planning*, vol. 30.1 (2007), pp. 45–48.

operate. Cultural differences may make this more difficult than it seems. For example, a recent study examined the impact of one standardized corporationwide safety policy on employees in three different countries: the United States, France, and Argentina. The results of this study indicated that the same policy was interpreted differently because of cultural differences. The individualistic, control-oriented culture of the United States stressed the role of top management in ensuring safety in a top-down fashion. However, this policy failed to work in Argentina, where the collectivist culture made employees feel that safety was everyone's joint concern; therefore, programs needed to be defined from the bottom up.[62]

At the beginning of this section we discussed a horrific accident at BP's Texas City refinery. After examining the causes of the explosion, the U.S. Chemical Safety and Hazard Investigation Board asked BP to set up an independent panel that would focus on overseeing radical changes in BP's safety procedures. This panel was tasked with investigating the safety culture at BP along with the procedures for inspecting equipment and reporting near-miss accidents. The panel's charter is not just to oversee the Texas City refinery, but also to look at the safety practices in refineries that BP has acquired over the years.[63]

The "Competing through Sustainability" box illustrates how The Gap has strategically managed a measurement and reporting system with regard to its suppliers to ensure that it is being socially responsible. This reporting system reveals The Gap's concern with human rights and safety in the workplace.

## A Look Back

At the beginning of the chapter we described the legal challenge Boeing faced with regard to potentially discriminating against women in their pay systems. The company already paid $4.5 million to the OFCCP in a fine, and faced a potential liability of over $1 billion if it lost the class action lawsuit. So, how did the lawsuit come out? In 1999 the company had settled for $11.3 million, but the agreement was thrown out because plaintiffs didn't believe the settlement was fair. In 2004 the suit was settled again for $72.5 million to be paid to the 17,960 current and former female Boeing employees who were named in the class action suit. And who made out in the settlement? The employee plaintiffs received between $500 and $26,000, with an average pretax payout of $3,000. The attorneys' and legal fees, on the other hand, comprised $15 million of the $72.5 million.

SOURCE: Josh Goodman, "Boeing Settles for $72 Million; 17,960 Plaintiffs in Gender-Bias Suit," Knight Ridder Tribune Business News, November 12, 2005, p.1.

### Questions

1. Based on what you read, do you think that Boeing will win or lose the class action pay discrimination case brought against it?
2. Assume that you have taken over the HR function at Boeing and want to make sure that your pay system is fair, so you commission a salary study that reveals pay differences between men and women. If you publicize the data and try to fix the problem, you open the company up to liability for past discrimination. What will you do?

Please see the Video Case that corresponds to this chapter online at www.mhhe.com/noe6e.

## Summary

Viewing employees as a source of competitive advantage results in dealing with them in ways that are ethical and legal as well as providing a safe workplace. An organization's legal environment—especially the laws regarding equal employment opportunity and safety—has a particularly strong effect on its HRM function. HRM is concerned with the management of people, and government is concerned with protecting individuals. One of HRM's major challenges, therefore, is to perform its function within the legal constraints imposed by the government. Given the multimillion-dollar settlements resulting from violations of EEO laws (and the moral requirement to treat people fairly regardless of their sex or race) as well as the penalties for violating OSHA, HR and line managers need a good understanding of the legal requirements and prohibitions in order to manage their businesses in ways that are sound, both financially and ethically. Organizations that do so effectively will definitely have a competitive advantage.

## Key Terms

Equal employment opportunity (EEO), 103
Americans with Disabilities Act (ADA) of 1990, 108
Equal Employment Opportunity Commission (EEOC), 110
Utilization analysis, 111
Goals and timetables, 111
Action steps, 111
Disparate treatment, 113
Bona fide occupational qualification (BFOQ), 114
Disparate impact, 116
Four-fifths rule, 117
Standard deviation rule, 117
Reasonable accommodation, 119
Occupational Safety and Health Act (OSHA), 129
General duty clause, 129
Safety awareness programs, 132
Job hazard analysis technique, 132
Technic of operations review (TOR), 132

## Discussion Questions

1. Disparate impact theory was originally created by the court in the *Griggs* case before finally being codified by Congress 20 years later in the Civil Rights Act of 1991. Given the system of law in the United States, from what branch of government should theories of discrimination develop?
2. Disparate impact analysis (the four-fifths rule, standard deviation analysis) is used in employment discrimination cases. The National Assessment of Education Progress conducted by the U.S. Department of Education found that among 21- to 25-year-olds (a) 60 percent of whites, 40 percent of Hispanics, and 25 percent of blacks could locate information in a news article or almanac; (b) 25 percent of whites, 7 percent of Hispanics, and 3 percent of blacks could decipher a bus schedule; and (c) 44 percent of whites, 20 percent of Hispanics, and 8 percent of blacks could correctly determine the change they were due from the purchase of a two-item restaurant meal. Do these tasks (locating information in a news article, deciphering a bus schedule, and determining correct change) have adverse impact? What are the implications?

3. Many companies have dress codes that require men to wear suits and women to wear dresses. Is this discriminatory according to disparate treatment theory? Why?
4. Cognitive ability tests seem to be the most valid selection devices available for hiring employees, yet they also have adverse impact against blacks and Hispanics. Given the validity and adverse impact, and considering that race norming is illegal under CRA 1991, what would you say in response to a recommendation that such tests be used for hiring?
5. How might the ADA's reasonable accommodation requirement affect workers such as law enforcement officers and firefighters?
6. The reasonable woman standard recognizes that women have different ideas than men of what constitutes appropriate behavior. What are the implications of this distinction? Do you think it is a good or bad idea to make this distinction?
7. Employers' major complaint about the ADA is that the costs of making reasonable accommodations will reduce their ability to compete with businesses (especially foreign ones) that do not face these requirements. Is this a legitimate concern? How should employers and society weigh the costs and benefits of the ADA?
8. Many have suggested that OSHA penalties are too weak and misdirected (aimed at employers rather than employees) to have any significant impact on employee safety. Do you think that OSHA-related sanctions need to be strengthened, or are existing penalties sufficient? Defend your answer.

## Self-Assessment Exercise

Take the following self-assessment quiz. For each statement, circle T if the statement is true or F is the statement is false.

### What do you know about sexual harassment?

1. A man cannot be the victim of sexual harassment. T F
2. The harasser can only be the victim's manager or a manager in another work area. T F
3. Sexual harassment charges can be filed only by the person who directly experiences the harassment. T F
4. The best way to discourage sexual harassment is to have a policy that discourages employees from dating each other. T F
5. Sexual harassment is not a form of sex discrimination. T F
6. After receiving a sexual harassment complaint, the employer should let the situation cool off before investigating the complaint. T F
7. Sexual harassment is illegal only if it results in the victim being laid off or receiving lower pay. T F

## Exercising Strategy: Home Depot's Bumpy Road to Equality

Home Depot is the largest home products firm selling home repair products and equipment for the "do-it-yourselfer." Founded 20 years ago, it now boasts 100,000 employees and more than 900 warehouse stores nationwide. The company's strategy for growth has focused mostly on one task: build more stores. In fact, an unwritten goal of Home Depot executives was to position a store within 30 minutes of every customer in the United States. They've almost made it. In addition, Home Depot has tried hard to implement a strategy of providing superior service to its customers. The company has prided itself on hiring people who are knowledgeable about home repair and who can teach customers how to do home repairs on their own. This strategy, along with blanketing the country with stores, has led to the firm's substantial advantage over competitors, including the now-defunct Home Quarters (HQ) and still-standing Lowe's.

But Home Depot has run into some legal problems. During the company's growth, a statistical anomaly has emerged. About 70 percent of the merchandise employees (those directly involved in selling lumber, electrical supplies, hardware, and so forth) are men, whereas about 70 percent of operations employees (cashiers, accountants, back office staff, and so forth) are women. Because of this difference, several years ago a lawsuit was filed on behalf of 17,000 current and former employees as well as up to 200,000 rejected applicants. Home Depot explained the disparity by noting that most female job applicants have experience as cashiers, so they are placed in cashier positions; most male applicants express an interest in or aptitude for home repair work such as carpentry or plumbing. However, attorneys argued that Home Depot was reinforcing gender stereotyping by hiring in this manner.

More recently, five former Home Depot employees sued the company, charging that it had discriminated against African American workers at two stores in southeast Florida. The five alleged that they were paid less than white workers, passed over for promotion, and given critical performance reviews based on race. "The company takes exception to the charges and believes they are without merit," said Home Depot spokesman Jerry Shields. The company has faced other racial discrimination suits as well, including one filed by the Michigan Department of Civil Rights.

To avoid such lawsuits in the future, Home Depot could resort to hiring and promoting by quota, ensuring an equal distribution of employees across all job categories—something that the company has wanted to avoid because it believes such action would undermine its competitive advantage. However, the company has taken steps to broaden and strengthen its own nondiscrimination policy by adding sexual orientation to the written policy. In addition, company president and CEO Bob Nardelli announced in the fall of 2001 that Home Depot would take special steps to protect benefits for its more than 500 employees who serve in the Army reserves and had been activated. "We will make up any difference between their Home Depot pay and their military pay if it's lower," said Nardelli. "When they come home [from duty], their jobs and their orange aprons are waiting for them."

In settling the gender discrimination suit the company agreed to pay $65 million to women who had been steered to cashiers' jobs and had been denied promotions. In addition, the company promised that every applicant would get a "fair shot." Home Depot's solution to this has been to leverage technology to make better hiring decisions that ensure the company is able to maximize diversity.

Home Depot instituted its Job Preference Program, an automated hiring and promotion system, across its 900 stores at a cost of $10 million. It has set up kiosks where potential applicants can log on to a computer, complete an application, and undergo a set of prescreening tests. This process weeds out unqualified applicants. Then the system prints out test scores along with structured interview questions and examples of good and bad answers for the managers interviewing those who make it through the prescreening. In addition, the Home Depot system is used for promotions. Employees are asked to constantly update their skills and career aspirations so they can be considered for promotions at nearby stores.

The system has been an unarguable success. Managers love it because they are able to get high-quality applicants without having to sift through mounds of résumés. In addition, the system seems to have accomplished its main purpose. The number of female managers has increased 30 percent and the number of minority managers by 28 percent since the introduction of the system. In fact, David Borgen, the co-counsel for the plaintiffs in the original lawsuit, states, "No one can say it can't be done anymore, because Home Depot is doing it bigger and better than anyone I know."

SOURCE: "Home Depot Says Thanks to America's Military; Extends Associates/Reservists' Benefits, Announces Military Discount," company press release, October 9, 2001; S. Jaffe, "New Tricks in Home Depot's Toolbox?" *BusinessWeek* Online, June 5, 2001, at www.businessweek.com; "HRC Lauds Home Depot for Adding Sexual Orientation to Its Non-discrimination Policy," Human Rights Campaign, May 14, 2001, at www.hrc.org; "Former Home Depot Employees File Racial Discrimination Lawsuit," Diversity at Work, June 2000, at www.diversityatwork.com; "Michigan Officials File Discrimination Suit against Home Depot," Diversity at Work, February 2000, at www.diversityatwork.com; M. Boot, "For Plaintiffs' Lawyers, There's No Place Like Home Depot," *The Wall Street Journal*, interactive edition, February 12, 1997.

### Questions

1. If Home Depot was correct in that it was not discriminating, but simply filling positions consistent with those who applied for them (and very few women were applying for customer service positions), given your reading of this chapter, was the firm guilty of discrimination? If so, under what theory?
2. How does this case illustrate the application of new technology to solving issues that have never been tied to technology? Can you think of other ways technology might be used to address diversity/EEO/affirmative action issues?

## MANAGING PEOPLE: FROM THE PAGES OF *BUSINESSWEEK*

BusinessWeek

### *Brown v. Board of Education:* A Bittersweet Birthday

**Decades of progress on integration have been followed by disturbing slippage** May 17 marks the 50th anniversary of *Brown v. Board of Education*, the landmark Supreme Court ruling that declared racially segregated "separate but equal" schools unconstitutional. The case is widely regarded as one of the court's most important decisions of the 20th century, but the birthday celebration will be something of a bittersweet occasion. There's no question that African Americans have made major strides since—economically, socially, and educationally. But starting in the late 1980s, political backlash brought racial progress to a halt. Since then, schools have slowly been resegregating, and the achievement gap between white and minority schoolchildren has been widening again. Can the United States ever achieve the great promise of integration? Some key questions follow.

**What did the Court strike down in 1954?** Throughout the South and in border states such as Delaware, black and white children were officially assigned to separate schools. In Topeka, Kansas, the lead city in the famous case, there were 18 elementary schools for whites and just 4 for blacks, forcing many African American children to travel a long way to school. The idea that black schools were "equal" to those for whites was a cruel fiction, condemning most black kids to a grossly inferior education.

**Surely we've come a long way since then?** Yes, though change took a long time. Over 99 percent of Southern black children were still in segregated schools in 1963. The 1960s civil rights movement eventually brought aggressive federal policies such as busing and court orders that forced extensive integration, especially in the South. So by 1988, 44 percent of Southern black children were attending schools where a majority of students were white, up from 2 percent in 1964. "We cut school desegregation almost in half between 1968 and 1990," says John Logan, director of the Lewis Mumford Center for Comparative Urban and Regional Research at State University of New York at Albany.

**What's the picture today?** There have been some real gains. The share of blacks graduating from high school has nearly quadrupled since *Brown*, to 88 percent today, while the share of those ages 25 to 29 with a college degree has increased more than sixfold, to 18 percent.

Another important trend is in housing, which in turn helps determine the characteristics of school districts. Residential integration is improving, albeit at a glacial pace. There's still high housing segregation in major metropolitan areas, but it has fallen four percentage points, to 65 percent, on an index developed by the Mumford Center. Some of the gains are happening in fast-growing new suburbs where race lines aren't so fixed. A few big cities have improved, too. In Dallas, for example, black–white residential segregation fell from 78 percent in 1980 to 59 percent in 2000.

**Why haven't schools continued to desegregate, too?** The increased racial mixing in housing hasn't been nearly large enough to offset the sheer increase in the ranks of minority schoolchildren. While the number of white elementary school kids remained flat, at 15.3 million, between 1990 and 2000, the number of black children climbed by 800,000, to 4.6 million, while Hispanic kids jumped by 1.7 million, to 4.3 million. The result: Minorities now comprise 40 percent of public school kids, vs. 32 percent in 1990. And as the nonwhite population has expanded, so have minority neighborhoods—and schools.

**So minorities have lost ground?** Yes, in some respects. By age 17, black students are still more than three years behind their white counterparts in reading and math. And whites are twice as likely to graduate from college. Taken as a whole, U.S. schools have been resegregating for 15 years or so, according to studies by the Harvard University Civil Rights Project. "We're celebrating [Brown] at a time when schools in all regions are becoming increasingly segregated," says project co-director Gary Orfield.

**What role has the political backlash against integration played?** The courts and politicians have been pulling back from integration goals for quite a while. In 1974, the Supreme Court ruled that heavily black Detroit didn't have to integrate its schools with the surrounding white suburbs. Then, in the 1980s, the growing backlash against busing and race-based school assignment led politicians and the courts to all but give up on those remedies, too.

**So what are the goals now?** The approach has shifted dramatically. Instead of trying to force integration, the United States has moved toward equalizing education. In a growing number of states, the courts have been siding with lawsuits that seek equal or "adequate" funding for minority and low-income schools.

The No Child Left Behind Act goes even further. It says that all children will receive a "highly qualified" teacher by 2006 and will achieve proficiency in math and reading by 2014. It specifically requires schools to meet these goals for racial subgroups. Paradoxically, it sounds like separate but equal again. Both the equal-funding suits and No Child Left Behind aim to improve all schools, whatever their racial composition. Integration is no longer the explicit goal.

**Can schools equalize without integrating?** It's possible in some cases, but probably not for the United States as a whole. The Education Trust, a nonprofit group in Washington, D.C., has identified a number of nearly all-black, low-income schools that have achieved exceptional test results. But such success requires outstanding leadership, good teachers, and a fervent commitment to high standards.

These qualities are far more difficult to achieve in large urban schools with many poor kids—the kind most black and Hispanic students attend. The average minority student goes to a school in which two-thirds of the students are low-income. By contrast, whites attend schools that are just 30 percent low-income.

**So are black–white achievement gaps as much about poverty as race?** Yes, which is why closing them is difficult with or without racial integration. Studies show that middle-class students tend to have higher expectations, more engaged parents, and better teachers. Poor children, by contrast, often come to school with far more personal problems. Yet poor schools are more likely to get inferior teachers, such as those who didn't major in the subject they teach. Many poor schools also lose as many as 20 percent of their teachers each year, while most middle-class suburban schools have more stable teaching staffs. "Research suggests that when low-income students attend middle-class schools, they do substantially better," says Richard Kahlenberg, senior fellow at the Century Foundation, a public policy think tank in New York City.

**Is it possible to achieve more economic integration?** There are a few shining examples, but they take enormous political commitment. One example that education-system reformers love to highlight is Wake County,

N.C., whose 110,000-student school district includes Raleigh. In 2000, it adopted a plan to ensure that low-income students make up no more than 40 percent of any student body. It also capped those achieving under grade level at 25 percent. Moreover, it used magnet schools offering specialized programs, such as one for gifted children, to help attract middle-income children to low-income areas.

Already, 91 percent of the county's third- to eighth-graders work at grade level in math and reading, up from 84 percent in 1999. More impressive, 75 percent of low-income kids are reading at grade level, up from just 56 percent in 1999, as are 78 percent of black children, up from 61 percent. "The academic payoff has been pretty incredible," says Walter C. Sherlin, a 28-year Wake County schools veteran and interim director of the nonprofit Wake Education Partnership.

**Could this serve as a national model?** For that to happen in many cities, school districts would have to merge with the surrounding suburbs. Wake County did this, but that was back in the 1970s and part of a long-term plan to bring about racial integration. In the metro Boston area, by contrast, students are balkanized into dozens of tiny districts, many of which are economically homogeneous. The result: Some 70 percent of white students attend schools that are over 90 percent white and overwhelmingly middle-class. Meanwhile, 97 percent of the schools that are over 90 percent minority are also high-poverty. Similar patterns exist in most major cities, but most affluent white suburbs aren't likely to swallow a move like Wake County's.

**How important is funding equality within states?** It's critical, especially if segregation by income and race persists. Massachusetts, for instance, has nearly tripled state aid to schools since 1993, with over 90 percent of the money going to the poorest towns. That has helped make Massachusetts a national leader in raising academic achievement.

Nationally, though, there are still huge inequities in school spending, with the poorest districts receiving less money than the richest—even though low-income children are more expensive to educate. Fixing these imbalances would be costly. Even in Massachusetts, a lower court judge ruled on April 26 that the system still shortchanges students in the poorest towns. Nationally, it would cost more than $50 billion a year in extra funding to correct inequities enough to meet the goals of No Child, figures Anthony P. Carnevale, a vice president at Educational Testing Service.

**If, somehow, the United States could achieve more economic integration, would racial integration still be necessary?** Proficiency on tests isn't the only aim. As the Supreme Court said last year in a landmark decision on affirmative action in higher education: "Effective participation by members of all racial and ethnic groups in the civic life of our nation is essential if the dream of one nation, indivisible, is to be realized." It's hard to see how students attending largely segregated schools, no matter how proficient, could be adequately prepared for life in an increasingly diverse country. In this sense, integrating America's educational system remains an essential, though still elusive, goal.

SOURCE: W. Symonds, "A Bittersweet Birthday," *BusinessWeek*, May 17, 2004, pp. 66–62.

### Questions

1. While segregation of public schools has been outlawed, the article notes that schools are not necessarily "desegregating" (i.e., there are still predominantly minority and predominantly nonminority schools). If students are to work in increasingly diverse workforces, is the current system failing them? Why or why not?
2. The black–white gap continues to exist with regard to reading, math, and graduation rates. What are the implications of this on organizations' selection systems (i.e., disparate impact)?
3. Given the lack of a "diverse" educational experience for a large percentage of black children, and the gap between them and their white counterparts, what must organizations do to leverage diversity as a source of competitive advantage?

## NOTES

1. J. Ledvinka, *Federal Regulation of Personnel and Human Resource Management* (Boston: Kent, 1982).
2. *Martin v. Wilks*, 49 FEP Cases 1641 (1989).
3. *Wards Cove Packing Co. v. Atonio*, FEPC 1519 (1989).
4. *Bakke v. Regents of the University of California*, 17 FEPC 1000 (1978).
5. *Patterson v. McLean Credit Union*, 49 FEPC 1814 (1987).
6. J. Friedman and G. Strickler, *The Law of Employment Discrimination: Cases and Materials*, 2nd ed. (Mineola, NY: Foundation Press, 1987).
7. "Labor Letter," *The Wall Street Journal*, August 25, 1987, p. 1.
8. J. Woo, "Ex-Workers Hit Back with Age-Bias Suits," *The Wall Street Journal*, December 8, 1992, p. B1.
9. W. Carley, "Salesman's Treatment Raises Bias Questions at Schering-Plough," *The Wall Street Journal*, May 31, 1995, p. A1.
10. http://www.eeoc.gov/press/1-8-07.html.
11. Special feature issue: "The New Civil Rights Act of 1991 and What It Means to Employers," *Employment Law Update* 6 (December 1991), pp. 1–12.
12. "ADA: The Final Regulations (Title I): A Lawyer's Dream/An Employer's Nightmare," *Employment Law Update* 16, no. 9 (1991), p. 1.

13. "ADA Supervisor Training Program: A Must for Any Supervisor Conducting a Legal Job Interview," *Employment Law Update* 7, no. 6 (1992), pp. 1–6.
14. Equal Employment Opportunity Commission, "Uniform Guidelines on Employee Selection Procedures," *Federal Register* 43 (1978), pp. 38290–315.
15. Ledvinka, *Federal Regulation*.
16. R. Pear, "The Cabinet Searches for Consensus on Affirmative Action," *The New York Times*, October 27, 1985, p. E5.
17. *McDonnell Douglas v. Green*, 411 U.S. 972 (1973).
18. *UAW v. Johnson Controls, Inc.* (1991).
19. Special feature issue: "The New Civil Rights Act of 1991," pp. 1–6.
20. *Washington v.Davis*, 12 FEP 1415 (1976).
21. *Albermarle Paper Company v. Moody*, 10 FEP 1181 (1975).
22. R. Reilly and G. Chao, "Validity and Fairness of Some Alternative Employee Selection Procedures," *Personnel Psychology* 35 (1982), pp. 1–63; J. Hunter and R. Hunter, "Validity and Utility of Alternative Predictors of Job Performance," *Psychological Bulletin* 96 (1984), pp. 72–98.
23. *Griggs v. Duke Power Company*, 401 U.S. 424 (1971).
24. B. Lindeman and P. Grossman, *Employment Discrimination Law* (Washington, DC: BNA Books, 1996).
25. M. Jacobs, "Workers' Religious Beliefs May Get New Attention," *The Wall Street Journal*, August 22, 1995, pp. B1, B8.
26. EEOC, "EEOC and Electrolux Reach Voluntary Resolution in Class Religious Accommodation Case," at www.eeoc.gov/press/9-24-03.
27. S. Sataline, "Who's Wrong when Rights Collide?" *The Wall Street Journal*, March 6, 2007, p. B1.
28. Lindeman and Grossman, *Employment Discrimination Law*.
29. J. Reno and D. Thornburgh, "ADA—Not a Disabling Mandate," *The Wall Street Journal*, July 26, 1995, p. A12.
30. Woo, "Ex-Workers Hit Back."
31. EEOC, "Target Corp. to Pay $775,000 for Racial Harassment: EEC Settles Suit for Class of African American Employees; Remedial Relief Included," at www.eeoc.gov/press/1-26-07.html.
32. W. Johnston and A. Packer, *Workforce 2000* (Indianapolis, IN: Hudson Institute, 1987).
33. *Bundy v. Jackson*, 641 F.2d 934, 24 FEP 1155 (D.C. Cir., 1981).
34. L. A. Graf and M. Hemmasi, "Risqué Humor: How It Really Affects the Workplace," *HR Magazine*, November 1995, pp. 64–69.
35. B. Carton, "At Jenny Craig, Men Are Ones Who Claim Sex Discrimination," *The Wall Street Journal*, November 29, 1995, p. A1; "Male-on-Male Harassment Suit Won," *Houston Chronicle*, August 12, 1995, p. 21A.
36. EEOC, "Texas Car Dealership to Pay $140,000 to Settle Same-Sex Harassment Suit by EEOC," at www.eeoc.gov/press/10-28-02.
37. EEOC, "Babies 'R' Us to Pay $205,000, Implement Training Due to Same-Sex Harassment of Male Employee," at www.eeoc.gov/press/1-15-03.
38. *Meritor Savings Bank v. Vinson* (1986).
39. R. Paetzold and A. O'Leary-Kelly, "The Implications of U.S. Supreme Court and Circuit Court Decisions for Hostile Environment Sexual Harassment Cases," in *Sexual Harassment: Perspectives, Frontiers, and Strategies*, ed. M. Stockdale (Beverly Hills, CA: Sage); R. B. McAfee and D. L. Deadrick, "Teach Employees to Just Say 'No'!" *HR Magazine*, February 1996, pp. 586–89.
40. C. Murray, "The Legacy of the 60's," *Commentary*, July 1992, pp. 23–30.
41. D. Kravitz and J. Platania, "Attitudes and Beliefs about Affirmative Action: Effects of Target and of Respondent Sex and Ethnicity," *Journal of Applied Psychology* 78 (1993), pp. 928–38.
42. J. Mathews, "Rash of Unintended Lawsuits Follows Passage of Disabilities Act," *Houston Chronicle*, May 16, 1995, p. 15A.
43. C. Bell, "What the First ADA Cases Tell Us," *SHRM Legal Report* (Winter 1995), pp. 4–7.
44. J. Fitzgerald, "Chatty IBMer Booted," *New York Post*, February 18, 2007.
45. National Organization on Disability 2006 Annual Report at www.nod.org.
46. K. Mills, "Disabilities Act: A Help, or a Needless Hassle," *B/CS Eagle*, August 23, 1995, p. A7.
47. C. Cummins and T. Herrick, "Investigators Fault BP for More Lapses in Refinery Safety," *The Wall Street Journal*, August 18, 2005, p. A3.
48. V. F. Estrada, "Are Your Factory Workers Know-It-All?" *Personnel Journal*, September 1995, pp. 128–34.
49. R. L. Simison, "Safety Last," *The Wall Street Journal*, March 18, 1986, p. 1.
50. J. Roughton, "Managing a Safety Program through Job Hazard Analysis," *Professional Safety* 37 (1992), pp. 28–31.
51. M. A. Verespec, "OSHA Reform Fails Again," *Industry Week*, November 2, 1992, p. 36.
52. R. G. Hallock and D. A. Weaver, "Controlling Losses and Enhancing Management Systems with TOR Analysis," *Professional Safety* 35 (1990), pp. 24–26.
53. H. Herbstman, "Controlling Losses the Burger King Way," *Risk Management* 37 (1990), pp. 22–30.
54. L. Bryan, "An Ounce of Prevention for Workplace Accidents," *Training and Development Journal* 44 (1990), pp. 101–2.
55. J. F. Mangan, "Hazard Communications: Safety in Knowledge," *Best's Review* 92 (1991), pp. 84–88.
56. T. Markus, "How to Set Up a Safety Awareness Program," *Supervision* 51 (1990), pp. 14–16.
57. J. Agnew and A. J. Saruda, "Age and Fatal Work-Related Falls," *Human Factors* 35 (1994), pp. 731–36.
58. R. King, "Active Safety Programs, Education Can Help Prevent Back Injuries," *Occupational Health and Safety* 60 (1991), pp. 49–52.
59. J. R. Hollenbeck, D. R. Ilgen, and S. M. Crampton, "Lower Back Disability in Occupational Settings: A Review of the Literature from a Human Resource Management View," *Personnel Psychology* 45 (1992), pp. 247–78.
60. T. W. Turriff, "NSPB Suggests 10-Step Program to Prevent Eye Injury," *Occupational Health and Safety* 60 (1991), pp. 62–66.
61. D. Hanson, "Chemical Plant Safety: OSHA Rule Addresses Industry Concerns," *Chemical and Engineering News* 70 (1992), pp. 4–5; K. Broscheit and K. Sawyer, "Safety Exhibit Teaches Customers and Employees about Electricity," *Transmission and Distribution* 43 (1992), pp. 174–79; R. Schuch, "Good Training Is Key to Avoiding Boiler Explosions," *National Underwriter* 95 (1992), pp. 21–22.
62. M. Janssens, J. M. Brett, and F. J. Smith, "Confirmatory Cross-Cultural Research: Testing the Viability of a Corporation-wide Safety Policy," *Academy of Management Journal* 38 (1995), pp. 364–82.
63. Cummins and Herrick, "Investigators Fault BP."

# 4

CHAPTER

# The Analysis and Design of Work

## LO LEARNING OBJECTIVES

After reading this chapter, you should be able to:

- **LO1** Analyze an organization's structure and work-flow process, identifying the output, activities, and inputs in the production of a product or service. *page 145*
- **LO2** Understand the importance of job analysis in strategic and human resource management. *page 158*
- **LO3** Choose the right job analysis technique for a variety of human resource activities. *page 161*
- **LO4** Identify the tasks performed and the skills required in a given job. *page 165*
- **LO5** Understand the different approaches to job design. *page 165*
- **LO6** Comprehend the trade-offs among the various approaches to designing jobs. *page 172*

# Enter the World of Business

## Designed to Be Number I: Toyota and BMW

In the first quarter of 2007, Toyota surpassed General Motors as the top auto producer in the world. This was a well-anticipated event, and the role that organizational design and job design played in Toyota's success has been publicized in many business case studies. Toyota developed an obsession for details, and after many years of study and continuous improvement, the company has developed thousands of pages of documentation that lays out precisely what needs to be done for every step of each job to ensure the highest level of reliability in its trucks and cars. As head of European operations, Shinichi Sasaki, notes, "Every decision at every stage must be done properly" and detailed organizational charts that plot where responsibility for various decisions rests are constantly scrutinized and updated.

A stark contrast to this approach to job design and organizational design can be found in Munich, Germany, home of BMW. Indeed, many have labeled BMW the "anti-Toyota" because whereas Toyota does all it can to simplify and standardize work procedures and decision making, BMW embraces complexity. This difference can be traced to BMW business strategy, where CEO Helmut Planke notes that "I cannot recall having seen a clear and convincing correlation between size and success. Our own goal is clear: to be the leader in every premium segment of the international automotive industry." This strategy to be the top producer in a niche category, and not the largest producer overall, leads BMW to take a different approach to how it structures work relative to Toyota.

First, in terms of organizational design, BMW is organized not in tall pyramid-shaped structures with many levels of management. Instead, its structure is very flat and structured around cellular networks that are constantly in flux. These networks are typically composed of project-oriented, cross-functional teams, and the emphasis is on lateral communication across various specializations, rather than vertical communications up and down the hierarchy. This is supported by the design of factories themselves, which are often filled with wide open spaces, flooded with natural light, and where the physical layout promotes movement patterns among line workers, engineers, and quality experts that result in spontaneous communication and collaboration. With a network you get the powerful ability to leverage knowledge quickly to bear on solving problems and this may be the only way to effectively manage BMW's kind of complexity.

Indeed, the choice of the larger organizational structure trickles down and strongly influences that nature of individual jobs. Unlike Toyota, which relies on highly detailed and formalized descriptions of processes that are written down and are to be closely adhered to, BMW teams are given wider ranging responsibilities for making their own decisions about work procedures, which often vary across different teams. Rather than finding the "one best way" and then incrementally improving this one method continuously, work teams at BMW are more entrepreneurial and often compete with each other to come up with the best methods for different tasks. Managers in this context are not presumed to have all the answers; instead, their central role is to ask the right questions, give the teams the resources to find the right answers themselves, and then judge them on the relative success.

In the end, the choices that BMW has made with respect to organizational design and job design have allowed it to become one of the most flexible producers of high-performance and highly customized automobiles serving the top end of the market. The fluid, bottom-up, approach to work practices motivates its workforce to come up with fresh new ideas that anticipate and shape customer preferences rather than simply respond to them. Thus, while Toyota was celebrating becoming number 1 in *volume*, with profit margins of over 8 percent in 2006, BMW is actually number 1 in terms of *profits*. As Ernst Bauman, head of personnel at BMW, states, "People talk about innovation in products, but what is underestimated is innovation in processes and organizations."

Sources: D. Kiley, "The Toyota Way to No. 1," *BusinessWeek*, April 27, 2007, pp. 21–24; I. Rowley, "Even Toyota Isn't Perfect," *BusinessWeek*, January 11, 2007, pp. 33–36; B. Breen, "BMW: Driven by Design," *Fast Company*, August 2002, pp. 123–125; G. Edmondson, "BMW's Dream Factory," *BusinessWeek*, October 16, 2006, pp. 70–80; G. Edmondson, "The Secret of BMW's Success," *BusinessWeek Online*, October 16, 2006, pp. 17–21.

## Introduction

In Chapter 2 we discussed the processes of strategy formulation and strategy implementation. Strategy formulation is the process by which a company decides how it will compete in the marketplace; this is often the energizing and guiding force for everything it does. Strategy implementation is the way the strategic plan gets carried out in activities of organizational members. We noted five important components in the strategy implementation process, three of which are directly related to the human resource management function and one of which we will discuss in this chapter: the task or job.[1]

Many central aspects of strategy formulation address how the work gets done, in terms of individual job design as well as the design of organizational structures that link individual jobs to each other and the organization as a whole. The way a firm competes can have a profound impact on the ways jobs are designed and how they are linked via organizational structure. In turn, the fit between the company's structure and environment can have a major impact on the firm's competitive success.

For example, like Toyota, if a company wants to compete via a low-cost, high-reliability strategy, it needs to maximize efficiency and coordination. Efficiency is maximized by breaking jobs down into small, simple components that are executed repetitively by low-wage, low-skilled workers who are focused on following written rules. Efficiency is also enhanced by eliminating any redundancy of support services, so that jobs are structured into functional clusters where everyone in the cluster is performing similar work. (Thus all marketing people work together in a single unit, all engineering personnel work together in a single unit, and so on.) People working together within these functional clusters learn a great deal about how the function can be used to leverage their skills into small amounts of increased efficiency via continuous, evolutionary improvements, and higher level managers focus exclusively on coordinating the different functional units.

On the other hand, if a company like BMW wants to compete via innovation, it needs to maximize flexibility. Flexibility is maximized by aggregating work into larger, holistic pieces that are executed by teams of higher-wage, higher-skilled workers. Flexibility is also enhanced by giving the units their own support systems and decision-making authority to take advantage of local opportunities in regional or specialized product markets. People working together in these cross-functional clusters generate a greater number of creative and novel ideas that can be leveraged into more discontinuous, revolutionary improvements.

Thus, it should be clear from the outset of this chapter that there is no "one best way" to design jobs and structure organizations. The organization needs to create a fit between its environment, competitive strategy, and philosophy on the one hand, with its jobs and organizational design on the other. Thus, in our opening story, we saw how Toyota became number 1 in sales volume by following one approach, whereas BMW became number 1 in profits by taking a different approach. Other automobile manufacturers like General Motors and Ford were struggling to compete with Toyota and BMW and were forced to slash payrolls and lay off workers. Many years ago, some believed that the difference between U.S. auto producers and their foreign competitors could be traced to American workers; however, when companies like Toyota and Honda came into the United States and demonstrated clearly that they could run profitable car companies with American workers, the focus shifted to processes and organization. It is now clear that the success of many of these non-U.S. firms was attributable to how they structured the work and designed their organizations. For example, Toyota's new plant in San Antonio, Texas differs in many ways from the General Motors plant in Arlington, Texas, but the nature of the workforce is not one of them.[2]

This chapter discusses the analysis and design of work and, in doing so, lays out some considerations that go into making informed decisions about how to create and link jobs. The chapter is divided into three sections, the first of which deals with "big-picture" issues related to work-flow analysis and organizational structure. The remaining two sections deal with more specific, lower-level issues related to job analysis and job design.

The fields of job analysis and job design have extensive overlap, yet in the past they have been treated differently.[3] Job analysis has focused on analyzing existing jobs to gather information for other human resource management practices such as selection, training, performance appraisal, and compensation. Job design, on the other hand, has focused on redesigning existing jobs to make them more efficient or more motivating to jobholders.[4] Thus job design has had a more proactive orientation toward changing the job, whereas job analysis has had a passive, information-gathering orientation. However, as we will show in this chapter, these two approaches are interrelated.

## Work-Flow Analysis and Organization Structure

**LO1**
Analyze an Organization's Structure and Work-Flow Process, Identifying the Output, Activities, and Inputs in the Production of a Product or Service

In the past, HR professionals and line managers have tended to analyze or design a particular job in isolation from the larger organizational context. *Work-flow design* is the process of analyzing the tasks necessary for the production of a product or service, prior to allocating and assigning these tasks to a particular job category or person. Only after we thoroughly understand work-flow design can we make informed decisions regarding how to initially bundle various tasks into discrete jobs that can be executed by a single person.

*Organization structure* refers to the relatively stable and formal network of vertical and horizontal interconnections among jobs that constitute the organization. Only after we understand how one job relates to those above (supervisors), below (subordinates), and at the same level in different functional areas (marketing versus production) can we make informed decisions about how to redesign or improve jobs to benefit the entire organization.

Finally, work-flow design and organization structure have to be understood in the context of how an organization has decided to compete. Both work-flow design and organization structure can be leveraged to gain competitive advantage for the firm, but how one does this depends on the firm's strategy and its competitive environment.

## Work-Flow Analysis

A theme common to nearly all organizations is the need to identify clearly the outputs of work, to specify the quality and quantity standards for those outputs, and to analyze the processes and inputs necessary for producing outputs that meet the quality standards.[5] This conception of the work-flow process is useful because it provides a means for the manager to understand all the tasks required to produce a number of high-quality products as well as the skills necessary to perform those tasks. This work-flow process is depicted in Figure 4.1. In this section we present an approach for analyzing the work process of a department as a means of examining jobs in the context of an organization.

### Analyzing Work Outputs

Every work unit—whether a department, team, or individual—seeks to produce some output that others can use. An output is the product of a work unit and is often an identifiable thing, such as a completed purchase order, an employment test, or a hot, juicy hamburger. However, an output can also be a service, such as the services provided by an airline that transports you to some destination, a housecleaning service that maintains your house, or a baby-sitter who watches over your children.

We often picture an organization only in terms of the product that it produces, and then we focus on that product as the output. So, for example, in our opening story, the products for Toyota and BMW are automobiles. Merely identifying an output or set of outputs is not sufficient. Once these outputs have been identified, it is necessary to specify standards for the quantity or quality of these outputs. For example, a productivity

figure 4.1
Developing a Work-Unit Activity Analysis

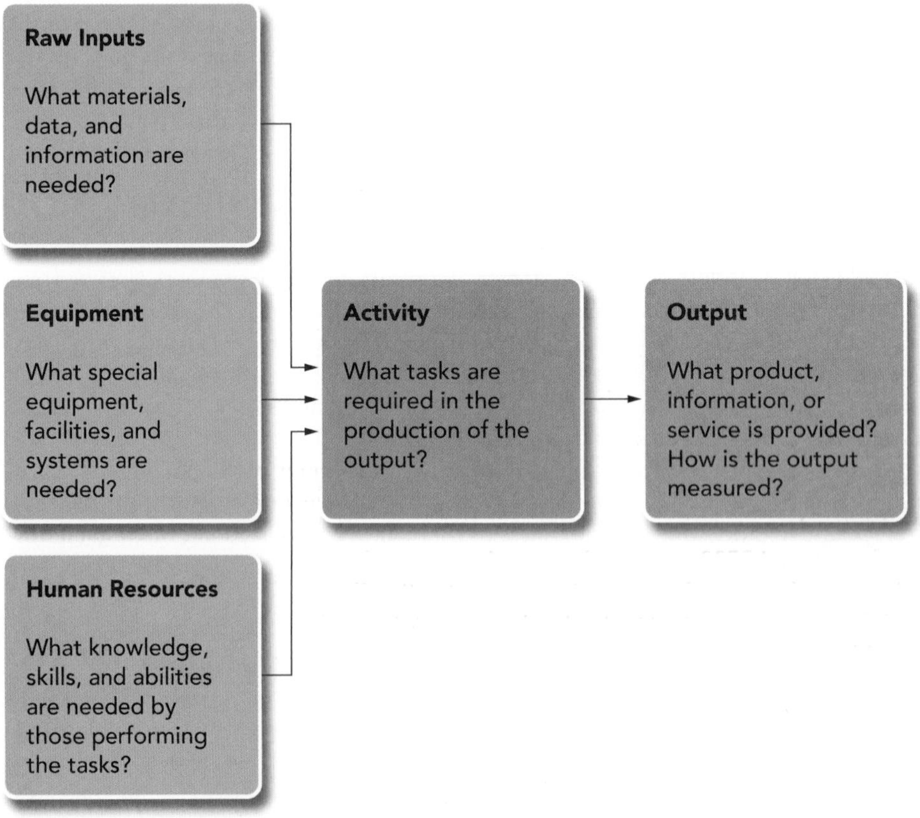

improvement technique known as ProMES (productivity measurement and evaluation system) focuses attention on both identifying work-unit outputs and specifying the levels of required performance for different levels of effectiveness.[6] With ProMES, the members of a work unit identify each of the products (outputs) of the work unit for the various customers. They then evaluate the effectiveness of each level of products in the eyes of their customers. Without an understanding of the output of a work unit, any attempt at increasing work-unit effectiveness will be futile.

## Analyzing Work Processes

Once the outputs of the work unit have been identified, it is possible to examine the work processes used to generate the output. The work processes are the activities that members of a work unit engage in to produce a given output. Every process consists of operating procedures that specify how things should be done at each stage of the development of the product. These procedures include all the tasks that must be performed in the production of the output. The tasks are usually broken down into those performed by each person in the work unit. Of course, in many situations where the work that needs to be done is highly complex, no single individual is likely to have all the required skills. In these situations, the work may be assigned to a team, and team-based job design is becoming increasingly popular in contemporary organizations.[7] In addition to providing a wider set of skills, team members can back each other up, share work when any member becomes overloaded, and catch each other's errors. Teams are not a panacea, however, and for teams to be effective, it is essential that the level of task interdependence (how much they have to cooperate) matches the level of outcome interdependence (how much they share the reward for task accomplishment).[8]

That is, if work is organized around teams, team bonuses rather than individual pay raises need to play a major role in terms of defining rewards. Teams also have to be given the autonomy to make their own decisions in order to maximize the flexible use of their skill and time and thus promote problem solving.[9]

For example, Louis Vuitton, the maker of top of the line bags and purses, used to design work processes centered on individuals. In this old system, each Vuitton worker did a highly specialized tasks (cutting leather and canvas, stitching seams, attaching the handle, and so on), and then, when each person was finished, he or she would sequentially send the bag to the next person in line. A typical line would be staffed by 20–30 people. In 2006, the company switched to a team-based design where teams of six to nine people all work together simultaneously to assemble the bags. Workers are cross-trained in multiple tasks and can flexibly change roles and shift production from one bag to another if any one bag becomes a "hit" and another becomes a "dud." The length of time it took to produce the same bags dropped from eight days to one day, and Vuitton customers, who had often had to be placed on waiting lists for their most popular products, were able to get their hands on the product much more quickly. This speed to market is critical given the emotional nature of this purchase—after all, if one is ready to spend $700 on a tote bag, it is best not to have to delay that decision.[10]

Again, to design work systems that are maximally efficient, a manager needs to understand the processes required in the development of the products for that work unit. Often, as workloads increase within a work group, the group will grow by adding positions to meet these new requirements. However, when the workload lightens, members may take on tasks that do not relate to the work unit's product in an effort to appear busy. Without a clear understanding of the tasks necessary to the production of an output, it is difficult to determine whether the work unit has become overstaffed. Understanding the tasks

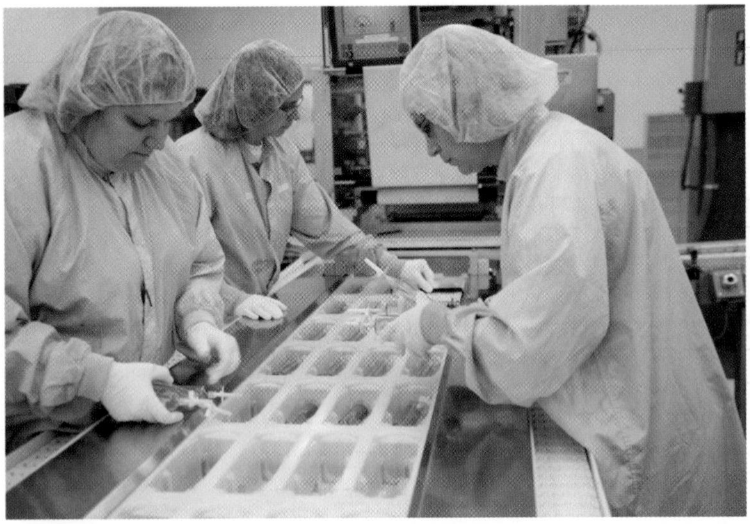

This job may look tedious or possibly even uninteresting. Considering how to engage employees in seeing the benefits of their work outside of the lab is an important way to motivate them through their day.

required allows the manager to specify which tasks are to be carried out by which individuals and eliminate tasks that are not necessary for the desired end. This ensures that the work group maintains a high level of productivity.

The notion of "lean production" was pioneered by Toyota, one of the companies in our opening vignette, but this idea has spread to many other companies that performed intense studies of their own work processes to find and eliminate waste, redundancies, and inefficiencies. For example, IBM shed 14,000 jobs between 2003 and 2006 in an effort to thin management ranks at its bureaucratic European operations. Much of the work of these former "managers" was pushed down to individual consultants who were given greater autonomy to make their own decisions. In addition to shedding layers of management, IBM shut down and sold corporate office space and workers were told to work at home, at the clients location, or at smaller satellite offices distributed throughout the world.[11] Indeed, as the "Competing through Technology" box illustrates, advances in new technology have made "closing down the headquarters" a viable option for more and more employers.

IBM is not the only company focused on eliminating midlevel managers. For example, at Unifi Inc., a textile producer, factory equipment is connected via high-speed data lines so that shop floor data can be relayed in real time to analysts at corporate headquarters, eliminating the need for local supervisors.[12] This kind of remote monitoring is becoming especially popular in multinational corporations as a means of standardizing work outputs. Although not all employees respond positively to technological changes in the nature of work, such changes are becoming increasingly critical in competing in the contemporary business environment.[13]

## Analyzing Work Inputs

The final stage in work-flow analysis is to identify the inputs used in the development of the work unit's product. As shown in Figure 4.1, these inputs can be broken down into the raw materials, equipment, and human skills needed to perform the tasks. *Raw materials* consist of the materials that will be converted into the work unit's product. *Equipment* refers to the technology and machinery necessary to transform the raw materials into the product. The final inputs in the work-flow process are the *human skills* and efforts necessary to perform the tasks.

To compete successfully, organizations often have to scour the world for the best raw materials, the best equipment, and the people with the best skills, and then try to integrate all of this seamlessly in the work processes that merge all these factors. As we have seen, IBM has been on the forefront of incorporating new technological equipment in the processes, in order to eliminate office space and reduce middle layers of management. This company has also searched high and wide for people with the best sets of skills as well. For example, symbolically, IBM's 2006 Annual Investors Meeting was held in Bangalore, India.

COMPETING THROUGH TECHNOLOGY

## Getting outside the Office—for Good

Seventeen years ago, when it separated from its parent company, Arthur Andersen, the consulting firm now known as Accenture was comprised of 40 locally owned partnerships operating in 47 different countries. With this as a starting point, one could imagine the difficulty of agreeing on where to locate the new company's headquarters. After a great deal of contentious, frustrating, and difficult internal debate, the answer was to locate the headquarters everywhere—or nowhere. That is, Accenture became the first major company to go virtual. Although incorporated in Bermuda for tax purposes, on any given day, Accenture's consultants could be anywhere in the world, operating out of their homes, on location with one of their clients, or at one of Accenture's many satellite branches located close to the world's major airports.

Although this decision was groundbreaking at that time, it is much more common today for employees to work off-site, and many well-known companies such as IBM, Sun Microsystems, Microsoft, and GE have adopted similar virtual arrangements. Current estimates indicate that 14 percent of the U.S. workforce operated off-site for at least two days a week in 2007, up from 11 percent in 2004, and projections are being made for 17 percent by the year 2009. This growth has been fueled by many benefits associated with virtual work: lower real estate costs, less commuting time, fewer office interruptions, better work/life balance, and enhanced customer contact, just to name a few. The key to effective use of virtual labor, however, relies on the critical interaction of good technology and good human resource management practices, which are both necessary but not sufficient for success.

Given its long experience with virtual work, an examination of how Accenture uses technology and human resource management is instructive for those thinking about increasing their virtual footprint. On any given day, the typical Accenture employee will log into the company's Web site to record where he or she is that day. If the consultant is not going to the client's office, and does not know where to find a desk, he or she will be directed to the closest Accenture office, where a fully networked cubicle is waiting. Each consultant has one single telephone number, and whenever a client calls that number, the call is forwarded automatically to the current location. Collaboration software downloaded on each employee's state-of-the-art laptop computer allows them to share data and manuscripts with colleagues, and most satellite offices have videoconferencing technology and whiteboards when graphic face-to-face communication is needed.

Still, technology can take one only so far, and Accenture managers must work harder and smarter when trying to manage such a widely distributed workforce, especially since they themselves are probably on the road on any given day. There are several keys to effective human resource management in this context. First, constant contact is a must, and most Accenture managers try to touch base with each and every consultant each and every day. Second, actual face-to-face meetings are essential to develop trusting relationships, and the home office tracks whenever two people who are connected in the organizational structure happen to be in the same city on the same day, in order to set up a real live personal encounter. Third, technology breakdowns occur frequently and need to be anticipated so that people can be quickly and painlessly directed to support centers so that valuable time is not lost due to hardware or software problems. Fourth, management by goal setting rather than direct performance monitoring is essential given the context, and managers have to be comfortable giving each employee wide latitude and autonomy. Fifth, some important personnel-related matters such as negative feedback really have to be conducted in person due to their emotional nature, and these special issues have to be segregated from more "run-of-the mill" operations. Finally, although technology is ever changing, some aspects of the world—such as time zones—simply cannot be changed. At Accenture, 1:00 PM London time is known as "The Magic Hour" because it is the single best time for cross-continent communications.

The internal difficulties caused by these arrangements are more than offset, however, by the ability this process affords Accenture consultants to get close to Accenture customers. Spending time with clients increases trust and understanding, and this is one of the primary reasons why 85 percent of Accenture clients have worked with the company for more than 10 years. As Bill Green, a grizzled veteran who logs over 165,000 miles a year, notes, "We get information we would never get if we were stuck back at some headquarters."

SOURCES: C. Hymowitz, "Have Advice, Will Travel," *The Wall Street Journal*, June 5, 2006, pp. B1, B5; R. King, "Working from Home: It's in the Details," *BusinessWeek*, February 12, 2007, pp. 39–40; A. Hesseldahl, "Tech Support for the Home Office," *BusinessWeek*, February 12, 2007, p. 40; R. King, "Virtual Workplace Dos and Don'ts," *BusinessWeek*, April 16, 2007, p. 30.

India is central to IBM's future because it is a source of high-skilled, low-cost talent, especially in the area of software development. Indeed, the size of IBM's staff in India surged from 9,000 to 43,000 between 2003 and 2006. However, this is just one part of the puzzle. Some of IBM operations require high-skill employees who have to work on-site with hardware issues in close proximity to U.S. customers, and hence IBM also opened a new center in Boulder, Colorado. IBM also needs the very narrow skills of people with doctorates in the hard sciences, and thus it opened a research lab in Yorktown Heights, New York. Some low-skill jobs that IBM needs are done by workers from China, Brazil, or eastern Europe, depending on where the call originates and the language spoken by the customer. The key to this strategy is not just going where one can get cheap labor, but, instead, going where one can get just the exact kind of labor needed at the best price. As noted by Robert Moffat, IBM's senior vice president, "Some people think the world is centered in India and that's it. Globalization is more than that. Our customers need the right skills, in the right place at the right time."[14]

Indeed research consistently shows that creating a good fit between the skills and values of workers and the tasks and missions they are assigned is a powerful determinant of organizational success that cannot be taken lightly.[15] Thus, the highly rationalized method for seamlessly integrating the skills of workers from different countries that characterizes IBM stands in stark contrast to other international ventures, where politics, rather than cold, hard business logic, seems to be the driving force behind who does what. As the "Competing through Globalization" box shows, nonrational methods for selecting work inputs and for defining work processes can often result in disastrous outcomes.

## Organization Structure

Whereas work-flow design provides a longitudinal overview of the dynamic relationships by which inputs are converted into outputs, organization structure provides a cross-sectional overview of the static relationships between individuals and units that create the outputs. Organization structure is typically displayed via organizational charts that convey both vertical reporting relationships and horizontal functional responsibilities.

**Centralization**
Degree to which decision-making authority resides at the top of the organizational chart.

### Dimensions of Structure

Two of the most critical dimensions of organization structure are centralization and departmentalization. **Centralization** refers to the degree to which decision-making authority resides at the top of the organizational chart as opposed to being distributed

## COMPETING THROUGH GLOBALIZATION

### Coordinating Work across Countries: How the Wires Can Get Crossed

The competition between Airbus and Boeing to dominate the market for commercial aviation is a fierce battle. The introduction of Boeing's highly successful 787 Dreamliner aircraft shifted the momentum in this fight to the Seattle-based manufacturer, and in 2006, Boeing outsold Airbus 723 to 226—a huge difference when the product is a commercial aircraft with a price tag of $200 million. The Airbus 380 double-decker jet was designed to be the strategic counterpunch to the Dreamliner; however, this punch had to be pulled due to problems managing the cross-border coordination that is required by the multinational nature of Airbus. Airbus, a joint venture between companies in Germany, France, Britain, and Italy, was originally hailed as a crowning achievement in European collaboration. In fact, funded partially with reduced-rate loans from the venture's respective governments, many in the industry felt this gave Airbus an unfair competitive advantage over its rivals. However, these loans came with political strings attached, and struggles in managing cross-border coordination have squandered this advantage.

The most recent example of this occurred when Airbus had to announce the indefinite delay of the Airbus 380 launch due to a wiring problem that some have labeled "the costliest blunder in the history of commercial aviation." This fiasco was directly caused by a lack of coordination between a plant in Hamburg, Germany, that produced the electrical wiring, and a plant in Toulouse, France, that served as the final assembly line for the aircraft. The two plants were using two different computer design systems that essentially could not "talk to each other," and hence the incompatibility was detected very, very late in the construction process.

Like the noncompatible computer systems, communications between the two plants were often lost in translation. Indeed, relationships between these two plants have been frosty from the beginning because most experts in aviation engineering agree that Hamburg was the most logical site for the final assembly line. Hamburg has an ideal waterfront location that would have allowed the oversized wings (too big for conventional land or air transport) to be delivered right to the line, whereas the plant in Toulouse was landlocked. To get the wings to Toulouse, Airbus had to order expensive, custom-built river barges and pay to have 100 miles of French highway widened and straightened. However, political maneuvering allowed France to obtain the rights for the more prestigious final assembly task, and Hamburg was delegated the wiring task.

The wiring task was not the best fit for Hamburg plant, however, because it was not using the most recent version computer-aided design software, which was a French system, but was instead using an older version of the same software. No one thought this would make a difference until it was too late, and at that point, each side pointed the finger at the other for not anticipating the problem. Much of the work performed at Hamburg was then shifted to Toulouse, which outraged the Germans, who stated that "the management screws up, and we take the blame." Airbus CEO Christian Streiff recognized that the overly political nature of the decision-making process contributed to the problem and concluded that "we have to ask questions about our assembly lines and how best to rationalize them," but he was ousted from his job long before such an analysis could take place.

Although who should really take the blame may not be clear, who will take the hit is perfectly clear. Shares in Airbus plummeted 34 percent on the day the announcement was made. In this industry, since 90 percent of an aircraft's purchase price is paid upon delivery, Airbus originally planned on having $2.5 billion in operating profits by 2007, but these were all lost to the delays. The lack of cash prompted yet further delays and some have estimated the overall cost of this one error to be in the $16 billion range. Most analysts believe that Airbus will have to come back yet again for more low-interest government loans, noting that "the fairy tale has turned into a nightmare that even the fiercest Euroskeptics wouldn't have imagined possible."

SOURCES: C. Matlack, "The Escalating Woes at Airbus," *BusinessWeek*, March 30, 2006, pp. 39–40; C. Matlack, "Airbus' Behemoth Hits Turbulence," *BusinessWeek*, June 14, 2006, pp. 48–49; C. Matlack, "Wayward Airbus," *BusinessWeek*, October 23, 2006, pp. 46–48.

**Departmentalization** Degree to which work units are grouped based on functional similarity or similarity of work flow.

throughout lower levels (in which case authority is *decentralized*). **Departmentalization** refers to the degree to which work units are grouped based on functional similarity or similarity of work flow.

For example, a school of business could be organized around functional similarity so that there would be a marketing department, a finance department, and an accounting department, and faculty within these specialized departments would each teach their area of expertise to all kinds of students. Alternatively, one could organize the same school around work-flow similarity, so that there would be an undergraduate unit, a graduate unit, and an executive development unit. Each of these units would have its own marketing, finance, and accounting professors who taught only their own respective students and not those of the other units.

## Structural Configurations

Although there are an infinite number of ways to combine centralization and departmentalization, two common configurations of organization structure tend to emerge in organizations. The first type, referred to as a *functional structure*, is shown in Figure 4.2. A functional structure, as the name implies, employs a functional departmentalization scheme with relatively high levels of centralization. High levels of

**figure 4.2**

The Functional Structure

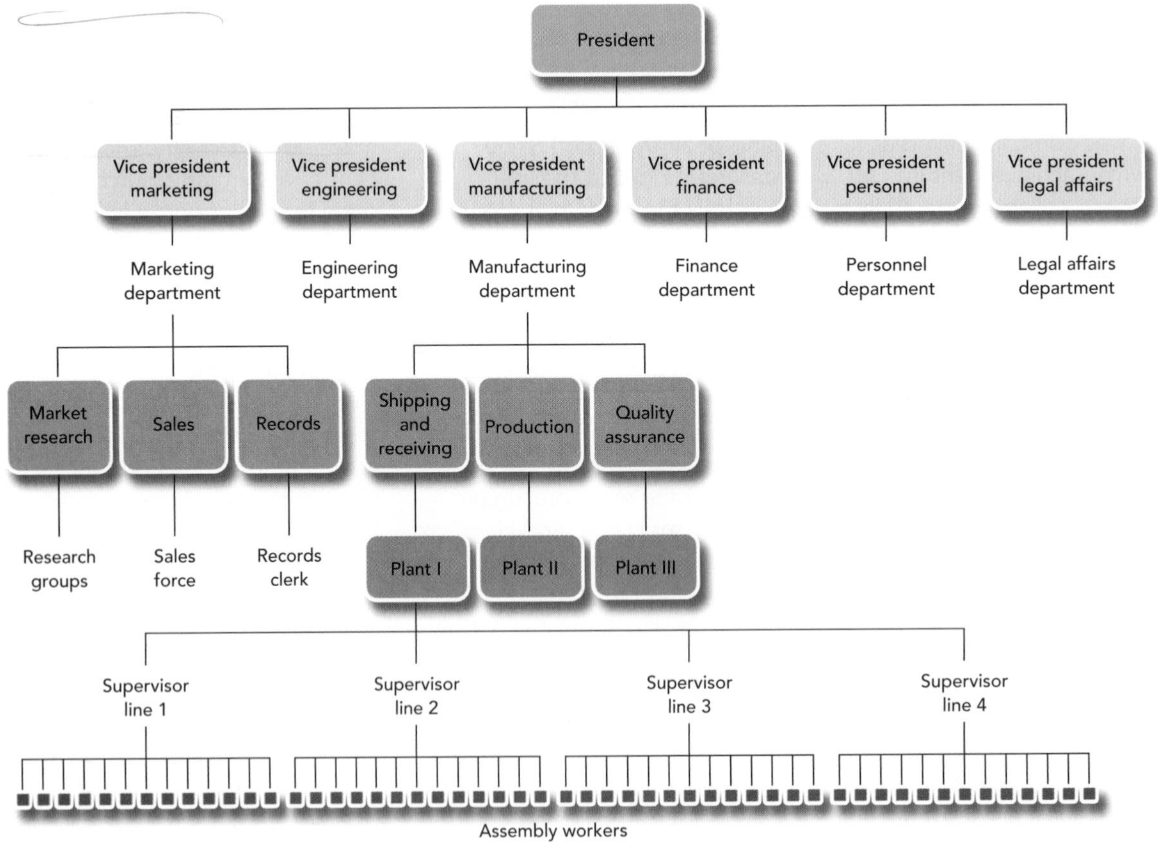


SOURCE: Adapted from J. A. Wagner and J. R. Hollenbeck, *Organizational Behavior: Securing Competitive Advantage*, 3rd ed. New York: Prentice Hall, 1998.

centralization tend to go naturally with functional departmentalization because individual units in the structures are so specialized that members of the unit may have a weak conceptualization of the overall organization mission. Thus, they tend to identify with their department and cannot always be relied on to make decisions that are in the best interests of the organization as a whole.

Alternatively, a second common configuration is a *divisional structure*, three examples of which are shown in Figures 4.3, 4.4, and 4.5. Divisional structures combine a divisional departmentalization scheme with relatively low levels of centralization. Units in these structures act almost like separate, self-sufficient, semi-autonomous organizations. The organization shown in Figure 4.3 is divisionally organized around different products; the organization shown in Figure 4.4 is divisionally organized around geographic regions; and the organization shown in Figure 4.5 is divisionally organized around different clients.

**figure 4.3**

Divisional Structure: Product Structure

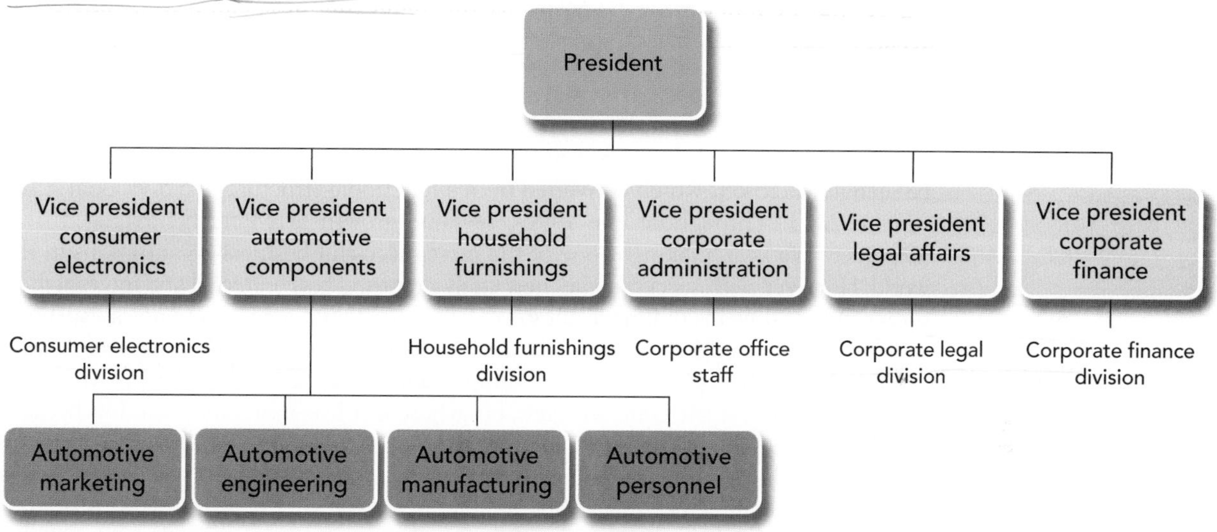


SOURCE: Adapted from J. A. Wagner and J. R. Hollenbeck, *Organizational Behavior: Securing Competitive Advantage*, 3rd ed. New York: Prentice Hall, 1998.

**figure 4.4**

Divisional Structure: Geographic Structure

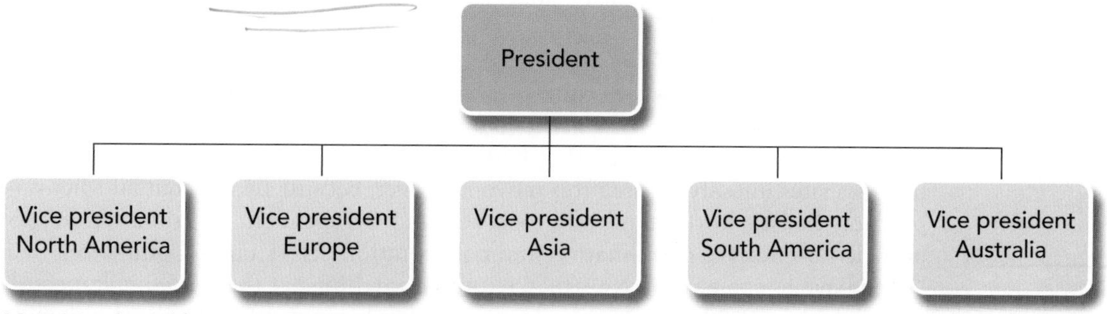


SOURCE: Adapted from J. A. Wagner and J. R. Hollenbeck, *Organizational Behavior: Securing Competitive Advantage*, 3rd ed. New York: Prentice Hall, 1998.

**figure 4.5**

Divisional Structure: Client Structure

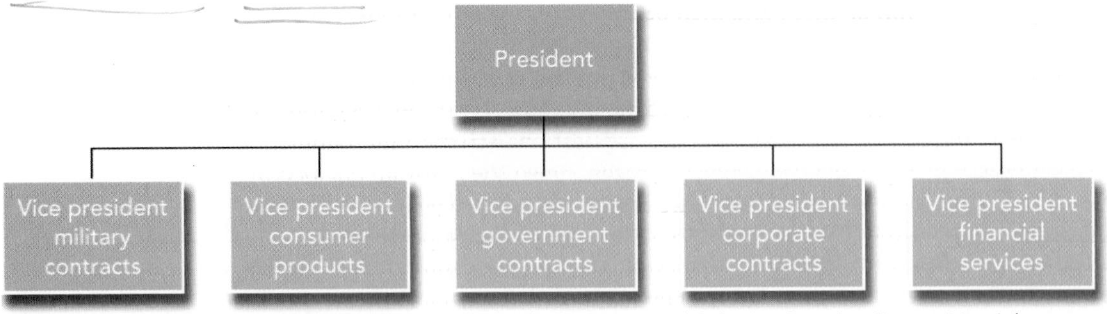


SOURCE: Adapted from J. A. Wagner and J. R. Hollenbeck, *Organizational Behavior: Securing Competitive Advantage,* 3rd ed. New York: Prentice Hall, 1998.

Because of their work-flow focus, their semi-autonomous nature, and their proximity to a homogeneous consumer base, divisional structures tend to be more flexible and innovative. They can detect and exploit opportunities in their respective consumer base faster than the more centralized functionally structured organizations. The perceived autonomy that goes along with this kind of structure also means that most employees prefer it and feel they are more fairly treated than when they are subject to centralized decision-making structures.[16] An example of this structure can be seen at Microsoft, which converted from a functional structure to a divisional structure in 2003. Throughout the 1990s, revenue growth at Microsoft averaged over 30 percent per year, making it one of the most successful business organizations in the world. However, with success comes new challenges, and both external and internal pressures created problems that have cut into Microsoft's dominance. Internally, as the organization increased in size and scope, the decision-making process at Microsoft was slowing to a crawl, and Microsoft experienced turnover among key personnel, many of whom became millionaires as the company grew, but whose intrinsic motivation was low because they did not feel that they had enough autonomy in their jobs. As one manager noted, "In the past, the system was optimized for people to get stuff done. Now, everybody is always preparing for a meeting."[17]

To turn this situation around, CEO Bill Ballmer took unprecedented steps in strategically restructuring the organization to respond to these new competitive pressures. The question guiding this reorganization was how best to divvy up the 55,000 Microsoft employees and define their jobs so that innovation and productivity could be maximized, while turnover and bureaucratic impediments could be minimized. Turning first to the organization's structure, it was clear that Microsoft was too centralized given its current size, and that too much decision-making authority rested with CEO and founder Bill Gates.

Ballmer wanted to decentralize the organization and create a large number of semi-autonomous business divisions (e.g., a Personal Computer Division, a Server Division, a Gaming Division) that had responsibility for their own profit and loss figures. Gates initially resisted this move, however, because he felt that all Microsoft products had to work seamlessly together, and independent divisions would not provide for effective coordination and collaboration across units. Ballmer realized, "We'd have to come up with a structure unlike anything out there, to simultaneously give divisions enough autonomy to manage themselves, yet make it easier for them to cooperate and integrate the technology."[18]

The solution was a structure that relied on seven autonomous divisions that were supported by a new concept in workflow design that formalized how product development would both proceed within divisions and then be transferred across divisions. The seven divisions divided the work up into separate units for operating systems (Windows Client), desktop applications (Information Worker), business services, (Business Solutions), servers systems (Server and Tools), mobile devices (Mobile and Embedded Devices), Internet services (MSN), and X-Box and other gaming applications (Home Entertainment). Within each unit, a new product development process called the Software Engineering Strategy laid out a universally applied procedure that dictated how a project moved from the "incubator phase" to the "definer phase" to the "owner phase," stipulating where the "participants," "reviewers," and "coaches" should provide input into the process. As Gates noted, "This is the first time we've really had a structure to formally deal with issues. So it's not just 'hey if you're confused, send an email to Bill.'"[19]

On the one hand, one of the immediate results of the new structure was that it clearly revealed how much money was being lost in certain divisions such as MSN and the Home Entertainment Divisions relative to the tried-and-true Windows Client Division. Although disheartening in some cases, this at least provided a benchmark from which to measure improvement as the divisions moved forward. More critically, however, these structural changes at the organization level spilled down to individual jobs, both clarifying who was supposed to do what and motivating individuals to sink or swim in their new, more autonomous roles. This helped reduce the turnover rates among the key players by increasing their intrinsic motivation. As one of Microsoft's new division leaders noted, all the new divisional managers "sense a chance to do one last great thing in their working lives," and this is the type of attitude that may help propel Microsoft back to the lofty rates of growth that it once enjoyed.

However, on the downside, divisional structures are not very efficient because of the redundancy associated with each group carrying its own functional specialists. Also, divisional structures can "self-cannibalize" if the gains achieved in one unit come at the expense of another unit. For example, Kinko's stores are structured divisionally with highly decentralized control. Each manager can set his or her own price and has autonomy to make his or her own decisions. But the drawback to this is lack of coordination in the sense that "every Kinko's store considers every other Kinko's store a competitor; they vie against each other for work, they bid against each other competing on price."[20] The exact same problem has been cited at Whole Foods Markets, which operates 189 stores throughout the United States. Whole Foods' stores emphasize organic produce, and individual store managers are encouraged to be entrepreneurial, with little guidance from central headquarters. Same-store sales growth at Whole Foods was averaging 15 percent in 2004 but was down to 6 percent in 2006, largely because of competition between one Whole Foods store and another.[21]

Lack of coordination caused by decentralized and divisional structures can be especially problematic with new and emerging organizations that do not have a great deal of history or firmly established culture. Higher levels of centralization and more functional design of work make it easier in this context to keep everyone on the same page while the business builds experience.[22]

Alternatively, functional structures are very efficient, with little redundancy across units, and provide little opportunity for self-cannibalization. Also, although the higher level of oversight in centralized structures tends to reduce the number of errors made by lower level workers, when errors do occur in overly centralized systems, they tend to cascade through the system as a whole more quickly, and can therefore be more debilitating. For example, when there was a blackout throughout a large part of the East and Midwest in the summer of 2003, many felt that the overly centralized nature of the nation's power grid was a major source of this crisis.[23] However, these structures tend to be inflexible and insensitive to subtle differences across products, regions, or clients.

Functional structures are most appropriate in stable, predictable environments, where demand for resources can be well anticipated and coordination requirements between jobs can be refined and standardized over consistent repetitions of activity. This type of structure also helps support organizations that compete on cost, because efficiency is central to make this strategy work. Divisional structures are most appropriate in unstable, unpredictable environments, where it is difficult to anticipate demands for resources, and coordination requirements between jobs are not consistent over time. This type of structure also helps support organizations that compete on differentiation or innovation, because flexible responsiveness is central to making this strategy work. Indeed, in the words of Microsoft founder Bill Gates, "we are now holding the leaders of our new business divisions accountable to think and act as if they are independent businesses so that will give us the flexibility to respond more quickly to changes in technology and the marketplace."[24] In order to increase their flexibility, many contemporary organizations are changing in the direction away from functional structures to more divisional structures, but this is often more difficult than it seems.[25] In many cases, norms and habits that are often created by the original structure persist even after the boxes on the organization chart have been rearranged, and the cultural influence can be as important as structural influences when it comes to determining outcomes of such transitions.[26]

## Structure and the Nature of Jobs

Finally, moving from big-picture issues to lower-level specifics, the type of organization structure also has implications for the design of jobs. Jobs in functional structures need to be narrow and highly specialized, and people tend to work alone. Workers in these structures (even middle managers) tend to have little decision-making authority or responsibility for managing coordination between themselves and others. Jobs in divisional structures need to be more holistic, with people working in teams that tend to have greater decision-making authority. For example, at Nucor Steel, production at its 30 minimill plants has doubled almost every two years and profit margins have pushed beyond 10 percent largely because of its flat, divisional structure. At Nucor, individual plant managers have wide autonomy in how to design work at their own mills. Nucor plants sometimes compete against each other, but the CEO makes sure that the competition is healthy, and that best practices are distributed throughout the organization as fast as possible, preventing any long-term sustainable advantage to any one plant. Moreover, the profit-sharing plan that makes up the largest part of people's pay operates at the organizational level, which also promotes collaboration among managers who want to make sure that every plant is successful. Thus, after taking over a new mill for the first time, one new plant manager got a call or visit from every other manager, offering advice and assistance. As the new manager noted, "It wasn't idle politeness. I took them up on it. My performance impacted their paycheck."[27]

Nucor employs just four levels of management and operates a headquarters of just 66 people, compared to one of its competitors, U.S. Steel, which has over 20 levels and 1,200 people at its headquarters. This gives Nucor a long-term sustainable competitive advantage, which it has held for close to 15 years. Sales at Nucor grew from $4.5 billion in 2000 to over $13 billion in 2006. During the same period, U.S. Steel's volume decreased by 6 percent. This has translated into success for both investors (roughly 400 percent return on investment in the last five years) and workers, whose wages average $100,000 a year, compared to $70,000 a year at U.S. Steel. As one industry analyst notes, "In terms of a business model, Nucor has won this part of the world," and much of that victory can be explained by their superior structure and process for managing work.[28]

The choice of structure also has implications for people who would assume the jobs created in functional versus divisional structures. For example, managers of divisional structures often need to be more experienced or high in cognitive ability relative to managers of functional structures.[29] The relatively smaller scope and routine nature of jobs created in centralized and functional structures make them less sensitive to individual differences between workers. The nature of the structure also has implications for relationships, in the sense that in centralized and functional structures people tend to think of fairness in terms or rules and procedures, whereas in decentralized and divisional structures, they tend to think of fairness in terms of outcomes and how they are treated interpersonally.[30]

Finally, flatter structures also have implications for organizational culture and the type of people that organizations attract and retain. For example, in 2004, in a highly public scandal, Putnam Investments was fined $110 million for engaging in "market timing," that is, jumping quickly in and out of funds in order to take advantage of momentary market inefficiencies. This is considered an unethical practice within the industry because it increases fund expenses which, in turn, harms long-term investors. Many long-term investors left the organization, some of whom had over $800 million being managed by Putnam.

According to Putnam insiders, the organization's tall and narrow organizational structure created a situation where too many people were managing other people and telling them what they had to do to get promoted. Since the only way to earn more money at Putnam was to climb the corporate ladder, too much pressure was put on managers and employees alike to boost short-term results in order to attract the attention of those high above. The culture was one where people tended to ask "What is the fine for this?" instead of "What does this do to help my clients?" When new CEO Ed Haldeman was brought in to repair the damage, one of his first steps was to remove hundreds of salespeople, and then flatten the structure. The goal was to attract a different kind of employee, who would be less interested in short-term gains and hierarchical promotions handed out by others and more interested in establishing personal long-term relationships with customers and more collaborative relationships with colleagues. In Haldeman's words, "To retain and attract the best people, it's necessary to provide them with autonomy and independence to make their own decisions."[31]

In our next section we cover specific approaches for analyzing and designing jobs. Although all of these approaches are viable, each focuses on a single, isolated job. These approaches do not necessarily consider how that single job fits into the overall work flow or structure of the organization. Thus, to use these techniques effectively, we have to understand the organization as a whole. Without this big-picture appreciation, we might redesign a job in a way that might be good for that one job but out of line with the work flow, structure, or strategy of the organization. In an effectively structured organization, people not only know how their job fits into the bigger picture, they know how everyone else fits as well. Thus, when one of Microsoft's managers says, "I'm not confused about who to go to in order to get something done—there's greater clarity now," this is a sign that the new structure may be meeting the internal needs of the organization's members.[32]

# Job Analysis

**Job Analysis**
The process of getting detailed information about jobs.

**LO2**
Understand the Importance of Job Analysis in Strategic and Human Resource Management.

**Job analysis** refers to the process of getting detailed information about jobs.[33] Job analysis has deep historical roots. For example, in his description of the "just" state, Socrates argued that society needed to recognize three things. First, there are individual differences in aptitudes for work, meaning that individuals differ in their abilities. Second, unique aptitude requirements exist for different occupations. Third, to achieve high-quality performance, society must attempt to place people in occupations that best suit their aptitudes. In other words, for society (or an organization) to succeed, it must have detailed information about the requirements of jobs (through job analysis) and it must ensure that a match exists between the job requirements and individuals' aptitudes (through selection).[34]

Whereas Socrates was concerned with the larger society, it is even more important for organizations to understand and match job requirements and people to achieve high-quality performance. This is particularly true in today's competitive marketplace. Thus the information gained through job analysis is of utmost importance; it has great value to both human resource and line managers.

## The Importance of Job Analysis to HR Managers

Job analysis is such an important activity to HR managers that it has been called the building block of everything that personnel does.[35] This statement refers to the fact that almost every human resource management program requires some type of information that is gleaned from job analysis: selection, performance appraisal, training and development, job evaluation, career planning, work redesign, and human resource planning.[36]

***Work Redesign.*** As previously discussed, job analysis and job design are interrelated. Often a firm will seek to redesign work to make it more efficient or effective. To redesign the work, detailed information about the existing job(s) must be available. In addition, redesigning a job will, in fact, be similar to analyzing a job that does not yet exist.

***Human Resource Planning.*** In human resource planning, planners analyze an organization's human resource needs in a dynamic environment and develop activities that enable a firm to adapt to change. This planning process requires accurate information about the levels of skill required in various jobs to ensure that enough individuals are available in the organization to meet the human resource needs of the strategic plan.[37]

***Selection.*** Human resource selection identifies the most qualified applicants for employment. To identify which applicants are most qualified, it is first necessary to determine the tasks that will be performed by the individual hired and the knowledge, skills, and abilities the individual must have to perform the job effectively. This information is gained through job analysis.[38]

***Training.*** Almost every employee hired by an organization will require training. Some training programs may be more extensive than others, but all require the trainer to have identified the tasks performed in the job to ensure that the training will prepare individuals to perform their jobs effectively.[39]

***Performance Appraisal.*** Performance appraisal deals with getting information about how well each employee is performing in order to reward those who are effective, improve the performance of those who are ineffective, or provide a written justification for why the poor performer should be disciplined. Through job analysis, the organization can identify the behaviors and results that distinguish effective performance from ineffective performance.[40]

***Career Planning.*** Career planning entails matching an individual's skills and aspirations with opportunities that are or may become available in the organization. This matching process requires that those in charge of career planning know the skill requirements of the various jobs. This allows them to guide individuals into jobs in which they will succeed and be satisfied.

***Job Evaluation.*** The process of job evaluation involves assessing the relative dollar value of each job to the organization to set up internally equitable pay structures. If pay structures are not equitable, employees will be dissatisfied and quit, or they will not see the benefits of striving for promotions. To put dollar values on jobs, it is necessary to get information about different jobs to determine which jobs deserve higher pay than others.[41]

## The Importance of Job Analysis to Line Managers

Job analysis is clearly important to the HR department's various activities, but why it is important to line managers may not be as clear. There are many reasons. First, managers must have detailed information about all the jobs in their work group to understand the work-flow process. Earlier in this chapter we noted the importance of understanding the work-flow process—specifically, identifying the tasks performed and the knowledge, skills, and abilities required to perform them. In addition, an understanding of this work-flow process is essential if a manager chooses to redesign certain aspects to increase efficiency or effectiveness.

Second, managers need to understand the job requirements to make intelligent hiring decisions. Very seldom do employees get hired by the human resource department without a manager's input. Managers will often interview prospective applicants and recommend who should receive a job offer. However, if the manager does not clearly understand what tasks are performed on the job and the skills necessary to perform them, the hiring decision may result in employees whom the manager "likes" but who are not capable of performing the job successfully.

Third, a manager is responsible for ensuring that each individual is performing satisfactorily (or better). This requires the manager to evaluate how well each person is performing and to provide feedback to those whose performance needs improvement. Again, this requires that the manager clearly understand the tasks required in every job. It is also the manager's responsibility to ensure that the work is being done safely, knowing where potential hazards might manifest themselves and creating a climate where people feel free to interrupt the production process if dangerous conditions exist.[42]

## Job Analysis Information

### Nature of Information

Two types of information are most useful in job analysis: job descriptions and job specifications. A **job description** is a list of the tasks, duties, and responsibilities (TDRs) that a job entails. TDRs are observable actions. For example, a clerical job requires the jobholder to type. If you were to observe someone in that position

TDRs

**Job Description**
A list of the tasks, duties, and responsibilities that a job entails.

for a day, you would certainly see some typing. When a manager attempts to evaluate job performance, it is most important to have detailed information about the work performed in the job (that is, the TDRs). This makes it possible to determine how well an individual is meeting each job requirement. Table 4.1 shows a sample job description.

**Job Specification**
A list of the knowledge, skills, abilities, and other characteristics (KSAOs) that an individual must have to perform a job.

A **job specification** is a list of the knowledge, skills, abilities, and other characteristics (KSAOs) that an individual must have to perform the job. *Knowledge* refers to factual or procedural information that is necessary for successfully performing a task. A *skill* is an individual's level of proficiency at performing a particular task. *Ability* refers to a more general enduring capability that an individual possesses. Finally, *other characteristics* might be personality traits such as one's achievement motivation or persistence. Thus KSAOs are characteristics about people that are not directly observable; they are observable only when individuals are carrying out the TDRs of the job. If someone applied for the clerical job discussed, you could not simply look at the individual to determine whether he or she possessed typing skills. However, if you were to observe that individual typing something, you could assess the level of typing skill. When a manager is attempting to fill a position, it is important to have accurate information about the characteristics a successful jobholder must have. This requires focusing on the KSAOs of each applicant.

**table 4.1**
A Sample Job Description

**Job Title:** Maintenance Mechanic

**General Description of Job:** General maintenance and repair of all equipment used in the operations of a particular district. Includes the servicing of company vehicles, shop equipment, and machinery used on job sites.

1. *Essential Duty (40%): Maintenance of Equipment*
   Tasks: Keep a log of all maintenance performed on equipment. Replace parts and fluids according to maintenance schedule. Regularly check gauges and loads for deviances that may indicate problems with equipment. Perform nonroutine maintenance as required. May involve limited supervision and training of operators performing maintenance.
2. *Essential Duty (40%): Repair of Equipment*
   Tasks: Requires inspection of equipment and a recommendation that a piece be scrapped or repaired. If equipment is to be repaired, mechanic will take whatever steps are necessary to return the piece to working order. This may include a partial or total rebuilding of the piece using various hand tools and equipment. Will primarily involve the overhaul and troubleshooting of diesel engines and hydraulic equipment.
3. *Essential Duty (10%): Testing and Approval*
   Tasks: Ensure that all required maintenance and repair has been performed and that it was performed according to manufacturer specifications. Approve or reject equipment as being ready for use on a job.
4. *Essential Duty (10%): Maintain Stock*
   Tasks: Maintain inventory of parts needed for the maintenance and repair of equipment. Responsible for ordering satisfactory parts and supplies at the lowest possible cost.

*Nonessential Functions*
Other duties as assigned.

## Sources of Job Analysis Information

In performing the job analysis, one question that often arises is, Who should make up the group of incumbents that are responsible for providing the job analysis information? Whatever job analysis method you choose, the process of job analysis entails obtaining information from people familiar with the job. We refer to these people as *subject-matter experts* because they are experts in their knowledge of the job.

In general, it will be useful to go to the job incumbent to get the most accurate information about what is actually done on the job. This is especially the case when it is difficult to monitor the person who does the job. However, particularly when the job analysis will be used for compensation purposes, incumbents might have an incentive to exaggerate their duties. Thus, you will also want to ask others familiar with the job, such as supervisors, to look over the information generated by the job incumbent. This serves as a check to determine whether what is being done is congruent with what is supposed to be done in the job. One conclusion that can be drawn from this research is that incumbents may provide the most accurate estimates of the actual time spent performing job tasks. However, supervisors may be a more accurate source of information about the importance of job duties. Incumbents also seem more accurate in terms of assessing safety-related risk factors associated with various aspects of work, and in general the further one moves up the organizational hierarchy, the less accurate the risk assessments.[43] Although job incumbents and supervisors are the most obvious and frequently used sources of job analysis information, other sources, such as customers, can be helpful, particularly for service jobs. Finally, when it comes to analyzing skill levels, external job analysts who have more experience rating a wide range of jobs may be the best source.[44]

## Job Analysis Methods

There are various methods for analyzing jobs and no "one best way." In this section we discuss three methods for analyzing jobs: the position analysis questionnaire, the task analysis inventory, and the job analysis system. Although most managers may not have time to use each of these techniques in the exact manner suggested, the three provide some anchors for thinking about broad approaches, task-focused approaches, and person-oriented approaches to conducting job analysis.

**LO3**
Choose the Right Job Analysis Technique for a Variety of Human Resource Activities.

### Position Analysis Questionnaire (PAQ)

We lead this section off with the PAQ because this is one of the broadest and most well-researched instruments for analyzing jobs. Moreover, its emphasis on inputs, processes, relationships, and outputs is consistent with the work-flow analysis approach that we used in leading off this chapter (Figure 4.1).

The PAQ is a standardized job analysis questionnaire containing 194 items.[45] These items represent work behaviors, work conditions, and job characteristics that can be generalized across a wide variety of jobs. They are organized into six sections:

1. *Information input*—Where and how a worker gets information needed to perform the job.
2. *Mental processes*—The reasoning, decision making, planning, and information processing activities that are involved in performing the job.

3. *Work output*—The physical activities, tools, and devices used by the worker to perform the job.
4. *Relationships with other persons*—The relationships with other people required in performing the job.
5. *Job context*—The physical and social contexts where the work is performed.
6. *Other characteristics*—The activities, conditions, and characteristics other than those previously described that are relevant to the job.

The job analyst is asked to determine whether each item applies to the job being analyzed. The analyst then rates the item on six scales: extent of use, amount of time, importance to the job, possibility of occurrence, applicability, and special code (special rating scales used with a particular item). These ratings are submitted to the PAQ headquarters, where a computer program generates a report regarding the job's scores on the job dimensions.

Research has indicated that the PAQ measures 32 dimensions and 13 overall dimensions of jobs (listed in Table 4.2) and that a given job's scores on these dimensions can be very useful. The significant database has linked scores on certain dimensions to scores on subtests of the General Aptitude Test Battery (GATB). Thus knowing the dimension scores provides some guidance regarding the types of abilities that are necessary to perform the job. Obviously, this technique provides information about the work performed in a format that allows for comparisons across jobs, whether those jobs are similar or dissimilar. Another advantage of the PAQ is that it covers the work context as well as inputs, outputs, and processes.

In spite of its widespread use, the PAQ is not without problems. One problem is that to fill out the test, an employee needs the reading level of a college graduate; this disqualifies some job incumbents from the PAQ. In fact, it is recommended that only job analysts trained in how to use the PAQ should complete the questionnaire, rather than job incumbents or supervisors. Indeed, the ratings of job incumbents tend to be lower in reliability relative to ratings from supervisors or trained job analysts.[46] A second problem associated with the PAQ is that its general, standardized format leads to rather abstract characterizations of jobs. Thus it does not lend itself well to describing the specific, concrete task activities that comprise the actual job, and it is not ideal for developing job descriptions or redesigning jobs. Methods that do focus on this aspect of the work are needed if this is the goal.

**table 4.2**

Overall Dimensions of the Position Analysis Questionnaire

| |
|---|
| Decision/communication/general responsibilities |
| Clerical/related activities |
| Technical/related activities |
| Service/related activities |
| Regular day schedule versus other work schedules |
| Routine/repetitive work activities |
| Environmental awareness |
| General physical activities |
| Supervising/coordinating other personnel |
| Public/customer/related contact activities |
| Unpleasant/hazardous/demanding environment |
| Nontypical work schedules |

## Fleishman Job Analysis System

Another job analysis technique that elicits information about the worker's characteristics is the Fleishman Job Analysis System (FJAS).[47] This approach defines *abilities* as enduring attributes of individuals that account for differences in performance. The system is based on a taxonomy of abilities that adequately represent all the dimensions relevant to work. This taxonomy includes 52 cognitive, psychomotor, physical, and sensory abilities, listed in Table 4.3.[48]

The actual FJAS scales consist of descriptions of the ability, followed by behavioral benchmark examples of the different levels of the ability along a seven-point scale. An example of the written comprehension ability scale from the FJAS is presented in Figure 4.6.

In using the job analysis technique, subject matter experts (SMEs) are presented with each of the 52 scales. These experts indicate the point on the scale that best represents the level of that ability required in a particular job. These ratings provide an accurate picture of the ability requirements of the job. Substantial research has shown the value of this general approach for human resource activities such as career development, selection, and training.[49]

## The Occupational Information Network (O*NET)

The *Dictionary of Occupational Titles* (DOT) was born during the 1930s and served as a vehicle for helping the new public employment system link the demand for skills and the supply of skills in the U.S. workforce. Although this system served the country well

**table 4.3**

Abilities Included in the Fleishman Job Analysis System

| | |
|---|---|
| 1. Oral comprehension | 27. Arm–hand steadiness |
| 2. Written comprehension | 28. Manual dexterity |
| 3. Oral expression | 29. Finger dexterity |
| 4. Written expression | 30. Wrist–finger speed |
| 5. Fluency of ideas | 31. Speed of limb movement |
| 6. Originality | 32. Static strength |
| 7. Memorization | 33. Explosive strength |
| 8. Problem sensitivity | 34. Dynamic strength |
| 9. Mathematical reasoning | 35. Trunk strength |
| 10. Number facility | 36. Extent flexibility |
| 11. Deductive reasoning | 37. Dynamic flexibility |
| 12. Inductive reasoning | 38. Gross body coordination |
| 13. Information ordering | 39. Gross body equilibrium |
| 14. Category flexibility | 40. Stamina |
| 15. Speed of closure | 41. Near vision |
| 16. Flexibility of closure | 42. Far vision |
| 17. Spatial orientation | 43. Visual color discrimination |
| 18. Visualization | 44. Night vision |
| 19. Perceptual speed | 45. Peripheral vision |
| 20. Selective attention | 46. Depth perception |
| 21. Time sharing | 47. Glare sensitivity |
| 22. Control precision | 48. Hearing sensitivity |
| 23. Multilimb coordination | 49. Auditory attention |
| 24. Response orientation | 50. Sound localization |
| 25. Rate control | 51. Speech recognition |
| 26. Reaction time | 52. Speech clarity |

figure 4.6
Example of an Ability from the Fleishman Job Analysis System

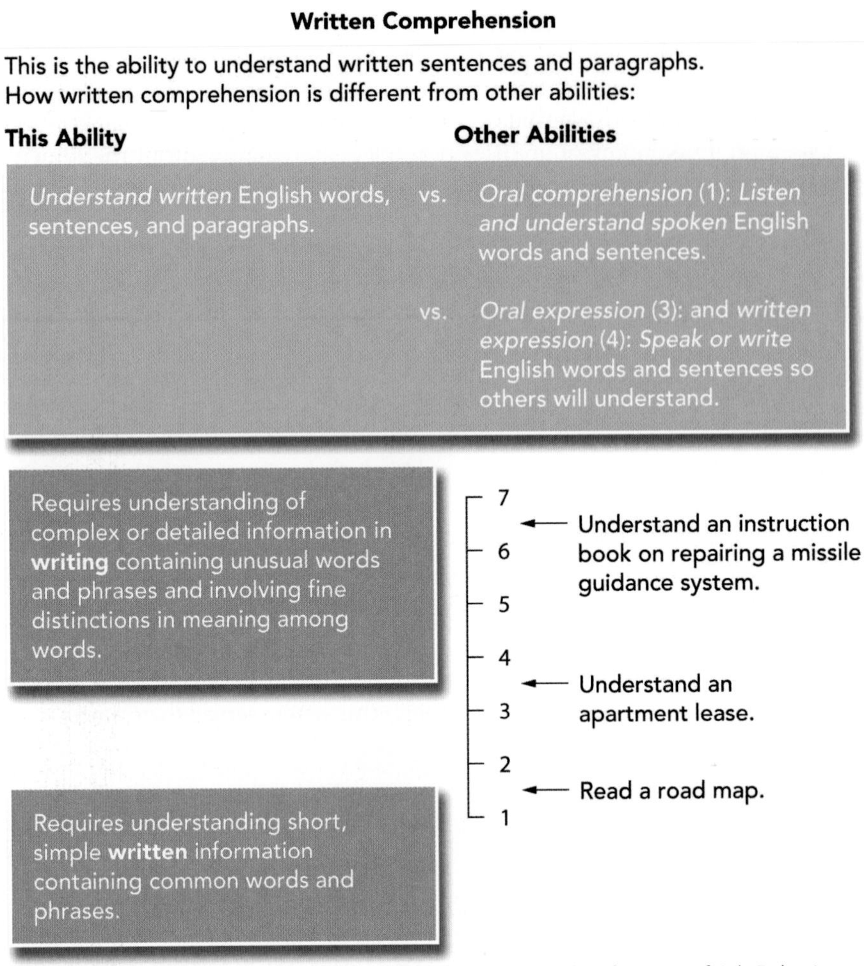

Written Comprehension
This is the ability to understand written sentences and paragraphs.
How written comprehension is different from other abilities:
This Ability
Other Abilities
Understand written English words, sentences, and paragraphs.
vs.
Oral comprehension (1): Listen and understand spoken English words and sentences.
vs.
Oral expression (3): and written expression (4): Speak or write English words and sentences so others will understand.
Requires understanding of complex or detailed information in writing containing unusual words and phrases and involving fine distinctions in meaning among words.
Requires understanding short, simple written information containing common words and phrases.
7
6
5
4
3
2
1
Understand an instruction book on repairing a missile guidance system.
Understand an apartment lease.
Read a road map.


SOURCE: E. A. Fleishman and M. D. Mumford, "Evaluating Classifications of Job Behavior: A Construct Validation of the Ability Requirements Scales," *Personnel Psychology* 44 (1991), pp. 523–76. The complete set of ability requirement scales, along with instructions for their use, may be found in E. A. Fleishman, *Fleishman Job Analysis Survey (F-JAS)* (Palo Alto, CA: Consulting Psychologists Press, 1992). Used with permission.

for over 60 years, it became clear to officials at the U.S. Department of Labor that jobs in the new economy were so qualitatively different from jobs in the old economy, that the DOT no longer served its purpose. Technological changes in the nature of work, global competition, and a shift from stable, fixed manufacturing jobs to a more flexible, dynamic, service-based economy were quickly making the system obsolete.[50]

For all these reasons, the Department of Labor abandoned the DOT in 1998 and developed an entirely new system for classifying jobs referred to as the Occupational Information Network, or O*NET. Instead of relying on fixed job titles and narrow task descriptions, the O*NET uses a common language that generalizes across jobs to describe the abilities, work styles, work activities, and work context required for various occupations that are more broadly defined (e.g., instead of the 12,000 jobs in the DOT, the O*NET describes only 1,000 occupations).[51]

The O*NET is being used by many employers and employment agencies. For example, after closing its Seattle-based headquarters, Boeing used the O*NET system to help find new jobs for the workers who were laid off because of the impending move.[52] The State of Texas has used the O*NET to identify emerging occupations within the state whose requisite knowledge, skills, and abilities are underrepresented in the current occupational system. This information will be used to help train Texas residents to be prepared for the jobs of the future. Finally, educational organizations like the Boys and Girls Clubs of America have used the O*NET to help design activities for children from disadvantaged backgrounds that would improve their standing on skills that are likely to be needed by future employers.[53]

Although these examples show its value for employers, the O*NET was also designed to help job seekers. To see if you think this new system meets the goal of promoting "the effective education, training, counseling, and employment needs of the American workforce," visit its Web site yourself at http://online.onetcenter.org/ and see if the skills it lists for your current job or your "dream job" match what you know from your own experiences and expectations.

## Dynamic Elements of Job Analysis

**LO4**
Identify the Tasks Performed and the Skills Required in a Given Job.

Although we tend to view jobs as static and stable, in fact, jobs tend to change and evolve over time. Those who occupy or manage the jobs often make minor, cumulative adjustments to the job that try to match either changing conditions in the environment or personal preferences for how to conduct the work.[54] Indeed, although there are numerous sources for error in the job analysis process,[55] most inaccuracy is likely to result from job descriptions simply being outdated. For this reason, in addition to statically defining the job, the job analysis process must also detect changes in the nature of jobs.

For example, in today's world of rapidly changing products and markets, some people have begun to question whether the concept of the job is simply a social artifact that has outlived its usefulness. Indeed, many researchers and practitioners are pointing to a trend referred to as "dejobbing" in organizations. This trend consists of viewing organizations as a field of work needing to be done rather than a set of discrete jobs held by specific individuals. For example, at Amazon.com, HR director Scott Pitasky notes, "Here, a person might be in the same 'job,' but three months later be doing completely different work."[56] This means Amazon.com puts more emphasis on broad worker specifications ("entrepreneurial and customer-focused") than on detailed job descriptions ("C++ programming") that may not be descriptive one year down the road.

# Job Design

**LO5**
Understand the Different Approaches to Job Design.

So far we have approached the issue of managing work in a passive way, focusing only on understanding what gets done, how it gets done, and the skills required to get it done. Although this is necessary, it is a very static view of jobs, in that jobs must already exist and that they are already assumed to be structured in the one best way. However, a manager may often be faced with a situation in which the work unit does not yet exist, requiring jobs within the work unit to be designed from scratch. Sometimes work loads within an existing work unit are increased, or work group size is decreased while the same work load is required, a trend increasingly observed with the movement toward downsizing.[57] Finally, sometimes the work is not being performed in the most efficient manner. In these cases, a manager may decide to change the way that work is done in order for the work unit to perform more effectively and efficiently. This requires redesigning the existing jobs.

## EVIDENCE-BASED HR

The biggest trend in job analysis today is a move to broaden job descriptions and minimize job classifications in order to support adaptability and flexibility. For example, consultants brought in to study Volkswagen AG found evidence that proved it took twice as long to build a car relative to Toyota. Much of this was attributable to highly detailed job classification systems that limited the work that different people could do. Thus, an engineer who was focused on axles could focus only on axles, which stifled communication across departments and made it difficult to trace the source of complex problems that resulted from interactions between departments. This and other problems associated with Volkswagen's work process contributed to a 60 percent loss in profits between 2001 and 2006. New CEO Wolfgang Bernhard was brought in to rectify this situation, and one of his first steps was to tear up existing narrow job descriptions and replace them with a more flexible cross-functional team arrangement.

A similar story can be found at Spirit AeroSystems. In 2005, as part of an effort to shed weak assets and underperforming units, Boeing sold its Wichita plant to Spirit. The Wichita plant was Boeing's biggest internal supplier of fuselages and nosecones, but it was consistently uncompetitive relative to other external suppliers that Boeing did not own. Based on the evidence collected by Boeing, it was cheaper for Boeing to get rid of this internal supplier than try to fix it; thus the Wichita plant and all of its employees became expendable. Spirit AeroSystems came in to purchase the plant, and the first step management took was to reduce the 160 job classifications and job descriptions down to 13. It also worked alongside the union to rewrite many inflexible work rules that created inefficiencies and redundancies throughout the work process. Within 18 months, the Wichita plant was turning a profit of over $250 million a year (much of it from Boeing) and raised $1.4 billion as part of an IPO in 2007. Each unionized employee at that point received a check for more than $60,000 as part of a profit-sharing arrangement. As one of the company's union workers noted, "This is what we are going to have to do to be globally competitive."

SOURCES: S. Power, "Top Volkswagon Executive Tries U.S.-Styled Turnaround Tactics," *The Wall Street Journal*, July 17, 2006, pp. A1, A11; S. Holmes, "Soaring Where Boeing Struggled," *BusinessWeek* February 19, 2007, pp. 72.

**Job Design**
The process of defining the way work will be performed and the tasks that will be required in a given job.

**Job Redesign**
The process of changing the tasks or the way work is performed in an existing job.

**Job design** is the process of defining how work will be performed and the tasks that will be required in a given job. **Job redesign** refers to changing the tasks or the way work is performed in an existing job. To effectively design jobs, one must thoroughly understand the job as it exists (through job analysis) and its place in the larger work unit's work-flow process (work-flow analysis). Having a detailed knowledge of the tasks performed in the work unit and in the job, a manager then has many alternative ways to design a job. This can be done most effectively through understanding the trade-offs between certain design approaches.

Research has identified four basic approaches that have been used among the various disciplines (such as psychology, management, engineering, and ergonomics) that have dealt with job design issues.[58] Although these four approaches comprehensively capture the historical approaches to this topic, one still needs to go below the category level to get a full appreciation of the exact nature of jobs and how they can be changed.[59] All jobs can be characterized in terms of how they fare according to each approach; thus a manager needs to understand the trade-offs of emphasizing one approach over another. In the next section we discuss each of these approaches and examine the implications of each for the design of jobs. Table 4.4 displays how jobs are characterized along each of these dimensions, and the Work Design Questionnaire (WDQ), a specific instrument that reliably measures these and other job design characteristics is available for use by companies wishing to comprehensively assess their jobs on these dimensions.[60]

## Mechanistic Approach

The mechanistic approach has roots in classical industrial engineering. The focus of the mechanistic approach is identifying the simplest way to structure work that maximizes efficiency. This most often entails reducing the complexity of the work to provide more human resource efficiency—that is, making the work so simple that anyone can be trained quickly and easily to perform it. This approach focuses on designing jobs around the concepts of task specialization, skill simplification, and repetition.

*Scientific management* was one of the earliest and best-known statements of the mechanistic approach.[61] According to this approach, productivity could be maximized by taking a scientific approach to the process of designing jobs. Scientific management first sought to identify the "one best way" to perform the job. This entailed performing time-and-motion studies to identify the most efficient movements for workers to make. Once the best way to perform the work is identified, workers should be selected based on their ability to do the job, they should be trained in the standard "one best way" to perform the job, and they should be offered monetary incentives to motivate them to work at their highest capacity.

The scientific management approach was built upon in later years, resulting in a mechanistic approach that calls for jobs to be designed so that they are very simple and lack any significant meaningfulness. By designing jobs in this way, the organization reduces its need for high-ability individuals and thus becomes less dependent on individual workers. Individuals are easily replaceable—that is, a new employee can be trained to perform the job quickly and inexpensively.

**table 4.4**

Major Elements of Various Approaches to Job Design

| |
|---|
| **The mechanistic approach** |
| Specialization |
| Skill variety |
| Work methods autonomy |
| **The motivational approach** |
| Decision-making autonomy |
| Task significance |
| Interdependence |
| **The biological approach** |
| Physical demands |
| Ergonomics |
| Work conditions |
| **The perceptual approach** |
| Job complexity |
| Information processing |
| Equipment use |

SOURCE: Adapted from *Organizational Dynamics*, Vol. 15, by M. A. Campion et al., "Job Design: Approaches, Outcomes, and Trade-Offs." Copyright © 1987, with permission from Elsevier.

## COMPETING THROUGH SUSTAINABILITY

### A Flawed System for Finding Bad Apples?

Many readers of this textbook probably own an Apple iPod and can attest to the fact that this is a very impressive piece of technology, especially in light of its incredibly low price. If you could be convinced that the low price of your iPod was attributable to the fact that the Chinese workers who manufactured it were exposed to miserable and inhumane working conditions, how this would make you feel? Would you be willing to pay more money for a competing product if you could be convinced that those who labored to produce it were treated fairly and with dignity? If so, how much extra would you pay: 100 percent 200 percent, or 300 percent more?

These were the types of questions that surfaced when Apple was charged with tolerating sweatshoplike conditions at the Hoh Hai Precision Industry factory in Langhua, China, where many of their iPods are manufactured. Even if it would not bother you, you can be sure that it did bother Apple. Apple is a company that has long associated itself with socially conscious causes, as well as people who have socially conscious reputations such as former vice president Al Gore and rock singer/political activist Bono. Moreover, many people in iPod's target market demographic are young, creative people who are very socially aware and willing to base purchasing decisions on their values. Finally, many socially responsible investment firms will also strike Apple from their portfolio if there are hints at impropriety in the conduct of those to whom they have outsourced work.

Apple launched an immediate investigation and reported that violations of its policies had indeed occurred at the Langhua plant, both in terms of the dormitory living conditions experienced by the workers (with hundreds of people living in a single building lined with row after row of triple bunk beds) and in the failure to pay overtime rates for workers who put in more than 60 hours a week or who had not gotten a day off from work in over a month. Although Apple vowed to take immediate steps to rectify this situation, this incident prompted many people to question the notion that simply setting standards and then monitoring the practices of offshore suppliers was sufficient for preventing abuse. Indeed, this incident and others have prompted serious reservations regarding the "standard setting and monitoring" paradigm currently used to control the behavior of offshore producers. Indeed, as Hannah Jones, Nike's vice president for corporate responsibility, notes, "We've come to realize that, while monitoring is crucial to measuring the performance of our suppliers, it doesn't lead to sustainable improvements."

This system is failing for many reasons. First, because of the lack of unions and weak government interest in enforcing labor laws, Chinese firms face little real pressure to comply. Second, a local industry has developed around these firms whose sole purpose is to help them deceive monitors and pass inspections without making any real changes (e.g., by showing companies how to manage two different sets of books and how to coach employees to answer specific questions that might arise in an interview). Third, many Chinese workers, especially those in rural locations, are hungry to work as many hours as possible, even if they are not paid overtime rates. Some have even been known to leave one employer for another simply because they can amass more hours, and they do not object to working overtime. Finally, many believe that Western companies really do not care about working conditions, as evidenced by the fact that they are constantly asking for lower prices from their Chinese subsidiaries, only to act shocked when labor violations are uncovered.

This last point—the lack of direct responsibility taken by Western firms—is an especially sore point for some observers. That is, the Western firms do not really run the factories or, in many cases, the investigations, which keeps them at arms length and gives them "plausible deniability" when an incident occurs. In contrast to this model, some firms like Motorola take direct responsibility for operations by building and running their own factories in China. For example, Motorola's Tianjin factory, which produces wireless phones, is owned and operated by Motorola. Monitoring and compliance with labor regulations and the ethical treatment of workers is not outsourced to others, as is so often the case with other Western firms. Under this model, firms that actually want to make sure that regulations are being met can make sure they are being met and need not act ignorant or naïve when unethical treatment of workers is uncovered.

SOURCES: P. Burrows, "High-Tech's 'Sweatshop' Wake-Up Call," *BusinessWeek*, June 15, 2006, pp. 34–35; A. Hesseldahl, "Fixing Apple's 'Sweatshop' Woes," *BusinessWeek*, June 29, 2006, pp. 37–40; A. Hesseldahl, "Apple Answers Sweatshop Claims," *BusinessWeek*, August 21, 2006, pp. 40–41; D. Roberts and P. Engardio, "Secrets, Lies, and Sweatshops," *BusinessWeek*, November, 27, 2006, pp. 50–58; P. Engardio, "Steamed over Sweatshops," *BusinessWeek*, December 18, 2006, pp. 18–19.

Many jobs structured this way are performed in developing countries where low-skilled and inexpensive labor is abundant. As one might expect, this includes a host of "low-tech" manufacturing and assembly jobs, but increasingly this also involves "digital factory jobs." For example, *ProQuest Historical Newspaper* provides a service where subscribers can access the contents of any article ever published by one of nine major U.S. newspapers simply by entering an author name, keyword, or image. You might wonder how all of this historical, nondigital information and text is entered into this digital database, and the answer would be found in Madras, Spain. Here workers take this material and enters the headline, author, major key words, and first paragraph of the work by hand into the database, and then run a program to attach a visual file to the rest of the article. This menial work is conducted by 850 workers, who comprise three 8-hour shifts that work 24 hours a day, 7 days a week.[62] It would be difficult, if not impossible to find workers in the United States willing to put up with work this boring, but as the "Competing through Sustainability" box shows, "boring" may be the least objectionable aspect to much of the work that is outsourced to developing nations.

## Motivational Approach

The motivational approach to job design has roots in organizational psychology and management literature and, in many ways, emerged as a reaction to mechanistic approaches to job design. It focuses on the job characteristics that affect psychological meaning and motivational potential, and it views attitudinal variables (such as satisfaction, intrinsic motivation, job involvement, and behavioral variables such as attendance and performance) as the most important outcomes of job design. The prescriptions of the motivational approach focus on increasing the meaningfulness of jobs through such interventions as job enlargement, job enrichment, and the construction of jobs around sociotechnical systems.[63]

A model of how job design affects employee reactions is the "Job Characteristics Model."[64] According to this model, jobs can be described in terms of five characteristics. *Skill variety* is the extent to which the job requires a variety of skills to carry out the tasks. *Task identity* is the degree to which a job requires completing a "whole" piece of work from beginning to end. *Task significance* is the extent to which the job has an important impact on the lives of other people. *Autonomy* is the degree to which the job allows an individual to make decisions about the way the work will be carried out. *Feedback* is the extent to which a person receives clear information about performance effectiveness from the work itself.

These five job characteristics determine the motivating potential of a job by affecting the three critical psychological states of "experienced meaningfulness," "responsibility," and "knowledge of results." According to the model, when the core job characteristics (and thus the critical psychological states) are high, individuals will have a high level of internal work motivation. This is expected to result in higher quantity and quality of work as well as higher levels of job satisfaction.[65] Of the three critical psychological states, research suggest that "experienced meaningfulness may be the most important when it comes to managing work-related stress."[66]

Job design interventions emphasizing the motivational approach tend to focus on increasing the meaningfulness of jobs. Much of the work on job enlargement (broadening the types of tasks performed), job enrichment (empowering workers by adding more decision-making authority to jobs), and self-managing work teams has its roots in the motivational approach to job design. The critical psychological state one needs to create in the mind of the job incumbent is that the work is meaningful and that it contributes to accomplishing goals that are important to the individual.[67]

In some cases, even work that may not be that interesting can be made significant by clarifying the link between what workers do and the outcomes of their work, perhaps far down the chain. For example, in medicine, a stent is an expandable wire form or perforated tube that is inserted into an artery to help promote blood flow after a heart operation. The actual work that goes into stent production is an assembly line process where each worker does a very small and, some might argue, boring task. To help increase the meaningfulness of this work, however, the company sponsors a party each year where line workers get to meet people whose lives were saved by the stents that were produced on that line. This is often a moving emotional experience for both parties and helps the employees see the impact of their work in a context where this would not naturally happen.[68] Thus, although at some point it might be necessary to pay workers, it is even more important to show job incumbents why their jobs are important. Indeed, one of the secrets behind effective transformational leaders is their ability to help workers see the larger meaning in what they are doing on a day-to-day basis.[69].

## Biological Approach

**Ergonomics**
The interface between individuals' physiological characteristics and the physical work environment.

The biological approach to job design comes primarily from the sciences of biomechanics (i.e., the study of body movements), work physiology, and occupational medicine, and it is usually referred to as *ergonomics*. **Ergonomics** is concerned with examining the interface between individuals' physiological characteristics and the physical work environment. The goal of this approach is to minimize physical strain on the worker by structuring the physical work environment around the way the human body works. It therefore focuses on outcomes such as physical fatigue, aches and pains, and health complaints. Research in this tradition looks a bit more on the context in which it takes place rather than the work itself, and hence issues like lighting, space, and hours worked become more salient from this perspective.[70]

The biological approach has been applied in redesigning equipment used in jobs that are physically demanding. Such redesign is often aimed at reducing the physical demands of certain jobs so that anyone can perform them. In addition, many biological interventions focus on redesigning machines and technology, such as adjusting the height of the computer keyboard to minimize occupational illnesses (like carpal tunnel syndrome). The design of chairs and desks to fit posture requirements is very important in many office jobs and is another example of the biological approach to job design. For example, one study found that having employees participate in an ergonomic redesign effort significantly reduced the number and severity of cumulative trauma disorders, lost production time, and restricted duty days.[71]

Often redesigning work to make it more worker-friendly also leads to increased efficiencies. For example, at International Truck and Engine Corporation, one of the most difficult aspects of truck production was pinning the axles to the truck frame. Traditionally, the frame was lowered onto the axle and a crew of six people, armed with oversized hammers and crowbars, forced the frame onto the axle. Because the workers could not see the bolts they had to tighten under the frame, the bolts were often not fastened properly, and many workers injured themselves in the process. After a brainstorming session, the workers and engineers figured that it would be better to flip the frame upside down and attach the axles from above instead of below. The result was a job that could be done twice as fast by half as many workers, who were much less likely to make mistakes or get injured.[72]

## Perceptual–Motor Approach

The perceptual–motor approach to job design has roots in human-factors literature.[73] Whereas the biological approach focuses on physical capabilities and limitations, the perceptual–motor approach focuses on human mental capabilities and limitations. The goal is to design jobs in a way that ensures they do not exceed people's mental capabilities and limitations. This approach generally tries to improve reliability, safety, and user reactions by designing jobs to reduce their information-processing requirements. In designing jobs, one looks at the least capable worker and then constructs job requirements that an individual of that ability level could meet. Similar to the mechanistic approach, this approach generally decreases the job's cognitive demands.

Recent changes in technological capacities hold the promise of helping to reduce job demands and errors, but in some cases, these developments have actually made the problem worse. The term "absence presence" has been coined to refer to the reduced attentive state that one might experience when simultaneously interacting with multiple media. For example, someone might be talking on a cell phone while driving a car, or surfing the net while attending a business meeting, or checking e-mail while preparing a presentation. In all these cases, the new technology serves as a source of distraction from the primary task, reducing performance and increasing the opportunities for errors.[74] Indeed, research shows that on complex tasks, even very short interruptions can break one's train of thought and derail performance. Thus, e-mail servers that have a feature that signals the arrival of each incoming message might best be turned off if the job incumbent cannot resist the temptation this creates to interrupt ongoing activity.[75]

In addition to external disruptions, information processing errors are also increased in any context that requires a "handoff" of information from one person to another. Indeed, problems with handoffs have become a major concern in the field of medicine. As Mike Leonard, physician leader for patient safety at Kaiser Colorado Hospital, notes, "In almost all serious avoidable episodes of patient harm, communication failures play a central role." This would include information that fails to get handed off from nurses, doctors, and medical technicians to one another (e.g., the results of the most recent test that was handed to the attending doctor does not get handed to the attending nurse) or information that fails to get handed off from one work shift to another (e.g., a patient who has already received medication from one shift gets it again from the next shift). Problems between shifts are especially likely due to fatigue and burnout, which may be present at the end of a shift for workers in stressful jobs.[76]

Increasingly, hospitals are borrowing the "SBAR" method, originally developed in commercial and military aviation as a means to hand off an airplane moving through different people's airspace, to standardize communication protocols at the handoff point in medical contexts. SBAR stands for situation, background, assessment, and recommendation, which constitute the four components of every successful handoff. That is, in a few seconds, the person handing off the patient needs to get control of the situation by demanding the listener's attention (situation), then relay enough information to establish the context or the problem (background), then give an overall evaluation of the condition (assessment), and finally make a specific suggestion about the next best course of action (recommendation). At one hospital that introduced this procedure, the rate of adverse events (i.e., unexpected medical problems that cause harm) was reduced by over half, from 90 to 40 for every 1,000 patients treated.[77]

## Trade-Offs among Different Approaches to Job Design

**LO6**
Comprehend the Trade-Offs among the Various Approaches to Designing Jobs.

A recent stream of research has aimed at understanding the trade-offs and implications of these different job design strategies.[78] Many authors have called for redesigning jobs according to the motivational approach so that the work becomes more psychologically meaningful. However, one study examined how the various approaches to job design are related to a variety of work outcomes. Table 4.5 summarizes the

**table 4.5**
Summary of Outcomes from the Job Design Approaches

| JOB DESIGN APPROACH | POSITIVE OUTCOMES | NEGATIVE OUTCOMES |
|---|---|---|
| Motivational | Higher job satisfaction<br>Higher motivation<br>Greater job involvement<br>Higher job performance<br>Lower absenteeism | Increased training time<br>Lower utilization levels<br>Greater likelihood of error<br>Greater chance of mental overload and stress |
| Mechanistic | Decreased training time<br>Higher utilization levels<br>Lower likelihood of error<br>Less chance of mental overload and stress | Lower job satisfaction<br>Lower motivation<br>Higher absenteeism |
| Biological | Less physical effort<br>Less physical fatigue<br>Fewer health complaints<br>Fewer medical incidents<br>Lower absenteeism<br>Higher job satisfaction | Higher financial costs because of changes in equipment or job environment |
| Perceptual–motor | Lower likelihood of error<br>Lower likelihood of accidents<br>Less chance of mental overload and stress<br>Lower training time<br>Higher utilization levels | Lower job satisfaction<br>Lower motivation |

SOURCE: Reprinted from *Organizational Dynamics*, Vol. 15, by M. A. Campion et al., "Job Design: Approaches, Outcomes, and Trade-Offs." Copyright © 1987, with permission from Elsevier.

results. For example, in this study, job incumbents expressed higher satisfaction with jobs scoring high on the motivational approach. Also, jobs scoring high on the biological approach were ones for which incumbents expressed lower physical requirements. Finally, the motivational and mechanistic approaches were negatively related to each other, suggesting that designing jobs to maximize efficiency very likely results in a lower motivational component to those jobs.

Another recent study demonstrated that enlarging clerical jobs made workers more satisfied, less bored, more proficient at catching errors, and better at providing customer service. However, these enlarged jobs also had costs, such as higher training requirements, higher basic skill requirements, and higher compensation requirements based on job evaluation compensable factors.[79]

Although the motivational and mechanistic approaches to job design do work against one another somewhat, at the same time there is not a tight, one-on-one correspondence between the two. Thus, not all efficiency-producing changes result in dissatisfying work, and not all changes that promote satisfaction create inevitable inefficiencies. By carefully and simultaneously attending to both efficiency and satisfaction aspects of job redesign, managers can sometimes achieve the best of both worlds.[80] For example, at the new Indiana Heart Hospital in Indianapolis, much of the work was digitized in order to create a paperless organization. There are over 600 computer terminals placed throughout the facility, and the doctors and staff directly enter or access information from these terminals as needed. This has eliminated the need for nurses' stations, chart racks, medical records departments, file storage rooms, and copiers and has cut down paperwork, resulting in an increase in efficiency, but also increased job satisfaction by eliminating bureaucracy, allowing the staff more immediate access to needed information. This has affected the bottom line by reducing the length of time a patient stays in the hospital from an average of five days at other hospitals to three days at Indiana Heart Hospital. This allows the hospital to process more patients per bed relative to the competition, giving them a direct source of competitive advantage.[81]

## A Look Back

The chapter opening vignette showed how two different companies producing the same product, Toyota and BMW, could each be successful in its own way, even though each had adopted a very different approach to how the organization is designed and work is carried out. Throughout the text, we also showed how other companies either gained or lost competitive advantage because of similar decisions.

### Questions

1. Based on this chapter, if you were the CEO of one of the less effective automakers, would you be tempted to copy the design of Toyota or BMW?
2. Based on this chapter, if you were a lower level operational worker, would you prefer to work for Toyota or BMW?
3. If BMW wanted to change so that it increased sales volume or if Toyota wanted to change to come up with more innovative designs, which transition do you think would be more difficult and why?

Please see the Video Case that corresponds to this chapter online at www.mhhe.com/noe6e.

## Summary

The analysis and design of work is one of the most important components to developing and maintaining a competitive advantage. Strategy implementation is virtually impossible without thorough attention devoted to work-flow analysis, job analysis, and job design. Managers need to understand the entire work-flow process in their work unit to ensure that the process maximizes efficiency and effectiveness. To understand this process, managers also must have clear, detailed information about the jobs that exist in the work unit, and the way to gain this information is through job analysis. Equipped with an understanding of the work-flow process and the existing job, managers can redesign jobs to ensure that the work unit is able to achieve its goals while individuals within the unit benefit on the various work outcome dimensions such as motivation, satisfaction, safety, health, and achievement. This is one key to competitive advantage.

## Key Terms

Centralization, 150
Departmentalization, 152
Job analysis, 158
Job description, 159
Job specification, 160
Job design, 166
Job redesign, 166
Ergonomics, 170

## Discussion Questions

1. Assume you are the manager of a fast-food restaurant. What are the outputs of your work unit? What are the activities required to produce those outputs? What are the inputs?
2. Based on Question 1, consider the cashier's job. What are the outputs, activities, and inputs for that job?
3. Consider the "job" of college student. Perform a job analysis on this job. What are the tasks required in the job? What are the knowledge, skills, and abilities necessary to perform those tasks? What environmental trends or shocks (like computers) might change the job, and how would that change the skill requirements?
4. Discuss how the following trends are changing the skill requirements for managerial jobs in the United States: (a) increasing use of computers, (b) increasing international competition, (c) increasing work–family conflicts.
5. Why is it important for a manager to be able to conduct a job analysis? What are the negative outcomes that would result from not understanding the jobs of those reporting to the manager?
6. What are the trade-offs between the different approaches to job design? Which approach do you think should be weighted most heavily when designing jobs?
7. For the cashier job in Question 2, which approach to job design was most influential in designing that job? In the context of the total work-flow process of the restaurant, how would you redesign the job to more heavily emphasize each of the other approaches?

## Self-Assessment Exercise

The chapter described how the Department of Labor's Occupational Information Network (O*NET) can help employers. The system was also designed to help job seekers. To see if you think this new system meets the goal of promoting "the effective education, training, counseling, and employment needs of the American workforce," visit O*NET's Web site at http://online.onetcenter.org/.

Look up the listing for your current job or dream job. List the skills identified for that job. For each skill, evaluate how well your own experiences and abilities enable you to match the job requirements.

## EXERCISING STRATEGY: FROM BIG BLUE TO EFFICIENT BLUE

IBM was long known as "Big Blue" because of its size, in terms of both the number of employees and the amount of revenue and costs associated with its operations. However, as the old saying goes, "the bigger they are, the harder they fall." In 1993 IBM racked up over $8 billion in losses when it was blindsided by the switch in consumer preferences from mainframe computers to smaller, networked personal computers.

The new incoming CEO, Lou Gerstner, needed to engineer one of the greatest turnarounds in modern business; he started with a new vision of what the company would become, as well as a strategy for getting where the company needed to be. The strategy had both an external aspect, focused on changing from an old-fashioned manufacturing company to a modern service provider, and an internal aspect of restructuring operations to reduce costs and promote efficiencies.

Nowhere was this internal strategy change felt more strongly than in the human resource division. In 1993, the HRM function at IBM was large, decentralized, and regionally based, with branch offices all over the world employing over 3,500 people. By the year 2000 there was only one single, centralized unit located in Raleigh, North Carolina, and this unit employed fewer than 1,000 people.

The key to the successful downsizing effort was its emphasis on matching size changes with changes in structure and the substitution of technology for labor. Instead of interacting face-to-face with the local human resources office, all communication would be technologically mediated and directed to the central Raleigh facility via telephone, e-mail, or fax. Moreover, user-friendly software was developed to help employees answer their questions without any other human involvement.

The sprawling, geographically dispersed units were replaced with an efficient three-tier system. The first tier was composed of broadly trained human resource generalists who received telephone calls from any of IBM's 700,000 HRM "customers" (employees) and tried to respond to any queries that could not be handled via the automated system. The second tier, a smaller number of highly trained specialists (such as in 401k plans, OSHA requirements, or selection standards), took any calls that exceeded the knowledge level of the generalists. Finally, the third tier consisted of even a smaller number of top executives charged with keeping the HRM practices in line with the overall corporate strategy being developed by Gerstner.

Amazingly, despite the radical downsizing of this unit, employee satisfaction with service actually increased to over 90 percent, and Gerstner singled out the reengineering of this department as a success story that should serve as a benchmark to the rest of the company's divisions. Moreover, the restructuring and redesign of these IBM jobs have formed a "blue"-print for many other HRM departments in other organizations.

SOURCES: S. N. Mehta, "What Lucent Can Learn from IBM," *Fortune*, June 25, 2001, p. 40; G. Flynn, "Out of the Red, Into the Blue," *Workforce*, March 2000, pp. 50–52; P. Gilster, "Making Online Self-Service Work," *Workforce*, January 2001, pp. 54–61; J. Hutchins, "The U.S. Postal Service Delivers an Innovative HR Strategy," *Workforce*, October 2000, pp. 116–18.

### Questions

1. In terms of our discussion of organizational structure, in what ways did the structure at IBM change under Lou Gerstner and what impact did this have on individual jobs?
2. Compare and contrast the direction of structural change at IBM with the direction of change we saw in the structural realignment at Microsoft (that was also discussed in the text).
3. Since both IBM and Microsoft achieved their goals by changing their structures and job design in opposite directions, what does this say about the relationship between organization structure and job design on the one hand and organizational performance and job satisfaction on the other?

## MANAGING PEOPLE: FROM THE PAGES OF *BUSINESSWEEK*

### BusinessWeek Giving the Boss the Big Picture

**A "dashboard" pulls up everything the CEO needs to run the show** It was New Year's Eve, 2003, and Oracle Corp. CEO Lawrence J. Ellison was on his honeymoon. He and his bride, romance novelist Melanie Craft, were relaxing on his 243-foot Katana yacht off St. Barts, the Caribbean island known as a haven for movie moguls and rock stars. But Ellison, for the umpteenth time, couldn't help himself. He climbed to his office on the upper deck of the Katana, fired up his computer, and logged on to the Web site of a small company called NetSuite Inc. It was the last day of the fiscal year, and Ellison, the co-founder of NetSuite and its largest investor, needed to know if the startup was going to meet its numbers.

Before the Internet, Ellison says, taking the pulse of a company was sort of ridiculous. To get the latest sales information, he would call several people and wait days for them to process financial reports that often were out of date by the time he got them. "You would use your cell phone and work on feelings," he says.

But thanks to a new Web-based management tool known as a dashboard, Ellision had the information he needed in seconds. Like the instrument panel in a car, the computer version displays critical info in easy-to-read graphics, assembled from data pulled in real time from corporate software programs. Logging on to his dashboard for NetSuite, Ellison reviewed the financial data and saw surprisingly strong sales. He quickly called NetSuite CEO Zachary A. Nelson. Recalls Nelson: "The first thing he screams is: 'Are the numbers on my dashboard right?'" Nelson looked at his own dashboard, but his sales data were lower. So he pushed a refresh button. "The information came up with the new orders, and it was the exact same number," says Nelson. "It was a very big high-five call."

Since the advent of the mainframe in the 1950s, companies have dreamed of using computers to manage their businesses. But early efforts came up short, with technology that was too costly or too clunky. Now, thanks to the Net and dashboards, those dreams are starting to come true. Forrester Research Inc. analyst Keith Gile estimates that 40 percent of the 2,000 largest companies use the technology. Some of the most prominent chief executives in the world are believers, from Steven A. Ballmer at Microsoft and Ivan G. Seidenberg at Verizon Communications to Robert L. Nardelli at Home Depot. "The dashboard puts me and more and more of our executives in real-time touch with the business," says Seidenberg. "The more eyes that see the results we're obtaining every day, the higher the quality of the decisions we can make."

The dashboard is the CEO's killer app, making the gritty details of a business that are often buried deep within a large organization accessible at a glance to senior executives. So powerful are the programs that they're beginning to change the nature of management, from an intuitive art into more of a science. Managers can see key changes in their businesses almost instantaneously—when salespeople falter or quality slides—and take quick, corrective action. At Verizon, Seidenberg and other executives can choose from among 300 metrics to put on their dashboards, from broadband sales to wireless subscriber defections. At General Electric Co., James P. Campbell, chief of the Consumer & Industrial division, which makes appliances and lighting products, tracks the number of orders coming in from each customer every day and compares that with targets. "I look at the digital dashboard the first thing in the morning so I have a quick global view of sales and service levels across the organization," says Campbell. "It's a key operational tool in our business."

The technology is particularly valuable to small companies, since most of them couldn't afford sophisticated software in the past. Up until about five years ago, dashboards had to be custom built, so the expense could run into the millions of dollars. Now, NetSuite and others offer products that run $1,000 to $2,000 a year per user. "NetSuite brought on a total change in the way the company works and thinks," says Nate Porter, vice-president of American Reporting Co., a Kirkland (Wash.) provider of credit reports and other mortgage services.

### Privacy Concerns

Still, dashboards have drawn some flak. Critics say CEOs can miss the big picture if they're glued to their computer screens. GE agrees with that point. While business unit chiefs such as Campbell are active dashboard users, CEO Jeffrey Immelt is not, since he focuses on issues such as broad strategy and dealmaking that the technology can't yet capture.

Other critics fear dashboards are an alluring but destructive force, the latest incarnation of Big Brother. The concern is that companies will use the technology to invade the privacy of workers and wield it as a whip to keep them in line. Even managers who use dashboards admit the tools can raise pressure on employees, create divisions in the office, and lead workers to hoard information.

One common concern is that dashboards can hurt morale. Consider the case of Little Earth Productions Inc., a Pittsburgh clothing manufacturer. The company uses NetSuite's tools to monitor the amount of business each salesperson has brought in and then displays it publicly. "You do feel bummed out sometimes if you are low on the list," says Ronisue Koller, a Little Earth salesperson.

Those pressures can lead to even bigger disruptions. NetSuite CEO Nelson says his dashboard allows him to read every e-mail sent by the sales staff and to inspect the leads of each salesperson. "It's frightening," he says. And it can have serious consequences. Once a month, Nelson plays "lead fairy" and looks at what sales leads have been followed up on and which ones haven't. One salesman quit when Nelson wrested away his sales leads that were not being used and gave them to others who were out of leads. "This raised enormous hackles in the company," says Nelson. "That's fine with me because he wasn't doing his job anyway."

Still, most management experts think the rewards are well worth the risks. They caution that executives should roll out the systems slowly and avoid highlighting individual performance, at least at first. They also underscore the need for business leaders to spend time up-front figuring out which metrics are the most useful to track. But that's a question of how to use the technology, not whether to implement it. "You can't manage something you can't measure," says Ken Rau, managing partner at Bay Area Consulting Group LLC in San Francisco. "Dashboards are one of management's key techniques to make sure an organization is performing according to its objectives."

The intellectual foundation for dashboards was laid down in the late 1970s with the academic field of decision support systems. DSS introduced the idea that computer systems could be used to aid the process of decision-making. But it wasn't until the late 1990s, as the Internet linked up computers around the world, that companies began building the dashboards of today. In 1998, GE was one of the first companies to cobble together its own proprietary technology. The trend picked up steam after the recession of 2001, when efficiency became a priority. In the past few years, a new wave of software makers—including NetSuite, Salesforce.com, and Hyperion Solutions—have begun making dashboards that are even cheaper and easier to use.

### A Must-Have

Netsuite, based in San Mateo, Calif., was founded in 1998 by Ellison and Evan Goldberg, a former top software engineer at Oracle. In 2002, Nelson took over the company after leaving Network Associates. Today the company offers everything from dashboards to marketing software to tools for setting up an e-commerce Web site. NetSuite claims more than 7,000 customers, most of them small and midsize businesses. In 2005, it was the second-fastest-growing technology company in North America based on five-year sales growth, according to consultant Deloitte. And last year it was on track to hit $70 million in sales, up from $41 million in 2004.

One big fan of dashboards is Microsoft Corp., which of course makes plenty of business software itself. Jeff Raikes, president of the Microsoft division that makes its Microsoft Office software, says that more than half of its employees use dashboards, including Ballmer and chief software architect William H. Gates III. "Every time I go to see Ballmer, it's an expectation that I bring my dashboard with me," says Raikes. Ballmer, he says, reviews the dashboards of his seven business heads during one-on-one meetings, zeroing in on such metrics as sales, customer satisfaction, and the status of key products under development.

As for Gates, Raikes says the Microsoft founder uses a dashboard during his "think week," when he leaves the office and reads more than 100 papers about the tech industry prepared by employees. "He uses the dashboard to track what he has read and the feedback and actions that should be taken," says Raikes.

### Troubleshooting

Dashboards are a natural for monitoring operations. In manufacturing, GE execs use them to follow the production of everything from lightbulbs to dishwashers, making sure production lines are running smoothly. In the software business. Raikes uses his dashboard to track the progress of the upcoming version of Office. Shaygan Kheradpir, the chief information officer at Verizon, has on his dashboard what co-workers call the Wall of Shaygan, a replica of every single node on the telecom giant's network. All green is good. Yellow or red merits a click. Red means an outage somewhere. "It makes you move where you need to move," he says.

Dashboard technology can help keep customers happy, too. Before NetSuite, American Reporting's Porter says customer-service reps just answered the phone and had no place to store client requests. Now the company's entire customer-service team uses the software. As a result, customer-service managers can see who is responding to calls. And service reps have access to every repair ticket, making it easier to handle customer problems. "It allows us to compete against some of the bigger boys," says Porter.

American Reporting isn't the only small fry that's benefiting. Jerry Driggs, chief operating officer of Little Earth, took four months last winter to move his business onto the NetSuite system. Little Earth sells funky eco-fashion products, such as a handbag made with recycled license plates. Today half of the company's 50 employees use the system to manage their production, sales, and financial operations. "Once you see it is so intuitive, you wonder how we ran the business before," says Driggs.

In fact, Driggs ran the business by the seat of his pants, and it showed. Because the company had no system to measure its production requirements or level of raw materials, much of which came from China, it took about six weeks to make and ship a handbag. And Little Earth constantly struggled with cash problems because Driggs would often buy more trim pieces and twist-knob closures than he needed: "You used to see dollars sitting on the shelves," he says. Now, using NetSuite, Driggs can monitor his purchase orders and inventory levels, and the system even alerts him when he is running low on closures and other parts. The result: Little Earth has slashed its shipping time to three days. "All of those things that used to drive us crazy are literally at our fingertips," says Driggs.

If it's near the end of a financial quarter, Oracle's Ellison tracks his customers like a hawk. "I want to know what our five biggest deals are three days before the quarter closes," he says. "I look at the [dashboard] several times a day. So much of our sales activity gets compressed into a few days." Ellison will then call the companies himself or figure out another way to seal the deal.

Since his honeymoon two years ago, Ellison has become more convinced than ever that dashboards are the way of the future. He just wishes more of his employees thought the way he does. One continuing frustration is that although all of Oracle's 20,000 salespeople use dashboards, Ellison says some 20 percent of them refuse to enter their sales leads into the system. Salespeople don't want to be held accountable for a lead that isn't converted into a sale. That makes it hard to get a true picture of the demand for Oracle's products.

Ellison has considered refusing to pay commissions on a sale if the order is not entered into a dashboard, but for now he thinks such a move might prove to be a bit draconian. "The salespeople are the last of the independents," says Ellison. "They think their Rolodex is private." Even Ellison, one of the world's richest men, concedes that technology—and the power it gives him—has it limits. "People have to be persuaded that it's right," he says.

SOURCE: S. E. Ante, "Giving the Boss the Big Picture," *BusinessWeek*, February 13, 2006, pp. 48–50.

### Questions

1. Typically, lower skilled work is often the target of technological innovation, but digital dashboards are aimed squarely at CEOs and top organizational officers. Why has digital technology been slow to work its way into the top echelons and what makes digital dashboard the exception to this general rule?
2. How does the availability of a dashboard change the nature of the CEO's job?
3. How does the availability of a dashboard change the nature of the jobs of people who report to the CEO?
4. Based upon the material in this chapter regarding organizational structure and job design, describe the conditions where the introduction of dashboards might harm organizational effectiveness as well as the conditions where it might promote effectiveness and explain why this is so.

## NOTES


1. J. Galbraith and R. Kazanjian, *Strategy Implementation: Structure, Systems, and Process* (St. Paul, MN: West, 1986).
2. L. Hawkins and N. Shirouzo, "A Tale of Two Auto Plants," *The Wall Street Journal*, May 24, 2006, pp. B1–B2.
3. D. Ilgen and J. Hollenbeck, "The Structure of Work: Job Design and Roles," in *Handbook of Industrial & Organizational Psychology*, 2nd ed., ed. M. Dunnette and L. Hough (Palo Alto, CA: Consulting Psychologists Press, 1991), pp. 165–208.
4. R. Griffin, *Task Design: An Integrative Approach* (Glenview, IL: Scott Foresman, 1982).
5. B. Brocka and M. S. Brocka, *Quality Management: Implementing the Best Ideas of the Masters* (Homewood, IL: Business One Irwin, 1992).
6. R. Pritchard, D. Jones, P. Roth, K. Stuebing, and S. Ekeberg, "Effects of Group Feedback, Goal Setting, and Incentives on Organizational Productivity," *Journal of Applied Psychology* 73 (1988), pp. 337–60.
7. G. L. Stewart and M. R. Barrick, "Team Structure and Performance: Assessing the Mediating Role of Intrateam Process and the Moderating Role of Task Type," *Academy of Management Journal* 43 (2000), pp. 135–48.
8. G. S. Van der Vegt, B. J. M. Emans, and E. Van de Vliert, "Patterns of Interdependence in Work Teams: A Two-Level Investigation of the Relations with Job and Team Satisfaction," *Personnel Psychology* 54 (2001), pp. 51–70.
9. F. P. Morgeson, M. D. Johnson, M. A. Campion, G. J. Medsker, and T. V. Mumford, "Understanding Reactions to Job Redesign: A Quasi-Experimental Investigation of the Moderating Effects of Organizational Context on Perceptions of Performance and Behavior," *Personnel Psychology* 59 (2006), pp. 333–63.
10. C. Passariello, "Louis Vuitton Tries Modern Methods on Factory Line," *The Wall Street Journal*, October 9, 2006, pp. A1, A15.
11. P. Glader, "It's Not Easy Being Lean," *The Wall Street Journal*, June 19, 2006, pp. B1, B3.
12. D. Little, "Even the Supervisor Is Expendable: The Internet Allows Factories to Be Managed from Anywhere," *BusinessWeek*, July 23, 2001, p. 78.
13. M. G. Morris and V. Venkatesh, "Age Differences in Technology Adoption Decisions: Implications for a Changing Workforce," *Personnel Psychology* 53 (2000), pp. 375–403.
14. S. Hamm, "Big Blue Shift," *BusinessWeek*, June 5, 2006, pp. 108–10.
15. A. L. Kristof-Brown, B. D. Zimmerman, and E. C. Johnson, "Consequences of Individuals' Fit at Work: A Meta-analysis of Person–Job, Person–Organization, Person–Group, and Person–Supervisor Fit," *Personnel Psychology* 58 (2005), pp. 281–342.
16. M. Schminke, M. L. Ambrose, and R. S. Cropanzano, "The Effect of Organizational Structure on Perceptions of Procedural Fairness," *Journal of Applied Psychology* 85 (2000), pp. 294–304.
17. J. Greene, "Microsoft's Midlife Crisis," *BusinessWeek*, April 19, 2004, pp. 88–98.
18. J. Kerstetter, "Gates and Ballmer on Making the Transition," *BusinessWeek*, April 19, 2004, pp. 96–97.
19. G. B. Schlender, "Ballmer Unbound: How Do You Impose Order on a Giant Runaway Mensa Meeting?" *Fortune*, January 26, 2004, pp. 117–24.
20. T. Neff and J. Citrin, "You're in Charge: Now What?" *Fortune*, January 24, 2005, pp. 109–20.
21. S. Gray, "Natural Competitor," *The Wall Street Journal*, December 4, 2006, pp. B1, B3.
22. W. D. Sine, H. Mitsuhashi, and D. A. Kirsch, "Revisiting Burns and Stalker: Formal Structure and New Venture Performance in Emerging Economic Sectors," *Academy of Management Journal* 49 (2006), pp. 121–32.
23. B. Nussaum, "Technology, Just Make It Simpler," *BusinessWeek*, September 8, 2003, p. 38.
24. K. Rebello, "Visionary-in-Chief: A Talk with Bill Gates on the World beyond Windows," *BusinessWeek*, May 17, 1999, pp. 114–16.
25. H. Moon, J. R. Hollenbeck, S. E. Humphrey, D. R. Ilgen, B. West, A. Ellis, and C.O.L.H. Porter, "Asymmetrical Adaptability: Dynamic Structures as One-Way Streets," *Academy of Management Journal* 47 (2006), pp. 681–96.
26. M. D. Johnson, J. R. Hollenbeck, D. R. Ilgen, S.E. Humphrey, C. J. Meyer, and D. K. Jundt, "Cutthroat Cooperation:

Asymmetrical Adaptation of Team Reward Structures," *Academy of Management Journal* 49 (2006), pp. 103–20.
27. P. Glader, "It's Not Easy Being Lean," *The Wall Street Journal*, June 19, 2006, pp. B1, B3.
28. N. Byrnes, "The Art of Motivation," *BusinessWeek*, May 1, 2006, pp. 57–62.
29. J. R. Hollenbeck, H. Moon, A. Ellis, B. West, D. R. Ilgen, L. Sheppard, C. O. Porter, and J. A. Wagner, "Structural Contingency Theory and Individual Differences: Examination of External and Internal Person–Team Fit," *Journal of Applied Psychology* 87 (2002), pp. 599–606.
30. M. L. Ambrose and M. Schminke, "Organization Structure as a Moderator of the Relationship between Procedural Justice, Interactional Justice, Perceived Organizational Support, and Supervisory Trust," *Journal of Applied Psychology* 88 (2003), pp. 295–305.
31. J. A. Marquez, "Taking a Longer View," *Workforce Management*, May 21, 2006, pp. 18–22.
32. B. Schlender, "Ballmer Unbound: How Do You Impose Order on a Giant Runaway Mensa Meeting?" *Fortune*, January 26, 2004, p. 123.
33. E. McCormick, "Job and Task Analysis," in *Handbook of Industrial & Organizational Psychology*, ed. M. Dunnette (Chicago: Rand McNalley, 1976), pp. 651–96.
34. E. Primoff and S. Fine, "A History of Job Analysis," in *The Job Analysis Handbook for Business, Industry, and Government*, ed. S. Gael (New York: Wiley, 1988), pp. 14–29.
35. W. Cascio, *Applied Psychology in Personnel Management*, 4th ed. (Englewood Cliffs, NJ: Prentice Hall, 1991).
36. P. Wright and K. Wexley, "How to Choose the Kind of Job Analysis You Really Need," *Personnel*, May 1985, pp. 51–55.
37. J. Walker, *Human Resource Strategy* (New York: McGraw-Hill, 1992).
38. R. Gatewood and H. Feild, *Human Resource Selection*, 2nd ed. (Hinsdale, IL: Dryden, 1990).
39. I. Goldstein, *Training in Organizations*, 3rd ed. (Pacific Grove, CA: Brooks/Cole, 1993).
40. K. Murphy and J. Cleveland, *Performance Appraisal: An Organizational Perspective* (Boston: Allyn & Bacon, 1991).
41. R. Harvey, L. Friedman, M. Hakel, and E. Cornelius, "Dimensionality of the Job Element Inventory (JEI): A Simplified Worker-Oriented Job-Analysis Questionnaire," *Journal of Applied Psychology* 73 (1988), pp. 639–46.
42. D. A. Hofmann, F. P. Morgeson, and S. J. Gerras, "Climate as a Moderator of the Relationship between Leader–Member Exchange and Content-Specific Citizenship: Safety Climate as an Exemplar," *Journal of Applied Psychology* 88 (2003), pp. 170–78.
43. A. K. Weyman, "Investigating the Influence of Organizational Role on Perceptions of Risk in Deep Coal Mines," *Journal of Applied Psychology* 88 (2003), pp. 404–12.
44. L. E. Baranowski and L. E. Anderson, "Examining Rater Source Variation in Work Behavior to KSA Linkages," *Personnel Psychology* 58 (2005), pp. 1041–54.
45. E. McCormick and R. Jeannerette, "The Position Analysis Questionnaire," in *The Job Analysis Handbook for Business, Industry, and Government*, pp. 880–901.
46. E. C. Dierdorff and M. A. Wilson, "A Meta-analysis of Job Analysis Reliability," *Journal of Applied Psychology* 88 (2003), pp. 635–46.
47. E. Fleishman and M. Reilly, *Handbook of Human Abilities* (Palo Alto, CA: Consulting Psychologists Press, 1992).
48. E. Fleishman and M. Mumford, "Ability Requirements Scales," in *The Job Analysis Handbook for Business, Industry, and Government*, pp. 917–35.
49. R. Christal, *The United States Air Force Occupational Research Project* (AFHRL-TR-73-75) (Lackland AFB, TX: Air Force Human Resources Laboratory, Occupational Research Division, 1974).
50. N. G. Peterson, M. D. Mumford, W. C. Borman, P. R. Jeanneret, and E. A. Fleishman, *An Occupational Information System for the 21st Century: The Development of O*NET* (Washington, DC: American Psychological Association, 1999).
51. N. G. Peterson, M. D. Mumford, W. C. Borman, P. R. Jeanneret, E. A. Fleishman, K. Y. Levin, M. A. Campion, M. S. Mayfield, F. P. Morgenson, K. Pearlman, M. K. Gowing, A. R. Lancaster, M. B. Silver, and D. M. Dye, "Understanding Work Using the Occupational Information Network (O*NET): Implications for Practice and Research," *Personnel Psychology* 54 (2001), pp. 451–92.
52. S. Holmes, "Lots of Green Left in the Emerald City," *BusinessWeek Online* (March 28, 2000).
53. D. Dyer, "O*NET in Action," O*NET Web site, http://online.onetcenter.org/.
54. M. K. Lindell, C. S. Clause, C. J. Brandt, and R. S. Landis, "Relationship between Organizational Context and Job Analysis Ratings," *Journal of Applied Psychology* 83 (1998), pp. 769–76.
55. F. P. Morgeson and M. A. Campion, "Social and Cognitive Sources of Potential Inaccuracy in Job Analysis," *Journal of Applied Psychology* 82 (1997), pp. 627–55.
56. S. Caudron, "Jobs Disappear When Work Becomes More Important," *Workforce*, January 2000, pp. 30–32.
57. K. Cameron, S. Freeman, and A. Mishra, "Best Practices in White Collar Downsizing: Managing Contradictions," *The Executive* 5 (1991), pp. 57–73.
58. M. Campion and P. Thayer, "Development and Field Evaluation of an Interdisciplinary Measure of Job Design," *Journal of Applied Psychology* 70 (1985), pp. 29–34.
59. J. R. Edwards, J. A. Scully, and M. D. Brtek, "The Measurement of Work: Hierarchical Representation of the Multimethod Job Design Questionnaire," *Personnel Psychology* 52 (1999), pp. 305–24.
60. F. P. Morgeson and S. E. Humphrey, "The Work Design Questionnaire (WDQ): Developing and Validating a Comprehensive Measure for Assessing Job Design and the Nature of Work," *Journal of Applied Psychology* 91 (2006), pp. 1312–39.
61. F. Taylor, *The Principles of Scientific Management* (New York: W. W. Norton, 1967) (originally published in 1911 by Harper & Brothers).
62. B. Helm, "Life on the Web's Factory Floor," *BusinessWeek*, May 22, 2006, pp. 70–71.
63. R. Griffin and G. McMahan, "Motivation through Job Design," in *OB: The State of the Science*, ed. J. Greenberg (Hillsdale, NJ: Lawrence Erlbaum Associates, 1993).
64. R. Hackman and G. Oldham, *Work Redesign* (Boston: Addison-Wesley, 1980).
65. M. Schrage, "More Power to Whom?" *Fortune* (July 23, 2001), p. 270.
66. A. A. Grandey, G. M. Fisk, and D. D. Steiner, "Must 'Service with a Smile' Be Stressful?" *Journal of Applied Psychology* 90, (2005), pp. 893–904.
67. R. C. Liden, S. J. Wayne, and R. T. Sparrowe, "An Examination of the Mediating Role of Psychological Empowerment on the Relations between the Job, Interpersonal Relationships, and Work Outcomes," *Journal of Applied Psychology* 85 (2000), pp. 407–16.
68. W. E. Byrnes, "Making the Job Meaningful All the Way Down the Line," *BusinessWeek*, May 1, 2006, p. 60.
69. J. A. Colquitt and R. F. Piccalo, "Transformational Leadership and Job Behaviors: The Mediating Role of Core Job

Characteristics," *Academy of Management Journal* 49 (2006), pp. 327–40.
70. S. Sonnentag and F. R. H. Zijistra, "Job Characteristics and Off-the-Job Activities as Predictors of Need for Recovery, Well-Being, and Fatigue," *Journal of Applied Psychology* 91 (2006), pp. 330–50.
71. D. May and C. Schwoerer, "Employee Health by Design: Using Employee Involvement Teams in Ergonomic Job Redesign," *Personnel Psychology* 47 (1994), pp. 861–86.
72. S. F. Brown, "International's Better Way to Build Trucks," *Fortune*, February 19, 2001, pp. 210k–210v.
73. W. Howell, "Human Factors in the Workplace," in *Handbook of Industrial & Organizational Psychology*, 2nd ed., pp. 209–70.
74. D. K. Berman, "Technology Has Us So Plugged into Data, We Have Turned Off," *The Wall Street Journal*, November 10, 2003, pp. A1–A2.
75. J. Baker, "From Open Doors to Gated Communities," *BusinessWeek*, September 8, 2003, p. 36.
76. L. E. LaBlanc, J. J. Hox, W. B. Schaufell, T. W. Taris, and M.C.W. Peters, "Take Care! The Evaluation of a Team-Based Burnout Intervention Program for Oncology Health Care Providers," *Journal of Applied Psychology* 92 (2007), pp. 213–27.
77. L. Landro, "Hospitals Combat Errors at the 'Hand-Off,'" *The Wall Street Journal*, June 28, 2006, pp. D1, D2.
78. J. R. Edwards, J. A. Scully, and M. D. Brteck, "The Nature and Outcomes of Work: A Replication and Extension of Interdisciplinary Work-Design Research," *Journal of Applied Psychology* 85 (2000), pp. 860–68.
79. M. Campion and C. McClelland, "Interdisciplinary Examination of the Costs and Benefits of Enlarged Jobs: A Job-Design Quasi-experiment," *Journal of Applied Psychology* 76 (1991), pp. 186–98.
80. F. P. Morgeson and M. A. Campion, "Minimizing Trade-Offs When Redesigning Work: Evidence from a Longitudinal Quasi-Experiment," *Personnel Psychology* 55 (2002), pp. 589–612.
81. E. Florian, "IT Takes on the ER," *Fortune*, November 24, 2003, pp. 193–200.

PART

# 2 Acquisition and Preparation of Human Resources

5

CHAPTER

# Human Resource Planning and Recruitment

LO

## LEARNING OBJECTIVES

After reading this chapter, you should be able to:

LO1 Discuss how to align a company's strategic direction with its human resource planning. *page 185*

LO2 Determine the labor demand for workers in various job categories. *page 186*

LO3 Discuss the advantages and disadvantages of various ways of eliminating a labor surplus and avoiding a labor shortage. *page 189*

LO4 Describe the various recruitment policies that organizations adopt to make job vacancies more attractive. *page 203*

LO5 List the various sources from which job applicants can be drawn, their relative advantages and disadvantages, and the methods for evaluating them. *page 206*

LO6 Explain the recruiter's role in the recruitment process, the limits the recruiter faces, and the opportunities available. *page 213*

# Enter the World of Business

## HR Recruiters at the Front Line of the Immigration Battle

Would you be willing to lay sewer pipe all day in the sweltering heat of a Mississippi summer for $7 an hour? Would you be willing to manually harvest lettuce for 12 hours a day for that same rate? Would you be willing to wash dishes in a restaurant well past midnight for that rate? If you are like most readers of this book, the answer to all three of those questions is probably "no"—but these are jobs that do have to be staffed by some employers. Finding workers willing to do these kinds of physically demanding, boring, low-status, low-paying jobs is not an easy proposition, and this difficulty creates both challenges and opportunities for competitive advantage as firms struggle to solve this problem.

One particularly tempting solution to this problem is the practice of hiring undocumented illegal immigrant workers. Indeed, it has been estimated that 24 percent of agricultural jobs, 14 percent of construction jobs, and 9 percent of manufacturing jobs are currently staffed with undocumented workers. If you are an employer in this industry, this source of labor is hard to resist, because most Americans would demand two or three times that rate to do this kind of work—if they would do it all. The pressure to go this direction becomes even more inviting when all of your competitors are doing it, and they get away with it because the authorities rarely prosecute employers engaging in this practice. If you abide by the law and hire only legal workers at two or three times the going rate for illegal workers, do you think customers will support you, or will they leave you and do business with your lower cost competitor? One employer who refused to hire illegal workers, Global Horizons, was being so devastated by competitors who were violating the law that it was forced to file suit against its competitors because it found this was the only option short of going out of business.

These are the kinds of questions that are fueling a national debate about what should be done in this country regarding the influx of illegal immigrant labor, and those who manage human resources are on the front line of this battle. On the one hand, some have argued for establishing "guest worker" programs or other provisions that would make these workers legal. Those forwarding these arguments note that this is simply recognizing the fact that the workers are already here, and the employers (and our economy) are already addicted to them, so why not find ways to make it legal? In addition, this group of people represents one of the largest areas of population growth in the United States, and they are increasingly targets not just in labor markets, but in product markets as well. For example, recognizing the need to service this large group of people, Wells Fargo Bank was the first to accept Mexican government-issued identification cards, called *matriculas*, as documentation to open bank accounts. This produced more than 500,000 new accounts and now represents 6 percent of Wells Fargo business—and over 50 percent of its new business growth in the last few years.

Firms that focus on employing illegal immigrants or marketing to them often state that this is a country built by immigrants, and that they are simply making the "American Dream" possible for the next wave of "poor, tired, huddled masses yearning to breathe free." In contrast, those who argue for a crackdown on illegal immigration (as well as a crackdown on employers who hire illegal immigrants), feel this is destroying the American Dream for those who are already legal residents. Research indicates that a 10 percent rise in labor supply typically results in a 3 percent drop in wages, and in some industries, such as the concrete industry, wages fell over 15 percent between 2000 and 2005. This drop was almost perfectly correlated with the proportion of illegal workers employed, leading many to conclude that this group is harming those already employed in the industry. Indeed, the backlash against immigrants can be seen most starkly by the formation of grassroots groups like the Minutemen, who are increasingly targeting employers that hire undocumented workers. This group notes that "if we can take one big employer down—handcuffs, federal prison terms, their property seized—we will make a great step forward to having our laws enforced."

In the midst of all this controversy, aggressive employers at the forefront of technology are finding competitive advantage by hiring immigrant workers that are *legal and documented.* For example, when she was unable to find enough workers for her construction firm, Ann Caroline typed in the words "Mexican construction workers" and "legal" into her Web browser, which then sent her to the site for Labormex Foreign Labor Solutions. This company specializes in finding legitimate foreign workers and has created a database that allows its clients access to this intersection of the "foreign but legal" labor market. Firms that compete by offering low costs, such as Super 8 Motels and Sonic Restaurants, have repeatedly gone to this source, and thus derive the benefits of low-priced labor without suffering the costs associated with illegal labor. With respect to finding and using Labormex as a source of employees, Gary Wilkerson, president of Sonic, states emphatically that "working with them has put us a step ahead of our competitors."

Sources: B. Grow, "A Body Blow to Illegal Labor," *BusinessWeek*, March 27, 2006, pp. 86–87; R. S. Dunham, "Reasons to Watch Whom You Hire," *BusinessWeek*, January 8, 2007, p. 11; B. Grow, "Embracing Illegals," *BusinessWeek*, July 18, 2005, pp. 56–64; S. McMillan, "If We Can Take Down Just One Employer . . .," *BusinessWeek*, August 21, 2006, pp. 30–32; M. Herbst, "Click for Foreign Labor," *BusinessWeek*, January 15, 2007, p. 71.

## Introduction

As the opening story illustrates, employers and human resource managers do not exist in a vacuum. In many cases, global movements, political pressures, cultural preferences, and product market developments all simultaneously influence what type of work is available, as well as who is available to provide labor at different prices. On the one hand, this dynamic nature of managing human resources makes the field challenging and difficult. On the other hand, however, this complexity provides a great opportunity to carve out unique and sustainable sources of competitive advantage if you or your human resource department can find a better way of doing business relative to your competitors. Thus, as in the example provided above, aggressive firms or creative individuals who are able to find legal and documented immigrant workers fill all their positions and do not face the risks of running afoul of the law or paying higher wages that they may not be able to pass on to the consumer in the form of higher costs. Firms that win out in this competition grow and prosper, while those that are too passive or make poor decisions lose out.

This kind of economic competition is what drives our U.S. capitalistic system toward higher levels of productivity and quality of life, and it is a continuing story. The immigration battles that one sees playing out in today's newspapers are not really new, and previous generations have come up with unique solutions to earlier problems that we now take for granted. For example, in the mid-1960s, in some U.S. industries, like tomato harvesting, almost all the workers were illegal immigrants and forces were working to restrict the use of immigrant workers. The solution for that generation was the technological development of machines that replace human labor, and farmers who invested in mechanical tomato harvesting machines eventually took over this industry. Those machines allowed for a fourfold increase in productivity while at the same time resulting in a 75 percent reduction of human labor. Today, almost all tomato harvesting is done this way and we take this for granted, but at the time, it was a new and creative idea that separated the winners and losers in this industry in a very efficient manner.[1]

The purpose of this chapter is to examine factors that influence the supply and demand for labor, and, in particular, focus on what human resources managers can do in terms of planning and executing human resource policies that give their firms competitive advantage in a dynamic environment.

Two of the major ways that societal trends and events affect employers are through (1) consumer markets, which affect the demand for goods and services, and (2) labor markets, which affect the supply of people to produce goods and services. In some cases, as we saw in the opening story, the market might be characterized by a labor shortage. In other cases, the market may be characterized by a surplus of labor. Reconciling the difference between the supply and demand for labor presents a challenge for organizations, and how they address this will affect their overall competitiveness.

There are three keys to effectively utilizing labor markets to one's competitive advantage. First, companies must have a clear idea of their current configuration of human resources. In particular, they need to know the strengths and weaknesses of their present stock of employees. Second, organizations must know where they are going in the future and be aware of how their present configuration of human resources relates to the configuration that will be needed. Third, where there are discrepancies between the present configuration and the configuration required for the future, organizations need programs that will address these discrepancies. Under conditions of a labor surplus, this may mean creating an effective downsizing intervention. Under conditions of a labor shortage, this may mean waging an effective recruitment campaign.

This chapter looks at tools and technologies that can help an organization develop and implement effective strategies for leveraging labor market "threats" into opportunities to gain competitive advantage. In the first half of the chapter, we lay out the actual steps that go into developing and implementing a human resource plan. Through each section, we focus especially on recent trends and practices (like downsizing, employing temporary workers, and outsourcing) that can have a major impact on the firm's bottom line and overall reputation. In the second half of the chapter, we familiarize you with the process by which individuals find and choose jobs and the role of personnel recruitment in reaching these individuals and shaping their choices.

## The Human Resource Planning Process

An overview of human resource planning is depicted in Figure 5.1. The process consists of forecasting, goal setting and strategic planning, and program implementation and evaluation. We discuss each of these stages in the next sections of this chapter.

**LO1**
Discuss How to Align a Company's Strategic Direction with Its Human Resource Planning.

**figure 5.1**
Overview of the Human Resource Planning Process

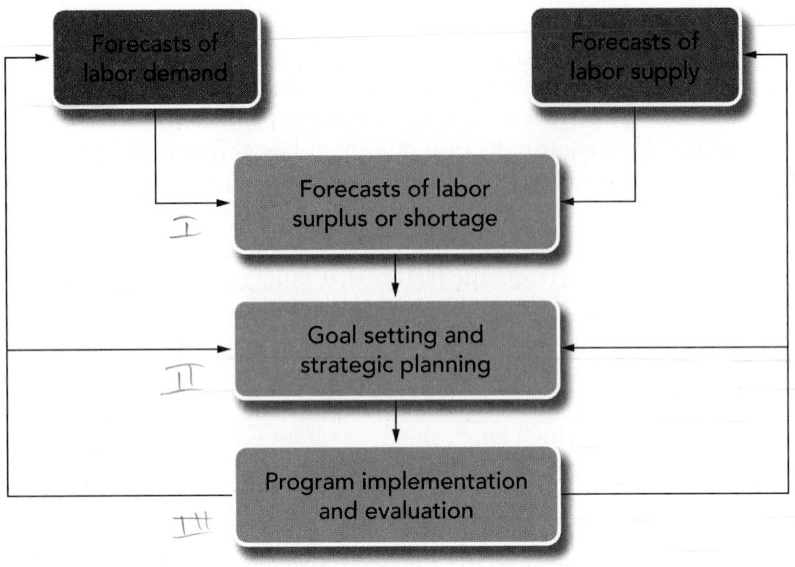


## Forecasting

**Forecasting**
The attempts to determine the supply of and demand for various types of human resources to predict areas within the organization where there will be future labor shortages or surpluses.

The first step in the planning process is **forecasting,** as shown in the top portion of Figure 5.1. In personnel forecasting, the HR manager attempts to ascertain the supply of and demand for various types of human resources. The primary goal is to predict areas within the organization where there will be future labor shortages or surpluses.

Forecasting, on both the supply and demand sides, can use either statistical methods or judgmental methods. Statistical methods are excellent for capturing historic trends in a company's demand for labor, and under the right conditions they give predictions that are much more precise than those that could be achieved through subjective judgments of a human forecaster. On the other hand, many important events that occur in the labor market have no historical precedent; hence, statistical methods that work from historical trends are of little use in such cases. For example, recall the story that opened this chapter. If the U.S. Congress were to pass legislation that allowed a guest worker program for Mexican workers to flow into the United States, there is no real historical way to estimate how many workers would avail themselves of this new opportunity.[2] With no historical precedent, one must rely on the pooled subjective judgments of experts, and their "best guesses" might be the only source from which to make inferences about the future. Typically, because of the complementary strengths and weaknesses of the two methods, companies that engage in human resource planning use a balanced approach that includes both statistical and judgmental components.

### Determining Labor Demand

**LO2**
Determine the Labor Demand for Workers in Various Job Categories.

Typically, demand forecasts are developed around specific job categories or skill areas relevant to the organization's current and future state. Once the job categories or skills are identified, the planner needs to seek information that will help predict whether the need for people with those skills or in that job category will increase or decrease in the future. Organizations differ in the sophistication with which such forecasts are derived.

At the most sophisticated level, an organization might have statistical models that predict labor demand for the next year given relatively objective statistics on leading indicators from the previous year. A **leading indicator** is an objective measure that accurately predicts future labor demand. For example, a manufacturer of automobile parts that sells its product primarily to the Big Three automakers would use several objective statistics on the Big Three automakers for one time period to predict how much demand there would be for the company's product at a later time period. Inventory levels, sales levels, employment levels, and profits at the Big Three in one year might predict the demand for labor in the production assembler job category in the next year.

**Leading Indicator**
An objective measure that accurately predicts future labor demand.

For example, using historical records, one might use multiple regression techniques to assess the best predictive model for estimating demand for production assemblers from information on sales levels, inventory levels, employment levels, and profits at the Big Three. This is not a statistics book, so a detailed explanation of regression techniques is beyond our scope. Rather, we simply note here that this technique will convert information of four or more leading indicators into a single predicted value for demand for production assemblers that is optimal—at least according to the historical data. For example, the demand for nurses in a community can historically be predicted very well by knowing the average age of the community members. Thus, if the average age of American citizens is going up, which it is, then one can expect an increase in the need for nurses. Studies based on these historical trends suggest that by the year 2014, our economy will need 1.2 million more nurses relative to what is available today.[3]

## EVIDENCE-BASED HR

Historical data are useful not only for making long-term predictions of labor demand in broad categories like nursing but also for more day-to-day specific predictions within a specific organization. For example, Wal-Mart has introduced a worker scheduling system that is based on extremely reliable predictions regarding how many customers are going to be in specific stores on specific days at specific times. That is, based on historical evidence, specific stores can predict the volume of traffic and schedule workers based on this evidence. Thus, rather than simply scheduling workers in straight eight-hour shifts, the stores can schedule people to work when they are most needed based on historical evidence. Other retailers like Radio Shack and Payless Shoes have developed similar software, which, according to HR director Larry Liebach, "optimizes our schedules to better anticipate when customers will be in our stores so that we can better engage them."

SOURCE: K. Maher, "Wal-Mart Seeks New Flexibility in Worker Shifts," *The Wall Street Journal*, January 3, 2007, p. A1.

Statistical planning models are useful when there is a long, stable history that can be used to reliably detect relationships among variables. However, these models almost always have to be complemented by subjective judgments of people who have expertise in the area. There are simply too many "once-in-a-lifetime" changes that have to be considered and that cannot be accurately captured in statistical models. For example, terrorism and instability in the Middle East, combined with an unprecedented demand for oil in emerging economies like China and India, have resulted in increasingly high and unpredictable energy prices. This in turn has led to a resurgence of interest in nuclear power in the United States, and more than 20 new nuclear plants are in the process of being built. Past concerns about the safety of nuclear power plants may resurface, however, and thus it is difficult to predict strictly from historical trends whether the demand for workers trained in nuclear power technology is going to increase.[4]

## Determining Labor Supply

Once a company has projected labor demand, it needs to get an indicator of the firm's labor supply. Determining the internal labor supply calls for a detailed analysis of how many people are currently in various job categories (or who have specific skills) within the company. This analysis is then modified to reflect changes in the near future caused by retirements, promotions, transfers, voluntary turnover, and terminations.

As in the case of labor demand, projections for labor supply can be derived either from historical statistical models or through judgmental techniques. One type of statistical procedure that can be employed for this purpose involves transitional matrices. **Transitional matrices** show the proportion (or number) of employees in different job categories at different times. Typically these matrices show how people move in one year from one state (outside the organization) or job category to another state or job category.[5]

**Transitional Matrix**
Matrix showing the proportion (or number) of employees in different job categories at different times.

Table 5.1 shows a hypothetical transitional matrix for our parts manufacturer, focusing on seven job categories. Although these matrices look imposing at first, you will see that they are easy to read and use in determining the internal labor supply. A matrix like the one in this table can be read in two ways. First, we can read the rows to answer the question "Where did people in this job category in 2004 go by 2007?" For example, 70 percent of those in the clerical job category (row 7) in 2004 were still in this job category in 2007, and the remaining 30 percent had left the organization. For the production assembler job category (row 6), 80 percent of those in this position in 2004 were still there in 2007. Of the remaining 20 percent, half (10 percent) were promoted to the production manager job category, and the other half (10 percent) left the organization. Finally, 75 percent of those in the production manager job category in 2004 were still there in 2007, while 10 percent were promoted to assistant plant manager and 15 percent left the organization.

Reading these kinds of matrices across rows makes it clear that there is a career progression within this firm from production assembler to production manager to assistant plant manager. Although we have not discussed rows 1 through 3, it might also be noted that there is a similar career progression from sales apprentice to sales

**table 5.1**

A Hypothetical Transitional Matrix for an Auto Parts Manufacturer

| | 2007 | | | | | | | |
|---|---|---|---|---|---|---|---|---|
| 2004 | (1) | (2) | (3) | (4) | (5) | (6) | (7) | (8) |
| (1) Sales manager | .95 | | | | | | | .05 |
| (2) Sales representative | .05 | .60 | | | | | | .35 |
| (3) Sales apprentice | | .20 | .50 | | | | | .30 |
| (4) Assistant plant manager | | | | .90 | .05 | | | .05 |
| (5) Production manager | | | | .10 | .75 | | | .15 |
| (6) Production assembler | | | | | .10 | .80 | | .10 |
| (7) Clerical | | | | | | | .70 | .30 |
| (8) Not in organization | .00 | .20 | .50 | .00 | .10 | .20 | .30 | |

representative to sales manager. In this organization, the clerical category is not part of any career progression. That is, this job category does not feed any other job categories listed in Table 5.1.

A transitional matrix can also be read from top to bottom (in the columns) to answer the question "Where did the people in this job category in 2007 come from (Where were they in 2004)?" Again, starting with the clerical job (column 7), 70 percent of the 2007 clerical positions were filled by people who were also in this position in 2004, and the remaining 30 percent were external hires (they were not part of the organization in 2004). In the production assembler job category (column 6), 80 percent of those occupying this job in 2007 occupied the same job in 2004, and the other 20 percent were external hires. The most diversely staffed job category seems to be that of production manager (column 5): 75 percent of those in this position in 2007 held the same position in 2004; however, 10 percent were former production assemblers who were promoted, 5 percent were former assistant plant managers who were demoted, and 10 percent were external hires who were not with the company in 2004.

Matrices such as these are extremely useful for charting historical trends in the company's supply of labor. More important, if conditions remain somewhat constant, they can also be used to plan for the future. For example, if we believe that we are going to have a surplus of labor in the production assembler job category in the next three years, we note that by simply initiating a freeze on external hires, the ranks of this position will be depleted by 20 percent on their own. Similarly, if we believe that we will have a labor shortage in the area of sales representatives, the matrix informs us that we may want to (1) decrease the amount of voluntary turnover in this position, since 35 percent of those in this category leave every three years, (2) speed the training of those in the sales apprentice job category so that they can be promoted more quickly than in the past, and/or (3) expand external recruitment of individuals for this job category, since the usual 20 percent of job incumbents drawn from this source may not be sufficient to meet future needs. As with labor demand, historical precedents for labor supply may not always be reliable indicators of future trends. Thus statistical forecasts of labor supply also need to be complemented with judgmental methods.

## Determining Labor Surplus or Shortage

**LO3**
Discuss the Advantages and Disadvantages of Various Ways of Eliminating a Labor Surplus and Avoiding a Labor Shortage.

Once forecasts for labor demand and supply are known, the planner can compare the figures to ascertain whether there will be a labor shortage or labor surplus for the respective job categories. When this is determined, the organization can determine what it is going to do about these potential problems. For example, we previously noted that it is relatively easy to predict from historical data that in the future, the United States is likely to experience a shortage of nurses and, perhaps, a shortage of workers with knowledge of nuclear power.

It is also easy to predict that the current shortage of skilled craftsmen is likely to get worse in the coming years. That is, jobs like ironworker, machinist, sheet metal worker, pipe fitter, plumber, and welder are in huge demand. Part of this is attributable to the fact that the production of heavy machinery is at all-time high levels and shows no sign of abating. In addition, the aging of the nation's infrastructure has created a vast need to repair bridges and tunnels. However, the average age of current workers in these job categories is 55, which, combined with the unwillingness of younger people to be attracted to such difficult and physically demanding work, has resulted in an undersupply of workers with these skills that is only going to get worse. Hal Connor, the human resource manager at a company that produces dehydration and compression machinery, notes that "we need welders like a starving person needs food." The competition to attract these workers will decide, more than any other factor, which firms will survive and prosper and which will go out of business.[6]

As the "Competing through Sustainability" box shows, these skilled trades are not the only job category that is likely to be characterized by a labor shortage. In the area of accounting, the battle is on now for future talent, and this battle is increasingly being waged early in the potential applicant's life.

## Goal Setting and Strategic Planning

The second step in human resource planning is goal setting and strategic planning, as shown in the middle of Figure 5.1. The purpose of setting specific quantitative goals is to focus attention on the problem and provide a benchmark for determining the relative success of any programs aimed at redressing a pending labor shortage or surplus. The goals should come directly from the analysis of labor supply and demand and should include a specific figure for what should happen with the job category or skill area and a specific timetable for when results should be achieved.

The auto parts manufacturer, for instance, might set a goal to reduce the number of individuals in the production assembler job category by 50 percent over the next three years. Similarly, the firm might set a goal to increase the number of individuals in the sales representative job category by 25 percent over the next three years.

Once these goals are established, the firm needs to choose from the many different strategies available for redressing labor shortages and surpluses. Table 5.2 shows some of the options for a human resource planner seeking to reduce a labor surplus. Table 5.3 shows some options available to the same planner intent on avoiding a labor shortage.

**table 5.2**

Options for Reducing an Expected Labor Surplus

| OPTION | SPEED | HUMAN SUFFERING |
|---|---|---|
| 1. Downsizing | Fast | High |
| 2. Pay reductions | Fast | High |
| 3. Demotions | Fast | High |
| 4. Transfers | Fast | Moderate |
| 5. Work sharing | Fast | Moderate |
| 6. Hiring freeze | Slow | Low |
| 7. Natural attrition | Slow | Low |
| 8. Early retirement | Slow | Low |
| 9. Retraining | Slow | Low |

**table 5.3**

Options for Avoiding an Expected Labor Shortage

| OPTION | SPEED | REVOCABILITY |
|---|---|---|
| 1. Overtime | Fast | High |
| 2. Temporary employees | Fast | High |
| 3. Outsourcing | Fast | High |
| 4. Retrained transfers | Slow | High |
| 5. Turnover reductions | Slow | Moderate |
| 6. New external hires | Slow | Low |
| 7. Technological innovation | Slow | Low |

## COMPETING THROUGH SUSTAINABILITY

### First Mover Advantage in Recruiting: Hitting Them in High School

Accounting is difficult and detailed work that demands a high level of education and dedication. At the same time, many people see this job as unglamorous at best, and uninteresting at worst. This combination has resulted in a chronic shortage of labor in this field, and every indication is that this is going to get worse. In fact, the Department of Labor recently predicted that this will become one of the fastest growing occupational categories in the next 10 years. Some estimates put the number of new openings in this field at over 50,000 positions in that time period.

As in every field that is characterized by a labor shortage, this creates real problems for employers in terms of attracting and retaining top talent. Experienced accountants often hop opportunistically from one job to another, pushing up pay rates and preventing the development of long-term experience with any one employer. This inability to sustain relationships with employees, in turn, tends to detract from the quality of service that can be provided to sustain long-term relationships with clients. Indeed, William Freda, a manager with over 30 years of experience at Deloitte & Touche USA LLP, notes that "I have never seen a tougher market for talent."

Employers in this market desperately need to both expand the size of their labor pool and increase the loyalty and long-term commitment of those that they draw from this pool. For many, both of these goals are met by establishing relationships with future employees early in life. That is, rather than waiting for candidates to earn an MBA and then recruit them, more and more employers are reaching out to undergraduate students and, in some cases, even high school students. As chief campus recruiter for Merrill Lynch, Elton Ndomo-Ogar, notes, "We're trying to build relationships earlier and turn these young people into professionals." By identifying the best students early, these firms can decide whether they are likely to be good employees for their company long before their competitors. Moreover, if this process is successful, the new employee is likely to hit the ground running since he or she is already familiar with the company's culture and procedures.

In terms of undergraduate students, one very traditional means of establishing such early relationships is through the use of college internship programs aimed at juniors and seniors. Although these programs are not new, what is new is the ever-growing yield ratio for this source of employees. According to one recent poll, one in four employers reported that over half of their new hires came out of college internship programs. What is also new is the degree to which these programs are increasingly aimed at college freshman. For example, for the first time in their history, Merrill Lynch has reached out with a recruitment program aimed at 300 college freshmen, with the hope that three-fourths of these interns will become new hires.

Not to be outdone in this competition for young talent, Price Waterhouse has bypassed college altogether and set its sights on high school students. Price Waterhouse's program includes workshops and conferences aimed at familiarizing young people both with accounting as a profession, and, of course, Price Waterhouse is one of the best employers in this profession. It follows up this broadly targeted message to large groups of students with more narrowly targeted internships, scholarships, and employment opportunities granted to those it considers to be the top students, with the goal of establishing long-term sustainable relationships. For example, Geovannie Concepcion was first recruited by Price Waterhouse when he was a junior at W.M. Young High School in Chicago. Concepcion, who hopes to work for Price Waterhouse when he graduates from DePaul University, states that "there is this feeling that they are investing in training me and my loyalty belongs with them," which, of course, is exactly the kind of emotional attachment that is the goal of such programs.

SOURCES: N. Byrnes, "Get 'Em While They're Young," *BusinessWeek*, May 22, 2006, p. 86–87; B. Leak, "The Draft Picks Get Younger," *BusinessWeek*, May 8, 2006, p. 96; A. Singh, "Firms Court New Hires—In High School," *The Wall Street Journal*, August 15, 2006, p. B5.

This stage is critical because the many options available to the planner differ widely in their expense, speed, effectiveness, amount of human suffering, and revocability (how easily the change can be undone). For example, if the organization can anticipate a labor surplus far enough in advance, it may be able to freeze hiring and then just let natural attrition adjust the size of the labor force. If successful, an organization may be able to avoid layoffs altogether, so that no one has to lose a job.

Unfortunately for many workers, in the past decade the typical organizational response to a surplus of labor has been downsizing, which is fast but high in human suffering. The widespread use of downsizing is a contributing factor in the largest number of personal bankruptcies ever recorded in the United States. Beyond this economic impact, the psychological impact spills over and affects families, increasing the rates of divorce, child abuse, and drug and alcohol addiction.[7] The typical organizational response to a labor shortage has been either hiring temporary employees or outsourcing, responses that are fast and high in revocability. Given the pervasiveness of these choices, we will devote special subsections of this chapter to each of these options.

Handling labor surplus

## Downsizing

**Downsizing** The planned elimination of large numbers of personnel designed to enhance organizational effectiveness.

We define **downsizing** as the planned elimination of large numbers of personnel designed to enhance organizational effectiveness. Many organizations adopted this strategic option in the 1990s, especially in the United States. In fact, over 85 percent of the Fortune 1000 firms downsized between 1987 and 2001, resulting in more than 8 million permanent layoffs—an unprecedented figure in U.S. economic history. The jobs eliminated in these downsizing efforts should not be thought of as temporary losses due to business cycle downturns or a recession but as permanent losses due to the changing competitive pressures faced by businesses today. In fact, in over 80 percent of the cases where downsizing took place, the organizations initiating the cutbacks were making a profit at the time.

4 major reasons

Rather than trying to stem current losses, the major reasons for most downsizing efforts dealt with promoting future competitiveness. Surveys indicate four major reasons that organizations engaged in downsizing. First, many organizations were looking to reduce costs, and because labor costs represent a big part of a company's total costs, this is an attractive place to start. For example, when the Dow Jones industrial average dropped from over 11,000 points to below 9,000 in the year 2001, many Wall Street firms were faced with high overhead costs that could be eliminated only by reducing head counts. Merrill Lynch, Bank of America, Paine Webber, J. P. Morgan Chase, and Deutsche Bank all laid off roughly 10 percent of their workforce in an effort to stay profitable.[8]

Second, in some organizations, closing outdated plants or introducing technological changes to old plants reduced the need for labor. For example, Eastman Machine is a Buffalo, New York–based manufacturer of equipment that is used for cutting fabric. In order to stave off low-priced competition from Chinese rivals, Eastman expanded heavily into the market for highly automated, computer-driven cutting machines that are not currently available in Asia. This eliminated much of the manual work that was formerly performed at the plant, and now, the same amount of product and revenue that was once generated by a 120-person workforce can be produced with a staff of 80, requiring a downsizing of one-third of the workforce.[9]

A third reason for downsizing was that, for economic reasons, many firms changed the location of where they did business. Some of this shift was from one region of the United States to another—in particular, many organizations moved from the Northeast, the Midwest, and California to the South and the mountain regions of the West. For example, Universal Studios moved many of its operations out of Los Angeles to Orlando, Florida, where the costs of producing television shows are over 40 percent less than in Los Angeles.[10] Some of this shift was also due to jobs moving out of the United States altogether. For example, close to 300,000 white-collar jobs were transferred from the United States to India in 2003 alone.[11]

Although the jury is still out on whether these downsizing efforts have enhanced organizational effectiveness, some early indications are that the results have not lived up to expectations. One study of 52 Fortune 100 firms shows that most firms that announce a downsizing campaign show worse, rather than better, financial performance in the following years.[12] The negative effect of downsizing on performance was especially high among firms that engaged in high-involvement work practices, such as employing teams and pay-for-performance incentives. Thus, the more a firm attempts to compete through its human resources, the more devastating the impact of layoffs is on productivity.[13]

The failure of many downsizing efforts to boost long-term performance led to a slight decrease in the use of this tactic by 2006, when the amount of downsizing in the U.S. economy on aggregate went back down to early 1990 levels.[14] Still, many employers engage in this tactic and hence it is important to understand what goes into an effective versus ineffective downsizing campaign. There seem to be a number of reasons for the failure of most downsizing efforts to live up to expectations in terms of enhancing firm performance. First, although the initial cost savings are a short-term plus, the long-term effects of an improperly managed downsizing effort can be negative. Downsizing not only leads to a loss of talent, but in many cases it disrupts the social networks needed to promote creativity and flexibility.[15] Second, many downsizing campaigns let go of people who turn out to be irreplaceable assets. In fact, one survey indicated that in 80 percent of the cases, firms wind up replacing some of the very people who were let go. Indeed, the practice of hiring back formerly laid-off workers has become so routine that many organizations are increasingly using software formerly used for tracking job applicants to track their laid-off employees.[16]

A third reason downsizing efforts often fail is that employees who survive the purges often become narrow-minded, self-absorbed, and risk-averse. Motivation levels drop off because any hope of future promotions—or even a future—with the company dies out. Many employees also start looking for alternative employment opportunities. The negative publicity associated with a downsizing campaign can also hurt the company's image in the labor market, making it more difficult to recruit employees later. The key to avoiding this kind of reputation damage is to ensure that the need for the layoff is well explained and that procedures for implementing the layoff are fair.[17] Although this may seem like common sense, many employers execute layoffs in ways that make matters worse. For example, in September 2006, Radio Shack human resource managers decided to inform 400 people that they were laid off by e-mail.[18] This makes a dehumanizing event even more dehumanizing, and the negative publicity that attended this decision will surely hurt the company's future recruitment efforts if business turns around.

The key to a successful downsizing effort is to avoid indiscriminant across-the-board cuts, and instead perform surgical strategic cuts that not only reduce costs, but also improve the firm's competitive position. For example, Raven Industries, a Sioux Falls manufacturer of a wide variety of plastic products, had to cut its workforce, but went about the process in a manner that would help make the company "China proof." They went from having 10 different divisions to 4, eliminating manufacturing of certain low-margin products that could be produced cheaper in China (e.g., generic plastic covers for pickup trucks) and pouring more resources into more profitable custom-made covers for widely different agricultural machines. In the process, the organization decreased in size almost by half (from 1,500 workers to 750), but revenue was off by less than 20 percent. Two years after this strategic downsizing effort, the company's share price increased from $4.50 to over $30.[19]

## Early Retirement Programs and Buyouts

Another popular means of reducing a labor surplus is to offer an early retirement program. As shown in Figure 5.2, the average age of the U.S. workforce is increasing. But although many baby boomers are approaching traditional retirement age, early indications are that this group has no intention of retiring any time soon.[20] Several forces fuel the drawing out of older workers' careers. First, the improved health of older people in general, in combination with the decreased physical labor in many jobs, has made working longer a viable option. Second, this option is attractive for many workers because they fear Social Security will be cut, and many have skimpy employer-sponsored pensions that may not be able to cover their expenses. Finally, age discrimination legislation and the outlawing of mandatory retirement ages have created constraints on organizations' ability to unilaterally deal with an aging workforce.

Although an older workforce has some clear advantages for employers in terms of experience and stability, it also poses problems. First, older workers are sometimes more costly than younger workers because of their higher seniority, higher medical costs, and higher pension contributions. When the value of the experience offsets

figure 5.2

Aging of the U.S. Population, 2000–2020

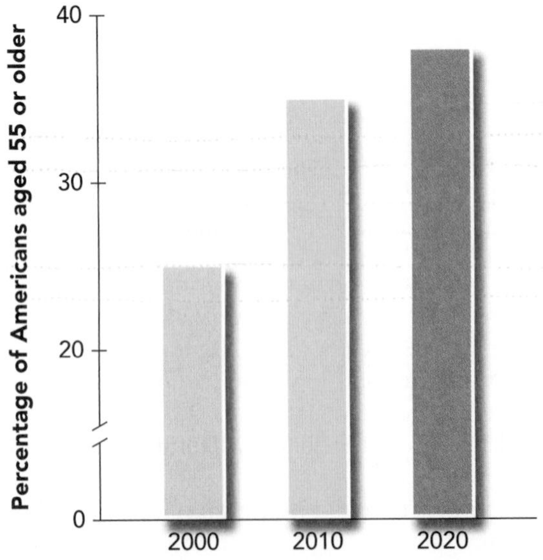

these costs, then employers are fine; but if it does not, it becomes difficult to pass these costs to consumers. Second, because older workers typically occupy the best-paid jobs, they sometimes prevent the hiring or block the advancement of younger workers. This is frustrating for the younger workers and leaves the organization in a perilous position whenever the older workers decide to retire.

In the face of such demographic pressures, many employers try to induce voluntary attrition among their older workers through early retirement incentive programs. These programs come in an infinite variety. Depending on how lucrative they are, they meet with varied success. Although some research suggests that these programs do induce attrition among lower-performing older workers, [21] to a large extent, such programs' success is contingent upon accurate forecasting. For example, at FedEx, the company had to scramble to find workers for the busy holiday season in 2003, when more people opted to take early retirement packages than anticipated. In contrast, at Electronic Data Systems, only one-third of the number of anticipated people opted to accept buyouts in a 2004 program that had to be reapplied in 2005 with a more lucrative set of enticements. Although mistakes in either direction can be costly, an underenrolled program creates an additional set of problems if employees start to think that they should wait it out and hope for an even better package further down the line. This makes the process of calculating one's future labor supply much more complex. As one HR manager notes, "It's a very dicey issue. You have to encourage people to leave and tell them this is the best offer you are going to get."[22]

For this and other reasons, many organizations are moving from early retirement programs to phased retirement programs. Phased retirement programs allow the organization to tap into the experience of older workers while reducing the number of hours they work (and hence reducing costs). This option is often helpful psychologically for the workers, who can ease into retirement rather than being thrust all at once into a markedly different way of life.[23]

Finally, many early retirement programs are simply converted into buyouts for specific workers that have nothing to do with age. For example, in 2006, Ford reduced the size of its unionized workforce by close to 50 percent using across-the-board buyouts of workers. Depending on the length of service, some employees received as little as $35,000 to leave, whereas those with the longest tenure receive as much as $145,000.[24]

HANDLING LABOR SHORTAGE

## Employing Temporary Workers

Whereas downsizing has been a popular method for reducing a labor surplus, hiring temporary workers and outsourcing has been the most widespread means of eliminating a labor shortage. Temporary employment affords firms the flexibility needed to operate efficiently in the face of swings in the demand for goods and services. In fact, a surge in temporary employment often precedes a jump in permanent hiring, and is often a leading indicator that the economy is expanding. For example, the number of temporary workers grew from 215 million to 230 million between 2003 and 2004, signaling to many the end of the recession.[25] In addition to flexibility, hiring temporary workers offers several other advantages:

- The use of temporary workers frees the firm from many administrative tasks and financial burdens associated with being the "employer of record."
- Small companies that cannot afford their own testing programs often get employees who have been tested by a temporary agency.

- Many temporary agencies train employees before sending them to employers, which reduces training costs and eases the transition for both the temporary worker and the company.
- Because the temporary worker has little experience in the host firm, she brings an objective perspective to the organization's problems and procedures that is sometimes valuable. Also, since the temporary worker may have a great deal of experience in other firms, she can sometimes identify solutions to the host organization's problems that were confronted at a different firm. Thus temporary employees can sometimes help employers to benchmark and improve their practices.

Certain disadvantages to employing temporary workers need to be overcome to effectively use this source of labor. For example, there is often tension between a firm's temporary employees and its full-time employees. Surveys indicate that 33 percent of full-time employees perceive the temporary help as a threat to their own job security. This can lead to low levels of cooperation and, in some cases, outright sabotage if not managed properly. Firms are more likely to derive the performance benefits from temporary employees when the current set of workers perceive their job security is high relative to when they feel threatened.[26]

There are several keys to managing this problem. First, the organization needs to have bottomed out in terms of any downsizing effort before it starts bringing in temporaries. A downsizing effort is almost like a death in the family for employees who survive, and a decent time interval needs to exist before new temporary workers are introduced into this context. Without this time delay, there will be a perceived association between the downsizing effort (which was a threat) and the new temporary employees (who may be perceived by some as outsiders who have been hired to replace old friends). Any upswing in demand for labor after a downsizing effort should probably first be met by an expansion of overtime granted to core full-time employees. If this demand persists over time, one can be more sure that the upswing is not temporary and that there will be no need for future layoffs. The extended stretches of overtime will eventually tax the full-time employees, who will then be more receptive to the prospect of hiring temporary employees to help lessen their load.

Second, if the organization is concerned about the reactions of full-time workers to the temporaries, it may want to go out of its way to hire "nonthreatening" temporaries. For example, although most temporary workers want their temporary assignments to turn into full-time work (75 percent of those surveyed expressed this hope), not all do. Some prefer the freedom of temporary arrangements. These workers are the ideal temporaries for a firm with fearful full-time workers. In many cases, temporary staffing firms have access to this type of employee, and this explains the massive growth rate for firms in that industry. For example, Manpower Inc., one of the larger temporary employment agencies, has seen an increase in stock price of more than 35 percent between 2005 and 2007.[27]

Of course, in attempting to convince full-time employees that they are valued and not about to be replaced by temporary workers, the organization must not create the perception that temporary workers are second-class organizational citizens. HR staff can also prevent feelings of a two-tiered society by ensuring that the temporary agency provides benefits to the temporaries that are at least minimally comparable to those enjoyed by the full-time workers with whom they interact. This not only reduces the benefit gap between the full-time and part-time workers but also helps attract the best part-time workers in the first place.

## Outsourcing and Offshoring

Whereas a temporary employee can be brought in to manage a single job, in other cases a firm may be interested in getting a much broader set of services performed by an outside organization; this is called **outsourcing.** Outsourcing is a logical choice when a firm simply does not have certain expertise and is not willing to invest time and effort into developing it. For example, ironically, companies increasingly outsource many of their human resource management tasks to outside vendors who specialize in efficiently performing many of the more routine administrative tasks associated with this function. Figure 5.3 shows a forecast for growth rates in the human resource outsourcing (HRO) industry. Cost savings in this area are easily obtained because rather than purchase and maintain their own specialized hardware and software, as well as specialized staff to support such systems, companies can time share the facilities and expertise of a firm that focuses on this technology.

**Outsourcing**
An organization's use of an outside organization for a broad set of services.

Thus, a moderate-size company that might otherwise need to have a 15- to 30-person HR staff can get by with just 5 to 7 people devoted to HR because they share services with outside firms like Accenture,[28] thus benefiting from economies of scale. In addition to managing the size of the HR unit, the hope is also that this frees up HR managers to focus on more strategic issues. As Samuel Borgese, VP of HR for Catalina Restaurant Group, notes, "This allows us to keep strategic tasks in-house with tactical support form the outsourcing vendor. It's very difficult for a VP of HR to be a strategic player if he or she is managing the HR infrastructure."[29]

figure 5.3
U.S. Multiprocess HR Outsourcing Forecast

NelsonHall puts the market for multiprocess HRO at $1.475 billion by 2010 for the midmarket, which it defines as companies with 1,000–10,000 employees. NelsonHall defines multiprocess HRO as two or more major HR tasks outsourced to a single vendor, so this market is broader than the market for comprehensive HRO.

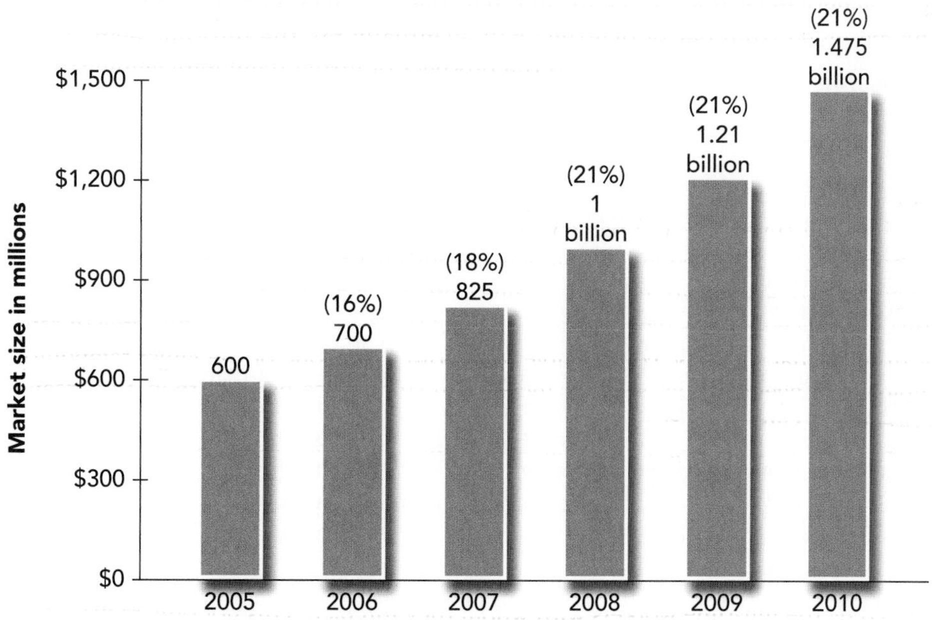


Note: Percentage = compound annual growth rate.
SOURCE: NelsonHall, "Multiple HR Outsourcing in the U.S.: Market Assessment," June 2006.

**Offshoring**
A special case of outsourcing where the jobs that move actually leave one country and go to another.

In other cases, outsourcing is aimed at simply reducing costs by hiring less expensive labor to do the work, and, more often than not, this means moving the work outside the country. **Offshoring** is a special case of outsourcing where the jobs that move actually leave one country and go to another. This kind of job migration has always taken place; however, rapid technological changes have made the current trends in this area historically unprecedented. Offshoring is controversial because close to 800,000 white-collar jobs have moved from the United States to India, eastern Europe, Southeast Asia, and China in the last eight years. In addition to restricting job growth in the United States this has also affected wages, in the sense that while the average rate of salary growth during an economic recovery is usually around 6–8 percent, because of offshoring, salary growth in the most recent recovery was actually negative (−1 percent)

Although initially many jobs that were outsourced were low scope and simple jobs, increasingly, higher skilled work is being done overseas. For example, in 2006, DuPont moved legal services associated with its $100 million asbestos case litigation to a team of lawyers working in the Philippines. Some of this work reflects the sort of tedious copying of documents (over 2 million pages) that is associated with a typical offshoring project, but much of the work requires actual legal judgments (e.g., determining the relevance of the document to the case or its need for confidentiality) that normally would be performed by U.S. lawyers. Paralegal work by U.S. firms can run up to $150 an hour versus $30 in the Philippines, and lawyers' salaries in the Philippines are one-fifth of their counterparts' in the United States.[30]

Do you know where the person you are speaking to is when you call a customer service line? You would be correct if you guessed a foreign country, but increasingly call center work is being done by individuals in a home office in the United States as well. What are the advantages and disadvantages of both of these settings?

Indeed, the stereotype that "call center" staffing is the only type of work being offshored is increasingly invalid, as countries like China, India, and those in eastern Europe try to climb the skill ladder of available work. In India alone, whereas 85 percent of the work offshored there in 2000 reflected call center work, by 2006 this was reduced to 35 percent. The growth in India is now in higher paying contracts dealing with business process improvement, processing mortgages, handling insurance claims, overseeing payrolls, and reading X-rays and other medical tests.[31] Many of the simple call center jobs that moved to India are either moving deeper into the rural Indian villages[32] or, ironically, moving back to the United States. Indeed, call center jobs are increasingly being performed by U.S. workers who are now operating out of their own homes instead of massive call centers like those run overseas. One recent survey indicated that 25 percent of call center employees are based in their own homes, and some have estimated that this will grow by another 25 percent between 2006 and 2010.[33]

Although this may seem problematic for U.S. employers, in fact, if effectively managed, firms that offshore certain aspects of work gain an undeniable competitive advantage over their rivals. Ignoring this source of advantage is self-defeating, and akin to putting one's head in the sand. For example, Levi-Strauss tried for years to compete against other low-cost jeans manufacturers who offshored their labor. However, after years of one plant shutdown after another, in 2003 the firm finally gave up and closed down all of its U.S. manufacturing plants. The move, which many saw as inevitable, was long overdue and had it been made earlier, the company might have been able to avoid losing over $20 million.

When making the decision to offshore some product or service, organizations should consider several critical factors. Many who failed to look before they leaped onto the offshoring bandwagon have been disappointed by their results. Quality control problems, security violations, and poor customer service experiences have in many cases wiped out all the cost savings attributed to lower wages and more. There are several steps a company should take to ensure the success of this strategy. First, when choosing an outsourcing vendor, it is usually the bigger and older the better. Small overseas upstarts often promise more than they can deliver and take risks that one is not likely to see in larger, more established contractors.[34] Second, do not offshore any work that is proprietary or requires tight security. One software developer that hired an Indian firm to debug its programs later found that the firm copied the software and sold it under its own brand name.[35] Third, it is generally a good idea to start small and then monitor the work very closely, especially in the beginning. Typically, if problems are going to develop, they manifest themselves quickly to those who are paying close attention.[36]

Finally, rather than treating offsourced work as just a cost-containment strategy, firms are increasingly looking for "transformational offshoring," which promotes growth and opens up avenues of new revenue. That is, the increased sophistication of outsourcing firms means that they are better able to partner with companies on an equal basis in developing innovative and unique ways to do business. This development has prompted one CEO to note that "I think we will end up with companies that deliver products faster, at lower cost, and are better able to compete against anyone in the world."[37]

### Altering Pay and Hours

Companies facing a shortage of labor may be reluctant to hire new full-time or part-time employees. Under some conditions, these firms may have the option of trying to garner more hours out of the existing labor force. Despite having to pay workers time-and-a-half for overtime production, employers see this as preferable to hiring and training new employees—especially if they are afraid that current demand for products or services may not extend to the future. Also, for a short time at least, many workers enjoy the added compensation. However, over extended periods, employees experience stress and frustration from being overworked in this manner. At some point, most employers in the U.S. will have to respond to a labor shortage with an increase in wages, which then has to be passed on to consumers in terms of an increase in price. However, as the "Competing through Globalization" box indicates, this simple causal chain does not seem to work the same way in China.

In the face of a labor surplus, organizations can sometimes avoid layoffs if they can get their employees to take pay cuts. For example, when DiamondCluster Inc., a Chicago-based technology consulting firm, experienced a downturn in demand for its services, rather than reduce the workforce, it instead convinced the workers to take an across-the-board 20 percent pay cut. Although painful, the workers eventually accepted the need for this move and perceived that it was better than a series of layoffs.[38] Alternatively one can avoid layoffs and hold the pay rate constant but reduce the number of hours of all the workers. Hilton Hotels took this strategy when faced with a diminished occupancy rate that occurred in the wake of the 9/11 terrorist attacks. Some employees went from working five days per week to two, and although the reduction in income was significant, many could file for partial unemployment compensation and everyone kept benefits.[39] This is a particularly good strategy if the employer feels the downturn is just a short-term phenomenon, as was the case with the post-9/11 dearth in travel.

## Program Implementation and Evaluation

The programs developed in the strategic-choice stage of the process are put into practice in the program-implementation stage, shown at the bottom of Figure 5.1. A critical aspect of program implementation is to make sure that some individual is

## COMPETING THROUGH GLOBALIZATION

### Why Labor Shortages Do Not Seem to Affect "The China Price"

Three words that often strike fear in the hearts of U.S. manufacturers are "the China price." Historically, China has had a vast oversupply of labor, resulting in extraordinarily low labor costs relative to what one would find in the United States. These low labor costs supported lower prices for goods produced in China, and this made it almost impossible for U.S. producers to compete with their Chinese rivals. The Chinese played to this advantage very well and the economic growth experienced by that country in the last 15 years has been unprecedented.

However, all good things must end, and in recent years Chinese firms have experienced labor shortages at all levels of the labor market. The major reason for this is not a shortage of bodies per se, which, with China's huge population, is nowhere near being tapped out. Rather the problem lies with the skill levels associated with all those bodies. Public education in China has lagged relative to other industrialized powers, and, in particular, the Cultural Revolution resulted in producing almost an entire generation of workers with low skill levels. As C.P. Lee, Motorola's chief of Human Resources, notes, "The skill base does not meet the demands of a rapidly growing market."

U.S. manufacturers might consider this development a sign of hope, because in the United States, labor shortages lead to increased wages, which in turn lead to higher prices through a usually strong and reliable causal chain. Unfortunately, this causal chain does not seem to operate the same way in China where, despite widespread labor shortages, one sees almost no increases in the price of Chinese goods. Understanding why this is the case provides a useful lesson in how to weather labor shortages and still maintain low prices.

One way to offset a labor shortage is to increase the efficiency of the current workforce. At Emerson Electric's Suzhou plant, for example, the company takes steps to automate work and reduce costs associated with running the plant, including raising the thermostats in summer, using reflective light fixtures, and even tapping excess heat from the factory to warm its worker dormitories. There is a limit to how far one can take efficiency gains, however, and as David Warth, a human resource manager at Emerson, notes, "So far it's an even trade-off between rising labor costs and efficiency gains." A second way to avoid this problem is to offer employees forms of compensation other than money, and many companies in China have been offering more intrinsically motivating jobs that give workers more autonomy and a greater chance at personal development. For example, when Sophia Zhu graduated from the People's University in Beijing, her dual major in economics and international relations made her a hot commodity in the labor market and she received over 20 job offers. In the end, she chose to work with a General Electric subsidiary not because it offered the most money, but instead because it "talked about development opportunities and gave a very clear path to career growth."

Despite these and other attempts to prevent wage spirals, inevitably these shortages did result in wage inflation across the economy, averaging close to 10 percent over the last three years. But even here, the reaction of Chinese firms differs from what one might see in the United States. Specifically, Chinese firms maintain prices in the face of higher labor costs by demonstrating a much greater willingness to take a hit in margins and profits. In fact, Chinese firms tend to pass on only about 20 percent of their cost hikes into prices relative to U.S. firms, allowing "the China price" to stay low even in the face of labor shortages.

SOURCE: B. Einhorn, "The Hunt for Chinese Talent," *BusinessWeek*, May 22, 2006, p. 104; D. Roberts, "How Rising Wages Are Changing the Game in China," *BusinessWeek*, March 27, 2006, pp. 32–35; D. Brady and D. Roberts, "Management Grab," *BusinessWeek*, August 21, 2006, pp. 88–90; C. Yang, "Imports from China Aren't Pricier—Yet," *BusinessWeek*, March 27, 2006, p. 35.

held accountable for achieving the stated goals and has the necessary authority and resources to accomplish this goal. It is also important to have regular progress reports on the implementation to be sure that all programs are in place by specified times and that the early returns from these programs are in line with projections.

The final step in the planning process is to evaluate the results. Of course, the most obvious evaluation involves checking whether the company has successfully avoided any potential labor shortages or surpluses. Although this bottom-line evaluation is critical, it is also important to go beyond it to see which specific parts of the planning process contributed to success or failure.

A good example of the necessary diagnostic work can be seen in Bell Atlantic's recent failed downsizing effort. Convinced that the company would need fewer workers, but facing a union (the Communication Workers of America) that staunchly opposed layoffs, Bell Atlantic developed a high-priced buyout plan. Almost a third of its unionized workforce (14,000 people) stood ready to take the company up on its offer. However, forecasts for product demand were grossly underestimated. The smaller workforce could not keep up with demand. To avert disaster, the company had to offer a 25 percent hike in its already generous pension plan to any employee who would stay. The overall effect was to create an extravagant bonus system that rewarded employees for either staying or leaving.[40]

## The Special Case of Affirmative Action Planning

We have argued that human resource planning is an important function that should be applied to an organization's entire labor force. It is also important to plan for various subgroups within the labor force. For example, affirmative action plans forecast and monitor the proportion of various protected group members, such as women and minorities, that are in various job categories and career tracks. The proportion of workers in these subgroups can then be compared with the proportion that each subgroup represents in the relevant labor market. This type of comparison is called a **workforce utilization review.** This process can be used to determine whether there is any subgroup whose proportion in the relevant labor market is substantially different from the proportion in the job category.

**Workforce Utilization Review**
A comparison of the proportion of workers in protected subgroups with the proportion that each subgroup represents in the relevant labor market.

If such an analysis indicates that some group—for example, African Americans—makes up 35 percent of the relevant labor market for a job category but that this same group constitutes only 5 percent of the actual incumbents in that job category in that organization, then this is evidence of underutilization. Underutilization could come about because of problems in selection or from problems in internal movement, and this could be seen via the transitional matrices discussed earlier in this chapter.

This kind of review is critical for many different reasons. First, many firms adopt "voluntary affirmative action programs" to make sure underutilization does not occur and to promote diversity. Second, companies might also engage in utilization reviews because they are legally required to do so. For example, Executive Order 11246 requires that government contractors and subcontractors maintain affirmative action programs. Third, affirmative action programs can be mandated by the courts as part of the settlement of discrimination complaints.

These kinds of affirmative programs are often controversial because they are seen as unfair by many nonminorities.[41] Indeed, even some minorities feel that these kinds of programs unfairly stigmatize the most highly qualified minority applicants because of perceptions that their hiring was based on something other than their skills and abilities.[42] However, when the evidence provided from a workforce utilization review makes it clear that a specific minority group has been historically underrepresented because of past discrimination, and that increasing the level of representation will benefit workforce diversity and competitiveness, then these kinds of programs are easier to justify to all involved.[43]

Regardless of the motivation for adopting affirmative action planning, the steps required to execute such a plan are identical to the steps in the generic planning process discussed earlier in this chapter. That is, the company needs to assess current utilization patterns and then forecast how these are likely to change in the near future. If these analyses suggest current underutilization and if forecasts suggest that this problem is not likely to change, then the company may need to set goals and timetables for changing this situation. Certain strategic choices need to be made in the pursuit of these goals that might affect recruitment or selection practices, and then the success of these strategies has to be evaluated against the goals established earlier in the process.

## The Human Resource Recruitment Process

**Human Resource Recruitment**
The practice or activity carried on by the organization with the primary purpose of identifying and attracting potential employees.

As the first half of this chapter shows, it is difficult to always anticipate exactly how many (if any) new employees will have to be hired in a given year in a given job category. The role of human resource recruitment is to build a supply of potential new hires that the organization can draw on if the need arises. Thus **human resource recruitment** is defined as any practice or activity carried on by the organization with the primary purpose of identifying and attracting potential employees.[44] It thus creates a buffer between planning and actual selection of new employees, which is the topic of our next chapter.

Recruitment activities are designed to affect (1) the number of people who apply for vacancies, (2) the type of people who apply for them, and/or (3) the likelihood that those applying for vacancies will accept positions if offered.[45] The goal of an organizational recruitment program is to ensure that the organization has a number of reasonably qualified applicants (who would find the job acceptable) to choose from when a vacancy occurs.

The goal of the recruiting is not simply to generate large numbers of applicants. If the process generates a sea of unqualified applicants, the organization will incur great expense in personnel selection (as discussed more fully in the next chapter), but few vacancies will actually be filled. This problem of generating too many applicants is often promulgated by the use of wide-reaching technologies like the Internet to reach people. For example, when Trend Micro was trying to fill a management position, it posted an advertisement on several online job boards, which resulted in a flood of nearly 1,000 resumes.[46]

The goal of personnel recruitment is not to finely discriminate among reasonably qualified applicants either. Recruiting new personnel and selecting new personnel are both complex processes. Each task is hard enough to accomplish successfully, even when one is well focused. Organizations explicitly trying to do both at the same time will probably not do either well. For example, research suggests that recruiters provide less information about the company when conducting dual-purpose interviews (interviews focused on both recruiting and selecting applicants).[47] Also, applicants apparently remember less information about the recruiting organization after dual-purpose interviews.[48] Finally, applicants respond less positively to highly structured interviews, and yet this is precisely the type of interview that has the highest validity in terms of making effective screening decisions.[49]

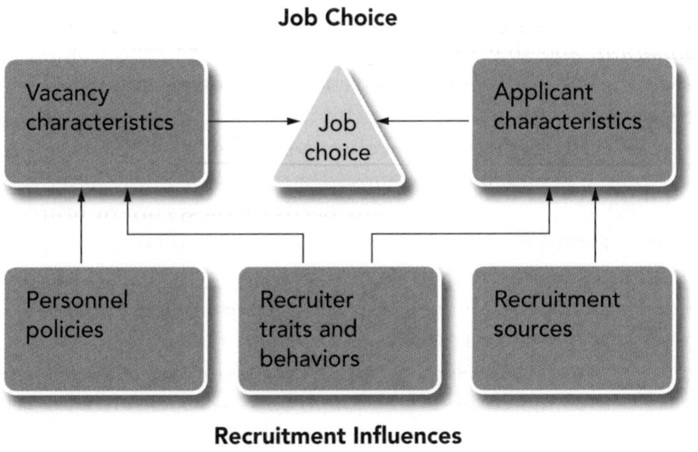


**figure 5.4**
Overview of the Individual Job Choice—Organizational Recruitment Process

Because of strategic differences among companies (see Chapter 2), the importance assigned to recruitment may differ.[50] In general, however, as shown in Figure 5.4, all companies have to make decisions in three areas of recruiting: (1) personnel policies, which affect the kinds of jobs the company has to offer; (2) recruitment sources used to solicit applicants, which affect the kinds of people who apply; and (3) the characteristics and behaviors of the recruiter. These, in turn, influence both the nature of the vacancies and the nature of the people applying for jobs in a way that shapes job choice decisions.[51]

## Personnel Policies

*Personnel policies* is a generic term we use to refer to organizational decisions that affect the nature of the vacancies for which people are recruited. If the research on recruitment makes one thing clear, it is that characteristics of the vacancy are more important than recruiters or recruiting sources when it comes to predicting job choice.[52]

**LO4**
Describe the Various Recruitment Policies That Organizations Adopt to Make Job Vacancies More Attractive.

### Internal versus External Recruiting

One desirable feature of a vacancy is that it provides ample opportunity for advancement and promotion. One organizational policy that affects this is the degree to which the company "promotes from within"—that is, recruits for upper-level vacancies internally rather than externally. Indeed, a 2001 survey of MBA students found that this was their top consideration when evaluating a company.[53]

We discuss internal versus external recruiting both here and in the section "Recruitment Sources" later in this chapter because this policy affects the nature of both the job and the individuals who apply. For now, we focus on the effects that promote-from-within policies have on job characteristics, noting that such policies make it clear to applicants that there are opportunities for advancement within the company. These opportunities spring not just from the first vacancy but from the vacancy created when a person in the company fills that vacancy. Similarly, during downtimes, organizations with strong internal recruiting orientations typically have developed information systems that support reassigning potentially dislocated workers to different jobs in the company. For example, at Wachovia Corporation, stock market slumps in 2003 created a labor surplus of investment bankers and many employees in this job category were threatened with a layoff. Because all the company's openings and résumés were in a common database, Wachovia could search for matches in skills sets and job requirements and in the process place over 50 percent of the investment bankers that would have been laid off into other positions in the organization.[54] Thus, internal staffing systems provide both opportunities for advancement during growth and opportunities for stable employment during declining periods.

The retailing industry is an example of an entire sector of the economy that is increasingly being perceived as an area with good opportunities for internal advancement. This is especially the case for the superstores, such as Wal-Mart, Home Depot, and Target, where thousands of managers must be hired and promoted each year to run new outlets. Applicants who used to shun retailing jobs are now attracted to them because of the opportunities for advancement. A new college graduate who goes to Target can have responsibility for 20 employees and an $8 million department just 12 weeks out of school. These trainees, if successful, can become managers of small stores in as little as three years. Some employees who started with Target at 24 years of age are regional senior vice presidents by the time they are 30.[55]

## Extrinsic and Intrinsic Rewards

Because pay is an important job characteristic for almost all applicants, companies that take a "lead-the-market" approach to pay—that is, a policy of paying higher-than-current-market wages—have a distinct advantage in recruiting. Pay can also make up for a job's less desirable features—for example, paying higher wages to employees who have to work midnight shifts. These kinds of specific shift differentials and other forms of more generic compensating differentials will be discussed in more detail in later chapters that focus on compensation strategies. We merely note here that "lead" policies make any given vacancy more attractive to applicants.

Increasingly, organizations that compete for applicants based on pay do so using pay forms other than wages and salary. In the 1990s many employers attempted to recruit employees with promises of stock option plans. However, the 2001 recession saw stock values drop sharply, thus reducing the attractiveness of this specific inducement. In addition, many people became aware of restrictions on stock option plans in the wake of the Enron bankruptcy in December 2001. Some low-level and midlevel Enron employees held stock options worth over $1 million. When Enron stock started to slide, the company prevented its employees from cashing out their options, leaving many to helplessly watch their stock become worthless. Other Enron employees whose 401(k) plans were entirely based on Enron stock (which they too could not sell) also suffered. It only made matters worse when the U.S. Securities and Exchange Commission suggested that Enron's top executives illegally made more than $1 billion off stock sales just prior to the bankruptcy announcement.

There are limits to what can be done in terms of using pay to attract people to certain jobs, however. For example, the U.S. Army, because of the ongoing wars in Iraq and Afghanistan, struggled and failed to meet its 2005 recruiting goals for new soldiers, despite offering a $20,000 signing bonus and a $400 a month raise in base pay for infantry positions. As General Michael Rochelle, head of Army recruiting, notes, "We can't get started down a slippery slope where we are depending on money to lure people in. The reality is that while we have to remain at least competitive, we're never going to be able to pay as much as the private sector." To offset this disadvantage in extrinsic financial rewards, the Army has to rely on more intrinsic rewards related to patriotism and personal growth opportunities that people associate with military service. For example, Rochelle suggests that "the idea that being a soldier strengthens you for today and for tomorrow, for whatever you go on to do in life, that clearly resonates with them," and thus this serves as an alternative means of appealing to recruits.[56] The Army's Partnership for Youth Success Program uses this idea to match recruits with private-sector employers who are interested in hiring former soldiers who have received the skills and experiences that the Army provides.

The Army also uses partnerships to help retain current soldiers, and one of these focuses on spouses. Because of the short-term nature of military deployments, spouses in the military have often struggled to find stable employment, and since marital discord is a primary negative influence on reenlistment, helping the spouses of soldiers can in turn promote retention. The Army partners with firms like Home Depot, Sprint, CVS, Sears, and Dell because these employers have many branches in different parts of the country. Thus, if the soldier is forced to redeploy from one base to another, the private company may well have openings that would allow the spouse to simply transfer from one branch to another. Partnerships like this help support soldiers but do not necessarily result in direct competition on pay with respect to private employers.[57]

Home Depot has this same type of recruiting partnership with other organizations such as the American Association of Retired Persons (AARP). The AARP signs up interested members as part of a database and then works with Home Depot to find suitable jobs for its members. Because many AARP members have outside income from pensions or Social Security, competition on wages is not as significant a factor for this segment of the labor force as it is for younger workers who are raising families. Moreover, Home Depot's own research makes it clear that the turnover and absenteeism rates are lower for older workers than for their younger colleagues. As Home Depot's CEO notes, "When you look at the knowledge and career experience, and the passion of the members of the AARP, this is a gold mine of resources to draw upon, and this helps us gain competitive advantage."[58]

## Employment-at-Will Policies

**Employment-at-will policies** state that either party in the employment relationship can terminate that relationship at any time, regardless of cause. Companies that do not have employment-at-will provisions typically have extensive due process policies. **Due process policies** formally lay out the steps an employee can take to appeal a termination decision. Recent court decisions have increasingly eroded employers' rights to terminate employees with impunity.[59] To protect themselves from wrongful discharge suits, employers have been encouraged to state explicitly, in all formal recruiting documentation, that the employment is "at will."

**Employment-at-Will Policies**
Policies which state that either an employer or an employee can terminate the employment relationship at any time, regardless of cause.

Some authors have gone so far as to suggest that all mention of due process should be eliminated from company handbooks, personnel manuals, and recruiting brochures.[60] Although this may have some legal advantages, job security is an important feature to many job applicants. Organizational recruiting materials that emphasize due process, rights of appeal, and grievance mechanisms send a message that job security is high; employment-at-will policies suggest the opposite. Research indicates that job applicants find companies with due process policies more attractive than companies with employment-at-will policies.[61]

**Due Process Policies**
Policies by which a company formally lays out the steps an employee can take to appeal a termination decision.

## Image Advertising

Organizations often advertise specific vacancies (discussed below in the section "Recruitment Sources"). Sometimes, however, organizations advertise just to promote themselves as a good place to work in general.[62] Image advertising is particularly important for companies in highly competitive labor markets that perceive themselves as having a bad image.[63] Indeed, research evidence suggests that the impact of company image on applicant reactions ranks second only to the nature of the work itself.[64]

Even though it does not provide any information about any specific job, image advertising is often effective because job applicants develop ideas about the general reputation of the firm (i.e., its brand image) and then this spills over to influence their expectations about the nature of specific jobs or careers at the organization.[65] Although someone once said that there is no such thing as bad publicity, this is not always true when it comes to recruiting. Although familiarity is better than lack of familiarity in general, applicants seem to be especially sensitive to bad publicity, and thus advertising campaigns are often used to try to send a positive message about the organization.[66] Although a firm can try to create an image using television advertisements or Web pages, research suggests that face-to-face contact (such as that provided by job fairs) is a much stronger avenue to enhance one's image.[67]

Research suggests that the language associated with the organization's brand image is often similar to personality trait descriptions that one might more commonly use to describe another person (such as innovative or competent or sincere).[68] These perceptions then influence the degree to which the person feels attracted to the organization, especially if there appears to be a good fit between the traits of the applicant and the traits that describe the organization.[69] Applicants seem particularly sensitive to issues of diversity and inclusion in these types of advertisements, and hence organizations that advertise their image need to go out of their way to ensure that the actors in their advertisements reflect the broad nature of the labor market constituencies that they are trying to appeal to in terms of race, gender, and culture.[70]

Whether the goal is to influence the perception of the public in general or specific segments of the labor market, research clearly shows that job seekers form beliefs about the nature of organizations well before they have any direct interviewing experience with those companies. Thus, it is critical for organizations to systematically assess their reputation in the labor market and redress any shortcomings they detect relative to their desired image.[71]

## Recruitment Sources

**LO5**
List the Various Sources from Which Job Applicants Can Be Drawn, Their Relative Advantages and Disadvantages, and the Methods for Evaluating Them.

The sources from which a company recruits potential employees are a critical aspect of its overall recruitment strategy. The total labor market is expansive; any single organization needs to draw from only a fraction of that total. The size and nature of the fraction that applies for an organization's vacancies will be affected by how (and to whom) the organization communicates its vacancies.[72] The type of person who is likely to respond to a job advertised on the Internet may be different from the type of person who responds to an ad in the classified section of a local newspaper. In this section we examine the different sources from which recruits can be drawn, highlighting the advantages and disadvantages of each.

### Internal versus External Sources

We discussed internal versus external sources of recruits earlier in this chapter and focused on the positive effects that internal recruiting can have on recruits' perceptions of job characteristics. We will now discuss this issue again, but with a focus on how using internal sources affects the kinds of people who are recruited.

In general, relying on internal sources offers a company several advantages.[73] First, it generates a sample of applicants who are well known to the firm. Second, these applicants are relatively knowledgeable about the company's vacancies, which minimizes the possibility of inflated expectations about the job. Third, it is generally cheaper and faster to fill vacancies internally.

A good example of the value of an internal recruitment system can be seen in the experience of Sun Trust. In 2000, Sun Trust, a large and diversified banking institution with close to 30,000 employees, was organized into 28 separate regional centers, each with its own Human Resource Department. Each department operated independently, and thus they all had different technologies, different services, and different forms and procedures for all sorts of HR activities including recruiting. This precluded any form of coordinated activity across regions and also created huge redundancies and inefficiencies. In 2002, the organization restructured its Human Resource Department and went from being a decentralized and divisional structure to a more centralized and functional structure (see Chapter 4 for a discussion of these different dimensions of structure), Job descriptions and recruiting practices were standardized, and all existing employees' skill sets were entered into a central database to promote internal movement within the organization. One year later, the time it took to fill a vacancy went from 30 days to 20 days, and the cost per hire dropped from $1,100 to $900. Much of this was attributed to the more efficient utilization of internal applicants.[74]

With all these advantages, you might ask why any organization would ever employ external recruiting methods. There are several good reasons why organizations might decide to recruit externally.[75] First, for entry-level positions and perhaps even for some specialized upper-level positions, there may not be any internal recruits from which to draw. Second, bringing in outsiders may expose the organization to new ideas or new ways of doing business. Using only internal recruitment can result in a workforce whose members all think alike and who therefore may be poorly suited to innovation.[76] For example, for most of its 100-year history, retailer J.C. Penney followed a practice of strictly promoting from within. This led to a very strong culture that in many ways was still closely related to the one first established by J.C. Penney himself in the late 1800s. The company's image was very conservative, and the behavior and attire of the employees was very formal. This culture made it difficult to attract and retain younger workers, however, and the accounting department estimated that turnover was costing the company $400 million a year. To stem the tide, J.C. Penney brought in an outsider, Mike Ullman, as the new CEO in 2006, and his first steps in redirecting the company were to loosen up the culture and hire more outsiders into key management positions. This was central to the CEO's new competitive strategy, in the sense that, in Ullman's own words, "In retailing today, you have to realize there is too much property and too much merchandise—what there isn't enough of is talent. If I had a choice to honor the past and lose, or move forward and win, I pick winning."[77]

**Direct Applicants**
People who apply for a job vacancy without prompting from the organization.

## Direct Applicants and Referrals

**Direct applicants** are people who apply for a vacancy without prompting from the organization. **Referrals** are people who are prompted to apply by someone within the organization. These two sources of recruits share some characteristics that make them excellent sources from which to draw.

**Referrals**
People who are prompted to apply for a job by someone within the organization.

First, many direct applicants are to some extent already "sold" on the organization. Most of them have done some homework and concluded that there is enough fit between themselves and the vacancy to warrant their submitting an application. This process is called *self-selection*. A form of aided self-selection occurs with referrals. Many job seekers look to friends, relatives, and acquaintances to help find employment, and evoking these social networks can greatly aid the job search process for both the job seeker and the organization.[78] Current employees (who are knowledgeable of both the vacancy and the person they are referring) do their homework and conclude that there is a fit between the person and the vacancy; they then sell the person on the job. Indeed, research shows that new hires that used at least one informal source reported having greater prehire knowledge of the organization than those who relied exclusively on formal recruitment sources. Those who report having multiple sources were even better, however, in terms of both prehire knowledge about the position and subsequent turnover. In fact, the turnover rate for applicants who came from multiple recruiting sources was half that of those recruited via campus interviews or newspaper advertisements.[79] Ironically, as more and more recruiting is accomplished via impersonal sources like the Internet, the ability to draw on personal sources of information on recruits is becoming even more valuable. At companies like Sprint, the percentage of new hires from this source has gone from 8 percent to 34 percent in the last three years alone.[80]

When one figures into these results the low costs of such sources, they clearly stand out as one of the best sources of new hires, and some employers even offer financial incentives to current employees for referring applicants who are accepted and perform acceptably on the job (stay 180 days, for example).[81] Other companies play off their good reputations in the labor market to generate direct applications. In the war for talent, some employers who try to entice one new employee from a competitor will often try to leverage that one person to try to entice even more people away. The term "liftout" has been coined for this practice of trying to recruit a whole team of people. For example, when Mike Mertz was recruited as the new chief executive at Optimus, a computer servicing outfit, within hours of leaving his former employer, he in turn recruited seven other former colleagues to join Optimus. Liftouts are seen as valuable because in recruiting a whole intact group, as Mertz notes, "You get the dynamics of a functioning team without having to create that yourself."[82] Indeed, the team chemistry and coordination that often takes years to build is already in place after a liftout, and this kind of speed provides competitive advantage. Of course, having a whole team lifted out of your organization is devastating, because customers are frequently next to leave, following the talent rather than standing pat, and hence firms have to work hard to make sure that they can retain their critical teams.

Of course, referrals do not necessarily have to come just from current employees. The importance of good community relations to recruitment can be seen in the experience of Papa John's Pizza, which was once rated number one on *BusinessWeek*'s list of 100 Best Small Companies in America. Papa John's, one of the fastest-growing companies in the United States, had relied on classified ads to find drivers and store employees. This method was highly unreliable, however, because the company did not have the facilities to develop sophisticated tests of people's skills and attitudes. Store managers are now encouraged to make professional contacts within their communities, such as with the principal or guidance counselor at the local high school, leaders of church groups, and coaches in youth sports leagues. Store managers can then use these contacts to help generate referrals among promising young applicants. These community relationships help connect Papa John's to youths who have established good reputations in their community for reliability and trustworthiness. As one industry analyst notes, "I think the greatest advantage for Papa John's is recruitment. Once you get your feet wet recruiting that way, you can move on to bigger and better things."[83]

## Advertisements in Newspapers and Periodicals

Advertisements to recruit personnel are ubiquitous, even though they typically generate less desirable recruits than direct applications or referrals—and do so at greater expense. However, because few employers can fill all their vacancies with direct applications and referrals, some form of advertising is usually needed. Moreover, an employer can take many steps to increase the effectiveness of this recruitment method.

The two most important questions to ask in designing a job advertisement are, What do we need to say? and To whom do we need to say it? With respect to the first question, many organizations fail to adequately communicate the specifics of the vacancy. Ideally, persons reading an ad should get enough information to evaluate the job and its requirements, allowing them to make a well-informed judgment regarding their qualifications. This could mean running long advertisements, which costs more. However, these additional costs should be evaluated against the costs of processing a huge number of applicants who are not reasonably qualified or who would not find the job acceptable once they learn more about it.

Perhaps the biggest problem with most advertisements is that they are often written to be overdemanding in terms of the actual skill requirements that are needed for the work, decreasing the number of legitimate applicants more than necessary. Some have estimated that roughly half of the labor shortage in certain engineering fields can be traced to this problem. For example, as one recruiter of software engineers noted with respect to his company's search policy, "I say smart people can learn sister applications, but there is a reluctance among hiring managers to see that. If they use a SAP database system, they won't even look at someone with experience with PeopleSoft."[84]

In terms of whom to reach with this message, the organization placing the advertisement has to decide which medium it will use. The classified section of local newspapers is the most common medium. It is a relatively inexpensive means of reaching many people within a specified geographic area who are currently looking for work (or at least interested enough to be reading the classifieds). On the downside, this medium does not allow an organization to target skill levels very well. Typically, classified ads are read by many people who are either over- or underqualified for the position. Moreover, people who are not looking for work rarely read the classifieds, and thus this is not the right medium for luring people away from their current employers. Specially targeted journals and periodicals may be better than general newspapers at reaching a specific part of the overall labor market. In addition, employers are increasingly using television—particularly cable television—as a reasonably priced way of reaching people.[85]

## Electronic Recruiting

The growth of the information superhighway has opened up new vistas for organizations trying to recruit talent. There are many ways to employ the Internet, and increasingly organizations are refining their use of this medium. In fact, a recent survey of HR executives indicated that electronic job boards were the most effective source of recruits for 36 percent of the respondents, well ahead of local newspapers (21 percent), job fairs (4 percent), and walk-ins and referrals (1 percent).[86]

Obviously, one of the easiest ways to get into "e-cruiting" is to simply use the organization's own Web page to solicit applications. By using their own Web page, organizations can highly tune their recruitment message and focus in on specific people. For example, the interactive nature of this medium allows individuals to fill out surveys that describe what they are looking for and what they have to offer the organizations. These surveys can be "graded" immediately and recruits can be given direct feedback about how well they are matched for the organization. Research shows that this type of immediate feedback regarding their fit is helpful both to recruits and to the organization, by quickly and cheaply eliminating misfits for either side.[87]

Of course, smaller and less well-known organizations may not attract any attention to their own Web sites, and thus for them this is not a good option. A second way for organizations to use the Web is to interact with the large, well-known job sites such as Monster.com, HotJobs.com, or CareerBuilder.com. These sites attract a vast array of applicants, who submit standardized résumés that can be electronically searched using key terms. Applicants can also search for companies in a similar fashion; the hope, of course, is that there may be a match between the employer and the applicant. The biggest downside to these large sites, however, is their sheer size and lack of differentiation. Because of this limitation of the large sites, smaller, more tailored Web sites called "niche boards" focus on certain industries, occupations, or geographic areas. For example, Telecommcareers.net is a site devoted to, as the name implies, the telecommunications industry. CIO.com, a companion site to *CIO Magazine*, is an occupational board that specializes in openings for chief information officers. The best evidence regarding the growing popularity and effectiveness of these niche boards can be seen in the behaviors of the larger sites, which are scrambling to create more focused subsections of their own.[88] Clearly this dynamic area of human resource management is one where innovative, forward-thinking managers can gain competitive advantage. Indeed, the "Competing through Technology" box illustrates some of the more recent technological developments that have been turned into recruitment vehicles.

## Public and Private Employment Agencies

The Social Security Act of 1935 requires that everyone receiving unemployment compensation be registered with a local state employment office. These state employment offices work with the U.S. Employment Service (USES) to try to ensure that unemployed individuals eventually get off state aid and back on employer payrolls. To accomplish this, agencies collect information from the unemployed about their skills and experiences.

Employers can register their job vacancies with their local state employment office, and the agency will attempt to find someone suitable using its computerized inventory of local unemployed individuals. The agency makes referrals to the organization at no charge, and these individuals can be interviewed or tested by the employer for potential vacancies. Because of certain legislative mandates, state unemployment offices often have specialized "desks" for minorities, handicapped individuals, and Vietnam-era veterans. Thus, this is an excellent source for employers who feel they are currently underutilizing any of these subgroups.

Public employment agencies serve primarily the blue-collar labor market; private employment agencies perform much the same service for the white-collar labor market. Unlike public agencies, however, private employment agencies charge the organization for the referrals. Another difference between private and public employment agencies is that one doesn't have to be unemployed to use a private employment agency.

One special type of private employment agency is the so-called executive search firm (ESF). These agencies are often referred to as *headhunters* because, unlike the other sources we have examined, they operate almost exclusively with people who are currently employed. Dealing with executive search firms is sometimes a sensitive process because executives may not want to advertise their availability for fear of their current employer's reaction. Thus, ESFs serve as an important confidentiality buffer between the employer and the recruit.

## COMPETING THROUGH TECHNOLOGY

### The Next Generation of Web-Based Recruiting Tools

The ability of the World Wide Web to grant access to large numbers of people has always made it a unique type of recruiting tool. In the beginning, this medium was used primarily as just another form of public relations as companies designed Web sites that would allow interested applicants to learn about their organization and then, if they felt there was a potential match, apply for work. Job posting boards such as Monster.com and CareerBuilder.com often supplemented these firm-specific sites and allowed applicants and employers a way to meet in cyberspace by listing résumés and job descriptions. As the Web has developed and evolved, the use of the Web by recruiters has become more sophisticated.

For example, the increased familiarity of Web devotees with Web logs, or "blogs," has created the opportunity for recruiters to reach out and have public or semipublic conversations with recruits. A blog is basically an online journal and different people can contribute to a streaming conversation and each contribution is recorded in chronological order. Microsoft's senior recruiter for marketing, Heather Hamilton, manages a blog that describes what it is like to work at a marketing career at Microsoft. Interested candidates can read what she posts and then ask questions or provide their own information. This allows many other "passive" applicants to see the answers to previous questions or what other people who are applying to the organization are like. In one week alone, this blog was viewed by over 25,000 people, and as Hamiton notes, "The big thing for me is reach . . . as a recruiter, I could be on the phone all day every day and not be able to reach that many people."

The growing use of iPods has also opened up a new and rich avenue to get information from employer to applicant via Podcasts. A Podcast is an audio or audiovisual program that can be placed on the Web by an employer and then downloaded onto a computer or an iPod for subsequent viewing. Podcasts are like e-mails in the sense that they can be used to reach out to a large number of people; however, the rich nature of the medium, which employs color, sound, and video, is much more powerful than a simple text-only e-mail. "Podcasts really make the job description come alive," notes Dan Finnigan, a general manager at HotJobs.com, "and the ability to describe the organization's culture is so much more emotionally charged with this medium relative to mere words on a page."

Social Networking sites such a Facebook and MySpace.com are yet another avenue for employers to reach out to younger workers in their own environments. Neither Facebook nor MySpace allows employers to create pages as members, but it does allow them to purchase pages in order to create what is called a "sponsored group." Ernst & Young's sponsored group page has been joined by over 5,000 Facebook users, who can access information about Ernst & Young and chat with recruiters from the company in a bloglike manner. Unlike more formal media, the conversations held here are very informal and serve as an easy first step for potential recruits to take in their relationship with the company.

As with any new and developing technology, all of these new approaches present their own unique challenges. From an employer's perspective, the interactive, dynamic, and unpredictable nature of blogs and social networking sites means that sometimes people who have negative things to say about the organization join in on the conversations, and this can be difficult to control. The biggest liability from the applicants' perspective is the need to protect their identity, because this medium has also been a haven for identity thieves, who post false openings in the hope of getting some applicant to provide personal information. In general, applicants interacting with these types of sites should never provide Social Security numbers or set up bank accounts or submit to security checks until they have visited the employer and had a personal meeting. These sites help employers and applicants take the first step toward building a relationship, and these other steps should not be taken until much, much later.

SOURCES: K.Maher, "Blogs Catch on As Recruiting Tool," *The Wall Street Journal*, September 28, 2004, p. B10; A. Singh, "Podcasts Extend Recruiters Reach," *The Wall Street Journal*, April 24, 2006, p. B3; E. White, "Ernst & Young Reaches Out to Recruits on Facebook," *The Wall Street Journal*, January 8, 2007, p. B5; D. Mattioli, "Who's Reading On-line Résumés? Identity Crooks," *The Wall Street Journal*, October 17, 2006, p. B9.

## Colleges and Universities

Most colleges and universities have placement services that seek to help their graduates obtain employment. Indeed, on-campus interviewing is the most important source of recruits for entry-level professional and managerial vacancies.[89] Organizations tend to focus especially on colleges that have strong reputations in areas for which they have critical needs (chemical engineering, public accounting, or the like).[90]

Many employers have found that to effectively compete for the best students, they need to do more than just sign prospective graduates up for interview slots. One of the best ways to establish a stronger presence on a campus is with a college internship program. For example, Dun & Bradstreet funds a summer intern program for minority MBA students and often hires these interns for full-time positions when they graduate.[91] These kinds of programs allow an organization to get early access to potential applicants and to assess their capacities directly.

Another way of increasing one's presence on campus is to participate in university job fairs. In general, a job fair is a place where many employers gather for a short time to meet large numbers of potential job applicants. Although job fairs can be held anywhere (such as at a hotel or convention center), campuses are ideal locations because of the many well-educated, yet unemployed, individuals who live there. Job fairs are a rather inexpensive means of generating an on-campus presence and can even provide one-on-one dialogue with potential recruits—dialogue that could not be achieved through less interactive media like newspaper ads.

Finally, as more organizations attempt to compete on a global level, the ability to recruit individuals who will be successful both at home and abroad is a growing concern. Many organizations feel that college campuses are one of the best places to search for this type of transportable talent. Molex Inc., for example, is a U.S. technology firm with 8,000 employees, only 2,000 of whom live in the United States. Molex derives 70 percent of its $950 million in annual sales from outside the United States, and thus the majority of workers are expatriates, local nationals, or foreign service employees. Three aspects of Molex's recruitment strategy are critical to its success in attaining an internationally talented workforce.

First, Molex focuses on recruiting college students. As one manager at Molex states, "We have had more success molding younger people into this company and into overseas assignments than taking more experienced people who've worked for other companies." Second, Molex recruits many foreigners (especially MBA candidates) who are studying in the United States for assignments back in their native country. These individuals have the best of both worlds in terms of having a formal education in U.S. business practices and also understanding both the language and culture of their home country. Finally, when recruiting U.S. students, Molex requires that each person hired be fluent in both English and one other language. This commitment to multilingual competency can be seen at the national headquarters, where 15 different languages are spoken.[92]

## Evaluating the Quality of a Source

Because there are few rules about the quality of a given source for a given vacancy, it is generally a good idea for employers to monitor the quality of all their recruitment sources. One means of accomplishing this is to develop and compare yield ratios for each source.[93] Yield ratios express the percentage of applicants who successfully move from one stage of the recruitment and selection process to the next. Comparing yield ratios for different sources helps determine which is best or most efficient for the type of vacancy being investigated. Data on cost per hire are also useful in establishing the efficiency of a given source.[94]

**table 5.4**

Hypothetical Yield Ratios for Five Recruitment Sources

| | RECRUITING SOURCE | | | | |
|---|---|---|---|---|---|
| | LOCAL UNIVERSITY | RENOWNED UNIVERSITY | EMPLOYEE REFERRALS | NEWSPAPER AD | EXECUTIVE SEARCH FIRMS |
| Résumés generated | 200 | 400 | 50 | 500 | 20 |
| Interview offers accepted | 175 | 100 | 45 | 400 | 20 |
| Yield ratio | 87% | 25% | 90% | 80% | 100% |
| Applicants judged acceptable | 100 | 95 | 40 | 50 | 19 |
| Yield ratio | 57% | 95% | 89% | 12% | 95% |
| Accept employment offers | 90 | 10 | 35 | 25 | 15 |
| Yield ratio | 90% | 11% | 88% | 50% | 79% |
| Cumulative yield ratio | 90/200<br>45% | 10/400<br>3% | 35/50<br>70% | 25/500<br>5% | 15/20<br>75% |
| Cost | $30,000 | $50,000 | $15,000 | $20,000 | $90,000 |
| Cost per hire | $333 | $5,000 | $428 | $800 | $6,000 |

Table 5.4 shows hypothetical yield ratios and cost-per-hire data for five recruitment sources. For the job vacancies generated by this company, the best two sources of recruits are local universities and employee referral programs. Newspaper ads generate the largest number of recruits, but relatively few of these are qualified for the position. Recruiting at nationally renowned universities generates highly qualified applicants, but relatively few of them ultimately accept positions. Finally, executive search firms generate a small list of highly qualified, interested applicants, but this is an expensive source compared with other alternatives.

## Recruiters

**LO6**
Explain the Recruiter's Role in the Recruitment Process, the Limits the Recruiter Faces, and the Opportunities Available.

The last part of the model presented in Figure 5.4 that we will discuss is the recruiter. We consider the recruiter this late in the chapter to reinforce our earlier observation that the recruiter often gets involved late in the process. In many cases, by the time a recruiter meets some applicants, they have already made up their minds about what they desire in a job, what the current job has to offer, and their likelihood of receiving a job offer.[95]

Moreover, many applicants approach the recruiter with some degree of skepticism. Knowing that it is the recruiter's job to sell them on a vacancy, some applicants may discount what the recruiter says relative to what they have heard from other sources (like friends, magazine articles, and professors). For these and other reasons, recruiters' characteristics and behaviors seem to have less impact on applicants' job choices than we might expect. Moreover, as shown in Figure 5.5, whatever impact a recruiter does have on an applicant lessens as we move from reaction criteria (how the applicant felt about the recruiter) toward job choice criteria (whether the applicant takes the job).[96]

***Recruiter's Functional Area.*** Most organizations must choose whether their recruiters are specialists in human resources or experts at particular jobs (supervisors or job incumbents). Some studies indicate that applicants find a job less attractive and the recruiter less credible when he is a personnel specialist.[97] This does not completely discount personnel specialists' role in recruiting, but it does indicate that such specialists need to take extra steps to ensure that applicants perceive them as knowledgeable and credible.

figure 5.5

Relative Impact of the Recruiter on Various Recruitment Interview Outcomes

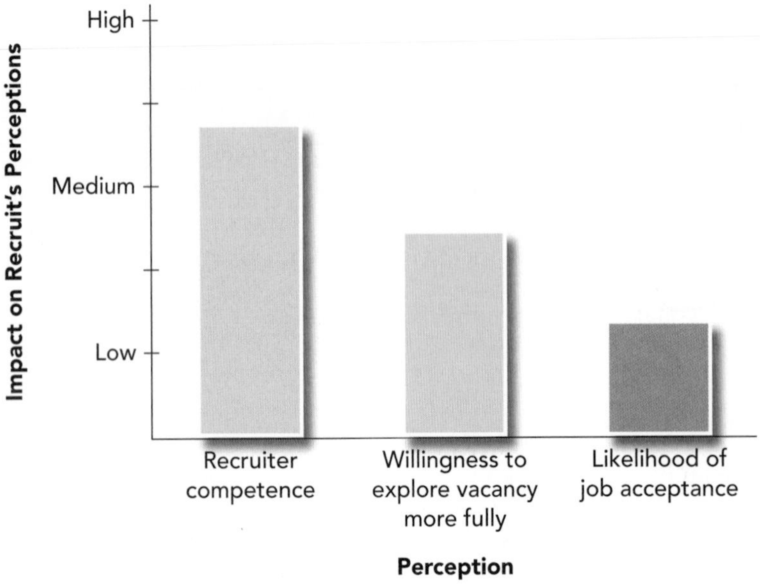


***Recruiter's Traits.*** Two traits stand out when applicants' reactions to recruiters are examined. The first, which could be called "warmth," reflects the degree to which the recruiter seems to care about the applicant and is enthusiastic about her potential to contribute to the company. The second characteristic could be called "informativeness." In general, applicants respond more positively to recruiters who are perceived as warm and informative. These characteristics seem more important than such demographic characteristics as age, sex, or race, which have complex and inconsistent effects on applicant responses.[98]

***Recruiter's Realism.*** Perhaps the most well-researched aspect of recruiting deals with the level of realism that the recruiter incorporates into his message. Since the recruiter's job is to attract candidates, there is some pressure to exaggerate the positive features of the vacancy while downplaying the negative features. Applicants are highly sensitive to negative information. Research suggests that the highest-quality applicants may be less willing to pursue jobs when this type of information comes out.[99] On the other hand, if the recruiter goes too far in a positive direction, the candidate can be misled and lured into taking the job under false pretenses.[100] This can lead to a serious case of unmet expectations and a high turnover rate.[101] In fact, unrealistic descriptions of a job may even lead new job incumbents to believe that the employer is deceitful.[102]

Many studies have looked at the capacity of "realistic job previews" to circumvent this problem and help minimize early job turnover. On the whole, the research indicates that realistic job previews do lower expectations and can help reduce future turnover in the workforce.[103] Certainly, the idea that one can go overboard in selling a vacancy to a recruit has merit. However, the belief that informing people about the negative characteristics of the job will totally "inoculate" them to such characteristics seems unwarranted, based on the research conducted to date.[104] Thus we return to the conclusion that an organization's decisions about personnel policies that directly affect the job's attributes (pay, security, advancement opportunities, and so on) will probably be more important than recruiter traits and behaviors in affecting job choice. Indeed, research indicates that structured interventions that help applicants simply make good decisions about which jobs are best for them may work out best for both employers and applicants. That is, helping applicants better understand their own needs and qualifications and then linking this to the current openings may be best in the long run for all concerned, even if it does not result in an immediate hire.[105]

***Enhancing Recruiter Impact.*** Although research suggests that recruiters do not have much influence on job choice, this does not mean recruiters cannot have an impact. For example, in contexts where applicants already have high awareness of the organization because its products are well known, the impact of the recruiter is weaker than in contexts where the applicant has low product awareness.[106] Organizations can take several steps to increase the impact that recruiters have on those they recruit. First, recruiters can provide timely feedback. Applicants react very negatively to delays in feedback, often making unwarranted attributions for the delays (such as, the organization is uninterested in my application). Second, recruiters need to avoid behaviors that might convey the wrong organizational impression.[107] Table 5.5 lists quotes from applicants who felt that they had had extremely bad experiences with recruiters. Third, recruiting can be done in teams rather than by individuals. As we have seen, applicants tend to view line personnel (job incumbents and supervisors) as more credible than personnel specialists, so these kinds of recruiters should be part of any team. On the other hand, personnel specialists have knowledge that is not shared by line personnel (who may perceive recruiting as a small part of their "real" jobs), so they should be included as well.

**table 5.5**

Quotes from Recruits Who Were Repelled by Recruiters

| |
|---|
| One firm I didn't think of talking to initially, but they called me and asked me to talk with them. So I did, and then the recruiter was very, very rude. Yes, very rude, and I've run into that a couple of times. (engineering graduate) |
| I had a very bad campus interview experience . . . the person who came was a last-minute fill-in. . . . I think he had a couple of "issues" and was very discourteous during the interview. He was one step away from yawning in my face. . . . The other thing he did was that he kept making these (nothing illegal, mind you) but he kept making these references to the fact that I had been out of my undergraduate and first graduate programs for more than 10 years now. (MBA with 10 years of experience) |
| ________ has a management training program which the recruiter had gone through. She was talking about the great presentational skills that ________ teaches you, and the woman was barely literate. She was embarrassing. If that was the best they could do, I did not want any part of them. Also, ________ and ________'s recruiters appeared to have real attitude problems. I also thought they were chauvinistic. (arts undergraduate) |
| ________ had a set schedule for me which they deviated from regularly. Times overlapped, and one person kept me too long, which pushed the whole day back. They almost seemed to be saying that it was my fault that I was late for the next one! I guess a lot of what they did just wasn't very professional. Even at the point when I was done, where most companies would have a cab pick you up, I was in the middle of a snowstorm in Chicago and they said, "You can get a cab downstairs." There weren't any cabs. I literally had to walk 12 or 14 blocks with my luggage, trying to find some way to get to the airport. They didn't book me a hotel for the night of the snowstorm so I had to sit in the airport for eight hours trying to get another flight. . . . They wouldn't even reimburse me for the additional plane fare. (industrial relations graduate student) |
| The guy at the interview made a joke about how nice my nails were and how they were going to ruin them there due to all the tough work. (engineering undergraduate) |

SOURCE: S. L. Rynes, R. D. Bretz Jr., and B. Gerhart, "The Importance of Recruitment in Job Choice: A Different Way of Looking," *Personnel Psychology* 44 (1991), pp. 487–521. Used by permission.

## A Look Back

Our chapter opening story on the immigration battle showed clearly how employers do not exist in a vacuum, and how changes in labor markets and product markets create a constant struggle to find and retain the most talented and motivated workers at the lowest cost. Managers and human resource professionals can help their firms win this struggle by doing an effective job in terms of human resource planning and recruitment. Early anticipation of a labor surplus allows a firm to use less disruptive labor reduction strategies, and early identification of labor shortages allows employers to use more creative and effective recruitment techniques.

**Questions**

1. At the national level, what steps can politicians and labor leaders take to help their citizens and members compete in an ever-changing labor market?
2. At the firm level, what steps can organizational leaders and human resource professionals take to help their companies prosper in times of rapid change and turbulence?
3. At the individual level, what can you and other job seekers do to ensure that you will always have access to a high-paying, secure job that you find interesting and challenging?

Please see the Video Case that corresponds to this chapter online at www.mhhe.com/noe6e.

## Summary

Human resource planning uses labor supply and demand forecasts to anticipate labor shortages and surpluses. It also entails programs that can be utilized to reduce a labor surplus (such as downsizing and early retirement programs) and eliminate a labor shortage (like bringing in temporary workers or expanding overtime). When done well, human resource planning can enhance the success of the organization while minimizing the human suffering resulting from poorly anticipated labor surpluses or shortages. Human resource recruiting is a buffer activity that creates an applicant pool that the organization can draw from in the event of a labor shortage that is to be filled with new hires. Organizational recruitment programs affect applications through personnel policies (such as promote-from-within policies or due process provisions) that affect the attributes of the vacancies themselves. They can also impact the nature of people who apply for positions by using different recruitment sources (like recruiting from universities versus advertising in newspapers). Finally, organizations can use recruiters to influence individuals' perceptions of jobs (eliminating misconceptions, clarifying uncertainties) or perceptions of themselves (changing their valences for various work outcomes).

## Key Terms

Forecasting, 186
Leading indicator, 187
Transitional matrix, 188
Downsizing, 192
Outsourcing, 197
Offshoring, 198
Workforce utilization review, 201
Human resource recruitment, 202
Employment-at-will policies, 205
Due process policies, 205
Direct applicants, 207
Referrals, 207

## Discussion Questions

1. Discuss the effects that an impending labor shortage might have on the following three subfunctions of human resource management: selection and placement, training and career development, and compensation and benefits. Which subfunction might be most heavily impacted? In what ways might these groups develop joint cooperative programs to avert a labor shortage?
2. Discuss the costs and benefits associated with statistical versus judgmental forecasts for labor demand and labor supply. Under what conditions might either of these techniques be infeasible? Under what conditions might both be feasible, but one more desirable than the other?
3. Some companies have detailed affirmative action plans, complete with goals and timetables, for women and minorities, and yet have no formal human resource plan for the organization as a whole. Why might this be the case? If you were a human resource specialist interviewing with this company for an open position, what would this practice imply for the role of the human resource manager in that company?
4. Recruiting people for jobs that entail international assignments is increasingly important for many companies. Where might one go to look for individuals interested in these types of assignments? How might recruiting practices aimed at these people differ from those one might apply to the "average" recruit?
5. Discuss the relative merits of internal versus external recruitment. What types of business strategies might best be supported by recruiting externally, and what types might call for internal recruitment? What factors might lead a firm to decide to switch from internal to external recruitment or vice versa?

## Self-Assessment Exercise

Most employers have to evaluate hundreds of résumés each week. If you want your résumé to have a good chance of being read by prospective employers, you must invest time and energy not only in its content, but also in its look. Review your résumé and answer yes or no to each of the following questions.

1. Does it avoid typos and grammatical errors?
2. Does it avoid using personal pronouns (such as I and me)?
3. Does it clearly identify what you have done and accomplished?
4. Does it highlight your accomplishments rather than your duties?
5. Does it exceed two pages in length?
6. Does it have correct contact information?
7. Does it have an employment objective that is specific and focuses on the employer's needs as well as your own?
8. Does it have at least one-inch margins?
9. Does it use a maximum of two typefaces or fonts?
10. Does it use bullet points to emphasize your skills and accomplishments?
11. Does it avoid use of underlining?
12. Is the presentation consistent? (Example: If you use all caps for the name of your most recent workplace, do you do that for previous workplaces as well?)

The more "yes" answers you gave, the more likely your résumé will attract an employer's attention and get you a job interview!

## Exercising Strategy: Southwest Airlines: Focused on Take-Offs, Not Layoffs

In the summer of 2001, the airline industry was facing severe problems due to slumping business travel and vacationer demand. In fact, Northwest Airlines announced draconian cuts in both schedules and service; Midway Airlines declared bankruptcy in August of that year, citing a "calamitous" decline in air traffic. However, as bad as things were, they soon got worse.

The September 11, 2001, terrorist attacks on New York and Washington, D.C., devastated the whole nation, but few segments of the economy felt the impact as dramatically as the already struggling airline industry. Even after reducing scheduled flights by more than 20 percent, most planes were taking off with fewer than half their seats filled, and airline shares lost a third of their value on the stock exchange. Most airlines needed to cut costs drastically in order to make ends meet, and over 100,000 employees were eventually laid off from American Airlines, United Airlines, US Airways, Continental Airlines, and America West.

Southwest Airlines bucked this trend, however. Indeed, despite the regular ups and downs of the airline industry, in its 30 years of operation, Southwest had never laid off employees; remarkably, it was able to maintain this record even during the difficult Fall 2001 period. Southwest's no-layoff policy is one of the core values that underlie its human resource strategy, and insiders stress that it is one of the main reasons why the Southwest workforce is so fiercely loyal, productive, and flexible.

The high productivity of these workers helps keep labor costs low, and these savings are passed on to consumers in the form of lower prices that are sometimes half those offered by competitors. High levels of job security also promote a willingness on the part of Southwest employees to be innovative on the job without fearing that they will be punished for any mistakes. Southwest also finds that satisfied employees help create satisfied customers and can even help in recruiting new employees when economic conditions are conducive to growth.

In order to keep this perfect no-layoff record in 2001, Southwest executives assembled into an emergency command and control center in Dallas and brainstormed methods other than layoffs that could reduce costs. Decisions were made to delay the planned purchase of new planes, as well as to scrap ongoing plans to renovate the company's headquarters. The company, which had no debt and over a billion dollars in cash, also leaned heavily on this "rainy-day" fund to help get through tough times. It was a difficult and painful process, but as CEO Jim Parker noted, "We are willing to suffer some damage, even to our stock price, to protect the jobs of our people."

SOURCES: M. Arndt, "Suddenly, Carriers Can't Get off the Ground," *BusinessWeek*, September 3, 2001, pp. 36–37; M. Arndt, "What Kind of Rescue?" *BusinessWeek*, October 1, 2001, pp. 36–37; W. Zeller, "Southwest: After Kelleher, More Blue Skies," *BusinessWeek*, April 2, 2001, p. 45; M. Conlin, "Where Layoffs Are a Last Resort," *BusinessWeek*, October 8, 2001, p. 42.

1. In this chapter, we explored several alternatives to layoffs as a means of reducing a labor surplus. Compare and contrast the list we generated with what was done at Southwest in the wake of the 9/11 attacks. How did the response at Southwest differ from the other airlines?
2. Southwest Airlines' "no-layoff policy" is an important component of its overall culture and strategy. In what ways does this no-layoff policy, which clearly hurts the airline in the short term, give Southwest a competitive advantage over other airlines in the long term?
3. In this chapter, we looked at the increased use of offshoring, where jobs are moved from the United States to other countries where labor rates are cheaper. In what ways is offshoring similar and different from a simple layoff? If there are some long-term benefits from avoiding layoffs, what might be the long-term advantages of trying to avoid offshoring?

## MANAGING PEOPLE: FROM THE PAGES OF *BUSINESSWEEK*

### BusinessWeek What's Really Propping Up the Economy

**Since 2001, the health-care industry has added 1.7 million jobs. The rest of the private sector? None** If you really want to understand what makes the U.S. economy tick these days, don't go to Silicon Valley, Wall Street, or Washington. Just take a short trip to your local hospital. Park where you don't block the ambulances, and watch the unending flow of doctors, nurses, technicians, and support personnel. You'll have a front-row seat at the health-care economy.

For years, everyone from politicians on both sides of the aisle to corporate execs to your Aunt Tilly have justifiably bemoaned American health care—the out-of-control costs, the vast inefficiencies, the lack of access, and the often inexplicable blunders.

But the very real problems with the health-care system mask a simple fact: Without it the nation's labor market would be in a deep coma. Since 2001, 1.7 million new jobs have been added in the health-care sector, which includes related industries such as pharmaceuticals and health insurance. Meanwhile, the number of private-sector jobs outside of health care is no higher than it was five years ago.

Sure, housing has been a bonanza for homebuilders, real estate agents, and mortgage brokers. Together they have added more than 900,000 jobs since 2001. But the pressures of globalization and new technology have wreaked havoc on the rest of the labor market: Factories are still closing, retailers are shrinking, and the finance and insurance sector, outside of real estate lending and health insurers, has generated few additional jobs.

Perhaps most surprising, information technology, the great electronic promise of the 1990s, has turned into one of the biggest job-growth disappointments of all time. Despite the splashy success of companies such as Google and Yahoo!, businesses at the core of the information economy—software, semiconductors, telecom, and the whole gamut of Web companies—have lost more than 1.1 million jobs in the past five years. Those businesses employ fewer Americans today than they did in 1998, when the Internet frenzy kicked into high gear.

#### Attitude Shift

Meanwhile, hospital administrators like Steven Altschuler, president of Children's Hospital of Philadelphia, are on a hiring spree. Altschuler has added the equivalent of 4,000 new full-time jobs since he took over six years ago, almost doubling the hospital's workforce. To put this in perspective, all the nonhealth-care businesses in the Philadelphia area combined added virtually no jobs over the same stretch.

Altschuler plans to add 3,000 more employees over the next five years as the hospital, one of the nation's leading pediatric centers, spends $1.7 billion to expand. Next up is a new 1.2 million-square-foot research facility that will be packed with well-paid scientists and support staff. "Health care is the major engine for the economy of the city of Philadelphia," says Altschuler.

The City of Brotherly Love is hardly alone. Across the country, state and local politicians, desperate for growth, are crafting their economic development strategies around biotech and health care. California will pour $3 billion into stem cell research over the next 10 years, and other areas are on the same path. "Our downtown business leaders and politicians have traditionally considered health care as a cost center, not as an economic engine," says Baiju R. Shah, a former McKinsey & Co. consultant who runs Cleveland's BioEnterprise, a nonprofit founded four years ago to stimulate the local health-care and bioscience industries. "But people are waking up."

What they're waking up to is the true underpinnings of the much vaunted American job machine. The U.S. unemployment rate is 4.7 percent, compared with 8.2 percent and 8.9 percent, respectively, in Germany and France. But the health-care systems of those two countries added very few jobs from 1997 to 2004, according to new data from the Organization for Economic Cooperation & Development, while U.S. hospitals and physician offices never stopped growing. Take away health-care hiring in the United States, and quicker than you can say cardiac bypass, the U.S. unemployment rate would be 1 to 2 percentage points higher.

Almost invisibly, health care has become the main American job program for the 21st century, replacing, at least for the moment, all the other industries that are vanishing from the landscape. With more than $2 trillion in spending—half public, half private—health care is propping up local job markets in the Northeast, Midwest, and South, the regions hit hardest by globalization and the collapse of manufacturing.

Health care is highly labor intensive, so most of that $2 trillion ends up in the pockets of workers. And at least so far, there's little leakage abroad in terms of patient care. "Health care is all home-produced," says Princeton University economist and health-care expert Uwe Reinhardt. The good news is that if the housing market falls into a deep swoon, health care could provide enough new jobs to prevent a wider recession. In August, health-services employment rose by 35,000, double the increase in construction and far outstripping any other sector.

John Maynard Keynes would nod approvingly if he were alive. Seventy years ago, the elegant British economist proposed that in tough times the government could and should spend large sums of money to create jobs and stimulate growth. His theories are out of fashion, but substitute "health care" for "government," and that's exactly what is happening today.

Make no mistake, though: The U.S. could eventually pay a big economic price for all these jobs. Ballooning government spending on health care is a major reason why Washington is running an enormous budget deficit, since federal outlays for health care totaled more than $600 billion in 2005, or roughly one quarter of the whole federal budget. Rising prices for medical care are making it harder for the average American to afford health insurance, leaving 47 million uninsured.

Moreover, as the high cost of health care lowers the competitiveness of U.S. corporations, it may accelerate the outflow of jobs in a self-reinforcing cycle. In fact, one explanation for the huge U.S. trade deficit is that the country is borrowing from overseas to fund creation of health-care jobs.

There's another enormous long-term problem: If current trends continue, 30 percent to 40 percent of all new jobs created over the next 25 years will be in health care. That sort of lopsided job creation is not the blueprint for a well-functioning economy. One solution would be to make health care less labor-intensive by investing a lot more in information technology. "Low productivity in health is mostly a product of low investment," says Harvard University economist Dale Jorgenson.

For now, though, health-care hiring is providing a safety net in areas where manufacturing and retailing are no longer dependable sources of jobs. Take Johnstown, Pa., a town that once hummed with activity from local steel mills, coal mines, and nearby factories. As most of these businesses closed, the town emptied out, going from a population of 63,000 in 1950 to 23,000 today.

Now, Conemaugh Health System, with about 5,000 workers, is the biggest employer in town. "Everyone has a Conemaugh parking sticker on their car," says Linda D. Suter, 48, who's in her second year at the nursing school Conemaugh operates. Suter's dad worked at a factory in a nearby town, now closed, that made backyard swing sets for kids.

Frank Kosnowsky sold appliances at the Sears in Johnstown for 10 years, starting right out of high school. But he got fed up with the way the company was changing and started thinking about going to nursing school. "One day I had a disagreement with my boss, and the application went right in," says Kosnowsky, 29. "I wanted something that had a future." He worked part-time at Sears while he went to nursing school. Now, three years later, he's the first and only male nurse working at Conemaugh's neonatal intensive-care unit—a career far different than that of his coal miner dad.

Suter and Kosnowsky live smack in the middle of the "Health Belt" that stretches from New England down through New York and Pennsylvania, across the Midwest and down through most of the South. These are areas where health care has been the major source of job growth over the past five years.

Nowhere is that truer than in Cleveland. There, Cleveland Clinic, with 29,000 employees, is the biggest employer by far. Next-largest is another hospital system. University Hospitals Health System, with 21,600 staffers. Then comes insurer Progressive Corp. and KeyCorp., each with fewer than 10,000 workers in the area. Cleveland

Clinic's performance is pretty good for an outfit that started in 1921 with four docs in a building they planned to turn into a hotel if their vision didn't pay off.

Beyond its immediate employment tallies, the Clinic has a huge multiplier effect on the local economy. CEO Dr. Delos M. Cosgrove says it supports perhaps 75,000 jobs in all in the area, ranging from Clinic staffers to workers at hotels and restaurants—which patients and their families use in more than 2.9 million patient visits per year—to 3,000 suppliers to the Clinic.

Only a few years ago manufacturers were Cleveland's job engines. Companies such as machine-tool giant Warner & Swasey Co. don't even exist anymore. Conglomerate TRW was sold in 2002, and parts of it moved away. Fittingly, the Clinic now occupies its former headquarters, which TRW donated.

Health care has been one of the few economic bright spots in the Detroit area, too. Nancy M. Schlichting heads the sprawling Henry Ford Health System, founded by the great man himself in 1915. Schlichting is overseeing the construction of a new 300-bed hospital in West Bloomfield, Mich., a suburb of Detroit, which will eventually generate the equivalent of 1,200 full-time jobs. This expansion comes at a time when Ford Motor Co. is considering big layoffs.

Then there's North Carolina. Since 2001 it has seen a total job increase of 24,000, or 0.6 percent. Meager enough—but take out the 60,000 jobs added by health care, and the state's jobs would have decreased by 36,000. Employment in manufacturing, retailing, trucking, utilities, and information all fell. And construction added only 5,000 jobs, a mere fraction of health care's contribution.

Oddly enough, the retirement meccas of Florida and Arizona are among the least dependent on health-care jobs for growth. Over the past five years the two states have gotten only 10 percent and 15 percent, respectively, of their new jobs from health-care services—hospitals, doctor's offices, and nursing homes. Phoenix showed a job gain of 240,000, but only 30,000 were in health care. That's partly because the influx of elderly has been balanced by a rise in younger workers, too.

Is the health-care economy a good deal for workers? It is for Patricia A. McDonald, a second-year student nurse at Conemaugh. Before going to nursing school, McDonald, 46, sold insurance door-to-door, often driving close to 1,000 miles a week in rural areas to make cold calls. Her take in sales commissions was $35,000 to $40,000 a year, but that was before deducting expenses. Registered nurses in the Johnstown area, by comparison, are paid an average of almost $43,000—with no traveling. "This will be much better," says McDonald.

Unlike many other industries, health care offers a full range of jobs, from home health aides making very low wages through technicians and nurses making middle-class salaries up to well-paid doctors. On average, annual pay in private health services is $43,700, slightly above the private-sector average of $42,600.

### Ripple Effect

Even more promising, health care has taken over the role manufacturing used to play in providing opportunities for less skilled workers to move up. Jeffrey Lites started as a part-time cashier in the cafeteria at Philadelphia's Children's Hospital in 1996 after being laid off as a computer operator. "I never envisioned working in a hospital," says Lites. But now, close to finishing his degree in early childhood education from Temple University, Lites works as a child-life assistant, providing recreation and activities for young patients who may stay for weeks or even months. "I have the best job in the entire hospital," says Lites, who moonlights as a musician on weekends.

The expansion of health care is also spinning off related jobs. Cleveland Clinic Innovations a unit that funds start-ups, has already created 19 companies in its five years of existence. Together they employ about 186 people, including more than 50 in the Cleveland area. One, Cleveland BioLabs Inc., went public in July and trades on NASDAQ. "We like to say that the New Economy is alive and well in the 40 blocks of the Cleveland Clinic," says Christopher Coburn, executive director of Cleveland Clinic Innovations.

James A. Martin is pursuing the same pot of gold in Shawnee, Kan., a city of almost 60,000 located just outside Kansas City. Martin, executive director of the Shawnee Economic Development Council, is helping the city set up a biosciences development district, the first in the state. He's hoping to build on the jobs already there, including the animal-health division of Bayer HealthCare. "The high growth potential of biosciences jumped out at us." says Martin. "We got the bug."

Scott Becker, CEO of Conemaugh, is leading the effort to develop a technology park in a prime location in the center of Johnstown, where a mammoth dairy used to be. Potential biotech and info tech tenants include a company dealing with electronic medical records and another that's involved with drug trials. "The goal is to bring a new, younger workforce back to town," says Becker.

### Unbalanced

Shah of Cleveland's BioEnterprise cautions that biotech may not be the right economic development strategy for many places. For one, it's hard to develop a local biotech industry from scratch. "I've seen a lot of regions that take a swing at that," says Shah. Besides, he says, biotech mainly provides jobs for a small number of highly paid workers. For many communities. Shah favors a broader strategy of encouraging health-care delivery and medical equipment and supplies.

Still, using health-care spending to create the vast majority of new jobs, while beneficial in the short run, is not desirable over the long run. A well-balanced economy needs to provide a wide variety of jobs, not just positions for doctors, nurses, and medical technicians.

The biggest worry is that demand for health care will absorb too much of the workforce and squeeze out other types of jobs. If medical spending rises to 25 percent of gross domestic product by 2030, as many economists expect, health care's share of jobs could grow to 15 percent or 16 percent of the labor market from today's 12 percent, based on historical patterns.

Such a shift in employment would require health care to be the single biggest creator of jobs in the economy for the foreseeable future. And while the United States could in theory afford to spend 25 percent of GDP on health care, it's hard to imagine a world in which our children have to choose between working for the local hospital or the local health insurer.

The real question, then, is whether it is possible to restructure the health-care system to provide equally good care with fewer workers. The answer is yes, say some experts. "What we have consistently found is that the supply of physicians, except at the low end, has rather little influence on patient outcomes," says David Goodman, a professor at Dartmouth Medical School who started his career as a pediatrician in a rural county in Northern New Hampshire. Jonathan Weiner, a professor at Johns Hopkins University's Bloomberg School of Public Health, agrees: "I am absolutely certain that we can provide quality health care with fewer doctors."

These assertions miss the point, says Richard Cooper, a professor at the University of Pennsylvania School of Medicine. Cooper, a former dean at the Medical College of Wisconsin, argues that the health-care workforce grows along with real incomes and GDP. "When you get richer, you aren't going to triple your food expenditures," says Cooper. "But there's much more that can be done to improve health." Princeton economist Reinhardt concurs, noting that "if you did geriatric health properly, you'd need a lot more geriatricians."

But both sides can agree that more spending on information technology could reduce the need for so many health-care workers. It's a truism in economics that investment boosts productivity, and the U.S. lags behind other countries in this area. One reason: "Every other country has the payers paying for IT," says Johns Hopkins' Gerard Anderson, an expert on the economics of health care. "In the U.S. we're asking the providers to pay for IT"—and they're not the ones who benefit.

Breakthroughs in technology offer other enticing possibilities for making health care less labor-intensive over the long run. Hakon Hakonarson just moved from Iceland to start up the new Center for Applied Genomics at Children's Hospital of Philadelphia. Hakonarson's group is using cutting-edge automated technology to analyze hundreds of DNA samples from hospital patients and their parents per day, something that wasn't possible until recently. His aim is to collect enough data within a short period of time to understand the genetic causes of childhood diseases and determine which children will respond best to which drugs. "If we go at this pace," says Hakonarson, "we will have something very powerful to analyze before yearend." The eventual result could be better, cheaper treatments, with fewer expensive side effects.

Meanwhile, Hakonarson employs 10 people in his lab as well as five nurses and medical assistants in the field who do nothing but ask families to participate in the study. For now, the health-care economy marches on.

SOURCE: M. Mandel, "What's Really Propping Up the Economy," *BusinessWeek*, September 25, 2006, pp. 55–62.

### Questions

1. In what sense have the factors associated with globalization that have decimated jobs in the manufacturing sector of the economy had less impact on the health care industry?
2. How have capital investment and the use of technology in the health care sector of the economy differed from the manufacturing sector, and what are the implications for the demand for labor?
3. In what sense is consumer demand for health care different from its demand for manufactured products, and what implications does this have for the demand for labor?
4. If one wanted to see expanded demand for labor in the manufacturing sector of the economy (and more job production), what lessons can be learned from job production in the health care arena?

## NOTES


1. J. Kronholz, "Immigrant Labor or Machines," *The Wall Street Journal*, December 19, 2006, p. A4.
2. A. Bernsstein, "Hiring Illegals: Inside the Deal Ahead," *BusinessWeek*, May 29, 2006, pp. 35–36.
3. K. Doheny, "Nursing Is in Critical Condition," *Workforce Management*, October 9, 2006, pp. 39–41.
4. A. Aston, "Who Will Run the Plants?" *BusinessWeek*, January 22, 2007, p. 78.
5. D. W. Jarrell, *Human Resource Planning: A Business Planning Approach* (Englewood Cliffs, NJ: Prentice Hall, 1993).
6. I. Brat, "Where Have All the Welders Gone, as Manufacturing and Repair Boom," *The Wall Street Journal*, August 15, 2006, pp. B2–3.
7. M. Conlin, "Savaged by the Slowdown," *BusinessWeek*, September 17, 2001, pp. 74–77.
8. A. Serwer, "What's Hot on Wall Street in 2001? Cost Cutting and Layoffs," *Fortune*, February 19, 2001, pp. 34–36.
9. N. D. Schwartz, "Will 'Made in the USA' Fade Away?" *Fortune*, November 24, 2003, pp. 98–110.
10. K. Labich, "The Geography of an Emerging America," *Fortune*, June 27, 1994, pp. 88–94.
11. J. E. Hilsenrath, "Behind the Outsourcing Debate: Surpsisingly, Few Hard Numbers," *The Wall Street Journal*, April 22, 2004, pp. A1–A3.
12. K. P. DeMeuse, P. A. Vanderheiden, and T. J. Bergmann, "Announced Layoffs: Their Effect on Corporate Financial

Performance," *Human Resource Management* 33 (1994), pp. 509–30.
13. C. D. Zatzick and R. D. Iverson, "High-Involvement Management and Workforce Reduction: Competitive Advantage or Disadvantage?" *Academy of Management Journal* 49, (2006), pp. 999–1015.
14. J. Mehring, " Laying Off the Layoffs," *BusinessWeek*, May 29, 2006, p. 28.
15. P. P. Shaw, "Network Destruction: The Structural Implications of Downsizing," *Academy of Management Journal* 43 (2000), pp. 101–12.
16. J. Schu, "Internet Helps Keep Goodwill of Downsized Employees," *Workforce*, July 2001, p. 15.
17. D. Skarlicki, J. H. Ellard, and B. R. C. Kellin, "Third Party Perceptions of a Layoff: Procedural, Derogation, and Retributive Aspects of Justice," *Journal of Applied Psychology* 83 (1998), pp. 119–27.
18. J. Holton, "You've Been Deleted," *Workforce Management*, September 11, 2006, p. 42.
19. J. E. Hilsenrath, "Adventures in Cost Cutting," *The Wall Street Journal*, May 10, 2004, pp. A1–A3.
20. R. Stodghill, "The Coming Job Bottleneck," *BusinessWeek*, March 24, 1997, pp. 184–85.
21. S. Kim and D. Feldman, "Healthy, Wealthy, or Wise: Predicting Actual Acceptances of Early Retirement Incentives at Three Points in Time," *Personnel Psychology* 51 (1998), pp. 623–42.
22. J. S. Lublin and S. Thurm, "How Companies Calculate Odds in Buyout Offers," *The Wall Street Journal*, March 27, 2006, pp. B1–B2.
23. D. Fandray, "Gray Matters," *Workforce*, July 2000, pp. 27–32.
24. S. Gustafson, "38,000 Took Buyouts, Ford Says," *Columbus* (Ohio) *Dispatch*, November 2006, pp. E1–E2.
25. J. Weber, "Not Just a Temporary Lift," *BusinessWeek*, January 19, 2004.
26. M. L. Kraimer, S. J. Wayne, R. C. Liden, and R. T. Sparrowe, "The Role of Job Securirty in Understanding the Relationship between Employees' Perceptions of Temporary Workers and Employees' Performance," *Journal of Applied Psychology* 90 (2005), pp. 389–398.
27. C. Hajim, "Bodies in Motion," *Fortune*, February 19, 2007, p. 114.
28. J. Marquez, "Inside Job," *Workforce Management*, February 12, 2006, pp. 19–21.
29. F. Hanson, "Special Report: Mid-market Outsourcing," *Workforce Management*, February 12, 2007, pp. 23–26.
30. P. Engardio, "Let's Offshore the Lawyers," *BusinessWeek*, September 18, 2006, pp. 42–43.
31. M. Kripalani, "Call Center? That's so 2004," *BusinessWeek*, August 7, 2006, pp. 40–41.
32. S. Hamm, "Outsourcing Heads to the Outskirts, "*BusinessWeek*, January 22, 2007, p. 56..
33. S. Shellenbarger, "Outsourcing Jobs to the Den, "*The Wall Street Journal*, January 2, 2006, p. D1.
34. W. Zellner, "Lessons from a Faded Levi-Strauss," *BusinessWeek*, December 15, 2003, p. 44.
35. A. Meisler, "Think Globally, Act Rationally," *Workforce*, January 2004, pp. 40–45.
36. S. E. Ante, "Shifting Work Offshore? Outsourcer Beware," *BusinessWeek*, January 12, 2004, pp. 36–37.
37. P. Engardio, "The Future of Outsourcing," *BusinessWeek*, January 30, 2006, pp. 50–58.
38. D. Foust, "A Smarter Squeeze?" *BusinessWeek*, December 31, 2001, pp. 42–44.
39. J. Eig, "Many Employers Cut Worker Hours to Avoid Layoffs," *The Wall Street Journal*, January 3, 2002, pp. A1–A2.
40. A. Bernstein, "Bell Atlantic North Faces a Monstrous Labor Crunch," *BusinessWeek*, June 8, 1998, p. 38.
41. K. Aquino, M. M. Steward, and A. Reed, "How Social Dominance Orientation and Job Status Influence Perceptions of African-American Affirmative Action Beneficiaries," *Personnel Psychology* 58 (2005), pp. 703–744.
42. R. Cropanzano, J. E. Slaughter, and P. D. Bachiochi, "Organizational Justice and Black Applicants Reactions to Affirmative Action," *Journal of Applied Psychology* 90 (2005), pp. 1168–84.
43. D. A. Harrison, D. A. Kravitz, D. M. Mayer, L. M. Leslie, and D. Lev-Arey, "Understanding Attitudes toward Affirmative Action Programs in Employment: Summary and Meta-analysis of 35 Years of Research," *Journal of Applied Psychology* 91 (2006), pp. 1013–36.
44. A. E. Barber, *Recruiting Employees* (Thousand Oaks, CA: Sage, 1998).
45. J. A. Breaugh, *Recruitment: Science and Practice* (Boston: PWS-Kent, 1992).
46. M. Totty, "New Tools for Frazzled Recruiters," *The Wall Street Journal*, October 23, 2006, p. C11.
47. C. K. Stevens, "Antecedents of Interview Interactions, Interviewers' Ratings, and Applicants' Reactions," *Personnel Psychology* 51 (1998), pp. 55–85.
48. A. E. Barber, J. R. Hollenbeck, S. L. Tower, and J. M. Phillips, "The Effects of Interview Focus on Recruitment Effectiveness: A Field Experiment," *Journal of Applied Psychology* 79 (1994), pp. 886–96.
49. D. S. Chapman and D. I. Zweig, "Developing a Nomological Network for Interview Structure: Antecedents and Consequences of the Structured Selection Interview," *Personnel Psychology* 58, (2005), pp. 673–702.
50. J. D. Olian and S. L. Rynes, "Organizational Staffing: Integrating Practice with Strategy," *Industrial Relations* 23 (1984), pp. 170–83.
51. R. Kanfer, C. R. Wanberg, and T. M. Kantrowitz, "Job Search and Employment: A Personality–Motivational Analysis and Meta-Analytic Review," *Journal of Applied Psychology* 86 (2001), pp. 837–55.
52. G. T. Milkovich and J. M. Newman, *Compensation* (Homewood, IL: Richard D. Irwin, 1990).
53. S. J. Marks, "After School," *Human Resources Executive*, June 15, 2001, pp. 49–51.
54. P. J. Kiger, "The Center of Attention," *Workforce*, March 2004, pp. 51–52.
55. K. Helliker, "Sold on the Job: Retailing Chains Offer a Lot of Opportunity, Young Managers Find," *The Wall Street Journal*, August 25, 1995, p. A1.
56. P. J. Kiker, "Recruitment Battles," *Workforce Management*, October 24, 2005, pp. 20–31.
57. S. Shellenbarger, "Military Recruits: Companies Make New Effort to Hire Spouses of Soldiers," *The Wall Street Journal*, December 15, 2005, p. D1.
58. K. Greene, "AARP Is to Recruit Older Workers for Home Depot," *The Wall Street Journal*, February 6, 2004, p. B5.
59. M. Leonard, "Challenges to the Termination-at-Will Doctrine," *Personnel Administrator* 28 (1983), pp. 49–56.
60. C. Schowerer and B. Rosen, "Effects of Employment-at-Will Policies and Compensation Policies on Corporate Image and Job Pursuit Intentions," *Journal of Applied Psychology* 74 (1989), pp. 653–56.
61. M. Magnus, "Recruitment Ads at Work," *Personnel Journal* 64 (1985), pp. 42–63.
62. S. L. Rynes and A. E. Barber, "Applicant Attraction Strategies: An Organizational Perspective," *Academy of Management Review* 15 (1990), pp. 286–310.
63. Breaugh, *Recruitment*.
64. D. S. Chapman, K. L. Uggerslev, S. A. Carroll, K. A. Piasentin, and D. A. Jones, "Applicant Attraction to Organizations and Job Choice: A Meta-analytic Review of the Correlates of Recruiting Outcomes," *Journal of Applied Psychology* 90 (2005), pp. 928–44.
65. C. Collins and C. K. Stevens, "The Relationship between Early Recruitment-Related Activities and the Application Decisions of New Labor Market Entrants: A Brand Equity Approach to Recruitment," *Journal of Applied Psychology* 87 (2002), pp. 1121–33.

66. M. E. Brooks, S. Highhouse, S. S. Russell, and D. C. Mohr, "Familiarity, Ambivalence, and Firm Reputation: Is Corporate Fame a Double-Edged Sword?" *Journal of Applied Psychology* 88 (2003), pp. 904–14.
67. D. N. Cable and K. Y. Yu, "Managing Job Seekers' Organizational Image Beliefs: The Role of Media Richness and Media Credibility," *Journal of Applied Psychology* 91 (2006), pp. 828–40.
68. F. Lievens and S. Highhouse, "The Relation of Instrumental and Symbolic Attributes to a Company's Attractiveness as an Employer," *Personnel Psychology* 56 (2003), pp. 75–102.
69. J. E. Slaughter, M. J. Zickar, S. Highhouse, and D. C. Mohr, "Personality Trait Inferences about Organizations: Development of a Measure and Assessment of Construct Validity," *Journal of Applied Psychology* 89 (2004), pp. 85–103.
70. D. R. Avery, "Reactions to Diversity in Recruitment Advertising—Are Differences Black and White?" *Journal of Applied Psychology* 88 (2003), pp. 672–79.
71. D. M. Cable, L. Aiman-Smith, P. Mulvey, and J. R. Edwards, "The Sources and Accuracy of Job Applicants' Beliefs about Organizational Culture," *Academy of Management Journal* 43 (2000), pp. 1076–85.
72. M. A. Conrad and S. D. Ashworth, "Recruiting Source Effectiveness: A Meta-analysis and Re-examination of Two Rival Hypotheses," paper presented at the annual meeting of the Society of Industrial/Organizational Psychology, Chicago, 1986.
73. Breaugh, *Recruitment*.
74. M. Hammers, "One Out of Many," *Workforce*, November 2003, pp. 59–60.
75. Breaugh, *Recruitment*.
76. R. S. Schuler and S. E. Jackson, "Linking Competitive Strategies with Human Resource Management Practices," *Academy of Management Executive* 1 (1987), pp. 207–19.
77. E. Byron, "Call Me Mike," *The Wall Street Journal*, March 27, 2006, pp. B1, B4.
78. C. R. Wanberg, R. Kanfer, and J.T. Banas, "Predictors and Outcomes of Networking Intensity among Job Seekers," *Journal of Applied Psychology* 85 (2000), pp. 491–503.
79. C. R. Williams, C. E. Labig, and T. H. Stone, "Recruitment Sources and Posthire Outcomes for Job Applicants and New Hires: A Test of Two Hypotheses," *Journal of Applied Psychology* 78 (1994), pp. 163–72.
80. J. Mintz, "Large Firms Increasingly Rely on Employee Job Referrals," *The Wall Street Journal*, March 1, 2005, p. B4.
81. A. Halcrow, "Employers Are Your Best Recruiters," *Personnel Journal* 67 (1988), pp. 42–49.
82. J. McGregor, " I Can't Believe They Took the Whole Team," *BusinessWeek*, December 18, 2006, pp. 120–22.
83. B. P. Sunoo, "Papa John's Rolls Out Hot HR Menu," *Personnel Journal*, September 1995, pp. 38–47.
84. S. Begley, "Behind 'Shortage' of Engineers: Employers Grow More Choosy," *The Wall Street Journal*, November 16, 2005, pp. A1, A12.
85. Breaugh, *Recruitment*.
86. J. Smith, "Is Online Recruiting Getting Easier?" *Workforce*, September 2, 2001, p. 25.
87. B. R. Dineen, S. R. Ash, and R. A. Noe, "A Web of Applicant Attraction: Person–Organization Fit in the Context of Web-Based Recruitment," *Journal of Applied Psychology* 87(2002), pp. 723–34.
88. A. Salkever, "A Better Way to Float Your Résumé," *Business-Week Online*, October 9, 2000, pp. 1–2.
89. P. Smith, "Sources Used by Employers When Hiring College Grads," *Personnel Journal*, February 1995, p. 25.
90. J. W. Boudreau and S. L. Rynes, "Role of Recruitment in Staffing Utility Analysis," *Journal of Applied Psychology* 70 (1985), pp. 354–66.
91. L. Winter, "Employers Go to School on Minority Recruiting," *The Wall Street Journal*, December 15, 1992, p. B1.
92. C. M. Solomon, "Navigating Your Search for Global Talent," *Personnel Journal*, May 1995, pp. 94–97.
93. R. Hawk, *The Recruitment Function* (New York: American Management Association, 1967).
94. K. D. Carlson, M. L. Connerly, and R. L. Mecham, "Recruitment Evaluation: The Case for Assessing the Quality of Applicants Attracted," *Personnel Psychology* 55 (2002), pp. 461–94.
95. C. K. Stevens, "Effects of Preinterview Beliefs on Applicants' Reactions to Campus Interviews," *Academy of Management Journal* 40 (1997), pp. 947–66.
96. C. D. Fisher, D. R. Ilgen, and W. D. Hoyer, "Source Credibility, Information Favorability, and Job Offer Acceptance," *Academy of Management Journal* 22 (1979), pp. 94–103; G. N. Powell, "Applicant Reactions to the Initial Employment Interview: Exploring Theoretical and Methodological Issues," *Personnel Psychology* 44 (1991), pp. 67–83; N. Schmitt and B. W. Coyle, "Applicant Decisions in the Employment Interview," *Journal of Applied Psychology* 61 (1976), pp. 184–92.
97. M. S. Taylor and T. J. Bergman, "Organizational Recruitment Activities and Applicants' Reactions at Different Stages of the Recruitment Process," *Personnel Psychology* 40 (1984), pp. 261–85; Fisher, Ilgen, and Hoyer, "Source Credibility."
98. L. M. Graves and G. N. Powell, "The Effect of Sex Similarity on Recruiters' Evaluations of Actual Applicants: A Test of the Similarity–Attraction Paradigm," *Personnel Psychology* 48 (1995), pp. 85–98.
99. R. D. Bretz and T. A. Judge, "Realistic Job Previews: A Test of the Adverse Self-Selection Hypothesis," *Journal of Applied Psychology* 83 (1998), pp. 330–37.
100. A. Meisler, "Little White Lies," *Workforce*, November 2003, pp. 88–89.
101. J. P. Wanous, *Organizational Entry: Recruitment, Selection and Socialization of Newcomers* (Reading, MA: Addison-Wesley, 1980).
102. P. Hom, R. W. Griffeth, L. E. Palich, and J. S. Bracker, "An Exploratory Investigation into Theoretical Mechanisms Underlying Realistic Job Previews," *Personnel Psychology* 51 (1998), pp. 421–51.
103. J. M. Phillips, "The Effects of Realistic Job Previews on Multiple Organizational Outcomes: A Meta-analysis," *Academy of Management Journal* 41 (1998), pp. 673–90.
104. P. G. Irving and J. P. Meyer, "Reexamination of the Met-Expectations Hypothesis: A Longitudinal Analysis," *Journal of Applied Psychology* 79 (1995), pp. 937–49.
105. Y. Ganzach, A. Pazy, Y. Hohayun, "Social Exchange and Organizational Commitment: Decision-Making Training for Job Choice as an Alternative to the Realistic Job Preview," *Personnel Psychology* 55 (2002), pp. 613–37.
106. C. Collins, "The Interactive Effects of Recruitment Practices and Product Awareness on Job Seekers' Employer Knowledge and Application Behaviors," *Journal of Applied Psychology* 92 (2007), pp. 180–90.
107. S. L. Rynes, R. D. Bretz, and B. Gerhart, "The Importance of Recruitment in Job Choice: A Different Way of Looking," *Personnel Psychology* 44 (1991), pp. 487–522.

# 6

CHAPTER

# Selection and Placement

LO

## LEARNING OBJECTIVES

**After reading this chapter, you should be able to:**

LO1 Establish the basic scientific properties of personnel selection methods, including reliability, validity, and generalizability. *page 227*

LO2 Discuss how the particular characteristics of a job, organization, or applicant affect the utility of any test. *page 236*

LO3 Describe the government's role in personnel selection decisions, particularly in the areas of constitutional law, federal laws, executive orders, and judicial precedent. *page 237*

LO4 List the common methods used in selecting human resources. *page 241*

LO5 Describe the degree to which each of the common methods used in selecting human resources meets the demands of reliability, validity, generalizability, utility, and legality. *page 241*

# Enter the World of Business

## Hiring Decisions: What You Don't Know Can Surely Hurt You

When John Anderson joined the staff at Putnam General Hospital in West Virginia, there was a lot the hospital did not know about him, and a lot of what the hospital's management thought they knew about him turned out not be true. They thought that he had worked in the prestigious Cleveland Clinic, but that was not the case. They thought he had graduated from Meharry Medical College in Nashville, but that was not true. They thought that he was a medical doctor certified in osteopathic surgery, but he was not (instead he was a doctor of osteopathy, an alternative school of medicine that emphasizes the muscular-skeletal system). They did know that he had failed to complete his residency in four out of five attempts. They did not know he had been essentially fired from three hospitals for conducting unnecessary surgeries, and that at one of them, he was arrested for stealing and destroying operating room log books that were part of an ongoing investigation. Of course, they learned all of these things eventually, but not until he had performed 500 operations, 100 of which resulted in malpractice suits that financially ruined the hospital.

Hiring strangers is perhaps one of the most dangerous, but inevitable, aspects of human resource management. Getting good information that helps you increase your familiarity with applicants is very difficult, however, for several reasons. First, the information that applicants provide on themselves is often exaggerated or inaccurate. According to ChoicePoint Inc., a background checking company headquartered in Georgia, 15 percent of résumés contain inaccuracies, and 9 percent of the 8 million background checks the company performs each year uncover an undisclosed felony. Second, past employers are rarely motivated to speak negatively regarding past hires for fear they will be sued for defamation of character. In fact, as one attorney in the Putnam General case described above noted, none of the hospitals that fired John Anderson shared this information with Putnam. In his words, "Often the hospital is grateful the problem has ended without having to take action for fear they may get sued." Finally, because many organizations do not have HR specialists in hiring on staff, they often outsource this work to external vendors. For example, in the John Anderson case, Putnam neither recruited nor interviewed Dr. Anderson, but instead paid an outsourcer, Comprehensive Healthcare Staffing of Norwalk, Connecticut, to find him and examine his qualifications.

Delegating the responsibility for this critical aspect of human resource management to outsiders may not be the best choice, however, because the companies, not the outsourcing firm, are most often the target of lawsuits charging "negligent hiring." That is, in many instances where an employee engages in violence, harassment, fraud, or identify theft, those harmed can sue the employer under a system where there are no caps on punitive damages. If a judge or jury finds that the employer did not "take reasonable care in hiring," plaintiffs often stand to win awards that average over $1 million per incident. For example, in the Putnam General Hospital case, the total value of all the potential awards associated with the John Anderson fiasco was well over $150 million. To put the size of the damage caused by this single hiring decision in context, Putnam General Hospital was eventually sold for less than $350 million.

Many organizations try to avoid such outcomes by performing criminal background checks on employees, and this is not a bad first step. However, this is hardly sufficient for a number of reasons. First, simply knowing that a person has a clean record in terms of convictions tells you little or nothing about that person's ability to actually perform the job in question. John Anderson was never convicted of a crime (he was only arrested), but he was still a poor hire because he was a poor surgeon who made unethical decisions. Second, these types of background checks often have a disparate impact on some minority groups, because of well-documented differences in conviction rates by sex, race, and ethnic background. Third, even if someone has been convicted of a crime, that does not mean that he or she has not paid a debt to society and is not deserving of a second chance. Indeed, many fear that the cheaper and more widespread use of criminal background checks is creating a class of unemployable people who have no choice but to return to a life of crime when they cannot obtain legitimate employment.

In the face of all of these issues, it is essential that employers turn strangers whom they are thinking of hiring into well-known entities who have been thoroughly and fairly vetted. This goes beyond just examining their criminal background and ensuring they have all the necessary skills and abilities for the specific job, as well as the traits and values embodied in the larger organization. The process needs to be systematic and documented so that even if one bad decision is made, the process would be viewed as "reasonable by a customer, fellow employee, judge or jury." As one human resource vice president notes, when it comes to hiring, "We want to be seen as being ultra-vigilant."

SOURCES: K. Maher, "Background Checks Stir Up Worries in Many Employees," *The Wall Street Journal*, January 20, 2004, p. A8; P. Davies, "A Doctor's Tale Shows Weakness in Medical Vetting," *The Wall Street Journal*, September 21, 2005, pp. A1, A8; F. Hansen, "Taking 'Reasonable' Action to Avoid Negligent Hiring Claims," *Workforce Management*, December 11, 2006, pp. 31–33; A. Joyce, "Checking Applicants' Backgrounds Easy, but Dicey," *The Wall Street Journal*, August 4, 2004, p. A8; A. Zimmerman and K. Stringer, "As Background Checks Proliferate, Ex-cons Face Jobs Lock," *The Wall Street Journal*, August 26, 2004, pp. B1, B3; J. McGregor, "Background Checks that Never End," *BusinessWeek*, March 20, 2006, p 40.

## Introduction

Any organization that intends to compete through people must take the utmost care with how it chooses organizational members, especially those at managerial ranks. These decisions have a critical impact on the organization's ability to compete, as well as each and every job applicant's life. These decisions are too important to be left to the whim of untrained individuals, and as you can see from the opening story, legal actions can be taken against employers who fail to adequately discharge this responsibility. However, on top of the legal price that may be paid by organizations that fail to make the best selection decisions is the price they pay in term of economic competitiveness. Jack Welch, the legendary former CEO at General Electric says it best:

> What could possibly be more important than who gets hired? Business is a game, and as with all games, the team that puts the best people on the field and gets them playing together wins. It's that simple.[1]

Thus the idea of taking this most important decision and outsourcing it to another firm, as was the case at Putnam General Hospital, is hard to defend both legally and economically.

This is true at the level of individual firms, as it is with respect to competition between nations. The United States has always been a magnet for talent from other nations, and this country grew economically powerful through the contributions of many different people who emigrated here from other countries. Some have suggested the United States is losing its edge in this regard, however, and that "this is America's most serious long-term threat."[2] That is, social and economic inequality, racial and ethnic bias, growing political intolerance, and a failing educational system are making the United States less attractive to a global class of mobile workers whose skills are rising in demand everywhere else in the world. Innovation and economic growth are fueled by people, and the firms or countries that bring in the best people will be the ones that compete most successfully.

The purpose of this chapter is to familiarize you with ways to minimize errors in employee selection and placement and, in doing so, improve your company's competitive position. The chapter first focuses on five standards that should be met by any selection method. The chapter then evaluates several common selection methods according to those standards.

## Selection Method Standards

Personnel selection is the process by which companies decide who will or will not be allowed into organizations. Several generic standards should be met in any selection process. We focus on five: (1) reliability, (2) validity, (3) generalizability, (4) utility, and (5) legality. The first four build off each other in the sense that the preceding standard is often necessary but not sufficient for the one that follows. This is less the case with legal standards. However, a thorough understanding of the first four standards helps us understand the rationale underlying many legal standards.

**LO1**
Establish the Basic Scientific Properties of Personnel Selection Methods, Including Reliability, Validity, and Generalizability.

FIVE STANDARDS

### Reliability

Much of the work in personnel selection involves measuring characteristics of people to determine who will be accepted for job openings. For example, we might be interested in applicants' physical characteristics (like strength or endurance), their cognitive abilities (such as mathematical ability or verbal reasoning capacity), or aspects of their personality (like their initiative or integrity). Whatever the specific focus, in the end we need to quantify people on these dimensions (assign numbers to them) so we can order them from high to low on the characteristic of interest. Once people are ordered in this way, we can decide whom to hire and whom to reject.

One key standard for any measuring device is its reliability. We define **reliability** as the degree to which a measure is free from random error.[3] If a measure of some supposedly stable characteristic such as intelligence is reliable, then the score a person receives based on that measure will be consistent over time and in different contexts.

**Reliability**
The consistency of a performance measure; the degree to which a performance measure is free from random error.

#### True Scores and the Reliability of Measurement

Most measurement in personnel selection deals with complex characteristics like intelligence, integrity, and leadership ability. However, to appreciate some of the complexities in measuring people, we will consider something concrete in discussing these concepts: the measurement of height. For example, if we were measuring an applicant's height, we might start by using a 12-inch ruler. Let's say the first person we measure turns out to be 6 feet 1 and 4⁄16 inches tall. It would not be surprising to find out that someone else measuring the same person a second time, perhaps an hour later, found this applicant's height to be 6 feet and 12⁄16 inches. The same applicant, measured a third time, maybe the next day, might be measured at 6 feet 1 and 8⁄16 inches tall.

As this example makes clear, even though the person's height is a stable characteristic, we get slightly different results each time he is assessed. This means that each time the person is assessed, we must be making slight errors. If a measurement device were perfectly reliable, there would be no errors of measurement. If we used a measure of height that was not as reliable as a ruler—for example, guessing someone's height after seeing her walk across the room—we might see an even greater amount of unreliability in the measure. Thus *reliability* refers to the measuring instrument (a ruler versus a visual guess) rather than to the characteristic itself.

Because one never really knows the true score for the person being measured, there is no direct way to capture the "true" reliability of the measure. We can estimate reliability in several different ways, however; and because most of these rely on computing a correlation coefficient, we will briefly describe and illustrate this statistic.

The *correlation coefficient* is a measure of the degree to which two sets of numbers are related. The correlation coefficient expresses the strength of the relationship in numerical form. A perfect positive relationship (as one set of numbers goes up, so does the other) equals +1.0; a perfect negative relationship (as one goes up, the other goes down) equals −1.0. When there is no relationship between the sets of numbers, the correlation equals .00. Although the actual calculation of this statistic goes beyond the scope of this book (see any introductory statistics book or spreadsheet program), it will be useful for us to conceptually examine the nature of the correlation coefficient and what this means in personnel selection contexts.

When assessing the reliability of a measure, for example, we might be interested in knowing how scores on the measure at one time relate to scores on the same measure at another time. Obviously, if the characteristic we are measuring is supposedly stable (like intelligence or integrity) and the time lapse is short, this relationship should be strong. If it were weak, then the measure would be inconsistent—hence unreliable. This is called assessing *test–retest reliability*.

Plotting the two sets of numbers on a two-dimensional graph often helps us to appreciate the meaning of various levels of the correlation coefficient. Figure 6.1, for example, examines the relationship between student scholastic aptitude in one's junior and senior years in high school, where aptitude for college is measured in three ways: (1) via the scores on the Scholastic Aptitude Test (SAT), (2) via ratings from a high school counselor on a 1-to-100 scale, and (3) via tossing dice. In this plot, each number on the graphs represents a person whose scholastic aptitude is assessed twice (in the junior and senior years), so in Figure 6.1a, $1_1$ represents a person who scored 1580 on the SAT in the junior year and 1500 in the senior year; $20_{20}$ represents a person who scored 480 in the junior year and 620 in the senior year.

Figure 6.1a shows a very strong relationship between SAT scores across the two years. This relationship is not perfect in that the scores changed slightly from one year to the next, but not a great deal. Indeed, if there were a perfect 1.0 correlation, the plot would show a straight line at a 45-degree angle. The correlation coefficient for this set of data is in the .90 range. In this case, .90 is considered the test–retest estimate of reliability.

Turning to Figure 6.1b, we see that the relationship between the high school counselors' ratings across the two years, while still positive, is not as strong. That is, the counselors' ratings of individual students' aptitudes for college are less consistent over the two years than their test scores. The correlation, and hence test–retest reliability, of this measure of aptitude is in the .50 range.

Finally, Figure 6.1c shows a worst-case scenario, where the students' aptitudes are assessed by tossing two six-sided dice. As you would expect, the random nature of the

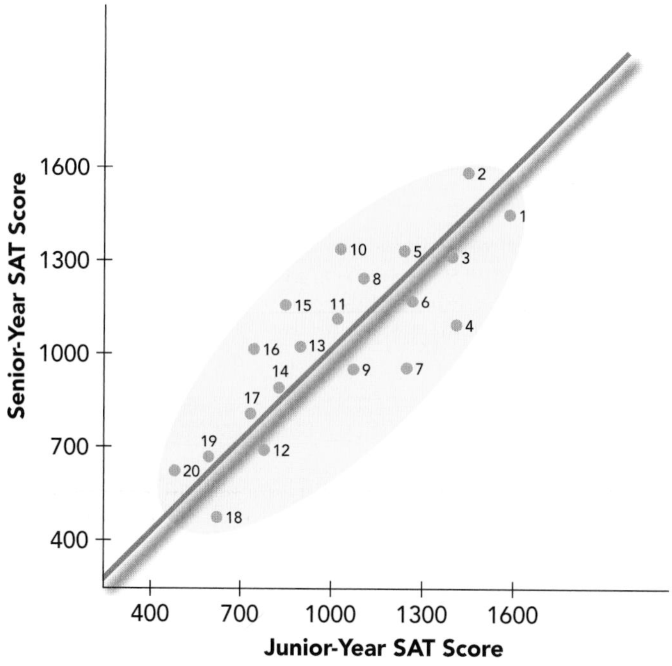


**figure 6.1a**

Measurements of a Student's Aptitude

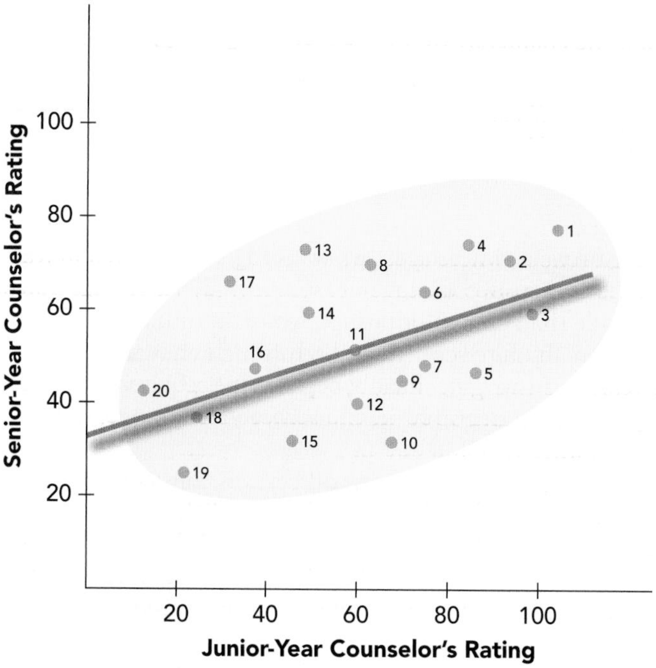


**figure 6.1b**

dice means that there is virtually no relationship between scores taken in one year and scores taken the next. Hence, in this instance, the correlation and test–retest estimate of reliability are .00. Although no one would seriously consider tossing dice to be a measure of aptitude, it is worth noting that research shows that the correlation of

figure 6.1c

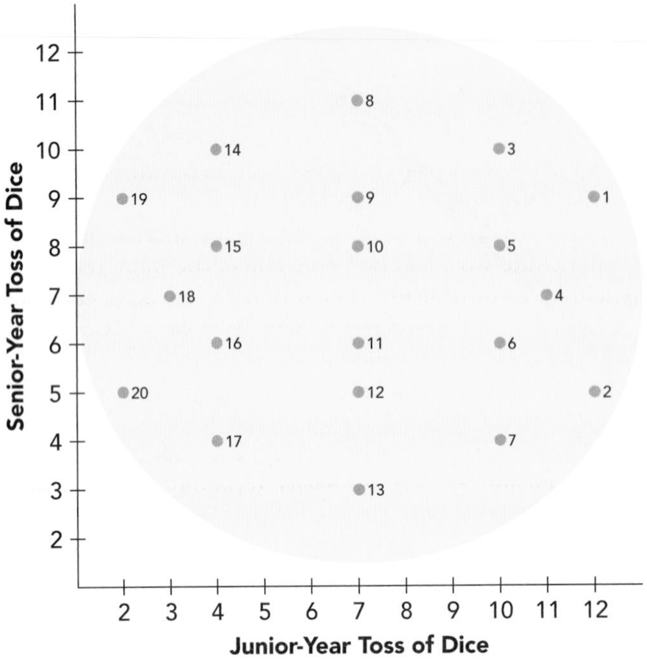


overall ratings of job applicants' suitability for jobs based on unstructured interviews is very close to .00. Thus, one cannot assume a measure is reliable without actually checking this directly. Novices in measurement are often surprised at exactly how unreliable many human judgments turn out to be.

## Standards for Reliability

Regardless of what characteristic we are measuring, we want highly reliable measures. Thus, in the previous example, when it comes to measuring students' aptitudes for college, the SAT is more reliable than counselor ratings, which in turn are more reliable than tossing dice. But in an absolute sense, how high is high enough—.50, .70, .90? This is a difficult question to answer specifically because the required reliability depends in part on the nature of the decision being made about the people being measured.

For example, let's assume some college admissions officer was considering several students depicted in Figures 6.1a and 6.1b. Turning first to Figure 6.1b, assume the admissions officer was deciding between Student 1 ($1_1$) and Student 20 ($20_{20}$). For this decision, the .50 reliability of the ratings is high enough because the difference between the two students is so large that one would make the same decision for admission regardless of the year in which the rating was taken. That is, Student 1 (with scores of 100 and 80 in the junior and senior year, respectively) is always admitted and Student 20 (with scores of 12 and 42 for junior and senior years, respectively) is always rejected. Thus, although the ratings in this case are not all that reliable in an absolute sense, their reliability is high enough for this decision.

On the other hand, let's assume the same college admissions officer was deciding between Student 1 ($1_1$) and Student 2 ($2_2$). Looking at Figure 6.1a, it is clear that even with the highly reliable SAT scores, the difference between these students is so small that one would make a different admission decision depending on what year one obtained the score. Student 1 would be selected over Student 2 if the junior-year score was used, but Student 2 would be chosen over Student 1 if the senior-year score was used. Thus, even though the reliability of the SAT exam is high in an absolute sense, it is not high enough for this decision. Under these conditions, the admissions officer needs to find some other basis for making the decision regarding these two students (like high school GPA or rank in graduating class).

Although these two scenarios clearly show that no specific value of reliability is always acceptable, they also demonstrate why, all else being equal, the more reliable a measure is, the better. For example, turning again to Figures 6.1a and 6.1b, consider Student 9 ($9_9$) and Student 14 ($14_{14}$). One would not be able to make a decision between these two students based on scholastic aptitude scores if assessed via counselor ratings, because the unreliability in the ratings is so large that scores across the two years conflict. That is, Student 9 has a higher rating than Student 14 in the junior year, but Student 14 has a higher rating than Student 9 in the senior year.

On the other hand, one would be able to base the decision on scholastic aptitude scores if assessed via the SAT, because the unreliability of the SAT scores is so low that scores across the two years point to the same conclusion. That is, Student 9's scores are always higher than Student 14's scores. Clearly, all else being equal, the more reliable the measure, the more likely it is that we can base decisions on the score differences that it reveals. Moreover, if there are differences between scores the first time someone takes a test and the second time, research evidence suggests that the second score is usually more predictive of future outcomes.[4]

There are many ways to increase the reliability of a test, including writing clear and unambiguous items and increasing the length of the test. In addition, new technologies that allow for the development of computer adaptive testing can generate highly reliable tests by tailoring the item sequencing and selection process differently for each individual. That is, with computer adaptive testing, there is no standard set of questions that everyone takes; instead, there is a massive pool of items, and the one that pops up on the test taker's screen depends partially on how that person did with past items. The program first sends some items of average difficulty, and if the respondent answers these correctly, the computer sends a set of more difficult items. If these are answered correctly, then a different set of even more difficult items is sent. If these are missed, then the program ratchets downs and sends easier items. The program continues iteratively until the exact level of difficulty is achieved where the respondent can get the items right about half the time. Although this process is incredibly efficient in terms of establishing the exact level of the person's ability, in the end, each test taker does not receive the exact same test, and some may feel this is unfair.[5] Indeed, this and other technological changes associated with the Internet have required people to think differently about exactly what is meant by various terms that have long been taken for granted in this area.

## Validity

We define **validity** as the extent to which performance on the measure is related to performance on the job. A measure must be reliable if it is to have any validity. On the other hand, we can reliably measure many characteristics (like height) that may have no relationship to whether someone can perform a job. For this reason, reliability is a necessary but insufficient condition for validity.

**Validity**
The extent to which a performance measure assesses all the relevant—and only the relevant—aspects of job performance.

figure 6.2
Relationship between 2006 SAT Scores and 2007 Freshman GPA

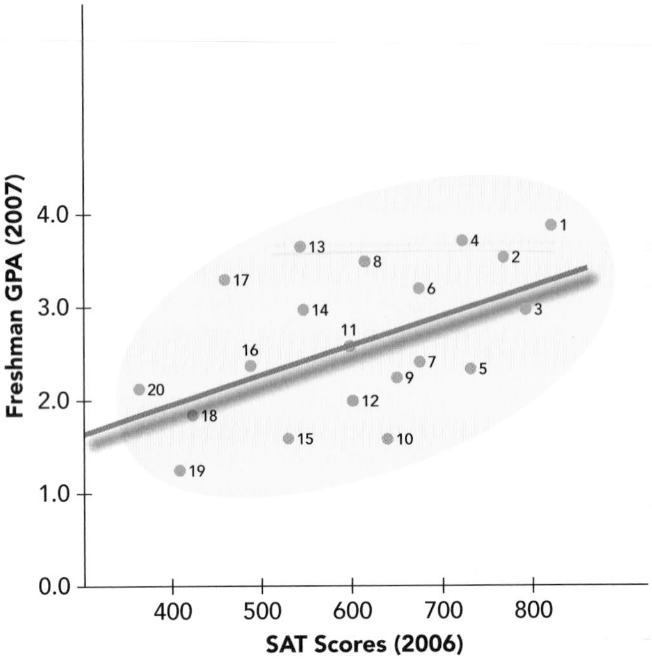


**Criterion-Related Validity**
A method of establishing the validity of a personnel selection method by showing a substantial correlation between test scores and job-performance scores.

**Predictive Validation**
A criterion-related validity study that seeks to establish an empirical relationship between applicants' test scores and their eventual performance on the job.

**Concurrent Validation**
A criterion-related validity study in which a test is administered to all the people currently in a job and then incumbents' scores are correlated with existing measures of their performance on the job.

## Criterion-Related Validation

One way of establishing the validity of a selection method is to show that there is an empirical association between scores on the selection measure and scores for job performance. If there is a substantial correlation between test scores and job-performance scores, **criterion-related validity** has been established. For example, Figure 6.2 shows the relationship between 2006 scores on the Scholastic Aptitude Test (SAT) and 2007 freshman grade point average (GPA). In this example, there is roughly a .50 correlation between the SAT and GPA. This .50 is referred to as a *validity coefficient*. Note that we have used the correlation coefficient to assess both reliability and validity, which may seem somewhat confusing. The key distinction is that the correlation reflects a reliability estimate when we are attempting to assess the same characteristic twice (such as SAT scores in the junior and senior years), but the correlation coefficient reflects a validity coefficient when we are attempting to relate one characteristic (SAT) to performance on some task (GPA).

Criterion-related validity studies come in two varieties. **Predictive validation** seeks to establish an empirical relationship between test scores taken prior to being hired and eventual performance on the job. Predictive validation requires one to administer tests to job applicants and then wait for some time after test administration to see how a subset of those applicants (those who were actually hired) performed.

Because of the time and effort required to conduct a predictive validation study, many employers are tempted to use a different design. **Concurrent validation** assesses the validity of a test by administering it to people already on the job and then correlating test scores with existing measures of each person's performance. The logic behind this strategy is that if the best performers currently on the job perform better on the test than those who are currently struggling on the job, the test has validity. (Figure 6.3 compares the two types of validation study.)

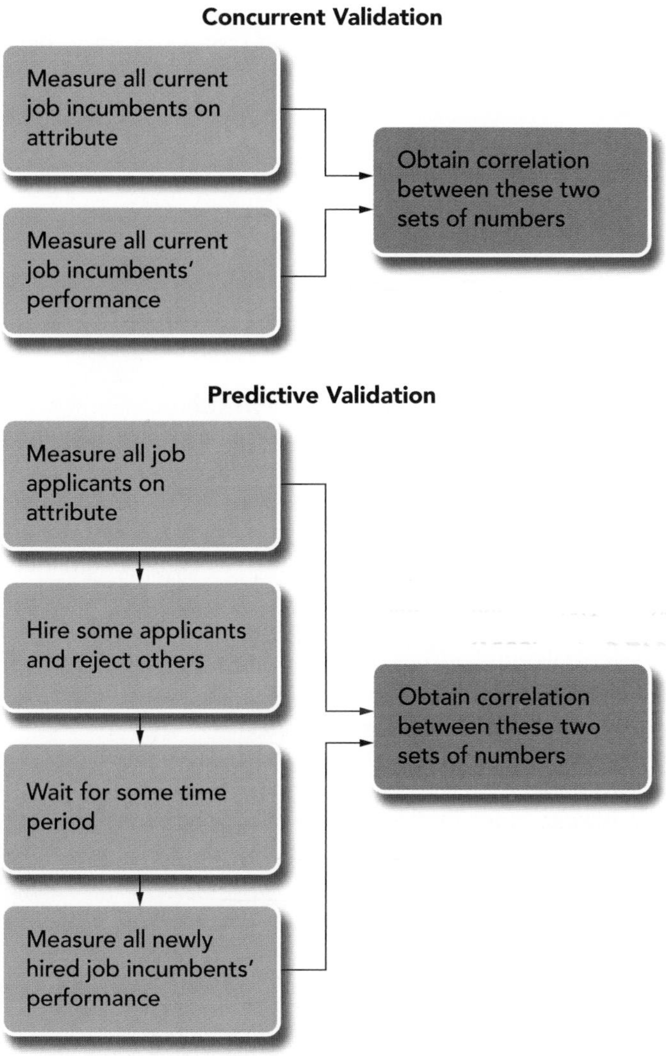


figure 6.3
Graphic Depiction of Concurrent and Predictive Validation Designs

Despite the extra effort and time needed for predictive validation, it is superior to concurrent validation for a number of reasons. First, job applicants (because they are seeking work) are typically more motivated to perform well on the tests than are current employees (who already have jobs). Second, current employees have learned many things on the job that job applicants have not yet learned. Therefore, the correlation between test scores and job performance for current employees may not be the same as the correlation between test scores and job performance for less knowledgeable job applicants. Third, current employees tend to be homogeneous—that is, similar to each other on many characteristics.[6] Thus, on many of the characteristics needed for success on the job, most current employees will show restriction in range. This restricted range makes it hard to detect a relationship between test scores and job-performance scores because few of the current employees will be very low on the characteristic you are trying to validate. For example, if emotional stability is required for a nursing career, it is quite likely that most nurses who have amassed five or six years' experience will score high on this characteristic. Yet to validate a test, you need both high test scorers (who

**table 6.1**

Required Level of Correlation to Reach Statistical Significance as a Function of Sample Size

| SAMPLE SIZE | REQUIRED CORRELATION |
|---|---|
| 5 | .75 |
| 10 | .58 |
| 20 | .42 |
| 40 | .30 |
| 80 | .21 |
| 100 | .19 |

should subsequently perform well on the job) and low test scorers (who should perform poorly on the job). Thus, although concurrent studies can sometimes help one anticipate the results of predictive studies, they do not serve as substitutes.[7]

Obviously, we would like our measures to be high in validity; but as with the reliability standard, we must also ask, how high is high enough? When trying to determine how much validity is enough, one typically has to turn to tests of statistical significance. A test of statistical significance answers the question, "How likely is it that a correlation of this size could have come about through luck or chance?"

Table 6.1 shows how big a correlation between a selection measure and a measure of job performance needs to be to achieve statistical significance at a level of .05 (that is, there is only a 5 out of 100 chance that one could get a correlation this big by chance alone). Although it is generally true that bigger correlations are better, the size of the sample on which the correlation is based plays a large role as well. Because many of the selection methods we examine in the second half of this chapter generate correlations in the .20s and .30s, we often need samples of 80 to 90 people.[8] A validation study with a small sample (such as 20 people) is almost doomed to failure from the start. Thus, many companies are too small to use a criterion-related validation strategy for most, if not all, of their jobs.

## Content Validation

**Content Validation**
A test-validation strategy performed by demonstrating that the items, questions, or problems posed by a test are a representative sample of the kinds of situations or problems that occur on the job.

When sample sizes are small, an alternative test validation strategy, content validation, can be used. **Content validation** is performed by demonstrating that the items, questions, or problems posed by the test are a representative sample of the kinds of situations or problems that occur on the job.[9] A test that is content valid exposes the job applicant to situations that are likely to occur on the job, and then tests whether the applicant currently has sufficient knowledge, skill, or ability to handle such situations.

For example, one general contracting firm that constructed tract housing needed to hire one construction superintendent.[10] This job involved organizing, supervising, and inspecting the work of many subcontractors involved in the construction process. The tests developed for this position attempted to mirror the job. One test was a scrambled subcontractor test, where the applicant had to take a random list of subcontractors (roofing, plumbing, electrical, fencing, concrete, and so on) and put them in the correct order that each should appear on the site. A second test measured construction error recognition. In this test, the applicant went into a shed that was specially constructed to have 25 common and expensive errors (like faulty wiring and upside-down windows) and recorded whatever problems she could detect. Because the content of these tests so closely parallels the content of the job, one can safely make inferences from one to the other. Although criterion-related validity is established by empirical means, content validity is achieved primarily through a process of expert judgment.

The ability to use content validation in small sample settings makes it generally more applicable than criterion-related validation. However, content validation has two limitations.[11] First, one assumption behind content validation is that the person who is to be hired must have the knowledge, skills, or abilities at the time she is hired. Thus it is not appropriate to use content validation in settings where the applicant is expected to learn the job in a formal training program conducted after selection.

Second, because subjective judgment plays such a large role in content validation, it is critical to minimize the amount of inference involved on the part of judges. Thus the judges' ratings need to be made with respect to relatively concrete and observable behaviors (for example, "applicant detects common construction errors" or "arranges optimal subcontractor schedules"). Content validation would be inappropriate for assessing more abstract characteristics such as intelligence, leadership capacity, and integrity.

## Generalizability

**Generalizability**
The degree to which the validity of a selection method established in one context extends to other contexts.

**Generalizability** is defined as the degree to which the validity of a selection method established in one context extends to other contexts. Thus, the SAT may be a valid predictor of someone's performance (e.g., as a measure of someone's GPA in an undergraduate program), but, does this same test predict performance in graduate programs? If the test does not predict success in this other situation, then it does not "generalize" to this other context. Thus, rather than rely on the SAT for all types of programs, separate tests like the GMAT, LSAT, MCAT, and GRE may be needed for particular types of graduate schools.

There are three primary "contexts" over which we might like to generalize: different situations (jobs or organizations), different samples of people, and different time periods. Just as reliability is necessary but not sufficient for validity, validity is necessary but not sufficient for generalizability.

It was once believed, for example, that validity coefficients were situationally specific—that is, the level of correlation between test and performance varied as one went from one organization to another, even though the jobs studied seemed to be identical. Subsequent research has indicated that this is largely false. Rather, tests tend to show similar levels of correlation even across jobs that are only somewhat similar (at least for tests of intelligence and cognitive ability). Correlations with these kinds of tests change as one goes across widely different kinds of jobs, however. Specifically, the more complex the job, the higher the validity of many tests.[12]

It was also believed that tests showed differential subgroup validity, which meant that the validity coefficient for any test–job performance pair was different for people of different races or genders. This belief was also refuted by subsequent research, and, in general, one finds very similar levels of correlations across different groups of people.[13]

Because the evidence suggests that test validity often extends across situations and subgroups, *validity generalization* stands as an alternative for validating selection methods for companies that cannot employ criterion-related or content validation. Validity generalization is a three-step process. First, the company provides evidence from previous criterion-related validity studies conducted in other situations that shows that a specific test (such as a test of emotional stability) is a valid predictor for a specific job (like nurse at a large hospital). Second, the company provides evidence from job analysis to document that the job it is trying to fill (nurse at a small hospital) is similar in all major respects to the job validated elsewhere (nurse at a large hospital). Finally, if the company can show that it uses a test that is the same as or similar to that used in the validated setting, then one can "generalize" the validity from the first context (large hospital) to the new context (small hospital).[14]

## Utility

**Utility**
The degree to which the information provided by selection methods enhances the effectiveness of selecting personnel in real organizations.

**Utility** is the degree to which the information provided by selection methods enhances the bottom-line effectiveness of the organization.[15] Strategic approaches to human resource management place a great deal of importance in determining the financial worth of their human capital, and great strides have been made in assessing this value.[16] In general, the more reliable, valid, and generalizable the selection method is, the more utility it will have. On the other hand, many characteristics of particular selection contexts enhance or detract from the usefulness of given selection methods, even when reliability, validity, and generalizability are held constant.

**LO2**
Discuss How the Particular Characteristics of a Job, Organization, or Applicant Affect the Utility of Any Test.

Figures 6.4a and 6.4b, for example, show two different scenarios where the correlation between a measure of extroversion and the amount of sales revenue generated by a sample of sales representatives is the same for two different companies: Company A and Company B. Although the correlation between the measure of extroversion and sales is the same, Company B derives much more utility or practical benefit from the measure. That is, as indicated by the arrows proceeding out of the boxes (which indicate the people selected), the average sales revenue of the three people selected by Company B (Figure 6.4b) is $850,000 compared to $780,000 from the three people selected by Company A (Figure 6.4a).

The major difference between these two companies is that Company B generated twice as many applicants as Company A. This means that the selection ratio (the percentage of people selected relative to the total number of people tested) is quite low for Company B (3/20) relative to Company A (3/10). Thus the people selected by Company B have higher amounts of extroversion than those selected by Company A; therefore, Company B takes better advantage of the relationship between extroversion and sales.

figure 6.4a

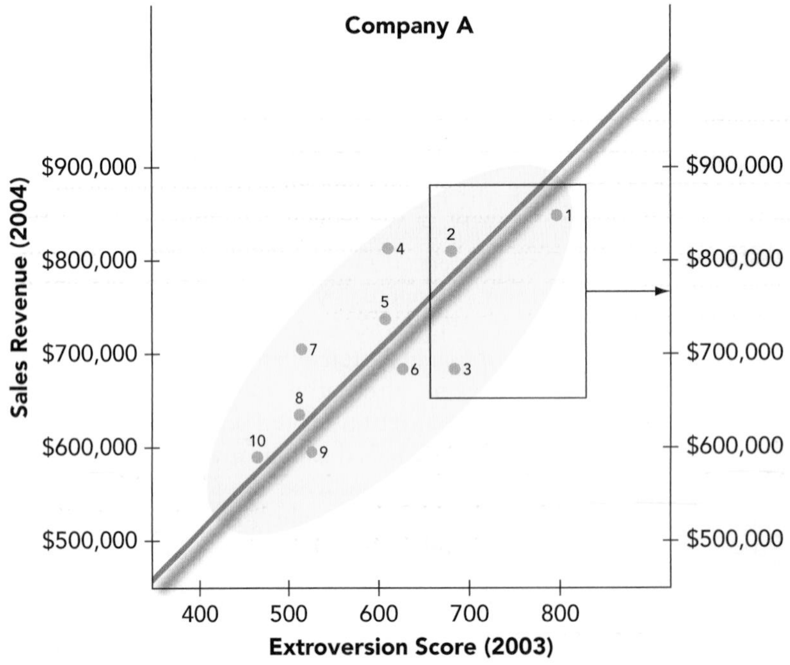

figure 6.4b

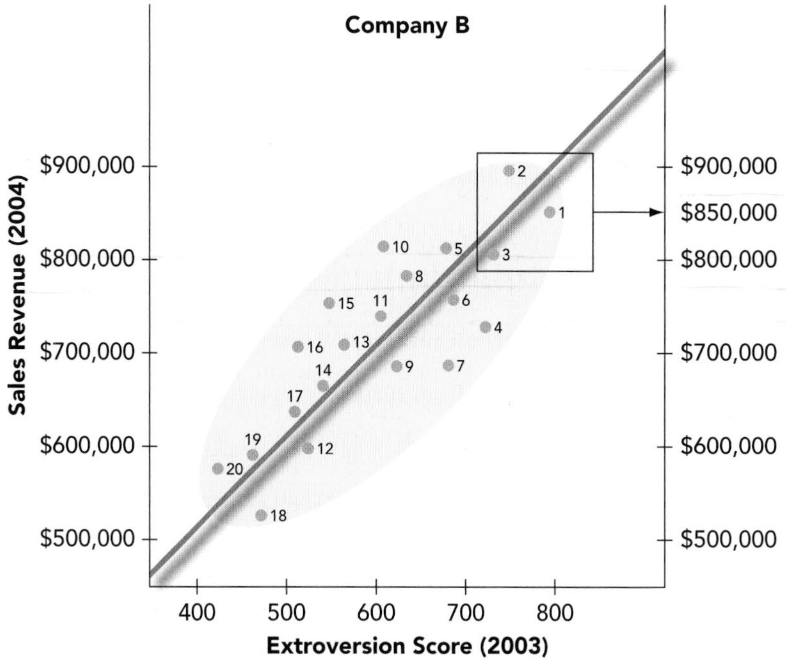


Although this might be somewhat offset by the cost of recruiting and measuring 20 more people, this added cost is probably trivial relative to the difference in revenue shown in this example ($70,000). Thus the utility of any test generally increases as the selection ratio gets lower, so long as the additional costs of recruiting and testing are not excessive.

Many other factors relate to the utility of a test. For example, the value of the product or service produced by the job incumbent plays a role: the more valuable the product or service, the more value there is in selecting the top performers. The cost of the test, of course, also plays a role. More expensive tests will on average have less utility unless they produce more valid predictions. A good recent example of this can be seen in the drug testing industry. Although few would dispute the reliability and validity of a properly conducted drug test, these can be relatively expensive, and employers are increasingly unwilling to pay the cost for these tests given the yield. Most drug tests yield few hard core drug abusers, and one study showed that given the hit rate of one test used in one department of the federal government, it cost the agency $77,000 per detected drug addict. Thus, although roughly 70 percent of companies were employing drug tests in 1996, that same figure is closer to 60 percent in 2003, due largely to cost/benefit questions such as this.[17]

## Legality

**LO3**
Describe the Government's Role in Personnel Selection Decisions, Particularly in the Areas of Constitutional Law, Federal Laws, Executive Orders, and Judicial Precedent.

The final standard that any selection method should adhere to is *legality*. All selection methods should conform to existing laws and existing legal precedents. Many issues related to selecting employees safely under U.S. law were discussed generically in Chapter 3. Our treatment there was broad and dealt with legal aspects in all areas of human resource management. In this chapter we focus more narrowly on issues that relate directly to personnel selection, bypassing constitutional amendments and focusing more squarely on federal legislation and executive orders.

## Federal Legislation

Three primary federal laws form the basis for a majority of the suits filed by job applicants. First, the Civil Rights Act of 1991 (discussed in Chapter 3), an extension of the Civil Rights Act of 1964, protects individuals from discrimination based on race, color, sex, religion, and national origin with respect to hiring as well as compensation and working conditions. The 1991 act differs from the 1964 act in three important areas.

First, it defines employers' explicit obligation to establish the business necessity of any neutral-appearing selection method that has had adverse impact on groups specified by the law. This is typically done by showing that the test has significant criterion-related or content validity. If the employer cannot show such a difference, which the research suggests will be difficult, then the process may be ruled illegal. It should also be noted that "customer preference" or "brand image" is not a legally defensible means of justifying a process that has adverse impact. For example, recently the retailer Abercrombie & Fitch was sued because it systematically screened out nonwhite applicants. Testimony in the trial suggested that one corporate representative visited a store, pointed to a blond-haired, blue-eyed model, and said, "This is the A&F look." She then told the manager that "she had better make the store look more like this."[18] This is not a legal defense, nor is the defense that "our customers prefer to buy from people of this or that race."

Second, the 1991 act allows the individual filing the complaint to have a jury decide whether he or she may recover punitive damages (in addition to lost wages and benefits) for emotional injuries caused by the discrimination.[19] This can generate large financial settlements as well as poor public relations that can hinder the organization's ability to compete. Finally, the 1991 act explicitly prohibits the granting of preferential treatment to minority groups. For example, it specifically prohibits adjusting scores upward on tests just because someone is in a group with lower average scores (sometimes referred to as *race norming*). Adjusting scores in this way has been found to have a number of negative effects, not only on the attitudes of white males who claim it causes reverse discrimination,[20] but on the proposed beneficiaries of such preferential treatment. Research shows that when selection decisions are perceived as being based partially on group membership, it undermines the confidence and hurts the job performance of the women or minority group members the program was designed to help.[21]

The Age Discrimination in Employment Act of 1967 is also widely used in personnel selection. Court interpretations of this act also mirror those of the Civil Rights Act, in the sense that if any neutral-appearing practice happens to have adverse impact on those over 40, the burden of proof shifts to the employer, who must show business necessity to avoid a guilty verdict.[22] The act does not protect younger workers (thus there is never a case for "reverse discrimination" here), and like the most recent civil rights act, it allows for jury trials and punitive damages. This act outlaws almost all "mandatory retirement" programs (company policies that dictate that everyone who reaches a set age must retire).

Litigation brought forward under this act surged in recent years. Two trends have combined to generate this increase: the general aging of the workforce and recent attempts by organizations to downsize. Together these trends have displaced many older workers, who have brought age discrimination suits against their former employers. The long list of companies sued under this act includes CBS Inc., McDonnell Douglas, Northwest Airlines, Disney, and Martin Marietta.[23] On the other hand, more recently, as the "Competing through Sustainability" box shows, many organizations have been

## COMPETING THROUGH SUSTAINABILITY

### The Y2Gray Crisis: Making Sure It Won't Happen

At the end of the last century, there was a flood of concern that computers would not roll over from 1999 to 2000 and that this would cause massive disruptions throughout U.S. society. In the end, this "Y2K" crisis never came to pass, and this may go down in history as one of the most overblown concerns to ever capture the national consciousness. A more recent crisis that has many of the markings of the same overhyped phenomenon relates to the aging of the U.S. workforce, or—as it is often referred to—the "Y2Gray" crisis. In this scenario, the predictions suggest that as the baby-boom generation creeps up on traditional retirement ages, massive retirement of skilled workers will result in crippling labor shortages that will disrupt the economy, bankrupt the Social Security system, and place an unsustainable burden on the rest of the working population. As one analyst noted, "We don't know if the shortage is 10 million or 14 million or 8 million, but the key is we are going to have a multimillion person shortage of skilled workers."

The primary basis for the Y2Gray crisis can be traced to data from the Bureau of Labor Statistics (BLS) that suggest that if past data regarding retirement practices and current data on the demographic makeup of the workforce are combined, the results point to a future labor shortage. However, this basic underlying demographic trend is then exacerbated by agism and biased perceptions in many businesses that limit the degree to which older workers are selected and placed in jobs that tap their true potential, increasing the exodus. Indeed, even in companies with no biased perceptions of older workers, neutral-appearing practices that are aimed at cutting costs, such as buyouts, are often disproportionately aimed at this set of workers due to their relatively high salaries. As Eugene Steuerle, senior fellow at the Urban Institute, noted, all of this combines to result in a situation where "people in their late 50s, 60s and 70s have now become the largest underutilized pool of human resources in the economy."

It does not have to be this way, and many organizations are recognizing the need to tap this source of graying talent in a way that creates sustainable competitive advantage. As we noted in our previous chapter, although historical trends are sometime useful in making projections, they assume that the past is a good predictor of the future. When it comes to retirement data, this does not seem to be the case. For example, the general level of health of this generation of workers is much better than any prior cohort of workers at similar ages in the past, thus reducing the need to retire early for health reasons. Moreover, the number of jobs in the current economy that are physically demanding has decreased dramatically, meaning that fewer older workers are facing insurmountable job demands that may be otherwise caused by physical limitations. Finally, the retirements of older workers today tend to be funded from 401(k) or defined contribution plans that reward staying in the workforce longer, as opposed to defined benefit plans, which make early retirements economically rational.

In addition to these factors that support working longer on the labor supply side, for many organizations, the skills and experience that this set of workers bring to the table also support working longer from the demand side. For example, this generation of older workers is perhaps the best educated cohort in history, and hence they have developed cognitive skills and human capital in specific fields that would take years to replace. In addition, in some businesses or industries, the long tenure of these workers has allowed them to build up personal relationships that may walk out the door with them should they retire from the organization. Finally, many organizations find that the unique experiences and values of this set of workers, when combined with unique experiences and values of younger generations, allow them to create diverse teams with flexible problem-solving strategies. Younger workers tend to work faster, but older workers tend to make fewer errors. Younger workers tend to face innovation with a radical revolutionary approach, whereas older workers tend to view innovation from a more incremental, evolutionary approach. When working together, this creates a vibrant team that can attack problems from a variety of angles.

To fully exploit the value of older workers, however, companies do have to recognize that their needs at this stage of life are different from those of younger workers and support them in unique ways. In many cases this is not happening. For example, a 2005 survey of personnel executives conducted by the Society of Human Resource Management revealed that 59 percent of the members do not actively recruit older workers and 65 percent have no specific policies to retain older workers. For example, older workers sometimes need to be targeted for on-the-job training on many technologies that younger workers are likely to pick up off-the-job, such as how to employ social networking or collaborative software. In addition, flexible work and pay policies need to be developed for some workers who are nearing retirement so they can reduce their hours in a way that is not a burden on the pay system or other workers. Finally, organizations need to fight explicit or implicit perceptual biases that unnecessarily constrain the nature of jobs in which these workers can be placed. All of this will be instrumental in securing increased competitive advantage for organizations as well as the U.S. economy as a whole, since people in many European countries are retiring at increasingly earlier ages.

SOURCES: E. Frauenheim, "False Alarm," *Workforce Management*, October 9, 2006, pp. 22–26; S. Jackson, "Supreme Court: Age Bias Need Not be Deliberate," *CNN.com*, March 30, 2005, p. 1; P. Coy, "Surprise! The Graying of the Workforce Is Better News than You Think," *BusinessWeek*, June 27, 2005, pp. 78–86; E. Frauenheim, "They Just Keep Going and Going . . .," *Workforce Management*, October 9, 2006. p. 26; A. Dunkin, "You're Older? So Sell Your Wisdom," *BusinessWeek*, February 19, 2007, p. 82; S. Berfield, "Walk 100 Miles in My Shoes," *BusinessWeek*, June 26, 2005, pp. 80–81.

reaching out to older workers as part of a strategic campaign to improve their performance and competitiveness.

Finally, the Americans with Disabilities Act (ADA) of 1991 protects individuals with physical and mental disabilities (or with a history of the same). It extends the Vocational Rehabilitation Act of 1973, requiring employers to make "reasonable accommodation" to disabled individuals whose handicaps may prevent them from performing essential functions of the job as currently designed. "Reasonable accommodation" could include restructuring jobs, modifying work schedules, making facilities accessible, providing readers, or modifying equipment. The ADA does not require an organization to hire someone whose disability prevents him or her from performing either critical or routine aspects of the job nor does it require accommodations that would cause "undue hardship."[24] However, technological advancements in the area of accommodations, along with the general shift in jobs from those that are physically demanding to those that are more mentally challenging, is increasing the percentage of jobs that disabled workers can hold.[25] Largely due to this act, the percentage of disabled people participating full-time in the U.S. workforce has increased from under 45 percent in 1986 to over 55 percent in 2001.[26]

## Executive Orders

As noted in Chapter 3, the executive branch of the government also regulates hiring decisions through the use of executive orders. Executive Order 11246 parallels the protections provided by the Civil Rights Act of 1964 but goes beyond the 1964 act in two important ways. First, not only do the executive orders prohibit discrimination, they actually mandate that employers take affirmative action to hire qualified minority applicants. Although many organizations attempt to promote diversity through training programs, the fact is that training programs are not very effective at creating a more integrated workforce. The best predictor of whether an organization becomes diverse is simply whether or not there is a person whose job it is to monitor and change hiring numbers (e.g., a diversity officer), and who is held strictly accountable for achieving quantifiable results in this regard.

Executive orders also allow the government to suspend all business with a contractor while an investigation is being conducted (rather than waiting for an actual finding), which puts a great deal of pressure on employers to comply with these orders. Executive orders are monitored by the Office of Federal Contract Compliance Procedures (OFCCP), which issues guidelines (like the Affirmative Action Program Guidelines published by the Bureau of National Affairs in 1983) to help companies comply.

## Types of Selection Methods

**LO4** List the Common Methods Used in Selecting Human Resources.

The first half of this chapter laid out the five standards by which we can judge selection measures. In the second half of this chapter, we examine the common selection methods used in various organizations and discuss their advantages and disadvantages in terms of these standards.

### Interviews

**LO5** Describe the Degree to Which Each of the Common Methods Used in Selecting Human Resources Meets the Demands of Reliability, Validity, Generalizability, Utility, and Legality.

A selection interview has been defined as "a dialogue initiated by one or more persons to gather information and evaluate the qualifications of an applicant for employment."[28] The selection interview is the most widespread selection method employed in organizations, and there have been literally hundreds of studies examining their effectiveness.[29]

Unfortunately, the long history of research on the employment interview suggests that, without proper care, it can be unreliable, low in validity,[30] and biased against a number of different groups.[31] Moreover, interviews are relatively costly because they require at least one person to interview another person, and these persons have to be brought to the same geographic location. Finally, in terms of legality, the subjectivity embodied in the process often makes applicants upset, particularly if they fail to get a job after being asked apparently irrelevant questions. Employers can also get into trouble in interview contexts when they do not pose the exact same questions to all applicants, since bias might be revealed in the nature of questions asked.[32] In the end, subjective selection methods like the interview must be validated by traditional criterion-related or content-validation procedures if they show any degree of adverse impact.[33]

Fortunately, more recent research has pointed to a number of concrete steps that one can employ to increase the utility of the personnel selection interview.[34] First, HR staff should keep the interview structured, standardized, and focused on accomplishing a small number of goals. That is, they should plan to come out of each interview with quantitative ratings on a small number of dimensions that are observable (like interpersonal style or ability to express oneself) and avoid ratings of abilities that may be better measured by tests (like intelligence). In addition to coming out of the interview with quantitative ratings, interviewers should also have a structured note-taking system that will aid recall when it comes to justifying the ratings.[35]

How to increase utility of selection interview

**table 6.2**

Examples of Experience-Based and Future-Oriented Situational Interview Items

| | |
|---|---|
| **Experience-based** | |
| Motivating employees: | "Think about an instance when you had to motivate an employee to perform a task that he or she disliked but that you needed to have done. How did you handle that situation?" |
| Resolving conflict: | "What was the biggest difference of opinion you ever had with a co-worker? How did you resolve that situation?" |
| Overcoming resistance to change: | "What was the hardest change you ever had to bring about in a past job, and what did you do to get the people around you to change their thoughts or behaviors?" |
| **Future-oriented** | |
| Motivating employees: | "Suppose you were working with an employee who you knew greatly disliked performing a particular task. You needed to get this task completed, however, and this person was the only one available to do it. What would you do to motivate that person?" |
| Resolving conflict: | "Imagine that you and a co-worker disagree about the best way to handle an absenteeism problem with another member of your team. How would you resolve that situation?" |
| Overcoming resistance to change: | "Suppose you had an idea for change in work procedures that would enhance quality, but some members of your work group were hesitant to make the change. What would you do in that situation?" |

**Situational Interview**
An interview procedure where applicants are confronted with specific issues, questions, or problems that are likely to arise on the job.

Second, ask questions dealing with specific situations that are likely to arise on the job, and use these to determine what the person is likely to do in that situation. These types of **situational interview** items have been shown to have quite high predictive validity.[36] Situational judgment items come in two varieties, as shown in Table 6.2. Some items are "experience-based" and require the applicant to reveal an actual experience he or she had in the past when confronting the situation. Other items are "future-oriented" and ask what the person is likely to do when confronting a certain hypothetical situation in the future. Research suggests that these types of items can both show validity but that experience-based items often outperform future-oriented items.[37] Experience-based items also appear to reduce some forms of impression management such as ingratiation better than future-oriented items.[38] Regardless of the past or future frame, an additional benefit of situational interview items is that their standardization and the concrete behavioral nature of the information that is collected mean that they can be effectively employed, even by those who have little training in psychological assessment.[39]

Situational interviews can be particularly effective when assessing sensitive issues dealing with the honesty and integrity of candidates. Clearly, simply asking people directly whether they have integrity will not produce much in the way of useful information. However, questions that pose ethical dilemmas and ask respondents to discuss how they dealt with such situations in the past are often revealing in terms of how different people deal with common dilemmas. For example, by stating "We have all observed someone stretching the rules at work, so give me two examples of situations in which you faced this dilemma and how you dealt with it," the interviewer forces the applicant to reveal how he or she deals with ethical dilemmas as an observer. Since the person is an observer and not the perpetrator in this case, he or she will be less defensive in terms of revealing how he or she deals with ethical issues. When assessing sensitive characteristics like this, research suggests that it is often best to wait until later in the interview to pose such questions, after some degree of rapport has been established and the candidate is less self-conscious.[40]

It is also important to use multiple interviewers who are trained to avoid many of the subjective errors that can result when one human being is asked to rate another. Many employers are now videotaping interviews and then sending the tapes (rather than the applicants) around from place to place. This is seen by some as a cost-effective means of allowing numerous raters to evaluate the candidate under standard conditions.[41]

When more than one person is able to interview a candidate for a position, there is significant advantage in removing any errors or biases that a single individual might make in choosing the correct person for the job. In today's technological world, it is becoming easier for multiple people to give their input in an interview by watching a video tape or listening via conference call if they cannot be there in person.

Limiting the subjectivity of the process is central to much of this training, and research suggests that it is best to ask interviewers to be "witnesses" of facts that can later be integrated via objective formulas, as opposed to being "judges" allowed to idiosyncratically weigh how various facts should be combined to form the final recommendation.[42] In addition to being a witness, the interviewer sometimes has to be the prosecuting attorney, since in some cases the interviewees may be motivated to try to present an overly positive, if not outright false, picture of their qualifications. Interviewers need to be critical and look for inconsistencies or gaps in stories or experiences in those who are providing information. Increasingly, interviewers are seeking training that helps them detect nonverbal signs that someone is trying to be deceptive, such as hand tremors, darting eyes, mumbled speech, and failing to maintain eye contact that may be a cause for concern and increased scrutiny.[43] In fact, one such trained observer in the U.S. Customs Department was credited with thwarting a terrorist mission aimed at disrupting the nation's Millennium Celebrations in Los Angeles. The officer spotted several behavioral manifestations of deceptiveness, then pulled the driver over for a detailed search that uncovered a substantial amount of bombmaking materials.[44]

## References, Biographical Data, and Application Blanks

Just as few employers would think of hiring someone without an interview, nearly all employers also use some method for getting background information on applicants before an interview. This information can be solicited from the people who know the candidate through reference checks.

The evidence on the reliability and validity of reference checks suggests that these are, at best, weak predictors of future success on the job.[45] The main reason for this low validity is that the evaluations supplied in most reference letters are so positive that it is hard to differentiate applicants. This problem with reference letters has two causes. First, the applicant usually gets to choose who writes the letter and can thus choose only those writers who think the highest of her abilities. Second, because letter writers can never be sure who will read the letters, they may fear that supplying damaging information about someone could come back to haunt them. This fear is well placed. For example, in 2003, a jury awarded $283,000 to a truck driver whose past employer told a would-be employer that he "was late most of the time, regularly missed two days a week, had a problem with authority and a poor work ethic."[46] In fact, there are even companies that provide a reference checking service for people who feel that they may be getting a damaging reference from an employer. For roughly $90, BadReferences.com will call and document what information past employers are providing for individuals who have such concerns. Applicants who are armed with this kind of evidence are in a strong legal position, and Michael Rankin, chief services officer at BadReferences, notes that "We haven't lost a case in twenty years."[47] Thus, it is clearly not in the past employers' interest to reveal too much information beyond job title and years of service.

The evidence on the utility of biographical information collected directly from job applicants is much more positive, especially for certain outcomes like turnover.[48] The low cost of obtaining such information significantly enhances its utility, especially when the information is used in conjunction with a well-designed, follow-up interview that complements, rather than duplicates, the biographical information bank.[49]

Again, as with the interview, the biggest concern with the use of biographical data, as we saw in our chapter opening vignette, is that applicants who supply the information may be motivated to misrepresent themselves. Background checks can help on this score, and many employers demand them.[50] In fact, as the "Competing through Technology" box shows, employers are increasingly performing their own background checks and uncovering a treasure trove of information by simply "Googling" an applicant's digital identity on the World Wide Web. However, background checks offer no guarantee, because of the increased sophistication of those in the dishonesty business. For example, there are now Web sites that will not only provide fake degrees, but also staffed telephone numbers that will provide further bogus information to callers. Some universities and state prison systems have even been hacked into by companies that try to insert or delete their clients' names from databases.[51] Even the U.S. Transportation Safety Administration, the organization in charge of national security at airports, struggles with this problem. In the ramp-up of hiring that followed the 9/11 attacks, the agency hired over 1,200 people for sensitive security jobs who later turned out to have criminal records.[52]

Although it is not a panacea, to some extent forcing applicants to elaborate on their responses to biodata questions can sometimes be helpful.[53] A good elaboration forces applicants to support their answers with evidence that includes names of other people involved, dates, locations, and objective evidence that would support a thorough cross-checking. Thus, rather than just asking someone if they have ever led a sales team, an elaborated item would force the applicant to name all members of the team, where and when the team was together, and what sales they accomplished citing specific products, figures, and customers. The evidence suggests that forced elaboration reduces the traditional measures of faking behavior.[54]

## Physical Ability Tests

Although automation and other advances in technology have eliminated or modified many physically demanding occupational tasks, many jobs still require certain physical abilities or psychomotor abilities.[55] In these cases, tests of physical abilities may be

## COMPETING THROUGH TECHNOLOGY

### Managing Your Digital Identity: "Dooce" and Don'ts

Heather Armstrong often struggled to quickly spell the word "dude" when instant messaging her friends. The word more typically came out "duce," which she later changed to "dooce" when setting up her blog, Dooce.com. When she was eventually fired by her employer for the content of what she posted on her blog, the term "dooced" was coined to refer to anyone who lost a job because of his or her digital identity. Thus, when former Delta Airlines flight attendant Ellen Simonetti was fired because she posted suggestive pictures in her work uniform on her personal Web site, it is fair to say "she was dooced."

It is also legitimate to use the term "dooced" to describe someone who was denied employment in the first place because of information the employer obtained from the Internet. Thus, when an employer "Googled" the name of a prospective job applicant and came across a description of a drunken binge the person just experienced, it is also fair to say he got dooced. Similarly, when another job applicant was not hired because potential co-workers did not think the "image" portrayed on his Web page (grandiose) matched the image of their work group (down-to-earth), it is fair to say he was dooced. Finally, if someone is discriminated against because the Internet was used to obtain information about him or her that would not be legal to ask in an interview, it is fair to say that person got dooced. In the new information age, it is dangerous to assume that the only information an employer has on you is what you provide on an application blank. Indeed, as Alice Marwick, a technology consultant, noted, "This takes people's own agency out of how they present themselves in an employment context."

The data from a 2006 survey of executive recruiters bears this out and reveals that employers commonly search the Web for information like this. In fact, 35 percent of respondents stated that they eliminated candidates based on what they learned from Web searches—up from 25 percent the year before. Some of this is attributable directly to content placed on blogs or social networking sites where the person may have disclosed information that a previous employer may have wanted to keep confidential (product launches, production problems, personnel matters, and so on). In other cases, the content of the person's digital identity may be at odds with the image or corporate culture that is being promoted by the organization. For example, in the Delta case, the company had previously been charged with sexism in the content of its marketing, and it was trying to move away from that image when Simonetti posed in her uniform.

The important point to take away from these lessons is that people need to manage their digital identity the same way they manage their résumés. For example, the first step, of course, is to know exactly what pops up on you if your name is searched. If your search turns up something potentially unflattering or embarrassing, remember that just removing it from your page may not be enough. The Internet does not come with an eraser, and others may have picked up and forwarded information, and so that information may still be out there. If possible, posting a correction may be a better approach because you can always point to that if some particular content becomes an issue. Since some information about you may have been posted by someone else, if this is inaccurate, it needs to be challenged, and a record of your challenge should be kept in hand so it too can be presented in the future. Finally, you may be able to manage any information that pops up for you (and in what order) by hiring a search engine optimization firm that will create both sites and hits for sites that will drive the incriminating information far, far down the list that is generated for you using various search algorithms.

If your digital record seems clear, then the next steps are much easier. First, try to minimize your "digital footprint" as much as possible, especially when it comes to information that is private. Second, make sure you do not post anything new that might portray you in a negative light. Although this may seem like common sense, for many people, blogging or managing their personal Web site is therapeutic, if not addictive, and this advice is thus, hard to take. Although it is possible to register with an online profile manager like LinkedIn, it is almost never safe to assume that you will be anonymous, and so the general rule should be that if you cannot say anything nice, don't say anything at all. Indeed, as Heather Armstrong, the original "dooce" notes, "I started this Web site in February 2001. A year later I was fired from my job for this Web site because I had written stories that included people in my workplace. My advice to you is BE YE NOT SO STUPID."

SOURCES: J. Twist "Pitfalls of Work Blogs," *BBC News*, May 15, 2006, p. 1; M. Conlin, "You Are What You Post," *BusinessWeek*, March 27 2006, pp. 52–53; D. Stead, "Just a Click Away," *BusinessWeek*, June 26, 2006, p. 9; O. Kharif, "Big Brother Is Reading Your Blog," *BusinessWeek*, February 28, 2006, p. 32.

relevant not only to predicting performance but to predicting occupational injuries and disabilities as well.[56] There are seven classes of tests in this area: ones that evaluate (1) muscular tension, (2) muscular power, (3) muscular endurance, (4) cardiovascular endurance, (5) flexibility, (6) balance, and (7) coordination.[57]

The criterion-related validities for these kinds of tests for certain jobs are quite strong.[58] Unfortunately, these tests, particularly the strength tests, are likely to have an adverse impact on some applicants with disabilities and many female applicants. For example, roughly two-thirds of all males score higher than the highest-scoring female on muscular tension tests.[59]

Because of this there are two key questions to ask in deciding whether to use these kinds of tests. First, is the physical ability essential to performing the job and is it mentioned prominently enough in the job description? Neither the Civil Rights Act nor the ADA requires employers to hire individuals who cannot perform essential job functions, and both accept a written job description as evidence of the essential functions of the job.[60] Second, is there a probability that failure to adequately perform the job would result in some risk to the safety or health of the applicant, co-workers, or clients? The "direct threat" clause of the ADA makes it clear that adverse impact against those with disabilities is warranted under such conditions.

**Cognitive Ability Tests**
Tests that include three dimensions: verbal comprehension, quantitative ability and reasoning ability.

**Verbal Comprehension**
Refers to a person's capacity to understand and use written and spoken language.

**Quantitative Ability**
Concerns the speed and accuracy with which one can solve arithmetic problems of all kinds.

**Reasoning Ability**
Refers to a person's capacity to invent solutions to many diverse problems.

## Cognitive Ability Tests

**Cognitive ability tests** differentiate individuals based on their mental rather than physical capacities. Cognitive ability has many different facets, although we will focus only on three dominant ones.[61] **Verbal comprehension** refers to a person's capacity to understand and use written and spoken language. **Quantitative ability** concerns the speed and accuracy with which one can solve arithmetic problems of all kinds. **Reasoning ability,** a broader concept, refers to a person's capacity to invent solutions to many diverse problems.

Some jobs require only one or two of these facets of cognitive ability. Under these conditions, maintaining the separation among the facets is appropriate. However, many jobs that are high in complexity require most, if not all, of the facets, and hence one general test is often as good as many tests of separate facets.[62] Highly reliable commercial tests measuring these kinds of abilities are widely available, and they are generally valid predictors of job performance in many different kinds of contexts, including widely different countries.[63] The validity of these kinds of tests is related to the complexity of the job, however, in that one sees higher criterion-related validation for complex jobs than for simple jobs.[64] The predictive validity for these tests is also higher in jobs that are dynamic and changing over time and thus require adaptability on the part of the job incumbent.[65]

As we saw in Chapter 4, organizational design and the specification of work processes reflect a strategic choice that involves how complex and dynamic individual jobs are going to be. This means that the strategic design of jobs has to be matched with strategic selection, so that when jobs are designed to be complex and dynamic, the selection system needs to emphasize cognitive ability. For example, although one generally thinks of football players as big and, perhaps, not so bright, the National Football League actually tests each player with a standardized cognitive ability test called the Wonderlic. Many teams use this device to select players, and this is especially the case for teams that strategically compete using complex offensive and defensive schemes described in playbooks that are over 200 pages long. For example, Mike Martz, former coach of the Superbowl champion St. Louis Cardinals, notes that, with respect to this test, "We have made a religion out of it in the last few years—as long as he plays at a high level, we'll choose a guy that is smarter." When brought in to help turn around the troubled Detroit Lions franchise, one of Martz's first moves was to draft players with high Wonderlic scores and cast off or trade players who scored low. Although it is too early to tell what effect this will have on the Lions, Martz can take comfort from the fact that 11 out of the last 14 Superbowl contenders have been in the top third overall in the league in general cognitive ability measured this way.[66]

Ironically, while the NFL is embracing cognitive ability testing, other institutions that one might think would find testing highly natural are abandoning the use of such tests. For example, the jobs of top-level executives could be fairly characterized as complex and dynamic, and analytic problem solving has consistently been shown to be a major predictor of success in this occupation.[67] Despite this, many of the top executive MBA programs, including 13 of the top 25 as ranked by *BusinessWeek,* have dropped the use of the GMAT in recent years.[68] The schools traditionally explain eliminating this screen in terms of placing more emphasis on diversity and experience relative to sheer brain power. However, due to the lucrative nature of these programs in terms of generating revenue for the schools, some have suggested that this is primarily a ploy to reduce barriers to entry, admit more students, and generate more revenue. This strategy may backfire, however, if the students who are eventually brought into these programs become a burden to their classmates or a liability to future employers. Indeed, there is some evidence that the ability to screen on general cognitive ability is the single greatest virtue associated with the most selective schools, and that controlling for this, the MBA degree itself is not a valid predictor for long-term executive success.[69]

One of the major drawbacks to these tests is that they typically have adverse impact on some minority groups. Indeed, the size of the differences is so large that some have advocated abandoning these types of tests for making decisions regarding who will be accepted for certain schools or jobs.[70] In the past, the difference between the means for blacks and whites meant that an average black would score at the 16th percentile of the distribution of white scores in some instances.[71] The notion of race norming, alluded to earlier, was born of the desire to use these high-utility tests in a manner that avoided adverse impact. Although race norming was made illegal by the recent amendments to the Civil Rights Act, some have advocated the use of banding to both achieve the benefits of testing and minimize its adverse impact. The concept of *banding* suggests that similar groups of people whose scores differ by only a small amount all be treated as having the same score. Then, within any band, preferential treatment is given to minorities. Most observers feel preferential treatment of minorities is acceptable when scores are tied, and banding simply broadens the definition of what constitutes a tied score.[72]

For example, in many classes a score of 90–100 percent may constitute a 4.0 for the course. This means that even though someone scoring 99 outperformed someone with a score of 91, each gets the same grade (a 4.0). Banding uses the same logic for all kinds of tests. Thus, if one was going to use the grade in the class as a selection standard, this would mean that the person with the 91 is equal to the person with the 99 (that is, they both score a 4.0), and if their scores are tied, preference should be given to the minority. Like race norming, banding is very controversial, especially if the bands are set too wide.[73]

## Personality Inventories

While ability tests attempt to categorize individuals relative to what they can do, personality measures tend to categorize individuals by what they are like. Two recent reviews of the personality literature independently arrived at five common aspects of personality.[74] We refer to these five major dimensions as "the Big Five": (1) extroversion, (2) adjustment, (3) agreeableness, (4) conscientiousness, and (5) inquisitiveness. Table 6.3 lists each of these with a corresponding list of adjectives that fit each dimension.

Although it is possible to find reliable, commercially available measures of each of these traits, the evidence for their validity and generalizability is mixed at best.[75] Despite this, the use of personality traits in selection contexts has risen over the years, and a 2006 study indicates that 35 percent of U.S. organizations employ these kinds of tests when selecting personnel.[76] Part of this is attributable to the wider use of team-based structures that put more emphasis on collaboration at work. In contexts where task interdependence between individuals is stressed, personality conflicts become more salient and disruptive relative to situations where individuals are working alone.[77] Team contexts require that people create and maintain roles and relationships, and several traits like agreeableness and conscientiousness seem to promote effective role taking.[78] On the other hand, people who are high in disagreeableness and low in conscientiousness are more prone to engage in counterproductive behavior in group contexts.[79]

**table 6.3**

The Five Major Dimensions of Personality Inventories

| | |
|---|---|
| 1. Extroversion | Sociable, gregarious, assertive, talkative, expressive |
| 2. Adjustment | Emotionally stable, nondepressed, secure, content |
| 3. Agreeableness | Courteous, trusting, good-natured, tolerant, cooperative, forgiving |
| 4. Conscientiousness | Dependable, organized, persevering, thorough, achievement-oriented |
| 5. Inquisitiveness | Curious, imaginative, artistically sensitive, broad-minded, playful |

The concept of "emotional intelligence" has been used to describe people who are especially effective in these kinds of fluid and socially intensive contexts. Emotional intelligence is traditionally conceived of having five aspects: (1) self-awareness (knowledge of one's strengths and weaknesses, (2) self-regulation (the ability to keep disruptive emotions in check), (3) self-motivation (how to motivate oneself and persevere in the face of obstacles), (4) empathy (the ability to sense and read emotions in others), and (5) social skills (the ability to manage the emotions of other people). Danial Goleman, one of the primary proponents of this construct, noted that "in the new workplace, with its emphasis on flexibility, teams and a strong customer orientation, this crucial set of emotional competencies is becoming increasingly essential for excellence in every job in every part of the world."[80] Although there is not a great deal of direct empirical research on emotional intelligence, there is a great deal of overlap between many of its dimensions and aspects of the Big Five, and there is a large body of evidence regarding these.

In addition to the development of team-based structures, the use of personality measures as screening devices has also increased because of the increased use of multinational structures and the increase in the number of jobs that require that people work in foreign locales. The number of people that are asked to work outside their own country has increased steadily over time, and more often than not, the decision of whom to send where is based primarily on technical skills. However, in one large study of expatriates working in Hong Kong, Japan, and Korea, high levels of emotional stability and openness to experience were two of the strongest predictors of adjustment and performance, and these tended to trump technical expertise when it came to predicting who would succeed and fail. In this study, the cost of an adjustment failure (i.e., someone who has to come home prior to finishing his or her assignment) was estimated at over $150,000 per person, and hence the stakes are high in this context.[81]

For example, conscientiousness, which captures the concepts of self-regulation and self-motivation, is one of the few factors that displays any validity across a number of different job categories, and many real-world managers rate this as one of the most important characteristics they look for in employees.[82] People high in conscientiousness show more stamina at work, which is helpful in many occupations. People who are high in conscientiousness strive to accomplish difficult goals and stand out relative to others, and hence are generally easier to motivate in work contexts.[83] Conscientiousness seems to be a particularly good predictor when teamed with tests of mental ability because there is a stronger relationship between this trait and performance when ability is high.[84] When jobs have a large customer service component or when ratings of job performance are taken in the form of subjective supervisory evaluations, it also helps if people who are high on conscientiousness are also high in social skills. This helps ensure that the achievement striving behaviors they exhibit are noticed by critical stakeholders.[85]

Although conscientiousness is the only dimension of personality that seems to show predictive validity across all situations, there are contexts where other components of the Big Five relate to job performance. First, extroversion and agreeableness seem to be related to performance in jobs such as sales or management; it is easy to see why these types of attributes would be required for such jobs.[86] These two factors also seem to be predictive of performance in team contexts, although in many cases it is the score of the lowest team member that determines the whole group outcome. That is, one highly disagreeable, introverted, or unconscientious member can ruin an entire team.[87]

Finally, the validity for almost all of the Big Five factors in terms of predicting job performance also seems to be higher when the scores are not obtained from the applicant but are instead taken from other people.[88] The lower validity associated with self-reports of personality can be traced to three factors. First, people sometimes lack insight into what their own personalities are actually like (or how they are perceived by others), so their scores are inaccurate or unreliable. Second, people's personalities sometimes vary across different contexts. Thus, someone may be very conscientious when it comes to social activities such as planning a family wedding or a fraternity party, but less conscientious when it comes to doing a paid job. Someone else may work hard at the office, and then not lift a finger to do household chores. Third, unlike intelligence tests, people are much better at "faking" their responses to personality items.[89] Research suggests that when people fill out these inventories when applying for a job, their scores on conscientiousness and emotional stability are much higher relative to when they are just filling out the same questionnaires anonymously for research purposes.[90]

Several steps can be used to try to reduce faking. For example, if employers simply warn applicants that they are going to cross-check the applicants' self-ratings with other people, this seems to reduce faking.[91] Also, the degree to which people can fake various personality traits is enhanced with questionnaires, and one sees much less faking of traits when interviewers are assessing the characteristics. [92] Finally, "Conditional Reasoning Tests," which try to tap personality traits indirectly by seeing how people resolve problems and make decisions, also seem to be less fakable relative to direct measures.[93]

Although these steps can be taken to try to reduce faking, they have had only mixed levels of success, and although a very low score on these traits is usually informative, a high score can come about in two ways—either the person is really high on the characteristics or he or she is faking.[94] All of this reinforces the idea that it is better to obtain this information from people other than the job applicant, and that it is better to use this information to reject low scorers but not necessarily hire all higher scores on the basis of self-reports alone.[95]

## EVIDENCE-BASED HR

It is essential to collect empirical evidence and validate personality tests in specific contexts rather than assuming that they will work because you were told that by a commercial developer of such tests. For example, one context where measures of personality have been validated with empirical evidence is in the context of franchise operations. A franchise operation is usually part of a national chain (e.g., Burger King, Kentucky Fried Chicken, World Gyms) but is run locally in an entrepreneurial fashion by a single individual. Evidence within this industry indicates that the amount of revenue each franchise generates varies widely, despite the similarity of product, advertising, and size across the corporation. To learn why this was the case, one franchise operator distributed a set of personality items to all current franchisees and identified each item that distinguished those generating revenue in the top 80th percentile from those whose revenue generation placed them in the bottom 20th percentile. The distinguishing items were then used to select future franchisees who tended to resemble the current high performers and not the current low performers (note this is what was referred to earlier as a concurrent design), resulting in an increase in annual royalties per franchise from $6,500 a month to $52,000.

SOURCE: J. Bennett, "Do You Have What It Takes?" *The Wall Street Journal*, September 19, 2006, p. R11.

## Work Samples

Work-sample tests attempt to simulate the job in a prehiring context to observe how the applicant performs in the simulated job.[96] The degree of fidelity in work samples can vary greatly. In some cases, applicants respond to a set of standardized hypothetical case studies and role play how they would react to certain situations.[97] Often these standardized role plays employ interactive video technology to create "virtual job auditions."[98] In other cases, the job applicants are brought to the employers' location and actually perform the job for a short time period as part of a "job tryout."[99] Finally, although not generally considered a test, the practice whereby employers hire someone on a temporary basis and then, after a rather long trial (six months to a year), hire that person permanently is in essence an extended work-sample test.[100]

In some cases, employers will sponsor competitions where contestants (who at this point are not even considered job applicants) vie for attention by going head-to-head in solving certain job-related problems. These sorts of competitions have been common in some industries like architecture and fashion design, but their use is spreading across many other business contexts. These competitions tend to be cost effective in generating a lot of interest, and some have attracted as many as 1,000 contestants who bring their talents to bear on specific problems faced by the employing organization.[101] Competitions are particularly well-suited for assessing and "discovering" young people who may not have extended track records or portfolios to evaluate.

As part of its own fight in the war for talent, Google sponsors an event called "Google Code Jam," which attracts more than 10,000 contestants a year from all over the world. This one-day competition requires contestants work to solve some very difficult programming problems under relatively high levels of time pressure. For example, finalists have to develop software that would perform unique and difficult searches employing a minimum number of "clicks" or develop a complex interactive war game from scratch in under two hours. The winner of the contest receives $7,000 and a guaranteed job at Google's prestigious Research and Development Center, but, in fact, Google usually winds up hiring over half of the 50 finalists each year (but that is not guaranteed). The finalists in this contest represent the best of the best in terms of world's top programmers, and as Robert Hughes, director of the Code Jam, notes, "Wherever the best talent is, Google wants them."[102] Moreover, as the Competing through Globalization Box illustrates, the winners of these competitions often come from what some would consider unlikely places.

The key in work-sample tests is the behavioral consistency between the requirements of the job and the requirements of the test.[103] Work-sample tests tend to be job specific—that is, tailored individually to each different job in each organization. On the positive side, this has resulted in tests that demonstrate a high degree of criterion-related validity. In addition, the obvious parallels between the test and the job make content validity high. In general, this reduces the likelihood that rejected applicants will challenge the procedure through litigation. Applicants who take work sample tests tend to see them as providing a clear "opportunity to perform," which promotes perceptions of fairness.[104] Available evidence also suggests that these tests are low in adverse impact.[105]

With all these advantages come two drawbacks. First, by their very nature the tests are job-specific, so generalizability is low. Second, partly because a new test has to be developed for each job and partly because of their nonstandardized formats, these tests are relatively expensive to develop. It is much more cost-effective to purchase a commercially available cognitive ability test that can be used for a number of different job categories within the company than to develop a test for each job. For this reason,

## COMPETING THROUGH GLOBALIZATION

### International Programming Competitions: Just Fun and Games?

In 1961, Russian Yuri Gagarin became the first person in world history to orbit the planet in a rocket-launched space vehicle. Because this occurred at the middle of the cold war, Americans were shocked and upset by this development and reacted by launching a national quest for space superiority, ending with the successful moon landing of 1969. Although not nearly as well known as Gagarin's flight, the results from the most recent programming competitions sponsored by companies like Google and Microsoft seem to be sending the same message. When it comes to international competitions that pit teams of technical problem solvers and computer programmers against one another in head-to-head competition, central and eastern Europeans are again dominating the field.

For example, the winning team at the 2006 ACM International Collegiate Programming Contest—who solved six complex programming puzzles in a grueling five-hour contest—hailed from Saratov State University in Russia. Only one U.S. team finished in the top 12 that year, and the next best U.S. team, from Duke University, solved only one of the puzzles that comprised the competition. The results from the 2005 competition, which was won by a team from Warsaw University in Poland, were even worse for the United States because no U.S. team finished in the top 12. Although one might dismiss these competitions as mere games, these games are pointing to an increasingly recognized fact that some of the best young minds are coming out of universities in central and eastern Europe. In the Soviet days, many workers from these countries would come to the United States to be educated and then stay but, increasingly, visa restrictions in the post-9/11 era and protectionist sentiments are making this more difficult, thus shifting the balance of power in the war for talent.

Indeed, although the Marxist regimes that ran these countries certainly created some problems, the systems of higher education were always quite good, especially when it came to mathematics and engineering. This emphasis on technical and applied skills often distinguishes these schools from their counterparts in western Europe, where the emphasis is more on management, economics, and law. Thus, although many Western companies first came into the regions of central and eastern Europe to take advantage of low-cost manufacturing labor, they soon realized how much more sophisticated the talent base really was once they were established there. "If you give them advanced tools and design knowledge, they bridge the gap between complex technology and low-cost systems," notes Hari Nair, the executive vice-president of operations for Tenneco Automotive.

In addition to having great technical skills, workers from this region also successfully compete against U.S. and western European students on price. The wages for engineers in countries like Romania, Poland, the Czech Republic, Hungary, and Bulgaria are one-tenth of what one would find in the United States or Germany. Cheaper rates can be found in Asia and India, but the greater proximity of central Europe to the United States and western Europe gives them a geographic advantage. As David Morgenstern, managing director of supply chain specialist Ariba Inc., notes, "Even if China is 5 percent cheaper, the location advantage swings the argument back to sourcing in Central Europe." Finally, the language skills of these students, who are often fluent in multiple languages beyond English and their native language, makes them unique when compared to U.S. or Asian workers.

Whether the United States can rebound from this trend the same way it rebounded from Gagarin's famous flight is yet to be seen. In responding to his team's loss in the international programming competition, the faculty adviser to Duke's team, Owen Astrachan, tried to cheer up the team, reassuring them that they should be proud of what they accomplished. Astrachan noted that even though they did not finish in the top 12, they were one of the top U.S. teams, and that they were competing against the best of the best. This pep talk did little to cheer up Duke senior Matt Edwards, however, who simply responded: "Yeah, we're the worst of the best of the best."

SOURCES: S. Hamm, "A Red Flag in the Brian Game," *BusinessWeek*, May 1, 2006, pp. 32–35; S. E. Ante, "Give Me Your Diligent, Your Smart," *BusinessWeek*, May 1, 2006, p. 35; J. Ewing and G. Edmondson, "The Rise of Central Europe," *BusinessWeek*, December 12, 2005, pp. 50–56; P. Kranz, "Sitting Pretty in Prague: DHL's Tech Triumph," *BusinessWeek*, December 12, 2005, p. 56.

some have rated the utility of cognitive ability tests higher than work-sample tests, despite the latter's higher criterion-related validity.[106]

In the area of managerial selection, work-sample tests are typically the cornerstone in assessment centers. Generically, the term **assessment center** is used to describe a wide variety of specific selection programs that employ multiple selection methods to rate either applicants or job incumbents on their managerial potential. Someone attending an assessment center would typically experience work-sample tests such as an in-basket test and several tests of more general abilities and personality. Because assessment centers employ multiple selection methods, their criterion-related validity tends to be quite high. Assessment centers seem to tap a number of different characteristics, but "problem-solving ability" stands out as probably the most important skill tapped via this method.[107] The idiosyncratic and unique nature of the different exercises, however, has led some to suggest that the exercises themselves should be scored for winners and losers without making any reference to higher order characteristics like skills, abilities, or traits.[108] Research indicates that one of the best combinations of selection methods includes work-sample tests with a highly structured interview and a measure of general cognitive ability. The validity coefficient expected from such a combined battery often exceeds .60.[109]

**Assessment Center**
A process in which multiple raters evaluate employees' performance on a number of exercises.

## Honesty Tests and Drug Tests

Many problems that confront society also exist within organizations, which has led to two new kinds of tests: honesty tests and drug-use tests. Many companies formerly employed polygraph tests, or lie detectors, to evaluate job applicants, but this changed with the passage of the Polygraph Act in 1988. This act banned the use of polygraphs in employment screening for most organizations. However, it did not eliminate the problem of theft by employees. As a result, the paper-and-pencil honesty testing industry was born.

Paper-and-pencil honesty tests come in a number of different forms. Some directly emphasize questions dealing with past theft admissions or associations with people who stole from employers. Other items are less direct and tap more basic traits such as social conformity, conscientiousness, or emotional stability.[110] Some sample items are shown in Table 6.4. A large-scale independent review of validity studies conducted by the publishers of many integrity tests suggests they can predict both theft and other disruptive behaviors.[111] Another positive feature of these tests is that one does not see large differences attributable to race or sex, so they are not likely to have adverse impact on these demographic groups.[112]

As is the case with measures of personality, some people are concerned that people confronting an honesty test can fake their way to a passing score. The evidence suggests that people instructed to fake their way to a high score (indicating honesty) can

**table 6.4**
Sample Items from a Typical Integrity Test

1. It's OK to take something from a company that is making too much profit.
2. Stealing is just a way of getting your fair share.
3. When a store overcharges its customers, it's OK to change price tags on merchandise.
4. If you could get into a movie without paying and not get caught, would you do it?
5. Is it OK to go around the law if you don't actually break it?

SOURCE: From *Inc.: The Magazine for Growing Companies.* Copyright © 1992 by Goldhirsh Group/Inc. Publishing. Reproduced with permission of Goldhirsh Group/Inc. Publishing via Copyright Clearance Center.

do so. However, it is not clear that this affects the validity of the predictions made using such tests. That is, it seems that despite this built-in bias, scores on the test still predict future theft. Thus, the effect of the faking bias is not large enough to detract from the test's validity.[113]

As with theft, there is a growing perception of the problems caused by drug use among employees. Indeed, 79 percent of *Fortune's* 1,000 chief executives cited substance abuse as a significant problem in their organizations, and 50 percent of medium-size and large organizations test applicants for drug use.[114] Because the physical properties of drugs are invariant and subject to highly rigorous chemical testing, the reliability and validity of drug tests are very high.

The major controversies surrounding drug tests involve not their reliability and validity but whether they represent an invasion of privacy, an unreasonable search and seizure, or a violation of due process. Urinalysis and blood tests are invasive procedures, and accusing someone of drug use is a serious matter. Employers considering the use of drug tests would be well advised to make sure that their drug-testing programs conform to some general rules. First, these tests should be administered systematically to all applicants for the same job. Second, testing seems more defensible for jobs that involve safety hazards associated with failure to perform.[115] Test results should be reported back to the applicant, who should be allowed an avenue of appeal (and perhaps retesting). Tests should be conducted in an environment that is as unintrusive as possible, and results from those tests should be held in strict confidence. Finally, when testing current employees, the program should be part of a wider organizational program that provides rehabilitation counseling.[116]

## A Look Back

In the vignette that opened this chapter, we saw how one poor hiring decision caused by lack of information regarding a specific job candidate resulted in a great deal of human suffering and essentially put a large hospital out of business. These are some of the most critical decisions that an organization will make, and thus leaving these decisions to the idiosyncratic and nonstandardized subjective judgments of uninformed local managers may not be the best method of making such choices. Thankfully, there are numerous alternatives to this for making such decisions, many of which have been validated and supported by years of research, and these were highlighted in this chapter.

### Questions

1. Based on this chapter, what are the best methods of obtaining information about job applicants?
2. What are the best characteristics to look for in applicants, and how does this depend on the nature of the job?
3. If you could use only two of the methods described in this chapter and could assess only two of the characteristics discussed, which would you choose, and why?

Please see the Video Case that corresponds to this chapter online at www. mhhe.com/noe6e.

standards

**table 6.5**

A Summary of Personnel Selection Methods

| METHOD | RELIABILITY | VALIDITY | GENERALIZABILITY | UTILITY | LEGALITY |
|---|---|---|---|---|---|
| Interviews | Low when unstructured and when assessing nonobservable traits | Low if unstructured and nonbehavioral | Low | Low, especially because of expense | Low because of subjectivity and potential interviewer bias; also, lack of validity makes job-relatedness low |
| Reference checks | Low, especially when obtained from letters | Low because of lack of range in evaluations | Low | Low, although not expensive to obtain | Those writing letters may be concerned with charges of libel |
| Biographical information | High test–retest, especially for verifiable information | High criterion-related validity; low in content validity | Usually job-specific, but have been successfully developed for many job types | High; inexpensive way to collect vast amounts of potentially relevant data | May have adverse impact; thus often develop separate scoring keys based on sex or race |
| Physical ability tests | High | Moderate criterion-related validity; high content validity for some jobs | Low; pertain only to physically demanding jobs | Moderate for some physical jobs; may prevent expensive injuries and disability | Often have adverse impact on women and people with disabilities; need to establish job-relatedness |
| Cognitive ability tests | High | Moderate criterion-related validity; content validation inappropriate | High; predictive for most jobs, although best for complex jobs | High; low cost and wide application across diverse jobs in companies | Often have adverse impact on race, especially for African Americans, though decreasing over time |
| Personality inventories | High | Low to moderate criterion-related validity for most traits; content validation inappropriate | Low; few traits predictive for many jobs, except conscientiousness | Low, although inexpensive for jobs where specific traits are relevant | Low because of cultural and sex differences on most traits, and low job-relatedness in general |
| Work-sample tests | High | High criterion and content validity | Usually job-specific, but have been successfully developed for many job types | High, despite the relatively high cost to develop | High because of low adverse impact and high job-relatedness |
| Honesty tests | Insufficient independent evidence | Insufficient independent evidence | Insufficient independent evidence | Insufficient independent evidence | Insufficient history of litigation, but will undergo scrutiny |
| Drug tests | High | High | High | Expensive, but may yield high payoffs for health-related costs | May be challenged on invasion-of-privacy grounds |

## SUMMARY

In this chapter we examined the five critical standards with which all personnel selection methods should conform: reliability, validity, generalizability, utility, and legality. We also looked at nine different selection methods currently used in organizations and evaluated each with respect to these five standards. Table 6.5 summarizes these selection methods and can be used as a guide in deciding which test to use for a specific purpose. Although we discussed each type of test individually, it is important to note in closing that there is no need to use only one type of test for any one job. Indeed, managerial assessment centers use many different forms of tests over a two- or three-day period to learn as much as possible about candidates for important executive positions. As a result, highly accurate predictions are often made, and the validity associated with the judicious use of multiple tests is higher than for tests used in isolation.

## KEY TERMS

Reliability, 227
Validity, 231
Criterion-related validity, 232
Prediction validation, 232
Concurrent validation, 232
Content validation, 234
Generalizability, 235
Utility, 236
Situational interview, 242
Cognitive ability tests, 246
Verbal comprehension, 246
Quantitative ability, 246
Reasoning ability, 246
Assessment center, 253

## DISCUSSION QUESTIONS

1. We examined nine different types of selection methods in this chapter. Assume that you were just rejected for a job based on one of these methods. Obviously, you might be disappointed and angry regardless of what method was used to make this decision, but can you think of two or three methods that might leave you most distressed? In general, why might the acceptability of the test to applicants be an important standard to add to the five we discussed in this chapter?
2. Videotaping applicants in interviews is becoming an increasingly popular means of getting multiple assessments of that individual from different perspectives. Can you think of some reasons why videotaping interviews might also be useful in evaluating the interviewer? What would you look for in an interviewer if you were evaluating one on videotape?
3. Distinguish between concurrent and predictive validation designs, discussing why the latter is preferred over the former. Examine each of the nine selection methods discussed in this chapter and determine which of these would have their validity most and least affected by the type of validation design employed.
4. Some have speculated that in addition to increasing the validity of decisions, employing rigorous selection methods has symbolic value for organizations. What message is sent to applicants about the organization through hiring practices, and how might this message be reinforced by recruitment programs that occur before selection and training programs that occur after selection?

## SELF-ASSESSMENT EXERCISE

Reviews of research about personality have identified five common aspects of personality, referred to as the Big Five personality traits. Find out which are your most prominent traits. Read each of the following statements, marking "Yes" if it describes you and "No" if it does not.

1. In conversations I tend to do most of the talking.
2. Often people look to me to make decisions.
3. I am a very active person.
4. I usually seem to be in a hurry.
5. I am dominant, forceful, and assertive.
6. I have a very active imagination.
7. I have an active fantasy life.
8. How I feel about things is important to me.
9. I find it easy to feel myself what others are feeling.

10. I think it's interesting to learn and develop new hobbies.
11. My first reaction is to trust people.
12. I believe that most persons are basically well intentioned.
13. I'm not crafty or shy.
14. I'd rather not talk about myself and my accomplishments.
15. I'd rather praise others than be praised myself.
16. I come into situations being fully prepared.
17. I pride myself on my sound judgment.
18. I have a lot of self-discipline.
19. I try to do jobs carefully so they don't have to be done again.
20. I like to keep everything in place so I know where it is.
21. I enjoy performing under pressure.
22. I am seldom sad or depressed.
23. I'm an even-tempered person.
24. I am levelheaded in emergencies.
25. I feel I am capable of coping with most of my problems.

The statements are grouped into categories. Statements 1–5 describe extroversion, 6–10 openness to experience, 11–15 agreeableness, 16–20 conscientiousness, and 21–25 emotional stability. The more times you wrote "Yes" for the statements in a category, the more likely you are to have the associated trait.

## EXERCISING STRATEGY: NEVER HAVING TO SAY "YOU NEVER KNOW"

Seymour Schlager had an impressive résumé. He had both MD and JD degrees, as well as a PhD in microbiology. He had experience as a director of established AIDS research at Abbott Laboratories, and as an entrepreneur in a small, upstart pharmaceutical company. He seemed like a perfect fit for the medical director job open at Becton Dickinson, a large medical device company, and was hired on the spot.

One fact about Schlager that did not come out of the application process was that he was convicted of attempted murder in 1991 and had spent several years in prison as a result of this crime. While any reader of this book could type Schlager's name into almost any Internet search engine and uncover at least one of the 24 articles written about his case—some of which were front-page material in the *Chicago Tribune*—apparently no one at Becton Dickinson felt this was necessary.

Although this is an extreme case, the practice of stretching, shading, spinning, and outright lying on one's résumé is hardly uncommon, and when one is in the business of hiring complete strangers, it pays to "be afraid—be very afraid." Although many firms fail to perform routine background checks on their hires, organizations that provide such checks can point to some startling statistics. For example, Kroll Associates, one of the leading investigative agencies for top-level executives, notes that of the 70 background checks it did in the year 2000, 39 percent turned up problems such as fraud, bankruptcy, and SEC violations that were serious enough to nix the employment offers being considered.

One reason for the lack of "due diligence" on the part of employers is that in a labor shortage, too many are in a rush to secure top talent. For example, when the firm Christian and Timbers narrowed the search for the new CEO of Pinpoint Networks Inc. down to six candidates, rather than let the firm finish its work, the young founders of this company were so infatuated with the résumé of one applicant that they immediately took over and closed the search. Unfortunately, when it became clear 13 weeks later that the new CEO, Anthony J. Blake, was not who he claimed to be, it was too late. Without a seasoned CEO, Pinpoint blew the opportunity to attract venture capital when it was still available. When the technology sector tanked later that year, Pinpoint was forced to lay off over a third of its workforce.

Experiences such as these are prompting other employers to slow down the hiring process so that they have a much better idea of exactly whom they are asking to join their organizational family. Some firms do not only background checks but also extensive psychological testing to ensure that a person is who he or she claims to be and also fits the culture of the organization. You never know what these kinds of investigations will uncover—unless, of course, you fail to perform them.

### Questions

1. People applying for jobs are always motivated to display themselves in the best light, and as a result, this can sometimes lead to inaccurate portrayals of abilities, skills, experiences, and personality. Based upon what you have read in this chapter, how should you approach a job applicant's written application and résumé if your goal is to make sure that they accurately reflect the person's past experiences and accomplishments?
2. In the face-to-face interview process, what steps can be taken to ensure that the applicant is being frank and honest with you, and what steps should you take if you feel that he or she is portraying an inaccurate picture of himself or herself?

3. Beyond the traditional approaches of going over the application and conducting face-to-face interviews, what other steps can you as an employer take to ensure that the person who is being hired for the job has the right abilities, skills, past experiences and personality?

SOURCES: G. David, "You Just Hired Him: Should You Have Known Better," *Fortune*, October 29, 2001, pp. 205–6; D. Foust, "When the CEO Is Too Good to Be True," *BusinessWeek*, July 16, 2001, pp. 62–63; C. Daniels, "Does This Man Need a Shrink?" *Fortune*, February 5, 2001.

## MANAGING PEOPLE: FROM THE PAGES OF *BUSINESSWEEK*

### BusinessWeek White Men Can't Help It

**Courts have been buying the idea that they have innate biases** Winning a big employment lawsuit these days often requires a bit of magic. After all, companies are awash in diversity training, equal opportunity policies, and 800 numbers aimed at rooting out bias. Managers have been well trained to keep their discriminatory thoughts to themselves, edit all hints of racism and sexism out of e-mail, and couch pay and promotion decisions in legally defensible language. So how do plaintiffs' lawyers prove their cases?

Enter the magician. Sociologist William T. Bielby is the leading courtroom proponent of a simple but powerful theory: "unconscious bias." He contends that white men will inevitably slight women and minorities because they just can't help themselves. So he tries to convince judges that no evidence of overt discrimination—no smoking gun memo, for instance—is needed to prove a case. As Allen G. King, an employment defense attorney at the Dallas office of Littler Mendelson, puts it: "I just have to leave you to your own devices, and because you are a white male," you will discriminate.

King and other defense attorneys have gotten to know Bielby well, having encountered him as an expert witness in dozens of major cases, including those currently pending against Wal-Mart, FedEx, Johnson & Johnson, and Cargill. For plaintiffs Bielby's fees—now $450 an hour, and totaling $30,000 or more per case—are often worth it. Numerous lawsuits in which he has been involved have ended in big dollar settlements, including suits against Merrill Lynch, Morgan Stanley, and Home Depot. In 2004 a federal judge in San Francisco cited Bielby's testimony when he agreed to let the largest-ever employment class action go forward against Wal-Mart Stores Inc. The company is appealing but could face gender bias claims on behalf of more than 1 million women.

Sitting in his quiet, dimly lit office at the University of Pennsylvania, Bielby, 58, explains his opinions and parries criticisms in a way that makes the provocative sound almost prosaic. An electric guitar propped in a stand on the floor hints at his other preoccupation: rock 'n' roll. A longtime guitar player, he's also made studying bands in the "post-Elvis, pre-Beatles" era part of his academic work. Every year, he joins colleagues to perform at the American Sociological Assn. convention.

#### Courtroom Celeb

Bielby's rock star turn, though, has been in the litigation arena. Now if an employer is faced with a class action based on gender or race, there is at least a 50 percent chance that plaintiffs will cite unconscious bias theory, says David A. Copus at Ogletree Deakins in Morristown, N.J. When corporations conduct "beauty contests" to hire law firms to represent them in these lawsuits, "if you can't go in and say how you're going to deal with an expert like Bielby, you can't get the case," says Littler Mendelson's King.

The key flaw that Bielby typically finds in the companies he testifies against is that they give managers too much discretion and let them rely on too many subjective factors in hiring, promotion, and pay. In that kind of unfettered atmosphere, he says, all people (not just white men) unknowingly revert to stereotypes in making decisions. "The tendency to invoke gender stereotypes in making judgments about people is rapid and automatic," Bielby wrote in a 2003 report on Wal-Mart that was filed with the court. "As a result, people are often unaware of how stereotypes affect their perceptions and behavior," including "individuals whose personal beliefs are relatively free of prejudice."

Bielby faulted Wal-Mart for the way it identifies candidates for management positions that often require a move. Without a "systematic mechanism" for determining who might be interested, he wrote in his report, managers may automatically assume women don't want jobs that require them to relocate.

Job postings are one way around this problem. But Bielby, citing deposition testimony of Wal-Mart executives, noted that store managers had authority to bypass the retailer's posting system and "informally approach" candidates. That can result in what he calls "tap-on-the-shoulder" promotions, typically favoring men. In its appeal, Wal-Mart says Bielby's testimony is unscientific and unreliable.

Certainly the idea that we all engage in stereotyping is well established among social psychologists, and it is percolating into the broader culture. In his 2005 book *Blink*, author Malcolm Gladwell discussed how stereotypes can influence the kind of split-second decision-making that takes place in police shootings. Business is also paying attention. The Implicit Assumption Test is a tool researchers have used to measure unconscious bias, and corporations, including BP PLC and Becton Dickinson & Co., are incorporating it into diversity training for managers. The February cover story of *HR Magazine*, published by the Society for Human Resource Management, was titled " Detecting Hidden Bias."

But Bielby's critics argue that stereotypes come into play primarily in interactions among strangers. When a supervisor has known an employee for months or years, "individuating information" takes over, allowing the manager to base decisions on specific traits he has come to know, not implicit assumptions, says Neal D. Mollen, an attorney in the Washington (D.C.) office of Paul, Hastings, Janofsky & Walker LLP, one of Wal-Mart's law firms.

Mark S. Dichter, an attorney at Morgan Lewis & Bockius LLP in Philadelphia, says that Bielby engages in the very practice that he finds so troublesome. "At the heart of his analysis is a stereotype statement that men are going to act in a certain way, without any analysis that men in [a] particular company are in fact acting that way," says Dichter. Adds Christopher Winship, a sociologist at Harvard University, who has opposed Bielby in seven cases. "If anybody came in and did that about women and blacks, all hell would break loose."

SOURCE: M. Orey, "White Men Can't Help It," *BusinessWeek*, May 15, 2006.

### Questions

1. What are the major elements of Dr. Bielby's "unconscious bias theory," and why is this theory controversial in the area of employment litigation?
2. What does the term "individuating information" mean and why might this make unconscious bias more of a problem in the area of personnel selection, as opposed to performance appraisal, career development, or pay raise decisions?
3. Wal-Mart and other companies that have had to face Dr. Bielby in court counter that his testimony is unscientific. How would you use the procedures that were discussed in this chapter under the headings of "Selection Method Standards" (reliability, validity, and so on) to either make or refute a case of bias in selection more scientifically?
4. If one considers the alternative selection methods discussed in this chapter under the heading of "Types of Selection Methods" (interviews, work-sample tests, and so on), which of these are more or less susceptible to the "unconscious bias" effects?

## NOTES


1. J. Welch and S. Welch, "So Many CEO's Get This Wrong,' *BusinessWeek*, July 17, 2006, p. 92.
2. A. Bernstein, "Talent: Will America Lose Out," *BusinessWeek*, May 16, 2005, p. 16.
3. J. C. Nunnally, *Psychometric Theory* (New York: McGraw-Hill, 1978).
4. F. Lievens, T. Buyse, and P. R. Sackett, "Retest Effects in Operational Selection Settings: Development and Test of a Framework," *Personnel Psychology* 58 (2005), pp. 981–1007.
5. D. Weichmann and A.M. Ryan, "Reactions to Computerized Testing in Selection Contexts," *International Journal of Selection and Assessment*, June 2003, pp. 215–29.
6. B. Schneider, "An Interactionist Perspective on Organizational Effectiveness," in *Organizational Effectiveness: A Comparison of Multiple Models*, ed. K. S. Cameron and D. A. Whetton (Orlando, FL: Academic Press, 1983), pp. 27–54.
7. N. Schmitt, R. Z. Gooding, R. A. Noe, and M. Kirsch, "Meta-Analysis of Validity Studies Published between 1964 and 1982 and the Investigation of Study Characteristics," *Personnel Psychology* 37 (1984), pp. 407–22.
8. J. Cohen, *Statistical Power Analysis for the Behavioral Sciences* (New York: Academic Press, 1977).
9. C. H. Lawshe, "Inferences from Personnel Tests and Their Validity," *Journal of Applied Psychology* 70 (1985), pp. 237–38.
10. D. D. Robinson, "Content-Oriented Personnel Selection in a Small Business Setting," *Personnel Psychology* 34 (1981), pp. 77–87.
11. P. R. Sackett, "Assessment Centers and Content Validity: Some Neglected Issues," *Personnel Psychology* 40 (1987), pp. 13–25.
12. F. L. Schmidt and J. E. Hunter, "The Future of Criterion-Related Validity," *Personnel Psychology* 33 (1980), pp. 41–60; F. L. Schmidt, J. E. Hunter, and K. Pearlman, "Task Differences as Moderators of Aptitude Test Validity: A Red Herring," *Journal of Applied Psychology* 66 (1982), pp. 166–85; R. L. Gutenberg, R. D. Arvey, H. G. Osburn, and R. P. Jeanneret, "Moderating Effects of Decision-Making/Information Processing Dimensions on Test Validities," *Journal of Applied Psychology* 68 (1983), pp. 600–8.
13. F. L. Schmidt, J. G. Berner, and J. E. Hunter, "Racial Differences in Validity of Employment Tests: Reality or Illusion," *Journal of Applied Psychology* 58 (1974), pp. 5–6.
14. Society for Industrial and Organizational Psychology, *Principles for the Validation and Use of Personnel Selection Procedures* (College Park, MD: University of Maryland Press, 1987).
15. J. W. Boudreau, "Utility Analysis for Decisions in Human Resource Management," in *Handbook of Industrial & Organizational Psychology*, ed. M. D. Dunnette and L. M. Hough (Palo Alto, CA: Consulting Psychologists Press, 1992).
16. E. Zimmerman, "What Are Employees Worth?" *Workforce*, February 2001, p. 36.
17. A. Meisler, "Negative Results," *Workforce*, October 2003, pp. 35–40.
18. A. Meisler, "When Bad Things Happen to Hot Brands," *Workforce*, July 2003, pp. 20–21.

19. K. F. Ebert, "New Civil Rights Act Invites Litigation," *Personnel Law* Update 6 (1991), p. 3.
20. G. Flynn, "The Reverse Discrimination Trap," *Workforce*, June 2003, pp. 106–7.
21. M. E. Heilman, W. S. Battle, C. E. Keller, and R. A. Lee, "Type of Affirmative Action Policy: A Determinant of Reactions to Sex-Based Preferential Selection," *Journal of Applied Psychology* 83 (1998), pp. 190–205.
22. A. Gutman, "Smith versus City of Jackson: Adverse Impact in the ADEA (Well Sort Of)," *Industrial Psychologist*, July 2005, pp. 31–32.
23. R. Ableson, "Fighting Discrimination Takes Will and Cash," *Taipei Times*, July 2, 2001, pp. 21–22.
24. S. Sonnenberg, "Unreasonable Accommodations," *Workforce*, August 2003, pp. 16–17.
25. J. Mullich, "Hiring without Limits," *Workforce*, June 2002, pp. 53–58.
26. B. P. Sunoo, "Accommodating Workers with Disabilities," *Workforce*, February 2001, p. 93.
27. L. T. Cullen, "The Diversity Delusion," *Time*, May 7, 2007, p. 45.
28. R. L. Dipboye, *Selection Interviews: Process Perspectives* (Cincinnati, OH: South-Western, 1991).
29. R. A. Posthuma, F. R. Morgeson, and M. A. Campion, "Beyond Employment Interview Validity: A Comprehensive Narrative Review of Recent Research and Trends over Time," *Personnel Psychology* 55 (2002), pp. 1–81.
30. J. E. Hunter and R. H. Hunter, "Validity and Utility of Alternative Predictors of Job Performance," *Psychological Bulletin* 96 (1984), pp. 72–98.
31. R. Pingitore, B. L. Dugoni, R. S. Tindale, and B. Spring, "Bias against Overweight Job Applicants in a Simulated Interview," *Journal of Applied Psychology* 79 (1994), pp. 909–17.
32. F. Hanson, "Keeping Interviews on Point to Stay Out of Legal Hot Water," *Workforce Management*, August 14, 2006, pp. 44–45.
33. *Watson v. Fort Worth Bank and Trust*, 108 Supreme Court 2791 (1988).
34. M. A. McDaniel, D. L. Whetzel, F. L. Schmidt, and S. D. Maurer, "The Validity of Employment Interviews: A Comprehensive Review and Meta-Analysis," *Journal of Applied Psychology* 79 (1994), pp. 599–616; A. I. Huffcutt and W. A. Arthur, "Hunter and Hunter (1984) Revisited: Interview Validity for Entry-Level Jobs," *Journal of Applied Psychology* 79 (1994), pp. 184–90.
35. C. H. Middendorf and T. H. Macan, "Note-Taking in the Interview: Effects on Recall and Judgments," *Journal of Applied Psychology* 87 (2002), pp. 293–303.
36. M. A. McDaniel, F. P. Morgeson, E. B. Finnegan, M. A. Campion, and E. P. Braverman, "Use of Situational Judgment Tests to Predict Job Performance: A Clarification of the Literature," *Journal of Applied Psychology* 86 (2001), pp. 730–40.
37. M. A. Campion, J. E. Campion, and J. P. Hudson, "Structured Interviewing: A Note of Incremental Validity and Alternative Question Types," *Journal of Applied Psychology* 79 (1994), pp. 998–1002; E. D. Pulakos and N. Schmitt, "Experience-Based and Situational Interview Questions: Studies of Validity," *Personnel Psychology* 48 (1995), pp. 289–308.
38. A. P. J. Ellis, B. J. West, A. M. Ryan, and R. P. DeShon, "The Use of Impression Management Tactics in Structured Interviews: A Function of Question Type?" *Journal of Applied Psychology* 87 (2002), pp. 1200–8.
39. S. Maurer, "A Practitioner-Based Analysis of Interviewer Job Expertise and Scale Format as Contextual Factors in Situational Interviews," *Personnel Psychology* 55 (2002), pp. 307–27.
40. W. C. Byham, "Can You Interview for Integrity?" *Across the Board*, March 2004, pp. 34–38.
41. T. Libby, "Surviving the Group Interview," *Forbes*, March 24, 1986, p. 190; Dipboye, *Selection Interviews*, p. 210.
42. Y. Ganzach, A. N. Kluger, and N. Klayman, "Making Decisions from an Interview: Expert Measurement and Mechanical Combination," *Personnel Psychology* 53 (2000), pp. 1–21.
43. S. F. Dingfelder, "To Tell the Truth," *Monitor on Psychology*, March 2004, pp. 22–23.
44. A. Davis, J. Pereira, and W. M. Bulkeley, "Security Concerns Bring Focus on Translating Body Language," *The Wall Street Journal*, August 15, 2002, pp. A1–A3.
45. Hunter and Hunter, "Validity and Utility."
46. D. D. Hatch, "Bad Reference for Ex-Employee Judged Defamatory," *Workforce*, December 2003, p. 20.
47. E. Zimmerman, "A Subtle Reference Trap for Unwary Employers," *Workforce*, April 2003, p. 22.
48. M. R. Barrick and R. D. Zimmerman, "Reducing Voluntary Turnover through Selection," *Journal of Applied Psychology* 90 (2005), pp. 159–66.
49. T. W. Dougherty, D. B. Turban, and J. C. Callender, "Confirming First Impressions in the Employment Interview: A Field Study of Interviewer Behavior," *Journal of Applied Psychology* 79 (1994), pp. 659–65.
50. C. Waxer, "Companies Demand that Staffing Agencies Check into Temps' Backgrounds," *Workforce*, June 2004, pp. 84–87.
51. S. Pustizzi, "Résumé Fraud Gets Slicker and Easier," *CNN.com*, March 11, 2004, p. 1.
52. K. Gordon, "Big, Fast and Easily Bungled," *Workforce*, August 2003, pp. 47–49.
53. N. Schmitt, F. L. Oswald, B. H. Kim, M. A. Gillespie, L. J. Ramsey, and T. Y. Yoo, "The Impact of Elaboration on Socially Desirable Responding and the Validity of Biodata Measures," *Journal of Applied Psychology* 88 (2003), pp. 979–88.
54. N. Schmitt and C. Kunce, "The Effects of Required Elaboration of Answers to Biodata Questions," *Personnel Psychology* 55 (2002), pp. 569–87.
55. L. C. Buffardi, E. A. Fleishman, R. A. Morath, and P. M. McCarthy, "Relationships between Ability Requirements and Human Errors in Job Tasks," *Journal of Applied Psychology* 85 (2000), pp. 551–64.
56. J. R. Hollenbeck, D. R. Ilgen, and S. M. Crampton, "Lower-Back Disability in Occupational Settings: A Human Resource Management View," *Personnel Psychology* 42 (1992), pp. 247–78.
57. J. Hogan, "Structure of Physical Performance in Occupational Tasks," *Journal of Applied Psychology* 76 (1991), pp. 495–507.
58. B. R. Blakely, M. A. Quinones, M. S. Crawford, and I. A. Jago, "The Validity of Isometric Strength Tests," *Personnel Psychology* 47 (1994), pp. 247–74.
59. J. Hogan, "Physical Abilities," in *Handbook of Industrial & Organizational Psychology*, 2nd ed., ed. M. D. Dunnette and L. M. Hough (Palo Alto, CA: Consulting Psychologists Press, 1991).
60. Americans with Disabilities Act of 1990, S. 933, Public Law 101-336 (1990).
61. Nunnally, *Psychometric Theory*.
62. M. J. Ree, J. A. Earles, and M. S. Teachout, "Predicting Job Performance: Not Much More Than g," *Journal of Applied Psychology* 79 (1994), pp. 518–24.
63. J. F. Salagado, N. Anderson, S. Moscoso, C. Bertua, and F. De Fruyt, "International Validity Generalization of GMA and Cognitive Abilities: A European Community Meta-Analysis," *Personnel Psychology* 56 (2003), pp. 573–605.

64. L. S. Gottfredson, "The g Factor in Employment," *Journal of Vocational Behavior* 29 (1986), pp. 293–96; Hunter and Hunter, "Validity and Utility"; Gutenberg et al., "Moderating Effects"; Schmidt, Berner, and Hunter, "Racial Differences in Validity."
65. J. A. LePine, J. A. Colquitt, and A. Erez, "Adaptability to Changing Task Contexts: Effects of General Cognitive Ability, Conscientiousness, and Openness to Experience," *Personnel Psychology* 53 (2000), pp. 563–93.
66. S. Walker, "The NFL's Smartest Team," *The Wall Street Journal*, September 30, 2005, pp. W1–W2.
67. D. Foust, "How to Pick a Business Brain," *BusinessWeek*, February 20, 2006, p. 104.
68. G. Gloeckler, "Sidestepping the GMAT," *BusinessWeek*, August 8, 2005, pp. 71–72.
69. L. Lavelle, "Is the MBA Overrated?" *BusinessWeek*, March 20, 2006, pp. 78–79.
70. R. J. Barro, "Why Colleges Shouldn't Dump the SAT," *BusinessWeek*, April 9, 2001, p. 20.
71. A. R. Jenson, "g: Artifact or Reality?" *Journal of Vocational Behavior* 29 (1986), pp. 301–31.
72. D. A. Kravitz and S. L. Klineberg, "Reactions to Versions of Affirmative Action among Whites, Blacks, and Hispanics," *Journal of Applied Psychology* (2000), pp. 597–611.
73. M. A. Campion, J. L. Outtz, S. Zedeck, F. S. Schmidt, J. E. Kehoe, K. R. Murphy, and R. M. Guion, "The Controversy over Score Banding in Personnel Selection: Answers to 10 Key Questions," *Personnel Psychology* 54 (2001), pp. 149–85.
74. M. R. Barrick and M. K. Mount, "The Big Five Personality Dimensions and Job Performance: A Meta-Analysis," *Personnel Psychology* 44 (1991), pp. 1–26; L. M. Hough, N. K. Eaton, M. D. Dunnette, J. D. Camp, and R. A. McCloy, "Criterion-Related Validities of Personality Constructs and the Effect of Response Distortion on Test Validities," *Journal of Applied Psychology* 75 (1990), pp. 467–76.
75. G. M. Hurtz and J. J. Donovan, "Personality and Job Performance: The Big Five Revisited," *Journal of Applied Psychology* 85 (2000), pp. 869–79.
76. E. Freudenheim, "Personality Testing Controversial, but Poised to Take Off," *Workforce Management*, August 14, 2006, p. 38.
77. V. Knight, "Personality Tests as Hiring Tools," *The Wall Street Journal*, March 15, 2006, p. B1.
78. G. L. Steward, I. S. Fulmer, and M. R. Barrick, "An Exploration of Member Roles as a Multilevel Linking Mechanism for Individual Traits and Team Outcomes," *Personnel Psychology* 58 (2005), pp. 343–65.
79. M. Mount, R. Ilies, and E. Johnson, "Relationship of Personality Traits and Counterproductive Work Behaviors: The Mediation Effects of Job Satisfaction," *Personnel Psychology* 59 (2006) pp. 591–622.
80. D. Goleman, "Sometimes, EQ Is More Important than IQ," *CNN.com*, January 14, 2005, p. 1.
81. M. A. Shaffer, D. A. Harrison, H. Gregersen, J. S. Black, L. A. Ferzandi, "You Can Take It With You: Individual Differences and Expatriate Effectiveness," *Journal of Applied Psychology* 91 (2006), 109–25.
82. N. M. Dudley, K. A. Orvis, J. E. Lebieki, and J. M. Cortina, "A Meta-analytic Investigation of Conscientiousness in the Prediction of Job Performance: Examining the Intercorrelation and the Incremental Validity of Narrow Traits," *Journal of Applied Psychology* 91 (2006), pp. 40–57.
83. M. R. Barrick, G. L. Stewart, and M. Piotrowski, "Personality and Job Performance: Test of the Mediating Effects of Motivation among Sales Representatives," *Journal of Applied Psychology* 87 (2002), pp. 43–51.
84. P. M. Wright, K. M. Kacmar, G. C. McMahan, and K. Deleeuw, "P = f(M × A): Cognitive Ability as a Moderator of the Relationship between Personality and Job Performance," *Journal of Management* 21 (1995), pp. 1129–39.
85. L. A. Witt and G. R. Ferris, "Social Skill as Moderator of the Conscientiousness–Performance Relationship: Convergent Results across Four Studies," *Journal of Applied Psychology* 88 (2003), pp. 809–20.
86. M. Mount, M. R. Barrick, and J. P. Strauss, "Validity of Observer Ratings of the Big Five Personality Factors," *Journal of Applied Psychology* 79 (1994), pp. 272–80.
87. M. R. Barrick, G. L. Stewart, M. J. Neubert, and M. K. Mount, "Relating Member Ability and Personality to Work Team Processes and Team Effectiveness," *Journal of Applied Psychology* 83 (1998), pp. 377–91; J. L. LePine, J. R. Hollenbeck, D. R. Ilgen, and J. Hedlund, "Effects of Individual Differences on the Performance of Hierarchical Decision Making Teams: Much More Than g," *Journal of Applied Psychology* 82 (1997), pp. 803–11.
88. Mount, Barrick, and Strauss, "Validity of Observer Ratings." J. M. Hunthausen, D. M. Truxillo, T. N. Bauer, and L. B. Hammer, "A Field Study of Frame of Reference Effects on Personality Test Validity," *Journal of Applied Psychology* 88 (2003), pp. 545–51.
89. N. Schmitt and F. L. Oswald, "The Impact of Corrections for Faking on the Validity of Non-cognitive Measures in Selection Contexts," *Journal of Applied Psychology*, 2006, pp. 613–21.
90. S. A. Birkland, T. M. Manson, J. L. Kisamore, M. T. Brannick, and M. A. Smith, "Faking on Personality Measures," *International Journal of Selection and Assessment* 14 (December 2006), pp. 317–35.
91. N. L Vasilopoulos, J. M. Cucina, and J. M. McElreath, "Do Warnings of Response Verification Moderate the Relationship between Personality and Cognitive Ability?" *Journal of Applied Psychology* 90 (2005), pp. 306–22.
92. C. H. Van Iddekinge, P. H. Raymark, and P. L. Roth, "Assessing Personality with a Structured Employment Interview: Construct-Related Validity and Susceptibility to Response Inflation," *Journal of Applied Psychology* 90 (2005), pp. 536–52.
93. J. M. LeBreton, C. D. Barksdale, J. Robin, and L. R. James, "Measurement Issues Associated with Conditional Reasoning Tests: Indirect Measurement and Test Faking," *Journal of Applied Psychology* 92 (2007), pp. 1–16.
94. E. White, "Personality Tests Aim to Stop 'Fakers,'" *The Wall Street Journal*, November 6, 2006, p. B3.
95. R. Mueller-Hanson, E. D., Heggestad, and G. C. Thornton, "Faking and Selection: Considering the Use of Personality from Select-In and Select-Out Perspectives," *Journal of Applied Psychology* 88 (2003), pp. 348–55.
96. P. L. Roth, P. Bobko, and M. L. McFarland, "A Meta-analysis of Work Sample Validity: Updating and Integrating Some Classic Literature," *Personnel Psychology* 58 (2005), pp. 1009–37.
97. C. Palmeri, "Putting Managers to the Test," *BusinessWeek*, November 20, 2006, p. 82.
98. C. Winkler, "Job Tryouts Go Virtual: Online Job Simulations Provide Sophisticated Candidate Assessments," *HR Magazine*, September 2006, pp. 10–15.
99. E. White, "Walk a Mile in My Shoes," *The Wall Street Journal*, January 16, 2006, B3.
100. A. Hedger, "Six Ways to Strengthen Staffing," *Workforce Management*, January 15, 2007.

101. K. Maher, "Win in a Competition, Land on Square that Offers Job," *The Wall Street Journal*, June 1, 2004, p. B10.
102. J. Puliyenthuruthel, "How Google Searches—For Talent," *BusinessWeek*, April 11, 2005, pp. 32–34.
103. P. F. Wernimont and J. P. Campbell, "Signs, Samples and Criteria," *Journal of Applied Psychology* 46 (1968), pp. 417–19.
104. D. J. Schleiger, V. Venkataramani, F. P. Morgeson, and M. A. Campion, "So You Didn't Get the Job . . . Now What Do You Think? Examining Opportunity to Perform Fairness Perceptions," *Personnel Psychology* 59 (2006), pp. 559–90.
105. N. Schmitt and A. E. Mills, "Traditional Tests and Job Simulations: Minority and Majority Performance and Test Validities," *Journal of Applied Psychology* 86 (2001), pp. 451–58.
106. Hunter and Hunter, "Validity and Utility."
107. W. Arthur, E. A. Day, T. L. McNelly and P. S. Edens, "Meta-Analysis of the Criterion-Related Validity of Assessment Center Dimensions," *Personnel Psychology* 56 (2003), pp. 125–54.
108. C. E. Lance, T. A. Lambert, A. G. Gewin, F. Lievens, and J. M. Conway, "Revised Estimates of Dimension and Exercise Variance Components in Assessment Center Postexercise Dimension Ratings," *Journal of Applied Psychology* 89 (2004), pp. 377–85.
109. F. L. Schmidt and J. E. Hunter, "The Validity and Utility of Selection Methods in Personnel Psychology: Practical and Theoretical Implications of 85 Years of Research Findings," *Psychological Bulletin* 124 (1998), pp. 262–74.
110. J. E. Wanek, P. R. Sackett, and D. S. Ones, "Toward an Understanding of Integrity Test Similarities and Differences: An Item-Level Analysis of Seven Tests," *Personnel Psychology* 56 (2003), pp. 873–94.
111. D. S. Ones, C. Viswesvaran, and F. L. Schmidt, "Comprehensive Meta-Analysis of Integrity Test Validities: Findings and Implications for Personnel Selection and Theories of Job Performance," *Journal of Applied Psychology* 78 (1993), pp. 679–703.
112. D. S. Ones and C. Viswesvaran, "Gender, Age, and Race Differences on Overt Integrity Tests: Results across Four Large-Scale Job Applicant Data Sets," *Journal of Applied Psychology* 83 (1998), pp. 35–42.
113. M. R. Cunningham, D. T. Wong, and A. P. Barbee, "Self-Presentation Dynamics on Overt Integrity Tests: Experimental Studies of the Reid Report," *Journal of Applied Psychology* 79 (1994), pp. 643–58.
114. M. Freudenheim, "Workers Substance Abuse Increasing, Survey Says," *The New York Times*, December 13, 1988, p. 2; J. P. Guthrie and J. D. Olian, "Drug and Alcohol Testing Programs: The Influence of Organizational Context and Objectives" (paper presented at the Fourth Annual Conference of the Society for Industrial/Organizational Psychology, Boston, 1989).
115. M. E. Paronto, D. M. Truxillo, T. N. Bauer, and M. C. Leo, "Drug Testing, Drug Treatment, and Marijuana Use: A Fairness Perspective," *Journal of Applied Psychology* 87 (2002), pp. 1159–66.
116. K. R. Murphy, G. C. Thornton, and D. H. Reynolds, "College Students' Attitudes toward Drug Testing Programs, *Personnel Psychology* 43 (1990), pp. 615–31.

7

CHAPTER

# Training

## LO LEARNING OBJECTIVES

**After reading this chapter, you should be able to:**

LO1 Discuss how training can contribute to companies' business strategy. *page 267*

LO2 Explain the role of the manager in identifying training needs and supporting training on the job. *page 269*

LO3 Conduct a needs assessment. *page 270*

LO4 Evaluate employees' readiness for training. *page 279*

LO5 Discuss the strengths and weaknesses of presentation, hands-on, and group training methods. *page 290*

LO6 Explain the potential advantages of e-learning for training. *page 301*

LO7 Design a training session to maximize learning. *page 308*

LO8 Choose an appropriate evaluation design based on training objectives and analysis of constraints. *page 309*

LO9 Design a cross-cultural preparation program. *page 314*

LO10 Develop a program for effectively managing diversity. *page 319*

# Enter the World of Business

## Learning Isn't Perishable at Wegmans Food Markets

At Wegmans Food Markets, learning is how the company differentiates itself from other supermarkets. Learning is not part of the competitive strategy: it *is* the competitive strategy.

Wegmans Food Markets is known as much for carrying 700 different types of cheeses as it is for being one of the best companies to work for. In 2007 Wegmans was named to *Fortune* magazine's 2006 list of the "100 Best Companies to Work For," ranked number 3. This marks the tenth consecutive year Wegmans has appeared on the annual list and its fifth year ranked among the top 10. Wegmans makes a considerable investment in training. The company recently branched out of its traditional locations in New York, Pennsylvania, and New Jersey to open two stores in Virginia. The company spent more than $1 million training staff.

Because the level of service is as important as is product knowledge, Wegmans offers classroom training as well as hands-on training. Because Wegmans is a food business, learning with the five senses is very important. Employees are put through rigorous courses in areas such as operations, product knowledge, and cooking. But employees first receive training about the products they are selling, what makes them good, and how to prepare them. Wegmans believes that with knowledge, employees can provide real value to customers. Part of the company's strategy is to help customers understand the products so they will buy a new product. Wegmans mails *Menu* magazine to about 1 million addresses four times a year. It has recipes, cooking techniques, and product advice. Customers come to the stores looking for products needed for the recipes and tips on how to prepare them. As a result, cooking coaches and sales staff go through a session each week on how to make a meal of the week. This training increases their product knowledge and makes them comfortable selling products.

Wegmans wants to teach people the company values. The values include caring and trust. Wegmans tries to find people who will care about the customers and care about their Wegmans teammates. High food safety standards are also important and are emphasized in technical training.

Wegmans also has special programs for teenagers who work in the stores. For example, the company has an apprenticeship program with about 250 people in it each year. The apprentices take on a team project on some aspect of the department they are working in. After studying for five months, the teams give presentations. The company also offers work-study programs. The three-year work-study program offers more than 1,500 hours of paid, school-supervised work experience, supported by related instruction at school. Students may receive high school credits for this experience. With the support of a mentor, students complete structured rotations through a variety of departments—bakery, produce, seafood, and other departments—based on career interests. The students learn and enhance their customer service, teamwork, product knowledge, food safety, and technical skills. Students in their last rotation during their senior year in high school focus on gaining new experiences in merchandising, product preparation, selling skills, and department sales concepts and finish off the program by completing a senior research project. Students who successfully finish the program receive either a full-time employment opportunity or, if attending college, a Scholarship Award and an opportunity to compete for the Store Operations Summer Internship program immediately after high school graduation. Why does Wegmans invest time and money in training students? Wegmans has a lot of young adults working in the stores and they are responsible for making a difference to customers by providing excellent service.

How does Wegmans Food Markets measure the return on its investment in training? CEO Danny Wegman says, "People are continuing to learn and have more confidence. We don't have a formula for measuring that, but we ask ourselves 'Are we being successful as a company? Are we getting good feedback from our people on the various courses we are offering? Do they feel they [the courses] are relevant to their success as individuals and part of the company?'"

Source: Based on www.wegmans.com Web site for Wegmans Food Markets and T. Bingham and P. Galagan, "A Higher Level of Learning," *TD*, September 2005, pp. 32–36.

## Introduction

As the chapter opening story shows, learning is an important part of Wegmans Food Markets' business strategy. Training helps employees at Wegmans develop specific skills that enable them to succeed in their current job and develop for the future. Wegmans also recognizes that learning involves not just formal training courses but also job experiences and interactions between employees. From Wegmans perspective, training leads to better customer service and product sales. Wegmans recognizes that its industry is becoming competitive—success will require smart, motivated employees who can delight customers and help sell products.

Why is the emphasis on strategic training important? Companies are in business to make money, and every business function is under pressure to show how it contributes to business success or face spending cuts and even outsourcing. To contribute to a company's success, training activities should help the company achieve its business strategy.

There is both a direct and an indirect link between training and business strategy and goals. Training can help employees develop skills needed to perform their jobs, which directly affects the business. Giving employees opportunities to learn and develop creates a positive work environment, which supports the business strategy by attracting talented employees as well as motivating and retaining current employees.

Why do Wegmans and many other companies believe that an investment in training can help them gain a competitive advantage? Training can

- Increase employees' knowledge of foreign competitors and cultures, which is critical for success in foreign markets.
- Help ensure that employees have the basic skills to work with new technology, such as robots and computer-assisted manufacturing processes.
- Help employees understand how to work effectively in teams to contribute to product and service quality.
- Ensure that the company's culture emphasizes innovation, creativity, and learning.
- Ensure employment security by providing new ways for employees to contribute to the company when their jobs change, their interests change, or their skills become obsolete.
- Prepare employees to accept and work more effectively with each other, particularly with minorities and women.[1]

In this chapter we emphasize the conditions through which training practices can help companies gain competitive advantage and how managers can contribute to a high-leverage training effort and create a learning organization. The chapter begins by discussing a systematic and effective approach to training design. Next we review training methods and training evaluation. The chapter concludes with a discussion of training issues including cross-cultural preparation, managing diversity, and socializing employees.

# High-Leverage Training Strategy: A Systematic Approach

**LO1**
Discuss How Training Can Contribute to Companies' Business Strategy.

In general, **training** refers to a planned effort by a company to facilitate employees' learning of job-related competencies. These competencies include knowledge, skills, or behaviors that are critical for successful job performance. The goal of training is for employees to master the knowledge, skill, and behaviors emphasized in training programs and to apply them to their day-to-day activities. Recently it has been acknowledged that to offer a competitive advantage, training has to involve more than just basic skill development.[2] Training is moving from a primary focus on teaching employees specific skills to a broader focus of creating and sharing knowledge.[3] That is, to use training to gain a competitive advantage, a firm should view training broadly as a way to create intellectual capital. Intellectual capital includes basic skills (skills needed to perform one's job), advanced skills (such as how to use technology to share information with other employees), an understanding of the customer or manufacturing system, and self-motivated creativity.

Traditionally most of the emphasis on training has been at the basic and advanced skill levels. But some estimate that 85 percent of the jobs in the United States and Europe require extensive use of knowledge. This requires employees to share knowledge and creatively use it to modify a product or serve the customer, as well as to understand the service or product development system.

Many companies have adopted this broader perspective, which is known as high-leverage training. **High-leverage training** is linked to strategic business goals and objectives, uses an instructional design process to ensure that training is effective, and compares or benchmarks the company's training programs against training programs in other companies.[4]

High-leverage training practices also help to create working conditions that encourage continuous learning. **Continuous learning** requires employees to understand the entire work system including the relationships among their jobs, their work units, and the company. (Continuous learning is similar to the idea of system understanding mentioned earlier.)[5] Employees are expected to acquire new skills and knowledge, apply them on the job, and share this information with other employees. Managers identify training needs and help to ensure that employees use training in their work. To facilitate the sharing of knowledge, managers may use informational maps that show where knowledge lies within the company (for example, directories that list what a person does as well as the specialized knowledge she possesses) and use technology such as groupware or the Internet that allows employees in various business units to work simultaneously on problems and share information.[6]

The emphasis on high-leverage training has been accompanied by a movement to link training to performance improvement or business strategy.[7] Companies have lost money on training because it is poorly designed, because it is not linked to a performance problem or business strategy, or because its outcomes are not properly evaluated.[8] That is, companies have been investing money into training simply because of beliefs that it is a good thing to do. The perspective that the training function exists to deliver programs to employees without a compelling business reason for doing so is being abandoned. Today, training is being evaluated not on the basis of the number of programs offered and training activity in the company but on how training addresses

**Training**
A planned effort to facilitate the learning of job-related knowledge, skills, and behavior by employees.

**High-Leverage Training**
Training practice that links training to strategic business goals, has top management support, relies on an instructional design model, and is benchmarked to programs in other organizations.

**Continuous Learning**
A learning system that requires employees to understand the entire work process and expects them to acquire new skills, apply them on the job, and share what they have learned with other employees.

business needs related to learning, behavior change, and performance improvement. In fact, training is becoming more performance-focused. That is, training is used to improve employee performance, which leads to improved business results. Training is seen as one of several possible solutions to improve performance. Other solutions can include such actions as changing the job or increasing employee motivation through pay and incentives. Today there is a greater emphasis on[9]

- Providing educational opportunities for all employees. These educational opportunities may include training programs, but they also include support for taking courses offered outside the company, self-study, and learning through job rotation.
- An ongoing process of performance improvement that is directly measurable rather than organizing one-time training events.
- The need to demonstrate to executives, managers, and trainees the benefits of training.
- Learning as a lifelong event in which senior management, trainer managers, and employees have ownership.
- Training being used to help attain strategic business objectives, which help companies gain a competitive advantage.

Figure 7.1 shows the strategic training and development process with examples of strategic initiatives, training activities, and metrics. The strategic training and development process involves identifying strategic training and development initiatives that will help achieve the business strategy. Employees participate in specific training and development activities that support these initiatives. The final step of the process involves collecting measures or metrics. The metrics are used to determine if training helped contribute to goals related to the business strategy.

IBM is a company that reinvented itself in 2002.[10] The new business strategy was to reshape the workforce so it could better meet clients' needs and expectations as IBM transformed itself from a high-tech industrial-age company to an information- and knowledge-driven company. This also required a massive organizational culture change—employees had to accept the strategy and make it work. Dedication to clients is the core foundation of the business strategy. To meet client needs requires employees who are adaptable and constantly adjusting. As a result, training has shifted to be about learning through work, on location based on client needs, rather than going to a

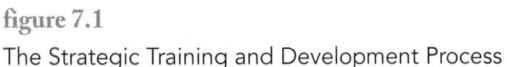

**figure 7.1**

The Strategic Training and Development Process

different location for a training course. Formal training courses are still used to teach managers, executives, and salespeople new skills or product lines at critical moments in their careers. "OnDemand learning," as IBM calls it, requires that learning teams responsible for designing the program understand the specific work being done by employees in different roles. IBM has defined more than 500 specific roles in the company and the expertise required for each role. The learning team designs learning opportunities into the work itself, a concept known as "work-embedded learning." Employees use computers to connect with experts, participate in an online community on a topic, or complete an online learning module. The amount of time spent on learning and training grew 32 percent from 2003 to 2004 through the expansion of work-embedded learning. The company committed more than $700 million to the learning initiatives which it believes are critical for achieving the business strategy.

This discussion is not meant to underestimate the importance of "traditional training" (a focus on acquisition of knowledge, skills, and abilities), but it should alert you that for many companies training is evolving from a focus on skills to an emphasis on learning and creating and sharing knowledge.

**LO2**
Explain the Role of the Manager in Identifying Training Needs and Supporting Training on the Job.

## Designing Effective Training Activities

A key characteristic of training activities that contribute to competitiveness is that they are designed according to the instructional design process.[11] **Training design process** refers to a systematic approach for developing training programs. Instructional System Design (ISD) and the ADDIE model (analysis, design, development, implementation, evaluation) are two specific types of training design processes you may know. Table 7.1 presents the six steps of this process, which emphasizes that

**Training Design Process**
A systematic approach for developing training programs.

**table 7.1**
The Training Process

1. Needs assessment
   - Organizational analysis
   - Person analysis
   - Task analysis
2. Ensuring employees' readiness for training
   - Attitudes and motivation
   - Basic skills
3. Creating a learning environment
   - Identification of learning objectives and training outcomes
   - Meaningful material
   - Practice
   - Feedback
   - Observation of others
   - Administering and coordinating program
4. Ensuring transfer of training
   - Self-management strategies
   - Peer and manager support
5. Selecting training methods
   - Presentational methods
   - Hands-on methods
   - Group methods
6. Evaluating training programs
   - Identification of training outcomes and evaluation design
   - Cost–benefit analysis

effective training practices involve more than just choosing the most popular or colorful training method.

Step 1 is to assess needs to determine if training is needed. Step 2 involves ensuring that employees have the motivation and basic skills to master training content. Step 3 addresses whether the training session (or the learning environment) has the factors necessary for learning to occur. Step 4 is to ensure that trainees apply the content of training to their jobs. This requires support from managers and peers for the use of training content on the job as well as getting the employee to understand how to take personal responsibility for skill improvement. Step 5 involves choosing a training method. As we shall see in this chapter, a variety of training methods are available ranging from traditional on-the-job training to newer technologies such as the Internet. The key is to choose a training method that will provide the appropriate learning environment to achieve the training objectives. Step 6 is evaluation—that is, determining whether training achieved the desired learning outcomes and/or financial objectives.

The training design process should be systematic yet flexible enough to adapt to business needs. Different steps may be completed simultaneously. Keep in mind that designing training unsystematically will reduce the benefits that can be realized. For example, choosing a training method before determining training needs or ensuring employees' readiness for training increases the risk that the method chosen will not be the most effective one for meeting training needs. Also, training may not even be necessary and may result in a waste of time and money! Employees may have the knowledge, skills, or behavior they need but simply not be motivated to use them. Next we will discuss important aspects of the training design process.

**Needs Assessment**
The process used to determine if training is necessary.

## Needs Assessment

**LO3**
Conduct a Needs Assessment.

The first step in the instructional design process, **needs assessment,** refers to the process used to determine if training is necessary. Figure 7.2 shows the causes and outcomes resulting from needs assessment. As we see, many different "pressure points" suggest that training is necessary. These pressure points include performance problems, new technology, internal or external customer requests for training, job redesign, new legislation, changes in customer preferences, new products, or

**figure 7.2**

The Needs Assessment Process

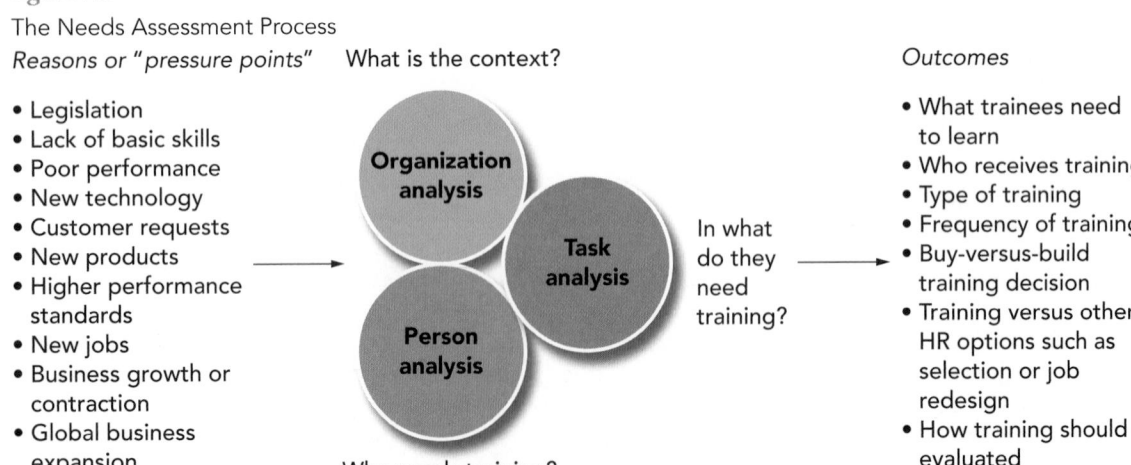

*Reasons or "pressure points"*

- Legislation
- Lack of basic skills
- Poor performance
- New technology
- Customer requests
- New products
- Higher performance standards
- New jobs
- Business growth or contraction
- Global business expansion

*Outcomes*

- What trainees need to learn
- Who receives training
- Type of training
- Frequency of training
- Buy-versus-build training decision
- Training versus other HR options such as selection or job redesign
- How training should be evaluated

employees' lack of basic skills as well as support for the company's business strategy (e.g., growth, global business expansion). Note that these pressure points do not guarantee that training is the correct solution. Consider, for example, a delivery truck driver whose job is to deliver anesthetic gases to medical facilities. The driver mistakenly hooks up the supply line of a mild anesthetic to the supply line of a hospital's oxygen system, contaminating the hospital's oxygen supply. Why did the driver make this mistake, which is clearly a performance problem? The driver may have done this because of a lack of knowledge about the appropriate line hookup for the anesthetic, anger over a requested salary increase that his manager recently denied, or mislabeled valves for connecting the gas supply. Only the lack of knowledge can be addressed by training. The other pressure points require addressing issues related to the consequence of good performance (pay system) or the design of the work environment.

Needs assessment typically involves organizational analysis, person analysis, and task analysis.[12] Organizational analysis considers the context in which training will occur. That is, **organizational analysis** involves determining the business appropriateness of training, given the company's business strategy, its resources available for training, and support by managers and peers for training activities.

**Organizational Analysis**
A process for determining the business appropriateness of training.

Person analysis helps identify who needs training. **Person analysis** involves (1) determining whether performance deficiencies result from a lack of knowledge, skill, or ability (a training issue) or from a motivational or work-design problem, (2) identifying who needs training, and (3) determining employees' readiness for training. **Task analysis** includes identifying the important tasks and knowledge, skill, and behaviors that need to be emphasized in training for employees to complete their tasks.

**Person Analysis**
A process for determining whether employees need training, who needs training, and whether employees are ready for training.

**Task Analysis**
The process of identifying the tasks, knowledge, skills, and behaviors that need to be emphasized in training.

In practice, organizational analysis, person analysis, and task analysis are usually not conducted in any specific order. However, because organizational analysis is concerned with identifying whether training fits with the company's strategic objectives and whether the company wants to devote time and money to training, it is usually conducted first. Person analysis and task analysis are often conducted at the same time because it is often difficult to determine whether performance deficiencies are a training problem without understanding the tasks and the work environment.

What outcomes result from a needs assessment? As shown in Figure 7.2, needs assessment shows who needs training and what trainees need to learn, including the tasks in which they need to be trained plus knowledge, skill, behavior, or other job requirements. Needs assessment helps determine whether the company will purchase training from a vendor or consultant or develop training using internal resources.

Steelcase spends considerable time and energy on needs assessment.[13] Course designers are responsible for ensuring that all of Steelcase University's training and development capabilities help drive business performance and lead strategic change for the company. The university helps to identify how behaviors need to change to align with new performance standards and future directions. The university tries to understand and provide solutions for critical business needs. Learning consultants serve as team members in key functional groups across the company. The learning consultant becomes aware of business challenges the function is facing and identifies the required business results. This helps identify a learning solution that can overcome behavior gaps. Consultants look for solutions that balance skill and knowledge development, management commitment, and demands of the work environment. If any of the three are missing, performance will not improve. The consultants serve as liaisons between the business unit and a team of project managers, instructional designers, and tech developers to communicate learning needs. The team may provide an already available course that meets the need or create a learning solution specific to the needs of the employees within the function.

## Organizational Analysis

Managers need to consider three factors before choosing training as the solution to any pressure point: the company's strategic direction, the training resources available, and support of managers and peers for training activities.

### Support of Managers and Peers

Various studies have found that peer and manager support for training is critical. The key factors to success are a positive attitude among peers and managers about participation in training activities; managers' and peers' willingness to tell trainees how they can more effectively use knowledge, skills, or behaviors learned in training on the job; and the availability of opportunities for the trainees to use training content in their jobs.[14] If peers' and managers' attitudes and behaviors are not supportive, employees are not likely to apply training content to their jobs.

### Company Strategy

In Chapter 2 we discussed the importance of business strategy for a company to gain a competitive advantage. Several types of strategies were discussed including growth and disinvestment. As Figure 7.1 highlights, training should help companies achieve the business strategy. Table 7.2 shows possible strategic training and development initiatives and their implications for training practices. **Strategic training and development initiatives** are learning-related actions that a company should take to help achieve its business strategy.[15] The initiatives are based on the business environment, an understanding of the company's goals and resources, and insight into potential training and development options. They provide the company with a road map to guide specific training and development activities. They also show how training will help the company reach its goals and add value. The plan or goal the company chooses to achieve strategic objectives has a major impact on whether resources (money, trainers' time, program development) should be devoted to addressing a training pressure point.

**Strategic Training and Development Initiatives**
Learning-related actions that a company takes to achieve its business strategy.

It is important to identify the prevailing business strategy to ensure that the company allocates enough of its budget to training, that employees receive training on relevant topics, and that employees get the right amount of training.[16] For example, Deluxe Corporation is a check printer based in Saint Paul, Minnesota. Factors such as electronic transactions, mergers and acquisitions among financial institutions, and a company reorganization resulted in downsizing and poor employee morale within the company.[17] Fewer than 140 of 400 account managers were still employed with the company. As a result of the downsizing, Deluxe lost many account managers with 5 to 10 years of experience. The account managers who remained had worked at Deluxe less than 3 years or more than 20 years. For

**table 7.2**

Strategic Training and Development Initiatives and Their Implications

| STRATEGIC TRAINING AND DEVELOPMENT INITIATIVES | IMPLICATIONS |
|---|---|
| Diversify the Learning Portfolio | • Use new technology such as the Internet for training<br>• Facilitate informal learning<br>• Provide more personalized learning opportunities |
| Expand Who Is Trained | • Train customers, suppliers, and employees<br>• Offer more learning opportunities to nonmanagerial employees |
| Accelerate the Pace of Employee Learning | • Quickly identify needs and provide a high-quality learning solution<br>• Reduce the time to develop training programs<br>• Facilitate access to learning resources on an as-needed basis |
| Improve Customer Service | • Ensure that employees have product and service knowledge<br>• Ensure that employees have skills needed to interact with customers<br>• Ensure that employees understand their roles and decision-making authority |
| Provide Development Opportunities and Communicate to Employees | • Ensure that employees have opportunities to develop<br>• Ensure that employees understand career opportunities and personal growth opportunities<br>• Ensure that training and development addresses employees' needs in current job as well as growth opportunities |
| Capture and Share Knowledge | • Capture insight and information from knowledgeable employees<br>• Logically organize and store information<br>• Provide methods to make information available (e.g., resource guides, Web sites) |
| Align Training and Development with the Company's Strategic Direction | • Identify needed knowledge, skills, abilities, or competencies<br>• Ensure that current training and development programs support the company's strategic needs |
| Ensure That the Work Environment Supports Learning and transfer of Training | • Remove constraints to learning, such as lack of time, resources, and equipment<br>• Dedicate physical space to encourage teamwork, collaboration, creativity, and knowledge sharing<br>• Ensure that employees understand the importance of learning<br>• Ensure that managers and peers are supportive of training, development, and learning |

SOURCE: Based on S. Tannenbaum, "A Strategic View of Organizational Training and Learning," in *Creating, Implementing and Managing Effective Training and Development,* ed. K. Kraiger (San Francisco: Jossey-Bass, 2002), pp. 10–52.

these account managers, sales training involved only product training. Deluxe used training to capture and retain not only business but also the hearts and minds of employees.

Account managers developed fundamental sales skills through a combination of online and workshop courses. To build credibility for the training, three high-performing account managers assisted two trainers from Deluxe's training department. Simultaneously with the account managers' training, all employees providing field support for the sales team participated in a one-day training session that emphasized the change from selling product to building relationships with customers. Sales managers and directors participated in a field-coaching program so they could reinforce the account managers' learning. The sales managers now "shadow" the account managers once every business quarter to observe their sales skills and to provide coaching. Another training program focused on strategic time management skills. As a result of the training, customer retention rates have improved to 95 percent, up from 85 percent two years ago.

For example, when Regions Financial Corporation, headquartered in Birmingham, Alabama, acquired Union Planters in 2004 the company faced postmerger challenges.[18] The new company now had 5 million customers through 1,400 branches located throughout the South, Midwest, and Texas. To serve such a large customer base, it was important that the workforce performed at the highest possible levels. As a result, early in the merger process, both online and instructor-led training programs were created to help familiarize employees with the new cultural values of the company and to provide product knowledge and learning related to specific financial systems and applications. To help ensure comprehension, learning coaches were used to answer questions, provide reinforcement, and offer help when needed.

A disinvestment strategy resulted in Edwards Lifesciences Corporation being spun off from another company.[19] The new company's management team's new strategic plan described goals for sales growth, new-product development, customer loyalty, and employee commitment and satisfaction. The company realized that it had to prepare leaders who could help the company meet its strategic goals. A review of leadership talent showed that leadership development was needed and a leadership program was developed. The program includes 20 participants from different functions and company locations. Part of the week-long program is devoted to a simulation in which teams of managers run their own business, including handling marketing, manufacturing, and financials. The sessions also include classes taught by company executives who speak about important topics like the company's business strategy.

## Training Resources

It is necessary to identify whether the company has the budget, time, and expertise for training. For example, if the company is installing computer-based manufacturing equipment in one of its plants, it has three possible strategies to have computer-literate employees. First, the company can use internal consultants to train all affected employees. Second, the company may decide that it is more cost-effective to identify computer-literate employees by using tests and work samples. Employees who fail the test or perform below standards on the work sample can be reassigned to other jobs. Choosing this strategy suggests that the company has decided to devote resources to selection and placement rather than training. Third, if it lacks time or expertise, the company may decide to purchase training from a consultant.

**Request for Proposal (RFP)**
A document that outlines for potential vendors and consultants the type of service the company is seeking, references needed, number of employees who should be trained, project funding, the follow-up process, expected completion date, and the date when proposals must be received by the company.

Many companies identify vendors and consultants who can provide training services by using requests for proposals.[20] A **request for proposal (RFP)** is a document that outlines for potential vendors and consultants the type of service the company is seeking, the type and number of references needed, the number of employees who need to be trained, funding for the project, the follow-up process used to determine level of satisfaction and service, the expected completion date of the project, and the date when proposals must be received by the company. The request for proposal may be mailed to potential consultants and vendors or posted on the company's Web site. The request for proposal is valuable because it provides a standard set of criteria

**table 7.3**

Questions to Ask Vendors and Consultants

| |
|---|
| How do your products and services fit our needs? |
| How much and what type of experience does your company have in designing and delivering training? |
| What are the qualifications and experiences of your staff? |
| Can you provide demonstrations or examples of training programs you have developed? |
| Would you provide references of clients for whom you worked? |
| What evidence do you have that your programs work? |
| Will the training program be customized to meet the company's needs? |
| How long will it take to develop the training program? |
| How much will your services cost? |
| What instructional design methods do you use? |

SOURCES: Adapted from R. Zemke and J. Armstrong, "Evaluating Multimedia Developers," *Training Magazine*, November 1996, pp. 33–38; B. Chapman, "How to Create the Ideal RFP," *Training*, January 2004, pp. 40–43.

against which all consultants will be evaluated. The RFP also helps eliminate the need to evaluate outside vendors who cannot provide the needed services.

Usually the RFP helps identify several vendors who meet the criteria. The next step is to choose the preferred provider. Table 7.3 provides examples of questions to ask vendors.

## Person Analysis

Person analysis helps the manager identify whether training is appropriate and which employees need training. In certain situations, such as the introduction of a new technology or service, all employees may need training. However, when managers, customers, or employees identify a problem (usually as a result of a performance deficiency), it is often unclear whether training is the solution.

A major pressure point for training is poor or substandard performance—that is, a gap between employees' current performance and their expected performance. Poor performance is indicated by customer complaints, low performance ratings, or on-the-job accidents or unsafe behavior. Another potential indicator of the need for training is if the job changes so current performance levels need improvement or employees must complete new tasks.

Figure 7.3 shows the factors that influence employees' performance and learning. These factors are person characteristics, input, output, consequences, and feedback.[21] **Person characteristics** refer to the employees' knowledge, skill, ability, and attitudes. **Input** relates to the instructions that tell employees what, how, and when to perform. Input also refers to the support given to employees to help them perform. This support includes resources such as equipment, time, or budget. Support also includes feedback and reinforcement from managers and peers. **Output** refers to the job's performance standards. **Consequences** are the incentives employees receive for performing well. **Feedback** is the information employees receive while they are performing.

From a manager's perspective, to determine if training is needed, for any performance problem you need to analyze characteristics of the performer, input, output, consequences, and feedback. How might this be done? Based on the model in

**Person Characteristics**
An employee's knowledge, skills, abilities, and attitudes.

**Input**
Instructions that tell employees what, how, and when to perform; also the support they are given to help them to perform.

**Output**
A job's performance standards.

**Consequences**
The incentives that employees receive for performing well.

**Feedback**
Information that employees receive while they are performing concerning how well they are meeting objectives.

figure 7.3

Factors That Influence Employee Performance and Learning

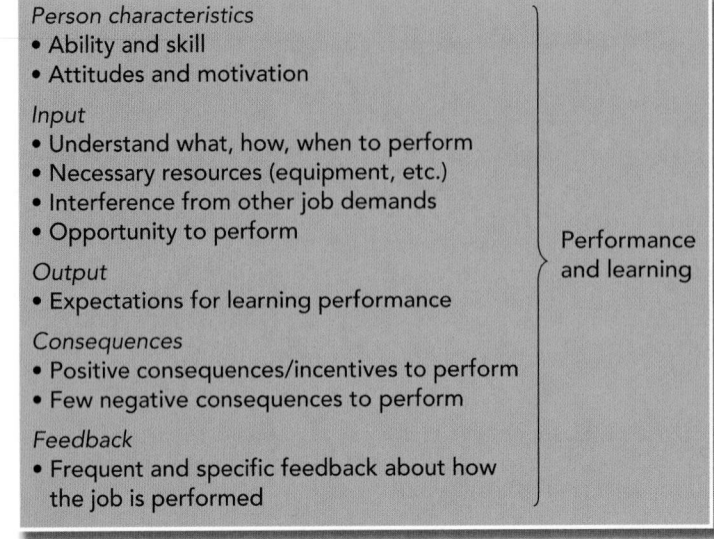

*Person characteristics*
- Ability and skill
- Attitudes and motivation

*Input*
- Understand what, how, when to perform
- Necessary resources (equipment, etc.)
- Interference from other job demands
- Opportunity to perform

*Output*
- Expectations for learning performance

*Consequences*
- Positive consequences/incentives to perform
- Few negative consequences to perform

*Feedback*
- Frequent and specific feedback about how the job is performed

→ Performance and learning

SOURCES: G. Rummler, "In Search of the Holy Performance Grail," *Training and Development,* April 1996, pp. 26–31; C. Reinhart, "How to Leap over Barriers to Performance," *Training and Development,* January 2000, pp. 20–24, G. Rummler and K. Morrill, "The Results Chain," *TD,* February 2005, pp. 27–35.

Figure 7.3, you should ask several questions to determine if training is the likely solution to a performance problem.[22] Assess whether

1. The performance problem is important and has the potential to cost the company a significant amount of money from lost productivity or customers.
2. Employees do not know how to perform effectively. Perhaps they received little or no previous training or the training was ineffective. (This problem is a characteristic of the person.)
3. Employees cannot demonstrate the correct knowledge or behavior. Perhaps they were trained but they infrequently or never used the training content (knowledge, skills, etc.) on the job. (This is an input problem.)
4. Performance expectations are clear (input) and there are no obstacles to performance such as faulty tools or equipment.
5. There are positive consequences for good performance, whereas poor performance is not rewarded. For example, if employees are dissatisfied with their compensation, their peers or a union may encourage them to slow down their pace of work. (This involves consequences.)
6. Employees receive timely, relevant, accurate, constructive, and specific feedback about their performance (a feedback issue).
7. Other solutions such as job redesign or transferring employees to other jobs are too expensive or unrealistic.

If employees lack the knowledge and skill to perform and the other factors are satisfactory, training is needed. If employees have the knowledge and skill to perform, but input, output, consequences, or feedback are inadequate, training may not be the best solution. For example, if poor performance results from faulty equipment, training cannot solve this problem, but repairing the equipment will! If poor performance results from lack of feedback, then employees may not need training, but their managers may need training on how to give performance feedback.

lc

## Task Analysis

A task analysis, defined on page 271, identifies the conditions in which tasks are performed. The conditions include identifying equipment and the environment the employee works in, time constraints (deadlines), safety considerations, or performance standards. Task analysis results in a description of work activities, including tasks performed by the employee and the knowledge, skills, and abilities required to successfully complete the tasks. A *job* is a specific position requiring the completion of specific tasks. A *task* is a statement of an employee's work activity in a specific job. There are four steps in task analysis:

1. Select the job(s) to be analyzed.
2. Develop a preliminary list of tasks performed on the job by interviewing and observing expert employees and their managers and talking with others who have performed a task analysis.
3. Validate or confirm the preliminary list of tasks. This involves having a group of subject matter experts (job incumbents, managers, and so on) answer in a meeting or on a written survey several questions regarding the tasks. The types of questions that may be asked include the following: How frequently is the task performed? How much time is spent performing each task? How important or critical is the task for successful performance of the job? How difficult is the task to learn? Is performance of the task expected of entry-level employees?[23]

   Table 7.4 presents a sample task analysis questionnaire. This information is used to determine which tasks will be focused on in the training program. The person or committee conducting the needs assessment must decide the level of ratings across dimensions that will determine that a task should be included in the training program. Tasks that are important, frequently performed, and of moderate-to-high levels of difficulty should be trained. Tasks that are not important and are infrequently performed will not be trained. It is difficult for managers and trainers to decide if tasks that are important, are performed infrequently, and require minimal difficulty should be included in training. Managers and trainers must determine whether important tasks—regardless of how frequently they are performed or their level of difficulty—will be included in training.
4. Identify the knowledge, skills, or abilities necessary to successfully perform each task. This information can be collected using interviews and questionnaires. Information concerning basic skill and cognitive ability requirements is critical for determining if certain levels of knowledge, skills, and abilities will be prerequisites for entrance to the training program (or job) or if supplementary training in underlying skills is needed. For training purposes, information concerning how difficult it is to learn the knowledge, skill, or ability is important—as is whether the knowledge, skill, or ability is expected to be acquired by the employee before taking the job.[24]

### Example of a Task Analysis

Each of the four steps of a task analysis can be seen in this example from a utility company. Trainers were given the job of developing a training system in six months.[25] The purpose of the program was to identify tasks and knowledge, skills, abilities, and other considerations that would serve as the basis for training program objectives and lesson plans.

**table 7.4**

Sample Task Statement Questionnaire

Name Date

Position

Please rate each of the task statements according to three factors: the *importance* of the task for effective performance, how *frequently* the task is performed, and the degree of *difficulty* required to become effective in the task. Use the following scales in making your ratings.

| *Importance* | *Frequency* |
|---|---|
| 4 = Task is critical for effective performance. | 4 = Task is performed once a day. |
| 3 = Task is important but not critical for effective performance. | 3 = Task is performed once a week. |
| 2 = Task is of some importance for effective performance. | 2 = Task is performed once every few months. |
| 1 = Task is of no importance for effective performance. | 1 = Task is performed once or twice a year. |
| 0 = Task is not performed. | 0 = Task is not performed. |

*Difficulty*

4 = Effective performance of the task requires extensive prior experience and/or training (12–18 months or longer).
3 = Effective performance of the task requires minimal prior experience and training (6–12 months).
2 = Effective performance of the task requires a brief period of prior training and experience (1–6 months).
1 = Effective performance of the task does not require specific prior training and/or experience.
0 = This task is not performed.

| *Task* | *Importance* | *Frequency* | *Difficulty* |
|---|---|---|---|
| 1. Ensuring maintenance on equipment, tools, and safety controls | | | |
| 2. Monitoring employee performance | | | |
| 3. Scheduling employees | | | |
| 4. Using statistical software on the computer | | | |
| 5. Monitoring changes made in processes using statistical methods | | | |

The first phase of the project involved identifying potential tasks for each job in the utility's electrical maintenance area. Procedures, equipment lists, and information provided by subject matter experts (SMEs) were used to generate the tasks. SMEs included managers, instructors, and senior technicians. The tasks were incorporated into a questionnaire administered to all technicians in the electrical maintenance department. The questionnaire included 550 tasks. Figure 7.4 shows sample items from the questionnaire for the electrical maintenance job. Technicians were asked to rate each task on importance, difficulty, and frequency of performance. The rating scale for frequency included zero. A zero rating indicated that the technician rating the task had never performed the task. Technicians who rated a task zero were asked not to evaluate the task's difficulty and importance.

Customized software was used to analyze the ratings collected via the questionnaire. The primary requirement used to determine whether a task required training was its importance rating. A task rated "very important" was identified as one requiring training regardless of its frequency or difficulty. If a task was rated moderately important but difficult, it also was designated for training. Tasks rated unimportant, not difficult, and done infrequently were not designated for training.

The list of tasks designated for training was reviewed by the SMEs to determine if it accurately described job tasks. The result was a list of 487 tasks. For each of the 487 tasks, two SMEs identified the necessary knowledge, skills, abilities, and other

figure 7.4

Sample Items from Task Analysis Questionnaires for the Electrical Maintenance Job

| Job: Electrical Maintenance Worker | | | | |
|---|---|---|---|---|
| | | Task Performance Ratings | | |
| **Task #s** | **Task Description** | **Frequency of Performance** | **Importance** | **Difficulty** |
| 199-264 | Replace a light bulb | 0 1 2 3 4 5 | 0 1 2 3 4 5 | 0 1 2 3 4 5 |
| 199-265 | Replace an electrical outlet | 0 1 2 3 4 5 | 0 1 2 3 4 5 | 0 1 2 3 4 5 |
| 199-266 | Install a light fixture | 0 1 2 3 4 5 | 0 1 2 3 4 5 | 0 1 2 3 4 5 |
| 199-267 | Replace a light switch | 0 1 2 3 4 5 | 0 1 2 3 4 5 | 0 1 2 3 4 5 |
| 199-268 | Install a new circuit breaker | 0 1 2 3 4 5 | 0 1 2 3 4 5 | 0 1 2 3 4 5 |
| | | **Frequency of Performance** 0=never 5=often | **Importance** 1=negligible 5=extremely high | **Difficulty** 1=easiest 5=most difficult |

SOURCE: E. F. Holton III and C. Bailey, "Top-to-Bottom Curriculum Redesign," *Training and Development*, March 1995, pp. 40–44. Reprinted with permission of *Training & Development*.

factors required for performance. This included information on working conditions, cues that initiate the task's start and end, performance standards, safety considerations, and necessary tools and equipment. All data were reviewed by plant technicians and members of the training department. More than 14,000 knowledge, skill, ability, and other considerations were clustered into common areas. An identification code was assigned to each group that linked groups to task and knowledge, skill, ability, and other factors. These groups were then combined into clusters that represented qualification areas. That is, the task clusters related to linked tasks that the employees must be certified in to perform the job. The clusters were used to identify training lesson plans and course objectives; trainers also reviewed the clusters to identify prerequisite skills.

## Ensuring Employees' Readiness for Training

**LO4** Evaluate Employees' Readiness for Training.

The second step in the training design process is to evaluate whether employees are ready to learn. *Readiness for training* refers to whether (1) employees have the personal characteristics (ability, attitudes, beliefs, and motivation) necessary to learn program content and apply it on the job and (2) the work environment will facilitate learning and not interfere with performance.

Although managers are not often trainers, they play an important role in influencing employees' readiness for training. **Motivation to learn** is the desire of the trainee to learn the content of the training program.[26] Various research studies have shown

**Motivation to Learn**
The desire of the trainee to learn the content of a training program.

that motivation is related to knowledge gain, behavior change, or skill acquisition in training programs.[27] Managers need to ensure that employees' motivation to learn is as high as possible. They can do this by ensuring employees' self-efficacy; understanding the benefits of training; being aware of training needs, career interests, and goals; understanding work environment characteristics; and ensuring employees' basic skill levels. Managers should also consider input, output, consequences, and feedback because these factors influence motivation to learn.

## Self-Efficacy

**Self-Efficacy**
The employees' belief that they can successfully learn the content of a training program.

**Self-efficacy** is the employees' belief that they can successfully learn the content of the training program. The training environment is potentially threatening to many employees who may not have extensive educational experience or who have little experience in the particular area emphasized by the training program. For example, training employees to use equipment for computer-based manufacturing represents a potential threat, especially if employees are intimidated by new technologies and do not have confidence in their ability to master the skills needed to use a computer. Research has demonstrated that self-efficacy is related to performance in training programs.[28] Managers can increase employees' self-efficacy level by

1. Letting employees know that the purpose of training is to try to improve performance rather than to identify areas in which employees are incompetent.
2. Providing as much information as possible about the training program and purpose of training prior to the actual training.
3. Showing employees the training success of their peers who are now in similar jobs.
4. Providing employees with feedback that learning is under their control and they have the ability and the responsibility to overcome any learning difficulties they experience in the program.

## Understanding the Benefits or Consequences of Training

Employees' motivation to learn can be enhanced by communicating to them the potential job-related, personal, and career benefits they may receive as a result of attending the training program. These benefits may include learning a more efficient way to perform a process or procedure, establishing contacts with other employees in the firm (networking), or increasing opportunities to pursue different career paths. The communication from the manager about potential benefits should be realistic. Unmet expectations about training programs have been shown to adversely affect motivation to learn.[29]

## Awareness of Training Needs, Career Interests, and Goals

To be motivated to learn in training programs, employees must be aware of their skill strengths and weaknesses and of the link between the training program and improvement of their weaknesses.[30] Managers should make sure that employees understand why they are asked to attend training programs, and they should communicate the link between training and improvement of skill weaknesses or knowledge deficiencies. This can be accomplished by sharing performance appraisal information with employees, holding career development discussions, or having employees complete self-evaluations of their skill strengths and weaknesses and career interests and goals.

If possible, employees need to choose programs to attend and must perceive how actual training assignments are made to maximize motivation to learn. Several recent studies have suggested that giving trainees a choice regarding which programs to attend and then honoring those choices maximizes motivation to learn. Giving employees choices but not necessarily honoring them can reduce motivation to learn.[31]

## Work Environment Characteristics

Employees' perceptions of two characteristics of the work environment—situational constraints and social support—are critical determinants of motivation to learn. *Situational constraints* include lack of proper tools and equipment, materials and supplies, budgetary support, and time. *Social support* refers to managers' and peers' willingness to provide feedback and reinforcement.[32]

To ensure that the work environment enhances trainees' motivation to learn, managers need to

1. Provide materials, time, job-related information, and other work aids necessary for employees to use new skills or behavior before participating in training programs.
2. Speak positively about the company's training programs to employees.
3. Let employees know they are doing a good job when they use training content in their work.
4. Encourage work group members to involve each other in trying to use new skills on the job by soliciting feedback and sharing training experiences and situations in which training content was helpful.
5. Give employees time and opportunities to practice and apply new skills or behaviors to their work.

## Basic Skills

Employees' motivation to learn in training activities can also be influenced by the degree to which they have **basic skills**—cognitive ability and reading and writing skills needed to understand the content of training programs. Recent forecasts of the skill levels of the U.S. workforce indicate that managers will likely have to work with employees who lack those skills.[33]

**Basic Skills**
Reading, writing, and communication skills needed to understand the content of a training program.

Managers need to conduct a literacy audit to determine employees' basic skill levels. Table 7.5 shows the activities involved in a literacy audit.

***Cognitive Ability.*** **Cognitive ability** includes verbal comprehension (understand and use written and spoken language), quantitative ability (speed and accuracy in solving math problems), and reasoning ability (logic in solving problems).[34] Research shows that cognitive ability is related to successful performance in all jobs.[35] The importance of cognitive ability for job success increases as the job becomes more complex.

**Cognitive Ability**
Includes three dimensions: verbal comprehension, quantitative ability, and reasoning ability.

Cognitive ability influences job performance and ability to learn in training programs. If trainees lack the cognitive ability level necessary to perform job tasks, they will not perform well. Also, trainees' level of cognitive ability can influence whether they can learn in training programs.[36] Trainees with low levels of cognitive ability are more likely to fail to complete training or (at the end of training) receive low grades on tests to measure how much they have learned.

As discussed in Chapter 6, to identify employees without the cognitive ability to succeed on the job or in training programs, companies use paper-and-pencil cognitive

**table 7.5**
Performing a Literacy Audit

| | |
|---|---|
| Step 1. | Observe employees to determine the basic skills they need to succeed in their jobs. Note the materials employees use on the job, the tasks performed, and the reading, writing, and computations completed by employees. |
| Step 2. | Collect all materials that are written and read on the job and identify computations that must be performed to determine the necessary level of basic skill proficiency. Materials include bills, memos, and forms such as inventory lists and requisition sheets. |
| Step 3. | Interview employees to determine the basic skills they believe are needed to do the job. Consider the basic-skill requirements of the job yourself. |
| Step 4. | Determine whether employees have the basic skills needed to successfully perform their jobs. Combine the information gathered by observing and interviewing employees and evaluating materials they use on their jobs. Write a description of each job in terms of reading, writing, and computation skills needed to perform successfully. |
| Step 5. | Develop or buy tests that ask questions relating specifically to the employees' jobs. Ask employees to complete the tests. |
| Step 6. | Compare test results with the description of the basic skills required for the job (from step 5). If the level of employees' reading, writing, and computation skills does not match the basic skills required by the job, then a basic skills problem exists. |

SOURCE: U.S. Department of Education, U.S. Department of Labor. *The Bottom Line: Basic Skills in the Workplace* (Washington, DC: 1988), pp. 14–15.

ability tests. Determining a job's cognitive ability requirement is part of the task analysis process discussed earlier in this chapter.

**Readability**
The difficulty level of written materials.

***Reading Ability.*** Lack of the appropriate reading level can impede performance and learning in training programs. Material used in training should be evaluated to ensure that its reading level does not exceed that required by the job. **Readability** refers to the difficulty level of written materials.[37] A readability assessment usually involves analysis of sentence length and word difficulty.

If trainees' reading level does not match the level needed for the training materials, four options are available. First, determine whether it is feasible to use video or on-the-job training, which involves learning by watching and practicing rather than by reading. Second, employees without the necessary reading level could be identified through reading tests and reassigned to other positions more congruent with their skill levels. Third, again using reading tests, identify employees who lack the necessary reading skills and provide them with remedial training. Fourth, determine whether the job can be redesigned to accommodate employees' reading levels. The fourth option is certainly most costly and least practical. Therefore, alternative training methods need to be considered, or you can elect a nontraining option. Nontraining options include selecting employees for jobs and training opportunities on the basis of reading, computation, writing, and other basic skill requirements.

The "Competing through Sustainability" box shows how companies are partnering with nonprofit groups to develop worker skills and in return get a motivated and committed workforce.

## COMPETING THROUGH SUSTAINABILITY
### Capitalizing on Local Talent

Many companies rely on welfare-to-work programs and nonprofit community groups to provide employment to the unemployed or low-income employees. The relationship is beneficial for the employees, the company, and the local community. Employees receive wage-paying jobs, companies get a committed and motivated workforce, and living and working standards are raised in the communities where the companies are located.

For example, TJX Companies, a discount clothing and home fashion retailer, has hired more than 36,000 employees from welfare rolls since 1997. TJX has found a qualified workforce with a retention rate that is 30 percent higher than average hires, which has resulted in better morale, customer service, and productivity. TJX believes that training has been critical to the company's success. English-language training is provided to employees in distribution centers and the corporate office. The First Step program includes classroom training, case management, internships, and job placement. TJX also has helped employees learn about the numerous state and federal assistance program benefits by printing and distributing a brochure explaining eligibility requirements for food stamp programs in Bosnian, Portuguese, Vietnamese, Spanish, and English.

CVS Corporation, a drug retailer, has hired more than 23,000 former welfare recipients with a retention rate of 60 percent. CVS operates regional training centers around the country. The centers provide new-hire training and also offer further training for jobs on the career path from entry-level jobs to higher paying jobs. The training centers include a simulated store where employees can learn entry-level jobs, pharmacy assistance, or how to be a pharmacy technician. CVS works with a government hiring team that works with city, state, and local government agencies (including Job Corps and Goodwill Industries).

Standard Aero San Antonio, a jet engine repair and overhaul company that provides services to the U.S. Navy and Air Force, needed new technicians to overhaul and repair jet engines but found few qualified employees. As a result, the company partnered with a local community college and a community-based organization that helps unemployed and underemployed people in the San Antonio, Texas, community. A local community college developed a five-month customized training program to help meet the company's need for technicians. Each student receives full wages and benefits from the beginning of training. The community organization provides child care and transportation to help the trainees finish the program. Out of 42 students, 37 completed the training program and were hired by Standard Aero. Standard Aero estimates a saving of $105,000 for the first class of employees, with a retention rate of 95 percent. The program provides benefits to the community by developing taxpaying workers and the company receives the advantage of access to trained, qualified workers.

SOURCE: Based on G. Johnson, "Grab Your Partner," *Training*, June 2004, pp. 32–38.

step 3

## Creating a Learning Environment

Learning permanently changes behavior. For employees to acquire knowledge and skills in the training program and apply this information in their jobs, the training program must include specific learning principles. Educational and industrial psychologists and instructional design specialists have identified several conditions under which employees learn best.[38] Table 7.6 shows the events that should take place for learning to occur in the training program and their implications for instruction.

Consider how several companies are creating a positive learning environment.[39] At Toshiba America Business Solutions in Irvine, California, a mobile flexible training

**table 7.6**

Conditions for Learning and Their Importance

| CONDITIONS FOR LEARNING | IMPORTANCE AND APPLICATION TO TRAINING |
|---|---|
| Need to know why they should learn | Employees need to understand the purpose or objectives of the training program to help them understand why they need training and what they are expected to accomplish. |
| Meaningful training content | Motivation to learn is enhanced when training is related to helping learner (such as related to current job tasks, problems, enhancing skills, or dealing with jobs or company changes). The training context should be similar to the work environment. |
| Opportunities for practice | Trainees need to demonstrate what is learned (knowledge, skill, behavior) to become more comfortable using it and to commit it to memory. Let trainees choose their practice strategy. |
| Feedback | Feedback helps learner modify behavior, skill, or use knowledge to meet objectives. Videotape, other trainees, and the trainer are useful feedback sources. |
| Observe experience, and interact with others | Adults learn best by doing. Gain new perspectives and insights by working with others. Can learn by observing the actions of models or sharing experiences with each other in communities of practice. |
| Good program coordination and administration | Eliminate distractions that could interfere with learning, such as cell-phone calls. Make sure the room is properly organized, comfortable, and appropriate for the training method (e.g., movable seating for team exercises). Trainees should receive announcements of the purpose of training, place, hour, and any pretraining materials such as cases or readings. |
| Commit training content to memory | Facilitate recall of training content after training. Examples, include using concept maps showing relationships among ideas, multiple types of review (e.g., writing, drawing, role plays), teach key words or provide a visual image. Limit instruction to manageable units that don't exceed memory limits, review and practice over multiple days (overlearning). |

SOURCES: Based on R. M. Gagne, "Learning Processes and Instruction," *Training Research Journal* 1 (1995/1996), pp. 17–28; M. Knowles, *The Adult Learner*, 4th ed. (Houston: Gulf, 1990); A. Bandura, *Social Foundations of Thought and Action* (Englewood Cliffs, NJ: Prentice Hall, 1986); E. A. Locke and G. D. Latham, *A Theory of Goal Setting and Task Performance* (Englewood Cliffs, NJ: Prentice Hall, 1990); B. Mager, *Preparing Instructional Objectives*, 2nd ed. (Belmont, CA: Lake, 1984); B.J. Smith and B. L. Delahaye, *How to Be an Effective Trainer*, 2nd ed. (New York: John Wiley and Sons, 1987); K. A. Smith-Jentsch, F. G. Jentsch, S. C. Payne, and E. Salas, "Can Pretraining Experience Explain Individual Differences in Learning?" *Journal of Applied Psychology* 81 (1996), pp. 110–16.

program was developed to train new dealers with no experience with the company's products. Training to Go is a blended learning approach with work-based and classroom learning sessions. Delivering the information in multiple ways engages the learners and aids in retention. Colorado Springs Utilities, a community-owned utility, provides natural gas, water, and electric services to more than 600,000 customers. All of the company executives issue public statements in support of learning, participate in learning events as instructors or speakers, and include learning objectives as part of their performance goals. Every training program begins with a brainstorming session to identify themes and activities that engage trainees, helping them enjoy training more and retain more of what they have learned. In a safety training class, students experience a simulated emergency and have to respond using skills they have learned along with their knowledge of an evacuation plan. The trainees perform different roles and activities in response to a power shutdown. The trainer then critiques their performance and trainees discuss what they have learned (or still need to learn). Trainees complete a written exam and review to ensure knowledge retention. Unisys Corporation, located in Blue Bell, Pennsylvania, helps businesses and governments apply information technology to achieve new levels of competitiveness and success. For example, Unisys provides information technology services to some of the world's most prestigious sports organizations, including the United States Golf Association and the Royal and Ancient Golf Club. Unisys's learning approach emphasizes training, feedback and coaching, and practice in its training programs, which include instructor-led, online learning, and blended learning (a mixture of online and instructor-led learning). For example, in a sales course the premise of *Mission Impossible* is used to send trainees on multiple missions with an agent to build and deliver persuasive presentations. After the online course, trainees attend an instructor-led course for one and a half days. On the job, a Web-based tool can be used to reinforce learning and create a presentation outline that can be used on the job.

Companies can facilitate both face-to-face and electronic communities of practice. **Communities of practice** are groups of employees who work together, learn from each other, and develop a common understanding of how to get work accomplished.[40] For example, at Siemens Power Transmission in Wendell, North Carolina, managers were wondering how to stop employees from gathering in the cafeteria for informal discussions during work time.[41] However, managers discovered that employees were developing problem-solving strategies, sharing product and procedural information, and providing career counseling to each other. As a result, they placed pads of paper and overhead projectors in the cafeteria as aides for informal meetings. Both Schlumberger and Intel have online communities of practice.[42] Schlumberger, an oilfield services provider headquartered in New York, uses online communities of practice to connect experts such as geologists, physicists, managers, and engineers in remote locations around the world to help each other solve problems. At Intel, a community of practice is used to connect trainers and training developers from the company's more than 90 groups of training employees so they can share resources, be introduced to new technology, and gain access to professional development opportunities.

**Communities of Practice**
Groups of employees who work together, learn from each other, and develop a common understanding of how to get work accomplished.

**Transfer of Training**
The use of knowledge, skills, and behaviors learned in training on the job.

## Ensuring Transfer of Training

**Transfer of training** refers to on-the-job use of knowledge, skills, and behaviors learned in training. As Figure 7.5 shows, transfer of training is influenced by the

figure 7.5
Work Environment Characteristics Influencing Transfer of Training

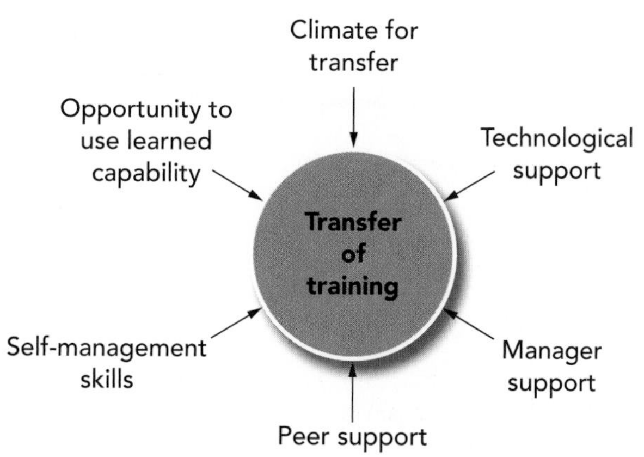

climate for transfer, manager support, peer support, opportunity to use learned capabilities, technology support, and self-management skills. As we discussed earlier, learning is influenced by the learning environment (such as meaningfulness of the material and opportunities for practice and feedback) and employees' readiness for training (for example, their self-efficacy and basic skill level). If no learning occurs in the training program, transfer is unlikely.

## Climate for Transfer

**Climate for Transfer** Trainees' perceptions of characteristics of the work environment (social support and situational constraints) that can either facilitate or inhibit use of trained skills or behavior.

One way to think about the work environment's influence on transfer of training is to consider the overall climate for transfer. **Climate for transfer** refers to trainees' perceptions about a wide variety of characteristics of the work environment that facilitate or inhibit use of trained skills or behavior. These characteristics include manager and peer support, opportunity to use skills, and the consequences for using learned capabilities.[43] Research has shown that transfer of training climate is significantly related to positive changes in behaviors following training.

## Manager Support

*Manager support* refers to the degree to which trainees' managers (1) emphasize the importance of attending training programs and (2) stress the application of training content to the job. Table 7.7 shows what managers should do to support training. For example, at Men's Wearhouse, managers are expected to spend part of their budget on training. A series of meetings are held with managers to explain the purpose of training and the manager's role in helping employees learn and use skills in the stores. At Johnson and Johnson managers learn online how to support training and development. Using a Web-based resource, managers can assess employees' skills and develop learning plans.[44]

Alltel Corporation, a telecommunications company, uses managers as trainers.[45] When changes in systems, products, or policies occur, managers are the primary trainers for employees. Alltel uses a series of monthly teleconferences to educate managers in the field about new marketing strategies, new rate plans, new wireless or data ser-

**table 7.7**

What Managers Should Do to Support Training

| |
|---|
| Understand the content of the training. |
| Know how training relates to what you need employees to do. |
| In performance appraisals, evaluate employees on how they apply training to their jobs. |
| Support employees' use of training when they return to work. |
| Ensure that employees have the equipment and technology needed to use training. |
| Prior to training, discuss with employees how they plan to use training. |
| Recognize newly trained employees who use training content. |
| Give employees release time from their work to attend training. |
| Explain to employees why they have been asked to attend training. |
| Give employees feedback related to skills or behavior they are trying to develop. |
| If possible, be a trainer. |

SOURCE: Based on A. Rossett, "That Was a Great Class, but . . ." *Training and Development*, July 1997, p. 21.

vices, and new offerings in products such as phone headsets. The emphasis in the sessions is not only on communicating changes but also on teaching the managers to effectively use learning principles to train employees. For example, the teleconferences might have managers participate in a role play designed to teach salespeople how to talk to customers about an equipment upgrade.

The greater the level of manager support, the more likely that transfer of training will occur.[46] The basic level of support that a manager should provide is acceptance, that is, allowing trainees to attend training. The highest level of support is to participate in training as an instructor (teaching in the program). Managers who serve as instructors are more likely to provide lower-level support functions such as reinforcing use of newly learned capabilities, discussing progress with trainees, and providing opportunities to practice. Managers can also facilitate transfer through use of action plans. An **action plan** is a written document that includes the steps that the trainee and manager will take to ensure that training transfers to the job. The action plan includes (1) a goal identifying what training content will be used and how it will be used (project, problem); (2) strategies for reaching the goal, including resources needed; (3) strategies for getting feedback (such as meetings with the manager); and (4) expected outcome (what will be different?). The action plan includes a schedule of specific dates and times when the manager and trainee agree to meet to discuss the progress being made in using learned capabilities on the job.

**Action Plan**
Document summarizing what the trainee and manager will do to ensure that training transfers to the job.

At a minimum, special sessions should be scheduled with managers to explain the purpose of the training and set expectations that they will encourage attendance at the training session, provide practice opportunities, reinforce use of training, and follow up with employees to determine the progress in using newly acquired capabilities.

## Peer Support

Transfer of training can also be enhanced by creating a support network among the trainees.[47] A **support network** is a group of two or more trainees who agree to meet and discuss their progress in using learned capabilities on the job. This could involve face-to-face meetings or communications via e-mail. Trainees can share successful experiences in using training content on the job; they can also discuss how they obtained resources needed to use training content or how they coped with a work environment that interfered with use of training content.

**Support Network**
Trainees who meet to discuss their progress in using learned capabilities on the job.

A newsletter might be written to show how trainees are dealing with transfer of training issues. Distributed to all trainees, the newsletter might feature interviews with trainees who were successful in using new skills. Managers may also provide trainees with a mentor—a more experienced employee who previously attended the same training program. The mentor, who may be a peer, can provide advice and support related to transfer of training issues (such as how to find opportunities to use the learned capabilities).

## Opportunity to Use Learned Capabilities

Opportunity to use learned capabilities **(opportunity to perform)** refers to the extent to which the trainee is provided with or actively seeks experience with newly learned knowledge, skill, and behaviors from the training program.[48] Opportunity to perform is influenced by both the work environment and trainee motivation. One way trainees can use learned capabilities is through assigned work experiences (problems or tasks) that require their use. The trainees' manager usually plays a key role in determining

**Opportunity to Perform**
Trainee is provided with or actively seeks experience using newly learned knowledge, skills, or behavior.

work assignments. Opportunity to perform is also influenced by the degree to which trainees take personal responsibility to actively seek out assignments that allow them to use newly acquired capabilities. Trainees given many opportunities to use training content on the job are more likely to maintain learned capabilities than trainees given few opportunities.[49]

## Technological Support: EPSS and Knowledge Management Systems

**Electronic Performance Support Systems (EPSS)**
Computer applications that can provide (as requested) skills training, information access, and expert advice.

**Electronic performance support systems (EPSS)** are computer applications that can provide, as requested, skills training, information access, and expert advice.[50] EPSSs may be used to enhance transfer of training by giving trainees an electronic information source that they can refer to as needed as they attempt to apply learned capabilities on the job.

For example, Atlanta-based poultry processor Cagle's Inc. uses an EPSS for employees who maintain the chicken-processing machines.[51] Because the machines that measure and cut chickens are constantly increasing in sophistication, it is impossible to continually train technicians so that they know the equipment's details. However, technicians are trained on the basic procedures they need to know to maintain these types of machines. When the machines encounter a problem, the technicians rely on what they have learned in training as well as on the EPSS, which provides more detailed instructions about the repairs. The EPSS also tells technicians the availability of parts and where in inventory to find replacement parts. The EPSS consists of a postage stamp–size computer monitor attached to a visor that magnifies the screen. The monitor is attached to a three-pound computer about half the size of a portable compact disc player. Attached to the visor is a microphone that the technician uses to give verbal commands to the computer. The EPSS helps employees diagnose and fix the machines very quickly. This is important given that the plant processes more than 100,000 chickens a day, and chicken is a perishable food product!

**Knowledge Management**
Process of enhancing company performance by designing and using tools, systems, and cultures to improve creation, sharing and use of knowledge.

**Knowledge management** refers to the process of enhancing company performance by designing and implementing tools, processes, systems, structures, and cultures to improve the creation, sharing, and use of knowledge.[52] Consider several examples of the methods companies use to share and create knowledge. At MWH Global, an engineering and environmental consulting company, a software program was used to analyze the data that employees provided about which colleagues they most frequently interacted with and whom they turned to for expertise.[53] The program plotted a web of interconnecting nodes and lines representing people and relationships. The web provides a corporate map of how works get done, lists the well-connected technical experts, and helps identify informal connections between people that are missing on a traditional organizational chart.

Caterpillar Inc. has moved toward becoming a learning organization with the help of knowledge management.[54] Thirty years ago Caterpillar Inc., a manufacturer of construction and mining equipment, engines, and gas turbines, had most of its value in plant and physical equipment. Today, intangible assets such as intellectual capital account for most of the company's value. Caterpillar's knowledge sharing system, a Web-based system known as Knowledge Network, has 3,000 communities of practice. They range in size from small teams to hundreds of employees from across the world. The communities of practice are used to distribute information, post questions, provide space for reference materials, and have links to standards and regulations relevant to the community. One community of practice focuses on bolted joints and fasteners.

The community of practice gives specialized engineers who generally work alone in manufacturing facilities the ability to ask other engineers questions or get second opinions on designs and problems. Caterpillar also has external communities of practice made up of dealers, suppliers, and customers.

Caterpillar's communities of practice using the Knowledge Network have resulted in improved decision making, increased collaboration and teamwork, improved work quality, and better product design and development. For example, members of the Bolted Joints and Fasteners community and the Dealer Service Training community saved more than $1.5 million from online discussions. The company also tracks participation using metrics such as number of discussions and number of people logged into the system, with the goal of increasing the amount of discussion and activity in the system.

## Self-Management Skills

Training programs should prepare employees to self-manage their use of new skills and behaviors on the job.[55] Specifically, within the training program, trainees should set goals for using skills or behaviors on the job, identify conditions under which they might fail to use them, identify the positive and negative consequences of using them, and monitor their use of them. Also, trainees need to understand that it is natural to encounter difficulty in trying to use skills on the job; relapses into old behavior and skill patterns do not indicate that trainees should give up. Finally, because peers and supervisors on the job may be unable to reward trainees using new behaviors or to provide feedback automatically, trainees need to create their own reward system and ask peers and managers for feedback.

Consider how Vanderbilt University Medical Center (VUMC) emphasizes transfer of training.[56] To improve patient safety and quality, VUMC initiated a team training program. The program teaches participants about patient safety mistakes and how to avoid them, team building, cross-checking and communications, decision making, and performance feedback. Participants are provided classroom training which shows how concepts from aviation flight crew training can be applied to patient safety and quality care by talking about how to create an effective team (crew), how to communicate effectively (briefings), how to recognize potential problems and what to do about them, how to make informed decisions, and how to critique performance (debrief). For example, the module on crew resource management focuses on how crew resource management is applied to health care and how it improves patient safety and quality of care.

Several steps are taken to make sure transfer of training occurs, that is, what is learned in the program is used and supported at work. Before the training starts, VUMC leaders are prepared to help the training succeed. Senior administrators, medical directors, and nursing staff attend a boot camp, which highlights the team training program. A safety climate survey is conducted to determine how each department perceives the VUMC attitudes toward safety practices and patient safety issues. Then, each department is reviewed to find built-in errors that are system problems and to evaluate how the team communicates and deals with conflict. After this, training, observation, coaching, and feedback are provided by medical supervisors. Checklists are provided for certain procedures such as patient handoffs, medication administration, and briefing and debriefing sessions to help participants use the strategies emphasized in training to improve safety and the quality of patient care. Patients also help ensure safety. They are asked to watch a video created by VUMC

figure 7.6
Overview of Use of Instructional Methods

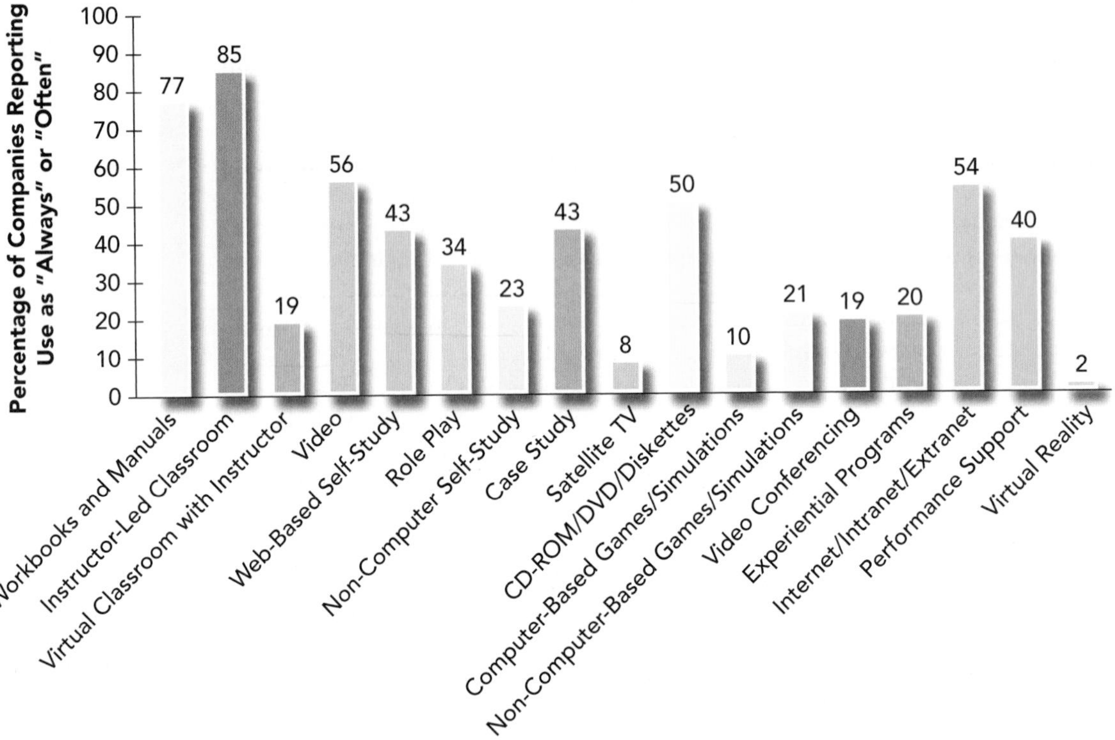


SOURCE: Based on H. Dolezalek, "Industry Report 2004," *Training*, October 2004, pp. 32, 34.

when they are admitted to the hospital. The video emphasizes the importance of asking questions about medications and medical procedures.

**LO5**
Discuss the Strengths and Weaknesses of Presentation, Hands-on, and Group Training Methods.

## Selecting Training Methods

A number of different methods can help employees acquire new knowledge, skills, and behaviors. Figure 7.6 shows the percentage of companies using different training methods. The figure shows that the instructor-led classroom is the most frequently used training method. Other common methods include the Internet, workbooks and manuals, and video. Figure 7.6 shows that traditional training methods, those that do not involve technology to deliver lessons, are more frequently used than is training that involves technology to deliver programs. For example, instructor-led classrooms, videos, workbooks and manuals, and role plays are used more frequently than virtual reality, computer-based games and simulations, and virtual classrooms with instructor. Note that there is one important exception: Technology-based programs involving CD-ROM/DVD/diskettes and Internet/intranet are frequently used by over 50 percent of the companies surveyed.

Regardless of whether the training method is traditional or technology based, for training to be effective it needs to be based on the training design model shown in Table 7.1. Needs assessment, a positive learning environment, and transfer of training are critical for training program effectiveness.

## Presentation Methods

**Presentation methods** refer to methods in which trainees are passive recipients of information. Presentation methods include traditional classroom instruction, distance learning, audiovisual techniques, and mobile technology such as iPods and PDAs. These are ideal for presenting new facts, information, different philosophies, and alternative problem-solving solutions or processes.

**Presentation Methods**
Training methods in which trainees are passive recipients of information.

***Instructor-Led Classroom Instruction.*** Classroom instruction typically involves having the trainer lecture a group. In many cases the lecture is supplemented with question-and-answer periods, discussion, or case studies. Classroom instruction remains a popular training method despite new technologies such as interactive video and computer-assisted instruction. Traditional classroom instruction is one of the least expensive, least time-consuming ways to present information on a specific topic to many trainees. The more active participation, job-related examples, and exercises that the instructor can build into traditional classroom instruction, the more likely trainees will learn and use the information presented on the job.

Distance learning is used by geographically dispersed companies to provide information about new products, policies, or procedures as well as skills training and expert lectures to field locations.[57] Distance learning features two-way communications between people. Distance learning currently involves two types of technology.[58] First, it includes teleconferencing. **Teleconferencing** refers to synchronous exchange of audio, video, and/or text between two or more individuals or groups at two or more locations. Trainees attend training programs in training facilities in which they can communicate with trainers (who are at another location) and other trainees using the telephone or personal computer. A second type of distance learning also includes individualized, personal-computer–based training.[59] Employees participate in training anywhere they have access to a personal computer. This type of distance learning may involve multimedia training methods such as Web-based training. Course material and assignments can be distributed using the company's intranet, video, or CD-ROM. Trainers and trainees interact using e-mail, bulletin boards, and conferencing systems.

**Teleconferencing**
Synchronous exchange of audio, video, or text between individuals or groups at two or more locations.

Teleconferencing usually includes a telephone link so that trainees viewing the presentation can call in questions and comments to the trainer. Also, satellite networks allow companies to link up with industry-specific and educational courses for which employees receive college credit and job certification. IBM, Digital Equipment, and Eastman Kodak are among the many firms that subscribe to the National Technological University, which broadcasts courses throughout the United States that technical employees need to obtain advanced degrees in engineering.[60]

An advantage of distance learning is that the company can save on travel costs. It also allows employees in geographically dispersed sites to receive training from experts who would not otherwise be available to visit each location. Intuit finds that a traditional classroom environment is good for introducing software and providing trainees with the opportunity to network. Virtual classroom training is used for courses on special software features, demonstrations, and troubleshooting using application-sharing features. General Mills uses virtual classrooms at smaller plants where offering a class on site is not cost effective.[61] Employees have access to courses in product-specific knowledge (e.g., cereal-producing), general technical skills (e.g., food chemistry) and functional-specific knowledge (e.g., maintenance).

Online learning also has disadvantages.[61] FileNeT Corporation was concerned with how its sales force was going to keep up with new software and software updates.[62] FileNeT tried self-paced online learning but discovered that salespeople did not like to read a lot of material about new products on the Web. Enrollment in online courses dwindled, and salespeople flooded the company's training department with requests for one-on-one assistance. To solve the training problem, the company decided to use webcasting. **Webcasting** involves classroom instructions that are provided online through live broadcasts. Webcasting helped spread the sales force training throughout the year rather than cramming it into twice-a-year sales meetings. Webcasting also helped ensure that the salespeople all received the same information. The salespeople liked the webcasts because of the timely information that helped them have conversations with customers. The live sessions were also popular because participants could ask questions. Webcasting has not replaced face-to-face training at FileNeT; classroom training is still about 80 percent of training, but that percentage has decreased by 10 percent. Webcasting has also resulted in savings of $500,000 annually (one of the twice-yearly sales meetings was canceled).

**Webcasting**
Classroom instruction provided online via live broadcasts.

The major disadvantage of distance learning is the potential for lack of interaction between the trainer and the audience. A high degree of interaction between trainees and the trainer is a positive learning feature that is missing from distance learning programs that merely use technology to broadcast a lecture to geographically dispersed employees. All that is done in this case is repurposing a traditional lecture (with its limitations for learning and transfer of training) for a new training technology! That's why establishing a communications link between employees and the trainer is important. Also, on-site instructors or facilitators should be available to answer questions and moderate question-and-answer sessions.

***Audiovisual Techniques.*** *Audiovisual instruction* includes overheads, slides, and video. As Figure 7.6 shows, video is a popular instructional method.[63] It has been used for improving communications skills, interviewing skills, and customer-service skills and for illustrating how procedures (such as welding) should be followed. Video is, however, rarely used alone. It is usually used in conjunction with lectures to show trainees real-life experiences and examples. Video is also a major component of behavior modeling and, naturally, interactive video instruction. Morse Bros., located in Tangent, Oregon, is one of only a few ready-mix firms in the Northwest that provide regular training for their drivers. Drivers play a key role in determining the success of the business. Excessive idling at construction sites, avoiding rollovers at construction sites, and product training can reduce costs and raise customer satisfaction. Morse Bros. produces training videos, which are presented by mentor-drivers. The mentor-driver's job is to select the weekly video, schedule viewing sessions, keep attendance records, and guide a wrap-up discussion following each video. The mentor-drivers are trained to call attention to key learning points covered in the video and relate the topics to issues the drivers deal with on the job. Because training sessions are scheduled early in the morning at the beginning of the drivers' shift, time is limited. Videos seldom run more than 10 minutes. For example, one called *Another Pair of Eyes* trains drivers to observe test procedures used by testing agencies at job sites. Samples are tested several times a month. A sample that fails can leave the company liable for demolition and removal of the concrete structure. Morse Bros. provides training on test procedures because samples often fail a test due to contamination (such as dirt) that gets into the test cylinder. At each training session, drivers answer several questions related to the content of the program. At the end of a session, drivers and the mentor-driver discuss anything that might be interfering with the quality of the product or timeliness of delivery. Mentor-drivers then share this information with company managers.[64]

The use of video in training has a number of advantages. First, the trainer can review, slow down, or speed up the lesson, which permits flexibility in customizing the session depending on trainees' expertise. Second, trainees can be exposed to equipment, problems, and events that cannot be easily demonstrated, such as equipment malfunctions, angry customers, or emergencies. Third, trainees get consistent instruction; program content is not affected by the interests and goals of a particular trainer. Fourth, videotaping trainees allows them to see and hear their own performance without the interpretation of the trainer. As a result, trainees cannot attribute poor performance to the bias of external evaluators such as the trainer or peers.

Most problems in video result from the creative approach used.[65] These problems include too much content for the trainee to learn, poor dialogue between the actors (which hinders the credibility and clarity of the message), overuse of humor or music, and drama that makes it confusing for the trainee to understand the important learning points emphasized in the video.

***Mobile Technologies: iPods and PDAs.*** Mobile technologies such as iPods and PDAs allow training and learning to occur naturally throughout the workday or at home, allow employees to be connected to communities of learning, and give employees the ability to learn at their own pace by reviewing material or skipping over content they know.[66] Capital One, a financial services company, provides iPods (portable audio players) for employees enrolled in training courses.[67] More than 2,000 iPods have been distributed as part of the Audio Learning program. The iPods can be used for business or personal reasons such as listening to music. Capital One decided that a new way to deliver training was needed based on employee surveys suggesting that employees did not have the time at work to attend classroom training. As a result, Capital One experimented with an audio channel for learning and found that employees liked learning on iPods and were able to gain access to programs that they would have been unable to attend in a classroom. Employees can access digitized audio, such as mp3 files, which are downloaded to their computers and can be transferred to their iPods. Approximately 30 training programs use the iPod. Employees can access a variety of programs including leadership development and workshops on conflict management. Books and Harvard Business School cases are provided to employees on the iPod and have been used in executive-level programs to discuss leadership and new-hire programs to understand customer service. Besides using the iPod as a primary training content delivery mechanism, some programs use the iPod to provide books or articles for employees for prework before they attend a classroom program, and others use it to enhance transfer of training. For example, scenarios and role plays discussed in classroom training are recorded and available for iPod upload. Employees can listen to the role plays, which reinforces the use of the training content on the job and motivates them to think about using what they have learned. Capital One has determined that despite the costs related to purchasing and providing each employee with an iPod, if employees were listening to four to six hours of training content outside the classroom, the company was breaking even. Some of the benefits of the iPod programs include employees'

Mobile technology is useful not only for entertainment, but can also be used for employees who travel and need to be in touch with the office. iPods and Personal Digital Assistants also give employees the ability to listen to and participate in training programs at their own leisure.

increased enthusiasm for learning (attending courses that use the iPod), employees' willingness to take on new roles and broader job responsibilities, and time savings over traditional learning methods.

Some of the challenges of using mobile technology for learning include ensuring that employees know when and how to take advantage of the technology; encouraging communication, collaboration, and interaction with other employees in communities of practice; and ensuring that employees can connect to a variety of networks no matter their location or mobile device they are using.[68] However, simply digitizing lectures and distributing them to employees will not facilitate learning. Thus, for example, Capital One creates simulated radio shows with phone-in questions and answers given by the announcers to create an audio learning environment that is enjoyable and interesting. The best approach may be to use iPods as part of a blended learning approach involving face-to-face interaction between trainees as well as audio learning.

## Hands-on Methods

**Hands-on Methods** Training methods that actively involve the trainee in learning.

**Hands-on methods** are training methods that require the trainee to be actively involved in learning. Hands-on methods include on-the-job training, simulations, business games and case studies, behavior modeling, interactive video, and Web-based training. These methods are ideal for developing specific skills, understanding how skills and behaviors can be transferred to the job, experiencing all aspects of completing a task, and dealing with interpersonal issues that arise on the job.

### On-the-Job Training (OJT)

**On-the-Job Training (OJT)** Peers or managers training new or inexperienced employees who learn the job by observation, understanding, and imitation.

**On-the-job training (OJT)** refers to new or inexperienced employees learning through observing peers or managers performing the job and trying to imitate their behavior. OJT can be useful for training newly hired employees, upgrading experienced employees' skills when new technology is introduced, cross-training employees within a department or work unit, and orienting transferred or promoted employees to their new jobs.

OJT takes various forms, including apprenticeships and self-directed learning programs. (Both are discussed later in this section.) OJT is an attractive training method because, compared to other methods, it needs less investment in time or money for materials, trainer's salary, or instructional design. Managers or peers who are job knowledge experts are used as instructors. As a result, it may be tempting to let them conduct the training as they believe it should be done.

This unstructured approach to OJT has several disadvantages[69] Managers and peers may not use the same process to complete a task. They may pass on bad habits as well as useful skills. Also, they may not understand that demonstration, practice, and feedback are important conditions for effective on-the-job training. Unstructured OJT can result in poorly trained employees, employees who use ineffective or dangerous methods to produce a product or provide a service, and products or services that vary in quality.

OJT must be structured to be effective. Table 7.8 shows the principles of structured OJT. Because OJT involves learning by observing others, successful OJT is based on the principles emphasized by social learning theory. These include the use of a credible trainer, a manager or peer who models the behavior or skill, communication of specific key behaviors, practice, feedback, and reinforcement. For example, at

**table 7.8**

Principles of On-the-Job Training

| PREPARING FOR INSTRUCTION | |
|---|---|
| 1. Break down the job into important steps.<br>2. Prepare the necessary equipment, materials, and supplies. | 3. Decide how much time you will devote to OJT and when you expect the employees to be competent in skill areas. |
| **ACTUAL INSTRUCTION** | |
| 1. Tell the trainees the objective of the task and ask them to watch you demonstrate it.<br>2. Show the trainees how to do it without saying anything.<br>3. Explain the key points or behaviors. (Write out the key points for the trainees, if possible.)<br>4. Show the trainees how to do it again.<br>5. Have the trainees do one or more single parts of the task and praise them for correct reproduction (optional). | 6. Have the trainees do the entire task and praise them for correct reproduction.<br>7. If mistakes are made, have the trainees practice until accurate reproduction is achieved.<br>8. Praise the trainees for their success in learning the task. |

SOURCES: Based on W. J. Rothwell and H. C. Kazanas, "Planned OJT Is Productive OJT," *Training and Development Journal*, October 1990, pp. 53–55; P. J. Decker and B. R. Nathan, *Behavior Modeling Training* (New York: Praeger Scientific, 1985).

Rochester Gas and Electric in Rochester, New York, radiation and chemistry instructors teach experienced employees how to conduct OJT.[70] While teaching these employees how to demonstrate software to new employees, the trainer may ask the employees to watch other OJT instructors as they train new recruits so they can learn new teaching techniques.

**Self-Directed Learning**
A program in which employees take responsibility for all aspects of learning.

**Self-directed learning** involves having employees take responsibility for all aspects of learning—when it is conducted and who will be involved. For example, at Corning Glass, new engineering graduates participate in an OJT program called SMART (self-managed, awareness, responsibility, and technical competence).[71] Each employee seeks the answers to a set of questions (such as "Under what conditions would a statistician be involved in the design of engineering experiments?") by visiting plants and research facilities and meeting with technical engineering experts and managers. After employees complete the questions, they are evaluated by a committee of peers who have already completed the SMART program. Evaluations have shown that the program cuts employees' start-up time in their new jobs from six weeks to three weeks. It is effective for a number of reasons. It encourages active involvement of the new employees in learning and allows flexibility in finding time for training. It has a peer-review evaluation component that motivates employees to complete the questions correctly. And, as a result of participating in the program, employees make contacts throughout the company and better understand the technical and personal resources available within the company.

There are several advantages and disadvantages of self-directed learning.[72] It allows trainees to learn at their own pace and receive feedback about the learning performance. For the company, self-directed learning requires fewer trainers, reduces costs associated with travel and meeting rooms, and makes multiple-site training more realistic. Self-directed learning provides consistent training content that captures the knowledge of experts. Self-directed learning also makes it easier for shift employees to gain access to training materials. A major disadvantage of self-directed learning is that trainees must be willing and comfortable learning on their own; that is, trainees must be motivated to learn. From the company perspective, self-directed learning results in higher development costs, and development time is longer than with other types of training programs. Self-directed learning will likely be more common in the future as companies seek to train staff flexibly, to take advantage of technology, and to encourage employees to be proactive in their learning rather than driven by the employer.[73]

The Four Seasons Regent Hotel and Resorts is a luxury hotel operations and management group with 22,000 employees worldwide, including approximately 13,000 in international locations. The Four Seasons faced the challenge of opening a new hotel and resort at Jambaran Bay, Bali. To address training needs, the human resources staff created a self-directed learning center. The Self Access Learning Center emphasizes communication skills as well as English language skills. Its purpose is to teach skills and improve employees' confidence in their communications. The center includes video recorders, training modules, books, and magazines. Besides English, the center also teaches Japanese (the language of 20 percent of hotel visitors) and provides training for foreign managers in Bahasa Indonesian, the native language of Indonesia. The training process begins by administering an English test to potential employees to gauge the level of English training they need. As employees complete each level of the training, they receive a monetary incentive.

How has the training paid dividends? Travel experts rated the Four Seasons Bali as one of the top hotels in the world. Business has increased steadily since the hotel opened, with guests from North America, Europe, Asia, Australia, and South America. As a result of the training, the Four Seasons is prepared for expansion. As the hotel industry expands in Asia, the Four Seasons now has a trained and talented staff that can be used to meet human resource needs as new resorts are developed. Four Seasons learned that the company must combine the training needs of the local culture with the standards of the company's culture to create a successful international business.[74]

**Apprenticeship**
A work-study training method with both on-the-job and classroom training.

**Apprenticeship** is a work-study training method with both on-the-job training and classroom training.[75] To qualify as a registered apprenticeship program under state or federal guidelines, at least 144 hours of classroom instruction and 2,000 hours, or one year, of on-the-job experience are required.[76] Apprenticeships can be sponsored by individual companies or by groups of companies cooperating with a union. The majority of apprenticeship programs are in the skilled trades, such as plumbing, carpentry, electrical work, and bricklaying.

The hours and weeks that must be devoted to completing specific skill units are clearly defined. OJT involves assisting a certified tradesperson (a journeyman) at the work site. The on-the-job training portion of the apprenticeship follows the guidelines for effective on-the-job training.[77] Modeling, practice, feedback, and evaluation are involved. First, the employer verifies that the trainee has the required knowledge of the operation or process. Next, the trainer (who is usually a more experienced, licensed employee) demonstrates each step of the process, emphasizing safety issues and key steps. The senior employee provides the apprentice with the opportunity to perform the process until all are satisfied that the apprentice can perform it properly and safely.

A major advantage of apprenticeship programs is that learners can earn pay while they learn. This is important because programs can last several years. Learners' wages usually increase automatically as their skills improve. Also, apprenticeships are usually effective learning experiences because they involve learning why and how a task is performed in classroom instruction provided by local trade schools, high schools, or community colleges. Apprenticeships also usually result in full-time employment for trainees when the program is completed. From the company's perspective, apprenticeship programs meet specific business needs and help to attract talented employees.

At its manufacturing facility in Toledo, Ohio, Libbey Glass has apprenticeship programs in mold making, machine repair, millwrighting, and maintenance repair.[78] Each apprentice requires the support of a journeyman for each work assignment. The program also requires apprentices to be evaluated every 1,000 hours to meet Department of Labor standards. The reviews are conducted by a committee including representatives of management and department journeymen. The committee also develops tests and other evaluation materials. The committee members cannot perform their normal duties during the time they are reviewing apprentices so their workload has to be spread among other employees or rescheduled for some other time. The benefits of the program include the development of employees who are more receptive to change in the work environment, the ability to perform work at Libbey instead of having to outsource jobs to contract labor, and an edge for Libbey in attracting talented employees who like the idea that after completing an apprenticeship they are eligible for promotions to other positions in the company, including management positions. Also, the apprenticeship program helps Libbey tailor training and work experiences to meet specific needs in maintenance repair, which is necessary to create and repair production mold equipment used in making glass products.

Apprentice-type programs are also used to prepare new managers. The president and chief executive officer of Goldcorp, Inc., a company in the mining industry, offers the chance for MBAs to apply for a nine-month apprenticeship.[79] The apprentice shadows Goldcorp's CEO, observing board meetings, negotiations, and the process of acquiring mines, and travels to learn important aspects of the mining industry. Goldcorp hopes the apprenticeships will attract more graduates to the mining industry, which many would not consider because of the mining industry's image as an unsafe, dirty business.

One disadvantage of many apprenticeship programs is limited access for minorities and women.[80] Another disadvantage is that there is no guarantee that jobs will be available when the program is completed. Finally, apprenticeship programs prepare trainees who are well trained in one craft or occupation. Due to the changing nature of jobs (thanks to new technology and use of cross-functional teams), many employers may be reluctant to employ workers from apprenticeship programs. Employers may believe that because apprentices are narrowly trained in one occupation or with one company, program graduates may have only company-specific skills and may be unable to acquire new skills or adapt their skills to changes in the workplace.

***Simulations.*** A **simulation** is a training method that represents a real-life situation, with trainees' decisions resulting in outcomes that mirror what would happen if the trainee were on the job. Simulations, which allow trainees to see the impact of their decisions in an artificial, risk-free environment, are used to teach production and process skills as well as management and interpersonal skills.

**Simulation**
A training method that represents a real-life situation, allowing trainees to see the outcomes of their decisions in an artificial environment.

New call center employees at American Express learn in a simulated environment that replicates a real call center.[81] Trainees go to a lab that contains cubicles identical to those in the call center. All materials (binders, reference materials, supplies) are exactly the same as they would be in the call center. The simulator uses a replica of the call center database and includes a role play that uses speech recognition software to simulate live calls. After the call center trainees learn transactions, they answer simulated calls that require them to practice the transactions. The simulator gives them feedback about errors they made during the calls and shows them the correct action. The simulator also tracks the trainees' performance and alerts the instructors if a trainee is falling behind. The simulator prepares call center employees in 32 days, an improvement over the previous 12-week program of classroom and on-the-job training. Turnover among call center employees is 50 percent lower since employees began training in the simulated environment. American Express believes that the reduction in turnover is because the training environment better prepares new employees to deal with the noise and pace of a real call center.

Rogers Wireless Communications, a cell phone company, uses a simulation to train sales skills and product knowledge.[82] An online role playing simulator that is used includes a variety of animated customers including a busy mother and a punk rocker, each providing a different customer service challenge. The simulation training has helped improve ratings of "mystery shoppers" at Rogers retail stores. Pitney Bowes, a mail-equipment and service company, uses an interactive spreadsheet program to simulate the company's product lines, key processes, and business culture. Executive teams are given a set of monthly revenue and product goals. They have to make a series of decisions including how many sales representatives to hire and how much time to invest in finding new clients. The decisions are plugged into the spreadsheet and both short- and long-term financial results are provided. The simulation has helped executives develop innovative ideas for transforming the sales organization with positive bottom-line dollar results.

**Avatars**
Computer depictions of humans that can be used as imaginary coaches, co-workers, and customers in simulations.

**Avatars** refer to computer depictions of humans that are being used as imaginary coaches, co-workers, and customers in simulations.[83] In second life (see www.secondlife.com), a virtual world built by its residents, avatars are used. Typically, trainees see the avatar who appears throughout the training course. For example, a sales training course at CDW Corporation, a technology products and service company, guides trainees through mock interviews with customers. The avatar introduces the customer situation, and the trainee hears the customer speaking in a simulated phone conversation. The trainee has to determine with help from the avatar what is happening in the sales process by reading the customer's voice. Loews Corporation's hotel chain uses "Virtual Leader," a program that helps participants learn how to be effective in meetings (e.g., how to build alliances, how to get a meeting agenda approved). As trainees attend the simulated meetings what they say (or don't say) results in scores that relate to their influence in the meeting.

**Virtual Reality**
Computer-based technology that provides trainees with a three-dimensional learning experience. Trainees operate in a simulated environment that responds to their behaviors and reactions.

A recent development in simulations is the use of virtual reality technology. **Virtual reality** is a computer-based technology that provides trainees with a three-dimensional learning experience. Using specialized equipment or viewing the virtual model on the computer screen, trainees move through the simulated environment and interact with its components.[84] Technology is used to stimulate multiple senses of the trainee.[85] Devices relay information from the environment to the senses. For example, audio interfaces, gloves that provide a sense of touch, treadmills, or motion platforms are used to create a realistic, artificial environment. Devices also communicate information about the trainee's movements to a computer. These devices allow the trainee to experience the perception of actually being in a particular environment. For example, Motorola's advanced manufacturing courses for employees learning to run the Pager Robotic Assembly facility use virtual reality. Employees are fitted with a head-mount display that allows them to view the virtual world, which includes the actual lab space, robots, tools, and the assembly operation. The trainees hear and see the actual sounds and sights as if they were using the real equipment. Also, the equipment responds to the employees' actions (such as turning on a switch or dial).

As you can see from the example, simulations can be effective for several reasons.[86] First, trainees can use them on their desktop, eliminating the need to travel to a central training location. Second, simulations are meaningful, get trainees involved in learning, and are emotionally engaging (they can be fun!). This helps increase employees' willingness to practice, retain, and improve their skills. Third, simulators provide a consistent message of what needs to be learned; trainees can work at their own pace; and, compared to face-to-face instruction, simulators can incorporate more situations or problems that a trainee might encounter. Fourth, simulations can safely put employees in situations that would be dangerous in the real world. Fifth, simulations have been found to result in positive outcomes such as training being completed in a shorter time compared to traditional training courses, and providing a positive return on investment. The use of simulations has been limited by their development costs. As the development costs of simulations continue to decrease they will likely become a more popular training method. One estimate is that products which once cost a half million dollars to develop can now be purchased from simulation developers for $150,000![87]

***Business Games and Case Studies.*** Situations that trainees study and discuss (case studies) and business games in which trainees must gather information, analyze it, and make decisions are used primarily for management skill development. One organization that has effectively used case studies is the Central Intelligence Agency (CIA).[88] The cases are historically accurate and use actual data. For example, "The Libyan Attack" is used in management courses to teach leadership qualities. "The Stamp Case" is used to teach new employees about the agency's ethics structure. The CIA uses approximately 100 cases. One-third are focused on management; the rest focus on operations training, counterintelligence, and analysis. The cases are used in the training curriculum where the objectives include teaching students to analyze and resolve complex, ambiguous situations. The CIA found that for the cases used in training programs to be credible and meaningful to trainees, the material had to be as authentic as possible and stimulate students to make decisions similar to those they must make in their work environment. As a result, to ensure case accuracy, the CIA uses retired officers to research and write cases. The CIA has even developed a case writing workshop to prepare instructors to use the case method.

Games stimulate learning because participants are actively involved and they mimic the competitive nature of business. The types of decisions that participants make in games include all aspects of management practice, including labor relations (such as agreement in contract negotiations), marketing (the price to charge for a new product), and finance (financing the purchase of new technology). For example, Harley-Davidson, the motorcycle company, uses a business game to help prospective dealers understand how dealerships make money.[89] The game involves 15 to 35 people working in teams. The game consists of five simulated rounds, each round challenging a team to manage a Harley dealership in competition with other teams. Between rounds of the game, lectures and case studies reinforce key concepts. The facilitators change the business situation in each round of the game. The facilitators can increase or decrease interest rates, add new products, cause employee turnover, or even set up a bad event such as a fire at the business. The game helps dealers develop skills needed for business success. Participants must work well as a team, listen to each other, and think strategically.

Documentation on learning from games is anecdotal.[90] Games may give team members a quick start at developing a framework for information and help develop cohesive groups. For some groups (such as senior executives) games may be more meaningful training activities (because the game is realistic) than presentation techniques such as classroom instruction.

Cases may be especially appropriate for developing higher-order intellectual skills such as analysis, synthesis, and evaluation. These skills are often required by managers, physicians, and other professional employees. Cases also help trainees develop the willingness to take risks given uncertain outcomes, based on their analysis of the situation. To use cases effectively, the learning environment must let trainees prepare and discuss their case analyses. Also, face-to-face or electronic communication among trainees must be arranged. Because trainee involvement is critical for the effectiveness of the case method, learners must be willing and able to analyze the case and then communicate and defend their positions.

There are a number of available sources for preexisting cases (e.g., Harvard Business School). It is especially important to review preexisting cases to determine how meaningful they will be to the trainee.

***Behavior Modeling.*** Research suggests that behavior modeling is one of the most effective techniques for teaching interpersonal skills.[91] Each training session, which typically lasts four hours, focuses on one interpersonal skill, such as coaching or communicating ideas. Each session presents the rationale behind key behaviors, a videotape of a model performing key behaviors, practice opportunities using role playing, evaluation of a model's performance in the videotape, and a planning session devoted to understanding how the key behaviors can be used on the job. In the practice sessions, trainees get feedback regarding how closely their behavior matches the key behaviors demonstrated by the model. The role playing and modeled performance are based on actual incidents in the employment setting in which the trainee needs to demonstrate success.

***Interactive Video.*** Interactive video combines the advantages of video and computer-based instruction. Instruction is provided one-on-one to trainees via a personal computer. Trainees use the keyboard or touch the monitor to interact with the program. Interactive video is used to teach technical procedures and interpersonal skills. The training program may be stored on a compact disc (CD-ROM) or the company intranet. For example, the Shoney's and Captain D's restaurant chains have more than 350 restaurants in more than 20 states.[92] Over 8,000 employees each year must be trained on the basics of the operational parts of the business, including how to make french fries, hush puppies, and coleslaw. Also, each year 600 new managers must be trained in business issues and back-office operations of the restaurants. The biggest challenge that Shoney's faced was how to consistently train geographically dispersed employees. Shoney's solution was to implement OneTouch, a live integrated video and two-way voice and data application that combines synchronous video, voice, and data and live Web pages so that team members can interact with trainers. OneTouch can be delivered to desktop PCs as well as to warehouses and repair bays. Desktop systems can be positioned in any appropriate locations in the restaurant. Individuals or groups of employees can gather around the PC for training. The training modules include such topics as orientation, kitchen, and dining room. Each module is interactive. Topics are introduced and are followed up by quizzes to ensure that learning occurs. For example, the coleslaw program shows trainees what the coleslaw ingredients are and where they can be found in the restaurant. The coleslaw program includes a video that trainees can watch and practice with. After they practice, they have to complete a quiz, and their manager has to verify that they completed the topic before they move on to the next program. The training is consistent and is easy to update so as to ensure it is current. The program also allows kitchen and counter staff to learn each other's skills, which gives Shoney's flexibility in its staffing (e.g., counter employees who know how to cook). The main disadvantage of interactive video is the high cost of developing the courseware. This may be a particular problem for courses in which frequent updates are necessary.[93]

**LO6**
Explain the Potential Advantages of E-Learning for Training.

***E-Learning.*** **E-learning** or online learning refers to instruction and delivery of training by computers through the Internet or company intranets.[94] E-learning includes Web-based training, distance learning, virtual classrooms, and use of CD-ROMs. E-learning can include task support, simulation training, distance learning, and learning portals. There are three important characteristics of e-learning. First, e-learning involves electronic networks that enable information and instruction to be delivered, shared, and updated instantly. Second, e-learning is delivered to the trainee via computers with Internet technology. Third, it focuses on learning solutions that go beyond traditional training to include information and tools that improve performance.

**E-Learning**
Instruction and delivery of training by computers through the Internet or company intranet.

Figure 7.7 depicts the features of e-learning, which include collaboration and sharing, links to resources, learner control, delivery, and administration. As Figure 7.7 shows, e-learning not only provides training content but lets learners control what they learn, the speed at which they progress through the program, how much they practice, and even when they learn. E-learning also allows learners to collaborate or interact with other trainees and experts, and it provides links to other learning resources such as reference materials, company Web sites, and other training programs. Text, video, graphics, and sound can present course content. E-learning may also include various aspects of training administration such as course enrollment, testing and evaluating trainees, and monitoring learning progress. Various delivery methods can be incorporated into e-learning including distance learning, CD-ROM, and the Internet.

These features of e-learning give it advantages over other training methods. E-learning initiatives are designed to contribute to strategic business objectives.[95] E-learning supports company initiatives such as attracting customers, devising new ways to operate such as e-business, or quickly developing products or new services. E-learning may involve a larger audience than traditional training programs, which focused on employees; it may involve partners, suppliers, vendors, and potential customers.

For example, Lucent Technologies, which designs and delivers communications network technologies, has devoted significant resources to ensure that customers and business partners have access to e-learning.[96] Training affects customer satisfaction with Lucent's products and solutions. It also influences employees' ability to sell to and service customers. Product training courses that deal with installing, repairing, and operating Lucent equipment are available to customers on the company's Web site. Users can take the courses, register and pay for the classes, and track their progress. Lucent also provides training to its business partners, who are required to be certified in Lucent's products before they can receive special discounts. As Lucent increases its electronically delivered courses, the company is also trying to increase the percentage of learners who take courses online. Today, about half of the users attend classroom-based training.

figure 7.7
Characteristics of E-Learning

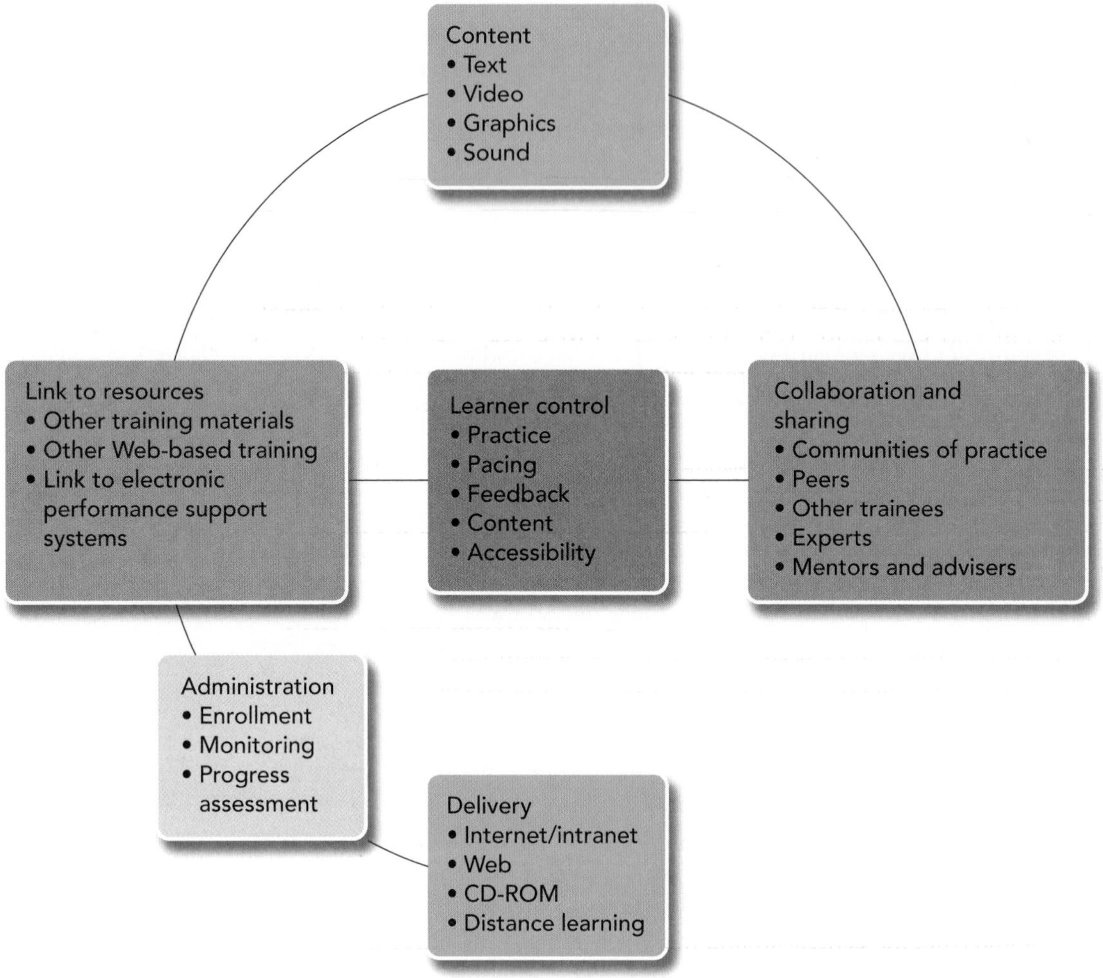


Learning is enhanced through e-learning because trainees are more engaged through the use of video, graphics, sound, and text, which appeal to multiple senses of the learner. Also, e-learning requires that learners actively participate in practice, questions, and interaction with other learners and experts.

Besides enhancing the training experience, e-learning can reduce training costs and time. E-learning brings training to geographically dispersed employees at their locations, reducing travel costs.

**Repurposing**
Directly translating instructor-led training online.

Effective e-learning is grounded on a thorough needs assessment and complete learning objectives. **Repurposing** refers to directly translating an instructor-led, face-to-face training program online. Online learning that merely repurposes an ineffective training program will remain ineffective. Unfortunately, in their haste to develop online learning, many companies are repurposing bad training! The best e-learning combines the advantages of the Internet with the principles of a good learning environment. Effective online learning takes advantage of the Web's dynamic nature and ability to use many positive learning features, including linking to other training sites and content through the use of hyperlinks, providing learner control, and allowing the trainee to collaborate with other learners. **Learner control** refers to the ability of trainees to actively learn through self-pacing, exercises, exploring links to other material, and conversations with other trainees and experts. That is, online learning allows activities typically led by the instructor (presentation, visuals, slides), trainees (discussion, questions), and group interaction (discussion of application of training content) to be incorporated into training without trainees or the instructor having to be physically present in a training room. Effective online learning gives trainees meaningful content, relevant examples, and the ability to apply content to work problems and issues. Also, trainees can practice and receive feedback through problems, exercises, assignments, and tests.

**Learner Control**
Ability of trainees to actively learn through self-pacing, exercises, links to other materials, and conversations with other trainees and experts.

***Blended Learning.*** Because of the limitations of online learning related to technology (e.g., insufficient bandwidth, lack of high-speed Web connections), because of trainee preference for face-to-face contact with instructors and other learners, and because of employees' inability to find unscheduled time during their workday to devote to learning from their desktops, many companies are moving to a hybrid, or blended, learning approach. *Blended learning* combines online learning, face-to-face instruction, and other methods for distributing learning content and instruction. The nearby "Competing through Technology" box shows how blended learning is benefiting several companies.

***Learning Management System.*** A **learning management system (LMS)** refers to a technology platform that can be used to automate the administration, development, and delivery of all of a company's training programs. An LMS can provide employees, managers, and trainers with the ability to manage, deliver, and track learning activities.[97] LMSs are becoming more popular for several reasons. An LMS can help companies reduce travel and other costs related to training, reduce time for program completion, increase employees' accessibility to training across the business, and provide administrative capabilities to track program completion and course enrollments. An LMS allows companies to track all of the learning activity in the business. For example, both FedEx Kinkos and Turner Construction have LMSs.[98] FedEx Kinkos has document and shipping centers around the world and employs more than 20,000 people. The LMS at FedEx includes a software package that allows creation of individualized training for each employee, schedules classrooms, tracks employee progress, manages all aspects of the training curriculum, and delivers e-learning courses. Employees have access via personal computer to their personal learning plans based on their job, what their manager requires, and their own personal interests. Turner Construction has a competency model that divides jobs into nine job families and divides the families into job levels (senior management, administrative/clerical, and management). Employees receive an online performance evaluation of their skills based on their job family and level. The performance management system links to the company's LMS. The LMS analyzes the employees' skill weaknesses and recommends courses that can improve those skills. The LMS system allows Turner Construction to identify skill gaps for entire levels, job families, or business units. The results can be used to identify where to spend moneys allocated for training to develop new courses.

**Learning Management System (LMS)**
Technology platform that automates the administration, development, and delivery of a company's training program.

***Group- or Team-Building Methods.*** **Group- or team-building methods** are training methods designed to improve team or group effectiveness. Training is directed at improving the trainees' skills as well as team effectiveness. In group-building methods, trainees share ideas and experiences, build group identity, understand the dynamics of

**Group- or Team-Building Methods**
Training techniques that help trainees share ideas and experiences, build group identity, understand the dynamics of interpersonal relationships, and get to know their own strengths and weaknesses and those of their co-workers.

## COMPETING THROUGH TECHNOLOGY
### A Blended Approach to Learning May Be Most Beneficial

Many companies, recognizing the strengths and weaknesses of face-to-face instruction and technology-based training methods, are using both in a blended learning approach. Technology-based training can be used to provide consistent delivery of training content involving transfer of information (knowledge and skills) to geographically dispersed employees who can work at their own pace, practice, and collaborate with the trainer and trainee online. Then, trainees can be brought to a central location for face-to-face training (classroom, action learning, games, and role plays), which can emphasize the application of knowledge and skills using cases and problems that require the application of training content. Face-to-face instruction is also more useful for facilitating interaction between trainees, collaboration, networking, and discussion.

For Union Pacific, the largest railroad in North America, about 40 percent of its employees work on locomotives and freight cars in different locations and on different work schedules. The company uses a blend of traditional training and e-learning. Web-based simulations are followed by review sessions conducted in classrooms. To educate engineers on train operations, Union Pacific uses desk-sized simulators that pull together satellite technology, terrain data, and track facts to create a graphic interface. However, maintenance worker training tends to involve more face-to-face instruction because these workers cannot learn how to use a wrench via computer. The company believes that blended learning is successful because it takes advantage of the realism of available simulations but still provides personal interaction between trainees and trainers in the classroom.

Express Personnel Services, a staffing company, found that managers can benefit from online material about hiring principles but need classroom instruction to learn how to apply those skills. Also, managers learn from others doing the same job but at a different location when they attend courses at one of the company's training centers. The company tried to use online forums to promote discussions between managers at different locations but found that they were too busy to use them. IBM uses a four-tier learning approach that includes e-learning in the first two tiers, blended learning in the third tier, and classroom learning in the fourth tier. The first tier is where knowledge or information is provided to trainees (what IBM calls information transfer). The second tier involves e-based testing of the concepts learned in the first tier. The third tier, called collaborative learning, involves both e-learning and the classroom to create an environment that facilitates collaboration between colleagues and learner and experts. The fourth tier includes face-to-face workshops, cases, and problem discussions where the skills learned in earlier stages are mastered through application and interaction with other learners.

SOURCES: Based on M. Tucker, "E-Learning Evolves," *HR Magazine*, October 2005, pp. 75–78; J. Mullich, "A Second Act for e-Learning," *Workforce Management*, February 2004, pp. 51–55; M. Weinstein, "Got Class," *Training*, December 2005, pp. 29–32.

interpersonal relationships, and get to know their own strengths and weaknesses and those of their co-workers. Group techniques focus on helping teams increase their skills for effective teamwork. A number of training techniques are available to improve work group or team performance, to establish a new team, or to improve interactions among different teams. They include trust falls, (in which each trainee stands on a table and falls backward into the arms of fellow group members), paintball games, NASCAR pit crews, cooking, obstacle canes, and even drumming! All involve examination of feelings, perceptions, and beliefs about the functioning of the team; discussion; and development of plans to apply what was learned in training to the team's performance in the work setting. Group-building methods fall into three categories: adventure learning, team training, and action learning.

Group-building methods often involve experiential learning. *Experiential learning* training programs involve gaining conceptual knowledge and theory; taking part in a behavioral simulation; analyzing the activity; and connecting the theory and activity with on-the-job or real-life situations.[99]

For experiential training programs to be successful, several guidelines should be followed. The program needs to tie in to a specific business problem. The trainees need to be moved outside their personal comfort zones but within limits so as not to reduce trainee motivation or ability to understand the purpose of the program. Multiple learning modes should be used, including audio, visual, and kinesthetic. When preparing activities for an experiential training program, trainers should ask trainees for input on the program goals. Clear expectations about the purpose, expected outcomes, and trainees' role in the program are important. Finally, training programs that include experiential learning should be linked to changes in employee attitudes, behaviors, and other business results.

California-based Quantum Corporation developed a project to overhaul the company's online infrastructure across global operations.[100] The project included a diverse group of team members from the information technology, engineering, marketing, and graphic design departments. The team consisted of very talented employees who were not used to working with each other. Many of the team members were geographically dispersed, which increased the difficulties in working together. Quantum hired an actors' group to lead the team through a series of improvisational activities designed to get the team members to share personal stories. Using music, props, lighting, and costumes, the actors interpreted the stories told by team members. The actors portrayed team members who, for example, expressed isolation and frustration. Other times, team members would play the parts. The sessions allowed each team member to ask questions of the actors or each other. The team came away from the activity with more empathy and understanding for each other. Development of the personal relationships created positive interpersonal bonds that helped the team meet deadlines and complete projects.

***Adventure Learning.*** **Adventure learning** develops teamwork and leadership skills using structured outdoor activities.[101] Adventure learning appears to be best suited for developing skills related to group effectiveness, such as self-awareness, problem solving, conflict management, and risk taking. Adventure learning may involve strenuous, challenging physical activities such as dogsledding or mountain climbing. It can also use structured individual and group outdoor activities such as climbing walls, going through rope courses, making trust falls, climbing ladders, and traveling from one tower to another using a device attached to a wire that connects the two towers.

**Adventure Learning**
Learning focused on the development of teamwork and leadership skills by using structured outdoor activities.

For example, a Chili's restaurant manager in adventure learning was required to scale a three-story-high wall.[102] About two-thirds away from the top of the wall the manager became very tired. She successfully reached the top of the wall using the advice and encouragement shouted from team members on the ground below. When asked to consider what she learned from the experience, she reported that the exercise made her realize that reaching personal success depends on other people. At her restaurant, everyone has to work together to make the customers happy.

Adventure learning can also include demanding activities that require coordination and place less of a physical strain on team members. For example, Cookin' Up Change is one of many team-building courses offered around the United States by chefs, caterers, hotels, and cooking schools.[103] These courses have been used by companies such as Honda and Microsoft. The underlying idea is that cooking classes help strengthen communications and networking skills by requiring team members to work together to create a full-course meal (a culinary feast!). Each team has to decide who does what kitchen tasks (e.g., cooking, cutting, cleaning) and prepares the main course, salads, or dessert. Often team members are required to switch assignments in midpreparation to see how the team reacts to change.

For adventure learning programs to succeed, the exercises should be related to the types of skills that participants are expected to develop. Also, after the exercises, a skilled facilitator should lead a discussion about what happened in the exercise, what was learned, how the exercise relates to the job situation, and how to set goals and apply what was learned on the job.[104]

Does adventure learning work? Rigorous evaluations of the impact of adventure learning on productivity and performance have not been conducted. However, participants often report that they gained a greater understanding of themselves and the ways they interact with their co-workers. One key to the success of an adventure learning program may be the insistence that whole work groups participate together so that group dynamics that inhibit effectiveness can emerge and be discussed.

The physically demanding nature of adventure learning and the requirement that trainees often have to touch each other in the exercises may increase the company's risk for negligence claims due to personal injury, intentional infliction of emotional distress, and invasion of privacy. Also, the Americans with Disabilities Act (discussed in Chapter 3) raises questions about requiring employees with disabilities to participate in physically demanding training experiences.[105]

***Team Training.*** Team training coordinates the performance of individuals who work together to achieve a common goal. Such training is an important issue when information must be shared and individuals affect the overall performance of the group. For example, in the military as well as the private sector (think of nuclear power plants or commercial airlines), much work is performed by crews, groups, or teams. Success depends on coordination of individual activities to make decisions, team performance, and readiness to deal with potentially dangerous situations (like an overheating nuclear reactor).

**Cross-Training**
Team members understand and practice each other's skills.

**Coordination Training**
Trains the team in how to share information and decisions.

**Team Leader Training**
Training the team manager or facilitator.

Team training strategies include cross-training and coordination training.[106] In **cross-training** team members understand and practice each other's skills so that members are prepared to step in and take another member's place. **Coordination training** trains the team in how to share information and decisions to maximize team performance. Coordination training is especially important for commercial aviation and surgical teams, who monitor different aspects of equipment and the environment but must share information to make the most effective decisions regarding patient care or aircraft safety and performance. **Team leader training** refers to training the team manager or facilitator. This may involve training the manager how to resolve conflict within the team or help the team coordinate activities or other team skills.

United Airlines (UAL) is having its supervisors "lead" ramp employees in attending Pit Instruction & Training (Pit Crew U), which focuses on the preparation, practice, and teamwork of NASCAR pit crews. United is using the training to develop standardized methods to safely and efficiently unload, load, and send off its airplanes.[107] Pit Instruction & Training, located outside of Charlotte, North Carolina, has a quarter-mile race track and a pit road with places for six cars. The school offers programs to train new racing pit crews, but most of its business comes from companies interested in having their teams work as safely, efficiently, and effectively as NASCAR pit crews. The training is part of a multimillion-dollar investment that includes updating equipment and providing luggage scanners. The purpose of the training is to reinforce the need for ramp teams to be orderly and communicate, and to help standardize tasks of ramp team members, along with increasing morale. Training has been optional for ramp employees and they have survived layoffs and been asked to make wage concessions to help the company get out of bankruptcy. United already has started scheduling shorter ground times at some airports, anticipating the positive results of the program. Shorter ground times translate into more daily flights without having to buy more airplanes. United hopes to cut the average airplane ground time by eight minutes to make the airline more competitive.

The keys for safety, speed, and efficiency for NASCAR pit crews is that each member knows what tasks to do (change tires, use air gun, add gasoline, clean up spills) and, when the crew has finished servicing the race car, moves new equipment into position anticipating the next pit stop. The training involves the ramp workers actually working as pit crews. They learn how to handle jacks, change tires, and fill fuel tanks on race cars. They are videotaped and timed just like real pit crews. They receive feedback from professional pit crew members who work on NASCAR teams and trainers Also, the training requires them to deal with circumstances they might encounter on the job. For one pit stop, lug nuts had been sprinkled intentionally in the area where the car stops to see if the United employees would notice them and clean them up. On their jobs ramp employees are responsible for removing debris from the tarmac so it doesn't get sucked into jet engines or harm equipment. For another pit stop, teams had to work with fewer members, as sometimes occurs when ramp crews are understaffed due to absences.

***Action Learning.*** In **action learning** teams or work groups get an actual business problem, work on solving it and commit to an action plan, and are accountable for carrying out the plan.[108] Typically, action learning involves between 6 and 30 employees; it may also include customers and vendors. There are several variations on the composition of the group. In one variation the group includes a single customer for the problem being dealt with. Sometimes the groups include cross-functional team members (members from different company departments) who all have a stake in the problem. Or the group may involve employees from multiple functions who all focus on their own functional problems, each contributing to helping solve the problems identified. For example, ATC, a public transportation services management company in Illinois, used action learning to help boost profitability by reducing operating costs.[109] Employees were divided into Action Workout Teams to identify ways of reducing costs and to brainstorm effective solutions. The process assumed that employees closest to where the work gets done have the best ideas about how to solve problems. Teams of five to seven employees met once a week for a couple of hours for 45 to 60 days. For example, a team working on parts inventory might have had a parts clerk, a couple of people from maintenance, a supervisor, and an operations employee. These teams studied problems and issues such as overtime, preventive maintenance, absenteeism, parts inventory, and inefficient safety inspection procedures. The teams brainstormed ideas, prioritized them according to their highest potential, developed action plans, installed them, tested them, and measured the outcomes. The solutions that the teams generated resulted in more than $1.8 million in savings for the company.

**Action Learning**
Teams work on an actual business problem, commit to an action plan, and are accountable for carrying out the plan.

**Six Sigma Training** An action training program that provides employees with defect-reducing tools to cut costs and certifies employees as green belts, champions, or black belts.

Six Sigma and black belt training programs involve principles of action learning. **Six Sigma Training** provides employees with measurement and statistical tools to help reduce defects and to cut costs.[110] Six Sigma is a quality standard with a goal of only 3.4 defects per million processes. There are several levels of Six Sigma training, resulting in employees becoming certified as green belts, champions, or black belts.[111] To become black belts, trainees must participate in workshops and written assignments coached by expert instructors. The training involves four 4-day sessions over about 16 weeks. Between training sessions, candidates apply what they learn to assigned projects and then use them in the next training session. Trainees are also required to complete not only oral and written exams but also two or more projects that have a significant impact on the company's bottom line. After completing black belt training, employees are able to develop, coach, and lead Six Sigma teams; mentor and advise management on determining Six Sigma projects; and provide Six Sigma tools and statistical methods to team members. After black belts lead several project teams, they can take additional training and be certified as master black belts. Master black belts can teach other black belts and help senior managers integrate Six Sigma into the company's business goals.

McKesson Corporation trained 15 to 20 black belts and reassigned them to their original business units as their team's Six Sigma representatives.[112] When the two-year commitment ends, the black belts return to the business at higher positions, helping to spread the approach throughout the organization and ensuring that key leaders are committed to the Six Sigma philosophy. In most divisions of the company, Six Sigma training is mandated for senior vice presidents, who attend training that introduces Six Sigma and details how to identify a potential Six Sigma project. Across the company, every manager and director is expected to attend basic training. The Six Sigma effort has shown benefits every year since the program started.

## Advice for Choosing a Training Method

**LO7**
Design a Training Session to Maximize Learning.

As a manager, you will likely be asked to choose a training method. Given the large number of training methods available to you, this task may seem difficult. One way to choose a training method is to compare methods. The first step in choosing a method is to identify the type of learning outcome that you want training to influence. These outcomes include verbal information, intellectual skills, cognitive strategies, attitudes, and motor skills. Training methods may influence one or several learning outcomes. Once you have identified a learning method, the next step is to consider the extent to which the method facilitates learning and transfer of training, the costs related to development and use of the method, and its effectiveness.

For learning to occur, trainees must understand the objectives of the training program, training content should be meaningful, and trainees should have the opportunity to practice and receive feedback. Also, a powerful way to learn is through observing and interacting with others. Transfer of training refers to the extent to which training will be used on the job. In general, the closer the training content and environment prepare trainees for use of learning outcomes on the job, the greater the likelihood that transfer will occur. Two types of costs are important: development costs and administrative costs. Development costs relate to design of the training program, including costs to buy or create the program. Administrative costs are incurred each time the training method is used. These include costs related to consultants, instructors, materials, and trainers.

Several trends are worth noting. First, there is considerable overlap between learning outcomes across the training methods. Group-building methods are unique because they focus on individual as well as team learning (e.g., improving group processes). If you are interested in improving the effectiveness of groups or teams, you should choose one of the group-building methods (e.g., action learning, team training, adventure learning). Second, comparing the presentation methods to the hands-on methods illustrates that most hands-on methods provide a better learning environment and transfer of training than do the presentation methods. The presentation methods are also less effective than the hands-on methods. E-learning or blended learning can be an effective training method for geographically dispersed trainees if it includes meaningful content, links to other resources, collaboration and sharing, and learner control. E-learning and other technology-driven training methods have higher development costs, but travel and housing cost savings will likely offset development costs over time. As the previous "Competing through Technology" box shows, many companies recognize the strengths and weaknesses of both technology-based training methods (such as iPods or e-learning) and face-to-face instruction. As a result, they are using both in a blended learning approach. The training budget for developing training methods can influence the method chosen. If you have a limited budget for developing new training methods, use structured on-the-job training—a relatively inexpensive yet effective hands-on method. If you have a larger budget, you might want to consider hands-on methods that facilitate transfer of training, such as simulators.

step 6

## Evaluating Training Programs

**LO8**
Choose an Appropriate Evaluation Design Based on Training Objectives and Analysis of Constraints.

Examining the outcomes of a program helps in evaluating its effectiveness. These outcomes should be related to the program objectives, which help trainees understand the purpose of the program. **Training outcomes** can be categorized as cognitive outcomes, skill-based outcomes, affective outcomes, results, and return on investment.[113] Table 7.9 shows the types of outcomes used in evaluating training programs and what is measured and how it is measured.

**Training Outcomes**
A way to evaluate the effectiveness of a training program based on cognitive, skill-based, affective, and results outcomes.

Which training outcomes measure is best? The answer depends on the training objectives. For example, if the instructional objectives identified business-related outcomes such as increased customer service or product quality, then results outcomes should be included in the evaluation. Both reaction and cognitive outcomes are usually collected before the trainees leave the training site. As a result, these measures do not help determine the extent to which trainees actually use the training content in their jobs (transfer of training). Skill-based, affective, and results outcomes measured following training can be used to determine transfer of training—that is, the extent to which training has changed behavior, skills, or attitudes or directly influenced objective measures related to company effectiveness (such as sales).

### Reasons for Evaluating Training

Many companies are beginning to invest millions of dollars in training programs to gain a competitive advantage. Firms with high-leverage training practices not only invest large sums of money in developing and administering training programs but also evaluate training programs. Why should training programs be evaluated?

1. To identify the program's strengths and weaknesses. This includes determining whether the program is meeting the learning objectives, the quality of the learning environment, and whether transfer of training to the job is occurring.

**table 7.9**

Outcomes Used in Evaluating Training Programs

| OUTCOME | WHAT IS MEASURED | HOW MEASURED | EXAMPLE |
|---|---|---|---|
| Cognitive Outcomes | • Acquisition of knowledge | • Pencil-and-paper tests<br>• Work sample | • Safety rules<br>• Electrical principles<br>• Steps in appraisal interview |
| Skill-Based Outcomes | • Behavior<br>• Skills | • Observation<br>• Work sample<br>• Ratings | • Jigsaw use<br>• Listening skills<br>• Coaching skills<br>• Airplane landings |
| Affective Outcomes | • Motivation<br>• Reaction to program<br>• Attitudes | • Interviews<br>• Focus groups<br>• Attitude surveys | • Satisfaction with training<br>• Beliefs regarding other cultures |
| Results | • Company payoff | • Observation<br>• Data from information system or performance records | • Absenteeism<br>• Accidents<br>• Patents |
| Return on Investment | • Economic value of training | • Identification and comparison of costs and benefits of the program | • Dollars |

2. To assess whether the content, organization, and administration of the program (including the schedule, accommodations, trainers, and materials) contribute to learning and the use of training content on the job.
3. To identify which trainees benefited most or least from the program.
4. To gather marketing data by asking participants whether they would recommend the program to others, why they attended the program, and their level of satisfaction with the program.
5. To determine the financial benefits and costs of the program.
6. To compare the costs and benefits of training to nontraining investments (such as work redesign or better employee selection).
7. To compare the costs and benefits of different training programs to choose the best program.

Walgreens is a good example of a company that has reconsidered the role of training based on evaluation data. A Walgreens training course for new technicians was developed to replace on-the-job training they received from the pharmacists who hired them. This course involved 20 hours of classroom training and 20 hours of supervision on the job. Because the company has several thousand stores, large amounts of money and time were invested in the training, so the company decided to evaluate the program.

The evaluation consisted of comparing technicians who had completed the program with some who had not. Surveys about new employees' performance were sent to the pharmacists who supervised the technicians. Some questions related to speed of entering patient and drug data into the store computer and how often the technician offered customers generic drug substitutes. The results showed that formally trained technicians were more efficient and wasted less of the pharmacist's time than those who received traditional on-the-job training. Sales in pharmacies with formally trained technicians exceeded sales in pharmacies with on-the-job–trained technicians by an average of $9,500 each year.[114]

## Evaluation Designs

As shown in Table 7.10, a number of different evaluation designs can be applied to training programs. Table 7.10 compares each evaluation design on the basis of who is involved (trainees and/or a comparison group that does not receive training), when outcome measures are collected (pretraining, posttraining), the costs, the time needed to conduct the evaluation, and the strength of the design for ruling out alternative explanations for the results (e.g., are improvements due to factors other than the training?). In general, designs that use pretraining and posttraining measures of outcomes and include a comparison group reduce the risk that factors other than training itself are responsible for the evaluation results. This builds confidence to use the results to make decisions. The trade-off is that evaluations using these designs are more costly and time-consuming to conduct than evaluations not using pretraining or posttraining measures or comparison groups.

There is no one appropriate evaluation design. Several factors need to be considered in choosing one:[115]

- Size of the training program.
- Purpose of training.
- Implications if a training program does not work.
- Company norms regarding evaluation.
- Costs of designing and conducting an evaluation.
- Need for speed in obtaining program effectiveness information.

For example, if a manager is interested in determining how much employees' communications skills have changed as a result of a behavior-modeling training program, a pretest/posttest comparison group design is necessary. Trainees should be randomly assigned to training and no-training conditions. These evaluation design features give the manager a high degree of confidence that any communication skill change is the result of participating in the training program.[116] This type of evaluation

**table 7.10**

Comparison of Evaluation Designs

| | | MEASURES | | | | |
|---|---|---|---|---|---|---|
| DESIGN | GROUPS | PRETRAINING | POSTTRAINING | COST | TIME | STRENGTH |
| Posttest only | Trainees | No | Yes | Low | Low | Low |
| Pretest/posttest | Trainees | Yes | Yes | Low | Low | Medium |
| Posttest only with comparison group | Trainees and comparison | No | Yes | Medium | Medium | Medium |
| Pretest/posttest with comparison group | Trainees and comparison | Yes | Yes | Medium | Medium | High |
| Time series | Trainees | Yes | Yes, several | Medium | Medium | Medium |

design is also necessary if the manager wants to compare the effectiveness of two training programs.

Consider the evaluation design that Mayo Clinic used to compare two methods for training new managers.[117] The Mayo Clinic, located in Rochester, Minnesota, is one of the world's leading centers of medical education and research. Recently, Mayo has undergone considerable growth, adding a new hospital and clinic in the Phoenix area. As a result, employees who were not fully prepared were moved into management positions. This resulted in increased employee dissatisfaction and employee turnover rates. After a needs assessment indicated that employees were leaving because of dissatisfaction with management, Mayo decided to initiate a new training program designed to help the new managers improve their skills. There was some debate whether the training would be best administered one-on-one with a coach or in a classroom. Because of the higher cost of using coaching instead of classroom training, Mayo decided to conduct an evaluation using a posttest comparison group design. Before training all managers, Mayo held three training sessions. No more than 75 managers were included in each session. Within each session managers were divided into three groups: a group that received four days of classroom training, a group that received one-on-one training from a coach, and a group that received no training (a comparison group). Mayo collected reaction (did the trainees like the program?), learning, transfer, and results outcomes. The evaluation found no statistically significant differences in the effects of the coaching compared to classroom training. As a result, Mayo decided to rely on classroom courses for new managers and consider coaching only for managers with critical and immediate job issues.

## Determining Return on Investment

**Cost–Benefit Analysis**
The process of determining the economic benefits of a training program using accounting methods.

**Cost–benefit analysis** is the process of determining the economic benefits of a training program using accounting methods, which involves determining training costs and benefits. Training cost information is important for several reasons:

1. To understand total expenditures for training, including direct and indirect costs.
2. To compare the costs of alternative training programs.
3. To evaluate the proportion of money spent on training development, administration, and evaluation, as well as to compare moneys spent on training for different groups of employees (such as exempt versus nonexempt).
4. To control costs.[118]

***Determining Costs.*** As we discussed earlier, training costs include direct and indirect costs.[119] One method for comparing costs of alternative training programs is the resource requirements model.[120] This model compares equipment, facilities, personnel, and materials costs across different stages of the training process (training design, implementation, needs assessment, development, and evaluation). The resource requirements model can help determine overall differences in costs between training programs. Also, costs incurred at different stages of the training process can be compared across programs.

***Determining Benefits.*** To identify the potential benefits of training, the company must review the original reasons for the training. For example, training may have been conducted to reduce production costs or overtime costs or to increase repeat business. A number of methods may help identify the benefits of training:

1. Technical, academic, and practitioner literature summarizes the benefits that have been shown to relate to a specific training program.
2. Pilot training programs assess the benefits for a small group of trainees before a company commits more resources.
3. Observing successful job performers can help a company determine what they do differently than unsuccessful job performers.[121]
4. Trainees and their managers can provide estimates of training benefits.

***Making the Analysis.*** To calculate return on investment, follow these steps:

1. Identify outcomes (e.g., quality, accidents).
2. Place a value on the outcomes.
3. Determine the change in performance after eliminating other potential influences on training results.
4. Obtain an annual amount of benefits (operational results) from training by comparing results after training to results before training (in dollars).
5. Determine the training costs (direct costs + indirect costs + development costs + overhead costs + compensation for trainees).
6. Calculate the total savings by subtracting the training costs from benefits (operational results).
7. Calculate the ROI by dividing benefits (operational results) by costs. The ROI gives an estimate of the dollar return expected from each dollar invested in training.

Recall our discussion earlier in the chapter on the evaluation of the new manager training program at Mayo Clinic.[122] To determine Mayo's return on investment, the human resource department calculated that one-third of the 84 employees retained (29 employees) would have left Mayo as a result of dissatisfaction. The department believed their retention was due to the impact of the training. The department calculated that the cost of a single employee turnover was 75 percent of average total compensation, or $42,000 per employee at Mayo. Multiplying $42,000 by 29 employees retained equals a savings of $609,000. However, the cost of the training program needs to be considered. If the annual cost of the training program ($125,000) was subtracted from the savings, the new savings were $484,000. These numbers were based on estimates but even if the net savings figure were cut in half, the ROI is still over 100 percent. Being able to quantify the benefits delivered by the program has given the human resource department greater credibility at Mayo.

## EVIDENCE-BASED HR

A training and development consultant at Apple Computer was concerned with the quality and consistency of the training program used in assembly operations. She wanted to show that training was not only effective but also resulted in financial benefits. To do this, the consultant chose an evaluation design that involved two separately trained groups—each consisting of 27 employees—and two untrained groups (comparison groups). The consultant collected a pretraining history of what was happening on the production line in each outcome she was measuring (productivity, quality, and labor efficiency). She determined the effectiveness of training by comparing performance between the comparison and training groups for two months after training. The consultant was able to show that the untrained comparison group had 2,000 more minutes of downtime than the trained group did. This finding meant that the trained employees built and shipped more products to customers—showing definitively that training was contributing to Apple's business objectives.

To conduct a cost–benefit analysis, the consultant had each employee in the training group estimate the effect of behavior change on a specific business measure (e.g., breaking down tasks will improve productivity or efficiency). The trainees assigned a confidence percentage to the estimates. To get a cost–benefit estimate for each group of trainees, the consultant multiplied the monthly cost–benefit by the confidence level and divided by the number of trainees. For example, one group of 20 trainees estimated a total overall monthly cost benefit of $336,000 related to business improvements and showed an average 70 percent confidence level with that estimate. Seventy percent multiplied by $336,000 gave a cost benefit of $235,200. This number was divided by 20 ($235,200/20 trainees) to give an average estimated cost benefit for the 20 trainees ($11,760).

SOURCE: A. Purcell, "20/20 ROI," *Training and Development*, July 2000, pp. 28–33.

## Special Training Issues

**LO9**
Design a Cross-Cultural Preparation Program.

To meet the competitive challenges of sustainability, globalization, and technology discussed in Chapter 1, companies must successfully deal with several special training issues. The special training issues include preparing employees to work in different cultures abroad, managing workforce diversity, and socializing and orienting new employees.

### Cross-Cultural Preparation

**Expatriate**
Employee sent by his or her company to manage operations in a different country.

As we mentioned in Chapter 1, companies today are challenged to expand globally. Because of the increase in global operations, employees often work outside their country of origin or work with employees from other countries. An **expatriate** works in a country other than his or her country of origin. For example, Microsoft is headquartered in the United States but has facilities around the world. To be effective, expatriates in the Microsoft Mexico operations in Mexico City must understand the region's business and social culture. Because of a growing pool of talented labor around the world, greater use of host-country nationals is occurring.[123] *Host-country nationals* are employees with citizenship in the country where a company is located. A key reason is that a host-country national can more easily understand the values and customs of the workforce than an expatriate can. Also, training and transporting U.S. employees and their families to a foreign assignment and housing them there tend to be more expensive than hiring a host-country national. We discuss international human resource management in detail in Chapter 15. Here the focus is on understanding how to prepare employees for expatriate assignments.

**Cross-Cultural Preparation**
The process of educating employees (and their families) who are given an assignment in a foreign country.

**Cross-cultural preparation** educates employees (expatriates) and their families who are to be sent to a foreign country. To successfully conduct business in the global marketplace, employees must understand the business practices and the cultural norms of different countries.

## Steps in Cross-Cultural Preparation

To prepare employees for cross-cultural assignments, companies need to provide cross-cultural training. Most U.S. companies send employees overseas without any preparation. As a result, the number of employees who return home before completing their assignments is higher for U.S. companies than for European and Japanese companies.[124] U.S. companies lose more than $2 billion a year as a result of failed overseas assignments.

To succeed overseas, expatriates (employees on foreign assignments) need to be

1. Competent in their areas of expertise.
2. Able to communicate verbally and nonverbally in the host country.
3. Flexible, tolerant of ambiguity, and sensitive to cultural differences.
4. Motivated to succeed, able to enjoy the challenge of working in other countries, and willing to learn about the host country's culture, language, and customs.
5. Supported by their families.[125]

One reason for U.S. expatriates' high failure rate is that companies place more emphasis on developing employees' technical skills than on preparing them to work in other cultures. Research suggests that the comfort of an expatriate's spouse and family is the most important determinant of whether the employee will complete the assignment.[126] Studies have also found that personality characteristics are related to expatriates' desire to terminate the assignment and performance in the assignment.[127] Expatriates who were extroverted (outgoing), agreeable (cooperative and tolerant), and conscientious (dependable, achievement oriented) were more likely to want to stay on the assignment and perform well. This suggests that cross-cultural training may be effective only when expatriates' personalities predispose them to be successful in assignments in other cultures.

The key to a successful foreign assignment is a combination of training and career management for the employee and family. The "Competing through Globalization" box shows the importance of language and cultural training. Foreign assignments involve three phases: predeparture, on-site, and repatriation (preparing to return home). Training is necessary in all three phases.

## Predeparture Phase

Before departure, employees need to receive language training and an orientation to the new country's culture and customs. It is critical that the family be included in orientation programs.[128] Expatriates and their families need information about housing, schools, recreation, shopping, and health care facilities in the areas where they will live. Expatriates also must discuss with their managers how the foreign assignment fits into their career plans and what types of positions they can expect upon return.

Cross-cultural training methods include presentational techniques, such as lectures that expatriates and their families attend on the customs and culture of the host country, immersion experiences, or actual experiences in the home country in culturally diverse communities.[129] Experiential exercises, such as miniculture experiences, allow expatriates to spend time with a family in the United States from the ethnic group of the host country. For example, an Indian trainer took 20 managers from Advanced Micro Devices on a two-week immersion trip during which the group traveled to New Delhi, Bangalore, and Mumbai, meeting with business persons and government officials.[130] The program required six months of planning, including providing the

## COMPETING THROUGH GLOBALIZATION

### Language Training Helps World Business

English is the common language at many multinational companies. But failing to speak the native language can cause employees to risk being misinterpreted or fail to understand informal conversations. Speaking and understanding the local language can help employees avoid misunderstandings and gain greater respect from business partners, subordinates, and customers. For example, a manager at ABB Ltd. oversees 7,000 employees in China and speaks basic Mandarin. Because Chinese employees are reluctant to say no to managers, conducting business is difficult. Because the manager isn't fluent in Chinese languages, he tries to read body language but often reaches the wrong conclusions.

At Intel, employees with a business need can take classes in Mandarin, Japanese, and Spanish at various offices throughout the United States, free of charge. The courses are not designed for expatriates destined for assignments abroad, but instead target employees who, through technology, are in direct contact with foreign clients or who work on cross-cultural teams within the company. With 78,000 employees in 294 offices in 48 countries, Intel has teams that are regularly made up of employees from different cultures working in different locations. The optional 12-week courses, taught at three levels by contracting companies, are designed to help minimize the culture gaps within these teams. The classes meet for two hours a week and cost the company approximately $300 per person. Employees are allowed to repeat courses.

Marcos Garciaacosta, a business alliance manager at Intel who is based in Arizona, has been taking Japanese classes since he joined the company seven years ago. He says that the "ease and flexibility of onsite classes" keep him motivated to continue to learn. And while he says he is far from fluent, he is now at a proficiency level that enables him to better communicate with business contacts and customers in Japan.

The in-house strategy is not new. Company spokeswoman Tracy Koon says that Intel offered its first language programs in Japanese in the 1980s. But despite its 20-year history, the program is still relatively small. Since January 2002, Intel has spent only $54,000 to train 180 employees in these three languages, a tiny fraction of its workforce, and one that does not include expatriates, who are compensated for language training outside these company classes. Without making a huge investment in the concept, Intel is receiving some positive results. Kathy Powell, the foundational development manager for Intel University, the division of the company that manages training, says the demand for foreign-language courses is increasing. Intel plans to expand the language-training program to overseas offices and to train 300 more employees by the end of this year.

The language classes are part of a larger in-house cultural-training curriculum for Intel employees. The company also offers optional one-day classes with titles such as "Working with Russia" and "Doing Business with the Japanese," which are designed to give employees basic information that they need to build relationships and do business cross-culturally. Class size is about 15 students, and subjects include culture, history and an overview of various countries and their business practices. Classes about other cultures are also becoming more popular. During the past 27 months, Intel has spent more than $762,000 on the program and has trained 2,495 employees. It plans to offer the classes to 2,300 more employees by the end of this year, at a cost of about $450,000.

"Our business is very global, and there are a large number of people here working across cultures," Koon says. "By having these language and cultural tools at your disposal when you work with employees from different countries, you can understand the do's and don'ts of the cultures. You're not going to be an effective team if you are constantly offending the other members without knowing it."

SOURCES: Based on G. Weber, "Intel's Internal Approach," *Workforce Management* 83 (2004), p. 49; K. Kranhold, D. Bileklan, M. Karnitschnig, and G. Parker, "Lost in Translation," *The Wall Street Journal*, May 18, 2004, pp. B1 and B6.

executives with information on foods to eat, potential security issues, how to interact in business meetings. For example, Indians prefer a relatively indirect way into business discussions, so the managers were advised to discuss current events and other subjects before talking business.

Research suggests that the degree of difference between the United States and the host country (cultural novelty), the amount of interaction with host country citizens and host nationals (interaction), and the familiarity with new job tasks and work environment (job novelty) all influence the "rigor" of the cross-cultural training method used.[131] Hands-on and group-building methods are most effective (and most needed) in assignments with a high level of cultural and job novelty that require a good deal of interpersonal interaction with host nationals.

## On-Site Phase

On-site training involves continued orientation to the host country and its customs and cultures through formal programs or through a mentoring relationship. Expatriates and their families may be paired with an employee from the host country who helps them understand the new, unfamiliar work environment and community.[132] Companies are also using the Web to help employees on expatriate assignments get answers to questions.[133] Expatriates can use a Web site to get answers to questions such as How do I conduct a meeting here? or What religious philosophy might have influenced today's negotiation behavior? Knowledge management software allows employees to contribute, organize, and access knowledge specific to their expatriate assignment.

A major reason that employees refuse expatriate assignments is that they can't afford to lose their spouse's income or are concerned that their spouse's career could be derailed by being out of the workforce for a few years.[134] Some "trailing" spouses decide to use the time to pursue educational activities that could contribute to their long-term career goals. But it is difficult to find these opportunities in an unfamiliar place. Pfizer, the pharmaceutical firm, is taking action to help trailing spouses. It provides a $10,000 allowance that the spouse can use in many different ways. A person at the expatriate location is assigned to help the spouse with professional development and locating educational or other resources. In countries where spouses are allowed to work, Pfizer tries to find them jobs within the company. Pfizer also provides cross-cultural counseling and language assistance. The company tries to connect the family with the expatriate community. Several multinational companies including Hewlett-Packard, Axalto, and Group Danon have partnered to develop partnerjob.com, an online employment resource that tries to get expatriate spouses jobs posted by other member companies.[135] However, work permit restrictions requiring potential employers to demonstrate that the spouse has skills that are not locally available remains a major restriction to spouse employment.

## Repatriation Phase

**Repatriation** prepares expatriates for return to the parent company and country from the foreign assignment. Expatriates and their families are likely to experience high levels of stress and anxiety when they return because of the changes that have occurred since their departure. Employees should be encouraged to self-manage the repatriation process.[136] Before they go on the assignment they need to consider

**Repatriation**
The preparation of expatriates for return to the parent company and country from a foreign assignment.

what skills they want to develop and the types of jobs that might be available in the company for an employee with those skills. Because the company changes and colleagues, peers, and managers may leave while the expatriate is on assignment, they need to maintain contact with key company and industry contacts. Otherwise, on return the employees' reentry shock will be heightened when they have to deal with new colleagues, a new job, and a company culture that may have changed. This includes providing expatriates with company newsletters and community newspapers and ensuring that they receive personal and work-related mail from the United States while they are on foreign assignment. It is also not uncommon for employees and their families to have to readjust to a lower standard of living in the United States than they had in the foreign country, where they may have enjoyed maid service, a limousine, private schools, and clubs. Salary and other compensation arrangements should be worked out well before employees return from overseas assignments.

Aside from reentry shock, many expatriates decide to leave the company because the assignments they are given upon returning to the United States have less responsibility, challenge, and status than their foreign assignments.[137] As noted earlier, career planning discussions need to be held before the employees leave the United States to ensure that they understand the positions they will be eligible for upon repatriation.

Royal Dutch Shell, a joint Dutch and United Kingdom oil and gas company, has one of the world's largest expatriate work forces. To avoid expatriates who feel undervalued and leave the company, Royal Dutch gets involved with expatriates and their career. Resource planners track workers abroad, helping to identify their next assignment. Most expatriates know their next assignment three to six months before the move, and all begin the next assignment with a clear job description. Expatriates who have the potential to reach top-level management positions are placed in the home office every third assignment to increase their visibility to company executives. Expatriates are also assigned technical mentors who evaluate their skills and help them improve their skills through training at Royal Dutch's training center.

Because of family issues, poor economic times, and security issues, many companies are using virtual expatriates, relying more on short-time assignments, frequent business travel, and international commutes in which an employee lives in one country and works in another.[138] *Virtual expatriates* have an assignment to manage an operation abroad without being located permanently in that country. The employees periodically travel to the overseas location, return, and later use videoconferencing and communications technology to manage the operation.[139] Virtual expatriates eliminate exposing the family to the culture shock of an overseas move. This setup also allows the employee to manage globally while keeping in close touch with the home office. Virtual expatriates are less expensive than traditional expatriates, who can cost companies over three times as much as a host national employee. One major disadvantage of virtual expatriates is that visiting a foreign operation on a sporadic basis may lengthen the time needed to build a local management team, so it will take longer to solve problems because of the lack of a strong personal relationship with local employees. One of the potential difficulties of short-term international assignments is that employees may be perceived as foreigners rather than colleagues because they haven't had the time to build relationships and develop trust among co-workers in their short-term location. Another is that traveling can take a physical and emotional toll on employees as they try to juggle business responsibilities with maintaining contact with family and friends. Procter & Gamble helps employees on short-term assignments by providing a trip fund that is based on the length of time an employee is on an extended business trip. For example, a U.S.-based employee working in western Europe for six months would get a fund containing the cost of five business-class round-trips. The employee can use money from the fund to take trips home or to cover family visits to the employee's location.

## Managing Workforce Diversity

**LIO**
Develop a Program for Effectively Managing Diversity.

The goals of diversity training are (1) to eliminate values, stereotypes, and managerial practices that inhibit employees' personal development and therefore (2) to allow employees to contribute to organizational goals regardless of their race, sexual orientation, gender, family status, religious orientation, or cultural background.[140] Because of Equal Opportunity Employment laws, companies have been forced to ensure that women and minorities are adequately represented in their labor force. That is, companies have focused on ensuring equal access to jobs. As was discussed in Chapter 1, the impact of culture on the workplace, and specifically on training and development, has received heightened attention. Cultural factors that companies need to consider include the terrorist attacks of 9/11; employees' fear of discussing cultural differences; more work being conducted in teams whose members have many different characteristics; the realization that people from diverse cultures represent an important customer market; and, especially for professional and technical jobs, the availability of highly trained employees that has many companies seeking workers from overseas. These new immigrants need diversity training to help them understand such facets of American culture as obsession with time, individualistic attitudes, and capitalistic ideas.[141]

**Managing diversity** involves creating an environment that allows all employees to contribute to organizational goals and experience personal growth. This environment includes access to jobs as well as fair and positive treatment of all employees. The company must develop employees who are comfortable working with people from a wide variety of ethnic, racial, and religious backgrounds. Managing diversity may require changing the company culture. It includes the company's standards and norms about how employees are treated, competitiveness, results orientation, innovation, and risk taking. The value placed on diversity is grounded in the company culture.

**Managing Diversity**
The process of creating an environment that allows all employees to contribute to organizational goals and experience personal growth.

### Managing Diversity through Adherence to Legislation

One approach to managing diversity is through affirmative action policies and by making sure that human resource management practices meet standards of equal employment opportunity laws.[142] This approach rarely changes employees' values, stereotypes, and behaviors that inhibit productivity and personal development. Figure 7.8 shows the cycle of disillusionment resulting from managing diversity by relying solely on adherence to employment laws. The cycle begins when the company realizes that it must change policies regarding women and minorities because of legal pressure or a discrepancy between the number or percentage of women and minorities in the company's workforce and the number available in the broader labor market. To address these concerns, a greater number of women and minorities are hired by the company. Managers see little need for additional action because women and minority employment rates reflect their availability in the labor market. However, as women and

figure 7.8
Cycle of Disillusionment Resulting from Managing Diversity through Adherence to Legislation

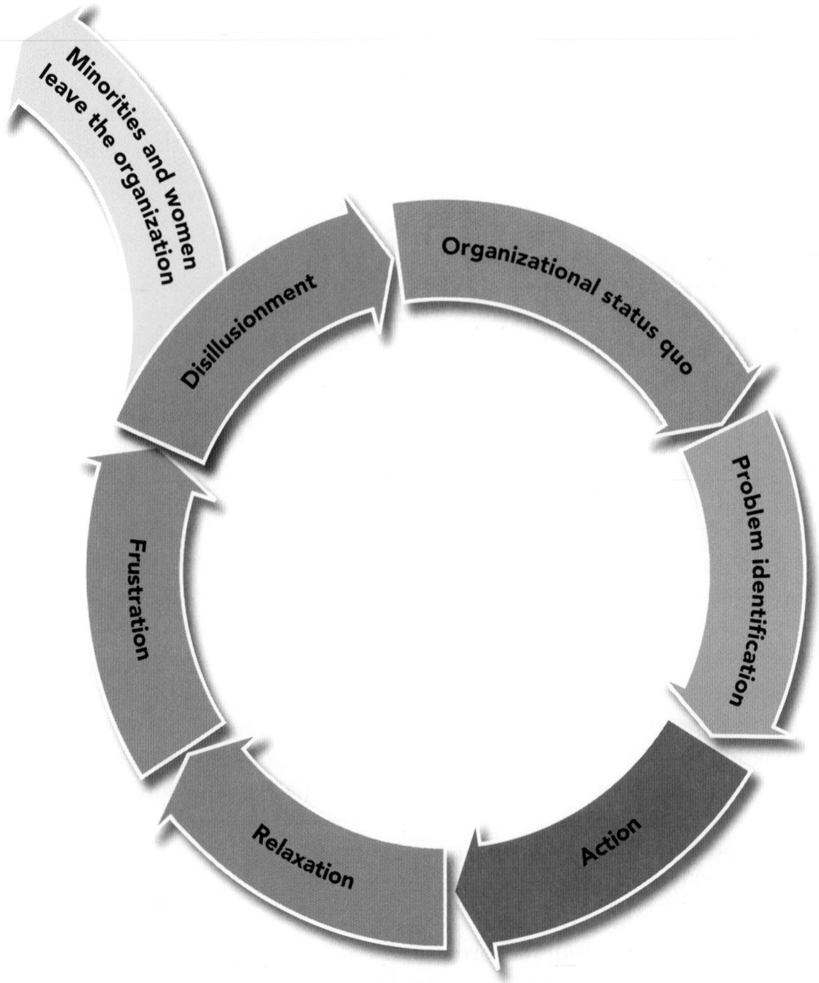


SOURCE: *HR Magazine* by Cresencio Torres and Mary Bruxelles. Copyright © 1992 by Society for Human Resource Management. Reproduced with permission of Society for Human Resource Management via Copyright Clearance Center.

minorities gain experience in the company, they may become frustrated. Managers and co-workers may avoid providing coaching or performance feedback to women and minorities because they are uncomfortable interacting with individuals from different gender, ethnic, or racial backgrounds. Co-workers may express beliefs that women and minorities are employed only because they received special treatment (hiring standards were lowered).[143] As a result of their frustration, women and minorities may form support groups to voice their concerns to management. Because of the work atmosphere, women and minorities may fail to fully utilize their skills and leave the company.

## Managing Diversity through Diversity Training Programs

The preceding discussion is not to suggest that companies should be reluctant to engage in affirmative action or pursue equal opportunity employment practices. However, affirmative action without additional supporting strategies does not deal with issues of assimilating women and minorities into the workforce. To successfully manage a diverse workforce, companies need to ensure that

- Employees understand how their values and stereotypes influence their behavior toward others of different gender, ethnic, racial, or religious backgrounds.
- Employees gain an appreciation of cultural differences among themselves.
- Behaviors that isolate or intimidate minority group members improve.

This can be accomplished through diversity training programs. **Diversity training** refers to training designed to change employee attitudes about diversity and/or develop skills needed to work with a diverse workforce. Diversity training programs differ according to whether attitude or behavior change is emphasized.[144]

**Diversity Training**
Training designed to change employee attitudes about diversity and/or develop skills needed to work with a diverse workforce.

## Attitude Awareness and Change Programs

**Attitude awareness and change programs** focus on increasing employees' awareness of differences in cultural and ethnic backgrounds, physical characteristics (such as disabilities), and personal characteristics that influence behavior toward others. The assumption underlying these programs is that, by increasing their awareness of stereotypes and beliefs, employees will be able to avoid negative stereotypes when interacting with employees of different backgrounds. The programs help employees consider the similarities and differences between cultural groups, examine their attitudes toward affirmative action, or analyze their beliefs about why minority employees are successful or unsuccessful in their jobs. Many of these programs use videotapes and experiential exercises to increase employees' awareness of the negative emotional and performance effects of stereotypes, values, and behaviors on minority group members. Sodexho serves millions of customers each day in the cafeterias it operates in companies and universities.[145] As a result it is important that Sodexho understand the needs of a diverse customer base. The company has mandatory classes that provide managers with an overview of equal opportunity and affirmative action laws. The classes relate to other initiatives, including courses on generational differences and body language that can be offensive. The courses involve group dialogues and scenarios. One game requires participants to wear labels such as "Hearing impaired" and interact with others based on that description.

**Attitude Awareness and Change Program**
Program focusing on increasing employees' awareness of differences in cultural and ethnic backgrounds, physical characteristics, and personal characteristics that influence behavior toward others.

The attitude awareness and change approach has been criticized for several reasons.[146] First, by focusing on group differences, the program may communicate that certain stereotypes and attitudes are valid. For example, in diversity training a male manager may learn that women employees prefer to work by building consensus rather than by arguing until others agree with their point. He might conclude that the training has validated his stereotype. As a result, he will continue to fail to give women important job responsibilities that involve heated negotiations with customers or clients. Second, encouraging employees to share their attitudes, feelings, and stereotypes toward certain groups may cause employees to feel guilty, angry, and less likely to see the similarities among racial, ethnic, or gender groups and the advantages of working together.

**Behavior-Based Program**
A program focusing on changing the organizational policies and individual behaviors that inhibit employees' personal growth and productivity.

## Behavior-Based Programs

**Behavior-based programs** focus on changing the organizational policies and individual behaviors that inhibit employees' personal growth and productivity. These programs can take three approaches.

One approach of these programs is to identify incidents that discourage employees from working up to their potential. Groups of employees are asked to identify specific promotion opportunities, sponsorship, training opportunities, or performance management practices that they believe were handled unfairly. Their views regarding how well the work environment and management practices value employee differences and provide equal opportunity may also be collected. Specific training programs may be developed to address the issues presented in the focus groups.

Another approach is to teach managers and employees basic rules of behavior in the workplace.[147] For example, managers and employees should learn that it is inappropriate to use statements and engage in behaviors that have negative racial, sexual, or cultural content. Companies that have focused on teaching rules and behavior have found that employees react less negatively to this type of training than to other diversity training approaches.

**Cultural Immersion**
A behavior-based diversity program that sends employees into communities where they interact with persons from different cultures, races, and nationalities.

A third approach is **cultural immersion:** sending employees directly into communities where they have to interact with persons from different cultures, races, and nationalities. The degree of interaction varies but may involve talking with community members, working in community organizations, or learning about religious, cultural, or historically significant events. For example, the United Parcel Service (UPS) Community Internship Program is designed to help UPS senior managers understand the needs of diverse customers and a diverse workforce through exposure to poverty and inequality.[148] UPS is the world's largest package delivery company and a leading global provider of transportation and logistic services. Since 1968, over 1,200 senior managers have completed the program, an internship that typically lasts four weeks. The internships take the managers to cities throughout the United States, where they work on the problems facing local populations. UPS managers may find themselves serving meals to the homeless, working in AIDS centers, helping migrant farm workers, building temporary housing and schools, and managing children in a Head Start program. These experiences take the managers outside their comfort zones, and the problems that they encounter—from transportation to housing to education to health care—help them better understand the issues that many UPS employees face daily. This enlightenment is a business necessity for UPS because three out of four managers are white whereas 35 percent of the employees are minorities. UPS has not formally evaluated the program, but the company continues to invest $10,000 per intern. The company has invested a total of more than $13.5 billion in the program since its start in 1968. Despite the lack of hard evaluation data, UPS managers report that the program helps them look for unconventional solutions to problems. One manager who spent a month working at a halfway house in New York was impressed by the creative ideas of uneducated addicts for keeping teens away from drugs. The manager realized that she had failed to capitalize on the creativity of the employees she supervised. As a result, when she returned to her job and faced problems, she started brainstorming with her entire staff, not just senior managers. Other managers report that the experience helped them empathize with employees facing crises at home.

## Characteristics of Successful Diversity Efforts

Is a behavior-based or an attitude awareness and change program most effective? Increasing evidence shows that attitude awareness programs are ineffective and that one-time diversity training programs are unlikely to succeed. For example,

R. R. Donnelley & Sons suspended its diversity awareness training program even though the company spent more than $3 million on it as a result of a racial discrimination lawsuit.[149]

At various training sessions participants were encouraged to voice their concerns. Many said that they were experiencing difficulty in working effectively due to abuse and harassment. The managers attending the training disputed the concerns. Also, after training, an employee who applied for an open position was rejected, because, she was told, she had been too honest in expressing her concerns during the diversity training session. Although R. R. Donnelley held many diversity training sessions, little progress was made in increasing the employment and promotion rates of women and minorities. Because of the low ratio of black employees to white employees, many black employees were asked to attend multiple training sessions to ensure diverse groups, which they resented. The company declined to release data requested by shareholders that it provided to the Equal Employment Opportunity Commission regarding female and minority representation in jobs throughout the company. The firm also failed to act on recommendations made by company-approved employee "diversity councils."

More generally, a survey of diversity training efforts found that[150]

- The most common area addressed through diversity efforts is the pervasiveness of stereotypes, assumptions, and biases.
- Fewer than one-third of companies do any kind of long-term evaluation or follow-up. The most common indicators of success were reduced grievances and lawsuits, increased diversity in promotions and hiring, increased self-awareness of biases, and increased consultation of HRM specialists on diversity-related issues.
- Most programs lasted only one day or less.
- Three-fourths of the survey respondents indicated that they believed the typical employee leaves diversity training with positive attitudes toward diversity. However, over 50 percent reported that the programs have no effect over the long term.

Little research addresses the impact of diversity or diversity-management practices on financial success. Diversity may enhance performance when organizations have an environment that promotes learning from diversity. There is no evidence to support the direct relationship between diversity and business.[151] Rather, a company will see the success of its diversity efforts only if it makes a long-term commitment to managing diversity. Successful diversity requires that it be viewed as an opportunity for employees to (1) learn from each other how to better accomplish their work, (2) be provided with a supportive and cooperative organizational culture, and (3) be taught leadership and process skills that can facilitate effective team functioning. Diversity is a reality in labor and customer markets and is a social expectation and value. Managers should focus on building an organizational environment, on human resource practices, and on managerial and team skills that all capitalize on diversity. As you will see in the discussion that follows, managing diversity requires difficult cultural change, not just slogans on the wall!

Table 7.11 shows the characteristics associated with the long-term success of diversity programs. It is critical that a diversity program be tied to business objectives. For example, cultural differences affect the type of skin cream consumers believe they need or the fragrance they may be attracted to. Understanding cultural differences is part of understanding the consumer (which is critical to the success of companies such as Avon). Top management support can be demonstrated by creating a structure to support the initiative.

**table 7.11**

Characteristics Associated with Diversity Programs' Long-Term Success

- Top management provides resources, personally intervenes, and publicly advocates diversity.
- The program is structured.
- Capitalizing on a diverse workforce is defined as a business objective.
- Capitalizing on a diverse workforce is seen as necessary to generate revenue and profits.
- The program is evaluated using metrics such as sales, retention, and promotion rates.
- Manager involvement is mandatory.
- The program is seen as a culture change, not a one-shot program.
- Managers and demographic groups are not blamed for problems.
- Behaviors and skills needed to successfully interact with others are taught.
- Managers are rewarded on progress toward meeting diversity goals.
- Management collects employee feedback and responds to it.

SOURCES: M. Jayne and R. Dipboye, "Leveraging Diversity to Improve Business Performance: Research Findings and Recommendations for Organizations," *Human Resource Management* 43 (2004); pp. 409–24; S. Rynes and B. Rosen, "What Makes Diversity Programs Work?" *HR Magazine,* October 1994, pp. 67–73; S. Rynes and B. Rosen, "A Field Survey of Factors Affecting the Adoption and Perceived Success of Diversity Training," *Personnel Psychology* 48 (1995), pp. 247–70; J. Gordon, "Different from What? Diversity as a Performance Issue," *Training,* May 1995, pp. 25–33; Corporate Leadership Council, *The Evolution of Corporate Diversity* (Washington, DC: Corporate Executive Board, 2002).

Pepsi's president believes that the full potential of diversity cannot be realized without employees being "comfortable being uncomfortable" so they are willing to share difficult issues in the workplace.[152] As a result, members of the senior management team were named sponsors for specific employee groups including African Americans, Latinos, Asians, women, women of color, white males, disabled, and gay, lesbian, and transgendered. The managers are expected to understand their group members' needs, identify talent, and mentor at least three employees in their group. Also, they are expected to provide updates to the president on their progress.

Consider Texaco's diversity effort, shown in Table 7.12. Prior to becoming a subsidiary of Chevron Texaco, Texaco developed a state-of-the-art diversity program after the company had to pay more than $175 million to settle a racial discrimination lawsuit.[153] The lawsuit made public accusations that company executives were using racial slurs. As Table 7.12 shows, managing diversity at Texaco went far beyond workshop attendance. Managing diversity became part of a culture change. Texaco's diversity effort included programs designed to stop discrimination in hiring, retention, and promotion. Managers were held accountable for diversity goals in their performance evaluations. The company also realized that to capitalize on diversity from a business perspective, it needed to give more opportunities to minority vendors, suppliers, and customers.

There is considerable evidence that the program has transformed the culture. From 2002 to 2004, Chevron Texaco spent more than $1 billion on products and services from supplier businesses owned by women and minorities.[154] Chevron Texaco also supports diversity networks, which are open to all employees. These formally structured organizations must show how they support the company's diversity objectives, vision, values, and strategy. More than 4,000 employees (approximately 5 percent of all employees) participate in these groups, which include a Native American network, a lesbian and gay network, a women's network, a black employees network, and a baby-boomer network. These networks are more than social clubs. Their goals are to

**table 7.12**

Texaco's Diversity Effort

**Recruitment and Hiring**
- Ask search firms to identify wider arrays of candidates.
- Enhance the interviewing, selection, and hiring skills of managers.
- Expand college recruitment at historically minority colleges.

**Identifying and Developing Talent**
- Form a partnership with INROADS, a nationwide internship program that targets minority students for management careers.
- Establish a mentoring process.
- Refine the company's global succession planning system to improve identification of talent.
- Improve the selection and development of managers and leaders to help ensure that they are capable of maximizing team performance.

**Ensuring Fair Treatment**
- Conduct extensive diversity training.
- Implement an alternative dispute resolution process.
- Include women and minorities on all human resources committees throughout the company.

**Holding Managers Accountable**
- Link managers' compensation to their success in creating "openness and inclusion in the workplace."
- Implement 360-degree feedback for all managers and supervisors.
- Redesign the company's employee attitude survey and begin using it annually to monitor employee attitudes.

**Improving Relationships with External Stakeholders**
- Broaden the company's base of vendors and suppliers to incorporate more minority- and women-owned businesses.
- Increase banking, investment, and insurance business with minority- and women-owned firms.
- Add more independent, minority retailers and increase the number of minority managers in company-owned gas stations and Xpress Lube outlets.

SOURCES: D. Hellriegel, S. E. Jackson, and J. W. Slocum Jr., *Management*, 8th ed. (Cincinnati, OH: South-Western College Publishing, 1999). Originally adapted from V. C. Smith, "Texaco Outlines Comprehensive Initiatives," *Human Resource Executive*, February 1997, p. 13; A. Bryant, "How Much Has Texaco Changed? A Mixed Report Card on Anti-bias Efforts," *The New York Times*, November 2, 1997, pp. 3-1, 3-16, 3-17; and "Texaco's Worldforce Diversity Plan," as reprinted in *Workforce*, March 1997, supp. from D. Daft and R. Noe, *Organizational Behavior* (Fort Worth, TX: Dryden Press, 2001), p. 58.

increase members' cultural awareness and leadership skills, to sponsor learning activities that help develop a more cross-culturally sensitive workforce, and to communicate new ideas. The company has also established alliances with organizations that promote equality and fairness for women and minorities.

Other companies, such as Denny's (in response to a lawsuit) and Weyerhaeuser (in response to a retiring workforce survey and survey results suggesting the need for a more accepting workplace) have established diversity programs with the same features as Texaco's program (recruitment and hiring, identifying and developing talent, etc.).[155] As should be apparent from this discussion, successful diversity programs involve more than just an effective training program. They require an ongoing process of culture change that includes top management support as well as diversity policies and practices in the areas of recruitment and hiring, training and development, and administrative structures, such as conducting diversity surveys and evaluating managers' progress on diversity goals.[156]

## Socialization and Orientation

**Organizational Socialization** The process used to transform new employees into effective company members.

**Organizational socialization** is the process by which new employees are transformed into effective members of the company. As Table 7.13 shows, effective socialization involves being prepared to perform the job effectively, learning about the organization, and establishing work relationships. Socialization involves three phases: anticipatory socialization, encounter, and settling in.[157] Figure 7.9 shows the three phases and the actions that should be taken to help employees at each phase.

**Anticipatory Socialization** Process that helps individuals develop expectations about the company, job, working conditions, and interpersonal relationships.

**Encounter Phase** Phase of socialization that occurs when an employee begins a new job.

**Settling-in Phase** Phase of socialization that occurs when employees are comfortable with job demands and social relationships.

Anticipatory socialization occurs before the individual joins the company. Through **anticipatory socialization,** expectations about the company, job, working conditions, and interpersonal relationships are developed through interactions with representatives of the company (recruiters, prospective peers, and managers) during recruitment and selection. The expectations are also based on prior work experiences in similar jobs. The **encounter phase** occurs when the employee begins a new job. No matter how realistic the information provided during interviews and site visits, individuals beginning new jobs will experience shock and surprise.[158] In the **settling-in phase,** employees begin to feel comfortable with their job demands and social relationships. They begin to resolve work conflicts (like too much work or conflicting job demands) and conflicts between work and nonwork activities. Employees are interested in the company's evaluation of their performance and in learning about potential career opportunities within the company.

Employees need to complete all three socialization phases to fully contribute to the company. For example, employees who do not feel that they have established good working relationships with co-workers will likely spend time and energy worrying about those relationships rather than being concerned with product development or customer service. Employees who experience successful socialization are more motivated, more committed to the company, and more satisfied with their jobs.[159]

**table 7.13**

What Employees Should Learn and Develop through the Socialization Process

| | |
|---|---|
| History | The company's traditions, customs, and myths; background of members |
| Company goals | Rules, values, or principles directing the company |
| Language | Slang and jargon unique to the company; professional technical language |
| Politics | How to gain information regarding the formal and informal work relationships and power structures in the company |
| People | Successful and satisfying work relationships with other employees |
| Performance proficiency | What needs to be learned; effectiveness in using and acquiring the knowledge, skills, and abilities needed for the job. |

SOURCE: Based on G. T. Chao, A. M. O'Leary-Kelly, S. Wolf, H. Klein, and P. D. Gardner, "Organizational Socialization: Its Content and Consequences," *Journal of Applied Psychology* 79 (1994), pp. 730–43.

figure 7.9

Phases of Socialization and Necessary Company Actions

**Anticipatory Socialization**
- Provide a realistic job preview as well as accurate information about the positive and negative aspects of the job, including working conditions, company, and location.

**Encounter**
- Provide training, challenging work, and orientation, thus reducing shock and surprise. Manager can help new employees understand their roles, provide information about the company, and empathize with stress of new job.

**Settling In**
- Provide performance evaluation and information on career opportunities.

SOURCES: Based on D. T. Hall, *Careers In and Out of Organizations* (Thousand Oaks, CA: Sage Publications, 2002), J. D. Kammeyer-Mueller and C. R. Wanberg, "Unwrapping the Organizational Entry Process: Disentangling Multiple Antecedents and Their Pathway to Adjustment," *Journal of Applied Psychology* 88 (2003), pp. 779–94; G. M. McEnvoy and W. F. Cascio, "Strategies for Reducing Employee Turnover: A Meta-analysis," *Journal of Applied Psychology* 70 (1985), pp. 342–53; M. R. Louis, "Surprise and Sensemaking: What Newcomers Experience in Entering Unfamiliar Organizational Settings," *Administrative Science Quarterly* 25 (1980), pp. 226–51; R. F. Morrison and T. M. Brantner, "What Enhances or Inhibits Learning a New Job? A Basic Career Issue,"*Journal of Applied Psychology* 77 (1992), pp. 926–40; D. A. Major, S. W. J. Kozlowski, G. T. Chao, and P. D. Gardner, "A Longitudinal Investigation of Newcomer Expectations, Early Socialization Outcomes, and the Moderating Effect of Role Development Factors," *Journal of Applied Psychology* 80 (1995), pp. 418–31.

## Socialization, Orientation, and Onboarding Programs

Socialization and orientation programs play an important role in socializing employees. Orientation involves familiarizing new employees with company rules, policies, and procedures. Typically, a program includes information about the company, department in which the employees will be working, and the community they will live in. Onboarding refers to the orientation process for newly hired managers.

Although the content of orientation programs is important, the process of orientation cannot be ignored. Too often, orientation programs consist of completing payroll forms and reviewing personnel policies with managers or human resource representatives. Although these are important activities, the new employee has little opportunity to ask questions, interact with peers and managers, or become familiar with the company's culture, products, and service.

Software and online tools are now available to help the company and its new employees complete the ordinary tasks related to taking a new job such as setting up e-mail accounts, distributing online employee handbooks, completing important documents such as tax and benefit forms, and scheduling orientation meetings.

This allows more orientation or "onboarding time" to be spent interacting with new peers and managers, as well as learning about the company culture and its products and services. For example, Pinnacle Entertainment used a Web-based system to create online files for newly hired casino employees.[160] The system allows employees to go online and complete forms and schedule two days of orientation. The new employees liked the system because it eliminated the need for them to write their personal information over and over on forms. The company found that the system reduced the time, paperwork, and hassles related to hiring new employees.

Effective orientation programs actively involve the new employee. Table 7.14 shows the characteristics of effective orientation. An important characteristic of effective orientation is that peers, managers, and senior co-workers are actively involved in helping new employees adjust to the work group.[161]

Several companies offer programs that include the characteristics shown in Table 7.14.[162] For example, through its "52 weeks" program, Qualcomm uses e-mail to distribute 52 short stories, written to share the company's history, factors that make it successful, and future business directions. Each new employee receives one story per week throughout his or her first year. Each story relates company history and demonstrates how the corporate culture was formed. The stories cover the first employee meeting in the company parking lot and the development of the chip division. The stories help employees understand that innovation, doing whatever it takes, and camaraderie are Qualcomm values.

Monster, the leader in online recruitment, uses a day-long orientation session in which education is mixed with fun, games, and prizes. The first part of the orientation session involves new employees meeting each other and discussing how they chose a job at Monster. Monster's founder and the North American president as well as other executives welcome the new hires either in person or via videotape. New employees receive information about Monster's business philosophy, its customers, and its products and services. New employees receive specialized badges and Monster prizes. The meeting room is decorated in Monster colors and includes a list of the company values. The second part of the orientation program helps employees get off to a good start in their new job. Each employee's manager receives a to-do list of things that need to be done before the new employee arrives (such as setting up a work area) and during that employee's first four weeks at Monster (such as training, completing paperwork, identifying peers). All new employees are also assigned departmental mentors. Mentors greet the new hires at the end of the orientation, introduce them to their managers, and serve as their key contact person until the new employee is comfortable. New hires reactions to the program have been positive.

**table 7.14**

Characteristics of Effective Orientation Programs

| |
|---|
| Employees are encouraged to ask questions. |
| Program includes information on both technical and social aspects of the job. |
| Orientation is the responsibility of the new employee's manager. |
| Debasing or embarrassing new employees is avoided. |
| Formal and informal interactions with managers and peers occur. |
| Programs involve relocation assistance (such as house hunting or information sessions on the community for employees and their spouses). |
| Employees learn about the company's products, services, and customers. |

For Randstad North America, a professional staffing services company, it is critical that new staffing agents who bring in clients quickly become as productive as possible. Randstad's orientation program took place in classroom sessions that were time consuming and overloaded new hires with information. Randstad changed the orientation program into a 16-week blended learning program that reduced classroom instruction and increased self-guided e-learning and on-the-job activities. New hires receive the basic information they need through e-learning or discussions with managers. Classroom instruction focuses on understanding the Randstad culture. The new program also includes presentations by district managers of the culture, job expectations, sales training, and performance and bonus plans, shadowing of experienced employees and managers on their jobs, and manager coaching. New employees spend more than 70 hours in job shadowing and training during their first month on the job. By the fourth month employees spend only five hours in training. At the end of the fourth month, employees take an exam. Evaluations of the new orientation program have been positive. New hires are satisfied with the new orientation program. The company estimates that $4 million of an increase in sales was directly due to the new orientation program.

An example of how orientation and socialization can reduce turnover and contribute to business is National City Corporation's Early Success program. National City Corporation, a bank and financial services company based in Cleveland, Ohio, was challenged by the high level of turnover that occurred among new employees within 90 days of being hired.[163] Turnover was 51 percent. Because it is difficult to provide excellent service and retain customers if customers are always dealing with a new employee, National City developed the National City Institute. Within the institute, the Early Success program provides a comfortable environment, a support network, and a series of classes where new hires learn product knowledge and customer service skills. For example, one course called Plus provides an overview of National City's corporate objectives, employee benefits, and information about the brand.

Another course, called People, Policies, and Practices, complements the employee handbook. Top-Notch Customer Care focuses on how to provide service and work in teams. New employees are matched with a peer (known as a buddy). The buddies are a support network for new hires that provides someone to answer their questions. The peer mentor is trained in coaching skills. The hiring managers also attend training designed to help them select buddy mentors, create a supportive work environment, communicate clearly, understand how to allow the new hire to gradually take on more responsibility, and help new hires achieve career goals. With the new program, new employees are 50 percent less likely to quit in the first three months on the job, resulting in a savings of approximately $1.35 million per year.

Onboarding gives new managers an introduction to the work they will be supervising and an understanding of the culture and operations of the entire company. For example, at Pella Corporation, an Iowa-based manufacturer of windows and doors, new managers are sent on a tour of production plants, meeting and observing employees and department heads. These tours ensure that the managers will get a better sense of the market and how the company's products are designed, built, and distributed.[164] At The Limited, the Columbus, Ohio, retail clothing company, new vice presidents and regional directors spend their days talking to customers, reading company history, working the floor of retail stores, investigating the competition, and studying the company's current and past operations. They spend a month with no responsibilities for the tasks related to their new positions. Limited's philosophy is that managers are better able to perform their job by first taking time to understand the people, customers, company, and operations they will be working with.

## A Look Back

As the chapter opener highlighted, Wegmans Food Markets uses training to support the company's business strategy. Wegmans provides extensive training focused on service and product knowledge.

**Questions**

1. Suppose a manager asked you to determine whether training was supporting a company's business strategy. How would you conduct this type of analysis? What kind of information would you look for?
2. Is there a difference between a company supporting learning and a company supporting training? Explain.

Please see the Video Case that corresponds to this chapter online at www.mhhe.com/noe6e.

## Summary

Technological innovations, new product markets, and a diverse workforce have increased the need for companies to reexamine how their training practices contribute to learning. In this chapter we discussed a systematic approach to training, including needs assessment, design of the learning environment, consideration of employee readiness for training, and transfer-of-training issues. We reviewed numerous training methods and stressed that the key to successful training was to choose a method that would best accomplish the objectives of training. We also emphasized how training can contribute to effectiveness through establishing a link with the company's strategic direction and demonstrating through cost–benefit analysis how training contributes to profitability. Managing diversity and cross-cultural preparation are two training issues that are relevant given company needs to capitalize on a diverse workforce and global markets.

## Key Terms

Training, 267
High-leverage training, 267
Continuous learning, 267
Training design process, 269
Needs assessment, 270
Organizational analysis, 271
Person analysis, 271
Task analysis, 271
Strategic training and development initiatives, 272
Request for proposal (RFP), 274
Person characteristics, 275
Input, 275
Output, 275
Consequences, 275
Feedback, 275
Motivation to learn, 279
Self-efficacy, 280
Basic skills, 281
Cognitive ability, 281
Readability, 282
Communities of practice, 285
Transfer of training, 285
Climate for transfer, 286
Action pan, 287
Support network, 287
Opportunity to perform, 287
Electronic performance support systems (EPSS), 288
Knowledge management, 288
Presentation methods, 291
Teleconferencing, 291
Webcasting, 292
Hands-on methods, 294
On-the-job training (OJT), 294
Self-directed learning, 295
Apprenticeship, 296
Simulation, 297
Avatar, 298
Virtual reality, 298
E-learning, 301
Repurposing, 302
Learner control, 303
Learning management system (LMS), 303

Group- or team-building methods, 303
Adventure learning, 305
Cross-training, 306
Coordination training, 306
Team leader training, 306
Action learning, 307
Six Sigma Training, 308
Training outcomes, 309
Cost-benefit analysis, 312
Expatriate, 314
Cross-cultural preparation, 314
Repatriation, 317
Managing diversity, 319
Diversity training, 321
Attitude awareness and change program, 321
Behavior-based program, 321
Cultural immersion, 322
Organizational socialization, 326
Anticipatory socialization, 326
Encounter phase, 326
Settling-in phase, 326

## Discussion Questions

1. Noetron, a retail electronics store, recently invested a large amount of money to train sales staff to improve customer service. The skills emphasized in the program include how to greet customers, determine their needs, and demonstrate product convenience. The company wants to know whether the program is effective. What outcomes should it collect? What type of evaluation design should it use?
2. "Melinda," bellowed Toran, "I've got a problem and you've got to solve it. I can't get people in this plant to work together as a team. As if I don't have enough trouble with the competition and delinquent accounts, now I have to put up with running a zoo. It's your responsibility to see that the staff gets along with each other. I want a human relations training proposal on my desk by Monday." How would you determine the need for human relations training? How would you determine whether you actually had a training problem? What else could be responsible?
3. Assume you are general manager of a small seafood company. Most training is unstructured and occurs on the job. Currently, senior fish cleaners are responsible for teaching new employees how to perform the job. Your company has been profitable, but recently wholesale fish dealers that buy your product have been complaining about the poor quality of your fresh fish. For example, some fillets have not had all the scales removed and abdomen parts remain attached to the fillets. You have decided to change the on-the-job training received by the fish cleaners. How will you modify the training to improve the quality of the product delivered to the wholesalers?
4. A training needs analysis indicates that managers' productivity is inhibited because they are reluctant to delegate tasks to their subordinates. Suppose you had to decide between using adventure learning and interactive video for your training program. What are the strengths and weaknesses of each technique? Which would you choose? Why? What factors would influence your decision?
5. To improve product quality, a company is introducing a computer-assisted manufacturing process into one of its assembly plants. The new technology is likely to substantially modify jobs. Employees will also be required to learn statistical process control techniques. The new technology and push for quality will require employees to attend numerous training sessions. Over 50 percent of the employees who will be affected by the new technology completed their formal education over 10 years ago. Only about 5 percent of the company's employees have used the tuition reimbursement benefit. How should management maximize employees' readiness for training?
6. A training course was offered for maintenance employees in which trainees were supposed to learn how to repair and operate a new, complex electronics system. On the job, maintenance employees were typically told about a symptom experienced by the machine operator and were asked to locate the trouble. During training, the trainer would pose various problems for the maintenance employees to solve. He would point out a component on an electrical diagram and ask, "What would happen if this component was faulty?" Trainees would then trace the circuitry on a blueprint to uncover the symptoms that would appear as a result of the problem. You are receiving complaints about poor troubleshooting from maintenance supervisors of employees who have completed the program. The trainees are highly motivated and have the necessary prerequisites. What is the problem with the training course? What recommendations do you have for fixing this course?
7. What factors contribute to the effectiveness of Web training programs?
8. Choose a job you are familiar with. Design a new employee orientation program for that job. Explain how your program contributes to effective socialization.
9. Why might employees prefer blended learning to training using iPods?
10. What learning condition do you think is most necessary for learning to occur? Which is least critical? Why?

## Self-Assessment Exercise:

In the chapter we discussed the need for learners to be motivated so that training will be effective. What is your motivation to learn? Find out by answering the following questions. Read each statement and indicate how much you agree with it, using the following scale:

5 = Strongly Agree
4 = Somewhat Agree
3 = Neutral
2 = Somewhat Disagree
1 = Strongly Disagree

| | | | | | |
|---|---|---|---|---|---|
| 1. I try to learn as much as I can from the courses I take. | 5 | 4 | 3 | 2 | 1 |
| 2. I believe I tend to learn more from my courses than other students do. | 5 | 4 | 3 | 2 | 1 |
| 3. When I'm involved in courses and can't understand something, I get so frustrated I stop trying to learn. | 5 | 4 | 3 | 2 | 1 |

## Exercising Strategy: "Knowledge Is Critical for the Rubber to Meet the Road"

Michelin manufactures and sells tires for all kinds of vehicles, publishes maps and guides, and operates a number of digital services in more than 170 countries. Michelin has identified that over half of its employees would be eligible to retire by 2014. Companies such as Michelin are challenged both to develop methods to acquire important knowledge from retiring employees and to determine how to link employees with one another and important knowledge.

### Questions

1. What steps should Michelin take to capture the knowledge from retiring employees and provide current employees with that knowledge?
2. How would you suggest that the company evaluate the effectiveness of its knowledge capturing and sharing system?

## Managing People: From the Pages of *BusinessWeek*

### BusinessWeek On-the-Job Video Gaming

**Interactive training tools are captivating employees and saving companies money** Laura Holshouser's favorite video games include *Halo*, *Tetris*, and an online training game developed by her employer. A training game? That's right. The 24-year-old graduate student, who manages a Cold Stone Creamery ice-cream store in Riverside, Calif., stumbled across the game on the corporate Web site in October.

It teaches portion control and customer service in a cartoon-like simulation of a Cold Stone store. Players scoop cones against the clock and try to avoid serving too much ice cream. The company says more than 8,000 employees, or about 30 percent of the total, voluntarily downloaded the game in the first week. "It's so much fun," says Holshouser. "I e-mailed it to everyone at work."

The military has used video games as a training tool since the 1980s. Now the practice is catching on with companies, too, ranging from Cold Stone to Cisco Systems Inc. to Canon Inc. Corporate trainers are betting that games' interactivity and fun will hook young, media-savvy employees like Holshouser and help them grasp and retain sales, technical, and management skills. "Video games teach resource management, collaboration, critical thinking, and tolerance for failure," says Ben Sawyer, who runs Digitalmill Inc., a game consultancy in Portland, Me.

The market for corporate training games is small but it's growing fast. Sawyer estimates that such games make up 15 percent of the "serious," or nonentertainment market, which also includes educational and medical training products. Over the next five years, Sawyer sees the serious-games market more than doubling, to $100 million, with trainers accounting for nearly a third of that. It's numbers like those that prompted Cyberlors Studios Inc., maker of *Playboy: The Mansion*, to refocus on training games—albeit based on its Playboy title. And training games will be top of mind at the Game Developers Conference in San Jose, Calif., this month.

Companies like video games because they are cost-effective. Why pay for someone to fly to a central training campus when you can just plunk them down in front of a computer? Even better, employees often play the games at home on their own time. Besides, by industry standards, training games are cheap to make. A typical military game costs up to $10 million, while sophisticated entertainment games can cost twice that. Since the corporate variety don't require dramatic, warlike explosions or complex 3D graphics, they cost a lot less. BreakAway Games Ltd., which designs simulation games for the military, is finishing its first corporate product, V-bank, to train bank auditors. Its budget? Just $500,000.

### Drag and Drop

Games are especially well-suited to training technicians. In one used by Canon, repairmen must drag and drop parts into the right spot on a copier. As in the board game *Operation*, a light flashes and a buzzer sounds if the repairman gets it wrong. Workers who played the game showed a 5 percent to 8 percent improvement in their training scores compared with older training techniques such as manuals, says Chuck Reinders, who trains technical support staff at Canon. This spring, the company will unveil 11 new training games.

Games are also being developed to help teach customer service workers to be more empathetic. Cyberlore, now rechristened Minerva Software Inc., is developing a training tool for a retailer by rejiggering its *Playboy Mansion* game. In the original, guests had to persuade models to pose topless. The new game requires players to use the art of persuasion to sell products, and simulates a store, down to the carpet and point-of-purchase display details.

Don Field, director of certifications at Cisco, says games won't entirely replace traditional training methods such as videos and classes. But he says they should be part of the toolbox. Last year, Cisco rolled out six new training games—some of them designed to teach technicians how to build a computer network. It's hard to imagine a drier subject. Not so in the virtual world. In one Cisco game, players must put the network together on Mars. In a sandstorm. "Our employees learn without realizing they are learning," says Field. Sounds suspiciously like fun.

SOURCE: Reena Jana, "On-the-Job Video Gaming," *BusinessWeek*, March 27, 2006.

### Questions

1. Considering the features of a good learning environment discussed in this chapter, how can video games enhance learning?
2. How can video games enhance transfer of training?
3. What features do you believe are essential for a video game to be used for training? Why?
4. What types of skills are best trained using video games? Why?

## NOTES

1. R. Hughes and K. Beatty, "Five Steps to Leading Strategically," *Training and Development*, July 2001, pp. 32–38; I. I. Goldstein and P. Gilliam, "Training Systems Issues in the Year 2000," *American Psychologist* 45 (1990), pp. 134–43; E. Salas and J. A. Cannon-Bowers, "The Science of Training: A Decade of Progress," *Annual Review of Psychology* 52 (2002), pp. 471–99.
2. J. B. Quinn, P. Anderson, and S. Finkelstein, "Leveraging Intellect," *Academy of Management Executive* 10 (1996), pp. 7–27; R. Brinkenhoff and A. Apking, *High Impact Learning* (Cambridge, MA: Perseus, 2001).
3. T. T. Baldwin, C. Danielson, and W. Wiggenhorn, "The Evolution of Learning Strategies in Organizations: From Employee Development to Business Redefinition," *Academy of Management Executive* 11 (1997), pp. 47–58; J. J. Martocchio and T. T. Baldwin, "The Evolution of Strategic Organizational Training," in *Research in Personnel and Human Resource Management* 15, ed. G. R. Ferris (Greenwich, CT: JAI Press, 1997), pp. 1–46.
4. A. P. Carnevale, "America and the New Economy," *Training and Development Journal*, November 1990, pp. 31–52.
5. J. M. Rosow and R. Zager, *Training: The Competitive Edge* (San Francisco: Jossey-Bass, 1988).
6. L. Thornburg, "Accounting for Knowledge," *HR Magazine*, October 1994, pp. 51–56; T. A. Stewart, "Mapping Corporate Brainpower," *Fortune*, October 30, 1995, p. 209.
7. D. Miller, "A Preliminary Typology of Organizational Learning: Synthesizing the Literature," *Strategic Management Journal* 22 (1996), pp. 484–505; ed. S. Jackson, M. Hitt, and A. DeNisi, *Managing Knowledge for Sustained Competitive Advantage* (San Francisco: Jossey-Bass, 2003).
8. D. Delong and L. Fahey, "Diagnosing Cultural Barriers to Knowledge Management," *Academy of Management Executive* 14 (2000), pp. 113–27; A. Rossett, "Knowledge Management Meets Analysis," *Training and Development*, May 1999, pp. 71–78.
9. I. Nonaka and H. Takeuchi, *The Knowledge Creating Company* (New York: Oxford University Press, 1995).

10. R. Davenport. "A New Shade of Big Blue," *TD*, May 2005, pp. 35–40.
11. R. Noe, *Employee Training and Development*, 4th ed. (New York: Irwin/McGraw-Hill, 2008.
12. Ibid.
13. Based on Steelcase company Web site, www.steelcase.com; G. Wolfe, "Steelcase: Demonstrating the Connection between Learning and Strategic Business Results," *TD*, April 2005, pp. 28–34; T. Bingham and P. Galagan, "At c-Level: James P. Hackett, President and CEO, Steelcase," *TD*, April 2005, pp. 22–26.
14. J. B. Tracey, S. I. Tannenbaum, and M. J. Kavanaugh, "Applying Trained Skills on the Job: The Importance of the Work Environment," *Journal of Applied Psychology* 80 (1995), pp. 239–52; E. Holton, R. Bates, and W. Ruona, "Development of a Generalized Learning Transfer System Inventory," *Human Resource Development Quarterly* 11(2001), pp. 333–60; E. Helton III and T. Baldwin, eds., *Improving Learning Transfer in Organizations* (San Francisco: Jossey-Bass, 2003); J. S. Russell, J. R. Terborg, and M. L. Powers, "Organizational Performance and Organizational Level Training and Support," *Personnel Psychology* 38 (1985), pp. 849–63.
15. S. Tannenbaum, "A Strategic View of Organizational Training and Learning," in *Creating, Implementing, and Managing Effective Training and Development*, ed. K. Kraiger (San Francisco: Jossey-Bass, 2002), pp. 10–52.
16. A. P. Carnevale, L. J. Gainer, and J. Villet, *Training in America* (San Francisco: Jossey-Bass, 1990).
17. K. Ellis, "Smarter, Faster, Better," *Training*, April 2003, pp. 27–31.
18. M. Pollard and T. Malcolm, "Rapid Integration Eases Bank Reinvention," *TD*, August 2005, pp. 40–42.
19. K. Ellis, "The Mindset That Matters: Linking Learning to the Business," *Training*, May 2005, pp. 38–43.
20. B. Chapman, "How to Create the Ideal RFP," *Training*, January 2004, pp. 20–23; B. Gerber, "How to Buy Training Programs," *Training*, June 1989, pp. 59–68.
21. C. Reinhart, "How to Leap over Barriers to Performance," *Training and Development*, January 2000, pp. 20–29; G. Rummler, "In Search of the Holy Performance Grail," *Training and Development*, April 1996, pp. 26–31; D. G. Langdon, "Selecting Interventions," *Performance Improvement* 36 (1997), pp. 11–15.
22. R. F. Mager and P. Pipe, *Analyzing Performance Problems: Or You Really Oughta Wanna*, 2nd ed. (Belmont, CA: Pittman Learning, 1984); A. P. Carnevale, L. J. Gainer, and A. S. Meltzer, *Workplace Basics Training Manual*, 1990 (San Francisco: Jossey-Bass, 1990); Rummler, "In Search of the Holy Performance Grail."
23. C. E. Schneier, J. P. Guthrie, and J. D. Olian, "A Practical Approach to Conducting and Using Training Needs Assessment," *Public Personnel Management*, Summer 1988, pp. 191–205.
24. I. Goldstein, "Training in Organizations," in *Handbook of Industrial/Organizational Psychology*, 2nd ed., ed. M. D. Dunnette and L. M. Hough (Palo Alto, CA: Consulting Psychologists Press, 1991), vol. 2, pp. 507–619.
25. E. F. Holton III and C. Bailey, "Top-to-Bottom Curriculum Redesign," *Training and Development*, March 1995, pp. 40–44.
26. R. A. Noe, "Trainees' Attributes and Attitudes: Neglected Influences on Training Effectiveness," *Academy of Management Review* 11 (1986), pp. 736–49.
27. T. T. Baldwin, R. T. Magjuka, and B. T. Loher, "The Perils of Participation: Effects of Choice on Trainee Motivation and Learning," *Personnel Psychology* 44 (1991), pp. 51–66; S. I. Tannenbaum, J. E. Mathieu, E. Salas, and J. A. Cannon-Bowers, "Meeting Trainees' Expectations: The Influence of Training Fulfillment on the Development of Commitment, Self-Efficacy, and Motivation," *Journal of Applied Psychology* 76 (1991), pp. 759–69.
28. M. E. Gist, C. Schwoerer, and B. Rosen, "Effects of Alternative Training Methods on Self-Efficacy and Performance in Computer Software Training," *Journal of Applied Psychology* 74 (1989), pp. 884–91; J. Martocchio and J. Dulebohn, "Performance Feedback Effects in Training: The Role of Perceived Controllability," *Personnel Psychology* 47 (1994), pp. 357–73; J. Martocchio, "Ability Conceptions and Learning," *Journal of Applied Psychology* 79 (1994), pp. 819–25.
29. W. D. Hicks and R. J. Klimoski, "Entry into Training Programs and Its Effects on Training Outcomes: A Field Experiment," *Academy of Management Journal* 30 (1987), pp. 542–52.
30. R. A. Noe and N. Schmitt, "The Influence of Trainee Attitudes on Training Effectiveness: Test of a Model," *Personnel Psychology* 39 (1986), pp. 497–523.
31. M. A. Quinones, "Pretraining Context Effects: Training Assignments as Feedback," *Journal of Applied Psychology* 80 (1995), pp. 226–38; Baldwin, Magjuka, and Loher, "The Perils of Participation."
32. L. H. Peters, E. J. O'Connor, and J. R. Eulberg, "Situational Constraints: Sources, Consequences, and Future Considerations," in *Research in Personnel and Human Resource Management*, ed. K. M. Rowland and G. R. Ferris (Greenwich, CT: JAI Press, 1985), vol. 3, pp. 79–114; E. J. O'Connor, L. H. Peters, A. Pooyan, J. Weekley, B. Frank, and B. Erenkranz, "Situational Constraints Effects on Performance, Affective Reactions, and Turnover: A Field Replication and Extension," *Journal of Applied Psychology* 69 (1984), pp. 663–72; D. J. Cohen, "What Motivates Trainees?" *Training and Development Journal*, November 1990, pp. 91–93; Russell, Terborg, and Powers, "Organizational Performance."
33. J. Casner-Lotto and L. Barrington, "Are They Ready to Work?" in (*United States: The Conference Board, Corporate Voices for Working Families, Partnerships for 21st Century Skills and Society for Human Resource Management*, 2006; R. Davenport, "Eliminate the Skills Gap," *TD*, February 2006, pp. 26–34; M. Schoeff, "Amid Calls to Bolster U.S. Innovation, Experts Lament Paucity of Basic Math Skills," *Workforce Management*, March 2006, pp. 46–49.
34. J. Nunally, *Psychometric Theory* (New York: McGraw-Hill, 1978).
35. L. Gottsfredson, "The g Factor in Employment," *Journal of Vocational Behavior* 19 (1986), pp. 293–96.
36. M. J. Ree and J. A. Earles, "Predicting Training Success: Not Much More Than g," *Personnel Psychology* 44 (1991), pp. 321–32.
37. D. R. Torrence and J. A. Torrence, "Training in the Face of Illiteracy," *Training and Development Journal*, August 1987, pp. 44–49.
38. C. E. Schneier, "Training and Development Programs: What Learning Theory and Research Have to Offer," *Personnel Journal*, April 1974, pp. 288–93; M. Knowles, "Adult Learning," in *Training and Development Handbook*, 3rd ed., ed. R. L. Craig (New York: McGraw-Hill, 1987), pp. 168–79; R. Zemke and S. Zemke, "30 Things We Know for Sure about Adult Learning," *Training*, June 1981, pp. 45–52; B. J. Smith and B. L. Delahaye, *How to Be an Effective Trainer*, 2nd ed. (New York: John Wiley and Sons, 1987).

39. Unisys Corporation Web site www.unisys.com; J. Salopek, "Unisys Corporation 2004 Best Award Winner," *TD*, October 2004, p. 3; J. Salopek, "Colorado Springs Utilities 2005 Best Award Winner," *TD*, October 2005, pp. 38–40; J. Salopek, "Toshiba America Business Solutions 2005 Best Award Winner," *TD*, October 2005, p. 67; J. Schettler, "Exelon Energy Delivery," *Training*, March 2003, p. 64; S. Caudron, "Learners Speak Out," *Training and Development*, April 2000, pp. 52–57.
40. D. Stamps, "Communities of Practice," *Training*, February 1997, pp. 35–42.
41. D. Goldwasser, "Me, a Trainer," *Training*, April 2001, pp. 61–66.
42. S. Allen, "Water Cooler Wisdom," *Training*, August 2005, pp. 30–34.
43. E. Holton III and T. Baldwin, eds, *Improving Learning Transfer in Organizations* (San Francisco: Jossey-Bass, 2003); J. B. Tracey, S. I. Tannenbaum, and M. J. Kavanaugh, "Applying Trained Skills on the Job: The Importance of the Work Environment," *Journal of Applied Psychology* 80 (1995), pp. 239–52; P. E. Tesluk, J. L. Farr, J. E. Mathieu, and R. J. Vance, "Generalization of Employee Involvement Training to the Job Setting: Individual and Situational Effects," *Personnel Psychology* 48 (1995), pp. 607–32; J. K. Ford, M. A. Quinones, D. J. Sego, and J. S. Sorra, "Factors Affecting the Opportunity to Perform Trained Tasks on the Job," *Personnel Psychology* 45 (1992), pp. 511–27.
44. D. Goldwasser, "Me, a Trainer."
45. J. Gordon, "Getting Serious about Supervisory Training," *Training*, February 2006, pp. 27–29.
46. J. M. Cusimano, "Managers as Facilitators," *Training and Development* 50 (1996), pp. 31–33.
47. C. M. Petrini, ed., "Bringing It Back to Work," *Training and Development Journal*, December 1990, pp. 15–21.
48. Ford, Quinones, Sego, and Sorra, "Factors Affecting the Opportunity to Perform Trained Tasks on the Job."
49. Ibid.; M. A. Quinones, J. K. Ford, D. J. Sego, and E. M. Smith, "The Effects of Individual and Transfer Environment Characteristics on the Opportunity to Perform Trained Tasks," *Training Research Journal* 1 (1995/96), pp. 29–48.
50. G. Stevens and E. Stevens, "The Truth about EPSS," *Training and Development* 50 (1996), pp. 59–61.
51. "In Your Face EPSSs," *Training*, April 1996, pp. 101–2.
52. S. E. Jackson, M. A. Hitt, and A. S. Denisi, eds., *Managing Knowledge for Sustained Competitive Advantage: Designing Strategies for Effective Human Resource Management* (San Francisco: Jossey-Bass, 2003); A. Rossett, "Knowledge Management Meets Analysis," *Training and Development*, May 1999, pp. 63–68; R. Davenport, "Why Does Knowledge Management Still Matter?" *T+D* 59 (2005), pp. 19–23.
53. J. MacGregor, "The Office Chart That Really Counts," *BusinessWeek*, February 27, 2006, pp. 48–49.
54. V. Powers, "Virtual Communities at Caterpillar Foster Knowledge Sharing," *TD*, June 2004, pp. 40–45.
55. R. D. Marx, "Relapse Prevention for Managerial Training: A Model for Maintenance of Behavior Change," *Academy of Management Review* 7 (1982), pp. 433–41; G. P. Latham and C. A. Frayne, "Self-Management Training for Increasing Job Attendance: A Follow-up and Replication," *Journal of Applied Psychology* 74 (1989), pp. 411–16.
56. P. Keller, "Soaring to New Safety Heights," *TD*, January 2006, pp. 51–54. Also see "About Us" on the Vanderbilt University Medical Center Web site at www.mc.vanderbilt.edu.
57. "Putting the Distance into Distance Learning," *Training*, October 1995, pp. 111–18.
58. D. Picard, "The Future Is Distance Training," *Training*, November 1996, pp. s3–s10.
59. A. F. Maydas, "On-line Networks Build the Savings into Employee Education," *HR Magazine*, October 1997, pp. 31–35.
60. J. M. Rosow and R. Zager, *Training: The Competitive Edge* (San Francisco: Jossey-Bass, 1988).
61. Training Top 100 Best Practices 2006, "General Mills," *Training*, March 2006, p. 61.
62. S. Alexander, "Reducing the Learning Burden," *Training*, September 2002, pp. 32–34.
63. H. Dolezalek, "Industry Training Report," *Training*, October 2004, pp. 33–34.
64. T. Skylar, "When Training Collides with a 35-Ton Truck," *Training*, March 1996, pp. 32–38.
65. R. B. Cohn, "How to Choose a Video Producer," *Training*, July 1996, pp. 58–61.
66. E. Wagner and P. Wilson, "Disconnected," *TD*, December 2005, pp. 40–43; J. Bronstein and A. Newman, "IM Learning," *TD*, February 2006, pp. 47–50.
67. M. Weinstein, "Ready or Not, Here Comes Podcasting," *Training*, January 2006, pp. 22–23; D. Sussman, "Now Here This," *TD*, September 2005, pp. 53–54; J. Pont, "Employee Training on iPod Playlist," *Workforce Management*, August 2005, p. 18.
68. E. Wagner and P. Wilson, "Disconnected," *TD*, December 2005, pp. 40–43.
69. B. Filipczak, "Who Owns Your OJT?" *Training*, December 1996, pp. 44–49.
70. Ibid.
71. D. B. Youst and L. Lipsett, "New Job Immersion without Drowning," *Training and Development Journal*, February 1989, pp. 73–75; G. M. Piskurich, *Self-Directed Learning* (San Francisco: Jossey-Bass, 1993).
72. G. M. Piskurich, "Self-Directed Learning," in *The ASTD Training and Development Handbook*, 4th ed., pp. 453–72; G. M. Piskurich, "Developing Self-Directed Learning," *Training and Development*, March 1994, pp. 31–36.
73. P. Warr and D. Bunce, "Trainee Characteristics and the Outcomes of Open Learning," *Personnel Psychology* 48 (1995), pp. 347–75.
74. C. M. Solomon, "When Training Doesn't Translate," *Workforce* 76, no. 3 (1997), pp. 40–44.
75. R. W. Glover, *Apprenticeship Lessons from Abroad* (Columbus, OH: National Center for Research in Vocational Education, 1986).
76. Commerce Clearing House, Inc., *Orientation–Training* (Chicago, IL: Personnel Practices Communications, Commerce Clearing House, 1981), pp. 501–905.
77. A. H. Howard III, "Apprenticeships," in *The ASTD Training and Development Handbook*, pp. 803–13.
78. M. Rowh, "The Rise of the Apprentice," *Human Resource Executive*, January 2006, pp. 38–43.
79. A. Ciaccio, "You're Hired: Goldcorp Stint Touts Opportunities in Mining," *The Wall Street Journal*, September 25, 2005, p. B6.
80. *Eldredge v. Carpenters JATC* (1981), 27 Fair Employment Practices (Bureau of National Affairs), p. 479.
81. M. Pramik, "Installers Learn on Practice Dwellings," *Columbus Dispatch*, February 7, 2003, p. F1.
82. C. Cornell, "Better than the Real Thing?" *Human Resource Executive*, August 2005, pp. 34–37.
83. J. Borzo, "Almost Human," *The Wall Street Journal*, May 24, 2004, pp. R1, R10; J. Hoff, "My Virtual Life," *BusinessWeek*, May 1, 2006, pp. 72–78.

84. N. Adams, "Lessons from the Virtual World," *Training*, June 1995, pp. 45–48.
85. Ibid.
86. Cornell, "Better than the Real Thing?"; E. Frauenheim," Can Video Games Win Points as Teaching Tools?" *Workforce Management*, April 10, 2006, pp. 12–14; S. Boehle, "Simulations: The Next Generation of e-Learning," *Training*, January 2005, pp. 22–31; Borzo, "Almost human."
87. Cornell, "Better than the Real Thing?"
88. T. W. Shreeve, "On the Case at the CIA," *Training and Development*, March 1997, pp. 53–54.
89. "Business War Games," *Training*, December 2002, p. 18.
90. M. Hequet, "Games That Teach," *Training*, July 1995, pp. 53–58.
91. G. P. Latham and L. M. Saari, "Application of Social Learning Theory to Training Supervisors through Behavior Modeling," *Journal of Applied Psychology* 64 (1979), pp. 239–46.
92. E. Hollis, "Shoney's: Workforce Development on the Side," *Chief Learning Officer*, March 2003, pp. 32–34.
93. Hannum, *Application of Emerging Training Technology*.
94. M. Rosenberg, *E-Learning: Strategies for Delivering Knowledge in the Digital Age* (New York: McGraw-Hill, 2001).
95. P. Galagan, "The E-Learning Revolution," *Training and Development*, December 2000, pp. 24–30; D. Khirallah, "A New Way to Learn," *Information Week Online* (May 22, 2000).
96. M. Gold, "E-Learning, the Lucent Way," *TD*, July 2003, pp. 46–50.
97. "Learning Management Systems: An Executive Summary," *Training*, March 2002, p. 4.
98. D. Sussman, "The LMS Value," *TD*, July 2005, pp. 43–45.
99. D. Brown and D. Harvey, *An Experiential Approach to Organizational Development* (Englewood Cliffs, NJ: Prentice Hall, 2000); J. Schettler, "Learning by Doing," *Training*, April 2002, pp. 38–43.
100. Schettler, "Learning by Doing."
101. R. J. Wagner, T. T. Baldwin, and C. C. Rowland, "Outdoor Training: Revolution or Fad?" *Training and Development Journal*, March 1991, pp. 51–57; C. J. Cantoni, "Learning the Ropes of Teamwork," *The Wall Street Journal*, October 2, 1995, p. A14.
102. C. Steinfeld, "Challenge Courses Can Build Strong Teams," *Training and Development*, April 1997, pp. 12–13.
103. D. Mishev, "Cooking for the Company," *Cooking Light*, August 2004, pp. 142–47.
104. P. F. Buller, J. R. Cragun, and G. M. McEvoy, "Getting the Most out of Outdoor Training," *Training and Development Journal*, March 1991, pp. 58–61.
105. C. Clements, R. J. Wagner, C. C. Roland, "The Ins and Outs of Experiential Training," *Training and Development*, February 1995, pp. 52–56.
106. Ibid.
107. S. Carey, "Racing to Improve," *The Wall Street Journal*, March 24, 2006, pp. B1, B6.
108. P. Froiland, "Action Learning," *Training*, January 1994, pp. 27–34.
109. "A Team Effort," *Training*, September 2002, p. 18.
110. H. Lancaster, "This Kind of Black Belt Can Help You Score Some Points at Work," *The Wall Street Journal*, September 14, 1999, p. B1; S. Gale, "Building Frameworks for Six Sigma Success," *Workforce*, May 2003, pp. 64–66.
111. J. DeFeo, "An ROI Story," *Training and Development*, July 2000, pp. 25–27.
112. S. Gale, "Six Sigma Is a Way of Life," *Workforce* May 2003, pp. 67–68.
113. K. Kraiger, J. K. Ford, and E. Salas, "Application of Cognitive, Skill-Based, and Affective Theories of Learning Outcomes to New Methods of Training Evaluation," *Journal of Applied Psychology* 78 (1993), pp. 311–28; J. J. Phillips, "ROI: The Search for Best Practices," *Training and Development*, February 1996, pp. 42–47; D. L. Kirkpatrick, "Evaluation of Training," in *Training and Development Handbook*, 2nd ed., ed. R. L. Craig (New York: McGraw-Hill, 1976), pp. 18-1 to 18–27.
114. B. Gerber, "Does Your Training Make a Difference? Prove It!" *Training*, March 1995, pp. 27–34.
115. A. P. Carnevale and E. R. Schulz, "Return on Investment: Accounting for Training," *Training and Development Journal*, July 1990, pp. S1–S32; P. R. Sackett and E. J. Mullen, "Beyond Formal Experimental Design: Toward an Expanded View of the Training Evaluation Process," *Personnel Psychology* 46 (1993), pp. 613–27; S. I. Tannenbaum and S. B. Woods, "Determining a Strategy for Evaluating Training: Operating within Organizational Constraints," *Human Resource Planning* 15 (1992), pp. 63–81; R. D. Arvey, S. E. Maxwell, and E. Salas, "The Relative Power of Training Evaluation Designs under Different Cost Configurations," *Journal of Applied Psychology* 77 (1992), pp. 155–60.
116. D. A. Grove and C. O. Ostroff, "Program Evaluation," in *Developing Human Resources*, ed. K. N. Wexley (Washington, DC: BNA Books, 1991), pp. 185–219.
117. D. Sussman, "Strong Medicine Required," *TD*, November 2005, pp. 34–38.
118. Carnevale and Schulz, "Return on Investment."
119. Ibid.; G. Kearsley, *Costs, Benefits, and Productivity in Training Systems* (Boston: Addison-Wesley, 1982).
120. Ibid.
121. D. G. Robinson and J. Robinson, "Training for Impact," *Training and Development Journal*, August 1989, pp. 30–42.
122. Sussman, "Strong Medicine Required."
123. B. Ettorre, "Let's Hear It for Local Talent," *Management Review*, October 1994, p. 9; S. Franklin, "A New World Order for Business Strategy," *Chicago Tribune*, May 15, 1994, sec. 19, pp. 7–8.
124. R. L. Tung, "Selection and Training of Personnel for Overseas Assignments," *Columbia Journal of World Business* 16 (1981), pp. 18–78.
125. W. A. Arthur Jr. and W. Bennett Jr., "The International Assignee: The Relative Importance of Factors Perceived to Contribute to Success," *Personnel Psychology* 48 (1995), pp. 99–114; G. M. Spreitzer, M. W. McCall Jr., and Joan D. Mahoney, "Early Identification of International Executive Potential," *Journal of Applied Psychology* 82 (1997), pp. 6–29.
126. J. S. Black and J. K. Stephens, "The Influence of the Spouse on American Expatriate Adjustment and Intent to Stay in Pacific Rim Overseas Assignments," *Journal of Management* 15 (1989), pp. 529–44; M. Shaffer and D. A. Harrison, "Forgotten Partners of International Assignments: Development and Test of a Model of Spouse Adjustment," *Journal of Applied Psychology* 86 (2001), pp. 238–54.
127. M. Shaffer, D. A. Harrison, H. Gregersen, J. S. Black, and L. A. Ferzandi, "You Can Take It with You: Individual Differences and Expatriate Effectiveness," *Journal of Applied Psychology* 91(2006), pp. 109–25; P. Caligiuri, "The Big Five Personality Characteristics as Predictors of Expatriate's Desire to Terminate the Assignment and Supervisor-Rated Performance," *Personnel Psychology* 53 (2000), pp. 67–88.

128. E. Dunbar and A. Katcher, "Preparing Managers for Foreign Assignments," *Training and Development Journal*, September 1990, pp. 45–47.
129. J. S. Black and M. Mendenhall, "A Practical but Theory-Based Framework for Selecting Cross-Cultural Training Methods," in *Readings and Cases in International Human Resource Management*, ed. M. Mendenhall and G. Oddou (Boston: PWS-Kent, 1991), pp. 177–204.
130. P. Tam, "Culture Course," *The Wall Street Journal*, May 25, 2004, pp. B1, B12.
131. S. Ronen, "Training the International Assignee," in *Training and Development in Organizations*, ed. I. L. Goldstein (San Francisco: Jossey-Bass, 1989), pp. 417–53.
132. P. R. Harris and R. T. Moran, *Managing Cultural Differences* (Houston: Gulf, 1991).
133. J. Carter, "Globe Trotters," *Training*, August 2005, pp. 22–28.
134. C. Solomon, "Unhappy Trails," *Workforce*, August 2000, pp. 36–41.
135. J. Ramirez, "Lost in the Shuffle," *Human Resource Executive*, January 2006, pp. 54–57.
136. H. Lancaster, "Before Going Overseas, Smart Managers Plan Their Homecoming," *The Wall Street Journal*, September 28, 1999, p. B1; A. Halcrow, "Expats: The Squandered Resource," *Workforce*, April 1999, pp. 42–48.
137. Harris and Moran, *Managing Cultural Differences*.
138. J. Cook, "Rethinking Relocation," *Human Resources Executive*, June 2, 2003, pp. 23–26.
139. J. Flynn, "E-Mail, Cellphones, and Frequent-Flier Miles Let 'Virtual' Expats Work Abroad but Live at Home," *The Wall Street Journal*, October 25, 1999, p. A26; J. Flynn, "Multinationals Help Career Couples Deal with Strains Affecting Expatriates," *The Wall Street Journal*, August 8, 2000, p. A19; C. Solomon, "The World Stops Shrinking," *Workforce*, January 2000, pp. 48–51.
140. S. E. Jackson and Associates, *Diversity in the Workplace: Human Resource Initiatives* (New York: Guilford Press, 1992).
141. M. Lee, "Post-9/11 Training," *TD*, September 2002, pp. 33–35.
142. R. R. Thomas, "Managing Diversity: A Conceptual Framework," in *Diversity in the Workplace* (New York: Guilford Press), pp. 306–18.
143. M. E. Heilman, C. J. Block, and J. A. Lucas, "Presumed Incompetent? Stigmatization and Affirmative Action Efforts," *Journal of Applied Psychology* 77 (1992), pp. 536–44.
144. B. Gerber, "Managing Diversity," *Training*, July 1990, pp. 23–30; T. Diamante, C. L. Reid, and L. Ciylo, "Making the Right Training Moves," *HR Magazine*, March 1995, pp. 60–65.
145. L. Egodigwe, "Back to Class," *The Wall Street Journal*, November 14, 2005, p. R4.
146. S. M. Paskoff, "Ending the Workplace Diversity Wars," *Training*, August 1996, pp. 43–47; H. B. Karp and N. Sutton, "Where Diversity Training Goes Wrong," *Training*, July 1993, pp. 30–34.
147. Paskoff, "Ending the Workplace Diversity Wars."
148. L. Lavelle, "For UPS Managers, a School of Hard Knocks," *BusinessWeek*, July 22, 2002, pp. 58–59; M. Berkley, "UPS Community Internship Program (CIP) Fact Sheet" (Atlanta, GA: United Parcel Service, 2003).
149. A. Markels, "Diversity Program Can Prove Divisive," *The Wall Street Journal*, January, 30, 1997, pp. B1–B2; "R. R. Donnelley Curtails Diversity Training Moves," *The Wall Street Journal*, February 13, 1997, p. B3.
150. S. Rynes and B. Rosen, "A Field Study of Factors Affecting the Adoption and Perceived Success of Diversity Training," *Personnel Psychology* 48 (1995), pp. 247–70.
151. T. Kochan, K. Bezrukova, R. Ely, S. Jackson, A. Joshi, K. Jehn, J. Leonard, D. Levine, and D. Thomas, "The Effects of Diversity on Business Performance: Report of the Diversity Research Network," *Human Resource Management* 42 (2003), pp. 8–21; F. Hansen, "Diversity's Business Case Just Doesn't Add Up," *Workforce*, June 2003, pp. 29–32; M. J. Wesson and C. I. Gogus, "Shaking Hands with the Computer: An Examination of Two Methods of Newcomer Socialization," *Journal of Applied Psychology* 90 (2005), pp. 1018–26; H. J. Klein and N. A., Weaver, "The Effectiveness of an Organizational-Level Orientation Training Program in the Socialization of New Hires," *Personnel Psychology* 53 (2000), pp. 47–66.
152. C. Terhune, "Pepsi, Vowing Diversity Isn't Just Image Polish, Seeks Inclusive Culture," *The Wall Street Journal*, April 19, 2005, p. B1.
153. H. Rosin, "Cultural Revolution at Texaco," *The New Republic*, February 2, 1998, pp. 15–18; K. Labich, "No More Crude at Texaco," *Fortune*, September 6, 1999, pp. 205–12.
154. See Social Responsibility section of www.chevrontexaco.com, Web site for Chevron Texaco.
155. I. Speizer, "Diversity on the Menu," *Workforce Management*, November 2004, pp. 41–45; F. Jossi, "Cultivating Diversity," *Human Resource Executive*, December 2004, pp. 37–40.
156. C. T. Schreiber, K. F. Price, and A. Morrison, "Workforce Diversity and the Glass Ceiling: Practices, Barriers, Possibilities," *Human Resource Planning* 16 (1994), pp. 51–69.
157. D. C. Feldman, "A Contingency Theory of Socialization," *Administrative Science Quarterly* 21 (1976), pp. 433–52; D. C. Feldman, "A Socialization Process That Helps New Recruits Succeed," *Personnel* 57 (1980), pp. 11–23; J. P. Wanous, A. E. Reichers, and S. D. Malik, "Organizational Socialization and Group Development: Toward an Integrative Perspective," *Academy of Management Review* 9 (1984), pp. 670–83; C. L. Adkins, "Previous Work Experience and Organizational Socialization: A Longitudinal Examination," *Academy of Management Journal* 38 (1995), pp. 839–62; E. W. Morrison, "Longitudinal Study of the Effects of Information Seeking on Newcomer Socialization," *Journal of Applied Psychology* 78 (1993), pp. 173–83.
158. M. R. Louis, "Surprise and Sense Making: What Newcomers Experience in Entering Unfamiliar Organizational Settings," *Administrative Science Quarterly* 25 (1980), pp. 226–51.
159. For example see J. D. Kammeyer-Mueller and C. R. Wanberg, "Unwrapping the Organizational Entry Process: Disentangling Multiple Antecedents and Their Pathway to Adjustment," *Journal of Applied Psychology* 88 (2003), pp. 779–94; M. R. Buckley, D. B. Fedor, J. G. Veres, D. S. Wiese, and S. M. Carraher, "Investigating Newcomer Expectations and Job-Related Outcomes," *Journal of Applied Psychology* 83 (1998), pp. 452–61; G. W. Maier and J. C. Brunstein, "The Role of Personal Work Goals in Newcomers' Job Satisfaction and Organizational Commitment: A Longitudinal Analysis," *Journal of Applied Psychology* 86 (2001), pp. 1034–42.
160. M. Kirk, "E-Orientation," *Human Resource Executive*, October 2005, pp. 40–43.
161. D. C. Feldman, *Managing Careers in Organizations* (Glenview, IL: Scott Foresman, 1988). D. Reed-Mendenhall and C. W. Millard, "Orientation: A Training and Development

Tool," *Personnel Administrator* 25, no. 8 (1980), pp. 42–44; M. R. Louis, B. Z. Posner, and G. H. Powell, "The Availability and Helpfulness of Socialization Practices," *Personnel Psychology* 36 (1983), pp. 857–66; C. Ostroff and S. W. J. Kozlowski Jr., "Organizational Socialization as a Learning Process: The Role of Information Acquisition," *Personnel Psychology* 45 (1992), pp. 849–74; D. R. France and R. L. Jarvis, "Quick Starts for New Employees," *Training and Development*, October 1996, pp. 47–50.

162. J. Schettler, "Welcome to ACME Inc." *Training*, August 2002, pp. 36–43; J. Salopek, "A Story to Tell," *TD*, October 2005, pp. 54–56; D. Sussman, "A Monstrous Welcome," *TD*, April 2005, pp. 401–41; D. Sussman, "Getting Up to Speed," *TD*, December 2005, pp. 49–51.
163. M. Hammers, "Quashing Quick Quits," *Workforce*, May 2003, p. 50.
164. K. Rhodes, "Breaking in the Top Dogs," *Training*, February 2000, pp. 67–71

PART 3

# Assessment and Development of HRM

# 8

CHAPTER

# Performance Management

## LO LEARNING OBJECTIVES

After reading this chapter, you should be able to:

LO1 Identify the major determinants of individual performance. *page 344*

LO2 Discuss the three general purposes of performance management. *page 346*

LO3 Identify the five criteria for effective performance management systems. *page 351*

LO4 Discuss the four approaches to performance management, the specific techniques used in each approach, and the way these approaches compare with the criteria for effective performance management systems. *page 355*

LO5 Choose the most effective approach to performance measurement for a given situation. *page 374*

LO6 Discuss the advantages and disadvantages of the different sources of performance information. *page 375*

LO7 Choose the most effective source(s) for performance information for any situation. *page 375*

LO8 Distinguish types of rating errors and explain how to minimize each in a performance evaluation. *page 381*

LO9 Conduct an effective performance feedback session. *page 383*

LO10 Identify the cause of a performance problem. *page 385*

# Enter the World of Business

## Lions . . . Tigers . . . and Bears . . . and Performance Management

The Zoological Society of San Diego, which operates the San Diego Zoo, the San Diego Zoo's Wild Animal Park, and the Conservation and Research for Endangered Species scientific center, employs 2,600 people and has revenues of more than $160 million per year. For many years, performance appraisals were not a high priority. Measurement metrics used to rate employees were inconsistent, and managers not completing appraisals faced no consequences. Different versions of the one-page appraisal form were used. Managers evaluated employees on how well they thought they were doing rather than specific goals. Managers received annual cost-of-living raises not linked to their performance.

As part of the Zoological Society's emphasis on accountability outlined in the strategic plan, a new performance management system for its 225 managerial employees was recently developed. The goals for the system were to establish employee goals related to the organization's goals, include both a midyear and end-of-year performance review, and require year-end-review ratings be used to determine performance-based pay increases. Employee teams were used to help design the system. One team evaluated vendors from which a new appraisal system could be purchased. The other team investigated skills characterizing an effective leader. Use of the teams led to performance appraisals based on two categories: goals and leadership competencies. Goals and leadership competencies each make up 50 percent of the overall employee appraisal. At the beginning of each year managers choose five goals, with three linked to the organization's objectives, such as visitor satisfaction or revenue, and the other two targeted to the manger's specific work area. Employees are rated on six leadership competencies, each including five subfactors. For example, "professionalism" includes ratings on teamwork, communications, interpersonal relations, Zoological Society mission, and customer focus.

The Zoological Society chose a Web-based system that helps guide managers through the appraisal process. The system allows employees to record accomplishments in an online journal they can share with their manager. This helps to ensure the accuracy of performance reviews. It is especially useful for employees of the Zoological Society who are involved with many different conservation and other projects that their manager may not know about. The system also includes tools such as a "comment helper," which provides phrases to use in giving feedback, and a "language sensitivity checker," which flags offensive words and suggests alternatives. Despite the use of the Web-based system, HR requires that the appraisal must be given in person, with the manager printing and reviewing it or discussing the results with the employee as they review it on the computer screen. The manager must certify that a personal meeting occurred.

HR believes that the Web-based appraisal process has helped the zoo attract talented employees. Employees are attracted to companies that have clearly defined performance goals and objectives, offer timely feedback, and determine salary based on performance. Long-time employees like the system because it helps encourage discussions with managers, goal setting, and raises based on performance. Michele Stancer, who has been working at the zoo for 28 years, says, "If you perform well, you will get more. I think people should be held accountable. I've been here a long time. You see people who are 'working in retirement,' and that's not good for anyone."

Source: Based on T. Henneman, "Employee Performance Management: What's Gnu at the Zoo?" *Workforce Management Online* (September 2006).

# Introduction

Companies that seek competitive advantage through employees must be able to manage the behavior and results of all employees. Traditionally, the formal performance appraisal system was viewed as the primary means for managing employee performance. Performance appraisal was an administrative duty performed by managers and was primarily the responsibility of the human resource function. Managers now view performance appraisal as an annual ritual—they quickly complete the form and use it to catalog all the negative information they have collected on an employee over the previous year. Because they may dislike confrontation and feel that they don't know how to give effective evaluations, some managers spend as little time as possible giving employees feedback. Not surprisingly, most managers and employees dislike performance appraisals! The major reasons for this dislike include the lack of ongoing review, lack of employee involvement, and lack of recognition for good performance.[1]

Some have argued that all performance appraisal systems are flawed to the point that they are manipulative, abusive, autocratic, and counterproductive. Table 8.1 shows some of the criticism of performance appraisals and how the problems can be fixed. It is important to realize that the deficiencies shown in Table 8.1 are not the result of evaluating employee performance. Rather, they result from how the appraisal system is developed and used. As the chapter opener illustrated, if done correctly, performance appraisal can provide several valuable benefits to both employees and the company. An important part of appraising performance is to establish employee goals, which should be tied to the company's strategic goals. The performance appraisal process tells top performers that they are valued by the company. It requires managers to at least annually communicate to employees their performance strengths and deficiencies. A good appraisal process ensures that all employees doing similar jobs are evaluated according to the same standards. The use of technology, such as the Web, can reduce the administrative burden of performance appraisal and improve the

**table 8.1**

Problems and Possible Solutions in Performance Management

| PROBLEM | SOLUTION |
|---|---|
| Discourages teamwork | Make collaboration a criterion on which employees will be evaluated. |
| Evaluators are inconsistent or use different criteria and standards | Provide training for managers; have the HR department look for patterns on appraisals that suggest bias or over- or underevaluation. |
| Only valuable for very good or very poor employees | Evaluate specific behaviors or results to show specifically what employees need to improve. |
| Encourages employees to achieve short-term goals | Include both long-term and short-term goals in the appraisal process. |
| Manager has complete power over the employee | Managers should be appraised for how they appraise their employees. |
| Too subjective | Evaluate specific behavior or results. |
| Produces emotional anguish | Focus on behavior; do not criticize employees; conduct appraisal on time. |

SOURCES: Based on G. Latham, J. Almost, S. Mann, and C. Moore, "New Developments in Performance Management," *Organizational Dynamics* 34 (2005), pp. 77–87; J. A. Siegel, "86 Your Appraisal Process?" *HR Magazine*, October 2000, pp. 199–202.

accuracy of performance reviews. Also, a properly conducted appraisal can help the company identify the strongest and weakest employees. It can help legally justify many HRM decisions such as promotions, salary increases, discipline, and layoffs. Annually, *Fortune* magazine ranks the most globally admired companies. The Hay Group, which produces the Global Most Admired report for *Fortune*, says the companies on the list have chief executive officers who understand that performance measurement is about learning how to motivate people and link performance to rewards.[2] Many of the executives report that performance measurement encourages collaboration and cooperation. They believe performance measures help companies focus on operational excellence, customer loyalty, and development of people.

We believe that performance appraisal is only one part of the broader process of performance management. We define **performance management** as the process through which managers ensure that employees' activities and outputs are congruent with the organization's goals. Performance management is central to gaining competitive advantage.

**Performance Management**
The means through which managers ensure that employees' activities and outputs are congruent with the organization's goals.

Our performance management system has three parts: defining performance, measuring performance, and feeding back performance information. First, a performance management system specifies which aspects of performance are relevant to the organization, primarily through *job analysis* (discussed in Chapter 4). Second, it measures those aspects of performance through **performance appraisal,** which is only one method for managing employee performance. Third, it provides feedback to employees through **performance feedback** sessions so they can adjust their performance to the organization's goals. Performance feedback is also fulfilled through tying rewards to performance via the compensation system (such as through merit increases or bonuses), a topic to be covered in Chapters 11 and 12.

**Performance Appraisal**
The process through which an organization gets information on how well an employee is doing his or her job.

**Performance Feedback**
The process of providing employees information regarding their performance effectiveness.

In this chapter we examine a variety of approaches to performance management. First we provide a brief summary of current performance management practices. Next, we present a model of performance that helps us examine the system's purposes. Then we discuss specific approaches to performance management and the strengths and weaknesses of each. We also look at various sources of performance information. The errors resulting from subjective assessments of performance are presented, as well as the means for reducing those errors. Then we discuss some effective components to performance feedback. Finally, we address components of a legally defensible performance management system.

## The Practice of Performance Management

Several recent surveys of human resource professionals suggest that most companies' performance management practices require annual paper-driven reviews that include both behaviors and business goals.[3] Figure 8.1 shows performance management practices. While many companies use performance management to manage employee performance and make pay decision, less than 25 percent of the companies use performance management to help manage talent through identifying training needs and developing leadership talent. Over half of companies do provide managers with a suggested distribution for their ratings; that is, they suggest the percentage of a percentage of employees that should be rated in each rating category. This is critical for ensuring that companies are able to provide pay, rewards, and development activities that differentiate excellent, average, and poor performers. Sixty-six percent of companies used the same performance management system across all levels of the organization. Three in four

figure 8.1

Performance Management Practices

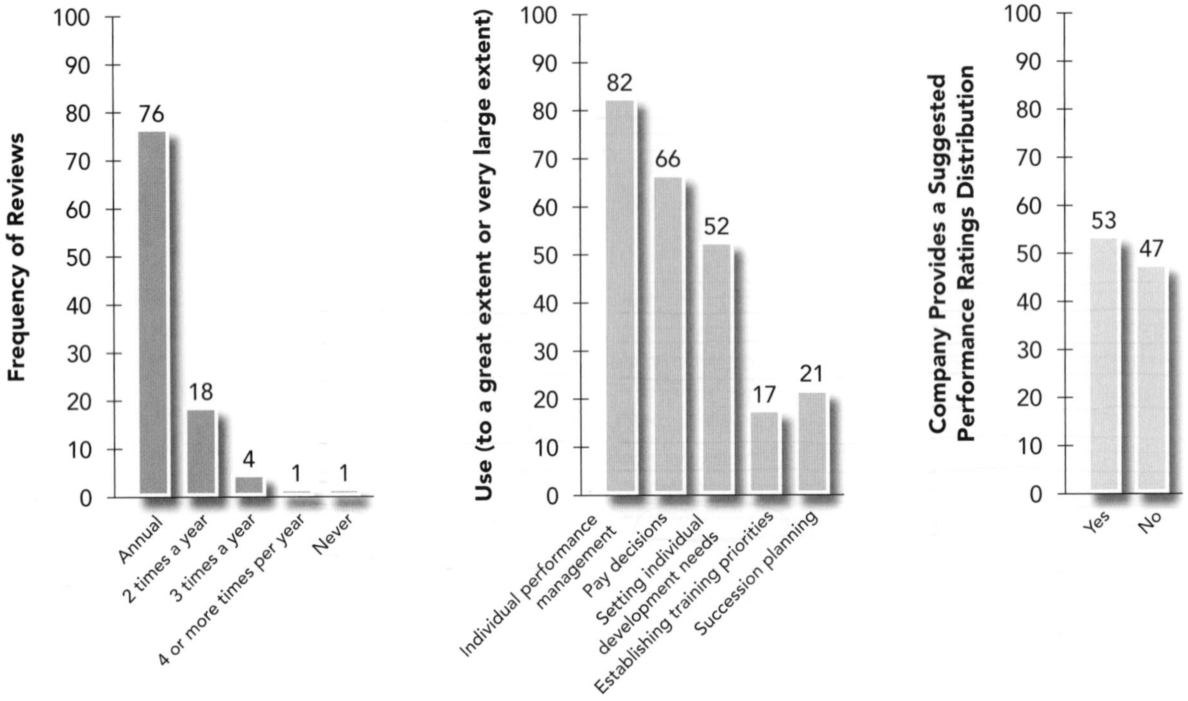


SOURCE: Based on A. Freedman, "Balancing Values, Results in Reviews," *Human Resource Executive*, August 2006, pp. 62–63.

companies' systems included a second-level review, with managers reviewing evaluations with their own manager before sharing results with employees. Only 28 percent of companies have automated their performance management system.

Because companies are interested in continuous improvement and creating engaged employees—employees who know what to do and are motivated to do it—many companies are moving to more frequent, streamlined performance reviews. For example, Green Mountain Coffee Roasters, which roasts, imports, and retails coffee beans to businesses, is moving toward more frequent reviews to ensure that employees know what they did well and what needs to be immediately changed so performance can improve. Whirlpool now requires managers to meet with employees at least quarterly to give feedback on how they are doing, how the company is doing, and how the business unit is performing. The new appraisal process requires completing a one-page online form that can be printed out for the meeting, if necessary.

## An Organizational Model of Performance Management

**LO1**
Identify the Major Determinants of Individual Performance.

For many years, researchers in the field of HRM and industrial–organizational psychology focused on performance appraisal as a measurement technique.[4] The goal of these performance appraisal systems was to measure individual employee performance reliably

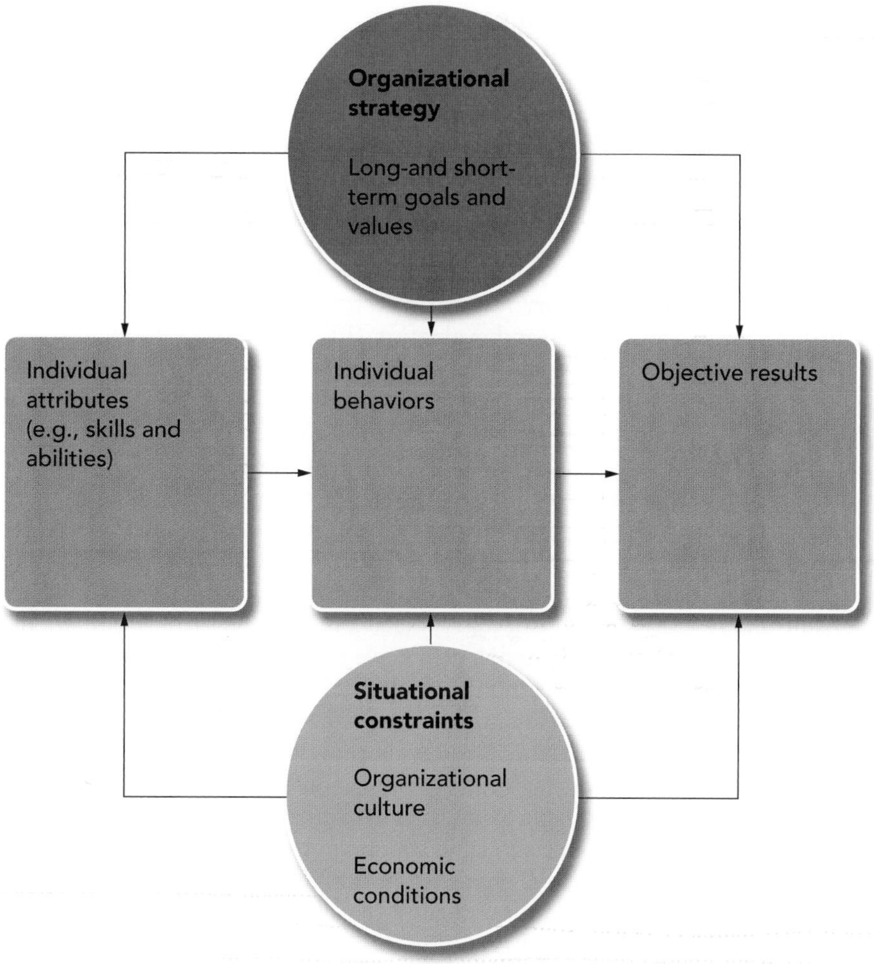


**figure 8.2**
Model of Performance Management in Organizations

and validly. This perspective, however, tended to ignore some important influences on the performance management process. Thus we begin this section by presenting the major purposes of performance management from an organizational rather than a measurement perspective. To do this, we need to understand the process of performance. Figure 8.2 depicts our process model of performance.

As the figure shows, individuals' attributes—their skills, abilities, and so on—are the raw materials of performance. For example, in a sales job, an organization wants someone who has good interpersonal skills and knowledge of the products. These raw materials are transformed into objective results through the employee's behavior. Employees can exhibit behaviors only if they have the necessary knowledge, skills, abilities, and other characteristics. Thus, employees with good product knowledge and interpersonal skills can talk about the advantages of various brands and can be friendly and helpful (not that they necessarily display those behaviors, only that they *can* display them). On the other hand, employees with little product knowledge or indifferent interpersonal skills cannot effectively display those behaviors. The objective results are the measurable, tangible outputs of the work, and they are a consequence of the employee's or the work group's behavior. In our example, a salesperson who displays the correct behaviors will likely make a number of sales.

**Performance Planning and Evaluation (PPE) System** Any system that seeks to tie the formal performance appraisal process to the company's strategies by specifying at the beginning of the evaluation period the types and level of performance that must be accomplished in order to achieve the strategy.

Another important component in our organizational model of the performance management system is the organization's strategy. The link between performance management and the organization's strategies and goals is often neglected. Chapter 2 pointed out that most companies pursue some type of strategy to attain their revenue, profit, and market share goals. Divisions, departments, work groups, and individuals within the company must align their activities with these strategies and goals. If they are not aligned, then the likelihood of achieving the goals becomes small. How is this link made in organizations? Primarily by specifying what needs to be accomplished and what behaviors must be exhibited for the company's strategy to be implemented. This link is being recognized as necessary more and more often, through the increasing popularity of **performance planning and evaluation (PPE) systems.** PPE systems seek to tie the formal performance appraisal process to the company's strategies by specifying at the beginning of the evaluation period the types and level of performance that must be accomplished to achieve the strategy. Then at the end of the evaluation period, individuals and groups are evaluated based on how closely their actual performance met the performance plan. In an ideal world, performance management systems would ensure that all activities support the organization's strategic goals.

Finally, our model notes that situational constraints are always at work within the performance management system. As discussed previously, an employee may have the necessary skills and yet not exhibit the necessary behaviors. Sometimes the organizational culture discourages the employee from doing effective things. Work group norms often dictate what the group's members do and the results they produce. On the other hand, some people are simply not motivated to exhibit the right behaviors. This often occurs if the employees do not believe their behaviors will be rewarded with pay raises, promotions, and so forth. Finally, people may be performing effective behaviors, and yet the right results do not follow. For example, an outstanding salesperson may not have a large dollar volume because the economy is bad and people are not buying.

Thus, as you can see in Figure 8.2, employees must have certain attributes to perform a set of behaviors and achieve some results. To gain competitive advantage, the attributes, behaviors, and results must be tied to the company's strategy. Regardless of the job or company, effective performance management systems measure performance criteria (such as behaviors or sales) as precisely as possible. Effective performance management systems also serve a strategic function by linking performance criteria to internal and external customer requirements. Effective performance management systems include a process for changing the system based on situational constraints. Besides serving a strategic purpose, performance management systems also have administrative and developmental purposes. We will next examine the various purposes of performance management systems.

## Purposes of Performance Management

**LO2**
Discuss the Three General Purposes of Performance Management.

The purposes of performance management systems are of three kinds: strategic, administrative, and developmental.

### Strategic Purpose

First and foremost, a performance management system should link employee activities with the organization's goals. One of the primary ways strategies are implemented is through defining the results, behaviors, and, to some extent, employee characteristics

Performance management is critical for executing a talent management system and involves one-on-one contact with managers to ensure that proper training and development are taking place.

that are necessary for carrying out those strategies, and then developing measurement and feedback systems that will maximize the extent to which employees exhibit the characteristics, engage in the behaviors, and produce the results.

Performance management is critical for companies to execute their talent management strategy, that is, to identify employees' strengths and weaknesses, link employees to appropriate training and development activity, and reward good performance with pay and other incentives. As we mentioned in Chapter 1, talent management is critical for competitiveness. At Just Born, the company that makes Peeps and Mike and Ike candy, the performance management system is part of the company's broader People Development System (PDS), which is designed to ensure both that learning and development align with business strategy and drive business results and that employees have the skills to succeed in their current and future jobs.[5] The PDS includes the performance management process, learning and career development processes, and succession planning process. Information from each of these systems is shared to ensure that, through training and on-the-job experiences, employees are developing the skills needed for their current jobs as well as preparing for their future career interests. Just Born's system starts with a planning meeting between the employee and his or her manager. At this meeting the employee's role and strategic goals of the department are discussed. The manager and employee agree on up to four personal objectives that will help the department meet its objectives and the employee achieve the specific items described in the job description. Two competencies that the employee needs to deliver or improve on are identified. The manager and employee work together to develop a learning plan to help the employee gain the competencies. During the year, the employee and manager meet to discuss the progress in meeting the goals and improving the competencies. Pay decisions made at the end of each fiscal year are based on the achievement of performance objectives and learning goals.

Performance management systems can even help develop global business (see the "Competing through Globalization" box on page 348).

## Administrative Purpose

Organizations use performance management information (performance appraisals, in particular) in many administrative decisions: salary administration (pay raises), promotions, retention–termination, layoffs, and recognition of individual performance.[6] Despite the importance of these decisions, however, many managers, who are the source of the information, see the performance appraisal process only as a necessary evil they must go through to fulfill their job requirements. They feel uncomfortable evaluating others and feeding those evaluations back to the employees. Thus, they tend to rate everyone high or at least rate them the same, making the performance appraisal information relatively useless. For example, one manager stated, "There is really no getting around the fact that whenever I evaluate one of my people, I stop and think about the impact—the ramifications of my

## COMPETING THROUGH GLOBALIZATION

### Going Global Requires a New Performance Management System

Kimberly-Clark developed a new performance management system to help support the company's business plan shift from a consumer products company to a global health and hygiene company. The base for the new system was a multidimensional rating that allowed human resources to set expectations and evaluate performance for business objectives and on-the job behaviors. The system focuses on what was accomplished and how it was accomplished. Employees provide a list of co-workers they want to be part of their rater team. The new system also includes a calibration process that brings managers together to jointly review the raters' assessment of their team members and to ensure that ratings across the company are consistent. All white-collar employees are asked to establish individual objectives that are aligned with the business sector and company objectives. Performance management for managers includes an evaluation of six global leadership qualities: visionary, inspirational, innovative, decisive, collaborative, and able to build talent. The entire system is online. Employee objectives can be found in a secure area of the company's intranet. Employees and managers can go online and review performance achievements. The most recent performance information, including results and behavioral observations, is available for appraisal meetings. All users have been trained to use the system through classroom and online meetings.

The results of the new system have been impressive. The online performance management system is available in 14 languages, making a common performance management system available worldwide to all Kimberly-Clark employees. A new leadership development competency model was developed. A new compensation system linked to the performance management system was introduced, giving managers the ability to better differentiate the pay and rewards of excellent, average, and poor performers. Employee surveys and focus groups have been used to evaluate the new process. Employees feel the system has helped them get more regular feedback and coaching from their managers and report that their performance objectives are aligned with the business strategy and more meaningful to them.

SOURCE: S. Miller, "Kimberly-Clark Corp.," *HR Magazine*, November 2006, pp. 64–68.

decisions on my relationship with the guy and his future here. . . . Call it being politically minded, or using managerial discretion, or fine-tuning the guy's ratings, but in the end, I've got to live with him, and I'm not going to rate a guy without thinking about the fallout."[7]

### Developmental Purpose

A third purpose of performance management is to develop employees who are effective at their jobs. When employees are not performing as well as they should, performance management seeks to improve their performance. The feedback given during a performance evaluation process often pinpoints the employee's weaknesses. Ideally, however, the performance management system identifies not only any deficient aspects of the employee's performance but also the causes of these deficiencies—for example, a skill deficiency, a motivational problem, or some obstacle holding the employee back.

Managers are often uncomfortable confronting employees with their performance weaknesses. Such confrontations, although necessary to the effectiveness of the work group, often strain everyday working relationships. Giving high ratings to all employees enables a manager to minimize such conflicts, but then the developmental purpose of the performance management system is not fully achieved.[8]

As you will see from this chapter there are many aspects to consider and a variety of choices for managers to make regarding performance management systems (e.g., source of performance information, approaches to measuring performance, and others). There is no one correct system that fits all companies. However, to make a performance management system that can best meet strategic, administrative, and developmental goals there are several things that should occur.[9] Table 8.2 provides recommendations for developing an effective performance management system that can meet strategic, administrative and developmental purposes. First, the system should ensure that values and beliefs are integrated into the system. For example, if

**table 8.2**

Recommendations for Developing an Effective Performance Management System

| |
|---|
| • Mirror the corporate culture and values. |
| • Have visible CEO and senior management support. |
| • Focus on the right company performance measures.<br>Vital or "critical few"—relate to strategy, mission, and goals.<br>Cascade company goals down the organization.<br>Goals are linked to business drivers. |
| • Link job descriptions to the performance management system.<br>Employees need to see the direct relationship between their job competencies, job description, and goals and objectives targeted in the performance plan.<br>Establish accountabilities. |
| • Differentiate performance fairly and effectively. |
| • Train managers in performance management. |
| • Link compensation to the performance management system.<br>Merit increases.<br>Annual incentives.<br>Long-term incentives.<br>Discretionary incentives. |
| • Communicate the total rewards system. |
| • Require managers to actively search out, offer, and acquire performance feedback on a regular basis.<br>Be involved in completing the performance cycle: planning, forecasting, progress review, end-of-year evaluation. |
| • Set clear expectations for employee development. |
| • Track effectiveness of the performance management system.<br>Is it able to identify trends in performance differentiation, pay differentiation, performance gaps/developmental needs?<br>Can data be shared with other applications (pay, training and development, workforce analysis, succession planning)? |
| • Adjust the system as required. |

SOURCES: Based on H. Aguinis, *Performance Management* (Upper Saddle River, NJ: Pearson Prentice Hall, 2007); A. Walker, "Is Performance Management as Simple as ABC?" *T+D,* February 2007, pp. 54–57; K . Oakes, "Performance Management Lacks Consistency," *T+D,* April 2007, pp. 50–53; L. Weatherly, *Performance Management: Getting It Right from the Start* (Alexandria, VA: Society for Human Resource Management, 2004); H. J. Bernardin, C. M. Hagan, J. S. Kane, and P. Villanova, "Effective Performance Management: A Focus on Precision Customers, and Situational Constraints," in *Performance Appraisal: State of the Art in Practice,* ed. J. S. Smither (San Francisco: Jossey-Bass, 1998), pp. 3–48.

employee involvement is an important value then self and/or peer appraisals should be part of the performance measurement process. Second, visible CEO and senior management support for the system is necessary. Studies show that senior management plays an important role in the design and implementation of the performance management system in most companies. The stronger the role of senior management the more likely lower level managers will take responsibility for ensuring that appraisals are completed and the system is used consistently across the company.[10] Third, the critical company performance measures should be identified. These should provide the best barometer of how the company is doing in relation to achieving its strategy and business goals. Fourth, job descriptions should be linked to the performance management system. Employees need to be able to see the link between their job requirements, their job descriptions, and the goals and objectives included in their performance plans. Fifth, be sure that the performance management system assesses employees fairly and objectively based on clearly understood standards of performance or in terms of their contribution relative to other employees. The system needs to identify poor, good, and excellent performance. Sixth, managers need to be trained in how to use the performance measurement system and how to give performance feedback on a daily basis as well as during the formal performance appraisal interview. Seventh, effective performance management systems link appraisals to financial rewards. Also, to effectively motivate employee performance with rewards, the program must be communicated and understood by employees. Eighth, employee training and development should be linked to the results of performance appraisals. Some companies establish a minimum number of training and development hours per year for each employee to set expectations. Finally, the effectiveness of the performance management system should be evaluated to make sure employee performance is linked to business goals and objectives and financial indicators such as return on investment. Based on the evaluation, the performance management system should be adjusted.

General Semiconductor has a workforce that is spread from North America to Asia and includes employees who speak five languages. Although General Semiconductor is headquartered on Long Island, New York, only 200 of its 5,600 employees are located in the United States. General Semiconductor makes power magnet components for the high-tech industry. These components power everything from automobiles to cell phones to dishwashers. It manufactures over 17 million parts each day in facilities in Europe, Taiwan, Ireland, and China.

The company's interest in growth created the need to identify a core set of company values and make sure these values were adhered to at all of the worldwide facilities. The company has eight values that are referred to as "culture points": integrity; a passion for customer satisfaction; respect for, responsiveness to, and empowerment of employees; technology and innovation; continual improvement; teamwork; job satisfaction; and a winning, competitive spirit. A leadership and problem-solving program developed by the company's HRM staff was used to spread these values throughout the company. The company also developed a program called People Plus that involves a 360-degree review of each employee, including an employee self-assessment matched with feedback from managers, peers, and subordinates chosen by the employee. Once the evaluations are completed, each employee meets with a psychologist to discuss the evaluations and make recommendations on how to improve the weaknesses identified.

Employees believe that the program brings the company together despite its global locations. The program focuses on identifying the unique talents and contributions of every employee. It also helps employees understand how others on the work team view them. The positive results of the program are measurable. Two years after the program was implemented, a survey of the senior management group showed that of 39 development areas, 36 showed improvement. The program has also contributed to a very stable workforce with a low turnover rate across all locations. This has helped General Semiconductor take pride in having the most knowledgeable and well-trained employees in its industry.[11]

An important step in performance management is to develop the measures by which performance will be evaluated. We next discuss the issues involved in developing and using different measures of performance.

## Performance Measures Criteria

**LO3**
Identify the Five Criteria for Effective Performance Management Systems.

In Chapter 4 we discussed how, through job analysis, one can analyze a job to determine exactly what constitutes effective performance. Once the company has determined, through job analysis and design, what kind of performance it expects from its employees, it needs to develop ways to measure that performance. This section presents the criteria underlying job performance measures. Later sections discuss approaches to performance measurement, sources of information, and errors.

Although people differ about criteria to use to evaluate performance management systems, we believe that five stand out: strategic congruence, validity, reliability, acceptability, and specificity.

### Strategic Congruence

**Strategic congruence** is the extent to which a performance management system elicits job performance that is congruent with the organization's strategy, goals, and culture. If a company emphasizes customer service, then its performance management system should assess how well its employees are serving the company's customers. Strategic congruence emphasizes the need for the performance management system to guide employees in contributing to the organization's success. This requires systems flexible enough to adapt to changes in the company's strategic posture.

**Strategic Congruence**
The extent to which the performance management system elicits job performance that is consistent with the organization's strategy, goals, and culture.

Many companies such as Hewlett-Packard, Federal Express, and Coca-Cola have introduced measures of critical success factors (CSFs) into their performance management systems.[12] CSFs are factors in a company's business strategy that give it a competitive edge. Companies measure employee behavior that relates to attainment of CSFs, which increases the importance of these behaviors for employees. Employees can be held accountable and rewarded for behaviors that directly relate to the company attaining the CSFs.

Take, for example, a drug company whose business strategy is to penetrate the North American market for dermatology compounds.[13] The company needs to shorten the drug development cycle, attract and retain research and development talent, and maximize the effectiveness of research teams. These are core competencies of the business; performance measures are linked directly to the core competencies. These include number of dermatology compound submissions to the Food and Drug Administration (FDA), number of compound approvals by the FDA, turnover of senior engineers, and team leadership and collaboration. The sources for information regarding these performance measures include FDA decisions, team member feedback on surveys, and turnover rates. Team and individual accountabilities are directly linked to the performance measures. For example, research teams' performance goals include FDA submission and approval of three compounds.

One challenge that companies face is how to measure customer loyalty, employee satisfaction, and other nonfinancial performance areas that affect profitability. To effectively use nonfinancial performance measures managers need to:[14]

- Develop a model of how nonfinancial performance measures link to the company's strategic goals. Identify the performance areas that are critical to success.
- Using already existing databases identify data that exists on key performance measures (e.g. customer satisfaction, employee satisfaction surveys). If data is not available, identify a performance area that affects the company's strategy and performance. Develop measures for those performance areas.
- Use statistical and qualitative methods for testing the relationship between the performance measures and financial outcomes. Regression and correlation analysis as well as focus groups and interviews can be used. For example, studies show that employees' involvement, satisfaction, and enthusiasm for work are significantly related to business performance including customer satisfaction, productivity, and profitability.[15]
- Revisit the model to ensure that the nonfinancial performance measures are appropriate and determine whether new measures should be added. This is important to understand the drivers of financial performance and to ensure that the model is appropriate as the business strategy and economic conditions change.
- Act on conclusions that the model demonstrates. For example, Sears found that employee attitudes about the supervision they received and the work environment had a significant impact on customer satisfaction and shareholder results. As a result, Sears invested in managerial training to help managers do a better job of holding employees accountable for their jobs while giving them autonomy to perform their roles.[16]
- Audit whether the actions taken and the investments made produced the desired result.

Most companies' appraisal systems remain constant over a long time and through a variety of strategic emphases. However, when a company's strategy changes, its employees' behavior needs to change too.[17] The fact that appraisal systems often do not change may account for why many managers see performance appraisal systems as having little impact on a firm's effectiveness.

## Validity

**Validity**
The extent to which a performance measure assesses all the relevant—and only the relevant—aspects of job performance.

**Validity** is the extent to which a performance measure assesses all the relevant—and only the relevant—aspects of performance. This is often referred to as "content validity." For a performance measure to be valid, it must not be deficient or contaminated. As you can see in Figure 8.3, one of the circles represents "true" job performance—all the aspects of performance relevant to success in the job. On the other hand, companies must use some measure of performance, such as a supervisory rating of performance on a set of dimensions or measures of the objective results on the job. Validity is concerned with maximizing the overlap between actual job performance and the measure of job performance (the green portion in the figure).

A performance measure is deficient if it does not measure all aspects of performance (the cranberry portion in the figure). An example is a system at a large university that

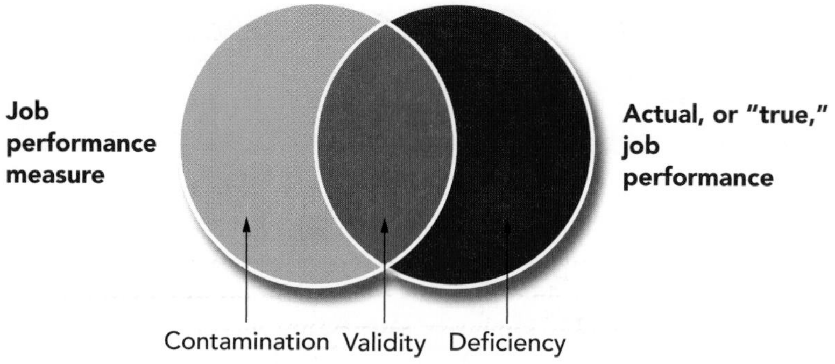


figure 8.3
Contamination and Deficiency of a Job Performance Measure

assesses faculty members based more on research than teaching, thereby relatively ignoring a relevant aspect of performance.

A contaminated measure evaluates irrelevant aspects of performance or aspects that are not job related (the gold portion in the figure). The performance measure should seek to minimize contamination, but its complete elimination is seldom possible. An example of a contaminated measure is the use of actual sales figures for evaluating salespersons across very different regional territories. Often sales are highly dependent upon the territory (number of potential customers, number of competitors, economic conditions) rather than the actual performance of the salesperson. A salesperson who works harder and better than others might not have the highest sales totals because the territory simply does not have as much sales potential as others. Thus, these figures alone would be a measure that is strongly affected by things beyond the control of the individual employee.

## Reliability

**Reliability** refers to the consistency of a performance measure. One important type of reliability is *interrater reliability:* the consistency among the individuals who evaluate the employee's performance. A performance measure has interrater reliability if two individuals give the same (or close to the same) evaluations of a person's job performance. Evidence seems to indicate that most subjective supervisory measures of job performance exhibit low reliability.[18] With some measures, the extent to which all the items rated are internally consistent is important (*internal consistency reliability*).

**Reliability**
The consistency of a performance measure; the degree to which a performance measure is free from random error.

In addition, the measure should be reliable over time (*test–retest reliability*). A measure that results in drastically different ratings depending on when the measures are taken lacks test–retest reliability. For example, if salespeople are evaluated based on their actual sales volume during a given month, it would be important to consider their consistency of monthly sales across time. What if an evaluator in a department store examined sales only during May? Employees in the lawn and garden department would have high sales volumes, but those in the men's clothing department would have somewhat low sales volumes. Clothing sales in May are traditionally lower than other months. One needs to measure performance consistently across time.

**Acceptability**
The extent to which a performance measure is deemed to be satisfactory or adequate by those who use it.

## Acceptability

**Acceptability** refers to whether the people who use a performance measure accept it. Many elaborate performance measures are extremely valid and reliable, but they

**table 8.3**
Categories of Perceived Fairness and Implications for Performance Management Systems

| FAIRNESS CATEGORY | IMPORTANCE FOR PERFORMANCE MANAGEMENT SYSTEM | IMPLICATIONS |
|---|---|---|
| Procedural fairness | Development | • Give managers and employees opportunity to participate in development of system.<br>• Ensure consistent standards when evaluating different employees.<br>• Minimize rating errors and biases. |
| Interpersonal fairness | Use | • Give timely and complete feedback.<br>• Allow employees to challenge the evaluation.<br>• Provide feedback in an atmosphere of respect and courtesy. |
| Outcome fairness | Outcomes | • Communicate expectations regarding performance evaluations and standards.<br>• Communicate expectations regarding rewards. |

SOURCE: Adapted from S. W. Gilliland and J. C. Langdon, "Creating Performance Management Systems That Promote Perceptions of Fairness," in *Performance Appraisal: State of the Art in Practice,* ed. J. W. Smither. Copyright © 1998 by Jossey-Bass, Inc. This material is used by permission of John Wiley & Sons, Inc.

consume so much of managers' time that they refuse to use it. Alternatively, those being evaluated by a measure may not accept it.

Acceptability is affected by the extent to which employees believe the performance management system is fair. As Table 8.3 shows, there are three categories of perceived fairness: procedural, interpersonal, and outcome fairness. The table also shows specifically how the performance management system's development, use, and outcomes affect perceptions of fairness. In developing and using a performance management system, managers should take the steps shown in the column labeled "Implications" in Table 8.3 to ensure that the system is perceived as fair. Research suggests that performance management systems that are perceived as unfair are likely to be legally challenged, be used incorrectly, and decrease employee motivation to improve.[19]

## Specificity

**Specificity**
The extent to which a performance measure gives detailed guidance to employees about what is expected of them and how they can meet these expectations.

**Specificity** is the extent to which a performance measure tells employees what is expected of them and how they can meet these expectations. Specificity is relevant to both the strategic and developmental purposes of performance management. If a measure does not specify what an employee must do to help the company achieve its strategic goals, it does not achieve its strategic purpose. Additionally, if the measure fails to point out employees' performance problems, it is almost impossible for the employees to correct their performance.

The "Competing through Sustainability" box shows how too much strategic emphasis on reaching short-term financial goals can hurt a company's sustainability.

## COMPETING THROUGH SUSTAINABILITY

### Strict Emphasis on Short-Term Goals Jeopardizes Long-Term Company Health

Shareholders and company owners expect the company's managers and employees to work to increase the company's value typically measured by its stock price. Other financial goals include greater profits through greater sales or lower costs. But can too much of a focus on these goals actually hurt rather than increase sustainability?

Companies' fixation on hitting quarterly financial targets often works against their producing sustainable profit growth. One study of 31 corporations found that the highest financial returns were achieved at companies whose CEOs had challenging financial goals and communicated a vision of the company beyond making profits, such as creating an innovative product, providing great customer service, or improving the quality of life. Another study concluded that the main cause of employees' difficulties in improving profits and innovating was an excessive focus on short-term financial results. Of the approximately 40 percent of employees who said they worked in nonperforming groups, one-third said their group had been high performing but began to fail when managers started raising their performance standards at the same time they were cutting budgets and staff.

Why does this happen? Managers may feel pressured to keep cutting costs to deliver greater profits in each quarterly financial statement. This can eliminate valuable employees, leaving their responsibilities to remaining employees who feel that their jobs are impossible to do. Organizational psychologist Richard Hagberg worked with a sales vice president who was urged to meet daily sales targets yet at the same time cut staff to meet profit goals. The vice president wanted to plan improvements to the product line and develop a new competitive strategy, but his time was spent figuring out how to squeeze more work from a shrinking staff. As a result of cutting training budgets and staff to meet short-term financial goals, long-term company success can be compromised because the most talented employees leave the company, taking clients and their human capital to competitors. The emphasis on short-term goals often encourages unethical practices such as faking performance data. Susan Annunzio of the Hudson Highland Center for High Performance in Chicago interviewed a factory manager who was given the goal of reducing operating costs. The manager identified ways to meet the target within a month, but he spread the improvements over a year so that his boss wouldn't immediately come back with a more difficult goal to meet.

The key to sustainable profit growth is not through steep cost cutting resulting from a fixation on short-term financial numbers. This erodes employee loyalty and teamwork along with innovation and risk taking—ingredients that are needed for sustainable profit growth. CEOs need to emphasize to shareholders and owners that sustainability comes from product differentiation and increased market share, goals that can be reached only with the help of talented employees.

SOURCE: Based on C. Hymowitz, "When Meeting Targets Becomes the Strategy, CEO Is on the Wrong Path," *The Wall Street Journal*, March 8, 2005, p. B1.

# Approaches to Measuring Performance

LO4
Discuss the Four Approaches to Performance Management, the Specific Techniques Used in Each Approach, and the Way These Approaches Compare with the Criteria for Effective Performance Management Systems.

The model of performance management presented in Figure 8.2 shows that we can manage performance by focusing on employee attributes, behaviors, or results. In addition, we can measure performance in a relative way, making overall comparisons among individuals' performance. Finally, we can develop a performance measurement system that incorporates some variety of the preceding measures, as evidenced by the quality approach to measuring performance. Various techniques combine these approaches. In this section we explore these approaches to measuring and managing performance, discussing the techniques that are associated with each approach and evaluating these approaches against the criteria of strategic congruence, validity, reliability, acceptability, and specificity.

## The Comparative Approach

The comparative approach to performance measurement requires the rater to compare an individual's performance with that of others. This approach usually uses some overall assessment of an individual's performance or worth and seeks to develop some ranking of the individuals within a work group. At least three techniques fall under the comparative approach: ranking, forced distribution, and paired comparison.

### Ranking

*Simple ranking* requires managers to rank employees within their departments from highest performer to poorest performer (or best to worst). *Alternation ranking*, on the other hand, consists of a manager looking at a list of employees, deciding who is the best employee, and crossing that person's name off the list. From the remaining names, the manager decides who the worst employee is and crosses that name off the list—and so forth.

Ranking is one method of performance appraisal that has received specific attention in the courts. In the *Albermarle v. Moody* case, the validation of the selection system was conducted using employee rankings as the measure of performance. The court actually stated, "There is no way of knowing precisely what criteria of job performance that supervisors were considering, whether each supervisor was considering the same criteria—or whether, indeed, any of the supervisors actually applied a focused and stable body of criteria of any kind."[20]

### Forced Distribution

The *forced distribution* method also uses a ranking format, but employees are ranked in groups. This technique requires the manager to put certain percentages of employees into predetermined categories. Forced distribution was popularized by former General Electric CEO Jack Welch, who insisted that GE annually identify and remove the bottom 10 percent of the workforce. Such performance ranking takes several forms. Most commonly, employees are grouped into three, four, or five categories usually of unequal size indicating the best workers, the worst workers, and one or more categories in between. For example, at General Electric managers were to place employees into top (20 percent), middle (70 percent), and bottom (10 percent) categories. The bottom 10 percent usually receive no bonuses and can be terminated. The forced distribution method forces managers to categorize employees based on distribution rules, not on their performance. For example, Charles Schwab has three possible ratings for employees but the bottom rating is never assigned.[21] Forced distribution systems force managers to distinguish between employees, which avoids an entitlement mentality for pay, rewards, and development activities. Even if a manager's employees are all above average performers, the manager is forced to rate some employees as "Not Acceptable."

Advocates of these systems say that they are the best way to identify high-potential employees who should be given training, promotions, and financial rewards and to identify the poorest performers who should be helped or asked to leave. Top level managers at many companies have observed that despite corporate performance and return to shareholders being flat or decreasing, compensation costs have continued to spiral upward and performance ratings continue to be high. They question how there can be such a disconnect between corporate performance and employees' evaluations and compensation. Forced distribution systems provide a mechanism to help align company performance and employee performance and compensation. Employees in the bottom 10 percent cause performance standards to be lowered, influence good employees to leave, and keep good employees from joining the company.

A forced distribution system helps managers tailor development activities to employees based on their performance. For example, as shown in Table 8.4, poor performers are given specific feedback about what they need to improve in their job and a timetable is set for their improvement. If they do not improve their performance, they are dismissed. Top performers are encouraged to participate in development activities such as job experiences, mentoring, and completion of leadership programs which will help prepare them for top management positions. The use of a forced

**table 8.4**
Performance and Development Based on Forced Distribution and Ranking

| RANKING OR DISTRIBUTION CATEGORY | PERFORMANCE AND DEVELOPMENT PLAN |
| --- | --- |
| A Above average<br>exceptional<br>A1 performer | • Accelerate development through challenging job assignments<br>• Provide mentor from leadership team<br>• Recognize and reward contributions<br>• Praise employees for strengths<br>• Consider leadership potential<br>• Nominate for leadership development programs |
| B Average<br>meets expectations<br>steady performer | • Offer feedback on how B can become a high performer<br>• Encourage development of strengths and improvement of weaknesses<br>• Recognize and reward employee contributions<br>• Consider enlarging job |
| C Below expectations<br>poor performance | • Give feedback and agree upon what specific skills, behavior, and/or results need to be improved with timetable for accomplishment<br>• Move to job that better matches skills<br>• Ask to leave the company |

SOURCES: Based on B. Axelrod, H. Handfield-Jones, and E. Michaels, "A New Game Plan for C Players," *HBR*, January 2002, pp. 80–88; A. Walker, "Is Performance Management as Simple as ABC?" *T+D*, February 2007, pp. 54–57; T. De Long and V. Vijayaraghavan, "Let's Hear It for B Players," *HBR*, June 2003, pp. 96–102.

distribution system is seen as a way for companies to increase performance, motivate employees, and open the door for new talent to join the company to replace poor performers.[22] Advocates say these systems force managers to make hard decisions about employee performance based on job-related criteria, rather than to be lenient in evaluating employees. Critics, on the other hand, say the systems in practice are arbitrary, may be illegal, and cause poor morale.[23] For example, one workgroup might have 20 percent poor performers while another might have only high performers, but the process mandates that 10 percent of employees be eliminated from both groups. Also, in many forced distribution systems an unintended consequence is the bottom category tends to consist of minorities, women, and people over 40 years of age, causing discrimination lawsuits. Finally, it is difficult to rank employees into distinctive categories when criteria are subjective or when it is difficult to differentiate employees on the criteria (such as teamwork or communications skills). For example, in 2002, Ford Motors settled two class action lawsuits for $10.5 million.[24] Ford said it needed the forced ranking system because its culture discouraged candor in performance evaluations. Ford Motors Performance Management System involved grading 1,800 middle managers as A, B, or C. Managers who received a C for one year received no bonus; two years at the C level meant possible demotion and termination. Ten percent of the managers were to be graded as C. But some employees claimed the system had a negative impact on older, white workers because they received a larger proportion of C grades. Eventually, Ford eliminated the forced ranking system.

Although there are many opinions on the pros and cons of forced distribution performance systems, few studies have examined their effectiveness. Research simulating different features of a forced system and other factors that influence company performance (e.g., voluntary turnover rate, validity of selection methods) suggests that forced distribution rating systems can improve the potential performance of a company's workforce.[25] Companies that have clear goals and management criteria, train evaluators, use the rankings along with other HR metrics, and reward good performance may find them useful. The majority of improvement appears to occur during the first several years the system is used, mainly because of the large number of poorly performing employees who are identified and fired. Keep in mind that despite the potential advantages of forced choice systems for improving a company's workforce performance, the potential negative side effects on morale, teamwork, recruiting, and shareholder perceptions should be considered before adopting such as system. Forced ranking is ethical as long as the system is clearly communicated, the system is part of a positive dimension of the organization culture (innovation, continuous improvement), and the employees have the chance to appeal decisions.

## Paired Comparison

The *paired comparison* method requires managers to compare every employee with every other employee in the work group, giving an employee a score of 1 every time he or she is considered the higher performer. Once all the pairs have been compared, the manager computes the number of times each employee received the favorable decision (that is, counts up the points), and this becomes the employee's performance score.

The paired comparison method tends to be time-consuming for managers and will become more so as organizations become flatter with an increased span of control. For example, a manager with 10 employees must make 45 (10 × 9⁄2) comparisons. However, if the group increases to 15 employees, 105 comparisons must be made.

### Evaluating the Comparative Approach

The comparative approach to performance measurement is an effective tool in differentiating employee performance; it virtually eliminates problems of leniency, central tendency, and strictness. This is especially valuable if the results of the measures are to be used in making administrative decisions such as pay raises and promotions. In addition, such systems are relatively easy to develop and in most cases easy to use; thus, they are often accepted by users.

One problem with these techniques, however, is their common failure to be linked to the strategic goals of the organization. Although raters can evaluate the extent to which individuals' performances support the strategy, this link is seldom made explicit. In addition, because of the subjective nature of the ratings, their actual validity and reliability depend on the raters themselves. Some firms use multiple evaluators to reduce the biases of any individual, but most do not. At best, we could conclude that their reliability and validity are modest.

These techniques lack specificity for feedback purposes. Based only on their relative rankings, individuals are completely unaware of what they must do differently to improve their ranking. This puts a heavy burden on the manager to provide specific feedback beyond that of the rating instrument itself. Finally, many employees and managers are less likely to accept evaluations based on comparative approaches. Evaluations depend on how employees' performance relates to other employees in a group, team, or department (normative standard) rather than on absolute standards of excellent, good, fair, and poor performance.

## The Attribute Approach

The attribute approach to performance management focuses on the extent to which individuals have certain attributes (characteristics or traits) believed desirable for the company's success. The techniques that use this approach define a set of traits—such as initiative, leadership, and competitiveness—and evaluate individuals on them.

### Graphic Rating Scales

The most common form that the attribute approach to performance management takes is the *graphic rating scale*. Table 8.5 shows a graphic rating scale used in a manufacturing company. As you can see, a list of traits is evaluated by a five-point (or some other number of points) rating scale. The manager considers one employee at a time, circling the number that signifies how much of that trait the individual has. Graphic rating scales can provide a number of different points (a discrete scale) or a continuum along which the rater simply places a check mark (a continuous scale).

The legal defensibility of graphic rating scales was questioned in the *Brito v. Zia* (1973) case. In this case Spanish-speaking employees had been terminated as a result of their performance appraisals. These appraisals consisted of supervisors' rating subordinates on a number of undefined dimensions such as volume of work, quantity of work, job knowledge, dependability, and cooperation. The court criticized the subjective

**table 8.5**

Example of a Graphic Rating Scale

The following areas of performance are significant to most positions. Indicate your assessment of performance on each dimension by circling the appropriate rating.

| PERFORMANCE DIMENSION | RATING | | | | |
|---|---|---|---|---|---|
| | DISTINGUISHED | EXCELLENT | COMMENDABLE | ADEQUATE | POOR |
| Knowledge | 5 | 4 | 3 | 2 | 1 |
| Communication | 5 | 4 | 3 | 2 | 1 |
| Judgment | 5 | 4 | 3 | 2 | 1 |
| Managerial skill | 5 | 4 | 3 | 2 | 1 |
| Quality performance | 5 | 4 | 3 | 2 | 1 |
| Teamwork | 5 | 4 | 3 | 2 | 1 |
| Interpersonal skills | 5 | 4 | 3 | 2 | 1 |
| Initiative | 5 | 4 | 3 | 2 | 1 |
| Creativity | 5 | 4 | 3 | 2 | 1 |
| Problem solving | 5 | 4 | 3 | 2 | 1 |

appraisals and stated that the company should have presented empirical data demonstrating that the appraisal was significantly related to actual work behavior.

## Mixed-Standard Scales

*Mixed-standard scales* were developed to get around some of the problems with graphic rating scales. To create a mixed-standard scale, we define the relevant performance dimensions and then develop statements representing good, average, and poor performance along each dimension. These statements are then mixed with the statements from other dimensions on the actual rating instrument. An example of a mixed-standard scale is presented in Table 8.6.

As we see in the table, the rater is asked to complete the rating instrument by indicating whether the employee's performance is above (+), at (0), or below (−) the statement. A special scoring key is then used to score the employee's performance for each dimension. Thus, for example, an employee performing above all three statements receives a 7. If the employee is below the good statement, at the average statement, and above the poor statement, a score of 4 is assessed. An employee below all three statements is given a rating of 1. This scoring is applied to all the dimensions to determine an overall performance score.

Note that mixed-standard scales were originally developed as trait-oriented scales. However, this same technique has been applied to instruments using behavioral rather than trait-oriented statements as a means of reducing rating errors in performance appraisal.[26]

## Evaluating the Attribute Approach

Attribute-based performance methods are the most popular methods in organizations. They are quite easy to develop and are generalizable across a variety of jobs, strategies,

**table 8.6**

An Example of a Mixed-Standard Scale

| | | | | |
|---|---|---|---|---|
| Three traits being assessed: Initiative (INTV), Intelligence (INTG), Relations with others (RWO) | | Levels of performance in statements: High (H), Medium (M), Low (L) | | |
| Instructions: Please indicate next to each statement whether the employee's performance is above (+), equal to (0), or below (−) the statement. | | | | |
| INTV | H | 1. | This employee is a real self-starter. The employee always takes the initiative and his/her superior never has to prod this individual. | + |
| INTG | M | 2. | While perhaps this employee is not a genius, s/he is a lot more intelligent than many people I know. | + |
| RWO | L | 3. | This employee has a tendency to get into unnecessary conflicts with other people. | 0 |
| INTV | M | 4. | While generally this employee shows initiative, occasionally his/her superior must prod him/her to complete work. | + |
| INTG | L | 5. | Although this employee is slower than some in understanding things, and may take a bit longer in learning new things, s/he is of average intelligence. | + |
| RWO | H | 6. | This employee is on good terms with everyone. S/he can get along with people even when s/he does not agree with them. | − |
| INTV | L | 7. | This employee has a bit of a tendency to sit around and wait for directions. | + |
| INTG | H | 8. | This employee is extremely intelligent, and s/he learns very rapidly. | − |
| RWO | M | 9. | This employee gets along with most people. Only very occasionally does s/he have conflicts with others on the job, and these are likely to be minor. | − |

Scoring Key:

| STATEMENTS | | | SCORE |
|---|---|---|---|
| HIGH | MEDIUM | LOW | |
| + | + | + | 7 |
| 0 | + | + | 6 |
| − | + | + | 5 |
| − | 0 | + | 4 |
| − | − | + | 3 |
| − | − | 0 | 2 |
| − | − | − | 1 |

Example score from preceding ratings:

| | STATEMENTS | | | SCORE |
|---|---|---|---|---|
| | HIGH | MEDIUM | LOW | |
| Initiative | + | + | + | 7 |
| Intelligence | 0 | + | + | 6 |
| Relations with others | − | − | 0 | 2 |

and organizations. In addition, if much attention is devoted to identifying those attributes relevant to job performance and carefully defining them on the rating instrument, they can be as reliable and valid as more elaborate measurement techniques.

However, these techniques fall short on several of the criteria for effective performance management. There is usually little congruence between the techniques and the company's strategy. These methods are used because of the ease in developing them and because the same method (list of traits, comparisons) is generalizable across any organization and any strategy. In addition, these methods usually have very vague performance standards that are open to different interpretations by different raters. Because of this, different raters often provide extremely different ratings and rankings. The result is that both the validity and reliability of these methods are usually low.

Virtually none of these techniques provides any specific guidance on how an employee can support the company's goals or correct performance deficiencies. In addition, when raters give feedback, these techniques tend to elicit defensiveness from employees. For example, how would you feel if you were told that on a five-point scale, you were rated a "2" in maturity? Certainly you might feel somewhat defensive and unwilling to accept that judgment, as well as any additional feedback. Also, being told you were rated a "2" in maturity doesn't tell you how to improve your rating.

## The Behavioral Approach

The behavioral approach to performance management attempts to define the behaviors an employee must exhibit to be effective in the job. The various techniques define those behaviors and then require managers to assess the extent to which employees exhibit them. We discuss five techniques that rely on the behavioral approach.

### Critical Incidents

The *critical incidents* approach requires managers to keep a record of specific examples of effective and ineffective performance on the part of each employee. Here's an example of an incident described in the performance evaluation of an appliance repair person:

> A customer called in about a refrigerator that was not cooling and was making a clicking noise every few minutes. The technician prediagnosed the cause of the problem and checked his truck for the necessary parts. When he found he did not have them, he checked the parts out from inventory so that the customer's refrigerator would be repaired on his first visit and the customer would be satisfied promptly.

These incidents give specific feedback to employees about what they do well and what they do poorly, and they can be tied to the company's strategy by focusing on incidents that best support that strategy. However, many managers resist having to keep a daily or weekly log of their employees' behavior. It is also often difficult to compare employees because each incident is specific to that individual.

### Behaviorally Anchored Rating Scales

A *behaviorally anchored rating scale* (BARS) builds on the critical incidents approach. It is designed to specifically define performance dimensions by developing behavioral anchors associated with different levels of performance.[27] An example of a BARS is presented in Figure 8.4. As you can see, the performance dimension has a number of examples of behaviors that indicate specific levels of performance along the dimension.

**Preparing for Duty**

7 — Always early for work, gathers all necessary equipment to go to work, fully dressed, uses time before roll call to review previous shift's activities and any new bulletins, takes notes of previous shift's activity mentioned during roll call.

6 — Always early for work, gathers all necessary equipment to go to work, fully dressed, checks activity from previous shifts before going to roll call.

5 — Early for work, has all necessary equipment to go to work, fully dressed.

4 — On time, has all necessary equipment to go to work, fully dressed.

3 — Not fully dressed for roll call, does not have all necessary equipment.

2 — Late for roll call, does not check equipment or vehicle for damage or needed repairs, unable to go to work from roll call, has to go to locker, vehicle, or home to get necessary equipment.

1 — Late for roll call majority of period, does not check equipment or vehicle, does not have necessary equipment to go to work.

SOURCE: Adapted from R. Harvey, "Job Analysis," in *Handbook of Industrial & Organizational Psychology,* 2nd ed., ed. M. Dunnette and L. Hough (Palo Alto, CA.: Consulting Psychologists Press, 1991), p. 138.

figure 8.4
Task-BARS Rating Dimension: Patrol Officer

To develop a BARS, we first gather a large number of critical incidents that represent effective and ineffective performance on the job. These incidents are classified into performance dimensions, and the ones that experts agree clearly represent a particular level of performance are used as behavioral examples (or anchors) to guide the rater. The manager's task is to consider an employee's performance along each dimension and determine where on the dimension the employee's performance fits using the behavioral anchors as guides. This rating becomes the employee's score for that dimension.

Behavioral anchors have advantages and disadvantages. They can increase interrater reliability by providing a precise and complete definition of the performance dimension. A disadvantage is that they can bias information recall—that is, behavior that closely approximates the anchor is more easily recalled than other behavior.[28] Research has also demonstrated that managers and their subordinates do not make much of a distinction between BARS and trait scales.[29]

## Behavioral Observation Scales

A *behavioral observation scale (BOS)* is a variation of a BARS. Like a BARS, a BOS is developed from critical incidents.[30] However, a BOS differs from a BARS in two basic ways. First, rather than discarding a large number of the behaviors that exemplify effective or ineffective performance, a BOS uses many of them to more specifically define all the behaviors that are necessary for effective performance (or that would be considered ineffective performance). Instead of using, say, 4 behaviors to define 4 levels of performance on a particular dimension, a BOS may use 15 behaviors. An example of a BOS is presented in Table 8.7.

A second difference is that rather than assessing which behavior best reflects an individual's performance, a BOS requires managers to rate the frequency with which the employee has exhibited each behavior during the rating period. These ratings are then averaged to compute an overall performance rating.

**table 8.7**

An Example of a Behavioral Observation Scale (BOS) for Evaluating Job Performance

| | | | | | | |
|---|---|---|---|---|---|---|
| Overcoming Resistance to Change | | | | | | |
| (1) Describes the details of the change to subordinates. | | | | | | |
| Almost Never | 1 | 2 | 3 | 4 | 5 | Almost Always |
| (2) Explains why the change is necessary. | | | | | | |
| Almost Never | 1 | 2 | 3 | 4 | 5 | Almost Always |
| (3) Discusses how the change will affect the employee. | | | | | | |
| Almost Never | 1 | 2 | 3 | 4 | 5 | Almost Always |
| (4) Listens to the employee's concerns. | | | | | | |
| Almost Never | 1 | 2 | 3 | 4 | 5 | Almost Always |
| (5) Asks the employee for help in making the change work. | | | | | | |
| Almost Never | 1 | 2 | 3 | 4 | 5 | Almost Always |
| (6) If necessary, specifies the date for a follow-up meeting to respond to the employee's concerns. | | | | | | |
| Almost Never | 1 | 2 | 3 | 4 | 5 | Almost Always |
| | | Total = ________ | | | | |
| Below Adequate 6–10 | Adequate 11–15 | | Full 16–20 | Excellent 21–25 | | Superior 26–30 |

Scores are set by management.

SOURCE: G. Latham and K. Wexley, *Increasing Productivity through Performance Appraisal*, p. 56. 

The major drawback of a BOS is that it may require more information than most managers can process or remember. A BOS can have 80 or more behaviors, and the manager must remember how frequently an employee exhibited each of these behaviors over a 6- or 12-month rating period. This is taxing enough for one employee, but managers often must rate 10 or more employees.

A direct comparison of BOS, BARS, and graphic rating scales found that both managers and employees prefer BOS for differentiating good from poor performers, maintaining objectivity, providing feedback, suggesting training needs, and being easy to use among managers and subordinates.[31]

## Organizational Behavior Modification

*Organizational behavior modification (OBM)* entails managing the behavior of employees through a formal system of behavioral feedback and reinforcement. This system builds on the behaviorist view of motivation, which holds that individuals' future behavior is determined by past behaviors that have been positively reinforced. The techniques vary, but most have four components. First, they define a set of key behaviors necessary for job performance. Second, they use a measurement system to assess whether these behaviors are exhibited. Third, the manager or consultant informs employees of those behaviors, perhaps even setting goals for how often the employees should exhibit those behaviors. Finally, feedback and reinforcement are provided to employees.[32]

Job analysis

OBM techniques have been used in a variety of settings. For example, OBM was used to increase the rates and timeliness of critical job behaviors by showing the connection between job behaviors and the accomplishments of a community mental health agency.[33] Job behaviors were identified that related to administration, record keeping, and service provided to clients. Feedback and reinforcement improved staff performance. Figure 8.5 shows increases in staff performance in record keeping following the feedback and reinforcement intervention. "Baseline" refers to measures of record keeping prior to the intervention. "Interview" refers to record keeping when interviews were being conducted with staff to better explain their jobs. Similar results have been observed with the frequency of safety behaviors in a processing plant.[34]

## Assessment Centers

Although assessment centers are usually used for selection and promotion decisions, they have also been used as a way of measuring managerial performance.[35] At an **assessment center,** individuals usually perform a number of simulated tasks, such as leaderless group discussions, in-basket management, and role playing. Assessors observe the individuals' behavior and evaluate their skill or potential as managers. We discuss assessment centers more in Chapter 9.

**Assessment Centers**
A process in which multiple raters evaluate employees' performance on a number of exercises.

The advantage of assessment centers is that they provide a somewhat objective measure of an individual's performance at managerial tasks. In addition, they allow specific performance feedback, and individualized developmental plans can be designed. For example, ARCO Oil & Gas Corporation sends its managers through assessment centers to identify their individual strengths and weaknesses and to create developmental action plans for each manager.

An interesting public sector application of assessment centers is in the state government of North Carolina. Managers there can be assessed to become "certified middle managers." This process includes an assessment center at the beginning of the certification program, from which an individualized developmental action plan is

figure 8.5

Increases in Record Keeping as a Result of OBM

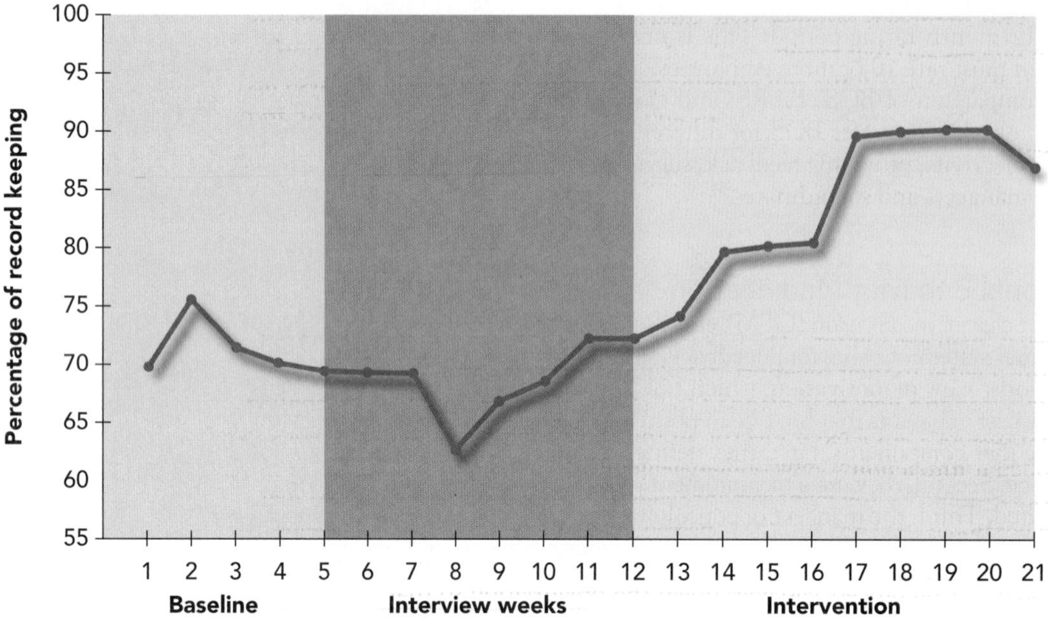


SOURCE: Based on K. L. Langeland, C. M. Johnson, and T. C. Mawhinney, "Improving Staff Performance in a Community Mental Health Setting: Job Analysis, Training, Goal Setting, Feedback, and Year of Data," *Journal of Organizational Behavior Management* 18 (1998), PP. 211–43.

created. The developmental plan, implemented over approximately two years, consists of training and on-the-job developmental experiences. At the end of the two years, the manager attends the certification assessment center. Those who successfully meet the criteria set forth then become certified.

## Evaluation of the Behavioral Approach

The behavioral approach can be very effective. It can link the company's strategy to the specific behavior necessary for implementing that strategy. It provides specific guidance and feedback for employees about the performance expected of them. Most of the techniques rely on in-depth job analysis, so the behaviors that are identified and measured are valid. Because those who will use the system develop the measures, the acceptability is also often high. Finally, with a substantial investment in training raters, the techniques are reasonably reliable.

The major weaknesses have to do with the organizational context of the system. Although the behavioral approach can be closely tied to a company's strategy, the behaviors and measures must be constantly monitored and revised to ensure that they are still linked to the strategic focus. This approach also assumes that there is "one best way" to do the job and that the behaviors that constitute this best way can be identified. One study found that managers seek to control behaviors when they perceive a clear relationship between behaviors and results. When this link is not clear, they tend to rely on managing results.[36] The behavioral approach might be best suited to less complex jobs (where the best way to achieve results is somewhat clear) and least suited to complex jobs (where there are multiple ways, or behaviors, to achieve success).

## The Results Approach

The results approach focuses on managing the objective, measurable results of a job or work group. This approach assumes that subjectivity can be eliminated from the measurement process and that results are the closest indicator of one's contribution to organizational effectiveness.[37] We will examine two performance management systems that use results: management by objectives and the productivity measurement and evaluation system.

### Management by Objectives

*Management by objectives* (MBO) is popular in both private and public organizations.[38] The original concept came from the accounting firm of Booz, Allen, and Hamilton and was called a "manager's letter." The process consisted of having all the subordinate managers write a letter to their superiors, detailing what their performance goals were for the coming year and how they planned to achieve them. Harold Smiddy applied and expanded this idea at General Electric in the 1950s, and Douglas McGregor has since developed it into a philosophy of management.[39]

In an MBO system, the top management team first defines the company's strategic goals for the coming year. These goals are passed on to the next layer of management, and these managers define the goals they must achieve for the company to reach its goals. This goal-setting process cascades down the organization so that all managers set goals that help the company achieve its goals.[40] These goals are used as the standards by which an individual's performance is evaluated.[41]

MBO systems have three common components.[42] They require specific, difficult, objective goals. (An example of MBO-based goals used in a financial service firm is presented in Table 8.8.) The goals are not usually set unilaterally by management but with the managers' and subordinates' participation. And the manager gives objective feedback throughout the rating period to monitor progress toward the goals.

Research on MBO has revealed two important findings regarding its effectiveness.[43] Of 70 studies examined, 68 showed productivity gains, while only 2 showed productivity losses, suggesting that MBO usually increases productivity. Also, productivity gains tend to be highest when there is substantial commitment to the MBO program from top management: an average increase of 56 percent when

**table 8.8**

An Example of a Management by Objectives (MBO) Measure of Job Performance

| KEY RESULT AREA | OBJECTIVE | % COMPLETE | ACTUAL PERFORMANCE |
|---|---|---|---|
| Loan portfolio management | Increase portfolio value by 10% over the next 12 months | 90 | Increased portfolio value by 9% over the past 12 months |
| Sales | Generate fee income of $30,000 over the next 12 months | 150 | Generated fee income of $45,000 over the past 12 months |

commitment was high, 33 percent when commitment was moderate, and 6 percent when commitment was low.

Clearly, MBO can have a very positive effect on an organization's performance. Considering the process through which goals are set (involvement of staff in setting objectives), it is also likely that MBO systems effectively link individual employee performance with the firm's strategic goals. SecureWorks Inc., a small, 100-employee company providing Internet security services, bases employees' pay on their performance.[44] Pay is rewarded on the basis of results, not effort. When linking pay to performance, it is critical that employees understand the performance goals and how to meet them, see that pay is really based on performance (i.e., poor performers receive fewer pay and other rewards than good performers), and believe the performance management system used to determine pay is fair. At SecureWorks, company goals are set by the management team at the beginning of each year. The goals are displayed throughout the company so employees can see them. Department goals in support of the corporate goals are set by managers and their teams. Each employee has a set of goals which are discussed and agreed upon with their manager. The goals are realistic, measurable, achievable, and aligned with the company goals. Employees have several chances throughout the year to receive rewards for their performance. These rewards include cost-of-living salary increases and the opportunity to earn restricted stock and a bonus. Employees can receive no rewards or all available rewards depending on their performance. The CEO reviews each employee's pay recommendation, which is based on a self- and manager performance evaluation and reviewed by the vice president of human resources.

### Productivity Measurement and Evaluation System (ProMES)

The main goal of ProMES is to motivate employees to higher levels of productivity.[45] It is a means of measuring and feeding back productivity information to personnel.

ProMES consists of four steps. First, people in an organization identify the products, or the set of activities or objectives, the organization expects to accomplish. The organization's productivity depends on how well it produces these products. At a repair shop, for example, a product might be something like "quality of repair." Second, the staff defines indicators of the products. Indicators are measures of how well the products are being generated by the organization. Quality of repair could be indicated by (1) return rate (percentage of items returned that did not function immediately after repair) and (2) percentage of quality-control inspections passed. Third, the staff establishes the contingencies between the amount of the indicators and the level of evaluation associated with that amount. Fourth, a feedback system is developed that provides employees and work groups with information about their specific level of performance on each of the indicators. An overall productivity score can be computed by summing the effectiveness scores across the various indicators.

Because this technique is somewhat new, it has been applied in only a few situations. However, research thus far strongly suggests it is effective in increasing productivity. (Figure 8.6 illustrates the productivity gains in the repair shop described previously.) The research also suggests the system is an effective feedback mechanism. However, users found it time-consuming to develop the initial system. Future research on ProMES needs to be conducted before we draw any firm conclusions, but the existing research indicates that this may be a useful performance management tool.

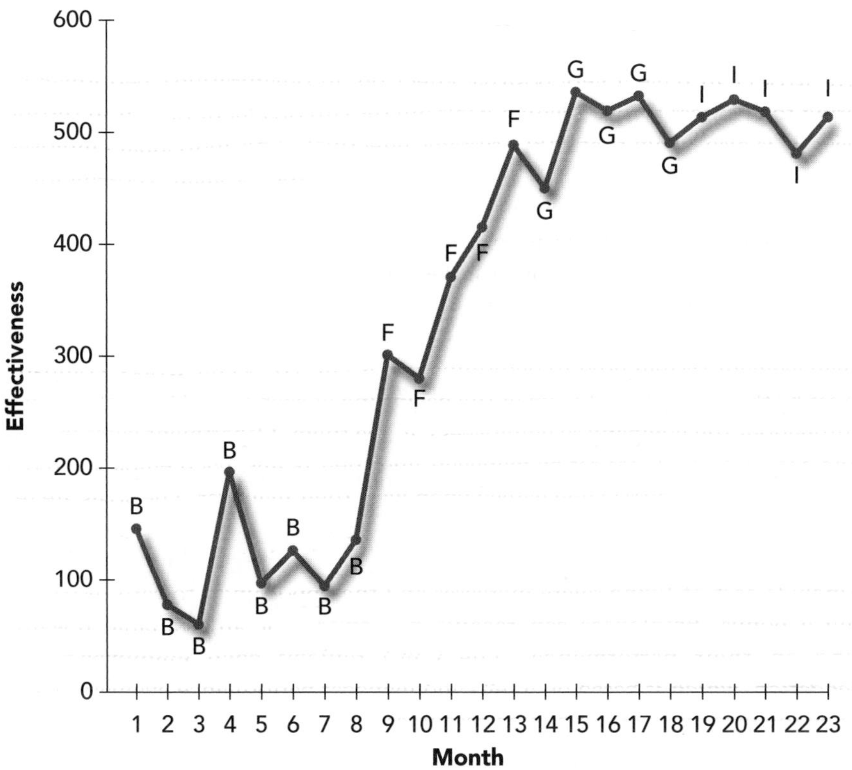


figure 8.6
Increases in Productivity for a Repair Shop Using ProMES Measures

SOURCE: R. Pritchard, S. Jones, P. Roth, K. Stuebing, and S. Ekeberg, "The Evaluation of an Integrated Approach to Measuring Organizational Productivity," *Personnel Psychology* 42 (1989), pp. 69–115. Used by permission.

## Evaluation of the Results Approach

The results approach minimizes subjectivity, relying on objective, quantifiable indicators of performance. Thus, it is usually highly acceptable to both managers and employees. Another advantage is that it links an individual's results with the organization's strategies and goals.

However, objective measurements can be both contaminated and deficient—contaminated because they are affected by things that are not under the employee's control, such as economic recessions, and deficient because not all the important aspects of job performance are amenable to objective measurement. Another disadvantage is that individuals may focus only on aspects of their performance that are measured, neglecting those that are not. For example, if the large majority of employees' goals relate to productivity, it is unlikely they will be concerned with customer service. One study found that objective performance goals led to higher performance but that they also led to helping co-workers less.[46] A final disadvantage is that, though results measures provide objective feedback, the feedback may not help employees learn how they need to change their behavior to increase their performance. If baseball players are in a hitting slump, simply telling them that their batting average is .190 may not motivate them to raise it. Feedback focusing on the exact behavior that needs to be changed (like taking one's eye off the ball or dropping one's shoulder) would be more helpful.[47]

John Deere takes specific actions to avoid these problems.[48] At the start of each fiscal year manager and employees meet to discuss objectives for the year. A midyear review then is conducted to check on the employees' progress in meeting the goals. The year-end review meeting focuses on evaluating goal accomplishment. Goal achievement at the end of the year is linked to pay increases and other rewards. All company objectives are supported by division objectives that are available for employees to view online. Employees also have available a learning and activities courseware catalog they can use to help develop skills needed to achieve their performance objectives.

## EVIDENCE-BASED HR

Children's Hospital in Boston wanted to improve cash flow and shorten the billing cycle (the time to receive payment of a bill). The hospital's accounts receivable department was taking more than 100 days to receive payment. To do this, the hospital decided to evaluate and reward team performance. Managers determine who will be rewarded and on what basis, and they have to communicate the plan and its benefits to employees. Team members have a set of three goals. In order of difficulty from least to greatest they are threshold, target, and optimal goals. These categories are defined in terms of how long a bill remains in accounts receivable. Teams receive a quarterly payment of $500 for meeting the threshold goal, $1,000 for meeting the target goal, or $1,500 for meeting the optimal goal. The payment is divided by team members according to the number of scheduled hours they worked. To reach the goals, team members must work together bill by bill, to process the paperwork faster.

To make sure employees understood the plan, the hospital held a series of meetings that presented information about the dollar value of each day a bill spends in accounts receivable and how the hospital is affected by poor cash flow. After employees understood how their work affects cash flow and how their efforts could improve it, they began working as a team. Employees started to take the initiative to follow up with patients, insurers, and medical records personnel. If any team members were not carrying their weight, peer pressure persuaded them to contribute more. Employees receive weekly progress reports so they can monitor their performance. The performance system has resulted in positive results. At the end of the first year, employees reduced the average number of days a bill spent in accounts receivable to just under 76. The plan also helped the hospital recruit and retain employees for its accounts payable team.

SOURCE: D. Cadrain, "Put Success in Sight," *HR Magazine*, May 2003, pp. 85–92.

## The Quality Approach

Thus far we have examined the traditional approaches to measuring and evaluating employee performance. Two fundamental characteristics of the quality approach are a customer orientation and a prevention approach to errors. Improving customer satisfaction is the primary goal of the quality approach. Customers can be internal or external to the organization. A performance management system designed with a strong quality orientation can be expected to

- Emphasize an assessment of both person and system factors in the measurement system.
- Emphasize that managers and employees work together to solve performance problems.
- Involve both internal and external customers in setting standards and measuring performance.
- Use multiple sources to evaluate person and system factors.[49]

Based on this chapter's earlier discussion of the characteristics of an effective performance management system, it should be apparent to you that these characteristics are not just unique to the quality approach but are characteristics of an effective appraisal system!

Advocates of the quality approach believe that most U.S. companies' performance management systems are incompatible with the quality philosophy for a number of reasons:

1. Most existing systems measure performance in terms of quantity, not quality.
2. Employees are held accountable for good or bad results to which they contribute but do not completely control.
3. Companies do not share the financial rewards of successes with employees according to how much they have contributed to them.
4. Rewards are not connected to business results.[50]

Sales, profit margins, and behavioral ratings are often collected by managers to evaluate employees' performance. These are person-based outcomes. An assumption of using these types of outcomes is that the employee completely controls them. However, according to the quality approach, these types of outcomes should not be used to evaluate employees' performance because they do not have complete control over them (that is, they are contaminated). For example, for salespersons, performance evaluations (and salary increases) are often based on attainment of a sales quota. Salespersons' abilities and motivation are assumed to be directly responsible for their performance. However, quality approach advocates argue that better determinants of whether a salesperson reaches the quota are "systems factors" (such as competitors' product price changes) and economic conditions (which are not under the salesperson's control).[51] Holding employees accountable for outcomes affected by systems factors is believed to result in dysfunctional behavior, such as falsifying sales reports, budgets, expense accounts, and other performance measures, as well as lowering employees' motivation for continuous improvement.

Quality advocates suggest that the major focus of performance evaluations should be to provide employees with feedback about areas in which they can improve. Two types of feedback are necessary: (1) subjective feedback from managers, peers, and customers about the personal qualities of the employee and (2) objective feedback based on the work process itself using statistical quality control methods.

Performance feedback from managers, peers, and customers should be based on such dimensions as cooperation, attitude, initiative, and communication skills. Performance evaluation should include a discussion of the employee's career plans. The quality approach also strongly emphasizes that performance appraisal systems should avoid providing overall evaluations of employees (like ratings such as excellent, good, poor). Categorizing employees is believed to encourage them to behave in ways that are expected based on their ratings. For example, "average" performers may not be motivated to improve their performance but rather may continue to perform at the expected level. Also, because employees do not have control over the quality of the system in which they work, employee performance evaluations should not be linked to compensation. Compensation rates should be based on prevailing market rates of pay, seniority, and business results, which are distributed equitably to all employees.

Statistical process control techniques are very important in the quality approach. These techniques provide employees with an objective tool to identify causes of problems and potential solutions. These techniques include process-flow analysis, cause-and-effect diagrams, Pareto charts, control charts, histograms, and scattergrams.

*Process-flow analysis* identifies each action and decision necessary to complete work, such as waiting on a customer or assembling a television set. Process-flow analysis is useful for identifying redundancy in processes that increase manufacturing or service time. For example, one business unit at Owens-Corning was able to confirm that customer orders were error-free only about 25 percent of the time (an unacceptable level of service). To improve the service level, the unit mapped out the process to identify bottlenecks and problem areas. As a result of this mapping, one simple change (installing an 800 number for the fax machine) increased overall accuracy of orders as well as transaction speed.[52]

In *cause-and-effect diagrams*, events or causes that result in undesirable outcomes are identified. Employees try to identify all possible causes of a problem. The feasibility of the causes is not evaluated, and as a result, cause-and-effect diagrams produce a large list of possible causes.

A *Pareto chart* highlights the most important cause of a problem. In a Pareto chart, causes are listed in decreasing order of importance, where *importance* is usually defined as the frequency with which that cause resulted in a problem. The assumption of Pareto analysis is that the majority of problems are the result of a small number of causes. Figure 8.7 shows a Pareto chart listing the reasons managers give for not selecting current employees for a job vacancy.

*Control charts* involve collecting data at multiple points in time. By collecting data at different times, employees can identify what factors contribute to an outcome and when they tend to occur. Figure 8.8 shows the percentage of employees hired internally for a company for each quarter between 1993 and 1995. Internal hiring increased dramatically during the third quarter of 1994. The use of control charts helps employees understand the number of internal candidates who can be expected to be hired each year. Also, the control chart shows that the amount of internal hiring conducted during the third quarter of 1994 was much larger than normal.

*Histograms* display distributions of large sets of data. Data are grouped into a smaller number of categories or classes. Histograms are useful for understanding the amount of

**figure 8.7**
Pareto Chart

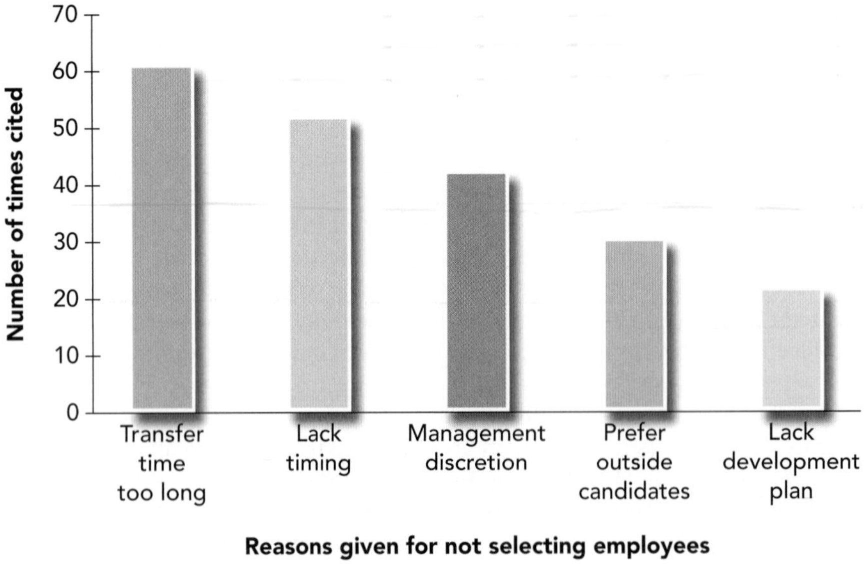


SOURCE: From *HR Magazine* by Clara Carter. Copyright 1992, by Society for Human Resource Management. Reprinted with permission of Society for Human Resource Management via Copyright Clearance Center.

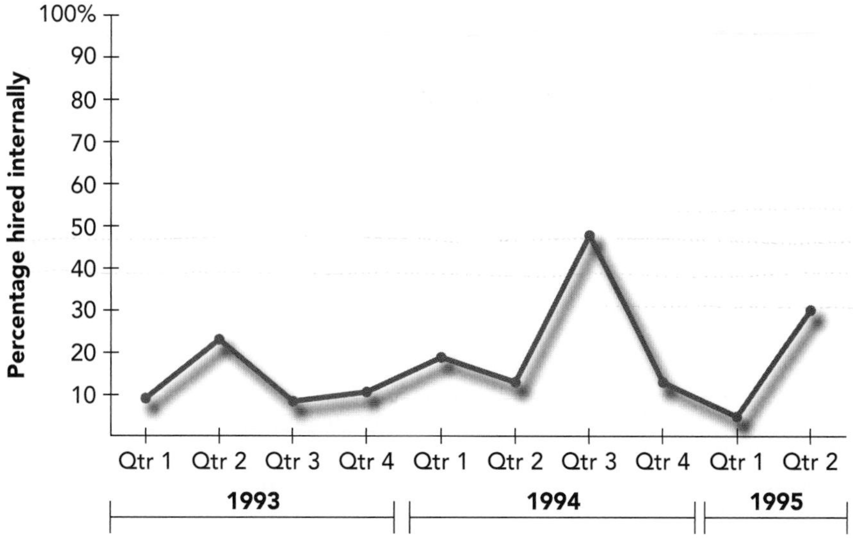


figure 8.8
Control Chart

SOURCE: From *HR Magazine* by Clara Carter. Copyright 1992, by Society for Human Resource Management. Reprinted with permission of Society for Human Resource Management via Copyright Clearance Center.

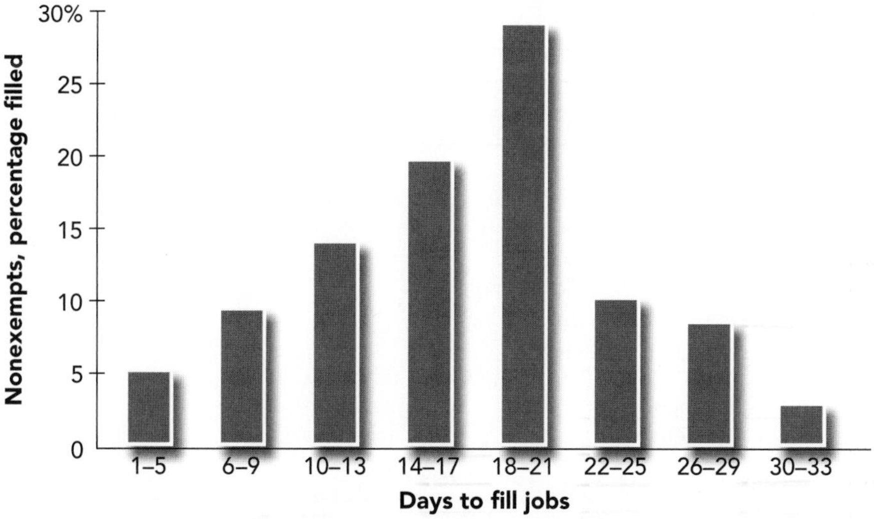


figure 8.9
Histogram

SOURCE: From *HR Magazine* by Clara Carter. Copyright 1992, by Society for Human Resource Management. Reprinted with permission of Society for Human Resource Management via Copyright Clearance Center.

variance between an outcome and the expected value or average outcome. Figure 8.9 is a histogram showing the number of days it took a company to fill nonexempt job vacancies. The histogram shows that most nonexempt jobs took from 18 to 21 days to fill, and the amount of time to fill nonexempt jobs ranged from 1 to 33 days. If an HR manager relied simply on data from personnel files on the number of days it took to fill nonexempt positions, it would be extremely difficult to understand the variation and average tendency in the amount of time to fill the positions.

*Scattergrams* show the relationship between two variables, events, or different pieces of data. Scattergrams help employees determine whether the relationship between two variables or events is positive, negative, or zero.

### Evaluation of the Quality Approach

**LO5**
Choose the Most Effective Approach to Performance Measurement for a Given Situation.

The quality approach relies primarily on a combination of the attribute and results approaches to performance measurement. However, traditional performance appraisal systems focus more on individual employee performance, while the quality approach adopts a systems-oriented focus.[53] Many companies may be unwilling to completely abandon their traditional performance management system because it serves as the basis for personnel selection validation, identification of training needs, or compensation decisions. Also, the quality approach advocates evaluation of personal traits (such as cooperation), which are difficult to relate to job performance unless the company has been structured into work teams.

In summary, organizations can take five approaches to measuring performance: comparative, attribute, behavioral, results, and quality. Table 8.9 summarizes the

**table 8.9**
Evaluation of Approaches to Performance Measurement

| | CRITERIA | | | | |
|---|---|---|---|---|---|
| APPROACH | STRATEGIC CONGRUENCE | VALIDITY | RELIABILITY | ACCEPTABILITY | SPECIFICITY |
| Comparative | Poor, unless manager takes time to make link | Can be high if ratings are done carefully | Depends on rater, but usually no measure of agreement used | Moderate; easy to develop and use but resistant to normative standard | Very low |
| Attribute | Usually low; requires manager to make link | Usually low; can be fine if developed carefully | Usually low; can be improved by specific definitions of attributes | High; easy to develop and use | Very low |
| Behavioral | Can be quite high | Usually high; minimizes contamination and deficiency | Usually high | Moderate; difficult to develop, but accepted well for use | Very high |
| Results | Very high | Usually high; can be both contaminated and deficient | High; main problem can be test–retest—depends on timing of measure | High; usually developed with input from those to be evaluated | High regarding results, but low regarding behaviors necessary to achieve them |
| Quality | Very high | High, but can be both contaminated and deficient | High | High; usually developed with input from those to be evaluated | High regarding results, but low regarding behaviors necessary to achieve them |

various approaches to measuring performance based on the criteria we set forth earlier and illustrates that each approach has strengths and weaknesses. As the quality approach illustrates, the most effective way of measuring performance is to rely on a combination of two or more alternatives. For example, performance management systems in many companies evaluate the extent to which managers reach specific performance goals or results as well as evaluate their behavior. Figure 8.10 shows an example of a performance management system that evaluates behavior and results. The results (project development) are linked to the goals of the business. The performance standards include behaviors that the employee can demonstrate to reach the results. The system provides for feedback to the employee and holds both the employee and manager accountable for changing behavior.

## Choosing a Source for Performance Information

Whatever approach to performance management is used, it is necessary to decide whom to use as the source of the performance measures. Each source has specific strengths and weaknesses. We discuss five primary sources: managers, peers, subordinates, self, and customers.

**LO6**
Discuss the Advantages and Disadvantages of the Different Sources of Performance Information.

### Managers

**LO7**
Choose the Most Effective Source(s) for Performance Information for Any Situation.

Managers are the most frequently used source of performance information. It is usually safe to assume that supervisors have extensive knowledge of the job requirements and that they have had adequate opportunity to observe their employees—in other words, that they have the ability to rate their employees. In addition, because supervisors have something to gain from the employees' high performance and something to lose from low performance, they are motivated to make accurate ratings.[54] Finally, feedback from supervisors is strongly related to performance and to employee perceptions of the accuracy of the appraisal if managers attempt to observe employee behavior or discuss performance issues in the feedback session.[55]

Burlington Northern Santa Fe Corporation of Fort Worth, Texas, improved its performance management process by holding leaders accountable in setting annual goals, creating individual development plans, providing feedback and coaching to employees, and self-evaluation.[56] An online performance management system supports the process. The company's executive team creates the overall company objectives, which cascade down to each department and individual employees who can now see how they contribute to the company's success. The online system allows managers and employees to see how they and the department are progressing on the objectives. Required to be engaged in the performance management process, managers are more focused on the necessary communications, coaching, and giving feedback, and they are more inclined to seek out training to be sure that they have the necessary communications, feedback, and coaching skills. Managers' effectiveness is monitored by periodic employee surveys that ask questions about whether the manager discusses performance, whether the dialogue with the manager is two-way, and whether the employee receives ongoing feedback.

Problems with using supervisors as the source of performance information can occur in particular situations. In some jobs, for example, the supervisor does not have an adequate opportunity to observe the employee performing his job duties. For example,

figure 8.10

Example of a Performance Management System That Includes Behavior and Results

| Accountabilities and Key Results | Performance Standards | Interim Feedback | Actual Results | Performance Rating | Areas for Development | Action |
|---|---|---|---|---|---|---|
| Key result areas that the employee will accomplish during the review period. Should align with company values, business goals, and job description. | How the key result area will be measured (quality, cost, quantity). Focus on work methods and accomplishments. | Employee and manager discuss performance on an ongoing basis. | Review actual performance for each key result. | Evaluate performance on each key result.<br><br>1 = Outstanding<br>2 = Highly effective<br>3 = Acceptable<br>4 = Unsatisfactory | Specific knowledge, skills, and behaviors to be developed that will help employee achieve key results. | What employee and manager will do to address development needs. |
| Project Development<br>Manage the development of project scope, cost estimate studies, and schedules for approval. | Develop preliminary project material for approval within four weeks after receiving project scope. Eighty percent of new projects receive approval. Initial cost estimates are within 5% of final estimates. | Preliminary project materials are developed on time. | By end of year, approvals were at 75%, 5% less than standard. | 3 | Increase knowledge of project management software. | Read articles, research, and meet with software vendors. |

in outside sales jobs, the supervisor does not have the opportunity to see the salesperson at work most of the time. This usually requires that the manager occasionally spend a day accompanying the salesperson on sales calls. However, on those occasions the employee will be on best behavior, so there is no assurance that performance that day accurately reflects performance when the manager is not around.

Also, some supervisors may be so biased against a particular employee that to use the supervisor as the sole source of information would result in less-than-accurate measures for that individual. Favoritism is a fact of organizational life, but it is one that must be minimized as much as possible in performance management.[57] Thus, the performance evaluation system should seek to minimize the opportunities for favoritism to affect ratings. One way to do this is not to rely on only a supervisor's evaluation of an employee's performance.

## Peers

Another source of performance information is the employee's co-workers. Peers are an excellent source of information in a job such as law enforcement, where the supervisor does not always observe the employee. Peers have expert knowledge of job requirements, and they often have the most opportunity to observe the employee in day-to-day activities. Peers also bring a different perspective to the evaluation process, which can be valuable in gaining an overall picture of the individual's performance. In fact, peers have been found to provide extremely valid assessments of performance in several different settings.[58]

One disadvantage of using peer ratings is the potential for friendship to bias ratings.[59] Little empirical evidence suggests that this is often a problem, however. Another disadvantage is that when the evaluations are made for administrative decisions, peers often find the situation of being both rater and ratee uncomfortable. When these ratings are used only for developmental purposes, however, peers react favorably.[60]

## Subordinates

Subordinates are an especially valuable source of performance information when managers are evaluated. Subordinates often have the best opportunity to evaluate how well a manager treats employees. **Upward feedback** refers to appraisals that involve collecting subordinates' evaluations of manager's behavior or skills. Dell Inc., the Texas-based computer company, recently took steps to focus not only on financial goals but also on making the company a great place to work to attract and keep talented employees.[61] To help develop what Dell calls a "winning culture," Dell added a people management component to its results-oriented performance management system. Managers are now rated by their employees on semiannual "Tell Dell" surveys. Managers who receive less than 50 percent favorable scores on five questions receive less favorable compensation, bonus, and promotion opportunities and are required to take additional training. Table 8.10 shows the five questions. Managers are expected to work continuously to improve their scores. Their goal is to receive at least 75 percent favorable ratings from employees on the five questions. One study found that managers viewed receiving upward feedback more positively when receiving feedback from subordinates who were identified, but subordinates preferred to provide anonymous feedback. When subordinates were identified, they inflated their ratings of the manager.[62]

**Upward Feedback**
Managerial performance appraisal that involves subordinates' evaluations of the manager's behavior or skills.

One problem with subordinate evaluations is that they give subordinates power over their managers, thus putting the manager in a difficult situation.[63] This can lead

**table 8.10**

Example of Upward Feedback Survey Questions from "Tell Dell" Surveys

- Even if I were offered a comparable position with similar pay and benefits at another company, I would stay at Dell.
- I receive ongoing feedback that helps me to improve my performance.
- My manager/supervisor supports my efforts to balance my work and personal life.
- My manager/supervisor is effective at managing people.
- I can be successful at Dell and still retain my individuality.

SOURCE: Based on A.Pomeroy, "Agent of Change," *HR Magazine*, May 2005, pp. 52–56.

to managers' emphasizing employee satisfaction over productivity. However, this happens only when administrative decisions are made from these evaluations. As with peer evaluations, it is a good idea to use subordinate evaluations only for developmental purposes. To assure subordinates that they need not fear retribution from their managers, it is necessary to use anonymous evaluations and at least three subordinates for each manager.

## Self

Although self-ratings are not often used as the sole source of performance information, they can still be valuable.[64] Obviously, individuals have extensive opportunities to observe their own behavior, and they usually have access to information regarding their results on the job. For example, hoping to quicken the pace of decision making and create a sense of urgency in its global workforce, General Motors has given salaried employees the chance to contribute to innovation and use of new technology.[65] Employees are given individual responsibility to contribute to corporate business results through a program known as the Performance Management Process (PMP). The PMP program established individual business objectives for salaried employees that must be linked to the employee's unit and to overall company goals. A recent survey indicates that 80 percent of GM's managers believe they are being held personally accountable for business results, compared to only 50 percent a few years ago.

One problem with self-ratings, however, is a tendency toward inflated assessments. This stems from two sources. If the ratings are going to be used for administrative decisions (like pay raises), it is in the employees' interests to inflate their ratings. And there is ample evidence in the social psychology literature that individuals attribute their poor performance to external causes, such as a co-worker who they think has not provided them with timely information. Although self-ratings are less inflated when supervisors provide frequent performance feedback, it is not advisable to use them for administrative purposes.[66] The best use of self-ratings is as a prelude to the performance feedback session to get employees thinking about their performance and to focus discussion on areas of disagreement.

## Customers

As discussed in Chapter 1, service industries are expected to account for a major portion of job growth.[67] As a result, many companies are involving customers in their evaluation systems. One writer has defined *services* this way: "Services is something which can be bought and sold but which you cannot drop on your foot."[68] Because of the unique nature of services—the product is often produced and consumed on the spot—supervisors, peers, and subordinates often do not have the opportunity to observe employee behavior. Instead, the customer is often the only person present to observe the employee's performance and thus is the best source of performance information.

Many companies in service industries have moved toward customer evaluations of employee performance. Marriott Corporation provides a customer satisfaction card in every room and mails surveys to a random sample of customers after their stay in a Marriott hotel. Whirlpool's Consumer Services Division conducts both mail and telephone surveys of customers after factory service technicians have serviced their appliances. These surveys allow the company to evaluate an individual technician's customer-service behaviors while in the customer's home.

Using customer evaluations of employee performance is appropriate in two situations.[69] The first is when an employee's job requires direct service to the customer or linking the customer to other services within the company. Second, customer evaluations are appropriate when the company is interested in gathering information to determine what products and services the customer wants. That is, customer evaluations serve a strategic goal by integrating marketing strategies with human resource activities and policies. Customer evaluations collected for this purpose are useful for both evaluating the employee and helping to determine whether changes in other HRM activities (such as training or the compensation system) are needed to improve customer service.

The weakness of customer surveys is their expense. Printing, postage, telephone, and labor can add up to hundreds of dollars for the evaluation of one individual. Thus many companies conduct such evaluations only once a year for a short time.

In conclusion, the best source of performance information often depends on the particular job. One should choose the source or sources that provide the best opportunity to observe employee behavior and results. Table 8.11 summarizes this information for most jobs. Often, eliciting performance information from a variety of sources results in a performance management process that is accurate and effective. In fact, one recent popular trend in organizations is called **360-degree appraisals.**[70] This technique consists of having multiple raters (boss, peers, subordinates, customers) provide input into a manager's evaluation. The major advantage of the technique is that it provides a means for minimizing bias in an otherwise subjective evaluation technique. It has been used primarily for strategic and developmental purposes and is discussed in greater detail in Chapter 9.[71]

The "Competing through Technology" box shows how several companies are using technology to increase acces to performance information for employees and managers.

**360-Degree Appraisal**
A performance appraisal process for managers that includes evaluations from a wide range of persons who interact with the manager. The process includes self-evaluations as well as evaluations from the manager's boss, subordinates, peers, and customers.

**table 8.11**
Frequency of Observation for Various Sources of Performance Information

| | SOURCE | | | | |
|---|---|---|---|---|---|
| | SUPERVISOR | PEERS | SUBORDINATES | SELF | CUSTOMERS |
| **Task** | | | | | |
| Behaviors | Occasional | Frequent | Rare | Always | Frequent |
| Results | Frequent | Frequent | Occasional | Frequent | Frequent |
| **Interpersonal** | | | | | |
| Behaviors | Occasional | Frequent | Frequent | Always | Frequent |
| Results | Occasional | Frequent | Frequent | Frequent | Frequent |

SOURCE: Adapted from K. Murphy and J. Cleveland, *Performance Appraisal: An Organizational Perspective* (Boston: Allyn & Bacon, 1991).

## COMPETING THROUGH TECHNOLOGY

### Going Paperless Increases the Effectiveness of Performance Management

Many companies are moving to Web-based and online paperless performance management systems. These systems have several advantages including helping companies ensure that performance goals at all levels of the organizations are aligned, providing managers with greater access to employee performance information and tools for understanding and using the data, and improving the efficiency of appraisal systems. Serono, a biotechnology company, uses an online performance management system that allows all managers to see the performance of any employee that they are responsible for as well as the total distribution of ratings. Senior managers can see how managers rated their people and analyze the relationship between department productivity and the total average performance of employees in the department. If a lack of relationship is shown, this suggests that employees are being overrated. At Amcor Sunclipse, a nationwide distribution company headquartered in southern California, annual appraisals were consistently late, they were inconsistent, they had little connection to company objectives, and they weren't useful in assigning employees to training programs or filling open positions. The new online process allows e-mail notification to employees and their manager to complete performance evaluations and makes it easier to weight the relative value of different performance goals. For example, all employees are measured on safety behaviors but safety is a more critical part of some jobs (such as manufacturing jobs) than others. The online system can be set up to automatically weight performance areas (safety, reduce waste, etc.) based on how important they are to the job. For example, for a manufacturing supervisor improving safety might count for 40 percent of the overall performance rating compared to 5 percent for an office worker.

Baxter Healthcare Corporation has an automated goal-alignment system that about half of its 55,000 employees participate in. At Baxter the process starts with the company's top strategic goals, known as the four B's (Best Team, Best Partner, Best Investments, Best Citizen). The executive team creates goals under each category. The top 150 executives then develop their goals, which are distributed to employees. The goals are collected in a performance management system. A Web site provides guidance on how to write goals, and achievement results are shared with the company's performance review and compensation systems. A manager of e-procurement of supplies at Baxter who reports to the VP of purchasing says, "The biggest value is the digitization and consistent fashion of performance information. Historically we'd put this information into filing cabinets and pull it out once or twice a year. What this process is, really, is a tool that provides me with an opportunity to better understand Baxter's expectations of me and my team."

Sandy Hill Community Health Centre (SHCSC) in Ottawa, Canada, valued using managers, peers, and self-evaluations as part of the performance management process but found that the administrative burden of such a system was overwhelming. Sandy Hill now uses a new software application that compiles performance evaluations for each employee and provides the employee's manager with a summary of results. The reporting format is flexible enough for the results to be easily importable into a database, spreadsheet, or HTML application. Matthew Garrison, the HR director at SHCSC, says, "The ability to conduct performance reviews online provides us with information that we would not have been able to gather through traditional paper means." The system also provides SHCSC with the capability to measure progress in meeting strategic goals and objectives, gather and analyze performance data, and use the data to drive organizational improvements.

SOURCES: K. Tyler, "Performance Art," *HR Magazine* August 2005, pp. 58–63; M. Hayes, "Goals Oriented," *Information Week* (March 10, 2003), from *Information Week* Web site at www.informationweek.com; D. Silverstone, "Paperless Performance Reviews," *HR Professional* (February 2005), from *HR Professional* Web site at www.hrpao.org/HRPAO/KnowledgeCentre/HRProfessional/newscluster/Paperless+Performance+Reviews.htm, retrieved February 19, 2005; M. Totty, "The Dreaded Performance Review," *The Wall Street Journal*, November 27, 2006, p. R7.

## Rater Errors in Performance Measurement

**LO8** Distinguish Types of Rating Errors and Explain How to Minimize Each in a Performance Evaluation.

Research consistently reveals that humans have tremendous limitations in processing information. Because we are so limited, we often use "heuristics," or simplifying mechanisms, to make judgments, whether about investments or about people.[72] These heuristics, which appear often in subjective measures of performance, can lead to rater errors. Performance evaluations may also be purposefully distorted. We discuss rater errors and appraisal politics next.

### Similar to Me

"Similar to me" is the error we make when we judge those who are similar to us more highly than those who are not. Research has demonstrated that this effect is strong, and when similarity is based on demographic characteristics such as race or sex, it can result in discriminatory decisions.[73] Most of us tend to think of ourselves as effective, and so if others are like us—in race, gender, background, attitudes, or beliefs—we assume that they too are effective.

### Contrast

Contrast error occurs when we compare individuals with one another instead of against an objective standard. Consider a completely competent performer who works with a number of peers who are outstanding. If the competent employee receives lower-than-deserved ratings because of the outstanding colleagues, that is contrast error.

### Distributional Errors

Distributional errors are the result of a rater's tendency to use only one part of the rating scale. *Leniency* occurs when a rater assigns high (lenient) ratings to all employees. *Strictness* occurs when a manager gives low ratings to all employees—that is, holds all employees to unreasonably high standards. *Central tendency* reflects that a manager rates all employees in the middle of the scale. These errors pose two problems. First, they make it difficult to distinguish among employees rated by the same person. Second, they create problems in comparing the performance of individuals rated by different raters. If one rater is lenient and the other is strict, employees of the strict rater will receive significantly fewer rewards than those rated by the lenient rater.

### Halo and Horns

These errors refer to a failure to distinguish among different aspects of performance. *Halo error* occurs when one positive performance aspect causes the rater to rate all other aspects of performance positively—for example, professors who are rated as outstanding researchers because they are known to be outstanding teachers. *Horns error* works in the opposite direction: one negative aspect results in the rater assigning low ratings to all the other aspects.

Halo and horns errors preclude making the necessary distinctions between strong and weak performance. Halo error leads to employees believing that no aspects of their performance need improvement. Horns error makes employees frustrated and defensive.

## Reducing Rater Errors

Two approaches to reducing rating errors have been offered.[74] *Rater error training* attempts to make managers aware of rating errors and helps them develop strategies for minimizing those errors.[75] These programs consist of having the participants view videotaped vignettes designed to elicit rating errors such as "contrast." They then make their ratings and discuss how the error influenced the rating. Finally, they get tips to avoid committing those errors. This approach has been shown to be effective for reducing errors, but there is evidence that reducing rating errors can also reduce accuracy.[76]

*Rater accuracy training*, also called *frame-of-reference training*, attempts to emphasize the multidimensional nature of performance and thoroughly familiarize raters with the actual content of various performance dimensions. This involves providing examples of performance for each dimension and then discussing the actual or "correct" level of performance that the example represents.[77] Accuracy training seems to increase accuracy, provided that in addition the raters are held accountable for ratings, job-related rating scales are used, and raters keep records of the behavior they observe.[78]

## Appraisal Politics

**Appraisal Politics**
A situation in which evaluators purposefully distort ratings to achieve personal or company goals.

**Appraisal politics** refer to evaluators purposefully distorting a rating to achieve personal or company goals. Research suggests that several factors promote appraisal politics. These factors are inherent in the appraisal system and the company culture. Appraisal politics are most likely to occur when raters are accountable to the employee being rated, there are competing rating goals, and a direct link exists between performance appraisal and highly desirable rewards. Also, appraisal politics are likely to occur if top executives tolerate distortion or are complacent toward it, and if distortion strategies are part of "company folklore" and are passed down from senior employees to new employees. For example, employees at King Pharmaceutical resisted development of a centralized performance system.[79] King Pharmaceuticals is built from smaller acquired companies, each with a unique culture. Each department within the company had developed its own way of figuring out how to evaluate performance and link it to pay.

It is unlikely that appraisal politics can be completely eliminated. Unfortunately, there is little research on the best methods to eliminate appraisal politics. To minimize appraisal politics, managers should keep in mind the characteristics of a fair appraisal system shown in Table 8.3. In addition, managers should

- Train raters on the appropriate use of the process as discussed previously.
- Build top management support for the appraisal system and actively discourage distortion.
- Give raters some latitude to customize performance objectives and criteria for their ratees.
- Recognize employee accomplishments that are not self-promoted.
- Provide employees with access to information regarding which behaviors are desired and acceptable at work.
- Encourage employees to actively seek and use feedback to improve performance.
- Make sure constraints such as budget do not drive the process.
- Make sure appraisal processes are consistent across the company.
- Foster a climate of openness to encourage employees to be honest about weaknesses.[80]

# Performance Feedback

**LO9**
Conduct an Effective Performance Feedback Session.

Once the expected performance has been defined and employees' performances have been measured, it is necessary to feed that performance information back to the employees so they can correct any deficiencies. The performance feedback process is complex and provokes anxiety for both the manager and the employee. Table 8.12 provides examples of feedback that managers have given employees. You be the judge as to these statements' effectiveness in improving employees' performance!

Few of us feel comfortable sitting in judgment of others. The thought of confronting others with what we perceive to be their deficiencies causes most of us to shake in our shoes. If giving negative feedback is painful, receiving it can be excruciating—thus the importance of the performance feedback process.

## The Manager's Role in an Effective Performance Feedback Process

If employees are not made aware of how their performance is not meeting expectations, their performance will almost certainly not improve. In fact, it may get worse. Effective managers provide specific performance feedback to employees in a way that elicits positive behavioral responses. To provide effective performance feedback managers should consider the following recommendations.[81]

***Feedback Should Be Given Frequently, Not Once a Year.*** There are two reasons for this. First, managers have a responsibility to correct performance deficiencies immediately on becoming aware of them. If performance is subpar in January, waiting until December to appraise the performance could mean an 11-month productivity loss. Second, a major determinant of the effectiveness of a feedback session is the degree to which the subordinate is not surprised by the evaluation. An easy rule to follow is that employees should receive such frequent performance feedback that they already know almost exactly what their formal evaluation will be.

***Create the Right Context for the Discussion.*** Managers should choose a neutral location for the feedback session. The manager's office may not be the best place for a constructive feedback session because the employee may associate the office with unpleasant

**table 8.12**
Examples of Performance Feedback

| |
|---|
| Since my last report; this employee has reached rock bottom and has started to dig. |
| His men would follow him anywhere, but only out of morbid curiosity. |
| I would not allow this employee to breed. |
| This associate is really not so much of a "has-been," but more of a "definitely won't-be." |
| Works well when under constant supervision and cornered like a rat in a trap. |
| When she opens her mouth, it seems that this is only to change whichever foot was previously in there. |
| He would be out of his depth in a parking-lot puddle. |
| This young lady has delusions of adequacy. |
| He sets low personal standards, then consistently fails to achieve them. |
| This employee should go far—and the sooner he starts, the better. |
| This employee is depriving a village somewhere of an idiot. |

SOURCE: Y. Harari, *The Daily Dose* (www.harari.org/index.html), July 22, 1997. Reprinted with permission.

conversations. Managers should describe the meeting as an opportunity to discuss the role of the employee, the role of the manager, and the relationship between them. Managers should also acknowledge that they would like the meeting to be an open dialogue.

***Ask the Employee to Rate His or Her Performance before the Session.*** Having employees complete a self-assessment before the feedback session can be very productive. It requires employees to think about their performance over the past rating period, and it encourages them to think about their weaknesses. Although self-ratings used for administrative decisions are often inflated, there is evidence that they may actually be lower than supervisors' ratings when done for developmental purposes. Another reason a self-assessment can be productive is that it can make the session go more smoothly by focusing discussion on areas where disagreement exists, resulting in a more efficient session. Finally, employees who have thought about past performance are more able to participate fully in the feedback session.

***Encourage the Subordinate to Participate in the Session.*** Managers can take one of three approaches in performance feedback sessions. In the "tell-and-sell" approach, managers tell the employees how they have rated them and then justify these ratings. In the "tell-and-listen" approach, managers tell employees how they have rated them and then let the employees explain their side of the story. In the "problem-solving" approach, managers and employees work together to solve performance problems in an atmosphere of respect and encouragement. In spite of the research demonstrating the superiority of the problem-solving approach, most managers still rely on the tell-and-sell approach.

When employees participate in the feedback session, they are consistently satisfied with the process. (Recall our discussion of fairness earlier in this chapter.) Participation includes allowing employees to voice their opinions of the evaluation, as well as discuss performance goals. One study found that, other than satisfaction with one's supervisor, participation was the single most important predictor of satisfaction with the feedback session.[82]

***Recognize Effective Performance through Praise.*** One usually thinks of performance feedback sessions as focusing on the employee's performance problems. This should never be the case. The purpose of the session is to give accurate performance feedback, which entails recognizing effective performance as well as poor performance. Praising effective performance provides reinforcement for that behavior. It also adds credibility to the feedback by making it clear that the manager is not just identifying performance problems.

***Focus on Solving Problems.*** A common mistake that managers make in providing performance feedback is to try to use the session as a chance to punish poorly performing employees by telling them how utterly lousy their performance is. This only reduces the employees' self-esteem and increases defensiveness, neither of which will improve performance.

To improve poor performance, a manager must attempt to solve the problems causing it. This entails working with the employee to determine the actual cause and then agreeing on how to solve it. For example, a salesperson's failure to meet a sales goal may be the result of lack of a proper sales pitch, lack of product knowledge, or stolen sales by another salesperson. Each of these causes requires a different solution. Without a problem-solving approach, however, the correct solution might never be identified.

***Focus Feedback on Behavior or Results, Not on the Person.*** One of the most important things to do when giving negative feedback is to avoid questioning the employee's worth as a person. This is best accomplished by focusing the discussion on the employee's behaviors or results, not on the employee. Saying "You're screwing up! You're just not motivated!" will bring about more defensiveness and ill feelings than stating "You did not meet the deadline that you agreed to because you spent too much time on another project."

***Minimize Criticism.*** Obviously, if an individual's performance is below standard, some criticism must take place. However, an effective manager should resist the temptation to reel off a litany of offenses. Having been confronted with the performance problem, an employee often agrees that a change is in order. However, if the manager continues to come up with more and more examples of low performance, the employee may get defensive.

***Agree to Specific Goals and Set a Date to Review Progress.*** The importance of goal setting cannot be overemphasized. It is one of the most effective motivators of performance.[83] Research has demonstrated that it results in increased satisfaction, motivation to improve, and performance improvement.[84] Besides setting goals, the manager must also set a specific follow-up date to review the employee's performance toward the goal. This provides an added incentive for the employee to take the goal seriously and work toward achieving it.

## What Managers Can Do to Diagnose Performance Problems and Manage Employees' Performance

**LO10**
Identify the Cause of a Performance Problem.

As we emphasized in the previous discussion, employees need performance feedback to improve their current job performance. As we will discuss in Chapter 9, "Employee Development," performance feedback is also needed for employees to develop their knowledge and skills for the future. In addition to understanding how to effectively give employees performance feedback, managers need to be able to diagnose the causes of performance problems and take actions to improve and maintain employee performance. For example, giving performance feedback to marginal employees may not be sufficient for improving their performance.

### Diagnosing the Causes of Poor Performance

Many different reasons can cause an employee's poor performance. For example, poor performance can be due to lack of employee ability, misunderstanding of performance expectations, lack of feedback, or the need for training an employee who does not have the knowledge and skills needed to meet the performance standards. When diagnosing the causes of poor performance it is important to consider whether the poor performance is detrimental to the business. That is, is poor performance critical to completing the job and does it affect business results? If it is detrimental, then the next step is to conduct a performance analysis to determine the cause of poor performance. The different factors that should be considered in analyzing poor performance are shown in Figure 8.11. For example, if an employee understands the expected level of performance, has been given sufficient feedback, understands the consequences, but lacks the knowledge and skills needed to meet the performance standard, this suggests that the manager may want to consider training the employee to improve

figure 8.11

Factors to Consider in Analyzing Poor Performance

**Input**

Does the employee recognize what he or she is supposed to do?
Are the job flow and procedures logical?
Do employees have the resources (tools, equipment, technology, time) needed for successful performance?
Are other job demands interfering with good performance in this area?

**Employee Characteristics**

Does the employee have the necessary skills and knowledge needed?
Does the employee know why the desired performance level is important?
Is the employee mentally, physically, and emotionally able to perform at the expected level?

**Feedback**

Has the employee been given information about his or her performance?
Is performance feedback relevant, timely, accurate, specific, and understandable?

**Performance Standard/Goals**

Do performance standards exist?
Does the employee know the desired level of expected performance?
Does the employee believe she or he can reach the performance standard?

**Consequences**

Are consequences (rewards, incentives) aligned with good performance?
Are the consequences of performance valuable to the employee?
Are performance consequences given in a timely manner?
Do work group or team norms encourage employees not to meet performance standards?

SOURCES: Based on G. Rummler, "In Search of the Holy Performance Grail," *Training and Development*, April 1996, pp. 26–31; C. Reinhart, "How to Leap over Barriers to Performance," *Training and Development*, January 2000, pp. 20–24; F. Wilmouth, C. Prigmore, and M. Bray, "HPT Models: An Overview of the Major Models in the Field," *Performance Improvement* 41 (2002), pp. 14–21.

performance, moving the employee to a different job that better fits that person's skills, or discharging the employee and making sure that selection methods to find a new employee measure the level of knowledge and skills needed to perform the job.

After conducting the performance analysis, managers should meet with the employee to discuss the results, agree to the next steps that the manager and employee will take to improve performance (e.g., training, providing resources, giving more feedback), discuss the consequences of failing to improve performance, and set a time line for improvement. This type of discussion is most beneficial if it occurs more frequently than the quarterly or yearly performance review, so performance issues can be quickly dealt with before they have adverse consequences for the company (and the employee). Below we discuss the actions that should be considered for different types of employees.

## Actions for Managing Employees' Performance

**Marginal employees** are those employees who are performing at a bare minimum level because of a lack of ability and/or motivation to perform well.[85] Table 8.13 shows actions for the manager to take with four different types of employees. As the table highlights, managers need to take into account whether employees lack ability, motivation, or both in considering ways to improve performance. To determine an employee's level of ability, a manager should consider if he or she has the knowledge, skills, and abilities needed to perform effectively. Lack of ability may be an issue if an employee is new or the job has recently changed. To determine employees' level of motivation, managers need to consider if employees are doing a job they want to do and if they feel they are being appropriately paid or rewarded. A sudden negative change in an employee's performance may indicate personal problems.

**Marginal Employee** An employee performing at a barely acceptable level because of lack of ability and/or motivation to perform well, not poor work conditions.

Employees with high ability and motivation are likely good performers *(solid performers)*. Table 8.13 emphasizes that managers should not ignore employees with high ability and high motivation. Managers should provide development opportunities

**table 8.13** Ways to Manage Employees' Performance

| | | ABILITY: HIGH | ABILITY: LOW |
|---|---|---|---|
| MOTIVATION | High | Solid performers<br>• Reward good performance<br>• Identify development opportunities<br>• Provide honest, direct feedback | Misdirected effort<br>• Coaching<br>• Frequent performance feedback<br>• Goal setting<br>• Training or temporary assignment for skill development<br>• Restructured job assignment |
| | Low | Underutilizers<br>• Give honest, direct feedback<br>• Provide counseling<br>• Use team building and conflict resolution<br>• Link rewards to performance outcomes<br>• Offer training for needed knowledge or skills<br>• Manage stress levels | Deadwood<br>• Withholding pay increases<br>• Demotion<br>• Outplacement<br>• Firing<br>• Specific, direct feedback on performance problems |

SOURCE: Based on M. London, *Job Feedback* (Mahwah, NJ: Lawrence Erlbaum Associates, 1997), pp. 96–97. Used by permission.

to keep them satisfied and effective. Poor performance resulting from lack of ability but not motivation *(misdirected effort)* may be improved by skill development activities such as training or temporary assignments. Managers with employees who have the ability but lack motivation *(underutilizers)* need to consider actions that focus on interpersonal problems or incentives. These actions include making sure that incentives or rewards that the employee values are linked to performance and making counseling available to help employees deal with personal problems or career or job dissatisfaction. Chronic poor performance by employees with low ability and motivation *(deadwood)* indicates that outplacement or firing may be the best solution.

## Developing and Implementing a System That Follows Legal Guidelines

We now discuss the legal issues and constraints affecting performance management. Because performance measures play a central role in such administrative decisions as promotions, pay raises, and discipline, employees who sue an organization over these decisions ultimately attack the measurement systems on which the decisions were made. Two types of cases have dominated: discrimination and unjust dismissal.

In discrimination suits, the plaintiff often alleges that the performance measurement system unjustly discriminated against the plaintiff because of race or gender. Many performance measures are subjective, and we have seen that individual biases can affect them, especially when those doing the measuring harbor racial or gender stereotypes.

In *Brito v. Zia,* the Supreme Court essentially equated performance measures with selection tests.[86] It ruled that the *Uniform Guidelines on Employee Selection Procedures* apply to evaluating the adequacy of a performance appraisal instrument. This ruling presents a challenge to those involved in developing performance measures, because a substantial body of research on race discrimination in performance rating has demonstrated that both white and black raters give higher ratings to members of their own racial group, even after rater training.[87] There is also evidence that the discriminatory biases in performance rating are worse when one group makes up a small percentage of the work group. When the vast majority of the group is male, females receive lower ratings; when the minority is male, males receive lower ratings.[88]

In the second type of suit, an unjust dismissal suit, the plaintiff claims that the dismissal was for reasons other than those the employer claims. For example, an employee who works for a defense contractor might blow the whistle on the company for defrauding the government. If the company fires the employee, claiming poor performance, the employee may argue that the firing was, in fact, because of blowing the whistle on the employer—in other words, that the dismissal was unjust. The court case will likely focus on the performance measurement system used as the basis for claiming the employee's performance was poor. Unjust dismissal also can result from terminating for poor performance an employee who has a history of favorable reviews and raises. Rewarding poor performers or giving poor performers positive evaluations because of an unwillingness to confront a performance issue undermines the credibility of any performance management system. This makes it difficult to defend termination decisions based on a performance appraisal system.

Because of the potential costs of discrimination and unjust dismissal suits, an organization needs to determine exactly what the courts consider a legally defensible performance management system. Based on reviews of such court decisions, we offer the following characteristics of a system that will withstand legal scrutiny.[89]

1. The system should be developed by conducting a valid job analysis that ascertains the important aspects of job performance. The requirements for job success should be clearly communicated to employees.
2. The system should be based on either behaviors or results; evaluations of ambiguous traits should be avoided.
3. Raters should be trained in how to use the system rather than simply given the materials and left to interpret how to conduct the appraisal.
4. There should be some form of review by upper-level managers of all the performance ratings, and there should be a system for employees to appeal what they consider to be an unfair evaluation.
5. The organization should provide some form of performance counseling or corrective guidance to help poor performers improve their performance before being dismissed. Both short- and long-term performance goals should be included.
6. Multiple raters should be used, particularly if an employee's performance is unlikely to be seen by only one rating source such as manager or customer. At a minimum, employees should be asked to comment on their appraisals. There should be a dialogue between the manager and the employee.

## Use of Technology for Performance Management: Electronic Monitoring

An increasing trend in companies is using sophisticated electronic tracking systems to ensure that employees are working when they should be. Electronic tracking systems include hand and fingerprint recognition systems, global positioning systems (GPSs), and systems that can track employees using handheld computers and cellphones. The systems are used on both blue-collar and white-collar employees.[90] For example, at the New York law firm Akin & Smith LLC, paralegals, receptionists, and clerks clock in by placing their finger on a sensor kept at a secretary's desk. The managing partners believe the system improves productivity and keeps everyone honest, holding them to their lunch times. At Mitsubishi Motors North American plant in Normal, Illinois, accounting managers can check from their desktop computers how many of the plant's 500 white-collar employees have shown up for work. The employees clock in using a Web-based system on their desk computers. The 2,600 assembly line workers are also tracked. They "clock in" for work with an identification badge instead of a paper time card.

Economic Advantages Corporation, a mortgage service company with offices in Vermont and New York, installed an attendance tracking system. The new system implies that the company's salaried workers, client services representatives, get paid by the hour. The company's president believes that most employees put in an honest day's work, but those employees who decide to take time off won't get paid for it. Illiana Financial Credit Union in Calumet City, Illinois, uses a fingerprint recognition system to track its tellers and loan officers. This has saved the company payroll costs by preventing employees from exaggerating their hours worked by staying late or starting early. Automated Waste Disposal, based in Danbury, Connecticut, was concerned with the amount of overtime hours of garbage collectors and sales staff. The operations manager installed a global positioning system (GPS) in garbage trucks and sales vehicles. The tracking technology has reduced the need for overtime hours to complete work, eliminating employees getting "lost" during the day and visiting friends or local restaurants during work hours.[91]

Despite the potential increased productivity benefits that can result from these systems, they still present privacy concerns. Critics argue that these system threaten to reduce the workplace to an electronic sweatshop in which employees are treated as robots that are monitored to maximize productivity for every second they are at work. Also, electronic monitoring systems such as GPS threaten employees' rights and dignity to work without being monitored.

Some argue that electronic tracking systems are needlessly surveilling and tracking employees when there is no reason to believe that anything is wrong. Good managers know what their employees are doing, and electronic systems should not be a substitute for good management. Critics also argue that such systems result in less productivity and motivation, demoralize employees, and create unnecessary stress. A mentality is created that employees have to always be at their desks to be productive. Advocates, on the other hand, counter that these systems ensure that time is not abused, they improve scheduling, and they help managers identify lazy workers. To avoid the potential negative effects of electronic monitoring, managers must communicate why employees are being monitored. Monitoring can also be used as a way for more experienced employees to coach less experienced employees.

In addition to monitoring, other types of electronic systems are being used to track attendance. TriB Nursery Inc., an Oklahoma plant wholesaler, is testing a hand recognition system to replace a punch time-clock to track employees who work across 300 acres during the company's busiest season. The hand readers make it easier for managers to figure out how many workers are on the job at any given time. The system allows the nursery to identify employees and to shift them to areas where they are most needed, increasing efficiency. The system also prevents friends' clocking in for each other.

## A Look Back

The chapter opener on the Zoological Society discussed its new Web-based appraisal system for managers.

### Questions

1. Consider the five criteria for effective performance appraisals discussed in the chapter. Evaluate the new appraisal system on each criterion. That is, decide whether the new appraisal system met the criterion, fell short of the criterion, or exceeded the criterion. Provide evidence for each.
2. What are the strengths and weaknesses of Web-based appraisal systems such as the one used by the Zoological Society? What changes would you recommend for the Zoological Society's system to improve its weaknesses?

Please see the Video Case that corresponds to this chapter online at www.mhhe.com/noe6e.

## Summary

Measuring and managing performance is a challenging enterprise and one of the keys to gaining competitive advantage. Performance management systems serve strategic, administrative, and developmental purposes—their importance cannot be overestimated. A performance measurement system should be evaluated against the criteria of strategic congruence, validity, reliability, acceptability, and specificity. Measured against these criteria, the comparative, attribute, behavioral, results, and quality approaches have different strengths and weaknesses. Thus, deciding which approach and which source of performance information are best depends on the job in question. Effective managers need to be aware of the issues involved in determining the best method or combination of methods for their particular situations. In addition, once performance has been measured, a major component of a manager's job is to feed that performance information back to employees in a way that results in improved performance rather than defensiveness and decreased motivation. Managers should take action based on the causes for poor performance: ability, motivation, or both. Managers must be sure that their performance management system can meet legal scrutiny, especially if it is used to discipline or fire poor performers.

## Key Terms

Performance management, 343
Performance appraisal, 343
Performance feedback, 343
Performance planning and evaluation (PPE) system, 346
Strategic congruence, 351
Validity, 352
Reliability, 353
Acceptability, 353
Specificity, 354
Assessment centers, 365
Upward feedback, 377
360-degree appraisal, 379
Appraisal politics, 382
Marginal employee, 387

## Discussion Questions

1. What are examples of administrative decisions that might be made in managing the performance of professors? Developmental decisions?
2. What would you consider the strategy of your university (e.g., research, undergraduate teaching, graduate teaching, a combination)? How might the performance management system for faculty members fulfill its strategic purpose of eliciting the types of behaviors and results required by this strategy?
3. If you were developing a performance measurement system for faculty members, what types of attributes would you seek to measure? Behaviors? Results?
4. What sources of performance information would you use to evaluate faculty members' performance?
5. The performance of students is usually evaluated with an overall results measure of grade point average. How is this measure contaminated? How is it deficient? What other measures might you use to more adequately evaluate student performance?
6. Think of the last time you had a conflict with another person, either at work or at school. Using the guidelines for performance feedback, how would you provide effective performance feedback to that person?
7. Explain what fairness has to do with performance management.
8. Why might a manager intentionally distort appraisal results? What would you recommend to minimize this problem?
9. Can computer monitoring of performance ever be acceptable to employees? Explain.
10. A delivery driver contaminated a hospital's oxygen supply by refilling the hospital's main oxygen supply line with trichloroethane, a mild anesthetic. Following detection of the contamination, all patients were switched to oxygen tanks and no patients were injured. How would you diagnose the cause of this performance problem? Explain.
11. One of the weaknesses of using customer evaluations of employee performance is their expense (postage, phone interviews, etc.). Can you think of other weaknesses? Strengths?

## Self-Assessment Exercise

How do you like getting feedback? To test your attitudes toward feedback, take the following quiz. Read each statement, and write A next to each statement you agree with. If you disagree with the statement, write D.

____ 1. I like being told how well I am doing on a project.
____ 2. Even though I may think I have done a good job, I feel a lot more confident when someone else tells me so.

____ 3. Even when I think I could have done something better, I feel good when other people think well of me for what I have done.

____ 4. It is important for me to know what people think of my work.

____ 5. I think my instructor would think worse of me if I asked him or her for feedback.

____ 6. I would be nervous about asking my instructor how she or he evaluates my behavior in class.

____ 7. It is not a good idea to ask my fellow students for feedback; they might think I am incompetent.

____ 8. It is embarrassing to ask other students for their impression of how I am doing in class.

____ 9. It would bother me to ask the instructor for feedback.

____ 10. It is not a good idea to ask the instructor for feedback because he or she might think I am incompetent.

____ 11. It is embarrassing to ask the instructor for feedback.

____ 12. It is better to try to figure out how I am doing on my own, rather than to ask other students for feedback.

For statements 1–4, add the total number of As: ________

For statements 5–12, add the total number of As: ________

For statements 1–4, the greater the number of As, the greater your preference for and trust in feedback from others. For statements 5–12, the greater the number of As, the greater the risk you believe there is in asking for feedback.

How might this information be useful in understanding how you react to feedback in school or on the job?

SOURCES: Based on D. B. Fedor, R. B. Rensvold, and S. M. Adams, "An Investigation of Factors Expected to Affect Feedback Seeking: A Longitudinal Field Study," *Personnel Psychology* 45 (1992), pp. 779–805; S. J. Asford, "Feedback Seeking in Individual Adaptation: A Resource Perspective," *Academy of Management Journal* 29 (1986), pp. 465–87.

## Exercising Strategy: A Customized Appraisal System

Equifax provides information solutions to businesses and consumers regarding credit reporting, fraud protection, and debt recovery services. Equifax created a customized performance system to integrate organizational and individual performance, increase accountability, and improve follow-up. Managers are required to create annual objectives in four areas: strategy, operations, people, and finances. The objectives are weighted along with needed competencies for workplace tasks. A midyear evaluation is completed to ensure that objectives are being met, identify any objectives that need to be changed, and ensure that managers are discussing performance with their employees. Ratings are not given at the midyear review but are provided at the end of the year. As part of the performance management process, employees must include a learning objective, which states how and when the employee intends to accomplish the objective and apply it in job or career development. The objective counts for 10 percent of the employee's overall evaluation.

SOURCE: Based on ASTD Best, "Equifax," *T+D*, October 2006, pp. 75–76.

### Questions

1. How does this type of performance management system affect training and development?
2. Do you think it is more important for performance management systems such as this one to focus more, less, or about the same on what gets accomplished (objectives) or how it is accomplished (behaviors, competencies)? Explain your choice.
3. What recommendations would you give to Equifax to make this system even more effective?

## Managing People: From the Pages of *BusinessWeek*

### BusinessWeek Cracking the Whip at Wyeth

**R&D chief Robert Ruffolo imposed tough targets on scientists—and it's working** When Robert R. Ruffolo Jr. signed on at Wyeth in 2000, his mandate was simple: shake up the drugmaker's mediocre research-and-development operation. He has certainly succeeded. One of Ruffolo's first moves as executive vice-president for R&D was conducting a top-to-bottom review of Wyeth's pipeline.

With the date of the meeting looming, Wyeth researcher Steven J. Projan all but gave up sleeping. For five straight days, Projan was so worried about the survival of a novel antibiotic he had been working on for seven years that he slept on his boss's couch and showered in the company gym when he wasn't fine-tuning the presentation for the drug. "There was a lot of fear and loathing about going through that process," Projan says. "Everybody was convinced this was a tool to kill off their favorite project."

### Shredding It Up

Since jumping ship at SmithKline Beecham in 2000, the 55-year-old Ruffolo, an avid fan of heavy-metal music, has ripped apart and reassembled Wyeth's $2.7 billion research operation. Among his controversial changes: a series of quotas for how many compounds must be churned out by company scientists. For some of them, having to hit a hard-and-fast number seemed anathema to the complex and at times serendipitous drug-development process.

But Ruffolo held bonuses hostage to managers' meeting that goal. More recently he began studying industries from aerospace to computer hardware manufacturing in a bid to better manage innovation. But don't expect him to steal from the playbooks of industry rivals. "Until recently, this industry didn't have to focus too much on productivity," he says. "The solutions to our problems aren't going to come from our competitors."

Wyeth's efforts to energize its labs reflect a major challenge in the drug business. In recent years the output from big-pharma R&D has been almost universally disappointing. According to the Tufts Center for the Study of Drug Development, only 58 new drugs were approved by the Food & Drug Administration from 2002 to 2004, down 47 percent from the peak of 110 from 1996 to 1998.

### Critical Transformation

The reasons are myriad, including a wealth of good treatments that are already available for many diseases and increased vigilance from regulators and physicians on safety. But with financial pressures building as more drugs go off-patent and as payers push back against rising drug costs, pharma companies can't afford to battle that problem by simply throwing bigger bucks at research.

That's why Ruffolo, who took over all of Wyeth R&D in mid-2002, is looking for ways to bring greater efficiency to the innovation process. His goal may not be unusual, but his hard-nosed approach to getting there is.

"A lot of companies at the senior level talk about transformational change, but it doesn't go very far down [the organization]," says Kenneth I. Kaitin, director of the Tufts Center. Ruffolo, he says, has been able to "instill across the entire R&D workforce the notion that it is critical for the company to transform itself."

### Rock 'n' Roll Fantasy

On the surface, Ruffolo may seem an unlikely radical. He spent 17 years as a researcher at SmithKline Beecham before it merged with Glaxo. At SmithKline he was credited with helping to push through the heart failure treatment Coreg in the face of sometimes stiff resistance.

But despite Ruffolo's Big Pharma pedigree, he's hardly the typical cerebral scientist. He spends much of his free time practicing electric guitar and playing in a band made up largely of other aging pharma execs. He hates classical music, and his favorite bands include Metallica, Megadeth, and Iron Maiden. In his free time, Ruffolo, who lives in Spring City, Pa., with his wife and three children, practices electric guitar in a basement complete with black light posters and a lava lamp. "It's a 14-year-old boy's fantasy," he says.

After signing on at Wyeth, Ruffolo followed Wyeth CEO Robert A. Essner's charge to "rattle the cage." Wyeth had a reputation for less-than-cutting-edge research and, at the time, was being buffeted by the fallout from the withdrawal of its diet drugs Pondimin (the "fen" in the fen-phen combo) and Redux. Ruffolo recalls that a scientist at another company laughed in his face when he said he was taking the job at Wyeth. "It was a strong motivator, to be laughed at," he recalls.

### Managing Resources

Ruffolo moved quickly to instill discipline. With the help of outside consultants, 70 scientists at the company took a hard look at recent projects that had succeeded and failed. They came to a stunning conclusion: Often, drugs with the lowest chance of paying off ended up with the most resources. Why? Scientists continued to plow money and staff into troubled projects in an attempt to rescue them.

So Ruffolo instituted the review process that sent Projan and everyone else scrambling. Under that system, a value is determined for every project in the pipeline based on a host of factors, including the cost of developing it, the likelihood of success, and expected future sales.

That culminates in an annual review that determines which projects move forward, which get put on the back burner, and which are killed. That new rigor made people more willing to terminate troubled projects. That's critical in the drug business since late-stage human trials are so expensive.

### Smart Decisions

Brenda Reis, an assistant vice-president in Wyeth R&D, had to make one of those tough calls. In 2004 her group was developing a new oral contraceptive. As part of Ruffolo's portfolio-review process they determined what sort of safety and effectiveness they would need from the drug in order to make it a hit.

In late summer of 2004, Reis recalls, the group of 12 people leading the project sat in stunned silence as they digested disappointing data from midstage human testing of the drug. The product was triggering a side effect that would seriously limit its potential. A few weeks later the group recommended the development of the compound be dropped. Her team was given an internal company award for stopping the project—a move that sent a clear signal that the company would reward good decision-making.

Ruffolo has set firm targets for how many compounds need to move forward at each stage of the development process. Take discovery scientists, the group that identifies new ways to attack diseases and creates compounds to be passed on to another group for more extensive testing. When Ruffolo came in, that group was moving just four drug candidates out of its labs every year. Ruffolo set the new target at 12—with no increases in resources or headcount. The target has been met every year since its 2001 implementation. This year, the bar has been raised to 15.

### Too Much Pressure?

Those targets forced big changes in the R&D operation. For one thing, scientists needed to standardize more of what they did in an effort to move compounds more quickly through their shop. Case in point: At the old Wyeth, researchers could design the early human safety studies—known as Phase one trials—in almost any way they wanted. Under the new regime, researchers pick from four or five standardized formats. That helped cut the time for a Phase one trial from 18 months to 6.

The approach has critics. Some former executives say he seemed out of touch with the anxiety his new demands created among scientists. Dr. Philip Frost, chief scientific officer at biotech ImClone Systems, describes Ruffolo as a "bully" at times. Ruffolo doesn't agree with that characterization, but he acknowledges that when it comes to the targets, "I forced it on them."

Critics also argue that Ruffolo went too far in trying to boost output. William J. Weiss, who left Wyeth in early 2004 and is now director of drug evaluation at biotech Cumbre in Dallas, says quotas like those set by Ruffolo can prompt scientists to "overlook problems with some compounds" in order to make their numbers. In fact, Wyeth has seen an increased failure rate for compounds in mid-stage testing recently.

Ruffolo says that this has occurred throughout the industry. Still, even supporters such as C. Richard Lyttle, CEO at pharmaceutical company Radius Health in Cambridge, Mass., point out that those sorts of productivity pressures can also force people to zero in on the projects that are the safest gambles. "If it's a sure bet for me, it is a sure bet for a lot of other people [at rival companies]," says Lyttle. "You don't get the real innovation."

### "Manage the Outcome"

Ruffolo dismisses such criticisms and says Wyeth took steps to ensure that only high-quality compounds move forward. For example, while discovery researchers used to have a lot of control over what moved into human testing, a council made up of scientists, regulatory experts, and marketing execs now make those decisions. That means discovery scientists can't simply pass a few questionable compounds out of their labs in order to meet targets.

Ruffolo says he specifically put fewer controls in at the so-called exploratory phase, when scientists tend to have eureka moments of, say, spotting a new cellular target they want to hit with a drug. "I don't think you can manage creativity," he says. "But I think you can manage the outcome after you have that creative effort."

Has Ruffolo's prescription worked? UBS Investment Research analyst Carl Seiden says Wyeth's pipeline has shown major improvement, with a number of potentially hot-selling products likely to hit in the next few years. Among them: a new antidepressant based on its current blockbuster Effexor and a new schizophrenia treatment.

According to Citigroup, Wyeth will generate 20 percent of revenues from new products in 2009, nearly double the industry average. A number of those were already in the works when Ruffolo came on board. But the company has also dramatically expanded the number of products that are moving through human testing.

### Fundamental Changes

The hunt for productivity boosts continues. Clinical trials, for example, are taking longer to do and costing more money than ever before. So early last year he tapped Dr. Evan Loh, a cardiologist by training and vice-president of Wyeth's clinical R&D, to come up with a new blueprint for human testing. Loh's team visited more than a dozen companies in industries such as aerospace and computer hardware, studying everything from how they manage complex projects to how they streamline manufacturing processes.

That, Loh says, will help "fundamentally change how we do things." For example, in the aerospace industry, the skills of project managers are usually matched specifically to the phase of that project's development. In pharma, Loh says, the same team of scientists often manage a project throughout its clinical development. But while the earlier part of that process requires great scientific insight, the latter demands more operational expertise and team leadership. As Wyeth revamps its clinical trial process, it will identify managers with the right skills for those different stages.

Ruffolo is also borrowing from the programming industry with a move toward global task-sharing. So when the lights go out at labs in places such as Collegeville, Pa., some tasks will be handed off to employees in other time zones. Steve Projan, who now oversees a group working on protein-based drugs in Cambridge, Mass., is already planning how to share work with a soon-to-be-opened lab in Dublin, Ireland. But Projan is the first to concede that this sort of thinking takes some getting used to. "Scientists love working in silos," he says. "We are all prima donnas."

SOURCE: Amy Barrett, "Cracking the Whip at Wyeth," *BusinessWeek Online*, February 6, 2006.

### Questions

1. Are there any downsides to an objective-based performance management system for scientists as described in the article? What are the potential dangers? What other types of outcomes should be included in scientists' performance management systems?
2. What strategic purpose does Wyeth's performance management system serve? Explain.

# NOTES


1. C. Lee, "Performance Appraisal: Can We Manage Away the Curse?" *Training*, May 1996, pp. 44–49.
2. "Measuring People Power," *Fortune*, October 2, 2000.
3. A. Freedman, "Balancing Values, Results in Reviews," *Human Resource Executive*, August 2006, pp. 62–63; G. Ruiz, "Performance Management Underperforms," *Workforce Management*, December 2006, pp. 47–49.
4. K. Murphy and J. Cleveland, *Performance Appraisal: An Organizational Perspective* (Boston: Allyn & Bacon, 1991).
5. M. Sallie-Dosunmu, "Born to Grow," *TD*, May 2006, pp. 33–37.
6. J. Cleveland, K. Murphy, and R. Williams, "Multiple Uses of Performance Appraisal: Prevalence and Correlates," *Journal of Applied Psychology* 74 (1989), pp. 130–35.
7. C. Longenecker, "Behind the Mask: The Politics of Employee Appraisal," *Academy of Management Executive* 1 (1987), p. 183.
8. M. Beer, "Note on Performance Appraisal," in *Readings in Human Resource Management*, ed. M. Beer and B. Spector (New York: Free Press, 1985).
9. L. Weatherly, *Performance Management: Getting It Right from the Start* (Alexandria, VA: Society for Human Resource Management, 2004).
10. E. Lawler and M. McDermott, "Current Performance Management Practices," *World at Work Journal* 12 no. 2 (2003), pp. 49–60.
11. C. Cole, "Eight Values Bring Unity to a Worldwide Force," *Workforce*, March 2001, pp. 44–45; General Semiconductor Web site, www.generalsemiconductor.com, September 2, 2001.
12. C. G. Banks and K. E. May, "Performance Management: The Real Glue in Organizations," in *Evolving Practices in Human Resource Management*, ed. A. Kraut and A. Korman (San Francisco: Jossey-Bass, 1999), pp. 118–45.
13. C. E. Schneier, D. G. Shaw, and R. W. Beatty, "Performance Measurement and Management: A Tool for Strategic Execution," *Human Resource Management* 30 (1991), pp. 279–301.
14. C. D. Ittner and D. F. Larcker, "Coming Up Short on Nonfinancial Performance Measurement," *Harvard Business Review*, December 2003, pp. 88–95.
15. J. K. Harter, F. Schmidt, and T. L. Hayes, "Business-Unit Level Relationships between Employee Satisfaction, Employee Engagement, and Business Outcomes: A Meta-Analysis," *Journal of Applied Psychology* 87 (2002), pp. 268–79.
16. A. J. Rucci, S. P. Kim, and R. T. Quinn, "The Employee-Customer-Profit Chain at Sears," *Harvard Business Review*, January–February 1998, pp. 82–97.
17. R. Schuler and S. Jackson, "Linking Competitive Strategies with Human Resource Practices," *Academy of Management Executive* 1 (1987), pp. 207–19.
18. L. King, J. Hunter, and F. Schmidt, "Halo in a Multidimensional Forced-Choice Performance Evaluation Scale," *Journal of Applied Psychology* 65 (1980), pp. 507–16.
19. B. R. Nathan, A. M. Mohrman, and J. Millman, "Interpersonal Relations as a Context for the Effects of Appraisal Interviews on Performance and Satisfaction: A Longitudinal Study," *Academy of Management Journal* 34 (1991), pp. 352–69; M. S. Taylor, K. B. Tracy, M. K. Renard, J. K. Harrison, and S. J. Carroll, "Due Process in Performance Appraisal: A Quasi-experiment in Procedural Justice," *Administrative Science Quarterly* 40 (1995), pp. 495–523; J. M. Werner and M. C. Bolino, "Explaining U.S. Courts of Appeals Decisions Involving Performance Appraisal: Accuracy, Fairness, and Validation," *Personnel Psychology* 50 (1997), pp. 1–24.
20. *Albermarle Paper Company v. Moody*, 10 FEP 1181 (1975).
21. G. Ruiz, "Lessons from the Front Lines," *Workforce Management*, December 2006, pp. 50–52.
22. S. Bates, "Forced Ranking," *HR Magazine*, June 2003, pp. 63–68; A. Meisler, "Deadman's Curve," *Workforce Management*, July 2003, pp. 44–49; M. Lowery, "Forcing the Issue," *Human Resource Executive* (October 16, 2003), pp. 26–29.
23. Ibid.
24. Ibid.
25. S. Scullen, P. Bergey, and L. Aiman-Smith, "Forced Choice Distribution Systems and the Improvement of Workforce Potential: A Baseline Simulation," *Personnel Psychology* 58 (2005), pp. 1–32.
26. F. Blanz and E. Ghiselli, "The Mixed Standard Scale: A New Rating System," *Personnel Psychology* 25 (1973), pp. 185–99; K. Murphy and J. Constans, "Behavioral Anchors as a Source of Bias in Rating," *Journal of Applied Psychology* 72 (1987), pp. 573–77.
27. P. Smith and L. Kendall, "Retranslation of Expectations: An Approach to the Construction of Unambiguous Anchors for Rating Scales," *Journal of Applied Psychology* 47 (1963), pp. 149–55.
28. Murphy and Constans, "Behavioral Anchors"; M. Piotrowski, J. Barnes-Farrel, and F. Esrig, "Behaviorally Anchored Bias: A Replication and Extension of Murphy and Constans," *Journal of Applied Psychology* 74 (1989), pp. 823–26.
29. U. Wiersma and G. Latham, "The Practicality of Behavioral Observation Scales, Behavioral Expectation Scales, and Trait Scales," *Personnel Psychology* 39 (1986), pp. 619–28.
30. G. Latham and K. Wexley, *Increasing Productivity through Performance Appraisal* (Boston: Addison-Wesley, 1981).
31. Wiersma and Latham, "The Practicality of Behavioral Observation Scales, Behavioral Expectation Scales, and Trait Scales."
32. D. C. Anderson, C. Crowell, J. Sucec, K. Gilligan, and M. Wikoff, "Behavior Management of Client Contacts in a Real Estate Brokerage: Getting Agents to Sell More," *Journal of Organizational Behavior Management* 4 (1983), pp. 67–96; A. D. Stajkovic and F. Luthans, "Differential Effects of Incentive Motivation on Work Performance," *Academy of Management Journal* 4 (2001), pp. 580–90; F. Luthans and R. Kreitner, *Organizational Behavior Modification and Beyond* (Glenview, IL: Scott Foresman, 1975).
33. K. L. Langeland, C. M. Jones, and T. C. Mawhinney, "Improving Staff Performance in a Community Mental Health Setting: Job Analysis, Training, Goal Setting, Feedback, and Years of Data," *Journal of Organizational Behavior Management* 18 (1998), pp. 21–43.
34. J. Komaki, R. Collins, and P. Penn, "The Role of Performance Antecedents and Consequences in Work Motivation," *Journal of Applied Psychology* 67 (1982), pp. 334–40.
35. Latham and Wexley, *Increasing Productivity through Performance Appraisal*.
36. S. Snell, "Control Theory in Strategic Human Resource Management: The Mediating Effect of Administrative Information," *Academy of Management Journal* 35 (1992), pp. 292–327.
37. T. Patten Jr., *A Manager's Guide to Performance Appraisal* (New York: Free Press, 1982).
38. M. O'Donnell and R. O'Donnell, "MBO—Is It Passe?" *Hospital and Health Services Administration* 28, no. 5 (1983), pp. 46–58; T. Poister and G. Streib, "Management Tools in Government: Trends over the Past Decade," *Public Administration Review* 49 (1989), pp. 240–48.

39. D. McGregor, "An Uneasy Look at Performance Appraisal," *Harvard Business Review* 35, no. 3 (1957), pp. 89–94.
40. E. Locke and G. Latham, *A Theory of Goal Setting and Task Performance* (Englewood Cliffs, NJ: Prentice Hall, 1990).
41. S. Carroll and H. Tosi, *Management by Objectives* (New York: Macmillan, 1973).
42. G. Odiorne, *MBO II: A System of Managerial Leadership for the 80's* (Belmont, CA: Pitman, 1986).
43. R. Rodgers and J. Hunter, "Impact of Management by Objectives on Organizational Productivity," *Journal of Applied Psychology* 76 (1991), pp. 322–26.
44. S. Wells, "No Results, No Raise," *HR Magazine*, May 2005, pp. 77–79.
45. R. Pritchard, S. Jones, P. Roth, K. Stuebing, and S. Ekeberg, "The Evaluation of an Integrated Approach to Measuring Organizational Productivity," *Personnel Psychology* 42 (1989), pp. 69–115.
46. P. Wright, J. George, S. Farnsworth, and G. McMahan, "Productivity and Extra-Role Behavior: The Effects of Goals and Incentives on Spontaneous Helping," *Journal of Applied Psychology* 78, no. 3 (1993), pp. 374–81.
47. Latham and Wexley, *Increasing Productivity through Performance Appraisal*.
48. J. Liedman, "The Ongoing Conversation," *Human Resource Executive*, November 2006, pp. 71–74; R. Davenport, "John Deere Champions Workforce Development," *TD*, April 2006, pp. 41–43.
49. R. L. Cardy, "Performance Appraisal in a Quality Context: A New Look at an Old Problem," in *Performance Appraisal: State of the Art in Practice*, ed. J. W. Smither (San Francisco: Jossey-Bass, 1998), pp. 132–62.
50. E. C. Huge, *Total Quality: An Executive's Guide for the 1990s* (Homewood, IL: Richard D. Irwin, 1990): see Chapter 5, "Measuring and Rewarding Performance," pp. 70–88; W. E. Deming, *Out of Crisis* (Cambridge, MA: MIT Center for Advanced Engineering Study, 1986).
51. M. Caroselli, *Total Quality Transformations* (Amherst, MA: Human Resource Development Press, 1991); Huge, *Total Quality*.
52. J. D. Cryer and R. B. Miller, *Statistics for Business: Data Analysis and Modeling* (Boston: PWS-Kent, 1991); C. Carter, "Seven Basic Quality Tools," *HR Magazine*, January 1992, pp. 81–83; D. K. Denton, "Process Mapping Trims Cycle Time," *HR Magazine*, February 1995, pp. 56–61.
53. D. E. Bowen and E. E. Lawler III, "Total Quality-Oriented Human Resource Management," *Organizational Dynamics* 21 (1992), pp. 29–41.
54. R. Heneman, K. Wexley, and M. Moore, "Performance Rating Accuracy: A Critical Review," *Journal of Business Research* 15 (1987), pp. 431–48.
55. T. Becker and R. Klimoski, "A Field Study of the Relationship between the Organizational Feedback Environment and Performance," *Personnel Psychology* 42 (1989), pp. 343–58; H. M. Findley, W. F. Giles, and K. W. Mossholder, "Performance Appraisal and Systems Facets: Relationships with Contextual Performance," *Journal of Applied Psychology* 85 (2000) pp. 634–40.
56. K. Ellis, "Developing for Dollars," *Training*, May 2003, pp. 34–39.
57. L. Axline, "Performance Biased Evaluations," *Supervisory Management*, November 1991, p. 3.
58. K. Wexley and R. Klimoski, "Performance Appraisal: An Update," in *Research in Personnel and Human Resource Management* (vol. 2), ed. K. Rowland and G. Ferris (Greenwich, CT: JAI Press, 1984).
59. F. Landy and J. Farr, *The Measurement of Work Performance: Methods, Theory, and Applications* (New York: Academic Press, 1983).
60. G. McEvoy and P. Buller, "User Acceptance of Peer Appraisals in an Industrial Setting," *Personnel Psychology* 40 (1987), pp. 785–97.
61. A. Pomeroy, "Agent of Change," *HR Magazine*, May 2005, pp. 52–56.
62. D. Antonioni, "The Effects of Feedback Accountability on Upward Appraisal Ratings," *Personnel Psychology* 47 (1994), pp. 349–56.
63. Murphy and Cleveland, *Performance Appraisal: An Organizational Perspective*.
64. J. Bernardin and L. Klatt, "Managerial Appraisal Systems: Has Practice Caught Up with the State of the Art?" *Public Personnel Administrator*, November 1985, pp. 79–86.
65. D. Shuit, "GM Goes Fast," *Workforce Management*, March 2004, pp. 36–38.
66. R. Steel and N. Ovalle, "Self-Appraisal Based on Supervisor Feedback," *Personnel Psychology* 37 (1984), pp. 667–85; L. E. Atwater, "The Advantages and Pitfalls of Self-Assessment in Organizations," in *Performance Appraisal: State of the Art in Practice*, pp. 331–65.
67. M. W. Horrigan, "Employment Projections to 2012: Concepts and Context," *Monthly Labor Review* 127 (2004), pp. 3–11.
68. E. Gummerson, "Lip Services—A Neglected Area of Service Marketing," *Journal of Services Marketing* 1 (1987), pp. 1–29.
69. J. Bernardin, B. Hagan, J. Kane, and P. Villanova, "Effective Performance Management: A Focus on Precision, Customers, and Situational Constraints," in *Performance Appraisal: State of the Art in Practice*, ed. J. W. Smither (San Francisco: Jossey-Bass, 1998), pp. 3–48.
70. R. Hoffman, "Ten Reasons You Should Be Using 360-Degree Feedback," *HR Magazine*, April 1995, pp. 82–84.
71. S. Sherman, "How Tomorrow's Best Leaders Are Learning Their Stuff," *Fortune*, November 27, 1995, pp. 90–104; W. W. Tornow, M. London, and Associates, *Maximizing the Value of 360-Degree Feedback* (San Francisco: Jossey-Bass, 1998); D. A. Waldman, L. E. Atwater, and D. Antonioni, "Has 360-Degree Feedback Gone Amok?" *Academy of Management Executive* 12 (1988), pp. 86–94.
72. A. Tversky and D. Kahneman, "Availability: A Heuristic for Judging Frequency and Probability," *Cognitive Psychology* 5 (1973), pp. 207–32.
73. K. Wexley and W. Nemeroff, "Effects of Racial Prejudice, Race of Applicant, and Biographical Similarity on Interviewer Evaluations of Job Applicants," *Journal of Social and Behavioral Sciences* 20 (1974), pp. 66–78.
74. D. Smith, "Training Programs for Performance Appraisal: A Review," *Academy of Management Review* 11 (1986), pp. 22–40.
75. G. Latham, K. Wexley, and E. Pursell, "Training Managers to Minimize Rating Errors in the Observation of Behavior," *Journal of Applied Psychology* 60 (1975), pp. 550–55.
76. J. Bernardin and E. Pence, "Effects of Rater Training: Creating New Response Sets and Decreasing Accuracy," *Journal of Applied Psychology* 65 (1980), pp. 60–66.
77. E. Pulakos, "A Comparison of Rater Training Programs: Error Training and Accuracy Training," *Journal of Applied Psychology* 69 (1984), pp. 581–88.
78. H. J. Bernardin, M. R. Buckley, C. L. Tyler, and D. S. Wiese, "A Reconsideration of Strategies in Rater Training," in *Research in Personnel and Human Resource Management*, vol. 18, ed. G. R. Ferris (Greenwich, CT: JAI Press, 2000), pp. 221–74.
79. G. Ruiz, "Lessons from the Front Lines," *Workforce Management*, December 2006, pp. 50–52.
80. S. W. J. Kozlowski, G. T. Chao, and R. F. Morrison, "Games Raters Play: Politics, Strategies, and Impression Management in Performance Appraisal," in *Performance Appraisal: State of the Art in Practice*, pp. 163–205; C. Rosen, P. Levy, and R. Hall, "Placing

Perceptions of Politics in the Context of the Feedback Environment, Employee Attitudes, and Job Performance," *Journal of Applied Psychology* 91 (2006), pp. 211–20.

81. K. Wexley, V. Singh, and G. Yukl, "Subordinate Participation in Three Types of Appraisal Interviews," *Journal of Applied Psychology* 58 (1973), pp. 54–57; K. Wexley, "Appraisal Interview," in *Performance Assessment*, ed. R. A. Berk (Baltimore: Johns Hopkins University Press, 1986), pp. 167–85; D. Cederblom, "The Performance Appraisal Interview: A Review, Implications, and Suggestions," *Academy of Management Review* 7 (1982), pp. 219–27; B. D. Cawley, L. M. Keeping, and P. E. Levy, "Participation in the Performance Appraisal Process and Employee Reactions: A Meta-analytic Review of Field Investigations," *Journal of Applied Psychology* 83, no. 3 (1998), pp. 615–63; H. Aguinis, *Performance Management* (Upper Saddle River, NJ: Pearson Prentice Hall, 2007); C. Lee, "Feedback, Not Appraisal," *HR Magazine*, November 2006, pp. 111–14.
82. W. Giles and K. Mossholder, "Employee Reactions to Contextual and Session Components of Performance Appraisal," *Journal of Applied Psychology* 75 (1990), pp. 371–77.
83. E. Locke and G. Latham, *A Theory of Goal Setting and Task Performance* (Englewood Cliffs, NJ: Prentice Hall, 1990).
84. H. Klein, S. Snell, and K. Wexley, "A Systems Model of the Performance Appraisal Interview Process," *Industrial Relations* 26 (1987), pp. 267–80.
85. M. London and E. M. Mone, "Managing Marginal Performance in Organizations Striving for Excellence," in *Human Resource Dilemmas in Work Organizations: Strategies for Resolution*, ed. A. K. Korman (New York: Guilford, 1993), pp. 95–124.
86. *Brito v. Zia Co.*, 478 F.2d 1200 (10th Cir 1973).
87. K. Kraiger and J. Ford, "A Meta-Analysis of Ratee Race Effects in Performance Rating," *Journal of Applied Psychology* 70 (1985), pp. 56–65.
88. P. Sackett, C. DuBois, and A. Noe, "Tokenism in Performance Evaluation: The Effects of Work Groups Representation on Male–Female and White–Black Differences in Performance Ratings," *Journal of Applied Psychology* 76 (1991), pp. 263–67.
89. G. Barrett and M. Kernan, "Performance Appraisal and Terminations: A Review of Court Decisions since *Brito v. Zia* with Implications for Personnel Practices," *Personnel Psychology* 40 (1987), pp. 489–503; H. Field and W. Holley, "The Relationship of Performance Appraisal System Characteristics to Verdicts in Selected Employment Discrimination Cases," *Academy of Management Journal* 25 (1982), pp. 392–406; J. M. Werner and M. C. Bolino, "Explaining U.S. Courts of Appeals Decisions Involving Performance Appraisal: Accuracy, Fairness, and Validation," *Personnel Psychology* 50 (1997), pp. 1–24; J. A. Segal, "86 Your Appraisal Process," *HR Magazine*, October 2000, pp. 199–202.
90. K. Maher, "Big Employer Is Watching," *The Wall Street Journal*, November 4, 2003, pp. B1 and B6.
91. D. Onley, "Technology Gives Big Brother Capability," *HR Magazine*, July 2005, pp. 99–102.

9

CHAPTER

# Employee Development

LO

## LEARNING OBJECTIVES

After reading this chapter, you should be able to:

LO1 Explain how employee development contributes to strategies related to employee retention, developing intellectual capital, and business growth. *page 400*

LO2 Discuss current trends in using formal education for development. *page 404*

LO3 Relate how assessment of personality type, work behaviors, and job performance can be used for employee development. *page 409*

LO4 Explain how job experiences can be used for skill development. *page 417*

LO5 Develop successful mentoring programs. *page 424*

LO6 Describe how to train managers to coach employees. *page 427*

LO7 Discuss the steps in the development planning process. *page 429*

LO8 Explain the employees' and company's responsibilities in planning development. *page 430*

LO9 Discuss what companies are doing for management development issues including succession planning, melting the glass ceiling, and helping dysfunctional managers. *page 433*

# Enter the World of Business

## Grit, Sweat, Heavy Equipment, and Employee Development Needed to Finish Projects on Time

Engineering, construction, and management company Washington Group International spends $50 million annually on employee development. Washington Group has approximately 25,000 employees working in over 40 states and more than 30 countries. Examples of the markets it serves include power generation, mining, manufacturing, and homeland security. The company is involved in diverse and difficult projects including destroying weapons of mass destruction in Russia and Ukraine, helping to rebuild Afghanistan and Iraq, helping to secure the United States from terrorist attacks at home, and upgrading coal-fired power plants in the United States with modern clean-air equipment. The company has merged and acquired many other companies, some of which were responsible for building the Hoover Dam, the San Francisco Bay Bridge, and the Trans-Alaska pipeline.

In 2001 the company was facing an employee shortage as the number of available engineering school graduates dropped and 25 percent of its workforce was becoming eligible for retirement in the next 5 to 10 years. The top executives believed that employee development had to become an important part of the company culture. As a result, employee development is one part of the company's three-part mission, along with operational excellence and financial results. Washington Group International believes that only through fully developing the skills of its employees can the company safely complete projects on time and at or below costs while providing high return for shareholders.

To facilitate employee development, the company first created a standard annual performance review for all salaried employees. Managers were asked to review 10 percent of their staffs each month. The focus of the reviews was changed from past performance to future goals. The process also includes having the company's top executives visit all of the Washington Group's business heads to review them, identify their top performers, and ask what they are doing to develop them. Thirty percent of managers' annual incentive compensation is based on their development efforts. The incentive compensation represents 15 to 50 percent of managers' base pay.

Washington Group's development efforts involve formal courses, job experiences, and mentoring. An important focus in the company's employee development program is training in management skills such as controlling costs and time management. Also, technical training is combined with job experiences to help employees better understand construction projects. One project manager worked on the construction of six auto plants, which helps him better understand each stage of the project. Several times each year managers are invited to the company's Leaders Forum. At the Leaders Forum, executives present current business challenges that the company is facing and ask participants to work in teams to generate solutions. For example, participants were presented with a business acquisition proposal. The experience gave managers the opportunity to understand how things work at the top of the company and helped them see all of the issues involved in making decisions such as considering labor unions and local government. The company's Leadership Excellence Program pairs managers with executive mentors for one year. For example, one manager who wants to develop his financial knowledge and presentation skills is working with his mentor to create a financial plan for another business unit and present it to financial executives.

Steve Hanks, CEO of Washington Group International, is involved in every aspect of employee development from reviewing courses to monitoring employee attendance and reviewing employee course feedback. Hanks believes that Washington Group is a constant learning organization, which is sufficient justification for the company's financial commitment to employee development. He is not concerned that competitors will lure his employees, fearing instead that if they don't train their employees, they will not stay with the company.

Source: Based on J. Marquez, "Building Knowledge," *Workforce Management,* February 2006, pp. 24–30; www.wgint.com, Web site for Washington Mutual International.

## Introduction

As the Washington Group International example illustrates, employee development is a key contributor to a company's competitive advantage, helps develop managerial talent, and allows employees to take responsibility for their careers. Employee development is a necessary component of a company's efforts to compete in the new economy, to meet the challenges of global competition and social change, and to incorporate technological advances and changes in work design. Employee development is key to ensuring that employees have the competencies necessary to serve customers and create new products and customer solutions. Employee development is also important to ensure that companies have the managerial talent needed to successfully execute a growth strategy. Regardless of the business strategy, development is important for retaining talented employees. Also because companies (and their employees) must constantly learn and change to meet customer needs and compete in new markets, the emphasis placed on both training and development has increased. As we noted in Chapter 1, employee commitment and retention are directly related to how employees are treated by their managers.

This chapter begins by discussing the relationship between development, training, and careers. Second, we look at development approaches, including formal education, assessment, job experiences, and interpersonal relationships. The chapter emphasizes the types of skills, knowledge, and behaviors that are strengthened by each development method. Choosing an approach is one part of development planning. Before one or multiple developmental approaches are used, the employee and the company must have an idea of the employee's development needs and the purpose of development. Identifying the needs and purpose of development is part of its planning. The third section of the chapter describes the steps of the development planning process. Employee and company responsibilities at each step of the process are emphasized. The chapter concludes with a discussion of special issues in employee development, including succession planning, dealing with dysfunctional managers, and using development to help women and minorities move into upper-level management positions (referred to as "melting the glass ceiling").

**Development**
The acquisition of knowledge, skills, and behaviors that improve an employee's ability to meet changes in job requirements and in client and customer demands.

## The Relationship between Development, Training, and Careers

**LO1**
Explain How Employee Development Contributes to Strategies Related to Employee Retention, Developing Intellectual Capital, and Business Growth.

### Development and Training

**Development** refers to formal education, job experiences, relationships, and assessment of personality and abilities that help employees prepare for the future. The Washington Group example illustrates that although development can occur through

**table 9.1**
Comparison between Training and Development

| | TRAINING | DEVELOPMENT |
|---|---|---|
| **Focus** | Current | Future |
| **Use of work experiences** | Low | High |
| **Goal** | Preparation for current job | Preparation for changes |
| **Participation** | Required | Voluntary |

participation in planned programs, it often results from work experiences. Because it is future-oriented, it involves learning that is not necessarily related to the employee's current job.[1] Table 9.1 shows the differences between training and development. Traditionally, training focuses on helping employees' performance in their current jobs. Development prepares them for other positions in the company and increases their ability to move into jobs that may not yet exist.[2] Development also helps employees prepare for changes in their current jobs that may result from new technology, work designs, new customers, or new product markets. Development is especially critical for talent management, particularly for senior managers and employees with leadership potential (recall our discussion of attracting and retaining talent in Chapter 1). Companies report that the most important talent management challenges they face include developing existing talent and attracting and retaining existing leadership talent.[3] Chapter 7 emphasized the strategic role of training. As training continues to become more strategic (that is, related to business goals), the distinction between training and development will blur. Both training and development will be required and will focus on current and future personal and company needs.

## Development and Careers

Traditionally, careers have been described in various ways.[4] Careers have been described as a sequence of positions held within an occupation. For example, a university faculty member can hold assistant, associate, and full professor positions. A career has also been described in the context of mobility within an organization. For example, an engineer may begin her career as a staff engineer. As her expertise, experience, and performance increase, she may move through advisory engineering, senior engineering, and senior technical positions. Finally, a career has been described as a characteristic of the employee. Each employee's career consists of different jobs, positions, and experiences.

Today's careers are known as protean careers.[5] A **protean career** is based on self-direction with the goal of psychological success in one's work. Employees take major responsibility for managing their careers. For example, an engineer may decide to take a sabbatical from her position to work in management at the United Way Agency for a year. The purpose of this assignment could be to develop her managerial skills as well as help her personally evaluate if she likes managerial work more than engineering.

**Protean Career**
A career that is based on self-direction with the goal of psychological success in one's work.

Changes in the psychological contract between employees and their companies have influenced the development of the protean career.[6] A **psychological contract** is the expectations that employers and employees have about each other. Today's psychological contract rarerly provides employees with job security even if they perform well. Instead, companies can offer employees opportunities to attend training

**Psychological Contract**
The expectations that employers and employees have about each other.

programs and participate in work experiences that can increase their employability with their current and future employers. For example, the term *blue-collar work* has always meant manufacturing work, but technology has transformed the meaning dramatically.[7] Traditional assembly-line jobs that required little skill and less education have been sent overseas. Today's blue-collar workers are more involved in customized manufacturing. At U.S. Steel employees make more than 700 different kinds of steel, requiring greater familiarity with additives and more understanding of customers and markets. Jobs once considered as lifetime employment are now more temporary, forcing employees to adapt by moving from one factory to another or by changing work shifts. Employees are taking classes to keep up with the latest developments in steelmaking, such as lathes and resins. Despite the lack of guaranteed lifetime employment, many blue-collar jobs are safer and better paying than they were 10 years ago.

**Psychological Success**
The feeling of pride and accomplishment that comes from achieving life goals.

The protean career has several implications for employee development. The goal of the new career is **psychological success:** the feeling of pride and accomplishment that comes from achieving life goals that are not limited to achievements at work (such as raising a family and having good physical health). Psychological success is more under the employee's control than the traditional career goals, which were not only influenced by employee effort but were controlled by the availability of positions in the company. Psychological success is self-determined rather than solely determined through signals the employee receives from the company (like salary increase and promotion). Psychological success appears to be especially important to the new generation of persons entering the workforce. For example, consider Jacqueline Strayer. Since graduating from college in 1976, she has held a series of positions with different companies including General Electric, GTE, United Technologies, and William Mercer.[8] At the same time, she earned a master's degree in professional studies in film and television and is currently working on a doctorate in management. Her motivation is finding interesting, challenging positions rather than trying to be promoted to a top management position. She is also passionate about running, so she wants to work with an employer that has a fitness center.

Employees need to develop new skills rather than rely on a static knowledge base. This has resulted from companies' need to be more responsive to customers' service and product demands. The types of knowledge an employee needs have changed.[9] In the traditional career, "knowing how" (having the appropriate skills and knowledge to provide a service or produce a product) was critical. Although knowing how remains important, employees also need to "know why" and "know whom." Knowing why refers to understanding the company's business and culture so the employee can develop and apply knowledge and skills that can contribute to the business. Knowing whom refers to relationships the employee may develop to contribute to company success. These relationships may include networking with vendors, suppliers, community members, customers, or industry experts. Learning to know whom and know why requires more than formal courses and training programs. Learning and development in the protean career are increasingly likely to involve relationships and job experiences rather than formal courses.

The emphasis on continuous learning and learning beyond knowing how as well as changes in the psychological contract are altering the direction and frequency of movement within careers (career pattern).[10] Traditional career patterns consisted of a series of steps arranged in a linear hierarchy, with higher steps related to increased authority, responsibility, and compensation. Expert career patterns involve a lifelong commitment to a field or specialization (such as law, medicine, or management). These types of career patterns will not disappear. Rather, career patterns involving movement across specializations or disciplines (a spiral career pattern) will become more prevalent. These new career patterns mean that developing employees (as well as employees taking control of their own careers) will require providing them with the opportunity to (a) determine their interests, skill strengths, and weaknesses and (b) based on this information, seek appropriate development experiences that will likely involve job experiences and relationships as well as formal courses.

The most appropriate view of a career is that it is "boundaryless."[11] It may include movement across several employers or even different occupations. Statistics indicate that the average employment tenure for all American workers is only five years.[12] One study found that 60 percent of employees of all ages rate time and flexibility as very important reasons for staying with a company.[13] But Gen Xers (those in their mid-20s to late 40s) were more likely to leave a job than baby boomers (those in their mid-40s to late 50s). Some 51 percent of employees under age 40 reported they were looking for a new job within the next year, compared to only 25 percent of those 40 or older. For example, Craig Matison, 33 years old, took a job with Cincinnati Bell Information System, a unit of Cincinnati Bell Corporation that manages billing for phone and cable companies.[14] Although he had been on the job only six months, he was already looking to make his next career move. Not wanting to stay on the technical career path, he regularly explored company databases for job postings, looking for sales and marketing opportunities within the company.

A career may also involve identifying more with a job or profession than with the present employer. A career can also be considered boundaryless in the sense that career plans or goals are influenced by personal or family demands and values. Finally, boundaryless may refer to the fact that career success may be tied not to promotions but to achieving goals that are personally meaningful to the employee rather than those set by parents, peers, or the company.

As this discussion shows, to retain and motivate employees companies need to provide a system to identify and meet employees' development needs. This is especially important to retain good performers and employees who have potential for managerial positions. This system is often known as a **career management** or **development planning system.** We will discuss these systems in detail later in the chapter.

**Career Management System**
A system to retain and motivate employees by identifying and meeting their development needs (also called *development planning systems*).

## Approaches to Employee Development

Four approaches are used to develop employees: formal education, assessment, job experiences, and interpersonal relationships.[15] Many companies use a combination of these approaches. Figure 9.1 shows the frequency of use of different employee development practices. Larger companies are more likely to use leadership training and development planning more frequently than smaller companies. Children's Healthcare of Atlanta, a medical system specializing in pediatric care, has a Center for Leadership that includes assessment, workshops, action learning, and personal coaches.[16] High-performing employees with potential to become managers complete a full day of assessment that includes participating in a business simulation requiring them to pretend they are managing a division of a major company. They also complete a personality inventory. Employees are given feedback about their behavior in the simulation and the results of the personality inventory. Employees attend five workshops each year that focus on helping employees work with the feedback they received during the assessment. The workshops cover topics such as leading change,

figure 9.1

Frequency of Use of Employee Development Practices

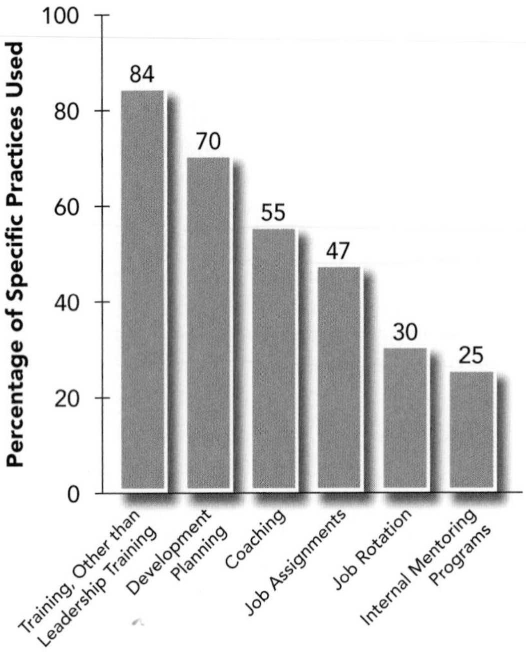


SOURCE: Based on E. Esen and J. Collison, *Employee Development* (Alexandria, VA: SHRM Research, 2005).

developing a business strategy, and creating a personal vision. Action learning requires participants to work in teams on a topic that is of strategic importance to the medical system. Coaches work with the employees to identify long-term improvement goals.

Keep in mind that although much development activity is targeted at managers, all levels of employees may be involved in development. For example, most employees typically receive performance appraisal feedback (a development activity related to assessment) at least once per year. As we discussed in Chapter 8, as part of the appraisal process they are asked to complete individual development plans outlining (1) how they plan to change their weaknesses and (2) their future plans (including positions or locations desired and education or experience needed). Next we explore each type of development approach.

**LO2**
Discuss Current Trends in Using Formal Education for Development.

## Formal Education

**Formal Education Programs**
Employee development programs, including short courses offered by consultants or universities, executive MBA programs, and university programs.

**Formal education programs** include off-site and on-site programs designed specifically for the company's employees, short courses offered by consultants or universities, executive MBA programs, and university programs in which participants actually live at the university while taking classes. These programs may involve lectures by business experts, business games and simulations, adventure learning, and meetings with customers.

Many companies such as Bank of Montreal and General Electric rely primarily on in-house development programs offered by training and development centers or corporate universities, rather than sending employees to programs offered by universities.[17] Companies rely on in-house programs because they can be tied directly to business needs, can be easily evaluated using company metrics, and can

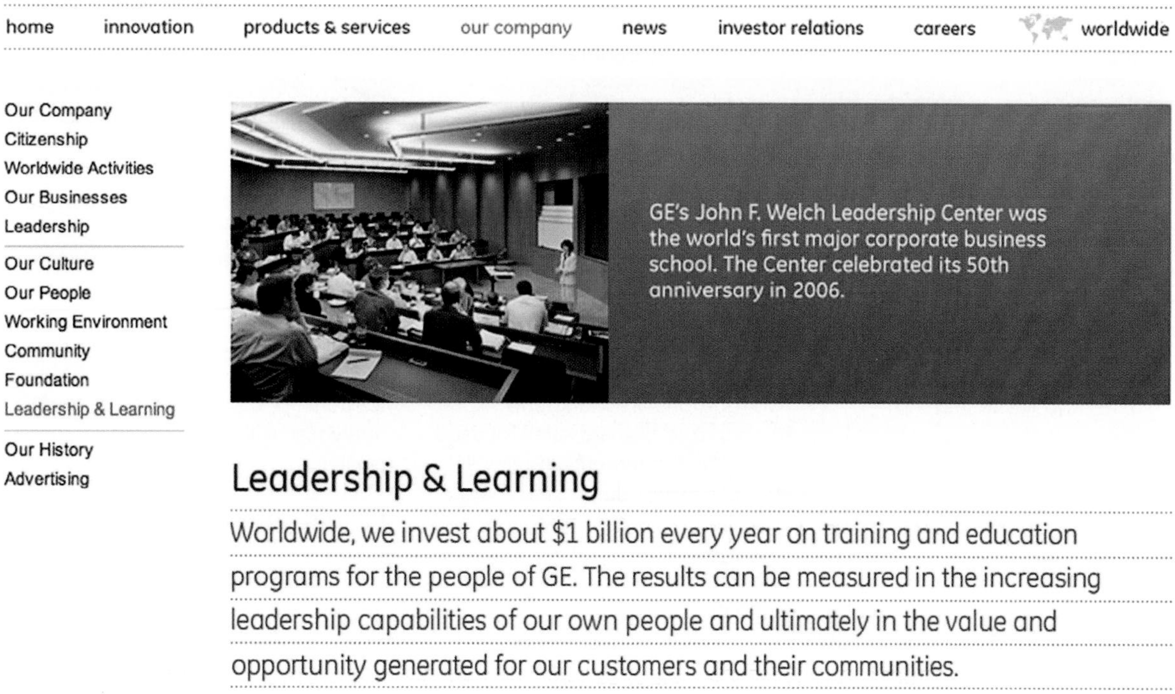
home
innovation
products & services
our company
news
investor relations
careers
worldwide
Our Company
Citizenship
Worldwide Activities
Our Businesses
Leadership
Our Culture
Our People
Working Environment
Community
Foundation
Leadership & Learning
Our History
Advertising
GE's John F. Welch Leadership Center was the world's first major corporate business school. The Center celebrated its 50th anniversary in 2006.
Leadership & Learning
Worldwide, we invest about $1 billion every year on training and education programs for the people of GE. The results can be measured in the increasing leadership capabilities of our own people and ultimately in the value and opportunity generated for our customers and their communities.

General Electric's Leadership Center is well known for being one of the great examples of leadership development in the world.

get senior-level management involved. The Bank of Montreal (BMO) has invested more than $400 million in training and development, including building the Institute for Learning, with high-tech classrooms, rooms to accommodate out-of-town employees, a presentation hall, restaurants, and a gym.[18] Each year 8,000 employees receive training at the Institute for Learning. A wide range of courses and programs are offered that are linked to the bank's business strategies. They include management leadership training, risk management training, project management programs, and a four-year MBA program in financial services offered through a partnership with the Dalhousie School of Management and the Institute for Canadian Bankers. BMO believes the programs provide immediate benefit to the company because they often require participants to provide solutions to issues the company is facing. Evaluation and feedback are used to determine the success of specific programs. BMO uses many different types of evaluation including skill tests and performance evaluations conducted by managers after the participant returns to the job to determine transfer of training. BMO also looks at the relationship between the bank's education spending and its performance. Employee surveys are used to determine the quality and relevance of programs.

General Electric (GE) has one of the oldest and most widely known management development centers in the world. GE develops managers at the John F. Welch Leadership Center at Crotonville, New York.[19] The facility has residence buildings where participants stay while attending programs as well as classrooms for courses, programs, and seminars. Each year GE employees chosen by their managers based on their performance and potential attend management development programs. The programs include professional skills development and specialized courses in areas such as risk analysis and loan structuring. All of the programs emphasize theory and practical application. Course time is spent discussing business issues facing GE. The programs

**table 9.2**

Examples of Leadership Development Programs at General Electric

| PROGRAM | SUMMARY | QUALIFICATIONS TO ATTEND |
| --- | --- | --- |
| Commercial Leadership Program: Sales and Marketing | Formal courses, including Selling@GE, Marketing@GE, and negotiation skills.<br>Challenging assignments in key sales and marketing roles within a business. | Undergraduate degree; minimum 3.0 GPA; less than 2 years full-time work experience, willingness to relocate; interest in sales and/or marketing. |
| Experienced Commercial Leadership Program (ECLP): Sales and Marketing | Four 6-month business rotations within a commercial segment; two rotations are marketing focused and two are sales focused.<br>Strengthen commercial business and leadership skills by completing classroom and online training and in-residence symposiums at the John F. Welch Learning Center. | MBA; 2–5 years marketing or sales experience; demonstrated leadership, communications, and analytical skills; willingness to relocate.<br>Bachelor's degree with 4+ years marketing or sales experience. |

SOURCE: Based on "Leadership Programs," www.gecareers.com (May 4, 2006).

are taught by in-house instructors, university faculty members, and even CEO Jeff Immelt. Examples of management development programs available at GE are shown in Table 9.2. As you can see, GE uses a combination of coursework and job experiences to develop entry-level and top levels of management. Other programs such as the Business Manager Course and the Executive Development Course involve action learning. As discussed in Chapter 7, action learning involves assigning a real problem that GE is facing to program participants who must present their recommendations to Jeff Immelt. Besides programs and courses for management development GE also holds seminars to better understand customer expectations and leadership conferences designed specifically for African-Americans, women, or Hispanic managers to discuss leading and learning.

Table 9.3 shows examples of institutions for executive education. There are several important trends in executive education. Leadership, entrepreneurship, and e-business are the most important topics in executive education programs. Programs directed at developing executives' understanding of global business issues and management of change are other important parts of executive development.[20] More and more companies and universities are using distance learning (which we discussed in Chapter 7) to reach executive audiences.[21] For example, Duke University's Fuqua School of Business offers an electronic executive MBA program in both Frankfurt, Germany, and Durham, North Carolina. Using their personal computers, students "attend" CD-ROM video lectures as well as traditional face-to-face lectures. They can download study aids and additional video and audio programs. Students discuss lectures and work on team projects using computer bulletin boards, e-mail, and live chat rooms. They use the Internet to research specific companies and class topics. Besides their work in the electronic learning environment students spend time in traditional face-to-face instructions for several weeks at home. They also attend courses held either in

**table 9.3**

Examples of Institutions That Provide Executive Education

| PROVIDER (LOCATION) | 2004–05 REVENUE (MILLIONS) | NO. OF EXECUTIVE NONDEGREE PROGRAMS | NO. OF EXECUTIVES ATTENDING PROGRAMS | RANGE OF COSTS FOR PROGRAMS | CORPORATE CLIENTS |
|---|---|---|---|---|---|
| London Business School (London, England) | 43.9 | 86 | 5,771 | $5,570–33,245 | Nokia<br>Shell<br>Michelin |
| University of Michigan (Ann Arbor) | 17.2 | 77 | 3,893 | 2,000–31,300 | TRW<br>Ford Motor<br>Pfizer |
| Stanford University (California) | 21.2 | 44 | 2,070 | 5,500–45,900 | Hewlett-Packard<br>Cisco Systems<br>Siemens AG |
| INSEAD (Fontainbleau, France) | 85.1 | 136 | 7,000 | 3,300–42,000 | IBM<br>Royal Dutch Shell<br>BASF |
| University of Virginia Darden School (Charlottesville) | 17.2 | 68 | 3,151 | 3,700–29,400 | U.S. Military<br>State Farm Insurance<br>Bacardi |

SOURCE: Based on "2005 Executive Education Profile," *BusinessWeek Online*, October 24, 2005, www.businessweek.com.

Germany or on the U.S. campus. The "Competing through Technology" box shows how IBM is using the Web for its management development programs.

Another trend in executive education is for companies and the education provider (business school or other educational institution) to create short custom courses with content designed specifically to meet the needs of the business. MetLife worked with Babson College to develop a course that included faculty and corporate executive participation and company project work.[22] The classes start with faculty members discussing a business principle, then the faculty member and corporate executive discuss how the principle works both in MetLife's industry (insurance and financial services) and within MetLife. Small teams of class participants work on business projects and provide recommendations to company executives, who decide whether to act on them. So far the company has found the program has been effective in addressing business issues. Eighty-two percent of projects have been implemented at the company.

Action Learning

The final important trend in executive education is to supplement formal courses from consultants or university faculty with other types of development activities. Avon Products' "Passport Program" is targeted at employees the company thinks can become general managers.[23] To learn Avon's global strategy, they meet for each session in a different country. The program brings a team of employees together for six-week periods spread over 18 months. Participants are provided with general background of a functional area by university faculty and consultants. The team then works with senior executives on a country project, such as how to penetrate a new market. The team projects are presented to Avon's top managers.

## COMPETING THROUGH TECHNOLOGY
### E-Learning Helps Build Management Talent

IBM believes that by utilizing e-learning and the classroom environment, managers participate in self-directed learning, try out skills in a "safe" environment, and gain access to communities of learning and just-in-time learning. The advantages of e-learning are complemented by the strengths of an interactive classroom experience and support from the manager's boss to create the best development program possible.

IBM's "Basic Blue for Managers" program replaces a successful New Managers School. The program includes e-learning and face-to-face classroom experiences. The program helps managers understand their responsibilities in managing performance, employee relations, diversity, and multicultural issues. It moves the learning of all basic management skills to the Web, using classroom experiences for more complex management issues. It also gives managers and their bosses greater responsibility for development, while the company provides support in the form of unlimited access to development activities and support networks. The learning model includes four levels:

- Management Quick Views: These provide practical information on over 40 common management topics related to how to conduct business, leadership and management competencies, productivity, and HRM issues.
- Interactive Learning Modules and Simulations: These interactive simulations emphasize people and task management. Employees learn by viewing videos, interacting with models and problem employees, deciding how to deal with a problem, issue, or request, and getting feedback on their decisions. Case studies are also available for review.
- Collaborative Learning: The learner can connect on the company intranet with tutors, team members, customers, or other learners to discuss problems, issues, and approaches to share learning.
- Learning Labs: Five-day class workshops build on the learning acquired during the previous phases of e-learning. The workshops emphasize peer learning and the development of a learning community. Through challenging activities and assignments managers gain increased awareness of themselves, their work teams, and IBM.

Management Quick Views, Interactive Learning Modules and Simulations, and Collaborative Learning are delivered by technology. Learning Labs is a face-to-face classroom experience.

The program recognizes the roles of the boss as coach, supporter, and role model. The boss is involved in the program through providing coaching and feedback, on-the-job learning experiences, assessment of the manager's development needs and progress, and assistance to complete individual development plans.

The role of the Manager @ IBM is an expert system that provides a customized learning portfolio for each manager based on their background, training, and management style. The expert system guides managers through prework that has to be completed prior to attending learning labs. Learning is reinforced through use of a knowledge management system that allows managers to post suggestions and store ideas.

Evaluations of both programs have been positive. Participants in the "Basic Blue for Managers" program report they are satisfied with the program content and delivery. Most of the participants have mastered the 15 subject areas included in the program. It is estimated that the business value related to leadership skill improvement averages $450,000 per employee. Managers who have completed the Role of the Manager @ IBM program have created action plans that have generated revenues of $184 million.

SOURCES: T. Barron, "IBM's New Fangled, Old-Fashioned Pep," *T+D*, (April 2004), pp. 64–65; D. Robb, Succeeding with Succession, *HR Magazine*, (January 2006), pp. 89–92; N. Lewis and P. Orton, "The Five Attributes of Innovative E-Learning," *Training and Development*, June 2000, pp. 47–51; K. Mantyla, *Blending E-learning* (Alexandria, VA: ASTD, 2001).

Managers who attend the Center for Creative Leadership development program take psychological tests; receive feedback from managers, peers, and direct reports; participate in group-building activities (like adventure learning, discussed in Chapter 7); receive counseling; and set improvement goals and write development plans.[24]

Enrollment in executive education programs or MBA programs may be limited to managers or employees identified to have management potential. As a result, many companies also provide tuition reimbursement as a benefit for all employees to encourage them to develop. **Tuition reimbursement** refers to the practice of reimbursing employees' costs for college and university courses and degree programs. Companies spend about $10 billion on tuition reimbursement for courses offered by nonprofit colleges and universities as well as for-profit universities like Capella University.[25] These courses include face-to-face classroom instruction, online learning, and blended learning. For example, United Technology's Employee Scholar Program allows employees to receive 100 percent tuition reimbursement of all educational costs including tuition, registration fees, and books. Courses do not have to be related to the employee's job. Employees receive three hours each week to study or attend class. Employees who earn a degree receive $10,000 of company stock. The company has paid more than $60 million for the program. About 15 percent of employees use the program.

**Tuition Reimbursement**
The practice of reimbursing employees' costs for college and university courses and degree programs.

## EVIDENCE-BASED HR

Given the costs of executive education and tuition reimbursement programs, companies are asking for evaluation data that show the value of the program. As a result, many universities offering executive education programs are beginning to measure programs' return on investment. For example, Columbia Business School uses performance measures to track the success of program participants. Leadership skills, team building, and strategic thinking are measured using self-assessment, manager evaluations, and peer reviews collected before the participant attends the program as well as up to a year following program completion. The University of Virginia's Graduate School of Business Administration asks participants in executive education programs to complete surveys three months after attending programs to judge the program's practical value. Some of Darden's programs use action learning (recall our discussion of action learning in Chapter 7), which requires employees to make presentations to top-level managers showing how participating in the program helped them to successfully deal with work problems. This demonstrates how learning has benefited the company. Kum and Go, a large convenience store chain, has a tuition reimbursement program that allows employees to obtain their college degrees while working full-time. The program reimburses students 100 percent of their tuition if they receive either an A or B, and 50 percent if they receive a C.

SOURCES: A. Meisler, "A Matter of Degree," *Workforce Management*, May 2004, pp. 32–38; K. Merriman, "Employers Warm Up to Online Education," *HR Magazine*, January 2006, pp. 79–82; "Flexibility Fuels Employee Development," *TD*, April 2006, pp. 96–97.

**Assessment**
Collecting information and providing feedback to employees about their behavior, communication style, or skills.

## Assessment

**LO3**
Relate How Assessment of Personality Type, Work Behaviors, and Job Performance Can Be Used for Employee Development.

**Assessment** involves collecting information and providing feedback to employees about their behavior, communication style, or skills.[26] The employees, their peers, managers, and customers may provide information. Assessment is most frequently used to identify employees with managerial potential and to measure current managers' strengths and weaknesses. Assessment is also used to identify managers with the potential to move into higher-level executive positions, and it can be used with work teams to identify the strengths and weaknesses of individual team members and the decision processes or communication styles that inhibit the team's productivity.

Companies vary in the methods and the sources of information they use in developmental assessment. Many companies appraise employee performance. Companies with sophisticated development systems use psychological tests to measure employees' skills, personality types, and communication styles. Self, peer, and managers' ratings of employees' interpersonal styles and behaviors may also be collected. Popular assessment tools include personality tests, the Myers-Briggs Type Indicator®, assessment centers, benchmarks, performance appraisal, and 360-degree feedback.

## Personality Tests

Tests are used to determine if employees have the personality characteristics necessary to be successful in specific managerial jobs or jobs involving international assignments. Personality tests typically measure five major dimensions: extroversion, adjustment, agreeableness, conscientiousness, and inquisitiveness (see Table 6.3 in Chapter 6). For example, Carmeuse North America uses personality tests in its leadership development program. The personality tests for employees who have been identified as having high potential for top management positions will be used to guide employees into development activities including coaching and formal courses.[27] Starwood Vacation Ownership, a subsidiary of Starwood Hotels and Resorts, uses several assessment tools to determine if the top managers value the commercial success of the business as well as tolerance for ambiguity, the ability to create and communicate a business strategy, the ability to build business partnerships, and the ability to develop staff. The assessment identifies managers who are ready for international assignments, may not fit their current position, or need coaching to better understand the company culture.[28]

## Myers-Briggs Type Indicator®

**Myers-Briggs Type Indicator (MBTI)®**
A psychological test used for team building and leadership development that identifies employees' preferences for energy, information gathering, decision making, and lifestyle.

**Myers-Briggs Type Indicator (MBTI)®** is the most popular psychological assessment tool for employee development. As many as 2 million people take the MBTI® in the United States each year. The test consists of more than 100 questions about how the person feels or prefers to behave in different situations (such as "Are you usually a good 'mixer' or rather quiet and reserved?"). The MBTI® is based on the work of Carl Jung, a psychiatrist who believed that differences in individuals' behavior resulted from preferences in decision making, interpersonal communication, and information gathering. The MBTI® identifies individuals' preference for energy (introversion versus extroversion), information gathering (sensing versus intuition), decision making (thinking versus feeling), and lifestyle (judging versus perceiving).[29] The energy dimension determines where individuals gain interpersonal strength and vitality. Extroverts (E) gain energy through interpersonal relationships. Introverts (I) gain energy by focusing on personal thoughts and feelings. The information-gathering preference relates to the actions individuals take when making decisions. Individuals with a Sensing (S) preference tend to gather facts and details. Intuitives (I) tend to focus less on facts and more on possibilities and relationships between ideas. Decision-making preferences differ based on the amount of consideration the person gives to others' feelings in making a decision. Individuals with a Thinking (T) preference tend to be objective in making decisions. Individuals with a Feeling (F) preference tend to evaluate the impact of potential decisions on others and be more subjective in making a decision. The lifestyle preference reflects an individual's tendency to be flexible and adaptable. Individuals with a Judging (J) preference focus on goals, establish deadlines, and prefer to be conclusive. Individuals with a Perceiving (P) preference tend to enjoy surprises, like to change decisions, and dislike deadlines.

Sixteen unique personality types result from the combination of the four MBTI® preferences. (See Table 9.4.) Each person has developed strengths and weaknesses as a result of using these preferences. For example, individuals who are Introverted, Sensing, Thinking, and Judging (known as ISTJs) tend to be serious, quiet, practical, orderly, and logical. These persons can organize tasks, be decisive, and follow through on plans and goals. ISTJs have several weaknesses because they have not used the opposite preferences: Extroversion, Intuition, Feeling, and Perceiving. Potential weaknesses for ISTJs include problems dealing with unexpected opportunities, appearing too task-oriented or impersonal to colleagues, and making overly quick decisions. Visit the Web site **www.keirsey.com** for more information on the personality types.

The MBTI® is used for understanding such things as communication, motivation, teamwork, work styles, and leadership. For example, it can be used by salespeople or executives who want to become more effective at interpersonal communication by learning about their own personality styles and the way they are perceived by others. The MBTI® can help develop teams by matching team members with assignments that allow them to capitalize on their preferences and helping employees understand how the different preferences of team members can lead to useful problem solving.[30] For example, employees with an Intuitive preference can be assigned brainstorming tasks. Employees with a Sensing preference can evaluate ideas.

Research on the validity, reliability, and effectiveness of the MBTI® is inconclusive.[31] People who take the MBTI® find it a positive experience and say it helps them change their behavior. MBTI® scores appear to be related to one's occupation. Analysis of managers' MBTI® scores in the United States, England, Latin America, and Japan suggests that a large majority of all managers have certain personality types (ISTJ, INTJ, ESTJ, or ENTJ). However, MBTI® scores are not necessarily stable over time. Studies in which the MBTI® was administered at two different times found that as few as 24 percent of those who took the test were classified as the same type the second time.

The MBTI® is a valuable tool for understanding communication styles and the ways people prefer to interact with others. Because it does not measure how well employees perform their preferred functions, it should not be used to appraise performance or evaluate employees' promotion potential. Furthermore, MBTI® types should not be viewed as unchangeable personality patterns.

**Assessment Center**
A process in which multiple raters evaluate employees' performance on a number of exercises.

## Assessment Center

At an **assessment center** multiple raters or evaluators (assessors) evaluate employees' performance on a number of exercises.[32] An assessment center is usually an off-site location such as a conference center. From 6 to 12 employees usually participate at one time. Assessment centers are primarily used to identify if employees have the personality characteristics, administrative skills, and interpersonal skills needed for managerial jobs. They are also increasingly being used to determine if employees have the necessary skills to work in teams.

**Leaderless Group Discussion**
Process in which a team of five to seven employees solves an assigned problem together within a certain time period.

The types of exercises used in assessment centers include leaderless group discussions, interviews, in-baskets, and role plays.[33] In a **leaderless group discussion,** a team

**table 9.4**

The 16 Personality Types Used in the Myers-Briggs Type Indicator Assessment

| | SENSING TYPES (S) | | INTUITIVE TYPES (N) | |
|---|---|---|---|---|
| | THINKING (T) | FEELING (F) | FEELING (F) | THINKING (T) |
| **Introverts (I)** Judging (J) | **ISTJ** Quiet, serious, earn success by thoroughness and dependability. Practical, matter-of-fact, realistic, and responsible. Decide logically what should be done and work toward it steadily, regardless of distractions. Take pleasure in making everything orderly and organized—their work, their home, their life. Value traditions and loyalty. | **ISFJ** Quiet, friendly, responsible, and conscientious. Committed and steady in meeting their obligations. Thorough, painstaking, and accurate. Loyal, considerate, notice and remember specifics about people who are important to them, concerned with how others feel. Strive to create an orderly and harmonious environment at work and at home. | **INFJ** Seek meaning and connection in ideas, relationships, and material possessions. Want to understand what motivates people and are insightful about others. Conscientious and committed to their firm values. Develop a clear vision about how best to serve the common good. Organized and decisive in implementing their vision. | **INTJ** Have original minds and great drive for implementing their ideas and achieving their goals. Quickly see patterns in external events and develop long-range explanatory perspectives. When committed, organize a job and carry it through. Skeptical and independent, have high standards of competence and performance—for themselves and others. |
| Perceiving (P) | **ISTP** Tolerant and flexible, quiet observers until a problem appears, then act quickly to find workable solutions. Analyze what makes things work and readily get through large amounts of data to isolate the core of practical problems. Interested in cause and effect, organize facts using logical principles, value efficiency. | **ISFP** Quiet, friendly, sensitive, and kind. Enjoy the present moment, what's going on around them. Like to have their own space and to work within their own time frame. Loyal and committed to their values and to people who are important to them. Dislike disagreements and conflicts, do not force their opinions or values on others. | **INFP** Idealistic, loyal to their values and to people who are important to them. Want an external life that is congruent with their values. Curious, quick to see possibilities, can be catalysts for implementing ideas. Seek to understand people and to help them fulfill their potential. Adaptable, flexible, and accepting unless a value is threatened. | **INTP** Seek to develop logical explanations for everything that interests them. Theoretical and abstract, interested more in ideas than in social interaction. Quiet, contained, flexible, and adaptable. Have unusual ability to focus in depth to solve problems in their area of interest. Skeptical, sometimes critical, always analytical. |
| **Extroverts (E)** Perceiving (P) | **ESTP** Flexible and tolerant, they take a pragmatic approach focused on immediate results. Theories and conceptual explanations bore them—they want to act energetically to solve the problem. Focus on the here-and-now, spontaneous, enjoy each moment that they can be active with others. Enjoy material comforts and style. Learn best through doing. | **ESFP** Outgoing, friendly, and accepting. Exuberant lovers of life, people, and material comforts. Enjoy working with others to make things happen. Bring common sense and a realistic approach to their work, and make work fun. Flexible and spontaneous, adapt readily to new people and environments. Learn best by trying a new skill with other people. | **ENFP** Warmly enthusiastic and imaginative. See life as full of possibilities. Make connections between events and information very quickly, and confidently proceed based on the patterns they see. Want a lot of affirmation from others, and readily give appreciation and support. Spontaneous and flexible, often rely on their ability to improvise and their verbal fluency. | **ENTP** Quick, ingenious, stimulating, alert, and outspoken. Resourceful in solving new and challenging problems. Adept at generating conceptual possibilities and then analyzing them strategically. Good at reading other people. Bored by routine, will seldom do the same thing the same way, apt to turn to one new interest after another. |
| Judging (J) | **ESTJ** Practical, realistic, matter-of-fact. Decisive, quickly move to implement decisions. Organize projects and people to get things done, focus on getting results in the most efficient way possible. Take care of routine details. Have a clear set of logical standards, systematically follow them and want others to also. Forceful in implementing their plans. | **ESFJ** Warmhearted, conscientious, and cooperative. Want harmony in their environment, work with determination to establish it. Like to work with others to complete tasks accurately and on time. Loyal, follow through even in small matters. Notice what others need in their day-by-day lives and try to provide it. Want to be appreciated for who they are and for what they contribute. | **ENFJ** Warm, empathetic, responsive, and responsible. Highly attuned to the emotions, needs, and motivations of others. Find potential in everyone, want to help others fulfill their potential. May act as catalysts for individual and group growth. Loyal, responsive to praise and criticism. Sociable, facilitate others in a group, and provide inspiring leadership. | **ENTJ** Frank, decisive, assume leadership readily. Quickly see illogical and inefficient procedures and policies, develop and implement comprehensive systems to solve organizational problems. Enjoy long-term planning and goal setting. Usually well informed, well read, enjoy expanding their knowledge and passing it on to others. Forceful in presenting their ideas. |

SOURCE: Reproduced with special permission of the publisher, Consulting Psychologists Press, Inc., Palo Alto, CA 94303, from *Manual: A Guide to the Development and Use of the Myers-Briggs Type Indicator* by Isabel Briggs-Myers and Mary H. McCaulley. Copyright 1985 by Peter Briggs-Myers and Katherine D. Myers. All rights reserved. Myers-Briggs Type Indicator and MBTI are registered trademarks of Consulting Psychologists Press, Inc. Further reproduction is prohibited without the publisher's consent.

of five to seven employees is assigned a problem and must work together to solve it within a certain time period. The problem may involve buying and selling supplies, nominating a subordinate for an award, or assembling a product. In the **interview,** employees answer questions about their work and personal experiences, skill strengths and weaknesses, and career plans. An **in-basket** is a simulation of the administrative tasks of the manager's job. The exercise includes a variety of documents that may appear in the in-basket on a manager's desk. The participants read the materials and decide how to respond to them. Responses might include delegating tasks, scheduling meetings, writing replies, or completely ignoring the memo! **Role plays** refer to the participant taking the part or role of a manager or other employee. For example, an assessment center participant may be asked to take the role of a manager who has to give a negative performance review to a subordinate. The participant is told about the subordinate's performance and is asked to prepare for and actually hold a 45-minute meeting with the subordinate to discuss the performance problems. The role of the subordinate is played by a manager or other member of the assessment center design team or company. The assessment center might also include interest and aptitude tests to evaluate an employee's vocabulary, general mental ability, and reasoning skills. Personality tests may be used to determine if employees can get along with others, their tolerance for ambiguity, and other traits related to success as a manager.

**Interview**
Employees are questioned about their work and personal experiences, skills, and career plans.

**In-Basket**
A simulation of the administrative tasks of a manager's job.

**Role Plays**
A participant taking the part or role of a manager or other employee.

Assessment center exercises are designed to measure employees' administrative and interpersonal skills. Skills typically measured include leadership, oral and written communication, judgment, organizational ability, and stress tolerance. Table 9.5 shows an example of the skills measured by the assessment center. As we see, each exercise gives participating employees the opportunity to demonstrate several different skills. For example, the exercise requiring scheduling to meet production demands

**table 9.5**

Examples of Skills Measured by Assessment Center Exercises

| | EXERCISES | | | | |
|---|---|---|---|---|---|
| | IN-BASKET | SCHEDULING EXERCISE | LEADERLESS GROUP DISCUSSION | PERSONALITY TEST | ROLE PLAY |
| SKILLS | | | | | |
| Leadership (Dominance, coaching, influence, resourcefulness) | X | | X | X | X |
| Problem solving (Judgment) | X | X | X | | X |
| Interpersonal (Sensitivity, conflict resolution, cooperation, oral communication) | | | X | X | X |
| Administrative (Organizing, planning, written communications) | X | X | X | | |
| Personal (Stress tolerance, confidence) | | | X | X | X |

X indicates skill measured by exercise.

evaluates employees' administrative and problem-solving ability. The leaderless group discussion measures interpersonal skills such as sensitivity toward others, stress tolerance, and oral communication skills.

Managers are usually used as assessors. The managers are trained to look for employee behaviors that are related to the skills that will be assessed. Typically, each assessor observes and records one or two employees' behaviors in each exercise. The assessors review their notes and rate each employee's level of skills (for example, 5 = high level of leadership skills, 1 = low level of leadership skills). After all employees have completed the exercises, the assessors discuss their observations of each employee. They compare their ratings and try to agree on each employee's rating for each of the skills.

As we mentioned in Chapter 6, research suggests that assessment center ratings are related to performance, salary level, and career advancement.[34] Assessment centers may also be useful for development because employees who participate in the process receive feedback regarding their attitudes, skill strengths, and weaknesses.[35] For example, Steelcase, the office furniture manufacturer based in Grand Rapids, Michigan, uses assessment centers for first-level managers.[36] The assessment center exercises include in-basket, interview simulation, and a timed scheduling exercise requiring participants to fill positions created by absences. Managers are also required to confront an employee on a performance issue, getting the employee to commit to improve. Because the exercises relate closely to what managers are required to do at work, feedback given to managers based on their performance in the assessment center can target specific skills or competencies that they need to be successful managers.

## Benchmarks

**Benchmarks©**
An instrument designed to measure the factors that are important to managerial success.

**Benchmarks©** is an instrument designed to measure the factors that are important to being a successful manager. The items measured by Benchmarks are based on research that examines the lessons executives learn at critical events in their careers.[37] This includes items that measure managers' skills in dealing with subordinates, acquiring resources, and creating a productive work climate. Table 9.6 shows the 16 skills and perspectives believed to be important for becoming a successful manager. These skills and perspectives have been shown to be related to performance evaluations, bosses' ratings of promotability, and actual promotions received.[38] To get a complete picture of managers' skills, the managers' supervisors, their peers, and the managers themselves all complete the instrument. A summary report presenting the self-ratings and ratings by others is provided to the manager, along with information about how the ratings compare with those of other managers. A development guide with examples of experiences that enhance each skill and how successful managers use the skills is also available.

## Performance Appraisals and 360-Degree Feedback Systems

**Performance Appraisal**
The process through which an organization gets information on how well an employee is doing his or her job.

As we mentioned in Chapter 8, **performance appraisal** is the process of measuring employees' performance. Performance appraisal information can be useful for employee development under certain conditions.[39] The appraisal system must tell employees specifically about their performance problems and how they can improve their performance. This includes providing a clear understanding of the differences between current performance and expected performance, identifying causes of the performance discrepancy, and developing action plans to improve performance. Managers must be

**table 9.6**

Skills Related to Managerial Success

| | |
|---|---|
| Resourcefulness | Can think strategically, engage in flexible problem solving, and work effectively with higher management. |
| Doing whatever it takes | Has perseverance and focus in the face of obstacles. |
| Being a quick study | Quickly masters new technical and business knowledge. |
| Building and mending relationships | Knows how to build and maintain working relationships with co-workers and external parties. |
| Leading subordinates | Delegates to subordinates effectively, broadens their opportunities, and acts with fairness toward them. |
| Compassion and sensitivity | Shows genuine interest in others and sensitivity to subordinates' needs. |
| Straightforwardness and composure | Is honorable and steadfast. |
| Setting a developmental climate | Provides a challenging climate to encourage subordinates' development. |
| Confronting problem subordinates | Acts decisively and fairly when dealing with problem subordinates. |
| Team orientation | Accomplishes tasks through managing others. |
| Balance between personal life and work | Balances work priorities with personal life so that neither is neglected. |
| Decisiveness | Prefers quick and approximate actions to slow and precise ones in many management situations. |
| Self-awareness | Has an accurate picture of strengths and weaknesses and is willing to improve. |
| Hiring talented staff | Hires talented people for the team. |
| Putting people at ease | Displays warmth and a good sense of humor. |
| Acting with flexibility | Can behave in ways that are often seen as opposites. |

SOURCE: Adapted with permission from C. D. McCauley, M. M. Lombardo, and C. J. Usher, "Diagnosing Management Development Needs: An Instrument Based on How Managers Develop," *Journal of Management* 15 (1989), pp. 389–403.

trained in frequent performance feedback. Managers also need to monitor employees' progress in carrying out action plans.

Recall our discussion in Chapter 8, Performance Management, of how Just Born uses performance appraisals for evaluation and development.[40] The appraisal starts with a planning meeting between employee and manager. The strategic initiatives of the department are discussed along with the employee's role. The employee and manager agree on four personal objectives that will help the department reach its goals as well as key performance outcomes related to the employee's job description. Competencies the employee needs to reach the personal objectives are identified. The manager and employee jointly develop a plan for improving or learning the competencies. During the year, the manager and employee monitor the progress toward reaching the performance and personal objectives and achievement of the learning plan. Pay decisions made at the end of each year are based on the achievement of both performance and learning objectives. General Electric has a unique process for reviewing top managers known as "Session C."[41] Session C includes full-day reviews at all major business locations and follow-up sessions. The sessions focus on evaluating managers' strengths and weaknesses. They also include presentations of business results and reviews of accomplishments.

**table 9.7**

Sample Competency and Items from a 360-Degree Feedback Instrument

| |
|---|
| **Decision Making** |
| Identifies the key decisions that have the greatest impact on business goals. |
| Understands and integrates conflicting or contradictory information. |
| Balances business sense with data and logic to make effective decisions. |
| Takes accountability for results of individual and team decisions. |
| Makes appropriate trade-offs between complete analysis and speed when making decisions. |

**Upward Feedback**
A performance appraisal process for managers that includes subordinates' evaluations.

**360-Degree Feed-Back Systems**
A performance appraisal system for managers that includes evaluations from a wide range of persons who interact with the manager. The process includes self-evaluations as well as evaluations from the manager's boss, subordinates, peers, and customers.

A recent trend in performance appraisals for management development is the use of upward feedback and 360-degree feedback. **Upward feedback** refers to appraisal that involves collecting subordinates' evaluations of managers' behaviors or skills. The 360-degree feedback process is a special case of upward feedback. In **360-degree feedback systems,** employees' behaviors or skills are evaluated not only by subordinates but by peers, customers, their bosses, and themselves. The raters complete a questionnaire asking them to rate the person on a number of different dimensions. Table 9.7 provides an example of the types of competencies that are rated in a 360-degree feedback questionnaire. This example evaluates the management competency of decision making. Each of the five items relates to a specific aspect of decision making (e.g., takes accountability for results of individual and team decisions). Typically, raters are asked to assess the manager's strength in a particular item or whether development is needed. Raters may also be asked to identify how frequently they observe a competency or skill (e.g., always, sometimes, seldom, never).

The results of a 360-degree feedback system show how the manager was rated on each item. The results also show how self-evaluations differ from evaluations from the other raters. Typically managers review their results, seek clarification from the raters, and set specific development goals based on the strengths and weaknesses identified.[42] Table 9.8 shows the type of activities involved in development planning using 360-degree feedback.[43]

The benefits of 360-degree feedback include collecting multiple perspectives of managers' performance, allowing employees to compare their own personal evaluations with the views of others, and formalizing communications about behaviors and skills ratings between employees and their internal and external customers. Several studies have shown that performance improves and behavior changes as a result of participating in

**table 9.8**

Activities in Development Planning

1. **Understand strengths and weaknesses.**
   Review ratings for strengths and weaknesses.
   Identify skills or behaviors where self and others' (manager, peer, customer) ratings agree and disagree.
2. **Identify a development goal.**
   Choose a skill or behavior to develop.
   Set a clear, specific goal with a specified outcome.
3. **Identify a process for recognizing goal accomplishment.**
4. **Identify strategies for reaching the development goal.**
   Establish strategies such as reading, job experiences, courses, and relationships.
   Establish strategies for receiving feedback on progress.
   Establish strategies for reinforcing the new skill or behavior.

upward feedback and 360-degree feedback systems.[44] The most change occurs in individuals who receive lower ratings from others than they gave themselves (overraters).

Potential limitations of 360-degree feedback include the time demands placed on the raters to complete the evaluations, managers seeking to identify and punish raters who provided negative information, the need to have a facilitator help interpret results, and companies' failure to provide ways that managers can act on the feedback they receive (development planning, meeting with raters, taking courses).

In effective 360-degree feedback systems, reliable or consistent ratings are provided, raters' confidentiality is maintained, the behaviors or skills assessed are job-related (valid), the system is easy to use, and managers receive and act on the feedback.[45]

Technology allows 360-degree questionnaires to be delivered to the raters via their personal computers. This increases the number of completed questionnaires returned, makes it easier to process the information, and speeds feedback reports to managers.

Regardless of the assessment method used, the information must be shared with the employee for development to occur. Along with assessment information, the employee needs suggestions for correcting skill weaknesses and using skills already learned. These suggestions might be to participate in training courses or develop skills through new job experiences. Based on the assessment information and available development opportunities, employees should develop action plans to guide their self-improvement efforts.

Capital One has developed effective 360-degree feedback systems.[46] Capitol One, a consumer credit company, has included a number of features in its 360-degree feedback system to minimize the chance that the ratings will be used as ways to get back at an employee or turned into popularity contests. The 360-degree assessments are based on the company's competency model, so raters are asked for specific feedback on a competency area. Rather than a lengthy form that places a large burden on raters to assess many different competencies, Capital One's assessment asks the raters to concentrate on three or four strengths or development opportunities. It also seeks comments rather than limiting raters to merely circling numbers corresponding to how much of each competency the employee has demonstrated. These comments often provide specific information about what aspect of a competency needs to be developed or identifies work situations in which a competency needs to be improved. This comment system helps tailor development activities to fit competency development. To increase the chances that the assessment will result in change, the feedback from the 360-degree assessment is linked to development plans, and the company offers coaching and training to help employees strengthen their competencies. Employees are encouraged to share feedback with their co-workers. This creates a work environment based on honest and open feedback that helps employees personally grow.

**Job Experiences**
The relationships, problems, demands, tasks, and other features that employees face in their jobs.

## Job Experiences

**LO4**
Explain How Job Experiences Can Be Used for Skill Development.

Most employee development occurs through **job experiences:**[47] relationships, problems, demands, tasks, or other features that employees face in their jobs. A major assumption of using job experiences for employee development is that development is most likely to occur when there is a mismatch between the employee's skills and past experiences and the skills required for the job. To succeed in their jobs, employees must stretch their skills—that is, they are forced to learn new skills, apply their skills and knowledge in a new way, and master new experiences.[48] New job assignments help take advantage of employees' existing skills, experiences, and contacts, while helping them develop new ones.[49] General Electric uses experienced managers to integrate newly acquired companies, which gives managers a new challenge and allows them to use a wide range of skills they have acquired over their career. Marriott International's information resources group has long-tenured employees who are highly competent but have little opportunity for promotion. Managers have been offered opportunities to take on a lateral assignment providing new challenges while giving junior employees some of their current responsibilities as part of their development plans.

Most of what we know about development through job experiences comes from a series of studies conducted by the Center for Creative Leadership.[50] Executives were asked to identify key career events that made a difference in their managerial styles and the lessons they learned from these experiences. The key events included those involving the job assignment (such as fixing a failing operation), those involving interpersonal relationships (getting along with supervisors), and the specific type of transition required (situations in which the executive did not have the necessary background). The job demands and what employees can learn from them are shown in Table 9.9.

**table 9.9**

Job Demands and the Lessons Employees Learn from Them

| | |
|---|---|
| Making transitions | *Unfamiliar responsibilities:* The manager must handle responsibilities that are new, very different, or much broader than previous ones.<br>*Proving yourself:* The manager has added pressure to show others she can handle the job. |
| Creating change | *Developing new directions:* The manager is responsible for starting something new in the organization, making strategic changes in the business, carrying out a reorganization, or responding to rapid changes in the business environment.<br>*Inherited problems:* The manager has to fix problems created by a former incumbent or take over problem employees.<br>*Reduction decisions:* Decisions about shutting down operations or staff reductions have to be made.<br>*Problems with employees:* Employees lack adequate experience, are incompetent, or are resistant. |
| Having high level of responsibility | *High stakes:* Clear deadlines, pressure from senior managers, high visibility, and responsibility for key decisions make success or failure in this job clearly evident.<br>*Managing business diversity:* The scope of the job is large with responsibilities for multiple functions, groups, products, customers, or markets.<br>*Job overload:* The sheer size of the job requires a large investment of time and energy.<br>*Handling external pressure:* External factors that affect the business (e.g., negotiating with unions or government agencies; working in a foreign culture; coping with serious community problems) must be dealt with. |
| Being involved in nonauthority relationships | *Influencing without authority:* Getting the job done requires influencing peers, higher management, external parties, or other key people over whom the manager has no direct authority. |
| Facing obstacles | *Adverse business conditions:* The business unit or product line faces financial problems or difficult economic conditions.<br>*Lack of top management support:* Senior management is reluctant to provide direction, support, or resources for current work or new projects.<br>*Lack of personal support:* The manager is excluded from key networks and gets little support and encouragement from others.<br>*Difficult boss:* The manager's opinions or management style differs from those of the boss, or the boss has major shortcomings. |

SOURCE: C. D. McCauley, L. J. Eastman, and J. Ohlott, "Linking Management Selection and Development through Stretch Assignments," *Human Resource Management* 84 (1995), pp. 93–115. 

One concern in the use of demanding job experiences for employee development is whether they are viewed as positive or negative stressors. Job experiences that are seen as positive stressors challenge employees to stimulate learning. Job challenges viewed as negative stressors create high levels of harmful stress for employees exposed to them. Recent research findings suggest that all of the job demands, with the exception of obstacles, are related to learning.[51] Managers reported that obstacles and job demands related to creating change were more likely to lead to negative stress than the other job demands. This suggests that companies should carefully weigh the potential negative consequences before placing employees in development assignments involving obstacles or creating change.

Although the research on development through job experiences has focused on executives and managers, line employees can also learn from job experiences. As we noted earlier, for a work team to be successful, its members now need the kinds of skills that only managers were once thought to need (such as dealing directly with customers, analyzing data to determine product quality, and resolving conflict among team members). Besides the development that occurs when a team is formed, employees can further develop their skills by switching work roles within the team.

Figure 9.2 shows the various ways that job experiences can be used for employee development. These include enlarging the current job, job rotation, transfers, promotions, downward moves, and temporary assignments. For companies with global operations (multinationals) it is not uncommon for employee development to involve international assignments that require frequent travel or relocation.

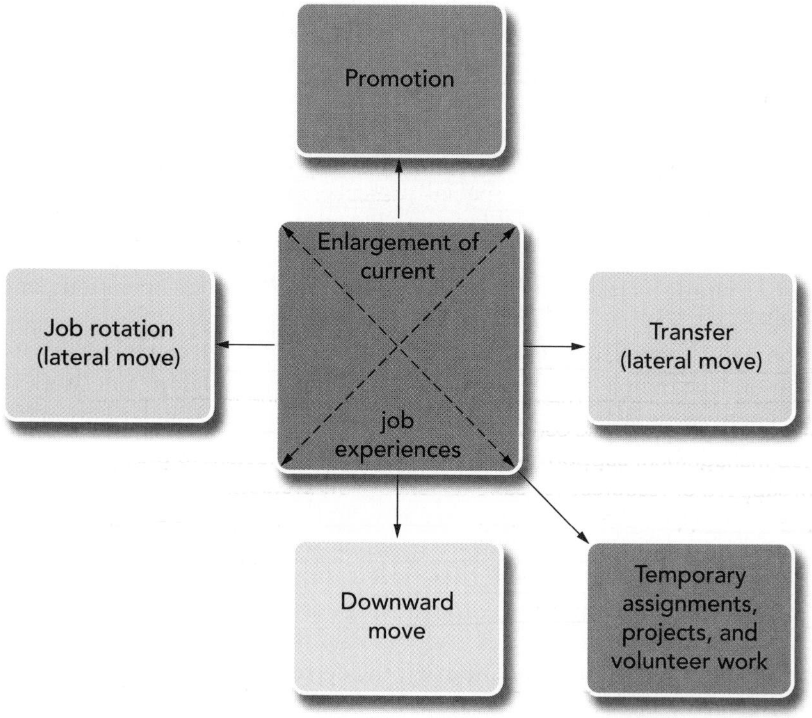


**figure 9.2**
How Job Experiences Are Used for Employee Development

## Enlarging the Current Job

**Job Enlargement** Adding challenges or new responsibilities to an employee's current job.

**Job enlargement** refers to adding challenges or new responsibilities to employees' current jobs. This could include special project assignments, switching roles within a work team, or researching new ways to serve clients and customers. For example, an engineering employee may join a task force developing new career paths for technical employees. Through this project work, the engineer may lead certain aspects of career path development (such as reviewing the company's career development process). As a result, the engineer not only learns about the company's career development system, but uses leadership and organizational skills to help the task force reach its goals. Some companies are enlarging jobs by giving two managers the same responsibilities and job title and allowing them to divide the work (two-in-a-box).[52] This helps managers learn from a more experienced employee; helps companies fill jobs that require multiple skills; and, for positions requiring extensive travel, ensures that one employee is always on site to deal with work-related issues. For example, at Cisco Systems, the head of the Cisco routing group, who was trained as an engineer but now works in business development, shared a job with an engineer. Each employee was exposed to the other's skills, which has helped both perform their jobs better.

## Job Rotation

**Job Rotation** The process of systematically moving a single individual from one job to another over the course of time. The job assignments may be in various functional areas of the company or movement may be between jobs in a single functional area or department.

**Job rotation** gives employees a series of job assignments in various functional areas of the company or movement among jobs in a single functional area or department. Arrow Electronics allows employees to take a 10-week sabbatical after seven years with the company.[53] While an employee is taking the sabbatical, the company uses the job vacancy as a job rotation for a different employee. Assignments to open positions are based on an employee's development needs. Employees who rotate to new positions are required to document their experiences and learning, especially emphasizing how the position helped them better understand the business. Regions Financial has two job rotation programs in information technology and regional banking.[54] The information technology program involves two full-time positions. Both positions require a 12- to 18-month job rotation within the six information technology departments to work on special projects. Employees participating in the company's Retail Leadership Development Program rotate to teller, financial service representative, and branch sales manager to complement instructor-led and computer-based training focusing on developing service, sales, branch operations, and leadership skills.

Job rotation helps employees gain an overall appreciation of the company's goals, increases their understanding of different company functions, develops a network of contacts, and improves problem-solving and decision-making skills.[55] Job rotation has also been shown to be related to skill acquisition, salary growth, and promotion rates. But there are several potential problems with job rotation for both the employee and the work unit. The rotation may create a short-term perspective on problems and solutions in rotating employees and their peers. Employees' satisfaction and motivation may be adversely affected because they find it difficult to develop functional specialties and they don't spend enough time in one position to receive a challenging assignment. Productivity losses and workload increases may be experienced by both the department gaining a rotating employee and the department losing the employee due to training demands and loss of a resource. Top-level managers may rotate jobs to

**table 9.10**
Characteristics of Effective Job Rotation Systems

| | |
|---|---|
| 1. | Job rotation is used to develop skills as well as give employees experience needed for managerial positions. |
| 2. | Employees understand specific skills that will be developed by rotation. |
| 3. | Job rotation is used for all levels and types of employees. |
| 4. | Job rotation is linked with the career management process so employees know the development needs addressed by each job assignment. |
| 5. | Benefits of rotation are maximized and costs are minimized through managing timing of rotations to reduce workload costs and helping employees understand job rotation's role in their development plans. |
| 6. | All employees have equal opportunities for job rotation assignments regardless of their demographic group. |

SOURCE: Based on L. Cheraskin and M. Campion, "Study Clarifies Job Rotation Benefits," *Personnel Journal*, November 1996, pp. 31–38.

get the experiences they need to be prepared for the top management job in the company—chief executive officer. For example, two top Citigroup managers, the chief financial officer and head of strategy and the chairman and the chief executive of the SmithBarney, Citigroup's stock-research and brokerage group, swapped jobs, so each could get the experiences needed to become a top leader in the company.[56] One manager needed financial experience and the other operations experience. Promotion of a chief financial officer to the company's top job requires experience in running a business unit.

The characteristics of effective job rotation systems are shown in Table 9.10. As we see, effective job rotation systems are linked to the company's training, development, and career management systems. Also, job rotation should be used for all types of employees, not just those with managerial potential.

## Transfers, Promotions, and Downward Moves

Upward, lateral, and downward mobility is available for development purposes in most companies.[57] In a **transfer,** an employee is assigned a job in a different area of the company. Transfers do not necessarily increase job responsibilities or compensation. They are likely lateral moves (a move to a job with similar responsibilities). **Promotions** are advancements into positions with greater challenges, more responsibility, and more authority than in the previous job. Promotions usually include pay increases.

**Transfer**
The movement of an employee to a different job assignment in a different area of the company.

**Promotions**
Advances into positions with greater challenge, more responsibility, and more authority than the employee's previous job.

Transfers may involve relocation within the United States or to another country. This can be stressful not only because the employee's work role changes, but if the employee is in a two-career family, the spouse must find new employment. Also, the family has to join a new community. Transfers disrupt employees' daily lives, interpersonal relationships, and work habits.[58] People have to find new housing, shopping, health care, and leisure facilities, and they may be many miles from the emotional support of friends and family. They also have to learn a new set of work norms and procedures; they must develop interpersonal relationships with their new managers and peers; and they are expected to be as productive in their new jobs as they were in their old jobs even though they may know little about the products, services, processes, or employees for whom they are responsible.

Because transfers can provoke anxiety, many companies have difficulty getting employees to accept them. Research has identified the employee characteristics associated with a willingness to accept transfers:[59] high career ambitions, a belief that one's future with the company is promising, and a belief that accepting a transfer is necessary for success in the company. Employees who are not married and not active in the community are generally most willing to accept transfers. Among married employees, the spouse's willingness to move is the most important influence on whether an employee will accept a transfer.

**Downward Move**
A job change involving a reduction in an employee's level of responsibility and authority.

A **downward move** occurs when an employee is given less responsibility and authority.[60] This may involve a move to another position at the same level (lateral demotion), a temporary cross-functional move, or a demotion because of poor performance. Temporary cross-functional moves to lower-level positions, which give employees experience working in different functional areas, are most frequently used for employee development. For example, engineers who want to move into management often take lower-level positions (like shift supervisor) to develop their management skills.

Because of the psychological and tangible rewards of promotions (such as increased feelings of self-worth, salary, and status in the company), employees are more willing to accept promotions than lateral or downward moves. Promotions are more readily available when a company is profitable and growing. When a company is restructuring or experiencing stable or declining profits—especially if numerous employees are interested in promotions and the company tends to rely on the external labor market to staff higher-level positions—promotion opportunities may be limited.[61]

Unfortunately, many employees have difficulty associating transfers and downward moves with development. They see them as punishments rather than as opportunities to develop skills that will help them achieve long-term success with the company. Many employees decide to leave a company rather than accept a transfer. Companies need to successfully manage transfers not only because of the costs of replacing employees but because of the costs directly associated with them. For example, GTE spends approximately $60 million a year on home purchases and other relocation costs such as temporary housing and relocation allowances.[62] One challenge companies face is learning how to use transfers and downward moves as development opportunities—convincing employees that accepting these opportunities will result in long-term benefits for them.

To ensure that employees accept transfers, promotions, and downward moves as development opportunities, companies can provide

- Information about the content, challenges, and potential benefits of the new job and location.
- Involvement in the transfer decision by sending the employees to preview the new location and giving them information about the community.
- Clear performance objectives and early feedback about their job performance.
- A host at the new location to help them adjust to the new community and workplace.
- Information about how the job opportunity will affect their income, taxes, mortgage payments, and other expenses.
- Reimbursement and assistance in selling and purchasing or renting a place to live.
- An orientation program for the new location and job.
- Information on how the new job experiences will support the employee's career plans.

- Assistance for dependent family members, including identifying schools and child care and elder care options.
- Help for the spouse in identifying and marketing skills and finding employment.[63]

**Externship** refers to a company allowing employees to take a full-time operational role at another company. Mercer Management, a consulting firm, uses externship to develop employees interested in gaining experience in a specific industry.[64] Mercer Management promises to employ the externs after their assignments end. For example, one employee who has been a Mercer consultant for five years is now vice president of Internet services for Binney & Smith, the maker of Crayola crayons. A year ago he was consulting on an Internet project for Binney & Smith. But he wanted to actually implement his recommendations rather than just give them to the client and move on to another project—so he started working at Binney & Smith. He remains on Mercer Management's payroll, though his salary comes from Binney & Smith. Mercer believes that employees who participate in the externship program will remain committed to the company because they have had the opportunity to learn and grow professionally and have not had to disrupt their personal and professional lives with a job search. Although externships give employees other employment options and some employees will leave, Mercer believes that it not only is a good development strategy but also helps in recruitment. The externship program signals to potential employees that Mercer is creative and flexible with its employees.

**Externship**
When a company allows an employee to take a full-time operational role at another company.

## Temporary Assignments, Projects, Volunteer Work, and Sabbaticals

Employee exchange is one type of temporary assignment. Two companies can agree to exchange employees. First Chicago National Bank and Kodak participated in an employee exchange program so that the two companies could better understand each other's business and how to improve the services provided.[65] For example, a First Chicago employee helped Kodak's business imaging division identify applications for compact disc technology. A Kodak employee helped First Chicago understand areas within the bank that could benefit from imaging technology.

Temporary assignments can include a **sabbatical** (a leave of absence from the company to renew or develop skills). Employees on sabbatical often receive full pay and benefits. Sabbaticals let employees get away from the day-to-day stresses of their jobs and acquire new skills and perspectives. Sabbaticals also allow employees more time for personal pursuits such as writing a book or spending more time with young children. Sabbaticals are common in a variety of industries ranging from consulting firms to the fast-food industry.[66] Fallon Worldwide, an advertising agency, offers a program called Dreamcatchers to staff members who want to work on a project or travel.[67] Dreamcatchers was developed to help the agency avoid having employees burn out and lose their creative edge. Employees have taken time off to write novels, kayak, and motorcyle through the Alps. Fallon Worldwide matches employee contributions of up to $1,000 annually for two years and offers up to two extra weeks of paid vacation. The agency partners believe that the program has helped in the retention of key employees and the recruiting of new ones. The partners also believe that the program helps recharge employees' creativity, which is key for employees to do their best work for customers.

**Sabbatical**
A leave of absence from the company to renew or develop skills.

Volunteer assignments can also be used for development. As part of their leadership development, General Mills managers serve as board members for nonprofit organizations.[68] Volunteer assignments may give employees opportunities to manage change, teach, have a high level of responsibility, and be exposed to other job demands shown in Table 9.9.

## COMPETING THROUGH GLOBALIZATION

### Going around the World Develops Leadership Skills

To prepare partners for top leadership positions, PricewaterhouseCoopers (PwC) sends them to developing areas of the world for eight weeks to use their business skills to benefit locals and learn how to overcome barriers, connect with clients from different cultures, and identify answers to very difficult problems. Partners are forced to take on projects outside their areas of expertise. The cost to PwC is $15,000 per participant for travel and expenses plus three months of salary. Each partner also spends two weeks in training to prepare for the trip and debriefing when they return. For example, one partner was sent to a village in Namibia, Africa, along with partners from Mexico and the Netherlands to help village leaders deal with the community's AIDS crisis (other projects have involved working with an ecotourism collective in Belize and small organic farmers in Zambia). The partner helped the village leaders understand what was needed to get support from the community for AIDS prevention programs. PwC has some evidence showing that the program is a success and is working on developing more measures such as impact on productivity rates.

Progress in meeting leadership goals set by program participants before they attend the program are evaluated. All 24 program participants are still working at PwC, half have been promoted, and most have new job responsibilities. The ability of program participants to win contracts with global clients appears to have improved. The partners who have participated believe that the experience has helped them better relate to their colleagues and clients. The partner who worked on the AIDS project has seen how slowly decisions are made in other places, which has helped him become more patient with his peers at work. Also, he now favors face-to-face conversations over e-mail because it is more valuable for building trust—a lesson learned in Namibia, where there was no electricity, e-mail, or PowerPoint presentations.

SOURCES: Based on J. Hempel, "It Takes a Village—and a Consultant," *BusinessWeek*, September 6, 2004, pp. 76–77; J. Marquez, "Companies Send Employees on Volunteer Projects Abroad to Cultivate Leadership Skills," *Workforce Management*, November 2005, pp. 50–51.

The "Competing through Globalization" box shows how PricewaterhouseCoopers is using project work to help improve managers' ability to work with global clients and benefit local communities in need.

### Interpersonal Relationships

**LO5**
Develop Successful Mentoring Programs.

Employees can also develop skills and increase their knowledge about the company and its customers by interacting with a more experienced organization member. Mentoring and coaching are two types of interpersonal relationships that are used to develop employees.

#### Mentoring

**Mentor**
An experienced, productive senior employee who helps develop a less experienced employee.

A **mentor** is an experienced, productive senior employee who helps develop a less experienced employee (the protégé). Most mentoring relationships develop informally as a result of interests or values shared by the mentor and protégé. Research suggests that employees with certain personality characteristics (like emotional stability, the ability to adapt their behavior based on the situation, and high needs for power and achievement) are most likely to seek a mentor and be an attractive protégé for a mentor.[69] Mentoring relationships can also develop as part of a planned company effort to bring together successful senior employees with less experienced employees.

***Developing Successful Mentoring Programs.*** Although many mentoring relationships develop informally, one major advantage of formalized mentoring programs is that they ensure access to mentors for all employees, regardless of gender or race. An additional advantage is that participants in the mentoring relationship know what is expected of them.[70] One limitation of formal mentoring programs is that mentors may not be able to provide counseling and coaching in a relationship that has been artificially created.[71]

Table 9.11 presents the characteristics of a successful formal mentoring program. Mentors should be chosen based on interpersonal and technical skills. They also need to be trained.[72]

A key to successful mentoring programs is that the mentor and protégé actually interact with each other face-to-face or virtually using videoconferencing.

Web-based matching systems are available to help match mentors and protégés. For example, both Dow Chemical and Intel have a Web system that allows protégés to input the qualities they want in a mentor. Then, similar to the results of a Google search, a list of names appears with the closest match to their qualities at the top.[73] Wyndham Hotels and Resorts found that a Web-based matching system has tripled the number of employees participating in mentoring. At Wyndham, once the list of names has been generated, the protégé selects the mentor who he or she believes is the best fit and has seven days to contact the mentor to arrange a meeting to decide if there is a good match. The mentor and protégé then sign a contract committing to meeting a certain amount of time each month. The system sends reminders of planned meetings to both the mentor and protégé.

**table 9.11**

Characteristics of Successful Formal Mentoring Programs

| |
|---|
| 1. Mentor and protégé participation is voluntary. Relationship can be ended at any time without fear of punishment. |
| 2. The mentor–protégé matching process does not limit the ability of informal relationships to develop. For example, a mentor pool can be established to allow protégés to choose from a variety of qualified mentors. |
| 3. Mentors are chosen on the basis of their past record in developing employees, willingness to serve as a mentor, and evidence of positive coaching, communication, and listening skills. |
| 4. Mentor–protégé matching is based on how the mentor's skills can help meet the protégé's needs. |
| 5. The purpose of the program is clearly understood. Projects and activities that the mentor and protégé are expected to complete are specified. |
| 6. The length of the program is specified. Mentor and protégé are encouraged to pursue the relationship beyond the formal period. |
| 7. A minimum level of contact between the mentor and protégé is specified. |
| 8. Protégés are encouraged to contact one another to discuss problems and share successes. |
| 9. The mentor program is evaluated. Interviews with mentors and protégés give immediate feedback regarding specific areas of dissatisfaction. Surveys gather more detailed information regarding benefits received from participating in the program. |
| 10. Employee development is rewarded, which signals managers that mentoring and other development activities are worth their time and effort. |

Professional services firm Ernst & Young has mentoring programs pairing high-potential employees with executive mentors (Executive Mentoring Program) and minority employees with senior leaders (Learning Partnerships). Mentors are not forced to serve; they volunteer their time. The programs require mentors and protégés to meet in person four times a year to set goals, for a six-month review, at a year-end evaluation session, and at one other time.[74] Any topics can be discussed in the confidential conversations including career goals, work–life balance, performance issues, and problems with managers. The mentors also introduce their protégés to senior managers whom they otherwise would not meet. Protégés grade their mentors using the company's performance appraisal system. The company has adjusted salaries and denied promotions to managers who were poor mentors.

**Career Support**
Coaching, protection, sponsorship, and providing challenging assignments, exposure, and visibility.

**Psychosocial Support**
Serving as a friend and role model, providing positive regard and acceptance, and creating an outlet for a protégé to talk about anxieties and fears.

***Benefits of Mentoring Relationships.*** Both mentors and protégés can benefit from a mentoring relationship. Research suggests that mentors provide career and psychosocial support to their protégés. **Career support** includes coaching, protection, sponsorship, and providing challenging assignments, exposure, and visibility. **Psychosocial support** includes serving as a friend and a role model, providing positive regard and acceptance, and creating an outlet for the protégé to talk about anxieties and fears. Additional benefits for the protégé include higher rates of promotion, higher salaries, and greater organizational influence.[75]

Mentoring relationships provide opportunities for mentors to develop their interpersonal skills and increase their feelings of self-esteem and worth to the organization. For individuals in technical fields such as engineering or health services, the protégé may help them gain knowledge about important new scientific developments in their field (and therefore prevent them from becoming technically obsolete). For example, General Electric recently launched an initiative in e-business. However, many veteran managers faced the challenge of trying to understand how to effectively use the Internet. Jack Welch, former CEO of General Electric, created a mentoring program for his top 600 managers.[76] The program involves having younger employees who have more experience with the Internet serving as mentors for the top managers. Welch generated interest in the program by getting his own mentor, who is approximately half his age and has much less business experience than he does—but is a Web expert who runs the company's Web site. The purpose of the program is to help managers become familiar with competitors' Web sites, experience the difficulty of ordering products online, and understand what the best Web sites are doing right. Welch started the program because he believes that e-business knowledge is generally inversely related to age and position in the company hierarchy. GE managers meet with their mentors for Web lessons, where they critique Web sites, discuss articles and books about e-commerce they have been given to read, and ask the mentors questions. The sessions benefit both the mentors and the protégés. The protégés learn about the Web, and the mentoring sessions make the younger employees more comfortable talking to their bosses. The mentors also learn about the skills that a manager needs to run a large business operation (such as the ability to communicate with different people).

***Purposes of Mentoring Programs.*** Mentor programs socialize new employees, increase the likelihood of skill transfer from training to the work setting, and provide opportunities for women and minorities to gain the exposure and skills needed to evolve into managerial positions. Consider the New York Hospital–Cornell Medical Center mentoring program.[77] The program is designed to help new employees more quickly learn housekeeping duties and understand the culture of the hospital. One benefit of the program is that new employees' performance deficiencies are more quickly corrected. Although the formal mentoring of new employees lasts only two weeks, mentors are available to provide support many months later.

At E. I. Du Pont de Nemours and Company's corporate headquarters, Steve Croft and Janet Graham have met at least once a month for the past seven years to share problems, information, and advice as part of Du Pont's mentoring program.[78] He is a planning manager in Du Pont's research division. She is an administrative assistant in the toxicology lab where Steve used to work. From a list of volunteers, protégés choose mentors (managers and executives) whose skills and experience they want to learn about. Croft, the mentor, has answered Graham's questions about corporate programs and given her the opportunity to meet scientists and managers in the company. Graham has also learned more about the role of other departments in the company and budgetary priorities. Croft too has benefited from the relationship. He has learned about how management decisions affect employees. For example, when the toxicology lab was forced to begin to charge departments for its services (rather than being supported from the company's general fund), Croft learned about employees' reactions and anxieties from Graham.

Because of the lack of potential mentors or a formal reward system supporting mentoring, and the belief that the quality of mentorships developed in a formal program is poorer than informal mentoring relationships, some companies have initiated group mentoring programs. In **group mentoring programs,** a successful senior employee is paired with a group of four to six less experienced protégés. One potential advantage of the mentoring group is that protégés can learn from each other as well as from a more experienced senior employee. The leader helps protégés understand the organization, guides them in analyzing their experiences, and helps them clarify career directions. Each member of the group may complete specific assignments, or the group may work together on a problem or issue.[79]

**Group Mentoring Program**
A program pairing a successful senior employee with a group of four to six less experienced protégés.

The "Competing through Sustainability" box shows how mentoring programs can lead to value for different company stakeholders.

## Coaching

A **coach** is a peer or manager who works with an employee to motivate him, help him develop skills, and provide reinforcement and feedback. There are three roles that a coach can play.[80] Part of coaching may be one-on-one with an employee (such as giving feedback). Another role is to help employees learn for themselves. This involves helping them find experts who can assist them with their concerns and teaching them how to obtain feedback from others. Third, coaching may involve providing resources such as mentors, courses, or job experiences that the employee may not be able to gain access to without the coach's help. Becton Dickinson uses peer coaching as part of its leadership development programs.[81] The topics discussed include job challenges as a development method, ambiguity as a change agent, and how to influence others. Evaluation of the peer coaching has found that coaches gain confidence in their abilities and participants learn about the topics discussed. Wachovia Corporation, a financial services company, has an executive coaching program that uses both internal and external coaches.[82] Participants in the executive leadership development program receive 360-degree assessments that they take to their internal coaches, who are from a different division in the company. Together the manager and coach review the assessment results and agree on an action plan.

**Coach**
A peer or manager who works with an employee to motivate her, help her develop skills, and provide reinforcement and feedback.

**LO6**
Describe How to Train Managers to Coach Employees.

## COMPETING THROUGH SUSTAINABILITY

### Mentoring Programs Have Potential to Pay Individual, Corporate, and Societal Dividends

A company's sustainability is determined by the extent to which it satisfies the needs of shareholders, customers, employees, community, and society. KLA-Tencor, Fannie Mae, and General Electric are using mentoring programs to help employees learn new skills, encourage women and minorities to move into management positions, and develop management talent that can help sustain a business strategy.

KLA-Tencor, a supplier of process control solutions for the semiconductor industry, uses mentoring to improve senior managers' skills. The senior managers receive mentoring from company board members as well as retired company executives. The senior managers are expected to increase their functional expertise, identify specific performance goals and developmental activities to address job-related weaknesses, and increase their understanding of the company's culture, vision, and political structure. KLA-Tencor also has an online mentoring program for managers identified as having high potential for upper-level positions. The program includes an automated relationship pairing function and a 360-degree assessment that is used in the mentoring relationship to improve skill weaknesses.

Fannie Mae provides financial products and services that make it possible for families to purchase homes. At Fannie Mae, the company's mentoring program is designed to encourage the advancement of high-potential employees, especially women and minorities. To ensure that the mentor and protégé are compatible, a pairing committee conducts detailed screening and matching based on the mentor's and protégé's interests and expectations (e.g., What skills, experiences, and knowledge would you like your mentor to possess?). Fannie Mae provides guidelines to both mentors and protégés that identify what is expected of the relationship. Orientation sessions help the mentor and protégé become acquainted with each other. Both mentor and protégé sign a confidentiality agreement to build trust between the parties. To help ensure the success of the mentoring program, Fannie Mae uses surveys to conduct formal and informal evaluations that help the company understand the strengths and weaknesses of the program.

Top females at General Electric are assigned leadership roles within GE's Women's Network (GEWN) local and regional groups so they can get leadership experience. The women also have the opportunity to meet and talk with members of GE's senior management team by attending speaker seminars, workshops, and networking dinners. The network opportunities help the women form an ongoing relationship with a senior leader, which can develop into a mentoring relationship.

SOURCES: Based on T. Galvin, "Best Practices: Mentoring, KLA-Tencor Corp.," *Training*, March 2003, p. 58; A. Poe, "Establishing Positive Mentoring Relationships," *HR Magazine*, February 2002, pp. 62–69; H. Dolezalek, "Got High Potentials?" *Training* 44 (2007), pp. 18–22.

The coaches are trained how to coach and understand the positive and negative aspects of 360-degree feedback. Research suggests that coaching improves managers' use of 360-degree feedback by helping them set specific improvement goals and solicit ideas for improvement, which results in improved performance.[83]

The best coaches should be empathetic, supportive, practical, and self-confident but not appear as someone who knows all the answers or wants to tell others what to do.[84] Employees who are going to be coached need to be open-minded and interested, not defensive, closed-minded, or concerned with their reputation. Both the coach and the employee to be coached take risks in the relationship. Coaches use their expertise and experiences to help an employee. Employees are vulnerable by honestly communicating about their weaknesses.

To develop coaching skills, training programs need to focus on four issues related to managers' reluctance to provide coaching.[85] First, managers may be reluctant to discuss performance issues even with a competent employee because they want to avoid confrontation. This is especially an issue when the manager is less of an expert than the employee. Second, managers may be better able to identify performance problems than to help employees solve them. Third, managers may also feel that the employee interprets coaching as criticism. Fourth, as companies downsize and operate with fewer employees, managers may feel that there is not enough time for coaching.

## Career Management and Development Planning Systems

Companies' career management systems vary in the level of sophistication and the emphasis they place on different components of the process. Steps and responsibilities in the career management system are shown in Figure 9.3.

**LO7**
Discuss the Steps in the Development Planning Process.

### Self-Assessment

*Self-assessment* refers to the use of information by employees to determine their career interests, values, aptitudes, and behavioral tendencies. It often involves psychological tests such as the Myers-Briggs Type Indicator (described earlier in the chapter), the Strong-Campbell Interest Inventory, and the Self-Directed Search. The Strong-Campbell helps employees identify their occupational and job interests; the Self-Directed Search identifies employees' preferences for working in different types of

**figure 9.3**
Steps and Responsibilities in the Career Management Process

| | Self-assessment → | Reality check → | Goal setting → | Action planning |
|---|---|---|---|---|
| **Employee responsibility** | Identify opportunities and needs to improve. | Identify what needs are realistic to develop. | Identify goal and method to determine goal progress. | Identify steps and timetable to reach goal. |
| **Company responsibility** | Provide assessment information to identify strengths, weaknesses, interests, and values. | Communicate performance evaluation, where employee fits in long-range plans of the company, changes in industry, profession, and workplace. | Ensure that goal is specific, challenging, and attainable; commit to help employee reach the goal. | Identify resources employee needs to reach goal, including courses, work experiences, relationships. |

**table 9.12**

Example of a Self-Assessment Exercise

| ACTIVITY (PURPOSE) |
|---|
| **Step 1: *Where am I?* (Examine current position of life and career.)**<br>Think about your life from past and present to the future. Draw a time line to represent important events. |
| **Step 2: *Who am I?* (Examine different roles.)**<br>Using 3 × 5 cards, write down one answer per card to the question "Who am I?" |
| **Step 3: *Where would I like to be and what would I like to happen?* (This helps in future goal setting.)**<br>Consider your life from present to future. Write an autobiography answering three questions: What do you want to have accomplished? What milestones do you want to achieve? What do you want to be remembered for? |
| **Step 4: *An ideal year in the future* (Identify resources needed.)**<br>Consider a one-year period in the future. If you had unlimited resources, what would you do? What would the ideal environment look like? Does the ideal environment match step 3? |
| **Step 5: *An ideal job* (Create current goal.)**<br>In the present, think about an ideal job for you with your available resources. Consider your role, resources, and type of training or education needed. |
| **Step 6: *Career by objective inventory* (Summarize current situation.)**<br>• What gets you excited each day?<br>• What do you do well? What are you known for?<br>• What do you need to achieve your goals?<br>• What could interfere with reaching your goals?<br>• What should you do now to move toward reaching your goals?<br>• What is your long-term career objective? |

SOURCE: Based on J. E. McMahon and S. K. Merman, "Career Development," in *The ASTD Training and Development Handbook,* 4th ed., ed. R. L. Craig. Copyright © 1996 The McGraw–Hill Companies. Reprinted with permission.

environments (like sales, counseling, landscaping, and so on). Tests may also help employees identify the relative values they place on work and leisure activities. Self-assessment can involve exercises such as the one in Table 9.12. This type of exercise helps an employee consider where she is now in her career, identify future plans, and gauge how her career fits with her current situation and available resources. In some companies, counselors assist employees in the self-assessment process and interpret the results of psychological tests.

**LO8**
Explain the Employees' and Company's Responsibilities in Planning Development.

Through the assessment, a development need can be identified. This need can result from gaps between current skills and/or interests and the type of work or position the employee wants. For example, at Lockheed Martin employees have the chance to receive online career assessment through the company's My LM Career Assessment.[86] Using the company's intranet, employees can take a career inventory that identifies their career interests and skills in different areas. The purpose of the inventory is to get employees thinking about the steps they are going to have to take to achieve career success. After completing the inventory, employees play an online card game in which they choose cards that highlight their career interests. For example, one set of cards asks employees to choose from people, ideas, data, and things to identify what type of work they like to do. Each card chosen helps the employee narrow his or her specific work style and preferences. Employees are encouraged to share and discuss their results with managers, mentors, or human resource representatives.

## Reality Check

*Reality check* refers to the information employees receive about how the company evaluates their skills and knowledge and where they fit into the company's plans (potential promotion opportunities, lateral moves). Usually this information is provided by the employee's manager as part of performance appraisal. It is not uncommon in well-developed career management systems for the manager to hold separate performance appraisals and career development discussions.

## Goal Setting

*Goal setting* refers to the process of employees developing short- and long-term career objectives. These goals usually relate to desired positions (such as becoming sales manager within three years), level of skill application (use one's budgeting skills to improve the unit's cash flow problems), work setting (move to corporate marketing within two years), or skill acquisition (learn how to use the company's human resource information system). These goals are usually discussed with the manager and written into a development plan. A development plan for a product manager is shown in Figure 9.4. Development plans usually include descriptions of strengths and weaknesses, career goals, and development activities for reaching the career goal.

Consider Just Born's Career Development Process (CDP) used by high-performing employees to identify their career path within the company and ready themselves for their next position.[87] The career development plan involves identifying both short- and long-term career goals. Employees commit to two goals to help them progress in their career. Just Born provides a competency dictionary on the company's intranet that can be used for identifying development needs. The CDP gives both employees and their managers the opportunity to discuss future career plans and becomes a reality check by raising expectations and increasing performance standards. Employees initiate the career development program by first defining future job interests, identifying work experiences that help prepare for the future job, and establishing the long-term career goal. The CDP is discussed with the employee's manager. The manager can support the CDP or suggest changes. If employees' future job interests are outside their current department, the interests are communicated to the manager of that department.

## Action Planning

During this phase, employees determine how they will achieve their short- and long-term career goals. Action plans may involve any one or combination of development approaches discussed in the chapter (such as enrolling in courses and seminars, getting additional assessment, obtaining new job experiences, or finding a mentor or coach).[88] The development approach used depends on the needs and developmental goal.

## Examples of Career Management and Development Systems

Effective career management and development systems include several important design features (see Table 9.13). Sprint's individual development plan is based on five core competencies: act with integrity, focus on the customer, deliver results, build relationships, and develop leadership.[89] These competencies are used by each business unit to establish its strategy as well as by each manager and employee in creating development plans. The competencies are the foundations for development

figure 9.4
Career Development Plan

**Name:** **Title:** Project Manager **Immediate Manager:**

**Competencies**
*Please identify your three greatest strengths and areas for improvement.*
**Strengths**
- Strategic thinking and execution (confidence, command skills, action orientation)
- Results orientation (competence, motivating others, perseverance)
- Spirit for winning (building team spirit, customer focus, respect colleagues)

**Areas for Improvement**
- Patience (tolerance of people or processes and sensitivity to pacing)
- Written communications (ability to write clearly and succinctly)
- Overly ambitious (too much focus on successful completion of projects rather than developing relationships with individuals involved in the projects)

**Career Goals**
*Please describe your overall career goals.*
- **Long-term:** Accept positions of increased responsibility to a level of general manager (or beyond). The areas of specific interest include but are not limited to product and brand management, technology and development, strategic planning, and marketing.
- **Short-term:** Continue to improve my skills in marketing and brand management while utilizing my skills in product management, strategic planning, and global relations.

**Next Assignments**
*Identify potential next assignments (including timing) that would help you develop toward your career goals.*
- Manager or director level in planning, development, product, or brand management. Timing estimated to be Spring 2009.

**Training and Development Needs**
*List both training and development activities that will either help you develop in your current assignment or provide overall career development.*
- Master's degree classes will allow me to practice and improve my written communications skills. The dynamics of my current position, teamwork, and reliance on other individuals allow me to practice patience and to focus on individual team members' needs along with the success of the projects.

**Employee** ______________________ **Date** __________
**Immediate Manager** ______________ **Date** __________
**Mentor** ________________________ **Date** __________

conversations between managers and employees. Among the resources available to support the development plan is a development activities guide, which includes audiotapes, books, and specific courses designed to improve each of the competencies, as well as a Web site where employees can learn about the process. General Mills' development plan follows the process shown in Figure 9.4. Each employee completes a development plan that asks employees to consider four areas:

- *Professional goals and motivation:* What professional goals do I have? What excites me to grow professionally?

**table 9.13**

Design Factors of Effective Career Management and Development Systems

| | |
|---|---|
| 1. | System is positioned as a response to a business need. |
| 2. | Employees and managers participate in development of the system. |
| 3. | Employees are encouraged to take an active role in career management and development. |
| 4. | Evaluation is ongoing and used to improve the system. |
| 5. | Business units can customize the system for their own purposes (with some constraints). |
| 6. | Employees have access to career information sources (including advisers and positions available). |
| 7. | Senior management supports the career system. |
| 8. | Career management is linked to other human resource practices such as performance management, training, and recruiting systems. |
| 9. | A large, diverse talent pool is created. |
| 10. | Career plan and talent evaluation information is available and accessible to all managers. |

SOURCE: Based on B. Baumann, J. Duncan, S. E. Former, and Z. Leibowitz, "Amoco Primes the Talent Pump," *Personnel Journal*, February 1996, pp. 79–84; D. Hall, *Careers In and Out of Organizations* (Thousand Oaks, CA: Sage 2002).

- *Talents or strengths:* What are my talents and strengths?
- *Development opportunities:* What development needs are important to improve?
- *Development objectives and action steps:* What will be my objective for this plan? What steps can I take to meet the objectives?

Managers and employees are encouraged to discuss the development plan at least once a year. Speakers, online tools, and workshops to help employees complete the development plan and prepare for a development discussion with their manager increase the visibility and emphasize the importance of the development planning process.

John Deere, the consumer and residential equipment provider, has an online career development program that encourages employees to manage their careers.[90] The online system includes a "job-fit analysis" to help employees compare themselves with positions they would like to have in the future. This gives employees control and responsibility for identifying skill deficiencies and encourages them to have discussions with their managers to design a development plan to help them reach their career goals. Employees can access job competencies for each position. Employees can prepare an online internal résumé for the company's job posting system. The résumés give employees' credentials exposure to managers throughout the company. In the first three months the online system was available, employees made more than 10,000 hits on the job catalogue. More than 6,000 internal résumés are posted in the system.

**Glass Ceiling**
A barrier to advancement to higher-level jobs in the company that adversely affects women and minorities. The barrier may be due to lack of access to training programs, development experiences, or relationships (e.g., mentoring).

## Special Issues in Employee Development

**LO9**
Discuss What Companies Are Doing for Management Development Issues Including Succession Planning, Melting the Glass Ceiling, and Helping Dysfunctional Managers.

### Melting the Glass Ceiling

A major development issue facing companies today is how to get women and minorities into upper-level management positions—how to break the **glass ceiling.** One estimate is that women hold only 10 percent of the 6,428 total line-corporate positions in *Fortune* 50 companies.[91] The glass ceiling is a barrier to advancement to the higher levels of the organization. This barrier may be due to stereotypes or company systems that adversely affect the development of women or minorities.[92] The glass ceiling is likely caused by lack of access to training programs, appropriate developmental job experiences, and developmental relationships (such as mentoring).[93] Research has found no gender differences in access to job experiences involving transitions or creating change.[94] However, male managers receive significantly more assignments involving high levels of responsibility (high stakes, managing business diversity, handling external pressure) than female managers of similar ability and managerial level. Also, female managers report experiencing more challenge due to lack of personal support (a type of job demand considered to be an obstacle that has been found to relate to harmful stress) than male managers. Career encouragement from peers and senior managers does help women advance to the higher management levels.[95] Managers making developmental assignments need to carefully consider whether gender biases or stereotypes are influencing the types of assignments given to women versus men.

Women and minorities often have trouble finding mentors because of their lack of access to the "old boy network," managers' preference to interact with other managers of similar status rather than with line employees, and intentional exclusion by managers who have negative stereotypes about women's and minorities' abilities, motivation, and job preferences.[96] Potential mentors may view minorities and women as a threat to their job security because they believe affirmative action plans give those groups preferential treatment.

Wal-Mart's strong corporate culture—emphasizing leadership, trust, willingness to relocate on short notice, and promotion from within—may have unintentionally created a glass ceiling.[97] Eighty-six percent of store manager positions are held by men. More than two-thirds of Wal-Mart managers started as hourly employees. Hourly job openings are posted at each store, but Wal-Mart never posted openings for management training positions that allowed hourly employees to move up into salaried, management positions. Part of the reason for this practice was that Wal-Mart values efficiency and never saw the need for job postings to fill open management positions. The other reason is that Wal-Mart trusts its managers to promote individuals who deserve promotion. However, women at Wal-Mart claim that it is difficult to find out about manager jobs. Traditionally, managers at Wal-Mart had to be willing to move with short notice. At Wal-Mart, this relocation requirement results in more opportunities for management jobs for men than for women. Male employees had more access to information about management job openings because they spent more time socializing and talking with management employees (who are primarily male). Wal-Mart is taking steps to ensure that the company remains a good place to work. For example, to give women more opportunities for management positions, Wal-Mart is developing a posting system for all management jobs. The company also plans on providing employees with a database that will notify them of job openings at stores across the country.

Consider Deloitte & Touche's efforts to melt the glass ceiling. Deloitte & Touche is an accounting, tax, and consulting firm with offices throughout the United States. The company had been experiencing high turnover of talented women and set out to understand why this was occurring and what the company could do to stop it.[98] Table 9.14 shows Deloitte & Touche's recommendations for melting the glass ceiling. Deloitte's Initiative for the Retention and Advancement of Women grew from a task force chaired by the company's chief executive officer. Deloitte & Touche made a

**table 9.14**

Deloitte & Touche's Recommendations for Melting the Glass Ceiling

| |
|---|
| Make sure senior management supports and is involved in the program. |
| Make a business case for change. |
| Make the change public. |
| Gather data on problems causing the glass ceiling using task forces, focus groups, and questionnaires. |
| Create awareness of how gender attitudes affect the work environment. |
| Force accountability through reviews of promotion rates and assignment decisions. |
| Promote development for all employees. |

SOURCE: Based on D. McCracken, "Winning the Talent War for Women," *Harvard Business Review*, November–December 2000, pp. 159–67.

business case for change by showing the senior partners of the company that half of the new hires were women, and half of them left the company before becoming candidates for upper management positions (partners). Data on the problem were gathered by having every management professional in the company attend a workshop designed to explore how gender attitudes affected the work environment (and led to the loss of talented women). The workshops included discussions, videos, and case studies. For example, a case scenario involved having partners evaluate two promising employees, one male and one female, with identical skills. One issue that was raised through the case analysis was that men get evaluated based on their potential, women based on their performance. Discussion suggested that the male could be expected to grow into the position through mentoring and other types of development. The female was evaluated based on performance in her current position. Her potential was not considered; rather, her past performance indicated that she was good in her current job but didn't have the necessary skills to move into executive management. The workshop also focused on how work assignments were allocated. High-profile, high-revenue assignments were important for advancement in the company. Workshop discussion showed that women were passed over for these desirable assignments because of false assumptions that male partners made about what women wanted, such as no travel. Also, women tended to get assigned to projects that were in the nonprofit, health care, and retail sectors—important segments but not as visible as areas like manufacturing, financial services, or mergers and acquisitions.

As a result of the workshops, Deloitte & Touche began discussing assignment decisions to make sure women had opportunities for highly visible assignments. Also, the company started formal career planning for both women and men. The company also sponsored networking events for women, where they had the opportunity to hear from successful women partners and meet other women at their level and higher in the company.

To measure the effectiveness of the program, Deloitte & Touche offices were given a menu of goals that they could choose from as evaluation criteria, including recruiting more women and reducing turnover. The compensation and promotability of office managers depended in part on their meeting these objectives. The company communicated to top management results on turnover and promotion rates for each office. Low-performing offices were visited by top managers to facilitate more progress.

Melting the glass ceiling takes time. Currently 14 percent of Deloitte & Touche's partners and directors are women, and women's and men's turnover rates are comparable. Reducing the turnover rate for women has saved the company an estimated $250 million in hiring and training costs. Deloitte is still striving to make sure that more women are partners and directors. In a global business world, one challenge is to extend the values of the initiative while respecting local cultural norms that might view women as less desirable employees or business partners.

Cigna Inc. has made a $2 million commitment to recruiting and developing executive women.[99] Cigna's leadership development program includes a week of "boot camp" where potential leaders attend leadership seminars and discussions. Women are rotated through a variety of supervisory jobs in different business units, assigned a mentor, and attend management training meetings run by senior executives. Cigna has seen the turnover rate of women executives drop 50 percent since 1998 due to development of the leadership programs in information technology, finance, and health care business specialties and the company's emphasis on bringing women candidates into consideration for executive job openings. Cigna now has a higher percentage of executive or senior management women (24 percent) than most other *Fortune* 500 companies. Women represent 40 percent of vice president and higher positions, an increase of 6 percent since 1999.

## Succession Planning

**Succession Planning**
The identification and tracking of high-potential employees capable of filling higher-level managerial positions.

**High-Potential Employees**
Employees the company believes are capable of being successful in high-level management positions.

Many companies are losing sizable numbers of upper-level managers due to retirement and company restructurings that reduced the number of potential upper-level managers. They are finding that their middle managers are not ready to move into upper management positions due to skill weaknesses or lack of needed experience. This creates the need for succession planning. Succession planning refers to the process of identifying and tracking high-potential employees. **Succession planning** helps organizations in several different ways.[100] It requires senior management to systematically review leadership talent in the company. It assures that top-level managerial talent is available. It provides a set of development experiences that managers must complete to be considered for top management positions; this avoids premature promotion of managers who are not ready for upper management ranks. Succession planning systems also help attract and retain managerial employees by providing them with development opportunities that they can complete if upper management is a career goal for them. **High-potential employees** are those the company believes are capable of being successful in higher-level managerial positions such as general manager of a strategic business unit, functional director (such as director of marketing), or chief executive officer (CEO).[101] High-potential employees typically complete an individual development program that involves education, executive mentoring and coaching, and rotation through job assignments. Job assignments are based on the successful career paths of the managers whom the high-potential employees are being prepared to replace. High-potential employees may also receive special assignments, such as making presentations and serving on committees and task forces.

Research suggests that the development of high-potential employees involves three stages.[102] A large pool of employees may initially be identified as high-potential employees, but the numbers are reduced over time because of turnover, poor performance, or a personal choice not to strive for a higher position. In stage 1, high-potential employees are selected. Those who have completed elite academic programs (like an MBA at Stanford) or who have been outstanding performers are identified. Psychological tests such as assessment centers may also be used.

In stage 2, high-potential employees receive development experiences. Those who succeed are the ones who continue to demonstrate good performance. A willingness to make sacrifices for the company is also necessary (such as accepting new assignments or relocating to a different region). Good oral and written communication skills, an ease in interpersonal relationships, and a talent for leadership are critical. In what is known as a "tournament model" of job transitions, high-potential employees who meet their senior managers' expectations in this stage advance into the next stage of the process.[103] Employees who do not meet the expectations are ineligible for higher-level managerial positions in the company.

To reach stage 3, high-potential employees usually have to be seen by top management as fitting into the company's culture and having the personality characteristics needed to successfully represent the company. These employees have the potential to occupy the company's top positions. In stage 3, the CEO becomes actively involved in developing the employees, who are exposed to the company's key personnel and are given a greater understanding of the company's culture. It is important to note that the development of high-potential employees is a slow process. Reaching stage 3 may take 15 to 20 years.

Table 9.15 shows the process used to develop a succession plan. The first step is to identify what positions are included in the succession plan, such as all management positions or only certain levels of management. The second step is to identify which employees are part of the succession planning system. For example, in some companies only high-potential employees are included in the succession plan. Third, the company needs to identify how positions will be evaluated. For example, will the emphasis be on competencies needed for each position or on the experiences an individual needs to have before moving into the position? Fourth, the company should identify how employee potential will be measured. That is, will employees' performance in their current jobs as well as ratings of potential be used? Will employees' position interests and career goals be considered? Fifth, the succession planning review process needs to be developed. Typically, succession planning reviews first involve employees' managers and human resources. A talent review could also include an overall assessment of leadership talent in the company, an identification of high-potential employees, and a discussion of plans to keep key managers from leaving the company. Sixth, succession planning is dependent on other human resource systems, including compensation, training and development, and staffing. Incentives and bonuses may be linked to completion of development opportunities. Activities such as training courses, job experiences, mentors, and 360-degree feedback can be used to meet development needs. Companies need to make decisions such as will they fill an open management position internally with a less-experienced

**table 9.15**

The Process of Developing a Succession Plan

1. Identify what positions are included in the plan.
2. Identify the employees who are included in the plan.
3. Develop standards to evaluate positions (e.g., competencies, desired experiences, desired knowledge, developmental value).
4. Determine how employee potential will be measured (e.g., current performance and potential performance).
5. Develop the succession planning review.
6. Link the succession planning system with other human resource systems, including training and development, compensation, and staffing systems.
7. Determine what feedback is provided to employees.

SOURCE: Based on B. Dowell, "Succession Planning," in *Implementing Organizational Interventions*, ed. J. Hedge and E. Pulaskos (San Francisco: Jossey-Bass, 2002), pp. 78–109.

employee who will improve in the role over time, or will they hire a manager from outside the company who can immediately deliver results. Finally, employees need to be provided with feedback on future moves, expected career paths, and development goals and experiences.

A good example of succession planning is the system at WellPoint, a health care company headquartered in Thousand Oaks, California.[104] WellPoint has a Web-based corporate database that identifies employees for management jobs throughout the company and tracks the development of employee talent. WellPoint has operations across the United States, including locations in California and Georgia. The succession planning system includes 600 managers and executives across five levels of the company. The Human Resource Planning System (HRPS) has detailed information on possible candidates, including performance evaluations, summaries of the candidates' accomplishments at the company, self-evaluations, information about career goals, and personal data such as the candidates' willingness to relocate to another part of the company. Part of the development of HRPS involved identifying the company's strength and weaknesses at each position. Senior management team members developed standards, or benchmarks, to use to identify the best candidates for promotion. The HRPS system allows managers and the human resource team to identify and evaluate candidates for every management position in the company. It helps identify and track the development of promising internal candidates and also identifies areas where internal candidates are weak, so that (1) external candidates can be recruited, (2) a special development program can be initiated to develop employee talent, and (3) the company can place more emphasis on developing the missing skills and competencies in internal candidates. For example, because WellPoint lacked candidates for two levels of management, the company created a special training program that used business case simulations for 24 managers and executives who had been identified as high-potential candidates for upper-level management positions.

WellPoint's process of succession planning includes several steps. First, each employee who is eligible for succession planning completes a self-evaluation that is sent to his or her manager. The manager adds a performance appraisal, a rating on the employee's core competencies, and a promotion assessment, that is, an assessment of the employee's potential for promotion. The promotion assessment includes the manager's opinion regarding what positions the employee might be ready for and when the employee should be moved. It also includes the manager's view on who could fill the open position if the employee is promoted. The information from the employee and the manager is used to create an online résumé for each eligible employee. The system has benefited the company's bottom line. WellPoint realized an 86 percent internal promotion rate, which exceeded its goal of filling 75 percent of management positions from within. By improving employees' opportunities for promotion, WellPoint has reduced its turnover rate by 6 percent since 1997 and has saved $21 million on recruitment and training expenses. The time to fill open management positions has been reduced from 60 days to 35 days.

## Helping Managers with Dysfunctional Behaviors

A number of studies have identified managerial behavior that can cause an otherwise competent manager to be a "toxic" or ineffective manager. Such behavior includes insensitivity to others, inability to be a team player, arrogance, poor conflict management skills, inability to meet business objectives, and inability to change or adapt during a transition.[105] For example, a skilled manager who is interpersonally abrasive, aggressive, and an autocratic leader may find it difficult to motivate subordinates, may alienate internal and external customers, and may have trouble getting ideas accepted by superiors. These managers are in jeopardy of losing their jobs and have little chance of future advancement because of the dysfunctional behavior. Typically, a combination of assessment, training, and counseling is used to help managers change the dysfunctional behavior.

For example, a middle manager at PG&E, an energy company, was hurting her relationships with her associates, and her career, by her brash personality.[106] PG&E hired a coach to work with her. The coach videotaped her as she role played an actual clash that she had had with another manager over a new information system. During the confrontation (and the role play) she was aloof, abrasive, cold, and condescending. The coach helped her see the limitations of her approach. She apologized to colleagues and listened to their ideas. Coaching helped this manager learn how to maintain her composure and focus on what is being said rather than on the person. Wachovia hires external coaches for top executives who have been identified as high-potential leaders who are facing a specific job challenge or problem such as moving into a new position after a merger. The coaching involves nine months to a year and includes 360-degree assessments, interviews, and psychological tests.[107]

## A Look Back

The chapter opener described the Washington Group's development program.

**Questions**

1. How might job experiences be useful for helping employees develop?
2. What should a development plan include that an employee at Washington Group would complete prior to participating in development activities?
3. Would the development activities for top employees differ from the activities used for average employees? Why? Explain the differences.

Please see the Video Case that corresponds to this chapter online at www.mhhe.com/noe6e.

## Summary

This chapter emphasized the various development methods that companies use: formal education, assessment, job experiences, and interpersonal relationships. Most companies use one or more of these approaches to develop employees. Formal education involves enrolling employees in courses or seminars offered by the company or educational institutions. Assessment involves measuring the employee's performance, behavior, skills, or personality characteristics. Job experiences include job enlargement, rotating to a new job, promotions, or transfers. A more experienced, senior employee (a mentor) can help employees better understand the company and gain exposure and visibility to key persons in the organization. Part of a manager's job responsibility may be to coach employees. Regardless of the development approaches used, employees should have a development plan to identify (1) the type of development needed, (2) development goals, (3) the best approach for development, and (4) whether development goals have been reached. For development plans to be effective, both the employee and the company have responsibilities that need to be completed.

## Key Terms

Development, 400
Protean career, 401
Psychological contract 401
Psychological success, 402
Career management system, 403
Formal education programs, 404
Tuition reimbursement, 409
Assessment, 409
Myers-Briggs Type Indicator (MBTI)®, 410
Assessment center, 411
Leaderless group discussion, 411
Interview, 413
In-basket, 413
Role plays, 413
Benchmarks©, 414
Performance appraisal, 414
Upward feedback, 416
360-degree feedback systems, 416
Job experiences, 417
Job enlargement, 420
Job rotation, 420
Transfer, 421
Promotions, 421
Downward move, 422
Externship, 423
Sabbatical, 423
Mentor, 424
Career support, 426
Psychosocial support, 426
Group mentoring programs, 427
Coach, 427
Glass ceiling, 433
Succession planning, 436
High-potential employees, 436

## Discussion Questions

1. How could assessment be used to create a productive work team?
2. List and explain the characteristics of effective 360-degree feedback systems.
3. Why do companies develop formal mentoring programs? What are the potential benefits for the mentor? For the protégé?
4. Your boss is interested in hiring a consultant to help identify potential managers among current employees of a fast-food restaurant. The manager's job is to help wait on customers and prepare food during busy times, oversee all aspects of restaurant operations (including scheduling, maintenance, on-the-job training, and food purchase), and help motivate employees to provide high-quality service. The manager is also responsible for resolving disputes that might occur between employees. The position involves working under stress and coordinating several activities at one time. She asks you to outline the type of assessment program you believe would do the best job of identifying employees who will be successful managers. What will you tell her?
5. Many employees are unwilling to relocate because they like their current community, and spouses and children prefer not to move. Yet employees need to develop new skills, strengthen skill weaknesses, and be exposed to new aspects of the business to prepare for management positions. How could an employee's current job be changed to develop management skills?
6. What is coaching? Is there one type of coaching? Explain.
7. Why are many managers reluctant to coach their employees?
8. Why should companies be interested in helping employees plan their careers? What benefits can companies gain? What are the risks?
9. What are the manager's roles in a career management system? Which role do you think is most difficult for the typical manager? Which is the easiest role? List the reasons why managers might resist involvement in career management.
10. What are the characteristics of the most effective company development strategies? Which characteristic do you believe is most important? Why?
11. Nationwide Financial, a 5,000-employee life insurance company based in Columbus, Ohio, found that its management development program contained four types of managers. One type, unknown leaders, have the right skills but their talents are unknown to top managers in the company. Another group, arrogant leaders, believe they have all the skills they need. What types of development program would you recommend for these managers?

## Self-Assessment Exercise

The Department of Labor's Occupational Information Network (O*NET) is designed to meet the goal of promoting the education, training, counseling, and employment needs of the American workforce. Go to http://online.onetcenter.org/. Click on Skills Search. Complete the skills search than click Go. What occupations match your skills? How might Skills Search be useful for career management?

## Exercising Strategy: Employees in Motion at EMC Corporation

At EMC Corporation, based in Hopkinton, Massachusetts, adapting to change is critical. EMC Corporation business has changed since the company was founded in 1989. The company's original focus was on proprietary data storage software. Today, only half of EMC's business is hardware. Much of the company's products and services focus on information management and storage. Also, the company has grown through acquiring new companies—20 in the last several years. Revenues have grown from $6.26 billion in 2003 to $11 billion in 2006. To help employees adapt to change, employees work with their managers to complete an individual development plan (IDP). Each IDP considers the employees' skills as well as business needs. This information is used to identify how e-learning, classroom training, mentoring, and job rotation can be used for learning.

### Questions

1. EMC is relying on job rotation as a development strategy. What things should EMC do to ensure this is a successful strategy? Are other development activities necessary? Why?
2. What data on outcomes should be collected to monitor the effectiveness of EMC's IDP and development program?

## Managing People: From the Pages of *BusinessWeek*

### BusinessWeek How to Groom the Next Boss

Of all the challenges confronting managers and directors, few are as difficult or as critical as finding and training a chief executive-in-waiting. At Coca-Cola, Xerox, and Procter & Gamble, CEO successions have been marked by long searches, poor choices, or fumbled transitions. But a company with a well-prepared No. 2 can quell uncertainty, even in the worst emergencies. When McDonald's Corp. CEO James Cantalupo died of a heart attack on April 19, the board named Chief Operating Officer Charles H. Bell to his post within hours.

Kenneth W. Freeman, CEO of Quest Diagnostics Inc., was determined not to leave his company in the lurch. He started grooming his handpicked successor five years ago. When he transfers management of the $4.7 billion medical-testing company to Surya N. Mohapatra at the May 4 annual meeting, it will be the culmination of a meticulous succession process that experts say is a case study in how to choose a future CEO and prepare him for the job. Marc S. Effron, global practice leader for consultants Hewitt Associates Inc., says the careful succession planning at the Teterboro (N.J.)–based company will pay off with a new CEO who can hit the ground running. "It's incredibly unusual," says Effron of Freeman's efforts. "They're going to see the benefits."

Freeman's search for a successor started in 1999. He was on the brink of an acquisition spree that would triple Quest's revenues in five years. But he knew the buying binge couldn't last and that Quest's next CEO would need a science background to exploit advances in medicine and technology to generate internal growth. To identify candidates, he put 200 executives from Quest and a recently acquired rival through an *Apprentice*-like challenge: daylong case assignments that allowed him to see their leadership skills in action. "This was his legacy," says Audrey B. Smith, a consultant with Development Dimensions International who worked with Freeman. "He felt huge pressure to make the right decision."

Of all the executives, one stood out: his new chief operating officer. Mohapatra came to Quest in February, 1999, from Picker International, a maker of medical imaging systems. He had extensive experience in cardiovascular disease and information technology—areas that would be crucial to Quest's future. What's more, he was CEO material. Says Freeman: "Here was a guy who was incredibly smart, who could balance a whole bunch of priorities at the same time, who could be incredibly focused, and who did not know the meaning of failure."

Four months after Mohapatra's arrival, Freeman named him president, giving him a clear—but by no means guaranteed—shot at the top job. The two men could not be more different. Mohapatra, a scientist with several patents to his name, grew up in India. Freeman, a New Yorker, had a long finance career at Corning Inc. When Corning Clinical Laboratories was spun off as Quest in 1996, Freeman became CEO, a position he says he had no intention of occupying for more than 10 years.

Front-runner or not, it quickly became clear that if Mohapatra was to be CEO he would need basic leadership skills. During his first week, one of the most glaring deficiencies, poor public speaking skills, became apparent. At a "town meeting" with employees in Baltimore, Mohapatra told the crowd of 800 that he was glad to be there—then clammed up. Freeman decided the best way to coax Mohapatra out of his shell was trial by fire. In the months that followed, he had Mohapatra make unscripted comments to employees, meet with shareholders, and field questions from analysts on conference calls. He is now a more polished, confident speaker.

As a scientist, Mohapatra had come to Quest with habits that Freeman felt could undermine him as a CEO. A deep thinker, he took weeks to make decisions that should only take days. And he was far more "hands-on" than he needed to be, sometimes reopening interviews for jobs that his subordinates were ready to fill. Freeman challenged Mohapatra to make faster decisions and give his executive team more authority. Every Sunday afternoon for five years, the two engaged in lengthy telephone conversations during which Freeman would analyze Mohapatra's evolving management style and suggest further improvements. It was, Freeman now concedes, "pure browbeating." Perhaps, but it worked. "Am I more ready now than I was four years ago? Absolutely," says Mohapatra.

Fine-tuning Mohapatra's management skills was only part of the challenge. Making him an active board participant was equally important. When he arrived, Mohapatra deferred to Freeman in board debates, contributing little. Freeman forced him to be more assertive—at first surreptitiously, by leaving the room during discussions, and later by asking him to conduct formal board presentations. Even after joining the board in 2002, Mohapatra continued to strike some directors as aloof. By changing the seating chart, Freeman was able to increase Mohapatra's face time with other directors. "You want someone to be able to speak their mind and participate," says Gail R. Wilensky, an independent director. "It helped."

When his long incubation ends, Mohapatra's success will be far from assured. Maintaining double-digit growth won't be easy as takeover targets become scarce. That's the way it is in business; the future is never assured. But Freeman has done about as much to increase the odds as a CEO can.

SOURCE: Reprinted from May 10, 2004, issue of *BusinessWeek*, by special permission. L. Lavelle, "How to Groom the Next Boss," *BusinessWeek*, May 10, 2004, pp. 93–94.

## Questions

1. What development activities did Kenneth Freeman use to strengthen the skills of Surya Mohapatra (his successor)? List the activities and the skills they were designed to improve. What other development activities could he have used? Identify the development activities and the skills they would be targeted to improve.
2. Could a coach help Mohapatra develop the skills needed to be an effective CEO? Explain.
3. What recommendations do you have for identifying and preparing managers for CEO positions? Indicate the succession planning process as well as the development activities you would recommend.

# Notes


1. M. London, *Managing the Training Enterprise* (San Francisco: Jossey-Bass, 1989); C. McCauley and S. Heslett, "Individual Development in the Workplace," in *Handbook of Industrial, Work, and Organizational Psychology*, Vol. 1, ed. N. Anderson, D. Ones, H. Sinangil, and C. Viswesveran (London: Sage Publications, 2001), pp. 313–35.
2. R. W. Pace, P. C. Smith, and G. E. Mills, *Human Resource Development* (Englewood Cliffs, NJ: Prentice Hall, 1991); W. Fitzgerald, "Training versus Development," *Training and Development Journal*, May 1992, pp. 81–84; R. A. Noe, S. L. Wilk, E. J. Mullen, and J. E. Wanek, "Employee Development: Issues in Construct Definition and Investigation of Antecedents," in *Improving Training Effectiveness in Work Organizations*, ed. J. K. Ford (Mahwah, NJ: Lawrence Erlbaum, 1997), pp. 153–89.
3. Towers Perrin HR Services, *Talent Management: The State of the Art* (Chicago, IL: Towers Perrin, 2005). Available at www.towersperrin.com.
4. J. H. Greenhaus and G. A. Callanan, *Career Management*, 2nd ed. (Fort Worth, TX: Dryden Press, 1994); D. C. Feldman, *Managing Careers in Organizations* (Glenview, IL: Scott Foresman, 1988); D. Hall, *Careers In and Out of Organizations* (Thousand Oaks, CA: Sage, 2002).
5. D. T. Hall, "Protean Careers of the 21st Century," *Academy of Management Executive* 11 (1996), pp. 8–16; Hall, *Careers In and Out of Organizations*.
6. D. M. Rousseau, "Changing the Deal while Keeping the People," *Academy of Management Executive* 11 (1996), pp. 50–61; D. M. Rousseau and J. M. Parks, "The Contracts of Individuals and Organizations," in *Research in Organizational Behavior* 15, ed. L. L. Cummings and B. M. Staw (Greenwich, CT: JAI Press, 1992), pp. 1–47.
7. C. Ansberry, "A New Blue-Collar World," *The Wall Street Journal*, June 30, 2003, p. B1.
8. K. Kathryn, "Three Generations, Three Perspectives," *The Wall Street Journal*, March 29, 2004, p. R8.
9. M. B. Arthur, P. H. Claman, and R. J. DeFillippi, "Intelligent Enterprise, Intelligent Careers," *Academy of Management Executive* 9 (1995), pp. 7–20.
10. K. R. Brousseau, M. J. Driver, K. Eneroth, and R. Larsson, "Career Pandemonium: Realigning Organizations and Individuals," *Academy of Management Executive* 11 (1996), pp. 52–66.
11. M. B. Arthur, "The Boundaryless Career: A New Perspective of Organizational Inquiry," *Journal of Organization Behavior* 15 (1994), pp. 295–309; P. H. Mirvis and D. T. Hall, "Psychological Success and the Boundaryless Career," *Journal of Organization Behavior* 15 (1994), pp. 365–80.
12. B. P. Grossman and R. S. Blitzer, "Choreographing Careers," *Training and Development*, January 1992, pp. 67–69.
13. Harris Interactive, Emerging workforce study, (Ft. Lauderdale, FL: Spherion, 2005); Available at www.spherion.com/pressroom/

L. Chao, "What GenXers Need to Be Happy at Work," *The Wall Street Journal*, November 29, 2005, p. B6; E. Kaplan-Leiserson, "The Changing Workforce," *TD*, February 2005, pp. 10–11.
14. J. S. Lubin and J. B. White, "Throwing Off Angst, Workers Are Feeling in Control of Their Careers," *The Wall Street Journal*, September 11, 1997, pp. A1, A6.
15. R. Noe *Employee Training and Development*, 4th ed. (New York: McGraw-Hill, Irwin 2008).
16. M. Weinstein, "Teaching the Top," *Training*, February 2005, pp. 30–33.
17. C. Waxer, "Course Review," *Human Resource Executive*, December 2005, pp. 46–48.
18. C. Waxer, "Bank of Montreal Opens Its Checkbook in the Name of Employee Development," *Workforce Management*, October 24, 2005, pp. 46–48.
19. R. Knight, "GE's Corporate Boot Camp cum Talent Spotting Venue," *Financial Times Business Education*, March 20, 2006, p. 2; J. Durett, "GE Hones Its Leaders at Crotonville," *Training*, May 2006, pp. 25–27.
20. J. Bolt, *Executive Development* (New York: Harper Business, 1989); M. A. Hitt, B. B. Tyler, C. Hardee, and D. Park, "Understanding Strategic Intent in the Global Marketplace," *Academy of Management Executive* 9 (1995), pp. 12–19.
21. J. A. Byrne, "Virtual Business Schools," *BusinessWeek*, October 23, 1995, pp. 64–68; T. Bartlett, "The Hottest Campus on the Internet," *BusinessWeek*, October 20, 1997, pp. 77–80.
22. I. Speizer, "Custom Fit," *Workforce Management*, March 2005, pp. 57–63.
23. J. Reingold, "Corporate America Goes to School," *BusinessWeek*, October 20, 1997, pp. 66–72.
24. L. Bongiorno, "How'm I Doing," *BusinessWeek*, October 23, 1995, pp. 72, 74.
25. Waxer, "Course Review."
26. A. Howard and D. W. Bray, *Managerial Lives in Transition: Advancing Age and Changing Times* (New York: Guilford, 1988); Bolt, *Executive Development;* J. R. Hinrichs and G. P. Hollenbeck, "Leadership Development," in *Developing Human Resources*, ed. K. N. Wexley (Washington, DC: BNA Books, 1991), pp. 5-221 to 5-237.
27. E. Krell, "Personality Counts," *HR Magazine*, November 2005, pp. 47–52.
28. C. Cornell, "The Value of Values," *Human Resource Executive*, November 2004, pp. 68–72.
29. S. K. Hirsch, *MBTI Team Member's Guide* (Palo Alto, CA: Consulting Psychologists Press, 1992); A. L. Hammer, *Introduction to Type and Careers* (Palo Alto, CA: Consulting Psychologists Press, 1993).
30. A. Thorne and H. Gough, *Portraits of Type* (Palo Alto, CA: Consulting Psychologists Press, 1991).
31. D. Druckman and R. A. Bjork, eds., *In the Mind's Eye: Enhancing Human Performance* (Washington, DC: National Academy Press, 1991); M. H. McCaulley, "The Myers-Briggs Type Indicator and Leadership," in *Measures of Leadership*, ed. K. E. Clark and M. B. Clark (West Orange, NJ: Leadership Library of America, 1990), pp. 381–418.
32. G. C. Thornton III and W. C. Byham, *Assessment Centers and Managerial Performance* (New York: Academic Press, 1982); L. F. Schoenfeldt and J. A. Steger, "Identification and Development of Management Talent," in *Research in Personnel and Human Resource Management*, ed. K. N. Rowland and G. Ferris (Greenwich, CT: JAI Press, 1989), vol. 7, pp. 151–81.
33. Thornton and Byham, *Assessment Centers and Managerial Performance*.
34. B. B. Gaugler, D. B. Rosenthal, G. C. Thornton III, and C. Bentson, "Metaanalysis of Assessment Center Validity," *Journal of Applied Psychology* 72 (1987), pp. 493–511; D. W. Bray, R. J. Campbell, and D. L. Grant, *Formative Years in Business: A Long-Term AT&T Study of Managerial Lives* (New York: Wiley, 1974).
35. R. G. Jones and M. D. Whitmore, "Evaluating Developmental Assessment Centers as Interventions," *Personnel Psychology* 48 (1995), pp. 377–88.
36. J. Schettler, "Building Bench Strength," *Training*, June 2002, pp. 55–58.
37. C. D. McCauley and M. M. Lombardo, "Benchmarks: An Instrument for Diagnosing Managerial Strengths and Weaknesses," in *Measures of Leadership*, pp. 535–45; "Benchmarks©—Overview," at www.ccl.org Web site for the Center for Creative Leadership, March 28, 2006.
38. C. D. McCauley, M. M. Lombardo, and C. J. Usher, "Diagnosing Management Development Needs: An Instrument Based on How Managers Develop," *Journal of Management* 15 (1989), pp. 389–403.
39. S. B. Silverman, "Individual Development through Performance Appraisal," in *Developing Human Resources*, pp. 5-120 to 5-151.
40. M. Sallie-Dosunmu, "Born to Grow," *TD*, May 2006, pp. 34–37.
41. "Master of HR at GE," *Human Resource Executive*, October 2004, pp. 16–24.
42. J. S. Lublin, "Turning the Tables: Underlings Evaluate Bosses," *The Wall Street Journal*, October 4, 1994, pp. B1, B14; B. O'Reilly, "360-Degree Feedback Can Change Your Life," *Fortune*, October 17, 1994, pp. 93–100; J. F. Milliman, R. A. Zawacki, C. Norman, L. Powell, and J. Kirksey, "Companies Evaluate Employees from All Perspectives," *Personnel Journal*, November 1994, pp. 99–103.
43. Center for Creative Leadership, *Skillscope for Managers: Development Planning Guide* (Greensboro, NC: Center for Creative Leadership, 1992); G. Yukl and R. Lepsinger, "360-Degree Feedback," *Training*, December 1995, pp. 45–50.
44. L. Atwater, P. Roush, and A. Fischthal, "The Influence of Upward Feedback on Self- and Follower Ratings of Leadership," *Personnel Psychology* 48 (1995), pp. 35–59; J. F. Hazucha, S. A. Hezlett, and R. J. Schneider, "The Impact of 360-Degree Feedback on Management Skill Development," *Human Resource Management* 32 (1993), pp. 325–51; J. W. Smither, M. London, N. Vasilopoulos, R. R. Reilly, R. E. Millsap, and N. Salvemini, "An Examination of the Effects of an Upward Feedback Program over Time," *Personnel Psychology* 48 (1995), pp. 1–34; J. Smither and A. Walker, "Are the Characteristics of Narrative Comments Related to Improvements in Multirater Feedback Ratings over Time?" *Journal of Applied Psychology* 89 (2004), pp. 575–81; J. Smither, M. London, and R. Reilly, "Does Performance Improve Following Multisource Feedback? A Theoretical Model, Meta-analysis, and Review of Empirical Findings," *Personnel Psychology* 58 (2005), pp. 33–66.
45. D. Bracken, "Straight Talk about Multirater Feedback," *Training and Development*, September 1994, pp. 44–51; K. Nowack, J. Hartley, and W. Bradley, "How to Evaluate Your 360-Feedback Efforts," *Training and Development*, April 1999, pp. 48–52.
46. A. Freedman, "The Evolution of 360s," *Human Resource Executive*, December 2002, pp. 47–51.
47. M. W. McCall Jr., M. M. Lombardo, and A. M. Morrison, *Lessons of Experience* (Lexington, MA: Lexington Books, 1988).
48. R. S. Snell, "Congenial Ways of Learning: So Near yet So Far," *Journal of Management Development* 9 (1990), pp. 17–23.

49. R. Morrison, T. Erickson, and K. Dychtwald, "Managing Middlescence," *Harvard Business Review*, March 2006, pp. 78–86.
50. McCall, Lombardo, and Morrison, *Lessons of Experience;* M. W. McCall, "Developing Executives through Work Experiences," *Human Resource Planning* 11 (1988), pp. 1–11; M. N. Ruderman, P. J. Ohlott, and C. D. McCauley, "Assessing Opportunities for Leadership Development," in *Measures of Leadership*, pp. 547–62; C. D. McCauley, L. J. Estman, and P. J. Ohlott, "Linking Management Selection and Development through Stretch Assignments," *Human Resource Management* 34 (1995), pp. 93–115.
51. C. D. McCauley, M. N. Ruderman, P. J. Ohlott, and J. E. Morrow, "Assessing the Developmental Components of Managerial Jobs," *Journal of Applied Psychology* 79 (1994), pp. 544–60.
52. S. Thurm, "Power-Sharing Prepares Managers," *The Wall Street Journal*, December 5, 2005, p. B4.
53. T. Galvin, "Best Practice: Job Rotation, Arrow Electronics," *Training*, March 2003, p. 59.
54. "Training Top 100 Best Practices: Regions Financial," *Training*, March 2006, p. 61.
55. M. London, *Developing Managers* (San Francisco: Jossey-Bass, 1985); M. A. Campion, L. Cheraskin, and M. J. Stevens, "Career-Related Antecedents and Outcomes of Job Rotation," *Academy of Management Journal* 37 (1994), pp. 1518–42; M. London, *Managing the Training Enterprise* (San Francisco: Jossey-Bass, 1989).
56. M. Pacelle, "Job Swap Is Meant to Groom 'next generation,'" *The Wall Street Journal*, September 28, 2004, pp. C1, C4.
57. D. C. Feldman, *Managing Careers in Organizations* (Glenview, IL: Scott Foresman, 1988).
58. J. M. Brett, L. K. Stroh, and A. H. Reilly, "Job Transfer," in *International Review of Industrial and Organizational Psychology: 1992*, ed. C. L. Cooper and I. T. Robinson (Chichester, England: John Wiley and Sons, 1992); D. C. Feldman and J. M. Brett, "Coping with New Jobs: A Comparative Study of New Hires and Job Changers," *Academy of Management Journal* 26 (1983), pp. 258–72.
59. R. A. Noe, B. D. Steffy, and A. E. Barber, "An Investigation of the Factors Influencing Employees' Willingness to Accept Mobility Opportunities," *Personnel Psychology* 41 (1988), pp. 559–80; S. Gould and L. E. Penley, "A Study of the Correlates of Willingness to Relocate," *Academy of Management Journal* 28 (1984), pp. 472–78; J. Landau and T. H. Hammer, "Clerical Employees' Perceptions of Intraorganizational Career Opportunities," Academy of Management Journal 29 (1986), pp. 385–405; R. P. Duncan and C. C. Perruci, "Dual Occupation Families and Migration," *American Sociological Review* 41 (1976), pp. 252–61; J. M. Brett and A. H. Reilly, "On the Road Again: Predicting the Job Transfer Decision," *Journal of Applied Psychology* 73 (1988), pp. 614–620.
60. D. T. Hall and L. A. Isabella, "Downward Moves and Career Development," *Organizational Dynamics* 14 (1985), pp. 5–23.
61. H. D. Dewirst, "Career Patterns: Mobility, Specialization, and Related Career Issues," in *Contemporary Career Development Issues*, ed. R. F. Morrison and J. Adams (Hillsdale, NJ: Lawrence Erlbaum, 1991), pp. 73–108.
62. N. C. Tompkins, "GTE Managers on the Move," *Personnel Journal*, August 1992, pp. 86–91.
63. J. M. Brett, "Job Transfer and Well-Being," *Journal of Applied Psychology* 67 (1992), pp. 450–63; F. J. Minor, L. A. Slade, and R. A. Myers, "Career Transitions in Changing Times," in *Contemporary Career Development Issues*, pp. 109–20; C. C. Pinder and K. G. Schroeder, "Time to Proficiency Following Job Transfers," *Academy of Management Journal* 30 (1987), pp. 336–53; G. Flynn, "Heck No—We Won't Go!" *Personnel Journal*, March 1996, pp. 37–43.
64. R. E. Silverman, "Mercer Tries to Keep Employees Through Its 'Externship' Program," *The Wall Street Journal*, November 7, 2000, p. B18.
65. D. Gunsch, "Customer Service Focus Prompts Employee Exchange," *Personnel Journal*, October 1992, pp. 32–38.
66. C. J. Bachler, "Workers Take Leave of Job Stress," *Personnel Journal*, January 1995, pp. 38–48.
67. F. Jossi, "Taking Time Off from Advertising," *Workforce*, April 2002, p. 15.
68. K. Ellis, "Pass It On," *Training*, June 2005, pp. 14–19.
69. D. B. Turban and T. W. Dougherty, "Role of Protégé Personality in Receipt of Mentoring and Career Success," *Academy of Management Journal* 37 (1994), pp. 688–702; E. A. Fagenson, "Mentoring: Who Needs It? A Comparison of Protégés' and Nonprotégés' Needs for Power, Achievement, Affiliation, and Autonomy," *Journal of Vocational Behavior* 41 (1992), pp. 48–60.
70. A. H. Geiger, "Measures for Mentors," *Training and Development Journal*, February 1992, pp. 65–67.
71. K. E. Kram, *Mentoring at Work: Developmental Relationships in Organizational Life* (Glenview, IL: Scott Foresman, 1985); K. Kram, "Phases of the Mentoring Relationship," *Academy of Management Journal* 26 (1983), pp. 608–25; G. T. Chao, P. M. Walz, and P. D. Gardner, "Formal and Informal Mentorships: A Comparison of Mentoring Functions and Contrasts with Nonmentored Counterparts," *Personnel Psychology* 45 (1992), pp. 619–36; C. Wanberg, E. Welsh, and S. Hezlett, "Mentoring Research: A Review and Dynamic Process Model," in *Research in Personnel and Human Resources Management*, ed. J. Martocchio and G. Ferris (New York: Elsevier Science, 2003), pp. 39–124.
72. L. Eby, M. Butts, A. Lockwood, and A. Simon "Protégés' Negative Mentoring Experiences: Construct Development and Nomological Validation," *Personnel Psychology* 57 (2004), pp. 411–47; M. Boyle, "Most Mentoring Programs Stink—but Yours Doesn't Have To," *Training*, August 2005, pp. 12–15.
73. E. Tahmincioglu, "Looking for a Mentor? Technology Can Help Make the Right Match," *Workforce Management*, December 2004, pp. 63–65; D. Owens, "Virtual Mentoring," *HR Magazine*, March 2006, pp. 105–7.
74. Boyle, "Most Mentoring Programs Stink."
75. G. F. Dreher and R. A. Ash, "A Comparative Study of Mentoring among Men and Women in Managerial, Professional, and Technical Positions," *Journal of Applied Psychology* 75 (1990), pp. 539–46; T. D. Allen, L. T. Eby, M. L. Poteet, E. Lentz, and L. Lima, "Career Benefits Associated with Mentoring for Protégés: A Meta-Analysis," *Journal of Applied Psychology* 89 (2004), pp. 127–36; R. A. Noe, D. B. Greenberger, and S. Wang, "Mentoring: What We Know and Where We Might Go," in *Research in Personnel and Human Resources Management*, ed. G. Ferris and J. Martucchio (New York: Elsevier Science, 2002), pp. 129–74; R. A. Noe, "An Investigation of the Determinants of Successful Assigned Mentoring Relationships," *Personnel Psychology* 41 (1988), pp. 457–79; B. J. Tepper, "Upward Maintenance Tactics in Supervisory Mentoring and Nonmentoring Relationships," *Academy of Management Journal* 38 (1995), pp. 1191–205; B. R. Ragins and T. A. Scandura, "Gender Differences in Expected Outcomes of Mentoring Relationships," *Academy of Management Journal* 37 (1994), pp. 957–71.

76. M. Murray, "GE Mentoring Program Turns Underlings into Teachers of the Web," *The Wall Street Journal*, February 15, 2000, pp. B1, B16.
77. C. M. Solomon, "Hotel Breathes Life Into Hospital's Customer Service," *Personnel Journal*, October 1995, p. 120.
78. F. Jossi, "Mentoring in Changing Times," *Training*, August 1997, pp. 50–54.
79. B. Kaye and B. Jackson, "Mentoring: A Group Guide," *Training and Development*, April 1995, pp. 23–27.
80. D. B. Peterson and M. D. Hicks, *Leader as Coach* (Minneapolis, MN: Personnel Decisions, 1996).
81. J. Toto, "Untapped World of Peer Coaching," *TD*, April 2006, pp. 69–71.
82. H. Johnson, "The Ins and Outs of Executive Coaching," *Training*, May 2004, pp. 36–41.
83. J. Smither, M. London, R. Flautt, Y. Vargas, and L. Kucine, "Can Working with an Executive Coach Improve Multisource Ratings over Time? A Quasi-Experimental Field Study," *Personnel Psychology* 56 (2003), pp. 23–44.
84. Toto, "Untapped World of Peer Coaching."
85. R. Zemke, " The Corporate Coach," *Training*, December 1996, pp. 24–28.
86. M. Weinstein, "Flying High," *Training*, March 2006, pp. 36–38; www.lockheedmartin.com, Web site for Lockheed Martin Corporation.
87. Sallie-Dosunmu, "Born to Grow."
88. D. T. Jaffe and C. D. Scott, "Career Development for Empowerment in a Changing Work World," in *New Directions in Career Planning and the Workplace*, ed. J. M. Kummerow (Palo Alto, CA: Consulting Psychologists Press, 1991), pp. 33–60; L. Summers, "A Logical Approach to Development Planning," *Training and Development* 48 (1994), pp. 22–31; D. B. Peterson and M. D. Hicks, *Development First* (Minneapolis, MN: Personnel Decisions, 1995).
89. K. Ellis, "Individual Development Plans: The Building Blocks of Development," *Training*, December 2004, pp. 20–25.
90. R. Davenport, "John Deere Champions Workforce Development," *TD*, April 2006, pp. 40–43.
91. *Women in U.S. Corporate Leadership: 2003* (New York: Catalyst, 2003).
92. U.S. Dept. of Labor, *A Report on the Glass Ceiling Initiative* (Washington, DC: U.S. Dept. of Labor, 1991).
93. P. J. Ohlott, M. N. Ruderman, and C. D. McCauley, "Gender Differences in Managers' Developmental Job Experiences," *Academy of Management Journal* 37 (1994), pp. 46–67; D. Mattioli, "Programs to Promote Female Managers Win Citations," *The Wall Street Journal*, January 30, 2007, p. B7.
94. L. A. Mainiero, "Getting Anointed for Advancement: The Case of Executive Women," *Academy of Management Executive* 8 (1994), pp. 53–67; J. S. Lublin, "Women at Top Still Are Distant from CEO Jobs," *The Wall Street Journal*, February 28, 1995, pp. B1, B5; P. Tharenov, S. Latimer, and D. Conroy, "How Do You Make It to the Top? An Examination of Influences on Women's and Men's Managerial Advancement," *Academy of Management Journal* 37 (1994), pp. 899–931.
95. P. Tharenou, "Going Up? Do Traits and Informal Social Processes Predict Advancement in Management? *Academy of Management Journal* 44 (2001), pp. 1005–17.
96. U.S. Dept. of Labor, *A Report on the Glass Ceiling Initiative;* R. A. Noe, "Women and Mentoring: A Review and Research Agenda," *Academy of Management Review* 13 (1988), pp. 65–78; B. R. Ragins and J. L. Cotton, "Easier Said Than Done: Gender Differences in Perceived Barriers to Gaining a Mentor," *Academy of Management Journal* 34 (1991), pp. 939–51.
97. C. Daniels, "Women vs. Wal-Mart," *Fortune*, July 21, 2003, pp. 78–82.
98. D. McCracken, "Winning the Talent War for Women," *Harvard Business Review*, November–December 2000, pp. 159–67.
99. E. Tahmincioglu, "When Women Rise," *Workforce Management*, September 2004, pp. 26–32.
100. W. J. Rothwell, *Effective Succession Planning*, 2nd ed. (New York: AMACOM, 2001).
101. C. B. Derr, C. Jones, and E. L. Toomey, "Managing High- Potential Employees: Current Practices in Thirty-Three U.S. Corporations," *Human Resource Management* 27 (1988), pp. 273–90.
102. Ibid.; K. M. Nowack, "The Secrets of Succession," *Training and Development* 48 (1994), pp. 49–54; J. S. Lublin, "An Overseas Stint Can Be a Ticket to the Top," *The Wall Street Journal*, January 29, 1996, pp. B1, B2.
103. Nowack, "The Secrets of Succession"; Lublin, "An Overseas Stint Can Be a Ticket to the Top."
104. P. Kiger, "Succession Planning Keeps WellPoint Competitive," *Workforce*, April 2002, pp. 50–54; E. Fravenheim, "Succession Progression," *Workforce Management*, January 2006, pp. 31–34.
105. M. W. McCall, Jr., and M. M. Lombardo, "Off the Track: Why and How Successful Executives Get Derailed," *Technical Report* no. 21 (Greensboro, NC: Center for Creative Leadership, 1983); E. V. Veslor and J. B. Leslie, "Why Executives Derail: Perspectives across Time and Cultures," *Academy of Management Executive* 9 (1995), pp. 62–72.
106. J. Lublin, "Did I Just Say That?! How You Can Recover from Foot-in-Mouth," *The Wall Street Journal*, June 18, 2002, p. B1.
107. Johnson, "The Ins and Outs of Executive Coaching."

10

CHAPTER

# Employee Separation and Retention

LO

## LEARNING OBJECTIVES

After reading this chapter, you should be able to:

LO1 Distinguish between involuntary and voluntary turnover, and discuss how each of these forms of turnover can be leveraged for competitive advantage. *page 449*

LO2 List the major elements that contribute to perceptions of justice and how to apply these in organizational contexts involving discipline and dismissal. *page 453*

LO3 Specify the relationship between job satisfaction and various forms of job withdrawal, and identify the major sources of job satisfaction in work contexts. *page 461*

LO4 Design a survey feedback intervention program and use this to promote retention of key organizational personnel. *page 471*

# Enter the World of Business

## Is Employee Privacy Going Up in Smoke?

Scott Rodrigues had worked at Scott's Miracle-Gro Company for less than one year when he was fired for failing a drug test. Although there is nothing remarkable about being fired when a drug test reveals the use of some illegal substance like cocaine or marijuana, what made Rodrigues's case unique was the fact that the drug detected in his system was nicotine. Rodrigues was fired for smoking cigarettes. Scott's Miracle-Gro Company is at the forefront of firms that are taking extreme steps to curtail rising health care costs, and its "no-tobacco policy," which is being challenged by Rodrigues's attorneys in court, is one controversial part of its program. As Rodrigues notes, "Five years ago if you would have told me, 'Hey, you better quit smoking or you might not a get a job' I would have laughed. Here I am five years later and I can't get a job."

Moreover, this is just the tip of the iceberg in terms of the comprehensiveness of the issues that Miracle-Gro's health assessment program delves into. In addition to smoking (or chewing tobacco, which was also common in some plants), employees are asked whether they drink alcohol and how much; do they suffer from high cholesterol or high blood pressure; are they depressed of burned-out; how stressful are their relationships with their spouse or children; what were the causes of death for their parents; and so on. All of this seems highly intrusive and an invasion of privacy on the part of the employer; however, the company took this step only after it became convinced that its workforce was in such bad physical shape that the costs it was incurring for health care expenses were destroying its ability to compete effectively. Indeed, Miracle-Gro's health care expenditures had essentially doubled from roughly $10 million in 1999 to $20 million in 2003 and were projected to go up another 20 percent the next year.

Although perhaps on the edge of how far companies are willing to go to reduce these costs, Miracle-Gro is certainly not alone in terms of its concerns about such costs. For example, cell phone service provider Sprint realized in 2004 that its annual increase for health care expenditures was going up $50 million a year, and that an increase in sales revenue of 12 percent each year would be needed to simply cover that cost—an increase that was twice the industry average. Delta Airlines performed a similar analysis and discovered that it was paying over $5,000 annually per employee for health care, and that this was going up close to 10 percent a year. More pointedly, Delta's analysis revealed that much of this cost was attributable to a small percentage of its workers. For example, as Lynn Zonakis, director of health strategy and resources, noted, "We saw that 1/10 of 1 percent of our participants were responsible for 10 percent of our health care costs, and that 1 percent was responsible for 33 percent of our cost."

Most employers that run the numbers come to a similar conclusion: a small percentage of workers drive a big percentage of costs, and predicting which workers are in this group is not difficult. Indeed, the very factors that Miracle-Gro screens for reflect this list of valid predictors. Thus, although this may seem invasive from the employees' perspective because a lot of the troublesome behavior occurs outside of work, much of this becomes job-related when the costs are borne by the employer. Some have argued that this is a sufficient reason for the United States to come up with some national plan for health care coverage, but it is not clear that this politically controversial idea will ever gain much ground in this country.

In the meantime, individual employers have to make their own decisions regarding how to balance privacy concerns with cost concerns, and how much pressure to place on employees whose lifestyles put them at risk. Although financial costs are often the driving force behind these programs, one should not lose sight of the fact that the quality of life enjoyed by employees both on and off the job is also affected. For example, while Scott Rodrigues was suing Miracle-Gro over its program, another employee, Joe Pellegrini, was celebrating the fact that the very same program saved his life. Although physically fit, Pellegrini's health assessment indicated a high level of cholesterol, and the company forced him to see a physician. That trip to the doctor revealed a 95 percent blockage in a heart valve that would probably have killed him within five days. Obviously, Pellegrini has a different perception of Miracle-Gro's policies than Rodrigues, noting that when it came to his own life, "It was that close."

Sources: M. Colin, "Get Healthy—Or Else," *BusinessWeek*, February 26, 2007, pp. 58–69; J. Marquez, "Being Healthy May Be Its Own Reward, but a Little Cash Can Also Help Keep Workers Fit," *Workforce Management*, September 2005, pp. 66–69; V. Leo, "Wellness—Or Orwellness?" *BusinessWeek*, March 19, 2007, p. 82.

## Introduction

Every executive recognizes the need for satisfied, loyal customers. If the firm is publicly held, it is also safe to assume that every executive appreciates the need to have satisfied, loyal investors. Customers and investors provide the financial resources that allow the organization to survive. Not every executive understands the need to generate satisfaction and loyalty among employees, however. Yet, retention rates among employees are related to retention rates among customers.[1] In fact, research has established a direct link between employee retention rates and sales growth[2] and companies that are cited as one of the "100 Best Companies to Work For" routinely outperform their competition on many other financial indicators of performance.[3] For example Figure 10.1 shows the average annual returns for the "100 Best Companies to Work For" over various time periods ending in 2005. The figure reveals that sustained (10 years) competitive advantage in capital markets is directly attributable to successfully managing the workforce.[4] Job satisfaction and retention are also related to organizational performance. Firms that fail to secure a loyal base of workers constantly place an inexperienced group of noncohesive units on the front lines of their organization, much to their own detriment.[5] This is especially the case in service industries, where disgruntled workers often create

**figure 10.1**
Stock Performance: Average Annual Return Best Companies to Work For vs. S&P 500

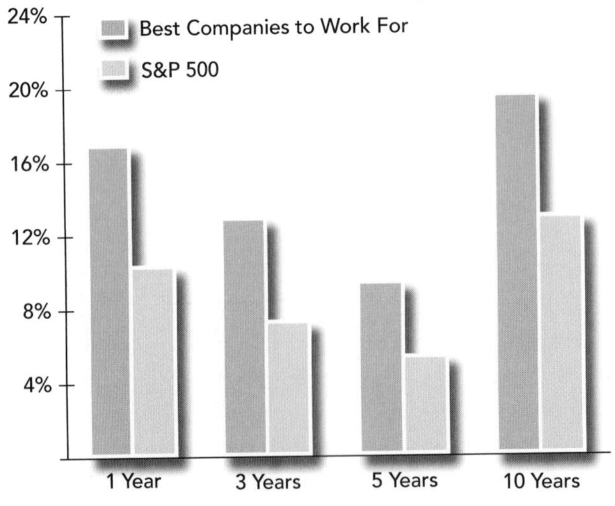


SOURCE: M. Boyle, "Happy People, Happy Returns," *BusinessWeek*, January 22, 2007, p. 100.

large numbers of dissatisfied customers.[6] Lack of experience and cohesiveness within work units destroys efficiency, and the costs associated with constantly replacing workers erodes a firm's competitive position.[7]

In addition to holding onto key personnel, another hallmark of successful firms is their ability and willingness to dismiss employees who are engaging in counterproductive behavior. Indeed, it is somewhat ironic that one of the keys to retaining productive employees is ensuring that these people are not being made miserable by supervisors or co-workers who are engaging in unproductive, disruptive, or dangerous behavior. As our opening vignette shows, the definition of what constitutes "counterproductive behavior" has expanded over the years. For employers who are responsible for covering the costs for workers' health and well-being, this may even include behaviors such as smoking, occurring outside the workplace. Whether this is perceived as paternalistic "tough love," where the employer is safeguarding workers' health and safety, or whether this is perceived as a Big Brother intervention that robs people of their rights will differ for different members of the labor pool. How will history judge companies like Miracle-Gro? If they continue to attract and retain productive employees while at the same time reducing their costs associated with health care expenditures, this will be seen as a visionary act. However, if talented people leave in droves to take jobs with competitors that promise to stay out of their personal lives, then this will be seen as a major strategic blunder.

Thus, to compete effectively, organizations must take steps to ensure that good performers are motivated to stay with the organization, whereas chronically low performers are allowed, encouraged, or, if necessary, forced to leave. Retaining top performers is not always easy, however. Competing organizations are constantly looking to steal top performers, and "poaching talent" has become an art form in the current tight labor market.[8] It is also not nearly as easy to fire employees as many people think. The increased willingness of people to sue their employer, combined with an unprecedented level of violence in the workplace, has made discharging employees who lack talent legally complicated and personally dangerous.[9]

The purpose of this chapter (the last in Part 3 of this book) is to focus on employee separation and retention. The material presented in Part 3's previous two chapters ("Performance Management" and "Employee Development") can be used to help establish who are the current effective performers as well as who is likely to respond well to future developmental opportunities. This chapter completes Part 3 by discussing what can be done to retain high-performing employees who warrant further development as well as managing the separation process for low-performing employees who have not responded well to developmental opportunities.

Since much of what needs to be done to retain employees involves compensation and benefits, this chapter also serves as a bridge to Part 4, which addresses these issues in more detail. The chapter is divided into two sections. The first examines **involuntary turnover,** that is, turnover initiated by the organization (often among people who would prefer to stay). The second deals with **voluntary turnover,** that is, turnover initiated by employees (often whom the company would prefer to keep). Although both types of turnover reflect employee separation, they are clearly different phenomena that need to be examined separately.[10]

**Involuntary Turnover**
Turnover initiated by the organization (often among people who would prefer to stay).

**Voluntary Turnover**
Turnover initiated by employees (often whom the company would prefer to keep).

## Managing Involuntary Turnover

**LO1**
Distinguish between Involuntary and Voluntary Turnover, and Discuss How Each of These Forms of Turnover Can Be Leveraged for Competitive Advantage.

Despite a company's best efforts in the area of personnel selection, training, and design of compensation systems, some employees will occasionally fail to meet performance requirements or will violate company policies while on the job. When this happens, organizations need to invoke a discipline program that could ultimately lead to the individual's discharge. For a number of reasons, discharging employees can be a very difficult task that needs to be handled with the utmost care and attention to detail.

First, legal aspects to this decision can have important repercussions for the organization. Historically, in the absence of a specified contract, either the employer or the employee could sever the employment relationship at any time. The severing of this relationship could be for "good cause," "no cause," or even "bad cause." Over time, this policy has been referred to as the **employment-at-will doctrine.** This employment-at-will doctrine has eroded significantly over time, however. Today employees who are fired sometimes sue their employers for wrongful discharge. Some judges have been willing to consider employees who meet certain criteria regarding longevity, promotions, raises, and favorable past performance reviews as having an implied contract to dismissal only for good cause—even in the face of direct language in the company handbook that states an employment-at-will relationship.[11]

**Employment-at-Will Doctrine**
The doctrine that, in the absence of a specific contract, either an employer or employee could sever the employment relationship at any time.

A wrongful discharge suit typically attempts to establish that the discharge either (1) violated an implied contract or covenant (that is, the employer acted unfairly) or (2) violated public policy (that is, the employee was terminated because he or she refused to do something illegal, unethical, or unsafe). Wrongful discharge suits can also be filed as a civil rights infringement if the person discharged is a member of a protected group. Indeed, as the "Competing through Sustainability" box shows, the number of people who can be considered "protected" has expanded over time, and this has made some organizations very skittish about firing anyone. Figure 10.2 shows

**figure 10.2**
Probable Outcomes of Wrongful Discharge Suits

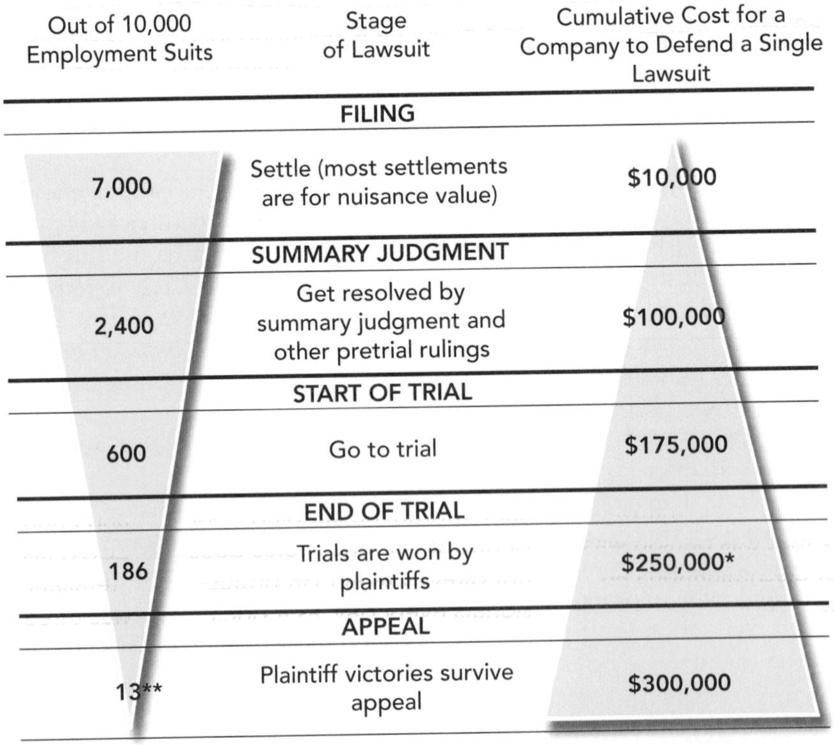

Out of 10,000 Employment Suits
Stage of Lawsuit
Cumulative Cost for a Company to Defend a Single Lawsuit
FILING
7,000
Settle (most settlements are for nuisance value)
$10,000
SUMMARY JUDGMENT
2,400
Get resolved by summary judgment and other pretrial rulings
$100,000
START OF TRIAL
600
Go to trial
$175,000
END OF TRIAL
186
Trials are won by plaintiffs
$250,000*
APPEAL
13**
Plaintiff victories survive appeal
$300,000


*Assumes a five-day trial

**Out of 22 trial losses typically appealed by companies

SOURCES: M. Orey, "Fear of Firing," *BusinessWeek*, April 23, 2007, p. 60. Cornell Law School; *Hofstra Labor & Employment Law Journal;* BW reporting.

## COMPETING THROUGH SUSTAINABILITY

### Laws with Unintended Consequences: Is It Legal to Fire Anyone?

Starting with the Civil Rights Act of 1964, the United States has seen a number of laws at the federal, state, and municipal level aimed at reducing the incidence of unfair treatment afforded to a number of different groups. These were well-intended efforts that, taken one at a time, are easy to defend, and have done a great deal to level the playing field for many individuals. However, the overall result of this legislation, when taken as a whole, is that it creates an environment where almost everyone in the workforce today is "protected" by one form of legislation or another. Thus, laws exist to protect racial minorities, women, older workers (over 40 years of age), homosexuals, disabled workers (including the obese), whistle-blowers, people who have filed workers' compensation claims, and—if one counts reverse discrimination claims—Caucasians. Indeed, as noted by Lisa Cassilly, a defense attorney for the firm Alston and Bird, "It's difficult to find someone who doesn't have some capacity to claim protected status." This means that in almost any instance when someone is fired for poor performance, the alternative possibility that this person was a victim of discrimination can be raised.

Not surprisingly, this has led to an increase in litigation: roughly 8,000 wrongful termination lawsuits were filed in 1991, but by 2006 the number of lawsuits filed annually was close to 15,000. Moreover, because the Civil Rights Act of 1991 allowed for jury trials and "punitive" damages, in some well-known cases the size of the awards are attention getting. For example, in a recent case at General Electric, an employee was awarded more than $11 million in a wrongful discharge suit. The vividness of these highly publicized cases often distorts the perceptions of how infrequently plaintiffs actually win such cases, and this led to a number of practices where the employer's short-term emphasis on staying out of court came into conflict with the long-term need to develop a competitive workforce.

For example, one reaction to this dilemma is enduring long stretches of poor performance in order to create the extensive "paper trail" that would support a negative action. While HR professionals often point the finger of blame at supervisors who have not done a diligent job documenting past performance problems, supervisors often turn around and accuse HR of being "nervous Nellies" who never seem satisfied with the amount of evidence provided by supervisors. Moreover, keeping poor performers in their roles does not directly affect HR professionals every day, as it does supervisors, who have to watch helplessly as the morale of the rest of the workforce erodes. Indeed, nothing is more corrosive to team-based structures than wide variability in effort and performance between different members, and hence it is somewhat ironic that the key to prompting and sustaining a collaborative and productive culture is maintaining the firm's right to at-will employment. As one member of a research team in a pharmaceutical firm noted with respect to the idea of "carrying" a poor performer for fear of litigation, "As a female and also of a minority race, I am appalled and saddened by this scenario as I must bear the weight of this constant underperformer."

Another questionable reaction is to initiate punitive actions short of termination, in an effort to get the employee to quit independently. This reaction is often a result of frustrated supervisors, who, unable to fire someone because of HR, resort to punishing the employee in other ways. This might include giving the person a low-level work assignment, a downsized office, or some other form of undesirable treatment. The problem with this approach, however, is that it might be construed as retaliation, and the employer could be sued for this, even if the original discrimination suit is dismissed. In 2005 and 2006, some 30 percent of EEOC filings were this type of "retaliation lawsuits," which was three times the percentage just 10 years ago. In fact, some attorneys advise any clients who are expecting a poor performance appraisal or some other adverse job event to file a discrimination suit as part of a preemptive attack that sets up the groundwork for a subsequent retaliation lawsuit.

Finally, a third unsustainable reaction is to pay off the employee with thousands of dollars in excess severance pay in return for waiving the right to sue for wrongful dismissal. That is, even if the employer feels the case is unwarranted, in order to avoid litigation itself, the employer may offer the terminated employee $20,000 or more to waive his or her right to sue. The problem with this strategy is that it sets the expectation that all poor performers are entitled to compensation on their way out the door, and this eventually increases the amount of potential future litigation by rewarding frivolous charges. As we have seen in this chapter, this strategy grossly overestimates the plaintiff's probability of winning such a case. A more effective and sustainable strategy for employers would be to develop a reputation for defending the firm's right to terminate low performers, rather than invite bullying by an overly aggressive attorney or employee. As defense attorney Mark Dichter notes, "I can design HR policies that can virtually eliminate your risk of facing employment claims, but you'll have a pretty lousy workforce. At the end of the day, you have to run your business."

SOURCES: M. Orey, "Fear of Firing," *BusinessWeek*, April 23, 2007, pp. 52–62; M. Conlin, "Litigation Innoculation," *BusinessWeek*, May 28, 2007, p. 35; G. Casellas, "Fired Up over Firing," *BusinessWeek*, May 14, 2007, p. 76; C. Holahan, "Virtually Addicted," *BusinessWeek*, December 14, 2006, p. 41.

the base rate probabilities for various outcomes in such cases. As you can see, a plaintiff rarely achieves a victory in this kind of case should it survive appeal (odds are roughly one-tenth of 1 percent). However, the high legal cost associated with winning the case is often enough to make some employers reluctant to fire workers.

The costs associated with letting poor performers stay on within the organization cannot be discounted. Organizations that introduce "rank and yank" systems where low performers are systematically identified and, where necessary, eliminated from payrolls often experience quick improvement gains in the range of 40 percent.[12] Over time, research shows that the gains achieved by such programs get smaller and smaller, but the initial jump illustrates how many organizations drift into a situation where tolerating low performance has become an unsustainable business practice.[13] This fact is even being realized in many European countries where worker protections embody a critical cultural value. Recent legislation passed in both France and Germany have simplified the procedures that firms have to go through to eliminate poor performers and lowered the bar for the evidence that has to be provided in such cases.[14] Paradoxically, one of the countries they are trying to compete against, China, is actually moving in the opposite direction, trying to make it more difficult for employers to fire workers, in an effort to become more "worker-friendly."[15]

In addition to the financial risks associated with having to legally defend a dismissal, there are issues related to personal safety. Although the fact that some former employees use the court system to get back at their former employers may be distressing, even more problematic are employees who respond to a termination decision with violence directed at the employer. Violence in the workplace has become a major organizational problem and workplace homicide is the fastest-growing form of murder in the United States.[16] Although any number of organizational actions or decisions may incite violence among employees, the "nothing else to lose" aspect of employee dismissal cases makes for a dangerous situation, especially in the presence of other risk factors associated with the nature of the work.[17]

Given the critical financial and personal risks associated with employee dismissal, it is easy to see why the development of a standardized, systematic approach to discipline and discharge is critical to all organizations. These decisions should not be left solely to the discretion of individual managers or supervisors. In the next section we explore aspects of an effective discipline and discharge policy.

## Principles of Justice

**LO2**
List the Major Elements That Contribute to Perceptions of Justice and How to Apply These in Organizational Contexts Involving Discipline and Dismissal.

In Chapter 8 ("Performance Management") we touched on the notion of justice, particularly as this relates to the notions of outcome justice, procedural justice, and interactional justice. There we noted that employees are more likely to respond positively to negative feedback regarding their performance if they perceive the appraisal process as being fair on these three dimensions. Obviously, if fairness is important with respect to ongoing feedback, this is even more critical in the context of a final termination decision. Therefore, we will explore the three types of fairness perceptions in greater detail here, with an emphasis on how these need to be operationalized in effective discipline and discharge policies that support the type of "psychological contracts" that tend to govern employer–employee relationships.[18]

As we noted earlier in Chapter 8, **outcome fairness** refers to the judgment that people make with respect to the *outcomes received* relative to the outcomes received by other people with whom they identify (referent others). Clearly, a situation where one person is losing his or her job while others are not is conducive to perceptions of outcome unfairness on the part of the discharged employee. The degree to which this potentially unfair act translates into the type of anger and resentment that might spawn retaliation in the form of violence or litigation, however, depends on perceptions of procedural and interactional justice.[19]

**Outcome Fairness**
The judgment that people make with respect to the outcomes received relative to the outcomes received by other people with whom they identify.

Whereas outcome justice focuses on the ends, procedural and interactional justice focus on means. If methods and procedures used to arrive at and implement decisions that impact the employee negatively are seen as fair, the reaction is likely to be much more positive than if this is not the case. **Procedural justice** focuses specifically on the *methods used to determine the outcomes received*. Table 10.1 details six key principles that determine whether people perceive procedures as being fair. Even given all the negative ramifications of being dismissed from one's job, the person being dismissed may accept the decision with minimum anger if the procedures used to arrive at the decision are consistent, unbiased, accurate, correctable, representative, and ethical.

**Procedural Justice**
A concept of justice focusing on the methods used to determine the outcomes received.

**table 10.1**
Six Determinants of Procedural Justice

| | |
|---|---|
| (1) | **Consistency.** The procedures are applied consistently across time and other persons. |
| (2) | **Bias suppression.** The procedures are applied by a person who has no vested interest in the outcome and no prior prejudices regarding the individual. |
| (3) | **Information accuracy.** The procedure is based on information that is perceived to be true. |
| (4) | **Correctabilty.** The procedure has built-in safeguards that allow one to appeal mistakes or bad decisions. |
| (5) | **Representativeness.** The procedure is informed by the concerns of all groups or stakeholders (co-workers, customers, owners) affected by the decision, including the individual being dismissed. |
| (6) | **Ethicality.** The procedure is consistent with prevailing moral standards as they pertain to issues like invasion of privacy or deception. |

**table 10.2**

Four Determinants of Interactional Justice

| | |
|---|---|
| (1) | **Explanation.** Emphasize aspects of procedural fairness that justify the decision. |
| (2) | **Social sensitivity.** Treat the person with dignity and respect. |
| (3) | **Consideration.** Listen to the person's concerns. |
| (4) | **Empathy.** Identify with the person's feelings. |

**Interactional Justice**
A concept of justice referring to the interpersonal nature of how the outcomes were implemented.

Whereas procedural justice deals with how a decision was made, **interactional justice** refers to the *interpersonal nature of how the outcomes were implemented*. Table 10.2 lists the four key determinants of interactional justice. When the decision is explained well and implemented in a fashion that is socially sensitive, considerate, and empathetic, this helps defuse some of the resentment that might come about from a decision to discharge an employee. As one human research director noted, the key is to ensure that the affected individual "walks out with their dignity and self-respect intact."[20] Going through these steps is especially important if the individual who is being managed is already high in hostility, and hence a threat to respond in violent fashion.[21] Indeed, beyond the context of employee termination, the use of systems that promote procedural and interactive justice across the organization results in both more satisfied employees[22] and a more productive workforce.[23]

## Progressive Discipline and Alternative Dispute Resolution

Except in the most extreme cases, employees should generally not be terminated for a first offense. Rather, termination should come about at the end of a systematic discipline program. Effective discipline programs have two central components: documentation (which includes specific publication of work rules and job descriptions that should be in place prior to administering discipline) and progressive punitive measures. Thus, as shown in Table 10.3, punitive measures should be taken in steps of increasing magnitude, and only after having been clearly documented. This may start with an unofficial warning for the first offense, followed by a written reprimand for additional offenses. At some point, later offenses may lead to a temporary suspension. Before a company suspends an employee, it may even want to issue a "last chance notification," indicating that the next offense will result in termination. Such procedures may seem exasperatingly slow, and they may fail to meet one's emotional need for quick and satisfying retribution. In the end, however, when problem employees are discharged, the chance that they can prove they were discharged for poor cause has been minimized.

**table 10.3**

An Example of a Progressive Discipline Program

| OFFENSE FREQUENCY | ORGANIZATIONAL RESPONSE | DOCUMENTATION |
|---|---|---|
| First offense | Unofficial verbal warning | Witness present |
| Second offense | Official written warning | Document filed |
| Third offense | Second official warning, with threat of temporary suspension | Document filed |
| Fourth offense | Temporary suspension and "last chance notification" | Document filed |
| Fifth offense | Termination (with right to go to arbitration) | Document filed |

**table 10.4**
Stages in Alternative Dispute Resolution

ADR

| |
|---|
| **Stage 1: Open-door policy**<br>The two people in conflict (e.g., supervisor and subordinate) attempt to arrive at a settlement together. If none can be reached, they proceed to |
| **Stage 2: Peer review**<br>A panel composed of representatives from the organization that are at the same level of those people in the dispute hears the case and attempts to help the parties arrive at a settlement. If none can be reached, they proceed to |
| **Stage 3: Mediation**<br>A neutral third party from outside the organization hears the case and, via a nonbinding process, tries to help the disputants arrive at a settlement. If none can be reached, the parties proceed to |
| **Stage 4: Arbitration**<br>A professional arbitrator from outside the organization hears the case and resolves it unilaterally by rendering a specific decision or award. Most arbitrators are experienced employment attorneys or retired judges. |

At various points in the discipline process, the individual or the organization might want to bring in outside parties to help resolve discrepancies or conflicts. As a last resort, the individual might invoke the legal system to resolve these types of conflicts, but in order to avoid this, more and more companies are turning to **alternative dispute resolution (ADR)** techniques that show promise in resolving disputes in a timely, constructive, cost-effective manner. Alternative dispute resolution can take on many different forms, but in general, ADR proceeds through the four stages shown in Table 10.4. Each stage reflects a somewhat broader involvement of different people, and the hope is that the conflict will be resolved at earlier steps. However, the last step may include binding arbitration, where an agreed upon neutral party resolves the conflict unilaterally if necessary.

**Alternative Dispute Resolution (ADR)**
A method of resolving disputes that does not rely on the legal system. Often proceeds through the four stages of open door policy, peer review, mediation, and arbitration.

Whereas ADR is effective in dealing with problems related to performance and interpersonal differences in the workplace, many of the problems that lead an organization to want to terminate an individual's employment relate to drug or alcohol abuse. In these cases, the organization's discipline and dismissal program should also incorporate an employee assistance program. Due to the increased prevalence of EAPs in organizations, we describe them in detail here.

## Employee Assistance and Wellness Programs

An **EAP** is a referral service that supervisors or employees can use to seek professional treatment for various problems. EAPs began in the 1950s with a focus on treating alcoholism, but in the 1980s they expanded into drug treatment as well. EAPs continue to evolve, and many are now fully integrated into companies' overall health benefits plans, serving as gatekeepers for health care utilization—especially for mental health.[24] EAPs vary widely, but most share some basic elements. First, the programs are usually identified in official documents published by the employer (such as employee handbooks). Supervisors (and union representatives, where relevant) are trained to use the referral service for employees whom they suspect of having health-related problems. Employees are also trained to use the system to make self-referrals when necessary. Finally, costs and benefits of the

**Employee Assistance Programs (EAPs)**
Employer programs that attempt to ameliorate problems encountered by workers who are drug dependent, alcoholic, or psychologically troubled.

programs (as measured in positive employee outcomes such as return-to-work rates) are evaluated, typically annually.

Given EAPs' wide range of options and evolving nature, we need to constantly analyze their effectiveness. For example, there is a current debate about the short-term versus long-term costs with respect to the area of treating depression. In the past, hospitalization plus psychiatric care was the main way to treat employees who were clinically depressed. However, the advent of managed care and the widespread effectiveness of Prozac and other pharmaceutical interventions for depression have made it possible for regular physicians to treat depression with medication.[25] By eliminating hospitalization and psychiatric care, employers can save a great deal of money in treating this problem, but some have questioned its long-term effectiveness relative to more traditional treatments.[26]

Indeed, when it comes to depression, as the "Competing through Globalization" box shows, cultural and generational differences often determine the degree to which employees seek the treatment they need. Hence, the role of the employer in assuring workplace well-being and health is especially pronounced in these contexts, and in some cases, governmental involvement is required to comprehensively deal with issues that become matters of public health.

Whereas EAPs deal with employees who have developed problems at work because of health-related issues, employee wellness programs take a proactive and preemptive focus on trying to prevent health-related problems in the first place. As we saw in the vignette that opened this chapter, some companies, like Miracle Gro, have taken this to an extreme, and are willing to fire workers who fail to develop healthier lifestyles. Unlike Miracle Gro's rather punitive approach, most employers try to use positive incentives to lure at-risk workers into healthier lifestyles, and they fund these incentives with cost savings that the programs produce.

## EVIDENCE-BASED HR

For example, Microsoft's weight management employee benefit offers employees $6,000 to use toward a comprehensive, clinically managed program that includes a counselor, personal trainer, medical supervision, and a support group. The $6,000 benefit was chosen because internal analyses produced evidence to suggest this would be exactly what the company would save in expenditures with the employees who were most at risk. The companywide result of this program from 2002 to 2006 was that the organization's 2,000 employees lost more than 60,000 pounds. As Cecily Hall, Microsoft's HR director of benefits, notes, "These people are coming off prescription drugs, they're seeing their primary physician less, and not having as much hospitalization." Moreover, the positive, incentive-laden, and voluntary approach taken by Microsoft is perceived as much less intrusive and controversial relative to programs like Miracle Gro's.

SOURCE: M. Conlin, "More Micro, Less Soft," *BusinessWeek*, November 27, 2006, p 42.

## Outplacement Counseling

The terminal nature of an employee discharge not only leaves the person angry, it also leads to confusion as to how to react and in a quandary regarding what happens next. If the person feels there is nothing to lose and nowhere else to turn, the potential for violence or litigation is higher than most organizations are willing to tolerate. Therefore,

## COMPETING THROUGH GLOBALIZATION

### Reclaiming the Lost Generation

After World War II, Japan's "baby-boom" generation experienced a period of rapid economic growth and expansion, and eventually Japan rose to become the second largest industrialized economy in the world. During this period, a great deal was expected of Japanese workers in terms of the number of hours they worked and their loyalty to their companies, but this was in turn rewarded with guarantees of good wages and lifetime job security. All of this changed in the 1990s, however, as Japan's economy went stagnant, and the country witnessed scores of bankruptcies and layoffs of workers. During this period, the country went through what is now referred to as its "Hiring Ice Age," where it was all but impossible for young workers to secure full-time positions.

By 2007, however, all evidence pointed to the fact that Japan had rebounded from this economic downturn and was once again on the road to economic prosperity. Productivity at manufacturing plants was up, profits at the corporate level were soaring, real estate was moving, and the economy was growing at a clip that was close to 3 percent annually. This even was evidenced in hiring, and many new college graduates were receiving multiple full-time offers. However, between the good fortune of this new generation of college graduates and the postwar baby-boom generation lies an entire generation of workers in their upper 20s and 30s who never experienced full-time employment. This group is often referred to as the "Lost Generation," and all evidence suggests that they may not benefit much from this most recent expansion.

In the current expansion, many Japanese companies are jumping past this cohort of workers to newly minted college graduates when it comes to full-time hiring. Members of the lost generation, in contrast, seem to be stuck in their roles as part-time contract laborers. As Toshihiro Nagahama, senior economist at a Tokyo research institute, notes, "No matter how much companies want to hire from among this pool, many in their early 30s just don't have the needed skills." The work histories of these individuals, who spent their early careers desperately hopping from one part-time assignment to another, are not consistent with what many employers value. The general concern is that they have not developed the depth of skills that comes from stable employment, and that they may not display the type of loyalty expected within Japanese firms.

It should come as no surprise that this has had a devastating psychological impact on this cohort of workers, and in 2006, Japan set the record for the number of work-related suicides. In fact, the suicide rate jumped by over 50 percent in a single year between 2005 and 2006, precisely at the moment when the economy was recovering and it was becoming clear that the Lost Generation was not going to take part in the turnaround. Most of these suicides marked the end of long bouts of depression for many workers, and compensation claims for depression have also reached all-time highs in Japan. Workers in their 30s accounted for roughly two-thirds of work-related mental disabilities in 2006, and as one counselor noted, "Before, people tried to hide that they were suffering from depression, but now it has become more widely known that people suffer and commit suicide from work-related depression, leading to more applications for workers compensation." Even among those not disabled by stress, their work experiences have had a major impact on their life choices, and this is reflected by statistics that show that members of this generation have the lowest rates of marriage and childbearing when compared to any previous generation in Japan.

The national implication of these statistics has not been lost on government officials, who are now making attempts to deal with these issues. The government is now offering $2,500 to any company willing to move a temporary or contract employee into full-time status. The government has also put direct pressure on some of the larger employers, and Toyota has responded with a promise to convert 1,200 contract workers to full-time status by the end of the year. The government has also doubled the number of outreach and training centers devoted to placing these workers, fully staffed with counselors and psychologists. As Yosaku Sato, director of one such federally funded training and placement center, notes, "The government is finally realizing that it has a crisis on its hands."

SOURCES: B. Aston, "Work-Related Suicide Claims Up 52 Percent in Japan," *FoxNews.com*, May 17, 2007; I. Rowley and K, Hall, "Japan's Lost Generation," *BusinessWeek*, May 28, 2007, pp. 40–41; T. Otake, "Preventing Suicide and Axing Overtime Pay Is a Risky Mix," *The Japan Times*, July 18, 2006.

**Outplacement Counseling**
Counseling to help displaced employees manage the transition from one job to another.

many organizations provide **outplacement counseling,** which tries to help dismissed employees manage the transition from one job to another.

Outplacement counseling is aimed at helping people realize that losing a job is not the end of the world and that other opportunities exist. Indeed, for many people, losing a job can be a critical learning experience that plants the seed for future success. For example, when John Morgridge was fired from his job as branch manager at Honeywell 20 years ago, it made him realize that his own assertiveness and need for independence were never going to cut it in a large, bureaucratic institution like Honeywell. Morgridge took his skills and went on to build computer network maker Cisco Systems, which is now worth over $1 billion.[27] This is a success story for Morgridge, but the fact that a major corporation like Honeywell let his talent go certainly reflects a lost opportunity for the company. Retaining people who can make such contributions is a key to gaining and maintaining competitive advantage. The second half of this chapter is devoted to issues related to retention.

## Managing Voluntary Turnover

In the first section of this chapter, our focus was on how to help employees who were not contributing to the organization's goal in a manner that protected the firm's ability to compete, and on how to support former employees' transition into alternative employment. In this second section, we focus on the other side of the separation equation—preventing employees who are highly valued by the organization from leaving (and perhaps even joining the competition). At the organizational level, turnover results in lowered work unit performance, which, in turn, harms the firm's financial performance.[28] This causal chain is especially strong when the organization is losing its top performers. Research suggests that some of the organization's top performers are up to 300 percent more productive than average employees, and retaining these workers is especially difficult.[29] Moreover, in organizations that rely on teams or long-term customer contacts, the loss of workers who are central to employee teams or customer networks can be especially disruptive.[30]

In 2007, Yahoo witnessed a mass exodus of engineers and vice presidents who left to either join small startups or even worse—Google, one of Yahoo's top competitors. The stream of attrition started with lower level workers, but as one former vice president notes, "Now it's the people who have institutional knowledge who are leaving."[31] Google was the top destination spot for most of this talent because the firm was widely recognized as being a great place to work; in fact, it was rated number 1 on *Fortune* magazine's 2007 list of "100 Best Places to Work." Google is renowned for its outrageous employee benefits, which include 11 free gourmet cafeterias, five fully staffed on-site doctors' offices, on-site car washes and oil changes, free on-site washers and dryers, unlimited sick days, all-expense-paid ski trips, free shuttles with WiFi for commuters, lap pool, climbing wall, and volleyball courts.

Google's employees respond to all of this by working incredibly long hours and by putting all headhunter calls into their autoreject bin. Most employees are committed to the organization's general well-being not for annual raises but because they are heavily vested in stock options that will make them all millionaires if the company can maintain its current trajectory. Teamwork is demanded and salaries, while not high for the industry, tend to be uniform in order to promote collaboration and teamwork while discouraging "lone wolves." Individuals are given autonomy to run their own experimental projects (up to 20 percent of their time can be devoted to these), but collective decisions on most large-scale group projects are arrived at via open and spirited public debates that tend to unfold very quickly. In contrast, many workers who are leaving Yahoo complain that most large Yahoo projects have to be signed off by multiple division heads, which both slows the process and minimizes the sense of employee ownership. As noted by one former Yahoo employee, who now works for Google, "Hard core geeks are here because there's no place they'd rather be," which is pretty convincing evidence with respect to who is winning and losing the war for talent in this industry.[32]

In this section of the chapter, we examine the job withdrawal process that characterizes voluntary employee turnover, and we illustrate the central role that job satisfaction plays in this process. One recent study showed that firms in the top quartile in terms of employee job satisfaction had profit rates that were 4 percent higher than firms in the bottom quartile. There is also a demonstrable relationship between employee satisfaction and customer satisfaction at the individual level,[33] and turnover rates and customer satisfaction at the organizational level.[34] Indeed, the whole employee satisfaction–firm performance relationship can become part of a virtuous cycle, where firms with more highly satisfied employees perform better and increase their profits, which in turn they use to shore up employee pay and benefits—further adding to their competitive advantage.[35] We will discuss what aspects of job satisfaction seem most critical to retention and how to measure these facets and we show how survey–feedback interventions, designed around these measures, can be used to strategically manage the voluntary turnover process.

## Process of Job Withdrawal

Job withdrawal is a set of behaviors that dissatisfied individuals enact to avoid the work situation. The right side of Figure 10.3 shows a model grouping the overall set of behaviors into three categories: behavior change, physical job withdrawal, and psychological job withdrawal.

We present the various forms of withdrawal in a progression, as if individuals try the next category only if the preceding is either unsuccessful or impossible to implement. This theory of **progression of withdrawal** has a long history and many adherents.[36] Others have suggested that there is no tight progression in that any one of the categories can compensate for another, and people choose the category that is most likely to redress the specific source of dissatisfaction.[37] Still other theories maintain that turnover is set up by a general level of persistent dissatisfaction that then is triggered abruptly by some single disruptive event at work that either pushes the employee away (such as a dispute with supervisor or co-worker) or pulls the employee away (an alternative employment opportunity).[38] This model focuses on "the straw that breaks the camel's back" but shares with all the other theories an emphasis on job dissatisfaction as the necessary

**Progression of Withdrawal**
Theory that dissatisfied individuals enact a set of behaviors in succession to avoid their work situation.

figure 10.3

An Overall Model of the Job Dissatisfaction–Job Withdrawal Process

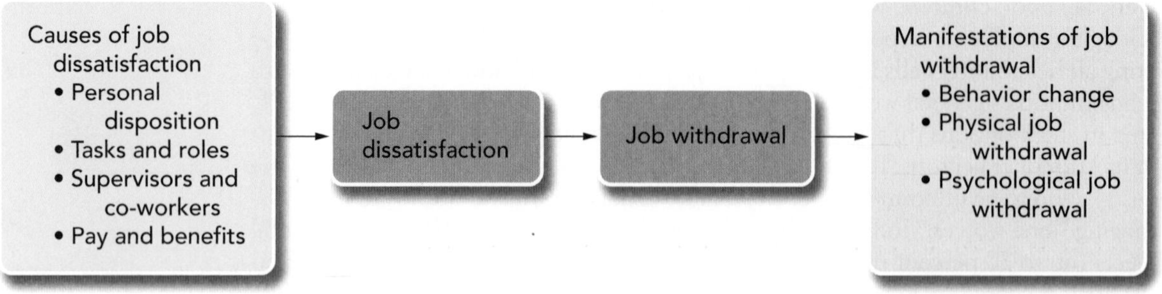


but insufficient cause of turnover.[39] Regardless of what specific theory one endorses, there is a general consensus that withdrawal behaviors are clearly related to one another, and they are all at least partially caused by job dissatisfaction.[40]

## Behavior Change

One might expect that an employee's first response to dissatisfaction would be to try to change the conditions that generate the dissatisfaction. This can lead to supervisor–subordinate confrontation, perhaps even conflict, as dissatisfied workers try to bring about changes in policy or upper-level personnel. Where employees are unionized, it can lead to an increased number of grievances being filed.[41] Although at first this type of conflict can feel threatening to the manager, on closer inspection, this is really an opportunity for the manager to learn about and perhaps solve an important problem. For example, Don McAdams, a manager at Johnsonville Foods, recalls an incident where one particular employee had been very critical of the company's incentive system. McAdams listened to the person's concerns and then asked him to head a committee charged with developing a better incentive system. At first the employee was taken aback, but he eventually accepted the challenge and became so enthusiastic about the project that he was the one who presented the new system to the general membership. Because this person was known to be highly critical of the old system, he had a high level of credibility with the other workers, who felt, "If this guy likes it, it must be pretty good." In the end, this critic-turned-champion was immensely successful in solving a specific organizational problem.[42]

**Whistle-blowing**
Making grievances public by going to the media or government.

Less constructively, employees can initiate change through **whistle-blowing** (making grievances public by going to the media).[43] Whistle-blowers are often dissatisfied individuals who cannot bring about internal change and, out of a sense of commitment or frustration, take their concerns to external constituencies. For example, Russell Tice was an employee of the U.S. National Security Agency (NSA) whose job was to electronically eavesdrop (i.e., spy) on our nation's enemies. He was devoted to his job and noted that "the mentality at NSA was we need to get these guys and we're going to do whatever it takes to get them." However, when his job was changed in the wake of 9/11 to focus on calls being made by U.S. citizens, he was concerned that without the proper warrants, this type of surveillance of his fellow Americans was illegal. No one at NSA would take Tice's concerns seriously, and so he took his concerns to the *New York Times*, which eventually published an article that accused the Bush administration of conducting widespread illegal wiretapping. The White House first denied the allegations, but when the evidence became too overwhelming to dispute, the administration admitted that the program was inappropriate and hence ended its existence. Tice eventually had his security clearance revoked, but he noted that it was worth it. "We need to clean up the intelligence community. We've had abuses and they need to be addressed."[44]

## Physical Job Withdrawal

If the job conditions cannot be changed, a dissatisfied worker may be able to solve the problem by leaving the job. This could take the form of an internal transfer if the dissatisfaction is job-specific (the result of an unfair supervisor or unpleasant working conditions). On the other hand, if the source of the dissatisfaction relates to organizationwide policies (lack of job security or below-market pay levels), organizational turnover is likely.

Many employees who would like to quit their jobs have to stay on if they have no other employment opportunities. For example, the weak job market that characterized the U.S. economy in the 2000–2003 time period meant that many dissatisfied employees could not quit even though job dissatisfaction levels were at historic highs.[45] In other cases, employees may want to leave because their firms are struggling, but they are stigmatized because other organizations are reluctant to hire individuals whose previous experience was all with an employer that was generally perceived to be uncompetitive. For example, one Midwest headhunter noted that "I get a call a week from someone at a high level at the Ford Motor Company saying they want to get out of the automotive world, but they are hard to place because people feel they are running away from something, not to something."[46] In these cases, another way of physically removing oneself from the dissatisfying work short of quitting altogether is to be absent.[47] One recent survey indicated that, on average, companies spend 15 percent of their payroll costs to make up for absent workers.[48] Short of missing the whole day, a dissatisfied employee may be late for work. Although not as disruptive as absenteeism, tardiness can be costly and is related to job satisfaction.[49]

**Job Involvement**
The degree to which people identify themselves with their jobs.

**Organizational Commitment**
The degree to which an employee identifies with the organization and is willing to put forth effort on its behalf.

**Job Satisfaction**
A pleasurable feeling that results from the perception that one's job fulfills or allows for the fulfillment of one's important job values.

## Psychological Withdrawal

When dissatisfied employees are unable to change their situation or remove themselves physically from their jobs, they may psychologically disengage themselves from their jobs. Although they are physically on the job, their minds may be somewhere else.

This psychological disengagement can take several forms. First, if the primary dissatisfaction has to do with the job itself, the employee may display a very low level of job involvement. **Job involvement** is the degree to which people identify themselves with their jobs. People who are uninvolved with their jobs consider their work an unimportant aspect of their lives. A second form of psychological disengagement, which can occur when the dissatisfaction is with the employer as a whole, is a low level of organizational commitment. **Organizational commitment** is the degree to which an employee identifies with the organization and is willing to put forth effort on its behalf.[50] Individuals who have low organizational commitment are often just waiting for the first good opportunity to quit their jobs.

**LO3**
Specify the Relationship between Job Satisfaction and Various Forms of Job Withdrawal, and Identify the Major Sources of Job Satisfaction in Work Contexts.

## Job Satisfaction and Job Withdrawal

As we see in Figure 10.3, the key driving force behind all the different forms of job withdrawal is **job satisfaction,** which we will define as a pleasurable feeling that results from the perception that one's job fulfills or allows for the fulfillment of one's important job values.[51] This definition reflects three important aspects of job satisfaction. First, job satisfaction is a function of *values*, defined as "what a person consciously or unconsciously desires to obtain." Second, this definition emphasizes that different employees have different views of which values are important, and this is critical in determining the nature and degree of their job satisfaction. One person may value high pay above all else; another may value the opportunity to travel; another may value staying within a specific geographic region. The third important aspect of job satisfaction is perception. An individual's perceptions may not be a completely accurate reflection of reality, and different people may view the same situation differently.

**Frame of Reference**
A standard point that serves as a comparison for other points and thus provides meaning.

In particular, people's perceptions are often strongly influenced by their frame of reference. A **frame of reference** is a standard point that serves as a comparison for other points and thus provides meaning. For example, an upper-level executive who offers a 6 percent salary increase to a lower-level manager might expect this to make the manager happy because inflation (the executive's frame of reference) is only 3 percent. The manager, on the other hand, might find the raise quite unsatisfactory because it is less than the 9 percent raise received by a colleague who does similar work (the manager's frame of reference). Thus values, perceptions, and importance are the three components of job satisfaction. People will be satisfied with their jobs as long as they perceive that their jobs meet their important values.

## Sources of Job Dissatisfaction

Many aspects of people and organizations can cause dissatisfaction among employees. Managers and HR professionals need to be aware of these because they are the levers which can raise job satisfaction and reduce employee withdrawal. This is an issue that is particularly salient in the current economy where pressures to raise productivity have pushed many workers to the limit, and the opportunity for changing jobs is enhanced by a market where the demand for labor is heating up.[52]

### Unsafe Working Conditions

Earlier in this chapter we discussed the employer's role in helping employees stay healthy via employee assistance programs for specific problems like drug addiction and alcohol dependency, as well as general wellness initiatives to promote health and reduce health care–related expenditures. As we saw in the vignette that opened this chapter, some companies are taking this very seriously, including monitoring activities that people engage in outside work, such as smoking cigarettes, and terminating employment in cases where the perception is employees are putting themselves (and hence the company's health benefits' costs) at risk. Obviously, if employers care this much about the risk employees are exposed to off the job, there needs to be an even more important emphasis on risk exposure that occurs on the job.

Of course, each employee has a right to safe working conditions, and previously in this book (see Chapter 3) we reviewed the Occupational Safety and Health Act of 1970 (OSHA), which spells out those rights in a very detailed fashion. We also discussed in that chapter how to develop safety awareness programs that identify and communicate job hazards, as well as how to reinforce safe work practices that would allow one to pass an OSHA inspection. Although our emphasis in that chapter on safety was primarily directed at legal compliance, we need to revisit the topic in this chapter, because OSHA is not the only audience that is likely to evaluate the safety of jobs. The perception and reaction of the organization's own employees to working conditions has implications for satisfaction, retention, and competitive advantage that go well beyond merely meeting the legal requirements. That is, if applicants or job incumbents conclude that their health or lives are at risk because of the job, attracting and retaining workers will be impossible.

Managing safety issues for jobs where risks are a daily part of the environment is a critical responsibility for Human Resources.

Not all jobs pose safety risks, but the nature of the work in a whole host of jobs makes managing safety-related perceptions critical. This includes jobs such as fishing boat operators, timber cutters, airline pilot/flight attendants, structural metal workers, garbage collectors, and taxi drivers/chauffeurs, which all have been identified as jobs where people are most likely to be involved in fatal accidents. In fact, in these job categories alone, close to 1,000 people die annually. Other jobs that rate low in terms of fatal accidents rate higher in nonfatal accidents, and this includes many jobs in eating establishments, hospitals, nursing homes, convenience stores, and the long-haul trucking industry. Still other jobs pose risks in terms of contracting occupational diseases due to exposure to chemicals. In industries like these, one of the foremost responsibilities of human resources is to ensure that workers and management both know and execute "best practices."

Although one would think that workers and managers would do this naturally, the fact is the longer one is exposed to a particular risk environment the more comfortable one gets in that environment and the less vigilant one becomes. Upper level management needs to continually emphasize and stress compliance with worker safety regulations and carefully monitor statistics related to workplace accidents. Many employers link financial bonuses to attaining specific safety-related goals, and this helps keep employees focused on doing the job the right way every day.[53] These programs more than pay for themselves over time. Research suggests that it is not unusual for a midsize company that reduces accidents by 10 percent to see a $50,000 reduction in premiums. Assuming that the firm has a profit margin of 5 percent, this is essentially the equivalent of bringing in another $1 million in sales. Based on these numbers, Jim Hatherley, a vice president at Liberty Mutual Group, notes that "the companies that have better profit-and-loss statements are the ones that take everything more seriously, including safety. When they look at safety as a business issue, they win."[54] Even beyond the straight financial characteristics, however, firms that emphasize safety send workers a clear signal that they care about them. This is an important aspect of organizational culture which strengthens the employee–employer relationship and promotes both attraction of new employees and retention of current employees.

## Personal Dispositions

Because dissatisfaction is an emotion that ultimately resides within the person, it is not surprising that many who have studied these outcomes have focused on individual differences. **Negative affectivity** is a term used to describe a dispositional dimension that reflects pervasive individual differences in satisfaction with any and all aspects of life. Individuals who are high in negative affectivity report higher levels of aversive mood states, including anger, contempt, disgust, guilt, fear, and nervousness across all contexts (work and nonwork).[55]

**Negative Affectivity**
A dispositional dimension that reflects pervasive individual differences in satisfaction with any and all aspects of life.

People who are high in negative affectivity tend to focus extensively on the negative aspects of themselves and others.[56] They also tend to persist in their negative attitudes even in the face of organizational interventions, such as increased pay levels, that generally increase the levels of satisfaction of other people.[57] Research has even shown that negative affectivity in early adolescence is predictive of overall job dissatisfaction in adulthood. There were also significant relationships between work attitudes measured over 5-year[58] and 10-year[59] periods, even for workers who changed employers and/or occupations. All of this implies that some individuals tend to bring low satisfaction with them to work. Thus these people may be relatively dissatisfied regardless of what steps the organization or the manager takes.

Another construct useful in understanding dispositional aspects of job satisfaction is the notion of core self-evaluations. *Core self-evaluations* have been defined as a basic positive or negative bottom-line opinion that individuals hold about themselves. A positive core evaluation reflects the person's self-image on a number of more specific traits, including high self-esteem, high self-efficacy, internal locus of control, and emotional stability. These factors, both alone and together, have been found to be quite predictive of job satisfaction.[60] Part of the reason why individuals with positive core self-evaluations have higher job satisfaction is that they tend to seek out and obtain jobs with more desirable characteristics, such as allowing discretion or dealing with complex tasks.[61] They also tend to take more socially approved proactive steps when it comes to trying to personally change a situation that is not to their liking. People with negative core self-evaluations tend to attribute dissatisfying features of their lives or work to the acts of other people, whom they blame for all their problems. They are less likely to work toward change, instead either doing nothing or acting aggressively toward those they blame for their misfortunes.[62]

The evidence on the linkage between these kinds of traits and job satisfaction suggests the importance of personnel selection as a way of raising overall levels of employee satisfaction. If job satisfaction remains relatively stable across time and jobs because of characteristics like negative affectivity or core self-evaluations, this suggests that transient changes in job satisfaction will be difficult to sustain in these individuals, who will typically revert to their "dispositional" or adaptation level over time.[63] Interviews should assess the degree to which any job applicant has a history of chronic dissatisfaction with employment. If an applicant states that he was dissatisfied with his past six jobs, what makes the employer think he won't be dissatisfied with this one?

### Tasks and Roles

As a predictor of job dissatisfaction, nothing surpasses the nature of the task itself.[64] Many aspects of a task have been linked to dissatisfaction. Several elaborate theories relating task characteristics to worker reactions have been formulated and extensively tested. We discussed several of these in Chapter 4. In this section we focus on four primary aspects of tasks that affect job satisfaction: the complexity of the task, the degree of physical strain and exertion on the job, the amount of flexibility in where and when the work is done, and, finally, the value the employee puts on the task.[65]

With a few exceptions, there is a strong positive relationship between task complexity and job satisfaction. That is, the boredom generated by simple, repetitive jobs that do not mentally challenge the worker leads to frustration and dissatisfaction.[66] One of the major interventions aimed at reducing job dissatisfaction by increasing job complexity is job enrichment. As the term suggests, this intervention is directed at jobs that are "impoverished" or boring because of their repetitive nature or low scope. Many job enrichment programs are based on the job characteristics theory discussed earlier in Chapter 4.

For example, at Xerox, work was once structured along four large functional units: manufacturing, research, marketing, and finance. Segmenting the work this way reduces the meaningfulness of many jobs. It also isolates workers from each other and distances them from customers. Thus CEO Paul Allaire restructured the organization into separate product divisions that each did its own manufacturing, research, marketing, and finance. Dan Cholish, a Xerox veteran, had been a "one-dimensional" engineer, but under the new system he has learned a little about manufacturing, finance, and marketing as he concentrates on customer needs. According to Cholish, "I've probably visited more customers in the last six months than I had in my last six years on my old assignment."[67]

**Job Rotation**
The process of systematically moving a single individual from one job to another over the course of time. The job assignments may be in various functional areas of the company or movement may be between jobs in a single functional area or department.

Another task-based intervention is **job rotation.** This is a process of systematically moving a single individual from one job to another over the course of time. Although employees may not feel capable of putting up with the dissatisfying aspects of a particular job indefinitely, they often feel they can do so temporarily. Job rotation can do more than simply spread out the dissatisfying aspects of a particular job. It can increase work complexity for employees and provide valuable cross-training in jobs so that employees eventually understand many different jobs. This makes for a more flexible workforce and increases workers' appreciation of the other tasks that have to be accomplished for the organization to complete its mission.[68] The second primary aspect of a task that affects job satisfaction is the degree to which the job involves physical strain and exertion.[69] This aspect is sometimes overlooked at a time when automation has removed much of the physical strain associated with jobs. Indeed, the fact that technology has aimed to lessen work-related physical exertion indicates that such exertion is almost universally considered undesirable. Nevertheless, many jobs can still be characterized as physically demanding.

Because of the degree to which nonwork roles often spill over and affect work roles, and vice versa, a third critical aspect of work that affects satisfaction and retention is the degree to which scheduling is flexible. In order to help employees manage their multiple roles, companies have turned to a number of family-friendly policies to both recruit new talent and hold onto the talent they already have. These policies may include provisions for child care, elder care, flexible work schedules, job sharing, telecommuting, and extended maternal and paternal leaves.[70] Although these programs create some headaches for managers in terms of scheduling work and reporting requirements, they have a number of demonstrable benefits. First, the provision of these sorts of benefits is a recruitment aid that helps employers attract potential job applicants.[71] Second, once hired, flexible work arrangements result in reduced absenteeism.[72] This is particularly true for firms that employ large numbers of women with children. In fact, one nonprofit company that could not compete on wages, was able to reduce its turnover rate from 30 percent to 7 percent just by initiating a program that let mothers bring their babies to work.[73] Third, over the long term, these programs result in higher levels of employee commitment to the organization.[74] They have also been linked to increased organizational citizenship behaviors on the part of individual employees,[75] as well as enhanced organizational performance, especially in organizations that employ a large percentage of female employees.[76] Indeed, the benefits of these kinds of programs are so well documented that the mere announcement that an organization is initiating some sort of flexible work policy has a positive impact on the share price of the company's stock.[77] Indeed, as the "Competing through Technology" box illustrates, some companies have taken the idea of flexible work arrangements to the limit.

## COMPETING THROUGH TECHNOLOGY

### Best Buy Breaks the Clock

In 2001, the specialists in human resources at Best Buy's headquarters in Minneapolis were aware that the company was experiencing a number of problems. Employee turnover was high, work satisfaction was low, and problems were particularly acute with some of the higher performing younger workers who felt that their jobs were being "micromanaged" by supervisors who cared more about "face time" and appearances than actual performance and innovation. HR specialists Cali Ressler and Jody Thompson considered nudging the organization toward the use of more flextime scheduling, but then rejected the idea when they concluded that it did not go far enough in terms of solving the current problems.

Traditional flextime programs presented several problems that limited their value to Best Buy. First, the main concern is that most flextime programs tinker with the problem on the edges and do not get at the core issue of restructuring work in a way that exploits current technology and radically expands worker freedom. Moving from a strict 9 to 5 schedule on one day to an 8 to 4 or 10 to 6 schedule on another day still leaves the worker in a largely fixed and inflexible time frame. Second, to make matters worse, moving to flextime adds a layer of scheduling complexity and bureaucracy to an administrative headache (scheduling) that is already overly complex and bureaucratic. Finally, because most flextime arrangements have to be approved by line supervisors or can be applied only to certain jobs, perceptions of favoritism associated with their use start to erode group cohesiveness, and those that take advantage of the program are often stigmatized by those who choose not to take advantage of the benefit.

Best Buy needed a more radical approach to solve its problems, and so Ressler and Thompson came up with the concept of the "Results-Oriented Work Environment" (ROWE), which essentially eliminated the use of time clocks and formal scheduling at Best Buy's headquarters. The wide availability of wireless broadband technology—a technology that was hardly foreign to Best Buy workers—had the potential to free workers from having to come into headquarters to do their own work or communicate with colleagues. Rather than counting the minutes that people were at their workstations, supervisors at Best Buy were charged with establishing and monitoring objective performance goals and metrics, and then letting the employees decide when, where, and how to accomplish those objectives. As Thompson notes, "We want people to stop thinking of work as a place you go to five days a week from 8 to 5, and start thinking of work as something you do."

Due to the revolutionary nature of this change, rather than try to force feed the program in a top-down fashion to the entire organization, Ressler and Thompson took a more grassroots approach, slowly introducing the program into units where the problems with satisfaction and retention were the worst or where supervisors and employees seemed most receptive. The initial results were impressive; however, the program soon began to spread like a virus from one department to another. Voluntary turnover dropped 90 percent, 50 percent and 75 percent in the Dot. Com, Logistics, and Sourcing Departments, respectively between 2005 and 2006, and, on average, productivity climbed 35 percent. Rather than working fewer hours, most employees, freed from the constraints of commuting and the general level of distraction created by the previous office environment, actually wound up working longer hours. Some workers struggled with their newfound freedom and had to be let go, but even those supervisors who were initially skeptical regarding the plan admitted that many of those same workers were not really carrying their own weight under the previous system. The new system did not cause those problems, but rather exposed them.

Many have questioned the degree to which this radical approach to scheduling would work in other contexts. Even Best Buy has not tried to take this approach, which was so successful at its headquarters, and apply it at its retail stores despite the fact that turnover is also a problem there. In a retail unit, the need to staff displays, work with customers, and manage cash registers works against the idea. Indeed, even other organizations might find it difficult to replicate Best Buy's success in their own corporate headquarters. In general, Best Buy is a company with a strong, technologically sophisticated culture, staffed primarily with younger workers. The system also puts a great deal of pressure on managers to come up with clear, objective performance metrics, and some fear that organizational citizenship behaviors will fall though the cracks. Finally, as flextime consultant Paul Rupert notes, "You can ridicule an obsession with face time, but some companies have a strong belief that having people in the same place at the same time creates synergy that is valuable to the company." Obviously, employers will have to answer this question for themselves, but at Best Buy, in the words of the CEO, "For years I have been focusing on the wrong currency. I was always looking to see if people were here. I should have been looking at what they were getting done."

SOURCES: J. McGregor, "Flextime, Honing the Balance" *BusinessWeek,* December 11, 2006, pp. 64-65; P. Kiger, "Throwing Out the Rules of Work," *Workforce Management,* September 25, 2006, pp. 16–23; A. Fisher, "Playing for Keeps," *BusinessWeek,* March 19, 2007, pp. 85–91; P. Kiger, "ROWE's Adaptability Questioned," *Workforce Management,* September 25, 2006, p. 20; M. Conlin, "Smashing the Clock," *BusinessWeek,* December 11, 2006, pp. 60–68.

Some organizations have also tried to create more flexible work arrangements by reclassifying job descriptions so that more workers are considered in the "managerial" class, but this sort of action is very controversial. Managers and professionals are supposedly "exempt" from the Fair Standards Act that dictates a 40-hour week, yet increasingly members of this group have been claiming they are misclassified and should be treated as nonexempt workers. Companies such as U-Haul, Taco Bell, PepsiCo, Auto Zone, Borders Books, Pacific Bell, Bridgestone, and Wal-Mart have been slapped with lawsuits by such workers seeking overtime pay. Plaintiffs argue that while their job titles may make it sound like they are managers, in reality their day-to-day activities have a lot more to do with production and much less with supervision. When the work starts taking longer than 40 hours a week, this becomes important. As one legal expert noted, "Companies that are not addressing these issues are sitting ducks waiting to get shot at."[78]

By far, the most important aspect of work in terms of generating satisfaction is the degree to which it is meaningfully related to core values of the worker. For example, Genentech is a small San Francisco–based biotech pharmaceutical company that competes directly with the largest and most well-funded pharmaceutical giants in the industry including Merck, Lilly, and Johnson & Johnson. From the outset, Genentech knew that the ultimate success of its venture depended on attracting and retaining the best minds within the field of bioscience, despite having less capital relative to the competition.

Genentech focused its mission on developing and testing "big ideas," particularly as this relates to life and death issues (e.g., drugs to fight cancer) in the field of health care. It then searched out scientists who had passionate feelings about work in this area, and surrounded them with a supportive corporate culture that was more like working in a small, close-knit research university than a large pharmaceutical company. Researchers were given the autonomy to pursue their own ideas in a context where every success was celebrated (often in a sophomoric fashion), and every failure was treated as a learning experience rather than a career-ending catastrophe. The strategy was a "swing for the fences" approach emphasizing hitting a few home runs, rather than trying to incrementally tinker with existing products. As CEO Art Levinson notes, "At the end of the day, we want to make drugs that really matter—that's the transcendent issue," and this is captured in the corporate motto: "In Business for Life."

This strategy was clearly a risky bet, since in this industry, up to $800 million may be spent to invent a new drug, only to have 90 percent of these drugs fail to reach the market, but so far this bet has paid off. According to Wall Street estimates, Genentech's year-end revenues for 2006 stood at $6.6 billion, three times what the company earned in 2002, and the stock price doubled from $47 to $95 a share between 2005 and 2006. The company has attracted many of the top graduating doctoral students, as well as many scientists who have left their larger, more conservative and hierarchical competitors. As one industry analyst noted, "From the day the company was founded, Genentech's culture has been its competitive advantage."[79]

## Supervisors and Co-workers

The two primary sets of people in an organization who affect job satisfaction are co-workers and supervisors. A person may be satisfied with her supervisor and co-workers for one of two reasons. First, she may have many of the same values, attitudes, and philosophies that the co-workers and supervisors have. Research shows the diversity in values and beliefs can create a "misfit" between the person and the work group that increases the likelihood of turnover.[80] Over time, this creates an environment where groups can become increasingly homogeneous, and this "attraction–selection–attrition" cycle can be a powerful determinant of the organization's culture.[81] Indeed, even if one cannot generate a unifying culture throughout an entire organization, it is worth noting that increases in job satisfaction can be derived simply from congruence among supervisors and subordinates at one level.[82]

Second, people may be satisfied with their supervisor and co-workers because they provide support that helps them achieve their own goals. Social support means the degree to which the person is surrounded by other people who are sympathetic and caring. Considerable research indicates that social support is a strong predictor of job satisfaction and lower employee turnover.[83] In contrast, abusive supervision is a major cause of turnover, and some organizations find that they can reduce turnover in some units by 25 percent to 33 percent in a single year simply by removing a specific supervisor who lacks interpersonal skills.[84] This is especially the case when individuals are promoted from operational roles to managerial roles because of their technical, rather than interpersonal skills. The lack of leadership skills and interpersonal sensitivity that was not a large part of the person's prior role is often exposed in that person's first managerial experience.[85]

Because of the powerful role played by supervisors and other more experienced workers in terms of supporting the organization's culture, some organizations are going to great lengths to develop the mentoring skills of their managers and other highly experienced workers.[86] In fact, recent statistics show that the number of Fortune 500 companies that provided formal mentoring programs jumped from 10 percent in 2002 to over 50 percent in 2007. Much of this is attributed to the fact that many organizations are facing a wave of retirements as baby boomers prepare to leave the workforce, and organizations are scrambling to develop systems that would promote critical knowledge transfer from older to younger workers. As William Arnone, a human capital consultant at Ernst & Young, notes, "Companies know there is a looming 'wisdom withdrawal' but they're putting off addressing it."[87]

This is not the case at the Tennessee Valley Authority, however, where the mentoring model provides a good generic example of how to transfer knowledge in a way that protects the organization's interests and helps to quickly develop the depth and breadth of younger workers' skills. The TVA provides nuclear-based electric power to much of the southern United States, but is faced with an aging workforce. The TVA program, based on interviews with the workforce, assigns workers a score from 1 to 5 that rates how impending their retirement might be (from 1, not within the next 6 years, to 5, within the next year). Then, based on interviews with senior managers, each person is rated on a 1 to 5 scale in terms of how much critical, irreplaceable knowledge he or she possesses.

If the resulting score for a unit or department indicates that there are three or four people with scores in the 20–25 range, this is a "red flag" that triggers a mentoring program where younger workers are assigned to shadow a longer term employee, in an effort to learn not just a role but the culture and norms of the organization as a whole.[88] Lockheed Martin has a very similar program in terms of transferring knowledge and culture, but its program places slightly more emphasis on the mentor's role in championing specific younger workers within the system. Turnover rates in jobs staffed primarily by younger workers dropped from 12 percent to 2.5 percent after the introduction of this program.[89]

Because a supportive environment reduces dissatisfaction, many organizations foster team building both on and off the job (such as via softball or bowling leagues). The idea is that group cohesiveness and support for individual group members will be increased through exposure and joint efforts. Although management certainly cannot ensure that each stressed employee develops friends, it can make it easier for employees to interact—a necessary condition for developing friendship and rapport. In fact, results of surveys indicate that endorsing the item "Most of my closest friendships are with people at work" is one of the most powerful tools for predicting turnover.[90]

## Pay and Benefits

We should not discount the influence of the job incumbent, the job itself, and the surrounding people in terms of influencing job satisfaction, but for most people, work is their primary source of income and financial security. Pay is also seen as an indicator of status within the organization as well as in society at large. Thus, for many individuals, the standing of their pay relative to those within their organization, or the standing of their pay relative to others doing similar work for other employers, becomes even more important than the level of pay itself.[91] Thus, for some people, pay is a reflection of self-worth, so pay satisfaction takes on critical significance when it comes to retention.[92] Indeed, the role of pay and benefits is so large that we devote the entire next part of this book to these topics. Within this chapter we focus primarily on satisfaction with two aspects of pay (pay levels and benefits) and how these are assessed within the organization. Methods for addressing these issues are discussed in Part 4 of this book.

One of the main dimensions of satisfaction with pay deals with pay levels relative to market wages. Indeed, when it comes to retention, employees being recruited away from one organization by another are often lured with promises of higher pay levels. In fact, exit surveys of high-performing employees who have left their organization indicate "better pay" as the reason in over 70 percent of the cases compared to only 33 percent who indicate "better opportunity." Ironically, when the managers of those same workers are polled, 68 percent cite "better opportunity" versus 45 percent who indicate it was "better pay," suggesting quite a difference of opinion.[93] Satisfaction with benefits is another important dimension of overall pay satisfaction. Because many individuals have a difficult time ascertaining the true dollar value of their benefits package, however, this dimension may not always be as salient to people as pay itself. In order to derive competitive advantage from benefits' expenditures, it is critical not only to make them highly salient to employees, however, but also link them to the organization's strategic direction.

In order to make costs better reflect revenues, organizations are increasingly adopting variable pay schemes that reward employees for specific accomplishments related to either individual or organizational performance.[94] Although "paying for performance" is an easy idea to express in general terms, it is often difficult to put into practice without creating certain negative side effects. For example, reward schemes that target the performance of individuals (merit raises or incentives for being the top salesperson) often detract from teamwork because the motivation to win the award makes it against the person's own self-interest to help colleagues succeed. On the other hand, incentives that are targeted at performance at the unit or organizational level often fail to recognize the difference between "star performers" and "social loafers," each of which gets the same reward. Thus, although simple in theory, organizations that opt for variable reward schemes need to think out these kinds of issues carefully to avoid negative side effects.

## Measuring and Monitoring Job Satisfaction

Most attempts to measure job satisfaction rely on workers' self-reports. There is a vast amount of data on the reliability and validity of many existing scales as well as a wealth of data from companies that have used these scales, allowing for comparisons across firms. Established scales are excellent places to begin if employers wish to assess the satisfaction levels of their employees. An employer would be foolish to "reinvent the wheel" by generating its own versions of measures of these broad constructs. Of course, in some cases, organizations want to measure their employees' satisfaction with aspects of their work that are specific to that organization (such as satisfaction with one particular health plan versus another). In these situations the organization may need to create its own scales, but this will be the exception rather than the rule.

One standardized, widely used measure of job satisfaction is the Job Descriptive Index (JDI). The JDI emphasizes various facets of satisfaction: pay, the work itself, supervision, co-workers, and promotions. Table 10.5 presents several items from the JDI scale. Other scales exist for those who want to get even more specific about different facets of satisfaction. For example, although the JDI we just examined assesses

**table 10.5**

Sample Items from a Standardized Job Satisfaction Scale (the JDI)

**Instructions:** Think of your present work. What is it like most of the time? In the blank beside each word given below, write

__Y__ for "Yes" if it describes your work
__N__ for "No" if it does NOT describe your work
__?__ if you cannot decide

| **Work Itself** | **Pay** | **Promotion Opportunities** |
|---|---|---|
| _____ Routine | _____ Less than I deserve | _____ Dead-end job |
| _____ Satisfying | _____ Highly paid | _____ Unfair policies |
| _____ Good | _____ Insecure | _____ Based on ability |

| **Supervision** | **Co-workers** |
|---|---|
| _____ Impolite | _____ Intelligent |
| _____ Praises good work | _____ Responsible |
| _____ Doesn't supervise enough | _____ Boring |

SOURCE: W. K. Balzar, D. C. Smith, D. E. Kravitz, S. E. Lovell, K. B. Paul, B. A. Reilly, and C. E. Reilly, *User's Manual for the Job Descriptive Index (JDI)* (Bowling Green, OH: Bowling Green State University, 1990).

satisfaction with pay, it does not break pay up into different dimensions.[95] The Pay Satisfaction Questionnaire (PSQ) focuses on these more specific dimensions (pay levels, benefits, pay structure, and pay raises); thus this measure gives a more detailed view of exactly what aspects of pay are most or least satisfying.[96] Taking this even further, we can find scales that take just one of these dimensions—benefits—and then break this down even further into multiple facets of satisfaction with benefits.

Clearly there is no end to the number of satisfaction facets that we might want to measure, but the key in operational contexts, where the main concern is retention, is making sure that scores on whatever measures taken truly relate to voluntary turnover among valued people. For example, satisfaction with co-workers might be low, but if this aspect of satisfaction is not too central to employees, it may not translate into voluntary turnover. Similarly, in an organization that bases raises on performance, low performers might report being dissatisfied with raises, but this may not reflect any operational problem. Indeed, the whole strategic purpose of many pay-for-performance plans is to create this type of dissatisfaction among low performers to motivate them to higher levels of performance.

## Survey-Feedback Interventions

**LO4** Design a Survey Feedback Intervention Program and Use This to Promote Retention of Key Organizational Personnel.

Regardless of what measures are used or how many facets of satisfaction are assessed, a systematic, ongoing program of *employee survey research* should be a prominent part of any human resource strategy for a number of reasons. First, it allows the company to monitor trends over time and thus prevent problems in the area of voluntary turnover before they happen. For example, Figure 10.4 shows the average profile for different

figure 10.4

Average Profile for Different Facets of Satisfaction over Time

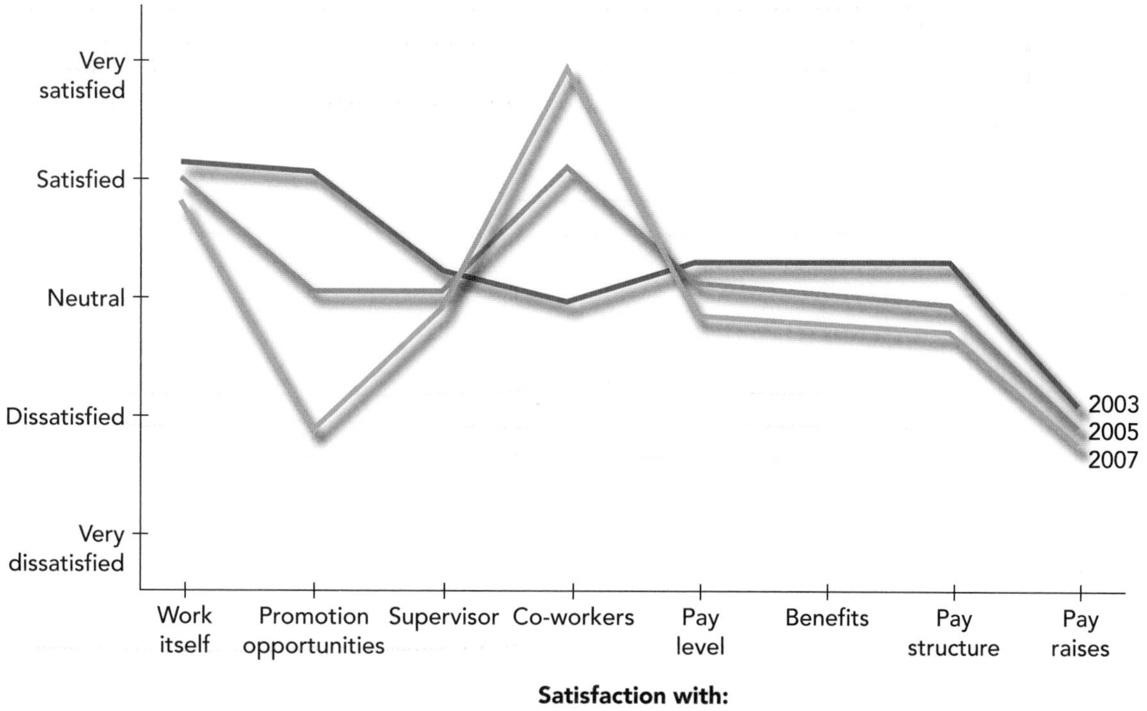

facets of satisfaction for a hypothetical company in 2003, 2005, and 2007. As the figure makes clear, the level of satisfaction with promotion opportunities in this company has eroded over time, whereas the satisfaction with co-workers has improved. If there was a strong relationship between satisfaction with promotion opportunities and voluntary turnover among high performers, this would constitute a threat that the organization might need to address via some of the techniques discussed in our previous chapter, "Employee Development." For example, First USA Bank saw exactly this kind of profile in its job satisfaction survey of all its managers. As Jeff Brown, vice president of organizational effectiveness, noted, "We already had a sense that career development was an issue, but the survey data really threw it in our faces and made us realize we had to do something about it." This led to First USA's "Opportunity Knocks" program, an employee-led career development effort that clarified the opportunities available within the firm as well as what skills and experiences were needed to take advantage of those opportunities. As a result of this program, two years later when the survey was conducted again, satisfaction with promotion opportunities increased by 40 percent.[97]

A second reason for engaging in an ongoing program of employee satisfaction surveys is that it provides a means of empirically assessing the impact of changes in policy (such as introduction of a new performance appraisal system) or personnel (introduction of a new CEO, for example) on worker attitudes. Figure 10.5 shows the average profile for different satisfaction facets for a hypothetical organization one year before and one year after a merger. An examination of the profile makes it clear that since the merger, satisfaction with supervision and pay structure have gone down dramatically, and this has not been offset by any increase in satisfaction along

**figure 10.5**

Average Profile for Different Facets of Satisfaction before and after a Major Event

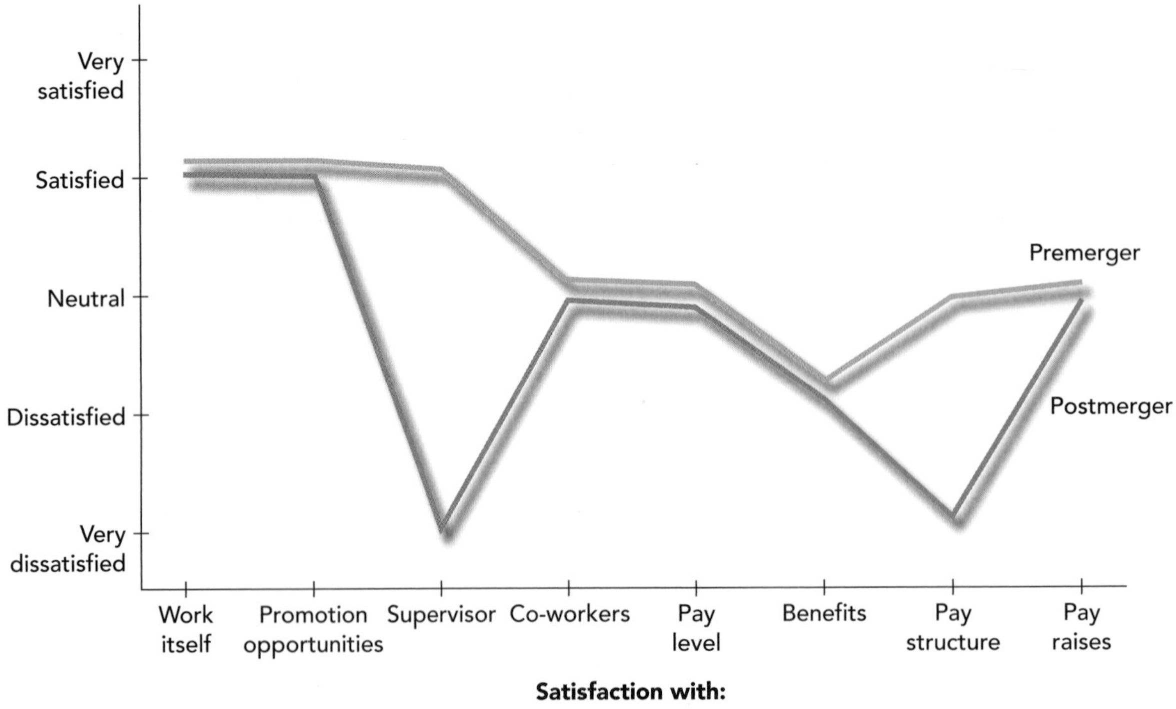

figure 10.6
Average Profile for Different Facets of Satisfaction versus the Industry Average

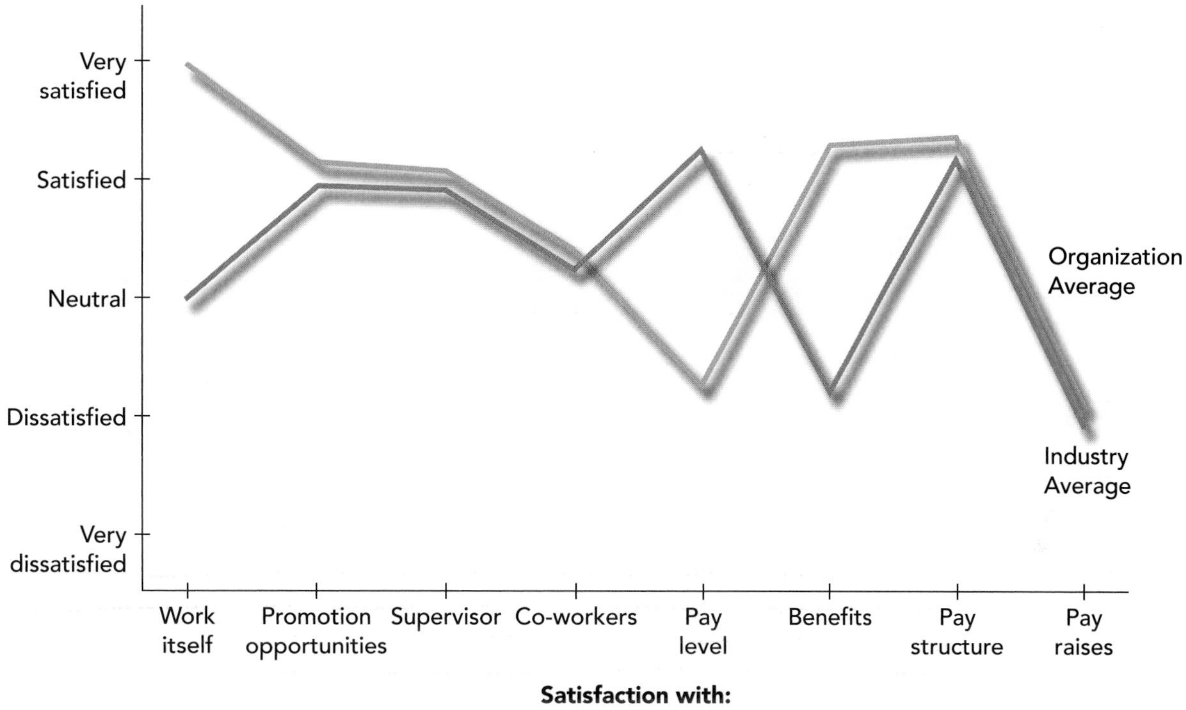


other dimensions. Again, this might point to the need for training programs for supervisors (like those discussed in Chapter 7) or changes in the job evaluation system (like those discussed in Chapter 11).

Third, when these surveys incorporate standardized scales like the JDI, they often allow the company to compare itself with others in the same industry along these dimensions. For example, Figure 10.6 shows the average profile for different satisfaction facets for a hypothetical organization and compares this to the industry average. Again, if we detect major differences between one organization and the industry as a whole (on overall pay levels, for example), this might allow the company to react and change its policies before there is a mass exodus of people moving to the competition.

According to Figure 10.6, the satisfaction with pay levels is low relative to the industry, but this is offset by higher-than-industry-average satisfaction with benefits and the work itself. As we showed in Chapter 6 ("Selection and Placement"), the organization might want to use this information to systematically screen people. That is, the fit between the person and the organization would be best if the company selected applicants who reported being most interested in the nature of the work itself and benefits, and rejected those applicants whose sole concern was with pay levels.

Within the organization, a systematic survey program also allows the company to check for differences between units and hence benchmark "best practices" that might be generalized across units. For example, Figure 10.7 shows the average profile for five different regional divisions of a hypothetical company. The figure shows that satisfaction with pay raises is much higher in one of the regions relative to the others. If the overall amount of money allocated to raises was equal through the entire company,

figure 10.7
Average Profile for Different Facets of Satisfaction for Different Regional Divisions

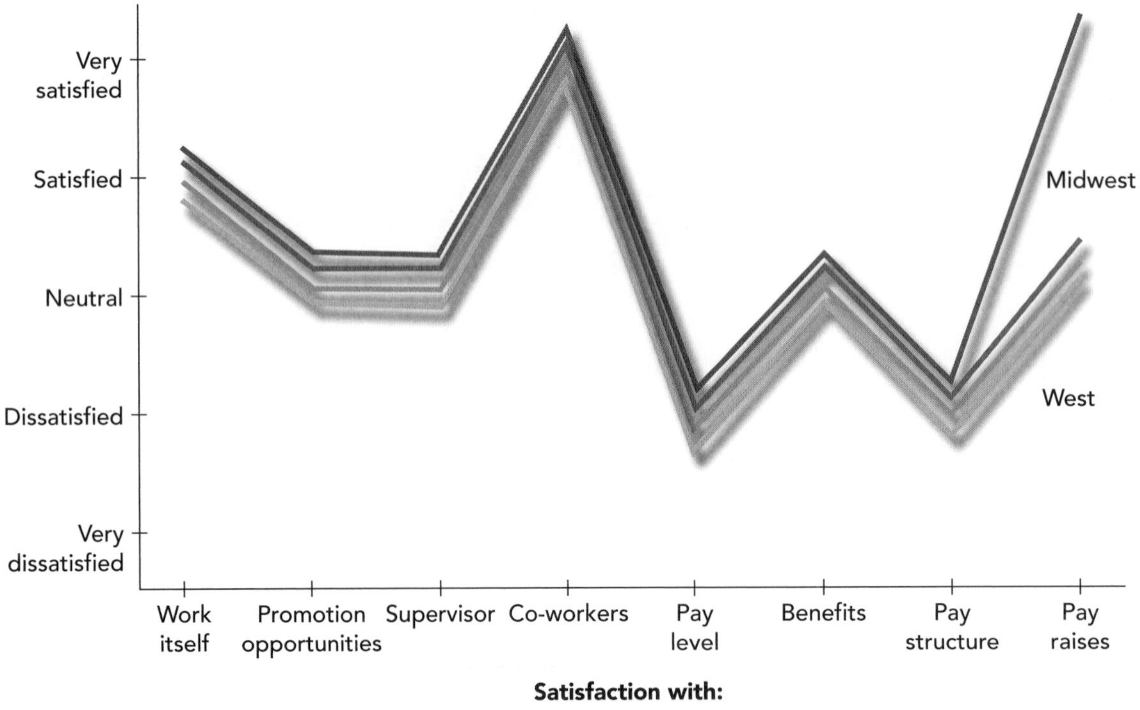


this implies that the manner in which raises are allocated or communicated in the Midwest region might be something that the other regions should look into.

Obviously a great deal can be learned from employee satisfaction surveys. It is surprising that many companies conducting regular consumer satisfaction surveys fail to show the same concern for employee satisfaction. Retention is an issue involving both customers and employees, however, and—as we've noted throughout this chapter—the two types of retention are substantially related. For example, sales agents at State Farm Insurance stay with the company for an average of 18 to 20 years—two to three times the average tenure in this industry. This kind of tenure allows the average State Farm agent to learn the job and develop long-term customer relations that cannot be matched by competitors who may lose half of their sales staff each year. State Farm also benefits from this experienced staff by systematically surveying its agents to get their views about where customer satisfaction is high, where it is low, and what can be done to improve service.[98] The result in terms of the bottom line is that State Farm achieves 40 percent higher sales per agent compared to the competition. In addition, as an indicator of quality of service, the retention rate among State Farm customers exceeds 95 percent.[99]

Although findings such as these are leading more companies to do such surveys, conducting an organizational opinion survey is not something that should be taken lightly. Especially in the beginning, surveys such as this often raise expectations. If people fail to see any timely actions taken on matters identified as problems in the survey, satisfaction is likely to be even lower than it would be in the absence of a survey.

Finally, although the focus in this section has been on surveys of current employees, any strategic retention policy also has to consider surveying people who are about to become ex-employees. Exit interviews with departing workers can be a valuable tool for uncovering systematic concerns that are driving retention problems. If properly conducted, an exit interview can reveal the reasons why people are leaving, and perhaps even set the stage for their later return.[100] Indeed, in the new economy, it is now so common for people who once left their firm to return that they are given a special name—"boomerangs."[101] A good exit interview sets the stage for this phenomenon because if a recruiter is armed with information about what caused a specific person to leave (such as an abusive supervisor or a lack of family-friendly policies), when the situation changes, the person may be willing to come back.[102] Indeed, in the war for talent, the best way to manage retention is to engage in a battle for every valued employee, even in situations when it looks like the battle may have been lost.

## A Look Back

In the story that opened this chapter, we saw how an organizational policy aimed at improving the general level of employee health was met with mixed reactions on the part of various employees. Some saw this as an intrusive invasion of privacy that ruined their lives, whereas others saw it as a needed prod to get them to take actions that in fact saved their lives.

### Questions

1. Based upon our discussion of outcome fairness, procedural fairness, and interactional fairness, do you think that aggressive wellness policies are unfair to employees? If so, what could be done to reduce this unfairness without significantly increasing costs?
2. What specific facets of job satisfaction are being targeted by these kinds of policies, and what facets or problems do they ignore?
3. Given the increased diversity of workers and their personal situations, how can a systematic employee survey process be used to quickly identify problems and solutions for different subgroups?

Please see the Video Case that corresponds to this chapter online at www.mhhe.com/noe6e.

## Summary

This chapter examined issues related to employee separation and retention. Involuntary turnover reflects a separation initiated by the organization, often when the individual would prefer to stay a member of the organization. Voluntary turnover reflects a separation initiated by the individual, often when the organization would prefer that the person stay a member. Organizations can gain competitive advantage by strategically managing the separation process so that involuntary turnover is implemented in a fashion that does not invite retaliation, and voluntary turnover among high performers is kept to a minimum. Retaliatory reactions to organizational discipline and dismissal decisions can be minimized by implementing these decisions in a manner that promotes feelings of procedural and interactive justice. Voluntary turnover can be minimized by measuring and monitoring employee levels of satisfaction with critical facets of job and organization, and then addressing any problems identified by such surveys.

## Key Terms

Involuntary turnover, 449
Voluntary turnover, 449
Employment-at-will doctrine, 450
Outcome fairness, 453
Procedural justice, 453
Interactional justice, 454
Alternative dispute resolution (ADR), 455
Employee assistance programs (EAPs), 455
Outplacement counseling, 458
Progression of withdrawal, 459
Whistle-blowing, 460
Job involvement, 461
Organizational commitment, 461
Job satisfaction, 461
Frame of reference, 462
Negative affectivity, 463
Job rotation, 465

## Discussion Questions

1. The discipline and discharge procedures described in this chapter are systematic but rather slow. In your opinion, should some offenses lead to immediate dismissal? If so, how would you justify this to a court if you were sued for wrongful discharge?
2. Organizational turnover is generally considered a negative outcome, and many organizations spend a great deal of time and money trying to reduce it. What situations would indicate that an increase in turnover might be just what an organization needs? Given the difficulty of terminating employees, what organizational policies might promote the retention of high-performing workers but voluntary turnover among low performers?
3. Three popular interventions for enhancing worker satisfaction are job enrichment, job rotation, and role analysis. What are the critical differences between these interventions, and under what conditions might one be preferable to the others?
4. If off-the-job stress and dissatisfaction begin to create on-the-job problems, what are the rights and responsibilities of the human resource manager in helping the employee to overcome these problems? Are intrusions into such areas an invasion of privacy, a benevolent and altruistic employer practice, or simply a prudent financial step taken to protect the firm's investment?
5. Discuss the advantages of using published, standardized measures in employee attitude surveys. Do employers ever need to develop their own measures for such surveys? Where would one turn to learn how to do this?

## Self-Assessment Exercise

The characteristics of your job influence your overall satisfaction with the job. One way to be satisfied at work is to find a job with the characteristics that you find desirable. The following assessment is a look at what kind of job is likely to satisfy you.

The following phrases describe different job characteristics. Read each phrase, then circle a number to indicate how much of the job characteristic you would like. Use the following scale: 1= very little; 2 = little; 3 = a moderate amount; 4 = much; 5 = very much.

1. The opportunity to perform a number of different activities each day 1 2 3 4 5
2. Contributing something significant to the company 1 2 3 4 5
3. The freedom to determine how to do my job 1 2 3 4 5
4. The ability to see projects or jobs through to completion, rather than performing only one piece of the job 1 2 3 4 5
5. Seeing the results of my work, so I can get an idea of how well I am doing the job 1 2 3 4 5
6. A feeling that the quality of my work is important to others in the company 1 2 3 4 5
7. The need to use a variety of complex skills 1 2 3 4 5
8. Responsibility to act and make decisions independently of managers or supervisors 1 2 3 4 5
9. Time and resources to do an entire piece of work from beginning to end 1 2 3 4 5
10. Getting feedback about my performance from the work itself 1 2 3 4 5

Add the scores for the pairs of items that measure each job characteristic. A higher score for a characteristic means that characteristic is more important to you.

*Skill Variety:* The degree to which a job requires you to use a variety of skills.

Item 1: ____ + Item 7: ____ = ____

*Task Identity:* The degree to which a job requires completion of a whole and identifiable piece of work.

Item 4: ____ + Item 9: ____ = ____

*Task Significance:* The degree to which a job has an impact on the lives or work of others.

Item 2: ____ + Item 6: ____ = ____

*Autonomy:* The degree to which a job provides freedom, empowerment, and discretion in scheduling the work and determining processes and procedures for completing the work.

Item 3: ____ + Item 8: ____ = ____

*Feedback:* The degree to which carrying out job-related tasks and activities provides you with direct and clear information about your effectiveness.

Item 5 ____ + Item 10: ____ = ____

SOURCE: Adapted from R. Daft and R. Noe, *Organizational Behavior* (New York: Harcourt, 2001).

## EXERCISING STRATEGY: FEELING INSECURE ABOUT AIRLINE SECURITY

Becoming an expert in any field takes some degree of training and on-the-job experience. When working as part of a team, it also takes some time to learn about the strengths and weaknesses of one's team members so that a unit can operate like a well-oiled machine. For this reason, turnover in just one position can drastically reduce the effectiveness of work units. However, imagine the case where the entire work unit changes *every four months!*

Although it may seem hard to believe, this was the turnover rate at the security checkpoints at Logan International Airport in September 2001, when two planes were hijacked and used as guided missiles in the attacks on the World Trade Center. And Logan was not even the worst airport in this regard. The turnover rates at both St. Louis and Atlanta were over 400 percent—meaning that the entire crew turned over every three months. Given the lack of experience that workers in these positions had on the job, as well as their lack of experience working together, it is not at all surprising that performance of these work units was abysmal. In fact, as Max Cleland, chairman of the Senate Armed Services Subcommittee on Personnel, noted, "This was our front line, and what we found is we didn't have security, we had a sieve."

A number of factors explain the incredibly high turnover rates in these jobs. First, the job is low in pay. Most airport security personnel make less than $6 an hour, well below the rate of even those who work in the airport's fast-food restaurants. Second, these are dead-end jobs. There is no career progression that would lead the incumbent to think that if he or she worked hard and stuck with it, he or she could climb into some managerial position. Third, the work itself is boring and monotonous. In addition, it is performed in a context of resentment, where hurried passengers look down on the security personnel who are perceived as being beneath those they are trying to serve. Finally, there is very little job security. A person can be fired for a single mistake, and the notion that a quality job is demanded is undermined by airline pressure to keep people moving during peak departure periods.

The airlines, which are currently responsible for security, blame this situation on the economics of the industry, where costs need to be kept low in order to maintain profitability. However, most airlines need to fill 65 percent of cabin capacity to clear a profit, and even two months after the terrorist attacks, fear of flying kept the capacity levels below 35 percent, putting even greater financial pressure on the carriers. As Cleland notes, as far as the industry is concerned, "Security is No. 1 in a series of confidence-building measures that will bring people back to fly."

Many of the security measures that are being considered will be imported from Europe and Israel, which have far better records than the United States in this area. There, airline security screening is treated as a police function, and the pay, training, and benefits are all much higher than what is seen in the United States. Moreover, a close emotional attachment between the security personnel and the airlines, many of which are nationalized, makes this work seem like a patriotic duty. This type of emotional attachment never develops in the revolving door that serves as the context for airline security work in the United States.

SOURCES: M. Fish, "Airport Security: A System Driven by the Minimum Wage," *CNN.com* (October 31, 2001), pp. 1–5; M. Fish, "Many Warnings over Security Preceded Terrorist Attacks," *CNN.com* (November 1, 2001), pp. 1–3; S. Candiotti, "FBI Arrests Man Who Tried to Board Flight Armed with Knives," *CNN.com* (November 5, 2001), pp. 1–2; M. Fish, "Outside the U.S., a Different Approach to Air Security," *CNN.com* (November 1, 2001), pp. 1–2.

### Questions

1. Many now look back at the way airport security was selected and managed prior to the 9/11 attacks with disbelief. What was the relationship between the airlines, the airports, the government, and the security agents prior to the attacks? How did the nature of these

relationships explain why airport security agents were managed so poorly?

2. How has the relationship between the airlines, airports, government, and security agents changed since 9/11, and in what ways has the new Transportation Safety Administration changed the nature of airport security work?

3. Much of the task in keeping air travel safe requires teamwork between the airlines, the airports, the government, and the security agents. In what way does high interdependence between people working together heighten the negative impact of employee turnover and performance?

## MANAGING PEOPLE: FROM THE PAGES OF *BUSINESSWEEK*

### BusinessWeek Getting Out of Dodge

**Top talent is fleeing the Big Three to escape declining morale and shaky prospects** Generous Motors it isn't. Not anymore. Just ask the several hundred General Motors Corp. managers who were fired on March 28. They were each taken aside and given a severance package, told to surrender their keys and badges, and allowed a month to turn in their cars. And while the hundreds of layoffs didn't amount to the "Black Tuesday" many managers expected, GM is just getting started. It plans many more such job cuts this year.

No sir, life in Motown isn't much fun these days. The rank and file of the United Auto Workers may be trembling in their steel-toed boots as GM and Ford Motor Co. gear up to impose tough new contracts and layoffs. But in the design studios, engineering labs, and corporate offices, the companies' white-collar professionals are experiencing the same kind of anxiety, gloom, and resignation as their blue-collar brothers and sisters.

GM Chairman G. Richard Wagoner and Ford Chairman William Clay "Bill" Ford Jr. exhort underlings to get jazzed about turning their companies around. But the troops are finding it hard to stay pumped. Executives get excited about new car projects only to watch them die before they get out of the studio. Middle managers find themselves reporting to a revolving roster of bosses. Pay, benefits, and perks aren't what they were.

And because the companies are erasing layers of management, the opportunities for advancement are dwindling. Many industry professionals believe the tough medicine will help their companies, but the turmoil is enough to wear down even the most determined optimist. "It's bad news after bad news," says a GM engineer. "It's not going to end anytime soon."

#### Résumés Are Flying

Is it any wonder that more and more Ford and GM executives are thinking about hitting the road? Headhunters report a steady flow of résumés from top Motown managers. "Not a week goes by without a Detroit executive telling me: 'If you see something outside the industry, I'd love to look at it,'" says Brad Marion, who runs the auto practice at executive search firm Korn/Ferry International.

Detroit's carmakers—even relatively healthy Chrysler Group—are already losing key talent. Ford lost its hybrid chief, Mary Ann Wright, to auto parts maker Collins & Aikman Corp. Levi Strauss & Co. snagged GM's chief financial officer for North America, Mary Boland. Dell Inc. got the auto maker's top quality officer, Annette Clayton. And Chrysler marketing whiz Julie Roehm fled to Wal-Mart Stores Inc. "If people at that level are leaving," says a GM product developer, "how bad are things going to get?"

It's hard to tell how worried Detroit should be. Kathleen S. Barclay, GM's vice-president of human resources, says they have no trouble fillings the jobs. She adds that those who stay are undeterred, even energized, by the challenges. The auto makers also say turnover isn't much higher than usual. Still, one Ford executive concedes "If this keeps happening, the talent pool will get pretty shallow."

How things have changed since Detroit's heyday. The Big Three had their pick of the brightest stars. Just five years ago GM and Ford were cherry-picking talent—swiping hot stylists from European carmakers and marketing bigs from the likes of Procter & Gamble Co. and General Electric Co.

Back in the day, Detroit also could afford to pay for its employees' loyalty: fat bonuses, union-caliber bennies, and a virtual guarantee of lifetime employment. It wasn't uncommon for Detroit professionals to stick around for 40 years. Or to find their sons and daughters climbing the ranks right behind them. That's Mary Ann Wright's story. "Ford took care of our family, "says Wright, whose father was a Ford engineer. "I thought 'God, I'm supposed to work for Ford forever.'"

Wright found huge satisfaction taking the Escape hybrid sport-utility vehicle from lab to showroom. And she was geared up to roll out a fleet of hybrids by 2010. But budget cuts and management chum meant "we weren't getting anything done." Wright also endured constant sniping that hybrids were a waste of time. In September a colleague sent an e-mail essentially asking: Why bother?

Soon after, Wright told Bill Ford she was quitting. He asked her to stay, but she was adamant. "When you're not having fun," Wright says, "it's time to go." She resurfaced in February as Collins & Aikman's vice-president of sales and program management. Her new employer is a fraction of Ford's size and struggling to emerge from bankruptcy. But there are compensations; including bonus, Wright, 43, could make more than $600,000, possibly double her take at Ford.

For executives overseeing the wholesale downsizing at GM, going to work can be especially draining. As the company's CFO for North America, Mary Boland spent her days scouring financial data, looking for ways to slash costs. That included figuring out which plants to close and dealing with the knowledge that these decisions had real-life consequences for families and communities. "It has been many years of downsizing at GM, but the last couple of years took its toll [on me] physically and mentally," Boland says. "I want to give 110 percent but I felt I couldn't keep up the pace."

Yet she found it hard tearing herself away from an industry that had also employed her father for decades as a tool-and-die maker. Before becoming CFO in 2004, Boland, now 48, had worked at the company for a quarter-century. Finally, though, her family nudged her into taking the CFO job at Levi's.

### "A Pretty Depressing Place"

When she finally took the plunge, Boland says, it was a big weight off her shoulders. Levi Strauss has completed its downsizing, having shifted its manufacturing offshore a few years ago. Now the company is looking for ways to grow rather than shrink.

Like Wright, Boland got a pretty decent package. She wouldn't give numbers, but says she got "a significant raise" to take the same job she had at GM. And every morning she wakes up in the tony San Francisco suburb of Tiburon, where she sips coffee and looks out over San Francisco Bay. Her morning commute takes her across the Golden Gate Bridge, a far cry from her old drive on Detroit's potholed John C. Lodge freeway. Says Boland: "Southeast Michigan is a pretty depressing place to be right now."

Detroit's rivals are only too aware of that, and they are taking advantage of the Motown malaise. The Japanese and Korean transplants are expanding, grabbing market share, and paying good salaries. So it's easy to see why Detroit professionals are going to work for the competition.

One is Joel T. Piaskowski. He's only 38, but he's the guy who designed the Buick Lucerne, one of GM's successful new models. Three years ago, Piaskowski quit GM and went to work for Hyundai Motor Co. in sunny Irvine, Calif. Today he's Hyundai's chief designer for North America, and other young Motown designers have followed in his wake.

GM wasn't in full downsizing mode when Piaskowski made the move. But he found it hard to make an impact. While GM was having trouble funding new car programs, Hyundai was adding models and even contemplating a luxury brand. Piaskowski saw an opportunity to put his stamp on an entire lineup.

Since he left GM, a dozen Big Three product developers have joined Piaskowski at Hyundai. And Cadillac designer Tom Kearns is now chief designer for North America at Hyundai sibling Kia. "I didn't recruit them," says Piaskowski. "They followed the buzz." And what about loyalty to his home town? Piaskowski's dad was a Chrysler designer, after all. "If it wasn't me," he says, "it would have been someone else." That's the last thing Detroit's auto makers need to hear.

SOURCE: D. Welch, "Getting Out of Dodge," *BusinessWeek*, April 17, 2006.

### Questions

1. Describe the nature of work at GM and Ford that makes high-performing employees want to leave voluntarily. In general, what are some of the unique challenges in retaining valued talent at the same time an organization is downsizing across the board?
2. How is the impact of these job conditions magnified because of the history of these employers and the expectations that were set up by these two employers? What does the future hold for these organizations if they continue to lose talent?
3. If you were an employer who was considering hiring a former Ford or General Motors employee, what unique concerns might you have relative to hiring someone with a similar background from a different company such as Toyota or BMW?
4. The picture painted in this article is a downward cycle where one problem creates another problem, which in turn creates yet another problem. What can leaders of organizations such as this do to reverse this self-perpetuating spiral? What can political leaders or leaders of labor organizations do to reverse this self-perpetuating spiral?

## NOTES

1. J. D. Shaw, M. K. Duffy, J. L. Johnson, and D. E. Lockhart, "Turnover, Social Capital Losses, and Performance," *Academy of Management Journal* 48 (2005), pp. 594–606.
2. R. Batt, "Managing Customer Services: Human Resource Practices, Quit Rates, and Sales Growth," *Academy of Management Journal* 45 (2002), pp. 587–97.
3. I. S. Fulmer, B. Gerhart, and K. S. Scott, "Are the 100 Best Better? An Empirical Investigation of the Relationship between Being a 'Great Place to Work' and Firm Performance," *Personnel Psychology* 56 (2003), pp. 965–93.
4. M. Boyle, "Happy People, Happy Returns," *Fortune*, January 22, 2007, p. 100.

5. J. P. Guthrie, "High-Involvement Work Practices, Turnover, and Productivity: Evidence from New Zealand," *Academy of Management Journal* 44 (2001), pp. 180–90.
6. S. S. Masterson, "A Trickle-Down Model of Organizational Justice: Relating Employees' and Customers' Perceptions of and Reactions to Fairness," *Journal of Applied Psychology* 86 (2001), pp. 594–604.
7. K. M. Kacmer, M. C. Andrews, D. L. Van Rooy, R. C. Steilberg, and S. Cerrone, "Sure Everyone Can Be Replaced . . . But at What Cost? Turnover as a Predictor of Unit-Level Performance," *Academy of Management Journal* 49 (2006), pp. 133–44.
8. F. Hanson, "'Poaching' Can Be Pricey, but Benefits May Outweigh Costs," *Workforce Management*, January 30, 2006, pp. 37–39.
9. S. A. Feeney, "The High Cost of Employee Violence," *Workforce*, August 2003, pp. 23–24.
10. J. D. Shaw, J. E. Delery, C. D. Jenkins, and N. Gupta, "An Organizational-Level Analysis of Voluntary Turnover," *Academy of Management Journal* 41 (1998), pp. 511–25.
11. M. Heller, "A Return to At-Will Employment," *Workforce*, May 2001, pp. 42–46.
12. D. Foust, "Tough Love at the Office," *BusinessWeek*, May 29, 2006, p. 106.
13. S. E. Scullen, P. K. Bergey, and L. Aimon-Smith, "Forced Distribution Rating Systems and the Improvement of Workforce Potential: A Baseline Simulation," *Personnel Psychology* 58 (2005), pp. 1–32.
14. J. Rossant and J. Ewing, "Every Little Reform Counts," *BusinessWeek*, March 7, 2005, pp. 54–55.
15. D. Roberts, "Rumbles Over Chinese Labor Reforms," *BusinessWeek*, March 12, 2007, p. 57.
16. J. McGregor, "Sweet Revenge," *BusinessWeek*, January 22, 2007, pp, 65–70.
17. M. M. Le Blanc and K. Kelloway, "Predictors and Outcomes of Workplace Violence and Aggression," *Journal of Applied Psychology* 87 (2002), pp. 444–53.
18. A. G. Tekleab, R. Takeuchi, and M. S. Taylor, "Extending the Chain of Relationships among Organizational Justice, Social Exchange, and Employee Reactions: The Role of Contract Violations," *Academy of Management Journal* 48 (2005), pp. 146–57.
19. D. P. Skarlicki and R. Folger, "Retaliation in the Workplace: The Roles of Distributive, Procedural, and Interactional Justice," *Journal of Applied Psychology* 82 (1997), pp. 434–43.
20. P. Dvorak, "Firing Workers Who Are a Bad Fit," *The Wall Street Journal*, May 1, 2006, p B5.
21. T. A. Judge, B. A. Scott, and R. Ilies, "Hostility, Job Attitudes and Workplace Deviance: A Test of a Multilevel Model," *Journal of Applied Psychology* 91 (2006), pp. 126–38.
22. B. J. Tepper, "Relationship among Supervisors' and Subordinates' Procedural Justice Perceptions and Organizational Citizenship Behaviors," *Academy of Management Journal* 46 (2003), pp. 97–105.
23. T. Simons and Q. Roberson, "Why Managers Should Care About Fairness: The Affects of Aggregate Justice Perceptions on Organizational Outcomes," *Journal of Applied Psychology* 88 (2003), pp. 432–43.
24. J. Smith, "EAPs Evolve to Health Plan Gatekeeper," *Employee Benefit Plan Review* 46 (1992), pp. 18–19.
25. A. Meisler, "Mind Field," *Workforce* (2003), pp. 57–60.
26. S. Sonnenberg and C. McEnerney, "Medical Leave: A Prescription," *Workforce*, April 2004, pp. 16–17.
27. J. Jones, "How to Bounce Back if You're Bounced Out," *BusinessWeek*, January 27, 1998, pp. 22–23.
28. J. D. Shaw, N. Gupta, and J. E. Delery, "Alternative Conceptualizations of the Relationship between Voluntary Turnover and Organizational Performance," *Academy of Management Journal* 48 (2005), pp. 50–68.
29. J. Sullivan, "Not All Turnover Is Equal," *Workforce Management*, May 21, 2007, p. 42.
30. J. Lublin, "Keeping Clients by Keeping Workers, *The Wall Street Journal*, November 20, 2006, p. B1.
31. R. Hof, "Even Yahoo Gets the Blues," *BusinessWeek*, May 28, 2007, p. 37.
32. A. Lashinsky, "Search and Enjoy," *Fortune*, January 22, 2007, pp. 70–82.
33. S. C. Payne and S. S. Weber, "Effects of Service Provider Attitudes and Employment Status on Citizenship Behaviors and Customer's Attitudes and Loyalty Behavior," *Journal of Applied Psychology* 91 (2006), pp. 365–78.
34. G. A. Gelade and M. Ivery, "The Impact of Human Resource Management and Work Climate on Organizational Performance," *Personnel Psychology* 56 (2003), pp. 383–404.
35. B. Schneider, P. J. Hanges, D. B. Smith, and A. N. Salvaggio, "Which Come First, Employee Attitudes or Organizational Financial and Market Performance?" *Journal of Applied Psychology* 88 (2003), pp. 838–51.
36. D. W. Baruch, "Why They Terminate," *Journal of Consulting Psychology* 8 (1944), pp. 35–46; J. G. Rosse, "Relations among Lateness, Absence and Turnover: Is There a Progression of Withdrawal?" *Human Relations* 41 (1988), pp. 517–31.
37. C. Hulin, "Adaptation, Persistence and Commitment in Organizations," in *Handbook of Industrial & Organizational Psychology* 2nd ed., ed. M. D. Dunnette and L. M. Hough (Palo Alto, CA: *Consulting Psychologists Press*, 1991), pp. 443–50.
38. C. Sablynski, T. Mitchell, T. Lee, J. Burton, and B. Holtom, "Turnover: An Integration of Lee and Mitchell's Unfolding Model and Job Embeddedness Construct and Hulin's Withdrawal Construct," in *The Psychology of Work*, ed. J. Brett and F. Drasgow (Mahwah, NJ: Lawrence Erlbaum Associates, 2002).
39. J. D. Kammeyer-Mueller, C. R. Wanberg, T. M. Glomb, and D. Ahlburg, "The Role of Temporal Shifts in Turnover Processes: It's About Time," *Journal of Applied Psychology* 90 (2005), pp. 644–58.
40. D. A. Harrison, D. A. Newman, and P. L. Roth, "How Important Are Job Attitudes? Meta-analytic Comparisons of Integrative Behavioral Outcomes and Time Sequences," *Academy of Management Journal* 49 (2006), pp. 305–25.
41. C. E. Labig and I. B. Helburn, "Union and Management Policy Influences on Grievance Initiation," *Journal of Labor Research* 7 (1986), pp. 269–84.
42. J. Cook, "Positively Negative," *Human Resource Executive* (June 15, 2001), pp. 101–4.
43. M. P. Miceli and J. P. Near, "Characteristics of Organizational Climate and Perceived Wrongdoing Associated with Whistle-Blowing Decisions," *Personnel Psychology* 38 (1985), pp. 525–44.
44. V. Walter, and A. Patel, "NSA Whistleblower Alleges Illegal Spying," *ABCNews.com*, January 10, 2006, p. 1.
45. L. Lavelle, "After the Jobless Recovery, a War for Talent," *BusinessWeek* (September 29, 2003), p. 92.
46. C. Jones, "As Ford Stumbles, More Managers See Leaving as the Way Forward," *The Wall Street Journal*, August 28, 2006, pp. B1, B2.
47. R. D. Hackett and R. M. Guion, "A Re-evaluation of the Job Satisfaction–Absenteeism Relation," *Organizational Behavior and Human Decision Processes* 35 (1985), pp. 340–81.

48. S. F. Gale, "Sickened by Costs of Absenteeism, Companies Look for Solutions," *Workforce*, September 2003, pp. 72–75.
49. J. G. Rosse and H. E. Miller, "Relationship between Absenteeism and Other Employee Behaviors," in *New Approaches to Understanding, Measuring, and Managing Employee Absence*, ed. P. S. Goodman and R. S. Atkin (San Francisco: Jossey-Bass, 1984).
50. R. T. Mowday, R. M. Steers, and L. W. Porter, "The Measurement of Organizational Commitment," *Journal of Vocational Behavior* 14 (1979), pp. 224–47.
51. E. A. Locke, "The Nature and Causes of Job Dissatisfaction," in *The Handbook of Industrial & Organizational Psychology*, ed. M. D. Dunnette (Chicago: Rand McNally, 1976), pp. 901–69.
52. E. Tahmincioglu, "More, More, More," *Workforce*, May 2004, pp. 41–44.
53. L. Woellert, "Does Welding Make You Sick?" *BusinessWeek*, July 10, 2006, p. 32.
54. J. Bailey, "Improving Safety for Workers Also Improves Company Health," *The Wall Street Journal*, May 1, 2006. p. B3.
55. D. Watson, L. A. Clark, and A. Tellegen, "Development and Validation of Brief Measures of Positive and Negative Affect: The PANAS Scales," *Journal of Personality and Social Psychology* 54 (1988), pp. 1063–70.
56. T. A. Judge, E. A. Locke, C. C. Durham, and A. N. Kluger, "Dispositional Effects on Job and Life Satisfaction: The Role of Core Evaluations," *Journal of Applied Psychology* 83 (1998), pp. 17–34.
57. T. Begley and C. Lee, "The Role of Negative Affectivity in Pay-at-Risk Reactions: A Longitudinal Study," *Journal of Applied Psychology*, 2005, pp. 382–88. G. E. Hardy, D. Woods, and T. D. Wall, "The Impact of Psychological Distress on Absence from Work," *Journal of Applied Psychology* 88 (2003), pp. 306–14.
58. B. M. Staw, N. E. Bell, and J. A. Clausen, "The Dispositional Approach to Job Attitudes: A Lifetime Longitudinal Test," *Administrative Science Quarterly* 31 (1986), pp. 56–78; B. M. Staw and J. Ross, "Stability in the Midst of Change: A Dispositional Approach to Job Attitudes," *Journal of Applied Psychology* 70 (1985), pp. 469–80.
59. R. P. Steel and J. R. Rentsch, "The Dispositional Model of Job Attitudes Revisited: Findings of a 10-Year Study," *Journal of Applied Psychology* 82 (1997), pp. 873–79.
60. T. A. Judge and J. E. Bono, "Relationship of Core Self-Evaluations Traits—Self-Esteem, Generalized Self-Efficacy, Locus of Control, and Emotional Stability—With Job Satisfaction and Job Performance: A Meta-Analysis," *Journal of Applied Psychology* 86 (2001), pp. 80–92.
61. T. A. Judge, J. E. Bono, and E. A. Locke, "Personality and Job Satisfaction: The Mediating Role of Job Characteristics," *Journal of Applied Psychology* 85 (2000), pp. 237–49.
62. S. C. Douglas and M. J. Martinko, "Exploring the Role of Individual Differences in the Prediction of Workplace Aggression," *Journal of Applied Psychology* 86 (2001), pp. 547–59.
63. N. A. Bowling, T. A. Beehr, S. H. Wagner, and T. M. Libkuman, "Adaptation-Level Theory, Opponent Process Theory, and Dispositions: An Integrated Approach to the Stability of Job Satisfaction," *Journal of Applied Psychology* 90 (2005), pp. 1044–53.
64. B. A. Gerhart, "How Important Are Dispositional Factors as Determinants of Job Satisfaction? Implications for Job Design and Other Personnel Programs," *Journal of Applied Psychology* 72 (1987), pp. 493–502.
65. E. F. Stone and H. G. Gueutal, "An Empirical Derivation of the Dimensions along Which Characteristics of Jobs Are Perceived," *Academy of Management Journal* 28 (1985), pp. 376–96.
66. L. W. Porter and R. M. Steers, "Organizational, Work and Personal Factors in Employee Absenteeism and Turnover," *Psychological Bulletin* 80 (1973), pp. 151–76.
67. L. Jones, "Xerox Is Rewriting the Book on Organization 'Architecture,'" *Chicago Tribune*, December 29, 1992, pp. 3-1, 3-2.
68. J. R. Hackman and G. R. Oldham, "Motivation through the Design of Work," *Organizational Behavior and Human Performance* 16 (1976), pp. 250–79.
69. Locke, "The Nature and Causes of Job Dissatisfaction."
70. B. Kaye, "Wake Up and Smell the Coffee: People Flock to Family Friendly," *BusinessWeek Online*, January 28, 2001, pp. 1–2.
71. B. L. Rau and M. M. Hyland, "Role Conflict and Flexible Work Arrangements: The Effects on Applicant Attraction," *Personnel Psychology* 55 (2002), pp. 111–36.
72. G. Weber, "Flexible Jobs Mean Fewer Absences," *Workforce*, November 2003, pp. 26–28.
73. M. Hammers, "Babies Deliver a Loyal Workforce," *Workforce*, April 2003, p. 52.
74. G. Flynn, "The Legalities of Flextime," *Workforce*, October 2001, pp. 62–66.
75. S. L. Lambert, "Added Benefits: The Link between Work–Life Benefits and Organizational Citizenship Behaviors," *Academy of Management Journal* 43 (2000), pp. 801–15.
76. J. E. Perry-Smith, "Work Family Human Resource Bundles and Perceived Organizational Performance," *Academy of Management Journal* 43 (2000), pp. 1107–17.
77. M. M. Arthur, "Share Price Reactions to Work-Family Initiatives: An Institutional Perspective," *Academy of Management Journal* 46 (2003), pp. 497–505.
78. M. Conlin, "Revenge of the Managers," *BusinessWeek*, March 12, 2001, pp. 60–61.
79. B. Morris, "The Best Place to Work Now," *Fortune*, January 20, 2006, pp. 79–86.
80. J. M. Sacco and N. Schmitt, "A Dynamic Multi-level Model of Demographic Diversity and Misfit Effects," *Journal of Applied Psychology* 90 (2005), pp. 203–31.
81. R. E. Ployhart, J. A. Weekley, and K. Baughman, "The Structure and Function of Human Capital Emergence: A Multilevel Examination of the Attraction–Selection–Attrition Model," *Academy of Management Journal* 49 (2006), pp. 661–77.
82. B. M. Meglino, E. C. Ravlin, and C. L. Adkins, "A Work Values Approach to Corporate Culture: A Field Test of the Value Congruence Process and Its Relationship to Individual Outcomes," *Journal of Applied Psychology* 74 (1989), pp. 424–33.
83. R. Eisenberger, F. Stinghamber, C. Vandenberghe, I. L. Sucharski, and L. Rhoades, "Perceived Supervisor Support: Contributions to Perceived Organizational Support and Employee Retention," *Journal of Applied Psychology* 87 (2002), pp. 565–73.
84. P. Lattman, "Does Thank You Help Keep Associates?" *The Wall Street Journal*, January 24, 2007.
85. S Aryee, Z. X. Chen, L. Y. Sun, and Y. A. Debrah, "Antecedents and Outcomes of Abusive Supervision: Test of a Trickle-Down Model," *Journal of Applied Psychology* 92 (2007), pp. 191–201.
86. S. C. Payne and A. H Huffman, "A Longitudinal Examination of the Influence of Mentoring on Organizational Commitment and Turnover," *Academy of Management Journal* 48 (2005), pp. 158–168.
87. S. Berfield, "Mentoring Can Be Messy," *BusinessWeek*, January 29, 2007, pp. 80–81.

88. A. Fisher, "Retain Your Brains," *Fortune*, July 24, 2006, pp. 49–50.
89. A. Fisher, "Have You Outgrown Your Job?" *Fortune*, August 21, 2006, pp. 46–54.
90. G. C. Ganster, M. R. Fusiler, and B. T. Mayes, "Role of Social Support in the Experience of Stress at Work," *Journal of Applied Psychology* 71 (1986), pp. 102–11.
91. C. O. Trevor and D. L. Wazeter, "Contingent View of Reactions to Objective Pay Conditions: Interdependence among Pay Structure Characteristics and Pay Relative to Internal and External Referents," *Journal of Applied Psychology* 91 (2006), pp. 1260–75.
92. S. C. Currall, A. J. Towler, T. A. Judge, and L. Kohn, "Pay Satisfaction and Organizational Outcomes," *Personnel Psychology* 58 (2005), pp. 613–40.
93. E. White, "Opportunity Knocks, and It Pays a Lot Better," *The Wall Street Journal*, November 13, 2006, p B3.
94. J. S. Lubin, "Bottom Up," *The Wall Street Journal*, April 14, 2003, pp. 1–3.
95. H. G. Heneman and D. S. Schwab, "Pay Satisfaction: Its Multidimensional Nature and Measurement," *International Journal of Applied Psychology* 20 (1985), pp. 129–41.
96. T. Judge and T. Welbourne, "A Confirmatory Investigation of the Dimensionality of the Pay Satisfaction Questionnaire," *Journal of Applied Psychology* 79 (1994), pp. 461–66.
97. P. K. Kiger, "At First USA Bank, Promotions and Job Satisfaction Are Up," *Workforce*, March 2001, pp. 54–56.
98. B. Schneider, S. D. Ashworth, A. C. Higgs, and L. Carr, "Design, Validity and Use of Strategically Focused Employee Attitude Surveys," *Personnel Psychology* 49 (1996), pp. 695–705.
99. M. Loeb, "Wouldn't It Be Good to Work for the Good Guys?" *Fortune*, October 14, 1996, pp. 223–24.
100. J. Applegaste, "Plan an Exit Interview," CNNMoney.com (November 13, 2000), pp. 1–2.
101. M. Conlin, "Job Security, No. Tall Latte, Yes," *BusinessWeek*, April 2, 2001, pp. 62–63.
102. J. Lynn, "Many Happy Returns," CNNMoney.com (March 2, 2001), pp. 1–2.

PART

# 4

# Compensation of Human Resources

11

CHAPTER

# Pay Structure Decisions

## LO LEARNING OBJECTIVES

After reading this chapter, you should be able to:

- **LO1** List the main decision areas and concepts in employee compensation management. *page 486*
- **LO2** Describe the major administrative tools used to manage employee compensation. *page 488*
- **LO3** Explain the importance of competitive labor market and product market forces in compensation decisions. *page 496*
- **LO4** Discuss the significance of process issues such as communication in compensation management. *page 500*
- **LO5** Describe new developments in the design of pay structures. *page 502*
- **LO6** Explain where the United States stands from an international perspective on pay issues. *page 505*
- **LO7** Explain the reasons for the controversy over executive pay. *page 509*
- **LO8** Describe the regulatory framework for employee compensation. *page 512*

# Enter the World of Business

## Toyota Sweats U.S. Labor Costs

Toyota Motor Corp. must hold down growth of its U.S. manufacturing wages and benefits, which are among the highest in the auto industry and are growing faster than the company's profit margin, according to a high-level company report obtained by the *Free Press.*

The report from Seiichi (Sean) Sudo, president of Toyota Engineering & Manufacturing in North America, said Toyota should strive to align hourly wages more closely with prevailing manufacturing pay in the state where each plant is located, "and not tie ourselves so closely to the U.S. auto industry, or other competitors."

Sudo's report to top managers said the Japan-based company projected a $900-million increase in U.S. manufacturing compensation by 2011, and human resources officials were working on trimming that by one-third.

The drive to hold down costs may boost UAW organizing efforts, if Toyota workers balk at the possibility of smaller raises, reduced benefits or greater demands for productivity gains. But the plan also illustrates that the world's most-profitable automaker is going to keep relentless pressure on Detroit and its signature industry.

The *Free Press* reported last week that at least some nonunion Toyota workers for the first time last year earned more than UAW assembly workers for Detroit's automakers.

Auto experts and Toyota's workers say it is ingrained in Toyota's culture to sweat over trying to save $300 million five years down the road even as the company rakes in more than $1 billion a month.

The root of Sudo's worry: Labor costs as a percentage of sales are growing faster than Toyota's profit margin. "This condition is not sustainable in the long term," he said in the report.

Sudo's 42-page report, which was left unsecured on computers at the Georgetown plant, says, "The U.S. auto industry pays among the highest manufacturing wages in the world. Compared with Japan and France, the U.S. auto industry pays 50 percent higher wages and over five times more than Mexico's auto manufacturers."

The company acknowledged that the documents supplied to the *Free Press* were authentic.

In a memo to workers at the plant after the report was circulated, Toyota noted that workers at Georgetown earned $3 an hour more than the U.S. auto industry standard. The *Free Press* reported last week the workers averaged $30 an hour, including bonuses. Currently, the median for comparable manufacturing jobs in Kentucky—half earn more, half earn less—is $12.64, according to the U.S. Department of Labor.

Toyota's strategy resembles what Hyundai Motor Co. uses at its plant in Montgomery, Ala. Assembly workers there make $14 an hour, about half the wages, bonuses and benefits of Toyota, Honda, Nissan and Detroit's automakers. But Hyundai's wages still are considerably higher than for comparable Alabama jobs, which pay $10.79 an hour.

Among the changes would be greater use of on-site medical clinics and the introduction of on-site pharmacies to combat rising health care costs. Toyota's language regarding North American health care inflation largely echoes that of Detroit's automakers.

The issues and solutions were laid out in a plan that also addressed quality, development of people and suppliers and the five-year production plan. The idea behind such a so-called hoshin plan is to ensure all employees understand and work toward the same long-term goals.

"Our challenge will be how to educate team members and managers about our condition, so that they can understand and accept change," Sudo said in the report.

Source: J. Roberson, "Toyota Sweats U.S. Labor Costs," *Detroit Free Press*, February 8, 2007.

# Introduction

LO1
List the Main Decision Areas and Concepts in Employee Compensation Management.

From the employer's point of view, pay is a powerful tool for furthering the organization's strategic goals. First, pay has a large impact on employee attitudes and behaviors. It influences the kind of employees who are attracted to (and remain with) the organization, and it can be a powerful tool for aligning current employees' interests with those of the broader organization. Second, employee compensation is typically a significant organizational cost and thus requires close scrutiny. As Table 11.1 shows, total compensation (cash and benefits) averages 22 percent of revenues and varies both within and across industries. In the chapter opener, Toyota's goal is to reduce its growth in labor costs, without jeopardizing its relationship with its workforce.

From the employees' point of view, policies having to do with wages, salaries, and other earnings affect their overall income and thus their standard of living. Both the level of pay and its seeming fairness compared with others' pay are important. Pay is also often considered a sign of status and success. Employees attach great importance to pay decisions when they evaluate their relationship with the organization. Therefore, pay decisions must be carefully managed and communicated.

**Pay Structure**
The relative pay of different jobs (job structure) and how much they are paid (pay level).

**Pay Level**
The average pay, including wages, salaries, and bonuses, of jobs in an organization.

**Job Structure**
The relative pay of jobs in an organization.

Pay decisions can be broken into two areas: pay structure and individual pay. In this chapter we focus on **pay structure,** which in turn entails a consideration of pay level and job structure. **Pay level** is defined here as the average pay (including wages, salaries, and bonuses) of jobs in an organization. (Benefits could also be included, but these are discussed separately in Chapter 13.) **Job structure** refers to the relative pay of jobs in an organization. Consider the same two jobs in two different organizations. In Organization 1, jobs A and B are paid an annual average compensation of $40,000 and $60,000, respectively. In Organization 2, the pay rates are $45,000 and $55,000, respectively. Organizations 1 and 2 have the same pay level ($50,000), but the job structures (relative rates of pay) differ.

Both pay level and job structure are characteristics of organizations and reflect decisions about jobs rather than about individual employees. This chapter's focus is on why and how organizations attach pay policies to jobs. In the next chapter we look within jobs to discuss the different approaches that can determine the pay of individual employees as well as the advantages and disadvantages of these different approaches.

Why is the focus on jobs in developing a pay structure? As the number of employees in an organization increases, so too does the number of human resource management decisions. In determining compensation, for example, each employee must be assigned a rate of pay that is acceptable in terms of external, internal, and individual equity (defined later) and in terms of the employer's cost. Although each employee is unique and thus requires some degree of individualized treatment, standardizing the

**table 11.1**
Total Compensation as a Percentage of Revenues

| | PERCENTILE | | |
|---|---|---|---|
| INDUSTRY | 25TH | 50TH | 75TH |
| Hospitals/health care | 43% | 46% | 49% |
| Manufacturing | 22 | 27 | 34 |
| Insurance/health care | 6 | 8 | 11 |
| All industries | 13 | 22 | 32 |

SOURCES: Data from Saratoga Institute, *Human Capital Benchmarking Report 2000* and Saratoga/PriceWaterhouseCoopers, *Key Trends in Human Capital: A Global Perspective, 2006.*

treatment of similar employees (those with similar jobs) can help greatly to make compensation administration and decision making more manageable and more equitable. Thus pay policies are often attached to particular jobs rather than tailored entirely to individual employees.

## Equity Theory and Fairness

In discussing the consequences of pay decisions, it is useful to keep in mind that employees often evaluate their pay relative to that of other employees. Equity theory suggests that people evaluate the fairness of their situations by comparing them with those of other people.[1] According to the theory, a person (P) compares her own ratio of perceived outcomes O (pay, benefits, working conditions) to perceived inputs I (effort, ability, experience) to the ratio of a comparison other (o).

$$O_P/I_P <, >, \text{or} = O_o/I_o?$$

If P's ratio ($O_P/I_P$) is smaller than the comparison other's ratio ($O_o/I_o$), underreward inequity results. If P's ratio is larger, overreward inequity results, although evidence suggests that this type of inequity is less likely to occur and less likely to be sustained because P may rationalize the situation by reevaluating her outcomes less favorably or inputs (self-worth) more favorably.[2]

The consequences of P's comparisons depend on whether equity is perceived. If equity is perceived, no change is expected in P's attitudes or behavior. In contrast, perceived inequity may cause P to restore equity. Some ways of restoring equity are counterproductive, including (1) reducing one's own inputs (not working as hard), (2) increasing one's outcomes (such as by theft), (3) leaving the situation that generates perceived inequity (leaving the organization or refusing to work or cooperate with employees who are perceived as overrewarded).

Equity theory's main implication for managing employee compensation is that to an important extent, employees evaluate their pay by comparing it with what others get paid, and their work attitudes and behaviors are influenced by such comparisons. Consider also the contract that shortstop Alex Rodriquez (now a New York Yankee) signed in 2000 with the Texas Rangers baseball team. Rodriguez will earn a minimum of $21 million to $27 million per year (plus incentives) during the 10-year span of the contract. However, two key provisions could result in him earning substantially more money. One provision states that during the 2001 to 2004 seasons, his base compensation must be at least $2 million higher than any other shortstop's in major league baseball. A second provision permits Rodriquez to void seasons after 2008 unless his 2009 and 2010 base compensation is at least $1 million higher than any position player's in major league baseball. Otherwise, Rodriguez is free to leave his current team. These provisions that peg Rodriguez's pay to other players' pay is a compelling example of the importance of being paid well in *relative* terms.

Another implication is that employee perceptions are what determine their evaluation. The fact that management believes its employees are paid well compared with those of other companies does not necessarily translate into employees' beliefs. Employees may have different information or make different comparisons than management. In the chapter opening story, Toyota's goal is to move from using wages in the U.S. auto industry as the standard of comparison to using the (lower) prevailing wages in the state where each plant is located. To do so, however, Toyota recognizes

**table 11.2**
Pay Structure Concepts and Consequences

| PAY STRUCTURE DECISION AREA | ADMINISTRATIVE TOOL | FOCUS OF EMPLOYEE PAY COMPARISONS | CONSEQUENCES OF EQUITY PERCEPTIONS |
|---|---|---|---|
| Pay level | Market pay surveys | External equity | External employee movement (attraction and retention of quality employees); labor costs; employee attitudes |
| Job structure | Job evaluation | Internal equity | Internal employee movement (promotion, transfer, job rotation); cooperation among employees; employee attitudes |

its "challenge will be how to educate team members and managers . . . so they can understand and accept [this] change."

Two types of employee social comparisons of pay are especially relevant in making pay level and job structure decisions. (See Table 11.2.) First, *external equity* pay comparisons focus on what employees in other organizations are paid for doing the same general job. Such comparisons are likely to influence the decisions of applicants to accept job offers as well as the attitudes and decisions of employees about whether to stay with an organization or take a job elsewhere. (See Chapters 5 and 10.) The organization's choice of pay level influences its employees' external pay comparisons and their consequences. A market pay survey is the primary administrative tool organizations use in choosing a pay level.

Second, *internal equity* pay comparisons focus on what employees within the same organization, but in different jobs, are paid. Employees make comparisons with lower-level jobs, jobs at the same level (but perhaps in different skill areas or product divisions), and jobs at higher levels. These comparisons may influence general attitudes of employees; their willingness to transfer to other jobs within the organization; their willingness to accept promotions; their inclination to cooperate across jobs, functional areas, or product groups; and their commitment to the organization. The organization's choice of job structure influences its employees' internal comparisons and their consequences. Job evaluation is the administrative tool organizations use to design job structures.

In addition, employees make internal equity pay comparisons with others performing the same job. Such comparisons are most relevant to the following chapter, which focuses on using pay to recognize individual contributions and differences.

We now turn to ways to choose and develop pay levels and pay structures, the consequences of such choices, and the ways two administrative tools—market pay surveys and job evaluation—help in making pay decisions.

# Developing Pay Levels

**LO2**
Describe the Major Administrative Tools Used to Manage Employee Compensation.

## Market Pressures

Any organization faces two important competitive market challenges in deciding what to pay its employees: product market competition and labor market competition.

## Product Market Competition

First, organizations must compete effectively in the product market. In other words, they must be able to sell their goods and services at a quantity and price that will bring a sufficient return on their investment. Organizations compete on multiple dimensions (quality, service, and so on), and price is one of the most important dimensions. An important influence on price is the cost of production.

An organization that has higher labor costs than its product market competitors will have to charge higher average prices for products of similar quality. Thus, for example, if labor costs are 30 percent of revenues at Company A and Company B, but Company A has labor costs that are 20 percent higher than those of Company B, we would expect Company A to have product prices that are higher by $(.30 \times .20) = 6$ percent. At some point, the higher price charged by Company A will contribute to a loss of its business to competing companies with lower prices (like Company B). In the automobile industry, labor-related expenses per vehicle (including retiree and active worker benefits such as health care) average $1,080–$1,335 higher for the Big Three (General Motors, Ford, Chrysler) than for Japanese producers in the United States, Toyota, Nissan, and Honda. This labor cost advantage is a major factor in the profit advantage per vehicle of $2,400 that these Japanese producers hold over the Big Three.[3]

Therefore, *product market competition* places an *upper bound* on labor costs and compensation. This upper bound is more constrictive when labor costs are a larger share of total costs and when demand for the product is affected by changes in price (that is, when demand is *elastic*). Although costs are only one part of the competitive equation (productivity is just as important), higher costs may result in a loss of business. In the absence of clear evidence on productivity differences, costs need to be closely monitored.

What components make up labor costs? A major component is the average cost per employee. This is made up of both direct payments (such as wages, salaries, and bonuses) and indirect payments (such as health insurance, Social Security, and unemployment compensation). A second component of labor cost is the staffing level (number of employees). Not surprisingly, financially troubled organizations often seek to cut costs by focusing on one or both components. Staff reductions, hiring freezes, wage and salary freezes, and sharing benefits costs with employees are several ways of enhancing the organization's competitive position in the product market.

## Labor Market Competition

A second important competitive market challenge is *labor market competition* Essentially, labor market competition is the amount an organization must pay to compete against other companies that hire similar employees. These labor market competitors typically include not only companies that have similar products but also those in different product markets that hire similar types of employees. If an organization is not competitive in the labor market, it will fail to attract and retain employees of sufficient numbers and quality. For example, even if a computer manufacturer offers newly graduated electrical engineers the same pay as other computer manufacturers, if automobile manufacturers and other labor market competitors offer salaries $5,000 higher, the computer company may not be able to hire enough qualified electrical engineers. Labor market competition places a *lower bound* on pay levels.

## Employees as a Resource

Because organizations have to compete in the labor market, they should consider their employees not just as a cost but as a resource in which the organization has invested and from which it expects valuable returns. Although controlling costs directly affects an organization's ability to compete in the product market, the organization's competitive position can be compromised if costs are kept low at the expense of employee productivity and quality. Having higher labor costs than your competitors is not necessarily bad if you also have the best and most effective workforce, one that produces more products of better quality.

Pay policies and programs are one of the most important human resource tools for encouraging desired employee behaviors and discouraging undesired behaviors. Therefore, they must be evaluated not just in terms of costs but in terms of the returns they generate—how they attract, retain, and motivate a high-quality workforce. For example, if the average revenue per employee in Company A is 20 percent higher than in Company B, it may not be important that the average pay in Company A is 10 percent higher than in Company B.

## Deciding What to Pay

Although organizations face important external labor and product market pressures in setting their pay levels, a range of discretion remains.[4] How large the range is depends on the particular competitive environment the organization faces. Where the range is broad, an important strategic decision is whether to pay above, at, or below the market average. The advantage of paying above the market average is the ability to attract and retain the top talent available, which can translate into a highly effective and productive workforce. The disadvantage, however, is the added cost.[5]

**Efficiency Wage Theory**
A theory stating that wages influence worker productivity.

Under what circumstances do the benefits of higher pay outweigh the higher costs? According to **efficiency wage theory,** one circumstance is when organizations have technologies or structures that depend on highly skilled employees. For example, organizations that emphasize decentralized decision making may need higher-caliber employees. Another circumstance where higher pay may be warranted is when an organization has difficulties observing and monitoring its employees' performance. It may therefore wish to provide an above-market pay rate to ensure the incentive to put forth maximum effort. The theory is that employees who are paid more than they would be paid elsewhere will be reluctant to shirk because they wish to retain their good jobs.[6]

## Market Pay Surveys

**Benchmarking**
Comparing an organization's practices against those of the competition.

To compete for talent, organizations use **benchmarking,** a procedure in which an organization compares its own practices against those of the competition. In compensation management, benchmarking against product market and labor market competitors is typically accomplished through the use of one or more pay surveys, which provide information on going rates of pay among competing organizations.

The use of pay surveys requires answers to several important questions:[7]

1. Which employers should be included in the survey? Ideally, they would be the key labor market and product market competitors.
2. Which jobs are included in the survey? Because only a sample of jobs is ordinarily used, care must be taken that the jobs are representative in terms of

level, functional area, and product market. Also, the job content must be sufficiently similar.

3. If multiple surveys are used, how are all the rates of pay weighted and combined? Organizations often have to weight and combine pay rates because different surveys are often tailored toward particular employee groups (labor markets) or product markets. The organization must decide how much relative weight to give to its labor market and product market competitors in setting pay.

Several factors affect decisions on how to combine surveys.[8] Product market comparisons that focus on labor costs are likely to deserve greater weight when (1) labor costs represent a large share of total costs, (2) product demand is elastic (it changes in response to product price changes), (3) the supply of labor is inelastic, and (4) employee skills are specific to the product market (and will remain so). In contrast, labor market comparisons may be more important when (1) attracting and retaining qualified employees is difficult and (2) the costs (administrative, disruption, and so on) of recruiting replacements are high.

As this discussion suggests, knowing what other organizations are paying is only one part of the story. It is also necessary to know what those organizations are getting in return for their investment in employees. To find that out, some organizations examine ratios such as revenues/employees and revenues/labor cost. The first ratio includes the staffing component of employee cost but not the average cost per employee. The second ratio, however, includes both. Note that comparing these ratios across organizations requires caution. For example, different industries rely on different labor and capital resources. So comparing the ratio of revenues to labor costs of a petroleum company (capital intensive, high ratio) to a hospital (labor intensive, low ratio) would be like comparing apples and oranges. But within industries, such comparisons can be useful. Besides revenues, other return-on-investment data might include product quality, customer satisfaction, and potential workforce quality (such as average education and skill levels).

## Rate Ranges

As the preceding discussion suggests, obtaining a single "going rate" of market pay is a complex task that involves a number of subjective decisions; it is both an art and a science. Once a market rate has been chosen, how is it incorporated into the pay structure? Typically—especially for white-collar jobs—it is used for setting the midpoint of pay ranges for either jobs or pay grades (discussed next). Market survey data are also often collected on minimum and maximum rates of pay as well. The use of **rate ranges** permits a company to recognize differences in employee performance, seniority, training, and so forth in setting individual pay (discussed in the next chapter). For some blue-collar jobs, however, particularly those covered by collective bargaining contracts, there may be a single rate of pay for all employees within the job.

**Rate Ranges**
Different employees in the same job may have different pay rates.

## Key Jobs and Nonkey Jobs

In using pay surveys, it is necessary to make a distinction between two general types of jobs: key jobs (or benchmark jobs) and nonkey jobs. **Key jobs** have relatively stable content and—perhaps most important—are common to many organizations. Therefore, it is possible to obtain market pay survey data on them. Note, however, that to avoid too much of an administrative burden, organizations may not gather market pay data on all

**Key Jobs**
Benchmark jobs, used in pay surveys, that have relatively stable content and are common to many organizations.

**Nonkey Jobs**
Jobs that are unique to organizations and that cannot be directly valued or compared through the use of market surveys.

such jobs. In contrast to key jobs, **nonkey jobs** are, to an important extent, unique to organizations; thus, by definition, they cannot be directly valued or compared through the use of market surveys. Therefore, they are treated differently in the pay-setting process.

## Developing a Job Structure

Although external comparisons of the sort we have been discussing are important, employees also evaluate their pay using internal comparisons. So, for example, a vice president of marketing may expect to be paid roughly the same amount as a vice president of information systems because they are at the same organizational level, with similar levels of responsibility and similar impacts on the organization's performance. A job structure can be defined as the relative worth of various jobs in the organization, based on these types of internal comparisons. We now discuss how such decisions are made.

### Job Evaluation

**Job Evaluation**
An administrative procedure used to measure internal job worth.

**Compensable Factors**
The characteristics of jobs that an organization values and chooses to pay for.

One typical way of measuring internal job worth is to use an administrative procedure called **job evaluation.** A job evaluation system is composed of compensable factors and a weighting scheme based on the importance of each **compensable factor** to the organization. Simply stated, compensable factors are the characteristics of jobs that an organization values and chooses to pay for. These characteristics may include job complexity, working conditions, required education, required experience, and responsibility. Most job evaluation systems use several compensable factors. Job analysis (discussed in Chapter 4) provides basic descriptive information on job attributes, and the job evaluation process assigns values to these compensable factors.

Scores can be generated in a variety of ways, but they typically include input from a number of people. A job evaluation committee commonly generates ratings. Although there are numerous ways to evaluate jobs, the most widely used is the point-factor system, which yields job evaluation points for each compensable factor.[9]

### The Point-Factor System

After generating scores for each compensable factor on each job, job evaluators often apply a weighting scheme to account for the differing importance of the compensable factors to the organization. Weights can be generated in two ways. First, *a priori* weights can be assigned, which means factors are weighted using expert judgments about the importance of each compensable factor. Second, weights can be derived empirically based on how important each factor seems in determining pay in the labor market. (Statistical methods such as multiple regression can be used for this purpose.) For the sake of simplicity, we assume in the following example that equal a priori weights are chosen, which means that the scores on the compensable factors can be simply summed.

Table 11.3 shows an example of a three-factor job evaluation system applied to three jobs. Note that the jobs differ in the levels of experience, education, and complexity required. Summing the scores on the three compensable factors provides an internally oriented assessment of relative job worth in the organization. In a sense, the computer programmer job is worth 41 percent (155/110 − 1) more than the computer operator job, and the systems analyst job is worth 91 percent (210/110 − 1) more than the computer operator job. Whatever pay level is chosen (based on

**table 11.3**

Example of a Three-Factor Job Evaluation System

| JOB TITLE | COMPENSABLE FACTORS | | | |
|---|---|---|---|---|
| | EXPERIENCE | EDUCATION | COMPLEXITY | TOTAL |
| Computer operator | 40 | 30 | 40 | 110 |
| Computer programmer | 40 | 50 | 65 | 155 |
| Systems analyst | 65 | 60 | 85 | 210 |

benchmarking and competitive strategy), we would expect the pay differentials to be somewhat similar to these percentages. The internal job evaluation and external survey-based measures of worth can, however, diverge.

## Developing a Pay Structure

In the example provided in Table 11.4, there are 15 jobs, 10 of which are key jobs. For these key jobs, both pay survey and job evaluation data are available. For the five nonkey jobs, by definition, no survey data are available, only job evaluation information. Note that, for simplicity's sake, we work with data from only two pay surveys and we use a weighted average that gives twice as much weight to survey 1. Also, our example works with a single structure. Many organizations have multiple structures that correspond to different job families (like clerical, technical, and professional) or product divisions.

How are the data in Table 11.4 combined to develop a pay structure? First, it is important to note that both internal and external comparisons must be considered in making compensation decisions. However, because the pay structures suggested by internal and

**table 11.4**

Job Evaluation and Pay Survey Data

| JOB | KEY JOB? | JOB TITLE | JOB EVALUATION | SURVEY 1 (S1) | SURVEY 2 (S2) | SURVEY COMPOSITE (2/3*S1 + 1/3*S2) |
|---|---|---|---|---|---|---|
| A | y | Computer operator | 110 | $2,012 | $1,731 | $1,919 |
| B | y | Engineering tech I | 115 | 2,206 | 1,908 | 2,106 |
| C | y | Computer programmer | 155 | 2,916 | 2,589 | 2,807 |
| D | n | Engineering tech II | 165 | — | — | — |
| E | n | Compensation analyst | 170 | — | — | — |
| F | y | Accountant | 190 | 3,613 | 3,099 | 3,442 |
| G | y | Systems analyst | 210 | 4,275 | 3,854 | 4,134 |
| H | n | Computer programmer—senior | 225 | — | — | — |
| I | y | Director of personnel | 245 | 4,982 | 4,506 | 4,823 |
| J | y | Accountant—senior | 255 | 5,205 | 4,270 | 4,893 |
| K | y | Systems analyst—senior | 270 | 5,868 | 5,652 | 5,796 |
| L | y | Industrial engineer | 275 | 5,496 | 4,794 | 5,262 |
| M | n | Chief accountant | 315 | — | — | — |
| N | y | Senior engineer | 320 | 7,026 | 6,572 | 6,875 |
| O | n | Senior scientist | 330 | — | — | — |

SOURCE: Adapted from S. Rynes, B. Gerhart, G. T. Milkovich, and J. Boudreau, *Current Compensation Professional Institute* (Scottsdale, AZ: American Compensation Association, 1988). Reprinted with permission.

external comparisons do not necessarily converge, employers must carefully balance them. Studies suggest that employers may differ significantly in the degree to which they place priority on internal- or external-comparison data in developing pay structures.[10]

At least three pay-setting approaches, which differ according to their relative emphasis on external or internal comparisons, can be identified.[11]

### Market Survey Data

**Pay Policy Line**
A mathematical expression that describes the relationship between a job's pay and its job evaluation points.

The approach with the greatest emphasis on external comparisons (market survey data) is achieved by directly basing pay on market surveys that cover as many key jobs as possible. For example, the rate of pay for job A in Table 11.5 would be \$1,919; for job B, \$2,106; and for job C, \$2,807. For nonkey jobs (jobs D, E, H, M, and O), however, pay survey information is not available, and we must proceed differently. Basically, we develop a market **pay policy line** based on the key jobs (for which there are both job evaluation and market pay survey data available). As Figure 11.1 shows, the data can be plotted with a line of best fit estimated. This line can be generated using a statistical procedure (regression analysis). Doing so yields the equation $-\$661 + \$22.69 \times$ job evaluation points. In other words, the predicted monthly salary (based on fitting a line to the key job data) is obtained by plugging the number of job evaluation points into this equation. Thus, for example, job D, a nonkey job, would have a predicted monthly salary of $-\$661 + \$22.69 \times 165 = \$3,083$.

As Figure 11.1 also indicates, it is not necessary to fit a straight line to the job evaluation and pay survey data. In some cases, a pay structure that provides increasing monetary rewards to higher-level jobs may be more consistent with the organization's goals or with the external market. For example, nonlinearity may be more appropriate

**table 11.5**
Pay Midpoints under Different Approaches

| JOB | KEY JOB? | JOB TITLE | JOB EVALUATION | (1) SURVEY + POLICY | (2) PAY MIDPOINTS POLICY | (3) GRADES |
|---|---|---|---|---|---|---|
| A | y | Computer operator | 110 | \$1,919 | \$1,835 | \$2,175 |
| B | y | Engineering tech I | 115 | 2,106 | 1,948 | 2,175 |
| C | y | Computer programmer | 155 | 2,807 | 2,856 | 3,310 |
| D | n | Engineering tech II | 165 | 3,083 | 3,083 | 3,310 |
| E | n | Compensation analyst | 170 | 3,196 | 3,196 | 3,310 |
| F | y | Accountant | 190 | 3,442 | 3,650 | 3,310 |
| G | y | Systems analyst | 210 | 4,134 | 4,104 | 4,444 |
| H | n | Computer programmer—senior | 225 | 4,444 | 4,444 | 4,444 |
| I | y | Director of personnel | 245 | 4,823 | 4,898 | 4,444 |
| J | y | Accountant—senior | 255 | 4,893 | 5,125 | 5,579 |
| K | y | Systems analyst—senior | 270 | 5,796 | 5,465 | 5,579 |
| L | y | Industrial engineer | 275 | 5,262 | 5,579 | 5,579 |
| M | n | Chief accountant | 315 | 6,486 | 6,486 | 6,713 |
| N | y | Senior engineer | 320 | 6,875 | 6,600 | 6,713 |
| O | n | Senior scientist | 330 | 6,826 | 6,826 | 6,713 |

SOURCE: Adapted from S. Rynes, B. Gerhart, G.T. Milkovich, and J. Boudreau, *Current Compensation Professional Institute* (Scottsdale, AZ: American Compensation Association, 1988). Reprinted with permission.

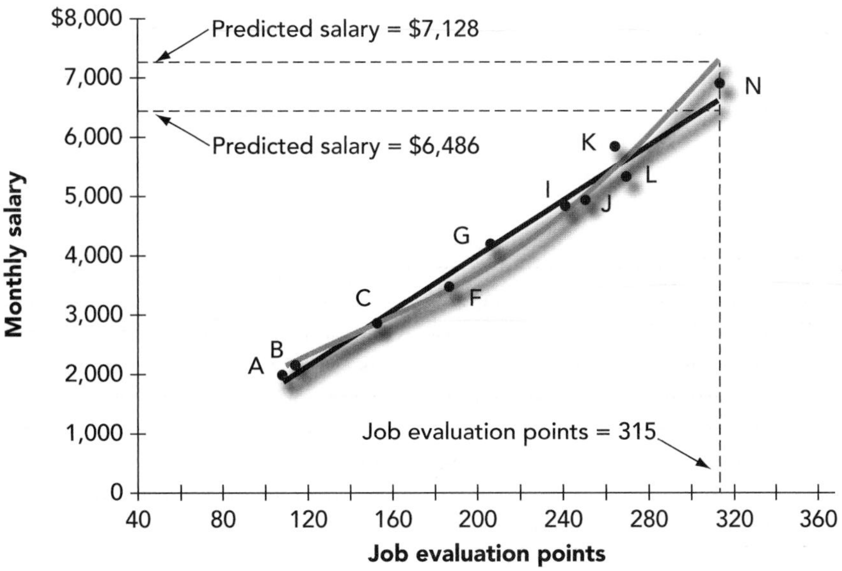


**figure 11.1**
Pay Policy Lines, Linear and Natural Logarithmic Functions

if higher-level jobs are especially valuable to organizations and the talent to perform such jobs is rare. The curvilinear function in Figure 11.1 is described by the equation

$$\text{Natural logarithm of pay} = \$6.98 + .006 \times \text{job evaluation points}$$

## Pay Policy Line

A second pay-setting approach that combines information from external and internal comparisons is to use the pay policy line to derive pay rates for both key and nonkey jobs. This approach differs from the first approach in that actual market rates are no longer used for key jobs. This introduces a greater degree of internal consistency into the structure because the pay of all the jobs is directly linked to the number of job evaluation points.

## Pay Grades

A third approach is to group jobs into a smaller number of pay classes or **pay grades.** Table 11.6 (see also Table 11.5, last column), for example, demonstrates one possibility: a five-grade structure. Each job within a grade would have the same rate range (that is,

**Pay Grades**
Jobs of similar worth or content grouped together for pay administration purposes.

**table 11.6**
Sample Pay Grade Structure

| | JOB EVALUATION POINTS RANGE | | MONTHLY PAY RATE RANGE | | |
|---|---|---|---|---|---|
| PAY GRADE | MINIMUM | MAXIMUM | MINIMUM | MIDPOINT | MAXIMUM |
| 1 | 100 | 150 | $1,740 | $2,175 | $2,610 |
| 2 | 150 | 200 | 2,648 | 3,310 | 3,971 |
| 3 | 200 | 250 | 3,555 | 4,444 | 5,333 |
| 4 | 250 | 300 | 4,463 | 5,579 | 6,694 |
| 5 | 300 | 350 | 5,370 | 6,713 | 8,056 |

would be assigned the same midpoint, minimum, and maximum). The advantage of this approach is that the administrative burden of setting separate rates of pay for hundreds (even thousands) of different jobs is reduced. It also permits greater flexibility in moving employees from job to job without raising concerns about, for example, going from a job having 230 job evaluation points to a job with 215 job evaluation points. What might look like a demotion in a completely job-based system is often a nonissue in a grade-based system. Note that the **range spread** (the distance between the minimum and maximum) is larger at higher levels, in recognition of the fact that performance differences are likely to have more impact on the organization at higher job levels. (See Figure 11.2.)

**Range Spread**
The distance between the minimum and maximum amounts in a pay grade.

The disadvantage of using grades is that some jobs will be underpaid and others overpaid. For example, job C and job F both fall within the same grade. The midpoint for job C under a grade system is $3,310 per month, or about $400 or so more than under the two alternative pay-setting approaches. Obviously, this will contribute to higher labor costs and potential difficulties in competing in the product market. Unless there is an expected return to this increased cost, the approach is questionable. Job F, on the other hand, is paid between $130 and $340 less per month under the grades system than it would be otherwise. Therefore, the company may find it more difficult to compete in the labor market.

## Conflicts between Market Pay Surveys and Job Evaluation

**LO3**
Explain the Importance of Competitive Labor Market and Product Market Forces in Compensation Decisions.

An examination of Table 11.5 suggests that the relative worth of jobs is quite similar overall, whether based on job evaluation or pay survey data. However, some inconsistencies typically arise, and these are usually indicated by jobs whose average survey pay is significantly below or above the pay policy line. The closest case in Table 11.5 is job L, for which the average pay falls significantly below the policy line. One possible explanation is that a relatively plentiful supply of people in the labor market are capable of performing this job, so the pay needed to attract and retain them is lower than would be expected given the job evaluation points. Another kind of inconsistency occurs when market surveys show that a job is paid higher than the policy line (like job K). Again, this may reflect relative supply and demand, in this case driving pay higher.

or lower

**figure 11.2**
Sample Pay Grade Structure

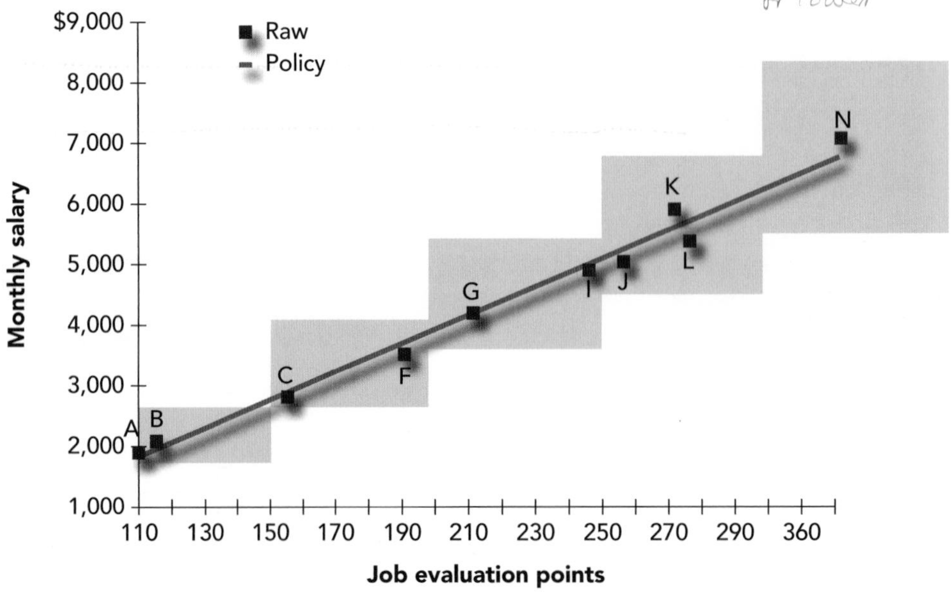

How are conflicts between external and internal equity resolved, and what are the consequences? The example of the vice presidents of marketing and information technology may help illustrate the type of choice faced. The marketing VP job may receive the same number of job evaluation points, but market survey data may indicate that it typically pays less than the information-technology VP job, perhaps because of tighter supply for the latter. Does the organization pay based on the market survey (external comparison) or on the job evaluation points (internal comparison)?

Emphasizing the internal comparison would suggest paying the two VPs the same. In doing so, however, either the VP of marketing would be "overpaid" or the VP of information technology would be "underpaid." The former drives up labor costs (product market problems); the latter may make it difficult to attract and retain a quality VP of information technology (labor market problems).

Another consideration has to do with the strategy of the organization. In some organizations (like Pepsi and Nike) the marketing function is critical to success. Thus, even though the market for marketing VPs is lower than that for information technology VPs, an organization may choose to be a pay leader for the marketing position (pay at the 90th percentile, for example) but only meet the market for the information technology position (perhaps pay at the 50th percentile). In other words, designing a pay structure requires careful consideration of which positions are most central to dealing with critical environmental challenges and opportunities in reaching the organization's goals.[12]

What about emphasizing external comparisons? Two potential problems arise. First, the marketing VP may be dissatisfied because she expects a job of similar rank and responsibility to that of the information technology VP to be paid similarly. Second, it becomes difficult to rotate people through different VP positions (for training and development) because going to the marketing VP position might appear as a demotion to the VP of information technology.

There is no one right solution to such dilemmas. Each organization must decide which objectives are most essential and choose the appropriate strategy. However, there seems to be a growing sentiment that external comparisons deserve greater weight because organizations are finding it increasingly difficult to ignore market competitive pressures.

## Monitoring Compensation Costs

Pay structure influences compensation costs in a number of ways. Most obviously, the pay level at which the structure is pegged influences these costs. However, this is only part of the story. The pay structure represents the organization's intended policy, but actual practice may not coincide with it. Take, for example, the pay grade structure presented earlier. The midpoint for grade 1 is $2,175, and the midpoint for grade 2 is $3,310. Now, consider the data on a group of individual employees in Table 11.7. One frequently used index of the correspondence between actual and intended pay is the **compa-ratio,** computed as follows:

Grade compa-ratio = Actual average pay for grade/Pay midpoint for grade

**Compa-Ratio**
An index of the correspondence between actual and intended pay.

The compa-ratio directly assesses the degree to which actual pay is consistent with the pay policy. A compa-ratio less than 1.00 suggests that actual pay is lagging behind the policy, whereas a compa-ratio greater than 1.00 indicates that pay (and costs) exceeds that of the policy. Although there may be good reasons for compa-ratios to differ from 1.00, managers should also consider whether the pay structure is allowing costs to get out of control.

**table 11.7**
Compa-Ratios for Two Grades

| EMPLOYEE | JOB | PAY | MIDPOINT | EMPLOYEE COMPA-RATIOS |
|---|---|---|---|---|
| | **Grade 1** | | | |
| 1 | Engineering tech I | $2,306 | $2,175 | 1.06 |
| 2 | Computer programmer | 2,066 | 2,175 | .95 |
| 3 | Engineering tech I | 2,523 | 2,175 | 1.16 |
| 4 | Engineering tech I | 2,414 | 2,175 | 1.11 |
| | | | | **1.07** |
| | **Grade 2** | | | |
| 5 | Computer programmer | 3,906 | 3,310 | 1.18 |
| 6 | Accountant | 3,773 | 3,310 | 1.14 |
| 7 | Accountant | 3,674 | 3,310 | 1.11 |
| | | | | **1.15** |

## Globalization, Geographic Region, and Pay Structures

As Figure 11.3 shows, market pay structures can differ substantially across countries both in terms of their level and in terms of the relative worth of jobs. Compared with the labor markets in Germany and the United States, markets in Slovakia and Korea provide much lower levels of pay overall and much lower payoffs to skill, education, and advancement.

**figure 11.3**
Earnings in Selected Occupations in Four Countries

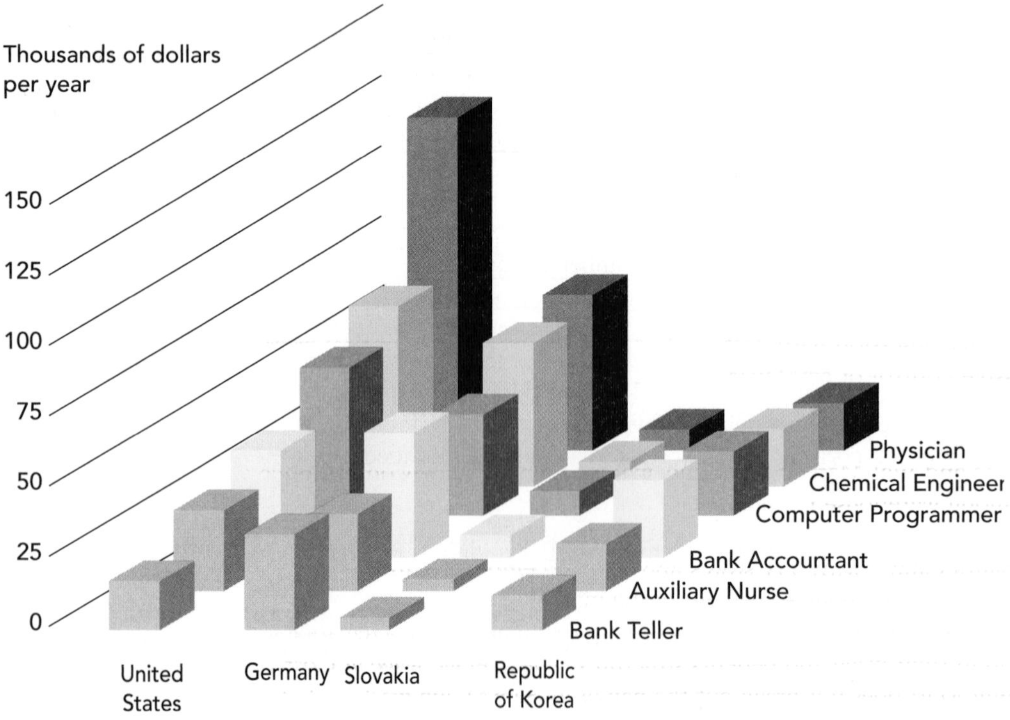


SOURCE: 2004 data from International Labor Organization Web site, at http://laborsta.ilo.org.

These differences create a dilemma for global companies. For example, should a German engineer posted to Korea be paid according to the standard in Germany or Korea? If the Germany standard is used, a sense of inequity is likely to exist among peers in Korea. If the Korea market standard is used, it may be all but impossible to find a German engineer willing to accept an assignment in Korea. Typically, expatriate pay and benefits (like housing allowance and tax equalization) continue to be linked more closely to the home country. However, this link appears to be slowly weakening and now depends more on the nature and length of the assignment.[13]

Geographic location is an important factor for Human Resources to consider when establishing a pay structure. Living in New York City is more expensive than other places, and employers need to factor in living costs when deciding upon salaries in order to hire a strong workforce.

Within the United States, Runzheimer International reports that 56 percent of companies have either a formal (30 percent) or informal (26 percent) policy that provides for pay differentials based on geographic location.[14] These differentials are intended to prevent inequitable treatment of employees who work in more expensive parts of the country. For example, according to Runzheimer, the cost of living index for New York City is 24 percent higher than in the average metropolitan area, whereas it is about average in Milwaukee. Therefore, an employee receiving annual pay of $50,000 in Milwaukee would require annual pay of more than $60,000 in New York City to retain the same purchasing power. The most common approach (74 percent of companies) is to move an employee higher in the pay structure to compensate for higher living costs. However, the drawback of this approach is that it may be difficult to adjust the salary downward if costs in that location fall or the employee moves to a lower-cost area. Thus 22 percent of the companies choose to pay an ongoing supplement that changes or disappears in the event of such changes.

## EVIDENCE-BASED HR

Wal-Mart's legendary obsession with cost containment shows up in countless ways, including aggressive control of employee benefits and wages. Managing labor costs isn't a crazy idea, of course. But stingy pay and benefits don't necessarily translate into lower costs in the long run.

Consider Costco and Wal-Mart's Sam's Club, which compete fiercely on low-price merchandise. Among warehouse retailers, Costco—with 338 stores and 67,600 full-time employees in the United States—is number one, accounting for about 50 percent of the market. Sam's Club—with 551 stores and 110,200 employees in the United States—is number two, with about 40 percent of the market.

Though the businesses are direct competitors and quite similar overall, a remarkable disparity shows up in their wage and benefits structures. The average wage at Costco is $17 an hour. Wal-Mart does not break out the pay of its Sam's Club workers, but a full-time worker at Wal-Mart makes $10.11 an hour on average, and a variety of sources suggest that Sam's Club's pay scale is similar to Wal-Mart's. A 2005 *New York Times* article by Steven Greenhouse reported that at $17 an hour, Costco's average pay is 42 percent higher than Sam's Club's ($9.86 an hour). Interviews that a colleague and I conducted with a dozen Sam's Club employees in San Francisco and Denver put the average hourly wage at about $10. And a 2004 *BusinessWeek* article by Stanley Holmes and Wendy Zellner estimated Sam's Club's average hourly wage at $11.52.

On the benefits side, 82 percent of Costco employees have health-insurance coverage, compared with less than half at Wal-Mart. And Costco workers pay just 8 percent of their health premiums, whereas Wal-Mart workers pay 33 percent of theirs. Ninety-one percent of Costco's employees are covered by retirement plans, with the company contributing an annual average of $1,330 per employee, while 64 percent of employees at Sam's Club are covered, with the company contributing an annual average of $747 per employee.

Costco's practices are clearly more expensive, but they have an offsetting cost-containment effect: Turnover is unusually low, at 17 percent overall and just 6 percent after one year's employment. In contrast, turnover at Wal-Mart is 44 percent a year—close to the industry average. In skilled and semiskilled jobs, the fully loaded cost of replacing a worker who leaves (excluding lost productivity) is typically 1.5 to 2.5 times the worker's annual salary. To be conservative, let's assume that the total cost of replacing an hourly employee at Costco or Sam's Club is only 60 percent of his or her annual salary. If a Costco employee quits, the cost of replacing him or her is therefore $21,216. If a Sam's Club employee leaves, the cost is $12,617. At first glance, it may seem that the low-wage approach at Sam's Club would result in lower turnover costs. But if its turnover rate is the same as Wal-Mart's, Sam's Club loses more than twice as many people as Costco does: 44 percent versus 17 percent. *By this calculation*, the total annual cost to Costco of employee churn is $244 million, whereas the total annual cost to Sam's Club is $612 million. That's $5,274 per Sam's Club employee, versus $3,628 per Costco employee.

In return for its generous wages and benefits, Costco gets one of the most loyal and productive workforces in all of retailing—and, probably not coincidentally, the lowest shrinkage (employee theft) figures in the industry. While Sam's Club and Costco generated $37 billion and $43 billion, respectively, in U.S. sales last year, Costco did it with 38 percent fewer employees—admittedly, in part by selling to higher-income shoppers and offering more high-end goods. As a result, Costco generated $21,805 in U.S. operating profit per hourly employee, compared with $11,615 at Sam's Club. Costco's stable, productive workforce more than offsets its higher costs.

These figures challenge the common assumption that labor rates equal labor costs. Costco's approach shows that when it comes to wages and benefits, a cost-leadership strategy need not be a race to the bottom.

SOURCE: W. F. Cascio, "The High Cost of Low Wages," *Harvard Business Review* 84 (December 2006) p. 23.

## The Importance of Process: Participation and Communication

**LO4**
Discuss the Significance of Process Issues Such as Communication in Compensation Management.

Compensation management has been criticized for following the simplistic belief that "if the right technology can be developed, the right answers will be found."[15] In reality, however, any given pay decision is rarely obvious to the diverse groups that make up organizations, regardless of the decision's technical merit or basis in theory. Of course, it is important when changing pay practices to decide which program or combination of programs makes most sense, but how such decisions are made and how they are communicated also matter.[16]

## Participation

Employee participation in compensation decision making can take many forms. For example, employees may serve on task forces charged with recommending and designing a pay program. They may also be asked to help communicate and explain its rationale. This is particularly true in the case of job evaluation as well as many of the programs discussed in the next chapter. To date, for what are perhaps obvious reasons, employee participation in pay level decisions remains fairly rare.

It is important to distinguish between participation by those affected by policies and those who must actually implement the policies. Managers are in the latter group (and often in the former group at the same time). As in other areas of human resource management, line managers are typically responsible for making policies work. Their intimate involvement in any change to existing pay practices is, of course, necessary.

## Communication

A dramatic example of the importance of communication was found in a study of how an organization communicated pay cuts to its employees and the effects on theft rates and perceived equity.[17] Two organization units received 15 percent across-the-board pay cuts. A third unit received no pay cut and served as a control group. The reasons for the pay cuts were communicated in different ways to the two pay-cut groups. In the "adequate explanation" pay-cut group, management provided a significant amount of information to explain its reasons for the pay cut and also expressed significant remorse. In contrast, the "inadequate explanation" group received much less information and no indication of remorse. The control group received no pay cut (and thus no explanation).

The control group and the two pay-cut groups began with the same theft rates and equity perceptions. After the pay cut, the theft rate was 54 percent higher in the "adequate explanation" group than in the control group. But in the "inadequate explanation" condition, the theft rate was 141 percent higher than in the control group. In this case communication had a large, independent effect on employees' attitudes and behaviors.

Communication is likely to have other important effects. We know, for example, as emphasized by equity theory that not only actual pay but the comparison standard influences employee attitudes.[18] Under two-tier wage plans, employees doing the same jobs are paid two different rates, depending on when they were hired. Moreover, the lower-paid employees do not necessarily move into the higher-paying tier. Common sense might suggest that the lower-paid employees would be less satisfied, but this is not necessarily true. In fact, a study by Peter Cappelli and Peter Sherer found that the lower-paid employees were more satisfied on average.[19] Apparently, those in the lower tier used different (lower) comparison standards than those in the higher tier. The lower-tier employees compared their jobs with unemployment or lower-paying jobs they had managed to avoid. As a result, they were more satisfied, despite being paid less money for the same work. This finding does not mean that two-tier wage plans are likely to be embraced by an organization's workforce. It does, however, support

## COMPETING THROUGH TECHNOLOGY
### UW Salary Data Taken Offline

The University of Wisconsin System has closed the book on making its salary data readily available online. As of December, only parts of the System's budget Redbook—the annual budget summaries for the System and all the individual campuses—are now posted.

System spokesman David Giroux says the move is primarily driven by institutional competitiveness and is part of an effort to stem the poaching of faculty members by other institutions who previously had easy access to salary information. "We see other universities around the country trying to pick off our young, up-and-coming faculty members and lure them away with more competitive offers. By making that information so widely available and even searchable . . . we were just making it much too easy for them," Giroux said.

Salary information, which by law is a matter of public record, is still available to anyone who asks, but getting it takes a little more effort than it used to. Ending a 10-year practice, it's no longer accessible at a click by anyone with an Internet connection.

Checking individual salaries now requires either a trip to the main library of any System institution, accessing the information through a System computer, contacting the human resources department of any System institution directly or plunking down $10 for the annual Redbook CD.

Giroux said the System is actually reverting to standards held by other state agencies. "We cannot and will not keep this information secret by law," Giroux said. "We will not, however, go above and beyond what's required by law. We're just taking reasonable steps to stem the flow of talent out of our universities."

SOURCE: H. LaRoi, "UW Salary Data Taken Offline," *Wisconsin State Journal*, March 7, 2007.

equity theory through its focus on the way employees compare their pay with other jobs and the need for managers to take this into consideration. Employees increasingly have access to salary survey information, which is likely to result in more comparisons and thus a greater need for effective communication.

Managers play the most crucial communication role because of their day-to-day interactions with their employees. Therefore, they must be prepared to explain why the pay structure is designed as it is and to judge whether employee concerns about the structure need to be addressed with changes to the structure. One common issue is deciding when a job needs to be reclassified because of substantial changes in its content. If an employee takes on more responsibility, she will often ask the manager for assistance in making the case for increased pay for the job.

# Current Challenges

## Problems with Job-Based Pay Structures

**LO5**
Describe New Developments in the Design of Pay Structures.

The approach taken in this chapter, that of defining pay structures in terms of jobs and their associated responsibilities, remains the most widely used in practice. However, job-based pay structures have a number of potential limitations.[20] First, they may encourage bureaucracy. The job description sets out specific tasks and activities for which the incumbent is responsible and, by implication, those for which the incumbent is not responsible. Although this facilitates performance evaluation and control by the manager, it can also encourage a lack of flexibility and a lack of initiative on the part of employees: "Why should I do that? It's not in my job description." Second, the structure's hierarchical nature reinforces a top-down decision making and information flow as well as status differentials, which do not lend themselves to taking advantage of the skills and knowledge of those closest to production. Third, the bureaucracy required to generate and update job descriptions and job evaluations can become a barrier to change because wholesale changes to job descriptions can involve a tremendous amount of time and cost. Fourth, the job-based pay structure may not reward desired behaviors, particularly in a rapidly changing environment where the knowledge, skills, and abilities needed yesterday may not be very helpful today and tomorrow. Fifth, the emphasis on job levels and status differentials encourages promotion-seeking behavior but may discourage lateral employee movement because employees are reluctant to accept jobs that are not promotions or that appear to be steps down.

## Responses to Problems with Job-Based Pay Structures

### Delayering and Banding

In response to the problems caused by job-based pay structures, some organizations are **delayering,** or reducing the number of job levels to achieve more flexibility in job assignments and in assigning merit increases. Pratt and Whitney, for example, changed from 11 pay grades and 3,000 job descriptions for entry-level through middle-management positions to 6 pay grades and several hundred job descriptions.[21] These broader groupings of jobs are also known as *broad bands*. Table 11.8 shows how banding might work for a small sample of jobs. IBM's change to broad bands was accompanied by a change away from a point-factor job evaluation system to a more streamlined approach to evaluating jobs, as Figure 11.4 shows.

**Delayering**
Reducing the number of job levels within an organization.

At the same time, IBM greatly reduced the bureaucratic nature of the system, going from 5,000 job titles and 24 salary grades to a simpler 1,200 jobs and 10 bands. Within their broad bands, managers were given more discretion to reward high performers and to choose pay levels that were competitive in the market for talent.

One possible disadvantage of delayering and banding is a reduced opportunity for promotion. Therefore, organizations need to consider what they will offer employees instead. In addition, to the extent that there are separate ranges within bands, the new structure may not represent as dramatic a change as it might appear. These distinctions can easily become just as entrenched as they were under the old system. Broad bands, with their greater spread between pay minimums and maximums, can also lead to weaker budgetary control and rising labor costs. Alternatively, the greater

**table 11.8**
Example of Pay Bands

| TRADITIONAL STRUCTURE | | BANDED STRUCTURE | |
|---|---|---|---|
| GRADE | TITLE | BAND | TITLE |
| 14 | Senior accountant | 6 | Senior accountant |
| 12 | Accountant III | | |
| 10 | Accountant II | 5 | Accountant |
| 8 | Accountant I | | |

SOURCE: P. LeBlanc, *Perspectives in Total Compensation 3*, no. 3 (March 1992), pp. 1–6. Used with permission of the National Practice Director, Sibson & Company, Inc.

**figure 11.4**

IBM's New Job Evaluation Approach

Below is an abbreviated schematic illustration of the new—and simple—IBM job evaluation approach:

**POSITION REFERENCE GUIDE**

| Band | Skills required | Leadership/Contribution | Scope/Impact |
|---|---|---|---|
| 1 | | | |
| 2 | | | |
| 3 | | | |
| 4 | | | |
| 5 | | | |
| 6 | | | |
| 7 | | | |
| 8 | | | |
| 9 | | | |
| 10 | | | |

**Factors: Leadership/Contribution**

Band 06: Understand the mission of the professional group and vision in own area of competence.

Band 07: Understand the departmental mission and vision.

Band 08: Understand departmental/functional mission and vision.

Band 09: Has vision of functional or unit mission.

Band 10: Has vision of overall strategies.

Both the bands and the approach are global. In the U.S., bands 1–5 are nonexempt; bands 6–10 are exempt. Each cell in the table contains descriptive language about key job characteristics. Position descriptions are compared to the chart and assigned to bands on a "best fit" basis. There are no points or scoring mechanisms. Managers assign employees to bands by selecting a position description that most closely resembles the work being done by an employee using an online position description library.

That's it!

SOURCE: A. S. Richter, "Paying the People in Black at Big Blue," *Compensation and Benefits Review,* May–June 1998, pp. 51–59. Copyright © 1998 by Sage Publications, Inc. Reprinted with permission of Sage Publications, Inc.

spread can permit managers to better recognize high performers with high pay. It can also permit the organization to reward employees for learning.

## Paying the Person: Pay for Skill, Knowledge, and Competency

A second, related response to job-based pay structure problems has been to move away from linking pay to jobs and toward building structures based on individual characteristics such as skill or knowledge.[22] Competency-based pay is similar but usually refers to a plan that covers exempt employees (such as managers). The basic idea is that if you want employees to learn more skills and become more flexible in the jobs they perform, you should pay them to do it. (See Chapter 7 for a discussion of the implications of skill-based pay systems on training.) According to Gerald Ledford, however, it is "a fundamental departure" because employees are now "paid for the skills they are capable of using, not for the job they are performing at a particular point in time."[23]

**Skill-Based Pay**
Pay based on the skills employees acquire and are capable of using.

**Skill-based pay** systems seem to fit well with the increased breadth and depth of skill that changing technology continues to bring.[24] For example, in a production environment, workers might be expected not only to operate machines but also to take responsibility for maintenance and troubleshooting, quality control, even modifying computer programs.[25] Toyota concluded years ago that "none of the specialists [e.g., quality inspectors, many managers, and foremen] beyond the assembly worker was actually adding any value to the car. What's more . . . assembly workers could probably do most of the functions of specialists much better because of their direct acquaintance with conditions on the line."[26]

In other words, an important potential advantage of skill-based pay is its contribution to increased worker flexibility, which in turn facilitates the decentralization of decision making to those who are most knowledgeable. It also provides the opportunity for leaner staffing levels because employee turnover or absenteeism can now be covered by current employees who are multiskilled.[27] In addition, multiskilled employees are important in cases where different products require different manufacturing processes or where supply shortages or other problems call for adaptive or flexible responses—characteristics typical, for example, of many newer so-called advanced manufacturing environments (like flexible manufacturing and just-in-time systems).[28] More generally, it has been suggested that skill-based plans also contribute to a climate of learning and adaptability and give employees a broader view of how the organization functions. Both changes should contribute to better use of employees' know-how and ideas. Consistent with the advantages just noted, a field study found that a change to a skill-based plan led to better quality and lower labor costs in a manufacturing plant.[29]

Of course, skill-based and competency-based approaches also have potential disadvantages.[30] First, although the plan will likely enhance skill acquisition, the organization may find it a challenge to use the new skills effectively. Without careful planning, it may find itself with large new labor costs but little payoff. In other words, if skills change, work design must change as quickly to take full advantage. Second, if pay growth is based entirely on skills, problems may arise if employees "top out" by acquiring all the skills too quickly, leaving no room for further pay growth. (Of course, this problem can also afflict job-based systems.) Third, and somewhat ironically, skill-based plans may generate a large bureaucracy—usually a criticism of job-based systems. Training programs need to be developed. Skills must be described, measured, and assigned monetary values. Certification tests must be developed to determine whether an employee has acquired a certain skill. Finally, as if the challenges in obtaining market rates under a job-based system were not enough, there is almost no body of knowledge regarding how to price combinations of skills (versus jobs) in the marketplace. Obtaining comparison data from other organizations will be difficult until skill-based plans become more widely used.

## Can the U.S. Labor Force Compete?

**LO6**
Explain Where the United States Stands from an International Perspective on Pay Issues.

We often hear that U.S. labor costs are simply too high to allow U.S. companies to compete effectively with companies in other countries. The average hourly labor costs (cash and benefits) for manufacturing production workers in the United States and in other advanced industrialized and newly industrialized countries are given in the following table in U.S. dollars:[31]

| | 1985 | 1990 | 1995 | 2000 | 2005 |
|---|---|---|---|---|---|
| **Industrialized** | | | | | |
| United States | $13.01 | $14.77 | $17.19 | $19.76 | $23.65 |
| Canada | 10.95 | 15.95 | 16.10 | 16.04 | 23.82 |
| Czech Republic | | | | 2.83 | 6.11 |
| Germany[a] | 9.57 | 21.53 | 30.26 | 23.38 | 33.00 |
| France | 7.52 | 15.49 | 20.01 | 15.70 | 24.63 |
| Japan | 6.43 | 12.64 | 23.82 | 22.27 | 21.76 |
| **Newly industrialized** | | | | | |
| Mexico | 1.60 | 1.80 | 1.51 | 2.08 | 2.63 |
| Hong Kong[b] | 1.73 | 3.20 | 4.82 | 5.63 | 5.65 |
| South Korea | 1.25 | 3.82 | 7.29 | 8.19 | 13.56 |
| China | | | | | 0.62[c] |

[a]West Germany for 1985 and 1990 data.
[b]Special Administrative Region of China.
[c]2004

Based solely on a cost approach, it would perhaps make sense to try to shift many types of production from a country like Germany to other countries, particularly the newly industrialized countries. Would this be a good idea? Not necessarily. There are several factors to consider.

## Instability of Country Differences in Labor Costs

First, note that relative labor costs are very unstable over time. For example, in 1985, U.S. labor costs were (13.01/9.57) or 36 percent greater than those of (West) Germany. But by 1990, the situation was reversed, with (West) German labor costs exceeding those of the United States by (21.53/14.77), or 46 percent, and remaining higher. Did German employers suddenly become more generous while U.S. employers clamped down on pay growth? Not exactly. Because all our figures are expressed in U.S. dollars, currency exchange rates influence such comparisons, and these exchange rates often fluctuate significantly from year to year. For example, in 1985, when German labor costs were 74 percent of those in the United States, the U.S. dollar was worth 2.94 German marks. But in 1990 the U.S. dollar was worth 1.62 German marks. If the exchange rate in 1990 were still 1 to 2.94, the average German hourly wage in U.S. dollars would have been $11.80, or about 80 percent of the U.S. average. In any event, relative to countries like Germany, U.S. labor costs are now a bargain; this explains, in part, decisions by BMW and Mercedes-Benz to locate production facilities in South Carolina and Alabama, respectively, where labor costs are lower than Germany's by a substantial amount. The euro, Germany's current currency, rose from €1 = US$.89 at the end of 2001 to €1 = US$1.19 by the end of 2005, reinforcing the rising labor cost in Germany relative to the United States (when expressed in U.S. dollars).

## Skill Levels

Second, the quality and productivity of national labor forces can vary dramatically. This is an especially important consideration in comparisons between labor costs in industrialized countries like the United States and developing countries like Mexico. For example, the high school graduation rate in the United States is 88 percent versus 25 percent in Mexico.[32] Thus, lower labor costs may reflect the lower average skill

## COMPETING THROUGH GLOBALIZATION

### Big Blue Shift: IBM Documents Give Rare Look at Sensitive Plans on "Offshoring"

In a rare look at the numbers and verbal nuances a big U.S. company chews over when moving jobs abroad, internal documents from International Business Machines Corp. show that it expects to save $168 million annually starting in 2006 by shifting several thousand high-paying programming jobs overseas.

Among other things, the documents indicate that for internal IBM accounting purposes, a programmer in China with three to five years experience would cost about $12.50 an hour, including salary and benefits. A person familiar with IBM's internal billing rates says that's less than one-fourth of the $56-an-hour cost of a comparable U.S. employee, which also includes salary and benefits.

According to the documents, which also provide managers with detailed advice on how to talk about the moves and their effect, IBM plans to shift the jobs from various U.S. locations to China, India and Brazil, where wages for skilled programmers are substantially lower.

But cheap labor is just part of the story. For IBM, globalization is about reorganizing its 200,000-strong services workforce along skill lines, not just geography, and about coordinating operations worldwide to deliver services that are better as well as cheaper. In essence, it's all about revamping the people supply chain.

Yes, this big shift is about Bangalore, but it's also about Tulsa, Okla., where modestly paid accounting specialists process paperwork for clients who want the tasks done in the United States; Boulder, Colo., where hard-to-find specialists fix problems in computers all over the world; and Yorktown Heights, N.Y., where scientists in IBM's unrivaled research labs dream up ways to take some of the labor out of tech services. "Some people think the world is centered in India, and that's it," says Senior Vice-President Robert W. Moffat Jr., who is in charge of the makeover. "Globalization is more than that. Our customers need us to put the right skills in the right place at the right time."

Here's how the thinking goes: In tech services, which account for half of IBM's $91 billion in annual revenues, low-cost labor is necessary but not sufficient. The company needs to bunch employees in competency centers (collections of people with specific skills) that are distributed around the world. That way it can take advantage of the low costs in some places, and in others have highly skilled employees in close proximity to customers. Rather than each country's business unit having its own workforce entirely, many people are drawn from the competency centers.

Here's just one example of how that can pay off: In the past, many software installations for clients' PCs were done for each machine individually by an IT employee who walked around from one machine to the next. The cost: about $70 per PC. Now, IBM has 200 people in Toronto running a software installation factory for clients worldwide. They assemble packages that are delivered to machines over the Net. The cost: 20 cents per PC.

The computing giant doesn't have the luxury of making these changes gradually. Indian tech companies, with their low costs and high quality, have rewritten the rules of competition in the $650 billion tech-services industry. Under this assault, IBM's services revenues declined 1.2 percent in the first quarter, to $11.6 billion. IBM and other Western tech-services giants are being forced to realign their workforces. "After years of putting their head in the sand, they're seeing it as a compelling threat," says Nandan M. Nilekani, chief executive of Infosys Technologies Ltd., one of the top Indian players. "They're acknowledging the megatrends but not moving fast enough."

It's too early to call the endgame. IBM and other Western outfits have deep ties with customers and vast resources of talent, so analysts expect the competition to be fierce. Most anticipate that IBM and Accenture will be among the winners, along with a handful of Indian companies. But they warn that IBM should take nothing for granted. "They still have a huge way to go to be cost- and price-competitive," says analyst Paul Roehrig of market researcher Forrester Research.

IBM's human resources department has prepared a draft "suggested script" for managers to use in telling employees that their jobs are being moved. The managers will tell the employees that "this is not a resource action"—IBM language for layoff—and that they will help the employees try to find a job elsewhere in IBM, although they can't promise to pay for any needed relocation.

IBM's competitors are making similar moves. Accenture Ltd., one of IBM's main rivals in the computer-services field, said recently it expects to double its workforce in India this year to nearly 10,000. Google Inc., the online search leader, said last month that it plans to open an engineering center in India this year as part of an expansion.

For all these companies, lower-cost labor is the biggest lure.

A chart of internal billing rates developed by IBM's Chinese group in Shanghai shows how dramatic the labor savings can be. The chart doesn't show actual wages, but instead reflects IBM's internal system by which one unit bills another for the work it does.

Besides the low-level programmers billing at $12.50 an hour, the chart shows that a Chinese senior analyst or application-development manager with more than five years experience would be billed at $18 an hour. The person familiar with IBM's operations said that person would be equivalent to a U.S. "Band 7" employee billed at about $66 an hour. And a Chinese project manager with seven years experience would be billed at $24 an hour, equivalent to a U.S. "Band 8" billed at about $81 hourly.

According to the IBM documents, the company expects severance costs for laying off U.S. employees in conjunction with the plan to be $30.6 million in 2004 and $47.4 million in 2005. Including other transition costs, the documents say, the offshoring plan will result in a loss of $19 million this year. Savings will amount to $40 million in 2005 and $168 million annually thereafter.

SOURCES: From *The Wall Street Journal, Online*, by William M. Bulkeley. Copyright 2004 by Dow Jones & Co., Inc. Reproduced with permission of Dow Jones & Co., Inc. via Copyright Clearance Center; and S. Hamm "Big Blue Shift," *BusinessWeek*, June 5, 2006.

level of the workforce; certain types of skilled labor may be less available in low-labor-cost countries. On the other hand, any given company needs only enough skilled employees for its own operations. Some companies have found that low labor costs do not necessarily preclude high quality.

## Productivity

Third, and most directly relevant, are data on comparative productivity and unit labor costs, essentially meaning labor cost per hour divided by productivity per hour worked. One indicator of productivity is gross domestic product (or total output of the economy) per person, adjusted for differences in purchasing power. On this measure, the United States fares well. These figures (in U.S. dollars) for 2005 are represented in Figure 11.5. The combination of lower labor costs and higher productivity translates into lower unit labor costs in the United States than in Japan and western Europe.[33]

## Nonlabor Considerations

Fourth, any consideration of where to locate production cannot be based on labor considerations alone. For example, although the average hourly labor cost in Country A may be $15 versus $10 in Country B, if labor costs are 30 percent of total operating costs and nonlabor operating costs are roughly the same, then the total operating costs might be $65 (50 + 15) in Country A and $60 (50 + 10) in Country B. Although labor costs in Country B are 33 percent less, total operating costs

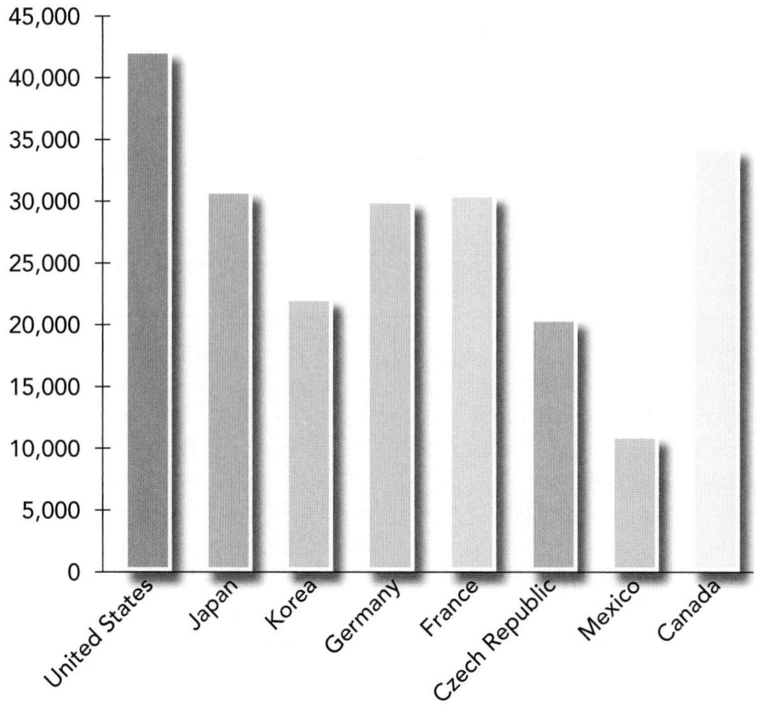


SOURCE: Annual National Accounts, www.oecd.org.

**figure 11.5**
Gross Domestic Product per Person, 2005

are only 7.7 percent less. This may not be enough to compensate for differences in skills and productivity, customer wait time, transportation costs, taxes, and so on. Further, the direct labor component of many products, particularly high-tech products (such as electronic components), may often be 5 percent or less. Thus the effect on product price competitiveness may be insignificant.[34]

In fact, an increasing number of organizations have decided that it is more important to focus on nonlabor factors in deciding where to locate production. Product development speed may be greater when manufacturing is physically close to the design group. Quick response to customers (like making a custom replacement product) is difficult when production facilities are on the other side of the world. Inventory levels can be dramatically reduced through the use of manufacturing methods like just-in-time production, but suppliers need to be in close physical proximity.

## Executive Pay

**LO7**
Explain the Reasons for the Controversy over Executive Pay.

The issue of executive pay has been given widespread attention in the press. In a sense, the topic has received more coverage than it deserves because there are very few top executives and their compensation accounts for only a small share of an organization's total labor costs. On the other hand, top executives have a disproportionate ability to influence organization performance, so decisions about their compensation are critical. Top executives also help set the tone or culture of the organization. If, for example, the top executive's pay seems unrelated to the organization's performance, staying high even when business is poor, employees may not understand why some of their pay should be at risk and depend on how the organization is performing.

## COMPETING THROUGH SUSTAINABILITY

### No Hair Shirts, but Still . . .

Susan Lyne knows the power of a public statement. As chief executive of Martha Stewart Living Omnimedia Inc. since late 2004, she has run the company through Stewart's jail term and much publicized comeback. With ad pages in the flagship magazine up 44 percent last year and a flurry of new deals sparking optimism for the brand, Lyne got a cash bonus of $625,500 last year. Instead of pocketing it, though, she asked the board to give $200,000 to a bonus pool for employees and convert the rest into restricted shares that won't fully vest until 2009.

Lyne says she wanted to recognize the efforts of employees because her plan to boost the company's long-term health cut into annual bonuses. More important, she felt the gesture would be a potent symbol. "There was a period of time in the 1990s when the bigger your pay package, the more people respected you," says Lyne, who earned a $900,000 salary in 2005. "I think that has changed—dramatically. There's a very different sense of what makes a good leader of a public company."

At a time when most news on CEO pay spotlights wretched excess, Lyne's move is an example of something far rarer: executive sacrifice. But she's not the only chief trying to earn some goodwill through compensation. General Electric Co.'s Jeffrey R. Immelt made $3.2 million in base pay in 2005 but converted his $6 million cash bonus into stock grants that materialize only if he meets cash flow and shareholder-return targets over the next two years. As Immelt wrote to share holders in GE's annual report: "I am totally aligned with you."

Other chiefs feel their recent performance doesn't warrant a raise. David Freeman, CEO of Lydall Inc., a Manchester (Conn.) maker of specially engineered products, asked that his salary not be raised and his maximum bonus be cut to 60 percent from 100 percent of his $420,000 base for 2006. More execs are trying to "flip the equation and turn their pay into an opportunity to make a positive statement," says Steve Harris, a worldwide partner at Mercer Human Resource Consulting LLC.

**More Scrutiny**

Could it be that a hint of shame is entering the corner office? Let's not be rash. Median CEO compensation at 200 of the country's largest companies rose 10 percent last year, to $8.4 million, according to pay consultant Pearl Meyer & Partners. But the give-backs may indicate a growing sensitivity surrounding pay. Compensation committees of increasingly independent boards don't want to be embarrassed. And the Securities and Exchange Commission is about to require more pay disclosure. Ira Kay, who heads the compensation practice for benefits consultant Watson Wyatt Worldwide Inc., predicts that the SEC's proposed rules will prompt "50 percent if not 75 percent" of companies to make noticeable changes to their pay practices.

Despite skepticism that more disclosure will have any impact on pay, there's growing evidence that CEOs and directors may be embarrassable. Some CEOs forgo pay after demanding big sacrifices of their workers. Robert S. Miller Jr. of bankrupt auto parts supplier Delphi Corp. cut his salary to $1 a year after asking for cuts of up to 40 percent from hourly workers. Doug Parker of US Airways Group Inc. declined a $770,000 bonus to reflect the pain many of his employees have endured.

Shareholder activists such as Brandon Rees, an analyst at the AFL-CIO, argue that seemingly noble gestures may be window dressing: "Too often it's a publicity stunt." And he thinks changes cast as voluntary may in fact be quietly forced by the board. "For once," Rees says, "I want to see a board of directors stand up and say: 'This CEO asked for too much money, and we said no.'"

SOURCE: D. Brady, "No Hair Shirts, but Still . . . The Uproar over CEO Pay Hits Home as Some Chiefs Take Less than They Could," *BusinessWeek*, May 1, 2006, p. 36.

**table 11.9**

CEO Compensation

| YEAR | SALARY PLUS BONUS | LONG-TERM COMPENSATION | TOTAL COMPENSATION | CHANGE IN PAY | CHANGE IN S&P 500* | CEO/WORKER** |
|---|---|---|---|---|---|---|
| 2005 | — | — | $10.9 million | 7% | 4.9% | 350[a] |
| 2004 | — | — | 10.2 million | —[b] | 10.9 | 337 |
| 2003 | — | — | 8.1 million | 9 | 29 | 276 |
| 2002 | — | — | 7.4 million | −33 | −22 | 259 |
| 2001 | — | — | 11.0 million | −16 | −12 | 397 |
| 2000 | $2.7 million[a] | $10.4 million[a] | 13.1 million | 6 | −9 | 484 |
| 1999 | 2.3 million | 10.1 million | 12.4 million | 17 | 21 | 475 |
| 1998 | 2.1 million | 8.5 million | 10.6 million | 36 | 27 | 419 |
| 1997 | 2.2 million | 5.6 million | 7.8 million | 35 | 31 | 326 |
| 1996 | 2.3 million | 3.2 million | 5.8 million | 54 | 23 | 209 |

*Change in market value of the Standard & Poor's 500 group of companies.

**Ratio of CEO pay to hourly employee pay.

[a]Estimated.

[b]Not computed because *Forbes* and *BusinessWeek* pay estimates not sufficiently comparable.

SOURCE: 1996–2003 data from annual special issue of *BusinessWeek;* 2004–2005 data from annual special issue of *Forbes.*

**table 11.10**

Highest-Paid CEOs

| | TOTAL COMPENSATION |
|---|---|
| Richard D. Fairbank, Capital One Financial | $249 million |
| Terry S. Semel, Yahoo | 230 million |
| Henry R. Silverman, Cendant | 140 million |

SOURCE: Data from April 20, 2006, issue of *Forbes.*

How much do executives make? Table 11.9 provides some data. Long-term compensation, typically in the form of stock plans, is the major component of CEO pay, which means that CEO pay varies with the performance of the stock market (see the "change in S&P 500" column). Table 11.10 shows that some CEOs are paid well above the averages shown in Table 11.9.

As Table 11.11 shows, U.S. top executives are also the highest paid in the world. (These figures are lower than those from *BusinessWeek* and *Forbes* because the latter reports pertain to larger companies.) The fact that the differential between top-executive pay and that of an average manufacturing worker is so much higher in the United States than in some other countries has been described as creating a "trust gap"—that is, in employees' minds, a "frame of mind that mistrusts senior management's intentions, doubts its competence, and resents its self-congratulatory pay." The issue becomes more salient when many of the same companies with high executive pay simultaneously engage in layoffs or other forms of employment reduction. Employees might ask, "If the company needs to cut costs, why not cut executive pay rather than our jobs?"[35] The issue is one of perceived fairness. One study, in fact, reported that business units with higher pay differentials between executives and rank-and-file

**table 11.11**

Total Remuneration of CEOs in Selected Countries (U.S. dollars)

| COUNTRY | CEO TOTAL REMUNERATION | CEO/MANUFACTURING EMPLOYEE TOTAL REMUNERATION MULTIPLE |
|---|---|---|
| United States | $2,160,000 | 39 |
| Canada | 1,100,000 | 24 |
| Mexico | 1,000,000 | 60 |
| Brazil | 849,000 | 60 |
| Argentina | 431,000 | 45 |
| France | 1,200,000 | 23 |
| Germany | 1,180,000 | 20 |
| China | 211,000 | 36 |
| India | 291,000 | 51 |
| Japan | 543,000 | 11 |
| Korea | 584,000 | 23 |

Notes: Data based on a company with $500 million in sales; total remuneration includes salary, bonus, company contributions, perquisites, and long-term incentives. Table 11.11 values are based on much smaller companies than those in Table 11.9, thus explaining the table differences.
SOURCE: Towers Perrin, "2005–2006 Worldwide Total Remuneration," Stamford, CT, 2006.

employees had lower customer satisfaction, which was speculated to result from employees' perceptions of inequity coming through in customer relations.[36] Perhaps more important than how much top executives are paid is how they are paid (i.e., whether performance-based). This is an issue we return to in the next chapter.

## Government Regulation of Employee Compensation

### Equal Employment Opportunity

**LO8**
Describe the Regulatory Framework for Employee Compensation.

Equal Employment Opportunity (EEO) regulation (such as Title VII and the Civil Rights Act) prohibits sex- and race-based differences in employment outcomes such as pay, unless justified by business necessity (like pay differences stemming from differences in job performance). In addition to regulatory pressures, organizations must deal with changing labor market and demographic realities. At least two trends are directly relevant in discussing EEO. First, women have gone from 33 percent of all employees in 1960 to 47 percent in 2007. Second, between 1960 and 2007, whites have gone from 90 percent to 82 percent of all employees. The percentage of white males in organizations will probably continue to decline, making attention to EEO issues in compensation even more important.

Is there equality of treatment in pay determination? Typically, the popular press focuses on raw earnings ratios. For example, in 2006, among full-time workers, the ratio of female-to-male median earnings was .81, the ratio of black-to-white earnings was .80, and Hispanic–Latino-to-white earnings was .70.[37] These percentages have generally risen over the last two to three decades, but significant race and sex differences in pay clearly remain.[38]

The usefulness of raw percentages is limited, however, because some portion of earnings differences arises from differences in legitimate factors: education, labor market experience, and occupation. Adjusting for such factors reduces earnings differences based on race and sex, but significant differences remain. With few exceptions, such adjustments rarely account for more than half of the earnings differential.[39]

What aspects of pay determination are responsible for such differences? In the case of women, it is suggested that their work is undervalued. Another explanation rests on the "crowding" hypothesis, which argues that women were historically restricted to entering a small number of occupations. As a result, the supply of workers far exceeded demand, resulting in lower pay for such occupations. If so, market surveys would only perpetuate the situation.

**Comparable Worth**
A public policy that advocates remedies for any undervaluation of women's jobs (also called *pay equity*).

**Comparable worth** (or pay equity) is a public policy that advocates remedies for any undervaluation of women's jobs. The idea is to obtain equal pay, not just for jobs of equal content (already mandated by the Equal Pay Act of 1963) but for jobs of equal value or worth. Typically, job evaluation is used to measure worth. Table 11.12, which is based on State of Washington data from one of the first comparable worth

**table 11.12**

Job Evaluation Points, Monthly Prevailing Market Pay Rates, and Proportion of Incumbents in Job Who Are Female

| BENCHMARK TITLE | MONTHLY EVALUATION POINTS | PREVAILING RATES[a] | PREVAILING RATE AS PERCENTAGE OF PREDICTED[b] | PERCENTAGE OF FEMALE INCUMBENTS |
|---|---|---|---|---|
| Warehouse worker | 97 | $1,286 | 109.1% | 15.4% |
| Truck driver | 97 | 1,493 | 126.6 | 13.6 |
| Laundry worker | 105 | 884 | 73.2 | 80.3 |
| Telephone operator | 118 | 887 | 71.6 | 95.7 |
| Retail sales clerk | 121 | 921 | 74.3 | 100.0 |
| Data entry operator | 125 | 1,017 | 82.1 | 96.5 |
| Intermediate clerk typist | 129 | 968 | 76.3 | 96.7 |
| Highway engineering tech | 133 | 1,401 | 110.4 | 11.1 |
| Word processing equipment operator | 138 | 1,082 | 83.2 | 98.3 |
| Correctional officer | 173 | 1,436 | 105.0 | 9.3 |
| Licensed practical nurse | 173 | 1,030 | 75.3 | 89.5 |
| Automotive mechanic | 175 | 1,646 | 120.4 | 0.0 |
| Maintenance carpenter | 197 | 1,707 | 118.9 | 2.3 |
| Secretary | 197 | 1,122 | 78.1 | 98.5 |
| Administrative assistant | 226 | 1,334 | 90.6 | 95.1 |
| Chemist | 277 | 1,885 | 116.0 | 20.0 |
| Civil engineer | 287 | 1,885 | 116.0 | 0.0 |
| Highway engineer 3 | 345 | 1,980 | 110.4 | 3.0 |
| Registered nurse | 348 | 1,368 | 76.3 | 92.2 |
| Librarian 3 | 353 | 1,625 | 90.6 | 84.6 |
| Senior architect | 362 | 2,240 | 121.8 | 16.7 |
| Senior computer systems analyst | 384 | 2,080 | 113.1 | 17.8 |
| Personnel representative | 410 | 1,956 | 101.2 | 45.6 |
| Physician | 861 | 3,857 | 128.0 | 13.6 |

[a]Prevailing market rate as of July 1, 1980. Midpoint of job range set equal to this amount.

[b]Predicted salary is based on regression of prevailing market rate on job evaluation points $2.43 × job evaluation points + 936.19, $r = .77$.

SOURCE: Reprinted with permission of *Public Personnel Management,* published by the International Personnel Management Association.

cases, suggests that measures of worth based on internal comparisons (job evaluation) and external comparisons (market surveys) can be compared. In this case many disagreements between the two measures appear. Internal comparisons suggest that women's jobs are underpaid, whereas external comparisons are less supportive of this argument. For example, although the licensed practical nurse job receives 173 job evaluation points and the truck driver position receives 97 points, the market rate (and thus the State of Washington employer rate) for the truck driver position is $1,493 per month versus only $1,030 per month for the nurse. The truck driver is paid nearly 127 percent more than the pay policy line would predict, whereas the nurse is paid only 75 percent of the pay policy line prediction.

One potential problem with using job evaluation to establish worth independent of the market is that job evaluation procedures were never designed for this purpose.[40] Rather, as demonstrated earlier, their major use is in helping to capture the market pay policy and then applying that to nonkey jobs for which market data are not available. In other words, job evaluation has typically been used to help apply the market pay policy, quite the opposite of replacing the market in pay setting.

As with any regulation, there are also concerns that EEO regulation obstructs market forces, which, according to economic theory, provide the most efficient means of pricing and allocating people to jobs. In theory, moving away from a reliance on market forces would result in some jobs being paid too much and others too little, leading to an oversupply of workers for the former and an undersupply for the latter. In addition, some empirical evidence suggests that a comparable worth policy would not have much impact on the relative earnings of women in the private sector.[41] One limitation of such a policy is that it targets single employers, ignoring that men and women tend to work for different employers.[42] To the extent that segregation by employer contributes to pay differences between men and women, comparable worth would not be effective. In other words, to the extent that sex-based pay differences are the result of men and women working in different organizations with different pay levels, such policies will have little impact.

Perhaps most important, despite potential problems with market rates, the courts have consistently ruled that using the going market rates of pay is an acceptable defense in comparable worth litigation suits.[43] The rationale is that organizations face competitive labor and product markets. Paying less or more than the market rate will put the organization at a competitive disadvantage. Thus there is no comparable worth legal mandate in the U.S. private sector. On the other hand, by the early 1990s, almost one-half of the states had begun or completed comparable worth adjustments to public-sector employees' pay. In addition, in 1988 the Canadian province of Ontario mandated comparable worth in both the private and public sectors. Further although comparable worth is not mandated in the U.S. private sector, the Department of Labor (Office of Federal Contracts Compliance) put into place new enforcement standards and guidelines in 2006 that prohibit race or sex-based "systemic compensation discrimination," which it defines as a situation "where there are statistically significant compensation disparities (as established by a regression analysis) between similarly situated employees, after taking into account the legitimate factors which influence compensation, such as: education, prior work experience, performance, productivity, and time in the job."[44]

Some work has focused on pinpointing where women's pay falls behind that of men. One finding is that the pay gap is wider where bonus and incentive payments (not just base salary) are examined. Other evidence indicates that women lose ground at the time they are hired and actually do better once they are employed for some time.[45] One interpretation is that when actual job performance (rather than the limited general qualification information available on applicants) is used in decisions, women may be less likely to encounter unequal treatment. If so, more attention needs to be devoted to ensuring fair treatment of applicants and new employees.[46] On the other hand, a "glass ceiling" is believed to exist in some organizations that allows women (and minorities) to come within sight of the top echelons of management, but not advance to them.

It is likely, however, that organizations will differ in terms of where women's earnings disadvantages arise. For example, advancement opportunities for women and other protected groups may be hindered by unequal access to the "old boy" or informal network. This, in turn, may be reflected in lower rates of pay. Mentoring programs have been suggested as one means of improving access. Indeed, one study found that mentoring was successful, having a significant positive effect on the pay of both men and women, with women receiving a greater payoff in percentage terms than men.[47]

## Minimum Wage, Overtime, and Prevailing Wage Laws

The 1938 **Fair Labor Standards Act (FLSA)** establishes a **minimum wage** for jobs that is $5.85 per hour as of July 2007, $6.25 per hour as of July 2008, and $7.25 per hour as of July 2009. State laws may specify higher minimum wages. The FLSA also permits a subminimum training wage that is approximately 85 percent of the minimum wage, which employers are permitted to pay most employees under the age of 20 for a period of up to 90 days.

**Fair Labor Standards Act (FLSA)**
The 1938 law that established the minimum wage and overtime pay.

**Minimum Wage**
The lowest amount that employers are legally allowed to pay; the 1990 amendment of the Fair Labor Standards Act permits a subminimum wage to workers under the age of 20 for a period of up to 90 days.

The FLSA also requires that employees be paid at a rate of one and a half times their hourly rate for each hour of overtime worked beyond 40 hours in a week. The hourly rate includes not only the base wage but also other components such as bonuses and piece-rate payments. The FLSA requires overtime pay for any hours beyond 40 in a week that an employer "suffers or permits" the employee to perform, regardless of whether the work is done at the workplace or whether the employer explicitly asked or expected the employee to do it. If the employer knows the employee is working overtime but neither moves to stop it nor pays time and a half, a violation of the FLSA may have occurred. A department store was the target of a lawsuit that claimed employees were "encouraged" to, among other things, write thank-you notes to customers outside of scheduled work hours but were not compensated for this work. Although the company denied encouraging this off-the-clock work, it reached an out-of-court settlement to pay between $15 million and $30 million in back pay (plus legal fees of $7.5 million) to approximately 85,000 sales representatives it employed over a three-year period.[48]

Executive, professional, administrative, outside sales and certain "computer employees" occupations are **exempt** from FLSA coverage. *Nonexempt* occupations are covered and include most hourly jobs. One estimate is that just over 20 percent of employees fall into the exempt category.[49] Exempt status depends on job responsibilities and salary. All exemptions (except for outside sales) require that an employee be paid no less than $455 per week. The job responsibility criteria vary. For example, the executive exemption is based on whether two or more people are supervised, whether there is authority to hire and fire (or whether particular weight is given to the employee's recommendations), and whether the employee's primary duty is managing the enterprise, recognized department, or subdivision of the enterprise. The Wage and Hour Division, Employment Standards Administration (www.dol.gov/esa), U.S. Department of Labor, and its local offices can provide further information on these definitions. (The exemptions do *not* apply to police, firefighters, paramedics, and first responders.)

**Exempt**
Employees who are not covered by the Fair Labor Standards Act. Exempt employees are not eligible for overtime pay.

Two pieces of legislation—the 1931 Davis-Bacon Act and the 1936 Walsh-Healy Public Contracts Act—require federal contractors to pay employees no less than the prevailing wages in the area. Davis-Bacon covers construction contractors receiving federal money of more than $2,000. Typically, prevailing wages have been based on relevant union contracts, partly because only 30 percent of the local labor force is required to be used in establishing the prevailing rate. Walsh-Healy covers all government contractors receiving $10,000 or more in federal funds.

Finally, employers must take care in deciding whether a person working on their premises is classified as an employee or independent contractor. We address this issue in Chapter 13.

## A Look Back

We began this chapter by showing how Toyota hopes to make its labor costs more competitive, while at the same time heading off employee relations problems and inequity perceptions through open communication. We also examined how IBM realigned its pay structure and global workforce to support changes to its strategy for competing in evolving markets. We have seen in this chapter that pay structure decisions influence the success of strategy execution by influencing costs, employee perceptions of equity, and the way that different structures provide flexibility and incentives for employees to learn and be productive.

**Questions**

1. What types of changes have the companies discussed in this chapter made to their pay structures to support execution of their business strategies?
2. Would other companies seeking to better align their pay structures with their business strategies benefit from imitating the changes made at these companies?

Please see the Video Case that corresponds to this chapter online at www.mhhe.com/noe6e.

## Summary

In this chapter we have discussed the nature of the pay structure and its component parts, the pay level, and the job structure. Equity theory suggests that social comparisons are an important influence on how employees evaluate their pay. Employees make external comparisons between their pay and the pay they believe is received by employees in other organizations. Such comparisons may have consequences for employee attitudes and retention. Employees also make internal comparisons between what they receive and what they perceive others within the organization are paid. These types of comparisons may have consequences for internal movement, cooperation, and attitudes (like organization commitment). Such comparisons play an important role in the controversy over executive pay, as illustrated by the focus of critics on the ratio of executive pay to that of lower-paid workers.

Pay benchmarking surveys and job evaluation are two administrative tools widely used in managing the pay level and job structure components of the pay structure, which influence employee social comparisons. Pay surveys also permit organizations to benchmark their labor costs against other organizations. Globalization is increasing the need for organizations to be competitive in both their labor costs and productivity.

The nature of pay structures is undergoing a fundamental change in many organizations. One change is the move to fewer pay levels to reduce labor costs and bureaucracy. Second, some employers are shifting from paying employees for narrow jobs to giving them broader responsibilities and paying them to learn the necessary skills.

Finally, a theme that runs through this chapter and the next is the importance of process in managing employee compensation. How a new program is designed, decided on, implemented, and communicated is perhaps just as important as its core characteristics.

## Key Terms

Pay structure, 486
Pay level, 486
Job structure, 486
Efficiency wage theory, 490
Benchmarking, 490
Rate ranges, 491
Key jobs, 491
Nonkey jobs, 492
Job evaluation, 492
Compensable factors, 492
Pay policy line, 494
Pay grades, 495
Range spread, 496
Compa-ratio, 497
Delayering, 503
Skill-based pay, 505
Comparable worth, 513
Fair Labor Standards Act (FLSA), 515
Minimum wage, 515
Exempt, 515

## Discussion Questions

1. You have been asked to evaluate whether your organization's current pay structure makes sense in view of what competing organizations are paying. How would you determine what organizations to compare your organization with? Why might your organization's pay structure differ from those in competing organizations? What are the potential consequences of having a pay structure that is out of line relative to those of your competitors?
2. Top management has decided that the organization is too bureaucratic and has too many layers of jobs to compete effectively. You have been asked to suggest innovative alternatives to the traditional "job-based" approach to employee compensation and to list the advantages and disadvantages of these new approaches.
3. If major changes of the type mentioned in question 2 are to be made, what types of so-called process issues need to be considered? Of what relevance is equity theory in helping to understand how employees might react to changes in the pay structure?
4. Are executive pay levels unreasonable? Why or why not?
5. Your company plans to build a new manufacturing plant but is undecided where to locate it. What factors would you consider in choosing in which country (or state) to build the plant?
6. You have been asked to evaluate whether a company's pay structure is fair to women and minorities. How would you go about answering this question?

## Self-Assessment Exercise

Consider your current job or a job you had in the past. For each of the following pay characteristics, indicate your level of satisfaction by using the following scale: 1 = very dissatisfied; 2 = somewhat dissatisfied; 3 = neither satisfied nor dissatisfied; 4 = somewhat satisfied; 5 = very satisfied.

____ 1. My take-home pay
____ 2. My current pay
____ 3. My overall level of pay
____ 4. Size of my current salary
____ 5. My benefit package
____ 6. Amount the company pays toward my benefits
____ 7. The value of my benefits
____ 8. The number of benefits I receive
____ 9. My most recent raise
____ 10. Influence my manager has over my pay
____ 11. The raises I have typically received in the past
____ 12. The company's pay structure
____ 13. Information the company gives about pay issues of concern to me
____ 14. Pay of other jobs in the company
____ 15. Consistency of the company's pay policies
____ 16. How my raises are determined
____ 17. Differences in pay among jobs in the company
____ 18. The way the company administers pay

These 18 items measure four dimensions of pay satisfaction. Find your total score for each set of item numbers to measure your satisfaction with each dimension.

*Pay Level*
Total of items 1, 2, 3, 4, 9, 11: ____________

*Benefits*
Total of items 5, 6, 7, 8: ____________

*Pay Structure and Administration*
Total of items 12, 13, 14, 15, 17, 18: ____________

*Pay Raises*
Total of items 10, 11, 16: ____________

Considering the principles discussed in this chapter, how could your company improve (or how could it have improved) your satisfaction on each dimension?

SOURCE: Based on H. G. Heneman III and D. P. Schwab, "Pay Satisfaction: Its Multidimensional Nature and Measurement," *International Journal of Psychology* 20 (1985), pp. 129–41.

## Exercising Strategy: Changing Compensation to Support Changes in Corporate Strategy

By realigning its strategy and compensation and benefits programs, Corning Inc., once a traditional economy company, hopes to compete successfully in the new economy. First, the company divested itself of several business units, including Corning Consumer Products. These divestitures reduced its annual revenues from $5 billion to $3 billion. Next Corning pursued a "high-octane" growth strategy in optical communications (optical fiber, cable systems, photo technologies, optical networking devices), environmental technologies, display technologies, and specialty materials. To support this shift in corporate strategy, Corning sought to support growth by creating an environment that bolstered innovation, risk taking, teaming, and speed. One major change was in its compensation system. The salary structure was streamlined from 11 grades to 5 broad bands for exempt employees and from 7 grades to 3 broad bands for nonexempt employees. In a new economy company, products have a short life cycle and change in markets is a way of life. This means that the nature of work also changes rapidly, so the detailed job descriptions and traditional promotion paths of the past may not fit this fluid environment. By changing its salary structure, Corning hopes to increase its ability to move quickly in responding to and anticipating customer needs in rapidly changing markets by encouraging flexibility, teamwork, and learning among its employees. Decentralizing more pay decisions to managers contributes to this flexibility, and giving employees an increasing stake in the success of the company by making more employees eligible for stock options contributes to the increased focus on teamwork. Finally, employee compensation is increasingly tied to individual employee learning and performance as the broad bands allow managers more flexibility to recognize outstanding achievements.

SOURCE: B. Parus, "How an Old Economy Company Became a New Economy Enterprise," *Workspan* 44:6 (June 2001), pp. 34–41.

### Questions

1. What are the pros and cons of Corning's new pay structure?
2. How did shifting product market conditions affect Corning's restructuring and its success?

## Managing People: From the Pages of *BusinessWeek*

BusinessWeek

### How Rising Wages Are Changing the Game in China

A labor shortage has pay soaring. That is sure to send ripples around the globe.

For years, Yongjin Group has earned a decent profit selling lamps and furniture to the likes of Wal-Mart, Home Depot, Target, and Pottery Barn. But lately the company has seen its margins shrink to 5 percent—half what Yongjin made when it opened its factory in the steamy southern Chinese city of Dongguan 14 years ago. Why? Labor shortages are forcing the company to boost wages. Last year salaries surged 40 percent, to an average of $160 a month, and Yongjin still can't find enough workers. "This business needs a lot of labor," says President Sam Lin. "This is a very tough challenge."

Some 1,500 miles northeast, in the city of Suzhou, Emerson Climate Technologies Co. is facing similar woes. The maker of air conditioner compressors has seen turnover for some jobs hit 20 percent annually, and Emerson General Manager David Warth says it's all he can do to keep his 800 employees from jumping ship to Samsung, Siemens, Nokia, and other multinationals that are now operating in the tech manufacturing hub. "It has gotten to the point that we are just swapping folks and raising salaries," says Warth.

Wait a minute. Doesn't China have an inexhaustible supply of cheap labor? Not any longer. From the textile and toy factories of the south to the corporate headquarters and research labs in Beijing and Shanghai, the No. 1 challenge today is finding and keeping good workers. Turnover in some low-tech industries approaches 50 percent, according to the Institute of Contemporary Observation, a Shenzhen labor research group. Guangdong Province says it has 2.5 million jobs that remain unfilled, while Jiangsu, Zhejiang, and Shandong provinces say they, too, face shortages of qualified workers. "Before, people talked about China's unlimited labor supply," says Zhang Juwei, deputy director of the Institute of Population & Labor Economics at the Chinese Academy of Social Sciences in Beijing. "We should revise that: China is facing a limited supply of labor."

Reports of labor shortages first cropped up in late 2004, but companies thought the phenomenon was temporary. Now a surge in both turnover and wage costs is convincing multinationals and their suppliers that the China game is changing permanently. With the gap between wages in China and those elsewhere gradually closing, the pressure to pass price increases on to consumers in the United States and other markets will start to build. As Citigroup noted in a February report: "The continuous growth of labor costs in China, even at a moderate pace . . . is likely to have implications for inflation worldwide." These factors eventually will force the Chinese to upgrade their entire industrial base to make higher-margin goods. And those bigger paychecks are building a consumer class in China that multinationals want to target.

### "There Is a Break Point"

The wage issue has started to affect how companies operate in China. U.S. corporations and their suppliers are starting to rethink where to locate facilities, whether deeper into the interior (where salaries and land values are smaller), or even farther afield, to lower-cost countries such as Vietnam or Indonesia. Already, higher labor costs are beginning to price some manufacturers out of more developed Chinese cities such as Shanghai and Suzhou. "There is a break point where people will say this is too expensive," says Michael Barbalas, general manager at the Suzhou plant of Andrew Corp., a Westchester (III.) maker of wireless networking gear. At his factory, he says, wages have been rising by 10 percent annually.

This is a slow process, to be sure. Imports from the mainland have yet to fuel inflation in the United States, while improved productivity in China has so far offset higher wages. But economists say those productivity gains are getting harder to find, and manufacturers who are seeing their margins hit, such as Yongjin, can hold out for only so long before they have to try to raise prices.

The pressure has as much to do with skills as it does with numbers. Although the total labor force is about 800 million, relatively few people have the qualifications employers want. For most textile, toy, and tech-assembly jobs, for example, export-oriented manufacturers prefer women from 18 to 25 years old or people with experience operating machinery. "The skills base does not meet the demands of a rapidly growing market," says C.P. Lee, Asia-Pacific human resources chief at Motorola Inc., which has 9,000 employees in China.

As a result, companies across the board are feeling the squeeze. Last year turnover at multinationals in China averaged 14 percent, up from 11.3 percent in 2004 and 8.3 percent in 2001. Salaries jumped by 8.4 percent, according to human resources consultant Hewitt Associates LLC. And a January report by the American Chamber of Commerce in China found that rising labor costs have pinched margins at 48 percent of U.S. manufacturers on the mainland. "China runs the risk of losing its advantage" of cheap labor, says Teresa Woodland, an author of the report.

That means managers can no longer simply provide eight-to-a-room dorms and expect laborers to toil 12 hours a day, seven days a week. When 30-year-old He Maofang first arrived in Dongguan in 2000, for instance, "work was hard to find." But now "there are plenty of choices," says He, who started at Yongjin last June. In addition to boosting salaries, Yongjin has upgraded its dormitories and improved the food in the company cafeteria. Despite those efforts, its five factories remain about 10 percent shy of the 6,000 employees they need.

Many companies are compensating for the shortages by penetrating deeper into China's vast heartland, where wages can be half what they are on the coast. General Motors, Honda, Motorola, and Intel, for instance, have all shifted some manufacturing or research to inland locations in recent years, both to tap lower costs and to open up new markets. But a two-year-old effort by the Chinese government to lift rural incomes through tax cuts is keeping some potential factory workers on the farm. So with investment growing in the interior, labor shortages are popping up there, too. "More and more multinationals are looking for opportunities in second-tier cities," boosting salaries there faster than in the traditional manufacturing strongholds farther east, says Jean Lin, head of the compensation practice at Hewitt.

### Better Training

The trend goes beyond the factory. Only about 10 percent of Chinese candidates for jobs in key areas such as finance, accounting, and engineering are qualified to work for a foreign company, estimates consultant McKinsey & Co. While China today has fewer than 5,000 managers with the skills needed by multinationals, 75,000 jobs for such managers are expected to be created over the next five years, McKinsey says. The talent crunch "is the No. 1 constraint on China's growth," says Andrew Grant, McKinsey's China chief. "It will hit earlier and be more powerful than any [other] constraint," such as raw materials shortages.

Some U.S. companies in China believe better education and training is the way to stay ahead of the game. Motorola regularly hires graduates straight from school and then trains them at its "Motorola University" in Beijing. Intel Corp., which has invested $1.3 billion in chip assembly, testing, and research and development in China, has backed initiatives that have trained 600,000 teachers there. "It helps contribute to our future workforce," says Intel China President Wee Theng Tan.

### Lower Energy Bills

Others are doing everything they can to retain employees. St. Louis-based Emerson has introduced flexible work hours at its Suzhou plant for workers with children. It has built a "green" office with solar power, ambitious recycling plans, and chargers for the electric bicycles used by many staffers. And to build loyalty the company holds quarterly parties for the entire staff and organizes free trips to resort areas. "I chose Emerson because it is a well-respected company," says 25-year-old Rocky Lu, who started as a technician at Emerson's Suzhou plant in February. He got a 50 percent raise from his last job, at a state enterprise, to nearly $400 a month.

Emerson is cutting costs elsewhere to ensure that rising wages don't price it out of Suzhou. It has lowered utility bills by raising the thermostat a couple of degrees in the summer and dropping the mercury in the winter while passing out long underwear to keep workers warm. It has added reflective light fixtures that can use lower-wattage bulbs. And it has recently tapped excess heat from its factory to warm dormitory showers. "So far it's an even tradeoff" between rising labor costs and efficiency gains, says Emerson manager Warth. "We have to deal with it if we want to remain in business."

Beijing realizes that it, too, needs to deal with the issue if it wants to stay in business. So the government is further loosening rules that prevent rural residents from moving to cities to work and is offering tax breaks to overseas Chinese who return to the mainland. The higher education system is also being overhauled to include more practical classes and vocational training in a bid to expand China's skilled workforce by a third, to 8 percent of the population. China will still be the world's workshop. But the world will need to adjust to the inexorable rise of the workshop's wages.

SOURCE: D. Roberts, "How Rising Wages Are Changing the Game in China," *BusinessWeek*, March 27, 2006, pp. 32ff.

### Questions

1. Is competing on the basis of labor cost a source of sustainable competitive advantage for a company? For a country? Why or why not?
2. For companies that use a motivational approach to job design and that involve workers in decisions, how important is the cost of a labor force relative to the skills of the labor force?
3. How are companies changing their human resource strategies and practices in an effort to control labor costs while at the same time improving worker skills?
4. As the competition for workers in China heats up, to what extent will employers need to change the terms and conditions (e.g., working hours) of the employment relationship they have with workers?

## NOTES


1. J. S. Adams, "Inequity in Social Exchange," in *Advances in Experimental Social Psychology*, ed. L. Berkowitz (New York: Academic Press, 1965); P. S. Goodman, "An Examination of Referents Used in the Evaluation of Pay," *Organizational Behavior and Human Performance* 12 (1974), pp. 170–95; C. O. Trevor and D. L. Wazeter, "A Contingent View of Reactions to Objective Pay Conditions: Interdependence among Pay Structure Characteristics and Pay Relative to Internal and External Referents," *Journal of Applied Psychology* 91 (2006), pp. 1260–1275.
2. J. B. Miner, *Theories of Organizational Behavior* (Hinsdale, IL: Dryden Press, 1980); B. Gerhart and S. L. Rynes, *Compensation: Theory, Evidence, and Strategic Implications* (Thousand Oaks, CA: Sage, 2003).
3. J. McCracken, "Desperate to Cut Costs, Ford Gets Union's Help," *The Wall Street Journal*, March 2, 2007; original data are from Harbour-FedEx Associates.
4. B. Gerhart and G. T. Milkovich, "Organizational Differences in Managerial Compensation and Financial Performance," *Academy of Management Journal* 33 (1990), pp. 663–91; E. L. Groshen, "Why Do Wages Vary among Employers?" *Economic Review* 24 (1988), pp. 19–38; Gerhart and Rynes, *Compensation*.
5. M. L. Williams, M. A. McDaniel, N. T. Nguyen, "A Meta-analysis of the Antecedents and Consequences of Pay Level Satisfaction," *Journal of Applied Psychology* 91 (2006), pp. 392–413; M. C. Sturman, C. O. Trevor, J. W. Boudreau, and B. Gerhart, "Is It Worth It to Win the Talent War? Evaluating the Utility of Performance-Based Pay," *Personnel Psychology* 56 (2003), pp. 997–1035; B. Klaas and J. A. McClendon, "To Lead, Lag or Match: Estimating the Financial Impact of Pay Level Policies," *Personnel Psychology* 49 (1996), pp. 121–41. S. C. Currall, A. J. Towler T. A. Judge, and L. Kohn, "Pay Satisfaction and Organizational Outcomes," *Personnel Psychology* 58 (2005), pp. 613–40; M. P. Brown, M. C. Sturman, and M. J. Simmering, "Compensation Policy and Organizational Performance: The Efficiency, Operational, and Financial Implications of Pay Levels and Pay Structures," *Academy of Management Journal* 46 (2003), pp. 752–62.
6. G. A. Akerlof, "Gift Exchange and Efficiency-Wage Theory: Four Views," *American Economic Review* 74 (1984), pp. 79–83; J. L. Yellen, "Efficiency Wage Models of Unemployment," *American Economic Review* 74 (1984), pp. 200–5.
7. S. L. Rynes and G. T. Milkovich, "Wage Surveys: Dispelling Some Myths about the 'Market Wage,'" *Personnel Psychology* 39 (1986), pp. 71–90.
8. B. Gerhart and G. T. Milkovich, "Employee Compensation: Research and Practice," in *Handbook of Industrial and Organizational Psychology*, 2nd ed., ed. M. D. Dunnette and L. M. Hough (Palo Alto, CA: Consulting Psychologists Press, 1992).
9. G. T. Milkovich and J. M. Newman, *Compensation*, 7th ed. (New York: Irwin/McGraw-Hill, 2002).
10. B. Gerhart, G. T. Milkovich, and B. Murray, "Pay, Performance, and Participation," in *Research Frontiers in Industrial Relations and Human Resources*, ed. D. Lewin, O. S. Mitchell, and P. D. Sherer (Madison, WI: IRRA, 1992).
11. C. H. Fay, "External Pay Relationships," in *Compensation and Benefits*, ed. L. R. Gomez-Mejia (Washington, DC: Bureau of National Affairs, 1989).
12. J. P. Pfeffer and A. Davis-Blake, "Understanding Organizational Wage Structures: A Resource Dependence Approach," *Academy of Management Journal* 30 (1987), pp. 437–55; M. A. Carpenter and J. B. Wade, "Micro-Level Opportunity Structures as Determinants of Non-CEO Executive Pay," *Academy of Management Journal* 45 (2002), pp. 1085–1103.
13. C. M. Solomon, "Global Compensation: Learn the ABCs," *Personnel Journal*, July 1995, p. 70; R. A. Swaak, "Expatriate Management: The Search for Best Practices," *Compensation and Benefits Review*, March–April 1995, p. 21.
14. *1997–1998 Survey of Geographic Pay Differential Policies and Practices* (Rochester, WI: Runzeimer International). Actually, data from the American Chamber of Commerce Research Association (ACCRA) estimate the cost of living in New York City (in 2001) to be 239.2, compared to 100 for the average metropolitan area.

15. E. E. Lawler III, *Pay and Organizational Development* (Reading, MA: Addison-Wesley, 1981).
16. R. Folger and M. A. Konovsky, "Effects of Procedural and Distributive Justice on Reactions to Pay Raise Decisions," *Academy of Management Journal* 32 (1989), pp. 115–30; H. G. Heneman III and T. A. Judge, "Compensation Attitudes," in S. L. Rynes and B. Gerhart, eds., *Compensation in Organizations* (San Francisco: Jossey-Bass (2002), pp. 61–103; J. Greenberg, "Determinants of Perceived Fairness of Performance Evaluations," *Journal of Applied Psychology* 71 (1986), pp. 340–42; H. G. Heneman III, "Pay Satisfaction," *Research in Personnel and Human Resource Management* 3 (1985), pp. 115–39.
17. J. Greenberg, "Employee Theft as a Reaction to Underpayment of Inequity: The Hidden Cost of Pay Cuts," *Journal of Applied Psychology* 75 (1990), pp. 561–68.
18. Adams, "Inequity in Social Exchange"; C. J. Berger, C. A. Olson, and J. W. Boudreau, "The Effect of Unionism on Job Satisfaction: The Role of Work-Related Values and Perceived Rewards," *Organizational Behavior and Human Performance* 32 (1983), pp. 284–324; P. Cappelli and P. D. Sherer, "Assessing Worker Attitudes under a Two-Tier Wage Plan," *Industrial and Labor Relations Review* 43 (1990), pp. 225–44; R. W. Rice, S. M. Phillips, and D. B. McFarlin, "Multiple Discrepancies and Pay Satisfaction," *Journal of Applied Psychology* 75 (1990), pp. 386–93.
19. Cappelli and Sherer, "Assessing Worker Attitudes."
20. R. M. Kanter, *When Giants Learn to Dance* (New York: Simon & Schuster, 1989); E. E. Lawler III, *Strategic Pay* (San Francisco: Jossey-Bass, 1990); "Farewell, Fast Track," *BusinessWeek*, December 10, 1990, pp. 192–200; R. L. Heneman, G. E. Ledford, Jr., and M. T. Gresham, "The Changing Nature of Work and Its Effects on Compensation Design and Delivery," in S. L. Rynes and B. Gerhart, eds., *Compensation in Organizations*.
21. P. R. Eyers, "Realignment Ties Pay to Performance," *Personnel Journal*, January 1993, p. 74.
22. Lawler, *Strategic Pay;* G. Ledford, "3 Cases on Skill-Based Pay: An Overview," *Compensation and Benefits Review*, March–April 1991, pp. 11–23; G. E. Ledford, "Paying for the Skills, Knowledge, Competencies of Knowledge Workers," *Compensation and Benefits Review*, July–August 1995, p. 55; Heneman et al., "The Changing Nature of Work."
23. Ledford, "3 Cases."
24. Heneman et al., "The Changing Nature of Work."
25. T. D. Wall, J. M. Corbett, R. Martin, C. W. Clegg, and P. R. Jackson, "Advanced Manufacturing Technology, Work Design, and Performance: A Change Study," *Journal of Applied Psychology* 75 (1990), pp. 691–97.
26. Womack et al., *The Machine That Changed the World*, p. 56.
27. Lawler, *Strategic Pay*.
28. Ibid.; Gerhart and Milkovich, "Employee Compensation."
29. B. C. Murray and B. Gerhart, "An Empirical Analysis of a Skill-Based Pay Program and Plant Performance Outcomes," *Academy of Management Journal* 41, no. 1 (1998), pp. 68–78.
30. Ibid.; N. Gupta, D. Jenkins, and W. Curington, "Paying for Knowledge: Myths and Realities," *National Productivity Review*, Spring 1986, pp. 107–23; J. D. Shaw, N. Gupta, A. Mitra, and G. E. Ledford, "Success and Survival of Skill-Based Pay Plans," *Journal of Management* 31 (2005), pp. 28–49.
31. Data from U.S. Bureau of Labor Statistics Web site, www.bls.gov.
32. *Education at a Glance—OECD Indicators 2001* (Paris: OECD, 2001).
33. C. Sparks and M. Greiner, "U.S. and Foreign Productivity and Labor Costs," *Monthly Labor Review*, February 1997, pp. 26–35.
34. E. Faltermayer, "U.S. Companies Come Back Home," *Fortune*, December 30, 1991, pp. 106ff; M. Hayes, "Precious Connection: Companies Thinking about Using Offshore Outsourcing Need to Consider More than Just Cost Savings," *Information Week Online*, www.informationweek.com (October 20, 2003).
35. A. Farnham, "The Trust Gap," *Fortune*, December 4, 1989, pp. 56ff; Scott McCartney, "AMR Unions Express Fury," *The Wall Street Journal*, April 17, 2003.
36. D. M. Cowherd and D. I. Levine, "Product Quality and Pay Equity between Lower-Level Employees and Top Management: An Investigation of Distributive Justice Theory," *Administrative Science Quarterly* 37 (1992), pp. 302–20.
37. Bureau of Labor Statistics, *Current Population Surveys* (Web site).
38. Bureau of Labor Statistics, U.S. Department of Labor, "Highlights of Women's Earnings in 2002," Report 972 (2003).
39. B. Gerhart, "Gender Differences in Current and Starting Salaries: The Role of Performance, College Major, and Job Title," *Industrial and Labor Relations Review* 43 (1990), pp. 418–33; G. G. Cain, "The Economic Analysis of Labor-Market Discrimination: A Survey," in *Handbook of Labor Economics*, ed. O. Ashenfelter and R. Layard (New York: North-Holland, 1986), pp. 694–785.
40. D. P. Schwab, "Job Evaluation and Pay-Setting: Concepts and Practices," in *Comparable Worth: Issues and Alternatives*, ed. E. R. Livernash (Washington, DC: Equal Employment Advisory Council, 1980).
41. B. Gerhart and N. El Cheikh, "Earnings and Percentage Female: A Longitudinal Study," *Industrial Relations* 30 (1991), pp. 62–78; R. S. Smith, "Comparable Worth: Limited Coverage and the Exacerbation of Inequality," *Industrial and Labor Relations Review* 61 (1988), pp. 227–39.
42. W. T. Bielby and J. N. Baron, "Men and Women at Work: Sex Segregation and Statistical Discrimination," *American Journal of Sociology* 91 (1986), pp. 759–99.
43. Rynes and Milkovich, "Wage Surveys"; G. T. Milkovich and J. Newman, *Compensation* (Homewood, IL: BPI/Irwin, 1993).
44. U.S. Department of Labor Web site, at www.dol.gov/esa/regs/compliance/ofccp/faqs/comstrds.htm.
45. Gerhart, "Gender Differences in Current and Starting Salaries"; B. Gerhart and G. T. Milkovich, "Salaries, Salary Growth, and Promotions of Men and Women in a Large, Private Firm," in *Pay Equity: Empirical Inquiries*, ed. R. Michael, H. Hartmann, and B. O'Farrell (Washington, DC: National Academy Press, 1989); K. W. Chauvin and R. A. Ash, "Gender Earnings Differentials in Total Pay, Base Pay, and Contingent Pay," *Industrial and Labor Relations Review* 47 (1994), pp. 634–49; M. M. Elvira and M. E. Graham, "Not Just a Formality: Pay System Formalization and Sex-Related Earnings Effects," *Organization Science* 13 (2002), pp. 601–17.
46. Gerhart, "Gender Differences in Current and Starting Salaries"; B. Gerhart and S. Rynes, "Determinants and Consequences of Salary Negotiations by Graduating Male and Female MBAs," *Journal of Applied Psychology* 76 (1991), pp. 256–62.
47. G. F. Dreher and R. A. Ash, "A Comparative Study of Mentoring among Men and Women in Managerial, Professional, and Technical Positions," *Journal of Applied Psychology* 75 (1990), pp. 539–46.
48. G. A. Patterson, "Nordstrom Inc. Sets Back-Pay Accord on Suit Alleging 'Off-the-Clock' Work," *The Wall Street Journal*, January 12, 1993, p. A2; for additional information on overtime legal issues, see A. Weintraub and J. Kerstetter, "Revenge of the Overworked Nerds," *BusinessWeek Online*, www.businessweek.com (December 8, 2003).
49. R. I. Henderson, *Compensation Management in a Knowledge-Based World* (Upper Saddle River, NJ: Prentice Hall, 2003).

12

CHAPTER

# Recognizing Employee Contributions with Pay

## LO LEARNING OBJECTIVES

After reading this chapter, you should be able to:

# Enter the World of Business

## Employers Increasingly Favor Bonuses to Raises

Employers are making employees work harder for their money. Most workers will receive modest raises this year and next, as employers reward employees with performance-linked bonuses rather than broad salary increases, according to a survey by consulting company Hewitt Associates Inc.

The economy and labor market are relatively strong, but employers are loath to increase fixed costs with raises. Employers are making more workers eligible for bonuses and have increased the share of their payroll devoted to variable pay in the past few years. The strategy parallels employers' efforts to vary raises based on employees' performance; bonuses have the advantage of not being permanent. "More companies are relying on bonuses as the basis for pay for performance than they are on merit increases," says Hewitt consultant Ken Abosch. Bonuses can help employers manage costs and are "very effective around creating focus" on business objectives, Mr. Abosch says. Hewitt's annual survey included about 1,000 large and midsize U.S. organizations this year.

Consider Whirlpool Corp., which overhauled its pay-for-performance and review system this year. As part of the changes, the Benton Harbor, Mich., appliance maker increased the maximum bonuses for high-performing employees. It also made a larger percentage of employees eligible for bigger bonuses. Whirlpool also awards merit raises based on performance. But it considers bonuses a more powerful motivator. "It starts breaking away at the notion of entitlement," says David Binkley, Whirlpool's human resources chief. With merit pay, "if you just spread it around, it just raises your costs." Across corporate America, he notes, "those days are coming to an end where everyone just automatically gets this 3.6 percent, 3.7 percent" merit raise.

Eighty percent of companies offer a bonus plan this year, up from 78 percent last year and from 67 percent in 1997, according to the Hewitt study. Nearly one-fourth of employers have expanded eligibility for their bonus plans since 2003, according to a survey of about 950 U.S. employers by Mercer Human Resource Consulting.

Even as bonus pools increase, some employers are making it harder for workers to earn top payouts. About 30 percent of employers surveyed by consulting company Watson Wyatt Worldwide said they are raising expectations for individual performance to earn bonuses, says Laura Sejen, a practice director at Watson Wyatt. Many companies have raised targets for company performance as well.

The trend toward variable pay also poses management challenges. Many companies struggle to create—and communicate—the objectives against which employees should be measured, compensation consultants say. "This sort of basic, foundational element is something that they still really struggle with," says Ms. Sejen.

Some companies set "stretch" goals so high that employees lose heart and motivation. Other firms clearly explain a new compensation system to the first round of employees, but neglect new hires. Consultants say they often field questions from employers about the effectiveness of their plans. Employees are confused: About 36 percent say supervisors do a good job linking individual performance to rewards, according to the Watson Wyatt survey.

KeySpan Corp., a New York gas-and-electricity company with 9,700 employees, is putting more emphasis on variable pay. In the last five years or so, the company has increasingly used larger bonus payments to reward top performers. A bonus "has to be re-earned every year; it's not an expectation that has been set in people's minds," notes Elaine Weinstein, KeySpan's senior vice president of human resources.

At first, employees found the changes "demoralizing," Ms. Weinstein says. So the company held seminars for managers on how to conduct fair and honest performance discussions, and gave employees information about pay in the industry. Today, morale has recovered. "They agree they're getting paid well," she says. "We've made it very clear." Last year, the approximately 60 percent to 70 percent of employees who fell within the satisfactory range received merit raises between 2 percent and 3.5 percent, they also were eligible for bonuses. The mentality, Ms. Weinstein says, has gone "from entitlement to meritocracy."

Source: E. White, "Employers Increasingly Favor Bonuses to Raises: Companies Aim to Motivate Workers, Lower Fixed Costs; Losing 'Entitlement' Notion," *The Wall Street Journal*, August 28, 2006, p. B3.

## Introduction

The opening story illustrates how companies seek to use compensation to motivate performance, while at the same time controlling fixed compensation costs.

The preceding chapter discussed setting pay for jobs. In this chapter we focus on using pay to recognize and reward employees' contributions to the organization's success. Employees' pay does not depend solely on the jobs they hold. Instead, differences in performance (individual, group, or organization), seniority, skills, and so forth are used as a basis for differentiating pay among employees.[1]

Several key questions arise in evaluating different pay programs for recognizing contributions. First, what are the costs of the program? Second, what is the expected return (in terms of influences on attitudes and behaviors) from such investments? Third, does the program fit with the organization's human resource strategy and its overall business strategy? Fourth, what might go wrong with the plan in terms of unintended consequences? For example, will the plan encourage managers and employees to pay more attention to some objectives (e.g., short-term sales) than to some others (e.g., customer service and long-term customer satisfaction)?

Organizations have a relatively large degree of discretion in deciding how to pay, especially compared with the pay level decisions discussed in the previous chapter. The same organizational pay level (or "compensation pie") can be distributed (shared) among employees in many ways. Whether each employee's share is based on individual performance, profits, seniority, or other factors, the size of the pie (and thus the cost to the organization) can remain the same.

Regardless of cost differences, different pay programs can have very different consequences for productivity and return on investment. Indeed, a study of how much 150 organizations paid found not only that the largest differences between organizations had to do with how they paid, but that these differences also resulted in different levels of profitability.[2]

## How Does Pay Influence Individual Employees?

**LO1**
Discuss How Pay Influences Individual Employees and Describe Three Theories That Explain the Effect of Compensation on Individuals.

Pay plans are typically used to energize, direct, or control employee behavior. Equity theory, described in the previous chapter, is relevant here as well. Most employees compare their own pay with that of others, especially those in the same job. Perceptions of inequity may cause employees to take actions to restore equity. Unfortunately, some of these actions (like quitting or lack of cooperation) may not help the organization.

Three additional theories also help explain compensation's effects: reinforcement, expectancy, and agency theories.

## Reinforcement Theory

E. L. Thorndike's Law of Effect states that a response followed by a reward is more likely to recur in the future. The implication for compensation management is that high employee performance followed by a monetary reward will make future high performance more likely. By the same token, high performance not followed by a reward will make it less likely in the future. The theory emphasizes the importance of a person's actual experience of a reward.

## Expectancy Theory

**Expectancy Theory**
The theory that says motivation is a function of valence, instrumentality, and expectancy.

Although **expectancy theory** also focuses on the link between rewards and behaviors, it emphasizes expected (rather than experienced) rewards. In other words, it focuses on the effects of incentives. Behaviors (job performance) can be described as a function of ability and motivation. In turn, motivation is hypothesized to be a function of expectancy, instrumentality, and valence perceptions. Compensation systems differ according to their impact on these motivational components. Generally speaking, the main factor is instrumentality: the perceived link between behaviors and pay. Valence of pay outcomes should remain the same under different pay systems. Expectancy perceptions (the perceived link between effort and performance) often have more to do with job design and training than pay systems. A possible exception would be skill-based pay, which directly influences employee training and thus expectancy perceptions.

Although expectancy theory implies that linking an increased amount of rewards to performance will increase motivation and performance, some authors have questioned this assumption, arguing that monetary rewards may increase extrinsic motivation but decrease intrinsic motivation. Extrinsic motivation depends on rewards (such as pay and benefits) controlled by an external source, whereas intrinsic motivation depends on rewards that flow naturally from work itself (like performing interesting work).[3] In other words, paying a child to read books may diminish the child's natural interest in reading, and the child may in the future be less likely to read books unless there are monetary incentives. Although monetary incentives may reduce intrinsic motivation in some settings (such as education), the evidence suggests that such effects are small and isolated in work settings.[4] Therefore, while it is important to keep in mind that money is not the only effective way to motivate behavior and that monetary rewards will not always be the answer to motivation problems, it does not appear that monetary rewards run much risk of compromising intrinsic motivation in most work settings.

Monetary rewards are not the only way to motivate employees, but they do play a key role in many workplaces.

## Agency Theory

This theory focuses on the divergent interests and goals of the organization's stakeholders and the ways that employee compensation can be used to align these interests and goals. We cover agency theory in some depth because it provides especially relevant implications for compensation design.

**Principal**
In agency theory, a person (e.g., an owner) who seeks to direct another person's behavior.

**Agent**
In agency theory, a person (e.g., a manager) who is expected to act on behalf of a principal (e.g., an owner).

Large Cos.

An important characteristic of the modern corporation is the separation of ownership from management (or control). Unlike the early stages of capitalism, where owner and manager were often the same, today, with some exceptions (mostly smaller companies), most stockholders are far removed from the day-to-day operation of companies. Although this separation has important advantages (like mobility of financial capital and diversification of investment risk), it also creates agency costs—the interests of the **principals** (owners) and their **agents** (managers) may no longer converge. What is best for the agent, or manager, may not be best for the owner.

Agency costs can arise from two factors. First, principals and agents may have different goals (goal incongruence). Second, principals may have less than perfect information on the degree to which the agent is pursuing and achieving the principal's goals (information asymetry).

Three examples of agency costs can occur in managerial compensation.[5] First, although shareholders seek to maximize their wealth, management may spend money on things such as perquisites (corporate jets, for example) or "empire building" (making acquisitions that do not add value to the company but may enhance the manager's prestige or pay). Second, managers and shareholders may differ in their attitudes toward risk. Shareholders can diversify their investments (and thus their risks) more easily than managers (whose only major source of income may be their jobs), so managers are typically more averse to risk. They may be less likely to pursue projects or acquisitions with high potential payoff. It also suggests a preference on the part of managers for relatively little risk in their pay (high emphasis on base salary, low emphasis on uncertain bonuses or incentives). Indeed, research shows that managerial compensation in manager-controlled firms is more often designed in this manner.[6] Third, decision-making horizons may differ. For example, if managers change companies more than owners change ownership, managers may be more likely to maximize short-run performance (and pay), perhaps at the expense of long-term success.

Agency theory is also of value in the analysis and design of nonmanagers' compensation. In this case, interests may diverge between managers (now in the role of principals) and their employees (who take on the role of agents).

In designing either managerial or nonmanagerial compensation, the key question is, How can such agency costs be minimized? Agency theory says that the principal must choose a contracting scheme that helps align the interests of the agent with the principal's own interests (that is, it reduces agency costs). These contracts can be classified as either behavior-oriented (such as merit pay) or outcome-oriented (stock options, profit sharing, commissions, and so on).[7]

At first blush, outcome-oriented contracts seem to be the obvious solution. If profits are high, compensation goes up. If profits drop, compensation goes down. The interests of "the company" and employees are aligned. An important drawback, however, is that such contracts increase the agent's risk. And because agents are averse to risk, they may require higher pay (a compensating wage differential) to make up for it.[8]

Behavior-based contracts, on the other hand, do not transfer risk to the agent and thus do not require a compensating wage differential. However, the principal must be able to overcome the information asymetry issue noted previously and monitor with little cost what the agent has done. Otherwise, the principal must either invest in monitoring (e.g., add more supervisors) and information or structure the contract so that pay is linked at least partly to outcomes.[9]

## COMPETING THROUGH GLOBALIZATION

### SAP Dangles a Big, Fat Carrot

The challenge to managers: Double market cap by 2010. The reward: Hundreds of millions.

Hasso Plattner, the sparkplug co-founder and former chief executive of SAP, always held annual executive retreats in the dead of winter at his thatch-roof cottage on the island of Sylt, a Martha's Vineyard look-alike on Germany's seacoast. The forbidding weather kept people focused on what transpired in his spartan living room. But the 2003 meeting, Plattner's last as CEO, was more intense than he would have preferred. SAP's software license revenues—a key measure of future health—had shrunk the previous year for the first time since the company broke them out. Was SAP over the hill?

Picture barrel-chested Plattner seated in a captain's chair at the head of a large wooden table that barely left room for the 10 colleagues pressed around it. Soft-spoken, professorial CEO Henning Kagermann, who was then co-CEO, sat beside him while others squirmed uncomfortably on wooden benches. Plattner, who just weeks later would become board chairman, made it clear just how dissatisfied he was. Rather than go conservative, Plattner said SAP should strive for a shockingly optimistic goal: 15 percent annual growth. "It was an extreme stretch," recalls Kagermann.

Amazingly, the company did even better than the two men had dared to hope. SAP achieved 18 percent software license growth last year, contributing to $10.8 billion in overall revenues. And SAP has become even more dominant as the leading supplier of enterprise software applications, which manage accounting, human resources, customer management, procurement, and manufacturing. No wonder its stock has shot up 40 percent in the past 12 months.

But Kagermann, 59, won't be able to take a breather. His pal Plattner has set another stretch goal for him: On May 9, SAP announced that it will pay $381 million to several hundred managers and key employees if they can double the company's market capitalization—from a $57 billion starting point—by the end of 2010. A third of that would go to the top seven executives.

The bonus plan, unveiled at the annual shareholders meeting in Germany, is way out of character for SAP, which has a reputation since Kagermann took over for being very well managed but unexciting. It's also out of character for a business in Germany, where executives are typically paid less than half as much as their American counterparts. "I don't think it's appropriate," says Heribert Fieber, former chairman of the employees' council at electronics giant Siemens, who is advising a group of restive SAP employees. "There are workers who haven't even gotten raises in line with inflation."

**"The Merlin Role"** Plattner argues that the bonus payout would be fair compensation for an impressive feat. SAP is already highly valued by investors, with a price-earnings ratio of 39. That compares with 24 for Oracle Corp. and 16 for IBM, the two largest players in the overall corporate-software sphere. Plattner has a ready-made argument for shareholders: "If you want extraordinary growth, you want to have an extraordinary bonus scheme."

The fiery 62-year-old executive, whose ultra-aggressive personality was forged in war-devastated Berlin, isn't likely to wither under criticism of the bonanza. He sees it as a way to inject entrepreneurial vim into a 34-year-old company with 35,000 employees and a vast array of products. Since he handed off his CEO duties, he has continued to play a vital role, helping shape technology strategy and pressing relentlessly to make products easier to use. He often rushes from his office at SAP headquarters in Walldorf, Germany, to present Kagermann with bold ideas. It was just such a Plattner brainstorm last summer that brought about the incentive plan.

SAP's top executives welcome the chance to prove they can accelerate growth yet again. "For me, the important impact is that the entire company understands we're on a journey to something special, and it's achievable," says Kagermann. "People want to be in a good company, and they want to have dreams."

Does it all add up to SAP being able to double its market capitalization? *Ein Slam Dunk,* it's not. But under Kagermann's leadership—and with a vigorous push in the back from Plattner—this is one mature software maker that may be up to the challenge.

SOURCE: S. Hamm, with S. Lacy and J. Ewing, "SAP Dangles a Big, Fat Carrot," *BusinessWeek,* May 22, 2006, p. 67.

Which type of contract should an organization use? It depends partly on the following factors:[10]

- *Risk aversion*. Risk aversion among agents makes outcome-oriented contracts less likely.
- *Outcome uncertainty*. Profit is an example of an outcome. Agents are less willing to have their pay linked to profits to the extent that there is a risk of low profits. They would therefore prefer a behavior-oriented contract.
- *Job programmability*. As jobs become less programmable (less routine), outcome-oriented contracts become more likely because monitoring becomes more difficult.[11]
- *Measurable job outcomes*. When outcomes are more measurable, outcome-oriented contracts are more likely.
- *Ability to pay*. Outcome-oriented contracts contribute to higher compensation costs because of the risk premium.
- *Tradition*. A tradition or custom of using (or not using) outcome-oriented contracts will make such contracts more (or less) likely.

In summary, the reinforcement, expectancy, and agency theories all focus on the fact that behavior–reward contingencies can shape behaviors. However, agency theory is of particular value in compensation management because of its emphasis on the risk–reward trade-off, an issue that needs close attention when companies consider variable pay plans, which can carry significant risk.

## How Does Pay Influence Labor Force Composition?

Traditionally, using pay to recognize employee contributions has been thought of as a way to influence the behaviors and attitudes of current employees, whereas pay level and benefits have been seen as a way to influence so-called membership behaviors: decisions about whether to join or remain with the organization. However, there is increasing recognition that individual pay programs may also affect the nature and composition of an organization's workforce.[12] For example, it is possible that an organization that links pay to performance may attract more high performers than an organization that does not link the two. There may be a similar effect with respect to job retention.[13]

Continuing the analysis, different pay systems appear to attract people with different personality traits and values.[14] Organizations that link pay to individual performance may be more likely to attract individualistic employees, whereas organizations relying more heavily on team rewards are more likely to attract team-oriented employees. The implication is that the design of compensation programs needs to be carefully coordinated with the organization and human resource strategy. Increasingly, both in the United States and abroad, employers are seeking to establish stronger links between pay and performance.

## Programs

**LO2**
Describe the Fundamental Pay Programs for Recognizing Employees' Contributions to the Organization's Success.

In compensating employees, an organization does not have to choose one program over another. Instead, a combination of programs is often the best solution. For example, one program may foster teamwork and cooperation but not enough individual initiative. Another may do the opposite. Used in conjunction, a balance may be attained. Such balancing of objectives, combined with careful alignment with the organization and human resource strategy, may help increase the probability that a pay for performance program has its intended effects and reduce the probability of unintended consequences and problems.[15]

Table 12.1 provides an overview of the programs for recognizing employee contributions. Each program shares a focus on paying for performance. The programs differ

**table 12.1**

Programs for Recognizing Employee Contributions

| | MERIT PAY | INCENTIVE PAY | PROFIT SHARING | OWNERSHIP | GAIN SHARING | SKILL-BASED |
|---|---|---|---|---|---|---|
| **Design features** | | | | | | |
| Payment method | Changes in base pay | Bonus | Bonus | Equity changes | Bonus | Change in base pay |
| Frequency of payout | Annually | Weekly | Semiannually or annually | When stock sold | Monthly or quarterly | When skill or competency acquired |
| Performance measures | Supervisor's appraisal of individual performance | Individual output, productivity, sales | Company profit | Company stock returns | Production or controllable costs of stand-alone work unit | Skill or competency acquisition of individuals |
| **Consequences** | | | | | | |
| Performance motivation | Relationship between pay and performance varies | Clear performance–reward connection | Stronger in smaller firms | Stronger in smaller firms | Stronger in smaller units | Encourages learning |
| Attraction | Over time pays better performers more | Pays higher performers more | Helps with all employees if plan pays out | Can help lock in employees | Helps with all employees if plan pays out | Attracts learning-oriented employees |
| Culture | Individual competition | Individual competition | Knowledge of business and cooperation | Sense of ownership and cooperation | Supports cooperation, problem solving | Learning and flexible organization |
| Costs | Requires well-developed performance appraisal system | Setting and maintaining acceptable standards | Relates costs to ability to pay | Relates costs to ability to pay | Setting and maintaining acceptable standards | Training and certification |
| **Contingencies** | | | | | | |
| Management style | Some participation desirable | Control | Fits participation | Fits participation | Fits participation | Fits participation |
| Type of work | Individual unless group appraisals done | Stable, individual, easily measurable | All types | All types | All types | Significant skill depth or breadth |

SOURCE: Adapted and modified from E. E. Lawler III, "Pay for Performance: A Strategic Analysis," in *Compensation and Benefits*, ed. L. R. Gomez-Mejia (Washington, DC: Bureau of National Affairs, 1989).

figure 12.1
Performance Dimensions for Lower to Midlevel Managers, Arrow Electronics

1. Exercises good business judgment
2. Inspires enthusiasm, energy, understanding, loyalty for company goals
3. Attracts, grows, and retains outstanding talent
4. Shows initiative
5. Has position-specific knowledge
6. Delivers results
7. Builds internal good will

SOURCE: From "Compensation and Performance Evaluation at Arrow Electronics" (Boston: Harvard Business School), Case 9-800-290. Copyright © 2000 by the President and Fellows of Harvard College. Reprinted with permission.

LO3
List the Advantages and Disadvantages of the Pay Programs.

according to three design features: (1) payment method, (2) frequency of payout, and (3) ways of measuring performance. In a perhaps more speculative vein, the table also suggests the potential consequences of such programs for (1) performance motivation of employees, (2) attraction of employees, (3) organization culture, and (4) costs. Finally, there are two contingencies that may influence whether each pay program fits the situation: (1) management style and (2) type of work. We now discuss the different programs and some of their potential consequences in more depth.

## Merit Pay

In merit pay programs, annual pay increases are usually linked to performance appraisal ratings. (See Chapter 8.) Some type of merit pay program exists in almost all organizations (although evidence on merit pay effectiveness is surprisingly scarce).[16] As the chapter opening demonstrated, some employers have moved toward a form of merit pay that relies on bonuses rather than increases to base pay. One reason for the widespread use of merit pay is its ability to define and reward a broad range of performance dimensions. (See Figure 12.1 for an example.) Indeed, given the pervasiveness of merit pay programs, we devote a good deal of attention to them here.

### Basic Features

**Merit Increase Grid**
A grid that combines an employee's performance rating with the employee's position in a pay range to determine the size and frequency of his or her pay increases.

Many merit pay programs work off of a **merit increase grid.** As Table 12.2 indicates, the size and frequency of pay increases are determined by two factors. The first factor is the individual's performance rating (because better performers should receive higher pay). The second factor is position in range (that is, an individual's compa-ratio). So, for example, an employee with a performance rating of EX and a compa-ratio of 120 would receive a pay increase of 9 to 11 percent. By comparison, an employee with a performance rating of EX and a compa-ratio of 85 would receive an increase of 13 to 15 percent. (Note that the general magnitude of increases in such a table is influenced by inflation rates. Thus the percentage increases in such a grid would have been considerably lower in recent years.) One reason for factoring in the compa-ratio is to control compensation costs and maintain the integrity of the pay structure. If a person with a compa-ratio of 120 received a merit increase of 13 to 15 percent, she would soon exceed the pay range maximum. Not factoring in the compa-ratio would also result in uncontrolled growth of compensation costs for employees who continue to perform the same job year after year. Instead, some organizations think in terms of assessing where the employee's pay is now and where it should be, given a particular performance level.

**table 12.2**

Example of Merit Increase Grid from Merck & Co., Inc.

| PERFORMANCE RATING | SUGGESTED MERIT INCREASE PERCENTAGE | | | |
|---|---|---|---|---|
| | COMPA-RATIO 80.00–95.00 | COMPA-RATIO 95.01–110.00 | COMPA-RATIO 110.01–120.00 | COMPA-RATIO 120.01–125.00 |
| EX (Exceptional within Merck) | 13–15% | 12–14% | 9–11% | To maximum of range |
| WD (Merck Standard with Distinction) | 9–11 | 8–10 | 7–9 | — |
| HS (High Merck Standard) | 7–9 | 6–8 | — | — |
| RI (Merck Standard Room for Improvement) | 5–7 | — | — | — |
| NA (Not Adequate for Merck) | — | — | — | — |

SOURCE: K. J. Murphy, "Merck & Co., Inc., (B)" (Boston: Harvard Business School), Case 491-006. Copyright © 1990 by the President and Fellows of Harvard College. Reprinted with permission.

Consider Table 12.3. An employee who consistently performs at the EX level should be paid at 115 to 125 percent of the market (that is, a compa-ratio of 115 to 125). To the extent that the employee is far from that pay level, larger and more frequent pay increases are necessary to move the employee to the correct position. On the other hand, if the employee is already at that pay level, smaller pay increases will be needed. The main objective in the latter case would be to provide pay increases that are sufficient to maintain the employee at the targeted compa-ratio.

In controlling compensation costs, another factor that requires close attention is the distribution of performance ratings. (See Chapter 8.) In many organizations, 60 to 70 percent of employees fall into the top two (out of four to five) performance rating categories.[17] This means tremendous growth in compensation costs because most employees will eventually be above the midpoint of the pay range, resulting in compa-ratios well over 100. To avoid this, some organizations provide guidelines regarding the percentage of employees who should fall into each performance category, usually limiting the percentage that can be placed in the top two categories. These guidelines are enforced differently, ranging from true guidelines to strict forced-distribution requirements.

In general, merit pay programs have the following characteristics. First, they identify individual differences in performance, which are assumed to reflect differences in ability or motivation. By implication, system constraints on performance are not

**table 12.3**

Performance Ratings and Compa-ratio Targets

| PERFORMANCE RATING | COMPA-RATIO TARGET |
|---|---|
| EX (Exceptional within Merck) | 115–125 |
| WD (Merck Standard with Distinction) | 100–120 |
| HS (High Merck Standard) | 90–110 |
| RI (Merck Standard Room for Improvement) | 80–95 |
| NA (Not Adequate for Merck) | None |

SOURCE: K. J. Murphy, "Merck & Co., Inc., (B)" (Boston: Harvard Business School), Case 491-006. Copyright © 1990 by the President and Fellows of Harvard College. Reprinted with permission.

seen as significant. Second, the majority of information on individual performance is collected from the immediate supervisor. Peer and subordinate ratings are rare, and where they exist, they tend to receive less weight than supervisory ratings.[18] Third, there is a policy of linking pay increases to performance appraisal results.[19] Fourth, the feedback under such systems tends to occur infrequently, often once per year at the formal performance review session. Fifth, the flow of feedback tends to be largely unidirectional, from supervisor to subordinate.

## Criticisms of Traditional Merit Pay Programs

Criticisms of this process have been raised. For example, W. Edwards Deming, a leader of the total quality management movement, argued that it is unfair to rate individual performance because "apparent differences between people arise almost entirely from the system that they work in, not from the people themselves."[20] Examples of system factors include co-workers, the job, materials, equipment, customers, management, supervision, and environmental conditions. These are believed to be largely outside the worker's control, instead falling under management's responsibility. Deming argued that the performance rating is essentially "the result of a lottery."[21]

Deming also argued that the individual focus of merit pay discourages teamwork: "Everyone propels himself forward, or tries to, for his own good, on his own life preserver. The organization is the loser."[22] As an example, if people in the purchasing department are evaluated based on the number of contracts negotiated, they may have little interest in materials quality, even though manufacturing is having quality problems.

Deming's solution was to eliminate the link between individual performance and pay. This approach reflects a desire to move away from recognizing individual contributions. What are the consequences of such a move? It is possible that fewer employees with individual-achievement orientations would be attracted to and remain with the organization. One study of job retention found that the relationship between pay growth and individual performance over time was weaker at higher performance levels. As a consequence, the organization lost a disproportionate share of its top performers.[23] In other words, too little emphasis on individual performance may leave the organization with average and poor performers.[24]

Thus, although Deming's concerns about too much emphasis on individual performance are well taken, one must be careful not to replace one set of problems with another. Instead, there needs to be an appropriate balance between individual and group objectives. At the very least, ranking and forced-distribution performance-rating systems need to be considered with caution, lest they contribute to behavior that is too individualistic and competitive.

Another criticism of merit pay programs is the way they measure performance. If the performance measure is not perceived as being fair and accurate, the entire merit pay program can break down. One potential impediment to accuracy is the almost exclusive reliance on the supervisor for providing performance ratings, even though peers, subordinates, and customers (internal and external) often have information on a person's performance that is as good as or better than that of the supervisor. A 360-degree performance feedback approach (discussed in Chapter 9) gathers feedback from each of these sources. To date, however, organizations have been reluctant to use these multisource data for making pay decisions.[25]

In general, process issues appear to be important in administering merit pay. In any situation where rewards are distributed, employees appear to assess fairness along

**table 12.4**

Aspects of Procedural Justice in Pay Raise Decisions

| | |
|---|---|
| Indicate the extent to which your supervisor did each of the following: | |
| 1. | Was honest and ethical in dealing with you. |
| 2. | Gave you an opportunity to express your side. |
| 3. | Used consistent standards in evaluating your performance. |
| 4. | Considered your views regarding your performance. |
| 5. | Gave you feedback that helped you learn how well you were doing. |
| 6. | Was completely candid and frank with you. |
| 7. | Showed a real interest in trying to be fair. |
| 8. | Became thoroughly familiar with your performance. |
| 9. | Took into account factors beyond your control. |
| 10. | Got input from you before a recommendation. |
| 11. | Made clear what was expected of you. |
| Indicate how much of an opportunity existed, after the last raise decision, for you to do each of the following things: | |
| 12. | Make an appeal about the size of a raise. |
| 13. | Express your feelings to your supervisor about the salary decision. |
| 14. | Discuss, with your supervisor, how your performance was evaluated. |
| 15. | Develop, with your supervisor, an action plan for future performance. |

SOURCE: From *Academy of Management Journal* by R. Folger and M. A. Konovsky. Reprinted with permission of *Academy of Management* via Copyright Clearance Center.

two dimensions: distributive (based on how much they receive) and procedural (what process was used to decide how much).[26] Some of the most important aspects of procedural fairness, or justice, appear in Table 12.4. These items suggest that employees desire clear and consistent performance standards, as well as opportunities to provide input, discuss their performance, and appeal any decision they believe to be incorrect.

Perhaps the most basic criticism is that merit pay does not really exist. High performers are not paid significantly more than mediocre or even poor performers in most cases.[27] For example, with a merit increase budget of 4 to 5 percent, suppose high performers receive 6 percent raises, versus 3.5 to 4 percent raises for average performers. On a salary of $40,000 per year, the difference in take-home pay would not be more than about $300 per year, or about $6 per week. Critics of merit pay point out that this difference is probably not significant enough to influence employee behaviors or attitudes. Indeed, as Figure 12.2 indicates, many employees do not believe there is any payoff to higher levels of performance.

Of course, small differences in pay can accumulate into large differences over time. The present value of the salary advantage would be $29,489 (based on a discount rate of 5 percent). For example, over a 30-year career, an initial annual salary difference of $740 with equal merit increases thereafter of 7 percent would accumulate into a career salary advantage of $75,738.[28] Whether employees think in these terms is open to question. But even if they do not, nothing prevents an organization from explaining to employees that what may appear to be small differences in pay can add up to large differences over time. It should also be kept in mind that merit ratings are often closely linked to promotions, which in turn are closely linked to salary. Thus, even in merit pay settings where performance differences are not recognized in the short run, high performers are likely to have significantly higher career earnings.

Finally, the accumulation effect just described can also be seen as a drawback if it contributes to an entitlement mentality. Here the concern is that a big merit increase

**figure 12.2**

Percentage of Employees Who Agree That Better Performance Leads to Better Increases

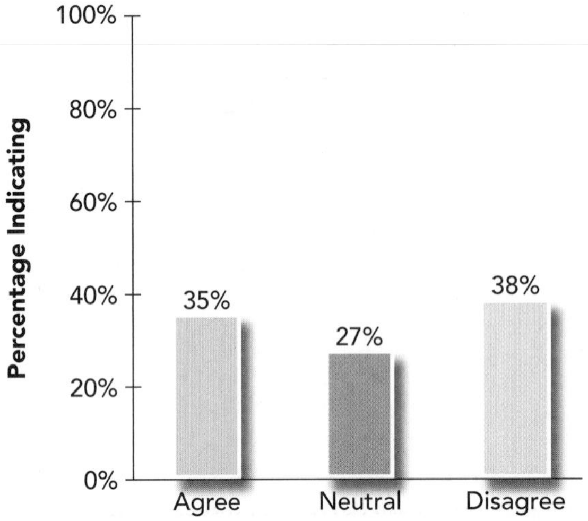


SOURCE: Hay Group, *Managing Performance: Survey of Employees in 335 companies*, Philadelphia: Hay Group, 2002. Reprinted with permission.

given early in an employee's career remains part of base salary "forever." It does not have to be re-earned each year, and the cost to the organization grows over time, perhaps more than either the employee's performance or the organization's profitability would always warrant. Merit bonuses (payouts that do not become part of base salary), in lieu of traditional merit increases, are thus used by some organizations instead.

## EVIDENCE-BASED HR

Applebee's International Inc. is trying to infuse a bit of General Electric Co. into the restaurant business. In a bid to reduce high turnover rates among restaurant employees. Applebee's, the U.S.'s biggest casual-dining chain by number of restaurants, reviews and ranks its hourly employees, and then rewards managers for retaining their better workers.

The tactic is an unusual combination of two more-common techniques: employee-ranking systems popularized by some large corporations such as GE and retention bonuses paid to managers in high-turnover industries such as retail and restaurants. In those industries, turnover rates among hourly workers can run as high as 200 percent, meaning that the average worker leaves after six months. For other midsize and large companies, annual employee turnover is typically about 10 percent to 15 percent.

At Applebee's, Overland Park, Kan., managers must divide hourly workers into "A" players, the top 20 percent; B, the middle 60 percent; the C, the bottom 20 percent. The managers then are eligible for merit raises and bonuses based on how well they retain employees in the top 80 percent. The practice is unusual in the restaurant industry, where managers tend to worry more about staffing the next shift than career development and performance evaluation. "Among the hourly retail or service employees, there is certainly a tendency to say, 'Let's bring warm bodies in here,' and then to just try to hold down turnover in general," says Rick Beal, a senior compensation consultant at Watson Wyatt Worldwide, a human resources consulting firm in

Washington, D.C. Mr. Beal says rewarding managers for retaining the better workers is a great idea in theory, but will prove effective only if employers develop straightforward, and simple, ways to judge hourly workers. "Otherwise you're going to burn more time than it's worth," he says.

Applebee's says the system is time-consuming, but worth the effort. Before introducing the system in 2001. Applebee's measured overall turnover but didn't use the numbers to evaluate managers. Then, executives realized, "there is a different value if you lose a top-20 person than if you lose a bottom-20 person," says John Prutsman, who is in charge of human resources for the restaurants. In order to reward managers for keeping the best people, the company had to develop a system for reviewing hourly workers, including the grading criteria. Today, Applebee's evaluates all hourly employees twice a year on nine counts, including reliability, attitude, guest service, and teamwork. First, employees complete a self-evaluation. Then, managers grade employees. Since employees can work for more than one manager, determining a final grade requires meeting to reconcile differing opinions. A typical Applebee's has about 60 hourly workers, one general manager, and three or four lower-level managers.

Brad Miller, general manager at an Applebee's in Albuquerque, N.M., recalls a discussion about one worker's tardiness. Managers couldn't agree on whether the worker, a college student, was too often blaming classes for his lateness. His "reliability" rating would determine whether the employee received an A or B grade. Mr. Miller asked other workers in the store, who said the worker's lateness often had little to do with his classes. He earned a B.

Managers, in turn, get rewarded on how well they retain the top 80 percent, or their A's and B's. To win employees' loyalty, managers can give out small raises; award them "Applebucks," points toward prizes such as bicycles, radios or DVD players; or distribute special pins for highly ranked employees. Workers generally aren't told their grades. Many managers also employ their own motivational tricks, such as displaying posters of employee photos or not scheduling employees to work on their birthdays and anniversaries. Applebee's credits the system with helping to reduce annual turnover among hourly employees at company-owned restaurants almost by half in four years, to 84 percent in 2004 from 146 percent in 2000. Applebee's owns 485 restaurants; a further 1,301 are franchises, where Applebee's doesn't control the retention practices but shares its techniques with the franchisees.

Linda Saleeby, general manager at an Applebee's in Chester, Va., for the past seven years, says the evaluation process takes her management team about six weeks from start to finish. But she says the benefits extend beyond reduced turnover. She says employees like knowing what is expected of them and generally where they stand. "They know what it is we're focusing on," she says. "I don't think any kind of time we spend on people is a waste of time or hassle, because it's such a huge portion of our business," she says.

Ms. Saleeby has benefited from the system, too, by earning raises and bonuses based partly on her high retention scores. Some of her techniques include giving out ice-cream bars to employees who work on Saturdays, meeting with parents of newly hired teen workers, and holding "round-table meetings" with employees to give them a say in things like scheduling. She likes the focus on the top 80 percent. "There's a certain number of people, despite all the tools you use to hire them, that just don't work out," she says.

SOURCE: E. White, "Theory & Practice: How to Reduce Turnover; Restaurant Chain Retains Workers Using Rankings and Rewards," *The Wall Street Journal*, November 21, 2005, p. B5.

## Individual Incentives

Like merit pay, individual incentives reward individual performance, but with two important differences. First, payments are not rolled into base pay. They must be continuously earned and re-earned. Second, performance is usually measured as physical output (such as number of water faucets produced) rather than by subjective ratings. Individual incentives have the potential to significantly increase performance. Locke and his colleagues found that monetary incentives increased production output by a median of 30 percent—more than any other motivational device studied.[29]

Nevertheless, individual incentives are relatively rare for a variety of reasons.[30] Most jobs (like those of managers and professionals) have no physical output measure. Instead, they involve what might be described as "knowledge work." Also, many potential administrative problems (such as setting and maintaining acceptable standards) often prove intractable. Third, individual incentives may do such a good job of motivating employees that they do whatever they get paid for and nothing else. (See the Dilbert cartoon in Figure 12.3.) Fourth, as the name implies, individual incentives typically do not fit well with a team approach. Fifth, they may be inconsistent with the goals of acquiring multiple skills and proactive problem solving. Learning new skills often requires employees to slow or stop production. If the employees are paid based on production volume, they may not want to slow down or stop. Sixth, some incentive plans reward output volume at the expense of quality or customer service.

Therefore, although individual incentives carry potential advantages, they are not likely to contribute to a flexible, proactive, problem-solving workforce. In addition, such programs may not be particularly helpful in the pursuit of total quality management objectives.

## Profit Sharing and Ownership

**Profit Sharing**
A compensation plan in which payments are based on a measure of organization performance (profits) and do not become part of the employees' base salary.

### Profit Sharing

At the other end of the individual–group continuum are profit sharing and stock ownership plans. Under **profit sharing,** payments are based on a measure of organization performance (profits), and the payments do not become part of the base salary. Profit sharing has two potential advantages. First, it may encourage employees to think more like owners, taking a broad view of what needs to be done to make the organization more effective. Thus, the sort of narrow self-interest encouraged by individual incentive plans (and perhaps also by merit pay) is presumably less of an issue. Instead, increased cooperation and citizenship are expected. Second, because payments do not

**figure 12.3**
How Incentives Sometimes "Work"

SOURCE: DILBERT reprinted by permission of United Feature Syndicate, Inc.

## COMPETING THROUGH SUSTAINABILITY

### Tech Companies Give Stock-Options Value, and Actually Survive

Your favorite stock might not be joining the party, but the Nasdaq composite is up double digits from a year ago. In some parts of technology, notably most things involving the Internet, we are in the midst of what might be termed Bubble II. Venture capitalists continue to find start-up companies they deem worthy of starting up. And the daily papers are full of tales of twentysomethings turned millionaires through acquisitions by companies like Google and Oracle.

If this is the end of the world as we know it, then I feel fine. The reason for suggesting an apocalypse averted is that we are nearly finished with the first fiscal quarter for which public companies are forced to fully expense the value of the stock options given as incentives to employees. This is a move the tech industry bitterly fought against for more than a decade, with tech trade groups warning of the consequences in news releases, one more dire than the other. Expensing options "will hurt competitiveness and economic growth," said one; another said it "would seriously undermine the robust health of the U.S. and global economies."

Now that expensing is occurring, the reaction is mostly a shrug. There are, as always, unintended consequences, but life goes on.

For one thing, the venture-capital industry has known for a while that expensing options was going to start this quarter, yet they kept funds flowing to U.S. companies. VentureOne, the Dow Jones unit that tracks venture financing, shows that 2,139 start-ups received some form of venture financing during 2005, compared with 2,120 the year before. The total amount invested, $22.1 billion, also topped the figure for 2004.

What's more, those start-ups continue to use stock options to recruit employees, despite predictions they'd be forced to abandon the practice. The fact that these start-ups might one day be post-IPO companies, and have lower earnings-per-share figures as they are forced to expense those options, is considered by most struggling start-ups to be the sort of problem you wouldn't mind having one day.

"When you are a start-up and losing money, it just doesn't enter into your discussions," said Shiv Tasker, CEO of Bluespec, a Waltham, Mass., start-up working on products for the chip-design market.

Even many established tech companies continue to give out options. For instance, every new hire at Cisco gets some options, the company says, with the amount depending on the position. That isn't to say the tech companies as a whole haven't cut back on options. According to the compensation-research firm, Equilar, 3.1 percent of all outstanding shares belonging to a representative group of 124 tech companies were given out as stock options in 2003. Last year, that figure fell to 2.4 percent a 23 percent decline.

Much of that decrease can be attributed to the fact that companies like Microsoft have switched from giving stock options—the right to buy a stock, sometimes at a reduced price—to actually giving out shares. For many rank and file, that latter deal might well be a better one, because even if the stock price falls, it will always be worth something. With options, if the stock's value falls below the "strike price" of your option, you're out of luck.

Another bit of data from Equilar would seem to support the tech industry's arguments that in a post-expensing world, only top executives would get options, on account of the expense that would become associated with them. In 2003, 19.5 percent of stock options went to too officers; last year, the figure rose to 21.5 percent, suggesting that fewer secretaries and stock-room employees were getting theirs.

It's hard to tell if there is a trend here; the 2004 figure was 18 percent. But many studies have noted the extent to which corporate profits are increasingly winding up in the hands of top officers. Pension funds sure aren't getting them. If corporate wealth is indeed being increasingly skewed toward top officers, it's hard to believe the expensing of options is the real culprit.

Of course, expensing options has its downside. Some say it's bringing back the practice from the bad old dot-com days of companies putting out two sets of numbers—one with their actual financial information, the other with the numbers the way the company itself would like them viewed. These days, that second number means with the options expensing removed. Indeed, to the extent that Wall Street has yawned about options expensing, it's because investors have learned to simply overlook the expenses associated with options. Then again, determined investors will always find something to overlook when they put their minds to it.

For many years, nearly every visitor to Silicon Valley got a fire- and-brimstone speech from tech leaders about the evils of stock-option expensing. It's now clear the reports of the imminent death of the tech sector were greatly exaggerated. Considering the real problems facing technology in America, like dwindling federal support for research, it's a shame that so much political capital was so badly spent.

SOURCE: L. Gomes, "Tech Companies Give Stock-Options Value, and Actually Survive," *The Wall Street Journal*, March 22, 2006, p. B1.

become part of base pay, labor costs are automatically reduced during difficult economic times, and wealth is shared during good times. Consequently, organizations may not need to rely on layoffs as much to reduce costs during tough times.[31]

Does profit sharing contribute to better organization performance? The evidence is not clear. Although there is consistent support for a correlation between profit sharing payments and profits, questions have been raised about the direction of causality.[32] For example, Ford, Chrysler, and GM all have profit sharing plans in their contracts with the United Auto Workers (UAW). (See Figure 12.4 for provisions of the GM–UAW plan.) The average profit sharing payment at Ford one year was $4,000 per

**figure 12.4**

Profit Sharing in the General Motors–UAW Contract

2.14 **"Profits"** . . . means income earned by U.S. operations before income taxes and "extraordinary" items. . . . Profits are before any profit sharing charges are deducted. Profits also are before incentive program charges for U.S. operations.

2.18 **"Total Profit Share"** . . . means an obligation of the corporation for any plan year in an amount equal to the sum of:
(a) 6 percent of the portion of profits . . . which exceeds 0.0 percent of sales and revenues . . . but does not exceed 1.8 percent . . .;
(b) 8 percent of the portion of profits . . . which exceeds 1.8 percent of sales and revenues . . . but does not exceed 2.3 percent . . .;
(c) 10 percent of the portion of profits . . . which exceeds 2.3 percent of sales and revenues . . . but does not exceed 4.6 percent . . .;
(d) 14 percent of the portion of profits . . . which exceeds 4.6 percent of sales and revenues . . . but does not exceed 6.9 percent . . .;
(e) 17 percent of the portion of profits . . . which exceeds 6.9 percent of sales and revenues.

4.02 **Allocation of Profit Sharing Amount to Participants**
The portion of the total profit share for the plan year allocated to this plan . . . will be allocated to each participant entitled to a distribution . . . in the proportion that (a) the participant's compensation hours for the plan year bears to (b) the total compensated hours for all participants in the plan entitled to a distribution for the plan year.

SOURCE: From J. A. Fossum, *Labor Relations: Development, Structure and Process*, 2002. 

worker versus an average of $550 per worker at GM and $8,000 at Chrysler. Given that the profit sharing plans are similar, it seems unlikely they caused Ford and Chrysler to be more profitable. Rather, it would appear that profits were higher at Ford for other reasons, resulting in higher profit sharing payments.

This example also helps illustrate the fundamental drawback of profit sharing. Why should automobile workers at GM receive profit sharing payments that are only 1/15 the size received by those doing the same type of work at Chrysler? Is it because Chrysler UAW members performed 15 times better than their counterparts at GM that year? Probably not. Rather, workers are likely to view top management decisions regarding products, engineering, pricing, and marketing as more important. As a result, with the exception of top (and perhaps some middle) managers, most employees are unlikely to see a strong connection between what they do and what they earn under profit sharing. This means that performance motivation is likely to change very little under profit sharing. Consistent with expectancy theory, motivation depends on a strong link between behaviors and valued consequences such as pay (instrumentality perceptions).

Another factor that reduces the motivational impact of profit sharing plans is that most plans are of the deferred type. Roughly 16 percent of full-time employees in medium-size and large private establishments participate in profit sharing plans, but only 1 percent of employees overall (about 6 percent of those in profit sharing plans) are in cash plans where profits are paid to employees during the current time period.[33]

Not only may profit sharing fail to increase performance motivation, but employees may also react very negatively when they learn that such plans do not pay out during business downturns.[34] First, they may not feel they are to blame because they have been performing their jobs well. Other factors are beyond their control, so why should they be penalized? Second, what seems like a small amount of risked pay for a manager earning $80,000 per year can be very painful to someone earning $15,000 or $20,000.

Consider the case of the Du Pont Fibers Division, which had a plan that linked a portion of employees' pay to division profits.[35] After the plan's implementation, employees' base salary was about 4 percent lower than similar employees in other divisions unless 100 percent of the profit goal (a 4 percent increase over the previous year's profits) was reached. Thus, there was what might be called downside risk. However, there was also considerable upside opportunity: if 100 percent of the profit goal was exceeded, employees would earn more than similar employees in other divisions. For example, if the division reached 150 percent of the profit goal (6 percent growth in profits), employees would receive 12 percent more than comparable employees in other divisions.

Initially, the plan worked fine. The profit goal was exceeded, and employees earned slightly more than employees in other divisions. In the following year, however, profits were down 26 percent, and the profit goal was not met. Employees received no profit sharing bonus; instead, they earned 4 percent less than comparable employees in other divisions. Profit sharing was no longer seen as a very good idea. Du Pont management responded to employee concerns by eliminating the plan and returning to a system of fixed base salaries with no variable (or risk) component. This outcome is perhaps not surprising from an agency theory perspective, which suggests that employees must somehow be compensated before they will be willing to assume increased risk.

One solution some organizations choose is to design plans that have upside but not downside risk. In such cases, when a profit sharing plan is introduced, base pay is not reduced. Thus, when profits are high, employees share in the gain, but when profits are low, they are not penalized. Such plans largely eliminate what is purported to be a major advantage of profit sharing: reducing labor costs during business downturns. During business upturns, labor costs will increase. Given that the performance benefits of such plans are not assured, an organization runs the risk under such plans of increasing its labor costs with little return on its investment.

In summary, although profit sharing may be useful as one component of a compensation system (to enhance identification with broad organizational goals), it may need to be complemented with other pay programs that more closely link pay to outcomes that individuals or teams can control (or "own"), particularly in larger companies. In addition, profit sharing runs the risk of contributing to employee dissatisfaction or higher labor costs, depending on how it is designed.

## Ownership

Employee ownership is similar to profit sharing in some key respects, such as encouraging employees to focus on the success of the organization as a whole. In fact, with ownership, this focus may be even stronger. Like profit sharing, ownership may be less motivational the larger the organization. And because employees may not realize any financial gain until they actually sell their stock (typically upon leaving the organization), the link between pay and performance may be even less obvious than under profit sharing. Thus, from a reinforcement theory standpoint (with its emphasis on actually experiencing rewards), performance motivation may be especially low.

**Stock Options**
An employee ownership plan that gives employees the opportunity to buy the company's stock at a previously fixed price.

One way of achieving employee ownership is through **stock options,** which give employees the opportunity to buy stock at a fixed price. Say the employees receive options to purchase stock at $10 per share in 2005, and the stock price reaches $30 per share in 2010. They have the option of purchasing stock ("exercising" their stock options) at $10 per share in 2010, thus making a tidy return on investment if the shares are then sold. If the stock price goes down to $8 per share in the year 2010, however, there will be no financial gain. Therefore, employees are encouraged to act in ways that will benefit the organization.

For many years, stock options had typically been reserved for executives in larger, established companies. More recently, there was a trend toward pushing eligibility farther down in the organization.[36] In fact, many companies, including PepsiCo, Merck, McDonald's, Wal-Mart, and Procter & Gamble, began granting stock options to employees at all levels. Among start-up companies like these in the technology sector, these broad-based stock option programs have long been popular and companies like Microsoft and Cisco Systems attribute much of their growth and success to these option plans. Some studies suggest that organization performance is higher when a large percentage of top and midlevel managers are eligible for long-term incentives such as stock options, which is consistent with agency theory's focus on the problem of encouraging managers to think like owners.[37] However, it is not clear whether these findings would hold up for lower-level employees, particularly in larger companies, who may see much less opportunity to influence overall organization performance.

The Golden Age of stock options may be coming to an end. Investors have long questioned the historically favorable tax treatment of stock options. In 2004, the Financial Accounting Standards Board (FASB) proposed a landmark change that would require companies to expense options on their financial statements, which reduces reported net income, dramatically in some cases. Microsoft, for example, decided to eliminate stock options in favor of actual stock grants. This is partly in response to the new accounting standards and partly in recognition of the fact that Microsoft's stock price is not likely to grow as rapidly as it once did, making options less effective in recruiting, retaining, and motivating its employees. It appears that many companies are cutting back on stock options overall, and especially for nonexecutive employees.

**Employee stock ownership plans (ESOPs),** under which employers give employees stock in the company, are the most common form of employee ownership, with the number of employees in such plans increasing from 4 million in 1980 to over 10 million in 1999 in the United States.[38] In Japan, 91 percent of companies listed on Japanese stock markets have an ESOP, and these companies appear to have higher average productivity than non-ESOP companies.[39] ESOPs raise a number of unique issues. On the negative side, they can carry significant risk for employees. An ESOP must, by law, invest at least 51 percent of assets in its company's stock, resulting in less diversification of investment risk (in some cases, no diversification). Consequently, when employees buy out companies in poor financial condition to save their jobs, or when the ESOP is used to fund pensions, employees risk serious financial difficulties if the company does poorly.[40] This is not just a concern for employees, because, as agency theory suggests, employees may require higher pay to offset increased risks of this sort.

**Employee Stock Ownership Plan (ESOP)**
An employee ownership plan that gives employers certain tax and financial advantages when stock is granted to employees.

ESOPs can be attractive to organizations because they have tax and financing advantages and can serve as a takeover defense (under the assumption that employee owners will be "friendly" to management). ESOPs give employees the right to vote their securities (if registered on a national exchange).[41] As such, some degree of participation in a select number of decisions is mandatory, but overall participation in decision making appears to vary significantly across organizations with ESOPs. Some studies suggest that the positive effects of ownership are larger in cases where employees have greater participation,[42] perhaps because the "employee–owner comes to psychologically experience his/her ownership in the organization."[43]

## Gainsharing, Group Incentives, and Team Awards

### Gainsharing

**Gainsharing** programs offer a means of sharing productivity gains with employees. Although sometimes confused with profit sharing plans, gainsharing differs in two key respects. First, instead of using an organization-level performance measure (profits), the programs measure group or plant performance, which is likely to be seen as more controllable by employees. Second, payouts are distributed more frequently and not deferred. In a sense, gainsharing programs represent an effort to pull out the best features of organization-oriented plans like profit sharing and individual-oriented plans like merit pay and individual incentives. Like profit sharing, gainsharing encourages pursuit of broader goals than individual-oriented plans do. But, unlike profit sharing, gainsharing can motivate employees much as individual plans do because of the more controllable nature of the performance measure and the frequency of payouts. Indeed, studies indicate that gainsharing improves performance.[44]

**Gainsharing**
A form of compensation based on group or plant performance (rather than organizationwide profits) that does not become part of the employee's base salary.

One type of gainsharing, the Scanlon plan (developed in the 1930s by Joseph N. Scanlon, president of a local union at Empire Steel and Tin Plant in Mansfield, Ohio), provides a monetary bonus to employees (and the organization) if the ratio of labor costs to the sales value of production is kept below a certain standard.

**table 12.5**

Example of Gainsharing (Modified Scanlon Plan) Report

| ITEMS | AVERAGE OF 1ST AND 2ND PERIODS | AVERAGE OF 2ND AND 3RD PERIODS |
|---|---|---|
| 1. Sales in dollars | $1,000,000 | $1,000,000 |
| 2. Inventory change and work in process | 100,000 | 100,000 |
| 3. Sales value of production | 1,100,000 | 1,100,000 |
| 4. Allowable costs (82.5% × 3 above) | 907,500 | 907,500 |
| 5. Actual costs | 850,000 | 917,500 |
| 6. Gain (4 – 5 above) | 57,500 | −10,000 |
| 7. Employee share (55% of 6 above) | 31,625 | −5,500 |
| 8. Monthly reserve (20% of 7 above) *If no bonus, 100% of 7 above | 6,325 | −5,500 |
| 9. Bonus to be distributed (7 – 8) | 25,300 | 0 |
| 10. Company share (45% of 6 above) | 25,875 | −4,500 |
| 11. Participating payroll | 132,000 | 132,000 |
| 12. Bonus percentage (9/11) | 19.2% | 0.0% |
| 13. Monthly reserve (8 above) | 6,325 | −5,500 |
| 14. Reserve at the end of last period | 0 | 6,325 |
| 15. Year-end reserve to date | 6,325 | 825 |

SOURCE: K. Mericle, and D. O. Kim, *Gainsharing and Goalsharing* (Westport, CT: Praeger, 2004).

Table 12.5 shows a modified (i.e., costs in addition to labor are included) Scanlon plan. Because actual costs ($850,000) were less than allowable costs ($907,500) in the first and second periods, there is a gain of $57,500. The organization receives 45 percent of the savings, and the employees receive the other 55 percent, although part of the employees' share is set aside in the event that actual costs exceed the standard in upcoming months (as Table 12.5 shows did occur).

Gainsharing plans like the Scanlon plan and pay-for-performance plans in general often encompass more than just a monetary component. As Table 12.6 indicates, there is often a strong emphasis on taking advantage of employee know-how to improve the production process through teams and suggestion systems. A number of recommendations have been made about the organization conditions that should be in place for gainsharing to succeed. Commonly mentioned factors include (1) management commitment, (2) a need to change or a strong commitment to continuous improvement, (3) management's acceptance and encouragement of employee input, (4) high levels of cooperation and interaction, (5) employment security, (6) information sharing on productivity and costs, (7) goal setting, (8) commitment of all involved parties to the process of change and improvement, and (9) agreement on a performance standard and calculation that is understandable, seen as fair, and closely related to managerial objectives.[45]

## Group Incentives and Team Awards

Whereas gainsharing plans are often plantwide, group incentives and team awards typically pertain to a smaller work group.[46] Group incentives (like individual

**table 12.6**

Employee Involvement Plans for Nonmanagement Employees

| TYPE OF EMPLOYEE INVOLVEMENT PROGRAM | PERCENTAGE USING PROGRAM | MEDIAN PERCENTAGE OF EMPLOYEES PARTICIPATING | MEDIAN NUMBER OF HOURS SPENT PER PARTICIPATING EMPLOYEE PER YEAR |
|---|---|---|---|
| Individual suggestion plans | 42% | 20% | 5 |
| Ad hoc problem solving groups | 44 | 20 | 22 |
| Team group suggestion plans | 28 | 25 | 10 |
| Employee–management teams | 19 | 15 | 40 |
| Quality circles | 26 | 16 | 50 |
| Percentage of all plans using any type of employee involvement program | 66 | | |

SOURCE: J. L. McAdams, "Design, Implementation, and Results: Employee Involvement and Performance Reward Plans," *Compensation and Benefits Review,* March–April 1995, pp. 45–55. Copyright © 1995 by Sage Publications, Inc. Reprinted with permission of Sage Publications, Inc.

incentives) tend to measure performance in terms of physical output, whereas team award plans may use a broader range of performance measures (like cost savings, successful completion of product design, or meeting deadlines). As with individual incentive plans, these plans have a number of potential drawbacks. Competition between individuals may be reduced, but it may be replaced by competition between groups or teams. Also, as with any incentive plan, a standard-setting process must be developed that is seen as fair by employees, and these standards must not exclude important dimensions such as quality.

see p. 24

## Balanced Scorecard

**LO4** Describe How Organizations Combine Incentive Plans in a Balanced Scorecard.

As the preceding discussion indicates, every pay program has advantages and disadvantages. Therefore, rather than choosing one program, some companies find it useful to design a mix of pay programs, one that has just the right chemistry for the situation at hand. Relying exclusively on merit pay or individual incentives may result in high levels of work motivation but unacceptable levels of individualistic and competitive behavior and too little concern for broader plant or organization goals. Relying too heavily on profit sharing and gainsharing plans may increase cooperation and concern for the welfare of the entire plant or organization, but it may reduce individual work motivation to unacceptable levels. However, a particular mix of merit pay, gainsharing, and profit sharing could contribute to acceptable performance on all these performance dimensions.

One approach that seeks to balance multiple objectives is the balanced scorecard (see Chapter 1), which Kaplan and Norton describe as a way for companies to "track financial results while simultaneously monitoring progress in building the capabilities and acquiring the intangible assets they would need for future growth."[47]

Table 12.7 shows how a mix of measures might be used by a manufacturing firm to motivate improvements in a balanced set of key business drivers.

**table 12.7**
Illustration of Balanced Scorecard Incentive Concept

| PERFORMANCE MEASURE | INCENTIVE SCHEDULE: TARGET INCENTIVE | PERFORMANCE | % TARGET | ACTUAL PERFORMANCE | INCENTIVE EARNED |
|---|---|---|---|---|---|
| Financial<br>• Return on capital employed | $100 | 20%+<br>16–20%<br>12–16%<br>Below 12% | 150%<br>100%<br>50%<br>0% | 18% | $100 |
| Customer<br>• Product returns | $ 40 | 1 in:<br>1,000 +<br>900–999<br>800–899<br>Below 800 | <br>150%<br>100%<br>50%<br>0% | 1 in 876 | $ 20 |
| Internal<br>• Cycle time reduction (%) | $ 30 | 9%+<br>6–9%<br>3–6%<br>0–3% | 150%<br>100%<br>50%<br>0% | 11% | $ 45 |
| Learning and growth<br>• Voluntary employee turnover | $ 30 | Below 5%<br>5–8%<br>8–12% | 150%<br>100%<br>50% | 7% | $ 30 |
| Total | $200 | | | | $195 |

SOURCE: F. C. McKenzie and M. P. Shilling, "Avoiding Performance Traps: Ensuring Effective Incentive Design and Implementation," *Compensation and Benefits Review,* July–August 1998, pp. 57–65. Copyright © 1998 by Sage Publications, Inc. Reprinted with permission of Sage Publications, Inc.

## Managerial and Executive Pay

**LO5**
Discuss Issues Related to Performance-Based Pay for Executives.

Because of their significant ability to influence organization performance, top managers and executives are a strategically important group whose compensation warrants special attention. In the previous chapter we discussed how much this group is paid. Here we focus on the issue of how their pay is determined.

Each year *BusinessWeek* publishes a list of top executives who did the most for their pay and those who did the least. The latter group has been the impetus for much of the attention to executive pay. The problem seems to be that in some companies, top executive pay is high every year, regardless of profitability or stock market performance. One study, for example, found that CEO pay changes by $3.25 for every $1,000 change in shareholder wealth. Although this relationship was interpreted to mean that "the compensation of top executives is virtually independent of corporate performance, later work suggests this is not the case in most companies."[48]

How can executive pay be linked to organization performance? From an agency theory perspective, the goal of owners (shareholders) is to encourage the agents (managers and executives) to act in the best interests of the owners. This may mean less emphasis on noncontingent pay, such as base salary, and more emphasis on outcome-oriented "contracts" that make some portion of executive pay contingent on the organization's profitability or stock performance.[49] Among midlevel and top managers, it is common to use both short-term bonus and long-term incentive plans to encourage

**table 12.8**
The Relationship between Managerial Pay and Organization Return on Assets

| | PREDICTED RETURN ON ASSETS | | |
|---|---|---|---|
| BONUS/BASE RATIO | LONG-TERM INCENTIVE ELIGIBILITY | % | $[a] |
| 10% | 28% | 5.2% | $250 million |
| 20 | 28 | 5.6 | 269 million |
| 10 | 48 | 5.9 | 283 million |
| 20 | 48 | 7.1 | 341 million |

[a]Based on the assets of the average *Fortune* 500 company in 1990.

SOURCE: B. Gerhart and G. T. Milkovich, "Organizational Differences in Managerial Compensation and Financial Performance," *Academy of Management Journal* 33 (1990), pp. 663–91.

the pursuit of both short- and long-term organization performance objectives. Indeed, in the *BusinessWeek* surveys discussed in Chapter 11, the bulk of executive compensation comes from stock options and other forms of long-term compensation.

To what extent do organizations use such pay-for-performance plans, and what are their consequences? Research suggests that organizations vary substantially in the extent to which they use both long-term and short-term incentive programs. Further, greater use of such plans among top and midlevel managers was associated with higher subsequent levels of profitability. As Table 12.8 indicates, greater reliance on short-term bonuses and long-term incentives (relative to base pay) resulted in substantial improvements in return on assets.[50]

Earlier, we saw how the balanced scorecard approach could be applied to paying manufacturing employees. It is also useful in designing executive pay. Table 12.9 shows how the choice of performance measures can be guided by a desire to balance shareholder, customer, and employee objectives. Sears sees financial results as a lagging indicator that tells the company how it has done in the past, whereas customer and employee metrics like those in Table 12.9 are leading indicators that tell the company how its financial results will be in the future. Thus, Sears ties its executive compensation to achievement of objectives to "(1) drive profitable growth, (2) become customer-centric, (3) foster the development of a diverse, high-performance culture, and (4) focus on productivity and returns."[51]

**table 12.9**
Whirlpool's Three-Stakeholder Scorecard

| STAKEHOLDER | MEASURES |
|---|---|
| Shareholder value | Economic value added<br>Earnings per share<br>Cash flow<br>Total cost productivity |
| Customer value | Quality<br>Market share<br>Customer satisfaction |
| Employee value | High-performance culture index<br>High-performance culture deployment<br>Training and development diversity |

SOURCE: From E. L. Gubman, *The Talent Solution*, 1998. Copyright © 1998 The McGraw-Hill Companies, Inc. Reproduced with permission of The McGraw-Hill Companies.

**table 12.10**
Guidelines for Board of Directors Structure and Effective Governance

| | |
|---|---|
| Interlocking boards | Top executives should not serve on each other's boards. Otherwise, there may be an incentive for executives to heed the Golden Rule too closely. |
| Outside versus inside directors | Inside directors are part of the management team and thus report to the top executive. Therefore, the number of inside directors should be kept to a minimum. Some committees, such as the nominating committee and the compensation committee, should be composed entirely of outside directors. |
| Outside directors meet without top executive | Such meetings permit directors to speak freely and consider actions that might be in the best interests of shareholders but unattractive to the top executive. |
| Director pensions | Directors with pensions may be reluctant to have conflicts with the top executive for fear of losing their directorships and thus their pensions. |
| Director pay | Directors should be required to own a minimum amount of stock to align their interests with those of shareholders. |

SOURCE: Adapted from J. A. Byrne, "The CEO and the Board," *BusinessWeek*, September 15, 1997, p. 12.

Finally, there is pressure from regulators and shareholders to better link pay and performance. The Securities and Exchange Commission (SEC) requires companies to report compensation levels for the five highest paid executives and the company's performance relative to that of competitors over a five-year period. In 2006, the SEC put additional rules into effect that require better disclosure of the value of executive perquisites and retirement benefits.

Large retirement fund investors such as TIAA-CREF and CalPERS have proposed guidelines to better ensure that boards of directors act in shareholders' best interests when making executive pay decisions, rather than being beholden to management. Some of the governance practices believed to be related to director independence from management are shown in Table 12.10. In addition, when a firm's future is at risk, the board may well need to demonstrate its independence from management by taking dramatic action, which may include removing the chief executive.

## Process and Context Issues

**LO6**
Explain the Importance of Process Issues Such as Communication in Compensation Management.

In Chapter 11 we discussed the importance of process issues such as communication and employee participation. Significant differences in how such issues are handled can be found both across and within organizations, suggesting that organizations have considerable discretion in this aspect of compensation management.[52] As such, it represents another strategic opportunity to distinguish one's organization from the competition.

### Employee Participation in Decision Making

Consider employee participation in decision making and its potential consequences. Involvement in the design and implementation of pay policies has been linked to higher pay satisfaction and job satisfaction, presumably because employees have a better understanding of and greater commitment to the policy when they are involved.[53]

What about the effects on productivity? Agency theory provides some insight. The delegation of decision making by a principal to an agent creates agency costs because employees may not act in the best interests of top management. In addition, the more agents there are, the higher the monitoring costs.[54] Together, these suggest that delegation of decision making can be very costly.

On the other hand, agency theory suggests that monitoring would be less costly and more effective if performed by employees because they have knowledge about the workplace and behavior of fellow employees that managers do not have. As such, the right compensation system might encourage self-monitoring and peer monitoring.[55]

Researchers have suggested that two general factors are critical to encouraging such monitoring: monetary incentives (outcome-oriented contracts in agency theory) and an environment that fosters trust and cooperation. This environment, in turn, is a function of employment security, group cohesiveness, and individual rights for employees—in other words, respect for and commitment to employees.[56]

## Communication

Another important process issue is communication. Earlier, we spoke of its importance in the administration of merit pay, both from the perspective of procedural fairness and as a means of obtaining the maximum impact from a merit pay program. More generally, a change in any part of the compensation system is likely to give rise to employee concerns. Rumors and assumptions based on poor or incomplete information are always an issue in administering compensation, partly because of its importance to employee economic security and well-being. Therefore, in making any changes, it is crucial to determine how best to communicate reasons for the changes to employees. Some organizations now rely heavily on video messages from the chief executive officer to communicate the rationale for major changes. Brochures that include scenarios for typical employees are also used, as are focus group sessions where small groups of employees are interviewed to obtain feedback about concerns that can be addressed in later communication programs.

## Pay and Process: Intertwined Effects

The preceding discussion treats process issues such as participation as factors that may facilitate the success of pay programs. At least one commentator, however, has described an even more important role for process factors in determining employee performance:

> Worker participation apparently helps make alternative compensation plans . . . work better—and also has beneficial effects of its own. . . . It appears that changing the way workers are treated may boost productivity more than changing the way they are paid.[57]

This suggestion raises a broader question: How important are pay decisions, per se, relative to other human resource practices? Although it may not be terribly useful to attempt to disentangle closely intertwined programs, it is important to reinforce the notion that human resource programs, even those as powerful as compensation systems, do not work alone.

Consider gainsharing programs. As described earlier, pay is often only one component of such programs. (See Table 12.6.) How important are the nonpay components?[58] There is ample evidence that gainsharing programs that rely almost exclusively on the monetary component can have substantial effects on productivity.[59] On the other hand, a study of an automotive parts plant found that adding a participation component (monthly meetings with management to discuss the gainsharing plan and ways to increase productivity) to a gainsharing pay incentive plan raised productivity. In a related study, employees were asked about the factors that motivated them to engage in active participation (such as suggestion systems). Employees reported that the desire to earn a monetary bonus was much less important than a number of nonpay factors, particularly the desire for influence and control in how their work was done.[60] A third study reported that productivity and profitability were both enhanced by the addition of employee participation in decisions, beyond the improvement derived from monetary incentives such as gainsharing.[61]

## Organization Strategy and Compensation Strategy: A Question of Fit

**LO7**
List the Major Factors to Consider in Matching the Pay Strategy to the Organization's Strategy.

Although much of our focus has been on the general, or average, effects of different pay programs, it is also useful to think in terms of matching pay strategies to organization strategies. To take an example from medicine, using the same medical treatment regardless of the symptoms and diagnosis would be foolish. In choosing a pay strategy, one must consider how effectively it will further the organization's overall business strategy. Consider again the findings reported in Table 12.8. The average effect of moving from a pay strategy with below-average variability in pay to one with above-average variability is an increase in return on assets of almost two percentage points (from 5.2 percent to 7.1 percent). But in some organizations, the increase could be smaller. In fact, greater variability in pay could contribute to a lower return on assets in some organizations. In other organizations, greater variability in pay could contribute to increases in return on assets of greater than two percentage points. Obviously, being able to tell where variable pay works and where it does not could have substantial consequences.

In Chapter 2 we discussed directional business strategies, two of which were growth (internal or external) and concentration ("sticking to the knitting"). How should compensation strategies differ according to whether an organization follows a growth strategy or a concentration strategy? Table 12.11 provides some suggested matches. Basically, a growth strategy's emphasis on innovation, risk taking, and new markets is linked to a

**table 12.11**
Matching Pay Strategy and Organization Strategy

| PAY STRATEGY DIMENSIONS | ORGANIZATION STRATEGY CONCENTRATION | ORGANIZATION STRATEGY GROWTH |
|---|---|---|
| Risk sharing (variable pay) | Low | High |
| Time orientation | Short-term | Long-term |
| Pay level (short run) | Above market | Below market |
| Pay level (long-run potential) | Below market | Above market |
| Benefits level | Above market | Below market |
| Centralization of pay decisions | Centralized | Decentralized |
| Pay unit of analysis | Job | Skills |

SOURCE: Adapted from L. R. Gomez-Mejia and D. B. Balkin, *Compensation, Organizational Strategy, and Firm Performance* (Cincinnati: South-Western, 1992), Appendix 4b.

## COMPETING THROUGH TECHNOLOGY

### Google Will Let Employees Sell Vested Options

Google Inc. plans to allow non-executive employees to sell vested stock options through an online-auction system, a move aimed at boosting the value of options for staff and potential hires that comes at a time when Google's shares have fallen back from their stratospheric ascent.

The Mountain View, Calif., Internet company said Morgan Stanley will manage the online-auction system and other unspecified financial institutions will participate as buyers. Under the program to begin in April, those institutions will be able to buy vested options from Google employees, presumably at a premium to the option's value based on the difference between the current share price and the strike, or purchase, price for shares under the option.

Compensation experts said Google's plan for transferable stock options, or TSOs, appears to be unique in offering an ongoing marketplace for vested stock options. The system could enable employees to make money by selling even options that are underwater, or priced below the current share price, Google said. That is because a financial institution might be willing to pay something for the right to buy Google shares at an option's strike price over the remainder of its duration, which resets to a maximum of two years when an employee sells the option.

The program represents an attempt by Google to add value to options, and make their value less theoretical for employees, the company said.

The move comes as Google's share price is trading barely above the $471.84 it hit January 11. In 4 P.M. trading on the Nasdaq Stock Market, Google was at $481.78, down 0.4 percent.

"It's helpful for us for recruiting purposes, retention purposes and just understanding purposes if every option we grant has a value, whether it's in the money, at the money or underwater," said Dave Rolefson, a Google equity and executive-compensation manager. Mr. Rolefson said it is possible that Google might be able to issue fewer options as a result of the new program, but said that isn't the primary aim. Company executives said a primary interest behind the TSOs is to narrow the gap between the theoretical value of stock options that Google expenses under new accounting rules and employees' lower perceptions of their value. Google will take unspecified charges related to modifying options under the plan, which applies to all non-executive options granted since the company's August 2004 initial public offering. Employees will still be able to exercise any vested options as before.

Compensation experts said it remains unknown what financial institutions would be willing to pay for the vested options, particularly given a restriction against the institutions' reselling them. Ted Buyniski, senior vice president at Radford Surveys + Consulting, a business unit of Aon Corp. specializing in compensation, described the TSO program as "a very smart move" with benefits outweighing any transaction costs and increased overhang of stock options. Mr. Buyniski was briefed on the news before its release.

SOURCE: K. J. Delaney, "Google Will Let Employees Sell Vested Options," *The Wall Street Journal*, December 13, 2006, p. C-3.

pay strategy that shares risk with employees but also gives them the opportunity for high future earnings by having them share in whatever success the organization has.[62] This means relatively low levels of fixed compensation in the short run but the use of bonuses and stock options, for example, that can pay off handsomely in the long run. Stock options have been described as the pay program "that built Silicon Valley," having been used by companies such as Apple, Microsoft, and others.[63] When such companies become successful, everyone from top managers to secretaries can become millionaires if they own stock. Growth organizations are also thought to benefit from a less bureaucratic orientation, in the sense of having more decentralization and flexibility in pay decisions and in recognizing individual skills, rather than being constrained by job or grade classification systems. On the other hand, concentration-oriented organizations are thought to require a very different set of pay practices by virtue of their lower rate of growth, more stable workforce, and greater need for consistency and standardization in pay decisions. As noted earlier, Microsoft has eliminated stock options in favor of stock grants to its employees, in part because it is not the growth company it once was.

## A Look Back

In this chapter, we discussed the potential advantages and disadvantages of different types of incentive or pay for performance plans. We also saw that these pay plans can have both intended and unintended consequences. Designing a pay for performance strategy typically seeks to balance the pros and cons of different plans and reduce the chance of unintended consequences. To an important degree, pay strategy will depend on the particular goals and strategy of the organization and its units. For example, Microsoft determined that its pay strategy needed to be revised (less emphasis on stock options, more on stock grants) to support a change in its business strategy and to recognize the slower-paced growth of its stock price. At the beginning of this chapter, we saw that many organizations are working to link pay to performance and reduce fixed labor costs.

### Questions

1. Does money motivate? Use the theories and examples discussed in this chapter to address this question.
2. Think of a job that you have held. Design an incentive plan. What would be the potential advantages and disadvantages of your plan? If your money was invested in the company, would you adopt the plan?

Please see the Video Case that corresponds to this chapter online at www.mhhe.com/noe6e.

## Summary

Our focus in this chapter has been on the design and administration of programs that recognize employee contributions to the organization's success. These programs vary as to whether they link pay to individual, group, or organization performance. Often, it is not so much a choice of one program or the other as it is a choice between different combinations of programs that seek to balance individual, group, and organization objectives.

Wages, bonuses, and other types of pay have an important influence on an employee's standard of living. This carries at least two important implications. First, pay can be a powerful motivator. An effective pay strategy can substantially promote an organization's success; conversely, a poorly conceived pay strategy can have detrimental effects. Second, the importance of pay means that employees care a great deal about the fairness of the pay process. A recurring theme is that pay programs must be explained and administered in such a way that employees understand their underlying rationale and believe it is fair.

The fact that organizations differ in their business and human resource strategies suggests that the most effective compensation strategy may differ from one organization to another. Although benchmarking programs against the competition is informative, what succeeds in some organizations may not be a good idea for others. The balanced scorecard suggests the need for organizations to decide what their key objectives are and use pay to support them.

## Key Terms

Expectancy theory, 525
Principal, 526
Agent, 526
Merit increase grid, 530
Profit sharing, 536
Stock options, 540
Employee stock ownership plan (ESOP), 541
Gainsharing, 541

## Discussion Questions

1. To compete more effectively, your organization is considering a profit sharing plan to increase employee effort and to encourage employees to think like owners. What are the potential advantages and disadvantages of such a plan? Would the profit sharing plan have the same impact on all types of employees? Is the size of your organization an important consideration? Why? What alternative pay programs should be considered?
2. Gainsharing plans have often been used in manufacturing settings but can also be applied in service organizations. How could performance standards be developed for gainsharing plans in hospitals, banks, insurance companies, and so forth?
3. Your organization has two business units. One unit is a long-established manufacturer of a product that competes on price and has not been subject to many technological innovations. The other business unit is just being started. It has no products yet, but it is working on developing a new technology for testing the effects of drugs on people via simulation instead of through lengthy clinical trials. Would you recommend that the two business units have the same pay programs for recognizing individual contributions? Why?
4. Beginning with the opening vignette and continuing throughout the chapter, we have seen many examples of companies (e.g., SAP, Google, Applebee's) making changes to how they pay for performance. Do you believe the changes at these companies make sense? What are the potential payoffs and pitfalls of their new pay strategies?

## Self-Assessment Exercise

Pay is only one type of incentive that can motivate you to perform well and contribute to your satisfaction at work. This survey will help you understand what motivates you at work. Consider each aspect of work and rate its importance to you, using the following scale: 5 = very important, 4 = somewhat important, 3 = neutral, 2 = somewhat unimportant, 1 = very unimportant.

| | | | | | |
|---|---|---|---|---|---|
| Salary or wages | 1 | 2 | 3 | 4 | 5 |
| Cash bonuses | 1 | 2 | 3 | 4 | 5 |
| Boss's management style | 1 | 2 | 3 | 4 | 5 |
| Location of workplace | 1 | 2 | 3 | 4 | 5 |
| Commute | 1 | 2 | 3 | 4 | 5 |
| Job security | 1 | 2 | 3 | 4 | 5 |
| Opportunity for advancement | 1 | 2 | 3 | 4 | 5 |
| Work environment | 1 | 2 | 3 | 4 | 5 |
| Level of independence in job | 1 | 2 | 3 | 4 | 5 |
| Level of teamwork required for job | 1 | 2 | 3 | 4 | 5 |
| Other (enter your own): | | | | | |
| ________________ | 1 | 2 | 3 | 4 | 5 |
| ________________ | 1 | 2 | 3 | 4 | 5 |
| ________________ | 1 | 2 | 3 | 4 | 5 |

Which aspects of work received a score of 5? A score of 4? These are the ones you believe motivate you to perform well and make you happy in your job. Which aspects of work received a score of 1 or 2? These are least likely to motivate you. Is pay the only way to motivate you?

SOURCE: Based on the "Job Assessor" found at www.salarymonster.com, accessed August 2002.

## Exercising Strategy: Paying for Good Employee Relations

Organizations understand that reaching financial objectives, or satisfying shareholders, depends to a considerable degree on how well they manage relationships with other important stakeholders such as customers and employees. One suggestion has been to link compensation, in part, to customer satisfaction and employee satisfaction. Is this a good idea in the case of employee satisfaction? There is some disagreement on this issue. Eastman Kodak has, since 1995, used employee opinion survey results as one factor in deciding executive bonuses. Likewise, United Airlines, which is employee-owned, is moving to a system where executive bonuses will depend to some degree on employee-satisfaction surveys. Although the idea of rewarding managers for good employee relations has some intuitive appeal, there may be unintended consequences. Indeed, Gordon Bethune, CEO of Continental Airlines, described such an idea as "absolutely stupid." Bethune argues, "Being an effective leader and having a company where people enjoy coming to work is not a popularity contest. When you run popularity contests, you tend to do things that may get you more points. That may not be good for shareholders and may not be good for the company." This is not to say that Bethune and Continental do not see employee relations as an important part of their competitive advantage. Continental was named the 2001 airline of the year by *Air Transport World* and number 18 on Fortune's 2001 list of best companies to work for in America. And many companies use employee opinion survey results to adjust their employee relations policies as needed. Rather, the issue is whether an incentive plan that explicitly rewards employee satisfaction will produce only intended positive consequences or might also produce unintended, less desirable consequences. Eastman Kodak and United are two examples of companies that have decided some direct incentive makes sense, even if it is small relative to other factors (like financial performance) that determine executive pay. Other companies, even those that use strong employee relations as an important source of competitive advantage, have been too concerned about unintended consequences to use explicit incentives.

SOURCE: "Bottom-up Pay: Companies Regularly Survey How Employees Feel about Their Bosses, But They Rarely Use Ratings to Set Compensation," *The Wall Street Journal*, April 6, 2000, pp. R5+.

### Questions

1. Should companies worry about employee attitudes? Why or why not?
2. If positive employee attitudes are an objective, should organizations directly link pay incentives to attitudes?

## MANAGING PEOPLE: FROM THE PAGES OF *BUSINESSWEEK*

### BusinessWeek The Art of Motivation

**What you can learn from a company that treats workers like owners. Inside the surprising performance culture of steelmaker Nucor** It was about 2 P.M. on March 9 when three Nucor Corp. electricians got the call from their colleagues at the Hickman (Ark.) plant. It was bad news: Hickman's electrical grid had failed. For a minimill steelmaker like Nucor, which melts scrap steel from autos, dishwashers, mobile homes, and the like in an electric arc furnace to make new steel, there's little that could be worse. The trio immediately dropped what they were doing and headed out to the plant. Malcolm McDonald, an electrician from the Decatur (Ala.) mill, was in Indiana visiting another facility. He drove down, arriving at 9 o'clock that night. Les Hart and Bryson Trumble, from Nucor's facility in Hertford County, N.C., boarded a plane that landed in Memphis at 11 P.M. Then they drove two hours to the troubled plant.

No supervisor had asked them to make the trip, and no one had to. They went on their own. Camping out in the electrical substation with the Hickman staff, the team worked 20-hour shifts to get the plant up and running again in three days instead of the anticipated full week. There wasn't any direct financial incentive for them to blow their weekends, no extra money in their next paycheck, but for the company their contribution was huge. Hickman went on to post a first-quarter record for tons of steel shipped.

What's most amazing about this story is that at Nucor it's not considered particularly remarkable. "It could have easily been a Hickman operator going to help the Crawfordsville [Ind.] mill," says Executive Vice-President John J. Ferriola, who oversees the Hickman plant and seven others. "It happens daily."

In an industry as Rust Belt as they come, Nucor has nurtured one of the most dynamic and engaged workforces around. The 11,300 nonunion employees at the Charlotte (N.C.) company don't see themselves as worker bees waiting for instructions from above. Nucor's flattened hierarchy and emphasis on pushing power to the front line lead its employees to adopt the mindset of owner-operators. It's a profitable formula: Nucor's 387 percent return to shareholders over the past five years handily beats almost all other companies in the Standard & Poor's 500-stock index, including New Economy icons Amazon.com, Starbucks, and eBay. And the company has become more profitable as it has grown: Margins, which were 7 percent in 2000, reached 10 percent last year.

Nucor gained renown in the late 1980s for its radical pay practices, which base the vast majority of most workers' income on their performance. An upstart nipping at the heels of the integrated steel giants, Nucor had a close-knit culture that was the natural outgrowth of its underdog identity. Legendary leader F. Kenneth Iverson's radical insight: that employees, even hourly clock-punchers, will make an extraordinary effort if you reward them richly, treat them with respect, and give them real power.

Nucor is an upstart no more, and the untold story of how it has clung to that core philosophy even as it has grown into the largest steel company in the United States is in many ways as compelling as the celebrated tale of its brash youth. Iverson retired in 1999. Under CEO Daniel R. DiMicco, a 23-year veteran, Nucor has snapped up 13 plants over the past five years while managing to instill its unique culture in all of the facilities it has bought, an achievement that makes him a more than worthy successor to Iverson.

Nucor's performance, propelled by a red-hot steel market, has been nothing less than sensational. It has grown into a company with 2005 sales of $12.7 billion, up from $4.6 billion when DiMicco took over in 2000. Last year net income was $1.3 billion, up from $311 million in 2000. In 2005 the company shipped more steel in the United States—20.7 million tons—than any other company. "In terms of a business model," says Louis L. Schorsch, president and CEO of Nucor rival Mittal Steel USA, "They've won in this part of the world."

At Nucor the art of motivation is about an unblinking focus on the people on the front line of the business. It's about talking to them, listening to them, taking a risk on their ideas, and accepting the occasional failure. It's a culture built in part with symbolic gestures. Every year, for example, every single employee's name goes on the cover of the annual report. And, like Iverson before him, DiMicco flies commercial, manages without an executive parking space, and really does make the coffee in the office when he takes the last cup. Although he has an Ivy League pedigree, including degrees from Brown University and the University of Pennsylvania, DiMicco retains the plain-talking style of a guy raised in a middle-class family in Mt. Kisco, N.Y. Only 65 people—yes, 65—work alongside him at headquarters.

At times, workers and managers exhibit a level of passion for the company that can border on the bizarre. Executive Vice-President Joseph A. Rutkowski, an engineer who came up through the mills, speaks of Nucor as a "magic" place, representing the best of American rebelliousness. He says "we epitomize how people should think, should be." EVP Ferriola goes even further: "I consider myself an apostle" for the gospel of Ken Iverson. "After Christ died, people still spread the word. Our culture is a living thing. It will not die because we will not let it die, ever."

### Strategic Highflier

Unusual? No doubt. But Vijay Govindarajan, a professor at Dartmouth College's Tuck School of Business, teaches Nucor as an example of outstanding strategic execution, placing it alongside highfliers such as JetBlue Airways and eBay. "My students say: 'I thought Nucor created steel.' And I say: 'No, Nucor creates knowledge.'"

At a time when many observers are busy hammering the final nail into the coffin of American heavy manufacturing, Nucor's business model is well worth considering. It raises the question of whether troubled companies such as General Motors and Ford—not to mention nonmanufacturers such as Delta Airlines or Verizon Communications—could energize their workers by adopting some version of this plan. But Nucor's path is hard to follow. It requires managers to abandon the command-and-control model that has dominated American business for the better part of a century, trust their people, and do a much better job of sharing corporate wealth.

Money is where the rubber meets the road. Nucor's unusual pay system is the single most daring element of the company's model and the hardest for outsiders and acquired companies to embrace. An experienced steelworker at another company can easily earn $16 to $21 an hour. At Nucor the guarantee is closer to $10. A bonus tied to the production of defect-free steel by an employee's entire shift can triple the average steelworker's take-home pay.

With demand for steel scorching these days, payday has become a regular cause for celebration. Nucor gave out more than $220 million in profit sharing and bonuses to the rank and file in 2005. The average Nucor steelworker took home nearly $79,000 last year. Add to that a $2,000 one-time bonus to mark the company's record earnings and almost $18,000, on average, in profit sharing. Not only is good work rewarded, but bad work is penalized. Bonuses are calculated on every order and paid out every week. At the Berkeley mill in Huger, S.C., if workers make a bad batch of steel and catch it before it has moved on, they lose the bonus they otherwise would have made on that shipment. But if it gets to the customer, they lose three times that.

Managers don't just ask workers to put a big chunk of their pay at risk. Their own take-home depends heavily on results as well. Department managers typically get a base pay that's 75 percent to 90 percent of the market average. But in a great year that same manager might get a bonus of 75 percent or even 90 percent, based on the return on assets of the whole plant. "In average-to-bad years, we earn less than our peers in other companies. That's supposed to teach us that we don't want to be average or bad. We want to be good," says James M. Coblin, Nucor's vice-president for human resources.

Compared with other U.S. companies, pay disparities are modest at Nucor. Today, the typical CEO makes more than 400 times what a factory worker takes home. Last year, Nucor's chief executive collected a salary and bonus precisely 23 times that of his average steelworker. DiMicco did well by any reasonable standard, making some $2.3 million in salary and bonus (plus long-term pay equaling $4.9 million), but that's because Nucor is doing well. When things are bad, DiMicco suffers, too. In 2003, as the company was dealing with an industry downturn and barely squeaked out a profit, DiMicco made $1.4 million. He gets few stock options, and most of his restricted stock and other longer-term bonuses don't materialize if the company doesn't beat the competition and outpace a sample group of other high-performing companies for good measure. Paul Hodgson, senior research associate at the Corporate Library, an organization that researches corporate governance issues, and an expert in the field who rarely has anything good to say about CEO compensation, calls Nucor's system a "best practice." Adds Hodgson: "Not too many companies get my vote of approval."

Executive pay is geared toward team building. The bonus of a plant manager, a department manager's boss, depends on the entire corporation's return on equity. So there's no glory in winning at your own plant if the others are failing. When EVP Ferriola became general manager of Nucor's Vulcraft plant in Grapeland, Tex., in 1995, he remembers he wasn't in the job two days before he received calls from every other general manager in the Vulcraft division offering to help however they could. (Vulcraft manufactures the steel joists and decks that hold up the ceilings of shopping centers and other buildings.) "It wasn't idle politeness. I took them up on it," says Ferriola. And they wanted him to, he notes. "My performance impacted their paycheck."

This high-stakes teamwork can be the hardest thing for a newly acquired plant to get used to. David Hutchins, a frontline supervisor or "lead man" in the rolling mill at Nucor's first big acquisition, its Auburn (N.Y.) plant, describes the old way of thinking. The job of a rolling mill is to thin out the steel made in the hot mill furnace, preparing it to be cut into sheets. In the days before the Nucor acquisition, if the cutting backed up, Hutchins would just take a break. "We'd sit back, have a cup of coffee, and complain: Those guys stink," he says. "At Nucor, we're not 'you guys' and 'us guys.' It's all of us guys. Wherever the bottleneck is, we go there, and everyone works on it."

It took six months to convince Auburn workers that they would do better under Nucor's pay system. During that time the company paid people based on their old formula but posted what they would have received under Nucor's formula. Pretty soon the numbers became a powerful argument to switch. Hutchins saw his pay climb from $53,000 the year before the sale to $67,000 in 2001 and to $92,000 last year. "It's like I got a second job, and I'm doing the same one," he says. Today it has become standard procedure for a team of Nucor vets, including people who work on the plant floor, to visit with their counterparts in any acquisition. They explain the system eye to eye.

The payoff for Nucor? In Auburn's second year of Nucor operation, with fewer people and no substantial capital investment, the plant saw a 14 percent improvement in total shipments. Other acquisitions have seen big jumps in production as well. A mill bought in Tuscaloosa, Ala., went from 800,000 tons a year to 1.2 million with Nucor in just two years. A bar mill in Marion, Ohio, acquired last year, has already pushed annual production from 400,000 tons to 450,000.

But to focus only on pay would be to miss something special about the culture Nucor has created. There's a healthy competition among facilities and even among shifts, balanced with a long history of cooperation and idea-sharing. Rick Ryan, the shipping department supervisor at the Auburn mill, has taken trips to study plants in Nebraska and South Carolina. Ryan had always used wood blocks as supports beneath the bundles of steel the plant produced. But after seeing other Nucor plants use steel blocks, he switched. Because they can be reused, Ryan figures the move saves $150,000 a year.

Since there's always room for improvement, plant managers regularly set up contests for shifts to try to outdo one another on a set goal, generally related to safety, efficiency, or output. Ryan says Nucor's Utah plant is the benchmark these days. It is the most profitable, with the lowest costs per ton. "They've got everything down to a science," says Ryan admiringly. "It gives you something to shoot for."

### In-House Entrepreneurs

As Nucor grows, existing facilities making products that overlap with those of acquired plants may need to find new businesses to branch into. So Nucor employees have to innovate themselves out of tough spots and into more profitable ones. The Crawfordsville plant is among those that have felt the squeeze. It's famous as the place that pioneered the commercialization of the thin-strip casting of steel that made it possible for minimills such as Nucor to compete with the industry's Old Guard. But Crawfordsville is not on a large waterway, a disadvantage at a time of high fuel costs. As Nucor's oldest sheet mill, it can't make sheets as wide as many of Nucor's other mills, including a giant plant in Decatur acquired in 2002.

So General Manager Ron Dickerson has focused more of Crawfordsville's output on types of steel that are harder to make, more profitable, and less threatened by imports. Now, Crawfordsville can make 160 different grades of steel. Those with a high carbon content, for example, are stronger and lighter and are particularly useful for steel ties for shipping and in car parts. It took a lot of work to figure out how to make this type of steel, which is prone to crack in mid-production, but workers agitated for the chance. They wanted more work for the plant so they could get more hours. Nucor's giant Berkeley mill has gone through a similar evolution, adding new machinery, including a $20 million vacuum degasser used for higher-margin ultraclean steels. The internal competition from Decatur "forced us to get better quicker," says Berkeley's general manager, Ladd Hall.

Like many employees, Hall sometimes sounds like a walking advertisement for Nucor. Whisking a visitor out of his office and onto the factory floor, he mentions that he often walks through the plant on Saturday mornings at 5 or 6 A.M. to chat with the line workers before having breakfast with his children at 9 A.M. "I can give you all the rhetoric you want," says Ladd, "but the people in the mills, that's what makes it Nucor."

SOURCE: N. Byrnes with M. Arndt, "The Art of Motivation," *BusinessWeek*, May 1, 2006, pp. 56+.

## Questions

1. What business is Nucor in and how is its business strategy different from that of its competitors?
2. What role does compensation play in creating the motivated workforce that seems to be a key to Nucor's business strategy execution? How does compensation at Nucor differ from compensation at its competitors?
3. Does Nucor's workforce productivity and impact stem entirely from its compensation system or are there other key aspects of human resource strategy that are also important. Explain.

# Notes


1. We draw freely in this chapter on several literature reviews: B. Gerhart and G. T. Milkovich, "Employee Compensation: Research and Practice," in *Handbook of Industrial and Organizational Psychology*, vol. 3, 2nd ed., ed. M. D. Dunnette and L. M. Hough (Palo Alto, CA: Consulting Psychologists Press, 1992); B. Gerhart and S. L. Rynes, *Compensation: Theory, Evidence, and Strategic Implications* (Thousand Oaks, CA: Sage, 2003); B. Gerhart, "Compensation Strategy and Organization Performance," in S. L. Rynes and B. Gerhart, eds., *Compensation in Organizations: Current Research and Practice* (San Francisco: Jossey-Bass, 2000), pp. 151–94.
2. B. Gerhart and G. T. Milkovich, "Organizational Differences in Managerial Compensation and Financial Performance," *Academy of Management Journal* 33 (1990), pp. 663–91.
3. E. Deci and R. Ryan, *Intrinsic Motivation and Self-Determination in Human Behavior* (New York: Plenum, 1985); A. Kohn, "Why Incentive Plans Cannot Work," *Harvard Business Review*, September–October 1993.
4. R. Eisenberger and J. Cameron "Detrimental Effects of Reward: Reality or Myth?" *American Psychologist* 51, no. 11 (1996), pp. 1153–66; S. L. Rynes, B. Gerhart, and L. Parks, "Personnel Psychology: Performance Evaluation and Compensation," *Annual Review of Psychology* (2005).
5. R. A. Lambert and D. F. Larcker, "Executive Compensation, Corporate Decision Making, and Shareholder Wealth," in *Executive Compensation*, ed. F. Foulkes (Boston: Harvard Business School Press, 1989), pp. 287–309.
6. L. R. Gomez-Mejia, H. Tosi, and T. Hinkin, "Managerial Control, Performance, and Executive Compensation," *Academy of Management Journal* 30 (1987), pp. 51–70; H. L. Tosi Jr. and L. R. Gomez-Mejia, "The Decoupling of CEO Pay and Performance: An Agency Theory Perspective," *Administrative Science Quarterly* 34 (1989), pp. 169–89.
7. K. M. Eisenhardt, "Agency Theory: An Assessment and Review," *Academy of Management Review* 14 (1989), pp. 57–74.
8. R. E. Hoskisson, M. A. Hitt, and C.W. L. Hill, "Managerial Incentives and Investment in R&D in Large Multiproduct Firms," *Organizational Science* 4 (1993), pp. 325–41; M. Bloom and G. T. Milkovich, "Relationships among Risk, Incentive Pay, and Organizational Performance," *Academy of Management Journal* 41 (1998), pp. 283–97.
9. Eisenhardt, "Agency Theory."
10. Ibid.; E. J. Conlon and J. M. Parks, "Effects of Monitoring and Tradition on Compensation Arrangements: An Experiment with Principal–Agent Dyads," *Academy of Management Journal* 33 (1990), pp. 603–22; K. M. Eisenhardt, "Agency- and Institutional-Theory Explanations: The Case of Retail Sales Compensation," *Academy of Management Journal* 31 (1988), pp. 488–511; Gerhart and Milkovich, "Employee Compensation."
11. G. T. Milkovich, J. Hannon, and B. Gerhart, "The Effects of Research and Development Intensity on Managerial Compensation in Large Organizations," *Journal of High Technology Management Research* 2 (1991), pp. 133–50.
12. G. T. Milkovich and A. K. Wigdor, *Pay for Performance* (Washington, DC: National Academy Press, 1991); Gerhart and Milkovich, "Employee Compensation"; Gerhart and Rynes, *Compensation: Theory, Evidence, and Strategic Implications*.
13. C. Trevor, B. Gerhart, and J. W. Boudreau, "Voluntary Turnover and Job Performance: Curvilinearity and the Moderating Influences of Salary Growth and Promotions," *Journal of Applied Psychology* 82 (1997), pp. 44–61; C. B. Cadsby, F. Song, and F. Tapon, "Sorting and Incentive Effects of Pay-for-Performance: An Experimental Investigation," *Academy of Management Journal* 50 (2007), pp. 387–405; A. Salamin and P. W. Hom, "In Search of the Elusive U-Shaped Performance-Turnover Relationship: Are High Performing Swiss Bankers More Liable to Quit?" *Journal of Applied Psychology* 90 (2005), pp. 1204–16.
14. R. D. Bretz, R. A. Ash, and G. F. Dreher, "Do People Make the Place? An Examination of the Attraction–Selection–Attrition Hypothesis," *Personnel Psychology* 42 (1989), pp. 561–81; T. A. Judge and R. D. Bretz, "Effect of Values on Job Choice Decisions," *Journal of Applied Psychology* 77 (1992), pp. 261–71; D. M. Cable and T. A. Judge, "Pay Performances and Job Search Decisions: A Person–Organization Fit Perspective," *Personnel Psychology* 47 (1994), pp. 317–48.
15. E. E. Lawler III, *Strategic Pay* (San Francisco: Jossey-Bass, 1990); Gerhart and Milkovich, "Employee Compensation"; Gerhart and Rynes, *Compensation: Theory, Evidence, and Strategic Implications;* B. Gerhart, C. Trevor, and M. Graham, "New Directions in Employee Compensation Research" in G. R. Ferris (ed.), *Research in Personnel and Human Resources Management* (London: JAI Press, 1996), pp. 143–203; M. Beer and M. D. Cannon, "Promise and Peril in Implementing Pay-for-Performance," *Human Resource Management* 43 (2004), pp. 3–20.
16. R. D. Bretz, G. T. Milkovich, and W. Read, "The Current State of Performance Appraisal Research and Practice," *Journal of Management* 18 (1992), pp. 321–52; R. L. Heneman, "Merit Pay Research," *Research in Personnel and Human Resource Management* 8 (1990), pp. 203–63; Milkovich and Wigdor, *Pay for Performance;* Rynes, Gerhart, and Parks, "Personnel Psychology: Performance Evaluation and Compensation."
17. Bretz et al., "Current State of Performance Appraisal."
18. Ibid.
19. Ibid.
20. W. E. Deming, *Out of the Crisis* (Cambridge, MA: Center for Advanced Engineering Study, Massachusetts Institute of Technology, 1986), p. 110.
21. Ibid.
22. Ibid.
23. Trevor et al., "Voluntary Turnover."

24. Rynes and Gerhart, *Compensation: Theory, Evidence, and Strategic Implications*.
25. Rynes, Gerhart, and Parks, "Personnel Psychology: Performance Evaluation and Compensation."
26. R. Folger and M. A. Konovsky, "Effects of Procedural and Distributive Justice on Reactions to Pay Raise Decisions," *Academy of Management Journal* 32 (1989), pp. 115–30; J. Greenberg, "Determinants of Perceived Fairness of Performance Evaluations," *Journal of Applied Psychology* 71 (1986), pp. 340–42.
27. Rynes, Gerhart, and Parks, "Personnel Psychology: Performance Evaluation and Compensation."
28. B. Gerhart and S. Rynes, "Determinants and Consequences of Salary Negotiations by Graduating Male and Female MBAs," *Journal of Applied Psychology* (1991), pp. 256–62; Gerhart and Rynes, *Compensation: Theory, Evidence, and Strategic Implications*.
29. E. A. Locke, D. B. Feren, V. M. McCaleb, K. N. Shaw, and A. T. Denny, "The Relative Effectiveness of Four Methods of Motivating Employee Performance," in *Changes in Working Life*, ed. K. D. Duncan, M. M. Gruenberg, and D. Wallis (New York: Wiley, 1980), pp. 363–88; for a summary of additional evidence, see also Gerhart and Rynes, *Compensation: Theory, Evidence, and Strategic Implications*.
30. Gerhart and Milkovich, "Employee Compensation."
31. This idea has been referred to as the "share economy." See M. L. Weitzman, "The Simple Macroeconomics of Profit Sharing," *American Economic Review* 75 (1985), pp. 937–53. For supportive empirical evidence, see the following studies: J. Chelius and R. S. Smith, "Profit Sharing and Employment Stability," *Industrial and Labor Relations Review* 43 (1990), pp. 256S–73S; B. Gerhart and L. O. Trevor, "Employment Stability under Different Managerial Compensation Systems," working paper 1995 (Cornell University: Center for Advanced Human Resource Studies); D. L. Kruse, "Profit Sharing and Employment Variability: Microeconomic Evidence on the Weitzman Theory," *Industrial and Labor Relations Review* 44 (1991), pp. 437–53.
32. Gerhart and Milkovich, "Employee Compensation"; M. L. Weitzman and D. L. Kruse, "Profit Sharing and Productivity," in *Paying for Productivity*, ed. A. S. Blinder (Washington, DC: Brookings Institution, 1990); D. L. Kruse, *Profit Sharing: Does It Make a Difference?* (Kalamazoo, MI: Upjohn Institute, 1993); M. Magnan and S. St-Onge, "The Impact of Profit Sharing on the Performance of Financial Services Firms," *Journal of Management Studies* 42 (2005), pp. 761–91.
33. "GM/UAW: The Battle Goes On," *Ward's Auto World* (May 1995), p. 40; E. M. Coates III, "Profit Sharing Today: Plans and Provisions," *Monthly Labor Review* (April 1991), pp. 19–25.
34. Gerhart and Rynes, *Compensation: Theory, Evidence, and Strategic Implications*.
35. American Management Association, *CompFlash*, April 1991, p. 3.
36. "Executive Compensation: Taking Stock," *Personnel* 67 (December 1990), pp. 7–8; "Another Day, Another Dollar Needs Another Look," *Personnel* 68 (January 1991), pp. 9–13; J. Blasi, D. Kruse, and A. Bernstein, *In the Company of Owners* (New York: Basic Books, 2003).
37. Gerhart and Milkovich, "Organizational Differences in Managerial Compensation."
38. *EBRI Databook on Employee Benefits* (Washington, DC: Employee Benefit Research Institute, 1995). www.nceo.org (National Center for Employee Ownership Web site).
39. D. Jones and T. Kato, "The Productivity Effects of Employee Stock Ownership Plans and Bonuses: Evidence from Japanese Panel Data," *American Economic Review* 185, no. 3 (June 1995), pp. 391–414.
40. "Employees Left Holding the Bag," *Fortune* (May 20, 1991), pp. 83–93; M. A. Conte and J. Svejnar, "The Performance Effects of Employee Ownership Plans," in *Paying for Productivity*, pp. 245–94.
41. Conte and Svejnar, "Performance Effects of Employee Ownership Plans."
42. Ibid.; T. H. Hammer, "New Developments in Profit Sharing, Gainsharing, and Employee Ownership," in *Productivity in Organizations*, ed. J. P. Campbell, R. J. Campbell and Associates (San Francisco: Jossey-Bass, 1988); K. J. Klein, "Employee Stock Ownership and Employee Attitudes: A Test of Three Models," *Journal of Applied Psychology* 72 (1987), pp. 319–32.
43. J. L. Pierce, S. Rubenfeld, and S. Morgan, "Employee Ownership: A Conceptual Model of Process and Effects," *Academy of Management Review* 16 (1991), pp. 121–44.
44. R. T. Kaufman, "The Effects of Improshare on Productivity," *Industrial and Labor Relations Review* 45 (1992), pp. 311–22; M. H. Schuster, "The Scanlon Plan: A Longitudinal Analysis," *Journal of Applied Behavioral Science* 20 (1984), pp. 23–28; M. M. Petty, B. Singleton, and D. W. Connell, "An Experimental Evaluation of an Organizational Incentive Plan in the Electric Utility Industry," *Journal of Applied Psychology* 77 (1992), pp. 427–36; W. N. Cooke, "Employee Participation Programs, Group-Based Incentives, and Company Performance: A Union–Nonunion Comparison," *Industrial and Labor Relations Review* 47 (1994), pp. 594–609; J. B. Arthur and L. Aiman-Smith, "Gainsharing and Organizational Learning: An Analysis of Employee Suggestions over Time," *Academy of Management Journal* 44 (2001), pp. 737–54; J. B. Arthur and G. S. Jelf, "The Effects of Gainsharing on Grievance Rates and Absenteeism over Time," *Journal of Labor Research* 20 (1999), pp. 133–45.
45. T. L. Ross and R. A. Ross, "Gainsharing: Sharing Improved Performance," in *The Compensation Handbook*, 3rd ed., ed. M. L. Rock and L. A. Berger (New York: McGraw-Hill, 1991).
46. T. M. Welbourne and L. R. Gomez-Mejia, "Team Incentives in the Workplace," in *The Compensation Handbook*, 3rd ed.
47. R. S. Kaplan and D. P. Norton "Using the Balanced Scorecard as a Strategic Management System," *Harvard Business Review*, January–February 1996, pp. 75–85.
48. M. C. Jensen and K. J. Murphy, "Performance Pay and Top-Management Incentives," *Journal of Political Economy* 98 (1990), pp. 225–64; A stronger relationship between CEO pay and performance was found by R. K. Aggarwal and A. A. Samwick, "The Other Side of the Trade-off: The Impact of Risk on Executive Compensation," *Journal of Political Economy* 107 (1999), pp. 65–105. Also, these observed relationships actually translate into significant changes in CEO pay in response to modest changes in financial performance of a company, as made clear by Gerhart and Rynes, *Compensation: Theory, Evidence, and Strategic Implications*.
49. M. C. Jensen and K. J. Murphy, "CEO Incentives—It's Not How Much You Pay, but How," *Harvard Business Review* 68 (May–June 1990), pp. 138–53. The definitive resource on executive pay is B. R. Ellis, *The Complete Guide to Executive Compensation* (New York: McGraw-Hill, 2002).
50. Gerhart and Milkovich, "Organizational Differences in Managerial Compensation."
51. Sears, Roebuck proxy statement to shareholders, March 22, 2004. Available at www.sec.gov.
52. J. Cutcher-Gershenfeld, "The Impact on Economic Performance of a Transformation in Workplace Relations," *Industrial and Labor Relations Review* 44 (1991), pp. 241–60; Irene Goll, "Environment, Corporate Ideology, and Involvement Programs," *Industrial Relations* 30 (1991), pp. 138–49.

53. L. R. Gomez-Mejia and D. B. Balkin, *Compensation, Organizational Strategy, and Firm Performance* (Cincinnati: South-Western, 1992); G. D. Jenkins and E. E. Lawler III, "Impact of Employee Participation in Pay Plan Development," *Organizational Behavior and Human Performance* 28 (1981), pp. 111–28.
54. D. I. Levine and L. D. Tyson, "Participation, Productivity, and the Firm's Environment," in *Paying for Productivity*.
55. T. Welbourne, D. Balkin, and L. Gomez-Mejia, "Gainsharing and Mutual Monitoring: A Combined Agency–Organizational Justice Interpretation," *Academy of Management Journal* 38 (1995), pp. 881–99.
56. Ibid.
57. Blinder, *Paying for Productivity*.
58. Hammer, "New Developments in Profit Sharing"; Milkovich and Wigdor, *Pay for Performance;* D. J. B. Mitchell, D. Lewin, and E. E. Lawler III, "Alternative Pay Systems, Firm Performance and Productivity," in *Paying for Productivity*.
59. Kaufman, "The Effects of Improshare on Productivity"; M. H. Schuster, "The Scanlon Plan: A Longitudinal Analysis," *Journal of Applied Behavioral Science* 20 (1984), pp. 23–28; J. A. Wagner III, P. Rubin, and T. J. Callahan, "Incentive Payment and Nonmanagerial Productivity: An Interrupted Time Series Analysis of Magnitude and Trend," *Organizational Behavior and Human Decision Processes* 42 (1988), pp. 47–74.
60. C. R. Gowen III and S. A. Jennings, "The Effects of Changes in Participation and Group Size on Gainsharing Success: A Case Study," *Journal of Organizational Behavior Management* 11 (1991), pp. 147–69.
61. L. Hatcher, T. L. Ross, and D. Collins, "Attributions for Participation and Nonparticipation in Gainsharing-Plan Involvement Systems," *Group and Organization Studies* 16 (1991), pp. 25–43; Mitchell et al., "Alternative Pay Systems."
62. B. R. Ellig, "Compensation Elements: Market Phase Determines the Mix," *Compensation and Benefits Review* 13 (3) (1981), pp. 30–38; L. R. Gomez-Mejia and D. B. Balkin, *Compensation, Organizational Strategy, and Firm Performance* (Cincinnati, Ohio: South-Western Publishing, 1992); M. K. Kroumova and J. C. Sesis, "Intellectual Capital, Monitoring, and Risk: What Predicts the Adoption of Employee Stock Options?" *Industrial Relations* 45 (2006), pp. 734–52; Y. Yanadori and J. H. Marler, "Compensation Strategy: Does Business Strategy Influence Compensation in High-Technology Firms?" *Strategic Management Journal* 27 (2006), pp. 559–70; B. Gerhart, "Compensation Strategy and Organizational Performance" in S. L. Rynes and B. Gerhart (eds.), *Compensation in Organizations* (San Francisco: Jossey-Bass, 2000).
63. A. J. Baker, "Stock Options—a Perk That Built Silicon Valley," *The Wall Street Journal*, June 23, 1993, p. A20.

13

CHAPTER

# Employee Benefits

## LO LEARNING OBJECTIVES

After reading this chapter, you should be able to:

- **LO1** Discuss the growth in benefits costs and the underlying reasons for that growth. *page 561*
- **LO2** Explain the major provisions of employee benefits programs. *page 564*
- **LO3** Discuss how employee benefits in the United States compare with those in other countries. *page 579*
- **LO4** Describe the effects of benefits management on cost and workforce quality. *page 583*
- **LO5** Explain the importance of effectively communicating the nature and value of benefits to employees. *page 590*
- **LO6** Describe the regulatory constraints that affect the way employee benefits are designed and administered. *page 594*

# Enter the World of Business

## The Boss Taketh Away and the Boss Giveth

**As health benefits shrink, companies add other perks; buying extra vacation days.**

Employers might appear stingy as a result of cuts to pensions and health-care, but recently, companies have been trying to lessen the pain by introducing other kinds of workplace benefits. Most of the added benefits are intended to help both employers and employees. For workers, new job benefits are increasingly important as the loss of others forces them to take on added responsibility for funding their own retirement savings and paying medical expenses. Companies needing to hire skilled workers are finding that more generous benefits can help lure applicants. And other companies are cutting worker turnover by making it easier for employees to juggle family and work life.

Faced with a shortage of engineers, defense contractor Raytheon Co. has begun extending benefits to partners and dependents of gay employees because "we don't want to be limited in our access to any of these talent pools," the company says. Indeed, one-third of companies in a recent survey by the Society for Human Resource Management, a professional organization, currently offer domestic-partner benefits for gay and other nontraditional families, up from 16 percent in 2001.

Tonie Moya, a test engineer in Raytheon's intelligence and information systems division, says the company's domestic-partner benefits lured her two years ago from her previous job with another defense contractor. Ms. Moya, whose three children already had health coverage, lives in Aurora, Colo., with her partner of 13 years. "The health benefits and being able to cover my domestic partner were most important," Ms. Moya says.

Service companies such as Hilton Hotels Corp. and Wachovia Corp. are battling absenteeism by allowing employees to lump vacation and sick days into a single bank of days off. Hewitt Associates, a human-resources consulting firm, found in a recent survey of workplace benefits that 18 percent of companies offered so-called paid-time-off banks last year, up from 10 percent five years earlier.

"It is one great benefit at the Hilton," says Margaret Carlos, an executive administrator for the hotel chain in North Glendale, Calif. "I grew up in the Philippines, and I can plan ahead and use the balance of banked time for when I go to my country," she says.

To appeal to younger workers, most companies have ditched casual Fridays in favor of casual full-time, a perk offered by nearly two-thirds of companies last year, compared with less than half in 2000, the Hewitt survey showed.

Other companies are offering more time off. Biotechnology firm Genentech Inc. starts out its workers with three weeks of paid vacation, instead of the traditional two weeks, and employees are eligible for a six-week sabbatical after six years on the job. Still, that isn't enough for some people, and 19 percent of companies surveyed by Hewitt allow their employees to buy additional vacation days, up from 14 percent five years earlier.

The new workplace perks come as employees are being squeezed in other areas. Many have been forced to pay a greater share of their medical expenses and to take responsibility for funding more of their retirement savings. Employers are eager to offload some of these expenses after facing years of soaring health-care costs and traditional pension plans that have become increasingly burdensome as the population ages.

Some companies have dropped health-care coverage altogether: The share of companies offering any type of medical plan has fallen to 61 percent from 69 percent since 2000, with most of the decline among smaller employers, according to the Hewitt study.

"Employers are focusing on what they can do to get the best people and keep them once they have found them. Where can they get a significant bang for their buck?" says Carol Sladek, work/life consultant for Hewitt.

Flexible work schedules, including variable hours and telecommuting, are another fast-expanding benefit, according to the Hewitt study. However, job sharing, which splits a position among multiple workers, peaked as a fad and is now offered by 18 percent of companies, down from 26 percent in 2001, according to the Society for Human Resource Management survey. Polly Heinen, an assistant manager at Principal Financial Group Inc. in Des Moines, Iowa, reduced her workweek to just four days, while keeping her full-time hours, after the birth of her third child. "Friday is my pretend-that-I-am-a-stay-at-home-mom day. We go to Chuck E. Cheese sometimes, or go to the park. It has been a lifesaver. I absolutely love it."

Among other expanding benefits: Companies increasingly are partnering junior workers with more senior employees to help them plan their careers and navigate the corporate culture, human-resources experts say. Ed Goings joined KPMG LLP in Chicago five years ago after a career in law enforcement, but he had difficulty adapting to the corporate world. The firm two years ago set him up with a mentor who he says taught him the ropes. Since then, Mr. Goings has been promoted twice and now is head of forensic technology in the Midwest for KPMG. "The field is very lucrative. I could leave this job at any time and possibly make more money," he says. The mentoring program is "one of the main reasons I am still at KPMG."

Discounted prices are another growing trend. By making available home and auto insurance in the workplace, companies are able to get group discounts for their employees. Entertainment discounts and ticket-purchasing services are now offered by 23 percent of companies surveyed by Hewitt, up from 14 percent in 2000. Still, some of these discounted services, like life insurance, replace ones that were formerly paid for by employers.

Even as many companies drop or scale back traditional pension plans, the number of employers offering some type of retirement program rose to 81 percent this spring from 73 percent in 2001, according to the Society for Human Resource Management survey. Bill Bland, owner of Nu-Lane Cargo Services of Visalia, Calif., a three-year-old transportation brokerage firm, started a 401 (k) plan recently to discourage turnover among his 25 employees. "It reduces their wanting to go out and explore other opportunities," he says.

Source: M. P. McQueen, "The Boss Taketh Away and the Boss Giveth," *The Wall Street Journal*, October 24, 2006, p. D1.

## Introduction

If we think of benefits as a part of total employee compensation, many of the concepts discussed in the two previous chapters on employee compensation apply here as well. This means, for example, that both cost and behavioral objectives are important. The cost of benefits adds an average of 37 percent to every dollar of payroll, thus accounting for about 27 percent of the total employee compensation package. Controlling labor costs is not possible without controlling benefits costs. When General Motors pays more than $1,700 in health care costs per car produced, more than it spends on steel, its ability to sell automobiles at a competitive price is challenged, when health care costs per vehicle are $180 at Toyota (U.S. plants), and $107 at Honda (U.S. plants).[1] On the behavioral side, benefits seem to influence whether potential employees come to work for a company, whether they stay, when they retire—perhaps even how they perform (although the empirical evidence, especially on the latter point, is surprisingly limited). Different employees look for different types of benefits. Employers need to regularly reexamine their benefits to see whether they fit the needs of today rather than yesterday. The chapter opening story indicates that while many employers continue to shift away from traditional pension plans and shift health care costs to control overall benefits costs, they are, at the same time, offering new benefits as needed to be competitive in the labor market.

Although it makes sense to think of benefits as part of total compensation, benefits have unique aspects. First, there is the question of legal compliance. Although direct compensation is subject to government regulation, the scope and impact of regulation on benefits is far greater. Some benefits, such as Social Security, are mandated by law. Others, although not mandated, are subject to significant regulation or must meet certain criteria to achieve the most favorable tax treatment; these include pensions and savings plans. The heavy involvement of government in benefits decisions reflects the central role benefits play in maintaining economic security.

A second unique aspect of benefits is that organizations so typically offer them that they have come to be institutionalized. Providing medical and retirement benefits of some sort remains almost obligatory for many (e. g., large) employers. A large employer that did not offer such benefits to its full-time employees would be highly unusual, and the employer might well have trouble attracting and retaining a quality workforce. Of course, as the chapter opening story indicates, norms regarding benefits programs also evolve and change.

A third unique aspect of benefits, compared with other forms of compensation, is their complexity. It is relatively easy to understand the value of a dollar as part of a salary, but not as part of a benefits package. The advantages and disadvantages of different types of medical coverage, pension provisions, disability insurance, and so forth are often difficult to grasp, and their value (beyond a general sense that they are good to have) is rarely as clear as the value of one's salary. Most fundamentally, employees may not even be aware of the benefits available to them; and if they are aware, they may not understand how to use them. When employers spend large sums of money on benefits but employees do not understand the benefits or attach much value to them, the return on employers' benefits investment will be fairly dismal.[2] Thus, another reason for giving more responsibility to employees for retirement planning and other benefits is to increase their understanding of the value of such benefits.

## Reasons for Benefits Growth

**LO1**
Discuss the Growth in Benefits Costs and the Underlying Reasons for That Growth.

In thinking about benefits as part of total compensation, a basic question arises: Why do employers choose to channel a significant portion of the compensation dollar away from cash (wages and salaries) into benefits? Economic theory tells us that people prefer a dollar in cash over a dollar's worth of any specific commodity because the cash can be used to purchase the commodity or something else.[3] Thus cash is less restrictive. Several factors, however, have contributed to less emphasis on cash and more on benefits in compensation. To understand these factors, it is useful to examine the growth in benefits over time and the underlying reasons for that growth.

figure 13.1

Growth of Employee Benefits, Percentage of Wages and Salaries and of Total Compensation, 1929–2006

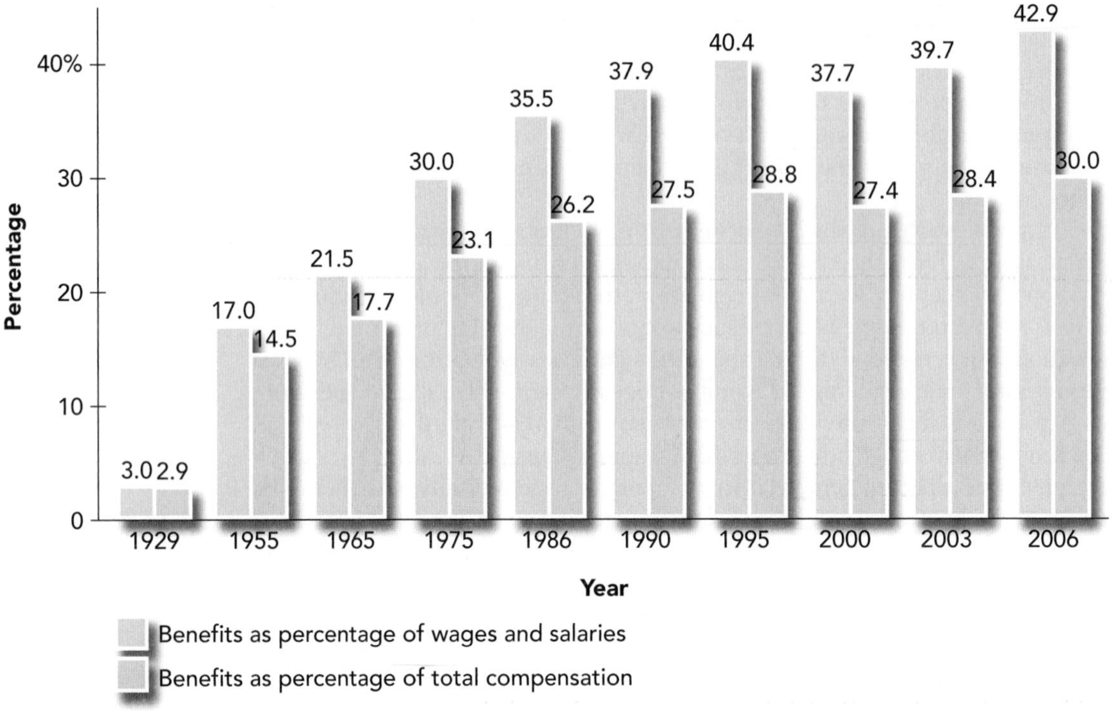


SOURCES: Data through 1990, U.S. Chamber of Commerce Research Center, *Employee Benefits 1990, Employee Benefits 1997, Employee Benefits 2000* (Washington, DC: U.S. Chamber of Commerce, 1991, 1997, and 2000). Data from 1995 onward, "Employer Cost for Employer Compensation," www.bls.gov.

Figure 13.1 gives an indication of the overall growth in benefits. Note that in 1929, on the eve of the Great Depression, benefits added an average of only 3 percent to every dollar of payroll. By 1955 this figure had grown to 17 percent, and it has continued to grow, now accounting for about 43 cents on top of every payroll dollar.

Many factors contributed to this tremendous growth.[4] First, during the 1930s several laws were passed as part of Franklin Roosevelt's New Deal, a legislative program aimed at buffering people from the devastating effects of the Great Depression. The Social Security Act and other legislation established legally required benefits (such as the Social Security retirement system) and modified the tax structure in such a way as to effectively make other benefits—such as workers' compensation (for work-related injuries) and unemployment insurance—mandatory. Second, wage and price controls instituted during World War II, combined with labor market shortages, forced employers to think of new ways to attract and retain employees. Because benefits were not covered by wage controls, employers channeled more resources in this direction. Once institutionalized, such benefits tended to remain even after wage and price controls were lifted.

Third, the tax treatment of benefits programs is often more favorable for employees than the tax treatment of wages and salaries, meaning that a dollar spent on benefits has the potential to generate more value for the employees than the same dollar

**table 13.1**

Example of Marginal Tax Rates for an Employee Salary of $50,000

| | NOMINAL TAX RATE | EFFECTIVE TAX RATE |
|---|---|---|
| Federal | 25.0% | 25.0% |
| State (New York) | 6.8 | 5.1 |
| City (New York) | 3.7 | 2.8 |
| Social Security | 6.2 | 6.2 |
| Medicare | 1.45 | 1.45 |
| Total tax rate | | 40.55 |

Note: State and city taxes are deductible on the federal tax return, reducing their effective tax rate.

**Marginal Tax Rate**
The percentage of an additional dollar of earnings that goes to taxes.

spent on wages and salaries. The **marginal tax rate** is the percentage of additional earnings that goes to taxes. Consider the hypothetical employee in Table 13.1 and the effect on take-home pay of a $1,000 increase in salary. The total effective marginal tax rate is higher for higher-paid employees and also varies according to state and city. (New York State and New York City are among the highest.) A $1,000 annual raise for the employee earning $50,000 per year would increase net pay $594.50 ($1,000 × [1 − .4055]). In contrast, an extra $1,000 put into benefits would lead to an increase of $1,000 in "take-home benefits."

Employers, too, realize tax advantages from certain types of benefits. Although both cash compensation and most benefits are deductible as operating expenses, employers (like employees) pay Social Security tax on salaries below a certain amount ($97,500 in 2007) and Medicare tax on the entire salary, as well as other taxes like workers' compensation and unemployment compensation. However, no such taxes are paid on most employee benefits. The bottom line is that the employer may be able to provide more value to employees by spending the extra $1,000 on benefits instead of salary.

The tax advantage of benefits also takes another form. Deferring compensation until retirement allows the employee to receive cash, but at a time (retirement) when the employee's tax rate is sometimes lower because of a lower income level. More important, perhaps, is that investment returns on the deferred money typically accumulate tax free, resulting in much faster growth of the investment.

A fourth factor that has influenced benefits growth is the cost advantage that groups typically realize over individuals. Organizations that represent large groups of employees can purchase insurance (or self-insure) at a lower rate because of economies of scale, which spread fixed costs over more employees to reduce the cost per person. Insurance risks can be more easily pooled in large groups, and large groups can also achieve greater bargaining power in dealing with insurance carriers or medical providers.

A fifth factor influencing the growth of benefits was the growth of organized labor from the 1930s through the 1950s. This growth was partly a result of another piece of New Deal legislation, the National Labor Relations Act, which greatly enhanced trade unions' ability to organize workers and negotiate contracts with employers. Benefits were often a key negotiation objective. (Indeed, they still are. It is estimated that more than half of workers who struck in the early 1990s did so over health care coverage issues.)[5] Unions were able to successfully pursue their members' interests in benefits, particularly when tax advantages provided an incentive for employers to shift money from

**table 13.2**

Differentiating via Benefits

| | |
|---|---|
| CMP Media | $30,000 for infertility treatments or adoption |
| Fannie Mae | 10 paid hours per month for volunteer work |
| Microstrategy | One-week Caribbean cruise each January |
| Eli Lilly | Free Lilly drugs (including Prozac) |
| Pfizer | Free Pfizer drugs (including Viagra) |
| Intel | Eight-week sabbatical after seven years |

SOURCE: From "100 Best Companies to Work For," *Fortune*. 

cash to benefits. For unions, a new benefit such as medical coverage was a tangible success that could have more impact on prospective union members than a wage increase of equivalent value, which might have amounted to only a cent or two per hour. Also, many nonunion employers responded to the threat of unionization by implementing the same benefits for their own employees, thus contributing to benefits growth.

Finally, employers may also provide unique benefits as a means of differentiating themselves in the eyes of current or prospective employees. In this way, employers communicate key aspects of their culture that set them apart from the rest of the pack. Table 13.2 shows some examples.

## Benefits Programs

**LO2**
Explain the Major Provisions of Employee Benefits Programs.

Most benefits fall into one of the following categories: social insurance, private group insurance, retirement, pay for time not worked, and family-friendly policies.[6] Table 13.3, based on Bureau of Labor Statistics (BLS) data, provides an overview of the prevalence of specific benefits programs. As Table 13.3 shows, the percentage of employees covered by these benefits programs increases with establishment size. Among the largest employers, these percentages would be higher still. Likewise, as shown in Table 13.4, benefits (and total compensation) costs also increase with establishment size.

**table 13.3**

Percentage of Full-Time Workers in U.S. Private Sector Who Participated in Selected Benefits Programs, 2006, by Establishment Size

| | ESTABLISHMENTS HAVING 100 WORKERS OR MORE | ESTABLISHMENTS HAVING LESS THAN 100 WORKERS |
|---|---|---|
| Medical care | 63% | 43% |
| Dental care | 50 | 24 |
| Short-term disability insurance | 52 | 25 |
| Long-term disability insurance | 42 | 18 |
| All retirement | 67 | 37 |
| Defined benefit pension | 33 | 9 |
| Defined contribution plan | 54 | 33 |
| Life insurance | 66 | 36 |
| Paid leave | | |
| Holidays | 86 | 68 |
| Vacation | 86 | 70 |
| Family | 10 | 6 |

SOURCE: http://stats.bls.gov/ebs/home.htm.

**table 13.4**
Total Hourly Compensation and Benefits Costs by Establishment Size

| | | ESTABLISHMENT SIZE | |
|---|---|---|---|
| | ALL | 1–99 EMPLOYEES | 500 OR MORE EMPLOYEES |
| Total compensation | $27.31 | $20.74 | $36.10 |
| Wages and salaries | 19.12 | 15.28 | 24.13 |
| Benefits | 8.18 | 5.45 | 11.97 |

SOURCE: "Employer Cost for Employee Compensation," September 2006, www.bls.gov.

## Social Insurance (Legally Required)

### Social Security

Among the most important provisions of the Social Security Act of 1935 was the establishment of old-age insurance and unemployment insurance. The act was later amended to add survivor's insurance (1939), disability insurance (1956), hospital insurance (Medicare Part A, 1965), and supplementary medical insurance (Medicare Part B, 1965) for the elderly. Together these provisions constitute the federal Old Age, Survivors, Disability, and Health Insurance (OASDHI) program. Over 90 percent of U.S. employees are covered by the program, the main exceptions being railroad and federal, state, and local government employees, who often have their own plans. Note, however, that an individual employee must meet certain eligibility requirements to receive benefits. To be fully insured typically requires 40 quarters of covered employment and minimum earnings of $1,000 per quarter in 2007. However, the eligibility rules for survivors' and disability benefits are somewhat different.

Social Security retirement (old-age insurance) benefits for fully insured workers begin at age 65 years and 6 months (full benefits) or age 62 (at a permanent reduction in benefits) for those born in 1940. The full retirement age now rises with birth year, reaching age 67 for those born in 1960 or later. Although the amount of the benefit depends on one's earnings history, benefits go up very little after a certain level (the maximum monthly benefit in 2007 was $2,116); thus high earners help subsidize benefit payments to low earners. Cost-of-living increases are provided each year that the consumer price index increases.

An important attribute of the Social Security retirement benefit is that it is free from state tax in about half of the states and entirely free from federal tax. However, the federal tax code has an earnings test for those who are still earning wages (and not yet at full retirement age). In 2007, beneficiaries between age 62 and the full retirement age were allowed to make $12,960; in the year an individual reaches full retirement age, the earnings test is $34,440. If these amounts are exceeded, the Social Security benefit is reduced $1 for every $2 in excess earnings for those under the full retirement age and $1 for every $3 in the year a worker reaches the full retirement age. These provisions are important because of their effects on the work decisions of those between 62 and full retirement age. The earnings test increases a person's incentive to retire (otherwise full Social Security benefits are not received), and if she continues to work, the incentive to work part-time rather than full-time increases.

A major change made in January 2000 is that there is no earnings test once full retirement age is reached. Therefore, these workers no longer incur any earnings penalty (and thus have no tax-related work disincentive).

How are retirement and other benefits financed? Both employers and employees are assessed a payroll tax. In 2007, each paid a tax of 7.65 percent (a total of 15.3 percent) on the first $87,900 of the employee's earnings. Of the 7.65 percent, 6.2 percent funds OASDHI, and 1.45 percent funds Medicare (Part A). In addition, the 1.45 percent Medicare tax is assessed on all earnings.

What are the behavioral consequences of Social Security benefits? Because they are legally mandated, employers do not have discretion in designing this aspect of their benefits programs. However, Social Security does affect employees' retirement decisions. The eligibility age for benefits and any tax penalty for earnings influence retirement decisions. The elimination of the tax penalty on earnings for those at full retirement age should mean a larger pool of older workers in the labor force for employers to tap into.

## Unemployment Insurance

Established by the 1935 Social Security Act, this program has four major objectives: (1) to offset lost income during involuntary unemployment, (2) to help unemployed workers find new jobs, (3) to provide an incentive for employers to stabilize employment, and (4) to preserve investments in worker skills by providing income during short-term layoffs (which allows workers to return to their employer rather than start over with another employer).

The unemployment insurance program is financed largely through federal and state taxes on employers. Although, strictly speaking, the decision to establish the program is left to each state, the Social Security Act created a tax incentive structure that quickly led every state to establish a program. The federal tax rate is currently 0.8 percent on the first $7,000 of wages. The state tax rate varies, the minimum being 5.4 percent on the first $7,000 of wages. Many states have a higher rate or impose the tax on a greater share of earnings.[7]

A very important feature of the unemployment insurance program is that no state imposes the same tax on every employer. Instead, the size of the tax depends on the employer's experience rating. Employers that have a history of laying off a large share of their workforces pay higher taxes than those who do not. In some states, an employer that has had very few layoffs may pay no state tax. In contrast, an employer with a poor experience rating could pay a tax as high as 5 to 10 percent, depending on the state.[8]

Unemployed workers are eligible for benefits if they (1) have a prior attachment to the workforce (often 52 weeks or four quarters of work at a minimum level of pay), (2) are available for work, (3) are actively seeking work (including registering at the local unemployment office), and (4) were not discharged for cause (such as willful misconduct), did not quit voluntarily, and are not out of work because of a labor dispute.

Benefits also vary by state, but they are typically about 50 percent of a person's earnings and last for 26 weeks. Extended benefits for up to 13 weeks are also available in states with a sustained unemployment rate above 6.5 percent. Emergency extended benefits are also sometimes funded by Congress. All states have minimum and maximum weekly benefit levels. In contrast to Social Security retirement benefits, unemployment benefits are taxed as ordinary income.

Because unemployment insurance is, in effect, legally required, management's discretion is limited here, too. Management's main task is to keep its experience rating low by avoiding unnecessary workforce reductions (by relying, for example, on the sorts of actions described in Chapter 5).

## Workers' Compensation

Workers' compensation laws cover job-related injuries and death.[9] Prior to enactment of these laws, workers suffering work-related injuries or diseases could receive compensation only by suing for damages. Moreover, the common-law defenses available to employers meant that such lawsuits were not usually successful. In contrast, these laws operate under a principle of no-fault liability, meaning that an employee does not need to establish gross negligence by the employer. In return, employers receive immunity from lawsuits. (One exception is the employer who intentionally contributes to a dangerous workplace.) Employees are not covered when injuries are self-inflicted or stem from intoxication or "willful disregard of safety rules."[10] Approximately 90 percent of all U.S. workers are covered by state workers' compensation laws, although again there are differences among states, with coverage ranging from 70 percent to over 95 percent.

Workers' compensation benefits fall into four major categories: (1) disability income, (2) medical care, (3) death benefits, and (4) rehabilitative services.

Disability income is typically two-thirds of predisability earnings, although each state has its own minimum and maximum. In contrast to unemployment insurance benefits, disability benefits are tax free. The system is financed differently by different states, some having a single state fund, most allowing employers to purchase coverage from private insurance companies. Self-funding by employers is also permitted in most states. The cost to the employer is based on three factors. The first factor is the nature of the occupations and the risk attached to each. Premiums for low-risk occupations may be less than 1 percent of payroll; the cost for some of the most hazardous occupations may be as high as 100 percent of payroll. The second factor is the state where work is located. For example, the loss of a leg may be worth $264,040 in Pennsylvania versus $67,860 in Colorado.[11] The third factor is the employer's experience rating.

The cost of the workers' compensation system to U.S. employers grew dramatically through 1992, leading to an increased focus on ways of controlling workers' compensation costs.[12] The experience rating system again provides an incentive for employers to make their workplaces safer. Dramatic injuries (like losing a finger or hand) are less prevalent than minor ones, such as sprains and strains. Back strain is the most expensive benign health condition in developed countries. Each year in the United States, 3–4 percent of the population is temporarily disabled and 1 percent is permanently and totally disabled.[13] Many actions can be taken to reduce workplace injuries, such as work redesign and training; and to speed the return to health, and thus to work (e.g., exercise).[14] Some changes can be fairly simple (such as permitting workers to sit instead of having them bend over). It is also important to hold managers accountable (in their performance evaluations) for making workplaces safer and getting employees back to work promptly following an injury. With the passage of the Americans with Disabilities Act, employers came under even greater pressure to deal effectively and fairly with workplace injuries. See the discussion in Chapter 3 on safety awareness programs for some of the ways employers and employees are striving to make the workplace safer.

## Private Group Insurance

As we noted earlier, group insurance rates are typically lower than individual rates because of economies of scale, the ability to pool risks, and the greater bargaining power of a group. This cost advantage, together with tax considerations and a concern for employee security, helps explain the prevalence of employer-sponsored insurance plans. We discuss two major types: medical insurance and disability insurance. Note that these programs are not legally required; rather, they are offered at the discretion of employers.

## To Retain Valued Women Employees, Companies Pitch Flextime as Macho

Here's a novel approach to keeping women in the work force: Focus on men.

Some employers are trying to overcome a perceived stigma on flexible work schedules—often viewed as a concession to women—by redefining the issue as a quality-of-life concern for everyone. The approach is gaining traction, especially in the male-dominated financial-services sector, where employers have long struggled to retain and promote women.

Among the techniques companies are testing: highlighting successful men who have tapped flexible work arrangements; encouraging more employees to work from home part of the time; and promoting alternative career paths. Many of the ideas aren't new, but it's the first time they have been aggressively pitched to men. Encouraging men to consider flexible work arrangements is a way of "making it legitimate," says Sylvia Ann Hewlett, president of the Center for Work-Life Policy, a New York research and advocacy group.

First Things First. People.
Rob McLeod, Senior Manager
When my wife and I were preparing for our second child, we were concerned about how we could manage two children under two years of age. The people at Ernst & Young overwhelmingly encouraged me to take parental leave. Not only did I take the leave, but I was able to add on some vacation time so I could spend a full month with my family. Working at Ernst & Young, I've always been able to utilize flexibility to meet my family commitments. This year, I was promoted to senior manager, and I'm looking forward to my career knowing that I can succeed professionally and meet the needs of my family...I know that Ernst & Young puts its people first. flexibility.iweb.ey.com
WORKING MOTHER
100 BEST COMPANIES 2006
top 10
Audit • Tax • Transaction Advisory Services
ERNST & YOUNG
Quality In Everything We Do


This poster took Ernst & Young's family-friendly message to Times Square.

This autumn, the New York office of accounting firm Ernst & Young LLP displayed a nine-foot poster—visible from the sidewalks of Times Square—highlighting Rob McLeod's promotion after taking a paternity leave. The poster, scaled down and sent to every office in the United States, was part of a campaign to spotlight successful men who value their personal lives. Ernst & Young also created four videos—two starring men—illustrating the firm's concern for employee needs.

Mr. McLeod, promoted to senior manager in October, endured teasing from co-workers. But he says he also received dozens of calls and e-mails from women co-workers who appreciated seeing a man who cares about balancing work with family life. He says Ernst & Young's culture is changing, as more employees leave early to be with their families and catch up on work from home. Managers, too, both men and women, are more open about leaving work to attend to their personal lives.

In Philadelphia one day last week, Ernst & Young audit partner Lisa Young told employees she'd be unavailable until 10 A.M., because she was going to build gingerbread houses at her daughter's school. When Ms. Young joined the firm, she says, she would have explained the absence as an "appointment." Ms. Young says an audit partner can work 12-hour days during busy season. The firm's flexibility push hasn't reduced her hours, but she feels more comfortable breaking up her workday.

Ernst & Young ramped up its flexibility push in the summer of 2005, when it encouraged its project teams to massage work schedules to suit personal needs. Employees could leave work early on Fridays, for example, or come in later in the mornings. At the end of the summer, managers asked for feedback. Two thousand people responded in 20 minutes; 10,000 employees, then half the firm's U.S. workforce, replied eventually. The biggest suggestion: Don't limit flexibility to summers. Executives say that's what they wanted to hear.

"We want to make flexibility gender-neutral, so everyone wants to take advantage," says Maryella Gockel, the firm's flexibility-strategy leader. Ms. Gockel says only about 10 percent of employees need to formally adjust their schedules; others just want more freedom to tend to an occasional personal need. Ernst & Young, like many firms, has long had a formal policy permitting such flexibility. But Ms. Gockel says many employees of both genders shied away from using it, fearing it would hurt career prospects.

Ms. Hewlett agrees. In a survey of 2,443 women college graduates released by her center and the *Harvard Business Review,* 35 percent of respondents thought they would be penalized for taking advantage of their employer's work-life policies. Citing other research, Ms. Hewlett says about two-thirds of professional women who stop working would stay if they had a "recognized and respectable" way to scale back.

Ernst & Young's new efforts to include men in flexible-work arrangements come on top of other programs aimed at retaining and promoting women, such as mentoring or concierge services that simplify personal lives. The firm's executives say the various initiatives appear to be having a cumulative impact: A smaller percentage of senior managers who are women leave the firm each year than men in the same group.

Rick Beal, a managing consultant at Watson Wyatt Worldwide, says he sees more employers aggressively marketing these flexibility options to all employees. Professional firms, in areas such as consulting, law and accounting, are most likely to try the tactic, he says.

Lehman Brothers Holdings Inc. is outfitting home offices and encouraging some employees to occasionally work from home. The investment-services company presents the initiative as contingency planning for a disaster, but Lehman executives say they're also hoping to convince both men and women that success doesn't require constant face time with the boss. "We're committed to destigmatizing flex" schedules, says Anne Erni, Lehman's chief diversity officer. Ms. Erni says the company believes it can retain more women and recruit younger workers if it makes the issue gender-neutral.

Heather Galler, founder of employment Web site JobKite.com, says that companies that promote flexibility to men and women tend to do better with job seekers.

Seymour Adler, a consultant for Chicago-based Aon Consulting, cites other benefits: Promoting quality-of-life programs to all employees can damp resentment from men who feel left out by women's programs. It can also address concerns of single people or non-parents who believe those with families have more flexible options.

Accounting firm Deloitte & Touche LLP is testing a program it calls "mass career customization" with 383 employees, 74 percent of whom are men. The firm, which estimates it costs an average of $150,000 to replace a lost worker, is aggressively pitching the idea that the traditional career path—focused on quickly becoming a partner—is not the only route to success. "The test employees are encouraged to consider alternatives, such as a reduced workload, a client mix with less travel, or an administrative job with less client pressure. "We're trying to get away from the notion that one size fits all," says Diane Davies, a principal at Deloitte's Los Angeles office.

SOURCE: J. Badal, "To Retain Valued Women Employees, Companies Pitch Flextime as Macho," *The Wall Street Journal*, December 11, 2006, p. B1.

## Medical Insurance

Not surprisingly, public opinion surveys indicate that medical benefits are by far the most important benefit to the average person.[15] As Table 13.3 indicates, most full-time employees in medium-size and large companies get such benefits. Three basic types of medical expenses are typically covered: hospital expenses, surgical expenses, and physicians' visits. Other benefits that employers may offer include dental care, vision care, birthing centers, and prescription drug programs. Perhaps the most important issue in benefits management is the challenge of providing quality medical benefits while controlling costs, a subject we return to in a later section.

The **Consolidated Omnibus Budget Reconciliation Act (COBRA)** of 1985 requires employers to permit employees to extend their health insurance coverage at group rates for up to 36 months following a "qualifying event" such as termination (except for gross misconduct), a reduction in hours that leads to the loss of health insurance, death, and other events. The beneficiary (whether the employee, spouse, or dependent) must have access to the same services as employees who have not lost their health insurance. Note

**Consolidated Omnibus Budget Reconciliation Act (COBRA)**
The 1985 act that requires employers to permit employees to extend their health insurance coverage at group rates for up to 36 months following a qualifying event, such as a layoff.

## EVIDENCE-BASED HR

When Cadmus Communications Corp. began requiring employees to undergo a health-risk assessment to qualify for medical coverage, some workers feared their medical conditions could cost them their jobs. But Stephanie Metzger credits the mandatory testing with possibly saving her life. Ms. Metzger, a Cadmus Communications accounts manager, says a screening revealed she had swollen thyroid nodules, one of which turned out to be cancerous. "If I had gone to my doctor, I could not have gotten that test because I didn't have any symptoms," says the Ephrata, Pa., resident. Because it was caught early, Ms. Metzger, who was then 32 years old, stayed in the hospital just 24 hours after surgery and then received outpatient treatment. Doctors now say she is cancer-free.

Like Cadmus, a growing number of companies in recent years have sought to cut medical costs by integrating so-called wellness programs into their health-care coverage. Though many programs are still in their early stages, a number of them are starting to show some positive results—both in terms of cost savings for employers and improved health for employees.

Cadmus, a publishing-services company in Richmond, Va., says its overall health-care costs grew $500,000 last year, after rising by $2 million in each of the preceding four years, an improvement the company attributes in part to its nearly two-year-old wellness program. As a result of the mandatory screenings, about 140 employees went on medication to control high blood pressure and an additional 150 went on cholesterol medication. Hospital stays fell sharply. Other companies, including supermarket chain Safeway Inc. and mortgage giant Freddie Mac, also say they have saved money through efforts to keep their workers healthier.

Many wellness programs make available free or low-cost health screenings. Some companies have installed on-site medical clinics to encourage workers to seek preventive care. Other companies require that workers undergo health-risk assessments in order to qualify for medical coverage. Employees deemed at risk, for conditions such as diabetes, heart disease and obesity, might then receive a phone call from a nurse suggesting follow-up action. A recent survey by consulting firm Hewitt Associates found that 42 percent of companies offered some type of health-risk assessment in 2005, up from 29 percent in 2001.

It might seem surprising that some companies are expanding the availability of medical services for workers. For years, employers instead have sought to control access to care, by such means as requiring primary-care physician referrals to see specialists and increasing employees' share of premiums and co-payments. A recent survey by Kaiser Family Foundation found that since 2000 the average annual worker health-care premium contribution jumped 83 percent to $2,973 for family coverage.

But in recent years a growing number of companies and insurers have been trying to remove some barriers to care based on evidence that suggests early detection and intervention will save money in the long run, especially for chronic diseases such as cancer and heart disease. "Catching something early is cheaper than a catastrophic event," says Cindy Ellis, Cadmus's benefits manager. Although the company's wellness program pushed costs up sharply last year for diagnostic screenings and prescription medicines, as more employees sought earlier intervention for health conditions, this was more than offset by savings in hospital fees. Cadmus says its employees last year spent half as many days in the hospital as compared with the previous year.

Safeway also says it has saved money as a result of new programs that eliminated certain co-payments to encourage more preventive health care, though it declined to provide detailed figures. The company last year began covering 100 percent of the cost of annual adult physicals, well-child exams, colonoscopies and mammograms for its 10,000 nonunionized employees.

And Freddie Mac says it has saved $900,000 a year in medical and lost-productivity costs from installing an in-house clinic for its 5,000 employees in 2004. The clinic, which offers such routine services as annual physicals, flu shots and allergy tests, saves the company $117 every time an employee is seen in-house instead of by an outside provider, a Freddie Mac spokeswoman says.

But some wellness programs have generated controversy for being autocratic, at least at first. To qualify for medical coverage, Cadmus last year began requiring a health-risk assessment of its 3,000 employees and their covered spouses. The assessment consisted of an online questionnaire, a blood-pressure check and a finger-prick blood test for cholesterol. Employees were assured the results would be known only to Cadmus's health insurer, Cigna Corp., and wouldn't lead to punitive premiums. Still, 17 employees dropped coverage rather than comply. "Associates were frightened and fearful. They thought that we were going to find out who was unhealthy and terminate those people," says Lisa Licata, Cadmus's senior vice president of human resources.

In return, employees got some new perks under the redesigned plan: Low-cost screenings for clogged arteries and thyroid problems, on-site mammograms, low-cost flu shots, and subsidized visits to a nutritionist. Cadmus installed blood pressure cuffs at work sites so employees could self-check. It gave away free pedometers to encourage exercise. The company even changed cafeteria and vending-machine offerings, charging more for regular soda than diet, for example.

The assessments yielded some surprises: Although only 28 percent of employees volunteered that they were overweight, tests showed 78 percent actually were. The screenings also turned up many cases of hypertension and high cholesterol. Cigna nurses contacted the at-risk employees and referred them to doctors for follow-up care. Employees weren't required to take prescriptions or change their lifestyles to keep their medical coverage.

"They used to discourage you from taking these expensive tests," says Ms. Metzger, the Cadmus employee treated for cancer. "But I paid $25 and look what happened; it was worth it. Then insurance kicked in and I paid very little out of my pocket," she says.

Ms. Ellis, the Cadmus benefits manager, says she believes a voluntary wellness program wouldn't have yielded so many positive results. "In the best scenario, you get maybe 40 percent participation" with a voluntary program, she says. Cigna says it recently instituted a similar program for its employees after seeing the results at Cadmus.

While Cadmus threatened to withhold health-care coverage from employees who didn't participate in the program, other, mostly larger, companies typically use incentives to encourage preventive care. Such programs usually apply to employees regardless of their choice of health-care plan, even those with high-deductible plans. At Molson Coors Brewing Co., for example, employees of the company's U.S. unit receive a $200 discount on their annual health-care premiums for filling out a health-risk appraisal form and following up on any medical advice. U.S. employees of AstraZeneca PLC, the pharmaceutical company, receive a $50 monthly discount on their health-insurance premiums in return for undergoing an annual health-risk assessment, a company spokeswoman says.

Dell Inc. last year started giving employees who agree to a health-risk assessment a deduction, currently $75, from their annual health-care premium. Those who complete a wellness program for managing health risks get an additional $225 deposited into an account that reimburses employees for medical expenses. While results aren't in yet, "we have every reason to believe it will be worth our investment and pay off for employees as well," said Kathleen Angel, Dell's global benefits director.

Companies also are setting up on-site medical clinics to provide primary and preventive health care for workers, at lower cost. Media group Discovery Communications, a unit of Discovery Holding Co., and casino operator Harrah's Entertainment Inc. contract with Whole Health Management Inc. to operate workplace clinics staffed with physicians and nurses. Discovery estimates it has saved $1 million a year since starting its clinic in 2004. The clinic is available to its 1,500 employees in Maryland and their dependents over the age of 14.

SOURCE: M. P. McQueen, "The Road to Wellness Is Starting at the Office; Employers' Efforts to Push Preventive Care Begin to Show Both Health and Cost Benefits," *The Wall Street Journal*, December 5, 2006, p, D1.

that the beneficiaries do not get free coverage. Rather, they receive the advantage of purchasing coverage at the group rather than the individual rate.

### Disability Insurance

Two basic types of disability coverage exist.[16] As Table 13.3 indicates, 25 to 52 percent of employees are covered by short-term disability plans and 18 to 42 percent are covered by long-term disability plans. Short-term plans typically provide benefits for six months or less, at which point long-term plans take over, potentially covering the person for life. The salary replacement rate is typically between 50 and 70 percent, although short-term plans are sometimes higher. There are often caps on the amount that can be paid each month. Federal income taxation of disability benefits depends on the funding method. Where employee contributions completely fund the plan, there is no federal tax. Benefits based on employer contributions are taxed. Finally, disability benefits, especially long-term ones, need to be coordinated with other programs, such as Social Security disability benefits.

## Retirement

Earlier we discussed the old-age insurance part of Social Security, a legally required source of retirement income. Although this remains the largest single component of the elderly's overall retirement income (39 percent), the combination of private pensions (18 percent) and earnings from assets (savings and other investments like stock) account for an even larger share (16 percent). The remainder of the elderly's income comes from earnings (24 percent) and other sources (3 percent).[17]

Employers have no legal obligation to offer private retirement plans, but many do. As we note later, if a private retirement plan is provided, it must meet certain standards set forth by the Employee Retirement Income Security Act.

### Defined Benefit

A *defined benefit plan* guarantees ("defines") a specified retirement benefit level to employees based typically on a combination of years of service and age as well as on the employee's earnings level (usually the five highest earnings years). For instance, an organization might guarantee a monthly pension payment of $1,500 to an employee retiring at age 65 with 30 years of service and an average salary over the final 5 years of $40,000. As Table 13.3 indicates, full-time employees in 33 percent of larger companies and 9 percent in smaller companies are covered by such plans. (As recently as the mid-1990s 50 percent of larger companies and 15 percent of smaller

## COMPETING THROUGH SUSTAINABILITY

### A Passion for the Planet

Patagonia aims to produce top-quality products while doing the least possible harm to the environment. It's a mission that attracts and holds top-notch talent.

Southern Californian Scott Robinson had quite a résumé when he returned from studying in France last Christmas. The 26-year-old had an undergraduate degree from Bucknell University, two MBAs, and internships at two of Europe's most respected corporations, Nestlé and Unilever Group. Yet, when it came time to take the next career step, he chose a job as a stock handler in a surf shop in Cardiff-by-the-Sea, Calif. Actually, he begged for the job. What gives? Simple, he says: "I wanted to work for a company that's driven by values."

The company is Patagonia Inc., a Ventura (Calif.) seller of outdoor clothing and equipment that has a reputation as an enlightened employer and champion of the environment. On his return from France, Robinson read *Let My People Go Surfing*, a memoir and manifesto of sustainable business practices by Patagonia founder and Chairman Yvon Chouinard. The company's goal is as simple as it is challenging: to produce the highest-quality products while doing the least possible harm to the environment.

That mission is a daily inspiration for Patagonia's 1,275 employees, from Chouinard to the flip-flop-wearing guy who answers the phone in the headquarters lobby. Most corporate mission statements are empty platitudes. This one guides every decision. And it's the centerpiece of a set of management practices that have helped Patagonia grow at a healthy rate and retain what is arguably the best reputation in its industry even while it faces increasing competition from much larger companies.

Patagonia's philosophy is the handiwork of Chouinard, a gruff yet funny outdoorsman who, despite his 67 years and arthritic hands, hasn't slowed down much. He helped pioneer modern rock-climbing techniques in his youth and now prowls the globe in search of outdoor adventures and product ideas. That is, when he's not shaking up his 33-year-old company, helping to preserve the environment, or advocating radical changes in the way Americans do business. "Most people want to do good things, but don't. At Patagonia, it's an essential part of your life," says Chouinard.

At a time when companies must adapt to an ever-quickening competitive pace, a highly motivated workforce can provide a crucial edge. Until now, there have been two primary approaches to keeping employees at the top of their game. At the high-stress workplace, bosses rule by fear, kicking ass and taking names. At feel-good places, managers try to motivate employees with kind words and generous benefits. Neither approach is optimal. In a recent Gallup Poll, only one-third of Americans considered themselves passionate about their jobs.

A few companies have found a better way. "There are companies that stress continuous improvement and being way better than the competition but also make people feel comfortable," says Stanford University professor Jeffrey Pfeffer. These companies range from publicly traded giants such as FedEx and Southwest Airlines to small fry like Patagonia. They are meritocracies with ambitious goals that trust their employees to do the right thing—and give them the tools and time they need to do it.

Patagonia, with 39 stores in seven countries, works hard at achieving that delicate balance. It offers an on-site day-care center at its headquarters and full medical benefits to all employees, including part-timers. When the surf's up, Chouinard himself urges people to hit the beach. At the same time, the company demands hard work, creativity, collaboration, and results. Management isn't shy about axing employees who aren't up to snuff.

**Reluctant Businessman**

Patagonia enjoys an unrivaled reputation among outdoor aficionados, and its green philosophy is gaining broader appeal as more Americans embrace sustainable consumption. Chouinard's goal for Patagonia's own sustainability: "I look at this company as an experiment to see if we can run it so it's here 100 years from now and always makes the best-quality stuff," he says. That means keeping growth relatively slow but steady, at about 5 percent per year. Revenues were up a healthy 7 percent last year, to $260 million. Operating margins typically come in at the high end of the 12 percent to 15 percent industry average, according to people who have seen the numbers, and that's after it donates 1 percent of revenues to environmental groups. Patagonia, which declined to comment on its financials, is owned by a Chouinard family trust.

Chouinard calls himself a reluctant businessman. He disdains cell phones and laptops as much as he does quarterly-earnings-obsessed executives. (As you might imagine, he's as likely to take the company public as he is to club baby seals.) Yet he finds that concern for quality and sustainability doesn't pose a conflict with running a highly successful business. "Every time we do the right thing, our profits go up," he says.

Odd as it may sound, Chouinard gets a lot of business done standing waist-deep in water. He has coined a term—MBA, or managing by absence—that sums up his leadership philosophy. At the office, he's totally plugged in. But he spends much of his time traveling around the world doing outdoor things and talking to outdoor people about their likes and dislikes. Sometimes the best way for new CEO Casey Sheahan to get face time with Chouinard is to meet him on the water. Last year, the two were fishing for steelhead in British Columbia when they noticed that their feet were cold. Clearly their Patagonia waders weren't up to the job. They decided to launch a series of quality meetings to review and improve the company's products.

Chouinard and Sheahan are hardly the only Patagonia employees to enjoy "Eureka!" moments in the great outdoors. Getting away from the office regularly is a job requirement—considered essential for dreaming up the next generation of products. Whenever employees play outdoors, they're testing the newest gear or coming up with improvements. Regularly, teams of 20 to 30 people, including outdoor professionals Patagonia calls its ambassadors, go on excursions where they climb, fish, ski, or surf.

During such an outing at Yosemite National Park two years ago, mountaineer Dean Potter snipped the legs off of a pair of climbing pants at mid-calf so he could see his feet as he climbed. The next year, Patagonia offered a successful line of pants based on his ideas. "We spend a lot of the time climbing and cooking and drinking excessively," says designer Carey Mullett. "It's hard for people who are used to a fixed itinerary to understand, but it's this kind of deconstruction that leads to the most creative work."

Patagonians like to say they don't have a corporate culture, they have an unconventional culture. That goes not just for product innovations but for new business ventures. You can see the effect of this philosophy in the company's major new strategic initiative, surf shops. It signed up three professional surfer brothers, Chris, Keith, and Dan Malloy, who had sponsorship contracts with larger surf outfitters, to help come up with a vision of what Patagonia surfing should be.

The Malloys, with their deep tans and unruly sun-bleached hair, are far from the usual corporate stiffs. Chris, 34, explains how they bonded with Chouinard, a crack surfer himself, during a trip to Chile in 2004. They discovered they shared concerns about water pollution and wastefulness. (Chouinard, Chris notes, wore the same shorts eight days straight. Now that's conservation!)

**Green Sabbaticals**

Ultimately, given the freedom to try something different, the Malloys and Patagonia's strategists came up with a new concept for a surf store. Rather than copying rivals and selling loud clothing and boards that break easily, it sells durable boards and wet suits, and simple, long-lasting clothing. The focus is on "authenticity" and building a solid community—one that will, they hope, give their shops a sustainable edge. Every store will have a space set aside for surfers and environmental groups to gather.

The strategy is off to a strong start. Sales at the first store, opened in June in Cardiff-by-the-Sea, have been running 50 percent higher than expected, says Chouinard. The Malloys are now scouting locations in Ventura and Santa Cruz, Calif., and in Hawaii. Patagonia plans on operating 10 surf stores within the next several years. "We took some big pay cuts to work for Patagonia, but we're not regretting it," says Keith Malloy, 31.

Few Patagonians are in it just for the money. The company recently raised salaries to adjust for the cost of living, and everybody gets an annual bonus based on profits, but, overall, Patagonia pays at, or just slightly above, the market rate. However, the most significant rewards aren't monetary. One popular perk is a program that allows employees to take off up to two months at full pay and work for environmental groups. Lisa Myers, who works on the company's giving programs, tracked wolves in Yellowstone National Park during her sabbatical. The company also pays 50 percent of her college expenses as she pursues a wildlife biology degree. "It's easy to go to work when you get paid to do what you love to do," she says.

Patagonia's culture makes it a magnet for talented people. The company receives an average of 900 résumés for every job opening, so it can afford to be picky. Top outdoor industry executives want to work there, too. Sheahan just lured Damien Huang from much larger rival North Face to run Patagonia's product development group.

Can others capture some of Patagonia's magic? Most companies—especially ones with demanding public shareholders—simply can't let employees take a surfing break. They can, however, foster creativity and provide a sense of purpose. Perhaps the most valuable and easily applied lesson from Patagonia's experience is this: To think outside the box, sometimes you need to get out of the cubicle.

SOURCE: S. Hamm, "A Passion for the Planet," *BusinessWeek Online*, August 21, 2006.

companies had such plans.) The replacement ratio (pension payment/final salary) ranges from about 21 percent for a worker aged 55 with 30 years of service who earned $35,000 in her last year to about 36 percent for a 65-year-old worker with 40 years of service who earned the same amount. With Social Security added in, the ratio for the 65-year-old worker increases to about 77 percent.[18]

Defined benefit plans insulate employees from investment risk, which is borne by the company. In the event of severe financial difficulties that force the company to terminate or reduce employee pension benefits, the **Pension Benefit Guaranty Corporation (PBGC)** provides some protection of benefits. Established by the **Employee Retirement Income Security Act (ERISA)** of 1974, the PBGC guarantees a basic benefit, not necessarily complete pension benefit replacement, for employees who were eligible for pensions at the time of termination. It insures the retirement benefits of 44 million workers in about 31,000 plans. The maximum monthly benefit is limited to the lesser of 1/12 of an employee's annual gross income during a PBGC-defined period or $3,712 in 2007. The PBGC is funded by an annual contribution of $30 per plan participant, plus an additional variable rate premium for underfunded plans.[19] Note that the PBGC does not guarantee health care benefits.

**Pension Benefit Guaranty Corporation (PBGC)**
The agency that guarantees to pay employees a basic retirement benefit in the event that financial difficulties force a company to terminate or reduce employee pension benefits.

**Employee Retirement Income Security Act (ERISA)**
The 1974 act that increased the fiduciary responsibilities of pension plan trustees, established vesting rights and portability provisions, and established the Pension Benefit Guaranty Corporation (PBGC).

## Defined Contribution

Unlike defined benefit plans, *defined contribution plans* do not promise a specific benefit level for employees upon retirement. Rather, an individual account is set up for each employee with a guaranteed size of contribution. The advantage of such plans for employers is that they shift investment risk to employees and present fewer administrative challenges because there is no need to calculate payments based on age and service and no need to make payments to the PBGC. As Table 13.3 indicates, defined contribution plans are especially preferred in smaller companies, perhaps because of small employers' desire to avoid long-term obligations or perhaps because small companies tend to be younger, often being founded since the trend toward defined contribution plans. Some companies have both defined benefit and defined contribution plans.

There is a wide variety of defined contribution plans, a few of which are briefly described here. One of the simplest is a money purchase plan, under which an employer specifies a level of annual contribution (such as 10 percent of salary). At retirement age, the employee is entitled to the contributions plus the investment returns. The term "money purchase" stems from the fact that employees often use the money to purchase an annuity rather than taking it as a lump sum. Profit sharing plans and employee stock ownership plans are also often used as retirement vehicles. Both permit contributions (cash and stock, respectively) to vary from year to year, thus allowing employers to avoid fixed obligations that may be burdensome in difficult financial times. Section 401(k) plans (named after the tax code section) permit employees to defer compensation on a pretax basis. Annual contributions in 2007 are limited to $15,500, increasing by up to $500 annually thereafter through 2010, depending on inflation.[20]

Defined contribution plans continue to grow in importance, while, as we saw above, defined benefit plans have become less common. An important implication is that defined contribution plans put the responsibility for wise investing squarely on the shoulders of the employee. These investment decisions will become more critical because 401(k) plans continue to grow rapidly, covering 64 million people in 2003, up from 16 million in 1978.[21] Several factors affect the amount of income that will be available to an employee upon retirement. First, the earlier the age at which investments are made, the longer returns can accumulate. As Figure 13.2 shows, an annual investment of $3,000 made between ages 21 and 29 will be worth much more at age 65 than a similar investment made between ages 31 and 39. Second, different investments have different historical rates of return. Between 1946 and 1990, the average annual return was 11.4 percent for stocks, 5.1 percent for bonds, and 5.3 percent for cash (bank savings accounts).[22] As Figure 13.2 shows, if historical rates of return were

figure 13.2
The Relationship of Retirement Savings to Age When Savings Begins and Type of Investment Portfolio

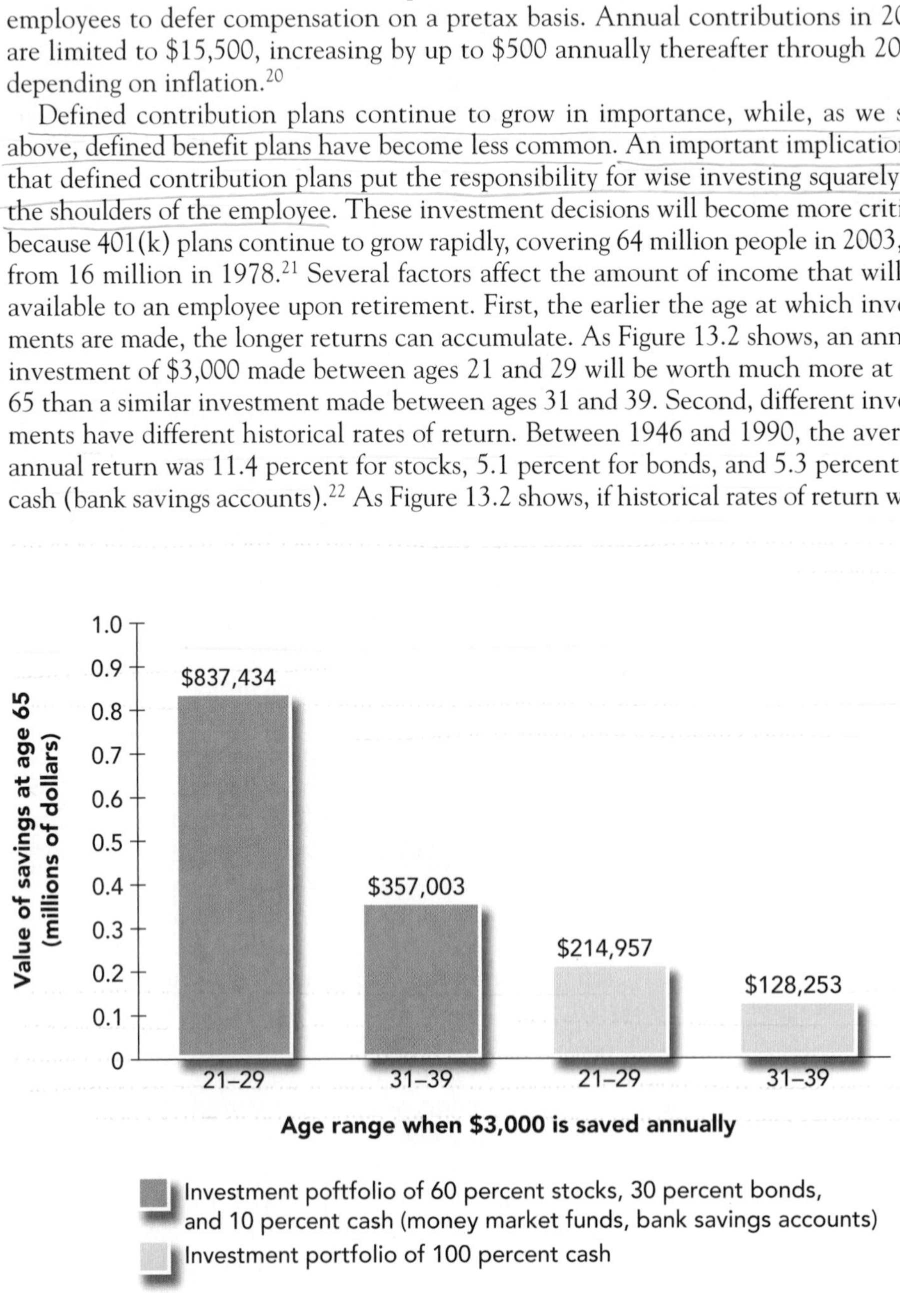

to continue, an investment in a mix of 60 percent stock, 30 percent bonds, and 10 percent cash between the ages of 21 and 29 would be worth almost four times as much at age 65 as would the same amount invested in a bank savings account. A third consideration is the need to counteract investment risk by diversification because stock and bond prices can be volatile in the short run. Although stocks have the greatest historical rate of return, that is no guarantee of future performance, particularly over shorter time periods. Thus some investment advisers recommend a mix of stock, bonds, and cash, as shown in Figure 13.2, to reduce investment risk. Younger investors may wish to have more stock, while those closer to retirement age typically have less stock in their portfolios. It's also important not to invest too heavily in any single stock. Some Enron employees had 100 percent of their 401k assets in Enron stock. When the price dropped from $90 to less than $1 in 2001, their retirement money was gone. Risk is further compounded by risk of job loss when one's employer struggles financially.

The Pension Protection Act of 2006 requires defined contribution plans holding publicly traded securities to provide employees with (1) the opportunity to divest employer securities and (2) at least three investment options other than employer securities.

## Cash Balance Plans

An increasingly popular way to combine the advantages of defined benefit plans and defined contribution plans is to use a **cash balance plan.** This type of retirement plan consists of individual accounts, as in a 401(k) plan. But in contrast to a 401(k), all the contributions come from the employer. Usually, the employer contributes a percentage of the employee's salary, say, 4 or 5 percent. The money in the cash balance plan earns interest according to a predetermined rate, such as the rate paid on U.S. Treasury bills. Employers guarantee this rate as in a defined benefit plan. This arrangement helps employers plan their contributions and helps employees predict their retirement benefits. If employees change jobs, they generally can roll over the balance into an individual retirement account.

**Cash Balance Plan**
Retirement plan in which the employer sets up an individual account for each employee and contributes a percentage of the employee's salary; the account earns interest at a predefined rate.

Many organizations have switched from traditional defined benefit plans to cash balance plans. The change, like any major change, requires employers to consider the effects on employees as well as on the organization's bottom line. Defined benefit plans are most generous to older employees with many years of service, and cash balance plans are most generous to young employees who will have many years ahead in which to earn interest. For an organization with many experienced employees, switching from a defined benefit plan can produce great savings in pension benefits. In that case, the older workers are the greatest losers, unless the organization adjusts the program to retain their benefits.

In recent years, however, few if any companies converted their defined benefit plans to cash balance plans because of legal uncertainties. In a closely watched case, IBM was sued for age discrimination after converting its plan in 1999. A district court ruled in 2003 that IBM had discriminated, but this was overturned in 2006 by the Seventh Circuit Court of Appeals. Also in 2006, the Pension Protection Act was passed; this act seeks to clarify the legal requirements of such plans. Thus, renewed movement to cash balance plans may occur. IBM, however, announced in 2006 that it would freeze its pension and cash balance plan benefits and instead place greater emphasis on its 401(k) plan.

## Funding, Communication, and Vesting Requirements

ERISA does not require organizations to have pension plans, but those that are set up must meet certain requirements. In addition to the termination provisions discussed

**Summary Plan Description (SPD)** A reporting requirement of the Employee Retirement Income Security Act (ERISA) that obligates employers to describe the plan's funding, eligibility requirements, risks, and so forth within 90 days after an employee has entered the plan.

earlier, plans must meet certain guidelines on management and funding. For example, employers are required to make yearly contributions that are sufficient to cover future obligations. (As noted previously, underfunded plans require higher premiums.) ERISA also specifies a number of reporting and disclosure requirements involving the IRS, the Department of Labor, and employees.[23] Employees, for example, must receive within 90 days after entering a plan a **summary plan description (SPD)** that describes the plan's funding, eligibility requirements, risks, and so forth. Upon request, an employer must also make available to an employee an individual benefit statement, which describes the employee's vested and unvested benefits. Obviously, employers may wish to provide such information on a regular basis anyway as a means of increasing the understanding and value employees attach to their benefits.

ERISA guarantees employees that when they become participants in a pension plan and work a specified minimum number of years, they earn a right to a pension upon retirement. These are referred to as *vesting rights*.[24] Vested employees have the right to their pension at retirement age, regardless of whether they remain with the employer until that time. Employee contributions to their own plans are always completely vested. The vesting of employer-funded pension benefits must take place under one of two schedules. Employers may choose to vest employees after five years; until that time, employers can provide zero vesting if they choose. Alternatively, employers may vest employees over a three- to seven-year period, with at least 20 percent vesting in the third year and each year thereafter. These two schedules represent minimum requirements; employers are free to vest employees more quickly. These are the two choices relevant to the majority of employers. However, so-called top-heavy plans, where pension benefits for "key" employees (like highly paid top managers) exceed a certain share of total pension benefits, require faster vesting for nonkey employees. On the other hand, multiemployer pension plans need not provide vesting until after 10 years of employment.

These requirements were put in place to prevent companies from terminating employees before they reach retirement age or before they reach their length-of-service requirements in order to avoid paying pension benefits. It should also be noted that transferring employees or laying them off as a means of avoiding pension obligations is not legal either, even if such actions are motivated partly by business necessity.[25] On the other hand, employers are free to choose whichever of the two vesting schedules is most advantageous. For example, an employer that experiences high quit rates during the fourth and fifth years of employment may choose five-year vesting to minimize pension costs.

The traditional defined benefit pension plan discourages employee turnover or delays it until the employer can recoup the training investment in employees.[26] Even if an employee's pension benefit is vested, it is usually smaller if the employee changes employers, mainly because the size of the benefit depends on earnings in the final years with an employer. Consider an employee who earns $30,000 after 20 years and $60,000 after 40 years.[27] The employer pays an annual retirement benefit equal to 1.5 percent of final earnings times the number of years of service. If the employee stays with the employer for 40 years, the annual benefit level upon retirement would be $36,000 (.015 × $60,000 × 40). If, instead, the employee changes employers after 20 years (and has the same earnings progression), the retirement benefit from the first employer would be $9,000 (.015 × $30,000 × 20). The annual benefit from the second employer would be $18,000 (.015 × $60,000 × 20). Therefore, staying with one employer for 40 years would yield an annual retirement benefit of $36,000, versus a combined annual retirement benefit of $27,000 ($9,000 + $18,000) if the employee changes employers once. It has also been suggested that pensions are designed to encourage long-service employees, whose earnings growth may eventually exceed their productivity growth, to retire. This is consistent with the fact that retirement benefits reach their maximum at retirement age.[28]

The fact that in recent years many employers have sought to reduce their workforces through early retirement programs is also consistent with the notion that pensions are used to retain certain employees while encouraging others to leave. One early retirement program approach is to adjust years-of-service credit upward for employees willing to retire, resulting in a higher retirement benefit for them (and less monetary incentive to work). These workforce reductions may also be one indication of a broader trend toward employees becoming less likely to spend their entire careers with a single employer.[29] On one hand, if more mobility across employers becomes necessary or desirable, the current pension system's incentives against (or penalties for) mobility may require modification. On the other hand, perhaps increased employee mobility will reinforce the continued trend toward defined contribution plans [like 401(k)s], which have greater portability (ease of transfer of funds) across employers.[30]

### International Comparisons

**LO3** Discuss How Employee Benefits in the United States Compare with Those in Other Countries.

About 45 percent of the U.S. private-sector labor force is covered by pension plans, compared with 100 percent in France, 92 percent in Switzerland, 42 percent in Germany, and 39 percent in Japan. Among those covered by pensions, U.S. workers are significantly less likely to be covered by defined benefit plans (see Table 13.3, page 564) than Japanese workers (100 percent) or German workers (90 percent).

## Pay for Time Not Worked

At first blush, paid vacation, holidays, sick leave, and so forth may not seem to make economic sense. The employer pays the employee for time not spent working, receiving no tangible production value in return. Therefore, some employers may see little direct advantage. Perhaps for this reason, a minimum number of vacation days (20) is mandated by law in the European Community. As many as 30 days of vacation is not uncommon for relatively new employees in Europe. By contrast, there is no legal minimum in the United States, but 10 days is typical for large companies. U.S. workers must typically be with an employer for 20 to 25 years before they receive as much paid vacation as their western European counterparts.[31]

Sick leave programs often provide full salary replacement for a limited period of time, usually not exceeding 26 weeks. The amount of sick leave is often based on length of service, accumulating with service (one day per month, for example). Sick leave policies need to be carefully structured to avoid providing employees with the wrong incentives. For example, if sick leave days disappear at the end of the year (rather than accumulate), a "use it or lose it" mentality may develop among employees, contributing to greater absenteeism. Organizations have developed a number of measures to counter this.[32] Some allow sick days to accumulate, then pay employees for the number of sick days when they retire or resign. Employers may also attempt to communicate to their employees that accumulated sick leave is better saved to use as a bridge to long-term disability, because the replacement rate (the ratio of sick leave or disability payments to normal salary) for the former is typically higher. Sick leave payments may equal 100 percent of usual salary, whereas the replacement ratio for long-term disability might be 50 percent, so the more sick leave accumulated, the longer an employee can avoid dropping to 50 percent of usual pay when unable to work.

LIST

# COMPETING THROUGH GLOBALIZATION

## Multicountry Benefits Require Delicate Touch: Understanding Local Differences Is Critical

Daunting complexities that are associated with developing any employee benefits program multiply as companies continue to globalize.

Different countries' cultures, laws, regulations and health care structures as well as firms' desire to compete for top talent while keeping an eye on costs are just a few of the factors that must be taken into account.

Other factors that must be considered in determining multinationals' global benefits strategy include whether the internationally based employees are local or expatriates, if the business is new to the country or is well-established, whether the local operation is a startup or an acquisition, the size of its presence in a particular country or region, and the local employees' benefits expertise, according to experts.

Meanwhile, the Sarbanes–Oxley Act's financial reporting requirements in the United States are leading many companies to centralize their benefit operations after many years of decentralization. But many are finding the crucial first step of data gathering—to determine what they already offer—a difficult task to accomplish, experts say.

"The first hurdle to get over is to understand that the world doesn't operate like the U.S. operates," said Richard Polak, president and chief executive officer of Los Angeles–based IBIS Advisors, an international HR consultancy.

Anthony Amato, VP of benefits and corporate travel for Silver Spring, Md–based Discovery Communications Inc., which has 900 employees in 30 countries outside the United States, agreed.

"I think the biggest challenge is shaking off your U.S.-centric, or your U.S. thinking, your U.S. mentality" in developing programs in other countries. Sensitivity to the local culture and business practices is a must, Mr. Amato said.

Mark Wood, VP, human resources for Novato, Calif–based BioMarin Pharmaceutical Inc., said, "There's a practical challenge of integrating the different ways of doing business in different countries with our kind of standard way of doing business here in the United States," whether that involves logistical, operational or compliance requirements. The firm produces biopharmaceuticals for rare diseases and medical conditions.

"We need to constantly remind ourselves of the international requirements of what we do and remind our international folks of the international implications of what they do," said Mr. Wood, whose firm has 20 international employees in seven nations.

Ford Motor Co. has developed five "books" that outline its strategy and procedures for its compensation and benefit programs, said Michael Bush, Ford's Dearborn, Mich–based director, income security programs, U.S. and global operations.

"We've tried to set up a system that is almost like a cookbook for the field," Mr. Bush explained. "It's all online now, and the HR people can pull this information up and see it."

### Interacting Locally

Firms must determine how their benefits programs intersect with the local national health system, said Bill Maloney, Phoenix-based world wide partner with Mercer Health & Benefits, a unit of Mercer Human Resource Consulting.

There are differences even among countries with national health systems, "so consequently the benefits that an employer's going to purchase are going to reflect how that health system is set up," said Mr. Maloney.

For instance, while Canada and the United Kingdom both have national health care, in the United Kingdom, employers can buy supplementary policies that give employees better access to the national health system and reduce waiting times. In Canada, regulations "prevent that kind of private insurance," Mr. Maloney said.

Meanwhile, particularly in Latin America and Asia, "there's a great shift away" from having the government provide benefits, said Greg Arms, New York–based chairman and executive VP of Willis Group Holdings Ltd.'s employee benefits practice.

Jayne Lux, director of the Global Health Benefits Institute, an initiative of the Washington–based National Business Group on Health, said a U.S. wellness program could be extended to and successfully rolled out in

Canada or Australia. "Can you then roll it out to Africa or Bangladesh, or one of the many countries that have what many would argue to have greater cultural and certainly greater language differences?" she asked. "I think the feeling now is, you can't."

In that case, the next step is whether to change the existing program or collaborate with local colleagues to develop something new, said Ms. Lux.

**Competitive Considerations**
Competition for talent is a factor as well.

Suzanne Wamba, director, world wide health and welfare benefits for New York–based White & Case L.L.P., which employs about 4,400 in 25 countries, said the law firm sees benefits "not only as part of remuneration, but as a very core component to attracting good talent."

In the United Kingdom, for instance, there is a "very established practice" of providing company vehicles to managers, "so to be competitive, any U.S. company operating in that marketplace has to offer a similarly competitive package of benefits," said Steve Rimmer, New York–based principal with PriceWaterhouseCoopers International Ltd.

SOURCE: J. Greenwald, "Multicountry Benefits Require Delicate Touch: Understanding Local Differences Is Critical," *Business Insurance*, December 11, 2006, p. 12.

Although vacation and other paid leave programs help attract and retain employees, there is a cost to providing time off with pay, especially in a global economy. The fact that vacation and other paid leave practices differ across countries contributes to the differences in labor costs described in Chapter 11. Consider that, on average, in manufacturing, German workers work 369 fewer hours per year than their U.S. counterparts, who work 1,804 hours per year, and over 500 fewer hours than workers in the Czech Republic, in central Europe. (See Figure 13.3.) In other words, German workers are at work approximately 9 fewer weeks per year than their U.S. counterparts and 12 to 13 fewer weeks than workers in the Czech Republic next door (and as of 2004, a member of the European Community). It is perhaps not surprising then that German manufacturers have looked outside Germany in many cases for alternative production sites.

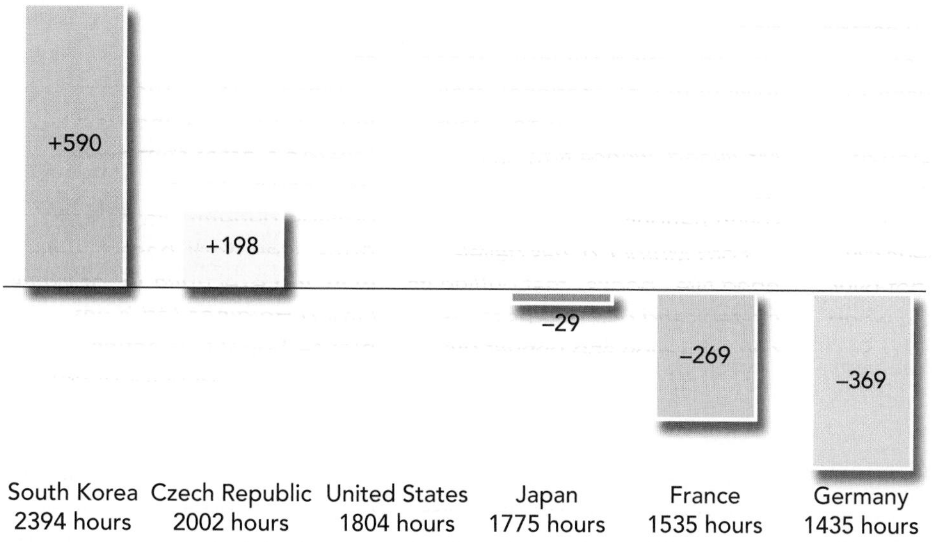


figure 13.3
Normal Annual Hours Worked Relative to United States

SOURCE: U.S. Department of Labor, *A Chartbook of International Labor Comparisons, January 2007.* Original data from Organization for Economic Cooperation and Development.

## Family-Friendly Policies

To ease employees' conflicts between work and nonwork, organizations may use *family-friendly policies* such as family leave policies and child care. Although the programs discussed here would seem to be targeted to a particular group of employees, these programs often have "spillover effects" on other employees, who see them as symbolizing a general corporate concern for human resources, thus promoting loyalty even among employee groups that do not use the programs possibly resulting in improved organizational performance.[33]

**Family and Medical Leave Act**
The 1993 act that requires employers with 50 or more employees to provide up to 12 weeks of unpaid leave after childbirth or adoption; to care for a seriously ill child, spouse, or parent; or for an employee's own serious illness.

Since 1993 the **Family and Medical Leave Act** requires organizations with 50 or more employees within a 75-mile radius to provide as much as 12 weeks of unpaid leave after childbirth or adoption; to care for a seriously ill child, spouse, or parent; or for an employee's own serious illness. Employees are guaranteed the same or a comparable job on their return to work. Employees with less than one year of service or who work under 25 hours per week or who are among the 10 percent highest paid are not covered.

Many employers had already taken steps to deal with this issue, partly to help attract and retain key employees. Less than 10 percent of American families fit the image of a husband working outside the home and a wife who stays home to take care of the children.[34]

The United States still offers significantly less unpaid leave than most western European countries and Japan. Moreover, paid family leave remains rare in the United States (fewer than 5 percent are eligible for paid leave, despite some state laws), in even sharper contrast to western Europe and Japan, where it is typically mandated by law.[35] Until the passage of the Americans with Disabilities Act, the only applicable law was the Pregnancy Discrimination Act of 1978, which requires employers that offer disability plans to treat pregnancy as they would any other disability.

Experience with the Family and Medical Leave Act suggests that a majority of those opting for this benefit fail to take the full allotment of time. This is especially the case among female executives. Many of these executives find they do not enjoy maternity leave as much as they expected they would and miss the challenges associated with their careers. Others fear that their careers would be damaged in the long run by missing out on opportunities that might arise while they are out on leave.[36]

### Child Care

U.S. companies increasingly provide some form of child care support to their employees. This support comes in several forms that vary in their degree of organizational involvement.[37] The lowest level of involvement, offered by 36 percent of companies, is when an organization supplies and helps employees collect information about the cost and quality of available child care. At the next level, organizations provide vouchers or discounts for employees to use at existing child care facilities (5 percent of companies). At the highest level, firms provide child care at or near their worksites (9 percent of companies). Toyota's Child Development Program provides 24-hours-a-day care for children of workers at its Georgetown, Kentucky, plant. This facility is designed to meet the needs of employees working evening and night shifts who want their children to be on the same schedule. In this facility, the children are kept awake all night. At the end of the night shift, the parents pick up their children and the whole family goes home to bed.[38]

An organization's decision to staff its own child care facility should not be taken lightly. It is typically a costly venture with important liability concerns. Moreover, the results, in terms of reducing absenteeism and enhancing productivity, are often mixed.[39] One reason for this is that many organizations are "jumping on the day care bandwagon" without giving much thought to the best form of assistance for their specific employees.

As an alternative example, Memphis-based First Tennessee Bank, which was losing 1,500 days of productivity a year because of child care problems, considered creating its own on-site day care center. Before acting, however, the company surveyed its employees. This survey indicated that the only real problem with day care occurred when the parents' regular day care provisions fell through because of sickness on the part of the child or provider. Based on these findings, the bank opted to establish a sick-child care center, which was less costly and smaller in scope than a full-time center and yet still solved the employees' major problem. As a result, absenteeism dropped so dramatically that the program paid for itself in the first nine months of operation.[40]

## Managing Benefits: Employer Objectives and Strategies

**LO4**
Describe the Effects of Benefits Management on Cost and Workforce Quality.

Although the regulatory environment places some important constraints on benefits decisions, employers retain significant discretion and need to evaluate the payoff of such decisions.[41] As discussed earlier, however, this evaluation needs to recognize that employees have come to expect certain things from employers. Employers who do not meet these expectations run the risk of violating what has been called an "implicit contract" between the employer and its workers. If employees believe their employers feel little commitment to their welfare, they can hardly be expected to commit themselves to the company's success.

Clearly, there is much room for progress in the evaluation of benefits decisions. Despite some of the obvious reasons for benefits—group discounts, regulation, and minimizing compensation-related taxes—organizations do not do as well as they could in spelling out what they want their benefits package to achieve and evaluating how well they are succeeding. Research suggests that most organizations do not have written benefits objectives.[42] Obviously, without clear objectives to measure progress, evaluation is difficult (and less likely to occur). Table 13.5 provides an example of one organization's written benefits objectives.

### Surveys and Benchmarking

As with cash compensation, an important element of benefits management is knowing what the competition is doing. Survey information on benefits packages is available from private consultants, the U.S. Chamber of Commerce, and the Bureau of Labor Statistics (BLS).[43] BLS data of the sort in Table 13.3 and the more detailed information on programs and provisions available from consultants are useful in designing competitive benefits packages. To compete effectively in the product market, cost information is also necessary. A good source is again the BLS, which provides information on benefits costs for specific categories as well as breakdowns by industry, occupation, union status, and organization size. Figure 13.4 shows some of these data for 2006.

**table 13.5**

One Company's Written Benefits Objectives

- To establish and maintain an employee benefit program that is based primarily on the employees' needs for leisure time and on protection against the risks of old age, loss of health, and loss of life.
- To establish and maintain an employee benefit program that complements the efforts of employees on their own behalf.
- To evaluate the employee benefit plan annually for its effect on employee morale and productivity, giving consideration to turnover, unfilled positions, attendance, employees' complaints, and employees' opinions.
- To compare the employee benefit plan annually with that of other leading companies in the same field and to maintain a benefit plan with an overall level of benefits based on cost per employee that falls within the second quintile of these companies.
- To maintain a level of benefits for nonunion employees that represents the same level of expenditures per employee as for union employees.
- To determine annually the costs of new, changed, and existing programs as percentages of salaries and wages and to maintain these percentages as much as possible.
- To self-fund benefits to the extent that a long-run cost savings can be expected for the firm and catastrophic losses can be avoided.
- To coordinate all benefits with social insurance programs to which the company makes payments.
- To provide benefits on a noncontributory basis except for dependent coverage, for which employees should pay a portion of the cost.
- To maintain continual communications with all employees concerning benefit programs.

SOURCE: *Employee Benefits*, 3rd ed., Burton T. Beam Jr. and John J. McFadden. © 1992 by Dearborn Financial Publishing, Inc. Published by Dearborn Financial Publishing, Inc., Chicago. All rights reserved.

**figure 13.4**

Employee Benefits Cost by Category, 2006

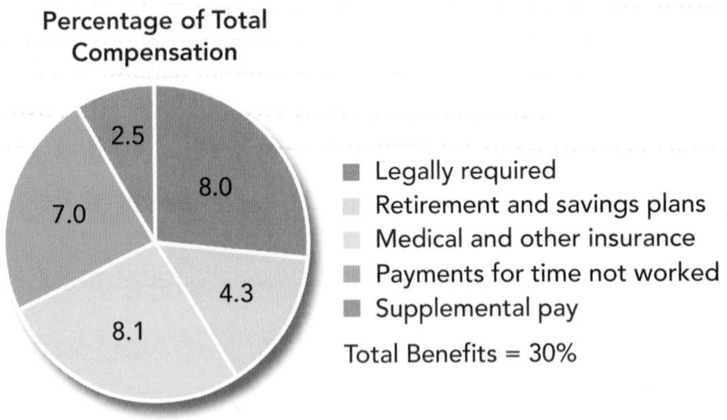


SOURCE: "Employer Cost for Employee Compensation," September 2006, www.bls.gov.

## Cost Control

In thinking about cost control strategies, it is useful to consider several factors. First, the larger the cost of a benefit category, the greater the opportunity for savings. Second, the growth trajectory of the benefit category is also important: even if costs are currently acceptable, the rate of growth may result in serious costs in the future. Third, cost containment efforts can only work to the extent that the employer has significant discretion in choosing how much to spend in a benefit category. Much of the cost of legally required benefits (like Social Security) is relatively fixed, which constrains cost reduction efforts. Even with legally required benefits, however, employers can take actions to limit costs because of "experience ratings," which impose higher taxes on employers with high rates of unemployment or workers' compensation claims.

One benefit—medical and other insurance—stands out as a target for cost control for two reasons. Its costs are substantial; they have, except for the 1994 to 1999 period, grown at a significant pace, and this growth is expected to continue. Second, employers have many options for attacking costs and improving quality.

## Health Care: Controlling Costs and Improving Quality

As Table 13.6 indicates, the United States spends more on health care than any other country in the world. U.S. health care expenditures have gone from 5.3 percent of the gross national product ($27 billion) in 1960 to 14 percent (approximately $1.45 trillion) recently. Yet the percentage of full-time workers receiving job-related health benefits has declined, with over 46 million Americans uninsured as of 2005.[44] The United States also trails Japan and western Europe on measures of life expectancy and infant mortality.

Unlike workers in most western European countries, who have nationalized health systems, the majority of Americans receiving health insurance get it through their (or a family member's) employers.[45] Consequently, health insurance, like pensions, discourages employee turnover because not all employers provide health insurance benefits.[46] Not surprisingly, the fact that many Americans receive coverage through their employers has meant that many efforts at controlling costs and increasing quality and coverage have been undertaken by employers. These efforts, broadly referred to as managed care, fall into six major categories: (1) plan design, (2) use of alternative providers, (3) use of alternative funding methods, (4) claims review, (5) education and prevention, and (6) external cost control systems.[47] Examples appear in Table 13.7.

One trend in plan design has been to shift costs to employees through the use of deductibles, coinsurance, exclusions and limitations, and maximum benefits.[48] These costs can be structured such that employees act on incentives to shift to less expensive plans.[49] Another trend has been to focus on reducing, rather than shifting, costs

**table 13.6**

Health Care Costs and Outcomes in Various Countries

| | LIFE EXPECTANCY AT BIRTH, FEMALE | UNDER-FIVE INFANT MORTALITY RATE (PER 1,000) | HEALTH EXPENDITURES AS A PERCENTAGE OF GDP |
|---|---|---|---|
| Japan | 73 | 4 | 8% |
| Korea | 81 | 6 | 6 |
| Canada | 83 | 6 | 10 |
| United Kingdom | 81 | 6 | 8 |
| France | 84 | 5 | 11 |
| Germany | 81 | 5 | 11 |
| Mexico | 78 | 28 | 7 |
| United States | 80 | 8 | 15 |

SOURCES: Organization for Economic Cooperation and Development, *OECD Health*. Data 2006, www.OECD.org and World Bank, *World Development Report 2007*, www.worldbank.org/wdr2007.

**table 13.7**
Ways Employers Use Managed Care to Control Health Care Costs

| |
|---|
| **Plan design** |
| Cost shifting to employees |
| Deductibles |
| Coinsurance |
| Exclusions and limitations |
| Maximum benefits |
| Cost reduction |
| Preadmission testing |
| Second surgical opinions |
| Coordination of benefits |
| Alternatives to hospital stays (such as home health care) |
| **Alternative providers** |
| Health maintenance organizations (HMOs) |
| Preferred provider organizations (PPOs) |
| **Alternative funding methods** |
| Self-funding |
| **Claims review** |
| **Health education and preventive care** |
| Wellness programs |
| Employee assistance programs (EAPs) |
| **Encouragement of external control systems** |
| National Council on Health Planning and Development |
| Employer coalitions |

SOURCE: Adapted from B. T. Beam Jr. and J. J. McFadden, *Employee Benefits*, 3rd ed. (Chicago: Dearborn Financial Publishing, 1992).

**Health Maintenance Organization (HMO)**
A health care plan that provides benefits on a prepaid basis for employees who are required to use only HMO medical service providers.

**Preferred Provider Organization (PPO)**
A group of health care providers who contract with employers, insurance companies, and so forth to provide health care at a reduced fee.

through such activities as preadmission testing and second surgical opinions. The use of alternative providers like **health maintenance organizations (HMOs)** and **preferred provider organizations (PPOs)** has also increased. HMOs differ from more traditional providers by focusing on preventive care and outpatient treatment, requiring employees to use only HMO services, and providing benefits on a prepaid basis. Many HMOs pay physicians and other health care workers a flat salary instead of using the traditional fee-for-service system, under which a physician's pay may depend on the number of patients seen. Paying on a salary basis is intended to reduce incentives for physicians to schedule more patient visits or medical procedures than might be necessary. (Of course, there is the risk that incentives will be reduced too much, resulting in inadequate access to medical procedures and specialists.) PPOs are essentially groups of health care providers that contract with employers, insurance companies, and so forth to provide health care at a reduced fee. They differ from HMOs in that they do not provide benefits on a prepaid basis and employees often are not required to use the preferred providers. Instead, employers may provide incentives for employees to choose, for example, a physician who participates in the plan. In general, PPOs seem to be less expensive than traditional delivery systems but more expensive than HMOs.[50] Another trend in employers' attempts to control costs has been to vary required employee contributions based on the employee's health and risk factors rather than charging each employee the same premium.

***Employee Wellness Programs.*** Employee wellness programs (EWPs) focus on changing behaviors both on and off work time that could eventually lead to future health problems. EWPs are preventive in nature; they attempt to manage health care costs by decreasing employees' needs for services. Typically, these programs aim at specific health risks such as high blood pressure, high cholesterol levels, smoking, and obesity. They also try to promote positive health influences such as physical exercise and good nutrition.[51]

EWPs are either passive or active. Passive programs use little or no outreach to individuals, nor do they provide ongoing support to motivate them to use the resources. Active wellness centers assume that behavior change requires not only awareness and opportunity but support and reinforcement.

One example of a passive wellness program is a health education program. Health education programs have two central goals: raising awareness levels of health-related issues and informing people on health-related topics. In these kinds of programs, a health educator usually conducts classes or lunchtime lectures (or coordinates outside speakers). The program may also have various promotions (like an annual mile run or a "smoke-out") and include a newsletter that reports on current health issues.

Another kind of passive employee wellness program is a fitness facility. In this kind of program, the company sets up a center for physical fitness equipped with aerobic and muscle-building exercise machines and staffed with certified athletic trainers. The facility is publicized within the organization, and employees are free to use it on their own time. Aetna, for example, has created five state-of-the-art health clubs that serve over 7,500 workers.[52] Northwestern Mutual Life's fitness facilities are open 24 hours a day to its 3,300 employees.[53] Health education classes related to smoking cessation and weight loss may be offered in addition to the facilities.

Although fitness facility programs are usually more expensive than health education programs, both are classified as passive because they rely on individual employees to identify their problems and take corrective action. In contrast, active wellness centers assume that behavior change also requires encouragement and assistance. One kind of active wellness center is the outreach and follow-up model. This type of wellness center contains all the features of a passive model, but it also has counselors who handle one-on-one outreach and provide tailored, individualized programs for employees. Typically, tailored programs obtain baseline measures on various indicators (weight, blood pressure, lung capacity, and so on) and measure individuals' progress relative to these indicators over time. The programs set goals and provide small, symbolic rewards to individuals who meet their goals.

This encouragement needs to be particularly targeted to employees in high-risk categories (like those who smoke, are overweight, or have high blood pressure) for two reasons. First, a small percentage of employees create a disproportionate amount of health care costs; therefore, targeted interventions are more efficient. Second, research shows that those in high-risk categories are the most likely to perceive barriers (like family problems or work overload)[54] to participating in company-sponsored fitness programs. Thus untargeted interventions are likely to miss the people that most need to be included.

Research on these different types of wellness centers leads to several conclusions.[55] First, the costs of health education programs are significantly less than those associated with either fitness facility programs or the follow-up model. Second, as indicated in Figure 13.5, all three models are effective in reducing the risk factors associated with cardiovascular disease (obesity, high blood pressure, smoking, and lack of exercise). However, the follow-up model is significantly better than the other two in reducing the risk factors.

figure 13.5
The Cost and Effectiveness of Three Different Types of Employee Wellness Designs

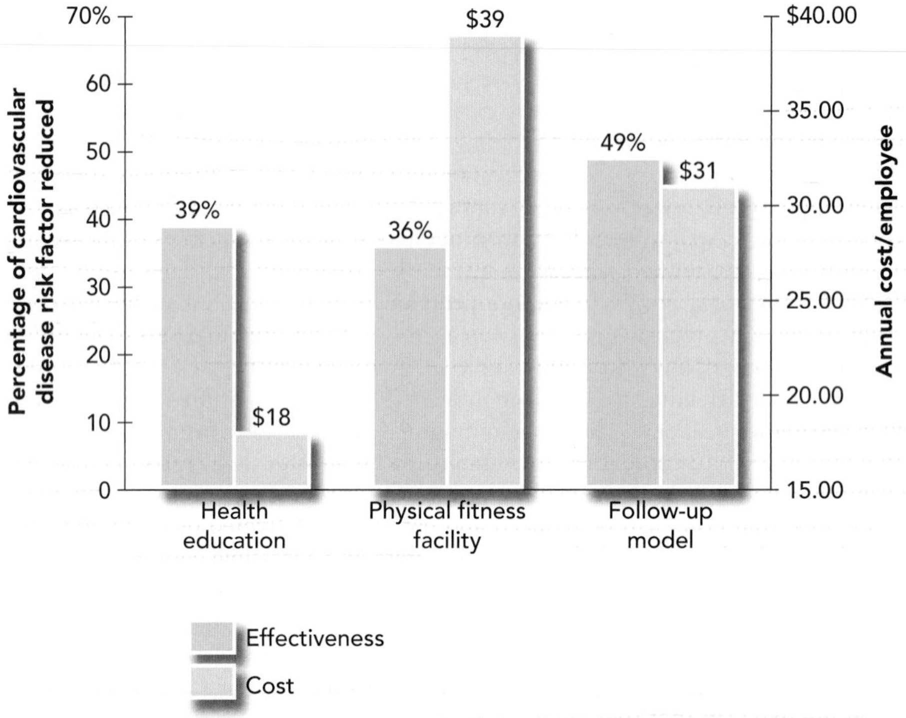


SOURCE: J. C. Erfurt, A. Foote, and M. A. Heirich, "The Cost Effectiveness of Worksite Wellness Programs for Hypertension Control, Weight Loss, Smoking Cessation and Exercise," *Personnel Psychology* 45 (1992), pp. 5–27. Used with permission.

Whether the added cost of follow-up programs compared with health education programs is warranted is a judgment that only employers, employees, and unions can make. However, employers like Sony and Quaker Oats believe that incentives are worth the extra cost, and their employees can receive up to several hundred dollars for reducing their risk factors. There appears to be no such ambiguity associated with the fitness facility model, however. This type of wellness center costs as much or more than the follow-up model but is only as effective as the health education model. Providing a fitness facility that does not include systematic outreach and routine long-term follow-up to assist people with risk factors is not cost-effective in reducing health risks. "Attendants may sit in the fitness center like the 'Maytag repairman' waiting for people to come."[56]

***Health Care Costs and Quality: Ongoing Challenges.*** In 2006, the average annual premium for family coverage was $11,480, with employers paying $8,508 (74 percent) and employees paying $2,973 (26 percent) on average.[57] (These numbers pertain only to employers that provide health care benefits.) Although premiums for employer-sponsored health care (family coverage) grew more slowly in 2006 (7.7 percent) than in any year since 2000, the cost increase was still double the overall inflation rate. Further, since 2000, health care premium costs increased by 87 percent. Thus, control of health care costs is an ongoing challenge.

Two important phenomena are often encountered in cost control efforts. First, piecemeal programs may not work well because steps to control one aspect (such as medical cost shifting) may lead employees to "migrate" to other programs that provide medical treatment at no cost to them (like workers' compensation). Second, there is often a so-called Pareto group, which refers to a small percentage (perhaps 20 percent) of employees being responsible for generating the majority (often 60 to 80 percent) of health care costs. Obviously, cost control efforts will be more successful to the extent that the costs generated by the Pareto group can be identified and managed effectively.[58]

Although cost control will continue to require a good deal of attention, there is a growing emphasis on monitoring health care quality, which has been described as "the next battlefield." A major focus is on identifying best medical practices by measuring and monitoring the relative success of alternative treatment strategies using large-scale databases and research.[59] In addition, employers increasingly cooperate with one another to develop "report cards" on health care provider organizations to facilitate better choices by their employers and to receive improved health care. General Motors, Ford, and Chrysler, for example, have developed this type of system and made it Web-accessible.[60]

In addition, several companies, including Intel, Wal-Mart, and British Petroleum, have announced a plan to provide digital health records to their employees. By doing so, they hope that costs will be reduced and better care delivered by providing consumers, hospitals, doctors, and pharmacies accurate and accessible data.[61]

## Staffing Responses to Control Benefits Cost Growth

Employers may change staffing practices to control benefits costs. First, because benefits costs are fixed (in that they do not usually go up with hours worked), the benefits cost per hour can be reduced by having employees work more hours. However, there are drawbacks to having employees work more hours. The Fair Labor Standards Act (FLSA), introduced in Chapter 11, requires that nonexempt employees be paid time-and-a-half for hours in excess of 40 per week. Yet the decline in U.S. work hours tapered off in the late 1940s; work hours have actually gone up since then. It is estimated that Americans were working the equivalent of one month longer in 1987 than they were in 1969, and these higher levels have continued.[62] Increased benefits were identified as one of the major reasons for this.

A second possible effect of FLSA regulations (though this is more speculative) is that organizations will try to have their employees classified as exempt whenever possible (though such attempts may run afoul of FLSA law). The growth in the number of salaried workers (many of whom are exempt) may also reflect an effort by organizations to limit the benefits cost per hour without having to pay overtime. A third potential effect is the growth in part-time employment and the use of temporary workers, which may be a response to rising benefits costs. Part-time workers are less likely to receive benefits than full-time workers although labor market shortages in recent years have reduced this difference.[63] Benefits for temporary workers are also usually quite limited.

Third, employers may be more likely to classify workers as independent contractors rather than employees, which eliminates the employer's obligation to provide legally required employee benefits. However, the Internal Revenue Service (IRS) scrutinizes such decisions carefully, as Microsoft and other companies have discovered. Microsoft was compelled to reclassify a group of workers as employees (rather than as independent contractors) and to grant them retroactive benefits. The IRS looks at several factors, including the permanency of the relationship between employer and worker, how much control the employer exercises in directing the worker, and whether the worker offers services to only that employer. Permanency, control, and dealing with a single employer are viewed by the IRS as suggestive of an employment relationship.

## Nature of the Workforce

Although general considerations such as cost control and "protection against the risks of old age and loss of health and life" (see Table 13.5) are important, employers must also consider the specific demographic composition and preferences of their current workforces in designing their benefits packages.

At a broad level, basic demographic factors such as age and sex can have important consequences for the types of benefits employees want. For example, an older workforce is more likely to be concerned about (and use) medical coverage, life insurance, and pensions. A workforce with a high percentage of women of childbearing age may care more about disability leave. Young, unmarried men and women often have less interest in benefits generally, preferring higher wages and salaries.

Although some general conclusions about employee preferences can be drawn based on demographics, more finely tuned assessments of employee benefit preferences need to be done. One approach is to use marketing research methods to assess employees' preferences the same way consumers' demands for products and services are assessed.[64] Methods include personal interviews, focus groups, and questionnaires. Relevant questions might include

- What benefits are most important to you?
- If you could choose one new benefit, what would it be?
- If you were given *x* dollars for benefits, how would you spend it?

As with surveys generally, care must be taken not to raise employee expectations regarding future changes. If the employer is not prepared to act on the employees' input, surveying may do more harm than good.

The preceding discussion may imply that the current makeup of the workforce is a given, but this is not the case. As discussed earlier, the benefits package may influence the composition of the workforce. For example, a benefits package that has strong medical benefits and pensions may be particularly attractive to older people or those with families. An attractive pension plan may be a way to attract workers who wish to make a long-term commitment to an organization. Where turnover costs are high, this type of strategy may have some appeal. On the other hand, a company that has very lucrative health care benefits may attract and retain people with high health care costs. Sick leave provisions may also affect the composition of the workforce. Organizations need to think about the signals their benefits packages send and the implications of these signals for workforce composition. In this vein, Table 13.8 shows the benefits used by Google, the number 1 ranked company on *Fortune*'s list of "100 Best Companies to Work For," to attract and retain its desired workforce.

## Communicating with Employees

**LO5**
Explain the Importance of Effectively Communicating the Nature and Value of Benefits to Employees.

Effective communication of benefits information to employees is critical if employers are to realize sufficient returns on their benefits investments. Research makes it clear that current employees and job applicants often have a very poor idea of what benefits provisions are already in place and the cost or market value of those benefits. One study asked employees to estimate both the amount contributed by the employer to their medical insurance and what it would cost the employees to provide their own health insurance. Table 13.9 shows that employees significantly underestimated both the cost and market value of their medical benefits. In the case of family coverage, employees estimated that the employer contributed $24, only 38 percent of the employer's

**table 13.8**

Employee Benefits at Google

- Up to $8,000/year in tuition reimbursement
- On-site perks include medical and dental facilities, oil change and bike repair, valet parking, free washers and dryers, and free breakfast, lunch, and dinner on a daily basis at 11 gourmet restaurants
- Unlimited sick leave
- 27 days of paid time off after one year of employment
- Global Education Leave program enables employees to take a leave of absence to pursue further education for up to 5 years and $150,000 in reimbursement.
- Free shuttles equipped with WiFi from locations around the Bay Area to headquarter offices.
- Classes on a variety of subjects from estate planning and home purchasing to foreign-language lessons in French, Spanish, Japanese and Mandarin.

SOURCE: The Great Place to Work® Institute, 2007, www.greatplacetowork.com.

**table 13.9**

Employee Perceptions versus Actual Cost and Market Value of Employer Contributions to Employee Medical Insurance

| | EMPLOYER CONTRIBUTION | | | MARKET VALUE[a] | | |
|---|---|---|---|---|---|---|
| COVERAGE | ACTUAL | EMPLOYEE PERCEPTION | RATIO | ACTUAL | EMPLOYEE PERCEPTION | RATIO |
| Individual | $34 | $23 | 68% | $ 61 | $37 | 61% |
| Family | 64 | 24 | 38 | 138 | 43 | 31 |

Note: Dollar values in table represent means across three different insurance carriers for individual coverage and three different carriers for family coverage.

[a]Defined as the amount a nonemployee would have to pay to obtain the same level of coverage.

SOURCE: Adapted from M. Wilson, G. B. Northcraft, and M. A. Neale, "The Perceived Value of Fringe Benefits," *Personnel Psychology* 38 (1985), pp. 309–20. Used with permission.

actual contribution. This employer was receiving a very poor return on its benefits investment: $0.38 for every $1.00 spent.[65] Other research shows that less than one-third of employees feel their employer benefit communications are effective.

The situation with job applicants is no better. One study of MBAs found that 46 percent believed that benefits added 15 percent or less on top of direct payroll. Not surprisingly, perhaps, benefits were dead last on the applicants' priority lists in making job choices.[66] A study of undergraduate business majors found similar results, with benefits ranked 15th (out of 18) in importance in evaluating jobs. These results must be interpreted with caution, however. Some research suggests that job attributes can be ranked low in importance, not because they are unimportant per se, but because all employers are perceived to be about the same on that attribute. If some employers offered noticeably poorer benefits, the importance of benefits could become much greater.

Organizations can help remedy the problem of applicants' and employees' lack of knowledge about benefits. One study found that employees' awareness of benefits information was significantly increased through several media, including memoranda, question-and-answer meetings, and detailed brochures. The increased awareness, in turn, contributed to significant increases in benefits satisfaction. Another study suggests, however, that increased employee knowledge of benefits can have a positive or negative effect, depending on the nature of the benefits package. For example, there was a negative, or inverse, correlation between cost to the employee and benefits satisfaction

**table 13.10**
Benefits Communication Media Examples for Different Audiences and Purposes

| MEDIA | AUDIENCE | PURPOSE |
|---|---|---|
| Enrollment package | All employees (English and Spanish) | Announce changes or new hire enrollment only by deadline |
| Meetings | Local employees | Provide information on benefits and changes |
| Teleconference messaging | Remote employees | Provide information on benefits and changes |
| Intranet | All employees (personalized) | Provide information on benefits, training, and employment policies |
| E-mail alerts | Supervisors | Provide employees with information |
| Summary plan descriptions | All employees | Make available compliance information |
| Paycheck attachments | All employees | Provide information on benefits |
| Webcasts | Regional managers | Share context for changes and their roles and responsibilities |

SOURCE: A. Parsons and K. Groh, "The New Road Effective Communications," *Compensation Benefits Review* 38 (2006) p. 57.

overall, but the correlation was more strongly negative among employees with greater knowledge of their benefits.[67] The implication is that employees will be least satisfied with their benefits if their cost is high and they are well informed.

One thing an employer should consider with respect to written benefits communication is that over 27 million employees in the United States may be functionally illiterate. Of course, there are many alternative ways to communicate benefits information. (See Table 13.10.) Nevertheless, most organizations spend little to communicate information about benefits, and much of this is spent on general written communications. Considering that Bureau of Labor Statistics data cited earlier indicate that organizations spend an average of over $17,000 per worker per year on benefits, together with the complex nature of many benefits and the poor understanding of most employees, the typical communication effort may be inadequate.[68] On a more positive note, organizations are increasingly using Web-based tools to personalize and tailor communications to individual employees. In addition, effective use of traditional approaches (e.g., booklets) can have a large effect on employee awareness.[69]

Cafeteria plans

Rather than a single standard benefits package for all employees, flexible benefit plans (flex-plans or cafeteria-style plans) permit employees to choose the types and amounts of benefits they want for themselves. The plans vary according to such things as whether minimum levels of certain benefits (such as health care coverage) are prescribed and whether employees can receive money for having chosen a "light" benefits package (or have to pay extra for more benefits). One example is vacation, where some plans permit employees to give up vacation days for more salary or, alternatively, purchase extra vacation days through a salary reduction.

Advantages

What are the potential advantages of such plans?[70] In the best case, almost all of the objectives discussed previously can be positively influenced. First, employees can gain a greater awareness and appreciation of what the employer provides them, particularly with plans that give employees a lump sum to allocate to benefits. Second, by permitting employee choice, there should be a better match between the benefits package and the employees' preferences. This, in turn, should improve employee attitudes and retention.[71] Third, employers may achieve overall cost reductions in their benefits programs. Cafeteria plans can be thought of as similar to defined contribution plans, whereas traditional plans are more like defined benefit plans. The employer can control the size of the contribution under the former, but not under the latter, because the cost and utilization of benefits is beyond the employer's control. Costs can also be controlled by designing the choices so that employees have an incentive to choose more efficient options. For example, in the case of a medical flex-plan, employees who do not wish to take advantage of the (presumably more cost-effective) HMO have to pay significant deductibles and other costs under the alternative plans.

One drawback of cafeteria-style plans is their administrative cost, especially in the initial design and start-up stages. However, software packages and standardized flex-plans developed by consultants offer some help in this regard. Another possible drawback to these plans is adverse selection. Employees are most likely to choose benefits that they expect to need the most. Someone in need of dental work would choose as much dental coverage as possible. As a result, employer costs can increase significantly as each employee chooses benefits based on their personal value. Another result of adverse selection is the difficulty in estimating benefits costs under such a plan, especially in small companies. Adverse selection can be controlled, however, by limiting coverage amounts, pricing benefits that are subject to adverse selection higher, or using a limited set of packaged options, which prevents employees from choosing too many benefits options that would be susceptible to adverse selection.

Drawbacks

## Flexible Spending Accounts

A flexible spending account permits pretax contributions to an employee account that can be drawn on to pay for uncovered health care expenses (like deductibles or copayments). A separate account of up to $5,000 per year is permitted for pretax contributions to cover dependent care expenses. The federal tax code requires that funds in the health care and dependent care accounts be earmarked in advance and spent during the plan year. Remaining funds revert to the employer. Therefore, the accounts work best to the extent that employees have predictable expenses. The major advantage of such plans is the increase in take-home pay that results from pretax payment of health and dependent care expenses. Consider again the hypothetical employee with annual earnings of $50,000 and an effective total marginal tax rate of 41 percent from Table 13.1. The take-home pay from an additional $10,000 in salary with and without a flexible dependent care account is as follows:

| | NO FLEXIBLE SPENDING CARE ACCOUNT | FLEXIBLE SPENDING CARE ACCOUNT |
|---|---|---|
| Salary portion | $10,000 | $10,000 |
| Pretax dependent care contribution | −$ 0 | −$ 5,000 |
| Taxable salary | $10,000 | $ 5,000 |
| Tax (41 percent) | −$ 4,100 | −$ 2,050 |
| Aftertax cost of dependent care | −$ 5,000 | −$ 0 |
| Take-home Pay | $ 900 | $ 2,950 |

Therefore, the use of a flexible spending account saves the employee $2,050 ($2,950 − $900) per year.

## General Regulatory Issues

**LO6**
Describe the Regulatory Constraints That Affect the Way Employee Benefits Are Designed and Administered.

Although we have already discussed a number of regulatory issues, some additional ones require attention.

### Nondiscrimination Rules and Qualified Plans

As a general rule, all benefits packages must meet certain rules to be classified as qualified plans. What are the advantages of a qualified plan? Basically, it receives more favorable tax treatment than a nonqualified plan. In the case of a qualified retirement plan, for example, these tax advantages include (1) an immediate tax deduction for employers for their contributions to retirement funds, (2) no tax liability for the employee at the time of the employer deduction, and (3) tax-free investment returns (from stocks, bonds, money markets, or the like) on the retirement funds.[72]

What rules must be satisfied for a plan to obtain qualified status? Each benefit area has different rules. It would be impossible to describe the various rules here, but some general observations are possible. Taking pensions as an example again, vesting requirements must be met. More generally, qualified plans must meet so-called nondiscrimination rules. Basically, this means that a benefit cannot discriminate in favor of "highly compensated employees." One rationale behind such rules is that the tax benefits of qualified benefits plans (and the corresponding loss of tax revenues for the U.S. government) should not go disproportionately to the wealthy.[73] Rather, the favorable tax treatment is designed to encourage employers to provide important benefits to a broad spectrum of employees. The nondiscrimination rules discourage owners or top managers from adopting plans that benefit them exclusively.

### Sex, Age, and Disability

Beyond the Pregnancy Discrimination Act's requirements that were discussed earlier in the chapter, a second area of concern for employers in ensuring legal treatment of men and women in the benefits area has to do with pension benefits. Women tend to live longer than men, meaning that pension benefits for women are more costly, all else being equal. However, in its 1978 *Manhart* ruling, the Supreme Court declared it illegal for employers to require women to contribute more to a defined benefit plan than men: Title VII protects individuals, and not all women outlive all men.[74]

Two major age-related issues have received attention under the Age Discrimination in Employment Act (ADEA) and later amendments such as the Older Workers Benefit Protection Act (OWBPA). First, employers must take care not to discriminate against workers over age 40 in the provision of pay or benefits. As one example, employers cannot generally cease accrual (stop the growth) of retirement benefits at some age (like 65) as a way of pressuring older employees to retire.[75] Second, early retirement incentive programs need to meet the following standards to avoid legal liability: (1) the employee is not coerced to accept the incentive and retire, (2) accurate information is provided regarding options, and (3) the employee is given adequate time (is not pressured) to make a decision.

Employers also have to comply with the Americans with Disabilities Act (ADA), which went into effect in 1992. The ADA specifies that employees with disabilities must have "equal access to whatever health insurance coverage the employer provides other employees." However, the act also notes that the terms and conditions of health insurance can be based on risk factors as long as this is not a subterfuge for denying the benefit to those with disabilities. Employers with risk-based programs in place would be in a stronger position, however, than employers who make changes after hiring employees with disabilities.[76]

## Monitoring Future Benefits Obligations

**Financial Accounting Statement (FAS) 106,** issued by the Financial Accounting Standards Board, became effective in 1993. This rule requires that any benefits (excluding pensions) provided after retirement (the major one being health care) can no longer be funded on a pay-as-you-go basis. Rather, they must be paid on an accrual basis, and companies must enter these future cost obligations on their financial statements. The effect on financial statements can be substantial. For AT&T, a company with a large retiree population, the initial effect of adopting FAS 106 was a reduction in net income of between $5.5 billion and $7.5 billion. General Motors (GM) took a $20.8 billion reduction in net income, resulting in a total loss of $23.5 billion in 1992, the largest loss in corporate history.[77] In 2002, GM's retiree health care cost was over 15 percent of its operating cash flow and it currently has an unfunded obligation here of more than $50 billion.[78]

**Financial Accounting Statement (FAS) 106**
The rule issued by the Financial Accounting Standards Board in 1993 requiring companies to fund benefits provided after retirement on an accrual rather than a pay-as-you-go basis and to enter these future cost obligations on their financial statements.

Increasing retiree health care costs (and the change in accounting standards) have led companies like GM to require its white-collar employees and retirees to pay insurance premiums for the first time in its history and to increase copayments and deductibles. Survey data indicate that some companies are ending retiree health care benefits altogether, while most have reduced benefits or increased retiree contributions. Obviously, such changes hit the elderly hard, especially those with relatively fixed incomes. Not surprisingly, legal challenges have arisen. The need to balance the interests of shareholders, current employees, and retirees in this area will be one of the most difficult challenges facing managers in the future.

## A Look Back

We have seen that many organizations have become less paternalistic in their employee benefits strategies. Employees now have more responsibility, and sometimes more risk, regarding their benefits choices. One change has been in the area of retirement income plans, where employers have moved toward greater reliance on defined contribution plans. Such plans require employees to understand investing; otherwise, their retirement years may not be so happy. The risk to employees is especially great when defined contribution plans invest a substantial portion of their assets in company stock. One reason companies do this is because they wish to move away from an entitlement mentality and instead link benefits to company performance. However, if the company has financial problems, employees risk losing not only their jobs, but also their retirement money. As we saw in the beginning of the chapter, another change has been in the area of health care benefits, where companies have reduced or sometimes eliminated such benefits. Again, the responsibility for anticipating this possibility increasingly falls with employees. In the health care area, employees are being asked to increase the proportion of costs that they pay and also to use data on health care quality to make better choices about health care. Finally, although these trends characterize many employers, some employers follow different benefit strategies as we saw in the Chapter opener.

### Questions

1. Why do employers offer benefits? Is it because the law requires it, because it makes good business sense, or because it is the right thing to do? How much responsibility should employers have for the health and well-being of their employees? Take the perspective of both a shareholder and an employee in answering this question.
2. If you were advising a new company on how to design its health care plan, what would you recommend?

Please see the Video Case that corresponds to this chapter online at www.mhhe.com/noe6e.

## Summary

Effective management of employee benefits is an important means by which organizations successfully compete. Benefits costs are substantial and continue to grow rapidly in some areas, most notably health care. Control of such costs is necessary to compete in the product market. At the same time, employers must offer a benefits package that permits them to compete in the labor market. Beyond investing more money in benefits, this attraction and retention of quality employees can be helped by better communication of the value of the benefits package and by allowing employees to tailor benefits to their own needs through flexible benefits plans.

Employers continue to be a major source of economic security for employees, often providing health insurance, retirement benefits, and so forth. Changes to benefits can have a tremendous impact on employees and retirees. Therefore, employers carry a significant social responsibility in making benefits decisions. At the same time, employees need to be aware that they will increasingly become responsible for their own economic security. Health care benefit design is changing to encourage employees to be more informed consumers, and retirement benefits will depend more and more on the financial investment decisions employees make on their own behalf.

## Key Terms

Marginal tax rate, 563
Consolidated Omnibus Budget Reconciliation Act (COBRA), 569
Pension Benefit Guaranty Corporation (PBGC), 575
Employee Retirement Income Security Act (ERISA), 575
Cash balance plan, 577
Summary plan description (SPD), 578
Family and Medical Leave Act, 582
Health maintenance organization (HMO), 586
Preferred provider organization (PPO), 586
Financial Accounting Statement (FAS) 106, 595

## Discussion Questions

1. The chapter opening story described how relationships between employers and employees are changing. What are the likely consequences of this change? Where does the social responsibility of employers end, and where does the need to operate more efficiently begin?
2. Your company, like many others, is experiencing double-digit percentage increases in health care costs. What suggestions can you offer that may reduce the rate of cost increases?
3. Why is communication so important in the employee benefits area? What sorts of programs can a company use to communicate more effectively? What are the potential positive consequences of more effective benefits communication?
4. What are the potential advantages of flexible benefits and flexible spending accounts? Are there any potential drawbacks?
5. Although benefits account for a large share of employee compensation, many feel there is little evidence on whether an employer receives an adequate return on the benefits investment. One suggestion has been to link benefits to individual, group, or organization performance. Explain why you would or would not recommend this strategy to an organization.

## Self-Assessment Exercise

One way companies determine which types of benefits to provide is to use a survey asking employees which types of benefits are important to them. Read the following list of employee benefits. For each benefit, mark an X in the column that indicates whether it is important to you or not.

| Benefit | Important to Have | Not Important to Have | % Employers Offering |
|---|---|---|---|
| Dependent-care flexible spending account | | | 70% |
| Flextime | | | 64 |
| Ability to bring child to work in case of emergency | | | 30 |
| Elder-care referral services | | | 21 |
| Adoption assistance | | | 21 |
| On-site child care center | | | 6 |
| Gym subsidy | | | 28 |
| Vaccinations on site (e.g., flu shots) | | | 61 |
| On-site fitness center | | | 26 |
| Casual dress days (every day) | | | 53 |
| Organization-sponsored sports teams | | | 39 |
| Food services/subsidized cafeteria | | | 29 |
| Travel-planning services | | | 27 |
| Dry-cleaning services | | | 15 |
| Massage therapy services at work | | | 12 |
| Self-defense training | | | 6 |
| Concierge services | | | 4 |

Compare your importance ratings for each benefit to the corresponding number in the right-hand column that indicates the percentage of employers that offer the benefit. Are you likely to find jobs that provide the benefits you want? Explain.

SOURCE: Based on Figure 2, "Percent of Employers Offering Work/Life Benefits (by Year)," in *Workplace Visions* 4 (2002), p. 3, published by the Society for Human Resource Management.

## Exercising Strategy: Companies Learn That It Pays to Keep Employees Fit

Physical fitness—or at least wellness—does matter, as more and more companies and their insurers are learning. A healthy workforce means better productivity and fewer workdays lost, not to mention reduced medical costs by keeping injuries and illnesses to a minimum. A study published by the Presidents' Council on Physical Fitness and Sports found that fitness programs provided by companies saved from $1.15 to $5.52 for every dollar spent.

At 3Com, the network communications company, employees spend their lunch hours at the WellCom Center, a 13,500-square-foot fitness facility right on site. There they can cycle, walk a treadmill, lift weights, take a fitness class, or relax in the sauna. Or they can play a game of basketball or beach volleyball outside. Afterward, they can cool off at the juice bar with a fruit smoothie. The center is open 24 hours a day, seven days a week, to meet the needs of employees who work at all hours. More than 40 percent of the 4,200 workers at 3Com are WellCom members, and 70 percent take advantage of the center's seminars on wellness, smoking cessation, or weight loss. "A healthy workforce is good for employees and good for 3Com," says Peter Sandman, a manager of strategic planning at the company. "It helps recruiting and it helps retention, especially in a competitive environment like Silicon Valley [California]."

Applied Materials Inc. of Santa Clara, California, conducted its own study that showed that for fitness center participants, medical payments were reduced by 20 percent, hospital admissions were 70 percent lower, costs for accident-related disability claims were 30 percent less, and workers' compensation claims were 79 percent less than those of employees who didn't use the company's fitness center. Even a five-minute stretch break has been shown to reduce strains and sprains by as much as 65 percent. "Just moving and getting away from their PC makes them feel better," says Judy Webster, director of corporate wellness for the company.

Boeing's health care package also includes access to its fitness centers as part of its overall recreation program. "When you're happy and healthy, you're able to perform at your best," explains the aircraft manufacturer's Web site. The recreation program includes indoor and outdoor facilities as well as discount packages for sports and cultural events. These companies have embraced the wisdom of the old adage, "an ounce of prevention is worth a pound of cure," and it has literally paid off.

SOURCES: Boeing Web site, www.boeing.com, accessed October 30, 2001; D. Beck, "Your Company Needs Its Own Best Practices," *Career Journal* from *The Wall Street Journal* (July 30–August 5, 2001), www.careerjournal.com; M. Chase, "Healthy Assets," *The Wall Street Journal* (May 1. 2000), http://interactive.wsj.

### Questions

1. Why don't more companies emphasize employee wellness? Does it work better for some companies than for others?
2. The companies here have on-site facilities. Is that the right model for all companies?

## MANAGING PEOPLE: FROM THE PAGES OF *BUSINESSWEEK*

### BusinessWeek Get Healthy-Or Else: Inside One Company's All-Out Attack on Medical Costs

In August, Joe Pellegrini got yet another nagging phone call. It was his health coach, a woman working on behalf of his employer, the $2.7 billion lawn-care company, Scotts Miracle-Gro Co. The 48-year-old executive knew the spiel by heart. "Have you been to your doctor yet? When are you going?" Then the prescription: "You need to lose weight and you really, really need to lower your cholesterol."

Pellegrini is a supply-chain executive at Scotts' headquarters in Marysville, Ohio, a land of all-you-can-eat buffets smack in the middle of America's obesity belt. At Scotts the hallways are filled with ldl-abusers and overweight diabetics. Pellegrini, by contrast, is an Armani-swaddled triathlete who often cycles 36 miles to and from work. Lose weight? "Give me a break," he thought. "It's all muscle, folks."

But a time bomb was ticking beneath the taut physique. Medical specialists working on behalf of Scotts had been scouring every aspect of Pellegrini's health. His profile—athletic, high body-mass index, and bad cholesterol (brought on by a love of 28-ounce sirloins)—triggered an alarm.

Eventually, Pellegrini succumbed to the company-applied pressure and agreed to abide by his health coach's action plan, which included an immediate visit to his doctor. A few weeks later, a specialist studying Pellegrini's angiogram spotted the heart value of what should have been a dead man. Within hours, two stents were installed. The surgeons later told him the 95 percent blockage would have killed him within five days. "It was that close," Pellegrini says.

About the time Pellegrini was cheating death, a lawn-care technician named Scott Rodrigues was having an entirely different experience with the Scotts wellness program. At the time, Rodrigues says he had been working at the company for about two weeks. He recalls a supervisor approaching him in the parking lot at the company's Cape Cod (Mass.) facility and urging him to get rid of the pack of Marlboro reds poking out of the dashboard of his decrepit Civic.

Rodrigues knew Scotts was going tobacco-free on Oct. 1 as part of its effort to improve employee health and cut medical costs. He recalls the company's interviewer saying that once Rodrigues passed the 60-day probation. Scotts would help him quit his 15-year habit—paying for counseling. Nicorette, prescription drugs, hypnosis. Whatever it took.

But on Sept. 1—which happened to be his 30th birthday—Rodrigues was fired. "Why?" he asked. "You failed your drug test," the boss replied. Rodrigues insisted it had to be a mistake. He didn't even keep beer in the fridge. Then his boss told him the drug was nicotine. "Five years ago, if you had told me, Hey, you better quit smoking or you might not get a job," I would have laughed. Here I am five years later, and I can't get a job."

In November, Rodrigues filed a lawsuit, now in federal court in Massachusetts. It alleges that Scotts discriminated against Rodrigues by firing him before he was eligible for health-care benefits and had a chance to take advantage of the stop-smoking initiative. The suit also seeks to prohibit Scotts from "enforcing or applying" its anti-nicotine program. The company hopes to have the suit dismissed. Citing its policy of not discussing pending litigation, Scotts declined to comment on the lawsuit.

Two stories—one man saved by the 11th-hour intervention of his employer; another fired on his 30th birthday for smoking—capture the dilemma facing companies around the country. How do executives looking to cut medical costs persuade employees to take better care of themselves without killing morale and spawning lawsuits? It's a question that's very much on the mind of Scotts CEO Jim Hagedorn, who acknowledges his company's wellness program is controversial. "Jack Welch told me: Man, you have balls of steel," says Hagedorn, "This is an area where CEOs are afraid to go. A lot of people are watching to see how badly we get sued."

Getting health insurance from your employer is sometimes seen as an entitlement, but the benefit owes its existence to a quirk of history. During World War II, employers desperate to attract workers began offering health insurance. Providing coverage has been an increasing burden for companies ever since. As a result, businesses have been forcing employees to shoulder more and more of the cost.

Some theorized that higher co-payments and pricier premiums would get people to take better care of themselves. It's not happening. "We have this notion that you can gorge on hot dogs, be in a pie-eating contest, and drink every day, and society will take care of you," says Harvard Business School Professor Michael E. Porter, who co-authored *Redefining Health Care*. "We can't afford to let individuals drive up costs because they're not willing to address their health problems."

Hence the wellness fixation at companies as varied as IBM, Microsoft, Harrah's Entertainment, and Scotts. Employees who voluntarily sing up for such programs often receive discounts on health-care premiums, free weight-loss and smoking-cessation programs, gratis gym memberships, counseling for emotional problems, and prizes like vacations or points that can be redeemed for gift cards.

Companies save money. Employees get healthier. What's not to like? But the wellness craze raises important issues. One is that people could start blaming unhealthy colleagues for helping push up premiums. Then there are the privacy and discrimination issues: How far should managers intrude into employees' lives? That's the essence of the Rodrigues lawsuit.

U.S. business has long evinced a paternalistic streak. Early last century. Ford Motor Co. sent investigators to workers' homes to make sure their sex lives were "unblemished" and they weren't imbibing one too many. Today, Scotts is in the vanguard of companies seeking to monitor and change employee behavior. The company's outlier status reflects the born-again zeal of its CEO. Hagedorn is a reformed nicotine addict himself. He smoked two packs a day for 20 years—until his mother, also a heavy smoker, died of lung cancer. Hagedorn quit the same day.

In the early 2000s, Hagedorn, like many other CEOs, watched health-care costs explode. From what he could see, the government and the health-insurance industry weren't doing anything to solve the crisis. At the same time, Hagedorn's employees were bingeing on care.

In February, 2003, Scotts doubled what workers paid for health insurance. Morale plummeted, and Hagedorn knew he had to do a better job selling the hike. Hagedorn is famous at Scotts for the "straight talk" sessions he holds with staff each quarter. A former F-16 fighter pilot who retains much of his military bravura, Hagedorn laces his sermons with salty language and unvarnished commentary. The CEO got right to the point: We were boneheaded, he told the crowd.

Then again, Hagedorn wanted employees to know what he was up against. Using a PowerPoint presentation, he showed that his annual health-care bill had soared 42 percent since 1999, to $20 million, which amounted to 20 percent of the company's net profits in 2003. Costs were projected to surge about 20 percent that year, vs. the national average of 9 percent and keep on climbing at a double-digit rate.

Toward the end of the talk, a young plant worker stood up and scolded Hagedorn. "You guys on the other side of the street, you got fancy financial advisers," he said. "How can you make me responsible for managing my finances and health care and not educate me? I only have a high school education." Hagedorn left the meeting thinking: "The guy's right."

A few months later, Hagedorn was watching CNN. A doctor was arguing that employers should get serious about obesity, smoking, and diabetes. Companies were paying the bills, he said, so they could do something. As it happens, Hagedorn had recently seen Scotts' health-risk assessment: Half of his 6,000 employees were overweight or morbidly obese; a quarter of them smoked.

The CNN program prompted an epiphany. Hagedorn wanted to share it right away with his human resources chief, Denise Stump. It was after 11 P.M., but he called her at home anyway. "Denise," he said, "we are moving into FEBA [forward-edge battle area]." Hagedorn told her he wanted to ban smoking and go after obesity. To achieve these aims, he proposed launching the kind of companywide intervention that families use to help an addicted relative.

Instituting such a policy wasn't a matter of saying, "Let it be so." Legal worried the plan might violate federal laws. Other advisers told the CEO point blank: Don't go there. And getting outside advice wasn't going to be easy. Many law firms were knee-deep in tobacco litigation and wouldn't go near Scotts' wellness initiative. Nor would board member Lynn Beasley. As chief operating officer for tobacco maker R.J. Reynolds, Beasley saw the conflict right away and quit the Scotts board. Stump recalls thinking: "We're going too fast."

Hagedorn isn't easily dissuaded. The 51-year-old CEO talks like a swaggering teenager, with "yo" this and "dude" that. A runaway at 15, Hagedorn still flies his rebel flag: A photo in his office features him giving the middle-finger salute.

Needless to say, Hagedorn got his way. Scotts hired a boutique law firm. And before long, the company had determined that in 21 states, including home-base Ohio, it wasn't illegal to hire and fire people based on their smoking habits. Scotts also realized it needed to create an arm's-length relationship with the wellness program. No one wanted to give managers an opportunity to discriminate against employees based on their health. That meant bringing in a third party to run the thing.

In 2005, Scotts hired Whole Health Management. The firm manages on-site primary care and fitness centers for dozens of corporations. Whole Health aggregates health and insurance claim data so Scotts can divine trends. But individual data are kept strictly confidential. Stump began selling the concept to employees. She held role-playing sessions to teach workers what to say if they bumped into each other in the clinic. On-site doctors told employees they would never betray confidences.

During one of Hagedorn's straight-talk sessions, workers told him a company gym would make wellness easier to swallow. "Done," Hagedorn said. But his vision went far beyond installing some StairMasters and throwing up health pointers on the Scotts intranet. Hagedorn built a soup-to-nuts medical and fitness center across the street from headquarters. Operated by Whole Health, the 24,000-square-foot facility cost $5 million and can meet pretty much any health-related need an employee might have, including a drive-thru for free prescription drugs. The clinic employs two full-time doctors, five nurses, a dietician, counselor, and two physical therapists. A team of fitness coaches provides personal training sessions for $30 an hour.

Scotts employees are now urged to take exhaustive health-risk assessments. Those who balk pay $40 a month more in premiums. Using data-mining software, Whole Health analysts scour the physical, mental, and family health histories of nearly every employee and cross-reference that information with insurance-claims data. Health coaches identify which employees are at moderate to high risk. All of them are assigned a health coach who draws up an action plan. Those who don't comply pay $67 a month on top of the $40. "We tried carrots," says Benefits Chief Pam Kuryla. "Carrots didn't work."

Many employees found Hagedorn's new policy intrusive. Topic A: the health assessment questionnaires, which asked things like: Do you smoke? Drink? What did your parents die of? Do you feel down, sad, hopeless? Burned out? How is your relationship with your spouse? Your kids? Are you pregnant, diabetic, suffering from high cholesterol? The tobacco ban was controversial, too, especially at the manufacturing plants, where Skoal chewers are common. Hagedorn wasn't unsympathetic. After all, it took his own wife three years to quit smoking. Scotts employees would get all the help they needed.

Workers told the CEO they were angry. Hagedorn concedes the program had Big Brother overtones. But he's adamant about bringing down health costs—even if it means being authoritarian. "If people understand the facts and still choose to smoke, it's suicidal," he says. "And we can't encourage suicidal behavior."

As chief wellness salesman, Hagedorn took it upon himself to motivate employees. He walks around campus joking, slapping guts, and exhorting people to work out. Hagedorn routinely teases Dave Overfield, who toils in the plant and whose weight has soared 40 pounds since he quit chewing tobacco.

"I'm working on it," Overfield tells his boss.

"You better be," Hagedorn shoots back.

The nudging begets peer pressure. Gym rats earn special pins they display on ID badge lanyards; these have become a coveted status object. Competition for trips to Hawaii, free massages and facials, and other cash and prizes is fierce. One group of employees started having lunch together every day to keep each other from peeling out of the parking lot for a smoke. Doughnuts have disappeared. "The message is: If you're not trying to do something to make yourself better, then you're going to pay more," says Kuryla.

Jim Lowe gets that. The 54-year-old forklift driver loved to eat. He started each day with two doughnuts. Lunch was a pair of Whoppers and fries. Nighttime involved a bag of chips, a couch, and a clicker. Lowe's philosophy was simple: "Let's don't go to a place that'll serve us a helping. Let's go to a buffet where you can eat all you want." He weighed 307 pounds.

He was the perfect candidate for the wellness crusade. Before long a dietician was telling Lowe exactly what to eat, and a personal trainer was showing him exactly how to work out. Soon Lowe was losing an average of four pounds a week. Co-workers at the plant began asking if he was taking diet pills. They gossiped that he had had gastric bypass surgery. Lowe proudly told them he was doing it "natural, working out and watching what I eat."

Lowe had always loved the way Wrangler jeans hung on his hero, country singer George Strait. But he couldn't get them in the Big & Tall catalog he ordered everything from. Lowe hadn't been in a clothing store for 15 years. The day he hit his goal of losing 137 pounds, he headed to Kohl's, where he tried on a pair of Wranglers; his eyes filled with tears. "I'm not trying to be Hercules," says Lowe as he pinches his gut between his fingers. "But as you can see, there's not a lot of flab."

So far, the company says, more than 70 percent of headquarters staff belongs to the fitness center. The smoking-cessation program has already had a 30 percent success rate. The wellness program, which costs $4 million a year to run, is a financial drain. But the company expects it to pay for itself in three to four years. Other large companies have seen a 3-to-1 return on investment in their wellness programs.

It's all pretty encouraging, except that if Rodrigues wins his case, it could set a precedent and then open the door to big-money lawsuits. So far, Scotts says it has not fired anyone else for using tobacco. In fact, because Rodrigues wasn't employed long enough to pass the probation period, the company argues that he was never officially an employee.

It's impossible to tell how the case will come out because there is so little case law. This much is certain: Rodrigues' lawyer, Harvey A. Schwartz, will argue that Scotts' wellness program amounts to a slippery slope. "Where will all this end?" he asks. "The consumption of alcohol, failure to exercise, skydiving, excessive television viewing, eating processed sugars, owning dangerous pets, flying private aircraft, mountain climbing, downhill ski racing, single-handed sailing, or spreading toxic chemicals on lawns?"

Where will it all end? Companies ask themselves the same question but from a different angle. In the absence of a solution to the health-care mess, businesses are on an unsustainable path. Hence the rush into wellness. Perhaps that's why Hagedorn is getting leeway from shareholders, including his own family, which controls 30 percent of the public shares. The stock is up 58 percent since Scotts launched its wellness program. If Hagedorn pulls this off, he'll be a hero in boardrooms around the country.

SOURCE: M. Conlin, "Get Healthy—Or Else: Inside One Company's All-Out Attack on Medical Costs," *BusinessWeek*, February 26, 2007, pp. 58+.

### Questions

1. Is it fair to fire someone for what they do when they are not at work? Why or why not?
2. What do you think would have happened to health care benefits at Scotts if it had not instituted an aggressive wellness program?
3. If an employer decides that hiring and firing employees based on whether they smoke is an effective policy, what other attributes of employees might employers consider? What, if any, ethical and legal issues come into play here?

## NOTES


1. D. Zoia, "DCC Attacks High Health Care Costs," *Ward's Auto World,* September 1999, p. 75; P. Welch, "A Small Reprieve for Detroit, But . . . ," *BusinessWeek,* September 22, 2003, p. 38; B. G. Hoffman, "Health Tab to Soar at GM," *Detroit News,* February 27, 2007.
2. H. W. Hennessey, "Using Employee Benefits to Gain a Competitive Advantage," *Benefits Quarterly* 5, no. 1 (1989), pp. 51–57; B. Gerhart and G.T. Milkovich, "Employee Compensation: Research and Practice," in *Handbook of Industrial and Organizational Psychology,* vol. 3, 2nd ed., ed. M. D. Dunnette and L. M. Hough (Palo Alto, CA: Consulting Psychologists Press, 1992); J. Swist, "Benefits Communications: Measuring Impact and Value," *Employee Benefit Plan Review,* September 2002, pp. 24–26.
3. R. Ehrenberg and R. S. Smith, *Modern Labor Economics: Theory and Public Policy,* 7th ed. (Upper Saddle River, NJ: Addison Wesley Longman, 2000).
4. B. T. Beam Jr. and J. J. McFadden, *Employee Benefits,* 6th ed. (Chicago: Dearborn Financial Publishing, 2000).
5. Bureau of National Affairs, "Most Workers Who Struck in 1990 Did So over Health Coverage, AFL–CIO Says," *Daily Labor Report,* August 20, 1991, p. A12; M. Herper, "GE Strike Sounds Health Care Alarm," *Forbes,* January 14, 2003, www.forbes.com.
6. The organization and description in this section draws heavily on Beam and McFadden, *Employee Benefits.*
7. See www.doleta.gov for further information.
8. J. A. Penczak, "Unemployment Benefit Plans," in *Employee Benefits Handbook,* 3rd ed., ed. J. D. Mamorsky (Boston: Warren, Gorham & Lamont, 1992).
9. J. V. Nackley, *Primer on Workers' Compensation* (Washington, DC: Bureau of National Affairs, 1989).
10. Beam and McFadden, *Employee Benefits,* p. 81.
11. www.dol.gov/esa.
12. M. D. Fefer, "What to Do about Workers' Comp," *Fortune,* June 29, 1992, pp. 80ff; National Academy of Social Insurance, "Recession Affects Workers' Compensation Trends," www.nasi.org (July 15, 2003).
13. A. H. Wheeler, "Pathophysiology of Chronic Back Pain," www.emedicine.com (2002).
14. J. R. Hollenbeck, D. R. Ilgen, and S. M. Crampton, "Lower Back Disability in Occupational Settings: A Review of the Literature from a Human Resource Management View," *Personnel Psychology* 45 (1992), pp. 247–78; J. J. Martocchio, D. A. Harrison, and H. Berkson, "Connections between Lower Back Pain, Interventions, and Absence from Work: A Time-Based Meta-Analysis," *Personnel Psychology* (2000), p. 595.
15. Employee Benefit Research Institute, "Value of Employee Benefits Constant in a Changing World," www.ebri.org (March 28, 2002).
16. Beam and McFadden, *Employee Benefits,* 6th ed.
17. Social Security Administration, "Fast Facts and Figures about Social Security." Data for 2001, published 2003, www.ssa.gov.
18. L. M. Dailey and J. A. Turner, "Private Pension Coverage in Nine Countries," *Monthly Labor Review,* May 1992, pp. 40–43; Hewitt Associates, *Salaried Employee Benefits Provided by Major Employers in 1990* (Lincolnshire, IL: Hewitt Associates, 1990); W. J. Wiatrowski, "New Survey Data on Pension Benefits," *Monthly Labor Review,* August 1991, pp. 8–21; K. A. Bender, "Pension Integration and Retirement Benefits," *Monthly Labor Review,* February 2001, pp. 49–58, http://stats.bls.gov/opub/mlr.
19. www.pbgc.gov.
20. www.irs.gov. Those age 50 and over have higher contribution limits.
21. R. A. Ippolito, "Toward Explaining the Growth of Defined Contribution Plans," *Industrial Relations* 34 (1995), pp. 1–20; Employee Benefit Research Institute, "Historical Statistics," EBRI May 2004 Policy Forum, www.ebri.org.
22. J. Fierman, "How Secure Is Your Nest Egg?" *Fortune,* August 12, 1991, pp. 50–54.
23. Beam and McFadden, *Employee Benefits.*
24. B. J. Coleman, *Primer on Employee Retirement Income Security Act,* 3rd ed. (Washington, DC: Bureau of National Affairs, 1989).
25. *Continental Can Company v. Gavalik,* summary in *Daily Labor Report* (December 8, 1987): "Supreme Court Lets Stand Third Circuit Ruling That Pension Avoidance Scheme Is ERISA Violation," No. 234, p. A-14.
26. A. L. Gustman, O. S. Mitchell, and T. L. Steinmeier, "The Role of Pensions in the Labor Market: A Survey of the Literature," *Industrial and Labor Relations* 47 (1994), pp. 417–38.
27. D. A. DeCenzo and S. J. Holoviak, *Employee Benefits* (Englewood Cliffs, NJ: Prentice-Hall, 1990).
28. E. P. Lazear, "Why Is There Early Retirement?" *Journal of Political Economy* 87 (1979), pp. 1261–84; Gustman et al., "The Role of Pensions."
29. P. Cappelli, *The New Deal at Work: Managing the Market-Driven Workforce* (Boston: Harvard Business School Press, 1999).
30. S. Dorsey, "Pension Portability and Labor Market Efficiency," *Industrial and Labor Relations* 48, no. 5 (1995), pp. 276–92.
31. Commission of the European Communities, European Community Directive 93/104/EC, issued November 23, 1993 and amended June 22, 2000, by Directive 2000/34/EC, http://europa/eu.int/comm/index_en.htm.
32. DeCenzo and Holoviak, *Employee Benefits,* 6th ed.
33. S. L. Grover and K. J. Crooker, "Who Appreciates Family Responsive Human Resource Policies: The Impact of Family-Friendly Policies on the Organizational Attachment of Parents and Nonparents," *Personnel Psychology* 48 (1995), pp. 271–88; T. J. Rothausen, J. A. Gonzalez, N. E. Clarke, and L. L. O'Dell, "Family-Friendly Backlash: Fact or Fiction? The Case of Organizations' On-Site Child Care Centers," *Personnel Psychology* 51 (1998), p. 685; M. A. Arthur, "Share Price Reactions to Work-Family Initiatives: An Institutional Perspective," *Academy of Management Journal* 46 (2003), p. 497; J. E. Perry-Smith and T. Blum, "Work-Family Human Resource Bundles and Perceived Organizational Performance," *Academy of Management Journal* 43 (2000), pp. 1107–17.
34. "The Employer's Role in Helping Working Families." For examples of child care arrangements in some well-known companies

(e.g., AT&T, Apple, Exxon, IBM, Merck), see "A Look at Child-Care Benefits," *USA Today*, March 14, 1989, p. 4B; U.S. Census Bureau, "America's Families and Living Arrangements," June 2001, www.census.gov.

35. J. Waldfogel, "International Policies toward Parental Leave and Child Care," *Future of Children* 11, no. 1 (2001), pp. 99–111.
36. P. Hardin, "Women Execs Should Feel at Ease about Taking Full Maternity Leave," *Personnel Journal*, September 1995, p. 19.
37. "The Families and Work Institute's 1998 Business Work–Life Study," www.familiesandwork.org. Results based on a nationally representative survey of employers having 100 or more employees.
38. J. Fierman, "It's 2 A.M.: Let's Go to Work," *Fortune*, August 21, 1995, pp. 82–88.
39. E. E. Kossek, "Diversity in Child Care Assistance Needs: Employee Problems, Preferences, and Work-Related Outcomes," *Personnel Psychology* 43 (1990), pp. 769–91.
40. "A Bank Profits from Its Work/Life Program," *Workforce*, February 1997, p. 49.
41. R. Broderick and B. Gerhart, "Nonwage Compensation," in *The Human Resource Management Handbook*, ed. D. Lewin, D. J. B. Mitchell, and M. A. Zadi (San Francisco: JAI Press, 1996).
42. Hennessey, "Using Employee Benefits to Gain a Competitive Advantage."
43. U.S. Bureau of Labor Statistics, "Employer Cost for Employee Compensation," www.bls.gov; U.S. Chamber of Commerce Research Center, Employee Benefits Study, annual (Washington, D.C.: U.S. Chamber of Commerce).
44. www.census.gov.
45. Employee Benefit Research Institute, "Health Care Reform."
46. A. C. Monheit and P. F. Cooper, "Health Insurance and Job Mobility: The Effects of Public Policy on Job-Lock," *Industrial and Labor Relations Review* 48 (1994), pp. 86–102.
47. Beam and McFadden, *Employee Benefits*.
48. R. Lieber, "New Way to Curb Medical Costs: Make Employees Feel the Sting," *The Wall Street Journal*, June 23, 2004, p. A1.
49. M. Barringer and O. S. Mitchell, "Workers' Preferences among Company-Provided Health Insurance Plans," *Industrial and Labor Relations Review* 48 (1994), pp. 141–52.
50. Beam and McFadden, *Employee Benefits*.
51. Wellness Councils of America, "101 Ways to Wellness," www.welcoa.org, 2001; Wellness Councils of America, "A Guide to Developing Your Worksite Wellness Program," www.welcoa.org, 1997.
52. S. Tully, "America's Healthiest Companies," *Fortune*, June 12, 1995, pp. 98–106.
53. G. Flynn, "Companies Make Wellness Work," *Personnel Journal*, February 1995, pp. 63–66.
54. D. A. Harrison and L. Z. Liska, "Promoting Regular Exercise in Organizational Fitness Programs: Health-Related Differences in Motivational Building Blocks," *Personnel Psychology* 47 (1994), pp. 47–71.
55. J. C. Erfurt, A. Foote, and M. A. Heirich, "The Cost-Effectiveness of Worksite Wellness Programs for Hypertension Control, Weight Loss, Smoking Cessation and Exercise," *Personnel Psychology* 45 (1992), pp. 5–27.
56. Ibid.
57. The Henry J. Kaiser Family Foundation and Health Research and Educational Trust, *Survey of Employer Health Benefits 2006*, www.kff.org.
58. H. Gardner, unpublished manuscript (Cheyenne, WY: Options & Choices, 1995).
59. H. B. Noble, "Quality Is Focus for Health Plans," *The New York Times*, July 3, 1995, p. A1; J. D. Klinke, "Medicine's Industrial Revolution," *The Wall Street Journal*, August 21, 1995, p. A8.
60. J. B. White, "Business Plan," *The Wall Street Journal*, October 19, 1998, p. R18.
61. G. McWilliams, "Big Employers Plan Electronic Health Records," *The Wall Street Journal*, November 29, 2006, p. B1.
62. J. Schor, *The Overworked American: The Unexpected Decline of Leisure* (New York: Basic Books, 1991); U.S. Bureau of Labor Statistics, "Workers Are on the Job More Hours over the Course of a Year," *Issues in Labor Statistics*, February 1997.
63. Hewitt Associates. http://www.hewitt.com.
64. Beam and McFadden, *Employee Benefits*.
65. M. Wilson, G. B. Northcraft, and M. A. Neale, "The Perceived Value of Fringe Benefits," *Personnel Psychology* 38 (1985), pp. 309–20. Similar results were found in other studies reviewed by H. W. Hennessey, P. L. Perrewe, and W. A. Hochwarter, "Impact of Benefit Awareness on Employee and Organizational Outcomes: A Longitudinal Field Experiment," *Benefits Quarterly* 8, no. 2 (1992), pp. 90–96; MetLife. Employee Benefits Benchmarking Report. www.metlife.com. Accessed June 24, 2007.
66. R. Huseman, J. Hatfield, and R. Robinson, "The MBA and Fringe Benefits," *Personnel Administrator* 23, no. 7 (1978), pp. 57–60. See summary in H. W. Hennessey Jr., "Using Employee Benefits to Gain a Competitive Advantage," *Benefits Quarterly* 5, no. 1 (1989), pp. 51–57.
67. Hennessey et al., "Impact of Benefit Awareness"; the same study found no impact of the increased awareness and benefits satisfaction on overall job satisfaction. G. F. Dreher, R. A. Ash, and R. D. Bretz, "Benefit Coverage and Employee Cost: Critical Factors in Explaining Compensation Satisfaction," *Personnel Psychology* 41 (1988), pp. 237–54.
68. M. C. Giallourakis and G. S. Taylor, "An Evaluation of Benefit Communication Strategy," *Employee Benefits Journal* 15, no. 4 (1991), pp. 14–18; Employee Benefits Research Institute, "How Readable Are Summary Plan Descriptions for Health Care Plans," *EBRI Notes*, October 2006, ebri.org.
69. J. Abraham, R. Feldman, and C. Carlin, "Understanding Employee Awareness of Health Care Quality Information: How Can Employers Benefit?" *Health Services Research* 39 (2004), pp. 1799–1816.
70. Beam and McFadden, *Employee Benefits*; M. W. Barringer and G. T. Milkovich, "A Theoretical Explanation of the Adoption and Design of Flexible Benefit Plans: A Case of Human Resource Innovation," *Academy of Management Review* 23 (1998), pp. 305–24.
71. For supportive evidence, see A. E. Barber, R. B. Dunham, and R. A. Formisano, "The Impact of Flexible Benefits on Employee Satisfaction: A Field Study," *Personnel Psychology* 45 (1992), pp. 55–75; E. E. Lawler, *Pay and Organizational Development* (Reading, MA: Addison-Wesley, 1981).
72. Beam and McFadden, *Employee Benefits*.
73. Ibid.
74. *Los Angeles Dept. of Water & Power v. Manhart*, 435 US SCt 702 (1978), 16 EPD, 8250.
75. S. K. Hoffman, "Discrimination Litigation Relating to Employee Benefits," *Labor Law Journal*, June 1992, pp. 362–81.
76. Ibid., p. 375.
77. W. A. Reimert, "Accounting for Retiree Health Benefits," *Compensation and Benefits Review* 23, no. 5 (September–October, 1991), pp. 49–55; D. P. Levin, "20.8 Billion G. M. Charge for Benefits," *The New York Times*, February 2, 1993, p. D4.
78. A. Tergesen, "The Hidden Bite of Retiree Health," *BusinessWeek*, January 19, 2004; D. Welch, "Has GM Outrun Its Pension Problems?" *BusinessWeek*, January 19, 2004.

PART

# 5

# Special Topics in Human Resource Management

# 14

CHAPTER

# Collective Bargaining and Labor Relations

LO

## LEARNING OBJECTIVES

After reading this chapter, you should be able to:

LO1 Describe what is meant by collective bargaining and labor relations. *page 607*

LO2 Identify the labor relations goals of management, labor unions, and society. *page 611*

LO3 Explain the legal environment's impact on labor relations. *page 622*

LO4 Describe the major labor–management interactions: organizing, contract negotiations, and contract administration. *page 626*

LO5 Describe new, less adversarial approaches to labor–management relations. *page 640*

LO6 Explain how changes in competitive challenges (e.g., product market competition and globalization) are influencing labor–management interactions. *page 647*

LO7 Explain how labor relations in the public sector differ from labor relations in the private sector. *page 648*

# Enter the World of Business

## Streamlined Model: Engine of Change

With its highly educated hourly workers, flexible structure and—perhaps most remarkable—blessing from the UAW, the Global Engine Manufacturing Alliance's plant in Michigan could be the workforce model for the future of U.S. automaking.

It's a Thursday morning in early April, and the Global Engine Manufacturing Alliance plant in Dundee, Michigan, is open as it always is, 21 hours a day, six days a week, 294 days a year. But a visitor to the plant might wonder where all the workers are.

True, for an auto engine plant, GEMA is more automated and thus leaner than most. The facility's total headcount is 275, significantly less than a typical engine plant, which has 600 to 2,000 workers. But that's not why the assembly lines seem empty, GEMA president Bruce Coventry says. "Since we're ahead of schedule, a lot of our people are in training," he says. Sure enough, down the hall are three rooms filled with employees being taught a wide array of subjects, ranging from how to assemble and engine to the study of mathematical formulas designed to teach problem-solving skills. Over the next several months, these employees will receive up to 1,160 hours of such training in class and on the assembly floor. "The fact that we are ahead of our production schedule allows us to focus our people on problem solving and continuous improvement," Coventry says. "That's luxury that most organizations don't usually have."

And that's why automakers from around the world, including GEMA's three owners—DaimlerChrysler, Mitsubishi, and Hyundai—are keeping close track of this facility, located 60 miles outside of Detroit. As General Motors and Ford seek to shed thousands of their union-represented employees, they are looking ahead to what kind of workforce they will need to compete in the increasingly global market. "They need a new business model for labor agreements and new kinds of workers," says Sean McAlinden, chief economist and vice president of research at the Center for Automotive Research in Ann Arbor, Michigan. Many are thinking that GEMA may prove to be that model, he says.

The Dundee facility, which opened in October, stands out from other auto plants in every aspect of how it manages its workforce. Its hourly employees are highly educated and rotate jobs and shifts to provide for greater flexibility. That's an unheard of concept in the traditional auto plant, where each worker is usually assigned to one and only one job.

Another unique aspect of GEMA's workforce model is that contractors, whom the plant refers to as "partners," work alongside assembly workers and engineers, sporting the same black-and-white uniforms. "We want everyone to feel like they are part of a team," Coventry says.

But the most unheard of thing for the auto industry is that the United Auto Workers has agreed to the concept. "This is an agreement that every automaker is looking at with laser eyes," McAlinden says.

GEMA expects to open a second facility in October on the same premises. At full capacity the Dundee plants will have 532 workers and produce 840,000 engines annually. Its goal is to be the most productive engine plant in the world, beating the industry standard of 1.8 hours of production per engine, says Mark Dunning, senior manager of human resources. The company says that so far GEMA is on track to hit those numbers, though it will not disclose preliminary data.

The initial investment for the two plants was $804 million, 50 percent less than DaimlerChrysler had ever invested in an engine plant, Coventry says.

The automakers' joint venture also has two non-GEMA plants in South Korea and one in Japan that produce engines for Hyundai and Mitsubishi, respectively. When all of the plants are operational by year's end, the venture will have the capacity to produce 1.8 million engines annually.

Coventry, who had been an engine plant manager for Chrysler since 1995, was the logical choice to come up with the idea for GEMA in 2001. Chrysler had recently bought a stake in Hyundai and Mitsubishi, and Thomas LaSorda, then head of DaimlerChrysler's engine and transmission division, wanted to come up with ways for the three companies to collaborate. All three organizations needed four-cylinder engines. Coventry was LaSorda's pick to help lead the project. A graduate of General Motors Institute, an engineering school established by General Motors and now called Kettering University, Coventry wanted to find a way to get rid of the waste and inefficiencies he had seen in traditional plants. "My pet peeves are bureaucracy, structure and management," he says.

Over the next several months, Coventry and a team of executives from the three automakers brainstormed over meetings in Korea and the United States. During these discussions, the group came up with a list of companies within and outside of the industry, such as Dell, Wal-Mart and Toyota, to serve as benchmarks for the business model they wanted.

Like its Japanese peers, the alliance wanted to focus on kaizen, the Japanese term for continuous improvement. But Coventry says that GEMA doesn't want to just replicate Toytoa, which he concedes is "the rabbit" all automakers are trying to catch. "We are doing many things that a Toyota employee would recognize, but the big differentiator is that our workforce has a much higher level of technical skill," he says.

GEMA's nonexempt workers, who start at $21 an hour and work up to $30 within five years, must have either a two-year technical degree, a skilled journeyman's card or five years' experience in advanced machining. This level of education is key to GEMA being more flexible, and thus faster than its competitors, Dunning says.

The other guiding principles of the plant's culture are problem solving and "the four A's": anyone can do anything anytime, anywhere. This means that workers rotate jobs—a model that is designed to give the plant more flexibility. Everyone on the floor has a similar title: They are "team members" and "team leaders."

By rotating jobs, the plant hopes to keep workers engaged and reduce the potential for injury, Coventry says. The chance of workers developing ergonomic injuries is lower if they aren't repeating the exact same motions all day long, he says. So far there have been no ergonomical injuries at the plant.

There are also no foremen overseeing the workers at GEMA. In their place are the team leaders. In contrast to foremen, the team leaders don't stand on the sidelines observing how the teams work. They work alongside six-person groups, each one including an engineer. Coventry bristles if he sees engineers at their desks while he's walking through the plant. "Having engineers on the floor enables us to solve problems right away when they happen," he says.

Bringing a new concept to the table is never easy in labor relations, but GEMA's management was ready to spend as much time as needed explaining the benefits of the workforce model. The UAW initially was concerned about the "four A's" concept, says Bruce Baumbach, the GEMA plant manager who helped oversee the negotiations. "Their concern was that it would give management the ability to pull out anybody, anytime," he says. Baumbach explained to the union leaders that the idea was to have a flexible model and that it would encompass all positions, including managers.

GEMA management also had to spend a lot of time making union leaders comfortable with the shift structure. "The UAW leadership understands the competitive situation that we are in," Coventry says. "None of us are happy about it, but they are realistic. The only reason they support this is because they believe it will allow us to be here in 40 years."

The question remains whether GEMA's workforce model is replicable. It's one thing to build a plant from scratch, but it's a completely different challenge to apply this model to an existing plant, where workers are already accustomed to doing things a certain way, analysts say.

The biggest hurdle for GEMA, though, may be persuading the local UAW chapters throughout the country to accept this new way of doing things. DaimlerChrysler, for one, is convinced this is the way to go, and it is implementing the GEMA model in new and existing plants as contracts come up for renewal, says Ed Saenz, a DaimlerChrysler spokesman.

In April, the automaker signed agreements to use the GEMA model at plants in Kenosha, Wisconsin, and Trenton, Michigan. "It's a question of survival," says Bruce Baumhower, president of UAW Local 12 in Toledo, Ohio. He has negotiated for a job classification structure and team approach similar to GEMA's at a DaimlerChrysler Jeep plant, "To compete, we need to be creative, or we lose our jobs."

Source: J. Marquez, "Streamlined Model: Engine of Change," *Workforce Management*, July 17, 2006, pp. 1, 20–30.

## Introduction

The events at GEMA illustrate both the important role of labor relations in running a business and the influence of competitive challenges on the nature of labor relations. Global competition has forced a rethinking of core strategies. To be more competitive, automakers must reduce cost but also improve quality. To do so, GEMA needed to convince UAW workers to cooperate in developing a new model of labor relations. Their employment depends on the company remaining financially viable. This common goal is what binds management and labor together in a search for improved competitiveness.

must be viable

## The Labor Relations Framework

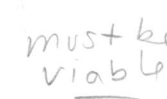

**LO1**
Describe What is Meant by Collective Bargaining and Labor Relations.

John Dunlop, former secretary of labor and a leading industrial relations scholar, suggested in the book *Industrial Relations Systems* (1958) that a successful industrial relations system consists of four elements: (1) an environmental context (technology, market pressures, and the legal framework, especially as it affects bargaining power); (2) participants, including employees and their unions, management, and the government; (3) a "web of rules" (rules of the game) that describe the process by which labor and management interact and resolve disagreements (such as the steps followed in settling contract grievances); and (4) ideology.[1] For the industrial relations system to operate properly, the three participants must, to some degree, have a common ideology (like acceptance of the capitalist system) and must accept the roles of the other participants. Acceptance does not translate into convergence of interests, however. To the contrary, some degree of worker–management conflict is inevitable because, although the interests of the two parties overlap, they also diverge in key respects (such as how to divide the economic profits).[2]

Therefore, according to Dunlop and other U.S. scholars of like mind, an effective industrial relations system does not eliminate conflict. Rather, it provides institutions (and a "web of rules") that resolve conflict in a way that minimizes its costs to management, employees, and society. The collective bargaining system is one such institution, as are related mechanisms such as mediation, arbitration, and participation in decision making. These ideas formed the basis for the development in the 1940s of schools and departments of industrial and labor relations to train labor relations professionals who, working in both union and management positions, would have the skills to minimize costly forms of conflict such as strikes (which were reaching record levels at the time) and maximize integrative (win–win) solutions to such disagreements.

A more recent industrial relations model, developed by Harry Katz and Thomas Kochan, is particularly helpful in laying out the types of decisions management and unions make in their interactions and the consequences of such decisions for attainment of goals in areas such as wages and benefits, job security, and the rights and responsibilities of unions and managements.[3] According to Katz and Kochan, these choices occur at three levels.

First, at the strategic level, management makes basic choices such as whether to work with its union(s) or to devote its efforts to developing nonunion operations. Environmental factors (or competitive challenges) offer both constraints and opportunities in implementing strategies. For example, if public opinion toward labor unions becomes negative during a particular time period, some employers may see that as an opportunity to rid themselves of unions, whereas other employers may seek a better working relationship with their unions. Similarly, increased competition may dictate the need to increase productivity or reduce labor costs, but whether this is accomplished by shifting work to nonunion facilities or by working with unions to become more competitive is a strategic choice that management faces.

Although management has often been the initiator of change in recent years, unions face a similar choice between fighting changes to the status quo and being open to new labor–management relationships (like less adversarial forms of participation in decision making, such as labor–management teams).

Katz and Kochan suggest that labor and management choices at the strategic level in turn affect the labor–management interaction at a second level, the functional level, where contract negotiations and union organizing occur, and at the final workplace level, the arena in which the contract is administered. In the opening story, GEMA's strategic-level choice was to work toward its labor unions being not part of the problem, but part of the solution. By doing so, they hope to have labor peace (functional level) and an effective day-to-day working relationship (workplace level). Although the relationships between labor and management at each of the three levels are somewhat interdependent, the relationship at the three levels may also differ. For example, while management may have a strategy of building an effective relationship with its unions at the strategic level, there may be significant day-to-day conflicts over work rules, grievances, and so forth at any given facility or bargaining unit (workplace level).

The labor relations framework depicted in Figure 14.1 incorporates many of the ideas discussed so far, including the important role of the environment (the competitive challenges); union, management, and societal goals; and a separation of union–management interactions into categories (union organizing, contract negotiation, contract administration) that can have important influences on one another but may also be analyzed somewhat independently. The model also highlights the important role that relative bargaining power plays in influencing goals, union–management interactions, and the degree to which each party achieves its goals. Relative bargaining power, in turn, is significantly influenced by the competitive environment (legal, social, quality, high-performance work systems, and globalization competitive challenges) and the size and depth of union membership.[4]

We now describe the components of this model in greater depth. The remainder of the chapter is organized into the following sections: the goals and strategies of society, management, and unions; union structure (including union administration and membership); the legal framework, perhaps the key aspect of the competitive environment for labor relations; union and management interactions (organizing, contract

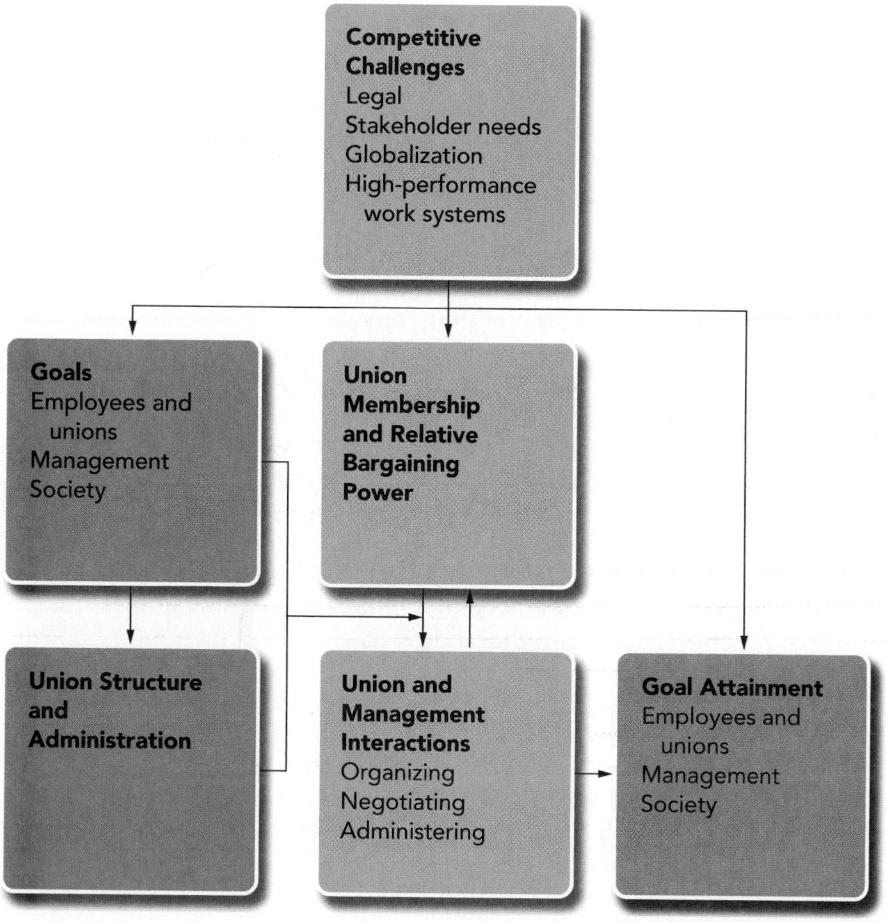


figure 14.1
A Labor Relations Framework

negotiation, contract administration); and goal attainment. Environmental factors (other than legal) and bargaining power are discussed in the context of these sections. In addition, two special topics, international comparisons and public sector labor relations, are discussed.

## EVIDENCE-BASED HR

For years, Jerry Sullivan, the head of the largest United Auto Workers local at Ford Motor Co., fought for higher pay, job protections and limits on the work his members had to do. But in the past year, as Ford teetered financially, the 59-year-old Vietnam veteran has changed course. These days he has urged his members to accept the outsourcing of company factory jobs to lower-paid workers, and to work new shifts without the tens of thousands of dollars in overtime they formerly would have earned. "Ford is in a desperate situation," sighs the burly, bearded Mr. Sullivan, who has spent 36 years at Ford, the last 10 as president of UAW Local 600 in suburban Dearborn. "If this company goes down, I want to be able to look in the mirror and say I did everything I could."

Mr. Sullivan's turnabout reflects the stark reality facing the UAW and the big U.S. car companies, which still employ roughly a third of the union's workers after years of job cuts. The Big Three auto makers acknowledge Japanese and Korean companies are out-earning them on each car by delivering more features for less cost. Now Detroit—with some help from the union—is trying to dismantle old business methods factory by factory in an effort to cut costs.

Ford, which lost $12.7 billion last year, so far has persuaded UAW locals at 33 of its 41 plants to accept new agreements aimed at transforming the way work is done on the factory floor. The "competitive operating agreements," all reached in the past 10 months, loosen some complex and often costly work rules.

An industry consultant's chart used by Ford during some negotiations with locals estimated Detroit's auto makers have an average "profit gap" of $2,400 per vehicle compared with the U.S. units of Toyota Motor Corp., Honda Motor Co. and Nissan Motor Co. That gap is so wide that Detroit is losing money on each car. Labor costs represent $1,080 to $1,335 of the gap, according to the consultant's figures. The biggest share of that, $490 to $705, is attributable to retiree's health-care costs. Next is $250 for work rules, edging out $220 for active workers' health care. Ford estimates it will save $1 billion a year if all plants adopt the various work-rule changes being asked of them.

DaimlerChrysler AG and General Motors Corp. have negotiated some similar changes, But generally only at new facilities, such as an engine plant that Chrysler opened in 2005 in Dundee, Mich. The UAW hasn't given Chrysler similar deals elsewhere, in part because Chrysler was seen as a profitable company until just a few months ago, say people familiar with the talks.

At Ford, the UAW is allowing locals to tear up existing deals months or years before they expire to put the new rules in place. Ford also has said it will close seven unidentified plants in the next few years, and subtly used that threat with its locals. The resulting changes have allowed Ford to cut 38,000 jobs through buyouts.

Ford, based in Dearborn, is navigating the worst financial crisis in its 103-year history. It expects to keep losing money until at least 2009 because it banked for too long on its sales of trucks and SUVs continuing to thrive. Instead they have begun sliding because of rising oil prices and increased competition. To avert disaster, Ford asked for the union's help, says Joe Hinrichs, Ford's head of North American manufacturing. Instead of just confronting UAW leaders with a list of work practices management wanted to change, Mr. Hinrichs and his staff have showed their union counterparts how big the cost gaps are at their factories, using the Harbour Report (on auto-manufacturing efficiency) figures and internal data. "We really need our people to realize we aren't competitive," says Mr. Hinrichs, a 40-year-old Harvard graduate who came to Ford after serving as one of the youngest plant managers in GM history. "No one has a right to be uncompetitive."

For many UAW members, some of the changes at Ford would have been unthinkable just a few years ago. The talks have ventured into sensitive areas, such as high UAW absentee rates. At Ford plants, workers only needed a doctor's note to be absent without using a vacation day, and Ford's absentee rate on plant floors has been about 11 percent—which the company asserts is about twice the rate of its Asian rivals. Each percentage point costs Ford about $20 million per year, say Ford executives. The new agreements cap the number of absences regardless of excuse, though the company would not discuss the figure.

Still, Ford and other U.S. makers are not nearly as efficient as their Japanese rivals. "Really they are just now getting to rules or processes that Toyota already had in place at their plants," said Laurie Harbour-Felax, the auto-efficiency consultant whose figures Ford used. "They have a long way to go."

At an engine plant in Lima, Ohio, workers were faced with the threat that engine work could be shifted south to Mexico or another plant. In addition to accepting outsourcing of work, they agreed to shift many managerial duties to union employees. This allowed Ford to cut the nonunion head count at Lima from 280 people to about 90. With the new agreement Lima's union workforce dropped to about 800 workers, from 1,100.

The UAW supervisors are called "team leaders," and work in a structure borrowed from Japanese assembly lines. Overseeing 8 to 12 other union members, the team leaders use big electronic scoreboards above their heads to track each day's target for assembling engines. If line speeds need to be increased or slowed, "rebalanced" in Ford parlance, the decision is made by UAW members instead of salaried engineers, who typically were paid $60,000 or more annually.

Ford had long given up on the union accepting such a move. "There are days I wonder why I am doing all this," says Brad Caskie, now a team leader and veteran of 22 years at the Lima plant. "It's pretty much like being a manager, and also a worker. Ford said to us this is what Toyota and Honda do, so it's what we need to do."

Until last summer, Mr. Caskie's job at Ford was to put timing components on car or truck engines as they chugged down the line, just under 100 of them an hour. When the plant adopted a competitive operating agreement last May and team leader jobs opened paying 50 cents more an hour, Mr. Caskie volunteered. Now the 49-year-old Ohio native manages 11 workers, scheduling vacations, overseeing quality of work, and arranging meetings to discuss safety or downtime problems. When he gets a chance, he jumps on the computer near the engine line to see how his team stacks up in terms of quality and speed compared with other teams. "I'm loyal to the company. They put my kids through college," said Mr. Caskie, who got his first Ford job in part because his stepfather and uncle, both UAW workers for Ford, helped him get in. "I feel like we had no choice, really, but to do this."

Plant manager Jan Allman says the Lima agreement saves the auto maker about $27 million a year overall. Her goal is for Lima to pass Toyota in the Harbour efficiency studies in 2008.

The process hasn't always gone smoothly. Earlier this year Ford, despite its continuing losses, said it was considering giving bonuses to white-collar workers—in part thanks to the cost savings it achieved in getting the new local agreements. At the Michigan Truck plant in Wayne, Mich., workers were furious that they were taking cuts while their managers were in line for bonuses. A vote on a cost-cutting deal there was delayed for weeks. After Ford acknowledged any bonus plan must include the union, the vote was rescheduled and the agreement passed.

"The bonus thing sent a bad message," says Mr. Sullivan. "This is a partnership, right? We are in this together, right? We made our concessions, so let's be fair." The company is still working out details of the bonus plan.

SOURCE: J. McCracken, "Desperate to Cut Costs, Ford Gets Union's Help," *The Wall Street Journal*, March 2, 2007, p. A1.

# Goals and Strategies

## Society

**LO2**
Identify the Labor Relations Goals of Management, Labor Unions, and Society.

In one sense, labor unions, with their emphasis on group action, do not fit well with the individualistic orientation of U.S. capitalism. However, industrial relations scholars such as Beatrice and Sidney Webb and John R. Commons argued in the late 1800s and early 1900s that individual workers' bargaining power was far smaller than that of employers, who were likely to have more financial resources and the ability to easily replace workers.[5] Effective institutions for worker representation (like labor unions) were therefore seen as a way to make bargaining power more equal.

Labor unions' major benefit to society is the institutionalization of industrial conflict, which is therefore resolved in the least costly way. Thus, although disagreements between management and labor continue, it is better to resolve disputes through discussion (collective bargaining) than by battling in the streets. As an influential group of industrial relations scholars put it in describing the future of advanced industrial relations around the world, "Class warfare will be forgotten. The battles will be in the corridors instead of the streets, and memos will flow instead of blood."[6] In this sense, collective bargaining not only has the potential to reduce economic losses caused by strikes but may also contribute to societal stability. For this reason, industrial relations scholars have often viewed labor unions as an essential component of a democratic society.[7] These were some of the beliefs that contributed to the enactment of the National Labor Relations Act (NLRA) in 1935, which sought to provide an environment conducive to collective bargaining and has since regulated labor and management activities and interactions.

Even Senator Orrin Hatch, described by *BusinessWeek* as "labor's archrival on Capitol Hill," has spoken of the need for unions:

> There are always going to be people who take advantage of workers. Unions even that out, to their credit. We need them to level the field between labor and management. If you didn't have unions, it would be very difficult for even enlightened employers not to take advantage of workers on wages and working conditions, because of [competition from] rivals. I'm among the first to say I believe in unions.[8]

Although an industrial relations system based on collective bargaining has drawbacks, so too do the alternatives. Unilateral control by management sacrifices workers' rights. Extensive involvement of government and the courts can result in conflict resolution that is expensive, slow, and imposed by someone (a judge) with much less firsthand knowledge of the circumstances than either labor or management.

## Management

One of management's most basic decisions is whether to encourage or discourage the unionization of its employees. It may discourage unions because it fears higher wage and benefit costs, the disruptions caused by strikes, and an adversarial relationship with its employees or, more generally, greater constraints placed on its decision-making flexibility and discretion. Historically, management has used two basic strategies to avoid unionization.[9] It may seek to provide employment terms and conditions that employees will perceive as sufficiently attractive and equitable so that they see little gain from union representation. Or it may aggressively oppose union representation, even where there is significant employee interest. Use of the latter strategy has increased significantly during the last 20 to 30 years.

If management voluntarily recognizes a union or if employees are already represented by a union, the focus is shifted from dealing with employees as individuals to employees as a group. Still, certain basic management objectives remain: controlling labor costs and increasing productivity (by keeping wages and benefits in check) and maintaining management prerogatives in important areas such as staffing levels and work rules. Of course, management always has the option of trying to decertify a union (that is, encouraging employees to vote out the union in a decertification election) if it believes that the majority of employees no longer wish to be represented by the union.

## Labor Unions

Labor unions seek, through collective action, to give workers a formal and independent voice in setting the terms and conditions of their work. Table 14.1 shows typical

**table 14.1**

Typical Provisions in Collective Bargaining Contracts

| | | |
|---|---|---|
| **Establishment and administration of the agreement**<br>Bargaining unit and plant supplements<br>Contract duration and reopening and renegotiation provisions<br>Union security and the checkoff<br>Special bargaining committees<br>Grievance procedures<br>Arbitration and mediation<br>Strikes and lockouts<br>Contract enforcement<br>**Functions, rights, and responsibilities**<br>Management rights clauses<br>Plant removal<br>Subcontracting<br>Union activities on company time and premises<br>Union–management cooperation<br>Regulation of technological change<br>Advance notice and consultation | **Wage determination and administration**<br>General provisions<br>Rate structure and wage differentials<br>Allowances<br>Incentive systems and production bonus plans<br>Production standards and time studies<br>Job classification and job evaluation<br>Individual wage adjustments<br>General wage adjustments during the contract period<br>**Job or income security**<br>Hiring and transfer arrangements<br>Employment and income guarantees<br>Reporting and call-in pay<br>Supplemental unemployment benefit plans<br>Regulation of overtime, shift work, etc.<br>Reduction of hours to forestall layoffs<br>Layoff procedures; seniority; recall<br>Worksharing in lieu of layoff<br>Attrition arrangements<br>Promotion practices<br>Training and retraining<br>Relocation allowances<br>Severance pay and layoff benefit plans<br>Special funds and study committees | **Plant operations**<br>Work and shop rules<br>Rest periods and other in-plant time allowances<br>Safety and health<br>Plant committees<br>Hours of work and premium pay practices<br>Shift operations<br>Hazardous work<br>Discipline and discharge<br>**Paid and unpaid leave**<br>Vacations and holidays<br>Sick leave<br>Funeral and personal leave<br>Military leave and jury duty<br>**Employee benefit plans**<br>Health and insurance plans<br>Pension plans<br>Profit-sharing, stock purchase, and thrift plans<br>Bonus plans<br>**Special groups**<br>Apprentices and learners<br>Workers with disabilities and older workers<br>Women<br>Veterans<br>Union representatives<br>Nondiscrimination clauses |

SOURCE: From H. C. Katz, T. A. Kochan, and A. J. S. Colvin, *An Introduction to Collective Bargaining and Industrial Relations*, 2008. Copyright © 2008 The McGraw-Hill Companies, Inc. Reprinted with permission.

provisions negotiated by unions in collective bargaining contracts. Labor unions attempt to represent their members' interests in these decisions.

A major goal of labor unions is bargaining effectiveness, because with it comes the power and influence to make the employees' voices heard and to effect changes in the workplace.[10] The right to strike is one important component of bargaining power. In turn, the success of a strike (actual or threatened) depends on the relative magnitude of the costs imposed on management versus those imposed on the union. A critical factor is the size of union membership. More members translate into a greater ability to halt or disrupt production and also into greater financial resources for continuing a strike in the face of lost wages.

## Union Structure, Administration, and Membership

A necessary step in discussing labor–management interactions is a basic knowledge of how labor and management are organized and how they function. Management has been described throughout this book. We now focus on labor unions.

### National and International Unions

Most union members belong to a national or international union. In turn, most national unions are composed of multiple local units, and most are affiliated with the American Federation of Labor and Congress of Industrial Organizations (AFL-CIO).

The largest national unions are listed in Table 14.2. (The National Education Association, with 2.5 million members, is not affiliated with the AFL-CIO.) An important characteristic of a union is whether it is a craft or industrial union. The electrical workers' and carpenters' unions are craft unions, meaning that the members all have a particular skill or occupation. Craft unions often are responsible for training their members (through apprenticeships) and for supplying craft workers to employers. Requests for carpenters, for example, would come to the union hiring hall, which would decide which carpenters to send out. Thus craft workers may work for many employers over time, their constant link being to the union. A craft union's bargaining power depends greatly on the control it can exercise over the supply of its workers.

In contrast, industrial unions are made up of members who are linked by their work in a particular industry (such as steelworkers and autoworkers). Typically they represent many different occupations. Membership in the union is a result of working for a particular employer in the industry. Changing employers is less common than it is among craft workers, and employees who change employers remain members of the same union only if they happen to move to other employers covered by that union. Whereas a craft union may restrict the number of, say, carpenters to maintain higher wages, industrial unions try to organize as many employees in as wide a range of skills as possible.

### Local Unions

Even when a national union plays the most critical role in negotiating terms of a collective bargaining contract, negotiation occurs at the local level as well as over work rules and other issues that are locally determined. In addition, administration of the contract

**table 14.2**

Largest Labor Unions in the United States

| ORGANIZATION | NUMBER OF MEMBERS |
|---|---|
| National Education Association | 2,731,419 |
| Service Employees International Union | 1,702,639 |
| American Federation of State, County and Municipal Employees | 1,350,000 |
| International Brotherhood of Teamsters | 1,350,000 |
| United Food and Commercial Workers International Union | 1,338,625 |
| American Federation to Teachers | 828,512 |
| International Brotherhood of Electrical Workers | 704,794 |
| Laborers' International Union of North America | 692,558 |
| International Union, United Automobile, Aerospace and Agricultural Implement Workers of America | 654,657 |
| International Association of Machinists and Aerospace Workers | 610,426 |
| Communications Workers of America | 545,638 |
| United Steel, Paper and Forestry, Rubber, Manufacturing, Energy, Allied Industrial and Service Workers International Union | 535,461 |
| United Brotherhood of Carpenters and Joiners of America | 524,237 |
| UNITE HERE | 441,276 |
| International Union of Operating Engineers | 388,804 |
| National Postal Mail Handlers Union | 357,000 |
| United Association of Journeymen and Apprentices of the Plumbing and Pipe Fitting Industry of the United States and Canada | 324,043 |
| National Association of Letter Carriers | 292,221 |
| International Association of Fire Fighters | 271,463 |
| American Postal Workers Union | 227,425 |
| American Federation of Government Employees | 226,599 |
| Amalgamated Transit Union | 180,598 |
| United American Nurses | 148,799 |
| Sheet Metal Workers International Association | 144,480 |
| International Union of Painters and Allied Trades | 128,351 |
| International Association of Bridge, Structural, Ornamental and Reinforcing Iron Workers | 125,437 |
| Transport Workers Union of America | 125,398 |
| American Association of Classified School Employees | 109,188 |
| Screen Actors Guild | 107,541 |
| Bakery, Confectionery, Tobacco Workers and Grain Millers International Union | 107,452 |
| National Rural Letter Carriers' Association | 105,460 |
| International Alliance of Theatrical Stage Employes, Moving Picture Technicians, Artists and Allied Crafts of the United States and Canada | 105,180 |
| United Mine Workers of America | 100,609 |

SOURCE: Reprinted with permission from Directory of U.S. Labor Organizations, 2006 edition by Courtesy D. Gifford. Copyright © 2006 by the Bureau of National Affairs Washington, DC 20037. For copies of BNA Books publications call toll free 1-800-960-1220.

is largely carried out at the local union level. Consequently, the bulk of day-to-day interaction between labor and management takes place at the local union level.

The local of an industrial-based union may correspond to a single large facility or to a number of small facilities. In a craft-oriented union, the local may cover a city or a region. The local union typically elects officers (like president, vice president, treasurer). Responsibility for contract negotiation may rest with the officers, or a bargaining committee may be formed for this purpose. Typically the national union provides assistance, ranging from background data about other settlements and technical advice to sending a representative to lead the negotiations.

Individual members' participation in local union meetings includes the election of union officials and strike votes. However, most union contact is with the shop steward, who is responsible for ensuring that the terms of the collective bargaining contract are enforced. The shop steward represents employees in contract grievances. Another union position, the business representative, performs some of the same functions, especially where the union deals with multiple employers, as is often the case with craft unions.

**Checkoff Provision**
A union contract provision that requires an employer to deduct union dues from employees' paychecks.

**Closed Shop**
A union security provision requiring a person to be a union member before being hired. Illegal under NLRA.

**Union Shop**
A union security provision that requires a person to join the union within a certain amount of time after being hired.

**Agency Shop**
A union security provision that requires an employee to pay union membership dues but not to join the union.

**Maintenance of Membership**
Union rules requiring members to remain members for a certain period of time (such as the length of the union contract).

**Right-to-Work Laws**
State laws that make union shops, maintenance of membership, and agency shops illegal.

## American Federation of Labor and Congress of Industrial Organizations (AFL-CIO)

The AFL-CIO is not a labor union but rather an association that seeks to advance the shared interests of its member unions at the national level, much as the Chamber of Commerce and the National Association of Manufacturers do for their member employers. As Figure 14.2 indicates, there are 54 affiliated national and international unions and thousands of locals. An important responsibility of the AFL-CIO is to represent labor's interests in public policy issues such as civil rights, economic policy, safety, and occupational health. It also provides information and analysis that member unions can use in their activities: organizing new members, negotiating new contracts, and administering contracts.

## Union Security

The survival and security of a union depends on its ability to ensure a regular flow of new members and member dues to support the services it provides. Therefore, unions typically place high priority on negotiating two contract provisions with an employer that are critical to a union's security or viability: checkoff provisions and union membership or contribution. First, under a **checkoff provision,** the employer, on behalf of the union, automatically deducts union dues from employees' paychecks.

A second union security provision focuses on the flow of new members (and their dues). The strongest union security arrangement is a **closed shop,** under which a person must be a union member (and thus pay dues) before being hired. A closed shop is, however, illegal under the NLRA. A **union shop** requires a person to join the union within a certain amount of time (30 days) after beginning employment. An **agency shop** is similar to a union shop but does not require union membership, only that dues be paid. **Maintenance of membership** rules do not require union membership but do require that employees who choose to join must remain members for a certain period of time (such as the length of the contract).

Under the 1947 Taft–Hartley Act (an amendment to the NLRA), states may pass so-called **right-to-work laws,** which make union shops, maintenance of membership, and agency shops illegal. The idea behind such laws is that compulsory union membership (or making employees pay union dues) infringes on the employee's right to freedom of association. From the union perspective, a big concern is "free riders," employees who benefit from union activities without belonging to a union. By law, all members of a bargaining unit, whether union members or not, must be represented by

**figure 14.2**
AFL-CIO Organization Chart

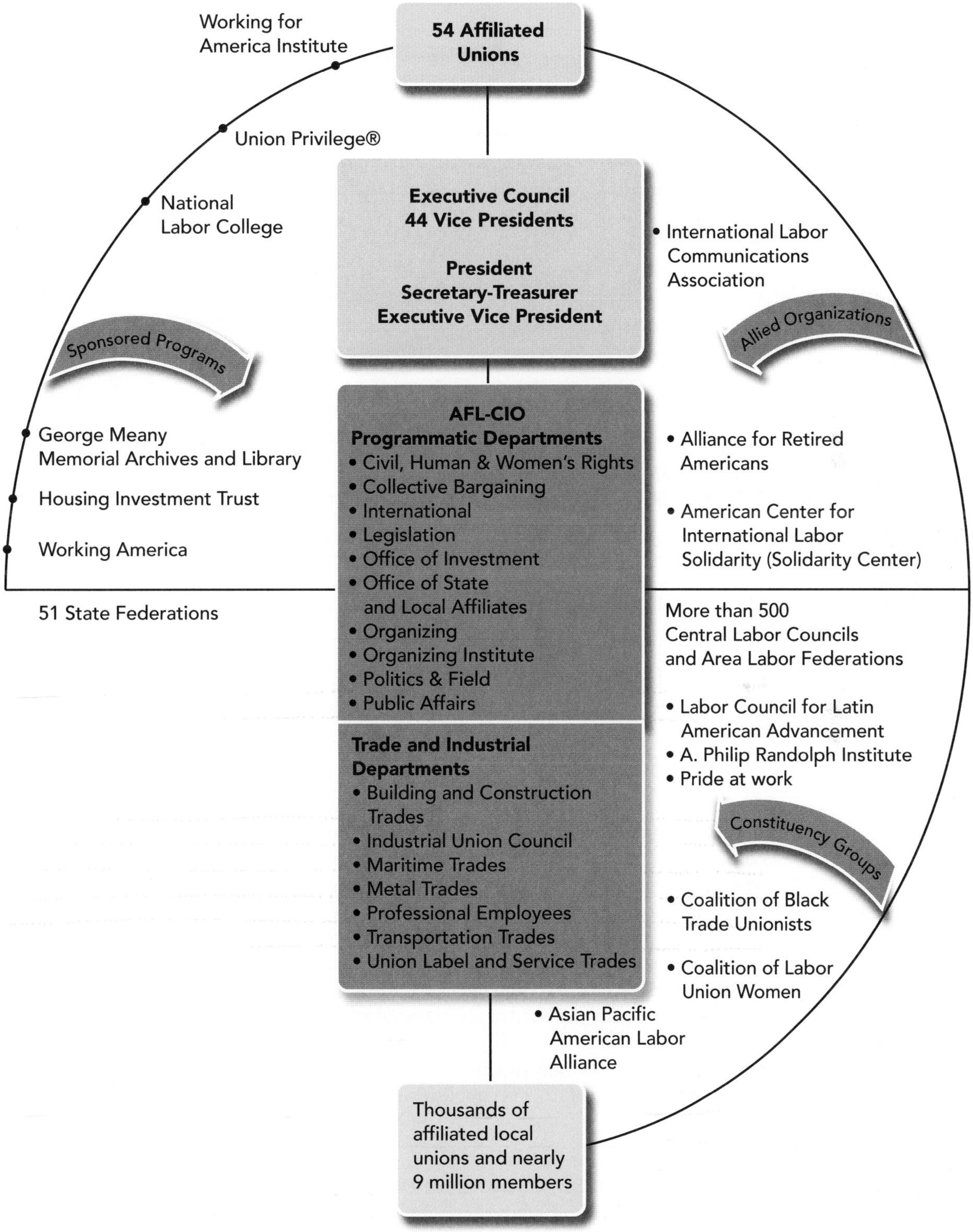


SOURCE: AFL-CIO, www.aflcio.org, accessed March 18, 2007.

figure 14.3

Union Membership Density among U.S. Wage and Salary Workers, 1973–2006

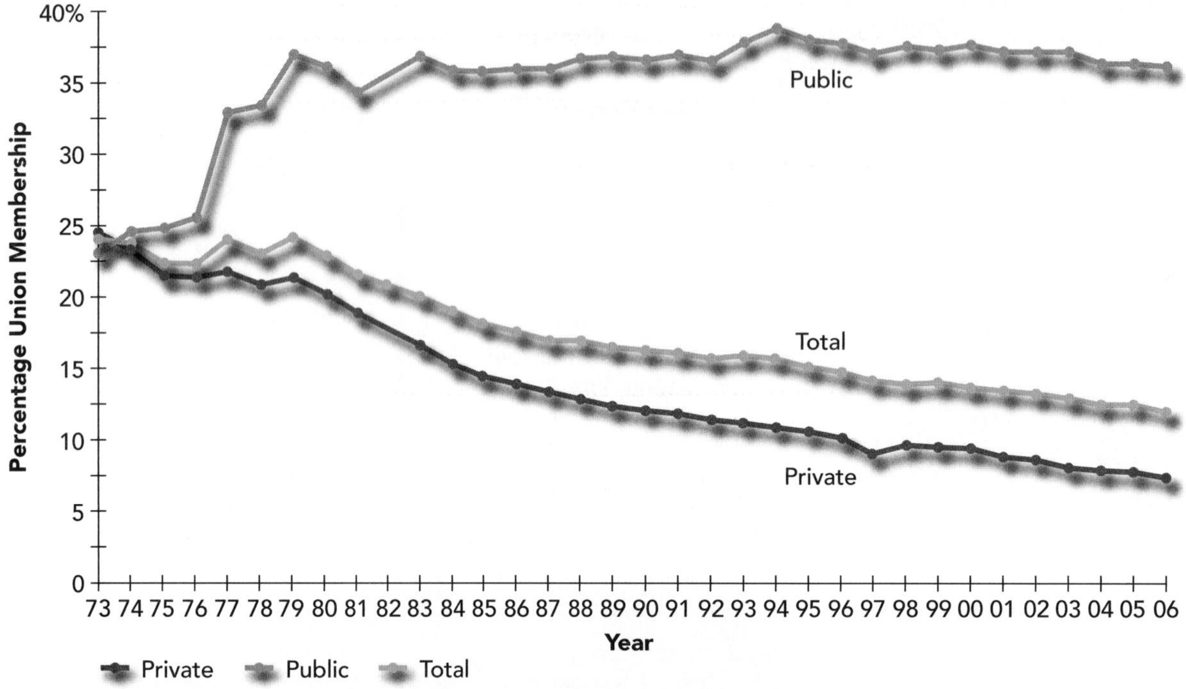


SOURCE: From B. T. Hirsch and D. A. MacPherson, *Union Membership and Earnings Data Book 2001* (Washington, DC: The Bureau of National Affairs, Inc., 2001). Reprinted with permission. Data for 2001 to 2006 obtained from U.S. Bureau of Labor Statistics, www.bls.gov.

the union. If the union is required to offer service to all bargaining unit members, even those who are not union members, it may lose its financial viability.

## Union Membership and Bargaining Power

At the strategic level, management and unions meet head-on over the issue of union organizing. Increasingly, employers are actively resisting unionization in an attempt to control costs and maintain their flexibility. Unions, on the other hand, must organize new members and hold on to their current members to have the kind of bargaining power and financial resources needed to achieve their goals in future organizing and to negotiate and administer contracts with management. For this reason we now discuss trends in union membership and possible explanations for those trends.

Since the 1950s, when union membership rose to 35 percent of employment, membership has consistently declined as a percentage of employment. It now stands at 12.0 percent of all employment and 7.4 percent of private-sector employment.[11] As Figure 14.3 indicates, this decline shows no indication of reversing (or even slowing down).[12]

What factors explain the decline in union membership? Several have been identified.[13]

Why union membership declining.

### Structural Changes in the Economy

At the risk of oversimplifying, we might say that unions have traditionally been strongest in urban workplaces (especially those outside the South) that employ middle-aged men in blue-collar jobs. However, much recent job growth has occurred among women and youth in the service sector of the economy. Although unionizing such groups is possible, unions have so far not had much success organizing these groups in the private sector. Despite the importance of structural changes in the economy, studies show that they account for no more than one-quarter of the overall union membership decline.[14] Also, Canada, which has been undergoing similar structural changes, has experienced growth in union membership since the early 1960s. Union membership in Canada now stands at over 30 percent of employment, compared with roughly 12 percent in the United States.

## Increased Employer Resistance

Almost one-half of large employers in a survey reported that their most important labor goal was to be union-free. This contrasts sharply with 50 years ago, when Jack Barbash wrote that "many tough bargainers [among employers] prefer the union to a situation where there is no union. Most of the employers in rubber, basic steel and the automobile industry fall in this category." The idea then was that an effective union could help assess and communicate the interests of employees to management, thus helping management make better decisions. But product-market pressures, such as foreign competition and deregulation (e.g., trucking, airlines, telecommunications), have contributed to increasing employer resistance to unions.[15] These changes in the competitive environment have contributed to a change in management's perspective and goals.[16]

In the absence of significant competition from foreign producers, unions were often able to organize entire industries. For example, the UAW organized all four major producers in the automobile industry (GM, Ford, Chrysler, and American Motors). The UAW usually sought and achieved the same union–management contract at each company. As a consequence, a negotiated wage increase in the industry could be passed on to the consumer in the form of higher prices. No company was undercut by its competitors because the labor cost of all major producers in the industry was determined by the same union–management contract, and the U.S. public had little option but to buy U.S.-made cars. However, the onset of foreign competition in the automobile market changed the competitive situation as well as the UAW's ability to organize the industry.[17] U.S. automakers were slow to recognize and respond to the competitive threat from foreign producers, resulting in a loss of market share and employment.

Competitive threats have contributed to increased employer resistance to union organizing and, in some cases, to an increased emphasis on ridding themselves of existing unions. Unionized workers receive, on average, 10 to 15 percent higher wages than their nonunion counterparts and this advantage is still larger if benefits are also included. Many employers have decided that they can no longer compete with these higher labor costs, and union membership has suffered as a result.[18] One measure of increased employer resistance is the dramatic increase in the late 1960s in the number of unfair employer labor practices (violations of sections of the NLRA such as section 8(a)(3), which prohibits firing employees for union organizing, as we discuss later) even though the number of elections held did not change much. (See Figure 14.4.) The use of remedies such as back pay for workers also grew, but the costs to employers of such penalties does not appear to have been sufficient to prevent the growth in employer unfair labor practices. Not surprisingly, the union victory rate in representation elections decreased from almost 59 percent in 1960 to

figure 14.4

Employer Resistance to Union Organizing, 1950–2005

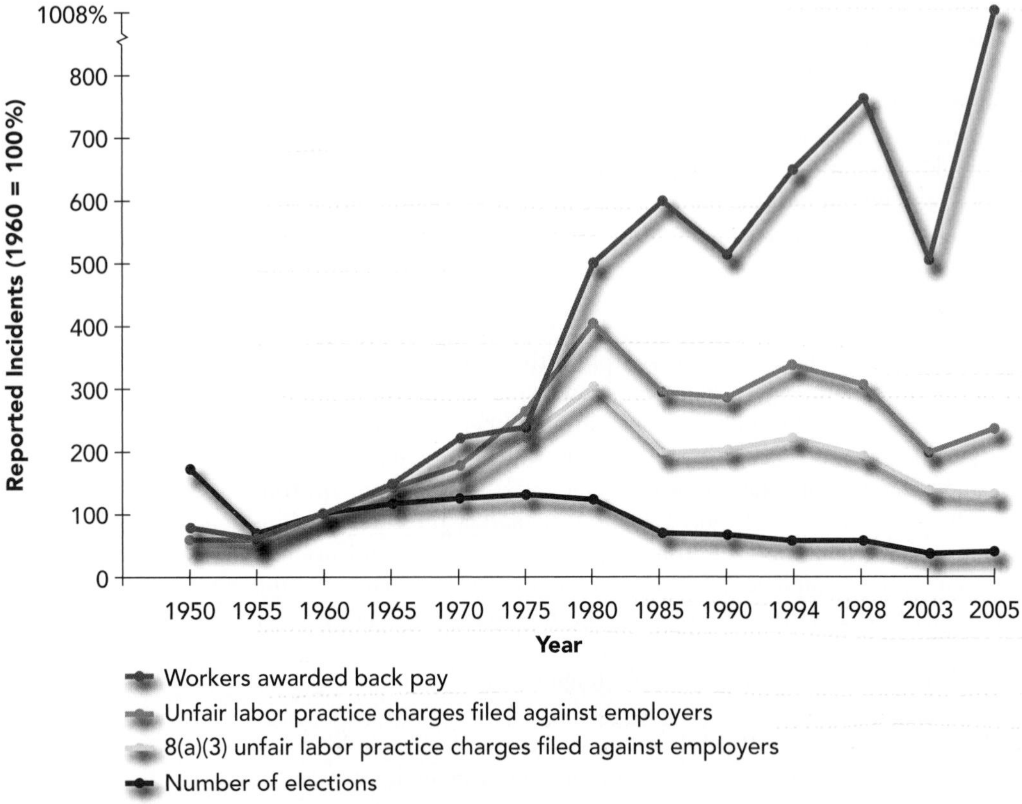


NOTE: 8(a)(3) charges refer to the section of the NLRA that makes it an unfair employer labor practice to discriminate against (e.g., fire) employees who engage in union activities such as union organizing.

SOURCE: Adapted and updated from R. B. Freeman and J. L. Medoff, *What Do Unions Do?* (New York: Basic Books, 1984). Data for 1985, 1989, 1990, 1994, 1998, 2003, and 2005 from National Labor Relations Board annual reports.

below 50 percent by 1975. Although the union victory rate in recent years has been over 50 percent, the number of elections has declined by more than 50 percent since the 1960s and 1970s. Moreover, decertification elections have gone from about 4 percent of elections in 1960 to about 14 percent of elections in 2005.[19] Given the significant decline in both elections and union membership percentage, the increases in the number of unfair labor practice charges and back pay awards is all the more notable.

Finally, even if a union wins the right to represent employees, its ability to successfully negotiate a contract with the employer is not guaranteed. Indeed, refusal to bargain by the employer is the unfair labor practice most frequently filed (over half of all charges) against employers.

At a personal level, some managers may face serious consequences if a union successfully organizes a new set of workers or mounts a serious organizing drive. One study indicated that 8 percent of the plant managers in companies with organizing drives were fired, and 10 percent of those in companies where the union was successful were fired (compared with 2 percent in a control group).[20] Furthermore, only 3 percent of the plant managers facing an organizing drive were promoted, and none of those ending up with a union contract were promoted (compared with 21 percent of the managers in the control group). Therefore, managers are often under intense pressure to oppose unionization attempts.

### Substitution with HRM

A major study of the human resource management strategies and practices among large, nonunion employers found that union avoidance was often an important employee relations objective.[21] Top management's values in such companies drive specific policies such as promotion from within, an influential personnel–human resource department, and above-average pay and benefits. These policies, in turn, contribute to a number of desirable outcomes such as flexibility, positive employee attitudes, and responsive and committed employees, which ultimately lead to higher productivity and better employee relations. In other words, employers attempt to remain nonunion by offering most of the things a union can offer, and then some, while still maintaining a productivity advantage over their competitors. Of course, one aspect of union representation that employers cannot duplicate is the independent employee voice that a union provides.

### Substitution by Government Regulation

Since the 1960s, regulation of many employment areas has increased, including equal employment opportunity, pensions, and worker displacement. Combined with existing regulations, this increase may result in fewer areas in which unions can provide worker rights or protection beyond those specified by law. Yet western European countries generally have more regulations and higher levels of union membership than the United States.[22]

### Worker Views

Industrial relations scholars have long argued that the absence in the United States of a history of feudalism and of strong class distinctions found in western Europe have contributed to a more pragmatic, business-oriented (versus class-conscious) unionism. Although this may help explain the somewhat lower level of union membership in the United States, its relevance in explaining the downward trend is not clear.

### Union Actions

In some ways, unions have hurt their own cause. First, corruption in unions such as the Teamsters may have had a detrimental effect. Second, questions have been raised about how well unions have adapted to recent changes in the economic structure. Employee groups and economic sectors with the fastest growth rates tend to have the lowest rates of unionization.[23] Women are less likely to be in unions than men (11 percent versus 14 percent), and nonmanufacturing industries such as finance, insurance, and real estate have a lower union representation (2 percent) than does manufacturing (14 percent). The South is also less heavily organized than the rest of the country, with, for example, South Carolina having a unionization rate of 4 percent, compared with 25 percent in New York State.[24]

## Legal Framework

**LO3**
Explain the Legal Environment's Impact on Labor Relations.

Although competitive challenges have a major impact on labor relations, the legal framework of collective bargaining is an especially critical determinant of union membership and relative bargaining power and, therefore, of the degree to which employers, employees, and society are successful in achieving their goals. The legal framework also constrains union structure and administration and the manner in which unions and employers interact. Perhaps the most dramatic example of labor laws' influence is the 1935 passage of the Wagner Act (also known as the National Labor Relations Act or NLRA), which actively supported collective bargaining rather than impeding it. As a result, union membership nearly tripled, from 3 million in 1933 (7.7 percent of all employment) to 8.8 million (19.2 percent of employment) by 1939.[25] With increased membership came greater union bargaining power and, consequently, more success in achieving union goals.

Before the 1930s, the legal system was generally hostile to unions. The courts generally viewed unions as coercive organizations that hindered free trade. Unions' focus on collective voice and collective action (strikes, boycotts) did not fit well with the U.S. emphasis on capitalism, individualism, freedom of contract, and property rights.[26]

The Great Depression of the 1930s, however, shifted public attitudes toward business and the free-enterprise system. Unemployment rates as high as 25 percent and a 30 percent drop in the gross national product between 1929 and 1933 focused attention on employee rights and on the shortcomings of the system as it existed then. The nation was in a crisis, and President Franklin Roosevelt responded with dramatic action, the New Deal. On the labor front, the 1935 NLRA ushered in a new era of public policy for labor unions, enshrining collective bargaining as the preferred mechanism for settling labor–management disputes.

The introduction to the NLRA states:

> It is in the national interest of the United States to maintain full production in its economy. Industrial strife among employees, employers, and labor organizations interferes with full production and is contrary to our national interest. Experience has shown that labor disputes can be lessened if the parties involved recognize the legitimate rights of each in their relations with one another. To establish these rights under the law, Congress enacted the National Labor Relations Act. Its purpose is to define and protect the rights of employees and employers, to encourage collective bargaining, and to eliminate certain practices on the part of labor and management that are harmful to the general welfare.[27]

The rights of employees are set out in Section 7 of the act, including the "right to self-organization, to form, join, or assist labor organizations, to bargain collectively through representatives of their own choosing, and to engage in other concerted activities for the purpose of collective bargaining. The act also gives employees the right to refrain from any or all of such activities except [in cases] requiring membership in a labor organization as a condition of employment."[28] Examples of protected activities include

- Union organizing.
- Joining a union, whether it is recognized by the employer or not.
- Going out on strike to secure better working conditions.
- Refraining from activity on behalf of the union.[29]

Although the NLRA has broad coverage in the private sector, Table 14.3 shows that there are some notable exclusions.

**table 14.3**

Are You Excluded from the NLRA's Coverage?

The NLRA specifically excludes from its coverage individuals who are

- Employed as a supervisor.
- Employed by a parent or spouse.
- Employed as an independent contractor.
- Employed in the domestic service of any person or family in a home.
- Employed as agricultural laborers.
- Employed by an employer subject to the Railway Labor Act.
- Employed by a federal, state, or local government.
- Employed by any other person who is not an employer as defined in the NLRA.

SOURCE: www.nlrb.gov/publications/engulp.html.

## Unfair Labor Practices—Employers

The NLRA prohibits certain activities by both employers and labor unions. Unfair labor practices by employers are listed in Section 8(a) of the NLRA. Section 8(a)(1) prohibits employers from interfering with, restraining, or coercing employees in exercising their rights to join or assist a labor organization or to refrain from such activities. Section 8(a)(2) prohibits employer domination of or interference with the formation or activities of a labor union. Section 8(a)(3) prohibits discrimination in any aspect of employment that attempts to encourage or discourage union-related activity. Section 8(a)(4) prohibits discrimination against employees for providing testimony relevant to enforcement of the NLRA. Section 8(a)(5) prohibits employers from refusing to bargain collectively with a labor organization that has standing under the act. Examples of employer unfair labor practices are listed in Table 14.4.

**table 14.4**

Examples of Employer Unfair Labor Practices

- Threatening employees with loss of their jobs or benefits if they join or vote for a union.
- Threatening to close down a plant if organized by a union.
- Questioning employees about their union membership or activities in a manner that restrains or coerces them.
- Spying or pretending to spy on union meetings.
- Granting wage increases that are timed to discourage employees from forming or joining a union.
- Taking an active part in organizing a union or committee to represent employees.
- Providing preferential treatment or aid to one of several unions trying to organize employees.
- Discharging employees for urging other employees to join a union or refusing to hire applicants because they are union members.
- Refusing to reinstate workers when job openings occur because the workers participated in a lawful strike.
- Ending operation at one plant and opening the same operation at another plant with new employees because employees at the first plant joined a union.
- Demoting or firing employees for filing an unfair labor practice or for testifying at an NLRB hearing.
- Refusing to meet with employees' representatives because the employees are on strike.
- Refusing to supply the employees' representative with cost and other data concerning a group insurance plan covering employees.
- Announcing a wage increase without consulting the employees' representative.
- Failing to bargain about the effects of a decision to close one of employer's plants.

SOURCE: National Labor Relations Board, *Basic Guide to the National Labor Relations Act* (Washington, DC: U.S. Government Printing Office, 1997). See also www.nlrb.gov.

**table 14.5**

Examples of Union Unfair Labor Practices

- Mass picketing in such numbers that nonstriking employees are physically barred from entering the plant.
- Acts of force or violence on the picket line or in connection with a strike.
- Threats to employees of bodily injury or that they will lose their jobs unless they support the union's activities.
- Fining or expelling members for crossing a picket line that is unlawful.
- Fining or expelling members for filing unfair labor practice charges or testifying before the NLRB.
- Insisting during contract negotiations that the employer agree to accept working conditions that will be determined by a group to which it does not belong.
- Fining or expelling union members for the way they apply the bargaining contract while carrying out their supervisory responsibilities.
- Causing an employer to discharge employees because they spoke out against a contract proposed by the union.
- Making a contract that requires an employer to hire only members of the union or employees "satisfactory" to the union.
- Insisting on the inclusion of illegal provisions in a contract.
- Terminating an existing contract and striking for a new one without notifying the employer, the Federal Mediation and Conciliation Service, and the state mediation service (where one exists).
- Attempting to compel a beer distributor to recognize a union (the union prevents the distributor from obtaining beer at a brewery by inducing the brewery's employees to refuse to fill the distributor's orders).
- Picketing an employer to force it to stop doing business with another employer who has refused to recognize the union (a "secondary boycott").

SOURCE: National Labor Relations Board, *A Guide to Basic Law and Procedures under the National Labor Relations Act* (Washington, DC: U.S. Government Printing Office, 1997). See also www.nlrb.gov.

## Unfair Labor Practices—Labor Unions

**Taft-Hartley Act, 1947**
The 1947 act that outlawed unfair union labor practices.

Originally the NLRA did not list any union unfair labor practices. These were added through the 1947 **Taft-Hartley Act.** The 1959 *Landrum-Griffin* Act further regulated unions' actions and their internal affairs (like financial disclosure and conduct of elections). Section 8(b)(1)(a) of the NLRA states that a labor organization is not to "restrain or coerce employees in the exercise of the rights guaranteed in section 7" (described earlier). Table 14.5 provides examples of union unfair labor practices.

## Enforcement

Enforcement of the NLRA rests with the National Labor Relations Board (NLRB), which is composed of a five-member board, the general counsel, and 33 regional offices. The basis for the NLRA is the commerce clause of the U.S. Constitution. Therefore, the NLRB's jurisdiction is limited to employers whose operations affect commerce generally and interstate commerce in particular. In practice, only purely local firms are likely to fall outside the NLRB's jurisdiction. Specific jurisdictional standards (nearly 20) that vary by industry are applied. Two examples of businesses that are covered (and the standards) are retail businesses that had more than $500,000 in annual business and newspapers that had more than $200,000 in annual business.

The NLRB's two major functions are to conduct and certify representation elections and prevent unfair labor practices. In both realms, it does not initiate action.

## A Whole New Game Ball?

N.B.A. players have been complaining for two months about the new synthetic basketball and the cuts on their fingers it has caused. The players were not given a chance to test it before the season, prompting their union to file a grievance last week with the National Labor Relations Board about the league's unilateral implementation.

Yesterday, David Stern, the N.B.A. commissioner, acknowledged the validity of the players' complaints and admitted regret over not consulting them beforehand. In a telephone interview, Stern said that balls were being sent back to the manufacturer, Spalding, for further testing. The league will continue to use the new balls, but Stern left open the possibility that they would be changed during the season. "I won't make a spirited defense with respect to the ball," Stern said. "In hindsight, we could have done a better job. I take responsibility for that."

He added: "If our players are unhappy with it, we have to analyze to the nth degree the cause of their unhappiness. Everything is on the table. I'm not pleased, but I'm realistic. We've got to do the right thing here. And of course the right thing is to listen to our players. Whether it's a day late or not, we're dealing with this."

Billy Hunter, the executive director of the union, said that it would not rescind its grievance until the league made a change. "It obviously is something that needs to be studied and reviewed," Hunter said in a telephone interview last night. "I would consider it a victory if they got the leather ball back, but we're going to let that run its course."

He said the grievance might not have prompted Stern's sudden reversal as much as "the general outcrying that he has gotten." "All these star players complaining," Hunter said, "it creates a problem."

Since the beginning of training camp, players have been upset with the switch to a ball that was supposed to have more consistency in the way it handles and bounces. Instead it has less. According to many players surveyed over the past two months, the new ball has stuck to the players' hands, become frequently lodged between the rim and the backboard, and has also not been able to absorb moisture as well as the leather ball.

Steve Nash, the Phoenix point guard and two-time league most valuable player, wore bandages on his fingers last week because of cuts caused by the new ball. The Nets' Jason Kidd, and the Dallas Mavericks' Jason Terry and Dirk Nowitzki have all spoken out against the material, complaining of cuts on their hands.

Jerry Stackhouse, the Mavericks guard who is the team's union representative, said he was encouraged to hear Stern's comments. "When that stuff is happening, then you really got to take a stronger look at it," Stackhouse said last night before the Mavericks played the Nets at Continental Arena in East Rutherford, N. J. "As players, we're going to adjust. It's not like the game has lost anything, that the scoring is down or we're not getting exciting finishes. The game's not been affected in that way.

"But it's one of those things where it is directly affecting our workplace. Unilateral, that's the word."

Mark Cuban, the outspoken Mavericks owner who has often been at odds with Stern, applauded Stern's admission of culpability. "That's smart," Cuban said last night. "In David Stern University, looking at the greater good sometimes means re-evaluating our decisions."

Stern said that every test showed that the synthetic ball was much more consistent. But, he said: "If our players are unhappy, then we're unhappy. We get every ball from every team. We go back. We have it taken apart. We do all kinds of tests. And that's a continuing process."

But the players wonder where the testing was before the season. Only three people, all retired players who are now analysts—Mark Jackson, Reggie Miller and Steve Kerr—tested the ball. Jackson, now a Nets television analyst, said that they spent less than an hour one day at Madison Square Garden shooting, passing and dribbling.

Jackson said he had no problem with it. "When I played, it

didn't matter," he said last night. "If it was round, let's get it on."

The only N.B.A. players who tested the ball in competition were the 2006 All-Stars, during last season's game in Houston. Stu Jackson, the N.B.A.'s vice president for basketball operations, said in October that the league made the change to be more consistent with other leagues in the world and also "because this is a better basketball."

But players and coaches have proof that says otherwise. One N.B.A. assistant coach, who did not want to be identified because he was not authorized to comment, tore a ligament in a finger when, in retrieving a ball that had bounced onto the sideline, his finger stuck at an odd angle on the surface of the ball.

The Knicks' Eddy Curry said: "The ball never leaves my hand the same way. It sticks to my middle finger. It bounces differently off the dribble and on the shot." He added, "I definitely notice a difference in the ball, but all my complaints won't change a thing."

Stackhouse said the players needed to be consulted earlier. "If it's something about the arenas and the fans and trying to enhance the game from a fan's perspective, use your expertise and business savvy to make unilateral decisions about that," he said. "When it comes to the actual game itself and when it comes to in between the lines, we should definitely have some input."

SOURCE: L. Robbins, "A Whole New Game Ball?" *The New York Times*, December 6, 2006.

Rather, it responds to requests for action. The NLRB's role in representation elections is discussed in the next section. Here we discuss unfair labor practices.

Unfair labor practice cases begin with the filing of a charge, which is investigated by a regional office. A charge must be filed within six months of the alleged unfair practice, and copies must be served on all parties. (Registered mail is recommended.) If the NLRB finds the charge to have merit and issues a complaint, there are two possible actions. It may defer to a grievance procedure agreed on by the employer and union. Otherwise, a hearing is held before an administrative law judge. The judge makes a recommendation, which can be appealed by either party. The NLRB has the authority to issue cease-and-desist orders to halt unfair labor practices. It can also order reinstatement of employees, with or without back pay. In 2005, for example, $84.3 million in back pay was awarded and 2,008 workers were offered reinstatement (of whom 79 percent accepted). Note, however, that the NLRA is not a criminal statute, and punitive damages are not available. If an employer or union refuses to comply with an NLRB order, the board has the authority to petition the U.S. Court of Appeals. The court can choose to enforce the order, remand it to the NLRB for modification, change it, or set it aside altogether.

## Union and Management Interactions: Organizing

**LO4**
Describe the Major Labor–Management Interactions: Organizing, Contract Negotiations, and Contract Administration.

To this point we have discussed macro trends in union membership. Here we shift our focus to the more micro questions of why individual employees join unions and how the organizing process works at the workplace level.

### Why Do Employees Join Unions?

Virtually every model of the decision to join a union focuses on two questions.[30] First, is there a gap between the pay, benefits, and other conditions of employment that employees actually receive versus what they believe they should receive? Second, if such a gap exists and is sufficiently large to motivate employees to try to remedy the situation, is union membership seen as the most effective or instrumental means of change? The outcome of an election campaign hinges on how the majority of employees answer these two questions.

## The Process and Legal Framework of Organizing

The NLRB is responsible for ensuring that the organizing process follows certain steps. At the most general level, the NLRB holds a union representation election if at least 30 percent of employees in the bargaining unit sign authorization cards (see Figure 14.5). If over 50 percent of the employees sign authorization cards, the union may request that the employer voluntarily recognize it. If 50 percent or fewer of the employees sign, or if the employer refuses to recognize the union voluntarily, the NLRB conducts a secret-ballot election. The union is certified by the NLRB as the exclusive representative of employees if over 50 percent of employees vote for the union. If more than one union appears on the ballot and neither gains a simple majority, a runoff election is held. Once a union has been certified as the exclusive representative of a group of employees, no additional elections are permitted for one year. After the negotiation of a contract, an election cannot be held for the contract's duration or for three years, whichever comes first. The parties to the contract may agree not to hold an election for longer than three years, but an outside party cannot be barred for more than three years.

As mentioned previously, union members' right to be represented by leaders of their own choosing was expanded under the Taft–Hartley Act to include the right to vote an existing union out—that is, to decertify it. The process follows the same steps as a representation election. A decertification election is not permitted when a contract is in effect. Research indicates that when decertification elections are held, unions typically do not fare well, losing about 65 percent of the time during 2005. Moreover, the number of such elections increased from roughly 5 percent of all elections in the 1950s and 1960s to about 14 percent in 2005.[31]

**figure 14.5**
Authorization Card

**YES, I WANT THE IAM**

I, the undersigned employee of

(Company) ______________________________

authorize the International Association of Machinists and Aerospace Workers (IAM) to act as my collective bargaining agent for wages, hours and working conditions. I agree that this card may be used either to support a demand for recognition or an NLRB election, at the discretion of the union.

Name (print)______________________ Date ______________

Home Address____________________ Phone______________

City__________________ State__________ Zip__________

Job Title________________ Dept.__________ Shift __________

Sign Here X______________________________________

Note: This authorization to be SIGNED and DATED in employee's own handwriting.
YOUR RIGHT TO SIGN THIS CARD IS PROTECTED BY FEDERAL LAW.

RECEIVED BY (Initial) ____________________

SOURCE: From J. A. Fossum, *Labor Relations: Development, Structure and Process*, 2002. Copyright © 2002 The McGraw-Hill Companies, Inc. Reprinted with permission.

The NLRB also is responsible for determining the appropriate bargaining unit and the employees who are eligible to participate in organizing activities. A unit may cover employees in one facility or multiple facilities within a single employer, or the unit may cover multiple employers. In general, employees on the payroll just prior to the ordering of an election are eligible to vote, although this rule is modified in some cases where, for example, employment in the industry is irregular. Most employees who are on strike and who have been replaced by other employees are eligible to vote in an election (such as a decertification election) that occurs within 12 months of the onset of the strike.

As shown in Table 14.3, the following types of employees cannot be included in bargaining units: agricultural laborers, independent contractors, supervisors, and managers. Beyond this, the NLRB attempts to group together employees who have a community of interest in their wages, hours, and working conditions. In many cases this grouping will be sharply contested, with management and the union jockeying to include or exclude certain employee subgroups in the hope of influencing the outcome of the election.

## Organizing Campaigns: Management and Union Strategies and Tactics

Tables 14.6 and 14.7 list common issues that arise during most campaigns. Unions attempt to persuade employees that their wages, benefits, treatment by employers, and opportunity to influence workplace decisions are not sufficient and that the union will be effective in obtaining improvements. Management emphasizes that it has provided a good package of wages, benefits, and so on. It also argues that, whereas a union is unlikely to provide improvements in such areas, it will likely lead to certain costs for employees, such as union dues and the income loss resulting from strikes.

**table 14.6**

Prevalence of Certain Union Issues in Campaigns

| UNION ISSUES | PERCENTAGE OF CAMPAIGNS |
|---|---|
| Union will prevent unfairness and will set up a grievance procedure and seniority system. | 82% |
| Union will improve unsatisfactory wages. | 79 |
| Union strength will give employees voice in wages, working conditions. | 79 |
| Union, not outsider, bargains for what employees want. | 73 |
| Union has obtained gains elsewhere. | 70 |
| Union will improve unsatisfactory sick leave and insurance. | 64 |
| Dues and initiation fees are reasonable. | 64 |
| Union will improve unsatisfactory vacations and holidays. | 61 |
| Union will improve unsatisfactory pensions. | 61 |
| Employer promises and good treatment may not be continued without union. | 61 |
| Employees choose union leaders. | 55 |
| Employer will seek to persuade or frighten employees to vote against union. | 55 |
| No strike without vote. | 55 |
| Union will improve unsatisfactory working conditions. | 52 |
| Employees have legal right to engage in union activity. | 52 |

SOURCE: From J. A. Fossum, *Labor Relations: Development, Structure and Process*, 1992. Copyright © 1992 The McGraw-Hill Companies, Inc. Reprinted with permission.

**table 14.7**

Prevalence of Certain Management Issues in Campaigns

| MANAGEMENT ISSUES | PERCENTAGE OF CAMPAIGNS |
|---|---|
| Improvements not dependent on unionization. | 85% |
| Wages good, equal to, or better than under union contract. | 82 |
| Financial costs of union dues outweigh gains. | 79 |
| Union is outsider. | 79 |
| Get facts before deciding; employer will provide facts and accept employee decision. | 76 |
| If union wins, strike may follow. | 70 |
| Loss of benefits may follow union win. | 67 |
| Strikers will lose wages; lose more than gain. | 67 |
| Unions not concerned with employee welfare. | 67 |
| Strike may lead to loss of jobs. | 64 |
| Employer has treated employees fairly and/or well. | 60 |
| Employees should be certain to vote. | 54 |

SOURCE: From J. A. Fossum, *Labor Relations: Development, Structure and Process*, 1992. Copyright © 1992 The McGraw-Hill Companies, Inc. Reprinted with permission.

As Table 14.8 indicates, employers use a variety of methods to oppose unions in organizing campaigns, some of which may go beyond what the law permits, especially in the eyes of union organizers. This perception is supported by our earlier discussion, which noted a significant increase in employer unfair labor practices since the late 1960s. (See Figure 14.4.)

Why would employers increasingly break the law? Fossum suggests that the consequences (like back pay and reinstatement of workers) of doing so are "slight."[32] His review

**table 14.8**

Percentage of Firms Using Various Methods to Oppose Union Organizing Campaigns

| | |
|---|---|
| **Survey of employers** | |
| Consultants used | 41% |
| Unfair labor practice charges filed against employer | 24 |
| **Survey of union organizers** | |
| Consultants and/or lawyers used | 70 |
| Unfair labor practices by employer | |
| Charges filed | 36 |
| Discharges or discriminatory layoffs | 42[a] |
| Company leaflets | 80 |
| Company letters | 91 |
| Captive audience speech | 91[b] |
| Supervisor meetings with small groups of employees | 92 |
| Supervisor intensity in opposing union | |
| Low | 14 |
| Moderate | 34 |
| High | 51 |

[a] This percentage is larger than the figure for charges filed because it includes cases in which no unfair labor practice charge was actually filed against the employer.

[b] Refers to management's requiring employees to attend a session on company time at which the disadvantages of union membership are emphasized.

SOURCE: R. B. Freeman and M. M. Kleiner, "Employer Behavior in the Face of Union Organizing Drives," *Industrial and Labor Relations Review* 43, no. 4 (April 1990), pp. 351–65. © Cornell University.

of various studies suggests that discrimination against employees involved in union organizing decreases union organizing success significantly and that the cost of back pay to union activists reinstated in their jobs is far smaller than the costs that would be incurred if the union managed to organize and gain better wages, benefits, and so forth.

Still, the NLRB attempts to maintain a noncoercive atmosphere under which employees feel they can exercise free choice. It will set aside an election if it believes that either the union or the employer has created "an atmosphere of confusion or fear of reprisals."[33] Examples of conduct that may lead to an election result being set aside include

- Threats of loss of jobs or benefits by an employer or union to influence votes or organizing activities.
- A grant of benefits or a promise of benefits as a means of influencing votes or organizing activities.
- An employer or union making campaign speeches to assembled groups of employees on company time less than 24 hours before an election.
- The actual use or threat of physical force or violence to influence votes or organizing activities.[34]

Supervisors have the most direct contact with employees. Thus, as Table 14.9 indicates, it is critical that they be proactive in establishing good relationships with

**table 14.9**
What Supervisors Should and Should Not Do to Stay Union-Free

| WHAT TO DO: |
|---|
| Report any direct or indirect signs of union activity to a core management group. |
| Deal with employees by carefully stating the company's response to pro-union arguments. These responses should be coordinated by the company to maintain consistency and to avoid threats or promises. |
| Take away union issues by following effective management practice all the time:<br>Deliver recognition and appreciation.<br>Solve employee problems.<br>Protect employees from harassment or humiliation.<br>Provide business-related information.<br>Be consistent in treatment of different employees.<br>Accommodate special circumstances where appropriate.<br>Ensure due process in performance management.<br>Treat all employees with dignity and respect. |

| WHAT TO AVOID: |
|---|
| Threatening employees with harsher terms and conditions of employment or employment loss if they engage in union activity. |
| Interrogating employees about pro-union or anti-union sentiments that they or others may have or reviewing union authorization cards or pro-union petitions. |
| Promising employees that they will receive favorable terms or conditions of employment if they forgo union activity. |
| Spying on employees known to be, or suspected of being, engaged in pro-union activities. |

SOURCE: *HR Magazine* by J. A. Segal. Copyright © 1998 by Society for Human Resource Management. Reproduced with permission of Society for Human Resource Management via Copyright Clearance Center.

employees if the company wishes to avoid union organizing attempts. It is also important for supervisors to know what not to do should a drive take place.

In response to organizing difficulties, the union movement has tried alternative approaches. **Associate union membership** is not linked to an employee's workplace and does not provide representation in collective bargaining. Instead the union provides other services, such as discounts on health and life insurance or credit cards.[35] In return, the union receives membership dues and a broader base of support for its activities. Associate membership may be attractive to employees who wish to join a union but cannot because their workplace is not organized by a union.

**Associate Union Membership**
A form of union membership by which the union receives dues in exchange for services (e.g., health insurance, credit cards) but does not provide representation in collective bargaining.

**Corporate campaigns** seek to bring public, financial, or political pressure on employers during the organizing (and negotiating) process.[36] For example, the Building and Construction Trades Department of the AFL-CIO successfully lobbied Congress to eliminate $100 million in tax breaks for a Toyota truck plant in Kentucky until Toyota agreed to use union construction workers and pay union wages.[37] The Amalgamated Clothing and Textile Workers Union (ACTWU) corporate campaign against J. P. Stevens during the late 1970s was one of the first and best known. The ACTWU organized a boycott of J. P. Stevens products and threatened to withdraw its pension funds from financial institutions where J. P. Stevens officers acted as directors. J. P. Stevens subsequently agreed to a contract with the ACTWU.[38]

**Corporate Campaigns**
Union activities designed to exert public, financial, or political pressure on employers during the union-organizing process.

Unions also hope to use their financial assets to influence companies. Prior to the rebound of the stock market in 2003, unions directly controlled roughly $250 billion in pension funds and shared control with employers over another $1.04 trillion.[39] In addition, public sector pension funds controlled another $2.0 trillion. The AFL-CIO and the United Steelworkers have also set up a separate fund, the Heartland Labor Capital Network, which invests in worker-friendly companies.[40]

In some recent success stories unions have eschewed elections in favor of strikes and negative publicity to pressure corporations to accept a union. The Hotel Employees and Restaurant Employees (HERE) organized 9,000 workers in 2001, with 80 percent of these memberships resulting from pressure on employers rather than a vote. The Union of Needletrade, Industrial and Textile Employees (UNITE), which organized 15,000 workers in 2001, has also succeeded with this approach. After losing an election by just two votes among employees of Up-to-Date Laundry, which cleans linens for Baltimore hotels and hospitals, UNITE decided to try other tactics, including a corporate campaign. It called a strike to demand that Up-to-Date recognize the union. It also persuaded several major customers of the laundry to threaten to stop using the laundry's services, shared claims of racial and sexual harassment with state agencies and the NAACP, and convinced the Baltimore city council to require testimony from Up-to-Date. Eventually, the company gave in, recognized the union, and negotiated a contract that raised the workers' $6-an-hour wages and gave them better benefits.

Another winning union organizing strategy is to negotiate employer neutrality and card-check provisions into a contract. Under a *neutrality provision*, the employer pledges not to oppose organizing attempts elsewhere in the company. A *card-check provision* is an agreement that if a certain percentage—by law, at least a majority—of employees sign an authorization card, the employer will recognize their union representation. An impartial outside agency, such as the American Arbitration Association, counts the cards. The Communication Workers of America negotiated these provisions in its dispute with Verizon. Evidence suggests that this strategy can be very effective for unions.

## Union and Management Interactions: Contract Negotiation

The majority of contract negotiations take place between unions and employers that have been through the process before. In most cases, management has come to accept the union as an organization that it must work with. But when the union has just been certified and is negotiating its first contract, the situation can be very different. In fact, unions are unable to negotiate a first contract in 27 to 37 percent of the cases.[41] As noted previously, more than half of all unfair labor practice charges filed against employers pertain to the refusal to negotiate.

Labor–management contracts differ in their bargaining structures—that is, the range of employees and employers that are covered. As Table 14.10 indicates, the contracts differ, first, according to whether narrow (craft) or broad (industrial) employee interests are covered. Second, they differ according to whether they cover multiple employers or multiple plants within a single employer. (A single employer may have multiple plants, some union and some nonunion.) Different structures have different implications for bargaining power and the number of interests that must be incorporated in reaching an agreement.

**Distributive Bargaining**
The part of the labor–management negotiation process that focuses on dividing a fixed economic "pie."

**Integrative Bargaining**
The part of the labor–management negotiation process that seeks solutions beneficial to both sides.

### The Negotiation Process

Richard Walton and Robert McKersie suggested that labor–management negotiations could be broken into four subprocesses: distributive bargaining, integrative bargaining, attitudinal structuring, and intraorganizational bargaining.[42] **Distributive bargaining** focuses on dividing a fixed economic "pie" between the two sides. A wage increase, for example, means that the union gets a larger share of the pie, management a smaller share. It is a win–lose situation. **Integrative bargaining** has a win–win focus; it seeks solutions beneficial to both sides. So if management needs to reduce

**table 14.10**
Types and Examples of Bargaining Structures

| EMPLOYEE INTERESTS COVERED | EMPLOYER INTERESTS COVERED: MULTIEMPLOYER (CENTRALIZED) | SINGLE-EMPLOYER—MULTIPLANT | SINGLE-EMPLOYER—SINGLE PLANT (DECENTRALIZED) |
|---|---|---|---|
| **Craft (Narrow)** | Construction trades<br>Interstate trucking<br>Longshoring<br>Hospital association | Airline<br>Teacher<br>Police<br>Firefighters<br>Railroad | Craft union in small manufacturing plant<br>Hospital |
| **Industrial or Multiskill (Broad)** | Coal mining (underground)<br>Basic steel (pre-1986)<br>Hotel association | Automobiles<br>Steel (post-1986)<br>Farm equipment<br>State government<br>Textile | Industrial union in small manufacturing plant |

SOURCE: Adapted from H. C. Katz and T. A. Kochan, *An Introduction to Collective Bargaining and Industrial Relations* (New York: McGraw-Hill, 2004). © 2004 The McGraw-Hill Companies, Inc. Used with permission.

labor costs, it could reach an agreement with the union to avoid layoffs in return for the union agreeing to changes in work rules that might enhance productivity.

**Attitudinal structuring** refers to the relationship and trust between labor and management negotiators. Where the relationship is poor, it may be difficult for the two sides to engage in integrative bargaining because each side hesitates to trust the other side to carry out its part of the deal. For example, the union may be reluctant to agree to productivity-enhancing work-rule changes to enhance job security if, in the past, it has made similar concessions but believes that management did not stick to its assurance of greater job security. Thus the long-term relationship between the two parties can have a very important impact on negotiations and their outcomes.

**Attitudinal Structuring**
The aspect of the labor–management negotiation process that refers to the relationship and level of trust between the negotiators.

**Intraorganizational bargaining** reminds us that labor–management negotiations involve more than just two parties. Within management, and to an even greater extent within the union, different factions can have conflicting objectives. High-seniority workers, who are least likely to be laid off, may be more willing to accept a contract that has layoffs (especially if it also offers a significant pay increase for those whose jobs are not at risk). Less senior workers would likely feel very differently. Thus negotiators and union leaders must simultaneously satisfy both the management side and their own internal constituencies. If they do not, they risk the union membership's rejecting the contract, or they risk being voted out of office in the next election. Management, too, is unlikely to be of one mind about how to approach negotiations. Some will focus more on long-term employee relations, others will focus on cost control, and still others will focus on what effect the contract will have on stockholders.

**Intraorganizational Bargaining**
The part of the labor–management negotiation process that focuses on the conflicting objectives of factions within labor and management.

## Management's Preparation for Negotiations

Clearly, the outcome of contract negotiations can have important consequences for labor costs and labor productivity and, therefore, for the company's ability to compete in the product market. Adapting Fossum's discussion, we can divide management preparation into the following seven areas, most of which have counterparts on the union side.[43]

1. *Establishing interdepartmental contract objectives:* The employer's industrial relations department needs to meet with the accounting, finance, production, marketing, and other departments and set contract goals that will permit each department to meet its responsibilities. As an example, finance may suggest a cost figure above which a contract settlement would seriously damage the company's financial health. The bargaining team needs to be constructed to take these various interests into account.
2. *Reviewing the old contract:* This step focuses on identifying provisions of the contract that might cause difficulties by hindering the company's productivity or flexibility or by leading to significant disagreements between management and the union.
3. *Preparing and analyzing data:* Information on labor costs and the productivity of competitors, as well as data the union may emphasize, needs to be prepared and analyzed. The union data might include cost-of-living changes and agreements reached by other unions that could serve as a target. Data on employee demographics and seniority are relevant for establishing the costs of such benefits as pensions, health insurance, and paid vacations. Finally, management needs to

know how much it would be hurt by a strike. How long will its inventory allow it to keep meeting customer orders? To what extent are other companies positioned to step in and offer replacement products? How difficult would it be to find replacement workers if the company decided to continue operations during a strike?

4. *Anticipating union demands:* Recalling grievances over the previous contract, having ongoing discussions with union leaders, and becoming aware of settlements at other companies are ways of anticipating likely union demands and developing potential counterproposals.
5. *Establishing the cost of possible contract provisions:* Wages have not only a direct influence on labor costs but often an indirect effect on benefit costs (such as Social Security and paid vacation). Recall that benefits add 35 to 40 cents to every dollar's worth of wages. Also, wage or benefit increases that seem manageable in the first year of a contract can accumulate to less manageable levels over time.
6. *Preparing for a strike:* If management intends to operate during a strike, it may need to line up replacement workers, increase its security, and figure out how to deal with incidents on the picket line and elsewhere. If management does not intend to operate during a strike (or if the company will not be operating at normal levels), it needs to alert suppliers and customers and consider possible ways to avoid the loss of their business. This could even entail purchasing a competitor's product in order to have something to sell to customers.
7. *Determining strategy and logistics:* Decisions must be made about the amount of authority the negotiating team will have. What concessions can it make on its own, and which ones require it to check with top management? On which issues can it compromise, and on which can it not? Decisions regarding meeting places and times must also be made.

## Negotiation Stages and Tactics

Negotiations go through various stages.[44] In the early stages, many more people are often present than in later stages. On the union side, this may give all the various internal interest groups a chance to participate and voice their goals. This, in turn, helps send a message to management about what the union feels it must do to satisfy its members, and it may also help the union achieve greater solidarity. Union negotiators often present an extensive list of proposals at this stage, partly to satisfy their constituents and partly to provide themselves with issues on which they can show flexibility later in the process. Management may or may not present proposals of its own; sometimes it prefers to react to the union's proposals.

During the middle stages, each side must make a series of decisions, even though the outcome is uncertain. How important is each issue to the other side? How likely is it that disagreement on particular issues will result in a strike? When and to what extent should one side signal its willingness to compromise on its position?

In the final stage, pressure for an agreement increases as the deadline for a strike approaches. Public negotiations may be only part of the process. Negotiators from each side may have one-on-one meetings or small-group meetings where public-relations pressures are reduced. In addition, a neutral third party may become involved, someone who can act as a go-between or facilitator. In some cases, the only way for the parties to convince each other of their resolve (or to convince their own constituents of the other party's resolve) is to allow an impasse to occur.

Various books suggest how to avoid impasses by using mutual gains or integrative bargaining tactics. For example, *Getting to Yes* (New York: Penguin Books, 1991), by Roger Fisher and William Ury, describes four basic principles:

1. Separate the people from the problem.
2. Focus on interests, not positions.
3. Generate a variety of possibilities before deciding what to do.
4. Insist that the results be based on some objective standard.

## Bargaining Power, Impasses, and Impasse Resolution

Employers' and unions' conflicting goals are resolved through the negotiation process just described. An important determinant of the outcome of this process is the relative bargaining power of each party, which can be defined as the "ability of one party to achieve its goals when faced with opposition from some other party to the bargaining process."[45] In collective bargaining, an important element of power is the relative ability of each party to withstand a strike. Although strikes are rare, the threat of a strike often looms large in labor–management negotiations. The relative ability to take a strike, whether one occurs or not, is an important determinant of bargaining power and, therefore, of bargaining outcomes.

## Management's Willingness to Take a Strike

Management's willingness to take a strike comes down to two questions:

1. *Can the company remain profitable over the long run if it agrees to the union's demands?* The answer is more likely to be yes to the extent that higher labor costs can be passed on to consumers without losing business. This, in turn, is most likely when (1) the price increase is small because labor costs are a small fraction of total costs or (2) there is little price competition in the industry. Low price competition can result from regulated prices, from competition based on quality (rather than price), or from the union's organizing all or most of the employers in the industry, which eliminates labor costs as a price factor.

   Unions share part of management's concern with long-term competitiveness because a decline in competitiveness can translate into a decline in employment levels. On the other hand, the majority of union members may prefer to have higher wages, despite employment declines, particularly if a minority of the members (those with low seniority) suffer more employment loss and the majority keep their employment with higher wages.
2. *Can the company continue to operate in the short run despite a strike?* Although "hanging tough" on its bargaining goals may pay off for management in the long run, the short-run concern is the loss of revenues and profits from production being disrupted. The cost to strikers is a loss of wages and possibly a permanent loss of jobs.

Under what conditions is management most able to take a strike? The following factors are important:[46]

1. *Product demand:* Management is less able to afford a strike when the demand for its product is strong because that is when more revenue and profits are lost.
2. *Product perishability:* A strike by certain kinds of employees (farm workers at harvest time, truckers transporting perishable food, airline employees at peak

Management has several factors to consider before taking a strike. Most negotiations do not result in a strike since it is often not in the best interest of either party.

travel periods) will result in permanent losses of revenue, thus increasing the cost of the strike to management.

3. *Technology:* An organization that is capital intensive (versus labor intensive) is less dependent on its employees and more likely to be able to use supervisors or others as replacements. Telephone companies are typically able to operate through strikes, even though installing new equipment or services and repair work may take significantly longer than usual.
4. *Availability of replacement workers:* When jobs are scarce, replacement workers are more available and perhaps more willing to cross picket lines. Using replacement workers to operate during a strike raises the stakes considerably for strikers who may be permanently replaced. Most strikers are not entitled to reinstatement until there are job openings for which they qualify. If replacements were hired, such openings may not occur for some time (if at all).
5. *Multiple production sites and staggered contracts:* Multiple sites and staggered contracts permit employers to shift production from the struck facility to facilities that, even if unionized, have contracts that expire at different times (so they are not able to strike at the same time).
6. *Integrated facilities:* When one facility produces something that other facilities need for their products, the employer is less able to take a strike because the disruption to production goes beyond that single facility. The just-in-time production system, which provides very little stockpiling of parts, further weakens management's ability to take a strike.
7. *Lack of substitutes for the product:* A strike is more costly to the employer if customers have a readily available alternative source from which to purchase the goods or services the company provides.

Bargaining outcomes also depend on the nature of the bargaining process and relationship, which includes the types of tactics used and the history of labor relations. The vast majority of labor–management negotiations do not result in a strike because a strike is typically not in the best interests of either party. Furthermore, both the union and management usually realize that if they wish to interact effectively in the future, the experience of a strike can be difficult to overcome. When strikes do occur, the conduct of each party during the strike can also have a lasting effect on labor–management relations. Violence by either side or threats of job loss by hiring replacements can make future relations difficult.

## Impasse Resolution Procedures: Alternatives to Strikes

Given the substantial costs of strikes to both parties, procedures that resolve conflicts without strikes have arisen in both the private and public sectors. Because many public sector employees do not have the right to strike, alternatives are particularly important in that arena.

Three often-used impasse resolution procedures are mediation, fact finding, and arbitration. All of them rely on the intervention of a neutral third party, most typically provided by the Federal Mediation and Conciliation Service (FMCS), which must be notified 60 days prior to contract expiration and 30 days prior to a planned change in contract terms (including a strike). **Mediation** is the least formal but most widely used of the procedures (in both the public and private sectors). One survey found it was used by nearly 40 percent of all large private sector bargaining units.[47] A mediator has no formal authority but, rather, acts as a facilitator and go-between in negotiations.

A **fact finder,** most commonly used in the public sector, typically reports on the reasons for the dispute, the views and arguments of both sides, and (in some cases) a recommended settlement, which the parties are free to decline. That these recommendations are made public may give rise to public pressure for a settlement. Even if a fact finder's settlement is not accepted, the hope is that he or she will identify or frame issues in such a way as to facilitate an agreement. Sometimes, for the simple reason that fact finding takes time, the parties reach a settlement during the interim.

The most formal type of outside intervention is **arbitration,** under which a solution is actually chosen by an arbitrator (or arbitration board). In some instances the arbitrator can fashion a solution (conventional arbitration). In other cases the arbitrator must choose either the management's or union's final offer (final offer arbitration) on either the contract as a whole or on an issue-by-issue basis. Traditionally, arbitrating the enforcement or interpretation of contract terms (rights arbitration) has been widely accepted, whereas arbitrating the actual writing or setting of contract terms (interest arbitration, our focus here) has been reserved for special circumstances. These include some public sector negotiations, where strikes may be especially costly (such as those by police or firefighters) and a very few private sector situations, where strikes have been especially debilitating to both sides (the steel industry in the 1970s).[48] One reason for avoiding greater use of interest arbitration is a strong belief that the parties closest to the situation (unions and management, not an arbitrator) are in the best position to effectively resolve their conflicts.

**Mediation**
A procedure for resolving collective bargaining impasses by which a mediator with no formal authority acts as a facilitator and go-between in the negotiations.

**Fact Finder**
A person who reports on the reasons for the labor–management dispute, the views and arguments of both sides, and a nonbinding recommendation for settling the dispute.

**Arbitration**
A procedure for resolving collective bargaining impasses by which an arbitrator chooses a solution to the dispute.

## Union and Management Interactions: Contract Administration

### Grievance Procedure

Although the negotiation process (and the occasional resulting strike) receive the most publicity, the negotiation process typically occurs only about every three years, whereas contract administration goes on day after day, year after year. The two processes—negotiation and administration—are linked, of course. Vague or incomplete contract language developed in the negotiation process can make administration of the contract difficult. Such difficulties can, in turn, create conflict that can spill over into the next negotiation process.[49] Furthermore, events during the negotiation process—strikes, the use of replacement workers, or violence by either side—can lead to management and labor difficulties in working successfully under a contract.

A key influence on successful contract administration is the grievance procedure for resolving labor–management disputes over the interpretation and execution of the contract. During World War II, the War Labor Board helped institutionalize the use of arbitration as an alternative to strikes to settle disputes that arose during the term of the contract. The soon-to-follow Taft–Hartley Act further reinforced this preference. Today the great majority of grievance procedures have binding arbitration as a final step, and only a minority of strikes occur during the term of a contract. (Most occur during the negotiation stage.) Strikes during the term of a contract can

## COMPETING THROUGH GLOBALIZATION

### Rumbles over Labor Reform: Beijing's Proposed Worker Protections Are Giving Multinationals the Jitters

One reason multinationals love China is its malleable workforce. That looks set to change with the impending passage of a new labor contract law that will make it harder to hire and fire, ultimately boosting the cost of doing business in the country. Under the law, "the hiring cost for employers will rise, the flow of labor will be further restricted, and the employment relationship will be more unstable," says Ma Jianjun, chairman of the Labor Committee of the Shanghai Bar Association.

The new law, likely to pass this spring, will usher in a raft of regulations similar to those in pro-labor European countries. Probationary periods for new hires will be shortened to as little as one month, while the use of short-term contracts will be restricted. And when companies are downsizing, they will have to base decisions not on workers' abilities but on factors such as whether they have dependents. "Distressed companies may be forced to lay off more qualified employees and employees in critical positions while retaining less essential personnel," the American Chamber of Commerce warned in a statement submitted to Chinese authorities.

That comment is one of more than 190,000 the government has received on the proposed law—an unprecedented level of public discussion of legislation in China. The debate spurred Beijing to tone down some of the measures. For instance, a second draft, released in December, no longer requires management to get China's official trade union to sign off on important staffing decisions, though labor bosses must still be consulted. "We have enough investment at stake that we can usually get someone to listen to us if we are passionate about an issue," says Scott D. Slipy, director of human resources in China for Microsoft Corp., which worked with the Chamber of Commerce to make its concerns heard.

Some foreign investors support the law. Those who buy goods from Chinese-owned factories hope it will cut down on worker abuse—and bad press. And they're hoping that turnover rates, which run as high as 100 percent a year, could come down if workers enjoy stronger protections. "We see it as a huge stabilizing force if there is an up-front contract enforced in factories," says Auret van Heerden, CEO of the Fair Labor Association, an industry group that represents the likes of Nike, Adidas, Liz Claiborne, and Eddie Bauer.

Many companies, meanwhile, are wondering how vigilant Beijing will be. "The current labor law already is stronger than many in the region," says William Anderson, who oversees social affairs in Asia for sportswear maker Adidas Group. "But it all comes down to enforcement."

SOURCE: D. Roberts, "Rumbles over Labor Reform: Beijing's Proposed Worker Protections Are Giving Multinationals the Jitters," *BusinessWeek*, March 12, 2007, p. 57.

be especially disruptive because they are more unpredictable than strikes during the negotiation phase, which occur only at regular intervals.

Beyond its ability to reduce strikes, a grievance procedure can be judged using three criteria.[30] First, how well are day-to-day contract questions resolved? Time delays and heavy use of the procedure may indicate problems. Second, how well does the grievance procedure adapt to changing circumstances? For example, if the company's business turns downward and the company needs to cut costs, how clear are the provisions relating to subcontracting of work, layoffs, and so forth? Third, in multiunit contracts, how well does the grievance procedure permit local contract issues (like work rules) to be included and resolved?

From the employees' perspective, the grievance procedure is the key to fair treatment in the workplace, and its effectiveness rests both on the degree to which employees feel they can use it without fear of recrimination and whether they believe their case will be carried forward strongly enough by their union representative. The **duty of fair representation** is mandated by the NLRA and requires that all bargaining unit members, whether union members or not, have equal access to and representation by the union in the grievance procedure. Too many grievances may indicate a problem, but so may too few. A very low grievance rate may suggest a fear of filing a grievance, a belief that the system is not effective, or a belief that representation is not adequate.

**Duty of Fair Representation**
The National Labor Relations Act requirement that all bargaining unit members have equal access to and representation by the union.

As Table 14.11 suggests, most grievance procedures have several steps prior to arbitration. Moreover, the majority of grievances are settled during the earlier steps of the process, which is desirable both to reduce time delays and to avoid the costs of arbitration. If the grievance does reach arbitration, the arbitrator makes the final ruling in the matter. A series of Supreme Court decisions in 1960, commonly known as the Steelworkers' Trilogy, established that the courts should essentially refrain from reviewing the merits of arbitrators' decisions and, instead, limit judicial review to the question of whether the issue was subject to arbitration under the contract.[51] Furthermore, unless the contract explicitly states that an issue is not subject to arbitration, it will be assumed that arbitration is an appropriate means of deciding the issue. Giving further strength to the role of arbitration is the NLRB's general policy of deferring to arbitration.

What types of issues most commonly reach arbitration? Data from the FMCS on a total of 2,473 grievances in 2006 show that discharge and disciplinary issues topped

**table 14.11**
Steps in a Typical Grievance Procedure

**Employee-initiated grievance**

**Step 1**

a. Employee discusses grievance or problem orally with supervisor.
b. Union steward and employee may discuss problem orally with supervisor.
c. Union steward and employee decide (1) whether problem has been resolved or (2) if not resolved, whether a contract violation has occurred.

**Step 2**

a. Grievance is put in writing and submitted to production superintendent or other designated line manager.
b. Steward and management representative meet and discuss grievance. Management's response is put in writing. A member of the industrial relations staff may be consulted at this stage.

**Step 3**

a. Grievance is appealed to top line management and industrial relations staff representatives. Additional local or international union officers may become involved in discussions. Decision is put in writing.

**Step 4**

a. Union decides on whether to appeal unresolved grievance to arbitration according to procedures specified in its constitution and/or bylaws.
b. Grievance is appealed to arbitration for binding decision.

**Discharge grievance**

a. Procedure may begin at step 2 or step 3.
b. Time limits between steps may be shorter to expedite the process.

**Union or group grievance**

a. Union representative initiates grievance at step 1 or step 2 on behalf of affected class of workers or union representatives.

SOURCE: H. C. Katz, T. A. Kochan, and A. J. S. Colvin, *An Introduction to Collective Bargaining and Industrial Relations,* 2008. Copyright © 2008 The McGraw-Hill Companies, Inc. Reprinted with permission.

the list with 913 cases.[52] Other frequent issues include the use of seniority in promotion, layoffs, transfers, work assignments, and scheduling (309 cases); wages (178); and benefits (127).

What criteria do arbitrators use to reach a decision? In the most common case—discharge or discipline—the following due process questions are important:[53]

1. *Did the employee know what the rule or expectation was and what the consequences of not adhering to it were?*
2. *Was the rule applied in a consistent and predictable way?* In other words, are all employees treated the same?
3. *Are facts collected in a fair and systematic manner?* An important element of this principle is detailed record keeping. Both employee actions (such as tardiness) and management's response (verbal or written warnings) should be carefully documented.
4. *Does the employee have the right to question the facts and present a defense?* An example in a union setting is a hearing with a shop steward present.
5. *Does the employee have the right to appeal a decision?* An example is recourse to an impartial third party, such as an arbitrator.
6. *Is there progressive discipline?* Except perhaps for severe cases, an arbitrator will typically look for evidence that an employee was alerted as early as possible that behavior was inappropriate and the employee was given a chance to change prior to some form of severe discipline, such as discharge.
7. *Are there unique mitigating circumstances?* Although discipline must be consistent, individuals differ in terms of their prior service, performance, and discipline record. All of these factors may need to be considered.

## New Labor–Management Strategies

**LO5**
Describe New, Less Adversarial Approaches to Labor–Management Relations.

Jack Barbash described the nature of the traditional relationship between labor and management (during both the negotiation and administration phases) as follows:

> Bargaining is a love–hate, cooperation–conflict relationship. The parties have a common interest in maximizing the total revenue which finances their respective returns. But they take on adversarial postures in debating how the revenue shall be divided as between wages and profits. It is the adversarial posture which has historically set the tone of the relationship.[54]

Although there have always been exceptions to the adversarial approach, there are signs of a more general transformation to less adversarial workplace relations (at least where the union's role is accepted by management).[55] This transformation has two basic objectives: (1) to increase the involvement of individuals and work groups in overcoming adversarial relations and increasing employee commitment, motivation, and problem solving and (2) to reorganize work so that work rules are minimized and flexibility in managing people is maximized. These objectives are especially important for companies that need to be able to shift production quickly in response to changes in markets and customer demands. The specific programs aimed at achieving these objectives include employee involvement in decision making, self-managing employee teams, labor–management problem-solving teams, broadly defined jobs, and sharing of financial gains and business information with employees.[56] Examples include the chapter opening story on GEMA and the UAW, as well as the labor-management relationships at Ford and Harley-Davidson, also described in the present chapter.

Union resistance to such programs has often been substantial, precisely because the programs seek to change workplace relations and the role that unions play. Without the union's support, these programs are less likely to survive and less likely to be effective if they do survive.[57] Union leaders have often feared that such programs will weaken unions' role as an independent representative of employee interests. Indeed, according to the NLRA, to "dominate or interfere with the formation or administration of any labor organization or contribute financial or other support to it" is an unfair labor practice. An example of a prohibited practice is "taking an active part in organizing a union or committee to represent employees."[58]

One case that has received much attention is that of Electromation, a small electrical parts manufacturer. In 1992 the NLRB ruled that the company had violated Section 8(a)(2) of the NLRA by setting up worker–management committees (typically about six workers and one or two managers) to solve problems having to do with absenteeism and pay scales.[59] The original complaint was filed by the Teamsters union, which was trying to organize the (nonunion) company and felt that the committees were, in effect, illegally competing with them to be workers' representatives. Similarly, Polaroid dissolved an employee committee that had been in existence for over 40 years in response to the U.S. Department of Labor's claim that it violated the NLRA. The primary functions of the employee committee had been to represent employees in grievances and to advise senior management on issues such as pay and company rules and regulations. In a third case, the NLRB ruled in 1993 that seven worker–management safety committees at DuPont were illegal under the NLRB because they were dominated by management. The committee members were chosen by management and their decisions were subject to the approval of the management members of the committees. Finally, the committees made decisions about issues that were mandatory subjects of bargaining with the employees' elected representative—the chemical workers' union.[60] The impact of such cases will be felt both in nonunion companies, as union organizers move to fill the worker representation vacuum, and in unionized companies, as managers find they must deal more directly and effectively with their unions.

In 1994 the Commission on the Future of Worker–Management Relations (also referred to as the Dunlop Commission, after its chair, former Secretary of Labor John Dunlop) recommended that Congress clarify Section 8(a)(2) and give employers more freedom to use employee involvement programs without risking legal challenges. In 1996 the U.S. Congress passed the Teamwork for Employees and Managers Act, which supporters said would remove legal roadblocks to greater employee involvement. Critics claimed the act went too far and would bring back employer-dominated labor organizations, which existed prior to the passage of the NLRA in 1935. The Clinton administration vetoed the bill, meaning that employers will continue to face some uncertainty about legal issues. Table 14.12 provides some guidance on when the use of teams might be illegal.

vetoed

**table 14.12**
When Teams May Be Illegal

| **Primary factors to look for that could mean a team violates national labor law:** | |
|---|---|
| Representation | Does the team address issues affecting nonteam employees? (Does it represent other workers?) |
| Subject matter | Do these issues involve matters such as wages, grievances, hours of work, and working conditions? |
| Management involvement | Does the team deal with any supervisors, managers, or executives on any issue? |
| Employer domination | Did the company create the team or decide what it would do and how it would function? |

SOURCE: From *BusinessWeek* January 25, 1993. Reprinted with permission.

Employers must take care that employee involvement meets the legal test, but the NLRB has clearly supported the legality of involvement in important cases. For example, in a 2001 ruling, the NLRB found that the use of seven employee participation committees at a Crown Cork & Seal aluminum can manufacturing plant did not violate federal labor law. The committees in question make and implement decisions regarding a wide range of issues, including production, quality, training, safety, and certain types of worker discipline. The NLRB determined that these committees were not employer-dominated labor organizations, which would have violated federal labor law. Instead of "dealing with" management in a bilateral manner where proposals are made that are either rejected or accepted by management, the teams and committees exercise authority, delegated by management, to operate the plant within certain parameters. Indeed, the NLRB noted that rather than "dealing with management," the evidence indicated that within delegated areas of authority, the teams and committees "are management." This authority was found to be similar to that delegated to a first-line supervisor. Thus the charge that the teams and committees did not have final decision-making authority (and so were not acting in a management capacity) did not weigh heavily with the NLRB, which noted, "Few, if any, supervisors in a conventional plant have authority that is final and absolute." Instead, it was noted that managers typically make recommendations that move up through "the chain of command."[61]

Although there are legal concerns to address, some evidence suggests that these new approaches to labor relations—incorporating greater employee participation in decisions, using employee teams, multiskilling, rotating jobs, and sharing financial gains—can contribute significantly to an organization's effectiveness.[62] One study, for example, compared the features of traditional and transformational approaches to labor relations at Xerox.[63] As Table 14.13 indicates, the transformational approach was characterized by better conflict resolution, more shop-floor cooperation, and greater worker autonomy and feedback in decision making. Furthermore, compared with the

**table 14.13**

Patterns in Labor–Management Relations Using Traditional and Transformational Approaches

| | PATTERN | |
|---|---|---|
| DIMENSION | TRADITIONAL | TRANSFORMATIONAL |
| **Conflict resolution** | | |
| Frequency of conflicts | High | Low |
| Speed of conflict resolution | Slow | Fast |
| Informal resolution of grievances | Low | High |
| Third- and fourth-step grievances | High | Low |
| **Shop-floor cooperation** | | |
| Formal problem-solving groups (such as quality, reducing scrap, employment security) | Low | High |
| Informal problem-solving activity | Low | High |
| **Worker autonomy and feedback** | | |
| Formal autonomous work groups | Low | High |
| Informal worker autonomous activity | Low | High |
| Worker-initiated changes in work design | Low | High |
| Feedback on cost, quality, and schedule | Low | High |

SOURCE: Adapted from J. Cutcher-Gershenfeld, "The Impact of Economic Performance of a Transformation in Workplace Relations," *Industrial and Labor Relations Review* 44 (1991), pp. 241–60. Reprinted with permission.

traditional approach, transformational labor relations were found to be associated with lower costs, better product quality, and higher productivity. The Commission on the Future of Worker–Management Relations concluded that the evidence is "overwhelming that employee participation and labor–management partnerships are good for workers, firms, and the national economy." National survey data also indicate that most employees want more influence in workplace decisions and believe that such influence leads to more effective organizations.[64]

## Labor Relations Outcomes

The effectiveness of labor relations can be evaluated from management, labor, and societal perspectives. Management seeks to control costs and enhance productivity and quality. Labor unions seek to raise wages and benefits and exercise control over how employees spend their time at work (such as through work rules). Each of the three parties typically seeks to avoid forms of conflict (like strikes) that impose significant costs on everyone. In this section we examine several outcomes.

### Strikes

Table 14.14 presents data on strikes in the United States that involved 1,000 or more employees. Because strikes are more likely in large units, the lack of data on smaller units is probably not a major concern, although such data would, of course, raise the figure on the estimated time lost to strikes. For example, for the 1960s, this estimate is .12 percent using data on strikes involving 1,000 or more employees versus .17 percent for all strikes. Although strikes impose significant costs on union members, employers, and society, it is clear from Table 14.14 that strikes are the exception rather than the rule. Very little working time is lost to strikes in the United States (with

**table 14.14**
Work Stoppages Involving 1,000 or More Workers

| YEAR | STOPPAGES | NUMBER OF WORKERS (THOUSANDS) | PERCENTAGE OF TOTAL WORKING TIME |
|---|---|---|---|
| 1950 | 424 | 1,698 | 0.26% |
| 1955 | 363 | 2,055 | 0.16 |
| 1960 | 222 | 896 | 0.09 |
| 1965 | 268 | 999 | 0.10 |
| 1970 | 381 | 2,468 | 0.29 |
| 1975 | 235 | 965 | 0.09 |
| 1980 | 187 | 795 | 0.09 |
| 1985 | 54 | 324 | 0.03 |
| 1990 | 44 | 185 | 0.02 |
| 1995 | 31 | 192 | 0.02 |
| 2000 | 39 | 394 | 0.06 |
| 2002 | 19 | 46 | <.005 |
| 2004 | 17 | 171 | 0.01 |
| 2006 | 20 | 70 | 0.01 |

SOURCE: http://stats.bls.gov.

annual work hours of 1,800, about 11 minutes per union member in 2005), and their frequency in recent years is generally low by historical standards. Does this mean that the industrial relations system is working well? Not necessarily. Some would view the low number of strikes as another sign of labor's weakness.

## Wages and Benefits

In 2006, private-sector unionized workers received, on average, wages 24 percent higher than their nonunion counterparts.[65] Total compensation was 44 percent higher for union-covered employees because of an even larger effect of unions on benefits.[66] However, these are raw differences. To assess the net effect of unions on wages more accurately, adjustments must be made. We now briefly highlight a few of these.

The union wage effect is likely to be overestimated to the extent that unions can more easily organize workers who are already highly paid or who are more productive. The gap is likely to be underestimated to the extent that nonunion employers raise wages and benefits in response to the perceived "union threat" in the hope that their employees will then have less interest in union representation. When these and other factors are taken into account, the net union advantage in wages, though still substantial, is reduced to 10 to 15 percent. The union benefits advantage is also reduced, but it remains larger than the union wage effect, and the union effect on total compensation is therefore larger than the wage effect alone.[67]

Beyond differences in pay and benefits, unions typically influence the way pay and promotions are determined. Whereas management often seeks to deal with employees as individuals, emphasizing performance differences in pay and promotion decisions, unions seek to build group solidarity and avoid the possibly arbitrary treatment of employees. To do so, unions focus on equal pay for equal work. Any differences among employees in pay or promotions, they say, should be based on seniority (an objective measure) rather than on performance (a subjective measure susceptible to favoritism). It is very common in union settings for there to be a single rate of pay for all employees in a particular job classification.

## Productivity

There has been much debate regarding the effects of unions on productivity.[68] Unions are believed to decrease productivity in at least three ways: (1) the union pay advantage causes employers to use less labor and more capital per worker than they would otherwise, which reduces efficiency across society; (2) union contract provisions may limit permissible workloads, restrict the tasks that particular workers are allowed to perform, and require employers to use more employees for certain jobs than they otherwise would; and (3) strikes, slowdowns, and working-to-rule (slowing down production by following every workplace rule to an extreme) result in lost production.[69]

On the other hand, unions can have positive effects on productivity.[70] Employees, whether members of a union or not, communicate to management regarding how good a job it is doing by either the "exit" or "voice" mechanisms. "Exit" refers to simply leaving the company to work for a better employer. "Voice" refers to communicating one's concerns to management without necessarily leaving the employer. Unions are believed to increase the operation and effectiveness of the voice mechanism.[71] This, in turn, is likely to reduce employee turnover and its associated costs. More broadly, voice can be seen as including the union's contribution to the success of

## COMPETING THROUGH SUSTAINABILITY

### Model Partnership: Automakers, Labor Could Learn from Harley-Davidson's Kansas City Operation

If there weren't three of them, Karl Eberle, Richard "Stick" Doyle and Tony Wilson could be an old married couple.

They bicker over money. They fret about the kids. They finish each other's sentences.

Together, they run the Harley-Davidson motorcycle factory here, although Eberle is the plant manager, while Doyle and Wilson run the local chapters of the United Steelworkers and International Association of Machinists and Aerospace Workers, respectively.

"It's as close to your marriage as you'd ever want to get," Eberle said recently, prompting a wry chuckle from the other two. At a time when Delphi Corp. and the United Auto Workers are threatening a war that could prove apocalyptic for both of them, Harley and its unions are hard at work demonstrating that American manufacturing doesn't have to implode just because workers get paid less in China or India.

Instead of laying people off or outsourcing jobs, Harley has embraced its workers as partners. And rather than fighting for every last "work rule" or job classification, the unions have accepted a major role in controlling their own destiny.

Harley's system, which has contributed to 20 consecutive years of record sales and earnings, has yet to be tested by a major, prolonged downturn. Organizational experts agree that few other companies could adopt it wholesale.

But in the mid-1980s, Harley-Davidson Inc. was in worse shape than General Motors Corp. or Ford Motor Co. are today. And the company's acceleration away from the abyss over the past two decades offers many lessons for any kind of company beset by growing competition from outside and management stagnation from within.

What it boils down to, said Jim Ziemer, Harley's CEO, is a lot of hard work and commitment, something that tests the patience of many companies pressured by Wall Street.

"You have to build trust, and it takes time; we're talking about years," Ziemer said. "Sometime it's easier to pick up the phone and call somebody in Mexico."

In some ways, Harley's labor-management detente is really nothing new. It depends on the sort of factory teams and worker-empowerment programs that have become commonplace in American manufacturing.

Countless companies, including the embattled automakers, have tried to institute the principles pioneered by Japan's Toyota Motor Corp. But many of those efforts have foundered on the shoals of bureaucracy, mutual recalcitrance and fear of anything new.

What is new is a growing recognition that getting the most out of U.S. labor requires more than just team-building and empowerment programs. It calls for a new way of thinking about management and work; one that emphasizes mutual trust instead of command and control.

Harley has discovered that allowing unions true participation in all aspects of running a plant provides a powerful lubricant for reducing costs, boosting productivity and ultimately giving customers more of what they want. Hiring good people and making full use of their ingenuity and intellect is the true promise of the "knowledge economy," management experts agree.

"We expect more than just your hands," said Harold Scott, Harley's chief of human resources. "You gotta have people who want to contribute and then train them to do it."

On a windblown March afternoon in Kansas City, Eberle, Doyle and Wilson gathered in the glass-walled office suite they share on the second floor of Harley's factory, and tried to explain how their unique arrangement works. The fact that management and labor share quarters is unusual enough, but these three also share responsibility for budgets, capital spending, and other aspects of running the plant.

Built from scratch and opened in 1998 to manufacture the company's smaller Sportster model, the Kansas City factory is a maze of articulated robots and noisy metal-bending machines. One measure of its success over the past decade is that the corporate office has given it four additional lines. In addition to

Sportsters, Kansas City now produces Dyna Glides, V-Rods, custom bikes and the Revolution V-Twin powertrain. Employment has exploded from a little more than 50 original employees to around 1,000 today.

"They used to call it 'an experiment in labor relations,' but I don't think they'd call it an experiment anymore," said the steelworkers' Doyle.

After Japanese competition and crippling quality problems nearly spelled its demise in the early 1980s, Harley rose from the near-dead, helped by import tariffs instituted by the Reagan administration. A tough-minded turnaround group seized the opportunity to slash jobs and install a radical new Toyota-style just-in-time manufacturing system. With the quality problems fixed, baby boomers flocked to Harley dealerships, looking to sow their wild oats.

For then-Harley CEO Rich Teerlink, however, the battle had just begun. How, he wondered, could the company keep its edge in the absence of an external crisis?

Unlike other manufacturing leaders, who were beginning to flee overseas or to "right-to-work" states in the South, Teerlink decided the way to inspire better performance was not by running from unions but by engaging them. He thought America's best companies were "effective, efficient and humane." But it also was likely that Harley's flag-waving customers wouldn't put up with a lot of outsourcing.

SOURCE: M. Oneal, "Model Partnership: Automakers, Labor Could Learn from Harley-Davidson's Kansas City Operation," *Columbus Dispatch*, May 27, 2006 (original article in *Chicago Tribune*).

labor–management cooperation programs that make use of employee suggestions and increased involvement in decisions. A second way that unions can increase productivity is (perhaps ironically) through their emphasis on the use of seniority in pay, promotion, and layoff decisions. Although management typically prefers to rely more heavily on performance in such decisions, using seniority has a potentially important advantage—namely, it reduces competition among workers. As a result, workers may be less reluctant to share their knowledge with less senior workers because they do not have to worry about less senior workers taking their jobs. Finally, the introduction of a union may have a "shock effect" on management, pressuring it into tightening standards and accountability and paying greater heed to employee input in the design and management of production.[72]

Although there is evidence that unions have both positive and negative effects on productivity, most studies have found that union workers are more productive than nonunion workers. Nevertheless, it is generally recognized that most of the findings on this issue are open to a number of alternative explanations, making any clear conclusions difficult. For example, if unions raise productivity, why has union representation of employees declined over time, even within industries?[73] A related concern is that unionized establishments are more likely to survive where there is some inherent productivity advantage unrelated to unionism that actually offsets a negative impact of unionism. If so, these establishments would be overrepresented, whereas establishments that did not survive the negative impact of unions would be underrepresented. Consequently, any negative impact of unions on productivity would be underestimated.

## Profits and Stock Performance

Even if unions do raise productivity, a company's profits and stock performance may still suffer if unions raise costs (such as wages) or decrease investment by a greater amount. Evidence shows that unions have a large negative effect on profits and that union coverage tends to decline more quickly in firms experiencing lower shareholder returns, suggesting that some firms become more competitive partly by reducing union strength.[74] Similarly, one study finds that each dollar of unexpected increase in collectively bargained labor costs results in a dollar reduction in shareholder wealth. Other research suggests that investment in research and development is lower in unionized firms.[75] Strikes, although infrequent, lower shareholder returns in both the struck companies and firms (like suppliers) linked to those companies.[76] These research findings describe the average effects of unions. The consequences of more innovative union–management relationships for profits and stock performance are less clear.

## The International Context

**LO6**
Explain How Changes in Competitive Challenges (e.g., Product Market Competition and Globalization) Are Influencing Labor–Management Interactions.

Except for China, Russia, and Ukraine, the United States has more union members than any other country. Yet, as Table 14.15 indicates, aside from France and Korea, the United States has the lowest unionization rate (union density) of any country in the table. Even more striking are differences in union coverage, the percentage of employees whose terms and conditions of employment are governed by a union contract. (See Table 14.15.) In parts of western Europe, it is not uncommon to have coverage rates of 80 to 90 percent, meaning that the influence of labor unions far outstrips what would be implied by their membership levels.[77] Why are the unionization rate and coverage comparatively low? One explanation is that the United States does not have as strong a history of deep class-based divisions in society as other countries do. For example, labor and social democratic political parties are commonplace in western Europe, and they are major players in the political process. Furthermore, the labor movement in western Europe is broader than that in the United States. It extends not just to the workplace but—through its own or closely related political parties—directly into the national political process.

– U.S.

What is the trend in union membership rates and coverage? In the United States, we saw earlier that the trend is clearly downward, at least in the private sector.

**table 14.15**
Union Membership and Union Coverage, Selected Countries

| | MEMBERSHIP | | COVERAGE |
|---|---|---|---|
| COUNTRY | NUMBER (THOUSANDS) | PERCENTAGE OF EMPLOYMENT (DENSITY) | PERCENTAGE OF EMPLOYMENT |
| United States | 15,776 | 12 | 14 |
| Canada | 4,037 | 30 | 32 |
| Japan | 10,531 | 20 | 24 |
| Korea | 1,606 | 11 | — |
| Australia | 1,867 | 23 | 50 |
| Netherlands | 1,575 | 25 | 82 |
| France | 1,830 | 8 | 95 |
| United Kingdom | 6,524 | 29 | 35 |

SOURCE: J. Visser, "Union Membership Statistics in 24 Countries," *Monthly Labor Review,* January 2006, pp. 38–49.

Although there have also been declines in membership rates in many other countries, coverage rates have stayed high in many of these countries. In the United States, deregulation and competition from foreign-owned companies have forced companies to become more efficient. Combined with the fact that the union wage premium in the United States is substantially larger than in other advanced industrialized countries, it is not surprising that management opposition would be higher in the United States than elsewhere.[78] This, in turn, may help explain why the decline in union influence has been especially steep in the United States.

It seems likely that—with the growing globalization of markets—labor costs and productivity will continue to be key challenges. The European Union (EU) added 10 new member countries in 2004, and 2 more in 2007 bringing its total to 27 countries and 490 million people, or about 60 percent larger than the United States. The newer EU countries (e.g., Bulgaria, the Czech Republic, Poland, Romania, Slovakia) have much lower wages than the existing EU countries. Closer to home, we have the North American Free Trade Agreement among the United States, Canada, and Mexico. These common market agreements mean that goods, services, and production will continue to move more freely across international borders. Where substantial differences in wages, benefits, and other costs of doing business (such as regulation) exist, there will be a tendency to move to areas that are less costly, unless skills are unavailable or productivity is significantly lower there. Unless labor unions can increase their productivity sufficiently or organize new production facilities, union influence is likely to decline.

In addition to membership and coverage, the United States differs from western Europe in the degree of formal worker participation in decision making. Works' councils (joint labor–management decision-making institutions at the enterprise level) and worker representation on supervisory boards of directors (codetermination) are mandated by law in countries such as Germany. The Scandinavian countries, Austria, and Luxembourg have similar legislation. German works' councils make decisions about changes in work or the work environment, discipline, pay systems, safety, and other human resource issues. The degree of codetermination on supervisory boards depends on the size and industry of the company. For example, in German organizations having more than 2,000 employees, half of the board members must be worker representatives. (However, the chairman of the board, a management representative, can cast a tie-breaking vote.) In contrast, worker representation on boards of directors in the United States is still rare.[79]

The works' councils exist in part because collective bargaining agreements in countries such as Germany tend to be oriented toward industrywide or regional issues, with less emphasis on local issues. However, competitive forces have led employers to increasingly opt out of centralized bargaining, even in the countries best known for centralized bargaining, like Sweden and Germany.[80]

## The Public Sector

**LO7**
Explain How Labor Relations in the Public Sector Differ from Labor Relations in the Private Sector.

Unlike the private sector, union membership in the public sector grew in the 1960s and 1970s and remained fairly stable through the 1980s. As we saw earlier, in Figure 14.3 in 2006 some 36 percent of government employees were union members. Like the NLRA in the private sector, changes in the legal framework contributed significantly to union growth in the public sector. One early step was the enactment in Wisconsin of collective bargaining legislation in 1959 for its state employees.[81] Executive Order 10988 provided collective bargaining rights for federal employees in 1962. By the end of the 1960s, most states had passed similar laws. The Civil Service Reform Act of 1978, Title VII, later established the Federal Labor Relations Authority (modeled after the NLRB). Many states have similar administrative agencies to administer their own laws.

An interesting aspect of public sector union growth is that much of it has occurred in the service industry and among white-collar employees—groups that have traditionally been viewed as difficult to organize. The American Federation of State, County, and Municipal Employees (AFSCME) with 1.4 million members, has about 325,000 members in health care, 325,000 in clerical jobs, and over 400,000 in all white-collar occupations.[82]

In contrast to the private sector, strikes are illegal at the federal level of the public sector and in most states. At the local level, all states prohibit strikes by police (Hawaii being a partial exception) and firefighters (Idaho being the exception). Teachers and state employees are somewhat more likely to have the right to strike, depending on the state. Legal or not, strikes nonetheless do occur in the public sector. In 2006, of the 20 strikes involving 1,000 or more workers, 8 were in state and local government.

## A Look Back

The membership rate, and thus influence, of labor unions in the United States and in many other countries has been on the decline in the private sector. In the meantime, however, as we saw in the opening to this chapter, there continue to be companies where labor unions represent a large share of employees and thus play a major role in the operation and success of those companies. In such companies, whatever the national trend, effective labor relations are crucial for both companies and workers.

### Questions

1. Many people picture labor union members as being men in blue-collar jobs in manufacturing plants. Is that accurate? Are there certain types of jobs where an employer can be fairly certain that employees will not join a union? Give examples.
2. Why do people join labor unions? Would you be interested in joining a labor union if given the opportunity? Why or why not? As a manager, would you prefer to work with a union or would you prefer that employees be unrepresented by a union? Explain.
3. What led to a change in labor relations at the Global Engine Manufacturing Alliance? What was the nature of the change and do you think it is an important and sustainable change?

Please see the Video Case that corresponds to this chapter online at www.mhhe.com/noe6e.

## Summary

Labor unions seek to represent the interests of their members in the workplace. Although this may further the cause of industrial democracy, management often finds that unions increase labor costs while setting limits on the company's flexibility and discretion in decision making. As a result, the company may witness a diminished ability to compete effectively in a global economy. Not surprisingly, management in nonunion companies often feels compelled to actively resist the unionization of its employees. This, together with a host of economic, legal, and other factors, has contributed to union losses in membership and bargaining power in the private sector. There are some indications, however, that managements and unions are seeking new, more effective ways of working together to enhance competitiveness while giving employees a voice in how workplace decisions are made.

## Key Terms

Checkoff provision, 616
Closed shop, 616
Union shop, 616
Agency shop, 616
Maintenance of membership, 616
Right-to-work laws, 616
Taft-Hartley Act, 1947, 624
Associate union membership, 631
Corporate campaigns, 631
Distributive bargaining, 632
Integrative bargaining, 632
Attitudinal structuring, 633
Intraorganizational bargaining, 633
Mediation, 637
Fact finder, 637
Arbitration, 637
Duty of fair representation, 639

## Discussion Questions

1. Why do employees join unions?
2. What has been the trend in union membership in the United States, and what are the underlying reasons for the trend?
3. What are the consequences for management and owners of having a union represent employees?
4. What are the general provisions of the National Labor Relations Act, and how does it affect labor–management interactions?
5. What are the features of traditional and nontraditional labor relations? What are the potential advantages of the "new" nontraditional approaches to labor relations?
6. How does the U.S. industrial and labor relations system compare with systems in other countries, such as those in western Europe?

## Self-Assessment Exercise

Would you join a union? Each of the following phrases expresses an opinion about the effects of a union on employees' jobs. For each phrase, circle a number on the scale to indicate whether you agree that a union would affect your job as described by the phrase.

| **Having a union would result in . . .** | **Strongly Disagree** | | | | **Strongly Agree** |
|---|---|---|---|---|---|
| 1. Increased wages | 1 | 2 | 3 | 4 | 5 |
| 2. Improved benefits | 1 | 2 | 3 | 4 | 5 |
| 3. Protection from being fired | 1 | 2 | 3 | 4 | 5 |
| 4. More promotions | 1 | 2 | 3 | 4 | 5 |
| 5. Better work hours | 1 | 2 | 3 | 4 | 5 |
| 6. Improved productivity | 1 | 2 | 3 | 4 | 5 |
| 7. Better working conditions | 1 | 2 | 3 | 4 | 5 |
| 8. Fewer accidents at work | 1 | 2 | 3 | 4 | 5 |
| 9. More interesting work | 1 | 2 | 3 | 4 | 5 |
| 10. Easier handling of employee problems | 1 | 2 | 3 | 4 | 5 |
| 11. Increased work disruptions | 5 | 4 | 3 | 2 | 1 |
| 12. More disagreements between employees and management | 5 | 4 | 3 | 2 | 1 |
| 13. Work stoppages | 5 | 4 | 3 | 2 | 1 |

Add up your total score. The highest score possible is 65, the lowest 13. The higher your score, the more you see value in unions, and the more likely you would be to join a union.

SOURCE: Based on S. A. Youngblood, A. S. DeNisi, J. L. Molleston, and W. H. Mobley, "The Impact of Work Environment, Instrumentality Beliefs, Perceived Union Image, and Subjective Norms on Union Voting Intentions," *Academy of Management Journal* 27 (1984), pp. 576–90.

## Exercising Strategy: How Nissan Laps Detroit

Jonathan Gates slaps a wide slab of tan-colored, hard foam rubber on his workbench. He fastens a numbered tag in one corner and some black foam insulation at the edges. As soon as he puts a number on the piece of foam, which will become the top of a dashboard for a Nissan Quest minivan, the vehicle has an identity. All of the parts for a big chunk of the minivan's interior, decked out with the customer's choice of colors, fabrics, and options, will come together in the next 42 minutes.

Gates and his co-workers fill a crucial role at Nissan Motor Co.'s new Canton, Mississippi, assembly plant: Almost everything a driver touches inside a new Quest, Titan pickup, or Armada sport-utility vehicle is put together in a single module, starting at Gates's workbench. "This is the most important job," he says. And yet, amazingly, Gates doesn't even work for Nissan. He works for Lextron/Visteon Automotive Systems, a parts supplier that also builds the center console between the front seats and a subassembly of the car's front end. The finished modules pass over a wall to be bolted into a car or truck body rolling down the assembly line. Lextron/Visteon does the work faster than Nissan could and pays $3 an hour less than the carmaker pays assembly workers. Nissan is using a similar strategy for its vehicle frames, seats, electrical systems, and completed doors.

It's a level of efficiency that Detroit auto makers are only beginning to attempt. Along with other features in Nissan's eight-month-old, $1.4 billion factory, the wholesale integration of outside suppliers is another reason why General Motors, Ford, and Chrysler are still playing catch-up with Japanese car manufacturers. The Big Three have made great strides in productivity in recent years: General Motors Corp.'s best plants now actually beat Toyota's factories. But overall, every time Detroit gets close, the competition seems to get a little better.

Nissan's secret? Sure, its plants use cheaper, nonunion labor. Besides lower wages, its Smyrna, Tennessee, workers get about $3 an hour less in benefits than Big Three assemblers represented by the United Auto Workers. But there's more to it. Outsourcing offers huge savings, whereas the Big Three must negotiate the outsourcing of subassembly work with the union. And Nissan's plants are far more flexible in adjusting to market twists and turns. Nissan's Canton plant can send a minivan, pickup truck, and sport-utility vehicle down the same assembly line, one after the other, without interruption. At first glance, a Nissan factory does not look much different than one you would see in Detroit or St. Louis. But talk to the workers, and it soon becomes clear how relentlessly the company squeezes mere seconds out of the assembly process.

The United Auto Workers is slowly allowing more outsourcing. But the UAW wants to outsource work only to union-friendly suppliers. And even then it has to be negotiated. Nissan, meanwhile, has free rein to outsource jobs. Two of Smyrna's vehicles—the Maxima and Altima sedans—were engineered to be built using modules built by suppliers. Every vehicle built in Canton was designed that way. All together, buying modules saves 15 percent to 30 percent on the total cost of that section of the car, according to the Center for Automotive Research (CAR) in Ann Arbor, Michigan. And the Big Three? GM is the most "modular" of the domestic manufacturers, but only a few of its plants have been designed to build cars using many big modules.

Detroit is slowly making headway. Prudential says half of GM's 35 North American assembly lines can make multiple vehicles. GM's two-year-old Cadillac plant in Lansing, Michigan, will make three luxury vehicles: the CTS and STS sedans and SRX SUV. It has also been designed to get some large, preassembled modules from suppliers. GM is using the Cadillac plant as a model for upgrading other plants. "We're getting much more flexible," says Gary L. Cowger, president of GM North America.

But it's much easier to design a new factory to be flexible from the ground up than to refurbish those built 30 or more years ago. And with so much excess capacity, the Big Three have no room to build new plants. Even if they could match the Japanese in productivity, they would have to account for the costs of laid-off workers, whose contracts entitle them to 75 percent of their pay.

By contrast, Nissan runs a tight ship and works its employees harder. During the UAW's failed attempt to organize Smyrna in 2001, workers told the union that line speeds were too fast and people were getting injured, says Bob King, the UAW's vice president of organizing. The union says that in 2001, Nissan reported 31 injuries per 1,000 workers—twice the average at Big Three plants—according to logs reported to the Occupational Safety and Health Administration.

Nissan does not dispute the OSHA figures, but it denies its assembly lines are any less safe than Detroit's. Although the company won't release current numbers, executives do say that they have taken steps to reduce injuries. For instance, the company has workers do four different jobs during a typical eight-hour shift, to try to cut down on repetitive-motion injuries. Nissan claims that injury rates have fallen 60 percent in the past two years.

SOURCE: From "How Nissan Laps Detroit," *BusinessWeek*, December 22, 2003. Reprinted with permission.

### Questions

1. Can unionized plants compete with Nissan's nonunion plants?
2. Why isn't there a union at Nissan? Would a union be a good thing or a bad thing for Nissan workers? Nissan shareholders?

## Managing People: From the Pages of *BusinessWeek*

### BusinessWeek Twilight of the UAW

**The Pressure to make wage and benefit concessions won't go away** For more than two decades, the United Auto Workers has grudgingly allowed Detroit carmakers to slash jobs as they have struggled to keep pace with the onslaught from foreign rivals. That's what UAW President Ron Gettelfinger agreed to when he signed off on General Motors Corp.'s buyout of more than 40,000 jobs at the No.1 carmaker and its former parts unit, bankrupt Delphi Corp. Where the union has always drawn the line is on bedrock issues: wages and benefits for workers and retirees.

This time, though, that line won't hold. GM's buyouts are the beginning, not the end, of the concessions the union will have to make over the next few years. Unless GM and Ford Motor Co. see miraculous sales rebounds, the UAW at last will have to give ground on pay and health care. Already, Delphi's tough-talking chairman, Robert S. "Steve" Miller Jr., has issued an ultimatum requiring pay cuts of nearly 40 percent for the remaining 12,000 Delphi workers who can't take GM's offer. If the union continues to refuse, Miller could impose a harsher labor deal in bankruptcy court.

Gettelfinger can't look for relief across town, either. Ford has already announced plans to slash 25,000 jobs and will likely do a buyout deal, too. Similarly, bankrupt auto parts makers—including Collins & Aikman, Dana, and Tower Automotive—are using the courts to cut pay or close factories, Says a high-level official at another union: "This is a leadership moment for the UAW. We've had to deal with this in steel and airlines; now it's autos' turn."

What's going on is nothing less than the slow death of what was once the country's most powerful industrial union. Despite years of relentless global pressure, the UAW has been able to maintain some of the best blue-collar posts in the United States. But like lumbering GM itself, the union failed to realize what it would take to compete in a world economy. In the 1980s and 1990s, it fought concessions that would have helped U.S. carmakers fend off imports. The upshot: Like GM and Ford, it's paying the price today.

This year alone, the UAW will lose about 70,000 of its 640,000 members as a result of cuts at Ford, GM, and Delphi, bringing total membership to well under 600,000, vs. 1.5 million in 1980. At the same time, wages at parts makers are plunging and the paid-layoff clause, known in Detroit as the JOBS bank, is certain to be vulnerable when Big Three executives and UAW leaders face off in bargaining next year. Add it all up, and "this is the decline of the UAW," says Sean McAlinden, chief economist with the Center for Automotive Research in Ann Arbor, Mich. "We're in the 21st century. It's over."

The UAW's setbacks highlight a broader challenge faced by blue-collar America. Just as union bargaining muscle helped make the middle class, so too does its weakening signal the stiffer barriers less-skilled workers face in today's globalized economy. Just 52 percent of households headed by someone with only a high school degree are middle-class in 2003, vs. 68 percent in 1969, according to the National Center on Education & the Economy in Washington. "There are still opportunities for those without higher education, but they're shrinking every year," says NCEE Senior Fellow Anthony Carnevale.

#### Bringing in Buyouts

UAW leaders bristle at the thought that they are losing clout. Gettelfinger told *BusinessWeek* in an interview last year that "every Labor Day there are stories written that we're going away. But we're still here." True, he does still wield tremendous power over the Big Three. He negotiated buyouts of $35,000 to $140,000 from GM rather than pink slips for workers. GM will fund the estimated $4 billion to $5 billion in total restructuring costs for its plants and those of Delphi by selling off parts of its General Motors Acceptance Corp. finance arm and its stakes in Japanese auto companies, which is what Gettelfinger really wanted. And so far, the cuts to health-care benefits still leave his retirees with a better medical deal than most employees have. Nor have hourly workers yet lost ground in health care.

But the UAW's grip on wages and benefits can't last. America's employer-paid medical insurance amounts to an ever-increasing tax on domestic manufacturers trying to compete with foreign rivals based in countries with nationalized health care. Meanwhile, foreign auto makers get state and local tax breaks to build new plants in the U.S. that in some cases amount to five years' worth of their wage bill, says AlixPartners LLC Managing Director John Hoffecker.

#### Chinese Autos on the Way

There's another buzzsaw coming: cars from China. Every big auto maker is expanding production in the Chinese market, and analysts expect most to start exporting vehicles to the United States in a few years. "Chinese cars are coming," says Harvard University economics professor Richard Freeman. "I don't know if the UAW can hold on to its wages and benefits [in the face of that]."

The UAW's prospects look eerily similar to those that once faced another oldline union, the United Steelworkers. In 2002, after decades of relentless battering from global rivals, most U.S. steelmakers were hopelessly uncompetitive. To salvage what was left of the industry, the Steelworkers agreed to cut wages and benefits as well as jobs.

Most dramatically, the union allowed players such as U.S. Steel Corp. and Bethlehem Steel Corp.—then headed by none other than Delphi's Miller—to all but wipe out their legacy costs. The companies ended retiree health plans and used bankruptcy court to dump pension plans onto the federal government, cleaning billions off their books and out of steelworker retirees' pockets.

The UAW appears to be headed down the same path. "We were told by our union that we can expect to see a very different Delphi," says Skip Dziedzic, shop committee chairman of UAW Local 1868 near Milwaukee. "And I think we will." UAW workers can also expect to see a very different auto industry, and because their fortunes are so intertwined, a vastly diminished union.

*–With Aaron Bernstein in Washington*

SOURCE: D. Welch, with A. Bernstein, "Twilight of the UAW," *BusinessWeek*, April 10, 2006, pp. 62–64.

## Questions

1. How did the UAW get into this position? Could it have done anything to avoid it?
2. Thinking of the UAW and, more broadly, labor unions in the private sector, what might unions do in the future to maintain (or increase) their influence?
3. Is the decline of the UAW and private sector unionism, should it continue, a good thing or a bad thing for workers, companies, and society? Explain.
4. Should nonunion workers care about what happens to the UAW and other unions? Why or why not?

# Notes


1. J. T. Dunlop, *Industrial Relations Systems* (New York: Holt, 1958).
2. C. Kerr, "Industrial Conflict and Its Mediation," *American Journal of Sociology* 60 (1954), pp. 230–45.
3. T. A. Kochan, *Collective Bargaining and Industrial Relations* (Homewood, IL: Richard D. Irwin, 1980), p. 25; H. C. Katz and T. A. Kochan, *An Introduction to Collective Bargaining and Industrial Relations*, 3rd ed. (New York: McGraw-Hill, 2004).
4. Katz and Kochan, *An Introduction to Collective Bargaining*.
5. S. Webb and B. Webb, *Industrial Democracy* (London: Longmans, Green, 1897); J. R. Commons, *Institutional Economics* (New York: Macmillan, 1934).
6. C. Kerr, J. T. Dunlop, F. Harbison, and C. Myers, "Industrialism and World Society," *Harvard Business Review*, February 1961, pp. 113–26.
7. T. A. Kochan and K. R. Wever, "American Unions and the Future of Worker Representation," in *The State of the Unions*, ed. G. Strauss et al. (Madison, WI: Industrial Relations Research Association, 1991).
8. "Why America Needs Unions, but Not the Kind It Has Now," *BusinessWeek*, May 23, 1994, p. 70.
9. Katz and Kochan, *An Introduction to Collective Bargaining*.
10. J. Barbash, *The Elements of Industrial Relations* (Madison, WI: University of Wisconsin Press, 1984).
11. U.S. Bureau of Labor Statistics, www.bls.gov.
12. J. T. Bennett and B. E. Kaufman, *The Future of Private Sector Unionism in the United States* (Armonk, NY: M. E. Sharpe, 2002).
13. Katz and Kochan, *An Introduction to Collective Bargaining*. Katz and Kochan in turn build on work by J. Fiorito and C. L. Maranto, "The Contemporary Decline of Union Strength," *Contemporary Policy Issues* 3 (1987), pp. 12–27.
14. G. N. Chaison and J. Rose, "The Macrodeterminants of Union Growth and Decline," in *The State of the Unions*, George Strauss et al. (eds.) (Madison, WI: Industrial Relations Research Association, 1991).
15. D. L. Belman and K. A. Monaco, "The Effects of Deregulation, Deunionization, Technology, and Human Capital on the Work and Work Lives of Truck Drivers," *Industrial and Labor Relations Review* 54 (2001), pp. 502–24.
16. T. A. Kochan, R. B. McKersie, and J. Chalykoff, "The Effects of Corporate Strategy and Workplace Innovations in Union Representation," *Industrial and Labor Relations Review* 39 (1986), pp. 487–501; Chaison and Rose, "The Macrodeterminants of Union Growth"; J. Barbash, *Practice of Unionism* (New York: Harper, 1956), p. 210; W. N. Cooke and D. G. Meyer, "Structural and Market Predictors of Corporate Labor Relations Strategies," *Industrial and Labor Relations Review* 43 (1990), pp. 280–93; T. A. Kochan and P. Cappelli, "The Transformation of the Industrial Relations and Personnel Function," in *Internal Labor Markets*, ed. P. Osterman (Cambridge, MA: MIT Press, 1984).
17. Kochan and Cappelli, "The Transformation of the Industrial Relations and Personnel Function."
18. S. B. Jarrell and T. D. Stanley, "A Meta-Analysis of the Union–Nonunion Wage Gap," *Industrial and Labor Relations Review* 44 (1990), pp. 54–67; P. D. Lineneman, M. L. Wachter, and W. H. Carter, "Evaluating the Evidence on Union Employment and Wages," *Industrial and Labor Relations Review* 44 (1990), pp. 34–53; L. Mischel and M. Walters, "How Unions Help All Workers," Economic Policy Institute Briefing Paper (2003).
19. National Labor Relations Board annual reports.
20. R. B. Freeman and M. M. Kleiner, "Employer Behavior in the Face of Union Organizing Drives," *Industrial and Labor Relations Review* 43 (1990), pp. 351–65.
21. F. K. Foulkes, "Large Nonunionized Employers," in *U.S. Industrial Relations 1950–1980: A Critical Assessment*, eds. J. Steiber et al. (Madison, WI: Industrial Relations Research Association, 1981).
22. Katz and Kochan, *An Introduction to Collective Bargaining*.
23. E. E. Herman, J. L. Schwarz, and A. Kuhn, *Collective Bargaining and Labor Relations* (Englewood Cliffs, NJ: Prentice Hall, 1992), p. 32.
24. BLS Web site; AFL-CIO Web site.
25. Herman et al., *Collective Bargaining*, p. 33.
26. Kochan, *Collective Bargaining and Industrial Relations*, p. 61.
27. National Labor Relations Board, *A Guide to Basic Law and Procedures under the National Labor Relations Act* (Washington, DC: U.S. Government Printing Office, 1991).
28. Ibid.
29. Ibid.
30. H. N. Wheeler and J. A. McClendon, "The Individual Decision to Unionize," in *The State of the Unions*.
31. National Labor Relations Board annual reports.

32. J. A. Fossum, *Labor Relations*, 8th ed. (New York: McGraw-Hill, 2002), p. 149.
33. National Labor Relations Board, *A Guide to Basic Law*, p. 17.
34. Ibid.
35. Herman et al., *Collective Bargaining*; P. Jarley and J. Fiorito, "Associate Membership: Unionism or Consumerism?" *Industrial and Labor Relations Review* 43 (1990), pp. 209–24.
36. Katz and Kochan, *An Introduction to Collective Bargaining*, R. L. Rose, "Unions Hit Corporate Campaign Trail," *The Wall Street Journal*, March 8, 1993, p. B1.
37. P. Jarley and C. L. Maranto, "Union Corporate Campaigns: An Assessment," *Industrial and Labor Relations Review* 44 (1990), pp. 505–24.
38. Katz and Kochan, *An Introduction to Collective Bargaining*.
39. A. Fung, T. Hebb, and J. Rogers (eds.), *Working Capital: The Power of Labor's Pensions* (Ithaca, NY: Cornell University Press, 2001).
40. A. Bernstein, "Working Capital: Labor's New Weapon?" *BusinessWeek*, September 27, 1997, A. Michaud, "Investments with the Union Label," *BusinessWeek*, August 22, 2001.
41. Chaison and Rose, "The Macrodeterminants of Union Growth."
42. R. E. Walton and R. B. McKersie, *A Behavioral Theory of Negotiations* (New York: McGraw-Hill, 1965).
43. Fossum, *Labor Relations*. See also C. S. Loughran, *Negotiating a Labor Contract: A Management Handbook*, 2nd ed. (Washington, DC: Bureau of National Affairs, 1990).
44. C. M. Steven, *Strategy and Collective Bargaining Negotiations* (New York: McGraw-Hill, 1963); Katz and Kochan, *An Introduction to Collective Bargaining*.
45. Kochan, *Collective Bargaining and Industrial Relations*.
46. Fossum, *Labor Relations*.
47. Kochan, *Collective Bargaining and Industrial Relations*, p. 272.
48. Herman et al., *Collective Bargaining*.
49. Katz and Kochan, *An Introduction to Collective Bargaining*.
50. Kochan, *Collective Bargaining and Industrial Relations*, p. 386.
51. *United Steelworkers v. American Manufacturing Co.*, 363 U.S. 564 (1960); *United Steelworkers v. Warrior Gulf and Navigation Co.*, 363 U.S. 574 (1960); *United Steelworkers v. Enterprise Wheel and Car Corp.*, 363 U.S. 593 (1960).
52. Original data from U.S. Federal Mediation and Conciliation Service, *Fiftieth Annual Report, Fiscal Year 2006* (Washington, DC: U.S. Government Printing Office, 2006); www.fmcs.gov.
53. J. R. Redecker, *Employee Discipline: Policies and Practices* (Washington, DC: Bureau of National Affairs, 1989).
54. Barbash, *The Elements of Industrial Relations*, p. 6.
55. T. A. Kochan, H. C. Katz, and R. B. McKersie, *The Transformation of American Industrial Relations* (New York: Basic Books, 1986), chap. 6.
56. J. B. Arthur, "The Link between Business Strategy and Industrial Relations Systems in American Steel Minimills," *Industrial and Labor Relations Review* 45 (1992), pp. 488–506; M. Schuster, "Union Management Cooperation," in *Employee and Labor Relations*, ed. J. A. Fossum (Washington, DC: Bureau of National Affairs, 1990); E. Cohen-Rosenthal and C. Burton, *Mutual Gains: A Guide to Union–Management Cooperation*, 2nd ed. (Ithaca, NY: ILR Press, 1993); T. A. Kochan and P. Osterman, *The Mutual Gains Enterprise* (Boston: Harvard Business School Press, 1994); E. Applebaum and R. Batt, *The New American Workplace* (Ithaca, NY: ILR Press, 1994).
57. A. E. Eaton, "Factors Contributing to the Survival of Employee Participation Programs in Unionized Settings," *Industrial and Labor Relations Review* 47, no. 3 (1994), pp. 371–89.
58. National Labor Relations Board, *A Guide to Basic Law*.
59. A. Bernstein, "Putting a Damper on That Old Team Spirit," *BusinessWeek*, May 4, 1992, p. 60.
60. Bureau of National Affairs, "Polaroid Dissolves Employee Committee in Response to Labor Department Ruling," *Daily Labor Report*, June 23, 1992, p. A3; K. G. Salwen, "DuPont Is Told It Must Disband Nonunion Panels," *The Wall Street Journal*, June 7, 1993, p. A2.
61. "NLRB 4-0 Approves Crown Cork & Seal's Use of Seven Employee Participation Committees," *HR News*, September 3, 2001.
62. Kochan and Osterman, *Mutual Gains*; J. P. MacDuffie, "Human Resource Bundles and Manufacturing Performance: Organizational Logic and Flexible Production Systems in the World Auto Industry," *Industrial and Labor Relations Review* 48, no. 2 (1995), pp. 197–221; W. N. Cooke, "Employee Participation Programs, Group-Based Incentives, and Company Performance: A Union–Nonunion Comparison," *Industrial and Labor Relations Review* 47, no. 4 (1994), pp. 594–609; C. Doucouliagos, "Worker Participation and Productivity in Labor-Managed and Participatory Capitalist Firms: A Meta-Analysis," *Industrial and Labor Relations Review* 49, no. 1 (1995), pp. 58–77; L. W. Hunter, J. P. MacDuffie, and L. Doucet, "What Makes Teams Take? Employee Reactions to Work Reforms," *Industrial and Labor Relations Review* 55 (2002), pp. 448–72; S. J. Deery and R. D. Iverson, "Labor-Management Cooperation: Antecedents and Impact on Organizational Performance," *Industrial and Labor Relations Review* 58 (2005), pp. 588–609.
63. J. Cutcher-Gershenfeld, "The Impact of Economic Performance of a Transformation in Workplace Relations," *Industrial and Labor Relations Review* 44 (1991), pp. 241–60.
64. R. B. Freeman and J. Rogers, *Proceedings of the Industrial Relations Research Association*, 1995. A survey of workers represented by the United Autoworkers at six Chrysler manufacturing plants found generally positive worker reactions to the implementation of work teams, streamlined job classifications, and skill-based pay. See L. W. Hunter, J. P. Macduffie, and L. Doucet, "What Makes Teams Take? Employee Reactions to Work Reforms," *Industrial and Labor Relations Review* 55 (2002), p. 448. A study of the airline industry, moreover, concludes that relational factors, such as conflict and workplace culture, also play an important role in firm performance. See J. H. Gittell, A. vonNordenflycht, and T. A. Kochan, "Mutual Gains or Zero Sum? Labor Relations and Firm Performance in the Airline Industry," *Industrial and Labor Relations Review* 57 (2004), p. 163.
65. http://stats.bls.gov.
66. Ibid.
67. Jarrell and Stanley, "A Meta-Analysis"; R. B. Freeman and J. Medoff, *What Do Unions Do?* (New York: Basic Books, 1984); L. Mishel and M. Walters, "How Unions Help All Workers," *Economic Policy Institute Briefing Paper*, August 2003, www.epinet.org.
68. J. T. Addison and B. T. Hirsch, "Union Effects on Productivity, Profits, and Growth: Has the Long Run Arrived?" *Journal of Labor Economics* 7 (1989), pp. 72–105.
69. R. B. Freeman and J. L. Medoff, "The Two Faces of Unionism," *Public Interest* 57 (Fall 1979), pp. 69–93.
70. Ibid., L. Mishel and P. Voos, *Unions and Economic Competitiveness* (Armonk, NY: M. E. Sharpe, 1991); M. Ash and J. A. Seago, "The Effect of Registered Nurses' Unions on Heart-Attack Mortality," *Industrial and Labor Relations Review* 57 (2004), p. 422; C. Doucouliagos and P. Laroche, "What Do Unions Do to Productivity? A Meta-Analysis," *Industrial Relations* 42 (2003), pp. 650–91.
71. Freeman and Medoff, "Two Faces."

72. S. Slichter, J. Healy, and E. R. Livernash, *The Impact of Collective Bargaining on Management* (Washington, DC: Brookings Institution, 1960); Freeman and Medoff, "Two Faces."
73. Freeman and Medoff, *What Do Unions Do?*; Herman et al., *Collective Bargaining;* Addison and Hirsch, "Union Effects on Productivity"; Katz and Kochan, *An Introduction to Collective Bargaining;* Lineneman et al., "Evaluating the Evidence."
74. B. E. Becker and C. A. Olson, "Unions and Firm Profits," *Industrial Relations* 31, no. 3 (1992), pp. 395–415; B. T. Hirsch and B. A. Morgan, "Shareholder Risks and Returns in Union and Nonunion Firms," *Industrial and Labor Relations Review* 47, no. 2 (1994), pp. 302–18.
75. Addison and Hirsch, "Union Effects on Productivity." See also B. T. Hirsch, *Labor Unions and the Economic Performance of Firms* (Kalamazoo, MI: W. E. Upjohn Institute, 1991); J. M. Abowd, "The Effect of Wage Bargains on the Stock Market Value of the Firm," *American Economic Review* 79 (1989), pp. 774–800; Hirsch, *Labor Unions*.
76. B. E. Becker, and C. A. Olson, "The Impact of Strikes on Shareholder Equity," *Industrial and Labor Relations Review* 39, no. 3 (1986), pp. 425–38; O. Persons, "The Effects of Automobile Strikes on the Stock Value of Steel Suppliers," *Industrial and Labor Relations Review* 49, no. 1 (1995), pp. 78–87.
77. C. Brewster, "Levels of Analysis in Strategic HRM: Questions Raised by Comparative Research," Conference on Research and Theory in HRM, Cornell University, October 1997.
78. C. Chang and C. Sorrentino, "Union Membership in 12 Countries," *Monthly Labor Review* 114, no. 12 (1991), pp. 46–53; D. G. Blanchflower and R. B. Freeman, "Going Different Ways: Unionism in the U.S. and Other Advanced O.E.C.D. Countries" (Symposium on the Future Role of Unions, Industry, and Government in Industrial Relations. University of Minnesota), cited in Chaison and Rose, "The Macrodeterminants of Union Growth," p. 23.
79. J. P. Begin and E. F. Beal, *The Practice of Collective Bargaining* (Homewood, IL: Richard D. Irwin, 1989); T. H. Hammer, S. C. Currall, and R. N. Stern, "Worker Representation on Boards of Directors: A Study of Competing Roles," *Industrial and Labor Relations Review* 44 (1991), pp. 661–80; Katz and Kochan, *An Introduction to Collective Bargaining;* H. Gunter and G. Leminsky, "The Federal Republic of Germany," in *Labor in the Twentieth Century*, ed. J. T. Dunlop and W. Galenson (New York: Academic Press, 1978), pp. 149–96.
80. "Adapt or Die," *The Economist*, July 1, 1995, p. 54; G. Steinmetz, "German Firms Sour on Stem That Keeps Peace with Workers: Centralized Bargaining, a Key to Postwar Gains, Inflates Costs, Companies Fear," *The Wall Street Journal*, October 17, 1995, p. A1; H. C. Katz, W. Lee, and J. Lee, *The New Structure of Labor Relations: Tripartism and Decentralization* (Ithaca, NY: ILR Press/ Cornell University, 2004).
81. J. F. Burton and T. Thomason, "The Extent of Collective Bargaining in the Public Sector," in *Public Sector Bargaining*, ed. B. Aaron, J. M. Najita, and J. L. Stern (Washington, DC: Bureau of National Affairs, 1988).
82. www.afscme.org.

15

CHAPTER

# Managing Human Resources Globally

## LO LEARNING OBJECTIVES

After reading this chapter, you should be able to:

- LO1 Identify the recent changes that have caused companies to expand into international markets. *page 659*
- LO2 Discuss the four factors that most strongly influence HRM in international markets. *page 662*
- LO3 List the different categories of international employees. *page 670*
- LO4 Identify the four levels of global participation and the HRM issues faced within each level. *page 670*
- LO5 Discuss the ways companies attempt to select, train, compensate, and reintegrate expatriate managers. *page 674*

# ENTER THE WORLD OF BUSINESS

## Global Sourcing of Talent: IBM's Dilemma

As the global economy becomes more and more interdependent, companies are forced to make tough decisions regarding the sourcing of their work. It used to be that when a company based in the United States needed to manufacture goods closer to their global customers, the rationale seemed obvious and few people balked. Then, as companies found that locating manufacturing overseas could capitalize on lower labor costs, enabling them to then ship those goods to the United States (consequently, not needing U.S. manufacturing plants as much), public sentiment began occasionally to turn negative. However, most recently, enabled by global telecommunications technology, companies have discovered that they can locate call center jobs and information technology jobs (such as software coding or computer chip design) in countries such as India or China and realize as much as a 75 percent labor cost savings. For instance, Stephanie Moore, vice president of outsourcing at Forrester Research, states "You can get crackerjack Java programmers in India right out of college for $5,000 a year versus $60,000 here. The technology is such, why be in New York City when you can be 9,000 miles away with far less expense?" Such savings cannot be ignored by companies whose customers want low costs and shareholders want high profits.

For instance, General Electric has thousands of call center, research and development, and information technology workers in India. Peter Stack, a G.E. spokesman, stated "The outsourcing presence in India definitely gives us a competitive advantage in the businesses that use it. Those businesses are some of our growth businesses, and I would say that they're businesses where our overall employment is increasing."

In addition to cost savings, the global sourcing of talent provides capability that is difficult to build within one country or one time zone. For instance, Oracle's spokesman David Samson argues "Our aim here is not cost driven. It's to build a 24/7 follow-the-sun model for development and support. When a software engineer goes to bed at night in the U.S., his or her colleague in India picks up development when they get into work. They're able to continually develop products."

However, in spite of the cost and capability advantages, offshoring of jobs can result in considerable negative publicity. For instance, IBM's efforts to develop offshore call center and information technology capability has elicited significant backlash in the United States. Internal IBM employees have recorded calls and released internal memos that provide negative grist for opponents to focus on. For instance, a recorded phone call of IBM's director of global employee relations, Tom Lynch, was released, in which he and other executives were suggesting they should move some jobs now done in the United States to India or other countries. "Our competitors are doing it, and we have to do it," he stated. He also suggested, "Governments are going to find out that they're fairly limited as to what they can do, so unionizing becomes an attractive option."

Ultimately the dilemma is what to do about those whose jobs are being replaced. In the call Mr. Lynch stated, "One of our challenges that we deal with every day is trying to balance what the business needs to do versus impact on people. This is one of these areas where this challenge hits us squarely between the eyes."

Source: From "IBM Explores Shift of White-Collar Jobs Overseas," by S. Greenhouse, *New York Times*, July 22, 2003. Copyright © 2003 by The New York Times Co. Reprinted with permission. W. Bulkeley (July 29, 2004) IBM now plans fewer layoffs from offshoring. http://online.wsj.com/article_print/0,,SB109105951415677179,00.html.

## Introduction

The environment in which business competes is rapidly becoming globalized. More and more companies are entering international markets by exporting their products overseas, building plants in other countries, and entering into alliances with foreign companies. Back in the middle of the 1980s, 61 of the top 100 organizations had their headquarters in the United States. By 2004, that number had dropped to 35, and, as you can see in Table 15.1, of the world's largest 25 organizations, only 9 are headquartered in the United States, with 13 in Europe and 3 in Asia. Of *Fortune* magazine's Global 500 (the 500 largest companies), 170 are headquartered in the United States, 70 in Japan, 38 in the United Kingdom, 38 in France, 35 in Germany, 20 in China, 14 in the Netherlands, and 12 in South Korea. In addition, for the first time in history, an automaker from outside the United States (Toyota) became the largest in worldwide sales, surpassing General Motors in the first quarter of 2007.

A survey of 12,000 managers from 25 different countries indicates how common international expansion has become, both in the United States and in other countries.[1] Of the U.S. managers surveyed, 26 percent indicated that their companies had recently expanded internationally. Among the larger companies (10,000 or more employees), 45 percent had expanded internationally during the previous two years. Currently, exports account for 11 percent of the gross domestic product

**table 15.1**

*Fortune* Global 500—25 Largest Organizations Ranked by Revenues

| RANK | COMPANY | REVENUES ($ MILLIONS) | PROFITS ($ MILLIONS) |
|---|---|---|---|
| 1 | ExxonMobil | 339,938.0 | 36,130.0 |
| 2 | Wal-Mart Stores | 315,654.0 | 11,231.0 |
| 3 | Royal Dutch Shell | 306,731.0 | 25,311.0 |
| 4 | BP | 267,600.0 | 22,341.0 |
| 5 | General Motors | 192,604.0 | −10,567.0 |
| 6 | Chevron | 189,481.0 | 14,099.0 |
| 7 | DaimlerChrysler | 186,106.3 | 3,536.3 |
| 8 | Toyota Motor | 185,805.0 | 12,119.6 |
| 9 | Ford Motor | 177,210.0 | 2,024.0 |
| 10 | ConocoPhillips | 166,683.0 | 13,529.0 |
| 11 | General Electric | 157,153.0 | 16,353.0 |
| 12 | Total | 152,360.7 | 15,250.0 |
| 13 | ING Group | 138,235.3 | 8,958.9 |
| 14 | Citigroup | 131,045.0 | 24,589.0 |
| 15 | AXA | 129,839.2 | 5,186.5 |
| 16 | Allianz | 121,406.0 | 5,442.4 |
| 17 | Volkswagen | 118,376.6 | 1,391.7 |
| 18 | Fortis | 112,351.4 | 4,896.3 |
| 19 | Credit Agricole | 110,764.6 | 7,434.3 |
| 20 | American International Group | 108,905.0 | 10,477.0 |
| 21 | Assicurazioni Generali | 101,403.8 | 2,384.0 |
| 22 | Siemens | 100,098.7 | 2,854.9 |
| 23 | Sinopec | 98,784.9 | 2,668.4 |
| 24 | Nippon Telegraph & Telephone | 94,869.3 | 4,404.6 |
| 25 | Carrefour | 94,454.5 | 1,784.3 |

SOURCE: http://money.cnn.com/magazines/fortune/global500/2006/full_list/.

in the United States, and they have been growing at a rate of 12 percent a year since 1987.[2]

Indeed, most organizations now function in the global economy. Thus U.S. businesses are entering international markets at the same time foreign companies are entering the U.S. market.

What is behind the trend toward expansion into global markets? Companies are attempting to gain a competitive advantage, which can be provided by international expansion in a number of ways. First, these countries are new markets with large numbers of potential customers. For companies that are producing below their capacity, they provide a means of increasing sales and profits. Second, many companies are building production facilities in other countries as a means of capitalizing on those countries' lower labor costs for relatively unskilled jobs. For example, many of the *maquiladora* plants (foreign-owned plants located in Mexico that employ Mexican laborers) provide low-skilled labor at considerably lower cost than in the United States. In 1999, the average manufacturing hourly wage in Mexico was $2.12.[3] Third, the rapid increase in telecommunications and information technology enables work to be done more rapidly, efficiently, and effectively around the globe. With the best college graduates available for $2.00 an hour in India versus $12–18 an hour in the United States, companies can hire the best talent (resulting in better work) at a lower cost. And because their day is our night, work done in the United States can be handed off to those in India for a 24/7 work process.[4]

According to a survey of almost 3,000 line executives and HR executives from 12 countries, international competition is the number one factor affecting HRM. The globalization of business structures and globalization of the economy ranked fourth and fifth, respectively.[5] Deciding whether to enter foreign markets and whether to develop plants or other facilities in other countries, however, is no simple matter, and many human resource issues surface.

This chapter discusses the human resource issues that must be addressed to gain competitive advantage in a world of global competition. This is not a chapter on international human resource management (the specific HRM policies and programs companies use to manage human resources across international boundaries).[6] The chapter focuses instead on the key factors that must be addressed to strategically manage human resources in an international context. We discuss some of the important events that have increased the global nature of business over the past few years. We then identify some of the factors that are most important to HRM in global environments. Finally, we examine particular issues related to managing expatriate managers. These issues present unique opportunities for firms to gain competitive advantage.

## Current Global Changes

**LOI**
Identify the Recent Changes That Have Caused Companies to Expand into International Markets.

Several recent social and political changes have accelerated the movement toward international competition. The effects of these changes have been profound and far-reaching. Many are still evolving. In this section we discuss the major developments that have accentuated the need for organizations to gain a competitive advantage through effectively managing human resources in a global economy.

### European Economic Community

European countries have managed their economies individually for years. Because of the countries' close geographic proximity, their economies have become intertwined. This created a number of problems for international businesses; for example, the regulations of one country, such as France, might be completely different from those of another country, such as Germany. In response, most of the European countries agreed to participate in the European Economic Community, which began in 1992. The EEC is a confederation of most of the European nations that agree to engage in free trade with one another, with commerce regulated by an overseeing body called the European Commission (EC). Under the EEC, legal regulation in the participating countries has become more, although not completely, uniform. Assuming the EEC's trend toward free trade among members continues, Europe has become one of the largest free markets in the world. In addition, as of 1999, all of the members of the European Economic Community share a common currency, the euro. This ties the members' economic fates even more closely with one another. In addition to the previous 15 EU states, as of May 1, 2004, 10 EU accession states—Cyprus, the Czech Republic, Estonia, Hungary, Latvia, Lithuania, Malta, Poland, Slovakia, and Slovenia—were added to the EU, expanding the economic zone covered by the European Union.

## North American Free Trade Agreement (NAFTA)

NAFTA is an agreement among Canada, the United States, and Mexico that has created a free market even larger than the European Economic Community. The United States and Canada already had a free trade agreement since 1989, but NAFTA brought Mexico into the consortium. The agreement was prompted by Mexico's increasing willingness to open its markets and facilities in an effort to promote economic growth.[7] As previously discussed, the *maquiladora* plants exemplify this trend. In addition, some efforts have been made to expand the membership of NAFTA to other Latin American countries, such as Chile.

NAFTA has increased U.S. investment in Mexico because of Mexico's substantially lower labor costs for low-skilled employees. This has had two effects on employment in the United States. First, many low-skilled jobs went south, decreasing employment opportunities for U.S. citizens who lack higher-level skills. Second, it has increased employment opportunities for Americans with higher-level skills beyond those already being observed.[8]

## The Growth of Asia

An additional global market that is of economic consequence to many firms lies in Asia. Whereas Japan has been a dominant economic force for over 20 years, recently countries such as Singapore, Hong Kong, and Malaysia have become significant economic forces. In addition, China, with its population of over 1 billion and trend toward opening its markets to foreign investors, presents a tremendous potential market for goods. In fact, a consortium of Singaporean companies and governmental agencies has jointly developed with China a huge industrial township in eastern China's Suzhou City that will consist of ready-made factories for sale to foreign companies.[9] Although Asia has recently been the victim of a large-scale economic recession termed the "Asian flu," it is fully expected to regain its stature as an attractive market for products and investment over the next few years.

## General Agreement on Tariffs and Trade (GATT)

GATT is an international framework of rules and principles for reducing trade barriers across countries around the world. It currently consists of over 100 member nations.

The most recent round of GATT negotiations resulted in an agreement to cut tariffs (taxes on imports) by 40 percent, reduce government subsidies to businesses, expand protection of intellectual property such as copyrights and patents, and establish rules for investing and trading in services. It also established the World Trade Organization (WTO) to resolve disputes among GATT members.

These changes—the European Economic Community, NAFTA, the growth of Asia, and GATT—all exemplify events that are pushing companies to compete in a global economy. These developments are opening new markets and new sources of technology and labor in a way that has never been seen in history. However, this era of increasing international competition accentuates the need to manage human resources effectively to gain competitive advantage in a global marketplace. This requires understanding some of the factors that can determine the effectiveness of various HRM practices and approaches.

The market in Asia presents a huge opportunity and will have a significant economic impact in future years.

## Factors Affecting HRM in Global Markets

Companies that enter global markets must recognize that these markets are not simply mirror images of their home country. Countries differ along a number of dimensions that influence the attractiveness of direct foreign investment in each country. These differences determine the economic viability of building an operation in a foreign location, and they have a particularly strong impact on HRM in that operation. Researchers in international management have identified a number of factors that can affect HRM in global markets, and we focus on four factors, as depicted in Figure 15.1: culture, education–human capital, the political–legal system, and the economic system.[10]

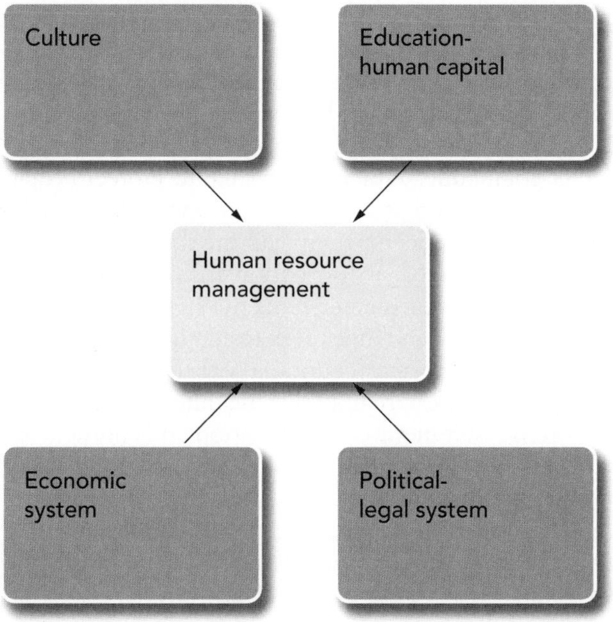


figure 15.1
Factors Affecting Human Resource Management in International Markets

LO2
Discuss the Four Factors That Most Strongly Influence HRM in International Markets.

## Culture

By far the most important factor influencing international HRM is the culture of the country in which a facility is located. Culture is defined as "the set of important assumptions (often unstated) that members of a community share."[11] These assumptions consist of beliefs about the world and how it works and the ideals that are worth striving for.[12]

Culture is important to HRM for two reasons. First, it often determines the other three factors affecting HRM in global markets. Culture can greatly affect a country's laws, in that laws are often the codification of right and wrong as defined by the culture. Culture also affects human capital, because if education is greatly valued by the culture, then members of the community try to increase their human capital. Finally, as we will discuss later, cultures and economic systems are closely intertwined.[13]

However, the most important reason that culture is important to HRM is that it often determines the effectiveness of various HRM practices. Practices found to be effective in the United States may not be effective in a culture that has different beliefs and values.[14] For example, U.S. companies rely heavily on individual performance appraisal, and rewards are tied to individual performance. In Japan, however, individuals are expected to subordinate their wishes and desires to those of the larger group. Thus, individual-based evaluation and incentives are not nearly as effective there and, in fact, are seldom observed among Japanese organizations.[15]

In this section we examine a model that attempts to characterize different cultures. This model illustrates why culture can have a profound influence on HRM.

### Hofstede's Cultural Dimensions

In a classic study of culture, Geert Hofstede identified four dimensions on which various cultures could be classified.[16] In a later study he added a fifth dimension that aids in characterizing cultures.[17] The relative scores for 10 major countries are provided in Table 15.2. **Individualism–collectivism** describes the strength of the relation between an individual and other individuals in the society—that is, the degree to which people act as individuals rather than as members of a group. In individualist cultures, such as the United States, Great Britain, and the Netherlands, people are expected to look after their own interests and the interests of their immediate families. The individual is expected to stand on her own two feet rather than be protected by the group. In collectivist cultures, such as Colombia, Pakistan, and Taiwan, people are expected to look after the interest of the larger community, which is expected to protect people when they are in trouble.

**Individualism–Collectivism**
One of Hofstede's cultural dimensions; describes the strength of the relation between an individual and other individuals in a society.

The second dimension, **power distance,** concerns how a culture deals with hierarchical power relationships—particularly the unequal distribution of power. It describes the degree of inequality among people that is considered to be normal. Cultures with small power distance, such as those of Denmark and Israel, seek to eliminate inequalities in power and wealth as much as possible, whereas countries with large power distances, such as India and the Philippines, seek to maintain those differences.

**Power Distance**
One of Hofstede's cultural dimensions; describes how a culture deals with hierarchical power relationships.

Differences in power distance often result in miscommunication and conflicts between people from different cultures. For example, in Mexico and Japan individuals are always addressed by their titles (Señor Smith or Smith-san, respectively). Individuals from the United States, however, often believe in minimizing power distances by using first names. Although this is perfectly normal, and possibly even advisable in the United States, it can be offensive and a sign of disrespect in other cultures.

**table 15.2**
Cultural Dimension Scores for 10 Countries

| | PD[a] | ID | MA | UA | LT |
|---|---|---|---|---|---|
| United States | 40 L[b] | 91 H | 62 H | 46 L | 29 L |
| Germany | 35 L | 67 H | 66 H | 65 M | 31 M |
| Japan | 54 M | 45 M | 95 H | 92 H | 80 H |
| France | 68 H | 71 H | 43 M | 86 H | 30[c] L |
| Netherlands | 38 L | 80 H | 14 L | 53 M | 44 M |
| Hong Kong | 68 H | 25 L | 57 H | 29 L | 96 H |
| Indonesia | 78 H | 14 L | 46 M | 48 L | 25[c] L |
| West Africa | 77 H | 20 L | 46 M | 54 M | 16 L |
| Russia | 95[c] H | 50[c] M | 40[c] L | 90[c] H | 10[c] L |
| China | 80[c] H | 20[c] L | 50[c] M | 60[c] M | 118 H |

[a]PD = power distance; ID = individualism; MA = masculinity; UA = uncertainty avoidance; LT = long-term orientation.

[b]H = top third; M = medium third; L = bottom third (among 53 countries and regions for the first four dimensions; among 23 countries for the fifth).

[c]Estimated.

SOURCE: From *Academy of Management Executive* by G. Hofstede. Copyright © 1993 by Academy of Management. Reproduced with permission of Academy of Management via Copyright Clearance Center.

The third dimension, **uncertainty avoidance,** describes how cultures seek to deal with the fact that the future is not perfectly predictable. It is defined as the degree to which people in a culture prefer structured over unstructured situations. Some cultures, such as those of Singapore and Jamaica, have weak uncertainty avoidance. They socialize individuals to accept this uncertainty and take each day as it comes. People from these cultures tend to be rather easygoing and flexible regarding different views. Other cultures, such as those of Greece and Portugal, socialize their people to seek security through technology, law, and religion. Thus these cultures provide clear rules as to how one should behave.

**Uncertainty Avoidance**
One of Hofstede's cultural dimensions; describes how cultures seek to deal with an unpredictable future.

The **masculinity–femininity** dimension describes the division of roles between the sexes within a society. In "masculine" cultures, such as those of Germany and Japan, what are considered traditionally masculine values—showing off, achieving something visible, and making money—permeate the society. These societies stress assertiveness, performance, success, and competition. "Feminine" cultures, such as those of Sweden and Norway, promote values that have been traditionally regarded as feminine, such as putting relationships before money, helping others, and preserving the environment. These cultures stress service, care for the weak, and solidarity.

**Masculinity–Femininity Dimension**
One of Hofstede's cultural dimensions; describes the division of roles between the sexes within a society.

Finally, the fifth dimension comes from the philosophy of the Far East and is referred to as the **long-term–short-term orientation.** Cultures high on the long-term orientation focus on the future and hold values in the present that will not necessarily provide an immediate benefit, such as thrift (saving) and persistence. Hofstede found that many Far Eastern countries such as Japan and China have a long-term orientation. Short-term orientations, on the other hand, are found in the United States, Russia, and West Africa. These cultures are oriented toward the past and present and promote respect for tradition and for fulfilling social obligations.

**Long-Term–Short-Term Orientation**
One of Hofstede's cultural dimensions; describes how a culture balances immediate benefits with future rewards.

The current Japanese criticism of management practices in the United States illustrates the differences in long-term–short-term orientation. Japanese managers, traditionally exhibiting a long-term orientation, engage in 5- to 10-year planning. This leads them to criticize U.S. managers, who are traditionally much more short-term in orientation because their planning often consists of quarterly to yearly time horizons.

These five dimensions help us understand the potential problems of managing employees from different cultures. Later in this chapter we will explore how these cultural dimensions affect the acceptability and utility of various HRM practices. However, it is important to note that these differences can have a profound influence on whether a company chooses to enter a given country. One interesting finding of Hofstede's research was the impact of culture on a country's economic health. He found that countries with individualist cultures were more wealthy. Collectivist cultures with high power distance were all poor.[18] Cultures seem to affect a country's economy through their promotion of individual work ethics and incentives for individuals to increase their human capital. Figure 15.2 maps the countries Hofstede studied on the two characteristics of individualism–collectivism and economic success.

## Implications of Culture for HRM

Cultures have an important impact on approaches to managing people. As we discuss later, the culture can strongly affect the education–human capital of a country, the political–legal system, and the economic system. As Hofstede found, culture also has a profound impact on a country's economic health by promoting certain values that either aid or inhibit economic growth.

More important to this discussion, however, is that cultural characteristics influence the ways managers behave in relation to subordinates, as well as the perceptions of the appropriateness of various HRM practices. First, cultures differ strongly on such things as how subordinates expect leaders to lead, how decisions are handled within the hierarchy, and (most important) what motivates individuals. For example, in Germany, managers achieve their status by demonstrating technical skills, so employees look to them to assign their tasks and resolve technical problems. In the Netherlands, on the other hand, managers focus on seeking consensus among all parties and must engage in an open-ended exchange of views and balancing of interests.[19] Clearly, these methods have different implications for selecting and training managers in the different countries.

Second, cultures strongly influence the appropriateness of HRM practices. For example, as previously discussed, the extent to which a culture promotes an individualistic versus a collectivist orientation will impact the effectiveness of individually oriented human resource management systems. In the United States, companies often focus selection systems on assessing an individual's technical skill and, to a lesser extent, social skills. In collectivist cultures, on the other hand, companies focus more on assessing how well an individual will perform as a member of the work group.

Similarly, cultures can influence compensation systems. Individualistic cultures such as those found in the United States often exhibit great differences between the highest- and lowest-paid individuals in an organization, with the highest-paid individual often receiving 200 times the salary of the lowest. Collectivist cultures, on the other hand, tend to have much flatter salary structures, with the top-paid individual receiving only about 20 times the overall pay of the lowest-paid one.

Cultural differences can affect the communication and coordination processes in organizations. Collectivist cultures, as well as those with less of an authoritarian orientation, value group decision making and participative management practices more highly than do individualistic cultures. When a person raised in an individualistic culture must work closely with those from a collectivist culture, communication problems and conflicts often appear. Much of the emphasis on "cultural diversity" programs in organizations focuses on understanding the cultures of others in order to better communicate with them.

figure 15.2

The Position of the Studied Countries on Their Individualism Index (IDV) versus Their 1970 National Wealth

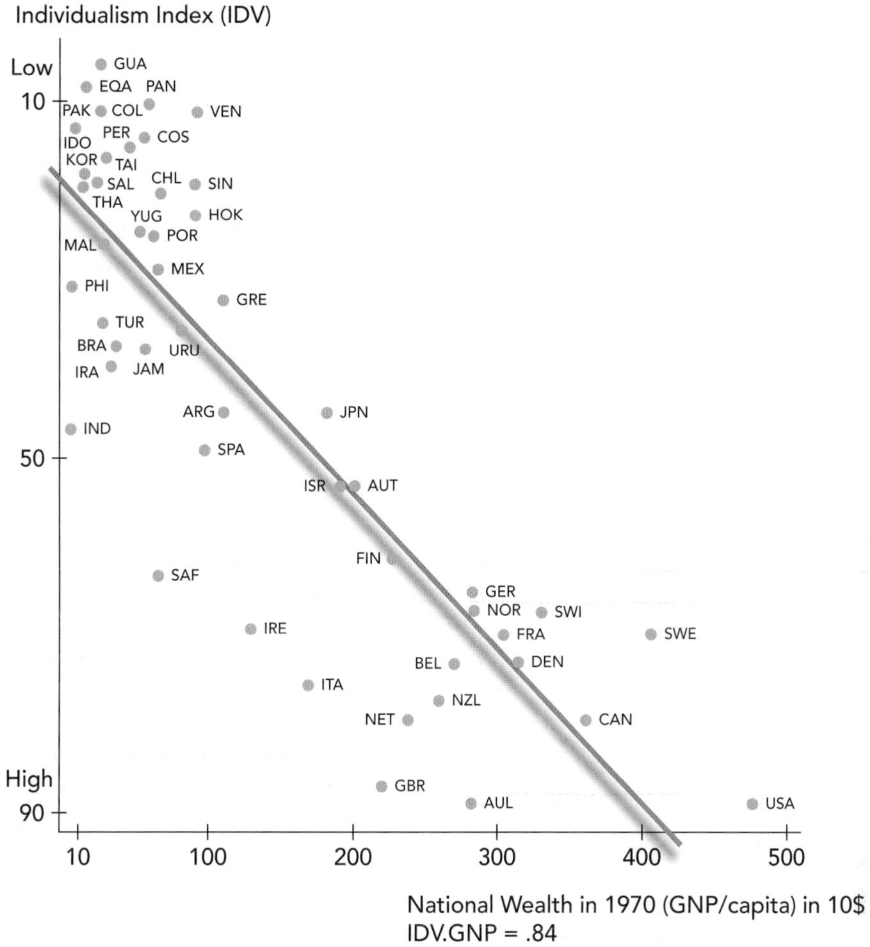


| | | | | | | | |
|---|---|---|---|---|---|---|---|
| ARG | Argentina | FIN | Finland | KOR | South Korea | SWE | Sweden |
| AUL | Australia | FRA | France | MAL | Malaysia | SWI | Switzerland |
| AUT | Austria | GBR | Great Britain | MEX | Mexico | TAI | Taiwan |
| BEL | Belgium | GER | Germany | NET | Netherlands | THA | Thailand |
| BRA | Brazil | GRE | Greece | NOR | Norway | TUR | Turkey |
| CAN | Canada | GUA | Guatemala | NZL | New Zealand | URU | Uruguay |
| CHL | Chile | HOK | Hong Kong | PAK | Pakistan | USA | United States |
| COL | Colombia | IDO | Indonesia | PAN | Panama | VEN | Venezuela |
| COS | Costa Rica | IND | India | PER | Peru | WAF | West Africa (Nigeria, Ghana, Sierra Leone) |
| DEN | Denmark | IRA | Iran | PHI | Philippines | YUG | Yugoslavia |
| EAF | East Africa (Kenya, Ethiopia, Zambia) | IRE | Ireland | POR | Portugal | | |
| | | ISR | Israel | SAF | South Africa | | |
| | | ITA | Italy | SAL | El Salvador | | |
| | | JAM | Jamaica | SIN | Singapore | | |
| EQA | Equador | JPN | Japan | SPA | Spain | | |

SOURCE: G. Hofstede, "The Cultural Relativity of Organizational Practices and Theories," *Journal of International Business Studies* 14, no. 2 (Fall 1983), p. 89. Reprinted with permission of Palgrave Macmillan.

## EVIDENCE-BASED HR

While national culture is important, recent research also suggests that its importance may be overstated. Researchers reexamining Hofstede's original work found that while differences existed across nations, significant cultural differences also existed within nations. They further found that the differences in cultures across organizations within countries was larger than the differences across countries. Their results imply that while one cannot ignore national culture, one must not think that certain HR practices may not be effective simply based on a regard for national culture. People of varying cultural backgrounds within a nation will be drawn to organizations whose cultures better match their individual, as opposed to national, value systems.

SOURCE: B. Gerhart and M. Fang, "National Culture and Human Resource Management: Assumptions and Evidence," *International Journal of Human Resource Management* 16, no. 6 (June 2005), pp. 971–86.

## Education–Human Capital

Def.

A company's potential to find and maintain a qualified workforce is an important consideration in any decision to expand into a foreign market. Thus a country's human capital resources can be an important HRM issue. *Human capital* refers to the productive capabilities of individuals—that is, the knowledge, skills, and experience that have economic value.[20]

Countries differ in their levels of human capital. For example, as discussed in Chapter 1, the United States suffers from a human capital shortage because the jobs being created require skills beyond those of most new entrants into the workforce.[21] In former East Germany, there is an excess of human capital in terms of technical knowledge and skill because of that country's large investment in education. However, East Germany's business schools did not teach management development, so there is a human capital shortage for managerial jobs.[22] Similarly, companies in what used to be West Germany have shifted toward types of production and service that require high-skilled workers; this is creating a human capital shortage for high-skill jobs, yet the unemployment rate remains high because of a large number of low-skilled workers.[23] However, the high skills and low wages of workers in many countries make their labor forces quite attractive.

A country's human capital is determined by a number of variables. A major variable is the educational opportunities available to the labor force. In the Netherlands, for instance, government funding of school systems allows students to go all the way through graduate school without paying.[24] Similarly, the free education provided to citizens in the former Soviet bloc resulted in high levels of human capital, in spite of the poor infrastructure and economy that resulted from the socialist economic systems. In contrast, some Third World countries, such as Nicaragua and Haiti, have relatively low levels of human capital because of a lack of investment in education.

A country's human capital may profoundly affect a foreign company's desire to locate there or enter that country's market. Countries with low human capital attract facilities that require low skills and low wage levels. This explains why U.S. companies desire to move their currently unionized low-skill–high-wage manufacturing and assembly jobs to Mexico, where they can obtain low-skilled workers for substantially lower wages. Similarly, Japan ships its messy, low-skill work to neighboring countries while maintaining its high-skill work at home.[25] Countries like Mexico, with relatively low levels of human capital, might not be as attractive for operations that consist of more high-skill jobs.

Countries with high human capital are attractive sites for direct foreign investment that creates high-skill jobs. In Ireland, for example, over 25 percent of 18-year-olds attend college, a rate much higher than other European countries. In addition, Ireland's economy supports only 1.1 million jobs for a population of 3.5 million. The combination of high education levels, a strong work ethic, and high unemployment makes the country attractive for foreign firms because of the resulting high productivity and low turnover. The Met Life insurance company set up a facility for Irish workers to analyze medical insurance claims. It has found the high levels of human capital and the high work ethic provide such a competitive advantage that the company is currently looking for other work performed in the United States to be shipped to Ireland. Similarly, as already discussed, the skills of newly graduated technology workers in India are as high or higher than those found among their counterparts in the United States. In addition, because jobs are not as plentiful in India, the worker attitudes are better in many of these locations.[26]

## Political–Legal System

The regulations imposed by a country's legal system can strongly affect HRM. The political–legal system often dictates the requirements for certain HRM practices, such as training, compensation, hiring, firing, and layoffs. In large part, the legal system is an outgrowth of the culture in which it exists. Thus the laws of a particular country often reflect societal norms about what constitutes legitimate behavior.[27]

For example, the United States has led the world in eliminating discrimination in the workplace. Because of the importance this has in our culture, we also have legal safeguards such as equal employment opportunity laws (discussed in Chapter 3) that strongly affect the hiring and firing practices of firms. As a society, we also have strong beliefs regarding the equity of pay systems; thus the Fair Labor Standards Act (discussed in Chapter 11), among other laws and regulations, sets the minimum wage for a variety of jobs. We have regulations that dictate much of the process for negotiation between unions and management. These regulations profoundly affect the ways human resources are managed in the United States.

Similarly, the legal regulations regarding HRM in other countries reflect their societal norms. For example, in Germany employees have a legal right to "codetermination" at the company, plant, and individual levels. At the company level, a firm's employees have direct influence on the important decisions that affect them, such as large investments or new strategies. This is brought about through having employee representatives on the supervisory council (*Aufsichtsrat*). At the plant level, codetermination exists through works councils. These councils have no rights in the economic management of the company, but they can influence HRM policies on such issues as working hours, payment methods, hirings, and transfers. Finally, at the individual level, employees have contractual rights, such as the right to read their personnel files and the right to be informed about how their pay is calculated.[28]

The EEC provides another example of the effects of the political–legal system on HRM. The EEC's Community Charter of December 9, 1989, provides for the fundamental social rights of workers. These rights include freedom of movement, freedom to choose one's occupation and be fairly compensated, guarantee of social protection via Social Security benefits, freedom of association and collective bargaining, equal treatment for men and women, and a safe and healthful work environment, among others.

## Economic System

A country's economic system influences HRM in a number of ways. As previously discussed, a country's culture is integrally tied to its economic system, and these systems provide many of the incentives for developing human capital. In socialist economic systems there are ample opportunities for developing human capital because the education system is free. However, under these systems, there is little economic incentive to develop human capital because there are no monetary rewards for increasing human capital. In addition, in former Soviet bloc countries, an individual's investment in human capital did not always result in a promotion. Rather, it was investment in the Communist Party that led to career advancements.

In capitalist systems the opposite situation exists. There is less opportunity to develop human capital without higher costs. (You have probably observed tuition increases at U.S. universities.) However, those who do invest in their individual human capital, particularly through education, are more able to reap monetary rewards, thus providing more incentive for such investment. In the United States, individuals' salaries usually reflect differences in human capital (high-skill workers receive higher compensation than low-skill workers). In fact, research estimates that an individual's wages increase by between 10 and 16 percent for each additional year of schooling.[29]

In addition to the effects of an economic system on HRM, the health of the system can have an important impact. For example, we referred earlier to lower labor costs in India. In developed countries with a high level of wealth, labor costs tend to be quite high relative to those in developing countries. While labor costs are related to the human capital of a country, they are not perfectly related, as shown by Figure 15.3. This

**figure 15.3**
Average Gross Hourly Compensation in Several Countries

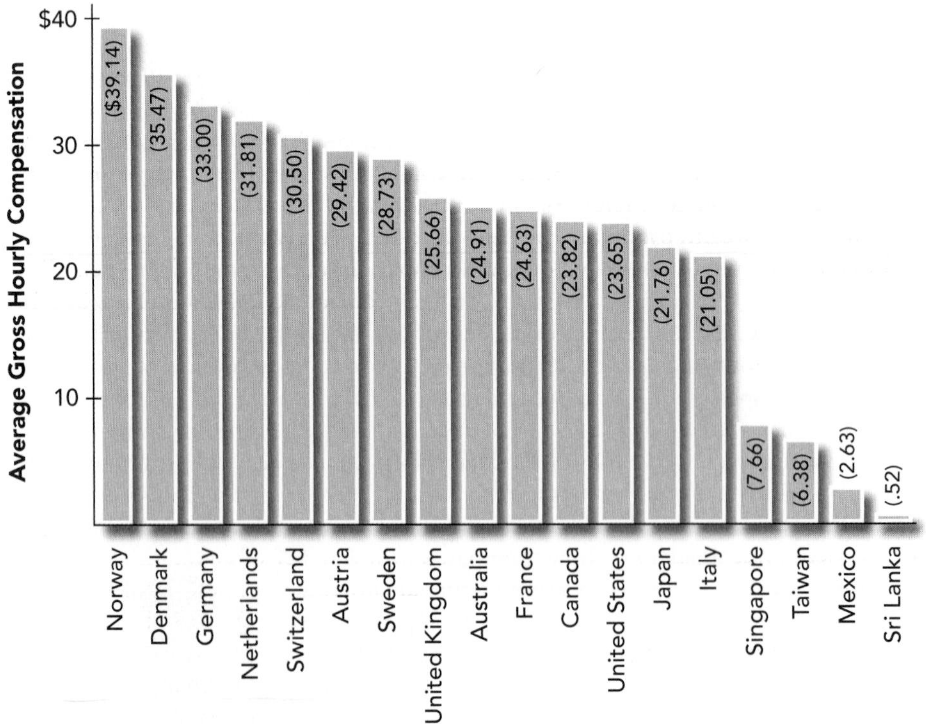


SOURCE: U.S. Bureau of Labor Statistics, ftp.bls.gov/pub/special.requests/ForeignLabor/ind3133naics.txt, 2007.

## COMPETING THROUGH GLOBALIZATION

### VW's 28-Hour Workweek Goes Kaput

While American autoworkers may negotiate over pay and benefits, they probably cannot even begin to understand the "plight" of Volkwagen's workers at its plant in Wolfsberg, Germany.

In 1994, while facing an economic downturn that made 20,000 employees redundant, rather than lay off those employees, VW decided to shorten the workweek instead. By cutting the workweek 20 percent, they were able to cut down on the cost of building a car. However, as the economy came back and VW produced more cars, the 28.8-hour workweek remained. The 28.8 hours compared quite favorably to General Motors' 40-hour workweek and the 35-hour standard at other German automakers.

However, as global competition heats up and new carmakers are making more inroads into the German market, VW had to ask its employees to increase the number of hours worked to 33 for the same weekly paycheck. While this will still be the shortest workweek in the industry, workers are not pleased. Ronald Wachendorf, a 50-year-old mechanic, states "We all knew something like this would come. The general mood among my colleagues is not good."

Before you begin to feel too sorry for them, you should also realize that not only do these workers have short workweeks, but they are also among the highest paid in the industry. In a country that has the highest paid autoworkers at an average of $44 per hour, VW's pay is set at $69 per hour. This compares even more favorably to the $34 per hour in the United States. This lack of empathy spills over to others around the Wolfsberg area. Carmen Stumpf, a bartender at a local watering hole, gets to hear the workers complain about their loss of privilege. "They don't see their situation in relation to others," she says. Rolf Schnellecke, Wolfsberg's mayor, agrees, saying "It was not a very just situation" that Volkswagen employees "worked four days a week and still wound up getting more money" than "normal people" in the town.

SOURCE: S. Wolf and A. Schoenfeld, "VW's 28-Hour Work Week Goes Kaput in Wolfsberg," *The Wall Street Journal,* January 5, 2007. http://online.wsj.com/article/SB116794740942867459.html.

chart provides a good example of the different hourly labor costs for manufacturing jobs in various countries.

An economic system also affects HRM directly through its taxes on compensation packages. Thus the differential labor costs shown in Figure 15.3 do not always reflect the actual take-home pay of employees. Socialist systems are characterized by tax systems that redistribute wealth by taking a higher percentage of a person's income as she moves up the economic ladder. Capitalist systems attempt to reward individuals for their efforts by allowing them to keep more of their earnings. Companies that do business in other countries have to present compensation packages to expatriate managers that are competitive in take-home, rather than gross, pay. HRM responses to these issues affecting expatriate managers will be discussed in more detail later in this chapter.

These differences in economies can have a profound impact on pay systems, particularly among global companies seeking to develop an international compensation and reward system that maintains cost controls while enabling local operations to compete in the war for talent. One recent study examining how compensation managers design these systems indicates that they look at a number of factors including the global firm strategy, the local regulatory/political context, institutions and stakeholders, local markets, and national culture. While they try to learn from the best practices that exist globally, they balance these approaches with the constraints imposed by the local environment.[30] However, not just the hourly labor costs, but also the total cost of employees, affect decisions about where to locate workers. The "Competing through Globalization" box describes the challenges that Volkswagen faces in trying to make its German workforce competitive from a cost perspective.

**Parent Country**
The country in which a company's corporate headquarters is located.

In conclusion, every country varies in terms of its culture, human capital, legal system, and economic systems. These variations directly influence the types of HRM systems that must be developed to accommodate the particular situation. The extent to which these differences affect a company depends on how involved the company is in global markets. In the next sections we discuss important concepts of global business and various levels of global participation, particularly noting how these factors come into play.

# Managing Employees in a Global Context

## Types of International Employees

**LO3**
List the Different Categories of International Employees.

**Host Country**
The country in which the parent country organization seeks to locate or has already located a facility.

**Third Country**
A country other than a host or parent country.

**Expatriate**
An employee sent by his or her company in one country to manage operations in a different country.

Before discussing the levels of global participation, we need to distinguish between parent countries, host countries, and third countries. A **parent country** is the country in which the company's corporate headquarters are located. For example, the United States is the parent country of General Motors. A **host country** is the country in which the parent country organization seeks to locate (or has already located) a facility. Thus Great Britain is a host country for General Motors because GM has operations there. A **third country** is a country other than the host country or parent country, and a company may or may not have a facility there.

There are also different categories of employees. **Expatriate** is the term generally used for employees sent by a company in one country to manage operations in a different country. With the increasing globalization of business, it is now important to distinguish among different types of expatriates. **Parent-country nationals (PCNs)** are employees who were born and live in the parent country. **Host-country nationals (HCNs)** are those employees who were born and raised in the host, as opposed to the parent, country. Finally, **third-country nationals (TCNs)** are employees born in a country other than the parent country and host country but who work in the host country. Thus a manager born and raised in Brazil employed by an organization located in the United States and assigned to manage an operation in Thailand would be considered a TCN.

Research shows that countries differ in their use of various types of international employees. One study revealed that Japanese multinational firms have more ethnocentric HRM policies and practices (they tend to use Japanese expatriate managers more than local host-country nationals) than either European or U.S. firms. This study also found that the use of ethnocentric HRM practices is associated with more HRM problems.[31]

## Levels of Global Participation

**LO4**
Identify the Four Levels of Global Participation and the HRM Issues Faced within Each Level.

We often hear companies referred to as "multinational" or "international." However, it is important to understand the different levels of participation in international markets. This is especially important because as a company becomes more involved in international trade, different types of HRM problems arise. In this section we examine Nancy Adler's categorization of the various levels of international participation from which a company may choose.[32] Figure 15.4 depicts these levels of involvement.

**Parent-Country Nationals (PCNs)**
Employees who were born and live in a parent country.

### Domestic

Most companies begin by operating within a domestic marketplace. For example, an entrepreneur may have an idea for a product that meets a need in the U.S. marketplace. This individual then obtains capital to build a facility that produces the product

figure 15.4
Levels of Global Participation

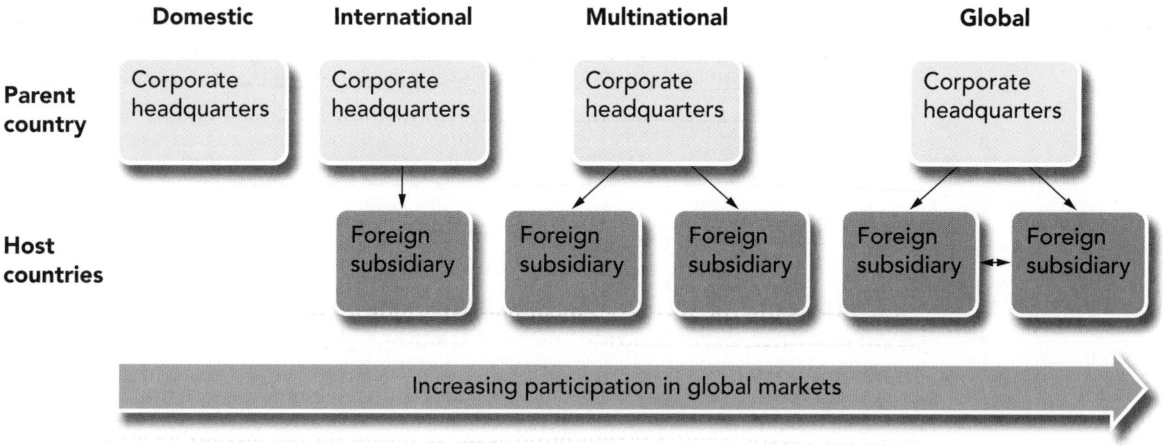


or service in a quantity that meets the needs of a small market niche. This requires recruiting, hiring, training, and compensating a number of individuals who will be involved in the production process, and these individuals are usually drawn from the local labor market. The focus of the selection and training programs is often on the employees' technical competence to perform job-related duties and to some extent on interpersonal skills. In addition, because the company is usually involved in only one labor market, determining the market rate of pay for various jobs is relatively easy.

**Host-Country Nationals (HCNs)**
Employees who were born and raised in the host, not the parent, country.

**Third-Country Nationals (TCNs)**
Employees born in a country other than the parent or host country.

As the product grows in popularity, the owner might choose to build additional facilities in different parts of the country to reduce the costs of transporting the product over large distances. In deciding where to locate these facilities, the owner must consider the attractiveness of the local labor markets. Various parts of the country may have different cultures that make those areas more or less attractive according to the work ethics of the potential employees. Similarly, the human capital in the different areas may vary greatly because of differences in educational systems. Finally, local pay rates may differ. It is for these reasons that the U.S. economy in the past 10 years has experienced a movement of jobs from northern states, which are characterized by strong unions and high labor costs, to the Sunbelt states, which have lower labor costs and are less unionized.

Incidentally, even domestic companies face problems with cultural diversity. In the United States, for example, the representation of women and minorities is increasing within the workforce. These groups come to the workplace with worldviews that differ from those of the traditional white male. Thus we are seeing more and more emphasis on developing systems for managing cultural diversity within single-country organizations, even though the diversity might be on a somewhat smaller scale than the diversity of cultures across national boundaries.[33]

It is important to note that companies functioning at the domestic level face an environment with very similar cultural, human capital, political–legal, and economic situations, although some variation might be observed across states and geographic areas.

## International

As more competitors enter the domestic market, companies face the possibility of losing market share; thus they often seek other markets for their products. This usually requires entering international markets, initially by exporting products but ultimately by building production facilities in other countries. The decision to participate in international competition raises a host of human resource issues. All the problems regarding locating facilities are magnified. One must consider whether a particular location provides an environment where human resources can be successfully acquired and managed.

Now the company faces an entirely different situation with regard to culture, human capital, the political–legal system, and the economic system. For example, the availability of human capital is of utmost importance, and there is a substantially greater variability in human capital between the United States and other countries than there is among the various states in the United States.

A country's legal system may also present HRM problems. For example, France has a relatively high minimum wage, which drives labor costs up. In addition, regulations make it extremely difficult to fire or lay off an employee. In Germany companies are legally required to offer employees influence in the management of the firm. Companies that develop facilities in other countries have to adapt their HRM practices to conform to the host country's laws. This requires the company to gain expertise in the country's HRM legal requirements and knowledge about how to deal with the country's legal system, and it often requires the company to hire one or more HCNs. In fact, some countries legally require companies to hire a certain percentage of HCNs for any foreign-owned subsidiary.

Finally, cultures have to be considered. To the extent that the country's culture is vastly different from that of the parent organization, conflicts, communication problems, and morale problems may occur. Expatriate managers must be trained to identify these cultural differences, and they must be flexible enough to adapt their styles to those of their host country. This requires an extensive selection effort to identify individuals who are capable of adapting to new environments and an extensive training program to ensure that the culture shock is not devastating.

### Multinational

Whereas international companies build one or a few facilities in another country, they become multinational when they build facilities in a number of different countries, attempting to capitalize on lower production and distribution costs in different locations. The lower production costs are gained by shifting production from higher-cost locations to lower-cost locations. For example, some of the major U.S. automakers have plants all over the world. They continue to shift their production from the United States, where labor unions have gained high wages for their members, to *maquiladora* facilities in Mexico, where the wages are substantially lower. Similarly, these companies minimize distribution costs by locating facilities in Europe for manufacturing and assembling automobiles to sell in the European market. They are also now expanding into some of the former Soviet bloc countries to produce automobiles for the European market.

The HRM problems multinational companies face are similar to those international companies face, only magnified. Instead of having to consider only one or two countries' cultural, human capital, legal, and economic systems, the multinational company must address these differences for a large number of countries. This accentuates the need to select managers capable of functioning in a variety of settings, give them necessary training, and provide flexible compensation systems that take into account the different market pay rates, tax systems, and costs of living.

## COMPETING THROUGH SUSTAINABILITY
### CEOs Begin to Embrace Sustainability

Jeff Immelt and Bob Nardelli were both considered potential successors to Jack Welch when he was to retire from GE. Immelt got the job and Nardelli took over as CEO at Home Depot. In spite of the fact that both delivered reasonably good operational results, neither company's stock price grew substantially in the six years that they have been in charge. However, Jeff Immelt sits securely at GE while Bob Nardelli was recently let go. Why? At least part of the reason was how they dealt with stakeholders besides the shareholders.

Mr. Immelt pushed GE into an "eco-imagination" strategy. This strategy seeks to build the internal capability to provide environmentally friendly products and services. GE has grown in the wind power part of the business as well as pushing water purification and desalination. And even in the parts of the business that might not be as "eco-friendly" he has pushed managers to find ways to reduce GE's emissions of greenhouse gases.

Mr. Immelt is not the only CEO embracing sustainability. Wal-Mart CEO Lee Scott has surprised a number of observers with his "green" strategy. Under Scott Wal-Mart has focused on building energy-efficient stores and doing so in a way that minimizes environmental damage to the location. In addition, Wal-Mart has begun offering a number of "green" products such as low-wattage light bulbs. Mr. Scott stated "The generation of people I work with—like A.G. Lafley (of Procter & Gamble) . . . and Jeff Immelt—feel there is a business reason to do this.

Nardelli, on the other hand, complained that the corporate system is under attack. "I am very concerned with the future of business and the capitalistic system in this country," he said. "Somebody has yelled fire in the auditorium. If you stand back, you've got to say that we as a country should share a growing concern as it relates to the capitalist system. The things that got us to where we are are under attack."

SOURCE: A. Murray, "Executive's Fatal Flaw: Failing to Understand the New Demands on CEO's," *The Wall Street Journal*, January 4, 2007, p. A1.

Multinational companies now employ many "inpatriates"—managers from different countries who become part of the corporate headquarters staff. This creates a need to integrate managers from different cultures into the culture of the parent company. In addition, multinational companies now take more expatriates from countries other than the parent country and place them in facilities of other countries. For example, a manager from Scotland, working for a U.S. company, might be assigned to run an operation in South Africa. This practice accentuates the need for cross-cultural training to provide managerial skills for interaction with individuals from different cultures. The "Competing through Sustainability" box describes how a number of U.S. CEOs are beginning to embrace a "green" strategy that looks more like policies favored by European CEOs.

### Global

Many researchers now propose a fourth level of integration: global organizations. Global organizations compete on state-of-the-art, top-quality products and services and do so with the lowest costs possible. Whereas multinational companies attempt to develop identical products distributed worldwide, global companies increasingly emphasize flexibility and mass customization of products to meet the needs of particular clients. Multinational companies are usually driven to locate facilities in a country as a means of reaching that country's market or lowering production costs, and the company must deal with the differences across the countries. Global firms, on the other hand, choose to locate a facility based on the ability to effectively, efficiently, and flexibly produce a product or service and attempt to create synergy through the cultural differences.

This creates the need for HRM systems that encourage flexible production (thus presenting a host of HRM issues). These companies proactively consider the cultures, human capital, political–legal systems, and economic systems to determine where production facilities can be located to provide a competitive advantage. Global companies have multiple headquarters spread across the globe, resulting in less hierarchically structured organizations that emphasize decentralized decision making. This results in the need for human resource systems that recruit, develop, retain, and use managers and executives who are competent transnationally.

**Transnational Scope**
A company's ability to make HRM decisions from an international perspective.

**Transnational Representation**
Reflects the multinational composition of a company's managers.

**Transnational Process**
The extent to which a company's planning and decision-making processes include representatives and ideas from a variety of cultures.

A transnational HRM system is characterized by three attributes.[34] **Transnational scope** refers to the fact that HRM decisions must be made from a global rather than a national or regional perspective. This creates the need to make decisions that balance the need for uniformity (to ensure fair treatment of all employees) with the need for flexibility (to meet the needs of employees in different countries). **Transnational representation** reflects the multinational composition of a company's managers. Global participation does not necessarily ensure that each country is providing managers to the company's ranks. This is a prerequisite if the company is to achieve the next attribute. **Transnational process** refers to the extent to which the company's planning and decision-making processes include representatives and ideas from a variety of cultures. This attribute allows for diverse viewpoints and knowledge associated with different cultures, increasing the quality of decision making.

These three characteristics are necessary for global companies to achieve cultural synergy. Rather than simply integrating foreigners into the domestic organization, a successful transnational company needs managers who will treat managers from other cultures as equals. This synergy can be accomplished only by combining selection, training, appraisal, and compensation systems in such a way that managers have a transnational rather than a parochial orientation. However, a survey of 50 companies in the United States and Canada found that global companies' HRM systems are far less transnational in scope, representation, and process than the companies' strategic planning systems and organizational structures.[35]

In conclusion, entry into international markets creates a host of HRM issues that must be addressed if a company is to gain competitive advantage. Once the choice has been made to compete in a global arena, companies must seek to manage employees who are sent to foreign countries (expatriates and third-country nationals). This causes the need to shift from focusing only on the culture, human capital, political–legal, and economic influences of the host country to examining ways to manage the expatriate managers who must be located there. Selection systems must be developed that allow the company to identify managers capable of functioning in a new culture. These managers must be trained to identify the important aspects of the new culture in which they will live as well as the relevant legal–political and economic systems. Finally, these managers must be compensated to offset the costs of uprooting themselves and their families to move to a new situation vastly different from their previous lives. In the next section we address issues regarding management of expatriates.

**LO5**
Discuss the Ways Companies Attempt to Select, Train, Compensate, and Reintegrate Expatriate Managers.

## Managing Expatriates in Global Markets

We have outlined the major macro-level factors that influence HRM in global markets. These factors can affect a company's decision whether to build facilities in a given country. In addition, if a company does develop such facilities, these factors strongly affect the HRM practices used. However, one important issue that has been recognized over the past few years is the set of problems inherent in selecting, training, compensating, and reintegrating expatriate managers.

According to a recent study by the National Foreign Trade Council (NFTC), there were 250,000 Americans on assignments overseas and that number was expected to increase. In addition, the NFTC estimates that the average one-time cost for relocating an expatriate is $60,000.[36] The importance to the company's profitability of making the right expatriate assignments should not be underestimated. Expatriate managers' average compensation package is approximately $250,000,[37] and the cost of an unsuccessful expatriate assignment (that is, a manager returning early) is approximately $100,000.[38] The failure rate for expatriate assignments among U.S. firms had been estimated at between 15 and 40 percent. However, more recent research suggests that the current figure is much lower. Some recent studies of European multinationals put the rate at 5 percent for most firms. While the failure rate is generally recognized as higher among U.S. multinationals, it is doubtful that the number reaches the 15–40 percent range.[39]

In the final section of the chapter, we discuss the major issues relevant to the management of expatriate managers. These issues cover the selection, training, compensation, and reacculturation of expatriates.

## Selection of Expatriate Managers

One of the major problems in managing expatriate managers is determining which individuals in the organization are most capable of handling an assignment in a different culture. Expatriate managers must have technical competence in the area of operations; otherwise they will be unable to earn the respect of subordinates. However, technical competence has been almost the sole variable used in deciding whom to send on overseas assignments, despite the fact that multiple skills are necessary for successful performance in these assignments.[40]

A successful expatriate manager must be sensitive to the country's cultural norms, flexible enough to adapt to those norms, and strong enough to make it through the inevitable culture shock. In addition, the manager's family must be similarly capable of adapting to the new culture. These adaptive skills have been categorized into three dimensions:[41] (1) the self dimension (the skills that enable a manager to maintain a positive self-image and psychological well-being); (2) the relationship dimension (the skills required to foster relationships with the host-country nationals); and (3) the perception dimension (those skills that enable a manager to accurately perceive and evaluate the host environment). One study of international assignees found that they considered the following five factors to be important in descending order of importance: family situation, flexibility and adaptability, job knowledge and motivation, relational skills, and extracultural openness.[42] Table 15.3 presents a series of considerations and questions to ask potential expatriate managers to assess their ability to adapt to a new cultural environment.

Little evidence suggests that U.S. companies have invested much effort in attempting to make correct expatriate selections. One researcher found that only 5 percent of the firms surveyed administered any tests to determine the degree to which expatriate candidates possessed cross-cultural skills.[43] More recent research reveals that only 35 percent of firms choose expatriates from multiple candidates and that those firms emphasize only technical job-related experience and skills in making these decisions.[44] These findings glaringly demonstrate that U.S. organizations need to improve their success rate in overseas assignments. As discussed in Chapter 6, the technology for assessing individuals' knowledge, skills, and abilities has advanced. The potential for selection testing to decrease the failure rate and productivity problems of U.S. expatriate managers

**table 15.3**

Interview Worksheet for International Candidates

**Motivation**
- Investigate reasons and degree of interest in wanting to be considered.
- Determine desire to work abroad, verified by previous concerns such as personal travel, language training, reading, and association with foreign employees or students.
- Determine whether the candidate has a realistic understanding of what working and living abroad requires.
- Determine the basic attitudes of the spouse toward an overseas assignment.

**Health**
- Determine whether any medical problems of the candidate or his or her family might be critical to the success of the assignment.
- Determine whether he or she is in good physical and mental health, without any foreseeable change.

**Language ability**
- Determine potential for learning a new language.
- Determine any previous language(s) studied or oral ability (judge against language needed on the overseas assignment).
- Determine the ability of the spouse to meet the language requirements.

**Family considerations**
- How many moves has the family made in the past among different cities or parts of the United States?
- What problems were encountered?
- How recent was the last move?
- What is the spouse's goal in this move?
- What are the number of children and the ages of each?
- Has divorce or its potential, or death of a family member, weakened family solidarity?
- Will all the children move? Why or why not?
- What are the location, health, and living arrangements of grandparents and the number of trips normally made to their home each year?
- Are there any special adjustment problems that you would expect?
- How is each member of the family reacting to this possible move?
- Do special educational problems exist within the family?

**Resourcefulness and initiative**
- Is the candidate independent; can he make and stand by his decisions and judgments?
- Does she have the intellectual capacity to deal with several dimensions simultaneously?
- Is he able to reach objectives and produce results with whatever personnel and facilities are available, regardless of the limitations and barriers that might arise?
- Can the candidate operate without a clear definition of responsibility and authority on a foreign assignment?
- Will the candidate be able to explain the aims and company philosophy to the local managers and workers?
- Does she possess sufficient self-discipline and self-confidence to overcome difficulties or handle complex problems?
- Can the candidate work without supervision?
- Can the candidate operate effectively in a foreign environment without normal communications and supporting services?

**Adaptability**
- Is the candidate sensitive to others, open to the opinions of others, cooperative, and able to compromise?
- What are his reactions to new situations, and efforts to understand and appreciate differences?
- Is she culturally sensitive, aware, and able to relate across the culture?
- Does the candidate understand his own culturally derived values?
- How does the candidate react to criticism?
- What is her understanding of the U.S. government system?
- Will he be able to make and develop contacts with peers in the foreign country?
- Does she have patience when dealing with problems?
- Is he resilient; can he bounce back after setbacks?

*(continues)*

**table 15.3**

Interview Worksheet for International Candidates *concluded*

| |
|---|
| **Career planning** |
| • Does the candidate consider the assignment anything other than a temporary overseas trip? |
| • Is the move consistent with her progression and that planned by the company? |
| • Is his career planning realistic? |
| • What is the candidate's basic attitude toward the company? |
| • Is there any history or indication of interpersonal problems with this employee? |
| **Financial** |
| • Are there any current financial and/or legal considerations that might affect the assignment, such as house purchase, children and college expenses, car purchases? |
| • Are financial considerations negative factors? Will undue pressures be brought to bear on the employee or her family as a result of the assignment? |

SOURCE: Reprinted with permission from *Multinational People Management,* pp. 55–57, by D. M. Noer. Copyright © 1989 by the Bureau of National Affairs, Inc., Washington, DC 20037.

seems promising. For instance, recent research has examined the "Big Five" personality dimensions as predictors of expatriate success (remember these from Chapter 6). For instance, one study distinguished between expatriate success as measured by not terminating the assignment and success as measured by supervisory evaluations of the expatriate. The researcher found that agreeableness, emotional stability, and extraversion were negatively related to the desire to terminate the assignment (i.e., they wanted to stay on the assignment longer), and conscientiousness was positively related to supervisory evaluations of the expatriate.[45]

A final issue with regard to expatriate selection is the use of women in expatriate assignments. For a long time U.S. firms believed that women would not be successful managers in countries where women have not traditionally been promoted to management positions (such as in Japan and other Asian countries). However, recent evidence indicates that this is not true. Robin Abrams, an expatriate manager for Apple Computer's Hong Kong office, states that nobody cares whether "you are wearing trousers or a skirt if you have demonstrated core competencies." In fact, some women believe that the novelty of their presence among a group of men increases their credibility with locals. In fact, some research suggests that male and female expatriates can perform equally well in international assignments, regardless of the country's cultural predispositions toward women in management. However, female expatriates self-rate their adjustment lower in countries that have few women in the workforce.[46] Also research has shown that female expatriates were perceived as being effective regardless of the cultural toughness of the host country.[47] And the fact is that female expatriates feel more strongly than their supervisors that prejudice does not limit women's ability to be successful.[48] The "Competing through Technology" box describes how IBM leverages technology to optimally manage its global workforce.

## Training and Development of Expatriates

Once an expatriate manager has been selected, it is necessary to prepare that manager for the upcoming assignment. Because these individuals already have job-related skills, some firms have focused development efforts on cross-cultural training. A review of the cross-cultural training literature found support for the belief that cross-cultural training has an impact on effectiveness.[49] However, in spite of this, cross-cultural training is

## COMPETING THROUGH TECHNOLOGY

### IBM Leverages Technology to Match Employees to Projects

As IBM moves more and more toward building its services capability, it increasingly enters the global labor market, competing against firms such as Wipro and Infosys that have considerably lower labor costs. These companies, based in the developing economy of India, have access to high-quality low-cost software engineering talent that can provide a significant cost advantage over IBM when bidding on projects. How does IBM compete? As you would expect a technology company to . . . through technology.

Certainly IBM is expanding its global footprint to compete with Wipro and Infosys in India. One estimate is that by the end of 2007 IBM will have over 50,000 employees in India, comprising almost one-sixth of its total workforce, and giving India the second highest number of IBM employees behind the United States. However, the global expansion is being aided by the information technology system.

Senior Vice President Bob Moffat has been tasked with finding efficiencies in how IBM can deliver services to clients, and he is doing so by tightening the services supply chain. He launched a project called Professional Marketplace, which is a database of IBM's talent. When complete, it will show the skills, salaries, location, and availability of all of IBM's 250,000 services, software, sales, and distribution employees. The database can ensure that IBM does not send overqualified consultants out on projects that could be filled by qualified consultants that cost less. Given that the system will include their global workforce, it will almost guarantee that if a job can be performed by a lower cost employee from India, Brazil, or China, it will be.

Another project is the Workforce Management Initiative, which resembles an internal Monster.com site. A database with over 33,000 résumés, it enables managers to search for employees with the precise skills required for any given project. For instance, when a health care client needed a consultant with a clinical background, the system was able to identify former registered nurse Lynn Yarbrough almost instantly, rather than the week it would have taken before.

Systems such as these enable IBM to identify the right person with the right skills to put them in the right place at the right time . . . and most importantly, at the right cost.

SOURCES: D. Kirkpatrick, "IBM Shares Its Secrets," *Fortune*, 152, no. 5 (September 5, 2005), pp. 128–33; "IBM: Pinpointing Inside Up-and-Comers," *BusinessWeek*, October 10, 2005, p. 72.

hardly universal. According to one 1995 survey, nearly 40 percent of the respondents offered no cross-cultural preparation to expatriates.[50]

What exactly is emphasized in cross-cultural training programs? The details regarding these programs were discussed in Chapter 7. However, for now, it is important to know that most attempt to create an appreciation of the host country's culture so that expatriates can behave appropriately.[51] This entails emphasizing a few aspects of cultural sensitivity. First, expatriates must be clear about their own cultural background, particularly as it is perceived by the host nationals. With an accurate cultural self-awareness, managers can modify their behavior to accentuate the effective characteristics while minimizing those that are dysfunctional.[52]

Second, expatriates must understand the particular aspects of culture in the new work environment. Although culture is an elusive, almost invisible phenomenon, astute expatriate managers must perceive the culture and adapt their behavior to it. This entails identifying the types of behaviors and interpersonal styles that are considered acceptable in both business meetings and social gatherings. For example, Germans value promptness for meetings to a much greater extent than do Latin Americans. Table 15.4 displays some ways body language conveys different messages in different countries.

**table 15.4**

International Body Language

| COUNTRY | NONVERBAL MESSAGES |
|---|---|
| Argentina | If the waiter approaches pointing to the side of his head and making a spinning gesture with their finger, don't think they've lost it—they're trying to say you have a phone call. |
| Bangladesh | Bursting to go to the toilet? Hold it. It is considered very rude to excuse yourself from the table to use the bathroom. |
| Bolivia | Don't make "the sign of the fig" (thumb protruding between index and middle finger), historically a sign that you couldn't care less—it is very insulting. |
| Bulgaria | Bulgarians nod the head up and down to mean no, not yes. To say yes, a Bulgarian nods the head back and forth. |
| China | In Eastern culture, silence really can be golden. So don't panic if long periods of silence form part of your meeting with Chinese clients. It simply means they are considering your proposal carefully. |
| Egypt | As across the Arab world the left hand is unclean, use your right to accept business cards and to greet someone. Use only your right hand for eating. |
| Fiji | To show respect to your Fijian hosts when addressing them, stand with your arms folded behind your back. |
| France | The French don't like strong handshakes, preferring a short, light grip or air kissing. If your French colleague is seen to be playing an imaginary flute, however, it means he thinks you are not being truthful. |
| Germany | When Germans meet across a large conference table and it is awkward to reach over and shake hands, they will instead rap their knuckles lightly on the table by way of a greeting. |
| Greece | Beware of making the okay sign to Greek colleagues as it signifies bodily orifices. A safer bet is the thumbs-up sign. The thumbs-down, however, is the kind of gesture reserved for when a Greek motorist cuts you off on the highway. |
| Hong Kong | When trying to attract someone's attention, don't use your index finger with palm extended upward. This is how the Cantonese call their dogs. |
| India | Beware of whistling in public—it is the height of rudeness here. |
| Japan | Japan is a real minefield for Western businesspeople, but one that always gets to them is the way the Japanese heartily slurp their noodles at lunch. Far from being rude, it actually shows appreciation of the food in Japanese culture. |
| Jordan | No matter how hungry you are, it is customary to refuse seconds from your host twice before finally accepting a third time. |
| Lebanon | Itchy eyebrow? Don't scratch it. Licking your little finger and brushing it across your eyebrow is provocative. |
| Malaysia | If you find a Malaysian standing with hands on hips before you, you've clearly said something wrong. It means he's livid. |
| Mexico | Mexicans are very tactile and often perform a bizarre handshake whereby, after pressing together the palms, they will slide their hands upward to grasp each other's thumbs. |
| Netherlands | The Dutch may seem open-minded, but if Dutch people tap the underside of their elbow, it means they think you're unreliable. |
| Pakistan | The overt display of a closed fist is an incitement to war. |
| Philippines | The "Roger Moore" is a common greeting here—a quick flash of the eyebrows supersedes the need for handshakes. |
| Russia | The Russians are highly tactile meet and greeters, with bear hugs and kisses direct on the lips commonplace. Don't take this habit to nearby Uzbekistan, however. They'd probably shoot you. |
| Saudi Arabia | If a Saudi man takes another's hand on the street, it's a sign of mutual respect. |
| Samoa | When your new Samoan host offers you a cup of the traditional drink, kava, make sure to deliberately spill a few drops on the ground before taking your first sip. |
| Turkey | Be careful not to lean back on your chair and point the sole of your foot at anyone in a meeting in Istanbul. Pointing with the underside of the foot is highly insulting. |

SOURCES: http://www.businesstravelerusa.com/articles.php?articleID=490 Business Traveler Center; R. Axtell, *Gestures: The Dos and Taboos of Body Language Around the World,* (New York: John Wiley and Sons, 1991); P. Harris and R. Moran, *Managing Cultural Differences,* 3rd ed. (Houston, TX: Gulf Publishing Company, 1991); R. Linowes, "The Japanese Manager's Traumatic Entry into the United States: Understanding the American-Japanese Cultural Divide," *Academy of Management Executive* 7, no. 4 (1993), p. 26; D. Doke, "Perfect Strangers," *HR Magazine,* December 2004, pp. 62–68.

Finally, expatriates must learn to communicate accurately in the new culture. Some firms attempt to use expatriates who speak the language of the host country, and a few provide language training. However, most companies simply assume that the host-country nationals all speak the parent-country's language. Although this assumption might be true, seldom do these nationals speak the parent-country language fluently. Thus expatriate managers must be trained to communicate with others when language barriers exist. Table 15.5 offers some tips for communicating across language barriers.

Effective cross-cultural training helps ease an expatriate's transition to the new work environment. It can also help avoid costly mistakes, such as the expatriate who attempted to bring two bottles of brandy into the Muslim country of Qatar. The brandy was discovered by customs; not only was the expatriate deported, the company was also "disinvited" from the country.[53]

**table 15.5**

Communicating across Language Barriers

**Verbal behavior**

- *Clear, slow speech.* Enunciate each word. Do not use colloquial expressions.
- *Repetition.* Repeat each important idea using different words to explain the same concept.
- *Simple sentences.* Avoid compound, long sentences.
- *Active verbs.* Avoid passive verbs.

**Nonverbal behavior**

- *Visual restatements.* Use as many visual restatements as possible, such as pictures, graphs, tables, and slides.
- *Gestures.* Use more facial and hand gestures to emphasize the meaning of words.
- *Demonstration.* Act out as many themes as possible.
- *Pauses.* Pause more frequently.
- *Summaries.* Hand out written summaries of your verbal presentation.

**Attribution**

- *Silence.* When there is a silence, wait. Do not jump in to fill the silence. The other person is probably just thinking more slowly in the nonnative language or translating.
- *Intelligence.* Do not equate poor grammar and mispronunciation with lack of intelligence; it is usually a sign of second-language use.
- *Differences.* If unsure, assume difference, not similarity.

**Comprehension**

- *Understanding.* Do not just assume that they understand; assume that they do not understand.
- *Checking comprehension.* Have colleagues repeat their understanding of the material back to you. Do not simply ask whether they understand or not. Let them explain what they understand to you.

**Design**

- *Breaks.* Take more frequent breaks. Second-language comprehension is exhausting.
- *Small modules.* Divide the material into smaller modules.
- *Longer time frame.* Allocate more time for each module than usual in a monolingual program.

**Motivation**

- *Encouragement.* Verbally and nonverbally encourage and reinforce speaking by nonnative language participants.
- *Drawing out.* Explicitly draw out marginal and passive participants.
- *Reinforcement.* Do not embarrass novice speakers.

SOURCE: From *International Dimensions of Organizational Behavior,* 2nd ed. by Nancy Adler, pp. 84–85. Copyright © 1991. Reprinted with permission of South-Western, a division of Thomson Learning: www.thomsonrights.com. Fax 800-730-2215.

## Compensation of Expatriates

One of the more troublesome aspects of managing expatriates is determining the compensation package. As previously discussed, these packages average $250,000, but it is necessary to examine the exact breakdown of these packages. Most use a balance sheet approach to determine the total package level. This approach entails developing a total compensation package that equalizes the purchasing power of the expatriate manager with that of employees in similar positions in the home country and provides incentives to offset the inconveniences incurred in the location. Purchasing power includes all of the expenses associated with the expatriate assignment. Expenses include goods and services (food, personal care, clothing, recreation, and transportation), housing (for a principal residence), income taxes (paid to federal and local governments), reserve (savings, payments for benefits, pension contributions), and shipment and storage (costs associated with moving and/or storing personal belongings). A typical balance sheet is shown in Figure 15.5.

As you can see from this figure, the employee starts with a set of costs for taxes, housing, goods and services, and reserve. However, in the host country, these costs are significantly higher. Thus the company must make up the difference between costs in the home and those in the host country, and then provide a premium and/or incentive for the employee to go through the trouble of living in a different environment.

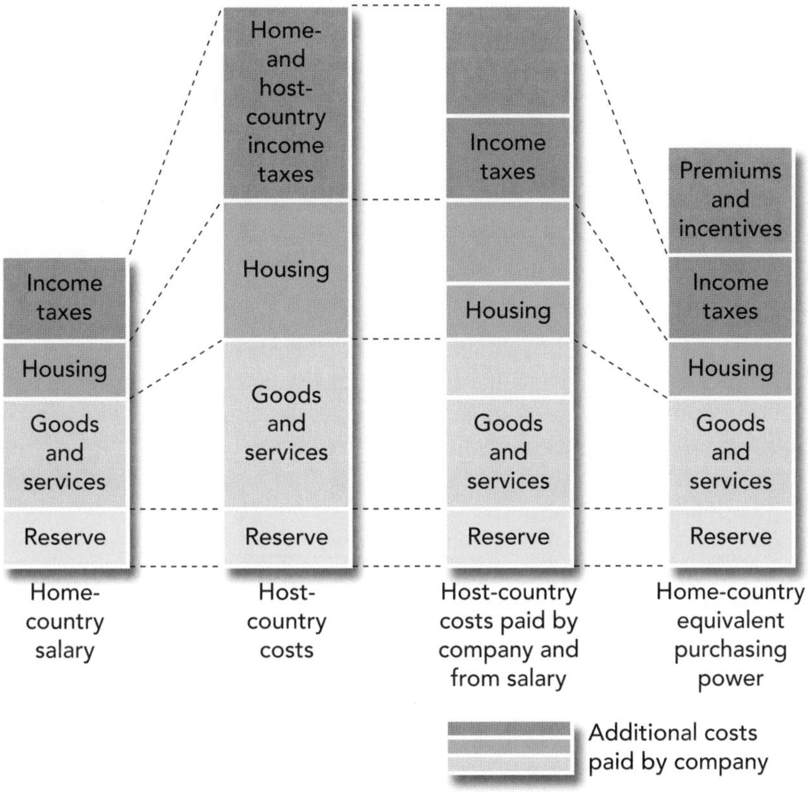


figure 15.5
The Balance Sheet for Determining Expatriate Compensation

SOURCE: C. Reynolds, "Compensation of Overseas Personnel," in J. J. Famularo, ed., *Handbook of Human Resource Administration*, 2nd ed., 1986. Copyright © 1986 The McGraw-Hill Companies, Inc. Reprinted with permission.

**table 15.6**

Average Amount of Allowance as a Percentage of Base Pay

| | |
|---|---|
| Housing (purchase) | 38% |
| Goods and services (cost of living) | 24 |
| Education | 22 |
| Position | 17 |
| Hardship | 13 |

SOURCE: From *HR Magazine* by B. Fitzgerald-Turner. Copyright © 1997 by Society for Human Resource Management. Reproduced with permission of Society for Human Resource Management via Copyright Clearance Center.

Table 15.6 provides an idea of just how much these add-ons can cost for an expatriate. As we see, these combined benefits amount to a 114 percent increase in compensation cost above the base pay.

Total pay packages have four components. First, there is the base salary. Determining the base salary is not a simple matter, however. Fluctuating exchange rates between countries may make an offered salary a raise some of the time, a pay cut at other times. In addition, the base salary may be based on comparable pay in the parent country, or it may be based on the prevailing market rates for the job in the host country. Expatriates are often offered a salary premium beyond that of their present salary as an inducement to accept the expatriate assignment.

Tax equalization allowances are a second component. They are necessary because of countries' different taxation systems in high-tax countries. For example, a senior executive earning $100,000 in Belgium (with a maximum marginal tax rate of 70.8 percent) could cost a company almost $1 million in taxes over five to seven years.[54] Under most tax equalization plans, the company withholds the amount of tax to be paid in the home country, then pays all of the taxes accrued in the host country.

A third component, benefits, presents additional compensation problems. Most of the problems have to do with the transportability of the benefits. For example, if an expatriate contributing to a pension plan in the United States is moved to a different country, does the individual have a new pension in the host country, or should the individual be allowed to contribute to the existing pension in her home country? What about health care systems located in the United States? How does the company ensure that expatriate employees have equal health care coverage? For example, in one company, the different health care plans available resulted in situations where it might cost significantly less to have the employee fly to the United States to have a procedure performed rather than to have it done in the host country. However, the health plans did not allow this alternative.

Finally, allowances are often offered to make the expatriate assignment less unattractive. Cost-of-living allowances are payments that offset the differences in expenditures on day-to-day necessities between the host country and the parent country. For instance, Table 15.7 shows the differences in cost of living among some of the larger international cities. Housing allowances ensure that the expatriate can maintain the same home-country living standard. Education allowances reimburse expatriates for the expense of placing their children in private English-speaking schools. Relocation allowances cover all the expenses of making the actual move to a new country, including transportation to and from the new location, temporary living expenses, and shipping and/or storage of personal possessions.

**table 15.7**

Global Cost of Living Survey: Ranking of Selected Cities among the Top 50 International Cities, 2005

| CITY | INDEX |
|---|---|
| 1 Tokyo, Japan | 134.7 |
| 2 London | 120.3 |
| 9 Hong Kong | 109.5 |
| 13 New York City | 100.0 |
| 14 Dublin | 100.0 |
| 20 Sydney | 95.2 |
| 30 Shanghai | 90.4 |
| 34 Singapore | 88.0 |
| 40 Glasgow | 87.5 |
| 47 Birmingham | 85.8 |

Note: Base city New York = 100.

SOURCE: Mercer Human Resource Consulting, "Worldwide Cost of Living—City Rankings, 2005," *Global Cost of Living Survey*, 2005.

Figure 15.6 illustrates a typical summary sheet for an expatriate manager's compensation package.

The cost of a U.S. expatriate working in another country is approximately three to four times that of a comparable U.S. employee.[55] In addition, "about 38 percent of multinational companies surveyed by KPMG LLP for its 2006 Global Assignment Policies and Practices say overseas assignment programs are 'more generous than they need to be.' "[56] These two facts combined have put pressure on global organizations to rethink their tax equalization strategy and expatriate packages.

## Reacculturation of Expatriates

A final issue of importance to managing expatriates is dealing with the reacculturation process when the managers reenter their home country. Reentry is no simple feat. Culture shock takes place in reverse. The individual has changed, the company has changed, and the culture has changed while the expatriate was overseas. According to one source, 60 to 70 percent of expatriates did not know what their position would be upon their return, and 46 percent ended up with jobs that gave them reduced autonomy and authority.[57] Twenty percent of workers want to leave the company when they return from an overseas assignment, and this presents potentially serious morale and productivity problems.[58] In fact, the most recent estimates are that 25 percent of expatriate managers leave the company within one year of returning from their expatriate assignments.[59] If these repatriates leave, the company has virtually no way to recoup its substantial investment in human capital.[60]

Companies are increasingly making efforts to help expatriates through reacculturation. Two characteristics help in this transition process: communication and validation.[61] *Communication* refers to the extent to which the expatriate receives information and recognizes changes while abroad. The closer the contact with the home organization while abroad, the more proactive, effective, and satisfied the expatriate will be upon reentry. *Validation* refers to the amount of recognition received by the expatriate upon return home. Expatriates who receive recognition from their peers and their bosses for their foreign work and their future potential

figure 15.6
International Assignment Allowance Form

| | | | |
|---|---|---|---|
| **Name** | John H. Doe | **Effective date** | 1 October 2004 |
| **Location of assignment** | Singapore | **Title** | Manager, SLS./Serv. AP/ME |

| **Home base** | **Emp. no.** | **LCA code** | **Tax code** |
|---|---|---|---|
| Houston, Texas | 1234 | 202 | 202 |

**Reason for Change:** International Assignment

| | Old | New |
|---|---|---|
| **Monthly base salary** | | $5,000.00 |
| **Living cost allowance** | | $1,291.00 |
| **Foreign service premium** | | $ 750.00 |
| **Area allowance** | | -0- |
| **Gross monthly salary** | | $7,041.00 |
| **Housing deduction** | | $ 500.00 |
| **Hypothetical tax** | | $ 570.00 |
| **Other** | | |
| **Net monthly salary** | | $5,971.00 |

**Prepared by** ____________ **Date** ____________

**Vice President, Human Resources** ____________ **Date** ____________

contribution to the company have fewer troubles with reentry compared with those who are treated as if they were "out of the loop." Given the tremendous investment that firms make in expatriate employees, usually aimed at providing global experience that will help the company, firms certainly do not want to lose expatriates after their assignments have concluded.

Finally, one research study noted the role of an expatriate manager's expectations about the expatriate assignment in determining repatriation adjustment and job performance. This study found that managers whose job expectations (constraints and demands in terms of volume and performance standards) and nonwork expectations (living and housing conditions) were met exhibited a greater degree of repatriation adjustment and higher levels of job performance.[62] Monsanto has an extensive repatriation program that begins long before the expatriate returns. The program entails providing extensive information regarding the potential culture shock of repatriation and information on how family members, friends, and the office environment might have changed. Then, a few months after returning, expatriate managers hold "debriefing" sessions with several colleagues to help work through difficulties. Monsanto believes that this program provides them with a source of competitive advantage in international assignments.[63]

In sum, a variety of HR practices can support effective expatriation. In general, the selection system must rigorously assess potential expatriates' skills and personalities and even focus on the candidate's spouse. Training should be conducted prior to and during the expatriate assignment, and the assignment itself should be viewed as a career development experience. Effective reward systems must go beyond salary and benefits, and while keeping the employee "whole" and even offering a monetary premium, should also provide access to career development and learning opportunities. Finally, serious efforts should be made to manage the repatriation process.[64] A summary of the key points is provided in Table 15.8.

Summary

**table 15.8**

Human Resource Practices That Support Effective Expatriation

**Staffing and Selection**
- Communicate the value of international assignments for the company's global mission.
- Ensure that those with the highest potential move internationally.
- Provide short-term assignments to increase the pool of employees with international experience.
- Recruit employees who have lived or who were educated abroad.

**Training and Career Development**
- Make international assignment planning a part of the career development process.
- Encourage early international experience.
- Create learning opportunities during the assignment.
- Use international assignments as a leadership development tool.

**Performance Appraisal and Compensation**
- Differentiate performance management based on expatriate roles.
- Align incentives with expatriation objectives.
- Tailor benefits to the expatriate's needs.
- Focus on equality of opportunities, not cash.
- Emphasize rewarding careers rather than short-term outcomes.

**Expatriation and Repatriation Activities**
- Involve the family in the orientation program at the beginning and the end of the assignment.
- Establish mentor relationships between expatriates and executives from the home location.
- Provide support for dual careers.
- Secure opportunities for the returning manager to use knowledge and skills learned while on the international assignment.

SOURCE: P. Evans, V. Pucik, and J. Barsoux, *The Global Challenge: Framework for International Human Resource Management*, 2002. Copyright © 2002 The McGraw-Hill Companies, Inc. Reprinted with permission.

## A Look Back

At the beginning of this chapter we examined the challenge that companies, in particular IBM, face as they seek to build global capability at low cost. Such efforts have potentially negative effects on their existing domestic workforce. How do they deal with these challenges?

IBM is increasing employment for the first time in three years, expecting to boost worldwide headcount by 15,000 to 330,000. Over 2,000 of that net increase will occur in the United States. In addition, IBM recently adopted a new internal-transfer policy which would enable employees who would otherwise be laid off to fill more open positions within IBM. IBM Vice President of Learning Ted Hoff states that this policy will result in fewer offshored jobs, and a person familiar with IBM suggests that IBM may lay off only 2,000 U.S. workers in 2004, down from the previous estimate of 3,000.

Some transfers may mean working for lower pay. The policy allows employees to transfer to "comparable jobs" but "comparable" is defined within IBM as up to a 10 percent pay cut and a shift or schedule change. IBM also says it will pay for retraining, allocating $25 million over the next two years, and give employees threatened by offshoring more time (60 days warning, as opposed to the previous 30 days) to find an in-house job.

Such a move will not only help alleviate insecurity among existing workers, but actually will help the bottom line. Stephanie Moore, an analyst at Forrester Research, suggests that IBM is not alone in this effort as companies increasingly discover some of the problems with offshoring. "Some people say they don't believe it, but the fact is it's less expensive to repurpose the people than it is to fire them and hire different ones."

### Questions

1. How does the issue of offshoring impact existing workforces? What can firms do to alleviate concerns or address potentially negative consequences?
2. Is offshoring the same thing as "global sourcing of talent"? While the strategy hurts U.S. workers, can and should a global company be patriotic in making its talent sourcing decisions?
3. What are some of the ethical concerns with regard to offshoring? Consider this question both from the standpoint of the parent country (e.g., the United States) and from that of the host country (e.g., India).

Please see the Video Case that corresponds to this chapter online at www.mhhe.com/noe6e.

## Summary

Today's organizations are more involved in international commerce than ever before, and the trend will continue. Recent historic events such as the development of the EEC, NAFTA, the economic growth of Asia, and GATT have accelerated the movement toward a global market. Companies competing in the global marketplace require top-quality people to compete successfully. This requires that managers be aware of the many factors that significantly affect HRM in a global environment, such as culture, human capital, and the political–legal and economic systems, and that they understand how these factors come into play in the various levels of global participation. Finally, it requires that they be adept at developing HRM systems that maximize the effectiveness of all human resources, particularly with regard to expatriate managers. Managers cannot overestimate the importance of effectively managing human resources to gain competitive advantage in today's global marketplace.

## Key Terms

Individualism–collectivism, 662
Power distance, 662
Uncertainty avoidance, 663
Masculinity–femininity dimension, 663
Long-term–short-term orientation, 663
Parent country, 670
Host country, 670
Third country, 670
Expatriate, 670
Parent-country nationals (PCNs), 670
Host-country nationals (HCNs), 671
Third-country nationals (TCNs), 671
Transnational scope, 674
Transnational representation, 674
Transnational process, 674

## Discussion Questions

1. What current trends and/or events (besides those mentioned at the outset of the chapter) are responsible for the increased internationalization of the marketplace?
2. According to Hofstede (in Table 15.2), the United States is low on power distance, high on individuality, high on masculinity, low on uncertainty avoidance, and low on long-term orientation. Russia, on the other hand, is high on power distance, moderate on individuality, low on masculinity, high on uncertainty avoidance, and low on long-term orientation. Many U.S. managers are transplanting their own HRM practices into Russia while companies seek to develop operations there. How acceptable and effective do you think the following practices will be and why? (a) Extensive assessments of individual abilities for selection? (b) Individually based appraisal systems? (c) Suggestion systems? (d) Self-managing work teams?
3. The chapter notes that political–legal and economic systems can reflect a country's culture. The former Eastern bloc countries seem to be changing their political–legal and economic systems. Is this change brought on by their cultures, or will culture have an impact on the ability to change these systems? Why?
4. Think of the different levels of global participation. What companies that you are familiar with exhibit the different levels of participation?
5. Think of a time when you had to function in another culture (on a vacation or job). What were the major obstacles you faced, and how did you deal with them? Was this a stressful experience? Why? How can companies help expatriate employees deal with stress?
6. What types of skills do you need to be able to manage in today's global marketplace? Where do you expect to get those skills? What classes and/or experiences will you need?

## Self-Assessment Exercise

The following list includes a number of qualities that have been identified as being associated with success in an expatriate assignment. Rate the degree to which you possess each quality, using the following scale:

1 = very low
2 = low
3 = moderate
4 = high
5 = very high

____ Resourcefulness/resilience
____ Adaptability/flexibility
____ Emotional stability
____ Ability to deal with ambiguity/uncertainty/differences
____ Desire to work with people who are different
____ Cultural empathy/sensitivity
____ Tolerance of others' views, especially when they differ from your own
____ Sensitivity to feelings and attitudes of others
____ Good health and wellness

Add up your total score for the items. The higher your score, the greater your likelihood of success. Qualities that you rated low would be considered weaknesses for an expatriate assignment. Keep in mind that you will also need to be technically competent for the assignment, and your spouse and family (if applicable) must be adaptable and willing to live abroad.

SOURCE: Based on "Rating Scale on Successful Expatriate Qualities," from P. R. Harris and R. T. Moran, *Managing Cultural Differences*, 3rd ed. (Houston: Gulf, 1991), p. 569.

## Exercising Strategy: Terrorism and Global Human Resource Management

Globalization has continued to increase as companies expand their operations in a number of countries, employing an increasingly global workforce. Although this process has resulted in a number of positive outcomes, it has also occasionally presented new types of problems for firms to face.

On September 11, 2001, terrorists with Middle Eastern roots (alleged to be part of Osama bin Laden's al-Qaida network) hijacked four U.S. planes, crashing two of them into the World Trade Center's twin towers and one into the Pentagon (a fourth was crashed in Pennsylvania in a scuffle with passengers). President Bush and U.K. Prime Minister Tony Blair, after their demands that the Taliban government in Afghanistan turn over bin Laden and his leaders were ignored, began military action against that country on October 7, 2001. At the writing of this chapter, we do not know what the ultimate result of this action will be, but we do know that both the terrorist acts and the subsequent war on terrorism have created a host of issues for multinational companies.

First, companies doing business overseas, particularly in Muslim-dominated countries such as the Arab states and Indonesia, must manage their expatriate workforce (particularly U.S. and British citizens) in what has the potential to become hostile territory. These employees fear for their security, and some have asked to return to their home countries.

Second, companies with global workforces must manage across what have become increasingly nationalistic boundaries. Those of us in the United States may view the terrorist attacks as an act of war and our response as being entirely justified. However, those in the Arab world, while not justifying the terrorist attacks, may similarly feel that the military response toward Afghanistan (and later Iraq) is hostile aggression. One executive at a global oil company noted the difficulty in managing a workforce that is approximately 25 percent Arab. He stated that many of the Arab executives have said, "While we know that you are concerned about the events of September 11, you should know that we are equally concerned about the events of October 7 and since."

### Questions

1. How can a global company manage the inevitable conflicts that will arise among individuals from different religious, racial, ethnic, and national groups who must work together within firms? How can these conflicts be overcome to create a productive work environment?
2. What will firms have to do differently in managing expatriates, particularly U.S. or British citizens who are asked to take assignments in predominantly Muslim countries?

## Managing People: From the Pages of *BusinessWeek*

### BusinessWeek The Toyota Way to No. I

**Toyota's top U.S. executive on how it managed to become the world's No. 1 carmaker and why the company can hang on to the top spot** It happened. Toyota passed General Motors in worldwide sales globally in the first quarter. We knew it was coming. It's ikely that the trend will continue and hold up for the entire year, and for years to come.

As the baton gets passed this year, there's a mix of opinions and perspectives in the auto industry about whether Toyota is succeeding fairly. Does its lack of health-care and pension responsibilities, which hobble GM, Ford, and DaimlerChrysler's Chrysler division, allow Toyota an advantage on an unlevel playing field? Does Japan's insular economy, which has made it so difficult for U.S. auto makers to achieve sales in Japan, offer an unfair advantage? Do charges that the Japanese government weakens the yen against the dollar to keep prices down and profit up abroad hold water?

Toyota isn't accepting the No. 1 position comfortably. It makes some of its executives nervous to be the chased, rather than the chaser. Yuki Funo is the chairman and CEO of Toyota Motor Sales USA—the top Japanese executive for Toyota in North America. He recently sat down with *BusinessWeek* Senior Correspondent David Kiley to discuss some of the issues confronting Toyota as it achieves top-dog status. Edited excerpts form their conversation follow:

**Have you been talking among yourselves about protecting your culture, which could be vulnerable to change as you become the world's largest auto maker?**

As far as Toyota culture goes . . . we regard ourselves as Japanese, but more important than the Japanese nature of our company is the "Toyota Way," which is embodied in our concepts and systems.

Toyota Way is more than just a Japanese Way. It's about constant improvement. If it was a Japanese Way only, then we wouldn't have Japanese companies that perform poorly or go into bankruptcy. Toyota doesn't monopolize this idea. And it has to translate beyond Japanese culture to be successful. We employ close to 400,000 worldwide, excluding dealers. If we include dealers, it might be about 1 million.

Of that, a significant number are Japanese. But there are people from every culture working for Toyota that share the concept and this way of doing business. From that viewpoint, growing larger doesn't suggest that we're stepping out of anything that's part of our culture.

**Someone I know says Toyota really believes and nurtures the idea that the company should be able to build a car with no problems or flaws. When this person does business with Ford and GM, it's different, they tell me. Those companies strive to be better, but you don't get the idea they think a perfect car is possible.**

With the Toyota Way . . . one of the key elements is *kaizen:* continuous improvement. There's no end to it. It's a never-ending journey. Respect for people is another important element. Employees. Customers. Suppliers. When it comes to consumers, they demand changes from time to time. We have to always keep watching what the consumer wants. If we base our business on what the customer wants, there's no end to the improvement we can achieve.

**I remember a story related to me by a supplier company: They entered into a contract to supply axles for pickup trucks. It was the first contract his company had with Toyota. He said he was awarded the contract with no discussion of price. It was all based on whether his company's processes and quality were acceptable to Toyota. He was flabbergasted. Is that a common way Toyota does business?**

Toyota's thinking based on the Toyota Way is teamwork with suppliers. This teamwork is going to be a long-lasting relationship. Price is only one element. Trust is a more important element. The relationship is a sharing concept, and should always be win-win. Price is important, too. But trust is perhaps more so. This is an idea that American business schools have come to preach. IBM, General Electric, and other companies talk about how important the mission of the company is. Toyota is only doing intelligently what the business schools are teaching.

In the church when you get married, the priest or minister doesn't ask each partner how much each will get from the other in terms of money. You're asked about how well you get along. What is your commitment to one another? Now, in real-life situations, some companies practice this, and some don't. Some practice this in the United States. Some don't. It's the same in Japan. So there are fantastic achievements in both countries, and there are bankruptcies in both countries. So, it isn't a Japanese issue or an American issue. It's a company-culture issue.

**Growth comes from both new products and boosting volume of existing products. Will your sales growth come more from new products or from existing products in new geographic markets?**

I think 15 percent global market share isn't low, but it's not that high either. There are a lot of opportunities for our product lineup as it is. But now that we have gone into full-size pickups with the new product, we fill in a significant segment.

I think we need to pursue more niches in the future. We had a car at the Detroit Auto Show that could be a replacement for the former Supra sports car. But what's more important is to keep improving the products we have. Like Camry—what consumers want out of Camry is always changing. That's my understanding of how to keep a product strong for the future. We will look after Camry customers by looking after Camry as a product. Same goes with RAV4 and others.

**From time to time, a GM or Ford exec will complain about an uneven playing field: a health-care advantage for Toyota, or monetary policy that favors Japanese products. Do you and your colleagues read that and pay attention?**

We always read the stuff in the newspapers. We know health care is very difficult situation for the Big Three. It's a fact of life that they incur more costs. That's the political and economic history of the United States. A decision was made some years back on what they would give to workers. To some degree, the problem is of their own creation.

Not all the workers in every industry receive as high a medical benefit as in the auto industry. Who decided that? It's their management. They complain sometimes about the currency valuation. It's very difficult. For example, the biggest economy in the world is the United States. Bigger than Japan. It's the Big Three who have an advantage in operating in the biggest economy in the world. For myself, I invested in my English education. If you're born here, there's no need to invest in that. So, that's not a level playing field. It's very difficult to define what a level playing field is.

**You would think that GM and Ford execs, given the fact they all grew up here, should have a better idea of how to design and package a family sedan and minivan, yet**

**these are two product segments where you and Honda have done especially well against the Big Three.**
Increasingly, we're doing the development of our vehicles in the States. The Camry chief engineer is a Japanese man. Why the heck does he develop the most favorite car in the United States? That Camry car doesn't sell in Japan. It's a failure Why? He applies himself to understanding what the customer wants. He visits here and learns things.

If we talk about the level playing field, what is it? He had to overcome such a big handicap being Japanese to create a car that's the top seller in America. It's very difficult to talk about what the level playing field is.

**U.S. companies are saying that while they're improving manufacturing processes, costs, etc. they will never out-Toyota Toyota. They have decided the best way to outdo you as they close the gap on those things is by out designing you. Do you feel a greater pressure to compete on expressive design than you once did?**
Toyota, if you look at the history, our design hasn't been very expressive. If we aren't careful, design could fall into the dull category. Our designers have been seeing design as a critical challenge. If you look at the last 5 to 10 years, designers have done a great job of advancing here.

Look at the FJ Crusier. People look at that and say, "Who designed that? Toyota? I can't believe it." Every organization has strengths and weaknesses. Twenty years ago. Toyota had no confidence in how we would operate manufacturing in the United States. That's why we regard the NUMMI joint-venture plant [where Toyota builds the Matrix and Corolla alongside the Pontiac Vibe] with GM as very beneficial. GM helped us a great deal.

**The corporate advertising you have been running seems to be quite effective. Some of your Detroit rivals resent the fact that you're acting and talking like an American company.**
We have a lot of dialogue about what should be the corporate message. That advertising is what we wanted to accomplish. We knew that many people didn't know what we have been doing in the United States for 50 years. In San Antonio, Texas, for example, we gave a lot of money to the local family-literacy program. We have been giving money to this organization nationally for 20 years. But we had never advertised it. People need to have a clearer and more correct image of Toyota.

**Is your decision to advertise more aggressively a response to those kinds of remarks by people like Ford President of the Americas Mark Fields or GM Vice-Chairman Bob Lutz?**
More important than the political consideration, Toyota is known as a product. No one knows what Toyota is. Toyota is a faceless organization. It doesn't have a human element in the eyes of the consumer. Toyota is just a car.

Toyota is bigger than that though. It's people. We have some 40,000 people working for us in the United States. We need to have more of a face. That we are people. That's the most critical thing we have been trying to achieve.

**Perhaps you would like to star in some ads yourself? DaimlerChrysler Chairman Dieter Zetsche did that last year as "Dr. Z." Do you want to be known as "Dr. T"?**
No We want to show everybody in the company. The heroes. Not one single person.

SOURCE: D. Kiley, "The Toyota Way to No.1," *BusinessWeek*, April 26, 2007.

## Questions

1. As you look at how Toyota has surpassed GM and the other U.S. automakers, in what ways do you think its workforce has provided a competitive advantage?
2. What do you think are the major HR issues that Toyota will face in the future?

# Notes


1. R. M. Kanter, "Transcending Business Boundaries: 12,000 World Managers View Change," *Harvard Business Review*, May–June 1991, pp. 151–64.
2. R. Norton, "Will a Global Slump Hurt the U.S.?" *Fortune*, February 22, 1993, pp. 63–64.
3. U.S. Department of Labor, "International Comparisons of Hourly Compensation Costs for Production Workers in Manufacturing, 1975–1999," Bureau of Labor Statistics news release, www.aoi.gov.
4. D. Kirkpatrick, "The Net Makes It All Easier—Including Exporting U.S. Jobs," *Fortune*, http://www.fortune.com/fortune/print/0,15935,450755,00.html (May 2003).
5. Towers Perrin, *Priorities for Competitive Advantage: A Worldwide Human Resource Study* (Valhalla, NY: Towers Perrin, 1991).
6. R. Schuler, "An Integrative Framework of Strategic International Human Resource Management," *Journal of Management* (1993), pp. 419–60.
7. L. Rubio, "The Rationale for NAFTA: Mexico's New 'Outward Looking' Strategy," *Business Economics* (1991), pp. 12–16.
8. H. Cooper, "Economic Impact of NAFTA: It's a Wash, Experts Say," *The Wall Street Journal*, interactive edition (June 17, 1997).
9. J. Mark, "Suzhou Factories Are Nearly Ready," *Asian Wall Street Journal*, August 14, 1995, p. 8.
10. R. Peiper, *Human Resource Management: An International Comparison* (Berlin: Walter de Gruyter, 1990).
11. V. Sathe, *Culture and Related Corporate Realities* (Homewood, IL: Richard D. Irwin, 1985).
12. M. Rokeach, *Beliefs, Attitudes, and Values* (San Francisco: Jossey-Bass, 1968).
13. L. Harrison, *Who Prospers? How Cultural Values Shape Economic and Political Success* (New York: Free Press, 1992).
14. N. Adler, *International Dimensions of Organizational Behavior*, 2nd ed. (Boston: PWS-Kent, 1991).

15. R. Yates, "Japanese Managers Say They're Adopting Some U.S. Ways," *Chicago Tribune*, February 29, 1992, p. B1.
16. G. Hofstede, "Dimensions of National Cultures in Fifty Countries and Three Regions," in *Expectations in Cross-Cultural Psychology*, eds. J. Deregowski, S. Dziurawiec, and R. C. Annis (Lisse, Netherlands: Swets and Zeitlinger, 1983).
17. G. Hofstede, "Cultural Constraints in Management Theories," *Academy of Management Executive* 7 (1993), pp. 81–90.
18. G. Hofstede, "The Cultural Relativity of Organizational Theories," *Journal of International Business Studies* 14 (1983), pp. 75–90.
19. G. Hofstede, "Cultural Constraints in Management Theories."
20. S. Snell and J. Dean, "Integrated Manufacturing and Human Resource Management: A Human Capital Perspective," *Academy of Management Journal* 35 (1992), pp. 467–504.
21. W. Johnston and A. Packer, *Workforce 2000: Work and Workers for the Twenty-first Century* (Indianapolis, IN: Hudson Institute, 1988).
22. H. Meyer, "Human Resource Management in the German Democratic Republic: Problems of Availability and the Use of Manpower Potential in the Sphere of the High-Qualification Spectrum in a Retrospective View," in *Human Resource Management: An International Comparison*, ed. R. Peiper (Berlin: Walter de Gruyter, 1990).
23. P. Conrad and R. Peiper, "Human Resource Management in the Federal Republic of Germany," in ibid.
24. N. Adler and S. Bartholomew, "Managing Globally Competent People," *The Executive* 6 (1992), pp. 52–65.
25. B. O'Reilly, "Your New Global Workforce," *Fortune*, December 14, 1992, pp. 52–66.
26. A. Hoffman, "Are Technology Jobs Headed Offshore?" *Monster.com*, http://technology.monster.com/articles/offshore.
27. J. Ledvinka and V. Scardello, *Federal Employment Regulation in Human Resource Management* (Boston: PWS-Kent, 1991).
28. Conrad and Peiper, "Human Resource Management in the Federal Republic of Germany."
29. R. Solow, "Growth with Equity through Investment in Human Capital," The George Seltzer Distinguished Lecture, University of Minnesota.
30. M. Bloom, G. Milkovich, and A. Mitra, "Toward a Model of International Compensation and Rewards: Learning from How Managers Respond to Variations in Local Host Contexts," working paper 00-14 (Center for Advance Human Resource Studies, Cornell University: 2000).
31. R. Kopp, "International Human Resource Policies and Practices in Japanese, European, and United States Multinationals," *Human Resource Management* 33 (1994), pp. 581–99.
32. Adler, *International Dimensions of Organizational Behavior*.
33. S. Jackson and Associates, *Diversity in the Workplace: Human Resource Initiatives* (New York: Guilford Press, 1991).
34. Adler and Bartholomew, "Managing Globally Competent People."
35. Ibid.
36. S. Dolianski, "Are Expats Getting Lost in the Translation?" *Workforce*, February 1997.
37. L. Copeland and L. Griggs, *Going International* (New York: Random House, 1985).
38. K. F. Misa and J. M. Fabriacatore, "Return on Investments of Overseas Personnel," *Financial Executive* 47 (April 1979), pp. 42–46.
39. N. Forster, "The Persistent Myth of High Expatriate Failure Rates: A Reappraisal," *International Journal of Human Resource Management* 8, no. 4 (1997), pp. 414–34.
40. M. Mendenhall, E. Dunbar, and G. R. Oddou, "Expatriate Selection, Training, and Career-Pathing: A Review and Critique," *Human Resource Management* 26 (1987), pp. 331–45.
41. M. Mendenhall and G. Oddou, "The Dimensions of Expatriate Acculturation," *Academy of Management Review* 10 (1985), pp. 39–47.
42. W. Arthur and W. Bennett, "The International Assignee: The Relative Importance of Factors Perceived to Contribute to Success," *Personnel Psychology* 48 (1995), pp. 99–114.
43. R. Tung, "Selecting and Training of Personnel for Overseas Assignments," *Columbia Journal of World Business* 16, no. 2 (1981), pp. 68–78.
44. Moran, Stahl, and Boyer, Inc., *International Human Resource Management* (Boulder, CO: Moran, Stahl, & Boyer, 1987).
45. P. Caligiuri, "The Big Five Personality Characteristics as Predictors of Expatriates' Desire to Terminate the Assignment and Supervisor Rated Performance," *Personnel Psychology* 53 (2000), pp. 67–88.
46. P. Caligiuri and R. Tung, "Comparing the Success of Male and Female Expatriates from a U.S.-based Multinational Company," *International Journal of Human Resource Management* 10, no. 5 (1999), pp. 763–82.
47. L. Stroh, A. Varma, and S. Valy-Durbin, "Why Are Women Left at Home? Are They Unwilling to Go on International Assignments?" *Journal of World Business* 35, no. 3 (2000), pp. 241–55.
48. A. Harzing, *Managing the Multinationals: An International Study of Control Mechanisms* (Cheltenham: Edward Elgar, 1999).
49. J. S. Black and M. Mendenhall, "Cross-Cultural Training Effectiveness: A Review and Theoretical Framework for Future Research," *Academy of Management Review* 15 (1990), pp. 113–36.
50. B. Fitzgerald-Turner, "Myths of Expatriate Life," *HRMagazine* 42, no. 6 (June 1997), pp. 65–74.
51. P. Dowling and R. Schuler, *International Dimensions of Human Resource Management* (Boston: PWS-Kent, 1990).
52. Adler, *International Dimensions of Organizational Behavior*.
53. Dowling and Schuler, *International Dimensions of Human Resource Management*.
54. R. Schuler and P. Dowling, *Survey of ASPA/I Members* (New York: Stern School of Business, New York University, 1988).
55. C. Joinson, "No Returns: Localizing Expats Saves Companies Big Money and Can Be a Smooth Transition with a Little Due Diligence by HR," *HRMagazine* 11, no. 47 (2002), p. 70.
56. J. J. Smith, "Firms Say Expats Getting Too Costly, but Few Willing to Act" (2006), *SHRM Online*, retrieved March 9, 2007, www.shrm.org/global/library_published/subject/nonIC/CMS_018300.asp.
57. C. Solomon, "Repatriation: Up, Down, or Out?" *Personnel Journal* (1995), pp. 28–37.
58. "Workers Sent Overseas Have Adjustment Problems, a New Study Shows," *The Wall Street Journal*, June 19, 1984, p. 1.
59. J. S. Black, "Repatriation: A Comparison of Japanese and American Practices and Results," *Proceedings of the Eastern Academy of Management Bi-annual International Conference* (Hong Kong, 1989), pp. 45–49.
60. J. S. Black, "Coming Home: The Relationship of Expatriate Expectations with Repatriation Adjustment and Job Performance," *Human Relations* 45 (1992), pp. 177–92.
61. Adler, *International Dimensions of Organizational Behavior*.
62. Black, "Coming Home."
63. C. Solomon, "Repatriation: Up, Down, or Out?"
64. P. Evans, V. Pucik, and J. Barsoux, *The Global Challenge: International Human Resource Management* (New York: McGraw-Hill, 2002), p. 137.

16

CHAPTER

# Strategically Managing the HRM Function

## LO LEARNING OBJECTIVES

After reading this chapter, you should be able to:

- **LO1** Describe the roles that HRM plays in firms today and the categories of HRM activities. *page* 694
- **LO2** Discuss how the HRM function can define its mission and market. *page* 697
- **LO3** Explain the approaches to evaluating the effectiveness of HRM practices. *page* 700
- **LO4** Describe the new structures for the HRM function. *page* 706
- **LO5** Describe how outsourcing HRM activities can improve service delivery efficiency and effectiveness. *page* 708
- **LO6** Relate how process reengineering is used to review and redesign HRM practices. *page* 709
- **LO7** Discuss the types of new technologies that can improve the efficiency and effectiveness of HRM. *page* 712
- **LO8** List the competencies the HRM executive needs to become a strategic partner in the company. *page* 721

# Enter the World of Business

## IBM's HR Function Restructures to Support the Business

When Sam Palmisano took over from Lou Gerstner as the CEO of IBM in 2003, he began implementing a radical restructuring of the organization through his Business Transformation Initiative. This called for IBM to create an "on-demand" global supply chain providing customers with software, hardware, business processing, and consulting wherever and whenever they needed it. Today this initiative has positioned IBM with over $90 billion in revenues with over 330,000 employees.

HR has played a critical role in this transformation, led by J. Randall MacDonald, the Senior Vice President of HR. Under his leadership IBM has cut costs, stood up to union drives, and restructured the pension and benefit systems to position IBM more competitively.

However, in December of 2006 MacDonald announced a worldwide, $100 million reorganization of the HR function called "the Workplace Management Initiative (WMI)." This initiative segments the 330,000 employees into three customer sets. The first set consists of executive and technical people, the second managerial talent, and the third the rank and file employees. Within each group there is a separate cross-functional HR team serving that group. As MacDonald says, "Blow it all up is my attitude. Don't think about silos; think about end-to-end process. We'll manage each person within each group as an asset and develop them accordingly. You'll have talent, learning and compensation people all managing people within their assigned levels."

This restructuring is demanded from the strategy of IBM's business. "If I look at a three-year plan and it says we're going to enter new markets, I have to decide what skills we'll need three years from now to compete in these markets," says MacDonald. "I have to look at what existing skills I have that will become obsolete. In three years 22 percent of our workforce will have obsolete skills. Of the 22 percent, 85 percent have fundamental competencies that we can build on to get them ready for the skills we'll need years from now.

"I don't mean to be arrogant about it, but this is leading-edge," says MacDonald. "My team is doing things in the 21st century that nobody else has done. It's the wave of the future."

Source: R. J. Grossman, "IBM's HR Takes a Risk," *HR Magazine*, April 2007, pp. 54–59.

## Introduction

Throughout this book we have emphasized how human resource management practices can help companies gain a competitive advantage. We identified specific practices related to managing the internal and external environment; designing work and measuring work outcomes; and acquiring, developing, and compensating human resources. We have also discussed the best of current research and practice to show how they may contribute to a company's competitive advantage.

As we said in Chapter 1, the role of the HRM function has been evolving over time. As we see in this chapter's opening story, it has now reached a crossroads. Although it began as a purely administrative function, most HR executives now see the function's major role as being much more strategic. However, this evolution has resulted in a misalignment between the skills and capabilities of members of the function and the new requirements placed on it. Virtually every HRM function in top companies is going through a transformation process to create a function that can play this new strategic role while successfully fulfilling its other roles. This transformation process is also going on globally. Managing this process is the subject of this chapter. First we discuss the various activities of the HRM function. Then we examine how to develop a market- or customer-oriented HRM function. We then describe the current structure of most HRM functions. Finally, we explore measurement approaches for assessing the effectiveness of the function.

## Activities of HRM

**LO1**
Describe the Roles That HRM Plays in Firms Today and the Categories of HRM Activities.

To understand the transformation going on in HRM, one must understand HRM activities in terms of their strategic value. One way of classifying these activities is depicted in Figure 16.1. Transactional activities (the day-to-day transactions such as benefits administration, record keeping, and employee services) are low in their strategic value. Traditional activities such as performance management, training, recruiting, selection, compensation, and employee relations are the nuts and bolts of HRM. These activities have moderate strategic value because they often form the practices and systems to ensure strategy execution. Transformational activities create long-term capability and adaptability for the firm. These activities include knowledge management, management development, cultural change, and strategic redirection and renewal. Obviously, these activities comprise the greatest strategic value for the firm.

As we see in the figure, most HRM functions spend the vast majority of their time on transactional activities, with substantially less on traditional and very little on transformational activities. However, virtually all HRM functions, in order to add value to the firm, must increase their efforts in the traditional and transformational activities. To do this, however, requires that HR executives (1) develop a strategy for the HRM function, (2) assess the current effectiveness of the HRM function, and (3) redesign, reengineer, or outsource HRM processes to improve efficiency and effectiveness. These issues will be discussed in the following sections.

## Strategic Management of the HRM Function

In light of the various roles and activities of the HRM function, we can easily see that it is highly unlikely that any function can (or should) effectively deliver on all roles and all activities. Although this is a laudable goal, resource constraints in terms of

figure 16.1

Categories of HRM Activities and Percentages of Time Spent on Them

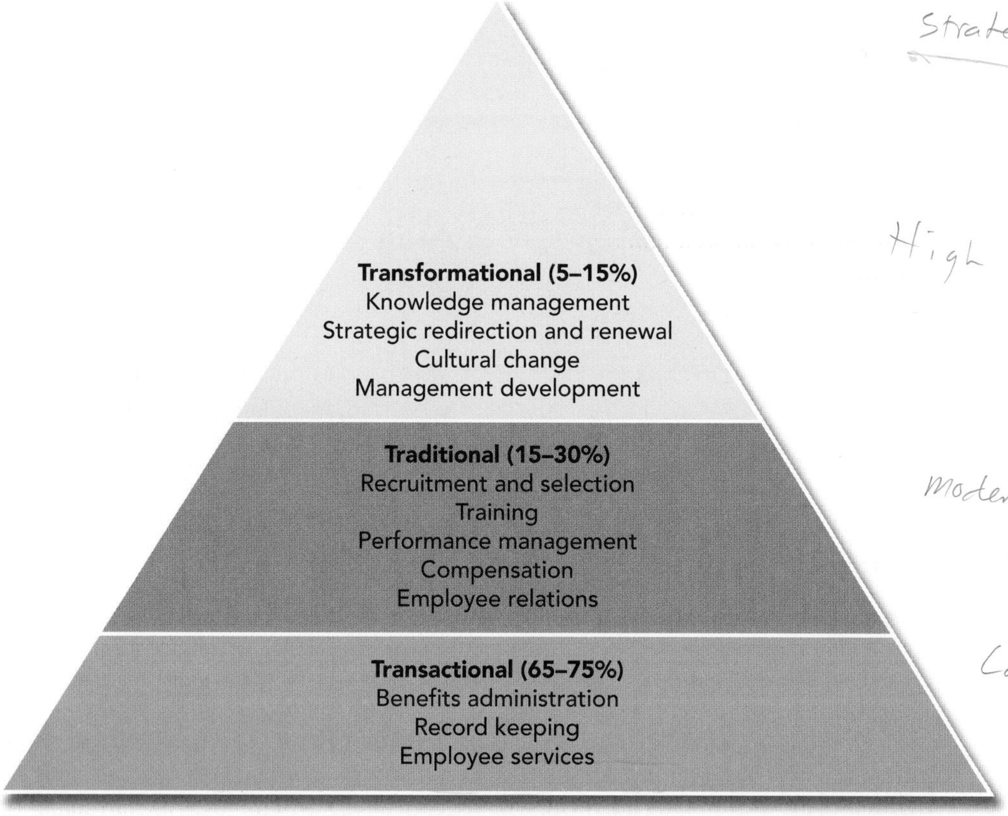


SOURCE: P. Wright, G. McMahan, S. Snell, and B. Gerhart, *Strategic Human Resource Management: Building Human Capital and Organizational Capability.* Technical report. Cornell University, 1998.

time, money, and head count require that the HR executive make strategic choices about where and how to allocate these resources for maximum value to the firm.

Chapter 2 explained the strategic management process that takes place at the organization level and discussed the role of HRM in this process. HRM has been seen as a strategic partner that has input into the formulation of the company's strategy and develops and aligns HRM programs to help implement the strategy. However, for the HRM function to become truly strategic in its orientation, it must view itself as a separate business entity and engage in strategic management in an effort to effectively serve the various internal customers.

In this respect, one recent trend within the field of HRM, consistent with the total quality management philosophy, is for the HR executive to take a customer-oriented approach to implementing the function. In other words, the strategic planning process that takes place at the level of the business can also be performed with the HRM function. HR executives in more progressive U.S. companies have begun to view the HRM function as a strategic business unit and have tried to define that business in terms of their customer base, their customers' needs, and the technologies required to satisfy customers' needs (Figure 16.2). For example, Weyerhaeuser Corporation's human resources department identified 11 characteristics

figure 16.2
Customer-Oriented Perspective of the HRM Function

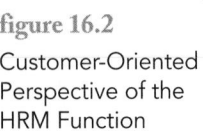

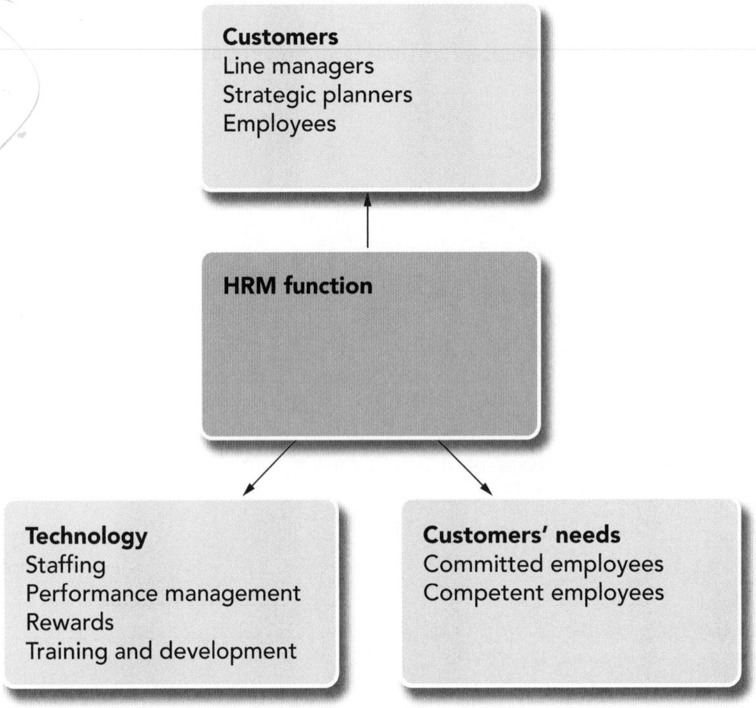


that would describe a quality human resource organization; these are presented in Table 16.1.

A customer orientation is one of the most important changes in the HRM function's attempts to become strategic. It entails first identifying customers. The most obvious example of HRM customers are the line managers who require HRM services. In addition, the strategic planning team is a customer in the sense that it requires the identification, analysis, and recommendations regarding people-oriented business problems. Employees are also HRM customers because the rewards they receive from the employment relationship are determined and/or administered by the HRM department.

**table 16.1**
Characteristics of HRM Quality at Weyerhaeuser Corporation

| |
|---|
| • Human resources products and service are linked to customer requirements. |
| • Customer requirements are translated into internal service applications. |
| • Processes for producing products and services are documented with cost/value relationships understood. |
| • Reliable methods and standardized processes are in place. |
| • Waste and inefficiency are eliminated. |
| • Problem solving and decision making are based on facts and data. |
| • Critical success variables are tracked, displayed, and maintained. |
| • Human resources employees are trained and educated in total quality tools and principles. |
| • Human resource systems have been aligned to total quality implementation strategies. |
| • Human resource managers provide leadership and support to organizations on large-scale organizational change. |
| • Human resource professionals function as "strategic partners" in managing the business and implementing total quality principles. |

In addition, the products of the HRM department must be identified. Line managers want to have high-quality employees committed to the organization. The strategic planning team requires information and recommendations for the planning process as well as programs that support the strategic plan once it has been identified. Employees want compensation and benefit programs that are consistent, adequate, and equitable, and they want fair promotion decisions. At Southwest Airlines, the "People" department administers customer surveys to all clients as they leave the department to measure how well their needs have been satisfied.

Finally, the technologies through which HRM meets customer needs vary depending on the need being satisfied. Selection systems ensure that applicants selected for employment have the necessary knowledge, skills, and abilities to provide value to the organization. Training and development systems meet the needs of both line managers and employees by giving employees development opportunities to ensure they are constantly increasing their human capital and, thus, providing increased value to the company. Performance management systems make clear to employees what is expected of them and assure line managers and strategic planners that employee behavior will be in line with the company's goals. Finally, reward systems similarly benefit all customers (line managers, strategic planners, and employees). These systems assure line managers that employees will use their skills for organizational benefit, and they provide strategic planners with ways to ensure that all employees are acting in ways that will support the strategic plan. Obviously, reward systems provide employees with an equitable return for their investment of skills and effort.

For example, Whirlpool Corporation's HR managers go through a formalized process of identifying their customer, the need/value they satisfy, and the technology used to satisfy the customer. As Whirlpool planned for start-up of a centralized service super-center, the plan called for hiring between 100 and 150 employees to serve as call takers who receive service requests from Whirlpool appliance owners and set up service appointments from these calls. The HR manager in charge of developing a selection system for hiring these call takers identified the operations manager in charge of phone service as the HRM department's customer, the delivery of qualified phone call takers as the need satisfied, and the use of a structured interview and paper-and-pencil tests as the technologies employed. This customer service orientation may be the trend of the future. It provides a means for the HRM function to specifically identify who its customers are, what customers' needs are being met, and how well those needs are being met.

# Building an HR Strategy

## The Basic Process

**LO2** Discuss How the HRM Function Can Define Its Mission and Market.

How do HR functions build their HR strategies? Recent research has examined how HR functions go about the process of building their HR strategies that should support the business strategies. Conducting case studies on 20 different companies, Wright and colleagues describe the generic approach as somewhat consistent with the process for developing a business strategy.[1]

As depicted in Figure 16.3, the function first scans the environment to determine the trends or events that might have an impact on the organization (e.g., future talent shortage, increasing immigrant population, aging of the workforce). It then examines the strategic business issues or needs (e.g., is the company growing, expanding internationally, needing to develop new technologies?). For instance, Figure 16.4 displays

figure 16.3
Basic Process for HR Strategy

figure 16.4
IBM Priorities and the On-Demand Era

**IBM Strategic Priorities on Demand**

1. Delivering business value
2. Offering world class open infrastructure
3. Developing innovative leadership technology
4. Exploiting new profitable growth opportunities
5. Creating brand leadership and a superior customer experience
6. ***Attracting, motivating, and retaining the best talent in our industry***

"An enterprise whose business processes—integrated end-to-end across the company and with key partners, suppliers, and customers—can respond with speed to any customer demand, market opportunity or external threat."

—Sam Palmisano, *IBM Chairman and CEO*

IBM's major business strategy priorities. As can be seen in this example, a clear strategic priority is the attraction, motivation, and retention of talent.

From these issues, the HR strategy team needs to identify the specific people issues that will be critical to address in order for the business to succeed (a potential leadership vacuum, lack of technological expertise, lack of diversity, etc.). All of this information is used in designing the HR strategy, which provides a detailed plan regarding the major priorities and the programs, policies, and processes that must be developed or executed. Finally, this HR strategy is communicated to the relevant parties, both internal and external to the function. Again, IBM's HR strategy, depicted in Figure 16.5,

figure 16.5
IBM HR Strategy

shows how IBM seeks to differentiate itself in the labor market as well as the major priority areas that the HR strategy seeks to address.

## Involving Line Executives

This generic process provides for the potential to involve line executives in a number of ways. Because the HR strategy seeks to address business issues, involving those in charge of running the business can increase the quality of information from which the HR strategy is created. This involvement can occur in a few ways. First, line executives could simply provide input, by either surveying or interviewing them regarding the business challenges and strategy. Second, they could be members of the team that actually develops the HR strategy. Third, once the strategy is developed, they could receive communications with the HR strategy information. Finally, they could have to formally approve the strategy, in essence "signing off" that the HR strategy fully supports the business strategy. The most progressive organizations use all four forms of involvement, asking a large group of executives for input, having one or two executives on the team, communicating the HR strategy broadly to executives, and having the senior executive team formally approve it.

## Characterizing HR Strategies

As you can see in Figure 16.6, the variety of ways that HR strategies can be generated results in various levels of linkage with the business. In general, four categories of this relationship can be identified.

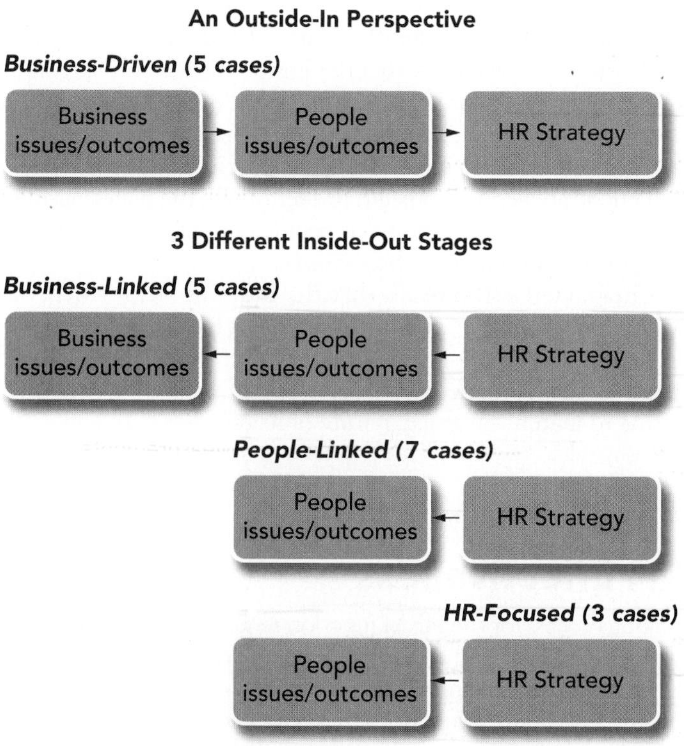


**figure 16.6**

Approaches to Developing an HR Strategy

## COMPETING THROUGH GLOBALIZATION
### Citigroup Matches Human Capital to Revenues

A lot of companies talk about "going global." Usually this means selling or setting up operations overseas. Particularly with U.S.-based companies, going global means sending a bunch of expatriates to the overseas locations to run whatever operations are there. However, if you are Citigroup, and you have one of the largest global operations in the world already, how do you get more global?

In Citi's case, this means building a management team that does not all come from the United States. Recently they announced a management shakeup that one seldom sees from a U.S.-based organization. The reshuffle entailed assigning a large number of their senior management positions in their Fixed Income, Commodities, and Currencies division to overseas business leaders which better reflects the proportion of revenues coming from overseas. After the reassignments, over half of the 21 senior managers will be from outside the United States.

Citigroup estimates that over half of the current revenues from this division come from outside the United States, and that this percentage will continue to grow. Geoff Coley, the co-head of the FICC group, stated "North America is and will always be an important market." But clearly the investment, the proliferation of products, the savings rates, and the development of emerging markets economies are creating huge growth rates in the underlying capital markets business outside North America.

Citi's decisions exemplify a trend to increasingly try to develop diversity in human capital that reflects the diversity of their markets.

SOURCE: P. Larsen and D. Wighton, "Citigroup Shakeup to Favor Executives Outside of New York," *Financial Times*, February 8, 2007.

First, at the most elementary level, "HR-focused" HR functions' articulation of people outcomes stems more from an analysis of what their functions currently do than from an understanding of how those people outcomes relate to the larger business. Second, "people-linked" functions have clearly identified, articulated, and aligned their HR activities around people issues and outcomes, but not business issues and outcomes. Third, "business-linked" HR functions begin with an assessment of what HR is doing, then identify the major people outcomes they should focus on, and, in a few cases, how those might translate into positive business outcomes. Finally, "business-driven" functions have fully developed HR strategies which begin by identifying the major business needs and issues, consider how people fit in and what people outcomes are necessary, and then build HR systems focused on meeting those needs.

The HR strategy must help address the issues that the business faces which will determine its success. As finding, attracting, and retaining talent has become a critical issue, virtually every HR function is addressing this as part of the HR strategy (as can be seen in IBM's HR strategy). The "Competing through Globalization" box discusses how Citigroup is attempting to match the global nature of its business with a globally representative workforce.

## Measuring HRM Effectiveness

**LO3**
Explain the Approaches to Evaluating the Effectiveness of HRM Practices.

The strategic decision-making process for the HRM function requires that decision makers have a good sense of the effectiveness of the current HRM function. This information provides the foundation for decisions regarding which processes, systems, and skills of HR employees need improvement. Often HRM functions that have been heavily involved in transactional activities for a long time tend to lack systems, processes, and skills for delivering state-of-the-art traditional activities and are thoroughly unable to contribute in the transformational arena. Thus diagnosis of the effectiveness of the HRM function provides critical information for its strategic management.

In addition, having good measures of the function's effectiveness provides the following benefits:[2]

- *Marketing the function:* Evaluation is a sign to other managers that the HRM function really cares about the organization as a whole and is trying to support operations, production, marketing, and other functions of the company. Information regarding cost savings and benefits is useful to prove to internal customers that HRM practices contribute to the bottom line. Such information is also useful for gaining additional business for the HRM function.
- *Providing accountability:* Evaluation helps determine whether the HRM function is meeting its objectives and effectively using its budget.

## Approaches for Evaluating Effectiveness

Two approaches are commonly used to evaluate the effectiveness of HRM practices: the audit approach and the analytic approach.

### Audit Approach

The **audit approach** focuses on reviewing the various outcomes of the HRM functional areas. Both key indicators and customer satisfaction measures are typically collected. Table 16.2 lists examples of key indicators and customer satisfaction measures for staffing, equal employment opportunity, compensation, benefits, training, performance management, safety, labor relations, and succession planning. The development of electronic employee databases and information systems has made it much easier to collect, store, and analyze the functional key indicators (more on this later in the chapter) than in the past, when information was kept in file folders.

**Audit Approach**
Type of assessment of HRM effectiveness that involves review of customer satisfaction or key indicators (like turnover rate or average days to fill a position) related to an HRM functional area (such as recruiting or training).

We previously discussed how HRM functions can become much more customer-oriented as part of the strategic management process. If, in fact, the function desires to be more customer-focused, then one important source of effectiveness data can be the customers. Just as firms often survey their customers to determine how effectively the customers feel they are being served, the HRM function can survey its internal customers.

One important internal customer is the employees of the firm. Employees often have both direct contact with the HRM function (through activities such as benefits administration and payroll) and indirect contact with the function through their involvement in activities such as receiving performance appraisals, pay raises, and training programs. Many organizations such as AT&T, Motorola, and General Electric use their regular employee attitude survey as a way to assess the employees as users/customers of the HRM programs and practices.[3] However, the problem with assessing effectiveness only from the employees' perspective is that often they are responding not from the standpoint of the good of the firm, but, rather, from their own individual perspective. For example, employees notoriously and consistently express dissatisfaction with pay level (who doesn't want more money?), but to simply ratchet up pay across the board would put the firm at a serious labor cost disadvantage.

**table 16.2**

Examples of Key Indicators and Customer Satisfaction Measures for HRM Functions

| KEY INDICATORS | CUSTOMER SATISFACTION MEASURES |
|---|---|
| **Staffing** | |
| Average days taken to fill open requisitions<br>Ratio of acceptances to offers made<br>Ratio of minority/women applicants to representation in local labor market<br>Per capita requirement costs<br>Average years of experience/education of hires per job family | Anticipation of personnel needs<br>Timeliness of referring qualified workers to line supervisors<br>Treatment of applicants<br>Skill in handling terminations<br>Adaptability to changing labor market conditions |
| **Equal employment opportunity** | |
| Ratio of EEO grievances to employee population<br>Minority representation by EEO categories<br>Minority turnover rate | Resolution of EEO grievances<br>Day-to-day assistance provided by personnel department in implementing affirmative action plan<br>Aggressive recruitment to identify qualified women and minority applicants |
| **Compensation** | |
| Per capita (average) merit increases<br>Ratio of recommendations for reclassification to number of employees<br>Percentage of overtime hours to straight time<br>Ratio of average salary offers to average salary in community | Fairness of existing job evaluation system in assigning grades and salaries<br>Competitiveness in local labor market<br>Relationship between pay and performance<br>Employee satisfaction with pay |
| **Benefits** | |
| Average unemployment compensation payment (UCP)<br>Average workers' compensation payment (WCP)<br>Benefit cost per payroll dollar<br>Percentage of sick leave to total pay | Promptness in handling claims<br>Fairness and consistency in the application of benefit policies<br>Communication of benefits to employees<br>Assistance provided to line managers in reducing potential for unnecessary claims |
| **Training** | |
| Percentage of employees participating in training programs per job family<br>Percentage of employees receiving tuition refunds<br>Training dollars per employee | Extent to which training programs meet the needs of employees and the company<br>Communication to employees about available training opportunities<br>Quality of introduction/orientation programs |
| **Employee appraisal and development** | |
| Distribution of performance appraisal ratings<br>Appropriate psychometric properties of appraisal forms | Assistance in identifying management potential<br>Organizational development activities provided by HRM department |
| **Succession planning** | |
| Ratio of promotions to number of employees<br>Ratio of open requisitions filled internally to those filled externally | Extent to which promotions are made from within<br>Assistance/counseling provided to employees in career planning |
| **Safety** | |
| Frequency/severity ratio of accidents<br>Safety-related expenses per $1,000 of payroll<br>Plant security losses per square foot (e.g., fires, burglaries) | Assistance to line managers in organizing safety programs<br>Assistance to line managers in identifying potential safety hazards<br>Assistance to line managers in providing a good working environment (lighting, cleanliness, heating, etc.) |

*continues*

**table 16.2 (concluded)**

Examples of Key Indicators and Customer Satisfaction Measures for HRM Functions *concluded*

| KEY INDICATORS | CUSTOMER SATISFACTION MEASURES |
|---|---|
| **Labor relations** | |
| Ratio of grievances by pay plan to number of employees | Assistance provided to line managers in handling grievances |
| Frequency and duration of work stoppages | Efforts to promote a spirit of cooperation in plant |
| Percentage of grievances settled | Efforts to monitor the employee relations climate in plant |
| **Overall effectiveness** | |
| Ratio of personnel staff to employee population | Accuracy and clarity of information provided to managers and employees |
| Turnover rate | Competence and expertise of staff |
| Absenteeism rate | Working relationship between organizations and HRM department |
| Ratio of per capita revenues to per capita cost | |
| Net income per employee | |

SOURCE: Reprinted with permission. Excerpts from Chapter 1.5, "Evaluating Human Resource Effectiveness," pp. 187–227, by Anne S. Tsui and Luis R. Gomez-Mejia, from *Human Resource Management: Evolving Roles and Responsibilities;* edited by Lee Dyer. Copyright © 1988 by The Bureau of National Affairs, Inc., Washington, DC 20037. To order BNA publications call toll free 1-800-960-1220.

Thus, many firms have gone to surveys of top line executives as a better means of assessing the effectiveness of the HRM function. The top-level line executives can see how the systems and practices are impacting both employees and the overall effectiveness of the firm from a strategic standpoint. This can also be useful for determining how well HR employees' perceptions of their function's effectiveness align with the views of their line colleagues. For example, a study of 14 firms revealed that HR executives and line executives agreed on the relative effectiveness of HR's delivery of services such as staffing and training systems (that is, which were most and least effectively delivered) but not on the absolute level of effectiveness. As Figure 16.7 shows, HR executives' ratings of their effectiveness in different roles also diverged significantly from line executives'. In addition, line executives viewed HRM as being significantly less effective with regard to HRM's actual contributions to the firm's overall effectiveness, as we see in Figure 16.8.[4]

## The Analytic Approach

**Analytic Approach**
Type of assessment of HRM effectiveness that involves determining the impact of, or the financial cost and benefits of, a program or practice.

The **analytic approach** focuses on either (1) determining whether the introduction of a program or practice (like a training program or a new compensation system) has the intended effect or (2) estimating the financial costs and benefits resulting from an HRM practice. For example, in Chapter 7 we discussed how companies can determine a training program's impact on learning, behavior, and results. Evaluating a training program is one strategy for determining whether the program works. Typically, in an overall evaluation of effectiveness, we are interested in determining the degree of change associated with the program.

The second strategy involves determining the dollar value of the training program, taking into account all the costs associated with the program. Using this strategy, we are not concerned with how much change occurred but rather with the dollar value

**figure 16.7**
Comparing HR and Line Executives' Evaluations of the Effectiveness of HRM Roles

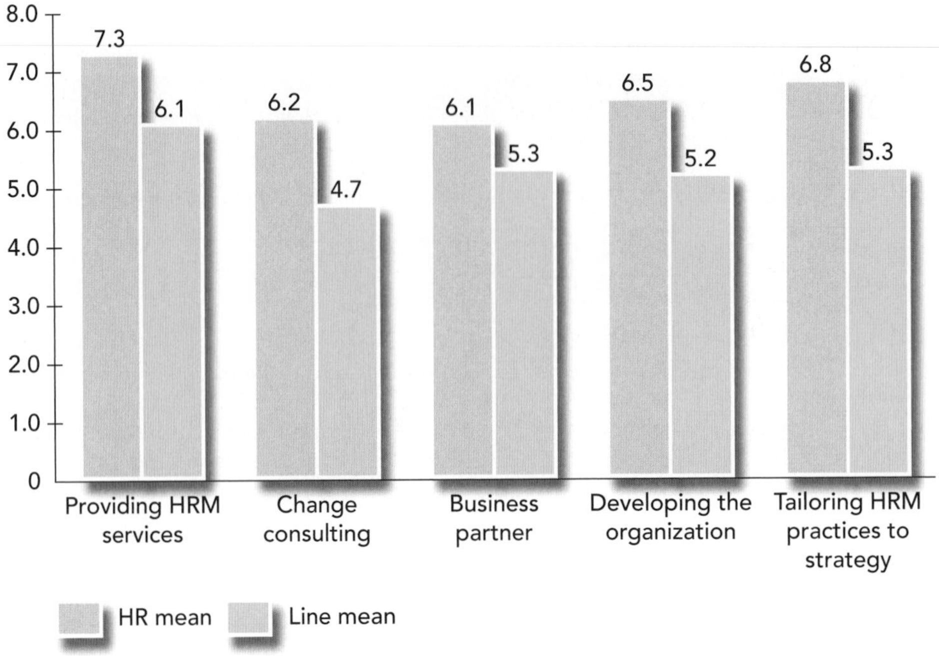


SOURCE: P. Wright, G. McMahan, S. Snell, and B. Gerhart, "Comparing Line and HR Executives' Perceptions of HR Effectiveness: Services, Roles, and Contributions." CAHRS (Center for Advanced Human Resource Studies) working paper 98-29, School of ILR, Cornell University, Ithaca, NY.

**figure 16.8**
Comparing HR and Line Executives' Evaluations of the Effectiveness of HRM Contributions

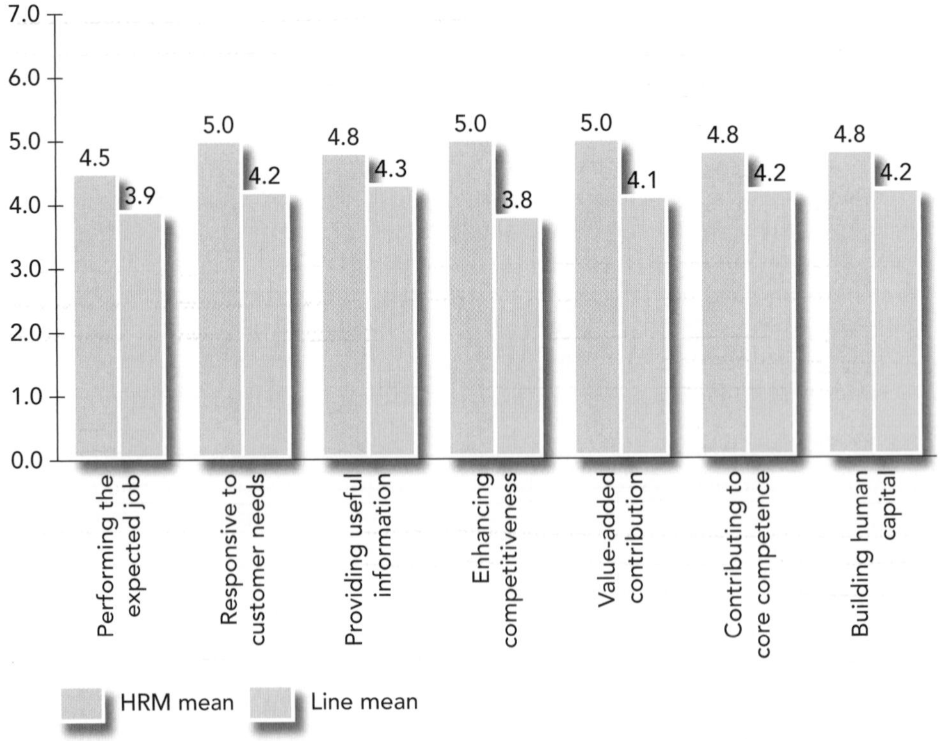


SOURCE: P. Wright, G. McMahan, S. Snell, and B. Gerhart, "Comparing Line and HR Executives' Perceptions of HR Effectiveness: Services, Roles, and Contributions." CAHRS (Center for Advanced Human Resource Studies) working paper 98-29, School of ILR, Cornell University, Ithaca, NY.

**table 16.3**
Types of Cost–Benefit Analysis

**Human resource accounting**
- Capitalization of salary
- Net present value of expected wage payments
- Returns on human assets and human investments

**Utility analysis**
- Turnover costs
- Absenteeism and sick leave costs
- Gains from selection programs
- Impact of positive employee attitudes
- Financial gains of training programs

SOURCE: Based on A. S. Tsui and L. R. Gomez-Mejia, "Evaluating HR Effectiveness," in *Human Resource Management: Evolving Roles and Responsibilities*, ed. L. Dyer (Washington, DC: Bureau of National Affairs, 1988), pp. 1–196.

(costs versus benefits) of the program. Table 16.3 lists the various types of cost–benefit analyses that are done. The human resource accounting approach attempts to place a dollar value on human resources as if they were physical resources (like plant and equipment) or financial resources (like cash). Utility analysis attempts to estimate the financial impact of employee behaviors (such as absenteeism, turnover, job performance, and substance abuse).

For example, wellness programs are a popular HRM program for reducing health care costs through reducing employees' risk of heart disease and cancer. One study evaluated four different types of wellness programs. Part of the evaluation involved determining the costs and benefits associated with the four programs over a three-year period.[5] A different type of wellness program was implemented at each site. Site A instituted a program involving raising employees' awareness of health risks (distributing news articles, blood pressure testing, health education classes). Site B set up a physical fitness facility for employees. Site C raised awareness of health risks and followed up with employees who had identified health risks. Site D provided health education and follow-up counseling and promoted physical competition and health-related events. Table 16.4 shows the effectiveness and cost-effectiveness of the Site C and Site D wellness models.

The analytic approach is more demanding than the audit approach because it requires the detailed use of statistics and finance. A good example of the level of sophistication that can be required for cost–benefit analysis is shown in Table 16.5. This table shows the types of information needed to determine the dollar value of a new selection test for entry-level computer programmers.

**table 16.4**
Effectiveness and Cost-Effectiveness of Two Wellness Programs for Four Cardiovascular Disease Risk Factors

| | SITE C | SITE D |
|---|---|---|
| Annual direct program costs, per employee per year | $30.96 | $38.57 |
| Percentage of cardiovascular disease risks[a] for which risk was moderately reduced or relapse prevented | 48% | 51% |
| Percentage of preceding entry per annual $1 spent per employee | 1.55% | 1.32% |
| Amount spent per 1% of risks reduced or relapse prevented | $.65 | $.76 |

[a]High blood pressure, overweight, smoking, and lack of exercise.

SOURCE: J. C. Erfurt, A. Foote, and M. A. Heirich, "The Cost-Effectiveness of Worksite Wellness Programs," *Personnel Psychology* 45 (1992), p. 22.

**table 16.5**

Example of Analysis Needed to Determine the Dollar Value of a Selection Test

| | |
|---|---|
| **Cost–benefit information** | |
| Current employment | 4,404 |
| Number separating | 618 |
| Number selected | 618 |
| Average tenure | 9.69 years |
| **Test information** | |
| Number of applicants | 1,236 |
| Testing cost per applicant | $10 |
| Total test cost | $12,360 |
| Average test score | .80 SD |
| Test validity | .76 |
| $SD_y$ (per year)[a] | $10,413 |
| **Computation** | |
| Quantity | = Average tenure × Applicants selected |
| | = 9.69 years × 618 applicants |
| | = 5,988 person-years |
| Quality | = Average test score × Test validity × $SD_y$ |
| | = .80 × .76 × $10,413 |
| | = $6,331 per year |
| Utility | = (Quantity × Quality) − Costs |
| | = (5,988 person-year × $6,331 per year) − $12,360 |
| | = $37.9 million |

[a] $SD_y$ = Dollar value of one standard difference in job performance. Approximately 40% of average salary.

SOURCES: From J. W. Boudreau, "Utility Analysis," in *Human Resource Management: Evolving Roles and Responsibilities*, ed. L. Dyer (Washington, DC: Bureau of National Affairs, 1988), p. 150; F. L. Schmidt, J. E. Hunter, R. C. McKenzie, and T. W. Muldrow, "Impact of Valid Selection Procedures on Work-Force Productivity," *Journal of Applied Psychology* 64 (1979), pp. 609–26.

## Improving HRM Effectiveness

**LO4**
Describe the New Structures for the HRM Function.

Once a strategic direction has been established and HRM's effectiveness evaluated, leaders of the HRM function can explore how to improve its effectiveness in contributing to the firm's competitiveness. Returning briefly to Figure 16.1, which depicted the different activities of the HRM function, often the improvement focuses on two aspects of the pyramid. First, within each activity, HRM needs to improve both the efficiency and effectiveness in performing each of the activities. Second, often there is a push to eliminate as much of the transactional work as possible (and some of the traditional work) to free up time and resources to focus more on the higher–value-added transformational work. Redesign of the structure (reporting relationships) and processes (through outsourcing and information technology) enables the function to achieve these goals simultaneously. Figure 16.9 depicts this process.

### Restructuring to Improve HRM Effectiveness

Traditional HRM functions were structured around the basic HRM subfunctions such as staffing, training, compensation, appraisal, and labor relations. Each of these areas had a director who reported to the VP of HRM, who often reported to a VP of finance and administration. However, for the HRM function to truly contribute strategically

figure 16.9
Improving HRM Effectiveness

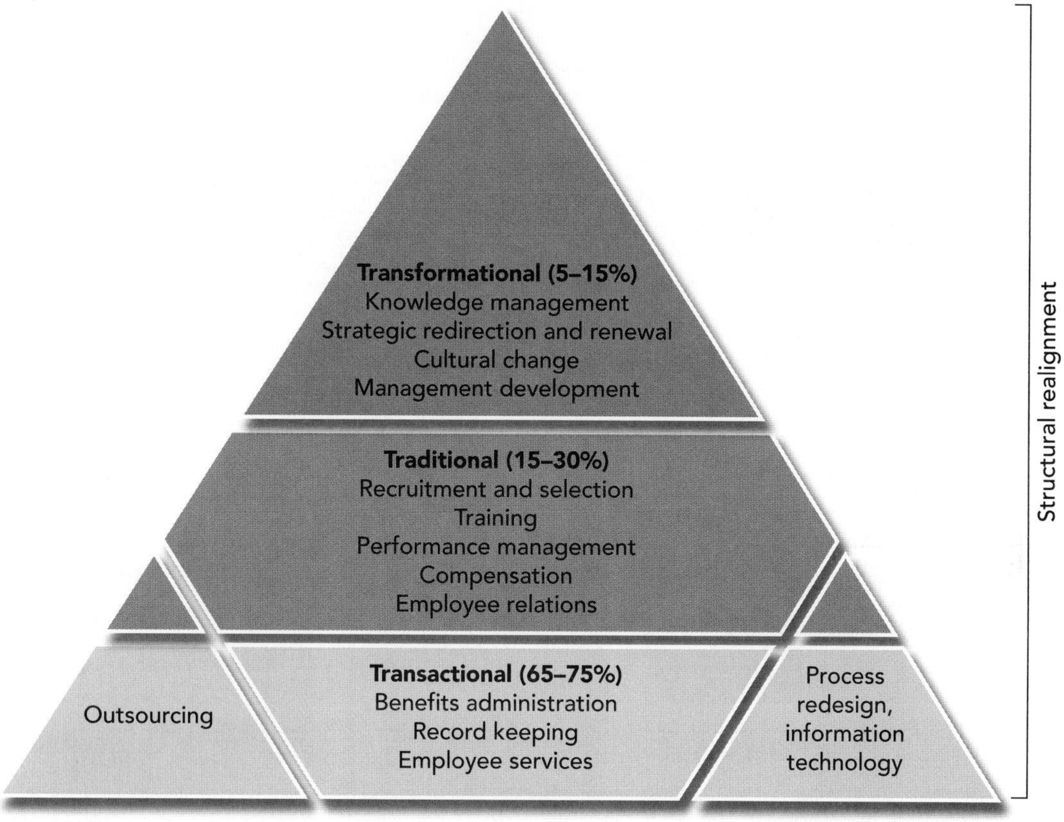


to firm effectiveness, the senior HR person must be part of the top management team (reporting directly to the chief executive officer), and there must be a different structural arrangement within the function itself.

A recent generic structure for the HRM function is depicted in Figure 16.10. As we see, the HRM function effectively is divided into three divisions: the centers for expertise, the field generalists, and the service center.[6] The centers for expertise usually consist of the functional specialists in the traditional areas of HRM such as recruitment, selection, training, and compensation. These individuals ideally act as consultants in the development of state-of-the-art systems and processes for use in the organization. The field generalists consist of the HRM generalists who are assigned to a business unit within the firm. These individuals usually have dual reporting relationships to both the head of the line business and the head of HRM (although the line business tends to take priority). They ideally take responsibility for helping the line executives in their business strategically address people issues, and they ensure that the HRM systems enable the business to execute its strategy. Finally, the service center consists of individuals who ensure that the transactional activities are delivered throughout the organization. These service centers often leverage information technology to efficiently deliver employee services. For example, organizations such as Chevron have created call-in service centers where employees can dial a central number where service center employees are available to answer their questions and process their requests and transactions.

figure 16.10
Old and New Structures for the HRM Organization

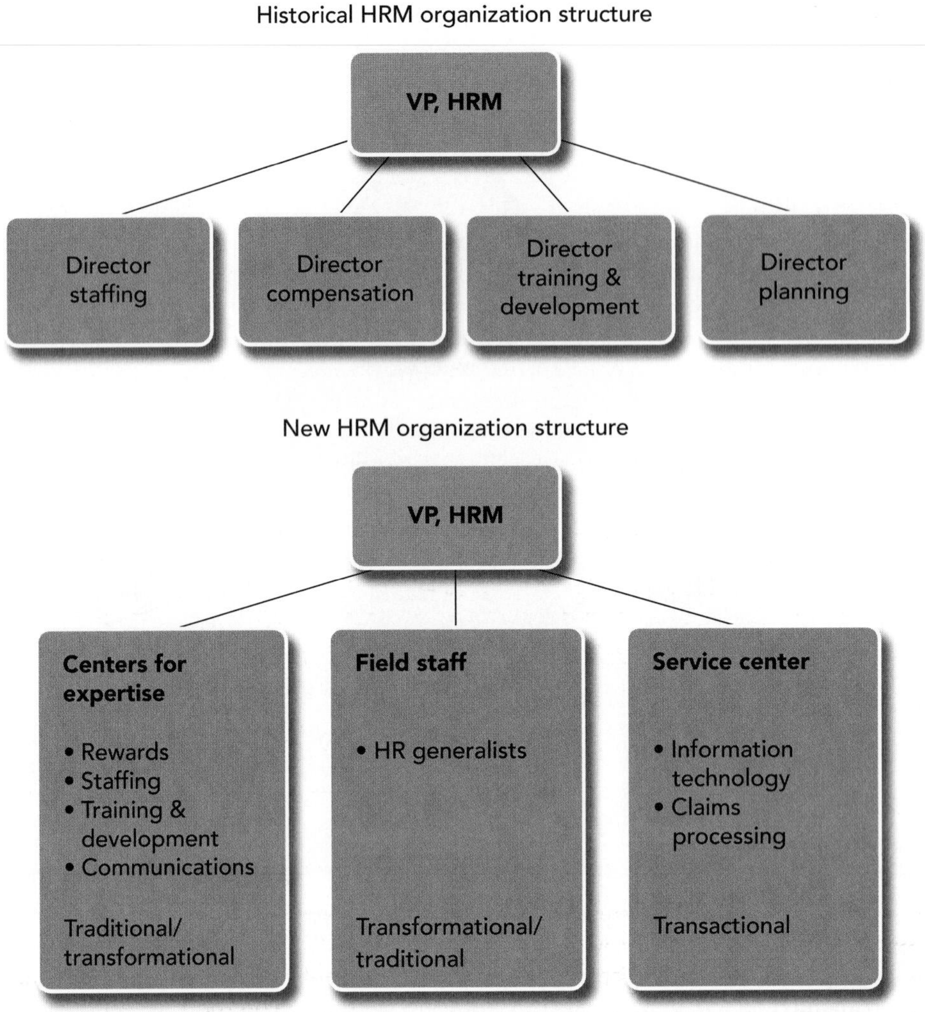


SOURCE: P. Wright, G. McMahan, S. Snell, and B. Gerhart, *Strategic Human Resource Management: Building Human Capital and Organizational Capability.* Technical report. Cornell University, 1998.

Such structural arrangements improve service delivery through specialization. Center for expertise employees can develop current functional skills without being distracted by transactional activities, and generalists can focus on learning the business environment without having to maintain expertise in functional specializations. Finally, service center employees can focus on efficient delivery of basic services across business units.

**LO5**
Describe How Outsourcing HRM Activities Can Improve Service Delivery Efficiency and Effectiveness.

## Outsourcing to Improve HRM Effectiveness

Restructuring the internal HRM function and redesigning the processes represent internal approaches to improving HRM effectiveness. However, increasingly HR executives are seeking to improve the effectiveness of the systems, processes, and services the function delivers through outsourcing. **Outsourcing** entails contracting with an outside vendor to provide a product or service to the firm, as opposed to producing the product using employees within the firm.

**Outsourcing**
An organization's use of an outside organization for a broad set of services.

Why would a firm outsource an HRM activity or service? Usually this is done for one of two reasons: Either the outsourcing partner can provide the service more cheaply than it would cost to do it internally, or the partner can provide it more effectively than it can be performed internally. Early on, firms resorted to outsourcing for efficiency reasons. Why would using an outsourced provider be more efficient than having internal employees provide a service? Usually it is because outsourced providers are specialists who are able to develop extensive expertise that can be leveraged across a number of companies.

For example, consider a relatively small firm that seeks to develop a pension system for employees. To provide this service to employees, the HRM function would need to learn all of the basics of pension law. Then it would need to hire a person with specific expertise in administering a pension system in terms of making sure that employee contributions are withheld and that the correct payouts are made to retired employees. Then the company would have to hire someone with expertise in investing pension funds. If the firm is small, requirements of the pension fund might not fill the time (80 hours per week) of these two new hires. Assume that it takes only 20 total hours a week for these people to do their jobs. The firm would be wasting 60 hours of employee time each week. However, a firm that specializes in providing pension administration services to multiple firms could provide the 20 hours of required time to that firm and three other firms for the same cost as had the firm performed this activity internally. Thus the specialist firm could charge the focal firm 50 percent of what it would cost the small firm to do the pensions internally. Of that 50 percent, 25 percent (20 hours) would go to paying direct salaries and the other 25 percent would be profit. Here the focal firm would save 50 percent of its expenses while the provider would make money.

Now consider the aspect of effectiveness. Because the outsourced provider works for a number of firms and specializes in pensions, its employees develop state-of-the-art knowledge of running pension plans. They can learn unique innovations from one company and transfer that learning to a new company. In addition, employees can be more easily and efficiently trained because all of them will be trained in the same processes and procedures. Finally, with experience in providing constant pension services, the firm is able to develop a capability to perform these services that could never be developed by two individuals working 25 percent of the time on these services.

What kind of services are being outsourced? Firms primarily outsource transactional activities and services of HRM such as pension and benefits administration as well as payroll. However, a number of traditional and some transformational activities have been outsourced as well. The "Competing through Technology" box describes how CIGNA's HR function outsourced many of its activities and transformed its HR processes as part of that company's turnaround.

**LO6**
Relate How Process Reengineering Is Used to Review and Redesign HRM Practices.

## Improving HRM Effectiveness through Process Redesign

In addition to structural arrangements, process redesign enables the HRM function to more efficiently and effectively deliver HRM services. Process redesign often uses information technology, but information technology applications are not a requirement. Thus we will discuss the general issue of process reengineering and then explore information technology applications that have aided HRM in process redesign.

**Reengineering**
Review and redesign of work processes to make them more efficient and improve the quality of the end product or service.

**Reengineering** is a complete review of critical work processes and redesign to make them more efficient and able to deliver higher quality. Reengineering is especially critical to ensuring that the benefits of new technology can be realized. Applying new technology to an inefficient process will not improve efficiency or effectiveness.

## COMPETING THROUGH TECHNOLOGY

### CIGNA's HR Uses Technology and Outsourcing to Deliver

In 2003 CIGNA was facing critical challenges, with the stock price at $40, down from $140 a few years before. CEO Edward Hanway brought in John Murabito to head up the HR function at CIGNA as part of the company's turnaround. "John played an important role in positioning CIGNA for success," says Hanway. "He helped move the company forward by personally contributing to the company's overall strategy and then ensuring human resources was an enabler to business success."

How did Murabito do this? "To one degree or another, we've changed nearly every critical people process and foundational people element that exists at CIGNA," says Murabito. He outsourced the vast majority of administrative work to IBM. Then, he sought to refocus a more streamlined function on the areas that had maximal value to the business.

He believes that in an era of increasing competition, all corporate functions, including HR, will face greater pressure to deliver services with greater efficiency as well as effectiveness. "Ultimately, I believe the company-owned HR function, which will be the nonoutsourced part of the function, will get smaller and smaller," he says. "And I think that's actually OK for HR people, who will become valued commodities within a company as they expertly advise their senior-level clients. That model will replace the approach of having an HR person for every 200 employees, responsible for solving small issues that can now be performed mainly through managers, employee self-service and outsourced arrangements.

SOURCE: E. Krell, "From Steel Yards to HR Stewardship," *HR Magazine*, April, 2007, pp. 60–65.

Instead, it will increase product or service costs related to the introduction of the new technology.

Reengineering can be used to review the HRM department functions and processes, or it can be used to review specific HRM practices such as work design or the performance management system. The reengineering process involves the four steps shown in Figure 16.11: identify the process to be reengineered, understand the process, redesign the process, and implement the new process.[7]

### Identifying the Process

Managers who control the process or are responsible for functions within the process (sometimes called "process owners") should be identified and asked to be part of the

**figure 16.11**
The Reengineering Process

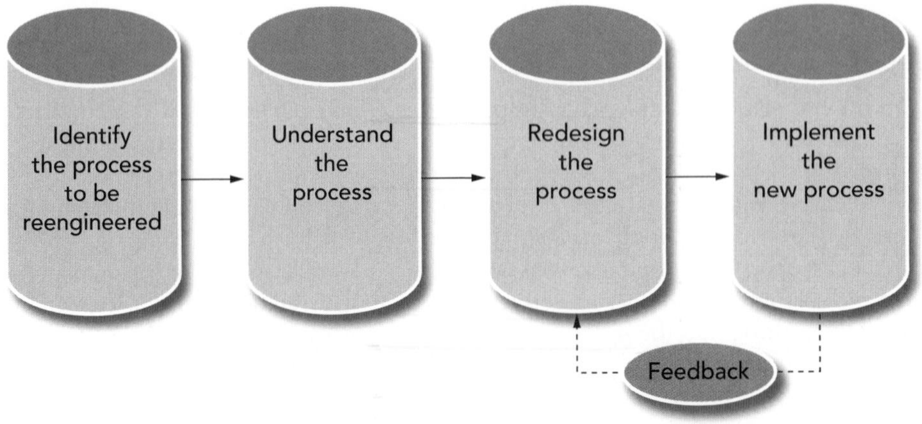

reengineering team. Team members should include employees involved in the process (to provide expertise) and those outside the process, as well as internal or external customers who see the outcome of the process.

## Understanding the Process

Several things need to be considered when evaluating a process:

- Can jobs be combined?
- Can employees be given more autonomy? Can decision making and control be built into the process through streamlining it?
- Are all the steps in the process necessary?
- Are data redundancy, unnecessary checks, and controls built into the process?
- How many special cases and exceptions have to be dealt with?
- Are the steps in the process arranged in their natural order?
- What is the desired outcome? Are all of the tasks necessary? What is the value of the process?

Various techniques are used to understand processes. Data-flow diagrams are useful to show the flow of data among departments. Figure 16.12 shows a data-flow diagram for payroll data and the steps in producing a paycheck. Information about the employee and department are sent to the general account. The payroll check is issued based on a payment voucher that is generated from the general accounting ledger. Data-entity relationship diagrams show the types of data used within a business function

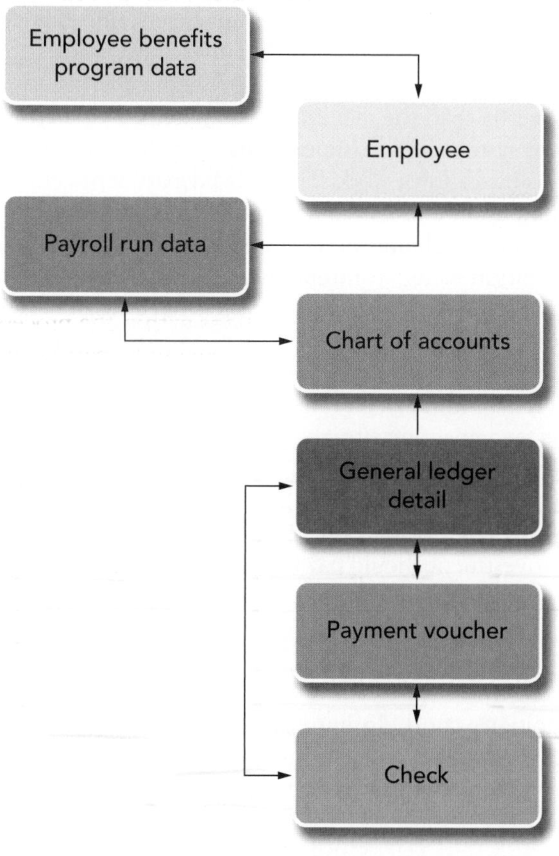


**figure 16.12**
A Data-Flow Diagram for Payroll Data

and the relationship among the different types of data. In scenario analysis, simulations of real-world issues are presented to data end users. The end users are asked to indicate how an information system could help address their particular situations and what data should be maintained to deal with those situations. Surveys and focus groups collect information about the data collected, used, and stored in a functional area, as well as information about time and information-processing requirements. Users may be asked to evaluate the importance, frequency, and criticality of automating specific tasks within a functional area. For example, how critical is it to have an applicant tracking system that maintains data on applicants' previous work experience? Cost–benefit analyses compare the costs of completing tasks with and without an automated system or software application. For example, the analysis should include the costs in terms of people, time, materials, and dollars; the anticipated costs of software and hardware; and labor, time, and material expenses.[8]

### Redesigning the Process

During the redesign phase, the team develops models, tests them, chooses a prototype, and determines how to integrate the prototype into the organization.

**LO7**
Discuss the Types of New Technologies That Can Improve the Efficiency and Effectiveness of HRM.

### Implementing the Process

The company tries out the process by testing it in a limited, controlled setting before expanding companywide. For example, J. M. Huber Corporation, a New Jersey–based conglomerate that has several operating divisions scattered throughout the United States, used reengineering to avoid installing new software onto inefficient processes.[9] HR staff began by documenting and studying the existing work flow and creating a strategy for improving efficiency. Top management, midlevel managers, and human resources staff worked together to identify the processes that they most wanted to improve. They determined that the most critical issue was to develop a client–server system that could access data more easily than the mainframe computer they were currently using. Also, the client–server system could eliminate many of the requisitions needed to get access to data, which slowed down work. The HRM department's efforts have streamlined record-keeping functions, eliminated redundant steps, and automated manual processes. The fully automated client–server system allows employees to sign up and change benefits information using an interactive voice-response system that is connected to the company's database. In addition, managers have easier access to employees' salary history, job descriptions, and other data. If an employee is eligible for a salary increase and the manager requests a change and it is approved, the system will process it (without entry by a clerical worker), and the changes will be seen on the employee's paycheck. Results of the reengineering effort are impressive. The redesigned processes have reduced the number of problems that HRM has to give to other departments by 42 percent, cut work steps by 26 percent, and eliminated 20 percent of the original work. Although the company is spending over $1 million to make the technology work, it estimates that the investment should pay for itself in five years.

**New Technologies**
Current applications of knowledge, procedures, and equipment that have not been previously used. Usually involves replacing human labor with equipment, information processing, or some combination of the two.

## Improving HRM Effectiveness through Using New Technologies—HRM Information Systems

Several new and emerging technologies can help improve the effectiveness of the HRM function. **New technologies** are current applications of knowledge, procedures, and equipment that have not been used previously. New technology usually involves automation—that is, replacing human labor with equipment, information processing, or some combination of the two.

In HRM, technology has already been used for three broad functions: transaction processing, reporting, and tracking; decision support systems; and expert systems.[10] **Transaction processing** refers to computations and calculations used to review and document HRM decisions and practices. This includes documenting relocation, training expenses, and course enrollments and filling out government reporting requirements (such as EEO-1 reports, which require companies to report information to the government regarding employees' race and gender by job category). **Decision support systems** are designed to help managers solve problems. They usually include a "what if" feature that allows users to see how outcomes change when assumptions or data change. These systems are useful, for example, for helping companies determine the number of new hires needed based on different turnover rates or the availability of employees with a certain skill in the labor market. **Expert systems** are computer systems incorporating the decision rules of people deemed to have expertise in a certain area. The system recommends actions that the user can take based on the information provided by the user. The recommended actions are those that a human expert would take in a similar situation (such as a manager interviewing a job candidate). We discuss expert systems in more detail later in this chapter.

Technology has helped employers find leaner, more flexible ways of working. Human Resource professionals are increasingly using new technology to streamline HR functions.

The newest technologies being applied to HRM include interactive voice technology, client–server architecture, relational databases, imaging, and development of specialized software. These technologies improve effectiveness through increasing access to information, improving communications, improving the speed with which HRM transactions and information can be gathered, and reducing the costs and facilitating the administration of HRM functions such as recruiting, training, and performance management. Technology enables

- Employees to gain complete control over their training and benefits enrollments (more self-service).
- The creation of a paperless employment office.
- Streamlining the HRM department's work.
- Knowledge-based decision support technology, which allows employees and managers to access knowledge as needed.
- Employees and managers to select the type of media they want to use to send and receive information.
- Work to be completed at any time and place.
- Closer monitoring of employees' work.[11]

There is evidence that new technology is related to improvements in productivity. Improvements in productivity have been credited largely to downsizing, restructuring, and reengineering. But technology is also responsible because new technology has allowed companies to find leaner, more flexible ways of operating.[12] A study of companies in a variety of industries found that investments in computers provided a better return than investments in other kinds of capital.[13] Technology requires companies to have appropriately skilled and motivated people and streamlined work processes. In some cases technology is replacing human capital.[14] For example, Statewide, the regional telephone unit

**Transaction Processing**
Computations and calculations used to review and document HRM decisions and practices.

**Decision Support Systems**
Problem-solving systems which usually include a "what-if" feature that allows users to see how outcomes change when assumptions or data change.

**Expert Systems**
Computer systems incorporating the decision rules of people recognized as experts in a certain area.

of Pacific Telesis Group, used to dispatch about 20,000 trucks a day to fix customers' lines. New technology has enabled the company to find broken lines using computer signals. As a result, fewer truck dispatches (and fewer drivers) are necessary.

## Interactive Voice Technology

Interactive voice technology uses a conventional personal computer to create an automated phone-response system. This technology is especially useful for benefits administration. For example, at Hannaford Brothers, a supermarket chain spread through the northeastern United States, the HRM department installed an interactive voice-response system that allows employees to get information on their retirement accounts, stock purchases, and benefits plans by using the touchtone buttons on their phone.[15] Employees can also directly enroll in programs and speak to an HRM representative if they have questions. As a result of the technology, the company was able to reduce the size of the HRM staff and more quickly serve employees' benefits needs.

## Networks and Client–Server Architecture

**Network**
A combination of desktop computers, computer terminals, and mainframes or minicomputers that share access to databases and a method to transmit information throughout the system.

**Client–Server Architecture**
Computer design that provides a method to consolidate data and applications into a single host system (the client).

Traditionally, different computer systems (with separate databases) are used for payroll, recruiting, and other human resource management functions. A **network** is a combination of desktop computers, computer terminals, and mainframes or minicomputers that share access to databases and a means to transmit information throughout the system. A common form of network involves client–server architecture. **Client–server architecture** provides the means of consolidating data and applications into a single system (the client).[16] The data can be accessed by multiple users. Also, software applications can be stored on the server and "borrowed" by other users. Client–server architecture allows easier access to data, faster response time, and maximum use of the computing power of the personal computer.

For example, a pharmaceutical company with 50,000 employees worldwide uses client–server technology to create an employee information system that integrates data from six databases.[17] The available data include financial, operational, and human resource information. A manager at a European location can compare her plant's human resource costs with those for the entire company or a plant in Ohio, and at the same time senior management can use the same data to compare the productivity of the Ohio plant with a plant in Maine.

## Relational Databases

**Relational database**
A database structure that stores information in separate files that can be linked by common elements.

Databases contain several data files (topics), which are made up of employee information (records) containing data fields. A data field is an element or type of information such as employee name, Social Security number, or job classification.

In a **relational database** information is stored in separate files, which look like tables. These files can be linked by common elements (fields) such as name, identification number, or location. This contrasts with the traditional file structure, in which all data associated with an employee was kept in one file. In the relational database shown in Figure 16.13, employees' personal information is located in one file and salary information in another, but both topics of information can be accessed via the employees' Social Security numbers.

Users of relational databases can file and retrieve information according to any field or multiple fields across different tables or databases. They provide an easy way

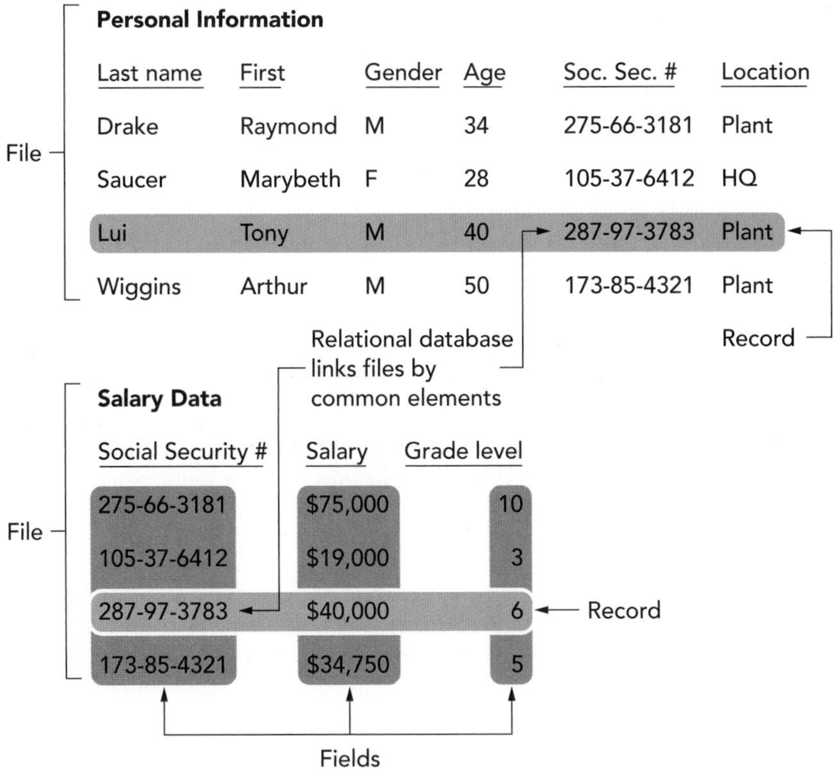


**figure 16.13**
Example of a Relational Database

to organize data. Also, the number of data fields that can be kept for any employee using a relational database is limitless. The ability to join or merge data from several different tables or to view only a subset of data is especially useful in human resource management. Databases that have been developed to track employee benefit costs, training courses, and compensation, for example, contain separate pieces of employee information that can be accessed and merged as desired by the user. Relational technology also allows databases to be established in several different locations. Users in one plant or division location can access data from any other company location. Consider an oil company. Human resources data—such as the names, salaries, and skills of employees working on an oil rig in the Gulf of Mexico—can be stored at company headquarters. Databases at the oil rig site itself might contain employee name, safety equipment issued, and appropriate skill certification. Headquarters and oil rig managers can access information on each database as needed.

## Imaging

**Imaging** refers to scanning documents, storing them electronically, and retrieving them.[18] Imaging is particularly useful because paper files take a large volume of space and are difficult to access. Imaging has been used in applicant tracking and in benefits management. Applicants' résumés can be scanned and stored in a database so they will be available for access at a later date. Some software applications (such as Resumix) allow the user to scan the résumé based on key items such as job history, education, or experience. At Warner-Lambert, the compensation and benefits department provides HR-related services for over 15,000 retirees.[19] Eight employees retire or die each

**Imaging**
A process for scanning documents, storing them electronically, and retrieving them.

month; approximately 100 employees terminate each month. This "exit" activity created a tremendous volume of paper for each employee, as well as requests for data from analysts in the department. Locating and refiling the data was very time-consuming and inefficient. Using imaging, the compensation and benefits department was able to better serve its customers by reducing the time needed to locate a file or handle a phone inquiry from a retiree, providing the ability for sharing files among analysts simultaneously, eliminating the need to refile, and reducing the physical space needed to store the files.

## Expert Systems

As we discussed earlier, expert systems are technologies that mimic a human expert. Expert systems have three elements:

- A knowledge base that contains facts, figures, and rules about a specific subject.
- A decision-making capability that draws conclusions from those facts and figures to solve problems and answer questions.
- A user interface that gathers and gives information to the person using the system.

The use of expert systems in HRM is relatively new. Some companies use expert systems to help employees decide how to allocate their money for benefits, help managers schedule the labor requirements for projects, and assist managers in conducting selection interviews. Pic 'n Pay stores (a chain of shoe stores) uses an expert system for the initial job interview. Candidates call a toll-free phone number. The candidates then respond to 100 questions, and the computer records the responses and scores them. At headquarters, a team of trained interviewers evaluates the responses and designs a list of follow-up questions, which are administered by the hiring manager. The expert system reduced employee turnover by 50 percent and reduced losses due to theft by 39 percent. Also, hiring of minorities has risen 8 percent, implying that decision biases may be less significant using the expert system.[20]

A large international food processor uses an expert system called Performer, designed to provide training and support to its plant operators. One of the problems the company was facing was determining why potato chips were being scorched in the fryer operation. An operator solved the problem using Performer. He selected the "troubleshooting" menu, then "product texture/flavor," then "off oil flavor." The program listed probable causes, beginning with high oxidation during frying. The operator chose that cause, and the system recommended adjusting the cooking line's oil flush, providing detailed steps for that procedure. Following those steps resolved the problem.[21]

Expert systems can deliver both high quality and lower costs. By using the decision processes of experts, the system enables many people to arrive at decisions that reflect the expert's knowledge. An expert system helps avoid the errors that can result from fatigue and decision biases. The efficiencies of an expert system can be realized if it can be operated by fewer employees or less skilled (and likely less costly) employees than the company would otherwise require.

**Groupware**
Software that enables multiple users to track, share, and organize information and to work on the same database or document simultaneously.

## Groupware

**Groupware** (electronic meeting software) is a software application that enables multiple users to track, share, and organize information and to work on the same document simultaneously.[22] Companies have been using groupware to improve business processes such as sales and account management, to improve meeting effectiveness, and to identify and share knowledge in the organization. (See our earlier discussion of creating a learning organization in Chapter 7.) Monsanto uses Lotus Notes to link salespeople, account managers, and competitor-intelligence analysts.[23] The database contains updated news on competitors and customers, information from public news sources, salespeople's reports, an in-house directory of experts, and attendees' notes from conventions and conferences. Many companies are also creating their own "intranet," a private company network that competes with groupware programs such as Lotus Notes. Intranets are cheaper and simpler to use than groupware programs but pose potential security problems because of the difficulty of keeping people out of the network.[24]

## Software Applications for HRM

### Improving HRM Effectiveness through New Technologies—E-HRM

Since the mid-1990s as HRM functions sought to play a more strategic role in their organizations, the first task was to eliminate transactional tasks in order to free up time to focus on traditional and transformational activities. Part of building a strategic HR function requires moving much of the transactional work away from being done by people so that the people can have time available to work on strategic activities. Consequently, the use of technology can both make HR more strategic and by doing so increase the value that HR adds to the business.[25] As indicated in Figure 16.9, outsourcing of many of these activities provided one mechanism for reducing this burden. However, more relevant today is the focus on the use of information technology to handle these tasks. Early on this was achieved by the development and implementation of information systems that were run by the HRM function but more recently have evolved into systems that allow employees to serve themselves. Thus, for example, employees can access the system and make their benefit enrollment, changes, or claims online. Clearly, technology has freed HRM functions from transactional activities to focus on more strategic actions.

However, the speed requirements of e-business force HRM functions to explore how to leverage technology for the delivery of traditional and transformational HRM activities. This does not imply that over time all of HRM will be executed over the Web, but that a number of HRM activities currently delivered via paper or face-to-face communications can be moved to the Web with no loss (and even gains) in effectiveness and efficiency. This is illustrated by Figure 16.14. We explore some examples next.

### Recruitment and Selection

Traditional recruitment and selection processes have required considerable face-to-face communications with recruitment firms and potential employees, labor-intensive assessment devices, and significant monitoring of managerial decisions to ensure that hiring patterns and decisions do not run afoul of regulatory requirements. However, technology has transformed these processes.

For example, online recruiting accounted for one of every eight hires last year, according to k-force.com's poll of 300 U.S. companies. IBM employees now fill out forms on the Web to identify contract help they need, and that information is immediately sent

figure 16.14
Change in Delivery

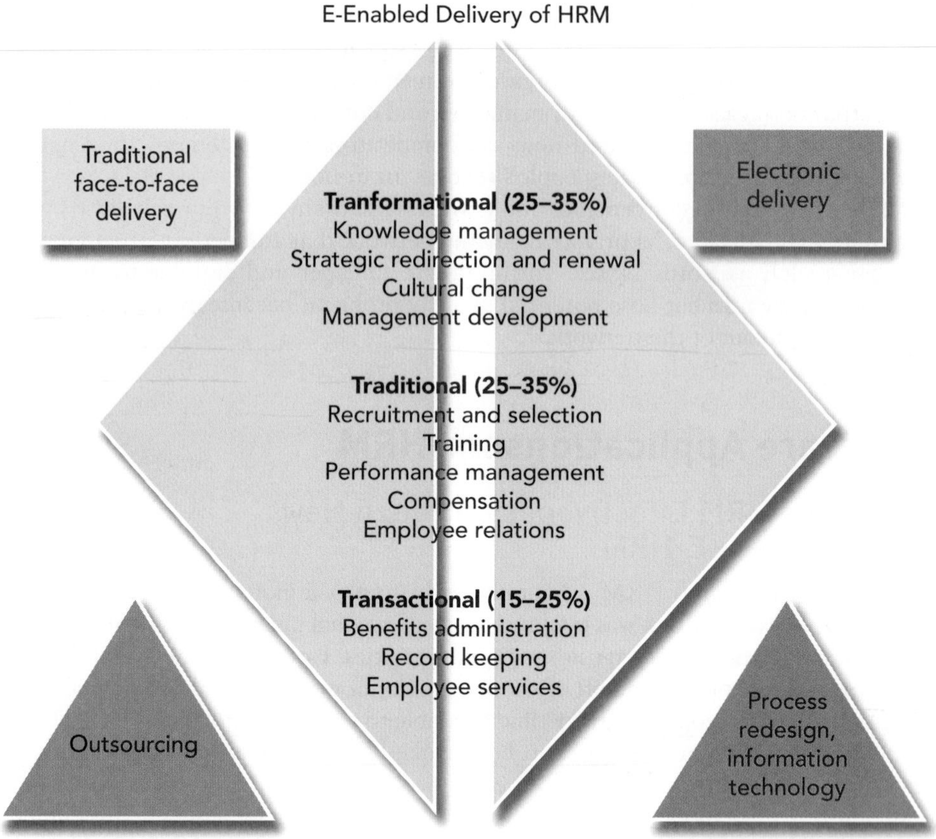


to 14 temp agencies. Within an hour agencies respond with résumés for review, allowing IBM to cut hiring time from 10 days to 3 and save $3 million per year.

In addition, firms such as Q-Hire in Austin, Texas, provide online testing services. Applicants for positions at a firm are directed to a Web site where they complete an assessment device. Their scores are immediately compared to an ideal profile, and this profile comparison is communicated to the company screening manager. Firms can gather considerable amounts of relevant information about potential employees long before they ever need to set foot on company premises.

Finally, technology has enabled firms to monitor hiring processes to minimize the potential for discriminatory hiring decisions. For example, Home Depot was accused of forcing female applicants into cashier jobs while reserving the customer service jobs for males. While not admitting guilt, as part of their consent decree Home Depot uses technology to identify people who have skills for jobs they are not applying for based on key words in their résumés. In addition, the technology forces managers to interview diverse candidate sets before making decisions.

### Compensation and Rewards

Compensation systems in organizations probably reflect the most pervasive form of bureaucracy within HRM. In spite of the critical role they play in attracting, motivating, and retaining employees, most systems consist of rigid, time-consuming, and ineffective processes. Managers fill out what they believe to be useless forms, ignore guidelines, and display a general disdain for the entire process.

Leveraging technology may allow firms to better achieve their compensation goals with considerably less effort. For example, one problem many merit or bonus pay plans face is that managers refuse to differentiate among performers, giving everyone similar pay increases. This allows them to spend less time thinking about how to manage (rate and review) performance as well as minimizes the potential conflict they might face. Thus employees do not see linkages between performance and pay, resulting in lower motivation among all employees and higher turnover among top performers (and possibly lower turnover among bottom performers). To minimize this, Cypress Semiconductors requires managers to distinguish between equity and merit and forces distributions with regard to both concepts.[26] For example, equity means that the top-ranked performer in any group of peers should make 50 percent more than the lowest-ranked performer, and people with comparable performance should receive comparable salaries. With regard to merit, there must be at least a 7 percent spread between the lowest and highest pay raises (if the lowest raise is 3 percent, then the highest must be at least 10 percent). If ratings and raises are input into a system, the firm can monitor and control the rating process to ensure that adequate differentiations are made consistent with the policy.

## Training and Development

Exploring different vehicles for delivering training (PC, video, and the like) certainly is not a new concept. In addition, a number of firms have begun delivering training via the Web. Their experience suggests that some types of training can be done effectively via the Internet or an intranet, whereas others might not. For example, companies such as IBM and Dell both boast that they have developed Internet-based training for some parts of their workforce.

Interestingly, the challenge of speedy delivery of HRM services brings the concept of Internet-based training to the forefront. In today's competitive environment, firms compete to attract and retain both customers and talented employees. How well a firm develops and treats existing employees largely determines how well it achieves these outcomes. Yet the challenges of speed, project focus, and changing technology create environments that discourage managers from managing their people, resulting in a situation where employees may not feel respected or valued.

This presents a challenge to firms to provide both the incentive and the skills for managers to treat employees as assets rather than commodities. Consider how Internet-based training might facilitate this. Assume that you work for Widget.com, a fast-growing, fast-paced e-business. You arrive at work Monday morning, and your e-mail contains a high-priority message with either an attachment or a link to a URL. It is your Monday morning challenge from the CEO, and you know that the system will track whether you link and complete this challenge. When you link to it, you see a digital video of your CEO telling you how people are Widget.com's competitive advantage, and that when they don't feel valued, they leave. Thus his challenge to you is to make your employees feel valued today. To do so, you will in the next 10 minutes learn how to express appreciation to an employee. You receive six learning points; you observe a digitized video model performing the learning points; you review the learning points again and take a quiz. You then see the CEO giving you the final challenge: that in the next 15 minutes you are to take one of your employees aside and express your appreciation using the skill you just developed.

Notice the advantages of this process. First, it was not time-consuming like most three-day or one-week training programs. The entire process (training and demonstration with a real employee) took less than 30 minutes; you have developed a skill; and an employee now probably feels better about the organization. It communicated a real organizational value or necessary competency. It didn't require any travel expenses to a training facility. It did not overwhelm you with so much information that you would be lucky to remember 10 percent of what you were exposed to. Finally, it was a push, rather than pull, approach to training. The firm did not wait for you to realize you had a deficiency and then go search and sign up for training. It pushed the training to you.

Thus technology allows firms to deliver training and development for at least some skills or knowledge faster, more efficiently, and probably more effectively. It can quickly merge training, communication, and immediate response to strategic contingencies.

Creating and nurturing a committed workforce presents a tremendous challenge to firms today. According to a recent survey conducted by Monster.com, 61 percent of Americans consider themselves overworked and 86 percent are not satisfied with their jobs.[27] Such findings suggest that firms need to find ways to monitor commitment levels, identify potential obstacles to commitment, and respond quickly to eliminate those obstacles. In large part, attitude surveys have constituted the platform from which these activities were managed in the past.

Consider the traditional attitude survey. Surveys are administered to employees over a period of four to six weeks. The data are entered and analyzed, requiring another six to eight weeks. A group interprets the results to identify the major problem areas, and task forces are formed to develop recommendations; this process easily takes another four to six months. Finally, decisions must be made about implementing the task force recommendations. In the end, at best employees might see responses to their concerns 12 to 18 months after the survey—and then the survey administrators cannot understand why employees think that completing the survey is a waste of time.

Now consider how technology can shorten that cycle. E-pulse represents one attempt to create a platform for almost real-time attitude surveys. Developed by Theresa Welbourne at the University of Michigan, E-pulse is a scalable survey device administered online. Normally three questions are asked regarding how employees feel about work, but more questions can be added to get feedback on any specific issue. The survey goes out online, and when employees complete it, the data are immediately entered and analyzed. In essence, the part of the process that took four months in the past has been reduced to a day.

Next the firm can decide how it wants to use the information. For example, it could be broken down by business, site, or work unit, with the relevant information going to the leader of the chosen unit of analysis. In essence, a supervisor could receive almost immediate feedback about the attitudes of his or her work group, or a general manager about his or her business unit. The supervisor or manager can respond immediately, even if only to communicate that she or he realizes a problem exists and will take action soon.

One must recognize that although the technology provides for faster HRM, only a more systemic approach will ensure better and smarter HRM. For example, disseminating the information to the supervisors and managers may be faster, but unless those individuals possess good problem-solving and communication skills, they may either ignore the information or, worse yet, exacerbate the problem with inappropriate responses. As we noted with regard to training, this systemic approach requires knocking down traditional functional walls to deliver organizational solutions rather than functional programs. Thus the challenge is to get beyond viewing the technology as a panacea or even as a functional tool, but rather as a catalyst for transforming the HRM organization. The "Competing through Sustainability" box describes how technology companies are trying to promote more environmentally friendly workplaces.

## COMPETING THROUGH SUSTAINABILITY
### Tech Companies Go Green

It's hard to imagine ourselves working without computers today. However, did you know that the power it takes for you to have your home computer tied to a Web application equals that of the total power usage of an individual in the developing world?

As technology companies increasingly recognize that their products are significant users of energy, many have attempted to engineer "greener" products. The Silicon Valley Leadership Group, a regional business booster association, has announced a 12-point campaign called Clean and Green that frames traditional issues such as ride-sharing and mass transit in the context of global warming. For instance, chipmaker Intel's official position is "Climate change is an important environmental issue. The broad consensus of established scientific experts is that warming can be attributed to human activities. Significant steps are needed to reduce greenhouse gas emissions."

With increasing power consumption not being met by increasing power supply, tech companies understand that their growth may be limited by a lack of electricity to power them. Thus, they know that they need to build more energy-efficient products if they are to be able to sell them. This has led the Environmental Protection Agency (EPA) to begin developing Energy Star standards for computer servers similar to those developed for refrigerators and washing machines. "When engineers look at an energy issue, they see it as a problem that can be overcome," says Andrew Fanara, the EPS official leading the Energy Star project. "They seem to have an ability to engineer their way our of anything."

SOURCE: L. Gomes, "It's Not That Easy Being Green, but Techs Are Trying This Year," *The Wall Street Journal*, January 3, 2007, p. B1.

# The Future for HR Professionals

**LO8**
List the Competencies the HRM Executive Needs to Become a Strategic Partner in the Company.

The future for careers in the human resource profession seems brighter than ever. An increasing number of successful companies such as Microsoft have made the top HR job a member of the senior management team, reporting directly to the chief executive officer. CEOs recognize the importance of their workforce in driving competitive success. Firms need to seek the balance between attracting, motivating, and retaining the very best talent and keeping labor and administrative costs as low as possible. Finding such a balance requires HR leaders who have a deep knowledge of the business combined with a deep knowledge of HR issues, tools, processes, and technologies.

For a reader who is just getting a first glimpse of the HRM function, to portray what a vastly different role HRM must play today compared to 20 or even 10 years ago is impossible. As noted earlier, HRM has traditionally played a largely administrative role—simply processing paperwork plus developing and administering hiring, training, appraisal, compensation, and benefits systems—and all of this has been unrelated to the strategic direction of the firm. In the early 1980s HRM took on more of a one-way linkage role, helping to implement strategy. Now strategic decision makers are realizing the importance of people issues and so are calling for HRM to become the "source of people expertise" in the firm.[28] This requires that HR managers possess and use knowledge of how people can and do play a role in competitive advantage as well as the policies, programs, and practices that can leverage the firm's people as a source of competitive advantage. This leads to an entirely new set of competencies for today's strategic HR executive.[29]

4 competencies needed

In the future, HR professionals will need four basic competencies to become partners in the strategic management process (see Figure 2.7).[30] First, they will need "business competence"—knowing the company's business and understanding its economic financial capabilities. This calls for making logical decisions that support the company's strategic plan based on the most accurate information possible. Because in almost all companies the effectiveness of decisions must be evaluated in terms of dollar values, the HR executive must be able to calculate the costs and benefits of each alternative in terms of its dollar impact.[31] In addition, it requires that the nonmonetary impact be considered. The HR executive must be fully capable of identifying the social and ethical issues attached to HRM practices.

Second, HR professionals will need "professional–technical knowledge" of state-of-the-art HRM practices in areas such as staffing, development, rewards, organizational design, and communication. New selection techniques, performance appraisal methods, training programs, and incentive plans are constantly being developed. Some of these programs can provide value whereas others may be no more than the products of today's HRM equivalent of snake oil. HR executives must be able to critically evaluate the new techniques offered as state-of-the-art HRM programs and use only those that will benefit the company.

Third, they must be skilled in the "management of change processes," such as diagnosing problems, implementing organizational changes, and evaluating results. Every time a company changes its strategy in even a minor way, the entire company has to change. These changes result in conflict, resistance, and confusion among the people who must implement the new plans or programs. The HR executive must have the skills to oversee the change in a way that ensures its success. In fact, one survey of Fortune 500 companies found that 87 percent of the companies had their organization development/change function as part of the HR department.[32]

Finally, these professionals must also have "integration competence," meaning the ability to integrate the three other competencies to increase the company's value. This requires that, although specialist knowledge is necessary, a generalist perspective must be taken in making decisions. This entails seeing how all the functions within the HRM area fit together to be effective and recognizing that changes in any one part of the HRM package are likely to require changes in other parts of the package. For example, a health care company in central Texas was attempting to fill a position in the X-ray department. It was able to identify qualified candidates for the position, but none of the candidates accepted the offer. It was not until the company examined its total package (pay, benefits, promotion opportunities, and so on) and changed the composition of the package that it was able to fill the position.

The new strategic role for HRM presents both opportunities and challenges. HRM has the chance to profoundly impact the way organizations compete through people. On the other hand, with this opportunity come serious responsibility and accountability.[33] HRM functions of the future must consist of individuals who view themselves as businesspeople who happen to work in an HRM function, rather than HRM people who happen to work in a business.

## A Look Back

The beginning of this chapter related a bit of how IBM's HR function is seeking to transform itself, particularly with regard to how it delivers services internally. To make IBM's HR restructuring work, Randy MacDonald had to assemble an HR team that is truly business oriented. For instance, Karen Barbar, vice president of learning, was an experienced hardware engineer who transferred into HR. "Five years ago I would not have considered leaving hardware development to move to HR," she says. "But now, I see that our ability to develop expertise is what distinguishes IBM from its competitors. In HR, I'm involved in driving the transition of the company."

MacDonald challenges other HR executives to follow his example. "I don't care if you're sitting on top at IBM or you're at a Fortune 1000 company. You are entrusted by the shareholders to protect the assets of the corporation that are human in nature. Don't worry about jargon like 'business partner.' You should be just like any other senior executive making a difference to your company."

SOURCE: R. J. Grossman. "IBM's HR Takes a Risk," *HR Magazine*, April, 2007, pp. 54–59.

### Questions

1. Do you think that IBM's approach to HR is a model for future HR functions? Why or why not?
2. In what ways does IBM's approach to HR model a business-driven approach?
3. How is IBM's approach to HR different from the approaches taken by HR functions that you have worked for or know of?

Please see the Video Case that corresponds to this chapter online at www.mhhe.com/noe6e.

## Summary

The roles required of the HRM function have changed as people have become recognized as a true source of competitive advantage. This has required a transformation of the HRM function from focusing solely on transactional activities to an increasing involvement in strategic activities. In fact, according to a recent study, 64 percent of HR executives said that their HRM function is in a process of transformation.[34] The strategic management of the HRM function will determine whether HRM will transform itself to a true strategic partner or simply be blown up.

In this chapter we have explored the various changing roles of the HRM function. HRM today must play roles as an administrative expert, employee advocate, change agent, and strategic partner. The function must also deliver transactional, traditional, and transformational services and activities to the firm, and it must be both efficient and effective. HR executives must strategically manage the HRM function just as the firm must be strategically managed. This requires that HRM develop measures of the function's performance through customer surveys and analytical methods. These measures can form the basis for planning ways to improve performance. HRM performance can increase through new structures for the function, through using reengineering and information technology, and through outsourcing.

## Key Terms

Audit approach, 701
Analytic approach, 703
Outsourcing, 708
Reengineering, 709
New technologies, 712
Transaction processing, 713
Decision support systems, 713
Expert systems, 714
Network, 714
Client–server architecture, 714
Relational database, 714
Imaging, 715
Groupware, 716

## Discussion Questions

1. Why have the roles and activities of the HRM function changed over the past 20 to 30 years? What has been driving this change? How effectively do you think HRM has responded?
2. How can the processes for strategic management discussed in Chapter 2 be transplanted to manage the HRM function?
3. Why do you think that few companies take the time to determine the effectiveness of HRM practices? Should a company be concerned about evaluating HRM practices? Why? What might people working in the HRM function gain by evaluating the function?
4. How might imaging technology be useful for recruitment? For training? For benefits administration? For performance management?
5. Employees in your company currently choose and enroll in benefits programs after reading communications brochures, completing enrollment forms, and sending them to their HR rep. A temporary staff has to be hired to process the large amount of paperwork that is generated. Enrollment forms need to be checked, sorted, batched, sent to data entry, keypunched, returned, and filed. The process is slow and prone to errors. How could you use process reengineering to make benefits enrollment more efficient and effective?
6. Some argue that outsourcing an activity is bad because the activity is no longer a means of distinguishing the firm from competitors. (All competitors can buy the same service from the same provider, so it cannot be a source of competitive advantage.) Is this true? If so, why would a firm outsource any activity?

## Self-Assessment Exercise

How ethical are you? Read each of the following descriptions. For each, circle whether you believe the behavior described is ethical or unethical.

1. A company president found that a competitor had made an important scientific discovery that would sharply reduce the profits of his own company. The president hired a key employee of the competitor in an attempt to learn the details of the discovery. — Ethical / Unethical
2. To increase profits, a general manager used a production process that exceeded legal limits for environmental pollution. — Ethical / Unethical
3. Because of pressure from her brokerage firm, a stockbroker recommended a type of bond that she did not consider to be a good investment. — Ethical / Unethical
4. A small business received one-fourth of its revenues in the form of cash. On the company's income tax forms, the owner reported only one-half of the cash receipts. — Ethical / Unethical
5. A corporate executive promoted a loyal friend and competent manager to the position of divisional vice president in preference to a better qualified manager with whom she had no close ties. — Ethical / Unethical
6. An employer received applications for a supervisor's position from two equally qualified applicants. The employer hired the male applicant because he thought some employees might resent being supervised by a female. — Ethical / Unethical
7. An engineer discovered what he perceived to be a product design flaw that constituted a safety hazard. His company declined to correct the flaw. The engineer decided to keep quiet, rather than taking his complaint outside the company. — Ethical / Unethical
8. A comptroller selected a legal method of financial reporting that concealed some embarrassing financial facts. Otherwise, those facts would have been public knowledge. — Ethical / Unethical
9. A company paid a $350,000 "consulting" fee to an official of a foreign country. In return, the official promised to help the company obtain a contract that should produce a $10 million profit for the company. — Ethical / Unethical
10. A member of a corporation's board of directors learned that his company intended to announce a stock split and increase its dividend. On the basis of this favorable information, the director bought additional shares of the company's stock. Following the announcement of the information, he sold the stock at a gain. — Ethical / Unethical

Now score your results. How many actions did you judge to be unethical?

All of these actions are unethical. The more of the actions you judged to be unethical, the better your understanding of ethical business behavior.

SOURCE: Based on S. Morris et al., "A Test of Environmental, Situational, and Personal Influences on the Ethical Intentions of CEOs," *Business and Society* 34 (1995), pp. 119–47.

## Exercising Strategy: Transforming the Business and HR at Xerox

In 1958, Xerox launched the Xerox 914, the first automatic, plain-paper office copier. This product went on to become the top-selling industrial product of all time. Xerox's successful xerography technology gave it a sustainable competitive advantage that endured for years. However, all good things must come to an end, and in Xerox's case, that end was the late 1990s. By 2000, Xerox experienced its biggest slide in history, and the consensus among analysts within the industry was that Xerox was working with "an unsustainable business model," meaning unless things changed drastically, Xerox would soon cease to exist. In 2000 Xerox had $17.1 billion in debt, with only $154 million in cash on hand. By 2001, Xerox's stock, which had peaked at $63, fell to about $4—a loss of 90 percent of its market capitalization. And as if that was not enough, it also faced an accounting investigation by the Securities and Exchange Commission for how it accounted for its customer leases on copiers.

Enter new VP of HR Pat Nazemetz in 1999 and new CEO Anne Mulcahy in 2000 to try to right a sinking ship. Mulcahy put the company on a starvation diet. This entailed selling major operations in China and Hong Kong, reducing global headcount to 61,100 from 91,500 through selloffs, early retirements, and layoffs, and implementing drastic cost controls. While Mulcahy's strategy has brought Xerox back to life (2003 saw Xerox triple its net income to $360 million) as an organization, the HR function had to drive the change in the business while simultaneously transforming the function.

While many HR functions look to outsource, Xerox transformed its HR function largely internally. According to Nazemetz, outsourcing providers say "'Let us in, let us take over your HR function and we can take 10 percent to 30 percent out of your cost base.' We began trimming down, finding synergies and opportunities to get more efficient. We found the savings ourselves."

The largest single savings came from consolidating and expanding the HR Service Center. The Center began with purely transactional work (e.g., address changes), then added Web-based processes to handle routine work. The Center now conducts research and analysis to HR operations and handles employee-relations issues. This has enabled HR to reduce headcount without reducing levels of service.

Also, as with any organization that has shed 30 percent of its workforce, employee morale was and continues to be an issue. Even before the fall, HR had been taking the pulse of employees through their "hearts and minds" surveys. This intranet-based survey taps into a number of employee attitudes and seeks to identify the problem areas for HR and line executives to focus on. Employees have noted concerns with items like "Company supports risk-taking," "Company considers impact on employees," "Senior-management behavior is consistent with words," and "Trust level is high."

"People often ask me how Xerox has found success" says Mulcahy. "My answer is that you have to have a strategy and a plan, but [more importantly], what you really need is excellence of execution, and that starts and ends with a talented, motivated group of people aligned around a common set of goals. Our HR people came through with a series of alignment workshops and retention incentives just when we needed them [to] make Xerox the stronger, better company it is today."

### Questions

1. After having gone through the massive downsizing, morale obviously has presented challenges. While Xerox employees seem to understand the need for change (minds), they may not emotionally embrace it (hearts). How can Xerox gain both "hearts" and "minds"?
2. Xerox's HR function focuses on three initiatives: (a) employee value proposition (what can employees expect from the company, and what can the company expect from employees?), (b) performance culture (how can the company develop a culture that encourages continuous improvement and high performance from all employees?), and (c) "three exceptional candidates" (how can HR deliver a pipeline of three-deep bench talent for every position within the organization?). From everything you have learned, how might Xerox address each of these issues?

## MANAGING PEOPLE: FROM THE PAGES OF *BUSINESSWEEK*

### BusinessWeek Saving Starbucks' Soul

**Chairman Howard Schultz is on a mission to take his company back to its roots. Oh, yeah—he also wants to triple sales in five years.** *"A heady aroma of coffee reached out and drew me in. I stepped inside and saw what looked like a temple for the worship of coffee . . . it was my Mecca. I had arrived."—Howard Schultz on his first visit to Starbucks in 1981*

On April 3, Starbucks launches a pair of confections called Dulce de Leche Latte and Dulce de Leche Frappuccino. A 16-oz. Grande latte has a robust 440 calories (about the same as two packages of M&M's) and costs about $4.50 in New York City—or about three times as much as McDonald's most expensive premium coffee. Starbucks Corp. describes its latest concoctions, which took 18 months to perfect, this way: "Topped with whipped cream and a dusting of toffee sprinkles, Starbucks' version of this traditional delicacy is a luxurious tasty treat."

If you find yourself at Starbucks in the next few weeks, letting a Dulce de Leche Latte slide over your taste buds, you might wonder how this drink came to be. It's a tale worth hearing. On the surface it's a story about how the Starbucks marketing machine conjures and sells café romance to millions of people around the world. On a deeper level it's a story about how a company, along with its messianic leader, is struggling to hold on to its soul.

Ask Schultz for the key to Starbucks and he'll tell you it's all about storytelling. Starbucks is centered on two oft-repeated tales: Schultz' trip to Seattle in 1981, where he first enjoyed gourmet coffee, and a 1983 trip to Milan, where he discovered espresso bar culture. Not only are these journeys useful touchstones for recruits, they also provide the original marketing story for a company that prides itself on giving customers an authentic experience. "The one common thread to the success of these stories and the company itself," says Schultz, "is that they have to be true—and they have to be authentic."

#### True Believers

Stories alone aren't enough, though, to fuel Starbucks' other obsession: to grow really, really big. By 2012, Schultz aims to nearly triple annual sales, to $23.3 billion. The company also plans to have 40,000 stores worldwide, up from 13,500 today, not long after that. To hit its profit targets. Starbucks has become expert at something that's decidedly unromantic—streamlining operations. Over the past 10 years the company has redesigned the space behind the counter to boost barista efficiency. Automatic espresso machines speed the time it takes to serve up a shot. Coffee is vacuum-sealed, making it easier to ship over long distances. To boost sales, the company sells everything from breath mints to CDs to notebooks. Add it up and you have an experience that's nothing like the worn wooden counters of the first store in Pike Place Market or an Italian espresso bar.

Somewhere along the way that disconnect began to gnaw at Schultz. Most recently it manifested itself in a note he wrote to his senior team. The Valentine's Day memo, which leaked to the Web, cut to the heart of what he sees as the company's dilemma. "We have had to make a series of decisions," Schultz wrote, "that, in retrospect, have led to the watering down of the Starbucks experience, and what some might call the commoditization of our brand."

Now, Schultz is asking his lieutenants to redouble their efforts to return to their roots. "We're constantly—I don't want to say battling—but we don't want to be that big company that's corporate and slick," says Michelle Gass, senior vice-president and chief merchant for global products. "We don't. We still think about ourselves as a small entrepreneurial company." That's a tricky business when you have 150,000 employees in 39 countries. But keeping that coffee joie de vivre alive inside Starbucks is crucial to Schultz' entire philosophy. Who better to sell something than a true believer?

In 2004, Starbucks introduced something called the Coffee Master program for its employees. It's a kind of extra-credit course that teaches the staff how to discern the subtleties of regional flavor. Graduates (there are now 25,000) earn a special black apron and an insignia on their business cards. The highlight is the "cupping ceremony," a tasting ritual traditionally used by coffee traders. After the grounds have steeped in boiling water, tasters "crest" the mixture, penetrating the crust on top with a spoon and inhaling the aroma. As employees slurp the brew, a Starbucks Coffee Educator encourages them to taste a Kenyan coffee's "citrusy" notes or the "mushroomy" flavor of a Sumatran blend.

If the ritual reminds you of a wine tasting, that's intentional. Schultz has long wanted to emulate the wine business. Winemakers, after all, command a premium by focusing on provenance: the region of origin, the vineyard, and, of course, the grape that gives the wine its particular notes—a story, in other words. Bringing wine's cachet to coffee would help take the brand upmarket and allow Starbucks to sell premium beans.

The product and marketing people call the strategy "Geography is a Flavor." And in 2005 they began selling this new story with whole-bean coffee. The company reorganized the menu behind the counter, grouping coffees by geography instead of by "smooth" or "bold." It replaced the colorful Starbucks coffee bags with clean white packages emblazoned with colored bands representing the region of origin. Later, for those connoisseurs willing to pay $28 a pound, Starbucks introduced single-origin beans called "Black Apron Exclusives."

The next step was to reach the masses who buy drinks in the stores. The team decided to launch a series of in-store promotions, each with a new set of drinks, that would communicate regional idiosyncrasies to customers. The first promotion, the team decided, would highlight Central and South America, where Starbucks buys more than 70 percent of its beans.

The sort of authenticity Schultz loves to talk about is hard to pull off when you're the size of Starbucks. Telling a story to a mass audience sometimes requires smoothing over inconvenient cultural nuances. Plus, the marketing folks have to work quickly to stay abreast of beverage trends, not to mention ahead of such rivals as Dunkin' Donuts and McDonald's. Diving deep is not an option.

A year ago, 10 Starbucks marketers and designers got on a plane and went looking for inspiration in Costa Rica. "It's being able to say: This is how and why this [drink] is made," says Angie McKenzie, who runs new product design. "Not because someone told us or we read it somewhere." The Starbucks team spent five days in Costa Rica, traveling on a minivan owned by TAM Tours. Later, a smaller group toured Mexico City and Oaxaca as well.

## Made in China

The mission was to find products that would evoke an authentic vibe in the United States. That's harder than it sounds. Philip Clark, a merchandising executive, wanted to sell traditional Costa Rican mugs. But the ones typically used to drink coffee were drab and brown; they wouldn't pop on store shelves. Plus, they broke easily. Then he found Cecilia de Figueres, who handpaints ceramic mugs in a mountainside studio an hour from the capital, San Jose. The artist favors bright floral patterns; they would pop nicely. Starbucks paid de Figueres a flat fee for her designs. Each mug will have a tag bearing her name and likeness; on the bottom it will say "Made in China."

Starbucks will weave artisans and other Costa Ricans into the in-store promotional campaign. Painter Eloy Zuñiga Guevara will appear on a poster with a decidedly homespun Latin aesthetic. (And if customers want some authenticity to take home with them, they can buy one of five paintings of Costa Rican farmers that Guevara produced for Starbucks. They will sell for $25 apiece.) A second poster will feature Costa Rican coffee farmers from whom Starbucks buys beans. A third will show a grandmotherly figure cooking up dulce de leche on a gas stove. (She's a paid model from Seattle.) Each poster will feature the tagline "I am Starbucks."

Having devised a story, Starbucks needed a drink that would say "Latin America." Beverage brainstorming takes place in the Liquid Lab, an airy space painted in Starbucks' familiar blue, green, and orange hues. The room features huge bulletin boards plastered with the latest beverage trends. In this case it didn't take an anthropologist to figure out which drink Starbucks should use to promote its Latin American theme.

Dulce de leche is a caramel-and-milk dessert enjoyed throughout much of the region. What's more, Häagen-Dazs introduced dulce de leche ice cream in 1998, and Starbucks followed suit with its own ice cream in 1999. So Americans are familiar with the flavor, says McKenzie, but "it still has a nice exotic edge to it." Besides, she adds, caramel and milk go great with coffee.

Even so, concocting a drink is never simple at Starbucks. The research-and-development department routinely tackles 70 beverage projects a year, with 8 of them leading to new drinks. A drink must not only appeal to a broad swath of coffee drinkers but also be easy for a barista to make quickly so as to maximize sales per store (hello, Wall Street). "The store . . . is a little manufacturing plant," says Gass, and yet it must seem as though the drink is being handcrafted specially for the customer (hello, Howard Schultz).

Creating the Dulce de Leche Latte and Frappuccino fell to Debbie Ismon, a 26-year-old beverage developer who holds a degree in food science and has worked at Starbucks for 2 1/2 years. In late June 2006, the design team brought her a small sample they'd whipped up that they felt embodied the right tastes, plus a written description of the characteristics they hoped to see. For the next four months, Ismon fiddled with various ratios of caramel, cooked milk, and sweetness "notes." After the design group decided which version tasted most "in-concept," Ismon mixed up three different flavors for the big taste test. One hundred or so random Starbucks employees filed in, sampled the drinks, and rated them on computer screens. The process was repeated two more times for each drink. Finally, 18 months after starting the process, Starbucks had its two latest premium beverages.

If previous drinks, such as Caramel Macchiato, are any guide, Starbucks' Dulce de Leche drinks will sell briskly. That should please Wall Street and perhaps even help perk up the stock, which is down 20 percent from its May 2006 high on worries that operating margins are falling and that Starbucks could miss its ambitious growth targets.

And as you wait in line for your Dulce de Leche Latte, you might ask yourself: Are you paying $4.50 for a caffeine jolt and caramel topping? Or have you simply been dazzled by Howard Schultz' storytelling magic?

SOURCE: B. Helm, "Saving Starbucks' Soul," *BusinessWeek*, April 9, 2007, pp. 56–61.

## Questions

1. What are some of the HRM issues inherent in Howard Schultz's concerns?
2. How would an effective strategic HRM function contribute to keeping Starbucks on track?

## NOTES


1. P. Wright, S. Snell, and P. Jacobsen, "Current Approaches to HR Strategies: Inside-Out vs. Outside-In," *Human Resource Planning* (in press).
2. A. S. Tsui and L. R. Gomez-Mejia, "Evaluating HR Effectiveness," in *Human Resource Management: Evolving Roles and Responsibilities*, ed. L. Dyer (Washington, DC: Bureau of National Affairs, 1988), pp. 1-187–1-227.
3. D. Ulrich, "Measuring Human Resources: An Overview of Practice and a Prescription for Results," *Human Resource Management* 36, no. 3 (1997), pp. 303–20.
4. P. Wright, G. McMahan, S. Snell, and B. Gerhart, "Comparing Line and HR Executives' Perceptions of HR Effectiveness: Services, Roles, and Contributions," CAHRS (Center for Advanced Human Resource Studies) working paper 98-29, School of ILR, Cornell University, Ithaca, NY.
5. J. C. Erfurt, A. Foote, and M. A. Heirich, "The Cost-Effectiveness of Worksite Wellness Programs," *Personnel Psychology* 15 (1992), p. 22.
6. P. Wright, G. McMahan, S. Snell, and B. Gerhart, *Strategic HRM: Building Human Capital and Organizational Capability*, Technical report. Cornell University, Ithaca, NY, 1998.
7. T. B. Kinni, "A Reengineering Primer," *Quality Digest*, January 1994, pp. 26–30; "Reengineering Is Helping Health of Hospitals and Its Patients," *Total Quality Newsletter*, February 1994, p. 5; R. Recardo, "Process Reengineering in a Finance Division," *Journal for Quality and Participation*, June 1994, pp. 70–73.
8. L. Quillen, "Human Resource Computerization: A Dollar and Cents Approach," *Personnel Journal*, July 1989, pp. 74–77.
9. S. Greengard, "New Technology Is HR's Route to Reengineering," *Personnel Journal*, July 1994, pp. 32c–32o.
10. R. Broderick and J. W. Boudreau, "Human Resource Management, Information Technology, and the Competitive Edge," *Academy of Management Executive* 6 (1992), pp. 7–17.
11. S. E. O'Connell, "New Technologies Bring New Tools, New Rules," *HRMagazine*, December 1995, pp. 43–48; S. F. O'Connell, "The Virtual Workplace Moves at Warp Speed," *HRMagazine*, March 1996, pp. 51–57.
12. E. Brynjolfsson and L. Hitt, "The Productivity Paradox of Information Technology," *Communications of the ACM*, December 1993, pp. 66–77.
13. "Seven Critical Success Factors for Using Information Technology," *Total Quality Newsletter*, February 1994, p. 6.
14. J. E. Rigdon, "Technological Gains Are Cutting Costs in Jobs and Services," *The Wall Street Journal*, February 24, 1995, pp. A1, A5, A6.
15. S. Greengard, "How Technology Is Advancing HR," *Personnel Journal*, September 1993, pp. 80–90.
16. T. L. Hunter, "How Client/Server Is Reshaping the HRIS," *Personnel Journal*, July 1992, pp. 38–46; B. Busbin, "The Hidden Costs of Client/Server," *The Review*, August–September 1995, pp. 21–24.
17. D. Drechsel, "Principles for Client/Server Success," *The Review*, August–September 1995, pp. 26–29.
18. A. L. Lederer, "Emerging Technology and the Buy–Wait Dilemma: Sorting Fact from Fantasy," *The Review*, June–July 1993, pp. 16–19.
19. D. L. Fowler, "Imaging in HR: A Case Study," *The Review*, October–November 1994, pp. 29–33.
20. "Dial a Job Interview," *Chain Store Age Executive*, July 1994, pp. 35–36.
21. P. A. Galagan, "Think Performance: A Conversation with Gloria Gery," *Training and Development*, March 1994, pp. 47–51.
22. J. Clark and R. Koonce, "Meetings Go High-Tech," *Training and Development*, November 1995, pp. 32–38; A. M. Townsend, M. E. Whitman, and A. R. Hendrickson, "Computer Support Adds Power to Group Processes," *HRMagazine*, September 1995, pp. 87–91.
23. T. A. Stewart, "Getting Real about Brainpower," *Fortune*, November 27, 1994, pp. 201–3.
24. B. Ziegler, "Internet Software Poses Big Threat to Notes, IBM's Stake in Lotus," *The Wall Street Journal*, November 7, 1995, pp. A1, A8.
25. S. Shrivastava and J. Shaw, "Liberating HR through Technology," *Human Resource Management* 42, no. 3 (2003), pp. 201–17.
26. C. O'Reilly and P. Caldwell, *Cypress Semiconductor (A): Vision, Values, and Killer Software* (Stanford University Case Study, HR-8A, 1998).
27. "61 Percent of Americans Consider Themselves Overworked and 86 Percent Are Not Satisfied with Their Job, According to Monster's 2004 Work/Life Balance Survey," *Business Wire*, August 3, 2004.
28. G. McMahan and R. Woodman, "The Current Practice of Organization Development within the Firm: A Survey of Large Industrial Corporations," Group and Organization Studies 17 (1992), pp. 117–34.
29. B. Becker, M. Huselid, and D. Ulrich, *The HR Scorecard: Linking People, Strategy, and Performance* (Cambridge, MA: HBS Press, 2001).
30. D. Ulrich and A. Yeung, "A Shared Mindset," *Personnel Administrator*, March 1989, pp. 38–45.
31. G. Jones and P. Wright, "An Economic Approach to Conceptualizing the Utility of Human Resource Management Practices," *Research in Personnel/Human Resources* 10 (1992), pp. 271–99.
32. R. Schuler and J. Walker, "Human Resources Strategy: Focusing on Issues and Actions," *Organizational Dynamics*, Summer 1990, pp. 5–19.
33. J. Paauwe, *Human Resource Management and Performance: Unique Approaches for Achieving Long-Term Viability* (Oxford: Oxford University Press, 2004).
34. S. Csoka and B. Hackett, *Transforming the HR Function for Global Business Success*, (New York: Conference Board, 1998), Report 1209-19RR.

# APPENDIX

## Human Resource Certification Institute PHR/SPHR Test Specifications

HRCI conducts two levels of certification testing, the Professional in Human Resources (PHR) and the Senior Professional in Human Resources (SPHR). Following is the body of knowledge that HRCI recommends studying in preparing to take the certification exam. This body of knowledge is divided into six categories or functional areas within HR: Strategic Management, Workforce Planning and Employment, Human Resource Development, Total Rewards, and Risk Management. After the heading for each functional area, the PHR and SPHR weighted percentages are given. The PHR exam deals more heavily with questions on an operational level, whereas the SPHR exam focuses more on strategy. Additionally, within each functional area, the information is split under the headings Responsibilities and Knowledge.

Your text is a helpful resource in mastering many of the concepts that are tested in the PHR/SPHR exam. Visit the text Web site at **www.mhhe.com/noe6e** for a complete listing of page references for each of the knowledge requirements in the HRCI body of knowledge.

### 01 STRATEGIC MANAGEMENT (12%, 29%)

Developing, contributing to, and supporting the organization's mission, vision, values, strategic goals, and objectives; formulating policies; guiding and leading the change process; and evaluating HR's contributions to organizational effectiveness.

**Responsibilities:**

01 Interpret information related to the organization's operations from internal sources, including financial/accounting, business development, marketing, sales, operations, and information technology, in order to contribute to the development of the organization's strategic plan.

02 Interpret information from external sources related to the general business environment, industry practices and developments, technological developments, economic environment, labor pool, and legal and regulatory environment, in order to contribute to the development of the organization's strategic plan.

03 Participate as a contributing partner in the organization's strategic planning process.

04 Establish strategic relationships with key individuals in the organization to influence organizational decision-making.

05 Establish relationships/alliances with key individuals and organizations in the community to assist in achieving the organization's strategic goals and objectives.

06 Develop and utilize metrics to evaluate HR's contributions to the achievement of the organization's strategic goals and objectives.

07 Develop and execute strategies for managing organizational change that balance the expectations and needs of the organization, its employees, and all other stakeholders.

08 Develop and align the organization's human capital management plan with its strategic plan.

09 Facilitate the development and communication of the organization's core values and ethical behaviors.

10 Reinforce the organization's core values and behavioral expectations through modeling, communication, and coaching.

11 Develop and manage the HR budget in a manner consistent with the organization's strategic goals, objectives, and values.

12 Provide information for the development and monitoring of the organization's overall budget.

13 Monitor the legislative and regulatory environment for proposed changes and their potential impact to the organization, taking appropriate proactive steps to support, modify, or oppose the proposed changes.

SOURCE: The PHR/SPHR test specifications are defined and updated by the Human Resource Certification Institute (HRCI) every three to five years to reflect actual HR practice.

14 Develop policies and procedures to support corporate governance initiatives (for example, board of directors training, whistleblower protection, code of conduct).
15 Participate in enterprise risk management by examining HR policies to evaluate their potential risks to the organization.
16 Identify and evaluate alternatives and recommend strategies for vendor selection and/or outsourcing (for example, HRIS, benefits, payroll).
17 Participate in strategic decision-making and due diligence activities related to organizational structure and design (for example, corporate restructuring, mergers and acquisitions [M&A], off shoring, divestitures). **SPHR ONLY**
18 Determine strategic application of integrated technical tools and systems (for example, HRIS, performance management tools, applicant tracking, compensation tools, employee self-service technologies).

### Knowledge of:

01 The organization's mission, vision, values, business goals, objectives, plans, and processes.
02 Legislative and regulatory processes.
03 Strategic planning process and implementation.
04 Management functions, including planning, organizing, directing, and controlling.
05 Techniques to promote creativity and innovation.
06 Corporate governance procedures and compliance (for example, Sarbanes-Oxley Act).
07 Transition techniques for corporate restructuring, M&A, offshoring, and divestitures. **SPHR ONLY**

## 02 WORKFORCE PLANNING AND EMPLOYMENT (26%, 17%)

Developing, implementing, and evaluating sourcing, recruitment, hiring, orientation, succession planning, retention, and organizational exit programs necessary to ensure the workforce's ability to achieve the organization's goals and objectives.

### Responsibilities:

01 Ensure that workforce planning and employment activities are compliant with applicable federal, state, and local laws and regulations.
02 Identify workforce requirements to achieve the organization's short- and long-term goals and objectives (for example, corporate restructuring, M&A activity, workforce expansion or reduction).
03 Conduct job analyses to create job descriptions and identify job competencies.
04 Identify and document essential job functions for positions.
05 Establish hiring criteria based on job descriptions and required competencies.
06 Analyze labor market for trends that impact the ability to meet workforce requirements (for example, SWOT analysis, environmental scan, demographic scan). **SPHR ONLY**
07 Assess skill sets of internal workforce and external labor market to determine the availability of qualified candidates, utilizing third party vendors or agencies as appropriate.
08 Identify internal and external recruitment sources (for example, employee referrals, online job boards, résumé banks) and implement selected recruitment methods.
09 Evaluate recruitment methods and sources for effectiveness (for example, return on investment [ROI], cost per hire, time to fill).
10 Develop strategies to brand/market the organization to potential qualified applicants.
11 Develop and implement selection procedures, including applicant tracking, interviewing, testing, reference and background checking, and drug screening.
12 Develop and extend employment offers and conduct negotiations as necessary.
13 Administer post-offer employment activities (for example, execute employment agreements, complete I-9 verification forms, coordinate relocations, schedule physical exams).
14 Implement and/or administer the process for non-U.S. citizens to legally work in the United States.
15 Develop, implement, and evaluate orientation processes for new hires, rehires, and transfers.
16 Develop, implement, and evaluate retention strategies and practices.
17 Develop, implement, and evaluate succession planning process.
18 Develop and implement the organizational exit process for both voluntary and involuntary terminations, including planning for reductions in force (RIF).
19 Develop, implement, and evaluate an AAP, as required.

### Knowledge of:

08 Federal/state/local employment-related laws and regulations related to workforce planning and employment (for example, Title VII, ADA, ADEA, USERRA, EEOC Uniform Guidelines on Employee Selection Procedures, Immigration Reform and Control Act, Internal Revenue Code).
09 Quantitative analyses required to assess past and future staffing effectiveness (for example, cost-benefit analysis, costs per hire, selection ratios, adverse impact).
10 Recruitment sources (for example, Internet, agencies, employee referral) for targeting passive, semi-active and active candidates.

11 Recruitment strategies.
12 Staffing alternatives (for example, temporary and contract, outsourcing, job sharing, part-time).
13 Planning techniques (for example, succession planning, forecasting).
14 Reliability and validity of selection tests/tools/methods.
15 Use and interpretation of selection tests (for example, psychological/personality, cognitive, motor/physical assessments, performance, assessment center).
16 Interviewing techniques (for example, behavioral, situational, panel).
17 Relocation practices.
18 Impact of total rewards on recruitment and retention.
19 International HR and implications of global workforce for workforce planning and employment. **SPHR ONLY**
20 Voluntary and involuntary terminations, downsizing, restructuring, and outplacement strategies and practices.
21 Internal workforce assessment techniques (for example, skills testing, skills inventory, workforce demographic analysis) and employment policies, practices, and procedures (for example, orientation and retention).
22 Employer marketing and branding techniques.
23 Negotiation skills and techniques.

## 03 HUMAN RESOURCE DEVELOPMENT (17%, 17%)

Developing, implementing, and evaluating activities and programs that address employee training and development, performance appraisal, talent and performance management, and the unique needs of employees, to ensure that the knowledge, skills, abilities, and performance of the workforce meet current and future organizational and individual needs.

### Responsibilities:

01 Ensure that human resource development programs are compliant with all applicable federal, state, and local laws and regulations.
02 Conduct a needs assessment to identify and establish priorities regarding human resource development activities. **SPHR ONLY**
03 Develop/select and implement employee training programs (for example, leadership skills, harassment prevention, computer skills) to increase individual and organizational effectiveness. Note that this includes training design and methods for obtaining feedback from training (e.g., surveys, pre- and post-testing).
04 Evaluate effectiveness of employee training programs through the use of metrics (for example, participant surveys, pre- and post-testing). **SPHR ONLY**
05 Develop, implement, and evaluate talent management programs that include assessing talent, developing talent, and placing high-potential employees. **SPHR ONLY**
06 Develop/select and evaluate performance appraisal process (for example, instruments, ranking and rating scales, relationship to compensation, frequency).
07 Implement training programs for performance evaluators. **PHR ONLY**
08 Develop, implement, and evaluate performance management programs and procedures (for example, goal setting, job rotations, promotions).
09 Develop/select, implement, and evaluate programs (for example, flexible work arrangements, diversity initiatives, repatriation) to meet the unique needs of employees. **SPHR ONLY**

### Knowledge of:

24 Applicable federal, state, and local laws and regulations related to human resources development activities (for example, Title VII, ADA, ADEA, USERRA, EEOC Uniform Guidelines on Employee Selection Procedures).
25 Career development and leadership development theories and applications.
26 OD theories and applications.
27 Training program development techniques to create general and specialized training programs.
28 Training methods, facilitation techniques, instructional methods, and program delivery mechanisms.
29 Task/process analysis.
30 Performance appraisal methods (for example, instruments, ranking and rating scales).
31 Performance management methods (for example, goal setting, job rotations, promotions).
32 Applicable global issues (for example, international law, culture, local management approaches/practices, societal norms). **SPHR ONLY**
33 Techniques to assess training program effectiveness, including use of applicable metrics (for example, participant surveys, pre- and post-testing).
34 E-learning.
35 Mentoring and executive coaching.

## 04 TOTAL REWARDS (16%, 12%)

Developing/selecting, implementing/administering, and evaluating compensation and benefits programs for all employee groups that support the organization's strategic goals, objectives, and values.

### Responsibilities:

01 Ensure that compensation and benefits programs are compliant with applicable federal, state, and local laws and regulations.

02 Develop, implement, and evaluate compensation policies/programs and pay structures based upon internal equity and external market conditions that support the organization's strategic goals, objectives, and values.
03 Administer payroll functions (for example, new hires, deductions, adjustments, terminations).
04 Conduct benefits programs needs assessments (for example, benchmarking, employee survey).
05 Develop/select, implement/administer, and evaluate benefit programs that support the organization's strategic goals, objectives, and values (for example, health and welfare, retirement, stock purchase, wellness, employee assistance programs [EAP], time-off).
06 Communicate and train the workforce in the compensation and benefits programs and policies (for example, self-service technologies).
07 Develop/select, implement/administer, and evaluate executive compensation programs (for example, stock purchase, stock options, incentive, bonus, supplemental retirement plans). **SPHR ONLY**
08 Develop, implement/administer, and evaluate expatriate and foreign national compensation and benefits programs. **SPHR ONLY**

**Knowledge of:**

36 Federal, state, and local compensation, benefits, and tax laws (for example, FLSA, ERISA, COBRA, HIPAA, FMLA, FICA).
37 Total rewards strategies (for example, compensation, benefits, wellness, rewards, recognition, employee assistance).
38 Budgeting and accounting practices related to compensation and benefits.
39 Job evaluation methods.
40 Job pricing and pay structures.
41 External labor markets and/or economic factors.
42 Pay programs (for example, incentive, variable, merit).
43 Executive compensation methods. **SPHR ONLY**
44 Non-cash compensation methods (for example, stock options, ESOPs). **SPHR ONLY**
45 Benefits programs (for example, health and welfare, retirement, wellness, EAP, time-off).
46 International compensation laws and practices (for example, expatriate compensation, entitlements, choice of law codes). **SPHR ONLY**
47 Fiduciary responsibility related to total rewards management. **SPHR ONLY**

## 05 EMPLOYEE AND LABOR RELATIONS (22%, 18%)

Analyzing, developing, implementing/administering, and evaluating the workplace relationship between employer and employee, in order to maintain relationships and working conditions that balance employer and employee needs and rights in support of the organization's strategic goals, objectives, and values.

**Responsibilities:**

01 Ensure that employee and labor relations activities are compliant with applicable federal, state, and local laws and regulations.
02 Assess organizational climate by obtaining employee input (for example, focus groups, employee surveys, staff meetings).
03 Implement organizational change activities as appropriate in response to employee feedback.
04 Develop employee relations programs (for example, awards, recognition, discounts, special events) that promote a positive organizational culture.
05 Implement employee relations programs that promote a positive organizational culture.
06 Evaluate effectiveness of employee relations programs through the use of metrics (for example, exit interviews, employee surveys).
07 Establish workplace policies and procedures (for example, dress code, attendance, computer use) and monitor their application and enforcement to ensure consistency.
08 Develop, administer, and evaluate grievance/dispute resolution and performance improvement policies and procedures.
09 Resolve employee complaints filed with federal, state, and local agencies involving employment practices, utilizing professional resources as necessary (for example, legal counsel, mediation/arbitration specialists, and investigators).
10 Develop and direct proactive employee relations strategies for remaining union-free in non-organized locations.
11 Participate in collective bargaining activities, including contract negotiation and administration. **SPHR ONLY**

**Knowledge of:**

48 Applicable federal, state and local laws affecting employment in union and nonunion environments, such as antidiscrimination laws, sexual harassment, labor relations, and privacy (for example, WARN Act, Title VII, NLRA).
49 Techniques for facilitating positive employee relations (for example, employee surveys, focus groups, dispute resolution, labor/management cooperative strategies and programs).
50 Employee involvement strategies (for example, employee management committees, self-directed work teams, staff meetings).

51 Individual employment rights issues and practices (for example, employment at will, negligent hiring, defamation, employees' rights to bargain collectively).
52 Workplace behavior issues/practices (for example, absenteeism and performance improvement).
53 Unfair labor practices (for example, employee communication strategies and management training).
54 The collective bargaining process, strategies, and concepts (for example, contract negotiation and administration). **SPHR ONLY**
55 Positive employee relations strategies and nonmonetary rewards.

## 06 RISK MANAGEMENT (7%, 7%)

Developing, implementing/administering, and evaluating programs, plans, and policies which provide a safe and secure working environment and to protect the organization from liability.

### Responsibilities:

01 Ensure that workplace health, safety, security, and privacy activities are compliant with applicable federal, state, and local laws and regulations.
02 Identify the organization's safety program needs.
03 Develop/select and implement/administer occupational injury and illness prevention, safety incentives, and training programs. **PHR ONLY**
04 Develop/select, implement, and evaluate plans and policies to protect employees and other individuals, and to minimize the organization's loss and liability (for example, emergency response, evacuation, workplace violence, substance abuse, return-to-work policies).
05 Communicate and train the workforce on the plans and policies to protect employees and other individuals, and to minimize the organization's loss and liability.
06 Develop and monitor business continuity and disaster recovery plans.
07 Communicate and train the workforce on the business continuity and disaster recovery plans.
08 Develop internal and external privacy policies (for example, identity theft, data protection, HIPAA compliance, workplace monitoring).
09 Administer internal and external privacy policies.

### Knowledge of:

56 Federal, state, and local workplace health, safety, security, and privacy laws and regulations (for example, OSHA, Drug-Free Workplace Act, ADA, HIPAA, Sarbanes-Oxley).
57 Occupational injury and illness compensation and programs.
58 Occupational injury and illness prevention programs.
59 Investigation procedures of workplace safety, health and security enforcement agencies (for example, OSHA, National Institute for Occupational Safety and Health [NIOSH]).
60 Workplace safety risks.
61 Workplace security risks (for example, theft, corporate espionage, asset and data protection, sabotage).
62 Potential violent behavior and workplace violence conditions.
63 General health and safety practices (for example, evacuation, hazard communication, ergonomic evaluations).
64 Incident and emergency response plans.
65 Internal investigation, monitoring, and surveillance techniques.
66 Issues related to substance abuse and dependency (for example, identification of symptoms, substance-abuse testing, discipline).
67 Business continuity and disaster recovery plans (for example, data storage and backup, alternative work locations and procedures).
68 Data integrity techniques and technology (for example, data sharing, firewalls).

## CORE KNOWLEDGE REQUIRED BY HR PROFESSIONALS

69 Needs assessment and analysis.
70 Third-party contract negotiation and management, including development of requests for proposals (RFPs).
71 Communication skills and strategies (for example, presentation, collaboration, influencing, diplomacy, sensitivity).
72 Organizational documentation requirements to meet federal and state requirements.
73 Adult learning processes.
74 Motivation concepts and applications.
75 Training techniques (for example, computer based, classroom, on-the-job).
76 Leadership concepts and applications.
77 Project management concepts and applications.
78 Diversity concepts and applications.
79 Human relations concepts and applications (for example, interpersonal and organizational behavior).
80 HR ethics and professional standards.
81 Technology to support HR activities (for example, HRIS, employee self-service, e-learning, ATS).
82 Qualitative and quantitative methods and tools for analysis, interpretation, and decision-making purposes (for example, metrics and measurements, cost/benefit analysis, financial statement analysis).

83 Change management methods.
84 Job analysis and job description methods.
85 Employee records management (for example, electronic/paper, retention, disposal).
86 The interrelationships among HR activities and programs across functional areas.
87 Types of organizational structures (for example, matrix, hierarchy).
88 Environmental scanning concepts and applications.
89 Methods for assessing employee attitudes, opinions, and satisfaction (for example, opinion surveys, attitude surveys, focus groups/panels).
90 Basic budgeting and accounting concepts.
91 Risk management techniques.

# GLOSSARY

**Acceptability** The extent to which a performance measure is deemed to be satisfactory or adequate by those who use it.

**Action learning** Teams work on an actual business problem, commit to an action plan, and are accountable for carrying out the plan.

**Action plan** Document summarizing what the trainee and manager will do to ensure that training transfers to the job.

**Action steps** The part of a written affirmative plan that specifies what an employer plans to do to reduce underutilization of protected groups.

**Adventure learning** Learning focused on the development of teamwork and leadership skills by using structured outdoor activities.

**Agency shop** A union security provision that requires an employee to pay union membership dues but not to join the union.

**Agent** In agency theory, a person (e.g., a manager) who is expected to act on behalf of a principal (e.g., an owner).

**Alternative dispute resolution (ADR)** A method of resolving disputes that does not rely on the legal system. Often proceeds through the four stages of open door policy, peer review, mediation, and arbitration.

**Alternative work arrangements** Independent contractors, on-call workers, temporary workers, and contract company workers who are not employed full-time by the company.

**Americans with Disabilities Act (ADA)** A 1990 act prohibiting individuals with disabilities from being discriminated against in the workplace.

**Analytic approach** Type of assessment of HRM effectiveness that involves determining the impact of, or the financial costs and benefits of, a program or practice.

**Anticipatory socialization** Process that helps individuals develop expectations about the company, job, working conditions, and interpersonal relationships.

**Appraisal politics** A situation in which evaluators purposefully distort a rating to achieve personal or company goals.

**Apprenticeship** A work-study training method with both on-the-job and classroom training.

**Arbitration** A procedure for resolving collective bargaining impasses by which an arbitrator chooses a solution to the dispute.

**Assessment** Collecting information and providing feedback to employees about their behavior, communication style, or skills.

**Assessment center** A process in which multiple raters evaluate employees' performance on a number of exercises.

**Associate union membership** A form of union membership by which the union receives dues in exchange for services (e.g., health insurance, credit cards) but does not provide representation in collective bargaining.

**Attitude awareness and change program** Program focusing on increasing employees' awareness of differences in cultural and ethnic backgrounds, physical characteristics, and personal characteristics that influence behavior toward others.

**Attitudinal structuring** The aspect of the labor–management negotiation process that refers to the relationship and level of trust between the negotiators.

**Audiovisual instruction** Includes overheads, slides, and video.

**Audit approach** Type of assessment of HRM effectiveness that involves review of customer satisfaction or key indicators (e.g., turnover rate, average days to fill a position) related to an HRM functional area (e.g., recruiting, training).

**Avatars** Computer depictions of humans that can be used as imaginary coaches, co-workers, and customers in simulations.

**Balanced scorecard** A means of performance measurement that gives managers a chance to look at their company from the perspectives of internal and external customers, employees, and shareholders.

**Basic skills** Reading, writing, and communication skills needed to understand the content of a training program.

**Behavior-based program** A program focusing on changing the organizational policies and individual behaviors that inhibit employees' personal growth and productivity.

**Benchmarking** Comparing an organization's practices against those of the competition.

**Benchmarks©** An instrument designed to measure the factors that are important to managerial success.

**Bona fide occupational qualification (BFOQ)** A job qualification based on race, sex, religion, and so on that an employer asserts is a necessary qualification for the job.

**Career management system** A system to retain and motivate employees by identifying and meeting their development needs (also called *development planning system*).

**Career support** Coaching, protection, sponsorship, and providing challenging assignments, exposure, and visibility.

**Cash balance plan** Retirement plan in which the employer sets up an individual account for each employee and contributes a percentage of the employee's salary; the account earns interest at a predetermined rate.

**Centralization** Degree to which decision-making authority resides at the top of the organizational chart.

**Checkoff provision** A union contract provision that requires an employer to deduct union dues from employees' paychecks.

**Client–server architecture** Computer design that provides a method to consolidate data and applications into a single host system (the client).

**Climate for transfer** Trainees' perceptions of characteristics of the work environment (social support and situational constraints) that can either facilitate or inhibit use of trained skills or behavior.

**Closed shop** A union security provision requiring a person to be a union member before being hired. Illegal under NLRA.

**Coach** A peer or manager who works with an employee to motivate her, help her develop skills, and provide reinforcement and feedback.

**Cognitive ability** Includes three dimensions: verbal comprehension, quantitative ability, and reasoning ability.

**Cognitive ability tests** Tests that include three dimensions: verbal comprehension, quantitative ability, and reasoning ability.

**Communities of practice** Groups of employees who work together, learn from each other, and develop a common understanding of how to get work accomplished.

**Comparable worth** A public policy that advocates remedies for any undervaluation of women's jobs (also called *pay equity*).

**Compa-ratio** An index of the correspondence between actual and intended pay.

**Compensable factors** The characteristics of jobs that an organization values and chooses to pay for.

**Competitiveness** A company's ability to maintain and gain market share in its industry.

**Concentration strategy** A strategy focusing on increasing market share, reducing costs, or creating and maintaining a market niche for products and services.

**Concurrent validation** A criterion-related validity study in which a test is administered to all the people currently in a job and then incumbents' scores are correlated with existing measures of their performance on the job.

**Consequences** The incentives that employees receive for performing well.

**Consolidated Omnibus Budget Reconciliation Act (COBRA)** The 1985 act that requires employers to permit employees to extend their health insurance coverage at group rates for up to 36 months following a qualifying event, such as a layoff.

**Content validation** A test validation strategy performed by demonstrating that the items, questions, or problems posed by a test are a representative sample of the kinds of situations or problems that occur on the job.

**Continuous learning** A learning system that requires employees to understand the entire work process and expects them to acquire new skills, apply them on the job, and share what they have learned with other employees.

**Coordination training** Training a team in how to share information and decision-making responsibilities to maximize team performance.

**Corporate campaigns** Union activities designed to exert public, financial, or political pressure on employers during the union-organizing process.

**Cost–benefit analysis** The process of determining the economic benefits of a training program using accounting methods.

**Criterion-related validity** A method of establishing the validity of a personnel selection method by showing a substantial correlation between test scores and job performance scores.

**Cross-cultural preparation** The process of educating employees (and their families) who are given an assignment in a foreign country.

**Cross-training** Training in which team members understand and practice each other's skills so that members are prepared to step in and take another member's place should he or she temporarily or permanently leave the team.

**Cultural immersion** A behavior-based diversity program that sends employees into communities where they interact with persons from different cultures, races, and nationalities.

**Decision support systems** Problem-solving systems that usually include a "what-if" feature that allows users to see how outcomes change when assumptions or data change.

**Delayering** Reducing the number of job levels within an organization.

**Departmentalization** Degree to which work units are grouped based on functional similarity or similarity of workflow.

**Development** The acquisition of knowledge, skills, and behaviors that improve an employee's ability to meet changes in job requirements and in client and customer demands.

**Direct applicants** People who apply for a job vacancy without prompting from the organization.

**Disparate impact** A theory of discrimination based on facially neutral employment practices that disproportionately exclude a protected group from employment opportunities.

**Disparate treatment** A theory of discrimination based on different treatment given to individuals because of their race, color, religion, sex, national origin, age, or disability status.

**Distributive bargaining** The part of the labor–management negotiation process that focuses on dividing a fixed economic "pie."

**Diversity training** Training designed to change employee attitudes about diversity and/or develop skills needed to work with a diverse workforce.

**Downsizing** The planned elimination of large numbers of personnel, designed to enhance organizational effectiveness.

**Downward move** A job change involving a reduction in an employee's level of responsibility and authority.

**Due process policies** Policies by which a company formally lays out the steps an employee can take to appeal a termination decision.

**Duty of fair representation** The National Labor Relations Act requirement that all bargaining unit members have equal access to and representation by the union.

**Efficiency wage theory** A theory stating that wage influences worker productivity.

**E-learning** Instruction and delivery of training by computers through the Internet or company intranet.

**Electronic business (e-business)** Any business that a company conducts electronically.

**Electronic human resource management (e-HRM)** The processing and transmission of digitized information used in HRM.

**Electronic performance support systems (EPSS)** Computer applications that can provide (as requested) skills training, information access, and expert advice.

**Employee assistance programs (EAPs)** Employer programs that attempt to ameliorate problems encountered by workers who are drug dependent, alcoholic, or psychologically troubled.

**Employee engagement** The degree to which employees are fully involved in their work and the strength of their job and company commitment.

**Employee Retirement Income Security Act (ERISA)** The 1974 act that increased the fiduciary responsibilities of pension plan trustees, established vesting rights and portability provisions, and established the Pension Benefit Guaranty Corporation (PBGC).

**Employee stock ownership plan (ESOP)** An employee ownership plan that provides employers certain tax and financial advantages when stock is granted to employees.

**Employment-at-will doctrine** The doctrine that, in the absence of a specific contract, either an employer or employee could sever the employment relationship at any time.

**Employment-at-will policies** Policies which state that either an employer or employee can terminate the employment relationship at any time, regardless of cause.

**Empowering** Giving employees the responsibility and authority to make decisions.

**Encounter phase** Phase of socialization that occurs when an employee begins a new job.

**Equal employment opportunity (EEO)** The government's attempt to ensure that all individuals have an equal opportunity for employment, regardless of race, color, religion, sex, age, disability, or national origin.

**Equal Employment Opportunity Commission (EEOC)** The government commission established to ensure that all individuals have an equal opportunity for employment, regardless of race, color, religion, sex, age, disability, or national origin.

**Ergonomics** The interface between individuals' physiological characteristics and the physical work environment.

**Exempt** Employees who are not covered by the Fair Labor Standards Act. Exempt employees are not eligible for overtime pay.

**Expatriate** Employee sent by his or her company to manage operations in a different country.

**Expectancy theory** The theory that says motivation is a function of valence, instrumentality, and expectancy.

**Expert systems** Computer systems incorporating the decision rules of people recognized as experts in a certain area.

**External analysis** Examining the organization's operating environment to identify strategic opportunities and threats.

**External growth strategy** An emphasis on acquiring vendors and suppliers or buying businesses that allow a company to expand into new markets.

**External labor market** Persons outside the firm who are actively seeking employment.

**Externship** When a company allows an employee to take a full-time operational role at another company.

**Evidence-based HR** Demonstrating that human resource practices have a positive influence on the company's bottom line or key stakeholders (employees, customers, community, shareholders).

**Fact finder** A person who reports on the reasons for a labor–management dispute, the views and arguments of both sides, and a nonbinding recommendation for settling the dispute.

**Fair Labor Standards Act (FLSA)** The 1938 law that established the minimum wage and overtime pay.

**Family and Medical Leave Act** The 1993 act that requires employers with 50 or more employees to provide up to 12 weeks of unpaid leave after childbirth or adoption; to care for a seriously ill child, spouse, or parent; or for an employee's own serious illness.

**Feedback** Information that employees receive while they are performing concerning how well they are meeting objectives.

**Financial Accounting Statement (FAS) 106** The rule issued by the Financial Accounting Standards Board in 1993 requiring companies to fund benefits provided after retirement on an accrual rather than a pay-as-you-go basis and to enter these future cost obligations on their financial statements.

**Forecasting** The attempts to determine the supply of and demand for various types of human resources to predict areas within the organization where there will be future labor shortages or surpluses.

**Formal education programs** Employee development programs, including short courses offered by consultants or universities, executive MBA programs, and university programs.

**Four-fifths rule** A rule that states that an employment test has disparate impact if the hiring rate for a minority group is less than four-fifths, or 80 percent, of the hiring rate for the majority group.

**Frame of reference** A standard point that serves as a comparison for other points and thus provides meaning.

**Gainsharing** A form of group compensation based on group or plant performance (rather than organizationwide profits) that does not become part of the employee's base salary.

**General duty clause** The provision of the Occupational Safety and Health Act that states an employer has an overall obligation to furnish employees with a place of employment free from recognized hazards.

**Generalizability** The degree to which the validity of a selection method established in one context extends to other contexts.

**Glass ceiling** A barrier to advancement to higher-level jobs in the company that adversely affects women and minorities. The barrier may be due to lack of access to training programs, development experiences, or relationships (e.g., mentoring).

**Goals** What an organization hopes to achieve in the medium- to long-term future.

**Goals and timetables** The part of a written affirmative action plan that specifies the percentage of women and minorities that an employer seeks to have in each job group and the date by which that percentage is to be attained.

**Group mentoring program** A program pairing a successful senior employee with a group of four to six less experienced protégés.

**Group- or team-building methods** Training methods that help trainees share ideas and experiences, build group identity, understand the dynamics of interpersonal relationships, and get to know their own strengths and weaknesses and those of their co-workers.

**Groupware** Software application that enables multiple users to track, share, and organize information and to work on the same database or document simultaneously.

**Hands-on methods** Training methods that require the trainee to be actively involved in learning.

**Health maintenance organization (HMO)** A health care plan that provides benefits on a prepaid basis for employees who are required to use only HMO medical service providers.

**High-leverage training** Training practice that links training to strategic business goals, has top management support, relies on an instructional design model, and is benchmarked to programs in other organizations.

**High-performance work systems** Work systems that maximize the fit between employees and technology.

**High-potential employees** Employees the company believes are capable of being successful in high-level management positions.

**Host country** The country in which the parent-country organization seeks to locate or has already located a facility.

**Host-country nationals (HCNs)** Employees born and raised in a host, not parent, country.

**HR dashboard** HR metrics (such as productivity and absenteeism) that are accessible by employees and managers through the company intranet or human resource information system.

**Human resource information system (HRIS)** A system used to acquire, store, manipulate, analyze, retrieve, and distribute information related to human resources.

**Human resource management (HRM)** The policies, practices, and systems that influence employees' behavior, attitudes, and performances.

**Human resource recruitment** The practice or activity carried on by the organization with the primary purpose of identifying and attracting potential employees.

**Imaging** A process for scanning documents, storing them electronically, and retrieving them.

**In-basket** A simulation of the administrative tasks of a manager's job.

**Individualism–collectivism** One of Hofstede's cultural dimensions; describes the strength of the relation between an individual and other individuals in a society.

**Input** Instructions that tell the employee what, how, and when to perform; also the support they are given to help them perform.

**Intangible assets** A type of company asset including human capital, customer capital, social capital, and intellectual capital.

**Integrative bargaining** The part of the labor–management negotiation process that seeks solutions beneficial to both sides.

**Intellectual capital** Creativity, productivity, and service provided by employees.

**Interactional justice** A concept of justice referring to the interpersonal nature of how the outcomes were implemented.

**Internal analysis** The process of examining an organization's strengths and weaknesses.

**Internal growth strategy** A focus on new market and product development, innovation, and joint ventures.

**Internal labor force** Labor force of current employees.

**Interview** Employees are questioned about their work and personal experiences, skills, and career plans.

**Intraorganizational bargaining** The part of the labor–management negotiation process that focuses on the conflicting objectives of factions within labor and management.

**Involuntary turnover** Turnover initiated by the organization (often among people who would prefer to stay).

**ISO 9000:2000** A series of quality assurance standards developed by the International Organization for Standardization in Switzerland and adopted worldwide.

**Job analysis** The process of getting detailed information about jobs.

**Job description** A list of the tasks, duties, and responsibilities that a job entails.

**Job design** The process of defining the way work will be performed and the tasks that will be required in a given job.

**Job enlargement** Adding challenges or new responsibilities to an employee's current job.

**Job enrichment** Ways to add complexity and meaningfulness to a person's work.

**Job evaluation** An administrative procedure used to measure internal job worth.

**Job experience** The relationships, problems, demands, tasks, and other features that employees face in their jobs.

**Job hazard analysis technique** A breakdown of each job into basic elements, each of which is rated for its potential for harm or injury.

**Job involvement** The degree to which people identify themselves with their jobs.

**Job redesign** The process of changing the tasks or the way work is performed in an existing job.

**Job rotation** The process of systematically moving a single individual from one job to another over the course of time. The job assignments may be in various functional areas of the company or movement may be between jobs in a single functional area or department.

**Job satisfaction** A pleasurable feeling that results from the perception that one's job fulfills or allows for the fulfillment of one's important job values.

**Job specification** A list of the knowledge, skills, abilities, and other characteristics (KSAOs) that an individual must have to perform a job.

**Job structure** The relative pay of jobs in an organization.

**Key jobs** Benchmark jobs, used in pay surveys, that have relatively stable content and are common to many organizations.

**Knowledge management** Process of enhancing company performance by designing and using tools, systems, and cultures to improve creation, sharing, and use of knowledge.

**Knowledge workers** Employees who own the intellectual means of producing a product or service.

**Leaderless group discussion** Process in which a team of five to seven employees solve an assigned problem together within a certain time period.

**Leading indicator** An objective measure that accurately predicts future labor demand.

**Learner control** Ability of trainees to actively learn through self-pacing, exercises, links to other materials, and conversations with other trainees and experts.

**Learning management system (LMS)** Technology platform that automates the administration, development, and delivery of a company's training program.

**Learning organization** An organization whose employees are continuously attempting to learn new things and apply what they have learned to improve product or service quality.

**Long-term–short-term orientation** One of Hofstede's cultural dimensions; describes how a culture balances immediate benefits with future rewards.

**Maintenance of membership** Union rules requiring members to remain members for a certain period of time (e.g., the length of the union contract).

**Malcolm Baldrige National Quality Award** An award established in 1987 to promote quality awareness, to recognize quality achievements of U.S. companies, and to publicize successful quality strategies.

**Managing diversity** The process of creating an environment that allows all employees to contribute to organizational goals and experience personal growth.

**Marginal employee** An employee performing at a barely acceptable level because of lack of ability and/or motivation to perform well, not poor work conditions.

**Marginal tax rate** The percentage of an additional dollar of earnings that goes to taxes.

**Masculinity–femininity dimension** One of Hofstede's cultural dimensions; describes the division of roles between the sexes within a society.

**Mediation** A procedure for resolving collective bargaining impasses by which a mediator with no formal authority acts as a facilitator and go-between in the negotiations.

**Mentor** An experienced, productive senior employee who helps develop a less experienced employee.

**Merit increase grid** A grid that combines an employee's performance rating with his or her position in a pay range to determine the size and frequency of his or her pay increases.

**Minimum wage** The lowest amount that employers are legally allowed to pay; the 1990 amendment of the Fair Labor Standards Act permits a subminimum wage to workers under the age of 20 for a period of up to 90 days.

**Motivation to learn** The desire of the trainee to learn the content of a training program.

**Myers-Briggs Type Indicator (MBTI)®** A psychological test used for team building and leadership development that identifies employees' preferences for energy, information gathering, decision making, and lifestyle.

**Needs assessment** The process used to determine if training is necessary.

**Negative affectivity** A dispositional dimension that reflects pervasive individual differences in satisfaction with any and all aspects of life.

**Network** A combination of desktop computers, computer terminals, and mainframes or minicomputers that share access to databases and a method to transmit information throughout the system.

**New technologies** Current applications of knowledge, procedures, and equipment that have not been previously used. Usually involves replacing human labor with equipment, information processing, or some combination of the two.

**Nonkey jobs** Jobs that are unique to organizations and that cannot be directly valued or compared through the use of market surveys.

**Objective** The purpose and expected outcome of training activities.

**Occupational Safety and Health Act (OSHA)** The 1970 law that authorizes the federal government to establish and enforce occupational safety and health standards for all places of employment engaging in interstate commerce.

**Offshoring** A special case of outsourcing where the jobs that move actually leave one country and go to another.

**Onshoring** Exporting jobs to rural parts of the United States.

**On-the-job training (OJT)** Peers or managers training new or inexperienced employees who learn the job by observation, understanding, and imitation.

**Opportunity to perform** The trainee is provided with or actively seeks experience using newly learned knowledge skills, or behavior.

**Organizational analysis** A process for determining the business appropriateness of training.

**Organizational commitment** The degree to which an employee identifies with the organization and is willing to put forth effort on its behalf.

**Organizational socialization** The process by which new employees are transformed into effective members of a company.

**Outcome fairness** The judgment that people make with respect to the outcomes received relative to the outcomes received by other people with whom they identify.

**Outplacement counseling** Counseling to help displaced employees manage the transition from one job to another.

**Output** A job's performance standards.

**Outsourcing** An organization's use of an outside organization for a broad set of services.

**Parent country** The country in which a company's corporate headquarters is located.

**Parent-country nationals (PCNs)** Employees who were born and live in a parent country.

**Pay grades** Jobs of similar worth or content grouped together for pay administration purposes.

**Pay level** The average pay, including wages, salaries, and bonuses, of jobs in an organization.

**Pay policy line** A mathematical expression that describes the relationship between a job's pay and its job evaluation points.

**Pay structure** The relative pay of different jobs (job structure) and how much they are paid (pay level).

**Pension Benefit Guaranty Corporation (PBGC)** The agency that guarantees to pay employees a basic retirement benefit in the event that financial difficulties force a company to terminate or reduce employee pension benefits.

**Performance appraisal** The process through which an organization gets information on how well an employee is doing his or her job.

**Performance feedback** The process of providing employees information regarding their performance effectiveness.

**Performance management** The means through which managers ensure that employees' activities and outputs are congruent with the organization's goals.

**Performance planning and evaluation (PPE) system** Any system that seeks to tie the formal performance appraisal process to the company's strategies by specifying at the beginning of the evaluation period the types and level of performance that must be accomplished in order to achieve the strategy.

**Person analysis** A process for determining whether employees need training, who needs training, and whether employees are ready for training.

**Person characteristics** An employee's knowledge, skills, abilities, and attitudes.

**Power distance** One of Hofstede's cultural dimensions; concerns how a culture deals with hierarchical power relationships—particularly the unequal distribution of power.

**Predictive validation** A criterion-related validity study that seeks to establish an empirical relationship between applicants' test scores and their eventual performance on the job.

**Preferred provider organization (PPO)** A group of health care providers who contract with employers, insurance companies, and so forth to provide health care at a reduced fee.

**Presentation methods** Training methods in which trainees are passive recipients of information.

**Principal** In agency theory, a person (e.g., the owner) who seeks to direct another person's behavior.

**Procedural justice** A concept of justice focusing on the methods used to determine the outcomes received.

**Profit sharing** A compensation plan in which payments are based on a measure of organization performance (profits) and do not become part of the employees' base salary.

**Progression of withdrawal** Theory that dissatisfied individuals enact a set of behaviors to avoid the work situation.

**Promotions** Advances into positions with greater challenge, more responsibility, and more authority than the employee's previous job.

**Protean career** A career that is frequently changing due to both changes in the person's interests, abilities, and values and changes in the work environment.

**Psychological contract** Expectations of employee contributions and what the company will provide in return.

**Psychological success** The feeling of pride and accomplishment that comes from achieving life goals.

**Psychosocial support** Serving as a friend and role model, providing positive regard and acceptance, and creating an outlet for a protégé to talk about anxieties and fears.

**Quantitative ability** Concerns the speed and accuracy with which one can solve arithmetic problems of all kinds.

**Range spread** The distance between the minimum and maximum amounts in a pay grade.

**Rate ranges** Different employees in the same job may have different pay rates.

**Readability** The difficulty level of written materials.

**Realistic job preview** Provides accurate information about the attractive and unattractive aspects of a job, working conditions, company, and location to ensure that potential employees develop appropriate expectations.

**Reasonable accommodation** Making facilities readily accessible to and usable by individuals with disabilities.

**Reasoning ability** Refers to a person's capacity to invent solutions to many diverse problems.

**Recruitment** The process of seeking applicants for potential employment.

**Reengineering** Review and redesign of work processes to make them more efficient and improve the quality of the end product or service.

**Referrals** People who are prompted to apply for a job by someone within the organization.

**Relational database** A database structure that stores information in separate files that can be linked by common elements.

**Reliability** The consistency of a performance measure; the degree to which a performance measure is free from random error.

**Repatriation** The preparation of expatriates for return to the parent company and country from a foreign assignment.

**Repurposing** Directly translating instructor-led training online.

**Request for proposal (RFP)** A document that outlines for potential vendors and consultants the type of service the company is seeking, references needed, number of employees who should be trained, project funding, the follow-up process, expected completion date, and the date when proposals must be received by the company.

**Right-to-work laws** State laws that make union shops, maintenance of membership, and agency shops illegal.

**Role behaviors** Behaviors that are required of an individual in his or her role as a job holder in a social work environment.

**Role play** A participant taking the part or role of a manager or other employee.

**Sabbatical** A leave of absence from the company to renew or develop skills.

**Safety awareness programs** Employer programs that attempt to instill symbolic and substantive changes in the organization's emphasis on safety.

**Sarbanes-Oxley Act of 2002** A congressional act passed in response to illegal and unethical behavior by managers and executives. The Act sets stricter rules for business, especially accounting practices including requiring more open and consistent disclosure of financial data, CEOs' assurance that data are completely accurate, and provisions that affect the employee–employer relationship (e.g., development of a code of conduct for senior financial officers).

**Selection** The process by which an organization attempts to identify applicants with the necessary knowledge, skills, abilities, and other characteristics that will help it achieve its goals.

**Self-directed learning** A program in which employees take responsibility for all aspects of learning.

**Self-efficacy** The employees' belief that they can successfully learn the content of a training program.

**Self-service** Giving employees online access to human resources information.

**Settling-in phase** Phase of socialization that occurs when employees are comfortable with job demands and social relationships.

**Simulation** A training method that represents a real-life situation, allowing trainees to see the outcomes of their decisions in an artificial environment.

**Situational interview** An interview procedure where applicants are confronted with specific issues, questions, or problems that are likely to arise on the job.

**Six Sigma process** System of measuring, analyzing, improving, and controlling processes once they meet quality standards.

**Six Sigma Training** An action training program that provides employees with defect-reducing tools to cut costs and certifies employees as green belts, champions, or black belts.

**Skill-based pay** Pay based on the skills employees acquire and are capable of using.

**Specificity** The extent to which a performance measure gives detailed guidance to employees about what is expected of them and how they can meet these expectations.

**Stakeholders** The various interest groups who have relationships with and, consequently, whose interests are tied to the organization (e.g., employees, suppliers, customers, shareholders, community).

**Standard deviation rule** A rule used to analyze employment tests to determine disparate impact; it uses the difference between the expected representation for minority groups and the actual representation to determine whether the difference between the two is greater than would occur by chance.

**Stock options** An employee ownership plan that gives employees the opportunity to buy the company's stock at a previously fixed price.

**Strategic choice** The organization's strategy; the ways an organization will attempt to fulfill its mission and achieve its long-term goals.

**Strategic congruence** The extent to which the performance management system elicits job performance that is consistent with the organization's strategy, goals, and culture.

**Strategic human resource management (SHRM)** A pattern of planned human resource deployments and activities intended to enable an organization to achieve its goals.

**Strategic training and development initiatives** Learning-related actions that a company takes to achieve its business strategy.

**Strategy formulation** The process of deciding on a strategic direction by defining a company's mission and goals, its external opportunities and threats, and its internal strengths and weaknesses.

**Strategy implementation** The process of devising structures and allocating resources to enact the strategy a company has chosen.

**Succession planning** The identification and tracking of high-potential employees capable of filling higher-level managerial positions.

**Summary plan description (SPD)** A reporting requirement of the Employee Retirement Income Security Act (ERISA) that obligates employers to describe the plan's funding, eligibility requirements, risks, and so forth within 90 days after an employee has entered the plan.

**Support network** Trainees who meet to discuss their progress in using learned capabilities on the job.

**Sustainability** The ability of a company to survive in a dynamic competitive environment. Based on an approach to organizational decision making that considers the long term impact of strategies on stakeholders (e.g., employees, shareholders, suppliers, community).

**Taft-Hartley Act** The 1947 act that outlawed unfair union labor practices.

**Task analysis** The process of identifying the tasks, knowledge, skills, and behaviors that need to be emphasized in training.

**Team leader training** Training of the team manager or facilitator.

**Technic of operations review (TOR)** Method of determining safety problems via an analysis of past accidents.

**Teleconferencing** Synchronous exchange of audio, video, or text between individuals or groups at two or more locations.

**Third country** A country other than a host or parent country.

**Third-country nationals (TCNs)** Employees born in a country other than a parent or host country.

**360-degree appraisal (feedback systems)** A performance appraisal process for managers that includes evaluations from a wide range of persons who interact with the manager. The process includes self-evaluations as well as evaluations from the manager's boss, subordinates, peers, and customers.

**Total quality management (TQM)** A cooperative form of doing business that relies on the talents and capabilities of both labor and management to continually improve quality and productivity.

**Training** A planned effort to facilitate the learning of job-related knowledge, skills, and behavior by employees.

**Training design process** A systematic approach for developing training programs.

**Training outcomes** A way to evaluate the effectiveness of a training program based on cognitive, skill-based, affective, and results outcomes.

**Transaction processing** Computations and calculations used to review and document HRM decisions and practices.

**Transfer** The movement of an employee to a different job assignment in a different area of the company.

**Transfer of training** The use of knowledge, skills, and behaviors learned in training on the job.

**Transitional matrix** Matrix showing the proportion or number of employees in different job categories at different times.

**Transnational process** The extent to which a company's planning and decision-making processes include representatives and ideas from a variety of cultures.

**Transnational representation** Reflects the multinational composition of a company's managers.

**Transnational scope** A company's ability to make HRM decisions from an international perspective.

**Tuition reimbursement** The practice of reimbursing employees' costs for college and university courses and degree programs.

**Uncertainty avoidance** One of Hofstede's cultural dimensions; describes how cultures seek to deal with an unpredictable future.

**Union shop** A union security provision that requires a person to join the union within a certain amount of time after being hired.

**Upward feedback** A performance appraisal process for managers that includes subordinates' evaluations.

**Utility** The degree to which the information provided by selection methods enhances the effectiveness of selecting personnel in real organizations.

**Utilization analysis** A comparison of the race, sex, and ethnic composition of an employer's workforce with that of the available labor supply.

**Validity** The extent to which a performance measure assesses all the relevant—and only the relevant—aspects of job performance.

**Verbal comprehension** Refers to a person's capacity to understand and use written and spoken language.

**Virtual reality** Computer-based technology that provides trainees with a three-dimensional learning experience. Trainees operate in a simulated environment that responds to their behaviors and reactions.

**Virtual teams** Teams that are separated by time, geographic distance, culture and/or organizational boundaries and rely exclusively on technology for interaction between team members.

**Voluntary turnover** Turnover initiated by employees (often whom the company would prefer to keep).

**Webcasting** Classroom instruction provided online via live broadcasts.

**Whistle-blowing** Making grievances public by going to the media or government.

**Workforce utilization review** A comparison of the proportion of workers in protected subgroups with the proportion that each subgroup represents in the relevant labor market.

# Photo Credits

| | |
|---|---|
| Page 24 | Photo Courtesy of Best Buy |
| Page 83 | Digital Vision/Getty Images |
| Page 130 | Courtesy of OSHA |
| Page 148 | MEDRAD INC. |
| Page 198 | © Ryan McVay/Getty Images |
| Page 243 | Digital Vision/Getty Images |
| Page 293 | © The McGraw-Hill Companies, Inc./Lars A. Niki, photographer |
| Page 347 | Ryan McVay/Getty Images |
| Page 405 | Courtesy of GE |
| Page 463 | Kim Steele/Getty Images |
| Page 499 | Grant V Faint/Digital Vision/Getty Images |
| Page 525 | Photodisc/Getty Images |
| Page 568 | Courtesy of Ernst & Young |
| Page 636 | The McGraw-Hill Companies, Inc./Andrew Resek, photographer |
| Page 661 | D Normark/PhotoLink/Getty Images |
| Page 713 | Ryan McVay/Getty Images |

# NAME AND COMPANY INDEX

# Subject Index

## COMPETING THROUGH GLOBALIZATION

## ALGEBRA'S COMMON GRAPHS

**Identity Function**

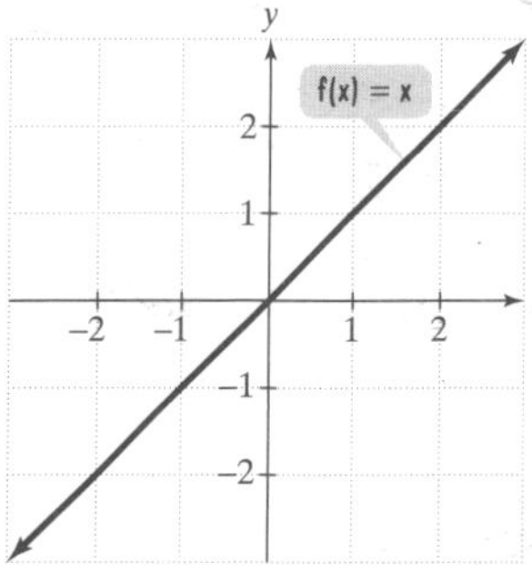


**Standard Quadratic Function**

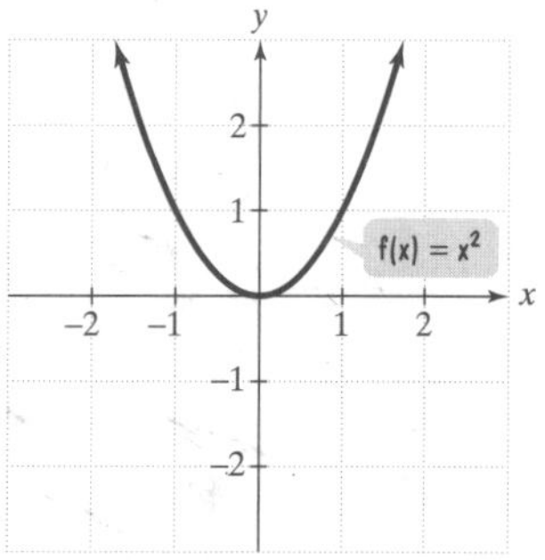


**Standard Cubic Function**

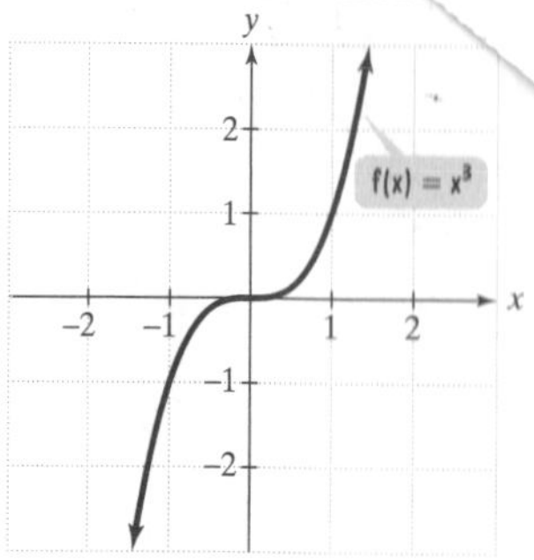


**Absolute Value Function**

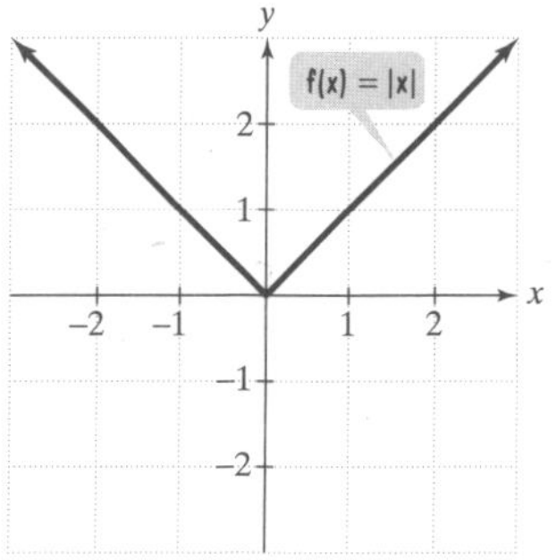


**Square Root Function**

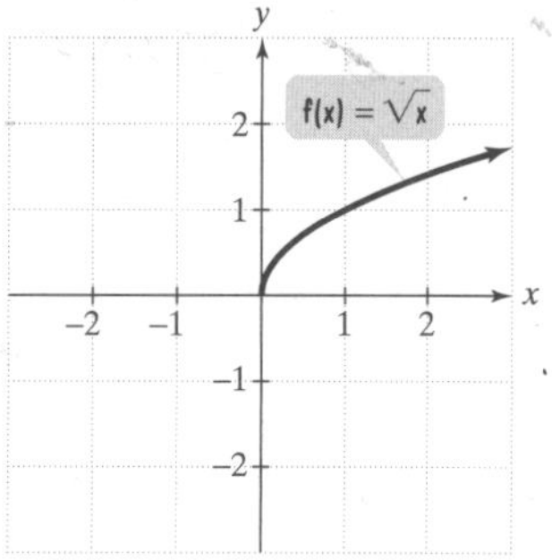


**Greatest Integer Function**

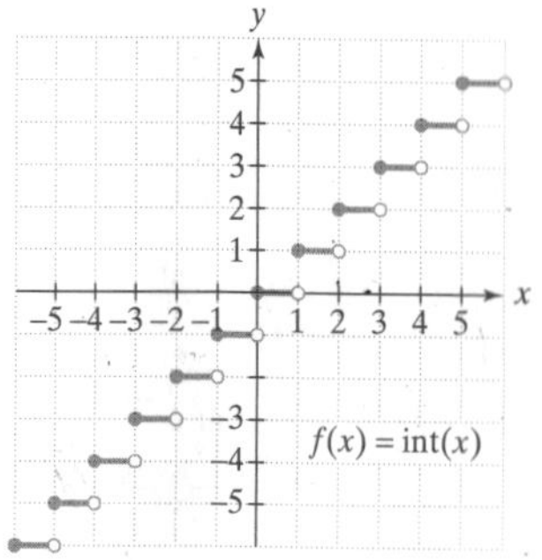


## TRANSFORMATIONS

In each case, $c$ represents a positive real number.

| Function | | Draw the graph of $f$ and: |
|---|---|---|
| Vertical translations | $y = f(x) + c$ | Shift $f$ upward $c$ units. |
| | $y = f(x) - c$ | Shift $f$ downward $c$ units. |
| Horizontal translations | $y = f(x - c)$ | Shift $f$ to the right $c$ units. |
| | $y = f(x + c)$ | Shift $f$ to the left $c$ units. |
| Reflections | $y = -f(x)$ | Reflect $f$ about the $x$-axis. |
| | $y = f(-x)$ | Reflect $f$ about the $y$-axis. |
| Stretching or Shrinking | $y = cf(x); c > 1$ | Stretch $f$, multiplying each of its $y$-values by $c$. |
| | $y = cf(x); 0 < x < 1$ | Shrink $f$, multiplying each of its $y$-values by $c$. |

## DISTANCE AND MIDPOINT FORMULAS

1. The distance from $(x_1, y_1)$ to $(x_2, y_2)$ is
$$\sqrt{(x_2 - x_1)^2 + (y_2 - y_1)^2}.$$
2. The midpoint of the line segment with endpoints $(x_1, y_1)$ and $(x_2, y_2)$ is
$$\left(\frac{x_1 + x_2}{2}, \frac{y_1 + y_2}{2}\right).$$

## QUADRATIC FORMULA

The solutions to $ax^2 + bx + c = 0$ with $a \neq 0$ are
$$x = \frac{-b \pm \sqrt{b^2 - 4ac}}{2a}.$$

## FUNCTIONS

1. Linear Function: $f(x) = mx + b$
   Graph is a line with slope $m$ and $y$-intercept $b$.

2. Quadratic Function: $f(x) = ax^2 + bx + c, a \neq 0$
   Graph is a parabola with vertex at $x = -\dfrac{b}{2a}$.
   Quadratic Function: $f(x) = a(x - h)^2 + k$
   In this form, the parabola's vertex is $(h, k)$.
3. $n$th-Degree Polynomial Function: $f(x) = a_n x^n + a_{n-1}x^{n-1} + a_{n-2}x^{n-2} + \cdots + a_1 x + a_0, a_n \neq 0$
   For $n$ odd and $a_n > 0$, graph falls to the left and rises to the right.
   For $n$ odd and $a_n < 0$, graph rises to the left and falls to the right.
   For $n$ even and $a_n > 0$, graph rises to the left and to the right.
   For $n$ even and $a_n < 0$, graph falls to the left and to the right.
4. Rational Function: $f(x) = \dfrac{p(x)}{q(x)}$, $p(x)$ and $q(x)$ are polynomials, $q(x) \neq 0$
5. Exponential Function: $f(x) = b^x, b > 0, b \neq 1$
   Graphs:

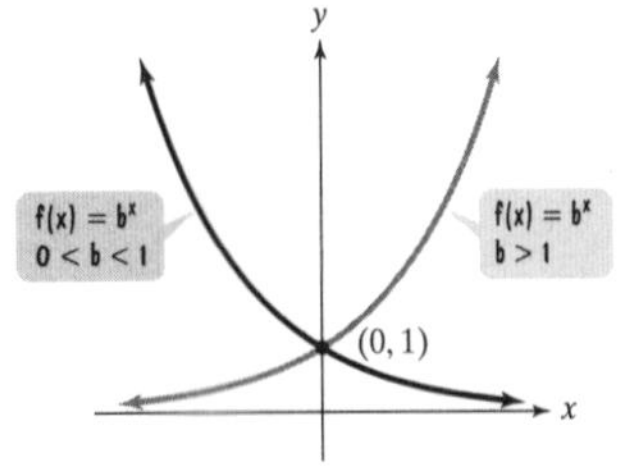


6. Logarithmic Function: $f(x) = \log_b x, b > 0, b \neq 1$
   $y = \log_b x$ is equivalent to $x = b^y$.
   Graph:

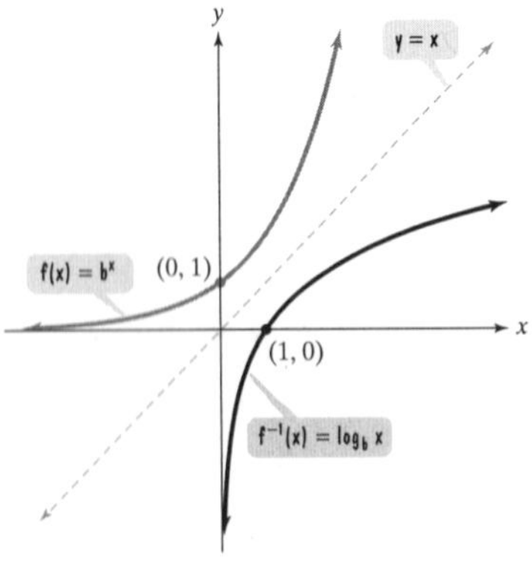


$b > 1$

## PROPERTIES OF LOGARITHMS

1. $\log_b(MN) = \log_b M + \log_b N$
2. $\log_b\left(\dfrac{M}{N}\right) = \log_b M - \log_b N$
3. $\log_b M^p = p \log_b M$
4. $\log_b M = \dfrac{\log_a M}{\log_a b} = \dfrac{\ln M}{\ln b} = \dfrac{\log M}{\log b}$
5. $\log_b b^x = x; \quad \ln e^x = x$
6. $b^{\log_b x} = x; \quad e^{\ln x} = x$

## INVERSE OF A 2 × 2 MATRIX

If $A = \begin{bmatrix} a & b \\ c & d \end{bmatrix}$, then $A^{-1} = \dfrac{1}{ad - bc}\begin{bmatrix} d & -b \\ -c & a \end{bmatrix}$, where $ad - bc \neq 0$.

## CRAMER'S RULE

If

$$\begin{aligned} a_{11}x_1 + a_{12}x_2 + a_{13}x_3 + \cdots + a_{1n}x_n &= b_1 \\ a_{21}x_1 + a_{22}x_2 + a_{23}x_3 + \cdots + a_{2n}x_n &= b_2 \\ a_{31}x_1 + a_{32}x_2 + a_{33}x_3 + \cdots + a_{3n}x_n &= b_3 \\ &\vdots \\ a_{n1}x_1 + a_{n2}x_2 + a_{n3}x_3 + \cdots + a_{nn}x_n &= b_n \end{aligned}$$

then $x_i = \dfrac{D_i}{D}, D \neq 0$.

$D$: determinant of the system's coefficients
$D_i$: determinant in which coefficients of $x_i$ are replaced by $b_1, b_2, b_3, \ldots, b_n$.

## CONIC SECTIONS

**Circle**

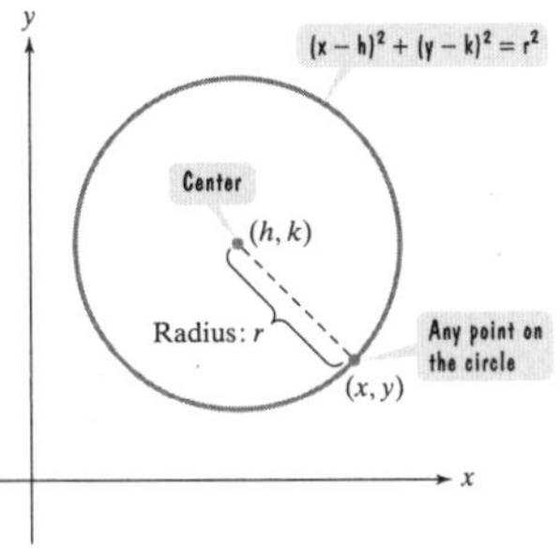


**Ellipse**

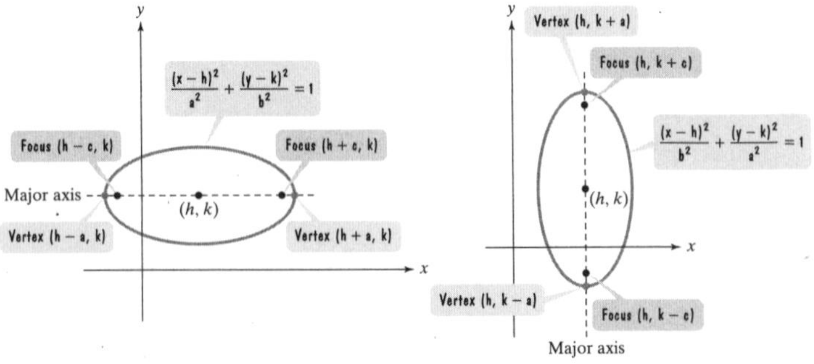


**Hyperbola**

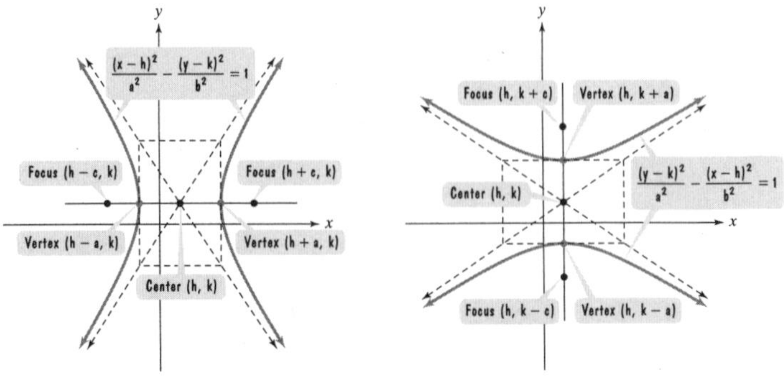


*(continued on inside back cover)*

# Precalculus

**Robert Blitzer**
*Miami-Dade Community College*

PRENTICE HALL
Upper Saddle River, NJ 07458

**Library of Congress Cataloging-in-Publication Data**

Blitzer, Robert.
Precalculus / Robert Blitzer.
p. cm.
Includes index.
ISBN 0-13-028153-0
1. Algebra. I. Title.
QA154.2.B556 2001
512--dc21 00-065224

Editor-in-Chief and Acquisitions Editor: ***Sally Yagan***
Senior Development Editor: ***Shana Ederer***
Editor-in-Chief, Development: ***Carol Trueheart***
Editorial/Production Supervision: ***Bayani Mendoza de Leon***
Vice President/Director of Production and Manufacturing: ***David W. Riccardi***
Senior Managing Editor: ***Linda Mihatov Behrens***
Executive Managing Editor: ***Kathleen Schiaparelli***
Manufacturing Buyer: ***Alan Fischer***
Manufacturing Manager: ***Trudy Pisciotti***
Director of Marketing: ***John Tweeddale***
Senior Marketing Manager: ***Patrice Lumumba Jones***
Marketing Assistant: ***Vince Jansen***
Associate Editor, Mathematics/Statistics Media: ***Audra J. Walsh***
Director of Creative Services: ***Paul Belfanti***
Art Director: ***Maureen Eide***
Assistant to the Art Director: ***John Christiana***
Art Editor: ***Grace Hazeldine***
Photo Researcher: ***Melinda Alexander***
Photo Editor: ***Beth Boyd***
Cover Designer: ***Maureen Eide***
Interior Design and Layout: ***Lorraine Castellano***
Editorial Assistant: ***Meisha Welch***
Cover image: *Tom Brakefield / BRAKE / Bruce Coleman Inc.*


Upper Saddle River, New Jersey 07458



Printed in the United States of America

10 9 8 7 6 5 4 3 2 1

ISBN 0-13-028153-0

Prentice-Hall International (UK) Limited, *London*
Prentice-Hall of Australia Pty. Limited, *Sydney*
Prentice-Hall Canada Inc., *Toronto*
Prentice-Hall Hispanoamericana, S.A., *Mexico*
Prentice-Hall of India Private Limited, *New Delhi*
Prentice-Hall of Japan, Inc., *Tokyo*
Pearson Education Asia Pte. Ltd.
Editora Prentice-Hall do Brasil, Ltda., *Rio de Janeiro*

# Contents

## Chapter 2

## Functions and Graphs 170



## Chapter 3

## Polynomial and Rational Functions 261



## Chapter 4

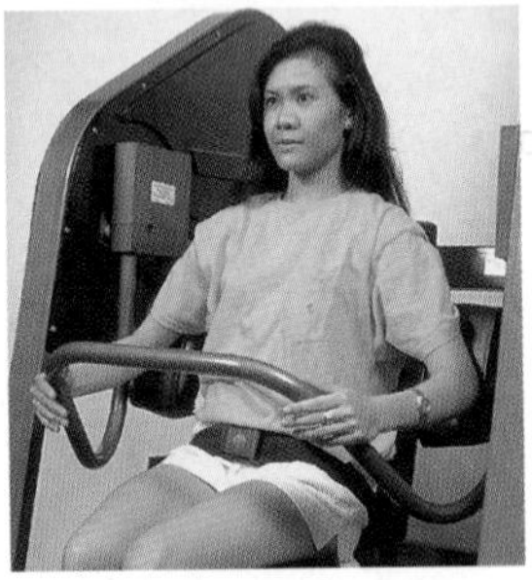

## Exponential and Logarithmic Functions 356



## Chapter 5

## Trigonometric Functions 424

## Chapter 6

## Chapter 7

## Chapter 8

## Chapter 9

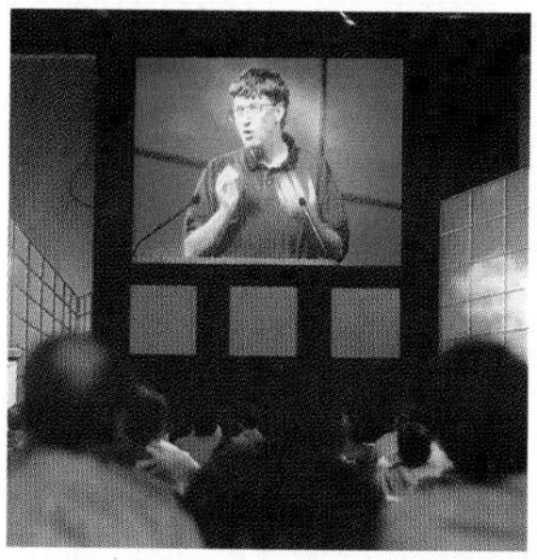

# Preface

*Precalculus* is designed and written to help students make the transition into calculus. The book has three fundamental goals:

1. To help students acquire a solid foundation in algebra and trigonometry, preparing them for calculus;
2. To show students how algebra and trigonometry can model and solve authentic real-world problems;
3. To enable students to develop problem-solving skills, fostering critical thinking within a varied and interesting setting.

*Precalculus* is not simply a condensed version of my *Algebra and Trigonometry* book. Precalculus students are different from algebra and trigonometry students, and this text reflects those differences. Here are a few specific examples:

- Factorizations involving fractional and negative exponents, as well as simplifying the kinds of fractional expressions that students encounter in calculus, have been added to Chapter P.
- Chapter 1 includes applications that are traditional calculus problems and that can be approached algebraically.
- Chapter 2 includes discussions of difference quotients, average rate of change, average velocity, and composite functions in calculus.
- Chapter 3 introduces an optimization strategy for solving word problems within the context of quadratic functions. Students will be able to use this strategy in calculus when solving similar problems with the derivative.
- Chapter 5 develops trigonometry from the perspective of the unit circle.
- Liberal arts applications are often replaced by more scientific applications. For example, Einstein's relativity models are discussed in Chapter 1, and Newton's Law of Cooling is developed in Chapter 4.
- Chapter 12, entitled "Introduction to Calculus," takes the student into calculus with discussions of limits, continuity, and derivatives.

A source of frustration for me and my colleagues is that very few students read their textbook. When I ask students why they do not take full advantage of the text, their responses generally fall into two categories:

- "I cannot follow the explanations."
- "The applications are not interesting."

I thought about both of these objections in writing every page of this book.

**"I can't follow the explanations."** For many of my students, textbook explanations are too compressed. The chapters in *Precalculus* have been written to make them extremely accessible. Every section contains a range of simple, intermediate, and challenging examples. Voice balloons allow for specific annotations in examples, further clarifying procedures and concepts.

**"The applications are not interesting."** One of the things I enjoy most about teaching in a large urban community college is the diversity of who my students are and what interests them. Real-world data that celebrate this variety are used to bring relevance to examples, discussions, and applications. I selected all updated real-world data to be interesting and intriguing to students. By connecting precalculus to the whole spectrum of their interests, it is my intent to show students that their world is profoundly mathematical and, indeed, $\pi$ is in the sky.

## Student Supplements

**Student Solutions Manual (0-13-028654-0); (2865D-2)** Includes fully worked out solutions to most of the odd-numbered exercises in the text as well as all exercises in chapter tests and all review exercises.

**MathPak Integrated Learning Environment (0-13-028247-2); (2824G-5)** Contains the College Algebra MathPro 4.0 along with a passcode-protected Website specifically designed to accompany this text. This product combines the series' key supplements into a comprehensive, easy-to-navigate package. Materials on the Website include but are not limited to: Section-by-section reading quizzes, Section-by-Section Powerpoint downloads, additional chapter projects, Chapter Quizzes and Tests, Student Solutions Manuals presented by chapter (exactly what is in the print version), Chapter Destinations and to interesting math Websites, and Graphing Calculator Manuals for the full line of TI's, Sharp, HP, and Casio Calculators.

**Review Videos (0-13-028240-5); (2824K-6)** Section-by-section videos written by and highlighting Jacquelyn White of St. Leo College. Each segment covers approximately 20 minutes of the key concepts and examples for each section. Each set of videos comes with a permissions letter allowing the school to duplicate for specific campus needs.

**Precalculus Investigations/Simundza, et. (0-13-010954-1); (1095D-6)** A three year NSF-funded project integrates an applied approach to the topics in the Precalculus curriculum via applied projects. The investigations reflect the AMATYC and NCTM Standards in both curriculum content and pedagogy.

**Companion Website** `www.prenhall.com/blitzer` This CW address will lead to the bridge page for all of the Blitzer titles. On the CW sites (which are different than the MathPak sites) are the following: Chapter Quizzes, Chapter Tests, Projects, Graphing Calculator Manual, Destinations, and PowerPoints.

**WebCT/Blackboard** Contains all the materials from the MathPak website (i.e., no MathPro) plus testing materials. Can be made available in Blackboard on adoption.

## Instructor Supplements

**Instructor's Resource Manual (0-13-028656-7) (2865F-7)** IRM contains the full solutions to the even-numbered exercises in the text.

**TestGen-EQ WIN/MAC CD (0-13-028249-9) (2824J-8)** New to Prentice Hall Mathematics is the use of TestGen EQ for our mathematics testing. TestGen-EQ is a fully algorithmic, easy-to-use software program written and based on the section objectives in the text.

**Test Item File (0-13-028676-1) (2867F-5)** A hard copy version of materials derived from the TestGen-EQ program.

## Acknowledgments

I wish to express my appreciation to all the reviewers for their helpful criticisms and suggestions, frequently transmitted with wit, humor, and intelligence. In particular, I would like to thank the following for reviewing *College Algebra* 2e, *Algebra & Trigonometry* 1e, and *Precalculus* 1e:

| | |
|---|---|
| Celeste Hernandez | *Richland College* |
| Christopher N. Hay-Jahans | *University of South Dakota* |
| Cynthia Glickman | *Community College of Southern Nevada* |
| Dan Van Peursem | *University of South Dakota* |
| David White | *The Victoria College* |
| David L. Gross | *University of Connecticut* |
| Debra A. Pharo | *Northwestern Michigan College* |
| Diana Colt | *University of Minnesota-Duluth* |
| Donald Gordon | *Manatee Community College* |
| Gloria Phoenix | *North Carolina Agricultural and Technical State University* |
| James Miller | *West Virginia University* |
| Joel K. Haack | *University of Northern Iowa* |
| Juha Pohjanpelto | *Oregon State University* |
| Kayoko Yates Barnhill | *Clark College* |
| Lloyd Best | *Pacific Union College* |
| Mike Hall | *University of Mississippi* |
| Nancy Raye Johnson | *Manatee Community College* |
| Richard E. Van Lommel | *California State University-Sacramento* |
| Sudhir Kumar Goel | *Valdosta State University* |
| Winfield A. Ihlow | *SUNY College at Oswego* |
| Yvelyne Germain-McCarthy | *University of New Orleans* |

Additional acknowledgments are extended to Jacquelyn White for creating the dynamic video series covering every section of the book; the team at Laurel Technical Services for the Herculean task of solving all the book's exercises, preparing the answer section and solutions manuals, as well as serving as accuracy checker; Melinda Alexander and Karen Pugliano, photo researchers, for obtaining the book's photographs; the team of graphic artists and mathematicians at Scientific Illustrators, whose superb illustrations and graphs provide visual support to the verbal portions of the text; Prepare Inc., the book's compositor, for inputting hundreds of pages with hardly an error; and Bayani Mendoza de Leon, whose talents as production editor contributed to the book's wonderful look.

Most of all, I wish to thank Sally Yagan and Shana Ederer. Shana, my development editor, contributed invaluable edits and suggestions that resulted in a finished product that is both accessible and up-to-date. Her influence on this book is extraordinary, guiding and coordinating every detail of this project. Sally, editor-in-chief of mathematics at Prentice Hall, is the key person in making this book a reality, and I am grateful to have had an editor with her experience, insight, and professionalism.

Sally Yagan and Shana Ederer are members of the terrific team at Prentice Hall who made this book possible, including Prentice Hall Co-President Tim Bozik and ESM President Paul Corey. Thank you Patrice Lumumba Jones, Senior Marketing Manager, for your innovative marketing efforts as well as the Prentice Hall sales force for your confidence in and enthusiasm for the book.

# To the Student

I've written this book so that you can learn about the power of algebra and trigonometry and how it relates directly to your life outside the classroom. All concepts are carefully explained, important definitions and procedures are set off in boxes, and worked-out examples that present solutions in a step-by-step manner appear in every section. Each example is followed by a similar matched problem, called a Check Point, for you to try so that you can actively participate in the learning process as you read the book. (Answers to all Check Points appear in the back of the book.) Study Tips offer hints and suggestions and often point out common errors to avoid. A great deal of attention has been given to applying algebra and trigonometry to your life to make your learning experience both interesting and relevant. As you begin your studies, I would like to offer some specific suggestions for using this book and for being successful in this course:

1. **Attend all lectures.** No book is intended to be a substitute for valuable insights and interactions that occur in the classroom. In addition to arriving for lecture on time and being prepared, you will find it useful to read the section before it is covered in lecture. This will give you a clear idea of the new material that will be discussed.
2. **Read the book.** Read each section with pen (or pencil) in hand. Move through the illustrative examples with great care. These worked-out examples provide a model for doing exercises in the exercise sets. As you proceed through the reading, do not give up if you do not understand every single word. Things will become clearer as you read on and see how various procedures are applied to specific worked-out examples.
3. **Work problems every day and check your answers.** The way to learn mathematics is by doing mathematics, which means working the Check Points and assigned exercises in the exercise sets. The more exercises you work, the better you will understand the material.
4. **Prepare for chapter exams.** After completing a chapter, study the summary, work the exercises in the Chapter Review, and work the exercises in the Chapter Test. Answers to all these exercises are given in the back of the book.
5. **Use the supplements available with this book.** A solutions manual containing worked-out solutions to the book's odd-numbered exercises and all review exercises, a dynamic web page, and video tapes created for every section of the book are among the supplements created to help you tap into the power of mathematics. Ask your instructor or bookstore what supplements are available and where you can find them.

It is my hope that that you will enjoy the pages of this book as you empower yourself with the algebra and trigonometry needed to succeed in calculus, your career, and in your life.

Regards,

*Bob*

Robert Blitzer

# A Guide to Using This Text

**Relevant Chapter Openers**
Every chapter highlights a scenario from everyday life and how the algebra relates to it. These scenarios are revisited later in the chapter.

## Functions and Graphs

**Chapter 2**

'Tis the season and you've waited until the last minute to mail your holiday gifts. Your only option is overnight express mail. You realize that the cost of mailing a gift depends on its weight, but the mailing costs seem somewhat odd. Your packages that weigh 1.1 pounds, 1.5 pounds, and 2 pounds cost \$15.75 each to send overnight. Packages that weigh 2.01 pounds and 3 pounds cost you \$18.50 each. Finally, your heaviest gift is barely over 3 pounds and its mailing cost is \$21.25. What sort of system is this in which costs increase by \$2.75, stepping from \$15.75 to \$18.50 and from \$18.50 to \$21.25?

The cost of mailing a package depends on its weight. The probability that you and another person in a room share the same birthday depends on the number of people in the room. In both these situations, the relationship between variables can be illustrated with the notion of a *function*. Understanding this concept will give you a new perspective on many ordinary situations.

170

Page 170

### Section Objectives

The learning objectives focus the students' study habits and also are the foundation for the algorithms found in MathPro (tutorial software) and in the Test-Gen-EQ (test generator software). Objectives reappear in the margin at their point of use.

### Section Openers

Each and every section opens with a unique application of algebra in students' lives outside the classroom. These scenarios are revisited later in the section.

## SECTION 5.7 Inverse Trigonometric Functions

**Objectives**

1. Understand and use the inverse sine function.
2. Understand and use the inverse cosine function.
3. Understand and use the inverse tangent function.
4. Use a calculator to evaluate inverse trigonometric functions.
5. Find exact values of composite functions with inverse trigonometric functions.

You watched *The Matrix* on video and were impressed by the elaborate computer-generated effects. The movie is being shown again at a local theater, where you can experience its stunning visual force on a large screen. Where in the theater should you sit to maximize the film's visual impact? In this section you will see how an inverse trigonometric function can enhance your movie-going experiences.

**Study Tip**

Here are some helpful things to remember from our discussion of inverse functions in Section 2.6.

- If no horizontal line intersects the graph of a function more than once, the function is one-to-one and has an inverse function.
- If the point $(a, b)$ is on the graph of $f$, then the point $(b, a)$ is on the graph of the inverse function, denoted $f^{-1}$. The graph of $f^{-1}$ is a reflection of the graph of $f$ about the line $y = x$.

**Page 510**

### Current Real-World Data

Relevant current data is used to illustrate the power of the algebra to real issues and contemporary information. It is used throughout the examples, exercises, and discussions. The data was selected to be interesting and intriguing to students.

### Discovery

These exercises found in the side columns of the text encourage students to explore problems in order to better understand them and their solutions. These are a great way to stimulate class-time exploration of concepts.

**Discovery**

The study of how changing a function's equation can affect its graph can be explored with a graphing utility. Use your graphing utility to verify the hand-drawn graphs as you read this section.

**Page 226**

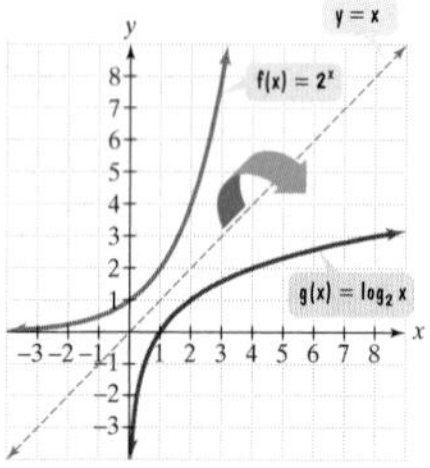


Figure 4.6 The graphs of $f(x) = 2^x$ and its inverse function

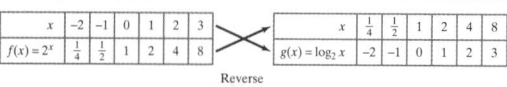

| $x$ | $-2$ | $-1$ | $0$ | $1$ | $2$ | $3$ |
|---|---|---|---|---|---|---|
| $f(x) = 2^x$ | $\frac{1}{4}$ | $\frac{1}{2}$ | $1$ | $2$ | $4$ | $8$ |

Reverse coordinates.

| $x$ | $\frac{1}{4}$ | $\frac{1}{2}$ | $1$ | $2$ | $4$ | $8$ |
|---|---|---|---|---|---|---|
| $g(x) = \log_2 x$ | $-2$ | $-1$ | $0$ | $1$ | $2$ | $3$ |

We now plot the ordered pairs in both tables, connecting them with smooth curves. Figure 4.6 shows the graphs of $f(x) = 2^x$ and its inverse function $g(x) = \log_2 x$. The graph of the inverse can also be drawn by reflecting the graph of $f(x) = 2^x$ about the line $y = x$.

**Check Point 6** Graph $f(x) = 3^x$ and $g(x) = \log_3 x$ in the same rectangular coordinate system.

Figure 4.7 illustrates the relationship between the graph of the exponential function, shown in blue and its inverse, the logarithmic function, shown in red, for bases greater than 1 and for bases between 0 and 1.

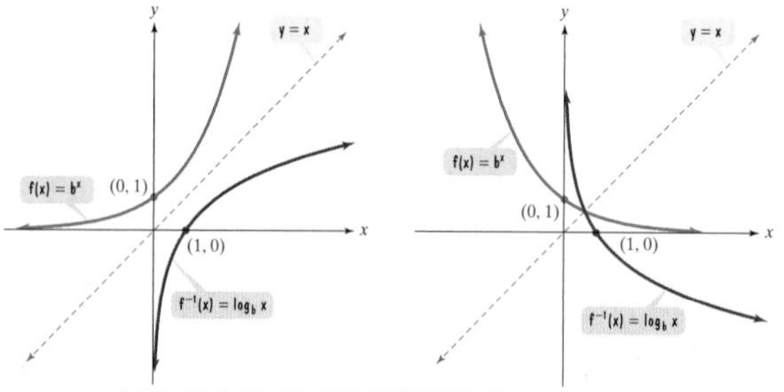


Figure 4.7 Gra

**Page 372**

## Explanatory Art

Much of the art program has text "balloons" that highlight what the numbers or graph "mean" in English. This helps students not lose sight of what the problem is asking for.

## Examples

Each example is titled—making clear the purpose of the example.

Examples are clearly written and provide students with detailed step-by-step solutions. No steps are omitted and each step is clearly explained.

## Essays

Enrichment Essays provide historical, interdisciplinary, and otherwise interesting connections throughout the text.

### Carbon Dating and Artistic Development

The artistic community was electrified by the discovery in 1995 of spectacular cave paintings in a limestone cavern in France. Carbon dating of the charcoal from the site showed that the images, created by artists of remarkable talent, were 30,000 years old, making them the oldest cave paintings ever found. The artists seemed to have used the cavern's natural contours to heighten a sense of perspective. The quality of the painting suggests that the art of early humans did not mature steadily from primitive to sophisticated in any simple linear fashion.

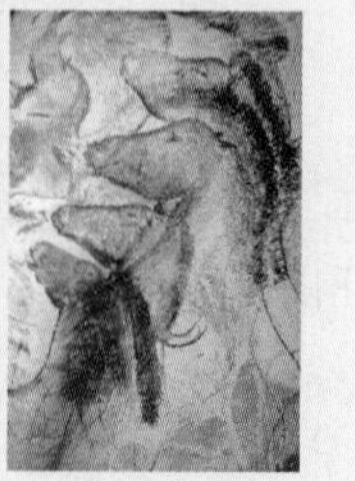

Our next example involves exponential decay and its use in determining the age of fossils and artifacts. The method is based on considering the percentage of carbon-14 remaining in the fossil or artifact. Carbon-14 decays exponentially with a *half-life* of approximately 5715 years. The **half-life** of a substance is the time required for half of a given sample to disintegrate. Thus, after 5715 years a given amount of carbon-14 will have decayed to half the original amount. Carbon dating is useful for artifacts or fossils up to 80,000 years old. Older objects do not have enough carbon-14 left to date age accurately.

**EXAMPLE 2 Carbon-14 Dating: The Dead Sea Scrolls**

**a.** Use the fact that after 5715 years a given amount of carbon-14 will have decayed to half the original amount to find the exponential decay model for carbon-14.

**b.** In 1947, earthenware jars containing what are known as the Dead Sea Scrolls were found by an Arab Bedouin herdsman. Analysis indicated that the scroll wrappings contained 76% of their original carbon-14. Estimate the age of the Dead Sea Scrolls.

**Solution** We begin with the exponential decay model $A = A_0e^{kt}$. We know that $k < 0$ because the problem involves the decay of carbon-14. After 5715 years ($t = 5715$), the amount of carbon-14 present, $A$, is half the original amount $A_0$. Thus we can substitute $\frac{A_0}{2}$ for $A$ in the exponential decay model. This will enable us to find $k$, the decay rate.

**a.** $\frac{A_0}{2} = A_0e^{k5715}$ — After 5715 years ($t = 5715$), $A = \frac{A_0}{2}$ (because the amount present, $A$, is half the original amount, $A_0$).

$\frac{1}{2} = e^{5715k}$ — Divide both sides of the equation by $A_0$.

$\ln\frac{1}{2} = \ln e^{5715k}$ — Take the natural logarithm of both sides.

$\ln\frac{1}{2} = 5715k$ — $\ln e^x = x$

$k = \frac{\ln\frac{1}{2}}{5715} \approx -0.000121$ — Solve for $k$.

Substituting for $k$ in the decay model, the model for carbon-14 is $A = A_0e^{-0.000121t}$.

**Page 405**

**Check Point 1** Find the domain and the range of the relation $\{(20, 157.4), (30, 231.8), (100, 752.6), (200, 1496.6)\}$.

As you worked Checkpoint 1, did you wonder if the numbers in each ordered pair represented anything? Think snakes! The first number in each ordered pair is a snake's tail length, in millimeters, and the second number is its body length, also in millimeters. Consider, for example, the ordered pair (30, 231.8).

(30, 231.8)

A snake whose tail length is 30 millimeters | has a body length of 231.8 millimeters.

The relation in the snake example can be pictured as follows:

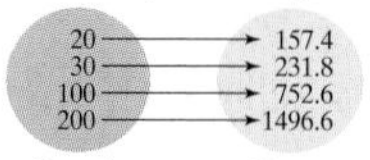


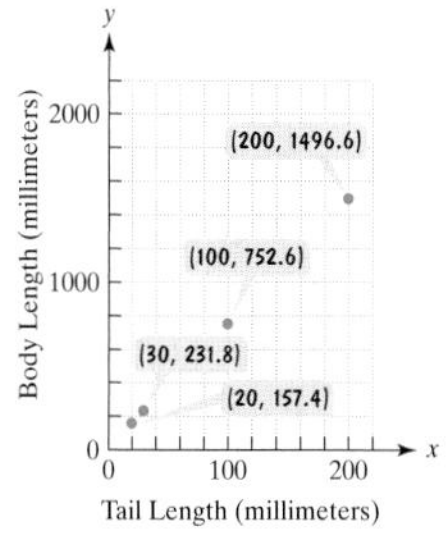


**Figure 2.19** The graph of a relation showing a correspondence between a snake's tail length and its body length

A scatter plot, like the one shown in Figure 2.19, is a way to represent the relation.

**Page 194**

## Check Points

Check Points offer students the opportunity to test their understanding of the example by working a similar exercise while they are reading the material. The answers to all the Check Points are given in the answer section

## Study Tips

Study Tip boxes offer suggestions for problem solving, point out common student errors, and provide informal tips and suggestions. These invaluable hints appear in abundance throughout the book.

### Study Tip

The word *range* can mean many things, from a chain of mountains to a cooking stove. For functions, it means the set of images of the domain. For graphing utilities, it means the setting used for the viewing rectangle. Try not to confuse these meanings.

**Page 196**

### Study Tip

The notation $f(x)$ does *not* mean "$f$ times $x$." The notation describes the value of the function at $x$.

**Page 198**

**Step 3 Find the values of $y$ for the five key points.** Take a few minutes and use your calculator to evaluate the function at each value of $x$ from step 2. Show that the key points are

$$\left(-\frac{\pi}{4}, \frac{1}{2}\right), \quad \left(-\frac{\pi}{8}, 0\right), \quad \left(0, -\frac{1}{2}\right), \quad \left(\frac{\pi}{8}, 0\right), \quad \text{and} \quad \left(\frac{\pi}{4}, \frac{1}{2}\right).$$

maximum point | x-intercept | minimum point | y-intercept | maximum point

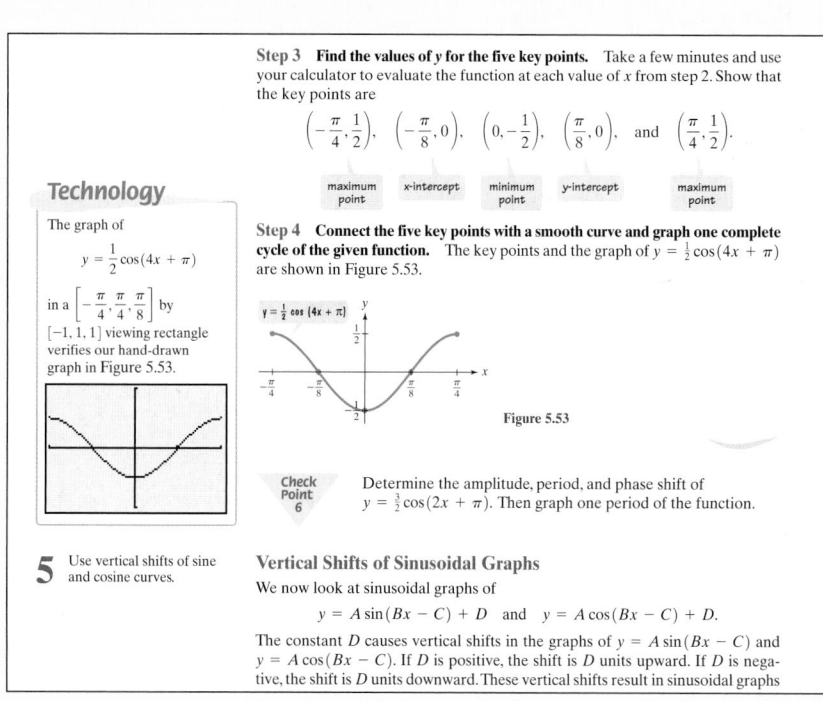

**Step 4 Connect the five key points with a smooth curve and graph one complete cycle of the given function.** The key points and the graph of $y = \frac{1}{2}\cos(4x + \pi)$ are shown in Figure 5.53.

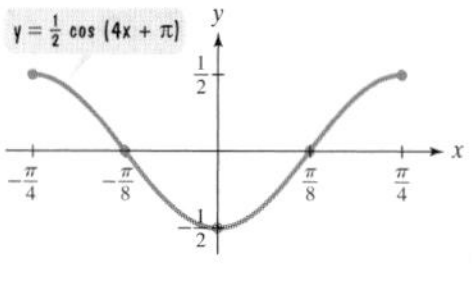


**Figure 5.53**

### Technology

The graph of

$$y = \frac{1}{2}\cos(4x + \pi)$$

in a $\left[-\frac{\pi}{4}, \frac{\pi}{4}, \frac{\pi}{8}\right]$ by $[-1, 1, 1]$ viewing rectangle verifies our hand-drawn graph in Figure 5.53.

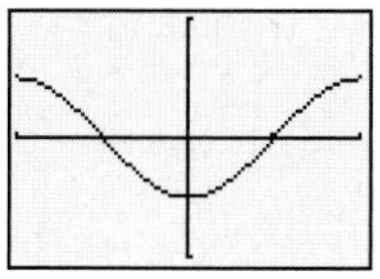

**Check Point 6** Determine the amplitude, period, and phase shift of $y = \frac{3}{2}\cos(2x + \pi)$. Then graph one period of the function.

**5** Use vertical shifts of sine and cosine curves.

**Vertical Shifts of Sinusoidal Graphs**

We now look at sinusoidal graphs of

$$y = A\sin(Bx - C) + D \quad \text{and} \quad y = A\cos(Bx - C) + D.$$

The constant $D$ causes vertical shifts in the graphs of $y = A\sin(Bx - C)$ and $y = A\cos(Bx - C)$. If $D$ is positive, the shift is $D$ units upward. If $D$ is negative, the shift is $D$ units downward. These vertical shifts result in sinusoidal graphs

**Page 482**

## Thorough, yet Optional Technology

Although the use of graphing utilities is optional, they are utilized in technology boxes to enable students to visualize, discover, and explore algebraic concepts. The use of graphing utilities is also reinforced in the technology exercises appearing in the exercise sets for those who want this option. With the book's early introduction to graphing, students can look at the calculator screens in the technology boxes and gain an increased understanding of an example's solution even if they are not using a graphing utility in the course.

## Exercise Sets

An extensive collection of exercises is included in all end-of-section and end-of-chapter materials. Within each category type, the exercises are organized by level. The category types found are: Practice Exercises, Application Exercises, Writing in Mathematics, Technology Exercises, Critical Thinking Exercises, and Group Exercises.

### EXERCISE SET 5.6

#### Practice Exercises

*In Exercises 1–4, the graph of a tangent function is given. Select the equation for each graph from the following options.*

$$y = \tan\left(x + \frac{\pi}{2}\right), \quad y = \tan(x + \pi), \quad y = -\tan x, \quad y = -\tan\left(x - \frac{\pi}{2}\right)$$

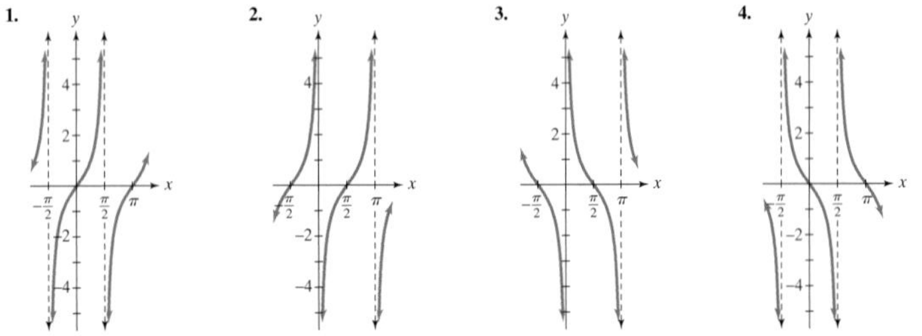


Pages 507–510

#### Application Exercises

**45.** An ambulance with a rotating beacon of light is parked 12 feet from a building. The function

$$d = 12 \tan 2\pi t$$

describes the distance, $d$, in feet, of the rotating beacon from point $C$ after $t$ seconds.

**a.** Graph the function on the interval $[0, 2]$.

**b.** For what values of $t$ in $[0, 2]$ is the function undefined? What does this mean in terms of the rotating beacon in the figure shown?

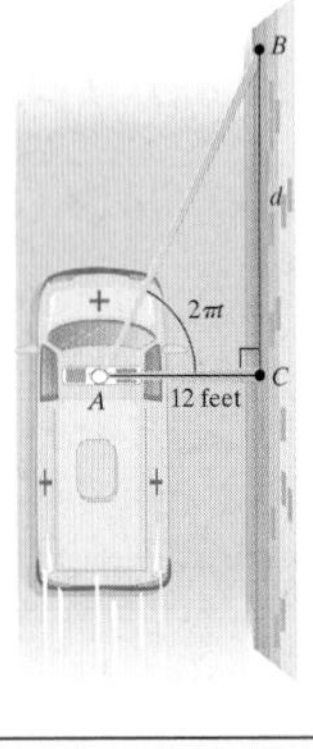


#### Writing in Mathematics

**51.** Without drawing a graph, describe the behavior of the basic tangent curve.

**52.** If you are given the equation of a tangent function, how do you find consecutive asymptotes?

**53.** If you are given the equation of a tangent function, how do you identify an $x$-intercept?

**54.** Without drawing a graph, describe the behavior of the basic cotangent curve.

**55.** If you are given the equation of a cotangent function, how do you find consecutive asymptotes?

**56.** Explain how to determine the range of $y = \csc x$ from the graph. What is the range?

**57.** Explain how to use a sine curve to obtain a cosecant curve. Why can the same procedure be used to obtain a secant curve from a cosine curve?

**58.** Scientists record brain activity by attaching electrodes to the scalp and then connecting these electrodes to a machine. The record of brain activity recorded with this machine is shown in the three graphs at the top of the next column. Which trigonometric functions would be most appropriate for describing the oscillations in brain activity? Describe similarities and differences among these functions when modeling brain activity when awake, during dreaming sleep, and during non-dreaming sleep.

#### Technology Exercises

*In working Exercises 59–62, describe what happens at the asymptotes on the graphing utility. Compare the graphs in the connected and dot modes.*

**59.** Use a graphing utility to verify any two of the tangent curves that you drew by hand in Exercises 5–12.

**60.** Use a graphing utility to verify any two of the cotangent curves that you drew by hand in Exercises 17–24.

**61.** Use a graphing utility to verify any two of the cosecant curves that you drew by hand in Exercises 29–44.

**62.** Use a graphing utility to verify any two of the secant curves that you drew by hand in Exercises 29–44.

*In Exercises 63–68, use a graphing utility to graph each function. Use a range setting so that the graph is shown for at least two periods.*

**63.** $y = \tan\frac{x}{4}$ **64.** $y = \tan 4x$

**65.** $y = \cot 2x$ **66.** $y = \cot\frac{x}{2}$

**67.** $y = \frac{1}{2}\tan \pi x$ **68.** $y = \frac{1}{2}\tan(\pi x + 1)$

*In Exercises 69–72, use a graphing utility to graph each pair of functions in the same viewing rectangle. Use a range setting so that the graphs are shown for at least two periods.*

**69.** $y = 0.8 \sin\frac{x}{2}$ and $y = 0.8 \csc\frac{x}{2}$

**70.** $y = 0.8 \sin\frac{x}{2}$ and $y = 0.8 \csc\frac{x}{2}$

**71.** $y = 4\cos\left(2x - \frac{\pi}{6}\right)$ and $y = 4\sec\left(2x - \frac{\pi}{6}\right)$

**72.** $y = -3.5\cos\left(\pi x - \frac{\pi}{6}\right)$ and $y = -3.5\sec\left(\pi x - \frac{\pi}{6}\right)$

**73.** Carbon dioxide particles in our atmosphere trap heat and raise the planet's temperature. The resultant gradually increasing temperature is called the greenhouse effect.

#### Critical Thinking Exercises

*In Exercises 75–76, write an equation for each blue graph.*

**75.**

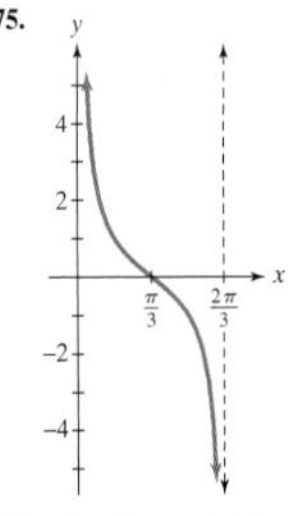


#### Group Exercise

**62.** Music and mathematics have been linked over the centuries. Group members should research and present a seminar to the class on music and mathematics. Be sure to include the role of trigonometric functions in the music-mathematics link.

Page 529

## End-of-Chapter Materials

**Chapter Summaries and Review Exercises**

Each section has its own focused summary and review exercises. These provide students with a good review for a chapter test.

**Pages 417–423**

### CHAPTER SUMMARY, REVIEW, AND TEST

#### Summary

**4.1 Exponential Functions**

a. The exponential function with base $b$ is defined by $f(x) = b^x$, where $b > 0$ and $b \neq 1$.

b. Characteristics of exponential functions and graphs for $0 < b < 1$ and $b > 1$ are shown in the box on page 354.

c. Transformations involving exponential functions are summarized in Table 4.1 on page 354.

d. The natural exponential function: $f(x) = e^x$. The irrational number $e$ is called the natural base, where $e \approx 2.7183$.

e. Formulas for compound interest: After $t$ years, the balance $A$ in an account with principal $P$ and annual interest rate $r$ (in decimal form) is given by one of the following formulas:

1. For $n$ compoundings per year: $A = P\left(1 + \frac{r}{n}\right)^{nt}$
2. For continuous compounding: $A = Pe^{rt}$

**4.2 Logarithmic Functions**

a. Definition of the logarithmic function: For $x > 0$ and $b > 0$, $b \neq 1$, $y = \log_b x$ is equivalent to $b^y = x$. The function $f(x) = \log_b x$ is the logarithmic function with base $b$. This function is the inverse function of the exponential function with base $b$.

b. Graphs of logarithmic functions for $b > 1$ and $0 < b < 1$ are shown in Figure 4.7 on page 366. Characteristics of the graphs are summarized in the box that follows the figure.

c. Transformations involving logarithmic functions are summarized in Table 4.3 on page 367.

d. The domain of a logarithmic function is the set of all positive real numbers. The domain of $f(x) = \log_b(x + c)$ consists of all $x$ for which $x + c > 0$.

e. Common and natural logarithms: $f(x) = \log x$ means $f(x) = \log_{10} x$ and is the common logarithmic function. $f(x) = \ln x$ means $f(x) = \log_e x$ and is the natural logarithmic function.

f. Basic Logarithmic Properties

| Base $b$ ($b > 0, b \neq 1$) | Base 10 (Common Logarithms) | Base $e$ (Natural Logarithms) |
|---|---|---|
| $\log_b 1 = 0$ | $\log 1 = 0$ | $\ln 1 = 0$ |
| $\log_b b = 1$ | $\log 10 = 1$ | $\ln e = 1$ |
| $\log_b b^x = x$ | $\log 10^x = x$ | $\ln e^x = x$ |
| $b^{\log_b x} = x$ | $10^{\log x} = x$ | $e^{\ln x} = x$ |

#### Chapter 4 Test

1. Graph $f(x) = 2^x$ and $g(x) = 2^{x+1}$ in the same rectangular coordinate system.
2. Graph $f(x) = \log_2 x$ and $g(x) = \log_2(x - 1)$ in the same rectangular coordinate system.
3. Write in exponential form: $\log_5 125 = 3$.
4. Write in logarithmic form: $\sqrt{36} = 6$.
5. Find the domain of $f(x) = \ln(3 - x)$.

*In Exercises 6–7, use properties of logarithms to expand each logarithmic expression as much as possible. Where possible, evaluate logarithmic expressions without using a calculator.*

6. $\log_4(64x^5)$
7. $\log_3 \frac{\sqrt[3]{x}}{81}$

*In Exercises 8–9, write each expression as a single logarithm.*

8. $6 \log x + 2 \log y$
9. $\ln 7 - 3 \ln x$
10. Use a calculator to evaluate $\log_{15} 71$ to four decimal places.

*In Exercises 11–16, solve each equation.*

11. $5^x = 1.4$
12. $400e^{0.005x} = 1600$
13. $e^{2x} - 6e^x + 5 = 0$
14. $\log_6(4x - 1) = 3$
15. $\log x + \log(x + 15) = 2$
16. $2 \ln 3x = 8$
17. Suppose you have \$3000 to invest. Which investment yields the greater return over 10 years: 6.5% compounded semianually or 6% compounded continuously? How much more (to the nearest dollar) is yielded by the better investment?
18. On the decibel scale, the loudness of a sound, in decibels, is given by $D = 10 \log \frac{I}{I_0}$, where $I$ is the intensity of the sound, in watts per meter$^2$, and $I_0$ is the intensity of a sound barely audible to the human ear. If the intensity of a sound is $10^{12}I_0$, what is its loudness in decibels? (Such a sound is potentially damaging to the ear.)
19. The percentage of married men in the United States who are employed is modeled by $P = 89.18e^{-0.004t}$. The model indicates that P% of married men were employed $t$ years after 1959.
    a. What percentage of married men were employed in 1959?
    b. Is the percentage of married men who are employed increasing or decreasing? Explain.
    c. In what year were 77% of U.S. married men employed?

#### Cumulative Review Exercises (Chapters 1–4)

*Solve each equation in Exercises 1–5.*

1. $|3x - 4| = 2$
2. $\sqrt{2x - 5} - \sqrt{x - 3} = 1$
3. $x^4 + x^3 - 3x^2 - x + 2 = 0$
4. $e^{5x} - 32 = 96$
5. $\log_2(x + 5) + \log_2(x - 1) = 4$

*Solve each inequality in Exercises 6–7. Express the answer in interval notation.*

6. $14 - 5x \geq -6$
7. $|2x - 4| \leq 2$
8. Write the point-slope form and the slope-intercept form of the line passing through $(1, 3)$ and $(3, -3)$.
9. If $f(x) = x^2$ and $g(x) = x + 2$, find $(f \circ g)(x)$ and $(g \circ f)(x)$.
10. If $f(x) = 2x - 7$, find $f^{-1}(x)$.
11. Divide $x^3 + 5x^2 + 3x - 10$ by $x + 2$.
12. Use the Rational Zero Theorem to list all possible rational zeros for $f(x) = 4x^3 - 7x - 3$.
13. The value of $y$ varies directly as the square of $x$. If $x = 3$ when $y = 12$, find $y$ when $x = 15$.
14. Solve $x^3 - 4x^2 + 6x - 4 = 0$ given that $1 + i$ is a root.

*In Exercises 15–18, graph each equation.*

15. $(x - 3)^2 + (y + 2)^2 = 4$
16. $f(x) = (x - 2)^2 - 1$
17. $f(x) = \frac{x^2 - 1}{x^2 - 4}$
18. $f(x) = (x - 2)^2(x + 1)$
19. You are paid time-and-a-half for each hour worked over 40 hours a week. Last week you worked 50 hours and earned \$660. What is your normal hourly salary?
20. The formula $F = 1 - k \ln(t + 1)$ models the fraction of people, $F$, who remember all the words in a list of nonsense words $t$ hours after memorizing the list. After 3 hours only half the people could remember all the words. Determine the value of $k$ and then predict the fraction of people in the group who will remember all the words after 6 hours.

# Applications Index

## D



## E



## F



## G

# Prerequisites: Fundamental Concepts of Algebra

## Chapter P

This chapter reviews fundamental concepts of algebra that are prerequisites for the study of precalculus. Algebra, like all of mathematics, provides the tools to help you recognize, classify, and explore the hidden patterns of your world, revealing its underling structure. Throughout the new millennium, literacy in algebra will be a prerequisite for functioning in a meaningful way personally, professionally, and as a citizen.

Listening to the radio on the way to work, you hear candidates in the upcoming election discussing the problem of the country's 5.5 trillion dollar deficit. It seems like this is a real problem, but then you realize that you don't really know what that number means. How can you look at this deficit in the proper perspective? If the national debt were evenly divided among all citizens of the country, how much would each citizen have to pay? Does the deficit seem like such a significant problem now?

## SECTION P.1 *Real Numbers and Algebraic Expressions*

### Objectives

1. Recognize subsets of the real numbers.
2. Use inequality symbols.
3. Evaluate absolute value.
4. Use absolute value to express distance.
5. Evaluate algebraic expressions.
6. Identity properties of the real numbers.
7. Simplify algebraic expressions.

The U.N. building is designed with three golden rectangles.

The United Nations Building in New York was designed to represent its mission of promoting world harmony. Viewed from the front, the building looks like three rectangles stacked upon each other. In each rectangle, the ratio of the width to height is $\sqrt{5} + 1$ to 2, approximately 1.618 to 1. The ancient Greeks believed that such a rectangle, called a **golden rectangle**, was the most visually pleasing of all rectangles.

The ratio 1.618 to 1 is approximate because $\sqrt{5}$ is an irrational number, a special kind of real number. Irrational? Real? Let's make sense of all this by describing the kinds of numbers you will encounter in this course.

**1** Recognize subsets of the real numbers.

### The Set of Real Numbers

Before we describe the set of real numbers, let's be sure you are familiar with some basic ideas about sets. A **set** is a collection of objects whose contents can be clearly determined. The objects in a set are called the **elements** of the set. For example, the set of numbers used for counting can be represented by

$$\{1, 2, 3, 4, 5, \ldots\}.$$

The braces, { }, indicate that we are representing a set. This form of representing a set uses commas to separate the elements of the set. The set of numbers used for counting is called the set of **natural numbers**. The three dots after the 5 indicate that there is no final element and that the listing goes on forever.

The sets that make up the real numbers are summarized in Table P.1. We refer to these sets as **subsets** of the real numbers, meaning that all elements in each subset are also elements in the set of real numbers.

Notice the use of the symbol $\approx$ in the examples of irrational numbers. The symbol means "is approximately equal to." Thus,

$$\sqrt{2} \approx 1.414214.$$

We can verify that this is only an approximation by multiplying 1.414214 by itself The product is very close to but not exactly 2:

$$1.414214 \times 1.414214 = 2.0000012378.$$

#### Technology

A calculator with a square root key gives a decimal approximation for $\sqrt{2}$, not the exact value.

Real numbers $\mathbb{R}$

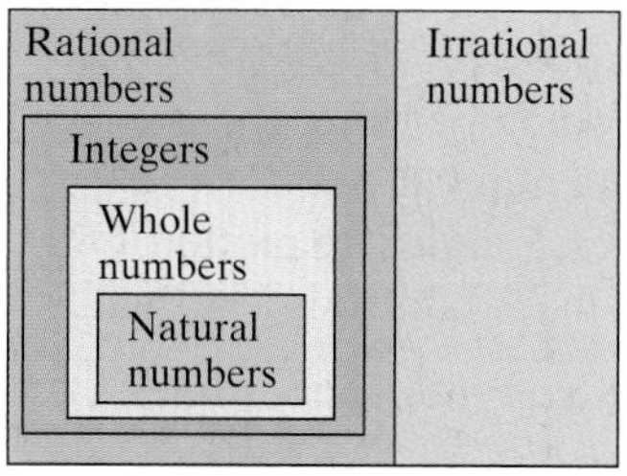


This diagram shows that every real number is rational or irrational.

**Table P.1 Important Subsets of the Real Numbers**

| Name | Description | Examples |
|---|---|---|
| Natural numbers $\mathbb{N}$ | $\{1, 2, 3, 4, 5, \ldots\}$ These numbers are used for counting. | $2, 3, 5, 17$ |
| Whole numbers $\mathbb{W}$ | $\{0, 1, 2, 3, 4, 5, \ldots\}$ The whole numbers add 0 to the set of natural numbers. | $0, 2, 3, 5, 17$ |
| Integers $\mathbb{Z}$ | $\{\ldots, -5, -4, -3, -2, -1, 0, 1, 2, 3, 4, 5, \ldots\}$ The integers add the negatives of the natural numbers to the set of whole numbers. | $-17, -5, -3, -2, 0, 2, 3, 5, 17$ |
| Rational numbers $\mathbb{Q}$ | These numbers can he expressed as an integer divided by a nonzero integer: $\frac{a}{b}$: $a$ and $b$ are integers: $b \neq 0$. Rational numbers can be expressed as terminating or repeating decimals. | $-17 = \frac{-17}{1}, -5 = \frac{-5}{1}, -3, -2,$ $0, 2, 3, 5, 17,$ $\frac{2}{5} = 0.4, \frac{-2}{3} = -0.6666\cdots = -0.\overline{6}$ |
| Irrational numbers $\mathbb{I}$ | This is the set of numbers whose decimal representations are neither terminating nor repeating. Irrational numbers cannot be expressed as a quotient of integers. | $\sqrt{2} \approx 1.414214$ $-\sqrt{3} \approx -1.73205$ $\pi \approx 3.142$ $-\frac{\pi}{2} \approx -1.571$ |

The set of **real numbers** is formed by combining the rational numbers and the irrational numbers. Thus, every real number is either rational or irrational.

## The Real Number Line

The **real number line** is a graph used to represent the set of real numbers. An arbitrary point, called the **origin**, is labeled 0; units to the right of the origin are **positive** and units to the left of the origin are **negative**. The real number line is shown in Figure P.1.

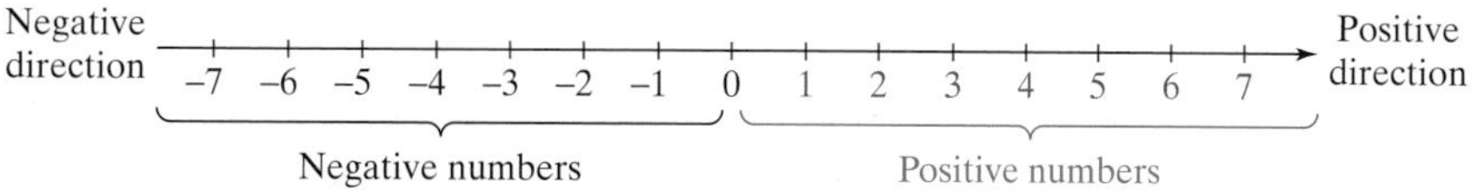


**Figure P.1** The real number line

Real numbers are **graphed** on a number line by placing a dot at the correct location for each number. The integers are easiest to locate. In Figure P.2 we've graphed the integers $-3$, 0, and 4.

**Figure P.2** Graphing $-3$, 0, and 4 on number line

Every real number corresponds to a point on the number line and every point on the number line corresponds to a real number. We say there is a **one-to-one correspondence** between all the real numbers and all points on a real number line. If you draw a point on the real number line corresponding to a real number, you are **plotting** the real number. In Figure P.2, we are plotting the real numbers $-3$, 0, and 4.

**2** Use inequality symbols.

## Ordering the Real Numbers

On the real number line, the real numbers increase from left to right. The lesser of two real numbers is the one farther to the left on a number line. The greater of two real numbers is the one farther to the right on a number line.

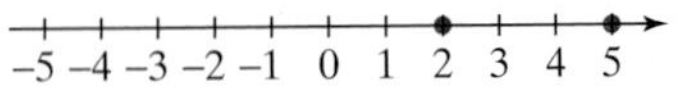


**Figure P.3**

Look at the number line in Figure P.3. The integers 2 and 5 are plotted. Observe that 2 is to the left of 5 on the number line. This means that 2 is less than 5:

$2 < 5$: 2 is less than 5 because 2 is to the *left* of 5 on the number line.

In Figure P.3, we can also observe that 5 is to the right of 2 on the number line. This means that 5 is greater than 2.

$5 > 2$: 5 is greater than 2 because 5 is to the right of 2 on the number line.

The symbols $<$ and $>$ are called **inequality symbols**. They may be combined with an equal sign, as shown in the following table.

| Symbols | Meaning | Example | Explanation |
|---|---|---|---|
| $a \leq b$ | $a$ is less than or equal to $b$. | $3 \leq 7$ | Because $3 < 7$ |
| | | $7 \leq 7$ | Because $7 = 7$ |
| $b \geq a$ | $b$ is greater than or equal to $a$. | $7 \geq 3$ | Because $7 > 3$ |
| | | $-5 \geq -5$ | Because $-5 = -5$ |

### Study Tip

The symbols $<$ and $>$ always point to the lesser of the two real numbers when the inequality is true.

$2 < 5$ The symbol points to 2, the lesser number.

$5 > 2$ The symbol points to 2, the lesser number.

**3** Evaluate absolute value.

## Absolute Value

**Absolute value** describes the distance from 0 on a real number line. If $a$ represents a real number, the symbol $|a|$ represents its absolute value, read "the absolute value of $a$." For example, the real number line in Figure P.4 shows that

$$|-3| = 3 \quad \text{and} \quad |5| = 5.$$

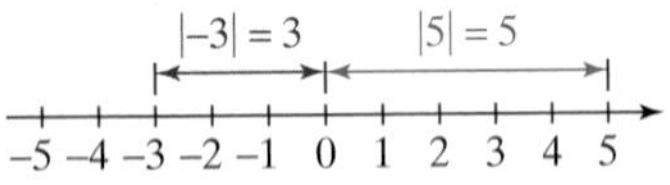


**Figure P.4** Absolute value as the distance from 0

The absolute value of $-3$ is 3 because $-3$ is 3 units from 0 on the number line. The absolute value of 5 is 5 because 5 is 5 units from 0 on the number line. The absolute value of a positive real number or 0 is the number itself. The absolute value of a negative real number, such as $-3$, is positive.

We can define the absolute value of the real number $x$ without referring to a number line. The algebraic definition of the absolute value of $x$ is given as follows:

**Definition of Absolute Value**

$$|x| = \begin{cases} x & \text{if } x \geq 0 \\ -x & \text{if } x < 0 \end{cases}$$

If $x$ is nonnegative (that is $x \geq 0$), the absolute value of $x$ is the number itself. For example:

$$|5| = 5 \qquad |\pi| = \pi \qquad \left|\frac{1}{3}\right| = \frac{1}{3} \qquad |0| = 0$$

Zero is the only number whose absolute value is 0.

If $x$ is a negative number (that is, $x < 0$), the absolute value of $x$ is the opposite of $x$. This makes the absolute value positive. For example,

$$|-3| = -(-3) = 3 \qquad |-\pi| = -(-\pi) = \pi \qquad \left|-\frac{1}{3}\right| = -\left(-\frac{1}{3}\right) = \frac{1}{3}.$$

This middle step is usually omitted.

## EXAMPLE 1 Evaluating Absolute Value

Rewrite each expression without absolute value bars.

**a.** $|\sqrt{3} - 1|$ **b.** $|2 - \pi|$ **c.** $\frac{|x|}{x}$ if $x < 0$

### Solution

**a.** Because $\sqrt{3} \approx 1.7$, the expression inside the absolute value bars is positive. The absolute value of a positive number is the number itself. Thus,

$$|\sqrt{3} - 1| = \sqrt{3} - 1.$$

**b.** Because $\pi \approx 3.14$, the number inside the absolute value bars is negative. The absolute value of $x$ when $x < 0$ is $-x$. Thus,

$$|2 - \pi| = -(2 - \pi) = \pi - 2.$$

**c.** If $x < 0$, then $|x| = -x$. Thus,

$$\frac{|x|}{x} = \frac{-x}{x} = -1.$$

**Check Point 1** Rewrite each expression without absolute value bars.

**a.** $|1 - \sqrt{2}|$ **b.** $|\pi - 3|$ **c.** $\frac{|x|}{x}$ if $x > 0$

**Discovery**

Verify the triangle inequality if $a = 4$ and $b = 5$. Verify the triangle inequality if $a = 4$ and $b = -5$.

When does equality occur in the triangle inequality and when does inequality occur? Verify your observation with additional number pairs.

Next, we list several basic properties of absolute value. Each of these properties can be derived from the definition of absolute value.

### Properties of Absolute Value

For all real numbers $a$ and $b$,

**1.** $|a| \geq 0$ **2.** $|-a| = |a|$ **3.** $a \leq |a|$

**4.** $|ab| = |a||b|$ **5.** $\left|\frac{a}{b}\right| = \frac{|a|}{|b|}$, $b \neq 0$

**6.** $|a + b| \leq |a| + |b|$ (called the triangle inequality)

**4** Use absolute value to express distance.

## Distance Between Points on a Real Number Line

Absolute value is used to find the distance between two points on a real number line. If $a$ and $b$ are any real numbers, the **distance between $a$ and $b$** is the absolute value of their difference. For example, the distance between 4 and 10 is 6. Using absolute value, we find this distance in one of two ways:

$$|10 - 4| = |6| = 6 \quad \text{or} \quad |4 - 10| = |-6| = 6.$$

The distance between 4 and 10 on the real number line is 6.

Notice that we obtain the same distance regardless of the order in which we subtract.

**Distance Between Two Points on the Real Number Line**

If $a$ and $b$ are any two points on a real number line, then the distance between $a$ and $b$ is given by

$$|a - b| \quad \text{or} \quad |b - a|.$$

## EXAMPLE 2 Distance Between Two Points on a Number Line

Find the distance between −5 and 3 on the real number line.

**Solution** Because the distance between $a$ and $b$ is given by $|a - b|$, the distance between −5 and 3 is

$$|-5 - 3| = |-8| = 8.$$

$a = -5$ $\quad$ $b = 3$

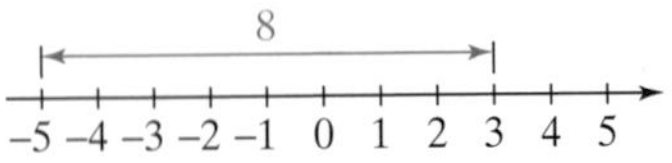


**Figure P.5** The distance between −5 and 3 is 8.

Figure P.5 verifies that there are 8 units between −5 and 3 on the real number line. We obtain the same distance if we reverse the order of the subtraction:

$$|3 - (-5)| = |8| = 8.$$

**Check Point 2** Find the distance between −4 and 5 on the real number line.

## Algebraic Expressions

Algebra uses letters, such as $x$ and $y$, to represent real numbers. Such letters are called **variables**. For example, imagine that you are basking in the sun on the beach. We can let $x$ represent the number of minutes that you can stay in the sun without burning with no sunscreen. With a number 6 sunscreen, exposure time without burning is six times as long, or 6 times $x$. This can be written $6 \cdot x$, but it is usually expressed as $6x$. Placing a number and a letter next to one another indicates multiplication.

Notice that $6x$ combines the number 6 and the variable $x$ using the operation of multiplication. A combination of variables and numbers using the operations of addition, subtraction, multiplication, or division, as well as powers or roots, is called an **algebraic expression**. Here are some examples of algebraic expressions:

$$x + 6, \quad x - 6, \quad 6x, \quad \frac{x}{6}, \quad 3x + 5, \quad \sqrt{x} + 7.$$

**5** Evaluate algebraic expressions.

## Evaluating Algebraic Expressions

**Evaluating an algebraic expression** means to find the value of the expression by substituting given values for each variable in the expression. For example, we can evaluate $6x$ (from the sun-screen example) when $x = 15$. We substitute 15 for $x$. We obtain $6 \cdot 15$, or 90. This means if you can stay in the sun for 15 minutes without burning when you don't put on any lotion, then with a number 6 lotion, you can "cook" for 90 minutes without burning.

### EXAMPLE 3 Evaluating an Algebraic Expression

Evaluate:

**a.** $(25t^2 + 125t) \div (t^2 + 1)$ for $t = 3$.

**b.** $\dfrac{-b + \sqrt{b^2 - 4ac}}{2a}$ for $a = 2$, $b = 9$, and $c = -5$.

**Solution**

| Expression | Value of the Variable (s) | Substitute | Evaluating the Expression |
|---|---|---|---|
| **a.** $(25t^2 + 125t) \div (t^2 + 1)$ | $t = 3$ | $(25 \cdot 3^2 + 125 \cdot 3) \div (3^2 + 1)$ | $= (25 \cdot 9 + 125 \cdot 3) \div (9 + 1)$ <br> $= (225 + 375) \div (9 + 1)$ <br> $= 600 \div 10$ <br> $= 60$ |
| **b.** $\dfrac{-b + \sqrt{b^2 - 4ac}}{2a}$ | $a = 2$ <br> $b = 9$ <br> $c = -5$ | $\dfrac{-9 + \sqrt{9^2 - 4(2)(-5)}}{2(2)}$ | $= \dfrac{-9 + \sqrt{81 - (-40)}}{4}$ <br> $= \dfrac{-9 + \sqrt{121}}{4}$ <br> $= \dfrac{-9 + 11}{4} = \dfrac{2}{4} = \dfrac{1}{2}$ |

**Check Point 3**

Evaluate:

**a.** $(3t^2 + 8t) \div (t^2 - 2)$ for t $= 2$.

**b.** $\dfrac{-b + \sqrt{b^2 - 4ac}}{2a}$ for $a = 1$, $b = -6$, and $c = 9$.

**6** Identify properties of the real numbers.

## Properties of Real Numbers and Algebraic Expressions

When you use your calculator to add two real numbers, you can enter them in any order. The fact that two real numbers can be added in any order is called the **commutative property of addition**. You probably use this property, as well as other properties of real numbers listed in Table P.2 on the next page, without giving it much thought. The properties of the real numbers are especially useful when working with algebraic expressions. For each property listed in Table P.2, $a$, $b$, and $c$ represent real numbers, variables, or algebraic expressions.

**Table P.2 Properties of the Real Numbers**

| Name | Meaning | Examples |
|---|---|---|
| Commutative Property of Addition | Two real numbers can be added in any order. $a + b = b + a$ | • $13 + 7 = 7 + 13$<br>• $13x + 7 = 7 + 13x$ |
| Commutative Property of Multiplication | Two real numbers can be multiplied in any order. $ab = ba$ | • $\sqrt{2} \cdot \sqrt{5} = \sqrt{5} \cdot \sqrt{2}$<br>• $x \cdot 6 = 6x$ |
| Associative Property of Addition | If three real numbers are added, it makes no difference which two are added first. $(a + b) + c = a + (b + c)$ | • $3 + (8 + x) = (3 + 8) + x = 11 + x$ |
| Associative Property of Multiplication | If three real numbers are multiplied, it makes no difference which two are multiplied first. $(a \cdot b) \cdot c = a \cdot (b \cdot c)$ | • $-2(3x) = (-2 \cdot 3)x = -6x$ |
| Distributive Property of Multiplication over Addition | Multiplication distributes over addition. $a \cdot (b + c) = a \cdot b + a \cdot c$ | • $7(4 + \sqrt{3}) = 7 \cdot 4 + 7 \cdot \sqrt{3} = 28 + 7\sqrt{3}$<br>• $5(3x + 7) = 5 \cdot 3x + 5 \cdot 7 = 15x + 35$ |
| Identity Property of Addition | Zero can be deleted from a sum. $a + 0 = a$ $0 + a = a$ | • $\sqrt{3} + 0 = \sqrt{3}$<br>• $0 + 6x = 6x$ |
| Identity Property of Multiplication | One can be deleted from a product. $a \cdot 1 = a$ $1 \cdot a = a$ | • $1 \cdot \pi = \pi$<br>• $13x \cdot 1 = 13x$ |
| Inverse Property of Addition | The sum of a real number and its additive inverse gives 0, the additive identity. $a + (-a) = 0$ $(-a) + a = 0$ | • $\sqrt{5} + (-\sqrt{5}) = 0$<br>• $6x + (-6x) = 0$<br>• $(-4y) + 4y = 0$ |
| Inverse Property of Multiplication | The product of a nonzero real number and its multiplicative inverse gives 1, the multiplicative identity. $a \cdot \frac{1}{a} = 1, \quad a \neq 0$ $\frac{1}{a} \cdot a = 1, \quad a \neq 0$ | • $7 \cdot \frac{1}{7} = 1$<br>• $\left(\frac{1}{x-3}\right)(x - 3) = 1, \ x \neq 3$ |

## Commutative Words and Sentences

The commutative property states that a change in order produces no change in the answer. The words and sentences listed here are commutative; they read the same from left to right and from right to left!

dad
repaper
never odd or even

Draw, o coward!
Dennis sinned.
Ma is a nun, as I am.

Revolting is error. Resign it, lover.
Naomi, did I moan?
Al lets Della call Ed Stella.

The properties in Table P.2 apply to the operations of addition and multiplication. Subtraction and division are defined in terms of addition and multiplication.

**Definitions of Subtraction and Division**

Let $a$ and $b$ represent real numbers.

**Subtraction:** $a - b = a + (-b)$

We call $-b$ the **additive inverse** or **opposite** of $b$.

**Division:** $a \div b = a \cdot \frac{1}{b}$, where $b \neq 0$

We call $\frac{1}{b}$ the **multiplicative inverse** or **reciprocal** of $b$. The quotient of $a$ and $b$, $a \div b$, can be written in the form $\frac{a}{b}$, where $a$ is the **numerator** and $b$ the **denominator** of the fraction.

Because subtraction is defined in terms of adding an inverse, the distributive property can be applied to subtraction:

$$a(b - c) = ab - ac$$

$$(b - c)a = ba - ca.$$

For example,

$$4(2x - 5) = 4 \cdot 2x - 4 \cdot 5 = 8x - 20.$$

**7** Simplify algebraic expressions.

## Simplifying Algebraic Expressions

The **terms** of an algebraic expression are those parts that are separated by addition. For example, consider the algebraic expression

$$7x - 9y - 3,$$

which can be expressed as

$$7x + (-9y) + (-3).$$

This expression contains three terms, namely $7x$, $-9y$, and $-3$.

The numerical part of a term is called its **numerical coefficient**. In the term $7x$, the 7 is the numerical coefficient. In the term $-9y$, the $-9$ is the numerical coefficient.

A term that consists of just a number is called a **constant term**. The constant term of $7x - 9y - 3$ is $-3$.

A term indicates a product. The expressions that are multiplied to form the term are called its **factors. Like terms** have the same variable factors with the same exponents on the variables. For example, $7x$ and $3x$ are like terms because they have the same variable factor, $x$. The distributive property (in reverse) can be used to add these terms:

$$7x + 3x = (7 + 3)x = 10x.$$

**Study Tip**

To add like terms, add their numerical coefficients. Use this result as the numerical coefficient of the terms' common variable(s).

An algebraic expression is **simplified** when parentheses have been removed and like terms have been combined.

### EXAMPLE 4 Simplifying an Algebraic Expression

Simplify: $6(2x - 4y) + 10(4x + 3y)$.

**Solution**

$$6(2x - 4y) + 10(4x + 3y)$$

$= 6 \cdot 2x - 6 \cdot 4y + 10 \cdot 4x + 10 \cdot 3y$ — Use the distributive property to remove the parentheses.

$= 12x - 24y + 40x + 30y$ — Multiply.

$= (12x + 40x) + (30y - 24y)$ — Group like terms.

$= 52x + 6y$ — Combine like terms.

**Check Point 4** Simplify: $7(4x - 3y) + 2(5x + y)$.

## Properties of Negatives

The distributive property can be extended to cover more than two terms within parentheses. For example,

This sign represents subtraction. This sign tells us that −3 is negative.

$$-3(4x - 2y + 6) = -3 \cdot 4x - (-3) \cdot 2y - 3 \cdot 6$$
$$= -12x - (-6y) - 18$$
$$= -12x + 6y - 18$$

The voice balloons illustrate that negative signs can appear side by side. They can represent the operation of subtraction or the fact that a real number is negative. Here is a list of properties of negatives and how they are applied to algebraic expressions.

**Properties of Negatives**

Let $a$ and $b$ represent real numbers, variables, or algebraic expressions.

| Property | Examples |
|---|---|
| **1.** $(-1)a = -a$ | $(-1)4xy = -4xy$ |
| **2.** $-(-a) = a$ | $-(-6y) = 6y$ |
| **3.** $(-a)b = -ab$ | $(-7)4xy = -7 \cdot 4xy = -28xy$ |
| **4.** $a(-b) = -ab$ | $5x(-3y) = -5x \cdot 3y = -15xy$ |
| **5.** $-(a + b) = -a - b$ | $-(7x + 6y) = -7x - 6y$ |
| **6.** $-(a - b) = -a + b = b - a$ | $-(3x - 7y) = -3x + 7y = 7y - 3x$ |

Do you notice that properties 5 and 6 in the box are related? In general, expressions within parentheses that are preceded by a negative can be simplified by dropping the parentheses and changing the sign of every term inside the parentheses.

For example,

$$-(3x - 2y + 5z - 6) = -3x + 2y - 5z + 6.$$

# EXERCISE SET P.1

## Practice Exercises

*In Exercises 1–4, list all numbers from the given set that are a. natural numbers, b. whole numbers, c. integers, d. rational numbers, e. irrational numbers.*

**1.** $\{-9, -\frac{4}{5}, 0, 0.25, \sqrt{3}, 9.2, \sqrt{100}\}$

**2.** $\{-7, -0.\overline{6}, 0, \sqrt{49}, \sqrt{50}\}$

**3.** $\{-11, -\frac{5}{6}, 0, 0.75, \sqrt{5}, \pi, \sqrt{64}\}$

**4.** $\{-5, -0.\overline{3}, 0, \sqrt{2}, \sqrt{4}\}$

**5.** Give an example of a whole number that is not a natural number.

**6.** Give an example of a rational number that is not an integer.

**7.** Give an example of a number that is an integer, a whole number, and a natural number.

**8.** Give an example of a number that is a rational number, an integer, and a real number.

*Determine whether each statement in Exercises 9–14 is true or false.*

**9.** $-13 \le -2$ **10.** $-6 > 2$

**11.** $4 \ge -7$ **12.** $-13 < -5$

**13.** $-\pi \ge -\pi$ **14.** $-3 > -13$

*In Exercises 15–22, rewrite each expression without absolute value bars.*

**15.** $|300|$ **16.** $|-203|$

**17.** $|12 - \pi|$ **18.** $|7 - \pi|$

**19.** $|\sqrt{2} - 5|$ **20.** $|\sqrt{5} - 13|$

**21.** $\frac{-3}{|-3|}$ **22.** $\frac{-7}{|-7|}$

*In Exercises 23–30, express the distance between the given numbers using absolute value. Then find the distance by evaluating the absolute value expression.*

**23.** 2 and 17 **24.** 4 and 15

**25.** −2 and 5 **26.** −6 and 8

**27.** −19 and −4 **28.** −26 and −3

**29.** −3.6 and −1.4 **30.** −5.4 and −1.2

*In Exercises 31–38, evaluate each algebraic expression for the given value of the variable.*

**31.** $5x + 7; \quad x = 4$ **32.** $9x + 6; \quad x = 5$

**33.** $4(x + 3) - 11; \quad x = -5$

**34.** $6(x + 5) - 13; \quad x = -7$

**35.** $\frac{1 - (x - 2)^2}{1 + (x - 2)^2}; \quad x = -1$ **36.** $\frac{2x^2 - 1}{2x^3 + 1}; \quad x = -\frac{1}{2}$

**37.** $\frac{-b + \sqrt{b^2 - 4ac}}{2a}; \quad a = 4, b = -20, c = 25$

**38.** $\frac{-b + \sqrt{b^2 - 4ac}}{2a}; \quad a = 3, b = 5, c = -2$

*In Exercises 39–46, state the name of the property illustrated.*

**39.** $6 + (-4) = (-4) + 6$

**40.** $11 \cdot (7 + 4) = 11 \cdot 7 + 11 \cdot 4$

**41.** $6 + (2 + 7) = (6 + 2) + 7$

**42.** $6 \cdot (2 \cdot 3) = 6 \cdot (3 \cdot 2)$

**43.** $(2 + 3) + (4 + 5) = (4 + 5) + (2 + 3)$

**44.** $7 \cdot (11 \cdot 8) = (11 \cdot 8) \cdot 7$

**45.** $2(-8 + 6) = -16 + 12$

**46.** $-8(3 + 11) = -24 + (-88)$

*In Exercises 47–52, simplify each algebraic expression.*

**47.** $5(3x + 4) - 4$ **48.** $2(5x + 4) - 3$

**49.** $5(3x - 2) + 12x$ **50.** $2(5x - 1) + 14x$

**51.** $7(3y - 5) + 2(4y + 3)$ **52.** $4(2y - 6) + 3(5y + 10)$

*In Exercises 53–58, write each algebraic expression without parentheses.*

**53.** $-(-14x)$ **54.** $-(-17y)$

**55.** $-(2x - 3y - 6)$ **56.** $-(5x - 13y - 1)$

**57.** $\frac{1}{3}(3x) + [(4y) + (-4y)]$ **58.** $\frac{1}{2}(2y) + [(-7x) + 7x]$

## Application Exercises

**59.** Are first putting on your left shoe and then putting on your right shoe commutative?

**60.** Are first getting undressed and then taking a shower commutative?

**61.** Give an example of two things that you do that are not commutative.

**62.** Give an example of two things that you do that are commutative.

**63.** The algebraic expression $962x + 18{,}667$ describes average yearly earnings in United States $x$ years after 1990. Evaluate the algebraic expression when $x = 7$. Describe what the answer means in practical terms.

**64.** The algebraic expression $1527x + 31{,}290$ describes average yearly earnings for elementary and secondary teachers in the United States $x$ years after 1990. Evaluate the algebraic expression when $x = 10$. Describe what the answer means in practical terms.

**65.** The optimum heart rate is the rate that a person should achieve during exercise for the exercise to be most beneficial. The algebraic expression

$$0.6(220 - a)$$

describes a person's optimum heart rate in beats per minute, where $a$ represents the age of the person.

**a.** Use the distributive property to rewrite the algebraic expression without parentheses.

**b.** Use each form of the algebraic expression to determine the optimum heart rate for a 20-year-old runner.

## Writing in Mathematics

*Writing about mathematics will help you to learn mathematics. For all writing exercises in this book, use complete sentences to respond to the question. Some writing exercises can be answered in a sentence; others require a paragraph or two. You can decide how much you need to write as long as your writing clearly and directly answers the question in the exercise. Standard references such as a dictionary and a thesaurus should be helpful.*

**66.** How do the whole numbers differ from the natural numbers?

**67.** Can a real number be both rational and irrational? Explain your answer.

**68.** If you are given two real numbers, explain how to determine which one is the lesser.

**69.** How can $\frac{|x|}{x}$ be equal to 1 or $-1$?

**70.** What is an algebraic expression? Give an example with your explanation.

**71.** Why is $3(x + 7) - 4x$ not simplified? What must be done to simplify the expression?

**72.** You can transpose the letters in the word "conversation" to form the phrase "voices rant on." From "total abstainers" we can form "sit not at ale bars." What two algebraic properties do each of these transpositions (called anagrams) remind you of? Explain your answer.

## Critical Thinking Exercises

**73.** Which one of the following statements is true?

**a.** Every rational number is an integer.

**b.** Some whole numbers are not integers.

**c.** Some rational numbers are not positive.

**d.** Irrational numbers cannot be negative.

**74.** Which of the following is true?

**a.** The term $x$ has no numerical coefficient.

**b.** $5 + 3(x - 4) = 8(x - 4) = 8x - 32$

**c.** $-x - x = -x + (-x) = 0$

**d.** $x - 0.02(x + 200) = 0.98x - 4$

*In Exercises 75–77, insert either $<$ or $>$ in the box between the numbers to make the statement true.*

**75.** $\sqrt{2}\,\square\,1.5$

**76.** $-\pi\,\square\,-3.5$

**77.** $-\frac{3.14}{2}\,\square\,-\frac{\pi}{2}$

**78.** A business that manufactures small alarm clocks has weekly fixed costs of \$5000. The average cost per clock for the business to manufacture $x$ clocks is described by

$$\frac{0.5x + 5000}{x}.$$

**a.** Find the average cost when $x = 100, 1000,$ and $10{,}000$.

**b.** Like all other businesses, the alarm clock manufacturer must make a profit. To do this, each clock must be sold for at least 50¢ more than what it costs to manufacture. Due to competition from a larger company, the clocks can be sold for \$1.50 each and no more. Our small manufacturer can only produce 2000 clocks weekly. Does this business have much of a future? Explain.

# SECTION P.2 Exponents and Scientific Notation

## Objectives

1. Evaluate exponential expressions.
2. Simplify exponential expressions.
3. Use scientific notation.

**1** Evaluate exponential expressions.

Although people do a great deal of talking, the total output since the beginning of gabble to the present day, including all baby talk, love songs, and congressional debates, only amounts to about 10 million billion words. This can be expressed as 16 factors of 10, or $10^{16}$ words.

Exponents such as 2, 3, 4, and so on are used to indicate repeated multiplication. For example,

$$10^2 = 10 \cdot 10 = 100,$$

$$10^3 = 10 \cdot 10 \cdot 10 = 1000,$$

$$10^4 = 10 \cdot 10 \cdot 10 \cdot 10 = 10{,}000.$$

The 10 that is repeated when multiplying is called the **base**. The small numbers above and to the right of the base are called **exponents**. The exponent tells the number of times the base is to be used when multiplying. In $10^3$, the base is 10 and the exponent is 3.

The formal algebraic definition of a natural number exponent summarizes our discussion.

### Powers Of Ten

| | |
|---|---|
| $10 = 10^1$ | |
| $100 = 10^2$ | |
| $1000 = 10^3$ | |
| $10{,}000 = 10^4$ | |
| $100{,}000 = 10^5$ | |
| $1{,}000{,}000 = 10^6$ | million |
| $10{,}000{,}000 = 10^7$ | |
| $100{,}000{,}000 = 10^8$ | |
| $1{,}000{,}000{,}000 = 10^9$ | billion |

### Technology

You can use a calculator to evaluate exponential expressions. For example, to evaluate $5^3$, press the following keys:

Scientific Calculator

5 [$x^y$] 3 [=]

Graphing Calculator

5 [∧] 3 [ENTER]

Although calculators have special keys to evaluate powers of ten and squaring bases, you can always use one of the sequences shown here.

### Definition of a Natural Number Exponent

If $b$ is a real number and $n$ is a natural number,

$$b^n = \underbrace{b \cdot b \cdot b \cdot \cdots \cdot b}_{b \text{ appears as a factor } n \text{ times.}}$$

(Exponent: $n$; Base: $b$)

$b^n$ is read "the $n$th power of $b$" or "$b$ to the $n$th power." Thus, the $n$th power of $b$ is defined as the product of $n$ factors of $b$.

Furthermore, $b^1 = b$.

## EXAMPLE 1 Evaluating an Exponential Expression

Evaluate: $(-2)^3 \cdot 3^2$.

**Solution**

$$(-2)^3 \cdot 3^2 = (-2)(-2)(-2) \cdot 3 \cdot 3 = -8 \cdot 9 = -72$$

This is $(-2)^3$, read "$-2$ cubed."

This is $3^2$, read "3 squared."

**Check Point 1** Evaluate: $(-4)^3 \cdot 2^2$.

2 Use properties of exponents.

## Properties of Exponents

The major properties of exponents are summarized in the box that follows.

### Properties of Exponents

| Property | Examples |
|---|---|
| **The Negative Exponent Rule**<br>If $b$ is any real number other than 0 and $n$ is a natural number, then $b^{-n} = \frac{1}{b^n}$. | • $5^{-3} = \frac{1}{5^3} = \frac{1}{125}$<br>• $\frac{1}{4^{-2}} = \frac{1}{\frac{1}{4^2}} = 4^2 = 16$ |
| **The Zero Exponent Rule**<br>If $b$ is any real number other than 0, $b^0 = 1$. | • $7^0 = 1$<br>• $(-5)^0 = 1$<br>• $-5^0 = -1$<br>Only 5 is raised to the zero power. |
| **The Product Rule**<br>If $b$ is a real number or algebraic expression, and $m$ and $n$ are integers, $b^m \cdot b^n = b^{m+n}$.<br>Add exponents when multiplying with the same base. | • $2^2 \cdot 2^3 = 2^{2+3} = 2^5 = 32$<br>• $x^{-3} \cdot x^7 = x^{-3+7} = x^4$ |
| **The Power Rule**<br>If $b$ is a real number or algebraic expression, and $m$ and $n$ are integers, $(b^m)^n = b^{mn}$.<br>Multiply exponents when an exponential expression is raised to a power. | • $(2^2)^3 = 2^{2 \cdot 3} = 2^6 = 64$<br>• $(x^{-3})^4 = x^{-3 \cdot 4} = x^{-12} = \frac{1}{x^{12}}$ |

**The Quotient Rule**

If $b$ is a nonzero real number or algebraic expression, and $m$ and $n$ are integers,

$$\frac{b^m}{b^n} = b^{m-n}.$$

Subtract exponents when dividing with the same base.

- $\frac{2^8}{2^4} = 2^{8-4} = 2^4 = 16$
- $\frac{x^3}{x^7} = x^{3-7} = x^{-4} = \frac{1}{x^4}$

**Products Raised to Powers**

If $a$ and $b$ are real number or algebraic expressions, and $n$ is an integer,

$$(ab)^n = a^n b^n.$$

When a product is raised to a power, raise each factor to the power.

- $(-2y)^4 = (-2)^4 y^4 = 16y^4$
- $(-2xy)^3 = (-2)^3 x^3 y^3 = -8x^3y^3$

**Quotients Raised to Powers**

If $a$ and $b$ are real numbers, $b \neq 0$, or algebraic expressions, and $n$ is an integer,

$$\left(\frac{a}{b}\right)^n = \frac{a^n}{b^n}.$$

When a quotient is raised to a power, raise the numerator and denominator to the power.

- $\left(\frac{2}{5}\right)^4 = \frac{2^4}{5^4} = \frac{16}{625}$
- $\left(-\frac{3}{x}\right)^3 = \frac{(-3)^3}{x^3} = -\frac{27}{x^3}$

**2** Simplify exponential expressions.

## Simplifying Exponential Expressions

Properties of exponents are used to simplify exponential expressions. An exponential expression is **simplified** when

- No parentheses appear.
- No powers are raised to powers.
- Each base occurs only once.
- No negative exponents appear.

### EXAMPLE 2 Simplifying Exponential Expressions

Simplify:

**a.** $(-3x^4y^5)^3$ **b.** $(-7xy^4)(-2x^5y^6)$ **c.** $\frac{-35x^2y^4}{5x^6y^{-8}}$ **d.** $\left(\frac{4x^2}{y}\right)^{-3}$

**Solution**

**a.** $(-3x^4y^5)^3 = (-3)^3(x^4)^3(y^5)^3$ Raise each factor in the product to the power.

$= (-3)^3 x^{4\cdot 3} y^{5\cdot 3}$ Multiply powers to powers.

$= -27x^{12}y^{15}$ $(-3)^3 = (-3)(-3)(-3) = -27$

**b.** $(-7xy^4)(-2x^5y^6) = (-7)(-2)xx^5y^4y^6$ Group factors with the same base.

$= 14x^{1+5}y^{4+6}$ When multiplying expressions with the same base, add the exponents.

$= 14x^6y^{10}$ Simplify.

**Visualizing Powers of 3**

The triangles contain 3, $3^2$, $3^3$, and $3^4$ circles.

**c.** $\dfrac{-35x^2y^4}{5x^6y^{-8}} = \left(\dfrac{-35}{5}\right)\left(\dfrac{x^2}{x^6}\right)\left(\dfrac{y^4}{y^{-8}}\right)$ Group factors with the same base.

$= -7x^{2-6}y^{4-(-8)}$ When dividing expression with the same base, subtract the exponents.

$= -7x^{-4}y^{12}$ Simplify. Notice that $4 - (-8) = 4 + 8 = 12$.

$= \dfrac{-7y^{12}}{x^4}$ Move $x^{-4}$, the factor with the negative exponent, from the numerator to the denominator.

**d.** $\left(\dfrac{4x^2}{y}\right)^{-3} = \dfrac{4^{-3}(x^2)^{-3}}{y^{-3}}$ Raise each factor inside the parentheses to the $-3$ power.

$= \dfrac{4^{-3}x^{-6}}{y^{-3}}$ Multiply powers to powers.

$= \dfrac{y^3}{4^3x^6}$ Move factors with negative exponents from the numerator to the denominator (or vice versa) by changing the sign of the exponent.

$= \dfrac{y^3}{64x^6}$ $4^3 = 4 \cdot 4 \cdot 4 = 64$

**Check Point 2** Simplify:

**a.** $(2x^3y^6)^4$ **b.** $(-6x^2y^5)(3xy^3)$ **c.** $\dfrac{100x^{12}y^2}{20x^{16}y^{-4}}$ **d.** $\left(\dfrac{5x}{y^4}\right)^{-2}$

## Study Tip

Try to avoid the following common errors that can occur when simplifying exponential expressions.

| Incorrect | Description of Error | Correct |
|---|---|---|
| $b^3b^4 = b^{12}$ | Exponents should be added, not multiplied. | $b^3b^4 = b^7$ |
| $3^n \cdot 3^m = 9^{n+m}$ | The common base should be retained, not multiplied. | $3^n \cdot 3^m = 3^{n+m}$ |
| $\dfrac{5^{16}}{5^4} = 5^4$ | Exponents should be subtracted, not divided. | $\dfrac{5^{16}}{5^4} = 5^{12}$ |
| $(4a)^3 = 4a^3$ | Both factors should be cubed. | $(4a)^3 = 64a^3$ |
| $b^{-n} = -\dfrac{1}{b^n}$ | Only the exponent should change sign. | $b^{-n} = \dfrac{1}{b^n}$ |
| $(a+b)^{-1} = \dfrac{1}{a} + \dfrac{1}{b}$ | The exponent applies to the entire expression $a + b$. | $(a+b)^{-1} = \dfrac{1}{a+b}$ |

**3** Use scientific notation.

## Scientific Notation

The national debt of the United States is about \$5.5 trillion. A stack of \$1 bills equaling the national debt would rise to twice the distance from the Earth to the moon. Because a trillion is $10^{12}$, the national debt can be expressed as

$$5.5 \times 10^{12}.$$

The number $5.5 \times 10^{12}$ is written in a form called **scientific notation**. A number in scientific notation is expressed as a number greater than or equal to 1 and less than 10 multiplied by some power of 10. It is customary to use the multiplication symbol, ×, rather than a dot in scientific notation.

Here are two examples of numbers in scientific notation:

Each day, $2.6 \times 10^7$ pounds of dust from the atmosphere settle on Earth.

The diameter of a hydrogen atom is $1.016 \times 10^{-8}$ centimeter.

We can use the exponent on the 10 to change a number in scientific notation to decimal notation. If the exponent is *positive*, move the decimal point in the number to the *right* the same number of places as the exponent. If the exponent is *negative*, move the decimal point in the number to the *left* the same number of places as the exponent.

## EXAMPLE 3 Converting from Scientific to Decimal Notation

Write each number in decimal notation.

**a.** $2.6 \times 10^7$ **b.** $1.016 \times 10^{-8}$

**Solution**

**a.** We express $2.6 \times 10^7$ in decimal notation by moving the decimal point in 2.6 seven places to the right. We need to add six zeros.

$$2.6 \times 10^7 = 26{,}000{,}000$$

**b.** We express $1.016 \times 10^{-8}$ in decimal notation by moving the decimal point in 1.016 eight places to the left. We need to add seven zeros to the right of the decimal point.

$$1.016 \times 10^{-8} = 0.00000001016$$

**Check Point 3** Write each number in decimal notation.

**a.** $7.4 \times 10^9$ **b.** $3.017 \times 10^{-6}$

To convert from decimal notation to scientific notation, we reverse the procedure of Example 3.

- Move the decimal point in the given number to obtain a number greater than or equal to 1 and less than 10.
- The number of places the decimal point moves gives the exponent on 10; the exponent is positive if the given number is greater than 10 and negative if the given number is between 0 and 1.

## EXAMPLE 4 Converting from Decimal Notation to Scientific Notation

Write each number in scientific notation.

**a.** 4,600,000 **b.** 0.00023

**Solution**

**a.** $4{,}600{,}000 = 4.6 \times 10^?$ $\xrightarrow{\text{Decimal point moves 6 places.}}$ $4.6 \times 10^6$

**b.** $0.00023 = 2.3 \times 10^{-?}$ $\xrightarrow{\text{Decimal point moves 4 places.}}$ $2.3 \times 10^{-4}$

**Check Point 4** Write each number in scientific notation.

**a.** 7,410,000,000 **b.** 0.000000092

## Computations with Scientific Notation

The product and quotient rules for exponents can be used to multiply or divide numbers that are expressed in scientific notation. For example, here's how to find the product of $3.4 \times 10^9$ and $2 \times 10^{-5}$.

$$(3.4 \times 10^9)(2 \times 10^{-5}) = (3.4 \times 2) \times (10^9 \times 10^{-5})$$
$$= 6.8 \times 10^{9+(-5)}$$
$$= 6.8 \times 10^4 \quad \text{or} \quad 68{,}000$$

**Technology**

On a graphing calculator, you can use the EE (enter exponent) key to find the product of $3.4 \times 10^9$ and $2 \times 10^{-5}$:

3.4 [EE] 9 [×] 2 [EE] [(−)] 5 [ENTER]

If your calculator is in the scientific notation mode, it will display 6.8 E4; in the normal mode it will display 68000.

In our next example, we use the quotient of two numbers in scientific notation to help put a number into perspective. The number is our national debt. The United States began accumulating large deficits in the 1980s. To finance the deficit, the government had borrowed \$5.5 trillion as of the end of 1998. The graph in Figure P.6 shows the national debt increasing over time.

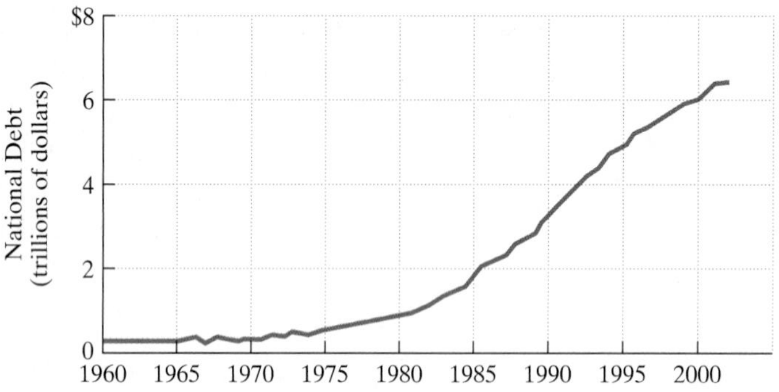


*Source*: Office of Management and Budget

**Figure P.6** The national debt

## EXAMPLE 5 The National Debt

As of the end of 1998, the national debt was \$5.5 trillion, or $5.5 \times 10^{12}$ dollars. At that time, the U.S. population was approximately 270,000,000 (270 million), or $2.7 \times 10^8$. If the national debt were evenly divided among every individual in the United States, how much would each citizen have to pay?

**Solution** The amount each citizen must pay is the total debt, $5.5 \times 10^{12}$ dollars, divided by the number of citizens, $2.7 \times 10^8$.

$$\frac{5.5 \times 10^{12}}{2.7 \times 10^8} = \left(\frac{5.5}{2.7}\right) \times \left(\frac{10^{12}}{10^8}\right)$$
$$\approx 2.04 \times 10^{12-8}$$
$$= 2.04 \times 10^4$$
$$= 20{,}400$$

**Technology**

Here is the keystroke sequence for solving Example 5 using a graphing calculator:

5.5 [EE] 12 [÷] 2.7 [EE] 8 [ENTER]

Every U.S. citizen would have to pay about \$20,400 to the federal government to pay off the national debt. A family of three would owe \$61,200!

**Check Point 5** Approximately $2 \times 10^4$ people run in the New York City Marathon each year. Each runner runs a distance of 26 miles. Write the total distance covered by all the runners (assuming that each person completes the marathon) in scientific notation.

## An Application: Black Holes in Space

The concept of a black hole, a region in space where matter appears to vanish, intrigues scientists and nonscientists alike. Scientists theorize that when massive stars run out of nuclear fuel, they begin to collapse under the force of their own gravity. As the star collapses, its density increases. In turn, the force of gravity increases so tremendously that even light cannot escape from the star. Consequently, it appears black.

A mathematical formula, called the Schwarzchild formula, describes the critical value to which the radius of a massive body must be reduced for it to become a black hole. This formula forms the basis of our next example.

### EXAMPLE 6 An Application of Scientific Notation

Use the Schwarzchild formula

$$R_s = \frac{2GM}{c^2}$$

where

$R_s$ = Radius of the star, in meters, that would cause it to become a black hole

$M$ = Mass of the star, in kilograms

$G$ = A constant, called the gravitational constant

$= 6.7 \times 10^{-11} \dfrac{\text{m}^3}{\text{kg}\cdot\text{s}^2}$

$c$ = Speed of light

$= 3 \times 10^8$ meters per second

to determine to what length the radius of the sun must be reduced for it to become a black hole. The sun's mass is approximately $2 \times 10^{30}$ kilograms.

**Solution**

$$R_s = \frac{2GM}{c^2}$$

$$= \frac{2 \times 6.7 \times 10^{-11} \times 2 \times 10^{30}}{(3 \times 10^8)^2}$$ Substitute the given values.

$$= \frac{(2 \times 6.7 \times 2) \times (10^{-11} \times 10^{30})}{(3 \times 10^8)^2}$$ Rearrange factors in the numerator.

$$= \frac{26.8 \times 10^{-11+30}}{3^2 \times (10^8)^2}$$ Add exponents in the numerator. Raise each factor in the denominator to the power.

$$= \frac{26.8 \times 10^{19}}{9 \times 10^{16}}$$ Multiply powers to powers: $(10^8)^2 = 10^{8 \cdot 2} = 10^{16}$.

$$= \frac{26.8}{9} \times 10^{19-16}$$ When dividing expressions with the same base, subtract the exponents.

$$\approx 2.978 \times 10^3$$

$$= 2978$$

Although the sun is not massive enough to become a black hole (its radius is approximately 700,000 kilometers), the Schwarzchild model theoretically indicates that if the sun's radius were reduced to approximately 2978 meters, that is, about $\frac{1}{235{,}000}$ its present size, it would become a black hole.

**Check Point 6** Pouiseville's law states that the speed of blood, $S$, in centimeters per second located $r$ centimeters from the central axis of an artery is

$$S = (1.76 \times 10^5)[(1.44 \times 10^{-2}) - r^2].$$

Find the speed of blood at the central axis of this artery.

## EXERCISE SET P.2

### Practice Exercises

*Evaluate each exponential expression in Exercises 1–22.*

**1.** $5^2 \cdot 2$

**2.** $6^2 \cdot 2$

**3.** $(-2)^6$

**4.** $(-2)^4$

**5.** $-2^6$

**6.** $-2^4$

**7.** $(-3)^0$

**8.** $(-9)^0$

**9.** $-3^0$

**10.** $-9^0$

**11.** $4^{-3}$

**12.** $2^{-6}$

**13.** $2^2 \cdot 2^3$

**14.** $3^3 \cdot 3^2$

**15.** $(2^2)^3$

**16.** $(3^3)^2$

**17.** $\frac{2^8}{2^4}$

**18.** $\frac{3^8}{3^4}$

**19.** $3^{-3} \cdot 3$

**20.** $2^{-3} \cdot 2$

**21.** $\frac{2^3}{2^7}$

**22.** $\frac{3^4}{3^7}$

*Simplify each exponential expression in Exercises 23–60.*

**23.** $x^{-2}y$

**24.** $xy^{-3}$

**25.** $x^0y^5$

**26.** $x^7y^0$

**27.** $x^3 \cdot x^7$

**28.** $x^{11} \cdot x^5$

**29.** $x^{-5} \cdot x^{10}$

**30.** $x^{-6} \cdot x^{12}$

**31.** $(x^3)^7$

**32.** $(x^{11})^5$

**33.** $(x^{-5})^3$

**34.** $(x^{-6})^4$

**35.** $\frac{x^{14}}{x^7}$

**36.** $\frac{x^{30}}{x^{10}}$

**37.** $\frac{x^{14}}{x^{-7}}$

**38.** $\frac{x^{30}}{x^{-10}}$

**39.** $(8x^3)^2$

**40.** $(6x^4)^2$

**41.** $\left(-\frac{4}{x}\right)^3$

**42.** $\left(-\frac{6}{y}\right)^3$

**43.** $(-3x^2y^5)^2$

**44.** $(-3x^4y^6)^3$

**45.** $(3x^4)(2x^7)$

**46.** $(11x^5)(9x^{12})$

**47.** $(-9x^3y)(-2x^6y^4)$

**48.** $(-5x^4y)(-6x^7y^{11})$

**49.** $\frac{8x^{20}}{2x^4}$

**50.** $\frac{20x^{24}}{10x^6}$

**51.** $\frac{25a^{13}b^4}{-5a^2b^3}$

**52.** $\frac{35a^{14}b^6}{-7a^7b^3}$

**53.** $\frac{14b^7}{7b^{14}}$

**54.** $\frac{20b^{10}}{10b^{20}}$

**55.** $(4x^3)^{-2}$

**56.** $(10x^2)^{-3}$

**57.** $\frac{24x^3y^5}{32x^7y^{-9}}$

**58.** $\frac{10x^4y^9}{30x^{12}y^{-3}}$

**59.** $\left(\frac{5x^3}{y}\right)^{-2}$

**60.** $\left(\frac{3x^4}{y}\right)^{-3}$

*In Exercises 61–68, write each number in decimal notation.*

**61.** $4.7 \times 10^3$

**62.** $9.12 \times 10^5$

**63.** $4 \times 10^6$

**64.** $7 \times 10^6$

**65.** $7.86 \times 10^{-4}$

**66.** $4.63 \times 10^{-5}$

**67.** $3.18 \times 10^{-6}$

**68.** $5.84 \times 10^{-7}$

*In Exercises 69–76, write each number in scientific notation.*

**69.** 3600

**70.** 2700

**71.** 220,000,000

**72.** 370,000,000,000

**73.** 0.027

**74.** 0.014

**75.** 0.000763

**76.** 0.000972

*In Exercises 77–84, perform the indicated operation and express the answer in decimal notation.*

**77.** $(2 \times 10^3)(3 \times 10^2)$

**78.** $(5 \times 10^2)(4 \times 10^4)$

**79.** $(4.1 \times 10^2)(3 \times 10^{-4})$

**80.** $(1.2 \times 10^3)(2 \times 10^{-5})$

**81.** $\frac{12 \times 10^6}{4 \times 10^2}$

**82.** $\frac{20 \times 10^{26}}{10 \times 10^{15}}$

**83.** $\frac{6.3 \times 10^3}{3 \times 10^5}$

**84.** $\frac{9.6 \times 10^2}{3 \times 10^{-3}}$

## Application Exercises

*In Exercises 85–88, use $10^6$ for one million and $10^9$ for one billion to rewrite the number in each statement in scientific notation.*

**85.** In 1999, the U.S. government collected $1,694,300 million.

**86.** In 1999, the U.S. government spent $1,751,800 million.

**87.** The federal government is expected to provide nearly $60 billion in student aid in 2002.

**88.** In 1998, U.S. consumers spent $5,493.7 billion.

**89.** If the population of the United States is $2.7 \times 10^8$ and each person spends about $120 per year on ice cream, express the total annual spending on ice cream in scientific notation.

*Use scientific notation to answer Exercises 90–94.*

**90.** The mass of Earth is approximately

5,976,000,000,000,000,000,000,000,000 grams

and the mass of the hydrogen atom is

0.000 000 000 000 000 000 000 001 66 gram.

If Earth were composed only of hydrogen atoms, how many hydrogen atoms would it contain?

**91.** If the length of a hydrogen atoms is 0.000 000 03 millimeter and the average human foot measures 200 millimeters, how many times as large as the hydrogen atom is the human foot?

**92.** The tallest tree known is the Howard Libbey redwood in Redwood Grove, California. The tree measures 100,000 millimeters. The distance from Earth to the sun is approximately 150,000,000,000,000 millimeters. How many of the tallest redwood trees would it take to span this distance?

**93.** Among the planets of the solar system, Pluto is the most distant from the sun, approximately $4.6 \times 10^9$ miles. How many seconds does it take the light of the sun to reach Pluto if light travels $1.86 \times 10^5$ miles per second?

**94.** Our galaxy measures approximately $1.2 \times 10^{17}$ kilometers across. If a space vehicle were capable of moving at half the speed of light (approximately $1.5 \times 10^5$ kilometers per second), how many years would it take for the vehicle to cross the galaxy?

## Writing in Mathematics

**95.** Describe what it means to raise a number to a power. In your description, include a discussion of the difference between $-5^2$ and $(-5)^2$.

**96.** Explain the product rule for exponents. Use $2^3 \cdot 2^5$ in your explanation.

**97.** Explain the power rule for exponents. Use $(3^2)^4$ in your explanation.

**98.** Explain the quotient rule for exponents. Use $\frac{5^8}{5^2}$ in your explanation.

**99.** Why is $(-3x^2)(2x^{-5})$ not simplified? What must be done to simplify the expression?

**100.** How do you know if a number is written in scientific notation?

**101.** Explain how to convert from scientific to decimal notation and give an example.

**102.** Explain how to convert from decimal to scientific notation and give an example.

## Critical Thinking Exercises

**103.** Which one of the following is true?

**a.** $4^{-2} < 4^{-3}$ **b.** $5^{-2} > 2^{-5}$

**c.** $(-2)^4 = 2^{-4}$ **d.** $5^2 \cdot 5^{-2} > 2^5 \cdot 2^{-5}$

**104.** The mad Dr. Frankenstein has gathered enough bits and pieces (so to speak) for $2^{-1} + 2^{-2}$ of his creature-to-be. Write a fraction that represents the amount of his creature that must still be obtained.

**105.** If $b^A = MN$, $b^C = M$, and $b^D = N$, what is the relationship among $A$, $C$, and $D$?

## Group Exercise

**106. Putting Numbers into Perspective.** A large number can be put into perspective by comparing it with another number. For example, we put the \$5.5 trillion national debt into perspective by comparing it to the number of U.S. citizens. The total distance covered by all the runners in the New York City Marathon (checkpoint Example 11 on page 22) can be put into perspective by comparing this distance with, say, the distance from New York to San Francisco.

For this project, each group member should consult an almanac, a newspaper, or the World Wide Web to find a number greater than one million. Explain to other members of the group the context in which the large number is used. Express the number in scientific notation. Then put the number into perspective by comparing it with another number.

# SECTION P.3 Radicals and Rational Exponents

## Objectives

1. Evaluate square roots.
2. Use the product rule to simplify square roots.
3. Use the quotient rule to simplify square roots.
4. Add and subtract square roots.
5. Rationalize denominators.
6. Evaluate and perform operations with higher roots.
7. Understand and use rational exponents.

What is the maximum speed at which a racing cyclist can turn a corner without tipping over? The answer, in miles per hour, is given by the algebraic expression $4\sqrt{x}$, where $x$ is the radius of the corner, in feet. Algebraic expressions containing roots describe phenomena as diverse as a wild animal's territorial area, evaporation on a lake's surface, and Albert Einstein's bizarre concept of how an astronaut moving close to the speed of light would barely age relative to friends watching from Earth. No description of your world can be complete without roots and radicals. In this section, we review the basics of radical expressions and the use of rational exponents to indicate radicals.

1 Evaluate square roots.

## Square Roots

The **principal square root** of a nonnegative real number $b$, written $\sqrt{b}$, is that number whose square equals $b$. For example,

$$\sqrt{100} = 10 \text{ because } 10^2 = 100 \quad \text{and} \quad \sqrt{0} = 0 \text{ because } 0^2 = 0.$$

Observe that the principal square root of a positive number is positive and the principal square root of 0 is 0.

The symbol $\sqrt{\phantom{x}}$ that we use to denote the principal square root is called a **radical sign**. The number under the radical sign is called the **radicand**. Together we refer to the radical sign and its radicand as a **radical**.

The following definition summarizes our discussion.

**Definition of the Principal Square Root**

If $a$ is a nonnegative real number, the nonnegative number $b$ such that $b^2 = a$, denoted by $b = \sqrt{a}$, is the **principal square root** of $a$.

In the real number system, negative numbers do not have square roots. For example, $\sqrt{-9}$ is not a real number because there is no real number whose square is $-9$.

If a number is nonnegative $(a \geq 0)$, then $(\sqrt{a})^2 = a$. For example,

$$(\sqrt{2})^2 = 2, \quad (\sqrt{3})^2 = 3, \quad (\sqrt{4})^2 = 4, \quad \text{and } (\sqrt{5})^2 = 5.$$

A number that is the square of a rational number is called a **perfect square**. For example,

64 is a perfect square because $64 = 8^2$.

$\frac{1}{9}$ is a perfect square because $\frac{1}{9} = \left(\frac{1}{3}\right)^2$.

The following rule can be used to find square roots of perfect squares.

**Square Roots of Perfect Squares**

$$\sqrt{a^2} = |a|$$

For example, $\sqrt{6^2} = 6$ and $\sqrt{(-6)^2} = |-6| = 6$.

2 Use the product rule to simplify square roots.

## The Product Rule for Square Roots

A square root is **simplified** when its radicand has no factors other than 1 that are perfect squares. For example, $\sqrt{500}$ is not simplified because it can be expressed as $\sqrt{100 \cdot 5}$ and $\sqrt{100}$ is a perfect square. The **product rule for square roots** can be used to simplify $\sqrt{500}$.

**The Product Rule for Square Roots**

If $a$ and $b$ represent nonnegative real numbers, then

$$\sqrt{ab} = \sqrt{a}\sqrt{b} \text{ and } \sqrt{a}\sqrt{b} = \sqrt{ab}.$$

The square root of a product is the product of the square roots.

Example 1 shows how the product rule is used to remove from the square root any perfect squares that occur as factors.

## EXAMPLE 1 Using the Product Rule to Simplify Square Roots

Simplify: **a.** $\sqrt{500}$ **b.** $\sqrt{6x} \cdot \sqrt{3x}$

**Solution**

**a.** $\sqrt{500} = \sqrt{100 \cdot 5}$ 100 is the largest perfect square factor of 500.

$= \sqrt{100}\sqrt{5}$ $\sqrt{ab} = \sqrt{a}\sqrt{b}$

$= 10\sqrt{5}$ $\sqrt{100} = 10$

**b.** $\sqrt{6x} \cdot \sqrt{3x} = \sqrt{6x \cdot 3x}$ $\sqrt{a}\sqrt{b} = \sqrt{ab}$

$= \sqrt{18x^2}$ Multiply.

$= \sqrt{9x^2 \cdot 2}$ 9 is the largest perfect square factor of 18.

$= \sqrt{9x^2}\sqrt{2}$ $\sqrt{ab} = \sqrt{a}\sqrt{b}$

$= \sqrt{9}\sqrt{x^2}\sqrt{2}$ Split $\sqrt{9x^2}$ into two square roots.

$= 3|x|\sqrt{2}$ $\sqrt{9} = 3$ (because $3^2 = 9$) and $\sqrt{x^2} = |x|$.

**Check Point 1** Simplify: **a.** $\sqrt{3^2}$ **b.** $\sqrt{5x} \cdot \sqrt{10x}$

**3** Use the quotient rule to simplify square roots.

## The Quotient Rule for Square Roots

Another property for square roots involves division.

**The Quotient Rule for Square Roots**

If $a$ and $b$ represent nonnegative real numbers and $b \neq 0$, then

$$\frac{\sqrt{a}}{\sqrt{b}} = \sqrt{\frac{a}{b}} \text{ and } \sqrt{\frac{a}{b}} = \frac{\sqrt{a}}{\sqrt{b}}.$$

The square root of a quotient is the quotient of the square roots.

## EXAMPLE 2 Using the Quotient Rule to Simplify Square Roots

Simplify: **a.** $\sqrt{\frac{100}{9}}$ **b.** $\frac{\sqrt{48x^3}}{\sqrt{6x}}$

**Solution**

**a.** $\sqrt{\frac{100}{9}} = \frac{\sqrt{100}}{\sqrt{9}} = \frac{10}{3}$

**b.** $\frac{\sqrt{48x^3}}{\sqrt{6x}} = \sqrt{\frac{48x^3}{6x}} = \sqrt{8x^2} = \sqrt{4x^2}\sqrt{2} = \sqrt{4}\sqrt{x^2}\sqrt{2} = 2|x|\sqrt{2}$

**Check Point 2** Simplify: **a.** $\sqrt{\frac{25}{16}}$ **b.** $\frac{\sqrt{150x^3}}{\sqrt{2x}}$

**4** Add and subtract square roots.

## Adding and Subtracting Square Roots

Two or more square roots can be combined provided that they have the same radicand. Such radicals are called **like radicals**. For example,

$$7\sqrt{11} + 6\sqrt{11} = (7 + 6)\sqrt{11} = 13\sqrt{11}.$$

### EXAMPLE 3 Adding and Subtracting Like Radicals

Add or subtract as indicated:

**a.** $7\sqrt{2} + 5\sqrt{2}$ **b.** $\sqrt{5x} - 7\sqrt{5x}$

**Solution**

**a.** $7\sqrt{2} + 5\sqrt{2} = (7 + 5)\sqrt{2}$ Apply the distributive property.

$= 12\sqrt{2}$ Simplify.

**b.** $\sqrt{5x} - 7\sqrt{5x} = 1\sqrt{5x} - 7\sqrt{5x}$ Write $\sqrt{5x}$ as $1\sqrt{5x}$.

$= (1 - 7)\sqrt{5x}$ Apply the distributive property.

$= -6\sqrt{5x}$ Simplify.

**Check Point 3** Add or subtract as indicated:

**a.** $8\sqrt{13} + 9\sqrt{13}$ **b.** $\sqrt{17x} - 20\sqrt{17x}$

In some cases, radicals can be combined once they have been simplified. For example, to add $\sqrt{2}$ and $\sqrt{8}$, we can write $\sqrt{8}$ as $\sqrt{4 \cdot 2}$ because 4 is a perfect square factor of 8.

$$\sqrt{2} + \sqrt{8} = \sqrt{2} + \sqrt{4 \cdot 2} = 1\sqrt{2} + 2\sqrt{2} = (1 + 2)\sqrt{2} = 3\sqrt{2}$$

### EXAMPLE 4 Combining Radicals That First Require Simplification

Add or subtract as indicated:

**a.** $7\sqrt{3} + \sqrt{12}$ **b.** $4\sqrt{50x} - 6\sqrt{32x}$

**Solution**

**a.** $7\sqrt{3} + \sqrt{12}$

$= 7\sqrt{3} + \sqrt{4 \cdot 3}$ Split 12 into two factors such that one is a perfect square.

$= 7\sqrt{3} + 2\sqrt{3}$ $\sqrt{4 \cdot 3} = \sqrt{4}\sqrt{3} = 2\sqrt{3}$

$= (7 + 2)\sqrt{3}$ Apply the distributive property. You will find that this step is usually done mentally.

$= 9\sqrt{3}$ Simplify.

## A Radical Idea: Time Is Relative

What does travel in space have to do with radicals? Imagine that in the future we will be able to travel at velocities approaching the speed of light (approximately 186,000 miles per second). According to Einstein's theory of relativity, time would pass more quickly on Earth than it would in the moving spaceship. The expression

$$R_f\sqrt{1 - \left(\frac{v}{c}\right)^2}$$

gives the aging rate of an astronaut relative to the aging rate of a friend on Earth, $R_f$. In the expression, $v$ is the astronaut's speed and $c$ is the speed of light. As the astronaut's speed approaches the speed of light, we can substitute $c$ for $v$:

$R_f\sqrt{1 - \left(\frac{v}{c}\right)^2}$ Let $v = c$.

$= R_f\sqrt{1 - 1^2}$

$= R_f\sqrt{0} = 0$

Close to the speed of light, the astronaut's aging rate relative to a friend on earth is nearly 0. What does this mean? As we age here on Earth, the space traveler would barely get older. The space traveler would return to a futuristic world in which friends and loved ones would be long dead.

**b.** $4\sqrt{50x} - 6\sqrt{32x}$

$= 4\sqrt{25 \cdot 2x} - 6\sqrt{16 \cdot 2x}$ — 25 is the largest perfect square factor of 50 and 16 is the largest perfect square factor of 32.

$= 4 \cdot 5\sqrt{2x} - 6 \cdot 4\sqrt{2x}$ — $\sqrt{25 \cdot 2} = \sqrt{25}\sqrt{2} = 5\sqrt{2}$ and $\sqrt{16 \cdot 2} = \sqrt{16}\sqrt{2} = 4\sqrt{2}$

$= 20\sqrt{2x} - 24\sqrt{2x}$ — Multiply.

$= (20 - 24)\sqrt{2x}$ — Apply the distributive property.

$= -4\sqrt{2x}$ — Simplify.

**Check Point 4** Add or subtract as indicated:

**a.** $5\sqrt{27} + \sqrt{12}$ **b.** $6\sqrt{18x} - 4\sqrt{8x}$

5 Rationalize denominators.

## Rationalizing Denominators

You can use a calculator to compare the approximate values for $\frac{1}{\sqrt{3}}$ and $\frac{\sqrt{3}}{3}$. The two approximations are the same. This is not a coincidence:

$$\frac{1}{\sqrt{3}} = \frac{1}{\sqrt{3}} \cdot \boxed{\frac{\sqrt{3}}{\sqrt{3}}} = \frac{\sqrt{3}}{\sqrt{9}} = \frac{\sqrt{3}}{3}.$$

Any number divided by itself is 1. Multiplication by 1 does not change the value of $\frac{1}{\sqrt{3}}$.

This process involves rewriting a radical to remove the square root from the denominator without changing the value of the radical. The process is called **rationalizing the denominator**. If the denominator contains the square root of a natural number that is not a perfect square, multiply the numerator and denominator by the smallest number that produces the square root of a perfect square in the denominator.

### EXAMPLE 5 Rationalizing Denominators

Rationalize the denominator: **a.** $\frac{15}{\sqrt{6}}$ **b.** $\frac{12}{\sqrt{8}}$

**Solution**

**a.** If we multiply numerator and denominator by $\sqrt{6}$, the denominator becomes $\sqrt{6} \cdot \sqrt{6} = \sqrt{36} = 6$. Therefore, we multiply by 1, choosing $\frac{\sqrt{6}}{\sqrt{6}}$ for 1:

$$\frac{15}{\sqrt{6}} = \frac{15}{\sqrt{6}} \cdot \frac{\sqrt{6}}{\sqrt{6}} = \frac{15\sqrt{6}}{\sqrt{36}} = \frac{15\sqrt{6}}{6} = \frac{5\sqrt{6}}{2}$$

Multiply by 1.

Simplify: $\frac{15}{6} = \frac{15 \div 3}{6 \div 3} = \frac{5}{2}$.

**b.** The *smallest* number that will produce a perfect square in the denominator of $\frac{12}{\sqrt{8}}$ is $\sqrt{2}$, because $\sqrt{8} \cdot \sqrt{2} = \sqrt{16} = 4$. We multiply by 1, choosing $\frac{\sqrt{2}}{\sqrt{2}}$ for 1.

$$\frac{12}{\sqrt{8}} = \frac{12}{\sqrt{8}} \cdot \frac{\sqrt{2}}{\sqrt{2}} = \frac{12\sqrt{2}}{\sqrt{16}} = \frac{12\sqrt{2}}{4} = 3\sqrt{2}$$

**Check Point 5** Rationalize the denominator: **a.** $\frac{5}{\sqrt{3}}$ **b.** $\frac{6}{\sqrt{12}}$

How can we rationalize a denominator if the denominator contains two terms? In general,

$$(\sqrt{a} + \sqrt{b})(\sqrt{a} - \sqrt{b}) = (\sqrt{a})^2 - (\sqrt{b})^2 = a - b.$$

Notice that the product does not contain a radical. Here are some specific examples.

| The Denominator Contains: | Multiply by: | The New Denominator Contains: |
|---|---|---|
| $7 + \sqrt{5}$ | $7 - \sqrt{5}$ | $7^2 - (\sqrt{5})^2 = 49 - 5 = 44$ |
| $\sqrt{3} - 6$ | $\sqrt{3} + 6$ | $(\sqrt{3})^2 - 6^2 = 3 - 36 = -33$ |
| $\sqrt{7} + \sqrt{3}$ | $\sqrt{7} - \sqrt{3}$ | $(\sqrt{7})^2 - (\sqrt{3})^2 = 7 - 3 = 4$ |

## EXAMPLE 6 Rationalizing a Denominator Containing Two Terms

Rationalize the denominator: $\frac{7}{5 + \sqrt{3}}$.

**Solution** If we multiply the numerator and denominator by $5 - \sqrt{3}$, the denominator will not contain a radical. Therefore, we multiply by 1, choosing $\frac{5 - \sqrt{3}}{5 - \sqrt{3}}$ for 1:

$$\frac{7}{5 + \sqrt{3}} = \frac{7}{5 + \sqrt{3}} \cdot \frac{5 - \sqrt{3}}{5 - \sqrt{3}} = \frac{7(5 - \sqrt{3})}{5^2 - (\sqrt{3})^2} = \frac{7(5 - \sqrt{3})}{25 - 3}$$

Multiply by 1.

$$= \frac{7(5 - \sqrt{3})}{22} \text{ or } \frac{35 - 7\sqrt{3}}{22}.$$

In either form of the answer, there is no radical in the denominator.

**Check Point 6** Rationalize the denominator: $\dfrac{8}{4+\sqrt{5}}$.

**6** Evaluate and perform operations with higher roots.

## Other Kinds of Roots

We define the **principal *n*th root** of a real number $a$, symbolized by $\sqrt[n]{a}$, as follows:

### Definition of the Principal *n*th Root of a Real Number

$$\sqrt[n]{a} = b \text{ means that } b^n = a.$$

If $n$, the **index**, is even, then $a$ is nonnegative $(a \geq 0)$ and $b$ is also nonnegative $(b \geq 0)$. If $n$ is odd, $a$ and $b$ can be any real numbers.

For example,

$$\sqrt[3]{64} = 4 \text{ because } 4^3 = 64 \quad \text{and} \quad \sqrt[5]{-32} = -2 \text{ because } (-2)^5 = -32.$$

The same vocabulary that we learned for square roots applies to $n$th roots. The symbol $\sqrt[n]{a}$ is called a **radical** and $a$ is called the **radicand.**

A number that is the $n$th power of a rational number is called a **perfect *n*th power**. For example, 8 is a perfect third power, or perfect cube, because $8 = 2^3$. In general, one of the following rules can be used to find $n$th roots of perfect $n$th powers.

### Finding *n*th Roots of Perfect *n*th Powers

If $n$ is odd, $\sqrt[n]{a^n} = a$.

If $n$ is even, $\sqrt[n]{a^n} = |a|$.

For example,

$$\sqrt[3]{(-2)^3} = -2 \quad \text{and} \quad \sqrt[4]{(-2)^4} = |-2| = 2.$$

Absolute value is not needed with odd roots, but is necessary with even roots.

## The Product and Quotient Rules for Other Roots

The product and quotient rules apply to cube roots, fourth roots, and all higher roots.

### The Product and Quotient Rules for *n*th Roots

For all real numbers, where the indicated roots represent real numbers,

$$\sqrt[n]{a} \cdot \sqrt[n]{b} = \sqrt[n]{ab} \quad \text{and} \quad \frac{\sqrt[n]{a}}{\sqrt[n]{b}} = \sqrt[n]{\frac{a}{b}}, \quad b \neq 0.$$

## EXAMPLE 7 Simplifying, Multiplying, and Dividing Higher Roots

Simplify: **a.** $\sqrt[3]{24}$ **b.** $\sqrt[4]{8} \cdot \sqrt[4]{4}$ **c.** $\sqrt[4]{\frac{81}{16}}$

### Solution

**a.** $\sqrt[3]{24} = \sqrt[3]{8 \cdot 3}$ Find the largest *perfect cube* that is a factor of 24. $\sqrt[3]{8} = 2$, so 8 is a perfect cube and is the largest perfect cube factor of 24.

$= \sqrt[3]{8} \cdot \sqrt[3]{3}$ $\sqrt[n]{ab} = \sqrt[n]{a}\sqrt[n]{b}$

$= 2\sqrt[3]{3}$

**b.** $\sqrt[4]{8} \cdot \sqrt[4]{4} = \sqrt[4]{8 \cdot 4}$ $\sqrt[n]{a} \cdot \sqrt[n]{b} = \sqrt[n]{ab}$

$= \sqrt[4]{32}$ Find the largest *perfect fourth power* that is a factor of 32.

$= \sqrt[4]{16 \cdot 2}$ $\sqrt[4]{16} = 2$, so 16 is a perfect fourth power and is the largest perfect fourth power that is a factor of 32.

$= \sqrt[4]{16} \cdot \sqrt[4]{2}$ $\sqrt[n]{ab} = \sqrt[n]{a} \cdot \sqrt[n]{b}$

$= 2\sqrt[4]{2}$

**c.** $\sqrt[4]{\frac{81}{16}} = \frac{\sqrt[4]{81}}{\sqrt[4]{16}}$ $\sqrt[n]{\frac{a}{b}} = \frac{\sqrt[n]{a}}{\sqrt[n]{b}}$

$= \frac{3}{2}$ $\sqrt[4]{81} = 3$ because $3^4 = 81$ and $\sqrt[4]{16} = 2$ because $2^4 = 16$.

**Check Point 7** Simplify: **a.** $\sqrt[3]{40}$ **b.** $\sqrt[5]{8} \cdot \sqrt[5]{8}$ **c.** $\sqrt[3]{\frac{125}{27}}$

We have seen that adding and subtracting square roots often involves simplifying terms. The same idea applies to adding and subtracting *n*th roots.

## EXAMPLE 8 Combining Cube Roots

Subtract: $5\sqrt[3]{16} - 11\sqrt[3]{2}$.

### Solution

$5\sqrt[3]{16} - 11\sqrt[3]{2}$

$= 5\sqrt[3]{8 \cdot 2} - 11\sqrt[3]{2}$ Because $\sqrt[3]{8} = 2$, 8 is the largest perfect cube that is a factor of 16.

$= 5 \cdot 2\sqrt[3]{2} - 11\sqrt[3]{2}$ $\sqrt[3]{8 \cdot 2} = \sqrt[3]{8}\sqrt[3]{2} = 2\sqrt[3]{2}$

$= 10\sqrt[3]{2} - 11\sqrt[3]{2}$ Multiply.

$= (10 - 11)\sqrt[3]{2}$ Apply the distributive property.

$= -1\sqrt[3]{2}$ or $-\sqrt[3]{2}$ Simplify.

**Check Point 8** Subtract: $3\sqrt[3]{81} - 4\sqrt[3]{3}$.

**7** Understand and use rational exponents.

## Rational Exponents

Animals in the wild have regions to which they confine their movement, called their territorial area. Territorial area, in square miles, is related to an animal's body weight. If an animal weighs $W$ pounds, its territorial area is

$$W^{141/100}$$

square miles.

$W$ to the *what* power?! How can we interpret the information given by this algebraic expression?

In the last part of this section, we turn our attention to rational exponents such as $\frac{141}{100}$ and their relationship to roots of real numbers.

**Definition of Rational Exponents**

If $\sqrt[n]{a}$ represents a real number and $n \geq 2$ is an integer, then

$$a^{1/n} = \sqrt[n]{a}.$$

Furthermore,

$$a^{-1/n} = \frac{1}{a^{1/n}} = \frac{1}{\sqrt[n]{a}}, \; a \neq 0.$$

### EXAMPLE 9 Using the Definition of $a^{1/n}$

Simplify: **a.** $64^{1/2}$ **b.** $8^{1/3}$ **c.** $64^{-1/3}$

**Solution**

**a.** $64^{1/2} = \sqrt{64} = 8$

**b.** $8^{1/3} = \sqrt[3]{8} = 2$

**c.** $64^{-1/3} = \dfrac{1}{64^{1/3}} = \dfrac{1}{\sqrt[3]{64}} = \dfrac{1}{4}$

**Check Point 9** Simplify: **a.** $81^{1/2}$ **b.** $27^{1/3}$ **c.** $32^{-1/5}$

Note that every rational exponent in Example 9 has a numerator of 1 or −1. We now define rational exponents with any integer in the numerator.

**Definition of Rational Exponents**

If $\sqrt[n]{a}$ represents a real number, $\dfrac{m}{n}$ is a rational number reduced to lowest terms, and $n \geq 2$ is an integer, then

$$a^{m/n} = (\sqrt[n]{a})^m = \sqrt[n]{a^m}.$$

The exponent $m/n$ consists of two parts: the denominator $n$ is the root and the numerator $m$ is the exponent. Furthermore,

$$a^{-m/n} = \frac{1}{a^{m/n}}.$$

### EXAMPLE 10 Using the Definition of $a^{m/n}$

Simplify: **a.** $27^{2/3}$ **b.** $9^{3/2}$ **c.** $16^{-3/4}$

**Solution**

**a.** $27^{2/3} = (\sqrt[3]{27})^2 = 3^2 = 9$

The denominator of $\frac{2}{3}$ is the root and the numerator is the exponent.

**b.** $9^{3/2} = (\sqrt{9})^3 = 3^3 = 27$

**c.** $16^{-3/4} = \dfrac{1}{16^{3/4}} = \dfrac{1}{(\sqrt[4]{16})^3} = \dfrac{1}{2^3} = \dfrac{1}{8}$

**A Radical Curiosity**

The expression

$$a^{m/n}$$

is not defined if $\sqrt[n]{a}$ is not a real number. This can lead to some strange results. For example,

$$(-125)^{2/6}$$

is not defined because $\sqrt[6]{-125}$ is not a real number. However,

$$(-125)^{1/3}$$

is defined because $\sqrt[3]{-125} = -5$.

**Check Point 10** Simplify: **a.** $4^{3/2}$ **b.** $32^{-2/5}$

Properties of exponents can be applied to expressions containing rational exponents.

### EXAMPLE 11 Simplifying Expressions with Rational Exponents

Simplify using properties of exponents:

**a.** $(5x^{1/2})(7x^{3/4})$ **b.** $\dfrac{32x^{5/3}}{16x^{3/4}}$

**Solution**

**a.** $(5x^{1/2})(7x^{3/4}) = 5 \cdot 7x^{1/2} \cdot x^{3/4}$ — Group factors with the same base.

$= 35x^{(1/2)+(3/4)}$ — When multiplying expressions with the same base, add the exponents.

$= 35x^{5/4}$ — $\frac{1}{2} + \frac{3}{4} = \frac{2}{4} + \frac{3}{4} = \frac{5}{4}$

**b.** $\dfrac{32x^{5/3}}{16x^{3/4}} = \left(\dfrac{32}{16}\right)\left(\dfrac{x^{5/3}}{x^{3/4}}\right)$ — Group factors with the same base.

$= 2x^{(5/3)-(3/4)}$ — When dividing expressions with the same base, subtract the exponents.

$= 2x^{11/12}$ — $\frac{5}{3} - \frac{3}{4} = \frac{20}{12} - \frac{9}{12} = \frac{11}{12}$

**Check Point 11** Simplify: **a.** $(2x^{4/3})(5x^{8/3})$ **b.** $\dfrac{20x^4}{5x^{3/2}}$

Rational exponents are sometimes useful for simplifying radicals by reducing their index.

**EXAMPLE 12 Reducing the Index of a Radical**

Simplify: $\sqrt[9]{x^3}$.

**Solution** $\sqrt[9]{x^3} = x^{3/9} = x^{1/3} = \sqrt[3]{x}$

**Check Point 12** Simplify: $\sqrt[6]{x^3}$.

## EXERCISE SET P.3

### Practice Exercises

*Evaluate each expression in Exercises 1–7 or indicate that the root is not a real number.*

1. $\sqrt{36}$
2. $\sqrt{25}$
3. $\sqrt{-36}$
4. $\sqrt{-25}$
5. $\sqrt{(-13)^2}$
6. $\sqrt{(-17)^2}$

*Use the product rule to simplify the expressions in Exercises 7–16.*

7. $\sqrt{50}$
8. $\sqrt{27}$
9. $\sqrt{45x^2}$
10. $\sqrt{125x^2}$
11. $\sqrt{2x} \cdot \sqrt{6x}$
12. $\sqrt{10x} \cdot \sqrt{8x}$
13. $\sqrt{x^3}$
14. $\sqrt{y^3}$
15. $\sqrt{2x^2} \cdot \sqrt{6x}$
16. $\sqrt{6x} \cdot \sqrt{3x^2}$

*Use the quotient rule to simplify the expressions in Exercises 17–24.*

17. $\sqrt{\frac{1}{81}}$
18. $\sqrt{\frac{1}{49}}$
19. $\sqrt{\frac{49}{16}}$
20. $\sqrt{\frac{121}{9}}$
21. $\frac{\sqrt{48x^3}}{\sqrt{3x}}$
22. $\frac{\sqrt{72x^3}}{\sqrt{8x}}$
23. $\frac{\sqrt{150x^4}}{\sqrt{3x}}$
24. $\frac{\sqrt{24x^4}}{\sqrt{3x}}$

*In Exercises 25–34, add or subtract terms whenever possible.*

25. $7\sqrt{3} + 6\sqrt{3}$
26. $8\sqrt{5} + 11\sqrt{5}$
27. $6\sqrt{17x} - 8\sqrt{17x}$
28. $4\sqrt{13x} - 6\sqrt{13x}$
29. $\sqrt{8} + 3\sqrt{2}$
30. $\sqrt{20} + 6\sqrt{5}$
31. $\sqrt{50x} - \sqrt{8x}$
32. $\sqrt{63x} - \sqrt{28x}$
33. $3\sqrt{18} + 5\sqrt{50}$
34. $4\sqrt{12} - 2\sqrt{75}$

*In Exercises 35–44, rationalize the denominator.*

35. $\frac{1}{\sqrt{7}}$
36. $\frac{2}{\sqrt{10}}$
37. $\frac{\sqrt{2}}{\sqrt{5}}$
38. $\frac{\sqrt{7}}{\sqrt{3}}$
39. $\frac{13}{3 + \sqrt{11}}$
40. $\frac{3}{3 + \sqrt{7}}$
41. $\frac{7}{\sqrt{5} - 2}$
42. $\frac{5}{\sqrt{3} - 1}$
43. $\frac{6}{\sqrt{5} + \sqrt{3}}$
44. $\frac{11}{\sqrt{7} - \sqrt{3}}$

*Evaluate each expression in Exercises 45–54 or indicate that the root is not a real number.*

45. $\sqrt[3]{125}$
46. $\sqrt[3]{8}$
47. $\sqrt[3]{-8}$
48. $\sqrt[3]{-125}$
49. $\sqrt[4]{-16}$
50. $\sqrt[4]{-81}$
51. $\sqrt[4]{(-3)^4}$
52. $\sqrt[4]{(-2)^4}$
53. $\sqrt[5]{(-3)^5}$
54. $\sqrt[5]{(-2)^5}$

*Simplify the radical expressions in Exercises 55–62.*

55. $\sqrt[3]{32}$
56. $\sqrt[3]{150}$
57. $\sqrt[3]{x^4}$
58. $\sqrt[3]{x^5}$
59. $\sqrt[3]{9} \cdot \sqrt[3]{6}$
60. $\sqrt[3]{12} \cdot \sqrt[3]{4}$
61. $\frac{\sqrt[5]{64x^6}}{\sqrt[5]{2x}}$
62. $\frac{\sqrt[4]{162x^5}}{\sqrt[4]{2x}}$

*In Exercises 63–70, evaluate each expression without using a calculator.*

63. $36^{1/2}$
64. $121^{1/2}$
65. $8^{1/3}$
66. $27^{1/3}$
67. $125^{2/3}$
68. $8^{2/3}$
69. $32^{-4/5}$
70. $16^{-5/2}$

*In Exercises 71–78, simplify using properties of exponents.*

71. $(7x^{1/3})(2x^{1/4})$
72. $(3x^{2/3})(4x^{3/4})$
73. $\frac{20x^{1/2}}{5x^{1/4}}$
74. $\frac{72x^{3/4}}{9x^{1/3}}$
75. $(x^{2/3})^3$
76. $(x^{4/5})^5$
77. $(25x^4y^6)^{1/2}$
78. $(125x^9y^6)^{1/3}$

*In Exercises 79–84, simplify by reducing the index of the radical.*

**79.** $\sqrt[4]{5^2}$

**80.** $\sqrt[4]{7^2}$

**81.** $\sqrt[3]{x^6}$

**82.** $\sqrt[4]{x^{12}}$

**83.** $\sqrt[6]{x^4}$

**84.** $\sqrt[9]{x^6}$

## Application Exercises

**85.** The algebraic expression $2\sqrt{5L}$ is used to estimate the speed of a car prior to an accident, in miles per hour, based on the length of its skid marks $L$, in feet. Find the speed of a car that left skid marks 40 feet long, and write the answer in simplified radical form.

**86.** The time, in seconds, that it takes an object to fall a distance $d$, in feet, is given by the algebraic expression $\sqrt{\frac{d}{16}}$. Find how long it will take a ball dropped from the top of a building 320 feet tall to hit the ground. Write the answer in simplified radical form.

**87.** The early Greeks believed that the most pleasing of all rectangles were golden rectangles whose ratio of width to height is

$$\frac{w}{h} = \frac{2}{\sqrt{5} - 1}.$$

Rationalize the denominator for this ratio and then use a calculator to approximate the answer correct to the nearest hundredth.

**88.** The amount of evaporation, in inches per day, of a large body of water can be described by the algebraic expression

$$\frac{w}{20\sqrt{a}}$$

where

$a$ = surface area of the water in square miles

$w$ = average wind speed of the air over the water, in miles per hour.

Determine the evaporation on a lake whose surface area is 9 square miles on a day when the wind speed over the water is 10 miles per hour.

**89.** In the Peanuts cartoon shown above, Woodstock appears to be working steps mentally. Fill in the missing steps that show how to go from $\frac{7\sqrt{2 \cdot 2 \cdot 3}}{6}$ to $\frac{7}{3}\sqrt{3}$.

PEANUTS reprinted by permission of United Feature Syndicate, Inc.

**90.** The algebraic expression $63.25x^{1/4}$ describes the average sale price, in thousands of dollars, of single-family homes in the U.S. Midwest $x$ years after 1981. Evaluate the algebraic expression when $x = 16$. Describe what the answer means in practical terms.

**91.** The algebraic expression $0.07d^{3/2}$ describes the duration of a storm, in hours, whose diameter is $d$ miles. Evaluate the algebraic expression when $d = 9$. Describe what the answer means in practical terms.

## Writing in Mathematics

**92.** Explain how to simplify $\sqrt{10} \cdot \sqrt{5}$.

**93.** Explain how to add $\sqrt{3} + \sqrt{12}$.

**94.** Describe what it means to rationalize a denominator. Use both $\frac{1}{\sqrt{5}}$ and $\frac{1}{5 + \sqrt{5}}$ in your explanation.

**95.** What difference is there in simplifying $\sqrt[3]{(-5)^3}$ and $\sqrt[4]{(-5)^4}$?

**96.** What does $a^{m/n}$ mean?

**97.** Describe the kinds of numbers that have rational fifth roots.

**98.** Why must $a$ and $b$ represent nonnegative numbers when we write $\sqrt{a} \cdot \sqrt{b} = \sqrt{ab}$? Is it necessary to use this restriction in the case of $\sqrt[3]{a} \cdot \sqrt[3]{b} = \sqrt[3]{ab}$? Explain.

## Technology Exercises

**99.** The algebraic expression $60.19x^{0.025}$ describes the expected lifespan of African American men $x$ years after 1969. Use a calculator to find the expected lifespan from 1970 through 2000. During what year did the expected lifespan of African American men first exceed 65 years?

**100.** The territorial area of an animal in the wild is defined to be the area of the region to which the animal confines its movements. The algebraic expression $W^{1.41}$ describes the territorial area, in square miles, of an animal that weighs $W$ pounds. Use a calculator to find the territorial area of animals weighing 25, 50, 150, 200, 250, and 300 pounds. What do the values that you obtain with your calculator indicate about the relationship between body weight and territorial area?

## Critical Thinking Exercises

**101.** Which one of the following is true?

**a.** Neither $(-8)^{1/2}$ nor $(-8)^{1/3}$ represent real numbers.

**b.** $\sqrt{x^2 + y^2} = x + y$

**c.** $8^{-1/3} = -2$  **d.** $2^{1/2} \cdot 2^{1/2} = 2$

*In Exercises 102–103, fill in each box to make the statement true.*

**102.** $(5 + \sqrt{\square})(5 - \sqrt{\square}) = 22$

**103.** $\sqrt{\square x^{\square}} = 5x^7$

**104.** Find exact value of $\sqrt{13 + \sqrt{2} + \frac{7}{3 + \sqrt{2}}}$ without the use of a calculator.

**105.** Place the correct symbol, > or <, in the box between each of the given numbers. *Do not use a calculator.* Then check your result with a calculator.

**a.** $3^{1/2} \square 3^{1/3}$  **b.** $\sqrt{7} + \sqrt{18} \square \sqrt{7 + 18}$

# SECTION P.4 Polynomials

## Objectives

1. Understand the vocabulary of polynomials.
2. Add and subtract polynomials.
3. Multiply polynomials.
4. Use FOIL in polynomial multiplication.
5. Use special products in polynomial multiplication.
6. Perform operations with polynomials in several variables.

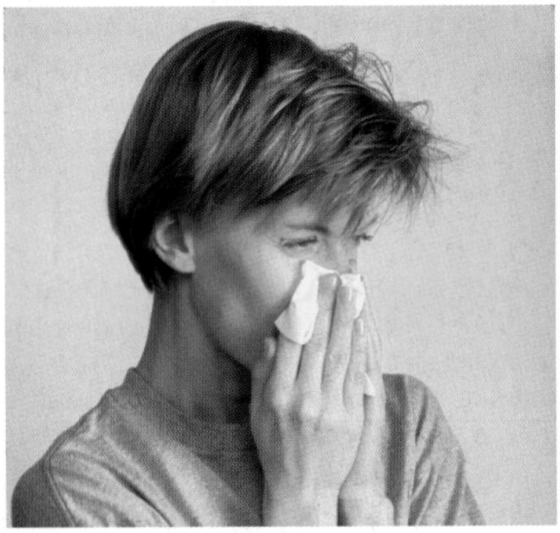

Runny nose? Sneezing? You are probably familiar with the unpleasant onset of a cold. We "catch cold" when the cold virus enters our bodies, where it multiplies. Fortunately, at a certain point the virus begins to die. The algebraic expression $-0.75x^4 + 3x^3 + 5$ describes the billions of viral particles in our bodies after $x$ days of invasion. The expression enables mathematicians to determine the day on which there is a maximum number of viral particles and, consequently, the day we feel sickest.

The algebraic expression $-0.75x^4 + 3x^3 + 5$ is an example of a polynomial. A **polynomial** is a single term or the sum of two or more terms containing variables with whole number exponents. This particular polynomial contains three terms. Equations containing polynomials are used in such diverse areas as science, business, medicine, psychology, and sociology. In this section, we review basic ideas about polynomials and their operations.

1 Understand the vocabulary of polynomials.

## The Vocabulary of Polynomials

Consider the polynomial

$$7x^3 - 9x^2 + 13x - 6.$$

We can express this polynomial as

$$7x^3 + (-9x^2) + 13x + (-6).$$

The polynomial contains four terms. It is customary to write the terms in the order of descending powers of the variables. This is the **standard form** of a polynomial.

We begin this section by limiting our discussion to polynomials containing only one variable. Each term of a polynomial in $x$ is of the form $ax^n$. The **degree** of $ax^n$ is $n$. For example, the degree of the term $7x^3$ is 3.

**Study Tip**

We can express 0 in many ways, including $0x$, $0x^2$, and $0x^3$. It is impossible to assign a single exponent on the variable. This is why 0 has no defined degree.

**The Degree of $ax^n$**

If $a \neq 0$, the degree of $ax^n$ is $n$. The degree of a nonzero constant is 0. The constant 0 has no defined degree.

Here is an example of a polynomial and the degree of each of its four terms.

$$6x^4 - 3x^3 + 2x - 5$$

degree 4 | degree 3 | degree 1 | degree of nonzero constant: 0

Notice that the exponent on $x$ for the term $2x$ is understood to be 1: $2x^1$. For this reason, the degree of $2x$ is 1. You can think of $-5$ as $-5x^0$; thus, its degree is 0.

A polynomial with exactly one term is called a **monomial**. A **binomial** is a polynomial that has two terms, each with a different exponent. A **trinomial** is a polynomial with three terms, each with a different exponent. Polynomials with four or more terms have no special names.

The **degree of a polynomial** is the highest degree of all the terms of the polynomial. For example, $4x^2 + 3x$ is a binomial of degree 2 because the degree of the first term is 2, and the degree of the other term is less than 2. Also, $7x^5 - 2x^2 + 4$ is a trinomial of degree 5 because the degree of the first term is 5, and the degrees of the other terms are less than 5.

Up to now, we have used $x$ to represent the variable in a polynomial. However, any letter can be used. For example,

$7x^5 - 3x^3 + 8$ is a polynomial (in $x$) of degree 5.

$6y^3 + 4y^2 - y + 3$ is a polynomial (in $y$) of degree 3.

$z^7 + \sqrt{2}$ is a polynomial (in $z$) of degree 7.

Not every algebraic expression is a polynomial. Algebraic expressions whose variables do not contain whole number exponents such as

$$3x^{-2} + 7 \quad \text{and} \quad 5x^{3/2} + 9x^{1/2} + 2$$

are not polynomials. Furthermore, a quotient of polynomials such as

$$\frac{x^2 + 2x + 5}{x^3 - 7x^2 + 9x - 3}$$

is not a polynomial because the form of a polynomial involves only addition and subtraction of terms, not division.

We can tie together the threads of our discussion with the formal definition of a polynomial in one variable. In this definition, the coefficients of the terms are represented by $a_n$ (read "$a$ sub $n$"), $a_{n-1}$ (read "$a$ sub $n$ minus 1"), $a_{n-2}$, and so on. The small letters to the lower right of each $a$ are called **subscripts** and are *not exponents*. Subscripts are used to distinguish one constant from another when a large and undetermined number of such constants are needed.

**Definition of a Polynomial in *x***

A **polynomial in *x*** is an algebraic expression of the form

$$a_n x^n + a_{n-1}x^{n-1} + a_{n-2}x^{n-2} + \cdots + a_1 x + a_0,$$

where $a_n, a_{n-1}, a_{n-2}, \ldots, a_1$ and $a_0$ are real numbers, $a_n \neq 0$, and $n$ is a nonnegative integer. The polynomial is of **degree *n***, $a_n$ is the **leading coefficient**, and $a_0$ is the **constant term**.

**2** Add and subtract polynomials.

## Adding and Subtracting Polynomials

Polynomials are added and subtracted by combining like terms. For example, we can combine the monomials $-9x^3$ and $13x^3$ using addition as follows:

$$-9x^3 + 13x^3 = (-9 + 13)x^3 = 4x^3.$$

### EXAMPLE 1 Adding and Subtracting Polynomials

Perform the indicated operations and simplify:

**a.** $(-9x^3 + 7x^2 - 5x + 3) + (13x^3 + 2x^2 - 8x - 6)$

**b.** $(7x^3 - 8x^2 + 9x - 6) - (2x^3 - 6x^2 - 3x + 9)$

**Solution**

**a.** $(-9x^3 + 7x^2 - 5x + 3) + (13x^3 + 2x^2 - 8x - 6)$

$= (-9x^3 + 13x^3) + (7x^2 + 2x^2) + (-5x - 8x) + (3 - 6)$ Group like terms.

$= 4x^3 + 9x^2 + (-13x) + (-3)$ Combine like terms.

$= 4x^3 + 9x^2 - 13x - 3$

**b.** $(7x^3 - 8x^2 + 9x - 6) - (2x^3 - 6x^2 - 3x + 9)$

$= (7x^3 - 8x^2 + 9x - 6) + (-2x^3 + 6x^2 + 3x - 9)$ Rewrite subtraction as addition of the additive inverse. Be sure to change the sign of each term inside parentheses preceded by the negative sign.

$= (7x^3 - 2x^3) + (-8x^2 + 6x^2) + (9x + 3x) + (-6 - 9)$ Group like terms.

$= 5x^3 + (-2x^2) + 12x + (-15)$ Combine like terms.

$= 5x^3 - 2x^2 + 12x - 15$

**Study Tip**

You can also arrange like terms in columns and combine vertically:

$$\begin{array}{r} 7x^3 - 8x^2 + \ 9x - 6 \\ -2x^3 + 6x^2 + \ 3x - 9 \\ \hline 5x^3 - 2x^2 + 12x - 15 \end{array}$$

The like terms can be combined by adding their coefficients.

**Check Point 1**

Perform the indicated operations and simplify:

**a.** $(-17x^3 + 4x^2 - 11x - 5) + (16x^3 - 3x^2 + 3x - 15)$

**b.** $(13x^3 - 9x^2 - 7x + 1) - (-7x^3 + 2x^2 - 5x + 9)$

**3** Multiply polynomials.

## Multiplying Polynomials

The product of two monomials is obtained by using properties of exponents. For example,

$$(-8x^6)(5x^3) = -8 \cdot 5x^{6+3} = -40x^9$$

Multiply coefficients and add exponents.

Furthermore, we can use the distributive property to multiply a monomial and a polynomial that is not a monomial. For example,

$$3x^4(2x^3 - 7x + 3) = 3x^4 \cdot 2x^3 - 3x^4 \cdot 7x + 3x^4 \cdot 3 = 6x^7 - 21x^5 + 9x^4.$$

monomial — trinomial

How do we multiply two polynomials if neither is a monomial? For example, consider

$$(2x + 3)(x^2 + 4x + 5).$$

binomial — trinomial

One way to perform this multiplication is to distribute $2x$ throughout the trinomial

$$2x(x^2 + 4x + 5)$$

and 3 throughout the trinomial

$$3(x^2 + 4x + 5).$$

Then combine the like terms that result. In general, the product of two polynomials is the polynomial obtained by multiplying each term of one polynomial by each term of the other polynomial and then combining like terms.

### EXAMPLE 2 Multiplying a Binomial and a Trinomial

Multiply: $(2x + 3)(x^2 + 4x + 5)$.

**Solution**

$(2x + 3)(x^2 + 4x + 5)$

$= 2x(x^2 + 4x + 5) + 3(x^2 + 4x + 5)$ — Use the distributive property to multiply the trinomial by each term of the binomial.

$= 2x \cdot x^2 + 2x \cdot 4x + 2x \cdot 5 + 3x^2 + 3 \cdot 4x + 3 \cdot 5$ — Use the distributive property.

$= 2x^3 + 8x^2 + 10x + 3x^2 + 12x + 15$ — Multiply the monomials.

$= 2x^3 + 11x^2 + 22x + 15$ — Combine like terms.

Another method for solving Example 2 is to use a vertical format similar to that used for multiplying whole numbers.

$$\begin{array}{rrrrl} & x^2 + & 4x + & 5 & \\ & & 2x + & 3 & \\ \hline & 3x^2 + & 12x + & 15 & \leftarrow 3(x^2+4x+5) \\ 2x^3 + & 8x^2 + & 10x & & \leftarrow 2x(x^2+4x+5) \\ \hline 2x^3 + & 11x^2 + & 22x + & 15 & \text{Combine like terms.} \end{array}$$

Write like terms in the same column.

**Check Point 2** Multiply: $(5x - 2)(3x^2 - 5x + 4)$.

**4** Use FOIL in polynomial multiplication.

## The Product of Two Binomials: FOIL

Frequently we need to find the product of two binomials. We can use a method called FOIL, which is based on the distributive property, to do so. For example, we can find the product of the binomials $3x + 2$ and $4x + 5$ as follows:

$$(3x + 2)(4x + 5) = 3x(4x + 5) + 2(4x + 5)$$ First, distribute $3x$ over $4x + 5$. Then distribute 2.

$$= 3x(4x) + 3x(5) + 2(4x) + 2(5)$$

$$= 12x^2 + 15x + 8x + 10.$$

Two binomials can be quickly multiplied by using the FOIL method, in which $F$ represents the product of the **first** terms in each binomial, $O$ represents the product of the **outside** terms, $I$ represents the product of the two **inside** terms, and $L$ represents the product of the **last**, or second, terms in each binomial.

first, last, inside, outside

$$(3x + 2)(4x + 5) = \underset{F}{12x^2} + \underset{O}{15x} + \underset{I}{8x} + \underset{L}{10}$$

$$= 12x^2 + 23x + 10$$ Combine like terms.

In general, here's how to use the FOIL method to find the product of $ax + b$ and $cx + d$:

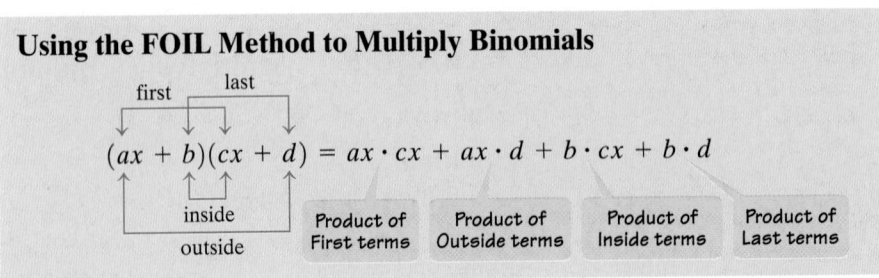

### Using the FOIL Method to Multiply Binomials

first, last, inside, outside

$$(ax + b)(cx + d) = ax \cdot cx + ax \cdot d + b \cdot cx + b \cdot d$$

Product of First terms; Product of Outside terms; Product of Inside terms; Product of Last terms

### EXAMPLE 3 Using the FOIL Method

Multiply: $(3x + 4)(5x - 3)$.

**Solution**

first, last, inside, outside — F O I L

$$(3x + 4)(5x - 3) = 3x \cdot 5x + 3x(-3) + 4 \cdot 5x + 4(-3)$$
$$= 15x^2 - 9x + 20x - 12$$
$$= 15x^2 + 11x - 12 \quad \text{Combine like terms.}$$

**Check Point 3** Multiply: $(7x - 5)(4x - 3)$.

**5** Use special products in polynomial multiplication.

## Special Products

There are several products that occur so frequently that it's convenient to memorize the form or pattern of these formulas.

**Special Products**

Let $A$ and $B$ represent real numbers, variables, or algebraic expressions.

| **Special Product** | **Example** |
|---|---|
| *Sum and Difference of Two Terms* | |
| $(A + B)(A - B) = A^2 - B^2$ | $(2x + 3)(2x - 3) = (2x)^2 - 3^2 = 4x^2 - 9$ |
| *Squaring a Binomial* | |
| $(A + B)^2 = A^2 + 2AB + B^2$ | $(y + 5)^2 = y^2 + 2 \cdot y \cdot 5 + 5^2 = y^2 + 10y + 25$ |
| $(A - B)^2 = A^2 - 2AB + B^2$ | $(3x - 4)^2 = (3x)^2 - 2 \cdot 3x \cdot 4 + 4^2 = 9x^2 - 24x + 16$ |
| *Cubing a Binomial* | |
| $(A + B)^3 = A^3 + 3A^2B + 3AB^2 + B^3$ | $(x + 4)^3 = x^3 + 3x^2(4) + 3x(4)^2 + 4^3 = x^3 + 12x^2 + 48x + 64$ |
| $(A - B)^3 = A^3 - 3A^2B + 3AB^2 - B^3$ | $(x - 2)^3 = x^3 - 3x^2(2) + 3x(2)^2 - 2^3 = x^3 - 6x^2 + 12x - 8$ |

**Study Tip**

Although it's convenient to memorize these forms, the FOIL method can be used on all five examples in the box. To cube $x + 4$, you can first square $x + 4$ using FOIL and then multiply this result by $x + 4$. In short, you do not necessarily have to utilize these special formulas. What is the advantage of knowing and using these forms?

**6** Perform operations with polynomials in several variables.

## Polynomials in Several Variables

The next time you visit the lumber yard and go rummaging through piles of wood, think *polynomials*, although polynomials a bit different from those we have encountered so far. The construction industry uses a polynomial in two variables to determine the number of board feet that can be manufactured from a tree with a diameter of $x$ inches and a length of $y$ feet. This polynomial is

$$\frac{1}{4}x^2y - 2xy + 4y.$$

### Visualizing a Special Products Formula

The formula

$$(A+B)^2 = A^2 + 2AB + B^2$$

can be interpreted geometrically.

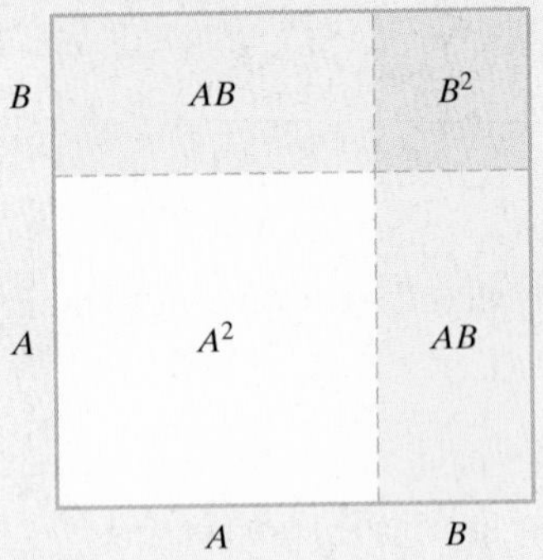


The area of the large rectangle is

$$(B+A)(A+B) = (A+B)^2.$$

The sum of the areas of the four smaller rectangles is

$$AB + B^2 + A^2 + AB$$
$$= A^2 + 2AB + B^2.$$

The area of the large rectangle equals the sum of the areas of the four smaller rectangles:

$$(A+B)^2 = A^2 + 2AB + B^2.$$

In general, a **polynomial in two variables**, $x$ and $y$, contains the sum of one or more monomials in the form $ax^ny^m$. The constant $a$ is the **coefficient**. The exponents $n$ and $m$ represent whole numbers. The **degree** of the monomial $ax^ny^m$ is $n + m$. We'll use the polynomial from the construction industry to illustrate these ideas.

The coefficients are $\frac{1}{4}$, −2, and 4.

$$\tfrac{1}{4}x^2y \quad -2xy \quad +4y$$

| Degree of monomial: $2 + 1 = 3$ | Degree of monomial: $1 + 1 = 2$ | Degree of monomial: $0 + 1 = 1$ |
|---|---|---|

The degree of a polynomial in two variables is the highest degree of all its terms. For the preceding polynomial, the degree is 3.

Polynomials containing two or more variables can be added, subtracted, and multiplied just like polynomials that contain only one variable.

## EXAMPLE 4 Multiplying Polynomials in Two Variables

Multiply: **a.** $(x + 4y)(3x - 5y)$ **b.** $(5x + 3y)^2$

**Solution** We will perform the multiplication in part (a) using the FOIL method. We will multiply in part (b) using the formula for the square of a binomial, $(A + B)^2$.

**a.** $(x + 4y)(3x - 5y)$ Multiply these binomials using the FOIL method.

F O I L

$$= (x)(3x) + (x)(-5y) + (4y)(3x) + (4y)(-5y)$$
$$= 3x^2 - 5xy + 12xy - 20y^2$$
$$= 3x^2 + 7xy - 20y^2 \quad \text{Combine like terms.}$$

$$(A + B)^2 = A^2 + 2 \cdot A \cdot B + B^2$$

**b.** $(5x + 3y)^2 = (5x)^2 + 2(5x)(3y) + (3y)^2$
$$= 25x^2 + 30xy + 9y^2$$

**Check Point 4** Multiply:

**a.** $(7x - 6y)(3x - y)$ **b.** $(x^2 + 5y)^2$

Special products can sometimes be used to find the products of certain trinomials, as illustrated in Example 5.

## EXAMPLE 5 Using the Special Products

Multiply: **a.** $(7x + 5 + 4y)(7x + 5 - 4y)$ **b.** $(3x + y + 1)^2$.

**Solution**

**a.** By grouping the first two terms within each of the parentheses, we can find the product using the form for the sum and difference of two terms:

$$(A + B) \cdot (A - B) = A^2 - B^2$$

$$[(7x + 5) + 4y] \cdot [(7x + 5) - 4y] = (7x + 5)^2 - (4y)^2$$
$$= (7x)^2 + 2 \cdot 7x \cdot 5 + 5^2 - (4y)^2$$
$$= 49x^2 + 70x + 25 - 16y^2$$

**b.** We can group the terms so that the formula for the square of a binomial can be applied:

$$(A + B)^2 = A^2 + 2 \cdot A \cdot B + B^2$$

$$[(3x + y) + 1]^2 = [(3x + y)^2 + 2 \cdot (3x + y) \cdot 1 + 1^2$$
$$= 9x^2 + 6xy + y^2 + 6x + 2y + 1$$

**Check Point 5** Multiply:

**a.** $(3x + 2 + 5y)(3x + 2 - 5y)$ **b.** $(2x + y + 3)^2$

## EXERCISE SET P.4

### Practice Exercises

*In Exercises 1–4, is the algebraic expression a polynomial? If it is, write the polynomial in standard form.*

**1.** $2x + 3x^2 - 5$
**2.** $2x + 3x^{-1} - 5$
**3.** $\dfrac{2x + 3}{x}$
**4.** $x^2 - x^3 + x^4 - 5$

*In Exercises 5–8, find the degree of the polynomial.*

**5.** $3x^2 - 5x + 4$
**6.** $-4x^3 + 7x^2 - 11$
**7.** $x^2 - 4x^3 + 9x - 12x^4 + 63$
**8.** $x^2 - 8x^3 + 15x^4 + 91$

*In Exercises 9–14, perform the indicated operations. Write the resulting polynomial in standard form and indicate its degree.*

**9.** $(-6x^3 + 5x^2 - 8x + 9) + (17x^3 + 2x^2 - 4x - 13)$
**10.** $(-7x^3 + 6x^2 - 11x + 13) + (19x^3 - 11x^2 + 7x - 17)$
**11.** $(17x^3 - 5x^2 + 4x - 3) - (5x^3 - 9x^2 - 8x + 11)$
**12.** $(18x^4 - 2x^3 - 7x + 8) - (9x^4 - 6x^3 - 5x + 7)$
**13.** $(5x^2 - 7x - 8) + (2x^2 - 3x + 7) - (x^2 - 4x - 3)$
**14.** $(8x^2 + 7x - 5) - (3x^2 - 4x) - (-6x^3 - 5x^2 + 3)$

*In Exercises 15–54, find each product.*

**15.** $(x + 1)(x^2 - x + 1)$
**16.** $(x + 5)(x^2 - 5x + 25)$
**17.** $(2x - 3)(x^2 - 3x + 5)$
**18.** $(2x - 1)(x^2 - 4x + 3)$
**19.** $(x + 7)(x + 3)$
**20.** $(x + 8)(x + 5)$
**21.** $(x - 5)(x + 3)$
**22.** $(x - 1)(x + 2)$
**23.** $(3x + 5)(2x + 1)$
**24.** $(7x + 4)(3x + 1)$
**25.** $(2x - 3)(5x + 3)$
**26.** $(2x - 5)(7x + 2)$
**27.** $(5x^2 - 4)(3x^2 - 7)$
**28.** $(7x^2 - 2)(3x^2 - 5)$
**29.** $(x + 3)(x - 3)$
**30.** $(x + 5)(x - 5)$
**31.** $(3x + 2)(3x - 2)$
**32.** $(2x + 5)(2x - 5)$
**33.** $(5 - 7x)(5 + 7x)$
**34.** $(4 - 3x)(4 + 3x)$
**35.** $(4x^2 + 5x)(4x^2 - 5x)$
**36.** $(3x^2 + 4x)(3x^2 - 4x)$
**37.** $(x + 2)^2$
**38.** $(x + 5)^2$
**39.** $(2x + 3)^2$
**40.** $(3x + 2)^2$
**41.** $(x - 3)^2$
**42.** $(x - 4)^2$
**43.** $(4x^2 - 1)^2$
**44.** $(5x^2 - 3)^2$
**45.** $(7 - 2x)^2$
**46.** $(9 - 5x)^2$
**47.** $(x + 1)^3$
**48.** $(x + 2)^3$
**49.** $(2x + 3)^3$
**50.** $(3x + 4)^3$
**51.** $(x - 3)^3$
**52.** $(x - 1)^3$
**53.** $(3x - 4)^3$
**54.** $(2x - 3)^3$

*In Exercises 55–78, find each product.*

**55.** $(x + 5y)(7x + 3y)$

**56.** $(x + 9y)(6x + 7y)$

**57.** $(x - 3y)(2x + 7y)$

**58.** $(3x - y)(2x + 5y)$

**59.** $(3xy - 1)(5xy + 2)$

**60.** $(7x^2y + 1)(2x^2y - 3)$

**61.** $(7x + 5y)^2$

**62.** $(9x + 7y)^2$

**63.** $(x^2y^2 - 3)^2$

**64.** $(x^2y^2 - 5)^2$

**65.** $(x - y)(x^2 + xy + y^2)$

**66.** $(x + y)(x^2 - xy + y^2)$

**67.** $(3x + 5y)(3x - 5y)$

**68.** $(7x + 3y)(7x - 3y)$

**69.** $(x + y + 3)(x + y - 3)$

**70.** $(x + y + 5)(x + y - 5)$

**71.** $(3x + 7 - 5y)(3x + 7 + 5y)$

**72.** $(5x + 7y - 2)(5x + 7y + 2)$

**73.** $[5y - (2x + 3)][5y + (2x + 3)]$

**74.** $[8y + (7 - 3x)][8y - (7 - 3x)]$

**75.** $(x + y + 1)^2$

**76.** $(x + y + 2)^2$

**77.** $(2x + y + 1)^2$

**78.** $(5x + 1 + 6y)^2$

*In Exercises 79–82, a geometric interpretation of a special products formula is illustrated. Select the formula for each illustration from the following options:*

$$(A + B)^2 = A^2 + 2AB + B^2,$$
$$(A + B)(A - B) = A^2 - B^2,$$
$$(A + 1)(B + 1) = AB + A + B + 1,$$
$$(A + 1)^2 = A^2 + 2A + 1$$

**79.**

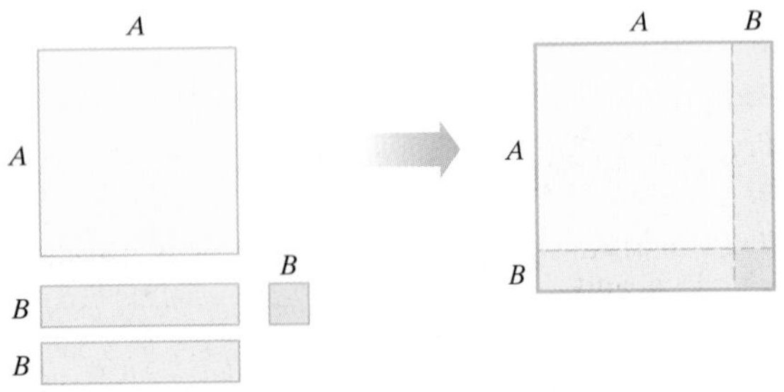

**80.**

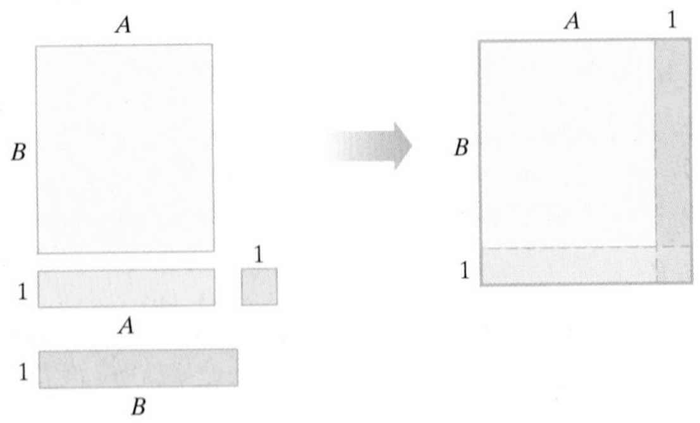

**81.**

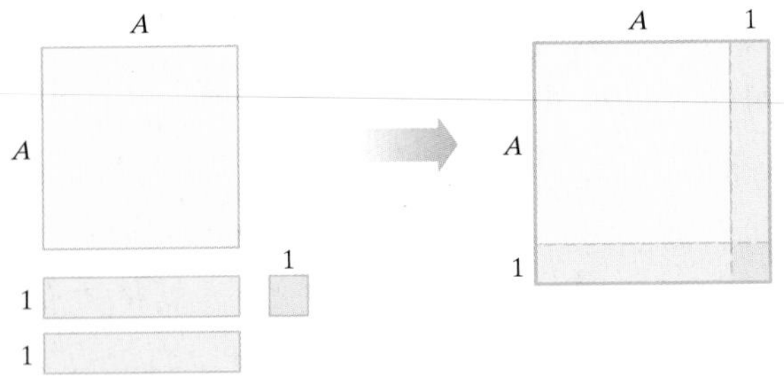

**82.**

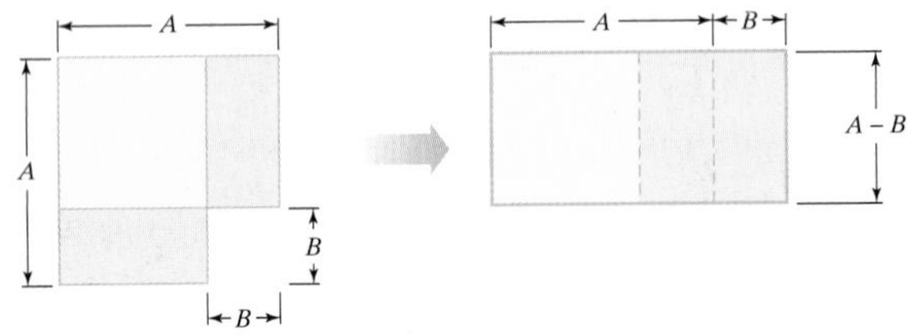

## Application Exercises

**83.** The polynomial $0.018x^2 - 0.757x + 9.047$ describes the amount, in thousands of dollars, that a person earning $x$ thousand dollars a year feels underpaid. Evaluate the polynomial when $x = 40$. Describe what the answer means in practical terms.

**84.** The polynomial $104.5x^2 - 1501.5x + 6016$ describes the death rate per year per 100,000 men for men averaging $x$ hours of sleep each night. Evaluate the polynomial when $x = 10$. Describe what the answer means in practical terms.

**85.** The polynomial $-0.02A^2 + 2A + 22$ is used by coaches to get athletes fired up so that they can perform well. The polynomial represents the performance level related to various levels of enthusiasm, from $A = 1$ (almost no enthusiasm) to $A = 100$ (maximum level of enthusiasm). Evaluate the polynomial when $A = 20$, $A = 50$, and $A = 80$. Describe what happens to performance as we get more and more fired up.

**86.** The polynomial

$$0.0001x^3 - 0.0043x^2 + 0.089x + 2.66$$

describes the number of pounds of waste produced each day by every American $x$ years after 1960. (The bar graph at the top of page 43 illustrates daily waste production for eight years.) Evaluate the polynomial when $x = 10$. Describe what the answer means in practical terms.

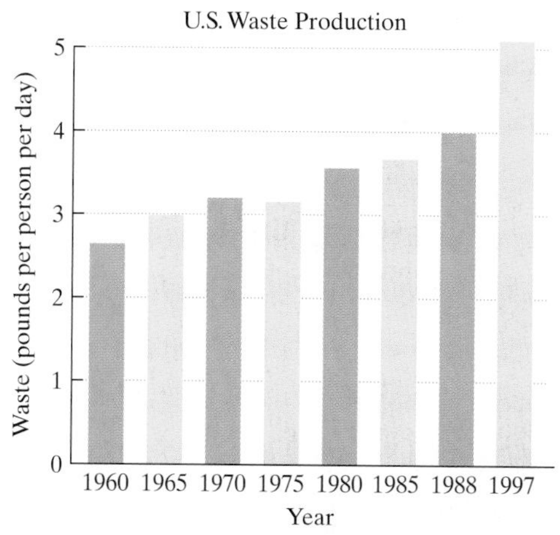


Source: U.S. Environmental Protection Agency.

**87.** The number of people who catch a cold $t$ weeks after January 1 is $5t - 3t^2 + t^3$. The number of people who recover $t$ weeks after January 1 is $t - t^2 + \frac{1}{3}t^3$. Write a polynomial in standard form for the number of people who are still ill with a cold $t$ weeks after January 1.

**88.** A rock on Earth and a rock on the moon are thrown into the air with a velocity of 48 feet per second by a 6-foot person. The height, $h$, in feet, reached by the rock after $t$ seconds is given by

$$h_{\text{Earth}} = -16t^2 + 48t + 6$$

$$h_{\text{Moon}} = -2.7t^2 + 48t + 6.$$

Write a polynomial in standard form expressing the difference between moon height and Earth height after $t$ seconds.

*In Exercises 89–90, write a polynomial in standard form that represents the area of the shaded region of each figure.*

**89.**

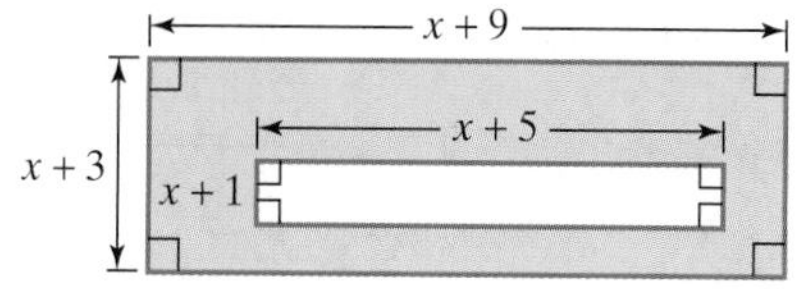


**90.**

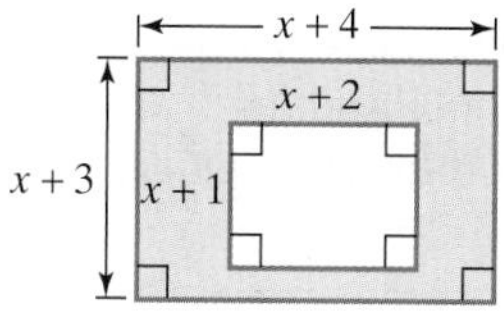


*In Exercises 91–92, write a polynomial in standard form that represents the volume of the open box in the figure shown.*

**91.**

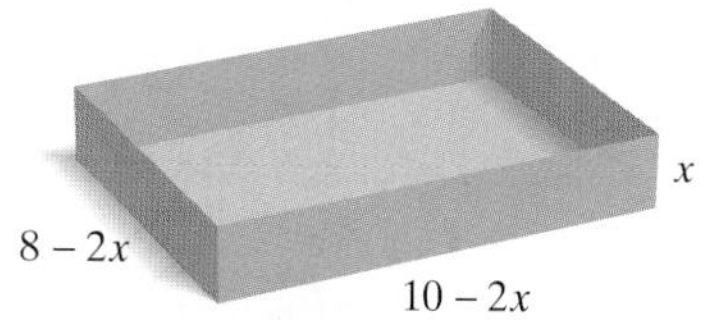


**92.**

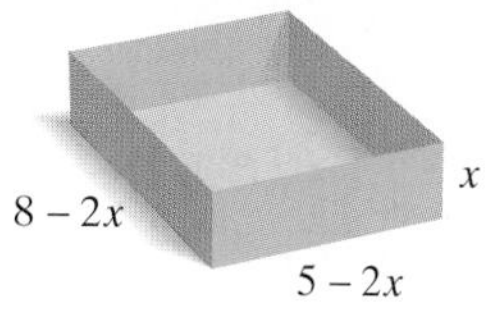


## Writing in Mathematics

**93.** What is a polynomial in $x$?

**94.** Explain how to subtract polynomials.

**95.** Explain how to multiply two binomials using the FOIL method. Give an example with your explanation.

**96.** Explain how to find the product of the sum and difference of two terms. Give an example with your explanation.

**97.** Explain how to square a binomial difference. Give an example with your explanation.

**98.** Explain how to find the degree of a polynomial in two variables.

**99.** For Exercise 85, explain why performance levels do what they do as we get more and more fired up. If possible, describe an example of a time when you were too enthused and thus did poorly at something you were hoping to do well.

## Technology Exercises

**100.** The common cold is caused by a rhinovirus. The polynomial

$$-0.75x^4 + 3x^3 + 5$$

describes the billions of viral particles in our bodies after $x$ days of invasion. Use a calculator to find the number of viral particles after 0 days (the time of the cold's onset), 1 day, 2 days, 3 days, and 4 days. After how many days is the number of viral particles at a maximum and consequently the day we feel the sickest? By when should we feel completely better?

**101.** The polynomial $-3.08x^2 + 40.35x + 305.89$ describes the annual number of aggravated assaults in the United States per 100,000 people $x$ years after 1986. Use a calculator to find the number of aggravated assaults per 100,000 people from 1986 to 2000. For this time period, during what year was the number of aggravated assaults per 100,000 people the greatest?

## Critical Thinking Exercises

**102.** Express the area of the plane figure shown as a polynomial in standard form.

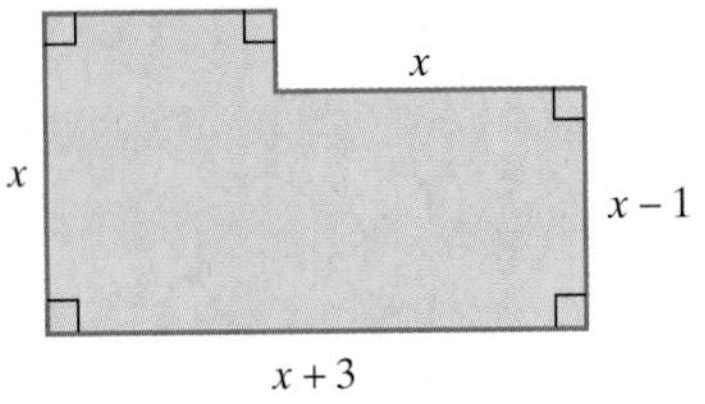


*In Exercises 103–104, represent the volume of each figure as a polynomial in standard form.*

**103.**

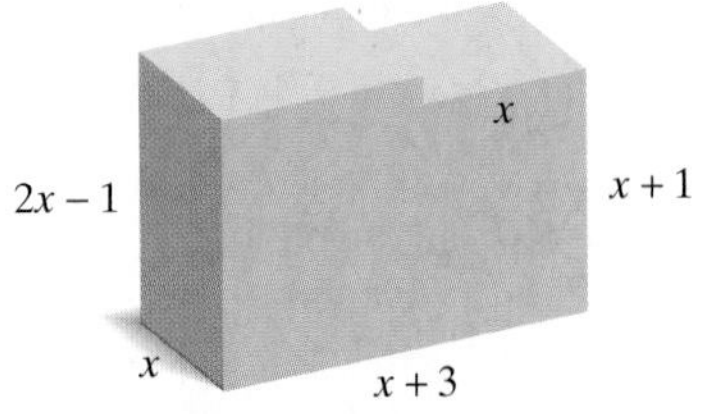


**104.**

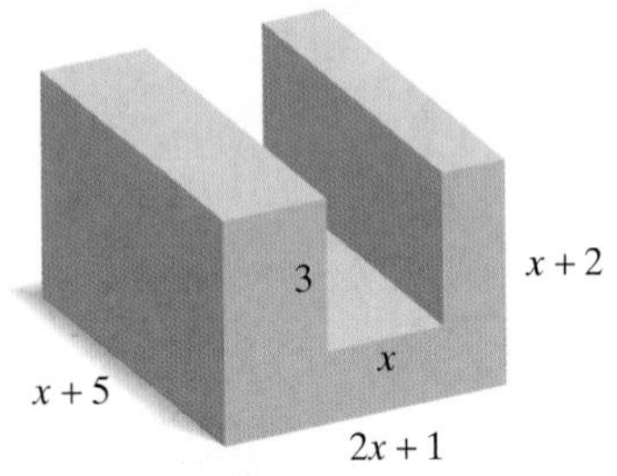


**105.** Simplify: $(y^n + 2)(y^n - 2) - (y^n - 3)^2$.

## SECTION P.5 *Factoring Polynomials*

### Objectives

1. Factor out the greatest common factor of a polynomial.
2. Factor by grouping.
3. Factor trinomials.
4. Factor the difference of squares.
5. Factor perfect square trinomials.
6. Factor the sum and difference of cubes.
7. Factor completely.
8. Factor algebraic expressions containing fractional and negative exponents.

A two-year-old boy is asked, "Do you have a brother?" He answers, "Yes." "What is your brother's name?" "Tom." Asked if Tom has a brother, the two-year-old replies, "No." The child can go in the direction from self to brother, but he cannot reverse this direction and move from brother back to self.

As our intellects develop, we learn to reverse the direction of our thinking. Reversibility of thought is found throughout algebra. For example, we can multiply polynomials and show that

$$(2x + 1)(3x - 2) = 6x^2 - x - 2.$$

We can also reverse this process and express the resulting polynomial as

$$6x^2 - x - 2 = (2x + 1)(3x - 2).$$

**Factoring** is the process of writing a polynomial as the product of two or more polynomials. The factors of $6x^2 - x - 2$ are $2x + 1$ and $3x - 2$.

In this section, we will be **factoring over the set of integers**, meaning that the coefficients in the factors are integers. Polynomials that cannot be factored using integer coefficients are called **irreducible over the integers**, or **prime**.

The goal in factoring a polynomial is to use one or more factoring techniques until each of the polynomial's factors is prime or irreducible. In this situation, the polynomial is said to be **factored completely**.

We will now discuss basic techniques for factoring polynomials.

**1** Factor out the greatest common factor of a polynomial.

## Common Factors

In any factoring problem, the first step is to look for the **greatest common factor**. The greatest common factor is an expression of the highest degree that divides each term of the polynomial. The distributive property in the reverse direction

$$ab + ac = a(b + c)$$

can be used to factor out the greatest common factor.

### EXAMPLE 1 Factoring out the Greatest Common Factor

Factor: **a.** $18x^3 + 27x^2$ **b.** $x^2(x + 3) + 5(x + 3)$

**Solution**

**a.** We begin by determining the greatest common factor. 9 is the greatest integer that divides 18 and 27. Furthermore, $x^2$ is the greatest expression that divides $x^3$ and $x^2$. Thus, the greatest common factor of the two terms in the polynomial is $9x^2$.

$18x^3 + 27x^2$

$= 9x^2(2x) + 9x^2(3)$ Express each term with the greatest common factor as a factor.

$= 9x^2(2x + 3)$ Factor out the greatest common factor.

**b.** In this situation, the greatest common factor is the common binomial factor $(x + 3)$. We factor out this common factor as follows.

$x^2(x + 3) + 5(x + 3) = (x + 3)(x^2 + 5)$ Factor out the common binomial factor.

**Check Point 1** Factor:

**a.** $10x^3 - 4x^2$ **b.** $2x(x - 7) + 3(x - 7)$

**2** Factor by grouping.

## Factoring by Grouping

Some polynomials have only a greatest common factor of 1. However, by a suitable rearrangement of the terms, it still may be possible to factor. This process, called **factoring by grouping**, is illustrated in Example 2.

### EXAMPLE 2 Factoring by Grouping

Factor: $x^3 + 4x^2 + 3x + 12$.

**Solution** Group terms that have a common factor:

$$\boxed{x^3 + 4x^2} + \boxed{3x + 12}.$$

Common factor is $x^2$.

Common factor is 3.

**Discovery**

In Example 2, group the terms as follows:

$$(x^3 + 3x) + (4x^2 + 12).$$

Factor out the greatest common factor from each group and complete the factoring process. Describe what happens. What can you conclude?

We now factor the given polynomial as follows.

$$x^3 + 4x^2 + 3x + 12$$

$$= (x^3 + 4x^2) + (3x + 12)$$ Group terms with common factors.

$$= x^2(x + 4) + 3(x + 4)$$ Factor out the greatest common factor from the grouped terms. The remaining two terms have $x + 4$ as a common binomial factor.

$$= (x + 4)(x^2 + 3)$$ Factor $(x + 4)$ out of both terms.

Thus, $x^3 + 4x^2 + 3x + 12 = (x + 4)(x^2 + 3)$. Check the factorization by multiplying the right side of the equation using the FOIL method. If the factorization is correct, you will obtain the original polynomial.

**Check Point 2** Factor: $x^3 + 5x^2 - 2x - 10.$

**3** Factor trinomials.

## Factoring Trinomials

To factor a trinomial of the form $ax^2 + bx + c$, a little trial and error may be necessary.

**A Strategy for Factoring $ax^2 + bx + c$**

(Assume, for the moment, that there is no greatest common factor.)

1. Find two **F**irst terms whose product is $ax^2$:

$$(\square x + \quad)(\square x + \quad) = ax^2 + bx + c$$

2. Find two **L**ast terms whose product is $c$:

$$(x + \square)(x + \square) = ax^2 + bx + c$$

3. By trial and error, perform steps 1 and 2 until the sum of the **O**utside product and **I**nside product is $bx$:

$$(\square x + \square)(\square x + \square) = ax^2 + bx + c$$

I

O

(sum of O + I)

If no such combinations exist, the polynomial is prime.

## EXAMPLE 3 Factoring Trinomials Whose Leading Coefficients Are 1

Factor: **a.** $x^2 + 6x + 8$ **b.** $x^2 + 3x - 18$

**Solution**

**a.** The factors of the first term are $x$ and $x$:

$$(x \quad)(x \quad)$$

To find the second term of each factor, we must find two numbers whose product is 8 and whose sum is 6.

| | | | | |
|---|---|---|---|---|
| **Factors of 8** | 8, 1 | 4, 2 | −8, −1 | −4, −2 |
| **Sum of Factors** | 9 | 6 | −9 | −6 |

This is the desired sum.

From the table in the margin, we see that 4 and 2 are the required integers. Thus,

$$x^2 + 6x + 8 = (x + 4)(x + 2) \quad \text{or} \quad (x + 2)(x + 4).$$

**b.** We begin with

$$x^2 + 3x - 18 = (x \qquad)(x \qquad).$$

| Factors of −18 | 18, −1 | −18, 1 | 9, −2 | −9, 2 | 6, −3 | −6, 3 |
|---|---|---|---|---|---|---|
| Sum of factors | 17 | −17 | 7 | −7 | 3 | −3 |

This is the desired sum.

To find the second term of each factor, we must find two numbers whose product is −18 and whose sum is 3. From the table in the margin, we see that 6 and −3 are the required integers. Thus,

$$x^2 + 3x - 18 = (x + 6)(x - 3)$$
$$\text{or} \quad (x - 3)(x + 6).$$

**Check Point 3** Factor:

**a.** $x^2 + 13x + 40$ **b.** $x^2 - 5x - 14$

## EXAMPLE 4 Factoring a Trinomial Whose Leading Coefficient Is Not 1

Factor: $8x^2 - 10x - 3$.

**Solution**

**Step 1 Find two First terms whose product is $8x^2$.**

$$8x^2 - 10x - 3 \stackrel{?}{=} (8x \qquad)(x \qquad)$$
$$8x^2 - 10x - 3 \stackrel{?}{=} (4x \qquad)(2x \qquad)$$

**Step 2 Find two Last terms whose product is −3.** The possible factors are $1(-3)$ and $-1(3)$.

**Step 3 Try various combinations of these factors.** The correct factorization of $8x^2 - 10x - 3$ is the one in which the sum of the *O*utside and *I*nside products is equal to $-10x$. Here is a list of the possible factors.

| Possible Factors of $8x^2 - 10x - 3$ | Sum of Outside and Inside Products (Should Equal $-10x$) |
|---|---|
| $(8x + 1)(x - 3)$ | $-24x + x = -23x$ |
| $(8x - 3)(x + 1)$ | $8x - 3x = 5x$ |
| $(8x - 1)(x + 3)$ | $24x - x = 23x$ |
| $(8x + 3)(x - 1)$ | $-8x + 3x = -5x$ |
| $(4x + 1)(2x - 3)$ | $-12x + 2x = -10x$ |
| $(4x - 3)(2x + 1)$ | $4x - 6x = -2x$ |
| $(4x - 1)(2x + 3)$ | $12x - 2x = 10x$ |
| $(4x + 3)(2x - 1)$ | $-4x + 6x = 2x$ |

This is the required middle term.

Thus,

$$8x^2 - 10x - 3 = (4x + 1)(2x - 3) \quad \text{or} \quad (2x - 3)(4x + 1).$$

Show that this factorization is correct by multiplying the factors using the FOIL method. You should obtain the original trinomial.

**Check Point 4** Factor: $6x^2 + 19x - 7$.

**4** Factor the difference of squares.

## Factoring the Difference of Two Squares

A method for factoring the difference of two squares is obtained by reversing the special product for the sum and difference of two terms.

> **The Difference of Two Squares**
>
> If $A$ and $B$ are real numbers, variables, or algebraic expressions, then
>
> $$A^2 - B^2 = (A + B)(A - B).$$
>
> In words: The difference of the squares of two terms factors as the product of a sum and the difference of those terms.

### EXAMPLE 5 Factoring the Difference of Two Squares

Factor: **a.** $x^2 - 4$ **b.** $81x^2 - 49$

**Solution** We must express each term as the square of some monomial. Then we use the formula for factoring $A^2 - B^2$.

**a.** $x^2 - 4^2 = x^2 - 2^2 = (x + 2)(x - 2)$

$A^2 - B^2 = (A + B)(A - B)$

**b.** $81x^2 - 49 = (9x)^2 - 7^2 = (9x + 7)(9x - 7)$

**Check Point 5** Factor:

**a.** $x^2 - 81$ **b.** $36x^2 - 25$

We have seen that a polynomial is factored completely when it is written as the product of prime polynomials. To be sure that you have factored completely, check to see whether the factors can be factored.

### EXAMPLE 6 A Repeated Factorization

Factor completely: $x^4 - 81$.

**Solution**

$x^4 - 81 = (x^2)^2 - 9^2$ Express as the difference of two squares.

$= (x^2 + 9)(x^2 - 9)$ The factors are the sum and difference of the squared terms.

$= (x^2 + 9)(x^2 - 3^2)$ The factor $x^2 - 9$ is the difference of two squares and can be factored.

$= (x^2 + 9)(x + 3)(x - 3)$ The factors of $x^2 - 9$ are the sum and difference of the squared terms.

> **Study Tip**
>
> Factoring $x^4 - 81$ as
>
> $$(x^2 + 9)(x^2 - 9)$$
>
> is not a complete factorization. The second factor $x^2 - 9$ is itself a difference of two squares and can be factored.

**Check Point 6** Factor completely: $81x^4 - 16$.

**5** Factor perfect square trinomials.

## Factoring Perfect Square Trinomials

Our next factoring technique is obtained by reversing the special products for squaring binomials. The trinomials that are factored using this technique are called **perfect square trinomials**.

### Factoring Perfect Square Trinomials

Let $A$ and $B$ be real numbers, variables, or algebraic expressions.

1. $A^2 + 2AB + B^2 = (A + B)^2$

   Same sign

2. $A^2 - 2AB + B^2 = (A - B)^2$

   Same sign

The two items in the box show that perfect square trinomials come in two forms: one in which the middle term is positive and one in which the middle term is negative. Here's how to recognize a perfect square trinomial:

1. The first and last terms are positive perfect squares.
2. The middle term is twice the product of the square roots of the first and last terms.

### EXAMPLE 7 Factoring Perfect Square Trinomials

Factor: **a.** $x^2 + 6x + 9$ **b.** $25x^2 - 60x + 36$

**Solution**

**a.** $x^2 + 6x + 9 = x^2 + 2 \cdot x \cdot 3 + 3^2 = (x + 3)^2$ The middle term has a positive sign.

$A^2 + 2AB + B^2 = (A + B)^2$

**b.** We suspect that $25x^2 - 60x + 36$ is a perfect square trinomial because $25x^2 = (5x)^2$ and $36 = 6^2$. The middle term can be expressed as twice the product of $5x$ and 6.

$$25x^2 - 60x + 36 = (5x)^2 - 2 \cdot 5x \cdot 6 + 6^2 = (5x - 6)^2$$

$A^2 - 2AB + B^2 = (A - B)^2$

**Check Point 7** Factor:

**a.** $x^2 + 14x + 49$ **b.** $16x^2 - 56x + 49$

**6** Factor the sum and difference of cubes.

## Factoring the Sum and Difference of Two Cubes

We can use the following formulas to factor the sum or the difference of two cubes.

**Factoring the Sum and Difference of Two Cubes**

**1.** Factoring the Sum of Two Cubes

$$A^3 + B^3 = (A + B)(A^2 - AB + B^2)$$

**2.** Factoring the Difference of Two Cubes

$$A^3 - B^3 = (A - B)(A^2 + AB + B^2)$$

### EXAMPLE 8 Factoring Sums and Differences of Two Cubes

Factor: **a.** $x^3 + 8$ **b.** $64x^3 - 125$

**Solution**

**a.** $x^3 + 8 = x^3 + 2^3 = (x + 2)(x^2 - x \cdot 2 + 2^2) = (x + 2)(x^2 - 2x + 4)$

$A^3 + B^3 = (A + B)(A^2 - AB + B^2)$

**b.** $64x^3 - 125 = (4x)^3 - 5^3 = (4x - 5)[(4x)^2 + (4x)(5) + 5^2]$

$A^3 - B^3 = (A - B)(A^2 + AB + B^2)$

$= (4x - 5)(16x^2 + 20x + 25)$

**Check Point 8** Factor:

**a.** $x^3 + 1$ **b.** $125x^3 - 8$

**7** Factor completely.

## Factoring Completely

Some polynomials can be factored using more than one technique. Always begin by trying to factor out the greatest common factor.

### EXAMPLE 9 Factoring Completely

Factor: **a.** $2a^3 + 8a^2 + 8a$ **b.** $x^3 - 5x^2 - 4x + 20$

**Solution**

**a.** $2a^3 + 8a^2 + 8a$

$= 2a(a^2 + 4a + 4)$ Factor out the greatest common factor.

$= 2a(a + 2)^2$ Factor the perfect square trinomial.

**b.** $x^3 - 5x^2 - 4x + 20$

$= (x^3 - 5x^2) + (-4x + 20)$ Group the terms with common factors.

$= x^2(x - 5) - 4(x - 5)$ Factor from each group.

$= (x - 5)(x^2 - 4)$ Factor out the common binomial factor, $(x - 5)$.

$= (x - 5)(x + 2)(x - 2)$ Factor completely by factoring $x^2 - 4$ as the difference of two squares.

**Check Point 9** Factor:

**a.** $2x^3 - 24x^2 + 72x$ **b.** $x^3 - 4x^2 - 9x + 36$

**8** Factor algebraic expressions containing fractional and negative exponents.

## Factoring Algebraic Expressions Containing Fractional and Negative Exponents

Algebraic expressions containing radicals and negative exponents occur frequently in calculus. Although these expressions are not polynomials, they can be simplified using factoring techniques.

### EXAMPLE 10 Factoring Involving Negative Fractional Exponents

Factor and simplify: $x(x + 1)^{-3/4} + (x + 1)^{1/4}$.

**Solution** The greatest common factor is $x + 1$ with the *smallest exponent* in the two terms. Thus, the greatest common factor is $(x + 1)^{-3/4}$.

$x(x + 1)^{-3/4} + (x + 1)^{1/4}$

$= (x + 1)^{-3/4}x + (x + 1)^{-3/4}(x + 1)$ Express each term with the greatest common factor as a factor.

$= (x + 1)^{-3/4}[x + (x + 1)]$ Factor out the greatest common factor.

$= \dfrac{2x + 1}{(x + 1)^{3/4}}$ $b^{-n} = \dfrac{1}{b^n}$

**Check Point 10** Factor and simplify: $x(x - 1)^{-1/2} + (x - 1)^{1/2}$.

# EXERCISE SET P.5

## Practice Exercises

*In Exercises 1–6, factor out the greatest common factor.*

**1.** $3x^2 + 6x$
**2.** $4x^2 - 8x$
**3.** $9x^4 - 18x^3 + 27x^2$
**4.** $6x^4 - 18x^3 + 12x^2$
**5.** $x^2(x - 3) + 12(x - 3)$
**6.** $x^2(2x + 5) + 17(2x + 5)$

*In Exercises 7–12, factor by grouping.*

**7.** $x^3 - 2x^2 + 5x - 10$
**8.** $x^3 - 3x^2 + 4x - 12$
**9.** $x^3 - x^2 + 2x - 2$
**10.** $x^3 + 6x^2 - 2x - 12$
**11.** $3x^3 - 2x^2 - 6x + 4$
**12.** $x^3 - x^2 - 5x + 5$

*In Exercises 13–26, factor each trinomial, or state that the trinomial is prime.*

**13.** $x^2 + 5x + 6$
**14.** $x^2 + 8x + 15$
**15.** $x^2 - 2x - 15$
**16.** $x^2 - 4x - 5$
**17.** $x^2 - 8x + 15$
**18.** $x^2 - 14x + 45$
**19.** $3x^2 - x - 2$
**20.** $2x^2 + 5x - 3$
**21.** $3x^2 - 25x - 28$
**22.** $3x^2 - 2x - 5$
**23.** $6x^2 - 11x + 4$
**24.** $6x^2 - 17x + 12$
**25.** $4x^2 + 16x + 15$
**26.** $8x^2 + 33x + 4$

*In Exercises 27–34, factor the difference of two squares.*

**27.** $x^2 - 100$
**28.** $x^2 - 144$
**29.** $9x^2 - 25y^2$
**30.** $36x^2 - 49y^2$
**31.** $x^4 - 16$
**32.** $x^4 - 1$
**33.** $16x^4 - 81$
**34.** $81x^4 - 1$

*In Exercises 35–40, factor any perfect square trinomials, or state that the polynomial is prime.*

**35.** $x^2 - 14x + 49$
**36.** $x^2 - 10x + 25$
**37.** $4x^2 + 4x + 1$
**38.** $25x^2 + 10x + 1$
**39.** $9x^2 - 6x + 1$
**40.** $64x^2 - 16x + 1$

*In Exercises 41–46, factor using the formula for the sum or difference of two cubes.*

**41.** $x^3 + 27$
**42.** $x^3 + 64$
**43.** $8x^3 - 1$
**44.** $27x^3 - 1$
**45.** $64x^3 + 27$
**46.** $8x^3 + 125$

*In Exercises 47–66, factor completely, or state that the polynomial is prime.*

**47.** $3x^3 - 3x$
**48.** $5x^3 - 45x$
**49.** $4x^2 - 4x - 24$
**50.** $6x^2 - 18x - 60$
**51.** $2x^4 - 162$
**52.** $7x^4 - 7$
**53.** $x^3 + 2x^2 - 9x - 18$
**54.** $x^3 + 3x^2 - 25x - 75$
**55.** $2x^2 - 2x - 112$
**56.** $6x^2 - 6x - 12$
**57.** $x^3 - 4x$
**58.** $9x^3 - 9x$
**59.** $x^2 + 64$
**60.** $x^2 + 36$
**61.** $x^3 + 2x^2 - 4x - 8$
**62.** $x^3 + 2x^2 - x - 2$
**63.** $y^5 - 81y$
**64.** $y^5 - 16y$
**65.** $20y^4 - 45y^2$
**66.** $48y^4 - 3y^2$

*In Exercises 67–76, factor and simplify each algebraic expression.*

**67.** $x^{3/2} - x^{1/2}$
**68.** $x^{3/4} - x^{1/4}$
**69.** $4x^{-2/3} + 8x^{1/3}$
**70.** $12x^{-3/4} + 6x^{1/4}$
**71.** $(x + 3)^{1/2} - (x + 3)^{3/2}$
**72.** $(x^2 + 4)^{3/2} + (x^2 + 4)^{7/2}$
**73.** $(x + 5)^{-1/2} - (x + 5)^{-3/2}$
**74.** $(x^2 + 3)^{-2/3} + (x^2 + 3)^{-5/3}$
**75.** $(4x - 1)^{1/2} - \frac{1}{3}(4x - 1)^{3/2}$
**76.** $-8(4x + 3)^{-2} + 10(5x + 1)(4x + 3)^{-1}$

## Application Exercises

**77.** You dive directly upward from a board that is 32 feet high. After $t$ seconds, your height above the water is described by the polynomial $-16t^2 + 16t + 32$. Factor the polynomial completely.

**78.** If $x$ represents a positive integer, factor $x^3 + 3x^2 + 2x$ to show that the trinomial represents the product of three consecutive integers.

*In Exercises 79–80, find the formula for the area of the shaded region and express it in factored form.*

**79.**

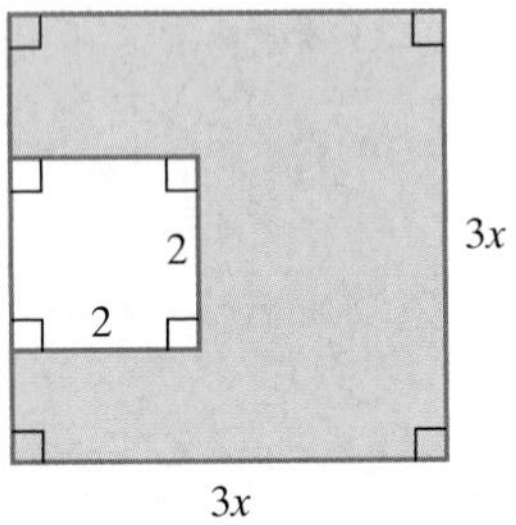


**80.**

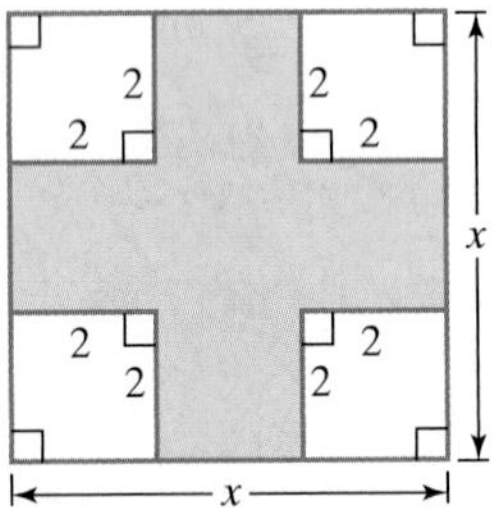


## Writing in Mathematics

**81.** Use an example and explain how to factor out the greatest common factor of a polynomial.

**82.** Suppose that a polynomial contains four terms. Explain how to use factoring by grouping to factor the polynomial.

**83.** Explain how to factor $3x^2 + 10x + 8$.

**84.** Explain how to factor the difference of two squares. Provide an example with your explanation.

**85.** What is a perfect square trinomial and how is it factored?

**86.** Explain how to factor $x^3 + 1$.

**87.** What does it mean to factor completely?

**88.** For Exercise 77, explain how to use your factored polynomial to figure out how many seconds it will take for you to hit the water.

## Technology Exercise

**89.** Computer algebra systems such as *Mathematica, Maple,* and *Derive* will factor polynomials. Graphing calculators, such as the TI-92 with *Derive*, will also allow you to enter a polynomial and use the F2 *Algebra* toolbar menu to display its factored form. Use a computer system or a calculator that can perform symbolic manipulations to verify any five of your factorizations in Exercises 47–66.

## Critical Thinking Exercises

**90.** Which one of the following is true?

**a.** Because $x^2 + 1$ is irreducible over the integers, it follows that $x^3 + 1$ is also irreducible.

**b.** One correct factored form for $x^2 - 4x + 3$ is $x(x - 4) + 3$.

**c.** $x^3 - 64 = (x - 4)^3$

**d.** None of the above is true.

*In Exercises 91–94, factor completely.*

**91.** $x^{2n} + 6x^n + 8$

**92.** $-x^2 - 4x + 5$

**93.** $x^2 + 8x + 16 - 25y^2$

**94.** $x^4 - y^4 - 2x^3y + 2xy^3$

*In Exercises 95–96, find all integers b so that the trinomial can be factored.*

**95.** $x^2 + bx + 15$

**96.** $x^2 + 4x + b$

## Group Exercise

**97.** Without looking at any factoring problems in the book, create five factoring problems. Make sure that some of your problems require at least two factoring strategies. Next, exchange problems with another person in your group. Work to factor your partner's problems. Evaluate the problems as you work: Are they too easy? Too difficult? Can the polynomials really be factored? Share your response with the person who wrote the problems. Finally, grade each other's work in factoring the polynomials. Each factoring problem is worth 20 points. You may award partial credit. If you take off points, explain why points are deducted and how you decided to take off a particular number of points for the error(s) that you found.

# SECTION P.6 Rational Expressions

## Objectives

1. Specify numbers that must be excluded from the domain of rational expressions.
2. Simplify rational expressions.
3. Multiply rational expressions.
4. Divide rational expressions.
5. Add and subtract rational expressions.
6. Simplify complex rational expressions.
7. Simplify fractional expressions that occur in calculus.
8. Rationalize numerators.

How do we describe the costs of reducing environmental pollution? We often use algebraic expressions involving quotients of polynomials. For example, the algebraic expression

$$\frac{250x}{100 - x}$$

describes the cost, in millions of dollars, to remove $x$ percent of the pollutants that are discharged into a river. Removing a modest percentage of pollutants, say 40%, is far less costly than removing a substantially greater percentage, such as 95%. We see this by evaluating the algebraic expression for $x = 40$ and $x = 95$.

**Discovery**

What happens if you try substituting 100 for $x$ in

$$\frac{250x}{100 - x}?$$

What does this tell you about the cost of cleaning up all of the river's pollutants?

Evaluating $\frac{250x}{100 - x}$ for

$x = 40$: Cost is $\frac{250(40)}{100 - 40} \approx 167$

$x = 95$: Cost is $\frac{250(95)}{100 - 95} = 4750$

The cost increases from approximately \$167 million to a possibly prohibitive \$4750 million, or \$4.75 billion. Costs spiral upward as the percentage of removed pollutants increases.

Many algebraic expressions that describe costs of environmental projects are examples of rational expressions. First we will define rational expressions. Then we will review how to perform operations with such expressions.

**1** Specify numbers that must be excluded from the domain of rational expressions.

## Rational Expressions

A **rational expression** is the quotient of two polynomials. Some examples are

$$\frac{x-2}{4}, \quad \frac{4}{x-2}, \quad \frac{x}{x^2-1}, \quad \text{and} \quad \frac{x^2+1}{x^2+2x-3}.$$

The set of real numbers for which an algebraic expression is defined is the **domain** of the expression. Because rational expressions indicate division and division by zero is undefined, we must exclude numbers from a rational expression's domain that make the denominator zero.

### EXAMPLE 1 Excluding Numbers from the Domain

Find all the numbers that must be excluded from the domain of each rational expression.

**a.** $\frac{4}{x-2}$ **b.** $\frac{x}{x^2-1}$

**Solution** To determine the numbers that must be excluded from each domain, examine the denominators.

**a.** $\frac{4}{x-2}$ **b.** $\frac{x}{x^2-1} = \frac{x}{(x+1)(x-1)}$

This denominator would equal zero if $x = 2$.

This factor would equal zero if $x = -1$.

This factor would equal zero if $x = 1$.

For the rational expression in part (a), we must exclude 2 from the domain. For the rational expression in part (b), we must exclude both −1 and 1 from the domain. These excluded numbers are often written to the right of a rational expression.

$$\frac{4}{x-2},\ x \neq 2 \qquad \frac{x}{x^2-1},\ x \neq -1,\ x \neq 1$$

**Check Point 1** Find all the numbers that must be excluded from each rational expression's domain.

**a.** $\frac{7}{x+5}$ **b.** $\frac{x}{x^2-36}$

2 Simplify rational expressions.

## Simplifying Rational Expressions

A rational expression is **simplified** if its numerator and denominator have no common factors other than 1 or −1. The following procedure can be used to simplify rational expressions.

**Simplifying Rational Expressions**

1. Factor the numerator and denominator completely.
2. Divide both the numerator and denominator by the common factors.

This procedure lets us cancel identical nonzero factors in the numerator and denominator. Thus, if $a$, $b$, and $c$ are real numbers or algebraic expressions such that $b \neq 0$ and $c \neq 0$,

$$\frac{ac}{bc} = \frac{a \cdot \cancel{c}}{a \cdot \cancel{c}} = \frac{a}{b}.$$

### EXAMPLE 2 Simplifying Rational Expressions

Simplify: **a.** $\frac{x^3 + x^2}{x + 1}$ **b.** $\frac{x^2 + 6x + 5}{x^2 - 25}$

**Solution**

**a.** $\frac{x^3 + x^2}{x + 1} = \frac{x^2(x + 1)}{x + 1}$ Factor the numerator. Because the denominator is x + 1, x ≠ −1.

$= \frac{x^2\overset{1}{\cancel{(x + 1)}}}{\underset{1}{\cancel{x + 1}}}$ Divide out the common factor of x + 1.

$= x^2, x \neq -1$ Denominators of 1 need not be written because $\frac{a}{1} = a$.

**b.** $\frac{x^2 + 6x + 5}{x^2 - 25} = \frac{(x + 5)(x + 1)}{(x + 5)(x - 5)}$ Factor the numerator and denominator. Because the denominator is (x + 5)(x − 5), x ≠ −5 and x ≠ 5.

$= \frac{\overset{1}{\cancel{(x + 5)}}(x + 1)}{\underset{1}{\cancel{(x + 5)}}(x - 5)}$ Divide out the common factor of x + 5.

$= \frac{x + 1}{x - 5}, \quad x \neq -5 \text{ and } x \neq 5$

**Check Point 2** Simplify:

**a.** $\frac{x^3 + 3x^2}{x + 3}$ **b.** $\frac{x^2 - 1}{x^2 + 2x + 1}$

3 Multiply rational expressions.

## Multiplying Rational Expressions

The product of two rational expressions is the product of their numerators over the product of their denominators. Thus, if $a$, $b$, $c$, and $d$ are real numbers or algebraic expressions such that $b \neq 0$ and $d \neq 0$,

$$\frac{a}{b} \cdot \frac{c}{d} = \frac{ac}{bd}.$$

Here is a step-by-step procedure for multiplying rational expressions.

**Multiplying Rational Expressions**

1. Factor all numerators and denominators completely.
2. Divide both the numerator and denominator by common factors.
3. Multiply the remaining factors in the numerator and multiply the remaining factors in the denominator.

## EXAMPLE 3 Multiplying Rational Expressions

Multiply and simplify:

$$\frac{x-7}{x-1} \cdot \frac{x^2-1}{3x-21}.$$

**Solution**

$$\frac{x-7}{x-1} \cdot \frac{x^2-1}{3x-21}$$

$$= \frac{x-7}{x-1} \cdot \frac{(x+1)(x-1)}{3(x-7)}$$

Factor all numerators and denominators. Because the denominator has factors of $x - 1$ and $x - 7$, $x \neq 1$ and $x \neq 7$.

$$= \frac{\overset{1}{\cancel{x-7}}}{\underset{1}{\cancel{x-1}}} \cdot \frac{(x+1)\overset{1}{\cancel{(x-1)}}}{3\underset{1}{\cancel{(x-7)}}}$$

Divide both the numerator and the denominator by common factors.

$$= \frac{x+1}{3}, x \neq 1, x \neq 7$$

Multiply the remaining factors in the numerator and denominator.

These excluded numbers from the domain must also be excluded from the simplified expression's domain.

**Check Point 3** Multiply and simplify:

$$\frac{x+3}{x^2-4} \cdot \frac{x^2-x-6}{x^2+6x+9}.$$

4 Divide rational expressions.

## Dividing Rational Expressions

We find the quotient of two rational expressions by inverting the divisor and multiplying. Thus, if $a$, $b$, $c$, and $d$ are real numbers or algebraic expressions such that $b \neq 0$, $c \neq 0$ and $d \neq 0$,

$$\frac{a}{b} \div \frac{c}{d} = \frac{a}{b} \cdot \frac{d}{c} = \frac{ad}{bc}.$$

## EXAMPLE 4 Dividing Rational Expressions

Divide and simplify:

$$\frac{x^2-2x-8}{x^2-9} \div \frac{x-4}{x+3}.$$

**Solution**

$$\frac{x^2-2x-8}{x^2-9} \div \frac{x-4}{x+3} = \frac{x^2-2x-8}{x^2-9} \cdot \frac{x+3}{x-4}$$ Invert the divisor and multiply.

$$= \frac{(x-4)(x+2)}{(x+3)(x-3)} \cdot \frac{x+3}{x-4}$$ Factor throughout. For nonzero denominators, $x \neq -3$, $x \neq 3$, and $x \neq 4$.

$$= \frac{\overset{1}{\cancel{(x-4)}}(x+2)}{\underset{1}{\cancel{(x+3)}}(x-3)} \cdot \frac{\overset{1}{\cancel{(x+3)}}}{\underset{1}{\cancel{(x-4)}}}$$ Divide both the numerator and denominator by common factors.

$$= \frac{x+2}{x-3}, x \neq -3, x \neq 3, x \neq 4$$ Multiply the remaining factors in the numerator and the denominator.

**Check Point 4** Divide and simplify:

$$\frac{x^2-2x+1}{x^3+x} \div \frac{x^2+x-2}{3x^2+3}.$$

**5** Add and subtract rational expressions.

## Adding and Subtracting Rational Expressions with the Same Denominator

We add or subtract rational expressions with the same denominator by (1) adding or subtracting the numerators, (2) placing this result over the common denominator, and (3) simplifying, if possible. Thus, if $a$, $b$, and $c$ are real numbers or algebraic expressions such that $b \neq 0$,

$$\frac{a}{b} + \frac{c}{b} = \frac{a+c}{b} \quad \text{and} \quad \frac{a}{b} - \frac{c}{d} = \frac{a-c}{b}.$$

### EXAMPLE 5 Subtracting Rational Expressions with the Same Denominator

Subtract: $\dfrac{5x+1}{x^2-9} - \dfrac{4x-2}{x^2-9}.$

**Study Tip**

Example 5 shows that when a numerator is being subtracted, we must subtract every term in that expression.

**Solution**

$$\frac{5x+1}{x^2-9} - \frac{4x-2}{x^2-9} = \frac{5x+1-(4x-2)}{x^2-9}$$ Subtract numerators and include parentheses to indicate that both terms are subtracted. Place this difference over the common denominator.

$$= \frac{5x+1-4x+2}{x^2-9}$$ Remove parentheses and then change the sign of each term.

$$= \frac{x+3}{x^2-9}$$ Combine like terms.

$$= \frac{\overset{1}{\cancel{x+3}}}{\underset{1}{\cancel{(x+3)}}(x-3)}$$ Factor and simplify ($x \neq -3$ and $x \neq 3$).

$$= \frac{1}{x-3}, x \neq -3, x \neq 3$$

**Check Point 5** Subtract: $\dfrac{x}{x+1} - \dfrac{3x+2}{x+1}.$

## Adding and Subtracting Rational Expressions with Different Denominators

Rational expressions that have no common factors in their denominators can be added or subtracted using one of the following properties:

$$\frac{a}{b}+\frac{c}{d}=\frac{ad+bc}{bd} \qquad \frac{a}{b}-\frac{c}{d}=\frac{ad-bc}{bd}, b \neq 0, d \neq 0.$$

The least common denominator, $bd$, is the product of the distinct factors in the two denominators.

### EXAMPLE 6 Subtracting Rational Expressions Having No Common Factors in Their Denominators

Subtract: $\frac{x+2}{2x-3}-\frac{4}{x+3}$.

**Solution** We need to find the least common denominator. This is the product of the distinct factors in each denominator, namely $(2x-3)(x+3)$. We can therefore use the subtraction property given above as follows:

$$\frac{a}{b} - \frac{c}{d} = \frac{ad-bc}{bd}$$

$$\frac{x+2}{2x-3}-\frac{4}{x+3}=\frac{(x+2)(x+3)-(2x-3)4}{(2x-3)(x+3)}$$

Observe that $a = x + 2$, $b = 2x - 3$, $c = 4$, and $d = x + 3$.

$$=\frac{x^2+5x+6-(8x-12)}{(2x-3)(x+3)}$$

Multiply.

$$=\frac{x^2+5x+6-8x+12}{(2x-3)(x+3)}$$

Remove parentheses and then change the sign of each term.

$$=\frac{x^2-3x+18}{(2x-3)(x+3)}, x \neq \frac{3}{2}, x \neq -3$$

Combine like terms in the numerator.

**Check Point 6** Add: $\frac{3}{x+1}+\frac{5}{x-1}$.

When adding and subtracting rational expressions that have different denominators with one or more common factors in the denominators, it is efficient to find the least common denominator first.

**Finding the Least Common Denominator**

1. Factor each denominator completely.
2. List the factors of the first denominator.
3. Add to the list in step 2 any factors of the second denominator that do not appear in the list.
4. Form the product of each different factor from the list in step 3. This product is the least common denominator.

## EXAMPLE 7 Finding the Least Common Denominator

Find the least common denominator that is needed to add or subtract the rational expressions

$$\frac{7}{5x^2 + 15x} \quad \text{and} \quad \frac{9}{x^2 + 6x + 9}.$$

### Solution

**Step 1** **Factor each denominator completely.**

$$5x^2 + 15x = 5x(x + 3)$$

$$x^2 + 6x + 9 = (x + 3)^2$$

**Step 2** **List the factors of the first denominator.**

$$5, x, (x + 3)$$

**Step 3** **Add any unlisted factors from the second denominator.** The second denominator is $(x + 3)^2$ or $(x + 3)(x + 3)$. One factor of $x + 3$ is already in our list, but the other factor is not. We add $x + 3$ to the list. We have

$$5, x, (x + 3), (x + 3).$$

**Step 4** **The least common denominator is the product of all factors in the final list.** Thus,

$$5x(x + 3)(x + 3)$$

is the least common denominator.

**Check Point 7** What is the least common denominator for denominators of $x^2 - 6x + 9$ and $x^2 - 9$?

Finding the least common denominator for two (or more) rational expressions is the first step needed to add or subtract the expressions.

### Adding and Subtracting Rational Expressions That Have Different Denominators With Shared Factors

1. Find the least common denominator.
2. Write all rational expressions in terms of the least common denominator. To do so, multiply both the numerator and the denominator of each rational expression by any factor(s) needed to convert the denominator into the least common denominator.
3. Add or subtract the numerators, placing the resulting expression over the least common denominator.
4. If necessary, simplify the resulting rational expression.

## EXAMPLE 8 Adding Rational Expressions with Different Denominators

Add: $\frac{x+3}{x^2+x-2}+\frac{2}{x^2-1}$.

**Solution**

**Step 1 Find the least common denominator.** Start by factoring the denominators.

$$x^2+x-2=(x+2)(x-1)$$
$$x^2-1=(x+1)(x-1)$$

The factors of the first denominator are $x+2$ and $x-1$. The only factor from the second denominator that is unlisted is $x+1$. Thus, the least common denominator is

$$(x+2)(x-1)(x+1).$$

**Step 2 Write all rational expressions in terms of the least common denominator.** We do so by multiplying both the numerator and the denominator by any factor(s) needed to convert the denominator into the least common denominator.

$$\frac{x+3}{x^2+x-2}+\frac{2}{x^2-1}$$

$$=\frac{x+3}{(x+2)(x-1)}+\frac{2}{(x+1)(x-1)}$$

The least common denominator is $(x+2)(x-1)(x+1)$.

$$=\frac{(x+3)(x+1)}{(x+2)(x-1)(x+1)}+\frac{2(x+2)}{(x+2)(x-1)(x+1)}$$

Rewrite each rational expression with the least common denominator. Multiply the numerator and the denominator by whatever extra factors are required to form $(x+2)(x-1)(x+1)$.

**Step 3 Add numerators, putting this sum over the least common denominator.**

$$=\frac{(x+3)(x+1)+2(x+2)}{(x+2)(x-1)(x+1)}$$

$$=\frac{x^2+4x+3+2x+4}{(x+2)(x-1)(x+1)}$$

Multiply in the numerator.

$$=\frac{x^2+6x+7}{(x+2)(x-1)(x+1)},\ x\neq-2,\ x\neq1,\ x\neq-1$$

Combine like terms in the numerator.

**Step 4 If necessary, simplify.** Because the numerator is prime, no further simplification is possible.

**Check Point 8** Subtract: $\frac{x}{x^2-10x+25}-\frac{x-4}{2x-10}$.

**6** Simplify complex rational expressions.

## Complex Rational Expressions

**Complex rational expressions** have numerators or denominators containing one or more rational expressions. Here are two examples of such expressions:

$$\frac{1+\frac{1}{x}}{1-\frac{1}{x}}$$

Separate rational expressions occur in the numerator and denominator.

$$\frac{\frac{1}{x+h}-\frac{1}{x}}{h}$$

Separate rational expressions occur in the numerator.

One method for simplifying a complex rational expression is to combine its numerator into a single expression and combine its denominator into a single expression. Then perform the division by inverting the denominator and multiplying.

### EXAMPLE 9 Simplifying a Complex Rational Expression

Simplify: $\dfrac{1+\frac{1}{x}}{1-\frac{1}{x}}$.

**Solution**

$$\frac{1+\frac{1}{x}}{1-\frac{1}{x}} = \frac{\frac{x}{x}+\frac{1}{x}}{\frac{x}{x}-\frac{1}{x}}, x \neq 0$$

The terms in the numerator and in the denominator are each combined by performing the addition and subtraction. The least common denominator is x.

$$= \frac{\frac{x+1}{x}}{\frac{x-1}{x}}$$

Perform the addition in the numerator and the subtraction in the denominator.

$$= \frac{x+1}{x} \div \frac{x-1}{x}$$

Rewrite the main fraction bar as ÷.

$$= \frac{x+1}{x} \cdot \frac{x}{x-1}$$

Invert the divisor and multiply ($x \neq 0$ and $x \neq 1$).

$$= \frac{x+1}{\overset{}{\cancel{x}}_{1}} \cdot \frac{\overset{1}{\cancel{x}}}{x-1}$$

Divide both the numerator and denominator by the common factor, x.

$$= \frac{x+1}{x-1}, x \neq 0, x \neq 1$$

Multiply the remaining factors in the numerator and in the denominator.

**Check Point 9** Simplify: $\dfrac{\frac{1}{x}-\frac{3}{2}}{\frac{1}{x}+\frac{3}{4}}$.

A second method for simplifying a complex rational expression is to find the least common denominator of all the rational expressions in its numerator and denominator. Then multiply each term in its numerator and denominator by this least common denominator. Here we use this method to simplify the complex rational expression in Example 9.

$$\frac{1+\frac{1}{x}}{1-\frac{1}{x}} = \frac{\left(1+\frac{1}{x}\right)}{\left(1-\frac{1}{x}\right)}\cdot\frac{x}{x}$$

The least common denominator of all the rational expressions is x. Multiply the numerator and denominator by x. Because $\frac{x}{x} = 1$, we are not changing the complex fraction ($x \neq 0$).

$$= \frac{1\cdot x + \frac{1}{x}\cdot x}{1\cdot x - \frac{1}{x}\cdot x}$$

Use the distributive property. Be sure to distribute x to every term.

$$= \frac{x+1}{x-1},\ x \neq 0,\ x \neq 1$$

Multiply. The complex rational expression is now simplified.

## EXAMPLE 10 Simplifying a Complex Rational Expression

Simplify: $\dfrac{\frac{1}{x+h}-\frac{1}{x}}{h}$.

**Solution** We will use the method of multiplying each of the three terms, $\frac{1}{x+h}$, $\frac{1}{x}$, and $h$ by the least common denominator. The least common denominator is $x(x+h)$.

$$\frac{\frac{1}{x+h}-\frac{1}{x}}{h}$$

$$= \frac{\left(\frac{1}{x+h}-\frac{1}{x}\right)x(x+h)}{h\,x(x+h)},$$

Multiply the numerator and denominator by $x(x+h)$, $h \neq 0$, $x \neq 0$, $x \neq -h$.

$$= \frac{\frac{1}{x+h}\cdot x(x+h) - \frac{1}{x}\cdot x(x+h)}{h\cdot x(x+h)}$$

Use the distributive property in the numerator.

$$= \frac{x-(x+h)}{hx(x+h)}$$

Simplify: $\frac{1}{\cancel{x+h}}\cdot x(\cancel{x+h}) = x$ and $\frac{1}{\cancel{x}}\cdot \cancel{x}(x+h) = x+h$.

$$= \frac{x-x-h}{hx(x+h)}$$

Subtract in the numerator.

$$= \frac{-\overset{1}{\cancel{h}}}{\underset{1}{\cancel{h}}x(x+h)}$$

Simplify: $x - x - h = -h$.

$$= -\frac{1}{x(x+h)},\ h \neq 0,\ x \neq 0,\ x \neq -h$$

Divide the numerator and denominator by $h$.

**Check Point 10** Simplify: $\dfrac{\frac{1}{x+7}-\frac{1}{x}}{7}$.

**7** Simplify fractional expressions that occur in calculus.

## Fractional Expressions in Calculus

Fractional expressions containing radicals occur frequently in calculus. Because of the radicals, these expressions are not rational expressions. However, they can often be simplified using the procedure for simplifying complex rational expressions.

### EXAMPLE 11 Simplifying a Fractional Expression Containing Radicals

Simplify: $\dfrac{\sqrt{9-x^2}+\dfrac{x^2}{\sqrt{9-x^2}}}{9-x^2}$.

**Solution**

$$\frac{\sqrt{9-x^2}+\dfrac{x^2}{\sqrt{9-x^2}}}{9-x^2}$$

The least common denominator of the denominators is $\sqrt{9-x^2}$.

$$=\frac{\sqrt{9-x^2}+\dfrac{x^2}{\sqrt{9-x^2}}}{9-x^2}\cdot\frac{\sqrt{9-x^2}}{\sqrt{9-x^2}}$$

Multiply the numerator and the denominator by $\sqrt{9-x^2}$.

$$=\frac{\sqrt{9-x^2}\sqrt{9-x^2}+\dfrac{x^2}{\sqrt{9-x^2}}\sqrt{9-x^2}}{(9-x^2)\sqrt{9-x^2}}$$

Use the distributive property in the numerator.

$$=\frac{(9-x^2)+x^2}{(9-x^2)^{3/2}}$$

In the denominator: $(9-x^2)^1(9-x^2)^{1/2}=(9-x^2)^{1+1/2}=(9-x^2)^{3/2}$.

$$=\frac{9}{\sqrt{(9-x^2)^3}}$$

Because the original expression was in radical form, write the denominator in radical form.

**Check Point 11** Simplify: $\dfrac{\sqrt{x}+\dfrac{1}{\sqrt{x}}}{x}$.

**8** Rationalize numerators.

Another fractional expression that you will encounter in calculus is

$$\frac{\sqrt{x+h}-\sqrt{x}}{h}.$$

Can you see that this expression is not defined if $h=0$? However, in calculus, you will ask the following question:

> What happens to the expression as $h$ takes on values that get closer and closer to 0, such as $h=0.1$, $h=0.01$, $h=0.001$, $h=0.0001$, and so on?

The question is answered by first **rationalizing the numerator**. This process involves rewriting the fractional expression to remove the square roots from the numerator.

## EXAMPLE 12 Rationalizing a Numerator

Rationalize the numerator:

$$\frac{\sqrt{x+h}-\sqrt{x}}{h}.$$

**Solution** If we multiply the numerator and denominator by $\sqrt{x+h}+\sqrt{x}$, the numerator will not contain radicals. Therefore, we multiply by 1, choosing $\frac{\sqrt{x+h}+\sqrt{x}}{\sqrt{x+h}+\sqrt{x}}$ for 1:

$$\frac{\sqrt{x+h}-\sqrt{x}}{h} = \frac{\sqrt{x+h}-\sqrt{x}}{h}\cdot\frac{\sqrt{x+h}+\sqrt{x}}{\sqrt{x+h}+\sqrt{x}}$$ Multiply by 1.

$$= \frac{(\sqrt{x+h})^2-(\sqrt{x})^2}{h(\sqrt{x+h}+\sqrt{x})}$$ $(\sqrt{a}-\sqrt{b})(\sqrt{a}+\sqrt{b}) = (\sqrt{a})^2-(\sqrt{b})^2$

$$= \frac{x+h-x}{h(\sqrt{x+h}+\sqrt{x})}$$ $(\sqrt{x+h})^2 = x+h$ and $(\sqrt{x})^2 = x$.

$$= \frac{h}{h(\sqrt{x+h}+\sqrt{x})}$$ Simplify: $x+h-x=h$.

$$= \frac{1}{\sqrt{x+h}+\sqrt{x}},\quad h \neq 0$$ Divide both the numerator and denominator by $h$.

What happens to $\frac{\sqrt{x+h}-\sqrt{x}}{h}$ as $h$ gets closer and closer to 0? In Example 12, we showed that

$$\frac{\sqrt{x+h}-\sqrt{x}}{h} = \frac{1}{\sqrt{x+h}+\sqrt{x}}.$$

As $h$ gets closer to 0, the expression on the right gets closer to $\frac{1}{\sqrt{x+0}+\sqrt{x}} = \frac{1}{\sqrt{x}+\sqrt{x}}$, or $\frac{1}{2\sqrt{x}}$. Thus, the fractional expression $\frac{\sqrt{x+h}-\sqrt{x}}{h}$ approaches $\frac{1}{2\sqrt{x}}$ as $h$ gets closer to 0.

**Check Point 12** Rationalize the numerator: $\frac{\sqrt{x+3}-\sqrt{x}}{3}$.

## EXERCISE SET P.6

### Practice Exercises

*In Exercises 1–6, find all numbers that must be excluded from the domain of each rational expression.*

**1.** $\dfrac{7}{x-3}$

**2.** $\dfrac{13}{x+9}$

**3.** $\dfrac{x+5}{x^2-25}$

**4.** $\dfrac{x+7}{x^2-49}$

**5.** $\dfrac{x-1}{x^2+11x+10}$

**6.** $\dfrac{x-3}{x^2+4x-45}$

*In Exercises 7–12, simplify each rational expression. Find all numbers that must be excluded from the domain of the simplified rational expression.*

**7.** $\dfrac{3x-9}{x^2-6x+9}$

**8.** $\dfrac{4x-8}{x^2-4x+4}$

**9.** $\dfrac{y^2+7y-18}{y^2-3y+2}$

**10.** $\dfrac{y^2-4y-5}{y^2+5y+4}$

**11.** $\dfrac{x^2+12x+36}{x^2-36}$

**12.** $\dfrac{x^2-14x+49}{x^2-49}$

*In Exercises 13–22, multiply or divide as indicated.*

**13.** $\dfrac{x^2-9}{x^2}\cdot\dfrac{x^2-3x}{x^2+x-12}$

**14.** $\dfrac{x^2-4}{x^2-4x+4}\cdot\dfrac{2x-4}{x+2}$

**15.** $\dfrac{x^2-5x+6}{x^2-2x-3}\cdot\dfrac{x^2-1}{x^2-4}$

**16.** $\dfrac{x^2+5x+6}{x^2+x-6}\cdot\dfrac{x^2-9}{x^2-x-6}$

**17.** $\dfrac{x^3-8}{x^2-4}\cdot\dfrac{x+2}{3x}$

**18.** $\dfrac{x^2+6x+9}{x^3+27}\cdot\dfrac{1}{x+3}$

**19.** $\dfrac{x^2-4}{x}\div\dfrac{x+2}{x-2}$

**20.** $\dfrac{x^2-4}{x-2}\div\dfrac{x+2}{4x-8}$

**21.** $\dfrac{x^2-25}{2x-2}\div\dfrac{x^2+10x+25}{x^2+4x-5}$

**22.** $\dfrac{x^2-4}{x^2+3x-10}\div\dfrac{x^2+5x+6}{x^2+8x+15}$

*In Exercises 23–40, add or subtract as indicated.*

**23.** $\dfrac{4x+1}{6x+5}+\dfrac{8x+9}{6x+5}$

**24.** $\dfrac{3x+2}{3x+4}+\dfrac{3x+6}{3x+4}$

**25.** $\dfrac{x^2-2x}{x^2+3x}+\dfrac{x^2+x}{x^2+3x}$

**26.** $\dfrac{x^2-4x}{x^2-x-6}+\dfrac{4x-4}{x^2-x-6}$

**27.** $\dfrac{x^2+3x}{x^2+x-12}-\dfrac{x^2-12}{x^2+x-12}$

**28.** $\dfrac{x^2-4x}{x^2-x-6}-\dfrac{x-6}{x^2-x-6}$

**29.** $\dfrac{3}{x+4}+\dfrac{6}{x+5}$

**30.** $\dfrac{8}{x-2}+\dfrac{2}{x-3}$

**31.** $\dfrac{3}{x+1}-\dfrac{3}{x}$

**32.** $\dfrac{4}{x}-\dfrac{3}{x+3}$

**33.** $\dfrac{2x}{x+2}+\dfrac{x+2}{x-2}$

**34.** $\dfrac{3x}{x-3}-\dfrac{x+4}{x+2}$

**35.** $\dfrac{x+5}{x-5}+\dfrac{x-5}{x+5}$

**36.** $\dfrac{x+3}{x-3}+\dfrac{x-3}{x+3}$

**37.** $\dfrac{4}{x^2+6x+9}+\dfrac{4}{x+3}$

**38.** $\dfrac{3}{5x+2}+\dfrac{5x}{25x^2-4}$

**39.** $\dfrac{3x}{x^2+3x-10}-\dfrac{2x}{x^2+x-6}$

**40.** $\dfrac{x}{x^2-2x-24}-\dfrac{x}{x^2-7x+6}$

*In Exercise 41–50, simplify each complex rational expression.*

**41.** $\dfrac{1+\dfrac{1}{x}}{3-\dfrac{1}{x}}$

**42.** $\dfrac{8+\dfrac{1}{x}}{4-\dfrac{1}{x}}$

**43.** $\dfrac{x-\dfrac{x}{x+3}}{x+2}$

**44.** $\dfrac{x-3}{x-\dfrac{3}{x-2}}$

**45.** $\dfrac{\dfrac{3}{x-2}-\dfrac{4}{x+2}}{\dfrac{7}{x^2-4}}$

**46.** $\dfrac{\dfrac{x}{x-2}+1}{\dfrac{3}{x^2-4}+1}$

**47.** $\dfrac{\dfrac{1}{x+1}}{\dfrac{1}{x^2-2x-3}+\dfrac{1}{x-3}}$

**48.** $\dfrac{\dfrac{6}{x^2+2x-15}-\dfrac{1}{x-3}}{\dfrac{1}{x+5}+1}$

**49.** $\dfrac{\dfrac{1}{(x+h)^2}-\dfrac{1}{x^2}}{h}$

**50.** $\dfrac{\dfrac{x+h}{x+h+1}-\dfrac{x}{x+1}}{h}$

*Exercises 51–56, contain fractional expressions that occur frequently in calculus. Simplify each expression.*

**51.** $\dfrac{\sqrt{x}-\dfrac{1}{3\sqrt{x}}}{\sqrt{x}}$

**52.** $\dfrac{\sqrt{x}-\dfrac{1}{4\sqrt{x}}}{\sqrt{x}}$

**53.** $\dfrac{\dfrac{x^2}{\sqrt{x^2+2}} - \sqrt{x^2+2}}{x^2}$ **54.** $\dfrac{\sqrt{5-x^2} + \dfrac{x^2}{\sqrt{5-x^2}}}{5-x^2}$

**55.** $\dfrac{\dfrac{1}{\sqrt{x+h}} - \dfrac{1}{\sqrt{x}}}{h}$ **56.** $\dfrac{\dfrac{1}{\sqrt{x+3}} - \dfrac{1}{\sqrt{x}}}{3}$

*In Exercises 57–60, rationalize the numerator.*

**57.** $\dfrac{\sqrt{x+5}-\sqrt{x}}{5}$ **58.** $\dfrac{\sqrt{x+7}-\sqrt{x}}{7}$

**59.** $\dfrac{\sqrt{x}+\sqrt{y}}{x^2-y^2}$ **60.** $\dfrac{\sqrt{x}-\sqrt{y}}{x^2-y^2}$

## Application Exercises

**61.** The polynomial $-0.14t^2 + 0.51t + 31.6$ describes the U.S. population (in millions) age 65 and older $t$ years after 1990. The polynomial $0.54t^2 + 12.64t + 107.1$ describes the total yearly cost of Medicare (in billions of dollars) $t$ years after 1990. Write a rational expression that describes the average cost of Medicare per person age 65 or older $t$ years after 1990.

**62.** The polynomial

$$6t^4 - 207t^3 + 2128t^2 - 6622t + 15{,}220$$

describes the annual number of drug convictions in the United States $t$ years after 1984. The polynomial

$$28t^4 - 711t^3 + 5963t^2 - 1695t + 27{,}424$$

describes the annual number of drug arrests in the United States $t$ years after 1984. Write a rational expression that describes the conviction rate for drug arrests in the United States $t$ years after 1984.

**63.** The rational expression

$$\frac{130x}{100-x}$$

describes the cost, in millions of dollars, to inoculate $x$ percent of the population against a particular strain of flu.

**a.** Evaluate the expression for $x = 40$, $x = 80$, and $x = 90$. Describe the meaning of each evaluation in terms of percentage inoculated and cost.

**b.** For what value of $x$ is the expression undefined?

**c.** What happens to the cost as $x$ approaches 100%? How can you interpret this observation?

**64.** Doctors use the rational expression

$$\frac{DA}{A+12}$$

to determine the dosage of a drug prescribed for children. In this expression, $A$ = child's age, and $D$ = adult dosage. What is the difference in the child's dosage for a 7-year-old child and a 3-year-old child? Express the answer as a single rational expression in terms of $D$. Then describe what your answer means in terms of the variables in the rational expression.

**65.** The average speed on a round-trip commute having a one-way distance $d$ is given by the complex rational expression

$$\frac{2d}{\dfrac{d}{r_1} + \dfrac{d}{r_2}}$$

in which $r_1$ and $r_2$ are the speeds on the outgoing and return trips, respectively. Simplify the expression. Then find the average speed for a person who drives from home to work at 30 miles per hour and returns on the same route averaging 20 miles per hour. Explain why the answer is not 25 miles per hour.

**66.** If three resistors with resistances $R_1$, $R_2$, and $R_3$ are connected in parallel, their combined resistance, $R$, is given by the equation

$$R = \frac{1}{\dfrac{1}{R_1} + \dfrac{1}{R_2} + \dfrac{1}{R_3}}.$$

Sinplify the complex rational expression on the right. Then find $R$ when $R_1$ is 4 ohms, $R_2$ is 8 ohms, and $R_3$ is 12 ohms.

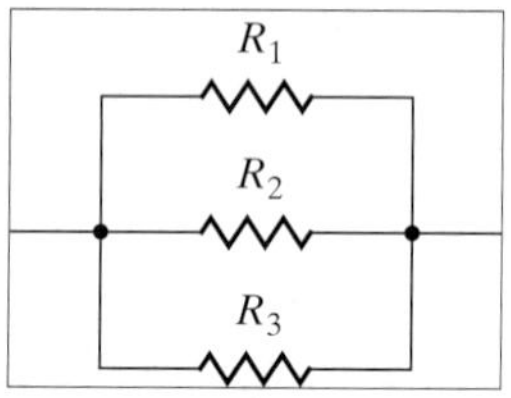


## Writing in Mathematics

**67.** What is a rational expression?

**68.** Explain how to determine what numbers must be excluded from the domain of a rational expression.

**69.** Explain how to simplify a rational expression.

**70.** Explain how to multiply rational expressions.

**71.** Explain how to divide rational expressions.

**72.** Explain how to add or subtract rational expressions with the same denominators.

**73.** Explain how to add rational expressions having no common factors in their denominators. Use $\dfrac{3}{x+5} + \dfrac{7}{x+2}$ in your explanation.

**74.** Explain how to find the least common denominator for denominators of $x^2 - 100$ and $x^2 - 20x + 100$.

**75.** Describe two ways to simplify $\dfrac{\frac{3}{x}+\frac{2}{x^2}}{\frac{1}{x^2}+\frac{2}{x}}$.

*Explain the error in Exercises 76–78. Then rewrite the right side of the equation to correct the error that now exists.*

**76.** $\frac{1}{a}+\frac{1}{b}=\frac{1}{a+b}$

**77.** $\frac{1}{x}+7=\frac{1}{x+7}$

**78.** $\frac{a}{x}+\frac{a}{b}=\frac{a}{x+b}$

**79.** A politician claims that each year the conviction rate for drug arrests in the United States is increasing. Explain how to use the polynomials in Exercise 62 to verify this claim.

## Technology Exercise

**80.** The polynomial

$$413.48t^2 + 185.72t + 24{,}031.95$$

describes the amount of Medicaid payments, in millions of dollars, $t$ years after 1980. The polynomial

$$0.004t^2 + 0.02t^3 + 0.01t^2 - 0.24t + 21.66$$

describes the annual number of Medicaid recipients in the United States $t$ years after 1980. Use a calculator to find the amount paid per recipient of Medicaid each year from 1988 to 2000. In what year did the amount paid per recipient fall below $900?

## Critical Thinking Exercises

**81.** Which one of the following is true?

**a.** $\frac{x^2-25}{x-5}=x-5$

**b.** $\frac{x}{y}\div\frac{y}{x}=1$, if $x\neq 0$ and $y\neq 0$.

**c.** The least common denominator needed to find $\frac{1}{x}+\frac{1}{x+3}$ is $x+3$.

**d.** The rational expression

$$\frac{x^2-16}{x-4}$$

is not defined for $x=4$. However, as $x$ gets closer and closer to 4, the value of the expression approaches 8.

*In Exercises 82–83, find the missing expression.*

**82.** $\frac{3x}{x-5}+\frac{\square}{5-x}=\frac{7x+1}{x-5}$

**83.** $\frac{4}{x-2}-\boxed{\frac{\phantom{x}}{\phantom{x}}}=\frac{2x+8}{(x-2)(x+1)}$

**84.** In one short sentence, five words or less, explain what

$$\frac{\frac{1}{x}+\frac{1}{x^2}+\frac{1}{x^3}}{\frac{1}{x^4}+\frac{1}{x^5}+\frac{1}{x^6}}$$

does to each number $x$.

# SECTION P.7 Complex Numbers

## Objectives

1. Add and subtract complex numbers.
2. Multiply complex numbers.
3. Divide complex numbers.
4. Perform operations with square roots of negative numbers.

Who is this kid warning us about our eyeballs turning black if we attempt to find the square root of −9? Don't believe what you hear on the street. Although square roots of negative numbers are not real numbers, they do play a significant role in algebra. In this section, we move beyond the real numbers and discuss square roots with negative radicands.

## The Imaginary Unit *i*

In Chapter 1, we'll be studying equations whose solutions involve the square roots of negative numbers. Because the square of a real number is never negative, there is no real number $x$ such that $x^2 = -1$. To provide a setting in which such equations have solutions, mathematicians invented an expanded system of numbers, the complex numbers. The imaginary number $i$, defined to be a solution to the equation $x^2 = -1$, is the basis of this new set.

**The Imaginary Unit *i***

The imaginary unit $i$ is defined as

$$i = \sqrt{-1}, \quad \text{where} \quad i^2 = -1.$$

Using the imaginary unit $i$, we can express the square root of any negative number as a real multiple of $i$. For example,

$$\sqrt{-25} = i\sqrt{25} = 5i.$$

We can check this result by squaring $5i$ and obtaining −25.

$$(5i)^2 = 5^2i^2 = 25(-1) = -25$$

A new system of numbers, called **complex numbers**, is based on adding multiples of $i$, such as $5i$, to the real numbers.

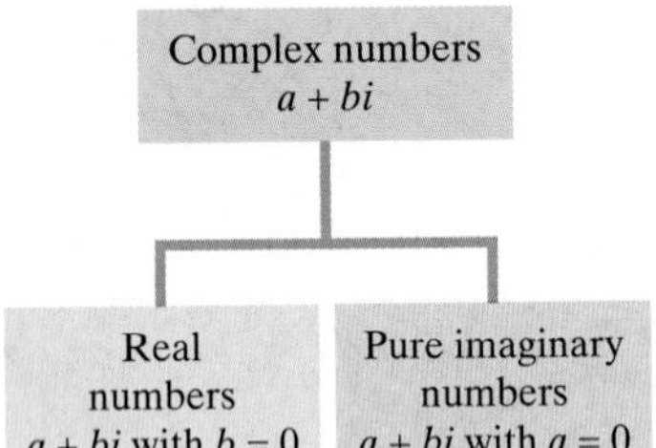


**Figure P.7** The complex number system

**Complex Numbers**

The set of all numbers in the form

$$a + bi$$

with real numbers $a$ and $b$, and $i$, the imaginary unit, is called the set of **complex numbers**. The real number $a$ is called the **real part**, and the real number $b$ is called the **imaginary part**, of the complex number $a + bi$. If $a = 0$ and $b \neq 0$, then the complex number $bi$ is called a **pure imaginary number** (Figure P.7).

A complex number is said to be **simplified** if it is expressed in the **standard form** $a + bi$. If $b$ is a radical, we usually write $i$ before $b$. For example, we write $7 + i\sqrt{5}$ rather than $7 + \sqrt{5}i$, which could easily be confused with $7 + \sqrt{5i}$.

Expressed in standard form, two complex numbers are equal if and only if their real parts are equal and their imaginary parts are equal.

**Equality of Complex Numbers**

$a + bi = c + di$ if and only if $a = c$ and $b = d$.

1 Add and subtract complex numbers.

## Operations with Complex Numbers

The form of a complex number $a + bi$ is like the binomial $a + bx$. Consequently, we can add, subtract, and multiply complex numbers using the same methods we used for binomials, remembering that $i^2 = -1$.

**Adding and Subtracting Complex Numbers**

1. $(a + bi) + (c + di) = (a + c) + (b + d)i$
   In words, this says that you add complex numbers by adding their real parts, adding their imaginary parts, and expressing the sum as a complex number.
2. $(a + bi) - (c + di) = (a - c) + (b - d)i$
   In words, this says that you subtract complex numbers by subtracting their real parts, subtracting their imaginary parts, and expressing the difference as a complex number.

**Study Tip**

The following examples, using the same integers as in Example 1, show how operations with complex numbers are just like operations with polynomials.

**a.** $(5 - 11x) + (7 + 4x)$
$= 12 - 7x$

**b.** $(-5 + 7x) - (-11 - 6x)$
$= -5 + 7x + 11 + 6x$
$= 6 + 13x$

### EXAMPLE 1 Adding and Subtracting Complex Numbers

Perform the indicated operations, writing the result in standard form.

**a.** $(5 - 11i) + (7 + 4i)$ **b.** $(-5 + 7i) - (-11 - 6i)$

**Solution**

**a.** $(5 - 11i) + (7 + 4i)$

$= 5 - 11i + 7 + 4i$ Remove the parentheses.

$= 5 + 7 - 11i + 4i$ Group real and imaginary terms.

$= (5 + 7) + (-11 + 4)i$

$= 12 - 7i$ Add real parts and add imaginary parts.

**b.** $(-5 + 7i) - (-11 - 6i)$

$= -5 + 7i + 11 + 6i$ Remove the parentheses.

$= -5 + 11 + 7i + 6i$ Group real and imaginary terms.

$= (-5 + 11) + (7 + 6)i$

$= 6 + 13i$

**Check Point 1** Add or subtract as indicated.

**a.** $(5 - 2i) + (3 + 3i)$ **b.** $(2 + 6i) - (12 - 4i)$

2 Multiply complex numbers.

Multiplication of complex numbers is performed the same way as multiplication of polynomials, using the distributive property and the FOIL method. After completing the multiplication, we replace $i^2$ with $-1$. This idea is illustrated in the next example.

## EXAMPLE 2 Multiplying Complex Numbers

Find the products: **a.** $4i(3 - 5i)$ **b.** $(7 - 3i)(-2 - 5i)$

### Solution

**a.**
$$\begin{aligned} 4i(3 - 5i) &= 4i(3) - 4i(5i) && \text{Distribute } 4i \text{ throughout the parentheses.} \\ &= 12i - 20i^2 && \text{Multiply.} \\ &= 12i - 20(-1) && \text{Replace } i^2 \text{ with } -1. \\ &= 20 + 12i && \text{Simplify to } 12i + 20 \text{ and write in standard form.} \end{aligned}$$

**b.** $(7 - 3i)(-2 - 5i)$

F O I L

$$\begin{aligned} &= -14 - 35i + 6i + 15i^2 && \text{Use the FOIL method.} \\ &= -14 - 35i + 6i + 15(-1) && i^2 = -1 \\ &= -14 - 15 - 35i + 6i && \text{Group real and imaginary terms.} \\ &= -29 - 29i && \text{Combine real and imaginary terms.} \end{aligned}$$

**Check Point 2** Find the products:

**a.** $7i(2 - 9i)$ **b.** $(5 + 4i)(6 - 7i)$

**3** Divide complex numbers.

**Complex Numbers on a Postage Stamp**

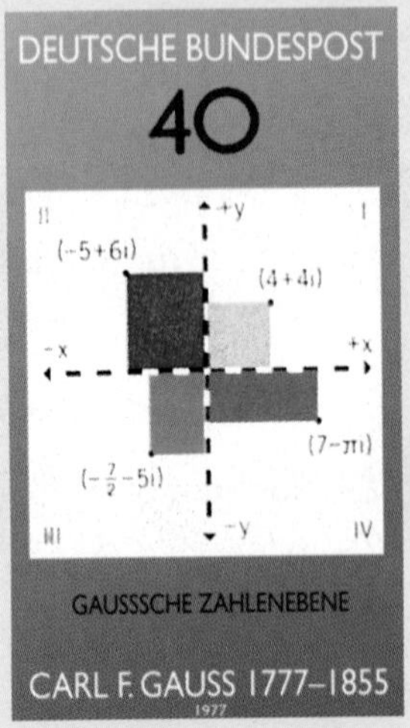


This stamp honors the work done by the German mathematician Carl Friedrich Gauss (1777–1855) with complex numbers. Gauss represented complex numbers as points in the plane.

## Complex Conjugates and Division

It is possible to multiply complex numbers and obtain a real number. This occurs when we multiply $a + bi$ and $a - bi$.

F O I L

$$\begin{aligned} (a + bi)(a - bi) &= a^2 - abi + abi - b^2i^2 && \text{Use the FOIL method.} \\ &= a^2 - b^2(-1) && i^2 = -1 \\ &= a^2 + b^2 && \text{Notice that this product eliminates } i. \end{aligned}$$

For the complex number $a + bi$, we define its **complex conjugate** to be $a - bi$. The multiplication of complex conjugates results in a real number.

**Conjugate of a Complex Number**

The **complex conjugate** of the number $a + bi$ is $a - bi$, and the complex conjugate of $a - bi$ is $a + bi$. The multiplication of complex conjugates gives a real number.

$$(a + bi)(a - bi) = a^2 + b^2$$
$$(a - bi)(a + bi) = a^2 + b^2$$

Complex conjugates are used to divide complex numbers. By multiplying the numerator and the denominator of the division by the complex conjugate of the denominator, you will obtain a real number in the denominator.

## EXAMPLE 3 Using Complex Conjugates to Divide Complex Numbers

Divide: $7 + 4i$ by $2 - 5i$.

**Solution** We first write the problem as $\frac{7 + 4i}{2 - 5i}$. The complex conjugate of the denominator, $2 - 5i$, is $2 + 5i$, so we multiply the numerator and the denominator by $2 + 5i$.

$$\frac{7 + 4i}{2 - 5i} = \frac{(7 + 4i)}{(2 - 5i)} \cdot \frac{(2 + 5i)}{(2 + 5i)}$$

Multiply the numerator and the denominator by the complex conjugate of the denominator.

F O I L

$$= \frac{14 + 35i + 8i + 20i^2}{2^2 + 5^2}$$

Use the FOIL method in the numerator and $(a - bi)(a + bi) = a^2 + b^2$ in the denominator.

$$= \frac{14 + 43i + 20(-1)}{29}$$

Replace $i^2$ by $-1$.

$$= \frac{-6 + 43i}{29}$$

Combine real terms in the numerator.

$$= -\frac{6}{29} + \frac{43}{29}i$$

Observe that the quotient is expressed in the standard form $a + bi$, with $a = -\frac{6}{29}$ and $b = \frac{43}{29}$.

**Check Point 3** Divide: $\frac{5 + 4i}{4 - 2i}$.

**4** Perform operations with square roots of negative numbers.

## Roots of Negative Numbers

The square of $4i$ and the square of $-4i$ both result in $-16$.

$$(4i)^2 = 16i^2 = 16(-1) = -16 \qquad (-4i)^2 = 16i^2 = -16$$

Consequently, in the complex number system $-16$ has two square roots, namely, $4i$ and $-4i$. We call $4i$ the **principal square root** of $-16$.

**Principal Square Root of a Negative Number**

For any positive number real number $b$, the **principal square root** of the negative number $-b$ is defined by

$$\sqrt{-b} = i\sqrt{b}.$$

## EXAMPLE 4 Operations Involving Square Roots of Negative Numbers

Perform the indicated operations and write the result in standard form:

**a.** $\sqrt{-18} - \sqrt{-8}$ **b.** $(-1 + \sqrt{-5})^2$ **c.** $\frac{-25 + \sqrt{-50}}{15}$

## Study Tip

Do not apply the properties

$$\sqrt{b}\sqrt{c} = \sqrt{bc}$$

and

$$\frac{\sqrt{b}}{\sqrt{c}} = \sqrt{\frac{b}{c}}$$

to the pure imaginary numbers because these properties can only be used when $b$ and $c$ are positive.

**Correct:**

$$\sqrt{-25}\sqrt{-4} = i\sqrt{25}\,i\sqrt{4} = (5i)(2i) = 10i^2 = 10(-1) = -10$$

**Incorrect:**

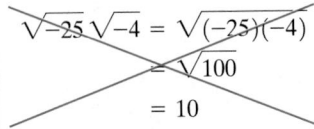

$$\sqrt{-25}\sqrt{-4} = \sqrt{(-25)(-4)} = \sqrt{100} = 10$$

One way to avoid confusion is to represent square roots of negative numbers in terms of $i$ before performing any operations.

**Solution** Begin by expressing all square roots of negative numbers in terms of $i$.

**a.** $\sqrt{-18} - \sqrt{-8} = i\sqrt{18} - i\sqrt{8} = i\sqrt{9 \cdot 2} - i\sqrt{4 \cdot 2}$
$= 3i\sqrt{2} - 2i\sqrt{2} = i\sqrt{2}$

$(A + B)^2 = A^2 + 2AB + B^2$

**b.** $(-1 + \sqrt{-5})^2 = (-1 + i\sqrt{5})^2 = (-1)^2 + 2(-1)(i\sqrt{5}) + (i\sqrt{5})^2$
$= 1 - 2i\sqrt{5} + 5i^2$
$= 1 - 2i\sqrt{5} + 5(-1)$
$= -4 - 2i\sqrt{5}$

**c.** $\dfrac{-25 + \sqrt{-50}}{15}$

$= \dfrac{-25 + i\sqrt{50}}{15}$ $\quad\sqrt{-b} = i\sqrt{b}$

$= \dfrac{-25 + 5i\sqrt{2}}{15}$ $\quad\sqrt{50} = \sqrt{25 \cdot 2} = 5\sqrt{2}$

$= \dfrac{-25}{15} + \dfrac{5i\sqrt{2}}{15}$ $\quad$ Write the complex number in standard form.

$= -\dfrac{5}{3} + i\dfrac{\sqrt{2}}{3}$ $\quad$ Simplify.

**Check Point 4** Perform the indicated operations and write the result in standard form.

**a.** $\sqrt{-27} + \sqrt{-48}$ **b.** $(-2 + \sqrt{-3})^2$ **c.** $\dfrac{-14 + \sqrt{-12}}{2}$

## EXERCISE SET P.7

### Practice Exercises

*In Exercises 1–8, add or subtract as indicated and write the result in standard form.*

**1.** $(7 + 2i) + (1 - 4i)$
**2.** $(-2 + 6i) + (4 - i)$
**3.** $(3 + 2i) - (5 - 7i)$
**4.** $(-7 + 5i) - (-9 - 11i)$
**5.** $6 - (-5 + 4i) - (-13 - 11i)$
**6.** $7 - (-9 + 2i) - (-17 - 6i)$
**7.** $8i - (14 - 9i)$
**8.** $15i - (12 - 11i)$

*In Exercises 9–20, find each product and write the result in standard form.*

**9.** $-3i(7i - 5)$
**10.** $-8i(2i - 7)$
**11.** $(-5 + 4i)(3 + 7i)$
**12.** $(-4 - 8i)(3 + 9i)$
**13.** $(7 - 5i)(-2 - 3i)$
**14.** $(8 - 4i)(-3 + 9i)$
**15.** $(3 + 5i)(3 - 5i)$
**16.** $(2 + 7i)(2 - 7i)$
**17.** $(-5 + 3i)(-5 - 3i)$
**18.** $(-7 - 4i)(-7 + 4i)$
**19.** $(2 + 3i)^2$
**20.** $(5 - 2i)^2$

*In Exercises 21–28, divide and express the result in standard form.*

**21.** $\dfrac{2}{3 - i}$
**22.** $\dfrac{3}{4 + i}$
**23.** $\dfrac{2i}{1 + i}$
**24.** $\dfrac{5i}{2 - i}$
**25.** $\dfrac{8i}{4 - 3i}$
**26.** $\dfrac{-6i}{3 + 2i}$
**27.** $\dfrac{2 + 3i}{2 + i}$
**28.** $\dfrac{3 - 4i}{4 + 3i}$

*In Exercises 29–44, perform the indicated operations and write the result in standard form.*

**29.** $\sqrt{-64} - \sqrt{-25}$
**30.** $\sqrt{-81} - \sqrt{-144}$
**31.** $5\sqrt{-16} + 3\sqrt{-81}$
**32.** $5\sqrt{-8} + 3\sqrt{-18}$
**33.** $(-2 + \sqrt{-4})^2$
**34.** $(-5 - \sqrt{-9})^2$
**35.** $(-3 - \sqrt{-7})^2$
**36.** $(-2 + \sqrt{-11})^2$

37. $\frac{-8 + \sqrt{-32}}{24}$

38. $\frac{-12 + \sqrt{-28}}{32}$

39. $\frac{-6 - \sqrt{-12}}{48}$

40. $\frac{-15 - \sqrt{-18}}{33}$

41. $\sqrt{-8}(\sqrt{-3} - \sqrt{5})$

42. $\sqrt{-12}(\sqrt{-4} - \sqrt{2})$

43. $(3\sqrt{-5})(-4\sqrt{-12})$

44. $(3\sqrt{-7})(2\sqrt{-8})$

### Writing in Mathematics

45. What is $i$?

46. Explain how to add complex numbers. Provide an example with your explanation.

47. Explain how to multiply complex numbers and give an example.

48. What is the complex conjugate of $2 + 3i$? What happens when you multiply this complex number by its complex conjugate?

49. Explain how to divide complex numbers. Provide an example with your explanation.

50. A stand-up comedian uses algebra in some jokes, including one about a telephone recording that announces "You have just reached an imaginary number. Please multiply by $i$ and dial again." Explain the joke.

*Explain the error in Exercises 51–52.*

51. $\sqrt{-9} + \sqrt{-16} = \sqrt{-25} = i\sqrt{25} = 5i$

52. $(\sqrt{-9})^2 = \sqrt{-9} \cdot \sqrt{-9} = \sqrt{81} = 9$

### Critical Thinking Exercises

53. Which one of the following is true?

**a.** Some irrational numbers are not complex numbers.

**b.** $(3 + 7i)(3 - 7i)$ is an imaginary number.

**c.** $\frac{7 + 3i}{5 + 3i} = \frac{7}{5}$

**d.** In the complex number system, $x^2 + y^2$ (the sum of two squares) can be factored as $(x + yi)(x - yi)$.

*In Exercises 54–56, perform the indicated operations and write the result in standard form.*

54. $(8 + 9i)(2 - i) - (1 - i)(1 + i)$

55. $\frac{4}{(2 + i)(3 - i)}$

56. $\frac{1 + i}{1 + 2i} + \frac{1 - i}{1 - 2i}$

57. Evaluate $x^2 - 2x + 2$ for $x = 1 + i$.

## SECTION P.8 *Graphs and Graphing Utilities*

### Objectives

1. Plot points in the rectangular coordinate system.
2. Graph equations in the rectangular coordinate system.
3. Interpret information about a graphing utility's viewing rectangle.
4. Use a graph to determine intercepts.
5. Find the distance between two points.
6. Find the midpoint of a line segment.
7. Interpret information given by graphs.

The beginning of the seventeenth century was a time of innovative ideas and enormous intellectual progress in Europe. English theatergoers enjoyed a succession of exciting new plays by Shakespeare. William Harvey proposed the radical notion that the heart was a pump for blood rather than the center of emotion. Galileo, with his new-fangled invention called the telescope, supported the theory of Polish astronomer Copernicus that the sun, not the Earth, was the center of the solar system. Monteverdi was writing the world's first grand operas. French mathematicians Pascal and Fermat invented a new field of mathematics called probability theory.

Into this arena of intellectual electricity stepped French aristocrat René Descartes (1596–1650). Descartes, propelled by the creativity surrounding him, developed a new branch of mathematics that brought together algebra and geometry in a unified way—a way that visualized numbers as points on a graph, equations as geometric figures, and geometric figures as equations. This new branch of mathematics, called *analytic geometry*, established Descartes as one of the founders of modern thought and among the most original mathematicians and philosophers of any age. We begin this section by looking at Descartes's deceptively simple idea, called the **rectangular coordinate system** or (in his honor) the **Cartesian coordinate system**.

**1** Plot points in the rectangular coordinate system.

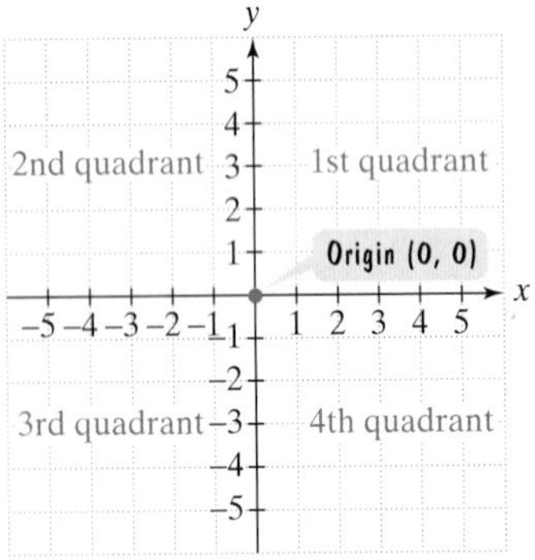


**Figure P.8** The rectangular coordinate system

## Points and Ordered Pairs

Descartes used two number lines that intersect at right angles at their zero points, as shown in Figure P.8. The horizontal number line is the **$x$-axis**. The vertical number line is the **$y$-axis**. The point of intersection of these axes is the **origin**. Positive numbers are shown to the right and above the origin. Negative numbers are shown to the left and below the origin. The axes divide the plane into four quarters, called **quadrants**. The points located on the axes are not in any quadrant.

Each point in the rectangular coordinate system corresponds to an **ordered pair** of real numbers, $(x, y)$. Examples of such pairs are $(4, 2)$ and $(-5, -3)$. The first number in each pair, called the **$x$-coordinate**, denotes the distance and direction from the origin along the $x$-axis. The second number, called the **$y$-coordinate**, denotes vertical distance and direction along a line parallel to the $y$-axis or along the $y$-axis itself.

Figure P.9 shows how we **plot**, or locate, the points corresponding to the ordered pairs $(4, 2)$ and $(-5, -3)$. We plot $(4, 2)$ by going 4 units from 0 to the right along the $x$-axis. Then we go 2 units up parallel to the $y$-axis. We plot $(-5, -3)$ by going 5 units from 0 to the left along the $x$-axis and 3 units down parallel to the $y$-axis. The phrase "the point corresponding to the ordered pair $(-5, -3)$" is often abbreviated as "the point $(-5, -3)$."

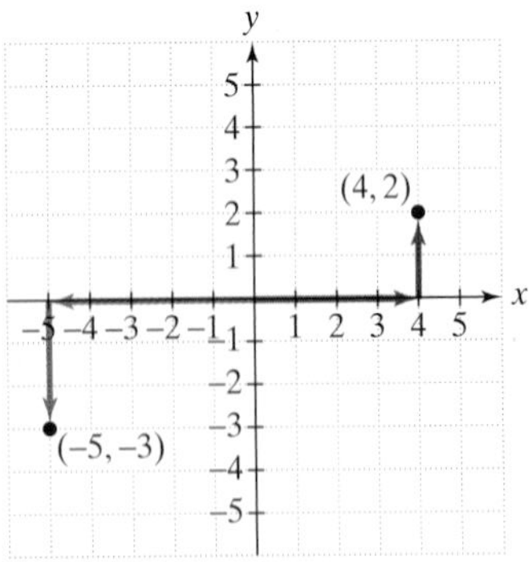


**Figure P.9** Plotting $(4, 2)$ and $(-5, -3)$

### EXAMPLE 1 Plotting Points in the Rectangular Coordinate System

Plot the points $A(-3, 5)$, $B(2, -4)$, $C(5, 0)$, $D(-5, -3)$, $E(0, 4)$, and $F(0, 0)$.

**Solution** See Figure P.10. We plot the points in the following way:

| | |
|---|---|
| $A(-3, 5)$: | 3 units left, 5 units up |
| $B(2, -4)$: | 2 units right, 4 units down |
| $C(5, 0)$: | 5 units right, 0 units up or down |
| $D(-5, -3)$: | 5 units left, 3 units down |
| $E(0, 4)$: | 0 units right or left, 4 units up |
| $F(0, 0)$: | 0 units right or left, 0 units up or down |

The origin is represented by $(0, 0)$.

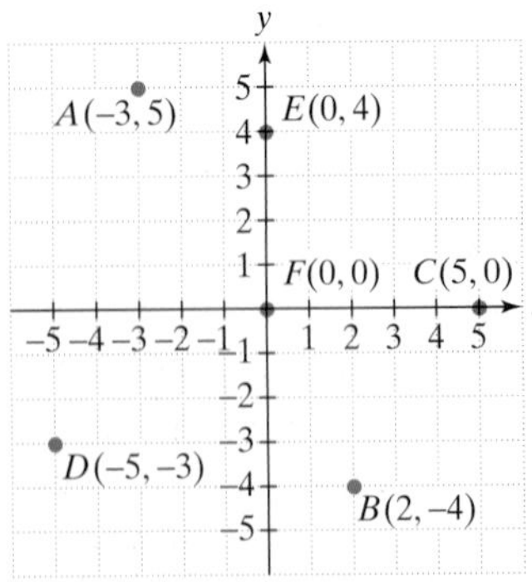


**Figure P.10** Plotting points

**Check Point 1** Plot the points

$A(-2, 4)$, $B(4, -2)$, $C(-3, 0)$, and $D(0, -3)$.

**2** Graph equations in the rectangular coordinate system.

## Graphs of Equations

A relationship between two quantities can be expressed as an **equation in two variables**, such as

$$y = x^2 - 4.$$

A **solution** to this equation is an ordered pair of real numbers with the following property: When the $x$-coordinate is substituted for $x$ and the $y$-coordinate is substituted for $y$ in the equation, we obtain a true statement. For example, if we let $x = 3$, then $y = 3^2 - 4 = 9 - 4 = 5$. The ordered pair $(3, 5)$ is a solution to the equation $y = x^2 - 4$. We also say that $(3, 5)$ **satisfies** the equation.

We can generate as many ordered-pair solutions as desired to $y = x^2 - 4$ by substituting numbers for $x$ and then finding the values for $y$. The **graph of the equation** is the set of all points whose coordinates satisfy the equation.

One method for graphing an equation such as $y = x^2 - 4$ is the **point-plotting method**. First, we find several ordered pairs that are solutions to the equation. Next, we plot these ordered pairs as points in the rectangular coordinate system. Finally, we connect the points with a smooth curve or line. This often gives us a picture of all ordered pairs that satisfy the equation.

### EXAMPLE 2 Graphing an Equation Using the Point-Plotting Method

Graph $y = x^2 - 4$. Select integers for $x$, starting with $-3$ and ending with 3.

**Solution** For each value of $x$ we find the corresponding value for $y$.

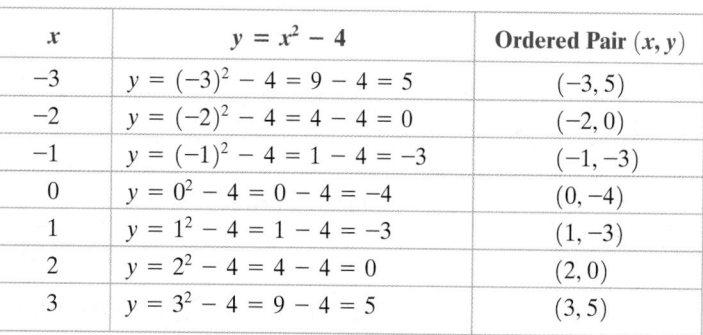

| $x$ | $y = x^2 - 4$ | **Ordered Pair** $(x, y)$ |
|---|---|---|
| $-3$ | $y = (-3)^2 - 4 = 9 - 4 = 5$ | $(-3, 5)$ |
| $-2$ | $y = (-2)^2 - 4 = 4 - 4 = 0$ | $(-2, 0)$ |
| $-1$ | $y = (-1)^2 - 4 = 1 - 4 = -3$ | $(-1, -3)$ |
| 0 | $y = 0^2 - 4 = 0 - 4 = -4$ | $(0, -4)$ |
| 1 | $y = 1^2 - 4 = 1 - 4 = -3$ | $(1, -3)$ |
| 2 | $y = 2^2 - 4 = 4 - 4 = 0$ | $(2, 0)$ |
| 3 | $y = 3^2 - 4 = 9 - 4 = 5$ | $(3, 5)$ |

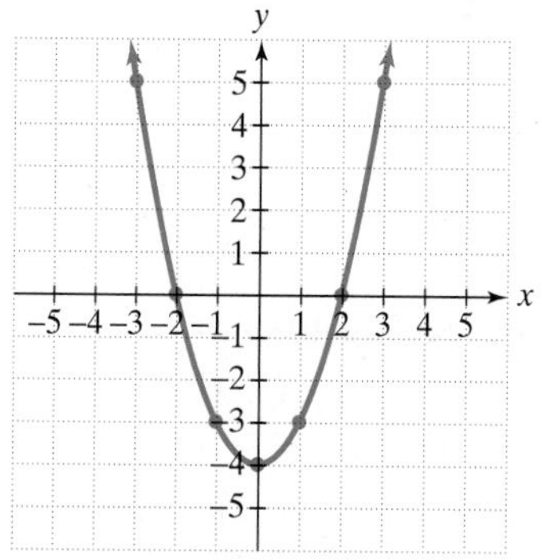


**Figure P.11** The graph of $y = x^2 - 4$

Now we plot the seven points and join them with a smooth curve, as shown in Figure P.11. The graph of $y = x^2 - 4$ is a curve where the part of the graph to the right of the $y$-axis is a reflection of the part to the left of it and vice versa. The arrows on the left and the right of the curve indicate that it extends indefinitely in both directions.

**Check Point 2** Graph $y = 2x - 4$. Select integers for $x$, starting with $-1$ and ending with 3.

**3** Interpret information about a graphing utility's viewing rectangle.

Graphing calculators or graphing software packages for computers are referred to as **graphing utilities** or graphers. A graphing utility is a powerful tool that quickly generates the graph of an equation in two variables. Figure P.12 on page 74 shows two such graphs for the equations in Example 2 and the checkpoint example.

What differences do you notice between these graphs and the graphs that we (and you) drew by hand? They do seem a bit "jittery." Arrows do not appear

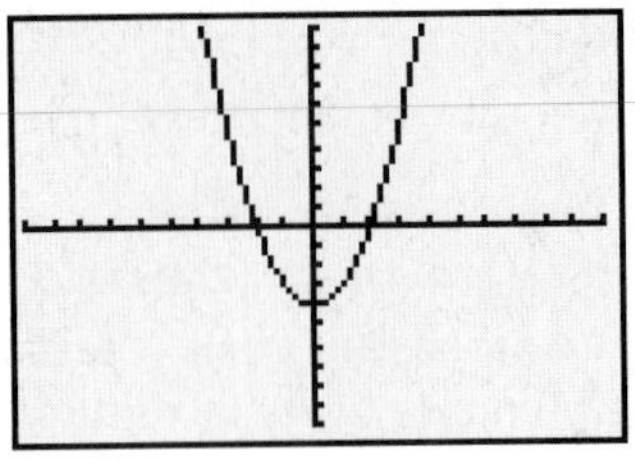

**Figure P.12(a)**
The graph of $y = x^2 - 4$

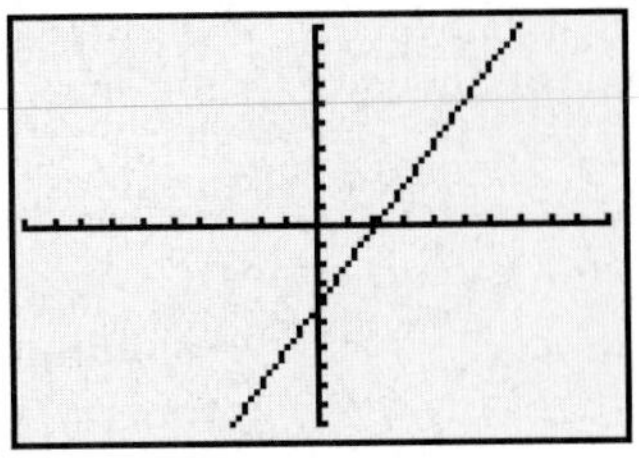

**Figure P.12(b)**
The graph of $y = 2x - 4$

on the left and right ends of the graphs. Furthermore, numbers are not given along the axes. For both graphs in Figure P.12, the $x$-axis extends from $-10$ to 10 and the $y$-axis also extends from $-10$ to 10. The distance represented by each consecutive tick mark is one unit. We say that the **viewing rectangle** is $[-10, 10, 1]$ by $[-10, 10, 1]$.

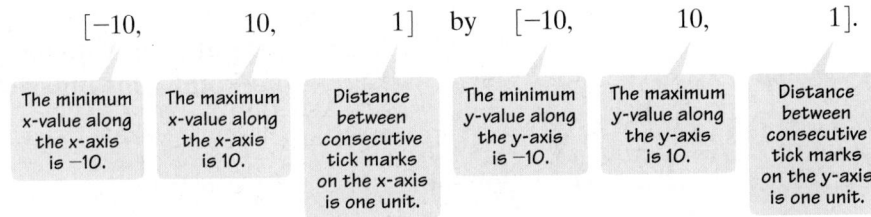

$[-10,$ $10,$ $1]$ by $[-10,$ $10,$ $1]$.

- The minimum $x$-value along the $x$-axis is $-10$.
- The maximum $x$-value along the $x$-axis is 10.
- Distance between consecutive tick marks on the $x$-axis is one unit.
- The minimum $y$-value along the $y$-axis is $-10$.
- The maximum $y$-value along the $y$-axis is 10.
- Distance between consecutive tick marks on the $y$-axis is one unit.

To graph an equation in $x$ and $y$ using a graphing utility, enter the equation and specify the size of the viewing rectangle. The size of the viewing rectangle sets minimum and maximum values for both the $x$- and $y$-axes. Enter these values, as well as the values between consecutive tick marks, on the respective axes. The $[-10, 10, 1]$ by $[-10, 10, 1]$ viewing rectangle used in Figure P.12 is called the **standard viewing rectangle**.

## EXAMPLE 3 Understanding the Viewing Rectangle

What is the meaning of a $[-2, 3, 0.5]$ by $[-10, 20, 5]$ viewing rectangle?

**Solution** We begin with $[-2, 3, 0.5]$, which describes the $x$-axis. The minimum $x$-value is $-2$ and the maximum $x$-value is 3. The distance between consecutive tick marks is 0.5.

Next, consider $[-10, 20, 5]$, which describes the $y$-axis. The minimum $y$-value is $-10$ and the maximum $y$-value is 20. The distance between consecutive tick marks is 5.

Figure P.13 illustrates a $[-2, 3, 0.5]$ by $[-10, 20, 5]$ viewing rectangle. To make things clearer, we've placed numbers by each tick mark. These numbers do not appear on the axes when you use a graphing utility to graph an equation.

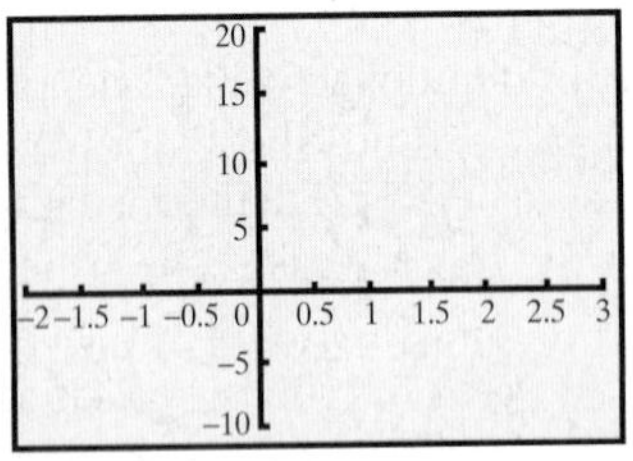


**Figure P.13** A $[-2, 3, 0.5]$ by $[-10, 20, 5]$ viewing rectangle

**Check Point 3** What is the meaning of a $[-100, 100, 50]$ by $[-100, 100, 10]$ viewing rectangle? Create a figure like the one in Figure P.13 that illustrates this viewing rectangle.

On most graphing utilities, the display screen is two-thirds as high as it is wide. By using a square setting, you can make the $x$ and $y$ tick marks be equally spaced. (This does not occur in the standard viewing rectangle.) Graphing utilities can also *zoom in* and *zoom out*. When you zoom in, you see a smaller portion of the graph, but you do so in greater detail. When you zoom out, you see a larger portion of the graph. Thus, zooming out may help you to develop a better understanding of the overall character of the graph. With practice, you will become more comfortable with graphing equations in two variables using your graphing utility. You will also develop a better sense of the size of the viewing rectangle that will reveal needed information about a particular graph.

**4** Use a graph to determine intercepts.

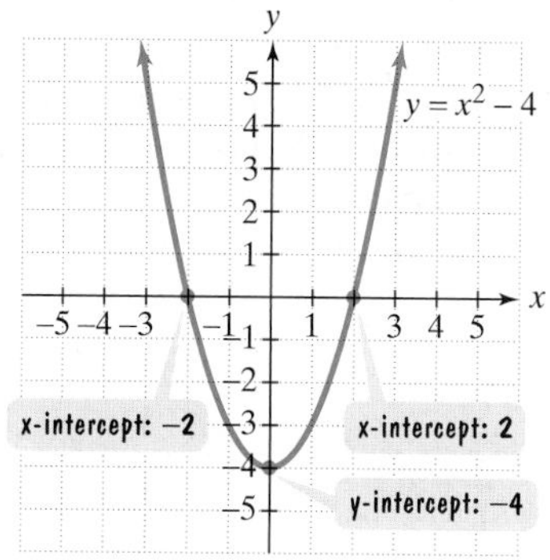


**Figure P.14** Intercepts of $y = x^2 - 4$

## Intercepts

An ***x*-intercept** of a graph is an $x$-coordinate of the point where the graph intersects the $x$-axis. For example, look at the graph of $y = x^2 - 4$ in Figure P.14. The graph crosses the $x$-axis at $(-2, 0)$ and $(2, 0)$. Thus, the $x$-intercepts are $-2$ and 2. **The *y*-coordinate corresponding to a graph's *x*-intercept is always zero.**

A ***y*-intercept** of a graph is a $y$-coordinate of the point where the graph intersects the $y$-axis. The graph of $y = x^2 - 4$ in Figure P.14 shows that the graph crosses the $y$-axis at $(0, -4)$. Thus, the $y$-intercept is $-4$. **The *x*-coordinate corresponding to a graph's *y*-intercept is always zero.**

Figure P.15 illustrates that a graph may have no intercepts or several intercepts.

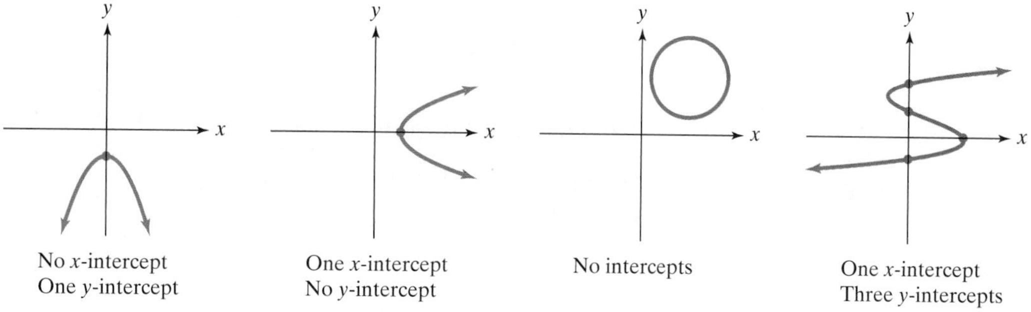


**Figure P.15**

**5** Find the distance between two points.

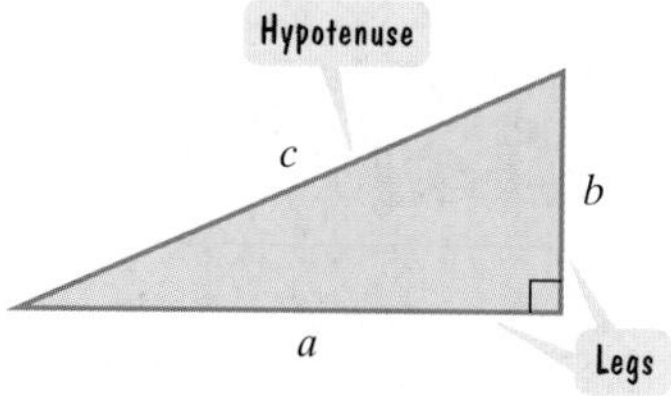


**Figure P.16** The Pythagorean Theorem: $a^2 + b^2 = c^2$

## The Distance Formula

We can use the **Pythagorean Theorem** to develop a formula that gives the distance between any two points in the rectangular coordinate system. Recall that the Pythagorean Theorem involves a triangle with a right (90°) angle, called a **right triangle**. The side opposite the right angle is called the **hypotenuse**. The other two sides are called the **legs**. In Figure P.16, $a$ and $b$ represent the lengths of the two legs of the triangle. Likewise, $c$ represents the length of the hypotenuse. Based on this figure, we express the Pythagorean Theorem as

$$a^2 + b^2 = c^2.$$

In any right triangle, the sum of the squares of the lengths of the legs is the square of the length of the hypotenuse.

Now we are ready to find the distance between the two points $P_1(x_1, y_1)$ and $P_2(x_2, y_2)$ in the rectangular coordinate system. The two points are illustrated in Figure P.17 on the next page.

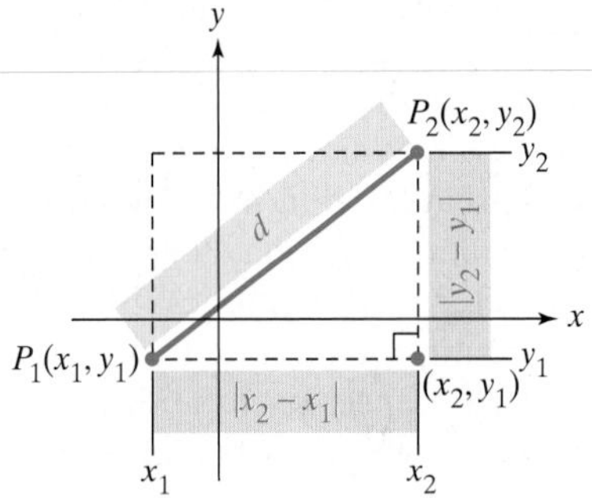


**Figure P.17**

The distance that we need to find is represented by $d$ and shown in blue. Notice that the distance between two points on the dashed horizontal line is the absolute value of the difference between the $x$-coordinates of the two points. This distance, $|x_2 - x_1|$, is shown in pink. Similarly, the distance between two points on the dashed vertical line is the absolute value of the difference between the $y$-coordinates of the two points. This distance, $|y_2 - y_1|$, is also shown in pink.

Because the dashed lines are horizontal and vertical, a right triangle is formed. Thus, we can use the Pythagorean Theorem to find distance $d$. By the Pythagorean Theorem,

$$d^2 = |x_2 - x_1|^2 + |y_2 - y_1|^2$$
$$d = \sqrt{|x_2 - x_1|^2 + |y_2 - y_1|^2}$$
$$d = \sqrt{(x_2 - x_1)^2 + (y_2 - y_1)^2}.$$

This result is the **distance formula**.

**The Distance Formula**

The distance $d$ between the points $(x_1, y_1)$ and $(x_2, y_2)$ in the rectangular coordinate system is

$$d = \sqrt{(x_2 - x_1)^2 + (y_2 - y_1)^2}.$$

When using the distance formula, it does not matter which point you call $(x_1, y_1)$ and which you call $(x_2, y_2)$.

## EXAMPLE 4 Using the Distance Formula

Find the distance between $(-1, -3)$ and $(2, 3)$.

**Solution** Letting $(x_1, y_1) = (-1, -3)$ and $(x_2, y_2) = (2, 3)$, we obtain

$d = \sqrt{(x_2 - x_1)^2 + (y_2 - y_1)^2}$ Use the distance formula.

$= \sqrt{[2 - (-1)]^2 + [3 - (-3)]^2}$ Substitute the given values.

$= \sqrt{(2 + 1)^2 + (3 + 3)^2}$ Perform subtractions within the grouping symbols.

$= \sqrt{3^2 + 6^2}$

$= \sqrt{9 + 36}$ Square 3 and 6.

$= \sqrt{45}$ Add.

$= 3\sqrt{5} \approx 6.7$ $\sqrt{45} = \sqrt{9 \cdot 5} = \sqrt{9}\sqrt{5} = 3\sqrt{5}$

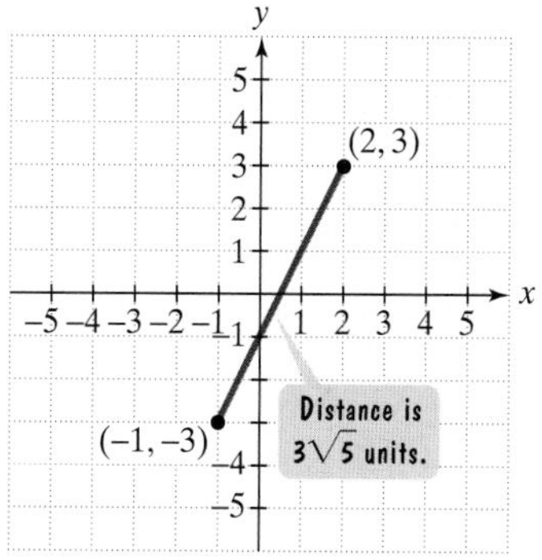


**Figure P.18** Finding the distance between two points

The distance between the given points is $3\sqrt{5}$ units, or approximately 6.7 units. The situation is illustrated in Figure P.18.

**Check Point 4** Find the distance between $(2, -2)$ and $(5, 2)$.

**6** Find the midpoint of a line segment.

## The Midpoint Formula

The distance formula can be used to prove a formula for finding the midpoint of a line segment between two given points. The formula is as follows.

> **The Midpoint Formula**
>
> Consider a line segment whose endpoints are $(x_1, y_1)$ and $(x_2, y_2)$. The coordinates of the segment's midpoint are
>
> $$\left(\frac{x_1 + x_2}{2}, \frac{y_1 + y_2}{2}\right).$$
>
> To find the midpoint, take the average of the two $x$-coordinates and of the two $y$-coordinates.

## EXAMPLE 5 Using the Midpoint Formula

Find the midpoint of the line segment with endpoints $(1, -6)$ and $(-8, -4)$.

**Solution** To find the coordinates of the midpoint, we average the coordinates of the endpoints.

$$\text{Midpoint} = \left(\frac{1 + (-8)}{2}, \frac{-6 + (-4)}{2}\right) = \left(\frac{-7}{2}, \frac{-10}{2}\right) = \left(-\frac{7}{2}, -5\right)$$

Average the $x$-coordinates. Average the $y$-coordinates.

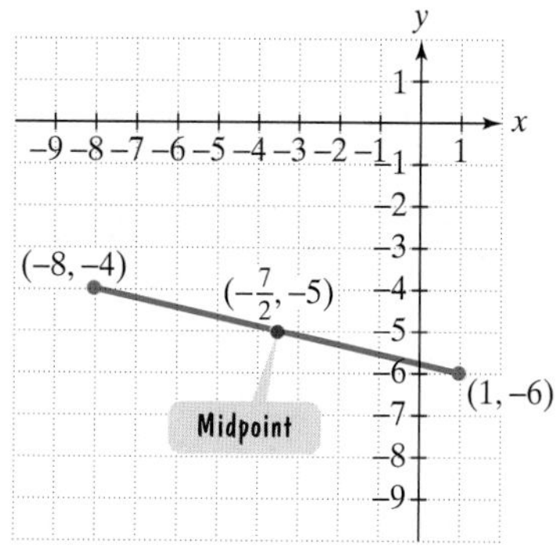


**Figure P.19** Finding a line segment's midpoint

Figure P.19 illustrates that the point $\left(-\frac{7}{2}, -5\right)$ is midway between the points $(1, -6)$ and $(-8, -4)$.

**Check Point 5** Find the midpoint of the line segment with endpoints $(1, 2)$ and $(7, -3)$.

**7** Interpret information given by graphs.

## Interpreting Information Given by Graphs

Singers Ricky Martin and Jennifer Lopez, television journalist Soledad O'Brien, boxer Oscar De La Hoya, Internet entrepreneur Carlos Cardona, actor John Leguizamo, and political organizer Luigi Crespo are members of a generation of young Hispanics that is changing the way America looks, feels, thinks, eats, dances, and votes. There are 31 million Hispanics in the United States, pumping \$300 billion a year into the economy. By 2050, the Hispanic population is expected to reach 96 million—an increase of more than 200 percent. Hispanics are also younger than the rest of the nation: A third are under 18. The graph in Figure P.20 shows

**Average Age of U.S. Whites, Blacks, and Hispanics**

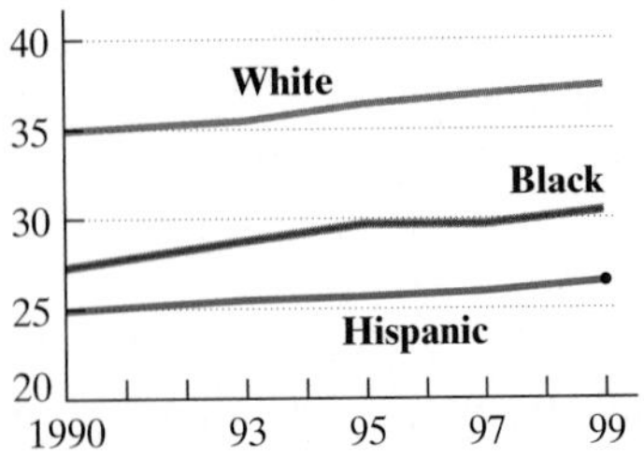


**Figure P.20** *Source:* U.S. Census Bureau

the average age of whites, African Americans, and Americans of Hispanic origin.

Magazines and newspapers often display information using **line graphs** like those in Figure P.20. Line graphs are often used to illustrate trends over time. Some measure of time, such as months or years, frequently appears on the horizontal axis. Amounts are generally listed on the vertical axis.

A line graph displays information in the first quadrant of a rectangular coordinate system. By identifying points on line graphs and their coordinates, you can interpret specific information given by the graph. For example, we've shown a point on the far right of the line graph in Figure P.20 for Hispanics. The point is directly above 1999 on the horizontal axis, so its $x$-coordinate is 1999. The point lies between 25 and 30, at approximately 27, in relation to the horizontal axis. Thus, its $y$-coordinate is 27. The coordinates (1999, 27) tell us that in 1999 the average age of U.S. Hispanics was approximately 27.

## EXAMPLE 6 Interpreting Information Given by Graphs

The graph in Figure P.21(a) shows the ticket sales from concert tours in North America from 1990 through 1997. For the period shown, in which year did sales reach a maximum? Estimate the sales for that year.

**Concert Ticket Sales in North America**

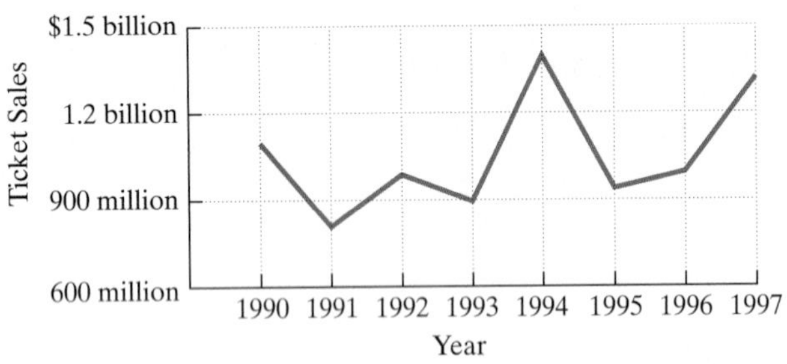


*Source:* Pollstar

**Figure P.21(a)**

**Concert Ticket Sales in North America**

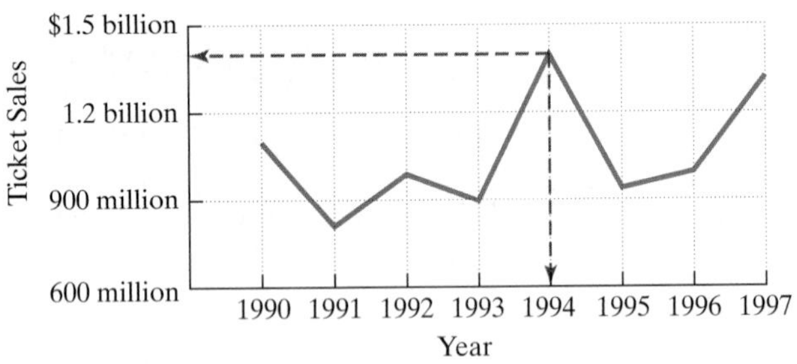


*Source:* Pollstar

**Figure P.21(b)**

**Solution** Maximum sales correspond to the highest point on the graph. This point is identified in Figure P.21(b). The coordinates of this point are approximately (1994, 1.4). This means that in 1994 ticket sales reached a maximum. The sales for that year were approximately $1.4 billion.

**Check Point 6** Use the graph in Figure P.21(a) to determine in which year sales reached a minimum. Estimate the sales for that year.

## EXERCISE SET P.8

### Practice Exercises

*In Exercises 1–10, plot the given point in a rectangular coordinate system.*

**1.** (1, 4)
**2.** (2, 5)
**3.** (−2, 3)
**4.** (−1, 4)
**5.** (−3, −5)
**6.** (−4, −2)
**7.** (4, −1)
**8.** (3, −2)
**9.** (−4, 0)
**10.** (0, −3)

*Graph each equation in Exercises 11–22. Let $x = -3, -2, -1, 0, 1, 2,$ and 3.*

**11.** $y = x^2 - 2$

**12.** $y = x^2 + 2$

**13.** $y = x - 2$

**14.** $y = x + 2$

**15.** $y = 2x + 1$

**16.** $y = 2x - 4$

**17.** $y = -\frac{1}{2}x$

**18.** $y = -\frac{1}{2}x + 2$

**19.** $y = x^3$

**20.** $y = x^3 - 1$

**21.** $y = |x|$

**22.** $y = |x| + 2$

*In Exercises 23–26, match the viewing rectangle with the correct figure. Then label the tick marks in the figure to illustrate this viewing rectangle.*

**23.** [−5, 5, 1] by [−5, 5, 1]

**24.** [−10, 10, 2] by [−4, 4, 2]

**25.** [−20, 80, 10] by [−30, 70, 10]

**26.** [−40, 40, 20] by [−1000, 1000, 100]

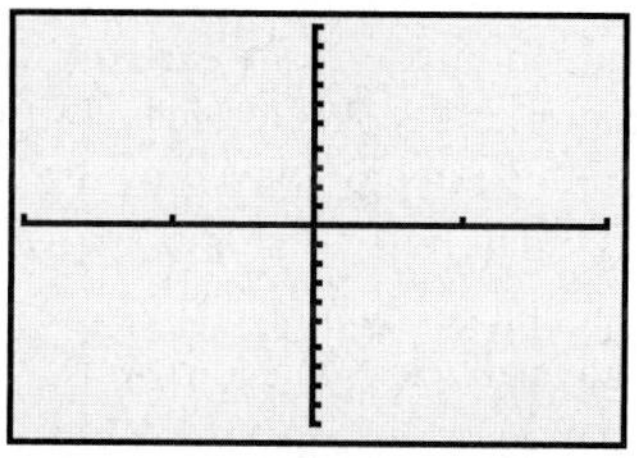
(a)

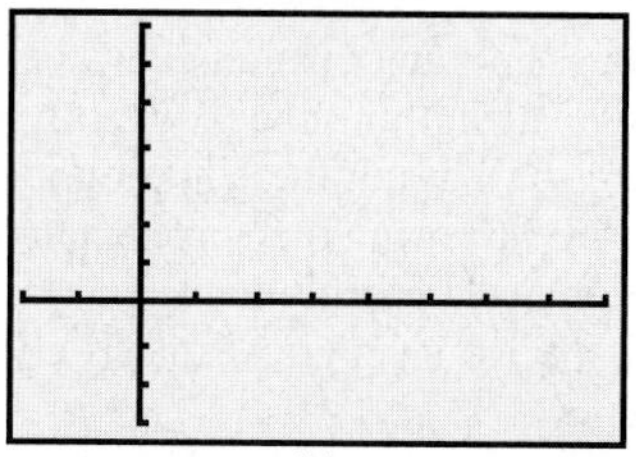
(b)

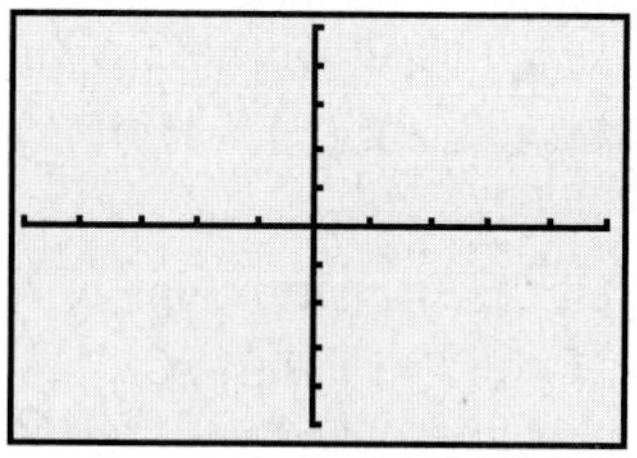
(c)

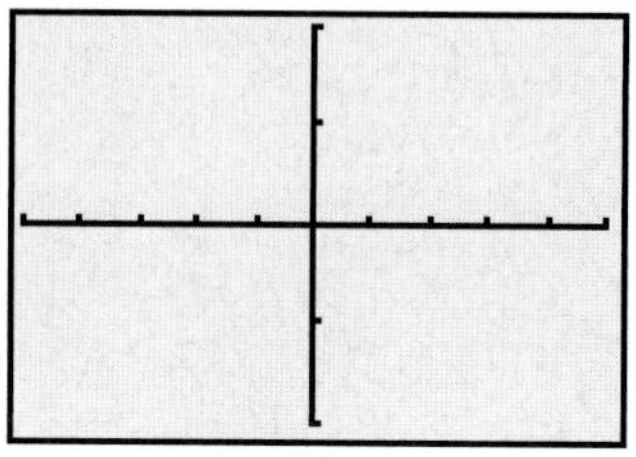
(d)

*In Exercises 27–32, use the graph and a. determine the x-intercepts, if any. b. Determine the y-intercepts, if any. For each graph, tick marks along the axes represent one unit each.*

**27.**

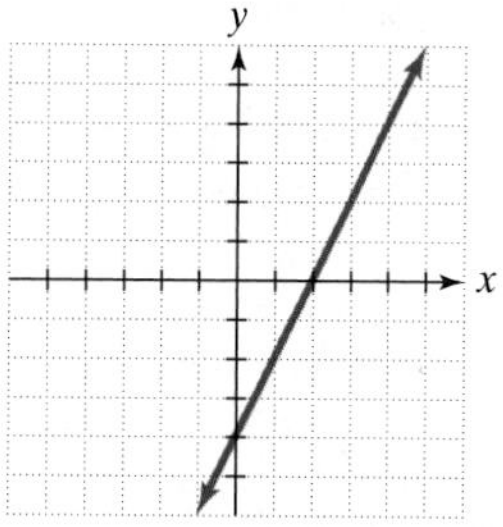


**28.**

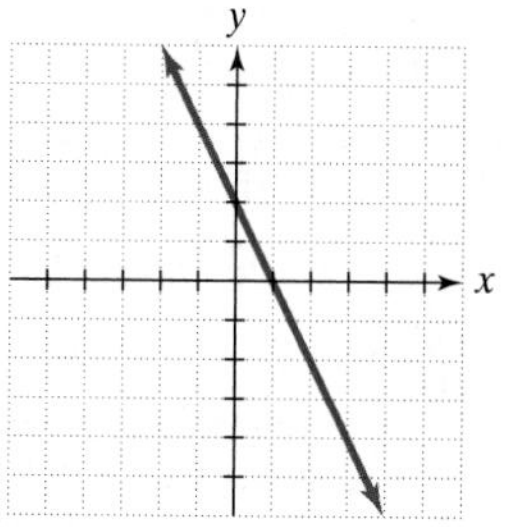


**29.**

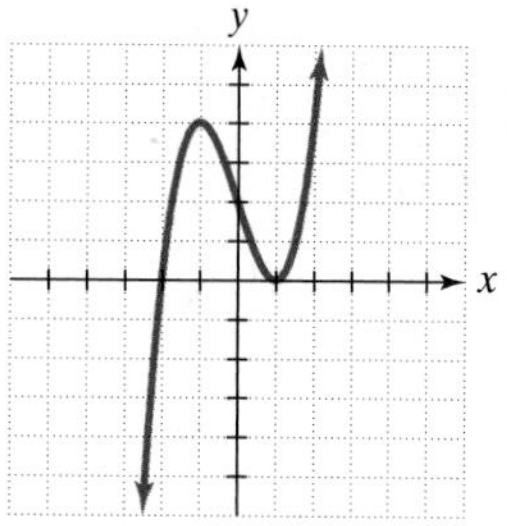


**30.**

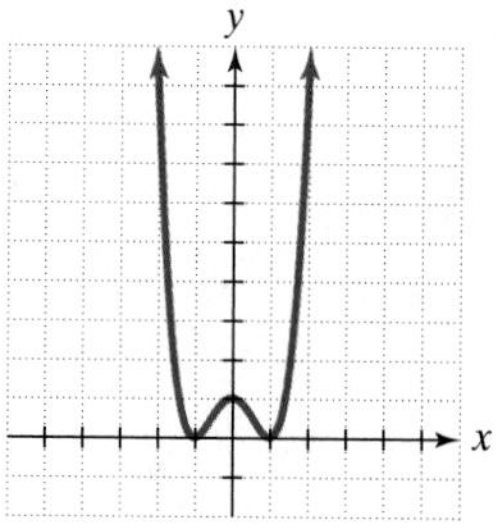


**31.**

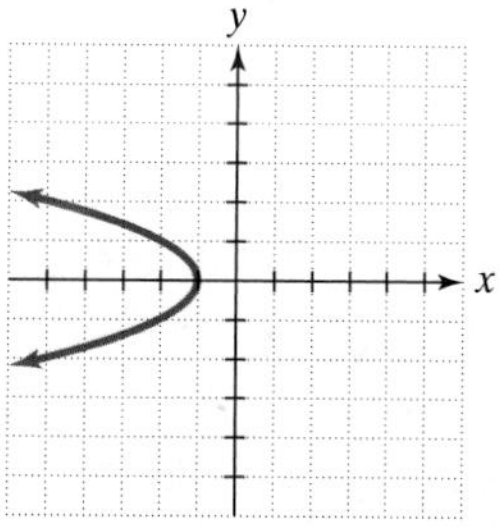


**32.**

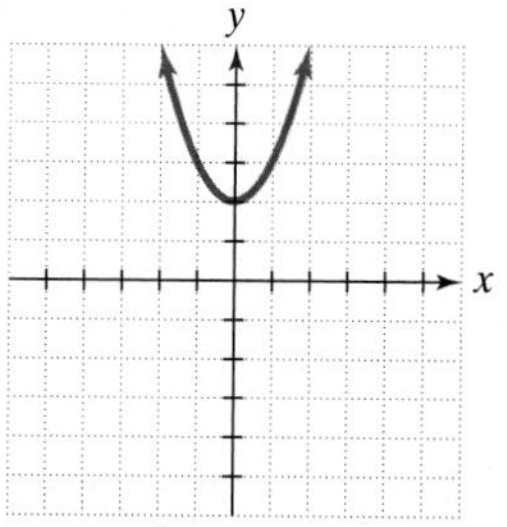


*In Exercises 33–38, a. Plot the points. b. Find the distance between the points. c. Find the midpoint of the line segment joining the points.*

**33.** (4, −3), (−6, 2)

**34.** (6, −3), (−4, −5)

**35.** (3, 2), (6, 7)

**36.** (−3, 6), (3, 4)

**37.** (1, −2), (−3, 6)

**38.** (5, 7), (2, 3)

## Application Exercises

*The line graph shows the U.S. unemployment rate from 1960 through 1997. Use the graph to solve Exercises 39–42.*

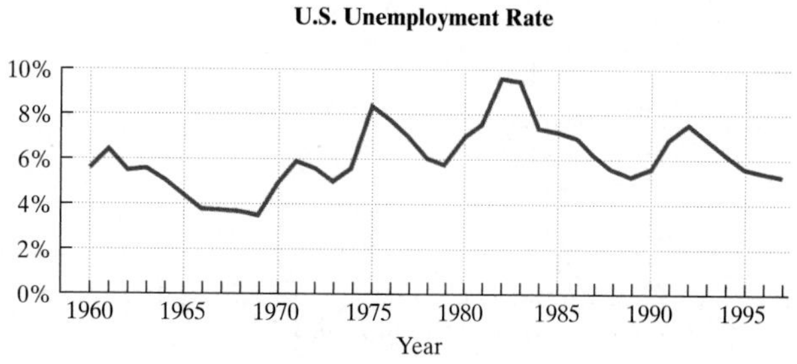


*Source:* U.S. Bureau of Labor Statistics

**39.** Find an estimate for the unemployment rate in 1970.

**40.** Find an estimate for the unemployment rate in 1980.

**41.** For the period shown, when did the unemployment rate reach a maximum? What is a reasonable estimate for the rate during that year?

**42.** For the period shown, when did the unemployment rate reach a minimum? What is a reasonable estimate for the rate during that year?

*The line graph shows the population of the United States from 1970 to 2000 for people under 16. In Exercises 43–46, find (or estimate) the coordinates of the given point. Then interpret the coordinates in terms of the information given by the graph.*

**U.S. Population for People Under 16**

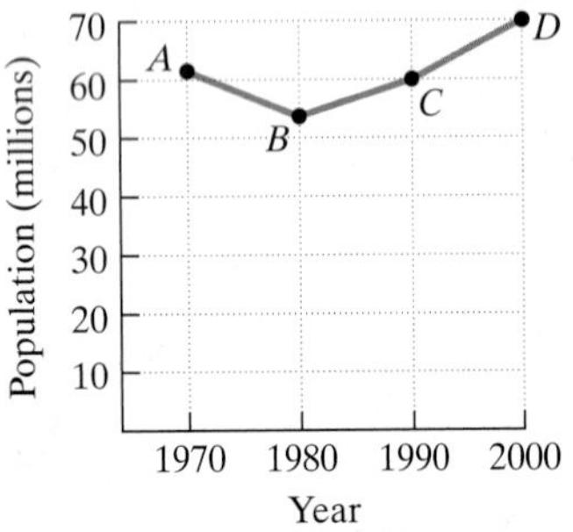


*Source:* U.S. Census Bureau

**43.** *A* **44.** *B* **45.** *C* **46.** *D*

**47.** The graph shows the height ($y$, in feet) of a ball dropped from the top of the Empire State Building at different times.

**a.** What is a reasonable estimate of the height of the Empire State Building?

**b.** What is a reasonable estimate, to the nearest tenth of a second, of how long it takes for the ball to hit the ground?

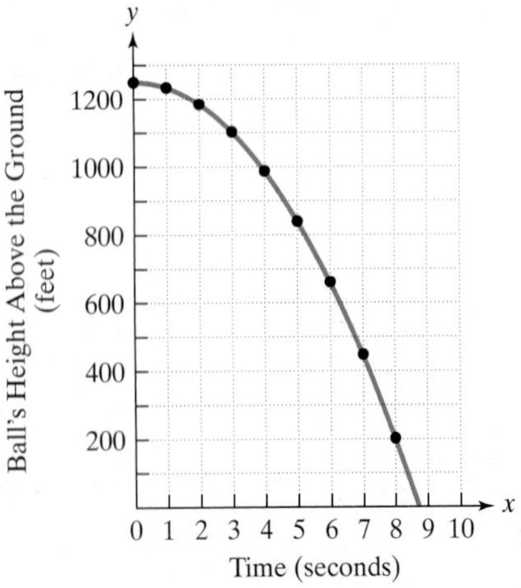


## Writing in Mathematics

**48.** What is the rectangular coordinate system?

**49.** Explain how to plot a point in the rectangular coordinate system. Give an example with your explanation.

**50.** Explain why $(5, -2)$ and $(-2, 5)$ do not represent the same point.

**51.** Explain how to graph an equation in the rectangular coordinate system.

**52.** What does a $[-20, 2, 1]$ by $[-4, 5, 0.5]$ viewing rectangle mean?

**53.** How is the distance formula used to find the distance between two given points?

**54.** How do you find the midpoint of a line segment if its endpoints are known?

## Technology Exercises

**55.** Use a graphing utility to verify each of your hand-drawn graphs in Exercises 11–22. Experiment with the range setting to make the graph displayed by the graphing utility resemble your hand-drawn graph as much as possible.

**56.** How many people are employed by the executive branch of the U.S. government? The equation

$$y = 0.09x^4 - 3.78x^3 + 50.06x^2 - 212.32x + 3101.16$$

approximates the number of civilians employed by the executive branch, in thousands, $x$ years after 1979. Use a graphing utility to graph the equation in a $[0, 20, 1]$ by $[2500, 3500, 500]$ viewing rectangle. Then describe something about the relationship between $x$ and $y$ that is revealed by looking at the graph that is not obvious from the equation.

*A graph of an equation is a* complete graph *if it shows all of the important features of the graph. Use a graphing utility to graph the equations in Exercises 57–60 in each of the given viewing rectangles. Then choose which viewing rectangle gives a complete graph.*

**57.** $y = x^2 + 10$

**a.** $[-5, 5, 1]$ by $[-5, 5, 1]$

**b.** $[-10, 10, 1]$ by $[-10, 10, 1]$

**c.** $[-10, 10, 1]$ by $[-50, 50, 1]$

**58.** $y = 0.1x^4 - x^3 + 2x^2$

**a.** $[-5, 5, 1]$ by $[-8, 2, 1]$

**b.** $[-10, 10, 1]$ by $[-10, 10, 1]$

**c.** $[-8, 16, 1]$ by $[-16, 8, 1]$

**59.** $y = \sqrt{x + 18}$

**a.** $[-10, 10, 1]$ by $[-10, 10, 1]$

**b.** $[-50, 50, 10]$ by $[-10, 10, 1]$

**c.** $[-10, 10, 1]$ by $[-50, 50, 10]$

**60.** $y = x^3 - 30x + 20$

**a.** $[-10, 10, 1]$ by $[-10, 10, 1]$

**b.** $[-10, 10, 1]$ by $[-50, 50, 10]$

**c.** $[-10, 10, 1]$ by $[-50, 100, 10]$

## Critical Thinking Exercises

**61.** Which one of the following is true?

**a.** If the coordinates of a point satisfy the inequality $xy > 0$, then $(x, y)$ must be in quadrant I.

**b.** The ordered pair $(2, 5)$ satisfies $3y - 2x = -4$.

**c.** If a point is on the $x$-axis, it is neither up nor down, so $x = 0$.

**d.** None of the above is true.

**62.** Show that the points $A(1, 1 + d)$, $B(3, 3 + d)$, and $C(6, 6 + d)$ are collinear (lie along a straight line) by showing that the distance from $A$ to $B$ plus the distance from $B$ to $C$ equals the distance from $A$ to $C$.

**63.** Prove the midpoint formula by using the following procedure.

**a.** Show that the distance between $(x_1, y_1)$ and $\left(\frac{x_1 + x_2}{2}, \frac{y_1 + y_2}{2}\right)$ is equal to the distance between $(x_2, y_2)$ and $\left(\frac{x_1 + x_2}{2}, \frac{y_1 + y_2}{2}\right)$.

**b.** Use the procedure from Exercise 62 and the distances from part (a) to show that the points $(x_1, y_1)$, $\left(\frac{x_1 + x_2}{2}, \frac{y_1 + y_2}{2}\right)$, and $(x_2, y_2)$ are collinear.

# CHAPTER SUMMARY, REVIEW, AND TEST

## Summary: Basic Formulas

### Definition of Absolute Value

$$|x| = \begin{cases} x & \text{if } x \ge 0 \\ -x & \text{if } x < 0 \end{cases}$$

### Distance Between Points *a* and *b* on a Number Line

$$|a - b| \quad \text{or} \quad |b - a|$$

### Properties of Algebra

| | |
|---|---|
| Commutative | $a + b = b + a, \quad ab = ba$ |
| Associative | $(a + b) + c = a + (b + c)$<br>$(ab)c = a(bc)$ |
| Distributive | $a(b + c) = ab + ac$ |
| Identity | $a + 0 = a \quad a \cdot 1 = a$ |
| Inverse | $a + (-a) = 0 \quad a \cdot \frac{1}{a} = 1, a \neq 0$ |

### Properties of Exponents

$$b^{-n} = \frac{1}{b^n}, \quad b^0 = 1, \quad b^m \cdot b^n = b^{m+n},$$

$$(b^m)^n = b^{mn}, \quad \frac{b^m}{b^n} = b^{m-n}, \quad (ab)^n = a^n b^n, \quad \left(\frac{a}{b}\right)^n = \frac{a^n}{b^n}$$

### Product and Quotient Rules for *n*th Roots

$$\sqrt[n]{a} \cdot \sqrt[n]{b} = \sqrt[n]{ab} \qquad \frac{\sqrt[n]{a}}{\sqrt[n]{b}} = \sqrt[n]{\frac{a}{b}}$$

### Rational Exponents

$$a^{1/n} = \sqrt[n]{a}, \quad a^{-1/n} = \frac{1}{a^{1/n}} = \frac{1}{\sqrt[n]{a}},$$

$$a^{m/n} = (\sqrt[n]{a})^m = \sqrt[n]{a^m}, \quad a^{-m/n} = \frac{1}{a^{m/n}}$$

### Special Products

$$(A + B)(A - B) = A^2 - B^2$$
$$(A + B)^2 = A^2 + 2AB + B^2$$
$$(A - B)^2 = A^2 - 2AB + B^2$$
$$(A + B)^3 = A^3 + 3A^2B + 3AB^2 + B^3$$
$$(A - B)^3 = A^3 - 3A^2B + 3AB^2 - B^3$$

### Factoring Formulas

$$A^2 - B^2 = (A + B)(A - B)$$
$$A^2 + 2AB + B^2 = (A + B)^2$$
$$A^2 - 2AB + B^2 = (A - B)^2$$
$$A^3 + B^3 = (A + B)(A^2 - AB + B^2)$$
$$A^3 - B^3 = (A - B)(A^2 + AB + B^2)$$

### Complex Numbers

$$i = \sqrt{-1} \text{ and } i^2 = -1, \quad (a + bi)(a - bi) = a^2 + b^2$$

### Distance and Midpoint Formulas

$$d = \sqrt{(x_2 - x_1)^2 + (y_2 - y_1)^2}$$

$$\text{midpoint} = \left(\frac{x_1 + x_2}{2}, \frac{y_1 + y_2}{2}\right)$$

## Review Exercises

*You can use these review exercises, like the review exercises at the end of each chapter, to test your understanding of the chapter's topics. However, you can also use these exercises as a prerequisite test to check your mastery of the fundamental algebra skills needed in this book.*

### P.1

**1.** Consider the set

$$\{-17, -\tfrac{9}{13}, 0, 0.75, \sqrt{2}, \pi, \sqrt{81}\}$$

List all numbers from the set that are a. natural numbers, b. whole numbers, c. integers, d. rational numbers, e. irrational numbers.

*In Exercises 2–4, rewrite each expressions without absolute value bars.*

**2.** $|-103|$ **3.** $|\sqrt{2} - 1|$

**4.** $|3 - \sqrt{17}|$

**5.** Express the distance between the numbers $-17$ and 4 using absolute value. Then evaluate the absolute value.

*In Exercises 6–7, evaluate each algebraic expression for the given value of the variable.*

**6.** $\frac{5}{9}(F - 32);\ F = 68$ **7.** $\frac{8(x + 5)}{3x + 8},\ x = 2$

*In Exercises 8–13, state the name of the property illustrated.*

**8.** $3 + 17 = 17 + 3$ **9.** $(6 \cdot 3) \cdot 9 = 6 \cdot (3 \cdot 9)$

**10.** $\sqrt{3}(\sqrt{5} + \sqrt{3}) = \sqrt{15} + 3$

**11.** $(6 \cdot 9) \cdot 2 = 2 \cdot (6 \cdot 9)$

**12.** $\sqrt{3}(\sqrt{5} + \sqrt{3}) = (\sqrt{5} + \sqrt{3})\sqrt{3}$

**13.** $(3 \cdot 7) + (4 \cdot 7) = (4 \cdot 7) + (3 \cdot 7)$

*In Exercises 14–15, simplify each algebraic expression.*

**14.** $3(7x - 5y) - 2(4y - x + 1)$

**15.** $\frac{1}{5}(5x) + [(3y) + (-3y)] - (-x)$

### P.2

*Evaluate each exponential expression in Exercises 16–19.*

**16.** $(-3)^3(-2)^2$ **17.** $2^{-4} + 4^{-1}$

**18.** $5^{-3} \cdot 5$ **19.** $\frac{3^3}{3^6}$

*Simplify each exponential expression in Exercises 20–23.*

**20.** $(-2x^4y^3)^3$ **21.** $(-5x^3y^2)(-2x^{-11}y^{-2})$

**22.** $(2x^3)^{-4}$ **23.** $\frac{7x^5y^6}{28x^{15}y^{-2}}$

*In Exercises 24–25, write each number in decimal notation.*

**24.** $3.74 \times 10^4$ **25.** $7.45 \times 10^{-5}$

*In Exercises 26–27, write each number in scientific notation.*

**26.** 3,590,000 **27.** 0.00725

*In Exercises 28–29, perform the indicated operation and write the answer in decimal notation.*

**28.** $(3 \times 10^3)(1.3 \times 10^2)$ **29.** $\frac{6.9 \times 10^3}{3 \times 10^5}$

**30.** If you earned \$1 million per year ($\$10^6$), how long would it take to accumulate \$1 billion ($\$10^9$)?

**31.** If the population of the United States is $2.7 \times 10^8$ and each person spends about \$150 per year going to the movies (or renting movies), express the total annual spending on movies in scientific notation.

### P.3

*Use the product rule to simplify the expressions in Exercises 32–35.*

**32.** $\sqrt{300}$ **33.** $\sqrt{12x^2}$

**34.** $\sqrt{10x} \cdot \sqrt{2x}$ **35.** $\sqrt{r^3}$

*Use the quotient rule to simplify the expressions in Exercises 36–37.*

**36.** $\sqrt{\frac{121}{4}}$ **37.** $\frac{\sqrt{96x^3}}{\sqrt{2x}}$

*In Exercises 38–40, add or subtract terms whenever possible.*

**38.** $7\sqrt{5} + 13\sqrt{5}$ **39.** $2\sqrt{50} + 3\sqrt{8}$

**40.** $4\sqrt{72} - 2\sqrt{48}$

*In Exercises 41–44, rationalize the denominator.*

**41.** $\frac{30}{\sqrt{5}}$ **42.** $\frac{\sqrt{2}}{\sqrt{3}}$

**43.** $\frac{5}{6 + \sqrt{3}}$ **44.** $\frac{14}{\sqrt{7} - \sqrt{5}}$

*Evaluate each expression in Exercises 45–48 or indicate that the root is not a real number.*

**45.** $\sqrt[3]{125}$ **46.** $\sqrt[5]{-32}$

**47.** $\sqrt[4]{-125}$ **48.** $\sqrt[4]{(-5)^4}$

*Simplify the radical expressions in Exercises 49–53.*

**49.** $\sqrt[3]{81}$ **50.** $\sqrt[3]{y^5}$

**51.** $\sqrt[4]{8} \cdot \sqrt[4]{10}$ **52.** $4\sqrt[3]{16} + 5\sqrt[3]{2}$

**53.** $\frac{\sqrt[4]{32x^5}}{\sqrt[4]{16x}}$

*In Exercises 54–59, evaluate each expression.*

**54.** $16^{1/2}$ **55.** $25^{-1/2}$

**56.** $125^{1/3}$ **57.** $27^{-1/3}$

**58.** $64^{2/3}$ **59.** $27^{-4/3}$

*In Exercises 60–62, simplify using properties of exponents.*

**60.** $(5x^{2/3})(4x^{1/4})$

**61.** $\dfrac{15x^{3/4}}{5x^{1/2}}$

**62.** $(125x^6)^{2/3}$

**63.** Simplify by reducing the index of the radical: $\sqrt[6]{y^3}$.

## P.4

*In Exercises 64–65, perform the indicated operations. Write the resulting polynomial in standard form and indicate its degree.*

**64.** $(-6x^3 + 7x^2 - 9x + 3) + (14x^3 + 3x^2 - 11x - 7)$

**65.** $(13x^4 - 8x^3 + 2x^2) - (5x^4 - 3x^3 + 2x^2 - 6)$

*In Exercises 66–72, find each product.*

**66.** $(3x - 2)(4x^2 + 3x - 5)$

**67.** $(3x - 5)(2x + 1)$

**68.** $(4x + 5)(4x - 5)$

**69.** $(2x + 5)^2$

**70.** $(3x - 4)^2$

**71.** $(2x + 1)^3$

**72.** $(5x - 2)^3$

*In Exercises 73–79, find each product.*

**73.** $(x + 7y)(3x - 5y)$

**74.** $(3x - 5y)^2$

**75.** $(3x^2 + 2y)^2$

**76.** $(7x + 4y)(7x - 4y)$

**77.** $(a - b)(a^2 + ab + b^2)$

**78.** $[5y - (2x + 1)][5y + (2x + 1)]$

**79.** $(x + 2y + 4)^2$

## P.5

*In Exercises 80–95, factor completely, or state that the polynomial is prime.*

**80.** $15x^3 + 3x^2$

**81.** $x^2 - 11x + 28$

**82.** $15x^2 - x - 2$

**83.** $64 - x^2$

**84.** $x^2 + 16$

**85.** $3x^4 - 9x^3 - 30x^2$

**86.** $20x^7 - 36x^3$

**87.** $x^3 - 3x^2 - 9x + 27$

**88.** $16x^2 - 40x + 25$

**89.** $x^4 - 16$

**90.** $y^3 - 8$

**91.** $x^3 + 64$

**92.** $3x^4 - 12x^2$

**93.** $27x^3 - 125$

**94.** $x^5 - x$

**95.** $x^3 + 5x^2 - 2x - 10$

*In Exercises 96–98, factor and simplify each algebraic expression.*

**96.** $16x^{-3/4} + 32x^{1/4}$

**97.** $(x^2 - 4)(x^2 + 3)^{1/2} - (x^2 - 4)^2(x^2 + 3)^{3/2}$

**98.** $12x^{-1/2} + 6x^{-3/2}$

## P.6

*In Exercises 99–101, simplify each rational expression. Also, list all numbers that must be excluded from the domain.*

**99.** $\dfrac{x^3 + 2x^2}{x + 2}$

**100.** $\dfrac{x^2 + 3x - 18}{x^2 - 36}$

**101.** $\dfrac{x^2 + 2x}{x^2 + 4x + 4}$

*In Exercises 102–104, multiply or divide as indicated.*

**102.** $\dfrac{x^2 + 6x + 9}{x^2 - 4} \cdot \dfrac{x + 3}{x - 2}$

**103.** $\dfrac{6x + 2}{x^2 - 1} \div \dfrac{3x^2 + x}{x - 1}$

**104.** $\dfrac{x^2 - 5x - 24}{x^2 - x - 12} \div \dfrac{x^2 - 10x + 16}{x^2 + x - 6}$

*In Exercises 105–108, add or subtract as indicated.*

**105.** $\dfrac{2x - 7}{x^2 - 9} - \dfrac{x - 10}{x^2 - 9}$

**106.** $\dfrac{3x}{x + 2} + \dfrac{x}{x - 2}$

**107.** $\dfrac{x}{x^2 - 9} + \dfrac{x - 1}{x^2 - 5x + 6}$

**108.** $\dfrac{4x - 1}{2x^2 + 5x - 3} - \dfrac{x + 3}{6x^2 + x - 2}$

*In Exercises 109–111, simplify each fractional expression.*

**109.** $\dfrac{3 + \dfrac{12}{x}}{1 - \dfrac{16}{x^2}}$

**110.** $\dfrac{3 - \dfrac{1}{x + 3}}{3 + \dfrac{1}{x + 3}}$

**111.** $\dfrac{\sqrt{25 - x^2} + \dfrac{x^2}{\sqrt{25 - x^2}}}{25 - x^2}$

## P.7

*In Exercises 112–121, perform the indicated operations and write the result in standard form.*

**112.** $(8 - 3i) - (17 - 7i)$

**113.** $4i(3i - 2)$

**114.** $(7 - 5i)(2 + 3i)$

**115.** $(3 - 4i)^2$

**116.** $(7 + 8i)(7 - 8i)$

**117.** $\dfrac{6}{5 + i}$

**118.** $\dfrac{3 + 4i}{4 - 2i}$

**119.** $\sqrt{-32} - \sqrt{-18}$

**120.** $(-2 + \sqrt{-100})^2$

**121.** $\dfrac{4 + \sqrt{-8}}{2}$

## P.8

*Graph each equation in Exercises 122–124. Let $x = -3, -2, -1, 0, 1, 2,$ and $3$.*

**122.** $y = 2x - 2$

**123.** $y = x^2 - 3$

**124.** $y = x$

**125.** What does a $[-20, 40, 10]$ by $[-5, 5, 1]$ viewing rectangle mean? Draw axes with tick marks and label the tick marks to illustrate this viewing rectangle.

*In Exercises 126–128, use the graph and determine the x-intercepts, if any, and the y-intercepts, if any. For each graph, tick marks along the axes represent one unit each.*

**126.**

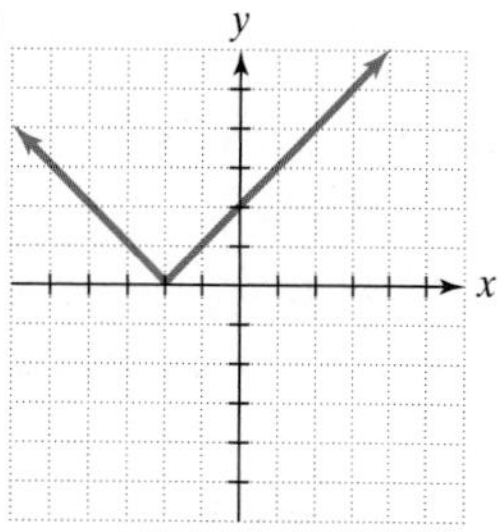


**127.**

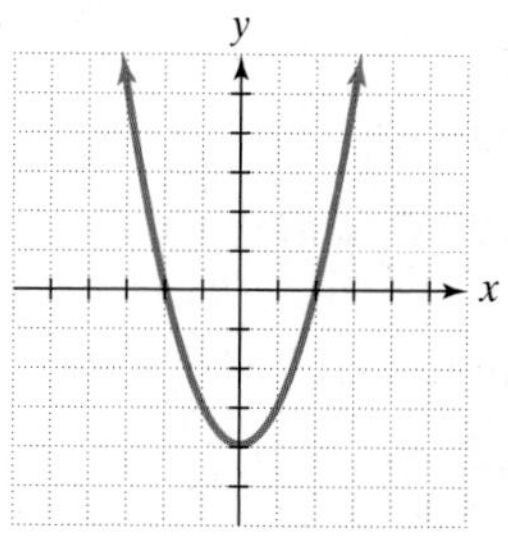

**128.**

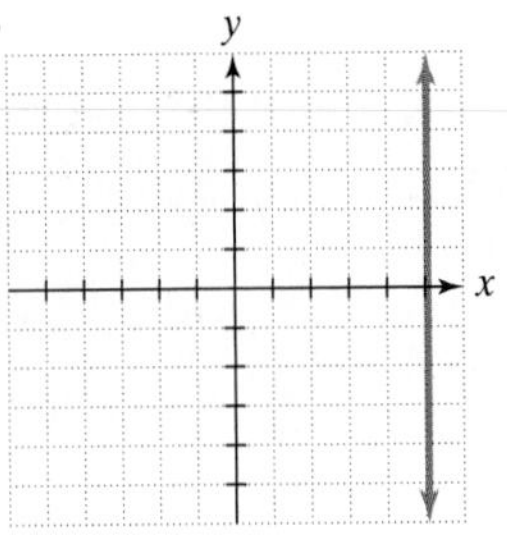


*In Exercises 129–130, a. Plot the points. b. Find the distance between the points. c. Find the midpoint of the line segment joining the points.*

**129.** $(-1, 0), (2, 4)$ **130.** $(2, -3), (4, 2)$

**131.** The line graphs show the number of applicants to U.S. law schools and medical schools.

**a.** For the period shown, when did the number of law school applicants reach a maximum? What is a reasonable estimate for the number of applicants during that year?

**b.** Find an estimate for the number of medical school applicants in 1990.

**c.** Estimate the coordinates of point $A$. Then interpret the coordinates in terms of the information given by the graph.

**Number of Applicants to U.S. Law and Medical Schools**

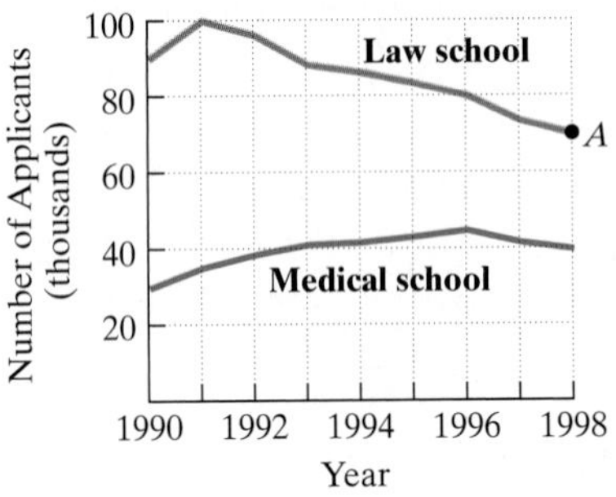


*Source:* U.S. Education Department

## Chapter P Test

**1.** List all the rational numbers in this set.

$$\{-7, -\tfrac{4}{5}, 0, 0.25, \sqrt{3}, \sqrt{4}, \tfrac{22}{7}, \pi\}$$

*In Exercises 2–3, state the name of the property illustrated.*

**2.** $3(2 + 5) = 3(5 + 2)$ **3.** $6(7 + 4) = 6 \cdot 7 + 6 \cdot 4$

**4.** Express in scientific notation: 0.00076.

*Simplify each expression in Exercises 5–11.*

**5.** $9(10x - 2y) - 5(x - 4y + 3)$

**6.** $\dfrac{30x^3y^4}{6x^9y^{-4}}$ **7.** $\sqrt{6r}\sqrt{3r}$

**8.** $4\sqrt{50} - 3\sqrt{18}$ **9.** $\dfrac{3}{5 + \sqrt{2}}$

**10.** $\sqrt[3]{16x^4}$ **11.** $\dfrac{x^2 + 2x - 3}{x^2 - 3x + 2}$

**12.** Evaluate: $27^{-5/3}$

*In Exercises 13–14, find each product.*

**13.** $(2x - 5)(x^2 - 4x + 3)$ **14.** $(5x + 3y)^2$

*In Exercises 15–20, factor completely.*

**15.** $x^2 - 9x + 18$ **16.** $x^3 + 2x^2 + 3x + 6$

**17.** $25x^2 - 9$ **18.** $36x^2 - 84x + 49$

**19.** $y^3 - 125$

**20.** $(x^2 - 9)(x^2 + 1)^{-1/2} - (x^2 - 9)(x^2 + 1)^{-3/2}$

*In Exercises 21–25, perform the operations and simplify, if possible.*

**21.** $\dfrac{2x + 8}{x - 3} \div \dfrac{x^2 + 5x + 4}{x^2 - 9}$ **22.** $\dfrac{x}{x + 3} + \dfrac{5}{x - 3}$

**23.** $\dfrac{2x + 3}{x^2 - 7x + 12} - \dfrac{2}{x - 3}$ **24.** $\dfrac{1 - \dfrac{x}{x + 2}}{1 + \dfrac{1}{x}}$

**25.** $\dfrac{2x\sqrt{x^2 + 5} - \dfrac{2x^3}{\sqrt{x^2 + 5}}}{x^2 + 5}$

*In Exercises 26–28, perform the indicated operations and write the result in standard form.*

**26.** $(6 - 7i)(2 + 5i)$ **27.** $\dfrac{5}{2 - i}$

**28.** $2\sqrt{-49} + 3\sqrt{-64}$

**29.** Graph $y = x^2 - 4$ by letting $x$ equal integers from $-3$ through 3.

**30.** Find the distance between $(2, 9)$ and $(6, 3)$ in simplified radical form.

# Equations, Inequalities, and Mathematical Models

# Chapter 1

Formulas like those that describe the height a child will attain as an adult are frequently obtained from actual data. Formulas can be used to explain what is happening in the present and to make predictions about what might occur in the future. Knowing how to create and use formulas will help you recognize patterns, logic, and order in a world that can appear chaotic to the untrained eye. In many ways, algebra will provide you with a new way of looking at your world.

Sitting in the biology department office, you overhear two of the professors discussing the possible adult heights of their respective children. Looking at the blackboard that they've been writing on, you see that there are formulas that can estimate the height a child will attain as an adult. If the child is $x$ years old and $h$ inches tall, that child's adult height, $H$, in inches, is approximated by one of the following formulas.

Girls: $$H = \frac{h}{0.00028x^3 - 0.0071x^2 + 0.0926x + 0.3524}$$

Boys: $$H = \frac{h}{0.00011x^3 - 0.0032x^2 + 0.0604x + 0.3796}$$

## SECTION 1.1 *Linear Equations*

### Objectives

1. Solve linear equations in one variable.
2. Solve equations with constants in denominators.
3. Solve equations with variables in denominators.
4. Recognize identities, conditional equations, and inconsistent equations.

Unfortunately, many of us have been fined for driving over the speed limit. The amount of the fine depends on how fast we are speeding. Suppose that a highway has a speed limit of 60 miles per hour. The amount that speeders are fined, $F$, is described by the statement of equality

$$F = 10x - 600,$$

where $x$ is the speed in miles per hour. We can use this statement to determine the fine, $F$, for a speeder traveling at, say, 70 miles per hour. We substitute 70 for $x$ in the given statement and then find the corresponding value for $F$.

$$F = 10(70) - 600 = 700 - 600 = 100$$

Thus, a person caught driving 70 miles per hour gets a \$100 fine.

A friend, whom we shall call Leadfoot, borrows your car and returns a few hours later with a \$400 speeding fine. Leadfoot is furious, protesting that the car was barely driven over the speed limit. Should you believe Leadfoot?

In order to decide if Leadfoot is telling the truth, use $F = 10x - 600$. Leadfoot was fined \$400, so substitute 400 for $F$:

$$400 = 10x - 600.$$

In Example 1, we will find the value for $x$. This variable represents Leadfoot's speed, which resulted in the \$400 fine.

An **equation** consists of two algebraic expressions joined by an equal sign. Thus, $400 = 10x - 600$ is an example of an equation. The equal sign divides the equation into two parts, the left side and the right side:

$$\underset{\text{Left side}}{\boxed{400}} = \underset{\text{Right side}}{\boxed{10x - 600}}$$

The two sides of an equation can be reversed. So, we can also express this equation as

$$10x - 600 = 400.$$

The form of this equation is $ax + b = c$, with $a = 10$, $b = -600$, and $c = 400$. Any equation in this form is called a **linear equation in one variable**. The exponent on the variable in such an equation is 1. In this section, we will study how to solve linear equations.

**1** Solve linear equations in one variable.

## Solving Linear Equations in One Variable

We begin by restating the definition of a linear equation in one variable.

### Definition of a Linear Equation

A **linear equation in one variable *x*** is an equation that can be written in the form

$$ax + b = c$$

where $a$ and $b$ are real numbers and $a \neq 0$.

An example of a linear equation in one variable is $4x + 12 = 0$. **Solving an equation** in $x$ involves determining all values of $x$ that result in a true statement when substituted into the equation. Such values are **solutions** or **roots** of the equation. For example, substitute $-3$ into $4x + 12 = 0$. We obtain $4(-3) + 12 = 0$, or $-12 + 12 = 0$. This simplifies to the true statement $0 = 0$. Thus, $-3$ is a solution of the equation $4x + 12 = 0$. We also say that $-3$ **satisfies** the equation $4x + 12 = 0$, because when we substitute $-3$ for $x$, a true statement results. The set of all such solutions is called the equation's **solution set**. For example, the solution set of the equation $4x + 12 = 0$ is $\{-3\}$.

Equations that have the same solution set are called **equivalent equations**. For example, the equations $4x + 12 = 0$, $4x = -12$, and $x = -3$ are equivalent equations because the solution set for each is $\{-3\}$. To solve a linear equation in $x$, we transform the equation into an equivalent equation one or more times. Our final equivalent equation should be in the form $x = d$, where $d$ is a real number. By inspection, we can see that the solution set for this equation is $\{d\}$.

To generate equivalent equations, we will use the following principles.

### Study Tip

We can solve equations such as $3(x - 6) = 5x$ for a variable. However, we cannot solve for a variable in an algebraic expression such as $3(x - 6)$. We *simplify* algebraic expressions.

**Correct**

Simplify: $3(x - 6)$.

$3(x - 6) = 3x - 18$

**Incorrect**

Simplify: $3(x - 6)$.

$3(x - 6) = 0$

$3x - 18 = 0$

$3x - 18 + 18 = 0 + 18$

$3x = 18$

$\frac{3x}{3} = \frac{18}{3}$

$x = 6$

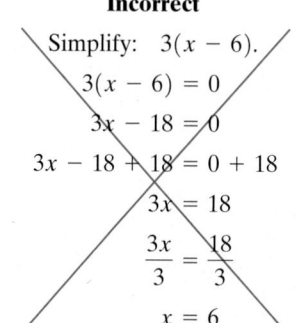

### Generating Equivalent Equations

An equation can be transformed into an **equivalent equation** by one or more of the following operations.

| | Example |
|---|---|
| **1.** Simplify an expression by removing grouping symbols and combining like terms. | $3(x - 6) = 6x - x$<br>$3x - 18 = 5x$ |
| **2.** Add (or subtract) the same real number or variable expression on *both* sides of the equation. | $3x - 18 = 5x$<br>$3x - 18 - 3x = 5x - 3x$<br>$-18 = 2x$<br>Subtract 3x from both sides of the equation. |
| **3.** Multiply (or divide) on *both* sides of the equation by the same *nonzero* quantity. | $-18 = 2x$<br>$\frac{-18}{2} = \frac{2x}{2}$<br>$-9 = x$<br>Divide both sides of the equation by 2. |
| **4.** Interchange the two sides of the equation. | $-9 = x$<br>$x = -9$ |

If you look closely at the equations in the box, you will notice that we have solved the equation $3(x - 6) = 6x - x$. The final equation, with $x$ isolated by itself on the left side, shows that $\{-9\}$ is the solution set. The idea in solving a linear equation is to get the variable by itself on one side of the equal sign and a number by itself on the other side.

**EXAMPLE 1 Solving a Linear Equation (Is Leadfoot Telling the Truth?)**

Solve the equation: $10x - 600 = 400$.

**Solution** Remember that $x$ represents Leadfoot's speed that resulted in the \$400 fine. Our goal is to get $x$ by itself on the left side. We do this by adding 600 to both sides to get $10x$ by itself. Then we isolate $x$ from $10x$ by dividing both sides of the equation by 10.

$$10x - 600 = 400 \quad \text{This is the given equation.}$$

$$10x - 600 + 600 = 400 + 600 \quad \text{Add 600 to both sides.}$$

$$10x = 1000 \quad \text{Combine like terms.}$$

$$\frac{10x}{10} = \frac{1000}{10} \quad \text{Divide both sides by 10.}$$

$$x = 100$$

Can this possibly be correct? Was Leadfoot doing 100 miles per hour in the car he borrowed from you? To find out, check the proposed solution, 100, in the original equation. In other words, evaluate when $x = 100$.

Check

$$10x - 600 = 400 \quad \text{This is the original equation.}$$

$$10(100) - 600 \stackrel{?}{=} 400 \quad \text{Substitute 100 for x.}$$

$$1000 - 600 \stackrel{?}{=} 400 \quad \text{Multiply: } 10(100) = 1000.$$

$$400 = 400 \quad \text{Subtract: } 1000 - 600 = 400.$$

The true statement $400 = 400$ indicates that 100 is the solution. This verifies that the solution set is $\{100\}$. Leadfoot was doing an outrageous 100 miles per hour, and lied by claiming that your car was barely driven over the speed limit.

### Study Tip

If your proposed solution is incorrect, you will get a false statement when you check your answer. For example, 65 is not a solution of $10x - 600 = 400$. Look what happens when we substitute 65 for $x$:

$$10x - 600 = 400$$

$$10(65) - 600 \stackrel{?}{=} 400$$

$$650 - 600 \stackrel{?}{=} 400$$

$$50 = 400 \quad \text{False.}$$

**Check Point 1** Solve and check: $5x - 8 = 72$.

We now present a step-by-step procedure for solving a linear equation in one variable. Not all of these steps are necessary to solve every equation.

**Solving a Linear Equation**

1. Simplify the algebraic expression on each side.
2. Collect all the variable terms on one side and all the constant terms on the other side.
3. Isolate the variable and solve.
4. Check the proposed solution in the original equation.

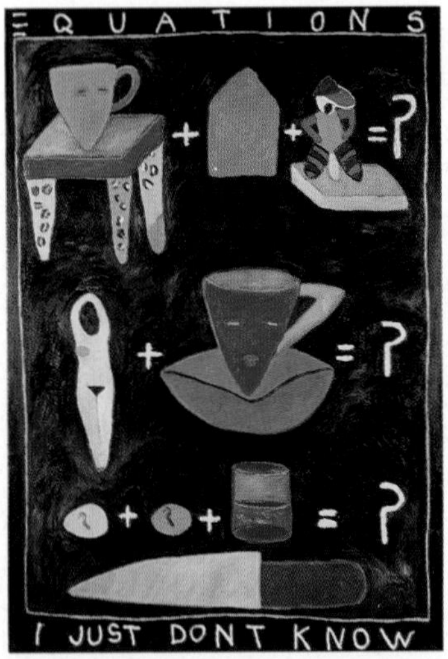


The compact, symbolic notation of algebra enables us to use a clear step-by-step method for solving equations, designed to avoid the confusion shown in the painting. *(Squeak Carnwath "Equations" 1981, oil on cotton canvas 96 in. h × 72 in. w.)*

## EXAMPLE 2 Solving a Linear Equation

Solve the equation: $2(x - 3) - 17 = 13 - 3(x + 2)$.

**Solution**

**Step 1 Simplify the algebraic expression on each side.**

| | |
|---|---|
| $2(x - 3) - 17 = 13 - 3(x + 2)$ | This is the given equation. |
| $2x - 6 - 17 = 13 - 3x - 6$ | Use the distributive property. |
| $2x - 23 = -3x + 7$ | Combine like terms. |

### Discovery

Solve the equation in Example 2 by collecting terms with the variable on the right and numerical terms on the left. What do you observe?

**Step 2 Collect variable terms on one side and constant terms on the other side.** We will collect variable terms on the left by adding $3x$ to both sides. We will collect the numbers on the right by adding 23 to both sides.

| | |
|---|---|
| $2x - 23 + 3x = -3x + 7 + 3x$ | Add 3x to both sides. |
| $5x - 23 = 7$ | Simplify. |
| $5x - 23 + 23 = 7 + 23$ | Add 23 to both sides. |
| $5x = 30$ | Simplify. |

**Step 3 Isolate the variable and solve.** We isolate the variable $x$ by dividing both sides by 5.

| | |
|---|---|
| $\frac{5x}{5} = \frac{30}{5}$ | Divide both sides by 5. |
| $x = 6$ | Simplify. |

**Step 4 Check the proposed solution in the original equation.** Substitute 6 for $x$ in the original equation.

| | |
|---|---|
| $2(x - 3) - 17 = 13 - 3(x + 2)$ | This is the original equation. |
| $2(6 - 3) - 17 \stackrel{?}{=} 13 - 3(6 + 2)$ | Substitute 6 for x. |
| $2(3) - 17 \stackrel{?}{=} 13 - 3(8)$ | Simplify inside parentheses. |
| $6 - 17 \stackrel{?}{=} 13 - 24$ | Multiply. |
| $-11 = -11$ ✓ | This true statement indicates that 6 is the solution. |

The solution set is $\{6\}$.

**Check Point 2** Solve and check: $4(2x + 1) - 29 = 3(2x - 5)$.

**2** Solve equations with constants in denominators.

## Linear Equations with Fractions

Equations are easier to solve when they do not contain fractions. How do we solve equations involving fractions? We begin by multiplying both sides of the equation by the least common denominator. The least common denominator is the smallest number that all the denominators will divide into. Example 3 shows how this is done.

## Technology

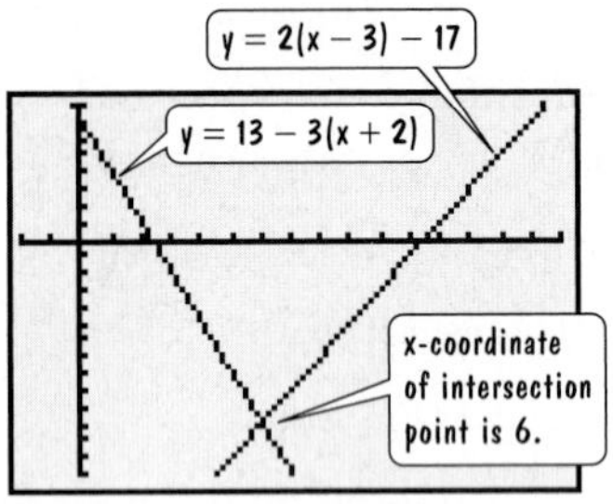


You can use a graphing utility to check the solution to a linear equation in one variable. **Graph the left side and graph the right side. The solution is the $x$-coordinate of the point where the graphs intersect.** For example, to verify that 6 is the solution of

$$2(x-3)-17=13-3(x+2),$$

graph these two equations in the same viewing rectangle:

$$y=2(x-3)-17$$

$$\text{and}\quad y=13-3(x+2)$$

Choose a large enough range setting so that you can see where the graphs intersect. The viewing rectangle on the left shows that the $x$-coordinate of the intersection point is 6, verifying that $\{6\}$ is the solution set for the given equation.

## EXAMPLE 3 Solving a Linear Equation Involving Fractions

Solve the equation: $\dfrac{3x}{2}=\dfrac{x}{5}-\dfrac{39}{5}$.

**Solution** The denominators are 2, 5, and 5. The smallest number that is divisible by 2, 5, and 5 is 10. We begin by multiplying both sides of the equation by 10, the least common denominator.

$$\frac{3x}{2}=\frac{x}{5}-\frac{39}{5}$$ This is the given equation.

$$10\cdot\frac{3x}{2}=10\left(\frac{x}{5}-\frac{39}{5}\right)$$ Multiply both sides by 10.

$$10\cdot\frac{3x}{2}=10\cdot\frac{x}{5}-10\cdot\frac{39}{5}$$ Use the distributive property. Be sure to multiply all terms by 10.

$$\overset{5}{\cancel{10}}\cdot\frac{3x}{\underset{1}{\cancel{2}}}=\overset{2}{\cancel{10}}\cdot\frac{x}{\underset{1}{\cancel{5}}}-\overset{2}{\cancel{10}}\cdot\frac{39}{\underset{1}{\cancel{5}}}$$ Divide out common factors in the multiplication.

$$15x=2x-78$$ Complete the multiplication. The fractions are now cleared.

At this point, we have an equation similar to those we previously solved. Collect the variable terms on one side and the constant terms on the other side.

$$15x-2x=2x-2x-78$$ Subtract $2x$ to get the $x$-terms on the left.

$$13x=-78$$ Simplify.

Isolate $x$ by dividing both sides by 13.

$$\frac{13x}{13}=\frac{-78}{13}$$ Divide both sides by 13.

$$x=-6$$ Simplify.

Check the proposed solution in the original equation. Substitute $-6$ for $x$ in the original equation. You should obtain $-9=-9$. This true statement verifies the solution set is $\{-6\}$.

**Check Point 3** Solve and check: $\frac{x}{4} = \frac{2x}{3} + \frac{5}{6}$.

**3** Solve equations with variables in denominators.

## Equations Involving Rational Expressions

In Example 3 we solved a linear equation with constants in denominators. Now, let's consider an equation such as

$$\frac{1}{x} = \frac{1}{5} + \frac{3}{2x}.$$

Can you see how this equation differs from the fractional equation that we solved earlier? The variable, $x$, appears in two of the denominators. The procedure for solving this equation still involves multiplying each side by the least common denominator. However, we must avoid any values of the variable that make a denominator zero. For example, examine the denominators in the equation

$$\frac{1}{x} = \frac{1}{5} + \frac{3}{2x}.$$

This denominator would equal zero if $x = 0$. This denominator would equal zero if $x = 0$.

We see that $x$ cannot equal zero. With this in mind, let's solve the equation.

### EXAMPLE 4 Solving an Equation Involving Rational Expressions

Solve: $\frac{1}{x} = \frac{1}{5} + \frac{3}{2x}$.

**Solution** The denominators are $x$, 5, and $2x$. The least common denominator is $10x$. We begin by multiplying both sides of the equation by $10x$. We will also write the restriction that $x$ cannot equal zero to the right of the equation.

$$\frac{1}{x} = \frac{1}{5} + \frac{3}{2x}, \quad x \neq 0$$ This is the given equation.

$$10x \cdot \frac{1}{x} = 10x\left(\frac{1}{5} + \frac{3}{2x}\right)$$ Multiply both sides by 10x.

$$10x \cdot \frac{1}{x} = 10x \cdot \frac{1}{5} + 10x \cdot \frac{3}{2x}$$ Use the distributive property. Be sure to multiply all terms by 10x.

$$\cancel{10x} \cdot \frac{1}{\cancel{x}} = \overset{2}{\cancel{10}}x \cdot \frac{1}{\underset{1}{\cancel{5}}} + \overset{5}{\cancel{10x}} \cdot \frac{3}{\underset{1}{\cancel{2x}}}$$ Divide out common factors in the multiplication.

$$10 = 2x + 15$$ Simplify.

Observe that the resulting equation,

$$10 = 2x + 15,$$

is now cleared of fractions. With the variable term, $2x$, already on the right, we will collect constant terms on the left by subtracting 15 from both sides.

$$10 - 15 = 2x + 15 - 15 \quad \text{Subtract 15 from both sides.}$$

$$-5 = 2x \quad \text{Simplify.}$$

Finally, we isolate the variable, $x$, by dividing both sides by 2.

$$\frac{-5}{2} = \frac{2x}{2} \quad \text{Divide both sides by 2.}$$

$$-\frac{5}{2} = x \quad \text{Simplify.}$$

We check our solution by substituting $-\frac{5}{2}$ into the original equation or by using a calculator. With a calculator, evaluate each side of the equation for $x = -\frac{5}{2}$, or for $x = -2.5$. Note that the original restriction that $x \neq 0$ is met. The solution set is $\{-\frac{5}{2}\}$.

**Check Point 4** Solve: $\frac{5}{2x} = \frac{17}{18} - \frac{1}{3x}$.

## EXAMPLE 5 Solving an Equation Involving Rational Expressions

Solve: $\frac{x}{x-3} = \frac{3}{x-3} + 9$.

**Solution** We must avoid any values of the variable $x$ that make a denominator zero.

$$\frac{x}{x-3} = \frac{3}{x-3} + 9$$

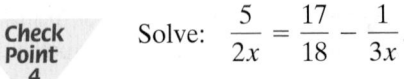

These denominators are zero if $x - 3 = 0$, or in other words, if $x = 3$.

We see that $x$ cannot equal 3. With denominators of $x - 3$, $x - 3$, and 1, the least common denominator is $x - 3$. We multiply both sides of the equation by $x - 3$. We also write the restriction that $x$ cannot equal 3 to the right of the equation.

$$\frac{x}{x-3} = \frac{3}{x-3} + 9, \quad x \neq 3 \quad \text{This is the given equation.}$$

$$(x-3) \cdot \frac{x}{x-3} = (x-3)\left[\frac{3}{x-3} + 9\right] \quad \text{Multiply both sides by } x - 3.$$

$$(x-3) \cdot \frac{x}{x-3} = (x-3) \cdot \frac{3}{x-3} + (x-3) \cdot 9 \quad \text{Use the distributive property.}$$

$$\cancel{(x-3)} \cdot \frac{x}{\cancel{x-3}} = \cancel{(x-3)} \cdot \frac{3}{\cancel{x-3}} + (x-3) \cdot 9 \quad \text{Divide out common factors in the multiplications.}$$

$$x = 3 + (x-3) \cdot 9 \quad \text{Simplify.}$$

The resulting equation, which can be expressed as

$$x = 3 + 9(x - 3),$$

is cleared of fractions. We now solve for $x$.

$$x = 3 + 9x - 27 \qquad \text{Use the distributive property.}$$

$$x = 9x - 24 \qquad \text{Combine numerical terms.}$$

$$x - 9x = 9x - 24 - 9x \qquad \text{Subtract } 9x \text{ from both sides.}$$

$$-8x = -24 \qquad \text{Simplify.}$$

$$\frac{-8x}{-8} = \frac{-24}{-8} \qquad \text{Solve for } x\text{, dividing both sides by } -8.$$

$$x = 3 \qquad \text{Simplify.}$$

The proposed solution, 3, is *not* a solution because of the restriction that $x \neq 3$. There is *no solution to this equation*. The solution set for this equation contains no elements and is called the empty set, written $\varnothing$.

**Check Point 5** Solve: $\dfrac{x}{x-2} = \dfrac{2}{x-2} - \dfrac{2}{3}$.

4 Recognize identities, conditional equations, and inconsistent equations.

## Types of Equations

We tend to place things in categories, allowing us to order and structure the world. For example, you can categorize yourself by your age group, your ethnicity, your academic major, or your gender. Equations can be placed into categories that depend on their solution sets.

An equation that is true for all real numbers for which both sides are defined is called an **identity**. An example of an identity is

$$x + 3 = x + 2 + 1.$$

Every number plus 3 is equal to that number plus 2 plus 1. Therefore, the solution set to this equation is the set of all real numbers. Another example of an identity is

$$\frac{2x}{x} = 2.$$

Because division by 0 is undefined, this equation is true for all real number values of $x$ except 0. The solution set is the set of nonzero real numbers.

An equation that is not an identity but that is true for at least one real number is called a **conditional equation**. The equation $10x - 600 = 400$ is an example of a conditional equation. The equation is not an identity and is true only if $x = 100$.

An **inconsistent equation** is an equation that is not true for even one real number. An example of an inconsistent equation is

$$x = x + 7.$$

There is no number that is equal to itself plus 7. Some inconsistent equations are less obvious than this. Consider the equation in Example 5,

$$\frac{x}{x-3} = \frac{2}{x-3} + 9.$$

This equation is not true for any real number and has no solution. Thus, it is inconsistent.

### EXAMPLE 6 Categorizing an Equation

Determine whether the equation

$$2(x + 1) = 2x + 3$$

is an identity, a conditional equation, or an inconsistent equation.

**Solution** Let's see what happens if we try solving the equation. Applying the distributive property on the left side, we obtain

$$2x + 2 = 2x + 3.$$

Does something look strange? Can doubling a number and increasing the product by 2 give the same result as doubling the same number and increasing the product by 3? No. Let's continue solving the equation by subtracting $2x$ from both sides.

$$2x + 2 - 2x = 2x + 3 - 2x$$
$$2 = 3$$

The false statement $2 = 3$ verifies that the given equation is inconsistent.

**Check Point 6** Determine whether the equation

$$2(x + 1) = 2x + 2$$

is an identity, a conditional equation, or an inconsistent equation.

## EXERCISE SET 1.1

### Practice Exercises

*In Exercises 1–16, solve and check each linear equation.*

1. $5x - 8 = 72$
2. $6x - 3 = 63$
3. $11x - (6x - 5) = 40$
4. $5x - (2x - 10) = 35$
5. $2x - 7 = 6 + x$
6. $3x + 5 = 2x + 13$
7. $7x + 4 = x + 16$
8. $13x + 14 = 12x - 5$
9. $3(x - 2) + 7 = 2(x + 5)$
10. $2(x - 1) + 3 = x - 3(x + 1)$
11. $3(x - 4) - 4(x - 3) = x + 3 - (x - 2)$
12. $2 - (7x + 5) = 13 - 3x$
13. $16 = 3(x - 1) - (x - 7)$
14. $5x - (2x + 2) = x + (3x - 5)$
15. $25 - [2 + 5y - 3(y + 2)] = -3(2y - 5) - [5(y - 1) - 3y + 3]$
16. $45 - [4 - 2y - 4(y + 7)] = -4(1 + 3y) - [4 - 3(y + 2) - 2(2y - 5)]$

*Exercises 17–30 contain equations with constants in denominators. Solve each equation by multiplying both sides by the least common denominator, thereby clearing fractions.*

17. $\frac{x}{3} = \frac{x}{2} - 2$
18. $\frac{x}{5} = \frac{x}{6} + 1$
19. $20 - \frac{x}{3} = \frac{x}{2}$
20. $\frac{x}{5} - \frac{1}{2} = \frac{x}{6}$
21. $\frac{3x}{5} = \frac{2x}{3} + 1$
22. $\frac{x}{2} = \frac{3x}{4} + 5$
23. $\frac{3x}{5} - x = \frac{x}{10} - \frac{5}{2}$
24. $2x - \frac{2x}{7} = \frac{x}{2} + \frac{17}{2}$
25. $\frac{x + 3}{6} = \frac{3}{8} + \frac{x - 5}{4}$
26. $\frac{x + 1}{4} = \frac{1}{6} + \frac{2 - x}{3}$
27. $\frac{x}{4} = 2 + \frac{x - 3}{3}$
28. $5 + \frac{x - 2}{3} = \frac{x + 3}{8}$
29. $\frac{x + 1}{3} = 5 - \frac{x + 2}{7}$
30. $\frac{3x}{5} - \frac{x - 3}{2} = \frac{x + 2}{3}$

*Exercises 31–50 contain equations with variables in denominators. For each equation,* **a.** *Write the value or values of the variable that make a denominator zero. These are the restrictions on the variable.* **b.** *Keeping the restrictions in mind, solve the equation by multiplying both sides by the least common denominator.*

31. $\frac{4}{x} = \frac{5}{2x} + 3$
32. $\frac{5}{x} = \frac{10}{3x} + 4$
33. $\frac{2}{x} + 3 = \frac{5}{2x} + \frac{13}{4}$
34. $\frac{7}{2x} - \frac{5}{3x} = \frac{22}{3}$

35. $\frac{2}{3x} + \frac{1}{4} = \frac{11}{6x} - \frac{1}{3}$

36. $\frac{5}{2x} - \frac{8}{9} = \frac{1}{18} - \frac{1}{3x}$

37. $\frac{x-2}{2x} + 1 = \frac{x+1}{x}$

38. $\frac{4}{x} = \frac{9}{5} - \frac{7x-4}{5x}$

39. $\frac{1}{x-1} + 5 = \frac{11}{x-1}$

40. $\frac{3}{x+4} - 7 = \frac{-4}{x+4}$

41. $\frac{8x}{x+1} = 4 - \frac{8}{x+1}$

42. $\frac{2}{x-2} = \frac{x}{x-2} - 2$

43. $\frac{3}{2x-2} + \frac{1}{2} = \frac{2}{x-1}$

44. $\frac{3}{x+3} = \frac{5}{2x+6} + \frac{1}{x-2}$

45. $\frac{3}{x+2} + \frac{2}{x-2} = \frac{8}{(x+2)(x-2)}$

46. $\frac{5}{x+2} + \frac{3}{x-2} = \frac{12}{(x+2)(x-2)}$

47. $\frac{2}{x+1} - \frac{1}{x-1} = \frac{2x}{x^2-1}$

48. $\frac{4}{x+5} + \frac{2}{x-5} = \frac{32}{x^2-25}$

49. $\frac{1}{x-4} - \frac{5}{x+2} = \frac{6}{x^2-2x-8}$

50. $\frac{6}{x+3} - \frac{5}{x-2} = \frac{-20}{x^2+x-6}$

*In Exercises 51–58, determine whether each equation is an identity, a conditional equation, or an inconsistent equation.*

51. $4(x-7) = 4x - 28$

52. $4(x-7) = 4x + 28$

53. $2x + 3 = 2x - 3$

54. $\frac{7x}{x} = 7$

55. $4x + 5x = 8x$

56. $8x + 2x = 9x$

57. $\frac{2x}{x-3} = \frac{6}{x-3} + 4$

58. $\frac{3}{x-3} = \frac{x}{x-3} + 3$

*The equations in Exercises 59–68 combine the types of equations we have discussed in this section. Solve each equation or state that it is true for all real numbers or no real numbers.*

59. $\frac{x+5}{2} - 4 = \frac{2x-1}{3}$

60. $\frac{x+2}{7} = 5 - \frac{x+1}{3}$

61. $\frac{2}{x-2} = 3 + \frac{x}{x-2}$

62. $\frac{6}{x+3} + 2 = \frac{-2x}{x+3}$

63. $8x - (3x+2) + 10 = 3x$

64. $2(x+2) + 2x = 4(x+1)$

65. $\frac{2}{x} + \frac{1}{2} = \frac{3}{4}$

66. $\frac{3}{x} - \frac{1}{6} = \frac{1}{3}$

67. $\frac{4}{x-2} + \frac{3}{x+5} = \frac{7}{(x+5)(x-2)}$

68. $\frac{1}{x-1} = \frac{1}{(2x+3)(x-1)} + \frac{4}{2x+3}$

## Application Exercises

69. The equation $d = 5000c - 525{,}000$ describes the relationship between the annual number of deaths ($d$) in the United States from heart disease and the average cholesterol level ($c$) of blood. (Cholesterol level, $c$, is expressed in milligrams per deciliter of blood.)
   a. In 1990, 500,000 Americans died from heart disease. Substitute 500,000 for $d$ in the given equation and then solve for $c$ to determine the average cholesterol level in 1990.
   b. Suppose that the average cholesterol level for people in the United States could be reduced to 180. Substitute 180 for $c$ in the given formula and then compute the value for $d$ to determine the number of annual deaths from heart disease with this reduced cholesterol level. Compared to the number of deaths in 1990, how many lives would be saved by this cholesterol reduction?

70. There is a relationship between the vocabulary of a child and its age. The equation $60A - V = 900$ describes this relationship, where $A$ is the age of the child in months and $V$ is the number of words that the child uses. Suppose that a child uses 1500 words. Substitute 1500 for $V$ in the equation to determine the child's age in months.

71. The equation

$$p = 15 + \frac{15d}{33}$$

describes the pressure of sea water ($p$, in pounds per square foot) at a depth of $d$ feet below the surface. The record depth for breath-held diving, by Francisco Ferreras (Cuba) off Grand-Bahama Island, on November 14,1993, involved pressure of 201 pounds per square foot. To what depth did Ferreras descend on this ill-advised venture? (He was underwater for 2 minutes and 9 seconds!)

72. The equation $P = -0.5d + 100$ describes the percentage ($P$) of lost hikers found in search and rescue missions when members of the search team walk parallel to one another separated by a distance of $d$ yards. If a search and rescue team finds 70% of lost hikers, substitute 70 for $P$ in the equation and find the parallel distance of separation between members of the search party.

## Writing in Mathematics

73. What is a linear equation in one variable? Give an example of this type of equation.
74. What does it mean to solve an equation?
75. What is the solution set of an equation?
76. What are equivalent equations? Give an example.
77. What is the difference between solving an equation such as $2(x-4) + 5x = 34$ and simplifying an algebraic expression such as $2(x-4) + 5x$? If there is a difference, which topic should be taught first? Why?

**78.** Suppose that you solve $\frac{x}{5} - \frac{x}{2} = 1$ by multiplying both sides by 20, rather than the least common denominator of 5 and 2 (namely, 10). Describe what happens. If you get the correct solution, why do you think we clear the equation of fractions by multiplying by the *least* common denominator?

**79.** Suppose you are an algebra teacher grading the following solution on an examination:

$$\begin{aligned} -3(x-6) &= 2 - x \\ -3x - 18 &= 2 - x \\ -2x - 18 &= 2 \\ -2x &= -16 \\ x &= 8 \end{aligned}$$

You should note that 8 checks, and the solution set is $\{8\}$. The student who worked the problem therefore wants full credit. Can you find any errors in the solution? If full credit is 10 points, how many points should you give the student? Justify your position.

**80.** Explain how to determine the restrictions on the variable for the equation

$$\frac{3}{x+5} + \frac{4}{x-2} = \frac{7}{(x+5)(x-2)}.$$

**81.** What is an identity? Give an example.

**82.** What is a conditional equation? Give an example.

**83.** What is an inconsistent equation? Give an example.

## Technology Exercises

*For Exercises 84–87, use your graphing utility to graph each side of the equations in the same viewing rectangle. Based on the resulting graph, label each equation as conditional, inconsistent, or an identity. If the equation is conditional, use the x-coordinate of the intersection point to find the solution set. Verify this value by direct substitution into the equation.*

**84.** $2(x - 6) + 3x = x + 6$

**85.** $9x + 3 - 3x = 2(3x + 1)$

**86.** $2(x + \frac{1}{2}) = 5x + 1 - 3x$

**87.** $\frac{2x-1}{3} - \frac{x-5}{6} = \frac{x-3}{4}$

## Critical Thinking Exercises

**88.** Which one of the following is true?

**a.** The equation $-7x = x$ has no solution.

**b.** The equations $\frac{x}{x-4} = \frac{4}{x-4}$ and $x = 4$ are equivalent.

**c.** The equations $3y - 1 = 11$ and $3y - 7 = 5$ are equivalent.

**d.** If $a$ and $b$ are any real numbers, then $ax + b = 0$ always has only one number in its solution set.

**89.** Solve for $x$: $ax + b = c$.

**90.** Write three equations that are equivalent to $x = 5$.

**91.** If $x$ represents a number, write an English sentence about the number that results in an inconsistent equation.

**92.** Find $b$ such that $\frac{7x+4}{b} + 13 = x$ will have a solution set given by $\{-6\}$.

**93.** Find $b$ such that $\frac{4x-b}{x-5} = 3$ will have a solution set given by $\varnothing$.

## Group Exercise

**94.** In your group, describe the best procedure for solving an equation like

$$0.47x + \frac{19}{4} = -0.2 + \frac{2}{5}x.$$

Use this procedure to actually solve the equation. Then compare procedures with other groups working on this problem. Which group devised the most streamlined method?

# SECTION 1.2 Formulas and Applications

## Objectives

1. Solve problems using formulas.
2. Use linear equations to solve problems.
3. Solve for a variable in a formula.

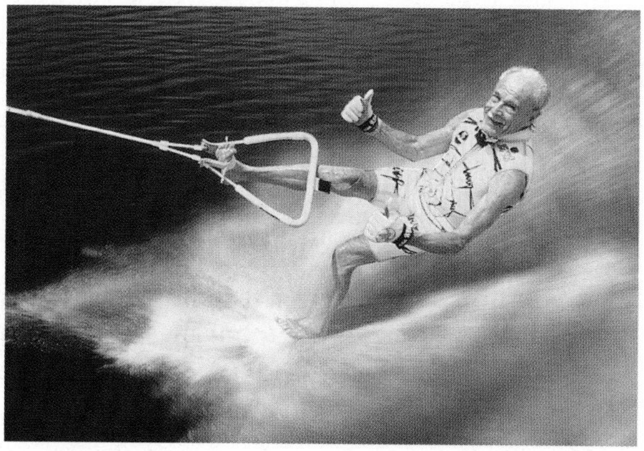

Could you live to be 125? The number of Americans ages 100 or older could approach 850,000 by 2050. Some scientists predict that by 2100, our descendants could live to be 200 years of age. In this section, we will see how equations can be used to make these kinds of predictions as we turn to applications of linear equations.

1 Solve problems using formulas.

### Formulas and Modeling Data

The graph in Figure 1.1 shows life expectancy in the United States by year of birth. For example, we can use the graph to find life expectancy for women born in 1980. Find the two bars for 1980 and then look at the bar on the right, representing females. The number printed on this bar is 77.4. Thus, the life expectancy for women born in 1980 is 77.4 years.

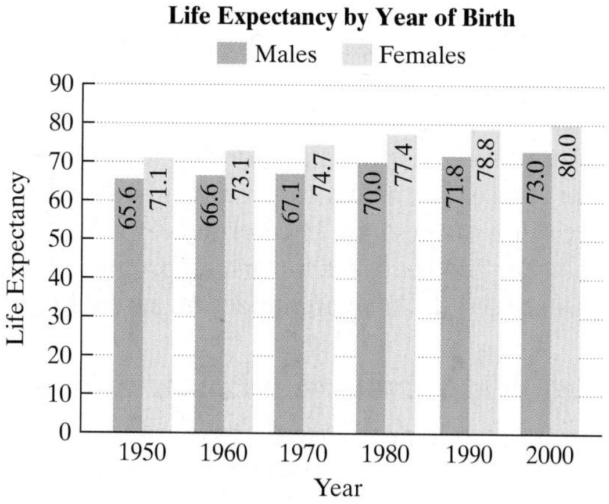


*Source*: U.S. Bureau of the Census

**Figure 1.1** Life expectancy by year of birth

The data for U.S. women in Figure 1.1 can be approximated by the equation

$$E = 0.215t + 71.05,$$

where the variable $E$ represents life expectancy for women born $t$ years after 1950. This equation is an example of a *formula*. A **formula** is an equation that uses letters to express relationships between two or more variables. The given formula expresses the relationship between the number of years born after 1950, $t$, and life expectancy for U.S. women, $E$.

## EXAMPLE 1 Using a Formula

Use the formula

$$E = 0.215t + 71.05$$

to determine the year of birth for which U.S. women can expect to live 77.5 years.

**Solution** We are given that the life expectancy for women is 77.5 years, so substitute 77.5 for $E$ in the formula and solve for $t$.

$$E = 0.215t + 71.05 \quad \text{This is the given formula.}$$

$$77.5 = 0.215t + 71.05 \quad \text{Replace } E \text{ by 77.5 and solve for } t.$$

$$77.5 - 71.05 = 0.215t + 71.05 - 71.05 \quad \text{Isolate the term containing } t \text{ by subtracting 71.05 from both sides.}$$

$$6.45 = 0.215t \quad \text{Simplify.}$$

$$\frac{6.45}{0.215} = \frac{0.215t}{0.215} \quad \text{Divide both sides by 0.215.}$$

$$30 = t \quad \text{Simplify.}$$

The formula indicates that U.S. women born 30 years after 1950, or in 1980, can expect to live 77.5 years.

**Table 1.1 Life Expectancy for U.S. Women**

| Birth Year | Actual Value | Value Predicted by $E = 0.215t + 71.05$ |
|---|---|---|
| 1950 | 71.1 | 71.05 |
| 1960 | 73.1 | 73.2 |
| 1970 | 74.7 | 75.35 |
| 1980 | 77.4 | 77.5 |
| 1990 | 78.8 | 79.65 |
| 2000 | 80.0 | 81.8 |

**Check Point 1** The formula $D = 0.2F - 1$ describes death rate from breast cancer per 100,000 women, $D$, and daily fat intake, $F$, in grams. The death rate of American women from breast cancer is 19 women per 100,000. What is the daily fat intake for women in America?

If you look back at the actual data in Figure 1.1, you will see that women born in 1980 can expect to live 77.4 years, not 77.5 as predicted by the formula. In developing formulas that describe, or *model*, data, mathematicians strive for both accuracy and simplicity. The formula $E = 0.215t + 71.05$ is relatively simple to use, but as we can see from Table 1.1, it is not an entirely accurate description of the data. Furthermore, we may not want to project the formula past the year 2000 because unforseen progress in conquering breast cancer and other diseases could have an impact on actual life expectancy.

**2** Use linear equations to solve problems.

## Problem Solving with Linear Equations

You are choosing between two kinds of heating systems for your home. Solar heating costs $29,700 to install, with operating costs of $150 per year. Electric heating costs $5000 to install, with operating costs of $1100 per year. After how many years will total costs for solar heating and electric heating be the same?

Before answering the question, let's see if we can write a critical sentence that describes, or *models*, the problem's conditions. The **verbal model** is

| The total costs for solar heating | must equal | the total costs for electric heating. |
|---|---|---|
| ? | = | ? |

The question marks under the voice balloons indicate that we need algebraic expressions for these unknowns. Once we obtain these expressions, we will have an equation that models the verbal conditions. We call this equation a *mathematical model*. A **mathematical model** is a formula or algebraic equation that can be formed from a verbal model. Earlier, we saw that a mathematical model can be formed using actual data.

Here is a step-by-step strategy for solving problems using mathematical models that are created from verbal models.

**Strategy for Problem Solving**

**Step 1** Read the problem carefully. Attempt to state the problem in your own words and state what the problem is looking for. Let $x$ (or any variable) represent one of the quantities in the problem.

**Step 2** If necessary, write expressions for any other unknown quantities in the problem in terms of $x$.

**Step 3** Form a verbal model of the problem's conditions and then write an equation in $x$ that translates the verbal model.

**Step 4** Solve the equation written in step 3 and answer the question in the problem.

**Step 5** Check the proposed solution in the original wording of the problem.

## EXAMPLE 2 Selecting a Heating System

Costs for two different kinds of heating systems for a three-bedroom home are given below.

| System | Cost to Install | Operating Cost per Year |
|---|---|---|
| Solar | \$29,700 | \$150 |
| Electric | \$5000 | \$1100 |

After how many years will total costs for solar heating and electric heating be the same?

### Solution

**Step 1 Let $x$ represent one of the quantities.**

Let $x$ = the number of years after which total costs for the two systems will be the same.

**Step 2 Represent other unknown quantities in terms of $x$.** There are no other unknown quantities to find, so we can skip this step.

**Step 3 Write an equation in $x$ that describes the conditions.** The total cost for the solar system is the installation cost, \$29,700, plus the yearly operating cost, \$150, times the number of years used, $x$. The total cost for the electric system is the installation cost, \$5000, plus the yearly operating cost, \$1100, times the number of years used, $x$.

| The total costs for solar heating | must equal | the total costs for electric heating. |
|---|---|---|
| $29{,}700 + 150x$ | $=$ | $5000 + 1100x$ |

**Step 4 Solve the equation and answer the question.**

$$29{,}700 + 150x = 5000 + 1100x$$ This is the equation that models the verbal conditions.

$$29{,}700 + 150x - 150x = 5000 + 1100x - 150x$$ Subtract 150x from both sides.

$$29{,}700 = 5000 + 950x$$ Simplify.

$$29{,}700 - 5000 = 5000 + 950x - 5000$$ Subtract 5000 from both sides.

$$24{,}700 = 950x$$ Simplify.

$$\frac{24{,}700}{950} = \frac{950x}{950}$$ Divide both sides by 950.

$$26 = x$$ Simplify.

Because $x$ represents the number of years after which total costs for the two systems will be the same, after 26 years, the total costs for solar heating and electric heating will be the same.

**Step 5 Check the proposed solution in the original wording of the problem.** The problem states that the total costs should be the same. Let's see if they are after 26 years:

$$\text{Total costs for solar heating} = \$29{,}700 + \$150(26) = \$33{,}600$$

Installation costs — yearly costs

$$\text{Total costs for electric heating} = \$5000 + \$1100(26) = \$33{,}600.$$

After 26 years, both systems will cost \$33,600. Thus, the proposed solution, 26 years, satisfies the problem's conditions.

**Check Point 2** Costs for two different fitness clubs are given below.

| Club | Yearly Fee | Cost per Hour to Use the Facility |
|---|---|---|
| Superfit | \$500 | \$1.00 |
| Healthy Bodies | \$400 | \$1.75 |

After how many hours of use each year will total costs for Superfit and Healthy Bodies be the same?

Our next example involves simple interest. The annual simple interest that an investment earns is given by the formula

$$I = Pr$$

where $I$ is the simple interest, $P$ is the principal, and $r$ is the simple interest rate, expressed in decimal form. Suppose, for example, that you deposit \$2000 ($P = 2000$) in a savings account that has a simple interest rate of 6% ($r = 0.06$). The annual simple interest is computed as follows:

$$I = Pr = (2000)(0.06) = 120.$$

The annual interest is \$120.

## EXAMPLE 3 Solving a Simple Interest Problem

You inherit \$16,000 with the stipulation that for the first year the money must be invested in two stocks paying 6% and 8% annual interest, respectively. How much should be invested at each rate if the total interest earned for the year is to be \$1180?

### Solution

**Step 1 Let $x$ represent one of the quantities.**

$$\text{Let } x = \text{the amount invested at 6\%.}$$

**Step 2 Represent other quantities in terms of $x$.** The other quantity that we seek is the amount to be invested at 8%. Because the total amount to be invested is \$16,000, and we already used up $x$,

$$16{,}000 - x = \text{the amount invested at 8\%.}$$

> **Study Tip**
>
> Look at the expression in step 2. Notice that when you add $x$ and $16{,}000 - x$, you get 16,000, the total investment. In many word problems, a total amount is divided into two parts.

**Step 3 Write an equation in $x$ that describes the conditions.** The interest for the two investments combined must be \$1180. Interest is $Pr$ or $rP$ for each investment.

| Interest from 6% investment | plus | interest from 8% investment | is | \$1180. |
|---|---|---|---|---|
| $0.06x$ | $+$ | $0.08(16{,}000 - x)$ | $=$ | $1180$ |
| rate times principal | | rate times principal | | |

**Step 4 Solve the equation and answer the question.**

| | |
|---|---|
| $0.06x + 0.08(16{,}000 - x) = 1180$ | This is the equation that models the verbal conditions. |
| $0.06x + 1280 - 0.08x = 1180$ | Use the distributive property. |
| $-0.02x + 1280 = 1180$ | Combine like terms. |
| $-0.02x + 1280 - 1280 = 1180 - 1280$ | Subtract 1280 from both sides. |
| $-0.02 = -100$ | Simplify. |
| $\dfrac{-0.02x}{-0.02} = \dfrac{-100}{-0.02}$ | Divide both sides by $-0.02$. |
| $x = 5000$ | Simplify. |

Because $x$ represents the amount invested at 6%, \$5000 should be invested at 6%. Because $16{,}000 - x$ represents the amount invested at 8%, \$16,000 − \$5000, or \$11,000, should be invested at 8%.

**Step 5 Check the proposed solution in the original wording of the problem.** The problem states that the total interest should be \$1180. The interest earned on \$5000 at 6% is (\$5000)(0.06), or \$300. The interest earned on \$11,000 at 8% is (\$11,000)(0.08), or \$880. The total interest is \$300 + \$880, or \$1180, exactly as it should be.

**Check Point 3** Suppose that you invest \$25,000, part at 9% simple interest and the remainder at 12%. If the total yearly interest from these investments was \$2550, find the amount invested at each rate.

Chemists and pharmacists often have to change the concentration of solutions and other mixtures. The five-step strategy can be used to solve problems in these situations.

## EXAMPLE 4 Solving a Solution Mixture Problem

A chemist needs to mix an 18% acid solution with a 45% acid solution to obtain 12 liters of a 36% acid solution. How many liters of each of the acid solutions must be used?

### Solution

**Step 1 Let $x$ represent one of the quantities.**

Let $x$ = the number of liters of the 18% acid solution to be used in the mixture.

**Step 2 Represent other quantities in terms of $x$.**
The other quantity that we seek is the number of liters of the 45% acid solution to be used in the mixture. Because the total to be obtained is 12 liters, and we already used up $x$,

$12 - x$ = the number of liters of the 45% acid solution to be used in the mixture.

**Step 3 Write an equation in $x$ that describes the conditions.** The situation is illustrated in Figure 1.2.

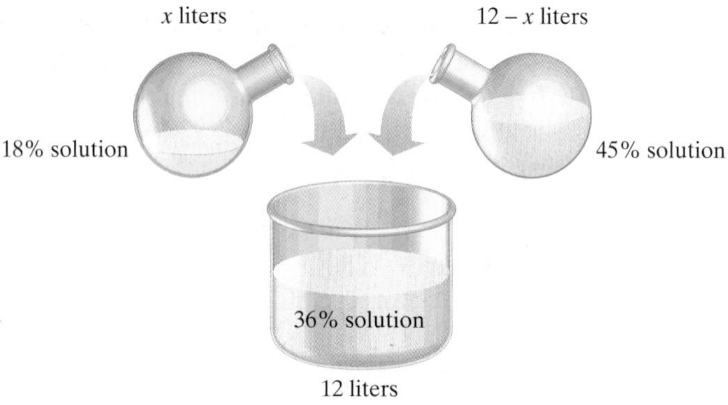


**Figure 1.2** Obtaining a 12-liter 36% acid mixture

The sum of the amounts of acid in the 18% solution and the 45% solution must equal the amount of acid in the 36%, 12 liter, mixture. We form a table that shows the amount of acid in each of the three solutions.

| | Number of Liters | × | Percent of Acid | = | Amount of Acid |
|---|---|---|---|---|---|
| **18% Acid Solution** | $x$ | | 18% = 0.18 | | $0.18x$ |
| **45% Acid Solution** | $12 - x$ | | 45% = 0.45 | | $0.45(12 - x)$ |
| **36% Acid Solution** | 12 | | 36% = 0.36 | | $0.36(12)$ |

| Amount of acid in the 18% solution | plus | Amount of acid in the 45% solution | equals | Amount of acid in the 36% mixture. |
|---|---|---|---|---|
| $0.18x$ | $+$ | $0.45(12 - x)$ | $=$ | $0.36(12)$ |

**Step 4 Solve the equation and answer the question.**

| | |
|---|---|
| $0.18x + 0.45(12 - x) = 0.36(12)$ | This is the equation that models the verbal conditions. |
| $0.18x + 5.4 - 0.45x = 4.32$ | Use the distributive property. |
| $-0.27x + 5.4 = 4.32$ | Combine like terms. |
| $-0.27x = -1.08$ | Subtract 5.4 from both sides. |
| $\frac{-0.27x}{-0.27} = \frac{-1.08}{-0.27}$ | Divide both sides by $-0.27$. |
| $x = 4$ | Simplify. |

Because $x$ represents the number of liters of the 18% solution, 4 liters of the 18% solution should be used in the mixture. Because $12 - x$ represents the number of liters of the 45% solution, $12 - 4$, or 8 liters of the 45% solution should be used in the mixture. Thus, the chemist should mix 4 liters of the 18% acid solution with 8 liters of the 45% acid solution.

**Step 5 Check the proposed solution in the original wording of the problem.** The problem states that the 12-liter mixture should be 36% acid. The amount of acid in this mixture is 0.36(12), or 4.32 liters of acid. The amount of acid in 4 liters of the 18% solution is 0.18(4), or 0.72 liter. The amount of acid in 8 liters of the 45% solution is 0.45(8), or 3.6 liters. The amount of acid in the two solutions used in the mixture is 0.72 liter + 3.6 liters, or 4.32 liters, exactly as it should be.

**Check Point 4** A chemist needs to mix a 10% acid solution with a 60% acid solution to obtain 50 milliliters of a 30% acid solution. How many milliliters of each of the acid solutions must be used?

Solving geometry problems usually requires a knowledge of basic geometric ideas and formulas. Formulas for area, perimeter, and volume are given in Table 1.2.

**Table 1.2 Common Formulas for Area, Perimeter, and Volume**

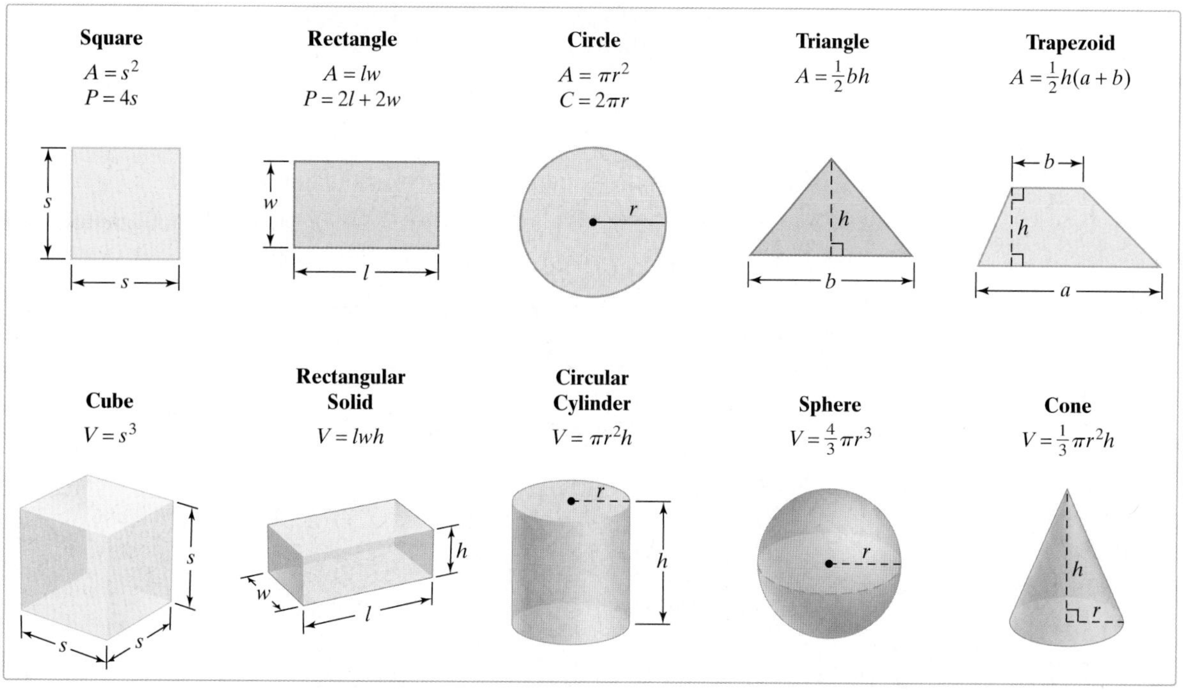

We will be using the formula for the perimeter of a rectangle, $P = 2l + 2w$, in our next example. A helpful verbal model for this formula is 2 times length plus 2 times width is a rectangle's perimeter.

## EXAMPLE 5 Finding the Dimensions of a Soccer Field

A rectangular soccer field is twice as long as it is wide. If the perimeter of a soccer field is 300 yards, what are the field's dimensions?

**Solution**

**Step 1 Let $x$ represent one of the quantities.** We know something about the length; the field is twice as long as it is wide. We will let

$$x = \text{the width.}$$

**Step 2 Represent other quantities in terms of $x$.** Because the field is twice as long as it is wide, let

$$2x = \text{the length.}$$

Figure 1.3 illustrates the soccer field and its dimensions.

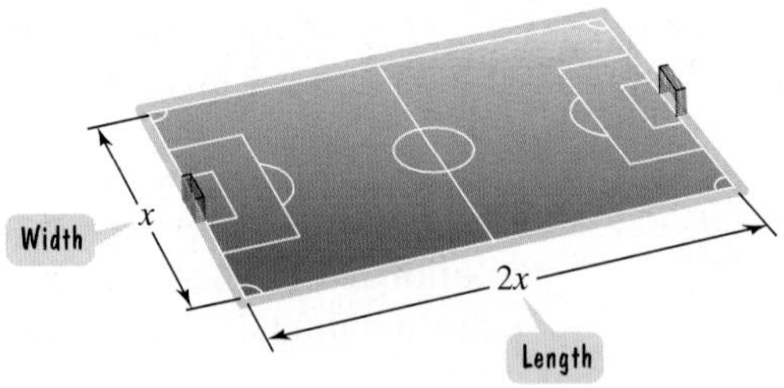


**Figure 1.3**

**Step 3 Write an equation in $x$ that describes the conditions.** Because the perimeter of a soccer field is 300 yards,

| Twice the length | plus | twice the width | is | the perimeter. |
|---|---|---|---|---|
| $2 \cdot 2x$ | $+$ | $2 \cdot x$ | $=$ | $300.$ |

**Step 4 Solve the equation and answer the question.**

$2 \cdot 2x + 2 \cdot x = 300$ This is the equation that models the verbal conditions.

$4x + 2x = 300$ Multiply.

$6x = 300$ Combine like terms.

$\frac{6x}{6} = \frac{300}{6}$ Divide both sides by 6.

$x = 50$ Simplify.

Thus,

$$\text{Width} = x = 50$$
$$\text{Length} = 2x = 2(50) = 100.$$

The dimensions of a soccer field are 50 yards by 100 yards.

**Step 5 Check the proposed solution in the original wording of the problem.** The perimeter of the soccer field using the dimensions that we found is 2(50 feet) + 2(100 feet) = 100 feet + 200 feet, or 300 feet. Because the problem's wording tells us that the perimeter is 300 feet, our dimensions are correct.

**Check Point 5** A rectangular swimming pool is three times as long as it is wide. If the perimeter of the pool is 320 feet, what are the pool's dimensions?

3 Solve for a variable in a formula.

## Solving for a Variable in a Formula

When working with formulas, such as the geometric formulas shown in Table 1.2, it is often necessary to solve for a specified variable. This is done by isolating the specified variable on one side of the equation. Begin by isolating all terms with the specified variable on one side of the equation and all terms without the specified variable on the other side. The next example shows how to do this.

### EXAMPLE 6 Solving for a Variable in a Formula

Solve the formula $2l + 2w = P$ for $w$.

**Solution** First, isolate $2w$ on the left by subtracting $2l$ from both sides. Then solve for $w$ by dividing both sides by 2.

We need to isolate $w$

$$2l + 2w = P$$ This is the given formula.

$$2l - 2l + 2w = P - 2l$$ Isolate $2w$ by subtracting $2l$ from both sides.

$$2w = P - 2l$$ Simplify.

$$\frac{2w}{2} = \frac{P - 2l}{2}$$ Isolate $w$ by dividing both sides by 2.

$$w = \frac{P - 2l}{2}$$ Simplify.

**Check Point 6** Solve $y = mx + b$ for $m$.

### EXAMPLE 7 Solving for a Variable That Occurs Twice in a Formula

Solve the formula $A = P + Prt$ for $P$.

**Solution** Notice that all terms with $P$ already occur on the right side of the equation. Factor $P$ from the two terms on the right to isolate $P$.

**Study Tip**

You cannot solve $A = P + Prt$ for $P$ by subtracting $Prt$ from both sides and writing

$$A - Prt = P.$$

When a formula is solved for a specified variable, that variable must be isolated on one side. The variable $P$ occurs on both sides of

$$A - Prt = P.$$

$$A = P + Prt \quad \text{This is the given formula.}$$

$$A = P(1 + rt) \quad \text{Factor } P \text{ on the right side of the equation.}$$

$$\frac{A}{1 + rt} = \frac{P(1 + rt)}{1 + rt} \quad \text{Divide both sides by } 1 + rt.$$

$$\frac{A}{1 + rt} = P \quad \text{Simplify: } \frac{P\cancel{(1 + rt)}}{1\cancel{(1 + rt)}} = \frac{P}{1} = P.$$

Equivalently,

$$P = \frac{A}{1 + rt}.$$

**Check Point 7** Solve the formula $P = C + MC$ for $C$.

## EXERCISE SET 1.2

### Practice Exercises

*In Exercises 1–4, use the five-step strategy given in the box on page 101 to solve each problem.*

1. During the 1998 baseball season, Mark McGwire hit four more home runs than Sammy Sosa. Combined, the two athletes hit 136 home runs. Determine the number of home runs hit by McGwire and Sosa.

2. In 1999, the most populous countries in the world were China and India. In that year, China's population exceeded India's by 269 million. Combined, the two countries had a population of 2265 million. Determine the 1999 population for China and India.

3. The first Super Bowl was played between the Green Bay Packers and the Kansas City Chiefs in 1967. Only once, in 1991, were the winning and losing scores in the Super Bowl consecutive integers. If the sum of the scores was 39, what were the scores?

4. The longest-lived U.S. presidents are John Adams (age 90), Herbert Hoover (also 90), and Harry Truman (88). Behind them are James Madison, Thomas Jefferson, and Richard Nixon. The latter three men lived a total of 249 years, and their ages at the time of death form consecutive odd integers. For how long did Nixon, Jefferson, and Madison live?

### Application Exercises

*Medical researchers have found that the desirable heart rate $R$, in beats per minute, for beneficial exercise is approximated by the formulas*

$$R = 143 - 0.65\,A \quad \text{for women}$$

$$R = 165 - 0.75\,A \quad \text{for men}$$

*where $A$ is the person's age. Use these formulas to solve Exercises 5–6.*

5. If the desirable heart rate for a woman is 117 beats per minute, how old is she? How is the solution shown on the line graph at the top of the next column?

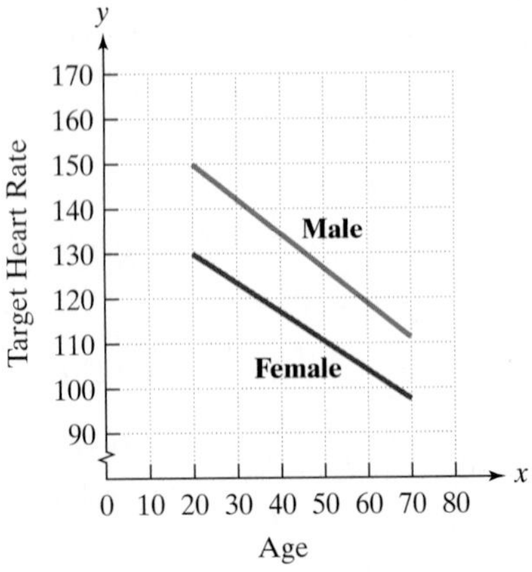

6. If the desirable heart rate for a man is 147 beats per minute, how old is he? How is the solution shown by the line graph?

7. The Indianapolis 500 is a car race in which specially built cars compete by racing 500 miles around the 2.5-mile track. Using the actual speeds of the winners from 1980 through 1992, mathematicians obtained the formula $y = 2.5x + 198.73$, in which $x$ represents the number of years after 1980 and $y$ represents the winning speed. How many years after 1980 is the winning speed predicted to be 273.73 miles per hour? What year will that be?

8. The International Panel on Climate Change is a U.N.-sponsored body made up of more than 1500 leading experts from 60 nations. According to their recent findings, increased levels of atmospheric carbon dioxide are affecting our climate. Global warming is under way and the effects could be catastrophic. The formula $C = 1.44t + 280$ describes carbon dioxide concentration $C$, in parts per million, $t$ years after 1939. The preindustrial carbon dioxide concentration of 280 parts per million remained fairly constant until World War II, increasing after that due primarily to the burning of fossil fuels related to energy consumption. When will the concentration be double the preindustrial level?

9. A woman's height $(h)$ is related to the length of the femur $(f)$ (the bone from the knee to the hip socket) by the formula $f = 0.432h - 10.44$. Both $h$ and $f$ are measured in inches. A partial skeleton is found of a woman in which the femur is 16 inches long. Police find the skeleton in an area where a woman slightly over 5 feet tall has been missing for over a year. Can the partial skeleton be that of the missing woman? Explain.

10. The formula

$$\frac{W}{2} - 3H = 53$$

describes the recommended weight $W$, in pounds, for a male, where $H$ represents the man's height in inches over 5 feet. What is the recommended weight for a man who is 6 feet, 3 inches tall?

*In Exercises 11–42, use the five-step strategy given in the box on page 101 to solve each problem.*

11. The bus fare in a city is \$1.25. People who use the bus have the option of purchasing a monthly coupon book for \$21.00. With the coupon book, the fare is reduced to \$0.50. Determine the number of times in a month the bus must be used so that the total monthly cost without the coupon book is the same as the total monthly cost with the coupon book.

12. A coupon book for a bridge costs \$21 per month. The toll for the bridge is normally \$2.50, but it is reduced to \$1 for people who have purchased the coupon book. Determine the number of times in a month the bridge must be crossed so that the total monthly cost without the coupon book is the same as the total monthly cost with the coupon book.

13. You can rent a car for \$30 per day with unlimited mileage or for \$25 per day plus 15¢ per mile. For what daily mileage do the two plans cost the same?

14. Numerous variables affect the relationship between education and income. A simplified form of two such models focuses on the effect of gender in these relationships. Yearly income for men increases by \$1600 with each year of education; men with no education earn \$6300 yearly. For women, yearly income increases by \$1200 for each year of education; women with no education earn \$2100 yearly. Using these models, how many years of education must a woman have to earn the same yearly salary as a man with 11 years of education?

15. You inherit \$25,000 with the stipulation that for the first year the money must be invested in two stocks paying 9% and 12% annual interest, respectively. How much should be invested at each rate if the total interest earned for the year is to be \$2250?

16. You inherit \$18,750 with the stipulation that for the first year the money must be invested in two stocks paying 10% and 12% annual interest, respectively. How much should be invested at each rate if the total interest earned for the year is to be \$2117?

17. You have \$70,000 to invest. Part of the money is to be placed in a Certificate of Deposit paying 8% per year. The rest is to be placed in corporate bonds paying 12% per year. If you wish to obtain an overall return of 9% per year, how much should you place in each investment?

18. A loan officer at a bank has \$1,000,000 to lend, lending at the rate of 19% per year or at the rate of 16% per year. If the officer is required to obtain an overall return of 18% per year, how much should be loaned at each rate?

19. You invest \$2500 in an account that pays 5.5% annual interest. How much additional money should you invest in an account that pays 8% annual interest so that your total interest is 7% of your total investment?

20. Money is invested at 8% and 9% annual interest, with \$5000 more invested at 8% than at 9%. If the accounts earn the same amount of yearly interest, how much was invested at each rate?

21. A chemist needs to mix a 30% acid solution with a 12% acid solution to obtain a 50 liter mixture consisting of 20% acid. How many liters of each of the acid solutions must be used?

22. A chemist needs to mix a 5% acid solution with a 10% acid solution to obtain a 50 liter mixture consisting of 8% acid. How many liters of each of the acid solutions must be used?

23. How many ounces of a 15% alcohol solution must be mixed with 4 ounces of a 20% alcohol solution to make a 17% alcohol solution?

24. How many liters of a 50% alcohol solution must be mixed with 80 liters of a 20% alcohol solution to make a 40% alcohol solution?

25. How many milliliters of pure water should a pharmacist add to 50 milliliters of a 15% minoxidil solution (used to treat male pattern baldness) to make a 10% minoxidil solution?

26. How many ounces of pure salt should be added to 40 ounces of a 20% salt solution to make a saline solution that is 36% salt?

27. At the north campus of a performing arts school, 10% of the students are music majors. At the south campus, 90% of the students are music majors. The campuses are merged into one east campus. If 42% of the 1000 students at the east campus are music majors, how many students did the north and south campuses have before the merger?

28. At the north campus of a small liberal arts college, 10% of the students are women. At the south campus, 50% of the students are women. The campuses are merged into one east campus. If 40% of the 1200 students at the east campus are women, how many students did the north and south campuses have before the merger?

29. The length of the rectangular tennis court at Wimbledon is 6 feet longer than twice the width. If the court's perimeter is 228 feet, what are the court's dimensions?

30. The length of a rectangular basketball court is 6 feet less than twice the width. If the court's perimeter is 288 feet, what are the court's dimensions?

31. A bookcase is to be constructed as shown in the figure. The length is to be 3 times the height. If 60 feet of lumber is available for the entire unit, find the length and height of the bookcase.

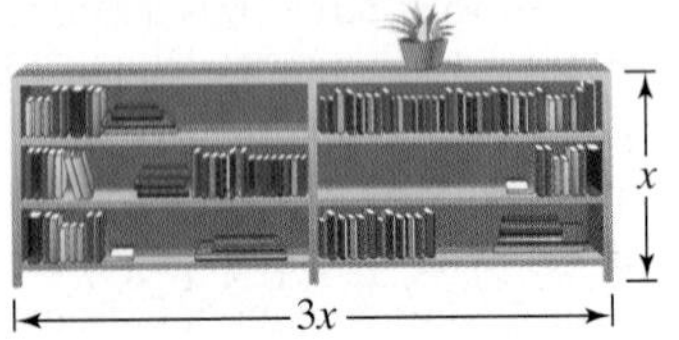


32. The height of the bookcase in the figure is 3 feet longer than the length of a shelf. If 18 feet of lumber is available for the entire unit, find the length and height of the unit.

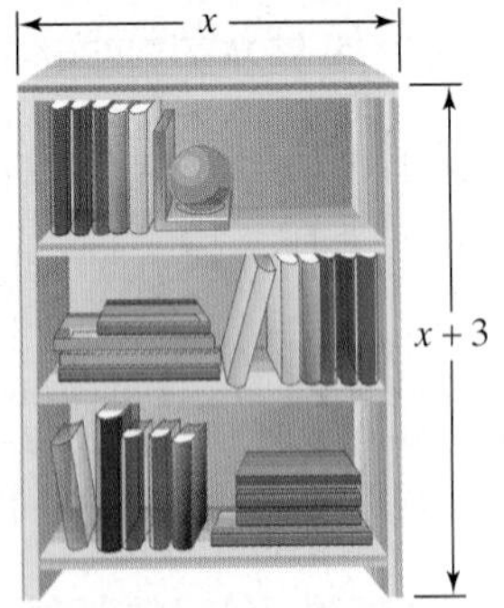


33. An automobile repair shop charged a customer $448, listing $63 for parts and the remainder for labor. If the cost of labor is $35 per hour, how many hours of labor did it take to repair the car?

34. A repair bill on a yacht came to $1603, including $532 for parts and the remainder for labor. If the cost of labor is $63 per hour, how many hours of labor did it take to repair the yacht?

35. After a 35% price reduction, a graphing calculator sold for $81.90. What was the calculator's price before the reduction?

36. After a 12% price reduction, a car sold for $17,600. What was the car's price before the reduction?

37. Inclusive of a 6.5% sales tax, a television sold for $788.10. Find the price of the television before the tax was added.

38. Inclusive of a 6.5% sales tax, a car sold for $17,466. Find the price of the car before the tax was added.

39. Markup is the amount added to the dealer's cost of an item to arrive at the selling price of that item. The selling price of a refrigerator is $584. If the markup is 25% of the dealer's cost, what is the dealer's cost of the refrigerator?

40. A calculator costs a dealer $80. Determine the selling price if the markup is 20% of the selling price.

41. An HMO pamphlet contains the following recommended weight for women: "Give yourself 100 pounds for the first 5 feet plus 5 pounds for every inch over 5 feet tall." Using this description, what height corresponds to an ideal weight of 135 pounds?

42. A job pays an annual salary of $33,150, which includes a holiday bonus of $750. If paychecks are issued twice a month, what is the gross amount for each paycheck?

*In Exercises 43–68, solve each formula for the specified variable.*

43. $A = lw$ for $w$

44. $D = RT$ for $R$

45. $A = \frac{1}{2}bh$ for $b$

46. $V = \frac{1}{3}Bh$ for $B$

47. $I = Prt$ for $P$

48. $C = 2\pi r$ for $r$

49. $E = mc^2$ for $m$

50. $V = \pi r^2 h$ for $h$

51. $T = D + pm$ for $p$

52. $P = C + MC$ for $M$

53. $A = \frac{1}{2}h(a + b)$ for $a$

54. $A = \frac{1}{2}h(a + b)$ for $b$

55. $S = P + Prt$ for $r$

56. $S = P + Prt$ for $t$

57. $B = \dfrac{F}{S - V}$ for $S$

58. $S = \dfrac{C}{1 - r}$ for $r$

59. $\dfrac{1}{p} + \dfrac{1}{q} = \dfrac{1}{f}$ for $f$

60. $\dfrac{1}{R} = \dfrac{1}{R_1} + \dfrac{1}{R_2}$ for $R_1$

61. $A = 2lw + 2lh + 2wh$ for $h$

62. $mv = Ft + mv_0$ for $m$

63. $I = \dfrac{nE}{R + nr}$ for $n$

64. $R = \dfrac{R_1 R_2}{R_1 + R_2}$ for $R_1$

65. $\dfrac{1}{cy} = \dfrac{1}{dy} - \dfrac{1}{e}$ for $y$

66. $\dfrac{1}{c} - \dfrac{1}{y} = \dfrac{1}{y} - \dfrac{1}{d}$ for $y$

**67.** $\frac{1}{s} = f + \frac{1 - f}{p}$ for $f$

**68.** $\frac{b}{ay - 1} - \frac{a}{by - 1} = 0$ for $y(a \neq b)$

## Writing in Mathematics

**69.** What is a formula?

**70.** We discussed formulas in this section after we considered procedures for solving linear equations. Doesn't working with a formula simply mean substituting given numbers into the formula and using the order of operations? Is it necessary to know how to solve equations to work with formulas? Explain.

**71.** In your own words, describe a step-by-step approach for solving algebraic word problems.

**72.** Did you have some difficulties solving some of the problems that were assigned in this exercise set? Discuss what you did if this happened to you. Did your course of action enhance your ability to solve algebraic word problems?

## Technology Exercises

**73.** The average hourly rate $(y)$ for public school cafeteria workers in the United States in 1980 was \$3.82 per hour. This rate has increased steadily by \$0.30 per hour each year since 1980.

**a.** Write a mathematical model for the hourly rate $x$ years after 1980.

**b.** Use a graphing utility to graph the model in a $[0, 12, 1]$ by $[0, 8, 1]$ viewing rectangle.

**c.** Use the trace feature to trace along the curve to determine in what year the hourly wage was \$6.22.

**d.** Verify your observation in part (c) algebraically by setting the model equal to 6.22 and solving for $x$.

**74.** A tennis club offers two payment options. Members can pay a monthly fee of \$30 plus \$5 per hour for court rental time. The second option has no monthly fee, but court time costs \$7.50 per hour.

**a.** Write a mathematical model representing total monthly costs for each option for $x$ hours of court rental time.

**b.** Use a graphing utility to graph the two models in a $[0, 15, 1]$ by $[0, 120, 6]$ viewing rectangle.

**c.** Use your utility's trace or intersection feature to determine where the two graphs intersect. Describe what the coordinates of this intersection point represent in practical terms.

**d.** Verify part (c) using an algebraic approach by setting the two models equal to one another and determining how many hours one has to rent the court so that the two plans result in identical monthly costs.

## Critical Thinking Exercises

**75.** The price of a dress is reduced by 40%. When the dress still does not sell, it is reduced by 40% of the reduced price. If the price of the dress after both reductions is \$72, what was the original price?

**76.** In a film, the actor Charles Coburn plays an elderly "uncle" character criticized for marrying a woman when he is 3 times her age. He wittily replies, "Ah, but in 20 years time I shall only be twice her age." How old is the "uncle" and the woman?

**77.** Suppose that we agree to pay you 8¢ for every problem in this chapter that you solve correctly and fine you 5¢ for every problem done incorrectly. If at the end of 26 problems we do not owe each other any money, how many problems did you solve correctly?

**78.** It was wartime when the Ricardos found out Mrs. Ricardo was pregnant. Ricky Ricardo was drafted and made out a will, deciding that \$14,000 in a savings account was to be divided between his wife and his child-to-be. Rather strangely, and certainly with gender bias, Ricky stipulated that if the child were a boy, he would get twice the amount of the mother's portion. If it were a girl, the mother would get twice the amount the girl was to receive. We'll never know what Ricky was thinking of, for (as fate would have it) he did not return from war. Mrs. Ricardo gave birth to twins—a boy and a girl. How was the money divided?

**79.** Solve for $C$: $V = C - \frac{C - S}{L}N$.

## Group Exercise

**80.** One of the best ways to learn how to *solve* a word problem in algebra is to *design* word problems of your own. Creating a word problem makes you very aware of precisely how much information is needed to solve the problem. You must also focus on the best way to present information to a reader and on how much information to give. As you write your problem, you gain skills that will help you solve problems created by others.

The group should design five different word problems that can be solved using an algebraic equation. All of the problems should be on different topics. For example, the group should not have more than one problem on simple interest. The group should turn in both the problems and their algebraic solutions.

# SECTION 1.3 *Quadratic Equations*

## Objectives

1. Solve quadratic equations by factoring.
2. Solve quadratic equations by the square root method.
3. Solve quadratic equations by completing the square.
4. Solve quadratic equations using the quadratic formula.
5. Use the discriminant to determine the kinds of solutions.
6. Solve problems modeled by quadratic equations.

The crocodile, an endangered species, was the subject of a protection program at Florida's Everglades National Park. Park rangers used the formula

$$P = -10x^2 + 475x + 3500$$

to estimate the crocodile population, $P$, after $x$ years of the protection program. Their goal was to bring the population up to 7250. To find out how long the program had to be continued for this to occur, we need to substitute 7250 for $P$ in the formula and solve for $x$:

$$7250 = -10x^2 + 475x + 3500.$$

Do you see how this equation differs from a linear equation? The exponent on $x$ is 2. Solving such an equation involves finding the set of numbers that will make the equation a true statement. In this section, we study a number of methods for solving equations in the form $ax^2 + bx + c = 0$. We also look at applications of these equations.

## The Standard Form of a Quadratic Equation

We begin by defining a quadratic equation.

**Definition of a Quadratic Equation**

A **quadratic equation** in $x$ is an equation that can be written in the **standard form**

$$ax^2 + bx + c = 0$$

where $a$, $b$, and $c$ are real numbers with $a \neq 0$. A quadratic equation in $x$ is also called a **second-degree polynomial equation** in $x$.

An example of a quadratic equation in standard form is $x^2 - 7x + 10 = 0$. The coefficient of $x^2$ is $1 (a = 1)$, the coefficient of $x$ is $-7 (b = -7)$, and the constant term is $10 (c = 10)$.

**1** Solve quadratic equations by factoring.

## Solving Quadratic Equations by Factoring

We can factor the left side of the quadratic equation $x^2 - 7x + 10 = 0$. We obtain $(x - 5)(x - 2) = 0$. If a quadratic equation has zero on one side and a factored expression on the other side, it can be solved using the **zero-product principle**.

**The Zero-Product Principle**

If the product of two algebraic expressions is zero, then at least one of the factors is equal to zero.

$$\text{If } AB = 0, \quad \text{then } A = 0 \text{ or } B = 0.$$

For example, consider the equation $(x - 5)(x - 2) = 0$. According to the zero-product principle, this product can be zero only if at least one of the factors is zero. We set each individual factor equal to zero and solve each resulting equation for $x$.

$$(x - 5)(x - 2) = 0$$

$$x - 5 = 0 \quad \text{or} \quad x - 2 = 0$$

$$x = 5 \qquad\qquad x = 2$$

**Solving a Quadratic Equation by Factoring**

1. If necessary, rewrite the equation in the form $ax^2 + bx + c = 0$, moving all terms to one side, thereby obtaining zero on the other side.
2. Factor.
3. Apply the zero-product principle, setting each factor equal to zero.
4. Solve the equations in step 3.
5. Check the solutions in the original equation.

## EXAMPLE 1 Solving Quadratic Equations by Factoring

Solve by factoring and then using the zero-product principle.

**a.** $4x^2 - 2x = 0$ **b.** $2x^2 + 7x = 4$

### Solution

**a.** We begin with $4x^2 - 2x = 0$.

**Step 1 Move all terms to one side and obtain zero on the other side.** All terms are already on the left and zero is on the other side, so we can skip this step.

**Step 2 Factor.** We factor out $2x$ from the two terms on the left side.

$$4x^2 - 2x = 0 \quad \text{This is the given equation.}$$

$$2x(2x - 1) = 0 \quad \text{Factor.}$$

**Steps 3 and 4 Set each factor equal to zero and solve the resulting equations.**

$$2x = 0 \quad \text{or} \quad 2x - 1 = 0$$

$$x = 0 \qquad\qquad 2x = 1$$

$$x = \tfrac{1}{2}$$

**Step 5 Check the solutions in the original equation.**

| **Check 0:** | **Check $\frac{1}{2}$:** |
|---|---|
| $4x^2 - 2x = 0$ | $4x^2 - 2x = 0$ |
| $4 \cdot 0^2 - 2 \cdot 0 \stackrel{?}{=} 0$ | $4\left(\frac{1}{2}\right)^2 - 2\left(\frac{1}{2}\right) \stackrel{?}{=} 0$ |
| $0 - 0 \stackrel{?}{=} 0$ | $4\left(\frac{1}{4}\right) - 2\left(\frac{1}{2}\right) \stackrel{?}{=} 0$ |
| $0 = 0$ ✓ | $1 - 1 \stackrel{?}{=} 0$ |
| | $0 = 0$ ✓ |

The solution set is $\left\{0, \frac{1}{2}\right\}$.

**b.** Next, we solve $2x^2 + 7x = 4$.

**Step 1 Move all terms to one side and obtain zero on the other side.** Subtract 4 from both sides and write the equation in standard form.

$$2x^2 + 7x - 4 = 4 - 4$$

$$2x^2 + 7x - 4 = 0$$

**Step 2 Factor.**

$$2x^2 + 7x - 4 = 0$$

$$(2x - 1)(x + 4) = 0$$

**Steps 3 and 4 Set each factor equal to zero and solve each resulting equation.**

$$2x - 1 = 0 \quad \text{or} \quad x + 4 = 0$$

$$2x = 1 \qquad\qquad x = -4$$

$$x = \frac{1}{2}$$

**Step 5 Check the solutions in the original equation.**

| **Check $\frac{1}{2}$:** | **Check $-4$:** |
|---|---|
| $2x^2 + 7x = 4$ | $2x^2 + 7x = 4$ |
| $2\left(\frac{1}{2}\right)^2 + 7\left(\frac{1}{2}\right) \stackrel{?}{=} 4$ | $2(-4)^2 + 7(-4) \stackrel{?}{=} 4$ |
| $\frac{1}{2} + \frac{7}{2} \stackrel{?}{=} 4$ | $32 + (-28) \stackrel{?}{=} 4$ |
| $4 = 4$ ✓ | $4 = 4$ ✓ |

The solution set is $\left\{-4, \frac{1}{2}\right\}$.

**Check Point 1** Solve by factoring and then using the zero-product principle.

**a.** $3x^2 - 9x = 0$ **b.** $2x^2 + x = 1$

## Technology

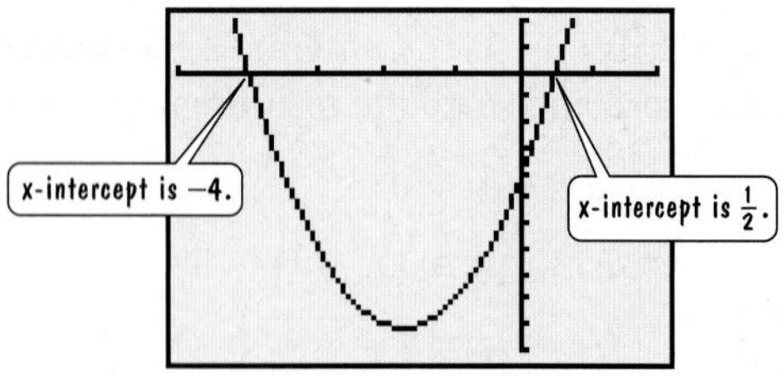


You can use a graphing utility to check the real solutions to a quadratic equation. **The solutions to $ax^2 + bx + c = 0$ correspond to the $x$-intercepts for the graph of $y = ax^2 + bx + c$.** For example, to check the solutions of $2x^2 + 7x = 4$, or $2x^2 + 7x - 4 = 0$, graph $y = 2x^2 + 7x - 4 = 0$, as shown on the left. Note that it is important to have all nonzero terms on one side of the quadratic equation before entering it into the graphing utility. The $x$-intercepts are $-4$ and $\frac{1}{2}$, verifying $\left\{-4, \frac{1}{2}\right\}$ as the solution set.

**2** Solve quadratic equations by the square root method.

## Solving Quadratic Equations by the Square Root Method

Quadratic equations of the form $u^2 = d$, where $d > 0$ and $u$ is an algebraic expression, can be solved by the **square root method**. First, isolate the squared expression $u^2$ on one side of the equation and the number $d$ on the other side. Then take the square root of both sides. Remember, there are two numbers whose square is $d$. One number is positive and one is negative.

We can use factoring to verify that $u^2 = d$ has two solutions.

$$u^2 = d$$ This is the given equation.

$$u^2 - d = 0$$ Move all terms to one side and obtain zero on the other side.

$$(u + \sqrt{d})(u - \sqrt{d}) = 0$$ Factor.

$$u + \sqrt{d} = 0 \quad \text{or} \quad u - \sqrt{d} = 0$$ Set each factor equal to zero.

$$u = -\sqrt{d} \qquad u = \sqrt{d}$$ Solve the resulting equations.

Because the solutions differ only in sign, we can write them in abbreviated notation as $u = \pm\sqrt{d}$. We read this as "$u$ equals positive or negative the square root of $d$."

Now that we have verified these solutions, we can solve $u^2 = d$ directly by taking square roots. This process is called **the square root method**.

### The Square Root Method

If $u$ is an algebraic expression and $d$ is a positive real number, then $u^2 = d$ has exactly two solutions:

$$\text{If } u^2 = d, \quad \text{then } u = \sqrt{d} \text{ or } u = -\sqrt{d}.$$

Equivalently,

$$\text{If } u^2 = d, \quad \text{then } u = \pm\sqrt{d}.$$

### EXAMPLE 2 Solving Quadratic Equations by the Square Root Method

Solve by the square root method:

**a.** $4x^2 = 20$ **b.** $(x - 2)^2 = 6$

**Solution**

**a.** In order to apply the square root method, we need a squared expression by itself on one side of the equation.

$$4x^2 = 20$$

We want $x^2$ by itself.

We can get $x^2$ by itself if we divide both sides by 4.

$$\frac{4x^2}{4} = \frac{20}{4}$$

$$x^2 = 5$$

Now, we can apply the square root method.

$$x = \pm\sqrt{5}$$

By checking both values in the original equation, we can confirm that the solution set is $\{-\sqrt{5}, \sqrt{5}\}$.

**b.** $(x - 2)^2 = 6$

The squared expression is by itself.

With the squared expression by itself, we can apply the square root method.

$$x - 2 = \pm\sqrt{6}$$

We solve for $x$ by adding 2 to both sides.

$$x = 2 \pm \sqrt{6}$$

By checking both values in the original equation, we can confirm that the solution set is $\{2 + \sqrt{6}, 2 - \sqrt{6}\}$.

**Check Point 2** Solve by the square root method:

**a.** $3x^2 = 21$ **b.** $(x + 5)^2 = 11$

**3** Solve quadratic equations by completing the square.

## Completing the Square

How do we solve an equation in the form $ax^2 + bx + c = 0$ if the equation cannot be factored? We cannot use the zero-product principle in such a case. However, we can convert the equation into an equivalent equation that can be solved using the square root method. This is accomplished by **completing the square**.

### Completing the Square

If $x^2 + bx$ is a binomial, then by adding $\left(\frac{b}{2}\right)^2$, which is the square of half the coefficient of $x$, a perfect square trinomial will result. That is,

$$x^2 + bx + \left(\frac{b}{2}\right)^2 = \left(x + \frac{b}{2}\right)^2.$$

We can solve any quadratic equation by completing the square. If the coefficient of the $x^2$ term is one, we add the square of half the coefficient of $x$ to both sides of the equation. **When you add a constant term to one side of the equation to complete the square, be certain to add the same constant to the other side of the equation.** These ideas are illustrated in Example 3.

## EXAMPLE 3 Solving a Quadratic Equation by Completing the Square

Solve by completing the square: $x^2 - 6x + 2 = 0$.

**Solution** We begin the procedure by isolating the binomial, $x^2 - 6x$, so that we can complete the square. Thus, we subtract 2 from both sides of the equation.

$$x^2 - 6x + 2 = 0$$
$$x^2 - 6x + 2 - 2 = 0 - 2$$
$$x^2 - 6x = -2$$

We need to add a constant to this binomial that will make it a perfect square trinomial.

What constant should we add? Add the square of half the coefficient of $x$.

$$x^2 - 6x = -2$$

$-6$ is the coefficient of $x$.
$\left(\frac{-6}{2}\right)^2 = (-3)^2 = 9$

Thus, we need to add 9 to $x^2 - 6x$. In order to keep the equation balanced, we must add 9 to both sides.

$x^2 - 6x = -2$ This is the quadratic equation with the binomial isolated.

$x^2 - 6x + 9 = -2 + 9$ Complete the square, adding 9 to both sides.

$(x - 3)^2 = 7$ Factor the perfect square trinomial.

$x - 3 = \pm\sqrt{7}$ Apply the square root method.

$x = 3 \pm \sqrt{7}$ Add 3 to both sides.

In this step we have converted our equation into one that can be solved by the square root method.

The solution set is $\{3 + \sqrt{7}, 3 - \sqrt{7}\}$.

**Check Point 3** Solve by completing the square: $x^2 - 2x - 2 = 0$.

If the coefficient of the $x^2$ term in a quadratic equation is not one, you must divide each side of the equation by this coefficient before completing the square. For example, to solve $3x^2 - 2x - 4 = 0$ by completing the square, first divide every term by 3:

$$\frac{3x^2}{3} - \frac{2x}{3} - \frac{4}{3} = \frac{0}{3}$$

$$x^2 - \frac{2}{3}x - \frac{4}{3} = 0.$$

Now that the coefficient of $x^2$ is one, we can solve by completing the square using the method of Example 3.

**4** Solve quadratic equations using the quadratic formula.

## Solving Quadratic Equations Using the Quadratic Formula

We can use the method of completing the square to derive a formula that can be used to solve all quadratic equations. The derivation given here also shows a particular quadratic equation, $3x^2 - 2x - 4 = 0$, to specifically illustrate each of the steps.

### Deriving the Quadratic Formula

| Standard Form of a Quadratic Equation | Comment | A Specific Example |
|---|---|---|
| $ax^2 + bx + c = 0, \quad a \neq 0$ | This is the given equation. | $3x^2 - 2x - 4 = 0$ |
| $x^2 + \frac{b}{a}x + \frac{c}{a} = 0$ | Divide both sides by the coefficient of $x^2$. | $x^2 - \frac{2}{3}x - \frac{4}{3} = 0$ |
| $x^2 + \frac{b}{a}x = -\frac{c}{a}$ | Isolate the binomial by adding $-\frac{c}{a}$ on both sides. | $x^2 - \frac{2}{3}x = \frac{4}{3}$ |
| $x^2 + \frac{b}{a}x + \left(\frac{b}{2a}\right)^2 = -\frac{c}{a} + \left(\frac{b}{2a}\right)^2$ (half)$^2$<br>$x^2 + \frac{b}{a}x + \frac{b^2}{4a^2} = -\frac{c}{a} + \frac{b^2}{4a^2}$ | Complete the square. Add the square of half the coefficient of $x$ to both sides. | $x^2 - \frac{2}{3}x + \left(\frac{1}{3}\right)^2 = \frac{4}{3} + \left(\frac{1}{3}\right)^2$ (half)$^2$<br>$x^2 - \frac{2}{3}x + \frac{1}{9} = \frac{4}{3} + \frac{1}{9}$ |
| $\left(x + \frac{b}{2a}\right)^2 = -\frac{c}{a} \cdot \frac{4a}{4a} + \frac{b^2}{4a^2}$ | Factor on the left and obtain a common denominator on the right. | $\left(x - \frac{1}{3}\right)^2 = \frac{4}{3} \cdot \frac{3}{3} + \frac{1}{9}$ |
| $\left(x + \frac{b}{2a}\right)^2 = \frac{-4ac + b^2}{4a^2}$<br>$\left(x + \frac{b}{2a}\right)^2 = \frac{b^2 - 4ac}{4a^2}$ | Add fractions on the right. | $\left(x - \frac{1}{3}\right)^2 = \frac{12 + 1}{9}$<br>$\left(x - \frac{1}{3}\right)^2 = \frac{13}{9}$ |
| $x + \frac{b}{2a} = \pm\sqrt{\frac{b^2 - 4ac}{4a^2}}$ | Apply the square root method. | $x - \frac{1}{3} = \pm\sqrt{\frac{13}{9}}$ |
| $x + \frac{b}{2a} = \pm\frac{\sqrt{b^2 - 4ac}}{2\lvert a\rvert}$ | Take the square root of the quotient, simplifying the denominator. | $x - \frac{1}{3} = \pm\frac{\sqrt{13}}{3}$ |
| $x = \frac{-b}{2a} \pm \frac{\sqrt{b^2 - 4ac}}{2\lvert a\rvert}$ | Solve for $x$ by subtracting $\frac{b}{2a}$ from both sides. | $x = \frac{1}{3} \pm \frac{\sqrt{13}}{3}$ |
| $x = \frac{-b \pm \sqrt{b^2 - 4ac}}{2\lvert a\rvert}$ | Combine fractions on the right. | $x = \frac{1 \pm \sqrt{13}}{3}$ |

## To Die at Twenty

Can the equations

$$7x^5 + 12x^3 - 9x + 4 = 0$$

and

$$8x^6 - 7x^5 + 4x^3 - 19 = 0$$

be solved using a formula similar to the quadratic formula? The first equation has five solutions and the second has six solutions, but they cannot be found using a formula. How do we know? In 1832, a 20-year-old Frenchman, Evariste Galois, wrote down a proof showing that there is no general formula to solve equations when the exponent on the variable is 5 or greater. Galois was jailed as a political activist several times while still a teenager. The day after his brilliant proof he fought a duel over a woman. The duel was a political setup. As he lay dying, Galois told his brother, Alfred, of the manuscript that contained his proof: "Mathematical manuscripts are in my room. On the table. Take care of my work. Make it known. Important. Don't cry, Alfred. I need all my courage—to die at twenty." (Our source is Leopold Infeld's biography of Galois, *Whom the Gods Love*. Some historians, however, dispute the story of Galois's ironic death the very day after his algebraic proof. Mathematical truths seem more reliable than historical ones!)

Because the same real numbers are represented by $\pm 2|a|$ and $\pm 2a$, we can omit the absolute value sign in the last step. The resulting formula is called the **quadratic formula**.

### The Quadratic Formula

The solutions of a quadratic equation in standard form $ax^2 + bx + c = 0$, with $a \neq 0$, are given by the **quadratic formula**

$$x = \frac{-b \pm \sqrt{b^2 - 4ac}}{2a}.$$

x equals negative b, plus or minus the square root of $b^2 - 4ac$, all divided by 2a.

To use the quadratic formula, write the quadratic equation in standard form if necessary. Then determine the numerical values for $a$ (the coefficient of the squared term), $b$ (the coefficient of the $x$ term), and $c$ (the constant term). Substitute the values of $a$, $b$, and $c$ in the quadratic formula and evaluate the expression. The $\pm$ sign indicates that there are two solutions of the equation.

### EXAMPLE 4 Solving a Quadratic Equation Using the Quadratic Formula

Solve using the quadratic formula: $2x^2 - 6x + 1 = 0$.

**Solution** The given equation is in standard form. Begin by identifying the values for $a$, $b$, and $c$.

$$2x^2 - 6x + 1 = 0$$

$a = 2$ $b = -6$ $c = 1$

$$x = \frac{-b \pm \sqrt{b^2 - 4ac}}{2a}$$ Use the quadratic formula: $a = 2$, $b = -6$, and $c = 1$.

$$= \frac{-(-6) \pm \sqrt{(-6)^2 - 4(2)(1)}}{2 \cdot 2}$$ Substitute the values for a, b, and c.

$$= \frac{6 \pm \sqrt{36 - 8}}{4}$$ $-(-6) = 6$ and $(-6)^2 = (-6)(-6) = 36$.

$$= \frac{6 \pm \sqrt{28}}{2}$$ Complete the subtraction under the radical.

$$= \frac{6 \pm 2\sqrt{7}}{4}$$ $\sqrt{28} = \sqrt{4 \cdot 7} = \sqrt{4}\sqrt{7} = 2\sqrt{7}$.

$$= \frac{2(3 \pm \sqrt{7})}{4}$$ Factor out 2 from the numerator.

$$= \frac{3 \pm \sqrt{7}}{2}$$ Divide the numerator and denominator by 2.

The solution set is $\left\{\frac{3 + \sqrt{7}}{2}, \frac{3 - \sqrt{7}}{2}\right\}$.

**Check Point 4** Solve using the quadratic formula:

$$2x^2 + 2x - 1 = 0.$$

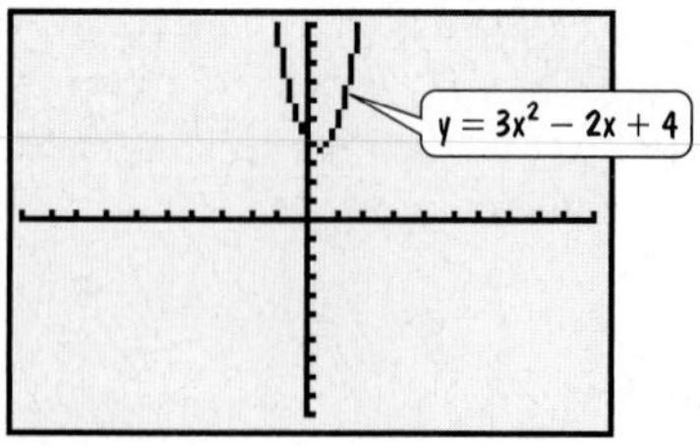


**Figure 1.4** This graph has no $x$-intercepts.

We have seen that a graphing utility can be used to check the solutions to the quadratic equation $ax^2 + bx + c = 0$. The $x$-intercepts of the graph of $y = ax^2 + bx + c$ are the solutions. However, take a look at the graph of $y = 3x^2 - 2x + 4$, shown in Figure 1.4. Notice that the graph has no $x$-intercepts. Can you guess what this means about the solutions of the quadratic equation $3x^2 - 2x + 4 = 0$? If you're not sure, we'll answer this question in the next example.

### EXAMPLE 5 Solving a Quadratic Equation Using the Quadratic Formula

Solve using the quadratic formula: $3x^2 - 2x + 4 = 0$.

**Study Tip**

See Section P.7, pages 67–72, to review complex numbers.

**Solution** The given equation is in standard form. Begin by identifying the values for $a$, $b$, and $c$.

$$3x^2 - 2x + 4 = 0$$

$a = 3$ $b = -2$ $c = 4$

$$x = \frac{-b \pm \sqrt{b^2 - 4ac}}{2a}$$ Use the quadratic formula $a = 3$, $b = -2$, and $c = 4$.

$$= \frac{-(-2) \pm \sqrt{(-2)^2 - 4(3)(4)}}{2(3)}$$ Substitute the values for $a$, $b$, and $c$.

$$= \frac{2 \pm \sqrt{4 - 48}}{6}$$ $-(-2) = 2$ and $(-2)^2 = (-2)(-2) = 4$.

$$= \frac{2 \pm \sqrt{-44}}{6}$$ Because the number under the radical sign is negative, the solutions will not be real numbers.

$$= \frac{2 \pm 2i\sqrt{11}}{6}$$ $\sqrt{-44} = \sqrt{4(11)(-1)} = 2i\sqrt{11}$

$$= \frac{2(1 \pm i\sqrt{11})}{6}$$ Factor 2 from the numerator.

$$= \frac{1 \pm i\sqrt{11}}{3}$$ Divide numerator and denominator by 2.

You can check that these solutions are correct using operations with complex numbers. The solutions are complex conjugates and the solution set is

$$\left\{\frac{1 + i\sqrt{11}}{3}, \frac{1 - i\sqrt{11}}{3}\right\}.$$

Hence, **complex imaginary solutions mean that the graph will not have any $x$-intercepts.**

**Check Point 5** Solve using the quadratic formula:

$$x^2 - 2x + 2 = 0.$$

**5** Use the discriminant to determine the kinds of solutions.

## The Discriminant

The quantity $b^2 - 4ac$, which appears under the radical sign in the quadratic formula, is called the **discriminant**. In Example 4 the discriminant was 28, a positive number that is not a perfect square. The equation had two solutions that were irrational numbers. In Example 5 the discriminant was −44, a negative number. The equation had solutions involving the imaginary number $i$. In this case our graph had no $x$-intercepts.

These observations are generalized in Table 1.3.

**Table 1.3 The Discriminant and the Nature of the Solutions to $ax^2 + bx + c = 0$**

| Discriminant $b^2 - 4ac$ | Kinds of Solutions to $ax^2 + bx + c = 0$ | Graph of $y = ax^2 + bx + c$ |
|---|---|---|
| $b^2 - 4ac > 0$ | two unequal real solutions | 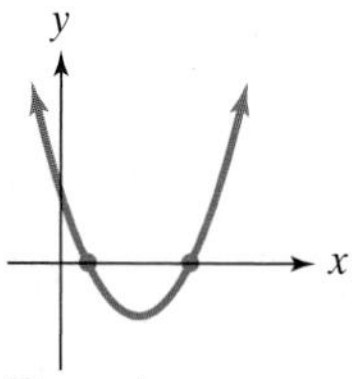 Two $x$-intercepts |
| $b^2 - 4ac = 0$ | one real solution (a repeated solution) | 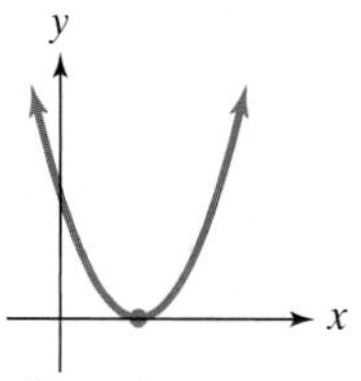 One $x$-intercept |
| $b^2 - 4ac < 0$ | No real solution; two complex imaginary solutions | 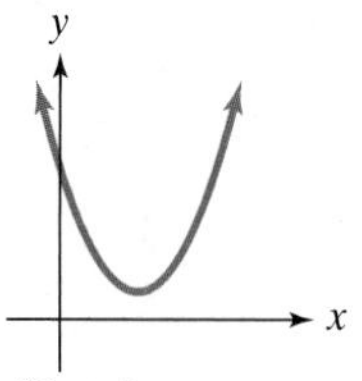 No $x$-intercepts |

## EXAMPLE 6 Using the Discriminant

Compute the discriminant of $4x^2 - 8x + 1 = 0$. What does the discriminant indicate about the kinds of solutions?

**Solution** Begin by identifying the values for $a$, $b$, and $c$.

$$4x^2 - 8x + 1 = 0$$

$a = 4$ $b = -8$ $c = 1$

Now, compute $b^2 - 4ac$, the discriminant.

$$b^2 - 4ac = (-8)^2 - 4 \cdot 4 \cdot 1 = 64 - 16 = 48$$

The discriminant is 48. Because the discriminant is positive, the equation $4x^2 - 8x + 1 = 0$ has two unequal real solutions.

**Check Point 6** Compute the discriminant of $3x^2 - 2x + 5 = 0$. What does the discriminant indicate about the kinds of solutions?

**6** Solve problems modeled by quadratic equations.

## Applications

### EXAMPLE 7 Using a Quadratic Equation to Answer a Question About the Variable in a Formula

A driver's age has something to do with his or her chances of getting into a car accident. The formula $N = 0.4x^2 - 36x + 1000$ approximates the number of accidents, $N$, per 50 million miles driven, for a driver who is $x$ years old. The formula models data for drivers ages 16 to 74, inclusive. What is the age of a driver predicted to have 312 accidents per 50 miles driven?

**Solution** We must find $x$, a driver's age, with $N = 312$ accidents per 50 million miles driven. Use the formula and substitute 312 for $N$.

$$N = 0.4x^2 - 36x + 1000 \qquad 312 = 0.4x^2 - 36x + 1000$$

Substitute 312 for N.

Let's write the quadratic equation on the right in standard form. Subtract 312 from both sides.

$$312 - 312 = 0.4x^2 - 36x + 1000 - 312$$

$$0 = 0.4x^2 - 36x + 688$$

Equivalently, $0.4x^2 - 36x + 1000 = 0$. The most efficient technique for solving this equation is the quadratic formula. Identify the values for $a$, $b$, and $c$.

$$0.4x^2 - 36x + 688 = 0$$

$a = 0.4$ $b = -36$ $c = 688$

Now, substitute these values into the quadratic formula.

$$x = \frac{-b \pm \sqrt{b^2 - 4ac}}{2a} = \frac{-(-36) \pm \sqrt{(-36)^2 - 4(0.4)(688)}}{2(0.4)}$$

$$= \frac{36 \pm \sqrt{195.2}}{0.8}$$

Thus,

$$x = \frac{36 + \sqrt{195.2}}{0.8} \quad \text{or} \quad x = \frac{36 - \sqrt{195.2}}{0.8}$$

$$\approx 62 \qquad\qquad \approx 28$$

Use a calculator to obtain an approximation to the nearest whole number.

Drivers who are about 28 and 62 years old are predicted to have 312 accidents per 50 million miles driven.

**Check Point 7** As we mentioned in the introduction to this section, rangers at a national park used the formula

$$P = -10x^2 + 475x + 3500$$

to estimate the crocodile population, $P$, after $x$ years of a protection program. How many years will it take to bring the population up to 7250?

In Example 7 we were given the mathematical model needed to solve the problem. In the next two examples, we need to form a verbal model to obtain the mathematical model needed to solve the problem. You will probably see these problems again in a slightly different form when you study calculus.

## EXAMPLE 8 Preview of a Calculus Problem

A machine produces open boxes using square sheets of metal. The machine cuts equal-sized squares measuring 2 inches on a side from each corner. Then the machine shapes the metal into an open box by turning up the sides. If each box must have a volume of 200 cubic inches, what should be the dimensions of the piece of sheet metal?

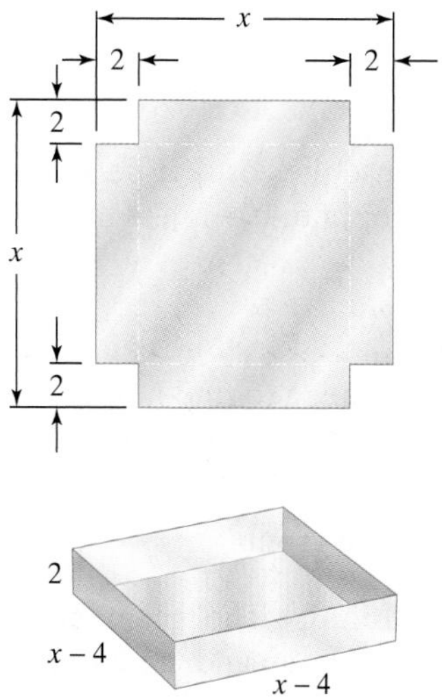


**Figure 1.5** Producing open boxes using square sheets of metal

**Solution** The situation is illustrated in Figure 1.5. Use this figure as a guide as we apply our five-step strategy for problem solving.

**Step 1 Let $x$ represent one of the quantities.** We let

$$x = \text{the length of a side of the sheet metal.}$$

**Step 2 Represent other quantities in terms of $x$.** Because the boxes are made from square sheets of metal, the width of the sheet metal is equal to its length. Thus,

$$x = \text{the width of a side of the sheet metal.}$$

**Step 3 Write an equation in $x$ that describes the conditions.** The volume of the box is 200 cubic inches. We use the formula $V = lwh$ to obtain a verbal model, shown below. Then we write our equation using the verbal model.

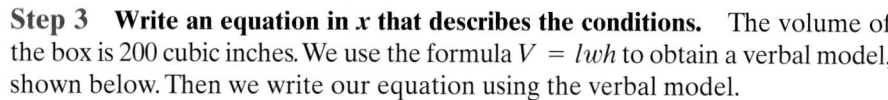

| Length of the box | times | width of the box | times | height of the box | equals | volume of the box. |
|---|---|---|---|---|---|---|
| $(x - 4)$ | $\cdot$ | $(x - 4)$ | $\cdot$ | 2 | $=$ | 200 |

**Step 4 Solve the equation and answer the question.**

| | |
|---|---|
| $2(x - 4)^2 = 200$ | This is the equation that models the verbal conditions. |
| $(x - 4)^2 = 100$ | Divide both sides by 2. |
| $x - 4 = \pm\sqrt{100}$ | Apply the square root method. |
| $x - 4 = \pm 10$ | Simplify. |
| $x = 14 \quad \text{or} \quad x = -6$ | Add 4 to both sides. |

Keep in mind that $x$ represents the width (and the length) of the sheet metal. No side can have a negative dimension, so we will not use −6. Thus, the sheet metal should be 14 inches by 14 inches.

**Step 5 Check the proposed solution in the original wording of the problem.** The problem states that the volume of the box should be 200 cubic inches. If we begin with a piece of sheet metal 14 inches by 14 inches, cut a 2-inch square from each corner, and fold up the edges, we get a box whose dimensions are 10 inches by 10 inches by 2 inches. The volume of the box is

$$V = lwh = (10\text{ in.})(10\text{ in.})(2\text{ in.}) = 200\text{ cubic inches.}$$

This volume checks with the given conditions for the problem.

**Check Point 8** A machine produces open boxes using square sheets of metal. The machine cuts equal-sized squares measuring 9 inches on a side from each corner. Then the machine shapes the metal into an open box by turning up the sides. If each box must have a volume of 144 cubic inches, what should be the dimensions of the piece of sheet metal?

## EXAMPLE 9 Preview of a Calculus Problem

An owner of a large diving boat that can carry as many as 70 people charges \$10 per passenger to groups of between 15 and 20 people. If more than 20 divers charter the boat, the fee per passenger is decreased by 10 cents times the number of people over 20. How many people must there be in a diving group to generate an income of \$323.90?

### Solution

**Step 1 Let $x$ represent one of the quantities.** Because the cost per person is computed differently depending on whether the number of divers is less than or equal to 20 or greater than 20, let

$$x = \text{the number of divers over 20.}$$

**Step 2 Represent other quantities in terms of $x$.** We need to find how many divers will generate an income of \$323.90. Because $x$ is the number of divers over 20,

$$20 + x = \text{the total number of divers in the group.}$$

**Step 3 Write an equation in $x$ that describes the conditions.** The income from each group is the product of the number of divers in the group and the cost per diver.

Total number of divers in the group | times | the cost per diver | equals | income.

$$(20 + x) \cdot (10 - 0.10x) = 323.90$$

The \$10 fee is decreased by 10 cents times the number of people over 20.

We must generate an income of \$323.90.

**Step 4 Solve the equation and answer the question.**

$$(20 + x)(10 - 0.10x) = 323.90$$ This is the equation that models the verbal conditions.

$$200 + 8x - 0.10x^2 = 323.90$$ Multiply using the FOIL method.

$$-0.10x^2 + 8x - 123.9 = 0$$ Subtract 323.90 from both sides and write the quadratic equation in standard form.

$a = -0.10$ $b = 8$ $c = -123.9$

$$x = \frac{-b \pm \sqrt{b^2 - 4ac}}{2a}$$ Use the quadratic formula: $a = -0.10$, $b = 8$, and $c = -123.9$.

$$= \frac{-8 \pm \sqrt{8^2 - 4(-0.10)(-123.9)}}{2(-0.10)}$$ Substitute the values for *a*, *b*, and *c*.

$$= \frac{-8 \pm \sqrt{14.44}}{-0.20}$$ Simplify under the radical.

$$x = \frac{-8 + 3.8}{-0.20} \quad \text{or} \quad x = \frac{-8 - 3.8}{-0.20}$$ $\sqrt{14.44} = 3.8$

$$= 21 \qquad\qquad = 59$$ Simplify.

Because $20 + x$ represents the total number of divers in the group, we see that $20 + 21$, or 41 divers, will generate an income of \$323.90. The second value for $x$ shows that $20 + 59$, or 79 divers, will also generate an income of \$323.90. However, we were told that the boat can carry as many as 70 passengers. Thus, 79 divers are too many. We conclude that with 41 divers in the group, an income of \$323.90 will be generated.

**Step 5 Check the proposed solution in the original wording of the problem.** With 41 divers, we should generate \$323.90. The group of 41 has 21 divers in excess of 20. Because the fee per diver is decreased by 10 cents times the number of people over 20, the cost per diver is

$$\$10 - \$0.10(21) = \$10 - \$2.10 = \$7.90.$$

The income is the number of divers, 41, times the cost per diver, \$7.90: 41(\$7.90) = \$323.90. This income checks with the given conditions for the problem.

## Technology

The graph of $y = -0.10x^2 + 8x + 200$, the model for income with $20 + x$ divers in the group, was obtained with a graphing utility using a [0, 50, 5] by [0, 400, 40] viewing rectangle. We can use the graph and the TRACE feature to find how many divers should be on the boat to maximize income. The graph indicates that income increases up to 40 divers (meaning that 20 + 40 or 60 passengers will maximize income). After 40, income starts to decrease, as shown in the table.

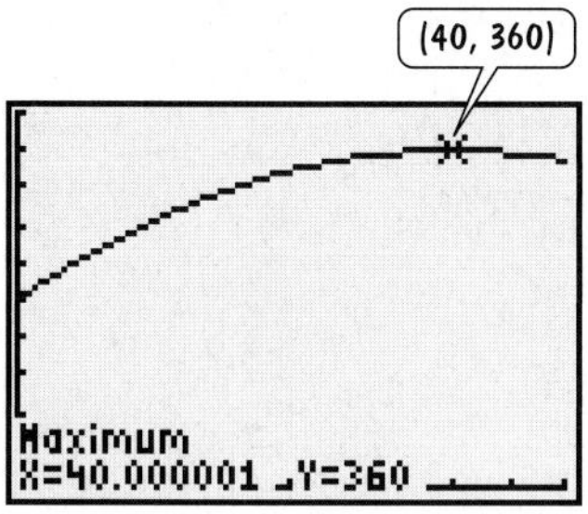


| Number of People in the Diving Group | Cost per Person | Income |
|---|---|---|
| 59 ($x = 39$) | \$6.10 | \$359.90 |
| 60 ($x = 40$) | \$6.00 | \$360.00 (maximum) |
| 61 ($x = 41$) | \$5.90 | 359.90 |

**Check Point 9** An owner of a large diving boat that can carry as many as 50 people charges \$8 per passenger to groups of between 5 and 10 people. If more than 10 divers charter the boat, the fee per passenger is decreased by 20 cents times the number of people over 10. How many people must there be in a diving group to generate an income of \$117.80?

# EXERCISE SET 1.3

## Practice Exercises

*Solve each equation in Exercises 1–10 by factoring and then using the zero-product principle.*

**1.** $x^2 - 3x - 10 = 0$
**2.** $x^2 - 13x + 36 = 0$
**3.** $6x^2 + 11x - 10 = 0$
**4.** $9x^2 + 9x + 2 = 0$
**5.** $3x^2 - 2x = 8$
**6.** $4x^2 - 13x = -3$
**7.** $3x^2 + 12x = 0$
**8.** $5x^2 - 20x = 0$
**9.** $2x(x - 3) = 5x^2 - 7x$
**10.** $16x(x - 2) = 8x - 25$

*Solve each equation in Exercises 11–18 by the square root method.*

**11.** $3x^2 = 27$
**12.** $5x^2 = 45$
**13.** $(x + 2)^2 = 25$
**14.** $(x - 3)^2 = 36$
**15.** $(3x + 2)^2 = 9$
**16.** $(4x - 1)^2 = 16$
**17.** $(5x - 1)^2 = 7$
**18.** $(8x - 3)^2 = 5$

*Solve each equation in Exercises 19–28 by completing the square.*

**19.** $x^2 - 2x = 2$
**20.** $x^2 + 4x = 12$
**21.** $x^2 - 6x - 11 = 0$
**22.** $x^2 - 2x - 5 = 0$
**23.** $x^2 + 3x - 1 = 0$
**24.** $x^2 - 3x - 5 = 0$
**25.** $2x^2 - 7x + 3 = 0$
**26.** $2x^2 + 5x - 3 = 0$
**27.** $4x^2 - 4x - 1 = 0$
**28.** $2x^2 - 4x - 1 = 0$

*Solve each equation in Exercises 29–38 using the quadratic formula.*

**29.** $x^2 + 8x + 15 = 0$
**30.** $x^2 + 8x + 12 = 0$
**31.** $x^2 + 5x + 3 = 0$
**32.** $x^2 + 5x + 2 = 0$
**33.** $3x^2 - 3x - 4 = 0$
**34.** $5x^2 + x - 2 = 0$
**35.** $4x^2 = 2x + 7$
**36.** $3x^2 = 6x - 1$
**37.** $x^2 - 6x + 10 = 0$
**38.** $x^2 - 2x + 17 = 0$

*Compute the discriminant of each equation in Exercises 39–46. What does the discriminant indicate about the kinds of solutions?*

**39.** $x^2 - 4x - 5 = 0$
**40.** $4x^2 - 2x + 3 = 0$
**41.** $2x^2 - 11x + 3 = 0$
**42.** $2x^2 + 11x - 6 = 0$
**43.** $x^2 - 2x + 1 = 0$
**44.** $3x^2 = 2x - 1$
**45.** $x^2 - 3x - 7 = 0$
**46.** $3x^2 + 4x - 2 = 0$

*Solve each equation in Exercises 47–68 by the method of your choice.*

**47.** $2x^2 - x = 1$
**48.** $3x^2 - 4x = 4$
**49.** $5x^2 + 2 = 11x$
**50.** $5x^2 = 6 - 13x$
**51.** $3x^2 = 60$
**52.** $2x^2 = 250$
**53.** $x^2 - 2x = 1$
**54.** $2x^2 + 3x = 1$
**55.** $(2x + 3)(x + 4) = 1$
**56.** $(2x - 5)(x + 1) = 2$
**57.** $(3x - 4)^2 = 16$
**58.** $(2x + 7)^2 = 25$
**59.** $3x^2 - 12x + 12 = 0$
**60.** $9 - 6x + x^2 = 0$
**61.** $4x^2 - 16 = 0$
**62.** $3x^2 - 27 = 0$
**63.** $x^2 - 6x + 13 = 0$
**64.** $x^2 - 4x + 29 = 0$
**65.** $x^2 = 4x - 7$
**66.** $5x^2 = 2x - 3$
**67.** $2x^2 - 7x = 0$
**68.** $2x^2 + 5x = 3$

## Application Exercises

**69.** The formula $M = 0.0075x^2 - 0.2676x + 14.8$ models the fuel efficiency of passenger cars, $M$, in miles per gallon, $x$ years after 1940. Environmentalists pressured automobile manufacturers for a fuel efficiency of 45 miles per gallon by the year 2000. In which year will fuel efficiency reach 45 miles per gallon according to the formula?

**70.** The formula $N = 0.036x^2 - 2.8x + 58.14$ models the number of deaths per year, $N$, per thousand people, for people who are $x$ years old, where $40 \le x \le 60$. Find, to the nearest whole number, the age at which 12 people per 1000 die annually.

*The Internet is the world's largest communications network. Although millions of computer owners access the Internet using phone lines, the process of downloading files can be slow and tedious. Cable-TV modems dramatically speed up this process. By contrast to phone modems, which transmit 56,000 bits per second, cable modems are capable of transmitting 10 million bits per second. The graph shows the millions of Internet users in the United States with this new technology. The data can be modeled by the formula $N = 0.4x^2 + 0.5$, where N represents the millions of people in the United States using cable modems x years after 1996. Use this formula to solve Exercises 71–72.*

**Number of People in the United States Using Cable TV Modems**

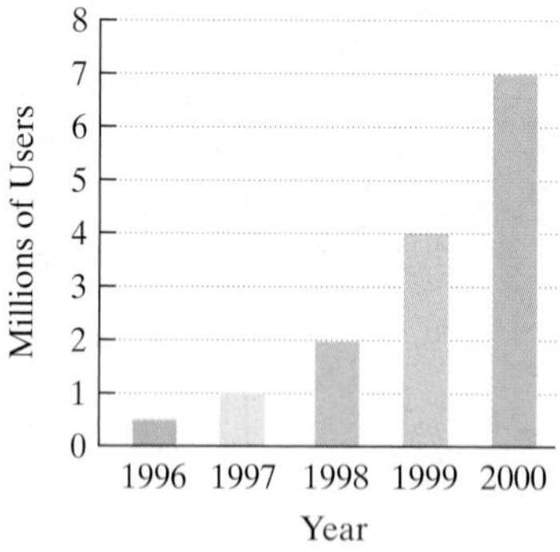


Source: *The New York Times*

**71.** According to the formula, in which year will 4.1 million Americans use cable TV modems? How well does the formula describe the actual number of users for that year?

**72.** According to the formula, in which year will 20.1 million Americans use cable TV modems?

**73.** The formula $N = 29{,}035t^2 + 429{,}200$ describes the leading golf winnings in the United States $t$ years after 1983. The leading golf winner for one of the years modeled by the formula was Greg Norman, who won $690,515. In what year did this occur?

**74.** The weight of a human fetus is given by the formula $W = 3t^2$, where $W$ is the weight in grams and $t$ is the time in weeks, $t \geq 0$ and $t \leq 39$. After how many weeks does the fetus weigh 300 grams?

*The data and the accompanying graph show the number of inmates in U.S. state and federal prisons from 1980 through 1998. The data can be modeled by the formula* $N = 2x^2 + 22x + 320$, *in which N represents the number of inmates, in thousands, in U.S. state and federal prisons x years after 1980. Use this formula to solve Exercises 75–76.*

**Number of Inmates in U.S. State and Federal Prisons**

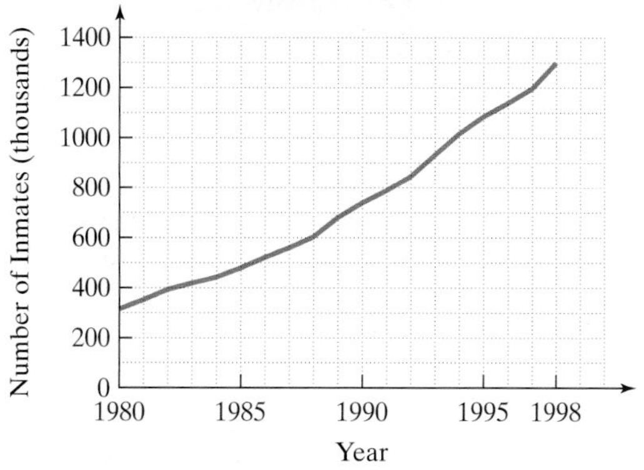


*Source:* U.S. Justice Department

| Year | Number of Inmates |
|---|---|
| 1980 | 315,974 |
| 1981 | 353,167 |
| 1982 | 394,374 |
| 1983 | 419,820 |
| 1984 | 443,398 |
| 1985 | 480,568 |
| 1986 | 522,084 |
| 1987 | 560,812 |
| 1988 | 603,732 |
| 1989 | 680,907 |
| 1990 | 739,980 |
| 1991 | 789,610 |
| 1992 | 846,277 |
| 1993 | 932,074 |
| 1994 | 1,016,691 |
| 1995 | 1,085,022 |
| 1996 | 1,138,984 |
| 1997 | 1,197,590 |
| 1998 | 1,302,019 |

**75.** According to the formula, in which year were there 740 thousand inmates in U.S. state and federal prisons? What was the actual number for that year? How well does the formula describe the actual number of inmates for that year?

**76.** According to the formula, in which year were there 1100 thousand inmates in U.S. state and federal prisons? What was the actual number for that year? How well does the formula describe the actual number of inmates for that year?

*The data and the accompanying graph show the cumulative number of deaths from AIDS in the United States from 1990 through 1998. The data can be modeled by the formula* $N = -1.65x^2 + 51.8x + 111.44$, *in which N represents the cumulative number of U.S. AIDS deaths, in thousands, x years after 1990. Use this formula to solve Exercises 77–78.*

**Cumulative Number of Deaths from AIDS in the United States**

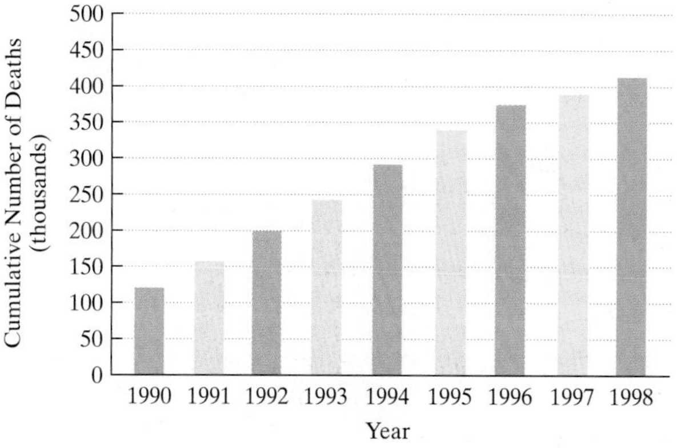


*Source*: Centers for Disease Control

| Year | Cumulative Number of Deaths from AIDS, in Thousands |
|---|---|
| 1990 | 121 |
| 1991 | 158 |
| 1992 | 199 |
| 1993 | 243 |
| 1994 | 292 |
| 1995 | 340 |
| 1996 | 375 |
| 1997 | 390 |
| 1998 | 414 |

**77.** According to the formula, in which year did the cumulative number of deaths from AIDS in the United States reach 330 thousand? What was the actual number for that year? How well does the formula describe the situation for that year?

**78.** According to the formula, in which year will the total number of U.S. AIDS deaths reach 500 thousand?

*In Exercises 79–90, use the five-step strategy to solve each problem. These problems appear in calculus in a slightly different form.*

**79.** A machine produces open boxes using square sheets of metal. The machine cuts equal-sized squares measuring 1 foot on a side from each corner. Then the machine shapes the metal into an open box by turning up the sides. If each box must have a volume of 4 cubic feet, what should be the dimensions of the piece of sheet metal?

**80.** A machine produces open boxes using rectangular sheets of metal. The length of each rectangular sheet is twice its width. The machine cuts equal-sized squares measuring 1 foot on a side from each corner. Then the machine shapes the metal into an open box by turning up the sides. If each box must have a volume of 4 cubic feet, what should be the dimensions of the piece of sheet metal?

**81.** A rectangular field is to be fenced on three sides with 1000 meters of fencing. As shown in the figure, the fourth side is a straight river's edge that will not be fenced.

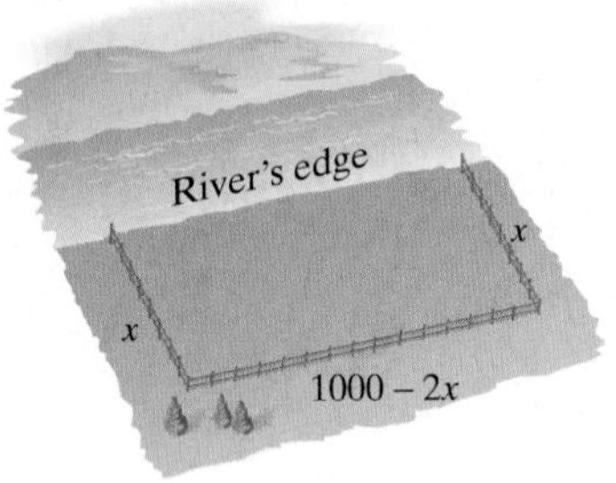


Find the dimensions of the field so that the area of the enclosure is 120,000 square meters.

**82.** You have 200 feet of fencing to build a rectangular enclosure. Determine the dimensions of the rectangle that make its area 1600 square feet.

**83.** A brick path of uniform width is constructed around the outside of a 6- by 10-yard rectangular garden. Find how wide the path should be if there is enough brick to cover 132 square yards.

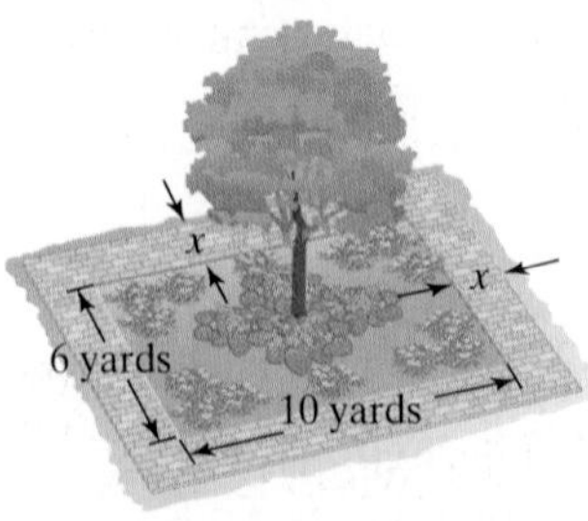


**84.** A picture is 20 inches long and 25 inches high. The picture is placed on a mat so that the mat's uniformly wide strip shows as a border for the picture. The perimeter of the mat is 114 inches. Find the width of the mat's strip that surrounds the picture.

**85.** A piece of wire is 8 inches long. The wire is cut into two pieces and then each piece is bent into a square. Find the length of each piece if the sum of the areas of these squares is to be 2 square inches.

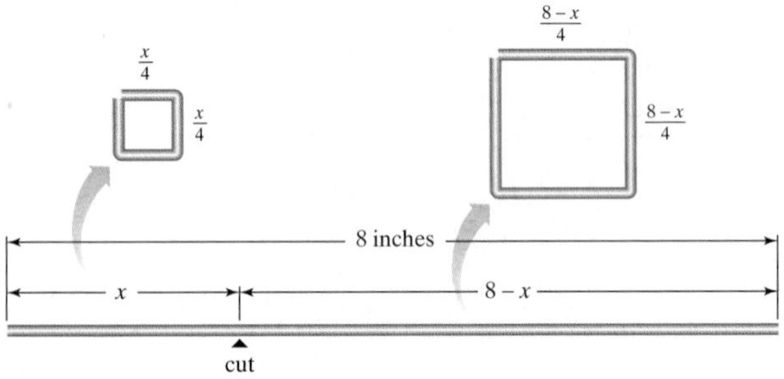


**86.** A piece of wire is 16 inches long. The wire is cut into two pieces and then each piece is bent into a square. Find the length of each piece if the sum of the areas of these squares is to be 8 square inches.

**87.** The annual yield per lemon tree is fairly constant at 320 pounds when the number of trees per acre is 50 or fewer. For each additional tree over 50, the annual yield per tree for all trees on the acre decreases by 4 pounds due to overcrowding. How many trees should be planted on an acre to yield 16,900 pounds of lemons?

**88.** The annual yield per pear tree is fairly constant at 160 pounds when the number of trees per acre is 40 or fewer. For each additional tree over 40, the annual yield per tree for all trees on the acre decreases by 2 pounds due to overcrowding. How many trees should be planted on an acre to yield 6912 pounds of pears?

**89.** The Norman window in the figure has a rectangular base and a semicircular top. If 2500 square centimeters of glass is used in making the window, what is the area of each of the four smaller rectangular regions?

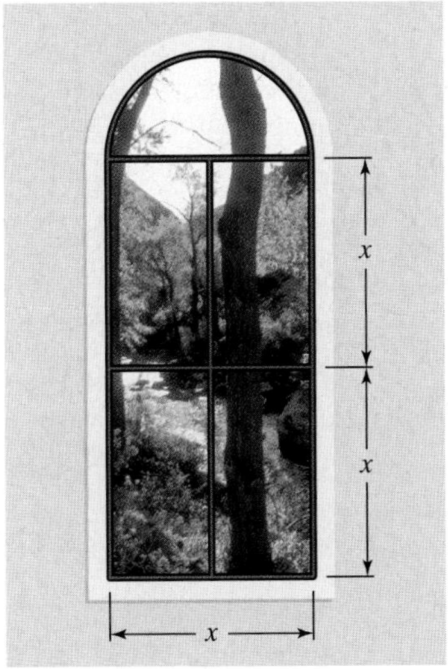


**90.** A storage bin consists of a cylinder and a roof that is a cone. The height of the roof is half the height of the cylinder, and the total volume of the bin is 11,200 $\pi$ cubic feet. Find the height of the cylinder.

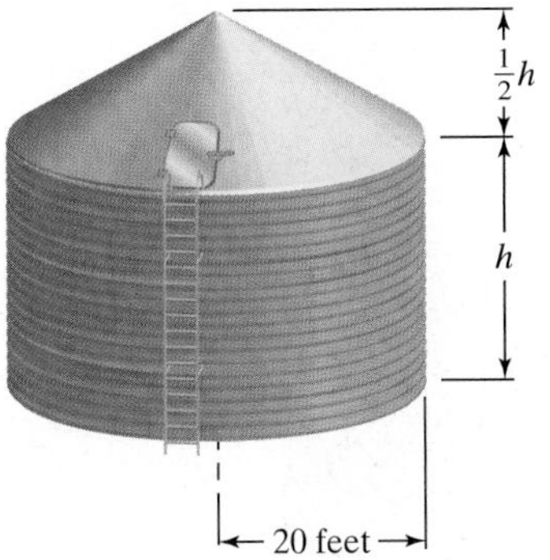


## Writing in Mathematics

**91.** What is a quadratic equation?

**92.** Explain how to solve $x^2 + 6x + 8 = 0$ using factoring and the zero-product principle.

**93.** Explain how to solve $x^2 + 6x + 8 = 0$ by completing the square.

**94.** Explain how to solve $x^2 + 6x + 8 = 0$ using the quadratic formula.

**95.** How is the quadratic formula derived?

**96.** What is the discriminant and what information does it provide about a quadratic equation?

**97.** If you are given a quadratic equation, how do you determine which method to use to solve it?

**98.** If $(x + 2)(x - 4) = 0$ indicates that $x + 2 = 0$ or $x - 4 = 0$, explain why $(x + 2)(x - 4) = 6$ does not mean $x + 2 = 6$ or $x - 4 = 6$. Could we solve the equation using $x + 2 = 3$ and $x - 4 = 2$ because $3 \cdot 2 = 6$?

## Technology Exercises

**99.** If you have access to a calculator that solves quadratic equations, consult the owner's manual to determine how to use this feature. Then use your calculator to solve any five of the equations in Exercises 29–38.

**100.** Graph the formula in Exercise 69,

$$y = 0.0075x^2 - 0.2676x + 14.8$$

using a [0, 80, 20] by [0, 50, 10] viewing rectangle. Move the cursor along the graph, using the TRACE and ZOOM features to estimate the year in which automobile fuel efficiency was the poorest. What was the gas mileage in that year? Use the Internet or your library to find pictures of the most popular cars for that year and write a sentence relating the most popular cars of the time with the fuel efficiency indicated by the formula's graph.

**101.** **a.** Use a graphing utility to graph the area model that you obtained in Exercise 81. Experiment with the range setting until your graph looks like the one shown in the figure. Then trace along the graph and find the points whose coordinates correspond to your algebraic solution in Exercise 81.

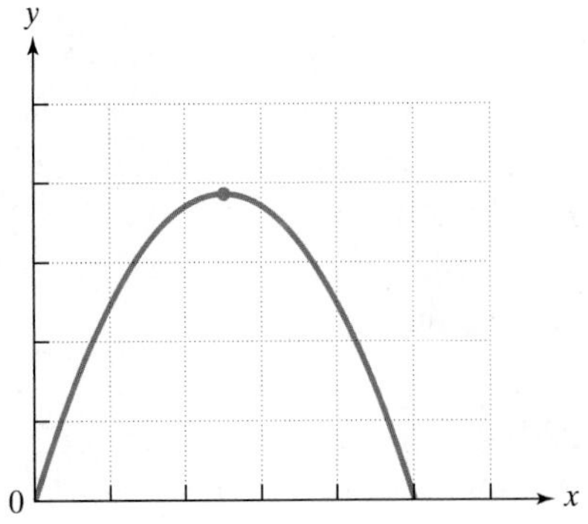


**b.** What is a reasonable estimate of the maximum area that can be enclosed? Trace along the graph and verify this estimate by finding the coordinates of the highest point on the graph. What are the dimensions of the rectangle of maximum area?

**c.** Does the rectangle enclosed in Exercise 81 make the best use of the 1000 meters of fencing? Explain.

## Critical Thinking Exercises

**102.** Which one of the following is true?

**a.** The equation $(2x - 3)^2 = 25$ is equivalent to $2x - 3 = 5$.

**b.** Every quadratic equation has two distinct numbers in its solution set.

**c.** A quadratic equation whose coefficients are real numbers can never have a solution set containing one real number and one complex nonreal number.

**d.** The equation $ax^2 + c = 0$ cannot be solved by the quadratic formula.

**103.** Solve the equation: $x^2 + 2\sqrt{3}x - 9 = 0$.

**104.** Write a quadratic equation in standard form whose solution set is $\{-3, 5\}$.

**105.** A person throws a rock upward from the edge of an 80-foot cliff. The height, $h$, in feet, of the rock above the water at the bottom of the cliff after $t$ seconds is described by the formula

$$h = -16t^2 + 64t + 80.$$

How long will it take for the rock to reach the water?

**106.** The personnel manager of a roller skate company knows that the company's weekly revenue is a function of the price of each pair of skates, modeled by $R = -2x^2 + 36x$, where $x$ represents the dollar price of a pair of skates and $R$ represents weekly revenue in tens of thousands of dollars. A job applicant promises the personnel manager an advertising campaign guaranteed to generate \$190,000 in weekly revenue. Substitute 19 for $R$ in the given model, compute the discriminant, and then explain why the applicant will or will not be hired in the advertising department.

### Group Exercise

**107.** Each group member should find an algebraic formula that contains an expression in the form $ax^2 + bx + c$ on one side that he or she finds intriguing. Consult college algebra books or liberal arts mathematics books to do so. Group members should select four of the formulas. For each formula selected, write and solve a problem similar to Exercises 95 and 96 in this exercise set.

## SECTION 1.4 *Other Types of Equations*

### Objectives

1. Solve polynomial equations by factoring.
2. Solve radical equations.
3. Solve equations with rational exponents.
4. Solve equations that are quadratic in form.
5. Solve equations involving absolute value.

The Galápagos Islands are a volcanic chain of islands lying 600 miles west of Ecuador. They are famed for their extraordinary wildlife, which includes a rare flightless cormorant, marine iguanas, and giant tortoises weighing more than 600 pounds. It was here that naturalist Charles Darwin began to formulate his theory of evolution. Darwin made an enormous collection of the islands' plant species. The formula

$$S = 28.5\sqrt[3]{x}$$

describes the number of plant species, $S$, on the various islands of the Galápagos chain in terms of the area, $x$, in square miles, of a particular island.

How can we find the area of a Galápagos island with 57 species of plants? Substitute 57 for $S$ in the formula and solve for $x$:

$$57 = 28.5\sqrt[3]{x}.$$

The resulting equation contains a variable in the radicand and is called a *radical equation*. In this section, in addition to radical equations, we will show you how to solve certain kinds of polynomial equations, equations involving rational exponents, and equations involving absolute value.

**1** Solve polynomial equations by factoring.

## Polynomial Equations

The linear and quadratic equations that we studied in the first three sections of this chapter can be thought of as polynomial equations of degrees 1 and 2, respectively. By contrast, consider the following polynomial equations of degree greater than 2.

$$3x^4 = 27x^2 \qquad\qquad x^3 + x^2 = 4x + 4$$

This equation is of degree 4 because 4 is the largest exponent.

This equation is of degree 3 because 3 is the largest exponent.

We can solve these equations by moving all terms to one side, thereby obtaining zero on the other side. We then use factoring and the zero-product principle.

### EXAMPLE 1 Solving a Polynomial Equation by Factoring

Solve by factoring: $3x^4 = 27x^2$.

**Solution**

**Step 1 Move all terms to one side and obtain zero on the other side.** Subtract $27x^2$ from both sides.

$$3x^4 - 27x^2 = 27x^2 - 27x^2$$
$$3x^4 - 27x^2 = 0$$

**Step 2 Factor.** We can factor $3x^2$ from each term.

$$3x^4 - 27x^2 = 0$$
$$3x^2(x^2 - 9) = 0$$

**Steps 3 and 4 Set each factor equal to zero and solve the resulting equations.**

$$3x^2 = 0 \quad \text{or} \quad x^2 - 9 = 0$$
$$x^2 = 0 \qquad x^2 = 9$$
$$x = \pm\sqrt{0} \qquad x = \pm\sqrt{9}$$
$$x = 0 \qquad x = \pm 3$$

**Step 5 Check the solutions in the original equation.** Check the three solutions, 0, −3, and 3, by substituting them into the original equation. Can you verify that the solution set is $\{-3, 0, 3\}$?

**Study Tip**

In solving $3x^4 = 27x^2$, be careful not to divide both sides by $x^2$. If you do, you'll lose 0 as a solution. In general, do not divide both sides of an equation by a variable because that variable might take on the value 0 and you cannot divide by 0.

**Check Point 1** Solve by factoring: $4x^4 = 12x^2$.

### EXAMPLE 2 Solving a Polynomial Equation by Factoring

Solve by factoring: $x^3 + x^2 = 4x + 4$.

**Solution**

**Step 1 Move all terms to one side and obtain zero on the other side.** Subtract $4x + 4$ from both sides.

$$x^3 + x^2 - 4x - 4 = 4x + 4 - 4x - 4$$
$$x^3 + x^2 - 4x - 4 = 0$$

**Step 2 Factor.** Use factoring by grouping. Group terms that have a common factor.

$$\boxed{x^3 + x^2} + \boxed{-4x - 4} = 0$$

Common factor is $x^2$. Common factor is $-4$.

$$x^2(x + 1) - 4(x + 1) = 0$$ Factor $x^2$ from the first two terms and $-4$ from the last two terms.

$$(x + 1)(x^2 - 4) = 0$$ Factor out the common binomial, $x + 1$, from each term.

**Steps 3 and 4 Set each factor equal to zero and solve the resulting equations.**

$$x + 1 = 0 \quad \text{or} \quad x^2 - 4 = 0$$
$$x = -1 \qquad\qquad x^2 = 4$$
$$x = \pm\sqrt{4} = \pm 2$$

**Step 5 Check the solutions in the original equation.** Check the three solutions, $-1, -2$, and 2, by substituting them into the original equation. Can you verify that the solution set is $\{-2, -1, 2\}$?

## Technology

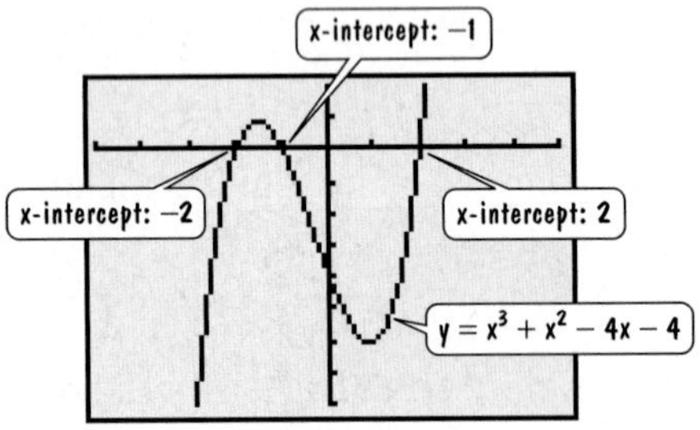


You can use a graphing utility to check the solutions to $x^3 + x^2 - 4x - 4 = 0$. Graph $y = x^3 + x^2 - 4x - 4$, as shown on the left. The $x$-intercepts are $-2, -1$, and 2, corresponding to the equation's solutions.

**Check Point 2** Solve by factoring: $2x^3 + 3x^2 = 8x + 12$.

**2** Solve radical equations.

## Equations Involving Radicals

A **radical equation** is an equation in which the variable occurs in a square root, cube root, or any higher root. An example of a radical equation is

$$28.5\sqrt[3]{x} = 57.$$

The variable occurs in a cube root.

This equation can be used to find the area, $x$, of a Galápagos island with 57 species of plants. First, we isolate the radical by dividing both sides of the equation by 28.5.

$$\frac{28.5\sqrt[3]{x}}{28.5} = \frac{57}{28.5}$$

$$\sqrt[3]{x} = 2$$

Next we eliminate the radical by raising each side of the equation to a power equal to the index of the radical. Because the index is 3, we cube both sides of the equation.

$$\left(\sqrt[3]{x}\right)^3 = 2^3$$

$$x = 8$$

Thus, a Galápagos island with 57 species of plants has an area of 8 square miles.

The Galápagos equation shows that solving equations involving radicals involves raising both sides of the equation to a power equal to the radical's index. All solutions of the original equation are also solutions of the resulting equation. However, the resulting equation may have some extra solutions that do not satisfy the original equation. Because the resulting equation may not be equivalent to the original equation, we must check each proposed solution by substituting it into the original equation. Let's see exactly how this works.

## EXAMPLE 3 Solving an Equation Involving a Radical

Solve: $x + \sqrt{26 - 11x} = 4$.

**Solution** To solve this equation, we isolate the radical expression $\sqrt{26 - 11x}$ on one side of the equation. By squaring both sides of the equation, we can then eliminate the square root.

$$x + \sqrt{26 - 11x} = 4 \quad \text{This is the given equation.}$$

$$x + \sqrt{26 - 11x} - x = 4 - x \quad \text{Isolate the radical by subtracting } x \text{ from both sides.}$$

$$\sqrt{26 - 11x} = 4 - x \quad \text{Simplify.}$$

$$\left(\sqrt{26 - 11x}\right)^2 = (4 - x)^2 \quad \text{Square both sides.}$$

$$26 - 11x = 16 - 8x + x^2 \quad \text{Use } (A - B)^2 = A^2 - 2AB + B^2 \text{ to square } 4 - x.$$

Next, we need to write this quadratic equation in standard form. We can obtain zero on the left side by subtracting 26 and adding $11x$ on both sides.

$$26 - 26 - 11x + 11x = 16 - 26 - 8x + 11x + x^2$$

$$0 = x^2 + 3x - 10 \quad \text{Simplify.}$$

$$0 = (x + 5)(x - 2) \quad \text{Factor.}$$

$$x + 5 = 0 \quad \text{or} \quad x - 2 = 0 \quad \text{Set each factor equal to zero.}$$

$$x = -5 \qquad\qquad x = 2 \quad \text{Solve for } x.$$

We have not completed the solution process. Although $-5$ and 2 satisfy the squared equation, there is no guarantee that they satisfy the original equation. Thus, we must check the proposed solutions. We can do this using a graphing utility (see the technology box in the margin) or by substituting both proposed solutions into the given equation

$$x + \sqrt{26 - 11x} = 4.$$

### Study Tip

Be sure to square *both sides* of an equation. Do *not* square each term.

**Correct:**

$$\left(\sqrt{26} - 11\right)^2 = (4 - x)^2$$

**Incorrect:**

$$\left(\sqrt{26} - 11\right)^2 = 4^2 - x^2$$

### Technology

The graph of

$$y = x + \sqrt{26 - 11x} - 4$$

is shown in a $[-10, 3, 1]$ by $[-4, 3, 1]$ viewing rectangle. The $x$-intercepts are $-5$ and 2, verifying $\{-5, 2\}$ as the solution set.

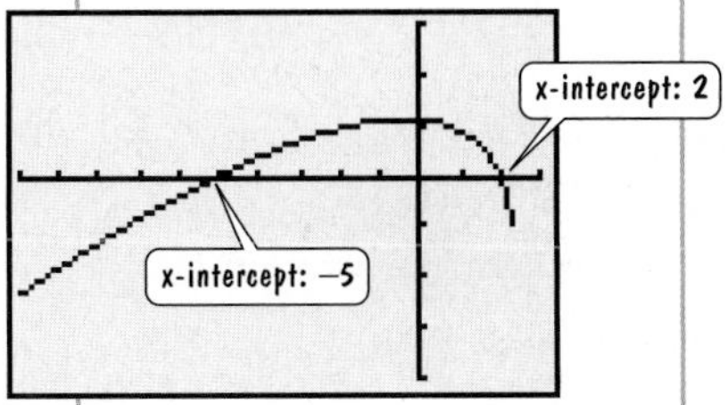

**Check −5:**

$-5 + \sqrt{26 - 11(-5)} \stackrel{?}{=} 4$

$-5 + \sqrt{81} \stackrel{?}{=} 4$

$-5 + 9 \stackrel{?}{=} 4$

$4 = 4$ ✓

**Check 2:**

$2 + \sqrt{26 - 11(2)} \stackrel{?}{=} 4$ — Substitute −5 and 2, respectively.

$2 + \sqrt{4} \stackrel{?}{=} 4$ — Simplify.

$2 + 2 \stackrel{?}{=} 4$

$4 = 4$ ✓ — Both −5 and 2 are solutions.

The solution set is $\{-5, 2\}$.

**Check Point 3** Solve and check: $\sqrt{6x + 7} - x = 2$.

## Study Tip

Don't forget to check for extraneous solutions when solving equations by raising both sides to an even power. Here's a simple example:

$x = 4$

$x^2 = 16$ — Square both sides.

$x = \pm\sqrt{16}$ — Use the square root method.

$x = \pm 4$

However, −4 does not check in $x = 4$. Thus, −4 is an extraneous solution.

When solving a radical equation, extra solutions may be introduced when you raise both sides of the equation to an even power. Such solutions are called **extraneous solutions**.

The solution of radical equations with two or more square root expressions involves isolating a radical, squaring both sides, and then repeating this process. Let's consider an equation containing two square root expressions.

## EXAMPLE 4 Solving an Equation Involving Two Radicals

Solve: $\sqrt{3x + 1} - \sqrt{x + 4} = 1$.

**Solution**

$\sqrt{3x + 1} - \sqrt{x + 4} = 1$ — This is the given equation.

$\sqrt{3x + 1} = \sqrt{x + 4} + 1$ — Isolate one of the radicals by adding $\sqrt{x + 4}$ to both sides.

$(\sqrt{3x + 1})^2 = (\sqrt{x + 4} + 1)^2$ — Square both sides.

Squaring the expression on the right side of the equation can be a bit tricky. We need to use the formula

$$(A + B)^2 = A^2 + 2AB + B^2.$$

Focusing on just the right side, here is how the squaring is done.

$$(A + B)^2 = A^2 + 2 \cdot A \cdot B + B^2$$

$$(\sqrt{x + 4} + 1)^2 = (\sqrt{x + 4})^2 + 2 \cdot \sqrt{x + 4} \cdot 1 + 1^2$$

This simplifies to $x + 4 + 2\sqrt{x + 4} + 1$. Thus, our equation can be written as follows.

$3x + 1 = x + 4 + 2\sqrt{x + 4} + 1$

$3x + 1 = x + 5 + 2\sqrt{x + 4}$ — Combine numerical terms on the right.

$2x - 4 = 2\sqrt{x + 4}$ — Isolate $2\sqrt{x + 4}$, the radical term, by subtracting $x + 5$ from both sides.

$x - 2 = \sqrt{x + 4}$ — Divide both sides by 2.

$(x - 2)^2 = (\sqrt{x + 4})^2$ — Square both sides.

$x^2 - 4x + 4 = x + 4$ — Multiply.

$x^2 - 5x = 0$ — Write the quadratic equation in standard form by subtracting x + 4 from both sides.

$x(x - 5) = 0$ — Factor.

$x = 0 \quad \text{or} \quad x - 5 = 0$ — Set each factor equal to zero.

$x = 0 \qquad\qquad x = 5$ — Solve for x.

Complete the solution process by checking both proposed solutions. We can do this using a graphing utility (see the technology box in the margin) or by substituting both proposed solutions in the given equation.

**Check 0:**

$$\sqrt{3x+1} - \sqrt{x+4} = 1$$
$$\sqrt{3 \cdot 0 + 1} - \sqrt{0+4} \stackrel{?}{=} 1$$
$$\sqrt{1} - \sqrt{4} \stackrel{?}{=} 1$$
$$1 - 2 \stackrel{?}{=} 1$$
$$-1 = 1 \quad \text{False}$$

**Check 5:**

$$\sqrt{3x+1} - \sqrt{x+4} = 1$$
$$\sqrt{3 \cdot 5 + 1} - \sqrt{5+4} \stackrel{?}{=} 1$$
$$\sqrt{16} - \sqrt{9} \stackrel{?}{=} 1$$
$$4 - 3 \stackrel{?}{=} 1$$
$$1 = 1 \ ✓$$

The check indicates that 0 is not a solution. It is an extraneous solution brought about by squaring each side of the equation. The only solution is 5, and the solution set is $\{5\}$.

**Technology**

The graph of

$y = \sqrt{3x+1} - \sqrt{x+4} - 1$

has only one $x$-intercept at 5. This verifies that the solution set for the given equation is $\{5\}$.

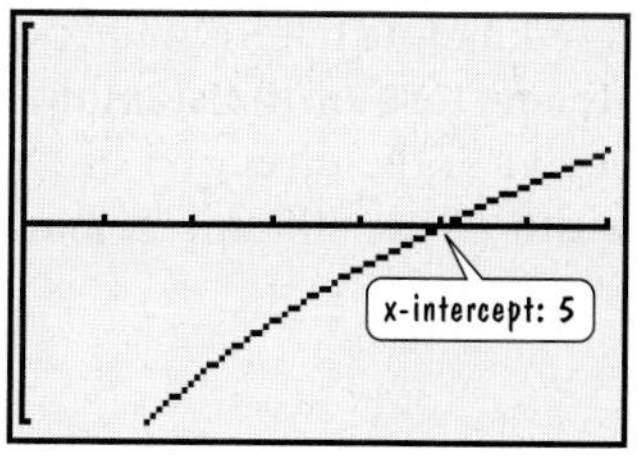


**Check Point 4** Solve and check: $\sqrt{x+5} - \sqrt{x-3} = 2$.

Radical equations are used to describe Albert Einstein's special theory of relativity. Suppose you are an observer watching an object moving at a velocity close to the speed of light, approximately 186,000 miles per second. According to this theory, time slows down, mass increases, and length in the direction of motion decreases from your point of view. Einstein's theory, verified with experiments in atomic physics, forms the basis of Example 5.

## EXAMPLE 5 Einstein's Special Relativity Models

Einstein's equations relate the mass, time, and length at rest $(M_0, T_0, L_0)$ to the mass, time, and length $(M, T, L)$ for a velocity $v$. The speed of light, $c$, is approximately 186,000 miles per second.

$$M = \frac{M_0}{\sqrt{1 - \frac{v^2}{c^2}}} \qquad T = \frac{T_0}{\sqrt{1 - \frac{v^2}{c^2}}} \qquad L = L_0\sqrt{1 - \frac{v^2}{c^2}}$$

How fast would a futuristic starship that is 600 meters tall have to move so that it would measure only 84 meters tall from the perspective of an observer who looks up and sees the ship pass by?

**Solution**

$$L = L_0\sqrt{1 - \frac{v^2}{c^2}}$$ This is Einstein's model for length.

$$84 = 600\sqrt{1 - \frac{v^2}{c^2}}$$ Substitute $L_0$ (length at rest) = 600 and $L$ (length at the velocity we must determine) = 84.

$$0.14 = \sqrt{1 - \frac{v^2}{c^2}}$$ Divide both sides by 600.

$$0.0196 = 1 - \frac{v^2}{c^2}$$ Square both sides.

$$0.0196c^2 = c^2 - v^2$$ Multiply both sides by $c^2$. Remember that $c$, the speed of light, is approximately 186,000 miles per second.

$$v^2 = 0.9804c^2$$ Isolate $v^2$ on the left.

$$v = \sqrt{0.9804c^2}$$ Assume that the starship is moving upward, so take only the positive root.

$$v \approx 0.99c$$

If the 600-meter tall futuristic starship moves at 99% the speed of light (approximately 184,140 miles per second), it will measure only 84 meters tall from the perspective of our stationary viewer. A before and after picture of the starship is shown in Figure 1.6. Observe that lengths perpendicular to the direction of motion are unchanged by the effect of speed, so the width of the starship remains unchanged.

**Figure 1.6**

**Check Point 5** How fast would a futuristic starship that is 600 meters tall have to move so that it would measure only half this length from the perspective of an observer who looks up and sees the ship pass by?

**3** Solve equations with rational exponents.

Because $\sqrt[n]{b}$ can be expressed as $b^{1/n}$, radical equations can be written using rational exponents. For example, the Galápagos equation

$$28.5\sqrt[3]{x} = 57$$

can be written

$$28.5x^{1/3} = 57.$$

We solve this equation exactly as we did when it was expressed in radical form. First, isolate $x^{1/3}$.

$$\frac{28.5x^{1/3}}{28.5} = \frac{57}{28.5}$$
$$x^{1/3} = 2$$

Complete the solution process by raising both sides to the third power.

$$\left(x^{1/3}\right)^3 = 2^3$$
$$x = 8$$

In general, a radical equation with rational exponents can be solved by: (1) isolating the expression with the rational exponent, and (2) raising both sides of the equation to a power that is the reciprocal of the rational exponent. Be sure to *complete the solution process* by *checking all proposed solutions in the original equation* to find out if they are actual solutions or extraneous solutions.

## EXAMPLE 6 Solving an Equation Involving a Rational Exponent

Solve: $3x^{3/4} - 6 = 0$.

**Solution** Our goal is to isolate $x^{3/4}$. Then we can raise both sides of the equation to the $\frac{4}{3}$ power because $\frac{4}{3}$ is the reciprocal of $\frac{3}{4}$.

$3x^{3/4} - 6 = 0$ This is the given equation; we will isolate $x^{3/4}$.

$3x^{3/4} = 6$ Add 6 to both sides.

$\frac{3x^{3/4}}{3} = \frac{6}{3}$ Divide both sides by 3.

$x^{3/4} = 2$ Simplify.

$\left(x^{3/4}\right)^{4/3} = 2^{4/3}$ Raise both sides to the $\frac{4}{3}$ power.

$x = 2^{4/3}$ Simplify the left side: $\left(x^{3/4}\right)^{4/3} = x^{\frac{3\cdot 4}{4\cdot 3}} = x^{\frac{12}{12}} = x^1 = x$.

The proposed solution is $2^{4/3}$. Complete the solution process by checking this value in the given equation.

$3x^{3/4} - 6 = 0$ This is the original equation.

$3\left(2^{4/3}\right)^{3/4} - 6 \stackrel{?}{=} 0$ Substitute the proposed solution.

$3 \cdot 2 - 6 \stackrel{?}{=} 0$ $\left(2^{4/3}\right)^{3/4} = 2^{\frac{4\cdot 3}{3\cdot 4}} = 2^{\frac{12}{12}} = 2^1 = 2$.

$0 = 0$ ✓ Thus, $2^{4/3}$ is a solution.

The solution is $2^{4/3} = \sqrt[3]{2^4} \approx 2.52$. The solution set is $\{2^{4/3}\}$.

**Check Point 6** Solve and check: $5x^{3/2} - 25 = 0$.

**4** Solve equations that are quadratic in form.

## Equations That Are Quadratic in Form

Some equations that are not quadratic can be written as quadratic equations using an appropriate substitution. Here are some examples.

| Given Equation | Substitution | New Equation |
|---|---|---|
| $x^4 - 8x^2 - 9 = 0$<br>or<br>$(x^2)^2 - 8x^2 - 9 = 0$ | $t = x^2$ | $t^2 - 8t - 9 = 0$ |
| $5x^{2/3} + 11x^{1/3} + 2 = 0$<br>or<br>$5(x^{1/3})^2 + 11x^{1/3} + 2 = 0$ | $t = x^{1/3}$ | $5t^2 + 11t + 2 = 0$ |

An equation that is **quadratic in form** is one that can be expressed as a quadratic equation using an appropriate substitution. Both of the preceding given equations are quadratic in form.

For equations that are quadratic in form, the exponent in one of the terms is half that of the other term. By letting $t$ equal the variable to the half power, a quadratic equation in $t$ will result. Now it's easy. Solve this quadratic equation for $t$. Finally, use your substitution to find the values for the variable in the given equation. Example 6 shows how this is done.

### EXAMPLE 7 Solving an Equation That Is Quadratic in Form

Solve: $x^4 - 8x^2 - 9 = 0$.

**Solution** Notice that the exponent on $x^2$ is half that of the exponent on $x^4$. We let $t$ equal the variable to the power that is half of 4. Thus,

$$\text{let } t = x^2.$$

Now we write the given equation as a quadratic equation in $t$ and solve for $t$.

$x^4 - 8x^2 - 9 = 0$ This is the given equation.

$(x^2)^2 - 8x^2 - 9 = 0$ The given equation contains $x^2$ and $x^2$ squared.

$t^2 - 8t - 9 = 0$ Replace $x^2$ by $t$.

$(t - 9)(t + 1) = 0$ Factor.

$t - 9 = 0$ or $t + 1 = 0$ Apply the zero-product principle.

$t = 9$ $t = -1$ Solve for $t$.

We're not done! Why not? We were asked to solve for $x$ and we have values for $t$. We use the original substitution, $t = x^2$, to solve for $x$. Replace $t$ by $x^2$ in each equation shown.

$$x^2 = 9 \qquad x^2 = -1$$
$$x = \pm\sqrt{9} \qquad x = \pm\sqrt{-1}$$
$$x = \pm 3 \qquad x = \pm i$$

The solution set is $\{-3, 3, -i, i\}$.

**Check Point 7** Solve: $x^4 - 5x^2 + 6 = 0$.

## EXAMPLE 8 Solving an Equation That Is Quadratic in Form

Solve: $5x^{2/3} + 11x^{1/3} + 2 = 0$.

**Solution** Notice that the exponent on $x^{1/3}$ is half that of the exponent on $x^{2/3}$. We let $t$ equal the variable to the power that is half of 4. Thus,

$$\text{let } t = x^{1/3}.$$

Now we write the given equation as a quadratic equation in $t$ and solve for $t$.

$$5x^{2/3} + 11x^{1/3} + 2 = 0 \quad \text{This is the given equation.}$$

$$5(x^{1/3})^2 + 11(x^{1/3}) + 2 = 0 \quad \text{The given equation contains } x^{1/3} \text{ and } x^{1/3} \text{ squared.}$$

$$5t^2 + 11t + 2 = 0 \quad \text{Replace } x^{1/3} \text{ by } t.$$

$$(5t + 1)(t + 2) = 0 \quad \text{Factor.}$$

$$5t + 1 = 0 \quad \text{or} \quad t + 2 = 0 \quad \text{Set each factor equal to 0.}$$

$$5t = -1 \qquad t = -2 \quad \text{Solve for } t.$$

$$t = -\tfrac{1}{5}$$

Use the original substitution, $t = x^{1/3}$, to solve for $x$. Replace $t$ by $x^{1/3}$ in each of the preceding equations.

$$x^{1/3} = -\frac{1}{5} \qquad x^{1/3} = -2 \quad \text{Replace } t \text{ with } x^{1/3}.$$

$$(x^{1/3})^3 = \left(-\frac{1}{5}\right)^3 \qquad (x^{1/3})^3 = (-2)^3 \quad \text{Solve for } x \text{ by cubing both sides of each equation.}$$

$$x = -\frac{1}{125} \qquad x = -8$$

Check these values to verify that the solution set is $\{-\frac{1}{125}, -8\}$.

**Check Point 8** Solve: $3x^{2/3} - 11x^{1/3} - 4 = 0$.

**5** Solve equations involving absolute value.

## Equations Involving Absolute Value

We solve equations containing absolute value using the fact that the expression inside the absolute value bars can be either positive or negative. For example, the equation

$$|2x - 3| = 11$$

is satisfied if $2x - 3$ is either 11 or $-11$, resulting in the two equations

$$2x - 3 = 11 \quad \text{or} \quad 2x - 3 = -11.$$

**Rewriting an Absolute Value Equation without Absolute Value Bars**

If $c$ is a positive real number and $X$ represents any algebraic expression, then $|X| = c$ is equivalent to $X = c$ or $X = -c$.

## EXAMPLE 9 Solving an Equation Involving Absolute Value

Solve: $|2x - 3| = 11$.

**Solution**

| | | |
|---|---|---|
| $|2x - 3| = 11$ | | This is the given equation. |
| $2x - 3 = 11$ | or $2x - 3 = -11$ | Rewrite the equation without absolute value bars. |
| $2x = 14$ | $2x = -8$ | Add 3 to both sides of each equation. |
| $x = 7$ | $x = -4$ | Divide both sides of each equation by 2. |

**Check**

| | | |
|---|---|---|
| $|2x - 3| = 11$ | | This is the original equation. |
| $|2(7) - 3| \stackrel{?}{=} 11$ | $|2(-4) - 3| \stackrel{?}{=} 11$ | Substitute the proposed solutions. |
| $|14 - 3| \stackrel{?}{=} 11$ | $|-8 - 3| \stackrel{?}{=} 11$ | Perform operations inside the absolute value bars. |
| $|11| \stackrel{?}{=} 11$ | $|-11| \stackrel{?}{=} 11$ | |
| $11 = 11$ ✓ | $11 = 11$ ✓ | These true statements indicate that 7 and −4 are solutions. |

The solution set is $\{-4, 7\}$.

### Discovery

Graph $y = |2x - 3|$ and $y = 11$ in a $[-10, 10, 1]$ by $[-1, 15, 1]$ viewing rectangle. How is the solution set of $|2x - 3| = 11$, namely $\{-4, 7\}$, shown by the graphs?

**Check Point 9** Solve: $|2x - 1| = 5$.

## EXERCISE SET 1.4

### Practice Exercises

*Solve each polynomial equation in Exercises 1–10 by factoring and then using the zero-product principle.*

**1.** $3x^4 - 48x^2 = 0$
**2.** $5x^4 - 20x^2 = 0$
**3.** $2x^4 = 16x$
**4.** $3x^4 = 81x$
**5.** $3x^3 + 2x^2 = 12x + 8$
**6.** $4x^3 - 12x^2 = 9x - 27$
**7.** $2x - 3 = 8x^3 - 12x^2$
**8.** $x + 1 = 9x^3 + 9x^2$
**9.** $4y^3 - 2 = y - 8y^2$
**10.** $9y^3 + 8 = 4y + 18y^2$

*Solve each radical equation in Exercises 11–28. Check all proposed solutions.*

**11.** $\sqrt{3x + 18} = x$
**12.** $\sqrt{20 - 8x} = x$
**13.** $\sqrt{x + 3} = x - 3$
**14.** $\sqrt{x + 10} = x - 2$
**15.** $\sqrt{2x + 13} = x + 7$
**16.** $\sqrt{6x + 1} = x - 1$
**17.** $x - \sqrt{2x + 5} = 5$
**18.** $x - \sqrt{x + 11} = 1$
**19.** $\sqrt{3x + 10} = x + 4$
**20.** $\sqrt{x} - 3 = x - 9$
**21.** $\sqrt{x + 8} - \sqrt{x - 4} = 2$
**22.** $\sqrt{x + 5} - \sqrt{x - 3} = 2$
**23.** $\sqrt{x - 5} - \sqrt{x - 8} = 3$
**24.** $\sqrt{2x - 3} - \sqrt{x - 2} = 1$
**25.** $\sqrt{2x + 3} + \sqrt{x - 2} = 2$
**26.** $\sqrt{x + 2} + \sqrt{3x + 7} = 1$
**27.** $\sqrt{3\sqrt{x + 1}} = \sqrt{3x - 5}$
**28.** $\sqrt{1 + 4\sqrt{x}} = 1 + \sqrt{x}$

*Solve and check each equation with rational exponents in Exercises 29–36.*

**29.** $x^{3/2} = 8$
**30.** $x^{3/2} = 27$
**31.** $(x - 4)^{3/2} = 27$
**32.** $(x + 5)^{3/2} = 8$
**33.** $6x^{5/2} - 12 = 0$
**34.** $8x^{5/3} - 24 = 0$
**35.** $(x^2 - x - 4)^{3/4} - 2 = 6$
**36.** $(x^2 - 3x + 3)^{3/2} - 1 = 0$

*Solve each equation in Exercises 37–56 by making an appropriate substitution.*

**37.** $x^4 - 5x^2 + 4 = 0$
**38.** $x^4 - 13x^2 + 36 = 0$
**39.** $9x^4 = 25x^2 - 16$
**40.** $4x^4 = 13x^2 - 9$
**41.** $x^6 + 8x^3 + 15 = 0$
**42.** $x^6 + 5x^3 + 6 = 0$
**43.** $5x^6 + x^3 = 18$
**44.** $3x^6 - 4x^3 = 15$

**45.** $x^{2/3} - x^{1/3} - 6 = 0$

**46.** $2x^{2/3} + 7x^{1/3} - 15 = 0$

**47.** $x^{3/2} - 2x^{3/4} + 1 = 0$

**48.** $x^{2/5} + x^{1/5} - 6 = 0$

**49.** $2x - 3x^{1/2} + 1 = 0$

**50.** $x + 3x^{1/2} - 4 = 0$

**51.** $(x - 5)^2 - 4(x - 5) - 21 = 0$

**52.** $(x + 3)^2 + 7(x + 3) - 18 = 0$

**53.** $(x^2 - x)^2 - 14(x^2 - x) + 24 = 0$

**54.** $(x^2 - 2x)^2 - 11(x^2 - 2x) + 24 = 0$

**55.** $\left(y - \frac{8}{y}\right)^2 + 5\left(y - \frac{8}{y}\right) - 14 = 0$

**56.** $\left(y - \frac{10}{y}\right)^2 + 6\left(y - \frac{10}{y}\right) - 27 = 0$

*Solve each equation in Exercises 57–62 by first rewriting the equation as two equations without absolute value bars.*

**57.** $|x| = 8$

**58.** $|x| = 6$

**59.** $|x - 2| = 7$

**60.** $|x + 1| = 5$

**61.** $|2x - 1| = 5$

**62.** $|2x - 3| = 11$

*Solve each equation in Exercises 63–72 by the method of your choice.*

**63.** $x + 2\sqrt{x} - 3 = 0$

**64.** $x^3 + 3x^2 - 4x - 12 = 0$

**65.** $(x + 4)^{3/2} = 8$

**66.** $(x^2 - 1)^2 - 2(x^2 - 1) = 3$

**67.** $\sqrt{4x + 15} - 2x = 0$

**68.** $x^{2/5} - 1 = 0$

**69.** $|x^2 + 2x - 36| = 12$

**70.** $\sqrt{3x + 1} - \sqrt{x - 1} = 2$

**71.** $x^3 - 2x^2 = x - 2$

**72.** $|x^2 + 6x + 1| = 8$

## Application Exercises

**73.** For a group of 50,000 births, the number of people, $N$, surviving to age $x$ is modeled by the formula $N = 5000\sqrt{100 - x}$. To what age will 40,000 people in the group survive?

**74.** Psychologists use the formula $N = 2\sqrt{Q} - 9$ to determine the number of nonsense syllables, $N$, that a subject with an IQ of $Q$ can repeat. If a subject can repeat 14 nonsense syllables, what is that person's IQ? Round to the nearest whole number.

**75.** The formula $N = 1220\sqrt[3]{x + 42} + 4900$ models the number of congressional aides in the House of Representatives $x$ years after 1930. In what year were approximately 9780 aides assigned to the House of Representatives?

**76.** Police use the model $v = \sqrt{24L}$ to estimate the speed of a car ($v$, in miles per hour) prior to an accident based on the length of its skid marks ($L$, in feet) on dry pavement. If a car is traveling at 60 miles per hour, what is the length of its skid marks?

**77.** The graph shows the remaining life expectancies for males and females in the United States in 1998. The formula $E = \sqrt{0.66A^2 - 110.55A + 4680.24}$ is an approximate model for some of the data in the graph, where $A$ represents current age and $E$ stands for remaining life expectancy (in years).

**Remaining Life Expectancies in the United States in 1998**

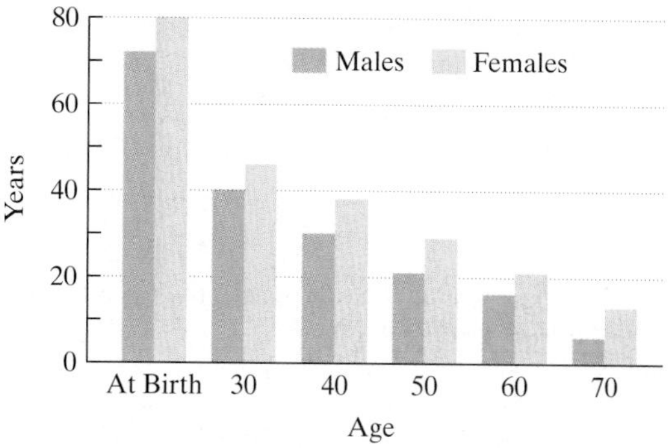


*Source*: Department of Health and Human Services

**a.** Is the formula a better model for males or for females?

**b.** If $E = 60$, find $A$ and describe what your result means in terms of the variables modeled by the formula.

**78.** Laser Records marketing research department determines that weekly demand for a boxed set of CDs by the Jumping Artichokes depends on the price per set, modeled by the formula $p = 30 - \sqrt{0.01x + 1}$, where $p$ represents the price of the set and $x$ represents the number of sets sold each week at price $p$.

**a.** At what price will there be no demand for the CD sets?

**b.** Approximately how many CD sets will sell weekly at a price of \$27.76?

*Use one of Einstein's models for mass, time, and length, given in Example 5 on page 135, to solve Exercises 79–82.*

**79.** How fast would a futuristic starship that is 800 meters tall have to move so that it would measure only 100 meters from the perspective of an observer who looks up and sees the ship pass by?

**80.** How fast would a futuristic starship that is 800 meters tall have to move so that it would measure only 300 meters from the perspective of an observer who looks up and sees the ship pass by?

**81.** How fast would a 120-pound person have to travel for that person's mass to double as perceived by an observer at rest?

**82.** A clock on board a futuristic starship traveling at $\frac{9}{10}$ of the speed of light measures a 10-second time period. How long is this time period from the perspective of an observer who looks up and sees the ship pass by?

*Use the Pythagorean Theorem to solve Exercises 83–84.*

**83.** Two vertical poles of lengths 6 feet and 8 feet stand 10 feet apart (see the figure). A cable reaches from the top of one pole to some point on the ground between the poles and then to the top of the other pole. Where should this point be located to use 18 feet of cable?

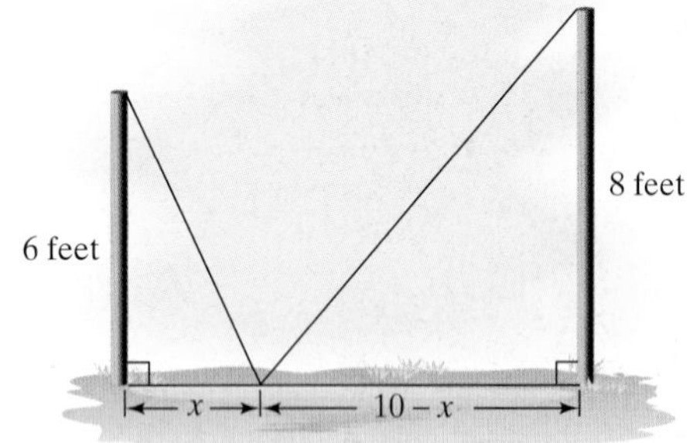


**84.** Twelve miles separate towns $A$ and $B$, located 6 miles and 3 miles, respectively, from a major expressway. Two new roads are to be built from $A$ to the expressway and then to $B$. (See the figure.)

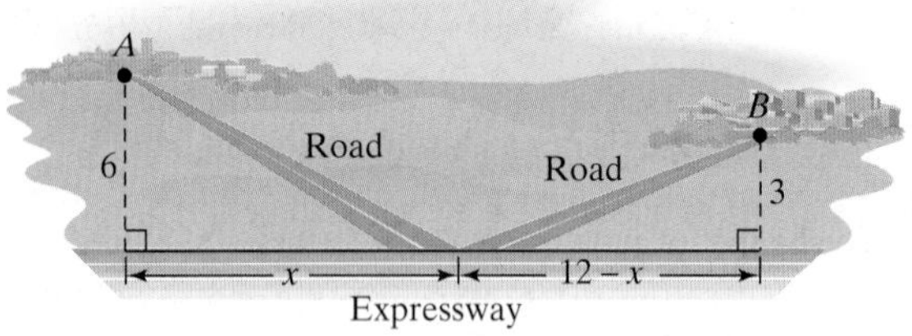


**a.** Find $x$ if the length of the new roads is 15 miles.
**b.** Write a verbal description for the road crew telling them where to position the new roads based on your answer to part (a).

## Writing in Mathematics

**85.** Without actually solving the equation, give a general description of how to solve $x^3 - 5x^2 - x + 5 = 0$

**86.** In solving $\sqrt{3x+4} - \sqrt{2x+4} = 2$, why is it a good idea to isolate a radical term? What if we don't do this and simply square each side? Describe what happens.

**87.** What is an extraneous solution to a radical equation?

**88.** Explain how to recognize an equation that is quadratic in form. Provide two original examples with your explanation.

**89.** Describe two methods for solving this equation: $x - 5\sqrt{x} + 4 = 0$.

**90.** Explain how to solve an equation involving absolute value.

**91.** Explain why the procedure that you explained in Exercise 90 does not apply to the equation $|x-2| = -3$. What is the solution set for this equation?

**92.** Reread Exercise 78. Suppose you are writing a report on the relationship between the price of the CDs and the units that will sell. Assume that you are the only one in the company who can understand the formula $p = 30 - \sqrt{0.01x + 1}$. Consequently, you must describe the relationship between $p$ and $x$ strictly using words. Write a description, minimizing the use of mathematical terminology.

## Technology Exercises

*Use a graphing utility to solve the equations in Exercises 93–97. Check by direct substitution.*

**93.** $x^3 + 3x^2 - x - 3 = 0$

**94.** $-x^4 + 4x^3 - 4x^2 = 0$

**95.** $x^4 - 2x^2 + 1 = 0$

**96.** $\sqrt{2x+13} - x - 5 = 0$

**97.** $\sqrt{4-x} - \sqrt{x+6} - 2 = 0$

**98.** Use a graphing utility to graph the formula in Exercise 73. In particular, graph $y = 5000\sqrt{100-x}$ in a $[0, 100, 10]$ by $[0, 50{,}000, 5000]$ viewing rectangle. Then use the TRACE feature to trace along the curve until you reach the point that visually shows the solution to Exercise 73.

**99.** Use a graphing utility to graph the formula in Exercise 74. In particular, graph $y = 2\sqrt{x} - 9$ in a $[0, 180, 10]$ by $[0, 20, 1]$ viewing rectangle. Then use the TRACE feature to trace along the curve until you reach the point that visually shows the solution to Exercise 74.

## Critical Thinking Exercises

**100.** Which one of the following is true?
**a.** Squaring both sides of $\sqrt{y+4} + \sqrt{y-1} = 5$ leads to $y + 4 + y - 1 = 25$, an equation with no radicals.
**b.** The equation $(x^2 - 2x)^9 - 5(x^2 - 2x)^3 + 6 = 0$ is quadratic in form and should be solved by letting

$$t = (x^2 - 2x)^3.$$

**c.** If a radical equation has two proposed solutions and one of these values is not a solution, the other value is also not a solution.
**d.** None of these statements is true.

**101.** Solve: $\sqrt{6x-2} = \sqrt{2x+3} - \sqrt{4x-1}$.

**102.** Solve *without* squaring both sides:

$$5 - \frac{2}{x} = \sqrt{5 - \frac{2}{x}}.$$

**103.** Solve for $x$: $\sqrt[3]{x\sqrt{x}} = 9$.

**104.** Solve for $x$: $x^{5/6} + x^{2/3} - 2x^{1/2} = 0$.

# SECTION 1.5 *Linear Inequalities*

## Objectives

1. Graph an inequality's solution set.
2. Use set-builder and interval notations.
3. Use properties of inequalities to solve inequalities.
4. Solve compound inequalities.
5. Solve inequalities involving absolute value.

Rent-a-Heap, a car rental company, charges \$125 per week plus \$0.20 per mile to rent one of their cars. Suppose you are limited by how much money you can spend for the week: You can spend at most \$335. If we let $x$ represent the number of miles you drive the heap in a week, we can write an inequality that models the given conditions.

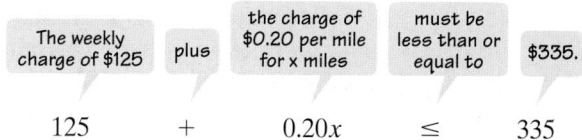

| The weekly charge of \$125 | plus | the charge of \$0.20 per mile for x miles | must be less than or equal to | \$335. |
|---|---|---|---|---|
| $125$ | $+$ | $0.20x$ | $\leq$ | $335$ |

Using the commutative property of addition, we can express this inequality as $0.20x + 125 \leq 335$. The form of this inequality is $ax + b \leq c$, with $a = 0.20$, $b = 125$, and $c = 335$. Any inequality in this form is called a **linear inequality in one variable**. The greatest exponent on the variable in such an equality is 1. The symbol between $ax + b$ and $c$ can be $\leq$ (is less than or equal to), $<$ (is less than), $\geq$ (is greater than or equal to), or $>$ (is greater than).

In this section, we will study how to solve linear inequalities such as $0.20x + 125 \leq 335$. **Solving an inequality** is the process of finding the set of numbers that make the inequality a true statement. These numbers are called the **solutions** of the inequality, and we say that they **satisfy** the inequality. The set of all solutions is called the **solution set** of the inequality. We begin by discussing how to graph and how to represent these solution sets.

1 Graph an inequality's solution set.

## Graphs of Inequalities; Interval Notation

There are infinitely many solutions to the inequality $x > -4$, namely all real numbers that are greater than $-4$. Although we cannot list all the solutions, we can make a drawing on a number line that represents these solutions. Such a drawing is called the **graph of the inequality**.

Graphs of solutions to linear inequalities are shown on a number line by shading all points representing numbers that are solutions. Parentheses indicate endpoints that are not solutions. Square brackets indicate endpoints that are solutions.

## EXAMPLE 1 Graphing Inequalities

Graph the solutions of:

**a.** $x < 3$ **b.** $x \geq -1$ **c.** $-1 < x \leq 3$.

### Study Tip

Because an inequality symbol points to the smaller number, $x < 3$ ($x$ is less than 3) may be expressed as $3 > x$ (3 is greater than $x$).

**Solution**

**a.** The solutions of $x < 3$ are all real numbers that are less than 3. They are graphed on a number line by shading all points to the left of 3. The parenthesis at 3 indicates that 3 is not a solution, but numbers such as 2.9999 and 2.6 are. The arrow shows that the graph extends indefinitely to the left.

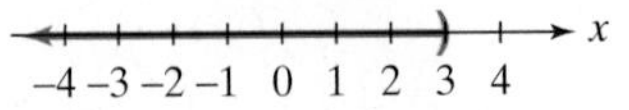


**b.** The solutions of $x \geq -1$ are all real numbers that are greater than or equal to $-1$. We shade all points to the right of $-1$ and the point for $-1$ itself. The bracket at $-1$ shows that $-1$ is a solution for the given inequality. The arrow shows that the graph extends indefinitely to the right.

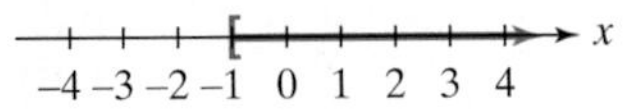


**c.** The inequality $-1 < x \leq 3$ is read "$-1$ is less than $x$ *and* $x$ is less than or equal to 3," or "$x$ is greater than $-1$ *and* less than or equal to 3." The solutions of $-1 < x \leq 3$ are all real numbers between $-1$ and 3, not including $-1$ but including 3. The parenthesis at $-1$ indicates that $-1$ is not a solution. By contrast, the bracket at 3 shows that 3 is a solution. Shading indicates the other solutions.

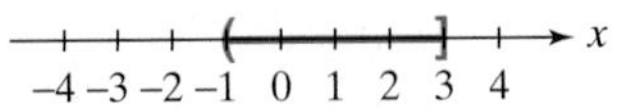


**Check Point 1** Graph the solutions of:

**a.** $x \leq 2$ **b.** $x > -4$ **c.** $2 \leq x < 6$

**2** Use set-builder and interval notations.

Now that we know how to graph the solution set for an inequality such as $x > -4$, let's see how to represent the solution set. One method is with **set-builder notation**. Using this method, the solution set for $x > -4$ can be expressed as

$$\{x \mid x > -4\}.$$

The set of all x — such that

We read this as "the set of all real numbers $x$ such that $x$ is greater than $-4$."

Another method used to represent solution sets for inequalities is **interval notation**. Using this notation, the solution set for $x > -4$ is expressed as $(-4, \infty)$. The parenthesis at $-4$ indicates that $-4$ is not included in the interval. The infinity symbol, $\infty$, does not represent a real number. It indicates that the interval extends indefinitely to the right.

Table 1.5 lists nine possible types of intervals used to describe subsets of real numbers.

**Table 1.5 Intervals on the Real Number Line**

**Let $a$ and $b$ be real numbers such that $a < b$.**

| Interval Notation | Set-Builder Notation | Graph |
|---|---|---|
| $(a, b)$ | $\{x \mid a < x < b\}$ | 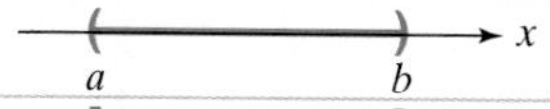 |
| $[a, b]$ | $\{x \mid a \leq x \leq b\}$ |  |
| $[a, b)$ | $\{x \mid a \leq x < b\}$ |  |
| $(a, b]$ | $\{x \mid a < x \leq b\}$ |  |
| $(a, \infty)$ | $\{x \mid x > a\}$ |  |
| $[a, \infty)$ | $\{x \mid x \geq a\}$ |  |
| $(-\infty, b)$ | $\{x \mid x < b\}$ | 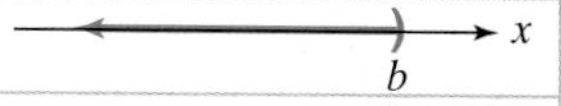 |
| $(-\infty, b]$ | $\{x \mid x \leq b\}$ |  |
| $(-\infty, \infty)$ | $\mathbb{R}$ (set of all real numbers) |  |

## EXAMPLE 2 Intervals and Inequalities

Express the intervals in terms of inequalities and graph:

**a.** $(-1, 4]$ **b.** $[2.5, 4]$ **c.** $(-4, \infty)$

### Solution

**a.** $(-1, 4] = \{x \mid -1 < x \leq 4\}$

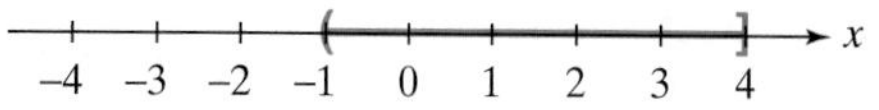


**b.** $[2.5, 4] = \{x \mid 2.5 \leq x \leq 4\}$

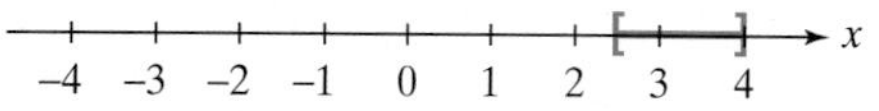


**c.** $(-4, \infty) = \{x \mid x > -4\}$

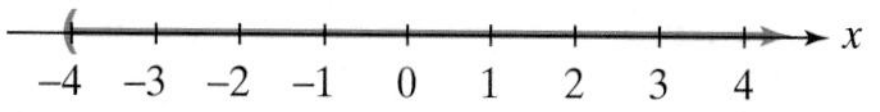


**Check Point 2** Express the intervals in terms of inequalities and graph:

**a.** $[-2, 5)$ **b.** $[1, 3.5]$ **c.** $(-\infty, -1)$

**3** Use properties of inequalities to solve inequalities.

## Solving Linear Inequalities

Inequalities with the same solution set are called **equivalent inequalities**. We can isolate a variable in a linear inequality the same way we can isolate a variable in a linear equation. The following properties are used to create equivalent inequalities.

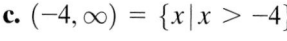

**Properties of Inequalities**

| Property | The Property in Words | Example |
|---|---|---|
| *Addition and Subtraction Properties*<br>If $a < b$, then $a + c < b + c$.<br>If $a < b$, then $a - c < b - c$. | If the same quantity is added to or subtracted from both sides of an inequality, the resulting inequality is equivalent to the original one. | $2x + 3 < 7$<br>Subtract 3:<br>$2x + 3 - 3 < 7 - 3$<br>Simplify:<br>$2x < 4$ |
| *Positive Multiplication and Division Properties*<br>If $a < b$ and $c$ is positive, then $ac < bc$.<br>If $a < b$ and $c$ is positive, then $\frac{a}{c} < \frac{b}{c}$. | If we multiply or divide both sides of an inequality by the same positive quantity, the resulting inequality is equivalent to the original one. | $2x < 4$<br>Divide by 2:<br>$\frac{2x}{2} < \frac{4}{2}$<br>Simplify:<br>$x < 2$ |
| *Negative Multiplication and Division Properties*<br>If $a < b$ and $c$ is negative, then $ac > bc$.<br>If $a < b$ and $c$ is negative, then $\frac{a}{c} > \frac{b}{c}$. | If we multiply or divide both sides of an inequality by the same negative quantity and reverse the direction of the inequality symbol, the result is an equivalent inequality. | $-4x < 20$<br>Divide by $-4$ and reverse the sense of the inequality:<br>$\frac{-4x}{-4} > \frac{20}{-4}$<br>Simplify:<br>$x > -5$ |

## EXAMPLE 3 Solving a Linear Inequality

Solve and graph the solution set: $7x + 15 \geq 13x + 51$.

**Solution** We will collect variable terms on the left and constant terms on the right.

$$7x + 15 \geq 13x + 51 \quad \text{This is the given inequality.}$$
$$7x + 15 - 13x \geq 13x + 51 - 13x \quad \text{Subtract 13x from both sides.}$$
$$-6x + 15 \geq 51 \quad \text{Simplify.}$$
$$-6x + 15 - 15 \geq 51 - 15 \quad \text{Subtract 15 from both sides.}$$
$$-6x \geq 36 \quad \text{Simplify.}$$
$$\frac{-6x}{-6} \leq \frac{36}{-6} \quad \text{Divide both sides by } -6 \text{ and reverse the sense of the inequality.}$$
$$x \leq -6 \quad \text{Simplify.}$$

The solution set consists of all real numbers that are less than or equal to $-6$, expressed as $\{x \mid x \leq -6\}$. The interval notation for this solution set is $(-\infty, -6]$. The graph of the solution set is shown as follows:

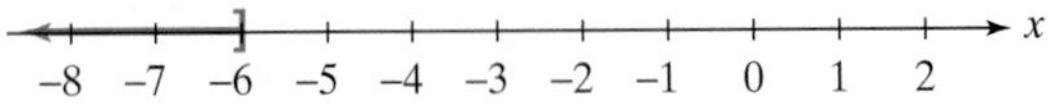


**Check Point 3** Solve and graph the solution set: $6 - 3x \leq 5x - 2$.

**Study Tip**

You can solve

$$7x + 15 \geq 13x + 51$$

by isolating $x$ on the right side. Subtract $7x$ from both sides:

$$7x + 15 - 7x \geq 13x + 51 - 7x$$
$$15 \geq 6x + 51$$

Now subtract 51 from both sides.

$$15 - 51 \geq 6x + 51 - 51$$
$$-36 \geq 6x$$

Finally, divide both sides by 6.

$$\frac{-36}{6} \geq \frac{6x}{6}$$
$$-6 \geq x$$

This last inequality means the same thing as

$$x \leq -6.$$

## Technology

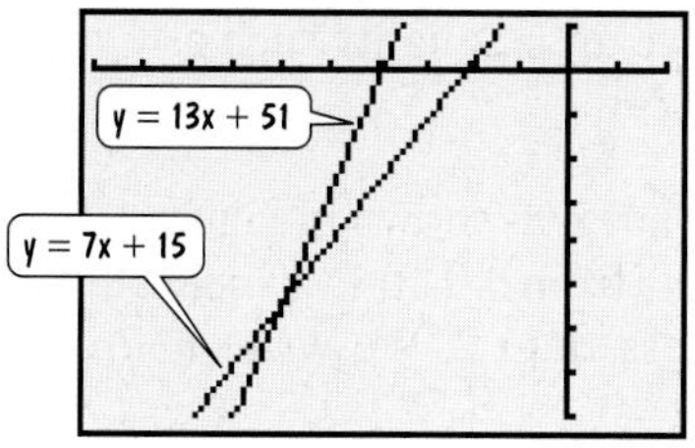


You can use a graphing utility to verify that $(-\infty, -6]$ is the solution set for

$$7x + 15 \geq 13x + 51.$$

For what values of x does the graph of y = 7x + 15 | lie above or on | the graph of y = 13x + 51?

The graphs are shown on the left in a $[-10, 2, 1]$ by $[-40, 5, 5]$ viewing rectangle. Notice that the graph of $y = 7x + 15$ lies above or on the graph of $y = 13x + 51$ when $x \leq -6$.

**4** Solve compound inequalities.

## Solving Compound Inequalities

We now consider two inequalities such as

$$-3 < 2x + 1 \text{ and } 2x + 1 \leq 3$$

expressed as a **compound inequality**

$$-3 < 2x + 1 \leq 3.$$

This double inequality form enables us to solve both inequalities at once. With three parts to a compound inequality, our goal is to **isolate *x* in the middle**.

### EXAMPLE 4 Solving a Compound Inequality

Solve and graph the solution set:

$$-3 < 2x + 1 \leq 3.$$

**Solution** We would like to isolate $x$ in the middle. We can do this by first subtracting 1 from all three parts of the compound inequality. Then we isolate $x$ from $2x$ by dividing all three parts of the inequality by 2.

$$-3 < 2x + 1 \leq 3 \quad \text{This is the given inequality.}$$

$$-3 - 1 < 2x + 1 - 1 \leq 3 - 1 \quad \text{Subtract 1 from all three parts.}$$

$$-4 < 2x \leq 2 \quad \text{Simplify.}$$

$$\frac{-4}{2} < \frac{2x}{2} \leq \frac{2}{2} \quad \text{Divide each part by 2.}$$

$$-2 < x \leq 1 \quad \text{Simplify.}$$

The solution set consists of all real numbers greater than $-2$ and less than or equal to 1, represented by $\{x \mid -2 < x \leq 1\}$ in set-builder notation and $(-2, 1]$ in interval notation. The graph is shown as follows:

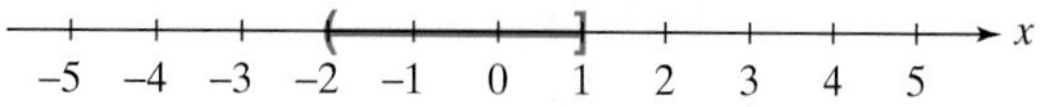


**Check Point 4** Solve and graph the solution set: $1 \leq 2x + 3 < 11$.

**5** Solve inequalities involving absolute value.

## Solving Inequalities with Absolute Value

We have seen that $|x|$ describes the distance of $x$ from zero on a real number line. We can use this geometric interpretation to solve an inequality such as

$$|x| < 2.$$

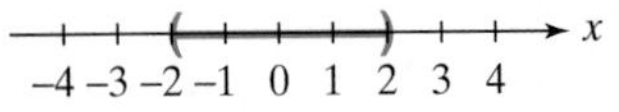


**Figure 1.7** $|x| < 2$, so $-2 < x < 2$.

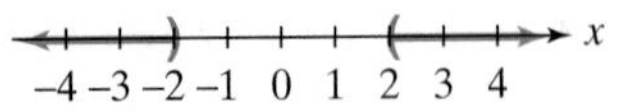


**Figure 1.8** $|x| > 2$, so $x < -2$ or $x > 2$.

This means that the distance of $x$ from 0 is *less than* 2, as shown in Figure 1.7. The interval shows values of $x$ that lie less than 2 units from 0. Thus, $x$ can lie between $-2$ and 2. That is, $x$ is greater than $-2$ and less than 2. We write $(-2, 2)$ or $\{x | -2 < x < 2\}$.

Some absolute value inequalities use the "greater than" symbol. For example, $|x| > 2$ means that the distance of $x$ from 0 is *greater than* 2, as shown in Figure 1.8. Thus, $x$ can be less than $-2$ *or* greater than 2. We write $x < -2$ or $x > 2$.

These observations suggest the following principles for solving inequalities with absolute value.

**Study Tip**

In the $|X| < c$ case, we have one compound inequality to solve. In the $|X| > c$ case, we have two separate inequalities to solve.

**Solving an Absolute Value Inequality**

If $X$ is an algebraic expression and $c$ is a positive number,

1. The solutions of $|X| < c$ are the numbers that satisfy $-c < X < c$.
2. The solutions of $|X| > c$ are the numbers that satisfy $X < -c$ or $X > c$.

These rules are valid if $<$ is replaced by $\leq$ and $>$ is replaced by $\geq$.

### EXAMPLE 5 Solving an Absolute Value Inequality with <

Solve and graph: $|x - 4| < 3$.

**Solution**

$|X| < c$ *means* $-c < X < c$.

$$|x - 4| < 3 \quad \text{means} \quad -3 < x - 4 < 3$$

We solve the compound inequality by adding 4 to all three parts.

$$-3 < x - 4 < 3$$
$$-3 + 4 < x - 4 + 4 < 3 + 4$$
$$1 < x < 7$$

The solution set is all real numbers greater than 1 and less than 7, denoted by $\{x | 1 < x < 7\}$ or $(1, 7)$. The graph of the solution set is shown as follows:

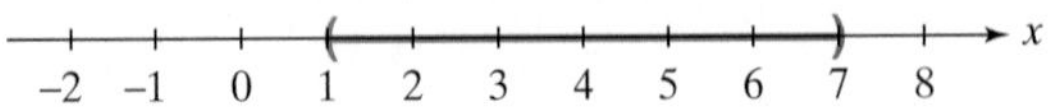


**Check Point 5** Solve and graph: $|x - 2| < 5$.

## EXAMPLE 6 Solving an Absolute Value Inequality with ≥

Solve and graph: $|2x + 3| \geq 5$.

### Solution

$|X| \geq c$ means $X \leq -c$ or $X \geq c$.

$|2x + 3| \geq 5$ means $2x + 3 \leq -5$ or $2x + 3 \geq 5$

We solve each of these inequalities separately.

| | | | |
|---|---|---|---|
| $2x + 3 \leq -5$ | or | $2x + 3 \geq 5$ | These are the inequalities without absolute value bars. |
| $2x + 3 - 3 \leq -5 - 3$ | or | $2x + 3 - 3 \geq 5 - 3$ | Subtract 3 from both sides. |
| $2x \leq -8$ | or | $2x \geq 2$ | Simplify. |
| $\frac{2x}{2} \leq \frac{-8}{2}$ | or | $\frac{2x}{2} \geq \frac{2}{2}$ | Divide both sides by 2. |
| $x \leq -4$ | or | $x \geq 1$ | Simplify. |

The solution set is $\{x \mid x \leq -4 \text{ or } x \geq 1\}$, that is, all $x$ in $(-\infty, -4]$ or $[1, \infty)$. The graph of the solution set is shown as follows:

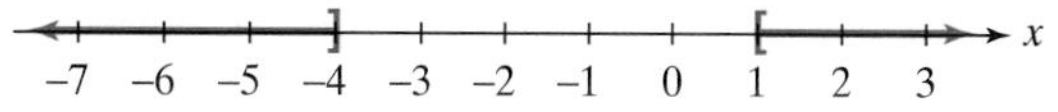


**Study Tip**

The graph of the solution set for $|X| > c$ will be divided into two intervals. The graph of the solution set for $|X| < c$ will be a single interval.

**Check Point 6** Solve and graph: $|2x - 5| \geq 3$.

## Applications

Our next example shows how to use an inequality to select the better deal between two pricing options. We will use our five-step strategy for solving problems using mathematical models.

## EXAMPLE 7 Creating and Comparing Mathematical Models

Acme Car rental agency charges \$4 a day plus \$0.15 a mile, whereas Interstate rental agency charges \$20 a day and \$0.05 a mile. How many miles must be driven to make the daily cost of an Acme rental a better deal than an Interstate rental?

### Solution

**Step 1 Let *x* represent one of the quantities.** We are looking for the number of miles that must be driven in a day to make Acme the better deal. Thus,

let $x$ = the number of miles driven in a day.

**Step 2 Represent other quantities in terms of $x$.** We are not asked to find another quantity, so we can skip this step.

**Step 3 Write an inequality in $x$ that describes the conditions.**

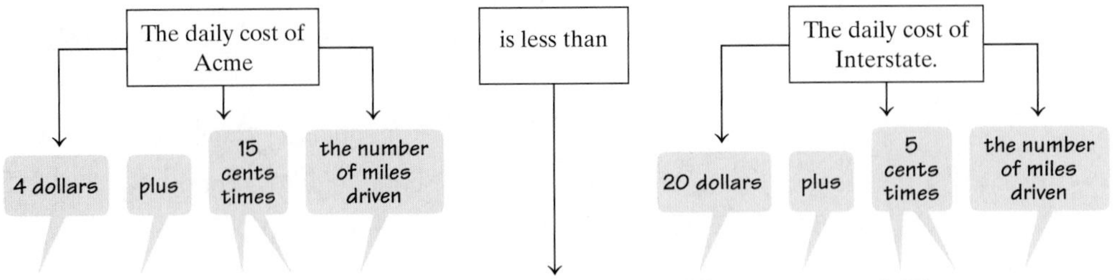


$$4 + 0.15 \cdot x < 20 + 0.05 \cdot x$$

**Step 4 Solve the inequality and answer the question.**

$$4 + 0.15x < 20 + 0.05x$$ This is the inequality that models the verbal conditions.

$$4 + 0.15x - 0.05x < 20 + 0.05x - 0.05x$$ Subtract 0.05x from both sides.

$$4 + 0.1x < 20$$ Simplify.

$$4 + 0.1x - 4 < 20 - 4$$ Subtract 4 from both sides.

$$0.1x < 16$$ Simplify.

$$\frac{0.1x}{0.1} < \frac{16}{0.1}$$ Divide both sides by 0.1.

$$x < 160$$ Simplify.

Thus, driving fewer than 160 miles per day makes Acme the better deal.

**Step 5 Check the proposed solution in the original wording of the problem.** One way to do this is to take a mileage less than 160 miles per day to see if Acme is the better deal. Suppose that 150 miles are driven in a day.

$$\text{Cost for Acme} = 4 + 0.15(150) = 26.50$$

$$\text{Cost for Interstate} = 20 + 0.05(150) = 27.50$$

and Acme has a lower daily cost, making Acme the better deal.

**Check Point 7** A car can be rented from Basic Rental for \$260 per week with no extra charge for mileage. Continental charges \$80 per week plus 25 cents for each mile driven to rent the same car. How many miles should be driven in a week to make the rental cost for Basic Rental a better deal than Continental's?

## EXERCISE SET 1.5

### Practice Exercises

*In Exercises 1–12, graph the solutions of each inequality on a number line.*

**1.** $x > 6$
**2.** $x > -2$
**3.** $x < -4$
**4.** $x < 0$
**5.** $x \ge -3$
**6.** $x \ge -5$
**7.** $x \le 4$
**8.** $x \le 7$
**9.** $-2 < x \le 5$
**10.** $-3 \le x < 7$
**11.** $-1 < x < 4$
**12.** $-7 \le x \le 0$

*In Exercises 13–26, express each interval in terms of an inequality and graph the interval on a number line.*

**13.** $(1, 6]$
**14.** $(-2, 4]$
**15.** $[-5, 2)$
**16.** $[-4, 3)$
**17.** $[-3, 1]$
**18.** $[-2, 5]$
**19.** $(2, \infty)$
**20.** $(3, \infty)$
**21.** $[-3, \infty)$
**22.** $[-5, \infty)$
**23.** $(-\infty, 3)$
**24.** $(-\infty, 2)$
**25.** $(-\infty, 5.5)$
**26.** $(-\infty, 3.5]$

*Solve each linear inequality in Exercises 27–48 and graph the solution set on a number line.*

**27.** $5x + 11 < 26$
**28.** $2x + 5 < 17$
**29.** $3x - 7 \ge 13$
**30.** $8x - 2 \ge 14$
**31.** $-9x \ge 36$
**32.** $-5x \le 30$
**33.** $8x - 11 \le 3x - 13$
**34.** $18x + 45 \le 12x - 8$
**35.** $4(x + 1) + 2 \ge 3x + 6$
**36.** $8x + 3 > 3(2x + 1) + x + 5$
**37.** $2x - 11 < -3(x + 2)$
**38.** $-4(x + 2) > 3x + 20$
**39.** $1 - (x + 3) \ge 4 - 2x$
**40.** $5(3 - x) \le 3x - 1$
**41.** $\frac{x}{4} - \frac{3}{5} \le \frac{x}{2} + 1$
**42.** $\frac{3x}{10} + 1 \ge \frac{1}{5} - \frac{x}{10}$
**43.** $1 - \frac{x}{2} > 4$
**44.** $7 - \frac{4}{5}x < \frac{3}{5}$
**45.** $\frac{x - 4}{6} \ge \frac{x - 2}{9} + \frac{5}{18}$
**46.** $\frac{4x - 3}{6} + 2 \ge \frac{2x - 1}{12}$
**47.** $4(3x - 2) - 3x < 3(1 + 3x) - 7$
**48.** $3(x - 8) - 2(10 - x) > 5(x - 1)$

*Solve each inequality in Exercises 49–56 by isolating the variable by itself in the middle. Graph the solution set on a number line.*

**49.** $6 < x + 3 < 8$
**50.** $7 < x + 5 < 11$
**51.** $-3 \le x - 2 < 1$
**52.** $-6 < x - 4 \le 1$
**53.** $-11 < 2x - 1 \le -5$
**54.** $3 \le 4x - 3 < 19$
**55.** $-3 \le \frac{2}{3}x - 5 < -1$
**56.** $-6 \le \frac{1}{2}x - 4 < -3$

*Solve each inequality in Exercises 57–84 by first rewriting each one as an equivalent inequality without absolute value bars. Graph the solution set on a number line.*

**57.** $|x| < 3$
**58.** $|x| < 5$
**59.** $|x - 1| \le 2$
**60.** $|x + 3| \le 4$
**61.** $|2x - 6| < 8$
**62.** $|3x + 5| < 17$
**63.** $|2(x - 1) + 4| \le 8$
**64.** $|3(x - 1) + 2| \le 20$
**65.** $\left|\frac{2y + 6}{3}\right| < 2$
**66.** $\left|\frac{3(x - 1)}{4}\right| < 6$
**67.** $|x| > 3$
**68.** $|x| > 5$
**69.** $|x - 1| \ge 2$
**70.** $|x + 3| \ge 4$
**71.** $|3x - 8| > 7$
**72.** $|5x - 2| > 13$
**73.** $\left|\frac{2x + 2}{4}\right| \ge 2$
**74.** $\left|\frac{3x - 3}{9}\right| \ge 1$
**75.** $\left|3 - \frac{2}{3}x\right| > 5$
**76.** $\left|3 - \frac{3}{4}x\right| > 9$
**77.** $3|x - 1| + 2 \ge 8$
**78.** $-2|4 - x| \ge -4$
**79.** $3 < |2x - 1|$
**80.** $5 \ge |4 - x|$
**81.** $12 < \left|-2x + \frac{6}{7}\right| + \frac{3}{7}$
**82.** $1 < \left|x - \frac{11}{3}\right| + \frac{7}{3}$
**83.** $4 + \left|3 - \frac{x}{3}\right| \ge 9$
**84.** $\left|2 - \frac{x}{2}\right| - 1 \le 1$

### Application Exercises

*The list on the next page shown ranks the ten best-educated cities in the United States measured by the percentage of the population with 16 or more years of education. Let x represent the percentage of the population with 16 or more years of education. In Exercises 85–90, write the name or names of the city or cities described by the given inequality or interval.*

**85.** $x \ge 34.4\%$
**86.** $x > 35.0\%$
**87.** $x < 30.0\%$
**88.** $x \le 30.3\%$

**89.** $[30.0\%, 34.4\%]$ **90.** $(30.6\%, 35.0\%]$

**Most Educated**

| City | % with 16+ Years of Education |
|---|---|
| 1. Raleigh, NC | 40.6% |
| 2. Seattle, WA | 37.9 |
| 3. San Francisco, CA | 35.0 |
| 4. Austin, TX | 34.4 |
| 5. Washington, DC | 33.3 |
| 6. Lexington-Fayette, KY | 30.6 |
| 7. Minneapolis, MN | 30.3 |
| 8. Boston, MA | 30.0 |
| 9. Arlington, TX | 30.0 |
| 10. San Diego, CA | 29.8 |

*Source:* U.S. Census Bureau

**91.** The bar graph shows the number of people in the United States with various disorders of mental illness. If $x$ represents millions of people, which disorders are described by $11 \leq 3x - 4 \leq 56$ cases?

**Mental Illness in America, by Disorder**

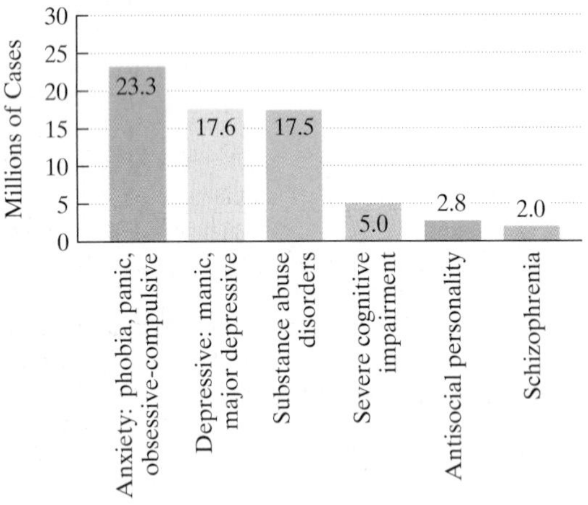


*Source*: National Institute of Mental Health.

**92.** The bar graph at the top of the next column shows revenues, in billions of dollars, for the pet pharmaceutical industry for three selected years. Let $x$ represent revenues in billions of dollars per year. Which year or years shown in the graph is/are described by the inequality

$$5 < 4x - 1 < 11?$$

**Pet Pharmaceutical Industry Revenues**

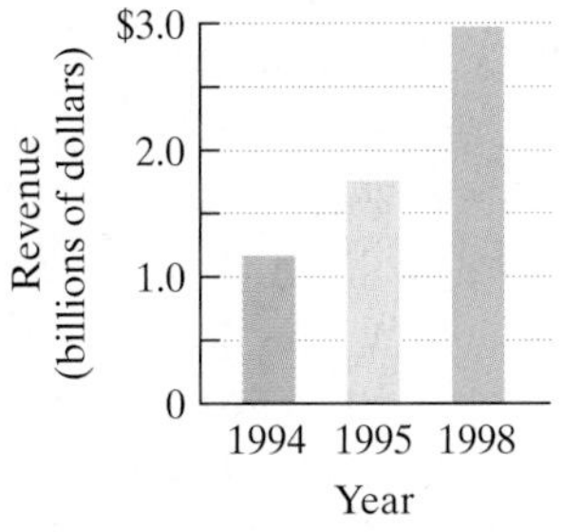


*Source*: American Veterinary Medical Association

**93.** Using data from 1996–1998, the number of liposuctions in the United States can be modeled by the formula $y = 30x + 113$, where $y$ is the number of liposuctions, in thousands, $x$ years after 1996. According to this formula, when will the number of liposuctions exceed 623 thousand?

**Liposuctions: U.S. Men and Women**

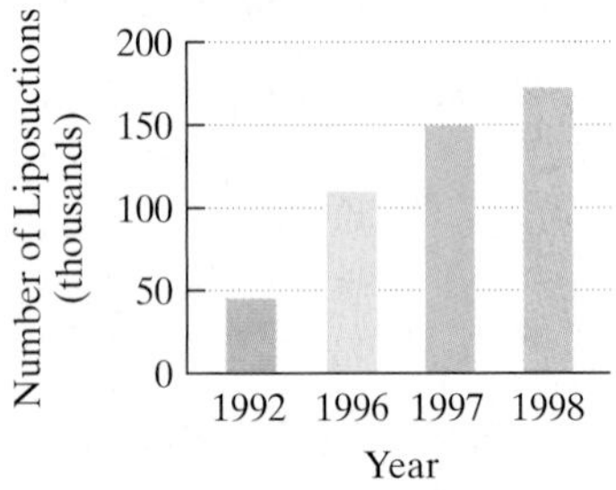


*Source:* U.S. Department of Health and Human Services

**94.** Lower interest rates have fueled larger mortgage loans. The formula $y = 3.5x + 58$ models the data shown in the graph, where $y$ is the size of the loan, in thousands of dollars, $x$ years after 1980. According to this formula, when will the average mortgage loan exceed $142 thousand?

**Average Mortgage Loan**

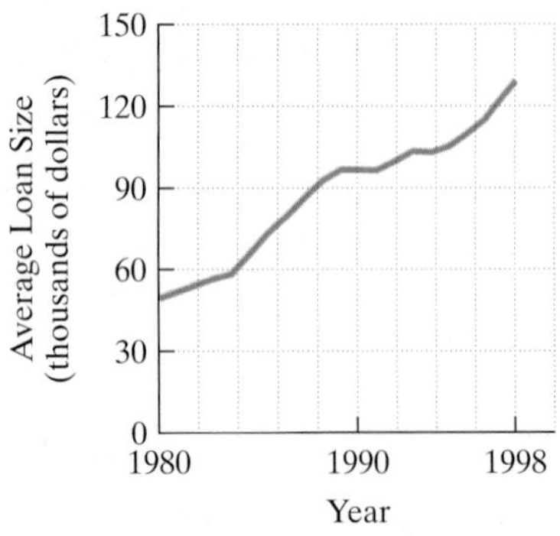


*Source:* Mortgage Bankers Association of America

**95.** Using current trends, future costs of Medicare can be modeled by $C = 18x + 250$, where $x$ represents the number of years after 2000 and $C$ represents the cost of Medicare, in billions of dollars. Use a compound inequality to determine the years when Medicare costs will range from 322 to 412 billion dollars.

**96.** The formula for converting Celsius temperature $(C)$ to Fahrenheit $(F)$ is $F = \frac{9}{5}C + 32$. If Fahrenheit temperature exceeds 77°, what does this mean in terms of Celsius temperature?

**97.** A local bank charges \$8 per month plus 5¢ per check. The credit union charges \$2 per month plus 8¢ per check. How many checks should be written each month to make the credit union a better deal?

**98.** A city commission has proposed two tax bills. The first bill requires that a homeowner pay \$1800 plus 3% of the assessed home value in taxes, The second bill requires taxes of \$200 plus 8% of the assessed home value. What price range of home assessment would make the first bill a better deal?

**99.** On two examinations, you have grades of 86 and 88. There is an optional final examination, which counts as one grade. You decide to take the final in order to get a course grade of A, meaning a final average of at least 90.

**a.** What must you get on the final to earn an A in the course?

**b.** By taking the final, if you do poorly, you might risk the B that you have in the course based on the first two exam grades. If your final average is less than 80, you will lose your B in the course. Describe the grades on the final that will cause this to happen.

**100.** A company that manufactures small clocks has fixed costs of \$75,000 per month. It costs the company \$3 to manufacture each clock. If the clocks sell for \$18 each, how many should be manufactured and sold monthly to make a profit?

**101.** A company that manufactures running shoes has fixed costs of \$65,000 per month. It costs the company \$20 to manufacture each pair of running shoes. If the shoes sell for \$85 a pair, how many should be manufactured and sold monthly to make a profit?

**102.** If a coin is tossed 100 times, we would expect approximately 50 of the outcomes to be heads. It can be demonstrated that a coin is unfair if $h$, the number of outcomes that result in heads, satisfies $\left|\frac{h - 50}{5}\right| \geq 1.645$. Describe the number of outcomes that determine an unfair coin that is tossed 100 times.

## Writing in Mathematics

**103.** When graphing the solutions of an inequality, what does a parenthesis signify? What does a bracket signify?

**104.** When solving an inequality, when is it necessary to change the sense of the inequality? Give an example.

**105.** Describe ways in which solving a linear inequality is similar to solving a linear equation.

**106.** Describe ways in which solving a linear inequality is different than solving a linear equation.

**107.** What is a compound inequality and how is it solved?

**108.** Describe how to solve an absolute value inequality involving the symbol $<$. Give an example.

**109.** Describe how to solve an absolute value inequality involving the symbol $>$. Give an example.

**110.** Explain why $|x| < -4$ has no solution.

**111.** Describe the solution set of $|x| > -4$.

## Technology Exercises

*In Exercises 112–113, solve each inequality using a graphing utility. Graph each side separately. Then determine the values of x for which the graph on the left side lies above the graph on the right side.*

**112.** $-3(x - 6) > 2x - 2$ **113.** $-2(x + 4) > 6x + 16$

*Use the same technique employed in Exercises 112–113 to solve each inequality in Exercises 114–115. In each case, what conclusion can you draw? What happens if you try solving the inequalities algebraically?*

**114.** $12x - 10 > 2(x - 4) + 10x$

**115.** $2x + 3 > 3(2x - 4) - 4x$

**116.** A bank offers two checking account plans. Plan A has a base service charge of \$4.00 per month plus 10¢ per check. Plan B charges a base service charge of \$2.00 per month plus 15¢ per check.

**a.** Write models for the total monthly costs for each plan if $x$ checks are written.

**b.** Use a graphing utility to graph the models in the same viewing rectangle. Use a [0, 50, 1] by [0, 10, 1] viewing rectangle.

**c.** Use the graphs (and the TRACE or intersection feature) to determine for what number of checks per month plan A will be better than plan B.

**d.** Verify the result of part (c) algebraically by solving an inequality.

## Critical Thinking Exercises

**117.** Which one of the following is true?

**a.** The first step in solving $|2x - 3| > -7$ is to rewrite the inequality as $2x - 3 > -7$ or $2x - 3 < 7$.

**b.** The smallest real number in the solution set of $2x > 6$ is 4.

**c.** All irrational numbers satisfy $|x - 4| > 0$.

**d.** None of these statements is true.

**118.** What's wrong with this argument? Suppose $x$ and $y$ represent two real numbers, where $x > y$:

| | |
|---|---|
| $2 > 1$ | This is a true statement. |
| $2(y - x) > 1(y - x)$ | Multiply both sides by $y - x$. |
| $2y - 2x > y - x$ | Use the distributive property. |
| $y > x$ | Subtract $y$ from both sides. Add $2x$ to both sides. |

The final inequality, $y > x$, is impossible because we were initially given $x > y$.

**119.** The graphs of $y = 6$, $y = 3(-x - 5) - 9$, and $y = 0$ are shown in the figure. The graph was obtained using a graphing utility with $x$ ranging from $-12$ to 1 and $y$ ranging from $-2$ to 8. Use the graph to write the solution set for the compound inequality

$$0 < 3(-x - 5) - 9 < 6.$$

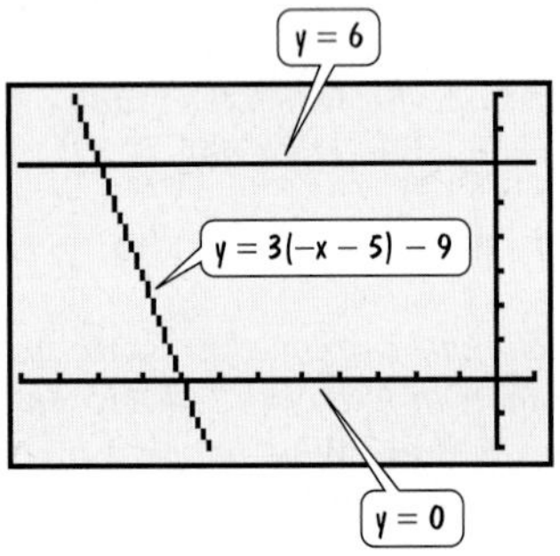


**120.** The percentage, $p$, of defective products manufactured by a company is given as $|p - 0.3\%| \le 0.2\%$. If 100,000 products are manufactured and the company offers a \$5 refund for each defective product, describe the company's cost for refunds.

## Group Exercise

**121.** Each group member should research one situation that provides two different pricing options. These can involve areas such as public transportation options (with or without coupon books) or long-distance telephone plans or anything of interest. Be sure to bring in all the details for each option. At a second group meeting, select the two pricing situations that are most interesting and relevant. Using each situation, write a word problem about selecting the better of the two options. The word problem should be one that can be solved using a linear inequality. The group should turn in the two problems and their solutions.

# SECTION 1.6 *Quadratic and Rational Inequalities*

### Objectives

1. Solve quadratic inequalities.
2. Solve rational inequalities.
3. Solve problems modeled by nonlinear inequalities.

Not afraid of heights and cutting-edge excitement? How about sky diving? Behind your exhilarating experience is the world of algebra. After you jump from the airplane, your height above the ground at every instant of your fall can be described by a formula involving a variable that is squared. At some point, you'll need to open your parachute. How can you determine when you must do so? Let $x$ represent the number of seconds you are falling. You can compute when to open the parachute by solving an inequality that takes on the form $ax^2 + bx + c < 0$. Such an inequality is called a **quadratic inequality**.

**Definition of a Quadratic Inequality**

A **quadratic inequality** is any inequality that can be put in one of the forms

$$ax^2 + bx + c < 0 \qquad ax^2 + bx + c > 0$$
$$ax^2 + bx + c \leq 0 \qquad ax^2 + bx + c \geq 0$$

where $a$, $b$, and $c$ are real numbers and $a \neq 0$.

In this section we establish the basic techniques for solving quadratic inequalities. We will use these techniques to solve inequalities containing quotients, called **rational inequalities**. Finally, we will consider a formula that models the position of any free-falling object. As a sky diver, you could be that free-falling object!

**1** Solve quadratic inequalities.

## Solving Quadratic Inequalities

Graphs can help us to estimate the solutions of quadratic inequalities. The graph of $y = x^2 - 7x + 10$ is shown in Figure 1.9. The $x$-intercepts, 2 and 5, are **boundary points** between where the graph lies above the $x$-axis, shown in blue, and where the graph lies below the $x$-axis, shown in red. These boundary points play a critical role in solving quadratic inequalities.

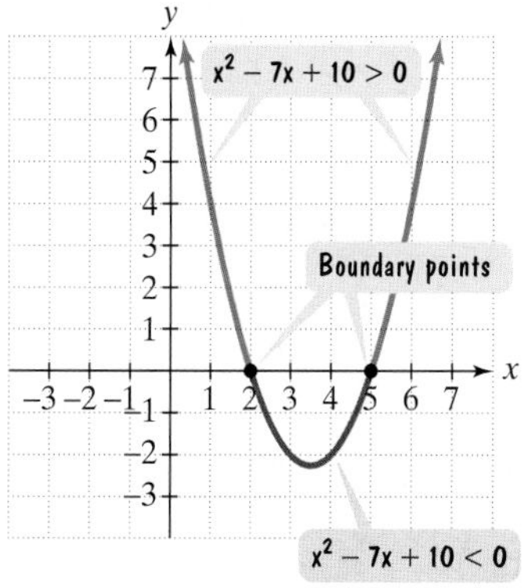


**Figure 1.9** The graph of $y = x^2 - 7x + 10$. The blue parts of the graph lie above the $x$-axis: $x^2 - 7x + 10 > 0$. By contrast, the red part lies below the $x$-axis: $x^2 - 7x + 10 < 0$.

**Procedure for Solving Quadratic Inequalities**

1. Express the inequality in the standard form
$$ax^2 + bx + c > 0 \quad \text{or} \quad ax^2 + bx + c < 0.$$
2. Solve the equation $ax^2 + bx + c = 0$. The real solutions are the **boundary points**.
3. Locate these boundary points on a number line, thereby dividing the number line into **test intervals**.
4. Choose one representative number within each test interval. If substituting that value into the original inequality produces a true statement, then all real numbers in the test interval belong to the solution set. If substituting that value into the original inequality produces a false statement, then no real numbers in the test interval belong to the solution set.
5. Write the solution set, selecting the interval(s) that produced a true statement. The graph of the solution set on a number line usually appears as

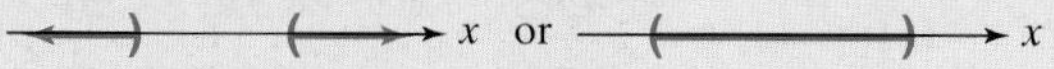


This procedure is valid if $<$ is replaced by $\leq$ and $>$ is replaced by $\geq$.

## EXAMPLE 1 Solving a Quadratic Inequality

Solve and graph the solution set on a real number line: $x^2 - 7x + 10 < 0$.

### Solution

**Step 1 Write the inequality in standard form.** The inequality is given in this form, so this step has been done for us.

**Step 2 Solve the related quadratic equation.** This equation is obtained by replacing the inequality sign by an equal sign. Thus, we will solve $x^2 - 7x + 10 = 0$.

$$x^2 - 7x + 10 = 0 \quad \text{This is the related quadratic equation.}$$

$$(x - 2)(x - 5) = 0 \quad \text{Factor.}$$

$$x - 2 = 0 \quad \text{or} \quad x - 5 = 0 \quad \text{Set each factor equal to 0.}$$

$$x = 2 \quad \text{or} \quad x = 5 \quad \text{Solve for x.}$$

The boundary points are 2 and 5.

**Step 3 Locate the boundary points on a number line.** The number line with the boundary points is shown as follows:

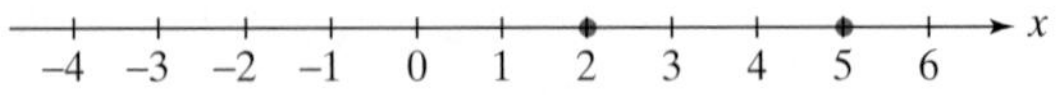


The boundary points divide the number line into three test intervals, namely $(-\infty, 2)$, $(2, 5)$, and $(5, \infty)$.

**Step 4 Take one representative number within each test interval and substitute that number into the original inequality.**

| Test Interval | Representative Number | Substitute into $x^2 - 7x + 10 < 0$ | Conclusion |
|---|---|---|---|
| $(-\infty, 2)$ | 0 | $0^2 - 7 \cdot 0 + 10 \overset{?}{<} 0$<br>$10 < 0,$<br>False | $(-\infty, 2)$ does not belong to the solution set. |
| $(2, 5)$ | 3 | $3^2 - 7 \cdot 3 + 10 \overset{?}{<} 0$<br>$9 - 21 + 10 \overset{?}{<} 0$<br>$-2 < 0,$<br>True | $(2, 5)$ belongs to the solution set. |
| $(5, \infty)$ | 6 | $6^2 - 7 \cdot 6 + 10 \overset{?}{<} 0$<br>$36 - 42 + 10 \overset{?}{<} 0$<br>$4 < 0,$<br>False | $(5, \infty)$ does not belong to the solution set. |

**Step 5 The solution set is the interval that produced a true statement.** Our analysis shows that the solution set is the interval $(2, 5)$. The graph in Figure 1.10 confirms that $x^2 - 7x + 10 < 0$ (lies below the $x$-axis) in this interval. The graph of the solution set on a number line is shown as follows:

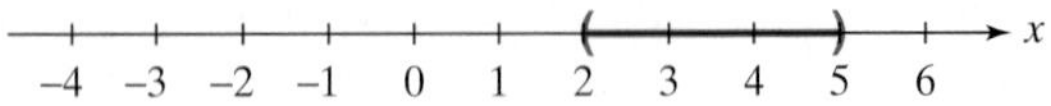


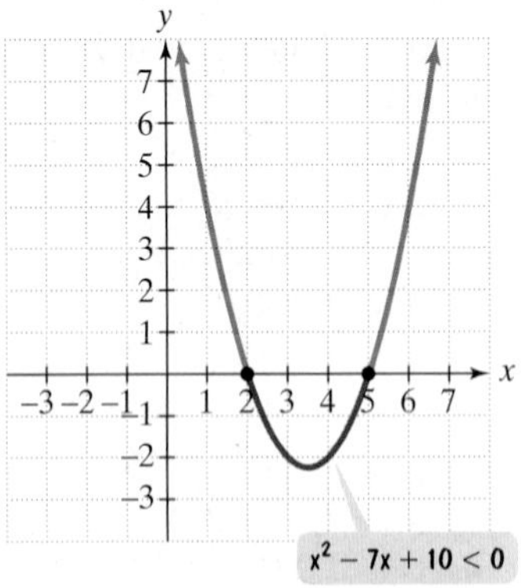


**Figure 1.10** The graph lies below the $x$-axis between the boundary points 2 and 5, in the interval $(2, 5)$

**Check Point 1** Solve and graph the solution set:

$$x^2 + 2x - 3 < 0.$$

## EXAMPLE 2 Solving a Quadratic Inequality

Solve and graph the solution set on a real number line: $2x^2 + x \geq 15$.

**Solution**

**Step 1 Write the inequality in standard form.** We can write $2x^2 + x \geq 15$ by subtracting 15 from both sides. This will give us zero on the right.

$$2x^2 + x - 15 \geq 15 - 15$$

$$2x^2 + x - 15 \geq 0$$

**Step 2 Solve the related quadratic equation.** This equation is obtained by replacing the inequality sign by an equal sign. Thus, we will solve $2x^2 + x - 15 = 0$.

$$2x^2 + x - 15 = 0 \quad \text{This is the related quadratic equation.}$$

$$(2x - 5)(x + 3) = 0 \quad \text{Factor.}$$

$$2x - 5 = 0 \quad \text{or} \quad x + 3 = 0 \quad \text{Set each factor equal to 0.}$$

$$x = \tfrac{5}{2} \quad \text{or} \quad x = -3 \quad \text{Solve for x.}$$

The boundary points are $-3$ and $\frac{5}{2}$.

**Step 3 Locate the boundary points on a number line.** The number line with the boundary points is shown as follows:

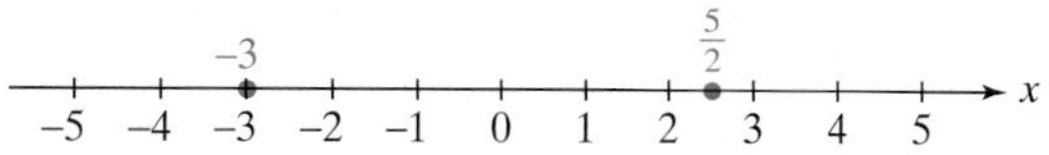


The boundary points divide the number line into three test intervals. Including the boundary points (because of the given greater than or equal to sign), the intervals are $(-\infty, -3]$, $[-3, \frac{5}{2}]$, and $[\frac{5}{2}, \infty)$.

**Step 4 Take one representative number within each test interval and substitute that number into the original inequality.**

| Test Interval | Representative Number | Substitute into $2x^2 + x \geq 15$ | Conclusion |
|---|---|---|---|
| $(-\infty, -3]$ | $-4$ | $2(-4)^2 + (-4) \overset{?}{\geq} 15$<br>$28 \geq 15$, True | $(-\infty, -3]$ belongs to the solution set. |
| $\left[-3, \frac{5}{2}\right]$ | 0 | $2 \cdot 0^2 + 0 \overset{?}{\geq} 15$<br>$0 \geq 15$, False | $\left[-3, \frac{5}{2}\right]$ does not belong to the solution set. |
| $\left[\frac{5}{2}, \infty\right)$ | 3 | $2 \cdot 3^2 + 3 \overset{?}{\geq} 15$<br>$21 \geq 15$, True | $\left[\frac{5}{2}, \infty\right)$ belongs to the solution set. |

**Step 5 The solution set are the intervals that produced a true statement.** Our analysis shows that the solution set is

$$(-\infty, -3] \text{ or } \left[\frac{5}{2}, \infty\right).$$

### Technology

The solution set for

$$2x^2 + x \geq 15$$

or, equivalently,

$$2x^2 + x - 15 \geq 0$$

can be verified with a graphing utility. The graph of $y = 2x^2 + x - 15$ was obtained using a $[-10, 10, 1]$ by $[-16, 6, 1]$ viewing rectangle. The graph lies above or on the $x$-axis, representing $\geq$, for all $x$ in $(-\infty, -3]$ or $[\frac{5}{2}, \infty)$.

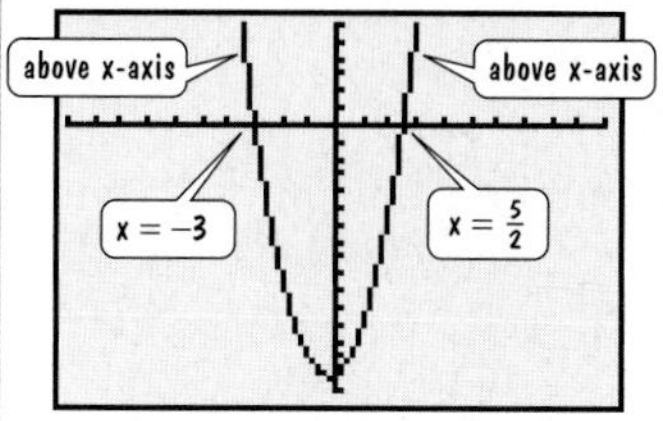

The graph of the solution set on a number line is shown as follows:

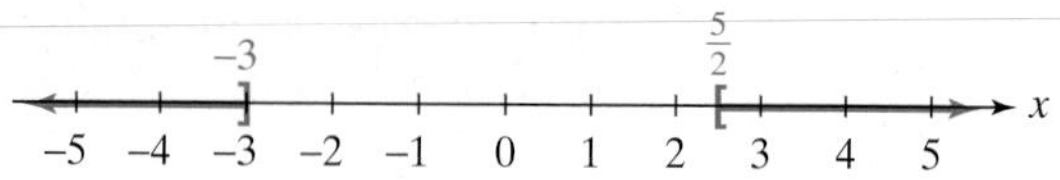


**Check Point 2** Solve and graph the solution set: $x^2 - x \geq 20$.

2 Solve rational inequalities.

## Solving Rational Inequalities

Inequalities that involve quotients can be solved in the same manner as quadratic inequalities. For example, the inequalities

$$(x + 3)(x - 7) > 0 \quad \text{and} \quad \frac{x + 3}{x - 7} > 0$$

are similar in that both are positive under the same conditions. To be positive, each of these inequalities must have two positive linear expressions

$$x + 3 > 0 \quad \text{and} \quad x - 7 > 0$$

or two negative linear expressions

$$x + 3 < 0 \quad \text{and} \quad x - 7 < 0.$$

Consequently, we use boundary points to divide the number line into test intervals. Then we select one representative number in each interval to determine whether that interval belongs to the solution set. Example 3 illustrates how this is done.

### EXAMPLE 3 Using Test Numbers to Solve a Rational Inequality

Solve and graph the solution set: $\dfrac{x + 3}{x - 7} > 0$.

**Solution** We begin by finding values of $x$ that make the numerator and denominator 0.

$x + 3 = 0 \qquad x - 7 = 0$ Set the numerator and denominator equal to 0.

$x = -3 \qquad x = 7$ Solve.

The boundary points are −3 and 7. We locate these numbers on a number line as follows:

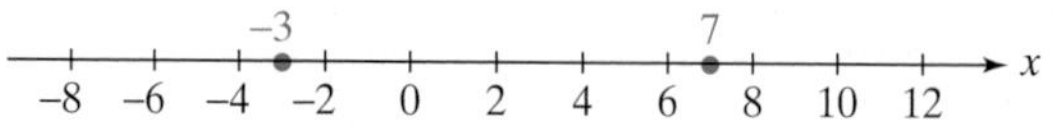


**Study Tip**

Many students want to solve

$$\frac{x + 3}{x - 7} > 0$$

by first multiplying both sides by $x - 7$ to clear fractions. This is incorrect. The problem is that $x - 7$ contains a variable and can be positive or negative, depending on the value of $x$. Thus, we do not know whether or not to reverse the sense of the inequality.

These boundary points divide the number line into three test intervals, namely $(-\infty, -3)$, $(-3, 7)$, and $(7, \infty)$. Now, we take one representative number from each test interval and substitute that number into the original inequality.

| Test Interval | Representative Number | Substitute into $\frac{x+3}{x-7} > 0$ | Conclusion |
|---|---|---|---|
| $(-\infty, -3)$ | $-4$ | $\frac{-4+3}{-4-7} \overset{?}{>} 0$ <br> $\frac{-1}{-11} \overset{?}{>} 0$ <br> $\frac{1}{11} > 0$, True | $(-\infty, -3)$ belongs to the solution set. |
| $(-3, 7)$ | $0$ | $\frac{0+3}{0-7} \overset{?}{>} 0$ <br> $-\frac{3}{7} > 0$, False | $(-3, 7)$ does not belong to the solution set. |
| $(7, \infty)$ | $8$ | $\frac{8+3}{8-7} \overset{?}{>} 0$ <br> $11 > 0$, True | $(7, \infty)$ belongs to the solution set. |

Our analysis shows that the solution set is

$$(-\infty, -3) \quad \text{or} \quad (7, \infty).$$

The graph of the solution set on a number line is shown as follows:

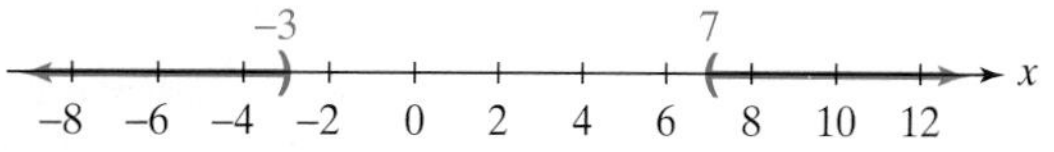


**Check Point 3** Solve and graph the solution set: $\frac{x-5}{x+2} > 0$.

The first step in solving a rational inequality is to bring all terms to one side, obtaining zero on the other side. Then express the nonzero side as a single quotient. At this point, we follow the same procedure as in Example 3.

## EXAMPLE 4 Solving a Rational Inequality

Solve and graph the solution set: $\frac{x+1}{x+3} \le 2$.

**Solution**

**Step 1 Express the inequality so that one side is zero and the other side is a single quotient.** We subtract 2 from both sides to obtain zero on the right.

$$\frac{x+1}{x+3} \le 2 \quad \text{This is the given inequality.}$$

$$\frac{x+1}{x+3} - 2 \le 0 \quad \text{Subtract 2 from both sides, obtaining 0 on the right.}$$

**Study Tip**

Do not begin solving

$$\frac{x+1}{x+3} \le 2$$

by multiplying both sides by $x + 3$. We do not know if $x + 3$ is positive or negative. Thus, we do not know whether or not to reverse the sense of the inequality.

$$\frac{x+1}{x+3} - \frac{2(x+3)}{x+3} \le 0$$ The least common denominator is x + 3. Express 2 in terms of this denominator.

$$\frac{x+1-2(x+3)}{x+3} \le 0$$ Subtract rational expressions.

$$\frac{x+1-2x-6}{x+3} \le 0$$ Apply the distributive property.

$$\frac{-x-5}{x+3} \le 0$$ Simplify.

**Step 2 Find boundary points by setting the numerator and the denominator equal to zero.**

$-x - 5 = 0 \qquad x + 3 = 0$ Set the numerator and denominator equal to 0. These are the values that make the previous quotient zero or undefined.

$x = -5 \qquad x = -3$ Solve for x.

The boundary points are −5 and −3. Because equality is included in the given less-than-or-equal-to symbol, we include the value of $x$ that causes the quotient $\frac{-x-5}{x+3}$ to be zero. Thus, −5 is included in the solution set. By contrast, we do not include −3 in the solution set because −3 makes the denominator zero.

**Step 3 Locate boundary points on a number line.** The number line, with the boundary points, is shown as follows:

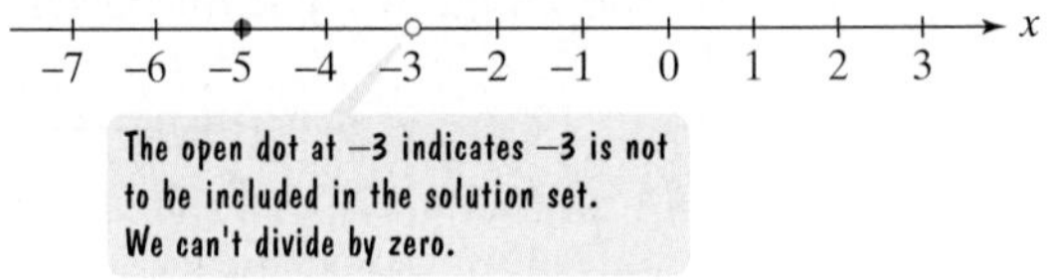
x
-7 -6 -5 -4 -3 -2 -1 0 1 2 3
The open dot at −3 indicates −3 is not to be included in the solution set. We can't divide by zero.

The boundary points divide the number line into three test intervals, namely $(-\infty, -5]$, $[-5, -3)$, and $(-3, \infty)$.

**Step 4 Take one representative number within each test interval and substitute that number into the original inequality.**

| Test Interval | Representative Number | Substitute into $\frac{x+1}{x+3} \le 2$ | Conclusion |
|---|---|---|---|
| $(-\infty, -5]$ | −6 | $\frac{-6+1}{-6+3} \overset{?}{\le} 2$<br>$\frac{5}{3} \le 2$, True | $(-\infty, -5]$ belongs to the solution set. |
| $[-5, -3)$ | −4 | $\frac{-4+1}{-4+3} \overset{?}{\le} 2$<br>$3 \le 2$, False | $[-5, -3)$ does not belong to the solution set. |
| $(-3, \infty)$ | 0 | $\frac{0+1}{0+3} \overset{?}{\le} 2$<br>$\frac{1}{3} \le 2$, True | $(-3, \infty)$ belongs to the solution set. |

**Discovery**

Because $(x + 3)^2$ is positive, it is possible so solve

$$\frac{x+1}{x+3} \leq 2$$

by first multiplying both sides by $(x + 3)^2$ (where $x \neq -3$). This will not reverse the sense of the inequality and will clear the fraction. Try using this solution method and compare it to the one on pages 156–158.

**Step 5** **The solution set consists of the intervals that produced a true statement.** Our analysis shows that the solution set is

$$(-\infty, -5] \quad \text{or} \quad (-3, \infty).$$

The graph of the solution set on a number line is shown as follows:

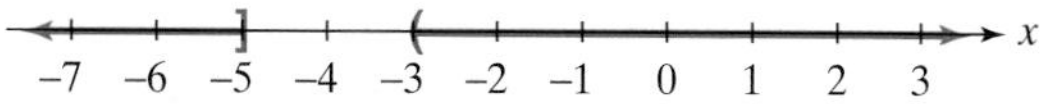


**Check Point 4** Solve and graph the solution set: $\frac{2x}{x+1} \leq 1.$

## Applications

**3** Solve problems modeled by nonlinear inequalities.

Intriguing signs point out that the world is profoundly mathematical. For example, did you know that every time you throw an object vertically upward, its changing height above the ground can be described by a mathematical formula? The same formula can be used to describe objects that are falling, such as the sky divers shown in the opening to this section.

**The Position Formula for a Free-Falling Object Near Earth's Surface**

An object that is falling or vertically projected into the air has its height in feet above the ground given by

$$s = -16t^2 + v_0 t + s_0$$

where $s$ is the height in feet, $v_0$ is the original velocity (initial velocity) of the object in feet per second, $t$ is the time that the object is in motion in seconds, and $s_0$ is the original height (initial height) of the object in feet.

In Example 5, we solve a quadratic inequality in a problem about the position of a free-falling object.

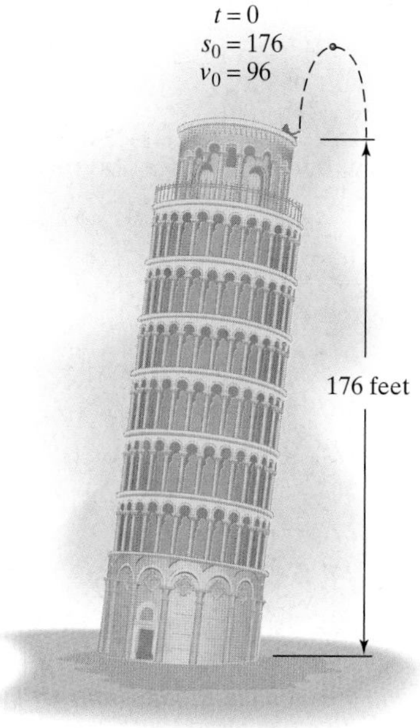


**Figure 1.11** Throwing a ball from 176 feet with a velocity of 96 feet per second

## EXAMPLE 5 Using the Position Model

A ball is thrown vertically upward from the top of the Leaning Tower of Pisa (176 feet high) with an initial velocity of 96 feet per second (Figure 1.11). During which time period will the ball's height exceed that of the tower?

**Solution**

$s = -16t^2 + v_0 t + s_0$ This is the position formula for a free-falling object.

$s = -16t^2 + 96t + 176$ Because $v_0$ (initial velocity) = 96 and $s_0$ (initial position) = 176, substitute these values into the formula.

When will the ball's height | exceed that | of the tower?

$$-16t^2 + 96t + 176 \quad > \quad 176$$

$-16t^2 + 96t + 176 > 176$ This is the inequality implied by the problem's question. We must find $t$.

$-16t^2 + 96t > 0$ Subtract 176 from both sides.

| | |
|---|---|
| $-16t^2 + 96t = 0$ | Solve the related quadratic equation. |
| $-16t(t - 6) = 0$ | Factor. |
| $-16t = 0$ or $t - 6 = 0$ | Set each factor equal to 0. |
| $t = 0$ $\quad$ $t = 6$ | Solve for t. The boundary points are 0 and 6. |

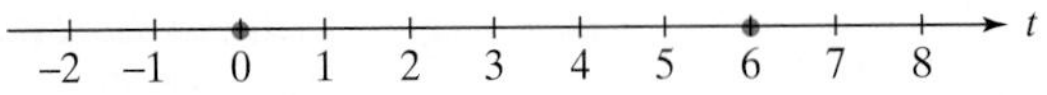

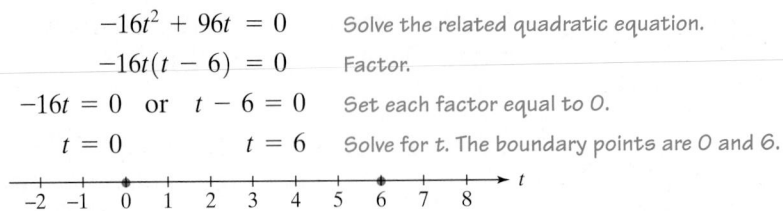

Locate these values on a number line, with $t \geq 0$.

The intervals are $(0, 6)$ and $(6, \infty)$, although the time interval should not extend to infinity but rather to the value of $t$ when the ball hits the ground. (By setting $-16t^2 + 96t + 176$ equal to zero, we find $t \approx 7.47$; the ball hits the ground after approximately 7.47 seconds.)

We use $(0, 6)$ and $(6, 7.47)$ for our test intervals.

| Test Interval | Representative Number | Substitute into $-16t^2 + 96t > 0$ | Conclusion |
|---|---|---|---|
| $(0, 6)$ | 1 | $-16 \cdot 1^2 + 96 \cdot 1 \overset{?}{>} 0$<br>$80 > 0$, True | $(0, 6)$ belongs to the solution set. |
| $(6, 7.47)$ | 7 | $-16 \cdot 7^2 + 96 \cdot 7 \overset{?}{>} 0$<br>$-112 > 0$, False | $(6, 7.47)$ does not belong to the solution set. |

The ball's height exceeds that of the tower between 0 and 6 seconds, excluding $t = 0$ and $t = 6$.

**Check Point 5** An object is propelled straight up from ground level with an initial velocity of 80 feet per second. Its height at time $t$ is described by

$$s = -16t^2 + 80t,$$

where the height, $s$, is measured in feet and the time, $t$, is measured in seconds. In which time interval will the object be more than 64 feet above the ground?

## EXERCISE SET 1.6

### Practice Exercises

*Solve each quadratic inequality in Exercises 1–26, and graph the solution set on a real number line. Express each solution set in interval notation.*

**1.** $(x - 4)(x + 2) > 0$
**2.** $(x + 3)(x - 5) > 0$
**3.** $(x - 7)(x + 3) \leq 0$
**4.** $(x + 1)(x - 7) \leq 0$
**5.** $x^2 - 5x + 4 > 0$
**6.** $x^2 - 4x + 3 < 0$
**7.** $x^2 + 5x + 4 > 0$
**8.** $x^2 + x - 6 > 0$
**9.** $x^2 - 6x + 9 < 0$
**10.** $x^2 - 2x + 1 > 0$
**11.** $x^2 - 6x + 8 \leq 0$
**12.** $x^2 - 2x - 3 \geq 0$
**13.** $3x^2 + 10x - 8 \leq 0$
**14.** $9x^2 + 3x - 2 \geq 0$
**15.** $2x^2 + x < 15$
**16.** $6x^2 + x > 1$
**17.** $4x^2 + 7x < -3$
**18.** $3x^2 + 16x < -5$
**19.** $5x \leq 2 - 3x^2$
**20.** $4x^2 + 1 \geq 4x$
**21.** $x^2 - 4x \geq 0$
**22.** $x^2 + 2x < 0$
**23.** $2x^2 + 3x > 0$
**24.** $3x^2 - 5x \leq 0$
**25.** $-x^2 + x \geq 0$
**26.** $-x^2 + 2x \geq 0$

*Solve each rational inequality in Exercises 27–42, and graph the solution set on a real number line. Express each solution set in interval notation.*

**27.** $\dfrac{x - 4}{x + 3} > 0$
**28.** $\dfrac{x + 5}{x - 2} > 0$

29. $\frac{x + 3}{x + 4} < 0$

30. $\frac{x + 5}{x + 2} < 0$

31. $\frac{-x + 2}{x - 4} \geq 0$

32. $\frac{-x - 3}{x + 2} \leq 0$

33. $\frac{4 - 2x}{3x + 4} \leq 0$

34. $\frac{3x + 5}{6 - 2x} \geq 0$

35. $\frac{x}{x - 3} > 0$

36. $\frac{x + 4}{x} > 0$

37. $\frac{x + 1}{x + 3} < 2$

38. $\frac{x}{x - 1} > 2$

39. $\frac{x + 4}{2x - 1} \leq 3$

40. $\frac{1}{x - 3} < 1$

41. $\frac{x - 2}{x + 2} \leq 2$

42. $\frac{x}{x + 2} \geq 2$

## Application Exercises

*Use the position formula*

$$s = -16t^2 + v_0t + s_0$$

$$(v_0 = \text{initial velocity}, s_0 = \text{initial position}, t = \text{time})$$

*to answer Exercises 43–46.*

**43.** A projectile is fired straight upward from ground level with an initial velocity of 80 feet per second. During which interval of time will the projectile's height exceed 96 feet?

**44.** A projectile is fired straight upward from ground level with an initial velocity of 128 feet per second. During which interval of time will the projectile's height exceed 128 feet?

**45.** A ball is thrown upward with a velocity of 64 feet per second from the top edge of a building 80 feet high. For how long is the ball higher than 96 feet?

**46.** A diver leaps into the air at 20 feet per second from a diving board that is 10 feet above the water. For how many seconds is the diver at least 12 feet above the water?

**47.** The formula

$$H = \frac{15}{8}x^2 - 30x + 200$$

describes heart rate, $H$, in beats per minute, $x$ minutes after a strenuous workout.

**a.** What is the heart rate immediately following the workout?

**b.** Describe the interval of time after a strenous workout in which heart rate exceeds 110 beats per minute.

**48.** The data in the bar graph at the top of the next column can be modeled by the formula

$$y = 0.6x^2 - 2.9x + 3.2$$

where $y$ represents the number of U.S. cellular telephone subscribers, in hundreds of thousands, $x$ years after 1985. When will the number of cellular subscribers exceed 185,200,000 or 185.2 hundred thousand?

**U.S. Cellular Telephone Subscribers**

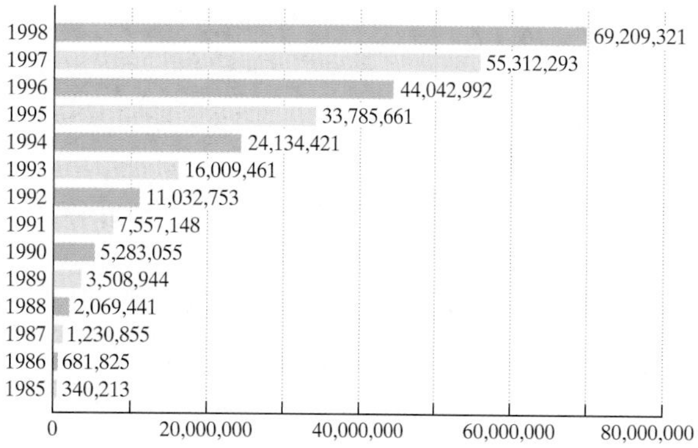


*Source*: Cellular Telephone Industry of America

**49.** The data in the bar graph shown below can be modeled by the formula

$$y = -0.22x^2 + 4.32x + 26$$

where $y$ represents the number of international visitors, in millions, $x$ years after 1986. According to this model, when will the number of international visitors to the United States be less than 41.3 million?

**International Visitors to the United States**

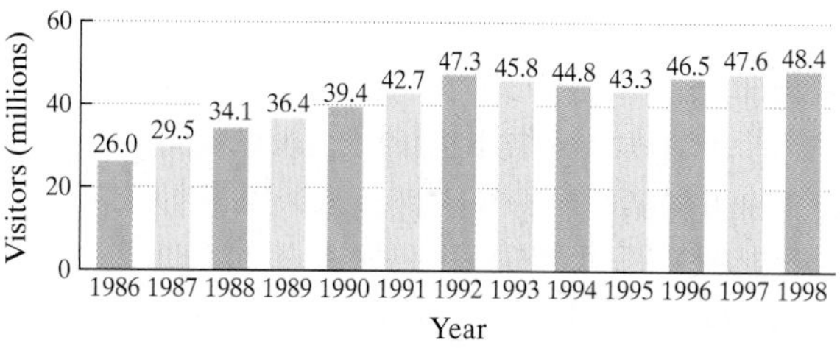


*Source*: U.S. Department of Commerce

**50.** The average cost per unit, $(\bar{C})$, of producing $x$ units of a product is modeled by

$$\bar{C} = \frac{150{,}000 + 0.25x}{x}.$$

How many units must be produced so that the average cost of producing each unit does not exceed $1.75?

**51.** The cost of removing $p\%$ of the bacteria from a river is given by the formula

$$C = \frac{4p}{100 - p}$$

where $C$ is measured in hundreds of thousands of dollars. If less than $600,000 is spent, what percentage of the bacteria can be removed?

## Writing in Mathematics

**52.** What is a quadratic inequality?

**53.** What is a rational inequality?

**54.** Describe similarities and differences between the solutions of

$$(x - 2)(x + 5) \geq 0 \quad \text{and} \quad \frac{x - 2}{x + 5} \geq 0.$$

## Technology Exercises

*Solve each inequality in Exercises 55–60 using a graphing utility.*

**55.** $x^2 + 3x - 10 > 0$

**56.** $2x^2 + 5x - 3 \leq 0$

**57.** $\dfrac{x - 4}{x - 1} \leq 0$

**58.** $\dfrac{x + 2}{x - 3} \leq 2$

**59.** $\dfrac{1}{x + 1} \leq \dfrac{2}{x + 4}$

**60.** $x^3 + 2x^2 - 5x - 6 > 0$

**61.** In a study of the winter moth in Nova Scotia, the number of eggs, $N$, in a female moth depended on her abdominal width, $W$, in millimeters, approximated by $N = 14W^3 - 17W^2 - 6W + 34$, where $1.5 \leq W \leq 3.5$. Graph the model on your graphing utility and use the TRACE and ZOOM features to describe the abdominal width of a moth with more than 46 eggs.

## Critical Thinking Exercises

**62.** Which one of the following is true?

**a.** The solution set to $x^2 > 25$ is $(5, \infty)$.

**b.** The inequality $\dfrac{x - 2}{x + 3} < 2$ can be solved by multiplying both sides by $x + 3$, resulting in the equivalent inequality $x - 2 < 2(x + 3)$.

**c.** $(x + 3)(x - 1) \geq 0$ and $\dfrac{x + 3}{x - 1} \geq 0$ have the same solution set.

**d.** None of these statements is true.

**63.** Write a quadratic inequality whose solution set is $[-3, 5]$.

**64.** Write a rational inequality whose solution set is $(-\infty, -4)$ or $[3, \infty)$.

*In Exercises 65–68, use inspection to describe each inequality's solution set. Do not solve any of the inequalities.*

**65.** $(x - 2)^2 > 0$

**66.** $(x - 2)^2 \leq 0$

**67.** $(x - 2)^2 < -1$

**68.** $\dfrac{1}{(x - 2)^2} > 0$

**69.** The graphing calculator screen at the top of the next column shows the graph of $y = 4x^2 - 8x + 7$.

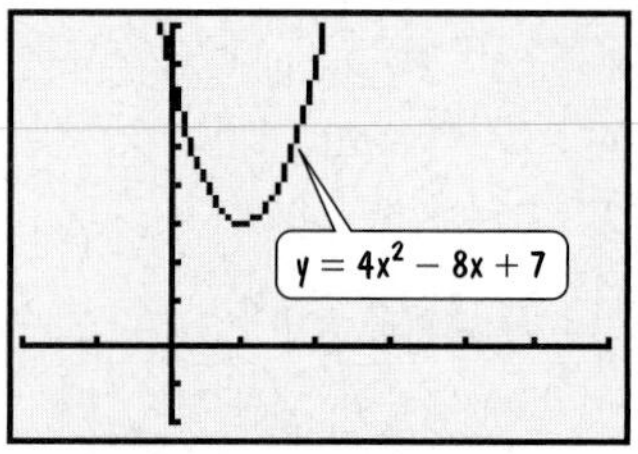


**a.** Use the graph to describe the solution set for $4x^2 - 8x + 7 > 0$.

**b.** Use the graph to describe the solution set for $4x^2 - 8x + 7 < 0$.

**c.** Use an algebraic approach to verify each of your descriptions in parts (a) and (b).

**70.** The graphing calculator screen shows the graph of $y = \sqrt{27 - 3x^2}$. Write and solve a quadratic inequality that explains why the graph only appears for $-3 \leq x \leq 3$.

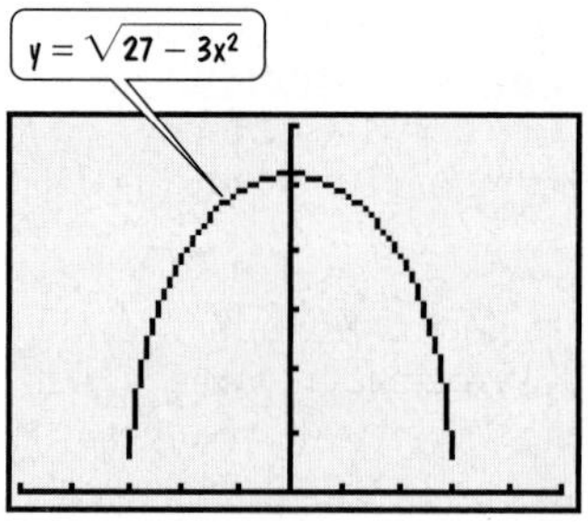


## Group Exercise

**71.** This exercise is intended as a group learning experience and is appropriate for groups of three to five people. Before working on the various parts of the problem, reread the description of the position formula on page 158.

**a.** Drop a ball from a height of 3 feet, 6 feet, and 12 feet. Record the number of seconds it takes for the ball to hit the ground.

**b.** For each of the three initial positions, use the position formula to determine the time required for the ball to hit the ground.

**c.** What factors might result in differences between the times that you recorded and the times indicated by the formula?

**d.** What appears to be happening to the time required for a free-falling object to hit the ground as its initial height is doubled? Verify this observation algebraically and with a graphing utility.

**e.** Repeat part (a) using a sheet of paper rather than a ball. What differences do you observe? What factor seems to be ignored in the position formula?

**f.** What is meant by the acceleration of gravity and how does this number appear in the position formula for a free-falling object?

# CHAPTER SUMMARY, REVIEW, AND TEST

## Summary

### 1.1 Linear Equations

a. A linear equation in one variable $x$ can be written in the form $ax + b = c, a \neq 0$.

b. The procedure for solving a linear equation is given in the box on page 90.

c. If an equation contains fractions, begin by multiplying both sides by the least common denominator, thereby clearing fractions.

d. If an equation contains rational expressions with variable denominators, avoid in the solution set any values of the variable that make a denominator zero.

e. An identity is an equation that is true for all real numbers for which both sides are defined. A conditional equation is not an identity and is true for at least one real number. An inconsistent equation is an equation that is not true for even one real number.

### 1.2 Formulas and Applications

a. A formula is an equation that uses letters to express relationships between two or more variables.

b. A mathematical model is a formula or algebraic equation that can be formed from a verbal model or from actual data.

c. A five-step procedure for solving problems using mathematical models is given in the box on page 101.

### 1.3 Quadratic Equations

a. A quadratic equation in $x$ can be written in the standard form $ax^2 + bx + c = 0, a \neq 0$.

b. The procedure for solving a quadratic equation by factoring and the zero-product principle is given in the box on page 113.

c. The procedure for solving a quadratic equation by the square root method is given in the box on page 115.

d. All quadratic equations can be solved by completing the square. Isolate the binomial with the two variable terms on one side of the equation. If the coefficient of the $x^2$ term is not one, divide each side of the equation by this coefficient. Then add the square of half the coefficient of $x$ to both sides.

e. All quadratic equations can be solved by the quadratic formula

$$x = \frac{-b \pm \sqrt{b^2 - 4ac}}{2a}.$$

The formula is derived by completing the square of the equation $ax^2 + bx + c = 0$.

f. The discriminant, $b^2 - 4ac$, indicates the kinds of solutions to the quadratic equation $ax^2 + bx + c = 0$, shown in Table 1.3 on page 121.

### 1.4 Other Types of Equations

a. Some polynomial equations of degree 3 or greater can be solved by moving all terms to one side, obtaining zero on the other side, factoring, and using the zero-product principle. Factoring by grouping is often used.

b. A radical equation is an equation in which the variable occurs in a square root, cube root, and so on. A radical equation can be solved by isolating the radical and raising both sides of the equation to a power equal to the radical's index. When raising both sides to an even power, check all proposed solutions in the original equation. Eliminate extraneous solutions from the solution set.

c. A radical equation with rational exponents can be solved by isolating the expression with the rational exponent and raising both sides of the equation to a power that is the reciprocal of the rational exponent. Check for possible extraneous solutions.

d. An equation is quadratic in form if it can be written in the form $at^2 + bt + c = 0$, where $t$ is an algebraic expression and $a \neq 0$. Solve for $t$ and use the substitution that resulted in this equation to find the values for the variable in the given equation.

e. Absolute value equations in the form $|X| = c, c > 0$, can be solved by rewriting the equation without absolute value bars: $X = c$ or $X = -c$.

### 1.5 Linear Inequalities

a. A linear inequality in one variable $x$ can be expressed as $ax + b \leq c$, $ax + b < c$, $ax + b \geq c$, or $ax + b > c$, $a \neq 0$.

b. Graphs of solutions to inequalities are shown on a number line by shading all points representing numbers that are solutions. Parentheses exclude endpoints and square brackets include endpoints.

c. Solution sets to inequalities can be expressed in set-builder or interval notation. Table 1.5 on page 145 compares the notations.

d. A linear inequality is solved using a procedure similar to solving a linear equation. However, when multiplying or dividing by a negative number, reverse the sense of the inequality.

e. A compound inequality with three parts can be solved by isolating $x$ in the middle.

f. Inequalities involving absolute value can be solved by rewriting the inequalities without absolute value bars. The ways to do this are shown in the box on page 148.

### 1.6 Quadratic and Rational Inequalities

a. A quadratic inequality can be expressed as $ax^2 + bx + c < 0$, $ax^2 + bx + c > 0$, $ax^2 + bx + c \le 0$, or $ax^2 + bx + c \ge 0$, $a \ne 0$.

b. A procedure for solving quadratic inequalities is given in the box on page 155.

c. Inequalities involving quotients are called rational inequalities. The procedure for solving such inequalities begins with expressing them so that one side is zero and the other side is a single quotient. Find boundary points by setting the numerator and denominator equal to zero. Then follow a procedure similar to that for solving quadratic inequalities.

## Review Exercises

### 1.1

*In Exercises 1–6, solve and check each linear equation.*

**1.** $2x - 5 = 7$

**2.** $5x + 20 = 3x$

**3.** $7(x - 4) = x + 2$

**4.** $1 - 2(6 - x) = 3x + 2$

**5.** $2(x - 4) + 3(x + 5) = 2x - 2$

**6.** $2x - 4(5x + 1) = 3x + 17$

*Exercises 7–11 contain equations with constants in denominators. Solve each equation and check by the method of your choice.*

**7.** $\frac{2x}{3} = \frac{x}{6} + 1$

**8.** $\frac{x}{2} - \frac{1}{10} = \frac{x}{5} + \frac{1}{2}$

**9.** $\frac{2x}{3} = 6 - \frac{x}{4}$

**10.** $\frac{x}{4} = 2 + \frac{x - 3}{3}$

**11.** $\frac{3x + 1}{3} - \frac{13}{2} = \frac{1 - x}{4}$

*Exercises 12–15 contain equations with variables in denominators. a. List the value or values representing restriction(s) on the variable. b. Solve the equation.*

**12.** $\frac{9}{4} - \frac{1}{2x} = \frac{4}{x}$

**13.** $\frac{7}{x - 5} + 2 = \frac{x + 2}{x - 5}$

**14.** $\frac{1}{x - 1} - \frac{1}{x + 1} = \frac{2}{x^2 - 1}$

**15.** $\frac{4}{x + 2} + \frac{2}{x - 4} = \frac{30}{x^2 - 2x - 8}$

*In Exercises 16–18, determine whether each equation is an identity, a conditional equation, or an inconsistent equation.*

**16.** $\frac{1}{x + 5} = 0$

**17.** $7x + 13 = 4x - 10 + 3x + 23$

**18.** $7x + 13 = 3x - 10 + 2x + 23$

**19.** The formula $M = 420x + 720$ models the data for the amount of money lost to credit card fraud worldwide, $M$, expressed in millions of dollars, $x$ years after 1989. In which year did losses amount to 4080 million dollars?

### 1.2

**20.** Suppose you were to list in order, from least to most, the family income for every U.S. family. The median income is the income in the middle of this list of ranked data. This income can be modeled by the formula

$$I = 1321.7(x - 1980) + 21{,}153.$$

In this formula, $I$ represents median family income in the United States and $x$ is the actual year, beginning in 1980. When was the median income \$47,587?

*In Exercises 21–27, use the five-step strategy given in the box on page 99 to solve each problem.*

**21.** The bus fare in a city is \$1.50. People who use the bus have the option of purchasing a monthly coupon book for \$25.00. With the coupon book, the fare is reduced to \$0.25. Determine the number of times in a month the bus must be used so that the total monthly cost without the coupon book is the same as the total monthly cost with the coupon book.

**22.** You inherit \$10,000 with the stipulation that for the first year the money must be invested in two stocks paying 8% and 12% annual interest, respectively. How much should be invested at each rate if the total interest earned for the year is to be \$950?

**23.** A chemist needs to mix a 75% saltwater solution with a 50% saltwater solution to obtain 10 gallons of a 60% saltwater solution. How many gallons of each of the solutions must be used?

**24.** The length of a rectangular football field is 14 meters more than twice the width. If the perimeter is 346 meters, find the field's dimensions.

**25.** A salesperson earns \$300 per week plus 5% commission of sales. How much must be sold to earn \$800 in a week?

**26.** After a 45% price reduction, a VCR sold for \$247.50. What was the price before the reduction?

**27.** A study entitled *Performing Arts—The Economic Dilemma* documents the relationship between the number of concerts given by a major orchestra and the attendance per concert. For each additional concert given per year, attendance per concert drops by approximately eight people. If 50 concerts are given, attendance per concert is 2987 people. How many concerts should be given to ensure an audience of 2627 people at each concert?

*In Exercises 28–29, solve each formula for the specified variable.*

**28.** $F = f(1 - M)$ for $M$ **29.** $R_T = \dfrac{R_1 R_2}{R_1 + R_2}$ for $R_1$

## 1.3

*Solve each equation in Exercises 30–31 by factoring and then using the zero-product principle.*

**30.** $2x^2 + 15x = 8$ **31.** $5x^2 + 20x = 0$

*Solve each equation in Exercises 32–33 by the square root method.*

**32.** $2x^2 - 3 = 125$ **33.** $(3x - 4)^2 = 18$

*Solve each equation in Exercises 33–34 by completing the square.*

**34.** $x^2 - 12x + 27 = 0$ **35.** $3x^2 - 12x + 11 = 0$

*Solve each equation in Exercises 36–38 using the quadratic formula.*

**36.** $x^2 = 2x + 4$ **37.** $x^2 - 2x + 19 = 0$

**38.** $2x^2 = 3 - 4x$

*Compute the discriminant of each equation in Exercises 39–40. What does the discriminant indicate about the kinds of solutions?*

**39.** $x^2 - 4x + 13 = 0$ **40.** $9x^2 = 2 - 3x$

*Solve each equation in Exercises 41–46 by the method of your choice.*

**41.** $2x^2 - 11x + 5 = 0$ **42.** $(3x + 5)(x - 3) = 5$

**43.** $3x^2 - 7x + 1 = 0$ **44.** $x^2 - 9 = 0$

**45.** $(x - 3)^2 - 25 = 0$ **46.** $3x^2 - x + 2 = 0$

**47.** The weight of a human fetus is modeled by the formula $W = 3t^2$, where $W$ is the weight in grams and $t$ is the time in weeks, $0 \le t \le 39$. After how many weeks does the fetus weigh 1200 grams?

**48.** The formula $N = 0.337x^2 - 2.265x + 3.962$ models the number of mountain bike owners $N$, in millions, in the United States $x$ years after 1980, where $3 \le x \le 20$. In which year (to the nearest year) did 10.9 million Americans own mountain bikes?

**49.** A billboard is 15 feet longer than it is high and has space for 324 square feet of advertising. What are the billboard's dimensions?

**50.** A machine produces open boxes using square sheets of metal. The machine cuts equal-sized squares measuring 3 inches on a side from each corner. Then the machine shapes the metal into an open box by turning up the sides. If each box must have a volume of 108 cubic inches, what should be the dimensions of the piece of sheet metal?

**51.** The annual yield per orange tree is fairly constant at 270 pounds when the number of trees per acre is 30 or fewer. For each additional tree over 30, the annual yield per tree for all trees on the acre decreases by 3 pounds due to overcrowding. How many trees should be planted on an acre to yield 9933 pounds of oranges?

## 1.4

*Solve each polynomial equation in Exercises 52–53.*

**52.** $2x^4 = 50x^2$ **53.** $2x^3 - x^2 - 18x + 9 = 0$

*Solve each radical equation in Exercises 54–55.*

**54.** $\sqrt{2x - 3} + x = 3$ **55.** $\sqrt{x - 4} + \sqrt{x + 1} = 5$

*Solve the equations with rational exponents in Exercises 56–57.*

**56.** $3x^{3/4} - 24 = 0$ **57.** $(x - 7)^{3/2} = 125$

*Solve each equation in Exercises 58–59 by making an appropriate substitution.*

**58.** $x^4 - 5x^2 + 4 = 0$ **59.** $x^{1/2} + 3x^{1/4} - 10 = 0$

*Solve the equations containing absolute value in Exercises 60–61.*

**60.** $|2x + 1| = 7$ **61.** $2|x - 3| - 7 = 10$

*Solve each equation in Exercises 62–65 by the method of your choice.*

**62.** $3x^{4/3} - 5x^{2/3} + 2 = 0$ **63.** $2\sqrt{x - 1} = x$

**64.** $|2x - 5| - 3 = 0$ **65.** $x^3 + 2x^2 = 9x + 18$

**66.** The distance to the horizon that you can see, measured in miles, on the top of a mountain $H$ feet high is modeled by the formula $D = \sqrt{2H}$. You've hiked to the top of a mountain with views extending 50 miles to the horizon. How high is the mountain?

**67.** Use Einstein's model

$$T = \frac{T_0}{\sqrt{1 - \dfrac{v^2}{c^2}}}$$

which relates time at rest, $T_0$, to time, $T$, at velocity $v$, to answer this question. A clock on board a futuristic starship traveling at 80% of the speed of light measures a 20-second time period. How long is this time period from the perspective of a stationary observer who looks up and sees the ship?

## 1.5

*In Exercises 68–70, graph the solutions of each inequality on a number line.*

**68.** $x > 5$ **69.** $x \le 1$

**70.** $-3 \le x < 0$

*In Exercises 71–73, express each interval in terms of an inequality, and graph the interval on a number line.*

**71.** $(-2, 3]$ **72.** $[-1.5, 2]$ **73.** $(-1, \infty)$

*Solve each linear inequality in Exercises 74–79 and graph the solution set on a number line.*

**74.** $-6x + 3 \le 15$

**75.** $6x - 9 \ge -4x - 3$

**76.** $\frac{x}{3} - \frac{3}{4} - 1 > \frac{x}{2}$

**77.** $6x + 5 > -2(x - 3) - 25$

**78.** $3(2x - 1) - 2(x - 4) \ge 7 + 2(3 + 4x)$

**79.** $7 < 2x + 3 \le 9$

*Solve each inequality in Exercises 80–82 by first rewriting each one as an equivalent inequality without absolute value bars. Graph the solution set on a number line.*

**80.** $|2x + 3| \le 15$

**81.** $\left|\frac{2x + 6}{3}\right| > 2$

**82.** $|2x + 5| - 7 \ge -6$

*The graph indicates that the United States has the world's highest incarceration rate. If x represents the incarceration rate per 100,000 population, list the country or countries that satisfy each inequality in Exercises 83–84.*

**Countries with the Highest Incarceration Rate**

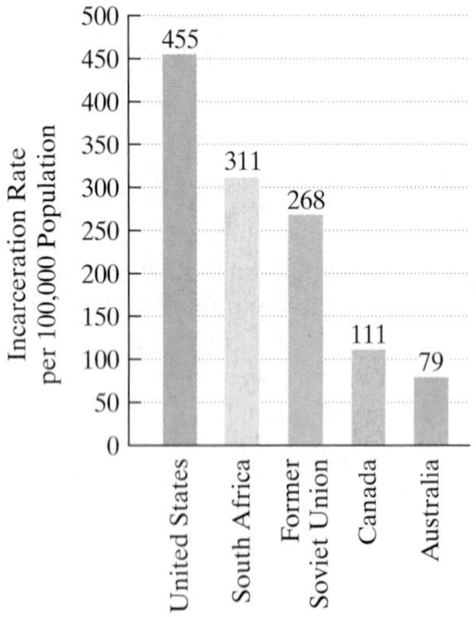


*Source:* FBI

**83.** $437 \le 4x - 7 \le 1229$

**84.** $|x - 320| > 80$

**85.** Approximately 90% of the population sleeps $h$ hours daily, where $h$ is modeled by the inequality $|h - 6.5| \le 1$. Write a sentence describing the range for the number of hours that most people sleep. Do *not* use the phrase "absolute value" in your description.

**86.** The formula for converting Fahrenheit temperature ($F$) to Celsius temperature ($C$) is $C = \frac{5}{9}(F - 32)$. If Celsius temperature ranges from 15° to 35°, inclusively, what is the range for the Fahrenheit temperature?

**87.** A person can choose between two charges on a checking account. The first method involves a fixed cost of \$11 per month plus 6¢ for each check written. The second method involves a fixed cost of \$4 per month plus 20¢ for each check written. How many checks should be written to make the first method a better deal?

**88.** In 1984, approximately 1644 thousand turntables were sold in the United States. This number has decreased by around 82 thousand each year since then. By contrast, annual sales of compact disc players has increased by 496 thousand each year, with approximately 284 thousand units sold in 1984. What was the first year in which the sales of compact disc players exceeded those of turntables?

## 1.6

*Solve each quadratic inequality in Exercises 89–90, and graph the solution set on a real number line. Express each solution set in interval notation.*

**89.** $2x^2 + 7x \le 4$

**90.** $2x^2 > 6x - 3$

*Solve each rational inequality in Exercises 91–92, and graph the solution set on a real number line. Express each solution set in interval notation.*

**91.** $\frac{x - 6}{x + 2} > 0$

**92.** $\frac{x + 3}{x - 4} \le 5$

**93.** Use the position formula

$$s = -16t^2 + v_0 t + s_0$$

initial velocity ($v_0$); initial height ($s_0$)

to solve this problem. A projectile is fired vertically upward from ground level with an initial velocity of 48 feet per second. During which time period will the projectile's height exceed 32 feet?

## Chapter 1 Test

*Find the solution set for each equation in Exercises 1–13.*

**1.** $7(x - 2) = 4(x + 1) - 21$

**2.** $\frac{2x - 3}{4} = \frac{x - 4}{2} - \frac{x + 1}{4}$

**3.** $\frac{2}{x - 3} - \frac{4}{x + 3} = \frac{8}{x^2 - 9}$

**4.** $2x^2 - 3x - 2 = 0$

**5.** $(3x - 1)^2 = 75$

**6.** $x(x - 2) = 4$

**7.** $4x^2 = 8x - 5$

**8.** $x^3 - 4x^2 - x + 4 = 0$

**9.** $\sqrt{x - 3} + 5 = x$

**10.** $\sqrt{x + 4} + \sqrt{x - 1} = 5$

**11.** $5x^{3/2} - 10 = 0$

**12.** $x^{2/3} - 9x^{1/3} + 8 = 0$

**13.** $\left|\frac{2}{3}x - 6\right| = 2$

*Solve each inequality in Exercises 14–19. Express the answer in interval notation and graph the solution set on a number line.*

**14.** $3(x + 4) \ge 5x - 12$

**15.** $\frac{x}{6} + \frac{1}{8} \le \frac{x}{2} - \frac{3}{4}$

**16.** $-3 \le \frac{2x + 5}{3} < 6$

**17.** $|3x + 2| \ge 3$

**18.** $x^2 < x + 12$

**19.** $\frac{2x + 1}{x - 3} > 3$

**20.** The monthly benefit ($B$) of a retirement plan is given by

$$B = \frac{2}{5}w + \frac{1}{125}n$$

where

$w$ = an employee's average monthly salary

$n$ = the number of years an employee worked for the company

**a.** Solve the formula for $n$.

**b.** Use your answer from part (a) to find the number of years an employee whose average monthly salary is \$800 must work to receive a monthly benefit of \$512.

**21.** Approximate population and growth figures for two states are given as follows.

| | **1980 Population (in Thousands)** | **Yearly Growth (in Thousands)** |
|---|---|---|
| **Arizona** | 2795 | 89 |
| **South Carolina** | 3071 | 43 |

When did Arizona have the same population as South Carolina?

**22.** The formula $y = 420x + 720$ describes the amount of money, $y$, in millions of dollars, lost to credit card fraud worldwide, $x$ years after 1989. In which year did losses amount to 4080 million dollars?

**23.** With a 9% raise, a physical therapist will earn \$45,780 annually. What is the therapist's salary prior to this raise?

**24.** You invest \$6000, part at 9% and the remainder at 6%. If the total yearly interest from the two investments is \$480, find the amount invested at each rate.

**25.** A machine produces open boxes using square sheets of metal. The machine cuts equal-sized squares measuring 3 inches on a side from each corner. Then the machine shapes the metal into an open box by turning up the sides. If each box must have a volume of 243 cubic inches, what should be the dimensions of the piece of sheet metal?

**26.** A chemist needs to mix a 50% acid solution with an 80% acid solution to obtain 100 milliliters of a 68% acid solution. How many milliliters of each of the acid solutions must be used?

**27.** A computer online service charges a flat monthly rate of \$20 or a monthly rate of \$5 plus 15 cents for every hour spent online. How many hours online each month will make the second option a better deal?

# Functions and Graphs

## Chapter 2

The cost of mailing a package depends on its weight. The probability that you and another person in a room share the same birthday depends on the number of people in the room. In both these situations, the relationship between variables can be illustrated with the notion of a *function*. Understanding this concept will give you a new perspective on many ordinary situations.

'Tis the season and you've waited until the last minute to mail your holiday gifts. Your only option is overnight express mail. You realize that the cost of mailing a gift depends on its weight, but the mailing costs seem somewhat odd. Your packages that weigh 1.1 pounds, 1.5 pounds, and 2 pounds cost $15.75 each to send overnight. Packages that weigh 2.01 pounds and 3 pounds cost you $18.50 each. Finally, your heaviest gift is barely over 3 pounds and its mailing cost is $21.25. What sort of system is this in which costs increase by $2.75, stepping from $15.75 to $18.50 and from $18.50 to $21.25?

# SECTION 2.1 *Lines and Slope*

## Objectives

1. Compute a line's slope.
2. Write the point-slope equation of a line.
3. Write and graph the slope-intercept equation of a line.
4. Recognize equations of horizontal and vertical lines.
5. Recognize and use the general form of a line's equation.
6. Model data with linear equations.

**Online Spending: Yearly Spending per Online Household**

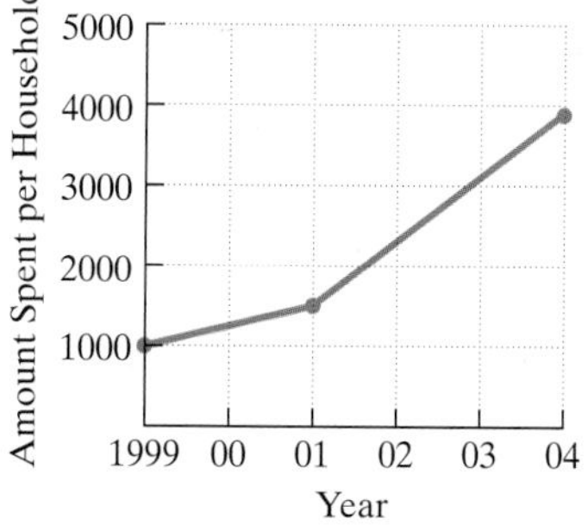


*Source*: Forrester Research

**Figure 2.1**

Good news: Projections indicate that in the next decades we'll live longer and move somewhere warmer where we'll shop online and chat on our tiny video cell phones. Figure 2.1 shows projected online shopping per U.S. online household through 2004. The graph is composed of two line segments. The segment on the right is steeper than the one on the left. This shows that online shopping is expected to increase more per year in 2001–2004 than in 1999–2001.

Data often fall on or near a line. In this section we will use equations to model such data and make predictions. We begin with a discussion of a line's steepness.

## The Slope of a Line

Mathematicians have developed a useful measure of the steepness of a line, called the **slope** of the line. Slope compares the vertical change (the **rise**) to the horizontal change (the **run**) when moving from one fixed point to another along the line. To calculate the slope of a line, mathematicians use a ratio comparing the change in $y$ (the rise) to the change in $x$ (the run).

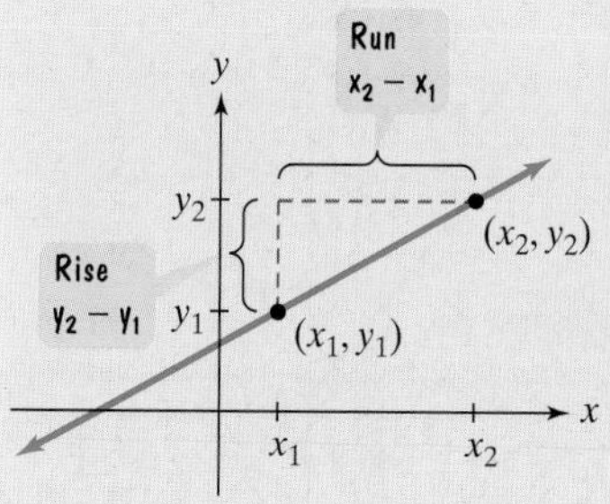


### Definition of Slope

The **slope** of the line through the distinct points $(x_1, y_1)$ and $(x_2, y_2)$ is

$$\frac{\text{Change in } y}{\text{Change in } x} = \frac{\text{Rise}}{\text{Run}}$$

$$= \frac{y_2 - y_1}{x_2 - x_1}$$

where $x_2 - x_1 \neq 0$.

It is common notation to let the letter $m$ represent the slope of a line. The letter $m$ is used because it is the first letter of the French verb *monter*, meaning to rise, or to ascend.

**1** Compute a line's slope.

## EXAMPLE 1 Using the Definition of Slope

Find the slope of the line passing through each pair of points.

**a.** $(-3, -1)$ and $(-2, 4)$ **b.** $(-3, 4)$ and $(2, -2)$

### Slope and the Streets of San Francisco

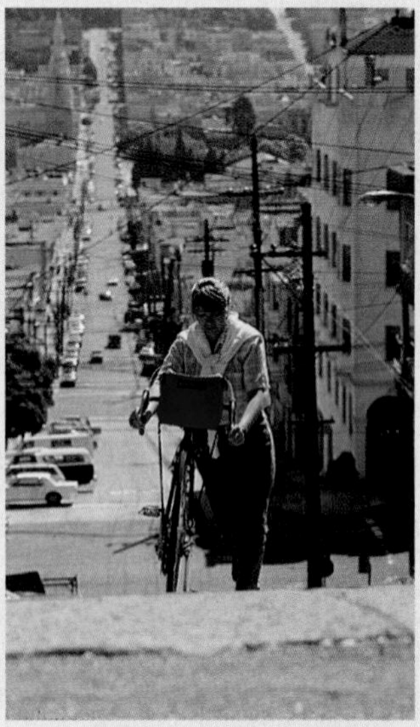

San Francisco's Filbert Street has a slope of 0.613, meaning that for every horizontal distance of 100 feet, the street ascends 61.3 feet vertically. With its 31.5° angle of inclination, the street is too steep to pave and is only accessible by wooden stairs.

**Solution**

**a.** Let $(x_1, y_1) = (-3, -1)$ and $(x_2, y_2) = (-2, 4)$. We obtain a slope of

$$m = \frac{\text{Change in } y}{\text{Change in } x} = \frac{y_2 - y_1}{x_2 - x_1} = \frac{4 - (-1)}{-2 - (-3)} = \frac{5}{1} = 5.$$

The situation is illustrated in Figure 2.2(a). The slope of the line is 5, indicating that there is a vertical change, a rise, of 5 units for each horizontal change, a run, of 1 unit. The slope is positive, and the line rises from left to right.

### Study Tip

When computing slope, it makes no difference which point you call $(x_1, y_1)$ and which point you call $(x_2, y_2)$. If we let $(x_1, y_1) = (-2, 4)$ and $(x_2, y_2) = (-3, -1)$, the slope is still 5:

$$m = \frac{y_2 - y_1}{x_2 - x_1} = \frac{-1 - 4}{-3 - (-2)} = \frac{-5}{-1} = 5.$$

However, you should not subtract in one order in the numerator $(y_2 - y_1)$ and then in a different order in the denominator $(x_1 - x_2)$. The slope is *not*

$$\frac{-1 - 4}{-2 - (-3)} = \frac{-5}{1} = -5. \quad \text{Incorrect.}$$

**b.** We can let $(x_1, y_1) = (-3, 4)$ and $(x_2, y_2) = (2, -2)$. The slope of the line shown in Figure 2.2(b) is computed as follows:

$$m = \frac{-2 - 4}{2 - (-3)} = \frac{-6}{5} = -\frac{6}{5}.$$

The slope of the line is $-\frac{6}{5}$. For every vertical change of $-6$ units (6 units down), there is a corresponding horizontal change of 5 units. The slope is negative and the line falls from left to right.

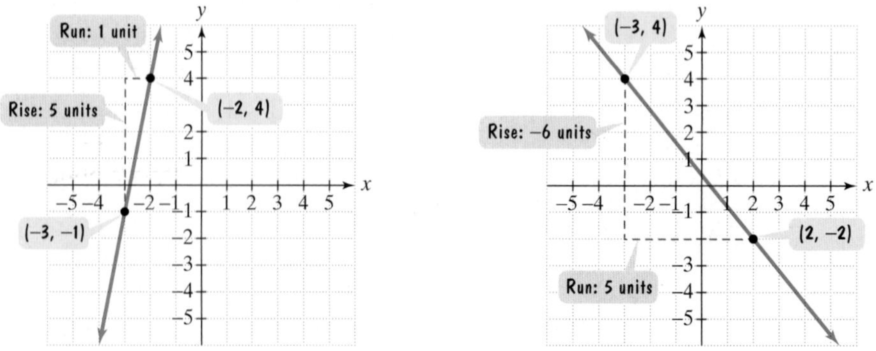


**Figure 2.2** Visualizing Slope (a) (b)

**Check Point 1** Find the slope of the line passing through each pair of points.

**a.** $(-3, 4)$ and $(-4, -2)$ **b.** $(4, -2)$ and $(-1, 5)$

Example 1 illustrates that a line with a positive slope is rising from left to right and a line with a negative slope is falling from left to right. By contrast, a horizontal line neither rises nor falls and has a slope of zero. A vertical line has no horizontal change, so $x_2 - x_1 = 0$ in the formula for slope. Because we cannot divide by zero, the slope of a vertical line is undefined. This discussion is summarized in Table 2.1.

**Table 2.1 Possibilities for a Line's Slope**

| Positive Slope | Negative Slope | Zero Slope | Undefined Slope |
| --- | --- | --- | --- |
| 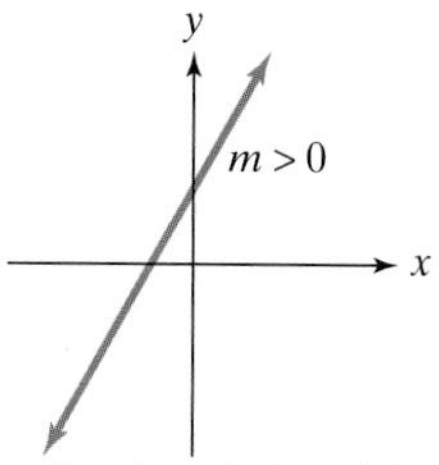  | 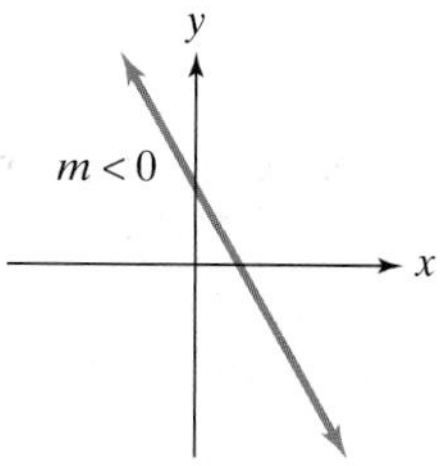  | 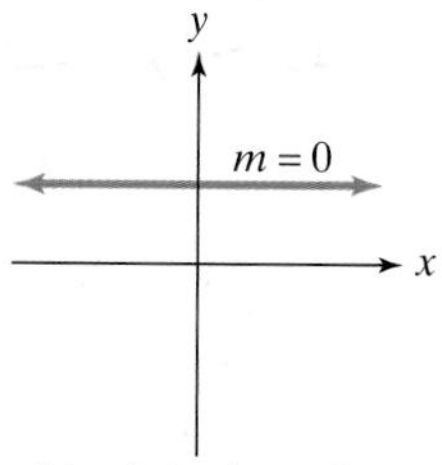  | 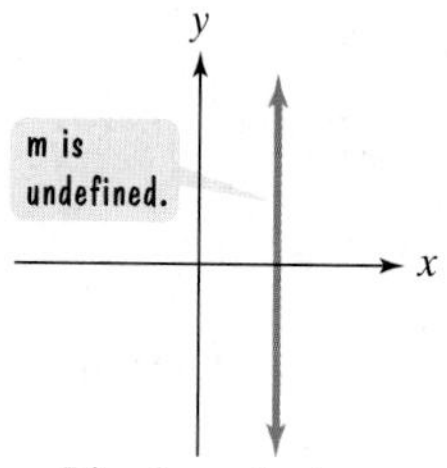  |
| Line rises from left to right. | Line falls from left to right. | Line is horizontal. | Line is vertical. |

**2** Write the point-slope equation of a line.

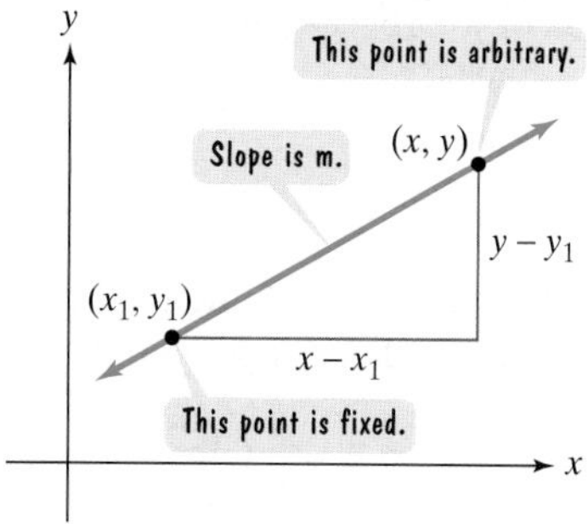


**Figure 2.3** A line passing through $(x_1, y_1)$ with slope $m$

## The Point-Slope Form of the Equation of a Line

We can use the slope of a line to obtain various forms of the line's equation. For example, consider a nonvertical line that has a slope of $m$ and contains the point $(x_1, y_1)$. Now, let $(x, y)$ represent any other point on the line, shown in Figure 2.3. Keep in mind that the point $(x, y)$ is arbitrary and is not in one fixed position. By contrast, the point $(x_1, y_1)$ is fixed. Regardless of where the point $(x, y)$ is located, the shape of the triangle in Figure 2.3 remains the same. Thus, the ratio for slope stays a constant $m$. This means that for all points along the line,

$$m = \frac{y - y_1}{x - x_1}, \quad x \neq x_1.$$

We can clear the fraction by multiplying both sides by $x - x_1$, the least common denominator.

$$m(x - x_1) = \frac{y - y_1}{\cancel{x - x_1}} \cdot \cancel{x - x_1}$$

$$m(x - x_1) = y - y_1 \qquad \text{Simplify.}$$

Now, if we reverse the two sides, we obtain the **point-slope form** of the equation of a line.

### Point-Slope Form of the Equation of a Line

**The point-slope equation** of a nonvertical line of slope $m$ that passes through the point $(x_1, y_1)$ is

$$y - y_1 = m(x - x_1).$$

For example, an equation of the line passing through $(1, 3)$ with a slope of 2 $(m = 2)$ is

$$y - 3 = 2(x - 1).$$

After we obtain the point-slope form of a line, it is customary to express the equation with $y$ isolated on one side of the equal sign. Example 2 illustrates how this is done.

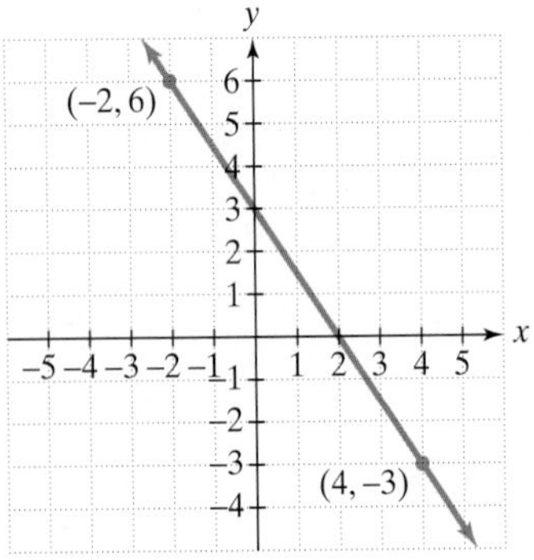


**Figure 2.4** Write the point-slope equation of this line.

## Discovery

You can use either point for $(x_1, y_1)$ when you write a line's point-slope equation. Rework Example 3 using $(-2, 6)$ for $(x_1, y_1)$. Once you solve for $y$, you should obtain the same equation as the one shown in the last line of the solution on page 172.

### EXAMPLE 2 Writing the Point-Slope Equation of a Line

Write the point-slope form of the equation of the line passing through the points $(4, -3)$ and $(-2, 6)$. (See Figure 2.4.) Then solve the equation for $y$.

**Solution** To use the point-slope form, we need to find the slope. The slope is the change in the $y$-coordinates divided by the corresponding change in the $x$-coordinates.

$$m = \frac{6 - (-3)}{-2 - 4} = \frac{9}{-6} = -\frac{3}{2}$$ This is the definition of slope using $(4, -3)$ and $(-2, 6)$.

We can take either point on the line to be $(x_1, y_1)$. Let's use $(x_1, y_1) = (4, -3)$. Now, we are ready to write the point-slope equation.

$$y - y_1 = m(x - x_1)$$ This is the point-slope form of the equation.

$$y - (-3) = -\tfrac{3}{2}(x - 4)$$ Substitute: $(x_1, y_1) = (4, -3)$ and $m = -\frac{3}{2}$.

$$y + 3 = -\tfrac{3}{2}(x - 4)$$ Simplify.

We now have the point-slope form of the equation of the line shown in Figure 2.4. Now, we solve this equation for $y$.

$$y + 3 = -\tfrac{3}{2}(x - 4)$$ This is the point-slope form of the equation.

$$y + 3 = -\tfrac{3}{2}x + 6$$ Use the distributive property.

$$y = -\tfrac{3}{2}x + 3$$ Subtract 3 from both sides.

**Check Point 2** Write the point-slope form of the equation of the line passing through the points $(-2, -1)$ and $(-1, -6)$. Then solve the equation for $y$.

**3** Write and graph the slope-intercept equation of a line.

### The Slope-Intercept Form of the Equation of a Line

Let's write the point-slope form of the equation of a line whose $y$-intercept is $b$ with slope $m$. The line is shown in Figure 2.5. Because the $y$-intercept is $b$, the line intersects the $y$-axis at $(0, b)$. We use the point-slope form with $x_1 = 0$ and $y_1 = b$.

$$y - y_1 = m(x - x_1)$$

Let $y_1 = b$. Let $x_1 = 0$.

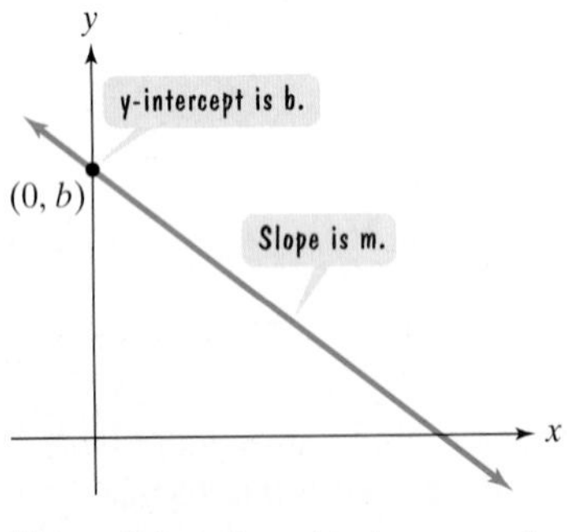


**Figure 2.5** A line with slope $m$ and $y$-intercept $b$

We obtain

$$y - b = m(x - 0).$$

Simplifying on the right side gives us

$$y - b = mx.$$

Finally, we solve for $y$ by adding $b$ to both sides.

$$y = mx + b$$

Thus, if a line's equation is written with $y$ isolated on one side, the $x$-coefficient is the line's slope and the constant term is the $y$-intercept. This form of a line's equation is called the **slope-intercept form** of a line.

### Slope-Intercept Form of the Equation of a Line

The **slope-intercept equation** of a nonvertical line with slope $m$ and $y$-intercept $b$ is

$$y = mx + b.$$

## EXAMPLE 3 Graphing by Using the Slope and $y$-Intercept

Graph the line whose equation is $y = \frac{2}{3}x + 2$.

**Solution** The equation of the line is in the form $y = mx + b$. We can find the slope, $m$, by identifying the coefficient of $x$. We can find the $y$-intercept, $b$, by identifying the constant term.

$$y = \frac{2}{3}x + 2$$

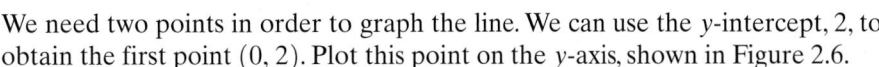

The slope is $\frac{2}{3}$.

The $y$-intercept is 2.

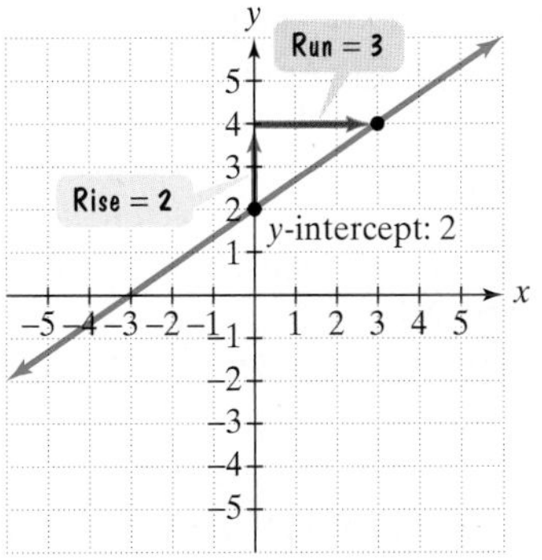


**Figure 2.6** The graph of $y = \frac{2}{3}x + 2$

We need two points in order to graph the line. We can use the $y$-intercept, 2, to obtain the first point (0, 2). Plot this point on the $y$-axis, shown in Figure 2.6.

We know the slope and one point on the line. We can use the slope, $\frac{2}{3}$, to determine a second point on the line. By definition,

$$m = \frac{2}{3} = \frac{\text{Rise}}{\text{Run}}.$$

We plot the second point on the line by starting at (0, 2), the first point. Based on the slope, we move 2 units *up* (the rise) and 3 units to the *right* (the run). This puts us at a second point on the line, shown in Figure 2.6.

We use a straightedge to draw a line through the two points. The graph of $y = \frac{2}{3}x + 2$ is shown in Figure 2.6.

### Graphing $y = mx + b$ by Using the Slope and $y$-Intercept

1. Plot the $y$-intercept on the $y$-axis. This is the point $(0, b)$.
2. Obtain a second point using the slope, $m$. Write $m$ as a fraction, and use rise over run starting at the $y$-intercept to plot this point.
3. Use a straightedge to draw a line through the two points. Draw arrowheads at the ends of the line to show that the line continues indefinitely in both directions.

**Check Point 3** Graph the line whose equation is $y = \frac{3}{5}x + 1$.

**4** Recognize equations of horizontal and vertical lines.

## Equations of Horizontal and Vertical Lines

Some things change very little. For example, from 1985 to the present, the number of Americans participating in downhill skiing has remained relatively constant, indicated by the graph shown in Figure 2.7. Shown in the figure is a horizontal line that passes through or near most of the data points.

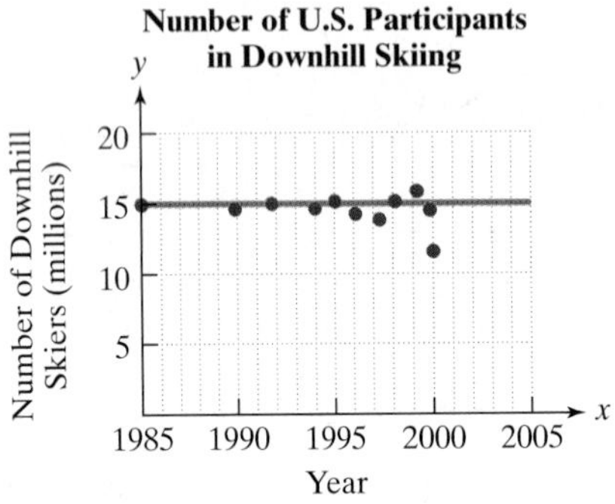


*Source*: National Ski Areas Association

**Figure 2.7**

We can use $y = mx + b$, the slope-intercept form of a line's equation, to write the equation of the horizontal line in Figure 2.7. We need the line's slope, $m$, and its $y$-intercept, $b$. Because the line is horizontal, $m = 0$. The line intersects the $y$-axis at 15, so $b = 15$. Thus, an equation that models the number of participants in downhill skiing for the period shown is

$$y = 0x + 15, \quad \text{or} \quad y = 15.$$

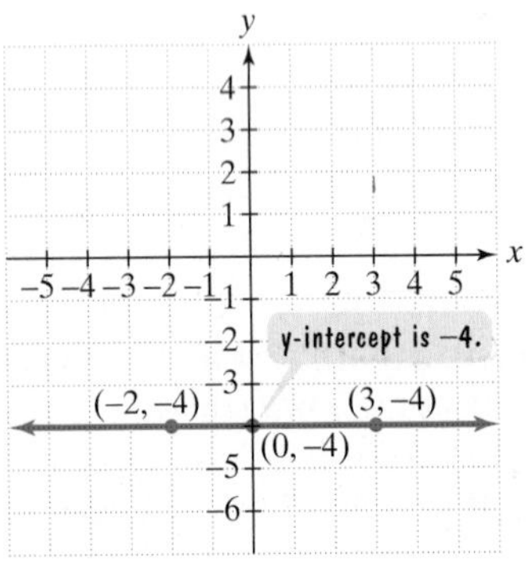


**Figure 2.8** The graph of $y = -4$

The popularity of downhill skiing remained relatively constant in the United States from 1985 to 2000 at approximately 15 million participants each year.

In general, if a line is horizontal, its slope is zero: $m = 0$. Thus, the equation $y = mx + b$ becomes $y = b$, where $b$ is the $y$-intercept. For example, the graph of $y = -4$ is a horizontal line with a $y$-intercept of $-4$. The graph is shown in Figure 2.8. Three of the points along the line are shown and labeled. No matter what the $x$-coordinate is, the corresponding $y$-coordinate for every point on line is $-4$.

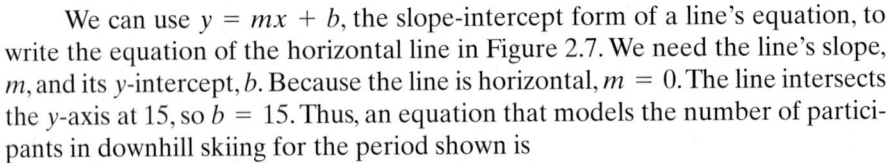

### Equation of a Horizontal Line

A horizontal line is given by an equation of the form

$$y = b$$

where $b$ is the $y$-intercept.

Next, let's see what we can discover about a vertical line by looking at an example.

## EXAMPLE 4 Graphing a Vertical Line

Graph $x = 5$ in the rectangular coordinate system.

**Solution** All points on the graph of $x = 5$ have a value of $x$ that is always 5. No matter what the $y$-coordinate is, the corresponding $x$-coordinate for every point on the line is 5. Let us select three of the possible values of $y$: −2, 0, and 3. So, three of the points on the graph of $x = 5$ are $(5, -2)$, $(5, 0)$, and $(5, 3)$. Plot each of these three points. Drawing a line that passes through the three points gives the vertical line shown in Figure 2.9.

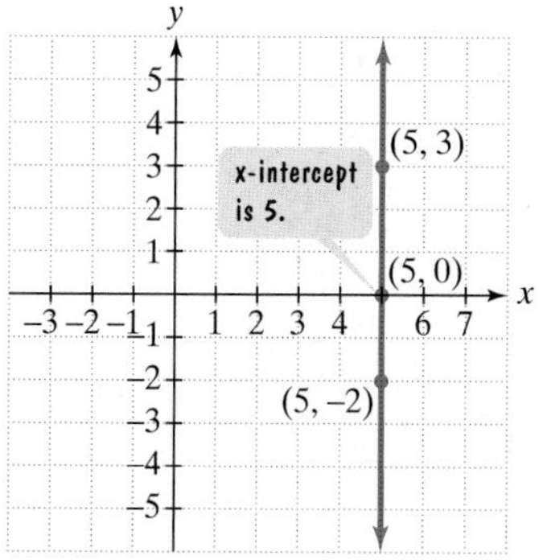


**Figure 2.9** The graph $x = 5$

### Equation of a Vertical Line

A vertical line is given by an equation of the form

$$x = a$$

where $a$ is the $x$-intercept.

**Check Point 4** Graph $x = -1$ in the rectangular coordinate system.

**5** Recognize and use the general form of a line's equation.

## The General Form of the Equation of a Line

The vertical line whose equation is $x = 5$ cannot be written in slope-intercept form, $y = mx + b$, because its slope is undefined. However, every line has an equation that can be expressed in the form $Ax + By + C = 0$. For example, $x = 5$ can be expressed as $1x + 0y - 5 = 0$, or $x - 5 = 0$. The equation $Ax + By + C = 0$ is called the **general form** of the equation of a line.

### General Form of the Equation of a Line

Every line has an equation that can be written in the **general form**

$$Ax + By + C = 0$$

where $A$, $B$, and $C$ are three real numbers, and $A$ and $B$ are not both zero.

If the equation of a line is given in general form, it is possible to find the slope, $m$, and the $y$-intercept, $b$, for the line. We solve the equation for $y$, transforming it into the slope-intercept form $y = mx + b$. In this form, the coefficient of $x$ is the slope of the line, and the constant term is its $y$-intercept.

## EXAMPLE 5 Finding the Slope and the y-Intercept

Find the slope and the $y$-intercept of the line whose equation is $2x - 3y + 6 = 0$.

**Solution** The equation is given in general form. We begin by rewriting it in the form $y = mx + b$. We need to solve for $y$.

$$2x - 3y + 6 = 0 \quad \text{This is the given equation.}$$

$$2x + 6 = 3y \quad \text{To isolate the } y\text{-term, add } 3y \text{ on both sides.}$$

$$3y = 2x + 6 \quad \text{Reverse the two sides. (This step is optional.)}$$

$$y = \frac{2}{3}x + 2 \quad \text{Divide both sides by 3.}$$

The coefficient of $x$, $\frac{2}{3}$, is the slope and the constant term, 2, is the $y$-intercept. This is the form of the equation that we graphed in Example 3 on page 175.

**Check Point 5** Find the slope and the $y$-intercept of the line whose equation is $3x + 6y - 12 = 0$. Then use the $y$-intercept and the slope to graph the equation.

We've covered a lot of territory. Let's take a moment to summarize the various forms for equations of lines.

### Equations of Lines

1. Point-slope form: $y - y_1 = m(x - x_1)$
2. Slope-intercept form: $y = mx + b$
3. Horizontal line: $y = b$
4. Vertical line: $x = a$
5. General form: $Ax + By + C = 0$

**6** Model data with linear equations.

## Applications

Linear equations are useful for modeling data that fall on or near a line. For example, Table 2.2 on page 176 gives the population of the United States, in millions, in the indicated year. The data are displayed as a set of five points in Figure 2.10.

**Table 2.2**

| Year | $x$ (Year after 1960) | $y$ (U.S. Population) (in millions) |
|---|---|---|
| 1960 | 0 | 179.3 |
| 1970 | 10 | 203.3 |
| 1980 | 20 | 226.5 |
| 1990 | 30 | 250.0 |
| 1998 | 38 | 268.9 |

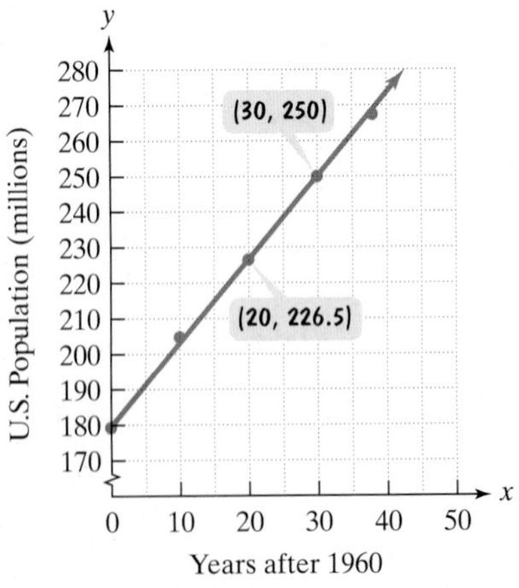


**Figure 2.10**

Data presented in a visual form as a set of points is called a **scatter plot**. Also shown in Figure 2.10 is a line that passes through or near the five points. By writing the equation of this line, we can obtain a model of the data and make predictions about the population of the United States in the future.

### Technology

You can use a graphing utility to obtain a model for a scatter plot in which the data points fall on or near a straight line. The line that best fits the data is called the **regression line**. After entering the data in Table 2.2, a graphing utility displays a scatter plot of the data and the regression line.

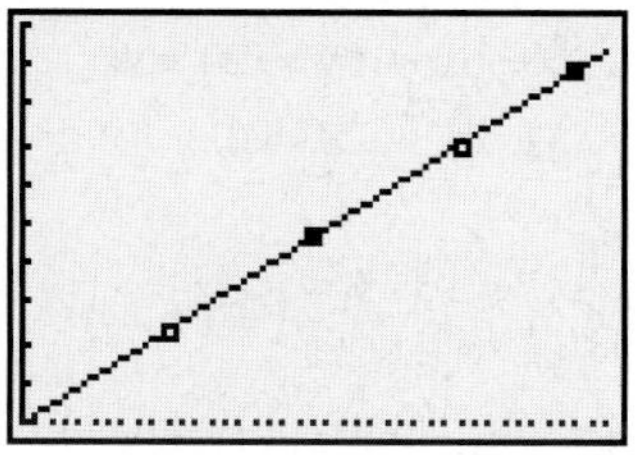

[0, 40, 1] by [180, 280, 10]

Also displayed is the regression line's equation.

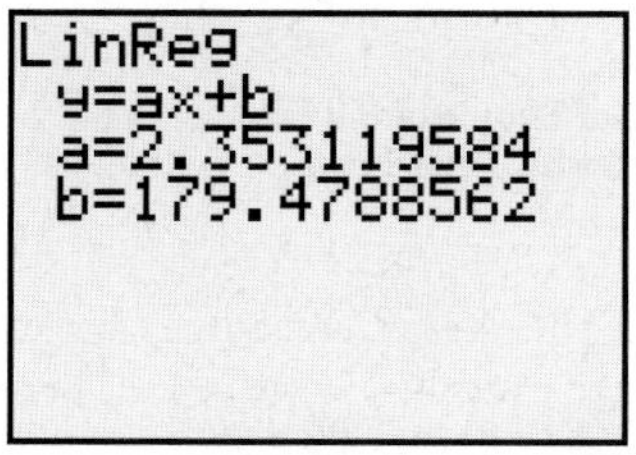


## EXAMPLE 6 Modeling U.S. Population

Write the equation of the line shown in Figure 2.10. Use the equation to predict U.S. population in 2010.

**Solution** The line in Figure 2.10 passes through (20, 226.5) and (30, 250). We start by finding the slope.

$$m = \frac{\text{change in } y}{\text{change in } x} = \frac{250 - 226.5}{30 - 20} = \frac{23.5}{10} = 2.35$$

Now, we write the line's equation.

$y - y_1 = m(x - x_1)$ Begin with the point-slope form.

$y - 250 = 2.35(x - 30)$ Either ordered pair can be $(x_1, y_1)$. Let $(x_1, y_1) = (30, 250)$. From above, $m = 2.35$.

$y - 250 = 2.35x - 70.5$ Apply the distributive property on the right.

$y = 2.35x + 179.5$ Add 250 to both sides and solve for $y$.

The linear equation that models U.S. population, $y$, in millions, $x$ years after 1960 is

$$y = 2.35x + 179.5.$$

Now, let's use this equation to predict U.S. population in 2010. Because 2010 is 50 years after 1960, substitute 50 for $x$ and compute $y$.

$$y = 2.35(50) + 179.5 = 297$$

Our equation predicts that the population of the United States in the year 2010 will be 297 million. (The projected figure from the U.S. Census Bureau is 297.716 million.)

If an equation in slope-intercept form describes some real-world situation, slope sometimes is interpreted as a **rate of change**. For example, $y = 2.35x + 179.5$ models U.S. population, $y$, in millions, $x$ years after 1960. The slope, 2.35, indicates that U.S. population is increasing by 2.35 million people per year. The rate of change of U.S. population with respect to time is 2.35 million people per year.

**Check Point 6** Use the data points (10, 203.3) and (20, 226.5) from Table 2.2 to write an equation that models U.S. population $x$ years after 1960. Use the equation to predict U.S. population in 2020.

# EXERCISE SET 2.1

## Practice Exercises

*In Exercises 1–10, find the slope of the line passing through each pair of points or state that the slope is undefined. Then indicate whether the line through the points rises, falls, is horizontal, or is vertical.*

**1.** $(4, 7)$ and $(8, 10)$
**2.** $(2, 1)$ and $(3, 4)$
**3.** $(-2, 1)$ and $(2, 2)$
**4.** $(-1, 3)$ and $(2, 4)$
**5.** $(4, -2)$ and $(3, -2)$
**6.** $(4, -1)$ and $(3, -1)$
**7.** $(-2, 4)$ and $(-1, -1)$
**8.** $(6, -4)$ and $(4, -2)$
**9.** $(5, 3)$ and $(5, -2)$
**10.** $(3, -4)$ and $(3, 5)$

*In Exercises 11–30, use the given conditions to write an equation for each line in point-slope form and slope-intercept form.*

**11.** Slope $= 2$, passing through $(3, 5)$
**12.** Slope $= 4$, passing through $(1, 3)$
**13.** Slope $= -3$, passing through $(-2, -3)$
**14.** Slope $= -5$, passing through $(-4, -2)$
**15.** Slope $= -4$, passing through $(-4, 0)$
**16.** Slope $= -2$, passing through $(0, -3)$
**17.** Slope $= \frac{1}{2}$, passing through the origin
**18.** Slope $= \frac{1}{3}$, passing through the origin
**19.** Passing through $(1, 2)$ and $(5, 10)$
**20.** Passing through $(3, 5)$ and $(8, 15)$
**21.** Passing through $(-3, 0)$ and $(0, 3)$
**22.** Passing through $(-2, 0)$ and $(0, 2)$
**23.** Passing through $(-3, -1)$ and $(2, 4)$
**24.** Passing through $(-2, -4)$ and $(1, -1)$
**25.** Passing through $(-3, -1)$ and $(4, -1)$
**26.** Passing through $(-2, -5)$ and $(6, -5)$
**27.** Passing through $(2, 4)$ with $x$-intercept $= -2$
**28.** Passing through $(1, -3)$ with $x$-intereept $= -1$
**29.** $x$-intercept $= -\frac{1}{2}$ and $y$-intercept $= 4$
**30.** $x$-intercept $= 4$ and $y$-intercept $= -2$

*In Exercises 31–38, give the slope and y-intercept of each line whose equation is given. Then graph the line.*

**31.** $y = 2x + 1$
**32.** $y = 3x + 2$
**33.** $y = -2x + 1$
**34.** $y = -3x + 2$
**35.** $y = \dfrac{3}{4}x - 2$
**36.** $y = \dfrac{3}{4}x - 3$
**37.** $y = -\dfrac{3}{5}x + 7$
**38.** $y = -\dfrac{2}{5}x + 6$

*In Exercises 39–44, graph each equation in the rectangular coordinate system.*

**39.** $y = -2$
**40.** $y = 4$
**41.** $x = -3$
**42.** $x = 5$
**43.** $y = 0$
**44.** $x = 0$

*In Exercises 45–52,*
**a.** *Rewrite the given equation in slope-intercept form.*
**b.** *Give the slope and y-intercept.*
**c.** *Graph the equation.*

**45.** $3x + y - 5 = 0$
**46.** $4x + y - 6 = 0$
**47.** $2x + 3y - 18 = 0$
**48.** $4x + 6y + 12 = 0$
**49.** $8x - 4y - 12 = 0$
**50.** $6x - 5y - 20 = 0$
**51.** $3x - 9 = 0$
**52.** $4y + 28 = 0$

## Application Exercises

**53.** As shown in the graph, the percentage of people in the United States satisfied with their lives remains relatively constant for all age groups. If $x$ represents a person's age and $y$ represents the percentage of people satisfied with their lives at that age, write an equation that reasonably models the data.

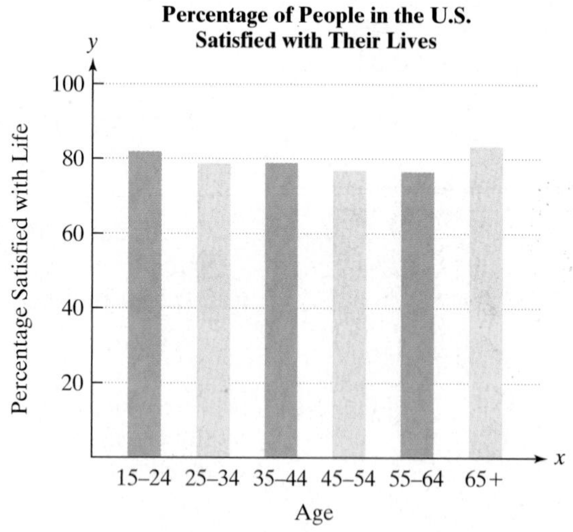


*Source: Culture Shift in Advanced Industrial Society,* Princeton University Press

**54.** The graph at the top of page 181 shows the life expectancy in years for U.S. women whose year of birth is indicated on the $x$-axis. Find the slope of the line passing through the points whose coordinates are shown on the graph. Describe what the slope represents.

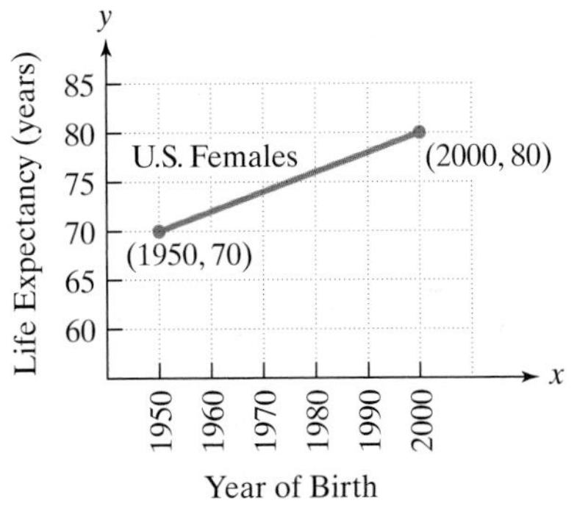


**55.** The graph shows U.S. population projections from 2000 through 2050. Use the equation $y = 2.35x + 179.5$, in which $x$ is the number of years after 1960 and $y$ is the U.S. population, in millions, to determine how well the equation models the projections for 2030, 2040, and 2050.

**U.S. Population Projections: 2000–2050**

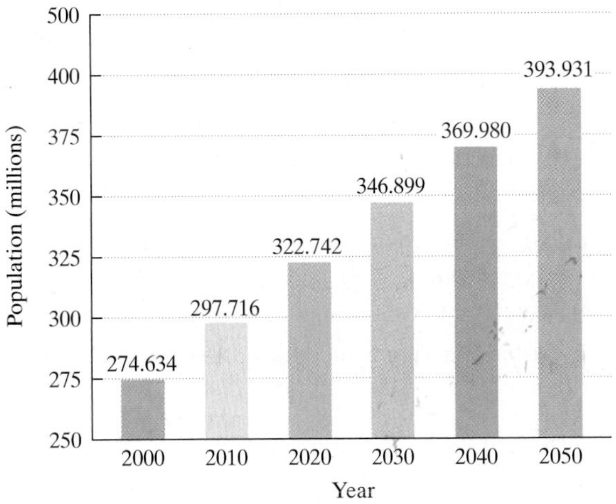


*Source*: U.S. Census Bureau

**56.** The figure shows projected online shopping per U.S. online household through 2004.

**Online Spending: Yearly Spending per Online Household**

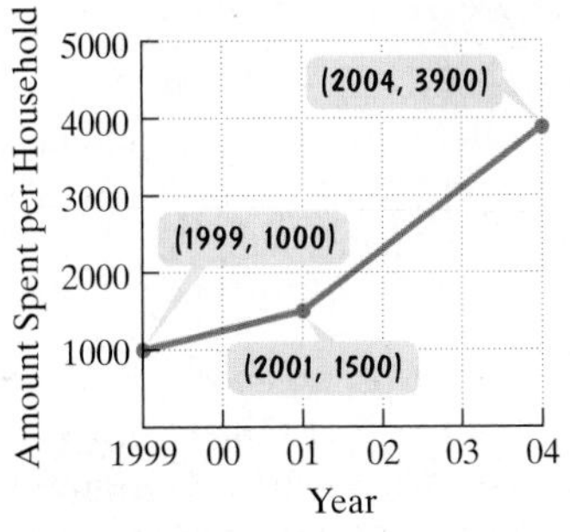


*Source*: Forrester Research

**a.** Find the slope of the line passing through (1999, 1000) and (2001, 1500). What does this represent in terms of the increase in online shopping per year?

**b.** Repeat part (a) for the data points (2001, 1500) and (2004, 3900).

**c.** Write the point-slope form of the equation of the line passing through (2001, 1500) and (2004, 3900).

**d.** Use the equation in part (c) to write the slope-intercept form of the equation.

**e.** Use the equation from part (c) to project the amount that will be spent shopping online per online household in 2010.

*In Exercises 57–58, two measurements are given for variables having a linear relationship. For each exercise, write the point-slope form of the equation of the line on which these measurements fall. Then use the point-slope form of the equation to write the slope-intercept form of the equation. Finally, use this equation to answer the question.*

**57.**

| $x$ (Number of Years after 1990) | $y$ (Total Consumer Spending in the United States, in Billions of Dollars) |
|---|---|
| 3 | 4459.2 |
| 7 | 5493.7 |

*Source*: U.S. Commerce Department

How much will consumers in the United States spend in the year 2020?

**58.**

| $x$ (Number of Years after 1985) | $y$ (Total of All Health-Care Expenditures in the United States, in Billions of Dollars) |
|---|---|
| 3 | 546 |
| 5 | 666 |

*Source*: U.S. Health Care Financing Administration

What will health-care expenditures in the United States be in the year 2010?

**59.** A business discovers a linear relationship between the number of shirts it can sell and the price per shirt. In particular, 20,000 shirts can be sold at \$19 each, and 2000 of the same shirts can be sold at \$55 each. Write the slope-intercept equation of the *demand line* through the ordered pairs (20,000 shirts, \$19) and (2000 shirts, \$55). Then determine the number of shirts that can be sold at \$50 each.

**60.** In 1965, radioactive wastes seeping into the Columbia River exposed citizens of eight Oregon counties and the city of Portland to radioactive contamination. In an article in the *Journal of Environmenial Health* (May–June, 1965), the authors formulated an index that measured the proximity of the residents to the contamination. The ordered pair for Columbia County (6.4, 178) indicates that its index is 6.4 and there are 178 cancer deaths per 100,000 residents. The corresponding ordered pair for Clatsop County is (8.3, 210). What is the predicted number of cancer deaths for Portland, with an index of 11.6?

**61.** Is there a relationship between education and prejudice? With increased education, does a person's level of prejudice tend to decrease? The scatter plot shows ten data points, each representing the number of years of school completed and the score on a test measuring prejudice for each subject. Higher scores on this 1-to-10 test indicate greater prejudice. Also shown is the regression line, the line that best fits the data. Use two points on this line to write both its point-slope and slope-intercept equations. Then use the slope-intercept equation to predict the score on the prejudice test for a person with seven years of education.

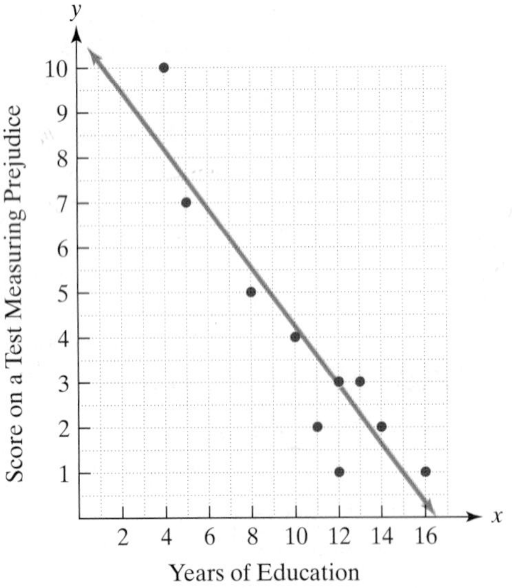


**62.** The scatter plot at the top of the next column shows the relationship between the percentage of married women of child-bearing age using contraceptives and the births per woman in selected countries. Also shown is the regression line. Use two points on this line to write both its point-slope and slope-intercept equations. Then find the number of births per woman if 90% of married women of child-bearing age use contraceptives.

**Contraceptive Prevalence and Births per Woman, Selected Countries**

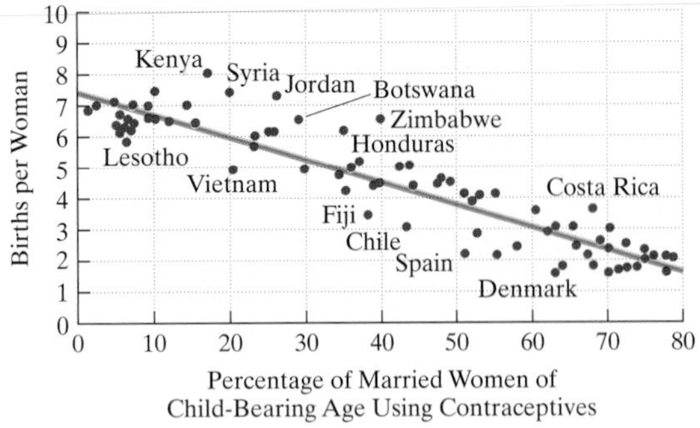


*Source*: Population Reference Bureau

## Writing in Mathematics

**63.** What is the slope of a line and how is it found?

**64.** Describe how to write the equation of a line if two points along the line are known.

**65.** Explain how to derive the slope-intercept form of a line's equation, $y = mx + b$, from the point-slope form

$$y - y_1 = m(x - x_1).$$

**66.** Explain how to graph the equation $x = 2$. Can this equation be expressed in slope-intercept form? Explain.

**67.** Explain how to use the general form of a line's equation to find the line's slope and $y$-intercept.

**68.** Look back at Figure 2.1 on page 168. Do you think that the line through the points corresponding to 2001 and 2004 will describe online spending per online household in 2040? Explain your answer.

**69.** Take a second look at the scatter plot in Exercise 61. Although there is a relationship between education and prejudice, we cannot necessarily conclude that increased education causes a person's level of prejudice to decrease. Offer two or more possible explanations for the data in the scatter plot.

## Technology Exercises

*Use a graphing utility to graph each equation in Exercises 70–73. Then use the* TRACE *feature to trace along the line and find the coordinates of two points. Use these points to compute the line's slope. Check your result by using the coefficient of x in the line's equation.*

**70.** $y = 2x + 4$

**71.** $y = -3x + 6$

**72.** $y = -\frac{1}{2}x - 5$

**73.** $y = \frac{3}{4}x - 2$

**74. a.** Use the statistical menu of your graphing utility to enter the ten data points shown in the scatter plot in Exercise 61.

b. Use the DRAW menu and the scatter plot capability to draw a scatter plot of the data points like the one shown in Exercise 61.

c. Select the linear regression option. Your utility should give you values for $a$ and $b$ for the equation of the regression line, $y = ax + b$. You may also be given a *correlation coefficient*, $r$. Values of $r$ close to 1 indicate that the points can be described by a linear relationship and the regression line has a positive slope. Values of $r$ close to $-1$ indicate that the points can be described by a linear relationship and the regression line has a negative slope. Values of $r$ close to 0 indicate no linear relationship between the variables.

d. Use the appropriate sequence (consult your manual) to graph the regression equation on top of the points in the scatter plot.

## Critical Thinking Exercises

**75.** Which one of the following is true?

a. A linear equation with nonnegative slope has a graph that rises from left to right.

b. The equations $y = 4x$ and $y = -4x$ have graphs that are perpendicular lines.

c. The line whose equation is $5x + 6y - 30 = 0$ passes through the point $(6, 0)$ and has slope $-\frac{5}{6}$.

d. The graph of $y = 7$ in the rectangular coordinate system is the single point $(7, 0)$.

**76.** Prove that the equation of a line passing through $(a, 0)$ and $(0, b)$ $(a \neq 0, b \neq 0)$ can be written in the form $\frac{x}{a} + \frac{y}{b} = 1$. Why is this called the *intercept form* of a line?

**77.** Use the figure at the top of the next column to make the following lists.

a. List the slopes $m_1$, $m_2$, $m_3$, and $m_4$ in order of decreasing size.

b. List the $y$-intercepts $b_1$, $b_2$, $b_3$, and $b_4$ in order of decreasing size.

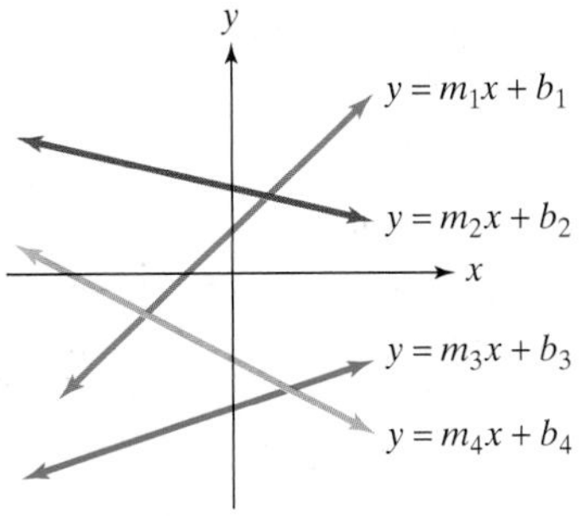


**78.** Excited about the success of celebrity stamps, post office officials were rumored to have put forth a plan to institute two new types of thermometers. On these new scales, °$E$ represents degrees Elvis and °$M$ represents degrees Madonna. If it is known that $40°E = 25°M$, $280°E = 125°M$, and degrees Elvis is linearly related to degrees Madonna, write an equation expressing $E$ in terms of $M$.

## Group Activity Exercise

**79.** Group members should consult an almanac, newspaper, magazine, or the Internet to find data that lie approximately on or near a straight line. Working by hand or using a graphing utility, construct a scatter plot for the data. If working by hand, draw a line that approximately fits the data and then write its equation. If using a graphing utility, obtain the equation of the regression line. Then use the equation of the line to make a prediction about what might happen in the future. Are there circumstances that might affect the accuracy of this prediction? List some of these circumstances.

# SECTION 2.2 Parallel and Perpendicular Lines and Circles

### Objectives

1. Find slopes and equations of parallel and perpendicular lines.
2. Write the standard form of a circle's equation.
3. Give the center and radius of a circle whose equation is in standard form.
4. Convert the general form of a circle's equation to standard form.

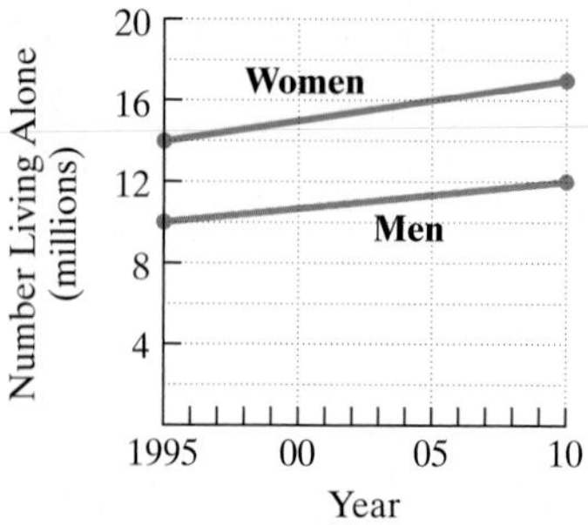

*Source*: Forrester Research

**Figure 2.11**

A best guess at the look of our nation in the next decades indicates that the number of men and women living alone will increase each year. Figure 2.11 shows that by 2010, approximately 12 million men and 17 million women will be living alone. Can you tell by the line graphs in the figure if the yearly increase for women is the same as the yearly increase for men? We begin this section by showing how we can use the slope of each line to answer this question.

## Parallel and Perpendicular Lines

Two nonintersecting lines that lie in the same plane are parallel. If two lines do not intersect, the ratio of the vertical change to the horizontal change is the same for each line. Because two parallel lines have the same "steepness," they must have the same slope.

**1** Find slopes and equations of parallel and perpendicular lines.

### Slope and Parallel Lines

1. If two nonvertical lines are parallel, then they have the same slope.
2. If two distinct nonvertical lines have the same slope, then they are parallel.
3. Two distinct vertical lines, both with undefined slopes, are parallel.

### EXAMPLE 1 Writing Equations of a Line Parallel to a Given Line

Write an equation of the line passing through $(-3, 2)$ and parallel to the line whose equation is $y = 2x + 1$. Express the equation in point-slope form and slope-intercept form.

**Solution** The situation is illustrated in Figure 2.12. We are looking for the equation of the line shown on the left. How do we obtain this equation? Notice that the line passes through the point $(-3, 2)$. Using the point-slope form of the line's equation, we have $x_1 = -3$ and $y_1 = 2$.

$$y - y_1 = m(x - x_1)$$

$y_1 = 2$ $\quad$ $x_1 = -3$

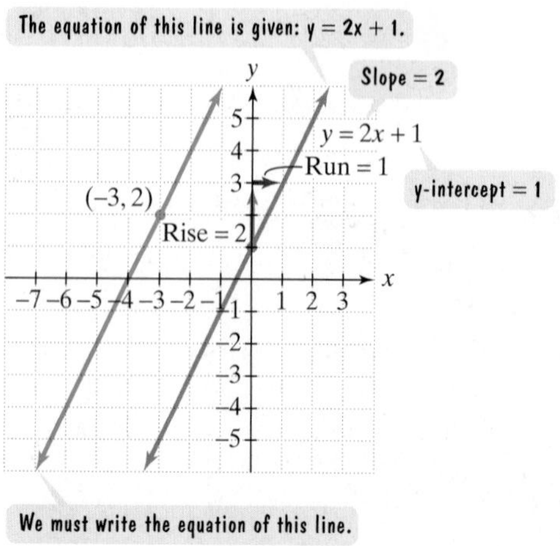


**Figure 2.12** Writing equations of a line parallel to a given line

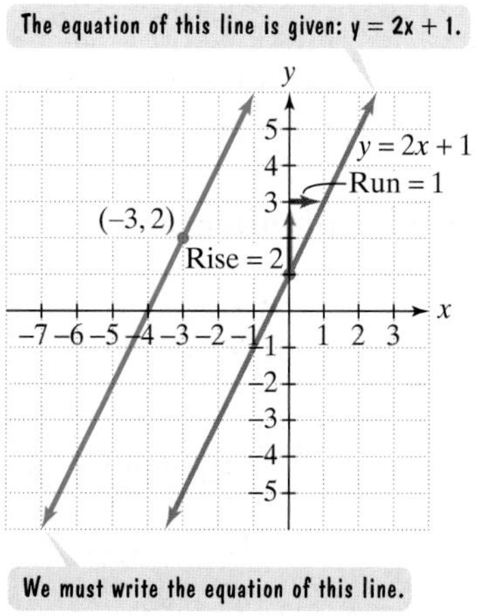


**Figure 2.12** Shown again so that you do not have to turn back a page

Now, the only thing missing from the equation is $m$, the slope of the line on the left. Do we know anything about the slope of either line in Figure 2.12? The answer is yes; we know the slope of the line on the right, whose equation is given.

$$y = 2x + 1$$

The slope of the line on the right in Figure 2.12 is 2.

Parallel lines have the same slope. Because the slope of the line with the given equation is 2, $m = 2$ for the line whose equation we must write.

$$y - y_1 = m(x - x_1)$$

$y_1 = 2$    $m = 2$    $x_1 = -3$

The point-slope form of the line's equation is

$$y - 2 = 2[x - (-3)] \text{ or}$$
$$y - 2 = 2(x + 3).$$

Solving for $y$, we obtain the slope-intercept form of the equation.

$$y - 2 = 2x + 6$$ Apply the distributive property.

$$y = 2x + 8$$ Add 2 to both sides. This is the slope-intercept form, $y = mx + b$, of the equation.

**Check Point 1** Write an equation of the line passing through $(-2, 5)$ and parallel to the line whose equation is $y = 3x + 1$. Express the equation in point-slope form and slope-intercept form.

Two lines that intersect at a right angle $(90°)$ are said to be **perpendicular**, shown in Figure 2.13. The relationship between the slopes of perpendicular lines is not as obvious as the relationship between parallel lines. Figure 2.13 shows line $AB$, with a slope of $\frac{c}{d}$. Rotate line $AB$ 90° to the left to obtain line $A'B'$ perpendicular to line $AB$. The figure indicates that the rise and the run of the new line are reversed from the original line, but the rise is now negative. This means that the slope of the new line is $-\frac{d}{c}$. Notice that the product of the slopes of the two perpendicular lines is $-1$:

$$\left(\frac{c}{d}\right)\left(-\frac{d}{c}\right) = -1.$$

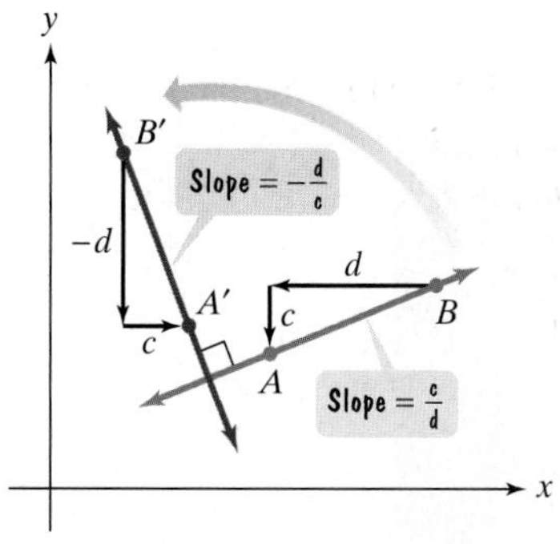


**Figure 2.13** Slopes of perpendicular lines

This relationship holds for all perpendicular lines and is summarized in the following box.

### Slope and Perpendicular Lines

1. If two nonvertical lines are perpendicular, then the product of their slopes is $-1$.
2. If the product of the slopes of two lines is $-1$, then the lines are perpendicular.
3. A horizontal line having zero slope is perpendicular to a vertical line having undefined slope.

An equivalent way of stating this relationship is to say that one line is perpendicular to another line if its slope is the *negative reciprocal* of the slope of the other. For example, if a line has slope 5, any line having slope $-\frac{1}{5}$ is perpendicular to it. Similarly, if a line has slope $-\frac{3}{4}$, any line having slope $\frac{4}{3}$ is perpendicular to it.

### EXAMPLE 2 Finding the Slope of a Line Perpendicular to a Given Line

Find the slope of any line that is perpendicular to the line whose equation is $x + 4y - 8 = 0$.

**Solution** We begin by writing the equation of the given line in slope-intercept form. Solve for $y$.

$x + 4y - 8 = 0$ This is the given equation.

$4y = -x + 8$ To isolate the y-term, subtract x and add 8 on both sides.

$y = -\frac{1}{4}x + 2$ Divide both sides by 4.

Slope is $-\frac{1}{4}$.

The given line has slope $-\frac{1}{4}$. Any line perpendicular to this line has a slope that is the negative reciprocal of $-\frac{1}{4}$. Thus, the slope of any perpendicular line is 4.

**Check Point 2** Find the slope of any line that is perpendicular to the line whose equation is $x + 3y - 12 = 0$.

## Circles

It's a good idea to know your way around a circle. Clocks, angles, maps, and compasses are based on circles. Circles occur everywhere in nature: in ripples on water, patterns on a butterfly's wings, and cross sections of trees. Some consider the circle to be the most pleasing of all shapes.

The rectangular coordinate system gives us a unique way of knowing a circle. It enables us to translate a circle's geometric definition into an algebraic equation. We begin with this geometric definition.

### Definition of a Circle

A **circle** is the set of all points in a plane that are equidistant from a fixed point called the **center**. The fixed distance from the circle's center to any point on the circle is called the **radius**.

Figure 2.14 is our starting point for obtaining a circle's equation. We've placed the circle into a rectangular coordinate system. The circle's center is $(h, k)$ and its radius is $r$. We let $(x, y)$ represent the coordinates of any point on the circle.

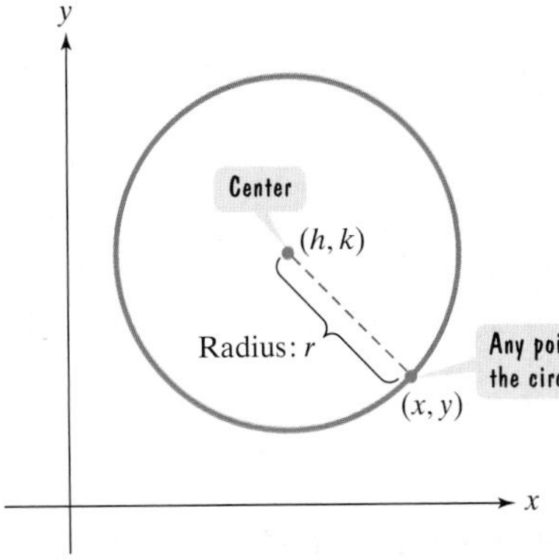


**Figure 2.14** A circle centered at $(h, k)$ with radius $r$

What does the geometric definition of a circle tell us about point $(x, y)$ in Figure 2.14? The point is on the circle if and only if its distance from the center is $r$. We can use the distance formula to express this idea algebraically:

The distance between $(x, y)$ and $(h, k)$ | is always | $r$.

$$\sqrt{(x-h)^2+(y-k)^2} \quad = \quad r$$

Squaring both sides of this equation yields the **standard form of the equation of a circle**.

### The Standard Form of the Equation of a Circle

The **standard form of the equation of a circle** with center $(h, k)$ and radius $r$ is

$$(x-h)^2+(y-k)^2=r^2.$$

**2** Write the standard form of a circle's equation.

## EXAMPLE 3 Finding the Standard Form of a Circle's Equation

Write the standard form of the equation of the circle with center $(0, 0)$ and radius 2. Graph the circle.

**Solution** The center is $(0, 0)$. Because the center is represented as $(h, k)$ in the standard form of the equation, $h = 0$ and $k = 0$. The radius is 2, so we will let $r = 2$ in the equation.

$(x-h)^2+(y-k)^2=r^2$ This is the standard form of a circle's equation.

$(x-0)^2+(y-0)^2=2^2$ Substitute 0 for h, 0 for k, and 2 for r.

$x^2+y^2=4$ Simplify.

The standard form of the equation of the circle is $x^2 + y^2 = 4$. Figure 2.15 shows the graph.

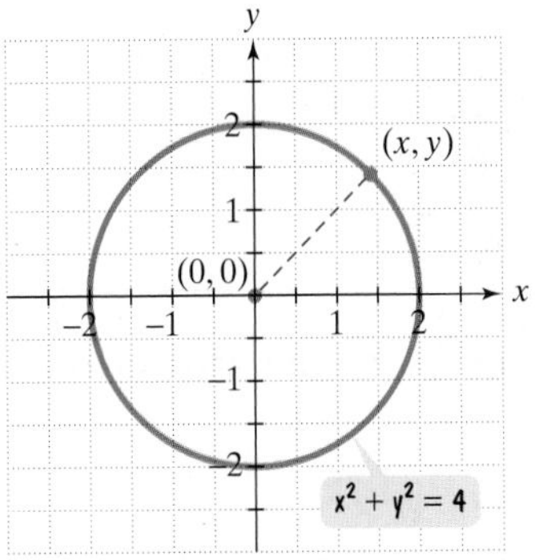


**Figure 2.15** The graph of $x^2 + y^2 = 4$

**Check Point 3** Write the standard form of the equation of the circle with center (0, 0) and radius 4.

## Technology

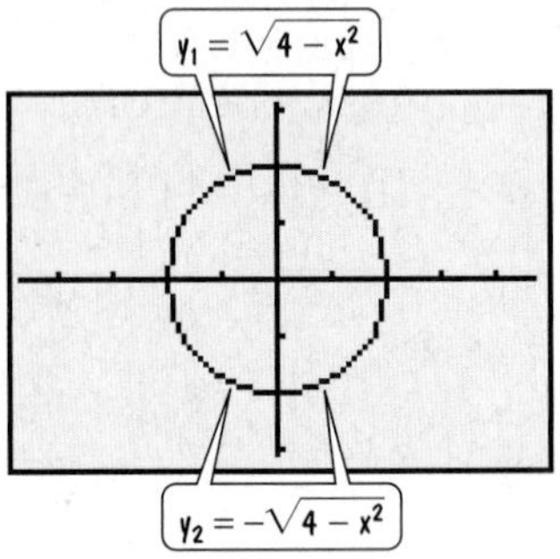


To graph a circle with a graphing utility, first solve the equation for $y$.

$$x^2 + y^2 = 4$$
$$y^2 = 4 - x^2$$
$$y = \pm\sqrt{4 - x^2}$$

Graph the two equations

$$y_1 = \sqrt{4 - x^2} \quad \text{and} \quad y_2 = -\sqrt{4 - x^2}$$

in the same viewing rectangle. The graph of $y_1 = \sqrt{4 - x^2}$ is the top semicircle because $y$ is always positive. The graph of $y_2 = -\sqrt{4 - x^2}$ is the bottom semicircle because $y$ is always negative. Use a ZOOM SQUARE setting so that the circle looks like a circle. (Many graphing utilities have problems connecting the two semicircles because the segments directly across horizontally from the center become nearly vertical.)

Example 3 and Check Point 3 involved circles centered at the origin. The standard form of the equation of all such circles is $x^2 + y^2 = r^2$, where $r$ is the circle's radius. Now, let's consider a circle whose center is not at the origin.

### EXAMPLE 4 Finding the Standard Form of a Circle's Equation

Write the standard form of the equation of the circle with center (−2, 3) and radius 4.

**Solution** The center is (−2, 3). Because the center is represented as $(h, k)$ in the standard form of the equation, $h = -2$ and $k = 3$. The radius is 4, so we will let $r = 4$ in the equation.

$$(x - h)^2 + (y - k)^2 = r^2 \quad \text{This is the standard form of a circle's equation.}$$
$$[x - (-2)]^2 + (y - 3)^2 = 4^2 \quad \text{Substitute } -2 \text{ for } h\text{, 3 for } k\text{, and 4 for } r.$$
$$(x + 2)^2 + (y - 3)^2 = 16 \quad \text{Simplify.}$$

The standard form of the equation of the circle is $(x + 2)^2 + (y - 3)^2 = 16$.

**Check Point 4** Write the standard form of the equation of the circle with center (5, −6) and radius 10.

**3** Give the center and radius of a circle whose equation is in standard form.

### EXAMPLE 5 Using the Standard Form of a Circle's Equation to Graph the Circle

Find the center and radius of the circle whose equation is

$$(x - 2)^2 + (y + 4)^2 = 9$$

and graph the equation.

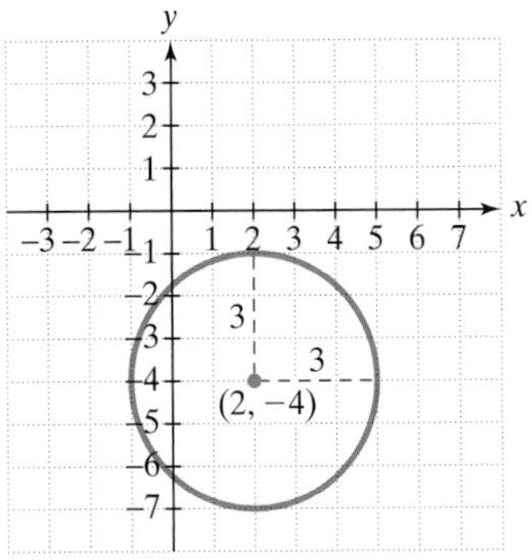

**Figure 2.16** The graph of $(x-2)^2+(y+4)^2=9$

**Solution** In order to graph the circle, we need to know its center, $(h, k)$, and its radius $r$. We can find the values for $h$, $k$, and $r$ by comparing the given equation to the standard form of the equation of a circle.

$$(x-2)^2+(y+4)^2=9$$
$$(x-2)^2+\left(y-(-4)\right)^2=3^2$$

This is $(x-h)^2$, with $h = 2$. This is $(y-k)^2$, with $k = -4$. This is $r^2$, with $r = 3$.

We see that $h = 2$, $k = -4$, and $r = 3$. Thus, the circle has center $(h, k) = (2, -4)$ and a radius of 3 units. To graph this circle, first plot the center $(2, -4)$. Because the radius is 3, you can locate at least four points on the circle by going out three units to the right, to the left, up, and down from the center.

Two such points, to the right and to the left of $(2, -4)$, are $(5, -4)$ and $(-1, -4)$, respectively.

Using these points, we obtain the graph in Figure 2.16.

**Check Point 5** Find the center and radius of the circle whose equation is

$$(x+3)^2+(y-1)^2=4$$

and graph the equation.

If we square $x-2$ and $y+4$ in the standard form of the equation of Example 5, we obtain another form for the circle's equation.

| | |
|---|---|
| $(x-2)^2+(y+4)^2=9$ | This is the standard form of the equation from Example 3. |
| $x^2-4x+4+y^2+8y+16=9$ | Square $x-2$ and $y+4$. |
| $x^2+y^2-4x+8y+20=9$ | Combine numerical terms and rearrange terms. |
| $x^2+y^2-4x+8y+11=0$ | Subtract 9 from both sides. |

This result suggests that an equation in the form $x^2+y^2+Dx+Ey+F=0$ can represent a circle. This is called the **general form of the equation of a circle.**

### The General Form of the Equation of a Circle

The **general form of the equation of a circle is**

$$x^2+y^2+Dx+Ey+F=0.$$

**4** Convert the general form of a circle's equation to standard form.

We can convert the general form of the equation of a circle to the standard form $(x-h)^2+(y-k)^2=r^2$. We do so by completing the square on $x$ and $y$. Let's see how this is done.

## EXAMPLE 6 Converting the General Form of a Circle's Equation to Standard Form and Graphing the Circle

Write in standard form and graph: $x^2+y^2+4x-6y-23=0$.

**Solution** Because we plan to complete the square on both $x$ and $y$, let's rearrange terms so that $x$-terms are arranged in descending order, $y$-terms are arranged in descending order, and the constant term appears on the right.

$$x^2 + y^2 + 4x - 6y - 23 = 0$$ This is the given equation.

$$(x^2 + 4x \quad\ ) + (y^2 - 6y \quad\ ) = 23$$ Rewrite in anticipation of completing the square.

$$(x^2 + 4x + 4) + (y^2 - 6y + 9) = 23 + 4 + 9$$ Complete the square on x: $\frac{1}{2} \cdot 4 = 2$ and $2^2 = 4$, so add 4 to both sides. Complete the square on y: $\frac{1}{2}(-6) = -3$ and $(-3)^2 = 9$, so add 9 to both sides.

Remember that numbers added on the left side must also be added on the right side.

$$(x + 2)^2 + (y - 3)^2 = 36$$ Factor on the left and add on the right.

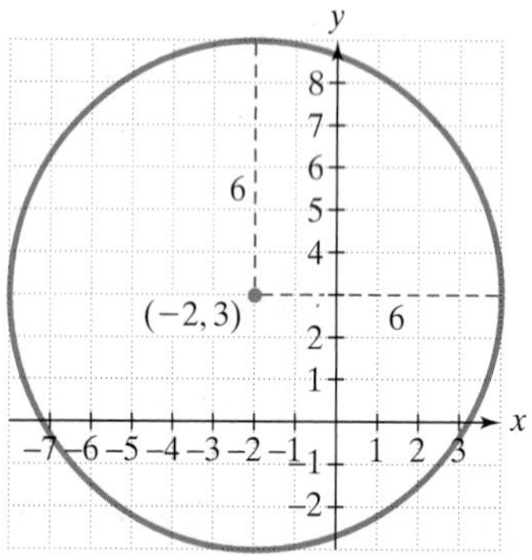


**Figure 2.17** The graph of $(x + 2)^2 + (y - 3)^2 = 36$

This last equation is in standard form. We can identify the circle's center and radius by comparing this equation to the standard form of the equation of a circle, $(x - h)^2 + (y - k)^2 = r^2$.

$$(x + 2)^2 + (y - 3)^2 = 36$$

$$(x - (-2))^2 + (y - 3)^2 = 6^2$$

This is $(x - h)^2$, with $h = -2$. This is $(y - k)^2$, with $k = 3$. This is $r^2$, with $r = 6$.

We use the center, $(h, k) = (-2, 3)$, and the radius, $r = 6$, to graph the circle. The graph is shown in Figure 2.17.

## Technology

To graph $x^2 + y^2 + 4x - 6y - 23 = 0$, rewrite the equation as a quadratic equation in $y$.

$$y^2 - 6y + (x^2 + 4x - 23) = 0$$

Now solve for $y$ using the quadratic formula, with $a = 1$, $b = -6$, and $c = x^2 + 4x - 23$.

$$y = \frac{-b \pm \sqrt{b^2 - 4ac}}{2a} = \frac{-(-6) \pm \sqrt{(-6)^2 - 4 \cdot 1(x^2 + 4x - 23)}}{2 \cdot 1} = \frac{6 \pm \sqrt{36 - 4(x^2 + 4x - 23)}}{2}$$

Because we will enter these equations, there is no need to simplify. Enter

$$y_1 = \frac{6 + \sqrt{36 - 4(x^2 + 4x - 23)}}{2}$$

and

$$y_2 = \frac{6 - \sqrt{36 - 4(x^2 + 4x - 23)}}{2}.$$

Use a ZOOM SQUARE setting. The graph is shown on the right.

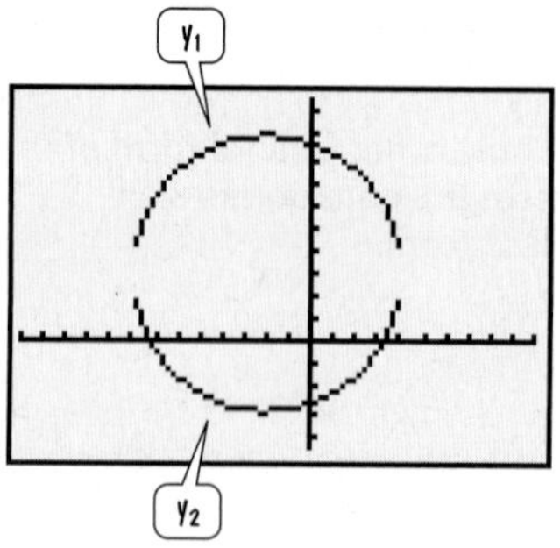


**Check Point 6** Write in standard form and graph:

$$x^2 + y^2 + 4x - 4y - 1 = 0.$$

## EXERCISE SET 2.2

### Practice Exercises

*In Exercises 1–16, the equation of a line is given. Find the slope of a line that is (a) parallel to the line with the given equation; and (b) perpendicular to the line with the given equation.*

**1.** $y = 5x$
**2.** $y = 3x$
**3.** $y = -7x$
**4.** $y = -9x$
**5.** $y = \frac{1}{2}x + 3$
**6.** $y = \frac{1}{4}x - 5$
**7.** $y = -\frac{2}{5}x - 1$
**8.** $y = -\frac{3}{7}x - 2$
**9.** $4x + y = 7$
**10.** $8x + y = 11$
**11.** $2x + 4y - 8 = 0$
**12.** $3x + 2y - 6 = 0$
**13.** $2x - 3y - 5 = 0$
**14.** $3x - 4y + 7 = 0$
**15.** $x = 6$
**16.** $y = 9$

*In Exercises 17–20, write an equation for line L in point-slope form and slope-intercept form.*

**17.**

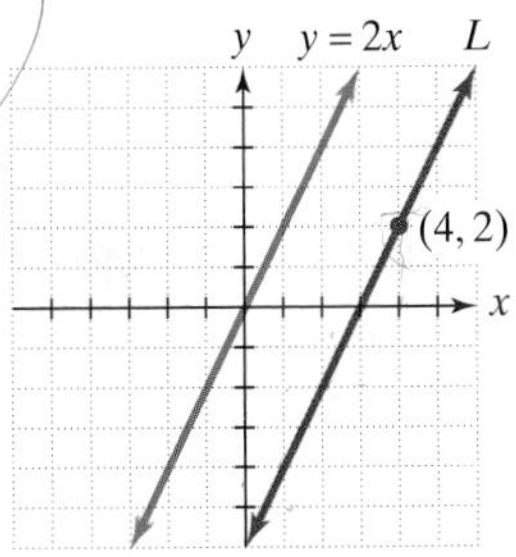


L is parallel to $y = 2x$.

**18.**

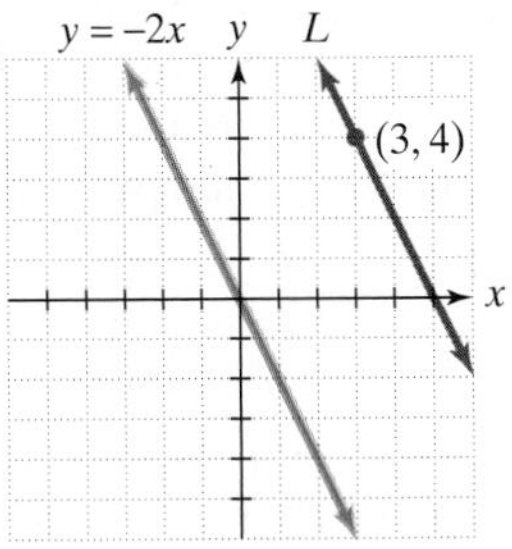


L is parallel to $y = -2x$.

**19.**

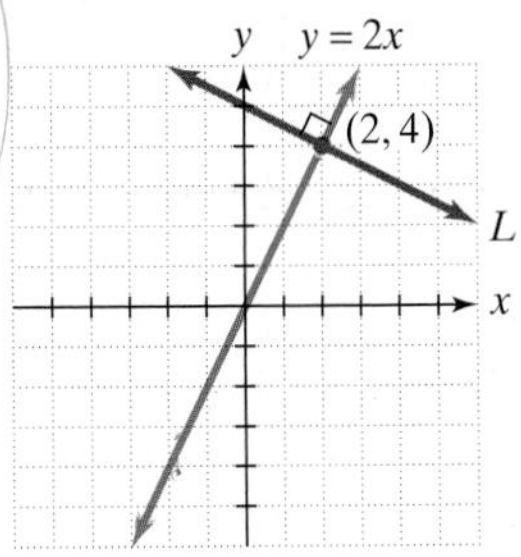


L is perpendicular to $y = 2x$.

**20.**

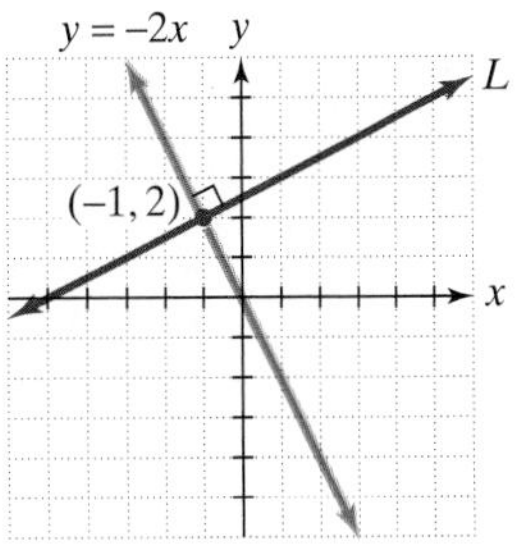


L is perpendicular to $y = -2x$.

*In Exercises 21–28, use the given conditions to write an equation for each line in point-slope form and slope-intercept form.*

**21.** Passing through $(-8, -10)$ and parallel to the line whose equation is $y = -4x + 3$

**22.** Passing through $(-2, -7)$ and parallel to the line whose equation is $y = -5x + 4$

**23.** Passing through $(2, -3)$ and perpendicular to the line whose equation is $y = \frac{1}{5}x + 6$

**24.** Passing through $(-4, 2)$ and perpendicular to the line whose equation is $y = \frac{1}{3}x + 7$

**25.** Passing through $(-2, 2)$ and parallel to the line whose equation is $2x - 3y - 7 = 0$

**26.** Passing through $(-1, 3)$ and parallel to the line whose equation is $3x - 2y - 5 = 0$

**27.** Passing through $(4, -7)$ and perpendicular to the line whose equation is $x - 2y - 3 = 0$

**28.** Passing through $(5, -9)$ and perpendicular to the line whose equation is $x + 7y - 12 = 0$

*In Exercises 29–38, write the standard form of the equation of the circle with the given center and radius.*

**29.** Center $(0, 0)$, $r = 7$
**30.** Center $(0, 0)$, $r = 8$
**31.** Center $(3, 2)$, $r = 5$
**32.** Center $(2, -1)$, $r = 4$
**33.** Center $(-1, 4)$, $r = 2$
**34.** Center $(-3, 5)$, $r = 3$
**35.** Center $(-3, -1)$, $r = \sqrt{3}$
**36.** Center $(-5, -3)$, $r = \sqrt{5}$
**37.** Center $(-4, 0)$, $r = 10$
**38.** Center $(-2, 0)$, $r = 6$

*In Exercises 39–46, give the center and radius of the circle described by the equation and graph each equation.*

**39.** $x^2 + y^2 = 16$
**40.** $x^2 + y^2 = 49$
**41.** $(x - 3)^2 + (y - 1)^2 = 36$
**42.** $(x - 2)^2 + (y - 3)^2 = 16$
**43.** $(x + 3)^2 + (y - 2)^2 = 4$
**44.** $(x + 1)^2 + (y - 4)^2 = 25$
**45.** $(x + 2)^2 + (y + 2)^2 = 4$
**46.** $(x + 4)^2 + (y + 5)^2 = 36$

*In Exercises 47–54, complete the square and write the equation in standard form. Then give the center and radius of each circle and graph the equation.*

47. $x^2 + y^2 + 6x + 2y + 6 = 0$
48. $x^2 + y^2 + 8x + 4y + 16 = 0$
49. $x^2 + y^2 - 10x - 6y - 30 = 0$
50. $x^2 + y^2 - 4x - 12y - 9 = 0$
51. $x^2 + y^2 + 8x - 2y - 8 = 0$
52. $x^2 + y^2 + 12x - 6y - 4 = 0$
53. $x^2 - 2x + y^2 - 15 = 0$
54. $x^2 + y^2 - 6y - 7 = 0$

## Application Exercises

55. The line graph shows the number of people in the United States projected to live alone through 2010.

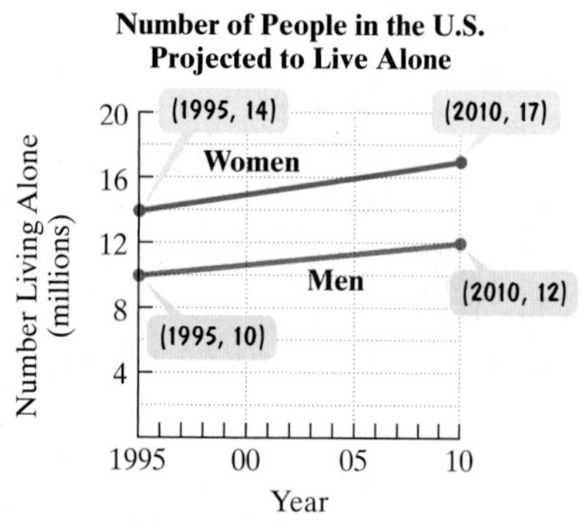


*Source*: Forrester Research

a. Find the slope of the line for U.S. women.
b. Find the slope of the line for U.S. men.
c. Are the lines parallel? What does this mean in terms of the yearly increase for women and the yearly increase for men?

56. The amount spent annually in college bookstores in the United States can be modeled by $y = 0.19x + 1.67$, where $x$ represents the number of years since 1982 and $y$ represents the amount spent in billions of dollars. If the graph of this equation is parallel to a line representing the amount spent annually in bookstores in the United States since 1982, what does this mean in terms of the yearly increase for spending on books?

57. We refer to the driveway in the figure shown at the top of the next column as being *circular*, meaning that it is bounded by two circles. The figure indicates that the radius of the larger circle is 52 feet and the radius of the smaller circle is 38 feet. All points on the circular driveway satisfy the following compound inequality:

| all points on the smaller circle | $\le$ | $(x, y)$ on the driveway | $\le$ | all points on the larger circle. |
|---|---|---|---|---|

a. Rewrite the left portion of this inequality by writing the equation of the smaller circle.

b. Rewrite the right portion of this inequality by writing the equation of the larger circle.

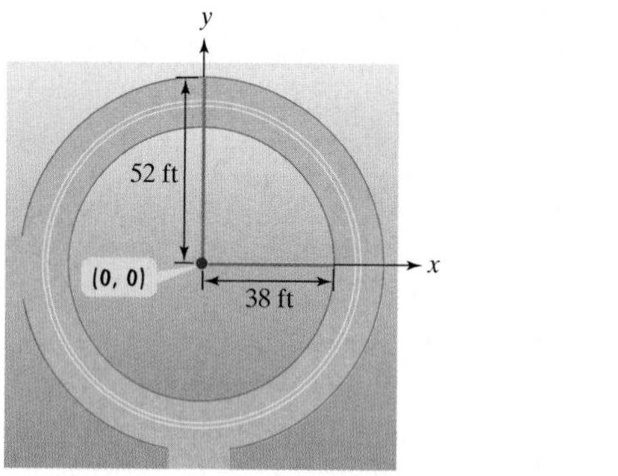


58. The circle formed by the middle lane of a circular running track can be described algebraically by $x^2 + y^2 = 4$, where all measurements are in miles. If you run around the track twice, approximately how many miles have you covered?

## Writing in Mathematics

59. If two lines are parallel, describe the relationship between their slopes.

60. If two lines are perpendicular, describe the relationship between their slopes.

61. The number of multiple births in the United States (twins, triplets, etc.) per 1000 live births can be modeled by $y = 0.463x + 18.888$, where $x$ represents the number of years since 1980 and $y$ represents multiple births per 1000 live births. Explain why the equation of this line cannot be parallel to the line representing the number of births in the United States since 1980.

62. If you know a point on a line and you know the equation of a line perpendicular to this line, explain how to write the line's equation.

63. What is a circle? Without using variables, describe how your definition of a circle can be used to obtain a form of its equation.

64. Give an example of a circle's equation in standard form. Describe how to find the center and radius for this circle.

65. How is the standard form of a circle's equation obtained from its general form?

66. Does $(x - 3)^2 + (y - 5)^2 = 0$ represent the equation of a circle? If not, describe the graph of this equation.

67. Does $(x - 3)^2 + (y - 5)^2 = -25$ represent the equation of a circle? What sort of set is the graph of this equation?

## Technology Exercises

**68.** The lines whose equations are $y = \frac{1}{3}x + 1$ and $y = -3x - 2$ are perpendicular because the product of their slopes, $\frac{1}{3}$ and $-3$, respectively, is $-1$.
**a.** Use a graphing utility to graph the equations. Do the lines appear to be perpendicular?
**b.** Now use the zoom square feature of your utility. Describe what happens to the graphs. Explain why this is so.

*In Exercises 69–71, use a graphing utility to graph each circle whose equation is given.*

**69.** $x^2 + y^2 = 25$

**70.** $(y + 1)^2 = 36 - (x - 3)^2$

**71.** $x^2 + 10x + y^2 - 4y - 20 = 0$

## Critical Thinking Exercises

**72.** Which one of the following is true?
**a.** The equation of the circle whose center is at the origin with radius 16 is $x^2 + y^2 = 16$.
**b.** The graph of $(x - 3)^2 + (y + 5)^2 = 36$ is a circle with a radius 6 centered at $(-3, 5)$.
**c.** The graph of $(x - 4) + (y + 6) = 25$ is a circle with a radius 5 centered at $(4, -6)$.
**d.** None of the above is true.

*In Exercises 73–74, write the point-slope form and the slope-intercept form of the equation for each line described.*

**73.** Having an $x$-intercept of $-3$ and perpendicular to the line passing through $(0, 0)$ and $(6, -2)$

**74.** Perpendicular to $3x - 2y = 4$ with the same $y$-intercept

*In Exercises 75–76, write the standard form and the general form of the equation of each circle.*

**75.** Center at $(3, -5)$ and passing through the point $(-2, 1)$

**76.** Passing through $(-7, 2)$ and $(1, 2)$; these points lie on the line that passes through the circle's center.

**77.** Find the area of the region bounded by the graphs of $(x - 2)^2 + (y + 3)^2 = 25$ and $(x - 2)^2 + (y + 3)^2 = 36$.

**78.** A **tangent line** to a circle is a line that intersects the circle at exactly one point. The tangent line is perpendicular to the radius of the circle at this point of contact. Write the point-slope equation of a line tangent to the circle whose equation is $x^2 + y^2 = 25$ at the point $(3, -4)$.

# SECTION 2.3 Introduction to Functions

## Objectives

1. Find the domain and range of a relation.
2. Determine whether a relation is a function.
3. Determine whether an equation represents a function.
4. Evaluate a function.
5. Find and simplify a function's difference quotient.
6. Understand and use piecewise functions.
7. Find the domain of a function.

Enjoy talking on the phone? In 1999, nearly 80 million Americans were chatting up a storm on their mobile phones, an increase of 300% from 1994, when only 20 million Americans were using mobile phones. And who can blame them? The graph in Figure 2.18 shows the decrease in the monthly average U.S. mobile-phone bills from 1994 through 1998. With video mobile phones by 2020, there seems to be no limit to the ways in which we keep in touch.

**U.S. Mobile-Phone Bills**

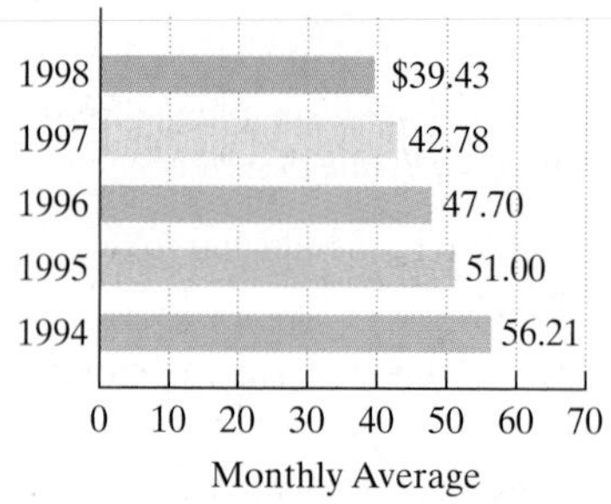


*Source*: Cellular Telephone Industry of America

**Figure 2.18**

If we let $x$ represent a year and $y$ the monthly average mobile-phone bill, the graph in Figure 2.18 shows a correspondence between the two variables $x$ and $y$. We can write this correspondence using a set of ordered pairs:

$$\{(1994, 56.21), (1995, 51.00), (1996, 47.70), (1997, 42.78), (1998, 39.43)\}$$

The mathematical term for a set of ordered pairs is a **relation**.

### Definition of a Relation

A **relation** is any set of ordered pairs. The set of all first components of the ordered pairs is called the **domain** of the relation, and the set of all second components is called the **range** of the relation.

**1** Find the domain and range of a relation.

## EXAMPLE 1 Analyzing U.S. Mobile-Phone Bills as a Relation

Find the domain and range of the relation

$$\{(1994, 56.21), (1995, 51.00), (1996, 47.70), (1997, 42.78), (1998, 39.43)\}.$$

**Solution** The domain is the set of all first components. Thus, the domain is

$$\{1994, 1995, 1996, 1997, 1998\}.$$

The range is the set of all second components. Thus, the range is

$$\{56.21, 51.00, 47.70, 42.78, 39.43\}.$$

**Check Point 1** Find the domain and the range of the relation $\{(20, 157.4), (30, 231.8), (100, 752.6), (200, 1496.6)\}$.

As you worked Check Point 1, did you wonder if the numbers in each ordered pair represented anything? Think snakes! The first number in each ordered pair is a snake's tail length, in millimeters, and the second number is its body length, also in millimeters. Consider, for example, the ordered pair (30, 231.8).

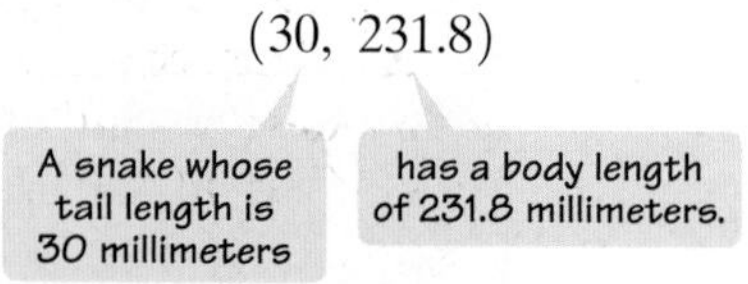


The relation in the snake example can be pictured as follows:

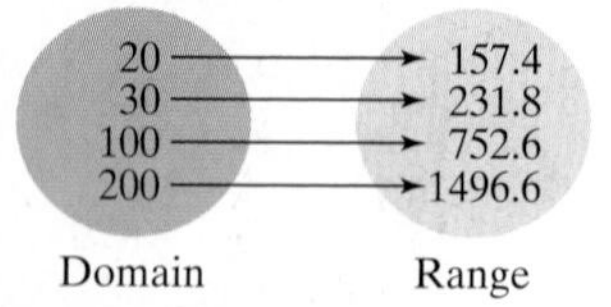


A scatter plot, like the one shown in Figure 2.19, is a way to represent the relation.

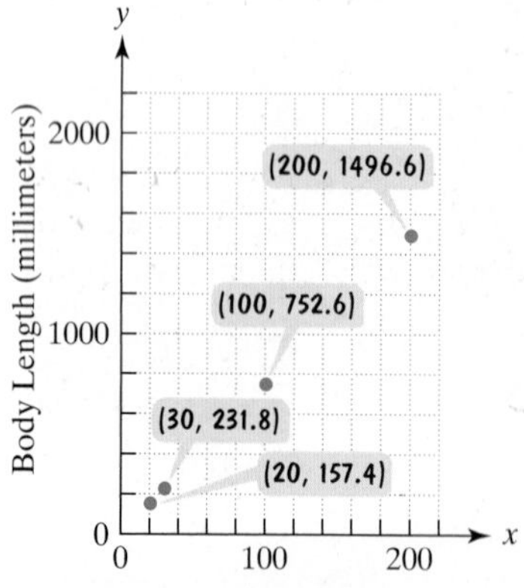


**Figure 2.19** The graph of a relation showing a correspondence between a snake's tail length and its body length

## Functions

The SAT is the test that everyone loves to hate. The scatter plot in Figure 2.20 on page 192 shows a relation indicating a correspondence between SAT scores and grade point averages for the first year in college for a group of randomly selected college students. The domain is the set of SAT scores for the students. The range is the set of their grade point averages. Is it possible for two students with the same SAT score to have different grade point averages? Look for two or more data points that are aligned vertically. We see that there are two students who have the same SAT score, 700, but their grade point averages are different. One student has a grade point average of approximately 2.4 and the other a grade point average of approximately 3.7. These students are represented by the following ordered pairs:

$$(700,\ 2.4) \qquad (700,\ 3.7).$$

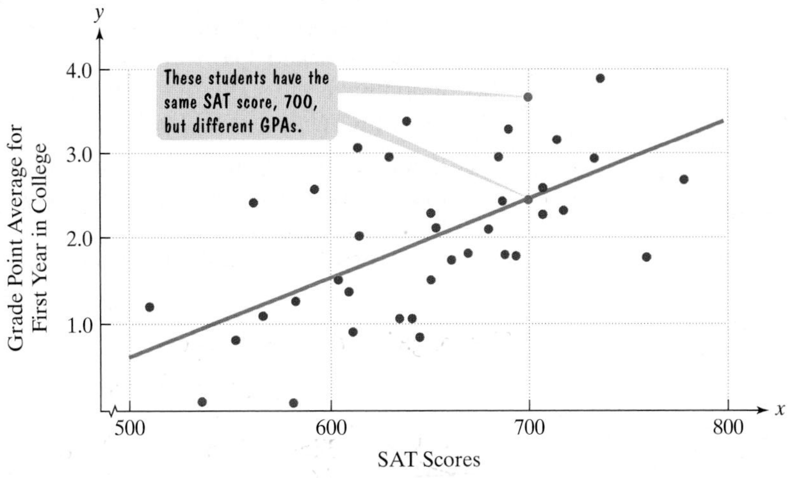


**Figure 2.20**

A relation in which each member of the domain corresponds to exactly one member of the range is a **function**. The relation in Figure 2.20, the SAT–grade point average scatter plot, is not a function because at least one member of the domain corresponds to two members of the range.

$$(700,\ 2.4) \qquad (700,\ 3.7)$$

The member of the domain, 700, corresponds to two members of the range, 2.4 and 3.7. Because a function is a relation in which **no two ordered pairs have the same first component and different second components**, the ordered pairs (700, 2.4) and (700, 3.7) are not ordered pairs of a function.

Same first components

$$(700,\ 2.4) \qquad (700,\ 3.7)$$

Different second components

### Definition of a Function

A **function** is a correspondence between two sets $X$ and $Y$ that assigns to each element $x$ of set $X$ exactly one element $y$ of set $Y$. For each element $x$ in $X$, the corresponding element $y$ in $Y$ is called the **value** of the function at $x$. The set $X$ is called the **domain** of the function, and the set of all function values, $Y$, is called the **range** of the function.

**2** Determine whether a relation is a function.

## EXAMPLE 2 Determining Whether a Relation is a Function

Determine whether each relation is a function.

**a.** $\{(1,6),(2,6),(3,8),(4,9)\}$ **b.** $\{(6,1),(6,2),(8,3),(9,4)\}$

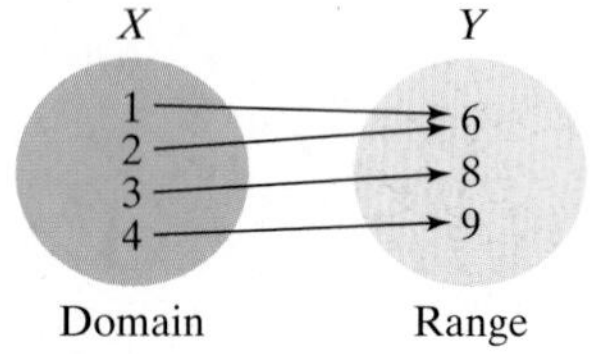


**(a)**

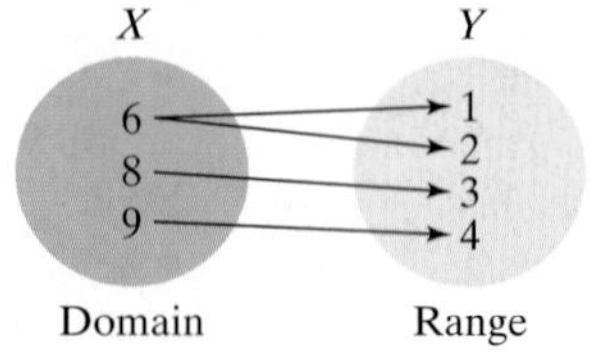


**(b)**

**Figure 2.21**

**Solution** We begin by making a figure for each relation that shows set $X$, the domain, and set $Y$, the range, shown in Figure 2.21.

**a.** Figure 2.21(a) shows that every element in the domain corresponds to exactly one element in the range. The element 1 in the domain corresponds to the element 6 in the range. Furthermore, 2 corresponds to 6, 3 corresponds to 8, and 4 corresponds to 9. No two ordered pairs in the given relation have the same first component and different second components. Thus, the relation is a function.

**b.** Figure 2.21(b) shows that 6 corresponds to both 1 and 2. If any element in the domain corresponds to more than one element in the range, the relation is not a function. This relation is not a function; two ordered pairs have the same first component and different second components.

Same first components

(6, 1) (6, 2)

Different second components

### Study Tip

The word *range* can mean many things, from a chain of mountains to a cooking stove. For functions, it means the set of all function values. For graphing utilities, it means the setting used for the viewing rectangle. Try not to confuse these meanings.

Look at Figure 2.21 again. The fact that 1 and 2 in the domain have the same image, 6, in the range does not violate the definition of a function. A function can have two different first components with the same second component. By contrast, a relation is not a function when two different ordered pairs have the same first component and different second components. Thus, the relation in Example 2(b) is not a function.

**Check Point 2** Determine whether each relation is a function.

**a.** $\{(1,2),(3,4),(5,6),(5,8)\}$

**b.** $\{(1,2),(3,4),(6,5),(8,5)\}$

## Functions as Equations

Functions are usually given in terms of equations rather than as sets of ordered pairs. Earlier we noted that, for a particular snake, its total body length is a function of its tail length. The function is modeled by the equation

$$y = 7.44x + 8.6.$$

The variable $x$ represents the snake's tail length, in millimeters. The variable $y$ represents the snake's total body length, in millimeters. The variable $y$ is a function of the variable $x$. For each value of $x$, there is one and only one value of $y$. The variable $x$ is called the **independent variable** because it can be assigned any value from the domain. Thus, $x$ can be assigned any positive number representing the snake's tail length. The variable $y$ is called the **dependent variable** because its value depends on $x$. A snake's total body length depends on its tail length. The value of the dependent variable, $y$, is calculated after selecting a value for the independent variable, $x$.

**3** Determine whether an equation represents a function.

We have seen that not every set of ordered pairs defines a function. Similarly, not all equations with the variables $x$ and $y$ define a function. If an equation is solved for $y$ and more than one value of $y$ can be obtained for a given $x$, then the equation does not define $y$ as a function of $x$.

## EXAMPLE 3 Determining Whether an Equation Represents a Function

Determine whether each equation defines $y$ as a function of $x$.

**a.** $x^2 + y = 4$ **b.** $x^2 + y^2 = 4$

**Solution** Solve each equation for $y$ in terms of $x$. If two or more values of $y$ can be obtained for a given $x$, the equation is not a function.

**a.**

$$x^2 + y = 4 \quad \text{This is the given equation.}$$
$$x^2 + y - x^2 = 4 - x^2 \quad \text{Solve for } y \text{ by subtracting } x^2 \text{ from both sides.}$$
$$y = 4 - x^2 \quad \text{Simplify.}$$

From this last equation we can see that for each value of $x$, there is one and only one value of $y$. For example, if $x = 1$, then $y = 4 - 1^2 = 3$. The equation defines $y$ as a function of $x$.

**b.**

$$x^2 + y^2 = 4 \quad \text{This given equation describes a circle.}$$
$$x^2 + y^2 - x^2 = 4 - x^2 \quad \text{Isolate } y^2 \text{ by subtracting } x^2 \text{ from both sides.}$$
$$y^2 = 4 - x^2 \quad \text{Simplify.}$$
$$y = \pm\sqrt{4 - x^2} \quad \text{Apply the square root method.}$$

The $\pm$ in this last equation shows that for certain values of $x$ (all values between $-2$ and 2), there are two values of $y$. For example, if $x = 1$, then $y = \pm\sqrt{4 - 1^2} = \pm\sqrt{3}$. For this reason, the equation does not define $y$ as a function of $x$.

**Check Point 3** Solve each equation for $y$ and then determine whether the equation defines $y$ as a function of $x$.

**a.** $2x + y = 6$ **b.** $x^2 + y^2 = 1$

**4** Evaluate a function.

## Function Notation

When an equation represents a function, the function is often named by a letter such as $f, g, h, F, G,$ or $H$. Any letter can be used to name a function. Suppose that $f$ names a function. Think of the domain as the set of the function's inputs and the range as the set of the function's outputs. As shown in Figure 2.22, the input is represented by $x$ and the output by $f(x)$. The special notation $\boldsymbol{f(x)}$, read "$f$ of $x$" or "$f$ at $x$," represents the **value of the function at the number $\boldsymbol{x}$**.

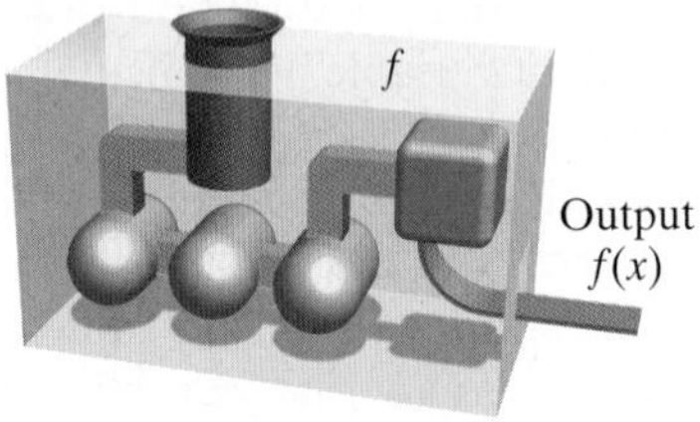


**Figure 2.22** A function as a machine with inputs and outputs

Let's make this clearer by considering a specific example. We know that the equation $y = 4 - x^2$ defines $y$ as a function of $x$. We'll name the function $f$. Now, we can apply our new function notation.

| Input | Output | Equation | |
|---|---|---|---|
| $x$ | $f(x)$ | $f(x) = 4 - x^2$ | We read this equation as "f of x equals $4 - x^2$." |

Suppose that we are interested in finding $f(3)$, the function's output when the input is 3. To find the value of the function at 3, we substitute 3 for $x$. We are **evaluating the function** at 3.

$$f(x) = 4 - x^2 \quad \text{This is the given function.}$$

$$f(3) = 4 - 3^2 \quad \text{The input is 3.}$$

$$= 4 - 9$$

$$= -5$$

**Study Tip**

The notation $f(x)$ does *not* mean "$f$ times $x$." The notation describes the value of the function at $x$.

The statement $f(3) = -5$ tells us that the value of the function at 3 is $-5$. When the function's input is 3, its output is $-5$. To find other function values, such as $f(-2), f(5),$ or $f(7)$, substitute the specified input values for $x$ into the function's equation.

If a function is named $f$ and $x$ represents the independent variable, the notation $f(x)$ corresponds to the $y$-value for a given $x$. Thus,

$$f(x) = 4 - x^2 \quad \text{and} \quad y = 4 - x^2$$

define the same function. This function may be written as

$$y = f(x) = 4 - x^2.$$

### EXAMPLE 4 Evaluating a Function

If $f(x) = x^2 + 3x + 5$, evaluate:

**a.** $f(2)$ **b.** $f(x + 3)$ **c.** $f(-x)$

**Solution** We substitute 2, $x + 3$, and $-x$ for $x$ in the definition of $f$. When replacing $x$ with a variable or an algebraic expression, you might find it helpful to think of the function's equation as

$$f(x) = x^2 + 3x + 5.$$

**a.** We find $f(2)$ by substituting 2 for $x$ in the equation.

$$f(2) = 2^2 + 3 \cdot 2 + 5 = 4 + 6 + 5 = 15$$

Thus, $f(2) = 15$.

**b.** We find $f(x + 3)$ by substituting $x + 3$ for $x$ in the equation.

$$f(x + 3) = (x + 3)^2 + 3(x + 3) + 5$$

Equivalently,

$$f(x + 3) = (x + 3)^2 + 3(x + 3) + 5$$
$$= x^2 + 6x + 9 + 3x + 9 + 5$$

Square $x + 3$ using $(A + B)^2 = A^2 + 2AB + B^2$. Distribute 3 throughout the parentheses.

$$= x^2 + 9x + 23.$$

Combine like terms.

**c.** We find $f(-x)$ by substituting $-x$ for $x$ in the equation.

$$f(-x) = (-x)^2 + 3(-x) + 5$$

Equivalently,

$$f(-x) = (-x)^2 + 3(-x) + 5$$
$$= x^2 - 3x + 5.$$

**Discovery**

Using $f(x) = x^2 + 3x + 5$ and the answers in parts (b) and (c):

1. Is $f(x + 3)$ equal to $f(x) + f(3)$?
2. Is $f(-x)$ equal to $-f(x)$?

**Check Point 4** If $f(x) = x^2 - 2x + 7$, evaluate:

**a.** $f(-5)$ **b.** $f(x + 4)$ **c.** $f(-x)$

**5** Find and simplify a function's difference quotient.

## Functions and Difference Quotients

**Definition of the Difference Quotient**

The expression

$$\frac{f(x + h) - f(x)}{h}$$

for $h \neq 0$ is called the **difference quotient.**

In the next section, we will see how the difference quotient is used to study the average rate of change of a function. In calculus, you will learn to use mathematics to describe the fluidity of the changing universe. The difference quotient plays an important role in this process. For now, the difference quotient gives us a chance to practice evaluating functions at expressions that involve more than one variable.

## EXAMPLE 5 Evaluating and Simplifying a Difference Quotient

If $f(x) = x^2 + 3x + 5$, find and simplify:

**a.** $f(x + h)$ **b.** $\frac{f(x+h) - f(x)}{h}$, $h \neq 0$.

### Solution

**a.** We find $f(x + h)$ by replacing $x$ with $x + h$ each time that $x$ appears in the equation.

$$f(x) = x^2 + 3x + 5$$

Replace x with x + h. | Replace x with x + h. | Replace x with x + h. | Copy the 5. There is no x in this term.

$$f(x+h) = (x+h)^2 + 3(x+h) + 5$$
$$= x^2 + 2xh + h^2 + 3x + 3h + 5$$

**b.** Using our result from part (a), we obtain the following:

This is $f(x+h)$ from part (a). This is $f(x)$ from the given equation.

$$\frac{f(x+h) - f(x)}{h} = \frac{x^2 + 2xh + h^2 + 3x + 3h + 5 - (x^2 + 3x + 5)}{h}$$

$$= \frac{x^2 + 2xh + h^2 + 3x + 3h + 5 - x^2 - 3x - 5}{h}$$ Remove parentheses and change the sign of each term in the parentheses.

$$= \frac{(x^2 - x^2) + (3x - 3x) + (5 - 5) + 2xh + h^2 + 3h}{h}$$ Group like terms.

$$= \frac{2xh + h^2 + 3h}{h}$$ Simplify.

$$= \frac{h(2x + h + 3)}{h}$$ Factor $h$ from the numerator.

$$= 2x + h + 3, h \neq 0$$ Cancel identical factors of $h$ in the numerator and denominator.

**Check Point 5** If $f(x) = x^2 - 7x + 3$, find and simplify:

**a.** $f(x + h)$ **b.** $\frac{f(x+h) - f(x)}{h}$, $h \neq 0$.

**6** Understand and use piecewise functions.

## Piecewise Functions

The early part of the twentieth century was the golden age of immigration in America. More than 13 million people migrated to the United States between 1900 and 1914. By 1910, foreign-born residents accounted for 15% of the total U.S. population. The graph in Figure 2.23 on the next page shows the percentage of Americans who were foreign born throughout the twentieth century.

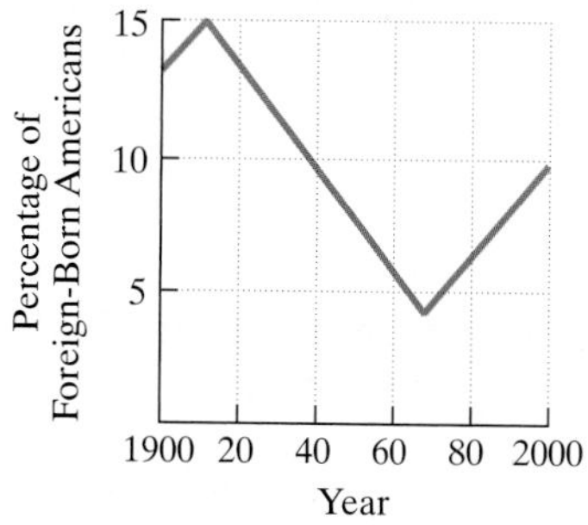

*Source*: U.S. Census Bureau

**Figure 2.23**

We can model the data from 1910 through 2000 with two functions, one from 1910 through 1970, years in which the percentage was decreasing, and one from 1970 through 2000, years in which the percentage was increasing. These two trends can be approximated by the function

$$P(t) = \begin{cases} -\dfrac{11}{60}t + 15 & \text{if } 0 \le t < 60 \\ \dfrac{1}{5}t - 8 & \text{if } 60 \le t \le 90 \end{cases}$$

in which $t$ represents the number of years after 1910 and $P(t)$ is the percentage of foreign-born Americans. A function such as this that is defined by two (or more) equations over a specified domain is called a **piecewise function**.

## EXAMPLE 6 Evaluating a Piecewise Function

Use the function $P(t)$, described previously, to find and interpret:

**a.** $P(30)$ **b.** $P(80)$

### Solution

**a.** To find $P(30)$, we let $t = 30$. Because 30 is less than 60, we use the first line of the piecewise function.

$$P(t) = -\tfrac{11}{60}t + 15 \quad \text{This is the function's equation for } 0 \le t < 60.$$

$$P(30) = -\tfrac{11}{60} \cdot 30 + 15 \quad \text{Replace } t \text{ with } 60.$$

$$= 9.5$$

This means that 30 years after 1910, in 1940, 9.5% of Americans were foreign born.

**b.** To find $P(80)$, we let $t = 80$. Because 80 is between 60 and 90, we use the second line of the piecewise function.

$$P(t) = \frac{1}{5}t - 8 \quad \text{This is the function's equation for } 60 \le t \le 90.$$

$$P(80) = \tfrac{1}{5} \cdot 80 - 8 \quad \text{Replace } t \text{ with } 80.$$

$$= 8$$

This means that 80 years after 1910, in 1990, 8% of Americans were foreign born.

**Check Point 6** If $f(x) = \begin{cases} x^2 + 3 & \text{if } x < 0 \\ 5x + 3 & \text{if } x \ge 0 \end{cases}$, find:

**a.** $f(-5)$ **b.** $f(6)$

**7** Find the domain of a function.

## The Domain of a Function

Let's reconsider the function that models the percentage of foreign-born Americans $t$ years after 1910, up through and including 2000. The domain of this function is

$$\{0,\ 1,\ 2,\ 3,\ \ldots,\ 90\}.$$

0 years after 1910 is 1910.

3 years after 1910 is 1913.

90 years after 1910 brings the domain up to the year 2000.

Functions that model data often have their domains explicitly given along with the function's equation. However, for most functions, only an equation is given, and the domain is not specified. In cases like this, the domain of $f$ is the largest set of real numbers for which the value of $f(x)$ is a real number. For example, consider the function

$$f(x) = \frac{1}{x - 3}.$$

Because division by 0 is undefined (and not a real number), the denominator $x - 3$ cannot be 0. Thus, $x$ cannot equal 3. The domain of the function consists of all real numbers other than 3, represented by $\{x \mid x \neq 3\}$.

Just as the domain of a function must exclude real numbers that cause division by zero, it must also exclude real numbers that result in an even root of a negative number. For example, consider the function

$$g(x) = \sqrt{x}.$$

The equation tells us to take the square root of $x$. Because only nonnegative numbers have real square roots, the expression under the radical sign, $x$, must be greater than or equal to 0. The domain of $g$ is $\{x \mid x \geq 0\}$ or the interval $[0, \infty)$.

**Finding a Function's Domain**

If a function $f$ does not model data or verbal conditions, its domain is the largest set of real numbers for which the value of $f(x)$ is a real number. Exclude from a function's domain real numbers that cause division by zero and real numbers that result in an even root of a negative number.

## EXAMPLE 7 Finding the Domain of a Function

Find the domain of each function:

**a.** $f(x) = x^2 - 7x$ **b.** $g(x) = \dfrac{6x}{x^2 - 9}$ **c.** $h(x) = \sqrt{3x + 12}$

**Solution**

**a.** The function $f(x) = x^2 - 7x$ contains neither division nor an even root. The domain of $f$ is the set of all real numbers.

**b.** The function $g(x) = \dfrac{6x}{x^2 - 9}$ contains division. Because division by 0 is undefined, we must exclude from the domain values of $x$ that cause $x^2 - 9$ to be 0. Thus, $x$ cannot equal $-3$ or 3. The domain of function $g$ is $\{x \mid x \neq -3, x \neq 3\}$.

**c.** The function $h(x) = \sqrt{3x + 12}$ contains an even root. Because only nonnegative numbers have real square roots, the quantity under the radical sign, $3x + 12$, must be greater than or equal to 0.

$$3x + 12 \geq 0$$
$$3x \geq -12$$
$$x \geq -4$$

The domain of $h$ is $\{x \mid x \geq -4\}$ or the interval $[-4, \infty)$.

### Technology

You can graph a function and visually determine its domain. For example, $h(x) = \sqrt{3x + 12}$, or $y = \sqrt{3x + 12}$, appears only for $x \geq -4$, verifying $[-4, \infty)$ as the domain.

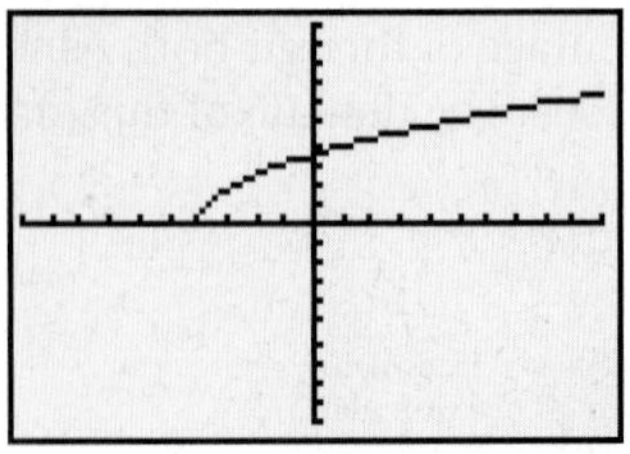

**Check Point 7** Find the domain of each function:

**a.** $f(x) = x^2 + 3x - 17$ **b.** $g(x) = \frac{5x}{x^2 - 49}$

**c.** $h(x) = \sqrt{9x - 27}$

## EXERCISE SET 2.3

### Practice Exercises

*In Exercises 1–8, determine whether each relation is a function. Give the domain and range for each relation.*

**1.** $\{(1, 2), (3, 4), (5, 5)\}$ **2.** $\{(4, 5), (6, 7), (8, 8)\}$

**3.** $\{(3, 4), (3, 5), (4, 4), (4, 5)\}$

**4.** $\{(5, 6), (5, 7)\ (6, 6), (6, 7)\}$

**5.** $\{(-3, -3), (-2, -2), (-1, -1), (0, 0)\}$

**6.** $\{(-7, -7), (-5, -5), (-3, -3), (0, 0)\}$

**7.** $\{(1, 4), (1, 5), (1, 6)\}$ **8.** $\{(4, 1), (5, 1), (6, 1)\}$

*In Exercises 9–20, determine whether each equation defines y as a function of x.*

**9.** $x + y = 16$ **10.** $x + y = 25$

**11.** $x^2 + y = 16$ **12.** $x^2 + y = 25$

**13.** $x^2 + y^2 = 16$ **14.** $x^2 + y^2 = 25$

**15.** $x = y^2$ **16.** $4x = y^2$

**17.** $y = \sqrt{x + 4}$ **18.** $y = -\sqrt{x + 4}$

**19.** $x + y^3 = 8$ **20.** $x + y^3 = 27$

*In Exercises 21–32, evaluate each function at the given values of the independent variable and simplify.*

**21.** $f(x) = 4x + 5$
**a.** $f(6)$ **b.** $f(x + 1)$ **c.** $f(-x)$

**22.** $f(x) = 3x + 7$
**a.** $f(4)$ **b.** $f(x + 1)$ **c.** $f(-x)$

**23.** $g(x) = x^2 + 2x + 3$
**a.** $g(-1)$ **b.** $g(x + 5)$ **c.** $g(-x)$

**24.** $g(x) = x^2 - 10x - 3$
**a.** $g(-1)$ **b.** $g(x + 2)$ **c.** $g(-x)$

**25.** $h(x) = x^4 - x^2 + 1$
**a.** $h(2)$ **b.** $h(-1)$
**c.** $h(-x)$ **d.** $h(3a)$

**26.** $h(x) = x^3 - x + 1$
**a.** $h(3)$ **b.** $h(-2)$
**c.** $h(-x)$ **d.** $h(3a)$

**27.** $f(r) = \sqrt{r + 6} + 3$
**a.** $f(-6)$ **b.** $f(10)$ **c.** $f(x - 6)$

**28.** $f(r) = \sqrt{25 - r} - 6$
**a.** $f(16)$ **b.** $f(-24)$ **c.** $f(25 - 2x)$

**29.** $f(x) = \frac{4x^2 - 1}{x^2}$
**a.** $f(2)$ **b.** $f(-2)$ **c.** $f(-x)$

**30.** $f(x) = \frac{4x^3 + 1}{x^3}$
**a.** $f(2)$ **b.** $f(-2)$ **c.** $f(-x)$

**31.** $f(x) = \frac{x}{|x|}$
**a.** $f(6)$ **b.** $f(-6)$ **c.** $f(r^2)$

**32.** $f(x) = \frac{|x + 3|}{x + 3}$
**a.** $f(5)$ **b.** $f(-5)$ **c.** $f(-9 - x)$

*In Exercises 33–44, find and simplify the difference quotient*

$$\frac{f(x + h) - f(x)}{h}, \quad h \neq 0$$

*for the given function.*

**33.** $f(x) = 3x + 7$ **34.** $f(x) = 6x + 1$

**35.** $f(x) = x^2$ **36.** $f(x) = 2x^2$

**37.** $f(x) = x^2 - 4x + 3$ **38.** $f(x) = x^2 - 5x + 8$

**39.** $f(x) = 6$ **40.** $f(x) = 7$

**41.** $f(x) = \frac{1}{x}$ **42.** $f(x) = \frac{1}{2x}$

**43.** $f(x) = \sqrt{x}$ Simplify the difference quotient by rationalizing the numerator.

**44.** $f(x) = \sqrt{x + 1}$ Simplify the difference quotient by rationalizing the numerator.

*In Exercises 45–50, evaluate each piecewise function at the given values of the independent variable.*

**45.** $f(x) = \begin{cases} 3x + 5 & \text{if } x < 0 \\ 4x + 7 & \text{if } x \geq 0 \end{cases}$
**a.** $f(-2)$ **b.** $f(0)$ **c.** $f(3)$

**46.** $f(x) = \begin{cases} 6x - 1 & \text{if } x < 0 \\ 7x + 3 & \text{if } x \geq 0 \end{cases}$
**a.** $f(-3)$ **b.** $f(0)$ **c.** $f(4)$

**47.** $g(x) = \begin{cases} x + 3 & \text{if } x \geq -3 \\ -(x + 3) & \text{if } x < -3 \end{cases}$
**a.** $g(0)$ **b.** $g(-6)$ **c.** $g(-3)$

**48.** $g(x) = \begin{cases} x + 5 & \text{if } x \geq -5 \\ -(x + 5) & \text{if } x < -5 \end{cases}$
**a.** $g(0)$ **b.** $g(-6)$ **c.** $g(-5)$

49. $h(x) = \begin{cases} \dfrac{x^2 - 9}{x - 3} & \text{if } x \neq 3 \\ 6 & \text{if } x = 3 \end{cases}$

**a.** $h(5)$ **b.** $h(0)$ **c.** $h(3)$

50. $h(x) = \begin{cases} \dfrac{x^2 - 25}{x - 5} & \text{if } x \neq 5 \\ 10 & \text{if } x = 5 \end{cases}$

**a.** $h(7)$ **b.** $h(0)$ **c.** $h(5)$

*In Exercises 51–72, find the domain of each function.*

**51.** $f(x) = 4x^2 - 3x + 1$ **52.** $f(x) = 8x^2 - 5x + 2$

**53.** $g(x) = \dfrac{3}{x - 4}$ **54.** $g(x) = \dfrac{2}{x + 5}$

**55.** $h(x) = \dfrac{7x}{x^2 - 16}$ **56.** $h(x) = \dfrac{12x}{x^2 - 36}$

**57.** $f(x) = \dfrac{2}{(x + 3)(x - 7)}$ **58.** $f(x) = \dfrac{15}{(x + 8)(x - 3)}$

**59.** $H(r) = \dfrac{4}{r^2 + 11r + 24}$ **60.** $H(r) = \dfrac{5}{6r^2 + r - 2}$

**61.** $f(t) = \dfrac{3}{t^2 + 4}$ **62.** $f(t) = \dfrac{5}{t^2 + 9}$

**63.** $f(x) = \sqrt{x - 3}$ **64.** $f(x) = \sqrt{x + 2}$

**65.** $f(x) = \dfrac{1}{\sqrt{x - 3}}$ **66.** $f(x) = \dfrac{1}{\sqrt{x + 2}}$

**67.** $g(x) = \sqrt{5x + 35}$ **68.** $g(x) = \sqrt{7x - 70}$

**69.** $f(x) = \sqrt{24 - 2x}$ **70.** $f(x) = \sqrt{84 - 6x}$

**71.** $f(x) = \sqrt{x^2 - 5x - 14}$ **72.** $f(x) = \sqrt{x^2 - 5x - 24}$

## Application Exercises

*It seems that Phideau's medical bills are costing us an arm and a paw. The graph shows veterinary costs, in billions of dollars, for dogs and cats in five selected years. Use the graph to solve Exercises 73–74.*

**Veterinary Costs in the U.S.**

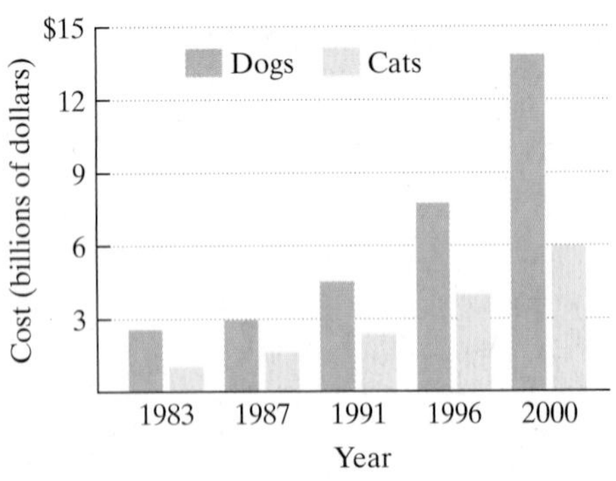


*Source*: American Veterinary Medical Association

**73.** Write five ordered pairs that approximate veterinary costs for dogs for the years shown. Find the domain and the range of the relation. Is this relation a function? Explain your answer.

**74.** Write five ordered pairs that approximate veterinary costs for cats for the years shown. Find the domain and the range of the relation. Is this relation a function? Explain your answer.

*The number of women enrolled in U.S. colleges can be modeled by the function $f(x) = 0.07x + 4.1$, where $x$ represents the number of years since 1984 and $f(x)$ represents enrollment in millions. The number of men enrolled in U.S. colleges can be modeled by the function $g(x) = 0.01x + 3.9$, where $x$ represents the number of years since 1984 and $g(x)$ represents enrollment, in millions. In Exercises 75–78, use these functions to find and interpret:*

**75.** $f(16)$ **76.** $g(16)$

**77.** $f(20) - g(20)$ **78.** $f(25) - g(25)$

**Enrollment in U.S. Colleges**

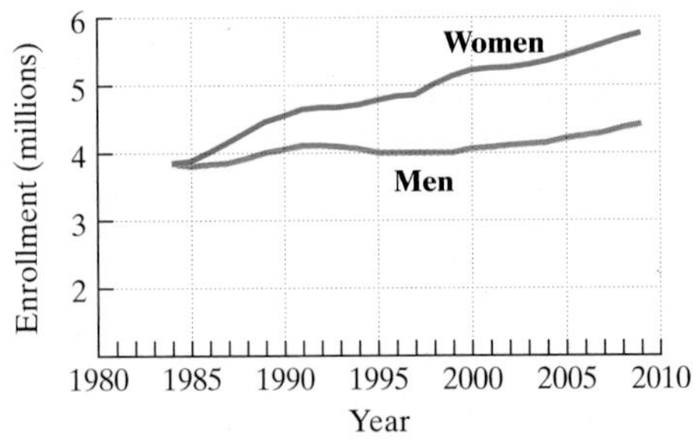


*Source*: Department of Education

*The number of lawyers in the United States can be modeled by the function*

$$f(x) = \begin{cases} 6.5x + 200 & \text{if } 0 \le x < 23 \\ 26.2x - 252 & \text{if } x \ge 23 \end{cases}$$

*where $x$ represents the number of years since 1951 and $f(x)$ represents the number of lawyers, in thousands. In Exercises 79–82, use this function to find and interpret:*

**79.** $f(0)$ **80.** $f(10)$

**81.** $f(50)$ **82.** $f(60)$

**Number of U.S. Lawyers**

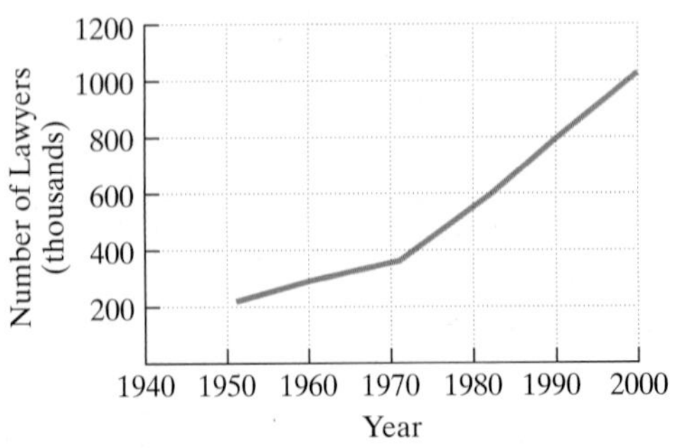


*Source*: Hudson Institute

**83.** On the average, infant girls weigh 7 pounds at birth and gain 1.5 pounds each month for the first six months. The function $f(x) = 1.5x + 7$ models this, where $x$ represents the infant's age, in months, $x \le 6$, and $f(x)$ describes the baby's weight, in pounds. Use the function to find $f(0)$, $f(2)$, $f(4)$, and $f(6)$. Describe what these results mean. Identify each of your computations as an appropriate point on the graph at the top of the next column.

**Average Weight for Infant Girls**

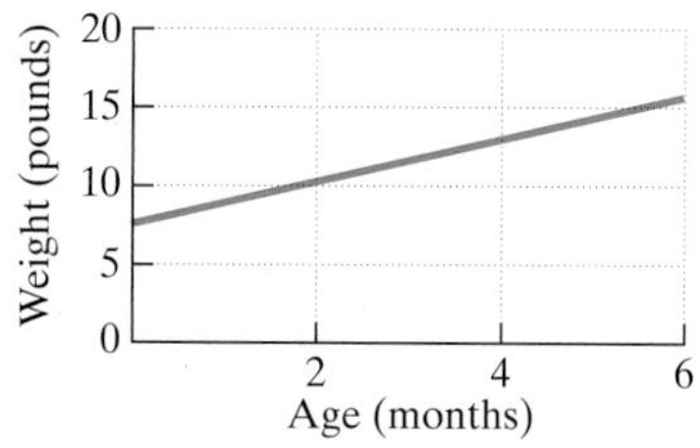


*We're eating more and getting heavier. The number of calories consumed each day per person in the United States can be modeled by*

$$f(x) = 0.89x^2 - 1.93x + 3306.27$$

*where $x$ is the number of years since 1974 and $f(x)$ represents the number of calories consumed each day per person. In Exercises 84–87, use this function to find and interpret:*

**84.** $f(0)$ **85.** $f(10)$

**86.** $f(15) - f(0)$ **87.** $f(15) - f(10)$

**Getting Heavier: Percentage of U.S. Men and Women Overweight**

| Men | 1999 | 2025 |
|---|---|---|
| Overweight | 62% | 73% |
| Obese | 19% | 37% |
| **Women** | | |
| Overweight | 47% | 75% |
| Obese | 19% | 35% |

*Source*: Beth Israel Medical Center

**88.** During a particular year, the taxes owed by a married person filing separately with an adjusted gross income of $x$ dollars is given by the piecewise function

$$T(x) = \begin{cases} 0.15x & \text{if } 0 \le x < 17{,}900 \\ 0.28(x - 17{,}900) + 2685 & \text{if } 17{,}900 \le x < 43{,}250 \\ 0.31(x - 43{,}250) + 9783 & \text{if } x \ge 43{,}250 \end{cases}$$

Find and interpret $T(70{,}000) - T(40{,}000)$.

**89.** The function

$$f(x) = \begin{cases} 0.0005x^2 + 0.025x + 8.8 & \text{if } 0 \le x < 30 \\ 0.0202x^2 - 1.58x + 39.2 & \text{if } x \ge 30 \end{cases}$$

models the average number of miles (in thousands) driven per car in the United States, per year, $x$ years after 1940. Find and interpret

**a.** $f(15)$ **b.** $f(50)$

**90.** A car was purchased for \$22,500. The value of the car decreases by \$3200 per year for the first seven years. Write a function $V$ that describes the value of the car after $x$ years, where $0 \le x \le 7$. Then find and interpret $V(3)$.

**91.** A car was purchased for \$17,900. The value of the car decreases by \$2100 per year for the first six years. Write a function $V$ that describes the value of the car after $x$ years, where $0 \le x \le 6$. Then find and interpret $V(4)$.

## Writing in Mathematics

**92.** If a relation is represented by a set of ordered pairs, explain how to determine whether the relation is a function.

**93.** How do you determine if an equation in $x$ and $y$ defines $y$ as a function of $x$?

**94.** A student in introductory algebra hears that functions are studied in subsequent algebra courses. The student asks you what a function is. Provide the student with a clear, relatively concise response.

**95.** Describe one advantage of using $f(x)$ rather than $y$ in a function's equation.

**96.** Explain how to find the difference quotient, $\frac{f(x+h) - f(x)}{h}$, if a function's equation is given.

**97.** What is a piecewise function?

**98.** How is the domain of a function determined?

**99.** For people filing a single return, federal income tax is a function of adjusted gross income because for each value of adjusted gross income there is a specific tax to be paid. On the other hand, the price of a house is not a function of the lot size on which the house sits because houses on same-sized lots can sell for many different prices.

**a.** Describe an everyday situation between variables that is a function.

**b.** Describe an everyday situation between variables that is not a function.

## Technology Exercises

*Use a graphing utility to find the domain of each function in Exercises 100–102. Then verify your observation algebraically.*

**100.** $f(x) = \sqrt{x - 1}$ **101.** $g(x) = \sqrt{2x + 6}$

**102.** $h(x) = \sqrt{15 - 3x}$

**103.** Graph $y = 0.89x^2 - 1.93x + 3306.27$, the model for caloric consumption used in Exercises 84–87, in a $[0, 15, 1]$ by $[3200, 3500, 15]$ viewing rectangle. Describe one bit of information revealed by the graph of the function that is not obvious by looking at its equation.

## Critical Thinking Exercises

**104.** Write a function defined by an equation in $x$ whose domain is $\{x \mid x \neq -4, x \neq 11\}$.

**105.** Write a function defined by an equation in $x$ whose domain is $[-6, \infty)$.

**106.** Give an example of an equation that does not define $y$ as a function of $x$ but that does define $x$ as a function of $y$.

**107.** If $f(x) = ax^2 + bx + c$ and $r_1 = \frac{-b + \sqrt{b^2 - 4ac}}{2a}$, find $f(r_1)$ without doing any algebra and explain how you arrived at your result.

## Group Exercise

**108.** Almanacs, newspapers, magazines, and the Internet contain bar graphs and line graphs that describe how things are changing over time. For example, the graph in Figure 2.18 on page 191 shows how mobile-phone bills are changing over time. Find a bar or line graph showing yearly changes that you find intriguing. Describe to the group what interests you about this data. The group should select their two favorite graphs. For each graph selected:

**a.** Rewrite the data so that they are presented as a relation in the form of a set of ordered pairs.

**b.** Determine whether the relation in part (a) is a function. Explain why the relation is a function, or why it is not.

# SECTION 2.4 *Graphs of Functions*

## Objectives

1. Graph functions by plotting points.
2. Obtain information about a function from its graph.
3. Use the vertical line test to identify functions.
4. Identify intervals on which a function increases, decreases, or is constant.
5. Find average rate of change and average velocity.
6. Identify even or odd functions and recognize their symmetries.
7. Recognize graphs of common functions.
8. Graph step functions.
9. Obtain information from graphs of functions in applied situations.

Have you ever seen a gas-guzzling car from the 1950s, with its huge fins and overstated design? The worst year for automobile fuel efficiency was 1958, when cars averaged a dismal 12.4 miles per gallon. We ended the last section with a function that modeled automobile fuel efficiency over time. If we graph the function's equation, we will get a much better idea of the relationship between time and fuel efficiency. In this section we will learn how to use the graph of a function to obtain useful information about the function.

## Graphs of Functions

A graph enables us to visualize a function's behavior. The graph shows the relationship between the function's two variables more clearly than the function's equation does. The **graph of a function** is the graph of its ordered pairs. For example, the graph of $f(x) = \sqrt{x}$ is the set of points $(x, y)$ in the rectangular coordinate system satisfying the equation $y = \sqrt{x}$. Thus, one way to graph a function is by plotting several of its ordered pairs and drawing a line or smooth curve through them. With the function's graph, we can picture its domain on the $x$-axis and its range on the $y$-axis. Our first example illustrates how this is done.

**1** Graph functions by plotting points.

### EXAMPLE 1 Graphing a Function by Plotting Points

Graph $f(x) = x^2 + 1$. To do so, use integer values of $x$ from the set $\{-3, -2, -1, 0, 1, 2, 3\}$ to obtain seven ordered pairs. Plot each ordered pair and draw a smooth curve through the points. Use the graph to specify the function's domain and range.

**Solution** The graph of $f(x) = x^2 + 1$ is, by definition, the graph of $y = x^2 + 1$. We begin by setting up a partial table of coordinates.

| $x$ | $f(x) = x^2 + 1$ | $(x, y)$ or $(x, f(x))$ |
|---|---|---|
| $-3$ | $f(-3) = (-3)^2 + 1 = 10$ | $(-3, 10)$ |
| $-2$ | $f(-2) = (-2)^2 + 1 = 5$ | $(-2, 5)$ |
| $-1$ | $f(-1) = (-1)^2 + 1 = 2$ | $(-1, 2)$ |
| 0 | $f(0) = 0^2 + 1 = 1$ | $(0, 1)$ |
| 1 | $f(1) = 1^2 + 1 = 2$ | $(1, 2)$ |
| 2 | $f(2) = 2^2 + 1 = 5$ | $(2, 5)$ |
| 3 | $f(3) = 3^2 + 1 = 10$ | $(3, 10)$ |

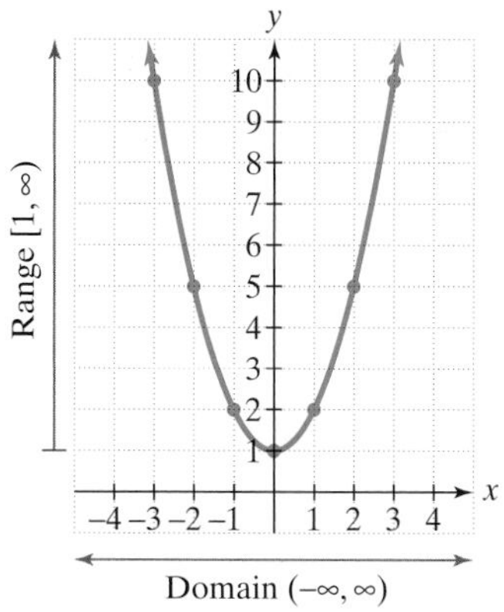


**Figure 2.24** The graph of $f(x) = x^2 + 1$

Now, we plot the seven points and draw a smooth curve through them, as shown in Figure 2.24. The graph of $f$ has a cuplike shape. The points on the graph of $f$ have $x$-coordinates that extend indefinitely far to the left and to the right. Thus, the domain consists of all real numbers, represented by $(-\infty, \infty)$. By contrast, the points on the graph have $y$-coordinates that start at 1 and extend indefinitely upward. Thus, the range consists of all real numbers greater than or equal to 1, represented by $[1, \infty)$.

**Check Point 1** Graph $f(x) = x^2 - 2$, using integers from $-3$ to 3 for $x$ in the partial table of coordinates. Use the graph to specify the function's domain and range.

### Technology

Does your graphing utility have a TABLE feature? If so, you can use it to create tables of coordinates for a function. You will need to enter the equation of the function and specify the starting value for $x$ TblStart and the increment between successive $x$-values ΔTbl. For the table of coordinates in Example 1, we start the table at $x = -3$ and increment by 1. Using the up- or down-arrow keys, you can scroll through the table and determine as many ordered pairs of the graph as desired.

**2** Obtain information about a function from its graph.

## Obtaining Information from Graphs

You can obtain information about a function from its graph. At the right or left of a graph, you will find closed dots, open dots, or arrows.

- A closed dot indicates that the graph does not extend beyond this point and the point belongs to the graph.
- An open dot indicates that the graph does not extend beyond this point and the point does not belong to the graph.
- An arrow indicates that the graph extends indefinitely in the direction in which the arrow points.

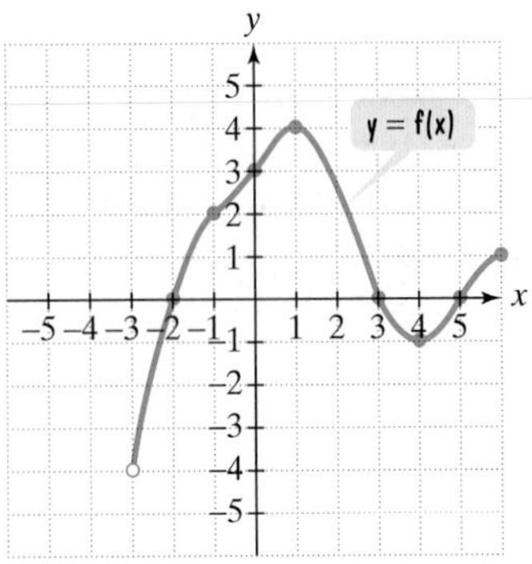


**Figure 2.25**

## EXAMPLE 2 Obtaining Information from a Function's Graph

Use the graph of the function $f$, shown in Figure 2.25, to answer the following questions.

**a.** What are the function values $f(-1)$ and $f(1)$?

**b.** What is the domain of $f$?

**c.** What is the range of $f$?

### Solution

**a.** Because $(-1, 2)$ is a point on the graph of $f$, the $y$-coordinate, 2, is the value of the function at the $x$-coordinate, $-1$. Thus, $f(-1) = 2$. Similarly, because $(1, 4)$ is also a point on the graph of $f$, this indicates that $f(1) = 4$.

**b.** The open dot on the left shows that $x = -3$ is not in the domain of $f$. By contrast, the closed dot on the right shows that $x = 6$ is in the domain of $f$. We determine the domain of $f$ by noticing that the points on the graph of $f$ have $x$-coordinates between $-3$, excluding $-3$, and 6, including 6. For each number $x$ between $-3$ and 6, there is a point $(x, f(x))$ on the graph. Thus, the domain of $f$ is $\{x \mid -3 < x \leq 6\}$ or the interval $(-3, 6]$.

**c.** The points on the graph all have $y$-coordinates between $-4$, not including $-4$, and 4, including 4. The graph does not extend below $y = -4$ or above $y = 4$. Thus, the range of $f$ is $\{y \mid -4 < y \leq 4\}$ or the interval $(-4, 4]$.

**Check Point 2** Use the graph of function $f$, shown below, to find $f(4)$, the domain, and the range.

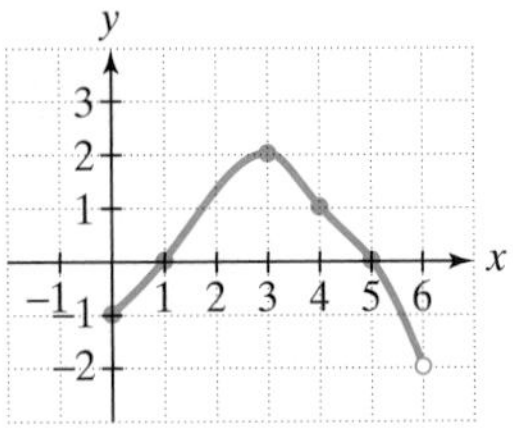

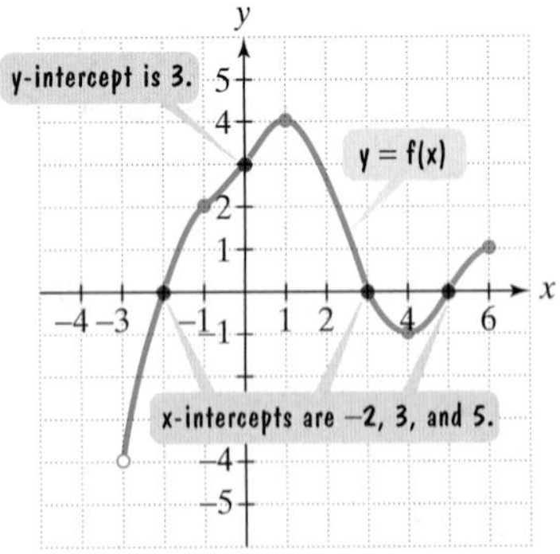


**Figure 2.26** Identifying intercepts

Figure 2.26 illustrates how we can identify a graph's intercepts. To find the $x$-intercepts, look for the points at which the graph crosses the $x$-axis. There are three such points: $(-2, 0)$, $(3, 0)$, and $(5, 0)$. Thus, the $x$-intercepts are $-2$, 3, and 5. We express this in function notation by writing $f(-2) = 0$, $f(3) = 0$, and $f(5) = 0$.

To find the $y$-intercept, look for the point at which the graph crosses the $y$-axis. This occurs at $(0, 3)$. Thus, the $y$-intercept is 3. We express this in function notation by writing $f(0) = 3$.

By the definition of a function, for each value of $x$ we can have at most one value for $y$. What does this mean in terms of intercepts? A function can have more than one $x$-intercept but at most one $y$-intercept.

**3** Use the vertical line test to identify functions.

## The Vertical Line Test

Not every graph in the rectangular coordinate system is the graph of a function. The definition of a function specifies that no value of $x$ can be paired with two or more different values of $y$. Consequently, if a graph contains two or more different points with the same first coordinate, the graph cannot represent a function. This is illustrated in Figure 2.27. Observe that points sharing a common first coordinate are vertically above or below each other.

This observation is the basis of a useful test for determining whether a graph defines $y$ as a function of $x$. The test is called the **vertical line test**.

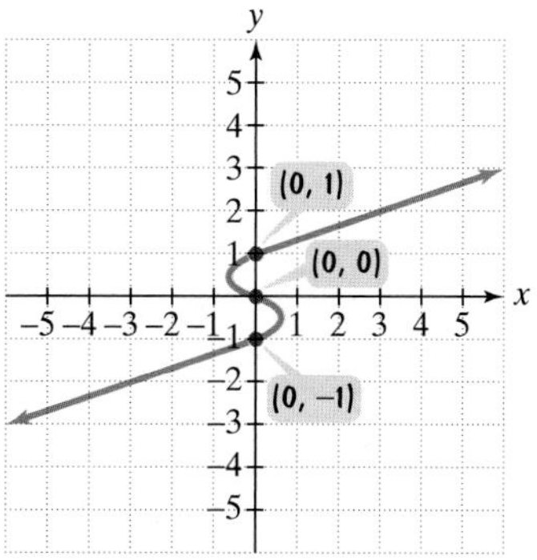


**Figure 2.27** $y$ is not a function of $x$ because 0 is paired with three values of $y$, namely, 1, 0, and $-1$.

> **The Vertical Line Test for Functions**
>
> If any vertical line intersects a graph in more than one point, the graph does not define $y$ as a function of $x$.

### EXAMPLE 3 Using the Vertical Line Test

Use the vertical line test to identify graphs in which $y$ is a function of $x$.

**a.**

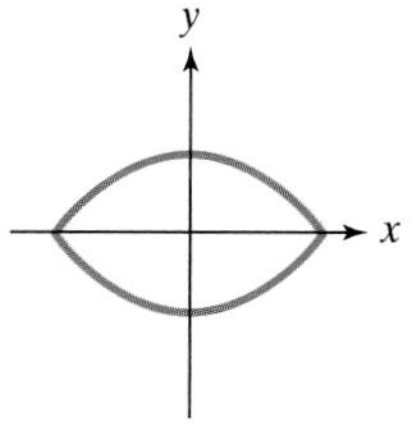

**b.**

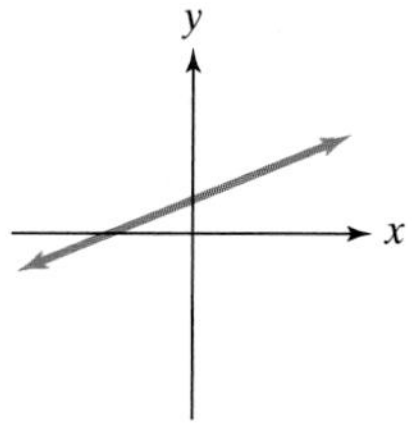

**c.**

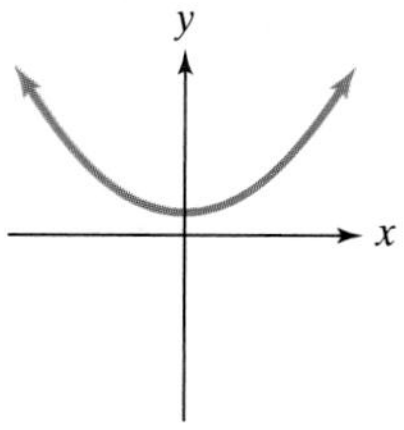

**d.**

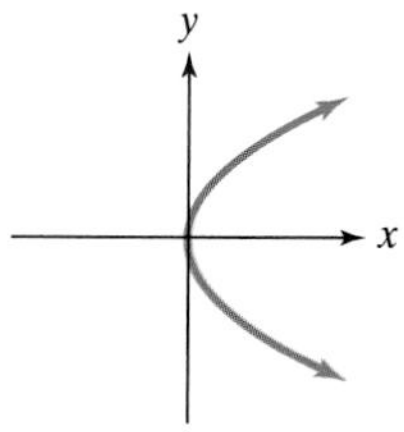

**Solution** $y$ is a function of $x$ for the graphs in (b) and (c).

**a.**

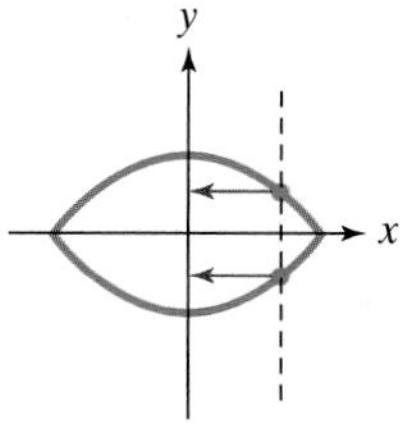

*y* **is not a function** of $x$. Two values of $y$ correspond to an $x$-value.

**b.**

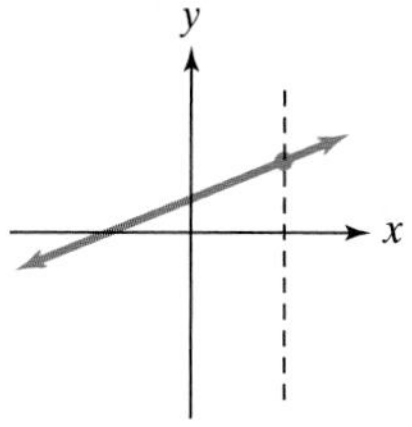

*y* **is a function** of $x$.

**c.**

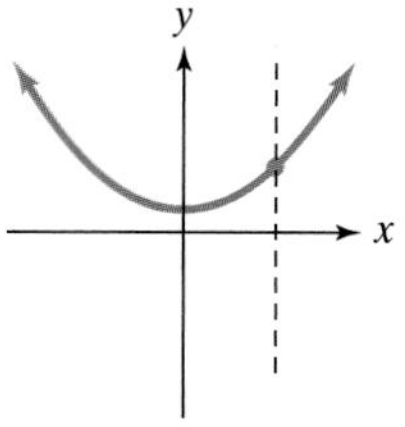

*y* **is a function** of $x$.

**d.**

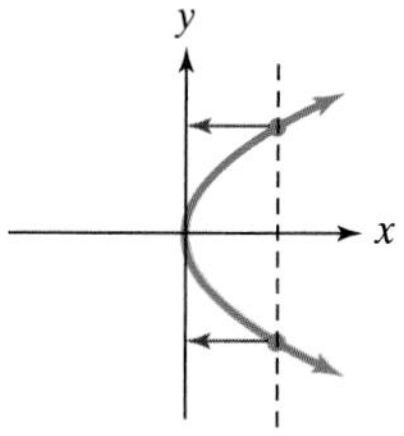

*y* **is not a function** of $x$. Two values of $y$ correspond to an $x$-value.

**Check Point 3** Use the vertical line test to identify graphs in which $y$ is a function of $x$.

**a.**

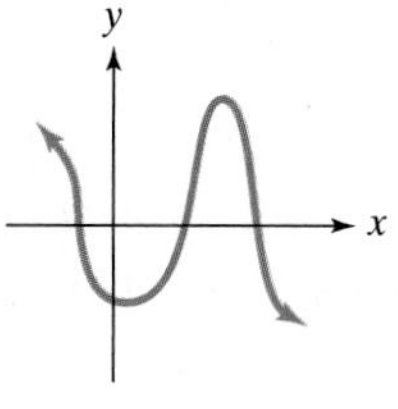

**b.**

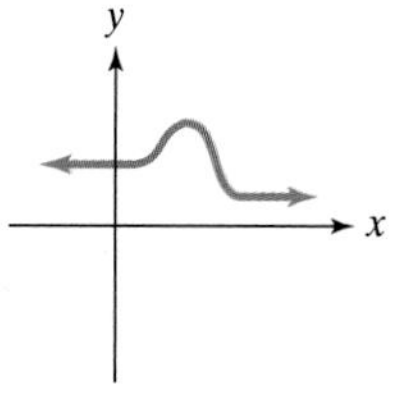

**c.**

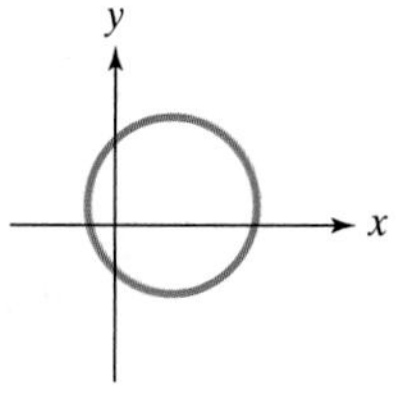

**4** Identify intervals on which a function increases, decreases, or is constant.

## Increasing and Decreasing Functions

A function $f$ is *increasing* when its graph rises, *decreasing* when its graph falls, and remains *constant* when its graph neither rises nor falls. We now provide a more algebraic description for these intuitive concepts.

### Increasing, Decreasing, and Constant Functions

1. A function is **increasing** on an interval if for any $x_1$ and $x_2$ in the interval, where $x_1 < x_2$, then $f(x_1) < f(x_2)$.
2. A function is **decreasing** on an interval if for any $x_1$ and $x_2$ in the interval, where $x_1 < x_2$, then $f(x_1) > f(x_2)$.
3. A function is **constant** on an interval if for any $x_1$ and $x_2$ in the interval, where $x_1 < x_2$, then $f(x_1) = f(x_2)$.

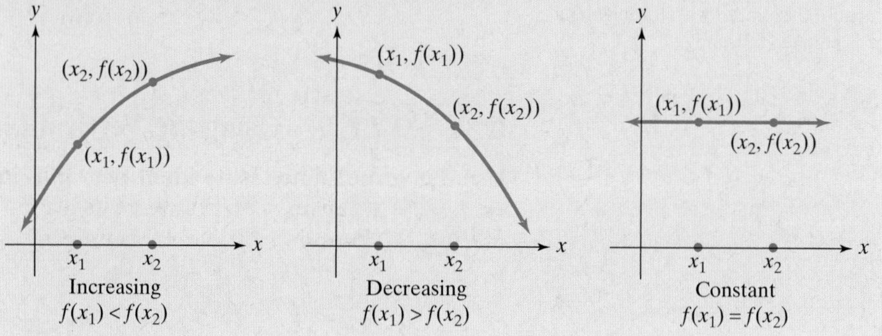


## EXAMPLE 4 Intervals on Which a Function Increases, Decreases, or Is Constant

Describe the increasing, decreasing, or constant behavior of each function whose graph is shown.

**a.**

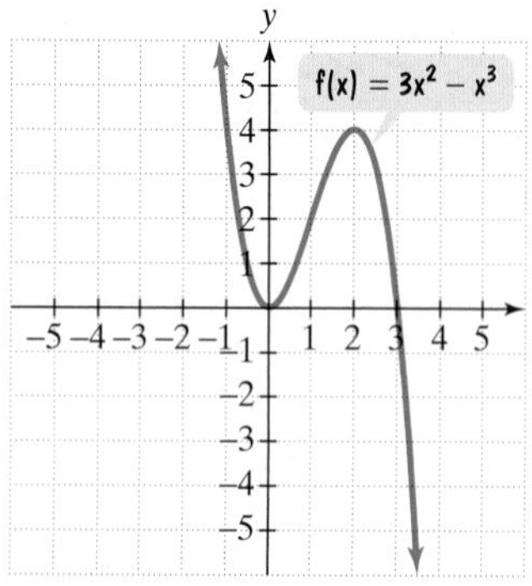


**b.**

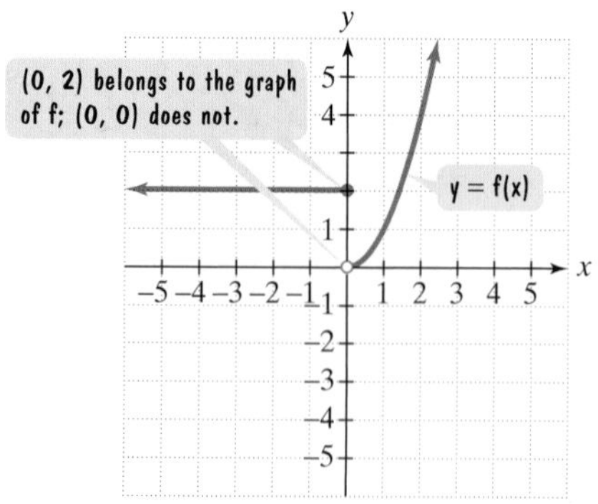


### Solution

**a.** The function is decreasing on the interval $(-\infty, 0)$, increasing on the interval $(0, 2)$, and decreasing on the interval $(2, \infty)$.

**b.** Although the function's equations are not given, the graph indicates that the function is defined in two pieces. The part of the graph to the left of the $y$-axis shows that the function is constant on the interval $(-\infty, 0)$. The part to the right of the $y$-axis shows that the function is increasing on the interval $(0, \infty)$.

**Check Point 4** Describe the increasing, decreasing, or constant behavior of the function whose graph is shown.

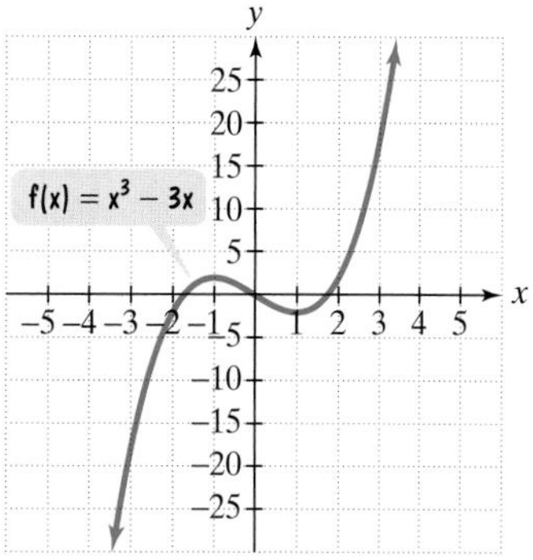


**5** Find average rate of change and average velocity.

## The Average Rate of Change of a Function

We have seen that the slope of a line can be interpreted as its rate of change. If the graph of a function is not a straight line, we speak of an **average rate of change** between any two points on its graph. To find the average rate of change, calculate the slope of the line containing the two points. This line is called a **secant line**.

### The Average Rate of Change of a Function

Let $(x_1, f(x_1))$ and $(x_2, f(x_2))$ be distinct points on the graph of a function $f$. (See Figure 2.28.) The **average rate of change of $f$** from $x_1$ to $x_2$, denoted by $\frac{\Delta y}{\Delta x}$ (read "*delta y divided by delta x*" or "*change in y divided by change in x*"), is

$$\frac{\Delta y}{\Delta x} = \frac{f(x_2) - f(x_1)}{x_2 - x_1}.$$

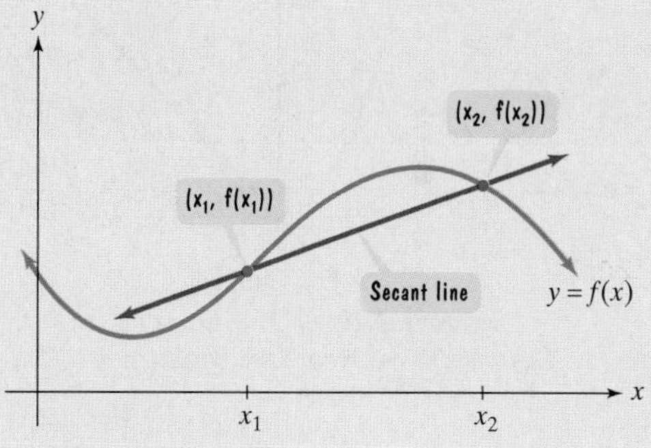


**Figure 2.28**

## EXAMPLE 5 Finding the Average Rate of Change

Find the average rate of change of $f(x) = x^2$ from:

**a.** $x_1 = 0$ to $x_2 = 1$ **b.** $x_1 = 1$ to $x_2 = 2$ **c.** $x_1 = -2$ to $x_2 = 0$.

### Solution

**a.** The average rate of change of $f(x) = x^2$ from $x_1 = 0$ to $x_2 = 1$ is

$$\frac{\Delta y}{\Delta x} = \frac{f(x_2) - f(x_1)}{x_2 - x_1} = \frac{f(1) - f(0)}{1 - 0} = \frac{1^2 - 0^2}{1} = 1.$$

Figure 2.29(a) shows the secant line of $f(x) = x^2$ from $x_1 = 0$ to $x_2 = 1$. The average rate of change is positive, and the function is increasing on the interval $(0, 1)$.

**b.** The average rate of change of $f(x) = x^2$ from $x_1 = 1$ to $x_2 = 2$ is

$$\frac{\Delta y}{\Delta x} = \frac{f(x_2) - f(x_1)}{x_2 - x_1} = \frac{f(2) - f(1)}{2 - 1} = \frac{2^2 - 1^2}{1} = 3.$$

Figure 2.29(b) shows the secant line of $f(x) = x^2$ from $x_1 = 1$ to $x_2 = 2$. The average rate of change is positive, and the function is increasing on the interval $(1, 2)$. Can you see that the graph rises more steeply on the interval $(1, 2)$ than on $(0, 1)$? This is because the average rate of change from $x_1 = 1$ to $x_2 = 2$ is greater than the average rate of change from $x_1 = 0$ to $x_2 = 1$.

**c.** The average rate of change of $f(x) = x^2$ from $x_1 = -2$ to $x_2 = 0$ is

$$\frac{\Delta y}{\Delta x} = \frac{f(x_2) - f(x_1)}{x_2 - x_1} = \frac{f(0) - f(-2)}{0 - (-2)} = \frac{0^2 - (-2)^2}{2} = \frac{-4}{2} = -2.$$

Figure 2.29(c) shows the secant line of $f(x) = x^2$ from $x_1 = -2$ to $x_2 = 0$. The average rate of change is negative, and the function is decreasing on the interval $(-2, 0)$.

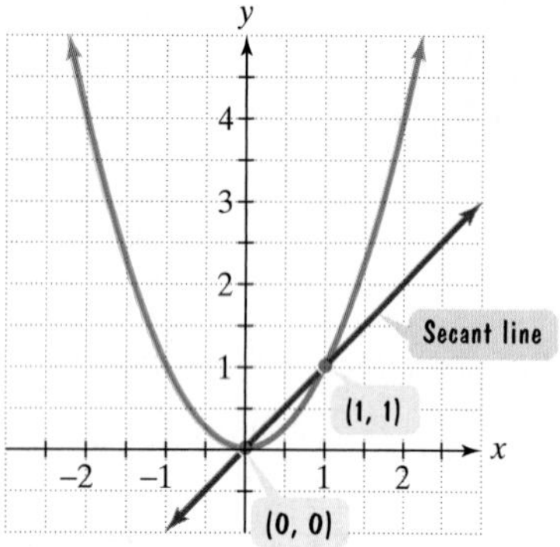


**Figure 2.29(a)** The secant line of $f(x) = x^2$ from $x_1 = 0$ to $x_2 = 1$

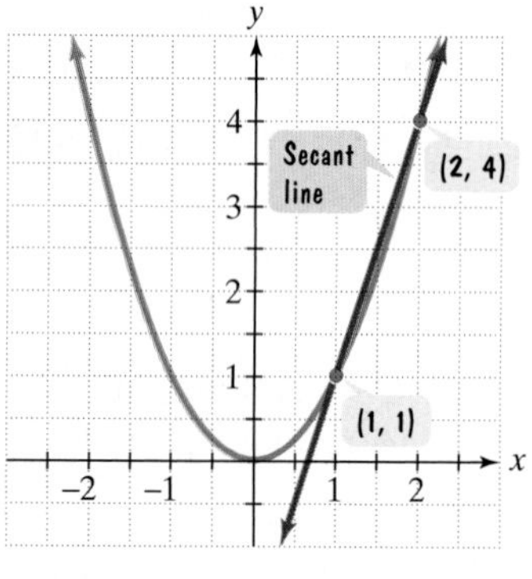


**Figure 2.29(b)** The secant line of $f(x) = x^2$ from $x_1 = 1$ to $x_2 = 2$

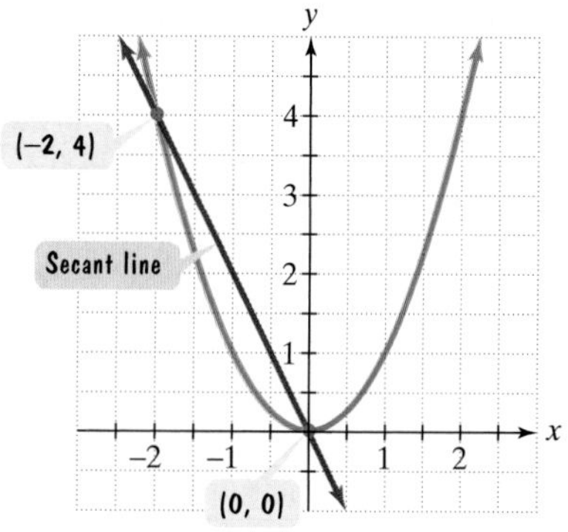


**Figure 2.29(c)** The secant line of $f(x) = x^2$ from $x_1 = -2$ to $x_2 = 0$

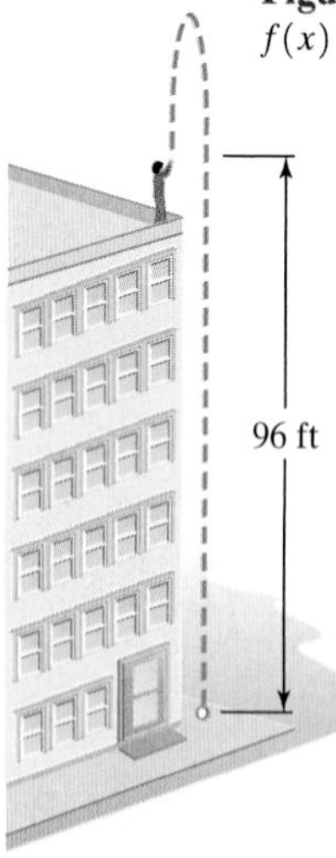


**Figure 2.30**

**Check Point 5**

Find the average rate of change of $f(x) = x^3$ from:

**a.** $x_1 = 0$ to $x_2 = 1$

**b.** $x_1 = 1$ to $x_2 = 2$

**c.** $x_1 = -2$ to $x_2 = 0$.

When working with applied functions, be sure to keep track of the units associated with the average rate of change. Consider, for example, a ball that is thrown straight up with an initial velocity of 80 feet per second from a height of 96 feet. (See Figure 2.30) The function

$$s(t) = -16t^2 + 80t + 96$$

describes the ball's height, $s(t)$, in feet, after $t$ seconds. For example, after 2 seconds, the ball is

$$s(2) = -16 \cdot 2^2 + 80 \cdot 2 + 96,$$

or 192 feet above the ground. The average rate of change from $t_1 = 0$ to $t_2 = 2$ is

$$\frac{\Delta s}{\Delta t} = \frac{s(t_2) - s(t_1)}{t_2 - t_1} = \frac{s(2) - s(0)}{2 \text{ sec} - 0 \text{ sec}} = \frac{192 \text{ ft} - 96 \text{ ft}}{2 \text{ sec}} = \frac{96 \text{ ft}}{2 \text{ sec}} = 48 \text{ ft/sec}.$$

Notice that the units have the form *distance, feet, per unit time, seconds*. Thus, $\frac{\Delta s}{\Delta t}$ gives us the *average velocity* of the ball. The ball's average velocity between the time it is thrown and 2 seconds later is 48 feet per second.

**Average Velocity of an Object**

Suppose that a function expresses an object's distance, $s(t)$, in terms of time, $t$. The **average velocity** of the object from $t_1$ to $t_2$ is

$$\frac{\Delta s}{\Delta t} = \frac{s(t_2) - s(t_1)}{t_2 - t_1}.$$

## EXAMPLE 6 Finding Average Velocity

The distance traveled by a ball rolling down a ramp is given by the function

$$s(t) = 5t^2,$$

where $t$ is the time, in seconds, after the ball is released, and $s(t)$ is measured in feet. Find the ball's average velocity from:

**a.** $t_1 = 2$ to $t_2 = 3$

**b.** $t_1 = 2$ to $t_2 = 2.5$

**c.** $t_1 = 2$ to $t_2 = 2.01$.

### Solution

**a.** The ball's average velocity between 2 and 3 seconds is

$$\frac{\Delta s}{\Delta t} = \frac{s(3) - s(2)}{3 - 2} = \frac{5 \cdot 3^2 - 5 \cdot 2^2}{1} = \frac{45 - 20}{1} = 25 \text{ ft/sec}.$$

**b.** The ball's average velocity between 2 and 2.5 seconds is

$$\frac{\Delta s}{\Delta t} = \frac{s(2.5) - s(2)}{2.5 - 2} = \frac{5(2.5)^2 - 5 \cdot 2^2}{0.5} = \frac{31.25 - 20}{0.5} = 22.5 \text{ ft/sec}.$$

**c.** The ball's average velocity between 2 and 2.01 seconds is

$$\frac{\Delta s}{\Delta t} = \frac{s(2.01) - s(2)}{2.01 - 2} = \frac{5(2.01)^2 - 5 \cdot 2^2}{0.01} = \frac{20.2005 - 20}{0.01} = 20.05 \text{ ft/sec}.$$

In Example 6, observe that each calculation begins at 2 seconds and involves shorter and shorter time intervals. In calculus, this procedure leads to the concept of *instantaneous*, as opposed to *average*, *velocity*.

**Check Point 6** The distance traveled by a ball rolling down a ramp is given by the function

$$s(t) = 4t^2,$$

where t is the time, in seconds, after the ball is released and $s(t)$ is measured in feet. Find the ball's average velocity from:

**a.** $t_1 = 1$ to $t_2 = 2$

**b.** $t_1 = 1$ to $t_2 = 1.5$

**c.** $t_1 = 1$ to $t_2 = 1.01$.

In calculus, you will study the average rate of change of $f$ from $x_1 = x$ to $x_2 = x + h$. In this case,

$$\frac{\Delta y}{\Delta x} = \frac{f(x_2) - f(x_1)}{x_2 - x_1} = \frac{f(x + h) - f(x)}{x + h - x} = \frac{f(x + h) - f(x)}{h}.$$

Do you recognize the last expression? It is the difference quotient that you used in the previous section to practice evaluating functions. Thus, the difference quotient gives the average rate of change of a function from $x$ to $x + h$. In the difference quotient, $h$ is thought of as a number very close to 0. In this way, the average rate of change can be found for a very short interval.

## Even and Odd Functions and Symmetry

Is beauty in the eye of the beholder? Or are there certain objects (or people) that are so well balanced and proportioned that they are universally pleasing to the eye? What constitutes an attractive human face? In Figure 2.31, we've drawn lines between paired features and marked the midpoints. Notice how the features line up almost perfectly. Each half of the face is a mirror image of the other half through the white vertical line.

Did you know that graphs of some equations exhibit exactly the kind of symmetry shown by the attractive face in Figure 2.31? The word *symmetry* comes from the Greek *symmetria*, meaning "the same measure." We can identify graphs with symmetry by looking at a function's equation and determining if the function is *even* or *odd*.

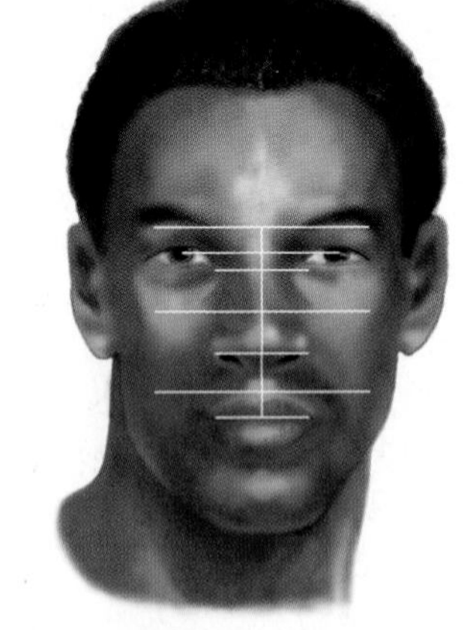

**Figure 2.31** To most people, an attractive face is one in which each half is an almost perfect mirror image of the other half.

**6** Identify even or odd functions and recognize their symmetries.

**Definition of Even and Odd Functions**

The function $f$ is an **even function** if

$$f(-x) = f(x) \quad \text{for all } x \text{ in the domain of } f.$$

The right side of the equation of an even function does not change if $x$ is replaced with $-x$.

The function $f$ is an **odd function** if

$$f(-x) = -f(x) \quad \text{for all } x \text{ in the domain of } f.$$

Every term in the right side of the equation of an odd function changes sign if $x$ is replaced by $-x$.

## EXAMPLE 7 Identifying Even or Odd Functions

Identify each of the following functions as even, odd, or neither.

**a.** $f(x) = x^3$ **b.** $g(x) = x^4 - 2x^2$ **c.** $h(x) = x^2 + 2x + 1$

**Solution** In each case, replace $x$ with $-x$ and simplify. If the right side of the equation stays the same, the function is even. If every term on the right changes sign, the function is odd.

**a.** We use the given function's equation, $f(x) = x^3$, to find $f(-x)$.

Use $f(x) = x^3$.

Replace x with −x. Replace x with −x.

$$f(-x) = (-x)^3 = (-x)(-x)(-x) = -x^3$$

There is only one term in the equation $f(x) = x^3$, and the term changed signs when we replaced $x$ with $-x$. Because $f(-x) = -f(x)$, $f$ is an odd function.

**b.** We use the given function's equation, $g(x) = x^4 - 2x^2$, to find $g(-x)$.

Use $g(x) = x^4 - 2x^2$.

Replace x with −x.

$$g(-x) = (-x)^4 - 2(-x)^2 = (-x)(-x)(-x)(-x) - 2(-x)(-x)$$
$$= x^4 - 2x^2.$$

The right side of the equation of the given function, $g(x) = x^4 - 2x^2$, did not change when we replaced $x$ with $-x$. Because $g(-x) = g(x)$, $g$ is an even function.

**c.** We use the given function's equation, $h(x) = x^2 + 2x + 1$, to find $h(-x)$.

Use $h(x) = x^2 + 2x + 1$.

Replace x with −x.

$$h(-x) = (-x)^2 + 2(-x) + 1 = x^2 - 2x + 1$$

The right side of the equation of the given function, $h(x) = x^2 + 2x + 1$, changed when we replaced $x$ with $-x$. Thus, $h(-x) \neq h(x)$, so $h$ is not an even function. The sign of *each* of the three terms in the equation for $h(x)$ did not change when we replaced $x$ with $-x$. Only the second term changed signs. Thus, $h(-x) \neq -h(x)$, so $h$ is not an odd function. We conclude that $h$ is neither an even nor an odd function.

**Check Point 7** Determine whether each of the following functions is even, odd, or neither.

**a.** $f(x) = x^2 + 6$ **b.** $g(x) = 7x^3 - x$ **c.** $h(x) = x^5 + 1$

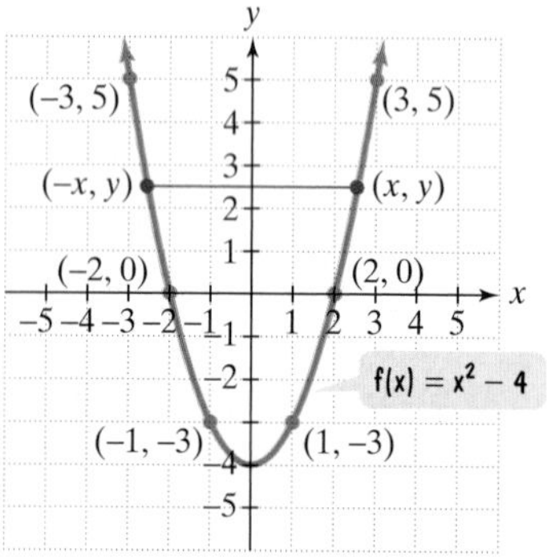


**Figure 2.32** *y*-axis symmetry with $f(-x) = f(x)$

Now, let's see what even and odd functions tell us about a function's graph. Begin with the even function $f(x) = x^2 - 4$, shown in Figure 2.32. The function is even because

$$f(-x) = (-x)^2 - 4 = x^2 - 4 = f(x).$$

Examine the pairs of points shown, such as (3, 5) and (−3, 5). Notice that we obtain the same $y$-coordinate whenever we evaluate the function at a value of $x$ and the value of $x$ equal to its opposite. Like the attractive face, each half of the graph is a mirror image of the other half through the $y$-axis. If we were to fold the paper along the $y$-axis, the two halves of the graph would coincide. This causes the graph to be *symmetric with respect to the y-axis*. A graph is **symmetric with respect to the *y*-axis** if, for every point $(x, y)$ on the graph, the point $(-x, y)$ is also on the graph. All even functions have graphs with this kind of symmetry.

### Even Functions and *y*-Axis Symmetry

The graph of an even function in which $f(-x) = f(x)$ is symmetric with respect to the $y$-axis.

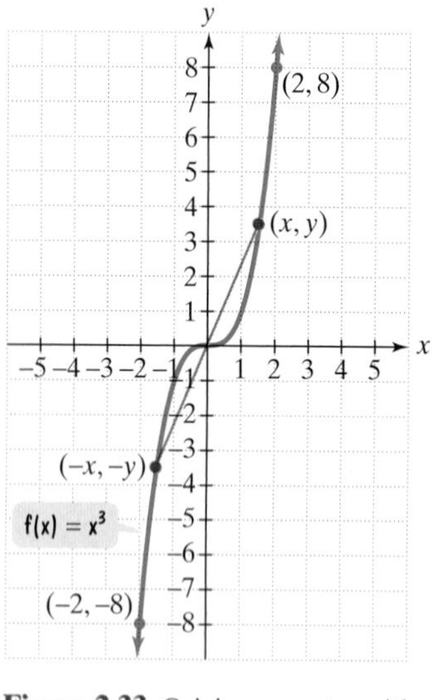


**Figure 2.33** Origin symmetry with $f(-x) = -f(x)$

Now, consider the graph of the function $f(x) = x^3$. In Example 7, we saw that $f(-x) = -f(x)$, so this is an odd function. Although the graph in Figure 2.33 is not symmetric with respect to the $y$-axis, it is symmetric in another way. Look at the pairs of points, such as (2, 8) and (−2, −8). For each point $(x, y)$ on the graph, the point $(-x, -y)$ is also on the graph. The points (2, 8) and (−2, −8) are reflections of one another in the origin. This means that

- the points are the same distance from the origin, and
- the points lie on a line through the origin.

A graph is **symmetric with respect to the origin** if, for every point $(x, y)$ on the graph, the point $(-x, -y)$ is also on the graph. Observe that the first- and third-quadrant portions of $f(x) = x^3$ are reflections of one another in the origin. Notice that $f(x)$ and $f(-x)$ have opposite signs, so that $f(-x) = -f(x)$. All odd functions have graphs with origin symmetry.

### Odd Functions and Origin Symmetry

The graph of an odd function in which $f(-x) = -f(x)$ is symmetric with respect to the origin.

**7** Recognize graphs of common functions.

## Graphs of Common Functions

Table 2.3 gives names to six frequently encountered functions in algebra. The table shows each function's graph and lists characteristics of the function. Study the shape of each graph and take a few minutes to verify the function's characteristics from its graph. Knowing these graphs is essential for understanding later graphing techniques.

**Table 2.3 Algebra's Common Graphs**

**Constant Function**

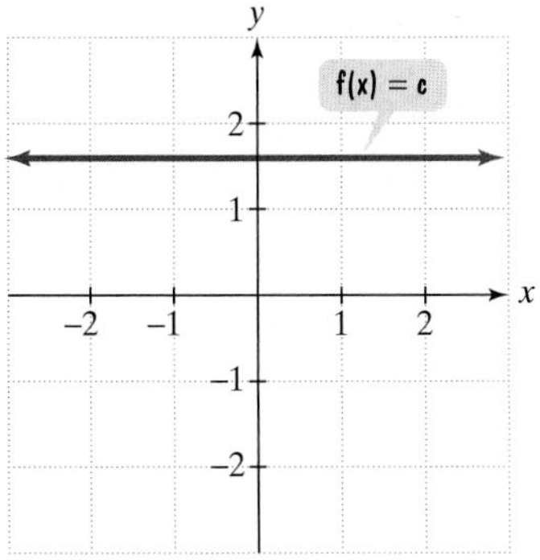


- Domain: $(-\infty, \infty)$
- Range: the single number $c$
- Constant on $(-\infty, \infty)$
- Even function

**Identity Function**

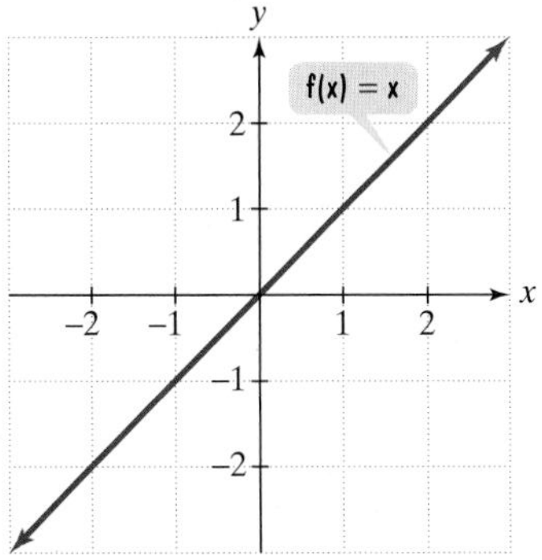


- Domain: $(-\infty, \infty)$
- Range: $(-\infty, \infty)$
- Increasing on $(-\infty, \infty)$
- Odd function

**Standard Quadratic Function**

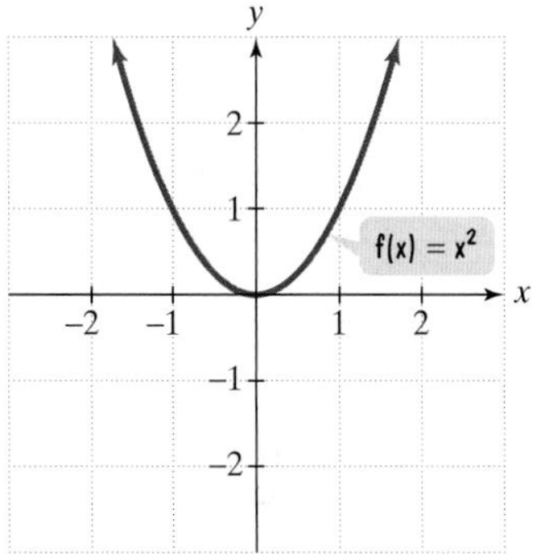


- Domain: $(-\infty, \infty)$
- Range: $[0, \infty)$
- Decreasing on $(-\infty, 0)$ and increasing on $(0, \infty)$
- Even function

**Standard Cubic Function**

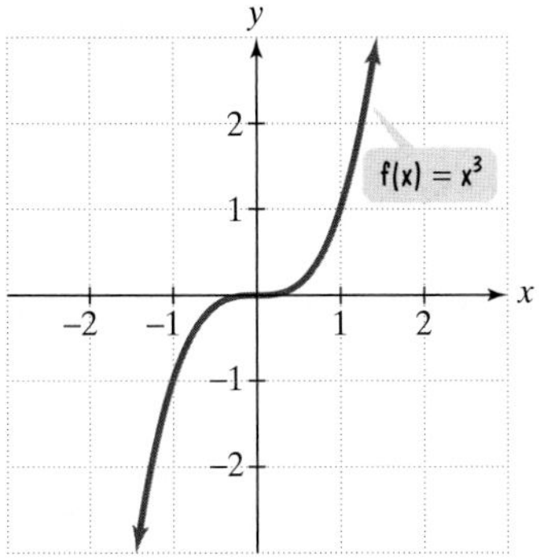


- Domain: $(-\infty, \infty)$
- Range: $(-\infty, \infty)$
- Increasing on $(-\infty, \infty)$
- Odd function

**Square Root Function**

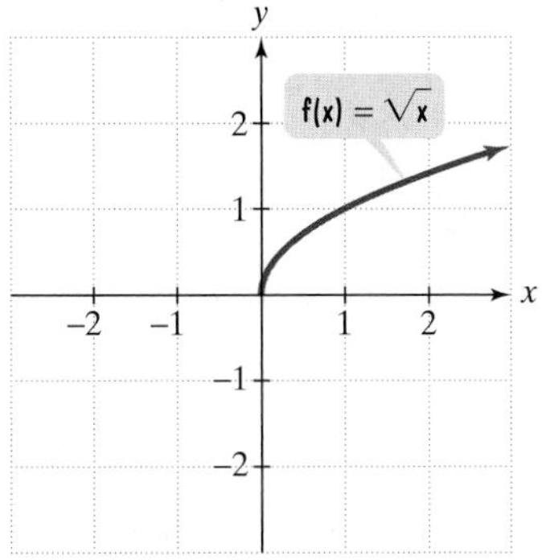


- Domain: $[0, \infty)$
- Range: $[0, \infty)$
- Increasing on $(0, \infty)$
- Neither even nor odd

**Absolute Value Function**

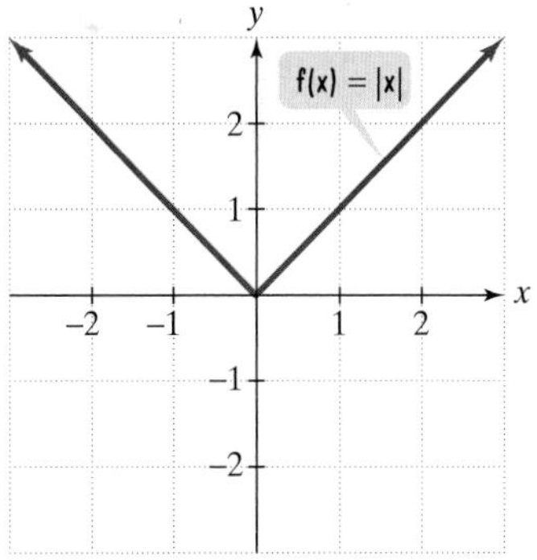


- Domain: $(-\infty, \infty)$
- Range: $[0, \infty)$
- Decreasing on $(-\infty, 0)$ and increasing on $(0, \infty)$
- Even function

### Discovery

Use a graphing utility to verify the six graphs shown in Table 2.3.

**8** Graph step functions.

## Step Functions

Have you ever mailed a letter that seemed heavier than usual? Perhaps you worried that the letter would not have enough postage. Costs for mailing a letter weighing up to 5 ounces are given in Table 2.4. If your letter weighs an ounce or less, the cost is \$0.33. If your letter weighs 1.05 ounces, 1.50 ounces, 1.90 ounces, or 2.00 ounces, the cost "steps" to \$0.55. The cost does not take on any value between \$0.33 and \$0.55. If your letter weighs 2.05 ounces, 2.50 ounces, 2.90 ounces, or 3 ounces, the cost "steps" to \$0.77. Cost increases are \$0.22 per step.

**Table 2.4 Cost of First-Class Mail (Effective January 10, 1999)**

| Weight Not Over | Cost |
|---|---|
| 1 ounce | \$0.33 |
| 2 ounces | 0.55 |
| 3 ounces | 0.77 |
| 4 ounces | 0.99 |
| 5 ounces | 1.21 |

*Source*: U.S. Postal Service

Now, let's see what the graph of the function that models this situation looks like. Let

$$x = \text{the weight of the letter in ounces, and}$$
$$y = f(x) = \text{the cost of mailing a letter weighing } x \text{ ounces.}$$

The graph is shown in Figure 2.34. Notice how it consists of a series of steps that jump vertically 22 units at each integer. The graph is constant between each pair of consecutive integers.

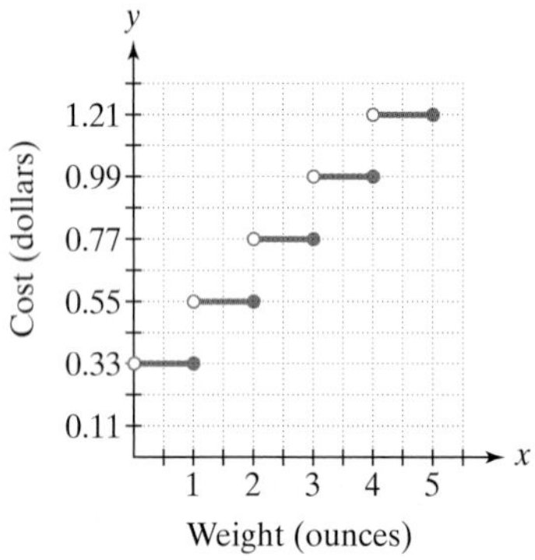


**Figure 2.34**

Mathematicians have a function that describes situations where function values graphically form discontinuous steps. The function is called the **greatest integer function**, symbolized by $\text{int}(x)$ or $[\![x]\!]$. And what is $\text{int}(x)$?

$$\text{int}(x) = \text{the greatest integer that is less than or equal to } x.$$

For example,

$$\text{int}(1) = 1, \quad \text{int}(1.3) = 1, \quad \text{int}(1.5) = 1, \quad \text{int}(1.9) = 1.$$

1 is the greatest integer that is less than or equal to 1, 1.3, 1.5, and 1.9.

Here are some additional examples:

$$\text{int}(2) = 2, \quad \text{int}(2.3) = 2, \quad \text{int}(2.5) = 2, \quad \text{int}(2.9) = 2.$$

2 is the greatest integer that is less than or equal to 2, 2.3, 2.5, and 2.9.

Notice how we jumped from 1 to 2 in the function values for $\text{int}(x)$. In particular,

$$\text{If } 1 \le x < 2, \quad \text{then} \quad \text{int}(x) = 1.$$
$$\text{If } 2 \le x < 3, \quad \text{then} \quad \text{int}(x) = 2.$$

The graph of $f(x) = \text{int}(x)$ is shown in Figure 2.35. The graph of the greatest integer function jumps vertically one unit at each integer. However, the graph is constant between each pair of consecutive integers. The rightmost of the horizontal steps shown in the graph illustrates that

$$\text{If } 5 \le x < 6, \quad \text{then} \quad \text{int}(x) = 5.$$

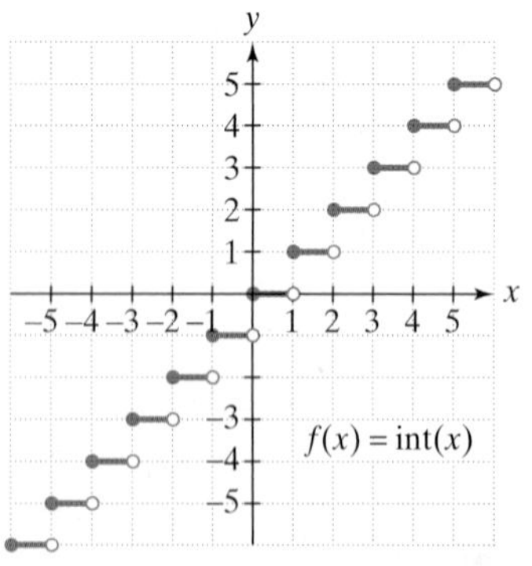


**Figure 2.35** The graph of the greatest integer function

In general,

$$\text{If } n \le x < n + 1, \text{where } n \text{ is an integer,} \quad \text{then} \quad \text{int}(x) = n.$$

By contrast to the graph for the cost of first-class mail, the graph of the greatest integer function includes the point on the left of each horizontal step, but does not include the point on the right. The domain of $f(x) = \text{int}(x)$ is the set of all real numbers, $(-\infty, \infty)$. The range is the set of all integers.

## Technology

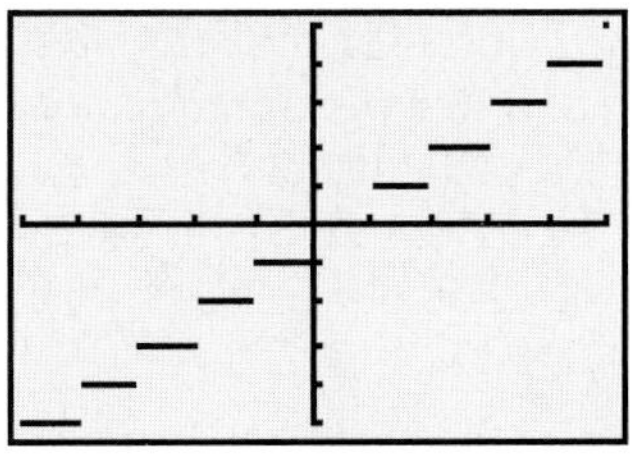

The graph of $f(x) = \text{int}(x)$, shown on the left, was obtained with a graphing utility. By graphing in "dot" mode, we can see the discontinuities at the integers. By looking at the graph, it is impossible to tell that, for each step, the point on the left is included and the point on the right is not. We must trace along the graph to obtain such information.

**9** Obtain information from graphs of functions in applied situations.

## Applications

We return to the function that models the fuel efficiency of U.S. automobiles over time. In the next example, we'll see what we can learn about this function from its graph.

### EXAMPLE 8 A Graph for the Fuel Efficiency Function

The function

$$f(x) = 0.0075x^2 - 0.2672x + 14.8$$

models the average number of miles per gallon of U.S. automobiles, $f(x)$, $x$ years after 1940. The graph of this function is shown as a continuous curve in Figure 2.36. (It can also be shown as a series of points, each point representing a year and miles per gallon for that year.)

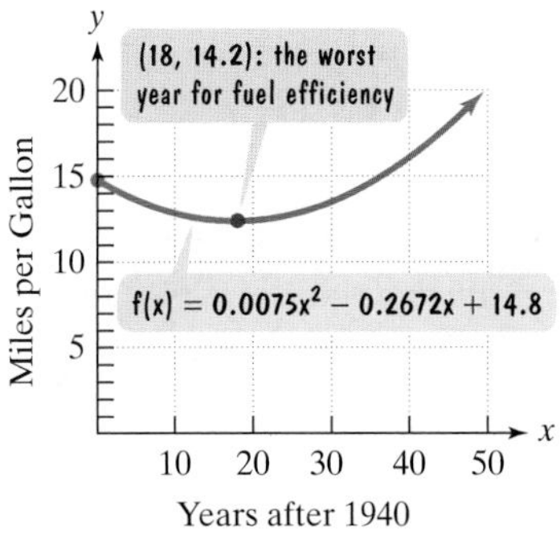


**Figure 2.36** Fuel efficiency of U.S. automobiles over time

**a.** On which interval is $f$ decreasing, and what does this mean?

**b.** On which interval is $f$ increasing, and what does this mean?

**Solution** Note the voice balloon pointing to (18, 14.2). It tells us that 18 years after 1940, in 1958, fuel efficiency was at its lowest point ever—a dismal 14.2 miles per gallon. This information, and the shape of the graph, enables us to find where $f$ is decreasing and where it is increasing.

**a.** Function $f$ is decreasing on the interval (0, 18).
This means that fuel efficiency was decreasing from 1940 through 1958.

**b.** Function $f$ is increasing on the interval (18, 50).
This means that fuel efficiency was increasing from 1958 through 1990.

**Check Point 8**

When a person receives a drug injected into a muscle, the concentration of the drug in the body, measured in milligrams per 100 milliliters, is a function of the time elapsed since the injection, measured in hours. Figure 2.37 on page 220 shows the graph of such a function, where $x$ = hours since the injection and $f(x)$ = drug concentration at time $x$.

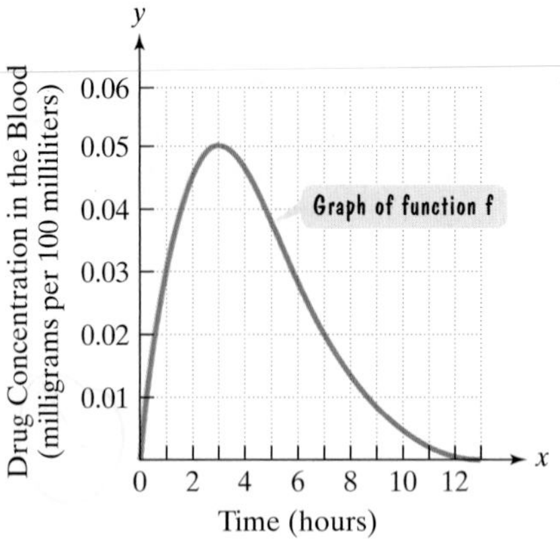


**Figure 2.37** Concentration of a drug as a function of time

**a.** On which interval is $f$ increasing, and what does this mean?

**b.** On which interval is $f$ decreasing, and what does this mean?

**c.** What is the drug's maximum concentration and when does this occur?

**d.** What happens by the end of 13 hours?

## EXERCISE SET 2.4

### Practice Exercises

*Graph the function in Exercises 1–14. Use the integer values of x given to the right of the function to obtain ordered pairs. Use the graph to specify the function's domain and range.*

**1.** $f(x) = x^2 + 2$ $\quad x = -3, -2, -1, 0, 1, 2, 3$

**2.** $f(x) = x^2 - 1$ $\quad x = -3, -2, -1, 0, 1, 2, 3$

**3.** $g(x) = \sqrt{x} - 1$ $\quad x = 0, 1, 4, 9$

**4.** $g(x) = \sqrt{x} + 2$ $\quad x = 0, 1, 4, 9$

**5.** $h(x) = \sqrt{x - 1}$ $\quad x = 1, 2, 5, 10$

**6.** $h(x) = \sqrt{x + 2}$ $\quad x = -2, -1, 2, 7$

**7.** $f(x) = |x| - 1$ $\quad x = -3, -2, -1, 0, 1, 2, 3$

**8.** $f(x) = |x| + 1$ $\quad x = -3, -2, -1, 0, 1, 2, 3$

**9.** $g(x) = |x - 1|$ $\quad x = -3, -2, -1, 0, 1, 2, 3$

**10.** $g(x) = |x + 1|$ $\quad x = -3, -2, -1, 0, 1, 2, 3$

**11.** $f(x) = 5$ $\quad x = -3, -2, -1, 0, 1, 2, 3$

**12.** $f(x) = 3$ $\quad x = -3, -2, -1, 0, 1, 2, 3$

**13.** $f(x) = x^3 - 2$ $\quad x = -2, -1, 0, 1, 2$

**14.** $f(x) = x^3 + 2$ $\quad x = -2, -1, 0, 1, 2$

*In Exercises 15–30, use the graph to determine* **a.** *the function's domain;* **b.** *the function's range;* **c.** *the x-intercepts, if any;* **d.** *the y-intercept, if any; and* **e.** *the function values indicated below some of the graphs.*

**15.**

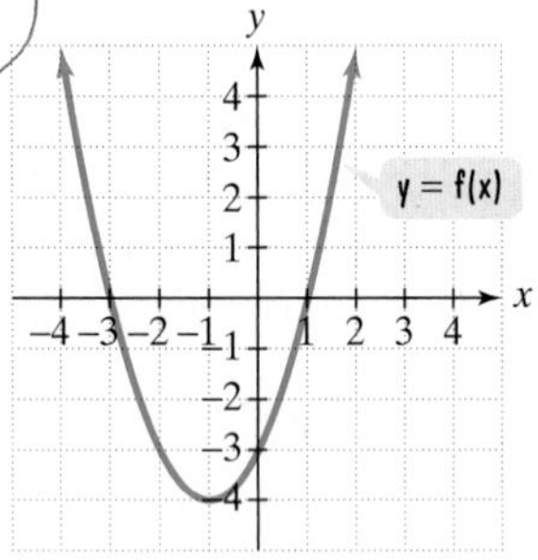


**16.**

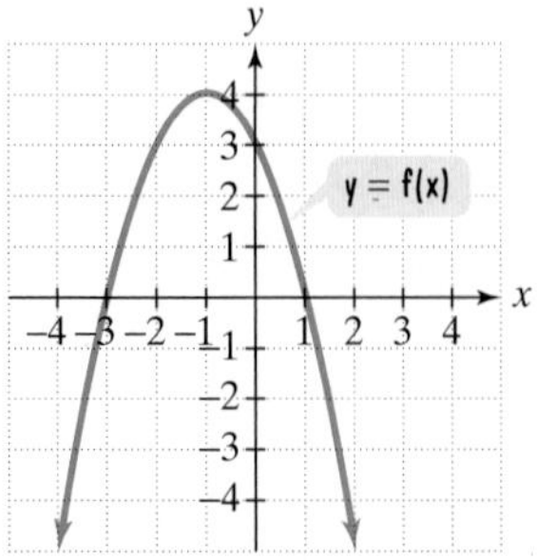

**17.**

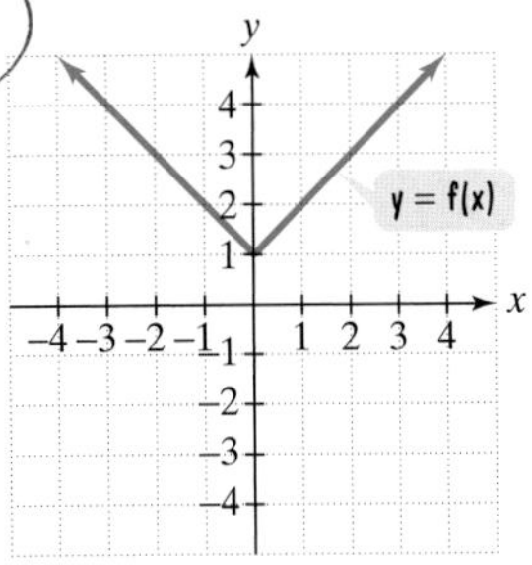


$f(-1) = ?$ $f(3) = ?$

**18.**

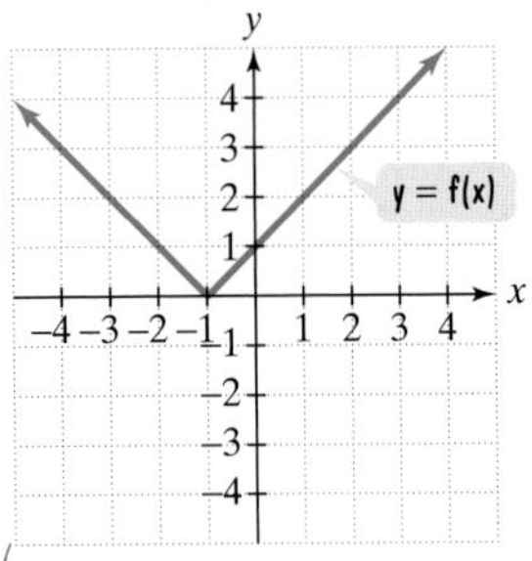


$f(-4) = ?$ $f(3) = ?$

**19.**

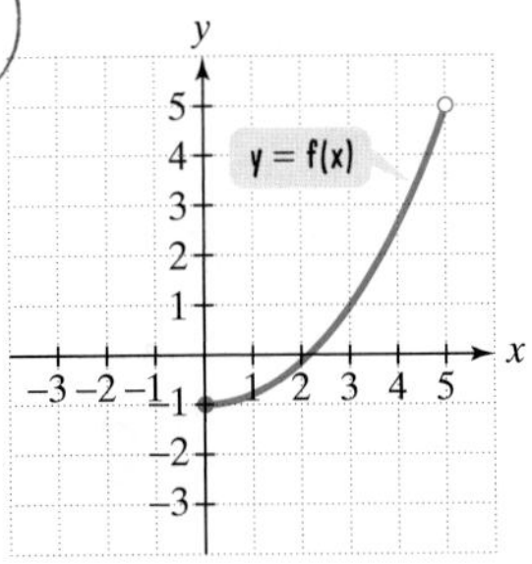


$f(3) = ?$

**20.**

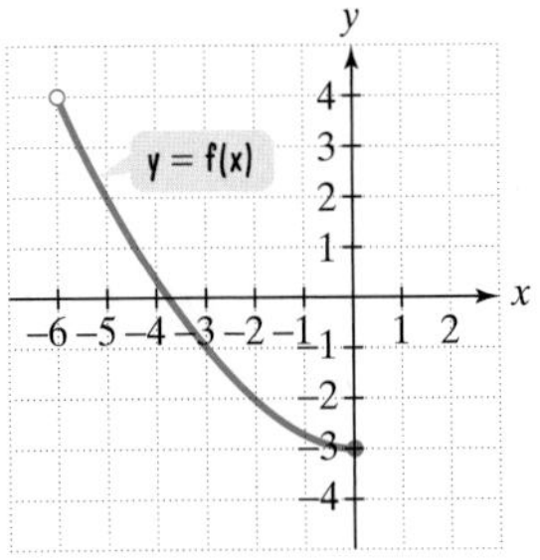


$f(-5) = ?$

**21.**

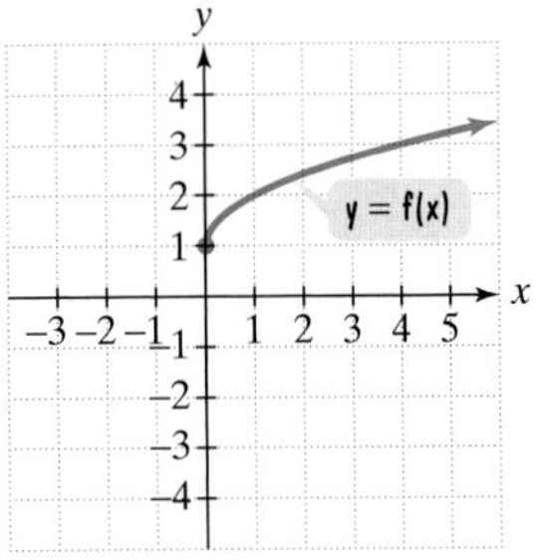


$f(4) = ?$

**22.**

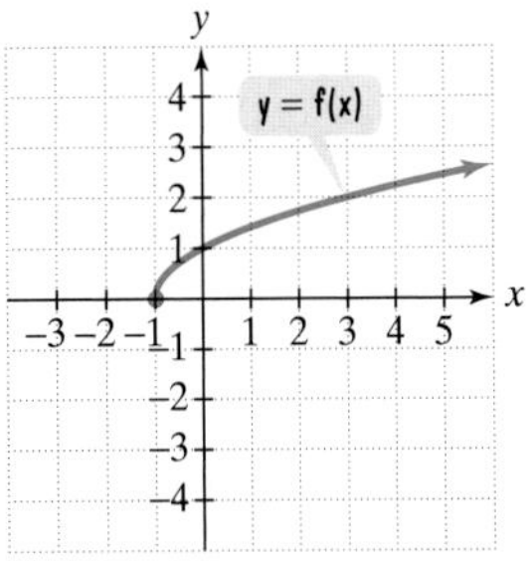


$f(3) = ?$

**23.**

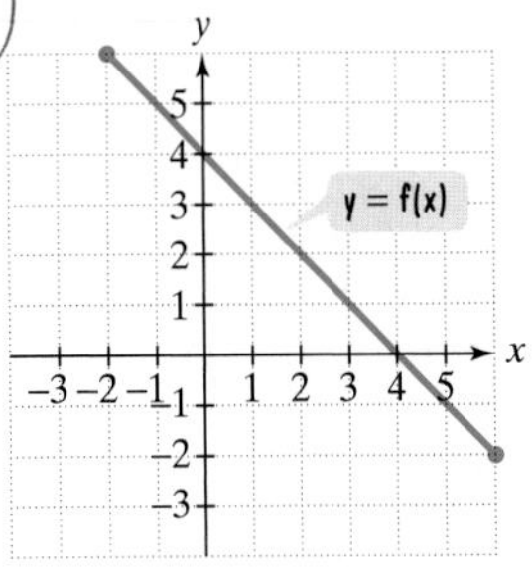


$f(-1) = ?$

**24.**

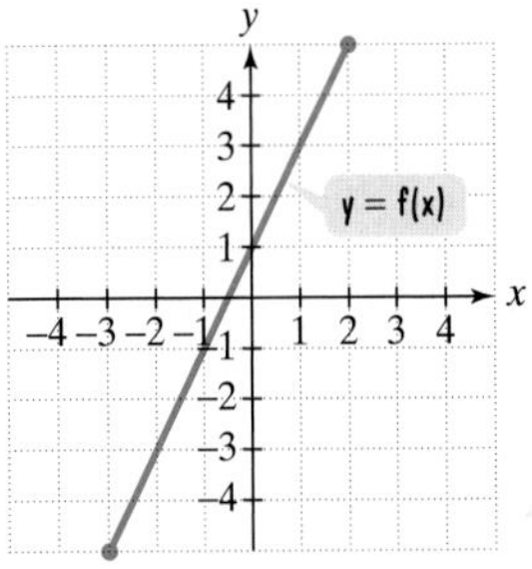


$f(-2) = ?$

**25.**

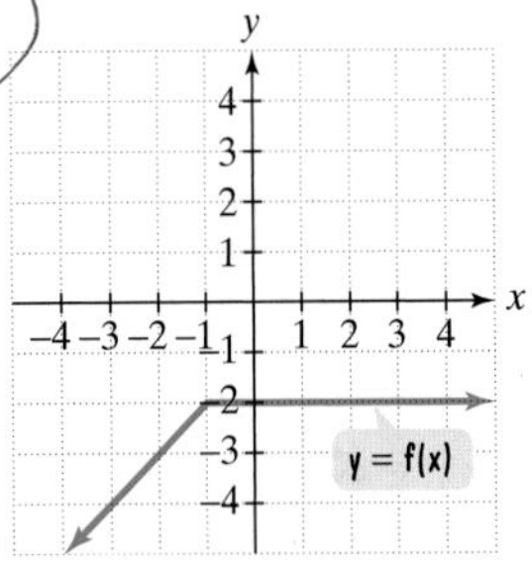


$f(-4) = ?$ $f(4) = ?$

**26.**

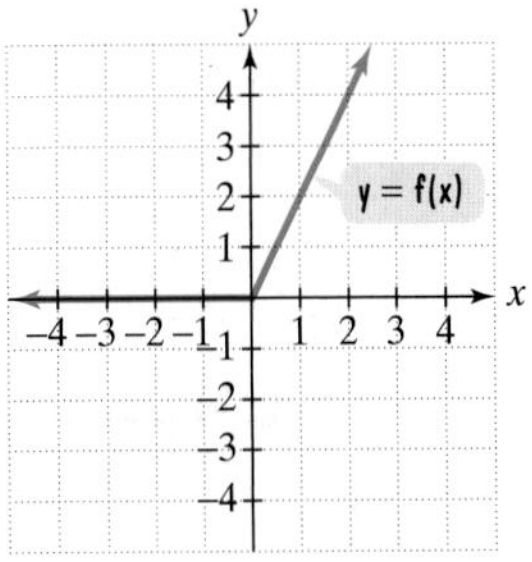


$f(-2) = ?$ $f(2) = ?$

**27.**

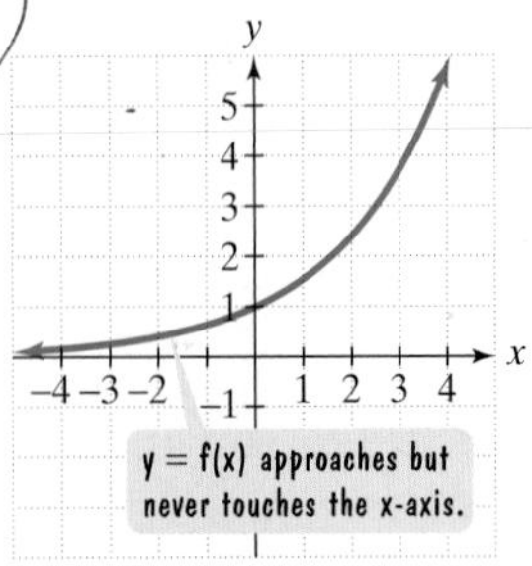
y = f(x) approaches but
never touches the x-axis.

**28.**

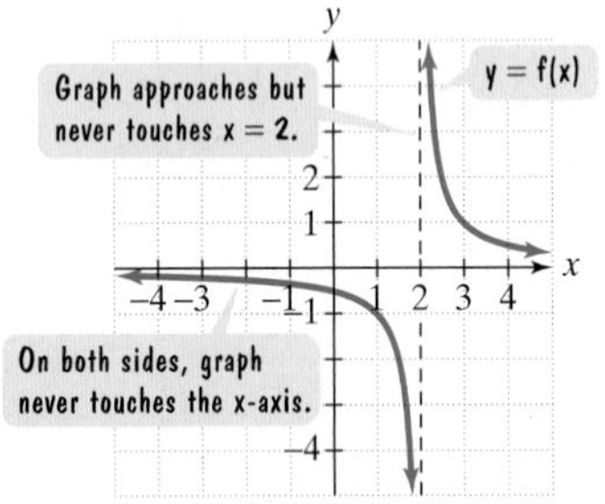
Graph approaches but
never touches x = 2.
y = f(x)
On both sides, graph
never touches the x-axis.

**29.**

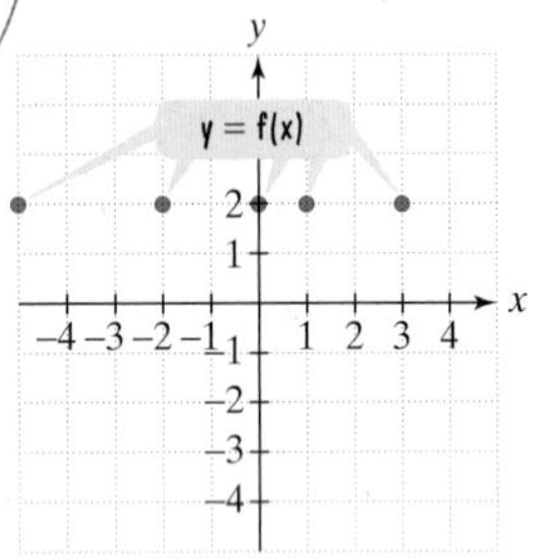
y = f(x)

**30.**

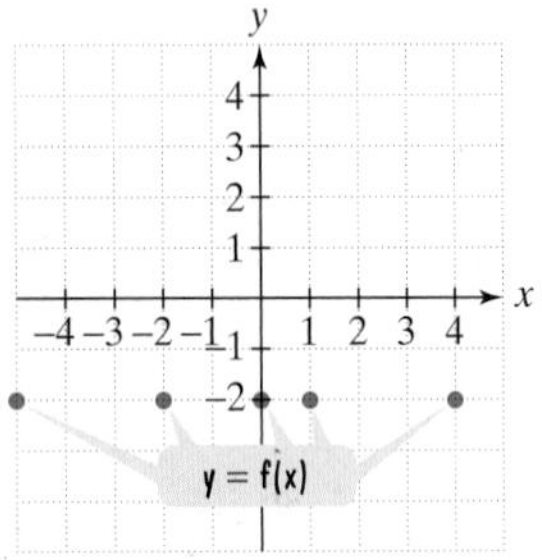
y = f(x)

*In Exercises 31–38, use the vertical line test to identify graphs in which y is a function of x.*

**31.**

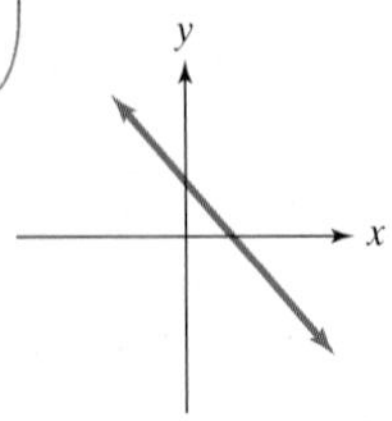

**32.**

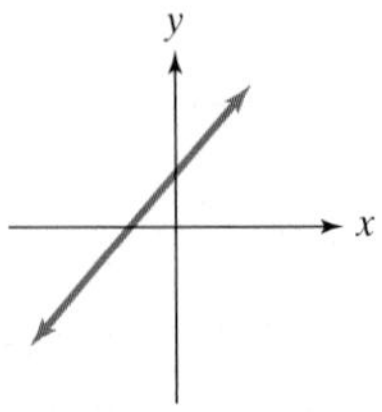

**33.**

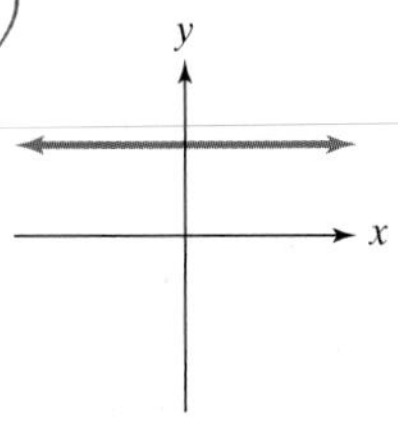

**34.**

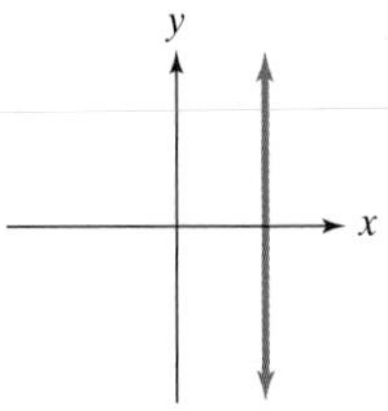

**35.**

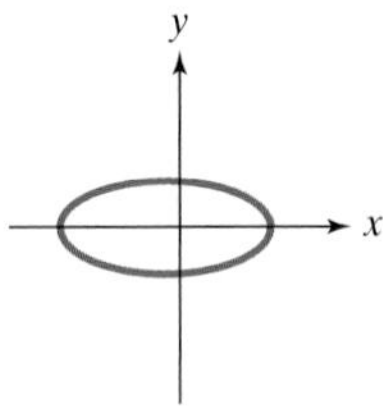

**36.**

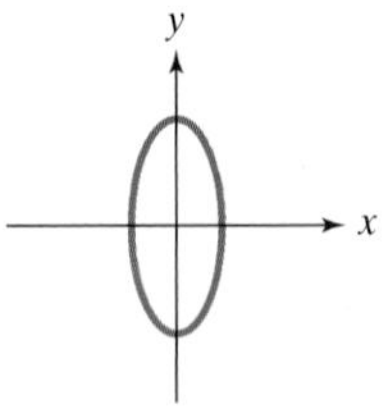

**37.**

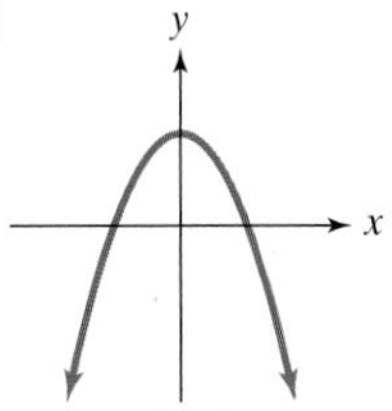

**38.**

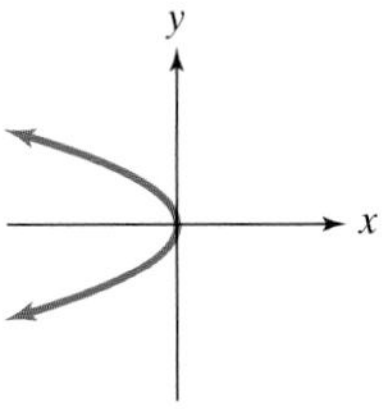

*In Exercises 39–50, use the graph to determine:*

**a.** *intervals on which the function is increasing, if any.*

**b.** *intervals on which the function is decreasing, if any.*

**c.** *intervals on which the function is constant, if any.*

**39.** Use the graph in Exercise 15.

**40.** Use the graph in Exercise 16.

**41.** Use the graph in Exercise 21.

**42.** Use the graph in Exercise 22.

**43.** Use the graph in Exercise 23.

**44.** Use the graph in Exercise 24.

**45.** Use the graph in Exercise 25.

**46.** Use the graph in Exercise 26.

**47.**

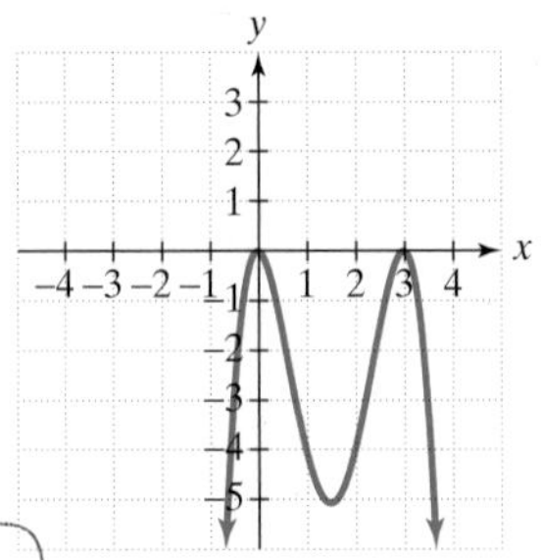

**48.**

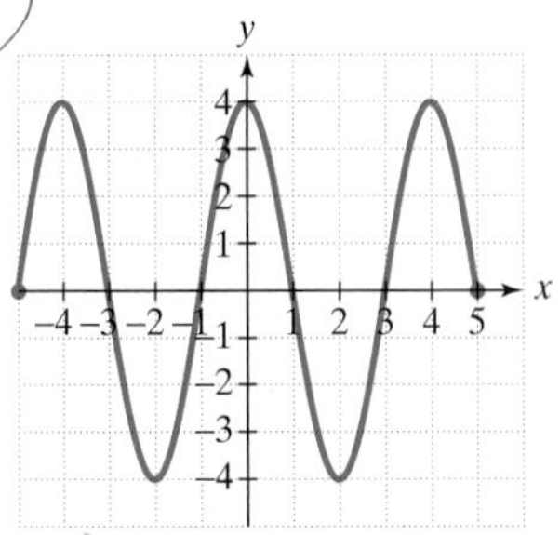

**49.**

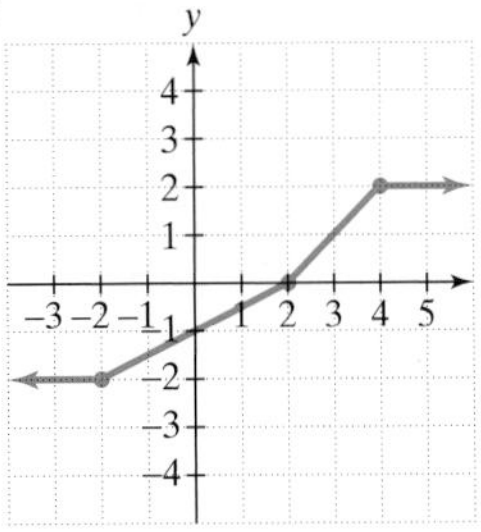

**50.**

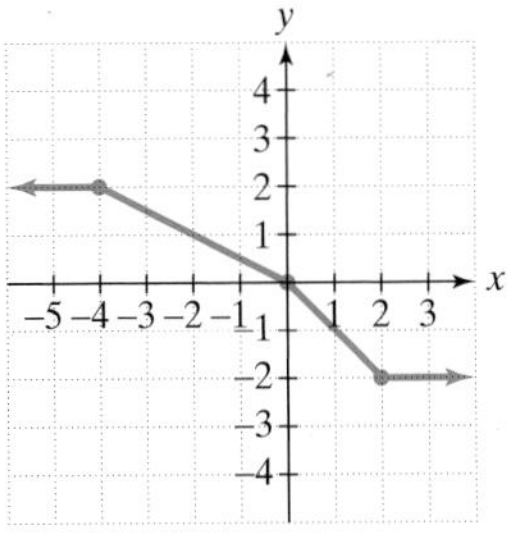

*In Exercises 51–56, find the average rate of change of the function from $x_1$ to $x_2$.*

**51.** $f(x) = 3x$ from $x_1 = 0$ to $x_2 = 5$

**52.** $f(x) = 6x$ from $x_1 = 0$ to $x_2 = 4$

**53.** $f(x) = x^2 + 2x$ from $x_1 = 3$ to $x_2 = 5$

**54.** $f(x) = x^2 - 2x$ from $x_1 = 3$ to $x_2 = 6$

**55.** $f(x) = \sqrt{x}$ from $x_1 = 4$ to $x_2 = 9$

**56.** $f(x) = \sqrt{x}$ from $x_1 = 9$ to $x_2 = 16$

*In Exercises 57–58, suppose that a ball is rolling down a ramp. The distance traveled by the ball is given by the function in each exercise, where t is the time, in seconds, after the ball is released, and s(t) is measured in feet. For each given function, find the ball's average velocity from* **a.** $t_1 = 3$ *to* $t_2 = 4$; **b.** $t_1 = 3$ *to* $t_2 = 3.5$; **c.** $t_1 = 3$ *to* $t_2 = 3.01$; *and* **d.** $t_1 = 3$ *to* $t_2 = 3.001$.

**57.** $s(t) = 10t^2$

**58.** $s(t) = 12t^2$

*In Exercises 59–70, determine whether each function is even, odd, or neither.*

**59.** $f(x) = x^3 + x$

**60.** $f(x) = x^3 - x$

**61.** $g(x) = x^2 + x$

**62.** $g(x) = x^2 - x$

**63.** $h(x) = x^2 - x^4$

**64.** $h(x) = 2x^2 + x^4$

**65.** $f(x) = x^2 - x^4 + 1$

**66.** $f(x) = 2x^2 + x^4 + 1$

**67.** $f(x) = \frac{1}{5}x^6 - 3x^2$

**68.** $f(x) = 2x^3 - 6x^5$

**69.** $f(x) = x\sqrt{1 - x^2}$

**70.** $f(x) = x^2\sqrt{1 - x^2}$

*In Exercises 71–74, use possible symmetry to determine whether each graph is the graph of an even function, an odd function, or a function that is neither even nor odd.*

**71.**

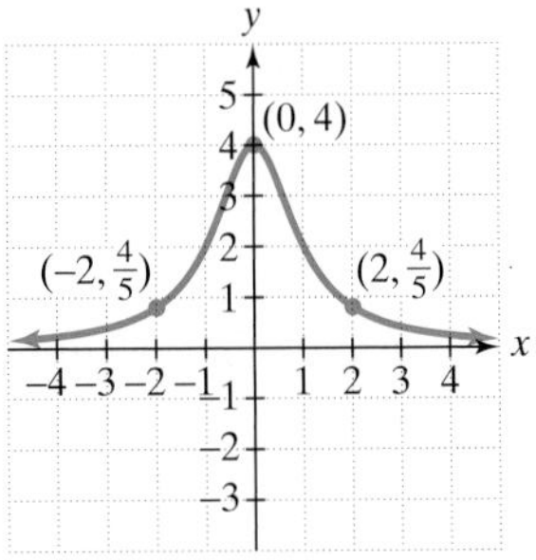


**72.**

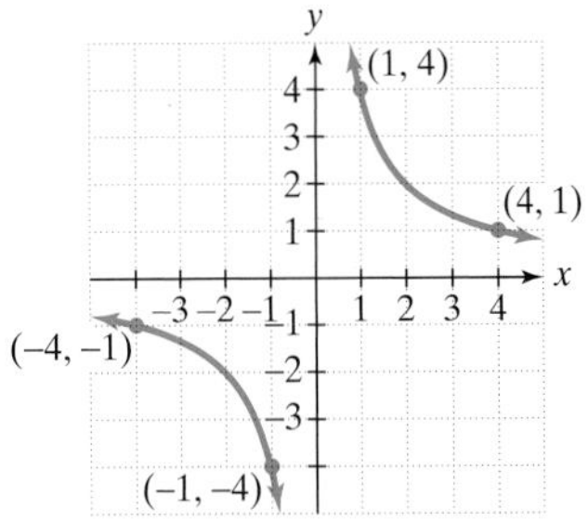


**73.**

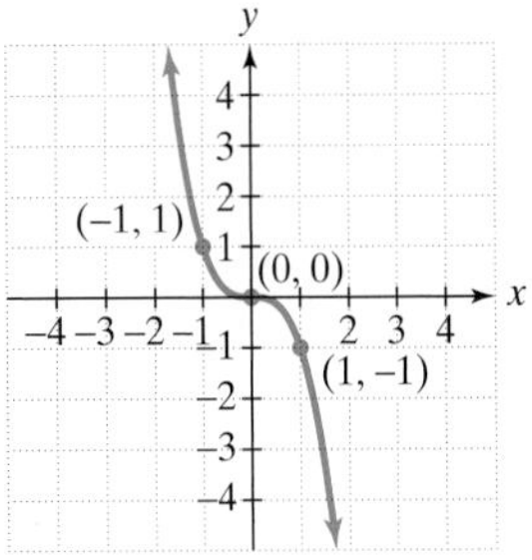


**74.**

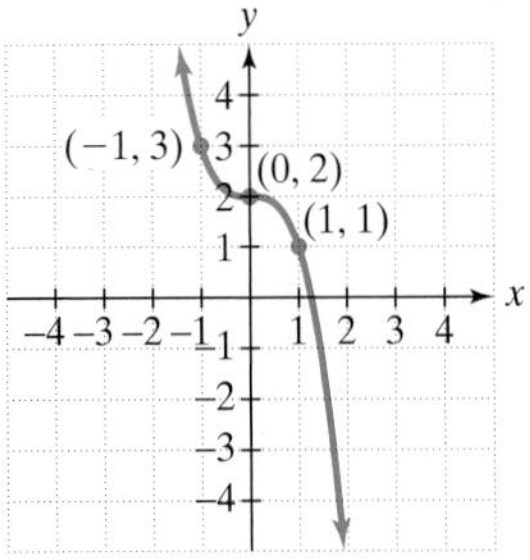


*In Exercises 75–80, if $f(x) = int(x)$, find each function value.*

**75.** $f(1.06)$

**76.** $f(2.99)$

**77.** $f(\frac{1}{3})$

**78.** $f(-1.5)$

**79.** $f(-2.3)$

**80.** $f(-99.001)$

## Application Exercises

*The graph shows the function $y = f(x)$, where $f(x)$ is defense spending in year x for $1988 \le x \le 1998$. Use the graph to solve Exercises 81–84.*

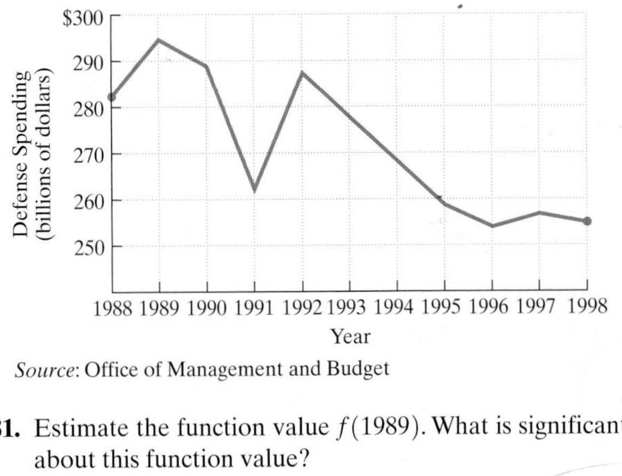


*Source*: Office of Management and Budget

**81.** Estimate the function value $f(1989)$. What is significant about this function value?

**82.** Estimate the function value $f(1996)$. What is significant about this function value?

**83.** In which time intervals is defense spending increasing?

**84.** In which time intervals is defense spending decreasing?

**85.** The function $f(x) = 0.4x^2 - 36x + 1000$ models the number of accidents per 50 million miles driven as a function of age, $x$, in years, where $16 \le x \le 74$. The graph of $f$ is shown.

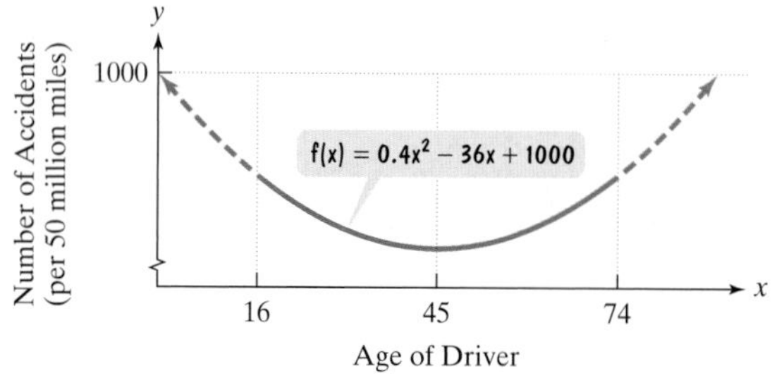


**a.** State the intervals on which the function is increasing and decreasing and describe what this means in terms of the variables modeled by the function.

**b.** For what value of $x$ does the graph reach its lowest point? What is the minimum value of $y$? Describe the practical significance of this minimum value.

**c.** The domain of $f$ is $[16, 74]$. Use the function's equation to determine the range of $f$. What is the practical significance of this range in terms of the meaning of $f(x)$ in the given function?

**86.** Based on a study by Vance Tucker (*Scientific American*, May 1969) the power expenditure of migratory birds in flight is a function of their flying speed, $x$, in miles per hour, modeled by $f(x) = 0.67x^2 - 27.74x + 387$. Power expenditure, $f(x)$, is measured in calories, and migratory birds generally fly between 12 and 30 miles per hour. The graph of $f$ is shown in the figure, with a domain of $[12, 30]$.

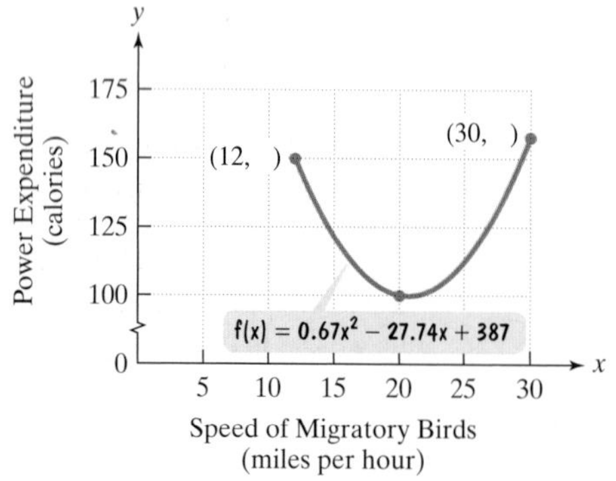


**a.** State the intervals on which the function is increasing and decreasing and describe what this means in terms of the variables modeled by the function.

**b.** For what approximate value of $x$ does the graph reach its lowest point? What is the minimum value of $y$? Describe the practical significance of this minimum value.

**c.** The domain of $f$ is $[12, 30]$. Use the function's equation to find the range of $f$. What is the practical significance of this range in terms of the meaning of $f(x)$ in the given function?

**87.** A model rocket is launched from a 3-foot platform with an initial velocity of 150 feet per second. The function

$$s(t) = -16t^2 + 150t + 3$$

describes the rocket's height, $s(t)$, in feet, $t$ seconds after launch.

**a.** Find the rocket's average velocity between 2 and 4 seconds.

**b.** Find the rocket's average velocity between 5 and 8 seconds.

**88.** A rock is thrown from the ground with an initial velocity of 80 feet per second. The function

$$s(t) = -16t^2 + 80t$$

describes the rock's height, $s(t)$, in feet, $t$ seconds after it was thrown.

**a.** Find the rock's average velocity between 1 and 3 seconds.

**b.** Find the rock's average velocity between 3 and 5 seconds.

**89.** Use Figure 2.37 on page 220 to solve this exercise.

**a.** Find the average rate of change of the drug concentration, in milligrams per 100 milliliters per hour, from $t = 0$ to $t = 2$. What does this mean in practical terms?

**b.** Find the average rate of change of the drug concentration, in milligrams per 100 milliliters per hour, from $t = 2$ to $t = 7$. What does this mean in practical terms?

**90.** The number of calories consumed per person per day in the United States, $f(x)$, can be modeled by

$$f(x) = 0.89x^2 - 1.93x + 3306.27,$$

where $x$ is the number of years since 1974.

**a.** Find the average rate of change of the function from $x = 6$ to $x = 16$. What does this mean in practical terms?

**b.** Find the average rate of change of the function from $x = 16$ to $x = 26$. What does this mean in practical terms?

**91.** The cost of a telephone call between two cities is \$0.10 for the first minute and \$0.05 for each additional minute or portion of a minute. Draw a graph of the cost, $C$, in dollars, of the phone call as a function of time, $t$, in minutes, on the interval $(0, 5]$.

**92.** A cargo service charges a flat fee of \$4 plus \$1 for each pound or fraction of a pound to mail a package. Let $C(x)$ represent the cost to mail a package that weighs $x$ pounds. Graph the cost function on the interval $(0, 5]$.

## Writing in Mathematics

**93.** Discuss one disadvantage to using point plotting as a method for graphing functions.

**94.** Explain how to use a function's graph to find the function's domain and range.

**95.** Explain how the vertical line test is used to determine whether a graph is a function.

**96.** What does it mean if function $f$ is increasing on an interval?

**97.** What is a secant line?

**98.** What is the average rate of change of a function?

**99.** If you are given a function's equation, how do you determine if the function is even, odd, or neither?

**100.** If you are given a function's graph, how do you determine if the function is even, odd, or neither?

**101.** What is a step function? Give an example of an everyday situation that can be modeled using such a function. Do not use the cost-of-mail example.

**102.** Explain how to find $\text{int}(-3.000004)$.

## Technology Exercises

**103.** The function $f(x) = -0.00002x^3 + 0.008x^2 - 0.3x + 6.95$ models the number of annual physician visits by a person of age $x$.

**a.** Use a graphing utility to graph the function in a $[0, 100, 5]$ by $[0, 60, 3]$ viewing rectangle.

**b.** What does the shape of the graph indicate about the relationship between one's age and the number of annual physician visits?

**c.** Use the TRACE or minimum function capability to find the coordinates of the lowest point on the graph of the function. What does this mean?

**104.** The function

$$C(x) = \begin{cases} -0.35x + 220 & \text{for } 0 \le x \le 20 \\ -0.80x + 229 & \text{for } x > 20 \end{cases}$$

describes the number of milligrams of cholesterol per deciliter of blood for American adults $x$ years after 1960.

**a.** Graph the function using a graphing utility in a $[0, 100, 20]$ by $[0, 250, 50]$ viewing rectangle.

**b.** What does the graph indicate about cholesterol level from 1960 to the present?

**c.** Was the goal of lowering cholesterol to a level under 200 reached before the year 2000?

*In Exercises 105–110, use a graphing utility to graph each function. Use a $[-5, 5, 1]$ by $[-5, 5, 1]$ viewing rectangle. Then find the intervals on which the function is increasing, decreasing, or constant.*

**105.** $f(x) = x^3 - 6x^2 + 9x + 1$

**106.** $g(x) = |4 - x^2|$

**107.** $h(x) = |x - 2| + |x + 2|$

**108.** $f(x) = x^{1/3}(x - 4)$

**109.** $g(x) = x^{2/3}$

**110.** $h(x) = 2 - x^{2/5}$

**111. a.** Graph the functions $f(x) = x^n$ for $n = 2, 4,$ and $6$ in a $[-2, 2, 1]$ by $[-1, 3, 1]$ viewing rectangle.

**b.** Graph the functions $f(x) = x^n$ for $n = 1, 3,$ and $5$ in a $[-2, 2, 1]$ by $[-2, 2, 1]$ viewing rectangle.

**c.** If $n$ is even, where is the graph of $f(x) = x^n$ increasing and where is it decreasing?

**d.** If $n$ is odd, what can you conclude about the graph of $f(x) = x^n$ in terms of increasing or decreasing behavior?

**e.** Graph all six functions in a $[-1, 3, 1]$ by $[-1, 3, 1]$ viewing rectangle. What do you observe about the graphs in terms of how flat or how steep they are?

## Critical Thinking Exercises

**112.** Which one of the following is true based on the graph of $f$ in the figure?

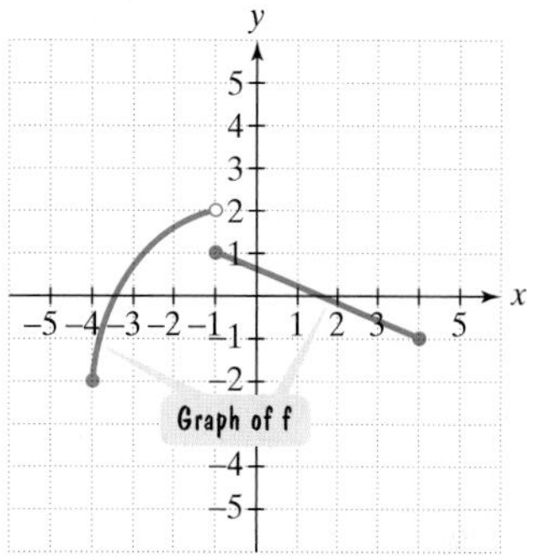


**a.** The domain of $f$ is $[-4, 1)$ or $(1, 4]$.

**b.** The range of $f$ is $[-2, 2]$.

**c.** $f(-1) - f(4) = 2$

**d.** $f(0) = 2.1$

**113.** Sketch the graph of $f$ using the following properties. (More than one correct graph is possible.) $f$ is a piecewise function that is decreasing on $(-\infty, 2)$, $f(2) = 0$, $f$ is increasing on $(2, \infty)$, and the range of $f$ is $[0, \infty)$.

**114.** Define a piecewise function on the intervals $(-\infty, 2]$, $(2, 5)$, and $[5, \infty)$ that does not "jump" at 2 or 5 such that one piece is a constant function, another piece is an increasing function, and the third piece is a decreasing function.

**115.** Use your work in Exercise 57 to solve this exercise. For the function $s(t) = 10t^2$, show that the average velocity from $t_1 = 3$ to $t_2 = 3 + \Delta t$ is $60 + 10(\Delta t)$. What does the average velocity seem to approach as $\Delta t$ gets very close to 0? How is this shown by the four values of average velocity that you found in Exercise 57?

**116.** Suppose that $h(x) = \dfrac{f(x)}{g(x)}$. The function $f$ can be even, odd, or neither. The same is true for the function $g$.

**a.** Under what conditions is $h$ definitely an even function?

**b.** Under what conditions is $h$ definitely an odd function?

**117.** Take another look at the cost of first-class mail and its graph (Table 2.4 and Figure 2.31 on pages 212–213). Change the description of the heading in the left column of Table 2.4 so that the graph includes the point on the left of each horizontal step, but does not include the point on the right.

# SECTION 2.5 Transformations and Combinations of Functions

## Objectives

1. Use vertical shifts to graph functions.
2. Use horizontal shifts to graph functions.
3. Use reflections to graph functions.
4. Use vertical stretching and shrinking to graph functions.
5. Graph functions involving a sequence of transformations.
6. Combine functions arithmetically, specifying domains.

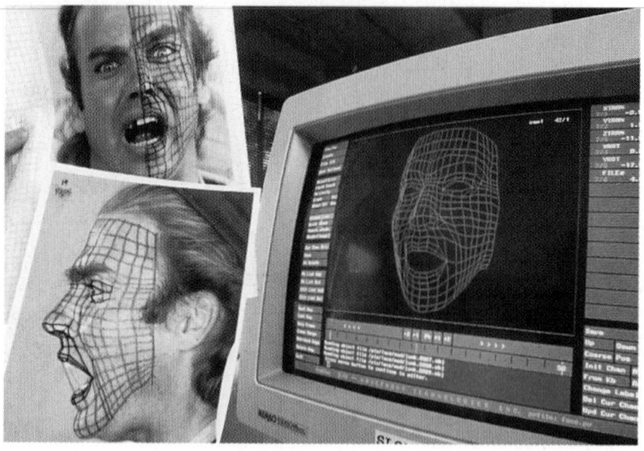

Have you seen *Terminator 2*, *The Mask*, or *The Matrix*? These were among the first films to use spectacular effects in which a character or object having one shape was transformed in a fluid fashion into a quite different shape. The name for such a transformation is **morphing**. The effect allows a real actor to be seamlessly transformed into a computer-generated animation. The animation can be made to perform impossible feats before it is morphed back to the conventionally filmed image.

Like transformed movie images, the graph of one function can be turned into the graph of a different function. To do this, we need to rely on a function's equation. Knowing that a graph is a transformation of a familiar graph makes graphing easier.

## Discovery

The study of how changing a function's equation can affect its graph can be explored with a graphing utility. Use your graphing utility to verify the hand-drawn graphs as you read this section.

**1** Use vertical shifts to graph functions.

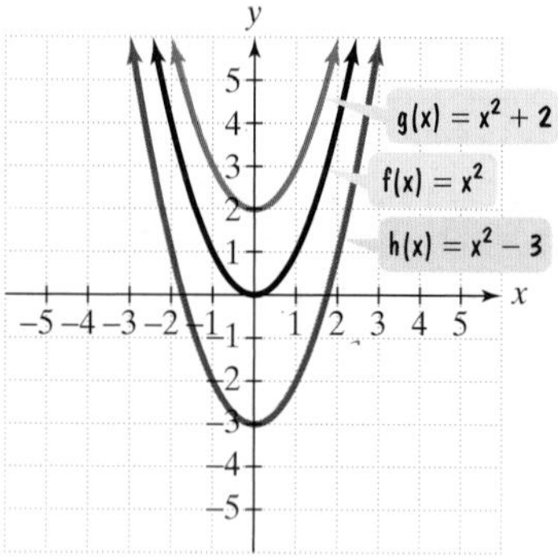


**Figure 2.38** Vertical shifts

The graph of $f(x) = x^2$ can be gradually morphed into the graph of $g(x) = x^2 + 2$ by using animation to graph $f(x) = x^2 + c$ for $0 \le c \le 2$. By selecting many values for $c$, we can create an animated sequence in which change appears to occur continuously.

### Vertical Shifts

Let's begin by looking at three graphs whose shapes are the same. Figure 2.38 shows the graphs. The black graph in the middle is the standard quadratic function $f(x) = x^2$. Now, look at the blue graph on the top. The equation of this graph, $g(x) = x^2 + 2$, adds 2 to the right side of $f(x) = x^2$. What effect does this have on the graph of $f$? It shifts the graph vertically up by 2 units.

$$g(x) = x^2 + 2 = f(x) + 2$$

The graph of $g$ — shifts the graph of $f$ up 2 units.

Finally, look at the red graph on the bottom of Figure 2.38. The equation of this graph, $h(x) = x^2 - 3$, subtracts 3 from the right side of $f(x) = x^2$. What effect does this have on the graph of $f$? It shifts the graph vertically down by 3 units.

$$h(x) = x^2 - 3 = f(x) - 3$$

The graph of $h$ — shifts the graph of $f$ down 3 units.

In general, if $c$ is positive, $y = f(x) + c$ shifts the graph of $f$ upward $c$ units and $y = f(x) - c$ shifts the graph of $f$ downward $c$ units. These are called **vertical shifts** of the graph of $f$.

### Vertical Shifts

Let $f$ be a function and $c$ a positive real number.

- The graph of $y = f(x) + c$ is the graph of $y = f(x)$ shifted $c$ units vertically upward.
- The graph of $y = f(x) - c$ is the graph of $y = f(x)$ shifted $c$ units vertically downward.

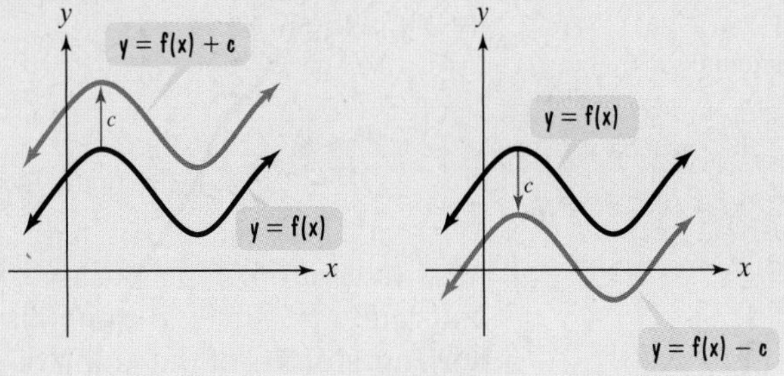


## EXAMPLE 1 Vertical Shift Down

Use the graph of $f(x) = |x|$ to obtain the graph of $g(x) = |x| - 4$.

**Solution** The graph of $g(x) = |x| - 4$ has the same shape as the graph of $f(x) = |x|$. However, it is shifted down vertically 4 units. We have constructed a table showing some of the coordinates for $f$ and $g$. The graphs of $f$ and $g$ are shown in Figure 2.39.

| $x$ | $y = f(x) = \|x\|$ | $y = g(x) = \|x\| - 4 = f(x) - 4$ |
|---|---|---|
| −2 | $\|-2\| = 2$ | $\|-2\| - 4 = -2$ |
| −1 | $\|-1\| = 1$ | $\|-1\| - 4 = -3$ |
| 0 | $\|0\| = 0$ | $\|0\| - 4 = -4$ |
| 1 | $\|1\| = 1$ | $\|1\| - 4 = -3$ |
| 2 | $\|2\| = 2$ | $\|2\| - 4 = -2$ |

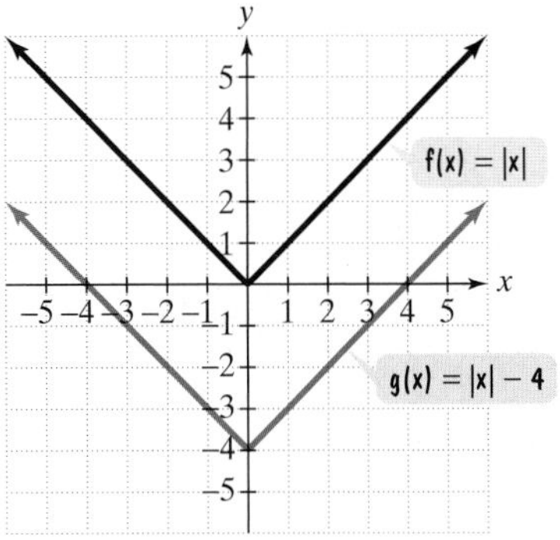


**Figure 2.39**

**Check Point 1** Use the graph of $f(x) = |x|$ to obtain the graph of $g(x) = |x| + 3$.

**2** Use horizontal shifts to graph functions.

### Horizontal Shifts

We return to the graph of $f(x) = x^2$, the standard quadratic function. In Figure 2.40, the graph of function $f$ is in the middle of the three graphs. Note that there are graphs to the right and left of $f$. By contrast to the vertical shift situation,

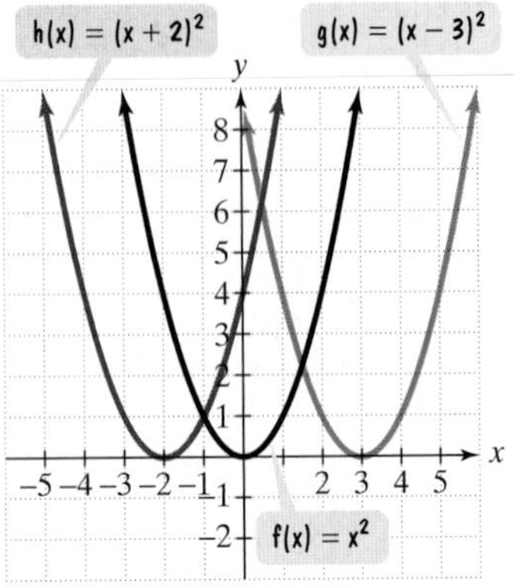


**Figure 2.40** Horizontal shifts

this time there are graphs to the left and to the right of the graph of $f$. Look at the blue graph on the right. The equation of this graph, $g(x) = (x - 3)^2$, subtracts 3 from each value of $x$ in the domain of $f(x) = x^2$. What effect does this have on the graph of $f$? It shifts the graph horizontally to the right by 3 units.

$$g(x) = (x - 3)^2 = f(x - 3)$$

The graph of $g$ | shifts the graph of $f$ 3 units to the right.

Now, look at the red graph on the left in Figure 2.40. The equation of this graph, $h(x) = (x + 2)^2$, adds 2 to each value of $x$ in the domain of $f(x) = x^2$. What effect does this have on the graph of $f$? It shifts the graph horizontally to the left by 2 units.

$$h(x) = (x + 2)^2 = f(x + 2)$$

The graph of $h$ | shifts the graph of $f$ 2 units to the left.

In general, if $c$ is positive, $y = f(x + c)$ shifts the graph of $f$ to the left $c$ units and $y = f(x - c)$ shifts the graph of $f$ to the right $c$ units. These are called **horizontal shifts** of the graph of $f$.

## Study Tip

We know that positive numbers are to the right of zero on a number line and negative numbers are to the left of zero. This positive-negative orientation does not apply to horizontal shifts. A *positive* number causes a shift to the *left* and a *negative* number causes a shift to the *right*.

### Horizontal Shifts

Let $f$ be a function and $c$ a positive real number.

- The graph of $y = f(x + c)$ is the graph of $y = f(x)$ shifted to the left $c$ units.
- The graph of $y = f(x - c)$ is the graph of $y = f(x)$ shifted to the right $c$ units.

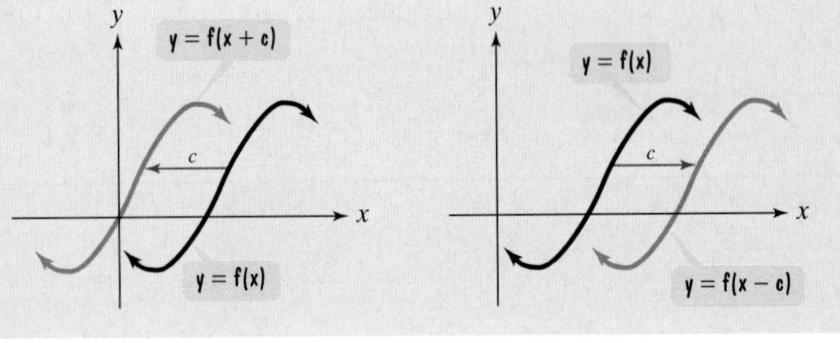


## EXAMPLE 2 Horizontal Shift to the Left

Use the graph of $f(x) = \sqrt{x}$ to obtain the graph of $g(x) = \sqrt{x + 5}$.

**Solution** Compare the equations for $f(x) = \sqrt{x}$ and $g(x) = \sqrt{x + 5}$. The equation for $g$ adds 5 to each value of $x$ in the domain of $f$.

$$y = g(x) = \sqrt{x + 5} = f(x + 5)$$

The graph of $g$ | shifts the graph of $f$ 5 units to the left.

The graph of $g(x) = \sqrt{x + 5}$ has the same shape as the graph of $f(x) = \sqrt{x}$. However, it is shifted horizontally to the left 5 units. We have created tables

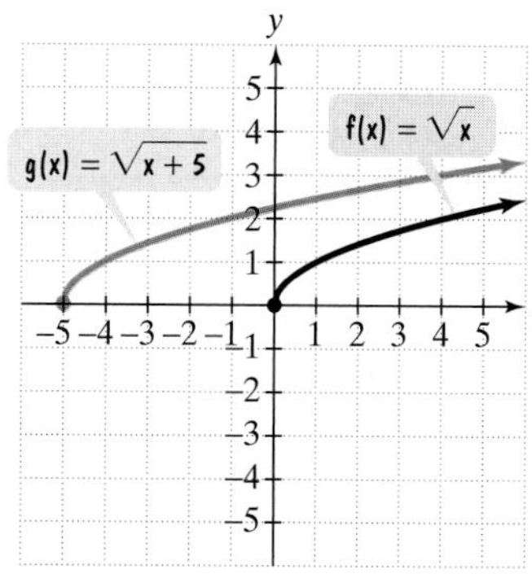


**Figure 2.41** Shifting $f(x) = \sqrt{x}$ five units left

showing some of the coordinates for $f$ and $g$. As shown in Figure 2.41, every point in the graph of $g$ is exactly 5 units to the left of a corresponding point on the graph of $f$.

| $x$ | $y = f(x) = \sqrt{x}$ |
|---|---|
| 0 | $\sqrt{0} = 0$ |
| 1 | $\sqrt{1} = 1$ |
| 4 | $\sqrt{4} = 2$ |

| $x$ | $y = g(x) = \sqrt{x+5}$ |
|---|---|
| −5 | $\sqrt{-5+5} = \sqrt{0} = 0$ |
| −4 | $\sqrt{-4+5} = \sqrt{1} = 1$ |
| −1 | $\sqrt{-1+5} = \sqrt{4} = 2$ |

**Check Point 2** Use the graph of $f(x) = \sqrt{x}$ to obtain the graph of $g(x) = \sqrt{x-4}$.

Some functions can be graphed by combining horizontal and vertical shifts. The function should be a variation of a function whose equation you know how to graph, such as the standard quadratic function, the standard cubic function, the square root function, or the absolute value function.

In our next example, we will use the graph of the standard quadratic function $f(x) = x^2$ to obtain the graph of $h(x) = (x+1)^2 - 3$. We will graph three functions:

$$f(x) = x^2 \qquad g(x) = (x+1)^2 \qquad h(x) = (x+1)^2 - 3$$

Start by graphing the standard quadratic function.

Shift the graph of f horizontally one unit to the left.

Shift the graph of g vertically down 3 units.

## EXAMPLE 3 Combining Horizontal and Vertical Shifts

Use the graph of $f(x) = x^2$ to obtain the graph of $h(x) = (x+1)^2 - 3$.

**Solution**

**Step 1 Graph $f(x) = x^2$.** The graph of the standard quadratic function is shown in Figure 2.42(a). We've identified three points on the graph.

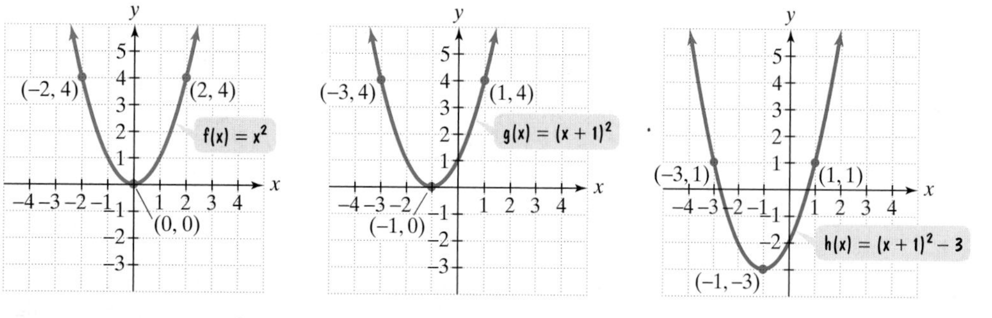


**(a)** The graph of $f(x) = x^2$ **(b)** The graph of $g(x) = (x+1)^2$ **(c)** The graph of $h(x) = (x+1)^2 - 3$

**Figure 2.42**

**Discovery**

Work Example 3 by first shifting the graph of $f(x) = x^2$ three units down, graphing $g(x) = x^2 - 3$. Now, shift this graph one unit left to graph $h(x) = (x + 1)^2 - 3$. Did you obtain the graph in Figure 2.39(c)? What can you conclude?

**Step 2 Graph $g(x) = (x + 1)^2$.** Because we add 1 to each value of $x$ in the domain of the standard quadratic function $f(x) = x^2$, we shift the graph of $f$ horizontally one unit to the left. This is shown in Figure 2.42(b). Notice that every point in the graph in Figure 2.42(b) has an $x$-coordinate that is one less than the $x$-coordinate for the corresponding point in the graph in Figure 2.42(a).

**Step 3 Graph $h(x) = (x + 1)^2 - 3$.** Because we subtract 3, we shift the graph in Figure 2.42(b) vertically down 3 units. The graph is shown in Figure 2.42(c). Notice that every point in the graph in Figure 2.42(c) has a $y$-coordinate that is three less than the $y$-coordinate of the corresponding point in the graph in Figure 2.42(b).

**Check Point 3** Use the graph of $f(x) = \sqrt{x}$ to obtain the graph of $h(x) = \sqrt{x - 1} - 2$.

**3** Use reflections to graph functions.

## Reflections of Graphs

This photograph shows a reflection of an old bridge in a Maryland river. This perfect reflection occurs because the surface of the water is absolutely still. A mild breeze rippling the water's surface would distort the reflection.

Is it possible for graphs to have mirror-like qualities? Yes. Figure 2.43 shows the graphs of $f(x) = x^2$ and $g(x) = -x^2$. The graph of $g$ is a **reflection about the $x$-axis** of the graph of $f$. In general, the graph of $y = -f(x)$ reflects the graph of $f$ about the $x$-axis. Thus, the graph of $g$ is a reflection of the graph of $f$ about the $x$-axis because

$$g(x) = -x^2 = -f(x).$$

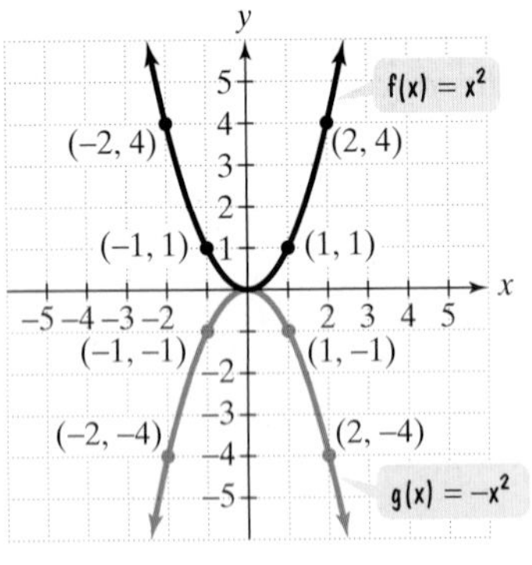


**Figure 2.43** Reflections about the $x$-axis

**Reflection About the $x$-Axis**

The graph of $y = -f(x)$ is the graph of $y = f(x)$ reflected about the $x$-axis.

## EXAMPLE 4 Reflection about the x-Axis

Use the graph of $f(x) = \sqrt{x}$ to obtain the graph of $g(x) = -\sqrt{x}$.

**Solution** Compare the equations for $f(x) = \sqrt{x}$ and $g(x) = -\sqrt{x}$. The graph of $g$ is a reflection about the $x$-axis of the graph of $f$ because

$$g(x) = -\sqrt{x} = -f(x).$$

We have created a table showing some of the coordinates for $f$ and $g$. The graphs of $f$ and $g$ are shown in Figure 2.44.

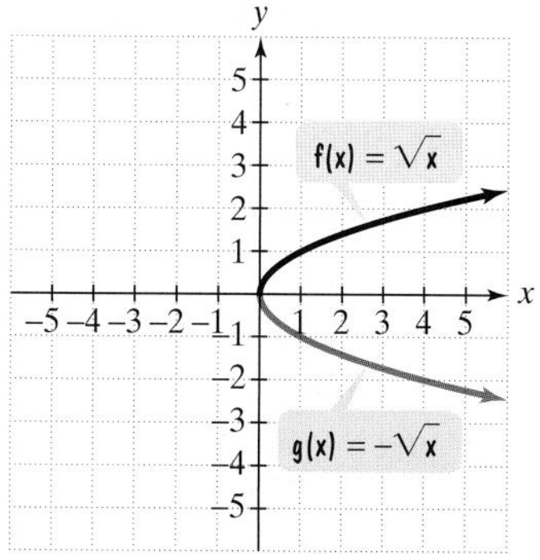


**Figure 2.44** Reflecting $f(x) = \sqrt{x}$ about the $x$-axis

| $x$ | $f(x) = \sqrt{x}$ | $g(x) = -\sqrt{x}$ |
|---|---|---|
| 0 | $\sqrt{0} = 0$ | $-\sqrt{0} = 0$ |
| 1 | $\sqrt{1} = 1$ | $-\sqrt{1} = -1$ |
| 4 | $\sqrt{4} = 2$ | $-\sqrt{4} = -2$ |

**Check Point 4** Use the graph of $f(x) = |x|$ to obtain the graph of $g(x) = -|x|$.

It is also possible to reflect graphs about the $y$-axis.

**Reflection about the y-Axis**

The graph of $y = f(-x)$ is the graph of $y = f(x)$ reflected about the $y$-axis.

## EXAMPLE 5 Reflection about the y-Axis

Use the graph of $f(x) = \sqrt{x}$ to obtain the graph of $h(x) = \sqrt{-x}$.

**Solution** Compare the equations for $f(x) = \sqrt{x}$ and $h(x) = \sqrt{-x}$. The graph of $h$ is a reflection about the $y$-axis of the graph of $f$ because

$$h(x) = \sqrt{-x} = f(-x).$$

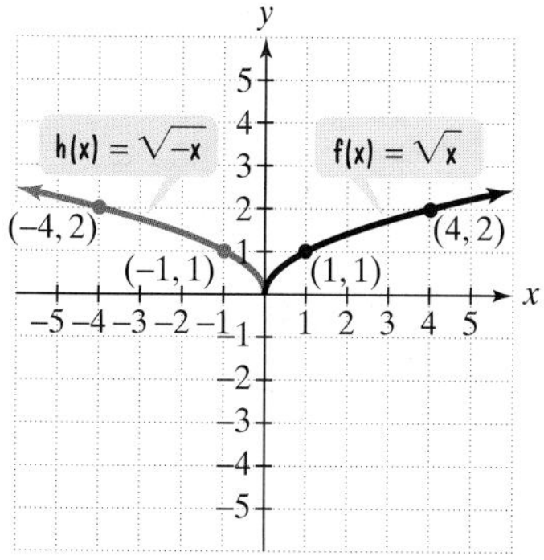


**Figure 2.45** Reflecting $f(x) = \sqrt{x}$ about the $y$-axis

We have created tables showing some of the coordinates for $f$ and $h$. The graphs of $f$ and $h$ are shown in Figure 2.45.

| $x$ | $f(x) = \sqrt{x}$ |
|---|---|
| 0 | $\sqrt{0} = 0$ |
| 1 | $\sqrt{1} = 1$ |
| 4 | $\sqrt{4} = 2$ |

| $x$ | $h(x) = \sqrt{-x}$ |
|---|---|
| 0 | $\sqrt{-0} = \sqrt{0} = 0$ |
| −1 | $\sqrt{-(-1)} = \sqrt{1} = 1$ |
| −4 | $\sqrt{-(-4)} = \sqrt{4} = 2$ |

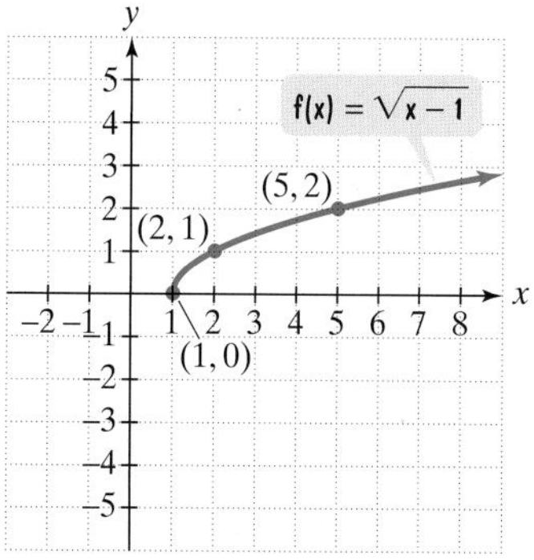


**Figure 2.46**

**Check Point 5** Use the graph of $f(x) = \sqrt{x - 1}$ in Figure 2.46 to obtain the graph of $h(x) = \sqrt{-x - 1}$.

**4** Use vertical stretching and shrinking to graph functions.

## Vertical Stretching and Shrinking

Morphing does much more than move an image horizontally, vertically, or about an axis. An object having one shape is transformed into a different shape. Horizontal shifts, vertical shifts, and reflections do not change the basic shape of a graph. How can we shrink and stretch graphs, thereby altering their basic shapes?

Look at the three graphs in Figure 2.47. The black graph in the middle is the graph of the standard quadratic function, $f(x) = x^2$. Now, look at the blue graph on the top. The equation of this graph is $g(x) = 2x^2$. Thus, for each $x$, the $y$-coordinate of $g$ is 2 times as large as the corresponding $y$-coordinate on the graph of $f$. The result is a narrower graph. We say that the graph of $g$ is obtained by vertically *stretching* the graph of $f$. Now, look at the red graph on the bottom. The equation of this graph is $h(x) = \frac{1}{2}x^2$, or $h(x) = \frac{1}{2}f(x)$. Thus, for each $x$, the $y$-coordinate of $h$ is one-half as large as the corresponding $y$-coordinate on the graph of $f$. The result is a wider graph. We say that the graph of $h$ is obtained by vertically *shrinking* the graph of $f$.

These observations can be summarized as follows.

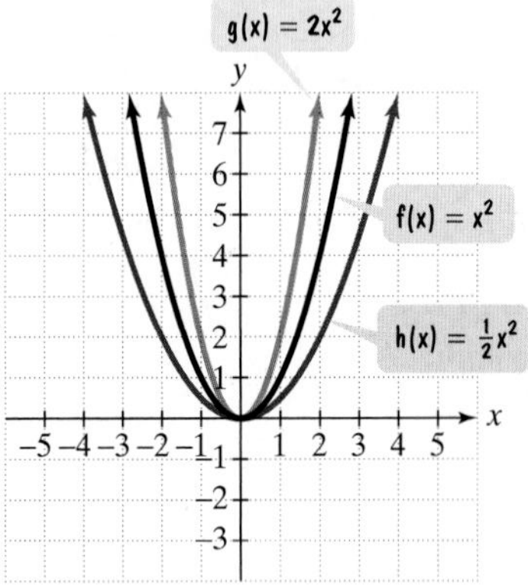

**Figure 2.47** Stretching and shrinking $f(x) = x^2$

### Stretching and Shrinking Graphs

Let $f$ be a function and $c$ a positive real number.

- If $c > 1$, the graph of $y = cf(x)$ is the graph of $y = f(x)$ vertically stretched by multiplying each of its $y$-coordinates by $c$.
- If $0 < c < 1$, the graph of $y = cf(x)$ is the graph of $y = f(x)$ vertically shrunk by multiplying each of its $y$-coordinates by $c$.

### EXAMPLE 6 Vertically Stretching a Graph

Use the graph of $f(x) = |x|$ to obtain the graph of $g(x) = 2|x|$.

**Solution** The graph of $g(x) = 2|x|$ is obtained by vertically stretching the graph of $f(x) = |x|$. We have constructed a table showing some of the coordinates for $f$ and $g$. Observe that the $y$-coordinate on the graph of $g$ is twice as large as the corresponding $y$-coordinate on the graph of $f$. The graphs of $f$ and $g$ are shown in Figure 2.48.

| $x$ | $f(x) = \|x\|$ | $g(x) = 2\|x\| = 2f(x)$ |
|---|---|---|
| −2 | $\|-2\| = 2$ | $2\|-2\| = 4$ |
| −1 | $\|-1\| = 1$ | $2\|-1\| = 2$ |
| 0 | $\|0\| = 0$ | $2\|0\| = 0$ |
| 1 | $\|1\| = 1$ | $2\|1\| = 2$ |
| 2 | $\|2\| = 2$ | $2\|2\| = 4$ |

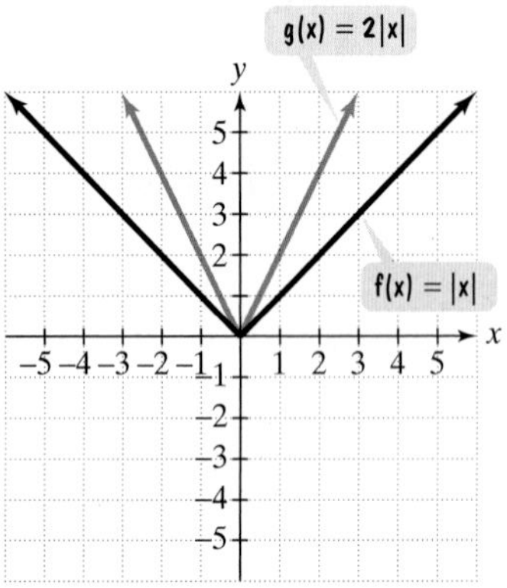

**Figure 2.48** Stretching $f(x) = |x|$

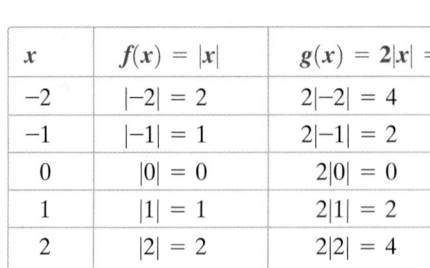

**Check Point 6** Use the graph of $f(x) = |x|$ to obtain the graph of $g(x) = 3|x|$.

## EXAMPLE 7 Vertically Shrinking a Graph

Use the graph of $f(x) = |x|$ to obtain the graph of $h(x) = \frac{1}{2}|x|$.

**Solution** The graph of $h(x) = \frac{1}{2}|x|$ is obtained by vertically shrinking the graph of $f(x) = |x|$. We have constructed a table showing some of the coordinates for $f$ and $h$. Observe that the $y$-coordinate on the graph of $h$ is one-half the corresponding $y$-coordinate on the graph of $f$. The graphs of $f$ and $h$ are shown in Figure 2.49.

| $x$ | $f(x) = \lvert x\rvert$ | $h(x) = \frac{1}{2}\lvert x\rvert = \frac{1}{2}f(x)$ |
|---|---|---|
| −2 | $\lvert -2\rvert = 2$ | $\frac{1}{2}\lvert -2\rvert = 1$ |
| −1 | $\lvert -1\rvert = 1$ | $\frac{1}{2}\lvert -1\rvert = \frac{1}{2}$ |
| 0 | $\lvert 0\rvert = 0$ | $\frac{1}{2}\lvert 0\rvert = 0$ |
| 1 | $\lvert 1\rvert = 1$ | $\frac{1}{2}\lvert 1\rvert = \frac{1}{2}$ |
| 2 | $\lvert 2\rvert = 2$ | $\frac{1}{2}\lvert 2\rvert = 1$ |

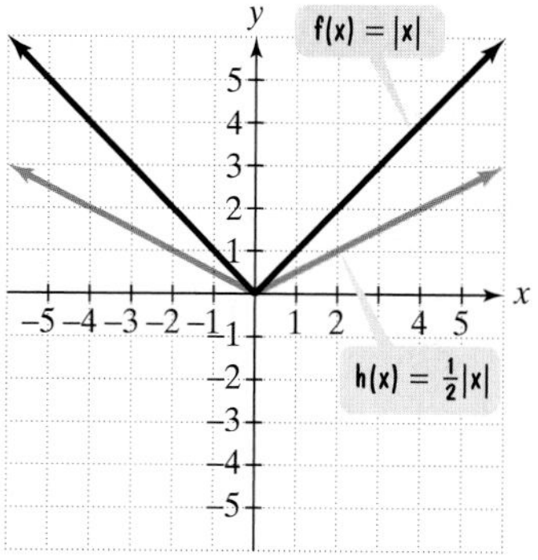


**Figure 2.49** Shrinking $f(x) = |x|$

**Check Point 7** Use the graph of $f(x) = |x|$ to obtain the graph of $h(x) = \frac{1}{4}|x|$.

**5** Graph functions involving a sequence of transformations.

## Sequences of Transformations

Table 2.5 summarizes the procedures for transforming the graph of $y = f(x)$.

**Table 2.5 Summary of Transformations**
**In each case, $c$ represents a positive real number.**

| To Graph: | Draw the Graph of $f$ and: | Changes in the Equation of $y = f(x)$ |
|---|---|---|
| Vertical shifts | | |
| $y = f(x) + c$ | Raise the graph of $f$ by $c$ units. | $c$ is added to $f(x)$. |
| $y = f(x) - c$ | Lower the graph of $f$ by $c$ units. | $c$ is subtracted from $f(x)$. |
| Horizontal shifts | | |
| $y = f(x + c)$ | Shift the graph of $f$ to the left $c$ units. | $x$ is replaced by $x + c$. |
| $y = f(x - c)$ | Shift the graph of $f$ to the right $c$ units. | $x$ is replaced by $x - c$. |
| Reflection about the $x$-axis $y = -f(x)$ | Reflect the graph of $f$ about the $x$-axis. | $f(x)$ is multiplied by −1. |
| Reflection about the $y$-axis $y = f(-x)$ | Reflect the graph of $f$ about the $y$-axis. | $x$ is replaced by $-x$. |
| Vertical stretching or shrinking | | |
| $y = cf(x), c > 1$ | Multiply each $y$-coordinate of $y = f(x)$ by $c$, vertically stretching the graph of $f$. | $f(x)$ is multiplied by $c$, $c > 1$. |
| $y = cf(x), 0 < c < 1$ | Multiply each $y$-coordinate of $y = f(x)$ by $c$, vertically shrinking the graph of $f$. | $f(x)$ is multiplied by $c$, $0 < c < 1$. |

A function involving more than one transformation can be graphed by performing transformations in the following order.

**1.** Horizontal shifting
**2.** Vertical stretching or shrinking
**3.** Reflecting
**4.** Vertical shifting

## EXAMPLE 8 Graphing Using a Sequence of Transformations

Use the graph of $f(x) = \sqrt{x}$ to graph $g(x) = \sqrt{1 - x} + 3$.

**Solution** The following sequence of steps is illustrated in Figure 2.50. We begin with the graph of $f(x) = \sqrt{x}$.

**Step 1 Horizontal Shifting** Graph $y = \sqrt{x + 1}$. Because $x$ is replaced by $x + 1$, the graph of $f(x) = \sqrt{x}$ is shifted 1 unit to the left.

**Step 2 Vertical Stretching or Shrinking** Because the equation $y = \sqrt{x + 1}$ is not multiplied by a constant in $g(x) = \sqrt{1 - x} + 3$, no stretching or shrinking is involved.

**Step 3 Reflecting** We are interested in graphing $y = \sqrt{1 - x} + 3$, or $y = \sqrt{-x + 1} + 3$. We have now graphed $y = \sqrt{x + 1}$. We can graph $y = \sqrt{-x + 1}$ by noting that $x$ is replaced by $-x$. Thus, we graph $y = \sqrt{-x + 1}$ by reflecting the graph of $y = \sqrt{x + 1}$ about the $y$-axis.

**Step 4 Vertical Shifting** We can use the graph of $y = \sqrt{1 - x}$ to get the graph of $g(x) = \sqrt{1 - x} + 3$. Because 3 is added, shift the graph of $y = \sqrt{1 - x}$ up by 3 units.

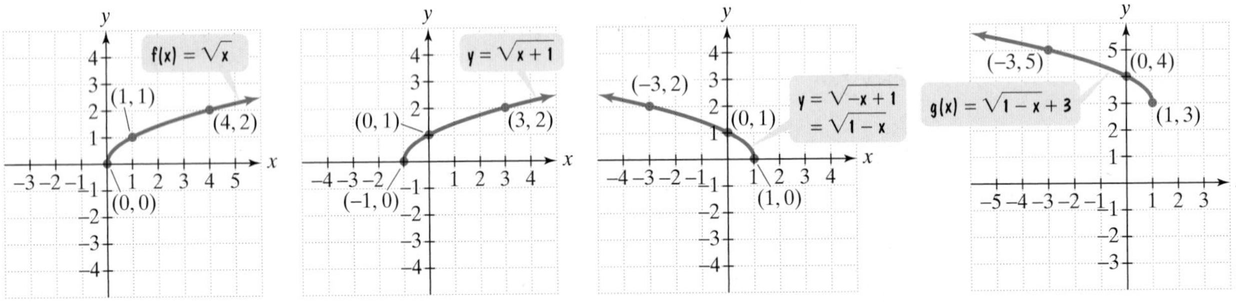


**Figure 2.50** Using $f(x) = \sqrt{x}$ to graph $g(x) = \sqrt{1 - x} + 3$.

**Check Point 8** Use the graph of $f(x) = x^2$ to graph $g(x) = -(x - 2)^2 + 3$.

**6** Combine functions arithmetically, specifying domains.

## Combinations of Functions

Functions, like numbers, can be added, subtracted, multiplied or divided. Because functions are usually given as equations, we perform these operations by performing operations with the algebraic expressions that appear on the right side of the equations. For example, we can combine the following two functions using addition:

$$f(x) = 2x + 1 \quad \text{and} \quad g(x) = x^2 - 4.$$

To do so, we add the terms to the right of the equal sign for $f(x)$ to the terms to the right of the equal sign for $g(x)$. Here is how it's done:

$$\begin{aligned}(f+g)(x) &= f(x)+g(x) \\ &= (2x+1)+(x^2-4) && \text{Add terms for } f(x) \text{ and } g(x). \\ &= 2x-3+x^2 && \text{Combine like terms.} \\ &= x^2+2x-3 && \text{Arrange terms in descending powers of } x.\end{aligned}$$

The name of this new function is $f + g$. Thus, the sum $f + g$ is the function defined by $(f + g)(x) = x^2 + 2x - 3$. The domain of $f + g$ consists of the numbers $x$ that are in the domain of $f$ and in the domain of $g$. Because neither $f$ nor $g$ contains division or even roots, the domain of each function is the set of all real numbers. Thus, the domain of $f + g$ is also the set of all real numbers.

## EXAMPLE 9 Finding the Sum of Two Functions

Let $f(x) = x^2 - 3$ and $g(x) = 4x + 5$. Find

**a.** $(f + g)(x)$ **b.** $(f + g)(3)$

### Solution

**a.** $(f + g)(x) = f(x) + g(x) = (x^2 - 3) + (4x + 5) = x^2 + 4x + 2$. Thus, $(f + g)(x) = x^2 + 4x + 2$.

**b.** We find $(f + g)(3)$ by substituting 3 for $x$ in the equation for $f + g$.

$$(f+g)(x) = x^2 + 4x + 2 \quad \text{This is the equation for } f+g.$$

Substitute 3 for x.

$$(f+g)(3) = 3^2 + 4\cdot 3 + 2 = 9 + 12 + 2 = 23$$

**Check Point 9** Let $f(x) = 3x^2 + 4x - 1$ and $g(x) = 2x + 7$. Find

**a.** $(f + g)(x)$ **b.** $(f + g)(4)$

Here is a general definition for function addition.

### The Sum of Functions

Let $f$ and $g$ be two functions. The **sum** $\boldsymbol{f + g}$ is the function defined by

$$(f+g)(x) = f(x) + g(x).$$

The domain of $f + g$ is the set of all real numbers that are common to the domain of $f$ and the domain of $g$.

## EXAMPLE 10 Adding Functions and Determining the Domain

Let $f(x) = \sqrt{x + 3}$ and $g(x) = \sqrt{x - 2}$. Find:

**a.** $(f + g)(x)$ **b.** the domain of $f + g$

**Solution**

**a.** $(f + g)(x) = f(x) + g(x) = \sqrt{x + 3} + \sqrt{x - 2}$.

**b.** The domain of $f + g$ is the set of all real numbers that are common to the domain of $f$ and the domain of $g$. Thus, we must find the domains of $f$ and $g$. We will do so for $f$ first.

Note that $f(x) = \sqrt{x + 3}$ is a function involving the square root of $x + 3$. Because the square root of a negative quantity is not a real number, the value of $x + 3$ must be nonnegative. Thus, the domain of $f$ is all $x$ such that $x + 3 \geq 0$. Equivalently, the the domain is $\{x | x \geq -3\}$, or $[-3, \infty)$.

Likewise, $g(x) = \sqrt{x - 2}$ is also a square root function. Because the square root of a negative quantity is not a real number, the value of $x - 2$ must be nonnegative. Thus, the domain of $g$ is all $x$ such that $x - 2 \geq 0$. Equivalently, the domain is $\{x | x \geq 2\}$, or $[2, \infty)$.

Now, we can use a number line to determine the the domain of $f + g$. Figure 2.51 shows the domain of $f$ in blue and the domain of $g$ in red. Can you see that all real numbers greater than or equal to 2 are common to both domains? This is shown in purple on the number line. Thus, the domain of $f + g$ is $[2, \infty)$.

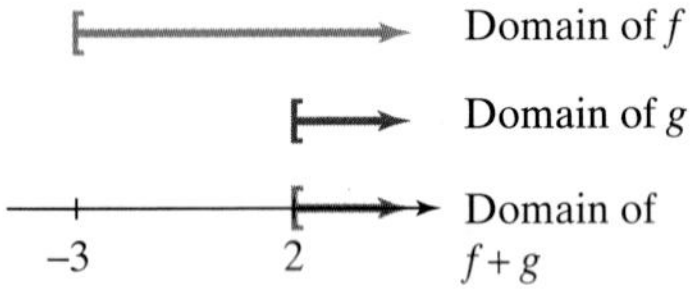


**Figure 2.51** Finding the domain of the sum $f + g$

**Check Point 10** Let $f(x) = \sqrt{x - 3}$ and $g(x) = \sqrt{x + 1}$. Find:

**a.** $(f + g)(x)$ **b.** the domain of $f + g$

We can also combine functions using subtraction, multiplication, and division by performing operations with the algebraic expressions that appear on the right side of the equations.

**Definitions: Sum, Difference, Product, and Quotient of Functions**

Let $f$ and $g$ be two functions. The **sum** $f + g$, the **difference** $f - g$, the **product** $fg$, and the **quotient** $\frac{f}{g}$ are functions whose domains are the set of all real numbers common to the domains of $f$ and $g$, defined as follows:

1. Sum: $(f + g)(x) = f(x) + g(x)$
2. Difference: $(f - g)(x) = f(x) - g(x)$
3. Product: $(fg)(x) = f(x) \cdot g(x)$
4. Quotient: $\left(\frac{f}{g}\right)(x) = \frac{f(x)}{g(x)}$, provided $g(x) \neq 0$

**Technology**

The graph shown below is the graph of

$$y = \sqrt{x + 3} + \sqrt{x - 2}$$

in a $[-3, 10, 1]$ by $[0, 8, 1]$ viewing rectangle. The graph reveals what we discovered algebraically in Example 10(b). The domain of this function is $[2, \infty)$.

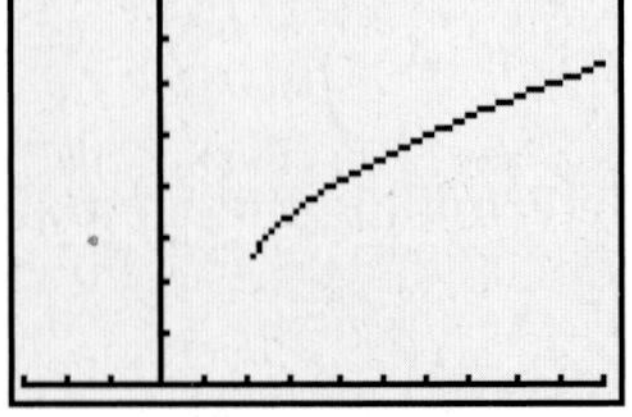

## EXAMPLE 11 Combining Functions

If $f(x) = 2x - 1$ and $g(x) = x^2 + x - 2$, find:

**a.** $(f - g)(x)$ **b.** $(fg)(x)$ **c.** $\left(\frac{f}{g}\right)(x)$

Determine the domain for each function.

**Solution**

**a.** $(f - g)(x) = f(x) - g(x)$ This is the definition of the difference $f - g$.

$= (2x - 1) - (x^2 + x - 2)$ Subtract $g(x)$ from $f(x)$.

$= 2x - 1 - x^2 - x + 2$ Perform the subtraction.

$= -x^2 + x + 1$ Combine like terms and arrange terms in descending powers of x.

**b.** $(fg)(x) = (2x - 1)(x^2 + x - 2)$ This is the definition of the product fg.

$= 2x(x^2 + x - 2) - 1(x^2 + x - 2)$ Multiply each term in the second factor by 2x and −1, respectively.

$= 2x^3 + 2x^2 - 4x - x^2 - x + 2$ Use the distributive property.

$= 2x^3 + (2x^2 - x^2) + (-4x - x) + 2$ Rearrange terms so that like terms are adjacent.

$= 2x^3 + x^2 - 5x + 2$ Combine like terms.

**c.** $\left(\frac{f}{g}\right)(x) = \frac{f(x)}{g(x)}$ This is the definition of the quotient $\frac{f}{g}$.

$= \frac{2x - 1}{x^2 + x - 2}$ Divide the algebraic expressions for f(x) and g(x).

Because the equations for $f$ and $g$ do not involve division or contain even roots, the domain of both $f$ and $g$ is the set of all real numbers. Thus, the domain of $f - g$ and $fg$ is the set of all real numbers. However, for $\frac{f}{g}$, the denominator cannot equal zero. We can factor the denominator as follows:

$$\left(\frac{f}{g}\right)(x) = \frac{2x - 1}{x^2 + x - 2} = \frac{2x - 1}{(x + 2)(x - 1)}$$

Because $x + 2 \neq 0$, $x \neq -2$.

Because $x - 1 \neq 0$, $x \neq 1$.

We see that the domain for $\frac{f}{g}$ is the set of all real numbers except −2 and 1: $\{x \mid x \neq -2 \text{ and } x \neq 1\}$.

**Check Point 11** If $f(x) = x - 5$ and $g(x) = x^2 - 1$, find:

**a.** $(f - g)(x)$ **b.** $(fg)(x)$ **c.** $\left(\frac{f}{g}\right)(x)$

Determine the domain for each function.

# EXERCISE SET 2.5

## Practice Exercises

*In Exercises 1–10, begin by graphing the standard quadratic function, $f(x) = x^2$. Then use transformations of this graph to graph the given function.*

1. $g(x) = x^2 - 2$
2. $g(x) = x^2 - 1$
3. $g(x) = (x - 2)^2$
4. $g(x) = (x - 1)^2$
5. $h(x) = -(x - 2)^2$
6. $h(x) = -(x - 1)^2$
7. $h(x) = (x - 2)^2 + 1$
8. $h(x) = (x - 1)^2 + 2$
9. $g(x) = 2(x - 2)^2$
10. $g(x) = \frac{1}{2}(x - 1)^2$

*In Exercises 11–22, begin by graphing the square root function, $f(x) = \sqrt{x}$. Then use transformations of this graph to graph the given function.*

11. $g(x) = \sqrt{x} + 2$
12. $g(x) = \sqrt{x} + 1$
13. $g(x) = \sqrt{x + 2}$
14. $g(x) = \sqrt{x + 1}$

**15.** $h(x) = -\sqrt{x+2}$

**16.** $h(x) = -\sqrt{x+1}$

**17.** $h(x) = \sqrt{-x+2}$

**18.** $h(x) = \sqrt{-x+1}$

**19.** $g(x) = \frac{1}{2}\sqrt{x+2}$

**20.** $g(x) = 2\sqrt{x+1}$

**21.** $h(x) = \sqrt{x+2} - 2$

**22.** $h(x) = \sqrt{x+1} - 1$

*In Exercises 23–34, begin by graphing the absolute value function, $f(x) = |x|$. Then use transformations of this graph to graph the given function.*

**23.** $g(x) = |x| + 4$

**24.** $g(x) = |x| + 3$

**25.** $g(x) = |x + 4|$

**26.** $g(x) = |x + 3|$

**27.** $h(x) = |x + 4| - 2$

**28.** $h(x) = |x + 3| - 2$

**29.** $h(x) = -|x + 4|$

**30.** $h(x) = -|x + 3|$

**31.** $g(x) = -|x + 4| + 1$

**32.** $g(x) = -|x + 4| + 2$

**33.** $h(x) = 2|x + 4|$

**34.** $h(x) = 2|x + 3|$

*In Exercises 35–44, begin by graphing the standard cubic function, $f(x) = x^3$. Then use transformations of this graph to graph the given function.*

**35.** $g(x) = x^3 - 3$

**36.** $g(x) = x^3 - 2$

**37.** $g(x) = (x - 3)^3$

**38.** $g(x) = (x - 2)^3$

**39.** $h(x) = -x^3$

**40.** $h(x) = -(x - 2)^3$

**41.** $h(x) = \frac{1}{2}x^3$

**42.** $h(x) = \frac{1}{4}x^3$

**43.** $r(x) = (x - 3)^3 + 2$

**44.** $r(x) = (x - 2)^3 + 1$

*In Exercises 45–52, use the graph of the function f to sketch the graph of the given function g.*

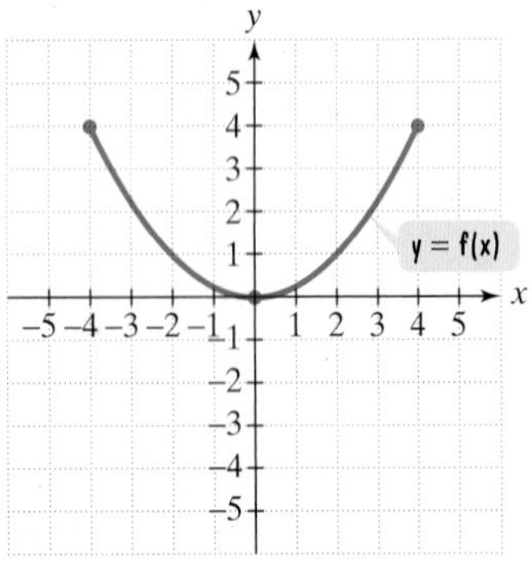


**45.** $g(x) = f(x) + 1$

**46.** $g(x) = f(x) + 2$

**47.** $g(x) = f(x + 1)$

**48.** $g(x) = f(x + 2)$

**49.** $g(x) = -f(x)$

**50.** $g(x) = \frac{1}{2}f(x)$

**51.** $g(x) = \frac{1}{2}f(x + 1)$

**52.** $g(x) = -f(x + 2)$

**53.** If $f(x) = 2x^2 - 5$ and $g(x) = 3x + 7$, find:
**a.** $(f + g)(x)$ **b.** $(f + g)(4)$.

**54.** If $f(x) = 3x^2 - 2x + 1$ and $g(x) = 4x - 1$, find:
**a.** $(f + g)(x)$ **b.** $(f + g)(5)$.

**55.** Let $f(x) = \sqrt{x - 6}$ and $g(x) = \sqrt{x + 2}$. Find:
**a.** $(f + g)(x)$ **b.** the domain of $f + g$.

**56.** Let $f(x) = \sqrt{x - 8}$ and $g(x) = \sqrt{x + 5}$. Find:
**a.** $(f + g)(x)$ **b.** the domain of $f + g$.

*In Exercises 57–68, find $f + g$, $f - g$, $fg$, and $\frac{f}{g}$. Determine the domain for each function.*

**57.** $f(x) = 2x + 3, \quad g(x) = x - 1$

**58.** $f(x) = 3x - 4, \quad g(x) = x + 2$

**59.** $f(x) = x - 5, \quad g(x) = 3x^2$

**60.** $f(x) = x - 6, \quad g(x) = 5x^2$

**61.** $f(x) = 2x^2 - x - 3, \quad g(x) = x + 1$

**62.** $f(x) = 6x^2 - x - 1, \quad g(x) = x - 1$

**63.** $f(x) = \sqrt{x}, \quad g(x) = x - 4$

**64.** $f(x) = \dfrac{1}{x}, \quad g(x) = x - 5$

**65.** $f(x) = 2 + \dfrac{1}{x}, \quad g(x) = \dfrac{1}{x}$

**66.** $f(x) = 6 - \dfrac{1}{x}, \quad g(x) = \dfrac{1}{x}$

**67.** $f(x) = \sqrt{x + 4}, \quad g(x) = \sqrt{x - 1}$

**68.** $f(x) = \sqrt{x + 6}, \quad g(x) = \sqrt{x - 3}$

## Application Exercises

*Consider the following functions:*

$f(x)$ = population of the world's more-developed regions in year $x$

$g(x)$ = the population of the world's less-developed regions in year $x$

$h(x)$ = total world population in year $x$.

*Use these functions and the graph shown to answer Exercises 69–72.*

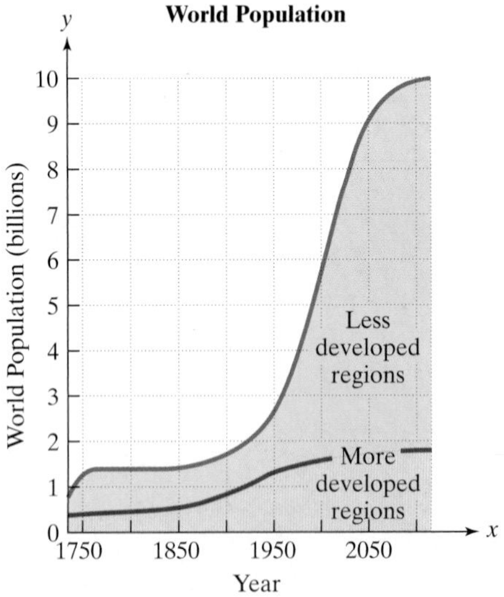


*Source*: Population Reference Bureau

**69.** What does the function $f + g$ represent?

**70.** What does the function $h - g$ represent?

**71.** Use the graph to estimate $(f + g)(2000)$.

**72.** Use the graph to estimate $(h - g)(2000)$.

**73.** A company that sells radios has yearly fixed costs of \$600,000. It costs the company \$45 to produce each radio. Each radio will sell for \$65. The company's costs and revenue are modeled by the functions

$C(x) = 600{,}000 + 45x$ This function models the company's costs.

$R(x) = 65x$ This function models the company's revenue.

Find and interpret $(R - C)(20{,}000)$, $(R - C)(30{,}000)$ and $(R - C)(40{,}000)$.

**74.** The function $f(t) = -0.14t^2 + 0.51t + 31.6$ models the U.S. population, $f(t)$, in millions, ages 65 and older $t$ years after 1990. The function $g(t) = 0.54t^2 + 12.64t + 107.1$ models the total yearly cost of Medicare, $g(t)$, in billions of dollars, $t$ years after 1990.

**a.** What does the function $\frac{g}{f}$ represent?

**b.** Find and interpret $\frac{g}{f}(10)$.

**75.** Consider two functions $M$ and $F$ that represent the number of male and female members of the House of Representatives for the years 1977, 1981, 1991, 1994, and 1999. Sketch the graphs of $M$ and $F$ in the same rectangular coordinate system, using the data in the bar graph. Each graph should consist of five points whose first coordinates are the years and second coordinates are the numbers of representatives, male or female. Now, add to the graphs in your coordinate system the graph of $M + F$. What constant function do you obtain? What is the significance of this constant?

**Gender Breakdown of the House of Representatives for Five Selected Years**

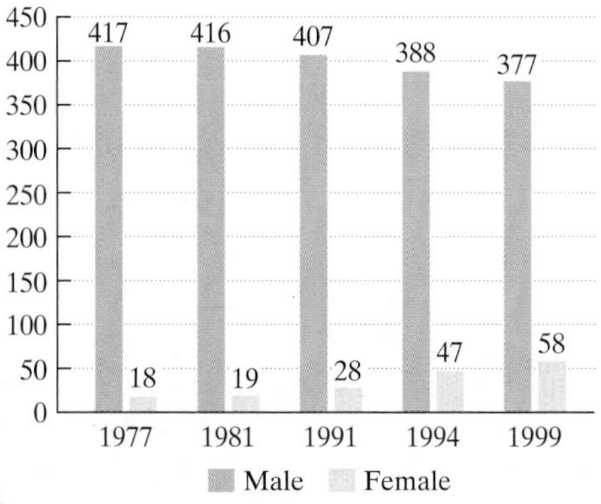


**76.** A department store has two locations in a city. From 1998 through 2002, the profits for each of the store's two branches are modeled by the functions $f(x) = -0.44x + 13.62$ and $g(x) = 0.51x + 11.14$. In each model, $x$ represents the number of years after 1998 and $f$ and $g$ represent the profit in millions of dollars.

**a.** What is the slope for $f$? Describe what this means.

**b.** What is the slope for $g$? Describe what this means.

**c.** Find $f + g$. What is the slope for this function? What does this mean?

## Writing in Mathematics

**77.** What must be done to a function's equation so that its graph is shifted vertically upward?

**78.** What must be done to a function's equation so that its graph is shifted horizontally to the right?

**79.** What must be done to a function's equation so that its graph is reflected about the $x$-axis?

**80.** What must be done to a function's equation so that its graph is reflected about the $y$-axis?

**81.** What must be done to a function's equation so that its graph is stretched?

**82.** If the equations of two functions are given, explain how to obtain the quotient function and its domain.

**83.** A company's profit is given by the function $y = P(x)$, where $x$ represents the amount spent on advertising and $P$ represents weekly profits, both expressed in hundreds of dollars.

**a.** Describe a situation that might occur in the company that would result in the graph of its profit function undergoing a vertical shift.

**b.** Now, consider the function $y = D(x)$, where $x$ represents the amount spent on advertising and $D$ represents weekly profits, both expressed in dollars rather than hundreds of dollars. If $D$ and $P$ are both graphed on the same axes, describe the relationship between the two graphs.

## Technology Exercises

**84. a.** Use a graphing utility to graph $f(x) = x^2 + 1$.

**b.** Graph $f(x) = x^2 + 1$, $g(x) = f(2x)$, $h(x) = f(3x)$, and $k(x) = f(4x)$ on the same viewing rectangle.

**c.** Describe the relationship among the graphs of $f, g, h$, and $k$ with emphasis on different values of $x$ for points on all four graphs that give the same $y$-coordinate.

**d.** Generalize by describing the relationship between the graph of $f$ and the graph of $g$, where $g(x) = f(cx)$ for $c > 1$.

**e.** Try out your generalization by sketching the graphs of $f(cx)$ for $c = 1$, $c = 2$, $c = 3$, and $c = 4$ for a function of your choice.

**85. a.** Use a graphing utility to graph $f(x) = x^2 + 1$.

**b.** Graph $f(x) = x^2 + 1$, and $g(x) = f(\frac{1}{2}x)$, and $h(x) = f(\frac{1}{4}x)$ on the same viewing rectangle.

**c.** Describe the relationship among the graphs of $f$, $g$, and $h$ with emphasis on different values of $x$ for points on all three graphs that give the same $y$-coordinate.

**d.** Generalize by describing the relationship between the graph of $f$ and the graph of $g$, where $g(x) = f(cx)$ for $0 < c < 1$.

**e.** Try out your generalization by sketching the graphs of $f(cx)$ for $c = 1$, and $c = \frac{1}{2}$, and $c = \frac{1}{4}$ for a function of your choice.

## Critical Thinking Exercises

**86.** Which one of the following is true?

**a.** If $f(x) = |x|$ and $g(x) = |x + 3| + 3$, then the graph of $g$ is a translation of three units to the right and three units upward of the graph of $f$.

**b.** If $f(x) = -\sqrt{x}$ and $g(x) = \sqrt{-x}$, then $f$ and $g$ have identical graphs.

**c.** If $f(x) = x^2$ and $g(x) = 5(x^2 - 2)$, then the graph of $g$ can be obtained from the graph of $f$ by stretching $f$ five units followed by a downward shift of two units.

**d.** If $f(x) = x^3$ and $g(x) = -(x - 3)^3 - 4$, then the graph of $g$ can be obtained from the graph of $f$ by moving $f$ three units to the right, reflecting in the $x$-axis, and then moving the resulting graph down four units.

*In Exercises 87–90, functions $f$ and $g$ are graphed in the same rectangular coordinate system. If $g$ is obtained from $f$ through a sequence of transformations, find an equation for $g$.*

**87.**

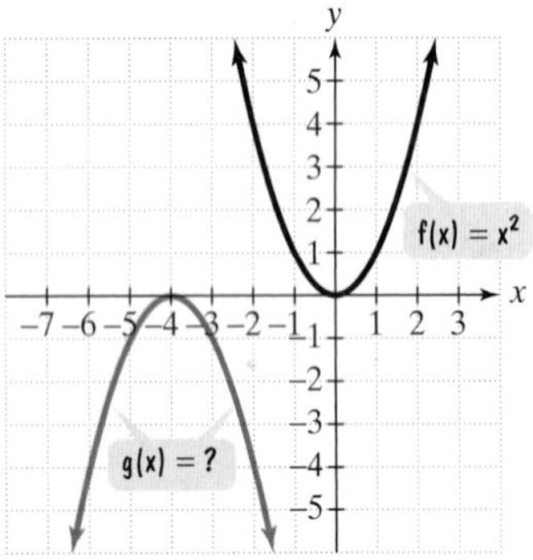


**88.**

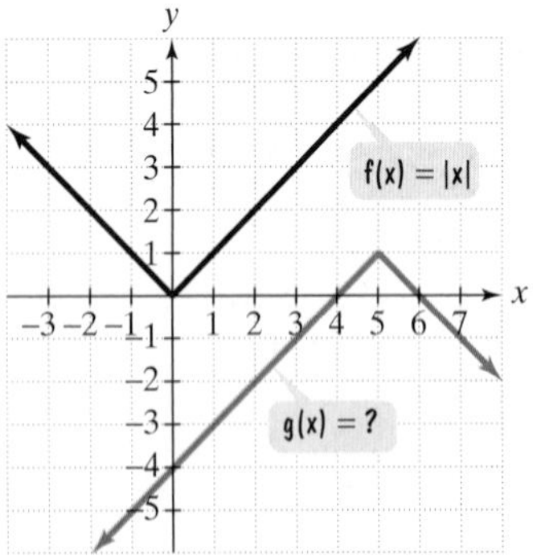


**89.**

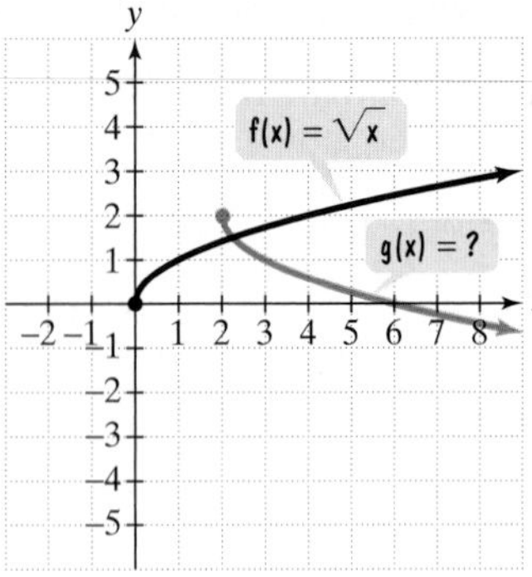


**90.**

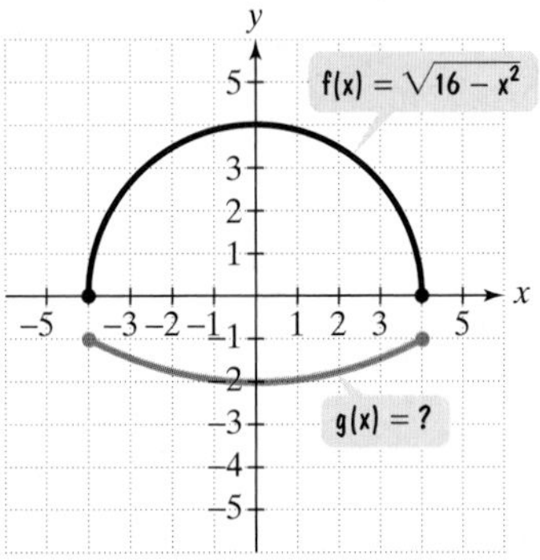


*For Exercises 91–94, assume that $(a, b)$ is a point on the graph of $f$. What is the corresponding point on the graph of each of the following functions?*

**91.** $y = f(-x)$

**92.** $y = 2f(x)$

**93.** $y = f(x - 3)$

**94.** $y = f(x) - 3$

## Group Exercise

**95.** This activity is a group research project on morphing and should result in a presentation made by group members to the entire class. Be sure to include morphing images that will intrigue class members. You should have no problem finding an array of fascinating images online. Also include a discussion of films using spectacular morphing effects. Rent videos of these films and show appropriate excerpts.

# SECTION 2.6 Composite and Inverse Functions

## Objectives

1. Form composite functions.
2. Write functions as compositions.
3. Verify inverse functions.
4. Find the inverse of a function.
5. Use the horizontal line test to determine if a function has an inverse function.
6. Use the graph of a one-to-one function to graph its inverse function.

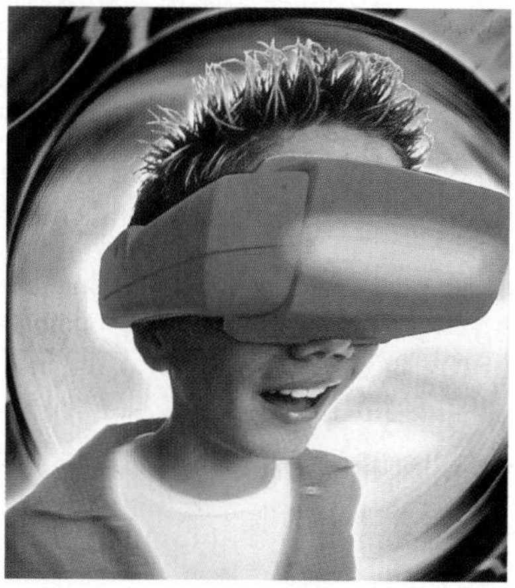

The time: the not-too-distant future. Your computer and its two-dimensional monitor have been replaced by a virtual reality system. You put on a headset and a virtual reality sensory suit. Suddenly you are skiing down a mountain. You feel the wind in your hair, the frost on your eyebrows, and the gentle heat of the sun on your face. Your heart races as you leap off cliffs, feeling the shudder through your ski boots as you race down the mountain.

Would you like to purchase a computer capable of helping you engage in virtual skiing? Luckily, your local computer store is having a sale right now. The models that are on sale cost either \$300 less than the regular price or 85% of the regular price. If $x$ represents the computer's regular price, both discounts can be described with the following functions.

$$f(x) = x - 300 \qquad\qquad g(x) = 0.85x$$

The computer is on sale for \$300 less than its regular price.

The computer is on sale for 85% of its regular price.

At the store, you bargain with the salesperson. Eventually, she makes an offer you can't refuse: The sale price is 85% of the regular price followed by a \$300 reduction:

$$0.85x - 300$$

85% of the regular price

followed by a \$300 reduction

In terms of functions $f$ and $g$, this offer can be obtained by taking the output of $g(x) = 0.85x$, namely $0.85x$, and using it as the input of $f$:

$$f(x) = x - 300$$

Replace $x$ by $0.85x$, the output of $g(x) = 0.85x$.

$$f(0.85x) = 0.85x - 300.$$

Because $0.85x$ is $g(x)$, we can write this last equation as

$$f(g(x)) = 0.85x - 300.$$

We read this equation as "$f$ of $g$ of $x$ is equal to $0.85x - 300$." We call $f(g(x))$ the **composition of the function $f$ with $g$**, or a **composite function**. This composite function is written $f \circ g$. Thus,

$$(f \circ g)(x) = f(g(x)) = 0.85x - 300.$$

Like all functions, we can evaluate $f \circ g$ for a specified value of $x$ in the function's domain. For example, here's how to find the value of this function at 1400:

$$(f \circ g)(x) = 0.85x - 300$$ This composite function describes the offer you cannot refuse.

Replace x by 1400.

$$(f \circ g)(1400) = 0.85(1400) - 300 = 1190 - 300 = 890.$$

This means that a computer that regularly sells for \$1400 is on sale for \$890 subject to both discounts.

In this section, we will focus on the composition of two functions. We will also study functions whose composition have a special relationship.

**1** Form composite functions.

Before you run out to buy a new computer, let's generalize our discussion of the computer's double discount and define the composition of any two functions.

**The Composition of Functions**

The **composition of the function $f$ with $g$** is denoted by $f \circ g$ and is defined by the equation

$$(f \circ g)(x) = f(g(x)).$$

The domain of the **composite function $f \circ g$** is the set of all $x$ such that

**1.** $x$ is in the domain of $g$ and

**2.** $g(x)$ is in the domain of $f$.

The composition of $f$ with $g$, $f \circ g$, is pictured as a machine with inputs and outputs in Figure 2.52. The diagram indicates that the output of $g$, or $g(x)$, becomes the input for "machine" $f$. If $g(x)$ is not in the domain of $f$, it cannot be input into machine $f$, and so $g(x)$ must be discarded.

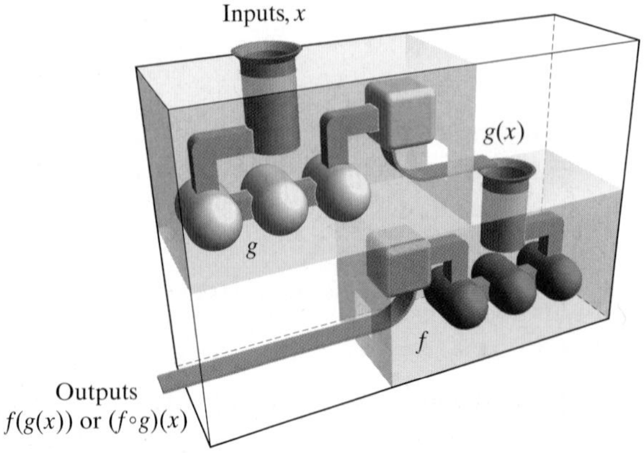


**Figure 2.52** Inputting one function into a second function

**EXAMPLE 1 Forming Composite Functions**

Given $f(x) = 3x - 4$ and $g(x) = x^2 + 6$, find:

**a.** $(f \circ g)(x)$ **b.** $(g \circ f)(x)$.

### Solution

**a.** We begin with $(f \circ g)(x)$, the composition of $f$ with $g$. Because $(f \circ g)(x)$ means $f(g(x))$, we must replace each occurrence of $x$ in the equation for $f$ by $g(x)$.

$f(x) = 3x - 4$ — This is the given equation for f.

Replace x by $g(x)$.

$$(f \circ g)(x) = f(g(x)) = 3g(x) - 4$$

$= 3(x^2 + 6) - 4$ — Because $g(x) = x^2 + 6$, replace $g(x)$ with $x^2 + 6$

$= 3x^2 + 18 - 4$ — Use the distributive property.

$= 3x^2 + 14$ — Simplify.

Thus, $(f \circ g)(x) = 3x^2 + 14$.

**b.** Next, we find $(g \circ f)(x)$, the composition of $g$ with $f$. Because $(g \circ f)(x)$ means $g(f(x))$, we must replace each occurrence of $x$ in the equation for $g$ by $f(x)$.

$g(x) = x^2 + 6$ — This is the given equation for g.

Replace x by $f(x)$.

$$(g \circ f)(x) = g(f(x)) = (f(x))^2 + 6$$

$= (3x - 4)^2 + 6$ — Because $f(x) = 3x - 4$, replace $f(x)$ with $3x - 4$.

$= 9x^2 - 24x + 16 + 6$ — Use $(A - B)^2 = A^2 - 2AB + B^2$ to square $3x - 4$.

$= 9x^2 - 24x + 22$ — Simplify.

Thus, $(g \circ f)(x) = 9x^2 - 24x + 22$. Notice that $(f \circ g)(x)$ is not the same function as $(g \circ f)(x)$.

**Check Point 1** Given $f(x) = 5x + 6$ and $g(x) = x^2 - 1$, find:

**a.** $(f \circ g)(x)$ **b.** $(g \circ f)(x)$.

**2** Write functions as compositions.

## Composite Functions in Calculus

Some techniques in calculus require that we be able to express a function as a composition of two functions. Although there is more than one way to do this, there is often a "natural" selection that comes to mind first. For example, consider the function $h$ defined by

$$h(x) = (3x^2 - 4x + 1)^5.$$

The function $h$ takes $3x^2 - 4x + 1$ and raises it to the power 5. A natural way to write $h$ as a composition of two functions is to raise the function $g(x) = 3x^2 - 4x + 1$ to the power 5. Thus, if we let

$$f(x) = x^5 \text{ and } g(x) = 3x^2 - 4x + 1, \text{then}$$

$$(f \circ g)(x) = f(g(x)) = f(3x^2 - 4x + 1) = (3x^2 - 4x + 1)^5.$$

## EXAMPLE 2 Writing a Function as a Composition

Express as a composition of two functions:

$$h(x) = \sqrt[3]{x^2 + 1}.$$

**Solution** The function $h$ takes $x^2 + 1$ and takes its cube root. A natural way to write $h$ as a composition of two functions is to take the cube root of the function $g(x) = x^2 + 1$. Thus, we let

$$f(x) = \sqrt[3]{x} \text{ and } g(x) = x^2 + 1.$$

We can check this composition by finding $(f \circ g)(x)$. This should give the original function, namely $h(x) = \sqrt[3]{x^2 + 1}$.

$$(f \circ g)(x) = f(g(x)) = f(x^2 + 1) = \sqrt[3]{x^2 + 1} = h(x)$$

**Check Point 2** Express as a composition of two functions:

$$h(x) = \sqrt{x^2 + 5}.$$

### Inverse Functions

Here are two functions that describe situations related to the price of a computer, $x$:

$$f(x) = x - 300 \qquad g(x) = x + 300.$$

Function $f$ subtracts \$300 from the computer's price and function $g$ adds \$300 to the computer's price. Let's see what $f(g(x))$ does. Put $g(x)$ into $f$:

$f(x) = x - 300$ This is the given equation for f.

Replace x by $g(x)$.

$f(g(x)) = g(x) - 300$

$= x + 300 - 300$ Because $g(x) = x + 300$, replace $g(x)$ by $x + 300$.

$= x$ This is the computer's original price.

Using $f(g(x))$, the computer's price, $x$, went through two changes: the first, an increase; the second, a decrease:

$$x + 300 - 300.$$

The final price of the computer, $x$, is identical to its starting price, $x$.

In general, if the changes made to $x$ by function $g$ are undone by the changes made by function $f$, then

$$f(g(x)) = x.$$

Assume, also, that this "undoing" takes place in the other direction:

$$g(f(x)) = x.$$

Under these conditions, we say that each function is the **inverse function** of the other. The fact that $g$ is the inverse of $f$ is expressed by renaming $g$ as $f^{-1}$, read "$f$-inverse." For example, the inverse functions

$$f(x) = x - 300 \qquad g(x) = x + 300$$

are usually named as follows:

$$f(x) = x - 300 \qquad f^{-1}(x) = x + 300.$$

With these ideas in mind, we present the formal definition of the inverse of a function.

**Study Tip**

The notation $f^{-1}$ represents the inverse function of $f$. The $-1$ is *not* an exponent. The notation $f^{-1}$ does *not* mean $\frac{1}{f}$:

$$f^{-1} \neq \frac{1}{f}$$

**Definition of the Inverse of a Function**

Let $f$ and $g$ be two functions such that

$$f(g(x)) = x \qquad \text{for every } x \text{ in the domain of } g$$

and

$$g(f(x)) = x \qquad \text{for every } x \text{ in the domain of } f.$$

The function $g$ is the **inverse** of the function $f$, and is denoted by $f^{-1}$ (read "$f$-inverse"). Thus, $f(f^{-1}(x)) = x$ and $f^{-1}(f(x)) = x$. The domain of $f$ is equal to the range of $f^{-1}$, and vice versa.

**3** Verify inverse functions.

## EXAMPLE 3 Verifying Inverse Functions

Show that each function is an inverse of the other:

$$f(x) = 3x + 2 \qquad \text{and} \qquad g(x) = \frac{x-2}{3}.$$

**Solution** To show that $f$ and $g$ are inverses of each other, we must show that $f(g(x)) = x$ and $g(f(x)) = x$. We begin with $f(g(x))$.

$$f(x) = 3x + 2$$ This is the equation for f.

Replace x by g(x).

$$f(g(x)) = 3g(x) + 2 = 3\left(\frac{x-2}{3}\right) + 2 = x - 2 + 2 = x$$

Next, we find $g(f(x))$.

$$g(x) = \frac{x-2}{3}$$ This is the equation for g.

Replace x by f(x).

$$g(f(x)) = \frac{f(x)-2}{3} = \frac{(3x+2)-2}{3} = \frac{3x}{3} = x$$

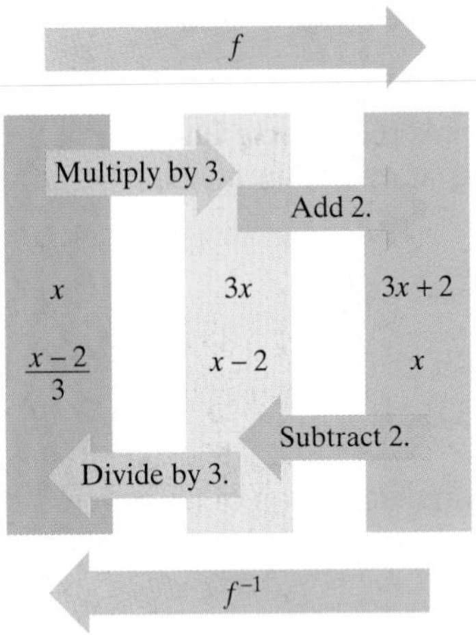


**Figure 2.53** $f^{-1}$ undoes the changes produced by $f$.

Because $g$ is the inverse of $f$ (and vice versa), we can use inverse notation and write

$$f(x) = 3x + 2 \quad \text{and} \quad f^{-1}(x) = \frac{x-2}{3}.$$

Notice how $f^{-1}$ undoes the changes produced by $f$: $f$ changes $x$ by *multiplying* by 3 and *adding* 2, and $f^{-1}$ undoes this by *subtracting* 2 and *dividing* by 3. This "undoing" process is illustrated in Figure 2.53.

**Check Point 3** Show that each function is an inverse of the other:

$$f(x) = 4x - 7 \quad \text{and} \quad g(x) = \frac{x+7}{4}.$$

**4** Find the inverse of a function.

## Finding the Inverse of a Function

The definition of the inverse of a function tells us that the domain of $f$ is equal to the range of $f^{-1}$, and vice versa. This means that if the function $f$ is the set of ordered pairs $(x, y)$, then the inverse of $f$ is the set of ordered pairs $(y, x)$. If a function is defined by an equation, we can obtain the equation for $f^{-1}$, the inverse of $f$, by interchanging the role of $x$ and $y$ in the equation for function $f$.

**Study Tip**

The procedure for finding a function's inverse uses a *switch-and-solve* strategy. Switch $x$ and $y$, then solve for $y$.

**Finding the Inverse of a Function**

The equation for the inverse of a function $f$ can be found as follows.

1. Replace $f(x)$ by $y$ in the equation for $f(x)$.
2. Interchange $x$ and $y$.
3. Solve for $y$. If this equation does not define $y$ as a function of $x$, the function $f$ does not have an inverse function and this procedure ends. If this equation does define $y$ as a function of $x$, the function $f$ has an inverse function.
4. If $f$ has an inverse function, replace $y$ in step 3 by $f^{-1}(x)$. We can verify our result by showing that $f(f^{-1}(x)) = x$ and $f^{-1}(f(x)) = x$.

### EXAMPLE 4 Finding the Inverse of a Function

Find the inverse of $f(x) = 7x - 5$.

**Solution**

**Step 1 Replace $f(x)$ by $y$:**

$$y = 7x - 5$$

**Step 2 Interchange $x$ and $y$:**

$$x = 7y - 5 \quad \text{This is the inverse function.}$$

**Step 3 Solve for $y$:**

$$x + 5 = 7y \quad \text{Add 5 to both sides.}$$

$$\frac{x+5}{7} = y \quad \text{Divide both sides by 7.}$$

**Discovery**

In Example 4, we found that if $f(x) = 7x - 5$, then

$$f^{-1}(x) = \frac{x+5}{7}.$$

Verify this result by showing that

$$f(f^{-1}(x)) = x$$

and

$$f^{-1}(f(x)) = x.$$

**Step 4 Replace $y$ by $f^{-1}(x)$:**

$$f^{-1}(x) = \frac{x+5}{7}$$ The equation is written with $f^{-1}$ on the left.

Thus, $f(x) = 7x - 5$ and $f^{-1}(x) = \frac{x+5}{7}$.

The inverse function, $f^{-1}$, undoes the changes produced by $f$. $f$ changes $x$ by multiplying by 7 and subtracting 5. $f^{-1}$ undoes this by adding 5 and dividing by 7.

**Check Point 4** Find the inverse of $f(x) = 2x + 7$.

## EXAMPLE 5 Finding the Equation of the Inverse

Find the inverse of $f(x) = x^3 + 1$.

**Solution**

**Step 1 Replace $f(x)$ with $y$:** $y = x^3 + 1$

**Step 2 Interchange $x$ and $y$:** $x = y^3 + 1$

**Step 3 Solve for $y$:**

$$x - 1 = y^3$$
$$\sqrt[3]{x-1} = \sqrt[3]{y^3}$$
$$\sqrt[3]{x-1} = y$$

**Step 4 Replace $y$ with $f^{-1}(x)$:** $f^{-1}(x) = \sqrt[3]{x-1}$.

Thus, the inverse of $f(x) = x^3 + 1$ is $f^{-1}(x) = \sqrt[3]{x-1}$.

**Check Point 5** Find the inverse of $f(x) = 4x^3 - 1$.

**5** Use the horizontal line test to determine if a function has an inverse function.

## The Horizontal Line Test and One-to-One Functions

Let's see what happens if we try to find the inverse of the standard quadratic function $f(x) = x^2$.

**Step 1 Replace $f(x)$ with $y$:** $y = x^2$.

**Step 2 Interchange $x$ and $y$:** $x = y^2$.

**Step 3 Solve for $y$:** We apply the square root method to solve $y^2 = x$ for $y$. We obtain

$$y = \pm\sqrt{x}.$$

The $\pm$ in this last equation shows that for certain values of $x$ (all positive real numbers), there are two values of $y$. Because this equation does not represent $y$ as a function of $x$, the standard quadratic function does not have an inverse function.

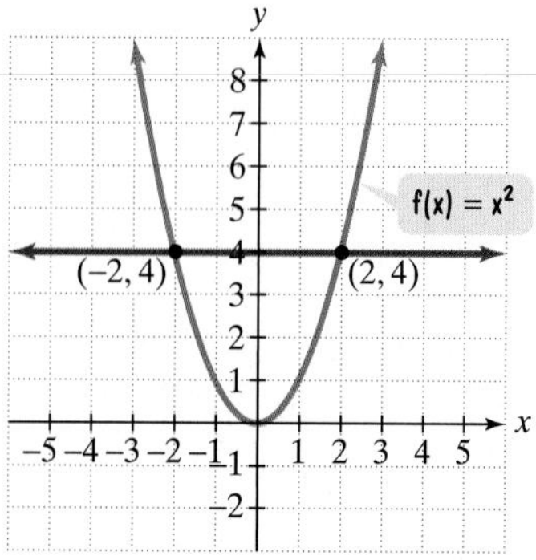


**Figure 2.54** The horizontal line intersects the graph twice.

## Discovery

How might you restrict the domain of $f(x) = x^2$, graphed in Figure 2.54, so that the remaining portion of the graph passes the horizontal line test?

Can we look at the graph of a function and tell if it represents a function with an inverse? Yes. The graph of the standard quadratic function is shown in Figure 2.54. Four units above the $x$-axis, a horizontal line is drawn. This line intersects the graph at two of its points, $(-2, 4)$ and $(2, 4)$. Because inverse functions have ordered pairs with the coordinates reversed, let's see what happens if we reverse these coordinates. We obtain $(4, -2)$ and $(4, 2)$. A function provides exactly one output for each input. However, the input 4 is associated with two outputs, $-2$ and 2. The points $(4, -2)$ and $(4, 2)$ do not define a function.

If any horizontal line, such as the one in Figure 2.54, intersects a graph at two or more points, these points will not define a function when their coordinates are reversed. This suggests the **horizontal line test** for inverse functions.

**The Horizontal Line Test For Inverse Functions**

A function $f$ has an inverse that is a function, $f^{-1}$, if there is no horizontal line that intersects the graph of the function $f$ at more than one point.

## EXAMPLE 6 Applying the Horizontal Line Test

Which of the following graphs represent functions that have inverse functions?

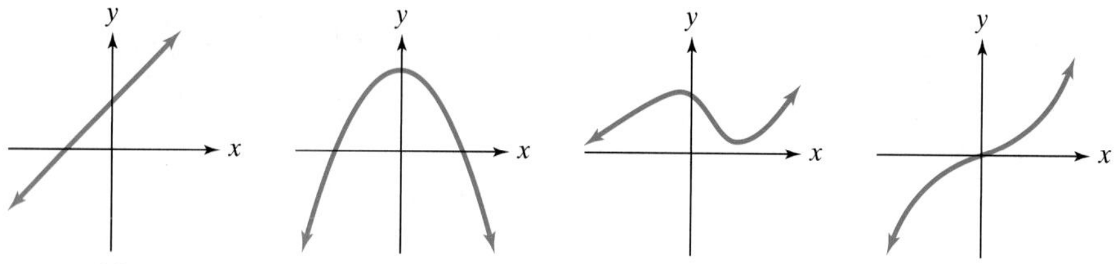


(a) (b) (c) (d)

**Solution** Notice that horizontal lines can be drawn in parts (b) and (c) that intersect the graphs more than once. These graphs do not pass the horizontal line test. These are not the graphs of functions with inverse functions. By contrast, no horizontal line can be drawn in parts (a) and (d) that intersect the graphs more than once. These graphs pass the horizontal line test. Thus, the graphs in parts (a) and (d) represent functions that have inverse functions.

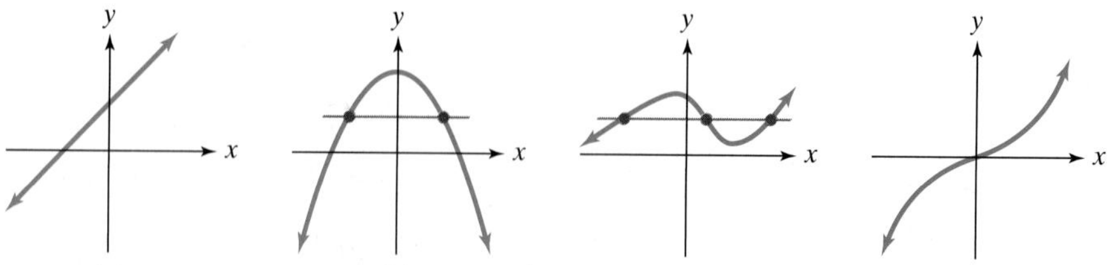


(a) Has an inverse function

(b)

(c)

(d) Has an inverse function

**Check Point 6** Which of the following graphs represent functions that have inverse functions?

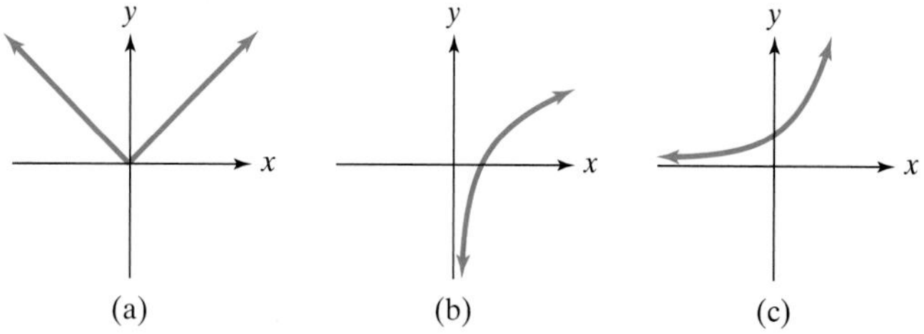

A function passes the horizontal line test when no two different ordered pairs have the same second component. This means that if $x_1 \neq x_2$, then $f(x_1) \neq f(x_2)$. Such a function is called a **one-to-one function**. Thus, a one-to-one function is a function in which no two different ordered pairs have the same second component. Only one-to-one functions have inverse functions. Any function that passes the horizontal line test is a one-to-one function. Any one-to-one function has a graph that passes the horizontal line test.

**6** Use the graph of a one-to-one function to graph its inverse function.

## Graphs of $f$ and $f^{-1}$

There is a relationship between the graph of a one-to-one function $f$ and its inverse $f^{-1}$. Because inverse functions have ordered pairs with the coordinates reversed, if the point $(a, b)$ is on the graph of $f$, then the point $(b, a)$ is on the graph of $f^{-1}$. The points $(a, b)$ and $(b, a)$ are symmetric with respect to the line $y = x$. Thus, **the graph of $f^{-1}$ is a reflection of the graph of $f$ about the line $y = x$.** This is illustrated in Figure 2.55.

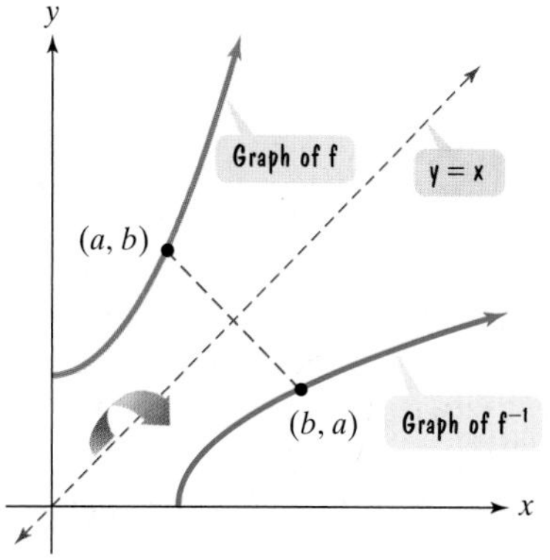


**Figure 2.55** The graph of $f^{-1}$ as a reflection of $f$ about $y = x$

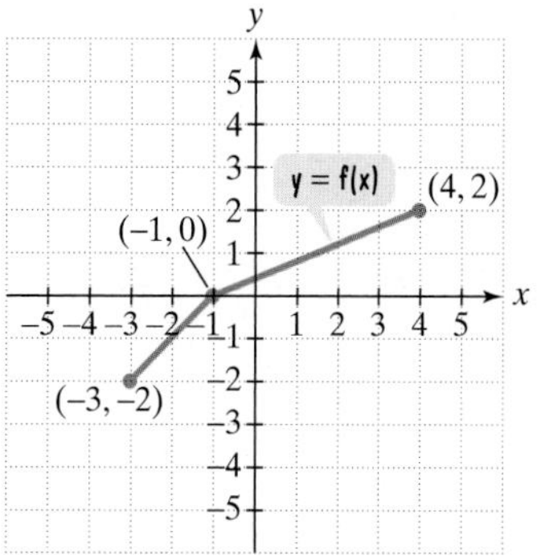


**Figure 2.56**

## EXAMPLE 7 Graphing the Inverse Function

Use the graph of $f$ in Figure 2.56 to draw the graph of its inverse function.

**Solution** We begin by noting that no horizontal line intersects the graph of $f$ at more than one point, so $f$ does have an inverse function. Because the points $(-3, -2)$, $(-1, 0)$, and $(4, 2)$ are on the graph of $f$, the graph of the inverse function, $f^{-1}$, has points with these ordered pairs reversed. Thus, $(-2, -3)$, $(0, -1)$, and $(2, 4)$ are on the graph of $f^{-1}$. We can use these points to graph $f^{-1}$.

The graph of $f^{-1}$ is shown in Figure 2.57. Note that the graph of $f^{-1}$ is the reflection of the graph of $f$ about the line $y = x$.

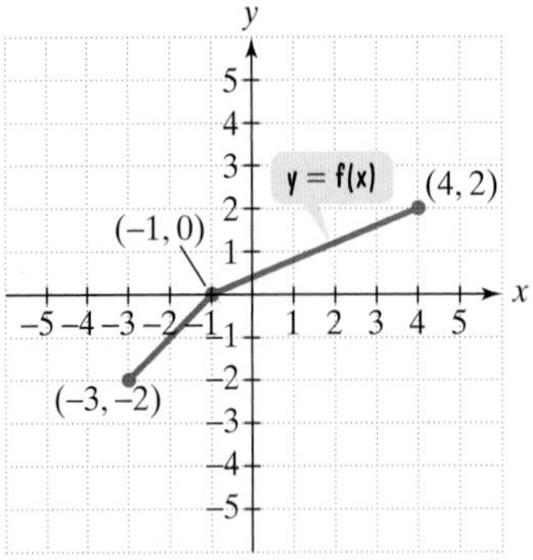


**Figure 2.56,** repeated

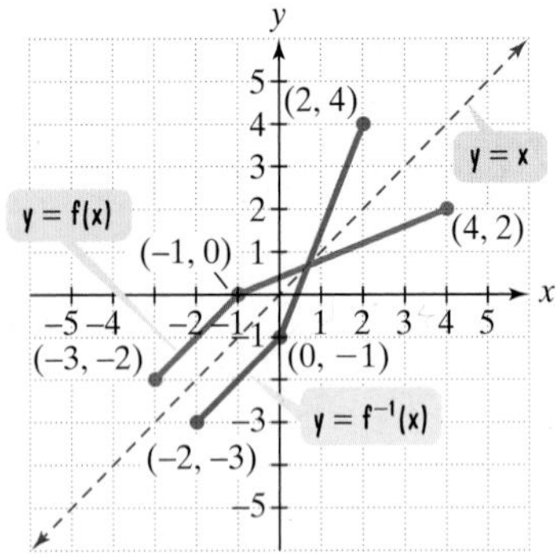


**Figure 2.57** The graph of $f$ and $f^{-1}$

**Check Point 7** Use the graph of $f$ in the figure to the right to draw the graph of its inverse function.

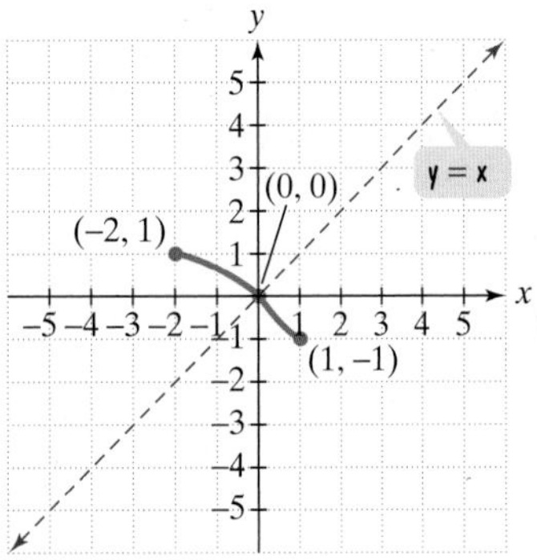


## EXERCISE SET 2.6

### Practice Exercises

*In Exercises 1–14, find*

a. $(f \circ g)(x)$;
b. $(g \circ f)(x)$;
c. $(f \circ g)(2)$.

1. $f(x) = 2x, \quad g(x) = x + 7$
2. $f(x) = 3x, \quad g(x) = x - 5$
3. $f(x) = x + 4, \quad g(x) = 2x + 1$
4. $f(x) = 5x + 2, \quad g(x) = 3x - 4$
5. $f(x) = 4x - 3, \quad g(x) = 5x^2 - 2$
6. $f(x) = 7x + 1, \quad g(x) = 2x^2 - 9$
7. $f(x) = x^2 + 2, \quad g(x) = x^2 - 2$
8. $f(x) = x^2 + 1, \quad g(x) = x^2 - 3$
9. $f(x) = \sqrt{x}, \quad g(x) = x - 1$
10. $f(x) = \sqrt{x}, \quad g(x) = x + 2$
11. $f(x) = 2x - 3, \quad g(x) = \dfrac{x + 3}{2}$
12. $f(x) = 6x - 3, \quad g(x) = \dfrac{x + 3}{6}$
13. $f(x) = \dfrac{1}{x}, \quad g(x) = \dfrac{1}{x}$
14. $f(x) = \dfrac{1}{x}, \quad g(x) = \dfrac{2}{x}$

*In Exercises 15–22, express the given function h as a composition of two functions f and g so that $h(x) = (f \circ g)(x)$.*

15. $h(x) = (3x - 1)^4$
16. $h(x) = (2x - 5)^3$
17. $h(x) = \sqrt[3]{x^2 - 9}$
18. $h(x) = \sqrt{5x^2 + 3}$
19. $h(x) = |2x - 5|$
20. $h(x) = |3x - 4|$
21. $h(x) = \dfrac{1}{2x - 3}$
22. $h(x) = \dfrac{1}{4x + 5}$

*In Exercises 23–32, find $f(g(x))$ and $g(f(x))$ and determine whether each pair of functions f and g are inverses of each other.*

23. $f(x) = 4x$ and $g(x) = \dfrac{x}{4}$

**24.** $f(x) = 6x$ and $g(x) = \frac{x}{6}$

**25.** $f(x) = 3x + 8$ and $g(x) = \frac{x - 8}{3}$

**26.** $f(x) = 4x + 9$ and $g(x) = \frac{x - 9}{4}$

**27.** $f(x) = 5x - 9$ and $g(x) = \frac{x + 5}{9}$

**28.** $f(x) = 3x - 7$ and $g(x) = \frac{x + 3}{7}$

**29.** $f(x) = \frac{3}{x - 4}$ and $g(x) = \frac{3}{x} + 4$

**30.** $f(x) = \frac{2}{x - 5}$ and $g(x) = \frac{2}{x} + 5$

**31.** $f(x) = -x$ and $g(x) = -x$

**32.** $f(x) = \sqrt[3]{x - 4}$ and $g(x) = x^3 + 4$

*The functions in Exercises 33–48 are all one-to-one. For each function:*

**a.** *Find an equation for $f^{-1}(x)$, the inverse function.*

**b.** *Verify that your equation is correct by showing that $f(f^{-1}(x)) = x$ and $f^{-1}(f(x)) = x$.*

**33.** $f(x) = 2x + 3$

**34.** $f(x) = 3x - 1$

**35.** $f(x) = x^3 + 2$

**36.** $f(x) = x^3 - 1$

**37.** $f(x) = (x + 2)^3$

**38.** $f(x) = (x - 1)^3$

**39.** $f(x) = \frac{1}{x}$

**40.** $f(x) = \frac{2}{x}$

**41.** $f(x) = \sqrt{x}$

**42.** $f(x) = \sqrt[3]{x}$

**43.** $f(x) = x^2 + 1$, for $x \geq 0$

**44.** $f(x) = x^2 - 1$, for $x \geq 0$

**45.** $f(x) = \frac{2x + 1}{x - 3}$

**46.** $f(x) = \frac{2x - 3}{x + 1}$

**47.** $f(x) = \sqrt[3]{x - 4} + 3$

**48.** $f(x) = x^{3/5}$

*Which graphs in Exercises 49–54 represent functions that have inverse functions?*

**49.**

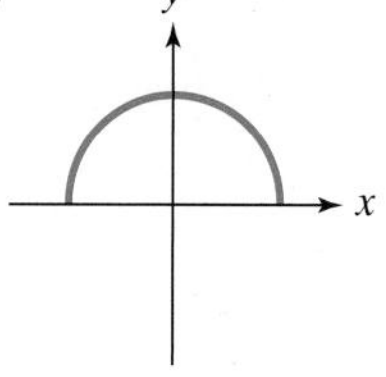


**50.**

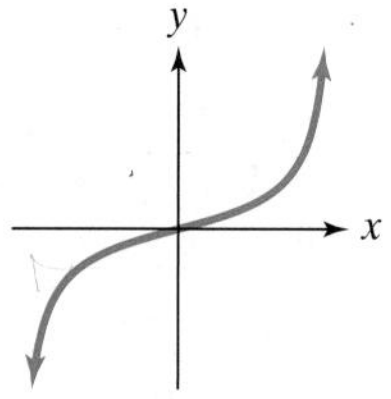


**51.**

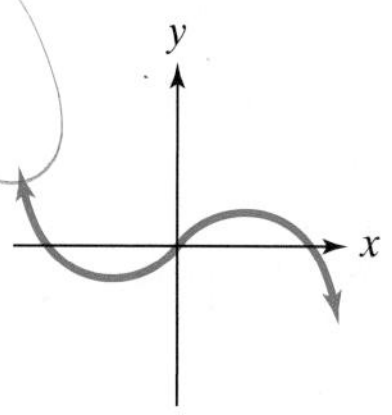


**52.**

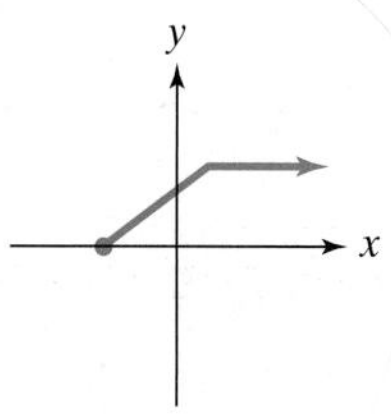


**53.**

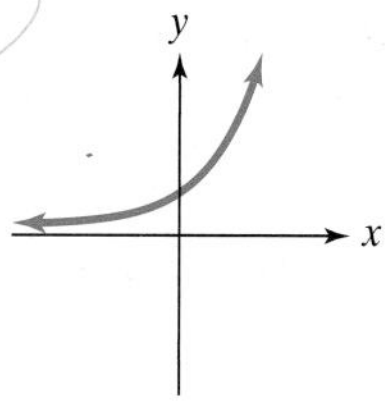


**54.**

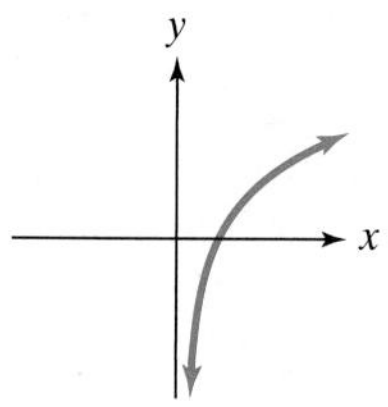


*In Exercises 55–58, use the graph of f to draw the graph of its inverse function.*

**55.**

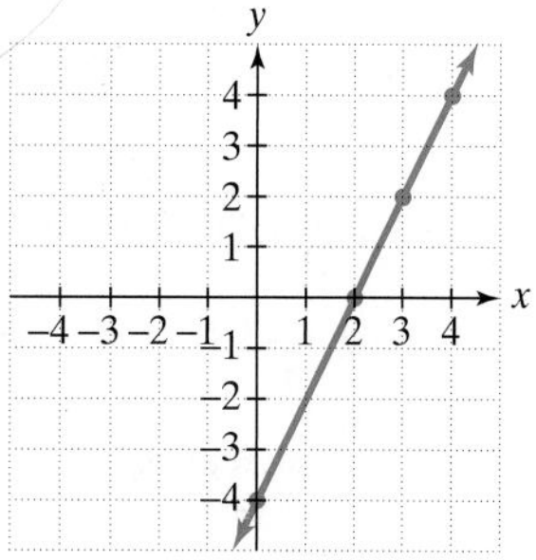


**56.**

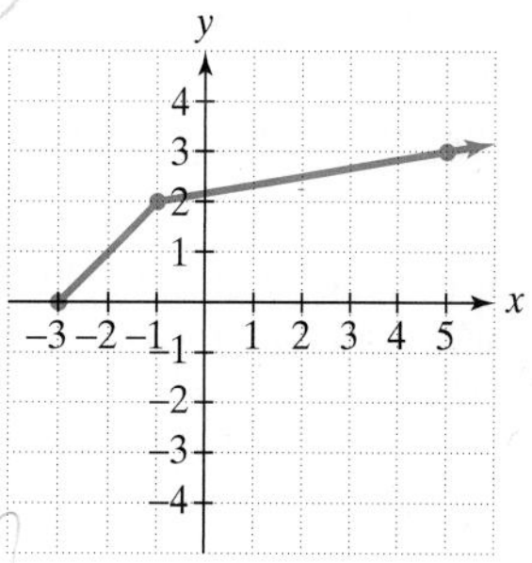


**57.**

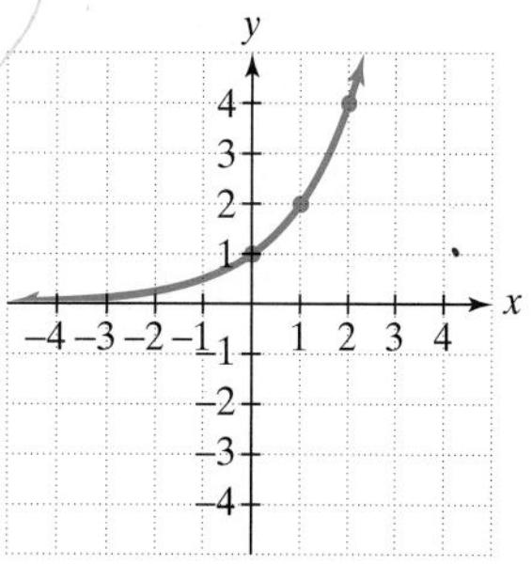


**58.**

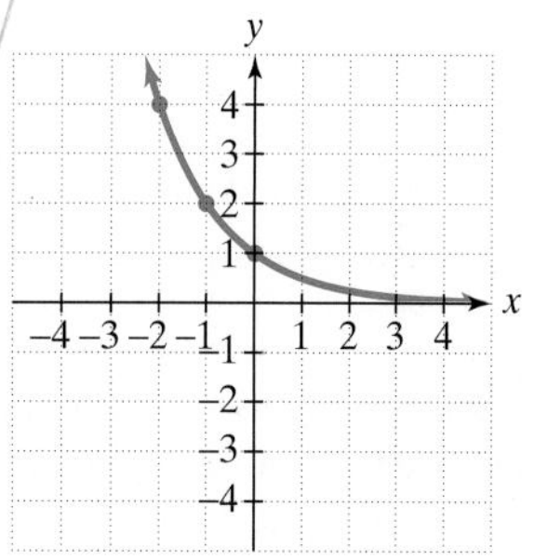

## Application Exercises

**59.** The regular price of a computer is $x$ dollars. Let $f(x) = x - 400$ and $g(x) = 0.75x$.

**a.** Describe what the functions $f$ and $g$ model in terms of the price of the computer.

**b.** Find $(f \circ g)(x)$ and describe what this models in terms of the price of the computer.

**c.** Repeat part (b) for $(g \circ f)(x)$.

**d.** Which composite function models the greater discount on the computer, $f \circ g$ or $g \circ f$? Explain.

**e.** Find $f^{-1}$ and describe what this models in terms of the price of the computer.

**60.** The regular price of a pair of jeans is $x$ dollars. Let $f(x) = x - 5$ and $g(x) = 0.6x$.

**a.** Describe what functions $f$ and $g$ model in terms of the price of the jeans.

**b.** Find $(f \circ g)(x)$ and describe what this models in terms of the price of the jeans.

**c.** Repeat part (b) for $(g \circ f)(x)$.

**d.** Which composite function models the greater discount on the jeans, $f \circ g$ or $g \circ f$? Explain.

**e.** Find $f^{-1}$ and describe what this models in terms of the price of the jeans.

**61.** The graph represents the probability of two people in the same room sharing a birthday as a function of the number of people in the room. Call the function $f$.

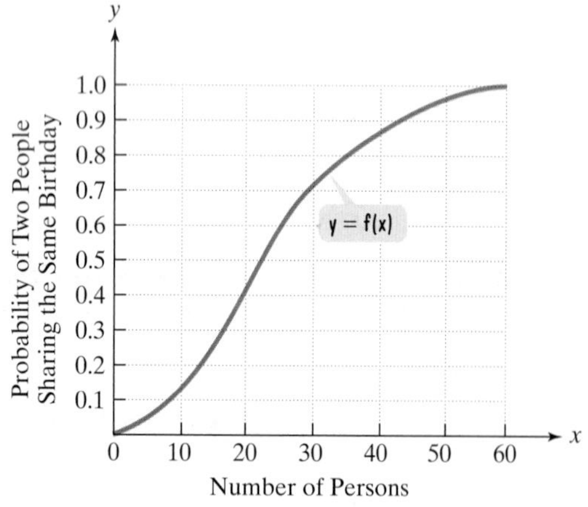


**a.** Explain why $f$ has an inverse that is a function.

**b.** Describe in practical terms the meaning of $f^{-1}(0.25)$, $f^{-1}(0.5)$, and $f^{-1}(0.7)$.

**62.** The line graph shown at the top of the next column is based on data from the World Health Organization.

**a.** Explain why $f$ has an inverse that is a function.

**b.** Describe in practical terms the meaning of $f^{-1}(20)$.

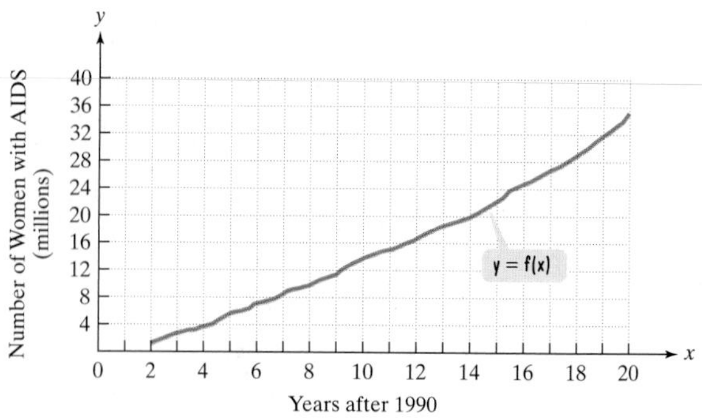


*Source*: Boston Globe

*The graph shows the average age at which women in the United States marry for the first time over a 110-year period. Use the graph to solve Exercises 63–64.*

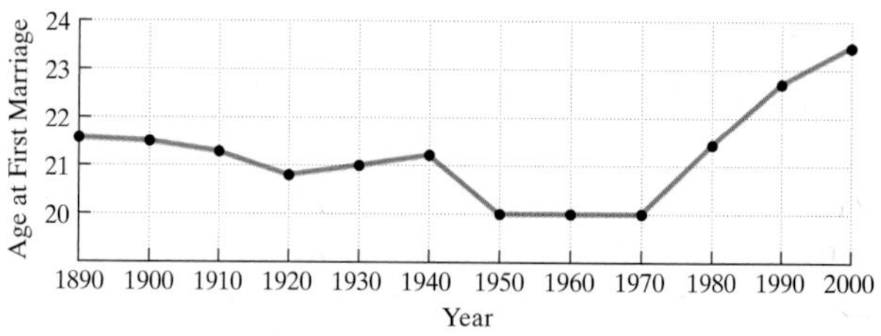


*Source*: U.S. Census Bureau

**63.** Does this graph have an inverse that is a function? What does this mean about the average age at which U.S. women marry during the period shown?

**64.** Identify two or more years in which U.S. women married for the first time at the same average age. What is this average age?

## Writing in Mathematics

**65.** Describe a procedure for finding $(f \circ g)(x)$.

**66.** Explain how to express $h(x) = (x^2 + 12)^9$ as a composition of two functions.

**67.** Explain how to determine if two functions are inverses of each other.

**68.** Describe how to find the inverse of a one-to-one function.

**69.** What is the horizontal line test and what does it indicate?

**70.** Describe how to use the graph of a one-to-one function to draw the graph of its inverse function.

**71.** How can a graphing utility be used to visually determine if two functions are inverses of each other?

**72.** Consider the following function:

(The Beatles, 20), (Elvis Presley, 18),

(Michael Jackson, 13)

(Mariah Carey, 13), (The Supremes, 12).

The domain is the set of the five recording artists with the most number 1 singles in the United States. The range is the set of the number of number 1 singles for each artist. Reverse each of the five ordered pairs. Is the resulting relation a function? Describe what this means in terms of whether or not the given function is one-to-one. (*Source: The Popular Music Database*)

### Technology Exercises

*In Exercises 73–81, use a graphing utility to graph the function. Use the graph to determine whether the function has an inverse that is a function (that is, whether the function is one-to-one).*

**73.** $f(x) = x^2 - 1$

**74.** $f(x) = \sqrt[3]{2 - x}$

**75.** $f(x) = \frac{x^3}{2}$

**76.** $f(x) = \frac{x^4}{4}$

**77.** $f(x) = \text{int}(x - 2)$

**78.** $f(x) = |x - 2|$

**79.** $f(x) = (x - 1)^3$

**80.** $f(x) = -\sqrt{16 - x^2}$

**81.** $f(x) = x^3 + x + 1$

*In Exercises 82–84, use a graphing utility to graph f and g in the same viewing rectangle. In addition, graph the line $y = x$ and visually determine if f and g are inverses.*

**82.** $f(x) = 4x + 4, \quad g(x) = 0.25x - 1$

**83.** $f(x) = \frac{1}{x} + 2, \quad g(x) = \frac{1}{x - 2}$

**84.** $f(x) = \sqrt[3]{x} - 2, \quad g(x) = (x + 2)^3$

### Critical Thinking Exercises

**85.** Which one of the following is true?

**a.** The inverse of $\{(1, 4), (2, 7)\}$ is $\{(2, 7), (1, 4)\}$.

**b.** The function $f(x) = 5$ is one-to-one.

**c.** If $f(x) = 3x$, then $f^{-1}(x) = \frac{1}{3x}$.

**d.** The domain of $f$ is the same as the range of $f^{-1}$.

**86.** If $h(x) = \sqrt{3x^2 + 5}$, find functions $f$ and $g$ so that $h(x) = (f \circ g)(x)$.

**87.** If $f(x) = 3x$ and $g(x) = x + 5$, find $(f \circ g)^{-1}(x)$ and $(g^{-1} \circ f^{-1})(x)$.

**88.** Show that

$$f(x) = \frac{3x - 2}{5x - 3}$$

is its own inverse.

**89.** Consider the two functions defined by $f(x) = m_1x + b_1$ and $g(x) = m_2x + b_2$. Prove that the slope of the composite function of $f$ with $g$ is equal to the product of the slopes of the two functions.

### Group Exercise

**90.** In Tom Stoppard's play *Arcadia*, the characters dream and talk about mathematics, including ideas involving graphing, composite functions, symmetry, and lack of symmetry in things that are tangled, mysterious, and unpredictable. Group members should rent and view the movie. Present a report on the ideas discussed by the characters that are related to concepts that we studied in this chapter. Bring in a copy of the video and show appropriate excerpts.

## CHAPTER SUMMARY, REVIEW, AND TEST

### Summary

#### 2.1 Lines and Slope

a. The slope, $m$, of the line through $(x_1, y_1)$ and $(x_2, y_2)$ is $m = \frac{y_2 - y_1}{x_2 - x_1}$.

b. Equations of lines include point-slope form, $y - y_1 = m(x - x_1)$, slope-intercept form, $y = mx + b$, and general form, $Ax + By + C = 0$. The equation of a horizontal line is $y = b$; a vertical line is $x = a$.

#### 2.2 Parallel and Perpendicular Lines; Circles

a. Parallel lines have equal slopes. Perpendicular lines have slopes that are negative reciprocals.

b. The standard form of the equation of a circle with center $(h, k)$ and radius $r$ is $(x - h)^2 + (y - k)^2 = r^2$.

c. The general form of the equation of a circle is $x^2 + y^2 + Dx + Ey + F = 0$.

d. To convert from the general form to the standard form of a circle's equation, complete the square on $x$ and $y$.

#### 2.3 Introduction to Functions

a. A relation is any set of ordered pairs. The set of first components is the domain and the set of second components is the range.

b. A function is a correspondence between two sets $X$ (the domain) and $Y$ (the range) that assigns to each element $x$ in the domain exactly one element $y$ in the range. If any element in a relation's domain corresponds to more than one element in the range, the relation is not a function.

c. Functions are usually given in terms of equations involving $x$ and $y$, in which $x$ is the independent variable and $y$ is the dependent variable. If an equation is solved for $y$ and more than one value of $y$ can be obtained for a given $x$, then the equation does not define $y$ as a function of $x$. If an equation defines a function, $f(x)$, the value of the function at $x$, often replaces $y$.

d. The difference quotient is

$$\frac{f(x+h)-f(x)}{h}, h \neq 0.$$

e. If a function $f$ does not model data or verbal conditions, its domain is the largest set of real numbers for which the value of $f(x)$ is a real number. Exclude from the function's domain real numbers that cause division by zero and real numbers that result in an even root of a negative number.

## 2.4 Graphs of Functions

a. The graph of a function is the graph of its ordered pairs.

b. The vertical line test for functions: If any vertical line intersects a graph in more than one point, the graph does not define $y$ as a function of $x$.

c. A function is increasing on intervals where its graph rises, decreasing on intervals where it falls, and constant on intervals where it neither rises nor falls. Precise definitions are given in the box on page 210.

d. The average rate of change of $f$ from $x_1$ to $x_2$ is

$$\frac{\Delta y}{\Delta x} = \frac{f(x_2) - f(x_1)}{x_2 - x_1}.$$

e. If a function expresses an object's distance, $s(t)$, in terms of time, $t$, the average velocity of the object from $t_1$ to $t_2$ is

$$\frac{\Delta s}{\Delta t} = \frac{s(t_2) - s(t_1)}{t_2 - t_1}.$$

f. The graph of an even function in which $f(-x) = f(x)$ is symmetric with respect to the $y$-axis. The graph of an odd function in which $f(-x) = -f(x)$ is symmetric with respect to the origin.

g. Table 2.3 on page 217 shows the graphs of the constant function, $f(x) = c$, the identity function, $f(x) = x$, the standard quadratic function, $f(x) = x^2$, the standard cubic function, $f(x) = x^3$, the square root function, $f(x) = \sqrt{x}$, and the absolute value function, $f(x) = |x|$. The table also lists characteristics of each function.

h. The graph of $f(x) = \text{int}(x)$, where $\text{int}(x)$ is the greatest integer that is less than or equal to $x$, has function values that form discontinuous steps, shown in Figure 2.35 on page 218. If $n \le x < n + 1$, where $n$ is an integer, then $\text{int}(x) = n$.

## 2.5 Transformations and Combinations of Functions

a. Table 2.5 on page 233 summarizes how to graph a function using vertical shifts, $y = f(x) \pm c$, horizontal shifts, $y = f(x \pm c)$, reflections about the $x$-axis, $y = -f(x)$, reflections about the $y$-axis, $y = f(-x)$, vertical stretching, $y = cf(x)$, $c > 1$, and vertical shrinking, $y = cf(x)$, $0 < c < 1$.

b. A function involving more than one transformation can be graphed in the following order: (1) horizontal shifting; (2) vertical stretching or shrinking; (3) reflecting; (4) vertical shifting.

c. When functions are given as equations, they can be added, subtracted, multiplied, or divided by performing operations with the algebraic expressions that appear on the right side of the equations. Definitions for the sum $f + g$, the difference $f - g$, the product $fg$, and the quotient $\frac{f}{g}$ functions are given in the box on page 236.

## 2.6 Composite and Inverse Functions

a. The composition of functions $f$ and $g$, $f \circ g$, is defined by $(f \circ g)(x) = f(g(x))$. The domain of the composite function $f \circ g$ is given in the box on page 242. This composite function is obtained by replacing each occurrence of $x$ in the equation for $f$ by $g(x)$.

b. If $f(g(x)) = x$ and $g(f(x)) = x$, function $g$ is the inverse of function $f$, denoted $f^{-1}$ and read "$f$ inverse." Thus, to show that $f$ and $g$ are inverses of each other, one must show $f(g(x)) = x$ and $g(f(x)) = x$.

c. The procedure for finding a function's inverse uses a switch-and-solve strategy. Switch $x$ and $y$, then solve for $y$. The procedure is given in the box on page 246.

d. The horizontal line test for inverse functions: A function $f$ has an inverse that is a function, $f^{-1}$, if there is no horizontal line that intersects the graph of the function $f$ at more than one point.

e. A one-to-one function is one in which no two different ordered pairs have the same second component. Only one-to-one functions have inverse functions.

f. If the point $(a, b)$ is on the graph of $f$, then the point $(b, a)$ is on the graph of $f^{-1}$. The graph of $f^{-1}$ is a reflection of the graph of $f$ about the line $y = x$.

# Review Exercises

## 2.1

*In Exercises 1–4, find the slope of the line passing through each pair of points or state that the slope is undefined. Then indicate whether the line through the points rises, falls, is horizontal, or is vertical.*

**1.** $(3, 2)$ and $(5, 1)$ **2.** $(-1, -2)$ and $(-3, -4)$

**3.** $\left(-3, \frac{1}{4}\right)$ and $\left(6, \frac{1}{4}\right)$ **4.** $(-2, 5)$ and $(-2, 10)$

*In Exercises 5–6, use the given conditions to write an equation for each line in point-slope form and slope-intercept form.*

**5.** Passing through $(-3, 2)$ with a slope of $-6$

**6.** Passing through $(1, 6)$ and $(-1, 2)$

*In Exercises 7–10, give the slope and y-intercept of each line whose equation is given. Then graph the line.*

**7.** $y = \frac{2}{5}x - 1$　　**8.** $y = -4x + 5$

**9.** $2x + 3y + 6 = 0$　　**10.** $2y - 8 = 0$

**11.** In 1900, the typical surfboard was 16 feet long. Since then, they have become shorter and shorter. Here are two data measurements for a typical surfboard's length. (A scatter plot of all such data measurements through 1980 would show all data points on or near a straight line.)

| $x$ (Years since 1900) | $y$ (Average Surfboard Length, in Feet) |
|---|---|
| 0 | 16 |
| 30 | 12.1 |

© Bishop Museum

**a.** Write the point-slope form of the equation of the line on which these measurements fall.
**b.** Use the point-slope form of the equation to write the slope-intercept form of the equation.
**c.** Use the equation in part (b) to find average surfboard length in 1970 and 1980.
**d.** Does the equation in part (b) reasonably describe reality in 2000?

**12.** The scatter plot shows the number of minutes each that 16 people exercise per week and the number of headaches per month each person experiences.

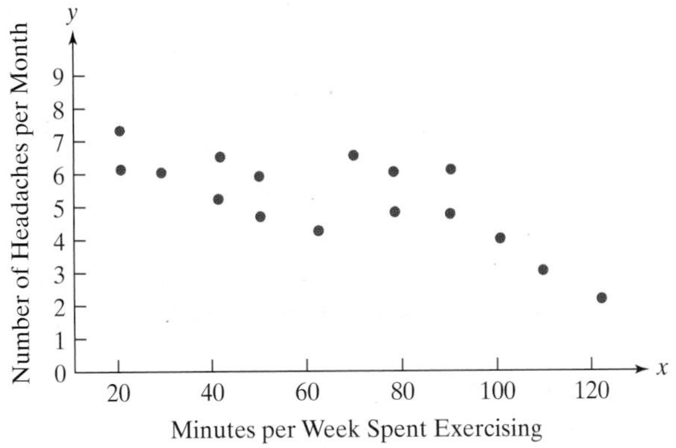


**a.** Draw a line that fits the data so that the spread of the data points around the line is as small as possible.
**b.** Use the coordinates of two points along your line to write its point-slope and slope-intercept equations.
**c.** Use the equation in part (b) to predict the number of headaches per month for a person exercising 130 minutes per week.

## 2.2

*In Exercises 13–14, use the given conditions to write an equation for each line in point-slope form and slope-intercept form.*

**13.** Passing through $(4, -7)$ and parallel to the line whose equation is $3x + y - 9 = 0$.

**14.** Passing through $(-3, 6)$ and perpendicular to the line whose equation is $y = \frac{1}{3}x + 4$.

*In Exercises 15–16, write the standard form of the equation of the circle with the given center and radius.*

**15.** Center $(0, 0), r = 3$　　**16.** Center $(-2, 4), r = 6$

*In Exercises 17–19, give the center and radius of each circle and graph its equation.*

**17.** $x^2 + y^2 = 1$　　**18.** $(x + 2)^2 + (y - 3)^2 = 9$

**19.** $x^2 + y^2 - 4x + 2y - 4 = 0$

## 2.3

*In Exercises 20–22, determine whether each relation is a function. Give the domain and range for each relation.*

**20.** $\{(2, 7), (3, 7), (5, 7)\}$　　**21.** $\{(1, 10)\ (2, 500), (13, \pi)\}$

**22.** $\{(12, 13), (14, 15), (12, 19)\}$

*In Exercises 23–25, determine whether each equation defines y as a function of x.*

**23.** $2x + y = 8$　　**24.** $3x^2 + y = 14$

**25.** $2x + y^2 = 6$

*In Exercises 26–29, evaluate each function at the given values of the independent variable and simplify.*

**26.** $f(x) = 5 - 7x$
**a.** $f(4)$　**b.** $f(x + 3)$　**c.** $f(-x)$

**27.** $g(x) = 3x^2 - 5x + 2$
**a.** $g(0)$　**b.** $g(-2)$
**c.** $g(x - 1)$　**d.** $g(-x)$

**28.** $g(x) = \begin{cases} \sqrt{x - 4} & \text{if } x \geq 4 \\ 4 - x & \text{if } x < 4 \end{cases}$

**a.** $g(13)$　**b.** $g(0)$　**c.** $g(-3)$

**29.** $f(x) = \begin{cases} \dfrac{x^2 - 1}{x - 1} & \text{if } x \neq 1 \\ 12 & \text{if } x = 1 \end{cases}$

**a.** $f(-2)$　**b.** $f(1)$　**c.** $f(2)$

*In Exercises 30–31, find and simplify the different quotient*

$$\frac{f(x+h)-f(x)}{h}, \qquad h \neq 0$$

*for the given function.*

**30.** $f(x) = 8x - 11$ **31.** $f(x) = x^2 - 13x + 5$

*In Exercises 32–36, find the domain of each function.*

**32.** $f(x) = x^2 + 6x - 3$ **33.** $g(x) = \dfrac{4}{x-7}$

**34.** $h(x) = \sqrt{8 - 2x}$ **35.** $f(x) = \dfrac{x}{x^2 - 1}$

**36.** $g(x) = \dfrac{\sqrt{x-2}}{x-5}$

## 2.4

*Graph the functions in Exercises 37–38. Use the integer values of x given to the right of the function to obtain the ordered pairs. Use the graph to specify the function's domain and range.*

**37.** $f(x) = x^2 - 4x + 4$ $x = -1, 0, 1, 2, 3, 4$

**38.** $f(x) = |2 - x|$ $x = -1, 0, 1, 2, 3, 4$

*In Exercises 39–41, use the graph to determine* **a.** *the function's domain;* **b.** *the function's range;* **c.** *the x-intercepts, if any;* **d.** *the y-intercept, if any;* **e.** *intervals on which, the function is increasing, decreasing, or constant; and* **f.** *the function values indicated below the graphs.*

**39.**

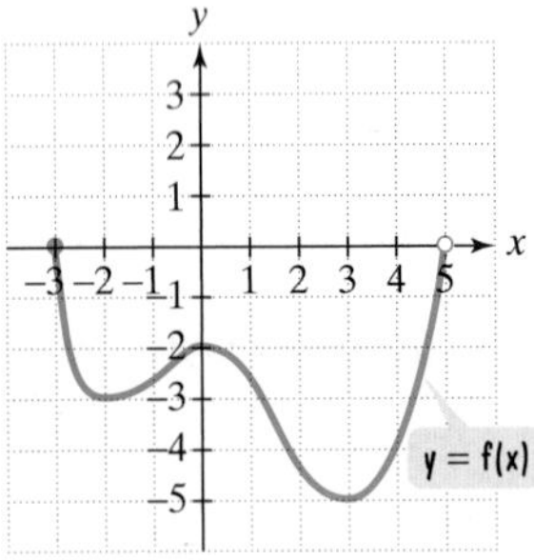


$f(-2) = ?$ $f(3) = ?$

**40.**

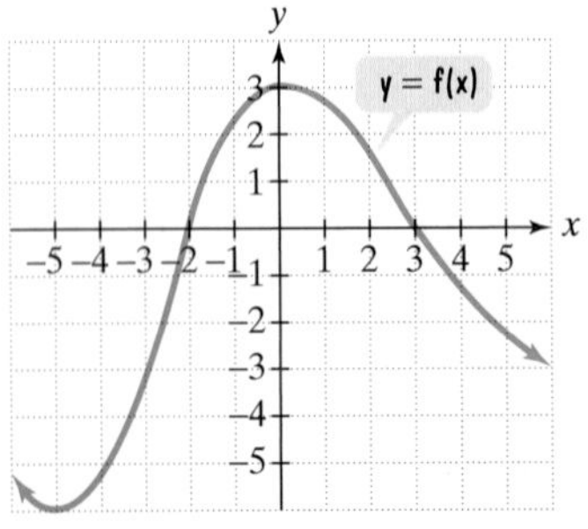


$f(-2) = ?$ $f(6) = ?$

**41.**

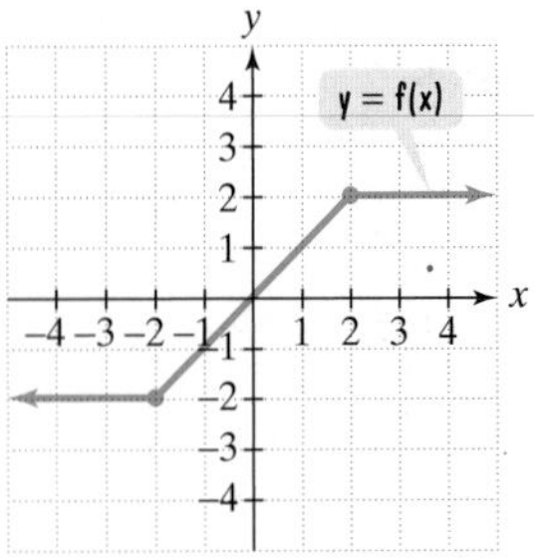


$f(-9) = ?$ $f(14) = ?$

*In Exercises 42–45, use the vertical line test to identify graphs in which y is a function of x.*

**42.**

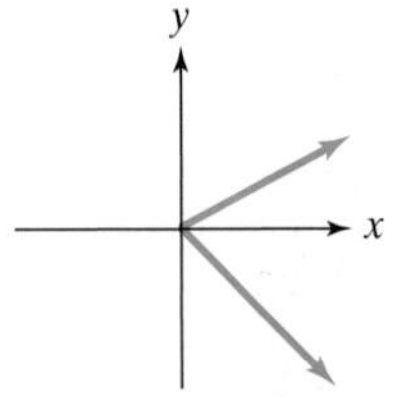

**43.**

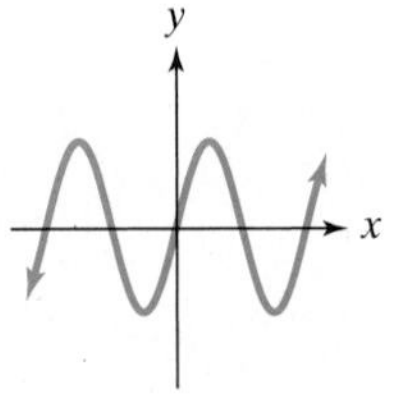

**44.**

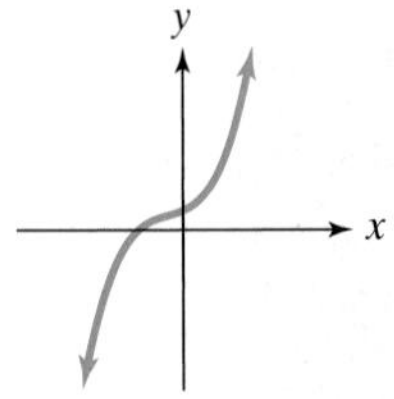

**45.**

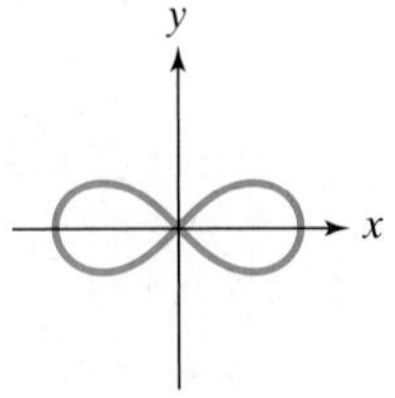

**46.** Find the average rate of change of $f(x) = x^2 - 4x$ from $x_1 = 5$ to $x_2 = 9$.

**47.** A person standing on the roof of a building throws a ball directly upward. The ball misses the rooftop on its way down and eventually strikes the ground. The function

$$s(t) = -16t^2 + 64t + 80$$

describes the ball's height above the ground, $s(t)$, $t$ seconds after it was thrown.

**a.** Find the ball's average velocity between the time it was thrown and 2 seconds later.

**b.** Find the ball's average velocity between 2 and 4 seconds after it was thrown.

**c.** What do the signs in your answers to parts (a) and (b) mean in terms of the direction of the ball's motion?

**48.** The function

$$f(x) = 0.32x^2 + 1.64x + 3.98$$

models the value, $f(x)$, in billions of dollars, of goods imported from China $x$ years after 1986. Find the average rate of change, in billions of dollars per year, in U.S. imports from China from 1991 to 1996.

*In Exercises 49–51, determine whether each function is even, odd, or neither. State each function's symmetry. If you are using a graphing utility, graph the function and verify its possible symmetry.*

**49.** $f(x) = x^3 - 5x$ **50.** $f(x) = x^4 - 2x^2 + 1$

**51.** $f(x) = 2x\sqrt{1 - x^2}$

**52.** The graph shows the height (in meters) of a vulture as a function of its time (in seconds) in flight.

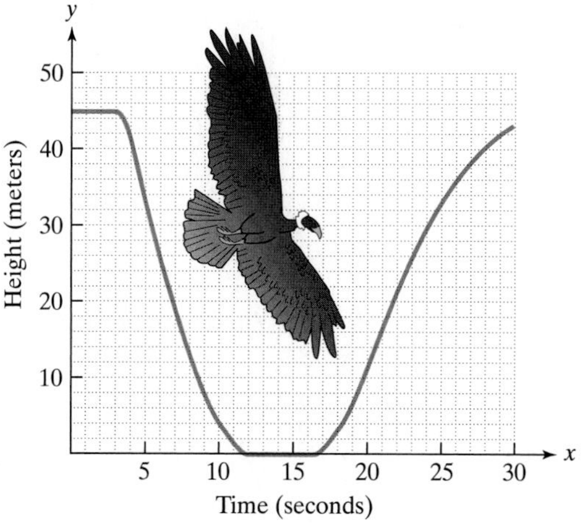


**a.** Is the vulture's height a function of time? Use the graph to explain why or why not.
**b.** On what interval is the function decreasing? Describe what this means in practical terms.
**c.** On what intervals is the function constant? What does this mean for each of these intervals?
**d.** On what interval is the function increasing? What does this mean?

**53.** A cargo service charges a flat fee of \$5 plus \$1.50 for each pound or fraction of a pound. Graph shipping cost (in dollars) as a function of weight ($x$, in pounds) for $0 < x \le 5$.

## 2.5

*In Exercises 54–56, begin by graphing the standard quadratic function, $f(x) = x^2$. Then use transformations of this graph to graph the given function.*

**54.** $g(x) = x^2 + 2$ **55.** $h(x) = (x + 2)^2$
**56.** $r(x) = -(x + 1)^2$

*In Exercises 57–59, begin by graphing the square root function, $f(x) = \sqrt{x}$. Then use transformations of this graph to graph the given function.*

**57.** $g(x) = \sqrt{x + 3}$ **58.** $h(x) = \sqrt{3 - x}$
**59.** $r(x) = 2\sqrt{x + 2}$

*In Exercises 60–62, begin by graphing the absolute value function, $f(x) = |x|$. Then use transformations of this graph to graph the given function.*

**60.** $g(x) = |x + 2| - 3$ **61.** $h(x) = -|x - 1| + 1$
**62.** $r(x) = \frac{1}{2}|x + 2|$

*In Exercises 63–65, begin by graphing the standard cubic function, $f(x) = x^3$. Then use transformations of this graph to graph the given function.*

**63.** $g(x) = \frac{1}{2}(x - 1)^3$ **64.** $h(x) = -(x + 1)^3$
**65.** $r(x) = \frac{1}{4}x^3 - 1$

*In Exercises 66–68, use the graph of the function $f$ to sketch the graph of the given function $g$.*

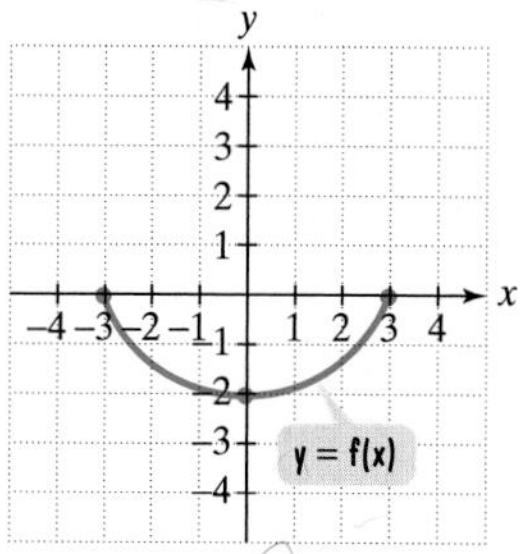


**66.** $g(x) = f(x + 2) + 3$ **67.** $g(x) = \frac{1}{2}f(x - 1)$
**68.** $g(x) = -2 + 2f(x + 2)$

*In Exercises 69–71, find $f + g$, $f - g$, $fg$, and $\frac{f}{g}$. Determine the domain for each function.*

**69.** $f(x) = 3x - 1, \quad g(x) = x - 5$
**70.** $f(x) = x^2 + x + 1, \quad g(x) = x^2 - 1$
**71.** $f(x) = \sqrt{x + 7}, \quad g(x) = \sqrt{x - 2}$

## 2.6

*In Exercises 72–73, find* **a.** $(f \circ g)(x)$; **b.** $(g \circ f)(x)$; **c.** $(f \circ g)(3)$.

**72.** $f(x) = x^2 + 3, \quad g(x) = 4x - 1$
**73.** $f(x) = \sqrt{x}, \quad g(x) = x + 1$

*In Exercises 74–75, express the given function $h$ as a composition of two functions $f$ and $g$ so that $h(x) = (f \circ g)(x)$.*

**74.** $h(x) = (x^2 + 2x - 1)^4$ **75.** $h(x) = \sqrt[3]{7x + 4}$

*In Exercises 76–77, find $f(g(x))$ and $g(f(x))$ and determine whether each pair of functions $f$ and $g$ are inverses of each other.*

**76.** $f(x) = \frac{3}{5}x + \frac{1}{2}$ and $g(x) = \frac{5}{3}x - 2$

**77.** $f(x) = 2 - 5x$ and $g(x) = \frac{2 - x}{5}$

*The functions in Exercises 78–80 are all one-to-one. For each function:*

**a.** *Find an equation of $f^{-1}(x)$, the inverse function.*
**b.** *Verify that your equation is correct by showing that $f(f^{-1}(x)) = x$ and $f^{-1}(f(x)) = x$.*

**78.** $f(x) = 4x - 3$ **79.** $f(x) = \sqrt{x + 2}$
**80.** $f(x) = 8x^3 + 1$

*Which graphs in Exercises 81–84 represent functions that have inverse functions?*

**81.**

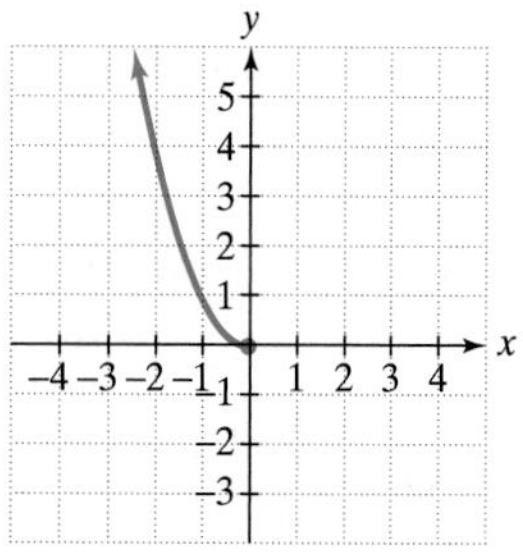

**82.**

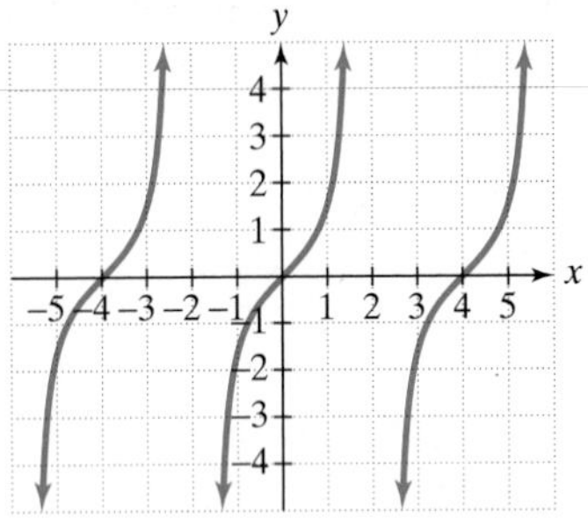

**83.**

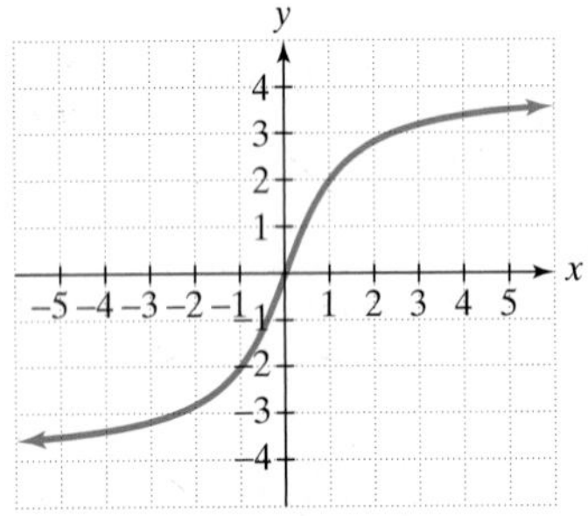

**84.**

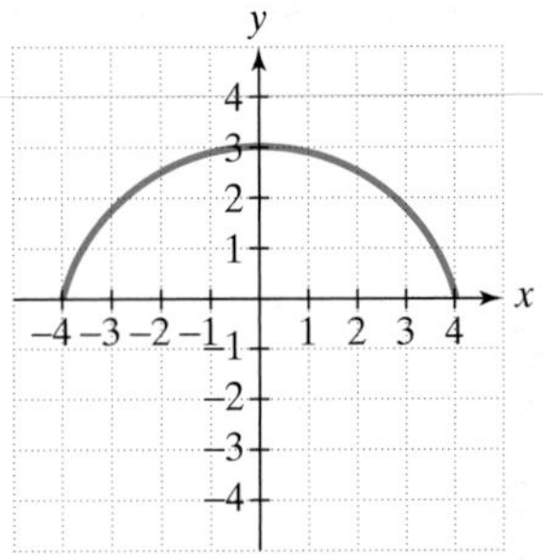

**85.** Use the graph of $f$ in the figure shown to draw the graph of its inverse function.

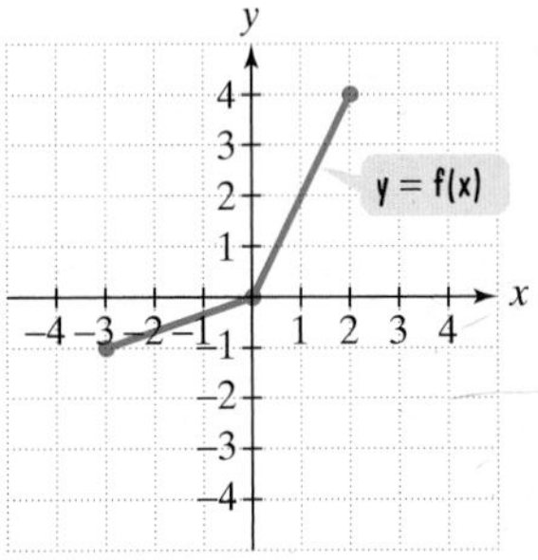


## Chapter 2 Test

*In Exercises 1–2, use the given conditions to write an equation for each line in point-slope form and slope-intercept form.*

1. Passing through $(2, 1)$ and $(-1, -8)$
2. Passing through $(-4, 6)$ and perpendicular to the line whose equation is $y = -\frac{1}{4}x + 5$
3. The data points $(4, 401.1)$ and $(9, 475.6)$, shown and described in the table, fall on a straight line.

| $x$ **(Number of Years after 1985)** | $y$ **(Average Weekly Earnings of U.S. Workers)** |
|---|---|
| 4 | 401.1 |
| 9 | 475.6 |

   a. Write the equation of the line on which these measurements fall in point-slope form and slope-intercept form.
   b. Use the slope-intercept form of the equation to predict the average weekly earnings for U.S. workers for the year 2005.

4. Give the center and radius of the circle whose equation is $x^2 + y^2 + 4x - 6y - 3 = 0$ and graph the equation.
5. List by letter all relations that are not functions.
   a. $\{(7, 5), (8, 5), (9, 5)\}$
   b. $\{(5, 7), (5, 8), (5, 9)\}$
   c.

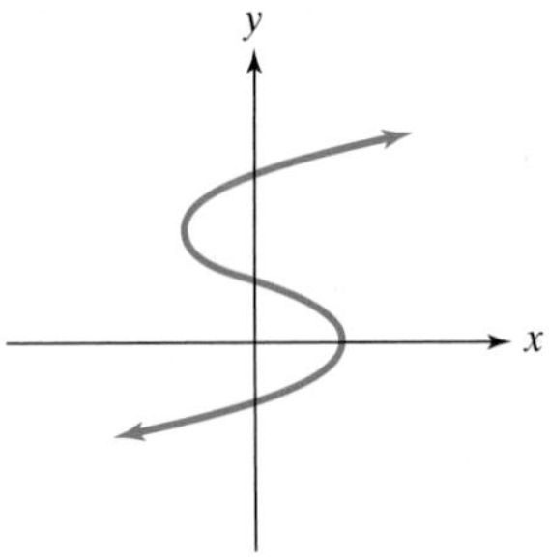

   d. $x^2 + y^2 = 100$
   e.

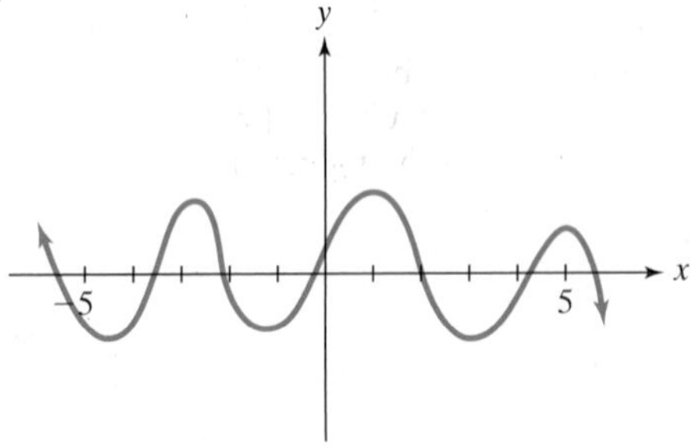

6. If $f(x) = x^2 - 2x + 5$, find $f(x - 1)$ and simplify.
7. If $g(x) = \begin{cases} \sqrt{x - 3} & \text{if } x \geq 3 \\ 3 - x & \text{if } x < 3 \end{cases}$, find $g(-1)$ and $g(7)$.
8. If $f(x) = \sqrt{12 - 3x}$, find the domain of $f$.

**9.** If $f(x) = x^2 + 11x - 7$, find and simplify the difference quotient $\frac{f(x+h) - f(x)}{h}$.

**10.** Use the graph of function $f$ to answer the following questions.

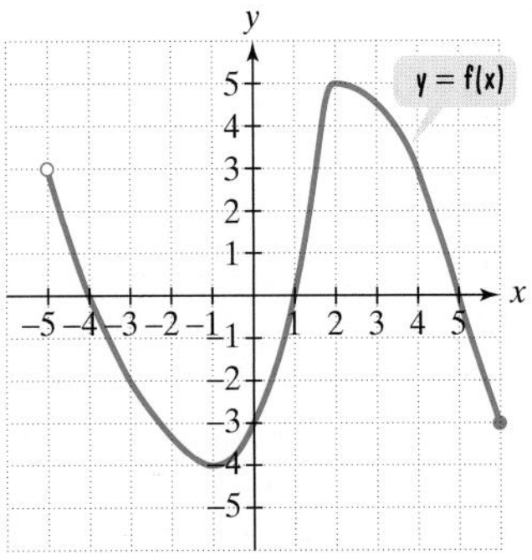


**a.** What is $f(4) - f(-3)$?
**b.** What is the domain of $f$?
**c.** What is the range of $f$?
**d.** On what interval or intervals is $f$ increasing?
**e.** On what interval or intervals is $f$ decreasing?
**f.** What are the $x$-intercepts?
**g.** What is the $y$-intercept?

**11.** Find the average rate of change of $f(x) = 3x^2 - 5$ from $x_1 = 6$ to $x_2 = 10$.

**12.** Determine whether $f(x) = x^4 - x^2$ is even, odd, or neither. Use your answer to explain why the graph in the figure shown cannot be the graph of $f$.

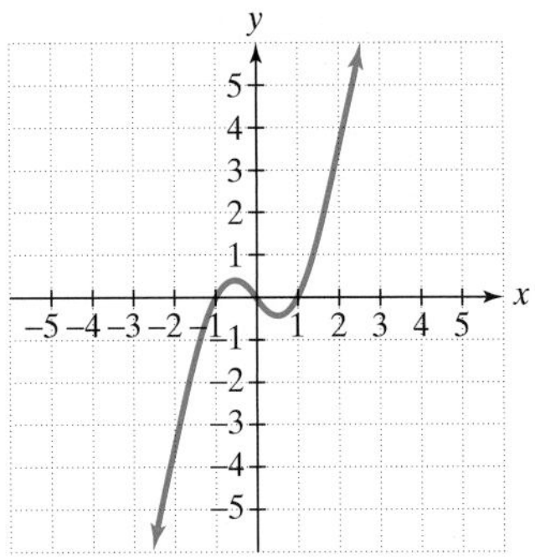

**13.** The figure shows how the graph of $h(x) = -2(x - 3)^2$ is obtained from the graph of $f(x) = x^2$. Describe this process, using the graph of $g$ in your description.

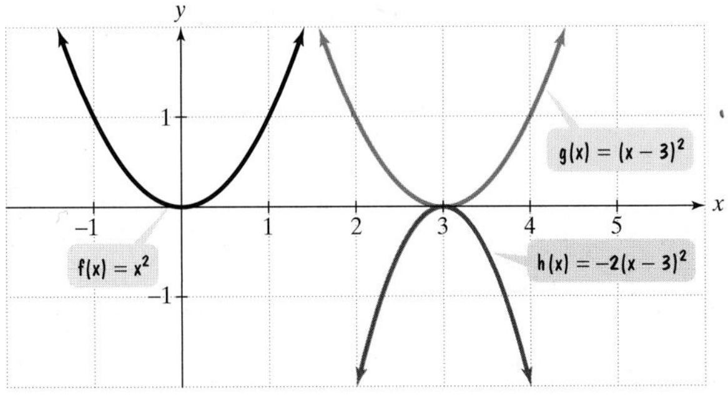


**14.** Begin by graphing the absolute value function, $f(x) = |x|$. Then use transformations of this graph to graph $g(x) = \frac{1}{2}|x + 1| + 3$.

*If $f(x) = x^2 + 3x - 4$ and $g(x) = 5x - 2$, find each function or function value in Exercises 15–19.*

**15.** $(f - g)(x)$

**16.** $\left(\frac{f}{g}\right)(x)$ and its domain

**17.** $(f \circ g)(x)$

**18.** $(g \circ f)(x)$

**19.** $f(g(2))$

**20.** Express $h(x) = (2x + 13)^7$ as a composition of two functions $f$ and $g$ so that $h(x) = (f \circ g)(x)$.

**21.** If $f(x) = \sqrt{x - 2}$, find the equation for $f^{-1}(x)$. Then verify that your equation is correct by showing that $f(f^{-1}(x)) = x$ and $f^{-1}(f(x)) = x$.

**22.** A function $f$ models the amount given to charity as a function of income. The graph of $f$ is shown in the figure.

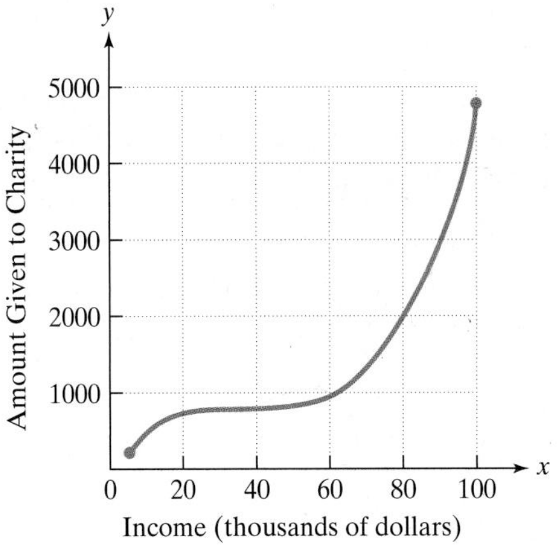


**a.** Explain why $f$ has an inverse that is a function.
**b.** Find $f(80)$.
**c.** Describe in practical terms the meaning of $f^{-1}(2000)$.

**23.** Use a graphing utility to graph $f(x) = \frac{x^3}{3} + x^2 - 15x + 3$ in a $[-10, 10, 1]$ by $[-30, 70, 10]$ viewing rectangle. Use the graph to answer the following questions.

**a.** Is $f$ one-to-one? Explain.
**b.** Is $f$ even, odd, or neither? Explain.
**c.** What is the range of $f$?
**d.** On what interval or intervals is $f$ increasing?
**e.** On what interval or intervals is $f$ decreasing?

## Cumulative Review Exercises (Chapters P–2)

*Simplify each expression in Exercises 1 and 2.*

1. $\dfrac{4x^2y}{2x^5y^{-3}}$

2. $\dfrac{5}{4\sqrt{2}}$

3. Factor: $x^3 - 4x^2 + 2x - 8$.

*In Exercises 4 and 5, perform the operations and simplify.*

4. $\dfrac{x-3}{x+4} + \dfrac{x}{x-2}$

5. $\dfrac{4 + \dfrac{2}{x}}{4 - \dfrac{2}{x}}$

*Solve each equation in Exercises 6–9.*

6. $(x+3)(x-4) = 8$

7. $3(4x-1) = 4 - 6(x-3)$

8. $\sqrt{x} + 2 = x$

9. $x^{2/3} - x^{1/3} - 6 = 0$

*Solve each inequality in Exercises 10 and 11. Express the answer in interval notation.*

10. $\dfrac{x}{2} - 3 \le \dfrac{x}{4} + 2$

11. $\dfrac{x+3}{x-2} \le 2$

12. Write the point-slope form and the slope-intercept form of the line passing through $(-2, 5)$ and perpendicular to the line whose equation is $y = -\frac{1}{4}x + \frac{1}{3}$.

13. Graph $f(x) = \sqrt{x}$ and then use transformations of this graph to graph $g(x) = \sqrt{x-3} + 4$ in the same rectangular coordinate system.

14. If $f(x) = 2 + \sqrt{x-3}$, find the equation for $f^{-1}(x)$.

15. If $f(x) = 3 - x^2$, find $\dfrac{f(x+h) - f(x)}{h}$ and simplify.

16. Solve for $r$: $G = \dfrac{a}{1-r}$.

17. The length of a rectangular garden is 2 feet more than twice its width. If 22 feet of fencing is needed to enclose the garden, what are its dimensions?

18. A bridge toll currently charges \$2.50 per car. The average number of cars crossing per day is 200. However, this number is expected to decrease by one car per day for every 5¢ increase over \$2.50. If the bridge needs to bring in an income of \$630 per day, what should the toll be?

19. On the first five tests you have scores of 61, 95, 71, 83, and 80. The last test, a final exam, counts as two grades. What score do you need on the final in order to have an average score of 80?

20. A rock is thrown from the ground with an initial velocity of 80 feet per second. The function

$$s(t) = -16t^2 + 80t$$

describes the rock's height, $s(t)$, $t$ seconds after it was thrown. Find the rock's average velocity between the time it was thrown and 2 seconds later.

# Polynomial and Rational Functions

## Chapter 3

There is a function that models the age in human years, $H(x)$, of a dog that is $x$ years old:

$$H(x) = -0.001183x^4 + 0.05495x^3 - 0.8523x^2 + 9.054x + 6.748.$$

The function contains variables to powers that are whole numbers and is an example of a **polynomial function**. In this chapter, we study polynomial functions and functions that consist of quotients of polynomials, called **rational functions**.

One of the joys of your life is your dog, your very special buddy. Lately, however, you've noticed that your companion is slowing down a bit. He's now 8 years old and you wonder how this translates into human years. You remember something about every year of a dog's life being equal to seven years for a human. Is there a more accurate description?

# SECTION 3.1 Quadratic Functions

## Objectives

1. Recognize characteristics of parabolas.
2. Graph parabolas.
3. Solve problems involving minimizing or maximizing quadratic functions.

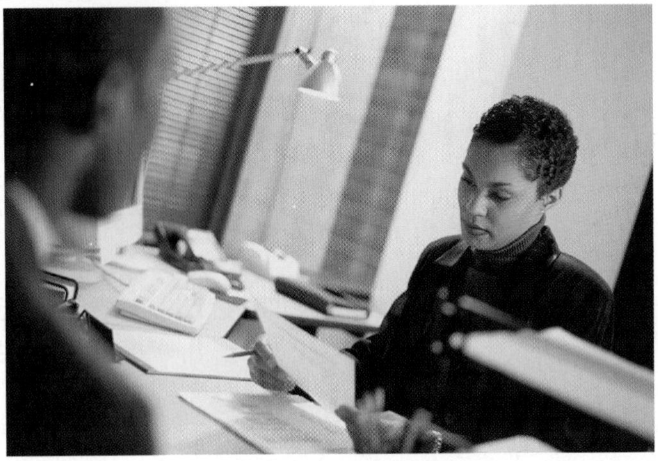

The wage gap is used to compare the status of women's earnings relative to men's. The wage gap is expressed as a percent and is calculated by dividing the median annual earnings for women by the median annual earnings for men. Based on data provided by the U.S. Women's Bureau, the function

$$f(x) = 0.022x^2 - 0.4x + 60.07$$

models women's earnings as a percentage of men's $x$ years after 1960. For example, to calculate the wage gap in 1998, substitute 38 for $x$ because 1998 is 38 years after 1960:

$$f(38) = 0.022(38)^2 - 0.4(38) + 60.07 \approx 76.6.$$

Thus, in 1998 women earned 76.6% as much as men. Since 1963, when the Equal Pay Act was signed, the wage gap between men and women has closed at a rate of less than half a penny per year.

The function $f(x) = 0.022x^2 - 0.4x + 60.07$ is an example of a *quadratic function*. A **quadratic function** is any function of the form

$$f(x) = ax^2 + bx + c$$

where $a$, $b$, and $c$ are real numbers and $a \neq 0$. A quadratic function is a polynomial function whose highest power is 2. In this section we will study quadratic functions and their graphs.

1 Recognize characteristics of parabolas.

## Graphs of Quadratic Functions

The graph of any quadratic function is called a **parabola**. Parabolas are shaped like cups, as shown in Figure 3.1 on page 263. If the coefficient of $x^2$ (the value of $a$ in $ax^2 + bx + c$) is positive, the parabola opens upward. When the coefficient of $x^2$ is negative, the graph opens downward. The **vertex** (or turning point) of the parabola is the minimum point on the graph when it opens upward, and the maximum point on the graph when it opens downward.

Look at the unusual image on page 263 of the word "mirror." The artist, Scott Kim, has created the image so that the two halves of the whole are mirror images of each other. A parabola shares this kind of symmetry, in which a line through the vertex divides the figure in half. Parabolas are symmetric to this line,

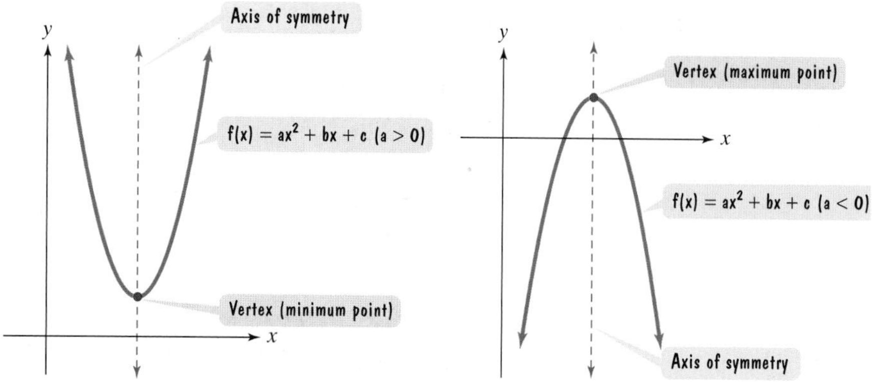


$a > 0$: Parabola opens upward. $a < 0$: Parabola opens downward.

**Figure 3.1** Characteristics of parabolas

called the **axis of symmetry**. The movements of gymnasts, divers, and swimmers can approximate this symmetry.

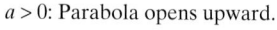

## Graphing Quadratic Functions in Standard Form

**2** Graph parabolas.

In Section 2.5, we applied a series of transformations to the graph of $f(x) = x^2$. The graph of this function is a parabola. The vertex for this parabola is at (0, 0). In Figure 3.2(a), the graph of $f(x) = ax^2$ for $a > 0$ is shown in black; it opens *upward*. In Figure 3.2(b), the graph of $f(x) = ax^2$ for $a < 0$ is shown in black; it opens *downward*.

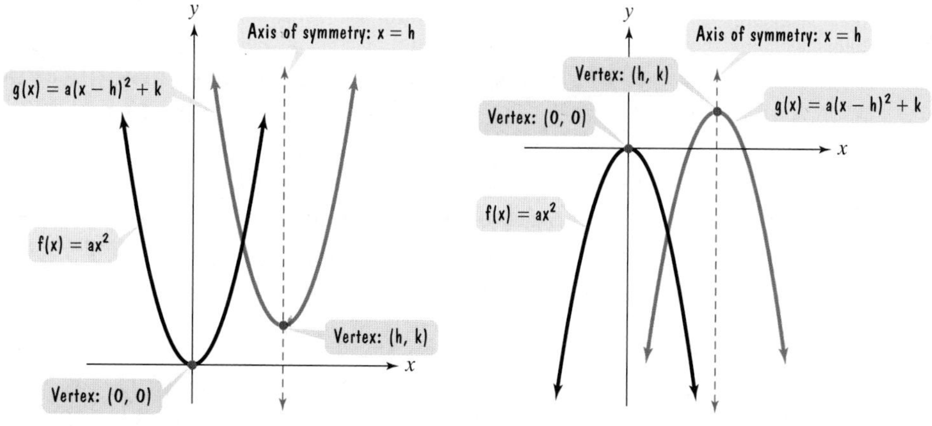


(a) $a > 0$: Parabola opens upward. (b) $a < 0$: Parabola opens downward.

**Figure 3.2** Transformations of $f(x) = ax^2$

Figure 3.2 also shows the graphs of $g(x) = a(x - h)^2 + k$ in blue. Compare these graphs to those of $f(x) = ax^2$. Observe that $h$ determines the horizontal shift and $k$ determines the vertical shift of the graph of $f(x) = ax^2$. Consequently, the vertex $(0, 0)$ on the graph of $f(x) = ax^2$ moves to the point $(h, k)$ on the graph of $g(x) = a(x - h)^2 + k$. The axis of symmetry is the vertical line whose equation is $x = h$.

The form of the expression for $g$ is convenient because it immediately identifies the vertex of the parabola as $(h, k)$. This is the **standard form** of a quadratic function.

**The Standard Form of a Quadratic Function**

The quadratic function

$$f(x) = a(x - h)^2 + k, \qquad a \neq 0$$

is in **standard form**. The graph of $f$ is a parabola whose vertex is the point $(h, k)$. The parabola is symmetric to the line $x = h$. If $a > 0$, the parabola opens upward; if $a < 0$, the parabola opens downward.

The sign of $a$ in $f(x) = a(x - h)^2 + k$ determines whether the parabola opens upward or downward. Furthermore, if $|a|$ is small, the parabola opens more widely than if $|a|$ is large. Here is a general procedure for graphing parabolas whose equations are in standard form.

**Graphing Parabolas With Equations in Standard Form**

To graph $f(x) = a(x - h)^2 + k$:

1. Determine whether the parabola opens upward or downward. If $a > 0$, it opens upward. If $a < 0$, it opens downward.
2. Determine the vertex of the parabola. The vertex is $(h, k)$.
3. Find any $x$-intercepts by replacing $f(x)$ with 0. Solve the resulting quadratic equation for $x$.
4. Find the $y$-intercept by replacing $x$ with 0.
5. Plot the intercepts and vertex. Connect these points with a smooth curve that is shaped like a cup.

## EXAMPLE 1 Graphing a Parabola Whose Equation Is in Standard Form

Graph the quadratic function $f(x) = -2(x - 3)^2 + 8$.

**Solution** We can graph this function by following the steps in the preceding box. We begin by identifying values for $a$, $h$, and $k$.

Standard form $\quad f(x) = a(x - h)^2 + k$

$a = -2 \quad h = 3 \quad k = 8$

Given equation $\quad f(x) = -2(x - 3)^2 + 8$

**Step 1 Determine how the parabola opens.** Note that $a$, the coefficient of $x^2$, is $-2$. Thus, $a < 0$; this negative value tells us that the parabola opens downward.

**Step 2** **Find the vertex.** The vertex of the parabola is at $(h, k)$. Because $h = 3$ and $k = 8$, the parabola has its vertex at $(3, 8)$.

**Step 3** **Find the *x*-intercepts.** Replace $f(x)$ with 0 in $f(x) = -2(x-3)^2 + 8$.

| | |
|---|---|
| $0 = -2(x-3)^2 + 8$ | Find x-intercepts, setting f(x) equal to 0. |
| $2(x-3)^2 = 8$ | Solve for x. Add $2(x-3)^2$ to both sides of the equation. |
| $(x-3)^2 = 4$ | Divide both sides by 2. |
| $(x-3) = \pm 2$ | Apply the square root method. If $(x-c)^2 = d$, then $x - c = \pm\sqrt{d}$. |
| $x - 3 = -2$ or $x - 3 = 2$ | Express as two separate equations. |
| $x = 1$ or $x = 5$ | Add 3 to both sides in each equation. |

The $x$-intercepts are 1 and 5. The parabola passes through $(1, 0)$ and $(5, 0)$.

**Step 4** **Find the *y*-intercept.** Replace $x$ with 0 in $f(x) = -2(x-3)^2 + 8$.

$$f(0) = -2(0-3)^2 + 8 = -2(-3)^2 + 8 = -2(9) + 8 = -10$$

The $y$-intercept is $-10$. The parabola passes through $(0, -10)$.

**Step 5** **Graph the parabola.** With a vertex at $(3, 8)$, $x$-intercepts at 1 and 5, and a $y$-intercept at $-10$, the graph of $f$ is shown in Figure 3.3. The axis of symmetry is the vertical line whose equation is $x = 3$.

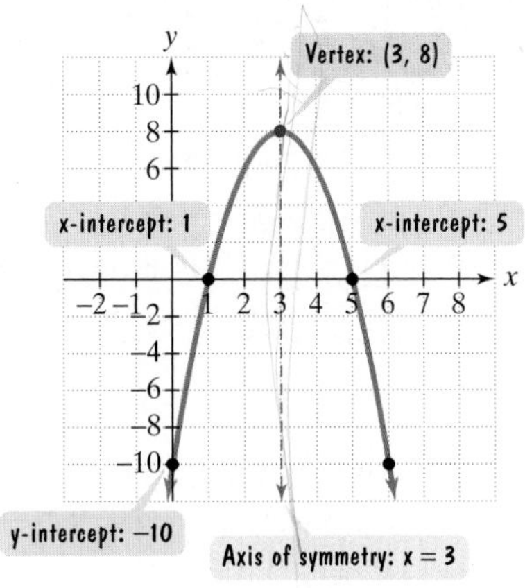


**Figure 3.3** The graph of $f(x) = -2(x-3)^2 + 8$

**Check Point 1** Graph the quadratic function $f(x) = -(x-1)^2 + 4$.

## EXAMPLE 2 Graphing a Parabola Whose Equation Is in Standard Form

Graph the quadratic function $f(x) = (x + 3)^2 + 1$.

**Solution** We begin by finding values for $a$, $h$, and $k$.

Standard form $\quad f(x) = a(x - h)^2 + k$

Given equation $\quad f(x) = (x + 3)^2 + 1$

or $\quad f(x) = 1(x - (-3))^2 + 1$

$a = 1 \quad h = -3 \quad k = 1$

**Step 1 Determine how the parabola opens.** Note that $a$, the coefficient of $x^2$, is 1. Thus, $a > 0$; this positive value tells us that the parabola opens upward.

**Step 2 Find the vertex.** The vertex of the parabola is at $(h, k)$. Because $h = -3$ and $k = 1$, the parabola has its vertex at $(-3, 1)$.

**Step 3 Find the $x$-intercepts.** Replace $f(x)$ with 0 in $f(x) = (x + 3)^2 + 1$. Because the vertex is at $(-3, 1)$, which lies above the $x$-axis, and the parabola opens upward, it appears that this parabola has no $x$-intercepts. We can verify this observation algebraically.

$0 = (x + 3)^2 + 1$ Find possible $x$-intercepts, setting $f(x)$ equal to 0.

$-1 = (x + 3)^2$ Solve for $x$. Subtract 1 from both sides.

$x + 3 = \pm\sqrt{-1}$ Apply the square root method.

$x + 3 = \pm i$ Recall that $\sqrt{-1} = i$, an imaginary number.

$x = -3 \pm i$ Subtract 3 from both sides.

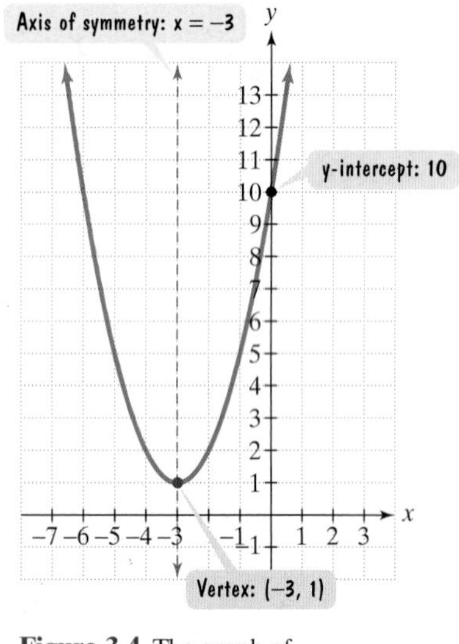


**Figure 3.4** The graph of $g(x) = (x + 3)^2 + 1$

Because this equation has no real solutions, the parabola has no $x$-intercepts.

**Step 4 Find the $y$-intercept.** Replace $x$ with 0 in $f(x) = (x + 3)^2 + 1$.

$$f(0) = (0 + 3)^2 + 1 = 3^2 + 1 = 9 + 1 = 10$$

The $y$-intercept is 10. The parabola passes through $(0, 10)$.

**Step 5 Graph the parabola.** With a vertex at $(-3, 1)$, no $x$-intercepts, and a $y$-intercept at 10, the graph of $f$ is shown in Figure 3.4. The axis of symmetry is the vertical line whose equation is $x = -3$.

**Check Point 2** Graph the quadratic function $f(x) = (x - 2)^2 + 1$.

## Graphing Functions in the Form $f(x) = ax^2 + bx + c$

Quadratic functions are frequently expressed in the form $f(x) = ax^2 + bx + c$. How can we identify the vertex of a parabola whose equation is in this form? Completing the square provides the answer to this question.

$$f(x) = ax^2 + bx + c$$

$$= a\left(x^2 + \frac{b}{a}x\right) + c \qquad \text{Factor out } a \text{ from } ax^2 + bx.$$

$$= a\left(x^2 + \frac{b}{a}x + \frac{b^2}{4a^2}\right) + c - a\left(\frac{b^2}{4a^2}\right)$$

Complete the square by adding the square of half the coefficient of x.

By completing the square, we added $a \cdot \frac{b^2}{4a^2}$. To avoid changing the function's equation, we must subtract this term.

$$= a\left(x + \frac{b}{2a}\right)^2 + c - \frac{b^2}{4a} \qquad \text{Write the trinomial as the square of a binomial and simplify the constant term.}$$

Compare the form of this equation with a quadratic function's standard form.

Standard form $\quad f(x) = a(x - h)^2 + k$

$h = -\frac{b}{2a}$ $\qquad$ $k = c - \frac{b^2}{4a}$

Equation under discussion $\quad f(x) = a\left(x - \left(-\frac{b}{2a}\right)\right)^2 + c - \frac{b^2}{4a}$

The important part of this observation is that $h$, the $x$-coordinate of the vertex, is $-\frac{b}{2a}$. The $y$-coordinate can be found by evaluating the function at $-\frac{b}{2a}$.

**The Vertex of a Parabola Whose Equation Is $f(x) = ax^2 + bx + c$**

Consider the parabola defined by the quadratic function $f(x) = ax^2 + bx + c$. The parabola's vertex is at $\left(-\frac{b}{2a}, f\left(-\frac{b}{2a}\right)\right)$.

We can apply our five-step procedure and graph parabolas in $f(x) = ax^2 + bx + c$ form. The only step that is different is how we determine the vertex.

## EXAMPLE 3 Graphing a Parabola in $f(x) = ax^2 + bx + c$ Form

Graph the quadratic function $f(x) = -x^2 + 4x - 1$.

### Solution

**Step 1 Determine how the parabola opens.** Note that $a$, the coefficient of $x^2$, is $-1$. Thus, $a < 0$; this negative value tells us that the parabola opens downward.

**Step 2 Find the vertex.** We know that the $x$-coordinate of the vertex is $x = -\frac{b}{2a}$. We identify $a$, $b$, and $c$ in $f(x) = ax^2 + bx + c$.

$$f(x) = -x^2 + 4x - 1$$

$a = -1$ $b = 4$ $c = -1$

Substitute the values of $a$ and $b$ into the equation for the $x$-coordinate:

$$x = -\frac{b}{2a} = -\frac{4}{2(-1)} = \frac{-4}{-2} = 2.$$

The $x$-coordinate of the vertex is 2. We substitute 2 for $x$ in the equation of the function to find the $y$-coordinate:

$$f(2) = -2^2 + 4 \cdot 2 - 1 = -4 + 8 - 1 = 3.$$

The vertex is at (2, 3).

**Step 3 Find the $x$-intercepts.** Replace $f(x)$ with 0 in $f(x) = -x^2 + 4x - 1$. We obtain $0 = -x^2 + 4x - 1$ or $-x^2 + 4x - 1 = 0$. This equation cannot be solved by factoring. We will use the quadratic formula to solve it.

$$a = -1, \quad b = 4, \quad c = -1$$

$$x = \frac{-b \pm \sqrt{b^2 - 4ac}}{2a} = \frac{-4 \pm \sqrt{4^2 - 4(-1)(-1)}}{2(-1)} = \frac{-4 \pm \sqrt{16 - 4}}{-2}$$

$$x = \frac{-4 - \sqrt{12}}{-2} \approx 3.7 \quad \text{or} \quad x = \frac{-4 + \sqrt{12}}{-2} \approx 0.3$$

The $x$-intercepts are approximately 0.3 and 3.7. The parabola passes through (0.3, 0) and (3.7, 0).

**Step 4 Find the $y$-intercept.** Replace $x$ with 0 in $f(x) = -x^2 + 4x - 1$.

$$f(0) = -0^2 + 4 \cdot 0 - 1 = -1$$

The $y$-intercept is $-1$. The parabola passes through $(0, -1)$.

**Step 5 Graph the parabola.** With a vertex at (2, 3), $x$-intercepts at 0.3 and 3.7, and a $y$-intercept at $-1$, the graph of $f$ is shown in Figure 3.5. The axis of symmetry is the vertical line whose equation is $x = 2$.

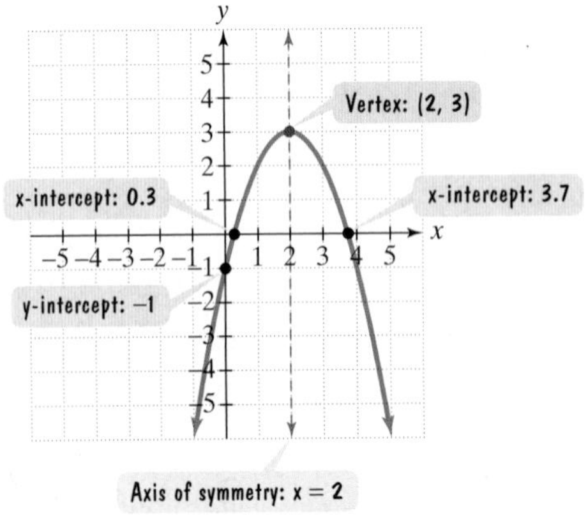


**Figure 3.5** The graph of $f(x) = -x^2 + 4x - 1$

**Check Point 3** Graph the quadratic function $f(x) = x^2 - 2x - 3$.

**3** Solve problems involving minimizing or maximizing quadratic functions.

## Applications of Quadratic Functions

When were women's earnings as a percentage of men's at the lowest? What is the age of a driver having the least number of car accidents? How much should a business spend on advertising to maximize its profits? The answers to these questions involve finding the maximum or minimum value of quadratic functions.

Consider the quadratic function $f(x) = ax^2 + bx + c$. If $a > 0$, the parabola opens upward and the vertex is its lowest point. If $a < 0$, the parabola opens downward and the vertex is its highest point. The $x$-coordinate of the vertex is $-\frac{b}{2a}$. Thus, we can find the minimum or maximum value of $f$ by evaluating the quadratic function at $x = -\frac{b}{2a}$.

**Minimum and Maximum: Quadratic Functions**

Consider $f(x) = ax^2 + bx + c$.

1. If $a > 0$, then $f$ has a minimum that occurs at $x = -\frac{b}{2a}$.
2. If $a < 0$, then $f$ has a maximum that occurs at $x = -\frac{b}{2a}$.

### EXAMPLE 4 An Application: The Wage Gap

The function

$$f(x) = 0.022x^2 - 0.4x + 60.07$$

models women's earnings as a percentage of men's $x$ years after 1960. In which year was this percentage at a minimum? What was the percentage for that year?

**Solution** The quadratic function is in the form $f(x) = ax^2 + bx + c$ with $a = 0.022$ and $b = -0.4$. With $a > 0$, the function has a minimum when $x = -\frac{b}{2a}$.

$$x = -\frac{b}{2a} = -\frac{(-0.4)}{2(0.022)} \approx 9$$

This means that women's earnings as a percentage of men's were at their lowest approximately 9 years after 1960, or in 1969. The percentage for that year was

$$f(9) = 0.022(9)^2 - 0.4(9) + 60.07 \approx 58.$$

In 1969, women earned approximately 58% as much as men.

**Check Point 4** The function $f(x) = 0.4x^2 - 36x + 1000$ models the number of accidents, $f(x)$, per 50 million miles driven, as a function of a driver's age, $x$, in years, where $16 \le x \le 74$. What is the age of a driver having the least number of car accidents? What is the minimum number of car accidents per 50 million miles driven?

## Modeling with Quadratic Functions

We've come a long way from the small nation of "embattled farmers" who launched the American Revolution. In the early years of our Republic, 95% of the population was involved in farming. Although U.S. agriculture is an integral part of the global economy, the number of U.S. farms has declined since the 1920s as individually owned family farms have been swallowed up by huge agribusinesses owned by corporations.

The graph in Figure 3.6 shows the number of farms in the United States from 1850 through 2010 (projected). Because the graph is shaped like a cup, with an increasing number of farms from 1850 to 1910 and a decreasing number of farms from 1910 to 2010, a quadratic function is an appropriate model for the data. You can use the statistical menu of a graphing utility to enter the data in Figure 3.6. We entered the data using

(number of decades after 1850, millions of U.S. farms).

Thus, we entered

$$(0, 2.3),\quad (2, 3.3),\quad (4, 5.1),\quad (6, 6.7),\quad (8, 6.4),$$
$$(10, 5.8),\quad (12, 3.6),\quad (14, 2.9),\quad (16, 2.3).$$

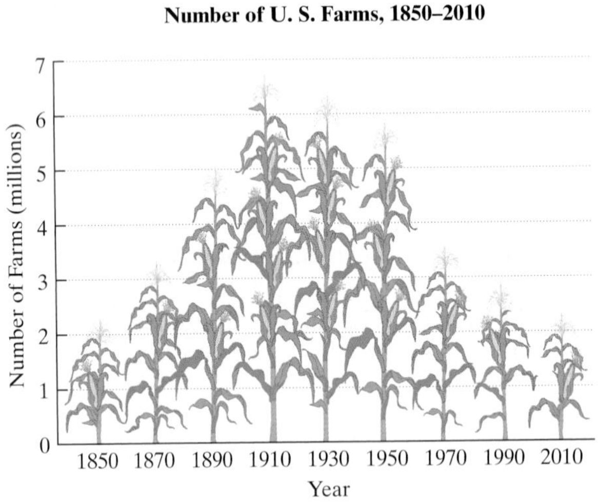


*Source*: U. S. Bureau of the Census

**Figure 3.6** The number of U.S. farms is declining.

**Figure 3.7** Executing the Quadratic Regression Program

Upon executing the QUADratic REGression program, we obtain the results shown in Figure 3.7. Thus, the quadratic function of best fit is

$$f(x) = -0.064x^2 + 0.99x + 2.2$$

where $x$ represents the number of decades after 1850 and $f(x)$ represents the number of U.S. farms, in millions.

Quadratic functions can also be formed from verbal conditions. Once we have obtained a quadratic function, we can then use the $x$-coordinate of the vertex to determine its maximum or minimum value. Here is a step-by-step strategy for solving these kinds of problems.

**Strategy for Solving Problems Involving Maximizing or Minimizing Quadratic Functions**

1. Read the problem carefully and decide which quantity is to be maximized or minimized.
2. Use the conditions of the problem to express the quantity as a function in one variable.
3. Rewrite the function in the form $f(x) = ax^2 + bx + c$.
4. If $a > 0$, $f$ has a minimum at $x = -\frac{b}{2a}$. If $a < 0$, $f$ has a maximum at $x = -\frac{b}{2a}$.
5. Answer the question posed in the problem.

## EXAMPLE 5 Solving a Number Problem

Among all pairs of numbers whose sum is 40, find a pair whose product is as large as possible. What is the maximum product?

### Solution

**Step 1 Decide what must be maximized or minimized.** We must maximize the product of two numbers. Calling the numbers $x$ and $y$, and calling the product $P$, we must maximize

$$P = xy.$$

**Step 2 Express this quantity as a function in one variable.** Right now, $P$ is expressed in terms of two variables, $x$ and $y$. However, because the sum of the numbers is 40, we can write

$$x + y = 40.$$

We can solve this equation for $y$ in terms of $x$ (or vice versa), substitute the result into $P = xy$, and obtain $P$ as a function of one variable. Solving for $y$, we get

$$y = 40 - x.$$

Now we substitute $40 - x$ for $y$ in $P = xy$.

$$P = xy = x(40 - x).$$

Because $P$ is now a function of $x$, we can write

$$P(x) = x(40 - x).$$

**Step 3 Write the function in the form $f(x) = ax^2 + bx + c$.** We apply the distributive property to obtain

$$P(x) = x(40 - x) = 40x - x^2$$

which can be expressed as

$$P(x) = -x^2 + 40x.$$

**Technology**

The graph of the product function

$$P(x) = x(40 - x)$$

was obtained with a graphing utility using a [0, 40, 4] by [0, 400, 20] viewing rectangle. The graphing utility's maximum function (FMAX) feature verifies that a maximum product of 400 occurs when one of the numbers is 20.

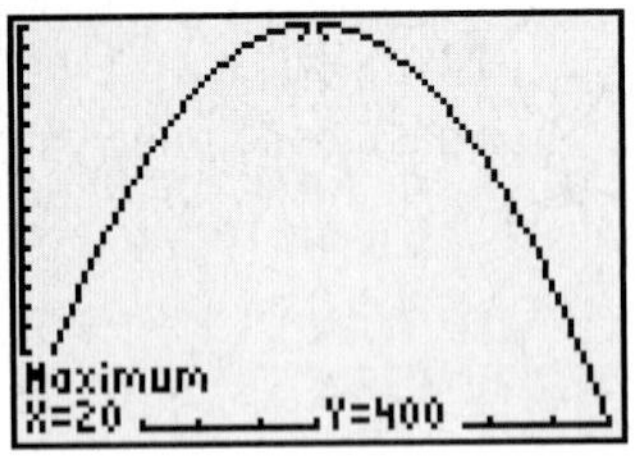


**Step 4 If $a < 0$, the function has a maximum at $x = -\frac{b}{2a}$.** Because $P(x) = -x^2 + 40x$, we see that $a = -1$ and $b = 40$. The function $P$ has a maximum at $x = -\frac{b}{2a}$.

$$x = -\frac{b}{2a}$$ *Remember that x represents one of the numbers.*

$$= -\frac{40}{2(-1)}$$ *Because $P(x) = -x^2 + 40x$, substitute −1 for a and 40 for b.*

$$= 20$$ *Simplify.*

**Step 5 Answer the question posed by the problem.** We found that $x = 20$. Now we must find the second number: $y = 40 - x = 40 - 20 = 20$. The number pair whose sum is 40 and whose product is as large as possible is 20, 20. The maximum product is $20 \cdot 20$, or 400.

**Check Point 5** Among all pairs of numbers whose sum is 8, find a pair whose product is as large as possible. What is the maximum product?

## EXAMPLE 6 Maximizing Area

You have 100 yards of fencing to enclose a rectangular region. Find the dimensions of the rectangle that maximize the enclosed area. What is the maximum area?

**Solution**

**Step 1 Decide what must be maximized or minimized.** We must maximize area. What we do not know are the rectangle's dimensions, $x$ and $y$.

**Step 2 Express this quantity as a function in one variable.** Because we must maximize area, we have $A = xy$. We need to transform this into a function in which $A$ is represented by one variable. Because you have 100 yards of fencing, the perimeter of the rectangle is 100 yards. This means that

$$2x + 2y = 100.$$

We can solve this equation for $y$ in terms of $x$, substitute the result into $A = xy$, and obtain $A$ as a function in one variable. Solving for $y$, we get

$$2y = 100 - 2x$$ *Subtract 2x from both sides.*

$$y = \frac{100 - 2x}{2}$$ *Divide both sides by 2.*

$$y = 50 - x$$ *Divide each term in the numerator by 2.*

Now we substitute $50 - x$ for $y$ in $A = xy$.

$$A = xy = x(50 - x).$$

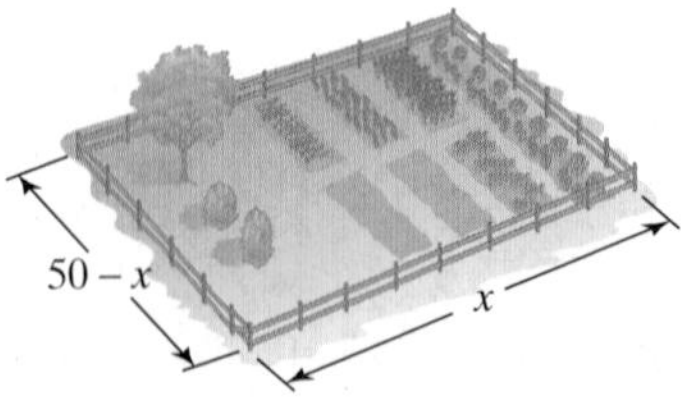


**Figure 3.8** What value of $x$ will maximize the rectangle's area?

The rectangle and its dimensions are illustrated in Figure 3.8. Because $A$ is now a function of $x$, we can write

$$A(x) = x(50 - x).$$

**Step 3 Write the function in the form $f(x) = ax^2 + bx + c$.** Applying the distributive property and rearranging terms, we obtain

$$A(x) = -x^2 + 50x.$$

**Step 4 If $a < 0$, the function has a maximum at $x = -\frac{b}{2a}$.** Using our formula for $A(x)$, we see that $a = -1$ and $b = 50$. The function has a maximum at $x = -\frac{b}{2a}$.

$$x = -\frac{b}{2a} = -\frac{50}{2(-1)} = 25$$

**Step 5 Answer the question posed by the problem.** We found that $x = 25$. Figure 3.8 on page 272 shows that the rectangle's other dimension is $50 - x = 50 - 25 = 25$. The dimensions that maximize area are 25 feet by 25 feet. The rectangle that gives the maximum area is actually a square with an area of 25 feet · 25 feet, or 625 square feet.

**Check Point 6** You have 120 feet of fencing to enclose a rectangular region. Find the dimensions of the rectangle that maximize the enclosed area. What is the maximum area?

The ability to express a quantity to be maximized or minimized as a function in one variable plays a critical role in solving max-min problems. In calculus, you will learn a technique for maximizing or minimizing all functions, not only quadratic functions.

## EXERCISE SET 3.1

### Practice Exercises

*In Exercises 1–4, the graph of a quadratic function is given. Write the function's equation, selecting from the following options.*

$f(x) = (x + 1)^2 - 1$ $g(x) = (x + 1)^2 + 1$ $h(x) = (x - 1)^2 + 1$ $j(x) = (x - 1)^2 - 1$

**1.**

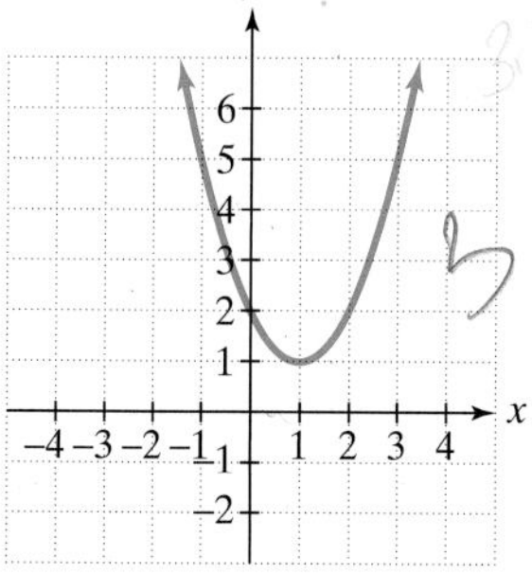

**2.**

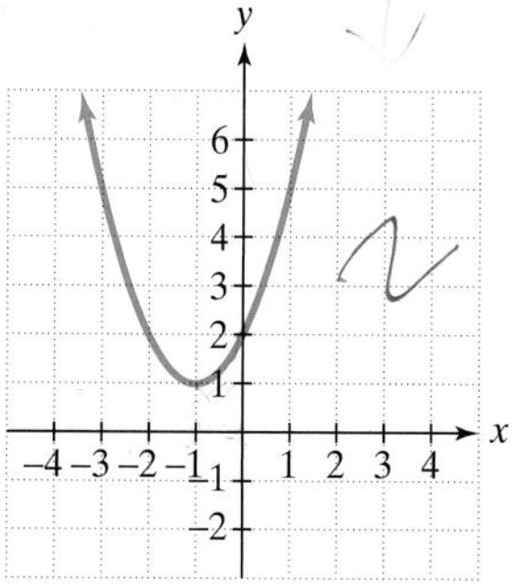

**3.**

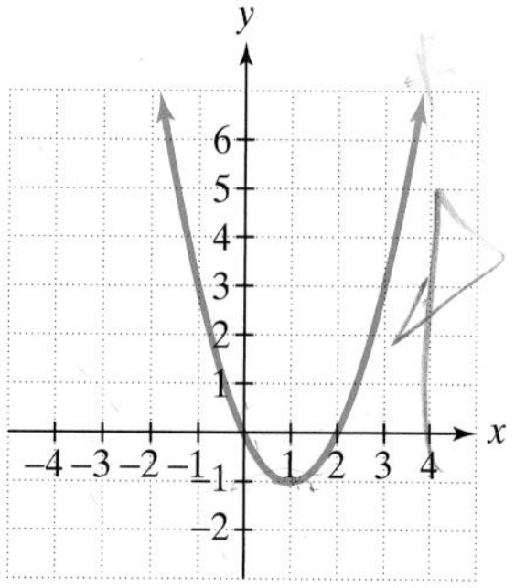

**4.**

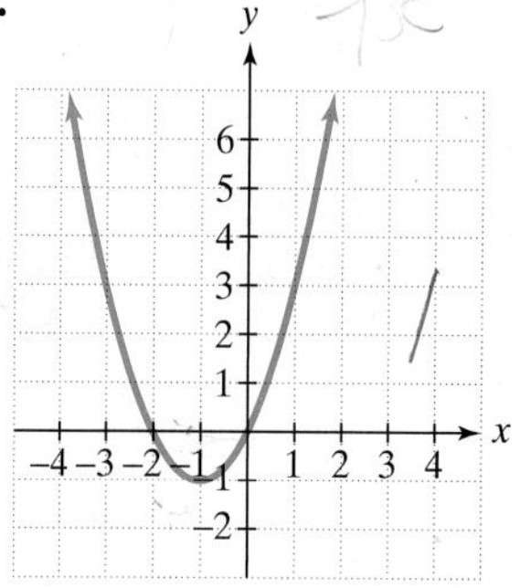

*In Exercises 5–8, the graph of a quadratic function is given. Write the function's equation, selecting from the following options.*

$f(x) = x^2 + 2x + 1 \qquad g(x) = x^2 - 2x + 1 \qquad h(x) = x^2 - 1 \qquad j(x) = -x^2 - 1$

**5.**

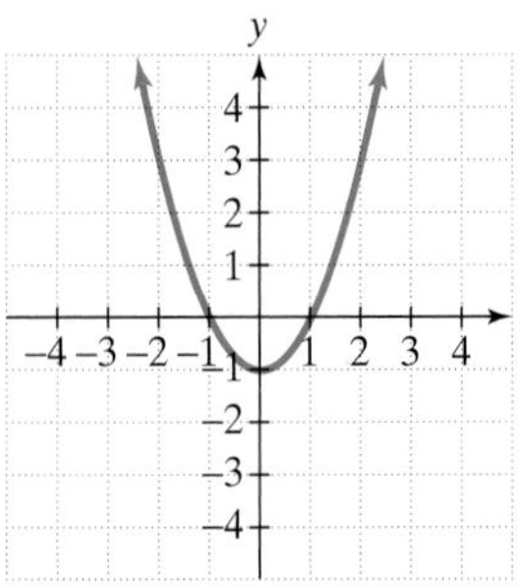


**6.**

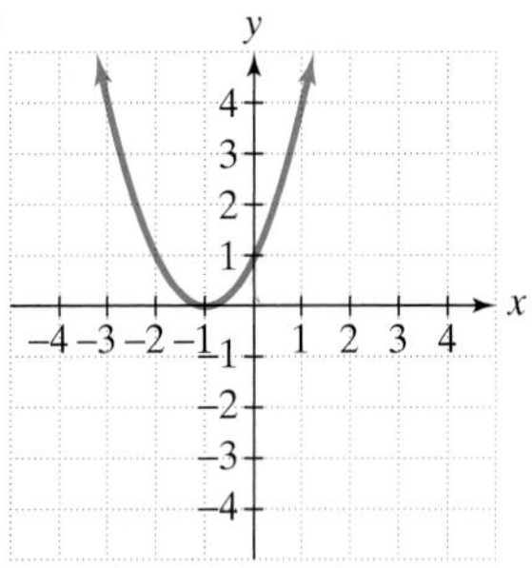


**7.**

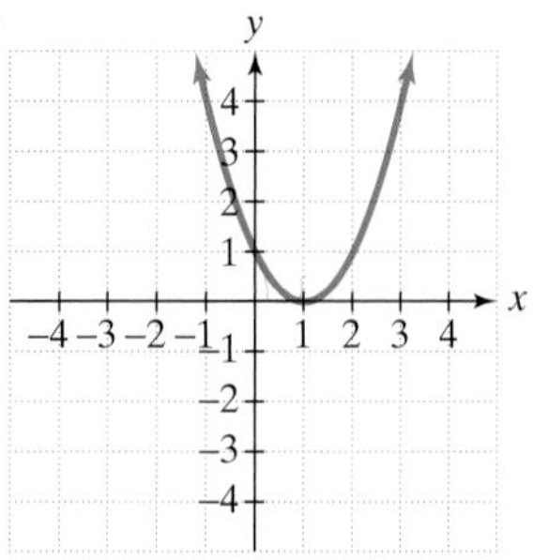


**8.**

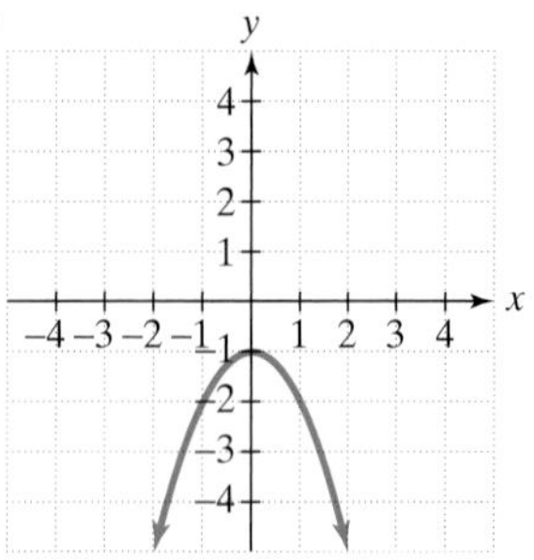


*In Exercises 9–16, find the coordinates of the vertex for the parabola defined by the given quadratic function.*

**9.** $f(x) = 2(x - 3)^2 + 1$

**10.** $f(x) = -3(x - 2)^2 + 12$

**11.** $f(x) = -2(x + 1)^2 + 5$

**12.** $f(x) = -2(x + 4)^2 - 8$

**13.** $f(x) = 2x^2 - 8x + 3$

**14.** $f(x) = 3x^2 - 12x + 1$

**15.** $f(x) = -x^2 - 2x + 8$

**16.** $f(x) = -2x^2 + 8x - 1$

*In Exercises 17–34, use the vertex and intercepts to sketch the graph of each quadratic function. Give the equation for the parabola's axis of symmetry.*

**17.** $f(x) = (x - 4)^2 - 1$

**18.** $f(x) = (x - 1)^2 - 2$

**19.** $f(x) = (x - 1)^2 + 2$

**20.** $f(x) = (x - 3)^2 + 2$

**21.** $y - 1 = (x - 3)^2$

**22.** $y - 3 = (x - 1)^2$

**23.** $f(x) = 2(x + 2)^2 - 1$

**24.** $f(x) = \frac{5}{4} - \left(x - \frac{1}{2}\right)^2$

**25.** $f(x) = 4 - (x - 1)^2$

**26.** $f(x) = 1 - (x - 3)^2$

**27.** $f(x) = x^2 - 2x - 3$

**28.** $f(x) = x^2 - 2x - 15$

**29.** $f(x) = x^2 + 3x - 10$

**30.** $f(x) = 2x^2 - 7x - 4$

**31.** $f(x) = 2x - x^2 + 3$

**32.** $f(x) = 5 - 4x - x^2$

**33.** $f(x) = 2x - x^2 - 2$

**34.** $f(x) = 6 - 4x + x^2$

*In Exercises 35–40, determine, without graphing, whether the given quadratic function has a minimum value or a maximum value. Then find the coordinates of the minimum or the maximum point.*

**35.** $f(x) = 3x^2 - 12x - 1$

**36.** $f(x) = 2x^2 - 8x - 3$

**37.** $f(x) = -4x^2 + 8x - 3$

**38.** $f(x) = -2x^2 - 12x + 3$

**39.** $f(x) = 5x^2 - 5x$

**40.** $f(x) = 6x^2 - 6x$

## Application Exercises

**41.** The U.S. Center for Disease Control modeled the average annual per capita consumption $C$ of cigarettes by Americans 18 and older as a function of time. The function is $C(t) = -3.1t^2 + 51.4t + 4024.5$, where $t$ represents years after 1960. According to this function, in which year did cigarette consumption per capita reach a maximum? What was the consumption for that year?

**Cigarette Consumption per U.S. Adult**

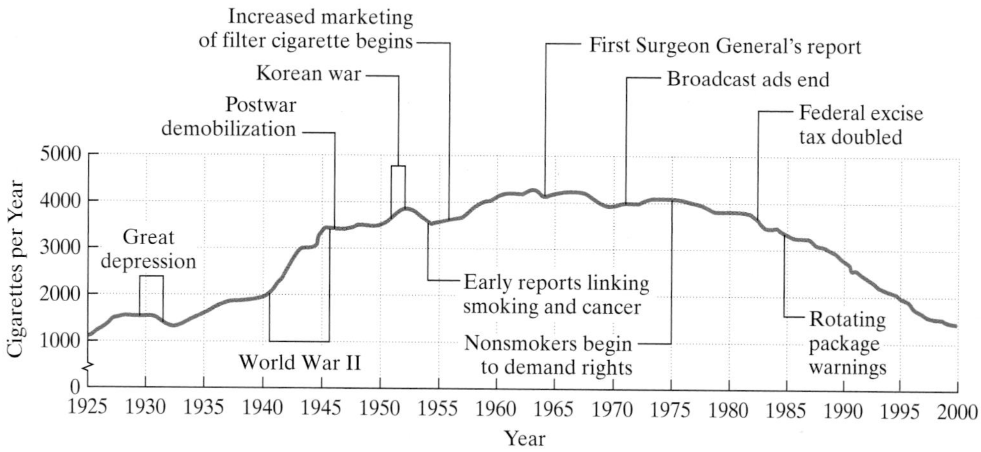


*Source*: U.S. Department of Health and Human Services

**42.** The function $R(x) = -0.0065x^2 + 0.23x + 8.47$ models the American marriage rate $R$ (the number of marriages per 1000 population) $x$ years after 1960. According to this function, in which year was the marriage rate the highest? What was the marriage rate for that year?

**43.** A person standing close to the edge of an 80-foot cliff throws a rock upward with an initial velocity of 64 feet per second. The height of the rock above the water at the bottom of the cliff, $s(t)$, in feet, after $t$ seconds is given by the quadratic function

$$s(t) = -16t^2 + 64t + 80.$$

After how many seconds will the rock reach its maximum height above the water? How many feet above the water is the rock at that time?

**44.** A person standing on a rooftop 112 feet high throws a ball directly upward. The ball misses the rooftop on its way down and eventually strikes the ground. The function

$$s(t) = -16t^2 + 96t + 112$$

describes the ball's height above the ground, $s(t)$, $t$ seconds after it was thrown. After how many seconds will the ball reach its maximum height above the ground? How many feet above the ground is the ball at that time?

**45.** Among all pairs of numbers whose sum is 16, find a pair whose product is as large as possible. What is the maximum product?

**46.** Among all pairs of numbers whose sum is 9, find a pair whose product is large as possible. What is the maximum product?

**47.** You have 120 feet of fencing to enclose a rectangular plot that borders on a river. If you do not fence the side along the river, find the length and width of the plot that will maximize the area. What is the largest area that can be enclosed?

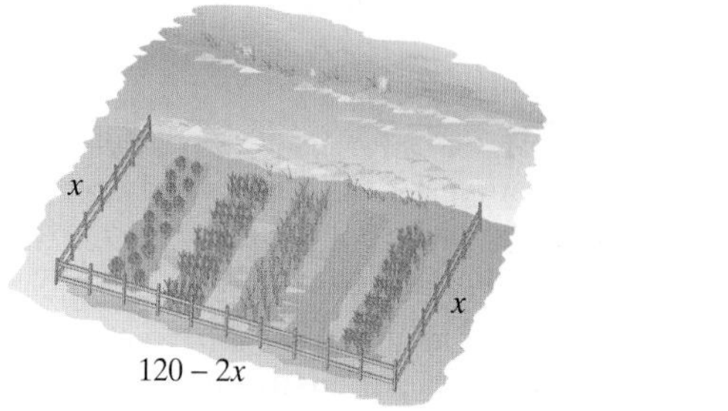


**48.** You have 600 feet of fencing to enclose a rectangular plot that borders on a river. If you do not fence the side along the river, find the length and width of the plot that will maximize the area. What is the largest area that can be enclosed?

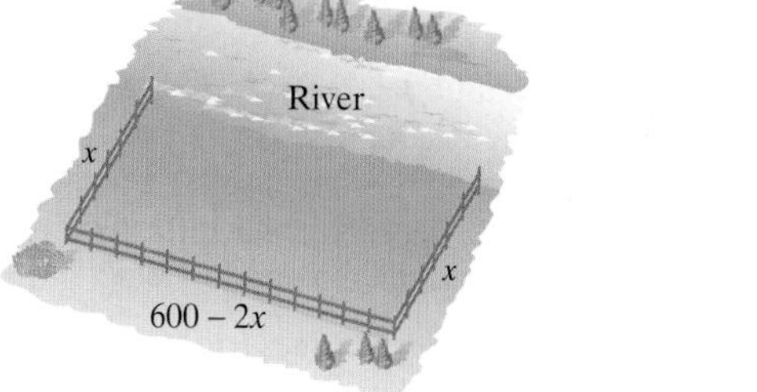

**49.** You have 20 yards of fencing to enclose a rectangular region. Find the dimensions of the rectangle that maximize the enclosed area. What is the maximum area?

**50.** You have 80 feet of fencing to enclose a rectangular region. Find the dimensions of the rectangle that maximize the enclosed area. What is the maximum area?

**51.** A rectangular playground is to be fenced off and divided in two by another fence parallel to one side of the playground. Six hundred feet of fencing is used. Find the dimensions of the playground that maximize the total enclosed area. What is the maximum area?

**52.** A rectangular playground is to be fenced off and divided into two by another fence parallel to one side of the playground. Four hundred feet of fencing is used. Find the dimensions of the playground that maximize the total enclosed area. What is the maximum area?

**53.** A rain gutter is made from sheets of aluminum that are 20 inches wide. As shown in the figure, the edges are turned up to form right angles. Determine the depth of the gutter that will maximize its cross-sectional area and allow the greatest amount of water to flow.

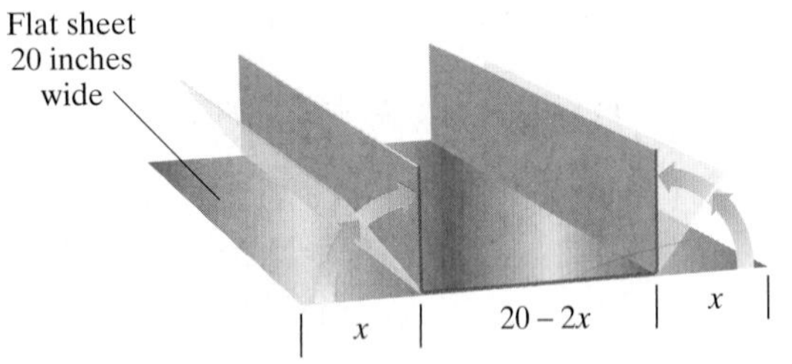


**54.** A rain gutter is made from sheets of aluminum that are 12 inches wide by turning up the edges to form right angles. Determine the depth of the gutter that will maximize its cross-sectional area and allow the greatest amount of water to flow.

**55.** A small cruising ship that can hold up to 50 people provides two-day excursions to groups of 34 or more. If there are 34 people in the group or fewer, each person pays \$60. If more than 34 people are in the group, the cost per person is decreased by \$1 times the number of people in excess of 34. Find the size of the group that maximizes income for the owners of the ship. What is the maximum income?

**56.** The annual yield per lemon tree is fairly constant at 320 pounds when the number of trees per acre is 50 or fewer. For each additional tree over 50, the annual yield per tree for all trees on the acre decreases by 4 pounds due to overcrowding. Find the number of trees that should be planted on an acre to produce the maximum yield. How many pounds is the maximum yield?

**57.** A piece of wire is 8 inches long. The wire is cut into two pieces and then each piece is bent into a square. Find the length of each piece that minimizes the sum of the areas of these squares.

**58.** A piece of wire is 16 inches long. The wire is cut into two pieces and then each piece is bent into a square. Find the length of each piece that minimizes the sum of the areas of these squares.

## Writing in Mathematics

**59.** What is a quadratic function?

**60.** What is a parabola? Describe its shape.

**61.** Explain how to decide whether a parabola opens upward or downward.

**62.** Describe how to find a parabola's vertex if its equation is expressed in standard form. Give an example.

**63.** Describe how to find a parabola's vertex if its equation is in the form $f(x) = ax^2 + bx + c$. Use $f(x) = x^2 - 6x + 8$ as an example.

**64.** A parabola that opens upward has its vertex at $(1, 2)$. Describe as much as you can about the parabola based on this information. Include in your discussion the number of $x$-intercepts (if any) for the parabola.

**65.** The quadratic function

$$f(x) = -0.018x^2 + 1.93x - 25.34$$

describes the miles per gallon of a Ford Taurus driven at $x$ miles per hour. Suppose that you own a Ford Taurus. Describe how you can use this function to save money.

## Technology Exercises

**66.** Use a graphing utility to verify any five of your hand-drawn graphs in Exercises 17–34.

**67.** **a.** Use a graphing utility to graph $y = 2x^2 - 82x + 720$ in a standard viewing rectangle. What do you observe?

**b.** Find the coordinates of the vertex for the given quadratic function.

**c.** The answer to part (b) is $(20.5, -120.5)$. Because the leading coefficient of the given function (2) is positive, the vertex is a minimum point on the graph. Use this fact to help find a viewing rectangle that will give a relatively complete picture of the parabola. With an axis of symmetry at $x = 20.5$, the setting for $x$ should extend past this, so try Xmin $= 0$ and Xmax $= 30$. The setting for $y$ should include (and probably go below) the $y$-coordinate of the graph's minimum point, so try Ymin $= -130$. Experiment with Ymax until your utility shows the parabola's major features.

**d.** In general, explain how knowing the coordinates of a parabola's vertex can help determine a reasonable viewing rectangle on a graphing utility for obtaining a complete picture of the parabola.

*In Exercises 68–71, find the vertex for each parabola. Then determine a reasonable viewing rectangle on your graphing utility and use it to graph the parabola.*

**68.** $y = -0.25x^2 + 40x$

**69.** $y = -4x^2 + 20x + 160$

**70.** $y = 5x^2 + 40x + 600$

**71.** $y = 0.01x^2 + 0.6x + 100$

**72.** The quadratic function $f(x) = 0.013x^2 - 0.96x + 25.4$ describes the average yearly consumption of whole milk per person in the United States $x$ years after 1970. The linear function $g(x) = 0.41x + 6.03$ describes the average yearly consumption of low-fat milk per person in the United States $x$ years after 1970.

**a.** Use a graphing utility to graph each function in the same viewing rectangle for the years 1970 through 2000.

**b.** Use the graphs to describe the trend in consumption for both types of milk. What possible explanations are there for these consumption patterns?

**73.** The function $y = 0.011x^2 - 0.097x + 4.1$ models the number of people in the United States, $y$, in millions, holding more than one job $x$ years after 1970. Use graphing utility to graph the function in a $[0, 20, 1]$ by $[3, 6, 1]$ viewing rectangle. TRACE along the curve or use your utility's minimum value feature to approximate the coordinates of the parabola's vertex. Describe what this represents in practical terms.

**74.** The following data show fuel efficiency, in miles per gallon, for all U.S. automobiles in the indicated year.

| $x$ (Years after 1940) | $y$ (Average Number of Miles per Gallon for U.S. Automobiles) |
|---|---|
| 1940: 0 | 14.8 |
| 1950: 10 | 13.9 |
| 1960: 20 | 13.4 |
| 1970: 30 | 13.5 |
| 1980: 40 | 15.5 |
| 1986: 46 | 18.3 |

*Source*: Statistical Abstract of the United States

**a.** Use a graphing utility to draw a scatter plot of the data. Explain why a quadratic function is appropriate for modeling these data.

**b.** Use the quadratic regression feature to find the quadratic function that best fits the data.

**c.** Use the equation in part (b) to determine the worst year for automobile fuel efficiency. What was the average number of miles per gallon for that year?

**d.** Use a graphing utility to draw a scatter plot of the data and graph the quadratic function of best fit on the scatter plot.

## Critical Thinking Exercises

**75.** Which one of the following is true?

**a.** No quadratic functions have a range of $(-\infty, \infty)$.

**b.** The vertex of the parabola described by $f(x) = 2(x - 5)^2 - 1$ is at $(5, 1)$.

**c.** The graph of $f(x) = -2(x + 4)^2 - 8$ has one $y$-intercept and two $x$-intercepts.

**d.** The maximum value of $y$ for the quadratic function $f(x) = -x^2 + x + 1$ is 1.

*In Exercises 76–77, find the axis of symmetry for each parabola whose equation is given. Use the axis of symmetry to find a second point on the parabola whose y-coordinate is the same as the given point.*

**76.** $f(x) = 3(x + 2)^2 - 5;\quad (-1, -2)$

**77.** $f(x) = (x - 3)^2 + 2;\quad (6, 11)$

**78.** The figure shows a Norman window that has the shape of a rectangle with a semicircle attached at the top. The diameter of the circle is equal to the width of the rectangle. If the window has a perimeter of 12 feet, find the dimensions of $h$ and $r$ that allow the maximum amount of light to enter. Round to two decimal places. (*Hint:* Maximize the window's area. You'll need to use the formulas for a circle's circumference and area: Circumference $= 2\pi r$; Area $= \pi r^2$).

## Group Exercise

**79.** Each group member should consult an almanac, newspaper, magazine, or the Internet to find data that can be modeled by a quadratic function. Group members should select the two sets of data that are most interesting and relevant. For each data set selected:

**a.** Use the quadratic regression feature of a graphing utility to find the quadratic function that best fits the data.

**b.** Use the equation of the quadratic function to make a prediction from the data. What circumstances might affect the accuracy of your prediction?

**c.** Use the equation of the quadratic function to write and solve a problem involving maximizing or minimizing the function.

# SECTION 3.2 Polynomial Functions and Their Graphs

## Objectives

1. Recognize characteristics of graphs of polynomial functions.
2. Determine end behavior.
3. Use factoring to find zeros of polynomial functions.
4. Identify the multiplicity of a zero.
5. Understand the relationship between degree and turning points.
6. Graph polynomial functions.

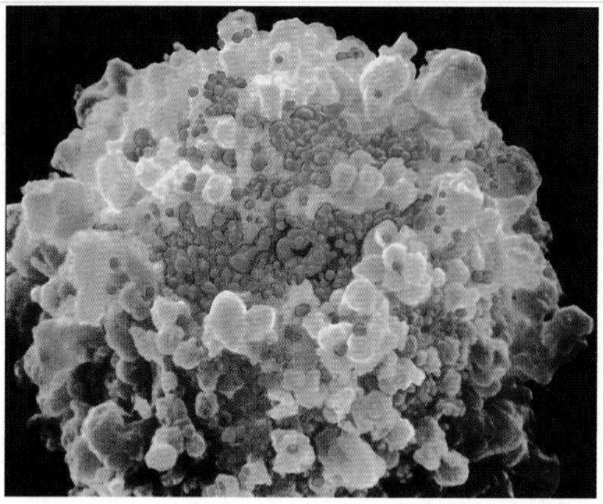

Magnified 6000 times, this color-scanned image shows a T-lymphocyte blood cell (green) infected with the HIV virus (red). Depletion of the number of T-cells causes destruction of the immune system.

In 1980, U.S. doctors diagnosed 41 cases of a rare form of cancer, Kaposi's sarcoma, that involved skin lesions, pneumonia, and severe immunological deficiencies. All cases involved gay men ranging in age from 26 to 51. By the end of 1998, approximately 680,000 Americans, straight and gay, male and female, old and young, were infected with the HIV virus.

Modeling AIDS-related data and making predictions about the epidemic's havoc is serious business. Changing circumstances and unforeseen events have resulted in models that are not particularly useful over long periods of time. For example, the function

$$f(x) = -143x^3 + 1810x^2 - 187x + 2331$$

models the number of AIDS cases diagnosed in the United States $x$ years after 1983. The model was obtained using cases diagnosed from 1983 through 1991. Figure 3.9 shows the graph of $f$ from 1983 through 1991 in a $[0, 8, 1]$ by $[0, 50{,}000, 5000]$ viewing rectangle. The function used to describe what was happening with new HIV infections over a limited period of time is an example of a **polynomial function**.

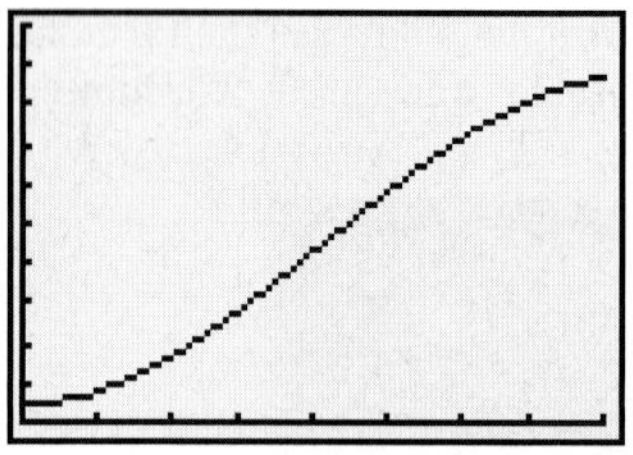

**Figure 3.9** The graph of a function modeling the number of AIDS cases from 1983 through 1991

### Definition of a Polynomial Function

Let $n$ be a nonnegative integer and let $a_n, a_{n-1}, \ldots, a_2, a_1, a_0$, be real numbers with $a_n \neq 0$. The function defined by

$$f(x) = a_n x^n + a_{n-1}x^{n-1} + \cdots + a_2 x^2 + a_1 x + a_0$$

is called a **polynomial function of $x$ of degree $n$.** The number $a_n$, the coefficient of the variable to the highest power, is called the **leading coefficient**.

A constant function $f(x) = a$, where $a \neq 0$, is a polynomial function of degree 0. A linear function $f(x) = ax + b$, where $a \neq 0$, is a polynomial function of degree 1. A quadratic function $f(x) = ax^2 + bx + c$, where $a \neq 0$, is a polynomial function of degree 2. In this section, we focus on polynomial functions of degree 3 or higher.

**1** Recognize characteristics of graphs of polynomial functions.

## Smooth, Continuous Graphs

Polynomial functions of degree 2 or less have graphs that are either parabolas or lines. We can graph such functions by plotting points. We can also graph polynomial functions of degree 3 or higher by plotting points. However, the process is rather tedious: Many points must be plotted. It may be easier to use a graphing utility for such functions. Regardless of the graphing method you use, you will find an ability to recognize the basic features of polynomial functions helpful. For example, they may help you choose an appropriate viewing rectangle for a graphing utility.

Two important features of the graphs of polynomial functions are that they are *smooth* and *continuous*. By **smooth**, we mean that the graph contains only rounded curves with no sharp corners. By **continuous**, we mean that the graph has no breaks and can be drawn without lifting your pencil from the rectangular coordinate system. These ideas are illustrated in Figure 3.10.

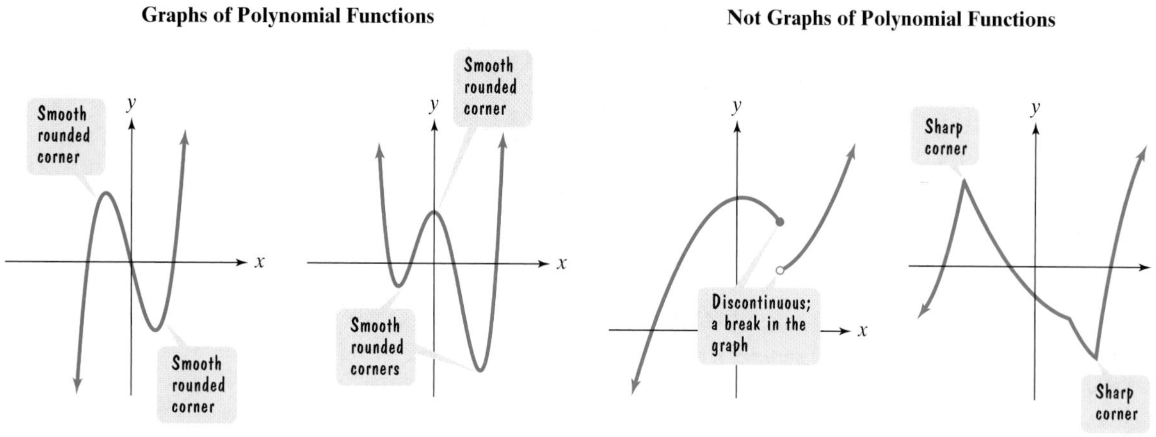


**Figure 3.10** Recognizing graphs of polynomial functions

**2** Determine end behavior.

## End Behavior of Polynomial Functions

Figure 3.11 shows the graph of the function

$$f(x) = -143x^3 + 1810x^2 - 187x + 2331,$$

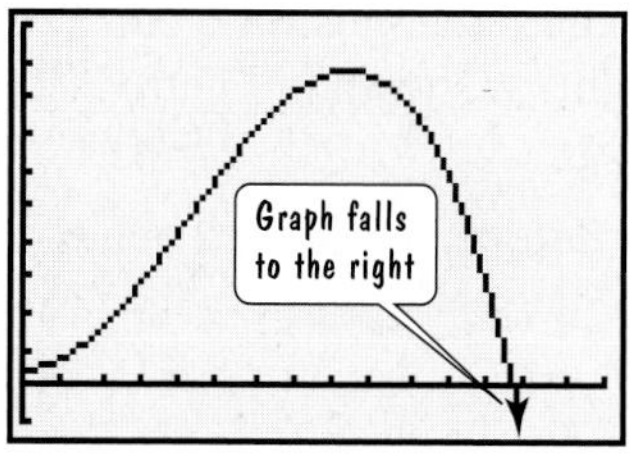


**Figure 3.11** By extending the viewing rectangle, $y$ is negative and the function no longer models the number of AIDS cases.

which models U.S. AIDS cases from 1983 through 1991. Look what happens to the graph when we extend the year up through 1998 with a $[0, 15, 1]$ by $[-5000, 50{,}000, 5000]$ viewing rectangle. By year 13 (1996), the values of $y$ are negative and the function no longer models AIDS cases. We've added an arrow to the graph at the far right to emphasize that it continues to decrease without bound. It is this far-right *end behavior* of the graph that makes it inappropriate for modeling AIDS cases into the future.

The behavior of a graph of a function to the far left or the far right is called its **end behavior**. Although the graph of a polynomial function may have intervals where it increases or decreases, the graph will eventually rise or fall without bound as it moves far to the left or far to the right.

How can you determine whether the graph of a polynomial function goes up or down at each end? The end behavior of a polynomial function

$$f(x) = a_n x^n + a_{n-1}x^{n-1} + \cdots + a_1 x + a_0$$

depends upon the leading term $a_n x^n$. In particular, the sign of the leading coefficient $a_n$, and the degree, $n$, of the polynomial function reveal its end behavior. In terms of end behavior, only the term of highest degree counts, summarized by the **Leading Coefficient Test**.

## The Leading Coefficient Test

As $x$ increases or decreases without bound, the graph of the polynomial function

$$f(x) = a_n x^n + a_{n-1}x^{n-1} + a_{n-2}x^{n-2} + \cdots + a_1 x + a_0 \quad (a_n \neq 0)$$

eventually rises or falls. In particular,

**1.** For $n$ odd:

If the leading coefficient is positive, the graph falls to the left and rises to the right.

$a_n > 0$

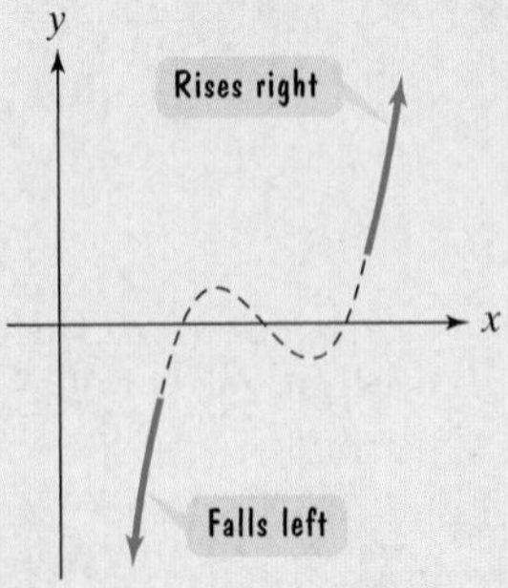


If the leading coefficient is negative, the graph rises to the left and falls to the right.

$a_n < 0$

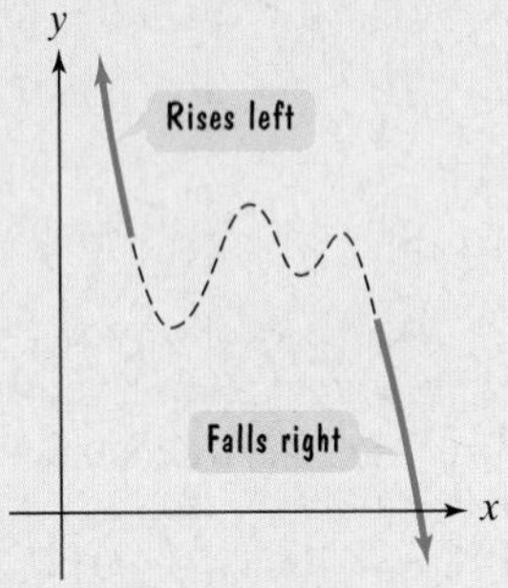


**2.** For $n$ even:

If the leading coefficient is positive, the graph rises to the left and to the right.

$a_n > 0$

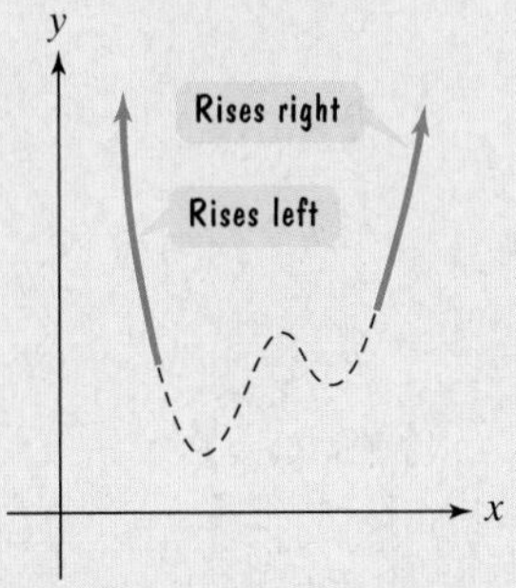


If the leading coefficient is negative, the graph falls to the left and to the right.

$a_n < 0$

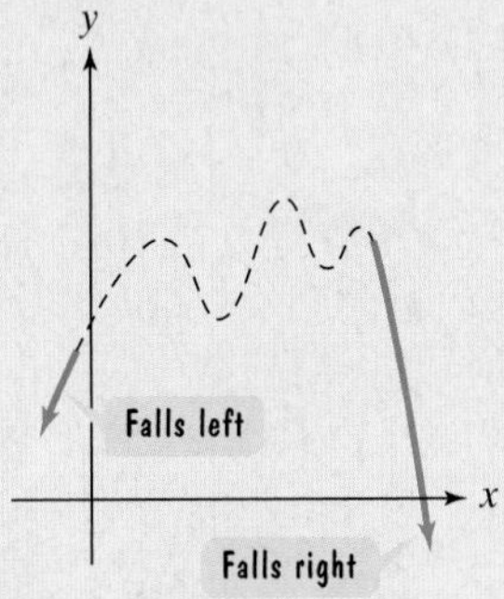


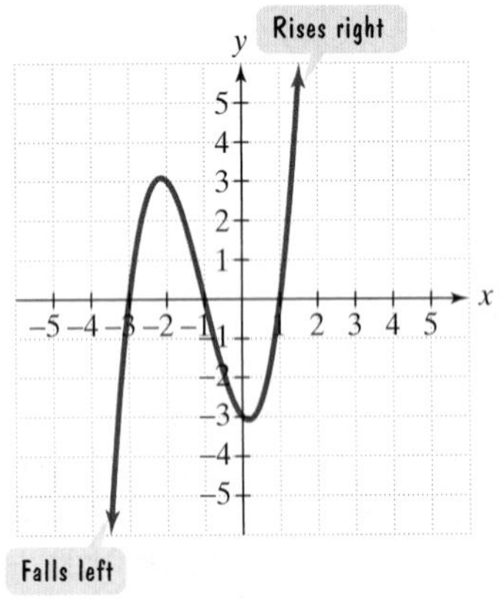


**Figure 3.12** The graph of $f(x) = x^3 + 3x^2 - x - 3$

### EXAMPLE 1 Using the Leading Coefficient Test

Use the Leading Coefficient Test to determine the end behavior of the graph of

$$f(x) = x^3 + 3x^2 - x - 3.$$

**Solution** Because the degree is odd ($n = 3$) and the leading coefficient, 1, is positive, the graph falls to the left and rises to the right, as shown in Figure 3.12.

**Check Point 1** Use the Leading Coefficient Test to determine the end behavior of the graph of $f(x) = x^4 - 4x^2$.

### EXAMPLE 2 Using the Leading Coefficient Test

Use end behavior to explain why

$$f(x) = -143x^3 + 1810x^2 - 187x + 2331$$

is only an appropriate model for AIDS cases for a limited time period.

**Solution** Because the degree is odd ($n = 3$) and the leading coefficient, $-143$, is negative, the graph rises to the left and falls to the right. The fact that it falls to the right indicates at some point the number of AIDS cases will be negative, an impossibility. No function with a graph that decreases without bound as $x$ (time) increases can model nonnegative real-world phenomena over a long period of time.

**Check Point 2**

The polynomial function

$$f(x) = -0.27x^3 + 9.2x^2 - 102.9x + 400$$

models the ratio of students to computers in U.S. public schools $x$ years after 1980. Use end behavior to determine whether this function could be an appropriate model for computers in the classroom well into the twenty-first century. Explain your answer.

If you use a graphing utility to graph a polynomial function, it is important to select a viewing rectangle that accurately reveals the graph's end behavior. If the viewing rectangle is too small, it may not accurately show end behavior.

### EXAMPLE 3 Using the Leading Coefficient Test

The graph of $f(x) = -x^4 + 8x^3 + 4x^2 + 2$ was obtained with a graphing utility using a $[-8, 8, 1]$ by $[-10, 10, 1]$ viewing rectangle. The graph is shown in Figure 3.13(a). Does the graph show the end behavior of the function?

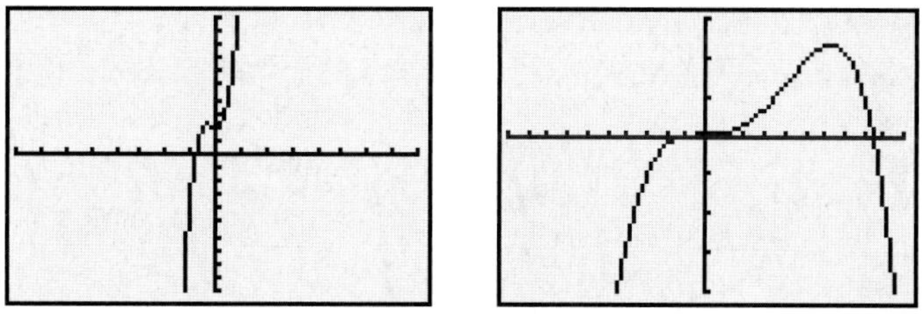

**Figure 3.13** **(a)** $[-8, 8, 1]$ by $[-10, 10, 1]$ **(b)** $[-10, 10, 1]$ by $[-1000, 750, 250]$

**Solution** Note that the degree is even $(n = 4)$ and the leading coefficient, $-1$, is negative. Thus, the Leading Coefficient Test indicates that the graph should fall to the left and the right. The graph in Figure 3.13(a) is falling to the left, but it is not falling to the right. Therefore, the graph is not complete enough to show end behavior. A more complete graph of the function is shown in a larger viewing rectangle in Figure 3.13(b).

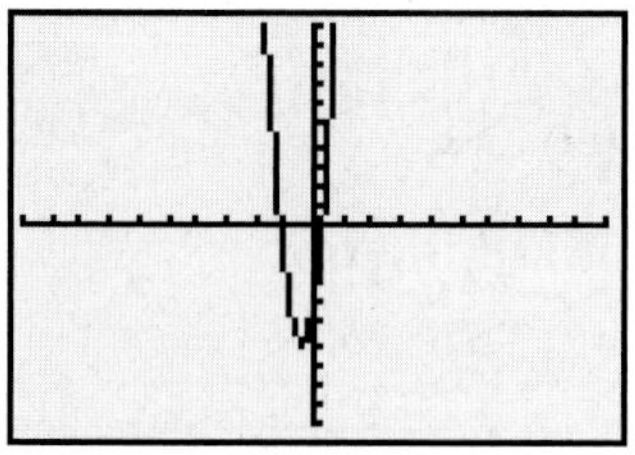

**Figure 3.14**

**Check Point 3**

The graph of $f(x) = x^3 + 13x^2 + 10x - 4$ is shown in a standard viewing rectangle in Figure 3.14. Use the Leading Coefficient Test to determine whether the graph shows the end behavior of the function. Explain your answer.

**3** Use factoring to find zeros of polynomial functions.

## Zeros of Polynomial Functions

If $f$ is a polynomial function, then the values of $x$ for which $f(x)$ is equal to 0 are called the **zeros** of $f$. These values of $x$ are the **roots** of the polynomial equation $f(x) = 0$. Each real root of the polynomial equation appears as an $x$-intercept of the graph of the polynomial function.

## EXAMPLE 4 Finding Zeros of a Polynomial Function

Find all zeros of $f(x) = x^3 + 3x^2 - x - 3$.

**Solution** By definition, the zeros are the values of $x$ for which $f(x)$ is equal to 0. Thus, we set $f(x)$ equal to 0:

$$f(x) = x^3 + 3x^2 - x - 3 = 0.$$

We solve the polynomial equation $x^3 + 3x^2 - x - 3 = 0$ for $x$ as follows:

$x^3 + 3x^2 - x - 3 = 0$ This is the equation needed to find the function's zeros.

$x^2(x + 3) - 1(x + 3) = 0$ Factor $x^2$ from the first two terms and −1 from the last two terms.

$(x + 3)(x^2 - 1) = 0$ A common factor of $x + 3$ is factored from the expression.

$x + 3 = 0$ or $x^2 - 1 = 0$ Set each factor equal to 0.

$x = -3$ $\quad x^2 = 1$ Solve for $x$.

$x = \pm 1$ Remember that if $x^2 = d$, then $x = \pm\sqrt{d}$.

The zeros of $f$ are −3, −1, and 1. The graph of $f$ in Figure 3.15 shows that each zero is an $x$-intercept.

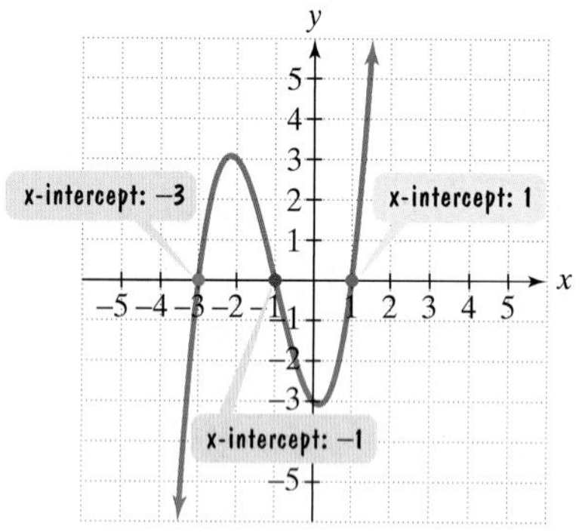


**Figure 3.15** The real zeros of $f(x) = x^3 + 3x^2 - x - 3$ are the $x$-intercepts for the graph of $f$.

**Check Point 4** Find all zeros of $f(x) = x^3 + 2x^2 - 4x - 8$.

## EXAMPLE 5 Finding Zeros of a Polynomial Function

Find all zeros of $f(x) = -x^4 + 4x^3 - 4x^2$.

**Solution** We find the zeros of $f$ by setting $f(x)$ equal to 0.

$-x^4 + 4x^3 - 4x^2 = 0$ We now have a polynomial equation.

$x^4 - 4x^3 + 4x^2 = 0$ Multiply both sides by −1. This step is optional.

$x^2(x^2 - 4x + 4) = 0$ Factor out $x^2$.

$x^2(x - 2)^2 = 0$ Factor completely.

$x^2 = 0$ or $(x - 2)^2 = 0$ Set each factor equal to 0.

$x = 0$ $\quad x = 2$ Solve for $x$.

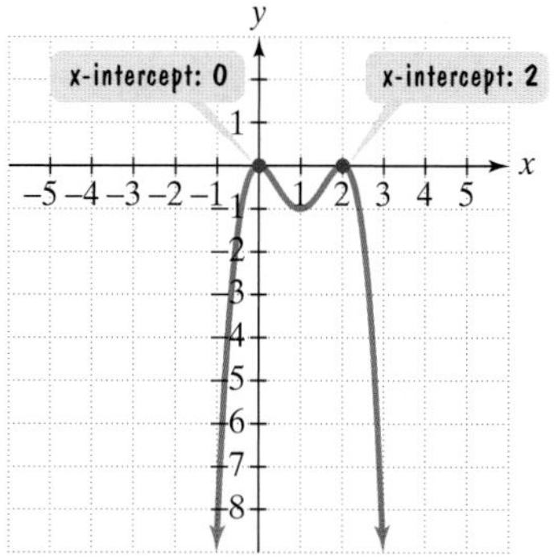


**Figure 3.16** The zeros of $f(x) = -x^4 + 4x^3 - 4x^2$, namely 0 and 2, are the $x$-intercepts for the graph of $f$.

The zeros of $f(x) = -x^4 + 4x^3 - 4x^2$ are 0 and 2. The graph of $f$, shown in Figure 3.16 has $x$-intercepts at 0 and 2.

**Check Point 5** Find all zeros of $f(x) = x^4 - 4x^2$.

In Example 5, we can use our factoring to express the function's equation as follows:

$$f(x) = -x^4 + 4x^3 - 4x^2 = -(x^4 - 4x^3 + 4x^2) = -x^2(x - 2)^2$$

The factor x occurs twice: $x^2 = x \cdot x$.

The factor $(x - 2)$ occurs twice: $(x - 2)^2 = (x - 2)(x - 2)$.

**4** Identify the multiplicity of a zero.

Notice that each factor occurs twice. In factoring the equation for the polynomial function $f$, if the same factor $x - r$ occurs $k$ times, but not $k + 1$ times, we call $r$ a **repeated zero with multiplicity *k***. For the polynomial

$$f(x) = -x^2(x - 2)^2,$$

0 and 2 are both repeated zeros with multiplicity 2. For the polynomial

$$f(x) = 4(x - 5)(x + 2)^3\left(x - \tfrac{1}{4}\right)^4,$$

5 is a zero with multiplicity 1, −2 is a repeated zero with multiplicity 3, and $\frac{1}{4}$ is a repeated zero with multiplicity 4.

The multiplicity of a zero tells us if the graph of a polynomial function touches the $x$-axis at the zero and turns around or crosses the $x$-axis at the zero. For example, look again at the graph of $f(x) = -x^4 + 4x^3 - 4x^2$ in Figure 3.15. Each zero, 0 and 2, is a repeated zero with multiplicity 2. The graph of $f$ touches, but does not cross, the $x$-axis at each of these zeros of even multiplicity. By contrast, a graph crosses the $x$-axis at zeros of odd multiplicity.

### Multiplicity and $x$-Intercepts

If $r$ is a zero of even multiplicity, then the graph **touches** the $x$-axis and turns around at $r$. If $r$ is a zero of odd multiplicity, then the graph **crosses** the $x$-axis at $r$. Regardless of whether a zero is even or odd, graphs tend to flatten out at zeros with multiplicity greater than one.

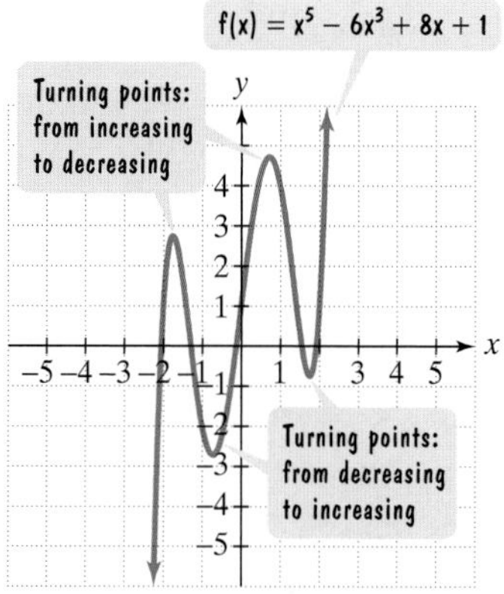


**Figure 3.17** Graph with four turning points

**5** Understand the relationship between degree and turning points.

## Turning Points of Polynomial Functions

The graph of $f(x) = x^5 - 6x^3 + 8x + 1$ is shown in Figure 3.17. The graph has four smooth **turning points**. At each turning point, the graph changes direction from increasing to decreasing or vice versa. In calculus, these points are called **local maxima** or **local minima**. The given equation has 5 as its greatest exponent and is therefore a polynomial function of degree 5. Notice that the graph has four turning points. In general, **if *f* is a polynomial of degree *n*, then the graph of *f* has at most *n* − 1 turning points.**

**6** Graph polynomial functions.

## A Strategy for Graphing Polynomial Functions

Here's a general strategy for graphing a polynomial function. A graphing utility is a valuable complement to this strategy. Some of the steps listed in the following box will help you to select a viewing rectangle that shows the important parts of the graph.

### Graphing a Polynomial Function

$$f(x) = a_n x^n + a_{n-1}x^{n-1} + a_{n-2}x^{n-2} + \cdots + a_1 x + a_0, \quad a_n \neq 0$$

1. Use the Leading Coefficient Test to determine the graph's end behavior.
2. Find $x$-intercepts by setting $f(x) = 0$ and solving the resulting polynomial equation. If there is an $x$-intercept at $r$ as a result of $(x - r)^k$ in the complete factorization of $f(x)$, then:
   **a.** If $k$ is even, the graph touches the $x$-axis at $r$ and turns around.
   **b.** If $k$ is odd, the graph crosses the $x$-axis at $r$.
   **c.** If $k > 1$, the graph flattens out at $(r, 0)$.
3. Find the $y$-intercept by setting $x$ equal to 0 and computing $f(0)$.
4. Use symmetry, if applicable, to help draw the graph:
   **a.** $y$-axis symmetry: $f(-x) = f(x)$
   **b.** Origin symmetry: $f(-x) = -f(x)$
5. Use the fact that the maximum number of turning points of the graph is $n - 1$ to check whether it is drawn correctly.

### EXAMPLE 6 Graphing a Polynomial Function

Graph: $f(x) = x^4 - 2x^2 + 1$.

**Solution**

**Step 1 Determine end behavior.** Because the degree is even ($n = 4$) and the leading coefficient, 1, is positive, the graph rises to the left and the right:

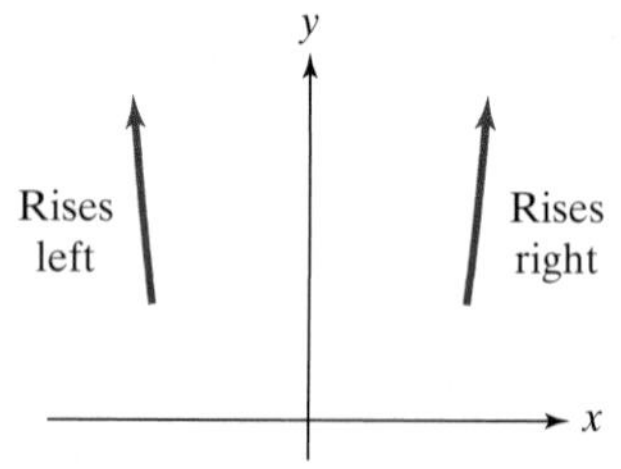


**Step 2 Find $x$-intercepts (zeros of the function) by setting $f(x) = 0$.**

$$x^4 - 2x^2 + 1 = 0$$

$$(x^2 - 1)(x^2 - 1) = 0 \quad \text{Factor.}$$

$$(x+1)(x-1)(x+1)(x-1) = 0 \quad \text{Factor completely.}$$

$$(x+1)^2(x-1)^2 = 0 \quad \text{Express the factoring in a more compact notation.}$$

$$(x+1)^2 = 0 \quad \text{or} \quad (x-1)^2 = 0 \quad \text{Set each factor equal to 0.}$$

$$x = -1 \qquad\qquad x = 1 \quad \text{Solve for } x.$$

We see that −1 and 1 are both repeated zeros with multiplicity 2. Because of the even multiplicity, the graph touches the $x$-axis at −1 and 1 and turns around. Furthermore, the graph tends to flatten out at these zeros with multiplicity greater than one:

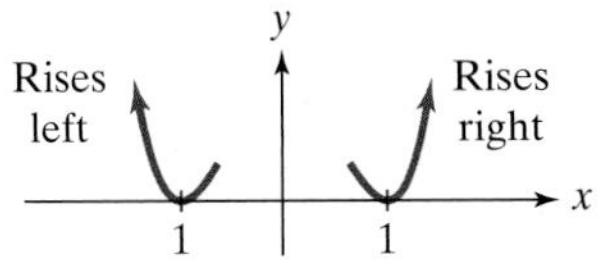


**Step 3 Find the $y$-intercept by setting $x$ equal to 0.**

$$f(0) = 0^4 - 2 \cdot 0^2 + 1 = 1$$

There is a $y$-intercept at 1, so the graph passes through $(0, 1)$:

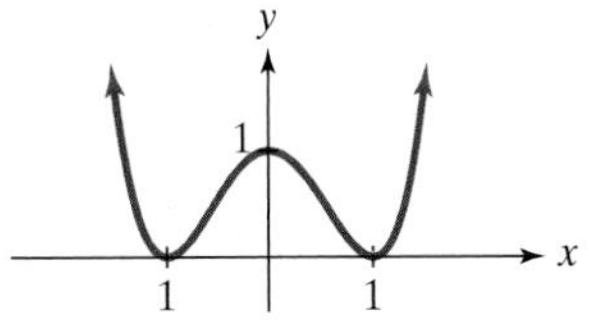


**Step 4 Use possible symmetry to help draw the graph.** Our partial graph suggests $y$-axis symmetry. Let's verify this by finding $f(-x)$.

$$f(x) = x^4 - 2x^2 + 1$$

Replace x with −x.

$$f(-x) = (-x)^4 - 2(-x)^2 + 1 = x^4 - 2x^2 + 1$$

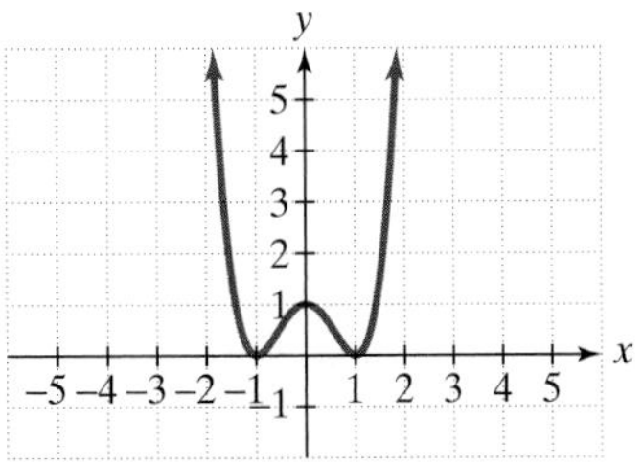


**Figure 3.18** The graph of $f(x) = x^4 - 2x^2 + 1$

Because $f(-x) = f(x)$, the graph of $f$ is symmetric with respect to the $y$-axis. Figure 3.18 shows the graph of $f(x) = x^4 - 2x^2 + 1$.

**Step 5 Use the fact that the maximum number of turning points of the graph is $n - 1$ to check whether it is drawn correctly.** Because $n = 4$, the maximum number of turning points is $4 - 1$, or 3. Because the graph in Figure 3.18 has three turning points, we have not violated the maximum number possible.

**Check Point 6** Use the five-step strategy to graph $f(x) = x^3 - 3x^2$.

## EXERCISE SET 3.2

### Practice Exercises

*In Exercises 1–10, determine which functions are polynomial functions. For those that are, identify the degree.*

1. $f(x) = 5x^2 + 6x^3$

2. $f(x) = 7x^2 + 9x^4$

3. $g(x) = 7x^5 - \pi x^3 + \frac{1}{5}x$

4. $g(x) = 6x^7 + \pi x^5 + \frac{2}{3}x$

5. $h(x) = 7x^3 + 2x^2 + \frac{1}{x}$

6. $h(x) = 8x^3 - x^2 + \frac{2}{x}$

7. $f(x) = x^{1/2} - 3x^2 + 5$

8. $f(x) = x^{1/3} - 4x^2 + 7$

9. $f(x) = \frac{x^2 + 7}{x^3}$

10. $f(x) = \frac{x^2 + 7}{3}$

*In Exercises 11–14, identify which graphs are not those of polynomial functions.*

**11.**

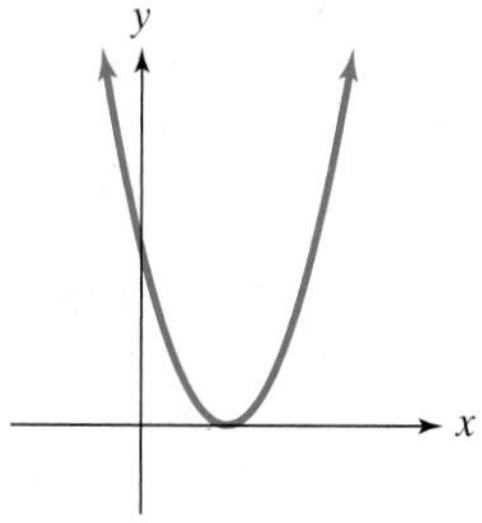


**12.**

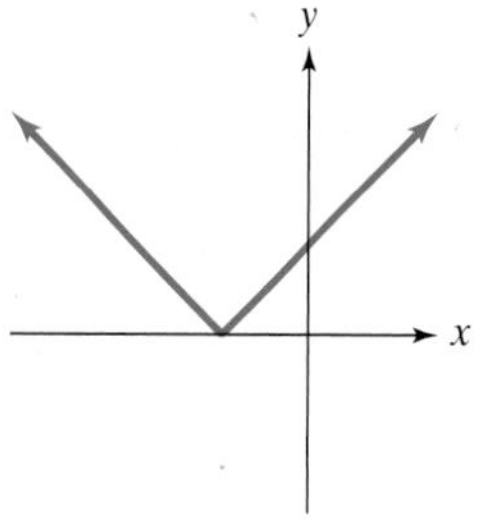


**13.**

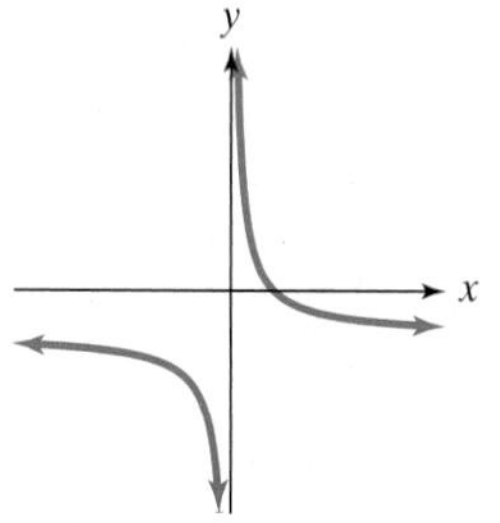


**14.**

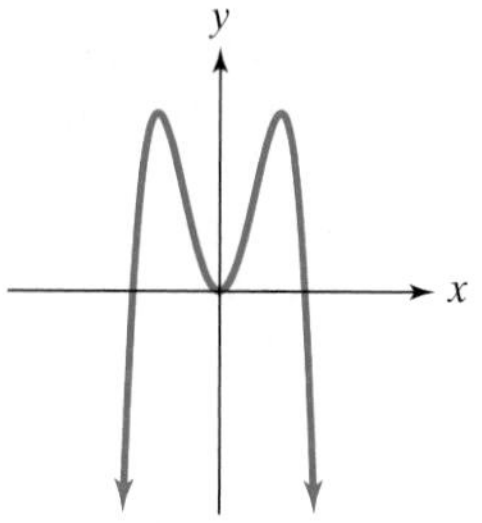


*In Exercises 15–20, use end behavior to match the polynomial function with its graph. [The graphs are labeled (a) through (f).]*

**(a)**

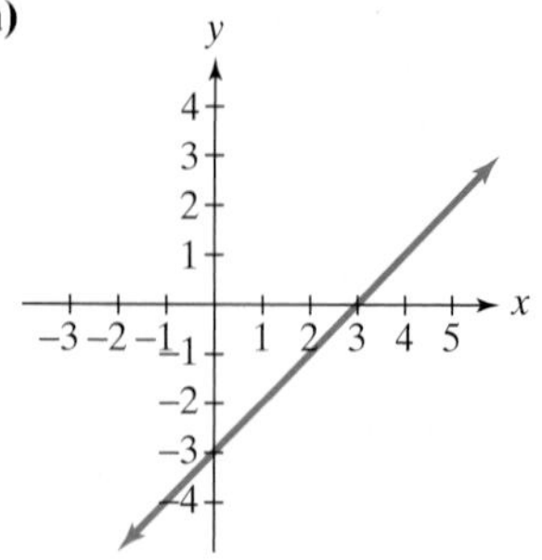


**(b)**

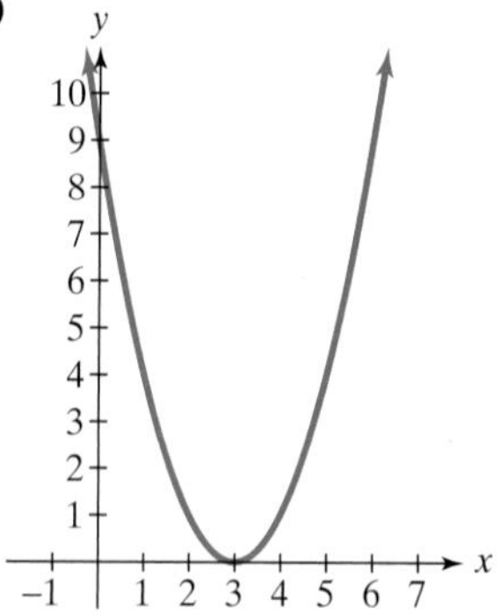


**(c)**

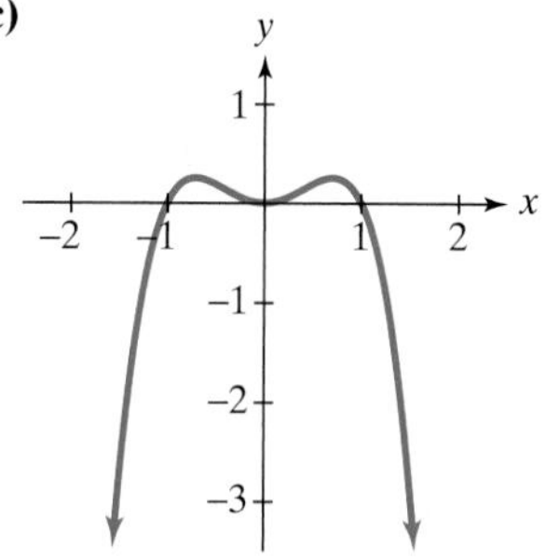


**(d)**

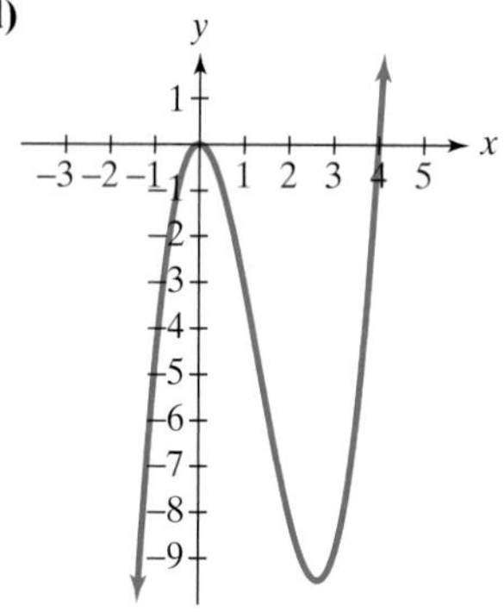


**(e)**

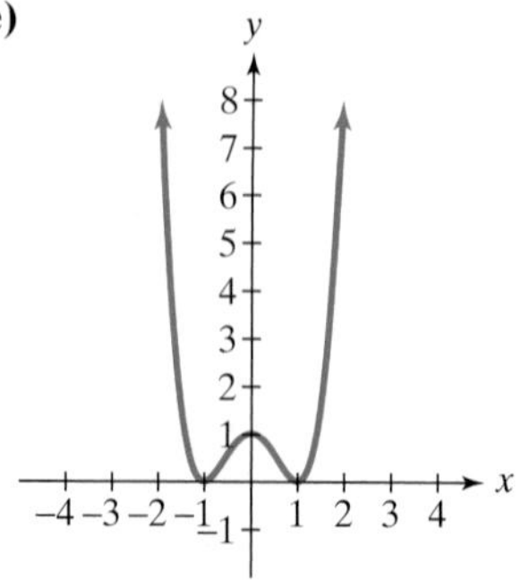

(f)

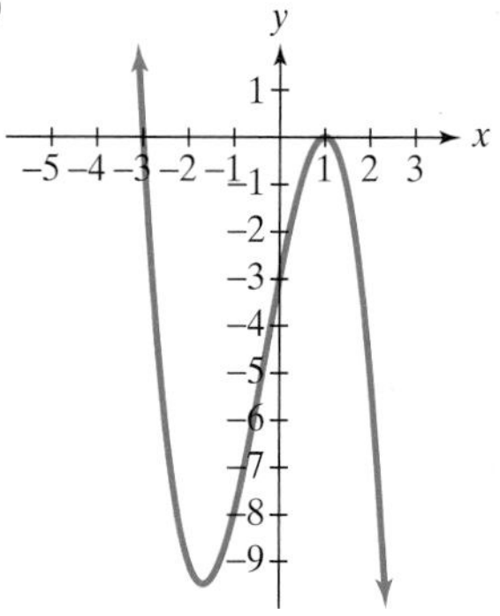


15. $f(x) = -x^4 + x^2$

16. $f(x) = x^3 - 4x^2$

17. $f(x) = (x - 3)^2$

18. $f(x) = -x^3 - x^2 + 5x - 3$

19. $f(x) = x - 3$

20. $f(x) = (x + 1)^2(x - 1)^2$

*In Exercises 21–26, use the Leading Coefficient Test to determine the end behavior of the graph of the polynomial function.*

21. $f(x) = 5x^3 + 7x^2 - x + 9$
22. $f(x) = 11x^3 - 6x^2 + x + 3$
23. $f(x) = 5x^4 + 7x^2 - x + 9$
24. $f(x) = 11x^4 - 6x^2 + x + 3$
25. $f(x) = -5x^4 + 7x^2 - x + 9$
26. $f(x) = -11x^4 - 6x^2 + x + 3$

*In Exercises 27–34, find the zeros for each polynomial function and give the multiplicity for each zero. State whether the graph crosses the x-axis or touches the x-axis and turns around at each zero.*

27. $f(x) = 2(x - 5)(x + 4)^2$
28. $f(x) = 3(x + 5)(x + 2)^2$
29. $f(x) = 4(x - 3)(x + 6)^3$
30. $f(x) = -3(x + \frac{1}{2})(x - 4)^3$
31. $f(x) = x^3 - 2x^2 + x$
32. $f(x) = x^3 + 4x^2 + 4x$
33. $f(x) = x^3 + 7x^2 - 4x - 28$
34. $f(x) = x^3 + 5x^2 - 9x - 45$

*In Exercises 35–50,*

**a.** *Use the Leading Coefficient Test to determine the graph's end behavior.*

**b.** *Find x-intercepts by setting $f(x) = 0$ and solving the resulting polynomial equation. State whether the graph crosses the x-axis or touches the x-axis and turns around at each intercept.*

**c.** *Find the y-intercept by setting x equal to 0 and computing $f(0)$.*

**d.** *Determine whether the graph has y-axis symmetry, origin symmetry, or neither.*

**e.** *If necessary, find a few additional points and graph the function. Use the fact that the maximum number of turning points of the graph is $n - 1$ to check whether it is drawn correctly.*

35. $f(x) = x^3 + 2x^2 - x - 2$
36. $f(x) = x^3 + x^2 - 4x - 4$
37. $f(x) = x^4 - 9x^2$
38. $f(x) = x^4 - x^2$
39. $f(x) = -x^4 + 16x^2$
40. $f(x) = -x^4 + 4x^2$
41. $f(x) = x^4 - 2x^3 + x^2$
42. $f(x) = x^4 - 6x^3 + 9x^2$
43. $f(x) = -2x^4 + 4x^3$
44. $f(x) = -2x^4 + 2x^3$
45. $f(x) = 6x^3 - 9x - x^5$
46. $f(x) = 6x - x^3 - x^5$
47. $f(x) = 3x^2 - x^3$
48. $f(x) = \frac{1}{2} - \frac{1}{2}x^4$
49. $f(x) = -3(x - 1)^2(x^2 - 4)$
50. $f(x) = -2(x - 4)^2(x^2 - 25)$

## Application Exercises

51. A herd of 100 elk is introduced to a small island. The number of elk, $N(t)$, after $t$ years is described by the polynomial function $N(t) = -t^4 + 21t^2 + 100$.
    **a.** Use the Leading Coefficient Test to determine the graph's end behavior to the right. What does this mean about what will eventually happen to the elk population?
    **b.** Graph the function.
    **c.** Graph only the portion of the function that serves as a realistic model for the elk population over time. When does the population become extinct?

52. The common cold is caused by a rhinovirus. After $t$ days of invasion by the viral particles, there are $N$ billion particles in our bodies, modeled by $N(t) = -\frac{3}{4}t^4 + 3t^3 + 5$. Use the Leading Coefficient Test to determine the graph's end behavior to the right. What does this mean about the number of viral particles in our bodies over time?

53. The following table shows the number of larceny thefts in the United States for the years 1988–1998, where 1 represents 1988, 2 represents 1989, and so on.

| Year, $x$ | Larceny Thefts, $T$, in thousands |
|---|---|
| 1988, 1 | 7706 |
| 1989, 2 | 7872 |
| 1990, 3 | 7946 |
| 1991, 4 | 8142 |
| 1992, 5 | 7915 |
| 1993, 6 | 7821 |
| 1994, 7 | 7880 |
| 1995, 8 | 7998 |
| 1996, 9 | 7905 |
| 1997, 10 | 7744 |
| 1998, 11 | 7374 |

Using the polynomial regression feature of a graphing utility, the third-degree polynomial function of best fit for the data is

$$T(x) = -0.87x^3 + 0.35x^2 + 81.62x + 7684.94.$$

**a.** Use this function to predict the number of larceny thefts in 2005.

**b.** Will this function be useful in modeling the number of larceny thefts over an extended period of time? Explain your answer.

**54.** Suppose that a polynomial function is used to model the data shown in the graph using

(number of years after 1900, murder rate per 100,000 people).

**Murders Per 100,000 People in the United States**

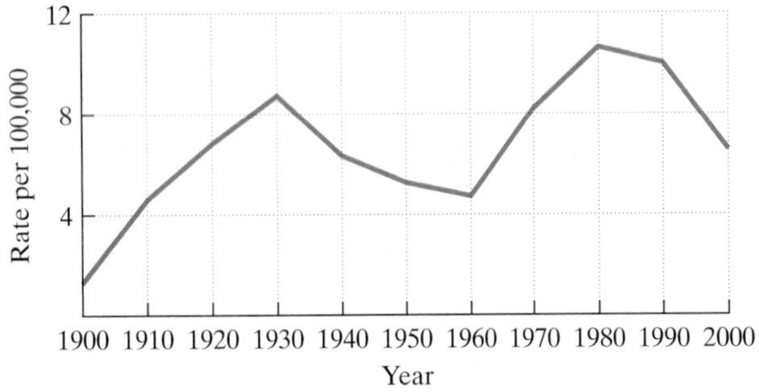


*Source*: National Center for Health Statistics

Determine the degree of the polynomial function of best fit. Should the leading coefficient be positive or negative? Explain your answers.

**55.** The polynomial function

$$H(x) = -0.001183x^4 + 0.05495x^3 - 0.8523x^2 + 9.054x + 6.748$$

models the age in human years, $H(x)$, of a dog that is $x$ years old, where $x \geq 1$.

**a.** Use this function to find the equivalent age in human years for a 10-year-old dog.

**b.** If dogs lived as long as humans, would this function be useful in modeling the dog's equivalent age in human years? Explain your answer.

## Writing in Mathematics

**56.** What is a polynomial function?

**57.** What do we mean when we describe the graph of a polynomial function as smooth and continuous?

**58.** What is meant by the end behavior of a polynomial function?

**59.** Explain how to use the Leading Coefficient Test to determine the end behavior of a polynomial function.

**60.** Why is a third-degree polynomial function with a negative leading coefficient not appropriate for modeling nonnegative real-world phenomena over a long period of time?

**61.** What are the zeros of a polynomial function and how are they found?

**62.** Explain the relationship between the multiplicity of a zero and whether or not the graph crosses or touches the $x$-axis at that zero.

**63.** Explain the relationship between the degree of a polynomial and the number of turning points on its graph.

**64.** Can the graph of a polynomial function have no $x$-intercepts? Explain.

**65.** Can the graph of a polynomial function have no $y$-intercept? Explain.

**66.** Describe a strategy for graphing a polynomial function. In your description, mention intercepts, the polynomial's degree, and turning points.

**67.** In a favorable habitat and without natural predators, a population of reindeer is introduced to an island preserve. The reindeer population $t$ years after their introduction is modeled by the polynomial function $f(t) = -0.125t^5 + 3.125t^4 + 4000$. Discuss the growth and decline of the reindeer population. Describe the factors that might contribute to this population model.

## Technology Exercises

**68.** Use a graphing utility to verify any five of the graphs that you drew by hand in Exercises 35–50.

*Write a polynomial function that imitates the end behavior of each graph in Exercises 69–72. The dashed portions of the graphs indicate that you should focus only on imitating the left and right behavior of the graph and can be flexible about what occurs between the left and right ends. Then use your graphing utility to graph the polynomial function and verify that you imitated the end behavior shown in the given graph.*

**69.**

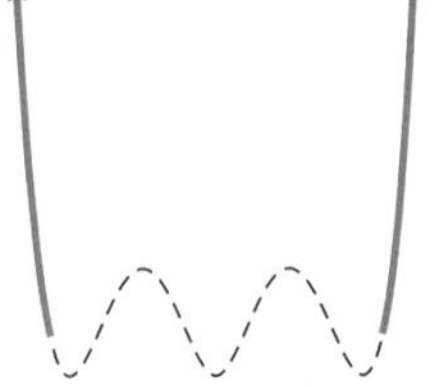

**70.**

**71.**

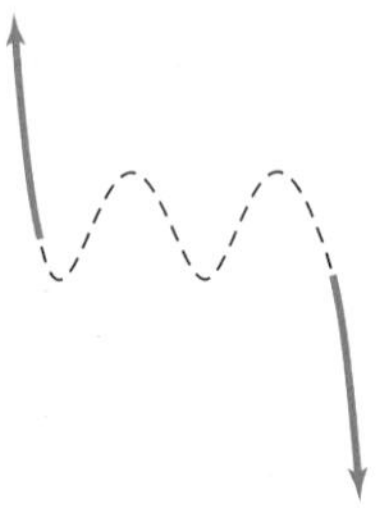

**72.**

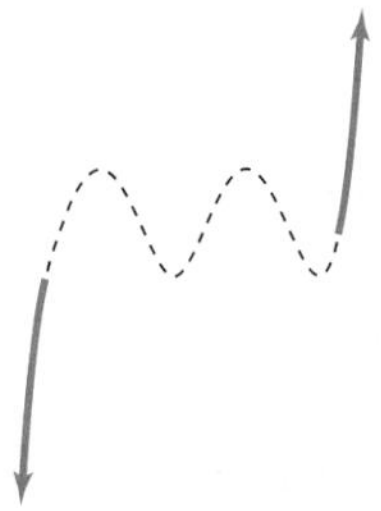

*In Exercises 73–76, use a graphing utility with a viewing rectangle large enough to show end behavior to graph each polynomial function.*

**73.** $f(x) = x^3 + 13x^2 + 10x - 4$

**74.** $f(x) = -2x^3 + 6x^2 + 3x - 1$

**75.** $f(x) = -x^4 + 8x^3 + 4x^2 + 2$

**76.** $f(x) = -x^5 + 5x^4 - 6x^3 + 2x + 20$

*For Exercises 77–78, use a graphing utility to graph f and g in the same viewing rectangle. Then use the* ZOOM OUT *feature to show that the end behavior of f and g is identical.*

**77.** $f(x) = x^3 - 6x + 1, \quad g(x) = x^3$

**78.** $f(x) = -x^4 + 2x^3 - 6x, \quad g(x) = -x^4$

## Critical Thinking Exercises

**79.** Which one of the following is true?

**a.** If $f(x) = -x^3 + 4x$, then the graph of $f$ falls to the left and to the right.

**b.** A mathematical model that is a polynomial of degree $n$ whose leading term is $a_n x^n$, $n$ odd and $a_n < 0$, is ideally suited to describe phenomena over unlimited periods of time.

**c.** There is more than one third-degree polynomial function with the same three $x$-intercepts.

**d.** The graph of a function with origin symmetry can rise to the left and to the right.

*Use the descriptions in Exercises 80–81 to write an equation of a polynomial function with the given characteristics. Use a graphing utility to graph your function to see if you are correct. If not, modify the function's equation and repeat this process.*

**80.** Crosses the $x$-axis at $-4$, 0, and 3; lies above the $x$-axis between $-4$ and 0; lies below the $x$-axis between 0 and 3

**81.** Touches the $x$-axis at 0 and crosses the $x$-axis at 2; lies below the $x$-axis between 0 and 2

## Group Exercise

**82.** This exercise is based on the group's work in Exercise 70 of Exercise Set 3.1. For the two data sets that the group selected:

**a.** Use the polynomial regression feature of a graphing utility to find the third-degree polynomial function that best fits the data.

**b.** Use this function to repeat the predictions that you made with the quadratic function. How do these predictions compare with those that you obtained previously?

**c.** For each data set, describe whether the quadratic function or the third-degree function is a better fit. Use a graphing utility, a scatter plot of the data, and the function of best fit drawn on the scatter plot to help determine which function is the better fit.

# SECTION 3.3 Dividing Polynomials; Remainder and Factor Theorems

### Objectives

1. Use long division to divide polynomials.
2. Use synthetic division to divide polynomials.
3. Evaluate a polynomial using the Remainder Theorem.
4. Use the Factor Theorem to solve a polynomial equation.

For those of you who are dog lovers, you might still be thinking of the polynomial function that models the age in human years, $H(x)$, of a dog that is $x$ years old, namely

$$H(x) = -0.001183x^4 + 0.05495x^3 - 0.8523x^2 + 9.054x + 6.748.$$

Suppose that you are in your twenties, say 25. What is Fido's equivalent age? To answer this question, we must substitute 25 for $H(x)$ and solve the resulting polynomial equation for $x$:

$$25 = -0.001183x^4 + 0.05495x^3 - 0.8523x^2 + 9.054x + 6.748.$$

How can we solve such an equation? You might begin by subtracting 25 from both sides to obtain zero on one side. But then what? The factoring that we used in the previous section will not work in this situation.

In Sections 3.4 and 3.5, we will present techniques for solving certain kinds of polynomial equations. These techniques will further enhance your ability to manipulate algebraically the formulas that model your world. Because these techniques are based on understanding polynomial division, in this section we look at two methods for dividing polynomials.

**1** Use long division to divide polynomials.

## Long Division of Polynomials and the Division Algorithm

We begin by looking at division by a polynomial containing more than one term, such as

$$x + 3\overline{)x^2 + 10x + 21}$$

Divisor has two terms. Dividend has three terms.

When a divisor has more than one term, the four steps used to divide whole numbers—**divide**, **multiply**, **subtract**, **bring down the next term**—form the repetitive procedure for polynomial long division.

### EXAMPLE 1 Long Division of Polynomials

Divide $x^2 + 10x + 21$ by $x + 3$.

**Solution** The following steps illustrate how polynomial division is very similar to numerical division.

$$x + 3\overline{)x^2 + 10x + 21}$$

Arrange the terms of the dividend $(x^2 + 10x + 21)$ and the divisor $(x + 3)$ in descending powers of x.

$$\begin{array}{r} x \\ x + 3\overline{)x^2 + 10x + 21} \end{array}$$

**Divide** $x^2$ (the first term in the dividend) by x (the first term in the divisor): $\frac{x^2}{x} = x$. Align like terms.

$$\begin{array}{r} x \\ x + 3\overline{)x^2 + 10x + 21} \\ \underline{x^2 + 3x\phantom{+21}} \end{array}$$

(times; equals)

**Multiply** each term in the divisor $(x + 3)$ by x, aligning terms of the product under like terms in the dividend.

$$\begin{array}{r} x \\ x + 3\overline{)x^2 + 10x + 21} \\ \underline{x^2 + 3x\phantom{+21}} \\ 7x\phantom{+21} \end{array}$$

**Subtract** $x^2 + 3x$ from $x^2 + 10x$ by changing the sign of each term in the lower expression and adding.

$$\begin{array}{r} x \\ x + 3\overline{)x^2 + 10x + 21} \\ \underline{x^2 + 3x\phantom{+21}}\downarrow \\ 7x + 21 \end{array}$$

**Bring down** 21 from the original dividend and add algebraically to form a new dividend.

$$\begin{array}{r} x + 7 \\ x+3\overline{)x^2 + 10x + 21} \\ \underline{x^2 + 3x} \quad\downarrow \\ 7x + 21 \end{array}$$

Find the second term of the quotient. **Divide** the first term of $7x + 21$ by $x$, the first term of the divisor: $\frac{7x}{x} = 7$.

$$\begin{array}{r} x + 7 \\ x+3\overline{)x^2 + 10x + 21} \\ \underline{x^2 + 3x} \\ 7x + 21 \\ \underline{7x + 21} \\ 0 \end{array}$$

times / equals

**Multiply** the divisor $(x + 3)$ by 7, aligning under like terms in the new dividend. Then **subtract** to obtain the remainder of 0.

Remainder

The quotient is $x + 7$. Because the remainder is 0, we can conclude that $x + 3$ is a factor of $x^2 + 10x + 21$ and

$$x^2 + 10x + 21 = (x + 3)(x + 7).$$

**Check Point 1** Divide $x^2 + 14x + 45$ by $x + 9$.

Before considering additional examples, let's summarize the general procedure for dividing one polynomial by another.

### Long Division of Polynomials

1. **Arrange the terms** of both the dividend and the divisor in descending powers of any variable.
2. **Divide** the first term in the dividend by the first term in the divisor. The result is the first term of the quotient.
3. **Multiply** every term in the divisor by the first term in the quotient. Write the resulting product beneath the dividend with like terms lined up.
4. **Subtract** the product from the dividend.
5. **Bring down** the next term in the original dividend and write it next to the remainder to form a new dividend.
6. Use this new expression as the dividend and repeat this process until the remainder can no longer be divided. This will occur when the degree of the remainder (the highest exponent on a variable in the remainder) is less than the degree of the divisor.

In our next long division, we will obtain a nonzero remainder.

## EXAMPLE 2 Long Division of Polynomials

Divide $4 - 5x - x^2 + 6x^3$ by $3x - 2$.

**Solution** We begin by writing the divisor and dividend in descending powers of $x$.

### Is It Hot in Here, or Is It Just Me?

In the 1980s, a rising trend in global surface temperature was observed and the term "global warming" was coined. Scientists are more convinced than ever that burning coal, oil, and gas results in a buildup of gases and particles that trap heat and raise the planet's temperature. The average increase in global surface temperature, in degrees Centigrade, $x$ years after 1980 can be modeled by the polynomial function

$$T(x) = \frac{21}{5{,}000{,}000}x^3 - \frac{127}{1{,}000{,}000}x^2 + \frac{1293}{50{,}000}x.$$

Use your graphing utility to graph the function in a [0, 60, 3] by [0, 2, 0.1] viewing rectangle. (Place parentheses around each fractional coefficient when you enter the equation.) What do you observe about global warming through the year 2040?

Multiply.

$$\begin{array}{r}
2x^2 \phantom{- 5x + 4} \\
3x - 2\overline{)6x^3 - x^2 - 5x + 4} \\
\ominus 6x^3 \oplus 4x^2 \phantom{- 5x + 4} \\
\hline
3x^2 - 5x \phantom{+ 4}
\end{array}$$

Divide: $\frac{6x^3}{3x} = 2x^2$.

Multiply: $2x^2(3x - 2) = 6x^3 - 4x^2$.

Subtract $6x^3 - 4x^2$ from $6x^3 - x^2$ and bring down $-5x$.

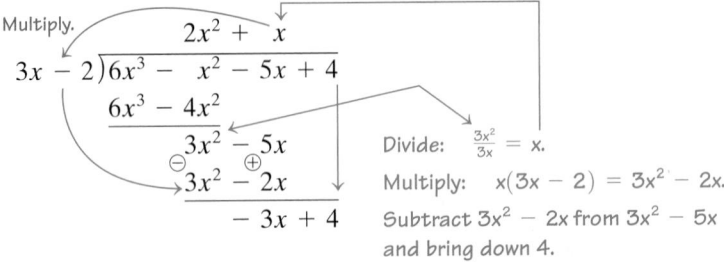

Now we divide $3x^2$ by $3x$ to obtain $x$, multiply $x$ and the divisor, and subtract.

Multiply.

$$\begin{array}{r}
2x^2 + x \phantom{+ 4} \\
3x - 2\overline{)6x^3 - x^2 - 5x + 4} \\
6x^3 - 4x^2 \phantom{- 5x + 4} \\
\hline
3x^2 - 5x \phantom{+ 4} \\
\ominus 3x^2 \oplus 2x \phantom{+ 4} \\
\hline
-3x + 4
\end{array}$$

Divide: $\frac{3x^2}{3x} = x$.

Multiply: $x(3x - 2) = 3x^2 - 2x$.

Subtract $3x^2 - 2x$ from $3x^2 - 5x$ and bring down 4.

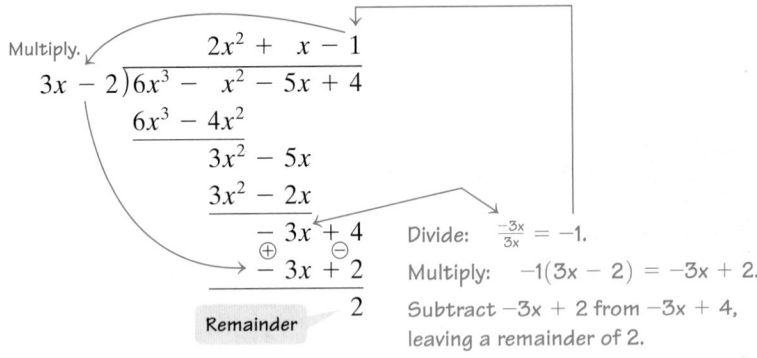

Now we divide $-3x$ by $3x$ to obtain $-1$, multiply $-1$ and the divisor, and subtract.

Multiply.

$$\begin{array}{r}
2x^2 + x - 1 \\
3x - 2\overline{)6x^3 - x^2 - 5x + 4} \\
6x^3 - 4x^2 \phantom{- 5x + 4} \\
\hline
3x^2 - 5x \phantom{+ 4} \\
3x^2 - 2x \phantom{+ 4} \\
\hline
-3x + 4 \\
\oplus 3x \ominus 2 \\
\hline
2
\end{array}$$

Remainder

Divide: $\frac{-3x}{3x} = -1$.

Multiply: $-1(3x - 2) = -3x + 2$.

Subtract $-3x + 2$ from $-3x + 4$, leaving a remainder of 2.

In Example 2, the quotient is $2x^2 + x - 1$ and the remainder is 2. This can be written in fractional form as follows:

$$\underbrace{\frac{6x^3 - x^2 - 5x + 4}{3x - 2}}_{\text{Dividend / Divisor}} = \underbrace{2x^2 + x - 1}_{\text{Quotient}} + \frac{\overset{\text{Remainder}}{2}}{\underset{\text{Divisor}}{3x - 2}}$$

Multiplying both sides of this equation by $3x - 2$ results in the following equation:

$$\underbrace{6x^3 - x^2 - 5x + 4}_{\text{Dividend}} = \underbrace{(3x - 2)}_{\text{Divisor}}\underbrace{(2x^2 + x - 1)}_{\text{Quotient}} + \underbrace{2}_{\text{Remainder}}$$

Polynomial long division is checked by multiplying the divisor with the quotient and then adding the remainder. This should give the dividend. The process illustrates the **Division Algorithm**.

**The Division Algorithm**

If $f(x)$ and $d(x)$ are polynomials, with $d(x) \neq 0$, and the degree of $d(x)$ is less than or equal to the degree of $f(x)$, then there exist unique polynomials $q(x)$ and $r(x)$ such that

$$\underset{\text{Dividend}}{f(x)} = \underset{\text{Divisor}}{d(x)} \cdot \underset{\text{Quotient}}{q(x)} + \underset{\text{Remainder}}{r(x)}.$$

The remainder, $r(x)$, equals 0 or it is of degree less than the degree of $d(x)$. If $r(x) = 0$, we say that $d(x)$ **divides evenly** into $f(x)$ and that $d(x)$ and $q(x)$ are **factors** of $f(x)$.

**Check Point 2** Divide $7 - 11x - 3x^2 + 2x^3$ by $x - 3$. Use the remainder to express your result in fractional form.

If a power of $x$ is missing in either a dividend or a divisor, add that power of $x$ with a coefficient of 0 and then divide. In this way, like terms will be aligned as you carry out the long division.

## EXAMPLE 3 Long Division of Polynomials

Divide $6x^4 + 5x^3 + 3x - 5$ by $3x^2 - 2x$.

**Solution** We write the dividend, $6x^4 + 5x^3 + 3x - 5$, as $6x^4 + 5x^3 + 0x^2 + 3x - 5$ so as to keep all like terms aligned.

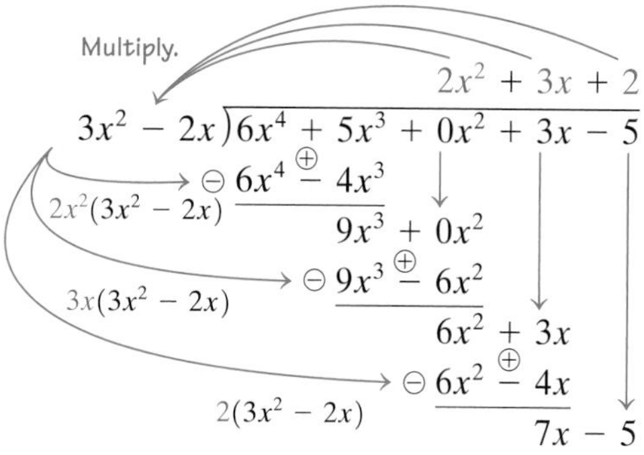


The division process is finished because the degree of $7x - 5$, which is 1, is less than the degree of the divisor $3x^2 - 2x$, which is 2. The answer is

$$\frac{6x^4 + 5x^3 + 3x - 5}{3x^2 - 2x} = 2x^2 + 3x + 2 + \frac{7x - 5}{3x^2 - 2x}.$$

**Check Point 3** Divide $2x^4 + 3x^3 - 7x - 10$ by $x^2 - 2x$.

**2** Use synthetic division to divide polynomials.

## Dividing Polynomials Using Synthetic Division

We can use **synthetic division** to divide polynomials if the divisor is of the form $x - c$. This method provides a quotient more quickly than long division. Let's compare the two methods showing $x^3 + 4x^2 - 5x + 5$ divided by $x - 3$.

**Long Division**

Quotient

$$
\begin{array}{r}
x^2 + \ 7x + 16 \\
x - 3\overline{\smash{)}x^3 + 4x^2 - 5x + 5} \\
\ominus x^3 \overset{\oplus}{-} 3x^2 \qquad\qquad \\
\hline
7x^2 \overset{}{-} 5x \qquad \\
\ominus 7x^2 \overset{\oplus}{-} 21x \qquad \\
\hline
16x + 5 \\
\ominus 16x \overset{\oplus}{-} 48 \\
\hline
53
\end{array}
$$

Divisor $x - c$; $c = 3$

Dividend

Remainder

**Synthetic Division**

$$
\begin{array}{r|rrrr}
3 & 1 & 4 & -5 & 5 \\
 & & 3 & 21 & 48 \\
\hline
 & 1 & 7 & 16 & 53
\end{array}
$$

Notice the relationship between the polynomials in the long division process and the numbers that appear in synthetic division.

These are the coefficients of the dividend $x^3 + 4x^2 - 5x + 5$.

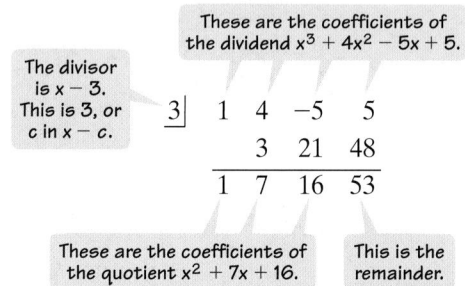

The divisor is $x - 3$. This is 3, or $c$ in $x - c$.

$$
\begin{array}{r|rrrr}
3 & 1 & 4 & -5 & 5 \\
 & & 3 & 21 & 48 \\
\hline
 & 1 & 7 & 16 & 53
\end{array}
$$

These are the coefficients of the quotient $x^2 + 7x + 16$.

This is the remainder.

Now let's look at the steps involved in synthetic division.

**Synthetic Division**

To divide a polynomial by $x - c$,

**Example**

1. Arrange polynomials in descending powers, with a 0 coefficient for any missing term.

$$x - 3\overline{\smash{)}x^3 + 4x^2 - 5x + 5}$$

2. Write $c$ for the divisor, $x - c$. To the right, write the coefficients of the dividend.

$$\begin{array}{r|rrrr} 3 & 1 & 4 & -5 & 5 \end{array}$$

3. Write the leading coefficient of the dividend on the bottom row.

$$
\begin{array}{r|rrrr}
3 & 1 & 4 & -5 & 5 \\
 & \downarrow & & & \\
\hline
 & 1 & & &
\end{array}
$$

Bring down 1.

4. Multiply $c$ (in this case, 3) times the value just written on the bottom row. Write the product in the next column in the second row.

$$
\begin{array}{r|rrrr}
3 & 1 & 4 & -5 & 5 \\
 & & 3 & & \\
\hline
 & 1 & & &
\end{array}
$$

Multiply by 3.

5. Add the values in this new column, writing the sum in the bottom row.

$$
\begin{array}{r|rrrr}
3 & 1 & 4 & -5 & 5 \\
 & & 3 & & \\
\hline
 & 1 & 7 & &
\end{array}
$$

Add.

**6.** Repeat this series of multiplications and additions until all columns are filled in.

$$\begin{array}{r|rrrr} 3 & 1 & 4 & -5 & 5 \\ & & 3 & 21 & \\ \hline & 1 & 7 & 16 & \end{array}$$

Add. Multiply by 3.

$$\begin{array}{r|rrrr} 3 & 1 & 4 & -5 & 5 \\ & & 3 & 21 & 48 \\ \hline & 1 & 7 & 16 & 53 \end{array}$$

Add. Multiply by 3.

**7.** Use the numbers in the last row to write the quotient and remainder in fractional form. **The degree of the first term of the quotient is one less than the degree of the first term of the dividend.** The final value in this row is the remainder.

Written from the last row of the synthetic division

$$x - 3\overline{)x^3 + 4x^2 - 5x + 5} \quad 1x^2 + 7x + 16 + \frac{53}{x - 3}$$

## EXAMPLE 4 Using Synthetic Division

Use synthetic division to divide $5x^3 + 6x + 8$ by $x + 2$.

**Solution** The divisor must be in the form $x - c$. Thus, we write $x + 2$ as $x - (-2)$. This means that $c = -2$. Writing a 0 coefficient for the missing $x^2$-term in the dividend, we can express the division as follows:

$$x - (-2)\overline{)5x^3 + 0x^2 + 6x + 8}.$$

Now we are ready to set up the problem so that we can use synthetic division.

Use the coefficients of the dividend $5x^3 + 0x^2 + 6x + 8$ in descending powers of $x$.

This is $c$ in $x-(-2)$.

$$\begin{array}{r|rrrr} -2 & 5 & 0 & 6 & 8 \end{array}$$

We begin the synthetic division process by bringing down 5. This is followed by a series of multiplications and additions.

**1. Bring down 5.**

$$\begin{array}{r|rrrr} -2 & 5 & 0 & 6 & 8 \\ & & & & \\ \hline & 5 & & & \end{array}$$

**2. Multiply: $-2(5) = -10$.**

$$\begin{array}{r|rrrr} -2 & 5 & 0 & 6 & 8 \\ & & -10 & & \\ \hline & 5 & & & \end{array}$$

Multiply by $-2$.

**3. Add: $0 + (-10) = -10$.**

$$\begin{array}{r|rrrr} -2 & 5 & 0 & 6 & 8 \\ & & -10 & & \\ \hline & 5 & -10 & & \end{array}$$

Add.

**4. Multiply: $-2(-10) = 20$.**

$$\begin{array}{r|rrrr} -2 & 5 & 0 & 6 & 8 \\ & & -10 & 20 & \\ \hline & 5 & -10 & & \end{array}$$

Multiply by $-2$.

**5. Add: $6 + 20 = 26$.**

$$\begin{array}{r|rrrr} -2 & 5 & 0 & 6 & 8 \\ & & -10 & 20 & \\ \hline & 5 & -10 & 26 & \end{array}$$

Add.

**6. Multiply: $-2(26) = -52$.**

$$\begin{array}{r|rrrr} -2 & 5 & 0 & 6 & 8 \\ & & -10 & 20 & -52 \\ \hline & 5 & -10 & 26 & \end{array}$$

Multiply by $-2$.

**7. Add: $8 + (-52) = -44$.**

$$\begin{array}{r|rrrr} -2 & 5 & 0 & 6 & 8 \\ & & -10 & 20 & -52 \\ \hline & 5 & -10 & 26 & -44 \end{array}$$

Add.

The numbers in the last row represent the coefficients of the quotient and the remainder. The degree of the first term of the quotient is one less than that of the dividend. Because the degree of the dividend is 3, the degree of the quotient is 2. This means that the 5 in the last row represents $5x^2$.

| | | | | |
|---|---|---|---|---|
| $-2$ | 5 | 0 | 6 | 8 |
| | | $-10$ | 20 | $-52$ |
| | 5 | $-10$ | 26 | $-44$ |

The quotient is $5x^2 - 10x + 26$. The remainder is $-44$.

Thus,

$$x + 2\overline{)5x^3 + 6x + 8} = 5x^2 - 10x + 26 - \frac{44}{x+2}$$

**Check Point 4** Use synthetic division to divide $x^3 - 7x - 6$ by $x + 2$.

**3** Evaluate a polynomial using the Remainder Theorem.

## The Remainder Theorem

Let's consider the Division Algorithm when the dividend, $f(x)$, is divided by $x - c$. In this case, the remainder must be a constant because its degree is less than one, the degree of $x - c$.

$$f(x) = d(x)q(x) + r(x)$$ This is the Division Algorithm.

Dividend Divisor Quotient Remainder

$$f(x) = (x - c)q(x) + r$$ The divisor is $x - c$. Call the constant remainder $r$.

Now let's evaluate $f$ at $c$.

$$f(c) = (c - c)q(c) + r$$ Find $f(c)$, setting $x = c$. This will give an expression for $r$.

$$f(c) = 0 \cdot q(c) + r$$ $c - c = 0$ and $0 \cdot q(c) = 0$.

$$f(c) = r$$ On the right, $0 + r = r$.

What does this last equation mean? If a polynomial is divided by $x - c$, the remainder is the value of the polynomial at $c$. This result is called the **Remainder Theorem**.

**The Remainder Theorem**

If the polynomial $f(x)$ is divided by $x - c$, then the remainder is $f(c)$.

Example 5 shows how we can use the Remainder Theorem to evaluate a polynomial function at 2. Rather than substituting 2 for $x$, we divide the function by $x - 2$. The remainder is $f(2)$.

**EXAMPLE 5** **Using the Remainder Theorem to Evaluate a Polynomial Function**

Given $f(x) = x^3 - 4x^2 + 5x + 3$, use the Remainder Theorem to find $f(2)$.

**Solution** By the Remainder Theorem, if $f(x)$ is divided by $x - 2$, then the remainder is $f(2)$. We'll use synthetic division to divide.

$$\begin{array}{r|rrrr} 2 & 1 & -4 & 5 & 3 \\ & & 2 & -4 & 2 \\ \hline & 1 & -2 & 1 & 5 \end{array}$$

Remainder

The remainder, 5, is the value of $f(2)$. Thus, $f(2) = 5$. We can verify that this is correct by evaluating $f(2)$ directly. Using $f(x) = x^3 - 4x^2 + 5x + 3$, we obtain

$$f(2) = 2^3 - 4 \cdot 2^2 + 5 \cdot 2 + 3 = 8 - 16 + 10 + 3 = 5.$$

**Check Point 5** Given $f(x) = 3x^3 + 4x^2 - 5x + 3$, use the Remainder Theorem to find $f(-4)$.

**4** Use the Factor Theorem to solve a polynomial equation.

## The Factor Theorem

Let's look again at the Division Algorithm when the divisor is of the form $x - c$.

$$f(x) = (x - c)q(x) + r$$

Dividend Divisor Quotient Constant remainder

By the Remainder Theorem, the remainder $r$ is $f(c)$, so we can substitute $f(c)$ for $r$:

$$f(x) = (x - c)q(x) + f(c).$$

Notice that if $f(c) = 0$, then

$$f(x) = (x - c)q(x)$$

so that $x - c$ is a factor of $f(x)$. This means that for the polynomial function $f(x)$, if $f(c) = 0$, then $x - c$ is a factor of $f(x)$.

Let's reverse directions and see what happens if $x - c$ is a factor of $f(x)$. This means that

$$f(x) = (x - c)q(x).$$

If we replace $x$ with $c$, we obtain

$$f(c) = (c - c)q(c) = 0.$$

Thus, if $x - c$ is a factor of $f(x)$, then $f(c) = 0$.

We have proved a result known as the **Factor Theorem**.

**The Factor Theorem**

Let $f(x)$ be a polynomial.

**a.** If $f(c) = 0$, then $x - c$ is a factor of $f(x)$.

**b.** If $x - c$ is a factor of $f(x)$, then $f(c) = 0$.

The example that follows shows how the Factor Theorem can be used to solve a polynomial equation.

## EXAMPLE 6 Using the Factor Theorem

Solve the equation $2x^3 - 3x^2 - 11x + 6 = 0$ given that 3 is a zero of $f(x) = 2x^3 - 3x^2 - 11x + 6$.

**Solution** We are given that $f(3) = 0$. The Factor Theorem tells us that $x - 3$ is a factor of $f(x)$. We'll use synthetic division to divide $f(x)$ by $x - 3$.

$$\begin{array}{r|rrrr} 3 & 2 & -3 & -11 & 6 \\ & & 6 & 9 & -6 \\ \hline & 2 & 3 & -2 & 0 \end{array} \qquad x - 3\overline{)2x^3 - 3x^2 - 11x + 6}^{\;2x^2 + 3x - 2}$$

Equivalently,

$$2x^3 - 3x^2 - 11x + 6 = (x - 3)(2x^2 + 3x - 2)$$

Now we can solve the polynomial equation.

$2x^3 - 3x^2 - 11x + 6 = 0$ — This is the given equation.

$(x - 3)(2x^2 + 3x - 2) = 0$ — Factor using the result from the synthetic division.

$(x - 3)(2x - 1)(x + 2) = 0$ — Factor the trinomial.

$x - 3 = 0$ or $2x - 1 = 0$ or $x + 2 = 0$ — Set each factor equal to 0.

$x = 3$ $\quad x = \frac{1}{2}$ $\quad x = -2$ — Solve for x.

The solution set is $\{-2, \frac{1}{2}, 3\}$.

### Technology

Because the solution set of

$$2x^3 - 3x^2 - 11x + 6 = 0$$

is $\{-2, \frac{1}{2}, 3\}$, this implies that the polynomial function

$$f(x) = 2x^3 - 3x^2 - 11x + 6$$

has $x$-intercepts (or zeros) at $-2, \frac{1}{2}$, and 3. This is verified by the graph of $f$.

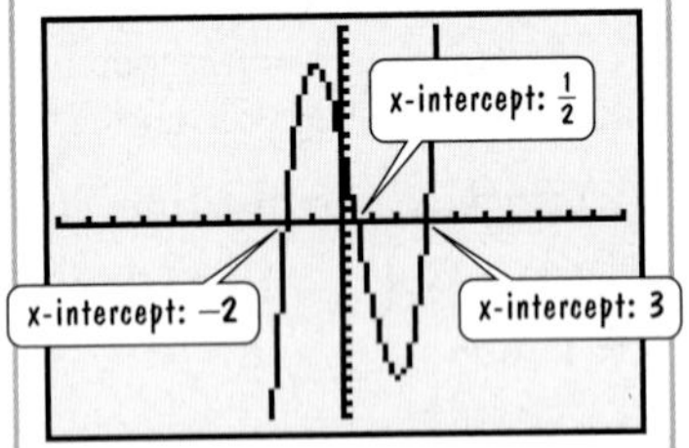


By the Factor Theorem, the following statements are useful in solving polynomial equations:

1. If $f(x)$ is divided by $x - c$ and the remainder is zero, then $c$ is a zero of $f$ and $c$ is a root of the polynomial equation $f(x) = 0$.
2. If $f(x)$ is divided by $x - c$ and the remainder is zero, then $x - c$ is a factor of $f(x)$.

**Check Point 6** Solve the equation $15x^3 + 14x^2 - 3x - 2 = 0$ given that $-1$ is a zero of $f(x) = 15x^3 + 14x^2 - 3x - 2$.

# EXERCISE SET 3.3

## Practice Exercises

*In Exercises 1–16, divide by long division.*

1. $(x^2 + 8x + 15) \div (x + 5)$
2. $(x^2 + 3x - 10) \div (x - 2)$
3. $(x^3 + 5x^2 + 7x + 2) \div (x + 2)$
4. $(x^3 - 2x^2 - 5x + 6) \div (x - 3)$
5. $(6x^3 + 7x^2 + 12x - 5) \div (3x - 1)$
6. $(6x^3 + 17x^2 + 27x + 20) \div (3x + 4)$
7. $(12x^2 + x - 4) \div (3x - 2)$
8. $(4x^2 - 8x + 6) \div (2x - 1)$
9. $\dfrac{2x^3 + 7x^2 + 9x - 20}{x + 3}$
10. $\dfrac{3x^2 - 2x + 5}{x - 3}$
11. $\dfrac{4x^4 - 4x^2 + 6x}{x - 4}$
12. $\dfrac{x^4 - 81}{x - 3}$
13. $\dfrac{6x^3 + 13x^2 - 11x - 15}{3x^2 - x - 3}$
14. $\dfrac{x^4 + 2x^3 - 4x^2 - 5x - 6}{x^2 + x - 2}$
15. $\dfrac{18x^4 + 9x^3 + 3x^2}{3x^2 + 1}$
16. $\dfrac{2x^5 - 8x^4 + 2x^3 + x^2}{2x^3 + 1}$

*In Exercises 17–32, divide by synthetic division.*

17. $(2x^2 + x - 10) \div (x - 2)$
18. $(x^2 + x - 2) \div (x - 1)$
19. $(3x^2 + 7x - 20) \div (x + 5)$
20. $(5x^2 - 12x - 8) \div (x + 3)$
21. $(4x^3 - 3x^2 + 3x - 1) \div (x - 1)$
22. $(5x^3 - 6x^2 + 3x + 11) \div (x - 2)$
23. $(6x^5 - 2x^3 + 4x^2 - 3x + 1) \div (x - 2)$
24. $(x^5 + 4x^4 - 3x^2 + 2x + 3) \div (x - 3)$
25. $(x^2 - 5x - 5x^3 + x^4) \div (5 + x)$
26. $(x^2 - 6x - 6x^3 + x^4) \div (6 + x)$
27. $\dfrac{x^5 + x^3 - 2}{x - 1}$
28. $\dfrac{x^7 + x^5 - 10x^3 + 12}{x + 2}$
29. $\dfrac{x^4 - 256}{x - 4}$
30. $\dfrac{x^7 - 128}{x - 2}$
31. $\dfrac{2x^5 - 3x^4 + x^3 - x^2 + 2x - 1}{x + 2}$
32. $\dfrac{x^5 - 2x^4 - x^3 + 3x^2 - x + 1}{x - 2}$
33. Given $f(x) = 2x^3 - 11x^2 + 7x - 5$, use the Remainder Theorem to find $f(4)$.
34. Given $f(x) = x^3 - 7x^2 + 5x - 6$, use the Remainder Theorem to find $f(3)$.
35. Given $f(x) = 7x^4 - 3x^3 + 6x + 9$, use the Remainder Theorem to find $f(-5)$.
36. Given $f(x) = 3x^4 + 6x^3 - 2x + 4$, use the Remainder Theorem to find $f(-4)$.
37. Use synthetic division to divide $f(x) = x^3 - 4x^2 + x + 6$ by $x + 1$. Use the result to find all zeros of $f$.
38. Use synthetic division to divide $f(x) = x^3 - 2x^2 - x + 2$ by $x + 1$. Use the result to find all zeros of $f$.
39. Solve the equation $2x^3 - 5x^2 + x + 2 = 0$ given that 2 is a zero of $f(x) = 2x^3 - 5x^2 + x + 2$.
40. Solve the equation $2x^3 - 3x^2 - 11x + 6 = 0$ given that $-2$ is a zero of $f(x) = 2x^3 - 3x^2 - 11x + 6$.
41. Solve the equation $12x^3 + 16x^2 - 5x - 3 = 0$ given that $-\frac{3}{2}$ is a root.
42. Solve the equation $3x^3 + 7x^2 - 22x - 8 = 0$ given that $-\frac{1}{3}$ is a root.

## Application Exercises

43. A rectangle with length $2x + 5$ inches has an area of $2x^4 + 15x^3 + 7x^2 - 135x - 225$ square inches. Write a polynomial that represents its width.
44. If you travel a distance of $x^3 + 3x^2 + 5x + 3$ miles at a rate of $x + 1$ miles per hour, write a polynomial that represents the number of hours you traveled.
45. Two people are 25 years old and 20 years old, respectively. In $x$ years from now, their ages can be represented by $x + 25$ and $x + 20$.
    a. Use long division to find $\dfrac{x + 25}{x + 20}$, the ratio of the older person's age in $x$ years to the younger person's age in $x$ years.
    b. Complete the following table.

| $x$ | 0 | 5 | 10 | 25 | 50 | 75 |
|---|---|---|---|---|---|---|
| $\dfrac{x + 25}{x + 20}$ | | | | | | |

    c. Describe what is happening to the ratio $\dfrac{x + 25}{x + 20}$ as $x$ increases. How can this be verified using the result of the long division in part (a)?

## Writing in Mathematics

46. Explain how to perform long division of polynomials. Use $2x^3 - 3x^2 - 11x + 7$ divided by $x - 3$ in your explanation.
47. In your own words, state the Division Algorithm.
48. How can the Division Algorithm be used to check the quotient and remainder in a long division problem?
49. Explain how to perform synthetic division. Use the division problem in Exercise 46 to support your explanation.
50. State the Remainder Theorem.

**51.** Explain how the Remainder Theorem can be used to find $f(-6)$ if $f(x) = x^4 + 7x^3 + 8x^2 + 11x + 5$. What advantage is there to using the Remainder Theorem in this situation rather than evaluating $f(-6)$ directly?

**52.** How can the Factor Theorem be used to determine if $x - 1$ is a factor of $x^3 - 2x^2 - 11x + 12$?

**53.** If you know that $-2$ is a zero of

$$f(x) = x^3 + 7x^2 + 4x - 12,$$

explain how to solve the equation

$$x^3 + 7x^2 + 4x - 12 = 0.$$

## Technology Exercises

*In Exercises 54–57, use a graphing utility to graph the function on each side of the given equation. If the graphs coincide, this verifies that the expressions are equivalent and the division has been performed correctly. If the graphs do not coincide, correct the expression on the right by performing the division. Then use your graphing utility to verify your result.*

**54.** $\dfrac{x^4 + 6x^3 + 6x^2 - 10x - 3}{x^2 + 2x - 3} = x^2 + 4x + 1,$ $\quad x \neq -3,\ x \neq 1$

**55.** $\dfrac{2x^3 - 3x^2 - 3x + 4}{x - 1} = 2x^2 - x + 4,\quad x \neq 1$

**56.** $\dfrac{3x^4 + 4x^3 - 32x^2 - 5x - 20}{x + 4} = 3x^3 + 8x^2 - 5,$ $\quad x \neq -4$

**57.** $\dfrac{10x^3 - 26x^2 + 17x - 13}{5x - 3} = 2x^2 - 4x + 1 - \dfrac{10}{5x - 3},$ $\quad x \neq \frac{3}{5}$

## Critical Thinking Exercises

**58.** Which one of the following is true?

**a.** If a trinomial in $x$ of degree 6 is divided by a trinomial in $x$ of degree 3, the degree of the quotient is 2.

**b.** Synthetic division could not be used to find the quotient of $10x^3 - 6x^2 + 4x - 1$ and $x - \frac{1}{2}$.

**c.** Any problem that can be done by synthetic division can also be done by the method for long division of polynomials.

**d.** If a polynomial long-division problem results in a remainder that is a whole number, then the divisor is a factor of the dividend.

**59.** Find $k$ so that $4x + 3$ is a factor of

$$20x^3 + 23x^2 - 10x + k.$$

**60.** When $2x^2 - 7x + 9$ is divided by a polynomial, the quotient is $2x - 3$ and the remainder is 3. Find the polynomial.

**61.** Find the quotient of $x^{3n} + 1$ and $x^n + 1$.

**62.** Synthetic division is a process for dividing a polynomial by $x - c$. The coefficient of $x$ is 1. How might synthetic division be used if you are dividing by $2x - 4$?

# SECTION 3.4 Zeros of Polynomial Functions

## Objectives

1. Use the Rational Zero Theorem to find possible rational zeros.
2. Find zeros of a polynomial function.
3. Solve polynomial equations.
4. Use Descartes's Rule of Signs.

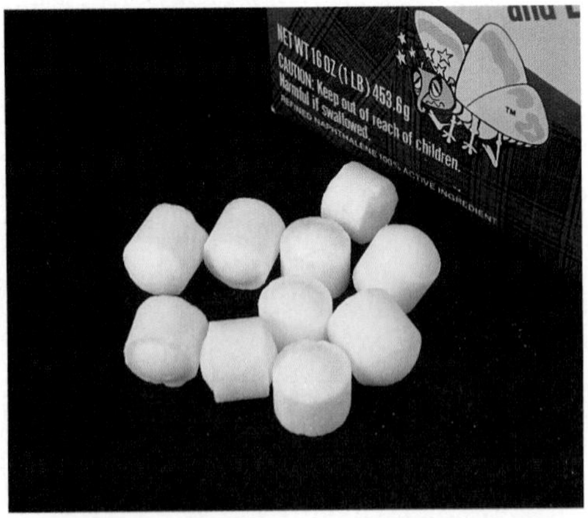


The solution to a multitude of moths?

A moth has moved into your closet. She appeared in your bedroom at night, but somehow her relatively stout body escaped your clutches. Within a few weeks swarms of moths in your tattered wardrobe suggest that Mama Moth was in the family way. There must be at least 200 critters nesting in every crevice of your clothing.

Two hundred plus moth-tykes from one female moth; is this possible? Indeed it is. The number of eggs, $N$, in a female moth is a function of her abdominal width, $W$, in millimeters, modeled by

$$N = 14W^3 - 17W^2 - 16W + 34$$

for $1.5 \leq W \leq 3.5$. Because there are 200 moths feasting on your favorite sweaters, Mama's abdominal width can be estimated by finding the roots of the polynomial equation

$$14W^3 - 17W^2 - 16W + 34 = 200.$$

With mathematics present even in your quickly disappearing attire, we move from rags to polynomial equations. The process of solving such equations begins with listing possibilities for Mama Moth's abdominal width. To do this, we turn to a theorem that plays an important role in finding zeros of polynomial functions.

**1** Use the Rational Zero Theorem to find possible rational zeros.

## The Rational Zero Theorem

The Rational Zero Theorem gives a list of possible rational zeros of a polynomial function. Equivalently, the theorem gives all possible rational roots of a polynomial equation. Not every number in the list will be a zero of the function, but every rational zero of the polynomial function will appear somewhere in the list.

**The Rational Zero Theorem**

If $f(x) = a_n x^n + a_{n-1}x^{n-1} + \cdots + a_1 x + a_0$ has *integer* coefficients and $\frac{p}{q}$ (where $\frac{p}{q}$ is reduced) is a rational zero, then $p$ is a factor of the constant term $a_0$ and $q$ is a factor of the leading coefficient $a_n$.

You can explore the "why" behind the Rational Zero Theorem in Exercise 64 of Exercise Set 3.4. For now, let's see if we can figure out what the theorem tells us about possible rational zeros. In order to use the theorem, list all the integers that are factors of the constant term, $a_0$. Then list all the integers that are factors of the leading coefficient, $a_n$. Finally list all possible rational zeros:

$$\text{Possible rational zeros} = \frac{\text{Factors of the constant term}}{\text{Factors of the leading coefficient}}.$$

### EXAMPLE 1 Using the Rational Zero Theorem

List all possible rational zeros of $f(x) = -x^4 + 4x^2 + 4$.

**Solution** The constant term is 4. We list all of its factors: $\pm1, \pm2, \pm4$. The leading coefficient is $-1$. Its factors are $\pm1$.

| | |
|---|---|
| Factors of the constant term: | $\pm1, \quad \pm2 \quad \pm4$ |
| Factors of the leading coefficient: | $\pm1$ |

Because

$$\text{Possible rational zeros} = \frac{\text{Factors of the constant term}}{\text{Factors of the leading coefficient}},$$

we must take each number in the first row, $\pm1, \pm2, \pm4$, and divide by each number in the second row, $\pm1$.

$$\text{Possible rational zeros} = \frac{\text{Factors of } 4}{\text{Factors of } -1} = \frac{\pm1, \pm2, \pm4}{\pm1} = \pm1, \quad \pm2, \quad \pm4$$

Divide ±1 by ±1. | Divide ±2 by ±1. | Divide ±4 by ±1.

There are six possible rational zeros. The graph of $f(x) = -x^4 + 4x^2 + 4$ is shown in Figure 3.19. The $x$-intercepts are $-2$ and 2. Thus, $-2$ and 2 are the actual rational zeros.

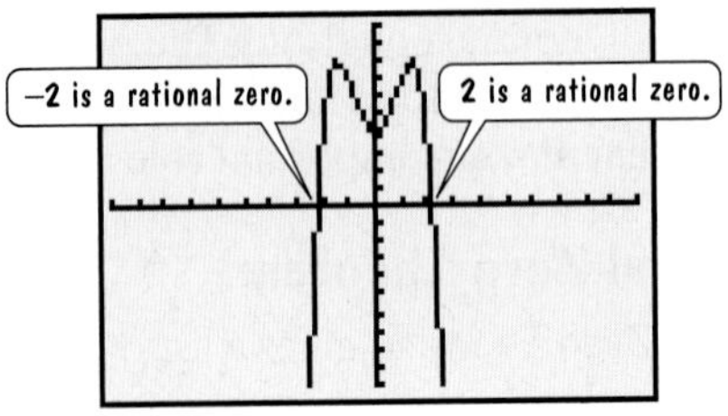
-2 is a rational zero.
2 is a rational zero.

**Figure 3.19** The graph of $f(x) = -x^4 + 4x^2 + 4$ shows that $-2$ and 2 are rational zeros.

**Check Point 1** List all possible rational zeros of $f(x) = x^3 + 2x^2 - 5x - 6$.

## EXAMPLE 2 Using the Rational Zero Theorem

List all possible rational zeros of $f(x) = 15x^3 + 14x^2 - 3x - 2$.

**Solution** The constant term is $-2$ and the leading coefficient is 15.

$$\text{Possible rational zeros} = \frac{\text{Factors of the constant term, } -2}{\text{Factors of the leading coefficient, } 15}$$

$$= \frac{\pm1, \pm2}{\pm1, \pm3, \pm5, \pm15}$$

$$= \pm1, \quad \pm2, \quad \pm\tfrac{1}{3}, \quad \pm\tfrac{2}{3}, \quad \pm\tfrac{1}{5}, \quad \pm\tfrac{2}{5}, \quad \pm\tfrac{1}{15}, \quad \pm\tfrac{2}{15}$$

Divide ±1 and ±2 by ±1. | Divide ±1 and ±2 by ±3. | Divide ±1 and ±2 by ±5. | Divide ±1 and ±2 by ±15.

There are 16 possible rational zeros. The actual solution set to $15x^3 + 14x^2 - 3x - 2 = 0$ is $\{-1, -\frac{1}{3}, \frac{2}{5}\}$, which contains 3 of the 16 possible zeros.

**Check Point 2** Find all possible rational zeros of $f(x) = 4x^5 + 12x^4 - x - 3$.

**2** Find zeros of a polynomial function.

How do we determine which (if any) of the possible rational zeros are rational zeros of the polynomial function? To find the first rational zero, we can use a trial-and-error process involving synthetic division. [Recall that if $f(x)$ is divided by $x - c$ and the remainder is zero, then $c$ is a zero of $f$.] After we identify the first rational zero, we use the result of the synthetic division to factor the original polynomial. Then we set each factor equal to zero to identify any additional rational zeros.

## EXAMPLE 3 Finding Zeros of a Polynomial Function

Find all rational zeros of $f(x) = x^3 + 2x^2 - 5x - 6$.

**Solution** We begin by listing all possible rational zeros.

Possible rational zeros

$$= \frac{\text{Factors of the constant term, } -6}{\text{Factors of the leading coefficient, } 1} = \frac{\pm 1, \pm 2, \pm 3, \pm 6}{\pm 1} = \pm 1, \pm 2, \pm 3, \pm 6$$

Divide the eight numbers in the numerator by $\pm 1$.

Now we will use synthetic division to see if we can find a rational root among the possible rational zeros $\pm 1$, $\pm 2$, $\pm 3$, $\pm 6$. Keep in mind that if $f(x)$ is divided by $x - c$ and the remainder is zero, then $c$ is a zero of $f$. Let's start by testing 1. If 1 is not a rational zero, then we will test other possible rational zeros.

**Test 1**

Coefficients of $f(x) = x^3 + 2x^2 - 5x - 6$

Possible rational zero

| | | | | |
|---|---|---|---|---|
| 1 | 1 | 2 | −5 | −6 |
| | | 1 | 3 | −2 |
| | 1 | 3 | −2 | −8 |

The nonzero remainder shows that 1 is not a zero.

**Test 2**

Coefficients of $f(x) = x^3 + 2x^2 - 5x - 6$

Possible rational zero

| | | | | |
|---|---|---|---|---|
| 2 | 1 | 2 | −5 | −6 |
| | | 2 | 8 | 6 |
| | 1 | 4 | 3 | 0 |

The zero remainder shows that 2 is a zero.

The zero remainder tells us that 2 is a zero of the polynomial function $f(x) = x^3 + 2x^2 - 5x - 6$. Equivalently, 2 is a solution, or root, of the polynomial equation $x^3 + 2x^2 - 5x - 6 = 0$. Thus, $x - 2$ is a factor of the polynomial.

$x^3 + 2x^2 - 5x - 6 = 0$ Finding the zeros of $f(x) = x^3 + 2x^2 - 5x - 6$ is the same as finding the roots of this equation.

$(x - 2)(x^2 + 4x + 3) = 0$ Factor using the result from the synthetic division.

$(x - 2)(x + 3)(x + 1) = 0$ Factor completely.

$x - 2 = 0$ or $x + 3 = 0$ or $x + 1 = 0$ Set each factor equal to zero.

$x = 2$ $\quad x = -3$ $\quad x = -1$ Solve for x.

The solution set is $\{-3, -1, 2\}$. The rational zeros of $f$ are $-3$, $-1$, and 2.

**Check Point 3** Find all rational zeros of $f(x) = x^3 + 8x^2 + 11x - 20$.

Our work in Example 3 involved solving a third-degree equation. We found one factor by synthetic division and factored the remaining quadratic factor using the FOIL method. If the degree of a polynomial function or equation is 4 or higher, it is often necessary to find more than one linear factor by synthetic division.

One way to speed up the process of finding the first zero is to graph the function. Any $x$-intercept is a zero.

**3** Solve polynomial equations.

## EXAMPLE 4 Solving a Polynomial Equation

Solve: $x^4 - 6x^2 - 8x + 24 = 0$.

**Solution** Recall that we refer to the zeros of a polynomial function and the roots of a polynomial equation. Because we are given an equation, we will use the word "roots," rather than "zeros," in the solution process. We begin by listing all possible rational roots.

$$\text{Possible rational roots} = \frac{\text{Factors of the constant term, 24}}{\text{Factors of the leading coefficient, 1}} = \frac{\pm1, \pm2, \pm3, \pm4, \pm6, \pm8, \pm12, \pm24}{\pm1} = \pm1, \pm2, \pm3, \pm4, \pm6, \pm8, \pm12, \pm24$$

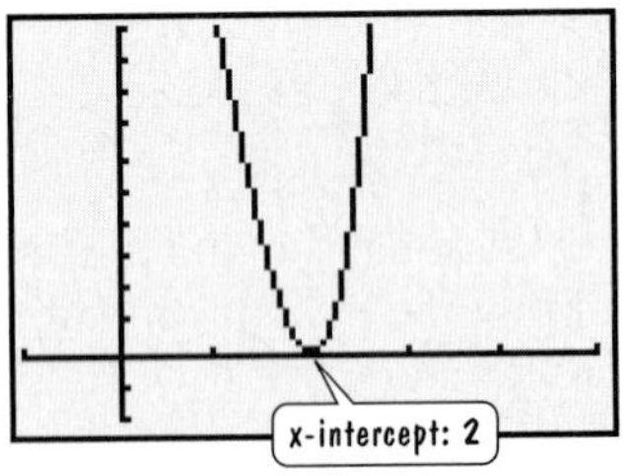


**Figure 3.20** The graph of $f(x) = x^4 - 6x^2 - 8x + 24$ in a $[-1, 5, 1]$ by $[-2, 10, 1]$ viewing rectangle

The graph of $f(x) = x^4 - 6x^2 - 8x + 24$ is shown in Figure 3.20. Because the $x$-intercept is 2, we will test 2 by synthetic division and show that it is a root of the given equation.

| | | | | | |
|---|---|---|---|---|---|
| 2 | 1 | 0 | −6 | −8 | 24 |
| | | 2 | 4 | −4 | −24 |
| | 1 | 2 | −2 | −12 | 0 |

Careful! $x^4 - 6x^2 - 8x + 24 = x^4 + 0x^3 - 6x^2 - 8x + 24$

The zero remainder indicates that 2 is a root of $x^4 - 6x^2 - 8x + 24 = 0$.

Now we can rewrite the given equation in factored form.

$x^4 - 6x^2 - 8x + 24 = 0$ This is the given equation.

$(x - 2)(x^3 + 2x^2 - 2x - 12) = 0$ This is the result obtained from the synthetic division.

$x - 2 = 0$ or $x^3 + 2x^2 - 2x - 12 = 0$ Set each factor equal to 0.

We can use the same approach to look for rational roots of the polynomial equation $x^3 + 2x^2 - 2x - 12 = 0$, listing all possible rational roots. However, take a second look at the graph in Figure 3.20. Because the graph turns around at 2, this means that 2 is a root of even multiplicity. Thus, 2 must also be a root of $x^3 + 2x^2 - 2x - 12 = 0$, confirmed by the following synthetic division.

| | | | | |
|---|---|---|---|---|
| 2 | 1 | 2 | −2 | −12 |
| | | 2 | 8 | 12 |
| | 1 | 4 | 6 | 0 |

These are the coefficients of $x^3 + 2x^2 - 2x - 12 = 0$.

The zero remainder indicates that 2 is a root of $x^3 + 2x^2 - 2x - 12 = 0$.

Now we can solve the original equation as follows:

$x^4 - 6x^2 - 8x + 24 = 0$ This is the given equation.

$(x - 2)(x^3 + 2x^2 - 2x - 12) = 0$ This was obtained from the first synthetic division.

$(x - 2)(x - 2)(x^2 + 4x + 6) = 0$ This was obtained from the second synthetic division.

$x - 2 = 0$ or $x - 2 = 0$ or $x^2 + 4x + 6 = 0$ Set each factor equal to 0.

$x = 2$ $\quad x = 2$ $\quad x^2 + 4x + 6 = 0$ Solve.

We can use the quadratic formula to solve $x^2 + 4x + 6 = 0$.

$$x = \frac{-b \pm \sqrt{b^2 - 4ac}}{2a}$$ We use the quadratic formula because $x^2 + 4x + 6$ cannot be factored.

$$= \frac{-4 \pm \sqrt{4^2 - 4(1)(6)}}{2(1)}$$ Let $a = 1$, $b = 4$, and $c = 6$.

$$= \frac{-4 \pm \sqrt{-8}}{2}$$ Multiply and subtract under the radical.

$$= \frac{-4 \pm 2i\sqrt{2}}{2}$$ $\sqrt{-8} = \sqrt{4(2)(-1)} = 2i\sqrt{2}$

$$= -2 \pm i\sqrt{2}$$ Simplify.

The solution set of the original equation is $\{2, -2 - i\sqrt{2}, -2 + i\sqrt{2}\}$.

In Example 4, 2 is a repeated root of the equation with multiplicity 2. The example illustrates two general properties.

**Properties of Polynomial Equations**

1. If a polynomial equation is of degree $n$, then counting multiple roots separately, the equation has $n$ roots.
2. If $a + bi$ is a root of a polynomial equation $(b \neq 0)$, then the nonreal complex number $a - bi$ is also a root. Nonreal complex roots, if they exist, occur in conjugate pairs.

These ideas will be developed in more detail in the next section.

**Check Point 4** Solve: $x^4 - 6x^3 + 22x^2 - 30x + 13 = 0$.

**4** Use Descartes's Rule of Signs.

An equation can have as many true [positive] roots as it contains changes of sign, from plus to minus or from minus to plus.... René Descartes (1596–1650) in *La Géométrie* (1637)

## Descartes's Rule of Signs

Because an $n$th-degree polynomial equation might have roots that are imaginary numbers, we should note that such an equation can have *at most n* real roots. **Descartes's Rule of Signs** provides even more specific information about the number of real zeros that a polynomial can have. The rule is based on considering *variations in sign* between consecutive coefficients. For example, the function

$$f(x) = 3x^7 - 2x^5 - x^4 + 7x^2 + x - 3$$

has three sign changes.

**Descartes's Rule of Signs**

Let $f(x) = a_n x^n + a_{n-1}x^{n-1} + \cdots + a_2 x^2 + a_1 x + a_0$ be a polynomial with real coefficients.

1. The number of *positive real zeros* of $f$ is either equal to the number of sign changes of $f(x)$ or is less than that number by an even integer. If

there is only one variation in sign, there is exactly one positive real zero.

2. The number of *negative real zeros* of $f$ is either equal to the number of sign changes of $f(-x)$ or is less than that number by an even integer. If $f(-x)$ has only one variation in sign, then $f$ has exactly one negative real zero.

## EXAMPLE 5 Using Descartes's Rule of Signs

Determine the possible number of positive and negative real zeros of $f(x) = x^3 + 2x^2 + 5x + 4$.

**Solution**

1. To find possibilities for positive real zeros, count the number of sign changes in the equation for $f(x)$. Because all the terms are positive, there are no variations in sign. Thus, there are no positive real zeros.
2. To find possibilities for negative real zeros, count the number of sign changes in the equation for $f(-x)$. We obtain this equation by replacing $x$ with $-x$ in the given function.

$$f(x) = x^3 + 2x^2 + 5x + 4$$ This is the given polynomial function.

Replace x with −x.

$$f(-x) = (-x)^3 + 2(-x)^2 + 5(-x) + 4$$
$$= -x^3 + 2x^2 - 5x + 4$$

Now count the sign changes.

$$f(-x) = -x^3 + 2x^2 - 5x + 4$$

1 2 3

There are three variations in sign. The number of negative real zeros of $f$ is either equal to the number of sign changes, 3, or is less than this number by an even integer. This means that there are either 3 negative real zeros or $3 - 2 = 1$ negative real zero.

What do the results of Example 5 mean in terms of solving

$$x^3 + 2x^2 + 5x + 4 = 0?$$

Without using Descartes's Rule of Signs, we list possible rational roots as follows:

Possible rational roots

$$= \frac{\text{Factors of the constant term, 4}}{\text{Factors of the leading coefficient, 1}} = \frac{\pm1, \pm2, \pm4}{\pm1} = \pm1, \quad \pm2, \quad \pm4.$$

However, Descartes's Rule of Signs informed us that $f(x) = x^3 + 2x^2 + 5x + 4$ has no positive real zeros. Thus, the polynomial equation $x^3 + 2x^2 + 5x + 4 = 0$ has no positive real roots. This means that we can eliminate the positive numbers from our list of possible rational roots. Possible rational roots include only $-1, -2,$ and $-4$. We can use synthetic division and test two of the three possible rational roots as follows:

| | | | | |
|---|---|---|---|---|
| $-1$ | 1 | 2 | 5 | 4 |
| | | $-1$ | $-1$ | $-4$ |
| | 1 | 1 | 4 | 0 |

The zero remainder shows that $-1$ is a root.

| | | | | |
|---|---|---|---|---|
| $-2$ | 1 | 2 | 5 | 4 |
| | | $-2$ | 0 | $-10$ |
| | 1 | 0 | 5 | $-6$ |

The nonzero remainder shows that $-2$ is not a root.

We do not need to test the third possible rational root using synthetic division. Based on our work in Example 5, we know that there are either one or three negative roots. If $-2$ is not a root and it is one of three possible negative roots, the polynomial equation cannot have three negative roots. Therefore, there is only one negative root, $-1$. The equation is of degree 3 and will have a total of three solutions. Two of the solutions will be nonreal complex numbers in a conjugate pair. (Verify this by completing the solution process.)

**Check Point 5** Determine the possible number of positive and negative real zeros of $f(x) = x^4 - 14x^3 + 71x^2 - 154x + 120$.

## EXERCISE SET 3.4

### Practice Exercises

*In Exercises 1–8, use the Rational Zero Theorem to list all possible rational zeros for each given function.*

1. $f(x) = x^3 + x^2 - 4x - 4$
2. $f(x) = x^3 + 3x^2 - 6x - 8$
3. $f(x) = 3x^4 - 11x^3 - x^2 + 19x + 6$
4. $f(x) = 2x^4 + 3x^3 - 11x^2 - 9x + 15$
5. $f(x) = 4x^4 - x^3 + 5x^2 - 2x - 6$
6. $f(x) = 3x^4 - 11x^3 - 3x^2 - 6x + 8$
7. $f(x) = x^5 - x^4 - 7x^3 + 7x^2 - 12x - 12$
8. $f(x) = 4x^5 - 8x^4 - x + 2$

*In Exercises 9–14,*

- **a.** *List all possible rational zeros.*
- **b.** *Use synthetic division to test the possible rational zeros and find an actual zero.*
- **c.** *Use the zero from part (b) to find all the zeros of the polynomial function.*

9. $f(x) = x^3 + x^2 - 4x - 4$
10. $f(x) = x^3 - 2x^2 - 11x + 12$
11. $f(x) = 2x^3 - 3x^2 - 11x + 6$
12. $f(x) = 2x^3 - 5x^2 + x + 2$
13. $f(x) = 3x^3 + 7x^2 - 22x - 8$
14. $f(x) = 3x^3 + 8x^2 - 15x + 4$

*In Exercises 15–22,*

- **a.** *List all possible rational roots.*
- **b.** *Use synthetic division to test the possible rational roots and find an actual root.*
- **c.** *Use the root from part (b) and solve the equation.*

15. $x^3 - 2x^2 - 11x + 12 = 0$
16. $x^3 - 2x^2 - 7x - 4 = 0$
17. $x^3 - 10x - 12 = 0$
18. $x^3 - 5x^2 + 17x - 13 = 0$
19. $6x^3 + 25x^2 - 24x + 5 = 0$
20. $2x^3 - 5x^2 - 6x + 4 = 0$
21. $x^4 - 2x^3 - 5x^2 + 8x + 4 = 0$
22. $x^4 - 2x^2 - 16x - 15 = 0$

*In Exercises 23–28, use Descartes's Rule of Signs to determine the possible number of positive and negative real zeros for each given function.*

23. $f(x) = x^3 + 2x^2 + 5x + 4$
24. $f(x) = x^3 + 7x^2 + x + 7$
25. $f(x) = 5x^3 - 3x^2 + 3x - 1$
26. $f(x) = -2x^3 + x^2 - x + 7$
27. $f(x) = 2x^4 - 5x^3 - x^2 - 6x + 4$
28. $f(x) = 4x^4 - x^3 + 5x^2 - 2x - 6$

*In Exercises 29–40, find all zeros of the polynomial function or solve the given polynomial equation. Use the Rational Zero Theorem and Descartes's Rule of Signs as an aid in obtaining the first zero or the first root.*

**29.** $f(x) = x^3 - 4x^2 - 7x + 10$

**30.** $f(x) = x^3 + 12x^2 + 21x + 10$

**31.** $2x^3 - x^2 - 9x - 4 = 0$

**32.** $3x^3 - 8x^2 - 8x + 8 = 0$

**33.** $x^4 - 3x^3 - 20x^2 - 24x - 8 = 0$

**34.** $x^4 - x^3 + 2x^2 - 4x - 8 = 0$

**35.** $f(x) = 3x^4 - 11x^3 - x^2 + 19x + 6$

**36.** $f(x) = 2x^4 + 3x^3 - 11x^2 - 9x + 15$

**37.** $4x^4 - x^3 + 5x^2 - 2x - 6 = 0$

**38.** $3x^4 - 11x^3 - 3x^2 - 6x + 8 = 0$

**39.** $2x^5 + 7x^4 - 18x^2 - 8x + 8 = 0$

**40.** $4x^5 + 12x^4 - 41x^3 - 99x^2 + 10x + 24 = 0$

## Application Exercises

**41.** Suppose that a polynomial function $f$ is used to model the data shown in the graph using

(number of years after 1993, thousands of deaths at the workplace).

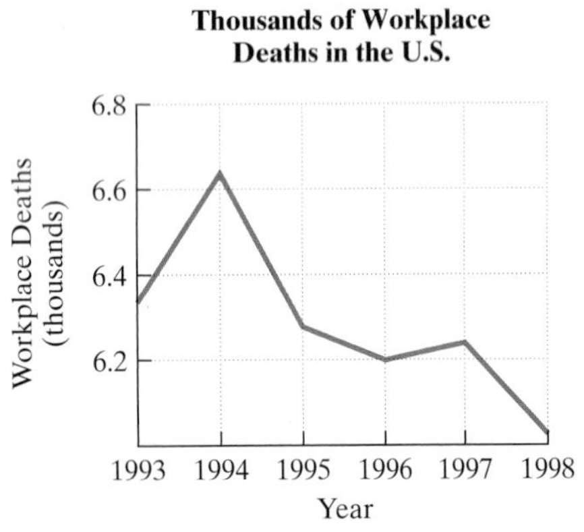


*Source*: F. B. I.

**a.** Use the graph to solve the polynomial equation $f(x) = 6.2$.

**b.** Describe the degree and the leading coefficient of the function $f$ that can be used to model the data in the graph.

**42.** Suppose that a polynomial function $f$ is used to model the data shown in the graph at the top of the next column using

(number of years after 1995, average cost of a computer in thousands of dollars).

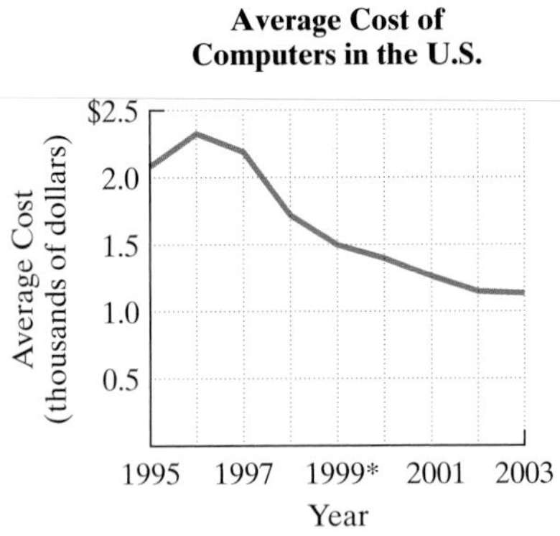


*Costs are projected from 1999 to 2003
*Source*: National Science Foundation

Use the graph to solve the polynomial equation $f(x) = 1.5$.

**43.** The number of eggs, $N$, in a female moth is a function of her abdominal width, $W$, in millimeters, modeled by $N = 14W^3 - 17W^2 - 16W + 34$, for $1.5 \le W \le 3.5$. What is the abdominal width when there are 211 eggs?

**44.** The concentration of a drug, in parts per million, in a patient's blood $x$ hours after the drug is administered is given by the function

$$f(x) = -x^4 + 12x^3 - 58x^2 + 132x.$$

How many hours after the drug is administered will it be eliminated from the bloodstream?

**45.** The width of a rectangular box is twice the height and the length is 7 inches more than the height. If the volume is 72 cubic inches, find the dimensions of the box.

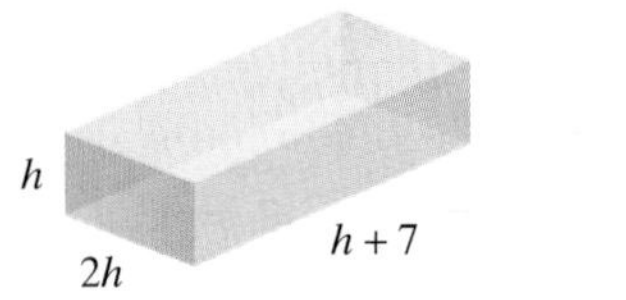


**46.** A box with an open top is formed by cutting squares out of the corners of a rectangular piece of cardboard 10 inches by 8 inches and then folding up the sides. If $x$ represents the length of the side of the square cut from each corner of the rectangle, what size square must be cut if the volume of the box is to be 48 cubic inches?

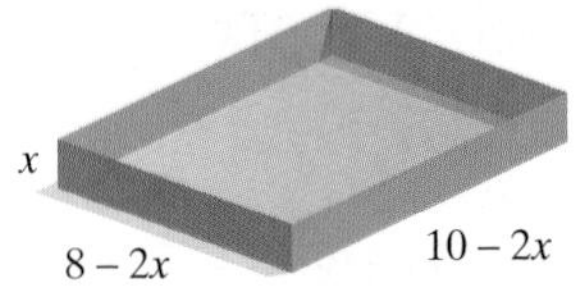

## Writing in Mathematics

**47.** Describe how to find the possible rational zeros of a polynomial function.

**48.** Describe how to use Descartes's Rule of signs to determine the possible number of positive real zeros of a polynomial function.

**49.** Describe how to use Descartes's rule of signs to determine the possible number of negative roots of a polynomial equation.

**50.** Why must every polynomial equation of degree 3 have at least one real root?

**51.** Explain why the equation $x^4 + 6x^2 + 2 = 0$ has no rational roots.

**52.** Suppose $\frac{3}{4}$ is a root of a polynomial equation. What does this tell us about the leading coefficient and the constant term in the equation?

**53.** The number of AIDS cases in the United States for the years 1983 through 1990 is approximated by the function

$$f(x) = -143x^3 + 1810x^2 - 187x + 2331$$

where $x$ represents the number of years after 1983. Use the Rational Zero Theorem to explain why, according to this formula, 14,199 cases could not have occurred 5 years after 1983.

## Technology Exercises

*The equations in Exercises 54–57 have real roots that are rational. Use the Rational Zero Theorem to list all possible rational roots. Then graph the polynomial function in the given viewing rectangle to determine which possible rational roots are actual roots of the equation.*

**54.** $2x^3 - 15x^2 + 22x + 15 = 0$; $[-1, 6, 1]$ by $[-50, 50, 1]$

**55.** $6x^3 - 19x^2 + 16x - 4 = 0$; $[0, 2, 1]$ by $[-3, 2, 1]$

**56.** $2x^4 + 7x^3 - 4x^2 - 27x - 18 = 0$; $[-4, 3, 1]$ by $[-45, 45, 1]$

**57.** $4x^4 + 4x^3 + 7x^2 - x - 2 = 0$; $[-2, 2, 1]$ by $[-5, 5, 1]$

**58.** Use Descartes's Rule of Signs to determine the possible number of positive and negative real zeros of $f(x) = 3x^4 + 5x^2 + 2$. What does this mean in terms of the graph of $f$? Verify your result by using a graphing utility to graph $f$.

**59.** Use Descartes's Rule of Signs to determine the possible number of positive and negative real zeros of $f(x) = x^5 - x^4 + x^3 - x^2 + x - 8$. Verify your result by using a graphing utility to graph $f$.

**60.** Make up a number of polynomial functions of odd degree and graph each function. Is it possible for the graph to have no real zeros? Explain. Try doing the same thing for polynomial functions of even degree. Now is it possible to have no real zeros?

## Critical Thinking Exercises

**61.** Which one of the following is true?

**a.** The equation $x^3 + 5x^2 + 6x + 1 = 0$ has one positive real root.

**b.** Descartes's Rule of Signs gives the exact number of positive and negative real roots for a polynomial equation.

**c.** Every polynomial equation of degree 3 has at least one rational root.

**d.** None of the above is true.

**62.** Give an example of a polynomial equation that has no real roots. Describe how you obtained the equation.

**63.** If the volume of the solid shown in the figure is 208 cubic inches, find the value of $x$.

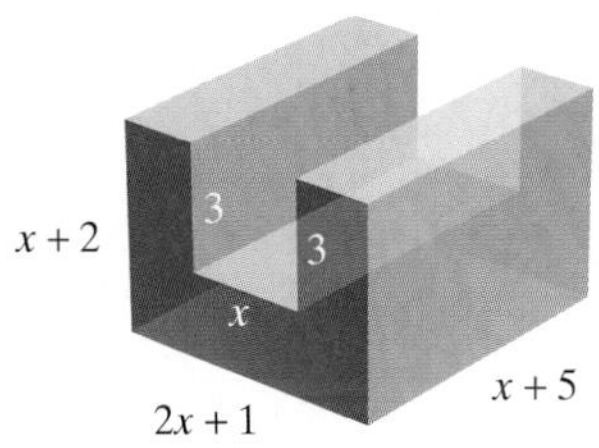


**64.** In this exercise, we lead you through the steps involved in the proof of the Rational Zero Theorem. Consider the polynomial equation

$$a_nx^n + a_{n-1}x^{n-1} + a_{n-2}x^{n-2} + \cdots + a_1x + a_0 = 0$$

where $\frac{p}{q}$ is a rational root reduced to lowest terms.

**a.** Substitute $\frac{p}{q}$ for $x$ in the equation and show that the equation can be written as

$$a_np^n + a_{n-1}p^{n-1}q + a_{n-2}p^{n-2}q^2 + \cdots + a_1pq^{n-1} = -a_0q^n.$$

**b.** Why is $p$ a factor of the left side of the equation?

**c.** Because $p$ divides the left side, it must also divide the right side. However, because $\frac{p}{q}$ is reduced to lowest terms, $p$ cannot divide $q$. Thus, $p$ and $q$ have no common factors other than $-1$ and 1. Because $p$ does divide the right side and it is not a factor of $q^n$, what can you conclude?

**d.** Rewrite the equation from part (a) with all terms containing $q$ on the left and the term that does not have a factor of $q$ on the right. Use an argument that parallels parts (b) and (c) to conclude that $q$ is a factor of $a_n$.

## SECTION 3.5 More On Zeros of Polynomial Functions

### Objectives

1. Find bounds for the roots of a polynomial equation.
2. Approximate real zeros.
3. Use conjugate roots to solve a polynomial equation.
4. Use the Linear Factorization Theorem to factor a polynomial.
5. Find polynomials with given zeros.

You stole my formula!

**Tartaglia's Secret Formula for One Solution of $x^3 + mx = n$**

$$x = \sqrt[3]{\sqrt{\left(\frac{n}{2}\right)^2 + \left(\frac{m}{3}\right)^3} + \frac{n}{2}} - \sqrt[3]{\sqrt{\left(\frac{n}{2}\right)^2 + \left(\frac{m}{3}\right)^3} - \frac{n}{2}}$$

Popularizers of mathematics are sharing bizarre stories that are giving math a secure place in popular culture. One episode, able to compete with the wildest fare served up by television talk shows and the tabloids, involves three Italian mathematicians and, of all things, zeros of polynomial functions.

Tartaglia (1499–1557), poor and starving, has found a formula that gives a root for a third-degree polynomial equation. Cardano (1501–1576) begs Tartaglia to reveal the secret formula, wheedling it from him with the promise he will find the impoverished Tartalia a patron. Then Cardano publishes his famous work *Ars Magna*, in which he presents Tartaglia's formula as his own. Cardano uses his most talented student, Ferrari (1522–1565), who derived a formula for a root of a fourth-degree polynomial equation, to falsely accuse Tartaglia of plagiarism. The dispute becomes violent and Tartaglia is fortunate to escape alive.

The noise from this "You Stole My Formula" episode is quieted by the work of French mathematician Evariste Galois (1811–1832). Galois proved that there is no general formula for finding roots of polynomial equations of degree 5 or higher. There are, of course, methods for finding roots. In this section, we continue our study of methods for finding zeros of polynomial functions.

**1** Find bounds for the roots of a polynomial equation.

### Upper and Lower Bounds for Roots

The **Upper and Lower Bound Theorem** helps us rule out many of a polynomial equation's possible rational roots. Figure 3.21 illustrates that $a$ is a **lower bound** and $b$ is an **upper bound** for the roots of $f(x) = 0$ because every real root $c$ of the equation satisfies $a \le c \le b$.

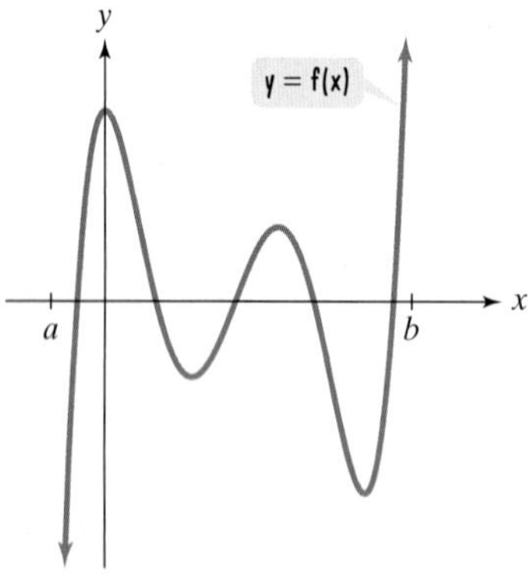

**Figure 3.21** $b$ is an upper bound and $a$ is a lower bound for the real roots of $f(x) = 0$.

**The Upper and Lower Bound Theorem**

Let $f(x)$ be a polynomial with real coefficients and a positive leading coefficient, and let $a$ and $b$ be nonzero real numbers.

1. Divide $f(x)$ by $x - b$ (where $b > 0$) using synthetic division. If the last row containing the quotient and remainder has no negative numbers, then $b$ is an **upper bound** for the real roots of $f(x) = 0$.
2. Divide $f(x)$ by $x - a$ (where $a < 0$) using synthetic division. If the last row containing the quotient and remainder has numbers that alternate in sign (zero entries count as positive or negative), then $a$ is a **lower bound** for the real roots of $f(x) = 0$.

## EXAMPLE 1 Finding Bounds for the Roots

Show that all the real roots of the equation $8x^3 + 10x^2 - 39x + 9 = 0$ lie between $-3$ and 2.

**Solution** We begin by showing that 2 is an upper bound. Divide the polynomial by $x - 2$. If all the numbers in the bottom row of the synthetic division are nonnegative, then 2 is an upper bound.

| | | | | |
|---|---|---|---|---|
| 2 | 8 | 10 | −39 | 9 |
| | | 16 | 52 | 26 |
| | 8 | 26 | 13 | 35 |

All numbers in this row are nonnegative.

The nonnegative entries in the last row verify that 2 is an upper bound. Next, we show that $-3$ is a lower bound. Divide the polynomial by $x - (-3)$, or $x + 3$. If the numbers in the bottom row of the synthetic division alternate in sign, then $-3$ is a lower bound. Remember that the number zero can be considered positive or negative.

| | | | | |
|---|---|---|---|---|
| −3 | 8 | 10 | −39 | 9 |
| | | −24 | 42 | −9 |
| | 8 | −14 | 3 | 0 |

Counting 0 as negative, the signs alternate: +, −, +, −.

By the Upper and Lower Bound Theorem, the alternating signs in the last row indicate that $-3$ is a lower bound for the roots. (The zero remainder indicates that $-3$ is also a root.)

**Check Point 1** Show that all the real roots of the equation $2x^3 + 11x^2 - 7x - 6 = 0$ lie between $-7$ and 2.

How might the Upper and Lower Bound Theorem be helpful in solving a polynomial equation? Consider the equation

$$x^4 + 3x^3 - 27x^2 + 3x - 28 = 0.$$

With a leading coefficient of 1 and a constant term of $-28$, the possible rational roots are

$$\pm 1, \quad \pm 2, \quad \pm 4, \quad \pm 7, \quad \pm 14, \quad \pm 28.$$

We begin testing for an actual root using synthetic division. The following divisions indicate that 1 and 2 are not roots because of the nonzero remainders. However, something interesting happens when testing 4.

| | | | | | |
|---|---|---|---|---|---|
| 1 | 1 | 3 | −27 | 3 | −28 |
| | | 1 | 4 | −23 | −20 |
| | 1 | 4 | −23 | −20 | −48 |

| | | | | | |
|---|---|---|---|---|---|
| 2 | 1 | 3 | −27 | 3 | −28 |
| | | 2 | 10 | −34 | −62 |
| | 1 | 5 | −17 | −31 | −90 |

| | | | | | |
|---|---|---|---|---|---|
| 4 | 1 | 3 | −27 | 3 | −28 |
| | | 4 | 28 | 4 | 28 |
| | 1 | 7 | 1 | 7 | 0 |

Nonnegative numbers

4 is a root of $f(x) = 0$ because the remainder is 0.

4 is an upper bound for the roots of $f(x) = 0$.

Notice that 4 is both a root and an upper bound for the roots. Should you take the time to use synthetic division and test 7, 14, and 28? There is no need to do this because all three numbers exceed 4, the upper bound for the roots. Thus, 7, 14, and 28 cannot be roots of the equation.

## Technology

The Upper and Lower Bound Theorem and your knowledge of polynomial functions can help you to find a reasonable range setting when using your graphing utility. Consider

$$f(x) = x^4 + 3x^3 - 27x^2 + 3x - 28.$$

Based on our discussion, 4 is a zero and an upper bound for the zeros. We can also use synthetic division to show that $-7$ is a zero and a lower bound for the zeros. We can use these lower and upper bounds to determine Xmin and Xmax. We'll go one unit to the left and to the right of these bounds and use $[-8, 5, 1]$. Now, how do we determine Ymin and Ymax? Let's see what kinds of values of $y$ we obtain when we evaluate the function between $-8$ and 5. Using synthetic division, direct substitution, or the table feature of some graphing utilities, we have $f(-6) = -370$, $f(-5) = -468$, $f(0) = -28$, and $f(3) = -100$. These evaluations suggest that we can use $-500$ for Ymin and 100 for Ymax. The graph of $f(x) = x^4 + 3x^3 - 27x^2 + 3x - 28$ is shown in a $[-8, 5, 1]$ by $[-500, 100, 20]$ viewing rectangle in Figure 3.22. Because the degree is even $(n = 4)$ and the leading coefficient, 1, is positive, the graph should rise to the left and right. This is precisely what occurs in Figure 3.22. Our work in obtaining this complete graph is an excellent illustration of the fact that technology complements human knowledge and is not intended to replace it.

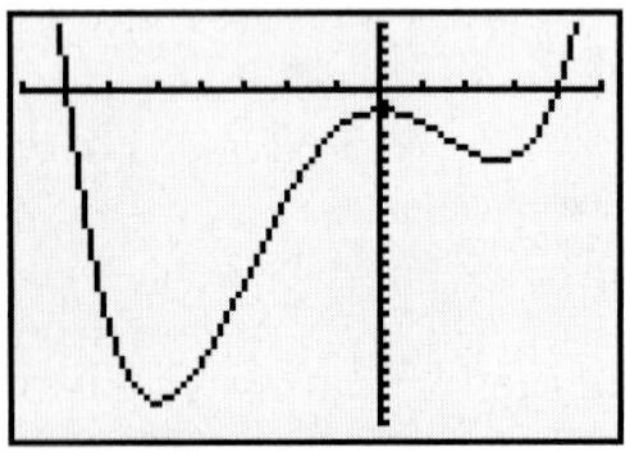

**Figure 3.22**

**2** Approximate real zeros.

## The Intermediate Value Theorem

We can find decimal approximations for real zeros of polynomial functions using a graphing utility. The **Intermediate Value Theorem** tells us of the existence of real zeros and how to approximate them. The idea behind the theorem is illustrated in Figure 3.23. The figure shows that if $(a, f(a))$ lies below the $x$-axis and $(b, f(b))$ lies above the $x$-axis, the smooth, continuous graph of a polynomial function $f$ must cross the $x$-axis at some value $c$ between $a$ and $b$. This value is a real zero for the function.

These observations are summarized in the **Intermediate Value Theorem**.

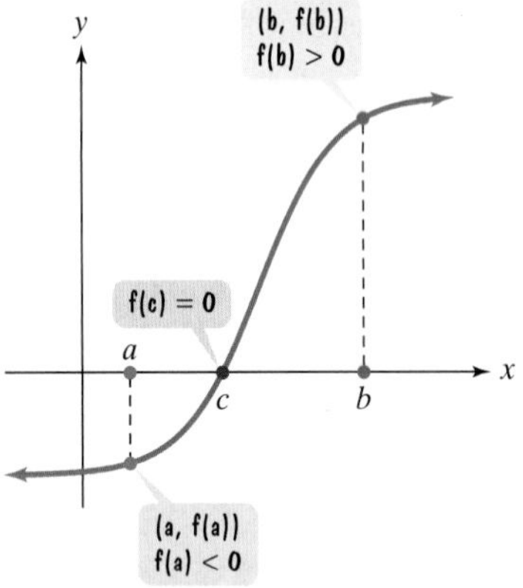


**Figure 3.23** The graph must cross the $x$-axis at some value between $a$ and $b$.

### The Intermediate Value Theorem for Polynomials

Let $f(x)$ be a polynomial function with real coefficients. If $f(a)$ and $f(b)$ have opposite signs, then there is at least one value of $c$ between $a$ and $b$ for which $f(c) = 0$. Equivalently, the equation $f(x) = 0$ has at least one real root between $a$ and $b$.

### EXAMPLE 2 Approximating a Real Zero

**a.** Show that the polynomial function $f(x) = x^3 - 2x - 5$ has a real zero between 2 and 3.

**b.** Use the Intermediate Value Theorem to find an approximation for this real zero to the nearest tenth.

**Solution**

**a.** Let us evaluate $f(x)$ at 2 and 3. If $f(2)$ and $f(3)$ have opposite signs, then there is a real zero between 2 and 3. Using $f(x) = x^3 - 2x - 5$, we obtain

$$f(2) = 2^3 - 2 \cdot 2 - 5 = 8 - 4 - 5 = -1$$

$f(2)$ is negative.

and

$$f(3) = 3^3 - 2 \cdot 3 - 5 = 27 - 6 - 5 = 16.$$

$f(3)$ is positive.

This sign change shows that the polynomial function has a real zero between 2 and 3.

**b.** A numerical approach is to evaluate $f$ at successive tenths between 2 and 3, looking for a sign change. This sign change will place the real zero between a pair of successive tenths.

| $x$ | $f(x) = x^3 - 2x - 5$ |
|---|---|
| 2 | $f(2) = 2^3 - 2(2) - 5 = -1$ |
| 2.1 | $f(2.1) = (2.1)^3 - 2(2.1) - 5 = 0.061$ |

Sign change

The sign change indicates that $f$ has a real zero between 2 and 2.1. We now follow a similar procedure to locate the real zero between successive hundredths. We divide the interval $[2, 2.1]$ into ten equal subintervals. Then we evaluate $f$ at each endpoint and look for a sign change.

$f(2.00) = -1$

$f(2.01) = -0.899399$

$f(2.02) = -0.797592$

$f(2.03) = -0.694573$

$f(2.04) = -0.590336$

$f(2.05) = -0.484875$

$f(2.06) = -0.378184$

$f(2.07) = -0.270257$

$f(2.08) = -0.161088$

$f(2.09) = -0.050671$

$f(2.1) = 0.061$

Sign change

The sign change indicates that $f$ has a real zero between 2.09 and 2.1. Correct to the nearest tenth, the zero is 2.1.

**Technology**

The following graph was obtained by entering

$$y = x^3 - 2x - 5$$

and

$$y = 0$$

and using the intersection feature in a $[-3, 3, 1]$ by $[-10, 10, 1]$ viewing rectangle. Correct to the nearest thousandth, the function's real zero is 2.095.

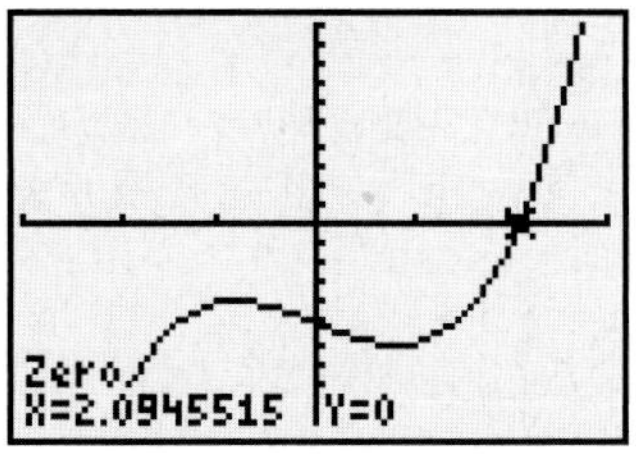


**Check Point 2** Show that the polynomial function $f(x) = 3x^3 - 10x + 9$ has a real zero between $-3$ and $-2$.

**3** Use conjugate roots to solve a polynomial equation.

## The Fundamental Theorem of Algebra

We have seen that if a polynomial equation is of degree $n$, then counting multiple roots separately, the equation has $n$ roots. Some of these roots may be nonreal complex numbers that occur in conjugate pairs, such as $2 + i$ and $2 - i$.

## EXAMPLE 3 Using Conjugate Roots to Solve a Polynomial Equation

Solve $x^4 - 4x^3 + 3x^2 + 8x - 10 = 0$ given that $2 + i$ is a root.

**Solution** The degree of the given equation is 4. This means that there are four roots. One of the roots is $2 + i$. Because complex nonreal roots come in conjugate pairs, we know that $2 - i$ is a second root. By the Factor Theorem, both

$$[x - (2 + i)] \text{ and } [x - (2 - i)]$$

are factors of the given polynomial. We multiply these known factors.

$$[x - (2 + i)][x - (2 - i)]$$

F O I L

$$= x^2 - x(2 - i) - x(2 + i) + (2 + i)(2 - i)$$ Multiply using the FOIL method.

$$= x^2 - 2x + ix - 2x - ix + (4 - i^2)$$ Continue multiplying.

$$= x^2 - 2x + ix - 2x - ix + [4 - (-1)]$$ Simplify using $i^2 = -1$.

$$= x^2 - 4x + 5$$ Combine like terms.

At this point we have only two of the four possible roots, $2 + i$ and $2 - i$. We can find the other two roots by factoring the given equation. We have found that $x^2 - 4x + 5$ is one of the factors. We can find the other factor(s) by dividing $x^2 - 4x + 5$ into the polynomial on the left side of the given equation.

$$\begin{array}{r}
x^2 \qquad\qquad - 2 \\
x^2 - 4x + 5 \overline{)\, x^4 - 4x^3 + 3x^2 + 8x - 10} \\
\underline{x^4 - 4x^3 + 5x^2 \qquad\qquad} \\
-2x^2 + 8x - 10 \\
\underline{-2x^2 + 8x - 10} \\
0
\end{array}$$

The zero remainder confirms that $x^2 - 4x + 5$ is a factor.

We can now solve the given equation.

$$x^4 - 4x^3 + 3x^2 + 8x - 10 = 0$$ This is the original equation.

$$(x^2 - 4x + 5)(x^2 - 2) = 0$$ Factor using the result of the polynomial long division.

$$x^2 - 4x + 5 = 0 \quad \text{or} \quad x^2 - 2 = 0$$ Set each factor equal to 0.

$$x = 2 \pm i \qquad\qquad x = \pm\sqrt{2}$$ Solve for x. We know the roots for the first equation, $x^2 - 4x + 5 = 0$, by our previous analysis.

The solution set is $\{2 \pm i, \pm\sqrt{2}\}$.

### Technology

The graph of

$f(x) =$

$x^4 - 4x^3 + 3x^2 + 8x - 10$

is shown in a $[-4, 4, 1]$ by $[-15, 5, 1]$ viewing rectangle. The real roots of $f(x) = 0$, the equation in Example 3, are $-\sqrt{2}$ and $\sqrt{2}$. These appear as $x$-intercepts at approximately $-1.4$ and $1.4$.

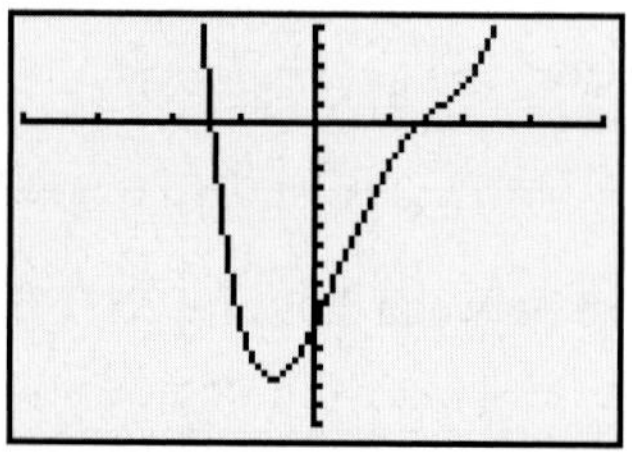

**Check Point 3** Solve $x^4 - 8x^3 + 64x - 105 = 0$ given that $2 - i$ is a root.

The fact that a polynomial equation of degree $n$ has $n$ roots is a consequence of a theorem proved in 1799 by a 22-year-old student named Carl Friedrich Gauss in his doctoral dissertation. His result is called the **Fundamental Theorem of Algebra**.

**The Fundamental Theorem of Algebra**

If $f(x)$ is a polynomial of degree $n$, where $n \geq 1$, then the equation $f(x) = 0$ has at least one complex root.

Suppose, for example, that $f(x) = 0$ represents a polynomial equation of degree $n$. By the Fundamental Theorem of Algebra, we know that this equation has at least one complex root; we'll call it $c_1$. By the Factor Theorem, we know that $x - c_1$ is a factor of $f(x)$. Therefore, we obtain

$$(x - c_1)q_1(x) = 0 \quad \text{The degree of the polynomial } q_1(x) \text{ is } n - 1.$$

$$x - c_1 = 0 \quad \text{or} \quad q_1(x) = 0 \quad \text{Set each factor equal to 0.}$$

If the degree of $q_1(x)$ is at least 1, by the Fundamental Theorem of Algebra the equation $q_1(x) = 0$ has at least one complex root. We'll call it $c_2$. The Factor Theorem gives us

$$q_1(x) = 0 \quad \text{The degree of } q_1(x) \text{ is } n - 1.$$

$$(x - c_2)q_2(x) = 0 \quad \text{The degree of } q_2(x) \text{ is } n - 2.$$

$$x - c_2 = 0 \quad \text{or} \quad q_2(x) = 0. \quad \text{Set each factor equal to 0.}$$

Let's see what we have up to this point, and then continue the process.

$$f(x) = 0 \quad \text{This is the original polynomial equation of degree } n.$$

$$(x - c_1)q_1(x) = 0 \quad \text{This is the result from our first application of the Fundamental Theorem.}$$

$$(x - c_1)(x - c_2)q_2(x) = 0 \quad \text{This is the result from our second application of the Fundamental Theorem.}$$

By continuing this process, we will obtain the product of $n$ linear factors. Setting each of these linear factors equal to zero results in $n$ complex roots. Thus, if $f(x)$ is a polynomial of degree $n$, where $n \geq 1$, then $f(x) = 0$ has exactly $n$ roots, where roots are counted according to their multiplicity.

**4** Use the Linear Factorization Theorem to factor a polynomial.

## The Linear Factorization Theorem

In Example 3, we found that $x^4 - 4x^3 + 3x^2 + 8x - 10 = 0$ has $\{2 \pm i, \pm\sqrt{2}\}$ as a solution set. The polynomial can be factored over the complex nonreal numbers as follows:

These are the four zeros.

$$f(x) = x^4 - 4x^3 + 3x^2 + 8x - 10$$

$$= [x - (2 + i)][x - (2 - i)](x + \sqrt{2})(x - \sqrt{2})$$

These are four linear factors.

This fourth-degree polynomial has four linear factors. Just as an $n$th-degree polynomial equation has $n$ roots, an $n$th-degree polynomial has $n$ linear factors. This is formally stated as the **Linear Factorization Theorem**.

**The Linear Factorization Theorem**

If $f(x) = a_nx^n + a_{n-1}x^{n-1} + \cdots + a_1x + a_0,$ where $n \geq 1$ and $a_n \neq 0$, then

$$f(x) = a_n(x - c_1)(x - c_2)\cdots(x - c_n)$$

where $c_1, c_2, \ldots, c_n$ are complex numbers (possibly real and not necessarily distinct). In words: An $n$th-degree polynomial can be expressed as the product of $n$ linear factors.

The Linear Factorization Theorem involves factors somewhat different than those you are used to seeing. For example, the polynomial $x^2 - 3$ is irreducible over the rational numbers. However, it can be factored over the real numbers as follows:

$$x^2 - 3 = (x + \sqrt{3})(x - \sqrt{3}).$$ Use $a^2 - b^2 = (a + b)(a - b)$ with $a = x$ and $b = \sqrt{3}$.

**Study Tip**

The sum of squares, irreducible over the real numbers, can be factored over the complex nonreal numbers as

$$a^2 + b^2 = (a + bi)(a - bi).$$

The polynomial $x^2 + 1$ is irreducible over the real numbers, but reducible over the complex nonreal numbers.

$$x^2 + 1 = (x + i)(x - i)$$

## EXAMPLE 4 Factoring a Polynomial

Factor $x^4 - 3x^2 - 28$:

**a.** As the product of factors that are irreducible over the rational numbers.
**b.** As the product of factors that are irreducible over the real numbers.
**c.** In completely factored form involving complex nonreal numbers.

**Solution**

**a.** $x^4 - 3x^2 - 28 = (x^2 - 7)(x^2 + 4)$ Both quadratic factors are irreducible over the rational numbers.

**b.** $= (x + \sqrt{7})(x - \sqrt{7})(x^2 + 4)$ The third factor is still irreducible over the real numbers.

**c.** $= (x + \sqrt{7})(x - \sqrt{7})(x + 2i)(x - 2i)$ This is the completely factored form using complex nonreal numbers.

**Check Point 4** Factor $x^4 - 4x^2 - 5$ as the product of factors that are irreducible over **a.** the rational numbers; **b.** the real numbers; **c.** the complex nonreal numbers.

**5** Find polynomials with given zeros.

## Reversing Things: Finding Polynomials When the Zeros Are Given

Many of our problems involving polynomial functions and polynomial equations dealt with the process of finding zeros and roots. The Linear Factorization Theorem enables us to reverse this process, finding a polynomial function when the zeros are given.

## EXAMPLE 5 Finding a Polynomial Function with Given Zeros

Find a fourth-degree polynomial function $f(x)$ with real coefficients that has $-2$, 2, and $i$ as zeros and such that $f(3) = -150$.

**Solution** Because $i$ is a zero and the polynomial has real coefficients, the conjugate must also be a zero. We can now use the Linear Factorization Theorem.

$f(x) = a_n(x - c_1)(x - c_2)(x - c_3)(x - c_4)$ This is the linear factorization for a fourth-degree polynomial.

$= a_n(x + 2)(x - 2)(x - i)(x + i)$ Use the given zeros: $c_1 = -2$, $c_2 = 2$, $c_3 = i$, and, from above, $c_4 = -i$.

$= a_n(x^2 - 4)(x^2 + 1)$ Multiply.

## Technology

The graph of $f(x) = -3x^4 + 9x^2 + 12$, shown in a $[-3, 3, 1]$ by $[-200, 20, 20]$ viewing rectangle, verifies that $-2$ and $2$ are real zeros. By tracing along the curve, we can check that $f(3) = -150$.

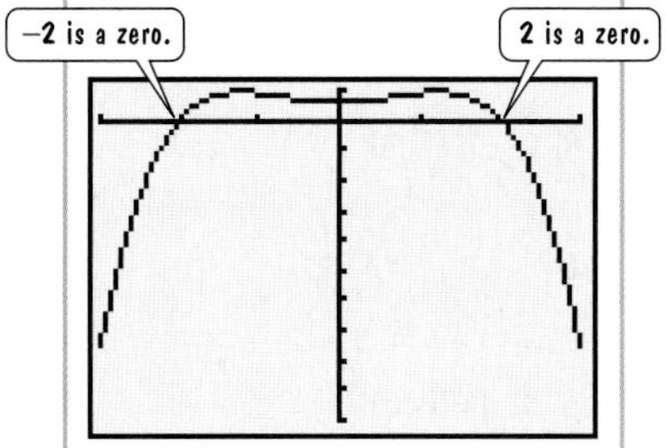


$$f(x) = a_n(x^4 - 3x^2 - 4)$$ Complete the multiplication.

$$f(3) = a_n(3^4 - 3 \cdot 3^2 - 4) = -150$$ To find $a_n$, use the fact that $f(3) = -150$.

$$a_n(81 - 27 - 4) = -150$$ Solve for $a_n$.

$$50a_n = -150$$

$$a_n = -3$$

Substituting $-3$ for $a_n$ in the formula for $f(x)$, we obtain

$$f(x) = -3(x^4 - 3x^2 - 4).$$

Equivalently,

$$f(x) = -3x^4 + 9x^2 + 12.$$

**Check Point 5** Find a third-degree polynomial function $f(x)$ with real coefficients that has $-3$ and $i$ as zeros and such that $f(1) = 8$.

## EXERCISE SET 3.5

### Practice Exercises

*Use the Upper and Lower Bound Theorem to solve Exercises 1–6.*

**1.** Show that all the real roots of the equation $x^4 - 5x^3 + 11x^2 + 33x - 18 = 0$ lie between $-4$ and 7.

**2.** Show that all the real roots of the equation $x^4 + 11x^3 - 12x^2 + 6 = 0$ lie between $-13$ and 1.

**3.** Show that all the real roots of the equation $2x^3 + 5x^2 - 8x - 7 = 0$ lie between $-4$ and 2.

**4.** Show that all the real roots of the equation $2x^5 - 13x^3 + 2x - 5 = 0$ lie between $-3$ and 3.

**5.** Consider the equation $x^4 + 3x^3 + 2x^2 - 5x + 12 = 0$.

**a.** List all possible rational roots.

**b.** Determine whether 1 is a root using synthetic division. What two conclusions can you draw?

**c.** Based on part (b), what possible rational roots can you eliminate?

**d.** Determine whether $-3$ is a root using synthetic division. What two conclusions can you draw?

**e.** Based on part (d), what possible rational roots can you eliminate?

**6.** Consider the equation
$2x^5 + 5x^4 - 8x^3 - 14x^2 + 6x + 9 = 0$.

**a.** List all possible rational roots.

**b.** Determine whether $\frac{3}{2}$ is a root using synthetic division. What two conclusions can you draw?

**c.** Based on part (b), what possible rational roots can you eliminate?

**d.** Determine whether $-3$ is a root using synthetic division. What two conclusions can you draw?

**e.** Based on part (d), what possible rational roots can you eliminate?

*In Exercises 7–14, show that each polynomial has a real zero between the given integers. Then use the Intermediate Value Theorem to find an approximation for this zero to the nearest tenth.*

**7.** $f(x) = x^3 - x - 1$; between 1 and 2

**8.** $f(x) = x^3 - 4x^2 + 2$; between 0 and 1

**9.** $f(x) = 2x^4 - 4x^2 + 1$; between $-1$ and 0

**10.** $f(x) = x^4 + 6x^3 - 18x^2$; between 2 and 3

**11.** $f(x) = x^3 + x^2 - 2x + 1$; between $-3$ and $-2$

**12.** $f(x) = x^5 - x^3 - 1$; between 1 and 2

**13.** $f(x) = 3x^3 - 10x + 9$; between $-3$ and $-2$

**14.** $f(x) = 3x^3 - 8x^2 + x + 2$; between 2 and 3

*In Exercises 15–22, use the given root to find the solution set of the polynomial equation.*

**15.** $x^3 - 2x^2 + 4x - 8 = 0$; $-2i$

**16.** $x^4 + 13x^2 + 36 = 0$; $3i$

**17.** $3x^3 - 7x^2 + 8x - 2 = 0$; $1 + i$

**18.** $x^3 - 7x^2 + 16x - 10 = 0$; $3 + i$

**19.** $x^4 - 6x^2 + 25 = 0$; $2 - i$

**20.** $x^4 - x^3 - 9x^2 + 29x - 60 = 0$; $1 + 2i$

**21.** $x^4 - 8x^3 + 64x - 105 = 0;\ 2 - i$

**22.** $4x^4 - 28x^3 + 129x^2 - 130x + 125 = 0;\ 3 - 4i$

*In Exercises 23–28, factor each polynomial:*

**a.** *as the product of factors that are irreducible over the rational numbers*

**b.** *as the product of factors that are irreducible over the real numbers*

**c.** *in completely factored form involving complex nonreal numbers*

**23.** $x^4 - x^2 - 20$

**24.** $x^4 + 6x^2 - 27$

**25.** $x^4 + x^2 - 6$

**26.** $x^4 - 9x^2 - 22$

**27.** $x^4 - 2x^3 + x^2 - 8x - 12$
(*Hint*: One factor is $x^2 + 4$.)

**28.** $x^4 - 4x^3 + 14x^2 - 36x + 45$
(*Hint*: One factor is $x^2 + 9$.)

*In Exercises 29–36, find an nth-degree polynomial function with real coefficients satisfying the given conditions. If you are using a graphing utility, use it to graph the function and verify the real zeros and the given function value.*

**29.** $n = 3$; 1 and $5i$ are zeros; $f(-1) = -104$

**30.** $n = 3$; 4 and $2i$ are zeros; $f(-1) = -50$

**31.** $n = 3$; $-5$ and $4 + 3i$ are zeros; $f(2) = 91$

**32.** $n = 3$; 6 and $-5 + 2i$ are zeros; $f(2) = -636$

**33.** $n = 4$; $i$ and $3i$ are zeros; $f(-1) = 20$

**34.** $n = 4$; $-2, -\frac{1}{2}$, and $i$ are zeros; $f(1) = 18$

**35.** $n = 4$; $-2, 5$, and $3 + 2i$ are zeros; $f(1) = -96$

**36.** $n = 4$; $-4, \frac{1}{3}$, and $2 + 3i$ are zeros; $f(1) = 100$

*In Exercises 37–44, find all the zeros of the function and write the polynomial as a product of linear factors.*

**37.** $f(x) = x^3 - x^2 + 25x - 25$

**38.** $f(x) = x^3 - 10x^2 + 33x - 34$

**39.** $f(x) = x^3 - 8x^2 + 25x - 26$

**40.** $f(x) = x^3 - 8x^2 + 17x - 4$

**41.** $f(x) = x^4 + 37x^2 + 36$

**42.** $f(x) = x^4 + 8x^3 + 9x^2 - 10x + 100$

**43.** $f(x) = 16x^4 + 36x^3 + 16x^2 + x - 30$

**44.** $f(x) = 2x^4 - x^3 + 7x^2 - 4x - 4$

## Application Exercises

*We have seen the polynomial function*

$$H(x) = -0.001183x^4 + 0.05495x^3 - 0.8523x^2 + 9.054x + 6.748$$

*that models the age in human years, $H(x)$, of a dog that is x years old, where $x \geq 1$. Although the coefficients make it difficult to solve equations algebraically using this function, a graph of the function makes approximate solutions possible. Use the graph shown to solve Exercises 45–46.*

**Dog's Age in Human Years**

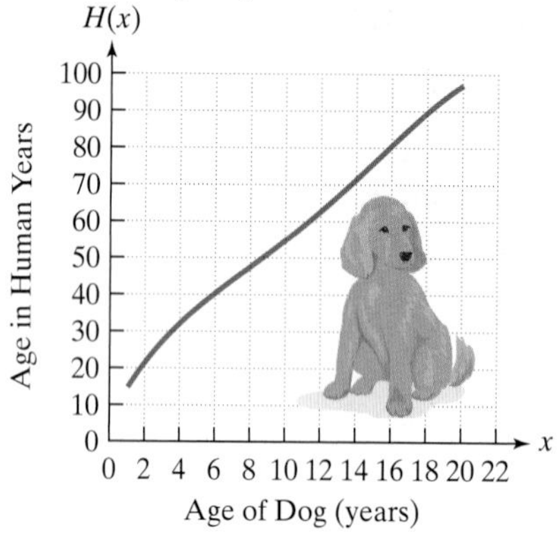


**45.** If you are 25, what is the equivalent age for dogs?

**46.** If you are 30, what is the equivalent age for dogs?

**47.** Set up an equation to answer the question in either Exercise 45 or 46. Bring all terms to one side and obtain zero on the other side. What are some of the difficulties involved in solving this equation? Explain how the Intermediate Value Theorem can be used to verify the approximate solution that you obtained from the graph.

*The bar graph shows the cost of Medicare, in billions of dollars, projected through 2005. Using the regression feature of a graphing utility, these data can be modeled by*

a linear function, $f(x) = 27x + 163$;

a quadratic function, $g(x) = 1.2x^2 + 15.2x + 181.4$;

a third-degree polynomial function,
$h(x) = 0.08x^3 - 0.06x^2 + 20.08x + 178.32$.

**Medicare Spending**

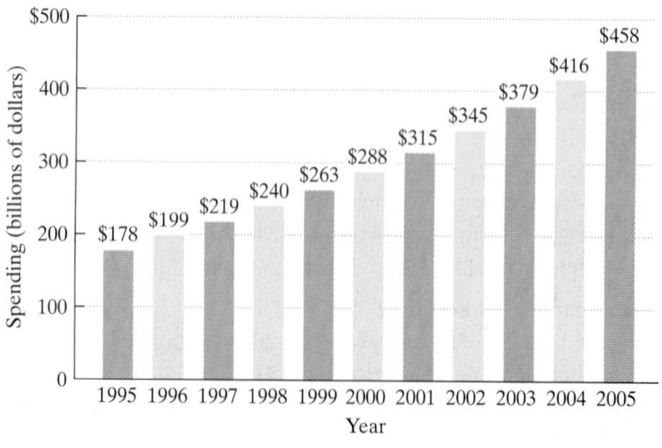


*Source*: Congressional Budget Office

*For each of these functions, x represents the number of years after 1995 and the function value represents Medicare spending, in billions of dollars, for that year.*

**48.** The graph indicates that Medicare spending will reach \$379 billion in 2003. Substitute 379 for $f(x)$, $g(x)$, and $h(x)$ in each of the three models. Then solve each resulting equation, if possible, to find how many years after 1995 spending will reach \$379 billion. Which of the three functions is the best model for 2003?

**49.** The graph indicates that Medicare spending will reach \$458 billion in 2005. Substitute 458 for $f(x)$, $g(x)$, and $h(x)$ in each of the three models. Then solve each resulting equation, if possible, to find how many years after 1995 spending will reach \$458 billion. Which of the three functions is the best model for 2005?

## Writing in Mathematics

**50.** When testing a number using synthetic division, how do you know if it is an upper bound for the real roots?

**51.** When testing a number using synthetic division, how do you know if it is a lower bound for the real roots?

**52.** How do you show that a polynomial function has a real zero between two given numbers?

**53.** How does the linear factorization of $f(x)$, that is,

$$f(x) = a_n(x - c_1)(x - c_2)\cdots(x - c_n),$$

show that a polynomial equation of degree $n$ has $n$ roots?

## Technology Exercises

**54.** Show that $-1$ is a lower bound of $f(x) = x^3 - 53x^2 + 103x - 51$. Show that 60 is an upper bound. Use this information and a graphing utility to draw a relatively complete graph of $f$.

*For Exercises 55–56, use a graphing utility to determine upper and lower bounds for the zeros of f. Does synthetic division verify your observations?*

**55.** $f(x) = 2x^3 + x^2 - 14x - 7$

**56.** $f(x) = 2x^4 - 7x^3 - 5x^2 + 28x - 12$

**57.** The function $f(x) = -0.00002x^3 + 0.008x^2 - 0.3x + 6.95$ models the number of annual physician visits, $f$, by a person of age $x$.

**a.** Graph the function for meaningful values of $x$ and discuss what the graph reveals in terms of the variables described by the model.

**b.** Use the polynomial root-finding capability of your graphing utility to find the age (to the nearest year) for the group that averages 13.43 annual physician visits.

**c.** Verify part (b) using the graph of $f$.

*Use a graphing utility to obtain a complete graph for each polynomial function in Exercises 58–61. Then determine the number of real zeros and the number of nonreal complex zeros for each function.*

**58.** $f(x) = x^3 - 6x - 9$

**59.** $f(x) = 3x^5 - 2x^4 + 6x^3 - 4x^2 - 24x + 16$

**60.** $f(x) = 3x^4 + 4x^3 - 7x^2 - 2x - 3$

**61.** $f(x) = x^6 - 64$

## Critical Thinking Exercises

*In Exercises 62–64, what is the smallest degree that each polynomial could have?*

**62.**

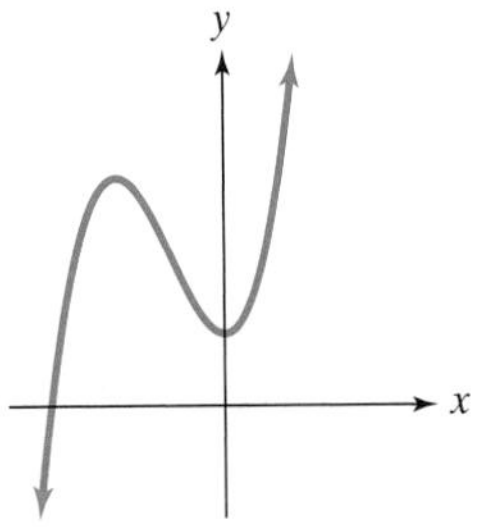


**63.**

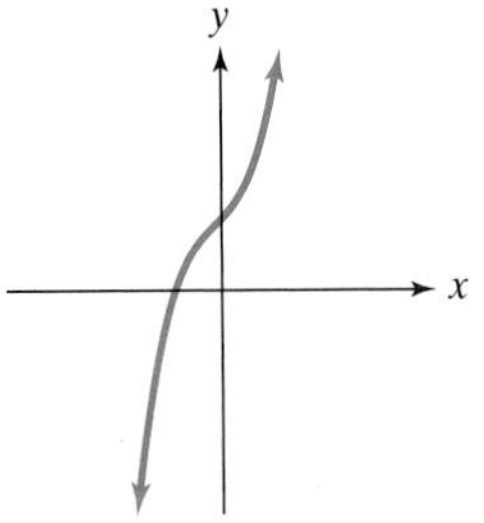


**64.**

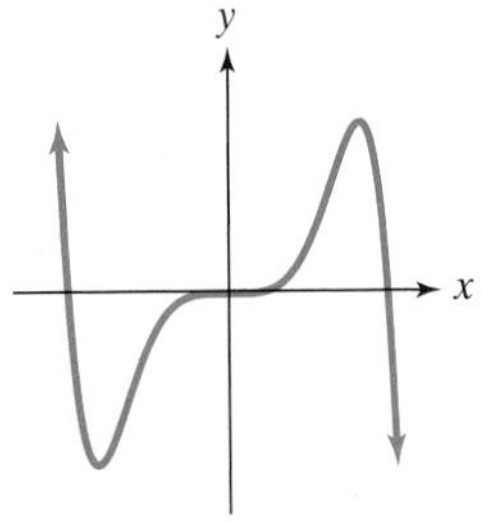


**65.** Explain why nonreal complex zeros are gained or lost in pairs in terms of graphs of polynomial functions.

**66.** Explain why a polynomial function of degree 20 cannot cross the $x$-axis exactly once.

**67.** Give an example of a function that is not subject to the Intermediate Value Theorem.

## Group Exercise

**68.** The graphs on page 314 show costs for private and public four-year colleges projected through the year 2017. According to these projections, your daughter's college education at a private four-year school could cost about \$250,000. This activity involves forming and using models from these data. Group members should begin by deciding whether to work with data for private or public colleges.

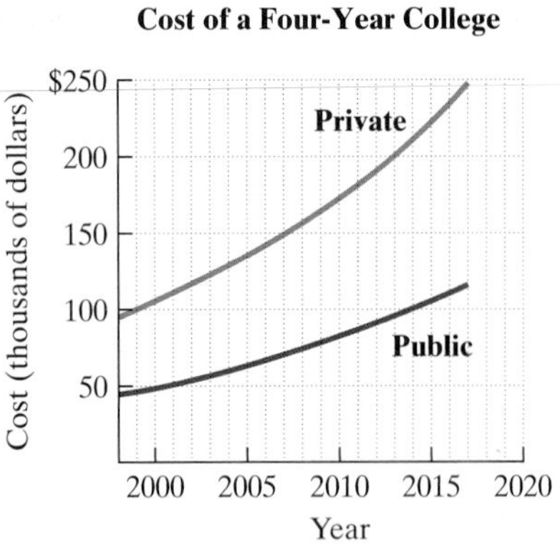


*Source*: U.S. Department of Education

**a.** Let $x = 0$ correspond to 1998, $x = 1$ to 1999, $x = 2$ to 2000, and so on up through $x = 19$ for 2017. Group members should use the chosen line graph to obtain a reasonable estimate for the cost of an education, $y$, in thousands of dollars, for each $x$.

**b.** Use the regression feature of a graphing utility to model the data for the cost of a four-year college $x$ years after 1998 using a linear function, a quadratic function, and a third-degree polynomial function.

**c.** Use these functions to write and solve a problem similar to Exercise 48 or 49.

**d.** Use these functions to make predictions well into the future. Which function, if any, seems to be most reasonable in its predicted cost? Of course, these are only predictions, subject to unforeseeable events. What events might render each of these models relatively useless over long periods of time?

# SECTION 3.6 *Rational Functions and Their Graphs*

## Objectives

1. Find the domain of rational functions.
2. Use arrow notation.
3. Identify vertical asymptotes.
4. Identify horizontal asymptotes.
5. Graph rational functions.
6. Identify slant asymptotes.
7. Solve applied problems involving rational functions.

Technology is now promising to bring light, fast, and beautiful wheelchairs to millions of disabled people. The cost of manufacturing these radically different wheelchairs can be modeled by rational functions. In this section we will see how graphs of these functions illustrate that low prices are possible with high production levels, urgently needed in this situation. There are more than half a billion people with disabilities in developing countries; an estimated 20 million need wheelchairs right now.

**1** Find the domain of rational functions.

## Rational Functions

**Rational functions** are quotients of polynomial functions. This means that rational functions can be expressed as

$$f(x) = \frac{p(x)}{q(x)}$$

where $p(x)$ and $q(x)$ are polynomial functions and $q(x) \neq 0$. The **domain** of a rational function is the set of all real numbers except the $x$-values that make the denominator zero. For example, the domain of the rational function

$$f(x) = \frac{x^2 + 7x + 9}{x(x-2)(x+5)}$$

This is $p(x)$.

This is $q(x)$.

is the set of all real numbers except 0, 2, and −5.

## EXAMPLE 1 Finding the Domain of a Rational Function

Find the domain of each rational function.

**a.** $f(x) = \dfrac{x^2 - 9}{x - 3}$ **b.** $g(x) = \dfrac{x}{x^2 - 9}$ **c.** $h(x) = \dfrac{x + 3}{x^2 + 9}$

**Solution** Rational functions contain division. Because division by 0 is undefined, we must exclude from the domain of each function values of $x$ that cause the polynomial function in the denominator to be 0.

**a.** The denominator of $f(x) = \dfrac{x^2 - 9}{x - 3}$ is 0 if $x = 3$. Thus, $x$ cannot equal 3. The domain of $f$ consists of all real numbers except 3, written $\{x \mid x \neq 3\}$.

**b.** The denominator of $g(x) = \dfrac{x}{x^2 - 9}$ is 0 if $x = -3$ or $x = 3$. Thus, the domain of $g$ consists of all real numbers except −3 and 3, written $\{x \mid x \neq -3, x \neq 3\}$.

**c.** No real numbers cause the denominator of $h(x) = \dfrac{x + 3}{x^2 + 9}$ to equal 0. The domain of $h$ consists of all real numbers.

**Check Point 1** Find the domain of each rational function.

**a.** $f(x) = \dfrac{x^2 - 25}{x - 5}$ **b.** $g(x) = \dfrac{x}{x^2 - 25}$ **c.** $h(x) = \dfrac{x + 5}{x^2 + 25}$

**2** Use arrow notation.

The most basic rational function is the **reciprocal function**, defined by $f(x) = \dfrac{1}{x}$. The denominator of the reciprocal function is zero when $x = 0$, so the domain of $f$ is the set of all real numbers except for 0.

Let's look at the behavior of $f$ near the excluded value 0. We start by evaluating $f(x)$ to the left of 0.

$x$ approaches 0 from the left.

| $x$ | −1 | −0.5 | −0.1 | −0.01 | −0.001 |
|---|---|---|---|---|---|
| $f(x) = \dfrac{1}{x}$ | −1 | −2 | −10 | −100 | −1000 |

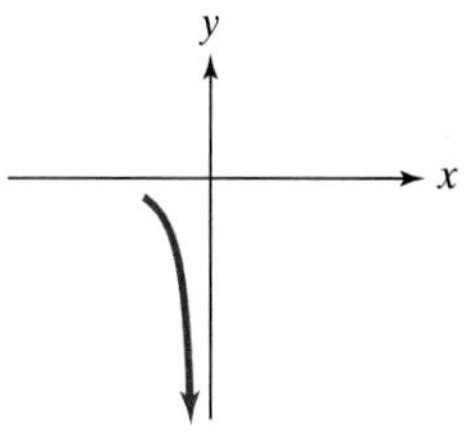

Mathematically, we say that "$x$ approaches 0 from the left." From the table and the accompanying graph, it appears that as $x$ approaches 0 from the left, the function values, $f(x)$, decrease without bound. We say that "$f(x)$ approaches negative infinity." We use a special arrow notation to describe this situation symbolically:

$$f(x) \to -\infty \quad \text{as} \quad x \to 0^-$$

f(x) approaches negative infinity (that is, the graph falls) as x approaches 0 from the left.

Observe that the minus $(-)$ superscript on the 0 $(x \to 0^-)$ is read "from the left."

Next, we evaluate $f(x)$ to the right of 0.

$x$ approaches 0 from the right.

| $x$ | 0.001 | 0.01 | 0.1 | 0.5 | 1 |
|---|---|---|---|---|---|
| $f(x) = \frac{1}{x}$ | 1000 | 100 | 10 | 2 | 1 |

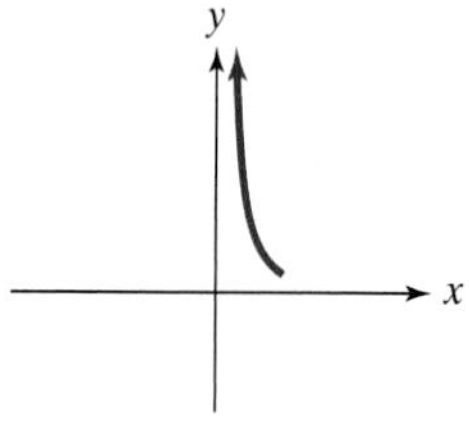


Mathematically, we say that "$x$ approaches 0 from the right." From the table and the accompanying graph, it appears that as $x$ approaches 0 from the right, the function values, $f(x)$, increase without bound. We say that "$f(x)$ approaches infinity." We again use a special arrow notation to describe this situation symbolically:

$$f(x) \to \infty \quad \text{as} \quad x \to 0^+$$

f(x) approaches infinity (that is, the graph rises) as x approaches 0 from the right.

Observe that the plus $(+)$ superscript on the 0 $(x \to 0^+)$ is read "from the right."

Now let's see what happens to the function values, $f(x)$, as $x$ gets farther away from the origin. The following tables suggest what happens to $f(x)$ as $x$ increases or decreases without bound.

**$x$ increases without bound:**

| $x$ | 1 | 10 | 100 | 1000 |
|---|---|---|---|---|
| $f(x) = \frac{1}{x}$ | 1 | 0.1 | 0.01 | 0.001 |

**$x$ decreases without bound:**

| $x$ | −1 | −10 | −100 | −1000 |
|---|---|---|---|---|
| $f(x) = \frac{1}{x}$ | −1 | −0.1 | −0.01 | −0.001 |

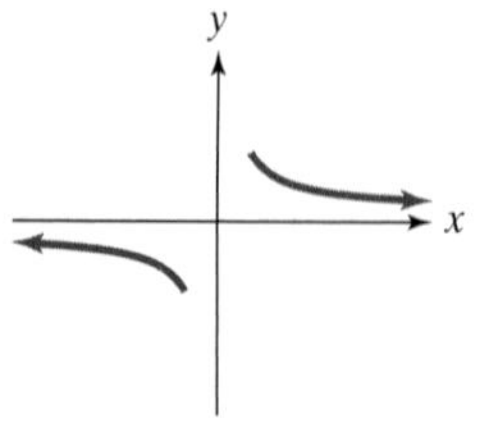


**Figure 3.24**
$f(x)$ approaches 0 as $x$ increases or decreases without bound

Figure 3.24 illustrates the end behavior of $f(x) = \frac{1}{x}$ as $x$ increases or decreases without bound. The function values, $f(x)$, are getting progressively closer to 0. This means that the graph of $f$ is approaching the horizontal line $y = 0$ (that is, the $x$-axis) as $x$ increases or decreases without bound. We use the arrow notation to describe this situation.

$$f(x) \to 0 \quad \text{as} \quad x \to \infty \qquad \text{and} \qquad f(x) \to 0 \quad \text{as} \quad x \to -\infty$$

f(x) approaches 0 as x increases without bound.

f(x) approaches 0 as x decreases without bound.

Thus, as $x$ approaches infinity ($x \to \infty$) or as $x$ approaches negative infinity ($x \to -\infty$), the function values are approaching zero: $f(x) \to 0$.

The graph of the reciprocal function $f(x) = \frac{1}{x}$ is shown in Figure 3.25. Unlike the graph of a polynomial function, the graph of the reciprocal function has a break in it and is composed of two distinct branches.

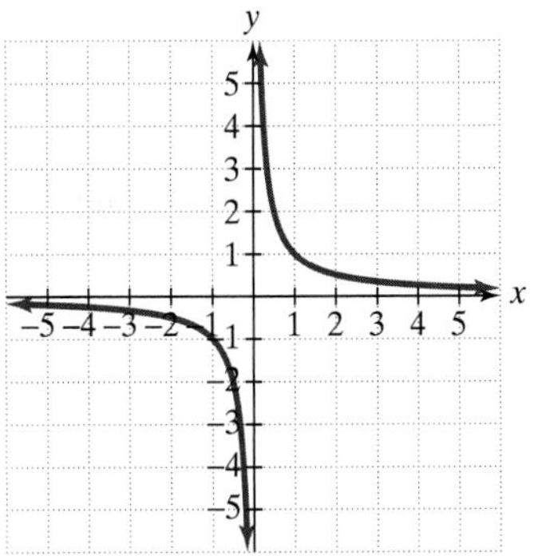


**Figure 3.25** The graph of the reciprocal function $f(x) = \frac{1}{x}$

The arrow notation used throughout our discussion of the reciprocal function is summarized in the following box.

### Arrow Notation

| **Symbol** | **Meaning** |
|---|---|
| $x \to a^+$ | $x$ approaches $a$ from the right. |
| $x \to a^-$ | $x$ approaches $a$ from the left. |
| $x \to \infty$ | $x$ approaches infinity; that is, $x$ increases without bound. |
| $x \to -\infty$ | $x$ approaches negative infinity; that is, $x$ decreases without bound. |

## Vertical Asymptotes of Rational Functions

**3** Identify vertical asymptotes.

Look again at the graph of $f(x) = \frac{1}{x}$. The curve approaches, but does not touch, the $y$-axis. The $y$-axis, or $x = 0$, is said to be a **vertical asymptote** of the graph. A rational function may have no vertical asymptotes, one vertical asymptote, or several vertical asymptotes. The graph of a rational function never intersects a vertical asymptote. We will use dashed lines to show asymptotes.

### Definition of a Vertical Asymptote

The line $x = a$ is a vertical asymptote of the graph of a function $f$ if $f(x)$ increases or decreases without bound as $x$ approaches $a$.

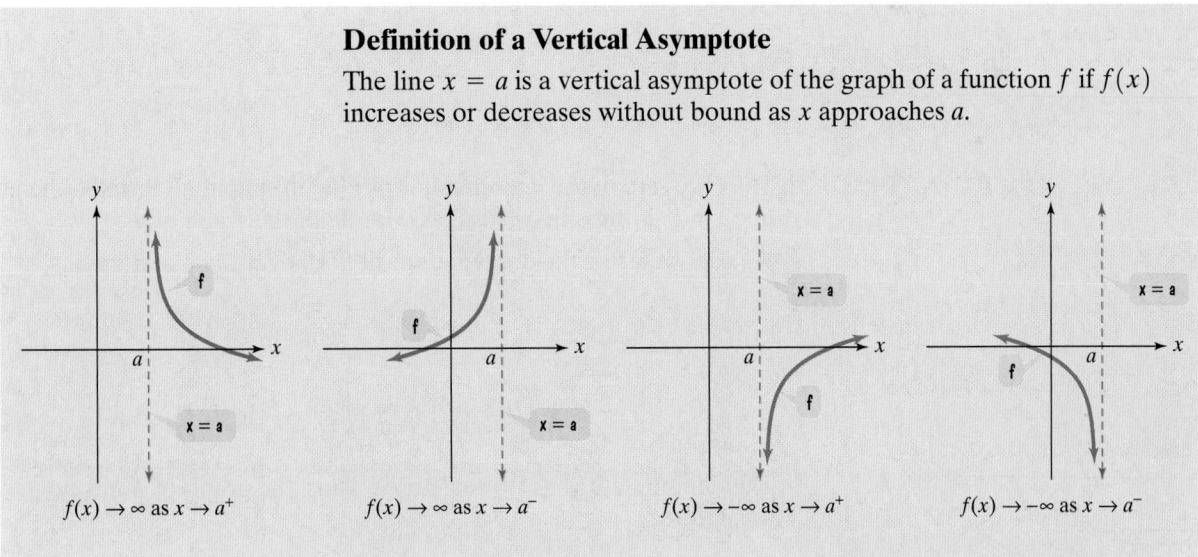

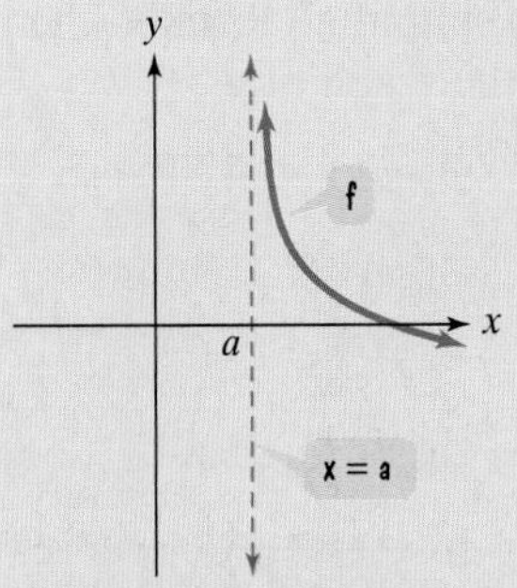


$f(x) \to \infty$ as $x \to a^+$

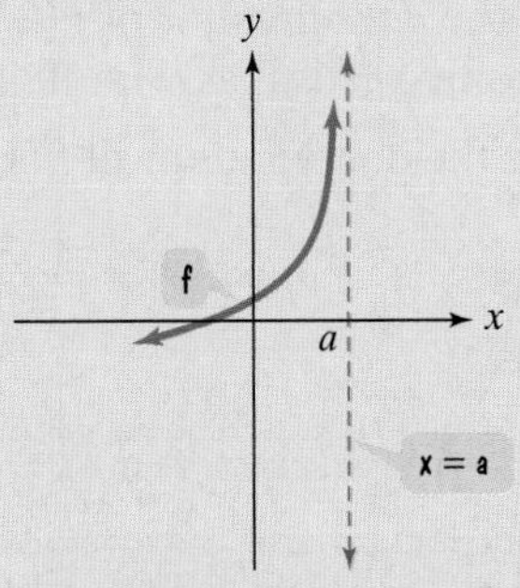


$f(x) \to \infty$ as $x \to a^-$

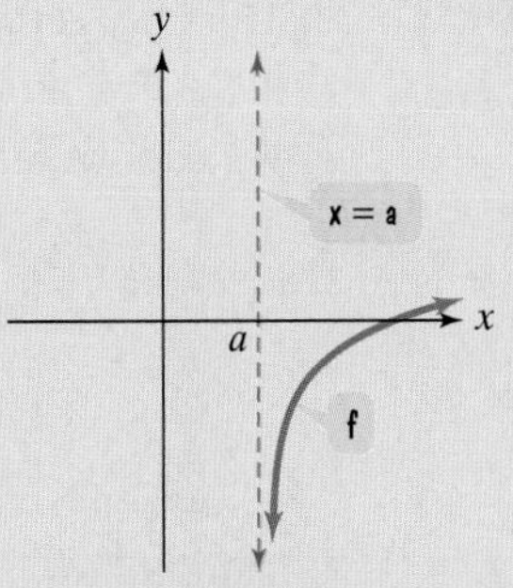


$f(x) \to -\infty$ as $x \to a^+$

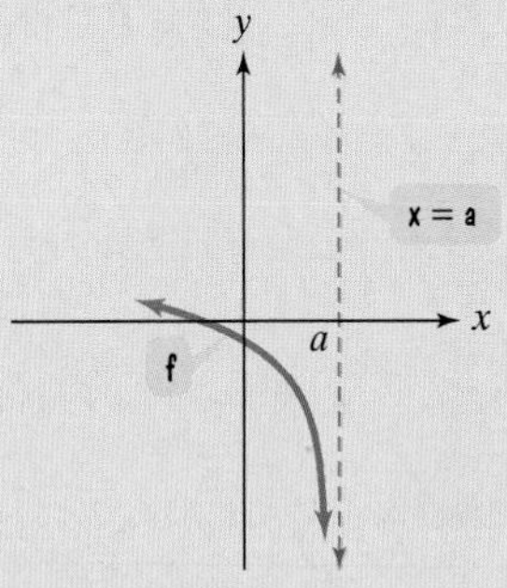


$f(x) \to -\infty$ as $x \to a^-$

Thus, $f(x) \to \infty$ or $f(x) \to -\infty$ as $x$ approaches $a$ from either the left or the right.

If the graph of a rational function has vertical asymptotes, they can be located by using the following theorem.

**Locating Vertical Asymptotes**

If $f(x) = \dfrac{p(x)}{q(x)}$ is a rational function in which $p(x)$ and $q(x)$ have no common factors and $a$ is a zero of $q(x)$, the denominator, then $x = a$ is a vertical asymptote of the graph of $f$.

## EXAMPLE 2 Finding the Vertical Asymptotes of a Rational Function

Find the vertical asymptotes, if any, of the graph of each rational function.

**a.** $f(x) = \dfrac{x}{x^2 - 9}$ **b.** $g(x) = \dfrac{x + 3}{x^2 - 9}$ **c.** $h(x) = \dfrac{x + 3}{x^2 + 9}$

**Solution** Factoring is usually helpful in identifying zeros of denominators.

**a.**
$$f(x) = \frac{x}{x^2 - 9} = \frac{x}{(x + 3)(x - 3)}$$

This factor is 0 if $x = -3$.

This factor is 0 if $x = 3$.

There are no common factors in the numerator and the denominator. The zeros of the denominator are $-3$ and 3. Thus, the lines $x = -3$ and $x = 3$ are the vertical asymptotes for the graph of $f$.

**b.** We will use factoring to see if there are common factors.

$$g(x) = \frac{x + 3}{x^2 - 9} = \frac{(x + 3)}{(x + 3)(x - 3)} = \frac{1}{x - 3}$$

There is a common factor, $x + 3$, so simplify.

This denominator is 0 if $x = 3$.

The only zero of the denominator of $g(x)$ in simplified form is 3. Thus, the line $x = 3$ is the only vertical asymptote of the graph of $g$.

**c.** We cannot factor the denominator of $h(x)$ over the real numbers.

$$h(x) = \frac{x + 3}{x^2 + 9}$$

No real numbers make this denominator 0.

The denominator has no real zeros. Thus, the graph of $h$ has no vertical asymptotes.

**Check Point 2** Find the vertical asymptotes, if any, of the graph of each rational function.

**a.** $f(x) = \dfrac{x}{x^2 - 1}$ **b.** $g(x) = \dfrac{x - 1}{x^2 - 1}$ **c.** $h(x) = \dfrac{x - 1}{x^2 + 1}$

A value where the denominator of a function is zero does not necessarily result in a vertical asymptote. There is a hole corresponding to $x = a$, and not a vertical asymptote, in the graph of a function under the following conditions: The value $a$ causes the denominator to be zero, but there is a reduced form of the function's equation in which $a$ does not cause the denominator to be zero.

Consider, for example, the function

$$f(x) = \frac{x^2 - 9}{x - 3}.$$

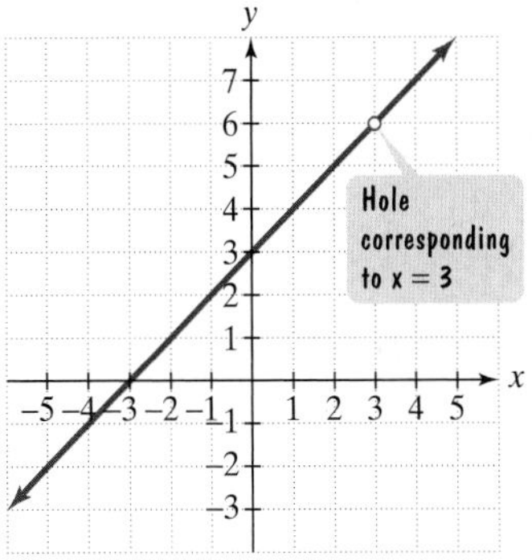


**Figure 3.26**

Because the denominator is zero when $x = 3$, the function's domain is all real numbers except 3. However, there is a reduced form of the equation in which 3 does not cause the denominator to be zero:

$$f(x) = \frac{x^2 - 9}{x - 3} = \frac{(x + 3)\cancel{(x - 3)}}{\cancel{x - 3}} = x + 3, \quad x \neq 3$$

Denominator is zero at $x = 3$.

In this reduced form, 3 does not result in a zero denominator.

Figure 3.26 shows that the graph has a hole corresponding to $x = 3$. Graphing utilities do not show this feature of the graph.

**4** Identify horizontal asymptotes.

## Horizontal Asymptotes of Rational Functions

Figure 3.25 shows the graph of the reciprocal function $f(x) = \frac{1}{x}$. As $x \to \infty$ and as $x \to -\infty$, the function values are approaching 0: $f(x) \to 0$. The line $y = 0$ (that is, the $x$-axis) is a **horizontal asymptote** of the graph. Many, but not all, rational functions have horizontal asymptotes.

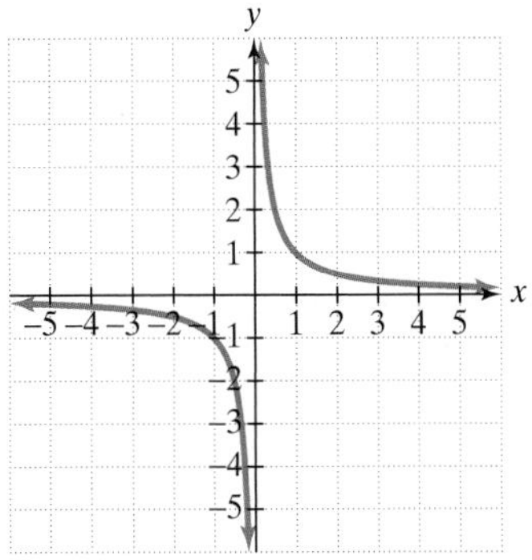

**Figure 3.25** The graph of the reciprocal function $f(x) = \frac{1}{x}$, repeated

### Definition of a Horizontal Asymptote

The line $y = b$ is a horizontal asymptote of the graph of a function $f$ if $f(x)$ approaches $b$ as $x$ increases or decreases without bound.

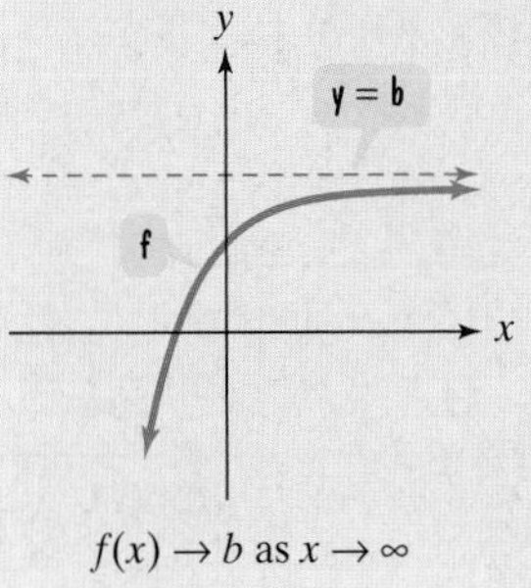


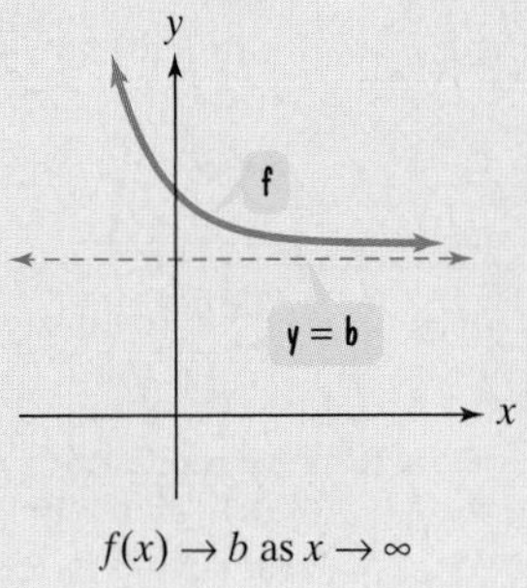


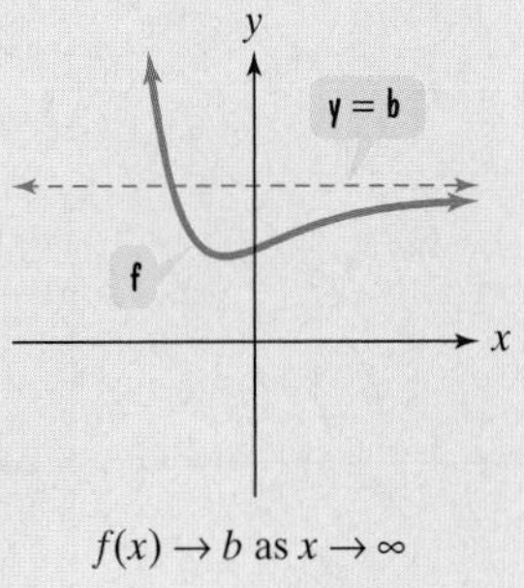


Recall that a rational function may have several vertical asymptotes. By contrast, it can have at most one horizontal asymptote. Although a graph can never intersect a vertical asymptote, it may cross its horizontal asymptote.

If the graph of a rational function has a horizontal asymptote, it can be located by using the following theorem.

**Locating Horizontal Asymptotes**

Let $f$ be the rational function given by

$$f(x) = \frac{a_n x^n + a_{n-1}x^{n-1} + \cdots + a_1 x + a_0}{b_m x^m + b_{m-1}x^{m-1} + \cdots + b_1 x + b_0}, \quad a_n \neq 0, b_m \neq 0.$$

The degree of the numerator is $n$. The degree of the denominator is $m$.

**1.** If $n < m$, the $x$-axis is the horizontal asymptote of the graph of $f$.

**2.** If $n = m$, the line $y = \frac{a_n}{b_m}$ is the horizontal asymptote of the graph of $f$.

**3.** If $n > m$, the graph of $f$ has no horizontal asymptote.

## EXAMPLE 3 Finding the Horizontal Asymptote of a Rational Function

Find the horizontal asymptote, if any, of the graph of each rational function.

**a.** $f(x) = \frac{4x}{2x^2 + 1}$ **b.** $g(x) = \frac{4x^2}{2x^2 + 1}$ **c.** $h(x) = \frac{4x^3}{2x^2 + 1}$

**Solution**

**a.** $f(x) = \frac{4x}{2x^2 + 1}$

The degree of the numerator, 1, is less than the degree of the denominator, 2. Thus, the graph of $f$ has the $x$-axis as a horizontal asymptote [see Figure 3.27(a)]. The equation of the horizontal asymptote is $y = 0$.

**b.** $g(x) = \frac{4x^2}{2x^2 + 1}$

The degree of the numerator, 2, is equal to the degree of the denominator, 2. The leading coefficients of the numerator and denominator, 4 and 2, are used to obtain the equation of the horizontal asymptote. The equation of the horizontal asymptote is $y = \frac{4}{2}$ or $y = 2$ [see Figure 3.27(b)].

**c.** $h(x) = \frac{4x^3}{2x^2 + 1}$

The degree of the numerator, 3, is greater than the degree of the denominator, 2. Thus, the graph of $h$ has no horizontal asymptote [see Figure 3.27(c)].

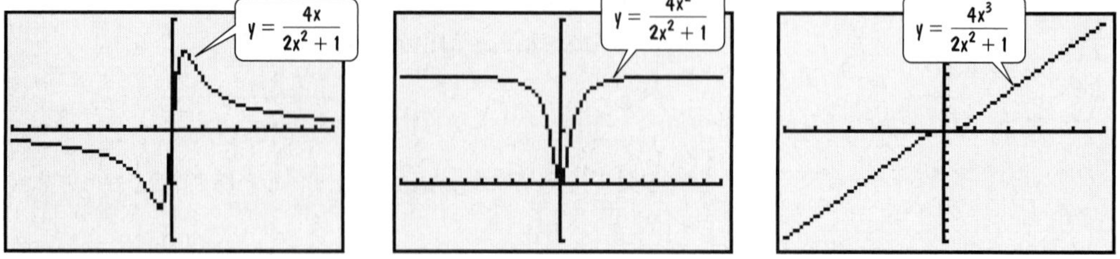


(a) The horizontal asymptote of the graph is $y = 0$.

(b) The horizontal asymptote of the graph is $y = 2$.

(c) The graph has no horizontal asymptote.

**Figure 3.27**

**Check Point 3** Find the horizontal asymptote, if any, of the graph of each rational function.

**a.** $f(x) = \dfrac{9x^2}{3x^2 + 1}$ **b.** $g(x) = \dfrac{9x}{3x^2 + 1}$ **c.** $h(x) = \dfrac{9x^3}{3x^2 + 1}$

**5** Graph rational functions.

## Graphing Rational Functions

Here are some suggestions for graphing rational functions.

**Strategy for Graphing a Rational Function**

Suppose that

$$f(x) = \frac{p(x)}{q(x)}$$

where $p(x)$ and $q(x)$ are polynomial functions with no common factors.

1. Determine whether the graph of $f$ has symmetry.
$$f(-x) = f(x)\text{: } y\text{-axis symmetry}$$
$$f(-x) = -f(x)\text{: origin symmetry}$$
2. Find the $y$-intercept (if there is one) by evaluating $f(0)$.
3. Find the $x$-intercepts (if there are any) by solving the equation $p(x) = 0$.
4. Find any vertical asymptote(s) by solving the equation $q(x) = 0$.
5. Find the horizontal asymptote (if there is one) using the rule for determining the horizontal asymptote of a rational function.
6. Plot at least one point between and beyond each $x$-intercept and vertical asymptote.
7. Use the information obtained previously to graph the function between and beyond the vertical asymptotes.

### EXAMPLE 4 Graphing a Rational Function

Graph: $f(x) = \dfrac{2x}{x - 1}$.

**Solution**

**Step 1 Determine symmetry.**

$$f(-x) = \frac{2(-x)}{-x - 1} = \frac{-2x}{-x - 1} = \frac{2x}{x + 1}$$

Because $f(-x)$ does not equal $f(x)$ or $-f(x)$, the graph has neither $y$-axis nor origin symmetry.

**Step 2 Find the $y$-intercept.** Evaluate $f(0)$.

$$f(0) = \frac{2 \cdot 0}{0 - 1} = \frac{0}{-1} = 0$$

The $y$-intercept is 0, and so the graph passes through the origin.

**Step 3** **Find $x$-intercept(s).** This is done by solving $p(x) = 0$.

$$2x = 0 \quad \text{Set the numerator equal to 0.}$$
$$x = 0$$

There is only one $x$-intercept. This verifies that the graph passes through the origin.

**Step 4** **Find the vertical asymptotes(s).** Solve $q(x) = 0$, thereby finding zeros of the denominator.

$$x - 1 = 0 \quad \text{Set the denominator equal to 0.}$$
$$x = 1$$

The equation of the vertical asymptote is $x = 1$.

**Step 5** **Find the horizontal asymptote.** Because the numerator and denominator have the same degree, the equation of the horizontal asymptote is

$$y = \frac{2}{1} = 2.$$

The equation of the horizontal asymptote is $y = 2$.

**Step 6** **Plot points between and beyond each $x$-intercept and vertical asymptote.** With an $x$-intercept at 0 and a vertical asymptote at $x = 1$, we evaluate the function at $-2, -1, \frac{1}{2}, 2$, and 4.

| $x$ | $-2$ | $-1$ | $\frac{1}{2}$ | 2 | 4 |
|---|---|---|---|---|---|
| $f(x) = \frac{2x}{x-1}$ | $\frac{4}{3}$ | 1 | $-2$ | 4 | $\frac{8}{3}$ |

Figure 3.28 shows these points, the $y$-intercept, the $x$-intercept, and the asymptotes.

**Step 7** **Graph the function.** The graph of $f(x) = \frac{2x}{x-1}$ is shown in Figure 3.29.

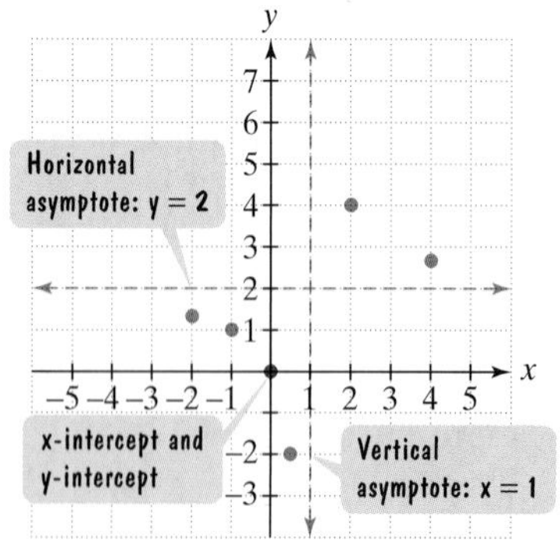


**Figure 3.28** Preparing to graph the rational function $f(x) = \frac{2x}{x-1}$

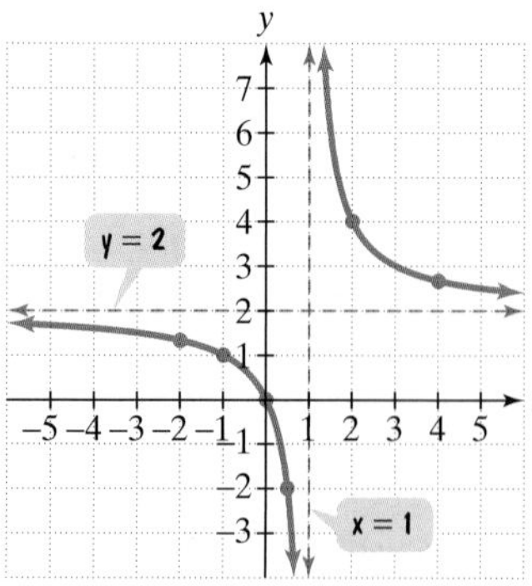


**Figure 3.29** The graph of $f(x) = \frac{2x}{x-1}$

## Technology

The graph of $y = \frac{2x}{x-1}$, obtained using the DOT mode in a $[-6, 6, 1]$ by $[-6, 6\ 1]$ viewing rectangle, verifies that our hand-drawn graph is correct.

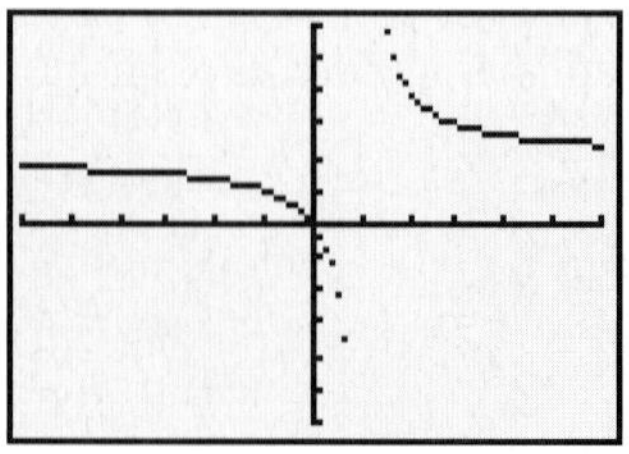

**Check Point 4** Graph: $f(x) = \frac{3x}{x-2}$.

## EXAMPLE 5 Graphing a Rational Function

Graph: $f(x) = \dfrac{3x^2}{x^2 - 4}$.

**Solution**

**Step 1 Determine symmetry:** $f(-x) = \dfrac{3(-x)^2}{(-x)^2 - 4} = \dfrac{3x^2}{x^2 - 4} = f(x)$: Symmetric with respect to the $y$-axis.

**Step 2 Find the $y$-intercept:** $f(0) = \dfrac{3 \cdot 0^2}{0^2 - 4} = \dfrac{0}{-4} = 0$: $y$-intercept is 0.

**Step 3 Find the $x$-intercept:** $3x^2 = 0$, so $x = 0$: $x$-intercepts is 0.

**Step 4 Find the vertical asymptotes:** Set $q(x) = 0$.

$$x^2 - 4 = 0 \quad \text{Set the denominator equal to 0.}$$
$$x^2 = 4$$
$$x = \pm 2$$

Vertical asymptotes: $x = -2$ and $x = 2$

**Step 5 Find the horizontal asymptote:** $y = \frac{3}{1} = 3$.

**Step 6 Plot points between and beyond the $x$-intercept and the vertical asymptotes.** With an $x$-intercept at 0 and vertical asymptotes at $x = -2$ and $x = 2$, we evaluate the function at $-3, -1, 1, 3$, and 4.

| $x$ | $-3$ | $-1$ | $1$ | $3$ | $4$ |
|---|---|---|---|---|---|
| $f(x) = \dfrac{3x^2}{x^2 - 4}$ | $\dfrac{27}{5}$ | $-1$ | $-1$ | $\dfrac{27}{5}$ | $4$ |

Figure 3.30 shows these points, the $y$-intercept, the $x$-intercept, and the asymptotes.

**Step 7 Graph the function.** The graph of $f(x) = \dfrac{3x^2}{x^2 - 4}$ is shown in Figure 3.31. The $y$-axis symmetry is now obvious.

**Technology**

The graph of $y = \dfrac{3x^2}{x^2 - 4}$ generated by a graphing utility verifies that our hand-drawn graph is correct.

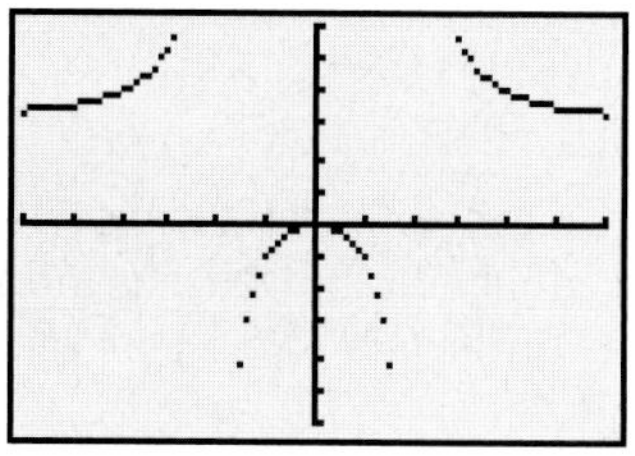

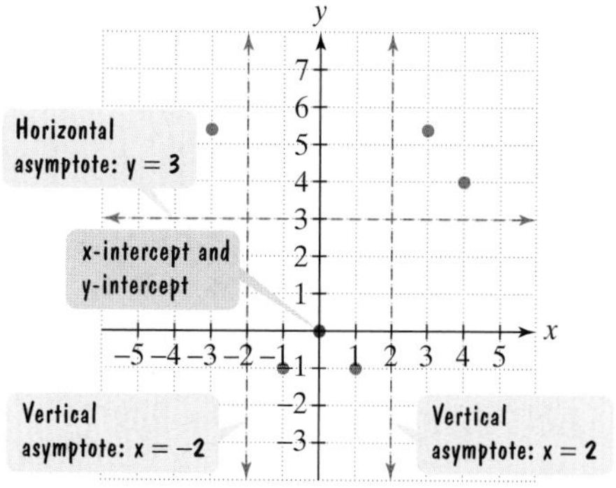


**Figure 3.30** Preparing to graph $f(x) = \dfrac{3x^2}{x^2 - 4}$

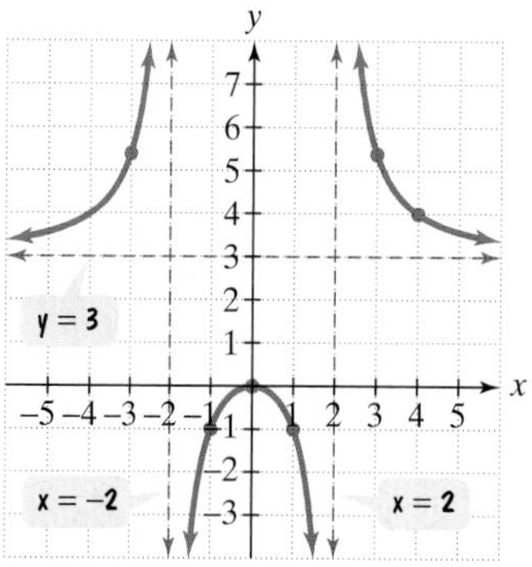


**Figure 3.31** The graph of $f(x) = \dfrac{3x^2}{x^2 - 4}$

**Check Point 5** Graph: $f(x) = \frac{2x^2}{x^2 - 9}$.

Example 6 illustrates that not every rational function has vertical and horizontal asymptotes.

## EXAMPLE 6 Graphing a Rational Function

Graph: $f(x) = \frac{x^4}{x^2 + 1}$.

### Solution

**Step 1 Determine symmetry:** $f(-x) = \frac{(-x)^4}{(-x)^2 + 1} = \frac{x^4}{x^2 + 1} = f(x)$: Symmetric with respect to the $y$-axis.

**Step 2 Find the $y$-intercept:** $f(0) = \frac{0^4}{0^2 + 1} = \frac{0}{1} = 0$: $y$-intercept is 0.

**Step 3 Find the $x$-intercept:** $x^4 = 0$, so $x = 0$: $x$-intercept is 0.

**Step 4 Find the vertical asymptote:** Set $q(x) = 0$.

$$x^2 + 1 = 0 \quad \text{Set the denominator equal to 0.}$$

$$x^2 = -1$$

Although this equation has imaginary roots ($x = \pm i$), there are no real roots. Thus, there is no vertical asymptote.

**Step 5 Find the horizontal asymptote:** Because the degree of the numerator, 4, is greater than the degree of the denominator, 2, there is no horizontal asymptote.

**Step 6 Plot points between and beyond the $x$-intercept and the vertical asymptotes.** With an $x$-intercept at 0 and no vertical asymptotes, we evaluate the function at −2, −1, 1, and 2.

| $x$ | −2 | −1 | 1 | 2 |
|---|---|---|---|---|
| $f(x) = \frac{x^4}{x^2 + 1}$ | $\frac{16}{5}$ | $\frac{1}{2}$ | $\frac{1}{2}$ | $\frac{16}{5}$ |

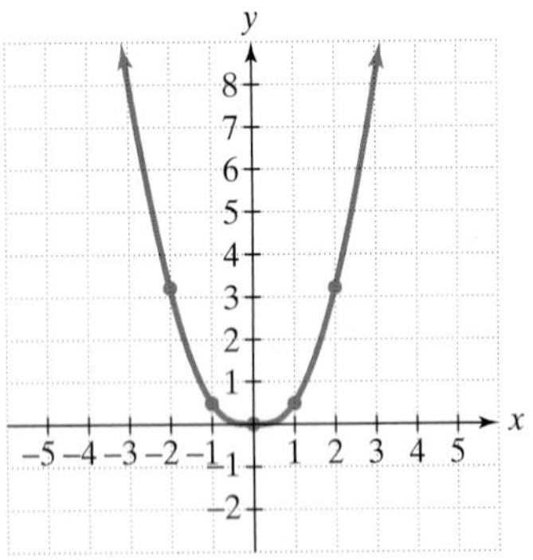


**Figure 3.32** The graph of $f(x) = \frac{x^4}{x^2 + 1}$

**Step 7 Graph the function.** Figure 3.32 shows the graph of $f$ using the points obtained from the table and $y$-axis symmetry. Notice that as $x$ approaches infinity or negative infinity ($x \to \infty$ or $x \to -\infty$), the function values, $f(x)$, are getting larger without bound $[f(x) \to \infty]$.

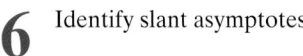

**Check Point 6** Graph: $f(x) = \dfrac{x^4}{x^2 + 2}$.

**6** Identify slant asymptotes.

## Slant Asymptotes

Examine the graph of

$$f(x) = \frac{x^2 + 1}{x - 1}$$

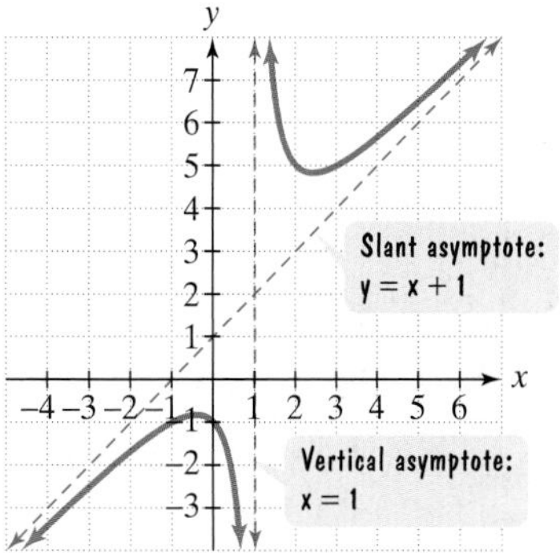


**Figure 3.33** The graph of $f(x) = \dfrac{x^2 + 1}{x - 1}$ with a slant asymptote

shown in Figure 3.33. Note that the degree of the numerator, 2, is greater than the degree of the denominator, 1. Thus, the graph of this function has no horizontal asymptote. However, the graph has a **slant asymptote**, $y = x + 1$.

**The graph of a rational function has a slant asymptote if the degree of the numerator is one more than the degree of the denominator.** The equation of the slant asymptote can be found by division. For example, to find the slant asymptote for the graph of $f(x) = \dfrac{x^2 + 1}{x - 1}$, divide $x - 1$ into $x^2 + 1$:

$$\begin{array}{r|rrr} 1 & 1 & 0 & 1 \\ & & 1 & 1 \\ \hline & 1 & 1 & 2 \end{array} \qquad x - 1 \overline{)\, x^2 + 0x + 1} \quad 1x + 1 + \frac{2}{x - 1}$$

Remainder

Observe that

$$f(x) = \frac{x^2 + 1}{x - 1} = \underbrace{x + 1}_{\text{Slant asymptote: } y = x + 1} + \frac{2}{x - 1}$$

If $|x| \to \infty$, the value of $\dfrac{2}{x - 1}$ is approximately 0. Thus, when $|x|$ is large, the function is very close to $y = x + 1 + 0$. This means that as $x \to \infty$ or as $x \to -\infty$, the graph of $f$ gets closer and closer to the line whose equation is $y = x + 1$. The line $y = x + 1$ is a slant asymptote of the graph.

In general, if $f(x) = \dfrac{p(x)}{q(x)}$ and the degree of $p$ is one greater than the degree of $q$, find the slant asymptote by dividing $q(x)$ into $p(x)$. The division will take the form

$$\frac{p(x)}{q(x)} = \underbrace{mx + b}_{\text{Slant asymptote: } y = mx + b} + \frac{\text{remainder}}{q(x)}.$$

The equation of the slant asymptote is $y = mx + b$.

## EXAMPLE 7 Finding the Slant Asymptote of a Rational Function

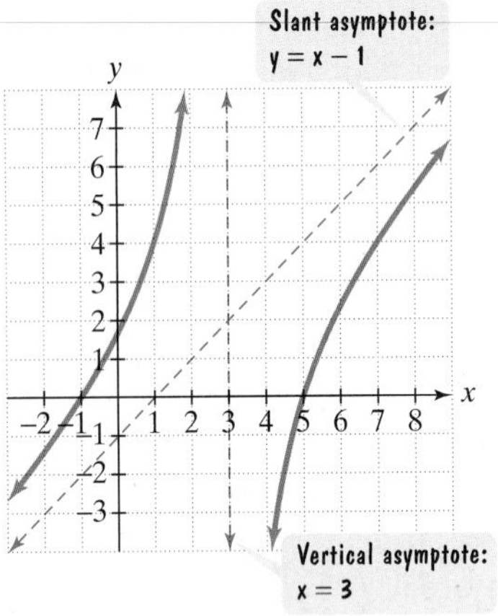


**Figure 3.34** The graph of $f(x) = \frac{x^2 - 4x - 5}{x - 3}$

Find the slant asymptote of $f(x) = \frac{x^2 - 4x - 5}{x - 3}$.

**Solution** Because the degree of the numerator, 2, is exactly one more than the degree of the denominator, 1, the graph of $f$ has a slant asymptote. To find the equation of the slant asymptote, divide $x - 3$ into $x^2 - 4x - 5$:

$$\begin{array}{r|rrr} 3 & 1 & -4 & -5 \\ & & 3 & -3 \\ \hline & 1 & -1 & -8 \end{array} \qquad 1x - 1 - \frac{8}{x-3} \text{ over } x - 3\overline{)x^2 - 4x - 5}$$

Remainder

The equation of the slant asymptote is $y = x - 1$. Using our strategy for graphing rational functions, the graph of $f(x) = \frac{x^2 - 4x - 5}{x - 3}$ is shown in Figure 3.34.

**Check Point 7** Find the slant asymptote of $f(x) = \frac{2x^2 - 5x + 7}{x - 2}$.

**7** Solve applied problems involving rational functions.

## Applications

There are numerous examples of asymptotic behavior in functions that describe real-world phenomena.

## EXAMPLE 8 Average Cost of Producing a Wheelchair

A company that manufactures wheelchairs has costs given by the function

$$C(x) = 400x + 500{,}000$$

where $x$ is the number of wheelchairs produced per month and $C(x)$ is measured in dollars. The average cost per wheelchair for the company is given by

$$\bar{C}(x) = \frac{400x + 500{,}000}{x}.$$

**a.** Find and interpret $\bar{C}(1000)$, $\bar{C}(10{,}000)$, and $\bar{C}(100{,}000)$.

**b.** What is the horizontal asymptote for the average cost function, $\bar{C}(x)$? Describe what this represents for the company.

**Solution**

**a.** $\bar{C}(1000) = \frac{400(1000) + 500{,}000}{1000} = 900$

The average cost per wheelchair of producing 1000 wheelchairs per month is $900.00.

$\bar{C}(10{,}000) = \frac{400(10{,}000) + 500{,}000}{10{,}000} = 450$

The average cost per wheelchair of producing 10,000 wheelchairs per month is $450.

$$\bar{C}(100{,}000) = \frac{400(100{,}000) + 500{,}000}{100{,}000} = 405$$

The average cost per wheelchair of producing 100,000 wheelchairs per month is \$405. Notice that with higher production levels, the cost of producing each wheelchair decreases.

**b.** We are given the average cost function

$$\bar{C}(x) = \frac{400x + 500{,}000}{x}$$

in which the degree of the numerator, 1, is equal to the degree of the denominator, 1. The leading coefficients of the numerator and denominator, 400 and 1, are used to obtain the equation of the horizontal asymptote. The equation of the horizontal asymptote is

$$y = \frac{400}{1} \quad \text{or} \quad y = 400.$$

The horizontal asymptote is shown in Figure 3.35. This means that the more wheelchairs produced per month, the closer the average cost per wheelchair for the company comes to \$400. The least possible cost per wheelchair is approaching \$400. Competitively low prices take place with high production levels, posing a major problem for small businesses.

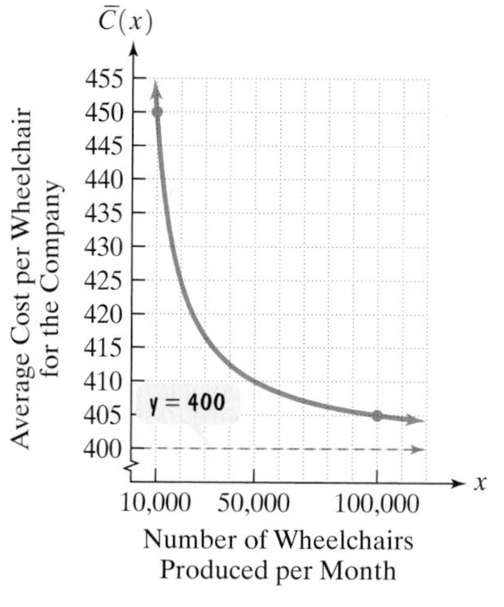


**Figure 3.35** As production level increases, the average cost per wheelchair approaches \$400.

**Check Point 8**

A company that manufactures running shoes has costs given by the function $C(x) = 30x + 300{,}000$, where $x$ is the number of pairs of shoes produced per week and $C(x)$ is measured in dollars. The average cost per pair for the company is given by

$$\bar{C}(x) = \frac{30x + 300{,}000}{x}.$$

**a.** Find and interpret $\bar{C}(1000)$, $\bar{C}(10{,}000)$, and $\bar{C}(100{,}000)$.

**b.** What is the horizontal asymptote for the average cost function, $\bar{C}(x)$? Describe what this represents for the company.

If an object moves at an average velocity, $v$, the distance, $s$, covered in time $t$ is given by the formula

$$s = vt.$$

Thus, *distance* $=$ *velocity* $\cdot$ *time*. Objects that move in accordance with this formula are said to be in **uniform motion**. In Example 9, we use a rational function to model time, $t$, in uniform motion. Solving the uniform motion formula for $t$, we obtain

$$t = \frac{s}{v}.$$

Thus, time is the quotient of distance and average velocity.

## EXAMPLE 9 Time Involved in Uniform Motion

Two commuters drove to work a distance of 40 miles and then returned again on the same route. The average velocity on the return trip was 30 miles per hour faster than the average velocity on the outgoing trip. Express the total time required to complete the round trip, $T$, as a function of the average velocity on the outgoing trip, $x$.

**Solution** As specified, the average velocity on the outgoing trip is represented by $x$. Because the average velocity on the return trip was 30 miles per hour faster than the average velocity on the outgoing trip, let

$x + 30 =$ the average velocity on the return trip.

The sentence that we use as a verbal model to write our rational function is

Total time on the round trip | equals | time on the outgoing trip | plus | time on the return trip.

$$T(x) = \frac{40}{x} + \frac{40}{x+30}.$$

This is outgoing distance, 40 miles, divided by outgoing velocity, x.

This is return distance, 40 miles, divided by return velocity, x + 30.

The function that expresses the total time required to complete the round trip is

$$T(x) = \frac{40}{x} + \frac{40}{x+30}.$$

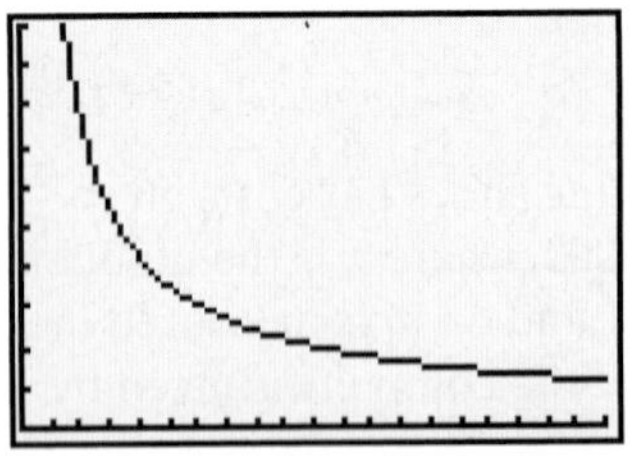

**Figure 3.36** The graph of $T(x) = \frac{40}{x} + \frac{40}{x+30}$. As average velocity increases, time for the trip decreases.

Once you have modeled a problem's conditions with a function, you can use a graphing utility to explore the function's behavior. For example, let's graph the function in Example 9. Because it seems unlikely that an average outgoing velocity exceeds 60 miles per hour with an average return velocity that is 30 miles per hour faster, we graph the function for $0 \le x \le 60$. Figure 3.36 shows the graph of $T(x) = \frac{40}{x} + \frac{40}{x+30}$ in a $[0, 60, 3]$ by $[0, 10, 1]$ viewing rectangle. Notice that the function is decreasing. This shows decreasing times with increasing average velocities. Can you see that the vertical asymptote is $x = 0$, or the $y$-axis? This indicates that close to an outgoing average velocity of zero miles per hour, the round trip will take nearly forever.

**Check Point 9**

Two commuters drove to work a distance of 20 miles and then returned again on the same route. The average velocity on the return trip was 10 miles per hour slower than the average velocity on the outgoing trip. Express the total time required to complete the round trip, $T$, as a function of the average velocity on the outgoing trip, $x$.

## EXERCISE SET 3.6

### Practice Exercises

*In Exercises 1–8, find the domain of each rational function.*

**1.** $f(x) = \dfrac{5x}{x - 4}$

**2.** $f(x) = \dfrac{7x}{x - 8}$

**3.** $g(x) = \dfrac{3x^2}{(x - 5)(x + 4)}$

**4.** $g(x) = \dfrac{2x^2}{(x - 2)(x + 6)}$

**5.** $h(x) = \dfrac{x + 7}{x^2 - 49}$

**6.** $h(x) = \dfrac{x + 8}{x^2 - 64}$

**7.** $f(x) = \dfrac{x + 7}{x^2 + 49}$

**8.** $f(x) = \dfrac{x + 8}{x^2 + 64}$

*Use the graph of the rational function in the figure shown to complete each statement in Exercises 9–14.*

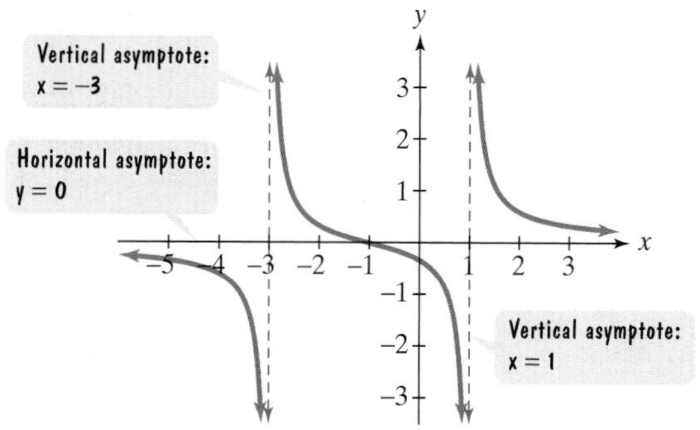


**9.** As $x \to -3^-$, $f(x) \to$ ______.

**10.** As $x \to -3^+$, $f(x) \to$ ______.

**11.** As $x \to 1^-$, $f(x) \to$ ______.

**12.** As $x \to 1^+$, $f(x) \to$ ______.

**13.** As $x \to -\infty$, $f(x) \to$ ______.

**14.** As $x \to \infty$, $f(x) \to$ ______.

*Use the graph of the rational function in the figure shown to complete each statement in Exercises 15–20.*

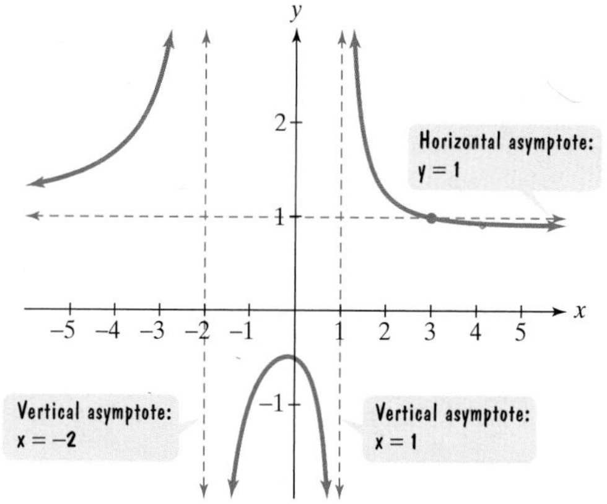


**15.** As $x \to 1^+$, $f(x) \to$ ______.

**16.** As $x \to 1^-$, $f(x) \to$ ______.

**17.** As $x \to -2^+$, $f(x) \to$ ______.

**18.** As $x \to -2^-$, $f(x) \to$ ______.

**19.** As $x \to \infty$, $f(x) \to$ ______.

**20.** As $x \to -\infty$, $f(x) \to$ ______.

*In Exercises 21–28, find the vertical asymptotes, if any, of the graph of each rational function.*

**21.** $f(x) = \dfrac{x}{x + 4}$

**22.** $f(x) = \dfrac{x}{x - 3}$

**23.** $g(x) = \dfrac{x + 3}{x(x + 4)}$

**24.** $g(x) = \dfrac{x + 3}{x(x - 3)}$

**25.** $h(x) = \dfrac{x}{x(x + 4)}$

**26.** $h(x) = \dfrac{x}{x(x - 3)}$

**27.** $r(x) = \dfrac{x}{x^2 + 4}$

**28.** $r(x) = \dfrac{x}{x^2 + 3}$

*In Exercises 29–36, find the horizontal asymptote, if any, of the graph of each rational function.*

**29.** $f(x) = \dfrac{12x}{3x^2 + 1}$ **30.** $f(x) = \dfrac{15x}{3x^2 + 1}$

**31.** $g(x) = \dfrac{12x^2}{3x^2 + 1}$ **32.** $g(x) = \dfrac{15x^2}{3x^2 + 1}$

**33.** $h(x) = \dfrac{12x^3}{3x^2 + 1}$ **34.** $h(x) = \dfrac{15x^3}{3x^2 + 1}$

**35.** $f(x) = \dfrac{-2x + 1}{3x + 5}$ **36.** $f(x) = \dfrac{-3x + 7}{5x - 2}$

*In Exercises 37–58, follow the seven steps on page 327 to graph each rational function.*

**37.** $f(x) = \dfrac{4x}{x - 2}$ **38.** $f(x) = \dfrac{3x}{x - 1}$

**39.** $f(x) = \dfrac{2x}{x^2 - 4}$ **40.** $f(x) = \dfrac{4x}{x^2 - 1}$

**41.** $f(x) = \dfrac{2x^2}{x^2 - 1}$ **42.** $f(x) = \dfrac{4x^2}{x^2 - 9}$

**43.** $f(x) = \dfrac{-x}{x + 1}$ **44.** $f(x) = \dfrac{-3x}{x + 2}$

**45.** $f(x) = -\dfrac{1}{x^2 - 4}$ **46.** $f(x) = -\dfrac{2}{x^2 - 1}$

**47.** $f(x) = \dfrac{2}{x^2 + x - 2}$ **48.** $f(x) = \dfrac{-2}{x^2 - x - 2}$

**49.** $f(x) = \dfrac{2x^2}{x^2 + 4}$ **50.** $f(x) = \dfrac{4x^2}{x^2 + 1}$

**51.** $f(x) = \dfrac{x + 2}{x^2 + x - 6}$ **52.** $f(x) = \dfrac{x - 4}{x^2 - x - 6}$

**53.** $f(x) = \dfrac{x^4}{x^2 + 2}$ **54.** $f(x) = \dfrac{2x^4}{x^2 + 1}$

**55.** $f(x) = \dfrac{x^2 + x - 12}{x^2 - 4}$ **56.** $f(x) = \dfrac{x^2}{x^2 + x - 6}$

**57.** $f(x) = \dfrac{3x^2 + x - 4}{2x^2 - 5x}$ **58.** $f(x) = \dfrac{x^2 - 4x + 3}{(x + 1)^2}$

*In Exercises 59–66,* **a.** *Find the slant asymptote of the graph of each rational function and* **b.** *Follow the seven-step strategy and use the slant asymptote to graph each rational function.*

**59.** $f(x) = \dfrac{x^2 - 1}{x}$ **60.** $f(x) = \dfrac{x^2 - 4}{x}$

**61.** $f(x) = \dfrac{x^2 + 1}{x}$ **62.** $f(x) = \dfrac{x^2 + 4}{x}$

**63.** $f(x) = \dfrac{x^2 + x - 6}{x - 3}$ **64.** $f(x) = \dfrac{x^2 - x + 1}{x - 1}$

**65.** $f(x) = \dfrac{x^3 + 1}{x^2 + 2x}$ **66.** $f(x) = \dfrac{x^3 - 1}{x^2 - 9}$

## Application Exercises

**67.** A company that manufactures small canoes has costs given by the function $C(x) = 20x + 20{,}000$, where $x$ is the number of canoes manufactured and $C(x)$ is measured in dollars. The average cost to manufacture each canoe is given by

$$\bar{C}(x) = \frac{20x + 20{,}000}{x}.$$

**a.** Find the average cost per canoe when $x = 100, 1000, 10{,}000$, and $100{,}000$.

**b.** What is the horizontal asymptote for the function $\bar{C}$, and what does it represent?

**68.** A company that manufactures bicycles has costs given by the function $C(x) = 100x + 100{,}000$, where $x$ is the number of bicycles manufactured and $C(x)$ is measured in dollars. The average cost to manufacture each bicycle is given by

$$\bar{C}(x) = \frac{100x + 100{,}000}{x}.$$

**a.** Find and interpret $\bar{C}(500)$, $\bar{C}(1000)$, $\bar{C}(2000)$, and $\bar{C}(4000)$.

**b.** What is the horizontal asymptote for the function $\bar{C}$? Describe what this means in practical terms.

**69.** The cost, in dollars, of removing $p$ percent of the air pollutants in the smokestack emission of a utility company that burns coal to generate electricity is given by

$$C(p) = \frac{60{,}000p}{100 - p}.$$

**a.** Current law requires that the company remove 80% of the pollutants from its smokestack emissions. A new law before the legislature would require increasing this amount by 5%. How much will it cost to remove another 5% of the pollutants?

**b.** Does this function indicate the possibility of removing 100% of the pollutants? Explain.

**70.** The rational function

$$C(x) = \frac{130x}{100 - x}, \quad 0 \le x < 100,$$

describes the cost $C$, in millions of dollars, to inoculate $x$% of the population against a particular strain of flu.

**a.** Find and interpret $C(80) - C(40)$.

**b.** Graph the function.

**c.** Describe the practical meaning of the observation that $x = 100$ is an asymptote.

**71.** The temperature, $F$, in degrees Fahrenheit, of a dessert placed in an icebox for $t$ hours is modeled by

$$F(t) = \frac{80}{t^2 + 4t + 1}.$$

**a.** Find and interpret $F(0)$.
**b.** Find the temperature of the dessert after 1 hour, 2 hours, 3 hours, 4 hours, and 5 hours.
**c.** What is the equation of the horizontal asymptote associated with this function? Describe what this means in terms of the dessert's temperature over time.
**d.** Graph the function.

**72.** The function $f(x) = \dfrac{72{,}900}{100x^2 + 729}$ models the percentage of people in the United States who are unemployed as a function of years of education, $x$.
**a.** Find and interpret $f(0)$.
**b.** Find and interpret $f(20)$.
**c.** Is there an education level that leads to guaranteed employment? If not, how is this indicated by the equation of the horizontal asymptote associated with this function?
**d.** Graph the function.

**73.** Rational functions are often used to model how much we remember over time. In an experiment on memory, students in a language class are asked to memorize 40 vocabulary words in Latin, a language with which the students are not familiar. After studying the words for one day, the class is tested each day thereafter to see how many words they remember. The class average is taken and the results are graphed as shown on page 330.

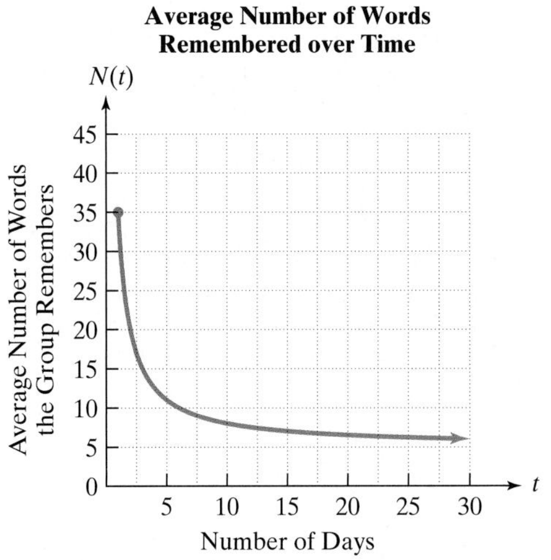


**a.** Use the graph to find a reasonable estimate of the number of Latin words remembered after 1 day, 5 days, and 15 days.
**b.** The function that models the number of Latin words remembered by the students after $t$ days is given by

$$N(t) = \frac{5t + 30}{t}, \quad \text{where } t \geq 1.$$

Find $N(1)$, $N(5)$, and $N(15)$, comparing these values with your estimates from part (a).
**c.** What does the graph indicate about the number of Latin words remembered by the group over time?
**d.** Use the function in part (b) to find the horizontal asymptote for the graph. Describe what this horizontal asymptote means in terms of the variables modeled in this situation.

**74.** A drug is injected into a patient and the concentration of the drug in the bloodstream is monitored. The drug's concentration, $C(t)$, in milligrams per liter, after $t$ hours is modeled by

$$C(t) = \frac{5t}{t^2 + 1}.$$

The graph of this rational function, obtained with a graphing utility, is shown in the figure.

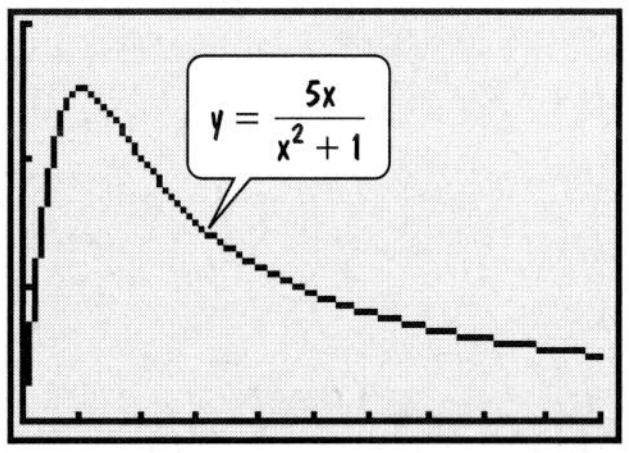


**a.** Use the graph to obtain a reasonable estimate of the drug's concentration after 3 hours. Then verify this estimate algebraically.
**b.** Use the function's equation to find the horizontal asymptote for the graph. Describe what this means about the drug's concentration in the patient's bloodstream as time increases.

*Exercises 75–78 involve writing functions that model a problem's conditions.*

**75.** You drive from your home to a vacation resort 600 miles away. You return on the same highway. The average velocity on the return trip is 10 miles per hour slower than the average velocity on the outgoing trip. Express the total time required to complete the round trip, $T$, as a function of the average velocity on the outgoing trip, $x$.

**76.** A tourist drives 90 miles along a scenic highway and then takes a 5-mile walk along a hiking trail. The average velocity driving is nine times that while hiking. Express the total time for driving and hiking, $T$, as a function of the average velocity on the hike, $x$.

**77.** A contractor is constructing the house shown in the figure. The cross section up to the roof is in the shape of a rectangle. The area of the rectangular floor of the house is 2500 square feet. Express the perimeter of the rectangular floor, $P$, as a function of the width of the rectangle, $x$.

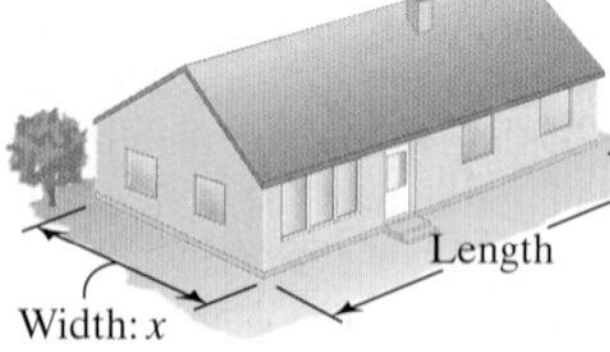


**78.** The figure shows a page with 1-inch margins at the top and the bottom and half-inch side margins. A publishing company is willing to vary the page dimensions subject to the condition that the printed area of the page is 50 square inches. Express the total area of the page, $A$, as a function of the width of the rectangle containing the print, $x$.

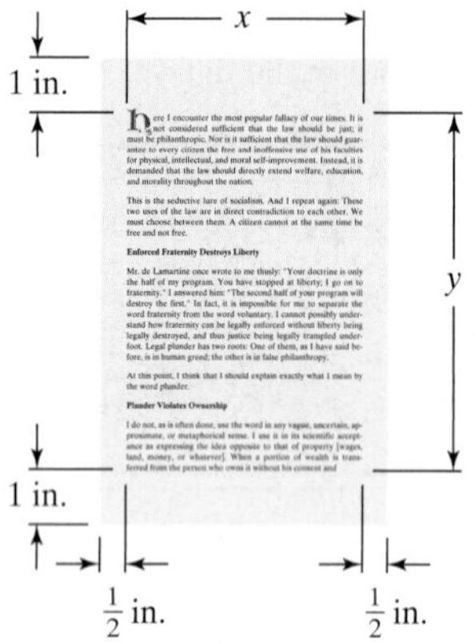


## Writing in Mathematics

**79.** What is a rational function?

**80.** Use everyday language to describe the graph of a rational function $f$ such that $f(x) \to 3$ as $x \to -\infty$.

**81.** Use everyday language to describe the behavior of a graph near its vertical asymptote if $f(x) \to \infty$ as $x \to -2^-$ and $f(x) \to -\infty$ as $x \to -2^+$.

**82.** If you are given the equation of a rational function, explain how to find the vertical asymptotes, if any, of the function's graph.

**83.** If you are given the equation of a rational function, explain how to find the horizontal asymptote, if any, of the function's graph.

**84.** Describe how to graph a rational function.

**85.** If you are given the equation of a rational function, how can you tell if the graph has a slant asymptote? If it does, how do you find its equation?

**86.** Is every rational function a polynomial function? Why or why not? Does a true statement result if the two adjectives rational and polynomial are reversed? Explain.

**87.** The function $f(x) = \frac{5000x}{x^2 + 36}$ describes the population density, $f(x)$, in people per square mile in a large city $x$ miles from the city's center. Describe what eventually happens to the population density as the distance from the city's center increases.

## Technology Exercises

**88.** Use a graphing utility to verify any five of your hand-drawn graphs in Exercises 37–66.

**89.** Use a graphing utility to verify your hand-drawn graphs in Exercises 71–72.

**90.** Use a graphing utility to graph $y = \frac{1}{x}$, $y = \frac{1}{x^3}$, and $\frac{1}{x^5}$ in the same viewing rectangle. For odd values of $n$, how does changing $n$ affect the graph of $y = \frac{1}{x^n}$?

**91.** Use a graphing utility to graph $y = \frac{1}{x^2}$, $y = \frac{1}{x^4}$, and $y = \frac{1}{x^6}$ in the same viewing rectangle. For even values of $n$, how does changing $n$ affect the graph of $y = \frac{1}{x^n}$?

**92.** A grocery store sells 4000 cases of canned soup per year. By averaging costs to purchase soup and pay storage costs, the owner has determined that if $x$ cases are ordered at a time, the inventory cost will be

$$C(x) = \frac{10{,}000}{x} + 3x.$$

**a.** Use a graphing utility to graph the inventory function.
**b.** Use the ZOOM and TRACE features or the minimum function feature of your graphing utility to approximate the number of cases that should be ordered to minimize inventory cost. What is the minimum cost?

**93.** Graph the time-on-a-round-trip-function from Example 9 on page 334, $T(x) = \frac{40}{x} + \frac{40}{x + 30}$, in a $[0, 60, 3]$ by $[0, 10, 1]$ viewing rectangle. If the commuters would like to complete the round trip in 2 hours, use the TRACE feature to determine what the average velocity on the outgoing trip should be. Set up and solve an equation that verifies this value for the average velocity.

**94.** In Exercise 77, use a graphing utility to graph the perimeter function that you obtained. A minimum perimeter for the 2500-square-foot house will reduce construction costs. Use the TRACE or minimum function feature to find the dimensions of the rectangle with the least possible perimeter.

**95.** In Exercise 78, use a graphing utility to graph the area function that you obtained. A minimum total page area containing 50 square inches of print will minimize the amount of paper that the company must use. Use the TRACE or minimum function feature to find the dimensions of the page with the least possible area.

**96.** Use a graphing utility to graph

$$f(x) = \frac{x^2 - 4x + 3}{x - 2}$$

and

$$g(x) = \frac{x^2 - 5x + 6}{x - 2}.$$

What differences do you observe between the graph of $f$ and $g$? How do you account for these differences?

## Critical Thinking Exercises

**97.** Which one of the following is true?

**a.** The graph of a rational function cannot have both a vertical and a horizontal asymptote.

**b.** It is not possible to have a rational function whose graph has no $y$-intercept.

**c.** The graph of a rational function can have three horizontal asymptotes.

**d.** The graph of a rational function can never cross a vertical asymptote.

**98.** Which one of the following is true?

**a.** The function $f(x) = \frac{1}{\sqrt{x - 3}}$ is a rational function.

**b.** The $x$-axis is a horizontal asymptote for the graph of $f(x) = \frac{4x - 1}{x + 3}$.

**c.** The number of televisions that a company can produce per week after $t$ weeks of production is given by

$$N(t) = \frac{3000t^2 + 30{,}000t}{t^2 + 10t + 25}.$$

Using this model, the company will eventually be able to produce 30,000 televisions in a single week.

**d.** None of the given statements is true.

*In Exercises 99–102, write the equation of a rational function $f(x) = \frac{p(x)}{q(x)}$ having the indicated properties, in which the degrees of $p$ and $q$ are as small as possible. More than one correct function may be possible. Graph your function using a graphing utility to verify that it has the required properties.*

**99.** $f$ has a vertical asymptote given by $x = 3$, a horizontal asymptote $y = 0$, $y$-intercept $= -1$, and no $x$-intercept.

**100.** $f$ has vertical asymptotes given by $x = -2$ and $x = 2$, a horizontal asymptote $y = 2$, $y$-intercept $= \frac{9}{2}$, $x$-intercepts of $-3$ and 3, and $y$-axis symmetry.

**101.** $f$ has a vertical asymptote given by $x = 1$, a slant asymptote whose equation is $y = x$, $y$-intercept $= 2$, and $x$-intercepts of $-1$ and 2.

**102.** $f$ has no vertical, horizontal, or slant asymptotes, and no $x$-intercepts.

## Group Exercise

**103.** Group members make up the sales team for a company that makes computer video games. It has been determined that the rational function

$$f(x) = \frac{200x}{x^2 + 100}$$

models the monthly sales, in thousands of games, of a new video game as a function of the number of months, $x$, after the game is introduced. The figure shows the graph of the function. What are the team's recommendations to the company in terms of how long the video game should be on the market before another new video game is introduced? What other factors might members want to take into account in terms of the recommendations? What will eventually happen to sales, and how is this indicated by the graph? What does this have to do with a horizontal asymptote? What could the company do to change the behavior of this function and continue generating sales? Would this be cost effective?

**Monthly Sales of a New Video Game**

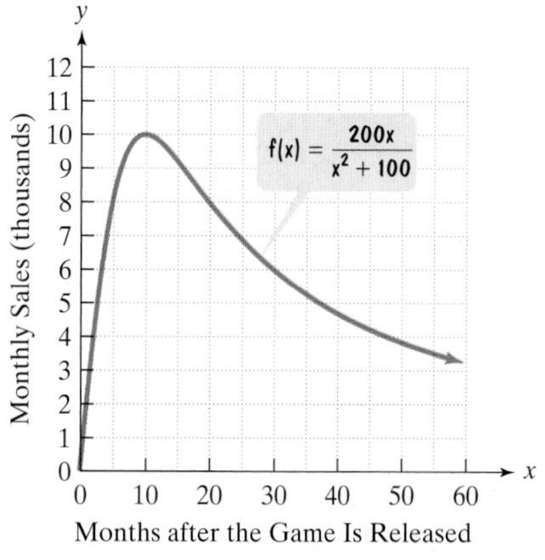

# SECTION 3.7 *Modeling Using Variation*

## Objectives

1. Solve direct variation problems.
2. Solve inverse variation problems.
3. Solve combined variation problems.
4. Solve problems involving joint variation.

Have you ever wondered how telecommunication companies estimate the number of phone calls expected per day between two cities? The formula

$$N = \frac{400P_1P_2}{d^2}$$

shows that the daily number of phone calls, $N$, increases as the populations of the cities, $P_1$ and $P_2$, in thousands, increase and decreases as the distance, $d$, between the cities increases.

Certain formulas occur so frequently in applied situations that they are given special names. Variation formulas show how one quantity changes in relation to other quantities. Quantities can vary *directly*, *inversely*, or *jointly*. In this section, we look at situations that can be modeled by each of these kinds of variation. And think of this: The next time you get one of those "all-circuits-are-busy" messages, you will be able to use a variation formula to estimate how many other callers you're competing with for those precious 5-cent minutes.

**1** Solve direct variation problems.

## Direct Variation

Because light travels faster than sound, during a thunderstorm we see lightning before we hear thunder. The formula

$$d = 1080t$$

describes the distance, in feet, of the storm's center if it takes $t$ seconds to hear thunder after seeing lightning. Thus,

If $t = 1$, $d = 1080 \cdot 1 = 1080$: If it takes 1 second to hear thunder, the storm's center is 1080 feet away.

If $t = 2$, $d = 1080 \cdot 2 = 2160$: If it takes 2 seconds to hear thunder, the storm's center is 2160 feet away.

If $t = 3$, $d = 1080 \cdot 3 = 3240$: If it takes 3 seconds to hear thunder, the storm's center is 3240 feet away.

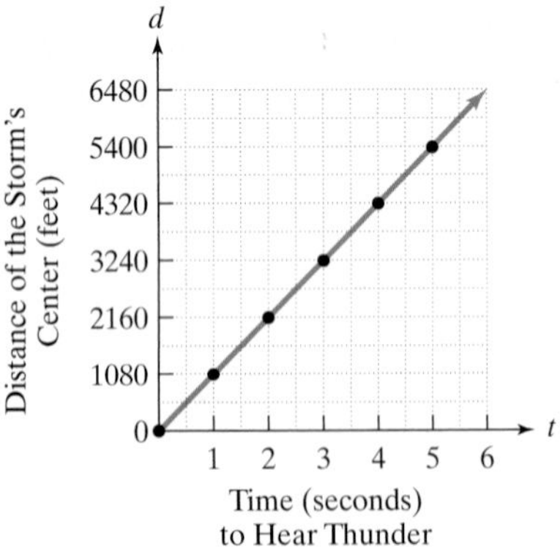


The graph of $d = 1080t$. Distance to a storm's center varies directly as the time it takes to hear thunder.

As the formula $d = 1080t$ illustrates, the distance to the storm's center is a constant multiple of how long it takes to hear the thunder. When the time is doubled, the storm's distance is doubled; when the time is tripled, the storm's distance is tripled; and so on. Because of this, the distance is said to **vary directly** as the time. The **equation of variation** is

$$d = 1080t.$$

Generalizing, we obtain the following statement.

**Direct Variation**

If a situation is described by an equation in the form

$$y = kx$$

where $k$ is a constant, we say that ***y* varies directly as *x***. The number $k$ is called the **constant of variation**.

Problems involving direct variation can be solved using the following procedure. This procedure applies to direct variation problems as well as to the other kinds of variation problems that we will discuss.

**Solving Variation Problems**

1. Write an equation that describes the given English statement.
2. Substitute the given pair of values into the equation in step 1 and find the value of $k$.
3. Substitute the value of $k$ into the equation in step 1.
4. Use the equation from step 3 to answer the problem's question.

## EXAMPLE 1 Solving a Direct Variation Problem

The amount of garbage, $G$, varies directly as the population, $P$. Allegheny County, Pennsylvania, has a population of 1.3 million and creates 26 million pounds of garbage each week. Find the weekly garbage produced by New York City with a population of 7.3 million.

### Solution

**Step 1 Write an equation.** We know that $y$ varies directly as $x$ is expressed as

$$y = kx.$$

By changing letters, we can write an equation that describes the following English statement: Garbage production, $G$, varies directly as the population, $P$.

$$G = kP$$

**Step 2 Use the given values to find *k*.** Allegheny County has a population of 1.3 million and creates 26 million pounds of garbage weekly. Substitute 26 for $G$ and 1.3 for $P$ in the direct variation equation. Then solve for $k$.

$$G = kP$$

$$26 = k \cdot 1.3$$

$$\frac{26}{1.3} = \frac{k \cdot 1.3}{1.3} \quad \text{Divide both sides by 1.3.}$$

$$20 = k \quad \text{Simplify.}$$

**Step 3 Substitute the value of *k* into the equation.**

$$G = kP \quad \text{Use the equation from step 1.}$$

$$G = 20P \quad \text{Replace } k \text{, the constant of variation, with 20.}$$

**Step 4 Answer the problem's question.** New York City has a population of 7.3 million. To find its weekly garbage production, substitute 7.3 for $P$ in $G = 20P$ and solve for $G$.

$$G = 20P \quad \text{Use the equation from step 3.}$$
$$G = 20(7.3) \quad \text{Substitute 7.3 for } P.$$
$$G = 146$$

The weekly garbage produced by New York City weighs approximately 146 million pounds.

**Check Point 1** The pressure, $P$, of water on an object below the surface varies directly as its distance, $D$, below the surface. If a submarine experiences a pressure of 25 pounds per square inch 60 feet below the surface, how much pressure will it experience 330 feet below the surface?

The direct variation equation $y = kx$ is a linear function. If $k > 0$, then the slope of the line is positive. Consequently, as $x$ increases, $y$ also increases.

A direct variation situation can involve variables to higher powers. For example, $y$ can vary directly as $x^2$ $(y = kx^2)$ or as $x^3$ $(y = kx^3)$.

### Direct Variation With Powers

***y* varies directly as the *n*th power of *x*** if there exists some nonzero constant $k$ such that

$$y = kx^n.$$

Direct variation with powers is modeled by polynomial functions. In our next example, the graph of the variation equation is the familiar parabola.

## EXAMPLE 2 Solving a Direct Variation Problem

The distance, $s$, that a body falls from rest varies directly as the square of the time, $t$, of the fall. If skydivers fall 64 feet in 2 seconds, how far will they fall in 4.5 seconds?

### Solution

**Step 1 Write an equation.** We know that $y$ varies directly as the square of $x$ is expressed as

$$y = kx^2.$$

By changing letters, we can write an equation that describes the following English statement: Distance, $s$, varies directly as the square of time, $t$, of the fall.

$$s = kt^2$$

**Step 2 Use the given values to find $k$.** Skydivers fall 64 feet in 2 seconds. Substitute 64 for $s$ and 2 for $t$ in the direct variation equation. Then solve for $k$.

$$s = kt^2$$
$$64 = k \cdot 2^2$$
$$64 = 4k$$
$$\frac{64}{4} = \frac{4k}{4}$$
$$16 = k$$

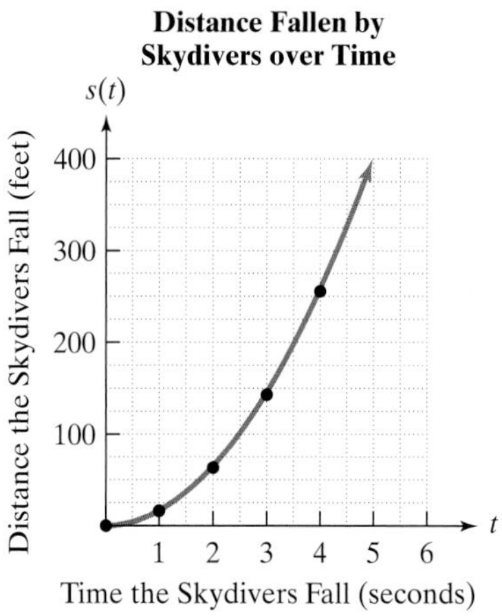


**Figure 3.37** The graph of $s(t) = 16t^2$

**Step 3 Substitute the value of $k$ into the equation.**

$$s = kt^2 \quad \text{Use the equation from step 1.}$$

$$s = 16t^2 \quad \text{Replace } k\text{, the constant of variation, with 16.}$$

**Step 4 Answer the problem's question.** How far will the skydivers fall in 4.5 seconds? Substitute 4.5 for $t$ in $s = 16t^2$ and solve for $s$.

$$s = 16(4.5)^2 = 16(20.25) = 324$$

Thus, in 4.5 seconds, skydivers will fall 324 feet.

We can express the variation equation from Example 4 in function notation, writing

$$s(t) = 16t^2.$$

The distance that a body falls from rest is a function of the time, $t$, of the fall. The parabola that is the graph of this quadratic function is shown in Figure 3.37. The graph increases rapidly from left to right, showing the effects of the acceleration of gravity.

**Check Point 2** The distance required to stop a car varies directly as the square of its speed. If 200 feet are required to stop a car traveling 60 miles per hour, how many feet are required to stop a car traveling 100 miles per hour?

**2** Solve inverse variation problems.

## Inverse Variation

The distance from Atlanta, Georgia, to Orlando, Florida, is 450 miles. The time that it takes to drive from Atlanta to Orlando depends on the rate at which one drives and is given by

$$\text{Time} = \frac{450}{\text{Rate}}.$$

For example, if you average 45 miles per hour, the time for the drive is

$$\text{Time} = \frac{450}{45} = 10,$$

or 10 hours. If you ignore speed limits and average 75 miles per hour, the time for the drive is

$$\text{Time} = \frac{450}{75} = 6,$$

or 6 hours. As your rate (or speed) increases, the time for the trip decreases and vice versa.

We can express the time for the Atlanta–Orlando trip using $t$ for time and $r$ for rate:

$$t = \frac{450}{r}.$$

This equation is an example of an **inverse variation** equation. Time, $t$, **varies inversely** as rate, $r$. When two quantities vary inversely, one quantity increases as the other decreases, and vice versa.

Generalizing, we obtain the following statement.

**Inverse Variation**

If a situation is described by an equation in the form

$$y = \frac{k}{x}$$

where $k$ is a constant, we say that **$y$ varies inversely as $x$.** The number $k$ is called the **constant of variation.**

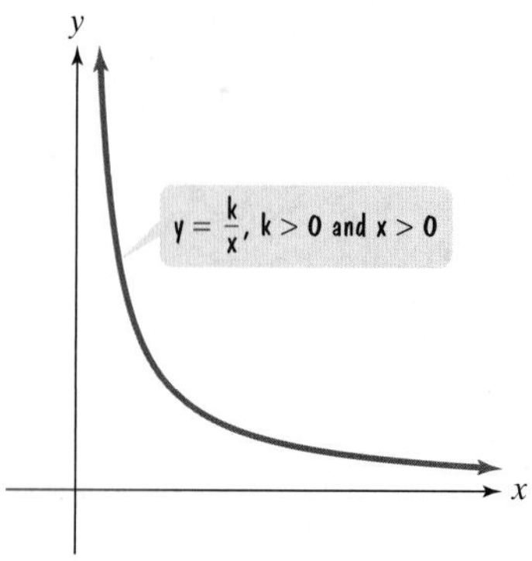


**Figure 3.38** The graph of the inverse variation equation

Notice that the inverse variation equation

$$y = \frac{k}{x}, \quad \text{or} \quad f(x) = \frac{k}{x},$$

is a rational function. For $k > 0$ and $x > 0$, the graph of the function takes on the shape shown in Figure 3.38.

We use the same procedure to solve inverse variation problems as we did to solve direct variation problems. Example 3 illustrates this procedure.

## EXAMPLE 3 Solving an Inverse Variation Problem

When you use a spray can and press the valve at the top, you decrease the pressure of the gas in the can. This decrease of pressure causes the volume of the gas in the can to increase. Because the gas needs more room than is provided in the can, it expands in spray form through the small hole near the valve. In general, if the temperature is constant, the pressure, $P$, of a gas in a container varies inversely as the volume, $V$, of the container. The pressure of a gas sample in a container whose volume is 8 cubic inches is 12 pounds per square inch. If the sample expands to a volume of 22 cubic inches, what is the new pressure of the gas?

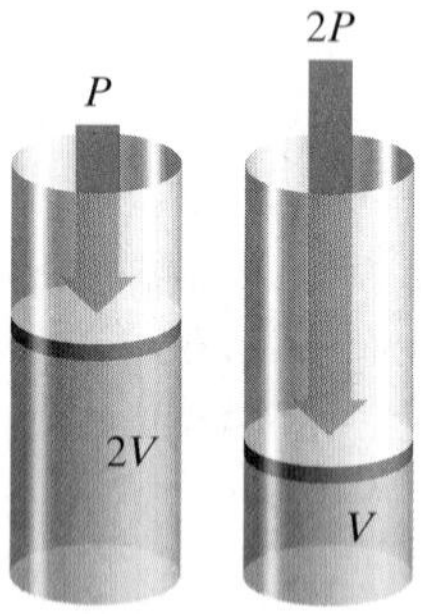


Doubling the pressure halves the volume.

**Solution**

**Step 1 Write an equation.** We know that $y$ varies inversely as $x$ is expressed as

$$y = \frac{k}{x}.$$

By changing letters, we can write an equation that describes the following English statement: The pressure, $P$, of a gas in a container varies inversely as the volume, $V$.

$$P = \frac{k}{V}.$$

**Step 2 Use the given values to find $k$.** The pressure of a gas sample in a container whose volume is 8 cubic inches is 12 pounds per square inch. Substitute 12 for $P$ and 8 for $V$ in the inverse variation equation. Then solve for $k$.

$$P = \frac{k}{V}$$

$$12 = \frac{k}{8}$$

$$12 \cdot 8 = \frac{k}{8} \cdot 8 \qquad \text{Multiply both sides by 8.}$$

$$96 = k \qquad \text{Simplify.}$$

**Step 3 Substitute the value of *k* into the equation.**

$$P = \frac{k}{V} \quad \text{Use the equation from step 1.}$$

$$P = \frac{96}{V} \quad \text{Replace } k\text{, the constant of variation, with 96.}$$

**Step 4 Answer the problem's question.** We need to find the pressure when the volume expands to 22 cubic inches. Substitute 22 for $V$ and solve for $P$.

$$P = \frac{96}{V} = \frac{96}{22} = 4\frac{4}{11}$$

When the volume is 22 cubic inches, the pressure of the gas is $4\frac{4}{11}$ pounds per square inch.

**Check Point 3** To continue making money, the number of new songs, $S$, a rock band needs to record each year varies inversely as the number of years, $N$, the band has been recording. After 4 years of recording, a band needs to record 15 new songs per year to be profitable. After 6 years, how many new songs will the band need to record in order to make a profit in the seventh year?

**3** Solve combined variation problems.

## Combined Variation

In a **combined variation** situation, direct and inverse variation occur at the same time. For example, as the advertising budget, $A$, of a company increases, its monthly sales, $S$, also increase. Monthly sales vary directly as the advertising budget:

$$S = kA.$$

By contrast, as the price of the company's product, $P$, increases, its monthly sales, $S$, decrease. Monthly sales vary inversely as the price of the product:

$$S = \frac{k}{P}.$$

We can combine these two variation equations into one combined equation:

$$S = \frac{kA}{P}.$$

The following example illustrates the application of combined variation.

### EXAMPLE 4 Solving a Combined Variation Problem

The owners of Rollerblades Now determine that the monthly sales, $S$, of its skates vary directly as its advertising budget, $A$, and inversely as the price of the skates, $P$. When \$60,000 is spent on advertising and the price of the skates is \$40, the monthly sales are 12,000 pairs of rollerblades.

**a.** Write an equation of variation that describes this situation.

**b.** Determine monthly sales if the amount of the advertising budget is increased to \$70,000.

**Solution**

**a.** Write an equation.

$$S = \frac{kA}{P}$$ Translate "sales vary directly as the advertising budget and inversely as the skates' price."

Use the given values to find $k$.

$$12{,}000 = \frac{k(60{,}000)}{40}$$ When \$60,000 is spent on advertising ($A = 60{,}000$) and the price is \$40 ($P = 40$), monthly sales are 12,000 units ($S = 12{,}000$).

$$12{,}000 = k \cdot 1500$$ Divide 60,000 by 40.

$$\frac{12{,}000}{1500} = \frac{k \cdot 1500}{1500}$$ Divide both sides of the equation by 1500.

$$8 = k$$ Simplify.

Therefore, the equation of variation that describes monthly sales is

$$S = \frac{8A}{P}.$$

**b.** The advertising budget is increased to \$70,000, so $A = 70{,}000$. The skates' price is still \$40, so $P = 40$.

$$S = \frac{8A}{P}$$ This is the equation from part (a).

$$S = \frac{8(70{,}000)}{40}$$ Substitute 70,000 for A and 40 for P.

$$S = 14{,}000$$

With a \$70,000 advertising budget and \$40 price, the company can expect to sell 14,000 pairs of rollerblades in a month (up from 12,000).

**Check Point 4** The number of minutes needed to solve an exercise set of variation problems varies directly as the number of problems and inversely as the number of people working to solve the problems. It takes 4 people 32 minutes to solve 16 problems. How many minutes will it take 8 people to solve 24 problems?

**4** Solve problems involving joint variation.

## Joint Variation

**Joint variation** is a variation in which a variable varies directly as the product of two or more other variables. Thus, the equation $y = kxz$ is read "$y$ varies jointly as $x$ and $z$."

Joint variation plays a critical role in Isaac Newton's formula for gravitation:

$$F = G\frac{m_1 m_2}{d^2}$$

The formula states that the force of gravitation, $F$, between two bodies varies jointly as the product of their masses, $m_1$ and $m_2$, and inversely as the square of the distance between them, $d$. ($G$ is the gravitational constant.) The formula indicates that gravitational force exists between any two objects in the universe, increasing as the distance between the bodies decreases. One practical result is that

the pull of the moon on the oceans is greater on the side of Earth closer to the moon. This gravitational imbalance is what produces tides.

### EXAMPLE 5 Modeling Centrifugal Force

The centrifugal force, $C$, of a body moving in a circle varies jointly with the radius of the circular path, $r$, and the body's mass, $m$, and inversely with the square of the time, $t$, it takes to move about one full circle. A 6-gram body moving in a circle with radius 100 centimeters at a rate of 1 revolution in 2 seconds has a centrifugal force of 6000 dynes. Find the centrifugal force of an 18-gram body moving in a circle with radius 100 centimeters at a rate of 1 revolution in 3 seconds.

**Solution**

$$C = \frac{krm}{t^2}$$ Translate "Centrifugal force, $C$, varies jointly with radius, $r$, and mass, $m$, and inversely with the square of time, $t$."

$$6000 = \frac{k(100)(6)}{2^2}$$ If $r = 100$, $m = 6$, and $t = 2$, then $C = 6000$.

$$40 = k$$ Solve for $k$.

$$C = \frac{40rm}{t^2}$$ Substitute 40 for $k$ in the model for centrifugal force.

$$= \frac{40(100)(18)}{3^2}$$ Find $C$ when $r = 100$, $m = 18$, and $t = 3$.

$$= 8000$$

The centrifugal force is 8000 dynes.

**Check Point 5** The volume of a cone, $V$, varies jointly as its height, $h$, and the square of its radius $r$. A cone with a radius measuring 6 feet and a height measuring 10 feet has a volume of $120\pi$ cubic feet. Find the volume of a cone having a radius of 12 feet and a height of 2 feet.

## EXERCISE SET 3.7

### Practice Exercises

*Use the four-step procedure for solving variation problems given on page 341 to solve Exercises 1–8.*

**1.** $y$ varies directly as $x$. $y = 35$ when $x = 5$. Find $y$ when $x = 12$.

**2.** $y$ varies directly as $x$. $y = 55$ when $x = 5$. Find $y$ when $x = 13$.

**3.** $y$ varies inversely as $x$. $y = 10$ when $x = 5$. Find $y$ when $x = 2$.

**4.** $y$ varies inversely as $x$. $y = 5$ when $x = 3$. Find $y$ when $x = 9$.

**5.** $y$ varies directly as $x$ and inversely as the square of $z$. $y = 20$ when $x = 50$ and $z = 5$. Find $y$ when $x = 3$ and $z = 6$.

**6.** $a$ varies directly as $b$ and inversely as the square of $c$. $a = 7$ when $b = 9$ and $c = 6$. Find $a$ when $b = 4$ and $c = 8$.

**7.** $y$ varies jointly as $x$ and $z$. $y = 25$ when $x = 2$ and $z = 5$. Find $y$ when $x = 8$ and $z = 12$.

**8.** $C$ varies jointly as $A$ and $T$. $C = 175$ when $A = 2100$ and $T = 4$. Find $C$ when $A = 2400$ and $T = 6$.

### Application Exercises

**9.** A person's fingernail length, $L$, in inches, varies directly as the number of weeks it has been growing, $W$.

**a.** Write an equation that expresses this relationship.

**b.** Fingernails grow at a rate of about 0.02 inch per week. Substitute 0.02 for $k$, the constant of variation, in the equation in part (a) and write the equation for fingernail length.

**c.** Substitute 52 for $W$ to determine your fingernail length at the end of one year if for some bizarre reason you decided not to cut them and they did not break.

**10.** A person's salary, $S$, varies directly as the number of hours worked, $h$.

**a.** Write an equation that expresses this relationship.

**b.** For a 40-hour work week, Gloria earned \$1400. Substitute 1400 for $S$ and 40 for $h$ in the equation from part (a) and find $k$, the constant of variation.

**c.** Substitute the value of $k$ into your equation in part (a) and write the equation that describes Gloria's salary in terms of the number of hours she works.

**d.** Use the equation from part (c) to find Gloria's salary for 25 hours of work.

*Use the four-step procedure for solving variation problems given on page 341 to solve Exercises 11–29.*

**11.** The cost, $C$, of an airplane ticket varies directly as the number of miles, $M$, in the trip. A 3000-mile trip costs \$400. What is the cost of a 450-mile trip?

**12.** An object's weight on the moon, $M$, varies directly as its weight on Earth, $E$. A person who weighs 55 kilograms on Earth weights 8.8 kilograms on the moon. What is the moon weight of a person who weighs 90 kilograms on Earth?

**13.** The Mach number is a measurement of speed named after the man who suggested it, Ernst Mach (1838–1916). The speed of an aircraft varies directly as its Mach number. Shown here are two aircraft. Use the figures for the Concord to determine the Blackbird's speed.

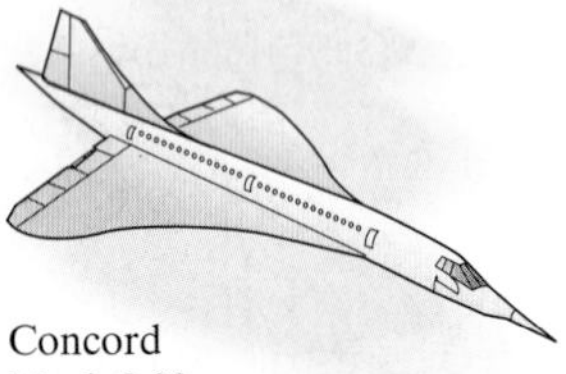

Concord
Mach 2.03
Speed = 1502.2 miles per hour

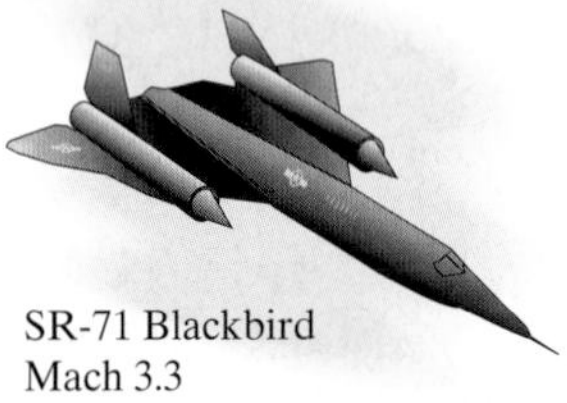

SR-71 Blackbird
Mach 3.3
Speed = ?

**14.** Do you still own records, or are you strictly a CD person? Record owners claim that the quality of sound on good vinyl surpasses that of a CD, although this is up for debate. This, however, is not debatable: The number of revolutions a record makes as it is being played varies directly as the time that it is on the turntable. A record that lasted 3 minutes made 135 revolutions. If a record takes 2.4 minutes to play, how many revolutions does it make?

**15.** If all men had identical body types, their weight would vary directly as the cube of their height. Shown is Robert Wadlow, who reached a record height of 8 feet 11 inches (107 inches) before his death at age 22. If a man who is 5 feet 10 inches tall (70 inches) with the same body type as Mr. Wadlow weighs 170 pounds, what was Robert Wadlow's weight shortly before his death?

**16.** The distance that an object falls varies directly as the square of the time it has been falling. An object falls 144 feet in 3 seconds. Find how far it will fall in 7 seconds.

**17.** The time that it takes you to get to campus varies inversely as your driving rate. Averaging 20 miles per hour in terrible traffic, it takes you 1.5 hours to get to campus. How long would the trip take averaging 60 miles per hour?

**18.** The weight that can be supported by a 2-inch by 4-inch piece of pine (called a 2-by-4) varies inversely as its length. A 10-foot 2-by-4 pine can support 500 pounds. What weight can be supported by a 125-foot 2-by-4 pine?

**19.** The volume of a gas in a container at a constant temperature varies inversely as the pressure. If the volume is 32 cubic centimeters at a pressure of 8 pounds, find the pressure when the volume is 40 cubic centimeters.

**20.** The current in a circuit varies inversely as the resistance. The current is 20 amperes when the resistance is 5 ohms. Find the current for a resistance of 16 ohms.

**21.** A person's body-mass index is used to assess levels of fatness, with an index from 20 to 26 considered in the desirable range. The index varies directly as one's weight, in pounds, and inversely as one's height, in inches. A person who weighs 150 pounds and is 70 inches tall has an index of 21. What is the body-mass index of a person who weighs 240 pounds and is 74 inches tall? Because the index is rounded to the nearest whole number, do so and then determine if this person's level of fatness is in the desirable range.

**22.** The volume of a gas varies directly as its temperature and inversely as its pressure. At a temperature of 100 Kelvin and a pressure of 15 kilograms per square meter, the gas occupies a volume of 20 cubic meters. Find the volume at a temperature of 150 Kelvin and a pressure of 30 kilograms per square meter.

**23.** The intensity of illumination on a surface varies inversely as the square of the distance of the light source from the surface. The illumination from a source is 25 foot-candles at a distance of 4 feet. What is the illumination when the distance is 6 feet?

**24.** The gravitational force with which Earth attracts an object varies inversely with the square of the distance from the center of Earth. A gravitational force of 160 pounds acts on an object 400 miles from Earth's center. Find the force of attraction on an object 6000 miles from the center of Earth.

**25.** Kinetic energy varies jointly as the mass and the square of the velocity. A mass of 8 grams and velocity of 3 centimeters per second has a kinetic energy of 36 ergs. Find the kinetic energy for a mass of 4 grams and velocity of 6 centimeters per second.

**26.** The electrical resistance of a wire varies directly as its length and inversely as the square of its diameter. A wire of 720 feet with $\frac{1}{4}$-inch diameter has a resistance of $1\frac{1}{2}$ ohms. Find the resistance for 960 feet of the same kind of wire if its diameter is doubled.

**27.** The average number of phone calls between two cities in a day varies jointly as the product of their populations and inversely as the square of the distance between them. The population of Minneapolis is 2538 thousand and the population of Cincinnati is 1818 thousand. Separated by 108 miles, the average number of telephone calls per day between the two cities is 158,233. Find the average number of telephone calls per day between Orlando, Florida (population 1225 thousand) and Seattle, Washington (population 2970 thousand), two cities that are 3403 miles apart.

**28.** The force of attraction between two bodies varies jointly as the product of their masses and inversely as the square of the distance between them. Two 1-kilogram masses separated by 1 meter exert a force of attraction of $6.67 \times 10^{-11}$ newton. What is the gravitational force exerted by Earth on a 1000-kilogram satellite orbiting at an altitude of 300 kilometers? (The mass of Earth is $5.98 \times 10^{24}$ kilograms and its radius is 6400 kilometers.)

**29.** The force of wind blowing on a window positioned at a right angle to its direction varies jointly with the area of the window and the square of the wind's speed. It is known that a wind of 30 miles per hour blowing on a window measuring 4 feet by 5 feet has a force of 150 pounds. During a storm with winds of 60 miles per hour, should hurricane shutters be placed on a window that measures 3 feet by 4 feet and is capable of withstanding 300 pounds of force?

**30.** The table of values shows the values for the current, $I$, in an electric circuit and the resistance, $R$, of the circuit.

| ***I* (amperes)** | 0.5 | 1.0 | 1.5 | 2.0 | 2.5 | 3.0 | 4.0 | 5.0 |
|---|---|---|---|---|---|---|---|---|
| ***R* (ohms)** | 12 | 6.0 | 4.0 | 3.0 | 2.4 | 2.0 | 1.5 | 1.2 |

**a.** Graph the ordered pairs in the table of values, with values of $I$ along the $x$-axis and values of $R$ along the $y$-axis. Connect the eight points with a smooth curve.
**b.** Does current vary directly or inversely as resistance? Use your graph and explain how you arrived at your answer.
**c.** Write an equation of variation for $I$ and $R$, using one of the ordered pairs in the table to find the constant of variation. Then use your variation equation to verify the other seven ordered pairs in the table.

## Writing in Mathematics

**31.** What does it mean if two quantities vary directly?

**32.** In your own words, explain how to solve a variation problem.

**33.** What does it mean if two quantities vary inversely?

**34.** Explain what is meant by combined variation. Give an example with your explanation.

**35.** Explain what is meant by joint variation. Give an example with your explanation.

*In Exercises 36–37, describe in words the variation shown by the given equation.*

**36.** $z = \dfrac{k\sqrt{x}}{y^2}$  **37.** $z = kx^2\sqrt{y}$

**38.** We have seen that the daily number of phone calls between two cities varies jointly as their populations and inversely as the square of the distance between them. This model, used by telecommunication companies to estimate the line capacities needed among various cities, is called the *gravity model*. Compare the model to Newton's formula for gravitation on page 346 and describe why the name *gravity model* is appropriate.

## Technology Exercise

**39.** Use a graphing utility to graph any three of the variation equations in Exercises 11–20. Then TRACE along each curve and identify the point that corresponds to the problem's solution.

## Critical Thinking Exercises

**40.** In a hurricane, the wind pressure varies directly as the square of the wind velocity. If wind pressure is a measure of a hurricane's destructive capacity, what happens to this destructive power when the wind speed doubles?

**41.** The illumination from a light source varies inversely as the square of the distance from the light source. If you raise a lamp from 15 inches to 30 inches over your desk, what happens to the illumination?

**42.** The heat generated by a stove element varies directly as the square of the voltage and inversely as the resistance. If the voltage remains constant, what needs to be done to triple the amount of heat generated?

**43.** Galileo's telescope brought about revolutionary changes in astronomy. A comparable leap in our ability to observe the universe took place as a result of the Hubble Space Telescope. The space telescope can see stars and galaxies whose brightness is $\frac{1}{50}$ of the faintest objects now observable using ground-based telescopes. Use the fact that the brightness of a point source, such as a star, varies inversely as the square of its distance from an observer to show that the space telescope can see about seven times farther than a ground-based telescope.

### Group Exercise

**44.** Begin by deciding on a product that interests the group because you are now in charge of advertising this product. Members were told that the demand for the product varies directly as the amount spent on advertising and inversely as the price of the product. However, as more money is spent on advertising, the price of your product rises. Under what conditions would members recommend an increased expense in advertising? Once you've determined what your product is, write formulas for the given conditions and experiment with hypothetical numbers. What other factors might you take into consideration in terms of your recommendation? How do these factor affect the demand for your product?

# CHAPTER SUMMARY, REVIEW, AND TEST

## Summary

### 3.1 Quadratic Functions

a. A quadratic function is of the form $f(x) = ax^2 + bx + c, a \neq 0$.

b. The standard form of a quadratic function is $f(x) = a(x - h)^2 + k, a \neq 0$.

c. The graph of a quadratic function is a parabola. The vertex is $(h, k)$ or $\left(-\frac{b}{2a}, f\left(-\frac{b}{2a}\right)\right)$. A procedure for graphing a parabola is given in the box on page 264.

d. A strategy for solving problems involving maximizing or minimizing quadratic functions is given in the box on page 271.

### 3.2 Polynomial Functions and Their Graphs

a. Polynomial Function of $x$ of Degree $n$: $f(x) = a_nx^n + a_{n-1}x^{n-1} + \cdots + a_2x^2 + a_1x + a_0, \quad a_n \neq 0$

b. The graphs of polynomial functions are smooth and continuous.

c. The end behavior of the graph of a polynomial function depends on the leading term, given by the Leading Coefficient Test in the box on page 280.

d. The values of $x$ for which $f(x)$ is equal to 0 are the zeros of the polynomial function $f$. These values are the roots of the polynomial equation $f(x) = 0$.

e. If $x - r$ occurs $k$ times in a polynomial function's factorization, $r$ is a repeated zero with multiplicity $k$. If $k$ is even, the graph touches the $x$-axis at $r$; if odd, it crosses the $x$-axis at $r$.

f. If $f$ is a polynomial of degree $n$, the graph of $f$ has at most $n - 1$ turning points.

g. A strategy for graphing a polynomial function is given in the box on page 284.

### 3.3 Dividing Polynomials; Remainder and Factor Theorems

a. Long division of polynomials is performed by dividing, multiplying, subtracting, bringing down the next term, and repeating this process until the degree of the remainder is less than the degree of the divisor. The details are given in the box on page 291.

b. The Division Algorithm: $f(x) = d(x)q(x) + r(x)$. The dividend is the product of the divisor and the quotient plus the remainder.

c. Synthetic division is used to divide a polynomial by $x - c$. The details are given in the box on pages 294–295.

d. The Remainder Theorem: If the polynomial $f(x)$ is divided by $x - c$, then the remainder is $f(c)$.

e. The Factor Theorem: If a polynomial function $f(x)$ is divided by $x - c$ and the remainder is zero, $c$ is a zero of $f$ and a root of $f(x) = 0$. If $c$ is a zero of $f$ or a root of $f(x) = 0$, then $x - c$ is a factor of $f(x)$.

### 3.4 Zeros of Polynomial Functions

a. The Rational Zero Theorem states that possible rational zeros of a polynomial function $= \frac{\text{Factors of the constant term}}{\text{Factors of the leading coefficient}}$. The theorem is stated in the box on page 301.

b. Descartes's Rule of Signs: The number of positive real zeros of $f$ equals the number of sign changes of $f(x)$ or is less than that number by an even integer. The number of negative real zeros of $f$ applies a similar statement to $f(-x)$.

## 3.5 More on Zeros of Polynomial Functions

a. The Upper and Lower Bound Theorem: The number $b > 0$ is an upper bound for the real roots of $f(x) = 0$ if synthetic division of $f(x)$ by $x - b$ results in no negative numbers. The number $a < 0$ is a lower bound if synthetic division by $x - a$ results in numbers that alternate in sign, counting zero entries as positive or negative.

b. The Intermediate Value Theorem: If $f(a)$ and $f(b)$ have opposite signs, there is at least one value of $c$ between $a$ and $b$ for which $f(c) = 0$.

c. Number of roots: If $f(x)$ is a polynomial of degree $n \geq 1$, then, counting multiple roots separately, the equation $f(x) = 0$ has $n$ roots.

d. If $a + bi$ is a root of $f(x) = 0$, then $a - bi$ is also a root.

e. The Linear Factorization Theorem: An $n$th-degree polynomial can be expressed as the product of $n$ linear factors. Thus,

$$f(x) = a_n(x - c_1)(x - c_2)\cdots(x - c_n).$$

## 3.6 Rational Functions and Their Graphs

a. Rational function: $f(x) = \dfrac{p(x)}{q(x)}$; $p(x)$ and $q(x)$ are polynomial functions and $q(x) \neq 0$. The domain of $f$ is the set of all real numbers excluding values of $x$ that make $q(x)$ zero.

b. Arrow notation is summarized in the box on page 323.

c. The line $x = a$ is a vertical asymptote of the graph of $f$ if $f(x)$ increases or decreases without bound as $x$ approaches $a$. Vertical asymptotes are identified using the location theorem in the box on page 324.

d. The line $y = b$ is a horizontal asymptote of the graph of $f$ if $f(x)$ approaches $b$ as $x$ increases or decreases without bound. Horizontal asymptotes are identified using the location theorem in the box on page 326.

e. A strategy for graphing rational functions is given in the box on page 327.

f. The graph of a rational functions has a slant asymptote when the degree of the numerator is one more than the degree of the denominator. The equation of the slant asymptote is found using division and ignoring the remainder term.

## 3.7 Modeling Using Variation

a.

| **English Statement** | **Equation** |
|---|---|
| $y$ varies directly as $x$. | $y = kx$ |
| $y$ varies directly as $x^n$. | $y = kx^n$ |
| $y$ varies inversely as $x$. | $y = \dfrac{k}{x}$ |
| $y$ varies inversely as $x^n$. | $y = \dfrac{k}{x^n}$ |
| $y$ varies jointly as $x$ and $z$. | $y = kxz$ |

b. A procedure for solving variation problems is given in the box on page 341.

# Review Exercises

## 3.1

*In Exercises 1–4, use the vertex and intercepts to sketch the graph of each quadratic function. Give the equation for the parabola's axis of symmetry.*

**1.** $f(x) = -2(x - 1)^2 + 3$ **2.** $f(x) = (x + 4)^2 - 2$

**3.** $f(x) = -x^2 + 2x + 3$ **4.** $f(x) = 2x^2 - 4x - 6$

**5.** The function $f(x) = 104.5x^2 - 1501.5x + 6016$ describes the death rate per year per 100,000 males, $f(x)$, for U.S. men who average $x$ hours of sleep each night. How many hours of sleep, to the nearest tenth of an hour, corresponds to the minimum death rate? What is this minimum death rate, to the nearest whole number?

**6.** A person standing close to the edge on the top of an 80-foot building throws a ball vertically upward with an initial velocity of 64 feet per second. The function $s(t) = -16t^2 + 64t + 80$ describes the ball's height above the ground, $s(t)$, in feet, $t$ seconds after it is thrown. After how many seconds does the ball reach its maximum height? What is the maximum height?

**7.** A field bordering a straight stream is to be enclosed. The side bordering the stream is not to be fenced. If 1000 yards of fencing material is to be used, what are the dimensions of the largest rectangular field that can be fenced? What is the maximum area?

**8.** An owner of a large diving boat that can hold as many as 70 people charges \$10 per passenger to groups between 15 and 20 people. If more than 20 divers charter the boat, the fee per passenger is decreased by 10¢ times the number of people in excess of 20. Find the size of the group that will maximize the boat owner's income. What is the maximum income?

## 3.2

*In Exercises 9–12, use end behavior and, if necessary, zeros to match each polynomial function with its graph on page 352.*

**9.** $f(x) = -x^3 + 12x^2 - x$

**10.** $g(x) = x^6 - 6x^4 + 9x^2$

**11.** $h(x) = x^5 - 5x^3 + 4x$

**12.** $r(x) = x^3 + 1$

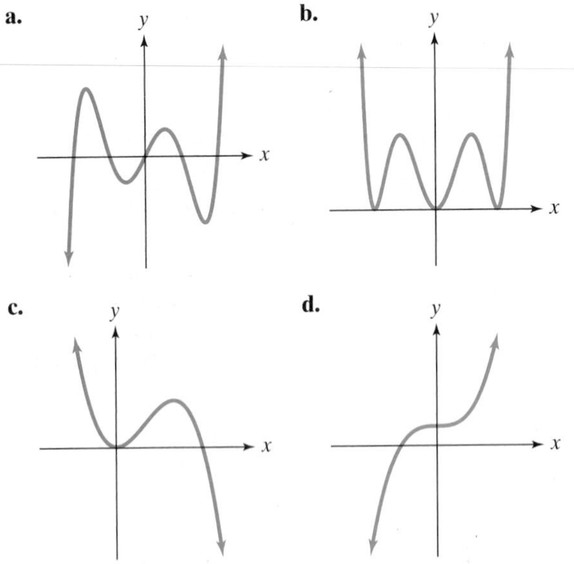


**13.** The function $f(x) = -0.0013x^3 + 0.78x^2 - 1.43x + 18.1$ models the percentage of U.S. families below the poverty level $x$ years after 1960. Use end behavior to explain why the model is valid only for a limited period of time.

**14.** Despite a combination of drugs used to inhibit the growth of the HIV virus, a patient dies as a result of the virus overwhelming his body. Could the function $N(t) = -\frac{3}{4}t^4 + 3t^3 + 5$ model the number of viral particles, in billions, in this patient's body over time? Use the graph's end behavior to the right to answer the question. Explain your answer.

*In Exercises 15–16, find the zeros for each polynomial function and give the multiplicity of each zero. State whether the graph crosses or touches the x-axis at each zero.*

**15.** $f(x) = -2(x - 1)(x + 2)^2(x + 5)^3$

**16.** $f(x) = x^3 - 5x^2 - 25x + 125$

*In Exercises 17–22,*

**a.** *Use the Leading Coefficient Test to determine the graph's end behavior.*

**b.** *Determine whether the graph has y-axis symmetry, origin symmetry, or neither.*

**c.** *Graph the function.*

**17.** $f(x) = x^3 - x^2 - 9x + 9$ **18.** $f(x) = 4x - x^3$

**19.** $f(x) = 2x^3 + 3x^2 - 8x - 12$ **20.** $f(x) = -x^4 + 25x^2$

**21.** $f(x) = -x^4 + 6x^3 - 9x^2$ **22.** $f(x) = 3x^4 - 15x^3$

## 3.3

*In Exercises 23–25, divide by long division.*

**23.** $(4x^3 - 3x^2 - 2x + 1) \div (x + 1)$

**24.** $(10x^3 - 26x^2 + 17x - 13) \div (5x - 3)$

**25.** $(4x^4 + 6x^3 + 3x - 1) \div (2x^2 + 1)$

*In Exercises 26–27, divide by synthetic division.*

**26.** $(3x^4 + 11x^3 - 20x^2 + 7x + 35) \div (x + 5)$

**27.** $(3x^4 - 2x^2 - 10x) \div (x - 2)$

**28.** Given $f(x) = 2x^3 - 7x^2 + 9x - 3$, use the Remainder Theorem to find $f(-13)$.

**29.** Use synthetic division to divide $f(x) = 2x^3 + x^2 - 13x + 6$ by $x - 2$. Use the result to find all zeros of $f$.

**30.** Solve the equation $x^3 - 17x + 4 = 0$ given that 4 is a root.

## 3.4

*In Exercises 31–32, use the Rational Zero Theorem to list all possible rational zeros for each given function.*

**31.** $f(x) = x^4 - 6x^3 + 14x^2 - 14x + 5$

**32.** $f(x) = 3x^5 - 2x^4 - 15x^3 + 10x^2 + 12x - 8$

*In Exercises 34–34, use Descartes's Rule of Signs to determine the possible number of positive and negative real zeros for each given function.*

**33.** $f(x) = 3x^4 - 2x^3 - 8x + 5$

**34.** $f(x) = 2x^5 - 3x^3 - 5x^2 + 3x - 1$

**35.** Use Descartes's Rule of Signs to explain why $2x^4 + 6x^2 + 8 = 0$ has no real roots.

*For Exercises 36–41,*

**a.** *List all possible rational roots or rational zeros.*

**b.** *Use Descartes's Rule of Signs to determine the possible number of positive and negative real roots or real zeros.*

**c.** *Use synthetic division to test the possible rational roots or zeros and find an actual root or zero.*

**d.** *Use the root or zero from part (c) to find all the zeros or roots.*

**36.** $f(x) = x^3 + 3x^2 - 4$

**37.** $f(x) = 6x^3 + x^2 - 4x + 1$

**38.** $8x^3 - 36x^2 + 46x - 15 = 0$

**39.** $x^4 - x^3 - 7x^2 + x + 6 = 0$

**40.** $4x^4 + 7x^2 - 2 = 0$

**41.** $f(x) = 2x^4 + x^3 - 9x^2 - 4x + 4$

## 3.5

**42.** Show that all real roots of the equation

$$2x^4 - 7x^3 - 5x^2 + 28x - 12 = 0$$

lie between −2 and 6. Use this result to list all possible rational roots.

**43.** Consider the equation $2x^4 - x^3 - 5x^2 + 10x + 12 = 0$.

**a.** List all possible rational roots.

**b.** Determine whether 2 is a root using synthetic division. In terms of bounds, what can you conclude?

**c.** Determine whether −2 is a root using synthetic division. In terms of bounds, what can you conclude?

**d.** Use the results of parts (b) and (c) to discard some of the possible rational roots from part (a). Now what are the possible rational roots?

*In Exercises 44–45, show that the polynomial has a zero between the given integers. Then use the Intermediate Value Theorem to find an approximation for this zero to the nearest tenth.*

**44.** $f(x) = x^3 - 2x - 1$; between 1 and 2

**45.** $f(x) = 3x^3 + 2x^2 - 8x + 7$; between $-3$ and $-2$

*In Exercises 46–48, use the given root to find the solution set of the polynomial equation.*

**46.** $4x^3 - 47x^2 + 232x + 61 = 0$; $6 + 5i$

**47.** $x^4 - 4x^3 + 16x^2 - 24x + 20 = 0$; $1 - 3i$

**48.** $2x^4 - 17x^3 + 137x^2 - 57x - 65 = 0$; $4 + 7i$

*In Exercises 49–51, find an nth-degree polynomial function with real coefficients satisfying the given conditions. If you are using a graphing utility, graph the function and verify the real zeros and the given function value.*

**49.** $n = 3$; 2 and $2 - 3i$ are zeros; $f(1) = -10$

**50.** $n = 4$; $i$ is a zero; $-3$ is a zero of multiplicity 2; $f(-1) = 16$

**51.** $n = 4$; $-2, 3$, and $1 + 3i$ are zeros; $f(2) = -40$

*In Exercises 52–53, find all the zeros of each polynomial function and write the polynomial as a product of linear factors.*

**52.** $f(x) = 2x^4 + 3x^3 + 3x - 2$

**53.** $g(x) = x^4 - 6x^3 + x^2 + 24x + 16$

*In Exercises 54–57, graphs of fifth-degree polynomial functions are shown. In each case, specify the number of real zeros and the number of nonreal complex zeros. Indicate whether there are any real zeros with multiplicity other than 1.*

**54.**

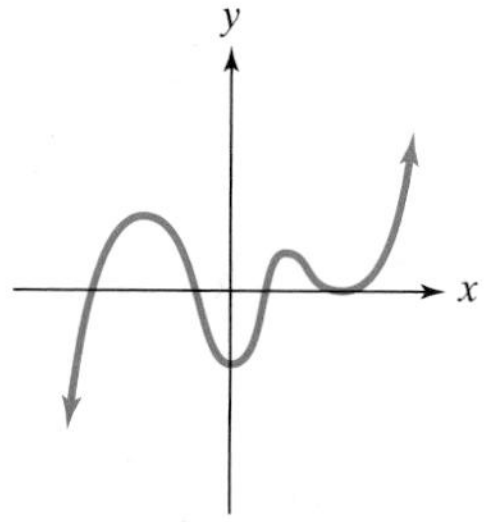


**55.**

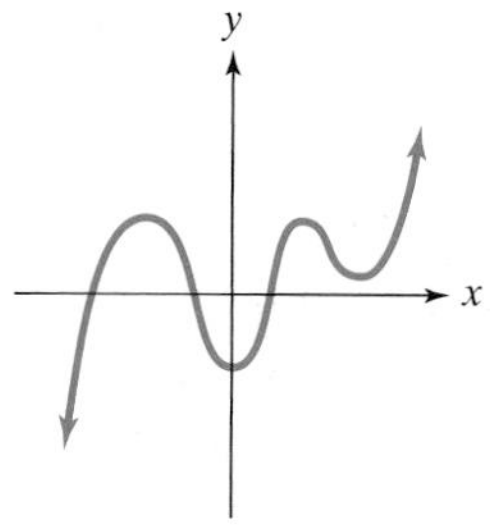


**56.**

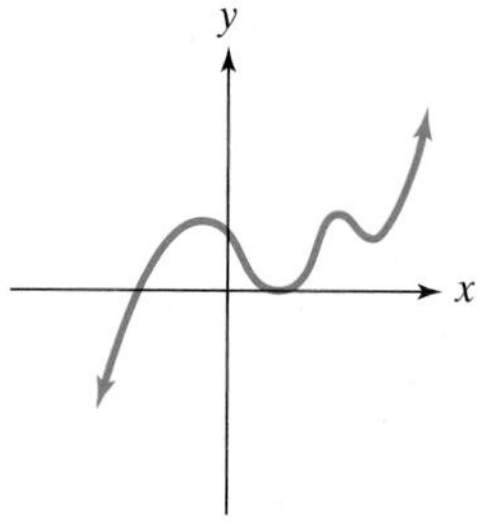


**57.**

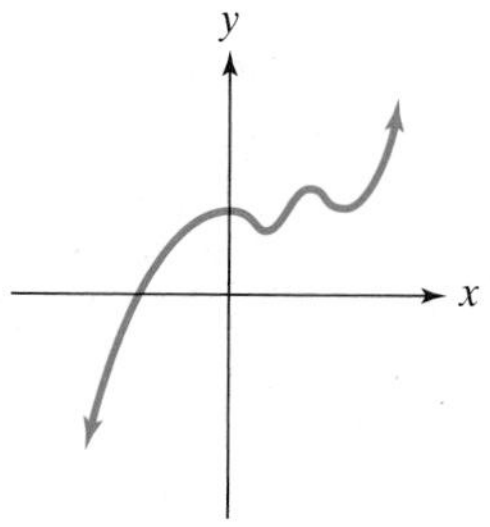


## 3.6

*In Exercises 58–65, find the vertical asymptotes, if any, the horizontal asymptote, if there is one, and the slant asymptote, if there is one, of the graph of each rational function. Then graph the rational function.*

**58.** $f(x) = \dfrac{2x}{x^2 - 9}$

**59.** $g(x) = \dfrac{2x - 4}{x + 3}$

**60.** $h(x) = \dfrac{x^2 - 3x - 4}{x^2 - x - 6}$

**61.** $r(x) = \dfrac{x^2 + 4x + 3}{(x + 2)^2}$

**62.** $y = \dfrac{x^2}{x + 1}$

**63.** $y = \dfrac{x^2 + 2x - 3}{x - 3}$

**64.** $f(x) = \dfrac{-2x^3}{x^2 + 1}$

**65.** $g(x) = \dfrac{4x^2 - 16x + 16}{2x - 3}$

**66.** A company that manufactures graphing calculators has costs given by the function $C(x) = 25x + 50{,}000$, where $x$ is the number of calculators manufactured and $C(x)$ is measured in dollars. The average cost to manufacture each calculator is given by

$$\bar{C}(x) = \frac{25x + 50{,}000}{x}.$$

**a.** Find and interpret $\bar{C}(50)$, $\bar{C}(100)$, $\bar{C}(1000)$, and $\bar{C}(100{,}000)$.

**b.** What is the horizontal asymptote for this function, and what does it represent?

**67.** In Silicon Valley, California, a government agency ordered computer-related companies to contribute to a monetary pool to clean up underground water supplies. (The companies had stored toxic chemicals in leaking underground containers.) The rational function

$$C(x) = \frac{200x}{100 - x}$$

models the cost, $C(x)$, in tens of thousands of dollars, for removing $x$ percent of the contaminants.

**a.** Find and interpret $C(90) - C(50)$.

**b.** What is the equation for the vertical asymptote? What does this mean in terms of the variables given by the function?

*Exercises 68–69 involve rational functions that model the given situations. In each case, find the horizontal asymptote as $x \to \infty$ and then describe what this means in practical terms.*

**68.** $F(x) = \dfrac{30(4 + 5x)}{1 + 0.05x}$; the number of fish, $F$, in thousands, after $x$ weeks in a lake that was stocked with 120,000 fish.

**69.** $P(x) = \dfrac{72{,}900}{100x^2 + 729}$; the percentage rate, $P$, of U.S. unemployment for groups with $x$ years of education.

**70.** In a get-tough drug policy, a politician promises to spend whatever it takes to seize all illegal drugs as they enter the country. If the cost of this venture is

$$C(p) = \frac{Ap}{100 - p}$$

where $A$ is a positive constant, $C$ is expressed in millions of dollars, and $p$ is the percentage of illegal drugs seized, use this function to evaluate the politician's promise.

**71.** A jogger ran 4 miles and then walked 2 miles. The average velocity running was 3 miles per hour faster than the average velocity walking. Express the total time for running and walking, $T$, as a function of the average velocity walking, $x$.

**72.** The area of a rectangular floor is 1000 square feet. Express the perimeter of the floor, $P$, as a function of the width of the rectangle, $x$.

## 3.7

*Solve the variation problems in Exercises 73–75.*

**73.** An electric bill varies directly as the amount of electricity used. The bill for 1400 kilowatts of electricity is \$98. What is the bill for 2200 kilowatts of electricity?

**74.** The distance that a body falls from rest varies directly as the square of the time of the fall. If skydivers fall 144 feet in 3 seconds, how far will they fall in 10 seconds?

**75.** The time it takes to drive a certain distance varies inversely as the rate of travel. If it takes 4 hours at 50 miles per hour to drive the distance, how long will it take at 40 miles per hour?

**76.** The loudness of a stereo speaker, measured in decibels, varies inversely as the square of your distance from the speaker. When you are 8 feet from the speaker, the loudness is 28 decibels. What is the loudness when you are 4 feet from the speaker?

**77.** The time required to assemble computers varies directly as the number of computers assembled and inversely as the number of workers. If 30 computers can be assembled by 6 workers in 10 hours, how long would it take 5 workers to assemble 40 computers?

**78.** The volume of a pyramid varies jointly as its height and the area of its base. A pyramid with a height of 15 feet and a base with an area of 35 square feet has a volume of 175 cubic feet. Find the volume of a pyramid with a height of 20 feet and a base with an area of 120 square feet.

# Chapter 3 Test

*In Exercises 1–2, use the vertex and intercepts to sketch the graph of each quadratic function. Give the equation for the parabola's axis of symmetry.*

**1.** $f(x) = (x + 1)^2 + 4$  **2.** $f(x) = x^2 - 2x - 3$

**3.** Determine, without graphing, whether the quadratic function $f(x) = -2x^2 + 12x - 16$ has a minimum value or a maximum value. Then find the coordinates of the minimum or the maximum point.

**4.** The function $f(x) = -x^2 + 46x - 360$ models the daily profit, $f(x)$, in hundreds of dollars, for a company that manufactures $x$ VCRs daily. How many VCRs should be manufactured each day to maximize profit? What is the maximum daily profit?

**5.** Consider the function $f(x) = x^3 - 5x^2 - 4x + 20$.

**a.** Use factoring to find all zeros of $f$.

**b.** Use the Leading Coefficient Test and the zeros of $f$ to graph the function.

**6.** Use end behavior to explain why the graph cannot be the graph of $f(x) = x^5 - x$. Then use intercepts to explain why the graph cannot represent $f(x) = x^5 - x$.

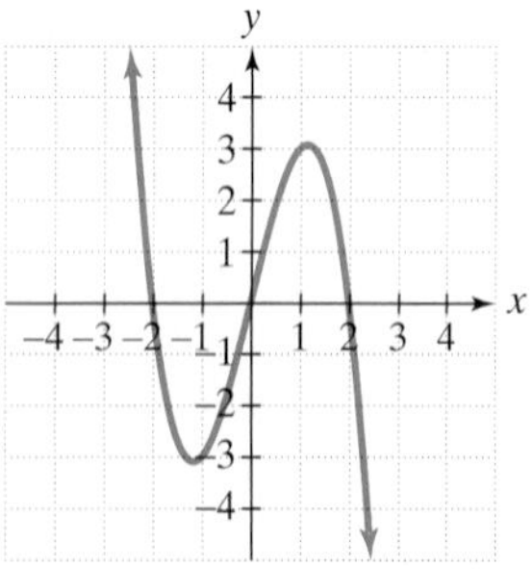

**7.** The graph of $f(x) = 6x^3 - 19x^2 + 16x - 4$ is shown in the figure at the top of the next column.

**a.** Based on the graph of $f$, find the root of the equation $6x^3 - 19x^2 + 16x - 4 = 0$ that is an integer.

**b.** Use synthetic division to find the other two roots of $6x^3 - 19x^2 + 16x - 4 = 0$.

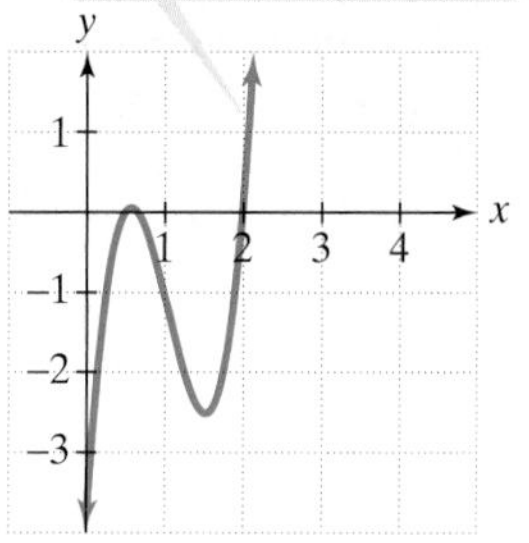


**8.** Use the Rational Zero Theorem to list all possible rational zeros of $f(x) = 2x^3 + 11x^2 - 7x - 6$.

**9.** Use Descartes's Rule of Signs to determine the possible number of positive and negative real zeros of

$$f(x) = 3x^5 - 2x^4 - 2x^2 + x - 1.$$

**10.** Solve: $x^3 + 6x^2 - x - 30 = 0$.

**11.** Consider the function whose equation is given by $f(x) = 2x^4 - x^3 - 13x^2 + 5x + 15$.

**a.** List all possible rational zeros.

**b.** Use the graph of $f$ in the figure shown and synthetic division to find all zeros of the function.

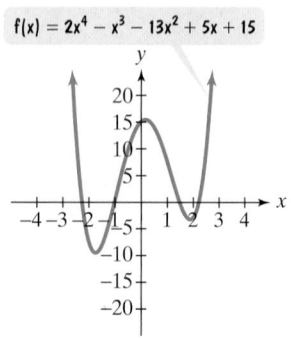

**12.** Use the graph of $f(x) = 3x^4 + 4x^3 - 7x^2 - 2x - 3$ in the figure shown to find the smallest positive integer that is an upper bound and the largest negative integer that is a lower bound for the real roots of

$$3x^4 + 4x^3 - 7x^2 - 2x - 3 = 0.$$

Then use synthetic division to show that all the real roots of the equation lie between these integers.

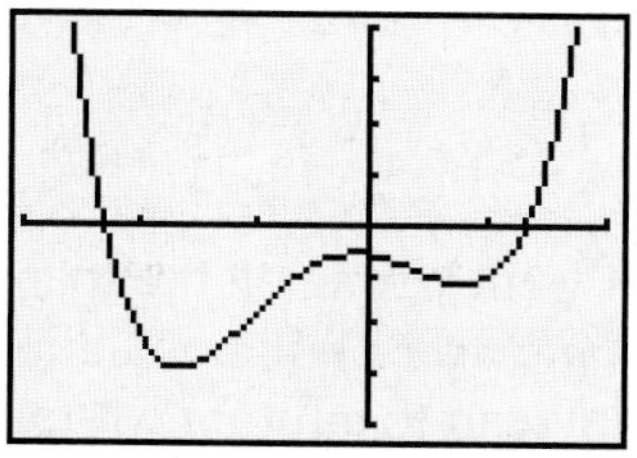

**13.** Solve $x^4 - 7x^3 + 18x^2 - 22x + 12 = 0$ given that $1 - i$ is a root.

**14.** Use the graph of $f(x) = x^3 + 3x^2 - 4$ in the figure shown to factor $x^3 + 3x^2 - 4$.

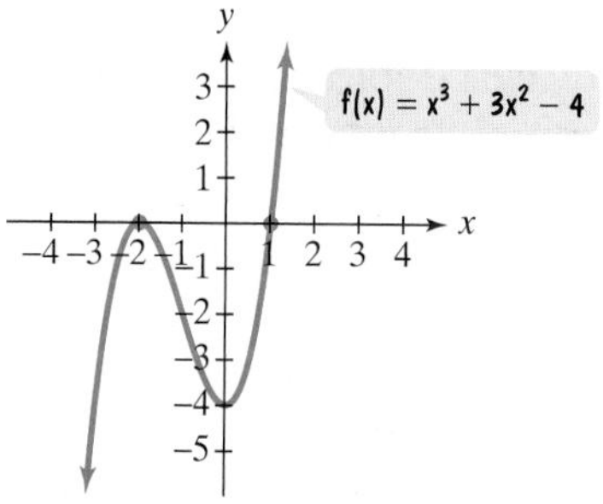


*In Exercises 15–18, find the domain of each rational function and graph the function.*

**15.** $f(x) = \dfrac{x}{x^2 - 16}$ **16.** $f(x) = \dfrac{x^2 - 9}{x - 2}$

**17.** $f(x) = \dfrac{x + 1}{x^2 + 2x - 3}$ **18.** $f(x) = \dfrac{4x^2}{x^2 + 3}$

**19.** A number of deer are placed into a newly acquired habitat. The deer population over time is modeled by a rational function whose graph is shown in the figure. Use the graph to answer each of the following questions.

**a.** How many deer were introduced into the habitat?

**b.** What is the population after 10 years?

**c.** What is the equation of the horizontal asymptote shown in the figure? What does this mean in terms of the deer population?

**Change in Deer Population over Time**

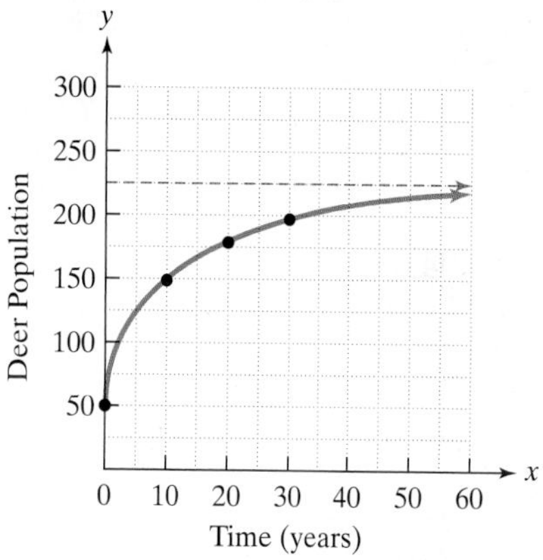


**20.** The intensity of light received at a source varies inversely as the square of the distance from the source. A particular light has an intensity of 20 foot-candles at 15 feet. What is the light's intensity at 10 feet?

## Cumulative Review Exercises (Chapters P–3)

*Simplify each expression in Exercises 1–3.*

**1.** $\dfrac{1}{2 - \sqrt{3}}$

**2.** $3(x^2 - 3x + 1) - 2(3x^2 + x - 4)$

**3.** $3\sqrt{8} + 5\sqrt{50} - 4\sqrt{32}$

**4.** Factor completely: $x^7 - x^5$.

*Solve each equation in Exercises 5–8.*

**5.** $|2x - 1| = 3$ **6.** $3x^2 - 5x + 1 = 0$

**7.** $9 + \dfrac{3}{x} = \dfrac{2}{x^2}$ **8.** $x^3 + 2x^2 - 5x - 6 = 0$

*Solve each inequality in Exercises 9–10. Express the answer in interval notation.*

**9.** $|2x - 5| > 3$ **10.** $3x^2 > 2x + 5$

**11.** Give the center and radius. Then graph the equation $x^2 + y^2 - 2x + 4y - 4 = 0$.

**12.** Solve for $t$: $V = C(1 - t)$.

**13.** If $f(x) = \sqrt{45 - 9x}$, find the domain of $f$.

*If $f(x) = x^2 + 2x - 5$ and $g(x) = 4x - 1$, find each function or function value in Exercises 14–16.*

**14.** $(f - g)(x)$ **15.** $(f \circ g)(x)$

**16.** $g(f(-3))$

**17.** Consider the function $f(x) = x^3 - 4x^2 - x + 4$.

**a.** Use factoring to find all zeros of $f$.

**b.** Use the Leading Coefficient Test and the zeros of $f$ to graph the function.

*Graph each function in Exercises 18–20.*

**18.** $f(x) = x^2 + 2x - 8$ **19.** $f(x) = x^2(x - 3)$

**20.** $f(x) = \dfrac{x - 1}{x - 2}$

# Exponential and Logarithmic Functions

## Chapter 4

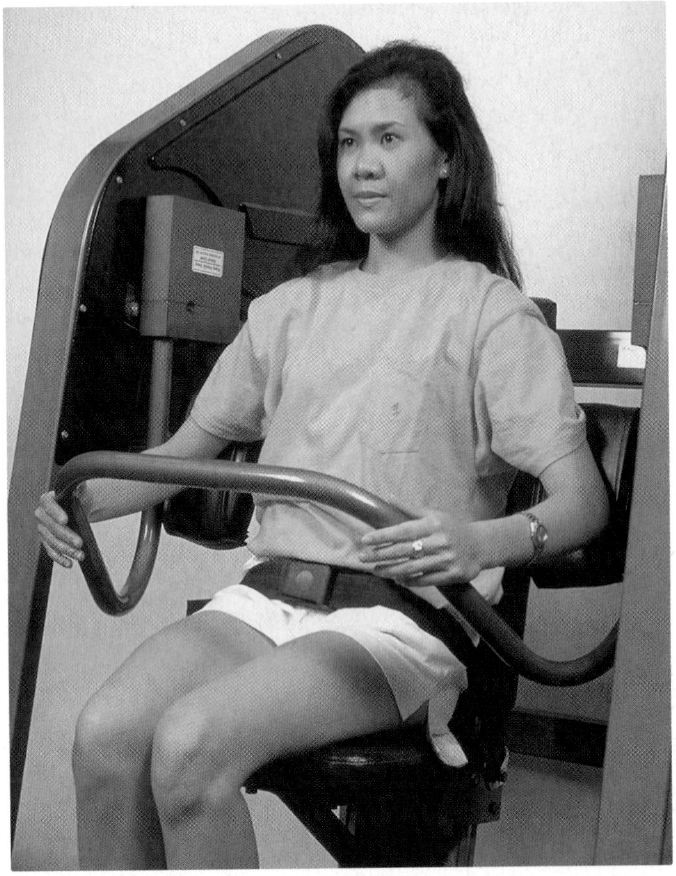

What went wrong on the space shuttle *Challenger*? Will population growth lead to a future without comfort or individual choice? Can I put aside a small amount of money and have millions for early retirement? Why did I feel I was walking too slowly on my visit to New York City? Why are people in California at far more risk from drunk drivers than from earthquakes? What is the difference between earthquakes measuring 6 and 7 on the Richter scale? And what can I hope to accomplish in weightlifting?

The functions that you will be learning about in this chapter will provide you with the mathematics for answering these questions. You will see how these remarkable functions enable us to predict the future and rediscover the past.

You've recently taken up weightlifting, recording the maximum number of pounds you can lift at the end of each week. At first your weight limit increases rapidly, but now you notice that this growth is beginning to level off. You wonder about a function that would serve as a mathematical model to predict the number of pounds you can lift as you continue the sport.

# SECTION 4.1 Exponential Functions

## Objectives

1. Evaluate exponential functions.
2. Graph exponential functions.
3. Evaluate functions with base $e$.
4. Use compound interest formulas.

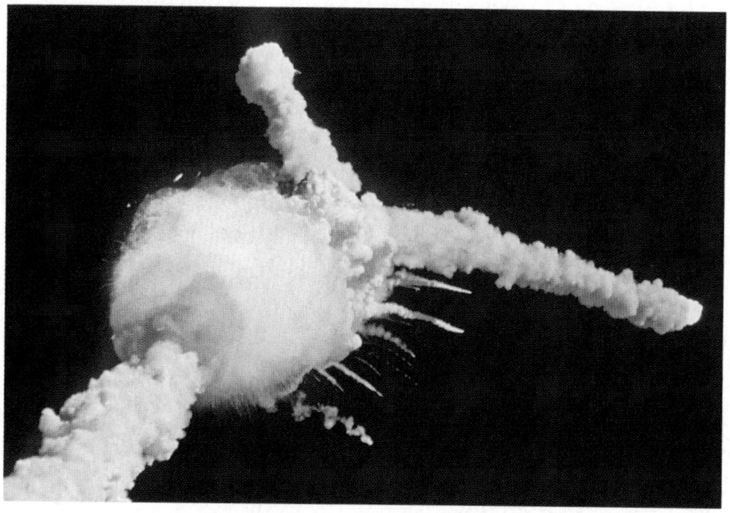

The space shuttle *Challenger* exploded approximately 73 seconds into flight on January 28, 1986. The tragedy involved damage to O-rings, which were used to seal the connections between different sections of the shuttle engines. The number of O-rings damaged increases dramatically as Fahrenheit temperature falls.

The function

$$f(x) = 13.49(0.967)^x - 1$$

models the number of O-rings expected to fail when the temperature is $x$°F. Can you see how this function is different from polynomial functions? The variable $x$ is in the exponent. Functions whose equations contain a variable in the exponent are called **exponential functions**. Many real-life situations, including population growth, growth of epidemics, radioactive decay, and other changes that involve rapid increase or decrease, can be described using exponential functions.

**Definition of the Exponential Function**

The **exponential function $f$ with base $b$** is defined by

$$f(x) = b^x \quad \text{or} \quad y = b^x$$

where $b$ is a positive constant other than $1 (b > 0$ and $b \neq 1)$ and $x$ is any real number.

Here are some examples of exponential functions.

$$f(x) = 2^x \qquad g(x) = 10^x \qquad h(x) = 3^{x+1}$$

Base is 2. Base is 10. Base is 3.

Each of these functions has a constant base and a variable exponent. By contrast, the following functions are not exponential.

$$F(x) = x^2 \qquad G(x) = 1^x \qquad H(x) = x^x$$

Variable is the base and not the exponent.

The base of an exponential function must be a positive constant other than 1.

Variable is both the base and the exponent.

Why is $G(x) = 1^x$ not classified as an exponential function? The number 1 raised to any power is 1. Thus, the function $G$ can be written as $G(x) = 1$, which is a constant function.

**1** Evaluate exponential functions.

You will need a calculator to evaluate exponential expressions. Most scientific calculators have an $\boxed{x^y}$ key. Graphing calculators have a $\boxed{\wedge}$ key. To evaluate expressions of the form $b^x$, enter the base $b$, press $\boxed{x^y}$ or $\boxed{\wedge}$, enter the exponent $x$, and finally press $\boxed{=}$ or $\boxed{\text{ENTER}}$.

## EXAMPLE 1 Evaluating an Exponential Function

The exponential function $f(x) = 13.49(0.967)^x - 1$ describes the number of O-rings expected to fail, $f(x)$, when the temperature is $x$°F. On the morning the *Challenger* was launched, the temperature was 31°F, colder than any previous experience. Find the number of O-rings expected to fail at this temperature.

**Solution** Because the temperature was 31°F, substitute 31 for $x$ and evaluate the function at 31.

$$f(x) = 13.49(0.967)^x - 1 \quad \text{This is the given function.}$$

$$f(31) = 13.49(0.967)^{31} - 1 \quad \text{Substitute 31 for x.}$$

Use a scientific or graphing calculator to evaluate $(0.967)^{31}$. Press the following keys on your calculator to do this:

Scientific calculator: .967 $\boxed{x^y}$ 31 $\boxed{=}$

Graphing calculator: .967 $\boxed{\wedge}$ 31 $\boxed{\text{ENTER}}$

The display should be approximately .353362693426. Multiplying this number by 13.49 and subtracting 1, we obtain

$$f(31) = 13.49(0.967)^{31} - 1 \approx 4.$$

Thus, four O-rings are expected to fail at a temperature of 31°F.

**Check Point 1** Use the function in Example 1 to find the number of O-rings expected to fail at a temperature of 60°F.

**2** Graph exponential functions.

## Graphing Exponential Functions

We are familiar with expressions involving $b^x$ where $x$ is a rational number. For example,

$$b^{1.7} = b^{17/10} = \sqrt[10]{b^{17}} \quad \text{and} \quad b^{1.73} = b^{173/100} = \sqrt[100]{b^{173}}.$$

However, note that the definition of $f(x) = b^x$ includes all real numbers for the domain $x$. You may wonder what $b^x$ means when $x$ is an irrational number, such as $b^{\sqrt{3}}$ or $b^{\pi}$. Using the nonrepeating and nonterminating approximation 1.73205 for $\sqrt{3}$, we can think of $b^{\sqrt{3}}$ as the value that has the successively closer approximations

$$b^{1.7}, b^{1.73}, b^{1.732}, b^{1.73205}, \ldots.$$

In this way, we can graph the exponential function with no holes, or points of discontinuity, at the irrational domain values.

## EXAMPLE 2 Graphing an Exponential Function

Graph: $f(x) = 2^x$.

**Solution** We begin by setting up a table of coordinates.

| $x$ | $f(x) = 2^x$ |
|---|---|
| $-3$ | $f(-3) = 2^{-3} = \frac{1}{8}$ |
| $-2$ | $f(-2) = 2^{-2} = \frac{1}{4}$ |
| $-1$ | $f(-1) = 2^{-1} = \frac{1}{2}$ |
| $0$ | $f(0) = 2^0 = 1$ |
| $1$ | $f(1) = 2^1 = 2$ |
| $2$ | $f(2) = 2^2 = 4$ |
| $3$ | $f(3) = 2^3 = 8$ |

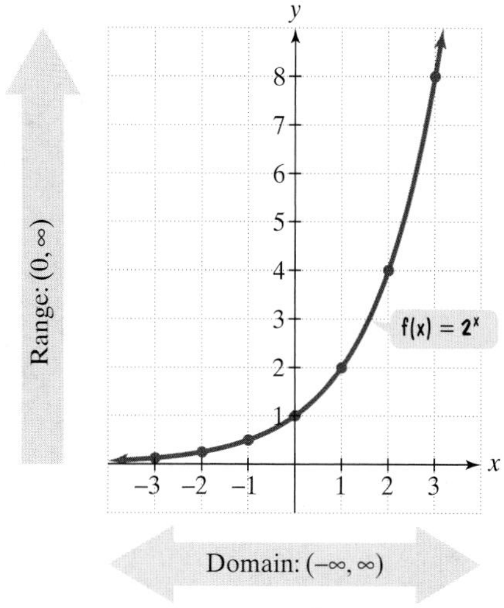


**Figure 4.1** The graph of $f(x) = 2^x$

We plot these points, connecting them with a continuous curve. Figure 4.1 shows the graph of $f(x) = 2^x$. Observe that the graph approaches but never touches the negative portion of the $x$-axis. Thus, the $x$-axis is a horizontal asymptote. The range is all positive real numbers. Although we used integers for $x$ in our table of coordinates, you can use a calculator to find additional points. For example, $f(0.3) = 2^{0.3} \approx 1.231$, $f(0.95) = 2^{0.95} \approx 1.932$. The points $(0.3, 1.231)$ and $(0.95, 1.932)$ fit the graph.

**Check Point 2** Graph $f(x) = 3^x$.

Four exponential functions have been graphed in Figure 4.2. Compare the graphs of functions where $b > 1$ to those where $b < 1$. When $b > 1$, the value of $y$ increases as the value of $x$ increases. When $b < 1$, the value of $y$ decreases as the value of $x$ increases. Notice that all four graphs pass through $(0, 1)$.

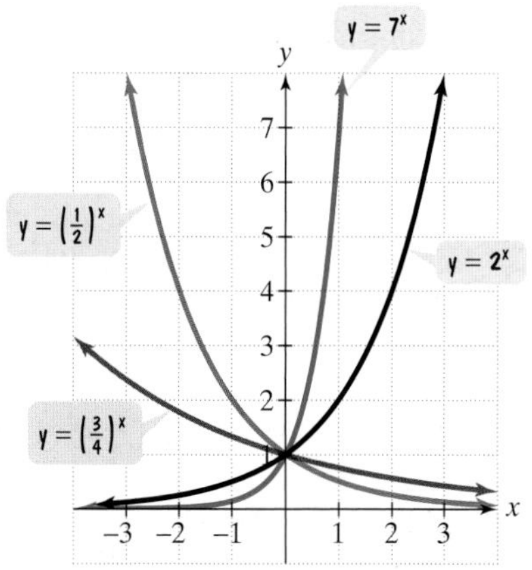


**Figure 4.2** Graphs of four exponential functions

These graphs illustrate the following general characteristics of exponential functions.

**Characteristics of Exponential Functions**

1. The domain of $f(x) = b^x$ consists of all real numbers. The range of $f(x) = b^x$ consists of all positive real numbers.
2. The graphs of all exponential functions pass through the point $(0, 1)$ because $f(0) = b^0 = 1 (b \neq 0)$.
3. If $b > 1$, $f(x) = b^x$ has a graph that goes up to the right and is an increasing function.
4. If $0 < b < 1$, $f(x) = b^x$ has a graph that goes down to the right and is a decreasing function.
5. $f(x) = b^x$ is one-to-one and has an inverse that is a function.
6. The graph of $f(x) = b^x$ approaches but does not cross the $x$-axis. The $x$-axis is a horizontal asymptote.

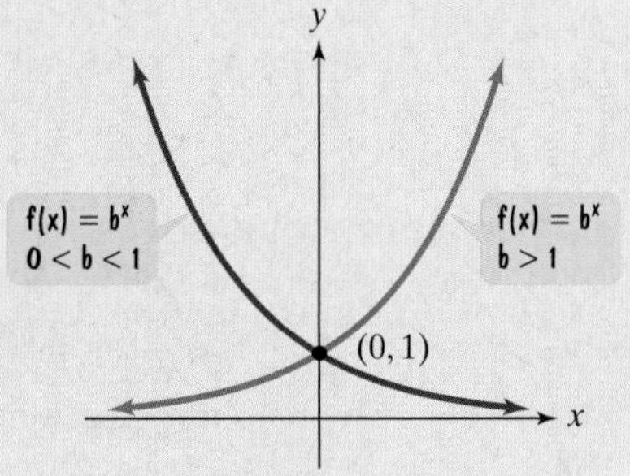


**Transformations of Exponential Functions** The graphs of exponential functions can be translated vertically or horizontally, reflected, stretched, or shrunk. We use the ideas of Section 2.5 to do so, as summarized in Table 4.1.

**Table 4.1 Transformations Involving Exponential Functions**

| Transformation | Equation | Description |
|---|---|---|
| Horizontal translation | $g(x) = b^{x+c}$ | • Shifts the graph of $f(x) = b^x$ to the left $c$ units if $c > 0$.<br>• Shifts the graph of $f(x) = b^x$ to the right $c$ units if $c < 0$. |
| Vertical stretching or shrinking | $g(x) = cb^x$ | Multiplying $y$-coordinates of $f(x) = b^x$ by $c$,<br>• Stretches the graph of $f(x) = b^x$ if $c > 1$.<br>• Shrinks the graph of $f(x) = b^x$ if $0 < c < 1$. |
| Reflecting | $g(x) = -b^x$<br><br>$g(x) = b^{-x}$ | • Reflects the graph of $f(x) = b^x$ about the $x$-axis.<br>• Reflects the graph of $f(x) = b^x$ about the $y$-axis. |
| Vertical translation | $g(x) = b^x + c$ | • Shifts the graph of $f(x) = b^x$ upward $c$ units if $c > 0$.<br>• Shifts the graph of $f(x) = b^x$ downward $c$ units if $c < 0$. |

Using the information in Table 4.1 and a table of coordinates, you will obtain relatively accurate graphs that can be verified using a graphing utility.

## EXAMPLE 3 Transformations Involving Exponential Functions

Use the graph of $f(x) = 3^x$ to obtain the graph of $g(x) = 3^{x+1}$.

**Solution** Examine Table 4.1. Note that the function $g(x) = 3^{x+1}$ has the general form $g(x) = b^{x+c}$, where $c = 1$. Because $c > 0$, we graph $g(x) = 3^{x+1}$ by shifting the graph of $f(x) = 3^x$ *one* unit to the *left*. We construct a table showing some of the coordinates for $f$ and $g$. The graphs of $f$ and $g$ are shown in Figure 4.3.

| $x$ | $f(x) = 3^x$ | $g(x) = 3^{x+1}$ |
|---|---|---|
| $-2$ | $3^{-2} = \frac{1}{9}$ | $3^{-2+1} = 3^{-1} = \frac{1}{3}$ |
| $-1$ | $3^{-1} = \frac{1}{3}$ | $3^{-1+1} = 3^0 = 1$ |
| $0$ | $3^0 = 1$ | $3^{0+1} = 3^1 = 3$ |
| $1$ | $3^1 = 3$ | $3^{1+1} = 3^2 = 9$ |
| $2$ | $3^2 = 9$ | $3^{2+1} = 3^3 = 27$ |

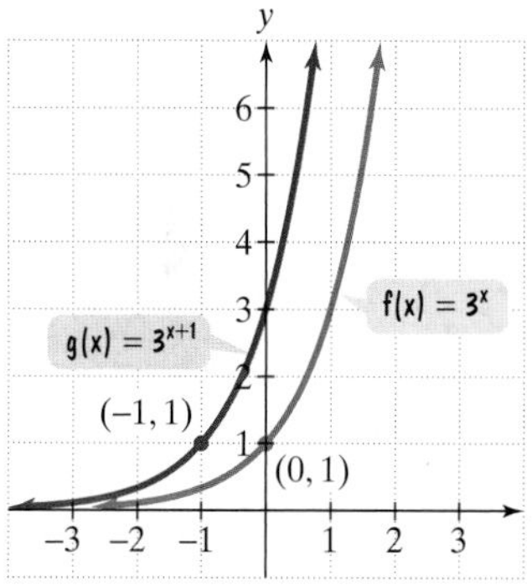


**Figure 4.3** The graph of $g(x) = 3^{x+1}$ shifts the graph of $f(x) = 3^x$ one unit to the left.

**Check Point 3** Use the graph of $f(x) = 3^x$ to obtain the graph of $g(x) = 3^{x-1}$.

If an exponential function is translated upward or downward, the horizontal asymptote is shifted by the amount of the vertical shift.

## EXAMPLE 4 Transformations Involving Exponential Functions

Use the graph of $f(x) = 2^x$ to obtain the graph of $g(x) = 2^x - 3$.

**Solution** Examine Table 4.1. Note that the function $g(x) = 2^x - 3$ has the general form $g(x) = b^x + c$, where $c = -3$. Because $c < 0$, we graph $g(x) = 2^x - 3$ by shifting the graph of $f(x) = 2^x$ *down three* units. We construct a table showing some of the coordinates for $f$ and $g$. The graphs of $f$ and $g$ are shown in Figure 4.4 on page 356. Notice that the horizontal asymptote for $f$, the $x$-axis, is shifted down three units for the horizontal asymptote for $g$. Thus, $y = -3$ is the horizontal asymptote for $g$.

| $x$ | $f(x) = 2^x$ | $g(x) = 2^x - 3$ |
|---|---|---|
| $-2$ | $\frac{1}{4}$ | $\frac{1}{4} - 3 = -2\frac{3}{4}$ |
| $-1$ | $\frac{1}{2}$ | $\frac{1}{2} - 3 = -2\frac{1}{2}$ |
| 0 | 1 | $1 - 3 = -2$ |
| 1 | 2 | $2 - 3 = -1$ |
| 2 | 4 | $4 - 3 = 1$ |

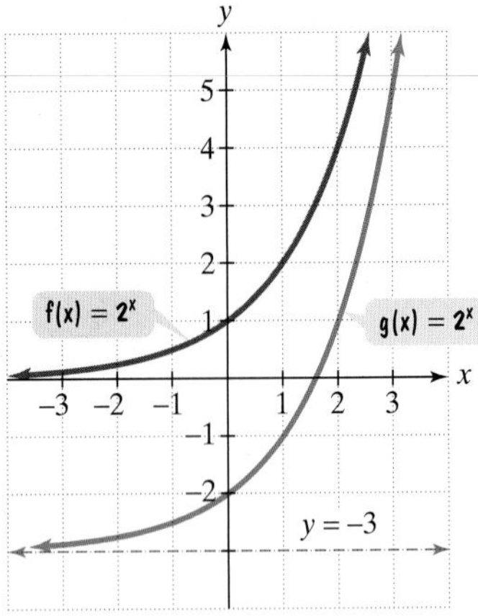


**Figure 4.4** The graph of $g(x) = 2^x - 3$ shifts the graph of $f(x) = 2^x$ down three units.

**Check Point 4** Use the graph of $f(x) = 2^x$ to obtain the graph of $g(x) = 2^x + 1$.

**3** Evaluate functions with base $e$.

## The Natural Base $e$

An irrational number, symbolized by the letter $e$, appears as the base in many applied exponential functions. This irrational number is approximately equal to 2.72. More accurately,

$$e \approx 2.71828\ldots.$$

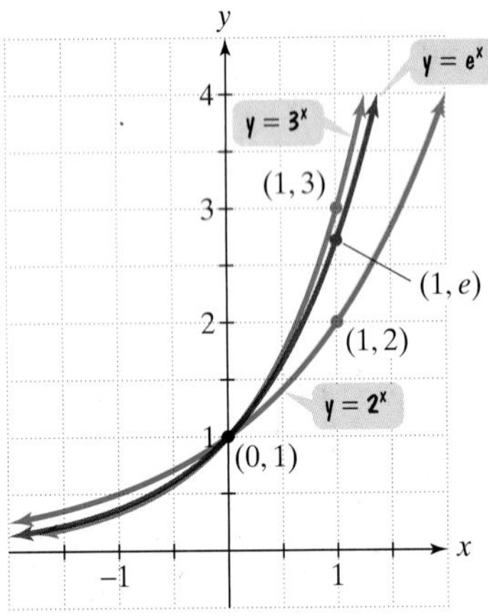

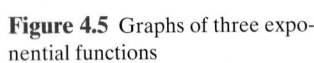

**Figure 4.5** Graphs of three exponential functions

The number $e$ is called the **natural base**. The function $f(x) = e^x$ is called the **natural exponential function**.

Use a scientific or graphing calculator with an $\boxed{e^x}$ key to evaluate $e$ to various powers. For example, to find $e^2$, press the following keys on most calculators:

Scientific calculator: $2\ \boxed{e^x}$

Graphing calculator: $\boxed{e^x}\ 2\ \boxed{\text{ENTER}}$

The display is approximately 7.389.

$$e^2 \approx 7.389$$

The number $e$ lies between 2 and 3. Because $2^2 = 4$ and $3^2 = 9$, it makes sense that $e^2$, approximately 7.389, lies between 4 and 9.

Because $2 < e < 3$, the graph of $y = e^x$ is between the graphs of $y = 2^x$ and $y = 3^x$, shown in Figure 4.5.

## EXAMPLE 5 World Population

In a report entitled *Resources and Man*, the U.S. National Academy of Sciences concluded that a world population of 10 billion "is close to (if not above) the maximum that an intensely managed world might hope to support with some degree of comfort and individual choice." At the time the report was issued in 1969,

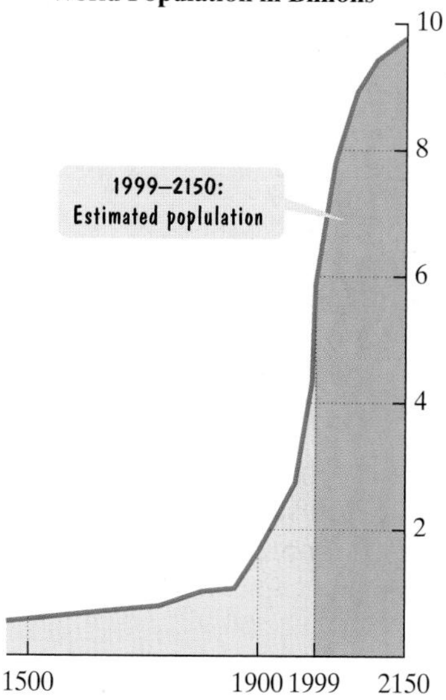

*Source*: U.N. Population Division

the world population was approximately 3.6 billion, with a growth rate of 2% per year. The function

$$f(x) = 3.6e^{0.02x}$$

describes world population, $f(x)$, in billions, $x$ years after 1969. Use the function to find world population in the year 2020. Is there cause for alarm?

**Solution** Because 2020 is 51 years after 1969, we substitute 51 for $x$:

$$f(51) = 3.6e^{0.02(51)}.$$

Although this computation can be done on your calculator in one step, we will break it down into smaller steps so that you can clearly see how we use the $\boxed{e^x}$ key. First find 0.02(51):

$$0.02(51) = 1.02.$$

Now find $e^{1.02}$:

Scientific calculator: 1.02 $\boxed{e^x}$

Graphing calculator: $\boxed{e^x}$ 1.02 $\boxed{\text{ENTER}}$

The display is approximately 2.7731948. Multiplying this number by 3.6, we obtain

$$f(51) = 3.6e^{0.02(51)} = 3.6e^{1.02} \approx 9.98.$$

This indicates that world population in the year 2020 will be approximately 9.98 billion. Because this number is quite close to 10 billion, the given function suggests that there may be cause for alarm.

World population in 1999 was 6 billion, but the growth rate was no longer 2%. It had slowed down to 1.3%. Using this current growth rate, exponential functions now predict a world population of 7.6 billion in the year 2020. Experts think the population may stabilize at 10 billion after 2200 if the deceleration in growth rate continues.

**Check Point 5** The function $f(x) = 6e^{0.013x}$ describes world population, $f(x)$, in billions, $x$ years after 1999 subject to a growth rate of 1.3% annually. Use the function to find world population in 2050.

**4** Use compound interest formulas.

## Compound Interest

We all want a wonderful life with fulfilling work, good health, and loving relationships. And let's be honest: Financial security wouldn't hurt! Achieving this goal depends on understanding how money in savings accounts grows in remarkable ways as a result of *compound interest*. **Compound interest** is interest computed on your original investment as well as on any accumulated interest.

Suppose a sum of money called the **principal**, $P$, is invested at an annual percentage rate $r$, in decimal form, compounded once per year. Because the interest is added to the principal at year's end, the accumulated value A is

$$A = P + Pr = P(1 + r).$$

The accumulated amount of money follows this pattern of multiplying the previous principal by $(1 + r)$ for each successive year, as indicated in Table 4.2.

**Table 4.2**

| Time in Years | Accumulated Value after Each Compounding |
|---|---|
| 0 | $A = P$ |
| 1 | $A = P(1 + r)$ |
| 2 | $A = P(1 + r)(1 + r) = P(1 + r)^2$ |
| 3 | $A = P(1 + r)^2(1 + r) = P(1 + r)^3$ |
| 4 | $A = P(1 + r)^3(1 + r) = P(1 + r)^4$ |
| ⋮ | ⋮ |
| $t$ | $A = P(1 + r)^t$ |

If money invested at a specified rate of interest is compounded more than once a year, then the formula $A = P(1 + r)^t$ can be adjusted to take into account the number of compounding periods in a year. If $n$ represents the number of compounding periods in a year, the formula becomes

$$A = P\left(1 + \frac{r}{n}\right)^{nt}.$$

Some banks use **continuous compounding**, where the number of compounding periods increases infinitely (compounding interest every trillionth of a second, every quadrillionth of a second, etc.). As $n$, the number of compounding periods in a year, increases without bound, the expression $\left(1 + \frac{1}{n}\right)^n$ approaches $e$. As a result, the formula for continuous compounding is $A = Pe^{rt}$. Although continuous compounding sounds terrific, it yields only a fraction of a percent more interest over a year than daily compounding.

| $n$ | $\left(1 + \frac{1}{n}\right)^n$ |
|---|---|
| 1 | 2 |
| 2 | 2.25 |
| 5 | 2.48832 |
| 10 | 2.59374246 |
| 100 | 2.704813829 |
| 1,000 | 2.716923932 |
| 10,000 | 2.718145927 |
| 100,000 | 2.718268237 |
| 1,000,000 | 2.718280469 |
| 1,000,000,000 | 2.718281827 |

As $n$ takes on increasingly large values, the expression $\left(1 + \frac{1}{n}\right)^n$ approaches $e$. Thus,

$$\left(1 + \frac{1}{n}\right)^n \to e \text{ as } n \to \infty.$$

**Formulas for Compound Interest**

After $t$ years, the balance $A$ in an account with principal $P$ and annual interest rate $r$ (in decimal form) is given by the following formulas:

1. For $n$ compoundings per year: $A = P\left(1 + \frac{r}{n}\right)^{nt}$
2. For continuous compounding: $A = Pe^{rt}$

## Technology

The graphs illustrate that as $x$ increases, $\left(1 + \frac{1}{x}\right)^x$ approaches $e$.

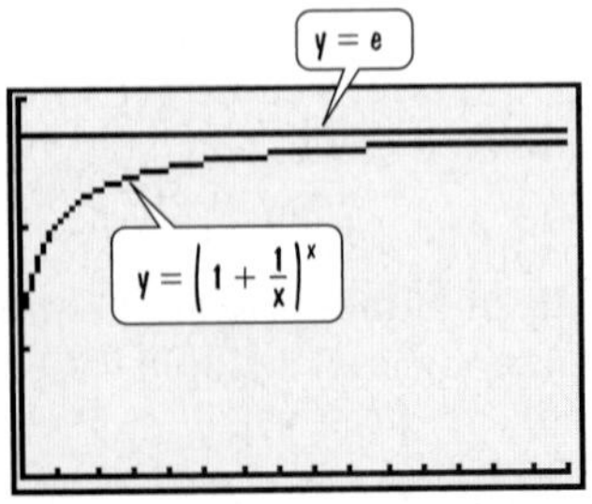


## EXAMPLE 6 Choosing Between Investments

You want to invest \$8000 for 6 years, and you have a choice between two accounts. The first pays 7% per year, compounded monthly. The second pays 6.85% per year, compounded continuously. Which is the better investment?

**Solution** The better investment is the one with the greater balance in the account after 6 years. Let's begin with the account with monthly compounding. We use the compound interest model with $P = 8000$, $r = 7\% = 0.07$, $n = 12$ (monthly compounding, means 12 compoundings per year), and $t = 6$.

$$A = P\left(1 + \frac{r}{n}\right)^{nt} = 8000\left(1 + \frac{0.07}{12}\right)^{12\cdot 6} \approx 12{,}160.84$$

The balance in this account after 6 years is \$12,160.84. For the second investment option, we use the model for continuous compounding with $P = 8000$, $r = 6.85\% = 0.0685$, and $t = 6$.

$$A = Pe^{rt} = 8000e^{0.0685(6)} \approx 12{,}066.60$$

The balance in this account after 6 years is \$12,066.60, slightly less than the previous amount. Thus, the better investment is the 7% monthly compounding option.

**Check Point 6** A sum of \$10,000 is invested at an annual rate of 8%. Find the balance in the account after 5 years subject to **a.** quarterly compounding and **b.** continuous compounding.

## EXERCISE SET 4.1

### Practice Exercises

*In Exercises 1–10, approximate each number using a calculator. Round your answer to three decimal places.*

**1.** $2^{3.4}$ **2.** $3^{2.4}$ **3.** $3^{\sqrt{5}}$ **4.** $5^{\sqrt{3}}$ **5.** $4^{-1.5}$

**6.** $6^{-1.2}$ **7.** $e^{2.3}$ **8.** $e^{3.4}$ **9.** $e^{-0.95}$ **10.** $e^{-0.75}$

*In Exercises 11–18, graph each function by making a table of coordinates. If applicable, use a graphing utility to confirm your hand-drawn graph.*

**11.** $f(x) = 4^x$ **12.** $f(x) = 5^x$

**13.** $g(x) = \left(\frac{3}{2}\right)^x$ **14.** $g(x) = \left(\frac{4}{3}\right)^x$

**15.** $h(x) = \left(\frac{1}{2}\right)^x$ **16.** $h(x) = \left(\frac{1}{3}\right)^x$

**17.** $f(x) = (0.6)^x$ **18.** $f(x) = (0.8)^x$

*In Exercises 19–24, the graph of an exponential function is given. Select the function for each graph from the following options:*

$$f(x) = 3^x,\ g(x) = 3^{x-1},\ h(x) = 3^x - 1,$$
$$F(x) = -3^x,\ G(x) = 3^{-x},\ H(x) = -3^{-x}.$$

**19.**

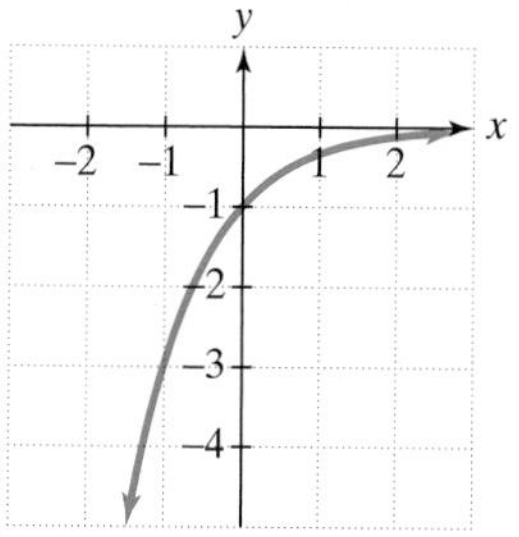

**20.**

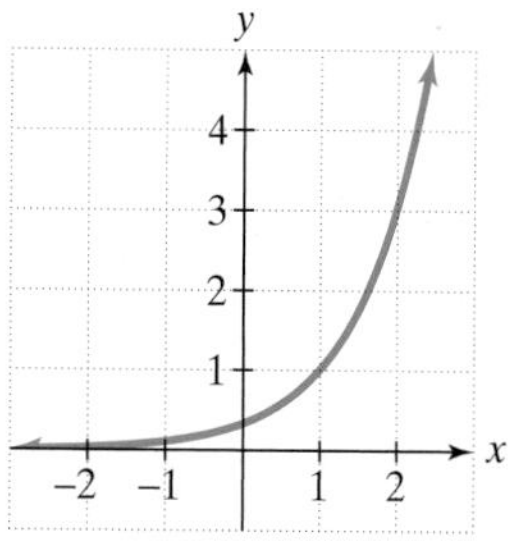

**21.**

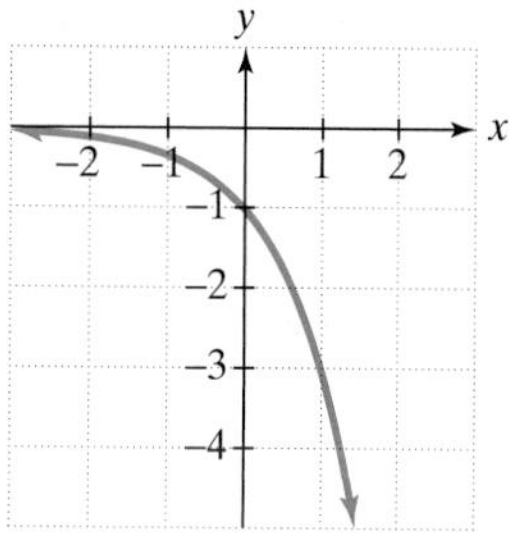

**22.**

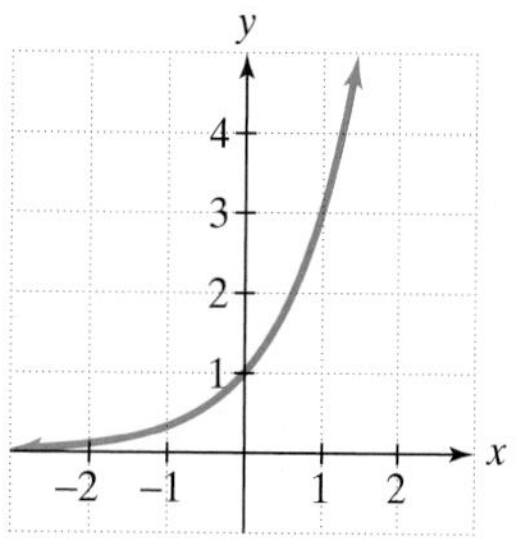

**23.**

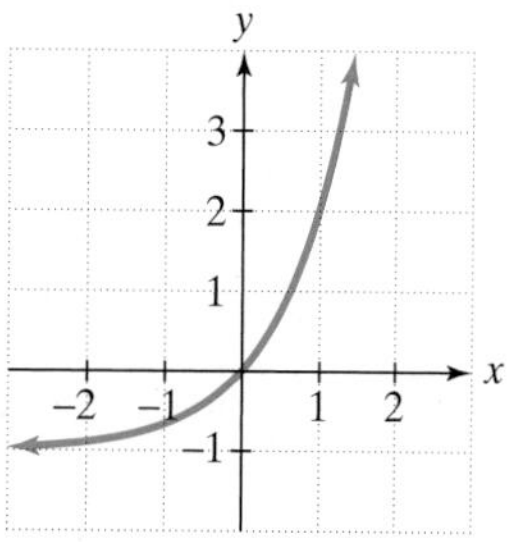

**24.**

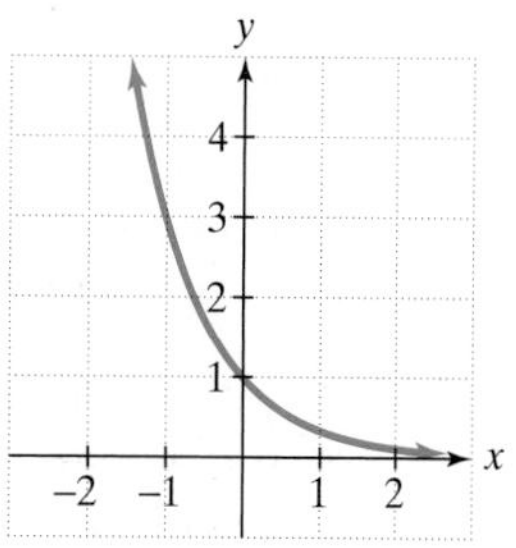

*In Exercises 25–34, begin by graphing $f(x) = 2^x$. Then use transformations of this graph and a table of coordinates to graph the given function.*

**25.** $g(x) = 2^{x+1}$

**26.** $g(x) = 2^{x+2}$

**27.** $g(x) = 2^x - 1$

**28.** $g(x) = 2^x + 2$

**29.** $h(x) = 2^{x+1} - 1$

**30.** $h(x) = 2^{x+2} - 1$

**31.** $g(x) = -2^x$

**32.** $g(x) = 2^{-x}$

**33.** $g(x) = 2 \cdot 2^x$

**34.** $g(x) = \frac{1}{2} \cdot 2^x$

*Use the compound interest formulas $A = P\left(1 + \frac{r}{n}\right)^{nt}$ and $A = Pe^{rt}$ to solve Exercises 35–38.*

**35.** Find the accumulated value of an investment of \$10,000 for 5 years at an interest rate of 5.5% if the money is **a.** compounded semiannually; **b.** compounded monthly; **c.** compounded continuously.

**36.** Find the accumulated value of an investment of \$5000 for 10 years at an interest rate of 6.5% if the money is **a.** compounded semiannually; **b.** compounded monthly; **c.** compounded continuously.

**37.** Suppose that you have \$12,000 to invest. Which investment yields the greatest return over 3 years: 7% compounded monthly or 6.85% compounded continuously?

**38.** Suppose that you have \$6000 to invest. Which investment yields the greatest return over 4 years: 8.25% compounded quarterly or 8.3% compounded semiannually?

## Application Exercises

*Use a calculator with an* $\boxed{x^y}$ *key or a* $\boxed{\wedge}$ *key to solve Exercises 39–46.*

**39.** The exponential function $f(x) = 67.38(1.026)^x$ describes the population of Mexico, $f(x)$, in millions, $x$ years after 1980.

**a.** Substitute 0 for $x$ and, without using a calculator, find Mexico's population in 1980.

**b.** Substitute 27 for $x$ and use your calculator to find Mexico's population in the year 2007 as predicted by this function.

**c.** Find Mexico's population in the year 2034 as predicted by this function.

**d.** Find Mexico's population in the year 2061 as predicted by this function.

**e.** What appears to be happening to Mexico's population every 27 years?

**40.** The 1986 explosion at the Chernobyl nuclear power plant in the former Soviet Union sent about 1000 kilograms of radioactive cesium–137 into the atmosphere. The function $f(x) = 1000(0.5)^{x/30}$ describes the amount, $f(x)$, in kilograms, of cesium-137 remaining in Chernobyl $x$ years after 1986. If even 100 kilograms of cesium-137 remain in Chernobyl's atmosphere, the area is considered unsafe for human habitation. Find $f(80)$ and determine if Chernobyl will be safe for human habitation by 2066.

*The function*

$$f(x) = \frac{0.9}{1 + 271(0.885)^x}$$

*models the fraction of people x years old with some coronary heart disease. Use this function to solve Exercises 41–42.*

**41.** Evaluate $f(25)$ and describe what this means in practical terms.

**42.** Evaluate $f(70)$ and describe what this means in practical terms.

*The formula $S = C(1 + r)^t$ models inflation, where $C$ = the value today, $r$ = the annual inflation rate, and $S$ = the inflated value $t$ years from now. Use this formula to solve Exercises 43–44.*

**43.** If the inflation rate is 6%, how much will a house now worth \$65,000 be worth in 10 years?

**44.** If the inflation rate is 3%, how much will a house now worth \$110,000 be worth in 5 years?

**45.** A decimal approximation for $\sqrt{3}$ is 1.7320508. Use a calculator to find $2^{1.7}$, $2^{1.73}$, $2^{1.732}$, $2^{1.73205}$, and $2^{1.7320508}$. Now find $2^{\sqrt{3}}$. What do you observe?

**46.** A decimal approximation for $\pi$ is 3.141593. Use a calculator to find $2^3$, $2^{3.1}$, $2^{3.14}$, $2^{3.141}$, $2^{3.1415}$, $2^{3.14159}$, and $2^{3.141593}$. Now find $2^{\pi}$. What do you observe?

*Use a calculator with an* $\boxed{e^x}$ *key to solve Exercises 47–51. The function $f(x) = 24{,}000e^{0.21x}$ describes the number of AIDS cases in the United States among intravenous drug users x years after 1989. Use this function to solve Exercises 47–48.*

**47.** Evaluate $f(11)$ and describe what this means in practical terms.

**48.** Evaluate $f(31)$ and describe what this means in practical terms.

**49.** In college, we study large volumes of information—information that, unfortunately, we do not often retain for very long. The function

$$f(x) = 80e^{-0.5x} + 20$$

describes the percentage of information, $f(x)$, that a particular person remembers $x$ weeks after learning the information.

**a.** Substitute 0 for $x$ and, without using a calculator, find the percentage of information remembered at the moment it is first learned.

**b.** Substitute 1 for $x$ and find the percentage of information that is remembered after 1 week.

**c.** Find the percentage of information that is remembered after 4 weeks.

**d.** Find the percentage of information that is remembered after one year (52 weeks).

**50.** In 1626, Peter Minuit convinced the Wappinger Indians to sell him Manhattan Island for \$24. If the Native Americans had put the \$24 into a bank account paying 5% interest, how much would the investment be worth in the year 2000 if interest were compounded

**a.** monthly? **b.** continuously?

**51.** The function

$$N(t) = \frac{30{,}000}{1 + 20e^{-1.5t}}$$

describes the number of people, $N(t)$, who become ill with influenza $t$ weeks after its initial outbreak in a town with 30,000 inhabitants. The horizontal asymptote in the graph indicates that there is a limit to the epidemic's growth.

**a.** How many people became ill with the flu when the epidemic began? (When the epidemic began, $t = 0$.)

**b.** How many people were ill by the end of the third week?

**c.** Why can't the spread of an epidemic simply grow indefinitely? What does the horizontal asymptote shown in the graph indicate about the limiting size of the population that becomes ill?

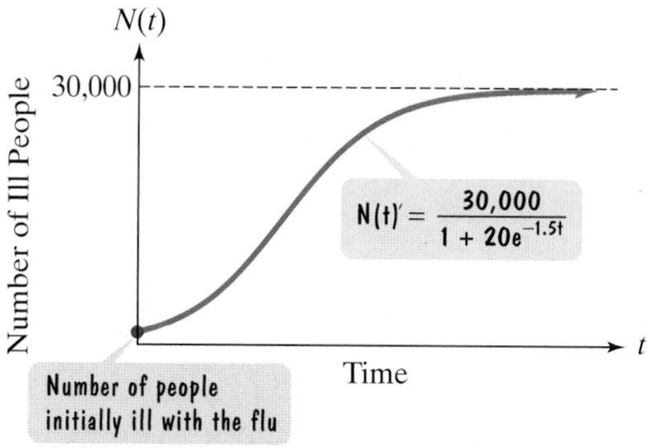


## Writing in Mathematics

**52.** What is an exponential function?

**53.** What is the natural exponential function?

**54.** Use a calculator to evaluate $\left(1 + \frac{1}{x}\right)^x$ for $x = 10$, 100, 1000, 10,000, 100,000, and 1,000,000. Describe what happens to the expression as $x$ increases.

**55.** Write an example similar to Example 6 on page 358 in which continuous compounding at a slightly lower yearly interest rate is a better investment than compounding $n$ times per year.

**56.** Describe how you could use the graph of $f(x) = 2^x$ to obtain a decimal approximation for $\sqrt{2}$.

**57.** The exponential function $y = 2^x$ is one-to-one and has an inverse function. Try finding the inverse function by exchanging $x$ and $y$ and solving for $y$. Describe the difficulty that you encounter in this process. What is needed to overcome this problem?

**58.** In 1999, world population was 6 billion with an annual growth rate of 1.3%. Discuss two factors that would cause this growth rate to slow down over the next ten years.

## Technology Exercises

**59.** Graph $y = 13.49(0.967)^x - 1$, the function for the number of O-rings expected to fail at $x$°F, in a [0, 90, 10] by [0, 20, 5] viewing rectangle. If NASA engineers had used this function and its graph, is it likely they would have allowed the *Challenger* to be launched when the temperature was 31°F? Explain.

**60.** The student–teacher ratio in U.S. elementary and secondary schools can be modeled by $y = 25.34\,(0.987)^x$, where $x$ represents the number of years since 1959 and $y$ represents the student–teacher ratio. Graph the function in a [1, 40, 1] by [0, 26, 1] viewing rectangle. When did the student–teacher ratio become less than 21 students per teacher?

**61.** You have \$10,000 to invest. One bank pays 5% interest compounded quarterly and the other pays 4.5% interest compounded monthly.

**a.** Use the formula for compound interest to write a function for the balance in each account at any time $t$.

**b.** Use a graphing utility to graph both functions in an appropriate viewing rectangle. Based on the graphs, which bank offers the better return on your money?

**62. a.** Graph $y = e^x$ and $y = 1 + x + \frac{x^2}{2}$ in the same viewing rectangle.

**b.** Graph $y = e^x$ and $y = 1 + x + \frac{x^2}{2} + \frac{x^3}{6}$ in the same viewing rectangle.

**c.** Graph $y = e^x$ and $y = 1 + x + \frac{x^2}{2} + \frac{x^3}{6} + \frac{x^4}{24}$ in the same viewing rectangle.

**d.** Describe what you observe in parts (a)–(c). Try generalizing this observation.

## Critical Thinking Exercises

**63.** Which one of the following is true?

**a.** As the number of compounding periods increases on a fixed investment, the amount of money in the account over a fixed interval of time will increase without bound.

**b.** The functions $f(x) = 3^{-x}$ and $g(x) = -3^x$ have the same graph.

**c.** $e = 2.718$.

**d.** The functions $f(x) = \left(\frac{1}{3}\right)^x$ and $g(x) = 3^{-x}$ have the same graph.

**64.** The graphs labeled (a)–(d) in the figure represent $y = 3^x$, $y = 5^x$, $y = \left(\frac{1}{3}\right)^x$, and $y = \left(\frac{1}{5}\right)^x$, but not necessarily in that order. Which is which? Describe the process that enables you to make this decision.

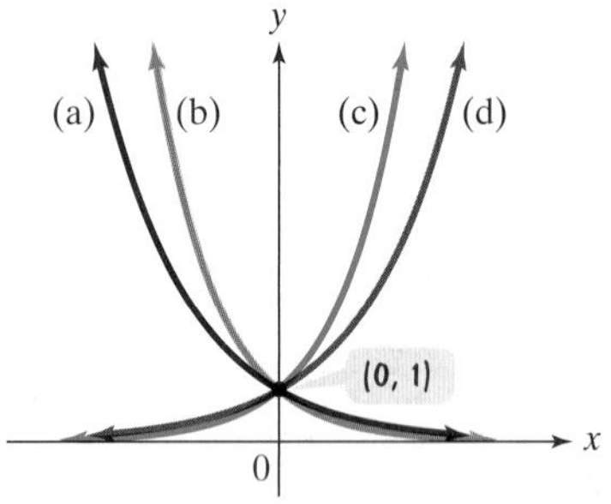


**65.** The hyperbolic cosine and hyperbolic sine functions are defined by

$$\cosh x = \frac{e^x + e^{-x}}{2} \quad \text{and} \quad \sinh x = \frac{e^x - e^{-x}}{2}.$$

Prove that $(\cosh x)^2 - (\sinh x)^2 = 1$.

# SECTION 4.2 Logarithmic Functions

## Objectives

1. Change from logarithmic to exponential form.
2. Change from exponential to logarithmic form.
3. Evaluate logarithms.
4. Use basic logarithmic properties.
5. Graph logarithmic functions.
6. Find the domain of a logarithmic function.
7. Use common logarithms.
8. Use natural logarithms.

The earthquake that ripped through northern California on October 17, 1989, measured 7.1 on the Richter scale, killed more than 60 people, and injured more than 2400. Shown here is San Francisco's Marina district, where shock waves tossed houses off their foundations and into the street.

The Richter scale is misleading because for each increase in one unit on the scale, there is a tenfold increase in the intensity of an earthquake. In this section our focus is on the inverse of the exponential function, called the logarithmic function. The logarithmic function will help you to understand diverse phenomena, including earthquake intensity, human memory, and the pace of life in large cities.

## Study Tip

In case you need to review inverse functions, they are discussed on pages 245–246. The horizontal line test appears on page 248.

## The Definition of Logarithmic Functions

No horizontal line can be drawn that intersects the graph of an exponential function at more than one point. This means that the exponential function is one-to-one and has an inverse. The inverse function of the exponential function with base $b$ is called the **logarithmic function with base $b$.**

**Definition of the Logarithmic Function**

For $x > 0$ and $b > 0$, $b \neq 1$,

$$y = \log_b x \quad \text{is equivalent to } b^y = x.$$

The function $f(x) = \log_b x$ is the **logarithmic function with base $b$.**

The equations

$$y = \log_b x \text{ and } b^y = x$$

are different ways of expressing the same thing. The first equation is in **logarithmic form** and the second equivalent equation is in **exponential form**.

Notice that a **logarithm**, $y$, **is an exponent**. You should learn the location of the base and exponent in each form.

**Location of Base and Exponent in Exponential and Logarithmic Forms**

Logarithmic Form: $y = \log_b x$ (Exponent: $y$; Base: $b$)    Exponential Form: $b^y = x$ (Exponent: $y$; Base: $b$)

1 Change from logarithmic to exponential form.

## EXAMPLE 1 Changing From Logarithmic to Exponential Form

Write each equation in its equivalent exponential form.

**a.** $2 = \log_5 x$ **b.** $3 = \log_b 64$ **c.** $\log_3 7 = y$

**Solution** We use the fact that $y = \log_b x$ means $b^y = x$.

**a.** $2 = \log_5 x$ means $5^2 = x$. **b.** $3 = \log_b 64$ means $b^3 = 64$.

Logarithms are exponents. Logarithms are exponents.

**c.** $\log_3 7 = y$ or $y = \log_3 7$ means $3^y = 7$.

**Check Point 1** Write each equation in its equivalent exponential form.

**a.** $3 = \log_7 x$ **b.** $2 = \log_b 25$ **c.** $\log_4 26 = y$

2 Change from exponential to logarithmic form.

## EXAMPLE 2 Changing From Exponential to Logarithmic Form

Write each equation in its equivalent logarithmic form.

**a.** $12^2 = x$ **b.** $b^3 = 8$ **c.** $e^y = 9$

**Solution** We use the fact that $b^y = x$ means $y = \log_b x$.

**a.** $12^2 = x$ means $2 = \log_{12} x$. **b.** $b^3 = 8$ means $3 = \log_b 8$.

Exponents are logarithms. Exponents are logarithms.

**c.** $e^y = 9$ means $y = \log_e 9$.

**Check Point 2** Write each equation in its equivalent logarithmic form.

**a.** $2^5 = x$ **b.** $b^3 = 27$ **c.** $e^y = 33$

**3** Evaluate logarithms.

Remembering that logarithms are exponents makes it possible to evaluate some logarithms by inspection. The logarithm of $x$ with base $b$, $\log_b x$, is the exponent to which $b$ must be raised to get $x$. For example, suppose we want to evaluate $\log_2 32$. We ask, 2 to what power gives 32? Because $2^5 = 32$, $\log_2 32 = 5$.

## EXAMPLE 3 Evaluating Logarithms

Evaluate:

**a.** $\log_2 16$ **b.** $\log_3 9$ **c.** $\log_{25} 5$

### Solution

| Logarithmic Expression | Question Needed for Evaluation | Logarithmic Expression Evaluated |
|---|---|---|
| **a.** $\log_2 16$ | 2 to what power gives 16? | $\log_2 16 = 4$ because $2^4 = 16$. |
| **b.** $\log_3 9$ | 3 to what power gives 9? | $\log_3 9 = 2$ because $3^2 = 9$. |
| **c.** $\log_{25} 5$ | 25 to what power gives 5? | $\log_{25} 5 = \frac{1}{2}$ because $25^{1/2} = \sqrt{25} = 5$. |

**Check Point 3** Evaluate:

**a.** $\log_{10} 100$ **b.** $\log_3 3$ **c.** $\log_{36} 6$

**4** Use basic logarithmic properties.

## Basic Logarithmic Properties

Because logarithms are exponents, they have properties that can be verified using properties of exponents.

### Basic Logarithmic Properties Involving One

1. $\log_b b = 1$ because 1 is the exponent to which $b$ must be raised to obtain $b$. $(b^1 = b)$
2. $\log_b 1 = 0$ because 0 is the exponent to which $b$ must be raised to obtain 1. $(b^0 = 1)$

## EXAMPLE 4 Using Properties of Logarithms

Evaluate:

**a.** $\log_7 7$ **b.** $\log_5 1$

### Solution

**a.** Because $\log_b b = 1$, we conclude $\log_7 7 = 1$.

**b.** Because $\log_b 1 = 0$, we conclude $\log_5 1 = 0$.

**Check Point 4** Evaluate:

**a.** $\log_9 9$ **b.** $\log_8 1$

The inverse of the exponential function is the logarithmic function. Thus, if $f(x) = b^x$, then $f^{-1}(x) = \log_b x$. In Chapter 2, we saw how inverse functions "undo" one another. In particular,

$$f(f^{-1}(x)) = x \text{ and } f^{-1}(f(x)) = x.$$

Applying these relationships to exponential and logarithmic functions, we obtain the following **inverse properties of logarithms**.

**Inverse Properties of Logarithms**

For $b > 0$ and $b \neq 1$,

| | |
|---|---|
| $\log_b b^x = x$ | The logarithm with base $b$ of $b$ raised to a power equals that power. |
| $b^{\log_b x} = x$ | $b$ raised to the logarithm with base $b$ of a number equals that number. |

## EXAMPLE 5 Using Inverse Properties of Logarithms

Evaluate:

**a.** $\log_4 4^5$ **b.** $6^{\log_6 9}$.

**Solution**

**a.** Because $\log_b b^x = x$, we conclude $\log_4 4^5 = 5$.

**b.** Because $b^{\log_b x} = x$, we conclude $6^{\log_6 9} = 9$.

**Check Point 5** Evaluate:

**a.** $\log_7 7^8$ **b.** $3^{\log_3 17}$

**5** Graph logarithmic functions.

## Graphs of Logarithmic Functions

How do we graph logarithmic functions? We use the fact that the logarithmic function is the inverse of the exponential function. This means that the logarithmic function reverses the coordinates of the exponential function. It also means that the graph of the logarithmic function is a reflection of the graph of the exponential function about the line $y = x$.

## EXAMPLE 6 Graphs of Exponential and Logarithmic Functions

Graph $f(x) = 2^x$ and $g(x) = \log_2 x$ in the same rectangular coordinate system.

**Solution** We first set up a table of coordinates for $f(x) = 2^x$. Reversing, these coordinates gives the coordinates for the inverse function $g(x) = \log_2 x$.

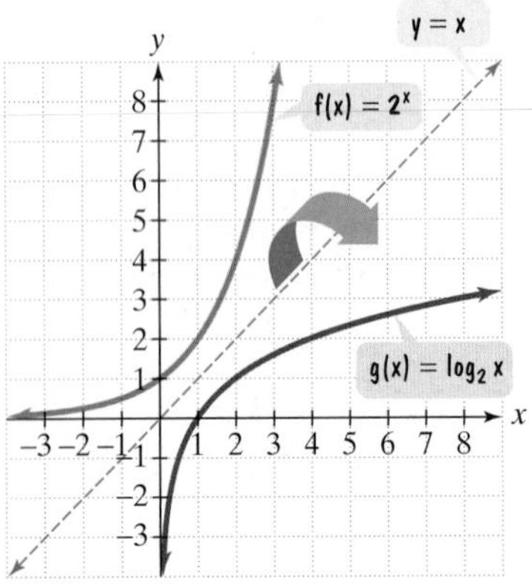


**Figure 4.6** The graphs of $f(x) = 2^x$ and its inverse function

| $x$ | $-2$ | $-1$ | $0$ | $1$ | $2$ | $3$ |
|---|---|---|---|---|---|---|
| $f(x) = 2^x$ | $\frac{1}{4}$ | $\frac{1}{2}$ | $1$ | $2$ | $4$ | $8$ |

Reverse coordinates.

| $x$ | $\frac{1}{4}$ | $\frac{1}{2}$ | $1$ | $2$ | $4$ | $8$ |
|---|---|---|---|---|---|---|
| $g(x) = \log_2 x$ | $-2$ | $-1$ | $0$ | $1$ | $2$ | $3$ |

We now plot the ordered pairs in both tables, connecting them with smooth curves. Figure 4.6 shows the graphs of $f(x) = 2^x$ and its inverse function $g(x) = \log_2 x$. The graph of the inverse can also be drawn by reflecting the graph of $f(x) = 2^x$ about the line $y = x$.

**Check Point 6** Graph $f(x) = 3^x$ and $g(x) = \log_3 x$ in the same rectangular coordinate system.

Figure 4.7 illustrates the relationship between the graph of the exponential function, shown in blue and its inverse, the logarithmic function, shown in red, for bases greater than 1 and for bases between 0 and 1.

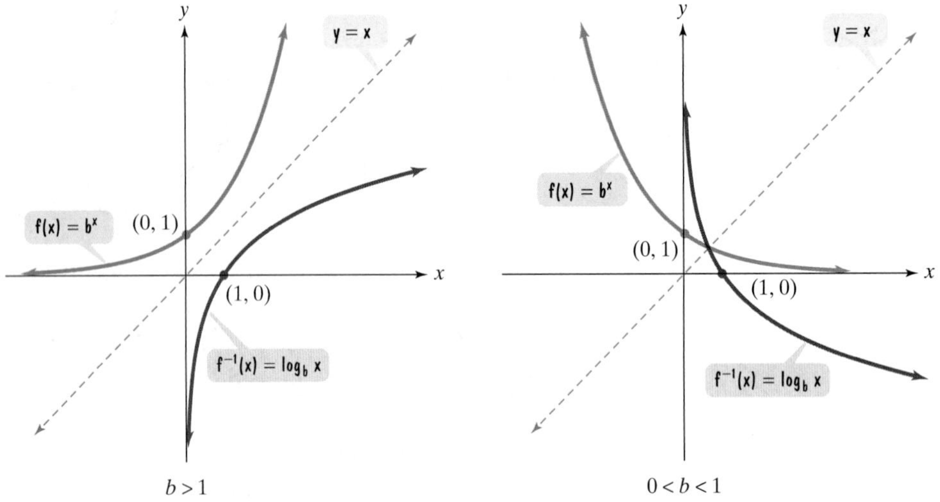


**Figure 4.7** Graphs of exponential and logarithmic functions

### Characteristics of the Graphs of Logarithmic Functions

- The $x$-intercept is 1. There is no $y$-intercept.
- The $y$-axis is a vertical asymptote.
- If $b > 1$, the function is increasing. If $0 < b < 1$, the function is decreasing.
- The graph is smooth and continuous. It has no sharp corners or gaps.

The graphs of logarithmic functions can be translated vertically or horizontally, reflected, stretched, or shrunk. We use the ideas of Section 2.5 to do so, as summarized in Table 4.3.

**Table 4.3 Transformations Involving Logarithmic Functions**

| Transformation | Equation | Description |
|---|---|---|
| Horizontal translation | $g(x) = \log_b(x + c)$ | • Shifts the graph of $f(x) = \log_b x$ to the left $c$ units if $c > 0$. Vertical asymptote: $x = -c$.<br>• Shifts the graph of $f(x) = \log_b x$ to the right $c$ units if $c < 0$. Vertical asymptote: $x = -c$. |
| Vertical stretching or shrinking | $g(x) = c \log_b x$ | Multiplying $y$-coordinates of $f(x) = \log_b x$ by $c$,<br>• Stretches the graph of $f(x) = \log_b x$ if $c > 1$.<br>• Shrinks the graph of $f(x) = \log_b x$ if $0 < c < 1$. |
| Reflecting | $g(x) = -\log_b x$<br>$g(x) = \log_b(-x)$ | • Reflects the graph of $f(x) = \log_b x$ about the $x$-axis.<br>• Reflects the graph of $f(x) = \log_b x$ about the $y$-axis. |
| Vertical translation | $g(x) = c + \log_b x$ | • Shifts the graph of $f(x) = \log_b x$ upward $c$ units if $c > 0$.<br>• Shifts the graph of $f(x) = \log_b x$ downward $c$ units if $c < 0$. |

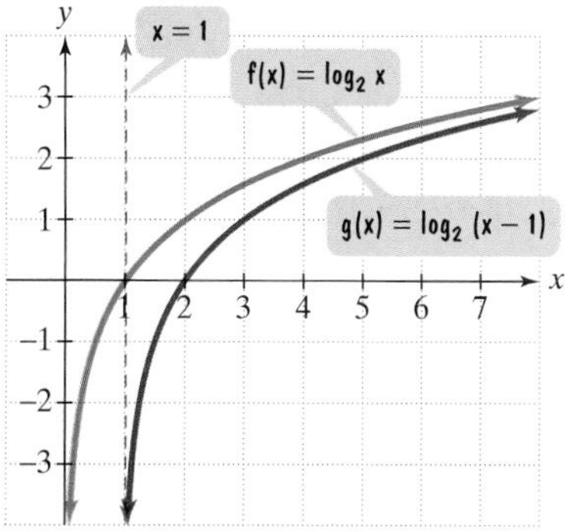


**Figure 4.8** Shifting $f(x) = \log_2 x$ one unit to the right

For example, Figure 4.8 illustrates that the graph of $g(x) = \log_2(x - 1)$ is the graph of $f(x) = \log_2 x$ moved one unit to the right. If a logarithmic function is translated to the left or to the right, both the $x$-intercept and the vertical asymptote are shifted by the amount of the horizontal shift. In Figure 4.8, the $x$-intercept of $f$ is 1. Because $g$ is shifted one unit to the right, its $x$-intercept is 2. Also observe that the vertical asymptote for $f$, the $y$-axis, is shifted one unit to the right for the vertical asymptote for $g$. Thus, $x = 1$ is the vertical asymptote for $g$.

Here are some other examples of transformations of graphs of logarithmic functions.

- The graph of $g(x) = 3 + \log_4 x$ is the graph of $f(x) = \log_4 x$ moved up three units, shown in Figure 4.9.
- The graph of $h(x) = -\log_2 x$ is the graph of $f(x) = \log_2 x$ reflected about the $x$-axis, shown in Figure 4.10.
- The graph of $r(x) = \log_2(-x)$ is the graph of $f(x) = \log_2 x$ reflected about the $y$-axis, shown in Figure 4.11.

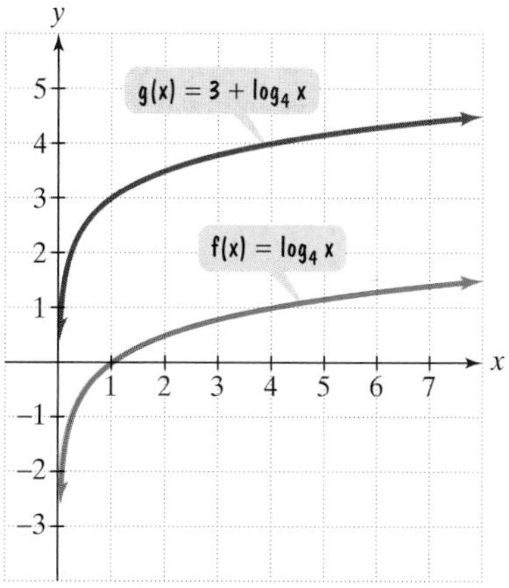


**Figure 4.9** Shifting vertically up three units

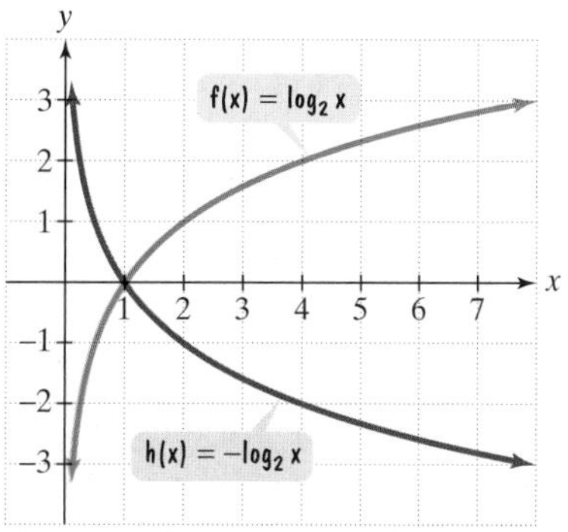


**Figure 4.10** Reflection about the $x$-axis

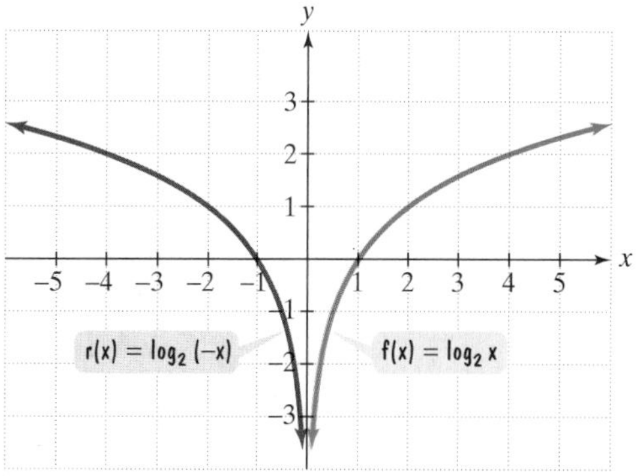


**Figure 4.11** Reflection about the $y$-axis

**6** Find the domain of a logarithmic function.

## The Domain of a Logarithmic Function

In Section 4.1 we learned that the domain of an exponential function includes all real numbers and its range is the set of positive real numbers. Because the logarithmic function reverses the domain and the range of the exponential function, the **domain of a logarithmic function is the set of all positive real numbers.** Thus, $\log_2 8$ is defined because the value of $x$ in the logarithmic expression, 8, is greater than zero and therefore is included in the domain of the logarithmic function $f(x) = \log_2 x$. However, $\log_2 0$ and $\log_2(-8)$ are not defined because 0 and $-8$ are not positive real numbers and therefore are excluded from the domain of the logarithmic function $f(x) = \log_2 x$. In general, the domain of $f(x) = \log_b(x + c)$ consists of all $x$ for which $x + c > 0$.

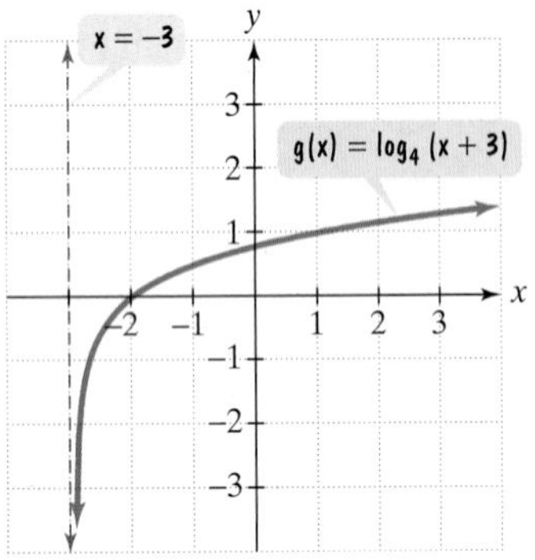


**Figure 4.12** The domain of $g(x) = \log_4(x + 3)$ is $(-3, \infty)$.

### EXAMPLE 7 Finding the Domain of a Logarithmic Function

Find the domain of $g(x) = \log_4(x + 3)$.

**Solution** The domain of $g$ consists of all $x$ for which $x + 3 > 0$. Solving this inequality for $x$, we obtain $x > -3$. Thus, the domain of $g$ is $(-3, \infty)$. This is illustrated in Figure 4.12. The vertical asymptote is $x = -3$, and all points on the graph of $g$ have $x$-coordinates that are greater than $-3$.

**Check Point 7** Find the domain of $h(x) = \log_4(x - 5)$.

**7** Use common logarithms.

## Common Logarithms

The logarithmic function with base 10 is called the **common logarithmic function.** The function $f(x) = \log_{10} x$ is usually expressed as $f(x) = \log x$. A calculator with a [LOG] key can be used to evaluate common logarithms. Here are some examples:

| Logarithm | Graphing Calculator Keystrokes | Display (or Approximate Display) |
|---|---|---|
| $\log 1000$ | [LOG] 1000 [ENTER] | 3 |
| $\log \frac{5}{2}$ | [LOG] [(] 5 [÷] 2 [)] [ENTER] | 0.39794 |
| $\frac{\log 5}{\log 2}$ | [LOG] 5 [÷] [LOG] 2 [ENTER] | 2.32192 |
| $\log(-3)$ | [LOG] [(−)] 3 [ENTER] | [ERROR] |

The error message given by many graphing calculators for $\log(-3)$ is a reminder that the domain of every logarithmic function, including the common logarithmic function, is the set of positive real numbers.

Many real-life phenomena start with rapid growth, and then the growth begins to level off. This type of behavior can be modeled by logarithmic functions.

## EXAMPLE 8 Modeling Height of Children

The percentage of adult height attained by a boy who is $x$ years old can be modeled by

$$f(x) = 29 + 48.8\log(x + 1)$$

where $x$ represents the boy's age and $f(x)$ represents the percentage of his adult height. Approximately what percentage of his adult height is a boy at age eight?

**Solution** We substitute the boy's age, 8, for $x$ and evaluate the function at 8.

$$f(x) = 29 + 48.8\log(x + 1) \quad \text{This is the given function.}$$

$$f(8) = 29 + 48.8\log(8 + 1) \quad \text{Substitute 8 for } x.$$

$$= 29 + 48.8\log 9 \quad \text{Graphing calculator keystrokes:}$$

$$\approx 76 \quad 29 \boxed{+} 48.8 \boxed{\times} \boxed{\text{LOG}}\ 9 \boxed{\text{ENTER}}$$

Thus, an 8-year-old boy is approximately 76% of his adult height.

**Check Point 8** Use the function in Example 8 to answer this question: Approximately what percentage of his adult height is a boy at age 10?

The basic properties of logarithms that were listed earlier in this section can be applied to common logarithms.

### Properties of Common Logarithms

| General Properties | Common Logarithms |
|---|---|
| **1.** $\log_b 1 = 0$ | **1.** $\log 1 = 0$ |
| **2.** $\log_b b = 1$ | **2.** $\log 10 = 1$ |
| **3.** $\log_b b^x = x$ | **3.** $\log 10^x = x$ |
| **4.** $b^{\log_b x} = x$ | **4.** $10^{\log x} = x$ |

The property $\log 10^x = x$ can be used to evaluate common logarithms involving powers of 10. For example,

$$\log 100 = \log 10^2 = 2, \quad \log 1000 = \log 10^3 = 3, \quad \log 10^{7.1} = 7.1.$$

## EXAMPLE 9 Earthquake Intensity

The magnitude $R$ on the Richter scale of an earthquake of intensity $I$ is given by

$$R = \log \frac{I}{I_0}$$

where $I_0$ is the intensity of a barely felt zero-level earthquake. The earthquake that destroyed San Francisco in 1906 was $10^{8.3}$ times as intense as a zero-level earthquake. What was its magnitude on the Richter scale?

**Solution** Because the earthquake was $10^{8.3}$ times as intense as a zero-level earthquake, the intensity $I$ is $10^{8.3}I_0$.

$$R = \log \frac{I}{I_0}$$ This is the formula for magnitude on the Richter scale.

$$R = \log \frac{10^{8.3} I_0}{I_0}$$ Substitute $10^{8.3}I_0$ for $I$.

$$= \log 10^{8.3}$$ Simplify.

$$= 8.3$$ Use the property $\log 10^x = x$.

San Francisco's 1906 earthquake registered 8.3 on the Richter scale.

**Check Point 9** Use the formula in Example 9 to solve this problem. If an earthquake is 10,000 times as intense as a zero-level quake ($I = 10{,}000I_0$), what is its magnitude on the Richter scale?

**8** Use natural logarithms.

## Natural Logarithms

The logarithmic function with base $e$ is called the **natural logarithmic function**. The function $f(x) = \log_e x$ is usually expressed as $f(x) = \ln x$, read "el en of $x$." A calculator with an LN key can be used to evaluate natural logarithms.

Like the domain of all logarithmic functions, the domain of the natural logarithmic function is the set of all positive real numbers. Thus, the domain of $f(x) = \ln(x + c)$ consists of all $x$ for which $x + c > 0$.

### EXAMPLE 10 Finding Domains of Natural Logarithmic Functions

Find the domain of each function.

**a.** $f(x) = \ln(3 - x)$ **b.** $g(x) = \ln(x - 3)^2$

**Solution**

**a.** The domain of $f$ consists of all $x$ for which $3 - x > 0$. Solving this inequality for $x$, we obtain $x < 3$. Thus, the domain of $f$ is $(-\infty, 3)$. This is verified by the graph in Figure 4.13.

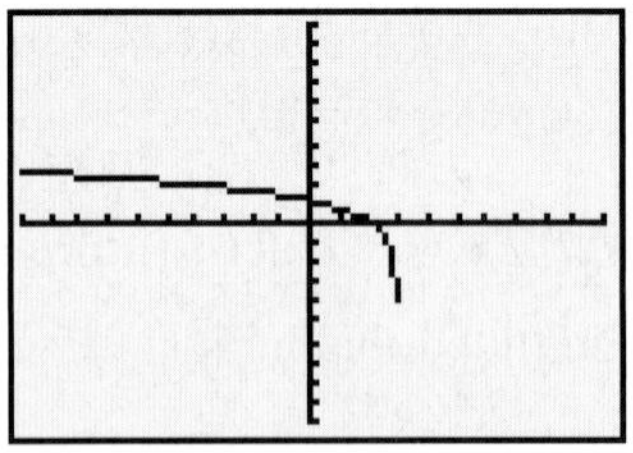

**Figure 4.13** The domain of $f(x) = \ln(3 - x)$ is $(-\infty, 3)$.

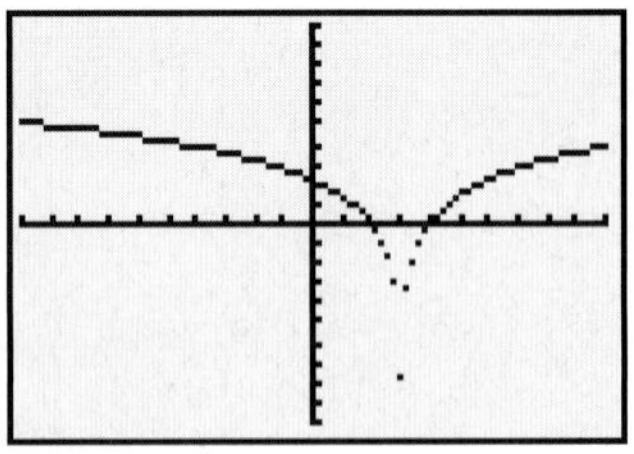

**Figure 4.14** 3 is excluded from the domain of $g(x) = \ln(x - 3)^2$.

**b.** The domain of $g$ consists of all $x$ for which $(x - 3)^2 > 0$. It follows that the domain of $g$ is all real numbers except 3. This is shown by the graph in Figure 4.14. If it is not obvious that 3 is excluded from the domain, try using a dot format.

**Check Point 10** Find the domain of each function.

**a.** $f(x) = \ln(4 - x)$ **b.** $g(x) = \ln x^2$

The basic properties of logarithms that were listed earlier in this section can be applied to natural logarithms.

**Properties of Natural Logarithms**

| General Properties | Natural Logarithms |
|---|---|
| **1.** $\log_b 1 = 0$ | **1.** $\ln 1 = 0$ |
| **2.** $\log_b b = 1$ | **2.** $\ln e = 1$ |
| **3.** $\log_b b^x = x$ | **3.** $\ln e^x = x$ |
| **4.** $b^{\log_b x} = x$ | **4.** $e^{\ln x} = x$ |

The property $\ln e^x = x$ can be used to evaluate natural logarithms involving powers of $e$. For example,

$$\ln e^2 = 2, \quad \ln e^3 = 3, \quad \ln e^{7.1} = 7.1, \quad \text{and} \quad \ln \frac{1}{e} = \ln e^{-1} = -1.$$

## EXAMPLE 11 Using Inverse Properties

Use inverse properties to simplify:

**a.** $\ln e^{7x}$ **b.** $e^{\ln 4x^2}$

**Solution**

**a.** Because $\ln e^x = x$, we conclude that $\ln e^{7x} = 7x$.

**b.** Because $e^{\ln x} = x$, we conclude $e^{\ln 4x^2} = 4x^2$.

**Check Point 11** Use inverse properties to simplify:

**a.** $\ln e^{25x}$ **b.** $e^{\ln \sqrt{x}}$

## EXAMPLE 12 Walking Speed and City population

As the population of a city increases, the pace of life also increases. The formula

$$W = 0.35 \ln P + 2.74$$

models average walking speed, $W$, in feet per second, for a resident of a city whose population is $P$ thousand. Find the average walking speed for people living in New York City with a population of 7323 thousand.

**Solution** We use the formula and substitute 7323 for $P$, the population in thousands.

| | |
|---|---|
| $W = 0.35 \ln P + 2.74$ | This is the given formula. |
| $W = 0.35 \ln 7323 + 2.74$ | Substitute 7323 for $P$. |
| $\approx 5.9$ | Graphing calculator keystrokes: 0.35 [×] [LN] 7323 [+] 2.74 [ENTER] |

The average walking speed in New York City is approximately 5.9 feet per second.

**Check Point 12** Use the formula $W = 0.35 \ln P + 2.74$ to find the average walking speed in Jackson, Mississippi with a population of 197 thousand.

# EXERCISE SET 4.2

## Practice Exercises

*In Exercises 1–8, write each equation in its equivalent exponential form.*

**1.** $4 = \log_2 16$
**2.** $6 = \log_2 64$
**3.** $2 = \log_3 x$
**4.** $2 = \log_9 x$
**5.** $5 = \log_b 32$
**6.** $3 = \log_b 27$
**7.** $\log_6 216 = y$
**8.** $\log_5 125 = y$

*In Exercises 9–20, write each equation in its equivalent logarithmic form.*

**9.** $2^3 = 8$
**10.** $5^4 = 625$
**11.** $2^{-4} = \frac{1}{16}$
**12.** $5^{-3} = \frac{1}{125}$
**13.** $\sqrt[3]{8} = 2$
**14.** $\sqrt[3]{64} = 4$
**15.** $13^2 = x$
**16.** $15^2 = x$
**17.** $b^3 = 1000$
**18.** $b^3 = 343$
**19.** $7^y = 200$
**20.** $8^y = 300$

*In Exercises 21–38, evaluate each expression without using a calculator.*

**21.** $\log_4 16$
**22.** $\log_7 49$
**23.** $\log_2 64$
**24.** $\log_3 27$
**25.** $\log_7 \sqrt{7}$
**26.** $\log_6 \sqrt{6}$
**27.** $\log_2 \frac{1}{8}$
**28.** $\log_3 \frac{1}{9}$
**29.** $\log_{64} 8$
**30.** $\log_{81} 9$
**31.** $\log_5 5$
**32.** $\log_{11} 11$
**33.** $\log_4 1$
**34.** $\log_6 1$
**35.** $\log_5 5^7$
**36.** $\log_4 4^6$
**37.** $8^{\log_8 19}$
**38.** $7^{\log_7 23}$

**39.** Graph $f(x) = 4^x$ and $g(x) = \log_4 x$ in the same rectangular coordinate system.

**40.** Graph $f(x) = 5^x$ and $g(x) = \log_5 x$ in the same rectangular coordinate system.

**41.** Graph $f(x) = (\frac{1}{2})^x$ and $g(x) = \log_{1/2} x$ in the same rectangular coordinate system.

**42.** Graph $f(x) = (\frac{1}{4})^x$ and $g(x) = \log_{1/4} x$ in the same rectangular coordinate system.

*In Exercises 43–48, the graph of a logarithmic function is given. Select the function for each graph from the following options.*

$$f(x) = \log_3 x,\ g(x) = \log_3 (x - 1),\ h(x) = \log_3 x - 1,$$
$$F(x) = -\log_3 x,\ G(x) = \log_3 (-x),\ H(x) = 1 - \log_3 x$$

**43.**

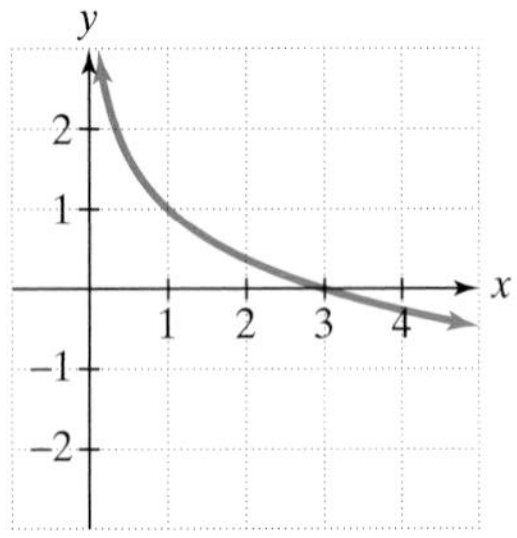


**44.**

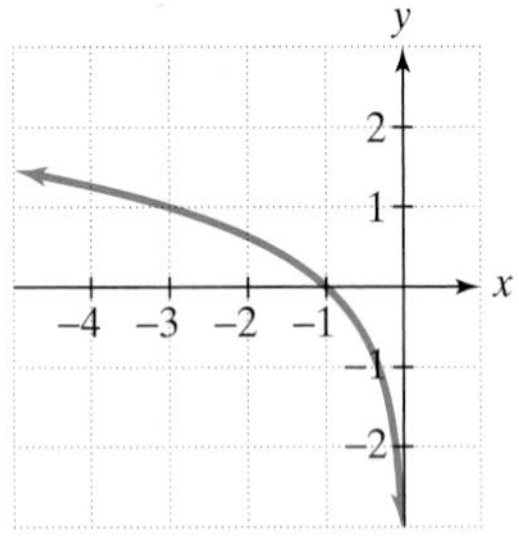


**45.**

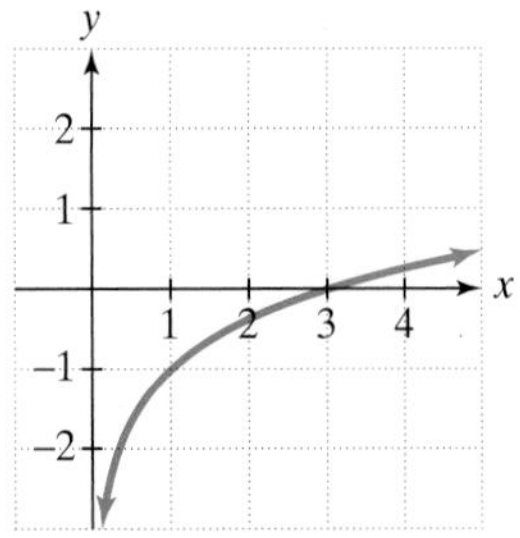

46.
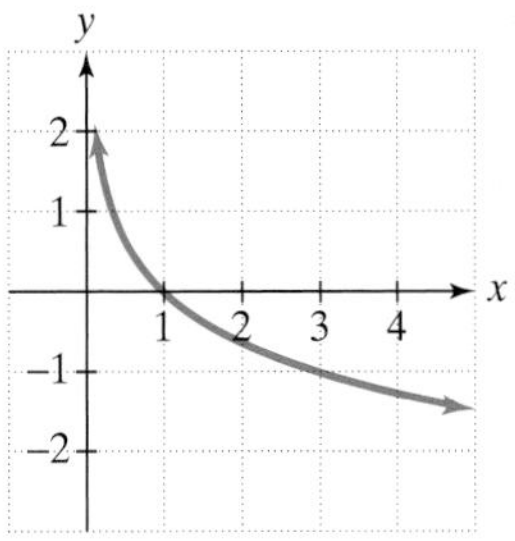


47.
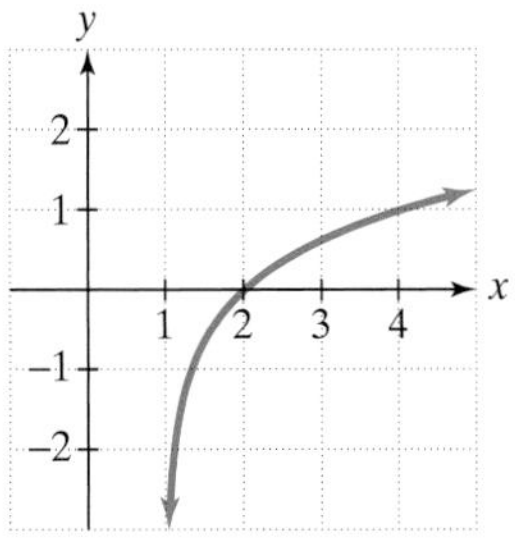


48.
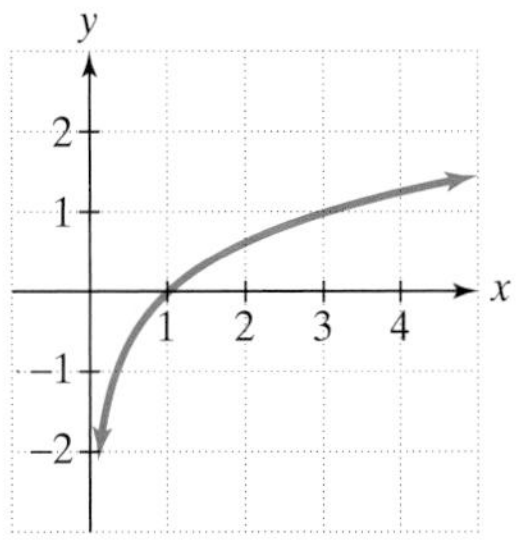


*In Exercises 49–54, begin by graphing $f(x) = \log_2 x$. Then use transformations of this graph to graph the given function. What is the graph's x-intercept? What is the vertical asymptote?*

**49.** $g(x) = \log_2(x + 1)$ **50.** $g(x) = \log_2(x + 2)$
**51.** $h(x) = 1 + \log_2 x$ **52.** $h(x) = 2 + \log_2 x$
**53.** $g(x) = \frac{1}{2}\log_2 x$ **54.** $g(x) = -2\log_2 x$

*In Exercises 55–60, find the domain of each logarithmic function.*

**55.** $f(x) = \log_5(x + 4)$ **56.** $f(x) = \log_5(x + 6)$
**57.** $f(x) = \log(2 - x)$ **58.** $f(x) = \log(7 - x)$
**59.** $f(x) = \ln(x - 2)^2$ **60.** $f(x) = \ln(x - 7)^2$

*In Exercises 61–74, evaluate each expression without using a calculator.*

**61.** $\log 100$ **62.** $\log 1000$ **63.** $\log 10^7$
**64.** $\log 10^8$ **65.** $10^{\log 33}$ **66.** $10^{\log 53}$
**67.** $\ln 1$ **68.** $\ln e$ **69.** $\ln e^6$
**70.** $\ln e^7$ **71.** $\ln\frac{1}{e^6}$ **72.** $\ln\frac{1}{e^7}$
**73.** $e^{\ln 125}$ **74.** $e^{\ln 300}$

*In Exercises 75–80, use inverse properties of logarithms to simplify each expression.*

**75.** $\ln e^{9x}$ **76.** $\ln e^{13x}$ **77.** $e^{\ln 5x^2}$
**78.** $e^{\ln 7x^2}$ **79.** $10^{\log\sqrt{x}}$ **80.** $10^{\log\sqrt[3]{x}}$

## Application Exercises

*The percentage of adult height attained by a girl who is x years old can be modeled by*

$$f(x) = 62 + 35\log(x - 4)$$

*where x represents the girl's age (from 5 to 15) and $f(x)$ represents the percentage of her adult height. Use the formula to solve Exercises 81–82.*

**81.** Approximately what percentage of her adult height is a girl at age 13?

**82.** Approximately what percentage of her adult height is a girl at age ten?

**83.** The annual amount that we spend to attend sporting events can be modeled by

$$f(x) = 2.05 + 1.3\ln x$$

where $x$ represents the number of years since 1984 and $f(x)$ represents the total annual expenditures for admission to spectator sports, in billions of dollars. In 2000, approximately how much was spent on admission to spectator sports?

**84.** The percentage of U.S. households with cable television can be modeled by

$$f(x) = 18.32 + 15.94\ln x$$

where $x$ represents the number of years since 1979 and $f(x)$ represents the percentage of U.S. households with cable television. What percentage of U.S. households had cable television in 1990?

*The loudness level of a sound, D, in decibels, is given by the formula*

$$D = 10\log(10^{12}I)$$

*where I is the intensity of the sound, in watts per meter². Decibel levels range from 0, a barely audible sound, to 160, a sound resulting in a ruptured eardrum. Use the formula to solve Exercises 85–86.*

**85.** The sound of a blue whale can be heard 500 miles away, reaching an intensity of $6.3 \times 10^6$ watts per meter². Determine the decibel level of this sound. At close range, can the sound of a blue whale rupture the human eardrum?

**86.** What is the decibel level of a normal conversation, $3.2 \times 10^{-6}$ watts per meter²?

**87.** Students in a psychology class took a final examination. As part of an experiment to see how much of the course content they remembered over time, they took equivalent forms of the exam in monthly intervals thereafter. The average score for the group, $f(t)$, after $t$ months was modeled by the function

$$f(t) = 88 - 15\ln(t + 1), \qquad 0 \le t \le 12.$$

**a.** What was the average score on the original exam?

**b.** What was the average score after 2 months? 4 months? 6 months? 8 months? 10 months? one year?

**c.** Sketch the graph of $f$ (either by hand or with a graphing utility). Describe what the graph indicates in terms of the material retained by the students.

## Writing in Mathematics

**88.** Describe the relationship between an equation in logarithmic form and an equivalent equation in exponential form.

**89.** What question can be asked to help evaluate $\log_3 81$?

**90.** Explain why the logarithm of 1 with base $b$ is 0.

**91.** Describe the following property using words: $\log_b b^x = x$.

**92.** Explain how to use the graph of $f(x) = 2^x$ to obtain the graph of $g(x) = \log_2 x$.

**93.** Explain how to find the domain of a logarithmic function.

**94.** New York City is one of the world's great walking cities. Use the formula in Example 12 on page 371 to describe what frequently happens to tourists exploring the city by foot.

**95.** Logarithmic models are well suited to phenomena in which growth is initially rapid but then begins to level off. Describe something that is changing over time that can be modeled using a logarithmic function.

**96.** Suppose that a girl is 4′ 6″ at age 10. Explain how to use the function in Exercises 81–82 to determine how tall she can expect to be as an adult.

## Technology Exercises

*In Exercises 97–100, graph f and g in the same viewing rectangle. Then describe the relationship of the graph of g to the graph of f.*

**97.** $f(x) = \ln x$, $g(x) = \ln(x + 3)$

**98.** $f(x) = \ln x$, $g(x) = \ln x + 3$

**99.** $f(x) = \log x$, $g(x) = -\log x$

**100.** $f(x) = \log x$, $g(x) = \log(x - 2) + 1$

**101.** Students in a mathematics class took a final examination. They took equivalent forms of the exam in monthly intervals thereafter. The average score, $f(t)$, for the group after $t$ months was modeled by the human memory function $f(t) = 75 - 10\log(t + 1)$, where $0 \le t \le 12$. Use a graphing utility to graph the function. Then determine how many months will elapse before the average score falls below 65.

**102.** Graph $f$ and $g$ in the same viewing rectangle.

**a.** $f(x) = \ln(3x)$, $g(x) = \ln 3 + \ln x$

**b.** $f(x) = \log(5x^2)$, $g(x) = \log 5 + \log x^2$

**c.** $f(x) = \ln(2x^3)$, $g(x) = \ln 2 + \ln x^3$

**d.** Describe what you observe in parts (a)–(c). Generalize this observation by writing an equivalent expression for $\log_b(MN)$, where $M > 0$ and $N > 0$.

**e.** Complete this statement: The logarithm of a product is equal to ________.

**103.** Graph each of the following functions in the same viewing rectangle and then place the functions in order from the one that increases most slowly to the one that increases most rapidly.

$$y = x,\ y = \sqrt{x},\ y = e^x,\ y = \ln x,\ y = x^x,\ y = x^2$$

## Critical Thinking Exercises

**104.** Which one of the following is true?

**a.** $\dfrac{\log_2 8}{\log_2 4} = \dfrac{8}{4}$

**b.** $\log(-100) = -2$.

**c.** The domain of $f(x) = \log_2 x$ is $(-\infty, \infty)$.

**d.** $\log_b x$ is the exponent to which $b$ must be raised to obtain $x$.

**105.** Without using a calculator, find the exact value of

$$\frac{\log_3 81 - \log_\pi 1}{\log_{2\sqrt{2}} 8 - \log 0.001}.$$

**106.** Solve for $x$: $\log_4[\log_3(\log_2 x)] = 0$.

**107.** Without using a calculator, determine which is the greater number: $\log_4 60$ or $\log_3 40$.

## Group Exercise

**108.** This group exercise involves exploring the way we grow. Group members should create a graph for the function that models the percentage of adult height attained by a boy who is $x$ years old, $f(x) = 29 + 48.8\log(x + 1)$. Let $x = 1, 2, 3, \ldots, 12$, find function values, and connect the resulting points with a smooth curve. Then create a function that models the percentage of adult height attained by a girl who is $x$ years old, $g(x) = 62 + 35\log(x - 4)$. Let $x = 5, 6, 7, \ldots, 15$, find function values, and connect the resulting points by a smooth curve. Group members should then discuss similarities and differences in the growth patterns for boys and girls based on the graphs.

# SECTION 4.3 Properties of Logarithms

## Objectives

1. Use the product rule.
2. Use the quotient rule.
3. Use the power rule.
4. Expand logarithmic expressions.
5. Condense logarithmic expressions.
6. Use the change-of-base property.

We all learn new things in different ways. In this section, we consider important properties of logarithms. What would be the most effective way for you to learn about these properties? Would it be helpful to use your graphing utility and discover one of these properties for yourself? To do so, work Exercise 102 in Exercise Set 4.2 before continuing. Would the properties become more meaningful if you could see exactly where they come from? If so, you will find details of the proofs of many of these properties in the appendix. The remainder of our work in this chapter will be based on the properties of logarithms that you learn in this section.

1 Use the product rule.

## The Product Rule

Properties of exponents correspond to properties of logarithms. For example, when we multiply with the same base, we add exponents:

$$b^M \cdot b^N = b^{M+N}.$$

This property of exponents, coupled with an awareness that a logarithm is an exponent, suggests the following property, called the **product rule**.

**The Product Rule**

Let $b$, $M$, and $N$ be positive real numbers with $b \neq 1$.

$$\log_b(MN) = \log_b M + \log_b N$$

The logarithm of a product is the sum of the logarithms.

When we use the product rule to write a single logarithm as the sum of two logarithms, we say that we are **expanding a logarithmic expression**. For example, we can use the product rule to expand $\ln(4x)$:

$$\ln(4x) = \ln 4 + \ln x$$

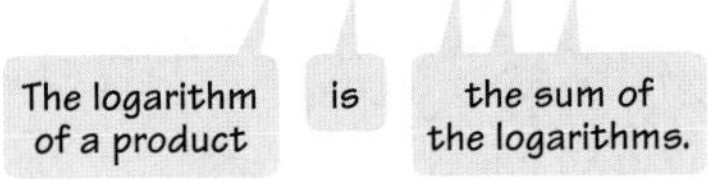
The logarithm of a product
is
the sum of the logarithms.

### EXAMPLE 1 Using the Product Rule

Use the product rule to expand

**a.** $\log_4(7 \cdot 9)$ **b.** $\log(10x)$

**Solution**

**a.** $\log_4(7 \cdot 9) = \log_4 7 + \log_4 9$ The logarithm of a product is the sum of the logarithms.

**b.** $\log(10x) = \log 10 + \log x$ The logarithm of a product is the sum of the logarithms. These are common logarithms with base 10 understood.

$= 1 + \log x$ Because $\log_b b = 1$, then $\log_{10} 10 = 1$.

**Check Point 1** Use the product rule to expand

**a.** $\log_6(10 \cdot 9)$ **b.** $\log(100x)$

## The Quotient Rule

2 Use the quotient rule.

When we divide with the same base, we subtract exponents:

$$\frac{b^M}{b^N} = b^{M-N}.$$

This property suggests the following property of logarithms, called the **quotient rule**.

> **The Quotient Rule**
>
> Let $b$, $M$, and $N$ be positive real numbers with $b \neq 1$.
>
> $$\log_b\left(\frac{M}{N}\right) = \log_b M - \log_b N$$
>
> The logarithm of a quotient is the difference of the logarithms.

When we use the quotient rule to write a single logarithm as the difference of two logarithms, we say that we are **expanding a logarithmic expression**. For example, we can use the quotient rule to expand $\log \frac{x}{2}$:

$$\log \frac{x}{2} = \log x - \log 2$$

The logarithm of a quotient | is | the difference of the logarithms.

### EXAMPLE 2 Using the Quotient Rule

Use the quotient rule to expand

**a.** $\log_7\left(\frac{14}{x}\right)$ **b.** $\ln\left(\frac{e^3}{7}\right)$

**Solution**

**a.** $\log_7\left(\frac{14}{x}\right) = \log_7 14 - \log_7 x$ — The logarithm of a quotient is the difference of the logarithms.

**b.** $\ln\left(\frac{e^3}{7}\right) = \ln e^3 - \ln 7$ — The logarithm of a quotient is the difference of the logarithms. These are natural logarithms with base *e* understood.

$= 3 - \ln 7$ — Because $\ln e^x = x$, then $\ln e^3 = 3$.

**Check Point 2** Use the quotient rule to expand

**a.** $\log_8\left(\frac{23}{x}\right)$ **b.** $\ln\left(\frac{e^5}{11}\right)$

**3** Use the power rule.

## The Power Rule

When an exponential expression is raised to a power, we multiply exponents:

$$(b^M)^p = b^{Mp}.$$

This property suggests the following property of logarithms, called the **power rule**.

**The Power Rule**

Let *b*, *M*, and *N* be positive real numbers with $b \neq 1$, and let *p* be any real number.

$$\log_b M^p = p \log_b M$$

The logarithm of a number with an exponent is the product of the exponent and the logarithm of that number.

When we use the power rule to "pull the exponent to the front," we say that we are **expanding a logarithmic expression**. For example, we can use the power rule to expand $\ln x^2$:

$$\ln x^2 = 2 \ln x.$$

The logarithm of a number with an exponent | is | the product of the exponent and the logarithm of that number.

Figure 4.15 shows the graphs of $y = \ln x^2$ and $y = 2\ln x$. Are $\ln x^2$ and $2 \ln x$ the same? The graphs illustrate that $y = \ln x^2$ and $y = 2\ln x$ have different domains. The graphs are only the same if $x > 0$. Thus, we should write

$$\ln x^2 = 2\ln x \text{ for } x > 0.$$

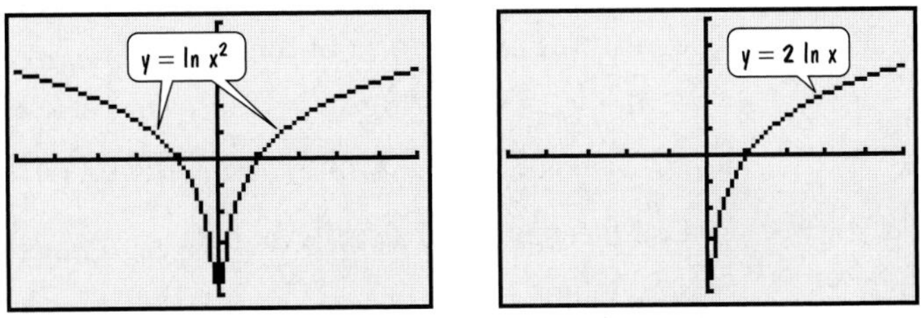


Domain: $(-\infty, 0)$ or $(0, \infty)$ Domain: $(0, \infty)$

**Figure 4.15** $\ln x^2$ and $2 \ln x$ have different domains.

When expanding a logarithmic expression, you might want to determine whether the rewriting has changed the domain of the expression.

**4** Expand logarithmic expressions.

### EXAMPLE 3 Using the Power Rule

Use the power rule to expand

**a.** $\log_5 7^4$ **b.** $\ln \sqrt{x}$

**Solution**

**a.** $\log_5 7^4 = 4\log_5 7$ The logarithm of a number with an exponent is the exponent times the logarithm of the number.

**b.** $\ln \sqrt{x} = \ln x^{1/2}$ Rewrite the radical using a rational exponent.

$= \frac{1}{2}\ln x$ Use the power rule to bring the exponent to the front.

**Check Point 3** Use the power rule to expand

**a.** $\log_6 8^9$ **b.** $\ln \sqrt[3]{x}$

## Study Tip

The graphs show

$$y_1 = \ln(x+3)$$

and $y_2 = \ln x + \ln 3$. The graphs are not the same. The graph of $y_1$ is the graph of the natural logarithmic function shifted 3 units to the left. By contrast, the graph of $y_2$ is the graph of the natural logarithmic function shifted upward by ln 3, or about 1.1 units. Thus we see that

$$\ln(x+3) \neq \ln x + \ln 3.$$

In general,

$$\log_b(M+N) \neq \log_b M + \log_b N.$$

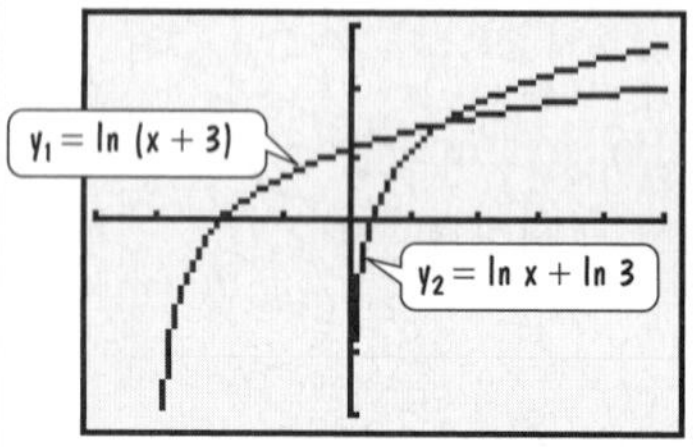


Try to avoid the following errors.

**INCORRECT**

$\log_b(M+N) = \log_b M + \log_b N$

$\log_b(M-N) = \log_b M - \log_b N$

$\log_b(M \cdot N) = \log_b M \cdot \log_b N$

$\log_b\left(\frac{M}{N}\right) = \frac{\log_b M}{\log_b N}$

$\frac{\log_b M}{\log_b N} = \log_b M - \log_b N$

## Expanding Logarithmic Expressions

It is sometimes necessary to use more than one property of logarithms when you expand a logarithmic expression. Properties for expanding logarithmic expressions are as follows:

**Properties for Expanding Logarithmic Expressions**

1. $\log_b(MN) = \log_b M + \log_b N$ Product rule
2. $\log_b\left(\frac{M}{N}\right) = \log_b M - \log_b N$ Quotient rule
3. $\log_b M^p = p\log_b M$ Power rule

In all cases, $M > 0$ and $N > 0$.

### EXAMPLE 4 Expanding Logarithmic Expressions

Use logarithmic properties to expand each expression as much as possible.

**a.** $\log_b x^2\sqrt{y}$ **b.** $\log_6\left(\frac{\sqrt[3]{x}}{36y^4}\right)$

**Solution** We will have to use two or more of the properties for expanding logarithms in each part of this example.

**a.** $\log_b x^2\sqrt{y} = \log_b x^2 y^{1/2}$ Use exponential notation.

$= \log_b x^2 + \log_b y^{1/2}$ Use the product rule.

$= 2\log_b x + \frac{1}{2}\log_b y$ Use the power rule.

**b.** $\log_6\left(\frac{\sqrt[3]{x}}{36y^4}\right) = \log_6 \frac{x^{1/3}}{36y^4}$ — Use exponential notation.

$= \log_6 x^{1/3} - \log_6 36y^4$ — Use the quotient rule.

$= \log_6 x^{1/3} - (\log_6 36 + \log_6 y^4)$ — Use the product rule on $\log_6 36y^4$.

$= \frac{1}{3}\log_6 x - (\log_6 36 + 4\log_6 y)$ — Use the power rule.

$= \frac{1}{3}\log_6 x - \log_6 36 - 4\log_6 y$ — Apply the distributive property.

$= \frac{1}{3}\log_6 x - 2 - 4\log_6 y$ — $\log_6 36 = 2$ because 2 is the power to which we must raise 6 to get 36. $(6^2 = 36)$

**Check Point 4** Use logarithmic properties to expand each expression as much as possible.

**a.** $\log_b x^4\sqrt[3]{y}$ **b.** $\log_5 \frac{\sqrt{x}}{25y^3}$

5 Condense logarithmic expressions.

## Condensing Logarithmic Expressions

To **condense a logarithmic expression**, we write the sum or difference of two or more logarithmic expressions as a single logarithmic expression. We use the properties of logarithms to do so.

### Properties for Condensing Logarithmic Expressions

1. $\log_b M + \log_b N = \log_b(MN)$ — Product rule
2. $\log_b M - \log_b N = \log_b\left(\frac{M}{N}\right)$ — Quotient rule
3. $p\log_b M = \log_b M^p$ — Power rule

In all cases, $M > 0$ and $N > 0$.

### EXAMPLE 5 Condensing Logarithmic Expressions

Write as a single logarithm:

**a.** $\log_4 2 + \log_4 32$ **b.** $\log(4x - 3) - \log x$

**Solution**

**a.** $\log_4 2 + \log_4 32 = \log_4(2 \cdot 32)$ — Use the product rule.

$= \log_4 64$ — We now have a single logarithm. However, we can simplify.

$= 3$ — $\log_4 64 = 3$ because $4^3 = 64$.

**b.** $\log(4x - 3) - \log x = \log \frac{4x - 3}{x}$ — Use the quotient rule.

**Check Point 5** Write as a single logarithm:

**a.** $\log 25 + \log 4$ **b.** $\log(7x + 6) - \log x$

Coefficients of logarithms must be 1 before you can condense them using the product and quotient rules. For example, to condense

$$2 \ln x + \ln(x + 1),$$

the coefficient of the first term must be 1. We use the power rule to rewrite the coefficient as an exponent:

1. Make the number in front an exponent.

$$2 \ln x + \ln(x + 1) = \ln x^2 + \ln(x + 1) = \ln x^2(x + 1)$$

2. Use the product rule. The sum of logarithms with coefficients 1 is the logarithm of the product.

## EXAMPLE 6 Condensing Logarithmic Expressions

**a.** $\frac{1}{2}\log x + 4\log(x - 1)$ **b.** $3\ln(x + 7) - \ln x$

**Solution**

**a.** $\frac{1}{2}\log x + 4\log(x - 1)$

$= \log x^{1/2} + \log(x - 1)^4$ Use the power rule so that all coefficients are 1.

$= \log x^{1/2}(x - 1)^4$ Use the product rule.

**b.** $3\ln(x + 7) - \ln x$

$= \ln(x + 7)^3 - \ln x$ Use the power rule so that all coefficients are 1.

$= \ln \dfrac{(x + 7)^3}{x}$ Use the quotient rule.

**Check Point 6** Write as a single logarithm:

**a.** $2\ln x + \frac{1}{3}\ln(x + 5)$ **b.** $2\log(x - 3) - \log x$

**6** Use the change-of-base property.

### The Change-of-Base Property

We have seen that calculators give the values of both common logarithms (base 10) and natural logarithms (base $e$). To find a logarithm with any other base, we can use the following change-of-base property.

**The Change-of-Base Property**

For any logarithmic bases $a$ and $b$, and any positive number $M$,

$$\log_b M = \frac{\log_a M}{\log_a b}.$$

The logarithm of $M$ with base $b$ is equal to the logarithm of $M$ with any new base divided by the logarithm of $b$ with that new base.

In the change-of-base property, base $b$ is the base of the original logarithm. Base $a$ is a new base that we introduce. Thus, the change-of-base property allows us to change from base $b$ to *any* new base $a$, as long as the newly introduced base is a positive number not equal to 1.

The change-of-base property is used to write a logarithm in terms of quantities that can be evaluated with a calculator. Because calculators contain keys for common (base 10) and natural (base $e$) logarithms, we will frequently introduce base 10 or base $e$.

| **Change-of-Base Property** | **Introducing Common Logarithms** | **Introducing Natural Logarithms** |
|---|---|---|
| $\log_b M = \dfrac{\log_a M}{\log_a b}$ | $\log_b M = \dfrac{\log_{10} M}{\log_{10} b}$ | $\log_b M = \dfrac{\log_e M}{\log_e b}$ |
| $a$ is the new introduced base. | 10 is the new introduced base. | $e$ is the new introduced base. |

Using the notations for common logarithms and natural logarithms, we have the following results.

**Discovery**

Find a reasonable estimate of $\log_5 140$ to the nearest whole number. 5 to what power is 140? Compare your estimate to the value obtained in Example 7.

**The Change-of-Base Property: Introducing Common and Natural Logarithms**

**Introducing Common Logarithms**

$$\log_b M = \frac{\log M}{\log b}$$

**Introducing Natural Logarithms**

$$\log_b M = \frac{\ln M}{\ln b}$$

## EXAMPLE 7 Changing Base to Common Logarithms

Use common logarithms to evaluate $\log_5 140$.

**Solution** Because $\log_b M = \dfrac{\log M}{\log b}$,

$$\log_5 140 = \frac{\log 140}{\log 5}$$

$$\approx 3.07.$$ Use a calculator: LOG 140 ÷ LOG 5 ENTER

This means that $\log_5 140 \approx 3.07$.

**Check Point 7** Use common logarithms to evaluate $\log_7 2506$.

## EXAMPLE 8 Changing Base to Natural Logarithms

Use natural logarithms to evaluate $\log_5 140$.

**Solution** Because $\log_b M = \dfrac{\ln M}{\ln b}$,

$$\log_5 140 = \frac{\ln 140}{\ln 5}$$

$$\approx 3.07.$$ Use a calculator: LN 140 ÷ LN 5 ENTER

We have again shown that $\log_5 140 \approx 3.07$.

**Check Point 8** Use natural logarithms to evaluate $\log_7 2506$.

We can use the change-of-base property to graph logarithmic functions with bases other than 10 or $e$ on a graphing utility.

### EXAMPLE 9 Using a Graphing Utility to Graph Logarithmic Functions

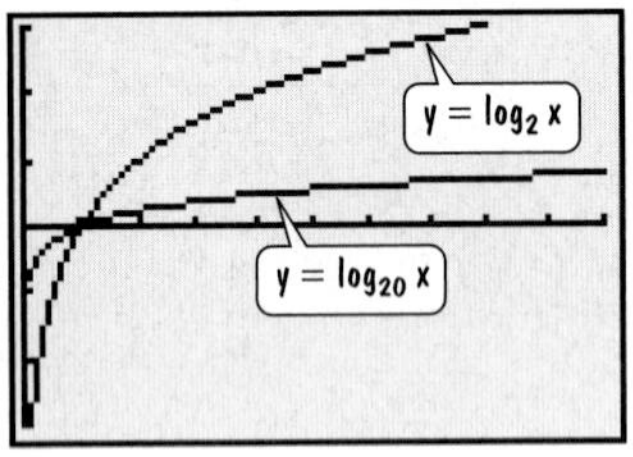


**Figure 4.16** Using the change-of-base property to graph logarithmic functions

Graph $y = \log_2 x$ and $y = \log_{20} x$ in the same viewing rectangle.

**Solution** Because $\log_2 x = \frac{\ln x}{\ln 2}$ and $\log_{20} x = \frac{\ln x}{\ln 20}$ the functions are entered as

$y_1$ = [LN] $x$ [÷] [LN] 2 [ENTER]

and $y_2$ = [LN] $x$ [÷] [LN] 20 [ENTER].

Using a $[0, 10, 1] \times [-3, 3, 1]$ viewing rectangle, the graphs are shown in Figure 4.16.

**Check Point 9** Graph $y = \log_3 x$ and $y = \log_{15} x$ in the same viewing rectangle.

## The Curious Number *e*

You will learn more about each curiosity mentioned below when you take calculus.

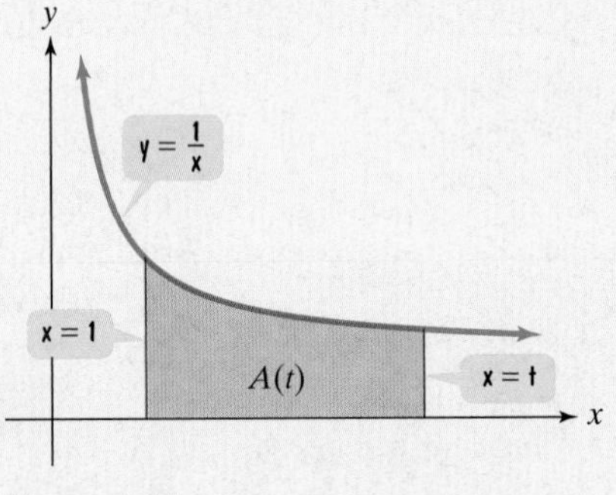


**Figure 4.17**

- The number $e$ was named by the Swiss mathematician Leonhard Euler (1707–1783), who proved that it is the limit as $n \to \infty$ of $\left(1 + \frac{1}{n}\right)^n$.
- $e$ features in Euler's remarkable relationship $e^{i\pi} = -1$, in which $i = \sqrt{-1}$.
- The first few decimal places of $e$ are fairly easy to remember: $e = 2.7\,1828\,1828\,45\,90\,45\ldots$.
- The best approximation of $e$ using numbers less than 1000 is also easy to remember: $e \approx \frac{878}{323} \approx 2.71826\ldots$.
- Isaac Newton (1642–1727), one of the cofounders of calculus, showed that $e^x = 1 + x + \frac{x^2}{2!} + \frac{x^3}{3!} + \frac{x^4}{4!} + \ldots$, from which we obtain $e = 1 + 1 + \frac{1}{2!} + \frac{1}{3!} + \frac{1}{4!} \ldots$, an infinite sum suitable for calculation because its terms decrease so rapidly. (*Note:* $n!$ ($n$ factorial) is the product of all the consecutive integers from $n$ down to 1: $n! = n(n-1)(n-2)(n-3)\cdot\ldots\cdot 3\cdot 2\cdot 1$.)
- The area of the region bounded by $y = \frac{1}{x}$, the $x$-axis, $x = 1$ and $x = t$ (shaded in Figure 4.17) is a function of $t$, designated by $A(t)$. Grégoire de Saint-Vincent, a Belgian Jesuit (1584–1667), spent his entire professional life attempting to find a formula for $A(t)$. With his student, he showed that $A(t) = \ln t$, becoming one of the first mathematicians to make use of the logarithmic function for something other than a computational device.

# EXERCISE SET 4.3

## Practice Exercises

*In Exercises 1–32, use properties of logarithms to expand each logarithmic expression as much as possible. Where possible, evaluate logarithmic expressions without using a calculator.*

**1.** $\log_5(12 \cdot 3)$

**2.** $\log_8(13 \cdot 9)$

**3.** $\log_7(7x)$

**4.** $\log_9(9x)$

**5.** $\log(1000x)$

**6.** $\log(10{,}000x)$

**7.** $\log_7\left(\frac{7}{x}\right)$

**8.** $\log_9\left(\frac{9}{x}\right)$

**9.** $\log\left(\frac{x}{100}\right)$

**10.** $\log\left(\frac{x}{1000}\right)$

**11.** $\log_4\left(\frac{64}{y}\right)$

**12.** $\log_5\left(\frac{125}{y}\right)$

**13.** $\ln\left(\frac{e^2}{5}\right)$

**14.** $\ln\left(\frac{e^4}{8}\right)$

**15.** $\log_b x^3$

**16.** $\log_b x^7$

**17.** $\log N^{-6}$

**18.** $\log M^{-8}$

**19.** $\ln \sqrt[5]{x}$

**20.** $\ln \sqrt[7]{x}$

**21.** $\log_b x^2 y$

**22.** $\log_b xy^3$

**23.** $\log_4\left(\frac{\sqrt{x}}{64}\right)$

**24.** $\log_5\left(\frac{\sqrt{x}}{25}\right)$

**25.** $\log_6\left(\frac{36}{\sqrt{x+1}}\right)$

**26.** $\log_8\left(\frac{64}{\sqrt{x+1}}\right)$

**27.** $\log_b \frac{x^2 y}{z^2}$

**28.** $\log_b \frac{x^3 y}{z^2}$

**29.** $\log \sqrt{100x}$

**30.** $\ln \sqrt{ex}$

**31.** $\log \sqrt[3]{\frac{x}{y}}$

**32.** $\log \sqrt[5]{\frac{x}{y}}$

*In Exercises 33–52, use properties of logarithms to condense each logarithmic expression. Write the expression as a single logarithm whose coefficient is 1. Where possible, evaluate logarithmic expressions.*

**33.** $\log 5 + \log 2$

**34.** $\log 250 + \log 4$

**35.** $\ln x + \ln 7$

**36.** $\ln x + \ln 3$

**37.** $\log_2 96 - \log_2 3$

**38.** $\log_3 405 - \log_3 5$

**39.** $\log(2x + 5) - \log x$

**40.** $\log(3x + 7) - \log x$

**41.** $\log x + 3 \log y$

**42.** $\log x + 7 \log y$

**43.** $\frac{1}{2} \ln x + \ln y$

**44.** $\frac{1}{3} \ln x + \ln y$

**45.** $2 \log_b x + 3 \log_b y$

**46.** $5 \log_b x + 6 \log_b y$

**47.** $5 \ln x - 2 \ln y$

**48.** $7 \ln x - 3 \ln y$

**49.** $3 \ln x - \frac{1}{3} \ln y$

**50.** $2 \ln x - \frac{1}{2} \ln y$

**51.** $4 \ln(x + 6) - 3 \ln x$

**52.** $8 \ln(x + 9) - 4 \ln x$

*In Exercises 53–60, use common logarithms or natural logarithms and a calculator to evaluate to four decimal places.*

**53.** $\log_5 13$

**54.** $\log_6 17$

**55.** $\log_{14} 87.5$

**56.** $\log_{16} 57.2$

**57.** $\log_{0.1} 17$

**58.** $\log_{0.3} 19$

**59.** $\log_\pi 63$

**60.** $\log_\pi 400$

## Application Exercises

**61.** The loudness level of a sound can be expressed by comparing the sound's intensity to the intensity of a sound barely audible to the human ear. The formula

$$D = 10(\log I - \log I_0)$$

describes the loudness level of a sound, $D$, in decibels, where $I$ is the intensity of the sound, in watts per meter$^2$, and $I_0$ is the intensity of a sound barely audible to the human ear.

**a.** Express the formula so that the expression in parentheses is written as a single logarithm.

**b.** Use the form of the formula from part (a) to answer this question. If a sound has an intensity 100 times the intensity of a softer sound, how much larger on the decibel scale is the loudness level of the more intense sound?

**62.** The formula

$$t = \frac{1}{c}[\ln A - \ln(A - N)]$$

describes the time, $t$, in weeks, that it takes to achieve mastery of a portion of a task, where $A$ is the maximum learning possible, $N$ is the portion of the learning that is to be achieved, and c is a constant used to measure an individual's learning style.

**a.** Express the formula so that the expression in brackets is written as a single logarithm.

**b.** The formula is also used to determine how long it will take chimpanzees and apes to master a task. For example, a typical chimpanzee learning sign language can master a maximum of 65 signs. Use the form of the formula from part (a) to answer this question. How many weeks will it take a chimpanzee to master 30 signs if $c$ for that chimp is 0.03?

## Writing in Mathematics

**63.** Describe the product rule for logarithms and give an example.

**64.** Describe the quotient rule for logarithms and give an example.

**65.** Describe the power rule for logarithms and give an example.

**66.** Without showing the details, explain how to condense $\ln x - 2\ln(x+1)$.

**67.** Describe the change-of-base property and give an example.

**68.** Explain how to use your calculator to find $\log_{14} 283$.

**69.** You overhear a student talking about a property of logarithms in which division becomes subtraction. Explain what the student means by this.

**70.** Find $\ln 2$ using a calculator. Then calculate each of the following: $1 - \frac{1}{2}$; $1 - \frac{1}{2} + \frac{1}{3}$; $1 - \frac{1}{2} + \frac{1}{3} - \frac{1}{4}$; $1 - \frac{1}{2} + \frac{1}{3} - \frac{1}{4} + \frac{1}{5}$; .... Describe what you observe.

## Technology Exercises

**71. a.** Use a graphing utility (and the change-of-base property) to graph $y = \log_3 x$.

**b.** Graph $y = 2 + \log_3 x$, $y = \log_3(x+2)$, and $y = -\log_3 x$ in the same viewing rectangle as $y = \log_3 x$. Then describe the change or changes that need to be made to the graph of $y = \log_3 x$ to obtain each of these three graphs.

**72.** Graph $y = \log x$, $y = \log(10x)$, and $y = \log(0.1x)$ in the same viewing rectangle. Describe the relationship among the three graphs. What logarithmic property accounts for this relationship?

**73.** Use a graphing utility and the change-of-base property to graph $y = \log_3 x$, $y = \log_{25} x$, and $y = \log_{100} x$ in the same viewing rectangle.

**a.** Which graph is on the top in the interval $(0, 1)$? Which is on the bottom?

**b.** Which graph is on the top in the interval $(1, \infty)$? Which is on the bottom?

**c.** Generalize by writing a statement about which graph is on top, which is on the bottom, and in which intervals, using $y = \log_b x$ where $b > 1$.

*Disprove each statement in Exercises 74–78 by*

**a.** *letting y equal a positive constant of your choice.*

**b.** *using a graphing utility to graph the function on each side of the equal sign. The two functions should have different graphs, showing that the equation is not true in general.*

**74.** $\log(x+y) = \log x + \log y$

**75.** $\log \frac{x}{y} = \frac{\log x}{\log y}$

**76.** $\ln(x-y) = \ln x - \ln y$

**77.** $\ln(xy) = (\ln x)(\ln y)$

**78.** $\frac{\ln x}{\ln y} = \ln x - \ln y$

## Critical Thinking Exercises

**79.** Which one of the following is true?

**a.** $\frac{\log_7 49}{\log_7 7} = \log_7 49 - \log_7 7$

**b.** $\log_b(x^3 + y^3) = 3\log_b x + 3\log_b y$

**c.** $\log_b(xy)^5 = (\log_b x + \log_b y)^5$

**d.** $\ln\sqrt{2} = \frac{\ln 2}{2}$

**80.** Use the change-of-base property to prove that

$$\log e = \frac{1}{\ln 10}$$

**81.** If $\log 3 = A$ and $\log 7 = B$, find $\log_7 9$ in terms of $A$ and $B$.

**82.** Write as a single term that does not contain a logarithm:

$$e^{\ln 8x^5 - \ln 2x^2}.$$

# SECTION 4.4 Exponential and Logarithmic Equations

## Objectives

1. Solve exponential equations.
2. Solve logarithmic equations.
3. Solve applied problems involving exponential and logarithmic equations.

Is an early retirement awaiting you?

You inherited \$30,000. You'd like to put aside \$25,000 and eventually have over half a million dollars for early retirement. Is this possible? In this section you will see how techniques for solving equations with variable exponents provide an answer to this question.

**1** Solve exponential equations.

## Exponential Equations

An **exponential equation** is an equation containing a variable in an exponent. Examples of exponential equations include

$$4^x = 15 \qquad \text{and} \qquad 40e^{0.6x} = 240.$$

Logarithms are extremely useful in solving such equations. The solution begins with isolating the exponential expression and taking the natural logarithm on both sides. Why can we do this? All logarithmic functions are one-to-one—that is, no two different ordered pairs have the same second component. Thus, if $M$ and $N$ are positive real numbers and $M = N$, then $\log_b M = \log_b N$.

**Using Natural Logarithms to Solve Exponential Equations**

1. Isolate the exponential expression.
2. Take the natural logarithm on both sides of the equation.
3. Simplify using one of the following properties:

$$\ln b^x = x \ln b \quad \text{or} \quad \ln e^x = x.$$

4. Solve for the variable.

### EXAMPLE 1 Solving an Exponential Equation

Solve: $4^x = 15$.

**Solution** Because the exponential expression, $4^x$, is already isolated on the left, we begin by taking the natural logarithm on both sides of the equation.

$$4^x = 15 \quad \text{This is the given equation.}$$

$$\ln 4^x = \ln 15 \quad \text{Take the natural logarithm on both sides.}$$

$$x \ln 4 = \ln 15 \quad \text{Use the power rule and bring the variable exponent to the front: } \ln b^x = x \ln b.$$

$$x = \frac{\ln 15}{\ln 4} \quad \text{Solve for } x \text{ by dividing both sides by } \ln 4.$$

We now have an exact value for $x$. We use the exact value for $x$ in the equation's solution set. Thus, the equation's solution set is $\left\{\frac{\ln 15}{\ln 4}\right\}$. We can obtain a decimal approximation by using a calculator:

[LN] 15 [÷] [LN] 4 [ENTER]

Using these keystrokes, $x \approx 1.95$. Because $4^2 = 16$, it seems reasonable that the solution to $4^x = 15$ is approximately 1.95.

**Check Point 1** Solve: $5^x = 134$. Find the solution set, and then use a calculator to obtain a decimal approximation to two decimal places for the solution.

## EXAMPLE 2 Solving an Exponential Equation

Solve: $40e^{0.6x} = 240$.

**Solution** We begin by dividing both sides by 40 to isolate the exponential expression, $e^{0.6x}$. Then we take the natural logarithm on both sides of the equation.

$$40e^{0.6x} = 240 \quad \text{This is the given equation.}$$

$$e^{0.6x} = 6 \quad \text{Isolate the exponential factor by dividing both sides by 40.}$$

$$\ln e^{0.6x} = \ln 6 \quad \text{Take the natural logarithm on both sides.}$$

$$0.6x = \ln 6 \quad \text{Use the inverse property } \ln e^x = x \text{ on the left.}$$

$$x = \frac{\ln 6}{0.6} \approx 2.99 \quad \text{Divide both sides by 0.6.}$$

Thus, the solution of the equation is $\frac{\ln 6}{0.6} \approx 2.99$. Try checking this approximate solution in the original equation, verifying that $\left\{\frac{\ln 6}{0.6}\right\}$ is the solution set.

**Check Point 2** Solve: $7e^{2x} = 63$. Find the solution set, and then use a calculator to obtain a decimal approximation to two decimal places for the solution.

## EXAMPLE 3 Solving an Exponential Equation

Solve: $5^{4x-7} - 3 = 10$

**Solution** We begin by adding 3 to both sides to isolate the exponential expression, $5^{4x-7}$. Then we take the natural logarithm on both sides of the equation.

| | |
|---|---|
| $5^{4x-7} - 3 = 10$ | This is the given equation. |
| $5^{4x-7} = 13$ | Add 3 to both sides. |
| $\ln 5^{4x-7} = \ln 13$ | Take the natural logarithm on both sides. |
| $(4x - 7)\ln 5 = \ln 13$ | Use the power rule to bring the exponent to the front: $\ln b^x = x \ln b$. |
| $4x\ln 5 - 7\ln 5 = \ln 13$ | Use the distributive property and distribute $\ln 5$ to both terms in parentheses. |
| $4x\ln 5 = \ln 13 + 7\ln 5$ | Isolate the variable term by adding $7\ln 5$ to both sides. |
| $x = \dfrac{\ln 13 + 7\ln 5}{4\ln 5}$ | Isolate $x$ by dividing both sides by $4\ln 5$. |

The solution set is $\left\{\dfrac{\ln 13 + 7\ln 5}{4\ln 5}\right\}$, approximately 2.15.

**Check Point 3** Solve: $6^{3x-4} - 7 = 2081$. Find the solution set, and then use a calculator to obtain a decimal approximation to two decimal places for the solution.

## EXAMPLE 4 Solving an Exponential Equation

Solve: $e^{2x} - 4e^x + 3 = 0$.

**Solution** The given equation is quadratic in form. If $t = e^x$, the equation can be expressed as $t^2 - 4t + 3 = 0$. Because this equation can be solved by factoring, we factor to isolate the exponential term.

| | | |
|---|---|---|
| $e^{2x} - 4e^x + 3 = 0$ | | This is the given equation. |
| $(e^x - 3)(e^x - 1) = 0$ | | Factor on the left. Notice that if $t = e^x$, $t^2 - 4t + 3 = (t - 3)(t - 1)$. |
| $e^x - 3 = 0$ | or $e^x - 1 = 0$ | Set each factor equal to 0. |
| $e^x = 3$ | $e^x = 1$ | Solve for $e^x$. |
| $\ln e^x = \ln 3$ | $x = 0$ | Take the natural logarithm on both sides of the first equation. The equation on the right can be solved by inspection. |
| $x = \ln 3$ | | $\ln e^x = x$ |

The solution set is $\{0, \ln 3\}$. The solutions are 0 and (approximately) 1.099.

### Technology

Shown below is the graph of $y = e^{2x} - 4e^x + 3$. There are two $x$-intercepts, one at 0 and one at approximately 1.099. These intercepts verify our algebraic solution.

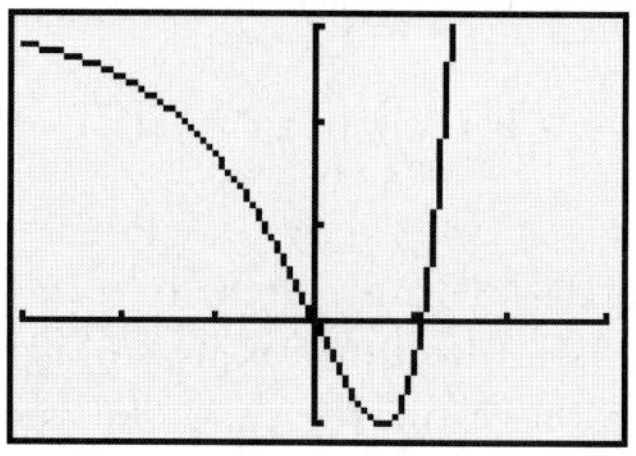

**Check Point 4** Solve: $e^{2x} - 8e^x + 7 = 0$. Find the solution set, and then use a calculator to obtain a decimal approximation to two decimal places, if necessary.

**2** Solve logarithmic equations.

## Logarithmic Equations

A **logarithmic equation** is an equation containing a variable in a logarithmic expression. Examples of logarithmic equations include

$$\log_4(x + 3) = 2 \quad \text{and} \quad \ln 2x = 3.$$

If a logarithmic equation is in the form $\log_b x = c$, we can solve the equation by rewriting it in its equivalent exponential form $b^c = x$. Example 5 illustrates how this is done.

### Technology

The graphs of

$$y_1 = \log_4(x + 3) \text{ and } y_2 = 2$$

have an intersection point whose $x$-coordinate is 13. This verifies that $\{13\}$ is the solution set for $\log_4(x + 3) = 2$.

*Note*:

Because

$$\log_b x = \frac{\ln x}{\ln b}$$

(change-of-base property),

we entered $y_1$ using

$$y_1 = \log_4(x + 3) = \frac{\ln(x + 3)}{\ln 4}$$

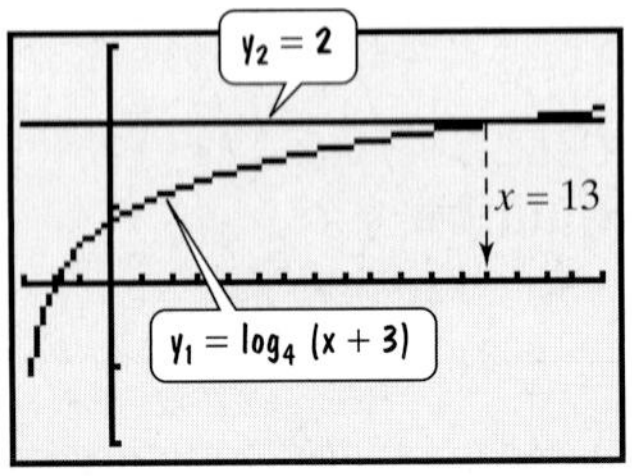


### EXAMPLE 5 Solving a Logarithmic Equation

Solve: $\log_4(x + 3) = 2$.

**Solution** We first rewrite the equation as an equivalent equation in exponential form using the fact that $\log_b x = c$ means $b^c = x$.

$$\log_4(x + 3) = 2 \quad \text{means} \quad 4^2 = x + 3$$

Logarithms are exponents.

Now we solve the equivalent equation for $x$.

$4^2 = x + 3$ — This is the equivalent equation.

$16 = x + 3$ — Square 4.

$13 = x$ — Subtract 3 from both sides.

**Check**

$\log_4(x + 3) = 2$ — This is the given logarithmic equation.

$\log_4(13 + 3) \stackrel{?}{=} 2$ — Substitute 13 for x.

$\log_4 16 \stackrel{?}{=} 2$

$2 = 2$ ✓ — $\log_4 16 = 2$ because $4^2 = 16$.

This true statement indicates that the solution set is $\{13\}$.

**Check Point 5** Solve: $\log_2(x - 4) = 3$.

Logarithmic expressions are defined only for logarithms of positive real numbers. Always check proposed solutions of a logarithmic equation in the original equation. Exclude from the solution set any proposed solution that produces the logarithm of a negative number or the logarithm of 0.

In order to rewrite the logarithmic equation $\log_b x = c$ in the equivalent exponential form $b^c = x$, we need a single logarithm whose coefficient is one. It is sometimes necessary to use properties of logarithms to condense logarithms into a single logarithm. In the next example we use the product rule for logarithms to obtain a single logarithmic expression on the left side.

## EXAMPLE 6 Using the Product Rule to Solve a Logarithmic Equation

Solve: $\log_2 x + \log_2(x - 7) = 3$.

**Solution**

$\log_2 x + \log_2(x - 7) = 3$ — This is the given equation.

$\log_2 x(x - 7) = 3$ — Use the product rule to obtain a single logarithm: $\log_b M + \log_b N = \log_b(MN)$.

$2^3 = x(x - 7)$ — $\log_b x = c$ means $b^c = x$.

$8 = x^2 - 7x$ — Apply the distributive property on the right.

$0 = x^2 - 7x - 8$ — Set the equation equal to 0.

$0 = (x - 8)(x + 1)$ — Factor.

$x - 8 = 0$ or $x + 1 = 0$ — Set each factor equal to 0.

$x = 8 \qquad x = -1$ — Solve for x.

**Check**

**Checking 8:**

$$\log_2 x + \log_2(x - 7) = 3$$
$$\log_2 8 + \log_2(8 - 7) \stackrel{?}{=} 3$$
$$\log_2 8 + \log_2 1 \stackrel{?}{=} 3$$
$$3 + 0 \stackrel{?}{=} 3$$
$$3 = 3 \checkmark$$

**Checking −1:**

$$\log_2 x + \log_2(x - 7) = 3$$
$$\log_2(-1) + \log_2(-1 - 7) \stackrel{?}{=} 3$$

The number −1 does not check. Negative numbers do not have logarithms.

The solution set is $\{8\}$.

**Check Point 6** Solve: $\log x + \log(x - 3) = 1$.

Equations involving natural logarithms can be solved using the inverse property $e^{\ln x} = x$. For example, to solve

$$\ln x = 5$$

we write both sides of the equation as exponents on base $e$:

$$e^{\ln x} = e^5$$

This is called **exponentiating both sides** of the equation. Using the inverse property $e^{\ln x} = x$, we simplify the left side of the equation and obtain the solution:

$$x = e^5.$$

### EXAMPLE 7 Solving an Equation with a Natural Logarithm

Solve: $3 \ln 2x = 12$.

**Solution**

| | |
|---|---|
| $3 \ln 2x = 12$ | This is the given equation. |
| $\ln 2x = 4$ | Divide both sides by 3. |
| $e^{\ln 2x} = e^4$ | Exponentiate both sides. |
| $2x = e^4$ | Use the inverse property to simplify the left side: $e^{\ln \square} = \square$. |
| $x = \frac{e^4}{2} \approx 27.30$ | Divide both sides by 2. |

**Check**

| | |
|---|---|
| $3 \ln 2x = 12$ | This is the given logarithmic equation. |
| $3 \ln 2\left(\frac{e^4}{2}\right) \stackrel{?}{=} 12$ | Substitute $\frac{e^4}{2}$ for x. |
| $3 \ln e^4 \stackrel{?}{=} 12$ | Simplify: $\frac{\cancel{2}}{1} \cdot \frac{e^4}{\cancel{2}} = e^4$. |
| $3 \cdot 4 \stackrel{?}{=} 12$ | Because $\ln e^x = x$, we conclude $\ln e^4 = 4$. |
| $12 = 12$ ✓ | |

This true statement indicates that the solution set is $\left\{\frac{e^4}{2}\right\}$.

**Check Point 7** Solve: $4 \ln 3x = 8$.

**3** Solve applied problems involving exponential and logarithmic equations.

## Applications

Our first applied example provides a mathematical perspective on the old slogan "Alcohol and driving don't mix." In California, where 38% of fatal traffic crashes involve drinking drivers, it is illegal to drive with a blood alcohol concentration of 0.08 or higher. At these levels, drivers may be arrested and charged with driving under the influence.

### EXAMPLE 8 Alcohol and Risk of a Car Accident

Medical research indicates that the risk of having a car accident increases exponentially as the concentration of alcohol in the blood increases. The risk is modeled by

$$R = 6e^{12.77x}$$

where $x$ is the blood alcohol concentration and $R$, given as a percent, is the risk of having a car accident. What blood alcohol concentration corresponds to a 17% risk of a car accident?

**Solution** For a risk of 17%, we let $R = 17$ in the equation and solve for $x$, the blood alcohol concentration.

| | |
|---|---|
| $R = 6e^{12.77x}$ | This is the given equation. |
| $6e^{12.77x} = 17$ | Substitute 17 for R and (optional) reverse the two sides of the equation. |
| $e^{12.77x} = \frac{17}{6}$ | Isolate the exponential factor by dividing both sides by 6. |
| $\ln e^{12.77x} = \ln\left(\frac{17}{6}\right)$ | Take the natural logarithm on both sides. |
| $12.77x = \ln\left(\frac{17}{6}\right)$ | Use the inverse property $\ln e^x = x$ on the left. |
| $x = \frac{\ln\left(\frac{17}{6}\right)}{12.77} \approx 0.08$ | Divide both sides by 12.77. |

For a blood alcohol concentration of 0.08, the risk of a car accident is 17%. In many states, it is illegal to drive at this blood alcohol concentration.

**Check Point 8** Use the formula in Example 8 to solve this problem. What blood alcohol concentration corresponds to a 7% risk of a car accident? (In many states, drivers under the age of 21 can lose their license for driving at this level.)

Suppose that you inherit \$30,000. Is it possible to invest \$25,000 and have over half a million dollars for early retirement? Our next example illustrates the power of compound interest.

## EXAMPLE 9 Revisiting the Formula for Compound Interest

The formula

$$A = P\left(1 + \frac{r}{n}\right)^{nt}$$

describes the accumulated value $A$ of a sum of money $P$, the principal, after $t$ years at annual percentage rate $r$ (in decimal form) compounded $n$ times a year. How long will it take \$25,000 to grow to \$500,000 at 9% annual interest compounded monthly?

**Solution**

| | |
|---|---|
| $A = P\left(1 + \frac{r}{n}\right)^{nt}$ | This is the given formula. |
| $500{,}000 = 25{,}000\left(1 + \frac{0.09}{12}\right)^{12t}$ | A (the desired accumulated value) = \$500,000, P (the principal) = \$25,000, r (the interest rate) = 9% = 0.09, and n = 12 (monthly compounding). |

### Playing Doubles: Interest Rates and Doubling Time

One way to calculate what your savings will be worth at some point in the future is to consider doubling time. Shown below is how long it takes for your money to double at different annual interest rates subject to continuous compounding.

| Annual Interest Rate | Years to Double |
|---|---|
| 5% | 13.9 years |
| 7% | 9.9 years |
| 9% | 7.7 years |
| 11% | 6.3 years |

Of course, the first problem is collecting some money to invest. The second problem is finding a reasonably safe investment with a return of 9% or more.

Our goal is to solve the equation for $t$. Let's reverse the two sides of the equation and then simplify within parentheses.

$$25{,}000\left(1 + \frac{0.09}{12}\right)^{12t} = 500{,}000$$

$$25{,}000(1 + 0.0075)^{12t} = 500{,}000 \quad \text{Divide within parentheses: } \frac{0.09}{12} = 0.0075.$$

$$25{,}000(1.0075)^{12t} = 500{,}000 \quad \text{Add within parentheses.}$$

$$(1.0075)^{12t} = 20 \quad \text{Divide both sides by 25,000.}$$

$$\ln(1.0075)^{12t} = \ln 20 \quad \text{Take the natural logarithm on both sides.}$$

$$12t \ln(1.0075) = \ln 20 \quad \text{Use the power rule to bring the exponent to the front: } \ln b^x = x \ln b.$$

$$t = \frac{\ln 20}{12 \ln 1.0075} \quad \text{Solve for } t\text{, dividing both sides by } 12 \ln 1.0075.$$

$$\approx 33.4 \quad \text{Use a calculator.}$$

After approximately 33.4 years, the \$25,000 will grow to an accumulated value of \$500,000. If you set aside the money at age 20, you can begin enjoying a life of leisure at about age 53.

**Check Point 9** How long, to the nearest tenth of a year, will it take \$1000 to grow to \$3600 at 8% annual interest compounded quarterly?

Yogi Berra, catcher and renowned hitter for the New York Yankees (1946–1963), said it best: "Prediction is very hard, especially when it's about the future." At the start of the twenty-first century, we are plagued by questions about the environment. Will we run out of gas? How hot will it get? Will there be neighborhoods where the air is pristine? Can we make garbage disappear? Will there be any wilderness left? Which wild animals will become extinct? These concerns have led to the growth of the environmental industry in the United States.

## EXAMPLE 10 The Growth of the Environmental Industry

The formula

$$N = 461.87 + 299.4 \ln x$$

models the thousands of workers, $N$, in the environmental industry in the United States $x$ years after 1979. By which year will there be 1,500,000, or 1500 thousand, U.S. workers in the environmental industry?

**Solution** We substitute 1500 for $N$ and solve for $x$, the number of years after 1979.

$$N = 461.87 + 299.4 \ln x \quad \text{This is the given formula.}$$

$$461.87 + 299.4 \ln x = 1500 \quad \text{Substitute 1500 for } N \text{ and reverse the two sides of the equation.}$$

Our goal is to isolate $\ln x$. We can then find $x$ by exponentiating both sides of the equation, using the inverse property $e^{\ln x} = x$.

$$299.4 \ln x = 1038.13 \quad \text{Subtract 461.87 from both sides.}$$

$$\ln x = \frac{1038.13}{299.4} \quad \text{Divide both sides by 299.4.}$$

$$e^{\ln x} = e^{1038.13/299.4} \quad \text{Exponentiate both sides.}$$

$$x = e^{1038.13/299.4} \quad e^{\ln x} = x$$

$$\approx 32 \quad \text{Use a calculator.}$$

Approximately 32 years after 1979, in the year 2011, there will be 1.5 million U.S. workers in the environmental industry.

**Check Point 10** Use the formula in Example 10 to find by what year there will be two million, or 2000 thousand, U.S. workers in the environmental industry.

## EXERCISE SET 4.4

### Practice Exercises

*Solve each exponential equation in Exercises 1–22. Express the solution set in terms of natural logarithms. Then use a calculator to obtain a decimal approximation, correct to two decimal places, for the solution.*

**1.** $10^x = 3.91$
**2.** $10^x = 8.07$
**3.** $e^x = 5.7$
**4.** $e^x = 0.83$
**5.** $5^x = 17$
**6.** $19^x = 143$
**7.** $5e^x = 23$
**8.** $9e^x = 107$
**9.** $3e^{5x} = 1977$
**10.** $4e^{7x} = 10{,}273$
**11.** $e^{1-5x} = 793$
**12.** $e^{1-8x} = 7957$
**13.** $e^{5x-3} - 2 = 10{,}476$
**14.** $e^{4x-5} - 7 = 11{,}243$
**15.** $7^{x+2} = 410$
**16.** $5^{x-3} = 137$
**17.** $7^{0.3x} = 813$
**18.** $3^{x/7} = 0.2$
**19.** $e^{2x} - 3e^x + 2 = 0$
**20.** $e^{2x} - 2e^x - 3 = 0$
**21.** $e^{4x} + 5e^{2x} - 24 = 0$
**22.** $e^{4x} - 3e^{2x} - 18 = 0$

*Solve each logarithmic equation in Exercises 23–36. Be sure to reject any value of x that produces the logarithm of a negative number or the logarithm of 0.*

**23.** $\log_3 x = 4$
**24.** $\log_5 x = 3$
**25.** $\log_4(x + 5) = 3$
**26.** $\log_5(x - 7) = 2$
**27.** $\log_3(x - 4) = -3$
**28.** $\log_7(x + 2) = -2$
**29.** $\log_4(3x + 2) = 3$
**30.** $\log_2(4x + 1) = 5$
**31.** $\log_5 x + \log_5(4x - 1) = 1$
**32.** $\log_6(x + 5) + \log_6 x = 2$
**33.** $\log_3(x - 5) + \log_3(x + 3) = 2$
**34.** $\log_2(x - 1) + \log_2(x + 1) = 3$
**35.** $\log_2(x + 2) - \log_2(x - 5) = 3$
**36.** $\log_4(x + 2) - \log_4(x - 1) = 1$

*Exercises 37–44 involve equations with natural logarithms. Solve each equation by isolating the natural logarithm and exponentiating both sides. Express the answer in terms of e. Then use a calculator to obtain a decimal approximation, correct to two decimal places, for the solution.*

**37.** $\ln x = 2$
**38.** $\ln x = 3$
**39.** $5 \ln 2x = 20$
**40.** $6 \ln 2x = 30$
**41.** $6 + 2 \ln x = 5$
**42.** $7 + 3 \ln x = 6$
**43.** $\ln \sqrt{x + 3} = 1$
**44.** $\ln \sqrt{x + 4} = 1$

### Application Exercises

*Use the formula $R = 6e^{12.77x}$, where x is the blood alcohol concentration and R, given as a percent, is the risk of having a car accident, to solve Exercises 45–46.*

**45.** What blood alcohol concentration corresponds to certainty, or a 100% risk, of a car accident?

**46.** What blood alcohol concentration corresponds to a 50% risk of a car accident?

**47.** The formula $A = 18.2e^{0.001t}$ models the population of New York State, in millions, $t$ years after 1994.
  **a.** What was the population of New York in 1994?
  **b.** When will the population of New York reach 18.5 million?

**48.** The formula $A = 14e^{0.168t}$ models the population of Florida, in millions, $t$ years after 1994.
  **a.** What was the population of Florida in 1994?
  **b.** When will the population of Florida reach 18.5 million?

*In Exercices 49–52, complete the table for a savings account subjected to n compoundings yearly* $\left(A = P\left(1 + \frac{r}{n}\right)^{nt}\right)$.

| | Amount Invested | Number of Compounding Periods | Annual Interest Rate | Accumulated Amount | Time $t$ in Years |
|---|---|---|---|---|---|
| **49.** | \$12,500 | 4 | 5.75% | \$20,000 | |
| **50.** | \$7250 | 12 | 6.5% | \$15,000 | |
| **51.** | \$1000 | 360 | | \$1400 | 2 |
| **52.** | \$5000 | 360 | | \$9000 | 4 |

*In Exercices 53–56, complete the table for a savings account subjected to continuous compounding* $(A = Pe^{rt})$.

| | Amount Invested | Annual Interest Rate | Accumulated Amount | Time $t$ in Years |
|---|---|---|---|---|
| **53.** | \$8000 | 8% | Double the amount invested | |
| **54.** | \$8000 | | \$12,000 | 2 |
| **55.** | \$2350 | | Triple the amount invested | 7 |
| **56.** | \$17,425 | 4.25% | \$25,000 | |

**57.** The formula $C = 15{,}557 + 5259 \ln x$ models the average cost of a new car $x$ years after 1989. When will the average cost of a new car be \$25,000?

**58.** The formula $C = 280 \ln(A + 1) + 1925$ models the number of calories, $C$, consumed each day by a person who owns $A$ acres of land in a developing country, where $0 \leq A \leq 4$. How many acres of land are owned by a person who consumes 2200 calories daily in a developing country? (Source: Grigg, D. *The World Food Problem*. Oxford: Blackwell Publishers, 1993.)

*The formula* $P = 95 - 30 \log_2 x$ *models the percentage, P, of students who could recall the important features of a classroom lecture as a function of time, where x represents the number of days that have elapsed since the lecture was given. The figure shows the graph of the formula. Use this information to solve Exercises 59–60.*

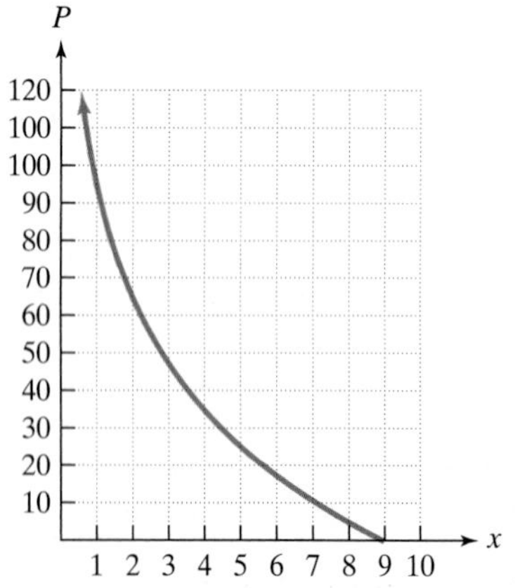


**59.** After how many days do only half the students recall the important features of the classroom lecture? (Let $P = 50$ and solve for $x$.) Can you approximately locate the point on the graph that conveys this information?

**60.** After how many days have all students forgotten the important features of the classroom lecture? (Let $P = 0$ and solve for $x$.) Can you approximately locate the point on the graph that conveys this information?

*The pH of a solution ranges from 0 to 14. An acid solution has a pH less than 7. Pure water is neutral and has a pH of 7. Normal, unpolluted rain has a pH of about 5.6. The pH of a solution is given by*

$$\text{pH} = -\log x$$

*where x represents the concentration of the hydrogen ions in the solution in moles per liter. Use the formula to solve Exercises 61–62.*

**61.** An environmental concern involves the destructive effects of acid rain. The most acidic rainfall ever had a pH of 2.4. What was the hydrogen ion concentration? Express the answer as a power of 10, and then round to the nearest thousandth.

**62.** The figure on page 401 shows very acidic rain in the northeast United States. What is the hydrogen ion concentration of rainfall with a pH of 4.2? Express the answer as a power of 10, and then round to the nearest hundred-thousandth.

**Acid Rain Over Canada and the United States**

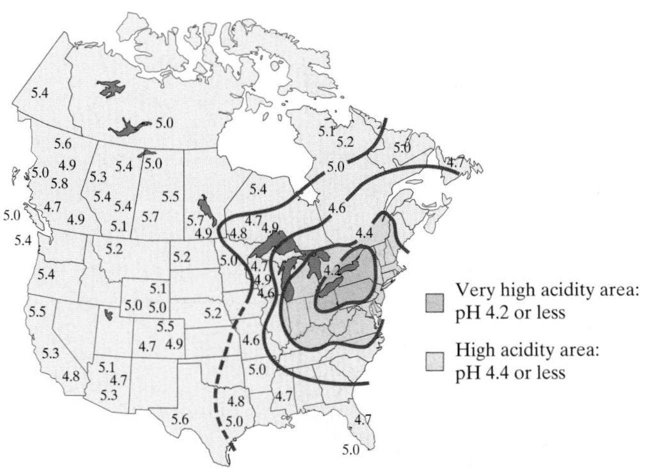


*Source*: National Atmospheric Program

## Writing in Mathematics

63. Explain how to solve an exponential equation. Use $3^x = 140$ in your explanation.

64. Explain how to solve a logarithmic equation. Use $\log_3(x - 1) = 4$ in your explanation.

65. In many states, a 17% risk of a car accident with a blood alcohol concentration of 0.08 is the lowest level for charging a motorist with driving under the influence. Do you agree with the 17% risk as a cutoff percentage, or do you feel that the percentage should be lower or higher? Explain your answer. What blood alcohol concentration corresponds to what you believe is an appropriate percentage?

66. Have you purchased a new or used car recently? If so, describe if the formula in Exercise 58 accurately models what you paid for your car. If there is a big difference between the figure given by the formula and the amount that you paid, how can you explain this difference?

## Technology Exercises

*In Exercises 67–74, use your graphing utility to graph each side of the equation in the same viewing rectangle. Then use the x-coordinate of the intersection point to find the equation's solution set. Verify this value by direct substitution into the equation.*

67. $2^{x+1} = 8$

68. $3^{x+1} = 9$

69. $\log_3(4x - 7) = 2$

70. $\log_3(3x - 2) = 2$

71. $\log(x + 3) + \log x = 1$

72. $\log(x - 15) + \log x = 2$

73. $3^x = 2x + 3$

74. $5^x = 3x + 4$

*Hurricanes are one of nature's most destructive forces. These low-pressure areas often have diameters of over 500 miles. The function $f(x) = 0.48 \ln(x + 1) + 27$ models the barometric air pressure, $f(x)$, in inches of mercury, at a distance of x miles from the eye of a hurricane. Use this function to solve Exercises 75–76.*

75. Graph the function in a $[0, 500, 50]$ by $[27, 30, 1]$ viewing rectangle. What does the shape of the graph indicate about barometric air pressure as the distance from the eye increases?

76. Use an equation to answer this question: How far from the eye of a hurricane is the barometric air pressure 29 inches of mercury? Use the TRACE and ZOOM features or the intersect command of your graphing utility to verify your answer.

77. The formula $P = 145e^{-0.092t}$ models a runner's pulse, $P$, in beats per minute, $t$ minutes after a race, where $0 \le t \le 15$. Graph the formula using a graphing utility. TRACE along the graph and determine after how many minutes the runner's pulse will be 70 beats per minute. Verify your observation algebraically.

78. The formula $W = 2600(1 - 0.51e^{-0.075t})^3$ models the weight, $W$, in kilograms, of a female African elephant at age $t$ years. (1 kilogram $\approx$ 2.2 pounds) Use a graphing utility to graph the formula. Then TRACE along the curve to estimate the age of an adult female elephant weighing 1800 kilograms.

## Critical Thinking Exercises

79. Which one of the following is true?
   **a.** If $\log(x + 3) = 2$, then $e^2 = x + 3$.
   **b.** If $\log(7x + 3) - \log(2x + 5) = 4$, then in exponential form $10^4 = (7x + 3) - (2x + 5)$.
   **c.** If $x = \frac{1}{k} \ln y$, then $y = e^{kx}$.
   **d.** Examples of exponential equations include $10^x = 5.71$, $e^x = 0.72$, and $x^{10} = 5.71$.

80. If \$4000 is deposited into an account paying 3% interest compounded annually and at the same time \$2000 is deposited into an account paying 5% interest compounded annually, after how long will the two accounts have the same balance?

*Solve each equation in Exercises 81–83. Check each proposed solution by direct substitution or with a graphing utility.*

81. $(\ln x)^2 = \ln x^2$

82. $(\log x)(2 \log x + 1) = 6$

83. $\ln(\ln x) = 0$

## Group Exercise

84. Research applications of logarithmic functions as mathematical models and plan a seminar based on your group's research. Each group member should research one of the following areas or any other area of interest: pH (acidity of solutions), intensity of sound (decibels), brightness of stars, consumption of natural resources, human memory, progress over time in a sport, profit over time. For the area that you select, explain how logarithmic functions are used and provide examples.

# SECTION 4.5 Modeling with Exponential and Logarithmic Functions

## Objectives

1. Model exponential growth and decay.
2. Use logistic growth models.
3. Use Newton's Law of Cooling.
4. Model data with exponential and logarithmic functions.
5. Express an exponential model in base *e*.

The most casual cruise on the Internet shows how people disagree when it comes to making predictions about the effects of the world's growing population. Some argue that there is a recent slowdown in the growth rate, economies remain robust, and famines in Biafra and Ethiopia are aberrations rather than signs of the future. Others say that the 6 billion people on Earth is twice as many as can be supported in middle-class comfort, and the world is running out of arable land and fresh water. Debates about entities that are growing exponentially can be approached mathematically: We can create functions that model data and use these functions to make predictions. In this section we will show you how this is done.

1 Model exponential growth and decay.

## Exponential Growth and Decay

One of algebra's many applications is to predict the behavior of variables. This can be done with **exponential growth** and **decay models.** With exponential growth and decay, quantities grow or decay at a rate directly proportional to their size. Populations that are growing exponentially grow extremely rapidly as they get larger because there are more adults to have offspring. For example, the **growth rate** for world population is 1.3%, or 0.013. This means that each year world population is 1.3% more than what it was in the previous year. In 1999, world population was 6 billion. Thus, we compute the world population in 2000 as follows:

$$6 \text{ billion} + 1.3\% \text{ of } 6 \text{ billion} = 6 + (0.013)(6) = 6.078.$$

This computation suggests that 6.078 billion people will populate the world in 2000. The 0.078 billion represents an increase of 78 million people from 1999 to 2000, the equivalent of the population of Germany. Using 1.3% as the annual growth rate, world population for 2001 is found in a similar manner:

$$6.078 \text{ billion} + 1.3\% \text{ of } 6.078 \text{ billion} = 6.078 + (0.013)(6.078) \approx 6.157.$$

This computation suggests that approximately 6.157 billion people will populate the world in 2001.

The explosive growth of world population may remind you of the growth of money in an account subject to compound interest. Just as the growth rate for world population is multiplied by the the population plus any increase in the population, a compound interest rate is multiplied by your original investment plus any accumulated interest. The balance in an account subject to continuous compounding and world population are special cases of an *exponential growth model.*

### Exponential Growth and Decay Models

The mathematical model for **exponential growth** or **decay** is given by

$$f(t) = A_0e^{kt} \quad \text{or} \quad A = A_0e^{kt}.$$

- **If $k > 0$, the function models the amount or size of a *growing* entity.** $A_0$ is the original amount or size of the growing entity at time $t = 0$, $A$ is the amount at time $t$, and $k$ is a constant representing the growth rate.
- **If $k < 0$, the function models the amount or size of a *decaying* entity.** $A_0$ is the original amount or size of the decaying entity at time $t = 0$, $A$ is the amount at time $t$, and $k$ is a constant representing the decay rate.

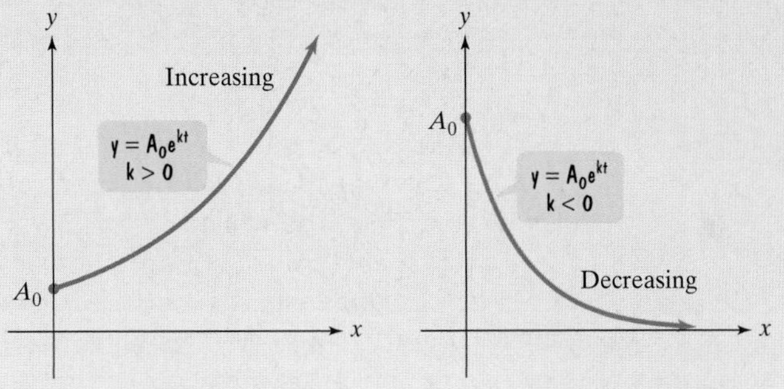


(a) Exponential growth (b) Exponential decay

Sometimes we need to use given data to determine $k$, the rate of growth or decay. After we compute the value of $k$, we can use the formula $A = A_0e^{kt}$ to make predictions. This idea is illustrated in our first two examples.

## EXAMPLE 1 Modeling Mexico City's Growth

The graph in Figure 4.18 shows the growth of the Mexico City metropolitan area from 1970 through 2000. In 1970, the population of Mexico City was 9.4 million. By 1990, it had grown to 20.2 million.

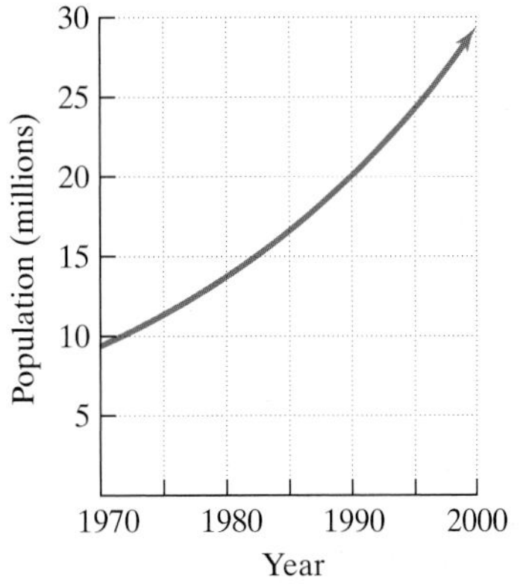


**Figure 4.18** Mexico City's population has grown exponentially.

**a.** Find the exponential growth function that models the data.

**b.** By what year will the population reach 40 million?

**Solution**

**a.** We use the exponential growth model

$$A = A_0 e^{kt}$$

in which $t$ is the number of years since 1970. This means that 1970 corresponds to $t = 0$. At that time there were 9.4 million inhabitants, so we substitute 9.4 for $A_0$ in the growth model.

$$A = 9.4e^{kt}$$

We are given that there were 20.2 million inhabitants in 1990. Because 1990 is 20 years after 1970, when $t = 20$ the value of $A$ is 20.2. Substituting these numbers into the growth model will enable us to find $k$, the growth rate. We know that $k > 0$ because the problem involves growth.

$$A = 9.4e^{kt}$$ Use the growth model with $A_0 = 9.4$.

$$20.2 = 9.4e^{k \cdot 20}$$ When $t = 20$, $A = 20.2$. Substitute these numbers into the model.

$$e^{20k} = \frac{20.2}{9.4}$$ Isolate the exponential factor by dividing both sides by 9.4. We also reversed the sides.

$$\ln e^{20k} = \ln \frac{20.2}{9.4}$$ Take the natural logarithm on both sides.

$$20k = \ln \frac{20.2}{9.4}$$ Simplify the left side using $\ln e^x = x$.

$$k = \frac{\ln \frac{20.2}{9.4}}{20} \approx 0.038$$ Divide both sides by 20 and solve for $k$.

We substitute 0.038 for $k$ in the growth model to obtain the exponential growth function for Mexico City. It is

$$A = 9.4e^{0.038t}$$

where $t$ is measured in years since 1970.

**b.** To find the year in which the population will reach 40 million, we substitute 40 for $A$ in the model from part (a) and solve for $t$.

$$A = 9.4e^{0.038t}$$ This is the model from part (a).

$$40 = 9.4e^{0.038t}$$ Substitute 40 for $A$.

$$e^{0.038t} = \frac{40}{9.4}$$ Divide both sides by 9.4.

$$\ln e^{0.038t} = \ln \frac{40}{9.4}$$ Take the natural logarithm on both sides.

$$0.038t = \ln \frac{40}{9.4}$$ Simplify on the left using $\ln e^x = x$.

$$t = \frac{\ln \frac{40}{9.4}}{0.038} \approx 38$$ Solve for $t$ by dividing both sides by 0.038.

Because 38 is the number of years after 1970, the model indicates that the population of Mexico City will reach 40 million by $1970 + 38$, or in the year 2008.

**Check Point 1** In 1980, the population of Africa was 491 million and by 1990 it had grown to 643 million.

**a.** Use the exponential growth model $A = A_0e^{kt}$, in which $t$ is the number of years since 1980, to find the exponential growth function that models the data.

**b.** By what year will Africa's population reach 1000 million, or one billion?

## Carbon Dating and Artistic Development

The artistic community was electrified by the discovery in 1995 of spectacular cave paintings in a limestone cavern in France. Carbon dating of the charcoal from the site showed that the images, created by artists of remarkable talent, were 30,000 years old, making them the oldest cave paintings ever found. The artists seemed to have used the cavern's natural contours to heighten a sense of perspective. The quality of the painting suggests that the art of early humans did not mature steadily from primitive to sophisticated in any simple linear fashion.

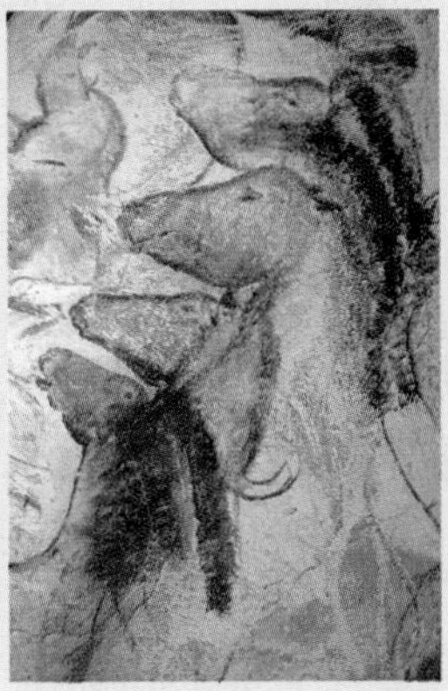

Our next example involves exponential decay and its use in determining the age of fossils and artifacts. The method is based on considering the percentage of carbon-14 remaining in the fossil or artifact. Carbon-14 decays exponentially with a *half-life* of approximately 5715 years. The **half-life** of a substance is the time required for half of a given sample to disintegrate. Thus, after 5715 years a given amount of carbon-14 will have decayed to half the original amount. Carbon dating is useful for artifacts or fossils up to 80,000 years old. Older objects do not have enough carbon-14 left to date age accurately.

## EXAMPLE 2 Carbon-14 Dating: The Dead Sea Scrolls

**a.** Use the fact that after 5715 years a given amount of carbon-14 will have decayed to half the original amount to find the exponential decay model for carbon-14.

**b.** In 1947, earthenware jars containing what are known as the Dead Sea Scrolls were found by an Arab Bedouin herdsman. Analysis indicated that the scroll wrappings contained 76% of their original carbon-14. Estimate the age of the Dead Sea Scrolls.

**Solution** We begin with the exponential decay model $A = A_0e^{kt}$. We know that $k < 0$ because the problem involves the decay of carbon-14. After 5715 years ($t = 5715$), the amount of carbon-14 present, $A$, is half the original amount $A_0$. Thus we can substitute $\frac{A_0}{2}$ for $A$ in the exponential decay model. This will enable us to find $k$, the decay rate.

**a.** $$\frac{A_0}{2} = A_0e^{k5715}$$ After 5715 years ($t = 5715$), $A = \frac{A_0}{2}$ (because the amount present, $A$, is half the original amount, $A_0$).

$$\frac{1}{2} = e^{5715k}$$ Divide both sides of the equation by $A_0$.

$$\ln\frac{1}{2} = \ln e^{5715k}$$ Take the natural logarithm of both sides.

$$\ln\frac{1}{2} = 5715k$$ $\ln e^x = x$

$$k = \frac{\ln\frac{1}{2}}{5715} \approx -0.000121$$ Solve for $k$.

Substituting for $k$ in the decay model, the model for carbon-14 is $A = A_0e^{-0.000121t}$.

**b.**

$$A = A_0 e^{-0.000121t}$$ This is the decay model for carbon-14.

$$0.76A_0 = A_0 e^{-0.000121t}$$ A, the amount present, is 76% of the original amount, so $A = 0.76A_0$.

$$0.76 = e^{-0.000121t}$$ Divide both sides of the equation by $A_0$.

$$\ln 0.76 = \ln e^{-0.000121t}$$ Take the natural logarithm on both sides.

$$\ln 0.76 = -0.000121t$$ $\ln e^x = x$

$$t = \frac{\ln 0.76}{-0.000121} \approx 2268$$ Solve for t.

The Dead Sea Scrolls are approximately 2268 years old plus the number of years between 1947 and the current year.

**Check Point 2** Strontium-90 is a waste product from nuclear reactors. As a consequence of fallout from atmospheric nuclear tests, we all have a measurable amount of strontium-90 in our bones.

**a.** Use the fact that after 28 years a given amount of strontium-90 will have decayed to half the original amount to find the exponential decay model for strontium-90.

**b.** Suppose that a nuclear accident occurs and releases 60 grams of strontium-90 into the atmosphere. How long will it take for strontium-90 to decay to a level of 10 grams?

**2** Use logistic growth models.

## Logistic Growth Models

From population growth to the spread of an epidemic, nothing on Earth can grow exponentially indefinitely. Growth is always limited. This is shown in Figure 4.19 by the horizontal asymptote. The **logistic growth model** is an exponential function used to model situations in which growth is limited.

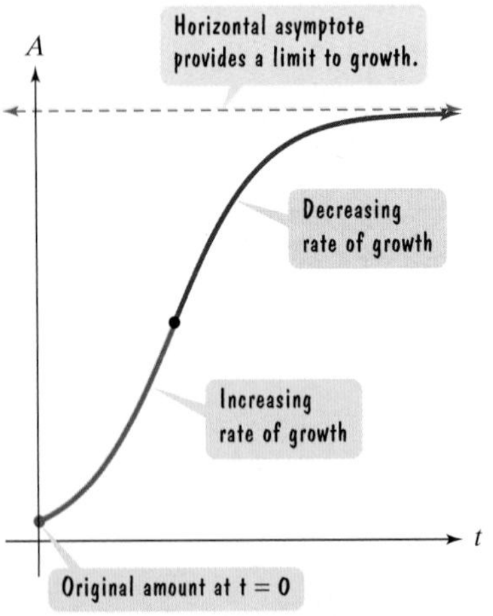


**Figure 4.19** The logistic growth curve has a horizontal asymptote that limits the growth of $A$ over time.

### Logistic Growth Model

The mathematical model for limited logistic growth is given by

$$f(t) = \frac{c}{1 + ae^{-bt}} \quad \text{or} \quad A = \frac{c}{1 + ae^{-bt}}$$

where $a$, $b$, and $c$ are constants with $c > 0$ and $b > 0$.

As time increases ($t \to \infty$), the expression $ae^{-bt}$ in the model approaches 0 and $A$ gets closer and closer to $c$. This means that $y = c$ is a horizontal asymptote for the graph of the function. Thus, the value of $A$ can never exceed $c$ and $c$ represents the limiting size that $A$ can attain.

## EXAMPLE 3 Modeling the Spread of the Flu

The function

$$f(t) = \frac{30{,}000}{1 + 20e^{-1.5t}}$$

describes the number of people, $f(t)$, who have become ill with influenza $t$ weeks after its initial outbreak in a town with 30,000 inhabitants.

**a.** How many people became ill with the flu when the epidemic began?

**b.** How many people were ill by the end of the fourth week?

**c.** What is the limiting size of $f(t)$, the population that becomes ill?

### Solution

**a.** The time at the beginning of the flu epidemic is $t = 0$. Thus, we can find the number of people who were ill at the beginning of the epidemic by substituting 0 for $t$.

$$f(t) = \frac{30{,}000}{1 + 20e^{-1.5t}}$$ This is the given logistic growth function.

$$f(0) = \frac{30{,}000}{1 + 20e^{-1.5(0)}}$$ When the epidemic began, $t = 0$.

$$= \frac{30{,}000}{1 + 20}$$ $e^{-1.5(0)} = e^0 = 1$

$$\approx 1429$$

Approximately 1429 people were ill when the epidemic began.

**b.** We find the number of people who were ill at the end of the fourth week by substituting 4 for $t$ in the logistic growth function.

$$f(t) = \frac{30{,}000}{1 + 20e^{-1.5t}}$$ Use the given logistic growth function.

$$f(4) = \frac{30{,}000}{1 + 20e^{-1.5(4)}}$$ To find the number of people ill by the end of week four, let $t = 4$.

$$= 28{,}583$$ Use a calculator.

Approximately 28,583 people were ill by the end of the fourth week. Compared with the number of people who were ill initially, this illustrates the virulence of the epidemic.

**c.** Recall that in the logistic growth model, $f(t) = \dfrac{c}{1 + ae^{-bt}}$, the constant $c$ represents the limiting size that $f(t)$ can attain. Thus, the number in the numerator, 30,000, is the limiting size of the population that becomes ill.

### Technology

The graph of the logistic growth function for the flu epidemic

$$y = \frac{30{,}000}{1 + 20e^{-1.5x}}$$

can be obtained using a graphing calculator. We started $x$ at 0 and ended at 10. This takes us to week 10. (In Example 3, we found that by week 4 approximately 28,583 people were ill.) We also know that 30,000 is the limiting size, so we took values of $y$ up to 30,000. Using a $[0, 10, 1]$ by $[0, 30{,}000, 3000]$ viewing rectangle, the graph of the logistic growth function is shown below.

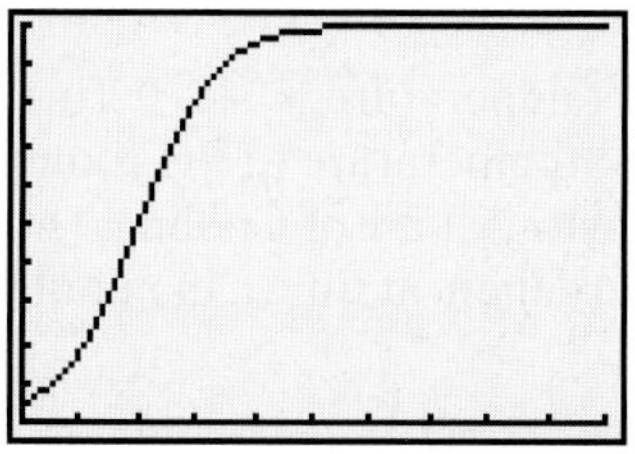

**Check Point 3**

In a learning theory project, psychologists discovered that

$$f(t) = \frac{0.8}{1 + e^{-0.2t}}$$

is a model for describing the proportion of correct responses after $t$ learning trials.

**a.** Find the proportion of correct responses prior to learning trials taking place.

**b.** Find the proportion of correct responses after 10 learning trials.

**c.** What is the limiting size of $f(t)$, the proportion of correct responses as continued learning trials take place?

**3** Use Newton's Law of Cooling

## Modeling Cooling

Over a period of time, a cup of hot coffee cools to the temperature of the surrounding air. **Newton's Law of Cooling**, named after Sir Isaac Newton, states that the temperature of a heated object decreases exponentially over time toward the temperature of the surrounding medium

**Newton's Law of Cooling**

The temperature, $T$, of a heated object at time $t$ is given by

$$T = C + (T_0 - C)e^{kt}$$

where $C$ is the constant temperature of the surrounding medium, $T_0$ is the initial temperature of the heated object, and $k$ is a negative constant that is associated with the cooling object.

## EXAMPLE 4 Using Newton's Law of Cooling

A cake removed from the oven has a temperature of 210°F. It is left to cool in a room that has a temperature of 70°F. After 30 minutes, the temperature of the cake is 140°F.

**a.** Use Newton's Law of Cooling to find a model for the temperature of the cake, $T$, after $t$ minutes.

**b.** What is the temperature of the cake after 40 minutes?

**c.** When will the temperature of the cake be 90°F?

### Solution

**a.** We use Newton's Law of Cooling

$$T = C + (T_0 - C)e^{kt}.$$

When the cake is removed from the oven, its temperature is 210°F. This is its initial temperature: $T_0 = 210$. The constant temperature of the room is 70°F: $C = 70$. Substitute these values into Newton's Law of Cooling. Thus, the temperature of the cake, $T$, in degrees Fahrenheit, at time $t$, in minutes, is

$$T = 70 + (210 - 70)e^{kt} = 70 + 140e^{kt}$$

After 30 minutes, the temperature of the cake is 140°F. This means that when $t = 30$, $T = 140$. Substituting these numbers into Newton's Law of

Cooling will enable us to find $k$, a negative constant.

| | |
|---|---|
| $T = 70 + 140e^{kt}$ | Use Newton's Law of Cooling from pag. 408. |
| $140 = 70 + 140e^{k \cdot 30}$ | When $t = 30$, $T = 140$. Substitute these numbers into the cooling model. |
| $70 = 140e^{30k}$ | Subtract 70 from both sides. |
| $e^{30k} = \frac{1}{2}$ | Isolate the exponential factor by dividing both sides by 140. We also reversed the sides. |
| $\ln e^{30k} = \ln \frac{1}{2}$ | Take the natural logarithm on both sides. |
| $30k = \ln \frac{1}{2}$ | Simplify the left side using $\ln e^x = x$. |
| $k = \frac{\ln \frac{1}{2}}{30} \approx -0.0231$ | Divide both sides by 30 and solve for $k$. |

We substitute $-0.0231$ for $k$ in Newton's Law of Cooling. The temperature of the cake, $T$, in degrees Fahrenheit, after $t$ minutes is modeled by

$$T = 70 + 140e^{-0.0231t}.$$

**b.** To find the temperature of the cake after 40 minutes, we substitute 40 for $t$ in the cooling model from part (a) and evaluate to find $T$.

$$T = 70 + 140e^{-0.0231(40)} \approx 126$$

After 40 minutes, the temperature of the cake will be approximately 126°F.

**c.** To find when the temperature of the cake will be 90°F, we substitute 90 for $T$ in the cooling model from part (a) and solve for $t$.

| | |
|---|---|
| $T = 70 + 140e^{-0.0231t}$ | This is the cooling model from part(a). |
| $90 = 70 + 140e^{-0.0231t}$ | Substitute 90 for $T$. |
| $20 = 140e^{-0.0231t}$ | Subtract 70 from both sides. |
| $e^{-0.0231t} = \frac{1}{7}$ | Divide both sides by 140. |
| $\ln e^{-0.0231t} = \ln \frac{1}{7}$ | Take the natural logarithm on both sides. |
| $-0.0231t = \ln \frac{1}{7}$ | Simplify the left side using $\ln e^x = x$. |
| $t = \frac{\ln \frac{1}{7}}{-0.0231} \approx 84$ | Solve for $t$ by dividing both sides by $-0.0231$. |

The temperature of the cake will be 90°F after approximately 84 minutes.

## Technology

The graphs illustrate how the temperature of the cake decreases exponentially over time toward the 70°F room temperature.

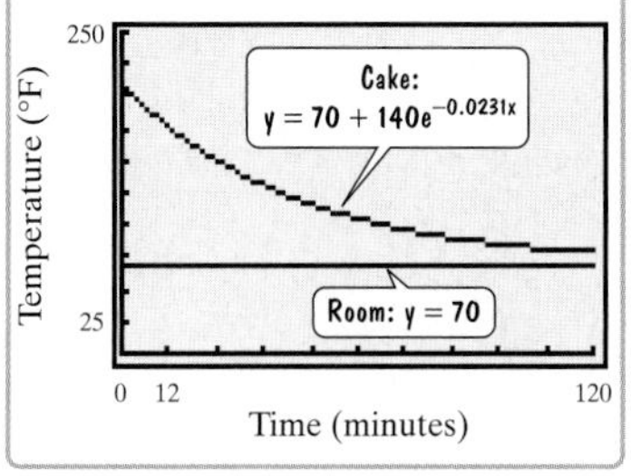


**Check Point 4**

An object is heated to 100°C. It is left to cool in a room that has a temperature of 30°C. After 5 minutes, the temperature of the object is 80°C.

**a.** Use Newton's Law of Cooling to find a model for the temperature of the object, $T$, after $t$ minutes.

**b.** What is the temperature of the object after 20 minutes?

**c.** When will the temperature of the object be 35°C?

**4** Model data with exponential and logarithmic functions.

## The Art of Modeling

Throughout this chapter, we have been working with models that were given. However, we can create functions that model data by observing patterns in scatter plots. Figure 4.20 shows scatter plots for data that are exponential or logarithmic.

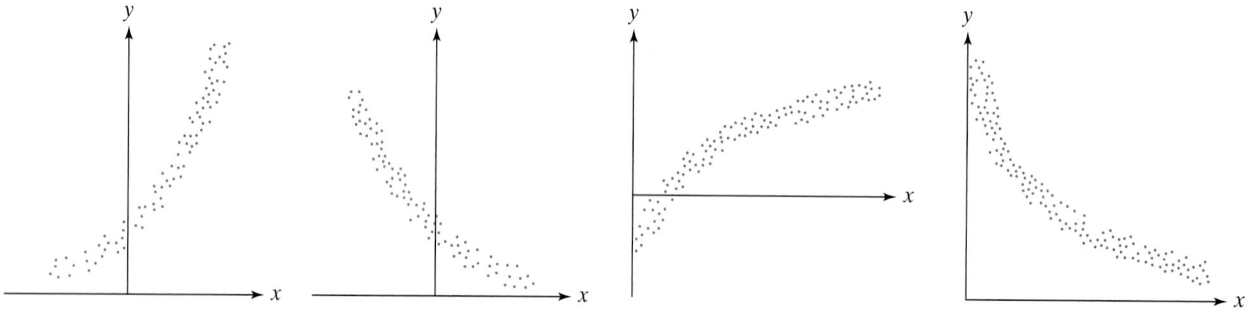

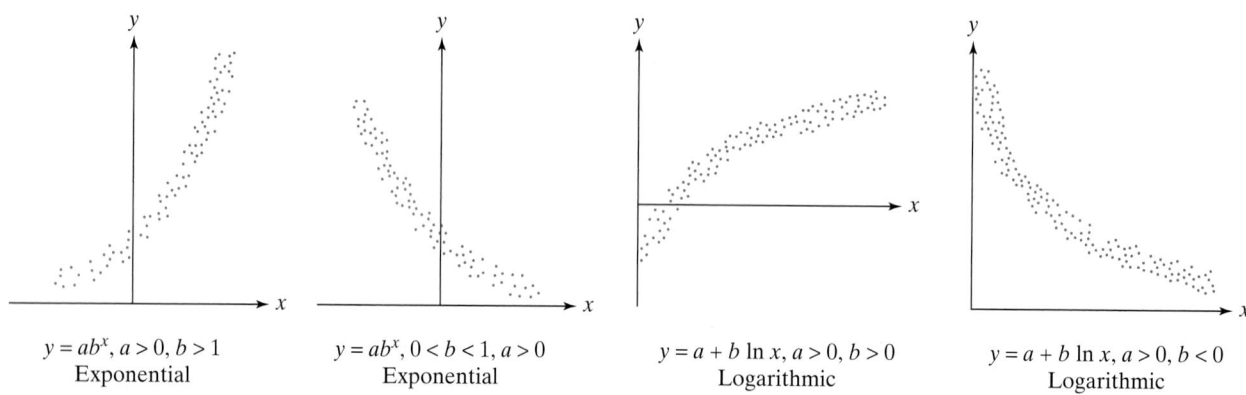

$y = ab^x, a > 0, b > 1$ Exponential | $y = ab^x, 0 < b < 1, a > 0$ Exponential | $y = a + b \ln x, a > 0, b > 0$ Logarithmic | $y = a + b \ln x, a > 0, b < 0$ Logarithmic

**Figure 4.20** Scatter plots for exponential or logarithmic models

Graphing utilities can be used to find the equation of a function that is derived from data. For example, earlier in the chapter we encountered a function that modeled the size of a city and the average walking speed, in feet per second, of pedestrians. The function was derived from the data in Table 4.4. The scatter plot is shown in Figure 4.21.

Because the data in this scatter plot increase rapidly at first and then begin to level off a bit, the shape suggests that a logarithmic model might be a good choice. A graphing utility fits the data in Table 4.4 to a logarithmic model of the form $y = a + b \ln x$ by using the Logarithmic REGression option (see Figure 4.22). From the figure, we see that the logarithmic model of the data, with numbers rounded to three decimal places, is

$$y = 2.735 + 0.352 \ln x.$$

**Table 4.4**

| *x*, Population (thousands) | *y*, Walking Speed (feet per second) |
|---|---|
| 5.5 | 3.3 |
| 14 | 3.7 |
| 71 | 4.3 |
| 138 | 4.4 |
| 342 | 4.8 |

*Source*: Mark and Helen Bornstein, "The Pace of Life"

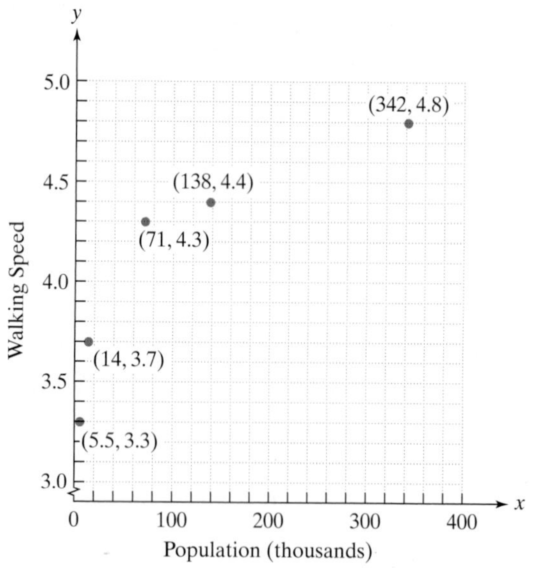


**Figure 4.21** Scatter plot for data in Table 4.4

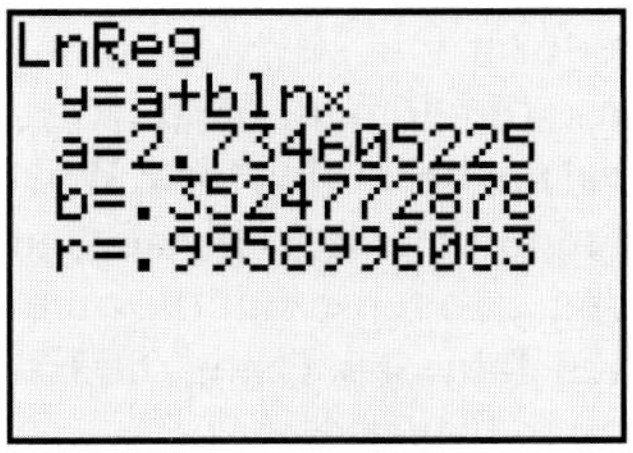


**Figure 4.22** A logarithmic model for the data in Table 4.4.

The number $r$ that appears in Figure 4.22 is called the **correlation coefficient** and is a measure of how well the model fits the data. The value of $r$ is such that $-1 \le r \le 1$. A positive $r$ means that as the $x$-values increase, so do the $y$-values. A negative $r$ means that as the $x$-values increase, the $y$-values decrease. **The closer that $r$ is to $-1$ or 1, the better the model fits the data.** Because $r$ is approximately 0.996, the model

$$y = 2.735 + 0.352 \ln x$$

fits the data very well.

Now let's look at data whose scatter plot suggests an exponential model. The data in Table 4.5 indicate world population for six years. The scatter plot is shown in Figure 4.23.

**Table 4.5**

| $x$, Year | $y$, World Population (billions) |
|---|---|
| 1950 | 2.6 |
| 1960 | 3.1 |
| 1970 | 3.7 |
| 1980 | 4.5 |
| 1989 | 5.3 |
| 1999 | 6.0 |

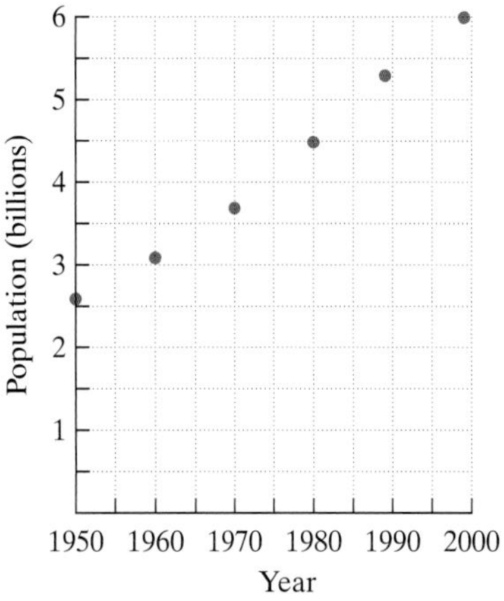


**Figure 4.23** A scatter plot for data in Table 4.5.

Because the data in this scatter plot have a rapidly increasing pattern, the shape suggests that an exponential model might be a good choice. (You might also want to try a linear model.) If you go with the exponential option, you will use a graphing utility's Exponential REGression option. With this feature, a graphing utility fits the data to an exponential model of the form $y = ab^x$.

## The Future of World Population

In the future, a new world order looms. The percentage of world population in less developed countries will increase, North America's will remain relatively stable, and Europe's will decrease.

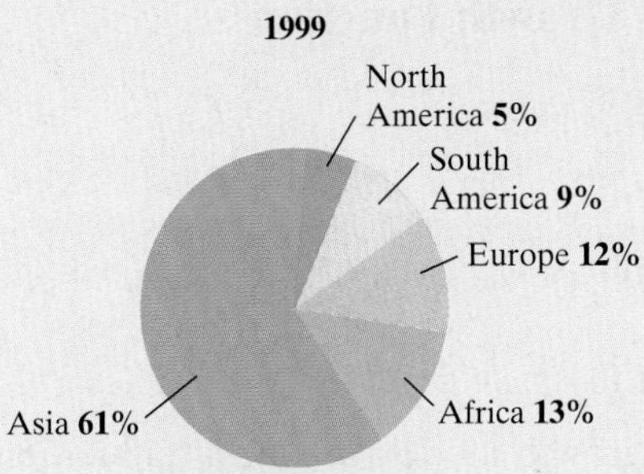


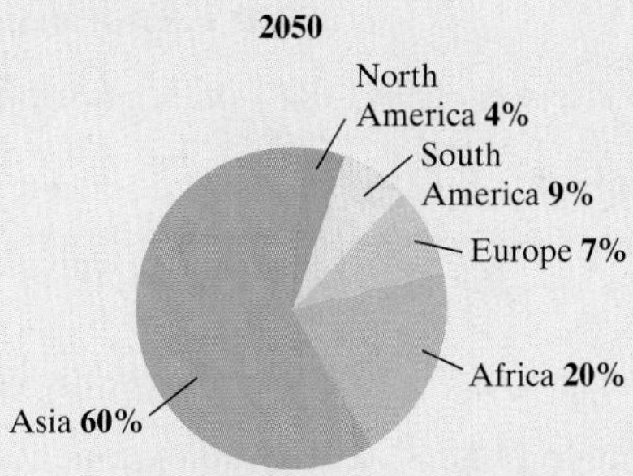


**Most Populous Countries, 2050**

| | |
|---|---|
| 1. India | 1529 million |
| 2. China | 1478 million |
| 3. U.S. | 349 million |
| 4. Pakistan | 345 million |
| 5. Indonesia | 312 million |
| 6. Nigeria | 244 million |
| 7. Brazil | 244 million |
| 8. Bangladesh | 212 million |
| 9. Ethiopia | 169 million |
| 10. Congo | 160 million |

*Source*: United Nations Population Fund

When computing an exponential model of the form $y = ab^x$, a graphing utility rewrites the equation using logarithms. Because the domain of the logarithmic function is the set of positive numbers, **zero must not be a value for $x$**. What does this mean in terms of our data for world population that starts in the year 1950? We must start values of $x$ after 0. Thus, we'll assign $x$ to represent the number of years since 1949. This gives us the data shown in Table 4.6. Using the Exponential REGression option, we obtain the equation in Figure 4.24.

**Table 4.6**

| $x$, Numbers of Years after 1949 | $y$, World Population (billions) |
|---|---|
| 1 (1950) | 2.6 |
| 11 (1960) | 3.1 |
| 21 (1970) | 3.7 |
| 31 (1980) | 4.5 |
| 40 (1989) | 5.3 |
| 50 (1999) | 6.0 |

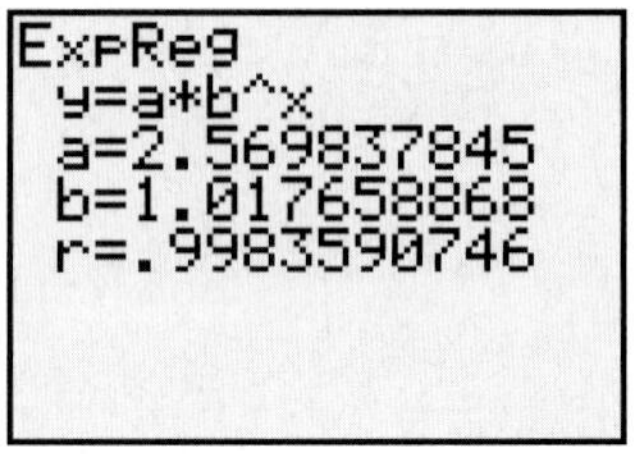

**Figure 4.24** An exponential model for the data in Table 4.6

From Figure 4.24, we see that the exponential model of the data for world population $x$ years after 1949, with numbers rounded to three decimal places, is

$$y = 2.570(1.018)^x.$$

The correlation coefficient, $r$, is close to 1, indicating that the model fits the data very well.

**5** Express an exponential model in base $e$.

Because $b = e^{\ln b}$, we can rewrite any model in the form $y = ab^x$ in terms of base $e$.

### Expressing an Exponential Model in Base $e$

$$y = ab^x \text{ is equivalent to } y = ae^{(\ln b)\cdot x}.$$

## EXAMPLE 5 Rewriting an Exponential Model as an Exponential Growth Function

Rewrite $y = 2.57(1.018)^x$ in terms of base $e$.

**Solution**

$y = ab^x$ is equivalent to $y = ae^{(\ln b)\cdot x}$.

$y = 2.57(1.018)^x$ is equivalent to $y = 2.57e^{(\ln 1.018)\cdot x}$.

Using $\ln 1.018 \approx 0.018$, the exponential growth model for world population $x$ years after 1949 is

$$y = 2.57e^{0.018x}.$$

In Example 5, we can replace $y$ by $A$ and $x$ by $t$ so that the model has the same letters as those in the exponential growth model $A = A_0e^{kt}$.

$$A = A_0 \; e^{kt} \quad \text{This is the exponential growth model.}$$

$$A = 2.57e^{0.018t} \quad \text{This is the model for world population.}$$

The value of $k$, 0.018, indicates a growth rate of 1.8%. Although this is an excellent model for the data, we must be careful about making projections about world population using this growth function. Why? World population growth rate is now 1.3%, not 1.8%, so our model will overestimate future populations.

**Check Point 5** Rewrite $y = 4(7.8)^x$ in terms of base $e$. Express the answer in terms of a natural logarithm, and then round to three decimal places.

When using a graphing utility to model data, begin with a scatter plot, drawn either by hand or with the graphing utility, to obtain a general picture for the shape of the data. It might be difficult to determine what model best fits the data—linear, logarithmic, exponential, quadratic, or something else. If necessary, use your graphing utility to fit several models to the data. The best model is the one that yields the value $r$, the correlation coefficient, closest to 1 or $-1$. Finding a proper fit for data can be almost as much art as it is mathematics. In this era of technology, the process of creating models that best fit data is one that involves more decision making than computation.

## EXERCISE SET 4.5

### Practice and Application Exercises

*The exponential growth model $A = 208e^{0.008t}$ describes the population of the United States, in millions, $t$ years after 1970. Use this model to solve Exercises 1–4.*

**1.** What was the population of the United States in 1970?

**2.** By what percentage is the population of the United States increasing each year?

**3.** When will the U.S. population be 300 million?

**4.** When will the U.S. population be 350 million?

*India is currently one of the world's fastest-growing countries. By 2040, the population of India will be larger than the population of China; by 2050, nearly one-third of the world's population will live in these two countries alone. The exponential growth model $A = 574e^{0.026t}$ describes the population of India, in millions, $t$ years after 1974. Use this model to solve Exercises 5–8.*

**5.** By what percentage is the population of India increasing each year?

**6.** What was the population of India in 1974?

**7.** When will India's population be 1624 million?

**8.** When will India's population be 2732 million?

*The value of houses in a neighborhood follows a pattern of exponential growth. In the year 2000, you purchased a house in this neighborhood. The value of your house, in thousands of dollars, $t$ years after 2000 is given by the exponential growth model $V = 140e^{0.068t}$. Use this model to solve Exercises 9–12.*

**9.** What did you pay for your house?

**10.** By what percentage is the price of houses in your neighborhood increasing each year?

**11.** When will your house be worth $200,000?

**12.** When will your house be worth $300,000?

**13.** Through the end of 1991, 200,000 cases of AIDS had been reported to the Centers for Disease Control in the United States. By the end of 1998, the number had grown to 680,000. The exponential growth function $A = 200e^{kt}$ describes the thousands of AIDS cases in the United States $t$ years after 1991. Use the fact that 7 years after 1991 there were 680 thousand cases to find $k$ to three decimal places. Then write the exponential growth function. According to your model, by what percentage is the number of AIDS cases in the United States increasing each year?

**14.** In 1980, China's population was 983 million; in 1990, it was 1154 million. The exponential growth function $A = 983e^{kt}$ describes the population of China, in millions, $t$ years after 1980. Use the fact that 10 years after 1980 the population was 1154 million to find $k$ to three decimal places. Then write the exponential growth function. According to your model, by what percentage is the population of China increasing each year?

*An artifact originally had 16 grams of carbon-14 present. The decay model $A = 16e^{-0.000121t}$ describes the amount of carbon-14 present after t years. Use this model to solve Exercises 15–16.*

**15.** How many grams of carbon-14 will be present in 5715 years?

**16.** How many grams of carbon-14 will be present in 11,430 years?

**17.** The half-life of the radioactive element krypton-91 is 10 seconds. If 16 grams of krypton-91 are initially present, how many grams are present after 10 seconds? 20 seconds? 30 seconds? 40 seconds? 50 seconds?

**18.** The half-life of the radioactive element plutonium-239 is 25,000 years. If 16 grams of plotonium-239 are initially present how many grams are present after 25,000 years? 50,000 years? 75,000 years? 100,000 years? 125,000 years?

*Use the exponential decay model for carbon-14, $A = A_0e^{-0.000121t}$, to solve Exercises 19–20.*

**19.** Prehistoric cave paintings were discovered in a cave in France. The paint contained 15% of the original carbon-14. Estimate the age of the paintings.

**20.** Skeletons were found at a construction site in San Francisco in 1989. The skeletons contained 88% of the expected amount of carbon-14 found in a living person. In 1989, how old were the skeletons?

**21.** The August 1978 issue of *National Geographic* described the 1964 find of dinosaur bones of a newly discovered dinosaur weighing 170 pounds, measuring 9 feet, with a 6-inch claw on one toe of each hind foot. The age of the dinosaur was estimated using potassium-40 dating of rocks surrounding the bones.

**a.** Potassium-40 decays exponentially with a half-life of approximately 1.31 billion years. Use the fact that after 1.31 billion years a given amount of potassium-40 will have decayed to half the original amount to show that the decay model for potassium-40 is given by $A = A_0e^{-0.52912t}$, where $t$ is in billions of years.

**b.** Analysis of the rocks surrounding the dinosaur bones indicated that 94.5% of the original amount of potassium-40 was still present. Let $A = 0.945A_0$ in the model in part (a) and estimate the age of the bones of the dinosaur.

**22.** A bird species in danger of extinction has a population that is decreasing exponentially $(A = A_0e^{kt})$. Five years ago the population was at 1400 and today only 1000 of the birds are alive. Once the population drops below 100, the situation will be irreversible. When will this happen?

**23.** Use the exponential growth model, $A = A_0e^{kt}$, to show that the time it takes a population to double (to grow from $A_0$ to $2A_0$) is given by $t = \frac{\ln 2}{k}$.

**24.** Use the exponential growth model, $A = A_0e^{kt}$, to show that the time it takes a population to triple (to grow from $A_0$ to $3A_0$) is given by $t = \frac{\ln 3}{k}$.

*Use the formula $t = \frac{\ln 2}{k}$ that gives the time for a population with a growth rate k to double to solve Exercises 25–26. Express each answer to the nearest whole year.*

**25.** China is growing at a rate of 1.1% per year. How long will it take China to double its population?

**26.** Japan is growing at a rate of 0.3% per year. How long will it take Japan to double its population?

**27.** The logistic growth function

$$f(t) = \frac{100{,}000}{1 + 5000e^{-t}}$$

describes the number of people who have become ill with influenza $t$ weeks after its initial outbreak in a particular community.

**a.** How many people became ill with the flu when the epidemic began?

**b.** How many people were ill by the end of the fourth week?

**c.** What is the limiting size of the population that becomes ill?

**28.** The logistic growth function

$$f(t) = \frac{500}{1 + 83.3e^{-0.162t}}$$

describes the population of an endangered species of birds $t$ years after they are introduced to a non-threatening habitat.

**a.** How many birds were initially introduced to the habitat?

**b.** How many birds are expected in the habitat after 10 years?

**c.** What is the limiting size of the bird population that the habitat will sustain?

*The logistic growth function*

$$P(x) = \frac{0.9}{1 + 271e^{-0.122x}}$$

*models the probability that an American who is x years old has some coronary heart disease. Use the function to solve Exercises 29–32.*

**29.** What is the probability that a 20-year-old has some coronary heart disease?

**30.** What is the probability that an 80-year-old has some coronary heart disease?

**31.** At what age is the probability of some coronary heart disease 0.5?

**32.** At what age is the probability of some coronary heart disease 0.7?

*Use Newton's Law of Cooling,* $T = C + (T_0 - C)e^{kt}$, *to solve Exercises 33–36.*

**33.** A bottle of juice initially has a temperature of 70°F. It is left to cool in a refrigerator that has a temperature of 45°F. After 10 minutes, the temperature of the juice is 55°F.

**a.** Use Newton's Law of Cooling to find a model for the temperature of the juice, $T$, after $t$ minutes.

**b.** What is the temperature of the juice after 15 minutes?

**c.** When will the temperature of the juice be 50°F?

**34.** A pizza removed from the oven has a temperature of 450°F. It is left sitting in a room that has a temperature of 70°F. After 5 minutes, the temperature of the pizza is 300°F.

**a.** Use Newton's Law of Cooling to find a model for the temperature of the pizza, $T$, after $t$ minutes.

**b.** What is the temperature of the pizza after 20 minutes?

**c.** When will the temperature of the pizza be 140°F?

**35.** A frozen steak initially has a temperature of 28°F. It is left to thaw in a room that has a temperature of 75°F. After 10 minutes, the temperature of the steak has risen to 38°F. After how many minutes will the temperature of the steak be 50°F?

**36.** A frozen steak initially has a temperature of 24°F. It is left to thaw in a room that has a temperature of 65°F. After 10 minutes, the temperature of the steak has risen to 30°F. After how many minutes will the temperature of the steak be 45°F?

*In Exercises 37–40, rewrite the equation in terms of base e. Express the answer in terms of a natural logarithm, and then round to three decimal places.*

**37.** $y = 100(4.6)^x$

**38.** $y = 1000(7.3)^x$

**39.** $y = 2.5(0.7)^x$

**40.** $y = 4.5(0.6)^x$

## Writing in Mathematics

**41.** Nigeria has a growth rate of 0.031 or 3.1%. Describe what this means.

**42.** How can you tell if an exponential model describes exponential growth or exponential decay?

**43.** Suppose that a population that is growing exponentially increases from 800,000 people in 1997 to 1,000,000 people in 2000. Without showing the details, describe how to obtain the exponential growth function that models this data.

**44.** What is the half-life of a substance?

**45.** Describe a difference between exponential growth and logistic growth.

**46.** Describe the shape of a scatter plot that suggests modeling the data with an exponential function.

**47.** You take up weightlifting and record the maximum number of pounds you can lift at the end of each week. You start off with rapid growth in terms of the weight you can lift from week to week, but then the growth begins to level off. Describe how to obtain a function that models the number of pounds you can lift at the end of each week. How can you use this function to predict what might happen if you continue the sport?

**48.** Would you prefer that your salary be modeled exponentially or logarithmically? Explain your answer.

**49.** One problem with all exponential growth models is that nothing can grow exponentially forever. Describe factors that might limit the size of a population.

## Technology Exercises

*The consumer price index measures changes in prices over time. The consumer price index for the bars shown in the graph on page 416 indicates that what cost \$1.00 in 1969 (the reference year) cost about \$1.16 in 1970, \$1.61 in 1975, \$2.49 in 1980, \$3.22 in 1985, \$3.91 in 1990,*

*$4.57 in 1995, and $4.96 in 1999. Use the data in the table to solve Exercises 50–54.*

**Consumer Price Index 1970–1999**

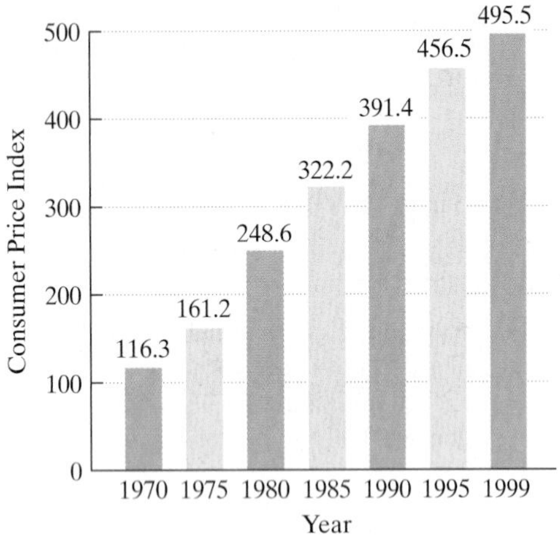


*Source*: U. S. Department of Labor

| *x*, Number of Years, after 1969 | *y*, Consumer Price Index |
|---|---|
| 1 | 116.3 |
| 6 | 161.2 |
| 11 | 248.8 |
| 16 | 322.2 |
| 21 | 391.4 |
| 26 | 456.5 |
| 30 | 495.5 |

**50.** Use your graphing utility's Exponential REGression option to obtain a model of the form $y = ab^x$ that fits the data. How well does the correlation coefficient, $r$, indicate that the model fits the data?

**51.** Use your graphing utility's Logarithmic REGression option to obtain a model of the form $y = a + b \ln x$ that fits the data. How well does the correlation coefficient, $r$, indicate that the model fits the data?

**52.** Use your graphing utility's Linear REGression option to obtain a model of the form $y = ax + b$ that fits the data. How well does the correlation coefficient, $r$, indicate that the model fits the data?

**53.** Use your graphing utility's Power REGression option to obtain a model of the form $y = ax^b$ that fits the data. How well does the correlation coefficient, $r$, indicate that the model fits the data?

**54.** Use the value of $r$ in Exercises 50–53 to select the model of best fit. Use this model to predict the consumer price index in 2007. How much will what cost $1.00 in 1969 cost in 2007?

**55.** In Exercises 29–32 you worked with the logistic growth function

$$P(x) = \frac{0.9}{1 + 271e^{-0.122x}}$$

that models the probability that an American who is $x$ years old has some coronary heart disease. Use your graphing utility to graph the function in a $[0, 100, 10]$ by $[0, 1, 0.1]$ viewing rectangle. Describe as specifically as possible what the logistic curve indicates about aging and the probability of coronary heart disease.

*In Exercises 56–57, use the data and a graphing utility to find the model that best fits the given data. Then use the model to make a prediction about what might occur in the future.*

**56.**

| *x*, Number of Years after 1984 | *y*, Millions of Computers in Use in the U.S. |
|---|---|
| 1 | 21.5 |
| 4 | 40.8 |
| 5 | 47.6 |
| 7 | 62.0 |
| 8 | 68.2 |
| 9 | 76.5 |
| 10 | 85.8 |
| 11 | 96.2 |
| 16 | 160.5 |

*Source:* Computer Industry Almanac

**57.**

| *x*, Number of Years after 1989 | *y*, Millions of CDs Sold in the U.S. |
|---|---|
| 1 | 286.5 |
| 2 | 333.3 |
| 3 | 407.5 |
| 4 | 495.4 |
| 5 | 662.1 |
| 6 | 722.9 |
| 7 | 778.9 |
| 8 | 753.1 |
| 9 | 847.0 |

*Source:* Recording Industry Association of America

## Critical Thinking Exercises

**58.** The World Health Organization makes predictions about the number of AIDS cases based on a compromise between a linear model and an exponential growth model. Explain why the World Health Organization does this.

**59.** Use Newton's Law of Cooling, $T = C + (T_0 - C)e^{kt}$, to solve this exercise. At 9:00 A.M., a coroner arrived at the home a person who had died during the night. The temperature of the room was 70°F, and at the time of death the person had a body temperature of 98.6°F. The coroner took the body's temperature at 9:30 A.M., at which time it was 85.6°F, and again at 10:00 A.M., when it was 82.7°F. At what time did the person die?

### Group Exercises

**60.** This activity is intended for three or four people who would like to take up weightlifting. Each person in the group should record the maximum number of pounds that he or she can lift at the end of each week for the first 10 consecutive weeks. Use the Logarithmic REGression option of a graphing utility to obtain a model showing the amount of weight that group members can lift from week 1 to week 10. Graph each of the models in the same viewing rectangle to observe similarities and differences among weight-growth patterns of each member. Use the functions to predict the amount of weight that group members will be able to lift in the future. If the group continues to work out together, check the accuracy of these predictions.

**61.** Each group member should consult an almanac, newspaper, magazine, or the Internet to find data that can be modeled by exponential or logarithmic functions. Group members should select the two sets of data that are most interesting and relevant. For each data set selected, find a model that best fits the data. Each group member should make one prediction based on the model and then discuss a consequence of this prediction. What factors might change the accuracy of each prediction?

## CHAPTER SUMMARY, REVIEW, AND TEST

### Summary

#### 4.1 Exponential Functions

a. The exponential function with base $b$ is defined by $f(x) = b^x$, where $b > 0$ and $b \neq 1$.

b. Characteristics of exponential functions and graphs for $0 < b < 1$ and $b > 1$ are shown in the box on page 360.

c. Transformations involving exponential functions are summarized in Table 4.1 on page 360.

d. The natural exponential function: $f(x) = e^x$. The irrational number $e$ is called the natural base, where $e \approx 2.7183$.

e. Formulas for compound interest: After $t$ years, the balance $A$ in an account with principal $P$ and annual interest rate $r$ (in decimal form) is given by one of the following formulas:

1. For $n$ compoundings per year: $A = P\left(1 + \frac{r}{n}\right)^{nt}$
2. For continuous compounding: $A = Pe^{rt}$

#### 4.2 Logarithmic Functions

a. Definition of the logarithmic function: For $x > 0$ and $b > 0$, $b \neq 1$, $y = \log_b x$ is equivalent to $b^y = x$. The function $f(x) = \log_b x$ is the logarithmic function with base $b$. This function is the inverse function of the exponential function with base $b$.

b. Graphs of logarithmic functions for $b > 1$ and $0 < b < 1$ are shown in Figure 4.7 on page 372. Characteristics of the graphs are summarized in the box that follows the figure.

c. Transformations involving logarithmic functions are summarized in Table 4.3 on page 373.

d. The domain of a logarithmic function is the set of all positive real numbers. The domain of $f(x) = \log_b(x + c)$ consists of all $x$ for which $x + c > 0$.

e. Common and natural logarithms: $f(x) = \log x$ means $f(x) = \log_{10} x$ and is the common logarithmic function. $f(x) = \ln x$ means $f(x) = \log_e x$ and is the natural logarithmic function.

f. Basic Logarithmic Properties

| Base $b$ ($b > 0, b \neq 1$) | Base 10 (Common Logarithms) | Base $e$ (Natural Logarithms) |
|---|---|---|
| $\log_b 1 = 0$ | $\log 1 = 0$ | $\ln 1 = 0$ |
| $\log_b b = 1$ | $\log 10 = 1$ | $\ln e = 1$ |
| $\log_b b^x = x$ | $\log 10^x = x$ | $\ln e^x = x$ |
| $b^{\log_b x} = x$ | $10^{\log x} = x$ | $e^{\ln x} = x$ |

## 4.3 Properties of Logarithms

a. *The Product Rule:* $\log_b(MN) = \log_b M + \log_b N$

b. *The Quotient Rule:* $\log_b\left(\frac{M}{N}\right) = \log_b M - \log_b N$

c. *The Power Rule:* $\log_b M^p = p \log_b M$

d. *The Change-of Base Property:*

| The General Property | Introducing Common Logarithms | Introducing Natural Logarithms |
|---|---|---|
| $\log_b M = \frac{\log_a M}{\log_a b}$ | $\log_b M = \frac{\log M}{\log b}$ | $\log_b M = \frac{\ln M}{\ln b}$ |

## 4.4 Exponential and Logarithmic Equations

a. An exponential equation is an equation containing a variable in an exponent. The solution procedure involves isolating the exponential expression and taking the natural logarithm on both sides. The box on page 387 provides the details.

b. A logarithmic equation is an equation containing a variable in a logarithmic expression. Logarithmic equations in the form $\log_b x = c$ can be solved by rewriting as $b^c = x$.

c. When checking logarithmic equations, reject proposed solutions that produce the logarithm of a negative number or the logarithm of 0 in the original equation.

d. Equations involving natural logarithms are solved by isolating the natural logarithm with coefficient 1 on one side and exponentiating both sides. Simplify using $e^{\ln x} = x$.

## 4.5 Modeling with Exponential and Logarithmic Functions

a. Exponential growth and decay models are given by $A = A_0 e^{kt}$ in which $t$ represents time, $A_0$ is the amount present at $t = 0$, and $A$ is the amount present at time $t$. If $k > 0$, the model describes growth and $k$ is the growth rate. If $k < 0$, the model describes decay and $k$ is the decay rate.

b. The logistic growth model, given by $A = \frac{c}{1 + ae^{-bt}}$, describes situations in which growth is limited. $y = c$ is a horizontal asymptote for the graph and growth, $A$, can never exceed $c$.

c. Newton's Law of Cooling: The temperature, $T$, of a heated object at time $t$ is given by

$$T = C + (T_0 - C)e^{kt},$$

where $C$ is the constant temperature of the surrounding medium, $T_0$ is the initial temperature of the heated object, and $k$ is a negative constant.

d. Scatter plots for exponential and logarithmic models are shown in Figure 4.20 on page 410. When using a graphing utility to model data, the closer that the correlation coefficient $r$ is to $-1$ or 1, the better the model fits the data.

e. Expressing an Exponential Model in Base $e$: $y = ab^x$ is equivalent to $y = ae^{(\ln b)\cdot x}$.

# Review Exercises

## 4.1

*In Exercises 1–4, the graph of an exponential function is given. Select the function for each graph from the following options:*

$$f(x) = 4^x,\ g(x) = 4^{-x},$$

$$h(x) = -4^{-x},\ r(x) = -4^{-x} + 3.$$

1.

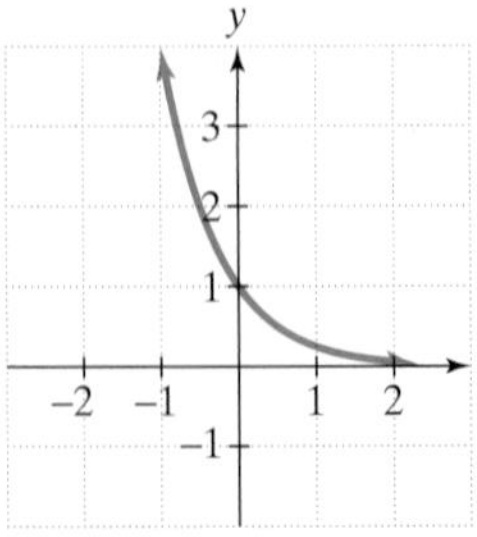


2.

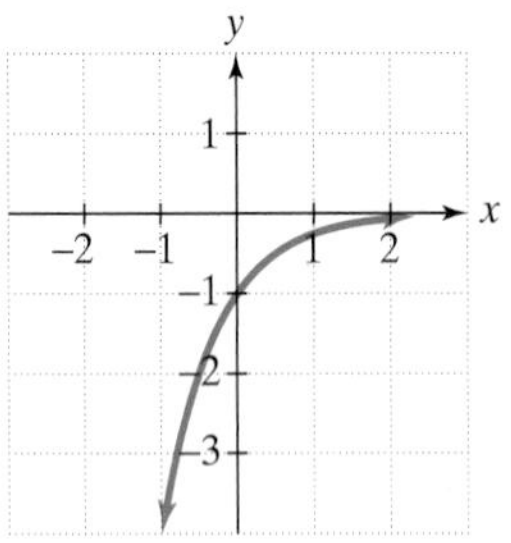


3.

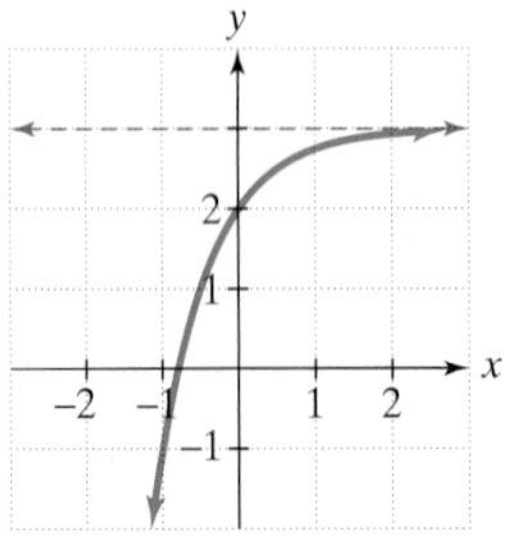

**4.**

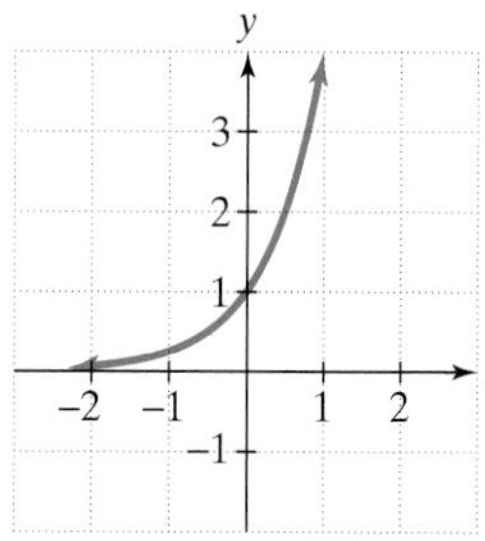


*In Exercises 5–8, sketch by hand the graphs of the two functions in the same rectangular coordinate system. Use a table of coordinates to sketch the first function and transformations of this function plus a table of coordinates to graph the second function.*

**5.** $f(x) = 2^x$ and $g(x) = 2^{x-1}$

**6.** $f(x) = 3^x$ and $g(x) = 3^x - 1$

**7.** $f(x) = 3^x$ and $g(x) = -3^x$

**8.** $f(x) = \left(\frac{1}{2}\right)^x$ and $g(x) = \left(\frac{1}{2}\right)^{-x}$

*Use the compound interest formulas to solve Exercises 9–10.*

**9.** Suppose that you have \$5000 to invest. Which investment yields the greater return over 5 years: 5.5% compounded semiannually or 5.25% compounded monthly?

**10.** Suppose that you have \$14,000 to invest. Which investment yields the greater return over 10 years: 7% compounded monthly or 6.85% compounded continuously?

**11.** A cup of coffee is taken out of a microwave oven and placed in a room. The temperature, $T$, in degrees Fahrenheit, of the coffee after $t$ minutes is modeled by the function $T = 70 + 130e^{-0.04855t}$. The graph of the function is shown in the figure. Use the graph to answer each of the following questions.

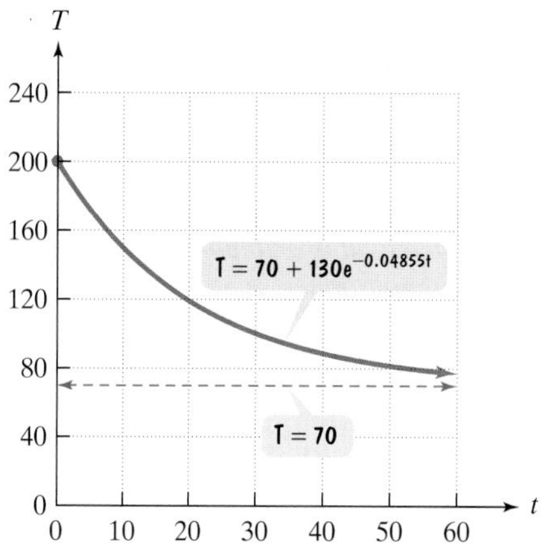


**a.** What was the temperature of the coffee when it was first taken out of the microwave?

**b.** What is a reasonable estimate of the temperature of the coffee after 20 minutes? Use your calculator to verify this estimate.

**c.** What is the limit of the temperature to which the coffee will cool? What does this tell you about the temperature of the room?

## 4.2

*In Exercises 12–14, write each equation in its equivalent exponential form.*

**12.** $\frac{1}{2} = \log_{49} 7$ **13.** $3 = \log_4 x$ **14.** $\log_3 81 = y$

*In Exercises 15–17, write each equation in its equivalent logarithmic form.*

**15.** $6^3 = 216$ **16.** $b^4 = 625$ **17.** $13^y = 874$

*In Exercises 18–25, evaluate each expression without using a calculator. If evaluation is not possible, state the reason.*

**18.** $\log_4 64$ **19.** $\log_5 \frac{1}{25}$ **20.** $\log_3(-9)$

**21.** $\log_{16} 4$ **22.** $\log_{17} 17$ **23.** $\log_3 3^8$

**24.** $\ln e^5$ **25.** $\log_3(\log_8 8)$

**26.** Graph $f(x) = 2^x$ and $g(x) = \log_2 x$ in the same rectangular coordinate system.

**27.** Graph $f(x) = \left(\frac{1}{3}\right)^x$ and $g(x) = \log_{1/3} x$ in the same rectangular coordinate system.

*In Exercises 28–31, the graph of a logarithmic function is given. Select the function for each graph from the following options:*

$$f(x) = \log x,\ g(x) = \log(-x),$$

$$h(x) = \log(2 - x),\ r(x) = 1 + \log(2 - x).$$

**28.**

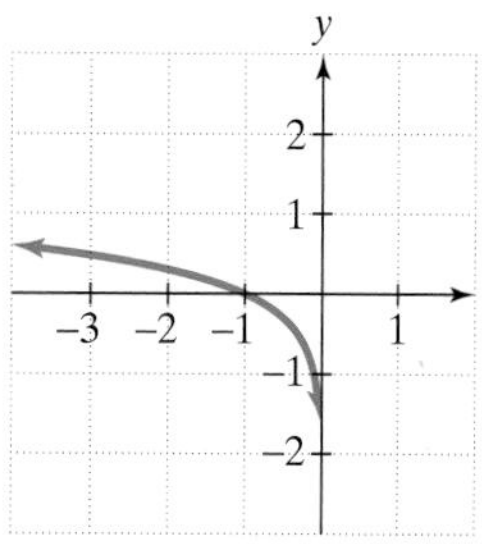


**29.**

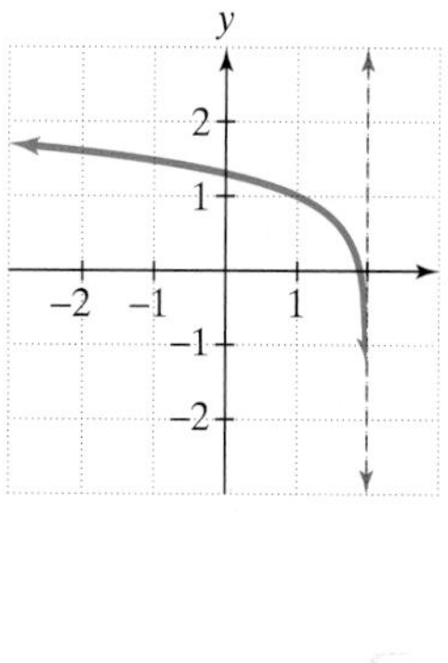

**30.**

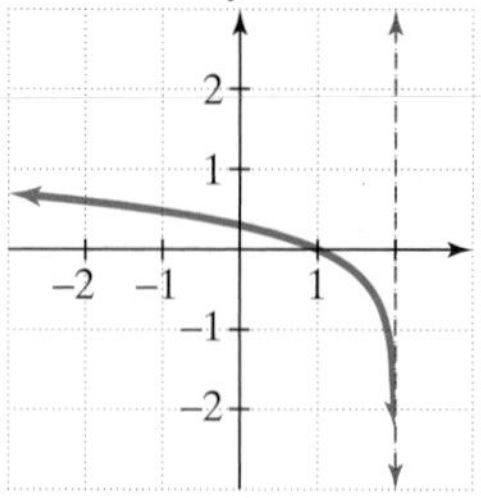


**31.**

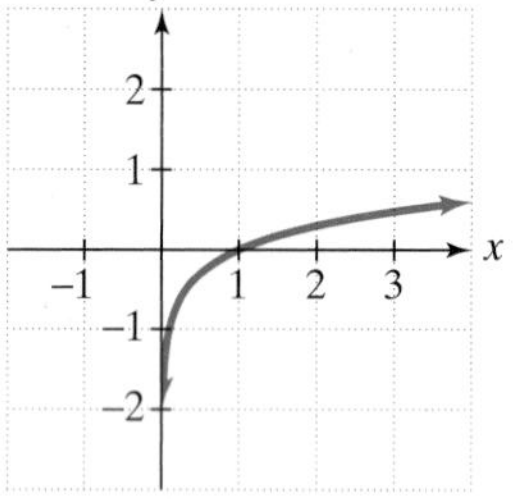


*In Exercises 32–34, begin by graphing $f(x) = \log_2 x$. Then use transformations of this graph to graph the given function. What is the graph's x-intercept? What is the vertical asymptote?*

**32.** $g(x) = \log_2(x - 2)$ **33.** $h(x) = -1 + \log_2 x$

**34.** $r(x) = \log_2(-x)$

*In Exercises 35–37, find the domain of each logarithmic function.*

**35.** $f(x) = \log_8(x + 5)$ **36.** $f(x) = \log(3 - x)$

**37.** $f(x) = \ln(x - 1)^2$

*In Exercises 38–40, use inverse properties of logarithms to simplify each expression.*

**38.** $\ln e^{6x}$ **39.** $e^{\ln \sqrt{x}}$ **40.** $10^{\log 4x^2}$

**41.** On the Richter scale, the magnitude, $R$, of an earthquake of intensity $I$ is given by $R = \log \frac{I}{I_0}$, where $I_0$ is the intensity of a barely felt zero-level earthquake. If the intensity of an earthquake is $1000I_0$, what is its magnitude on the Richter scale?

**42.** Students in a psychology class took a final examination. As part of an experiment to see how much of the course content they remembered over time, they took equivalent forms of the exam in monthly intervals thereafter. The average score, $f(t)$, for the group after $t$ months was modeled by the function $f(t) = 76 - 18\log(t + 1)$, where $0 \le t \le 12$.

**a.** What was the average score when the exam was first given?

**b.** What was the average score after 2 months? 4 months? 6 months? 8 months? one year?

**c.** Use the results from parts (a) and (b) to graph $f$. Describe what the shape of the graph indicates in terms of the material retained by the students.

**43.** The formula

$$t = \frac{1}{c}\ln\left(\frac{A}{A - N}\right)$$

describes the time, $t$, in weeks, that it takes to achieve mastery of a portion of a task. In the formula, $A$ represents maximum learning possible, $N$ is the portion of the learning that is to be achieved, and $c$ is a constant used to measure an individual's learning style. A 50-year-old man decides to start running as a way to maintain good health. He feels that the maximum rate he could ever hope to achieve is 12 miles per hour. How many weeks will it take before the man can run 5 miles per hour if $c = 0.06$ for this person?

## 4.3

*In Exercises 44–47, use properties of logarithms to expand each logarithmic expression as much as possible. Where possible, evaluate logarithmic expressions without using a calculator.*

**44.** $\log_6(36x^3)$ **45.** $\log_4 \frac{\sqrt{x}}{64}$

**46.** $\log_2 \frac{xy^2}{64}$ **47.** $\ln \sqrt[3]{\frac{x}{e}}$

*In Exercises 48–51, use properties of logarithms to condense each logarithmic expression. Write the expression as a single logarithm whose coefficient is 1.*

**48.** $\log_b 7 + \log_b 3$ **49.** $\log 3 - 3\log x$

**50.** $3\ln x + 4\ln y$ **51.** $\frac{1}{2}\ln x - \ln y$

*In Exercises 52–53, use common logarithms or natural logarithms and a calculator to evaluate to four decimal places.*

**52.** $\log_6 72{,}348$ **53.** $\log_4 0.863$

## 4.4

*Solve each exponential equation in Exercises 54–58. Express the answer in terms of natural logarithms. Then use a calculator to obtain a decimal approximation, correct to the nearest thousandth, for the solution.*

**54.** $8^x = 12{,}143$ **55.** $9e^{5x} = 1269$

**56.** $e^{12-5x} - 7 = 123$ **57.** $5^{4x+2} = 37{,}500$

**58.** $e^{2x} - e^x - 6 = 0$

*Solve each logarithmic equation in Exercises 59–63.*

**59.** $\log_4(3x - 5) = 3$

**60.** $\log_2(x + 3) + \log_2(x - 3) = 4$

**61.** $\log_3(x-1) - \log_3(x+2) = 2$

**62.** $\ln x = -1$ **63.** $3 + 4\ln 2x = 15$

**64.** The formula $A = 10.1e^{0.005t}$ models the population of Los Angeles, California, in millions, $t$ years after 1992. If the growth rate continues into the future, when will the population reach 13 million?

**65.** The amount of carbon dioxide in the atmosphere, measured in parts per million, has been increasing as a result of the burning of oil and coal. The buildup of gases and particles trap heat and raise the planet's temperature, a phenomenon called the greenhouse effect. Carbon dioxide accounts for about half of the warming. The formula $A = 364(1.005)^t$ projects carbon dioxide concentration, $A$, in parts per million, $t$ years after 2000. Using the projections given by the formula, when will the carbon dioxide concentration be double the preindustrial level of 280 parts per million?

**66.** The formula $C = 15{,}557 + 5259 \ln x$ models the average cost of a new car $x$ years after 1989. When will the average cost of a new car be $30,000?

**67.** Use the formula for compound interest with $n$ compoundings each year to solve this problem. How long, to the nearest tenth of a year, will it take $12,500 to grow to $20,000 at 6.5% annual interest compounded quarterly?

*Use the formula for continuous compounding to solve Exercises 68–69.*

**68.** How long, to the nearest tenth of a year, will it take $50,000 to triple in value at 7.5% annual interest compounded continuously?

**69.** What interest rate is required for an investment subject to continuous compounding to triple in 5 years?

## 4.5

**70.** According to the U.S. Bureau of the Census, in 1980 there were 14.6 million residents of Hispanic origin living in the United States. By 1997, the number had increased to 29.3 million. The exponential growth function $A = 14.6e^{kt}$ describes the U.S. Hispanic population, in millions, $t$ years after 1980.

**a.** Find $k$, correct to three decimal places.

**b.** Use the resulting model to project the Hispanic resident population in 2005.

**c.** In what year will the Hispanic resident population reach 50 million?

**71.** Use the exponential decay model for carbon-14, $A = A_0e^{-0.000121t}$, to solve this exercise. Prehistoric cave paintings were discovered in the Lascaux cave in France. The paint contained 15% of the original carbon-14. Estimate the age of the paintings at the time of the discovery.

**72.** Europe's Great Plague of 1666 devastated Eyam, England. There were 261 people in the village; only 83 survived. The logistic growth function

$$f(t) = \frac{171}{1 + 18.6e^{-0.0747t}}$$

models the number of people in Eyam who were infected $t$ days after the outbreak. (Source: Raggett, G. "Modeling the Eyam Plague." *The Institute of Mathematics and Its Application* 18:221–226.)

**a.** How many people were infected when the outbreak began?

**b.** How many people were infected after 45 days?

**c.** According to the model, what is the limiting size of Eyam's population that can become infected? With 83 survivors among 261 people, does this mean that the size of the infected population surpassed the limit set by the model? Explain your answer.

**73.** Use Newton's Law of Cooling, $T = C + (T_0 - C)e^{kt}$ to solve this exercise. You are served a cup of coffee that has a temperature of 185°F. The room temperature is 65°F. After 2 minutes, the temperature of the coffee is 155°F.

**a.** Write a model for the temperature of the coffee, $T$, after $t$ minutes.

**b.** When will the temperature of the coffee be 105°F?

*In Exercises 74–75, rewrite the equation in terms of base e. Express the answer in terms of a natural logarithm, and then round to three decimal places.*

**74.** $y = 73(2.6)^x$ **75.** $y = 6.5(0.43)^x$

**76.** The figure shows world population projections through the year 2150. The data are from the United Nations Family Planning Program and are based on optimistic or pessimistic expectations for successful control of human population growth. Suppose that you are interested in modeling these data using exponential, logarithmic, linear, and quadratic functions. Which function would you use to model each of the projections? Explain your choices. For the choice corresponding to a quadratic model, would your formula involve one with a positive or negative leading coefficient? Explain.

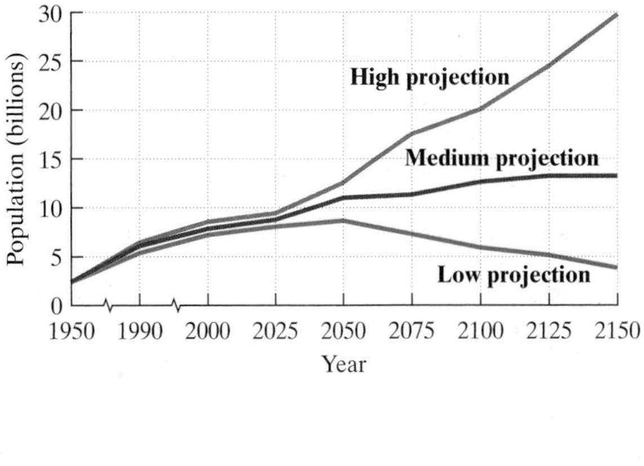

**77.** The figure shows the number of people in the United States age 65 and over, with projected figures for the year 2000 and beyond.

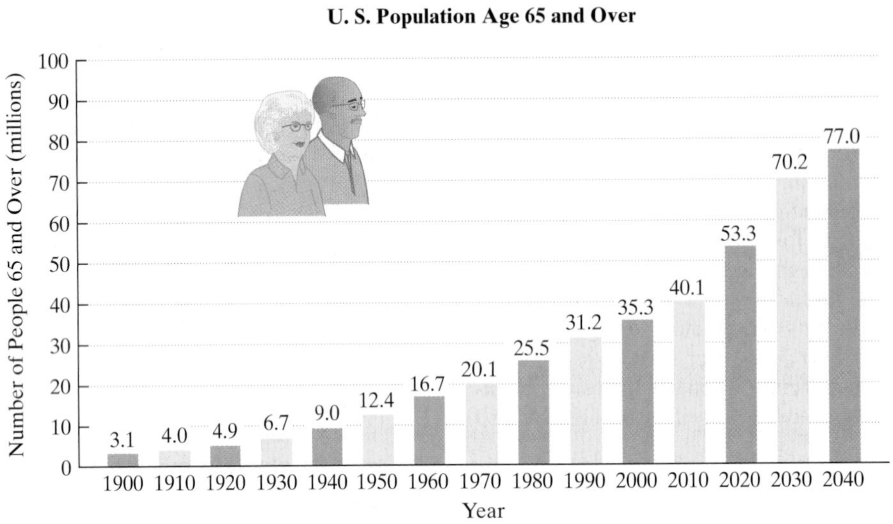


*Source*: U. S. Bureau of the Census

Let $x$ represent the number of years since 1899 and let $y$ represent the U.S. population, in millions. Use your graphing utility to find the model that best fits the data in the bar graph. Then use the model to find the U.S. population age 65 and over in 2050.

## Chapter 4 Test

**1.** Graph $f(x) = 2^x$ and $g(x) = 2^{x+1}$ in the same rectangular coordinate system.

**2.** Graph $f(x) = \log_2 x$ and $g(x) = \log_2(x - 1)$ in the same rectangular coordinate system.

**3.** Write in exponential form: $\log_5 125 = 3$.

**4.** Write in logarithmic form: $\sqrt{36} = 6$.

**5.** Find the domain of $f(x) = \ln(3 - x)$.

*In Exercises 6–7, use properties of logarithms to expand each logarithmic expression as much as possible. Where possible, evaluate logarithmic expressions without using a calculator.*

**6.** $\log_4(64x^5)$ **7.** $\log_3 \frac{\sqrt[3]{x}}{81}$

*In Exercises 8–9, write each expression as a single logarithm.*

**8.** $6 \log x + 2 \log y$ **9.** $\ln 7 - 3 \ln x$

**10.** Use a calculator to evaluate $\log_{15} 71$ to four decimal places.

*In Exercises 11–16, solve each equation.*

**11.** $5^x = 1.4$ **12.** $400e^{0.005x} = 1600$

**13.** $e^{2x} - 6e^x + 5 = 0$ **14.** $\log_6(4x - 1) = 3$

**15.** $\log x + \log(x + 15) = 2$ **16.** $2 \ln 3x = 8$

**17.** Suppose you have \$3000 to invest. Which investment yields the greater return over 10 years: 6.5% compounded semianually or 6% compounded continuously? How much more (to the nearest dollar) is yielded by the better investment?

**18.** On the decibel scale, the loudness of a sound, in decibels, is given by $D = 10 \log \frac{I}{I_0}$, where $I$ is the intensity of the sound, in watts per meter$^2$, and $I_0$ is the intensity of a sound barely audible to the human ear. If the intensity of a sound is $10^{12}I_0$, what is its loudness in decibels? (Such a sound is potentially damaging to the ear.)

**19.** The percentage of married men in the United States who are employed is modeled by $P = 89.18e^{-0.004t}$. The model indicates that P% of married men were employed $t$ years after 1959.

**a.** What percentage of married men were employed in 1959?

**b.** Is the percentage of married men who are employed increasing or decreasing? Explain.

**c.** In what year were 77% of U.S. married men employed?

**20.** The 1980 population of Europe was 484 million; in 1990, it was 509 million. Write the exponential growth function that describes the population of Europe, in millions, $t$ years after 1980.

**21.** Use the exponential decay model for carbon-14, $A = A_0e^{-0.000121t}$, to solve this exercise. Bones of a prehistoric man were discovered and contained 5% of the original amount of carbon-14. How long ago did the man die?

**22.** The logistic growth function

$$f(t) = \frac{140}{1 + 9e^{-0.165t}}$$

describes the population of an endangered species of elk $t$ years after they were introduced to a nonthreatening habitat.

**a.** How many elk were initially introduced to the habitat?
**b.** How many elk are expected in the habitat after 10 years?
**c.** What is the limiting size of the elk population that the habitat will sustain?

## Cumulative Review Exercises (Chapters 1–4)

*Solve each equation in Exercises 1–5.*

**1.** $|3x - 4| = 2$

**2.** $\sqrt{2x - 5} - \sqrt{x - 3} = 1$

**3.** $x^4 + x^3 - 3x^2 - x + 2 = 0$

**4.** $e^{5x} - 32 = 96$

**5.** $\log_2(x + 5) + \log_2(x - 1) = 4$

*Solve each inequality in Exercises 6–7. Express the answer in interval notation.*

**6.** $14 - 5x \geq -6$

**7.** $|2x - 4| \leq 2$

**8.** Write the point-slope form and the slope-intercept form of the line passing through $(1, 3)$ and $(3, -3)$.

**9.** If $f(x) = x^2$ and $g(x) = x + 2$, find $(f \circ g)(x)$ and $(g \circ f)(x)$.

**10.** If $f(x) = 2x - 7$, find $f^{-1}(x)$.

**11.** Divide $x^3 + 5x^2 + 3x - 10$ by $x + 2$.

**12.** Use the Rational Zero Theorem to list all possible rational zeros for $f(x) = 4x^3 - 7x - 3$.

**13.** The value of $y$ varies directly as the square of $x$. If $x = 3$ when $y = 12$, find $y$ when $x = 15$.

**14.** Solve $x^3 - 4x^2 + 6x - 4 = 0$ given that $1 + i$ is a root.

*In Exercises 15–18, graph each equation.*

**15.** $(x - 3)^2 + (y + 2)^2 = 4$

**16.** $f(x) = (x - 2)^2 - 1$

**17.** $f(x) = \dfrac{x^2 - 1}{x^2 - 4}$

**18.** $f(x) = (x - 2)^2(x + 1)$

**19.** You are paid time-and-a-half for each hour worked over 40 hours a week. Last week you worked 50 hours and earned \$660. What is your normal hourly salary?

**20.** The formula $F = 1 - k\ln(t + 1)$ models the fraction of people, $F$, who remember all the words in a list of nonsense words $t$ hours after memorizing the list. After 3 hours only half the people could remember all the words. Determine the value of $k$ and then predict the fraction of people in the group who will remember all the words after 6 hours.

# Trigonometric Functions

## Chapter 5

Have you had days where your physical, intellectual, and emotional potentials were all at their peak? Then there are those other days when we feel we should not even bother getting out of bed. Do our potentials run in oscillating cycles like the tides? Can they be described mathematically? In this chapter you will encounter functions that enable us to model phenomena that occur in cycles.

What a day! It started when you added two miles to your morning run. You've experienced a feeling of peak physical well-being ever since. College was wonderful: You actually enjoyed two difficult lectures and breezed through a math test that had you worried. Now you're having dinner with an old group of friends. You experience the warmth from bonds of friendship filling the room.

# SECTION 5.1 *Angles and Their Measure*

## Objectives

1. Recognize and use the vocabulary of angles.
2. Use degree measure.
3. Draw angles in standard position.
4. Find coterminal angles.
5. Find complements and supplements.
6. Use radian measure.
7. Convert between degrees and radians.
8. Find the length of a circular arc.
9. Use linear and angular speed to describe motion on a circular path.

The San Francisco Museum of Modern Art was constructed in 1996 to illustrate how art and architecture can enrich one another. The exterior involves geometric shapes, symmetry, and unusual facades. Although there are no windows, natural light streams in through a truncated cylindrical skylight that crowns the building. The architect worked with a scale model of the museum at the site and observed how light hit it during different times of the day. These observations were used to cut the cylindrical skylight at an angle that maximizes sunlight entering the interior.

Angles play a critical role in creating modern architecture. They are also fundamental in trigonometry. In this section, we begin our study of trigonometry by looking at angles and methods for measuring them.

**1** Recognize and use the vocabulary of angles.

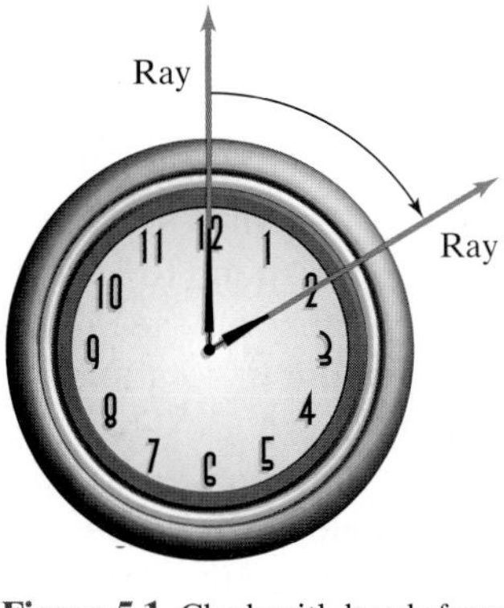


**Figure 5.1** Clock with hands forming an angle

## Angles

The hour hand of a clock suggests a **ray**, a part of a line that has only one endpoint and extends forever in the opposite direction. An **angle** is formed by two rays that have a common endpoint. One ray is called the **initial side** and the other the **terminal side**.

A rotating ray is often a useful way to think about angles. The ray in Figure 5.1 rotates from 12 to 2. The ray pointing to 12 is the **initial side** and the ray pointing to 2 is the **terminal side**. The common endpoint of an angle's initial side and terminal side is the **vertex** of the angle.

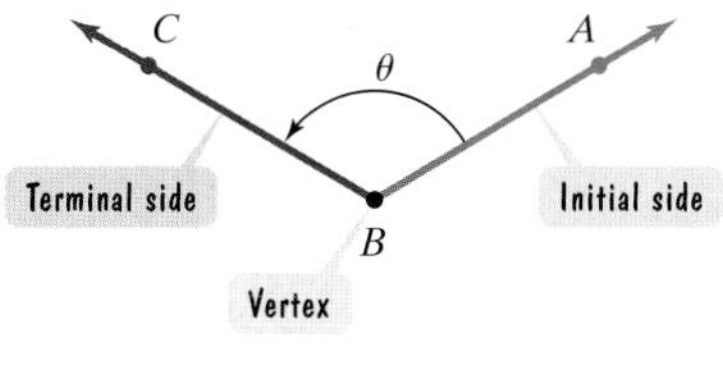


**Figure 5.2** An angle; two rays with a common endpoint

Figure 5.2 shows an angle. The arrow near the vertex shows the direction and the amount of rotation from the initial side to the terminal side. Several methods can be used to name an angle. Lowercase Greek letters, such as $\alpha$ (alpha), $\beta$ (beta), $\gamma$ (gamma), and $\theta$ (theta), are often used.

An angle is in **standard position** if

- its vertex is at the origin of a rectangular coordinate system

and

- its initial side lies along the positive $x$-axis.

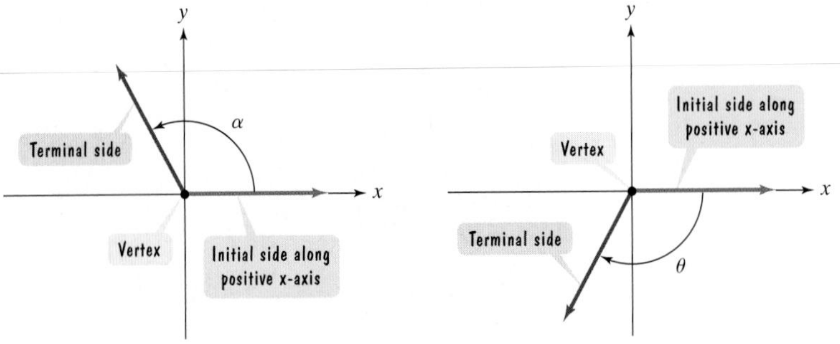


(a) $\alpha$ in standard position; $\alpha$ positive

(b) $\theta$ in standard position; $\theta$ negative

**Figure 5.3** Two angles in standard position

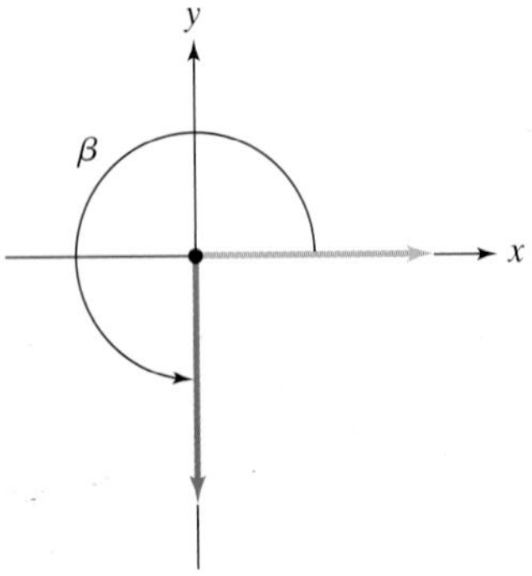


**Figure 5.4** $\beta$ is a quadrantal angle.

The angles in Figure 5.3 are both in standard position.

When we see an initial side and a terminal side in place, there are two kinds of rotation that could have generated it. The arrow in Figure 5.3(a) indicates that the rotation from the initial side to the terminal side is in the counterclockwise direction. **Positive angles** are generated by counterclockwise rotation. Thus, angle $\alpha$ is positive. By contrast, the arrow in Figure 5.3(b) shows that the rotation from the initial side to the terminal side is in the clockwise direction. **Negative angles** are generated by clockwise rotation. Thus, angle $\theta$ is negative.

When an angle is in standard position, its terminal side can lie in a quadrant. We say that the angle **lies in that quadrant**. For example, in Figure 5.3(a), the terminal side of angle $\alpha$ lies in quadrant II. Thus, angle $\alpha$ lies in quadrant II. By contrast, in Figure 5.3(b), the terminal side of angle $\theta$ lies in quadrant III. Thus, angle $\theta$ lies in quadrant III.

Must all angles in standard position lie in a quadrant? The answer is no. The terminal side can lie on the $x$-axis or the $y$-axis. For example, angle $\beta$ in Figure 5.4 has a terminal side that lies on the negative $y$-axis. An angle is called a **quadrantal angle** if its terminal side lies on the $x$-axis or the $y$-axis. Angle $\beta$ in Figure 5.4 is an example of a quadrantal angle.

**2** Use degree measure.

A complete 360° rotation

## Measuring Angles Using Degrees

Angles are measured by determining the amount of rotation from the initial side to the terminal side. One way to measure angles is in **degrees**, symbolized by a small, raised circle °. Think of the hour hand of a clock. From 12 noon to 12 midnight, the hour hand moves around in a complete circle. By definition, the ray has rotated through 360 degrees, or 360°. Using 360° as the amount of rotation of a ray back onto itself, a degree, 1°, is $\frac{1}{360}$ of a complete rotation.

Figure 5.5 shows angles classified by their degree measurement. An **acute angle** measures less than 90° [see Figure 5.5(a)]. A **right angle**, one quarter of a complete rotation, measures 90° [Figure 5.5(b)]. Examine the right angle—do you see a small square at the vertex? This symbol is used to indicate a right angle. An **obtuse angle** measures more than 90°, but less than 180° [Figure 5.5(c)]. Finally, a **straight angle**, one-half a complete rotation, measures 180° [Figure 5.5(d)].

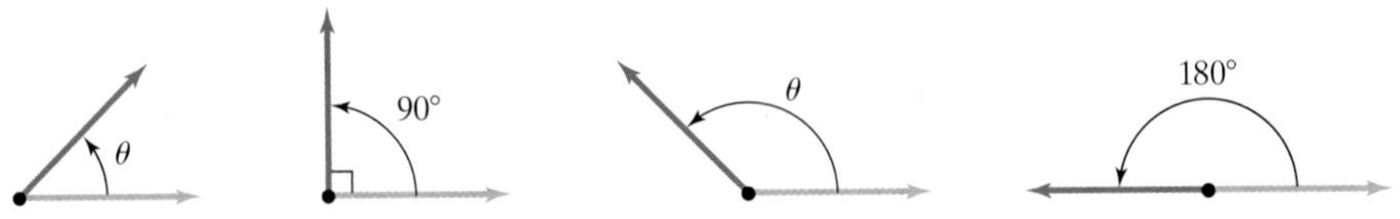


(a) **Acute angle** ($0° < \theta < 90°$)

(b) **Right angle** ($\frac{1}{4}$ rotation)

(c) **Obtuse angle** ($90° < \theta < 180°$)

(d) **Straight angle** ($\frac{1}{2}$ rotation)

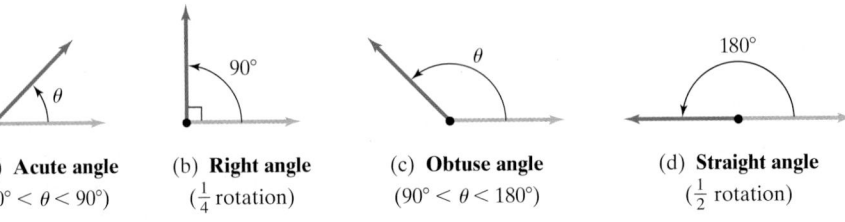

**Figure 5.5** Classifying angles by their degree measurement

**3** Draw angles in standard position.

We will be using notation such as $\theta = 60°$ to refer to an angle $\theta$ whose measure is 60°. We also refer to *an angle of 60°* or a *60°angle*, instead of using the more precise (but cumbersome) phrase *an angle whose measure is 60°*.

**Technology**

Fractional parts of degrees are measured in minutes and seconds. One minute, written $1'$, is $\frac{1}{60}$ degree.

One second, written $1''$, is $\frac{1}{3600}$ degree.

For example,

$$31°47'12'' = \left(31 + \frac{47}{60} + \frac{12}{3600}\right)^{\circ} = 31.787°.$$

Many calculators have keys for changing an angle from degree, minute, second notation (D°M′S″) to a decimal form and vice versa.

## EXAMPLE 1 Drawing Angles in Standard Position

Draw each angle in standard position.

**a.** a 45° angle **b.** a 225° angle **c.** a −135° angle **d.** a 405° angle

**Solution** Because we are drawing angles in standard position, each vertex is at the origin and each initial side lies along the positive $x$-axis.

**a.** A 45° angle is half of a right angle. The angle lies in quadrant I and is shown in Figure 5.6(a).

**b.** A 225° angle is a positive angle. It has a counterclockwise rotation of 180° followed by a counterclockwise rotation of 45°. The angle lies in quadrant III and is shown in Figure 5.6(b).

**c.** A −135° angle is negative angle. It has a clockwise rotation of 90° followed by a clockwise rotation of 45°. The angle lies in quadrant III and is shown in Figure 5.6(c).

**d.** A 405° angle is a positive angle. It has a counterclockwise rotation of 360°, one complete rotation, followed by a counterclockwise rotation of 45°. The angle lies in quadrant I and is shown in Figure 5.6(d).

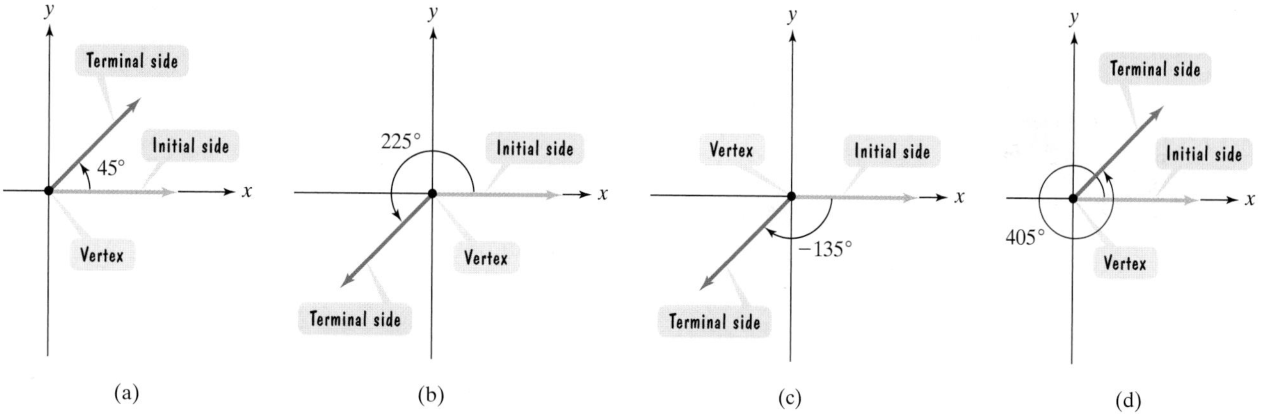


**Figure 5.6** Four angles in standard position

**Check Point 1** Draw each angle in standard position.

**a.** a 30° angle **b.** a 210° angle

**c.** a −120° angle **d.** a 390° angle

**4** Find coterminal angles.

Look at Figure 5.6 again. The 45° and 405° angles in parts (a) and (d) have the same initial and terminal sides. Similarly, the 225° and −135° angles in parts (b) and (c) have the same initial and terminal sides. Two angles with the same initial and terminal sides are called **coterminal angles**.

Every angle has infinitely many coterminal angles. Why? Think of an angle in standard position. One or more complete rotations of 360°, clockwise or counterclockwise, result in angles with the same initial and terminal sides as the original angle.

**Coterminal Angles**

An angle of $x°$ is coterminal with angles of

$$x° + k \cdot 360°$$

where $k$ is an integer.

Two coterminal angles for an angle of $x°$ can be found by adding 360° to $x°$ and subtracting 360° from $x°$.

### EXAMPLE 2 Finding Coterminal Angles

Assume the following angles are in standard position. Find a positive angle less than 360° that is coterminal with:

**a.** a 420° angle **b.** a −120° angle.

**Solution** We obtain the coterminal angle by adding or subtracting 360°. Our need to obtain a positive angle less than 360° determines whether we should add or subtract.

**a.** For a 420° angle, subtract 360° to find a positive coterminal angle.

$$420° - 360° = 60°$$

A 60° angle is coterminal with a 420° angle. Figure 5.7(a) illustrates that these angles have the same initial and terminal sides.

**b.** For a −120° angle, add 360° to find a positive coterminal angle.

$$-120° + 360° = 240°$$

A 240° angle is coterminal with a −120° angle. Figure 5.7(b) illustrates that these angles have the same initial and terminal sides.

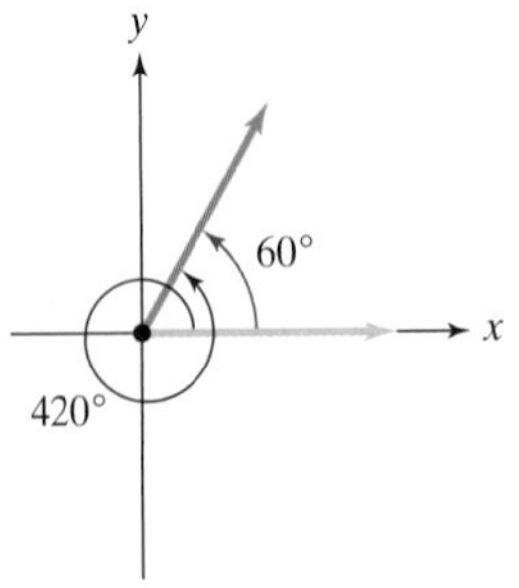


(a) Angles of 420° and 60° are coterminal.

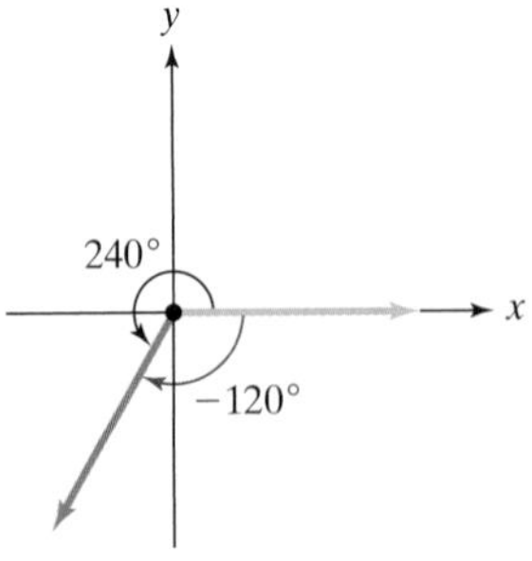


(b) Angles of −120° and 240° are coterminal.

**Figure 5.7** Pairs of coterminal angles

**Counterclockwise Clocks**

The counterclockwise rotation associated with positive angles was used in England to manufacture counterclockwise clocks. They ran backward but told the time perfectly correctly.

**Check Point 2** Find a positive angle less than 360° that is coterminal with:
**a.** a 400° angle **b.** a −135° angle.

**5** Find complements and supplements.

Two positive angles are **complements** if their sum is 90°. For example, angles of 70° and 20° are complements because $70° + 20° = 90°$.

Two positive angles are **supplements** if their sum is 180°. For example, angles of 130° and 50° are supplements because $130° + 50° = 180°$.

**Finding Complements and Supplements**

- For an $x°$ angle, the complement is a $90° - x°$ angle. Thus, the complement's measure is found by subtracting the angle's measure from 90°.
- For an $x°$ angle, the supplement is a $180° - x°$ angle. Thus, the supplement's measure is found by subtracting the angle's measure from 180°.

Because we use only positive angles for complements and supplements, some angles do not have complements and supplements.

## EXAMPLE 3 Complements and Supplements

If possible, find the complement and the supplement of the given angle.

**a.** $\theta = 62°$ **b.** $\alpha = 123°$

**Solution** We find the complement by subtracting the angle's measure from 90°. We find the supplement by subtracting the angle's measure from 180°.

**a.** We begin with $\theta = 62°$.

$$\text{complement} = 90° - 62° = 28°$$

$$\text{supplement} = 180° - 62° = 118°$$

For a 62° angle, the complement is a 28° angle and the supplement is a 118° angle.

**b.** Now we turn to $\alpha = 123°$. For the angle's complement, we consider subtracting 123° from 90°. The difference is negative. Because we use only positive angles for complements, a 123° angle has no complement. It does, however, have a supplement.

$$\text{supplement} = 180° - 123° = 57°$$

The supplement of a 123° angle is a 57° angle.

**Check Point 3** If possible, find the complement and the supplement of the given angle.
**a.** $\theta = 78°$ **b.** $\alpha = 150°$

**6** Use radian measure.

## Measuring Angles Using Radians

Another way to measure angles is in *radians*. Let's first define an angle measuring **1 radian**. We use a circle of radius $r$. In Figure 5.8, we've constructed an angle

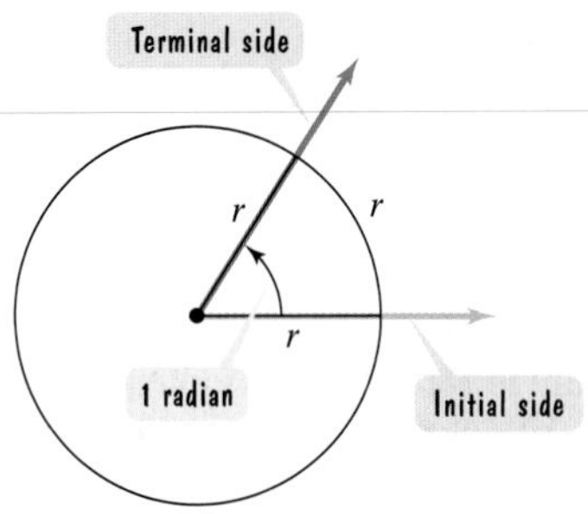


**Figure 5.8** For a 1-radian angle, the intercepted arc and the radius are equal.

whose vertex is at the center of the circle. Such an angle is called a **central angle**. Notice that the central angle intercepts an arc along the circle measuring $r$ units. The radius of the circle is also $r$ units. The measure of such an angle is 1 radian.

### Definition of a Radian

**One radian** is the measure of the central angle of a circle that intercepts an arc equal in length to the radius of the circle.

The **radian measure** of any central angle is the length of the intercepted arc divided by the circle's radius. In Figure 5.9(a), the length of the arc intercepted by angle $\beta$ is double the radius, $r$. We find the measure of angle $\beta$ in radians by dividing the length of the intercepted arc by the radius.

$$\beta = \frac{\text{length of the intercepted arc}}{\text{radius}} = \frac{2r}{r} = 2$$

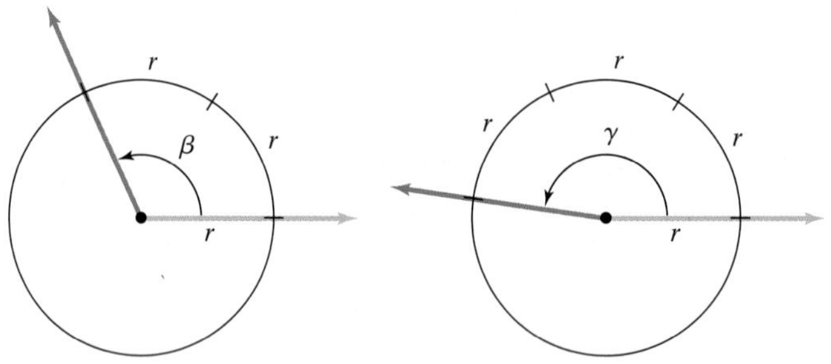


(a) $\beta = 2$ radians (b) $\gamma = 3$ radians

**Figure 5.9** Two central angles measured in radians

Thus, angle $\beta$ measures 2 radians. In Figure 5.9(b), the length of the intercepted arc is triple the radius, $r$. Let us find the measure of angle $\gamma$:

$$\gamma = \frac{\text{length of the intercepted arc}}{\text{radius}} = \frac{3r}{r} = 3$$

Thus, angle $\gamma$ measures 3 radians.

### Radian Measure

Consider an arc of length $s$ on a circle of radius $r$. The measure of the central angle $\theta$ that intercepts the arc is

$$\theta = \frac{s}{r} \text{ radians.}$$

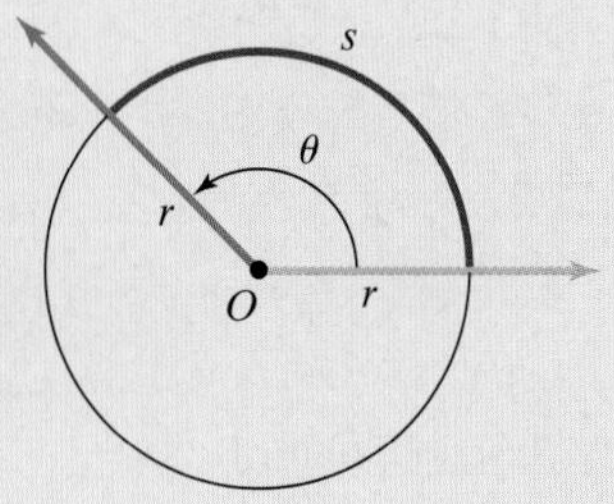

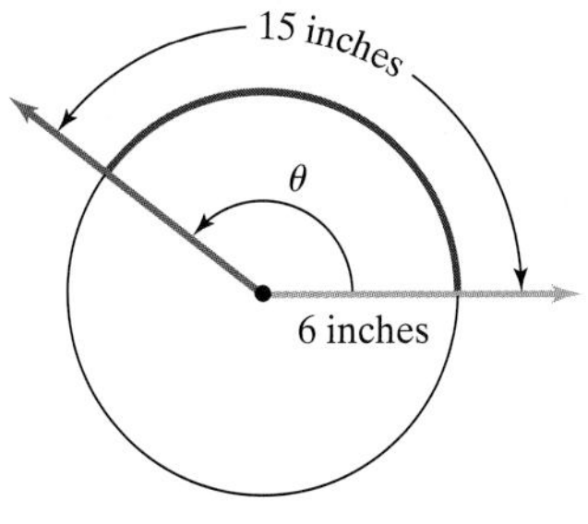


**Figure 5.10**

## EXAMPLE 4 Computing Radian Measure

A central angle $\theta$ in a circle of radius 6 inches intercepts an arc of length 15 inches. What is the radian measure of $\theta$?

**Solution** Angle $\theta$ is shown in Figure 5.10. The radian measure of a central angle is the length of the intercepted arc, $s$, divided by the circle's radius, $r$. The length of the intercepted arc is 15 inches: $s = 15$ inches. The circle's radius is 6 inches: $r = 6$ inches. Now we use the formula for radian measure to find the radian measure of $\theta$.

$$\theta = \frac{s}{r} = \frac{15 \text{ inches}}{6 \text{ inches}} = 2.5$$

Thus, the radian measure of $\theta$ is 2.5.

### Study Tip

Before applying the formula for radian measure, be sure that the same unit of length is used for the intercepted arc, $s$, and the radius, $r$.

In Example 4, notice that the units (inches) cancel when we use the formula for radian measure. We are left with a number with no units. Thus, if an angle $\theta$ has a measure of 2.5 radians, we can write $\theta = 2.5$ radians or $\theta = 2.5$. We will often include the word *radians* simply for emphasis. There should be no confusion as to whether radian or degree measure is being used. Why is this so? If $\theta$ has degree measure 2.5°, we must include the degree symbol and write $\theta = 2.5°$, and *not* $\theta = 2.5$.

**Check Point 4** A central angle $\theta$ in a circle of radius 12 feet intercepts an arc of length 42 feet. What is the radian measure of $\theta$?

**7** Convert between degrees and radians.

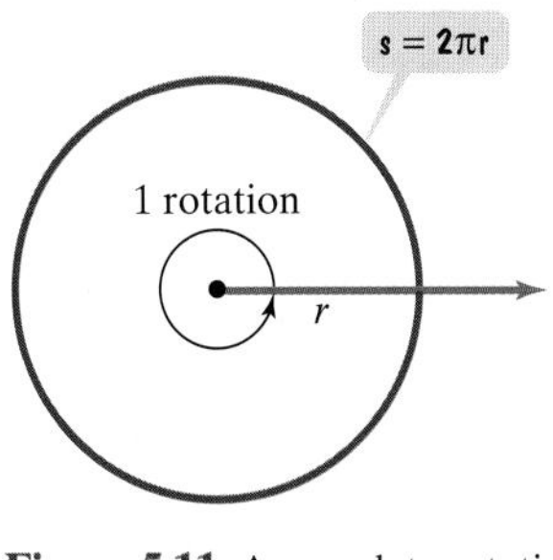


**Figure 5.11** A complete rotation

## Relationship between Degrees and Radians

How can we obtain a relationship between degrees and radians? We compare the number of degrees and the number of radians in one complete rotation, shown in Figure 5.11. We know that 360° is the amount of rotation of a ray back onto itself. The length of the intercepted arc is equal to the circumference of the circle. Thus, the radian measure of this central angle is the circumference of the circle divided by the circle's radius, $r$. The circumference of a circle of radius $r$ is $2\pi r$. We use the formula for radian measure to find the radian measure of the 360° angle.

$$\theta = \frac{s}{r} = \frac{\text{the circle's circumference}}{r} = \frac{2\pi r}{r} = 2\pi$$

Because one complete rotation measures 360° and $2\pi$ radians,

$$360° = 2\pi \text{ radians.}$$

Dividing both sides by 2, we have

$$180° = \pi \text{ radians.}$$

Dividing this last equation by 180° or $\pi$ gives the following conversion rules.

**Study Tip**

The unit you are converting *to* appears in the *numerator* of the conversion factor.

**Conversion between Degrees and Radians**

Using the basic relationship $\pi$ radians $= 180°$,

1. To convert degrees to radians, multiply degrees by $\frac{\pi \text{ radians}}{180°}$.
2. To convert radians to degrees, multiply radians by $\frac{180°}{\pi \text{ radians}}$.

Angles that are fractions of a complete rotation are usually expressed in radian measure as fractional multiples of $\pi$, rather than as decimal approximations. For example, we write $\theta = \frac{\pi}{2}$ rather than using the decimal approximation $\theta \approx 1.57$.

## EXAMPLE 5 Converting from Degrees to Radians

Convert each angle in degrees to radians.

**a.** $30°$ **b.** $90°$ **c.** $-135°$

**Solution** To convert degrees to radians, multiply by $\frac{\pi \text{ radians}}{180°}$. Observe how the degree units cancel.

**a.** $30° = 30° \cdot \frac{\pi \text{ radians}}{180°} = \frac{30\pi}{180} \text{ radians} = \frac{\pi}{6} \text{ radians}$

**b.** $90° = 90° \cdot \frac{\pi \text{ radians}}{180°} = \frac{90\pi}{180} \text{ radians} = \frac{\pi}{2} \text{ radians}$

**c.** $-135° = -135° \cdot \frac{\pi \text{ radians}}{180°} = -\frac{135\pi}{180} \text{ radians} = -\frac{3\pi}{4} \text{ radians}$

Divide the numerator and denominator by 45.

**Check Point 5** Convert each angle in degrees to radians.

**a.** $60°$ **b.** $270°$ **c.** $-300°$

## EXAMPLE 6 Converting from Radians to Degrees

Convert each angle in radians to degrees.

**a.** $\frac{\pi}{3}$ radians **b.** $-\frac{5\pi}{3}$ radians **c.** 1 radian

**Solution** To convert radians to degrees, multiply by $\frac{180°}{\pi \text{ radians}}$. Observe how the radian units cancel.

**Study Tip**

In Example 6(c), we see that 1 radian is approximately 57°. Keep in mind that a radian is much larger than a degree.

**a.** $\frac{\pi}{3}$ radians $= \frac{\pi \text{ radians}}{3} \cdot \frac{180°}{\pi \text{ radians}} = \frac{180°}{3} = 60°$

**b.** $-\frac{5\pi}{3}$ radians $= -\frac{5\pi \text{ radians}}{3} \cdot \frac{180°}{\pi \text{ radians}} = -\frac{5 \cdot 180°}{3} = -300°$

**c.** 1 radian $= 1 \text{ radian} \cdot \frac{180°}{\pi \text{ radians}} = \frac{180°}{\pi} \approx 57.3°$

**Check Point 6** Convert each angle in radians to degrees.

**a.** $\frac{\pi}{4}$ radians **b.** $-\frac{4\pi}{3}$ radians **c.** 6 radians

Figure 5.12 illustrates the degree and radian measures of angles that you will commonly see in trigonometry. Each angle is in standard position, so that the initial side lies along the positive $x$-axis. We will be using both degree and radian measure for these angles.

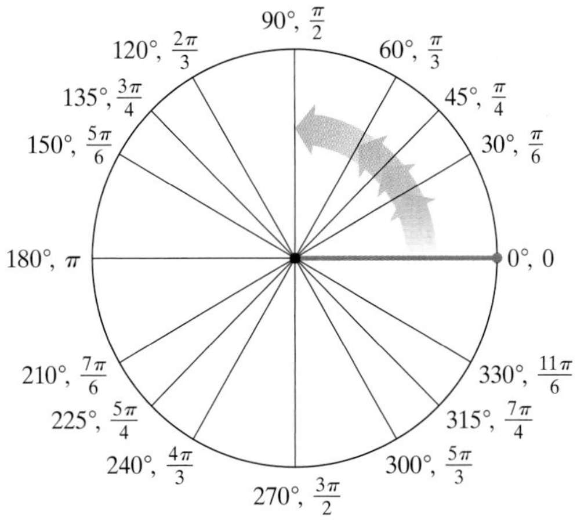


**Figure 5.12** Degree and radian measures of selected angles

**8** Find the length of a circular arc.

## The Length of a Circular Arc

We can use the radian measure formula, $\theta = \frac{s}{r}$, to find the length of the arc of a circle. How do we do this? Remember that $s$ represents the length of the arc intercepted by the central angle $\theta$. Thus, by solving the formula for $s$, we have an equation for arc length.

**The Length of a Circular Arc**

Let $r$ be the radius of a circle and $\theta$ the nonnegative radian measure of a central angle of the circle. The length of the arc intercepted by the central angle is

$$s = r\theta.$$

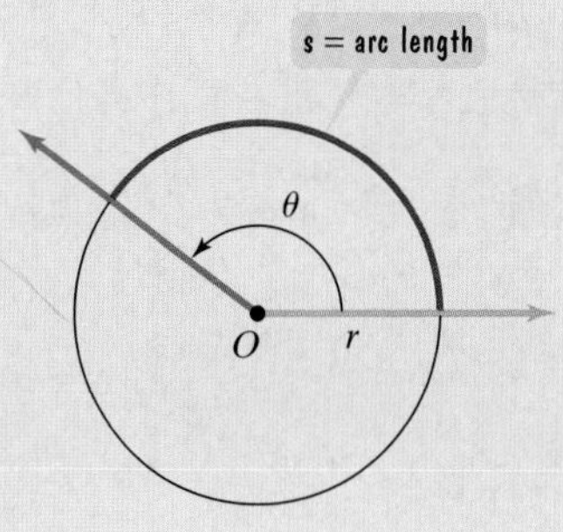

## EXAMPLE 7 Finding the Length of a Circular Arc

A circle has a radius of 10 inches. Find the length of the arc intercepted by a central angle of 120°.

**Study Tip**

The unit used to describe the length of a circular arc is the same unit that is given in the circle's radius.

**Solution** The formula $s = r\theta$ can be used only when $\theta$ is expressed in radians. Thus, we begin by converting 120° to radians. Multiply by $\frac{\pi \text{ radians}}{180°}$.

$$120° = 120° \cdot \frac{\pi \text{ radians}}{180°} = \frac{120\pi}{180} \text{ radians} = \frac{2\pi}{3} \text{ radians}$$

Now we can use the formula $s = r\theta$ to find the length of the arc. The circle's radius is 10 inches: $r = 10$ inches. The measure of the central angle, in radians, is $\frac{2\pi}{3}$: $\theta = \frac{2\pi}{3}$. The length of the arc intercepted by this central angle is

$$s = r\theta = (10 \text{ inches})\left(\frac{2\pi}{3}\right) = \frac{20\pi}{3} \text{ inches} \approx 20.94 \text{ inches.}$$

**Check Point 7** A circle has a radius of 6 inches. Find the length of the arc intercepted by a central angle of 45°. Express arc length in terms of $\pi$. Then round your answer to two decimal places.

**9** Use linear and angular speed to describe motion on a circular path.

## Linear and Angular Speed

A carousel contains four circular rows of animals. As the carousel revolves, the animals in the outer row travel a greater distance per unit of time than those in the inner rows. These animals have a greater *linear speed* than those in the inner rows. By contrast, all animals, regardless of the row, complete the same number of revolutions per unit of time. All animals in the four circular rows travel at the same *angular speed.*

Using $v$ for linear speed and $\omega$ (omega) for angular speed, we define these two kinds of speeds along a circular path as follows.

### Definitions of Linear and Angular Speed

If a point is in motion on a circle of radius $r$ through an angle of $\theta$ radians in time $t$, then its **linear speed** is

$$v = \frac{s}{t},$$

where $s$ is the arc length given by $s = r\theta$, and its **angular speed** is

$$\omega = \frac{\theta}{t}.$$

The hard drive in a computer rotates at 3600 revolutions per minute. This angular speed, expressed in revolutions per minute, can also be expressed in revolutions per second, radians per minute, and radians per second. Using $2\pi$

radians = 1 revolution, we express the angular speed of a hard drive in radians per minute as follows:

$$3600 \text{ revolutions per minute}$$

$$= \frac{3600 \text{ ~~revolutions~~}}{1 \text{ minute}} \cdot \frac{2\pi \text{ radians}}{1 \text{ ~~revolution~~}} = \frac{7200\pi \text{ radians}}{1 \text{ minute}}$$

$$= 7200\pi \text{ radians per minute.}$$

We can establish a relationship between the two kinds of speed by dividing both sides of the arc length formula, $s = r\theta$, by $t$:

$$\frac{s}{t} = \frac{r\theta}{t} = r\frac{\theta}{t}.$$

This expression defines linear speed. (for $\frac{s}{t}$)

This expression defines angular speed. (for $\frac{\theta}{t}$)

Thus, linear speed is the product of the radius and the angular speed.

**Linear Speed in Terms of Angular Speed**

The linear speed, $v$, of a point a distance $r$ from the center of rotation is given by

$$v = r\omega$$

where $\omega$ is the angular speed in radians per unit of time.

## EXAMPLE 8 Finding Linear Speed

A wind machine used to generate electricity has blades that are 10 feet in length (see Figure 5.13). The propeller is rotating at four revolutions per second. Find the linear speed, in feet per second, of the tips of the blades.

**Figure 5.13**

**Solution** We are given $\omega$, the angular speed.

$$\omega = 4 \text{ revolutions per second}$$

We use the formula $v = r\omega$ to find $v$, the linear speed. Before applying the formula, we must express $\omega$ in radians per second.

$$\omega = \frac{4 \cancel{\text{revolutions}}}{1 \text{ second}} \cdot \frac{2\pi \text{ radians}}{1 \cancel{\text{revolution}}} = \frac{8\pi \text{ radians}}{1 \text{ second}} \quad \text{or} \quad \frac{8\pi}{1 \text{ second}}$$

The angular speed of the propeller is $8\pi$ radians per second. The linear speed is

$$v = r\omega = 10 \text{ feet} \cdot \frac{8\pi}{1 \text{ second}} = \frac{80\pi \text{ feet}}{\text{second}}.$$

The linear speed of the tips of the blades is $80\pi$ feet per second, which is approximately 251 feet per second.

**Check Point 8** A 45-rpm record has an angular speed of 45 revolutions per minute. Find the linear speed, in inches per minute, at the point where the needle is 1.5 inches from the record's center.

## EXERCISE SET 5.1

### Practice Exercises

*In Exercises 1–6, each angle is in standard position. Determine the quadrant in which the angle lies.*

**1.** 145° **2.** 285°

**3.** −100° **4.** −110°

**5.** 362° **6.** 364°

*In Exercises 7–10, classify the angle as acute, right, straight, or obtuse.*

**7.**

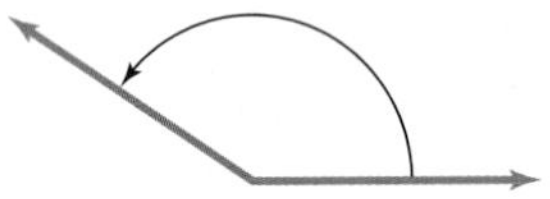

**8.**

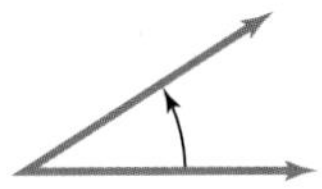

**9.**

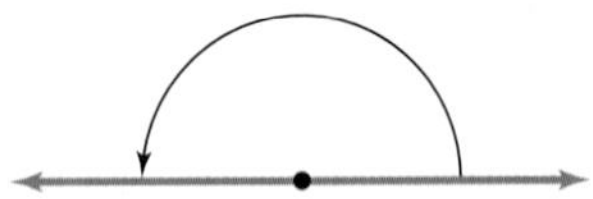

**10.**

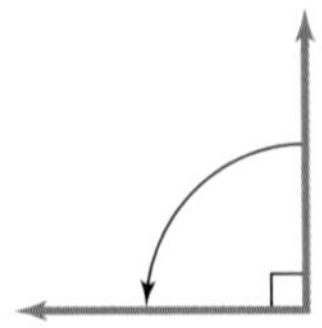

*In Exercises 11–18, draw each angle in standard position.*

**11.** 135° **12.** 120°

**13.** −150° **14.** −240°

**15.** 420° **16.** 450°

**17.** −90° **18.** −270°

*In Exercises 19–24, find a positive angle less than 360° that is coterminal with the given angle.*

**19.** 395° **20.** 415°

**21.** −150° **22.** −160°

**23.** −45° **24.** −40°

*In Exercises 25–30, if possible, find the complement and the supplement of the given angle.*

**25.** 52° **26.** 85°

**27.** 37.4° **28.** 47.6°

**29.** 111° **30.** 95°

*In Exercises 31–36, find the radian measure of the central angle of a circle of radius r that intercepts an arc of length s.*

| Radius, *r* | Arc length, *s* |
|---|---|
| **31.** 10 inches | 40 inches |
| **32.** 5 feet | 30 feet |
| **33.** 6 yards | 8 yards |
| **34.** 8 yards | 18 yards |
| **35.** 1 meter | 400 centimeters |
| **36.** 1 meter | 600 centimeters |

*In Exercises 37–44, convert each angle in degrees to radians. Express your answer as a multiple of $\pi$.*

**37.** $45°$ **38.** $18°$

**39.** $135°$ **40.** $150°$

**41.** $300°$ **42.** $330°$

**43.** $-225°$ **44.** $-270°$

*In Exercises 45–52, convert each angle in radians to degrees.*

**45.** $\frac{\pi}{2}$ **46.** $\frac{\pi}{9}$

**47.** $\frac{2\pi}{3}$ **48.** $\frac{3\pi}{4}$

**49.** $\frac{7\pi}{6}$ **50.** $\frac{11\pi}{6}$

**51.** $-3\pi$ **52.** $-4\pi$

*In Exercises 53–58, convert each angle in degrees to radians. Round to two decimal places.*

**53.** $18°$ **54.** $76°$

**55.** $-40°$ **56.** $-50°$

**57.** $200°$ **58.** $250°$

*In Exercises 59–64, convert each angle in radians to degrees. Round to two decimal places.*

**59.** 2 radians **60.** 3 radians

**61.** $\frac{\pi}{13}$ radians **62.** $\frac{\pi}{17}$ radians

**63.** $-4.8$ radians **64.** $-5.2$ radians

*In Exercises 65–68, find the length of the arc on a circle of radius r intercepted by a central angle $\theta$. Express arc length in terms of $\pi$. Then round your answer to two decimal places.*

| | **Radius, $r$** | **Central angle, $\theta$** |
|---|---|---|
| **65.** | 12 inches | $\theta = 45°$ |
| **66.** | 16 inches | $\theta = 60°$ |
| **67.** | 8 feet | $\theta = 225°$ |
| **68.** | 9 yards | $\theta = 315°$ |

*In Exercises 69–70, express each angular speed in radians per second.*

**69.** 6 revolutions per second

**70.** 20 revolutions per second

## Application Exercises

**71.** The minute hand of a clock moves from 12 to 2 o'clock, or $\frac{1}{6}$ of a complete revolution. Through how many degrees does it move? Through how many radians does it move?

**72.** The minute hand of a clock moves from 12 to 4 o'clock, or $\frac{1}{3}$ of a complete revolution. Through how many degrees does it move? Through how many radians does it move?

**73.** The minute hand of a clock is 8 inches long and moves from 12 to 2 o'clock. How far does the tip of the minute hand move? Express your answer in terms of $\pi$ and then round to two decimal places.

**74.** The minute hand of a clock is 6 inches long and moves from 12 to 4 o'clock. How far does the tip of the minute hand move? Express your answer in terms of $\pi$ and then round to two decimal places.

**75.** The figure shows a highway sign that warns of a railway crossing. The lines that form the cross pass through the circle's center and intersect at right angles. If the radius of the circle is 24 inches, find the length of each of the four arcs formed by the cross. Express your answer in terms of $\pi$ and then round to two decimal places.

**76.** The radius of a wheel is 80 centimeters. If the wheel rotates through an angle of $60°$, how many centimeters does it move? Express your answer in terms of $\pi$ and then round to two decimal places.

*How do we measure the distance between two points A and B on Earth? We measure along a circle with a center, C, at the center of Earth. The radius of the circle is equal to the distance from C to the surface. Use the fact that Earth is a sphere of radius equal to approximately 4000 miles to solve Exercises 77–80.*

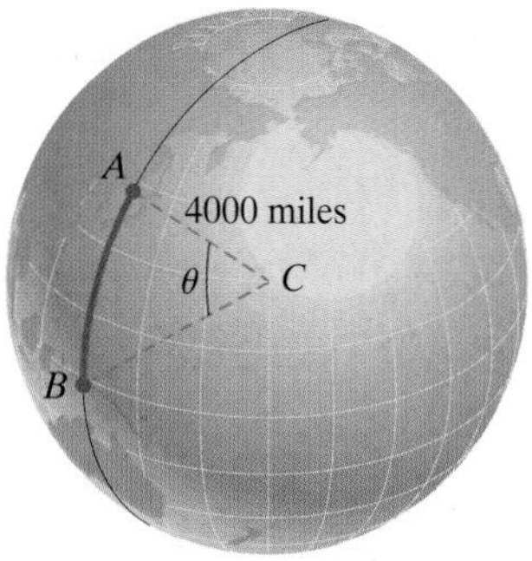

**77.** If two points $A$ and $B$ are 8000 miles apart, express angle $\theta$ in radians and in degrees.

**78.** If two points $A$ and $B$ are 10,000 miles apart, express angle $\theta$ in radians and in degrees.

**79.** If $\theta = 30°$, find the distance between $A$ and $B$ to the nearest mile.

**80.** If $\theta = 10°$, find the distance between $A$ and $B$ to the nearest mile.

**81.** The angular velocity of a point on the Earth is $\frac{\pi}{12}$ radians per hour. The Equator lies on a circle of radius approximately 4000 miles. Find the linear velocity, in miles per hour, of a point on the Equator.

**82.** A Ferris wheel has a radius of 25 feet. The wheel is rotating at three revolutions per minute. Find the linear speed, in feet per minute, of this Ferris wheel.

**83.** A water wheel has a radius of 12 feet. The wheel is rotating at 20 revolutions per minute. Find the linear speed, in feet per minute, of the water.

**84.** On a carousel, the outer row of animals is 20 feet from the center. The inner row of animals is 10 feet from the center. The carousel is rotating at 2.5 revolutions per minute. What is the difference, in feet per minute, in the linear speeds of the animals in the outer and inner rows? Round to the nearest foot per second.

## Writing in Mathematics

**85.** What is an angle?

**86.** What determines the size of an angle?

**87.** Describe an angle in standard position.

**88.** Explain the difference between positive and negative angles. What are coterminal angles?

**89.** Explain what is meant by one radian.

**90.** Explain how to find the radian measure of a central angle.

**91.** Describe how to convert an angle in degrees to radians.

**92.** Explain how to convert an angle in radians to degrees.

**93.** Explain how to find the length of a circular arc.

**94.** If a carousel is rotating at 2.5 revolutions per minute, explain how to find the linear speed of a child seated on one of the animals.

**95.** The angular velocity of a point on the Earth is $\frac{\pi}{12}$ radians per hour. Describe what happens every 24 hours.

**96.** Have you ever noticed that we use the vocabulary of angles in everyday speech? Here is an example:

> My opinion about art museums took a 180° turn after visiting the San Francisco Museum of Modern Art.

Explain what this means. Then give another example of the vocabulary of angles in everyday use.

## Technology Exercises

*In Exercises 97–100, use the keys on your calculator or graphing utility for converting an angle in degrees, minutes, and seconds (D°M′S″) into decimal form, and vice versa.*

*In Exercises 97–98, convert each angle to a decimal in degrees. Round your answer to two decimal places.*

**97.** $30°15'10''$

**98.** $65°45'20''$

*In Exercises 99–100, convert each angle to D°M′S″ form. Round your answer to the nearest second.*

**99.** 30.42°

**100.** 50.42°

## Critical Thinking Exercises

**101.** If $\theta = \frac{3}{2}$, is this angle larger or smaller than a right angle?

**102.** A railroad curve is laid out on a circle. What radius should be used if the track is to change direction by 20° in a distance of 100 miles? Round your answer to the nearest mile.

**103.** Assuming the Earth to be a sphere of radius 4000 miles, how many miles north of the Equator is Miami, Florida, if it is 26° north from the Equator? Round your answer to the nearest mile.

# SECTION 5.2 Trigonometric Functions: The Unit Circle

## Objectives

1. Use a unit circle to define trigonometric functions of real numbers.
2. Use a unit circle to find values of the trigonometric functions.
3. Recognize the domain and range of sine and cosine functions.
4. Find exact values of the trigonometric functions at $\frac{\pi}{4}$.
5. Use even and odd trigonometric functions.
6. Recognize and use fundamental identities.
7. Use periodic properties.
8. Evaluate trigonometric functions with a calculator.

There is something comforting in the repetition of some of nature's patterns. The ocean level at a beach varies between high and low tide approximately every 12 hours. The number of hours of daylight oscillates from a maximum on the summer solstice, June 21; it decreases slowly until the minimum daylight occurs on the winter solstice, December 21, and then increases to the same maximum the following June 21. Some believe that cycles, called biorhythms, represent physical, emotional, and intellectual aspects of our lives. In this chapter, we study six functions, the six *trigonometric functions*, that are used to model phenomena that occur again and again.

## Calculus and the Unit Circle

The word *trigonometry* means measurement of triangles. Trigonometric functions, with domains consisting of sets of angles, were first defined using right triangles. By contrast, problems in calculus are solved using functions whose domains are sets of real numbers. Therefore, we introduce the trigonometric functions using unit circles and radians, rather than right triangles and degrees.

A **unit circle** is a circle of radius 1, with center at the origin of a rectangular coordinate system. The equation of this unit circle is $x^2 + y^2 = 1$. Figure 5.14 shows a unit circle in which the central angle measures $t$ radians. We can use the formula for the length of a circular arc, $s = r\theta$, to find the length of the intercepted arc.

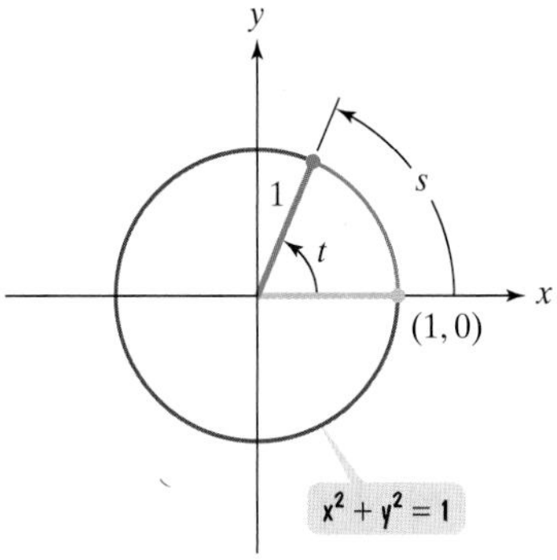


**Figure 5.14** A unit circle with a central angle measuring $t$ radians

$$s = r\theta = 1t = t$$

The radius of a unit circle is 1.

The radian measure of the central angle is t.

Thus, the length of the intercepted arc is $t$. This is also the radian measure of the central angle. **In a unit circle, the radian measure of the angle is equal to the measure of the intercepted arc.** Both are given by the same *real number t*.

In Figure 5.15, the radian measure of the angle and the length of the intercepted arc are both shown by $t$. Let $P = (x, y)$ denote the point on the unit circle that has arc length $t$ from $(1, 0)$. Figure 5.15(a) shows that if $t$ is positive, point $P$ is reached by moving counterclockwise along the unit circle from $(1,0)$. Figure 5.15(b) shows that if $t$ is negative, point $P$ is reached by moving clockwise along the unit circle from $(1, 0)$. For each real number $t$, there corresponds a point $P(x, y)$ on the unit circle.

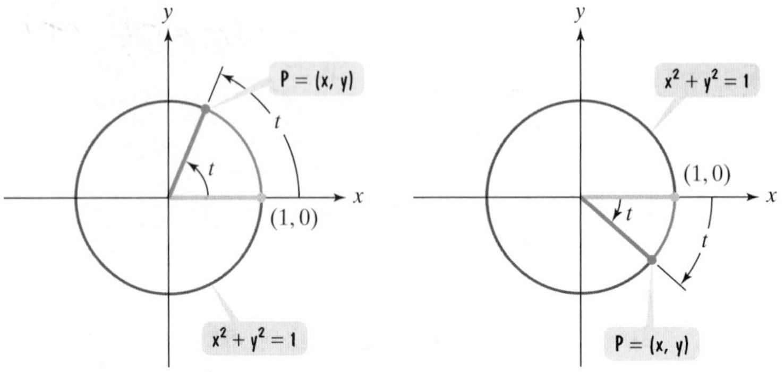


**Figure 5.15** (a) $t$ is positive. (b) $t$ is negative.

**1** Use a unit circle to define trigonometric functions of real numbers.

## The Six Trigonometric Functions

We begin the study of trigonometry by defining the six trigonometric functions. The inputs of these functions are real numbers, represented by $t$ in Figure 5.15. The outputs involve point $P = (x, y)$ on the unit circle that corresponds to $t$ and the coordinates of this point.

The trigonometric functions have names that are words, rather than single letters such as $f$, $g$, and $h$. For example, the **sine of $t$** is the $y$-coordinate of point $P$ on the unit circle:

$$\sin t = y.$$

Input is the real number $t$.

Output is the $y$-coordinate of a point on the unit circle.

The value of $y$ depends on the real number $t$ and thus is a function of $t$. The expression $\sin t$ really means $\sin(t)$, where sine is the name of the function and $t$, a real number, is an input.

For example, a point $P = (x, y)$ on the unit circle corresponding to a real number $t$ is shown in Figure 5.16, for $\pi < t < \frac{3\pi}{2}$. We see that the coordinates of $P = (x, y)$ are $x = -\frac{3}{5}$ and $y = -\frac{4}{5}$. Because the sine function is the $y$-coordinate of $P$, the value of this trigonometric function at the real number $t$ is

$$\sin t = -\frac{4}{5}.$$

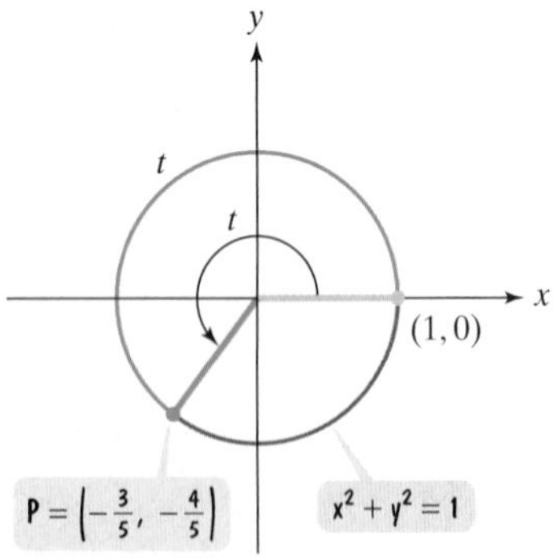


**Figure 5.16**

Here are the names of the six trigonometric functions, along with their abbreviations.

| Name | Abbreviation | Name | Abbreviation |
|---|---|---|---|
| sine | sin | cosecant | csc |
| cosine | cos | secant | sec |
| tangent | tan | cotangent | cot |

**Definitions of the Trigonometric Functions in Terms of a Unit Circle**

If $t$ is a real number and $P = (x, y)$ is a point on the unit circle that corresponds to $t$, then

$$\sin t = y \qquad \cos t = x \qquad \tan t = \frac{y}{x}, x \neq 0$$

$$\csc t = \frac{1}{y}, y \neq 0 \quad \sec t = \frac{1}{x}, x \neq 0 \quad \cot t = \frac{x}{y}, y \neq 0.$$

Because this definition expresses function values in terms of coordinates of a point on a unit circle, the trigonometric functions are sometimes called the **circular functions**. Observe that the functions in the second row in the box are the reciprocals of the corresponding functions in the first row.

**2** Use a unit circle to find values of the trigonometric functions.

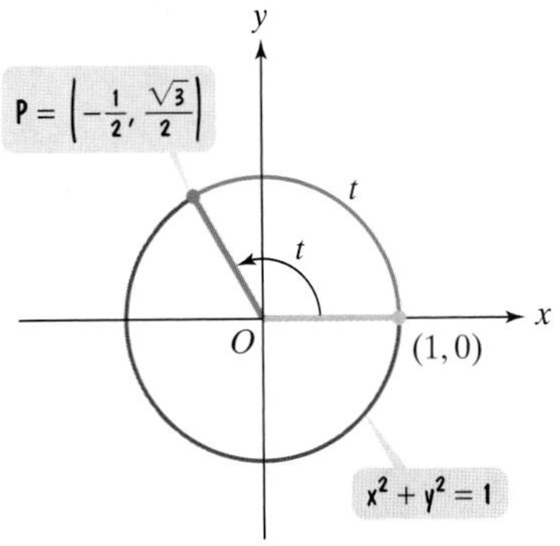


**Figure 5.17**

## EXAMPLE 1 Finding Values of the Trigonometric Functions

In Figure 5.17, $t$ is a real number and $P = \left(-\frac{1}{2}, \frac{\sqrt{3}}{2}\right)$ is a point on the unit circle that corresponds to $t$. Use the figure to find the values of the trigonometric functions at $t$.

**Solution** The point $P$ on the unit circle that corresponds to $t$ has coordinates $\left(-\frac{1}{2}, \frac{\sqrt{3}}{2}\right)$. We use $x = -\frac{1}{2}$ and $y = \frac{\sqrt{3}}{2}$ to find the values of the trigonometric functions.

$$\sin t = y = \frac{\sqrt{3}}{2} \qquad \cos t = x = -\frac{1}{2} \qquad \tan t = \frac{y}{x} = \frac{\frac{\sqrt{3}}{2}}{-\frac{1}{2}} = -\sqrt{3}$$

$$\csc t = \frac{1}{y} = \frac{1}{\frac{\sqrt{3}}{2}} = \frac{2}{\sqrt{3}} \qquad \sec t = \frac{1}{x} = \frac{1}{-\frac{1}{2}} = -2 \qquad \cot t = \frac{x}{y} = \frac{-\frac{1}{2}}{\frac{\sqrt{3}}{2}} = -\frac{1}{\sqrt{3}}$$

You can rationalize the denominator: $\frac{2}{\sqrt{3}} \cdot \frac{\sqrt{3}}{\sqrt{3}} = \frac{2\sqrt{3}}{3}$.

You can rationalize the denominator: $-\frac{1}{\sqrt{3}} \cdot \frac{\sqrt{3}}{\sqrt{3}} = -\frac{\sqrt{3}}{3}$.

**Check Point 1** Use the figure on the right to find the values of the trigonometric functions at $t$.

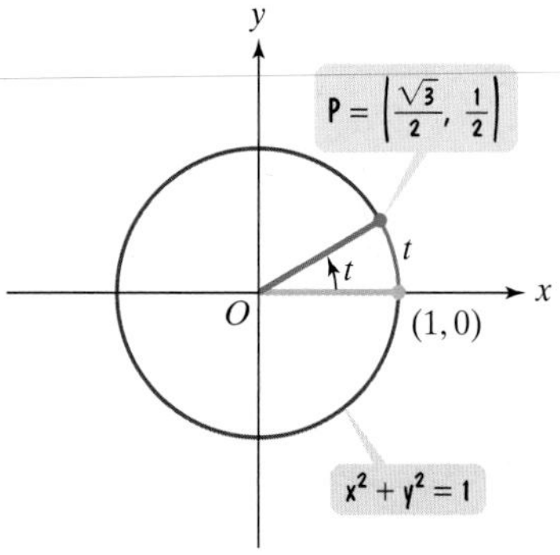


## EXAMPLE 2 Finding Values of the Trigonometric Functions

Use Figure 5.18 to find the values of the trigonometric functions at $t = \frac{\pi}{2}$.

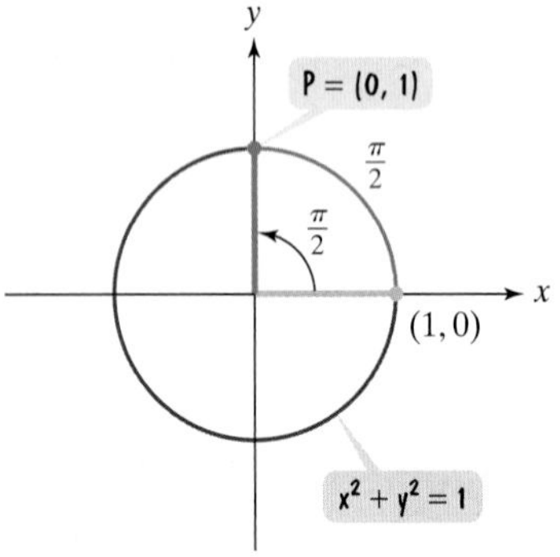


**Figure 5.18**

**Solution** The point $P$ on the unit circle that corresponds to $t = \frac{\pi}{2}$ has coordinates $(0, 1)$. We use $x = 0$ and $y = 1$ to find the values of the trigonometric functions.

$$\sin\frac{\pi}{2} = y = 1 \qquad \cos\frac{\pi}{2} = x = 0$$

$$\csc\frac{\pi}{2} = \frac{1}{y} = \frac{1}{1} = 1 \qquad \cot\frac{\pi}{2} = \frac{x}{y} = \frac{0}{1} = 0$$

By definition, $\tan t = \frac{y}{x}$ and $\sec t = \frac{1}{x}$. Because $x = 0$, $\tan\frac{\pi}{2}$ and $\sec\frac{\pi}{2}$ are undefined.

**Check Point 2** Use the figure on the right to find the values of the trigonometric functions at $t = \pi$.

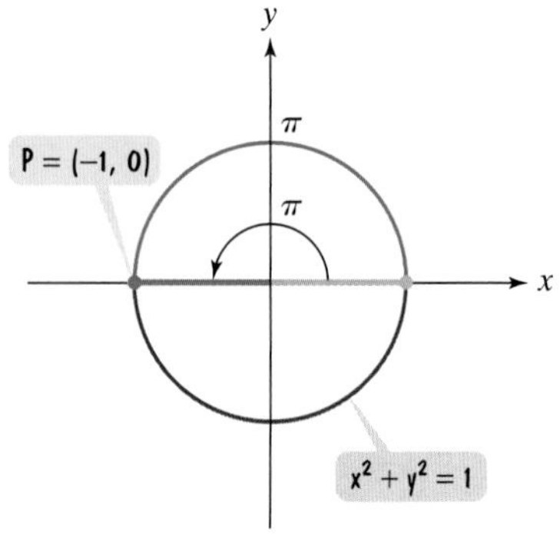


**3** Recognize the domain and range of sine and cosine functions.

## Domain and Range of Sine and Cosine Functions

The domain and range of each trigonometric function can be found from the unit circle definition. At this point, let's look only at the sine and cosine functions,

$$\sin t = y \quad \text{and} \quad \cos t = x.$$

Because $t$ can be any real number, the domain of the sine function and the cosine function is the set of all real numbers. Because the radius of the unit circle is 1, we have

$$-1 \le x \le 1 \quad \text{and} \quad -1 \le y \le 1.$$

Therefore, with $x = \cos t$ and $y = \sin t$, we obtain

$$-1 \le \cos t \le 1 \quad \text{and} \quad -1 \le \sin t \le 1.$$

The range of the cosine and sine functions is $[-1, 1]$.

**The Domain and Range of the Sine and Cosine Functions**

The domain of the sine function and the cosine function is the set of all real numbers. The range of these functions is the set of all real numbers from $-1$ to 1, inclusive.

**4** Find exact values of the trigonometric functions at $\frac{\pi}{4}$.

## Exact Values of Trigonometric Functions at $t = \frac{\pi}{4}$

Trigonometric functions at $t = \frac{\pi}{4}$ occur frequently. How do we use the unit circle to find values of the trigonometric functions at $t = \frac{\pi}{4}$? Look at Figure 5.19. We must find the coordinates of point $P = (a, b)$ on the unit circle that correspond to $t = \frac{\pi}{4}$. Can you see that $P$ lies on the line $y = x$? Thus, point $P$ has equal $x$- and $y$-coordinates: $a = b$. We find these coordinates as follows.

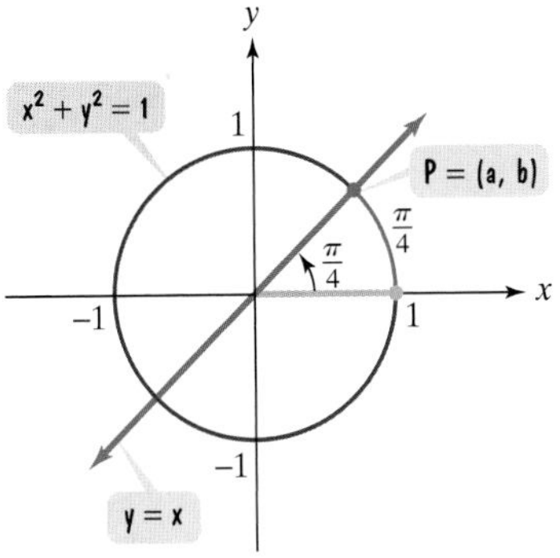

**Figure 5.19**

| | |
|---|---|
| $x^2 + y^2 = 1$ | This is the equation of the unit circle. |
| $a^2 + b^2 = 1$ | Point $P = (a, b)$ lies on the unit circle. Thus, its coordinates satisfy the circle's equation. |
| $a^2 + a^2 = 1$ | Because $a = b$, substitute $a^2$ for $b^2$ in the equation. |
| $2a^2 = 1$ | Add like terms. |
| $a^2 = \frac{1}{2}$ | Divide both sides of the equation by 2. |
| $a = \sqrt{\frac{1}{2}}$ | Because $a > 0$, take the positive square root of both sides. |

We see that $a = \frac{1}{\sqrt{2}}$. Because $a = b$, we also have $b = \frac{1}{\sqrt{2}}$. Thus, if $t = \frac{\pi}{4}$, point $P = \left(\frac{1}{\sqrt{2}}, \frac{1}{\sqrt{2}}\right)$ is the point on the unit circle that corresponds to $t$. We use these coordinates to find the values of the trigonometric functions at $t = \frac{\pi}{4}$.

## EXAMPLE 3 Finding Values of the Trigonometric Functions at $t = \frac{\pi}{4}$

Find $\sin\frac{\pi}{4}$, $\cos\frac{\pi}{4}$, and $\tan\frac{\pi}{4}$.

**Solution** The point $P$ on the unit circle that corresponds to $t = \frac{\pi}{4}$ has coordinates $\left(\frac{1}{\sqrt{2}}, \frac{1}{\sqrt{2}}\right)$. We use $x = \frac{1}{\sqrt{2}}$ and $y = \frac{1}{\sqrt{2}}$ to find the values the three trigonometric functions at $\frac{\pi}{4}$.

$$\sin\frac{\pi}{4} = y = \frac{1}{\sqrt{2}} \qquad \cos\frac{\pi}{4} = x = \frac{1}{\sqrt{2}} \qquad \tan\frac{\pi}{4} = \frac{y}{x} = \frac{\frac{1}{\sqrt{2}}}{\frac{1}{\sqrt{2}}} = 1$$

**Check Point 3** Find $\csc\frac{\pi}{4}$, $\sec\frac{\pi}{4}$, and $\cot\frac{\pi}{4}$.

When you worked Check Point 3, did you use the $x$- and $y$-coordinates of $P = \left(\frac{1}{\sqrt{2}}, \frac{1}{\sqrt{2}}\right)$, or did you use reciprocals to find the values?

$$\csc\frac{\pi}{4} = \sqrt{2} \qquad \sec\frac{\pi}{4} = \sqrt{2} \qquad \cot\frac{\pi}{4} = 1$$

Take the reciprocal of $\sin\frac{\pi}{4} = \frac{1}{\sqrt{2}}$.

Take the reciprocal of $\cos\frac{\pi}{4} = \frac{1}{\sqrt{2}}$.

Take the reciprocal of $\tan\frac{\pi}{4} = 1$.

We found that $\sin\frac{\pi}{4} = \frac{1}{\sqrt{2}}$ and $\cos\frac{\pi}{4} = \frac{1}{\sqrt{2}}$. This value is often expressed by rationalizing the denominator:

$$\frac{1}{\sqrt{2}} = \frac{1}{\sqrt{2}} \cdot \frac{\sqrt{2}}{\sqrt{2}} = \frac{\sqrt{2}}{2}.$$

We are multiplying by 1 and not changing the value of $\frac{1}{\sqrt{2}}$.

Thus, $\sin\frac{\pi}{4} = \frac{\sqrt{2}}{2}$ and $\cos\frac{\pi}{4} = \frac{\sqrt{2}}{2}$.

Because you will often see the trigonometric functions at $\frac{\pi}{4}$, it is a good idea to memorize the values shown in the following box. In the next section, you will learn to use a right triangle to obtain these values.

**Trigonometric Functions at $\frac{\pi}{4}$**

$$\sin\frac{\pi}{4} = \frac{\sqrt{2}}{2} \qquad \cos\frac{\pi}{4} = \frac{\sqrt{2}}{2} \qquad \tan\frac{\pi}{4} = 1$$

$$\csc\frac{\pi}{4} = \sqrt{2} \qquad \sec\frac{\pi}{4} = \sqrt{2} \qquad \cot\frac{\pi}{4} = 1$$

**5** Use even and odd trigonometric functions.

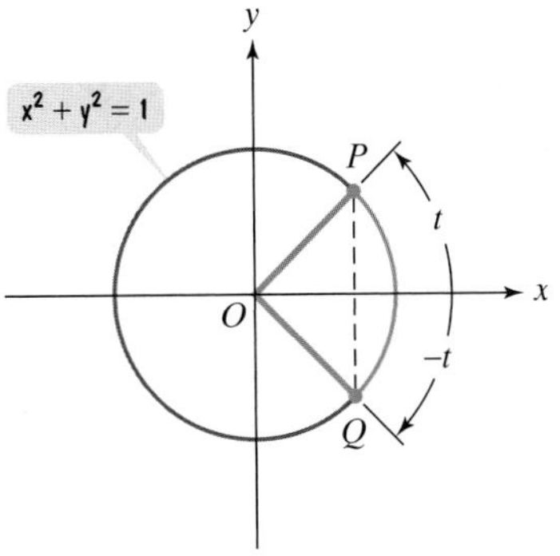


**Figure 5.20**

## Even and Odd Trigonometric Functions

In Chapter 2, we saw that a function is even if $f(-t) = f(t)$ and odd if $f(-t) = -f(t)$. We can use Figure 5.20 to show that the cosine is an even function and the sine is an odd function. By definition, the coordinates of the points $P$ and $Q$ in Figure 5.20 are as follows:

$$P\colon\ (\cos t, \sin t)$$
$$Q\colon\ (\cos(-t), \sin(-t))$$

In Figure 5.20, the $x$-coordinates of $P$ and $Q$ are the same. Thus,

$$\cos(-t) = \cos t.$$

This shows that cosine is an even function. By contrast, the $y$-coordinates of $P$ and $Q$ are negatives of each other. Thus,

$$\sin(-t) = -\sin t.$$

This shows that the sine is an odd function.

This argument is valid regardless of the length of $t$. Thus, the arc may terminate in any of the four quadrants. Using the unit circle definition of the trigonometric functions, we obtain the following results.

**Even and Odd Trigonometric Functions**

The cosine and secant functions are *even*.

$$\cos(-t) = \cos t \qquad \sec(-t) = \sec t$$

The sine, cosecant, tangent, and cotangent functions are *odd*.

$$\sin(-t) = -\sin t \qquad \csc(-t) = -\csc t$$
$$\tan(-t) = -\tan t \qquad \cot(-t) = -\cot t$$

**EXAMPLE 4 Using Even and Odd Functions to Find Values of the Trigonometric Functions**

**Table 5.1**

| $t$ | $\sin t$ | $\cos t$ | $\tan t$ |
|---|---|---|---|
| $\frac{\pi}{4}$ | $\frac{\sqrt{2}}{2}$ | $\frac{\sqrt{2}}{2}$ | 1 |
| $t$ | $\csc t$ | $\sec t$ | $\cot t$ |
| $\frac{\pi}{4}$ | $\sqrt{2}$ | $\sqrt{2}$ | 1 |

Table 5.1 shows the values of the trigonometric functions at $t = \frac{\pi}{4}$. Use these values to find:

**a.** $\cos\left(-\frac{\pi}{4}\right)$ **b.** $\tan\left(-\frac{\pi}{4}\right)$.

**Solution**

**a.** $\cos\left(-\frac{\pi}{4}\right) = \cos\frac{\pi}{4} = \frac{\sqrt{2}}{2}$ **b.** $\tan\left(-\frac{\pi}{4}\right) = -\tan\frac{\pi}{4} = -1$

**Check Point 4** Use the values in Table 5.1 to find:

**a.** $\sec\left(-\frac{\pi}{4}\right)$ **b.** $\sin\left(-\frac{\pi}{4}\right)$.

**6** Recognize and use fundamental identities.

## Fundamental Identities

Many relationships exist among the six trigonometric functions. These relationships are described using **trigonometric identities**. Trigonometric identities are equations that are true for all real numbers for which the trigonometric expressions in the equations are defined. For example, the definitions of the cosine and secant functions are given by

$$\cos t = x \quad \text{and} \quad \sec t = \frac{1}{x}, \; x \neq 0.$$

Substituting $\cos t$ for $x$ in the equation on the right, we see that

$$\sec t = \frac{1}{\cos t}, \quad \cos t \neq 0.$$

This identity is one of six **reciprocal identities**.

### Reciprocal Identities

$$\sin t = \frac{1}{\csc t} \qquad \cos t = \frac{1}{\sec t} \qquad \tan t = \frac{1}{\cot t}$$

$$\csc t = \frac{1}{\sin t} \qquad \sec t = \frac{1}{\cos t} \qquad \cot t = \frac{1}{\tan t}$$

Two other relationships that follow from the definitions of the trigonometric functions are called the **quotient identities**.

### Quotient Identities

$$\tan t = \frac{\sin t}{\cos t} \qquad \cot t = \frac{\cos t}{\sin t}$$

If $\sin t$ and $\cos t$ are known, a quotient identity and three reciprocal identities make it possible to find the value of each of the four remaining trigonometric functions.

### EXAMPLE 5 Using Quotient and Reciprocal Identities

Given $\sin t = \frac{1}{2}$ and $\cos t = \frac{\sqrt{3}}{2}$, find the value of each of the four remaining trigonometric functions.

**Solution** We can find $\tan t$ by using the quotient identity that describes $\tan t$ as the quotient of $\sin t$ and $\cos t$.

$$\tan t = \frac{\sin t}{\cos t} = \frac{\frac{1}{2}}{\frac{\sqrt{3}}{2}} = \frac{1}{2} \cdot \frac{2}{\sqrt{3}} = \frac{1}{\sqrt{3}} = \frac{1}{\sqrt{3}} \cdot \frac{\sqrt{3}}{\sqrt{3}} = \frac{\sqrt{3}}{3}$$

Rationalize the denominator.

We use the reciprocal identities to find the value of each of the remaining three functions.

$$\csc t = \frac{1}{\sin t} = \frac{1}{\frac{1}{2}} = 2$$

$$\sec t = \frac{1}{\cos t} = \frac{1}{\frac{\sqrt{3}}{2}} = \frac{2}{\sqrt{3}} = \frac{2}{\sqrt{3}} \cdot \frac{\sqrt{3}}{\sqrt{3}} = \frac{2\sqrt{3}}{3}$$

Rationalize the denominator.

$$\cot t = \frac{1}{\tan t} = \frac{1}{\frac{1}{\sqrt{3}}} = \sqrt{3}$$

**Check Point 5** Given $\sin t = \frac{2}{3}$ and $\cos t = \frac{\sqrt{5}}{3}$, find the value of each of the four remaining trigonometric functions.

Other relationships among trigonometric functions follow from the equation of the unit circle

$$x^2 + y^2 = 1.$$

Because $\cos t = x$ and $\sin t = y$, we see that

$$(\cos t)^2 + (\sin t)^2 = 1.$$

We will eliminate the parentheses in this identity by writing $\cos^2 t$ instead of $(\cos t)^2$ and $\sin^2 t$ instead of $(\sin t)^2$. With this notation, we can write the identity as

$$\cos^2 t + \sin^2 t = 1$$

or

$$\sin^2 t + \cos^2 t = 1.$$

The identity usually appears in this form.

Two additional identities can be obtained from $x^2 + y^2 = 1$ by dividing both sides by $x^2$ and $y^2$, respectively. The three identities are called the **Pythagorean identities**.

**Pythagorean Identities**

$\sin^2 t + \cos^2 t = 1 \qquad 1 + \tan^2 t = \sec^2 t \qquad 1 + \cot^2 t = \csc^2 t$

## EXAMPLE 6 Using a Pythagorean Identity

Given that $\sin t = \frac{3}{5}$ and $0 \le t < \frac{\pi}{2}$, find the value of $\cos t$ using a trigonometric identity.

**Solution** We can find the value of $\cos t$ by using the Pythagorean identity

$$\sin^2 t + \cos^2 t = 1.$$

$$\left(\frac{3}{5}\right)^2 + \cos^2 t = 1 \qquad \text{We are given that } \sin t = \frac{3}{5}.$$

$$\frac{9}{25} + \cos^2 t = 1 \qquad \text{Square } \frac{3}{5}: \left(\frac{3}{5}\right)^2 = \frac{3^2}{5^2} = \frac{9}{25}.$$

$$\cos^2 t = 1 - \frac{9}{25} \qquad \text{Subtract } \frac{9}{25} \text{ from both sides.}$$

$$\cos^2 t = \frac{16}{25} \qquad \text{Simplify: } 1 - \frac{9}{25} = \frac{25}{25} - \frac{9}{25} = \frac{16}{25}.$$

$$\cos t = \sqrt{\frac{16}{25}} = \frac{4}{5} \qquad \text{Because } 0 \le t < \frac{\pi}{2}, \cos t \text{ is positive.}$$

Thus, $\cos t = \frac{4}{5}$.

**Check Point 6** Given that $\sin t = \frac{1}{2}$ and $0 \le t < \frac{\pi}{2}$, find the value of $\cos t$ using a trigonometric identity.

**7** Use periodic properties.

## Periodic Functions

Certain patterns in nature repeat again and again. For example, the ocean level at a beach varies between low tide and high tide approximately every 12 hours. If low tide occurs at noon, then high tide will be around 6 P.M. and low tide will occur again around midnight, and so on infinitely. If $f(t)$ represents the ocean level at the beach at any time $t$, then the level is the same 12 hours later. Thus,

$$f(t + 12) = f(t).$$

The word *periodic* means that this tidal behavior repeats infinitely. The *period*, 12 hours, is the time it takes to complete one full cycle.

**Definition of a Periodic Function**

A function $f$ is **periodic** if there exists a positive number $p$ such that

$$f(t + p) = f(t)$$

for all $t$ in the domain of $f$. The smallest number $p$ for which $f$ is periodic is called the **period** of $f$.

The trigonometric functions are used to model periodic phenomena. Why? If we begin at any point $P$ on the unit circle and travel a distance of $2\pi$ units along the perimeter, we will return to the same point $P$. Because the trigonometric functions are defined in terms of the coordinates of that point $P$, we obtain the following results.

**Periodic Properties of the Sine and Cosine Functions**

$$\sin(t + 2\pi) = \sin t \qquad \text{and} \qquad \cos(t + 2\pi) = \cos t$$

The sine and cosine functions are periodic functions and have period $2\pi$.

## EXAMPLE 7 Using Periodic Properties to Find Values of the Trigonometric Functions

**Table 5.1**

| $t$ | $\sin t$ | $\cos t$ | $\tan t$ |
|---|---|---|---|
| $\frac{\pi}{4}$ | $\frac{\sqrt{2}}{2}$ | $\frac{\sqrt{2}}{2}$ | 1 |
| $t$ | $\csc t$ | $\sec t$ | $\cot t$ |
| $\frac{\pi}{4}$ | $\sqrt{2}$ | $\sqrt{2}$ | 1 |

The values of the trigonometric functions at $t = \frac{\pi}{4}$ are repeated in Table 5.1. Use a value in the table to find $\sin \frac{9\pi}{4}$.

**Solution**

$$\sin \frac{9\pi}{4} = \sin\left(2\pi + \frac{\pi}{4}\right) = \sin \frac{\pi}{4} = \frac{\sqrt{2}}{2}$$

**Check Point 7** Use a value in Table 5.1 to find $\tan \frac{9\pi}{4}$.

Like the sine and cosine functions, the secant and cosecant functions have period $2\pi$. However, this is not true for the tangent and cotangent functions. If we begin at any point $P(x, y)$ on the unit circle and travel a distance of $\pi$ units along the perimeter, we arrive at the point $(-x, -y)$. The tangent function, defined in terms of the coordinates of a point, is the same at $(x, y)$ and $(-x, -y)$.

Tangent function at (x, y) $\qquad \frac{y}{x} = \frac{-y}{-x} \qquad$ Tangent function $\pi$ radians later

We see that $\tan(t + \pi) = \tan t$. The same observations apply to the cotangent function.

**Periodic Properties of the Tangent and Cotangent Functions**

$$\tan(t + \pi) = \tan t \quad \text{and} \quad \cot(t + \pi) = \cot t$$

The tangent and cotangent functions are periodic functions and have period $\pi$.

Why do the trigonometric functions model phenomena that repeat *infinitely*? By starting at point $P$ on the unit circle and traveling a distance of $2\pi$ units, $4\pi$ units, $6\pi$ units, and so on, we return to the starting point $P$. Because the trigonometric functions are defined in terms of the coordinates of that point $P$, if we add (or subtract) multiples of $2\pi$, the trigonometric values do not change. Furthermore, the trigonometric values for the tangent and cotangent functions do not change if we add (or subtract) multiples of $\pi$.

**Repetitive Behavior of the Sine, Cosine, and Tangent Functions**

For any integer $n$ and real number $t$,

$$\sin(t + 2\pi n) = \sin t, \quad \cos(t + 2\pi n) = \cos t, \quad \text{and} \quad \tan(t + \pi n) = \tan t$$

**8** Evaluate trigonometric functions with a calculator.

## Using a Calculator to Evaluate Trigonometric Functions

We used a unit circle to find values of the trigonometric functions at $\frac{\pi}{4}$. These are exact values. We can find approximate values of the trigonometric functions using a calculator.

The first step in using a calculator to evaluate trigonometric functions is to set the calculator to the correct *mode*, degrees or radians. The domains of the trigonometric functions in the unit circle are sets of real numbers. Therefore, we use the radian mode.

Most calculators have keys marked [SIN], [COS], and [TAN]. For example, to find the value of $\sin 1.2$, set the calculator to the radian mode and enter 1.2 [SIN] on most scientific calculators and [SIN] 1.2 [ENTER] on most graphing calculators. Consult the manual for your calculator.

To evaluate the cosecant, secant, and cotangent functions, use the key for the respective reciprocal function, [SIN], [COS], or [TAN], and then use the reciprocal key. The reciprocal key is [$1/x$], on most scientific calculators and [$x^{-1}$] on most graphing calculators. For example, we can evaluate $\sec\frac{\pi}{12}$ using the following reciprocal relationship:

$$\sec\frac{\pi}{12} = \frac{1}{\cos\frac{\pi}{12}}.$$

Using the radian mode, enter one of the following keystroke sequences:

**Most Scientific Calculators**

[π] [÷] 12 [=] [COS] [1/x]

**Most Graphing Calculators**

[(] [COS] [(] [π] [÷] 12 [)] [)] [$x^{-1}$] [ENTER]

Rounding the display to four decimal places, we obtain $\sec \frac{\pi}{12} = 1.0353$.

## EXAMPLE 8 Evaluating Trigonometric Functions with a Calculator

Use a calculator to find the value to four decimal places of:

**a.** $\cos \frac{\pi}{4}$ **b.** $\cot 1.2$.

### Solution

**Scientific Calculator Solution**

| Function | Mode | Keystrokes | Display, rounded to four decimal places |
|---|---|---|---|
| **a.** $\cos \frac{\pi}{4}$ | Radian | [π] [÷] 4 [=] [COS] | 0.7071 |
| **b.** $\cot 1.2$ | Radian | 1.2 [TAN] [1/x] | 0.3888 |

**Graphing Calculator Solution**

| Function | Mode | Keystrokes | Display, rounded to four decimal places |
|---|---|---|---|
| **a.** $\cos \frac{\pi}{4}$ | Radian | [COS] [(] [π] [÷] 4 [)] [ENTER] | 0.7071 |
| **b.** $\cot 1.2$ | Radian | [(] [TAN] 1.2 [)] [$x^{-1}$] [ENTER] | 0.3888 |

**Check Point 8**

Use a calculator to find the value to four decimal places of:

**a.** $\sin \frac{\pi}{4}$ **b.** $\csc 1.5$.

## EXERCISE SET 5.2

### Practice Exercises

*In Exercises 1–4, a point $P(x, y)$ is shown on the unit circle corresponding to a real number t. Find the values of the trigonometric functions at t.*

**1.**

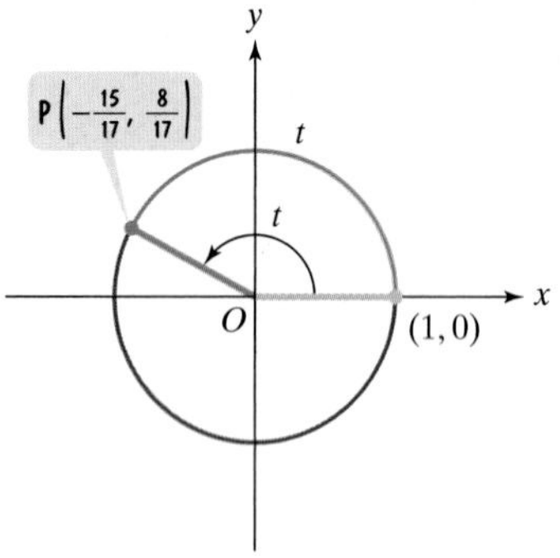


**2.**

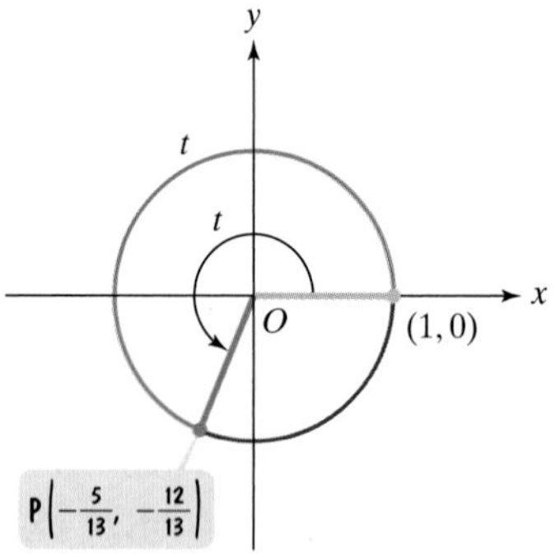


**3.**

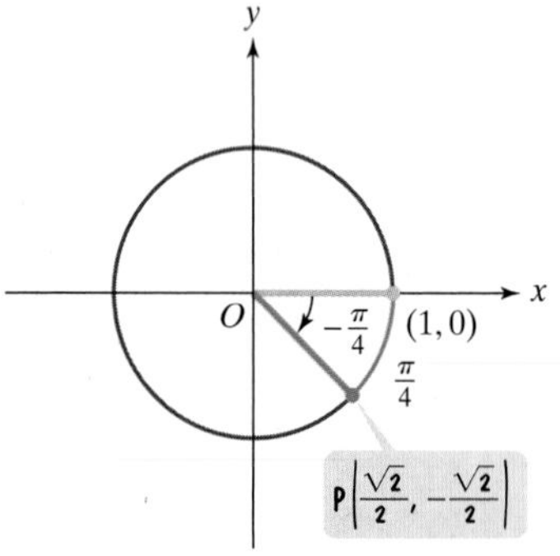


**4.**

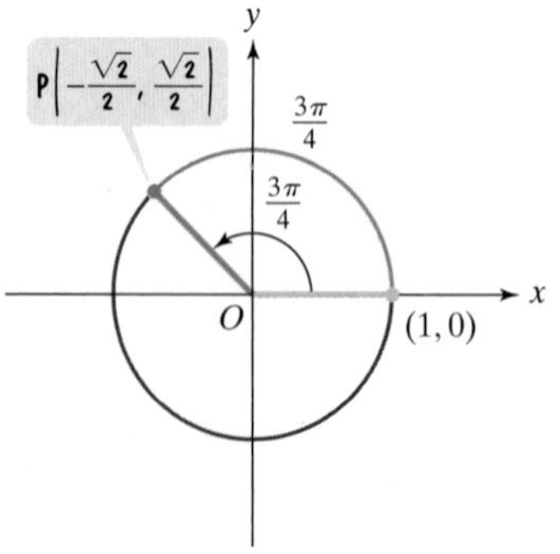


*In Exercises 5–18, the unit circle has been divided into twelve equal arcs, corresponding to t-values of*

$$0, \frac{\pi}{6}, \frac{\pi}{3}, \frac{\pi}{2}, \frac{2\pi}{3}, \frac{5\pi}{6}, \pi, \frac{7\pi}{6}, \frac{4\pi}{3}, \frac{3\pi}{2}, \frac{5\pi}{3}, \frac{11\pi}{6}, \text{ and } 2\pi.$$

*Use the $(x, y)$ coordinates in the figure to find the value of each trigonometric function at the indicated real number, t, or state that the expression is undefined.*

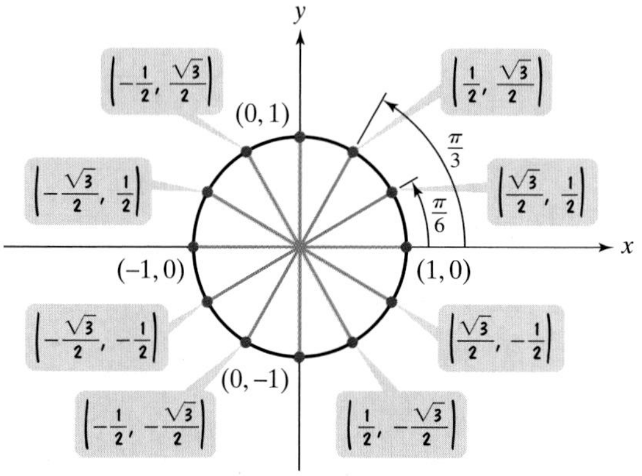


**5.** $\sin \frac{\pi}{6}$

**6.** $\sin \frac{\pi}{3}$

**7.** $\cos \frac{5\pi}{6}$

**8.** $\cos \frac{2\pi}{3}$

**9.** $\tan \pi$

**10.** $\tan 0$

**11.** $\csc \frac{7\pi}{6}$

**12.** $\csc \frac{4\pi}{3}$

**13.** $\sec \frac{11\pi}{6}$

**14.** $\sec \frac{5\pi}{3}$

**15.** $\sin \frac{3\pi}{2}$

**16.** $\cos \frac{3\pi}{2}$

**17.** $\sec \frac{3\pi}{2}$

**18.** $\tan \frac{3\pi}{2}$

*In Exercises 19–24:*

**a.** *Use the unit circle shown for Exercises 5–18 to find the value of the trigonometric function.*

**b.** *Use even and odd trigonometric functions and your answer from part (a) to find the value of the same trigonometric function at the indicated real number.*

**19. a.** $\cos \frac{\pi}{6}$ **b.** $\cos\left(-\frac{\pi}{6}\right)$

**20.** **a.** $\cos \frac{\pi}{3}$ **b.** $\cos\left(-\frac{\pi}{3}\right)$

**21.** **a.** $\sin \frac{5\pi}{6}$ **b.** $\sin\left(-\frac{5\pi}{6}\right)$

**22.** **a.** $\sin \frac{2\pi}{3}$ **b.** $\sin\left(-\frac{2\pi}{3}\right)$

**23.** **a.** $\tan \frac{5\pi}{3}$ **b.** $\tan\left(-\frac{5\pi}{3}\right)$

**24.** **a.** $\tan \frac{11\pi}{6}$ **b.** $\tan\left(-\frac{11\pi}{6}\right)$

*In Exercises 25–28,* $\sin t$ *and* $\cos t$ *are given. Use identities to find* $\tan t$, $\csc t$, $\sec t$, *and* $\cot t$. *Where necessary, rationalize denominators.*

**25.** $\sin t = \frac{8}{17}, \cos t = \frac{15}{17}$

**26.** $\sin t = \frac{3}{5}, \cos t = \frac{4}{5}$

**27.** $\sin t = \frac{1}{3}, \cos t = \frac{2\sqrt{2}}{3}$

**28.** $\sin t = \frac{2}{3}, \cos t = \frac{\sqrt{5}}{3}$

*In Exercises 29–32,* $0 \le t < \frac{\pi}{2}$ *and* $\sin t$ *is given. Use the Pythagorean identity* $\sin^2 t + \cos t = 1$ *to find cos t.*

**29.** $\sin t = \frac{6}{7}$

**30.** $\sin t = \frac{7}{8}$

**31.** $\sin t = \frac{\sqrt{39}}{8}$

**32.** $\sin t = \frac{\sqrt{21}}{5}$

*In Exercises 33–38, use an identity to find the value of each expression. Do not use a calculator.*

**33.** $\sin 1.7 \csc 1.7$

**34.** $\cos 2.3 \sec 2.3$

**35.** $\sin^2 \frac{\pi}{6} + \cos^2 \frac{\pi}{6}$

**36.** $\sin^2 \frac{\pi}{3} + \cos^2 \frac{\pi}{3}$

**37.** $\sec^2 \frac{\pi}{3} - \tan^2 \frac{\pi}{3}$

**38.** $\csc^2 \frac{\pi}{6} - \cot^2 \frac{\pi}{6}$

*In Exercises 39–46, the unit circle has been divided into eight equal arcs, corresponding to t-values of*

$$0, \frac{\pi}{4}, \frac{\pi}{2}, \frac{3\pi}{4}, \pi, \frac{5\pi}{4}, \frac{3\pi}{2}, \frac{7\pi}{4}, \text{ and } 2\pi.$$

**a.** *Use the* $(x, y)$ *coordinates in the figure to find the value of the trigonometric function.*

**b.** *Use periodic properties and your answer from part (a) to find the value of the same trigonometric function at the indicated real number.*

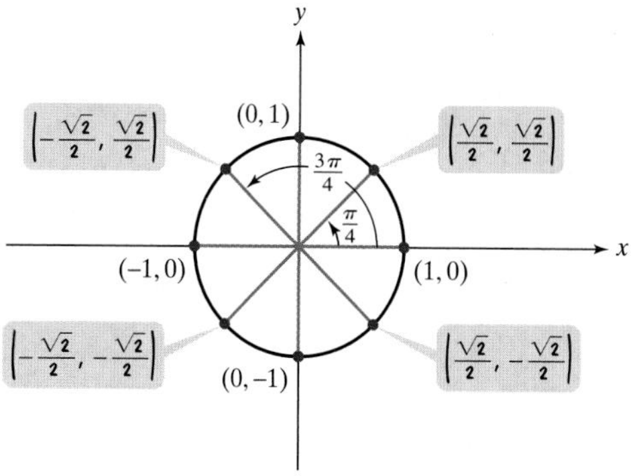


**39.** **a.** $\sin \frac{3\pi}{4}$ **b.** $\sin \frac{11\pi}{4}$

**40.** **a.** $\cos \frac{3\pi}{4}$ **b.** $\cos \frac{11\pi}{4}$

**41.** **a.** $\cos \frac{\pi}{2}$ **b.** $\cos \frac{9\pi}{2}$

**42.** **a.** $\sin \frac{\pi}{2}$ **b.** $\cos \frac{9\pi}{2}$

**43.** **a.** $\tan \pi$ **b.** $\tan 17\pi$

**44.** **a.** $\cot \frac{\pi}{2}$ **b.** $\cot \frac{15\pi}{2}$

**45.** **a.** $\sin \frac{7\pi}{4}$ **b.** $\sin \frac{47\pi}{4}$

**46.** **a.** $\cos \frac{7\pi}{4}$ **b.** $\cos \frac{47\pi}{4}$

*In Exercises 47–56, use a calculator to find the value of the trigonometric function to four decimal places.*

**47.** $\sin 0.8$

**48.** $\cos 0.6$

**49.** $\tan 3.4$

**50.** $\tan 3.7$

**51.** $\csc 1$

**52.** $\sec 1$

**53.** $\cos \frac{\pi}{10}$

**54.** $\sin \frac{3\pi}{10}$

**55.** $\cot \frac{\pi}{12}$

**56.** $\cot \frac{\pi}{18}$

## Application Exercises

**57.** The number of hours of daylight, $H$, on day $t$ of any given year (on January 1, $t = 1$) in Fairbanks, Alaska, can be modeled by the function

$$H = 12 + 8.3 \sin\left[\frac{2\pi}{365}(t - 80)\right].$$

**a.** March 21, the 80th day of the year, is the spring equinox. Find the number of hours of daylight in Fairbanks on this day.

b. June 21, the 172nd day of the year, is the summer solstice, the day with the maximum number of hours of daylight. To the nearest tenth of an hour, find the number of hours of daylight in Fairbanks on this day.
c. December 21, the 355th day of the year, is the winter solstice, the day with the minimum number of hours of daylight. Find, to the nearest tenth of an hour, the number of hours of daylight in Fairbanks on this day.

58. The number of hours of daylight, $H$, on day $t$ of any given year (on January 1, $t = 1$) in San Diego, California, can be modeled by the function

$$H = 12 + 2.4 \sin\left[\frac{2\pi}{365}(t - 80)\right].$$

a. March 21, the 80th day of the year, is the spring equinox. Find the number of hours of daylight in San Diego on this day.
b. June 21, the 172nd day of the year, is the summer solstice, the day with the maximum number of hours of daylight. Find, to the nearest tenth of an hour, the number of hours of daylight in San Diego on this day.
c. December 21, the 355th day of the year, is the winter solstice, the day with the minimum number of hours of daylight. To the nearest tenth of an hour, find the number of hours of daylight in San Diego on this day.

59. People who believe in biorhythms claim that there are three cycles that rule our behavior—the physical, emotional, and mental. Each is a sine function of a certain period. The function for our emotional fluctuations is

$$E = \sin\frac{\pi}{14}t$$

where $t$ is measured in days starting at birth. Emotional fluctuations, $E$, are measured from $-1$ to 1, inclusive, with 1 representing peak emotional well-being, $-1$ representing the low for emotional well-being, and 0 representing feeling neither emotionally high or low.
a. Find $E$ corresponding to $t = 7, 14, 21, 28,$ and 35. Describe what you observe.
b. What is the period of the emotional cycle?

60. The height of the water, $H$ in feet, at a boat dock $t$ hours after 6 A.M. is given by

$$H = 10 + 4\sin\frac{\pi}{6}t.$$

a. Find the height of the water at the dock at 6 A.M., 9 A.M., noon, 6 P.M., midnight, and 3 A.M.
b. When is low tide and when is high tide?
c. What is the period of this function and what does this mean about the tides?

## Writing in Mathematics

61. Why are the trigonometric functions sometimes called circular functions?

62. Define the sine of $t$.

63. Given a point on the unit circle that corresponds to $t$, explain how to find $\tan t$.

64. What is the range of the sine function? Use the unit circle to explain where this range comes from.

65. Explain how to use the unit circle to find values of the trigonometric functions at $\frac{\pi}{4}$.

66. What do we mean by even trigonometric functions? Which of the six functions fall into this category?

67. Use words (not an equation) to describe one of the reciprocal identities.

68. Use words (not an equation) to describe one of the quotient identities.

69. Use words (not an equation) to describe one of the Pythagorean identities.

70. What is a periodic function? Why are the sine and cosine functions periodic?

71. Explain how you can use the function for emotional fluctuations in Exercise 59 to determine good days for having dinner with your moody boss.

72. Describe a phenomenon that repeats again and again. What is its period?

## Critical Thinking Exercises

73. If $f(x) = \sin x$ and $f(a) = \frac{1}{4}$, find the value of
$$f(a) + f(a + 2\pi) + f(a + 4\pi) + f(a + 6\pi).$$

74. If $f(x) = \sin x$ and $f(a) = \frac{1}{4}$, find the value of $f(a) + 2f(-a)$.

75. The seats of a ferris wheel are 40 feet from the wheel's center. When you get on the ride, your seat is 5 feet above the ground. How far above the ground are you after rotating through an angle of $\frac{17\pi}{4}$ radians?

# SECTION 5.3 Right Triangle Trigonometry

## Objectives

1. Use right triangles to evaluate trigonometric functions.
2. Find function values for $30°\left(\frac{\pi}{6}\right)$, $45°\left(\frac{\pi}{4}\right)$, and $60°\left(\frac{\pi}{3}\right)$.
3. Use equal cofunctions of complements.
4. Use right triangle trigonometry to solve applied problems.

In the last century, Ang Rita Sherpa climbed Mount Everest eight times, all without the use of bottled oxygen.

Mountain climbers have forever been fascinated by reaching the top of Mount Everest, sometimes with tragic results. The mountain, on Asia's Tibet-Nepal border, is Earth's highest, peaking at an incredible 29,029 feet. The heights of mountains can be found using trigonometric functions. Remember that the word *trigonometry* means *measurement of triangles*. Trigonometry is used in navigation, building, and engineering. For centuries, Muslims have used trigonometry and the stars to navigate across the Arabian desert to Mecca, the birthplace of the prophet Muhammad, the founder of Islam. The ancient Greeks used trigonometry to record the locations of thousands of stars and worked out the motion of the Moon relative to the Earth. These applications involve looking at the trigonometric functions from the perspective of a right triangle.

**1** Use right triangles to evaluate trigonometric functions.

## Right Triangle Definitions of Trigonometric Functions

We have seen that in a unit circle, the radian measure of a central angle is equal to the measure of the intercepted arc. Thus, the value of a trigonometric function at the real number $t$ is its value at an angle of $t$ radians.

Figure 5.21(a) shows a central angle that measures $\frac{\pi}{3}$ radians and an intercepted arc of length $\frac{\pi}{3}$. Interpret $\frac{\pi}{3}$ as the measure of the central angle. In Figure 5.21(b) we construct a right triangle by dropping a perpendicular line

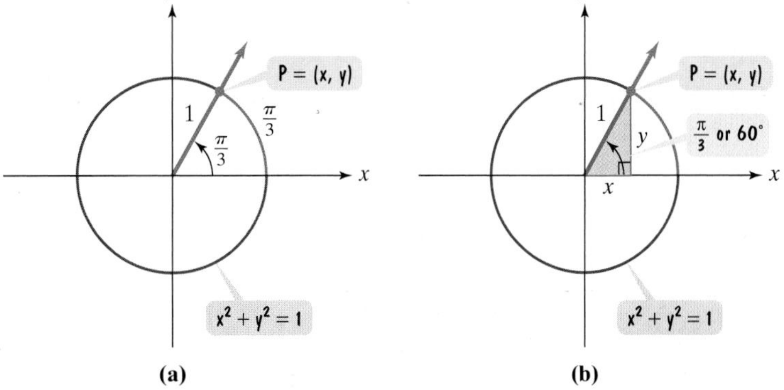


**Figure 5.21** Interpreting trigonometric functions using a unit circle and a right triangle

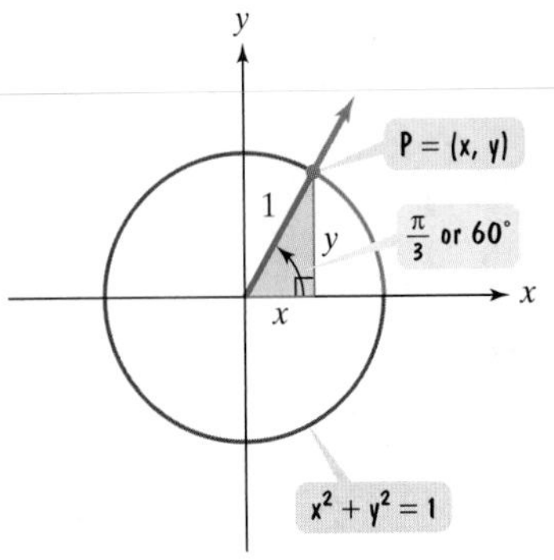


**Figure 5.21(b),** repeated

segment from point $P$ to the $x$-axis. Now we can think of $\frac{\pi}{3}$, or 60°, as the measure of an acute angle in this triangle. Because $\sin t$ is the second coordinate of point $P$ and $\cos t$ is the first coordinate of point $P$, we see that

$$\sin\frac{\pi}{3} = \sin 60^\circ = y = \frac{y}{1}$$

This is the length of the side opposite the 60° angle in the right triangle.

This is the length of the hypotenuse in the right triangle.

$$\cos\frac{\pi}{3} = \cos 60^\circ = x = \frac{x}{1}$$

This is the length of the side adjacent to the 60° angle.

This is the length of the hypotenuse.

In solving certain kinds of problems, it is helpful to interpret trigonometric functions in right triangles where angles are limited to acute angles. Figure 5.22 shows a right triangle with one of its acute angles labeled $\theta$. The side opposite the right angle, the hypotenuse, has length $c$. The other sides of the triangle are described by their position relative to the acute angle $\theta$. One side is opposite $\theta$. The length of this side is $a$. One side is adjacent to $\theta$. The length of this side is $b$.

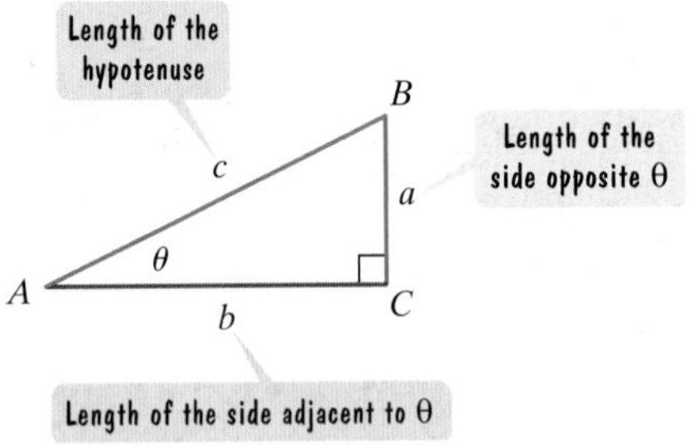


**Figure 5.22**

## Right Triangle Definitions of Trigonometric Functions

See Figure 5.22. The six **trigonometric functions of the acute angle $\theta$** are defined as follows.

$$\sin\theta = \frac{\text{length of side opposite angle }\theta}{\text{length of hypotenuse}} = \frac{a}{c} \qquad \csc\theta = \frac{\text{length of hypotenuse}}{\text{length of side opposite angle }\theta} = \frac{c}{a}$$

$$\cos\theta = \frac{\text{length of side adjacent to angle }\theta}{\text{length of hypotenuse}} = \frac{b}{c} \qquad \sec\theta = \frac{\text{length of hypotenuse}}{\text{length of side adjacent angle }\theta} = \frac{c}{b}$$

$$\tan\theta = \frac{\text{length of side opposite angle }\theta}{\text{length of side adjacent to angle }\theta} = \frac{a}{b} \qquad \cot\theta = \frac{\text{length of side adjacent to angle }\theta}{\text{length of side opposite angle }\theta} = \frac{b}{a}$$

Each of the trigonometric functions of the acute angle $\theta$ is positive. Observe that the functions in the second column in the box are the reciprocals of the corresponding functions in the first column.

Figure 5.23 on page 457 shows four right triangles of varying sizes. In each of the triangles, $\theta$ is the same acute angle, measuring approximately 56.3°. All four of these similar triangles have the same shape and the lengths of corresponding sides are in the same ratio. In each triangle, the tangent function has the same value: $\tan\theta = \frac{3}{2}$.

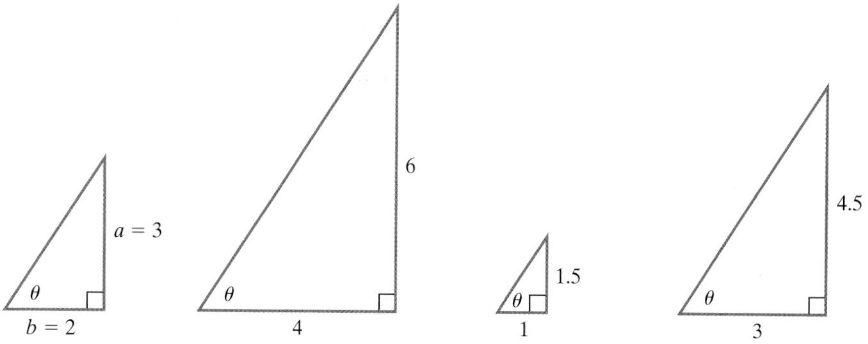


$\tan\theta = \frac{a}{b} = \frac{3}{2}$ $\tan\theta = \frac{6}{4} = \frac{3}{2}$ $\tan\theta = \frac{1.5}{1} = \frac{3}{2}$ $\tan\theta = \frac{4.5}{3} = \frac{3}{2}$

**Figure 5.23** A particular acute angle always gives the same ratio of opposite to adjacent sides.

In general, **the trigonometric function values of $\theta$ depend only on the size of angle $\theta$, and not on the size of the triangle.**

## EXAMPLE 1 Evaluating Trigonometric Functions

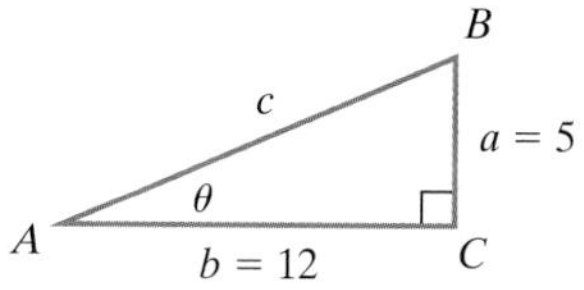


**Figure 5.24**

Find the value of each of the six trigonometric functions of $\theta$ in Figure 5.24.

**Solution** We need to find the values of the six trigonometric functions of $\theta$. However, we must know the lengths of all three sides of the triangle ($a$, $b$, and $c$) to evaluate all six functions. The values of $a$ and $b$ are given. We can use the Pythagorean Theorem, $c^2 = a^2 + b^2$, to find $c$.

$a = 5$ $b = 12$

$$c^2 = a^2 + b^2 = 5^2 + 12^2 = 25 + 144 = 169$$
$$c = \sqrt{169} = 13$$

Now that we know the lengths of the three sides of the triangle, we apply the definitions of the six trigonometric functions of $\theta$. Referring to these lengths as opposite, adjacent, and hypotenuse, we have

$$\sin\theta = \frac{\text{opposite}}{\text{hypotenuse}} = \frac{5}{13} \qquad \csc\theta = \frac{\text{hypotenuse}}{\text{opposite}} = \frac{13}{5}$$

$$\cos\theta = \frac{\text{adjacent}}{\text{hypotenuse}} = \frac{12}{13} \qquad \sec\theta = \frac{\text{hypotenuse}}{\text{adjacent}} = \frac{13}{12}$$

$$\tan\theta = \frac{\text{opposite}}{\text{adjacent}} = \frac{5}{12} \qquad \cot\theta = \frac{\text{adjacent}}{\text{opposite}} = \frac{12}{5}.$$

**Study Tip**

The functions in the second column are reciprocals of those in the first column. You can obtain their values by exchanging the numerator and denominator of the corresponding ratios in the first column.

**Check Point 1** Find the value of each of the six trigonometric functions of $\theta$ in the figure.

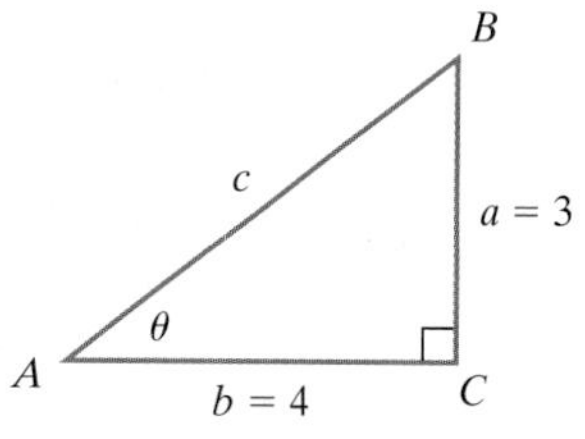

**2** Find function values for $30°\left(\frac{\pi}{6}\right)$, $45°\left(\frac{\pi}{4}\right)$, and $60°\left(\frac{\pi}{3}\right)$.

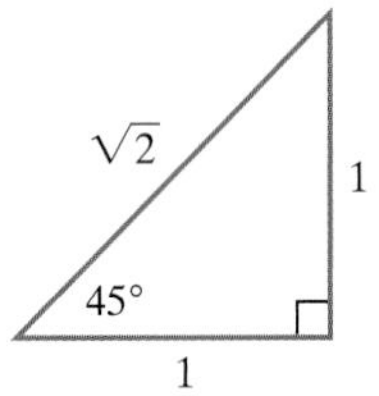

**Figure 5.25** An isosceles right triangle

## Function Values for Some Special Angles

In Section 5.2, we used the unit circle to find values of the trigonometric functions at $\frac{\pi}{4}$. How can we find the values of the trigonometric functions at $\frac{\pi}{4}$, or 45°, using a right triangle? We construct a right triangle with a 45° angle, shown in Figure 5.25. The triangle actually has two 45° angles. Thus, the triangle is isosceles—that is, it has two sides of the same length. Assume that each leg of the triangle has a length equal to 1. We can find the length of the hypotenuse using the Pythagorean Theorem.

$$(\text{length of hypotenuse})^2 = 1^2 + 1^2 = 2$$
$$\text{length of hypotenuse} = \sqrt{2}$$

With Figure 5.25, we can determine the trigonometric function values for 45°.

### EXAMPLE 2 Evaluating Trigonometric Functions of 45°

Use Figure 5.25 to find sin 45°, cos 45°, and tan 45°.

**Solution** We apply the definitions of these three trigonometric functions.

$$\sin 45° = \frac{\text{length of side opposite } 45°}{\text{length of hypotenuse}} = \frac{1}{\sqrt{2}} \text{ or } \frac{\sqrt{2}}{2}$$
$$\cos 45° = \frac{\text{length of side adjacent to } 45°}{\text{length of hypotenuse}} = \frac{1}{\sqrt{2}} \text{ or } \frac{\sqrt{2}}{2}$$
$$\tan 45° = \frac{\text{length of side opposite } 45°}{\text{length of side adjacent to } 45°} = \frac{1}{1} = 1$$

**Check Point 2** Use Figure 5.25 to find csc 45°, sec 45°, and cot 45°.

Two other angles that occur frequently in trigonometry are 30°, or $\frac{\pi}{6}$ radians, and 60°, or $\frac{\pi}{3}$ radians. We can find the values of the trigonometric functions of 30° and 60° by using a right triangle. To form this right triangle, draw an equilateral triangle—that is a triangle with all sides the same length. Assume that each side has a length equal to 2. Now take half of the equilateral triangle. We obtain the solid blue triangle in Figure 5.26. This right triangle has a hypotenuse of length 2 and a leg of length 1. The other leg has length $a$, which can be found using the Pythagorean Theorem.

$$a^2 + 1^2 = 2^2$$
$$a^2 + 1 = 4$$
$$a^2 = 3$$
$$a = \sqrt{3}$$

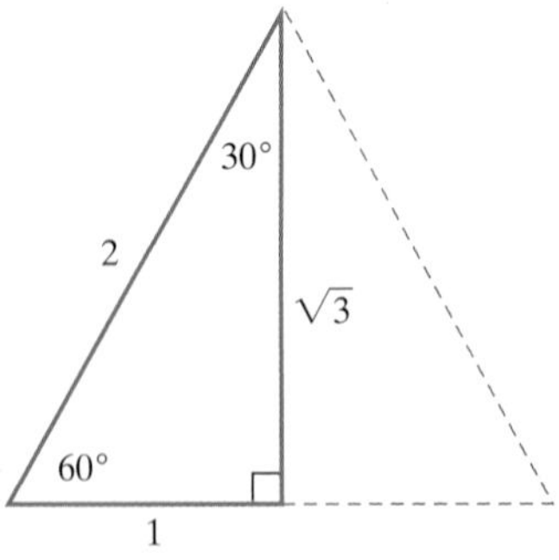

**Figure 5.26** A 30°-60°-90° triangle

With the blue right triangle in Figure 5.26, we can determine the trigonometric functions for 30° and 60°.

## EXAMPLE 3 Evaluating Trigonometric Functions of 30° and 60°

Use Figure 5.26 to find $\sin 60°$, $\cos 60°$, $\sin 30°$, and $\cos 30°$.

**Solution** We begin with 60°. Use the angle on the lower left in Figure 5.26.

$$\sin 60° = \frac{\text{length of side opposite } 60°}{\text{length of hypotenuse}} = \frac{\sqrt{3}}{2}$$

$$\cos 60° = \frac{\text{length of side adjacent to } 60°}{\text{length of hypotenuse}} = \frac{1}{2}$$

To find $\sin 30°$ and $\cos 30°$, use the angle on the upper right, in Figure 5.26.

$$\sin 30° = \frac{\text{length of side opposite } 30°}{\text{length of hypotenuse}} = \frac{1}{2}$$

$$\cos 30° = \frac{\text{length of side adjacent to } 30°}{\text{length of hypotenuse}} = \frac{\sqrt{3}}{2}$$

**Check Point 3** Use Figure 5.26 to find $\tan 60°$ and $\tan 30°$. If necessary, express the value without a square root in the denominator by rationalizing the denominator.

Because we will often use the function values of 30°, 45°, and 60°, you should learn to construct the right triangles shown in Figures 5.25 and 5.26. With sufficient practice, you will memorize the values shown in the following box.

### Sines, Cosines, and Tangents of Special Angles

| | | |
|---|---|---|
| $\sin 30° = \sin\frac{\pi}{6} = \frac{1}{2}$ | $\cos 30° = \cos\frac{\pi}{6} = \frac{\sqrt{3}}{2}$ | $\tan 30° = \tan\frac{\pi}{6} = \frac{\sqrt{3}}{3}$ |
| $\sin 45° = \sin\frac{\pi}{4} = \frac{\sqrt{2}}{2}$ | $\cos 45° = \cos\frac{\pi}{4} = \frac{\sqrt{2}}{2}$ | $\tan 45° = \tan\frac{\pi}{4} = 1$ |
| $\sin 60° = \sin\frac{\pi}{3} = \frac{\sqrt{3}}{2}$ | $\cos 60° = \cos\frac{\pi}{3} = \frac{1}{2}$ | $\tan 60° = \tan\frac{\pi}{3} = \sqrt{3}$ |

**3** Use equal cofunctions of complements.

## Trigonometric Functions and Complements

In Section 5.2, we used the unit circle to establish fundamental trigonometric identities. Another relationship among trigonometric functions is based on angles that are complements. We use a right triangle to establish this relationship. Refer to Figure 5.27. Because the sum of the angles of any triangle is 180°, in a right triangle the sum of the acute angles is 90°. Thus, the acute angles are complements. If the degree measure of one acute angle is $\theta$, then the degree measure of the other acute angle is $(90° - \theta)$. This angle is shown on the upper right in Figure 5.27.

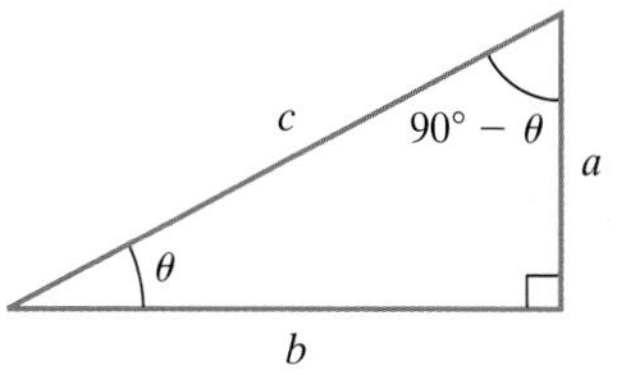


**Figure 5.27**

Let's use Figure 5.27 to compare $\sin\theta$ and $\cos(90° - \theta)$.

$$\sin\theta = \frac{\text{length of side opposite } \theta}{\text{length of hypotenuse}} = \frac{a}{c}$$

$$\cos(90° - \theta) = \frac{\text{length of side adjacent to } (90° - \theta)}{\text{length of hypotenuse}} = \frac{a}{c}$$

Thus, $\sin\theta = \cos(90° - \theta)$. If two angles are complements, the sine of one equals the cosine of the other. Because of this relationship, the sine and cosine are called *cofunctions* of each other. The name *cosine* is a shortened form of the phrase *complement's sine*.

Any pair of trigonometric functions $f$ and $g$ for which

$$f(\theta) = g(90° - \theta) \quad \text{and} \quad g(\theta) = f(90° - \theta)$$

are called **cofunctions**. Using Figure 5.27, we can show that the tangent and cotangent are cofunctions of each other. So are the secant and cosecant.

### Cofunction Identities

The value of a trigonometric function of $\theta$ is equal to the cofunction of the complement of $\theta$.

$$\sin\theta = \cos(90° - \theta) \qquad \cos\theta = \sin(90° - \theta)$$
$$\tan\theta = \cot(90° - \theta) \qquad \cot\theta = \tan(90° - \theta)$$
$$\sec\theta = \csc(90° - \theta) \qquad \csc\theta = \sec(90° - \theta)$$

If $\theta$ is in radians, replace 90° with $\frac{\pi}{2}$.

## EXAMPLE 4

Find a cofunction with the same value as the given expression.

**a.** $\sin 72°$ **b.** $\csc\frac{\pi}{3}$

**Solution** Because the value of a trigonometric function of $\theta$ is equal to the cofunction of the complement of $\theta$, we need to find the complement of each angle. We do this by subtracting the angle's measure from 90° or its radian equivalent, $\frac{\pi}{2}$.

**a.** $\sin 72° = \cos(90° - 72°) = \cos 18°$

We have a function and its cofunction.

**b.** $\csc\frac{\pi}{3} = \sec\left(\frac{\pi}{2} - \frac{\pi}{3}\right) = \sec\left(\frac{3\pi}{6} - \frac{2\pi}{6}\right) = \sec\frac{\pi}{6}$

We have a cofunction and its function.

Perform the subtraction using the least common denominator, 6.

**Check Point 4** Find a cofunction with the same value as the given expression.

**a.** $\sin 46°$ **b.** $\cot\frac{\pi}{12}$

4 Use right triangle trigonometry to solve applied problems.

## Applications

Many applications of right triangle trigonometry involve the angle made with an imaginary horizontal line. As shown in Figure 5.28, an angle formed by a horizontal line and the line of sight to an object that is above the horizontal line is

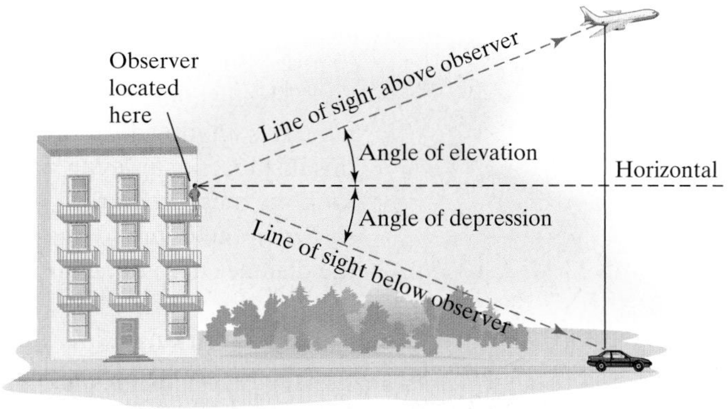


**Figure 5.28**

called the **angle of elevation**. The angle formed by a horizontal line and the line of sight to an object that is below the horizontal line is called the **angle of depression**. Transits and sextants are instruments used to measure such angles.

## EXAMPLE 5 Problem Solving Using an Angle of Elevation

Sighting the top of a building, a surveyor measured the angle of elevation to be 22°. The transit is 5 feet above the ground and 300 feet from the building. Find the building's height.

**Solution** The situation is illustrated in Figure 5.29. Let $a$ be the height of the portion of the building that lies above the transit. The height of the building is the transit's height, 5 feet, plus $a$. Thus, we need to identify a trigonometric function that will make it possible to find $a$. In terms of the 22° angle, we are looking for the side opposite the angle. The transit is 300 feet from the building, so the side adjacent to the 22° angle is 300 feet. Because we have a known angle, an unknown opposite side, and a known adjacent side, we select the tangent function.

$$\tan 22^\circ = \frac{a}{300}$$

Length of side opposite the 22° angle (numerator); Length of side adjacent to the 22° angle (denominator)

$$a = 300 \tan 22^\circ$$ Multiply both sides of the equation by 300.

$$a = 300(0.4040) \approx 121$$ Find tan 22° with a calculator in the degree mode.

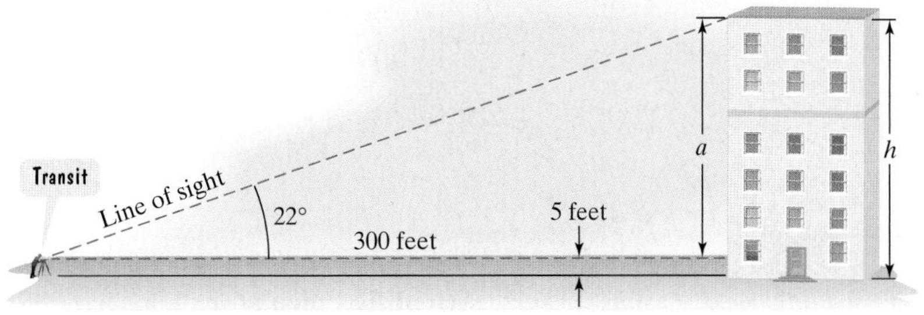


**Figure 5.29**

The height of the part of the building above the transit is 121 feet. Thus, the height of the building is determined by adding the transit's height, 5 feet, to 121 feet.

$$h = 5 + 121 = 126$$

The building's height is 126 feet.

**Check Point 5** The irregular blue shape in Figure 5.30 represents a lake. The distance across the lake, $a$, is unknown. To find this distance, a surveyor took the measurements shown in the figure. What is the distance across the lake?

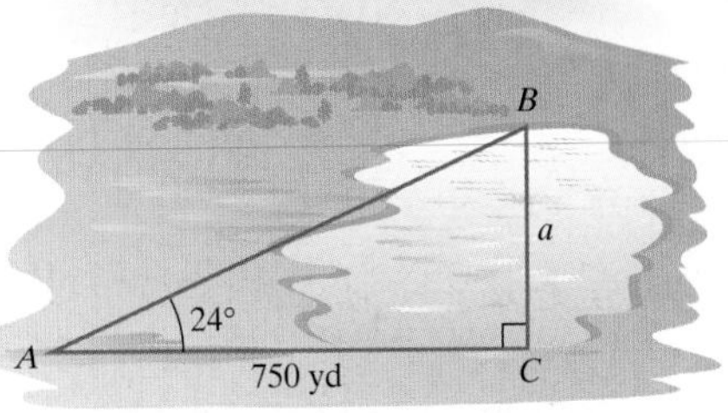

**Figure 5.30**

If two sides of a right triangle are known, an appropriate trigonometric function can be used to find an acute angle $\theta$ in the triangle. You will also need to use the *inverse key* on a calculator. This key uses a function value to display the acute angle $\theta$. For example, suppose that $\sin\theta = 0.866$. We can find $\theta$ in the degree mode by using the *inverse sine* key, usually labeled $\boxed{\text{SIN}^{-1}}$.

| **Scientific Calculator** | **Graphing Calculator** |
|---|---|
| .866 $\boxed{\text{SIN}^{-1}}$ | $\boxed{\text{SIN}^{-1}}$ .866 $\boxed{\text{ENTER}}$ |

The display shows approximately 59.99, which we can round to 60. Thus, if $\sin\theta = 0.866$, then $\theta \approx 60°$.

## EXAMPLE 6 Determining the Angle of Elevation

A building that is 21 meters tall casts a shadow 25 meters long. Find the angle of elevation of the sun to the nearest degree.

**Solution** The situation is illustrated in Figure 5.31. We are asked to find $\theta$. We begin with the tangent function.

$$\tan\theta = \frac{\text{side opposite } \theta}{\text{side adjacent to } \theta} = \frac{21}{25}$$

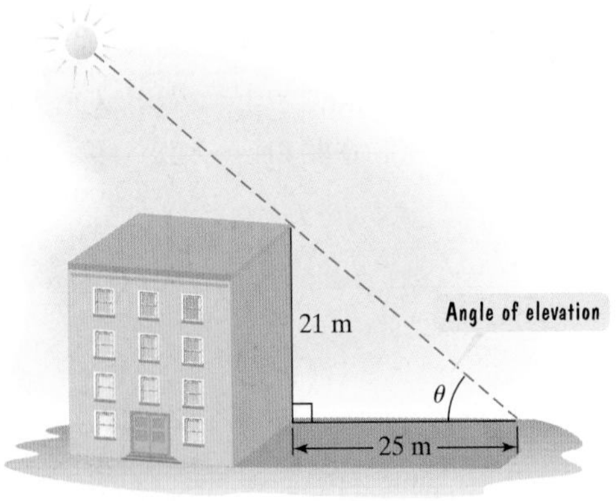

**Figure 5.31**

We use a calculator in the degree mode to find $\theta$.

| **Scientific Calculator** | **Graphing Calculator** |
|---|---|
| 21 $\boxed{\div}$ 25 $\boxed{=}$ $\boxed{\text{TAN}^{-1}}$ | $\boxed{\text{TAN}^{-1}}$ $\boxed{(}$ 21 $\boxed{\div}$ 25 $\boxed{)}$ $\boxed{\text{ENTER}}$ |

The display should show approximately 40. Thus, the angle of elevation of the sun is approximately 40°.

**Check Point 6** A flagpole that is 14 meters tall casts a shadow 10 meters long. Find the angle of elevation of the sun to the nearest degree.

## The Mountain Man

In the 1930s, a *National Geographic* team headed by Brad Washburn used trigonometry to create a map of the 5000-square-mile region of the Yukon, near the Canadian border. The team started with aerial photography. By drawing a network of angles on the photographs, the approximate locations of the major mountains and their rough heights were determined. The expedition then spent three months on foot to find the exact heights. Team members established two base points a known distance apart, one directly under the mountain's peak. By measuring the angle of elevation from one of the base points to the peak, the tangent function was used to determine the peak's height. The Yukon expedition was a major advance in the way maps are made.

# EXERCISE SET 5.3

### Practice Exercises

*In Exercises 1–8, use the Pythagorean Theorem to find the length of the missing side of each right triangle. Then find the value of each of the six trigonometric functions of θ.*

**1.**

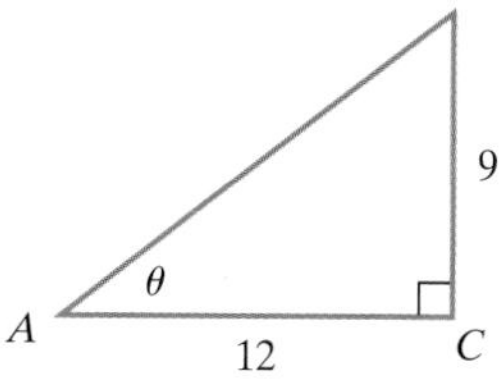


**2.**

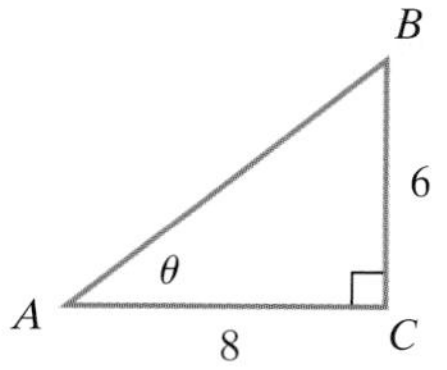


**3.**

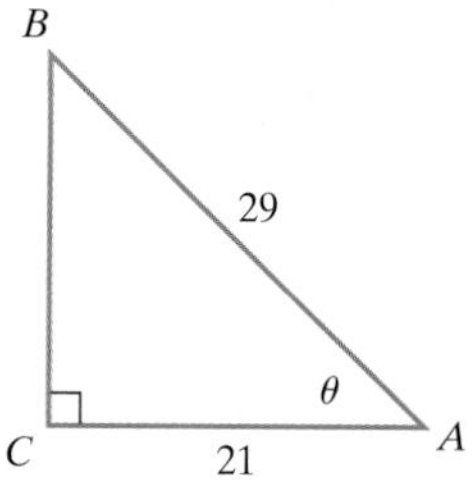


**4.**

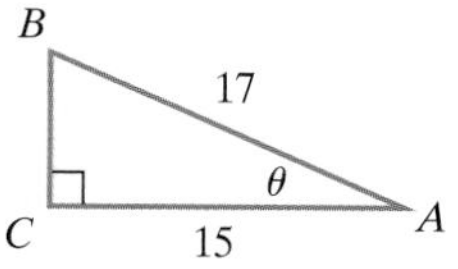


**5.**

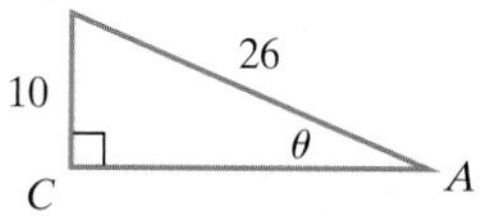


**6.**

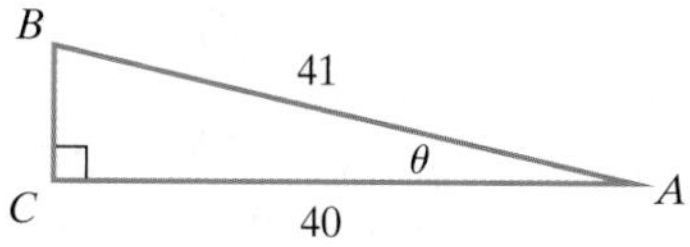


**7.**

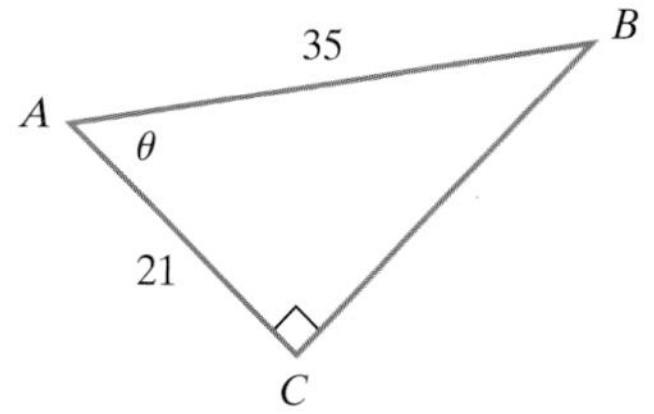


**8.**

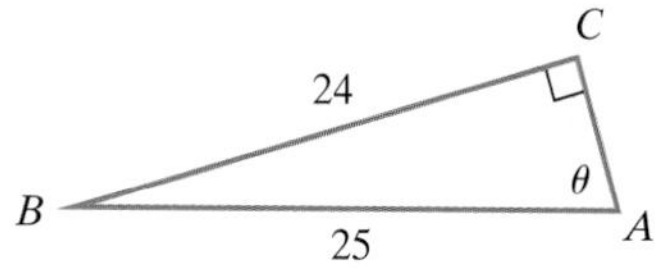


*In Exercises 9–20, use the given triangles to evaluate each expression. If necessary, express the value without a square root in the denominator by rationalizing the denominator.*

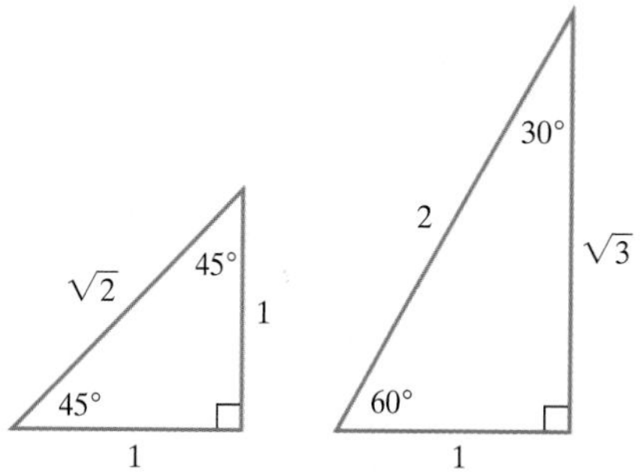


**9.** $\cos 30°$

**10.** $\tan 30°$

**11.** $\sec 45°$

**12.** $\csc 45°$

**13.** $\tan \frac{\pi}{3}$

**14.** $\cot \frac{\pi}{3}$

**15.** $\sin \frac{\pi}{4} - \cos \frac{\pi}{4}$

**16.** $\tan \frac{\pi}{4} + \csc \frac{\pi}{6}$

**17.** $\sin\frac{\pi}{3}\cos\frac{\pi}{4} - \tan\frac{\pi}{4}$

**18.** $\cos\frac{\pi}{3}\sec\frac{\pi}{3} - \cot\frac{\pi}{3}$

**19.** $2\tan\frac{\pi}{3} + \cos\frac{\pi}{4}\tan\frac{\pi}{6}$

**20.** $6\tan\frac{\pi}{4} + \sin\frac{\pi}{3}\sec\frac{\pi}{6}$

*In Exercises 21–28, find a cofunction with the same value as the given expression.*

**21.** $\sin 7°$

**22.** $\sin 19°$

**23.** $\csc 25°$

**24.** $\csc 35°$

**25.** $\tan\frac{\pi}{9}$

**26.** $\tan\frac{\pi}{7}$

**27.** $\cos\frac{2\pi}{5}$

**28.** $\cos\frac{3\pi}{8}$

*In Exercises 29–34, find the measure of the side of the right triangle whose length is designated by a lowercase letter. Round answers to the nearest whole number.*

**29.**

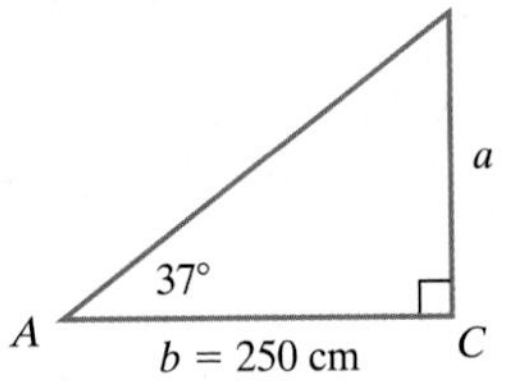


**30.**

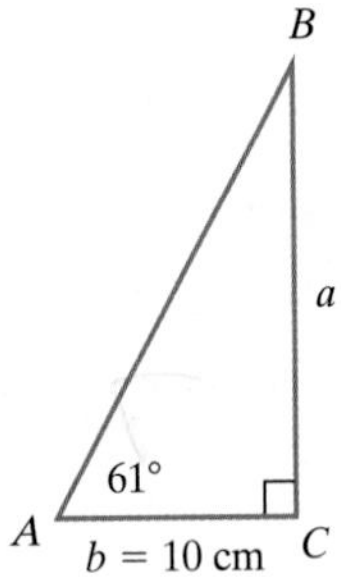


**31.**

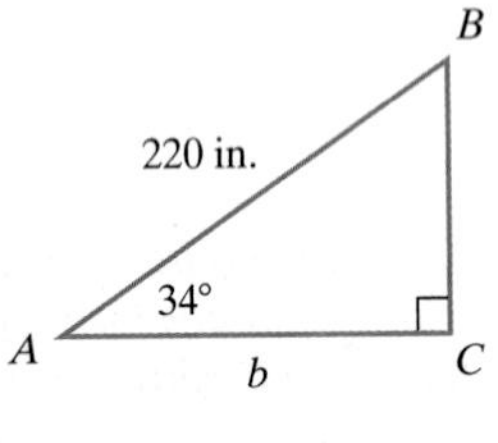


**32.**

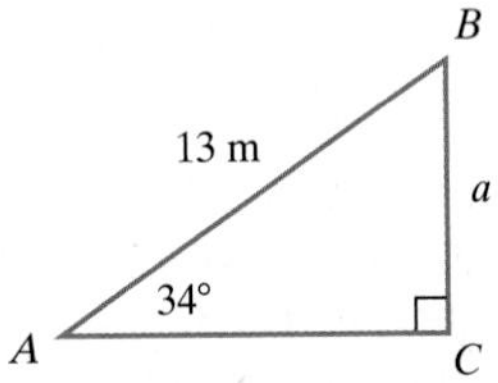


**33.**

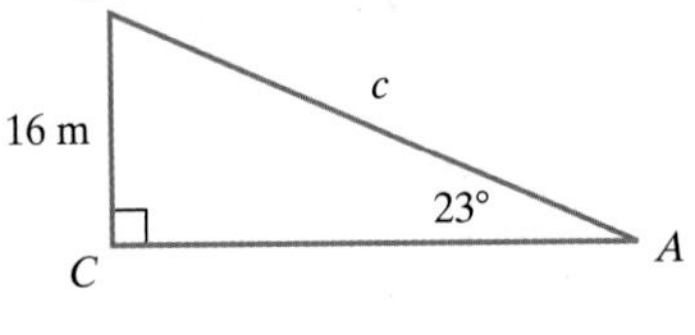


**34.**

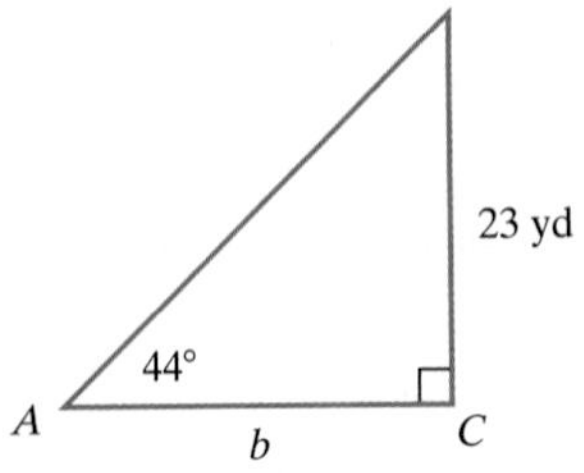


*In Exercises 35–38, use a calculator to find the value of the acute angle θ to the nearest degree.*

**35.** $\sin\theta = 0.2974$

**36.** $\cos\theta = 0.8771$

**37.** $\tan\theta = 4.6252$

**38.** $\tan\theta = 26.0307$

*In Exercises 39–42, use a calculator to find the value of the acute angle θ in radians, rounded to three decimal places.*

**39.** $\cos\theta = 0.4112$

**40.** $\sin\theta = 0.9499$

**41.** $\tan\theta = 0.4169$

**42.** $\tan\theta = 0.5117$

## Application Exercises

**43.** To find the distance across a lake, a surveyor took the measurements in the figure shown. Use these measurements to determine how far it is across the lake. Round to the nearest yard.

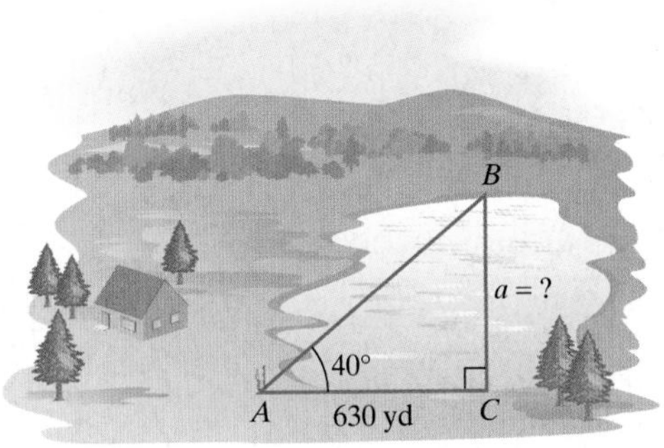


**44.** At a certain time of day, the angle of elevation of the sun is 40°. To the nearest foot, find the height of a tree whose shadow is 35 feet long.

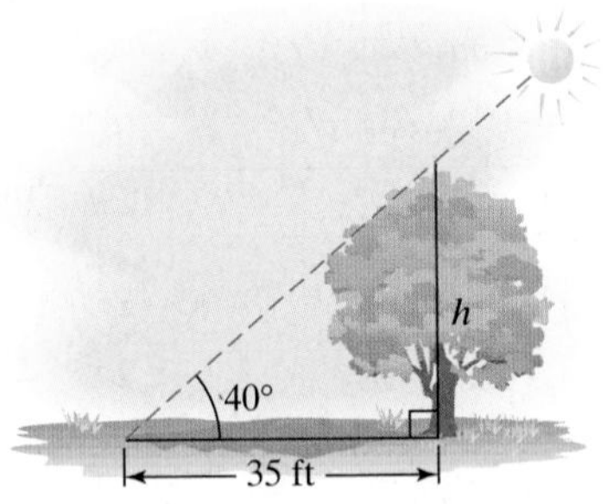


**45.** A tower that is 125 feet tall casts a shadow 172 feet long. Find the angle of elevation of the sun to the nearest degree.

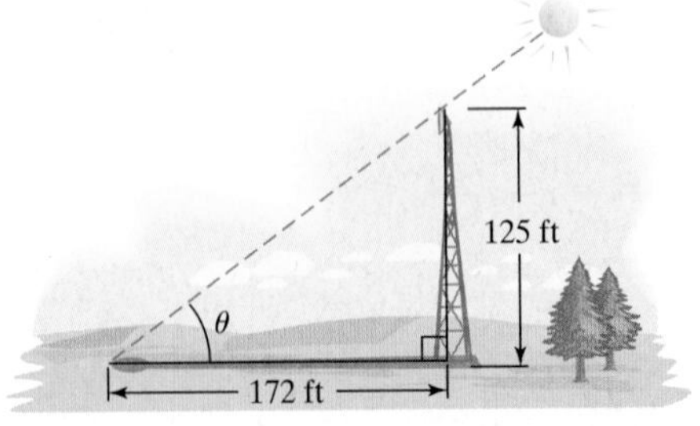

**46.** The Washington Monument is 555 feet high. If you stand one quarter of a mile, or 1320 feet, from the base of the monument and look to the top, find the angle of elevation to the nearest degree.

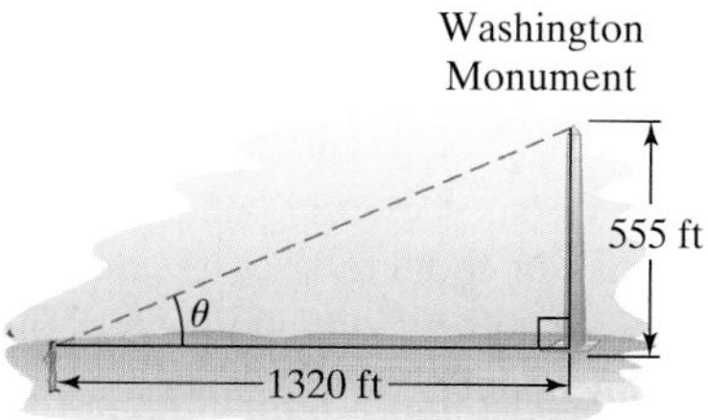


**47.** A plane rises from a take-off and flies at an angle of 10° with the horizontal runway. When it has gained 500 feet, find the distance, to the nearest foot, the plane has flown.

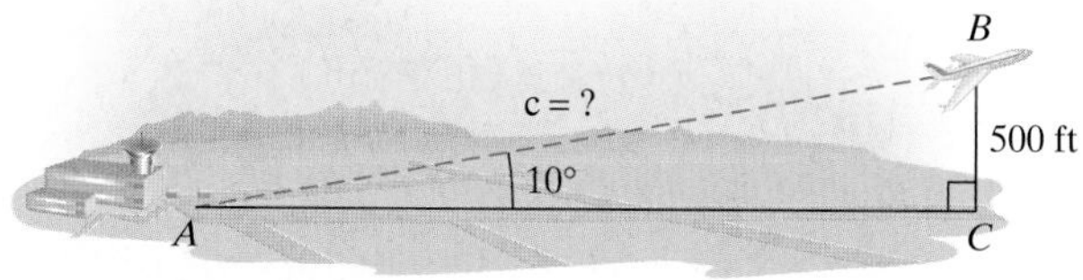


**48.** A road is inclined at an angle of 5°. After driving 5000 feet along this road, find the driver's increase in altitude. Round to the nearest foot.

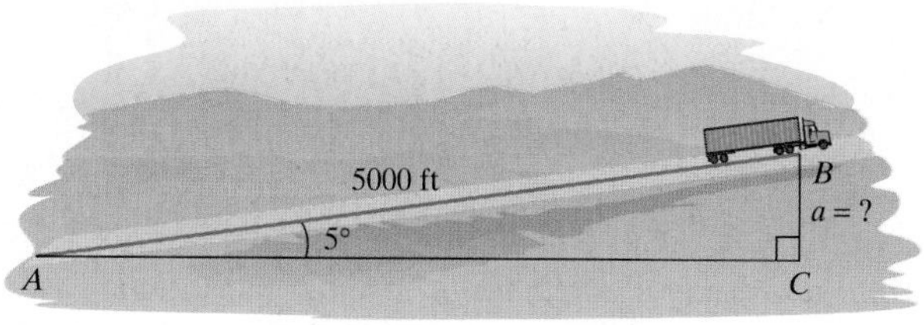


**49.** A telephone pole is 60 feet tall. A guy wire 75 feet long is attached from the ground to the top of the pole. Find the angle between the wire and the pole to the nearest degree.

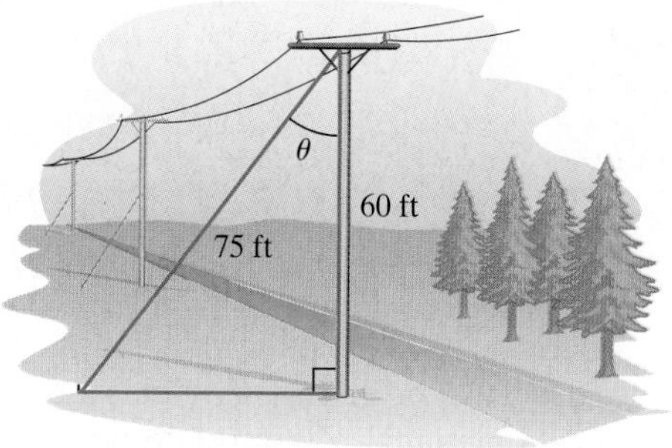


**50.** A telephone pole is 55 feet tall. A guy wire 80 feet long is attached from the ground to the top of the pole. Find the angle between the wire and the pole to the nearest degree.

## Writing in Mathematics

**51.** If you are given the lengths of the sides of a right triangle, describe how to find the sine of either acute angle.

**52.** Describe one similarity and one difference between the definitions of $\sin\theta$ and $\cos\theta$, where $\theta$ is an acute angle of a right triangle.

**53.** Describe the triangle used to find the trigonometric functions of 45°.

**54.** Describe the triangle used to find the trigonometric functions of 30° and 60°.

**55.** Describe a relationship among trigonometric functions that is based on angles that are complements.

**56.** Describe what is meant by an angle of elevation and an angle of depression.

**57.** Stonehenge, the famous "stone circle" in England, was built between 2750 B.C. and 1300 B.C. using solid stone blocks weighing over 99,000 pounds each. It required 550 people to pull a single stone up a ramp inclined at a 9° angle. Describe how right triangle trigonometry can be used to determine the distance the 550 workers had to drag a stone in order to raise it to a height of 30 feet.

## Technology Exercises

**58.** Use a calculator in the radian mode to fill in the values in the following table. Then draw a conclusion about $\frac{\sin\theta}{\theta}$ as $\theta$ approaches 0.

| $\theta$ | 0.4 | 0.3 | 0.2 | 0.1 | 0.01 | 0.001 | 0.0001 | 0.00001 |
|---|---|---|---|---|---|---|---|---|
| $\sin\theta$ | | | | | | | | |
| $\frac{\sin\theta}{\theta}$ | | | | | | | | |

**59.** Use a calculator in the radian mode to fill in the values in the following table. Then draw a conclusion about $\frac{\cos\theta - 1}{\theta}$ as $\theta$ approaches 0.

| $\theta$ | 0.4 | 0.3 | 0.2 | 0.1 | 0.01 | 0.001 | 0.0001 | 0.00001 |
|---|---|---|---|---|---|---|---|---|
| $\cos\theta$ | | | | | | | | |
| $\frac{\cos\theta - 1}{\theta}$ | | | | | | | | |

## Critical Thinking Exercises

**60.** Which one of the following is true?

**a.** $\frac{\tan 45°}{\tan 15°} = \tan 3°$ **b.** $\tan^2 15° - \sec^2 15° = -1$

**c.** $\sin 45° + \cos 45° = 1$ **d.** $\tan^2 5° = \tan 25°$

**61.** Explain why the sine or cosine of an acute angle cannot be greater than or equal to 1.

**62.** Describe what happens to the tangent of an acute angle as the angle gets close to 90°. What happens at 90°?

**63.** From the top of a 250-foot lighthouse, a plane is sighted overhead and a ship is observed directly below the plane. The angle of elevation of the plane is 22° and the angle of depression of the ship is 35°. Find a. the distance of the ship from the lighthouse; b. the plane's height above the water. Round to the nearest foot.

# SECTION 5.4 Trigonometric Functions of Any Angle

## Objectives

1. Use the definitions of trigonometric functions of any angle.
2. Use the signs of the trigonometric functions.
3. Find reference angles.
4. Use reference angles to evaluate trigonometric functions.

Cycles govern many aspects of life—heartbeats, sleep patterns, seasons, and tides all follow regular, predictable cycles. Because of their periodic nature, trigonometric functions are used to model phenomena that occur in cycles. It is helpful to apply these models regardless of whether we think of the domains of trigonometric functions as sets of real numbers or sets of angles. In order to understand and use models for cyclic phenomena from an angle perspective, we need to move beyond right triangles.

**1** Use the definitions of trigonometric functions of any angle.

## Trigonometric Functions of Any Angle

In the last section we evaluated trigonometric functions of acute angles, such as that shown in Figure 5.32(a). Note that this angle is in standard position. The point $P = (x, y)$ is a point $r$ units from the origin on the terminal side of $\theta$. A right triangle is formed by drawing a perpendicular from $P = (x, y)$ to the $x$-axis. Note that $y$ is the length of the side opposite $\theta$ and $x$ is the length of the side adjacent to $\theta$.

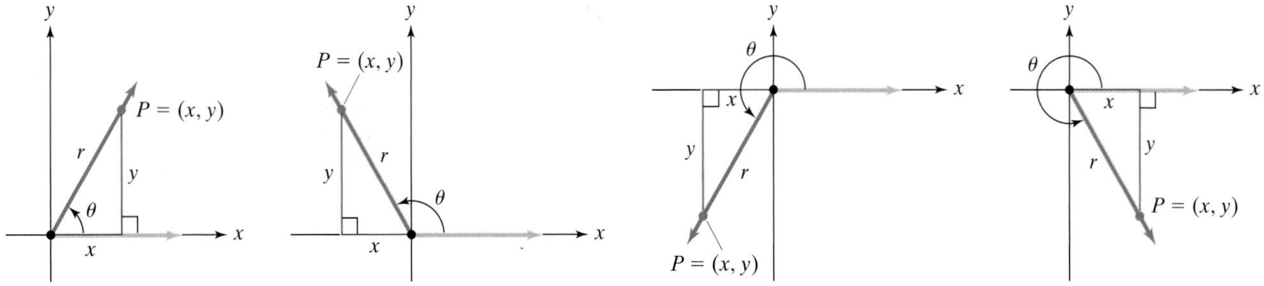


(a) $\theta$ lies in quadrant I. (b) $\theta$ lies in quadrant II. (c) $\theta$ lies in quadrant III. (d) $\theta$ lies in quadrant IV.

**Figure 5.32**

Figures 5.32(b), (c), and (d) show angles in standard position, but they are not acute. We can extend our definitions of the six trigonometric functions to include such angles, as well as quadrantal angles. (Recall that a quadrantal angle has its terminal side on the $x$-axis or $y$-axis; such angles are *not* shown in Figure 5.32.) The point $P = (x, y)$ may be any point on the terminal side of the angle $\theta$ other than the origin $(0, 0)$.

**Study Tip**

If $\theta$ is acute, we have the right triangle shown in Figure 5.32(a). In this situation, the definitions in the box are the right triangle definitions of the trigonometric functions. This should make it easier for you to remember the six definitions.

**Definitions of Trigonometric Functions of Any Angle**

Let $\theta$ be any angle in standard position, and let $P = (x, y)$ be a point on the terminal side of $\theta$. If $r = \sqrt{x^2 + y^2}$ is the distance from $(0, 0)$ to $(x, y)$, as shown in Figure 5.32, the **six trigonometric functions of $\theta$** are defined by the following ratios.

$$\sin\theta = \frac{y}{r} \qquad \cos\theta = \frac{x}{r} \qquad \tan\theta = \frac{y}{x},\ x \neq 0$$

$$\csc\theta = \frac{r}{y},\ y \neq 0 \qquad \sec\theta = \frac{r}{x},\ x \neq 0 \qquad \cot\theta = \frac{x}{y},\ y \neq 0$$

Because the point $P = (x, y)$ is any point on the terminal side of $\theta$ other than the origin $(0, 0)$, $r = \sqrt{x^2 + y^2}$ cannot be zero. Examine the six trigonometric functions defined previously. Note that the denominator of the sine and cosine functions is $r$. Because $r \neq 0$, the sine and cosine functions are defined for any real value of the angle $\theta$. This is not true for the other four trigonometric functions. Note that the denominator of the tangent and secant functions is $x$. These functions are not defined if $x = 0$. If the point $P = (x, y)$ is on the $y$-axis, then $x = 0$. Thus, the tangent and secant functions are undefined for all quadrantal angles with terminal sides on the positive or negative $y$-axis. Likewise, if $P = (x, y)$ is on the $x$-axis, then $y = 0$, and the cotangent and cosecant functions are undefined. The cotangent and cosecant functions are undefined for all quadrantal angles with terminal sides on the positive or negative $x$-axis.

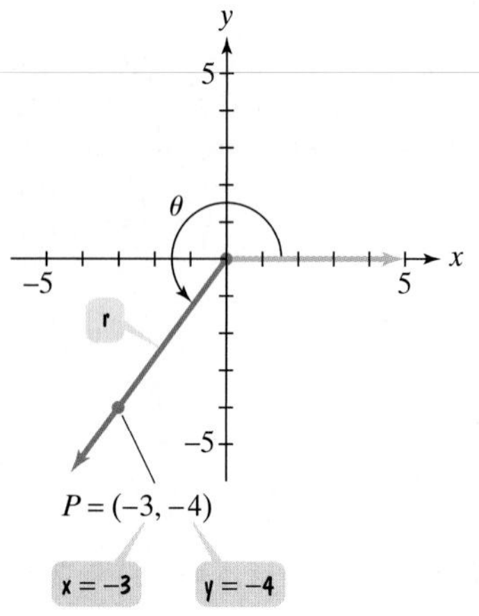


**Figure 5.33**

## EXAMPLE 1 Evaluating Trigonometric Functions

Let $P = (-3, -4)$ be a point on the terminal side of $\theta$. Find each of the six trigonometric functions of $\theta$.

**Solution** The situation is shown in Figure 5.33. We need values for $x$, $y$, and $r$ to evaluate all six trigonometric functions. We are given the values of $x$ and $y$. Because $P = (-3, -4)$ is a point on the terminal side of $\theta$, $x = -3$ and $y = -4$. Furthermore,

$$r = \sqrt{x^2 + y^2} = \sqrt{(-3)^2 + (-4)^2} = \sqrt{9 + 16} = \sqrt{25} = 5.$$

Now that we know $x$, $y$, and $r$, we can find the six trigonometric functions of $\theta$.

$$\sin\theta = \frac{y}{r} = \frac{-4}{5} = -\frac{4}{5}, \quad \cos\theta = \frac{x}{r} = \frac{-3}{5} = -\frac{3}{5}, \quad \tan\theta = \frac{y}{x} = \frac{-4}{-3} = \frac{4}{3}$$

$$\csc\theta = \frac{r}{y} = \frac{5}{-4} = -\frac{5}{4}, \quad \sec\theta = \frac{r}{x} = \frac{5}{-3} = -\frac{5}{3}, \quad \cot\theta = \frac{x}{y} = \frac{-3}{-4} = \frac{3}{4}$$

These ratios are the reciprocals of those shown directly above.

**Check Point 1** Let $P = (4, -3)$ be a point on the terminal side of $\theta$. Find each of the six trigonometric functions of $\theta$.

How do we find the values of the trigonometric functions for a quadrantal angle? First, draw the angle in standard position. Second, choose a point $P$ on the angle's terminal side. The trigonometric function values of $\theta$ depend only on the size of $\theta$ and not on the distance of point $P$ from the origin. Thus, we choose a point that is 1 unit from the origin. Finally, apply the definition of the appropriate trigonometric function.

## EXAMPLE 2 Trigonometric Functions of Quadrantal Angles

Evaluate, if possible, the sine function and the tangent function at the following four quadrantal angles:

**a.** $\theta = 0° = 0$ **b.** $\theta = 90° = \frac{\pi}{2}$ **c.** $\theta = 180° = \pi$ **d.** $\theta = 270° = \frac{3\pi}{2}$

**Solution**

**a.** If $\theta = 0° = 0$ radians, then the terminal side of the angle is on the positive $x$-axis. Let us select the point $P = (1, 0)$ with $x = 1$ and $y = 0$. This point is 1 unit from the origin, so $r = 1$. Now that we know $x$, $y$, and $r$, we can apply the definitions of the sine and tangent functions.

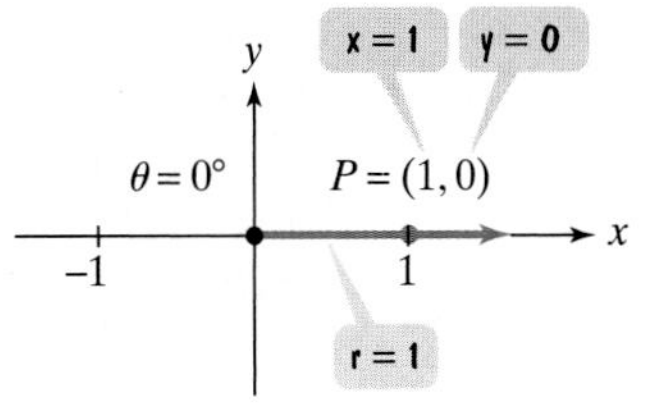


$$\sin 0° = \sin 0 = \frac{y}{r} = \frac{0}{1} = 0$$

$$\tan 0° = \tan 0 = \frac{y}{x} = \frac{0}{1} = 0$$

**b.** If $\theta = 90° = \frac{\pi}{2}$ radians, then the terminal side of the angle is on the positive $y$-axis. Let us select the point $P = (0, 1)$ with $x = 0$ and $y = 1$. This point is 1 unit from the origin, so $r = 1$. Now that we know $x$, $y$, and $r$, we can apply the definitions of the sine and tangent functions.

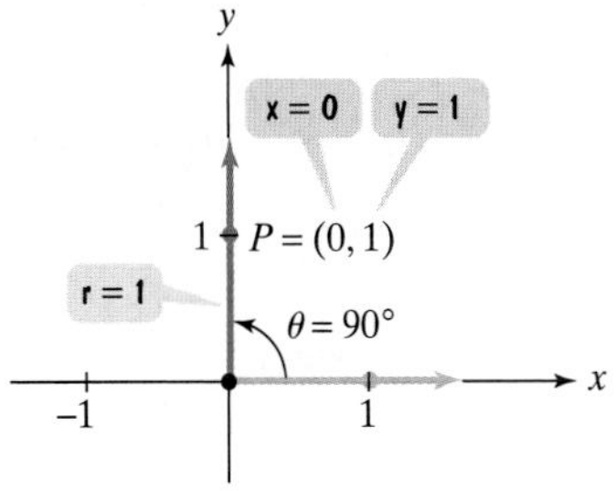


$$\sin 90° = \sin\frac{\pi}{2} = \frac{y}{r} = \frac{1}{1} = 1$$

$$\tan 90° = \tan\frac{\pi}{2} = \frac{y}{x} = \cancel{\frac{1}{0}}$$

Because division by 0 is undefined, tan 90° is undefined.

**c.** If $\theta = 180° = \pi$ radians, then the terminal side of the angle is on the negative $x$-axis. Let us select the point $P = (-1, 0)$ with $x = -1$ and $y = 0$. This point is 1 unit from the origin, so $r = 1$. Now that we know $x$, $y$, and $r$, we can apply the definitions of the sine and tangent functions.

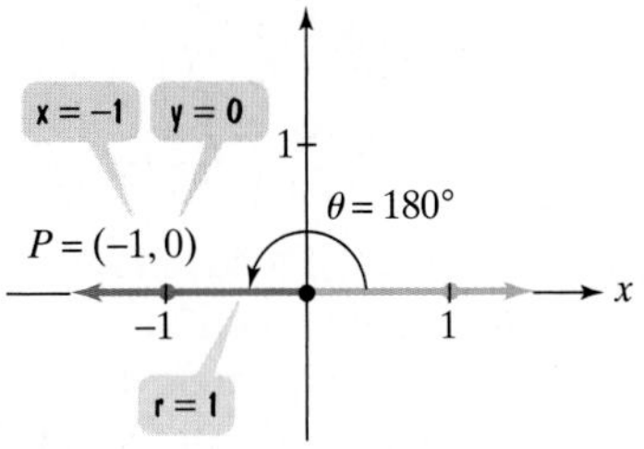


$$\sin 180° = \sin \pi = \frac{y}{r} = \frac{0}{1} = 0$$

$$\tan 180° = \tan \pi = \frac{y}{x} = \frac{0}{-1} = 0$$

**Discovery**

Try finding tan 90° and tan 270° with your calculator. Describe what occurs.

**d.** If $\theta = 270° = \frac{3\pi}{2}$ radians, then the terminal side of the angle is on the negative $y$-axis. Let us select the point $P = (0, -1)$ with $x = 0$ and $y = -1$. This point is 1 unit from the origin, so $r = 1$. Now that we know $x$, $y$, and $r$, we can apply the definitions of the sine and tangent functions.

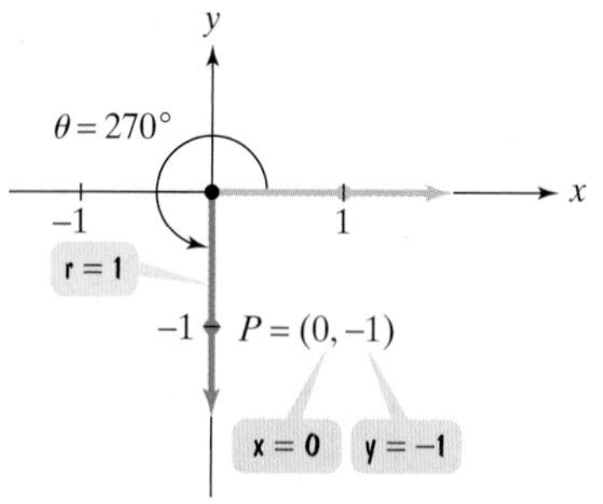


$$\sin 270° = \sin\frac{3\pi}{2} = \frac{y}{r} = \frac{-1}{1} = -1$$

$$\tan 270° = \tan\frac{3\pi}{2} = \frac{y}{x} = \frac{-1}{0}$$

Because division by 0 is undefined, tan 270° is undefined.

**Check Point 2** Evaluate, if possible, the cosine function and the cosecant function at the following four quadrantal angles:

**a.** $\theta = 0° = 0$ **b.** $\theta = 90° = \frac{\pi}{2}$

**c.** $\theta = 180° = \pi$ **d.** $\theta = 270° = \frac{3\pi}{2}$

**2** Use the signs of the trigonometric functions.

## The Signs of the Trigonometric Functions

In Example 2, we evaluated trigonometric functions of quadrantal angles. However, we will now return to the trigonometric functions of nonquadrantal angles. **If $\theta$ is not a quadrantal angle, the sign of a trigonometric function depends on the quadrant in which $\theta$ lies.** In all four quadrants, $r$ is positive. However, $x$ and $y$ can be positive or negative. For example, if $\theta$ lies in quadrant II, $x$ is negative and $y$ is positive. Thus, the only positive ratios in this quadrant are $\frac{y}{r}$ and its reciprocal, $\frac{r}{y}$. These ratios are the function values for the sine and cosecant, respectively. In short, if $\theta$ lies in quadrant II, $\sin\theta$ and $\csc\theta$ are positive. The other four trigonometric functions are negative.

Figure 5.34 summarizes the signs of the trigonometric functions. If $\theta$ lies in quadrant I, all six functions are positive. If $\theta$ lies in quadrant II, only $\sin\theta$ and $\csc\theta$ are positive. If $\theta$ lies in quadrant III, only $\tan\theta$ and $\cot\theta$ are positive. Finally, if $\theta$ lies in quadrant IV, only $\cos\theta$ and $\sec\theta$ are positive. Observe that the positive functions in each quadrant occur in reciprocal pairs.

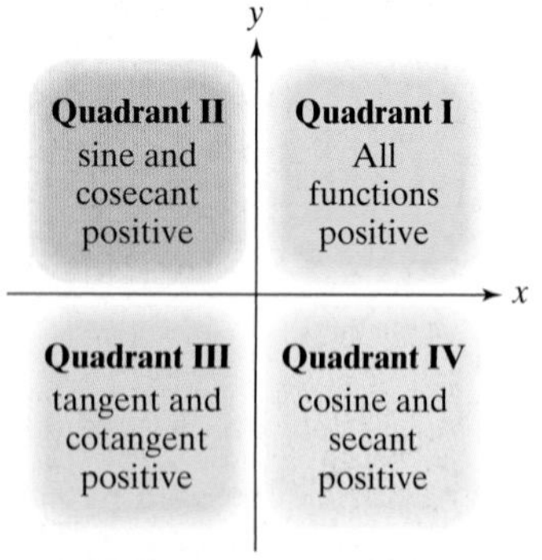


**Figure 5.34** The signs of the trigonometric functions

## EXAMPLE 3 Finding the Quadrant in Which an Angle Lies

If $\tan\theta < 0$ and $\cos\theta > 0$, name the quadrant in which angle $\theta$ lies.

**Solution** Because $\tan\theta < 0$, $\theta$ cannot lie in quadrant I; all the functions are positive in quadrant I. Furthermore, $\theta$ cannot lie in quadrant III; $\tan\theta$ is positive in quadrant III. Thus, with $\tan\theta < 0$, $\theta$ lies in quadrant II or quadrant IV. We are also given that $\cos\theta > 0$. Because quadrant IV is the only quadrant in which the cosine is positive and the tangent is negative, we conclude that $\theta$ lies in quadrant IV.

**Check Point 3** If $\sin\theta < 0$ and $\cos\theta < 0$, name the quadrant in which angle $\theta$ lies.

## EXAMPLE 4 Evaluating Trigonometric Functions

Given $\tan\theta = -\frac{2}{3}$ and $\cos\theta > 0$, find $\cos\theta$ and $\csc\theta$.

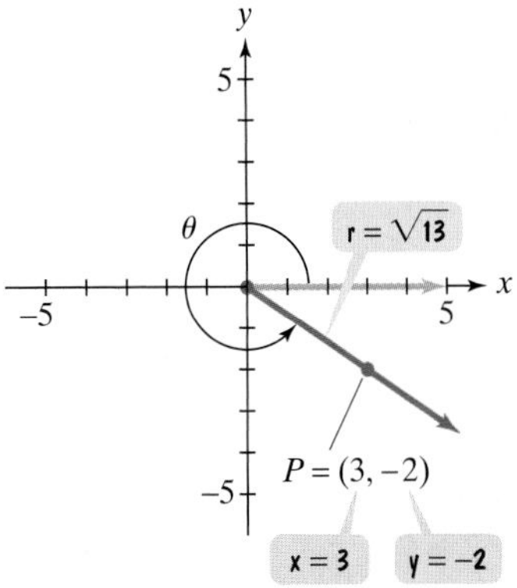


**Figure 5.35** $\tan\theta = -\frac{2}{3}$ and $\cos\theta > 0$

**Solution** Because the tangent is negative and the cosine is positive, $\theta$ lies in quadrant IV. This will help us to determine whether the negative sign in $\tan\theta = -\frac{2}{3}$ should be associated with the numerator or the denominator. Keep in mind that in quadrant IV, $x$ is positive and $y$ is negative. Thus,

In quadrant IV, y is negative.

$$\tan\theta = -\frac{2}{3} = \frac{y}{x} = \frac{-2}{3}$$

(See Figure 5.35). Thus, $x = 3$ and $y = -2$. Furthermore,

$$r = \sqrt{x^2 + y^2} = \sqrt{3^2 + (-2)^2} = \sqrt{9+4} = \sqrt{13}.$$

Now that we know $x$, $y$, and $r$, we can find $\cos\theta$ and $\csc\theta$.

$$\cos\theta = \frac{x}{r} = \frac{3}{\sqrt{13}} = \frac{3}{\sqrt{13}} \cdot \frac{\sqrt{13}}{\sqrt{13}} = \frac{3\sqrt{13}}{13} \qquad \csc\theta = \frac{r}{y} = \frac{\sqrt{13}}{-2} = -\frac{\sqrt{13}}{2}$$

**Check Point 4** Given $\tan\theta = -\frac{1}{3}$ and $\cos\theta < 0$, find $\sin\theta$ and $\sec\theta$.

**3** Find reference angles.

## Reference Angles

We will often evaluate trigonometric functions of positive angles greater than 90° and all negative angles by making use of a positive acute angle. This positive acute angle is called a *reference angle*.

**Definition of a Reference Angle**

Let $\theta$ be a nonacute angle in standard position that lies in a quadrant. Its **reference angle** is the positive acute angle $\theta'$ formed by the terminal side of $\theta$ and the $x$-axis.

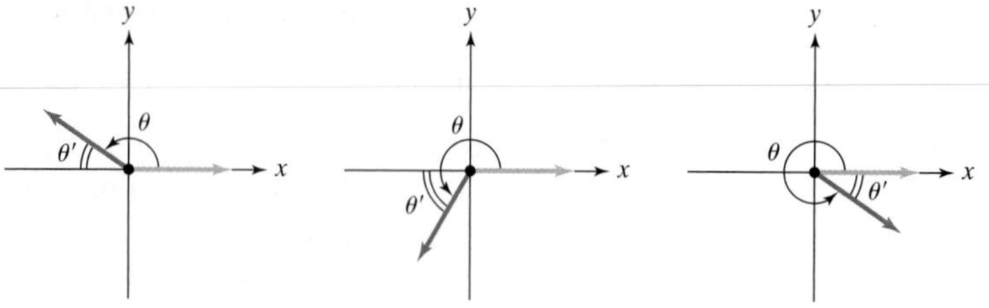


**Figure 5.36** Reference angles for positive angles in quadrants II, III, and IV

If $90° < \theta < 180°$, then $\theta' = 180° - \theta$.

If $180° < \theta < 270°$, then $\theta' = \theta - 180°$.

If $270° < \theta < 360°$, then $\theta' = 360° - \theta$.

Figure 5.36 shows the reference angle for $\theta$ lying in quadrants II, III, and IV. Notice that the formula used to find $\theta$, the reference angle, varies according to the quadrant in which $\theta$ lies. You may find it easier to find the reference angle for a given angle by making a figure that shows the angle in standard position. The acute angle formed by the terminal side of this angle and the $x$-axis is the reference angle.

## EXAMPLE 5 Finding Reference Angles

Find the reference angle, $\theta'$, for each of the following angles:

**a.** $\theta = 345°$ **b.** $\theta = \dfrac{5\pi}{6}$ **c.** $\theta = -135°$ **d.** $\theta = 2.5$.

### Solution

**a.** A 345° angle in standard position is shown in Figure 5.37. Because 345° lies in quadrant IV, the reference angle is

$$\theta' = 360° - 345° = 15°.$$

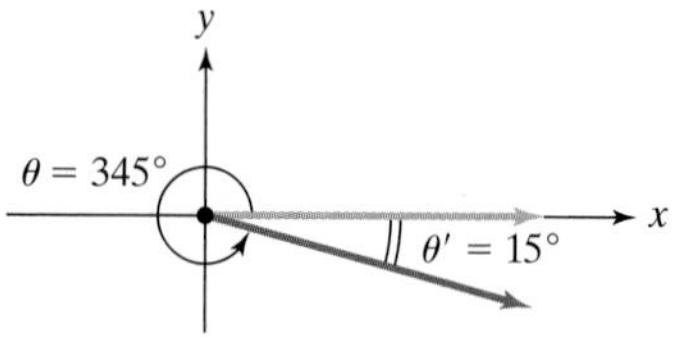


**Figure 5.37**

**b.** Because $\dfrac{5\pi}{6}$ lies between $\dfrac{\pi}{2} = \dfrac{3\pi}{6}$ and $\pi = \dfrac{6\pi}{6}$, $\theta = \dfrac{5\pi}{6}$ lies in quadrant II. The angle is shown in Figure 5.38. The reference angle is

$$\theta' = \pi - \frac{5\pi}{6} = \frac{6\pi}{6} - \frac{5\pi}{6} = \frac{\pi}{6}.$$

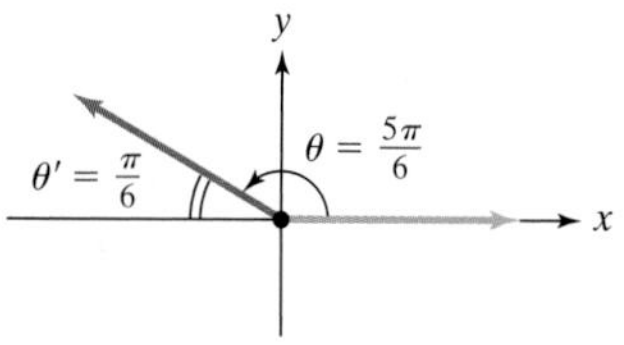


**Figure 5.38**

**c.** A $-135°$ angle in standard position is shown in Figure 5.39. The figure indicates that the positive acute angle formed by the terminal side of $\theta$ and the $x$-axis is 45°. The reference angle is

$$\theta' = 45°.$$

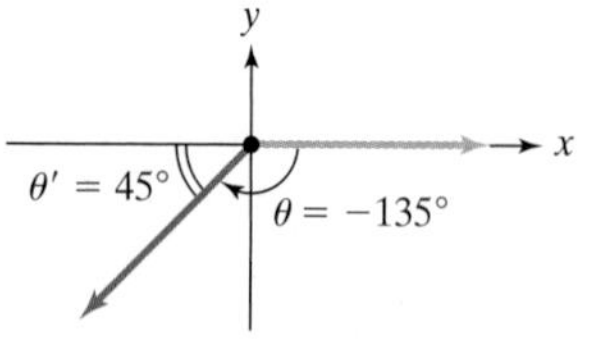


**Figure 5.39**

**d.** The angle $\theta = 2.5$ lies between $\dfrac{\pi}{2} \approx 1.57$ and $\pi \approx 3.14$. This means that $\theta = 2.5$ is in quadrant II, shown in Figure 5.40. The reference angle is

$$\theta' = \pi - 2.5 \approx 0.64.$$

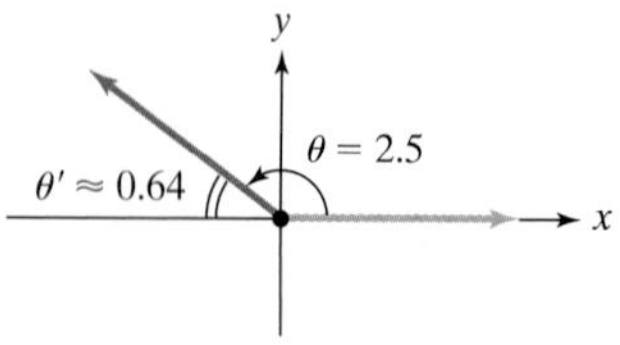


**Figure 5.40**

**Check Point 5**

Find the reference angle, $\theta'$, for each of the following angles:

**a.** $\theta = 210°$ **b.** $\theta = \dfrac{7\pi}{4}$ **c.** $\theta = -240°$ **d.** $\theta = 3.6$

**4** Use reference angles to evaluate trigonometric functions.

The way that reference angles are defined makes them useful in evaluating trigonometric functions.

**Using Reference Angles to Evaluate Trigonometric Functions**

The values of the trigonometric functions of a given angle, $\theta$, are the same as the values of the trigonometric functions of the reference angle, $\theta'$, except possibly for the sign. A function value of the acute angle, $\theta'$, is always positive. However, the same function value for $\theta$ may be positive or negative.

For example, we can use a reference angle, $\theta'$, to obtain an exact value for $\tan 120°$. The reference angle for $\theta = 120°$ is $\theta' = 180° - 120° = 60°$. We know the exact value for the tangent function of the reference angle: $\tan 60° = \sqrt{3}$. We also know that the value of a trigonometric function for a given angle, $\theta$, is the same as that for its reference angle, $\theta'$, except possibly for the sign. Thus, we can conclude that $\tan 120°$ equals $-\sqrt{3}$ or $\sqrt{3}$.

What sign should we attach to $\sqrt{3}$? A 120° angle lies in quadrant II, where sine and cosecant are positive. Thus, the tangent function is negative for a 120° angle. Therefore,

Prefix by a negative sign to show tangent is negative in quadrant II.

$$\tan 120° = -\tan 60° = -\sqrt{3}.$$

The reference angle for 120° is 60°.

In the previous section, we used two right triangles to find exact trigonometric values of 30°, 45°, and 60°. Using a procedure similar to finding $\tan 120°$, we can now find the function values of all angles for which 30°, 45°, or 60° are reference angles.

**A Procedure for Using Reference Angles to Evaluate Trigonometric Functions**

The value of a trigonometric function of any angle $\theta$ is found as follows:

1. Find the associated reference angle, $\theta'$, and the function value for $\theta'$.
2. Use the quadrant in which $\theta$ lies to prefix the appropriate sign to the function value in step 1.

**Discovery**

Draw the two right triangles involving 30°, 45°, and 60°. Indicate the length of each side. Use these lengths to verify the function values for the reference angles in the solution to Example 6.

## EXAMPLE 6 Using Reference Angles to Evaluate Trigonometric Functions

Use reference angles to find the exact value of each of the following trigonometric functions.

**a.** $\sin 135°$ **b.** $\cos \frac{4\pi}{3}$ **c.** $\cot\left(-\frac{\pi}{3}\right)$

**Solution**

**a.** We use our two-step procedure to find $\sin 135°$.

**Step 1 Find the reference angle, $\theta'$, and $\sin \theta'$.** Figure 5.41 shows 135° lies in quadrant II. The reference angle is

$$\theta' = 180° - 135° = 45°.$$

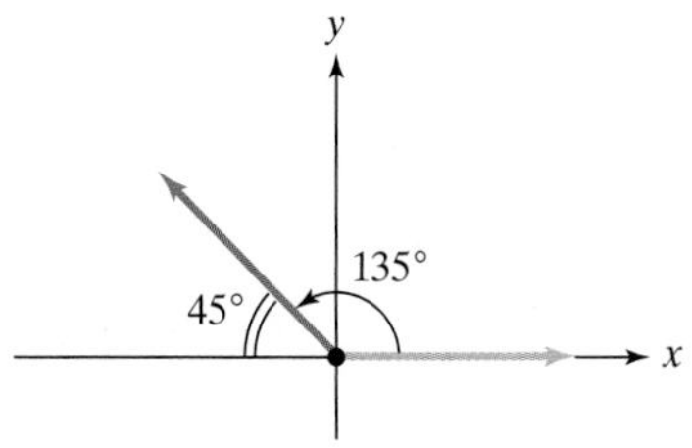


**Figure 5.41** Reference angle for 135°

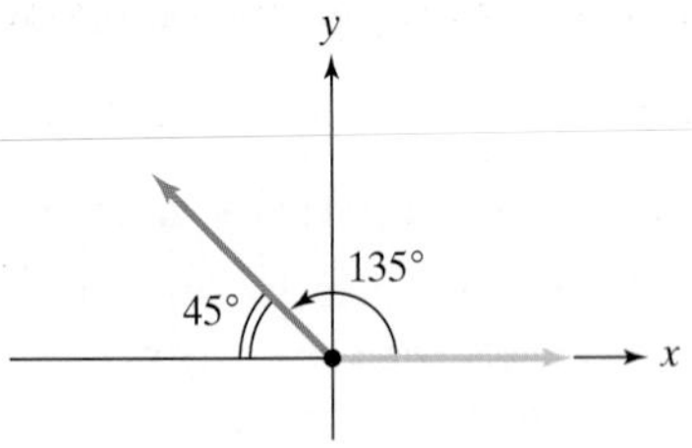


**Figure 5.41,** repeated

The function value for the reference angle is $\sin 45° = \frac{\sqrt{2}}{2}$.

**Step 2 Use the quadrant in which $\theta$ lies to prefix the appropriate sign to the function value in step 1.** The angle $\theta = 135°$ lies in quadrant II. Because the sine is positive in quadrant II, we put a + sign before the function value of the reference angle. Thus,

The sine is positive in quadrant II.

$$\sin 135° = +\sin 45° = \frac{\sqrt{2}}{2}.$$

The reference angle for 135° is 45°.

**b.** We use our two-step procedure to find $\cos \frac{4\pi}{3}$.

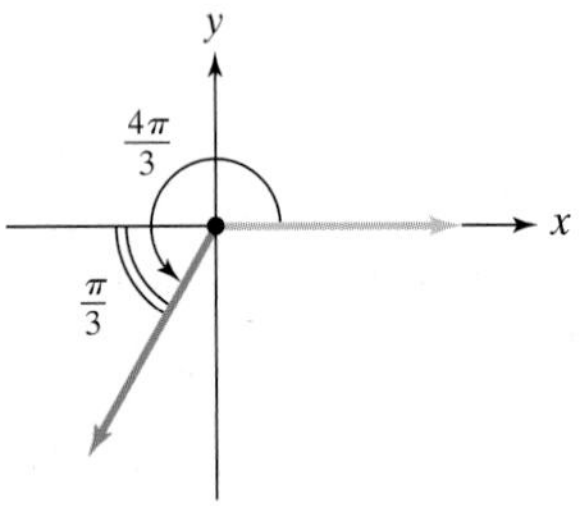


**Figure 5.42** Reference angle for $\frac{4\pi}{3}$

**Step 1 Find the reference angle, $\theta'$, and $\cos \theta'$.** Figure 5.42 shows that $\theta = \frac{4\pi}{3}$ lies in quadrant III. The reference angle is

$$\theta' = \frac{4\pi}{3} - \pi = \frac{4\pi}{3} - \frac{3\pi}{3} = \frac{\pi}{3}.$$

The function value for the reference angle is

$$\cos \frac{\pi}{3} = \frac{1}{2}.$$

**Step 2 Use the quadrant in which $\theta$ lies to prefix the appropriate sign to the function value in step 1.** The angle $\theta = \frac{4\pi}{3}$ lies in quadrant III. Because only the tangent and cotangent are positive in quadrant III, the cosine is negative in this quadrant. We put a − sign before the function value of the reference angle. Thus,

The cosine is negative in quadrant III.

$$\cos \frac{4\pi}{3} = -\cos \frac{\pi}{3} = -\frac{1}{2}.$$

The reference angle for $\frac{4\pi}{3}$ is $\frac{\pi}{3}$.

**c.** We use our two-step procedure to find $\cot\left(-\frac{\pi}{3}\right)$.

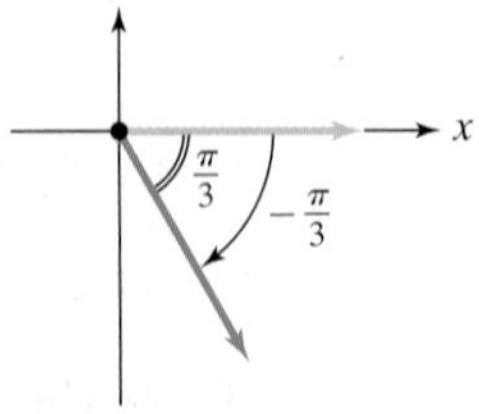


**Figure 5.43** Reference angle for $-\frac{\pi}{3}$

**Step 1 Find the reference angle, $\theta'$, and $\cot \theta'$.** Figure 5.43 shows that $\theta = -\frac{\pi}{3}$ lies in quadrant IV. The reference angle is $\theta' = \frac{\pi}{3}$. The function value for the reference angle is $\cot \frac{\pi}{3} = \frac{\sqrt{3}}{3}$.

**Step 2 Use the quadrant in which $\theta$ lies to prefix the appropriate sign to the function value in step 1.** The angle $\theta = -\frac{\pi}{3}$ lies in quadrant IV. Because only the cosine and secant are positive in quadrant IV, the cotangent is negative in this quadrant. We put a – sign before the function value of the reference angle. Thus,

The cotangent is negative in quadrant IV.

$$\cot\left(-\frac{\pi}{3}\right) = -\cot\frac{\pi}{3} = -\frac{\sqrt{3}}{3}.$$

The reference angle for $-\frac{\pi}{3}$ is $\frac{\pi}{3}$.

**Check Point 6** Use reference angles to find the exact value of the following trigonometric functions.

**a.** $\sin 300°$ **b.** $\tan\frac{5\pi}{4}$ **c.** $\sec\left(-\frac{\pi}{6}\right)$

## EXERCISE SET 5.4

### Practice Exercises

*In Exercises 1–8, a point on the terminal side of angle $\theta$ is given. Find the exact value of each of the six trigonometric functions of $\theta$.*

**1.** $(-4, 3)$ **2.** $(-12, 5)$ **3.** $(2, 3)$ **4.** $(3, 7)$
**5.** $(3, -3)$ **6.** $(5, -5)$ **7.** $(-2, -5)$ **8.** $(-1, -3)$

*In Exercises 9–16, evaluate the trigonometric function at the quadrantal angle, or state that the expression is undefined.*

**9.** $\cos\pi$ **10.** $\tan\pi$ **11.** $\sec\pi$ **12.** $\csc\pi$
**13.** $\tan\frac{3\pi}{2}$ **14.** $\cos\frac{3\pi}{2}$ **15.** $\cot\frac{\pi}{2}$ **16.** $\tan\frac{\pi}{2}$

*In Exercises 17–22, let $\theta$ be an angle in standard position. Name the quadrant in which $\theta$ lies.*

**17.** $\sin\theta > 0, \quad \cos\theta > 0$ **18.** $\sin\theta < 0, \quad \cos\theta > 0$
**19.** $\sin\theta < 0, \quad \cos\theta < 0$ **20.** $\tan\theta < 0, \quad \sin\theta < 0$
**21.** $\tan\theta < 0, \quad \cos\theta < 0$ **22.** $\cot\theta > 0, \quad \sec\theta < 0$

*In Exercises 23–34, find the exact value of each of the remaining trigonometric functions of $\theta$.*

**23.** $\cos\theta = -\frac{3}{5}$, $\theta$ in quadrant III
**24.** $\sin\theta = -\frac{12}{13}$, $\theta$ in quadrant III
**25.** $\sin\theta = \frac{5}{13}$, $\theta$ in quadrant II
**26.** $\cos\theta = \frac{4}{5}$, $\theta$ in quadrant IV
**27.** $\cos\theta = \frac{8}{17}$, $270° < \theta < 360°$
**28.** $\cos\theta = \frac{1}{3}$, $270° < \theta < 360°$
**29.** $\tan\theta = -\frac{2}{3}$, $\sin\theta > 0$ **30.** $\tan\theta = -\frac{1}{3}$, $\sin\theta > 0$
**31.** $\tan\theta = \frac{4}{3}$, $\cos\theta < 0$ **32.** $\tan\theta = \frac{5}{12}$, $\cos\theta < 0$
**33.** $\sec\theta = -3$, $\tan\theta > 0$ **34.** $\csc\theta = -4$, $\tan\theta > 0$

*In Exercises 35–50, find the reference angle for each angle.*

**35.** $160°$ **36.** $170°$ **37.** $205°$ **38.** $210°$
**39.** $355°$ **40.** $351°$ **41.** $\frac{7\pi}{4}$ **42.** $\frac{5\pi}{4}$
**43.** $\frac{5\pi}{6}$ **44.** $\frac{5\pi}{7}$ **45.** $-150°$ **46.** $-250°$
**47.** $-335°$ **48.** $-359°$ **49.** $4.7$ **50.** $5.5$

*In Exercises 51–66, use reference angles to find the exact value of each expression. Do not use a calculator.*

**51.** $\cos 225°$ **52.** $\sin 300°$ **53.** $\tan 210°$ **54.** $\sec 240°$
**55.** $\tan 420°$ **56.** $\tan 405°$ **57.** $\sin\frac{2\pi}{3}$ **58.** $\cos\frac{3\pi}{4}$
**59.** $\csc\frac{7\pi}{6}$ **60.** $\cot\frac{7\pi}{4}$ **61.** $\tan\frac{9\pi}{4}$ **62.** $\tan\frac{9\pi}{2}$
**63.** $\sin(-240°)$ **64.** $\sin(-225°)$
**65.** $\tan\left(-\frac{\pi}{4}\right)$ **66.** $\tan\left(-\frac{\pi}{6}\right)$

### Writing in Mathematics

**67.** If you are given a point on the terminal side of angle $\theta$, explain how to find $\sin\theta$.
**68.** Explain why $\tan 90°$ is undefined.
**69.** If $\cos\theta > 0$ and $\tan\theta < 0$, explain how to find the quadrant in which $\theta$ lies.
**70.** What is a reference angle? Give an example with your description.
**71.** Explain how reference angles are used to evaluate trigonometric functions. Give an example with your description.

# SECTION 5.5 *Graphs of Sine and Cosine Functions*

## Objectives

1. Understand the graph of $y = \sin x$.
2. Graph variations of $y = \sin x$.
3. Understand the graph of $y = \cos x$.
4. Graph variations of $y = \cos x$.
5. Use vertical shifts of sine and cosine curves.
6. Model periodic behavior.

Take a deep breath and relax. Many relaxation exercises involve slowing down our breathing. Some people suggest that the way we breathe affects every part of our lives. Did you know that graphs of trigonometric functions can be used to analyze the breathing cycle, which is our closest link to both life and death?

In this section, we use graphs of sine and cosine functions to visualize their properties. We use the traditional symbol $x$, rather than $\theta$ or $t$, to represent the independent variable. We use the symbol $y$ for the dependent variable, or the function's value at $x$. Thus, we will be graphing $y = \sin x$ and $y = \cos x$ in rectangular coordinates. In all graphs of trigonometric functions, the independent variable, $x$, is measured in radians.

**1** Understand the graph of $y = \sin x$.

## The Graph of $y = \sin x$

The trigonometric functions can be graphed in a rectangular coordinate system by plotting points whose coordinates belong to the function. Thus, we graph $y = \sin x$ by listing some points on the graph. Because the period of the sine function is $2\pi$, we will graph the function on the interval $[0, 2\pi]$. The rest of the graph is made up of repetitions of this portion.

Table 5.2 lists some values of $(x, y)$ on the graph of $y = \sin x, 0 \le x \le 2\pi$.

**Table 5.2 Values of $(x, y)$ on $y = \sin x$**

| $x$ | 0 | $\frac{\pi}{6}$ | $\frac{\pi}{3}$ | $\frac{\pi}{2}$ | $\frac{2\pi}{3}$ | $\frac{5\pi}{6}$ | $\pi$ | $\frac{7\pi}{6}$ | $\frac{4\pi}{3}$ | $\frac{3\pi}{2}$ | $\frac{5\pi}{3}$ | $\frac{11\pi}{6}$ | $2\pi$ |
|---|---|---|---|---|---|---|---|---|---|---|---|---|---|
| $y = \sin x$ | 0 | $\frac{1}{2}$ | $\frac{\sqrt{3}}{2}$ | 1 | $\frac{\sqrt{3}}{2}$ | $\frac{1}{2}$ | 0 | $-\frac{1}{2}$ | $-\frac{\sqrt{3}}{2}$ | $-1$ | $-\frac{\sqrt{3}}{2}$ | $-\frac{1}{2}$ | 0 |

As x increases from 0 to $\frac{\pi}{2}$, y increases from 0 to 1.

As x increases from $\frac{\pi}{2}$ to $\pi$, y decreases from 1 to 0.

As x increases from $\pi$ to $\frac{3\pi}{2}$, y decreases from 0 to $-1$.

As x increases from $\frac{3\pi}{2}$ to $2\pi$, y increases from $-1$ to 0.

In plotting the points obtained in Table 5.2, we will use the approximation $\frac{\sqrt{3}}{2} \approx 0.87$. Rather than approximating $\pi$, we will mark off units on the $x$-axis in terms of $\pi$. If we connect these points with a smooth curve, we obtain the graph shown in Figure 5.44 at the top of the next page. The figure shows one period of the graph of $y = \sin x$.

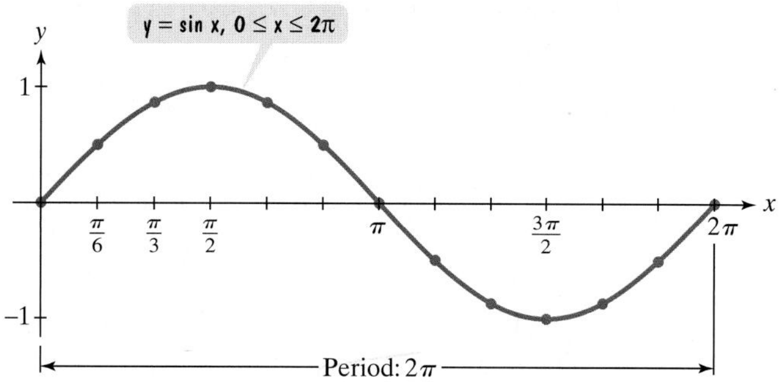


**Figure 5.44** One period of the graph of $y = \sin x$

We can obtain a more complete graph of $y = \sin x$ by continuing the portion shown in Figure 5.44 to the left and right. The graph of the sine function, called a **sine curve**, is shown in Figure 5.45. Any part of the graph that corresponds to one period $(2\pi)$ is one cycle of the graph of $y = \sin x$.

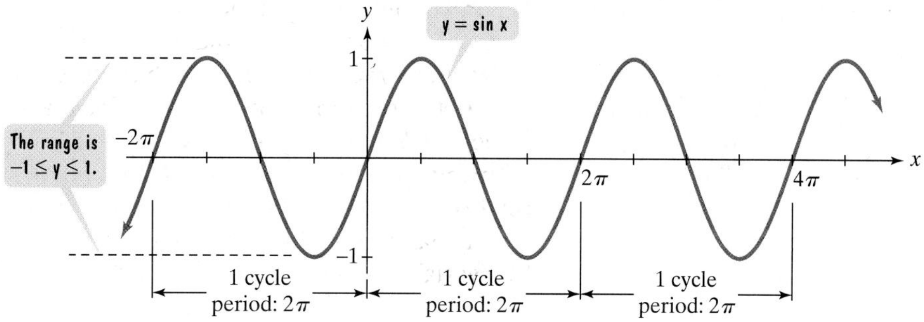


**Figure 5.45** The graph of $y = \sin x$

The graph of $y = \sin x$ allows us to visualize some of the properties of the sine function.

- The domain is the set of all real numbers. The graph extends indefinitely to the left and to the right with no gaps or holes.
- The range consists of all numbers between $-1$ and 1 inclusive. The graph never rises above 1 or falls below $-1$.
- The period is $2\pi$. The graph's pattern repeats in every interval of length $2\pi$.
- The function is an odd function: $\sin(-x) = -\sin x$. This can be seen by observing that the graph is symmetric with respect to the origin.

**2** Graph variations of $y = \sin x$.

## Graphing Variations of $y = \sin x$

To graph variations of $y = \sin x$ by hand, it is helpful to find $x$-intercepts, maximum points, and minimum points. One complete cycle of the sine curve includes three $x$-intercepts, one maximum point, and one minimum point. The graph of $y = \sin x$ has $x$-intercepts at the beginning, middle, and end of its full period, shown in Figure 5.46. The curve reaches its maximum point $\frac{1}{4}$ of the way through the period. It reaches its minimum point $\frac{3}{4}$ of the way through the period. Thus, key points in graphing sine functions are obtained by dividing the

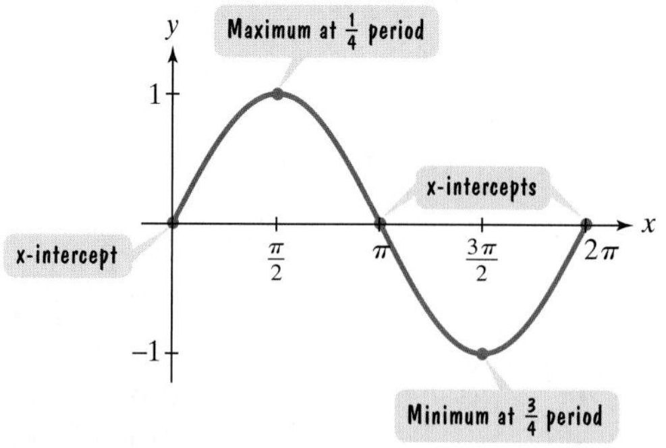


**Figure 5.46** Key points in graphing the sine function

period into four equal parts. The $x$-coordinates of the five key points are as follows:

$$x_1 = \text{value of } x \text{ where the cycle begins}$$

$$x_2 = x_1 + \frac{\text{period}}{4}$$

$$x_3 = x_2 + \frac{\text{period}}{4}$$

$$x_4 = x_3 + \frac{\text{period}}{4}$$

$$x_5 = x_4 + \frac{\text{period}}{4}.$$

Add "quarter-periods" to find successive value of x.

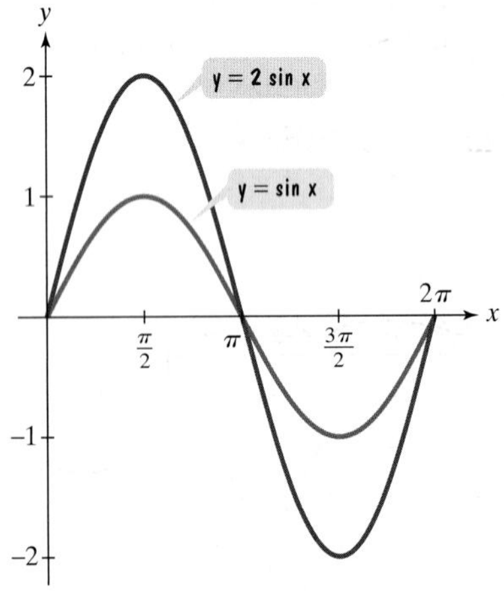


**Figure 5.47** Comparing the graphs of $y = \sin x$ and $y = 2\sin x$

The $y$-coordinates of the five key points are obtained by evaluating the given function at each of these values of $x$.

The graph of $y = \sin x$ forms the basis for graphing functions of the form

$$y = A\sin x.$$

For example, consider $y = 2\sin x$, in which $A = 2$. We can obtain the graph of $y = 2\sin x$ from that of $y = \sin x$ if we multiply each $y$-coordinate on the graph of $y = \sin x$ by 2. Figure 5.47 shows the graphs. The basic sine curve is *stretched* and ranges between $-2$ and 2 rather than between $-1$ and 1. However, both $y = \sin x$ and $y = 2\sin x$ have a period of $2\pi$.

In general, the graph of $y = A\sin x$ ranges between $-A$ and $A$. Thus, the range of the function is $-A \leq y \leq A$. If $A > 1$, the basic sine curve is *stretched*, as in Figure 5.47. If $A < 1$, the basic sine curve is *shrunk*. We call $|A|$ the **amplitude** of $y = A\sin x$. The maximum value of $y$ on the graph of $y = A\sin x$ is $|A|$, the amplitude.

**Graphing Variations of $y = \sin x$**

1. Identify the amplitude and the period.
2. Find the values of $x$ for the five key points—the three $x$-intercepts, the maximum point, and the minimum point. Start with the value of $x$ where the cycle begins and add quarter-periods—that is, $\frac{\text{period}}{4}$—to find successive values of $x$.
3. Find the values of $y$ for the five key points by evaluating the function at each value of $x$ from step 2.
4. Connect the five key points with a smooth curve and graph one complete cycle of the given function.
5. Extend the graph in step 4 to the left or right as desired.

## EXAMPLE 1 Graphing a Variation of $y = \sin x$

Determine the amplitude of $y = \frac{1}{2}\sin x$. Then graph $y = \sin x$ and $y = \frac{1}{2}\sin x$ for $0 \leq x \leq 2\pi$.

### Solution

**Step 1 Identify the amplitude and the period.** The equation $y = \frac{1}{2}\sin x$ is of the form $y = A\sin x$ with $A = \frac{1}{2}$. Thus, the amplitude is $|A| = \frac{1}{2}$. This means that the maximum value of $y$ is $\frac{1}{2}$ and the minimum value of $y$ is $-\frac{1}{2}$. The period for both $y = \frac{1}{2}\sin x$ and $y = \sin x$ is $2\pi$.

**Step 2 Find the values of $x$ for the five key points.** We need to find the three $x$-intercepts, the maximum point, and the minimum point on the interval $[0, 2\pi]$. To do so, we begin by dividing the period, $2\pi$, by 4.

$$\frac{\text{period}}{4} = \frac{2\pi}{4} = \frac{\pi}{2}$$

We start with the value of $x$ where the cycle begins: $x = 0$. Now we add quarter-periods, $\frac{\pi}{2}$, to generate $x$-values for each of the key points. The five $x$-values are

$$x = 0, \quad x = 0 + \frac{\pi}{2} = \frac{\pi}{2}, \quad x = \frac{\pi}{2} + \frac{\pi}{2} = \pi,$$

$$x = \pi + \frac{\pi}{2} = \frac{3\pi}{2}, \quad x = \frac{3\pi}{2} + \frac{\pi}{2} = 2\pi.$$

**Step 3 Find the values of $y$ for the five key points.** We evaluate the function at each value of $x$ from step 2.

| Value of $x$ | Value of $y$: $y = \frac{1}{2}\sin x$ | Coordinates of key point |
|---|---|---|
| 0 | $y = \frac{1}{2}\sin 0 = \frac{1}{2} \cdot 0 = 0$ | $(0, 0)$ |
| $\frac{\pi}{2}$ | $y = \frac{1}{2}\sin \frac{\pi}{2} = \frac{1}{2} \cdot 1 = \frac{1}{2}$ | $\left(\frac{\pi}{2}, \frac{1}{2}\right)$ maximum point |
| $\pi$ | $y = \frac{1}{2}\sin \pi = \frac{1}{2} \cdot 0 = 0$ | $(\pi, 0)$ |
| $\frac{3\pi}{2}$ | $y = \frac{1}{2}\sin \frac{3\pi}{2} = \frac{1}{2}(-1) = -\frac{1}{2}$ | $\left(\frac{3\pi}{2}, -\frac{1}{2}\right)$ minimum point |
| $2\pi$ | $y = \frac{1}{2}\sin 2\pi = \frac{1}{2} \cdot 0 = 0$ | $(2\pi, 0)$ |

There are $x$-intercepts at $0, \pi$, and $2\pi$. The maximum and minimum points are indicated by the voice balloons.

**Step 4 Connect the five key points with a smooth curve and graph one complete cycle of the given function.** The five key points for $y = \frac{1}{2}\sin x$ are shown in Figure 5.48. By connecting the points with a smooth curve, the figure shows one complete cycle of $y = \frac{1}{2}\sin x$. Also shown is the graph of $y = \sin x$. The graph of $y = \frac{1}{2}\sin x$ shrinks the graph of $y = \sin x$.

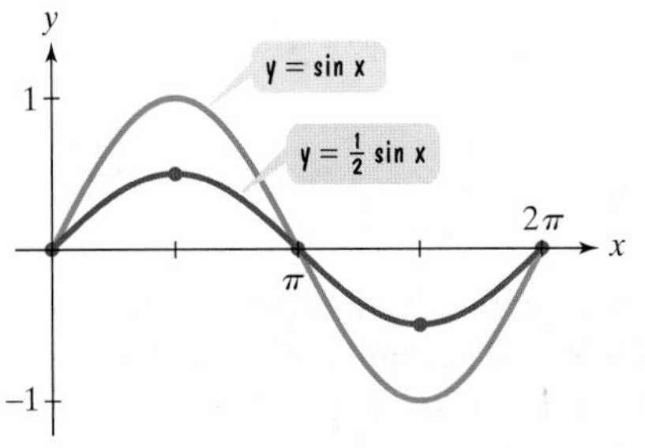


**Figure 5.48** The graphs of $y = \sin x$ and $y = \frac{1}{2}\sin x, 0 \le x \le 2\pi$

**Check Point 1** Determine the amplitude of $y = 3 \sin x$. Then graph $y = \sin x$ and $y = 3 \sin x$ for $0 \leq x \leq 2\pi$.

## EXAMPLE 2 Graphing a Variation of $y = \sin x$

Determine the amplitude of $y = -2 \sin x$. Then graph $y = \sin x$ and $y = -2 \sin x$ for $-\pi \leq x \leq 3\pi$.

### Solution

**Step 1 Identify the amplitude and the period.** The equation $y = -2 \sin x$ is of the form $y = A \sin x$ with $A = -2$. Thus, the amplitude is $|A| = |-2| = 2$. This means that the maximum value of $y$ is 2 and the minimum value of $y$ is $-2$. Both $y = \sin x$ and $y = -2 \sin x$ have a period of $2\pi$.

**Step 2 Find the $x$-values for the five key points.** Begin by dividing the period, $2\pi$, by 4.

$$\frac{\text{period}}{4} = \frac{2\pi}{4} = \frac{\pi}{2}$$

Start with the value of $x$ where the cycle begins: $x = 0$. Adding quarter-periods, $\frac{\pi}{2}$, the five $x$-values for the key points are

$$x = 0, \quad x = 0 + \frac{\pi}{2} = \frac{\pi}{2}, \quad x = \frac{\pi}{2} + \frac{\pi}{2} = \pi,$$

$$x = \pi + \frac{\pi}{2} = \frac{3\pi}{2}, \quad x = \frac{3\pi}{2} + \frac{\pi}{2} = 2\pi.$$

**Step 3 Find the values of $y$ for the five key points.** We evaluate the function at each value of $x$ from step 2.

| Value of $x$ | Value of $y$: $y = -2 \sin x$ | Coordinates of key point | |
|---|---|---|---|
| 0 | $y = -2 \sin 0 = -2 \cdot 0 = 0$ | $(0, 0)$ | |
| $\frac{\pi}{2}$ | $y = -2 \sin \frac{\pi}{2} = -2 \cdot 1 = -2$ | $\left(\frac{\pi}{2}, -2\right)$ | minimum point |
| $\pi$ | $y = -2 \sin \pi = -2 \cdot 0 = 0$ | $(\pi, 0)$ | |
| $\frac{3\pi}{2}$ | $y = -2 \sin \frac{3\pi}{2} = -2(-1) = 2$ | $\left(\frac{3\pi}{2}, 2\right)$ | maximum point |
| $2\pi$ | $y = -2 \sin 2\pi = -2 \cdot 0 = 0$ | $(2\pi, 0)$ | |

There are $x$-intercepts at 0, $\pi$, and $2\pi$. The minimum and maximum points are indicated by the voice balloons.

**Step 4 Connect the five key points with a smooth curve and graph one complete cycle of the given function.** The five key points for $y = -2 \sin x$ are shown in Figure 5.49. By connecting the points with a smooth curve, the red portion shows one complete cycle of $y = -2 \sin x$. Also shown in blue is one complete cycle of the graph of $y = \sin x$.

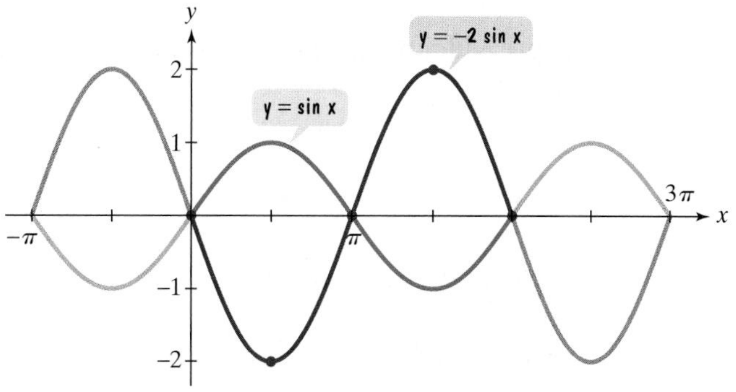


**Figure 5.49** The graphs of $y = \sin x$ and $y = -2\sin x, -\pi \le x \le 3\pi$

**Step 5 Extend the graph in step 4 to the left or right as desired.** The red and blue portions of the graphs in Figure 5.49 are from 0 to $2\pi$. In order to graph for $-\pi \le x \le 3\pi$, continue the pattern of each graph to the left and right. These extensions are shown in the lighter colors in Figure 5.49.

**Check Point 2** Determine the amplitude of $y = -\frac{1}{2}\sin x$. Then graph $y = \sin x$ and $y = -\frac{1}{2}\sin x$ for $-\pi \le x \le 3\pi$.

Now let us examine the graphs of functions of the form $y = A\sin Bx$, where $B$ is the coefficient of $x$. How do such graphs compare to those of functions of the form $y = A\sin x$? We know that $y = A\sin x$ completes one cycle from $x = 0$ to $x = 2\pi$. Thus, $y = A\sin Bx$ completes one cycle from $Bx = 0$ to $Bx = 2\pi$. Solve each of these equations for $x$.

$$Bx = 0 \qquad Bx = 2\pi$$

$$x = 0 \qquad x = \frac{2\pi}{B}$$ Divide both sides of each equation by $B$.

This means that $y = A\sin Bx$ completes one cycle from 0 to $\frac{2\pi}{B}$. The period is $\frac{2\pi}{B}$.

**Amplitudes and Periods**

The graph of $y = A\sin Bx$ has

$$\text{amplitude} = |A|$$

$$\text{period} = \frac{2\pi}{B}.$$

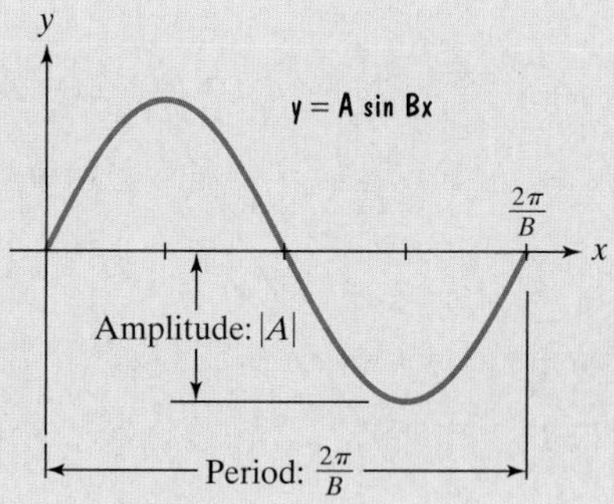

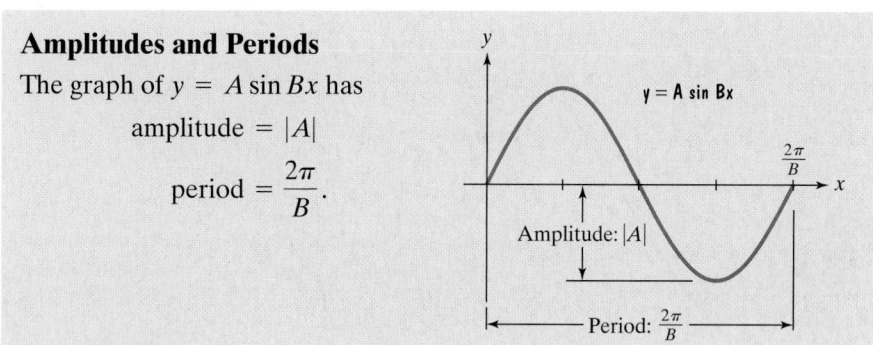

## EXAMPLE 3 Graphing a Function of the Form $y = A\sin Bx$

Determine the amplitude and period of $y = 3\sin 2x$. Then graph the function for $0 \le x \le 2\pi$.

**Solution**

**Step 1 Identify the amplitude and the period.** The equation $y = 3\sin 2x$ is of the form $y = A\sin Bx$ with $A = 3$ and $B = 2$.

$$\text{amplitude:} \quad |A| = |3| = 3$$

$$\text{period:} \quad \frac{2\pi}{B} = \frac{2\pi}{2} = \pi$$

The amplitude, 3, tells us that the maximum value of $y$ is 3 and the minimum value of $y$ is $-3$.

**Step 2 Find the $x$-values for the five key points.** Begin by dividing the period, $\pi$, by 4.

$$\frac{\text{period}}{4} = \frac{\pi}{4}$$

Start with the value of $x$ where the cycle begins: $x = 0$. Adding quarter-periods, $\frac{\pi}{4}$, the five $x$-values for the key points are

$$x = 0, \quad x = 0 + \frac{\pi}{4} = \frac{\pi}{4}, \quad x = \frac{\pi}{4} + \frac{\pi}{4} = \frac{\pi}{2},$$

$$x = \frac{\pi}{2} + \frac{\pi}{4} = \frac{3\pi}{4}, \quad x = \frac{3\pi}{4} + \frac{\pi}{4} = \pi.$$

**Step 3 Find the values of $y$ for the five key points.** We evaluate the function at each value of $x$ from step 2.

| Value of $x$ | Value of $y$: $y = 3\sin 2x$ | Coordinates of key point |
|---|---|---|
| 0 | $y = 3\sin 2 \cdot 0$ $= 3\sin 0 = 3 \cdot 0 = 0$ | $(0, 0)$ |
| $\frac{\pi}{4}$ | $y = 3\sin 2 \cdot \frac{\pi}{4}$ $= 3\sin\frac{\pi}{2} = 3 \cdot 1 = 3$ | $\left(\frac{\pi}{4}, 3\right)$ maximum point |
| $\frac{\pi}{2}$ | $y = 3\sin 2 \cdot \frac{\pi}{2}$ $= 3\sin\pi = 3 \cdot 0 = 0$ | $\left(\frac{\pi}{2}, 0\right)$ |
| $\frac{3\pi}{4}$ | $y = 3\sin 2 \cdot \frac{3\pi}{4}$ $= 3\sin\frac{3\pi}{2} = 3(-1) = -3$ | $\left(\frac{3\pi}{4}, -3\right)$ minimum point |
| $\pi$ | $y = 3\sin 2 \cdot \pi$ $= 3\sin 2\pi = 3 \cdot 0 = 0$ | $(\pi, 0)$ |

In the interval $[0, \pi]$, there are $x$-intercepts at $0, \frac{\pi}{2}$, and $\pi$. The maximum and minimum points are indicated by the voice balloons.

**Step 4 Connect the five key points with a smooth curve and graph one complete cycle of the given function.** The five key points for $y = 3\sin 2x$ are shown in

## Technology

The graph of $y = 3 \sin 2x$ in a $\left[0, 2\pi, \frac{\pi}{2}\right]$ by $[-4, 4, 1]$ viewing rectangle verifies our hand-drawn graph in Figure 5.50.

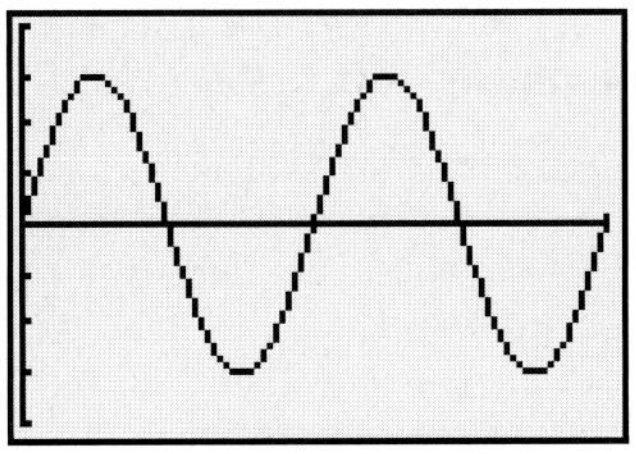

Figure 5.50. By connecting the points with a smooth curve, the blue portion shows one complete cycle of $y = 3 \sin 2x$ from 0 to $\pi$.

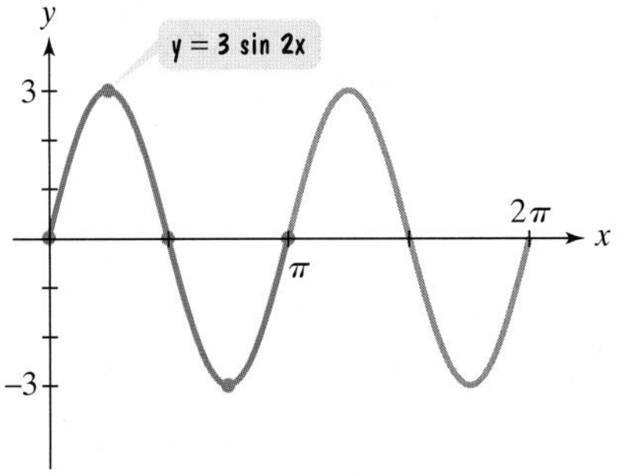


**Figure 5.50**

**Step 5 Extend the graph in step 4 to the left or right as desired.** The blue portion of the graph in Figure 5.50 is from 0 to $\pi$. In order to graph for $0 \le x \le 2\pi$, we continue this portion and extend the graph another full period to the right. This extension is shown in black in Figure 5.50.

**Check Point 3** Determine the amplitude and period of $y = 2 \sin \frac{1}{2}x$. Then graph the function for $0 \le x \le 8\pi$.

Now let us examine the graphs of functions of the form $y = A \sin(Bx - C)$. How do such graphs compare to those of functions of the form $y = A \sin Bx$? In both cases, the amplitude is $|A|$ and the period is $\frac{2\pi}{B}$. One complete cycle occurs if $Bx - C$ increases from 0 to $2\pi$. This means that we can find an interval containing one cycle by solving the equations

$$Bx - C = 0 \quad \text{and} \quad Bx - C = 2\pi$$

$$Bx = C \qquad Bx = C + 2\pi \qquad \text{Add } C \text{ to both sides in each equation.}$$

$$x = \frac{C}{B} \qquad x = \frac{C}{B} + \frac{2\pi}{B}. \qquad \text{Divide both sides by } B \text{ in each equation.}$$

This is the x-coordinate on the left where the cycle begins.

This is the x-coordinate on the right where the cycle ends. $\frac{2\pi}{B}$ is the period.

The voice balloon on the left indicates that $y = A \sin(Bx - C)$ shifts the graph of $y = A \sin Bx$ horizontally by $\frac{C}{B}$. Thus, the number $\frac{C}{B}$ is the **phase shift** associated with the graph.

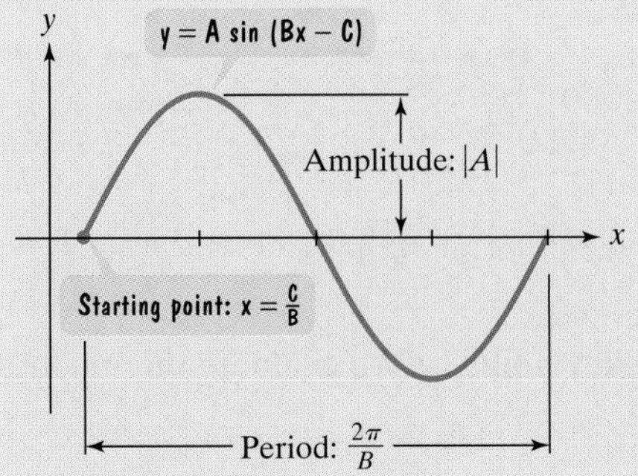


### The Graph of $y = A \sin(Bx - C)$

The graph of $y = A \sin(Bx - C)$ is obtained by horizontally shifting the graph of $y = A \sin Bx$ so that the starting point of the cycle is shifted from $x = 0$ to $x = \frac{C}{B}$. The number $\frac{C}{B}$ is called the **phase shift**.

$$\text{amplitude} = |A|$$

$$\text{period} = \frac{2\pi}{B}$$

## EXAMPLE 4 Graphing a Function of the Form $y = A\sin(Bx - C)$

Determine the amplitude, period, and phase shift of $y = 4\sin\left(2x - \frac{2\pi}{3}\right)$. Then graph one period of the function.

### Solution

**Step 1 Identify the amplitude, the period, and the phase shift.** We must first identify values for $A$, $B$, and $C$.

This equation is of the form $y = A\sin(Bx - C)$.

$$y = 4\sin\left(2x - \frac{2\pi}{3}\right)$$

Using the voice balloon, we see that $A = 4$, $B = 2$, and $C = \frac{2\pi}{3}$.

amplitude: $|A| = |4| = 4$ — The maximum $y$ is 4 and the minimum is $-4$.

period: $\frac{2\pi}{B} = \frac{2\pi}{2} = \pi$ — Each cycle is completed in $\pi$ radians.

phase shift: $\frac{C}{B} = \frac{\frac{2\pi}{3}}{2} = \frac{2\pi}{3} \cdot \frac{1}{2} = \frac{\pi}{3}$ — A cycle starts at $x = \frac{\pi}{3}$.

**Step 2 Find the $x$-values for the five key points.** Begin by dividing the period, $\pi$, by 4.

$$\frac{\text{period}}{4} = \frac{\pi}{4}$$

Start with the value of $x$ where the cycle begins: $x = \frac{\pi}{3}$. Adding quarter-periods, $\frac{\pi}{4}$, the five $x$-values for the key points are

$$x = \frac{\pi}{3}, \quad x = \frac{\pi}{3} + \frac{\pi}{4} = \frac{4\pi}{12} + \frac{3\pi}{12} = \frac{7\pi}{12},$$

$$x = \frac{7\pi}{12} + \frac{\pi}{4} = \frac{7\pi}{12} + \frac{3\pi}{12} = \frac{10\pi}{12} = \frac{5\pi}{6},$$

$$x = \frac{5\pi}{6} + \frac{\pi}{4} = \frac{10\pi}{12} + \frac{3\pi}{12} = \frac{13\pi}{12},$$

$$x = \frac{13\pi}{12} + \frac{\pi}{4} = \frac{13\pi}{12} + \frac{3\pi}{12} = \frac{16\pi}{12} = \frac{4\pi}{3}.$$

**Study Tip**

You can speed up the additions on the right by first writing the starting point and the quarter-period with a common denominator.

starting point

$$= \frac{\pi}{3} = \frac{4\pi}{12}$$

quarter-period

$$= \frac{\pi}{4} = \frac{3\pi}{12}$$

**Step 3 Find the values of $y$ for the five key points.** We evaluate the function at each value of $x$ from step 2.

| Value of $x$ | Value of $y$: $y = 4\sin\left(2x - \frac{2\pi}{3}\right)$ | Coordinates of key point |
|---|---|---|
| $\frac{\pi}{3}$ | $y = 4\sin\left(2 \cdot \frac{\pi}{3} - \frac{2\pi}{3}\right)$ $= 4\sin 0 = 4 \cdot 0 = 0$ | $\left(\frac{\pi}{3}, 0\right)$ |
| $\frac{7\pi}{12}$ | $y = 4\sin\left(2 \cdot \frac{7\pi}{12} - \frac{2\pi}{3}\right)$ $= 4\sin\left(\frac{7\pi}{6} - \frac{2\pi}{3}\right)$ $= 4\sin\frac{3\pi}{6} = 4\sin\frac{\pi}{2} = 4 \cdot 1 = 4$ | $\left(\frac{7\pi}{12}, 4\right)$ maximum point |
| $\frac{5\pi}{6}$ | $y = 4\sin\left(2 \cdot \frac{5\pi}{6} - \frac{2\pi}{3}\right)$ $= 4\sin\left(\frac{5\pi}{3} - \frac{2\pi}{3}\right)$ $= 4\sin\frac{3\pi}{3} = 4\sin\pi = 4 \cdot 0 = 0$ | $\left(\frac{5\pi}{6}, 0\right)$ |
| $\frac{13\pi}{12}$ | $y = 4\sin\left(2 \cdot \frac{13\pi}{12} - \frac{2\pi}{3}\right)$ $= 4\sin\left(\frac{13\pi}{6} - \frac{4\pi}{6}\right)$ $= 4\sin\frac{9\pi}{6} = 4\sin\frac{3\pi}{2} = 4(-1) = -4$ | $\left(\frac{13\pi}{12}, -4\right)$ minimum point |
| $\frac{4\pi}{3}$ | $y = 4\sin\left(2 \cdot \frac{4\pi}{3} - \frac{2\pi}{3}\right)$ $= 4\sin\frac{6\pi}{3} = 4\sin 2\pi = 4 \cdot 0 = 0$ | $\left(\frac{4\pi}{3}, 0\right)$ |

In the interval $\left[\frac{\pi}{3}, \frac{4\pi}{3}\right]$, there are $x$-intercepts at $\frac{\pi}{3}$, $\frac{5\pi}{6}$, and $\frac{4\pi}{3}$. The maximum and minimum points are indicated by the voice balloons.

**Step 4 Connect the five key points with a smooth curve and graph one complete cycle of the given function.** The key points and the graph of $y = 4\sin\left(2x - \frac{2\pi}{3}\right)$ are shown in Figure 5.51.

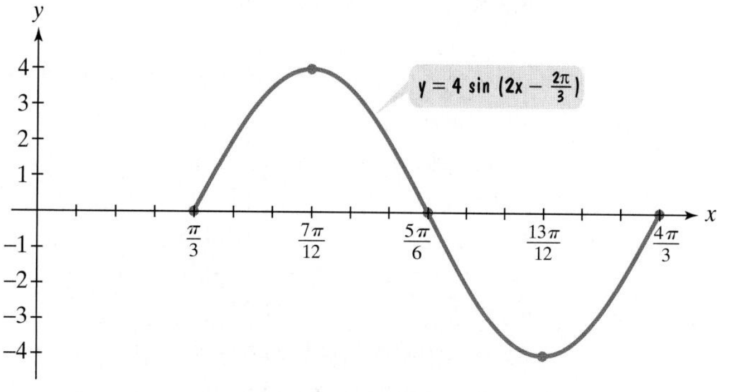


**Figure 5.51**

**Check Point 4** Determine the amplitude, period, and phase shift of $y = 3\sin\left(2x - \frac{\pi}{3}\right)$. Then graph one period of the function.

**3** Understand the graph of $y = \cos x$.

## The Graph of $y = \cos x$

We graph $y = \cos x$ by listing some points on the graph. Because the period of the cosine function is $2\pi$, we will concentrate on the graph of the basic cosine curve on the interval $[0, 2\pi]$. The rest of the graph is made up of repetitions of this portion. Table 5.3 lists some values of $(x, y)$ on the graph of $y = \cos x$.

**Table 5.3 Values of $(x, y)$ on $y = \cos x$**

| $x$ | $0$ | $\frac{\pi}{6}$ | $\frac{\pi}{3}$ | $\frac{\pi}{2}$ | $\frac{2\pi}{3}$ | $\frac{5\pi}{6}$ | $\pi$ | $\frac{7\pi}{6}$ | $\frac{4\pi}{3}$ | $\frac{3\pi}{2}$ | $\frac{5\pi}{3}$ | $\frac{11\pi}{6}$ | $2\pi$ |
|---|---|---|---|---|---|---|---|---|---|---|---|---|---|
| $y = \cos x$ | $1$ | $\frac{\sqrt{3}}{2}$ | $\frac{1}{2}$ | $0$ | $-\frac{1}{2}$ | $-\frac{\sqrt{3}}{2}$ | $-1$ | $-\frac{\sqrt{3}}{2}$ | $-\frac{1}{2}$ | $0$ | $\frac{1}{2}$ | $\frac{\sqrt{3}}{2}$ | $1$ |

As x increases from 0 to $\frac{\pi}{2}$, y decreases from 1 to 0.

As x increases from $\frac{\pi}{2}$ to $\pi$, y decreases from 0 to −1.

As x increases from $\pi$ to $\frac{3\pi}{2}$, y increases from −1 to 0.

As x increases from $\frac{3\pi}{2}$ to $2\pi$, y increases from 0 to 1.

Plotting the points in Table 5.3 and connecting them with a smooth curve, we obtain the graph shown in Figure 5.52. The portion of the graph in dark blue shows one complete period. We can obtain a more complete graph of $y = \cos x$ by extending this dark blue portion to the left and right.

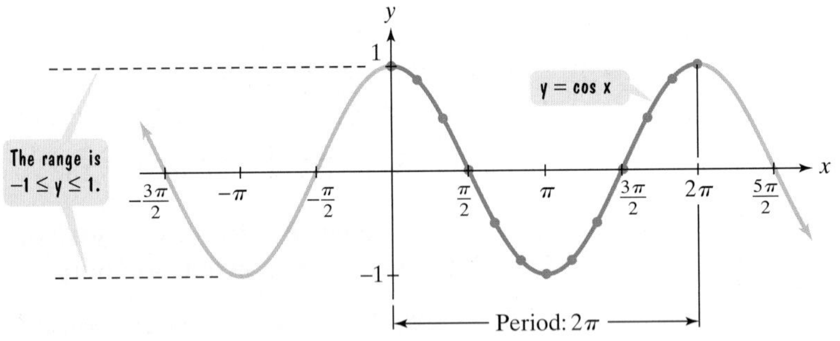


**Figure 5.52** The graph of $y = \cos x$

The graph of $y = \cos x$ allows us to visualize some of the properties of the cosine function.

- The domain is the set of all real numbers. The graph extends indefinitely to the left and to the right with no gaps or holes.
- The range consists of all numbers between $-1$ and $1$ inclusive. The graph never rises above 1 or falls below $-1$.
- The period is $2\pi$. The graph's pattern repeats in every interval of length $2\pi$.
- The function is an even function: $\cos(-x) = \cos x$. This can be seen by observing that the graph is symmetric with respect to the $y$-axis.

Take a second look at Figure 5.52. Can you see that the graph of $y = \cos x$ is the graph of $y = \sin x$ with a phase shift of $-\frac{\pi}{2}$ radians? If you trace along the curve from $x = -\frac{\pi}{2}$ to $x = \frac{3\pi}{2}$, you are tracing one complete cycle of the sine curve. This can be expressed as an identity:

$$\cos x = \sin\left(x + \frac{\pi}{2}\right).$$

Because of this similarity, the graphs of sine functions and cosine functions are called **sinusoidal graphs**.

**4** Graph variations of $y = \cos x$.

## Graphing Variations of $y = \cos x$

We use the same steps to graph variations of $y = \cos x$ as we did for graphing variations of $y = \sin x$. We will continue finding key points by dividing the period into four equal parts. Amplitudes, periods, and phase shifts play an important role when graphing by hand.

**The Graph of $y = A\cos Bx$**

The graph of $y = A\cos Bx$ has

$$\text{amplitude} = |A|$$

$$\text{period} = \frac{2\pi}{B}.$$

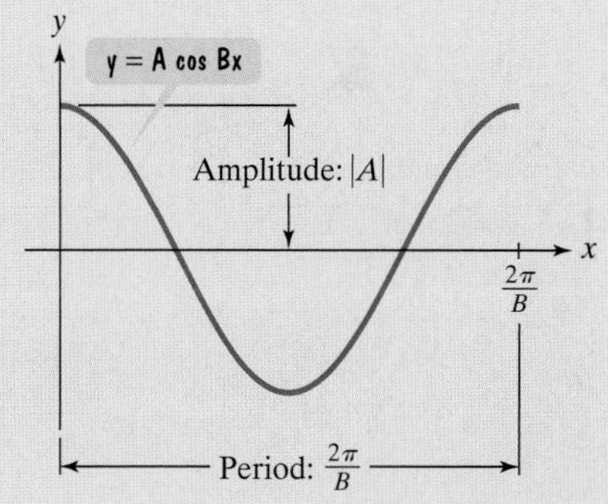


## EXAMPLE 5 Graphing a Function of the Form $y = A\cos Bx$

Determine the amplitude and period of $y = -3\cos\frac{\pi}{2}x$. Then graph the function for $-4 \le x \le 4$.

**Solution**

**Step 1 Identify the amplitude and the period.** The equation $y = -3\cos\frac{\pi}{2}x$ is of the form $y = A\cos Bx$ with $A = -3$ and $B = \frac{\pi}{2}$.

amplitude: $|A| = |-3| = 3$ — The maximum y is 3 and the minimum is −3.

period: $\frac{2\pi}{B} = \frac{2\pi}{\frac{\pi}{2}} = 2\pi \cdot \frac{2}{\pi} = 4$ — Each cycle is completed in 4 radians.

**Step 2 Find the $x$-values for the five key points.** Begin by dividing the period, 4, by 4.

$$\frac{\text{period}}{4} = \frac{4}{4} = 1$$

Start with the value of $x$ where the cycle begins: $x = 0$. Adding quarter-periods, 1, the five $x$-values for the key points are

$$x = 0, \quad x = 0 + 1 = 1, \quad x = 1 + 1 = 2, \quad x = 2 + 1 = 3, \quad x = 3 + 1 = 4$$

**Step 3 Find the values of $y$ for the five key points.** We evaluate the function at each value of $x$ from step 2.

| Value of $x$ | Value of $y$: $y = -3\cos\frac{\pi}{2}x$ | Coordinates of key point | |
|---|---|---|---|
| 0 | $y = -3\cos\frac{\pi}{2}\cdot 0$ $= -3\cos 0 = -3\cdot 1 = -3$ | $(0, -3)$ | minimum point |
| 1 | $y = -3\cos\frac{\pi}{2}\cdot 1$ $= -3\cos\frac{\pi}{2} = -3\cdot 0 = 0$ | $(1, 0)$ | |
| 2 | $y = -3\cos\frac{\pi}{2}\cdot 2$ $= -3\cos\pi = -3(-1) = 3$ | $(2, 3)$ | maximum point |
| 3 | $y = -3\cos\frac{\pi}{2}\cdot 3$ $= -3\cos\frac{3\pi}{2} = -3(0) = 0$ | $(3, 0)$ | |
| 4 | $y = -3\cos\frac{\pi}{2}\cdot 4$ $= -3\cos 2\pi = -3(1) = -3$ | $(4, -3)$ | minimum point |

In the interval $[0, 4]$, there are $x$-intercepts at 1 and 3. The minimum and maximum points are indicated by the voice balloons.

**Step 4 Connect the five key points with a smooth curve and graph one complete cycle of the given function.** The five key points for $y = -3\cos\frac{\pi}{2}x$ are shown in Figure 5.53. By connecting the points with a smooth curve, the blue portion shows one complete cycle of $y = -3\cos\frac{\pi}{2}x$ from 0 to 4.

## Technology

The graph of $y = -3\cos\frac{\pi}{2}x$ in a $[-4, 4, 1]$ by $[-4, 4, 1]$ viewing rectangle verifies our hand-drawn graph in Figure 5.53.

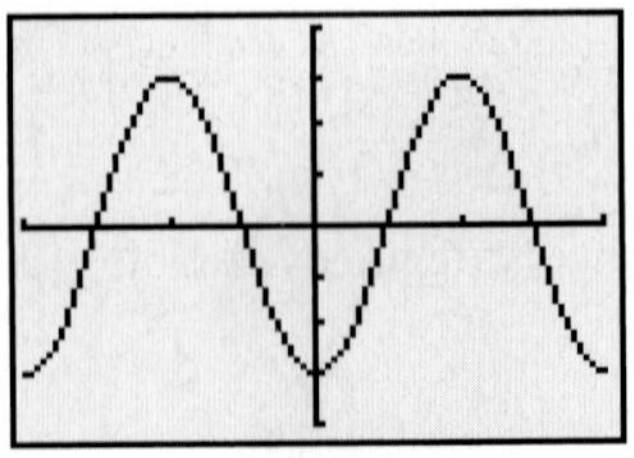

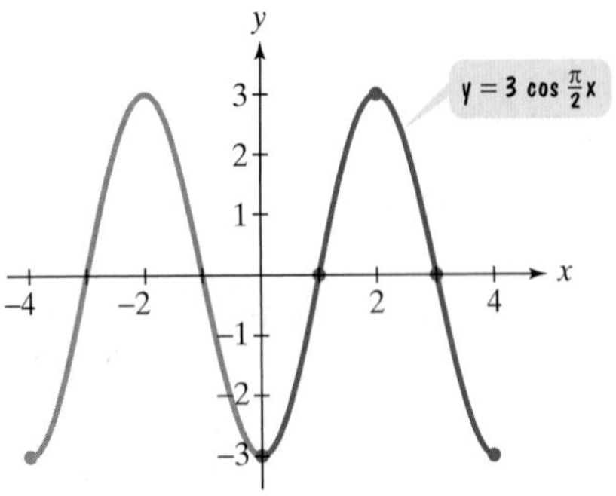


Figure 5.53

**Step 5 Extend the graph in step 4 to the left or right as desired.** The blue portion of the graph in Figure 5.53 is from 0 to 4. In order to graph for $-4 \leq x \leq 4$, we continue this portion and extend the graph another full period to the left. This extension is shown in black in Figure 5.53.

**Check Point 5** Determine the amplitude and period of $y = -4\cos\pi x$. Then graph the function for $-2 \leq x \leq 2$.

Finally, let us examine the graphs of functions of the form $y = A\cos(Bx - C)$. Graphs of these functions shift the graph of $y = A\cos Bx$ horizontally by $\frac{C}{B}$.

### The Graph of $y = A\cos(Bx - C)$

The graph of $y = A\cos(Bx - C)$ is obtained by horizontally shifting the graph of $y = A\cos Bx$ so that the starting point of the cycle is shifted from $x = 0$ to $x = \frac{C}{B}$. The number $\frac{C}{B}$ is called the **phase shift**.

$$\text{amplitude} = |A|$$

$$\text{period} = \frac{2\pi}{B}$$

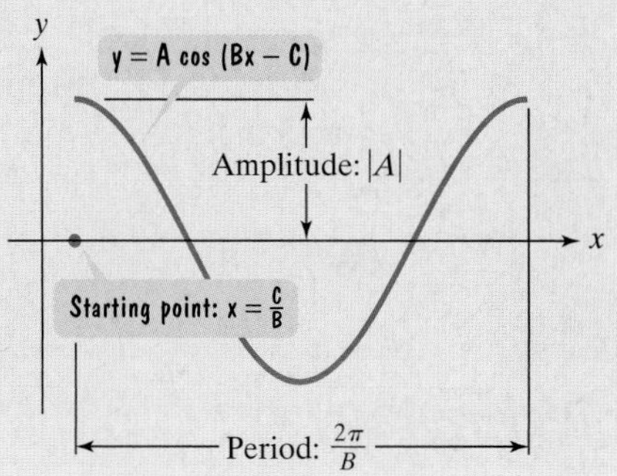


## EXAMPLE 6 Graphing a Function of the Form $y = A\cos(Bx - C)$

Determine the amplitude, period, and phase shift of $y = \frac{1}{2}\cos(4x + \pi)$. Then graph one period of the function.

**Solution**

**Step 1 Identify the amplitude, the period, and the phase shift.** We must first identify values for $A$, $B$, and $C$. To do this, we need to express the equation in the form $y = A\cos(Bx - C)$. Thus, we write $y = \frac{1}{2}\cos(4x + \pi)$ as $y = \frac{1}{2}\cos(4x - (-\pi))$. Now we can identify values for $A$, $B$, and $C$.

This equation is of the form $y = A\cos(Bx - C)$.

$$y = \frac{1}{2}\cos(4x - (-\pi))$$

Using the voice balloon, we see that $A = \frac{1}{2}$, $B = 4$, and $C = -\pi$.

$$\text{amplitude: } |A| = \left|\frac{1}{2}\right| = \frac{1}{2}$$

The maximum $y$ is $\frac{1}{2}$ and the minimum is $-\frac{1}{2}$.

$$\text{period: } \frac{2\pi}{B} = \frac{2\pi}{4} = \frac{\pi}{2}$$

Each cycle is completed in $\frac{\pi}{2}$ radians.

$$\text{phase shift: } \frac{C}{B} = -\frac{\pi}{4}$$

A cycle starts at $x = -\frac{\pi}{4}$.

**Step 2 Find the $x$-values for the five key points.** Begin by dividing the period, $\frac{\pi}{2}$, by 4.

$$\frac{\text{period}}{4} = \frac{\frac{\pi}{2}}{4} = \frac{\pi}{8}$$

Start with the value of $x$ where the cycle begins: $x = -\frac{\pi}{4}$. Adding quarter-periods, $\frac{\pi}{8}$, the five $x$-values for the key points are

$$x = -\frac{\pi}{4}, \quad x = -\frac{\pi}{4} + \frac{\pi}{8} = -\frac{2\pi}{8} + \frac{\pi}{8} = -\frac{\pi}{8}, \quad x = -\frac{\pi}{8} + \frac{\pi}{8} = 0,$$

$$x = 0 + \frac{\pi}{8} = \frac{\pi}{8}, \quad x = \frac{\pi}{8} + \frac{\pi}{8} = \frac{2\pi}{8} = \frac{\pi}{4}.$$

**Step 3 Find the values of $y$ for the five key points.** Take a few minutes and use your calculator to evaluate the function at each value of $x$ from step 2. Show that the key points are

$$\left(-\frac{\pi}{4}, \frac{1}{2}\right), \quad \left(-\frac{\pi}{8}, 0\right), \quad \left(0, -\frac{1}{2}\right), \quad \left(\frac{\pi}{8}, 0\right), \quad \text{and} \quad \left(\frac{\pi}{4}, \frac{1}{2}\right).$$

maximum point | x-intercept | minimum point | y-intercept | maximum point

**Step 4 Connect the five key points with a smooth curve and graph one complete cycle of the given function.** The key points and the graph of $y = \frac{1}{2}\cos(4x + \pi)$ are shown in Figure 5.54.

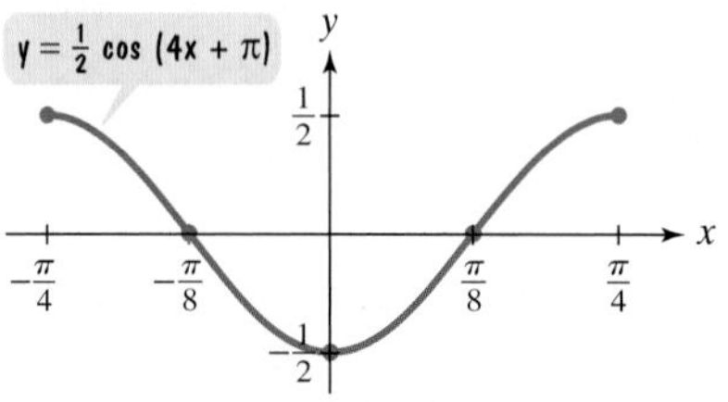


**Figure 5.54**

**Technology**

The graph of

$$y = \frac{1}{2}\cos(4x + \pi)$$

in a $\left[-\frac{\pi}{4}, \frac{\pi}{4}, \frac{\pi}{8}\right]$ by $[-1, 1, 1]$ viewing rectangle verifies our hand-drawn graph in Figure 5.54.

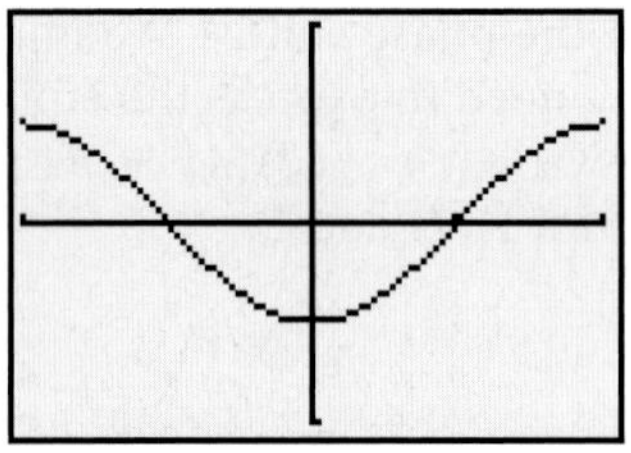

**Check Point 6** Determine the amplitude, period, and phase shift of $y = \frac{3}{2}\cos(2x + \pi)$. Then graph one period of the function.

**5** Use vertical shifts of sine and cosine curves.

## Vertical Shifts of Sinusoidal Graphs

We now look at sinusoidal graphs of

$$y = A\sin(Bx - C) + D \quad \text{and} \quad y = A\cos(Bx - C) + D.$$

The constant $D$ causes vertical shifts in the graphs of $y = A\sin(Bx - C)$ and $y = A\cos(Bx - C)$. If $D$ is positive, the shift is $D$ units upward. If $D$ is negative, the shift is $D$ units downward. These vertical shifts result in sinusoidal graphs oscillating about the horizontal line $y = D$ rather than about the $x$-axis. Thus, the maximum $y$ is $D + |A|$ and the minimum $y$ is $D - |A|$.

## EXAMPLE 7 A Vertical Shift

Graph one period of the function $y = \frac{1}{2}\cos x - 1$.

**Solution** The graph of $y = \frac{1}{2}\cos x - 1$ is the graph of $y = \frac{1}{2}\cos x$ shifted one unit downward. The period of $y = \frac{1}{2}\cos x$ is $2\pi$, which is also the period for the vertically shifted graph. The key points on the interval $[0, 2\pi]$ for $y = \frac{1}{2}\cos x - 1$ are found by first determining their $x$-coordinates. The quarter-period is $\frac{2\pi}{4}$ or $\frac{\pi}{2}$. The cycle begins at $x = 0$. As always, we add quarter-periods to generate $x$-values for each of the key points. The five $x$-values are

$$x = 0, \quad x = 0 + \frac{\pi}{2} = \frac{\pi}{2}, \quad x = \frac{\pi}{2} + \frac{\pi}{2} = \pi,$$

$$x = \pi + \frac{\pi}{2} = \frac{3\pi}{2}, \quad x = \frac{3\pi}{2} + \frac{\pi}{2} = 2\pi.$$

The values of $y$ for the five key points and their coordinates are determined as follows.

| **Value of $x$** | **Value of $y$: $y = \frac{1}{2}\cos x - 1$** | **Coordinates of key point** |
|---|---|---|
| $0$ | $y = \frac{1}{2}\cos 0 - 1$ $= \frac{1}{2}\cdot 1 - 1 = -\frac{1}{2}$ | $\left(0, -\frac{1}{2}\right)$ |
| $\frac{\pi}{2}$ | $y = \frac{1}{2}\cos\frac{\pi}{2} - 1$ $= \frac{1}{2}\cdot 0 - 1 = -1$ | $\left(\frac{\pi}{2}, -1\right)$ |
| $\pi$ | $y = \frac{1}{2}\cos\pi - 1$ $= \frac{1}{2}(-1) - 1 = -\frac{3}{2}$ | $\left(\pi, -\frac{3}{2}\right)$ |
| $\frac{3\pi}{2}$ | $y = \frac{1}{2}\cos\frac{3\pi}{2} - 1$ $= \frac{1}{2}\cdot 0 - 1 = -1$ | $\left(\frac{3\pi}{2}, -1\right)$ |
| $2\pi$ | $y = \frac{1}{2}\cos 2\pi - 1$ $= \frac{1}{2}\cdot 1 - 1 = -\frac{1}{2}$ | $\left(2\pi, -\frac{1}{2}\right)$ |

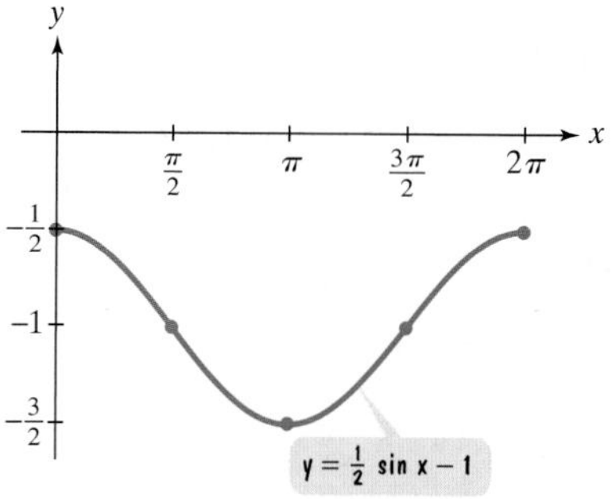


**Figure 5.55**

The five key points for $y = \frac{1}{2}\cos x - 1$ are shown in Figure 5.55. By connecting the points with a smooth curve, we obtain one period of the graph.

**Check Point 7** Graph one period of the function $y = 2\cos x + 1$.

**6** Model periodic behavior.

## Modeling Periodic Behavior

Our breathing consists of alternating periods of inhaling and exhaling. Each complete pumping cycle of the human heart can be described using a sine function. Our brain waves during deep sleep are sinusoidal. Viewed in this way, trigonometry becomes an intimate experience.

Some graphing utilities have a SINe REGression feature. This feature gives the sine function of best fit of wavelike data with the form of a sinusoidal function. However, it is not always necessary to use technology. In our next example, we use our understanding of sinusoidal graphs to model the process of breathing.

### EXAMPLE 8 A Trigonometric Breath of Life

The graph in Figure 5.56 shows one complete normal breathing cycle. The cycle consists of inhaling and exhaling. It takes place every 5 seconds. Velocity of air flow is positive when we inhale and negative when we exhale. It is measured in liters per second. If $y$ represents velocity of air flow after $x$ seconds, find a function of the form $y = A \sin Bx$ that models air flow in a normal breathing cycle.

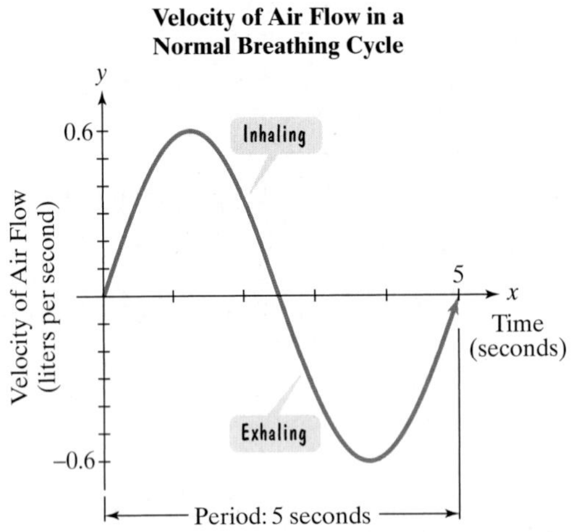


**Figure 5.56**

**Solution** We need to determine values for $A$ and $B$ in the equation $y = A \sin Bx$. $A$, the amplitude, is the maximum value of $y$. Figure 5.56 shows that this maximum value is 0.6. Thus, $A = 0.6$.

The value of $B$ in $y = A \sin Bx$ can be found using the formula for the period: period $= \frac{2\pi}{B}$. The period of our breathing cycle is 5 seconds. Thus,

$$5 = \frac{2\pi}{B} \quad \text{Our goal is to solve this equation for } B.$$

$$5B = 2\pi \quad \text{Multiply both sides of the equation by } B.$$

$$B = \frac{2\pi}{5} \quad \text{Divide both sides of the equation by 5.}$$

We see that $A = 0.6$ and $B = \frac{2\pi}{5}$. Substitute these values into $y = A \sin Bx$. The breathing cycle is modeled by

$$y = 0.6 \sin \frac{2\pi}{5} x.$$

**Check Point 8**

Find an equation of the form $y = A \sin Bx$ that produces the graph shown in the figure on the right.

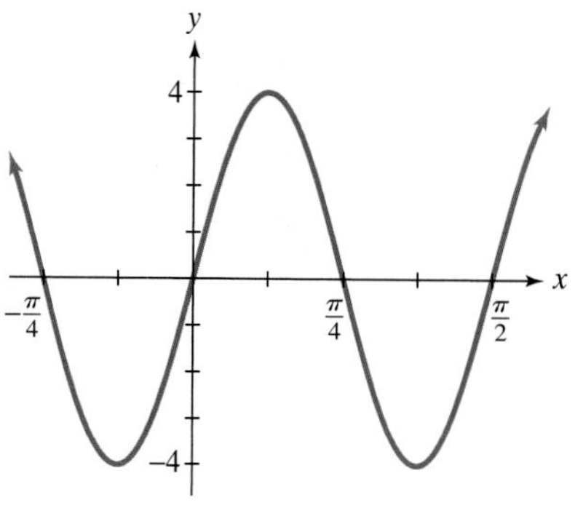


## EXAMPLE 9 Modeling a Tidal Cycle

Figure 5.56 shows that the depth of water at a boat dock varies with the tides. The depth is 5 feet at low tide and 13 feet at high tide. On a certain day, low tide occurs at 4 A.M. and high tide at 10 A.M. If $y$ represents the depth of the water $x$ hours after midnight, use a sine function of the form $y = A\sin(Bx - C) + D$ to model the water's depth.

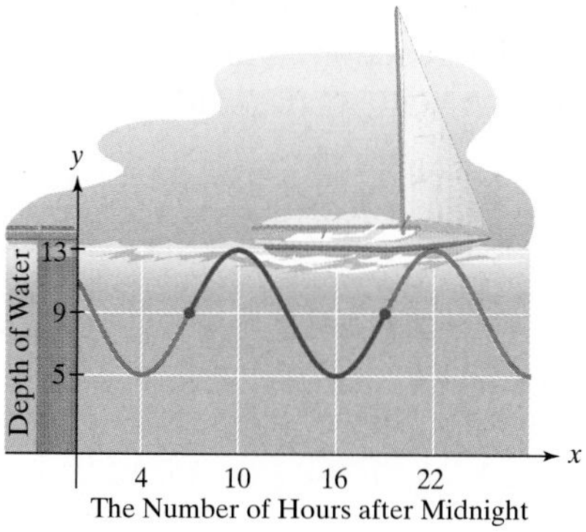


**Figure 5.57**

**Solution** We need to determine values for $A$, $B$, $C$, and $D$ in the equation $y = A\sin(Bx - C) + D$. We can find these values using Figure 5.57. We begin with D.

To find $D$, we use the vertical shift. Because the water's depth ranges from a minimum of 5 feet to a maximum of 13 feet, the curve oscillates about the middle value, 9 feet. Thus, $D = 9$, which is the vertical shift.

At maximum depth, the water is 4 feet above 9 feet. Thus, $A$, the amplitude, is 4: $A = 4$.

To find $B$, we use the period. The blue portion of the graph shows that one complete tidal cycle occurs in $19 - 7$, or 12 hours. The period is 12. Thus,

$$12 = \frac{2\pi}{B} \quad \text{Our goal is to solve this equation for } B.$$

$$12B = 2\pi \quad \text{Multiply both sides by } B.$$

$$B = \frac{2\pi}{12} = \frac{\pi}{6}. \quad \text{Divide both sides by 12.}$$

To find $C$, we use the phase shift. The blue portion of the graph shows that the starting point of the cycle is shifted from 0 to 7. The phase shift, $\frac{C}{B}$, is 7.

$$7 = \frac{C}{B} \quad \text{The phase shift of } y = A\sin(Bx - C) \text{ is } \frac{C}{B}.$$

$$7 = \frac{C}{\frac{\pi}{6}} \quad \text{From above, we have } B = \frac{\pi}{6}.$$

$$\frac{7\pi}{6} = C \quad \text{Multiply both sides of the equation by } \frac{\pi}{6}.$$

We see that $A = 4$, $B = \frac{\pi}{6}$, $C = \frac{7\pi}{6}$, and $D = 9$. Substitute these values into $y = A\sin(Bx - C) + D$. The water's depth $x$ hours after midnight is modeled by

$$y = 4\sin\left(\frac{\pi}{6}x - \frac{7\pi}{6}\right) + 9.$$

**Check Point 9**

The figure shows the number of hours of daylight for a region that is 30° north of the equator. Hours of daylight are at a minimum of 10 hours in January and December. Hours of daylight are at a maximum of 14 hours in June. Let $x$ represent the month of the year, with 1 for January, 2 for February, 3 for March, and 12 for December. If $y$ represents the number of hours of daylight in month $x$, use a sine function of the form $y = A\sin(Bx - C) + D$ to model the hours of daylight.

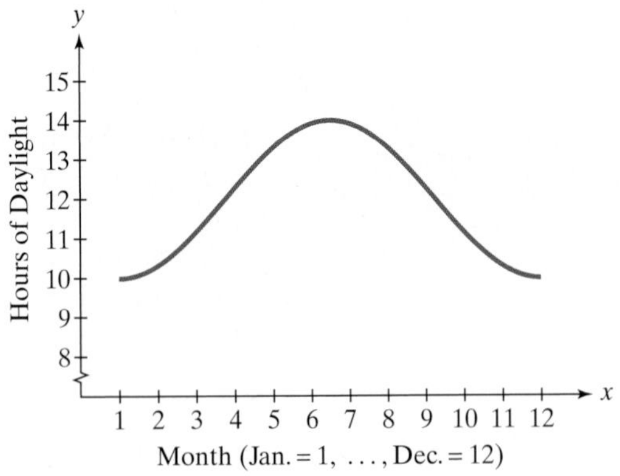


## EXERCISE SET 5.5

### Practice Exercises

*In Exercises 1–6, determine the amplitude of each function. Then graph the function and $y = \sin x$ in the same rectangular coordinate system for $0 \le x \le 2\pi$.*

**1.** $y = 4\sin x$

**2.** $y = 5\sin x$

**3.** $y = \frac{1}{3}\sin x$

**4.** $y = \frac{1}{4}\sin x$

**5.** $y = -3\sin x$

**6.** $y = -4\sin x$

*In Exercises 7–16, determine the amplitude and period of each function. Then graph one period of the function.*

**7.** $y = \sin 2x$

**8.** $y = \sin 4x$

**9.** $y = 3\sin\frac{1}{2}x$

**10.** $y = 2\sin\frac{1}{4}x$

**11.** $y = 4\sin\pi x$

**12.** $y = 3\sin 2\pi x$

**13.** $y = -3\sin 2\pi x$

**14.** $y = -2\sin\pi x$

**15.** $y = -\sin\frac{2}{3}x$

**16.** $y = -\sin\frac{4}{3}x$

*In Exercises 17–30, determine the amplitude, period, and phase shift of each function. Then graph one period of the function.*

**17.** $y = \sin(x - \pi)$

**18.** $y = \sin\left(x - \frac{\pi}{2}\right)$

**19.** $y = \sin(2x - \pi)$

**20.** $y = \sin\left(2x - \frac{\pi}{2}\right)$

**21.** $y = 3\sin(2x - \pi)$

**22.** $y = 3\sin\left(2x - \dfrac{\pi}{2}\right)$

**23.** $y = \frac{1}{2}\sin\left(x + \dfrac{\pi}{2}\right)$

**24.** $y = \frac{1}{2}\sin(x + \pi)$

**25.** $y = -2\sin\left(2x + \dfrac{\pi}{2}\right)$

**26.** $y = -3\sin\left(2x + \dfrac{\pi}{2}\right)$

**27.** $y = 3\sin(\pi x + 2)$

**28.** $y = 3\sin(2\pi x + 4)$

**29.** $y = -2\sin(2\pi x + 4\pi)$

**30.** $y = -3\sin(2\pi x + 4\pi)$

*In Exercises 31–34, determine the amplitude of each function. Then graph the function and $y = \cos x$ in the same rectangular coordinate system for $0 \le x \le 2\pi$.*

**31.** $y = 2\cos x$

**32.** $y = 3\cos x$

**33.** $y = -2\cos x$

**34.** $y = -3\cos x$

*In Exercises 35–42, determine the amplitude and period of each function. Then graph one period of the function.*

**35.** $y = \cos 2x$

**36.** $y = \cos 4x$

**37.** $y = 4\cos 2\pi x$

**38.** $y = 5\cos 2\pi x$

**39.** $y = -4\cos\frac{1}{2}x$

**40.** $y = -3\cos\frac{1}{3}x$

**41.** $y = -\frac{1}{2}\cos\dfrac{\pi}{3}x$

**42.** $y = -\frac{1}{2}\cos\dfrac{\pi}{4}x$

*In Exercises 43–50, determine the amplitude, period, and phase shift of each function. Then graph one period of the function.*

**43.** $y = 3\cos(2x - \pi)$

**44.** $y = 4\cos(2x - \pi)$

**45.** $y = \frac{1}{2}\cos\left(3x + \dfrac{\pi}{2}\right)$

**46.** $y = \frac{1}{2}\cos(2x + \pi)$

**47.** $y = -3\cos\left(2x - \dfrac{\pi}{2}\right)$

**48.** $y = -4\cos\left(2x - \dfrac{\pi}{2}\right)$

**49.** $y = 2\cos(2\pi x + 8\pi)$

**50.** $y = 3\cos(2\pi x + 4\pi)$

*In Exercises 51–58, use a vertical shift to graph one period of the function.*

**51.** $y = \sin x + 2$

**52.** $y = \sin x - 2$

**53.** $y = \cos x - 3$

**54.** $y = \cos x + 3$

**55.** $y = 2\sin\frac{1}{2}x + 1$

**56.** $y = 2\cos\frac{1}{2}x + 1$

**57.** $y = -3\cos 2\pi x + 2$

**58.** $y = -3\sin 2\pi x + 2$

## Application Exercises

*In the theory of biorhythms, sine functions are used to measure a person's potential. You can obtain your biorhythm chart online by simply entering your date of birth, the date you want your biorhythm chart to begin, and the number of months you wish to be included in the plot. The following is your author's chart, beginning January 25, 2000, when he was 19,998 days old. We all have cycles with the same amplitudes and periods as those shown here. Each of our three basic cycles begins at birth. Use the biorhythm chart shown to solve Exercises 59–66.*

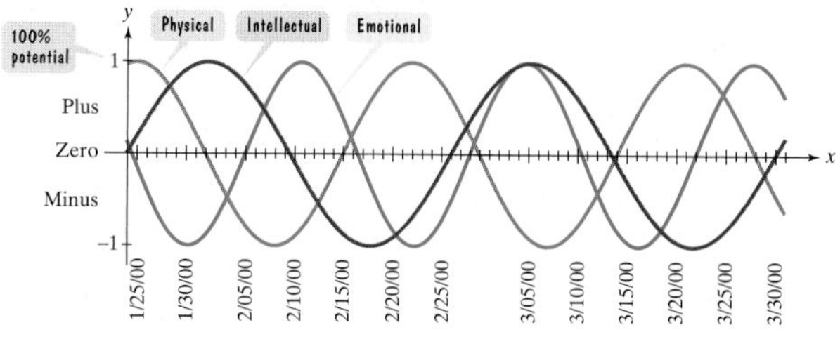


**59.** What is the period of the physical cycle?

**60.** What is the period of the emotional cycle?

**61.** What is the period of the intellectual cycle?

**62.** For the period shown, what is the worst day in February for your author to run in a marathon?

**63.** For the period shown, what is the best day in March for your author to meet an online friend for the first time?

**64.** For the period shown, what is the best day in January for your author to begin writing this trigonometry chapter?

**65.** If you extend these sinusoidal graphs to the end of the year, is there a day when your author should not even bother getting out of bed?

**66.** If you extend these sinusoidal graphs to the end of the year, are there any days where your author is at near-peak physical, emotional, and intellectual potential?

**67.** Rounded to the nearest hour, Los Angeles averages 14 hours of daylight in June, 10 hours in December, and 12 hours in March and September. Let $x$ represent the number of months after June and $y$ represent the number of hours of daylight in month $x$. Make a graph that displays the information from June of one year to June of the following year.

**68.** A clock with an hour hand that is 15 inches long is hanging on a wall. At noon, the distance between the tip of the hour hand and the ceiling is 23 inches. At 3 P.M., the distance is 38 inches; at 6 P.M. 53 inches; at 9 P.M. 38 inches; and at midnight the distance is again 23 inches. If $y$ represents the distance between the tip of the hour hand and the ceiling $x$ hours after noon, make a graph that displays the information for $0 \le x \le 24$.

**69.** The number of hours of daylight in Boston is given by

$$y = 3\sin\frac{2\pi}{365}(x - 79) + 12$$

where $x$ is the number of days after January 1.

**a.** What is the amplitude of this function?

**b.** What is the period of this function?

**c.** How many hours of daylight are there on the longest day of the year?

**d.** How many hours of daylight are there on the shortest day of the year?

**e.** Graph the function for one period, starting on January 1.

**70.** The average monthly temperature, $y$, in degrees Fahrenheit, for Juneau, Alaska, can be modeled by $y = 16\sin\left(\frac{\pi}{6}x - \frac{2\pi}{3}\right) + 40$, where $x$ is the month of the year (January = 1, February = 2, ..., December = 12). Graph the function for $1 \le x \le 12$. What is the highest average monthly temperature? In which month does this occur?

**71.** The figure shows the depth of water at the end of a boat dock. The depth is 6 feet at low tide and 12 feet at high tide. On a certain day, low tide occurs at 6 A.M. and high tide at noon. If $y$ represents the depth of the water $x$ hours after midnight, use a cosine function of the form $y = A\cos Bx + D$ to model the water's depth.

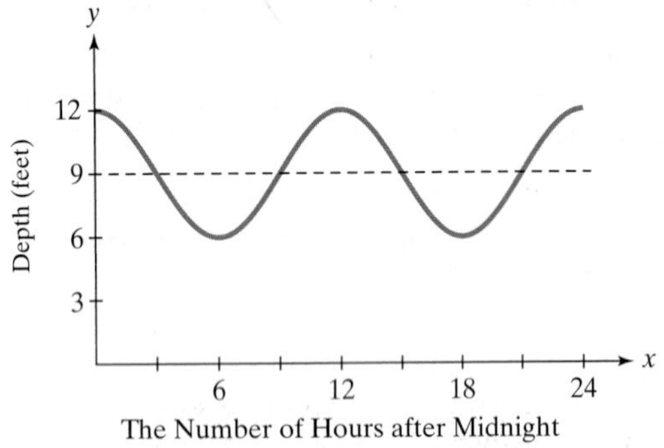


**72.** The figure shows the depth of water at the end of a boat dock. The depth is 5 feet at high tide and 3 feet at low tide. On a certain day, high tide occurs at noon and low tide at 6 P.M. If $y$ represents the depth of the water $x$ hours after noon, use a cosine function of the form $y = A\cos Bx + D$ to model the water's depth.

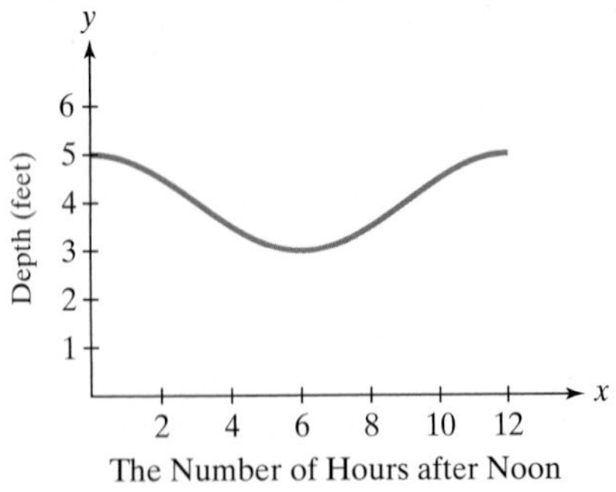


## Writing in Mathematics

**73.** Without drawing a graph, describe the behavior of the basic sine curve.

**74.** What is the amplitude of the sine function? What does this tell you about the graph?

**75.** If you are given the equation of a sine function, how do you determine the period?

**76.** What does a phase shift indicate about the graph of a sine function? How do you determine the phase shift from the function's equation?

**77.** Describe a general procedure for obtaining the graph of $y = A\sin(Bx - C)$.

**78.** Without drawing a graph, describe the behavior of the basic cosine curve.

**79.** Describe a relationship between the graphs of $y = \sin x$ and $y = \cos x$.

**80.** Describe the relationship between the graphs of $y = A\cos(Bx - C)$ and $y = A\cos(Bx - C) + D$.

**81.** Biorhythm cycles provide interesting applications of sinusoidal graphs. But do you believe in the validity of biorhythms? Write a few sentences explaining why or why not.

## Technology Exercises

**82.** Use a graphing utility to verify any five of the sine curves that you drew by hand in Exercises 7–30. The amplitude, period, and phase shift should help you to determine appropriate range settings.

**83.** Use a graphing utility to verify any five of the cosine curves that you drew by hand in Exercises 31–50.

**84.** Use a graphing utility to verify any two of the sinusoidal curves with vertical shifts that you drew in Exercises 51–58.

*In Exercises 85–88, use a graphing utility to graph two periods of the function.*

**85.** $y = 3\sin(2x + \pi)$

**86.** $y = -2\cos\left(2\pi x - \frac{\pi}{2}\right)$

**87.** $y = 0.2\sin\left(\frac{\pi}{10}x + \pi\right)$

**88.** $y = 3\sin(2x - \pi) + 5$

**89.** Use a graphing utility to graph $y = \sin x$ and $y = x - \frac{x^3}{6} + \frac{x^5}{120}$ in a $\left[-\pi, \pi, \frac{\pi}{2}\right]$ by $[-2, 2, 1]$ viewing rectangle. How do the graphs compare?

**90.** Use a graphing utility to graph $y = \cos x$ and $y = 1 - \frac{x^2}{2} + \frac{x^4}{24}$ in a $\left[-\pi, \pi, \frac{\pi}{2}\right]$ by $[-2, 2, 1]$ viewing rectangle. How do the graphs compare?

**91.** Use a graphing utility to graph

$$y = \sin x + \frac{\sin 2x}{2} + \frac{\sin 3x}{3} + \frac{\sin 4x}{4}$$

in a $\left[-2\pi, 2\pi, \frac{\pi}{2}\right]$ by $[-2, 2, 1]$ viewing rectangle. How do these waves compare to the smooth rolling waves of the basic sine curve?

**92.** Use a graphing utility to graph

$$y = \sin x - \frac{\sin 3x}{9} + \frac{\sin 5x}{25}$$

in a $\left[-2\pi, 2\pi, \frac{\pi}{2}\right]$ by $[-2, 2, 1]$ viewing rectangle. How do these waves compare to the smooth rolling waves of the basic sine curve?

**93.** The data show the average monthly temperatures for Washington, D.C.

**a.** Use your graphing utility to draw a scatter plot of the data from $x = 1$ through $x = 12$.

**b.** Use the SINe REGression feature to find the sinusoidal function of the form $y = A\sin(Bx + C) + D$ that best fits the data.

**c.** Use your graphing utility to draw the sinusoidal function of best fit on the scatter plot.

| $x$ | Month | Average Monthly Temperature, °F |
|---|---|---|
| 1 | (January) | 34.6 |
| 2 | (February) | 37.5 |
| 3 | (March) | 47.2 |
| 4 | (April) | 56.5 |
| 5 | (May) | 66.4 |
| 6 | (June) | 75.6 |
| 7 | (July) | 80.0 |
| 8 | (August) | 78.5 |
| 9 | (September) | 71.3 |
| 10 | (October) | 59.7 |
| 11 | (November) | 49.8 |
| 12 | (December) | 39.4 |

*Source:* U.S. National Oceanic and Atmospheric Administration.

**94.** Repeat Exercise 93 for data of your choice. The data can involve the average monthly temperatures for the region where you live or any data whose scatter plot takes the form of a sinusoidal function.

## Critical Thinking Exercises

*Graph the function in Exercises 95–96 by hand.*

**95.** $y = \sin x + \cos x \quad$ for $0 \le x \le 2\pi$

**96.** $y = x + \cos x \quad$ for $0 \le x \le \frac{5\pi}{2}$

**97.** Use the cosine function to find an equation of the graph in the figure shown.

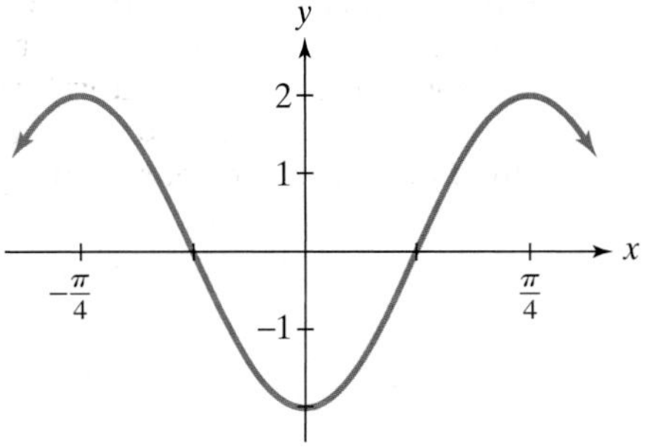


## Group Exercise

**98.** This exercise is intended to provide some fun with biorhythms, regardless of whether you believe they have any validity. We will use each member's chart to determine biorhythmic compatibility. Before meeting, each group member should go online and obtain his or her biorhythm chart. The date of the group meeting is the date on which your chart should begin. Include 12 months in the plot. At the meeting, compare differences and similarities among the intellectual sinusoidal curves. Using these comparisons, each person should find the one other person with whom he or she would be most intellectually compatible.

## SECTION 5.6 Graphs of Other Trigonometric Functions

### Objectives

1. Understand the graph of $y = \tan x$.
2. Graph variations of $y = \tan x$.
3. Understand the graph of $y = \cot x$.
4. Graph variations of $y = \cot x$.
5. Understand the graphs of $y = \csc x$ and $y = \sec x$.
6. Graph variations of $y = \csc x$ and $y = \sec x$.

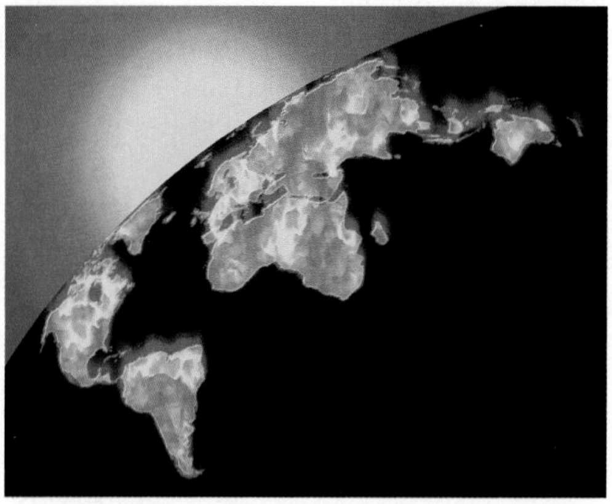

Recent advances in our understanding of climate have changed global warming from a subject for a disaster movie (the Statue of Liberty up to its chin in water) to a serious but manageable scientific and policy issue. Global warming may be related to the burning of fossil fuels, which adds carbon dioxide to the atmosphere. In the new millennium, we will see whether our use of fossil fuels will add enough carbon dioxide to the atmosphere to change it (and our climate) in significant ways. In this section's exercise set, you will see how trigonometric graphs reveal interesting patterns in carbon dioxide concentration from 1990 to 2000. In the section itself, trigonometric graphs will reveal patterns involving the tangent, cotangent, secant, and cosecant functions.

**1** Understand the graph of $y = \tan x$.

### The Graph of $y = \tan x$

The properties of the tangent function discussed in Section 5.2 will help us determine its graph. Because the tangent function has properties that are different from sinusoidal functions, its graph differs significantly from those of sine and cosine. Properties of the tangent function include the following:

- The period is $\pi$. It is only necessary to graph $y = \tan x$ over an interval of length $\pi$. The remainder of the graph consists of repetitions of that graph at intervals of $\pi$.
- The tangent function is an odd function: $\tan(-x) = -\tan x$. The graph is symmetric with respect to the origin.
- The tangent function is undefined at $\frac{\pi}{2}$. The graph of $y = \tan x$ has a vertical asymptote at $x = \frac{\pi}{2}$.

We obtain the graph of $y = \tan x$ using some points on the graph and origin symmetry. Table 5.4 lists some values of $(x, y)$ on the graph of $y = \tan x$ on the interval $\left[0, \frac{\pi}{2}\right)$.

**Table 5.4 Values of $(x, y)$ on $y = \tan x$**

| $x$ | 0 | $\frac{\pi}{6}$ | $\frac{\pi}{4}$ | $\frac{\pi}{3}$ | $\frac{5\pi}{12}$ (75°) | $\frac{17\pi}{36}$ (85°) | $\frac{89\pi}{180}$ (89°) | 1.57 | $\frac{\pi}{2}$ |
|---|---|---|---|---|---|---|---|---|---|
| $y = \tan x$ | 0 | $\frac{\sqrt{3}}{3} \approx 0.6$ | 1 | $\sqrt{3} \approx 1.7$ | 3.7 | 11.4 | 57.3 | 1255.8 | undefined |

As $x$ increases from 0 to $\frac{\pi}{2}$, $y$ increases slowly at first, then more and more rapidly.

The graph in Figure 5.58(a) is based on our observation in the voice balloon. Notice that $y$ increases without bound as $x$ approaches $\frac{\pi}{2}$. As the figure shows, the graph of $y = \tan x$ has a vertical asymptote at $x = \frac{\pi}{2}$.

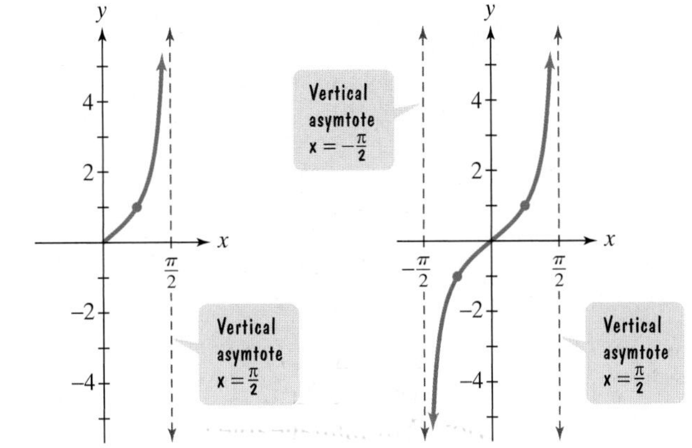


(a) $y = \tan x, 0 \le x < \frac{\pi}{2}$

(b) $y = \tan x, -\frac{\pi}{2} < x < \frac{\pi}{2}$

**Figure 5.58** Graphing the tangent function

The graph of $y = \tan x$ can be completed for the interval $\left(-\frac{\pi}{2}, \frac{\pi}{2}\right)$ by using origin symmetry. Figure 5.57(b) shows the result of reflecting the graph in Figure 5.58(a) about the origin. The graph of $y = \tan x$ has another vertical asymptote at $x = -\frac{\pi}{2}$. Notice that $y$ decreases without bound as $x$ approaches $-\frac{\pi}{2}$.

Because the period of the tangent function is $\pi$ radians, the graph in Figure 5.58(b) shows one complete period of $y = \tan x$. We obtain the complete graph of $y = \tan x$ by repeating the graph in Figure 5.58(b) to the left and right over intervals of $\pi$. The resulting graph and its main characteristics are shown in the following box.

### The Tangent Curve: The Graph of $y = \tan x$ and Its Characteristics

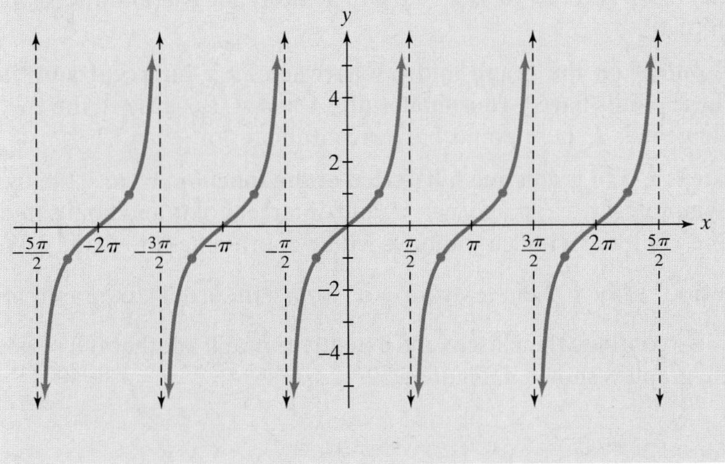


**Characteristics**

- **Period**: $\pi$
- **Domain**: All real numbers except odd multiples of $\frac{\pi}{2}$
- **Range**: All real numbers
- **Vertical asymptotes**: at odd multiples of $\frac{\pi}{2}$
- **An $x$-intercept** occurs midway between each pair of consecutive asymptotes.
- **Odd function** with origin symmetry
- Points on the graph midway between $x$-intercepts and consecutive asymptotes have $y$-coordinates of $-1$ and 1.

**2** Graph variations of $y = \tan x$.

## Graphing Variations of $y = \tan x$

We use the characteristics of the tangent curve to graph tangent functions of the form $y = A\tan(Bx - C)$.

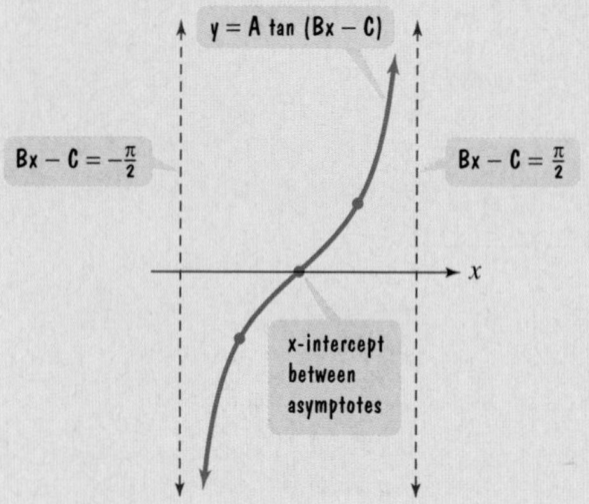


**Graphing $y = A\tan(Bx - C)$**

1. Find two consecutive asymptotes by setting the variable expression in the tangent equal to $-\frac{\pi}{2}$ and $\frac{\pi}{2}$ and solving

$$Bx - C = -\frac{\pi}{2} \text{ and } Bx - C = \frac{\pi}{2}.$$

2. Identify an $x$-intercept, midway between consecutive asymptotes.
3. Find the points on the graph midway between an $x$-intercept and the asymptotes. These points have $y$-coordinates of $-A$ and $A$.
4. Use steps 1–3 to graph one full period of the function. Add additional cycles to the left or right as needed.

### EXAMPLE 1 Graphing a Tangent Function

Graph $y = 2\tan\frac{x}{2}$ for $-\pi < x < 3\pi$.

**Solution**

**Step 1 Find two consecutive asymptotes.** We solve the equations

$$\frac{x}{2} = -\frac{\pi}{2} \quad \text{and} \quad \frac{x}{2} = \frac{\pi}{2}.$$ Set the variable expression in the tangent equal to $-\frac{\pi}{2}$ and $\frac{\pi}{2}$.

$$x = -\pi \qquad x = \pi$$ Multiply both sides of each equation by 2.

Thus, two consecutive asymptotes occur at $x = -\pi$ and $x = \pi$.

**Step 2 Identify an $x$-intercepts, midway between consecutive asymptotes.** Midway between $x = -\pi$ and $x = \pi$ is $x = 0$. An $x$-intercept is 0 and the graph passes through $(0, 0)$.

**Step 3 Find points on the graph midway between an $x$-intercept and the asymptotes. These points have $y$-coordinates of $-A$ and $A$.** Because $A$, the coefficient of the tangent, is 2, these points have $y$-coordinates of $-2$ and 2.

**Step 4 Use steps 1–3 to graph one full period of the function.** We use the two consecutive asymptotes, $x = -\pi$ and $x = \pi$, an $x$-intercept of 0, and points midway between the $x$-intercept and asymptotes with $y$-coordinates of $-2$ and 2. We graph one period of $y = 2\tan\frac{\pi}{2}$ from $-\pi$ to $\pi$. In order to graph for $-\pi < x < 3\pi$, we continue the pattern and extend the graph another full period to the right. The graph is shown in Figure 5.59.

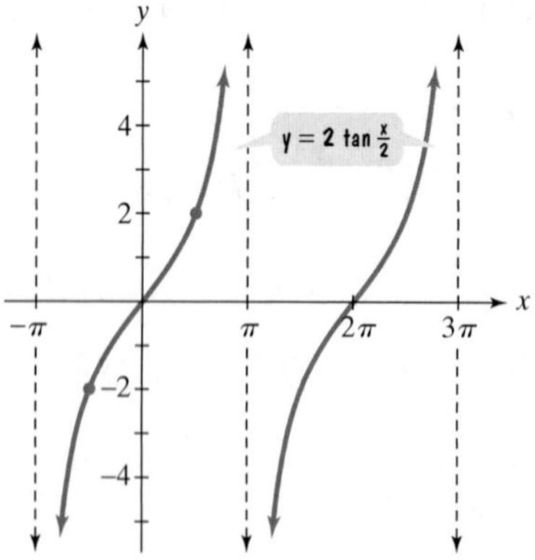


**Figure 5.59** The graph is shown for two full periods

**Check Point 1** Graph $y = 3\tan 2x$ for $-\frac{\pi}{4} < x < \frac{3\pi}{4}$.

## EXAMPLE 2 Graphing a Tangent Function

Graph two full periods of $y = \tan\left(x + \frac{\pi}{4}\right)$.

**Solution** The graph of $y = \tan\left(x + \frac{\pi}{4}\right)$ is the graph of $y = \tan x$ shifted horizontally to the left $\frac{\pi}{4}$ units.

**Step 1 Find two consecutive asymptotes.** We solve the equations

$$x + \frac{\pi}{4} = -\frac{\pi}{2} \quad \text{and} \quad x + \frac{\pi}{4} = \frac{\pi}{2}$$ Set the variable expression in the tangent equal to $-\frac{\pi}{2}$ and $\frac{\pi}{2}$.

$$x = -\frac{\pi}{4} - \frac{\pi}{2} \qquad x = -\frac{\pi}{4} + \frac{\pi}{2}$$ Subtract $\frac{\pi}{4}$ from both sides in each equation.

$$x = -\frac{3\pi}{4} \qquad x = \frac{\pi}{4}$$ Simplify.

Thus, two consecutive asymptotes occur at $x = -\frac{3\pi}{4}$ and $x = \frac{\pi}{4}$.

**Step 2 Identify an $x$-intercept, midway between consecutive asymptotes.**

$$x\text{-intercept} = \frac{-\frac{3\pi}{4} + \frac{\pi}{4}}{2} = \frac{-\frac{2\pi}{4}}{2} = -\frac{2\pi}{8} = -\frac{\pi}{4}$$

An $x$-intercept is $-\frac{\pi}{4}$ and the graph passes through $\left(-\frac{\pi}{4}, 0\right)$.

**Step 3 Find points on the graph midway between an $x$-intercept and the asymptotes.** Because $A$, the coefficient of the tangent, is 1, these points have $y$-coordinates of $-1$ and 1.

**Step 4 Use steps 1–3 to graph one full period of the function.** We use the two consecutive asymptotes, $x = -\frac{3\pi}{4}$ and $x = \frac{\pi}{4}$, to graph one full period of $y = \tan\left(x + \frac{\pi}{4}\right)$ from $-\frac{3\pi}{4}$ to $\frac{\pi}{4}$. We graph two full periods by continuing the pattern and extending the graph another full period to the right. The graph is shown in Figure 5.60.

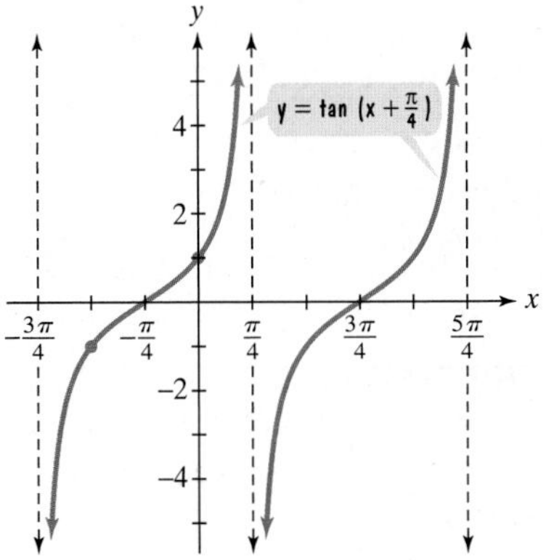


**Figure 5.60** The graph is shown for two full periods.

**Check Point 2** Graph two full periods of $y = \tan\left(x - \frac{\pi}{2}\right)$.

**3** Understand the graph of $y = \cot x$.

## The Graph of $y = \cot x$

Like the tangent function, the cotangent function, $y = \cot x$, has a period of $\pi$. The graph and its main characteristics are shown in the following box.

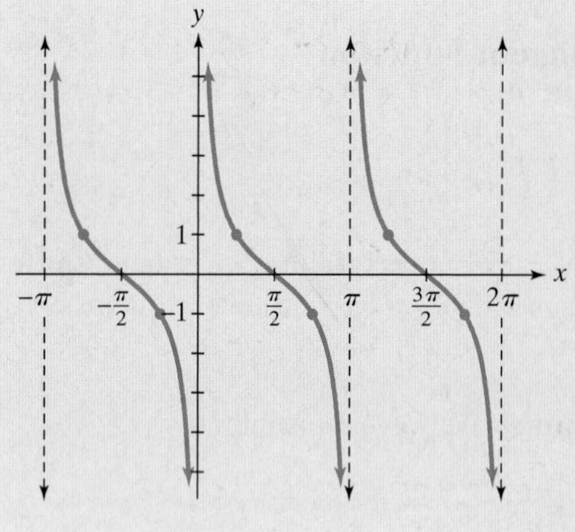


### The Cotangent Curve: The Graph of $y = \cot x$ and Its Characteristics

**Characteristics**

- **Period**: $\pi$
- **Domain**: All real numbers except integral multiples of $\pi$
- **Range**: All real numbers
- **Vertical asymptotes** at integral multiples of $\pi$
- **An $x$-intercept** occurs midway between each pair of consecutive asymptotes.
- **Odd function** with origin symmetry
- Points on the graph midway between $x$-intercepts and consecutive asymptotes have $y$-coordinates of 1 and −1.

**4** Graph variations of $y = \cot x$.

## Graphing Variations of $y = \cot x$

We use the characteristics of the cotangent curve to graph cotangent functions of the form $y = A\cot(Bx - C)$.

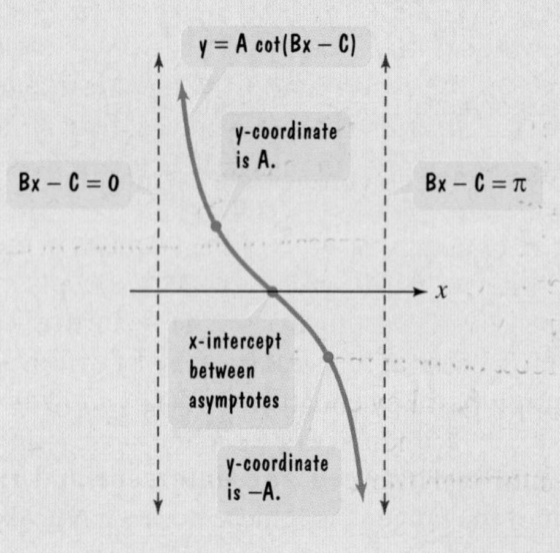


### Graphing $y = A\cot(Bx - C)$

1. Find two consecutive asymptotes by setting the variable expression in the cotangent equal to 0 and $\pi$ and solving

$$Bx - C = 0 \text{ and } Bx - C = \pi.$$

2. Identify an $x$-intercept, midway between consecutive asymptotes.
3. Find the points on the graph midway between an $x$-intercept and the asymptotes. These points have $y$-coordinates of $A$ and $-A$.
4. Use steps 1-3 to graph one full period of the function. Add additional cycles to the left or right as needed.

## EXAMPLE 3 Graphing a Cotangent Function

Graph $y = 3\cot 2x$.

### Solution

**Step 1** **Find two consecutive asymptotes.** We solve the equations

$$2x = 0 \quad \text{and} \quad 2x = \pi. \qquad \text{Set the variable expression in the cotangent equal to 0 and } \pi.$$

$$x = 0 \qquad x = \frac{\pi}{2} \qquad \text{Divide both sides of each equation by 2.}$$

Two consecutive asymptotes occur at $x = 0$ and $x = \frac{\pi}{2}$.

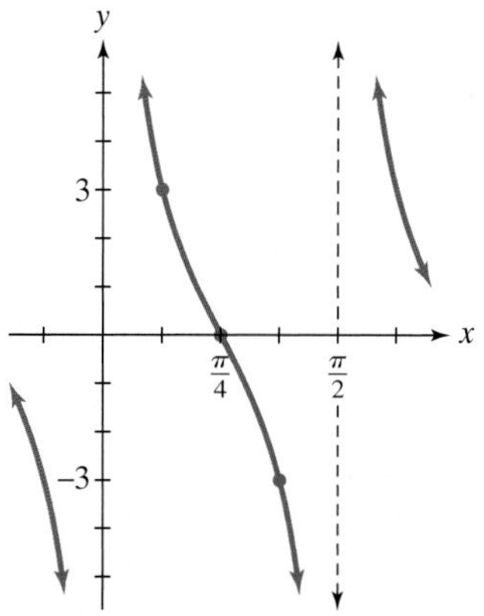


**Figure 5.61** The graph of $y = 3\cot 2x$

**Step 2 Identify an $x$-intercept, midway between consecutive asymptotes.** Midway between $x = 0$ and $x = \frac{\pi}{2}$ is $x = \frac{\pi}{4}$. An $x$-intercept is $\frac{\pi}{4}$ and the graph passes through $\left(\frac{\pi}{4}, 0\right)$.

**Step 3 Find points on the graph midway between an $x$-intercept and the asymptotes. These points have $y$-coordinates of $A$ and $-A$.** Because $A$, the coefficient of the cotangent, is 3, these points have $y$-coordinates of 3 and −3.

**Step 4 Use steps 1–3 to graph one full period of the function.** We use the two consecutive asymptotes, $x = 0$ and $x = \frac{\pi}{2}$, to graph one full period of $y = 3\cot 2x$. This curve is repeated to the left and right, as shown in Figure 5.61.

**Check Point 3** Graph $y = \frac{1}{2}\cot\frac{\pi}{2}x$.

**5** Understand the graphs of $y = \csc x$ and $y = \sec x$.

## The Graphs of $y = \csc x$ and $y = \sec x$

We obtain the graphs of the cosecant and secant curves by using the reciprocal identities

$$\csc x = \frac{1}{\sin x} \quad \text{and} \quad \sec x = \frac{1}{\cos x}.$$

The identity on the left tells us that the value of the cosecant function $y = \csc x$ at a given value of $x$ equals the reciprocal of the corresponding value of the sine function, provided that the value of the sine function is not 0. If the value of $\sin x$ is 0, then at each of these values of $x$, the cosecant function is not defined. A vertical asymptote is associated with each of these values on the graph of $y = \csc x$.

We obtain the graph of $y = \csc x$ by taking reciprocals of the $y$-values in the graph of $y = \sin x$. Vertical asymptotes of $y = \csc x$ occur at the $x$-intercepts of $y = \sin x$. Likewise, we obtain the graph of $y = \sec x$ by taking the reciprocal of $y = \cos x$. Vertical asymptotes of $y = \sec x$ occur at the $x$-intercepts of $y = \cos x$. The graphs of $y = \csc x$ and $y = \sec x$ and their key characteristics are shown in the following boxes. We have used dashed red lines to first graph $y = \sin x$ and $y = \cos x$, drawing vertical asymptotes through the $x$-intercepts.

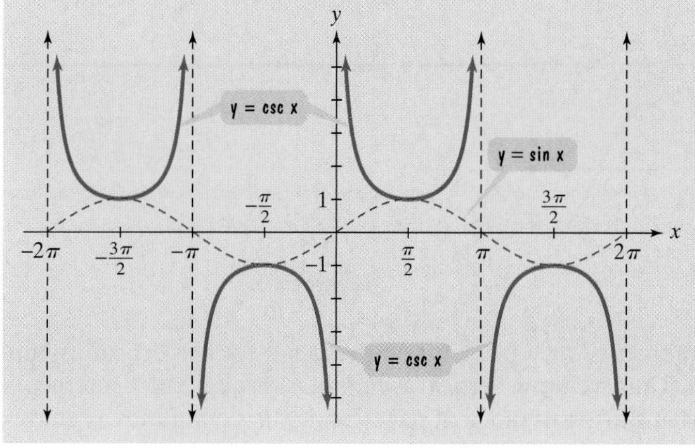


### The Cosecant Curve: The Graph of $y = \csc x$ and Its Characteristics

**Characteristics**

- **Period**: $2\pi$
- **Domain**: All real numbers except integral multiples of $\pi$
- **Range**: All real numbers $y$ such that $y \le -1$ or $y \ge 1$
- **Vertical asymptotes** at integral multiples of $\pi$
- **Odd function**, $\csc(-x) = -\csc x$, with origin symmetry

### The Secant Curve: The Graph of $y = \sec x$ and Its Characteristics

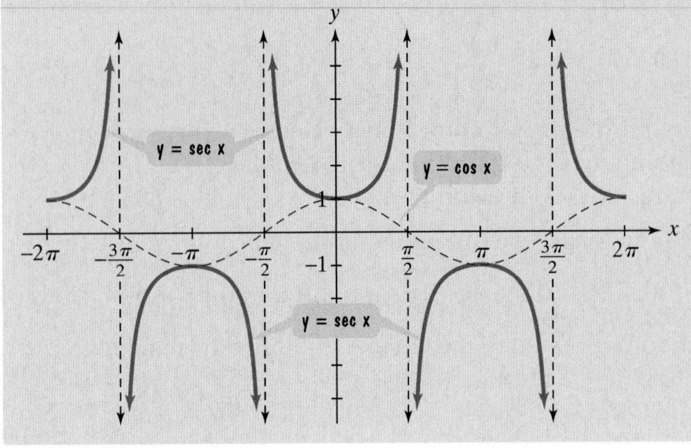


**Characteristics**

- **Period**: $2\pi$
- **Domain**: All real numbers except odd multiples of $\frac{\pi}{2}$
- **Range**: All real numbers $y$ such that $y \leq -1$ or $y \geq 1$
- **Vertical asymptotes** at odd multiples of $\frac{\pi}{2}$
- **Even function**, $\sec(-x) = \sec x$, with $y$-axis symmetry

**6** Graph variations of $y = \csc x$ and $y = \sec x$.

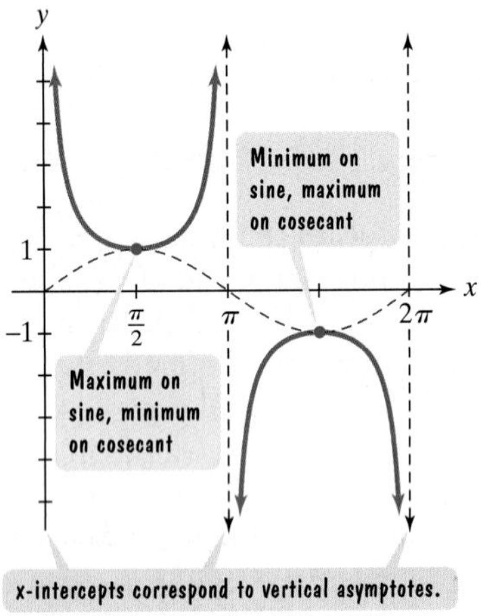


**Figure 5.62**

## Graphing Variations of $y = \csc x$ and $y = \sec x$

We use graphs of reciprocal functions to obtain graphs of cosecant and secant functions. To graph a cosecant or secant curve, begin by graphing the reciprocal function. For example, to graph $y = 2\csc 2x$, we use the graph of $y = 2\sin 2x$. Likewise, to graph $y = -3\sec\frac{x}{2}$, we use the graph of $y = -3\cos\frac{x}{2}$.

Figure 5.62 illustrates how we use a sine curve to obtain a cosecant curve. Notice that

- $x$-intercepts on the sine curve correspond to vertical asymptotes of the cosecant curve.
- A maximum point on the sine curve corresponds to a minimum point on a continuous portion of the cosecant curve.
- A minimum point on the sine curve corresponds to a maximum point on a continuous portion of the cosecant curve.

### EXAMPLE 4 Using a Sine Curve to Obtain a Cosecant Curve

Use the graph of $y = 2\sin 2x$ in Figure 5.63 to obtain the graph of $y = 2\csc 2x$.

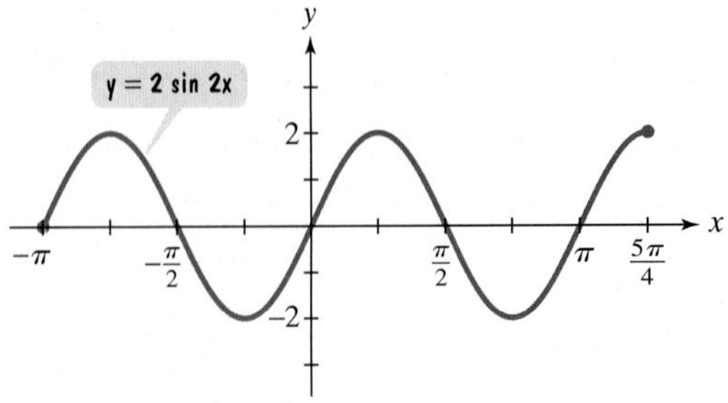


**Figure 5.63**

**Solution** The $x$-intercepts on $y = 2\sin 2x$ correspond to the vertical asymptotes of $y = 2\csc 2x$. Thus, we draw vertical asymptotes through the $x$-intercepts, shown in Figure 5.64 at the top of the next page. Using the asymptotes as guides, we sketch the graph of $y = 2\csc 2x$ in Figure 5.64.

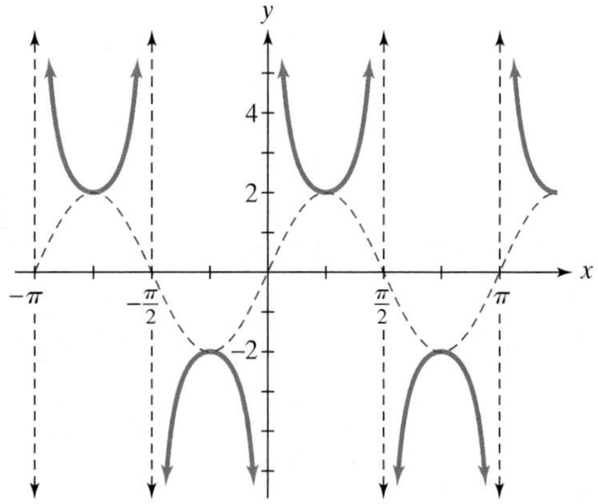


**Figure 5.64** Using a sine curve to graph $y = 2\csc 2x$

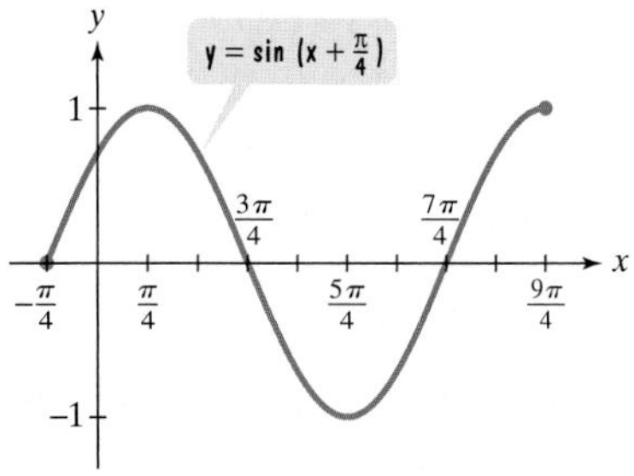


**Check Point 4** Use the graph of $y = \sin\left(x + \frac{\pi}{4}\right)$ shown on the left to obtain the graph of $y = \csc\left(x + \frac{\pi}{4}\right)$.

We use a cosine curve to obtain a secant curve in exactly the same way we used a sine curve to obtain a cosecant curve. Thus,

- $x$-intercepts on the cosine curve correspond to vertical asymptotes on the secant curve.
- A maximum point on the cosine curve corresponds to a minimum point on a continuous portion of the secant curve.
- A minimum point on the cosine curve corresponds to a maximum point on a continuous portion of the secant curve.

## EXAMPLE 5 Graphing a Secant Function

Graph $y = -3\sec\frac{x}{2}$ for $-\pi < x < 5\pi$.

**Solution** We begin by graphing the reciprocal cosine function, $y = -3\cos\frac{x}{2}$. This equation is of the form $y = A\cos Bx$ with $A = -3$ and $B = \frac{1}{2}$.

amplitude: $|A| = |-3| = 3$ — The maximum $y$ is 3 and the minimum is $-3$.

period: $\frac{2\pi}{B} = \frac{2\pi}{\frac{1}{2}} = 4\pi$ — Each cycle is completed in $4\pi$ radians.

We use quarter-periods, $\frac{4\pi}{4}$ or $\pi$, to find the $x$-values for the five key points. Starting with $x = 0$, the $x$-values are $0, \pi, 2\pi, 3\pi$, and $4\pi$. Evaluating the function at each of these values of $x$, the key points are

$$(0, -3), (\pi, 0), (2\pi, 3), (3\pi, 0), \text{ and } (4\pi, -3).$$

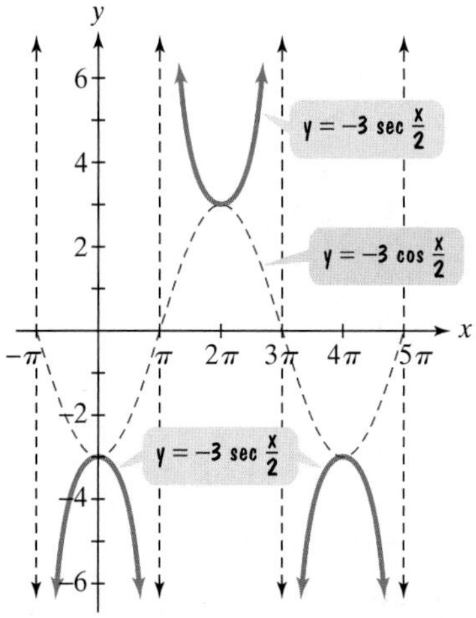


**Figure 5.65** Using a cosine curve to graph $y = -3\sec\frac{x}{2}$

We use these key points to graph $y = -3\cos\frac{x}{2}$ from 0 to $4\pi$. In order to graph for $-\pi \le x \le 5\pi$, extend the graph $\pi$ units to the left and $\pi$ units to the right. The graph is shown using a dashed red line in Figure 5.65. Now use this dashed red graph to obtain the graph of the reciprocal function. Draw vertical asymptotes through the $x$-intercepts. Using these asymptotes as guides, the graph of $y = -3\sec\frac{x}{2}$ is shown in blue in Figure 5.65.

**Check Point 5** Graph $y = 2\sec 2x$ for $-\frac{3\pi}{4} < x < \frac{3\pi}{4}$.

## The Six Curves of Trigonometry

Table 5.5 summarizes the graphs of the six trigonometric functions. Below each of the graphs is a description of the domain, range, and period of the function.

**Table 5.5 Graphs of the Six Trigonometric Functions**

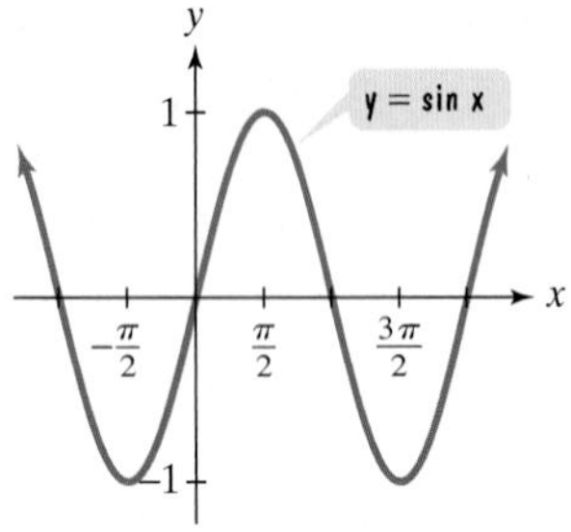


**Domain**: all real numbers

**Range**: $[-1, 1]$
**Period**: $2\pi$

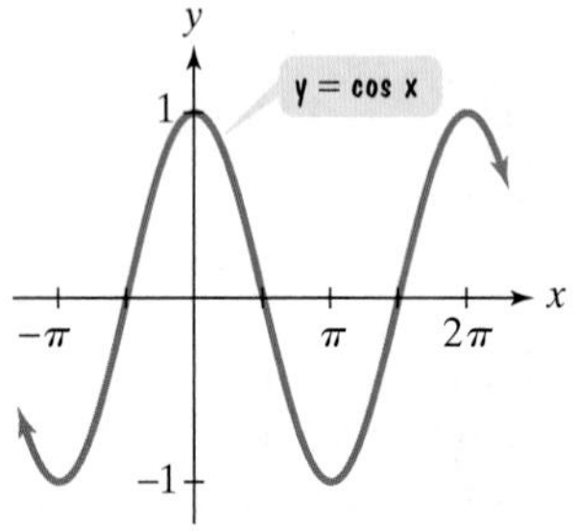


**Domain**: all real numbers

**Range**: $[-1, 1]$
**Period**: $2\pi$

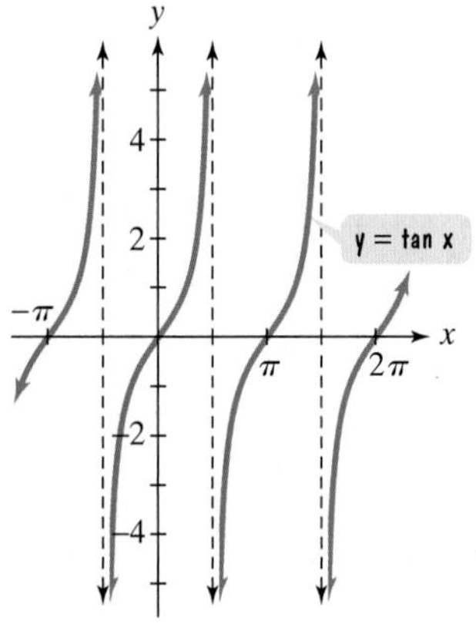


**Domain**: all real numbers except odd multiples of $\frac{\pi}{2}$

**Range**: all real numbers
**Period**: $\pi$

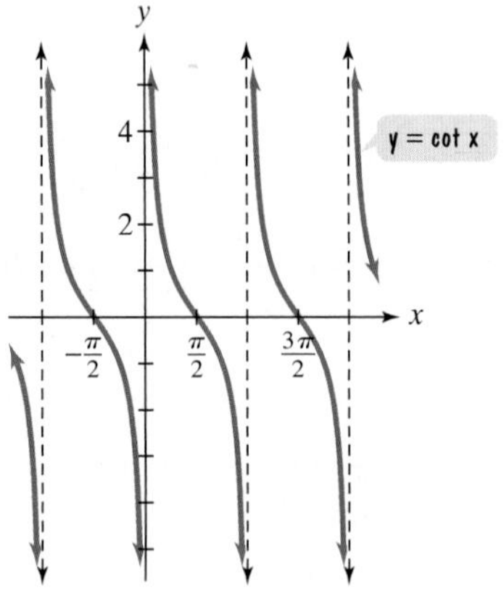


**Domain**: all real numbers except integral multiples of $\pi$

**Range**: all real numbers
**Period**: $\pi$

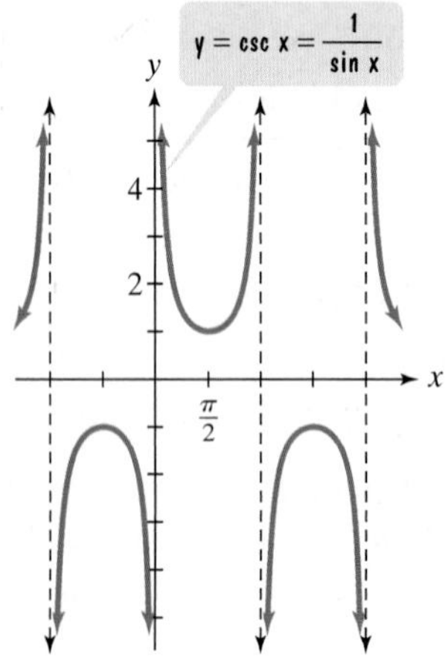


**Domain**: all real numbers except integral multiples of $\pi$

**Range**: $(-\infty, -1]$ or $[1, \infty)$
**Period**: $2\pi$

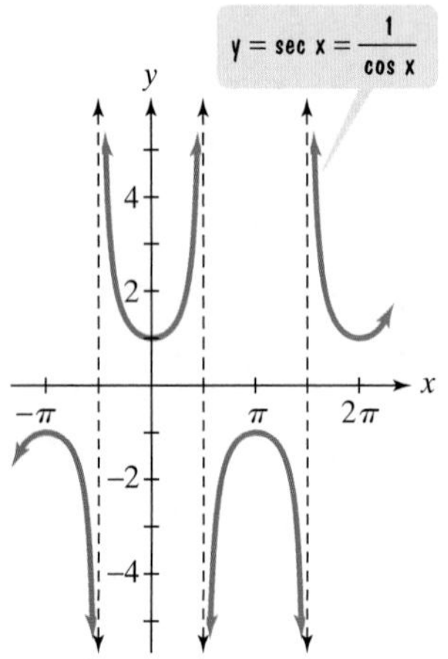


**Domain**: all real numbers except odd multiples of $\frac{\pi}{2}$

**Range**: $(-\infty, -1]$ or $[1, \infty)$
**Period**: $2\pi$

# EXERCISE SET 5.6

## Practice Exercises

*In Exercises 1–4, the graph of a tangent function is given. Select the equation for each graph from the following options.*

$$y = \tan\left(x + \frac{\pi}{2}\right), \quad y = \tan(x + \pi), \quad y = -\tan x, \quad y = -\tan\left(x - \frac{\pi}{2}\right)$$

**1.**

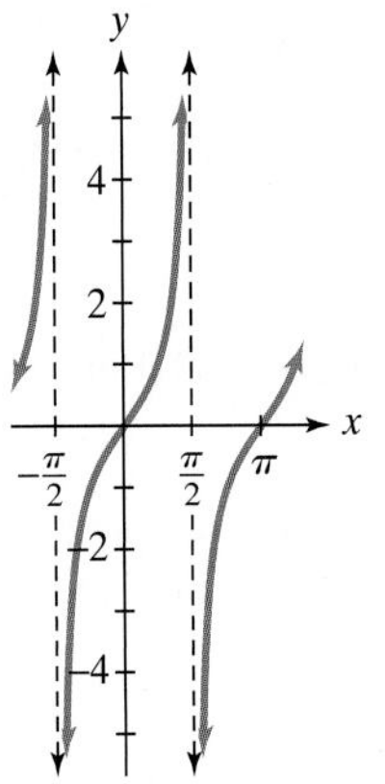


**2.**

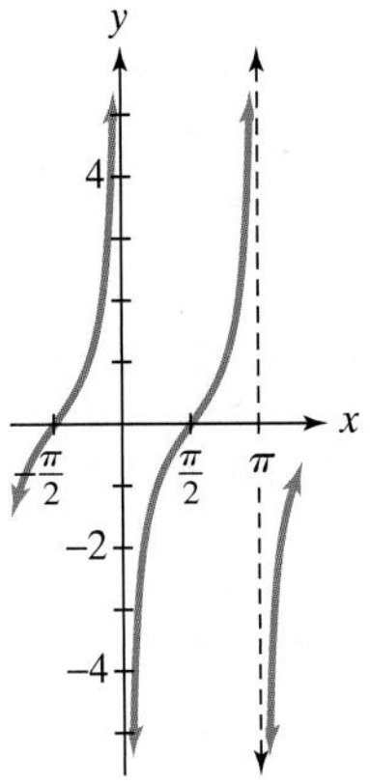


**3.**

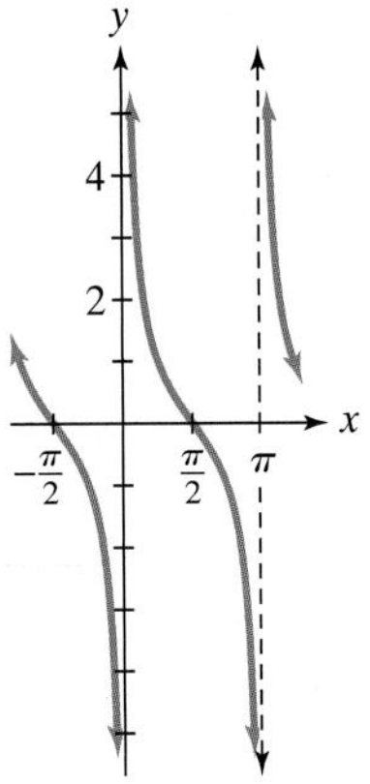


**4.**

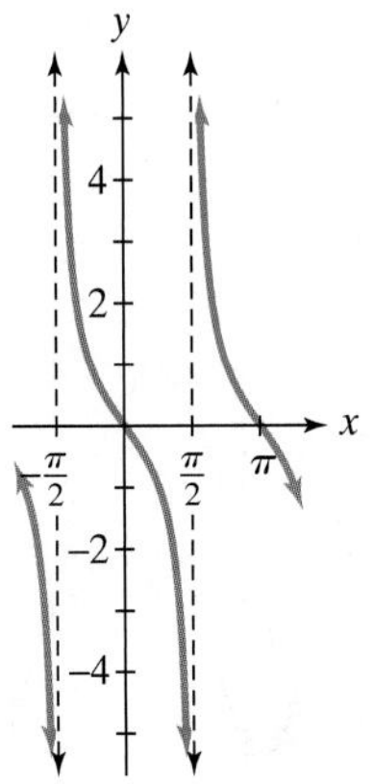


*In Exercises 5–12, graph two periods of the given tangent function.*

**5.** $y = 3\tan\dfrac{x}{4}$

**6.** $y = 2\tan\dfrac{x}{4}$

**7.** $y = \frac{1}{2}\tan 2x$

**8.** $y = 3\tan 2x$

**9.** $y = -2\tan\frac{1}{2}x$

**10.** $y = -3\tan\frac{1}{2}x$

**11.** $y = \tan(x - \pi)$

**12.** $y = \tan\left(x + \dfrac{\pi}{2}\right)$

*In Exercises 13–16, the graph of a cotangent function is given. Select the equation for each graph from the following options.*

$$y = \cot\left(x + \frac{\pi}{2}\right), \quad y = \cot(x + \pi), \quad y = -\cot x, \quad y = -\cot\left(x - \frac{\pi}{2}\right)$$

**13.**

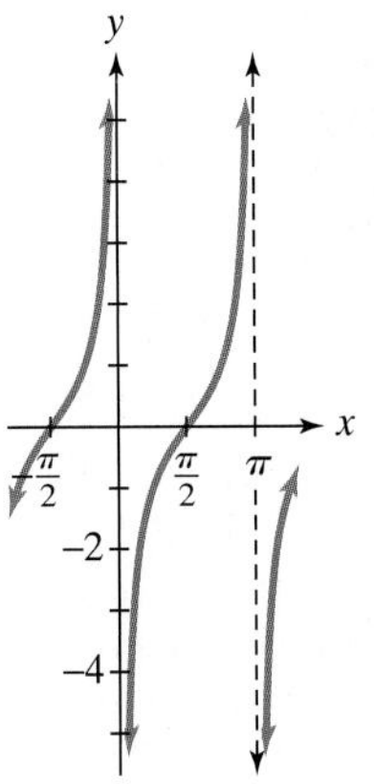


**14.**

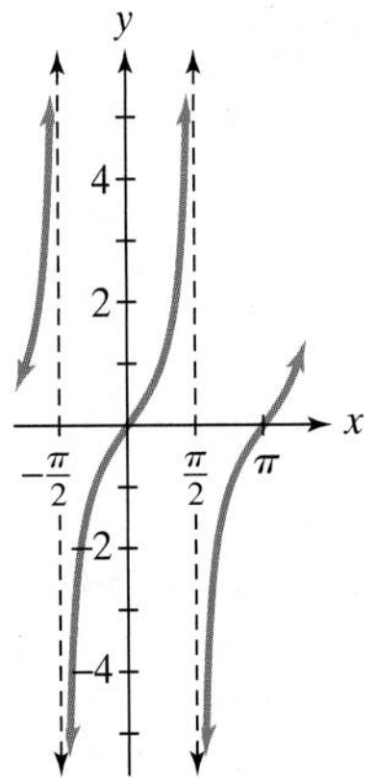


**15.**

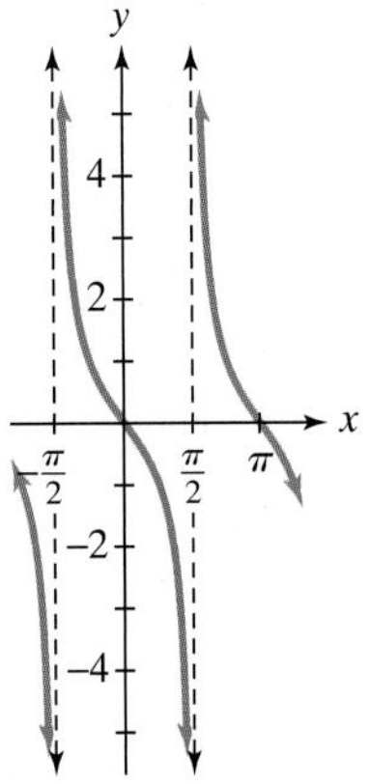


**16.**

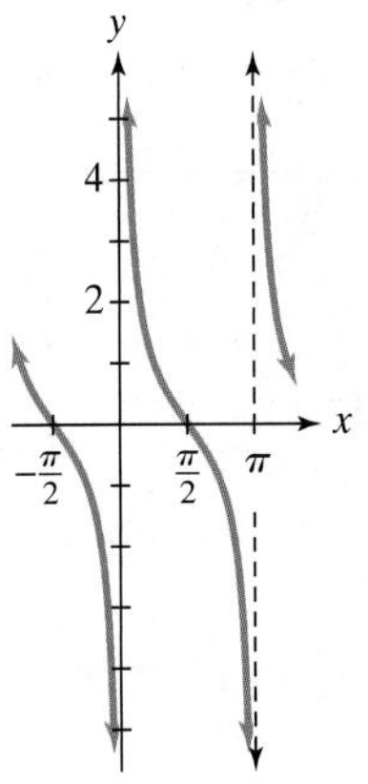


*In Exercises 17–24, graph two periods of the given cotangent function.*

**17.** $y = 2\cot x$

**18.** $y = \frac{1}{2}\cot x$

**19.** $y = \frac{1}{2}\cot 2x$

**20.** $y = 2\cot 2x$

**21.** $y = -3\cot\dfrac{\pi}{2}x$

**22.** $y = -2\cot\dfrac{\pi}{4}x$

**23.** $y = 3\cot\left(x + \dfrac{\pi}{2}\right)$

**24.** $y = 3\cot\left(x + \dfrac{\pi}{4}\right)$

*In Exercises 25–28, use each graph to obtain the graph of the reciprocal function. Give the equation of the function for the graph that you obtain.*

**25.**

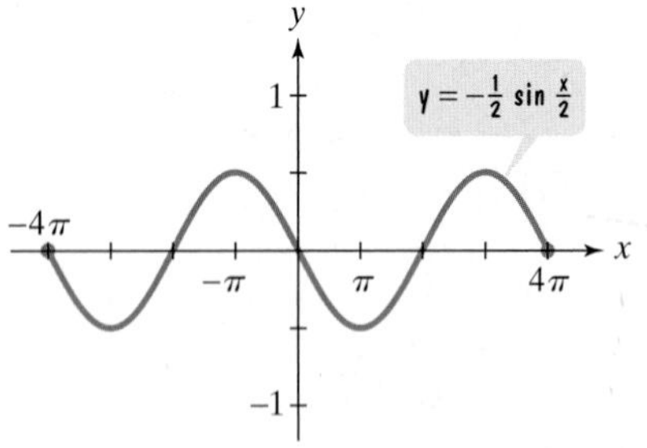


**26.**

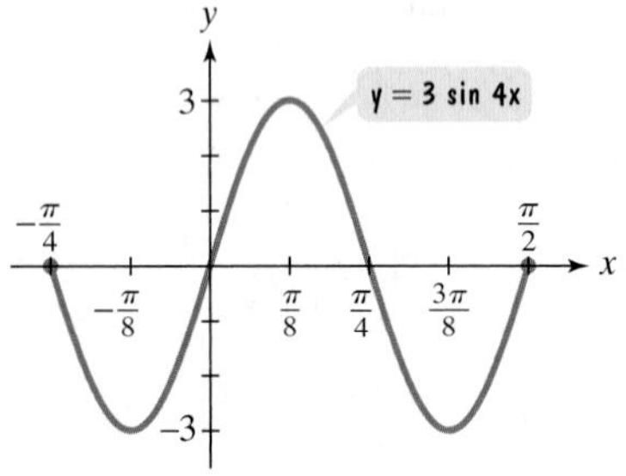


**27.**

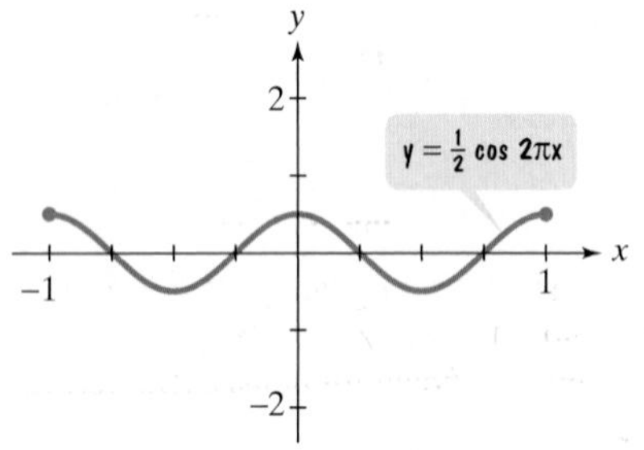


**28.**

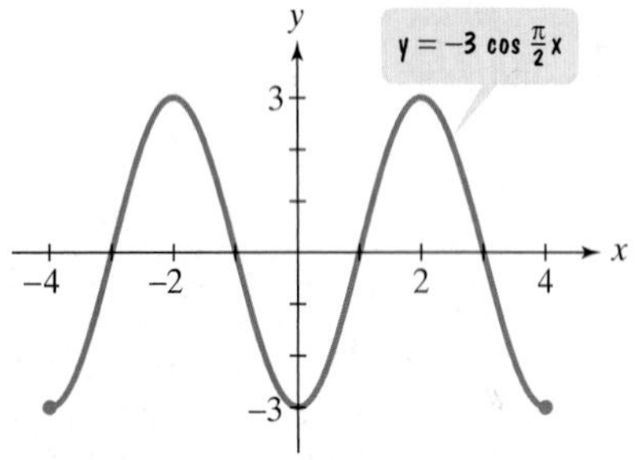


*In Exercises 29–44, graph two periods of the given cosecant or secant function.*

**29.** $y = 3\csc x$

**30.** $y = 2\csc x$

**31.** $y = \frac{1}{2}\csc\frac{x}{2}$

**32.** $y = \frac{3}{2}\csc\frac{x}{4}$

**33.** $y = 2\sec x$

**34.** $y = 3\sec x$

**35.** $y = \sec\frac{x}{3}$

**36.** $y = \sec\frac{x}{2}$

**37.** $y = -2\csc \pi x$

**38.** $y = -\frac{1}{2}\csc \pi x$

**39.** $y = -\frac{1}{2}\sec \pi x$

**40.** $y = -\frac{3}{2}\sec \pi x$

**41.** $y = \csc(x - \pi)$

**42.** $y = \csc\left(x - \frac{\pi}{2}\right)$

**43.** $y = 2\sec(x + \pi)$

**44.** $y = 2\sec\left(x + \frac{\pi}{2}\right)$

## Application Exercises

**45.** An ambulance with a rotating beacon of light is parked 12 feet from a building. The function

$$d = 12\tan 2\pi t$$

describes the distance, $d$, in feet, of the rotating beacon from point $C$ after $t$ seconds.

**a.** Graph the function on the interval $[0, 2]$.

**b.** For what values of $t$ in $[0, 2]$ is the function undefined? What does this mean in terms of the rotating beacon in the figure shown?

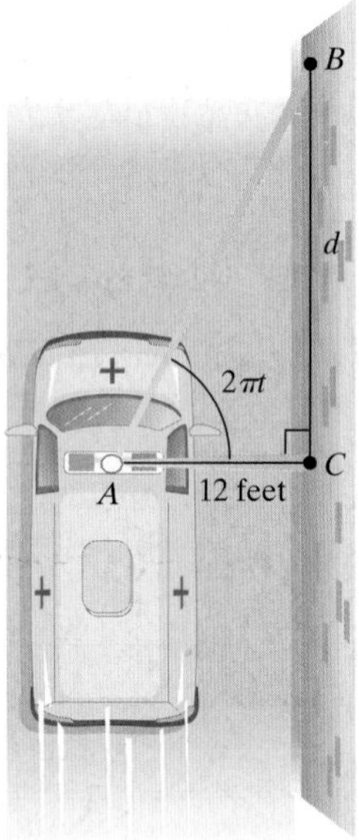


**46.** The angle of elevation from the top of a house to a jet flying 2 miles above the house is $x$ radians. If $d$ represents the horizontal distance of the jet from the house, express $d$ in terms of a trigonometric function of $x$. Then graph the function for $0 < x < \pi$.

**47.** Your best friend is marching with a band and has asked you to film her. The figure on page 497 shows that you have set yourself up 10 feet from the street where your friend will be passing from left to right. If $d$ represents your distance from your friend and $x$ is the radian measure of the angle shown, express $d$ in terms of a trigonometric function of

$x$. Then graph the function for $-\frac{\pi}{2} < x < \frac{\pi}{2}$. Negative angles indicate that your marching buddy is on your left.

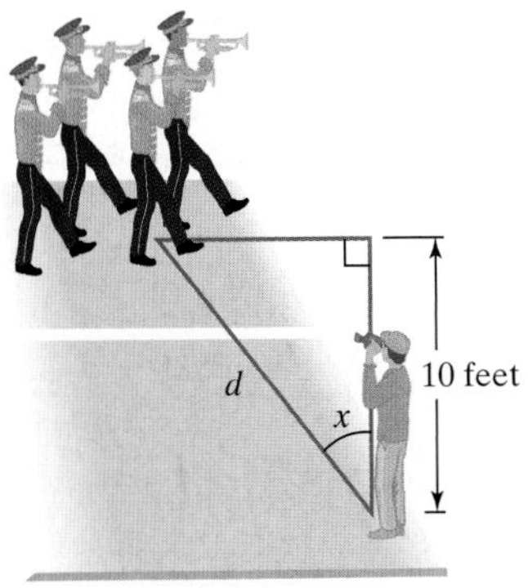


*In Exercises 48–50, sketch a reasonable graph that models the given situation.*

**48.** The number of hours of daylight per day in your hometown over a two-year period

**49.** The motion of a diving board vibrating 10 inches in each direction per second just after someone has dived off

**50.** The distance of a rotating beacon of light from a point on a wall (See the figure for Exercise 45.)

## Writing in Mathematics

**51.** Without drawing a graph, describe the behavior of the basic tangent curve.

**52.** If you are given the equation of a tangent function, how do you find consecutive asymptotes?

**53.** If you are given the equation of a tangent function, how do you identify an $x$-intercept?

**54.** Without drawing a graph, describe the behavior of the basic cotangent curve.

**55.** If you are given the equation of a cotangent function, how do you find consecutive asymptotes?

**56.** Explain how to determine the range of $y = \csc x$ from the graph. What is the range?

**57.** Explain how to use a sine curve to obtain a cosecant curve. Why can the same procedure be used to obtain a secant curve from a cosine curve?

**58.** Scientists record brain activity by attaching electrodes to the scalp and then connecting these electrodes to a machine. The record of brain activity recorded with this machine is shown in the three graphs at the top of the next column. Which trigonometric functions would be most appropriate for describing the oscillations in brain activity? Describe similarities and differences among these functions when modeling brain activity when awake, during dreaming sleep, and during non-dreaming sleep.

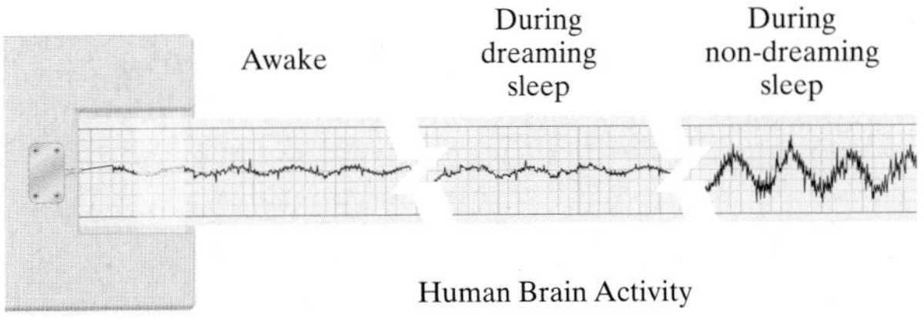


Human Brain Activity

## Technology Exercises

*In working Exercises 59–62, describe what happens at the asymptotes on the graphing utility. Compare the graphs in the connected and dot modes.*

**59.** Use a graphing utility to verify any two of the tangent curves that you drew by hand in Exercises 5–12.

**60.** Use a graphing utility to verify any two of the cotangent curves that you drew by hand in Exercises 17–24.

**61.** Use a graphing utility to verify any two of the cosecant curves that you drew by hand in Exercises 29–44.

**62.** Use a graphing utility to verify any two of the secant curves that you drew by hand in Exercises 29–44.

*In Exercises 63–68, use a graphing utility to graph each function. Use a range setting so that the graph is shown for at least two periods.*

**63.** $y = \tan \frac{x}{4}$

**64.** $y = \tan 4x$

**65.** $y = \cot 2x$

**66.** $y = \cot \frac{x}{2}$

**67.** $y = \frac{1}{2} \tan \pi x$

**68.** $y = \frac{1}{2} \tan(\pi x + 1)$

*In Exercises 69–72, use a graphing utility to graph each pair of functions in the same viewing rectangle. Use a range setting so that the graphs are shown for at least two periods.*

**69.** $y = 0.8 \sin \frac{x}{2}$ and $y = 0.8 \csc \frac{x}{2}$

**70.** $y = -2.5 \sin \frac{\pi}{3} x$ and $y = -2.5 \csc \frac{\pi}{3} x$

**71.** $y = 4 \cos\left(2x - \frac{\pi}{6}\right)$ and $y = 4 \sec\left(2x - \frac{\pi}{6}\right)$

**72.** $y = -3.5 \cos\left(\pi x - \frac{\pi}{6}\right)$ and $y = -3.5 \sec\left(\pi x - \frac{\pi}{6}\right)$

**73.** Carbon dioxide particles in our atmosphere trap heat and raise the planet's temperature. The resultant gradually increasing temperature is called the greenhouse effect. Carbon dioxide accounts for about half of global warming. The function

$$y = 2.5 \sin 2\pi x + 0.0216x^2 + 0.654x + 316$$

models carbon dioxide concentration, $y$, in parts per million, where $x = 0$ represents January 1960; $x = \frac{1}{12}$, February 1960; $x = \frac{2}{12}$, March 1960; … , $x = 1$, January 1961; $x = \frac{13}{12}$, February 1961; and so on. Use a graphing utility to graph the function in a [30, 40, 5] by [310, 380, 5] viewing rectangle. Describe what the graph reveals about carbon dioxide concentration from 1990 to 2000.

**74.** Graph $y = \sin \frac{1}{x}$ in a $[-0.2, 0.2, 0.01]$ by $[-1.2, 1.2, 0.01]$ viewing rectangle. What is happening as $x$ approaches 0 from the left or the right? Explain this behavior.

## Critical Thinking Exercises

*In Exercises 75–76, write an equation for each blue graph.*

**75.**

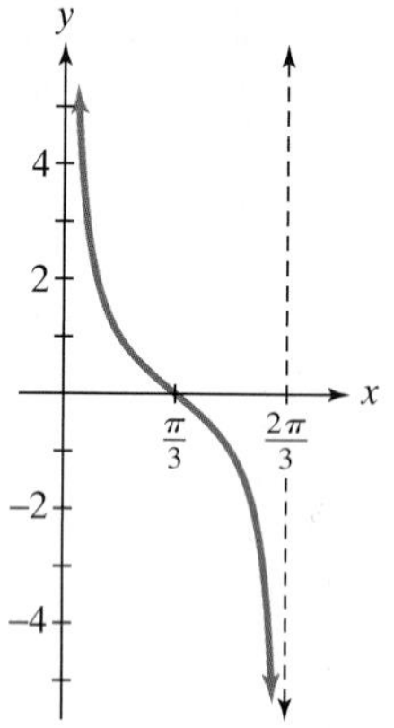


**76.**

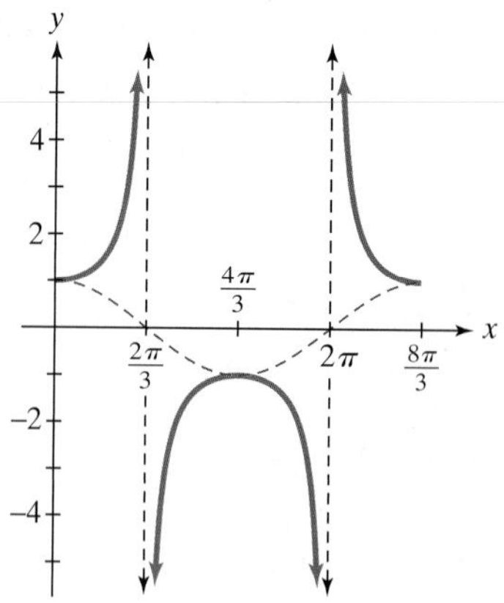


**77.** For $x > 0$, what effect does $2^{-x}$ in $y = 2^{-x} \sin x$ have on the graph of $y = \sin x$? What kind of behavior can be modeled by a function such as $y = 2^{-x} \sin x$?

# SECTION 5.7 Inverse Trigonometric Functions

## Objectives

1. Understand and use the inverse sine function.
2. Understand and use the inverse cosine function.
3. Understand and use the inverse tangent function.
4. Use a calculator to evaluate inverse trigonometric functions.
5. Find exact values of composite functions with inverse trigonometric functions.

You watched *The Matrix* on video and were impressed by the elaborate computer-generated effects. The movie is being shown again at a local theater, where you can experience its stunning visual force on a large screen. Where in the theater should you sit to maximize the film's visual impact? In this section you will see how an inverse trigonometric function can enhance your movie-going experiences.

### Study Tip

Here are some helpful things to remember from our discussion of inverse functions in Section 2.6.

- If no horizontal line intersects the graph of a function more than once, the function is one-to-one and has an inverse function.
- If the point $(a, b)$ is on the graph of $f$, then the point $(b, a)$ is on the graph of the inverse function, denoted $f^{-1}$. The graph of $f^{-1}$ is a reflection of the graph of $f$ about the line $y = x$.

**1** Understand and use the inverse sine function.

## The Inverse Sine Function

Figure 5.66 shows the graph of $y = \sin x$. Can you see that every horizontal line that can be drawn between $-1$ and 1 intersects the graph infinitely many times? Thus, the sine function is not one-to-one and has no inverse function.

In Figure 5.67, we have taken a portion of the sine curve, restricting the domain of the sine function to $-\frac{\pi}{2} \le x \le \frac{\pi}{2}$. With this restricted domain, every horizontal line that can be drawn between $-1$ and 1 intersects the graph exactly once. Thus, the restricted function passes the horizontal line test and is one-to-one.

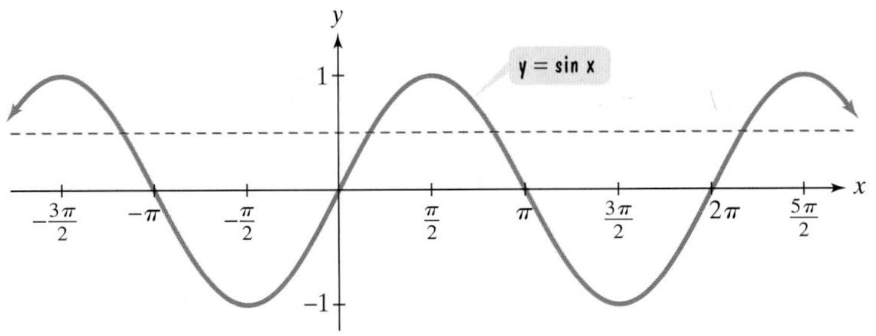


**Figure 5.66** The horizontal line test shows that the sine function is not one to one and has no inverse function.

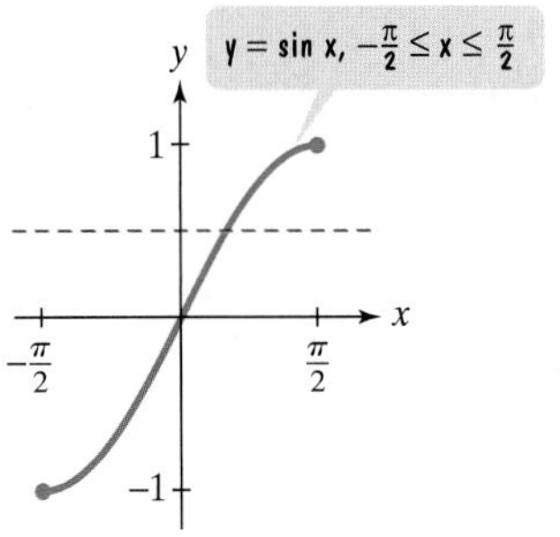


**Figure 5.67** The restricted sine function passes the horizontal line test. It is one-to-one and has an inverse function.

On the restricted domain $-\frac{\pi}{2} \le x \le \frac{\pi}{2}$, $y = \sin x$ has an inverse function. The inverse of the restricted sine function is called the **inverse sine function.** Two notations are commonly used to denote the inverse sine function:

$$y = \sin^{-1} x \quad \text{or} \quad y = \arcsin x.$$

In this book, we will use $y = \sin^{-1} x$. This notation has the same symbol as the inverse function notation $f^{-1}(x)$.

### The Inverse Sine Function

The **inverse sine function**, denoted by $\sin^{-1}$, is the inverse of the restricted sine function $y = \sin x$, $-\frac{\pi}{2} \le x \le \frac{\pi}{2}$. Thus,

$$y = \sin^{-1} x \quad \text{means} \quad \sin y = x,$$

where $-\frac{\pi}{2} \le y \le \frac{\pi}{2}$ and $-1 \le x \le 1$. We read $y = \sin^{-1} x$ as "$y$ equals the inverse sine at $x$."

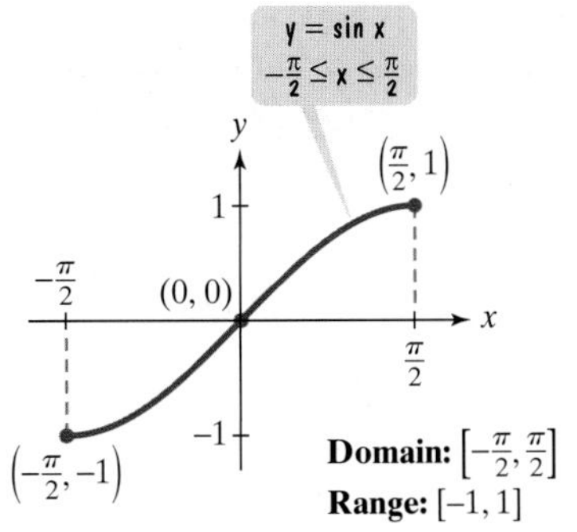


**Figure 5.68** The restricted sine function

One way to graph $y = \sin^{-1} x$ is to take points on the graph of the restricted sine function and reverse the order of the coordinates. For example, Figure 5 shows that $\left(-\frac{\pi}{2}, -1\right)$, $(0, 0)$, and $\left(\frac{\pi}{2}, 1\right)$ are on the graph of the restrict function. Reversing the order of the coordinates gives $\left(-1, -\frac{\pi}{2}\right)$.

$\left(1, \frac{\pi}{2}\right)$. We now use these three points to sketch the inverse sine function. The graph of $y = \sin^{-1} x$ is shown in Figure 5.69.

Another way to obtain the graph of $y = \sin^{-1} x$ is to reflect the graph of the restricted sine function about the line $y = x$, shown in Figure 5.70. The blue graph is the graph of $y = \sin^{-1} x$.

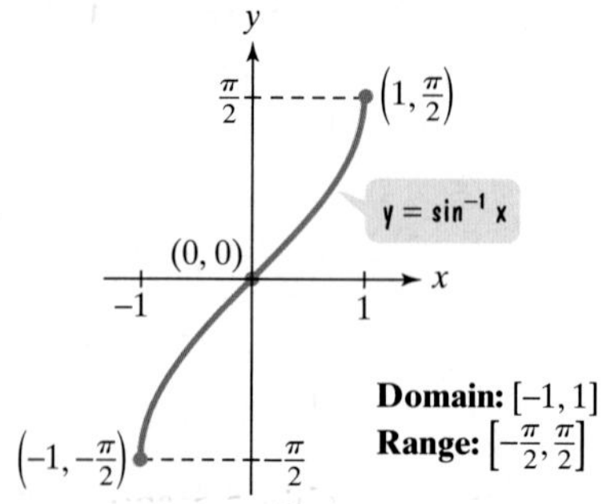


**Figure 5.69** The graph of the inverse sine function

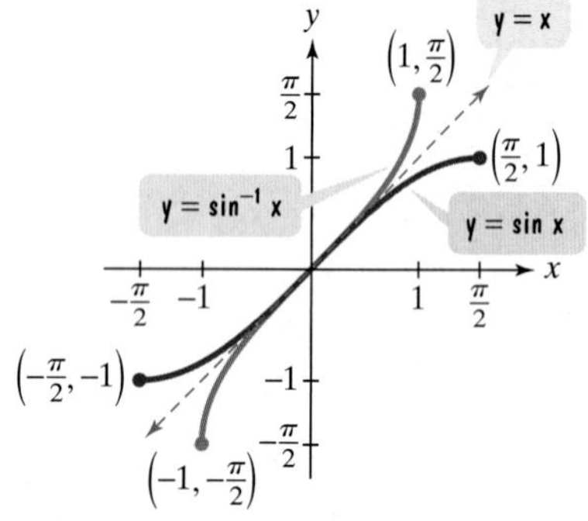


**Figure 5.70** Using a reflection to obtain the graph of the inverse sine function

Exact values of $\sin^{-1} x$ can be found by thinking of $\mathbf{sin^{-1}}x$ **as the angle in the interval** $\left[-\frac{\pi}{2}, \frac{\pi}{2}\right]$ **whose sine is** $x$. For example, we can use the two points on the blue graph of the inverse sine function in Figure 5.70 and write

$$\sin^{-1}(-1) = -\frac{\pi}{2} \quad \text{and} \quad \sin^{-1} 1 = \frac{\pi}{2}.$$

The angle whose sine is −1 is $-\frac{\pi}{2}$.

The angle whose sine is 1 is $\frac{\pi}{2}$.

Because we are thinking of $\sin^{-1} x$ in terms of an angle, we will represent such an angle by $\theta$.

**Table 5.6 Exact Values for $\sin\theta, -\frac{\pi}{2} \le \theta \le \frac{\pi}{2}$**

| $\theta$ | $\sin\theta$ |
|---|---|
| $-\frac{\pi}{2}$ | $-1$ |
| $-\frac{\pi}{3}$ | $-\frac{\sqrt{3}}{2}$ |
| $-\frac{\pi}{4}$ | $-\frac{\sqrt{2}}{2}$ |
| $-\frac{\pi}{6}$ | $-\frac{1}{2}$ |
| $0$ | $0$ |
| $\frac{\pi}{6}$ | $\frac{1}{2}$ |
| $\frac{\pi}{4}$ | $\frac{\sqrt{2}}{2}$ |
| $\frac{\pi}{3}$ | $\frac{\sqrt{3}}{2}$ |
| $\frac{\pi}{2}$ | $1$ |

**Finding Exact Values of $\sin^{-1} x$.**

1. Let $\theta = \sin^{-1} x$.
2. Rewrite step 1 as $\sin\theta = x$.
3. Use the exact values in Table 5.6 to find the value of $\theta$ in $\left[-\frac{\pi}{2}, \frac{\pi}{2}\right]$ that satisfies $\sin\theta = x$.

## EXAMPLE 1 Finding the Exact Value of an Inverse Sine Function

Find the exact value of $\sin^{-1} \frac{\sqrt{2}}{2}$.

**Solution**

**Step 1** **Let $\theta = \sin^{-1} x$.** Thus,

$$\theta = \sin^{-1}\frac{\sqrt{2}}{2}.$$

We must find the angle $\theta$, $-\frac{\pi}{2} \le \theta \le \frac{\pi}{2}$, whose sine equals $\frac{\sqrt{2}}{2}$.

**Step 2** **Rewrite $\theta = \sin^{-1} x$ as $\sin\theta = x$.** Using the definition of the inverse sine function, we rewrite $\theta = \sin^{-1}\frac{\sqrt{2}}{2}$ as

$$\sin\theta = \frac{\sqrt{2}}{2}.$$

**Step 3** **Use the exact values in Table 5.6 to find the value of $\theta$ in $\left[-\frac{\pi}{2}, \frac{\pi}{2}\right]$ that satisfies $\sin\theta = x$.** Table 5.5 shows that the only angle in the interval $\left[-\frac{\pi}{2}, \frac{\pi}{2}\right]$ that satisfies $\sin\theta = \frac{\sqrt{2}}{2}$ is $\frac{\pi}{4}$. Thus, $\theta = \frac{\pi}{4}$. Because $\theta$, in step 1, represents $\sin^{-1}\frac{\sqrt{2}}{2}$, we conclude that

$$\sin^{-1}\frac{\sqrt{2}}{2} = \frac{\pi}{4}.$$ The angle in $\left[-\frac{\pi}{2}, \frac{\pi}{2}\right]$ whose sine is $\frac{\sqrt{2}}{2}$ is $\frac{\pi}{4}$

**Study Tip**

If you have not already done so, you should memorize the values in Table 5.6, as well as those in the forthcoming Tables 5.7 and 5.8.

**Check Point 1** Find the exact value of $\sin^{-1}\frac{\sqrt{3}}{2}$.

## EXAMPLE 2 Finding the Exact Value of an Inverse Sine Function

Find the exact value of $\sin^{-1}\left(-\frac{1}{2}\right)$.

**Solution**

**Step 1** **Let $\theta = \sin^{-1} x$. Thus,**

$$\theta = \sin^{-1}\left(-\frac{1}{2}\right).$$

We must find the angle $\theta$, $-\frac{\pi}{2} \le \theta \le \frac{\pi}{2}$, whose sine equals $-\frac{1}{2}$.

**Step 2** **Rewrite $\theta = \sin^{-1}x$ as $\sin\theta = x$.** We obtain

$$\sin\theta = -\frac{1}{2}$$

**Step 3** **Use the exact values in Table 5.6 to find the value of $\theta$ in $\left[-\frac{\pi}{2}, \frac{\pi}{2}\right]$ that satisfies $\sin\theta = x$.** The table on page 500 shows that the only angle in the interval $\left[-\frac{\pi}{2}, \frac{\pi}{2}\right]$ that satisfies $\sin\theta = -\frac{1}{2}$ is $-\frac{\pi}{6}$. Thus,

$$\sin^{-1}\left(-\frac{1}{2}\right) = -\frac{\pi}{6}$$

**Check Point 2** Find the exact value of $\sin^{-1}\left(-\frac{\sqrt{2}}{2}\right)$.

Some inverse sine expressions cannot be evaluated. Because the domain of the inverse sine function is $[-1, 1]$, it is only possible to evaluate $\sin^{-1}x$ for values of $x$ in this domain. Thus, $\sin^{-1}3$ cannot be evaluated. There is no angle whose sine is 3.

**2** Understand and use the inverse cosine function.

## The Inverse Cosine Function

Figure 5.71 shows how we restrict the domain of the cosine function so that it becomes one-to-one and has an inverse function. Restrict the domain to the interval $[0, \pi]$, shown by the dark blue graph. Over this interval, the restricted cosine function passes the horizontal line test and has an inverse function.

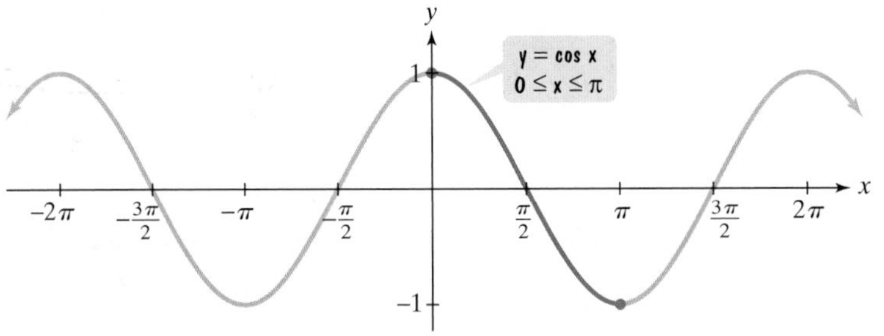


**Figure 5.71** $y = \cos x$ is one-to-one on the interval $[0, \pi]$.

### The Inverse Cosine Function

The **inverse cosine function**, denoted by $\cos^{-1}$, is the inverse of the restricted cosine function $y = \cos x$, $0 \le x \le \pi$. Thus,

$$y = \cos^{-1}x \quad \text{means} \quad \cos y = x,$$

where $0 \le y \le \pi$ and $-1 \le x \le 1$.

One way to graph $y = \cos^{-1} x$ is to take points on the graph of the restricted cosine function and reverse the order of the coordinates. For example, Figure 5.72 shows that $(0, 1)$, $\left(\frac{\pi}{2}, 0\right)$ and $(\pi, -1)$ are on the graph of the restricted cosine function. Reversing the order of the coordinates gives $(1, 0)$, $\left(0, \frac{\pi}{2}\right)$, and $(-1, \pi)$. We now use these three points to sketch the inverse cosine function. The graph of $y = \cos^{-1} x$ is shown in Figure 5.73. You can also obtain this graph by reflecting the graph of the restricted cosine function about the line $y = x$.

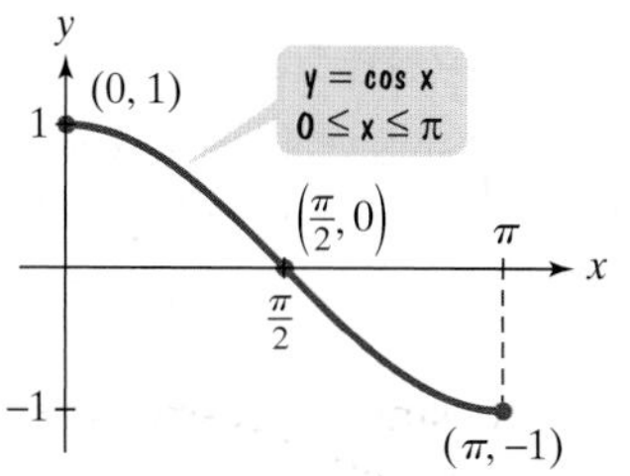


**Domain:** $[0, \pi]$
**Range:** $[-1, 1]$

**Figure 5.72** The restricted cosine function

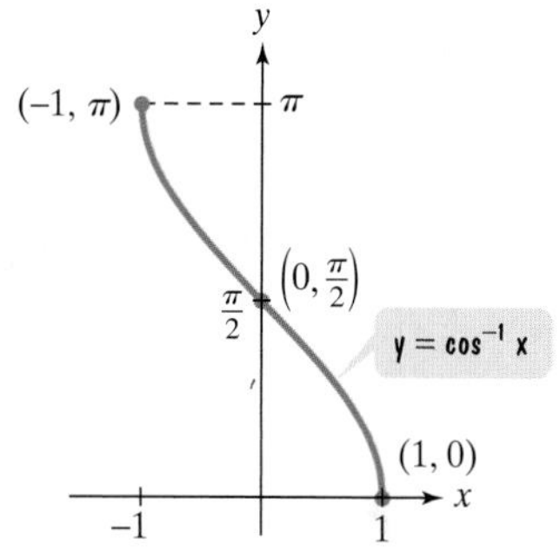


**Domain:** $[-1, 1]$
**Range:** $[0, \pi]$

**Figure 5.73** The graph of the inverse cosine function

**Table 5.7 Exact Values for $\cos\theta$, $0 \le \theta \le \pi$**

| $\theta$ | $\cos\theta$ |
|---|---|
| $0$ | $1$ |
| $\frac{\pi}{6}$ | $\frac{\sqrt{3}}{2}$ |
| $\frac{\pi}{4}$ | $\frac{\sqrt{2}}{2}$ |
| $\frac{\pi}{3}$ | $\frac{1}{2}$ |
| $\frac{\pi}{2}$ | $0$ |
| $\frac{2\pi}{3}$ | $-\frac{1}{2}$ |
| $\frac{3\pi}{4}$ | $-\frac{\sqrt{2}}{2}$ |
| $\frac{5\pi}{6}$ | $-\frac{\sqrt{3}}{2}$ |
| $\pi$ | $-1$ |

Exact values of $\cos^{-1} x$ can be found by thinking of $\cos^{-1}x$ as **the angle in the interval $[0, \pi]$ whose cosine is $x$.** This time we will use Table 5.7, which shows exact values for $\cos\theta$ for $\theta$ in the interval $[0, \pi]$.

## EXAMPLE 3 Finding the Exact Value of an Inverse Cosine Function

Find the exact value of $\cos^{-1}\left(-\frac{\sqrt{3}}{2}\right)$.

**Solution**

**Step 1 Let $\theta = \cos^{-1}x$.** Thus,

$$\theta = \cos^{-1}\left(-\frac{\sqrt{3}}{2}\right).$$

We must find the angle $\theta$, $0 \le \theta \le \pi$, whose cosine equals $-\frac{\sqrt{3}}{2}$.

**Step 2 Rewrite $\theta = \cos^{-1}x$ as $\cos\theta = x$.** We obtain

$$\cos\theta = -\frac{\sqrt{3}}{2}.$$

**Step 3 Use the exact values in Table 5.7 to find the value of $\theta$ in $[0, \pi]$ that satisfies $\cos\theta = x$.** The table on page 503 shows that the only angle in the interval $[0, \pi]$ that satisfies $\cos\theta = -\frac{\sqrt{3}}{2}$ is $\frac{5\pi}{6}$. Thus, $\theta = \frac{5\pi}{6}$ and

$$\cos^{-1}\left(-\frac{\sqrt{3}}{2}\right) = \frac{5\pi}{6}.$$ The angle in $[0, \pi]$ whose cosine is $-\frac{\sqrt{3}}{2}$ is $\frac{5\pi}{6}$.

**Check Point 3** Find the exact value of $\cos^{-1}\left(-\frac{1}{2}\right)$.

**3** Understand and use the inverse tangent function.

## The Inverse Tangent Function

Figure 5.74 shows how we restrict the domain of the tangent function so that it becomes one-to-one and has an inverse function. Restrict the domain to the interval $\left(-\frac{\pi}{2}, \frac{\pi}{2}\right)$, shown by the solid blue graph. Over this interval, the restricted tangent function passes the horizontal line test and has an inverse function.

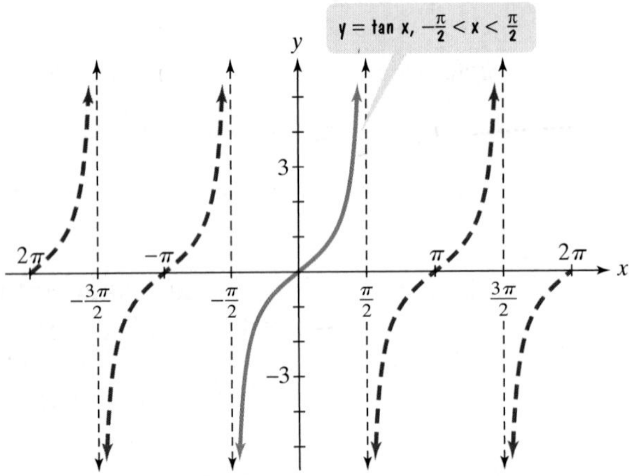


**Figure 5.74** $y = \tan x$ is one-to-one on the interval $\left(-\frac{\pi}{2}, \frac{\pi}{2}\right)$.

### The Inverse Tangent Function

The **inverse tangent function**, denoted by $\tan^{-1}$, is the inverse of the restricted tangent function $y = \tan x, -\frac{\pi}{2} < x < \frac{\pi}{2}$. Thus,

$$y = \tan^{-1}x \quad \text{means } \tan y = \infty,$$

where $-\frac{\pi}{2} < y < \frac{\pi}{2}$ and $-\infty < x < \infty$.

We graph $y = \tan^{-1}x$ by taking points on the graph of the restricted function and reversing the order of the coordinates. Figure 5.75 at the top of the next page shows that $\left(-\frac{\pi}{4}, -1\right)$, $(0, 0)$, and $\left(\frac{\pi}{4}, 1\right)$ are on the graph of the restricted tangent function. Reversing the order gives $\left(-1, -\frac{\pi}{4}\right)$, (0, 0), and $\left(1, \frac{\pi}{4}\right)$. We now use these three points to graph the inverse tangent function. The graph of $y = \tan^{-1} x$ is shown in Figure 5.76. Notice that the vertical asymptotes become horizontal asymptotes for the graph of the inverse function.

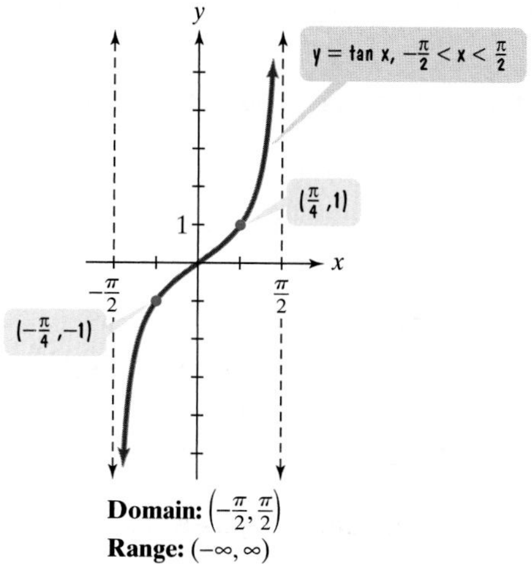


**Figure 5.75** The restricted tangent function

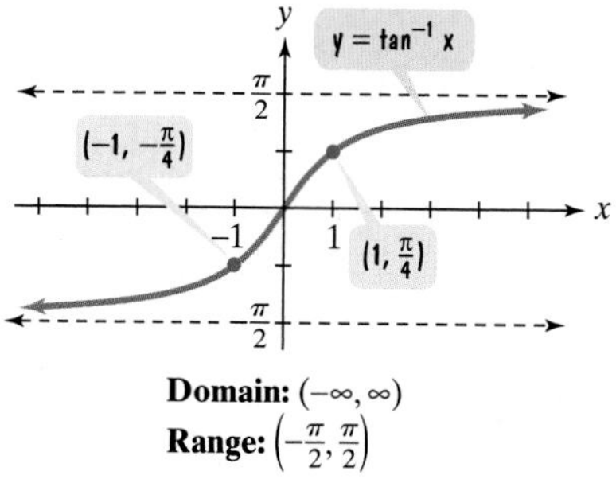


**Figure 5.76** The graph of the inverse tangent function

Exact values of $\tan^{-1} x$ can be found by thinking of $\tan^{-1} x$ as **the angle in the interval** $\left(-\frac{\pi}{2}, \frac{\pi}{2}\right)$ **whose tangent is *x*.** We use Table 5.8, which shows exact values for $\tan\theta$ for $\theta$ in the interval $\left(-\frac{\pi}{2}, \frac{\pi}{2}\right)$.

**Table 5.8 Exact Values for $\tan\theta, -\frac{\pi}{2} < \theta < \frac{\pi}{2}$**

| $\theta$ | $\tan\theta$ |
|---|---|
| $-\frac{\pi}{2}$ | Undefined |
| $-\frac{\pi}{3}$ | $-\sqrt{3}$ |
| $-\frac{\pi}{4}$ | $-1$ |
| $-\frac{\pi}{6}$ | $-\frac{\sqrt{3}}{3}$ |
| 0 | 0 |
| $\frac{\pi}{6}$ | $\frac{\sqrt{3}}{3}$ |
| $\frac{\pi}{4}$ | 1 |
| $\frac{\pi}{3}$ | $\sqrt{3}$ |
| $\frac{\pi}{2}$ | Undefined |

## EXAMPLE 4 Finding the Exact Value of an Inverse Tangent Function

Find the exact value of $\tan^{-1}\sqrt{3}$.

**Solution**

**Step 1 Let $\theta = \tan^{-1} x$.** Thus,

$$\theta = \tan^{-1}\sqrt{3}.$$

We must find the angle $\theta$, $-\frac{\pi}{2} < \theta < \frac{\pi}{2}$, whose tangent equals $\sqrt{3}$.

**Step 2 Rewrite $\theta = \tan^{-1} x$ as $\tan\theta = x$.** We obtain $\tan\theta = \sqrt{3}$.

**Step 3 Use the exact values in Table 5.8 to find the value of $\theta$ in $\left(-\frac{\pi}{2}, \frac{\pi}{2}\right)$ that satisfies $\tan\theta = x$.** The table shows that the only angle in the interval $\left(-\frac{\pi}{2}, \frac{\pi}{2}\right)$ that satisfies $\tan\theta = \sqrt{3}$ is $\frac{\pi}{3}$. Thus, $\theta = \frac{\pi}{3}$ and

$$\tan^{-1}\sqrt{3} = \frac{\pi}{3}.$$ The angle in $\left(-\frac{\pi}{2}, \frac{\pi}{2}\right)$ whose tangent is $\sqrt{3}$ is $\frac{\pi}{3}$.

**Check Point 4** Find the exact value of $\tan^{-1}(-1)$.

Table 5.9 summarizes the graphs of the three basic inverse trigonometric functions. Below each of the graphs is a description of the function's domain and range.

**Table 5.9 Graphs of the Three Basic Inverse Trigonometric Functions**

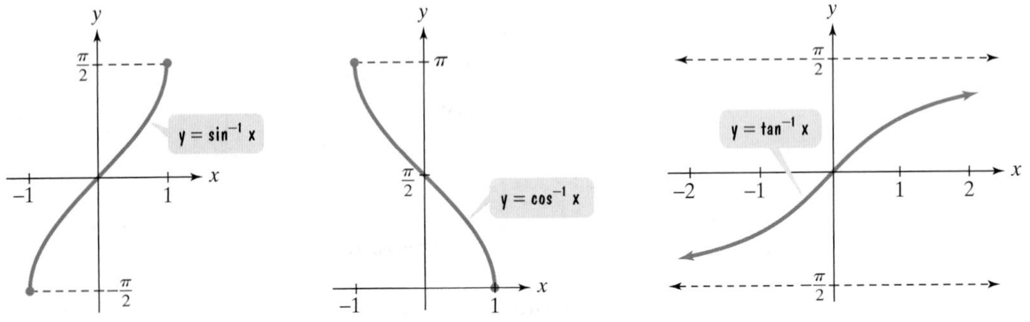


| | | |
|---|---|---|
| **Domain:** $[-1, 1]$ | **Domain:** $[-1, 1]$ | **Domain:** $(-\infty, \infty)$ |
| **Range:** $\left[-\frac{\pi}{2}, \frac{\pi}{2}\right]$ | **Range:** $[0, \pi]$ | **Range:** $\left(-\frac{\pi}{2}, \frac{\pi}{2}\right)$ |

**4** Use a calculator to evaluate inverse trigonometric functions.

## Using a Calculator to Evaluate Inverse Trigonometric Functions

Calculators give approximate values of inverse trigonometric functions. Use the keys marked [SIN⁻¹], [COS⁻¹], and [TAN⁻¹]. Consult your manual for the location of this feature.

### EXAMPLE 5 Calculators and Inverse Trigonometric Functions

Use a calculator to find the value to four decimal places of:

**a.** $\sin^{-1}\frac{1}{4}$ **b.** $\tan^{-1}(-9.65)$.

**Solution**

**Scientific Calculator Solution**

| Function | Mode | Keystrokes | Display, rounded to four places |
|---|---|---|---|
| **a.** $\sin^{-1}\frac{1}{4}$ | Radian | 1 [÷] 4 [=] [SIN⁻¹] | 0.2527 |
| **b.** $\tan^{-1}(-9.65)$ | Radian | 9.65 [+/−] [TAN⁻¹] | −1.4675 |

**Graphing Calculator Solution**

| Function | Mode | Keystrokes | Display, rounded to four places |
|---|---|---|---|
| **a.** $\sin^{-1}\frac{1}{4}$ | Radian | [SIN⁻¹] [(] 1 [÷] [4] [)] [ENTER] | 0.2527 |
| **b.** $\tan^{-1}(-9.65)$ | Radian | [TAN⁻¹] [(−)] 9.65 [ENTER] | −1.4675 |

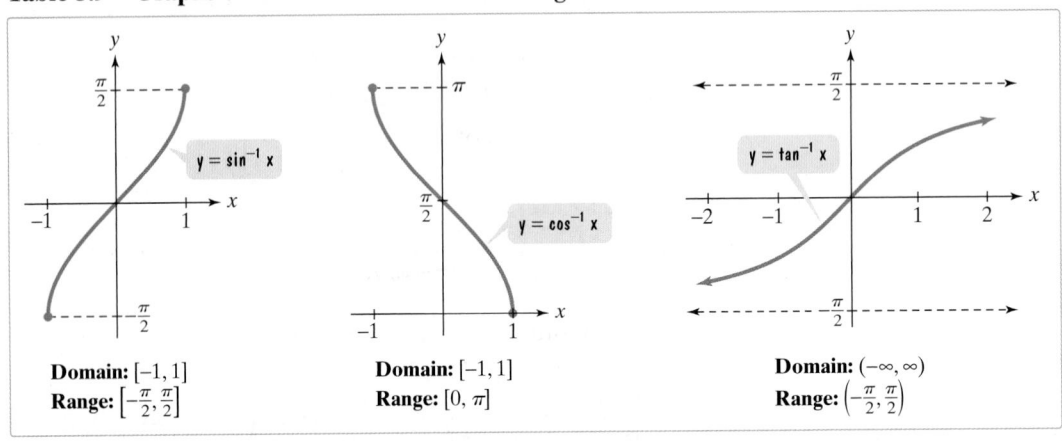

**Check Point 5** Use a calculator to find the value to four decimal places of:

**a.** $\cos^{-1}\frac{1}{3}$ **b.** $\tan^{-1}(-35.85)$.

What happens if you attempt to evaluate an inverse trigomometric function at a value that is not in its domain? In real number mode, most calculators will display an error message. For example, an error message can result if you attempt to approximate $\cos^{-1}3$. There is no angle whose cosine is 3. The domain of the inverse cosine function is $[-1, 1]$, and 3 does not belong to this domain.

**5** Find exact values of composite functions with inverse trigonometric functions.

## Composition of Functions Involving Inverse Trigonometric Functions

In our discussion of functions and their inverses in Section 2.6, we saw that

$$f(f^{-1}(x)) = x \quad \text{and} \quad f^{-1}(f(x)) = x.$$

x must be in the domain of $f^{-1}$.

x must be in the domain of f.

We apply these properties to the sine, cosine, tangent, and their inverse functions to obtain the following properties.

### Inverse Properties

**The Sine Function and Its Inverse**

$\sin(\sin^{-1}x) = x$ for every $x$ in the interval $[-1, 1]$

$\sin^{-1}(\sin x) = x$ for every $x$ in the interval $\left[-\frac{\pi}{2}, \frac{\pi}{2}\right]$

**The Cosine Function and Its Inverse**

$\cos(\cos^{-1}x) = x$ for every $x$ in the interval $[-1, 1]$

$\cos^{-1}(\cos x) = x$ for every $x$ in the interval $[0, \pi]$

**The Tangent Function and Its Inverse**

$\tan(\tan^{-1}x) = x$ for every real number $x$

$\tan^{-1}(\tan x) = x$ for every $x$ in the interval $\left(-\frac{\pi}{2}, \frac{\pi}{2}\right)$

The restrictions on $x$ in the inverse properties are a bit tricky. For example,

$$\sin^{-1}\left(\sin\frac{\pi}{4}\right) = \frac{\pi}{4}$$

$\sin^{-1}(\sin x) = x$ for $x$ in $\left[-\frac{\pi}{2}, \frac{\pi}{2}\right]$. Observe that $\frac{\pi}{4}$ is in this interval.

Can we use $\sin^{-1}(\sin x) = x$ to find the exact value of $\sin^{-1}\left(\sin\frac{5\pi}{4}\right)$? Is $\frac{5\pi}{4}$ in the interval $\left[-\frac{\pi}{2}, \frac{\pi}{2}\right]$? No. Thus to evaluate $\sin^{-1}\left(\sin\frac{5\pi}{4}\right)$, we must first find $\sin\frac{5\pi}{4}$.

$\frac{5\pi}{4}$ is in quadrant III where the sine is negative.

$$\sin\frac{5\pi}{4} = -\sin\frac{\pi}{4} = -\frac{\sqrt{2}}{2}$$

The reference angle for $\frac{5\pi}{4}$ is $\frac{\pi}{4}$.

We evaluate $\sin^{-1}\left(\sin\frac{5\pi}{4}\right)$ as follows.

$$\sin^{-1}\left(\sin\frac{5\pi}{4}\right) = \sin^{-1}\left(-\frac{\sqrt{2}}{2}\right) = -\frac{\pi}{4}$$ If necessary, see Table 5.5 on page 500.

To determine how to evaluate the composition of functions involving inverse trigonometric functions, first examine the value of $x$. You can use the inverse properties in the box on page 507 only if $x$ is in the specified interval.

## EXAMPLE 6 Evaluating Compositions of Functions and Their Inverses

Find the exact value, if possible, of:

**a.** $\cos(\cos^{-1}0.6)$ **b.** $\sin^{-1}\left(\sin\frac{3\pi}{2}\right)$ **c.** $\cos(\cos^{-1}2\pi)$.

### Solution

**a.** The inverse property $\cos(\cos^{-1}x) = x$ applies for every $x$ in $[-1, 1]$. To evaluate $\cos(\cos^{-1}0.6)$, observe that $x = 0.6$. This value of $x$ lies in $[-1, 1]$, which is the domain of the inverse cosine function. This means that we can use the inverse property $\cos(\cos^{-1}x) = x$. Thus,

$$\cos(\cos^{-1}0.6) = 0.6.$$

**b.** The inverse property $\sin^{-1}(\sin x) = x$ applies for every $x$ in $\left[-\frac{\pi}{2}, \frac{\pi}{2}\right]$. To evaluate $\sin^{-1}\left(\sin\frac{3\pi}{2}\right)$, observe that $x = \frac{3\pi}{2}$. This value of $x$ does not lie in $\left[-\frac{\pi}{2}, \frac{\pi}{2}\right]$. To evaluate this expression, we first find $\sin\frac{3\pi}{2}$.

$$\sin^{-1}\left(\sin\frac{3\pi}{2}\right) = \sin^{-1}(-1) = -\frac{\pi}{2}$$ The angle in $\left[-\frac{\pi}{2}, \frac{\pi}{2}\right]$ whose sine is $-1$ is $-\frac{\pi}{2}$.

**c.** The inverse property $\cos(\cos^{-1}x) = x$ applies for every $x$ in $[-1, 1]$. To attempt to evaluate $\cos(\cos^{-1}2\pi)$, observe that $x = 2\pi$. This value of $x$ does not lie in $[-1, 1]$, which is the domain of the inverse cosine function. Thus, the expression $\cos(\cos^{-1}2\pi)$ is not defined because $\cos^{-1}2\pi$ is not defined.

**Check Point 6** Find the exact value, if possible, of:

**a.** $\cos(\cos^{-1}0.7)$ **b.** $\sin^{-1}(\sin\pi)$ **c.** $\cos(\cos^{-1}\pi)$.

We can use points on terminal sides of angles in standard position to find exact values of expressions involving the composition of a function and a different inverse function. Here are two examples.

$$\cos\left(\tan^{-1}\frac{5}{12}\right) \qquad\qquad \cot\left[\sin^{-1}\left(-\frac{1}{3}\right)\right]$$

Inner part involves the angle in $\left(-\frac{\pi}{2}, \frac{\pi}{2}\right)$ whose tangent is $\frac{5}{12}$.

Inner part involves the angle in $\left(-\frac{\pi}{2}, \frac{\pi}{2}\right)$ whose sine is $-\frac{1}{3}$.

The inner part of each expression involves an angle. To evaluate such expressions, we represent such angles by $\theta$. Then we use a sketch that illustrates our representation. Examples 7 and 8 show how to carry out such evaluations.

## EXAMPLE 7 Evaluating a Composite Trigonometric Expression

Find the exact value of $\cos\left(\tan^{-1}\frac{5}{12}\right)$.

**Solution** We let $\theta$ represent the angle in $\left(-\frac{\pi}{2}, \frac{\pi}{2}\right)$ whose tangent is $\frac{5}{12}$. Thus,

$$\theta = \tan^{-1}\frac{5}{12}.$$

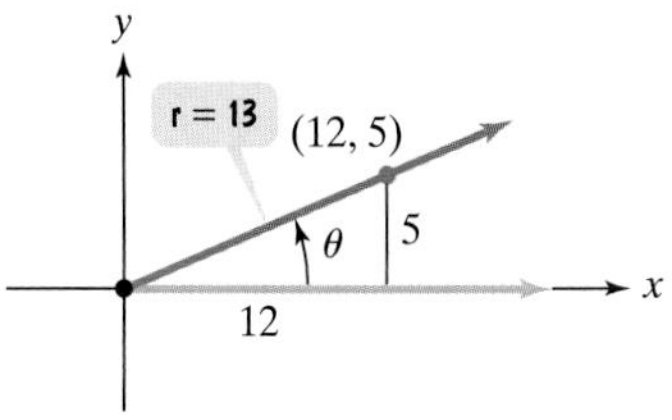

**Figure 5.77** Representing $\tan\theta = \frac{5}{12}$

Using the definition of the inverse tangent function, we can rewrite this as

$$\tan\theta = \frac{5}{12}.$$

Because $\tan\theta$ is positive, $\theta$ must be an angle in $\left(0, \frac{\pi}{2}\right)$. Thus, $\theta$ is a first-quadrant angle. Figure 5.77 shows a right triangle in quadrant I with

$$\tan\theta = \frac{5}{12}$$

Side opposite $\theta$. (5)
Side adjacent to $\theta$. (12)

The hypotenuse of the triangle can be found using the Pythagorean Theorem.

$$r^2 = 12^2 + 5^2 = 144 + 25 = 169 \quad \text{and} \quad r = \sqrt{169} = 13$$

We use this right triangle to find the exact value of $\cos\left(\tan^{-1}\frac{5}{12}\right)$.

$$\cos\left(\tan^{-1}\frac{5}{12}\right) = \cos\theta = \frac{\text{side adjacent to } \theta}{\text{hypotenuse}} = \frac{12}{13}$$

**Check Point 7** Find the exact value of $\sin\left(\tan^{-1}\frac{3}{4}\right)$.

## EXAMPLE 8 Evaluating a Composite Trigonometric Expression

Find the exact value of $\cot\left[\sin^{-1}\left(-\frac{1}{3}\right)\right]$.

**Solution** We let $\theta$ represent the angle in $\left[-\frac{\pi}{2}, \frac{\pi}{2}\right]$ whose sine is $-\frac{1}{3}$. Thus,

$$\theta = \sin^{-1}\left(-\frac{1}{3}\right) \quad \text{and} \quad \sin\theta = -\frac{1}{3}.$$

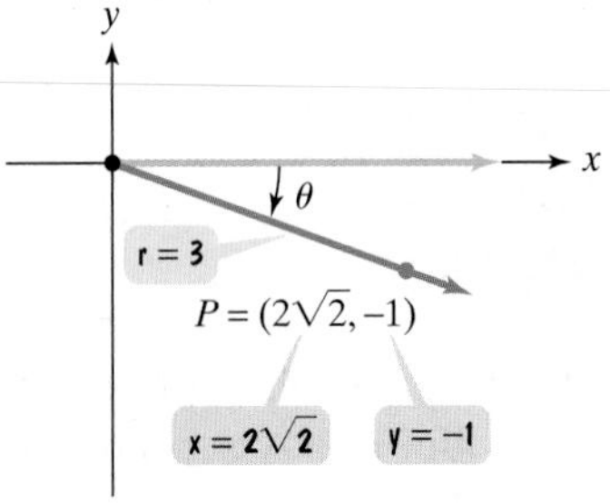


**Figure 5.78** Representing $\sin\theta = -\frac{1}{3}$

Because $\sin\theta$ is negative, $\theta$ must be an angle in $\left[-\frac{\pi}{2}, 0\right)$. Thus, $\theta$ is a negative angle that lies in quadrant IV. Figure 5.78 shows angle $\theta$ in quadrant IV with

In quadrant IV, y is negative

$$\sin\theta = -\frac{1}{3} = \frac{y}{r} = \frac{-1}{3}.$$

The value of $x$ can be found using $x^2 + y^2 = r^2$.

$$x^2 + (-1)^2 = 3^2$$

$$x^2 + 1 = 9$$

$$x^2 = 8$$

$$x = \sqrt{8} = \sqrt{4 \cdot 2} = 2\sqrt{2}$$ Remember that x is positive in quadrant IV.

We use values for $x$ and $y$ to find the exact value of $\cot\left[\sin^{-1}\left(-\frac{1}{3}\right)\right]$.

$$\cot\left[\sin^{-1}\left(-\frac{1}{3}\right)\right] = \cot\theta = \frac{x}{y} = \frac{2\sqrt{2}}{-1} = -2\sqrt{2}$$

**Check Point 8** Find the exact value of $\cos\left[\sin^{-1}\left(-\frac{1}{2}\right)\right]$.

Some composite functions with inverse trigonometric functions can be simplified to algebraic expressions. To simplify such an expression, we represent the inverse trigonometric function in the expression by $\theta$. Then we use a right triangle.

## EXAMPLE 9 Simplifying an Expression Involving $\sin^{-1} x$

If $0 < x \leq 1$, write $\cos(\sin^{-1} x)$ as an algebraic expression in $x$.

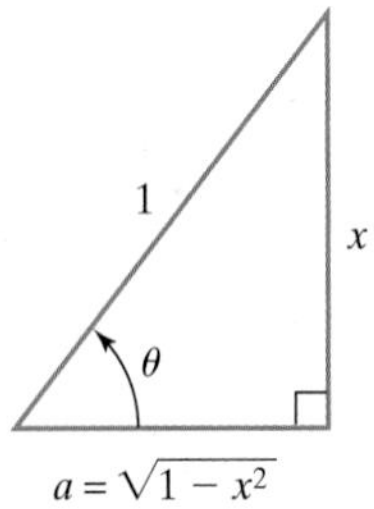


**Figure 5.79** Representing $\sin\theta = x$

**Solution** We let $\theta$ represent the angle in $\left[-\frac{\pi}{2}, \frac{\pi}{2}\right]$ whose sine is $x$. Thus,

$$\theta = \sin^{-1} x, \quad \text{and} \quad \sin\theta = x.$$

Because $0 < x \leq 1$, $\sin\theta$ is positive. Thus, $\theta$ is a first-quadrant angle. Figure 5.79 shows a right triangle in quadrant I with

$$\sin\theta = x = \frac{x}{1}.$$

Side opposite $\theta$

Hypotenuse

The third side, $a$, can be found using the Pythagorean Theorem.

$$a^2 + x^2 = 1^2$$ Apply the Pythagorean Theorem to the right triangle in Figure 5.78.

$$a^2 = 1 - x^2$$ Subtract $x^2$ from both sides.

$$a = \sqrt{1 - x^2}$$ Solve for $a$.

We use the right triangle in Figure 5.79 to write $\cos(\sin^{-1} x)$ as an algebraic expression.

$$\cos(\sin^{-1} x) = \cos\theta = \frac{\text{side adjacent to } \theta}{\text{hypotenuse}} = \frac{\sqrt{1-x^2}}{1} = \sqrt{1-x^2}$$

**Check Point 9** If $x > 0$, write $\sec(\tan^{-1} x)$ as an algebraic expression in $x$.

The inverse secant function, $y = \sec^{-1} x$, is used in calculus. However, inverse cotangent and inverse cosecant functions are rarely used. Two of these remaining inverse trigonometric functions are briefly developed in the exercise set that follows.

## EXERCISE SET 5.7

### Practice Exercises

*In Exercises 1–18, use the values in the table shown to find the exact value of each expression.*

| $\theta$ | $-\frac{\pi}{2}$ | $-\frac{\pi}{3}$ | $-\frac{\pi}{4}$ | $-\frac{\pi}{6}$ | 0 | $\frac{\pi}{6}$ | $\frac{\pi}{4}$ | $\frac{\pi}{3}$ | $\frac{\pi}{2}$ | $\frac{2\pi}{3}$ | $\frac{3\pi}{4}$ | $\frac{5\pi}{6}$ | $\pi$ |
|---|---|---|---|---|---|---|---|---|---|---|---|---|---|
| **sin $\theta$** | $-1$ | $-\frac{\sqrt{3}}{2}$ | $-\frac{\sqrt{2}}{2}$ | $-\frac{1}{2}$ | 0 | $\frac{1}{2}$ | $\frac{\sqrt{2}}{2}$ | $\frac{\sqrt{3}}{2}$ | 1 | $\frac{\sqrt{3}}{2}$ | $\frac{\sqrt{2}}{2}$ | $\frac{1}{2}$ | 0 |
| **cos $\theta$** | 0 | $\frac{1}{2}$ | $\frac{\sqrt{2}}{2}$ | $\frac{\sqrt{3}}{2}$ | 1 | $\frac{\sqrt{3}}{2}$ | $\frac{\sqrt{2}}{2}$ | $\frac{1}{2}$ | 0 | $-\frac{1}{2}$ | $-\frac{\sqrt{2}}{2}$ | $-\frac{\sqrt{3}}{2}$ | $-1$ |
| **tan $\theta$** | undef. | $-\sqrt{3}$ | $-1$ | $-\frac{\sqrt{3}}{3}$ | 0 | $\frac{\sqrt{3}}{3}$ | 1 | $\sqrt{3}$ | undef. | $-\sqrt{3}$ | $-1$ | $\frac{-\sqrt{3}}{3}$ | 0 |

**1.** $\sin^{-1}\frac{1}{2}$
**2.** $\sin^{-1} 0$
**3.** $\sin^{-1}\frac{\sqrt{2}}{2}$
**4.** $\sin^{-1}\frac{\sqrt{3}}{2}$
**5.** $\sin^{-1}\left(-\frac{1}{2}\right)$
**6.** $\sin^{-1}\left(-\frac{\sqrt{3}}{2}\right)$
**7.** $\cos^{-1}\frac{\sqrt{3}}{2}$
**8.** $\cos^{-1}\frac{\sqrt{2}}{2}$
**9.** $\cos^{-1}\left(-\frac{\sqrt{2}}{2}\right)$
**10.** $\cos^{-1}\left(-\frac{\sqrt{3}}{2}\right)$
**11.** $\cos^{-1} 0$
**12.** $\cos^{-1} 1$
**13.** $\tan^{-1}\frac{\sqrt{3}}{3}$
**14.** $\tan^{-1} 1$
**15.** $\tan^{-1} 0$
**16.** $\tan^{-1}(-1)$
**17.** $\tan^{-1}(-\sqrt{3})$
**18.** $\tan^{-1}\left(-\frac{\sqrt{3}}{3}\right)$

*In Exercises 19–30, use a calculator to find the value of each expression rounded to two decimal places.*

**19.** $\sin^{-1} 0.3$
**20.** $\sin^{-1} 0.47$
**21.** $\sin^{-1}(-0.32)$
**22.** $\sin^{-1}(-0.625)$
**23.** $\cos^{-1}\frac{3}{8}$
**24.** $\cos^{-1}\frac{4}{9}$
**25.** $\cos^{-1}\frac{\sqrt{5}}{7}$
**26.** $\cos^{-1}\frac{\sqrt{7}}{10}$
**27.** $\tan^{-1}(-20)$
**28.** $\tan^{-1}(-30)$
**29.** $\tan^{-1}(-\sqrt{473})$
**30.** $\tan^{-1}(-\sqrt{5061})$

*In Exercises 31–46, find the exact value of each expression, if possible. Do not use a calculator.*

**31.** $\sin(\sin^{-1} 0.9)$
**32.** $\cos(\cos^{-1} 0.57)$
**33.** $\sin^{-1}\left(\sin\frac{\pi}{3}\right)$
**34.** $\cos^{-1}\left(\cos\frac{2\pi}{3}\right)$
**35.** $\sin^{-1}\left(\sin\frac{5\pi}{6}\right)$
**36.** $\cos^{-1}\left(\cos\frac{4\pi}{3}\right)$
**37.** $\tan(\tan^{-1} 125)$
**38.** $\tan(\tan^{-1} 380)$
**39.** $\tan^{-1}\left[\tan\left(-\frac{\pi}{6}\right)\right]$
**40.** $\tan^{-1}\left[\tan\left(-\frac{\pi}{3}\right)\right]$

**41.** $\tan^{-1}\left(\tan\dfrac{2\pi}{3}\right)$

**42.** $\tan^{-1}\left(\tan\dfrac{3\pi}{4}\right)$

**43.** $\sin^{-1}(\sin\pi)$

**44.** $\cos^{-1}(\cos 2\pi)$

**45.** $\sin(\sin^{-1}\pi)$

**46.** $\cos(\cos^{-1}3\pi)$

*In Exercises 47–60, use a sketch to find the exact value of each expression.*

**47.** $\cos\left(\sin^{-1}\frac{4}{5}\right)$

**48.** $\sin\left(\tan^{-1}\frac{7}{24}\right)$

**49.** $\tan\left(\cos^{-1}\frac{5}{13}\right)$

**50.** $\cot\left(\sin^{-1}\frac{5}{13}\right)$

**51.** $\tan\left[\sin^{-1}\left(-\frac{3}{5}\right)\right]$

**52.** $\cos\left[\sin^{-1}\left(-\frac{4}{5}\right)\right]$

**53.** $\sin\left(\cos^{-1}\dfrac{\sqrt{2}}{2}\right)$

**54.** $\cos\left(\sin^{-1}\frac{1}{2}\right)$

**55.** $\sec\left[\sin^{-1}\left(-\frac{1}{4}\right)\right]$

**56.** $\sec\left[\sin^{-1}\left(-\frac{1}{2}\right)\right]$

**57.** $\tan\left[\cos^{-1}\left(-\frac{1}{3}\right)\right]$

**58.** $\tan\left[\cos^{-1}\left(-\frac{1}{4}\right)\right]$

**59.** $\csc\left[\cos^{-1}\left(-\dfrac{\sqrt{3}}{2}\right)\right]$

**60.** $\sec\left[\sin^{-1}\left(-\dfrac{\sqrt{2}}{2}\right)\right]$

*In Exercises 61–66, use a right triangle to write each expression as an algebraic expression. Assume that x is positive and in the domain of the given inverse trigonometric function.*

**61.** $\tan(\cos^{-1}x)$

**62.** $\sin(\tan^{-1}x)$

**63.** $\cos\left(\sin^{-1}\dfrac{1}{x}\right)$

**64.** $\sec\left(\cos^{-1}\dfrac{1}{x}\right)$

**65.** $\sec\left(\sin^{-1}\dfrac{x}{\sqrt{x^2+4}}\right)$

**66.** $\cot\left(\sin^{-1}\dfrac{\sqrt{x^2-9}}{x}\right)$

**67.** **a.** Graph the restricted secant function, $y = \sec x$, by restricting $x$ to the intervals $\left[0, \dfrac{\pi}{2}\right)$ and $\left(\dfrac{\pi}{2}, \pi\right]$.

**b.** Use the horizontal line test and explain why the restricted secant function has an inverse function.

**c.** Use the graph of the restricted secant function to graph $y = \sec^{-1}x$.

**68.** **a.** Graph the restricted cotangent function, $y = \cot x$, by restricting $x$ to the interval $(0, \pi)$.

**b.** Use the horizontal line test and explain why the restricted cotangent function has an inverse function.

**c.** Use the graph of the restricted cotangent function to graph $y = \cot^{-1}x$.

## Application Exercises

**69.** Your neighborhood movie theater has a 25-foot-high screen located 8 feet above your eye level. If you sit too close to the screen, your viewing angle is too small, resulting in a distorted picture. By contrast, if you sit too far back, the image is quite small, diminishing the movie's visual impact. If you sit $x$ feet back from the screen, your viewing angle $\theta$ is given by

$$\theta = \tan^{-1}\frac{33}{x} - \tan^{-1}\frac{8}{x}.$$

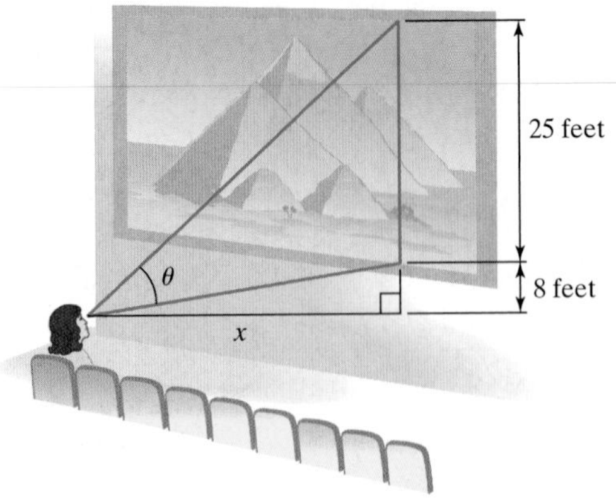


Find the viewing angle, in radians, at distances of 5 feet, 10 feet, 15 feet, 20 feet, and 25 feet.

**70.** The function $\theta = \tan^{-1}\dfrac{33}{x} - \tan^{-1}\dfrac{8}{x}$ is graphed below in a $[0, 50, 10]$ by $[0, 1, 0.1]$ viewing rectangle. Use the graph to describe what happens to your viewing angle as you move farther back from the screen. How far back from the screen, to the nearest foot, should you sit to maximize your viewing angle? Verify this observation by finding the viewing angle one foot closer to the screen and one foot farther from the screen for this ideal viewing distance.

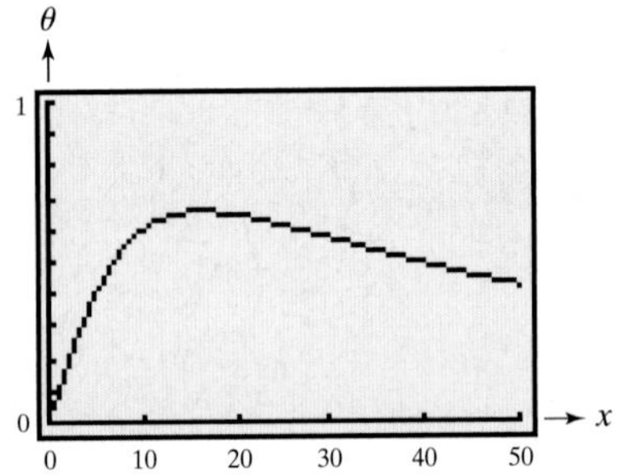


*The formula*

$$\theta = 2\tan^{-1}\frac{21.634}{x}$$

*gives the viewing angle, in radians, for a camera whose lens is x millimeters wide. Use this formula to solve Exercises 71–72.*

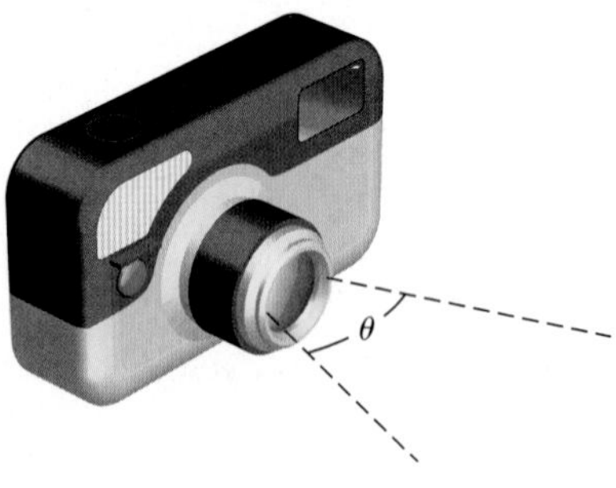


**71.** Find the viewing angle, in radians and in degrees (to the nearest tenth of a degree), of a 28-millimeter lens.

**72.** Find the viewing angle, in radians and degrees (to the nearest tenth of a degree), of a 300-millimeter telephoto lens.

*For years, mathematicians were challenged by the following problem: What is the area of a region under a curve between two values of x? The problem was solved in the seventeenth century with the development of integral calculus. Using calculus, the area of the region under* $y = \frac{1}{x^2+1}$, *above the x-axis, and between* $x = a$ *and* $x = b$ *is* $\tan^{-1} b - \tan^{-1} a$. *Use this result, shown in the figure, to find the area of the region under* $y = \frac{1}{x^2+1}$ *and between a and b given in Exercises 73–74.*

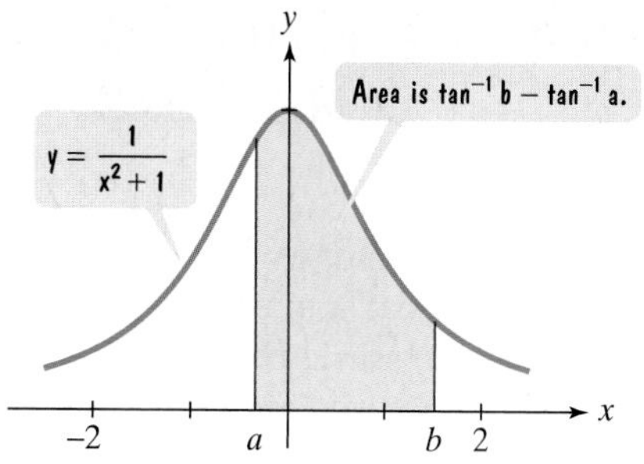


**73.** $a = 0$ and $b = 2$

**74.** $a = -2$ and $b = 1$

## Writing in Mathematics

**75.** Explain why, without restrictions, no trigonometric function has an inverse function.

**76.** Describe the restriction on the sine function so that it has an inverse function.

**77.** How can the graph of $y = \sin^{-1} x$ be obtained from the graph of the restricted sine function?

**78.** Without drawing a graph, describe the behavior of the graph of $y = \sin^{-1} x$. Mention the function's domain and range in your description.

**79.** Describe the restriction on the cosine function so that it has an inverse function.

**80.** Without drawing a graph, describe the behavior of the graph of $y = \cos^{-1} x$. Mention the function's domain and range in your description.

**81.** Describe the restriction on the tangent function so that it has an inverse function.

**82.** Without drawing a graph, describe the behavior of the graph of $y = \tan^{-1} x$. Mention the function's domain and range in your description.

**83.** If $\sin^{-1}\left(\sin \frac{\pi}{3}\right) = \frac{\pi}{3}$, is $\sin^{-1}\left(\sin \frac{5\pi}{6}\right) = \frac{5\pi}{6}$? Explain your answer.

**84.** Explain how a right triangle can be used to find the exact value of $\sec\left(\sin^{-1}\frac{4}{5}\right)$.

**85.** Find the height of the screen and the number of feet that it is located above eye level in your favorite movie theater. Modify the formula given in Exercise 69 so that it applies to your theater. Then describe where in the theater you should sit so that a movie creates the greatest visual impact.

## Technology Exercises

*In Exercises 86–89, graph each pair of functions in the same viewing rectangle. Use your knowledge of the domain and range for the inverse trigonometric functions to select an appropriate viewing rectangle. What does the graph of the second equation in each exercise do to the graph of the first equation?*

**86.** $y = \sin^{-1} x$ and $y = \sin^{-1} x + 2$

**87.** $y = \cos^{-1} x$ and $y = \cos^{-1}(x - 1)$

**88.** $y = \tan^{-1} x$ and $y = -2\tan^{-1} x$

**89.** $y = \sin^{-1} x$ and $y = \sin^{-1}(x + 2) + 1$

**90.** Graph $y = \tan^{-1} x$ and its two horizontal asymptotes in a $[-3, 3, 1]$ by $\left[-\pi, \pi, \frac{\pi}{2}\right]$ viewing rectangle. Then change the range setting to $[-50, 50, 5]$ by $\left[-\pi, \pi, \frac{\pi}{2}\right]$. What do you observe?

**91.** Graph $y = \sin^{-1} x + \cos^{-1} x$ in a $[-2, 2, 1]$ by $[0, 3, 1]$ viewing rectangle. What appears to be true about the sum of the inverse sine and inverse cosine for values between −1 and 1 inclusive?

## Critical Thinking Exercises

**92.** Solve $y = 2\sin^{-1}(x - 5)$ for $x$ in terms of $y$.

**93.** Solve for $x$: $2\sin^{-1} x = \frac{\pi}{4}$.

**94.** Prove that if $x > 0$, $\tan^{-1} x + \tan^{-1}\frac{1}{x} = \frac{\pi}{2}$.

**95.** Derive the formula for $\theta$, your viewing angle at the movie theater, in Exercise 69. *Hint*: Use the figure shown and represent the acute angle on the left in the smaller right triangle by $\alpha$. Find expressions for $\tan \alpha$ and $\tan(\alpha + \theta)$.

# SECTION 5.8 Applications of Trigonometric Functions

## Objectives

1. Solve a right triangle.
2. Solve problems involving bearings.
3. Model simple harmonic motion.

In the late 1960s, popular musicians were searching for new sounds. Film composers were looking for ways to create unique sounds as well. From these efforts, synthesizers that electronically reproduce musical sounds were born. From providing the backbone of today's most popular music to providing the strange sounds for the most experimental music, synthesizers are at the forefront of today's music technology.

If we did not understand the periodic nature of sinusoidal functions, the synthesizers used in almost all forms of music would not exist. In this section, we look at applications of trigonometric functions in right triangles and in modeling periodic phenomena such as sound.

**1** Solve a right triangle.

## Solving Right Triangles

**Solving a right triangle** means finding the missing lengths of its sides and the measurements of its angles. We will label right triangles so that side $a$ is opposite angle $A$, side $b$ is opposite angle $B$, and side $c$ is the hypotenuse opposite right angle $C$. Figure 5.80 illustrates this labeling.

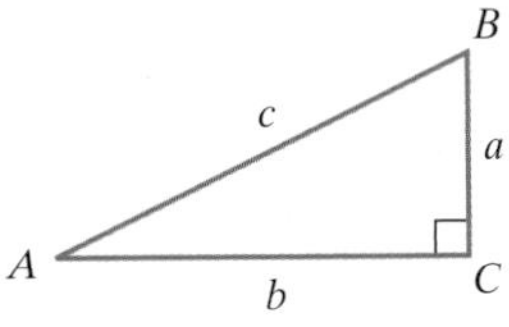


**Figure 5.80** Labeling right triangles

When solving a right triangle, we will use the sine, cosine, and tangent functions, rather than their reciprocals. Example 1 shows how to solve a right triangle when we know the length of a side and the measure of an acute angle.

### EXAMPLE 1 Solving a Right Triangle

Solve the right triangle shown in Figure 5.81.

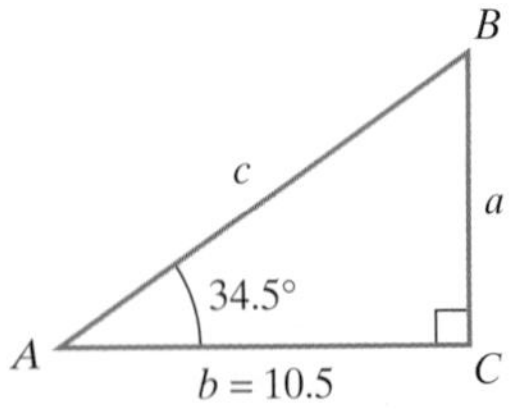


**Figure 5.81** Find $B$, $a$, and $c$

**Solution** We begin by finding the measure of angle $B$. We do not need a trigonometric function to do so. Because $C = 90°$ and the sum of a triangle's angles is 180°, we see that $A + B = 90°$. Thus,

$$B = 90° - A = 90° - 34.5° = 55.5°.$$

Now we need to find $a$. Because we have a known angle, an unknown opposite side, and a known adjacent side, we use the tangent function.

$$\tan 34.5° = \frac{a}{10.5}$$

Side opposite the 34.5° angle

Side adjacent to the 34.5° angle

**Discovery**

There is often more than one correct way to solve a right triangle. In Example 1, find $a$ using angle $B = 55.5°$. Find $c$ using the Pythagorean Theorem.

Now we solve for $a$.

$$a = 10.5 \tan 34.5° \approx 7.22$$

Finally, we need to find $c$. Because we have a known angle, a known adjacent side, and an unknown hypotenuse, we use the cosine function.

$$\cos 34.5° = \frac{10.5}{c}$$

Side adjacent to the 34.5° angle

hypotenuse

Now we solve for $c$.

$$c = \frac{10.5}{\cos 34.5°} \approx 12.74$$

In summary, $B = 55.5°$, $a \approx 7.22$, and $c \approx 12.74$.

**Check Point 1** In Figure 5.80, let $A = 62.7°$ and $a = 8.4$. Solve the right triangle, rounding lengths to two decimal places.

Trigonometry was first developed to measure heights and distances that are inconvenient or impossible to measure. In solving application problems, begin by making a sketch involving a right triangle that illustrates the problem's conditions. Then put your knowledge of solving right triangles to work and find the required distance or height.

## EXAMPLE 2 Finding the Side of a Triangle

From a point on level ground 125 feet from the base of a tower, the angle of elevation is 57.2°. Approximate the height of the tower to the nearest foot.

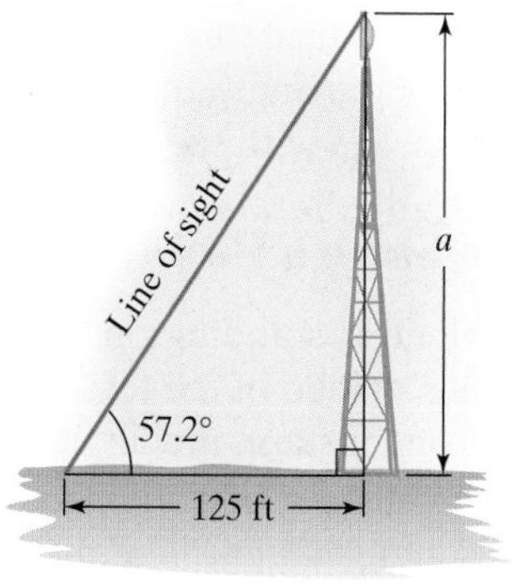


**Figure 5.82** Determining height without using direct measurement

**Solution** A sketch is shown in Figure 5.82, where $a$ represents the height of the tower. In the right triangle, we have a known angle, an unknown opposite side, and a known adjacent side. Therefore, we use the tangent function.

$$\tan 57.2° = \frac{a}{125}$$

Side opposite the 57.2° angle

Side adjacent to the 57.2° angle

Solving for $a$,

$$a = 125 \tan 57.2° \approx 194.$$

The tower is approximately 194 feet high.

**Check Point 2** From a point on level ground 80 feet from the base of the Eiffel Tower, the angle of elevation is 85.4°. Approximate the height of the Eiffel Tower to the nearest foot.

Example 3 illustrates how to find the measure of an acute angle of a right triangle if the length of two sides is known.

## EXAMPLE 3 Finding the Angle of a Triangle

A kite flies at a height of 30 feet when 65 feet of string is out. If the string is in a straight line, find the angle that it makes with the ground. Round to the nearest tenth of a degree.

**Solution** A sketch is shown in Figure 5.83, where $A$ represents the angle the string makes with the ground. In the right triangle, we have an unknown angle, a known opposite side, and a known hypotenuse. Therefore, we use the sine function.

$$\sin A = \frac{30}{65}$$

Side opposite A

hypotenuse

$$A = \sin^{-1}\frac{30}{65} \approx 27.5°$$

The string makes an angle of approximately 27.5° with the ground.

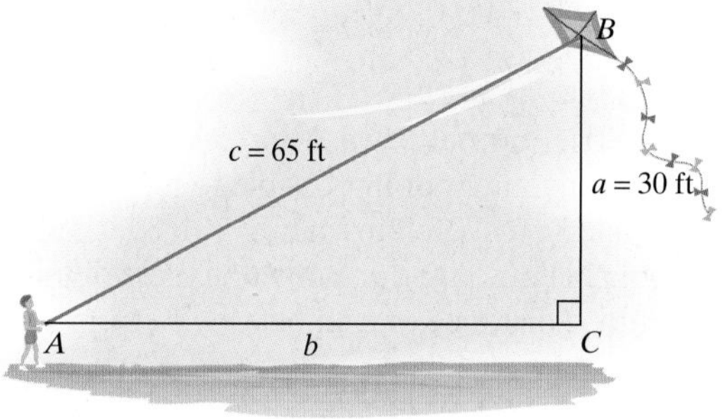


**Figure 5.83** Flying a kite

**Check Point 3** A guy wire is 13.8 yards long and is attached from the ground to a pole 6.7 yards above the ground. Find the angle, to the nearest tenth of a degree, that the wire makes with the ground.

## EXAMPLE 4 Using Two Right Triangles to Solve a Problem

You are taking your first hot-air balloon ride. Your friend is standing on level ground, 100 feet away from your point of launch, making a video of the terrified look on your rapidly ascending face. How rapidly? At one instant, the angle of elevation from the video camera to your face is 31.7°. One minute later, the angle of elevation is 76.2°. How far did you travel during that minute?

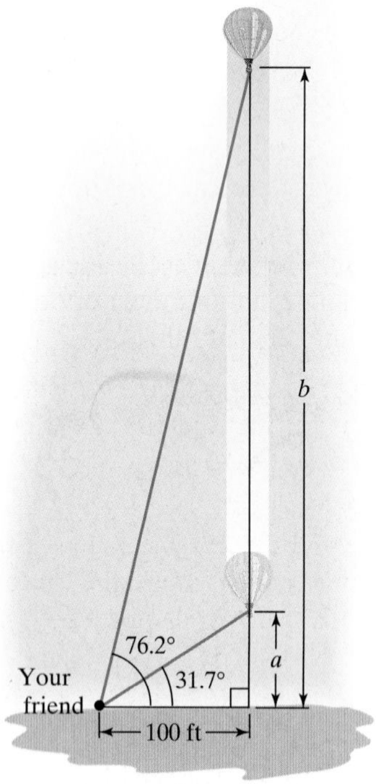


**Figure 5.84** Ascending in a hot-air balloon

**Solution** A sketch that illustrates the problem is shown in Figure 5.84. We need to determine $b - a$, the distance traveled during the one-minute period. We find $a$ using the small right triangle. Because we have a known angle, an unknown opposite side, and a known adjacent side, we use the tangent function.

$$\tan 31.7° = \frac{a}{100}$$

Side opposite the 31.7° angle

Side adjacent to the 31.7° angle

$$a = 100 \tan 31.7° \approx 61.8$$

We find $b$ using the tangent function in the large right triangle.

$$\tan 76.2° = \frac{b}{100}$$

Side opposite the 76.2° angle

Side adjacent to the 76.2° angle

$$b = 100 \tan 76.2° \approx 407.1$$

The balloon traveled 407.1 − 61.8, or approximately 345.3 feet, during the minute.

**Check Point 4** You are standing on level ground 800 feet from Mt. Rushmore, looking at the sculpture of Abraham Lincoln's face. The angle of elevation to the bottom of the sculpture is 32° and the angle of elevation to the top is 35°. Find the height of the sculpture of Lincoln's face to the nearest tenth of a foot.

**2** Solve problems involving bearings.

## Trigonometry and Bearings

In navigation and surveying problems, the term *bearing* is used to specify the location of one point relative to another. The **bearing** from point $O$ to point $P$ is the acute angle between ray $OP$ and a north-south line. Figure 5.85 illustrates some examples of bearings. The north-south line and the east-west line intersect at right angles.

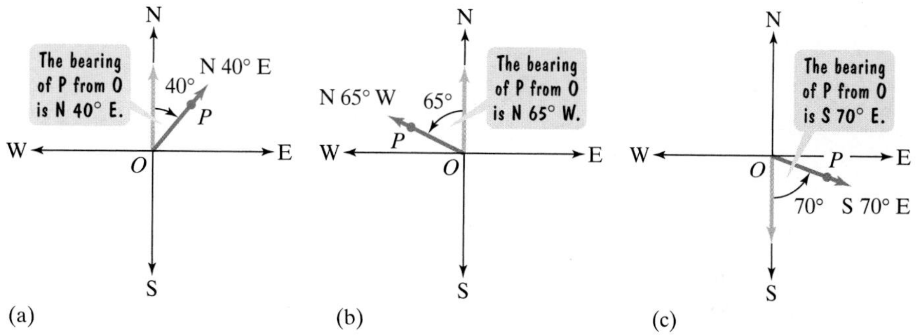


**Figure 5.85** An illustration of three bearings

Each bearing has three parts: a letter (N or S), the measure of an acute angle, and a letter (E or W). Here's how we write a bearing:

- If the acute angle is measured from the *north side* of the north-south line, then we write N first. [See Figure 5.85(a).] If the acute angle is measured from the *south side* of the north-south line, then we write S first. [See Figure 5.85(c).]
- Second, we write the measure of the acute angle.
- If the acute angle is measured on the *east side* of the north-south line, then we write E last. [See Figure 5.85(a)]. If the acute angle is measured on the *west side* of the north-south line, then we write W last. [See Figure 5.85(b).]

## EXAMPLE 5 Understanding Bearings

Use Figure 5.86 on page 530 to find:

**a.** the bearing from $O$ to $B$.

**b.** the bearing from $O$ to $A$.

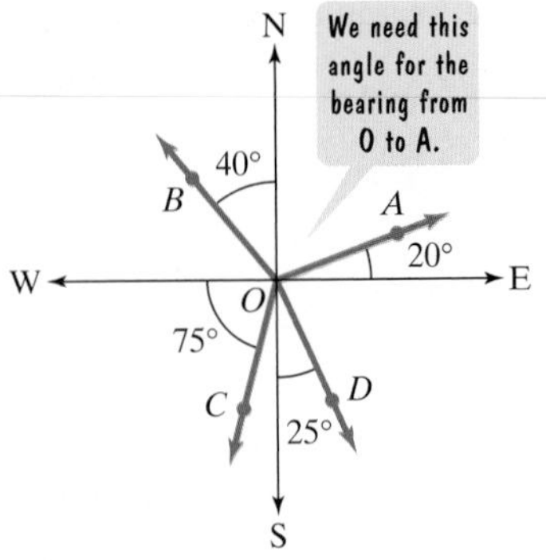


**Figure 5.86** Finding bearings

**Solution**

**a.** To find the bearing from $O$ to $B$, we need the acute angle between the ray $OB$ and the north-south line through $O$. The measurement of this angle is given to be 40°. Figure 5.86 shows that the angle is measured from the north side of the north-south line and lies west of the north-south line. Thus, the bearing from $O$ to $B$ is N 40° W.

**b.** To find the bearing from $O$ to $A$, we need the acute angle between the ray $OA$ and the north-south line through O. This angle is specified by the voice balloon in Figure 5.86. The figure shows that this angle measures $90° - 20°$, or 70°. This angle is measured from the north side of the north-south line. This angle is also east of the north-south line. Thus, the bearing from $O$ to $A$ is N 70° E.

**Check Point 5** Use Figure 5.86 to find:

**a.** the bearing from $O$ to $D$.

**b.** the bearing from $O$ to $C$.

## EXAMPLE 6 Finding the Bearing of a Boat

A boat leaves the entrance to a harbor and travels 25 miles on a bearing of N 42° E. Figure 5.87 shows that the captain then turns the boat 90° and travels 18 miles on a bearing of S 48° E. At that time:

**a.** How far is the boat from the harbor entrance?

**b.** What is the bearing of the boat from the harbor entrance?

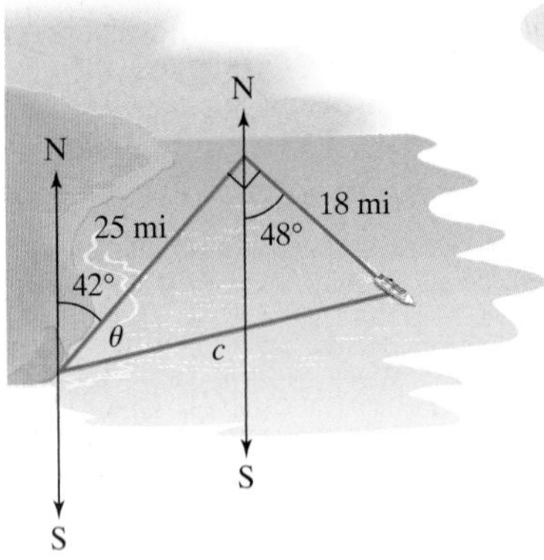


**Figure 5.87** Finding a boat's bearing from the harbor entrance

### Study Tip

When making a diagram showing bearings, draw a north-south line through each point at which a change in course occurs. The north side of the line lies above each point. The south side of the line lies below each point.

**Solution**

**a.** The boat's distance from the harbor entrance is represented by $c$ in Figure 5.87. Because we know the length of two sides of the right triangle, we find $c$ using the Pythagorean Theorem. We have

$$c^2 = a^2 + b^2 = 25^2 + 18^2 = 949$$

$$c = \sqrt{949} \approx 30.8.$$

The boat is approximately 30.8 miles from the harbor entrance.

**b.** To find the bearing of the boat from the harbor entrance, look at the north-south line passing through the harbor entrance on the left in Figure 5.87. The acute angle from this line to the ray on which the boat lies is $42° + \theta$. Because we are measuring the angle from the north side of the line and the boat is east of the harbor, its bearing from the harbor entrance is $\mathrm{N}(42° + \theta)\mathrm{E}$. To find $\theta$, we use the right triangle shown in Figure 5.87 and the tangent function.

$$\tan\theta = \frac{\text{side opposite } \theta}{\text{side adjacent to } \theta} = \frac{18}{25}$$

$$\theta = \tan^{-1}\frac{18}{25}$$

We can use a calculator in degree mode to find the value of $\theta$: $\theta \approx 35.8°$. Thus, $42° + \theta = 42° + 35.8° = 77.8°$. The bearing of the boat from the harbor entrance is N 77.8° E.

**Check Point 6** You leave the entrance to a system of hiking trails and hike 2.3 miles on a bearing of S 31° W. You then turn and hike 3.5 miles on a bearing of N 59° W. At that time:

**a.** How far are you from the entrance to the trail system?

**b.** What is your bearing from the entrance to the trail system?

**3** Model simple harmonic motion.

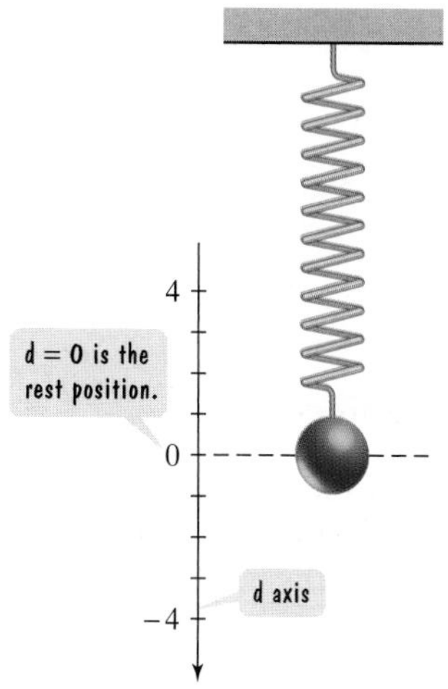


**Figure 5.88** Using a $d$-axis to describe a ball's distance from its rest position

## Simple Harmonic Motion

Because of their periodic nature, trigonometric functions are used to model phenomena that occur again and again. This includes vibratory or oscillatory motion, such as the motion of a vibrating guitar string, the swinging of a pendulum, or the bobbing of an object attached to a spring. Trigonometric functions are also used to describe radio waves from your favorite FM station, television waves from your not-to-be-missed weekly sitcom, and sound waves from your most-prized CDs.

To see how trigonometric functions are used to model vibratory motion, consider this: A ball is attached to a spring hung from the ceiling. You pull the ball down 4 inches and then release it. If we neglect the effects of friction and air resistance, the ball will continue bobbing up and down on the end of the spring. These up-and-down oscillations are called **simple harmonic motion.**

To better understand this motion, we use a $d$-axis, where $d$ represents distance. This axis is shown in Figure 5.88. On this axis, the position of the ball before you pull it down is $d = 0$. This rest position is called the **equilibrium position**. Now you pull the ball down 4 inches to $d = -4$ and release it. Figure 5.89 shows a sequence of "photographs" taken at one-second time intervals illustrating the distance of the ball from its rest position, $d$.

The curve in Figure 5.89 shows how the ball's distance from its rest position changes over time. The curve is sinusoidal and the motion can be described using a cosine or a sine function.

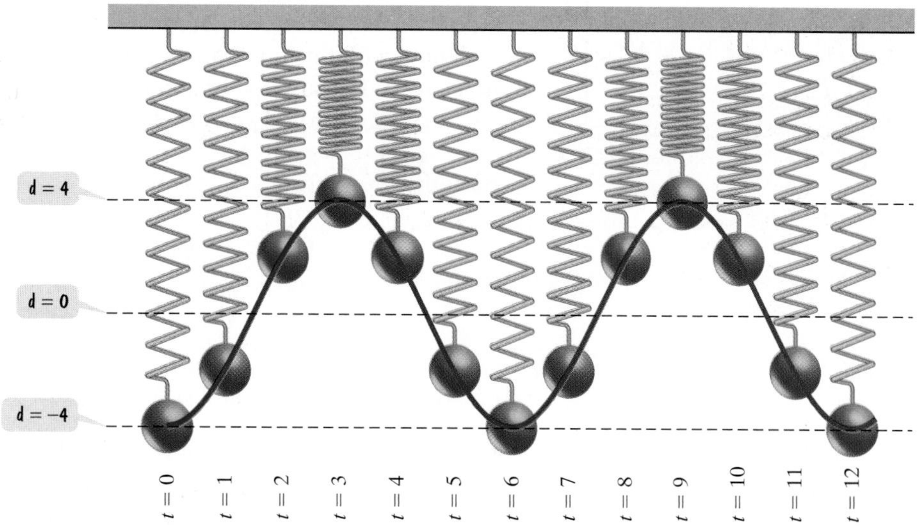


**Figure 5.89** A sequence of "photographs" showing the bobbing ball's distance from the rest position, taken at one-second intervals

**Simple Harmonic Motion**

An object that moves on a coordinate axis is in **simple harmonic motion** if its distance from the origin, $d$, at time $t$ is given by either

$$d = a\cos\omega t \text{ or } d = a\sin\omega t.$$

The motion has **amplitude** $|a|$, the maximum displacement of the object from its rest position. The **period** of the motion is $\frac{2\pi}{\omega}$, where $\omega > 0$. The period gives the time it takes for the motion to go through one complete cycle.

In describing simple harmonic motion, the equation with the cosine function is used if the object is at its greatest distance from rest position, the origin, at $t = 0$. By contrast, the equation with the sine function is used if the object is at its rest position, the origin, at $t = 0$.

## Diminishing Motion with Increasing Time

Due to friction and other resistive forces, the motion of an oscillating object decreases over time. The function

$$d = 3e^{-0.1t}\cos 2t$$

models this type of motion. The graph of the function is shown in a $t = [0, 10, 1]$ by $d = [-3, 3, 1]$ viewing rectangle. Notice how the amplitude is decreasing with time as the moving object loses energy.

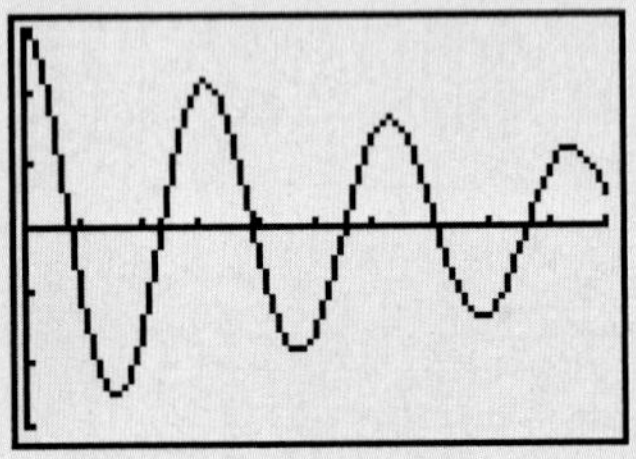

## EXAMPLE 7 Finding an Equation for an Object in Simple Harmonic Motion

A ball on a spring is pulled 4 inches below its rest position and then released. The period of the motion is 6 seconds. Write the equation for the ball's simple harmonic motion.

**Solution** We need to write an equation that describes $d$, the distance of the ball from its rest position, after $t$ seconds. (The motion is illustrated by the "photo" sequence in Figure 5.88 on page 519.) When the object is released ($t = 0$), the ball's distance from its rest position is 4 inches down. Because it is *down* 4 inches, $d$ is negative: When $t = 0$, $d = -4$. Notice the greatest distance from rest position occurs at $t = 0$. Thus, we will use the equation with the cosine function,

$$d = a\cos\omega t,$$

to model the ball's simple harmonic motion.

Now we determine values for $a$ and $\omega$. Recall that $|a|$ is the maximum displacement. Because the ball initially moves down, $a = -4$.

The value of $\omega$ in $d = a\cos\omega t$ can be found using the formula for the period.

$$\text{period} = \frac{2\pi}{\omega} = 6$$ We are given that the period of the motion is 6 seconds.

$$2\pi = 6\omega$$ Multiply both sides by $\omega$.

$$\omega = \frac{2\pi}{6} = \frac{\pi}{3}$$ Divide both sides by 6 and solve for $\omega$.

We see that $a = -4$ and $\omega = \frac{\pi}{3}$. Substitute these values into $d = a\cos\omega t$.

The equation for the ball's simple harmonic motion is

$$d = -4\cos\frac{\pi}{3}t.$$

## Modeling Music

Sounds are caused by vibrating objects that result in variations in pressure in the surrounding air. Areas of high and low pressure moving through the air are modeled by the harmonic motion formulas. When these vibrations reach our eardrums, the eardrums' vibrations send signals to our brains which create the sensation of hearing.

French mathematician John Fourier (1768–1830) proved that all musical sounds—instrumental and vocal—could be modeled by sums involving sine functions. Modeling musical sounds with sinusoidal functions is used by synthesizers to electronically produce sounds unobtainable from ordinary musical instruments.

**Check Point 7** A ball on a spring is pulled 6 inches below its rest position and then released. The period for the motion is 4 seconds. Write the equation for the ball's simple harmonic motion.

The period of the harmonic motion in Example 7 was 6 seconds. It takes 6 seconds for the moving object to complete one cycle. Thus, $\frac{1}{6}$ of a cycle is completed every second. We call $\frac{1}{6}$ the *frequency* of the moving object. **Frequency** describes the number of complete cycles per unit time and is the reciprocal of the period.

**Frequency of an Object in Simple Harmonic Motion**

An object in simple harmonic motion given by

$$d = a\cos\omega t \text{ or } d = a\sin\omega t$$

has **frequency** $f$ given by

$$f = \frac{\omega}{2\pi},\ \omega > 0.$$

Equivalently,

$$f = \frac{1}{\text{period}}.$$

## EXAMPLE 8 Analyzing Simple Harmonic Motion

Figure 5.90 shows a mass on a smooth table attached to a spring. The mass moves in simple harmonic motion described by

$$d = 10\cos\frac{\pi}{6}t$$

with $t$ measured in seconds and $d$ in centimeters. Find (a) the maximum displacement, (b) the frequency, and (c) the time required for one cycle.

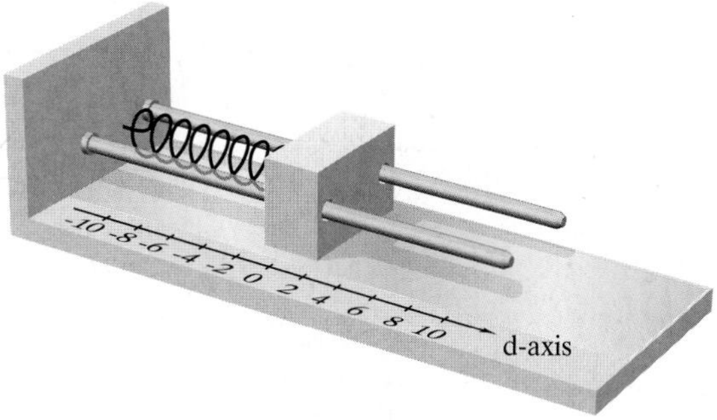


**Figure 5.90** A mass attached to a spring, moving in simple harmonic motion

**Solution** We begin by identifying values for $a$ and $\omega$.

$$d = 10\cos\frac{\pi}{6}t$$

The form of this equation is $d = a\cos\omega t$ with $a = 10$ and $\omega = \frac{\pi}{6}$.

**a.** The maximum displacement from the rest position is the amplitude. Because $a = 10$, the maximum displacement is 10 centimeters.

**b.** The frequency, $f$, is

$$f = \frac{\omega}{2\pi} = \frac{\frac{\pi}{6}}{2\pi} = \frac{\pi}{6} \cdot \frac{1}{2\pi} = \frac{1}{12}.$$

The frequency is $\frac{1}{12}$ cycle (or oscillation) per second.

**c.** The time required for one cycle is the period.

$$\text{period} = \frac{2\pi}{\omega} = \frac{2\pi}{\frac{\pi}{6}} = 2\pi \cdot \frac{6}{\pi} = 12$$

The time required for one cycle is 12 seconds.

**Check Point 8** An object moves in simple harmonic motion described by $d = 12 \cos \frac{\pi}{4} t$, where $t$ is measured in seconds and $d$ in centimeters. Find (a) the maximum displacement, (b) the frequency, and (c) the time required for one cycle.

## Resisting Damage of Simple Harmonic Motion

Simple harmonic motion from an earthquake caused this highway in Oakland, California to collapse. By studying the harmonic motion of the soil under the highway, engineers learn to build structures that can resist damage.

# EXERCISE SET 5.8

## Practice Exercises

*In Exercises 1–12, solve the right triangle shown in the figure. Round lengths to two decimal places and express angles to the nearest tenth of a degree.*

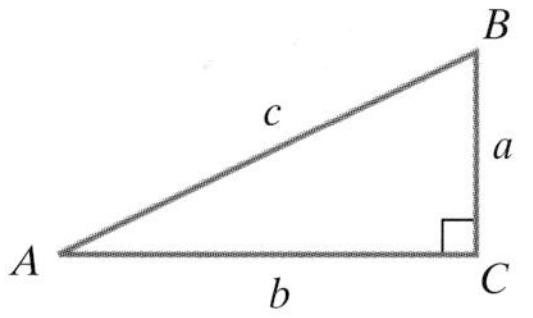


**1.** $A = 23.5°, b = 10$

**2.** $A = 41.5°, b = 20$

**3.** $A = 52.6°, c = 54$

**4.** $A = 54.8°, c = 80$

**5.** $B = 16.8°, b = 30.5$

**6.** $B = 23.8°, b = 40.5$

**7.** $a = 30.4, c = 50.2$

**8.** $a = 11.2, c = 65.8$

**9.** $a = 10.8, b = 24.7$

**10.** $a = 15.3, b = 17.6$

**11.** $b = 2, c = 7$

**12.** $b = 4, c = 9$

*Use the figure shown to solve Exercises 13–16.*

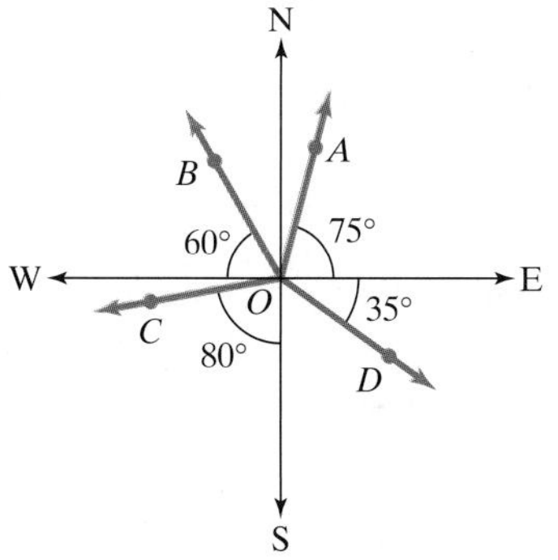


**13.** Find the bearing from $O$ to $A$.

**14.** Find the bearing from $O$ to $B$.

**15.** Find the bearing from $O$ to $C$.

**16.** Find the bearing from $O$ to $D$.

*In Exercises 17–20, an object is attached to a coiled spring. The object is pulled down (negative direction from the rest position) and then released. Write an equation for the distance of the object from its rest position after t seconds.*

| | Distance from rest position at $t = 0$ | Amplitude | Period |
|---|---|---|---|
| **17.** | 6 centimeters | 6 centimeters | 4 seconds |
| **18.** | 8 inches | 8 inches | 2 seconds |
| **19.** | 0 | 3 inches | 1.5 seconds |
| **20.** | 0 | 5 centimeters | 2.5 seconds |

*In Exercises 21–28, an object moves in simple harmonic motion described by the given equation, where t is measured in seconds and d in inches. In each exercise, find:*

**a.** *the maximum displacement.*

**b.** *the frequency.*

**c.** *the time required for one cycle.*

**21.** $d = 5\cos\frac{\pi}{2}t$

**22.** $d = 10\cos 2\pi t$

**23.** $d = -6\cos 2\pi t$

**24.** $d = -8\cos\frac{\pi}{2}t$

**25.** $d = \frac{1}{2}\sin 2t$

**26.** $d = \frac{1}{3}\sin 2t$

**27.** $d = -5\sin\frac{2\pi}{3}t$

**28.** $d = -4\sin\frac{3\pi}{2}t$

## Application Exercises

**29.** The tallest television transmitting tower in the world is in North Dakota. From a point on level ground 5280 feet (one mile) from the base of the tower, the angle of elevation is 21.3°. Approximate the height of the tower to the nearest foot.

**30.** From a point on level ground 30 yards from the base of a building, the angle of elevation is 38.7°. Approximate the height of the building to the nearest foot.

**31.** The Statue of Liberty is approximately 305 feet tall. If the angle of elevation of a ship to the top of the statue is 23.7°, how far, to the nearest foot, is the ship from the statue's base?

**32.** A 200-foot cliff drops vertically into the ocean. If the angle of elevation of a ship to the top of the cliff is 22.3°, how far off shore, to the nearest foot, is the ship?

**33.** A helicopter hovers 1000 feet above a small island. The figure shows that the angle of depression from the helicopter to point $P$ is 36°. How far off the coast, to the nearest foot, is the island?

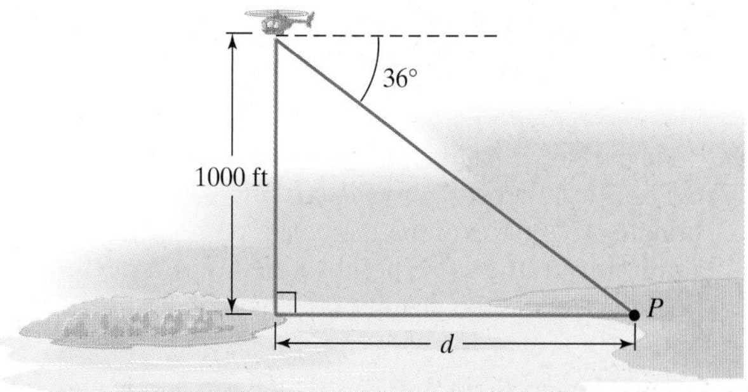

**34.** A police helicopter is flying at 800 feet. A stolen car is sighted at an angle of depression of 72°. Find the distance of the stolen car, to the nearest foot, from a point directly below the helicopter.

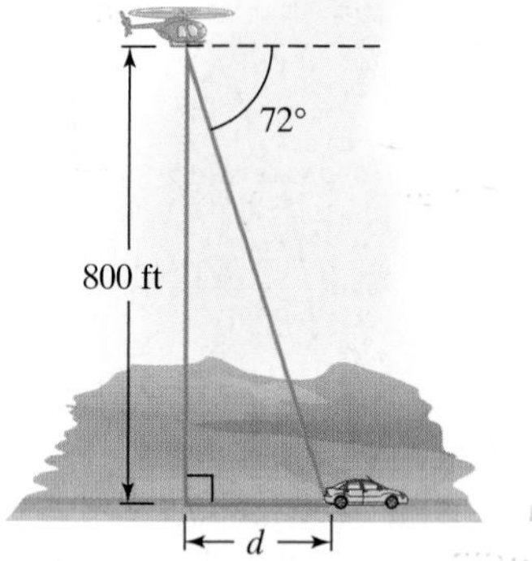


**35.** A wheelchair ramp is to be built beside the steps to the campus library. Find the angle of elevation of the 23-foot ramp, to the nearest tenth of a degree, if its final height is 6 feet.

**36.** A building that is 250 feet high casts a shadow 40 feet long. Find the angle of elevation, to the nearest tenth of a degree, of the sun at this time.

**37.** A hot-air balloon is rising vertically. The angle of elevation from a point on level ground 125 feet from the balloon to a point directly under the passenger compartment changes from 19.2° to 31.7°. How far, to the nearest tenth of a foot, does the balloon rise during this period?

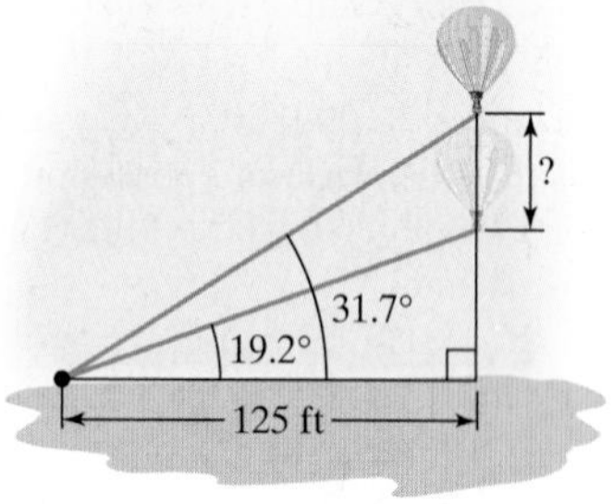


**38.** A flagpole is situated on top of a building. The angle of elevation from a point on level ground 330 feet from the building to the top of the flagpole is 63°. The angle of elevation from the same point to the bottom of the flagpole is 53°. Find the height of the flagpole to the nearest tenth of a foot.

**39.** A boat leaves the entrance to a harbor and travels 150 miles on a bearing of N 53° E. How many miles north and how many miles east from the harbor has the boat traveled?

**40.** A boat leaves the entrance to a harbor and travels 40 miles on a bearing of S 64° E. How many miles south and how many miles east from the harbor has the boat traveled?

**41.** A forest ranger sights a fire directly to the south. A second ranger, 7 miles east of the first ranger, also sights the fire. The bearing from the second ranger to the fire is S 28° W. How far, to the nearest tenth of a mile, is the first ranger from the fire?

**42.** A ship sights a lighthouse directly to the south. A second ship, 9 miles east of the first ship, also sights the lighthouse. The bearing from the second ship to the lighthouse is S 34° W. How far,to the nearest tenth of a mile, is the first ship from the lighthouse?

**43.** You leave your house and run 2 miles due west followed by 1.5 miles due north. At that time, what is your bearing from your house?

**44.** A ship is 9 miles east and 6 miles south of a harbor. What bearing should be taken to sail directly to the harbor?

**45.** A jet leaves a runway whose bearing is N 35° E from the control tower. After flying 5 miles, the jet turns 90° and flies on a bearing of S 55° E for 7 miles. At that time, what is the bearing of the jet from the control tower?

**46.** A ship leaves port with a bearing of S 40° W. After traveling 7 miles, the ship turns 90° and travels on a bearing of N 60° W for 11 miles. At that time, what is the bearing of the ship from port?

**47.** An object in simple harmonic motion has a frequency of $\frac{1}{2}$ oscillation per minute and an amplitude of 6 feet. Write an equation in the form $d = a \sin \omega t$ for the object's simple harmonic motion.

**48.** An object in simple harmonic motion has a frequency of $\frac{1}{4}$ oscillation per minute and an amplitude of 8 feet. Write an equation in the form $d = a \sin \omega t$ for the object's simple harmonic motion.

**49.** A piano tuner uses a tuning fork. If middle C has a frequency of 264 vibrations per second, write an equation in the form $d = a \sin \omega t$ for the simple harmonic motion.

**50.** A radio station, 98.1 on the FM dial, has radio waves with a frequency of 98.1 million cycles per second. Write an equation in the form $d = a \sin \omega t$ for the simple harmonic motion of the radio waves.

## Writing in Mathematics

**51.** What does it mean to solve a right triangle?

**52.** Explain how to find one of the acute angles of a right triangle if two sides are known.

**53.** Describe a situation in which a right triangle and a trigonometric function are used to measure a height or distance that would otherwise be inconvenient or impossible to measure.

**54.** What is meant by the bearing from point $O$ to point $P$? Give an example with your description.

**55.** What is simple harmonic motion? Give an example with your description.

**56.** Explain the period and the frequency of simple harmonic motion. How are they related?

**57.** Explain how the photograph of the damaged highway on page 522 illustrates simple harmonic motion.

## Technology Exercises

*The functions in Exercises 58–59 model motion in which the amplitude decreases with time due to friction or other resistive forces. Graph each function in the given viewing rectangle. How many complete oscillations occur on the time interval $0 \le x \le 10$?*

**58.** $y = 4e^{-0.1x} \cos 2x \quad [0, 10, 1]$ by $[-4, 4, 1]$

**59.** $y = -6e^{-0.09x} \cos 2\pi x \quad [0, 10, 1]$ by $[-6, 6, 1]$

## Critical Thinking Exercises

**60.** The figure shows a satellite circling 112 miles above Earth. When the satellite is directly above point $B$, angle $A$ measures 76.6°. Find Earth's radius to the nearest mile.

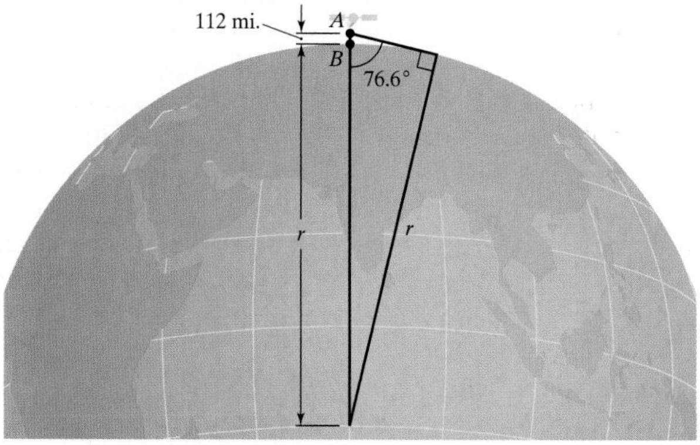


**61.** The figure shows that the angle of elevation to the top of the building changes from 20° to 40° as an observer advances 75 feet toward the building. Find the height of the building to the nearest foot.

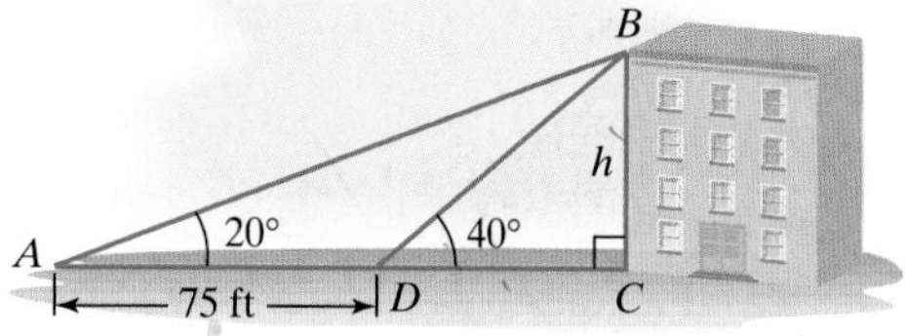


## Group Exercise

**62.** Music and mathematics have been linked over the centuries. Group members should research and present a seminar to the class on music and mathematics. Be sure to include the role of trigonometric functions in the music-mathematics link.

# CHAPTER SUMMARY, REVIEW, AND TEST

## Summary

### 5.1 Angles and Their Measure

a. An angle consists of two rays with a common endpoint, the vertex.

b. An angle is in standard position if its vertex is at the origin and its initial side lies along the positive $x$-axis. Figure 5.3 on page 426 shows positive and negative angles in standard position.

c. A quadrantal angle is one with its terminal side on the $x$-axis or the $y$-axis.

d. Angles can be measured in degrees. 1° is $\frac{1}{360}$ of a complete rotation.

e. Acute angles measure less than 90°, right angles 90°, obtuse angles more than 90° but less than 180°, and straight angles 180°.

f. Two angles with the same initial and terminal sides are called coterminal angles.

g. Two angles are complements if their sum is 90° and supplements if their sum is 180°. Only positive angles are used.

h. Angles can be measured in radians. One radian is the measure of the central angle if the intercepted arc and radius have the same length. In general, the radian measure of a central angle is the length of the intercepted arc divided by the circle's radius: $\theta = \frac{s}{r}$.

i. To convert degrees to radians, multiply degrees by $\frac{\pi \text{ radians}}{180°}$. To convert from radians to degrees, multiply radians by $\frac{180°}{\pi \text{ radians}}$.

j. The arc length formula, $s = r\theta$, is described in the box on page 000.

k. The definitions of linear speed, $v = \frac{s}{t}$, and angular speed, $\omega = \frac{\theta}{t}$, are given in the box on page 434.

l. Linear speed is expressed in terms of angular speed by $v = r\omega$, where $v$ is the linear speed of a point a distance $r$ from the center of rotation and $\omega$ is the angular speed in radians per unit of time.

## 5.2 Trigonometry Functions: The Unit Circle

a. Definitions of the trigonometric functions in terms of a unit circle are given in the box on page 441.

b. The cosine and secant functions are even:
$\cos(-t) = \cos t,\ \sec(-t) = \sec t.$
The other trigonometric functions are odd:
$\sin(-t) = -\sin t,\ \tan(-t) = -\tan t,$
$\cot(-t) = -\cot t,\ \csc(-t) = -\csc t.$

c. Fundamental Identities

1. Reciprocal Identities

$$\sin t = \frac{1}{\csc t} \qquad \cos t = \frac{1}{\sec t} \qquad \tan t = \frac{1}{\cot t}$$
$$\csc t = \frac{1}{\sin t} \qquad \sec t = \frac{1}{\cos t} \qquad \cot t = \frac{1}{\tan t}$$

2. Quotient Identities

$$\tan t = \frac{\sin t}{\cos t} \qquad \cot t = \frac{\cos t}{\sin t}$$

3. Pythagorean Identities

$$\sin^2 t + \cos^2 t = 1 \quad 1 + \tan^2 t = \sec^2 t \quad 1 + \cot^2 t = \csc^2 t$$

d. If $f(t + p) = f(t)$, function $f$ is periodic. The smallest $p$ for which $f$ is periodic is the period of $f$. The tangent and cotangent functions have period $\pi$. The other four trigonometric functions have period $2\pi$.

## 5.3 Right Triangle Trigonometry

a. The right triangle definitions of the six trigonometric functions are given in the box on page 456.

b. Function values for 30°, 45°, and 60° can be obtained using these special triangles.

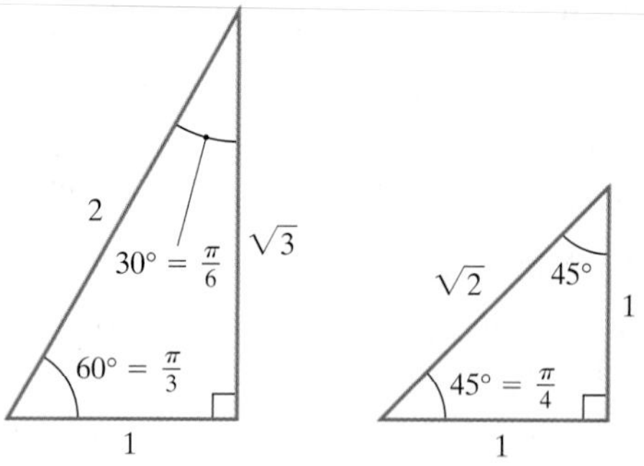


c. The value of a trigonometric function of $\theta$ is equal to the cofunction of the complement of $\theta$. Cofunction identities are listed in the box on page 460.

## 5.4 Trigonometric Functions of Any Angle

a. Definitions of the trigonometric functions of any angle are given in the box on page 467.

b. Signs of the trigonometric functions: All functions are positive in quadrant I. If $\theta$ lies in quadrant II, $\sin\theta$ and $\csc\theta$ are positive. If $\theta$ lies in quadrant III, $\tan\theta$ and $\cot\theta$ are positive. If $\theta$ lies in quadrant IV, $\cos\theta$ and $\sec\theta$ are positive.

c. If $\theta$ is a nonacute angle in standard position that lies in a quadrant, its reference angle is the positive acute angle $\theta'$ formed by the terminal side of $\theta$ and the $x$-axis. The reference angle for a given angle can be found by making a sketch that shows the angle in standard position. Figure 5.36 on page 472 shows reference angles for $\theta$ in quadrants II, III, and IV.

d. The values of the trigonometric functions of a given angle are the same as the values of the functions of the reference angle, except possibly for the sign. A procedure for using reference angles to evaluate trigonometric functions is given in the box on page 473.

## 5.5 and 5.6 Graphs of the Trigonometric Functions

a. Graphs of the six trigonometric functions with a description of the domain, range, and period of each function are given in Table 5.5 on page 506.

b. The graph of $y = A\sin(Bx - C)$ can be obtained using amplitude $= |A|$, period $= \frac{2\pi}{B}$ and phase shift $= \frac{C}{B}$. See the illustration in the box on page 483.

c. The graph of $y = A\cos(Bx - C)$ can be obtained using amplitude $= |A|$, period $= \frac{2\pi}{B}$, and phase shift $= \frac{C}{B}$. See the illustration in the box on page 489.

d. The constant $D$ in $y = A\sin(Bx - C) + D$ and $y = A\cos(Bx - C) + D$ causes vertical shifts in the graphs in the preceding items (b) and (c). If $D > 0$, the shift is $D$ units upward and if $D < 0$, the shift is $D$ units downward. Oscillation is about $y = D$.

e. The graph of $y = A\tan(Bx - C)$ is obtained using the procedure in the box on page 500. Consecutive asymptotes (solve $Bx - C = -\frac{\pi}{2}$ and $Bx - C = \frac{\pi}{2}$) and an $x$-intercept midway between them play a key role in the graphing process.

f. The graph of $y = A\cot(Bx - C)$ is obtained using the procedure in the box on page 502. Consecutive asymptotes (solve $Bx - C = 0$ and $Bx - C = \pi$) and an $x$-intercept midway between them play a key role in the graphing process.

g. To graph a cosecant curve, begin by graphing the reciprocal sine curve. Draw vertical asymptotes through $x$-intercepts, using asymptotes as guides to sketch the graph. To graph a secant curve, first graph the reciprocal cosine curve and use the same procedure.

### 5.7 Inverse Trigonometric Functions

a. On the restricted domain $-\frac{\pi}{2} \le x \le \frac{\pi}{2}$, $y = \sin x$ has an inverse function, defined in the box on page 511. Think of $\sin^{-1} x$ as the angle in $\left[-\frac{\pi}{2}, \frac{\pi}{2}\right]$ whose sine is $x$.

b. On the restricted domain $0 \le x \le \pi$, $y = \cos x$ has an inverse function, defined in the box on page 514. Think of $\cos^{-1} x$ as the angle in $[0, \pi]$ whose cosine is $x$.

c. On the restricted domain $-\frac{\pi}{2} < x < \frac{\pi}{2}$, $y = \tan x$ has an inverse function, defined in the box on page 516. Think of $\tan^{-1} x$ as the angle in $\left(-\frac{\pi}{2}, \frac{\pi}{2}\right)$ whose tangent is $x$.

d. Graphs of the three basic inverse trigonometric functions, with a description of the domain and range of each function, is given in Table 5.9 on page 518.

e. Inverse properties are given in the box on page 519. Points on terminal sides of angles in standard position are used to find exact values of the composition of a function and a different inverse function.

### 5.8 Applications of Trigonometric Functions

a. Solving a right triangle means finding the missing lengths of its sides and the measurements of its angles. The Pythagorean Theorem, two acute angles whose sum is 90°, and appropriate trigonometric functions are used in this process.

b. The bearing from point $O$ to point $P$ is the acute angle between ray $OP$ and a north-south line.

c. Simple harmonic motion, described in the box on page 532, is modeled by $d = a\cos\omega t$ or $d = a\sin t$, with amplitude $= |a|$, period $= \frac{2\pi}{\omega}$ and frequency $= \frac{\omega}{2\pi} = \frac{1}{\text{period}}$.

## Review Exercises

### 5.1

*In Exercises 1–4, draw each angle in standard position.*

**1.** 190° **2.** −135° **3.** $\frac{5\pi}{6}$ **4.** $-\frac{2\pi}{3}$

*In Exercises 5–6, find a positive angle less than 360° that is coterminal with the given angle.*

**5.** 400° **6.** −85°

*In Exercises 7–8, if possible, find the complement and the supplement of the given angle.*

**7.** 73° **8.** $\frac{2\pi}{3}$

**9.** Find the radian measure of the central angle of a circle of radius 6 centimeters that intercepts an arc of length 27 centimeters.

*In Exercises 10–12, convert each angle in degrees to radians. Express your answer as a multiple of $\pi$.*

**10.** 15° **11.** 120° **12.** 315°

*In Exercises 13–15, convert each angle in radians to degrees.*

**13.** $\frac{5\pi}{3}$ **14.** $\frac{7\pi}{5}$ **15.** $-\frac{5\pi}{6}$

**16.** Find the length of the arc on a circle of radius 10 feet intercepted by a 135° central angle. Express arc length in terms of $\pi$. Then round your answer to two decimal places.

**17.** The angular speed of a propeller on a wind generator is 10.3 revolutions per minute. Express this angular speed in radians per minute.

**18.** The propeller of an airplane has a radius of 3 feet. The propeller is rotating at 2250 revolutions per minute. Find the linear speed, in feet per minute, of the tip of the propeller.

## 5.2

*In Exercises 19–20, a point $P(x, y)$ is shown on the unit circle corresponding to a real number t. Find the values of the trigonometric functions at t.*

**19.**

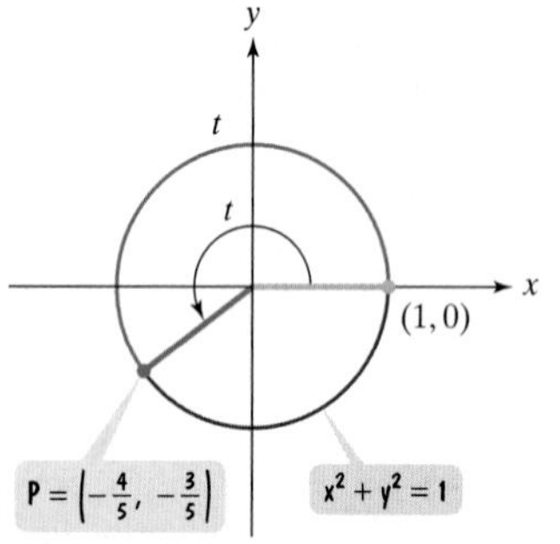


**20.**

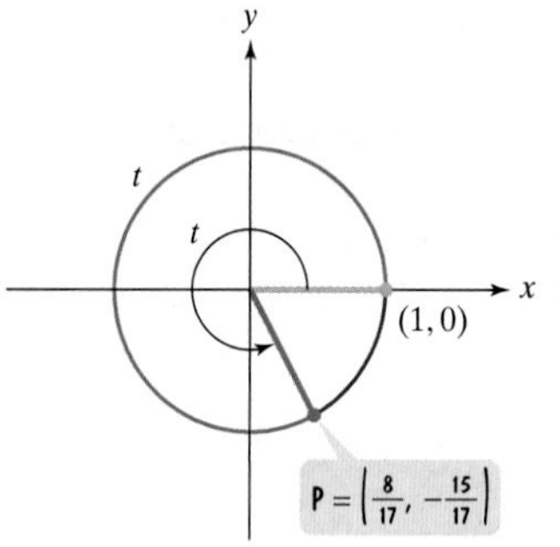


*In Exercises 21–24, use the figure shown to find the value of each trigonometric function at the indicated real number or state that the expression is undefined.*

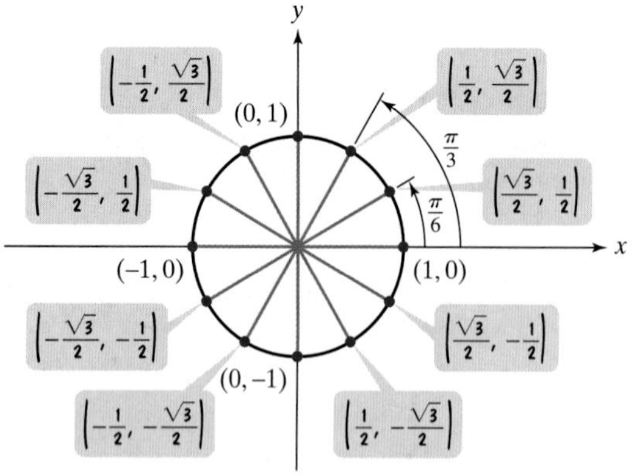


**21.** $\sec \frac{5\pi}{6}$ **22.** $\tan \frac{4\pi}{3}$ **23.** $\sec \frac{\pi}{2}$ **24.** $\cot \pi$

**25.** If $\sin t = \frac{2}{\sqrt{7}}$, $0 \le t < \frac{\pi}{2}$, use identities to find the remaining trigonometric functions.

*In Exercises 26–28, evaluate each expression without using a calculator.*

**26.** $\tan 4.7 \cot 4.7$

**27.** $\sin^2 \frac{\pi}{17} + \cos^2 \frac{\pi}{17}$

**28.** $\cot^2 1.4 - \csc^2 1.4$

## 5.3

**29.** Use the triangle to find each of the six trigonometric functions of $\theta$.

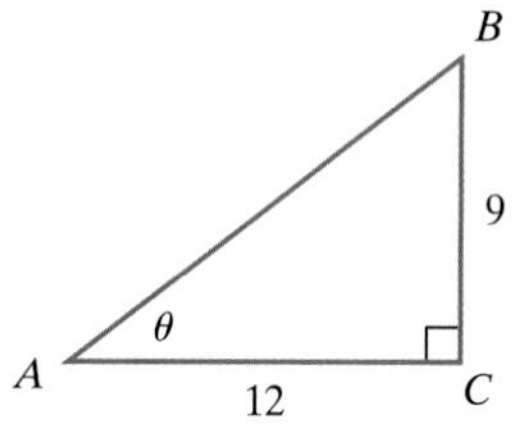


*In Exercises 30–31, find the exact value of each expression.*

**30.** $4 \cot \frac{\pi}{4} + \cos \frac{\pi}{3} \csc \frac{\pi}{6}$

**31.** $\cos \frac{\pi}{6} \sin \frac{\pi}{4} - \tan \frac{\pi}{4}$

*In Exercises 32–33, find a cofunction with the same value as the given expression.*

**32.** $\sin 70°$

**33.** $\cos \frac{\pi}{2}$

*In Exercises 34–36, find the measure of the side of the right triangle whose length is designated by a lowercase letter. Round answers to the nearest whole number.*

**34.**

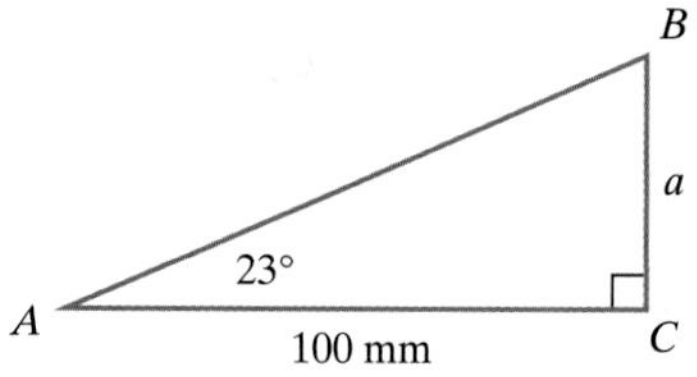


**35.**

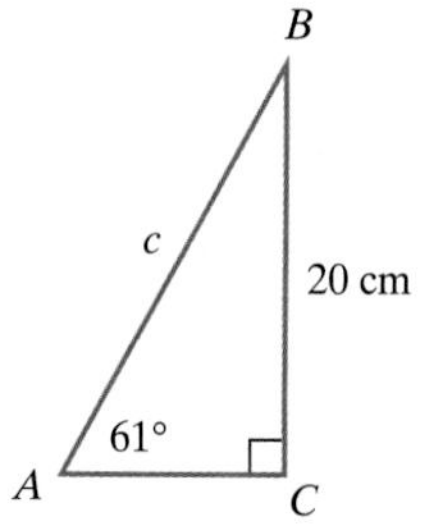


**36.**

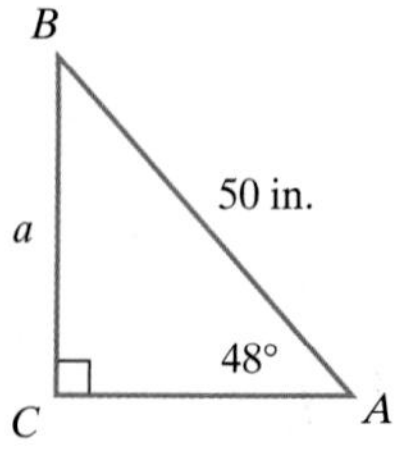


**37.** A hiker climbs for a half mile up a slope whose inclination is 17°. How many feet of altitude, to the nearest foot, does the hiker gain?

**38.** To find the distance across a lake, a surveyor took the measurements in the figure shown. What is the distance across the lake? Round to the nearest meter.

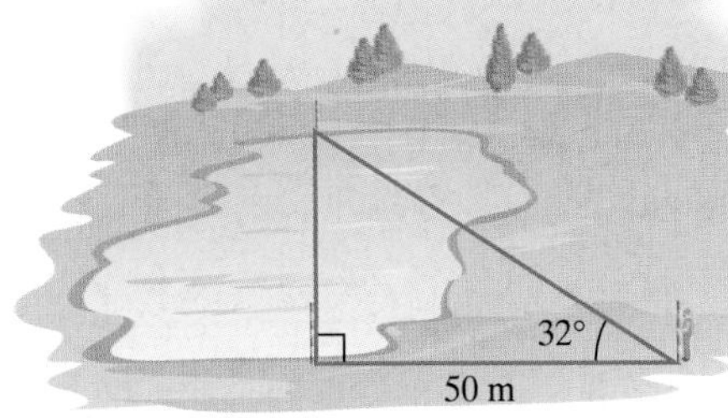


**39.** When a six-foot pole casts a four-foot shadow, what is the angle of elevation of the sun? Round to the nearest whole degree.

## 5.4

*In Exercises 40–41, a point on the terminal side of angle $\theta$ is given. Find the exact value of each of the six trigonometric functions of $\theta$, or state that the function is undefined.*

**40.** $(-1, -5)$ **41.** $(0, -1)$

*In Exercises 42–43, let $\theta$ be an angle in standard position. Name the quadrant in which $\theta$ lies.*

**42.** $\tan\theta > 0$ and $\sec\theta > 0$ **43.** $\tan\theta > 0$ and $\cos\theta < 0$

*In Exercises 44–45, find the exact value of each of the remaining trigonometric functions of $\theta$.*

**44.** $\cos\theta = \frac{2}{5}$, $\sin\theta < 0$ **45.** $\tan\theta = -\frac{1}{3}$, $\sin\theta > 0$

*In Exercises 46–48, find the reference angle for each angle.*

**46.** $265°$ **47.** $\frac{5\pi}{8}$ **48.** $-410°$

*In Exercises 49–57, find the exact value of each expression. Do not use a calculator.*

**49.** $\sin 240°$ **50.** $\tan 120°$ **51.** $\sec\frac{7\pi}{4}$

**52.** $\cos\frac{11\pi}{6}$ **53.** $\cot(-210°)$ **54.** $\csc\left(-\frac{2\pi}{3}\right)$

**55.** $\sin\left(-\frac{\pi}{3}\right)$ **56.** $\sin 495°$ **57.** $\tan\frac{13\pi}{4}$

## 5.5

*In Exercises 58–63, determine the amplitude and period of each function. Then graph one period of the function.*

**58.** $y = 3\sin 4x$ **59.** $y = -2\cos 2x$

**60.** $y = 2\cos\frac{1}{2}x$ **61.** $y = \frac{1}{2}\sin\frac{\pi}{3}x$

**62.** $y = -\sin\pi x$ **63.** $y = 3\cos\frac{x}{3}$

*In Exercises 64–68, determine the amplitude, period, and phase shift of each function. Then graph one period of the function.*

**64.** $y = 2\sin(x - \pi)$ **65.** $y = -3\cos(x + \pi)$

**66.** $y = \frac{3}{2}\cos\left(2x + \frac{\pi}{4}\right)$ **67.** $y = \frac{5}{2}\sin\left(2x + \frac{\pi}{2}\right)$

**68.** $y = -3\sin\left(\frac{\pi}{3}x - 3\pi\right)$

*In Exercises 69–70, use a vertical shift to graph one period of the function.*

**69.** $y = \sin 2x + 1$ **70.** $y = 2\cos\frac{1}{3}x - 2$

**71.** The equation

$$y = 98.6 + 0.3\sin\left(\frac{\pi}{12}x - \frac{11\pi}{12}\right)$$

models variation in body temperature, $y$, in °F, $x$ hours after midnight.

**a.** What is body temperature at midnight?
**b.** What is the period of the body temperature cycle?
**c.** When is body temperature highest? What is the body temperature at this time?
**d.** When is body temperature lowest? What is the body temperature at this time?
**e.** Graph one period of the body temperature function.

## 5.6

*In Exercises 72–78, graph two full periods of the given tangent or cotangent function.*

**72.** $y = 4\tan 2x$ **73.** $y = -2\tan\frac{\pi}{4}x$

**74.** $y = \tan(x + \pi)$ **75.** $y = -\tan\left(x - \frac{\pi}{4}\right)$

**76.** $y = 2\cot 3x$ **77.** $y = -\frac{1}{2}\cot\frac{\pi}{2}x$

**78.** $y = 2\cot\left(x + \frac{\pi}{2}\right)$

*In Exercises 79–82, graph two full periods of the given cosecant or secant function.*

**79.** $y = 3\sec 2\pi x$ **80.** $y = -2\csc\pi x$

**81.** $y = 3\sec(x + \pi)$ **82.** $y = \frac{5}{2}\csc(x - \pi)$

## 5.7

*In Exercises 83–100, find the exact value of each expression. Do not use a calculator.*

**83.** $\sin^{-1}1$ **84.** $\cos^{-1}1$

**85.** $\tan^{-1}1$ **86.** $\sin^{-1}\left(-\frac{\sqrt{3}}{2}\right)$

**87.** $\cos^{-1}\left(-\frac{1}{2}\right)$ **88.** $\tan^{-1}\left(-\frac{\sqrt{3}}{3}\right)$

**89.** $\cos\left(\sin^{-1}\frac{\sqrt{2}}{2}\right)$ **90.** $\sin(\cos^{-1}0)$

**91.** $\tan\left[\sin^{-1}\left(-\frac{1}{2}\right)\right]$ **92.** $\tan\left[\cos^{-1}\left(-\frac{\sqrt{3}}{2}\right)\right]$

**93.** $\csc\left(\tan^{-1}\frac{\sqrt{3}}{3}\right)$ **94.** $\cos\left(\tan^{-1}\frac{3}{4}\right)$

**95.** $\sin\left(\cos^{-1}\frac{3}{5}\right)$ **96.** $\tan\left[\sin^{-1}\left(-\frac{3}{5}\right)\right]$

**97.** $\tan\left[\cos^{-1}\left(-\frac{4}{5}\right)\right]$ **98.** $\sin^{-1}\left(\sin\frac{\pi}{3}\right)$

**99.** $\sin^{-1}\left(\sin\frac{2\pi}{3}\right)$ **100.** $\sin^{-1}\left(\cos\frac{2\pi}{3}\right)$

*In Exercises 101–102, use a right triangle to write each expression as an algebraic expression. Assume that x is positive and in the domain of the given inverse trigonometric function.*

**101.** $\cos\left(\tan^{-1}\frac{x}{2}\right)$ **102.** $\sec\left(\sin^{-1}\frac{1}{x}\right)$

## 5.8

*In Exercises 103–106, solve the right triangle shown in the figure. Round lengths to two decimal places and express angles to the nearest tenth of a degree.*

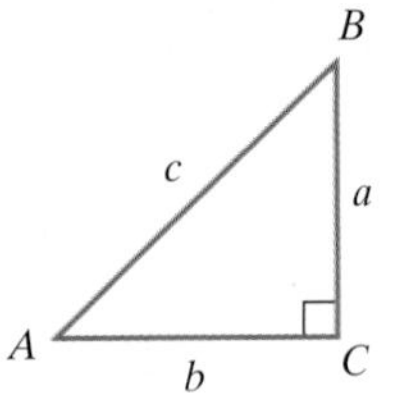


**103.** $A = 22.3°, c = 10$ **104.** $B = 37.4°, b = 6$

**105.** $a = 2, c = 7$ **106.** $a = 1.4, b = 3.6$

**107.** From a point on level ground 80 feet from the base of a building, the angle of elevation is 25.6°. Approximate the height of the building to the nearest foot.

**108.** Two buildings with flat roofs are 60 yards apart. The height of the shorter building is 40 yards. From its roof, the angle of elevation to the edge of the roof of the taller building is 40°. Find the height of the taller building to the nearest yard.

**109.** You want to measure the height of an antenna on the top of a 125-foot building. From a point in front of the building, you measure the angle of elevation to the top of the building to be 68° and the angle of elevation to the top of the antenna to be 71°. How tall is the antenna, to the nearest tenth of a foot?

*In Exercises 110–111, use the figure shown to find the bearing from O to A.*

**110.**

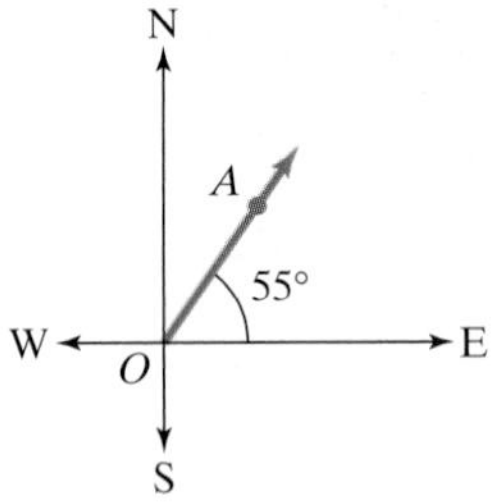


**111.**

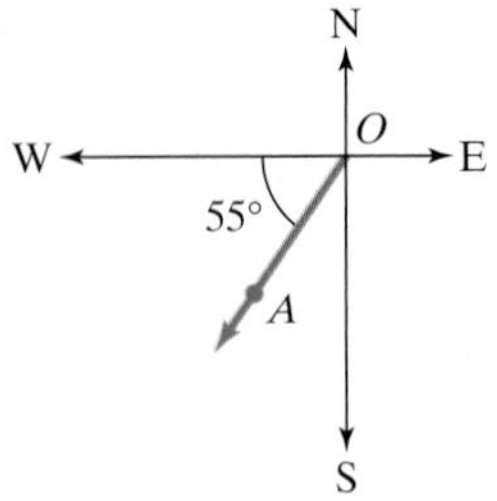


**112.** A ship is due west of a lighthouse. A second ship is 12 miles south of the first ship. The bearing from the second ship to the lighthouse is N 64° E. How far, to the nearest tenth of a mile, is the first ship from the lighthouse?

**113.** From city A to city B, a plane flies 850 miles at a bearing of N 58° E. From city B to city C, the plane flies 960 miles at a bearing of S 72° E.

**a.** Find, to the nearest tenth of a mile, the distance from city A to city C.

**b.** What is the bearing from city A to city C?

*In Exercises 114–115, an object moves in simple harmonic motion described by the given equation, where t is measured in seconds and d in centimeters. In each exercise, find*

**a.** *the maximum displacement.*

**b.** *the frequency.*

**c.** *the time required for one cycle.*

**114.** $d = 20\cos\frac{\pi}{4}t$ **115.** $d = \frac{1}{2}\sin 4t$

*In Exercises 116–117, an object is attached to a coiled spring. The object is pulled down (negative direction from the rest position) and then released. Write an equation for the distance of the object from its rest position after t seconds.*

| | Distance from rest position at $t = 0$ | Amplitude | Period |
|---|---|---|---|
| **116.** | 30 inches | 30 inches | 2 seconds |
| **117.** | 0 | $\frac{1}{4}$ inches | 5 seconds |

## Chapter 5 Test

1. Convert 135° to exact radian measure.
2. Find the supplement of the angle whose radian measure is $\frac{9\pi}{13}$. Express the answer in terms of $\pi$.
3. Find the length of the arc on a circle of radius 20 feet intercepted by a 75° central angle. Express arc length in terms of $\pi$. Then round your answer to two decimal places.
4. If $(-2, 5)$ is a point on the terminal side of angle $\theta$, find the exact value of each of the six trigonometric functions of $\theta$.
5. Determine the quadrant in which $\theta$ lies if $\cos < 0$ and $\cot\theta > 0$.

6. If $\cos\theta = \frac{1}{3}$ and $\tan\theta < 0$, find the exact value of each of the remaining trigonometric functions of $\theta$.

*In Exercises 7–9, find the exact value of each expression. Do not use a calculator.*

7. $\tan\frac{\pi}{6}\cos\frac{\pi}{3} - \cos\frac{\pi}{2}$

8. $\tan 300°$

9. $\sin\frac{7\pi}{4}$

*In Exercises 10–13, graph one period of each function.*

10. $y = 3\sin 2x$

11. $y = -2\cos\left(x - \frac{\pi}{2}\right)$

12. $y = 2\tan\frac{x}{2}$

13. $y = -\frac{1}{2}\csc\pi x$

14. Find the exact value of $\tan\left[\cos^{-1}\left(-\frac{1}{2}\right)\right]$.

15. Solve the right triangle in the figure shown. Round lengths to one decimal place.

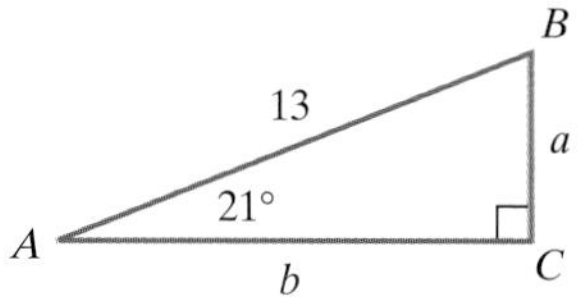


16. The angle of elevation of a building from a point on the ground 30 yards from its base is 37°. Find the height of the building to the nearest yard.

17. A 73-foot rope from the top of a circus tent pole is anchored to the flat ground 43 feet from the bottom of the pole. Find the angle, to the nearest tenth of a degree, that the rope makes with the pole.

18. Use the figure to find the bearing from $O$ to $P$.

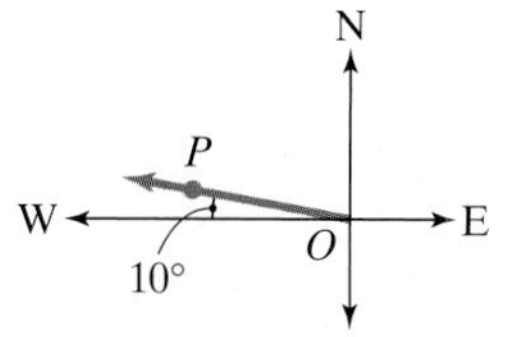


19. An object moves in simple harmonic motion described by $d = -6\cos\pi t$, where $t$ is measured in seconds and $d$ in inches. Find (a) the maximum displacement, (b) the frequency, and (c) the time required for one oscillation.

20. Why are trigonometric functions ideally suited to model phenomena that repeat in cycles?

## Cumulative Review Exercises (Chapters 1–5)

*Solve each equation or inequality in Exercises 1–6.*

1. $x^2 = 18 + 3x$

2. $x^3 + 5x^2 - 4x - 20 = 0$

3. $\log_2 x + \log_2(x - 2) = 3$

4. $\sqrt{x - 3} + 5 = x$

5. $x^3 - 4x^2 + x + 6 = 0$

6. $|2x - 5| \le 11$

7. If $f(x) = \sqrt{x - 6}$, find $f^{-1}(x)$.

8. Divide $20x^3 - 6x^2 - 9x + 10$ by $5x + 2$.

9. Write as a single logarithm and evaluate: $\log 25 + \log 40$.

10. Convert $\frac{14\pi}{9}$ radians to degrees.

11. Find the maximum number of positive and negative real roots of the equation $3x^4 - 2x^3 + 5x^2 + x - 9 = 0$.

*In Exercises 12–16, graph each equation.*

12. $f(x) = \frac{x}{x^2 - 1}$

13. $(x - 2)^2 + y^2 = 1$

14. $y = (x - 1)(x + 2)^2$

15. $y = \sin\left(2x + \frac{\pi}{2}\right)$, from 0 to $2\pi$

16. $y = 2\tan 3x$; graph two complete cycles.

17. You invest in a new play. The cost includes an overhead of \$30,000, plus production costs of \$2500 per performance. A sold-out performance brings you \$3125. How many sold-out performances must be played in order for you to break even?

18. Use the exponential growth model $A = A_0e^{kt}$ to solve this exercise. Data from the Federal Communication Commission show that the use of toll-free 800 numbers has grown exponentially. In 1991 there were 10.2 billion such calls and by 1998, there were 86.7 billion.
    a. Find the exponential function that models the data.
    b. By what year will the number of toll-free 800 numbers reach 200 billion?

19. The rate of heat lost through insulation varies inversely as the thickness of the insulation. The rate of heat lost through a 3.5-inch thickness of insulation is 2200 Btu per hour. What is the rate of heat lost through a 5-inch thickness of the same insulation?

20. A tower is 200 feet tall. To the nearest degree, find the angle of elevation from a point 50 feet from the base of the tower to the top of the tower.

# Analytic Trigonometry

Chapter 6

This chapter emphasizes the algebraic aspects of trigonometry. We derive important categories of identities involving trigonometric functions. These identities are used to simplify and analyze expressions that model phenomena as diverse as the distance achieved when throwing an object and musical sounds on a touch-tone phone. For example, we can find out critical information about an athlete's performance by using an identity to analyze an expression involving throwing distance. You will learn how to use trigonometric identities to better understand your periodic world.

You enjoy watching your friend participate in the shot put at college track and field events. After a few full turns in a circle, she throws ("puts") a 16-pound shot from the shoulder. The range of her throwing distance continues to improve. Knowing that you are studying trigonometry, she asks if there is some way that a trigonometric expression might help achieve the best distance possible in the event.

# SECTION 6.1 Verifying Trigonometric Identities

## Objective

1. Use the fundamental trigonometric identities to verify identities.

Do you enjoy solving puzzles? The process is a natural way to develop problem-solving skills that are important to every area of our lives. Engaging in problem solving for sheer pleasure releases chemicals in the brain that enhance our feeling of well-being. Perhaps this is why puzzles date back 12,000 years.

Thousands of relationships exist among the six trigonometric functions. Verifying these relationships is like solving a puzzle. Why? There are no rigid rules for the process. Thus, proving a trigonometric relationship requires you to be creative in your problem-solving abilities. By learning to establish these relationships, you will become a better, more confident problem solver. Furthermore, you may enjoy the feeling of satisfaction that accompanies solving each "puzzle."

## The Fundamental Identities

In Chapter 5, we used the unit circle to establish relationships among trigonometric functions. The fundamental identities summarized in the following box are expressed in terms of $x$, rather than $t$, although any letter can be used to represent the variable. These identities are true for all values of $x$ for which the expressions are defined.

### Study Tip

Memorize the identities in the box. You may need to use variations of these fundamental identities. For example, instead of

$$\sin^2 x + \cos^2 x = 1,$$

you might want to use

$$\sin^2 x = 1 - \cos^2 x$$

or

$$\cos^2 x = 1 - \sin^2 x.$$

Therefore, it is important to know each relationship well so that mental algebraic manipulation is possible.

### Fundamental Trigonometric Identities

**Reciprocal Identities**

$$\sin x = \frac{1}{\csc x} \qquad \cos x = \frac{1}{\sec x} \qquad \tan x = \frac{1}{\cot x}$$

$$\csc x = \frac{1}{\sin x} \qquad \sec x = \frac{1}{\cos x} \qquad \cot x = \frac{1}{\tan x}$$

**Quotient Identities**

$$\tan x = \frac{\sin x}{\cos x} \qquad \cot x = \frac{\cos x}{\sin x}$$

**Pythagorean Identities**

$$\sin^2 x + \cos^2 x = 1 \qquad 1 + \tan^2 x = \sec^2 x \qquad 1 + \cot^2 x = \csc^2 x$$

**Even-Odd Identities**

$$\sin(-x) = -\sin x \qquad \cos(-x) = \cos x \qquad \tan(-x) = -\tan x$$

$$\csc(-x) = -\csc x \qquad \sec(-x) = \sec x \qquad \cot(-x) = -\cot x$$

**1** Use the fundamental trigonometric identities to verify identities.

## Using Fundamental Identities to Verify Other Identities

The fundamental trigonometric identities are used to establish other relationships among trigonometric functions. To **verify an identity**, we show that one side of the identity can be simplified so that it is identical to the other side. Each side of the equation is manipulated independently of the other side of the equation. Start with the side containing the more complicated expression. If you substitute one or more fundamental identities on the more complicated side, you will often be able to rewrite it in a form identical to that of the other side.

No one method can be used to verify every identity. Some identities can be verified by rewriting the more complicated side so that it contains only sines and cosines.

### EXAMPLE 1 Changing to Sines and Cosines to Verify an Identity

Verify the identity: $\sec x \cot x = \csc x$.

**Solution** The left side of the equation contains the more complicated expression. Thus, we work with the left side. Let us express this side of the identity in terms of sines and cosines. Perhaps this strategy will enable us to transform the left side into $\csc x$, the expression on the right.

$$\sec x \cot x = \frac{1}{\cos x} \cdot \frac{\cos x}{\sin x}$$

Apply a reciprocal identity: $\sec x = \frac{1}{\cos x}$ and a quotient identity: $\cot x = \frac{\cos x}{\sin x}$.

$$= \frac{1}{\cancel{\cos x}} \cdot \frac{\cancel{\cos x}}{\sin x}$$

Divide both the numerator and the denominator by $\cos x$, the common factor.

$$= \frac{1}{\sin x}$$

Multiply the remaining factors in the numerator and denominator.

$$= \csc x$$

Apply a reciprocal identity: $\csc x = \frac{1}{\sin x}$.

By working with the left side and simplifying it so that it is identical to the right side, we have verified the given identity.

## Technology

You can use a graphing utility to provide evidence of an identity. For example, consider the equation in Example 1,

$$\sec x \cot x = \csc x.$$

Graph

$$y = \sec x \cot x$$

and

$$y = \csc x$$

in the same viewing rectangle. The screen shown indicates that the graphs appear to be the same. Example 1 shows the equivalence algebraically.

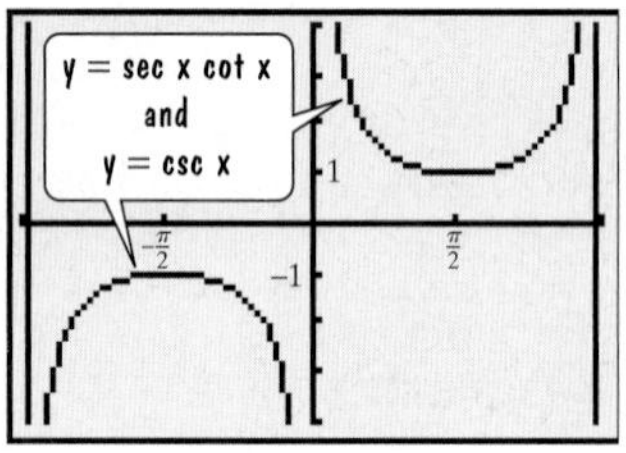


**Check Point 1** Verify the identity: $\csc x \tan x = \sec x$.

In verifying an identity, stay focused on your goal. When manipulating one side of the equation, continue to look at the other side to keep in mind the desired form of the result.

## Study Tip

Verifying that an equation is an identity is different from solving an equation. You cannot verify an identity by adding, subtracting, multiplying, or dividing each side by the same expression. If you do this, you assume that the given statement is true. You do not know that it is true until after you have verified it.

## EXAMPLE 2 Changing to Sines and Cosines to Verify an Identity

Verify the identity: $\sin x \tan x + \cos x = \sec x$.

**Solution** The left side is more complicated, so we so we start with it. Let us express this side of the identity so that it contains only sines and cosines. Thus, we use a quotient identity and replace $\tan x$ by $\frac{\sin x}{\cos x}$. Perhaps this strategy will enable us to transform the left side into $\sec x$, the expression on the right.

| | |
|---|---|
| $\sin x \tan x + \cos x = \sin x\left(\frac{\sin x}{\cos x}\right) + \cos x$ | Apply a quotient identity: $\tan x = \frac{\sin x}{\cos x}$. |
| $= \frac{\sin^2 x}{\cos x} + \cos x.$ | Multiply. |
| $= \frac{\sin^2 x}{\cos x} + \cos x \cdot \frac{\cos x}{\cos x}$ | The least common denominator is $\cos x$. Write the second expression with a denominator of $\cos x$. |
| $= \frac{\sin^2 x}{\cos x} + \frac{\cos^2 x}{\cos x}$ | Multiply. |
| $= \frac{\sin^2 x + \cos^2 x}{\cos x}$ | Add numerators, putting this sum over the least common denominator. |
| $= \frac{1}{\cos x}$ | Apply a Pythagorean identity: $\sin^2 x + \cos^2 x = 1$. |
| $= \sec x$ | Apply a reciprocal identity: $\sec x = \frac{1}{\cos x}$. |

By working with the left side and arriving at the right side, the identity is verified.

**Check Point 2** Verify the identity: $\cos x \cot x + \sin x = \csc x$.

Some identities are verified by using factoring to simplify a trigonometric expression.

## EXAMPLE 3 Using Factoring to Verify an Identity

Verify the identity: $\cos x - \cos x \sin^2 x = \cos^3 x$.

**Solution** We start with the more complicated side, the left side. Factor out the greatest common factor, $\cos x$, from each of the two terms.

| | |
|---|---|
| $\cos x - \cos x \sin^2 x = \cos x(1 - \sin^2 x)$ | Factor $\cos x$ from the two terms. |
| $= \cos x \cdot \cos^2 x$ | Use a variation of $\sin^2 x + \cos^2 x = 1$. Solving for $\cos^2 x$, we obtain $\cos^2 x = 1 - \sin^2 x$. |
| $= \cos^3 x$ | Multiply. |

We worked with the left side and arrived at the right side. Thus, the identity is verified.

**Check Point 3** Verify the identity: $\sin x - \sin x \cos^2 x = \sin^3 x$.

How do we verify identities in which sums or differences of fractions with trigonometric functions appear on one side? Use the least common denominator and combine the fractions. This technique is especially useful when the other side of the identity contains only one term.

## EXAMPLE 4 Combining Fractional Expressions to Verify an Identity

Verify the identity: $\dfrac{\cos x}{1 + \sin x} + \dfrac{1 + \sin x}{\cos x} = 2 \sec x$.

**Solution** We start with the more complicated side, the left side. The least common denominator of the fractions is $(1 + \sin x)(\cos x)$. We express each fraction in terms of this least common denominator by multiplying the numerator and denominator by the extra factor needed to form $(1 + \sin x)(\cos x)$.

$$\frac{\cos x}{1 + \sin x} + \frac{1 + \sin x}{\cos x}$$
The least common denominator is $(1 + \sin x)(\cos x)$.

$$= \frac{\cos x(\cos x)}{(1 + \sin x)(\cos x)} + \frac{(1 + \sin x)(1 + \sin x)}{(1 + \sin x)(\cos x)}$$
Rewrite each fraction with the least common denominator.

$$= \frac{\cos^2 x}{(1 + \sin x)(\cos x)} + \frac{1 + 2\sin x + \sin^2 x}{(1 + \sin x)(\cos x)}$$
Use the FOIL method to multiply $(1 + \sin x)(1 + \sin x)$.

$$= \frac{\cos^2 x + 1 + 2\sin x + \sin^2 x}{(1 + \sin x)(\cos x)}$$
Add numerators. Put this sum over the least common denominator.

$$= \frac{(\sin^2 x + \cos^2 x) + 1 + 2\sin x}{(1 + \sin x)(\cos x)}$$
Regroup terms to apply a Pythagorean identity.

$$= \frac{1 + 1 + 2\sin x}{(1 + \sin x)(\cos x)}$$
Apply a Pythagorean identity: $\sin^2 x + \cos^2 x = 1$.

$$= \frac{2 + 2\sin x}{(1 + \sin x)(\cos x)}$$
Add constant terms in the numerator: $1 + 1 = 2$.

$$= \frac{2\cancel{(1 + \sin x)}}{\cancel{(1 + \sin x)}(\cos x)}$$
Factor and simplify.

$$= \frac{2}{\cos x}$$

$$= 2\sec x$$
Apply a reciprocal identity: $\sec x = \dfrac{1}{\cos x}$.

We worked with the left side and arrived at the right side. Thus, the identity is verified.

**Study Tip**

Some students have difficulty verifying identities due to problems working with fractions. If this applies to you, review the material on rational expressions in Chapter P, Section P.6.

**Check Point 4** Verify the identity: $\dfrac{\sin x}{1 + \cos x} + \dfrac{1 + \cos x}{\sin x} = 2 \csc x$.

Some identities are verified using a technique that may remind you of rationalizing the denominator.

## EXAMPLE 5 Multiplying the Numerator and Denominator by the Same Factor to Verify an Identity

Verify the identity: $\dfrac{\sin x}{1 + \cos x} = \dfrac{1 - \cos x}{\sin x}$.

**Solution** The suggestions given in the previous examples do not apply here. Everything is already expressed in terms of sines and cosines. Furthermore, there are no fractions to combine and neither side looks more complicated than the other. Let's solve the puzzle by working with the left side and making it look like the expression on the right. The expression on the right contains $1 - \cos x$ in the numerator. This suggests multiplying the numerator and denominator of the left side by $1 - \cos x$. By doing this, we obtain $1 - \cos x$ in the numerator, the same as the numerator on the right.

$$\frac{\sin x}{1 + \cos x} = \frac{\sin x}{1 + \cos x} \cdot \frac{1 - \cos x}{1 - \cos x}$$
Multiply numerator and denominator by $1 - \cos x$.

$$= \frac{\sin x(1 - \cos x)}{1 - \cos^2 x}$$
Multiply. Use $(A + B)(A - B) = A^2 - B^2$, with $A = 1$ and $B = \cos x$, to multiply denominators.

$$= \frac{\sin x(1 - \cos x)}{\sin^2 x}$$
Use a variation of $\sin^2 x + \cos^2 x = 1$. Solving for $\sin^2 x$, we obtain $\sin^2 x = 1 - \cos^2 x$.

$$= \frac{1 - \cos x}{\sin x}$$
Simplify: $\dfrac{\sin x}{\sin^2 x} = \dfrac{\cancel{\sin x}}{\cancel{\sin x} \cdot \sin x} = \dfrac{1}{\sin x}$.

We worked with the left side and arrived at the right side. Thus, the identity is verified.

### Discovery

Verify the identity in Example 5 by making the right side look like the left side. Start with the expression on the right. Multiply the numerator and denominator by $1 + \cos x$.

**Check Point 5** Verify the identity: $\dfrac{\cos x}{1 + \sin x} = \dfrac{1 - \sin x}{\cos x}$.

## EXAMPLE 6 Changing to Sines and Cosines to Verify an Identity

Verify the identity: $\dfrac{\tan x - \sin(-x)}{1 + \cos x} = \tan x$.

**Solution** We begin with the left side. Our goal is to obtain $\tan x$, the expression on the right.

$$\frac{\tan x - \sin(-x)}{1 + \cos x} = \frac{\tan x - (-\sin x)}{1 + \cos x}$$ The sine function is odd: $\sin(-x) = -\sin x$.

$$= \frac{\tan x + \sin x}{1 + \cos x}$$ Simplify.

$$= \frac{\frac{\sin x}{\cos x} + \sin x}{1 + \cos x}$$ Apply a quotient identity: $\tan x = \frac{\sin x}{\cos x}$.

$$= \frac{\frac{\sin x}{\cos x} + \frac{\sin x \cos x}{\cos x}}{1 + \cos x}$$ Express the terms in the numerator with the least common denominator, $\cos x$.

$$= \frac{\frac{\sin x + \sin x \cos x}{\cos x}}{1 + \cos x}$$ Add in the numerator.

$$= \frac{\sin x + \sin x \cos x}{\cos x} \div \frac{1 + \cos x}{1}$$ Rewrite the main fraction bar as ÷.

$$= \frac{\sin x + \sin x \cos x}{\cos x} \cdot \frac{1}{1 + \cos x}$$ Invert the divisor and multiply.

$$= \frac{\sin x \overset{1}{\cancel{(1 + \cos x)}}}{\cos x} \cdot \frac{1}{\underset{1}{\cancel{1 + \cos x}}}$$ Factor and simplify.

$$= \frac{\sin x}{\cos x}$$ Multiply the remaining factors in the numerator and the denominator.

$$= \tan x$$ Apply a quotient identity.

The left side simplifies to $\tan x$, the right side. Thus, the identity is verified.

## Discovery

Try simplifying

$$\frac{\frac{\sin x}{\cos x} + \sin x}{1 + \cos x}$$

by multiplying the two terms in the numerator and the two terms in the denominator by $\cos x$. This method for simplifying the complex fraction involves multiplying the numerator and denominator by the least common denominator of all fractions in the expression. Do you prefer this simplification procedure over the method used on the right?

**Check Point 6** Verify the identity: $\frac{\sec x + \csc(-x)}{\sec x \csc x} = \sin x - \cos x$.

Is every identity verified by working with only one side? No. You can sometimes work with each side separately and show that both sides are equal to the same trigonometric expression. This is illustrated in Example 7.

### EXAMPLE 7 Working With Both Sides Separately to Verify an Identity

Verify the identity: $\frac{1}{1 + \cos\theta} + \frac{1}{1 - \cos\theta} = 2 + 2\cot^2\theta$.

**Solution** We begin by working with the left side.

$$\frac{1}{1+\cos\theta}+\frac{1}{1-\cos\theta}$$

The least common denominator is $(1+\cos\theta)(1-\cos\theta)$.

$$=\frac{1(1-\cos\theta)}{(1+\cos\theta)(1-\cos\theta)}+\frac{1(1+\cos\theta)}{(1+\cos\theta)(1-\cos\theta)}$$

Rewrite each fraction with the least common denominator.

$$=\frac{1-\cos\theta+1+\cos\theta}{(1+\cos\theta)(1-\cos\theta)}$$

Add numerators putting this sum over the least common denominator.

$$=\frac{2}{(1+\cos\theta)(1-\cos\theta)}$$

Simplify the numerator: $-\cos\theta+\cos\theta=0$ and $1+1=2$.

$$=\frac{2}{1-\cos^2\theta}$$

Multiply the factors in the denominator.

Now we work with the right side. Our goal is to transform this side into the simplified form attained for the left side, $\frac{2}{1-\cos^2\theta}$.

$$2+2\cot^2\theta=2+2\left(\frac{\cos^2\theta}{\sin^2\theta}\right)$$

Use a quotient identity: $\cot\theta=\frac{\cos\theta}{\sin\theta}$.

$$=\frac{2\sin^2\theta}{\sin^2\theta}+\frac{2\cos^2\theta}{\sin^2\theta}$$

Rewrite each fraction with the least common denominator, $\sin^2\theta$.

$$=\frac{2\sin^2\theta+2\cos^2\theta}{\sin^2\theta}$$

Add numerators. Put this sum over the least common denominator.

$$=\frac{2(\sin^2\theta+\cos^2\theta)}{\sin^2\theta}$$

Factor out the greatest common factor, 2.

$$=\frac{2}{\sin^2\theta}$$

Apply a Pythagorean identity: $\sin^2\theta+\cos^2\theta=1$.

$$=\frac{2}{1-\cos^2\theta}$$

Use a variation of $\sin^2\theta+\cos^2\theta=1$ and solve for $\sin^2\theta$: $\sin^2\theta=1-\cos^2\theta$.

The identity is verified because both sides are equal to $\frac{2}{1-\cos^2\theta}$.

**Check Point 7** Verify the identity: $\frac{1}{1+\sin\theta}+\frac{1}{1-\sin\theta}=2+2\tan^2\theta$.

## Guidelines for Verifying Trigonometric Identities

There is often more than one correct way to solve a puzzle, although one method may be shorter and more efficient than another. The same is true for verifying an identity. For example, how would you verify

$$\frac{\csc^2 x - 1}{\csc^2 x} = \cos^2 x?$$

One approach is to use a Pythagorean identity, $1 + \cot^2 x = \csc^2 x$, on the left side. Then change the resulting expression to sines and cosines.

$$\frac{\csc^2 x - 1}{\csc^2 x} = \frac{(1 + \cot^2 x) - 1}{\csc^2 x} = \frac{\cot^2 x}{\csc^2 x} = \frac{\frac{\cos^2 x}{\sin^2 x}}{\frac{1}{\sin^2 x}} = \frac{\cos^2 x}{\cancel{\sin^2 x}} \cdot \frac{\cancel{\sin^2 x}}{1} = \cos^2 x$$

Apply a Pythagorean identity: $1 + \cot^2 x = \csc^2 x$.

Use $\cot x = \frac{\cos x}{\sin x}$ and $\csc x = \frac{1}{\sin x}$ to change to sines and cosines.

Invert the divisor and multiply.

A more efficient strategy for verifying this identity may not be apparent at first glance. Work with the left side and divide each term in the numerator by the denominator, $\csc^2 x$.

$$\frac{\csc^2 x - 1}{\csc^2 x} = \frac{\csc^2 x}{\csc^2 x} - \frac{1}{\csc^2 x} = 1 - \sin^2 x = \cos^2 x$$

Apply a reciprocal identity: $\sin x = \frac{1}{\csc x}$.

Use $\sin^2 x + \cos^2 x = 1$ and solve for $\cos^2 x$.

With this strategy, we do obtain $\cos^2 x$, the expression on the right side, and it takes fewer steps than the first approach.

An even longer strategy, but one that works, is to replace each of the two occurrences of $\csc^2 x$ on the left side by $\frac{1}{\sin^2 x}$. This may be the approach that you first consider, particularly if you become accustomed to rewriting the more complicated side in terms of sines and cosines. The selection of an appropriate fundamental identity to solve the puzzle most efficiently is learned through lots of practice.

The more identities you prove, the more confident and efficient you will become. Although practice is the only way to learn how to verify identities, there are some guidelines developed throughout the section that should help you get started.

**Guidelines for Verifying Trigonometric Identities**

1. Work with each side of the equation independently of the other side. Start with the more complicated side and transform it in a step-by-step fashion until it looks exactly like the other side.
2. Analyze the identity and look for opportunities to apply the fundamental identities. Rewriting the more complicated side of the equation in terms of sines and cosines is often helpful.
3. If sums or differences of fractions appear on one side, use the least common denominator and combine the fractions.
4. Don't be afraid to stop and start over again if you are not getting anywhere. Creative puzzle solvers know that strategies leading to dead ends often provide good problem-solving ideas.

## EXERCISE SET 6.1

### Practice Exercises

*In Exercises 1–60, verify each identity.*

**1.** $\sin x \sec x = \tan x$

**2.** $\cos x \csc x = \cot x$

**3.** $\tan(-x)\cos x = -\sin x$

**4.** $\cot(-x)\sin x = -\cos x$

**5.** $\tan x \csc x \cos x = 1$

**6.** $\cot x \sec x \sin x = 1$

**7.** $\sec x - \sec x \sin^2 x = \cos x$

**8.** $\csc x - \csc x \cos^2 x = \sin x$

**9.** $\cos^2 x - \sin^2 x = 1 - 2\sin^2 x$

**10.** $\cos^2 x - \sin^2 x = 2\cos^2 x - 1$

**11.** $\csc\theta - \sin\theta = \cot\theta\cos\theta$

**12.** $\tan\theta + \cot\theta = \sec\theta\csc\theta$

**13.** $\dfrac{\tan\theta\cot\theta}{\csc\theta} = \sin\theta$

**14.** $\dfrac{\cos\theta\sec\theta}{\cot\theta} = \tan\theta$

**15.** $\sin^2\theta(1 + \cot^2\theta) = 1$

**16.** $\cos^2\theta(1 + \tan^2\theta) = 1$

**17.** $\sin t \tan t = \dfrac{1 - \cos^2 t}{\cos t}$

**18.** $\cos t \cot t = \dfrac{1 - \sin^2 t}{\sin t}$

**19.** $\dfrac{\csc^2 t}{\cot t} = \csc t \sec t$

**20.** $\dfrac{\sec^2 t}{\tan t} = \sec t \csc t$

**21.** $\dfrac{\tan^2 t}{\sec t} = \sec t - \cos t$

**22.** $\dfrac{\cot^2 t}{\csc t} = \csc t - \sin t$

**23.** $\dfrac{\sin t}{\csc t} + \dfrac{\cos t}{\sec t} = 1$

**24.** $\dfrac{\sin t}{\tan t} + \dfrac{\cos t}{\cot t} = \sin t + \cos t$

**25.** $\tan t + \dfrac{\cos t}{1 + \sin t} = \sec t$

**26.** $\cot t + \dfrac{\sin t}{1 + \cos t} = \csc t$

**27.** $1 - \dfrac{\sin^2 x}{1 + \cos x} = \cos x$

**28.** $1 - \dfrac{\cos^2 x}{1 + \sin x} = \sin x$

**29.** $\dfrac{\cos x}{1 - \sin x} + \dfrac{1 - \sin x}{\cos x} = 2\sec x$

**30.** $\dfrac{\sin x}{\cos x + 1} + \dfrac{\cos x - 1}{\sin x} = 0$

**31.** $\sec^2 x \csc^2 x = \sec^2 x + \csc^2 x$

**32.** $\csc^2 x \sec x = \sec x + \csc x \cot x$

**33.** $\dfrac{\sec x - \csc x}{\sec x + \csc x} = \dfrac{\tan x - 1}{\tan x + 1}$

**34.** $\dfrac{\csc x - \sec x}{\csc x + \sec x} = \dfrac{\cot x - 1}{\cot x + 1}$

**35.** $\dfrac{\sin^2 x - \cos^2 x}{\sin x + \cos x} = \sin x - \cos x$

**36.** $\dfrac{\tan^2 x - \cot^2 x}{\tan x + \cot x} = \tan x - \cot x$

**37.** $\tan^2 2x + \sin^2 2x + \cos^2 2x = \sec^2 2x$

**38.** $\cot^2 2x + \cos^2 2x + \sin^2 2x = \csc^2 2x$

**39.** $\dfrac{\tan 2\theta + \cot 2\theta}{\csc 2\theta} = \sec 2\theta$

**40.** $\dfrac{\tan 2\theta + \cot 2\theta}{\sec 2\theta} = \csc 2\theta$

**41.** $\dfrac{\tan x + \tan y}{1 - \tan x \tan y} = \dfrac{\sin x \cos y + \cos x \sin y}{\cos x \cos y - \sin x \sin y}$

**42.** $\dfrac{\cot x + \cot y}{1 - \cot x \cot y} = \dfrac{\cos x \sin y + \sin x \cos y}{\sin x \sin y - \cos x \cos y}$

**43.** $(\sec x - \tan x)^2 = \dfrac{1 - \sin x}{1 + \sin x}$

**44.** $(\csc x - \cot x)^2 = \dfrac{1 - \cos x}{1 + \cos x}$

**45.** $\dfrac{\sec t + 1}{\tan t} = \dfrac{\tan t}{\sec t - 1}$

**46.** $\dfrac{\csc t - 1}{\cot t} = \dfrac{\cot t}{\csc t + 1}$

**47.** $\dfrac{1 + \cos t}{1 - \cos t} = (\csc t + \cot t)^2$

**48.** $\dfrac{1 - \sin t}{1 + \sin t} = (\sec t - \tan t)^2$

**49.** $\cos^4 t - \sin^4 t = 1 - 2\sin^2 t$

**50.** $\sin^4 t - \cos^4 t = 1 - 2\cos^2 t$

**51.** $\dfrac{\sin\theta - \cos\theta}{\sin\theta} + \dfrac{\cos\theta - \sin\theta}{\cos\theta} = 2 - \sec\theta\csc\theta$

**52.** $\dfrac{\sin\theta}{1 - \cot\theta} - \dfrac{\cos\theta}{\tan\theta - 1} = \sin\theta + \cos\theta$

**53.** $(\tan^2\theta + 1)(\cos^2\theta + 1) = \tan^2\theta + 2$

**54.** $(\cot^2\theta + 1)(\sin^2\theta + 1) = \cot^2\theta + 2$

**55.** $(\cos\theta - \sin\theta)^2 + (\cos\theta + \sin\theta)^2 = 2$

**56.** $(3\cos\theta - 4\sin\theta)^2 + (4\cos\theta + 3\sin\theta)^2 = 25$

**57.** $\dfrac{\cos^2 x - \sin^2 x}{1 - \tan^2 x} = \cos^2 x$

**58.** $\dfrac{\sin x + \cos x}{\sin x} - \dfrac{\cos x - \sin x}{\cos x} = \sec x \csc x$

**59.** $(\sec x - \tan x)^2 = \dfrac{1 - \sin x}{1 + \sin x}$

**60.** $(\cot x - \csc x)^2 = \dfrac{1 - \cos x}{1 + \cos x}$

## Writing in Mathematics

**61.** Explain how to verify an identity.

**62.** Describe two strategies that can be used to verify identities.

**63.** Describe how you feel when you successfully verify a difficult identity. What other activities do you engage in that evoke the same feelings?

**64.** A 10-point question on a quiz asks students to verify the identity

$$\frac{\sin^2 x - \cos^2 x}{\sin x + \cos x} = \sin x - \cos x.$$

One student begins with the left side and obtains the right side as follows:

$$\frac{\sin^2 x - \cos^2 x}{\sin x + \cos x} = \frac{\sin^2 x}{\sin x} - \frac{\cos^2 x}{\cos x} = \sin x - \cos x.$$

How many points (out of 10) would you give this student? Explain your answer.

## Technology Exercises

*In Exercises 65–73, graph each side of the equation in the same viewing rectangle. If the graphs appear to coincide, verify that the equation is an identity. If the graphs do not appear to coincide, this indicates the equation is not an identity. In these exercises, find a value of x for which both sides are defined but not equal.*

**65.** $\tan x = \sec x(\sin x - \cos x) + 1$

**66.** $\sin x = -\cos x \tan(-x)$

**67.** $\sin\left(x + \dfrac{\pi}{4}\right) = \sin x + \sin\dfrac{\pi}{4}$

**68.** $\cos\left(x + \dfrac{\pi}{4}\right) = \cos x + \cos\dfrac{\pi}{4}$

**69.** $\cos(x + \pi) = \cos x$

**70.** $\sin(x + \pi) = \sin x$

**71.** $\dfrac{\sin x}{1 - \cos^2 x} = \csc x$

**72.** $\sin x - \sin x \cos^2 x = \sin^3 x$

**73.** $\sqrt{\sin^2 x + \cos^2 x} = \sin x + \cos x$

## Critical Thinking Exercises

*In Exercises 74–76, verify each identity.*

**74.** $\dfrac{\sin^3 x - \cos^3 x}{\sin x - \cos x} = 1 + \sin x \cos x$

**75.** $\dfrac{\sin x - \cos x + 1}{\sin x + \cos x - 1} = \dfrac{\sin x + 1}{\cos x}$

**76.** $\ln|\sec x| = -\ln|\cos x|$

**77.** Use one of the fundamental identities in the box on page 533 to create an original identity.

## Group Exercise

**78.** Group members are to write a helpful list of items for a pamphlet called "The Underground Guide to Verifying Identities." The pamphlet will be used primarily by students who sit, stare, and freak out every time they are asked to verify an identity. List easy ways to remember the fundamental identities. What helpful guidelines can you offer from the perspective of a student that you probably won't find in math books? If you have your own strategies that work particularly well, include them in the pamphlet.

# SECTION 6.2 *Sum and Difference Formulas*

## Objectives

1. Use the formula for the cosine of the difference of two angles.
2. Use sum and difference formulas for cosines and sines.
3. Use sum and difference formulas for tangents.

Listen to the same note played on a piano and a violin. The notes have a different quality or "tone." Tone depends on the way an instrument vibrates. However, the less than 1% of the population with amusia, or true tone deafness, cannot tell the two sounds apart. Even simple, familiar tunes such as *Happy Birthday* and *Jingle Bells* are mystifying to amusics.

When a note is played, it vibrates at a specific frequency and has a particular amplitude. Amusics cannot tell the difference between sounds from a tuning fork modeled by $p = 3\sin 2t$ and $p = 2\sin(2t + \pi)$. However, they can recognize the difference between the two equations. Notice that the second equation contains the sine of the sum of two angles. In this section, we will be developing identities involving the sums or differences of two angles. These formulas are called the **sum and difference formulas**. We begin with $\cos(\alpha - \beta)$, the cosine of the difference of two angles.

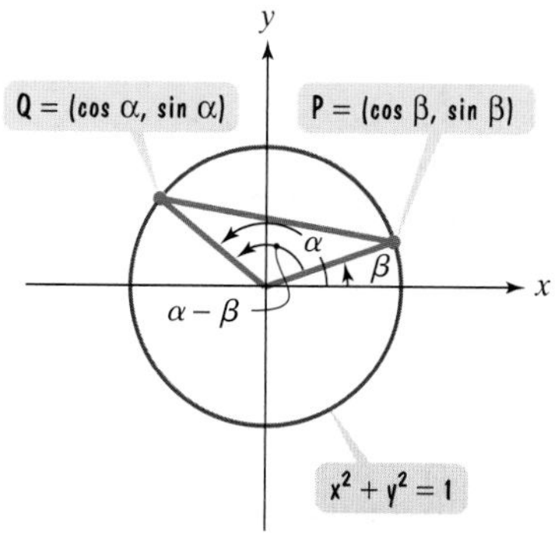


(a)

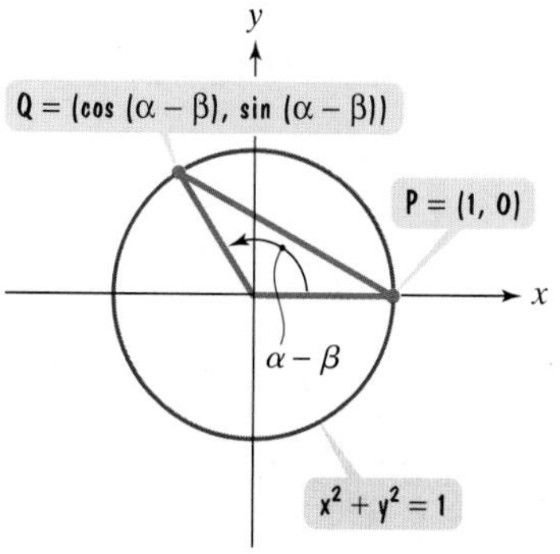


(b)

**Figure 6.1** Using the unit circle and $QP$ to develop a formula for $\cos(\alpha - \beta)$

## The Cosine of the Difference of Two Angles

### The Cosine of the Difference of Two Angles

$$\cos(\alpha - \beta) = \cos\alpha\cos\beta + \sin\alpha\sin\beta$$

The cosine of the difference of two angles equals the cosine of the first angle times the cosine of the second angle plus the sine of the first angle times the sine of the second angle.

We use Figure 6.1 to prove the identity in the box. The graph in Figure 6.1(a) shows a unit circle, $x^2 + y^2 = 1$. The figure uses the definitions of the cosine and sine functions as the $x$- and $y$-coordinates of points along the unit circle. For example, point $P$ corresponds to angle $\beta$. By definition, the $x$-coordinate of $P$ is $\cos\beta$ and the $y$-coordinate is $\sin\beta$. Similarly, point $Q$ corresponds to angle $\alpha$. By definition, the $x$-coordinate of $Q$ is $\cos\alpha$ and the $y$-coordinate is $\sin\alpha$.

Note that if we draw a line segment between points $P$ and $Q$, a triangle is formed. Angle $\alpha - \beta$ is one of the angles of this triangle. What happens if we rotate this triangle so that point $P$ falls on the $x$-axis at $(1, 0)$? The result is shown in Figure 6.1(b). This rotation changes the coordinates of points $P$ and $Q$. However, it has no effect on the length of line segment $PQ$.

We can use the distance formula, $d = \sqrt{(x_2 - x_1)^2 + (y_2 - y_1)^2}$, to find an expression for $PQ$ in Figure 6.1(a) and in Figure 6.1(b). By equating the two expressions for $PQ$, we will obtain the identity for the cosine of the difference of two angles, $\alpha - \beta$. We first apply the distance formula in Figure 6.1(a).

$$PQ = \sqrt{(\cos\alpha - \cos\beta)^2 + (\sin\alpha - \sin\beta)^2}$$

Apply the distance formula, $d = \sqrt{(x_2 - x_1)^2 + (y_2 - y_1)^2}$, to find the distance between $(\cos\beta, \sin\beta)$ and $(\cos\alpha, \sin\alpha)$.

$$= \sqrt{\cos^2\alpha - 2\cos\alpha\cos\beta + \cos^2\beta + \sin^2\alpha - 2\sin\alpha\sin\beta + \sin^2\beta}$$

Square each expression using $(A - B)^2 = A^2 - 2AB + B^2$.

$$= \sqrt{(\sin^2\alpha + \cos^2\alpha) + (\sin^2\beta + \cos^2\beta) - 2\cos\alpha\cos\beta - 2\sin\alpha\sin\beta}$$

Regroup terms to apply a Pythagorean identity.

$$= \sqrt{1 + 1 - 2\cos\alpha\cos\beta - 2\sin\alpha\sin\beta}$$

Because $\sin^2 x + \cos^2 x = 1$, each expression in parentheses equals 1.

$$= \sqrt{2 - 2\cos\alpha\cos\beta - 2\sin\alpha\sin\beta}$$

Simplify.

Next, we apply the distance formula in Figure 6.1(b) to obtain a second expression for $PQ$. We let $(x_1, y_1) = (1, 0)$ and $(x_2, y_2) = (\cos(\alpha - \beta), \sin(\alpha - \beta))$.

$$PQ = \sqrt{[\cos(\alpha - \beta) - 1]^2 + [\sin(\alpha - \beta) - 0]^2}$$

Apply the distance formula to find the distance between $(1, 0)$ and $(\cos(\alpha - \beta), \sin(\alpha - \beta))$.

$$= \sqrt{\cos^2(\alpha - \beta) - 2\cos(\alpha - \beta) + 1 + \sin^2(\alpha - \beta)}$$

Square each expression.

Using a Pythagorean identity, $\sin^2(\alpha - \beta) + \cos^2(\alpha - \beta) = 1$

$$= \sqrt{1 - 2\cos(\alpha - \beta) + 1}$$

Use a Pythagorean identity.

$$= \sqrt{2 - 2\cos(\alpha - \beta)}$$

Simplify.

Now we equate the two expressions for $PQ$.

$$\sqrt{2 - 2\cos(\alpha - \beta)} = \sqrt{2 - 2\cos\alpha\cos\beta - 2\sin\alpha\sin\beta}$$

The rotation does not change the length of $PQ$.

$$2 - 2\cos(\alpha - \beta) = 2 - 2\cos\alpha\cos\beta - 2\sin\alpha\sin\beta$$

Square both sides to eliminate radicals.

$$-2\cos(\alpha - \beta) = -2\cos\alpha\cos\beta - 2\sin\alpha\sin\beta$$

Subtract 2 from both sides of the equation.

$$\cos(\alpha - \beta) = \cos\alpha\cos\beta + \sin\alpha\sin\beta$$

Divide both sides of the equation by $-2$.

**1** Use the formula for the cosine of the difference of two angles.

Now that we see where the identity for the cosine of the difference of two angles comes from, let's look at some applications of this result.

## Sound Quality and Amusia

People with true tone deafness cannot hear the difference among tones produced by a tuning fork, a flute, an oboe, and a violin. They cannot dance or tell the difference between harmony and dissonance. People with amusia appear to have been born without the wiring necessary to process music. Intriguingly, they show no overt signs of brain damage and their brain scans appear normal. Thus, they can visually recognize the difference among sound waves that produce varying sound qualities.

**Varing Sound Qualities**

- Tuning Fork: Sound waves are rounded and regular, giving a pure and gentle tone.

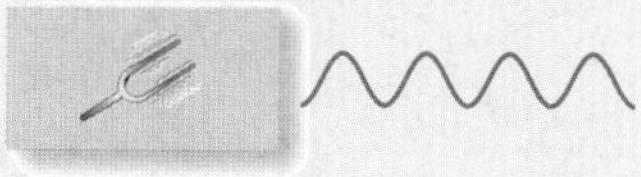

- Flute: Sound waves are smooth and give a fluid tone.

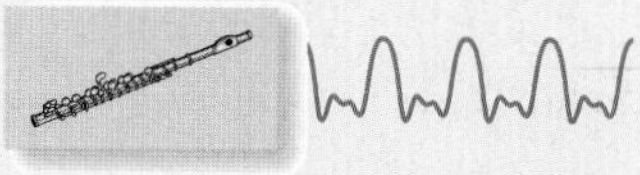

- Oboe: Rapid wave changes give a richer tone.

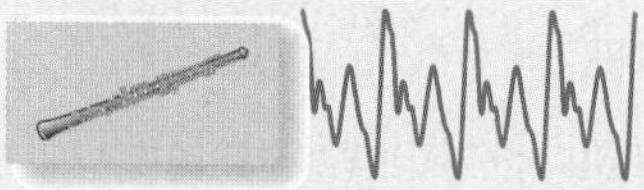

- Violin: Jagged waves give a brighter harsher tone.

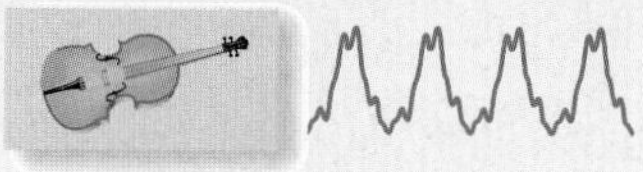

### EXAMPLE 1 Using the Difference Formula for Cosines to Find Exact Values

Find the exact value of $\cos 15°$.

**Solution** We know exact values for trigonometric functions of 60° and 45°. Thus, we write 15° as $60° - 45°$ and use the difference formula for cosines.

$$\cos 15° = \cos(60° - 45°)$$

$$= \cos 60° \cos 45° + \sin 60° \sin 45° \qquad \cos(\alpha - \beta) = \cos\alpha\cos\beta + \sin\alpha\sin\beta$$

$$= \frac{1}{2}\cdot\frac{\sqrt{2}}{2} + \frac{\sqrt{3}}{2}\cdot\frac{\sqrt{2}}{2} \qquad \text{Substitute exact valves from memory or use special right triangles.}$$

$$= \frac{\sqrt{2}}{4} + \frac{\sqrt{6}}{4} \qquad \text{Multiply.}$$

$$= \frac{\sqrt{2} + \sqrt{6}}{4} \qquad \text{Add.}$$

**Check Point 1** We know that $\cos 30° = \frac{\sqrt{3}}{2}$. Obtain this exact value using $\cos 30° = \cos(90° - 60°)$ and the difference formula for cosines.

### EXAMPLE 2 Using the Difference Formula for Cosines to Find Exact Values

Find the exact value of $\cos 80° \cos 20° + \sin 80° \sin 20°$.

**Solution** The given expression is the right side of the formula for $\cos(\alpha - \beta)$ with $\alpha = 80°$ and $\beta = 20°$.

$\cos(\alpha - \beta) = \cos\alpha\cos\beta + \sin\alpha\sin\beta$

$$\cos 80° \cos 20° + \sin 80° \sin 20° = \cos(80° - 20°) = \cos 60° = \frac{1}{2}$$

**Check Point 2** Find the exact value of

$$\cos 70° \cos 40° + \sin 70° \sin 40°.$$

### EXAMPLE 3 Verifying an Identity

Verify the identity: $\dfrac{\cos(\alpha - \beta)}{\sin\alpha\cos\beta} = \cot\alpha + \tan\beta$.

**Solution** We work with the left side.

$$\frac{\cos(\alpha - \beta)}{\sin\alpha\cos\beta} = \frac{\cos\alpha\cos\beta + \sin\alpha\sin\beta}{\sin\alpha\cos\beta}$$ Use the formula for $\cos(\alpha - \beta)$.

$$= \frac{\cos\alpha}{\sin\alpha}\frac{\cos\beta}{\cos\beta} + \frac{\sin\alpha}{\sin\alpha}\frac{\sin\beta}{\cos\beta}$$ Divide each term in the numerator by $\sin\alpha\cos\beta$.

$$= \cot\alpha \cdot 1 + 1 \cdot \tan\beta$$ Use quotient identities.

$$= \cot\alpha + \tan\beta$$ Simplify.

We worked with the left side and arrived at the right side. Thus, the identity is verified.

**Technology**

The graphs of

$$y = \cos\left(\frac{\pi}{2} - x\right)$$

and

$$y = \sin x$$

are shown in the same viewing rectangle. The graphs are the same. The voice balloon and the displayed math on the right show the equivalence algebraically.

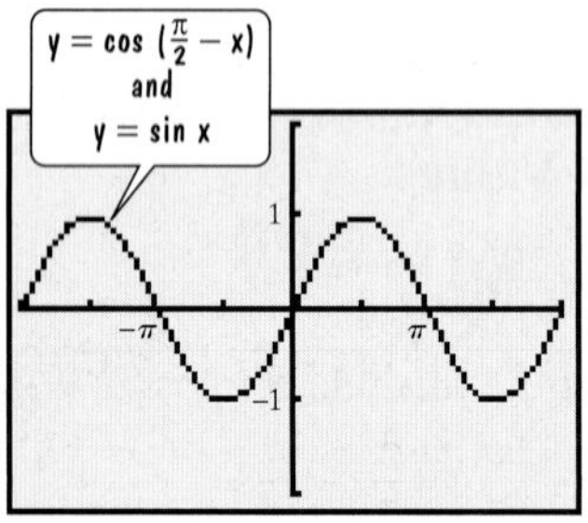


**Check Point 3** Verify the identity: $\dfrac{\cos(\alpha - \beta)}{\cos\alpha\cos\beta} = 1 + \tan\alpha\tan\beta$.

The difference formula for cosines is used to establish other identities. For example, in our work with right triangles we noted that cofunctions of complements are equal. Thus, because $90° - \theta$ and $\theta$ are complements,

$$\cos(90° - \theta) = \sin\theta.$$

We can use the formula for $\cos(\alpha - \beta)$ to prove this cofunction identity.

Apply $\cos(\alpha - \beta)$ with $\alpha = 90°$ and $\theta = \beta$.
$\cos(\alpha - \beta) = \cos\alpha\cos\beta + \sin\alpha\sin\beta$

$$\cos(90° - \theta) = \cos 90°\cos\theta + \sin 90°\sin\theta$$
$$= 0 \cdot \cos\theta + 1 \cdot \sin\theta$$
$$= \sin\theta$$

**2** Use sum and difference formulas for cosines and sines.

## Sum and Difference Formulas for Cosines and Sines

Our formula for $\cos(\alpha - \beta)$ can be used to verify an identity for a sum involving cosines, as well as identities for a sum and a difference for sines.

**Sum and Difference Formulas for Cosines and Sines**

1. $\cos(\alpha + \beta) = \cos\alpha\cos\beta - \sin\alpha\sin\beta$
2. $\cos(\alpha - \beta) = \cos\alpha\cos\beta + \sin\alpha\sin\beta$
3. $\sin(\alpha + \beta) = \sin\alpha\cos\beta + \cos\alpha\sin\beta$
4. $\sin(\alpha - \beta) = \sin\alpha\cos\beta - \cos\alpha\sin\beta$

Up to now, we have concentrated on the second formula in the box. The first identity gives a formula for the cosine of the sum of two angles. It is proved as follows.

| | |
|---|---|
| $\cos(\alpha + \beta) = \cos[\alpha - (-\beta)]$ | Express addition as subtraction of an inverse. |
| $= \cos\alpha\cos(-\beta) + \sin\alpha\sin(-\beta)$ | Use the second formula in the box. |
| $= \cos\alpha\cos\beta + \sin\alpha(-\sin\beta)$ | Cosine is even: $\cos(-\beta) = \cos\beta$. Sine is odd: $\sin(-\beta) = -\sin\beta$. |
| $= \cos\alpha\cos\beta - \sin\alpha\sin\beta$ | Simplify. |

Thus, the cosine of the sum of two angles equals the cosine of the first angle times the cosine of the second angle minus the sine of the first angle times the sine of the second angle.

The third identity in the box gives a formula for $\sin(\alpha + \beta)$, the sine of the sum of two angles. It is proved as follows.

| | |
|---|---|
| $\sin(\alpha + \beta) = \cos\left[\frac{\pi}{2} - (\alpha + \beta)\right]$ | Use a cofunction identity: $\sin\theta = \cos\left(\frac{\pi}{2} - \theta\right)$. |
| $= \cos\left[\left(\frac{\pi}{2} - \alpha\right) - \beta\right]$ | Regroup. |
| $= \cos\left(\frac{\pi}{2} - \alpha\right)\cos\beta + \sin\left(\frac{\pi}{2} - \alpha\right)\sin\beta$ | Use the formula for the cosine of a difference. |
| $= \sin\alpha\cos\beta + \cos\alpha\sin\beta$ | Use cofunction identities. |

Thus, the sine of the sum of two angles equals the sine of the first angle times the cosine of the second angle plus the cosine of the first angle times the sine of the second angle.

The final identity in the box gives a formula for $\sin(\alpha - \beta)$, the sine of the difference of two angles. It is proved by writing $\sin(\alpha - \beta)$ as $\sin[\alpha + (-\beta)]$ and then using the formula for the sine of a sum.

## EXAMPLE 4 Using the Sine of a Sum to Find an Exact Value

Find the exact value of $\sin\frac{7\pi}{12}$ by using the fact that $\frac{7\pi}{12} = \frac{\pi}{3} + \frac{\pi}{4}$.

**Solution** We apply the formula for the sine of a sum.

| | |
|---|---|
| $\sin\frac{7\pi}{12} = \sin\left(\frac{\pi}{3} + \frac{\pi}{4}\right)$ | |
| $= \sin\frac{\pi}{3}\cos\frac{\pi}{4} + \cos\frac{\pi}{3}\sin\frac{\pi}{4}$ | $(\sin\alpha + \beta) = \sin\alpha\cos\beta + \cos\alpha\sin\beta$ |
| $= \frac{\sqrt{3}}{2}\cdot\frac{\sqrt{2}}{2} + \frac{1}{2}\cdot\frac{\sqrt{2}}{2}$ | Substitute exact values. |
| $= \frac{\sqrt{6} + \sqrt{2}}{4}$ | |

**Check Point 4** Find the exact value of $\sin \frac{5\pi}{12}$ by using the fact that $\frac{5\pi}{12} = \frac{\pi}{6} + \frac{\pi}{4}$.

## EXAMPLE 5 Finding Exact Values

Suppose that $\sin\alpha = \frac{12}{13}$ for a quadrant II angle $\alpha$ and $\sin\beta = \frac{3}{5}$ for a quadrant I angle $\beta$. Find the exact value of:

**a.** $\cos\alpha$ **b.** $\cos\beta$ **c.** $\cos(\alpha + \beta)$ **d.** $\sin(\alpha + \beta)$.

### Solution

**a.** We find $\cos\alpha$ using a sketch that illustrates

$$\sin\alpha = \frac{12}{13} = \frac{y}{r}.$$

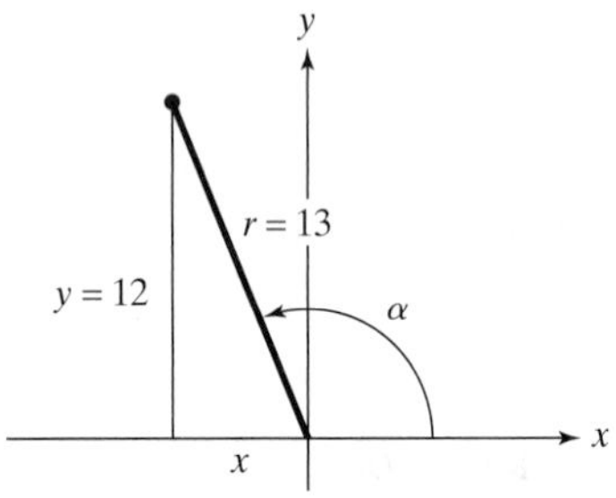


**Figure 6.2** $\sin\alpha = \frac{12}{13}$: $\alpha$ lies in quadrant II.

Figure 6.2 shows a quadrant II angle $\alpha$ and $\sin\alpha = \frac{12}{13}$. We find $x$ using $x^2 + y^2 = r^2$. Because $\alpha$ lies in quadrant II, $x$ is negative.

$$x^2 + 12^2 = 13^2 \quad x^2 + y^2 = r^2$$

$$x^2 + 144 = 169 \quad \text{Square 12 and 13, respectively.}$$

$$x^2 = 25 \quad \text{Subtract 144 from both sides.}$$

$$x = -\sqrt{25} = -5 \quad \text{In quadrant II, } x \text{ is negative.}$$

Thus,

$$\cos\alpha = \frac{x}{r} = \frac{-5}{13} = -\frac{5}{13}.$$

**b.** We find $\cos\beta$ using a sketch that illustrates

$$\sin\beta = \frac{3}{5} = \frac{y}{r}.$$

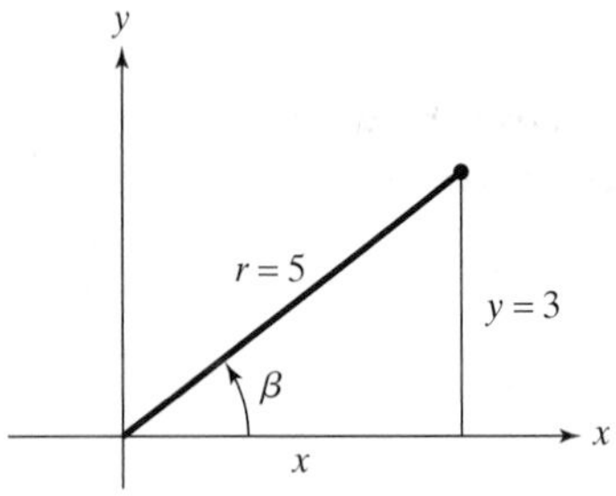


**Figure 6.3** $\sin\beta = \frac{3}{5}$, $\beta$ lies in quadrant I

Figure 6.3 shows a quadrant I angle $\beta$ and $\sin\beta = \frac{3}{5}$. We find $x$ using $x^2 + y^2 = r^2$.

$$x^2 + 3^2 = 5^2$$

$$x^2 = 25 - 9 = 16$$

$$x = \sqrt{16} = 4 \quad \text{In quadrant I, } x \text{ is positive.}$$

Thus,

$$\cos\beta = \frac{x}{r} = \frac{4}{5}.$$

We use the given values and the exact values that we determined to find exact values for $\cos(\alpha + \beta)$ and $\sin(\alpha + \beta)$.

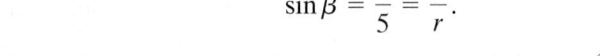

These values are given. These are the values we found.

$$\sin\alpha = \frac{12}{13},\ \sin\beta = \frac{3}{5} \qquad \cos\alpha = -\frac{5}{13},\ \cos\beta = \frac{4}{5}$$

**c.** We use the formula for the cosine of a sum.

$$\cos(\alpha + \beta) = \cos\alpha\cos\beta - \sin\alpha\sin\beta$$

$$= -\frac{5}{13}\left(\frac{4}{5}\right) - \frac{12}{13}\left(\frac{3}{5}\right) = -\frac{56}{65}$$

**d.** We use the formula for the sine of a sum.

$$\sin(\alpha + \beta) = \sin\alpha\cos\beta + \cos\alpha\sin\beta$$

$$= \frac{12}{13}\cdot\frac{4}{5} + \left(-\frac{5}{13}\right)\cdot\frac{3}{5} = \frac{33}{65}$$

**Check Point 5**

Suppose that $\sin\alpha = \frac{4}{5}$ for a quadrant II angle $\alpha$ and $\sin\beta = \frac{1}{2}$ for a quadrant I angle $\beta$. Find the exact value of:

**a.** $\cos\alpha$ **b.** $\cos\beta$

**c.** $\cos(\alpha + \beta)$ **d.** $\sin(\alpha + \beta)$.

## EXAMPLE 6 Verifying Observations On a Graphing Utility

Figure 6.4 shows the graph of $y = \sin\left(x - \frac{3\pi}{2}\right)$ in a $\left[0, 2\pi, \frac{\pi}{2}\right]$ by $[-2, 2, 1]$ viewing rectangle

**a.** Describe the graph using another equation.

**b.** Verify that the two equations are equivalent.

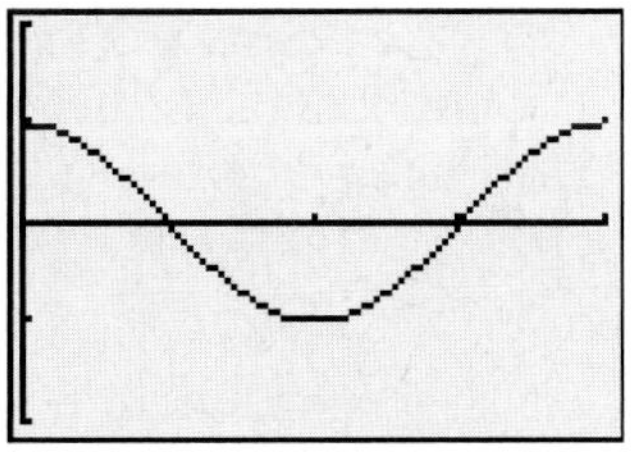

**Figure 6.4** The graph of $y = \sin\left(x - \frac{3\pi}{2}\right)$ in a $\left[0, 2\pi, \frac{\pi}{2}\right]$ by $[-2, 2, 1]$ viewing rectangle

### Solution

**a.** The graph appears to be the cosine curve $y = \cos x$. It cycles through maximum, intercept, minimum, intercept, and back to maximum. Thus, $y = \cos x$ also describes the graph.

**b.** We must show that

$$\sin\left(x - \frac{3\pi}{2}\right) = \cos x.$$

We apply the formula for the sine of a difference on the left side.

$$\sin\left(x - \frac{3\pi}{2}\right) = \sin x\cos\frac{3\pi}{2} - \cos x\sin\frac{3\pi}{2}$$ $\sin(\alpha - \beta) = \sin\alpha\cos\beta - \cos\alpha\sin\beta$

$$= \sin x \cdot 0 - \cos x(-1)$$ $\cos\frac{3\pi}{2} = 0$ and $\sin\frac{3\pi}{2} = -1$

$$= \cos x$$ Simplify.

This verifies our observation that $y = \sin\left(x - \frac{3\pi}{2}\right)$ and $y = \cos x$ describe the same graph.

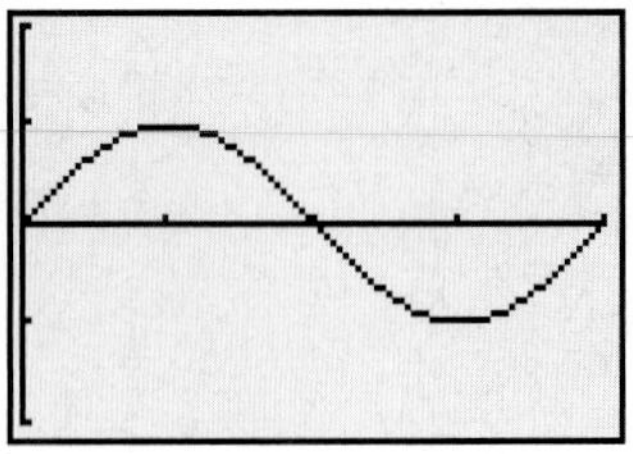

Figure 6.5

**Check Point 6** Figure 6.5 shows the graph of $y = \cos\left(x + \frac{3\pi}{2}\right)$ in a $\left[0, 2\pi, \frac{\pi}{2}\right]$ by $[-2, 2, 1]$ viewing rectangle.

**a.** Describe the graph using another equation.

**b.** Verify that the two equations are equivalent.

**3** Use sum and difference formulas for tangents.

## Sum and Difference Formulas for Tangents

By writing $\tan(\alpha + \beta)$ as the quotient of $\sin(\alpha + \beta)$ and $\cos(\alpha + \beta)$, we can develop a formula for the tangent of a sum. Writing subtraction as addition of an inverse leads to a formula for the tangent of a difference.

**Discovery**

Derive the sum and difference formulas for tangents by working Exercises 55 and 56 in Exercise Set 6.2.

**Sum and Difference Formulas for Tangents**

$$\tan(\alpha + \beta) = \frac{\tan\alpha + \tan\beta}{1 - \tan\alpha\tan\beta}$$

The tangent of the sum of two angles equals the tangent of the first angle plus the tangent of the second angle divided by 1 minus their product.

$$\tan(\alpha - \beta) = \frac{\tan\alpha - \tan\beta}{1 + \tan\alpha\tan\beta}$$

The tangent of the difference of two angles equals the tangent of the first angle minus the tangent of the second angle divided by 1 plus their product.

## EXAMPLE 7 Verifying an Identity

Verify the identity: $\tan\left(x - \frac{\pi}{4}\right) = \frac{\tan x - 1}{\tan x + 1}$.

**Solution** We work with the left side.

$$\tan\left(x - \frac{\pi}{4}\right) = \frac{\tan x - \tan\frac{\pi}{4}}{1 + \tan x \tan\frac{\pi}{4}} \qquad \tan(\alpha - \beta) = \frac{\tan\alpha - \tan\beta}{1 + \tan\alpha\tan\beta}$$

$$= \frac{\tan x - 1}{1 + \tan x \cdot 1} \qquad \tan\frac{\pi}{4} = 1$$

$$= \frac{\tan x - 1}{1 + \tan x}$$

**Check Point 7** Verify the identity: $\tan(x + \pi) = \tan x$.

## EXERCISE SET 6.2

### Practice Exercises

*Use the formula for the cosine of the difference of two angles to solve Exercises 1–12.*

*In Exercises 1–4, find the exact value of each expression.*

1. $\cos(45° - 30°)$
2. $\cos(120° - 45°)$
3. $\cos\left(\frac{3\pi}{4} - \frac{\pi}{6}\right)$
4. $\cos\left(\frac{2\pi}{3} - \frac{\pi}{6}\right)$

*In Exercises 5–8, each expression is the right side of the formula for $\cos(\alpha - \beta)$ with particular values for $\alpha$ and $\beta$.*

**a.** *Identify $\alpha$ and $\beta$ in each expression.*

**b.** *Write the expression as the cosine of an angle.*

**c.** *Find the exact value of the expression.*

5. $\cos 50° \cos 20° + \sin 50° \sin 20°$
6. $\cos 50° \cos 5° + \sin 50° \sin 5°$
7. $\cos\frac{5\pi}{12}\cos\frac{\pi}{12} + \sin\frac{5\pi}{12}\sin\frac{\pi}{12}$
8. $\cos\frac{5\pi}{18}\cos\frac{\pi}{9} + \sin\frac{5\pi}{18}\sin\frac{\pi}{9}$

*In Exercises 9–12, verify each identity.*

9. $\frac{\cos(\alpha - \beta)}{\cos\alpha\sin\beta} = \tan\alpha + \cot\beta$
10. $\frac{\cos(\alpha - \beta)}{\sin\alpha\sin\beta} = \cot\alpha\cot\beta + \cot\beta + 1$
11. $\cos\left(x - \frac{\pi}{4}\right) = \frac{\sqrt{2}}{2}(\cos x + \sin x)$
12. $\cos\left(x - \frac{5\pi}{4}\right) = -\frac{\sqrt{2}}{2}(\cos x + \sin x)$

*Use one or more of the six sum and difference identities to solve Exercises 13–54.*

*In Exercises 13–24, find the exact value of each expression.*

13. $\sin(45° - 30°)$
14. $\sin(60° - 45°)$
15. $\sin 105°$
16. $\sin 75°$
17. $\tan(30° + 45°)$
18. $\tan(60° + 45°)$
19. $\tan(240° - 45°)$
20. $\tan(300° - 45°)$
21. $\cos\left(\frac{3\pi}{4} + \frac{\pi}{6}\right)$
22. $\cos\left(\frac{4\pi}{3} + \frac{\pi}{4}\right)$
23. $\cos\frac{5\pi}{12}$
24. $\cos\frac{7\pi}{12}$

*In Exercises 25–32, write each expression as the sine, cosine, or tangent of an angle. Then find the exact value of the expression.*

25. $\sin 25° \cos 5° + \cos 25° \sin 5°$
26. $\sin 40° \cos 20° + \cos 40° \sin 20°$
27. $\frac{\tan 10° + \tan 35°}{1 - \tan 10° \tan 35°}$
28. $\frac{\tan 50° - \tan 20°}{1 + \tan 50° \tan 20°}$
29. $\sin\frac{5\pi}{12}\cos\frac{\pi}{4} - \cos\frac{5\pi}{12}\sin\frac{\pi}{4}$
30. $\sin\frac{7\pi}{12}\cos\frac{\pi}{12} - \cos\frac{7\pi}{12}\sin\frac{\pi}{12}$
31. $\dfrac{\tan\frac{\pi}{5} - \tan\frac{\pi}{30}}{1 + \tan\frac{\pi}{5}\tan\frac{\pi}{30}}$
32. $\dfrac{\tan\frac{\pi}{5} + \tan\frac{4\pi}{5}}{1 - \tan\frac{\pi}{5}\tan\frac{4\pi}{5}}$

*In Exercises 33–54, verify each identity.*

33. $\sin\left(x + \frac{\pi}{2}\right) = \cos x$
34. $\sin\left(x + \frac{3\pi}{2}\right) = -\cos x$
35. $\cos\left(x - \frac{\pi}{2}\right) = \sin x$
36. $\cos(\pi - x) = -\cos x$
37. $\tan(2\pi - x) = -\tan x$
38. $\tan(\pi - x) = -\tan x$
39. $\sin(\alpha + \beta) + \sin(\alpha - \beta) = 2\sin\alpha\cos\beta$
40. $\cos(\alpha + \beta) + \cos(\alpha - \beta) = 2\cos\alpha\cos\beta$
41. $\frac{\sin(\alpha - \beta)}{\cos\alpha\cos\beta} = \tan\alpha - \tan\beta$
42. $\frac{\sin(\alpha + \beta)}{\cos\alpha\cos\beta} = \tan\alpha + \tan\beta$
43. $\tan\left(\theta + \frac{\pi}{4}\right) = \frac{\cos\theta + \sin\theta}{\cos\theta - \sin\theta}$
44. $\tan\left(\frac{\pi}{4} - \theta\right) = \frac{\cos\theta - \sin\theta}{\cos\theta + \sin\theta}$
45. $\cos(\alpha + \beta)\cos(\alpha - \beta) = \cos^2\beta - \sin^2\alpha$
46. $\sin(\alpha + \beta)\sin(\alpha - \beta) = \cos^2\beta - \cos^2\alpha$
47. $\frac{\sin(\alpha + \beta)}{\sin(\alpha - \beta)} = \frac{\tan\alpha + \tan\beta}{\tan\alpha - \tan\beta}$
48. $\frac{\cos(\alpha + \beta)}{\cos(\alpha - \beta)} = \frac{1 - \tan\alpha\tan\beta}{1 + \tan\alpha\tan\beta}$
49. $\frac{\cos(x + h) - \cos x}{h} = \cos x\frac{\cos h - 1}{h} - \sin x\frac{\sin h}{h}$

**50.** $\dfrac{\sin(x+h)-\sin x}{h} = \cos x \dfrac{\sin h}{h} + \sin x \dfrac{\cos h - 1}{h}$

**51.** $\sin 2\alpha = 2\sin\alpha\cos\alpha$
*Hint*: Write $\sin 2\alpha$ as $\sin(\alpha+\alpha)$.

**52.** $\cos 2\alpha = \cos^2\alpha - \sin^2\alpha$
*Hint*: Write $\cos 2\alpha$ as $\cos(\alpha+\alpha)$.

**53.** $\tan 2\alpha = \dfrac{2\tan\alpha}{1-\tan^2\alpha}$
*Hint*: Write $\tan 2\alpha$ as $\tan(\alpha+\alpha)$.

**54.** $\tan\left(\dfrac{\pi}{4}+\alpha\right) - \tan\left(\dfrac{\pi}{4}-\alpha\right) = 2\tan 2\alpha$
*Hint*: Use the result in Exercise 53.

**55.** Derive the identity for $\tan(\alpha+\beta)$ using

$$\tan(\alpha+\beta) = \frac{\sin(\alpha+\beta)}{\cos(\alpha+\beta)}.$$

After applying the formulas for sums of sines and cosines, divide the numerator and denominator by $\cos\alpha\cos\beta$.

**56.** Derive the identity for $\tan(\alpha-\beta)$ using

$$\tan(\alpha-\beta) = \tan[\alpha+(-\beta)].$$

After applying the formula for the tangent of the sum of two angles, use the fact that the tangent is an odd function.

*In Exercises 57–62, find the exact value of the following under the given conditions:*

**a.** $\cos(\alpha+\beta)$ **b.** $\sin(\alpha+\beta)$ **c.** $\tan(\alpha+\beta)$

**57.** $\sin\alpha = \frac{3}{5}$, $\alpha$ lies in quadrant I, and $\sin\beta = \frac{5}{13}$, $\beta$ lies in quadrant II.

**58.** $\sin\alpha = \frac{4}{5}$, $\alpha$ lies in quadrant I, and $\sin\beta = \frac{7}{25}$, $\beta$ lies in quadrant II.

**59.** $\tan\alpha = -\frac{3}{4}$, $\alpha$ lies in quadrant II, and $\cos\beta = \frac{1}{3}$, $\beta$ lies in quadrant I.

**60.** $\tan\alpha = -\frac{4}{3}$, $\alpha$ lies in quadrant II, and $\cos\beta = \frac{2}{3}$, $\beta$ lies in quadrant I.

**61.** $\cos\alpha = \frac{8}{17}$, $\alpha$ lies in quadrant IV, and $\sin\beta = -\frac{1}{2}$, $\beta$ lies in quadrant III.

**62.** $\cos\alpha = \frac{1}{2}$, $\alpha$ lies in quadrant IV, and $\sin\beta = -\frac{1}{3}$, $\beta$ lies in quadrant III.

*In Exercises 63–66, the graph with the given equation is shown in a* $\left[0, 2\pi, \dfrac{\pi}{2}\right]$ *by* $[-2, 2, 1]$ *viewing rectangle.*

**a.** *Describe the graph using another equation.*

**b.** *Verify that the two equations are equivalent.*

**63.**

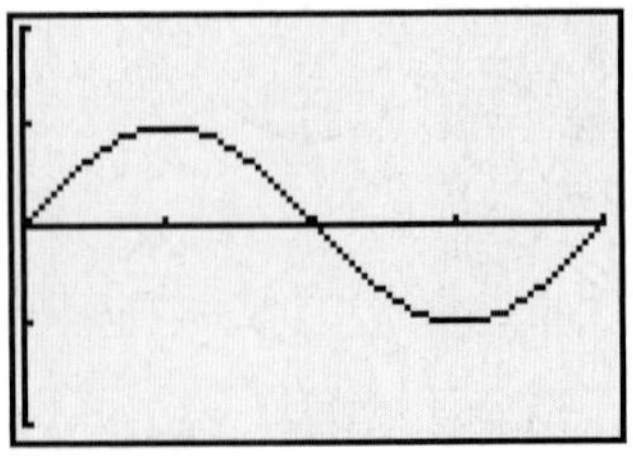

$y = \sin(\pi - x)$

**64.**

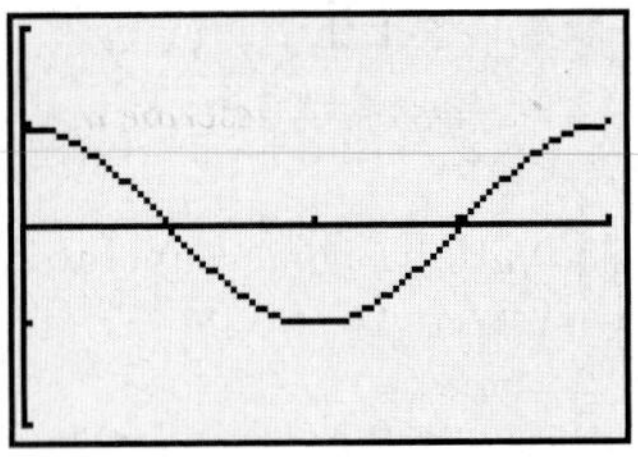

$y = \cos(x - 2\pi)$

**65.**

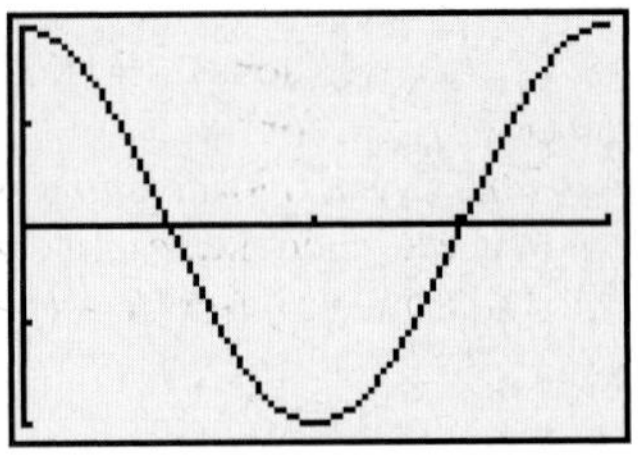

$y = \sin\left(x + \dfrac{\pi}{2}\right) + \sin\left(\dfrac{\pi}{2} - x\right)$

**66.**

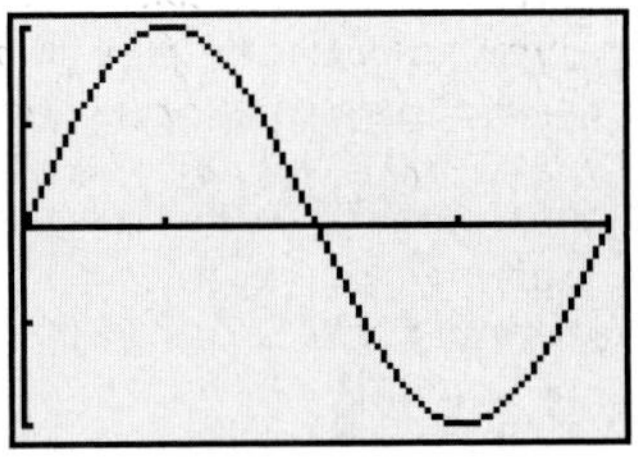

$y = \cos\left(x - \dfrac{\pi}{2}\right) - \cos\left(x + \dfrac{\pi}{2}\right)$

## Application Exercises

**67.** A ball attached to a spring is raised 2 feet and released with an initial vertical velocity of 3 feet per second. The distance of the ball from its rest position after $t$ seconds is given by $d = 2\cos t + 3\sin t$. Show that

$$2\cos t + 3\sin t = \sqrt{13}\cos(t - \theta),$$

where $\theta$ lies in quadrant I and $\tan\theta = \frac{3}{2}$. Use the identity to find the amplitude and the period of the ball's motion.

**68.** A tuning fork is held a certain distance from your ears and struck. Your eardrums' vibrations after $t$ seconds are given by $p = 3\sin 2t$. When a second tuning fork is struck, the formula $p = 2\sin(2t + \pi)$ describes the effects of the sound on the eardrums' vibrations. The total vibrations are given by $p = 3\sin 2t + 2\sin(2t + \pi)$.

**a.** Express $p$ using a single occurrence of the sine.

**b.** If the amplitude of $p$ is zero, no sound is heard. Based on your equation in part (a), does this occur with the two tuning forks in this exercise? Explain your answer.

### Writing in Mathematics

*In Exercises, 69–74, use words to describe the formula for:*

**69.** the cosine of the difference of two angles.
**70.** the cosine of the sum of two angles.
**71.** the sine of the sum of two angles.
**72.** the sine of the difference of two angles.
**73.** the tangent of the difference of two angles.
**74.** the tangent of the sum of two angles.
**75.** The distance formula and the definitions for cosine and sine are used to prove the formula for the cosine of the difference of two angles. This formula logically leads the way to the other sum and difference identities. Using this development of ideas and formulas, describe a characteristic of mathematical logic.

### Technology Exercises

*In Exercises 76–81, graph each side of the equation in the same viewing rectangle. If the graphs appear to coincide, verify that the equation is an identity. If the graphs do not appear to coincide, this indicates that the equation is not an identity. In these exercises, find a value of x for which both sides are defined but not equal.*

**76.** $\cos\left(\frac{3\pi}{2} - x\right) = -\sin x$

**77.** $\tan(\pi - x) = -\tan x$

**78.** $\sin\left(x + \frac{\pi}{2}\right) = \sin x + \sin\frac{\pi}{2}$

**79.** $\cos\left(x + \frac{\pi}{2}\right) = \cos x + \cos\frac{\pi}{2}$

**80.** $\cos 1.2x \cos 0.8x - \sin 1.2x \sin 0.8x = \cos 2x$

**81.** $\sin 1.2x \cos 0.8x + \cos 1.2x \sin 0.8x = \sin 2x$

### Critical Thinking Exercises

**82.** Graph $y = \sin 5x \cos 3x - \cos 5x \sin 3x$ from 0 to $2\pi$.

**83.** Verify the identity:

$$\frac{\sin(x-y)}{\cos x \cos y} + \frac{\sin(y-z)}{\cos y \cos z} + \frac{\sin(z-x)}{\cos z \cos x} = 0.$$

**84.** Without using a calculator, find the exact value of

$$\cos\left[\cos^{-1}\left(-\frac{\sqrt{3}}{2}\right) - \sin^{-1}\left(-\frac{1}{2}\right)\right].$$

**85.** Use right triangles to write

$$\cos(\sin^{-1} x - \cos^{-1} y)$$

as an algebraic expression. Assume that $x$ and $y$ are positive and in the domain of the given inverse trigonometric function.

### Group Exercise

**86.** Remembering the six sum and difference identities can be difficult. Did you have problems with some exercises because the identity you were using in your head turned out to be an incorrect formula? Are there easy ways to remember the six new identities presented in this section? Group members should address this question, considering one identity at a time. For each formula, list ways to make it easier to remember.

## SECTION 6.3 Double-Angle and Half-Angle Formulas

### Objectives

1. Use the double-angle formulas.
2. Use the power-reducing formulas.
3. Use the half-angle formulas.

We have a long history of throwing things. Prior to 400 B.C., the Greeks competed in games that included discus throwing. In the seventeenth century, English soldiers organized cannonball-throwing competitions. In 1827, a Yale University student, disappointed over failing an exam, took out his frustrations at the passing of a collection plate in chapel. Upon seizing the monetary tray, he flung it in the direction of a large open space on campus. Yale students see this act of frustration as the origin of the Frisbee.

In this section, we develop other important classes of identities called the double-angle and half-angle formulas. We will see how one of these formulas can be used by athletes to increase throwing distance.

**1** Use the double-angle formulas.

## Double-Angle Formulas

A number of basic identities follow from the sum formulas for sine, cosine, and tangent. The first category of identities involves **double-angle formulas.**

**Study Tip**

The 2 that appears in each of the double-angle expressions cannot be pulled to the front and written as a coefficient.

**INCORRECT**

$\sin 2\theta = 2\sin\theta$

$\cos 2\theta = 2\cos\theta$

$\tan 2\theta = 2\tan\theta$

The figure shows, in a $\left[0, 2\pi, \frac{\pi}{2}\right]$ by $[-3, 3, 1]$ viewing rectangle, that the graphs of

$$y = \sin 2x$$

and

$$y = 2\sin x$$

do not coincide.

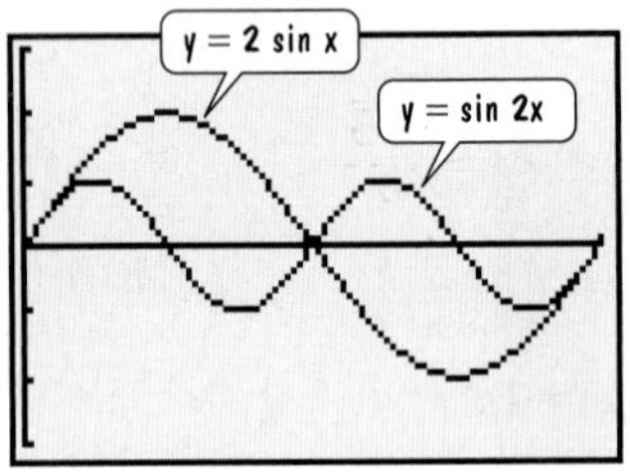


**Double-Angle Formulas**

$$\sin 2\theta = 2\sin\theta\cos\theta$$

$$\cos 2\theta = \cos^2\theta - \sin^2\theta$$

$$\tan 2\theta = \frac{2\tan\theta}{1-\tan^2\theta}$$

To prove each of these formulas, we replace $\alpha$ and $\beta$ by $\theta$ in the sum formulas for $\sin(\alpha+\beta)$, $\cos(\alpha+\beta)$, and $\tan(\alpha+\beta)$.

- $\sin 2\theta = \sin(\theta+\theta) = \sin\theta\cos\theta + \cos\theta\sin\theta = 2\sin\theta\cos\theta$

  We use $\sin(\alpha+\beta) = \sin\alpha\cos\beta + \cos\alpha\sin\beta$.

- $\cos 2\theta = \cos(\theta+\theta) = \cos\theta\cos\theta - \sin\theta\sin\theta = \cos^2\theta - \sin^2\theta$

  We use $\cos(\alpha+\beta) = \cos\alpha\cos\beta - \sin\alpha\sin\beta$.

- $\tan 2\theta = \tan(\theta+\theta) = \dfrac{\tan\theta+\tan\theta}{1-\tan\theta\tan\theta} = \dfrac{2\tan\theta}{1-\tan^2\theta}$

  We use $\tan(\alpha+\beta) = \dfrac{\tan\alpha+\tan\beta}{1-\tan\alpha\tan\beta}$.

**EXAMPLE 1 Using Double-Angle Formulas to Find Exact Values**

If $\sin\theta = \frac{5}{13}$ and $\theta$ lies in quadrant II, find the exact value of:

**a.** $\sin 2\theta$ **b.** $\cos 2\theta$ **c.** $\tan 2\theta$.

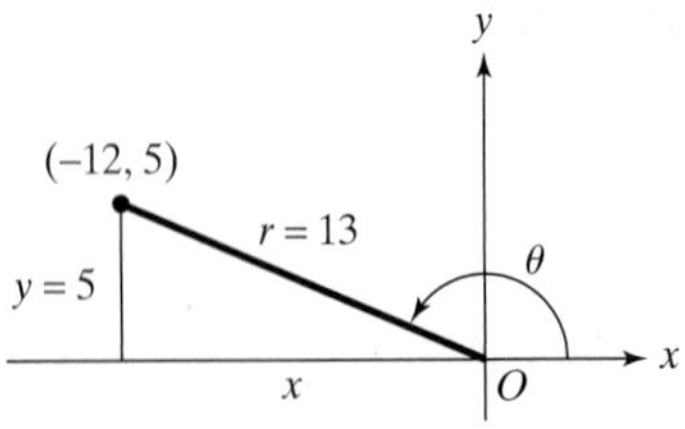


**Figure 6.6** $\sin\theta = \frac{5}{13}$ and $\theta$ lies in quadrant II.

**Solution** We begin with a sketch that illustrates

$$\sin\theta = \frac{5}{13} = \frac{y}{r}.$$

Figure 6.6 shows a quadrant II angle $\theta$ and $\sin\theta = \frac{5}{13}$. We find $x$ using $x^2 + y^2 = r^2$. Because $\theta$ lies in quadrant II, $x$ is negative.

$$x^2 + 5^2 = 13^2 \qquad x^2 + y^2 = r^2$$

$$x^2 = 13^2 - 5^2 = 144 \qquad \text{Solve for } x^2.$$

$$x = -\sqrt{144} = -12 \qquad \text{In quadrant II, } x \text{ is negative.}$$

Now we can use values for $x$, $y$, and $r$ to find the required values.

**a.** $\sin 2\theta = 2\sin\theta\cos\theta = 2\left(\frac{5}{13}\right)\left(-\frac{12}{13}\right) = -\frac{120}{169}$

**b.** $\cos 2\theta = \cos^2\theta - \sin^2\theta = \left(-\frac{12}{13}\right)^2 - \left(\frac{5}{13}\right)^2 = \frac{144}{169} - \frac{25}{169} = \frac{119}{169}$

**c.** $\tan 2\theta = \dfrac{2\tan\theta}{1-\tan^2\theta} = \dfrac{2\left(-\frac{5}{12}\right)}{1-\left(-\frac{5}{12}\right)^2} = \dfrac{-\frac{5}{6}}{1-\frac{25}{144}} = \dfrac{-\frac{5}{6}}{\frac{119}{144}} = \left(-\frac{5}{6}\right)\left(\frac{144}{119}\right) = -\frac{120}{119}$

**Check Point 1** If $\sin\theta = \frac{4}{5}$ and $\theta$ lies in quadrant II, find the exact value of:

**a.** $\sin 2\theta$ **b.** $\cos 2\theta$ **c.** $\tan 2\theta$.

## EXAMPLE 2 Using the Double Angle Formula for Tangents to Find an Exact Value

Find the exact value of $\dfrac{2\tan 15^\circ}{1-\tan^2 15^\circ}$.

**Solution** The given expression is the right side of the formula for $\tan 2\theta$ with $\theta = 15^\circ$.

$$\tan 2\theta = \frac{2\tan\theta}{1-\tan^2\theta}$$

$$\frac{2\tan 15^\circ}{1-\tan^2 15^\circ} = \tan(2\cdot 15^\circ) = \tan 30^\circ = \frac{\sqrt{3}}{3}$$

**Check Point 2** Find the exact value of $\cos^2 15^\circ - \sin^2 15^\circ$.

There are three forms of the double-angle formula for $\cos 2\theta$. The form we have seen involves both the cosine and the sine:

$$\cos 2\theta = \cos^2\theta - \sin^2\theta.$$

Using the Pythagorean identity $\sin^2\theta + \cos^2\theta = 1$, we can write this last formula in terms of the cosine only. We substitute $1 - \cos^2\theta$ for $\sin^2\theta$.

$$\cos 2\theta = \cos^2\theta - \sin^2\theta = \cos^2\theta - (1 - \cos^2\theta)$$

$$= \cos^2\theta - 1 + \cos^2\theta = 2\cos^2\theta - 1$$

We can also use a Pythagorean identity to write $\cos 2\theta$ in terms of sine only. We substitute $1 - \sin^2\theta$ for $\cos^2\theta$.

$$\cos 2\theta = \cos^2\theta - \sin^2\theta = 1 - \sin^2\theta - \sin^2\theta = 1 - 2\sin^2\theta$$

**Three Forms of the Double-Angle Formula for cos 2θ**

$$\cos 2\theta = \cos^2\theta - \sin^2\theta$$
$$\cos 2\theta = 2\cos^2\theta - 1$$
$$\cos 2\theta = 1 - 2\sin^2\theta$$

## EXAMPLE 3 Verifying an Identity

Verify the identity: $\cos 3\theta = 4\cos^3\theta - 3\cos\theta$.

**Solution** We begin by working with the left side. In order to obtain an expression for $\cos 3\theta$, we use the sum formula and write $3\theta$ as $2\theta + \theta$.

$\cos 3\theta = \cos(2\theta + \theta)$ — Write $3\theta$ as $2\theta + \theta$.

$= \cos 2\theta \cos\theta - \sin 2\theta \sin\theta$ — $\cos(\alpha + \beta) = \cos\alpha\cos\beta - \sin\alpha\sin\beta$

$2\cos^2\theta - 1$    $2\sin\theta\cos\theta$ — Substitute double-angle formulas. Because the right side of the given equation involves cosines only, use this form for $\cos 2\theta$.

$= (2\cos^2\theta - 1)\cos\theta - 2\sin\theta\cos\theta\sin\theta$

$= 2\cos^3\theta - \cos\theta - 2\sin^2\theta\cos\theta$ — Multiply.

$1 - \cos^2\theta$

$= 2\cos^3\theta - \cos\theta - 2(1 - \cos^2\theta)\cos\theta$ — To get cosines only, use $\sin^2\theta + \cos^2\theta = 1$ and substitute $1 - \cos^2\theta$ for $\sin^2\theta$.

$= 2\cos^3\theta - \cos\theta - 2\cos\theta + 2\cos^3\theta$ — Multiply.

$= 4\cos^3\theta - 3\cos\theta$ — Simplify: $2\cos^3\theta + 2\cos^3\theta = 4\cos^3\theta$ and $-\cos\theta - 2\cos\theta = -3\cos\theta$.

By working with the left side and expressing it in a form identical to the right side, we have verified the identity.

**Check Point 3** Verify the identity: $\sin 3\theta = 3\sin\theta - 4\sin^3\theta$.

**2** Use the power-reducing formulas.

## Power-Reducing Formulas

The double-angle formulas are used to derive the **power-reducing formulas**.

**Power-Reducing Formulas**

$$\sin^2\theta = \frac{1 - \cos 2\theta}{2} \qquad \cos^2\theta = \frac{1 + \cos 2\theta}{2} \qquad \tan^2\theta = \frac{1 - \cos 2\theta}{1 + \cos 2\theta}$$

We can prove the first two formulas in the box by working with two forms of the double-angle formula for $\cos 2\theta$.

This is the form with sine only. / This is the form with cosine only.

$$\cos 2\theta = 1 - 2\sin^2\theta \qquad \cos 2\theta = 2\cos^2\theta - 1$$

Solve the formula on the left for $\sin^2\theta$. Solve the formula on the right for $\cos^2\theta$.

$$2\sin^2\theta = 1 - \cos 2\theta \qquad 2\cos^2\theta = 1 + \cos 2\theta$$

$$\sin^2\theta = \frac{1-\cos 2\theta}{2} \qquad \cos^2\theta = \frac{1+\cos 2\theta}{2}$$ Divide both sides of each equation by 2.

These are the first two formulas in the box. The third formula in the box is proved by writing the tangent as the quotient of the sine and the cosine.

$$\tan^2\theta = \frac{\sin^2\theta}{\cos^2\theta} = \frac{\frac{1-\cos 2\theta}{2}}{\frac{1+\cos 2\theta}{2}} = \frac{1-\cos 2\theta}{\cancel{2}_1} \cdot \frac{\cancel{2}^1}{1+\cos 2\theta} = \frac{1-\cos 2\theta}{1+\cos 2\theta}$$

Power-reducing formulas are quite useful in calculus. By reducing the power of trigonometric functions, calculus can better explore the relationship between a function and how it is changing at every single instant in time.

## EXAMPLE 4 Reducing the Power of a Trigonometric Function

Write an equivalent expression for $\cos^4 x$ that does not contain powers of trigonometric functions greater than 1.

**Solution** We will apply the formula for $\cos^2\theta$ twice.

$$\cos^4 x = (\cos^2 x)^2$$

$$= \left(\frac{1+\cos 2x}{2}\right)^2$$ Use $\cos^2\theta = \frac{1+\cos 2\theta}{2}$ with $\theta = x$.

$$= \frac{1 + 2\cos 2x + \cos^2 2x}{4}$$ Square the numerator: $(A+B)^2 = A^2 + 2AB + B^2$. Square the denominator.

$$= \frac{1}{4} + \frac{1}{2}\cos 2x + \frac{1}{4}\cos^2 2x$$ Divide each term in the numerator by 4.

We can reduce the power of $\cos^2 2x$ using $\cos^2\theta = \frac{1+\cos 2\theta}{2}$ with $\theta = 2x$.

$$= \frac{1}{4} + \frac{1}{2}\cos 2x + \frac{1}{4}\left[\frac{1+\cos 2(2x)}{2}\right]$$ Use the power-reducing formula for $\cos^2\theta$ with $\theta = 2x$.

$$= \frac{1}{4} + \frac{1}{2}\cos 2x + \frac{1}{8}(1 + \cos 4x) \qquad \text{Multiply.}$$

$$= \frac{1}{4} + \frac{1}{2}\cos 2x + \frac{1}{8} + \frac{1}{8}\cos 4x \qquad \text{Distribute } \tfrac{1}{8} \text{ throughout parentheses.}$$

$$= \frac{3}{8} + \frac{1}{2}\cos 2x + \frac{1}{8}\cos 4x \qquad \text{Simplify: } \tfrac{1}{4} + \tfrac{1}{8} = \tfrac{2}{8} + \tfrac{1}{8} = \tfrac{3}{8}.$$

Thus, $\cos^4 x = \frac{3}{8} + \frac{1}{2}\cos 2x + \frac{1}{8}\cos 4x$. The expression for $\cos^4 x$ does not contain powers of trigonometric functions greater than 1.

**Check Point 4** Write an equivalent expression for $\sin^4 x$ that does not contain powers of trigonometric functions greater than 1.

**3** Use the half-angle formulas.

## Study Tip

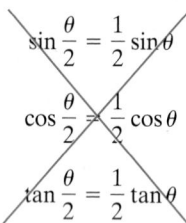

The $\frac{1}{2}$ that appears in each of the half-angle formulas cannot be pulled to the front and written as a coefficient

**INCORRECT**

$$\sin\frac{\theta}{2} = \frac{1}{2}\sin\theta$$

$$\cos\frac{\theta}{2} = \frac{1}{2}\cos\theta$$

$$\tan\frac{\theta}{2} = \frac{1}{2}\tan\theta$$

The figure shows, in a $\left[0, 2\pi, \frac{\pi}{2}\right]$ by $[-2, 2, 1]$ viewing rectangle, that the graphs of

$$y = \sin\frac{x}{2}$$

and

$$y = \frac{1}{2}\sin x$$

do not coincide.

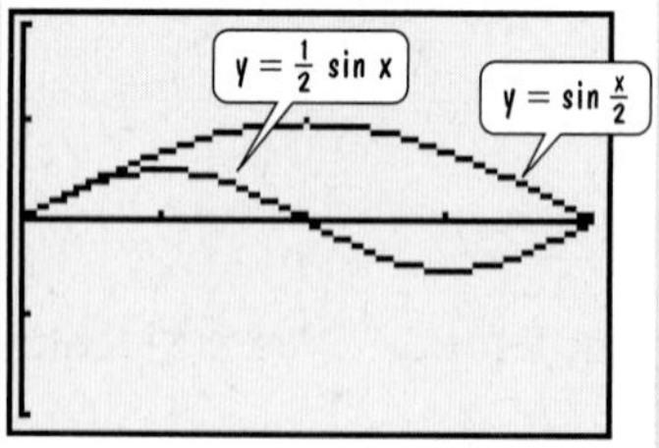


## Half-Angle Formulas

Useful equivalent forms of the power-reducing formulas can be obtained by replacing $\theta$ by $\frac{\alpha}{2}$. Then solve for the trigonometric function on the left sides of the equations. The resulting identities are called the **half-angle formulas**.

### Half-Angle Formulas

$$\sin\frac{\alpha}{2} = \pm\sqrt{\frac{1 - \cos\alpha}{2}}$$

$$\cos\frac{\alpha}{2} = \pm\sqrt{\frac{1 + \cos\alpha}{2}}$$

$$\tan\frac{\alpha}{2} = \pm\sqrt{\frac{1 - \cos\alpha}{1 + \cos\alpha}}$$

The + or − in each formula is determined by the quadrant in which $\frac{\alpha}{2}$ lies.

If we know the exact value for the sine, cosine, or tangent of an angle, we can use the half-angle formulas to find exact values for half that angle. For example, we know that $\cos 225° = -\frac{\sqrt{2}}{2}$. In the next example, we find the exact value of the cosine of half of 225°, or cos 112.5°.

## EXAMPLE 5 Using a Half-Angle Formula to Find an Exact Value

Find the exact value of cos 112.5°.

**Solution** Because $112.5° = \frac{225°}{2}$, we use the half-angle formula for $\cos\frac{\alpha}{2}$ with $\alpha = 225°$. What sign should we use when we apply the formula? Because 112.5° lies quadrant II, where only the sine and cosecant are positive, $\cos 112.5° < 0$. Thus, we use the − sign in the half-angle formula.

## Discovery

Use your calculator to find approximations for

$$-\frac{\sqrt{2-\sqrt{2}}}{2}$$

and $\cos 112.5°$. What do you observe?

$$\cos 112.5° = \cos\frac{225°}{2}$$

$$= -\sqrt{\frac{1+\cos 225°}{2}}$$ Use $\cos\frac{\alpha}{2} = -\sqrt{\frac{1+\cos\alpha}{2}}$ with $\alpha = 225°$.

$$= -\sqrt{\frac{1+\left(-\frac{\sqrt{2}}{2}\right)}{2}}$$ $\cos 225° = -\frac{\sqrt{2}}{2}$

$$= -\sqrt{\frac{2-\sqrt{2}}{4}}$$ Multiply the radicand by $\frac{2}{2}$: $\frac{1+\left(-\frac{\sqrt{2}}{2}\right)}{2}\cdot\frac{2}{2} = \frac{2-\sqrt{2}}{4}$.

$$= -\frac{\sqrt{2-\sqrt{2}}}{2}$$ Simplify: $\sqrt{4} = 2$.

**Check Point 5** Use $\cos 210° = -\frac{\sqrt{3}}{2}$ to find the exact value of $\cos 105°$.

There are alternate formulas for $\tan\frac{\alpha}{2}$ that do not require us to determine what sign to use when applying the formula. These formulas are logically connected to the identities in Example 6 and the Check Point.

## EXAMPLE 6 Verifying an Identity

Verify the identity: $\tan\theta = \frac{1-\cos 2\theta}{\sin 2\theta}$.

**Solution** We work with the right side.

$$\frac{1-\cos 2\theta}{\sin 2\theta} = \frac{1-(1-2\sin^2\theta)}{2\sin\theta\cos\theta}$$ The form $\cos 2\theta = 1 - 2\sin^2\theta$ is used because it produces only one term in the numerator. Use the double-angle formula for sine in the denominator.

$$= \frac{2\sin^2\theta}{2\sin\theta\cos\theta}$$ Simplify the numerator.

$$= \frac{\sin\theta}{\cos\theta}$$ Divide the numerator and denominator by $2\sin\theta$.

$$= \tan\theta$$ Use a quotient identity: $\tan\theta = \frac{\sin\theta}{\cos\theta}$.

The right side simplifies to $\tan\theta$, the expression on the left side. Thus, the identity is verified.

**Check Point 6** Verify the identity: $\tan\theta = \dfrac{\sin 2\theta}{1 + \cos 2\theta}$.

Half-angle formulas for $\tan\dfrac{\alpha}{2}$ can be obtained using the identities in Example 6 and the Check Point. Do you see how to do this? Replace each occurrence of $\theta$ by $\dfrac{\alpha}{2}$. This results in the following identities.

**Half-Angle Formulas for $\tan\dfrac{\alpha}{2}$**

$$\tan\frac{\alpha}{2} = \frac{1 - \cos\alpha}{\sin\alpha}$$

$$\tan\frac{\alpha}{2} = \frac{\sin\alpha}{1 + \cos\alpha}$$

## EXAMPLE 7 Verifying an Identity

Verify the identity: $\tan\dfrac{\alpha}{2} = \csc\alpha - \cot\alpha$.

**Solution** We begin with the right side.

$$\csc\alpha - \cot\alpha = \frac{1}{\sin\alpha} - \frac{\cos\alpha}{\sin\alpha} = \frac{1 - \cos\alpha}{\sin\alpha} = \tan\frac{\alpha}{2}$$

Express functions in terms of sines and cosines.

This is the first of the two half-angle formulas in the preceding box.

We worked with the right side and arrived at the left side. Thus, the identity is verified.

**Check Point 7** Verify the identity: $\tan\dfrac{\alpha}{2} = \dfrac{\sec\alpha}{\sec\alpha\csc\alpha + \csc\alpha}$.

We conclude with a summary of the principal trigonometric identities developed in this section and the previous section. The fundamental identities can be found in the box on page 533.

**Principal Trigonometric Identities**

Sum and Difference Formulas

$$\sin(\alpha+\beta)=\sin\alpha\cos\beta+\cos\alpha\sin\beta \qquad \sin(\alpha-\beta)=\sin\alpha\cos\beta-\cos\alpha\sin\beta$$

$$\cos(\alpha+\beta)=\cos\alpha\cos\beta-\sin\alpha\sin\beta \qquad \cos(\alpha-\beta)=\cos\alpha\cos\beta+\sin\alpha\sin\beta$$

$$\tan(\alpha+\beta)=\frac{\tan\alpha+\tan\beta}{1-\tan\alpha\tan\beta} \qquad \tan(\alpha-\beta)=\frac{\tan\alpha-\tan\beta}{1+\tan\alpha\tan\beta}$$

Double-Angle Formulas

$$\sin 2\theta = 2\sin\theta\cos\theta$$

$$\cos 2\theta = \cos^2\theta-\sin^2\theta = 2\cos^2\theta-1 = 1-2\sin^2\theta$$

$$\tan 2\theta = \frac{2\tan\theta}{1-\tan^2\theta}$$

Power-Reducing Formulas

$$\sin^2\theta=\frac{1-\cos 2\theta}{2} \qquad \cos^2\theta=\frac{1+\cos 2\theta}{2} \qquad \tan^2\theta=\frac{1-\cos 2\theta}{1+\cos 2\theta}$$

Half-Angle Formulas

$$\sin\frac{\alpha}{2}=\pm\sqrt{\frac{1-\cos\alpha}{2}} \qquad \cos\frac{\alpha}{2}=\pm\sqrt{\frac{1+\cos\alpha}{2}}$$

$$\tan\frac{\alpha}{2}=\pm\sqrt{\frac{1-\cos\alpha}{1+\cos\alpha}}=\frac{1-\cos\alpha}{\sin\alpha}=\frac{\sin\alpha}{1+\cos\alpha}$$

## Study Tip

To help remember the correct sign between the first two power-reducing formulas and the first two half-angle formulas, remember *sinus-minus*—the sine is minus.

## EXERCISE SET 6.3

### Practice Exercises

*In Exercises 1–6, use the figures to find the exact value of the trigonometric function.*

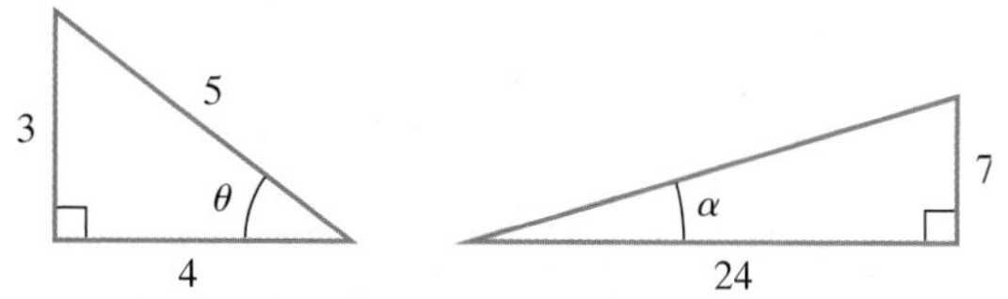


**1.** $\sin 2\theta$ **2.** $\cos 2\theta$ **3.** $\tan 2\theta$

**4.** $\sin 2\alpha$ **5.** $\cos 2\alpha$ **6.** $\tan 2\alpha$

*In Exercises 7–14, use the given information to find the exact value of:*

**a.** $\sin 2\theta$ **b.** $\cos 2\theta$ **c.** $\tan 2\theta$.

**7.** $\sin\theta=\frac{15}{17}$, $\theta$ lies in quadrant II.

**8.** $\sin\theta=\frac{12}{13}$, $\theta$ lies in quadrant II.

**9.** $\cos\theta=\frac{24}{25}$, $\theta$ lies in quadrant IV.

**10.** $\cos\theta=\frac{40}{41}$, $\theta$ lies in quadrant IV.

**11.** $\cot\theta=2$, $\theta$ lies in quadrant III.

**12.** $\cot\theta=3$, $\theta$ lies in quadrant III.

**13.** $\sin\theta=-\frac{9}{41}$, $\theta$ lies in quadrant III.

**14.** $\sin\theta=-\frac{2}{3}$, $\theta$ lies in quadrant III.

*In Exercises 15–22, write each expression as the sine, cosine, or tangent of a double angle. Then find the exact value of the expression.*

**15.** $2\sin 15^\circ\cos 15^\circ$ **16.** $2\sin 22.5^\circ\cos 22.5^\circ$

**17.** $\cos^2 75^\circ-\sin^2 75^\circ$ **18.** $\cos^2 105^\circ-\sin^2 105^\circ$

**19.** $2\cos^2\frac{\pi}{8}-1$ **20.** $1-2\sin^2\frac{\pi}{12}$

**21.** $\dfrac{2\tan\frac{\pi}{12}}{1-\tan^2\frac{\pi}{12}}$ **22.** $\dfrac{2\tan\frac{\pi}{8}}{1-\tan^2\frac{\pi}{8}}$

*In Exercises 23–34, verify each identity.*

**23.** $\sin 2\theta=\dfrac{2\tan\theta}{1+\tan^2\theta}$ **24.** $\sin 2\theta=\dfrac{2\cot\theta}{1+\cot^2\theta}$

**25.** $(\sin\theta+\cos\theta)^2=1+\sin 2\theta$

**26.** $(\sin\theta-\cos\theta)^2=1-\sin 2\theta$

**27.** $\sin^2 x+\cos 2x=\cos^2 x$

**28.** $1 - \tan^2 x = \dfrac{\cos 2x}{\cos^2 x}$

**29.** $\cot x = \dfrac{\sin 2x}{1 - \cos 2x}$

**30.** $\cot x = \dfrac{1 + \cos 2x}{\sin 2x}$

**31.** $\sin 2t - \tan t = \tan t \cos 2t$

**32.** $\sin 2t - \cot t = -\cot t \cos 2t$

**33.** $\sin 4t = 4 \sin t \cos^3 t - 4 \sin^3 t \cos t$

**34.** $\cos 4t = 8 \cos^4 t - 8 \cos^2 t + 1$

*In Exercises 35–38, use the power-reducing formulas to rewrite each expression as an equivalent expression that does not contain powers of trigonometric functions greater than 1.*

**35.** $6 \sin^2 x$

**36.** $10 \cos^2 x \cos^2 x$

**37.** $\sin^2 x \cos^2 x$

**38.** $8 \sin^2 x \cos^2 x$

*In Exercises 39–46, use a half-angle formula to find the exact value of each expression.*

**39.** $\sin 15°$

**40.** $\cos 22.5°$

**41.** $\cos 157.5°$

**42.** $\sin 105°$

**43.** $\tan 75°$

**44.** $\tan 112.5°$

**45.** $\tan \dfrac{7\pi}{8}$

**46.** $\tan \dfrac{3\pi}{8}$

*In Exercises 47–54, use the figures to find the exact value of the trigonometric function.*

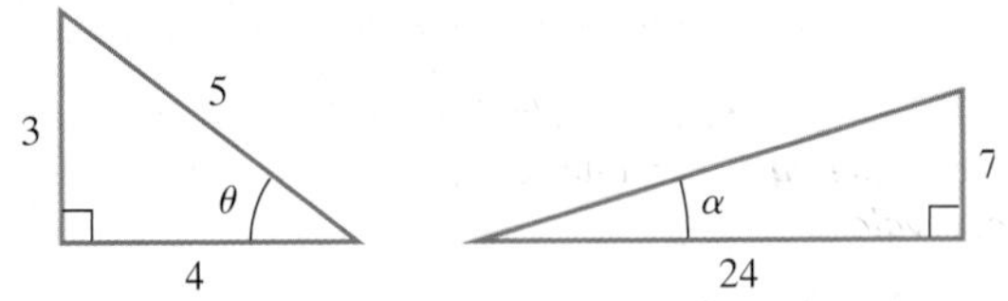


**47.** $\sin \dfrac{\theta}{2}$

**48.** $\cos \dfrac{\theta}{2}$

**49.** $\tan \dfrac{\theta}{2}$

**50.** $\sin \dfrac{\alpha}{2}$

**51.** $\cos \dfrac{\alpha}{2}$

**52.** $\tan \dfrac{\alpha}{2}$

**53.** $2 \sin \dfrac{\theta}{2} \cos \dfrac{\theta}{2}$

**54.** $2 \sin \dfrac{\alpha}{2} \cos \dfrac{\alpha}{2}$

*In Exercises 55–58, use the given information to find the exact value of:*

**a.** $\sin \dfrac{\alpha}{2}$ **b.** $\cos \dfrac{\alpha}{2}$ **c.** $\tan \dfrac{\alpha}{2}$.

**55.** $\tan \alpha = \frac{4}{3}$, $\alpha$ lies in quadrant III.

**56.** $\tan \alpha = \frac{8}{15}$, $\alpha$ lies in quadrant III.

**57.** $\sec \alpha = -\frac{13}{5}$, $\alpha$ lies in quadrant II.

**58.** $\sec \alpha = -3$, $\alpha$ lies in quadrant II.

*In Exercises 59–68, verify each identity.*

**59.** $\sin^2 \dfrac{\theta}{2} = \dfrac{\sec \theta - 1}{2 \sec \theta}$

**60.** $\sin^2 \dfrac{\theta}{2} = \dfrac{\csc \theta - \cot \theta}{2 \csc \theta}$

**61.** $\cos^2 \dfrac{\theta}{2} = \dfrac{\sin \theta + \tan \theta}{2 \tan \theta}$

**62.** $\cos^2 \dfrac{\theta}{2} = \dfrac{\sec \theta + 1}{2 \sec \theta}$

**63.** $\tan \dfrac{\alpha}{2} = \dfrac{\tan \alpha}{\sec \alpha + 1}$

**64.** $2 \tan \dfrac{\alpha}{2} = \dfrac{\sin^2 \alpha + 1 - \cos^2 \alpha}{\sin \alpha (1 + \cos \alpha)}$

**65.** $\cot \dfrac{x}{2} = \dfrac{\sin x}{1 - \cos x}$

**66.** $\cot \dfrac{x}{2} = \dfrac{1 + \cos x}{\sin x}$

**67.** $\tan \dfrac{x}{2} + \cot \dfrac{x}{2} = 2 \csc x$

**68.** $\tan \dfrac{x}{2} - \cot \dfrac{x}{2} = -2 \cot x$

## Application Exercises

**69.** Throwing events in track and field include the shot put, the discus throw, the hammer throw, and the javelin throw. The distance that the athlete can achieve depends on the initial speed of the object thrown and the angle above the horizontal at which the object leaves the hand. This angle is represented by $\theta$ in the figure shown. The distance $d$ in feet, that the athlete throws is modeled by the formula

$$d = \frac{v_o^2}{16} \sin \theta \cos \theta$$

in which $v_o$ is the initial speed of the object thrown, in feet per second, and $\theta$ is the angle, in degrees, at which the object leaves the hand.

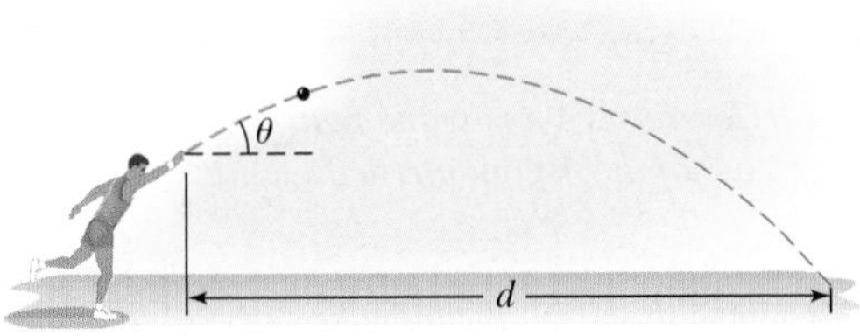


**a.** Use an identity to express the formula so that it contains the sine function only.

**b.** Use your formula from part (a) to find the angle, $\theta$, that produces the maximum distance, $d$, for a given initial speed, $v_o$.

*Use this information to solve Exercises 70–71.*

*The speed of a supersonic aircraft is usually represented by a Mach number, named after Austrian physicist Ernst Mach (1838–1916). A Mach number is the speed of the aircraft, in miles per hour, divided by the speed of sound, approximately 740 miles per hour. Thus, a plane flying at twice the speed of sound has a speed, M, of Mach 2. If an aircraft has a speed greater than Mach 1, a sonic boom is heard, created by sound waves that form a cone with a vertex angle $\theta$, shown in the* *figure. The relationship between the cone's vertex angle, $\theta$, and the Mach speed, $M$, of an aircraft that is flying faster than the speed of sound is given by*

$$\sin\frac{\theta}{2} = \frac{1}{M}.$$

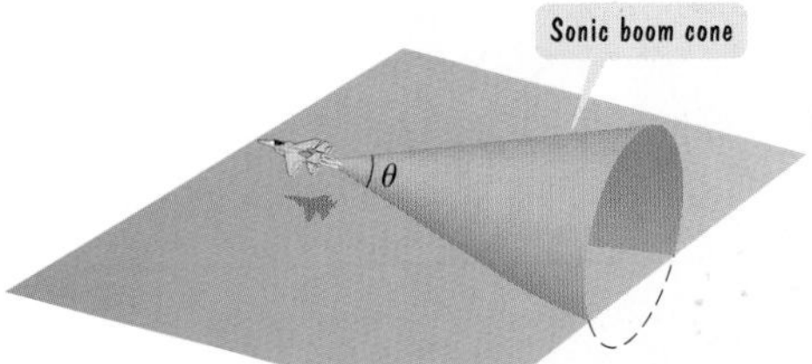


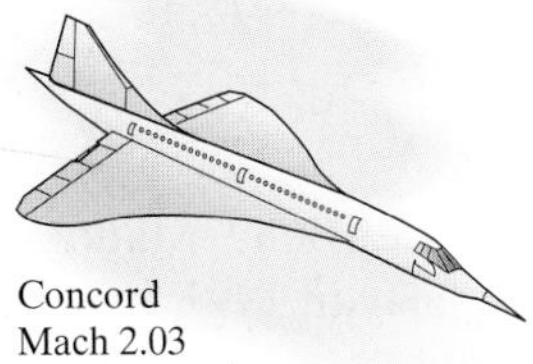

Concord
Mach 2.03

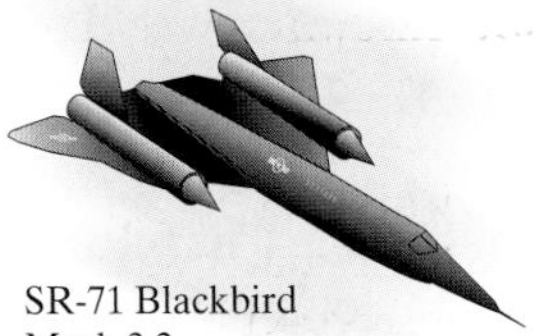

SR-71 Blackbird
Mach 3.3

**70.** If $\theta = \frac{\pi}{6}$, determine the Mach speed, $M$, of the aircraft. Express the speed as an exact value and as a decimal to the nearest tenth.

**71.** If $\theta = \frac{\pi}{4}$, determine the Mach speed, $M$, of the aircraft. Express the speed as an exact value and as a decimal to the nearest tenth.

## Writing in Mathematics

*In Exercises 72–79, use words to describe the formula for:*

**72.** the sine of double an angle.

**73.** the cosine of double an angle. (Describe one of the three formulas.)

**74.** the tangent of double an angle.

**75.** the power-reducing formula for the sine squared of an angle.

**76.** the power-reducing formula for the cosine squared of an angle.

**77.** the sine of half an angle.

**78.** the cosine of half an angle.

**79.** the tangent of half an angle. (Describe one of the two formulas that does not involve a square root.)

**80.** Explain how the double-angle formulas are derived.

**81.** How can there be three forms of the double-angle formula for $\cos 2\theta$?

**82.** Without showing algebraic details, describe in words how to reduce the power of $\cos^4 x$.

**83.** Describe one or more of the techniques you use to help remember the identities in the box on page 561.

**84.** Your friend is about to compete as a shot-putter in a college field event. Using Exercise 69(b), write a short description to your friend on how to achieve the best distance possible in the throwing event.

## Technology Exercises

*In Exercises 85–88, graph each side of the equation in the same viewing rectangle. If the graphs appear to coincide, verify that the equation is an identity. If the graphs do not appear to coincide, find a value of x for which both sides are defined but not equal.*

**85.** $3 - 6\sin^2 x = 3\cos 2x$

**86.** $4\cos^2\frac{x}{2} = 2 + 2\cos x$

**87.** $\sin\frac{x}{2} = \frac{1}{2}\sin x$

**88.** $\cos\frac{x}{2} = \frac{1}{2}\cos x$

*In Exercises 89–91, graph each equation in a* $\left[-2\pi, 2\pi, \frac{\pi}{2}\right]$ *by* $[-3, 3, 1]$ *viewing rectangle. Then **a.** Describe the graph using another equation, and **b.** Verify that the two equations are equivalent.*

**89.** $y = \dfrac{1 - 2\cos 2x}{2\sin x - 1}$

**90.** $y = \dfrac{2\tan\frac{x}{2}}{1 + \tan^2\frac{x}{2}}$

**91.** $y = \csc x - \cot x$

## Critical Thinking Exercises

**92.** Verify the identity:

$$\sin^3 x + \cos^3 x = (\sin x + \cos x)\left(1 - \frac{\sin 2x}{2}\right)$$

**93.** Use the power-reducing formulas to rewrite $\sin^6 x$ as an equivalent expression that does not contain powers of trigonometric functions greater than 1.

**94.** Use a right triangle to write $\sin(2\sin^{-1} x)$ as an algebraic expression. Assume that $x$ is positive and in the domain of the given inverse trigonometric function.

## SECTION 6.4 Product-to-Sum and Sum-to-Product Formulas

### Objectives

1. Use the product-to-sum formulas.
2. Use the sum-to-product formulas.

Dennis Hopper. Shirley MacLaine. Cher. Roseanne. Patti LaBelle. Madonna. They all attended Elizabeth Taylor's sixty-fifth birthday party in 1997, raising a total of \$1 million for AIDS causes. Hope it's not too late to send our birthday best and add:

112, 163-, 112, 196-, 110, 8521-, 008, 121-.

Relax, Roseanne. Bet you didn't know that each button on your touch-tone phone produces a unique sound. If we treat the commas as pauses and the hyphens as held notes, this sequence of numbers is *Happy Birthday* on a touch-tone phone.

Although *Happy Birthday* isn't Mozart or Sondheim, it is sinusoidal. Each of its touch-tone musical sounds can be described by the sum of two sine functions or the product of sines and cosines. In this section, we develop identities that enable us to use both descriptions. They are called the product-to-sum and sum-to-product formulas. We'll even apply this to musical sophistication at its best, including Mary's infamous lamb and those jingling bells.

**1** Use the product-to-sum formulas.

### The Product-to-Sum Formulas

How do we write the products of sines and/or cosines as sums or differences? We use the following identities, which are called **product-to-sum formulas.**

**Study Tip**

You may not need to memorize the formulas in this section. When you need them, you can either refer to one of the two boxes in the section or derive them using the methods shown.

**Product-to-Sum Formulas**

$$\sin\alpha\sin\beta = \tfrac{1}{2}[\cos(\alpha-\beta) - \cos(\alpha+\beta)]$$

$$\cos\alpha\cos\beta = \tfrac{1}{2}[\cos(\alpha-\beta) + \cos(\alpha+\beta)]$$

$$\sin\alpha\cos\beta = \tfrac{1}{2}[\sin(\alpha+\beta) + \sin(\alpha-\beta)]$$

$$\cos\alpha\sin\beta = \tfrac{1}{2}[\sin(\alpha+\beta) - \sin(\alpha-\beta)]$$

Although these formulas are difficult to remember, they are fairly easy to derive. For example, let's derive the first identity in the box,

$$\sin\alpha\sin\beta = \tfrac{1}{2}\left[\cos(\alpha-\beta) - \cos(\alpha+\beta)\right].$$

We begin with the difference and sum formulas for the cosine and subtract the second identity from the first:

$$\begin{aligned} \cos(\alpha-\beta) &= \cos\alpha\cos\beta + \sin\alpha\sin\beta \\ -[\cos(\alpha+\beta) &= \cos\alpha\cos\beta - \sin\alpha\sin\beta] \quad \text{Subtract the identities.} \\ \cos(\alpha-\beta) - \cos(\alpha+\beta) &= 0 + 2\sin\alpha\sin\beta \end{aligned}$$

Subtract terms on the left side.

Subtract terms on the right side: $\cos\alpha\cos\beta - \cos\alpha\cos\beta = 0$.

Subtract terms on the right side: $\sin\alpha\sin\beta - (-\sin\alpha\sin\beta) = 2\sin\alpha\sin\beta$.

Now we use this result to derive the product-to-sum formula for $\sin\alpha\sin\beta$.

$$2\sin\alpha\sin\beta = \cos(\alpha-\beta) - \cos(\alpha+\beta) \quad \text{Reverse the sides in the preceding equation.}$$

$$\sin\alpha\sin\beta = \tfrac{1}{2}\left[\cos(\alpha-\beta) - \cos(\alpha+\beta)\right] \quad \text{Multiply each side by } \tfrac{1}{2}.$$

This last equation is the desired formula. Likewise, we can derive the product-to-sum formula for cosine, $\cos\alpha\cos\beta = \frac{1}{2}\left[\cos(\alpha-\beta) + \cos(\alpha+\beta)\right]$. As we did for the previous derivation, begin with the difference and sum formulas for cosine. However, we *add* the formulas rather than subtracting them. Reversing both sides of this result and multiplying each side by $\frac{1}{2}$ produces the formula for $\cos\alpha\cos\beta$. The last two product-to-sum formulas, $\sin\alpha\cos\beta$ and $\cos\alpha\sin\beta$, are derived using the sum and difference formulas for sine in a similar manner.

## EXAMPLE 1 Using the Product-to-Sum Formulas

Express each of the following products as a sum or difference.

**a.** $\sin 8x \sin 3x$ **b.** $\sin 4x \cos x$

**Solution** The product-to-sum formula that we are using is shown in each of the voice balloons.

**a.** $\sin\alpha\sin\beta = \frac{1}{2}[\cos(\alpha-\beta) - \cos(\alpha+\beta)]$

$$\sin 8x\sin 3x = \tfrac{1}{2}\left[\cos(8x-3x) - \cos(8x+3x)\right] = \tfrac{1}{2}(\cos 5x - \cos 11x)$$

**b.** $\sin\alpha\cos\beta = \frac{1}{2}[\sin(\alpha+\beta) + \sin(\alpha-\beta)]$

$$\sin 4x\cos x = \tfrac{1}{2}\left[\sin(4x+x) + \sin(4x-x)\right] = \tfrac{1}{2}(\sin 5x + \sin 3x)$$

**Technology**

The graphs of

$$y = \sin 8x \sin 3x$$

and

$$y = \tfrac{1}{2}(\cos 5x - \cos 11x)$$

are shown in a $\left[-2\pi, 2\pi, \frac{\pi}{2}\right]$ by $[-1, 1, 1]$ viewing rectangle. The graphs coincide. This verifies our algebraic work in Example 1(a).

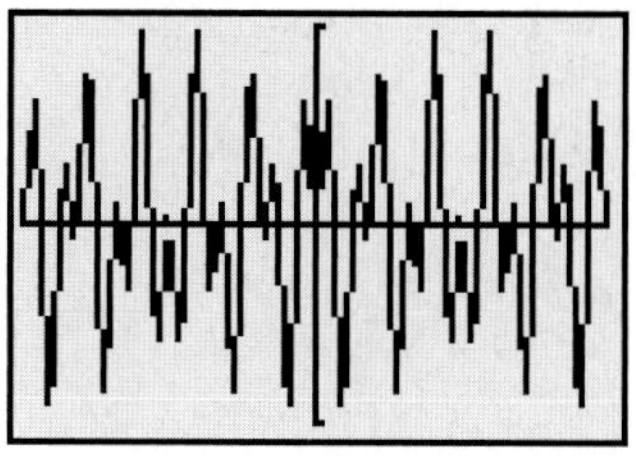

**Check Point 1** Express each of the following products as a sum or difference.

**a.** $\sin 5x \sin 2x$ **b.** $\cos 7x \cos x$

**2** Use the sum-to-product formulas.

## The Sum-to-Product Formulas

How do we write the sum or difference of sines and/or cosines as products? We use the following identities, which are called the **sum-to-product formulas.**

**Sum-to-Product Formulas**

$$\sin\alpha + \sin\beta = 2\sin\frac{\alpha+\beta}{2}\cos\frac{\alpha-\beta}{2}$$

$$\sin\alpha - \sin\beta = 2\sin\frac{\alpha-\beta}{2}\cos\frac{\alpha+\beta}{2}$$

$$\cos\alpha + \cos\beta = 2\cos\frac{\alpha+\beta}{2}\cos\frac{\alpha-\beta}{2}$$

$$\cos\alpha - \cos\beta = -2\sin\frac{\alpha+\beta}{2}\sin\frac{\alpha-\beta}{2}$$

We verify these formulas using the product-to-sum formulas. Let's verify the first sum-to-product formula

$$\sin\alpha + \sin\beta = 2\sin\frac{\alpha+\beta}{2}\cos\frac{\alpha-\beta}{2}.$$

We start with the right side of the formula, the side with the product. We can apply the product-to-sum formula for $\sin\alpha\cos\beta$ to this expression. By doing so, we obtain the left side of the formula, $\sin\alpha + \sin\beta$. Here's how:

$$\sin\alpha\cos\beta = \tfrac{1}{2}[\sin(\alpha+\beta) + \sin(\alpha-\beta)]$$

$$2\sin\frac{\alpha+\beta}{2}\cos\frac{\alpha-\beta}{2} = 2\cdot\frac{1}{2}\left[\sin\left(\frac{\alpha+\beta}{2}+\frac{\alpha-\beta}{2}\right)+\sin\left(\frac{\alpha+\beta}{2}-\frac{\alpha-\beta}{2}\right)\right]$$

$$= \sin\left(\frac{\alpha+\beta+\alpha-\beta}{2}\right) + \sin\left(\frac{\alpha+\beta-\alpha+\beta}{2}\right)$$

$$= \sin\frac{2\alpha}{2} + \sin\frac{2\beta}{2} = \sin\alpha + \sin\beta$$

The three other sum-to-product formulas in the box are verified in a similar manner. Start with the right side and obtain the left side using an appropriate product-to-sum formula.

### EXAMPLE 2 Using the Sum-to-Product Formulas

Express each sum or difference as a product.

**a.** $\sin 9x + \sin 5x$ **b.** $\cos 4x - \cos 3x$

**Solution** The sum-to-product formula that we are using is shown in each of the voice balloons.

**a.** $\sin\alpha + \sin\beta = 2\sin\frac{\alpha+\beta}{2}\cos\frac{\alpha-\beta}{2}$

$$\sin 9x + \sin 5x = 2\sin\frac{9x+5x}{2}\cos\frac{9x-5x}{2}$$
$$= 2\sin\frac{14x}{2}\cos\frac{4x}{2}$$
$$= 2\sin 7x\cos 2x$$

**b.** $\cos\alpha - \cos\beta = -2\sin\frac{\alpha+\beta}{2}\sin\frac{\alpha-\beta}{2}$

$$\cos 4x - \cos 3x = -2\sin\frac{4x+3x}{2}\sin\frac{4x-3x}{2}$$
$$= -2\sin\frac{7x}{2}\sin\frac{x}{2}$$

**Check Point 2**

Express each sum or difference as a product.

**a.** $\sin 7x + \sin 3x$ **b.** $\cos 3x + \cos 2x$

Some identities contain a fraction on one side with sums and differences of sines and/or cosines. Applying the sum-to-product formulas in the numerator and the denominator is often helpful in verifying these identities.

## EXAMPLE 3 Using Sum-to-Product Formulas to Verify an Identity

Verify the identity: $\dfrac{\cos 3x - \cos 5x}{\sin 3x + \sin 5x} = \tan x.$

**Solution** Because the left side is more complicated, we will work with it. We use sum-to-product formulas for the numerator and the denominator of the fraction on this side.

$$\frac{\cos 3x - \cos 5x}{\sin 3x + \sin 5x}$$

$\cos\alpha - \cos\beta = -2\sin\frac{\alpha+\beta}{2}\sin\frac{\alpha-\beta}{2}$

$$= \frac{-2\sin\frac{3x+5x}{2}\sin\frac{3x-5x}{2}}{\sin 3x + \sin 5x}$$

$\sin\alpha + \sin\beta = 2\sin\frac{\alpha+\beta}{2}\cos\frac{\alpha-\beta}{2}$

$$= \frac{-2\sin\frac{3x+5x}{2}\sin\frac{3x-5x}{2}}{2\sin\frac{3x+5x}{2}\cos\frac{3x-5x}{2}}$$

$$= \frac{-2\sin\frac{8x}{2}\sin\left(\frac{-2x}{2}\right)}{2\sin\frac{8x}{2}\cos\left(\frac{-2x}{2}\right)}$$ Perform the indicated additions.

$$= \frac{-2\sin 4x\sin(-x)}{2\sin 4x\cos(-x)}$$ Simplify.

$$= \frac{-(-\sin x)}{\cos x}$$ The sine function is odd: $\sin(-x) = -\sin x$. The cosine function is even: $\cos(-x) = \cos x$.

$$= \frac{\sin x}{\cos x}$$ Simplify.

$$= \tan x$$ Apply a quotient identity: $\tan x = \frac{\sin x}{\cos x}$.

We worked with the left side and arrived at the right side. Thus, the identity is verified.

**Check Point 3** Verify the identity: $\frac{\cos 3x - \cos x}{\sin 3x + \sin x} = -\tan x$.

## Sinusoidal Sounds

Music is all around us. A mere snippet of a song from the past can trigger vivid memories, inducing emotions ranging from unabashed joy to deep sorrow. Trigonometric functions can explain how sound travels from its source and describe its pitch, loudness, and quality. Still unexplained is the remarkable influence music has on the brain, including the deepest question of all: Why do we appreciate music?

When a note is played, it disturbs nearby air molecules, creating regions of higher-than-normal pressure and regions of lower-than-normal pressure. If we graph pressure, $y$, versus time, $t$, we get a sine wave that represents the note. The frequency of the sine wave is the number of high-low disturbances, or vibrations, per second. The greater the frequency, the higher the pitch; the lesser the frequency, the lower the pitch.

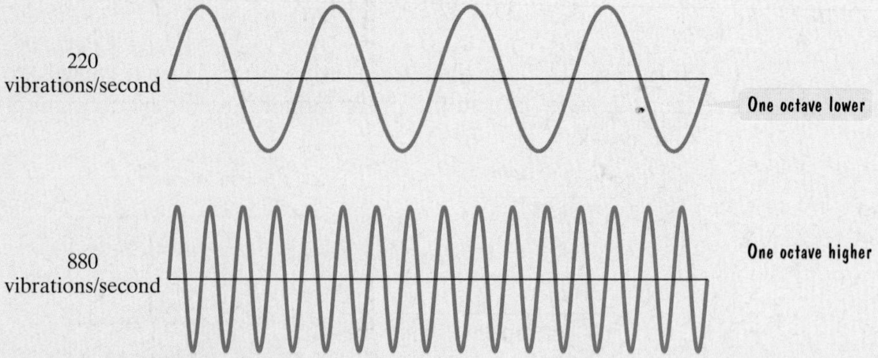


The amplitude of a note's sine wave is related to its loudness. The amplitude for the two sine waves shown is the same. Thus, the notes have the same loudness, although they differ in pitch. The greater the amplitude, the louder the sound; the lesser the amplitude, the softer the sound. The amplitude and frequency are characteristic of every note—and thus of its graph—until the note dissipates.

# EXERCISE SET 6.4

## Practice Exercises

*In Exercises 1–8, express each product as a sum or difference.*

1. $\sin 6x \sin 2x$
2. $\sin 8x \sin 4x$
3. $\cos 7x \cos 3x$
4. $\cos 9x \cos 2x$
5. $\sin x \cos 2x$
6. $\sin 2x \cos 3x$
7. $\cos \frac{3x}{2} \sin \frac{x}{2}$
8. $\cos \frac{5x}{2} \sin \frac{x}{2}$

*In Exercises 9–22, express each sum or difference as a product. If possible, find this product's exact value.*

9. $\sin 6x + \sin 2x$
10. $\sin 8x + \sin 2x$
11. $\sin 7x - \sin 3x$
12. $\sin 11x - \sin 5x$
13. $\cos 4x + \cos 2x$
14. $\cos 9x - \cos 7x$
15. $\sin x + \sin 2x$
16. $\sin x - \sin 2x$
17. $\cos \frac{3x}{2} + \cos \frac{x}{2}$
18. $\sin \frac{3x}{2} + \sin \frac{x}{2}$
19. $\sin 75° + \sin 15°$
20. $\cos 75° - \cos 15°$
21. $\sin \frac{\pi}{12} - \sin \frac{5\pi}{12}$
22. $\cos \frac{\pi}{12} - \cos \frac{5\pi}{12}$

*In Exercises 23–30, verify each identity.*

23. $\frac{\sin 3x - \sin x}{\cos 3x - \cos x} = -\cot 2x$
24. $\frac{\sin x + \sin 3x}{\cos x + \cos 3x} = \tan 2x$
25. $\frac{\sin 2x + \sin 4x}{\cos 2x + \cos 4x} = \tan 3x$
26. $\frac{\cos 4x - \cos 2x}{\sin 2x - \sin 4x} = \tan 3x$
27. $\frac{\sin x - \sin y}{\sin x + \sin y} = \tan \frac{x - y}{2} \cot \frac{x + y}{2}$
28. $\frac{\sin x + \sin y}{\sin x - \sin y} = \tan \frac{x + y}{2} \cot \frac{x - y}{2}$
29. $\frac{\sin x + \sin y}{\cos x + \cos y} = \tan \frac{x + y}{2}$
30. $\frac{\sin x - \sin y}{\cos x - \cos y} = -\cot \frac{x + y}{2}$

*In Exercises 31–34, the graph with the given equation is shown in a $\left[0, 2\pi, \frac{\pi}{2}\right]$ by $[-2, 2, 1]$ viewing rectangle.*

**a.** *Describe the graph using another equation.*

**b.** *Verify that the two equations are equivalent.*

31.
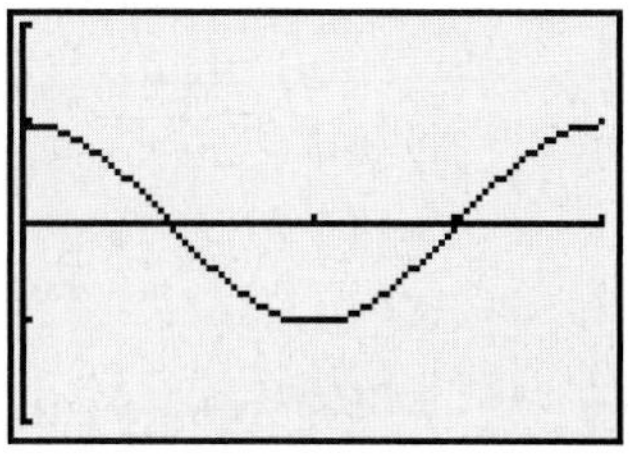

$y = \frac{\sin x + \sin 3x}{2 \sin 2x}$

32.
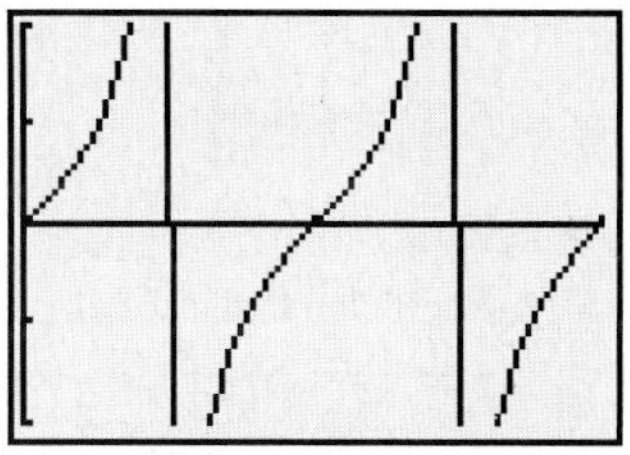

$y = \frac{\cos x - \cos 3x}{\sin x + \sin 3x}$

33.
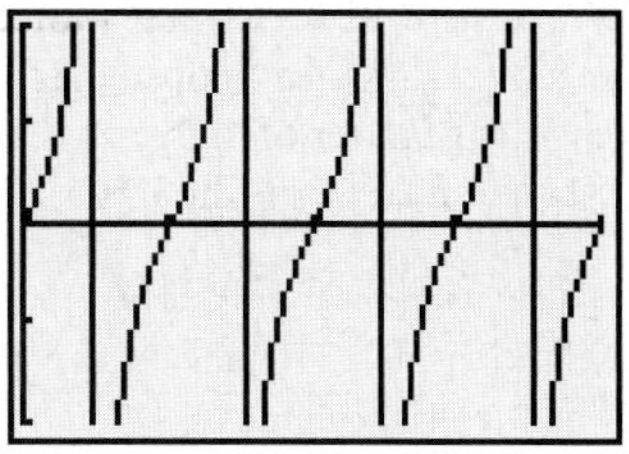

$y = \frac{\cos x - \cos 5x}{\sin x + \sin 5x}$

34.
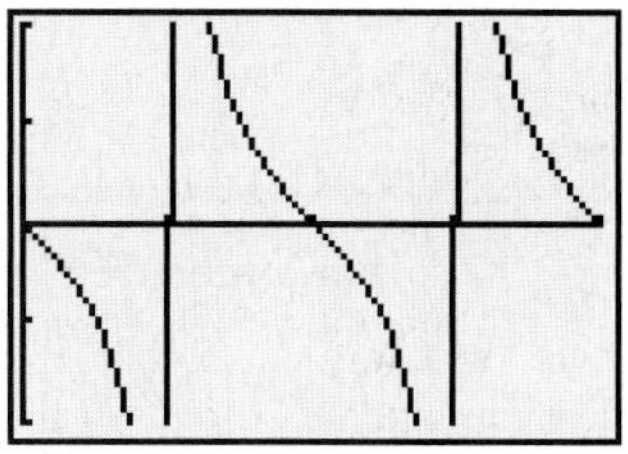

$y = \frac{\cos 5x - \cos 3x}{\sin 5x + \sin 3x}$

## Application Exercises

*Use this information to solve Exercises 35–36. The sound produced by touching each button on a touch-tone phone is described by*

$$y = \sin 2\pi lt + \sin 2\pi ht,$$

*where $l$ and $h$ are the low and high frequencies in the figure shown. For example, what sound is produced by touching 5? The low frequency is $l = 770$ cycles per second and the high frequency is $h = 1336$ cycles per second. The sound produced by touching 5 is described by*

$$y = \sin 2\pi(770)t + \sin 2\pi(1336)t.$$

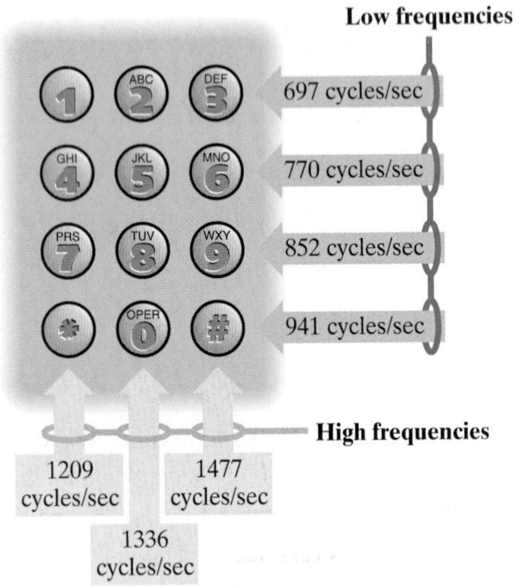


**35.** The touch-tone phone sequence for that most naive of melodies is given as follows.

**Mary Had A Little Lamb**

**3212333,222,399,3212333322321**

**a.** Many numbers do not appear in this sequence, including 7. If you accidently touch 7 for one of the notes, describe this sound as the sum of sines.

**b.** Describe this accidental sound as a product of sines and cosines.

**36.** The touch-tone phone sequence for *Jingle Bells* is given as follows.

**Jingle Bells**

**333,333,39123,666-663333322329,333,333,39123,666-6633,399621**

**a.** The first six notes of the song are produced by repeatedly touching 3. Describe this repeated sound as the sum of sines.

**b.** Describe the repeated sound as a product of sines and cosines.

## Writing in Mathematics

*In Exercises 37–40, use words to describe the given formula.*

**37.** $\sin\alpha\sin\beta = \frac{1}{2}[\cos(\alpha - \beta) - \cos(\alpha + \beta)]$

**38.** $\cos\alpha\cos\beta = \frac{1}{2}[\cos(\alpha - \beta) + \cos(\alpha + \beta)]$

**39.** $\sin\alpha + \sin\beta = 2\sin\frac{\alpha + \beta}{2}\cos\frac{\alpha - \beta}{2}$

**40.** $\cos\alpha + \cos\beta = 2\cos\frac{\alpha + \beta}{2}\cos\frac{\alpha - \beta}{2}$

**41.** Describe identities that can be verified using the sum-to-product formulas.

**42.** Why do the sounds produced by touching each button on a touch-tone phone have the same loudness? Answer the question using the equation described for Exercises 35 and 36, $y = \sin 2\pi lt + \sin 2\pi ht$, and determine the maximum value of $y$ for each sound.

## Technology Exercises

*In Exercises 43–46, graph each side of the equation in the same viewing rectangle. If the graphs appear to coincide, verify that the equation is an identity. If the graphs do not appear to coincide, find a value of $x$ for which both sides are defined but not equal.*

**43.** $\sin x + \sin 2x = \sin 3x$

**44.** $\cos x + \cos 2x = \cos 3x$

**45.** $\sin x + \sin 3x = 2\sin 2x\cos x$

**46.** $\cos x + \cos 3x = 2\cos 2x\cos x$

**47.** In Exercise 35(a), you wrote an equation for the sound produced by touching 7 on a touch-tone phone. Graph the equation in a $[0, 0.01, 0.001]$ by $[-2, 2, 1]$ viewing rectangle.

**48.** In Exercise 36(a), you wrote an equation for the sound produced by touching 3 on a touch-tone phone. Graph the equation in a $[0, 0.01, 0.001]$ by $[-2, 2, 1]$ viewing rectangle.

**49.** In this section, we saw how sums could be expressed as products. Sums of trigonometric functions can also be used to describe functions that are not trigonometric. French mathematician Jean Fourier (1768–1830) showed that *any function* can be described by a series of trigonometric functions. For example, the basic linear function $f(x) = x$ can also be represented by

$$f(x) = 2\left(\frac{\sin x}{1} - \frac{\sin 2x}{2} + \frac{\sin 3x}{3} - \frac{\sin 4x}{4} + \cdots\right).$$

**a.** Graph

$$y = 2\left(\frac{\sin x}{1}\right),$$

$$y = 2\left(\frac{\sin x}{1} - \frac{\sin 2x}{2}\right),$$

$$y = 2\left(\frac{\sin x}{1} - \frac{\sin 2x}{2} + \frac{\sin 3x}{3}\right)$$

and

$$y = 2\left(\frac{\sin x}{1} - \frac{\sin 2x}{2} + \frac{\sin 3x}{3} - \frac{\sin 4x}{4}\right)$$

in a $\left[-\pi, \pi, \frac{\pi}{2}\right]$ by $[-3, 3, 1]$ viewing rectangle. What patterns do you observe?

**b.** Graph

$$y = 2\left(\frac{\sin x}{1} - \frac{\sin 2x}{2} + \frac{\sin 3x}{3} - \frac{\sin 4x}{4} + \frac{\sin 5x}{5} - \frac{\sin 6x}{6} + \frac{\sin 7x}{7} - \frac{\sin 8x}{8} + \frac{\sin 9x}{9} - \frac{\sin 10x}{10}\right)$$

in a $\left[-\pi, \pi, \frac{\pi}{2}\right]$ by $[-3, 3, 1]$ viewing rectangle. Is a portion of the graph beginning to look like the graph of $f(x) = x$? Obtain a better approximation for the line by graphing functions that contain more and more terms involving sines of multiple angles.

**c.** Use

$$x = 2\left(\frac{\sin x}{1} - \frac{\sin 2x}{2} + \frac{\sin 3x}{3} - \frac{\sin 4x}{4} + \cdots\right)$$

and substitute $\frac{\pi}{2}$ for $x$ to obtain a formula for $\frac{\pi}{2}$. Show at least four nonzero terms. Then multiply both sides of your formula by 2 to write a nonending series of subtractions and additions that approaches $\pi$. Use this series to obtain an approximation for $\pi$ that is more accurate than the one given by your graphing utility.

## Critical Thinking Exercises

*Use the identities for $\sin(\alpha + \beta)$ and $\sin(\alpha - \beta)$ to solve Exercises 50–51.*

**50.** Add the left and right sides of the identities and derive the product-to-sum formula for $\sin\alpha\cos\beta$.

**51.** Subtract the left and right sides of the identities and derive the product-to-sum formula for $\cos\alpha\sin\beta$.

*In Exercises 52–53, verify the given sum-to-product formula. Start with the right side and obtain the expression on the left side by using an appropriate product-to-sum formula.*

**52.** $\sin\alpha - \sin\beta = 2\sin\frac{\alpha - \beta}{2}\cos\frac{\alpha + \beta}{2}$

**53.** $\cos\alpha + \cos\beta = 2\cos\frac{\alpha + \beta}{2}\cos\frac{\alpha - \beta}{2}$

*In Exercises 54–55, verify each identity.*

**54.** $\dfrac{\sin 2x + (\sin 3x + \sin x)}{\cos 2x + (\cos 3x + \cos x)} = \tan 2x$

**55.** $4\cos x\cos 2x\sin 3x = \sin 2x + \sin 4x + \sin 6x$

## Group Exercise

**56.** This activity should result in an unusual group display entitled "*Frere Jacques*, a New Perspective." Here is the touch-tone phone sequence.

**Frere Jacques**

**4564,4564,69#,69#,#*#964,#*#964,414,414**

Group members should write every sound in the sequence as both the sum of sines and the product of sines and cosines. Use the sum of sines form and a graphing utility with a $[0, 0.01, 0.001]$ by $[-2, 2, 1]$ viewing rectangle to obtain a graph for every sound. Download these graphs. Use the graphs and equations to create your display in such a way that adults find the trigonometry of this naive melody interesting.

# SECTION 6.5 Trigonometric Equations

## Objectives

1. Find all solutions of a trigonometric equation.
2. Solve equations with multiple angles.
3. Solve trigonometric equations quadratic in form.
4. Use factoring to separate different functions in trigonometric equations.
5. Use identities to solve trigonometric equations.

Exponential functions display the manic energies of uncontrolled growth. By contrast, trigonometric functions repeat their behavior. Do they embody in their regularity some basic rhythm of the universe? The cycles of periodic phenomena provide events that we can comfortably count on. When will the moon look just as it does at this moment? When can I count on 13.5 hours of daylight? When will my breathing be exactly as it is right now? Models with trigonometric functions embrace the periodic rhythms of our world. Equations containing trigonometric functions are used to answer questions about these models.

**1** Find all solutions of a trigonometric equation.

## Trigonometric Equations and Their Solutions

A **trigonometric equation** is an equation that contains a trigonometric expression with a variable, such as $\sin x$. We have seen that some trigonometric equations are identities, such as $\sin^2 x + \cos^2 x = 1$. These equations are true for every value of the variable for which the expressions are defined. In this section, we consider trigonometric equations that are true for only some values of the variable. The values that satisfy the equation are its **solutions**. (There are trigonometric equations that have no solution.)

An example of a trigonometric equation is

$$\sin x = \tfrac{1}{2}.$$

A solution of this equation is $\frac{\pi}{6}$ because $\sin\frac{\pi}{6} = \frac{1}{2}$. By contrast, $\pi$ is not a solution because $\sin \pi = 0 \neq \frac{1}{2}$.

Is $\frac{\pi}{6}$ the only solution of $\sin x = \frac{1}{2}$? The answer is no. Because of the periodic nature of the sine function, there are infinitely many values of $x$ for which $\sin x = \frac{1}{2}$. Figure 6.7 on page 573 shows five of the solutions, including $\frac{\pi}{6}$, for $-\frac{3\pi}{2} \leq x \leq \frac{7\pi}{2}$. Notice that the $x$-coordinates of the points where the graph of $y = \sin x$ intersects the line $y = \frac{1}{2}$ are the solutions of the equation $\sin x = \frac{1}{2}$.

How do we represent all solutions to $\sin x = \frac{1}{2}$? Because the period of the sine function is $2\pi$, first find all solutions in $[0, 2\pi)$. The solutions are

$$x = \frac{\pi}{6} \quad \text{and} \quad x = \pi - \frac{\pi}{6} = \frac{5\pi}{6}.$$

The sine is positive in quadrants I and II.

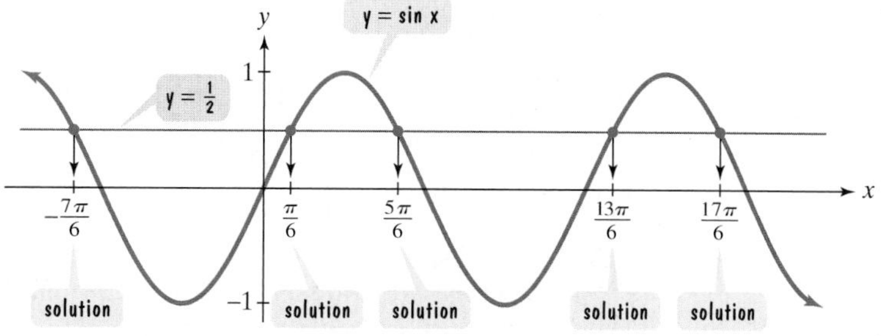


**Figure 6.7** The equation $\sin x = \frac{1}{2}$ has five solutions when $x$ is restricted to the interval $\left[-\frac{3\pi}{2}, \frac{7\pi}{2}\right]$.

Any multiple of $2\pi$ can be added to these values and the sine is still $\frac{1}{2}$. Thus, all solutions of $\sin x = \frac{1}{2}$ are given by

$$x = \frac{\pi}{6} + 2n\pi \quad \text{or} \quad x = \frac{5\pi}{6} + 2n\pi$$

where $n$ is any integer. By choosing any two integers, such as $n = 0$ and $n = 1$, we can find some solutions of $\sin x = \frac{1}{2}$. Thus, four of the solutions are

Let $n = 0$.

$$x = \frac{\pi}{6} + 2 \cdot 0\pi = \frac{\pi}{6} \qquad x = \frac{5\pi}{6} + 2 \cdot 0\pi = \frac{5\pi}{6}$$

Let $n = 1$.

$$x = \frac{\pi}{6} + 2 \cdot 1\pi = \frac{\pi}{6} + 2\pi = \frac{\pi}{6} + \frac{12\pi}{6} = \frac{13\pi}{6} \qquad x = \frac{5\pi}{6} + 2 \cdot 1\pi = \frac{5\pi}{6} + 2\pi = \frac{5\pi}{6} + \frac{12\pi}{6} = \frac{17\pi}{6}$$

These four solutions are shown among the five solutions in Figure 6.7.

## Equations Involving a Single Trigonometric Function

To solve an equation containing a single trigonometric function:

- Isolate the function on one side of the equation.
- Solve for the variable.

## EXAMPLE 1 Finding All Solutions of a Trigonometric Equation

Solve the equation: $3 \sin x - 2 = 5 \sin x - 1$.

**Solution** The equation contains a single trigonometric function, $\sin x$.

**Step 1 Isolate the function on one side of the equation.** We can solve for $\sin x$ by collecting all terms with $\sin x$ on the left side, and all the constant terms on the right side.

| | |
|---|---|
| $3 \sin x - 2 = 5 \sin x - 1$ | This is the given equation. |
| $3 \sin x - 5 \sin x - 2 = 5 \sin x - 5 \sin x - 1$ | Subtract $5 \sin x$ from both sides. |
| $-2 \sin x - 2 = -1$ | Simplify. |
| $-2 \sin x = 1$ | Add 2 to both sides. |
| $\sin x = -\frac{1}{2}$ | Divide both sides by $-2$ and solve for $\sin x$. |

### Urban Canyons

A city's tall buildings and narrow streets reduce the amount of sunlight. If $h$ is the average height of the buildings and $w$ is the width of the street, the angle of elevation from the street to the top of the buildings is given by the trigonometric equation

$$\tan \theta = \frac{h}{w}.$$

A value of $\theta = 63°$ can result in an 85% loss of illumination.

**Step 2 Solve for the variable.** Because $\sin\frac{\pi}{6} = \frac{1}{2}$, the solutions of $\sin x = -\frac{1}{2}$ in $[0, 2\pi)$ are

$$x = \pi + \frac{\pi}{6} = \frac{6\pi}{6} + \frac{\pi}{6} = \frac{7\pi}{6} \qquad x = 2\pi - \frac{\pi}{6} = \frac{12\pi}{6} - \frac{\pi}{6} = \frac{11\pi}{6}.$$

The sine is negative in quadrant III.

The sine is negative in quadrant IV.

Because the period of the sine function is $2\pi$, the solutions of the equation are given by

$$x = \frac{7\pi}{6} + 2n\pi \quad \text{and} \quad x = \frac{11\pi}{6} + 2n\pi$$

where $n$ is any integer.

**Check Point 1** Solve the equation: $5\sin x = 3\sin x + \sqrt{3}$.

Now we will concentrate on finding solutions of trigonometric equations for $0 \le x < 2\pi$. You can use a graphing utility to check the solutions of these equations. Graph the left side and graph the right side. The solutions are the $x$-coordinates of the points where the graphs intersect.

**2** Solve equations with multiple angles.

## Equations Involving Multiple Angles

Here are examples of two equations that include multiple angles.

$$\tan 3x = 1 \qquad \sin\frac{x}{2} = \frac{\sqrt{3}}{2}$$

This angle is a multiple of 3.

This angle is a multiple of $\frac{1}{2}$.

We will solve each equation for $0 \le x < 2\pi$. The period of the function plays an important role in ensuring that we do not leave out any solutions.

## EXAMPLE 2 Solving an Equation with a Multiple Angle

Solve the equation: $\tan 3x = 1, \quad 0 \le x < 2\pi$.

**Solution** The period of the tangent function is $\pi$. In the interval $[0, \pi)$, the only value for which the tangent function is 1 is $\frac{\pi}{4}$. This means that $3x = \frac{\pi}{4}$. Because the period is $\pi$, all the solutions to $\tan 3x = 1$ are given by

$$3x = \frac{\pi}{4} + n\pi \qquad \text{$n$ is any integer.}$$

$$x = \frac{\pi}{12} + \frac{n\pi}{3} \qquad \text{Divide both sides by 3 and solve for x.}$$

**Technology**

Shown below are the graphs of

$$y = \tan 3x$$

and

$$y = 1$$

in a $\left[0, 2\pi, \frac{\pi}{2}\right]$ by $[-3, 3, 1]$ viewing rectangle. The solutions of

$$\tan 3x = 1$$

in $[0, 2\pi)$ are shown by the $x$-coordinates of the six intersection points.

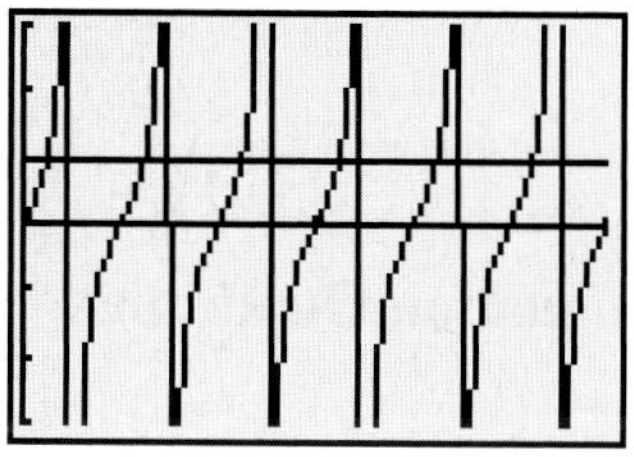

In the interval $[0, 2\pi)$, we obtain the solutions of $\tan 3x = 1$ as follows:

| Let $n = 0$. | Let $n = 1$. | Let $n = 2$. |
|---|---|---|
| $x = \frac{\pi}{12} + \frac{0\pi}{3} = \frac{\pi}{12}$ | $x = \frac{\pi}{12} + \frac{1\pi}{3} = \frac{\pi}{12} + \frac{4\pi}{12} = \frac{5\pi}{12}$ | $x = \frac{\pi}{12} + \frac{2\pi}{3} = \frac{\pi}{12} + \frac{8\pi}{12} = \frac{9\pi}{12} = \frac{3\pi}{4}$ |
| Let $n = 3$. | Let $n = 4$. | Let $n = 5$. |
| $x = \frac{\pi}{12} + \frac{3\pi}{3} = \frac{\pi}{12} + \frac{12\pi}{12} = \frac{13\pi}{12}$ | $x = \frac{\pi}{12} + \frac{4\pi}{3} = \frac{\pi}{12} + \frac{16\pi}{12} = \frac{17\pi}{12}$ | $x = \frac{\pi}{12} + \frac{5\pi}{3} = \frac{\pi}{12} + \frac{20\pi}{12} = \frac{21\pi}{12} = \frac{7\pi}{4}$ |

If you let $n = 6$, you will obtain $x = \frac{29\pi}{12}$. This value exceeds $2\pi$. In the interval $[0, 2\pi)$, the solutions of $\tan 3x = 1$ are $\frac{\pi}{12}, \frac{5\pi}{12}, \frac{3\pi}{4}, \frac{13\pi}{12}, \frac{17\pi}{12}$, and $\frac{7\pi}{4}$. These solutions are illustrated by the six intersection points in the technology box.

**Check Point 2** Solve the equation: $\tan 2x = \sqrt{3}, 0 \le x < 2\pi$.

## EXAMPLE 3 Solving an Equation with a Multiple Angle

Solve the equation: $\sin \frac{x}{2} = \frac{\sqrt{3}}{2}, \quad 0 \le x < 2\pi$.

**Solution** The period of the sine function is $2\pi$. In the interval $[0, 2\pi)$, there are two values at which the sine function is $\frac{\sqrt{3}}{2}$. One of these values is $\frac{\pi}{3}$. The sine is positive in quadrant II; thus, the other value is $\pi - \frac{\pi}{3}$, or $\frac{2\pi}{3}$. This means that $\frac{x}{2} = \frac{\pi}{3}$ or $\frac{x}{2} = \frac{2\pi}{3}$. Because the period is $2\pi$, all the solutions to $\sin \frac{x}{2} = \frac{\sqrt{3}}{2}$ are given by

$$\frac{x}{2} = \frac{\pi}{3} + 2n\pi \quad \text{or} \quad \frac{x}{2} = \frac{2\pi}{3} + 2n\pi. \quad n \text{ is any integer.}$$

$$x = \frac{2\pi}{3} + 4n\pi \qquad x = \frac{4\pi}{3} + 4n\pi. \quad \text{Multiply both sides by 2 and solve for } x.$$

If $n = 0$, we obtain $x = \frac{2\pi}{3}$ from the equation on the left and $x = \frac{4\pi}{3}$ from the equation on the right. If we let $n = 1$, we are adding $4 \cdot 1 \cdot \pi$, or $4\pi$, to each of these expressions. These values of $x$ exceed $2\pi$. Thus, in the interval $[0, 2\pi)$, the only solutions of $\sin \frac{x}{2} = \frac{\sqrt{3}}{2}$ are $\frac{2\pi}{3}$ and $\frac{4\pi}{3}$.

**Check Point 3** Solve the equation: $\sin\frac{x}{3} = \frac{1}{2}, 0 \le x < 2\pi.$

**3** Solve trigonometric equations quadratic in form.

## Trigonometric Equations Quadratic in Form

Some trigonometric equations are in the form of a quadratic equation $at^2 + bt + c = 0$, where $t$ is a trigonometric function. Here are two examples of trigonometric equations that are quadratic in form.

$$2\cos^2 x + \cos x - 1 = 0 \qquad 2\sin^2 x - 3\sin x + 1 = 0$$

The form of this equation is $2t^2 + t - 1 = 0$ with $t = \cos x$.

The form of this equation is $2t^2 - 3t + 1 = 0$ with $t = \sin x$.

To solve this kind of equation, try using factoring. If the trigonometric expression does not factor, use the quadratic formula.

### EXAMPLE 4 Solving a Trigonometric Equation Quadratic in Form

Solve the equation: $2\cos^2 x + \cos x - 1 = 0, \quad 0 \le x < 2\pi.$

**Solution** The given equation is in quadratic form $2t^2 + t - 1 = 0$ with $t = \cos x$. Let us attempt to solve the equation using factoring.

$$2\cos^2 x + \cos x - 1 = 0$$ This is the given equation.

$$(2\cos x - 1)(\cos x + 1) = 0$$ Factor. Notice that $2t^2 + t - 1$ factors as $(2t - 1)(t + 1)$.

$$2\cos x - 1 = 0 \quad \text{or} \quad \cos x + 1 = 0$$ Set each factor equal to 0.

$$2\cos x = 1 \qquad \cos x = -1$$ Solve for $\cos x$.

$$\cos x = \tfrac{1}{2}$$

$$x = \frac{\pi}{3} \qquad x = 2\pi - \frac{\pi}{3} = \frac{5\pi}{3} \qquad x = \pi$$ Solve each equation for $x$, $0 \le x < 2\pi$.

The cosine is positive in quadrants I and IV.

The solutions in the interval $[0, 2\pi)$ are $\frac{\pi}{3}$, $\pi$, and $\frac{5\pi}{3}$.

#### Technology

The graph of

$$y = 2\cos^2 x + \cos x - 1$$

is shown in a

$$\left[0, 2\pi, \frac{\pi}{2}\right] \text{ by } [-3, 3, 1]$$

viewing rectangle. The $x$-intercepts,

$$\frac{\pi}{3}, \pi, \text{ and } \frac{5\pi}{3},$$

verify the three solutions of

$$2\cos^2 x + \cos x - 1 = 0$$

in $[0, 2\pi)$.

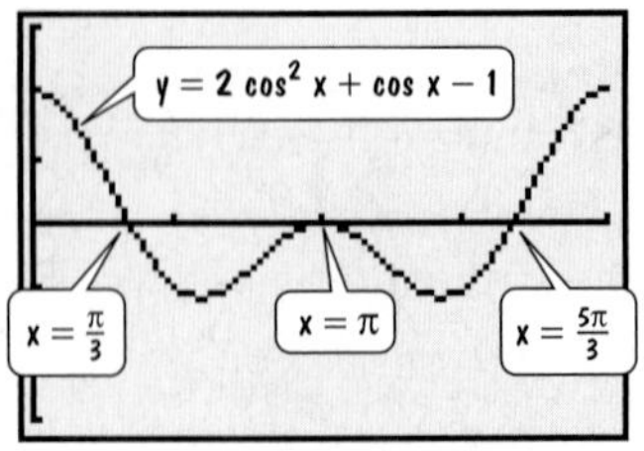


**Check Point 4** Solve the equation: $2\sin^2 x - 3\sin x + 1 = 0, 0 \le x < 2\pi.$

4 Use factoring to separate different functions in trigonometric equations.

## Using Factoring to Separate Two Different Trigonometric Functions in an Equation

We have seen that factoring is used to solve some trigonometric equations that are quadratic in form. Factoring can also be used to solve some trigonometric equations that contain two different functions such as

$$\tan x \sin^2 x = 3 \tan x.$$

In such a case, move all terms to one side and obtain zero on the other side. Then try to use factoring to separate the different functions. Example 5 shows how this is done.

### Study Tip

In solving

$$\tan x \sin^2 x = 3 \tan x,$$

do not begin by dividing both sides by $\tan x$. Division by zero is undefined. If you divide by $\tan x$, you lose the two solutions for which $\tan x = 0$, namely 0 and $\pi$.

### EXAMPLE 5 Using Factoring to Separate Different Functions

Solve the equation: $\tan x \sin^2 x = 3 \tan x, \quad 0 \le x < 2\pi$.

**Solution**

**Move all terms to one side and obtain zero on the other side.**

$$\tan x \sin^2 x = 3 \tan x \quad \text{This is the given equation.}$$

$$\tan x \sin^2 x - 3 \tan x = 0 \quad \text{Subtract } 3 \tan x \text{ from both sides.}$$

**Use factoring to separate the two functions.**

$$\tan x(\sin^2 x - 3) = 0 \quad \text{Factor out } \tan x \text{ from the two terms on the left side.}$$

$$\tan x = 0 \quad \text{or} \quad \sin^2 x - 3 = 0 \quad \text{Set each factor equal to 0.}$$

$$x = 0 \quad x = \pi \qquad \sin^2 x = 3 \quad \text{Solve for } x.$$

$$\sin x = \pm\sqrt{3}$$

This equation has no solution because sin x cannot be greater than 1 or less than −1.

The solutions in the interval $[0, 2\pi)$ are 0 and $\pi$.

**Check Point 5** Solve the equation: $\sin x \tan x = \sin x, \ 0 \le x < 2\pi$.

5 Use identities to solve trigonometric equations.

## Using Identities to Solve Trigonometric Equations

Some trigonometric equations contain more than one function on the same side and these functions cannot be separated by factoring. For example, consider the equation

$$2 \sin^2 x - \cos x - 1 = 0.$$

How can we obtain an equivalent equation that has only one trigonometric function? We use the identity $\sin^2 x + \cos^2 x = 1$ and substitute $1 - \cos^2 x$ for $\sin^2 x$.

$$2 \sin^2 x - \cos x - 1 = 0 \quad \text{This is the given equation.}$$

$$2(1 - \cos^2 x) - \cos x - 1 = 0 \quad \sin^2 x = 1 - \cos^2 x$$

$$2 - 2\cos^2 x - \cos x - 1 = 0 \quad \text{Use the distributive property.}$$

$$-2\cos^2 x - \cos x + 1 = 0 \quad \text{Combine like terms.}$$

Multiplying both sides of the equation by −1, we obtain

$$2\cos^2 x + \cos x - 1 = 0.$$

This equivalent equation contains only the cosine function. This is the equation that we solved in Example 4.

## EXAMPLE 6 Using an Identity to Solve a Trigonometric Equation

Solve the equation: $\cos 2x + 3\sin x - 2 = 0, 0 \leq x < 2\pi$.

**Solution** The given equation contains a cosine function and a sine function. The cosine is a function of $2x$ and the sine is a function of $x$. We want one trigonometric function of the same angle. This can be accomplished by using the double-angle identity $\cos 2x = 1 - 2\sin^2 x$ to obtain an equivalent equation involving $\sin x$ only.

$$\cos 2x + 3\sin x - 2 = 0 \quad \text{This is the given equation.}$$

$$1 - 2\sin^2 x + 3\sin x - 2 = 0 \quad \cos 2x = 1 - 2\sin^2 x$$

$$-2\sin^2 x + 3\sin x - 1 = 0 \quad \text{Combine like terms.}$$

$$2\sin^2 x - 3\sin x + 1 = 0 \quad \text{Multiply both sides by } -1.$$

The equation is now in quadratic form $2t^2 - 3t + 1 = 0$ with $t = \sin x$. We solve using factoring.

$$(2\sin x - 1)(\sin x - 1) = 0 \quad \text{Factor. Notice that } 2t^2 - 3t + 1 \text{ factors as } (2t - 1)(t - 1).$$

$$2\sin x - 1 = 0 \quad \text{or} \quad \sin x - 1 = 0 \quad \text{Set each factor equal to 0.}$$

$$\sin x = \tfrac{1}{2} \qquad \sin x = 1 \quad \text{Solve for } \sin x.$$

$$x = \frac{\pi}{6} \quad x = \pi - \frac{\pi}{6} = \frac{5\pi}{6} \qquad x = \frac{\pi}{2} \quad \text{Solve each equation for } x, 0 \leq x < 2\pi.$$

The solutions in the interval $[0, 2\pi)$ are $\frac{\pi}{6}, \frac{\pi}{2}$, and $\frac{5\pi}{6}$.

**Check Point 6** Solve the equation: $\cos 2x + \sin x = 0,\ 0 \leq x < 2\pi$.

Sometimes it is necessary to do something to both sides of a trigonometric equation to substitute an identity. For example, consider the equation

$$\sin x \cos x = \tfrac{1}{2}.$$

This equation contains both a sine and a cosine function. How can we obtain a single function? Multiply both sides by 2. In this way, we can use the double-angle identity $\sin 2x = 2\sin x \cos x$ and obtain $\sin 2x$, a single function, on the left side.

## EXAMPLE 7 Using an Identity to Solve a Trigonometric Equation

Solve the equation: $\sin x \cos x = \frac{1}{2}, 0 \le x < 2\pi$.

**Solution**

$$\sin x \cos x = \tfrac{1}{2} \quad \text{This is the given equation.}$$

$$2 \sin x \cos x = 1 \quad \text{Multiply both sides by 2 in anticipation of using } \sin 2x = 2 \sin x \cos x.$$

$$\sin 2x = 1 \quad \text{Use a double-angle identity.}$$

Notice that we have an equation with $2x$, a multiple angle. The period of the sine function is $2\pi$. In the interval $[0, 2\pi)$, the only value for which the sine function is 1 is $\frac{\pi}{2}$. This means that $2x = \frac{\pi}{2}$. Because the period is $2\pi$, all the solutions to $\sin 2x = 1$ are given by

$$2x = \frac{\pi}{2} + 2n\pi \quad n \text{ is any integer.}$$

$$x = \frac{\pi}{4} + n\pi \quad \text{Divide both sides by 2 and solve for } x.$$

The solutions in the interval $[0, 2\pi)$ are obtained by letting $n = 0$ and $n = 1$. The solutions are $\frac{\pi}{4}$ and $\frac{5\pi}{4}$.

### Technology

Shown below are the graphs of

$$y = \sin x \cos x$$

and

$$y = \tfrac{1}{2}$$

in a $\left[0, 2\pi, \frac{\pi}{2}\right]$ by $[-1, 1, 1]$ viewing rectangle. The solutions of

$$\sin x \cos x = \tfrac{1}{2}$$

are shown by the $x$-coordinates of the two intersection points.

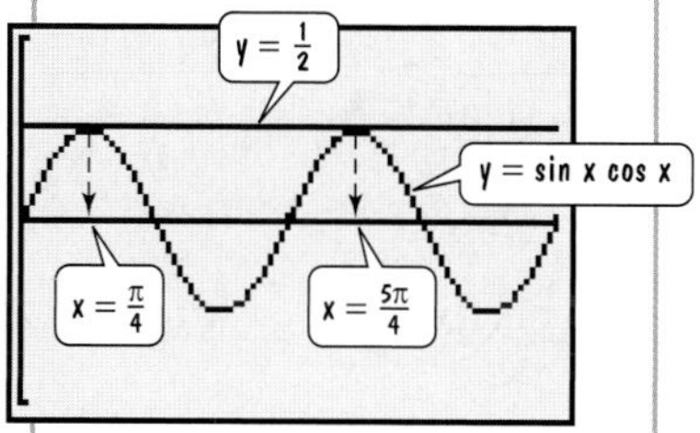


**Check Point 7** Solve the equation: $\sin x \cos x = -\frac{1}{2}, \ 0 \le x < 2\pi$.

Let's look at another equation that contains two different functions, $\sin x - \cos x = 1$. Can you think of an identity that can be used to produce only one function? Perhaps $\sin^2 x + \cos^2 x = 1$ might be helpful. The next example shows how we use this identity by squaring both sides of the given equation. Remember that if we raise both sides of an equation to an even power, we have the possibility of introducing extraneous solutions. Thus, we must check each proposed solution in the given equation. Alternatively, we can use a graphing utility to verify actual solutions.

## EXAMPLE 8 Using an Identity to Solve a Trigonometric Equation

Solve the equation: $\sin x - \cos x = 1, 0 \le x < 2\pi$.

**Solution** We square both sides of the equation in anticipation of using $\sin^2 x + \cos^2 x = 1$.

$$\sin x - \cos x = 1 \quad \text{This is the given equation.}$$

$$(\sin x - \cos x)^2 = 1^2 \quad \text{Square both sides.}$$

$$\sin^2 x - 2 \sin x \cos x + \cos^2 x = 1 \quad \text{Square the left side using } (A - B)^2 = A^2 - 2AB + B^2.$$

## Technology

A graphing utility can be used instead of the algebraic check on the right. Shown are the graphs of

$$y = \sin x - \cos x$$

and

$$y = 1$$

in a $\left[0, 2\pi, \frac{\pi}{2}\right]$ by $[-2, 2, 1]$ viewing rectangle. The actual solutions of

$$\sin x - \cos x = 1$$

are shown by the $x$-coordinates of the two intersection points, $\frac{\pi}{2}$ and $\pi$.

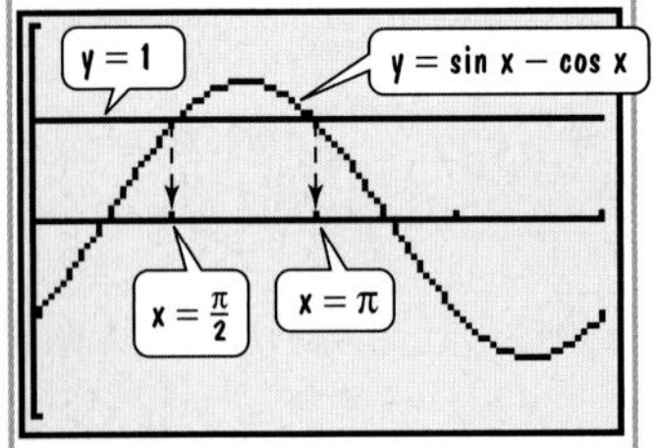


$$\sin^2 x + \cos^2 x - 2\sin x\cos x = 1 \quad \text{Rearrange terms.}$$

$$1 - 2\sin x\cos x = 1 \quad \text{Apply a Pythagorean identity: } \sin^2 x + \cos^2 x = 1.$$

$$-2\sin x\cos x = 0 \quad \text{Subtract 1 from both sides of the equation.}$$

$$\sin x\cos x = 0 \quad \text{Divide both sides of the equation by } -2.$$

$$\sin x = 0 \quad \text{or} \quad \cos x = 0 \quad \text{Set each factor equal to 0.}$$

$$x = 0 \quad x = \pi \quad x = \frac{\pi}{2} \quad x = \frac{3\pi}{2} \quad \text{Solve for } x \text{ in } [0, 2\pi).$$

We check these proposed solutions to see if any are extraneous.

**Check 0:**

$$\sin x - \cos x = 1$$
$$\sin 0 - \cos 0 \stackrel{?}{=} 1$$
$$0 - 1 \stackrel{?}{=} 1$$
$$-1 = 1 \text{ False}$$

**Check $\frac{\pi}{2}$:**

$$\sin x - \cos x = 1$$
$$\sin\frac{\pi}{2} - \cos\frac{\pi}{2} \stackrel{?}{=} 1$$
$$1 - 0 \stackrel{?}{=} 1$$
$$1 = 1 \text{ True}$$

**Check $\pi$:**

$$\sin x - \cos x = 1$$
$$\sin\pi - \cos\pi \stackrel{?}{=} 1$$
$$0 - (-1) \stackrel{?}{=} 1$$
$$1 = 1 \text{ True}$$

**Check $\frac{3\pi}{2}$:**

$$\sin x - \cos x = 1$$
$$\sin\frac{3\pi}{2} - \cos\frac{3\pi}{2} \stackrel{?}{=} 1$$
$$(-1) - 0 \stackrel{?}{=} 1$$
$$-1 = 1 \text{ False}$$

0 and $\frac{3\pi}{2}$ are extraneous.

The actual solutions in the interval $[0, 2\pi)$ are $\frac{\pi}{2}$ and $\pi$.

**Check Point 8** Solve the equation: $\cos x - \sin x = -1,\ 0 \le x < 2\pi$.

# EXERCISE SET 6.5

## Practice Exercises

*In Exercises 1–10, use substitution to determine whether the given x-value is a solution of the equation.*

1. $\cos x = \frac{\sqrt{2}}{2}, \quad x = \frac{\pi}{4}$
2. $\tan x = \sqrt{3}, \quad x = \frac{\pi}{3}$
3. $\sin x = \frac{\sqrt{3}}{2}, \quad x = \frac{\pi}{6}$
4. $\sin x = \frac{\sqrt{2}}{2}, \quad x = \frac{\pi}{3}$
5. $\cos x = -\frac{1}{2}, \quad x = \frac{2\pi}{3}$
6. $\cos x = -\frac{1}{2}, \quad x = \frac{4\pi}{3}$
7. $\tan 2x = -\frac{\sqrt{3}}{3}, \quad x = \frac{5\pi}{12}$
8. $\cos\frac{2x}{3} = -\frac{1}{2}, \quad x = \pi$
9. $\cos x = \sin 2x, x = \frac{\pi}{3}$
10. $\cos x + 2 = \sqrt{3}\sin x, \quad x = \frac{\pi}{6}$

*In Exercises 11–24, find all solutions of each equation.*

11. $\sin x = \frac{\sqrt{3}}{2}$
12. $\cos x = \frac{\sqrt{3}}{2}$
13. $\tan x = 1$
14. $\tan x = \sqrt{3}$
15. $\cos x = -\frac{1}{2}$
16. $\sin x = -\frac{\sqrt{2}}{2}$
17. $\tan x = 0$
18. $\sin x = 0$
19. $2\cos x + \sqrt{3} = 0$
20. $2\sin x + \sqrt{3} = 0$
21. $4\sin\theta - 1 = 2\sin\theta$
22. $5\sin\theta + 1 = 3\sin\theta$
23. $3\sin\theta + 5 = -2\sin\theta$
24. $7\cos\theta + 9 = -2\cos\theta$

*Exercises 25–38 involve equations with multiple angles. Solve each equation on the interval $[0, 2\pi)$.*

**25.** $\sin 2x = \frac{\sqrt{3}}{2}$ **26.** $\cos 2x = \frac{\sqrt{2}}{2}$

**27.** $\cos 4x = -\frac{\sqrt{3}}{2}$ **28.** $\sin 4x = -\frac{\sqrt{2}}{2}$

**29.** $\tan 3x = \frac{\sqrt{3}}{3}$ **30.** $\tan 3x = \sqrt{3}$

**31.** $\tan \frac{x}{2} = \sqrt{3}$ **32.** $\tan \frac{x}{2} = \frac{\sqrt{3}}{3}$

**33.** $\sin \frac{2\theta}{3} = -1$ **34.** $\cos \frac{2\theta}{3} = -1$

**35.** $\sec \frac{3\theta}{2} = -2$ **36.** $\cot \frac{3\theta}{2} = -\sqrt{3}$

**37.** $\sin\left(2x + \frac{\pi}{6}\right) = \frac{1}{2}$ **38.** $\sin\left(2x - \frac{\pi}{4}\right) = \frac{\sqrt{2}}{2}$

*Exercises 39–46 involve trigonometric equations quadratic in form. Solve each equation on the interval $[0, 2\pi)$.*

**39.** $2\sin^2 x - \sin x - 1 = 0$

**40.** $2\sin^2 x + \sin x - 1 = 0$

**41.** $2\cos^2 x + 3\cos x + 1 = 0$

**42.** $\cos^2 x + 2\cos x - 3 = 0$

**43.** $2\sin^2 x = \sin x + 3$ **44.** $2\sin^2 x = 4\sin x + 6$

**45.** $\sin^2\theta - 1 = 0$ **46.** $\cos^2\theta - 1 = 0$

*In Exercises 47–56, solve each equation on the interval $[0, 2\pi)$.*

**47.** $(\tan x - 1)(\cos x + 1) = 0$

**48.** $(\tan x + 1)(\sin x - 1) = 0$

**49.** $(2\cos x + \sqrt{3})(2\sin x + 1) = 0$

**50.** $(2\cos x - \sqrt{3})(2\sin x - 1) = 0$

**51.** $\cot x(\tan x - 1) = 0$ **52.** $\cot x(\tan x + 1) = 0$

**53.** $\sin x + 2\sin x\cos x = 0$ **54.** $\cos x - 2\sin x\cos x = 0$

**55.** $\tan^2 x\cos x = \tan^2 x$ **56.** $\cot^2 x\sin x = \cot^2 x$

*In Exercises 57–78, use an identity to solve each equation on the interval $[0, 2\pi)$.*

**57.** $2\cos^2 x + \sin x - 1 = 0$

**58.** $2\cos^2 x - \sin x - 1 = 0$

**59.** $\sin^2 x - 2\cos x - 2 = 0$

**60.** $4\sin^2 x + 4\cos x - 5 = 0$

**61.** $4\cos^2 x = 5 - 4\sin x$ **62.** $3\cos^2 x = \sin^2 x$

**63.** $\sin 2x = \cos x$ **64.** $\sin 2x = \sin x$

**65.** $\cos 2x = \cos x$ **66.** $\cos 2x = \sin x$

**67.** $\cos 2x + 5\cos x + 3 = 0$

**68.** $\cos 2x + \cos x + 1 = 0$

**69.** $\sin x\cos x = \frac{\sqrt{2}}{4}$ **70.** $\sin x\cos x = \frac{\sqrt{3}}{4}$

**71.** $\sin x + \cos x = 1$ **72.** $\sin x + \cos x = -1$

**73.** $\sin\left(x + \frac{\pi}{4}\right) + \sin\left(x - \frac{\pi}{4}\right) = 1$

**74.** $\sin\left(x + \frac{\pi}{3}\right) + \sin\left(x - \frac{\pi}{3}\right) = 1$

**75.** $\sin 2x\cos x + \cos 2x\sin x = \frac{\sqrt{2}}{2}$

**76.** $\sin 3x\cos 2x + \cos 3x\sin 2x = 1$

**77.** $\tan x + \sec x = 1$ **78.** $\tan x - \sec x = 1$

## Application Exercises

*Use this information to solve Exercises 79–80. Our cycle of normal breathing takes place every 5 seconds. Velocity of air flow, y, measured in liters per second, after x seconds is modeled by*

$$y = 0.6 \sin \frac{2\pi}{5} x.$$

*Velocity of air flow is positive when we inhale and negative when we exhale.*

**79.** Within each breathing cycle, when are we inhaling at 0.3 liter per second? Round to the nearest tenth of a second.

**80.** Within each breathing cycle, when are we exhaling at 0.3 liter per second? Round to the nearest tenth of a second.

*Use this information to solve Exercises 81–82. The number of hours of daylight in Boston is given by*

$$y = 3 \sin\left[\frac{2\pi}{365}(x - 79)\right] + 12$$

*where x is the number of days after January 1.*

**81.** How many days after January 1 does Boston have 10.5 hours of daylight? Round to the nearest day.

**82.** How many days after January 1 does Boston have 13.5 hours of daylight? Round to the nearest day.

*Use this information to solve Exercises 83–84. A ball on a spring is pulled 4 inches below its rest position and then released. After t seconds, the ball's distance from its rest position is given by*

$$d = -4 \cos \frac{\pi}{3} t.$$

**83.** Find all values of $t$ for which the ball is 2 inches above its rest position.

**84.** Find all values of $t$ for which the ball is 2 inches below its rest position.

*Use this information to solve Exercises 85–86. When throwing an object, the distance achieved depends on initial velocity, $v_o$, and the angle above the horizontal at which the* *object is thrown, $\theta$. The distance, d, in feet, that describes the range covered is given by*

$$d = \frac{v_o^2}{16}\sin\theta\cos\theta,$$

*where $v_o$ is measured in feet per second.*

**85.** You and your friend are throwing a baseball back and forth. If you throw the ball with an initial velocity of $v_o = 90$ feet per second, at what angle of elevation, $\theta$, should you direct your throw so that it can be easily caught by your friend located 170 feet away?

**86.** In Exercise 85, you increase the distance between you and your friend to 200 feet. With this increase, at what angle of elevation, $\theta$, should you direct your throw?

## Writing in Mathematics

**87.** What are the solutions of a trigonometric equation?

**88.** Describe the difference between verifying a trigonometric identity and solving a trigonometric equation.

**89.** Without actually solving the equation, describe how to solve

$$3\tan x - 2 = 5\tan x - 1.$$

**90.** In the interval $[0, 2\pi)$, the solutions of $\sin x = \cos 2x$ are $\frac{\pi}{6}, \frac{5\pi}{6}$, and $\frac{3\pi}{2}$. Explain how to use graphs generated by a graphing utility to check these solutions.

**91.** Suppose you are solving equations in the interval $[0, 2\pi)$. Without actually solving equations, what is the difference between the number of solutions of $\sin x = \frac{1}{2}$ and $\sin 2x = \frac{1}{2}$? How do you account for this difference?

*In Exercises 92–93, describe a general strategy for solving each equation. Do not solve the equation.*

**92.** $2\sin^2 x + 5\sin x + 3 = 0$

**93.** $\sin 2x = \sin x$

**94.** Describe a natural periodic phenomenon. Give an example of a question that can be answered by a trigonometric equation in the study of this phenomenon.

**95.** Some people experience depression with loss of sunlight. Use the essay on page 573 to determine whether such a person should live on a city street that is 80 feet wide with buildings whose height averages 400 feet. Explain your answer and include $\theta$, to the nearest degree, in your argument.

**96.** Use a graphing utility to verify the solutions of any five equations that you solved in Exercises 57–78.

## Technology Exercises

*In Exercises 97–101, use a graphing utility to approximate the solutions of each equation in the interval $[0, 2\pi)$. Round to the nearest hundredth of a radian.*

**97.** $15\cos^2 x + 7\cos x - 2 = 0$

**98.** $\cos x = x$

**99.** $2\sin^2 x = 1 - 2\sin x$

**100.** $\sin 2x = 2 - x^2$

**101.** $\sin x + \sin 2x + \sin 3x = 0$

## Critical Thinking Exercises

**102.** Which one of the following is true?

**a.** The equation $(\sin x - 3)(\cos x + 2) = 0$ has no solution.

**b.** The equation $\tan x = \frac{\pi}{2}$ has no solution.

**c.** A trigonometric equation with an infinite number of solutions is an identity.

**d.** The equations $\sin 2x = 1$ and $\sin 2x = \frac{1}{2}$ have the same number of solutions on the interval $[0, 2\pi)$.

*In Exercises 103–105, solve each equation on the interval $[0, 2\pi)$. Do not use a calculator.*

**103.** $2\cos x - 1 + 3\sec x = 0$

**104.** $\sin 3x + \sin x + \cos x = 0$

**105.** $\sin x + 2\sin\frac{x}{2} = \cos\frac{x}{2} + 1$

# CHAPTER SUMMARY, REVIEW, AND TEST

## Summary

### 6.1 Verifying Trigonometric Identities

a. Identities are trigonometric equations that are true for all values of the variable for which the expressions are defined.

b. Fundamental trigonometric identities are given in the box on page 545.

c. Guidelines for verifying trigonometric identities are given in the box on page 553.

### 6.2 and 6.3 Sum, Difference, Double-Angle, and Half-Angle Formulas

a. Sum and difference formulas, double-angle formulas, power-reducing formulas, and half-angle formulas are given in the box on page 573.

### 6.4 Product-to-Sum and Sum-to-Product Formulas

a. The product-to-sum formulas are given in the box on page 576.
b. The sum-to-product formulas are given in the box on page 578. These formulas are useful to verify identities with fractions that contain sums and differences of sines and/or cosines.

### 6.5 Trigonometric Equations

a. The values that satisfy a trigonometric equation are its solutions.
b. Algebraic techniques such as isolating an expression on one side of the equation and factoring are useful in solving trigonometric equations. Identities are also used to solve some trigonometric equations.

## Review Exercises

### 6.1

*In Exercises 1–12, verify each identity.*

1. $\sec x - \cos x = \tan x \sin x$
2. $\cos x + \sin x \tan x = \sec x$
3. $\sin^2\theta(1 + \cot^2\theta) = 1$
4. $(\sec\theta - 1)(\sec\theta + 1) = \tan^2\theta$
5. $\dfrac{1}{\sin t - 1} + \dfrac{1}{\sin t + 1} = -2\tan t \sec t$
6. $\dfrac{1 + \sin t}{\cos^2 t} = \tan^2 t + 1 + \tan t \sec t$
7. $\dfrac{\cos x}{1 - \sin x} = \dfrac{1 + \sin x}{\cos x}$
8. $1 - \dfrac{\cos^2 x}{1 + \sin x} = \sin x$
9. $(\tan\theta + \cot\theta)^2 = \sec^2\theta + \csc^2\theta$
10. $\dfrac{1}{\sin\theta + \cos\theta} + \dfrac{1}{\sin\theta - \cos\theta} = \dfrac{2\sin\theta}{\sin^4\theta - \cos^4\theta}$
11. $\dfrac{\cos t}{\cot t - 5\cos t} = \dfrac{1}{\csc t - 5}$
12. $\dfrac{1 - \cos t}{1 + \cos t} = (\csc t - \cot t)^2$

### 6.2 and 6.3

*In Exercises 13–18, use a sum or difference formula to find the exact value of each expression.*

13. $\cos(45° + 30°)$
14. $\sin 195°$
15. $\tan\left(\dfrac{4\pi}{3} - \dfrac{\pi}{4}\right)$
16. $\tan\dfrac{5\pi}{12}$
17. $\cos 65° \cos 5° + \sin 65° \sin 5°$
18. $\sin 80° \cos 50° - \cos 80° \sin 50°$

*In Exercises 19–30, verify each identity.*

19. $\sin\left(x + \dfrac{\pi}{6}\right) - \cos\left(x + \dfrac{\pi}{3}\right) = \sqrt{3}\sin x$
20. $\tan\left(x + \dfrac{3\pi}{4}\right) = \dfrac{\tan x - 1}{1 + \tan x}$
21. $\sec(\alpha + \beta) = \dfrac{\sec\alpha \sec\beta}{1 - \tan\alpha \tan\beta}$
22. $\dfrac{\cos(\alpha - \beta)}{\cos\alpha \cos\beta} = 1 + \tan\alpha \tan\beta$
23. $\cos^4 t - \sin^4 t = \cos 2t$
24. $\sin t - \cos 2t = (2\sin t - 1)(\sin t + 1)$
25. $\dfrac{\sin 2\theta - \sin\theta}{\cos 2\theta + \cos\theta} = \dfrac{1 - \cos\theta}{\sin\theta}$
26. $\dfrac{\sin 2\theta}{1 - \sin^2\theta} = 2\tan\theta$
27. $\tan 2t = 2\sin t \cos t \sec 2t$
28. $\cos 4t = 1 - 8\sin^2 t \cos^2 t$
29. $\tan\dfrac{x}{2}(1 + \cos x) = \sin x$
30. $\tan\dfrac{x}{2} = \dfrac{\sec x - 1}{\tan x}$

*In Exercises 31–33, the graph with the given equation is shown in a $\left[0, 2\pi, \dfrac{\pi}{2}\right]$ by $[-2, 2, 1]$ viewing rectangle.*

**a.** *Describe the graph using another equation.*
**b.** *Verify that the two equations are equivalent.*

31.

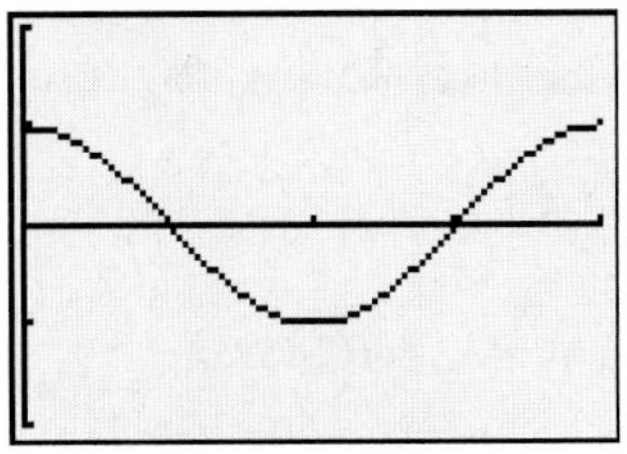

$y = \sin\left(x - \dfrac{3\pi}{2}\right)$

**32.**

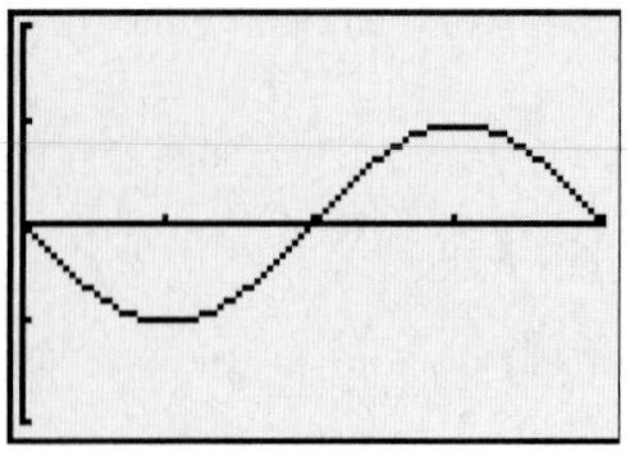

$y = \cos\left(x + \frac{\pi}{2}\right)$

**33.**

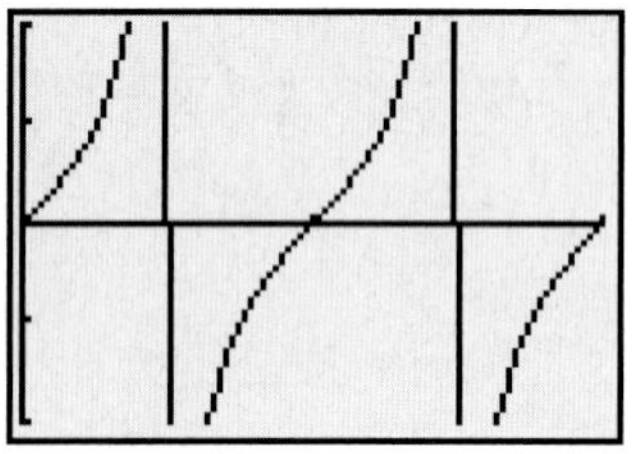

$y = \frac{\tan x - 1}{1 - \cot x}$

*In Exercises 34–37, find the exact value of the following under the given conditions:*

**a.** $\sin(\alpha + \beta)$ **b.** $\cos(\alpha - \beta)$ **c.** $\tan(\alpha + \beta)$

**d.** $\sin 2\alpha$ **e.** $\cos\frac{\beta}{2}$

**34.** $\sin\alpha = \frac{3}{5}$, $\alpha$ lies in quadrant I, and $\sin\beta = \frac{12}{13}$, $\beta$ lies in quadrant II.

**35.** $\tan\alpha = \frac{4}{3}$, $\alpha$ lies in quadrant III, and $\tan\beta = \frac{5}{12}$, $\beta$ lies in quadrant I.

**36.** $\tan\alpha = -3$, $\alpha$ lies in quadrant II, and $\cot\beta = -3$, $\beta$ lies in quadrant III.

**37.** $\sin\alpha = -\frac{1}{3}$, $\alpha$ lies in quadrant III, and $\cos\beta = -\frac{1}{3}$, $\beta$ lies in quadrant IV.

*In Exercises 38–41, use double- and half-angle formulas to find the exact value of each expression.*

**38.** $\cos^2 15° - \sin^2 15°$

**39.** $\dfrac{2\tan\frac{5\pi}{12}}{1 - \tan^2\frac{5\pi}{12}}$

**40.** $\sin 22.5°$

**41.** $\tan\frac{\pi}{12}$

## 6.4

*In Exercises 42–43, express each product as a sum or difference.*

**42.** $\sin 6x \sin 4x$

**43.** $\sin 7x \cos 3x$

*In Exercises 44–45, express each sum or difference as a product. If possible, find this product's exact value.*

**44.** $\sin 2x - \sin 4x$

**45.** $\cos 75° + \cos 15°$

*In Exercises 46–47, verify each identity.*

**46.** $\dfrac{\cos 3x + \cos 5x}{\cos 3x - \cos 5x} = \cot x \cot 4x$

**47.** $\dfrac{\sin 2x + \sin 6x}{\sin 2x - \sin 6x} = -\tan 4x \cot 2x$

**48.** The graph with the given equation is shown in a $\left[0, 2\pi, \frac{\pi}{2}\right]$ by $[-2, 2, 1]$ viewing rectangle.

$$y = \frac{\cos 3x + \cos x}{\sin 3x - \sin x}$$

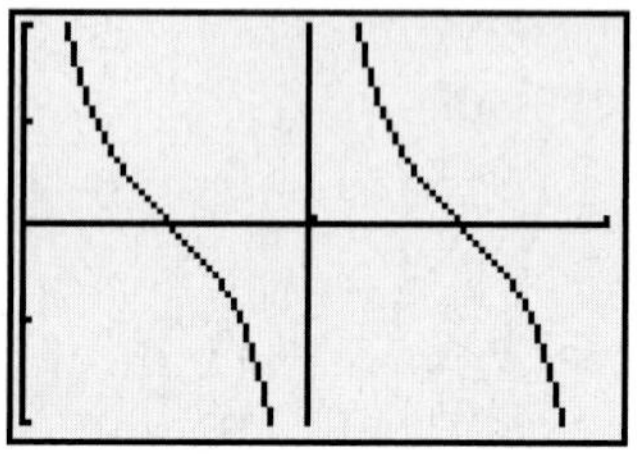

**a.** Describe the graph using another equation.

**b.** Verify that the two equations are equivalent.

## 6.5

*In Exercises 49–52, find all solutions of each equation.*

**49.** $\cos x = -\frac{1}{2}$

**50.** $\sin x = \frac{\sqrt{2}}{2}$

**51.** $2\sin x + 1 = 0$

**52.** $\sqrt{3}\tan x - 1 = 0$

*In Exercises 53–62, solve each equation on the interval $[0, 2\pi)$.*

**53.** $\cos 2x = -1$

**54.** $\sin 3x = 1$

**55.** $\tan\frac{x}{2} = -1$

**56.** $\tan x = 2\cos x \tan x$

**57.** $\cos^2 x - 2\cos x = 3$

**58.** $3\cos^2 x + \sin x = 1$

**59.** $4\sin^2 x = 1$

**60.** $\cos 2x + 2\cos x = 0$

**61.** $\sin 2x = \sqrt{3}\sin x$

**62.** $\sin x = \tan x$

**63.** A ball on a spring is pulled 6 inches below its rest position and then released. After $t$ seconds, the ball's distance from its rest position is given by

$$d = -6\cos\frac{\pi}{2}t.$$

Find all values of $t$ for which the ball is 3 inches below its rest position.

**64.** You are playing catch with a friend located 100 feet away. If you throw the ball with an initial velocity of $v_o = 90$ feet per second, at what angle of elevation $\theta$ should you direct your throw so that it can be caught easily? Use the formula

$$d = \frac{v_o^2}{16}\sin\theta\cos\theta.$$

## Chapter 6 Test

*Use the following conditions to solve Exercises 1–4.*

$\sin\alpha = \frac{4}{5}$, $\alpha$ lies in quadrant II

and $\cos\beta = \frac{5}{13}$, $\beta$ lies in quadrant I.

*Find the exact value of:*

**1.** $\cos(\alpha + \beta)$

**2.** $\tan(\alpha - \beta)$

**3.** $\sin 2\alpha$

**4.** $\cos\frac{\beta}{2}$

**5.** Use $105° = 135° - 30°$ to find the exact value of $\sin 105°$.

*In Exercises 6–11, verify each identity.*

**6.** $\cos x \csc x = \cot x$

**7.** $\frac{\sec x}{\cot x + \tan x} = \sin x$

**8.** $1 - \frac{\cos^2 x}{1 + \sin x} = \sin x$

**9.** $\cos\left(\theta + \frac{\pi}{2}\right) = -\sin\theta$

**10.** $\frac{\sin(\alpha - \beta)}{\sin\alpha\cos\beta} = 1 - \cot\alpha\tan\beta$

**11.** $\sin t\cos t(\tan t + \cot t) = 1$

*In Exercises 12–15, solve each equation on the interval* $[0, 2\pi)$.

**12.** $\sin 3x = -\frac{1}{2}$

**13.** $\sin 2x + \cos x = 0$

**14.** $2\cos^2 x - 3\cos x + 1 = 0$

**15.** $2\sin^2 x + \cos x = 1$

## Cumulative Review Exercises (Chapters 1–6)

*Solve each equation or inequality in Exercises 1–4.*

**1.** $x^3 + x^2 - x + 15 = 0$

**2.** $11^{x-1} = 125$

**3.** $x^2 + 2x - 8 > 0$

**4.** $\cos 2x + 3 = 5\cos x, \quad 0 \le x < 2\pi$

*In Exercises 5–10, graph each equation.*

**5.** $y = \sqrt{x + 2} - 1$; Use transformations of the graph of $y = \sqrt{x}$.

**6.** $(x - 1)^2 + (y + 2)^2 = 9$

**7.** $y + 2 = \frac{1}{3}(x - 1)$

**8.** $y = 3\cos 2x, \quad -2\pi \le x \le 2\pi$

**9.** $y = 2\sin\frac{x}{2} + 1, \quad -2\pi \le x \le 2\pi$

**10.** $f(x) = (x - 1)^2(x - 3)$

**11.** If $f(x) = x^2 + 3x - 1$, find $\frac{f(a + h) - f(a)}{h}$.

**12.** Find the exact value of $\sin 225°$.

**13.** Verify the identity: $\sec^4 x - \sec^2 x = \tan^4 x + \tan^2 x$.

**14.** Convert 320° to radians.

**15.** How long would it take for any amount of money, compounded continuously at 5.75% per year, to triple? Round to the nearest tenth of a year.

**16.** If $f(x) = \frac{2x + 1}{x - 3}$, find $f^{-1}(x)$.

**17.** If $C$ is a right angle in triangle $ABC$ with $A = 23°$ and $a = 12$, solve the triangle.

**18.** A formula for calculating an infant's dosage for medication is

$$\text{Infant's dose} = \frac{\text{age of infant in months}}{150} \times \text{adult dose}.$$

If a 12-month-old infant is to receive 8.5 mg of medication, find the equivalent adult dose to the nearest milligram.

**19.** From a point on the ground 12 feet from the base of a flagpole, the angle of elevation to the top of the pole is 53°. Approximate the height of the flagpole to the nearest tenth of a foot.

**20.** In *A Tour of the Calculus*, David Berlinski describes trigonometric identities in the following way. "An invisible inner connection exists among the trigonometric functions, one revealed in various identities, strange places where the trigonometric functions appear fluidly to exchange identities or to resolve themselves into unlikely numbers." What does Berlinski mean by this? Use two fundamental trigonometric identities to illustrate your answer.

# Additional Topics in Trigonometry

Chapter 7

These days, computers and trigonometric functions are everywhere. Trigonometry plays a critical role in analyzing the forces that surround your every move. Using trigonometry to understand how forces are measured is one of the topics in this chapter that focuses on additional applications of trigonometry.

You enjoy running, although lately you experience discomfort at various points of impact. Your doctor suggests a computer analysis. By attaching sensors to your running shoes as you jog along a treadmill, the computer provides a printout of the magnitude and direction of the forces as your feet hit the ground. Based on this analysis, customized orthotics can be made to fit inside your shoes to minimize the impact of your feet with the ground.

# SECTION 7.1 *The Law of Sines*

## Objectives

1. Use the Law of Sines to solve oblique triangles.
2. Use the Law of Sines to solve, if possible, the triangle or triangles in the ambiguous case.
3. Find the area of an oblique triangle using the sine function.
4. Solve applied problems using the Law of Sines.

Point Reyes National Seashore, 40 miles north of San Francisco, consists of 75,000 acres with miles of pristine surf-pummeled beaches, forested ridges, and bays flanked by white cliffs. A few people, inspired by nature in the raw, live on private property adjoining the National Seashore. In 1995, a fire in the park covered 12,350 acres and destroyed 45 of their homes.

Fire is a necessary part of the life cycle in many wilderness areas. It is also an ongoing threat to those kept inspired and alive on private paradises surrounded by nature's unspoiled beauty. In this section, we see how trigonometry can be used to locate small wilderness fires before they become major tragedies. To do this, we begin by considering triangles other than right triangles.

## The Law of Sines and Its Derivation

An **oblique triangle** is a triangle that does not contain a right angle. Figure 7.1 shows that an oblique triangle has either three acute angles or two acute angles and one obtuse angle. Notice that the angles are labeled $A$, $B$, and $C$. The sides opposite each angle are labeled as $a$, $b$, and $c$, respectively.

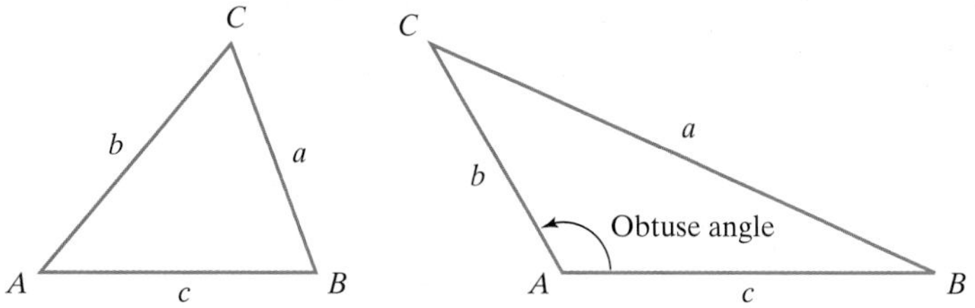


**Figure 7.1** Oblique triangles

Many relationships exist among the sides and angles in an oblique triangle. One such relationship is called the **Law of Sines**.

**Study Tip**

The Law of Sines can be expressed with the sines in the numerator:

$$\frac{\sin A}{a} = \frac{\sin B}{b} = \frac{\sin C}{c}.$$

**The Law of Sines**

If $A$, $B$, and $C$ are the measures of the angles of a triangle, and $a$, $b$, and $c$ are the lengths of the sides opposite these angles, then

$$\frac{a}{\sin A} = \frac{b}{\sin B} = \frac{c}{\sin C}.$$

The ratio of the length of the side of any triangle to the sine of the angle opposite that side is the same for all three sides of the triangle.

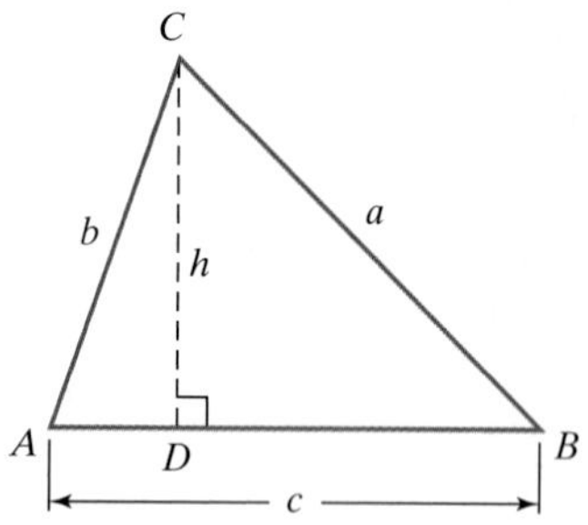


**Figure 7.2** Drawing an altitude to prove the Law of Sines

To prove the Law of Sines, we draw an altitude of length $h$ from one of the vertices of the triangle. In Figure 7.2, the altitude is drawn from vertex $C$. Two smaller triangles are formed, triangles $ACD$ and $BCD$. Note that both are right triangles. Thus, we can use the definition of the sine of an angle of a right triangle.

$$\sin B = \frac{h}{a} \qquad \sin A = \frac{h}{b} \qquad \sin\theta = \frac{\text{opposite}}{\text{hypotenuse}}.$$

$$h = a\sin B \qquad h = b\sin A \qquad \text{Solve each equation for } h.$$

Because we have found two expressions for $h$, we can set these expressions equal to each other.

$$a\sin B = b\sin A \qquad \text{Equate the expressions for } h.$$

$$\frac{a\sin B}{\sin A\sin B} = \frac{b\sin A}{\sin A\sin B} \qquad \text{Divide both sides by } \sin A\sin B.$$

$$\frac{a}{\sin A} = \frac{b}{\sin B} \qquad \text{Simplify.}$$

This proves part of the Law of Sines. If we use the same process and draw an altitude of length $h$ from vertex $A$, we obtain the following result:

$$\frac{b}{\sin B} = \frac{c}{\sin C}.$$

When this equation is combined with the previous equation, we obtain the Law of Sines. Because the sine of an angle is equal to the sine of 180° minus that angle, the Law of Sines is derived in a similar manner if the oblique triangle contains an obtuse angle.

**1** Use the Law of Sines to solve oblique triangles.

## Solving Oblique Triangles

**Solving an oblique triangle** means finding the lengths of its sides and the measurement of its angles. The Law of Sines can be used to solve a triangle in which one side and two angles are known. The three known measurements can be abbreviated using SAA (a side and two angles are known) or ASA (two angles and a side between them are known).

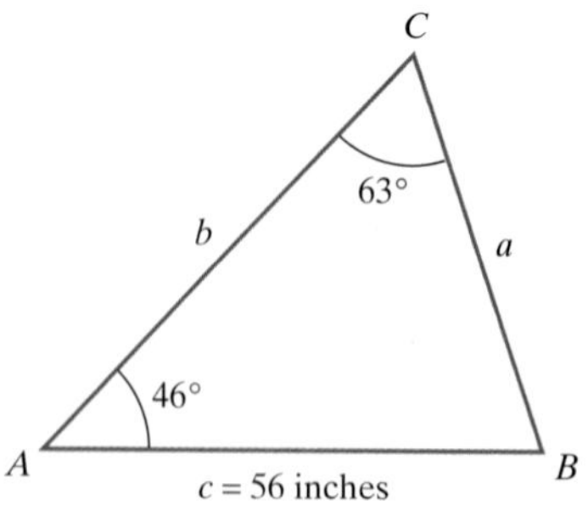


**Figure 7.3** Solving an oblique SAA triangle

### EXAMPLE 1 Solving a SAA Triangle Using the Law of Sines

Solve the triangle shown in Figure 7.3 with $A = 46°$, $C = 63°$, and $c = 56$ inches.

**Solution** We begin by finding $B$, the third angle of the triangle. We do not need the Law of Sines to do this. Instead, we use the fact that the sum of the measures of the interior angles of a triangle is 180°.

$$A + B + C = 180°$$

$$46° + B + 63° = 180° \quad \text{Substitute the given values: } A = 46° \text{ and } C = 63°.$$

$$109° + B = 180° \quad \text{Add.}$$

$$B = 71° \quad \text{Subtract } 109° \text{ from both sides.}$$

When we use the Law of Sines, we must be given one of the three ratios. In this example, we are given $c$ and $C$: $c = 56$ and $C = 63°$. Thus, we use the ratio $\frac{c}{\sin C}$, or $\frac{56}{\sin 63°}$, to find the other two sides. Use the Law of Sines to find $a$.

$$\frac{a}{\sin A} = \frac{c}{\sin C} \quad \text{The ratio of any side to the sine of its opposite angle equals the ratio of any other side to the sine of its opposite angle.}$$

$$\frac{a}{\sin 46°} = \frac{56}{\sin 63°} \quad A = 46°,\ c = 56, \text{ and } C = 63°.$$

$$a = \frac{56 \sin 46°}{\sin 63°} \quad \text{Multiply both sides by } \sin 46° \text{ and solve for } a.$$

$$a \approx 45 \text{ inches} \quad \text{Use a calculator.}$$

Use the Law of Sines again, this time to find $b$.

$$\frac{b}{\sin B} = \frac{c}{\sin C} \quad \text{We use the given ratio, } \frac{c}{\sin C}, \text{ to find } b.$$

$$\frac{b}{\sin 71°} = \frac{56}{\sin 63°} \quad \text{We found that } B = 71°. \text{ We are given } c = 56 \text{ and } C = 63°.$$

$$b = \frac{56 \sin 71°}{\sin 63°} \quad \text{Multiply both sides by } \sin 71° \text{ and solve for } b.$$

$$b \approx 59 \text{ inches} \quad \text{Use a calculator.}$$

The solution is $B = 71°$, $a \approx 45$ inches, and $b \approx 59$ inches.

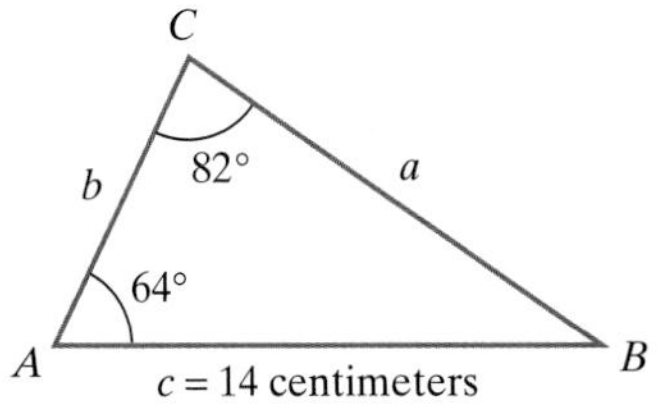


**Figure 7.4**

**Check Point 1** Solve the triangle shown in Figure 7.4 with $A = 64°$, $C = 82°$, and $c = 14$ centimeters.

## EXAMPLE 2 Solving an ASA Triangle Using the Law of Sines

Solve triangle $ABC$ if $A = 50°$, $C = 33.5°$, and $b = 76$.

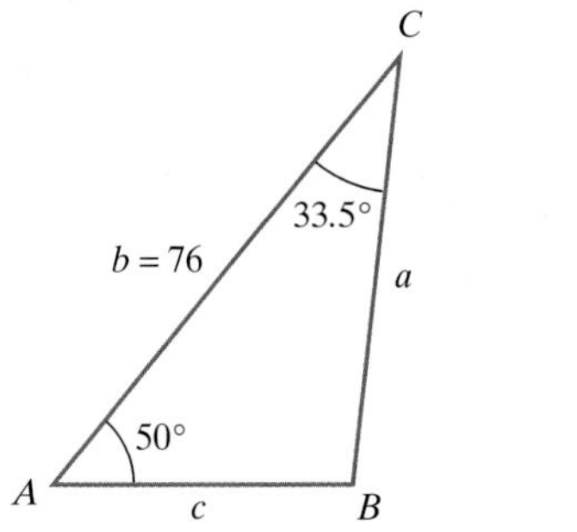


**Figure 7.5** Solving an ASA triangle

**Solution** We begin by drawing a picture of triangle $ABC$ and labeling it with the given information. Figure 7.5 shows the triangle that we must solve. We begin by finding $B$.

$$A + B + C = 180° \quad \text{The sum of the measures of a triangle's interior angles is } 180°.$$

$$50° + B + 33.5° = 180° \quad A = 50° \text{ and } C = 33.5°$$

$$83.5° + B = 180° \quad \text{Add.}$$

$$B = 96.5° \quad \text{Subtract } 83.5° \text{ from both sides.}$$

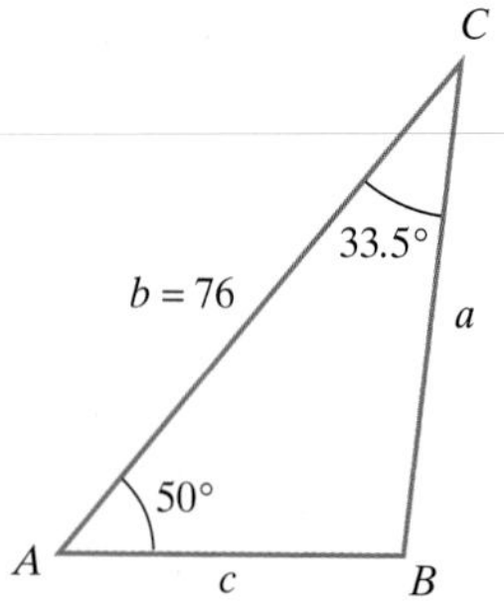


**Figure 7.5,** shown again.

Keep in mind that we must be given one of the three ratios to apply the Law of Sines. In this example, we are given that $b = 76$ and we found that $B = 96.5°$. Thus, we use the ratio $\frac{b}{\sin B}$, or $\frac{76}{\sin 96.5°}$, to find the other two sides. Use the Law of Sines to find $a$ and $c$.

**Find $a$:**

$$\frac{a}{\sin A} = \frac{b}{\sin B}$$

$$\frac{a}{\sin 50°} = \frac{76}{\sin 96.5°}$$

$$a = \frac{76 \sin 50°}{\sin 96.5°} \approx 59$$

This is the known ratio.

**Find $c$:**

$$\frac{c}{\sin C} = \frac{b}{\sin B}$$

$$\frac{c}{\sin 33.5°} = \frac{76}{\sin 96.5°}$$

$$c = \frac{76 \sin 33.5°}{\sin 96.5°} \approx 42$$

The solution is $B = 96.5°$, $a \approx 59$, and $c \approx 42$.

**2** Use the Law of Sines to solve, if possible, the triangle or triangles in the ambiguous case.

**Check Point 2** Solve triangle $ABC$ if $A = 40°$, $C = 22.5°$, and $b = 12$.

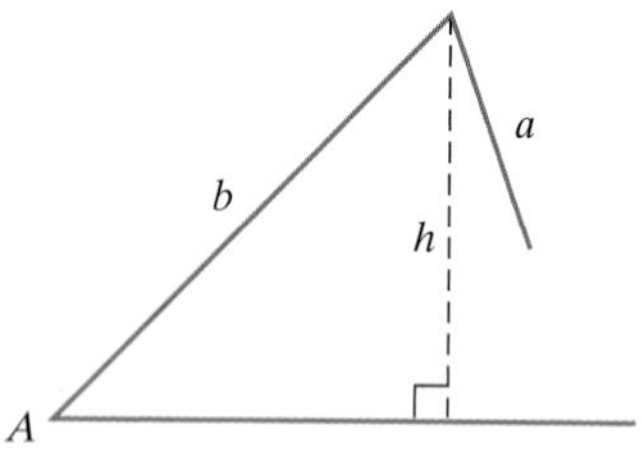


**Figure 7.6** Given SSA, no triangle may result.

## The Ambiguous Case (SSA)

If we are given two sides and an angle opposite one of them (SSA), does this determine a unique triangle? Can we solve this case using the Law of Sines? Such a case is called the **ambiguous case** because the given information may result in one triangle, two triangles, or no triangle at all. For example, in Figure 7.6, we are given $a$, $b$, and $A$. Because $a$ is shorter than $h$, it is not long enough to form a triangle. The number of possible triangles, if any, that can be formed in the SSA case depends on $h$, the length of the altitude, where $h = b \sin A$.

### The Ambiguous Case (SSA)

Consider a triangle in which $a$, $b$, and $A$ are given. This information may result in:

**No Triangle** | **One Right Triangle** | **Two Triangles** | **One Triangle**

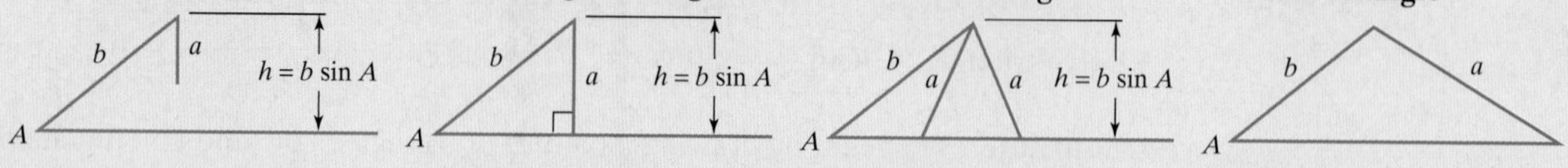


No Triangle: $a$ is less than $h$ and not long enough to form a triangle.

One Right Triangle: $a = h$ and just the right length to form a right triangle.

Two Triangles: $a$ is greater than $h$ and $a$ is less than $b$. Two distinct triangles are formed.

One Triangle: $a$ is greater than $h$ and $a$ is greater than $b$. One triangle is formed.

In a SSA situation, it is not necessary to draw an accurate sketch like those shown in the box. The Law of Sines determines the number of triangles, if any, and gives the solution for each triangle.

## EXAMPLE 3 Solving a SSA Triangle Using the Law of Sines (One Solution)

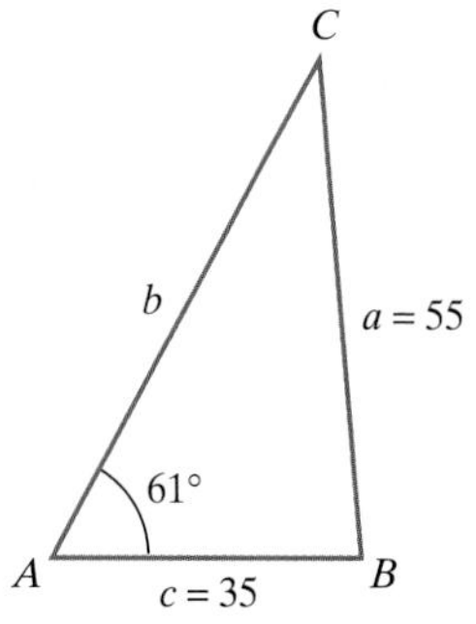


**Figure 7.7** Solving a SSA triangle; the ambiguous case

Solve triangle $ABC$ if $A = 61°$, $a = 55$, and $c = 35$.

**Solution** We begin with the sketch in Figure 7.7. The known ratio is $\frac{a}{\sin A}$, or $\frac{55}{\sin 61°}$. Because side $c$ is given, we use the Law of Sines to find angle $C$.

$$\frac{a}{\sin A} = \frac{c}{\sin C}$$ Apply the Law of Sines.

$$\frac{55}{\sin 61°} = \frac{35}{\sin C}$$ $a = 55$, $c = 35$, and $A = 61°$.

$$55 \sin C = 35 \sin 61°$$ Cross multiply: If $\frac{a}{b} = \frac{c}{d}$, then $ad = bc$.

$$\sin C = \frac{35 \sin 61°}{55}$$ Divide both sides by 55 and solve for $\sin C$.

$$\sin C \approx 0.5566$$ Use a calculator.

There are two angles $C$ between 0° and 180° for which $\sin C \approx 0.5566$.

$$C_1 \approx 34° \qquad C_2 \approx 180° - 34° \approx 146°$$

Obtain the acute angle with your calculator: $\sin^{-1} .5566$

The sine is positive in quadrant II.

Look at Figure 7.7. Given that $A = 61°$, can you see that $C_2 \approx 146°$ is impossible? By adding 146° to the given angle, 61°, we exceed a 180° sum:

$$61° + 146° = 207°.$$

Thus, the only possibility is that $C_1 \approx 34°$. We find $B$ using $C_1$ and the given information $A = 61°$.

$$B = 180° - C_1 - A \approx 180° - 34° - 61° = 85°$$

Side $b$ that lies opposite this 85° angle can now be found using the Law of Sines.

$$\frac{b}{\sin B} = \frac{a}{\sin A}$$ Apply the Law of Sines.

$$\frac{b}{\sin 85°} = \frac{55}{\sin 61°}$$ $a = 55$, $B \approx 85°$, and $A = 61°$.

$$b = \frac{55 \sin 85°}{\sin 61°} \approx 63$$ Multiply both sides by sin 85° and solve for $b$.

There is one triangle and the solution is $C_1$ (or $C$) $\approx 34°$, $B \approx 85°$, and $b \approx 63$.

**Check Point 3** Solve triangle $ABC$ if $A = 123°$, $a = 47$, and $c = 23$.

## EXAMPLE 4 Solving a SSA Triangle Using the Law of Sines (No Solution)

Solve triangle $ABC$ if $A = 75°$, $a = 51$, and $b = 71$.

**Solution** The known ratio is $\frac{a}{\sin A}$, or $\frac{51}{\sin 75°}$. Because side $b$ is given, we use the Law of Sines to find angle $B$.

$$\frac{a}{\sin A} = \frac{b}{\sin B} \quad \text{Use the Law of Sines.}$$

$$\frac{51}{\sin 75°} = \frac{71}{\sin B} \quad \text{Substitute the given values.}$$

$$51 \sin B = 71 \sin 75° \quad \text{Cross multiply.}$$

$$\sin B = \frac{71 \sin 75°}{51} \approx 1.34 \quad \text{Divide by 51 and solve for } \sin B.$$

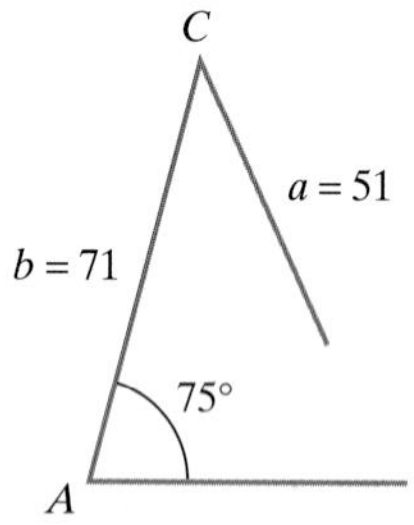


**Figure 7.8** $a$ is not long enough to form a triangle.

Because the sine can never exceed 1, there is no angle $B$ for which $\sin B \approx 1.34$. There is no triangle with the given measurements, illustrated in Figure 7.8.

**Check Point 4** Solve triangle $ABC$ if $A = 50°$, $a = 10$, and $b = 20$.

## EXAMPLE 5 Solving a SSA Triangle Using the Law of Sines (Two Solutions)

Solve triangle $ABC$ if $A = 40°$, $a = 54$, and $b = 62$.

**Solution** The known ratio is $\frac{a}{\sin A}$, or $\frac{54}{\sin 40°}$. We use the Law of Sines to find angle $B$.

$$\frac{a}{\sin A} = \frac{b}{\sin B} \quad \text{Use the Law of Sines.}$$

$$\frac{54}{\sin 40°} = \frac{62}{\sin B} \quad \text{Substitute the given values.}$$

$$54 \sin B = 62 \sin 40° \quad \text{Cross multiply.}$$

$$\sin B = \frac{62 \sin 40°}{54} \approx 0.7380 \quad \text{Divide by 54 and solve for } \sin B.$$

There are two angles $B$ between 0° and 180° for which $\sin B \approx 0.7380$.

$$B_1 \approx 48° \qquad B_2 \approx 180° - 48° = 132°$$

Find $\sin^{-1} .7380$ with your calculator.

The sine is positive in quadrant II.

If you add either angle to the given angle, 40°, the sum does not exceed 180°. Thus, there are two triangles with the given conditions, shown in Figure 7.9(a). The triangles, $AB_1C_1$ and $AB_2C_2$, are shown separately in Figures 7.9(b) and (c).

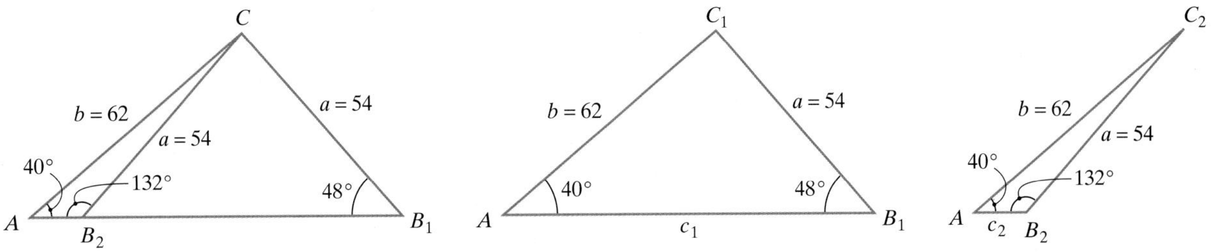


**(a)** Two triangles are possible with $A = 40°$, $a = 54$, and $b = 62$.

**(b)** In one possible triangle, $B_1 = 48°$.

**(c)** In the second possible triangle, $B_2 = 132°$.

**Figure 7.9**

**Study Tip**

The two triangles shown in Figure 7.9 are helpful in organizing the solutions. However, if you keep track of the two triangles, one with the given information and $B_1 = 48°$, and the other with the given information and $B_2 = 132°$, you do not have to draw the figure to solve the triangles.

We find angles $C_1$ and $C_2$ using a 180° angle sum in each of the two triangles.

$$C_1 = 180° - A - B_1 \qquad C_2 = 180° - A - B_2$$
$$\approx 180° - 40° - 48° \qquad \approx 180° - 40° - 132°$$
$$= 92° \qquad = 8°$$

We use the Law of Sines to find $c_1$ and $c_2$.

$$\frac{c_1}{\sin C_1} = \frac{a}{\sin A} \qquad \frac{c_2}{\sin C_2} = \frac{a}{\sin A}$$

$$\frac{c_1}{\sin 92°} = \frac{54}{\sin 40°} \qquad \frac{c_2}{\sin 8°} = \frac{54}{\sin 40°}$$

$$c_1 = \frac{54 \sin 92°}{\sin 40°} \approx 84 \qquad c_2 = \frac{54 \sin 8°}{\sin 40°} \approx 12$$

There are two triangles. In one triangle, the solution is $B_1 \approx 48°$, $C_1 \approx 92°$, and $c_1 \approx 84$. In the other triangle $B_2 \approx 132°$, $C_2 \approx 8°$, and $c_2 \approx 12$.

**Check Point 5** Solve triangle $ABC$ if $A = 35°$, $a = 12$, and $b = 16$.

**3** Find the area of an oblique triangle using the sine function.

## The Area of an Oblique Triangle

A formula for the area of an oblique triangle can be obtained using the procedure for proving the Law of Sines. We draw an altitude of length $h$ from one of the vertices of the triangle, shown in Figure 7.10. We apply the definition of the sine of angle $A$, $\frac{\text{opposite}}{\text{hypotenuse}}$, in right triangle $ACD$.

$$\sin A = \frac{h}{b} \quad \text{or} \quad h = b \sin A.$$

The area of a triangle is $\frac{1}{2}$ the product of any side and the altitude drawn to that side. Using the altitude $h$ in Figure 7.10, we have

$$\text{Area} = \tfrac{1}{2}ch = \tfrac{1}{2}cb \sin A.$$

Use the result from above: $h = b \sin A$.

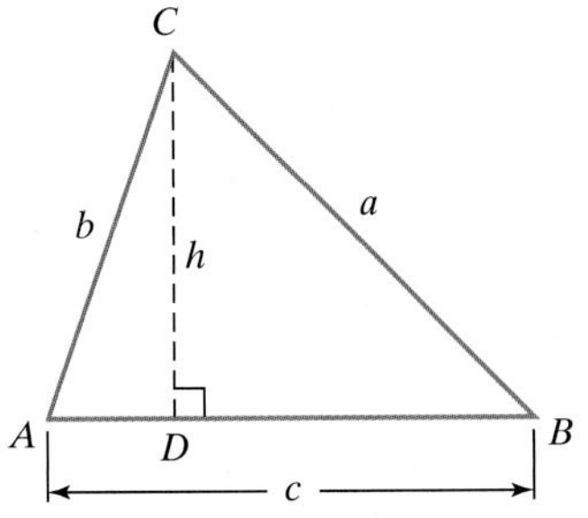


**Figure 7.10**

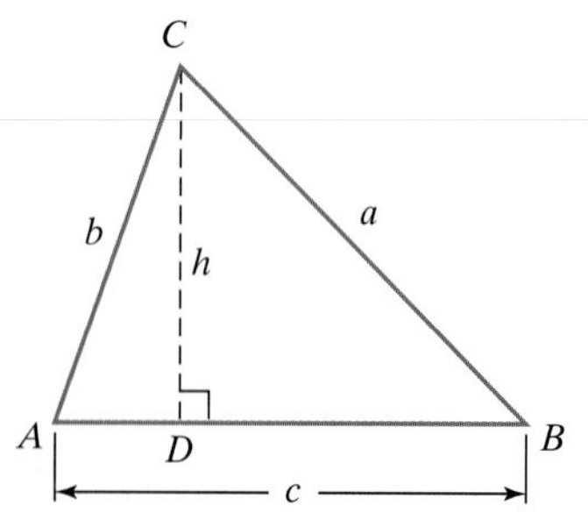


**Figure 7.10,** shown again

This result indicates that the area of the triangle is one-half the product of $b$ and $c$ times the sine of their included angle. If we draw altitudes from the other two vertices, we can use any two sides to compute the area.

**Area of An Oblique Triangle**

The area of a triangle equals one-half the product of the lengths of two sides times the sine of their included angle. In Figure 7.10, this wording can be expressed by the formulas

$$\text{Area} = \tfrac{1}{2}bc\sin A = \tfrac{1}{2}ab\sin C = \tfrac{1}{2}ac\sin B.$$

## EXAMPLE 6 Finding the Area of an Oblique Triangle

Find the area of a triangle having two sides of lengths 24 meters and 10 meters and an included angle of 62°.

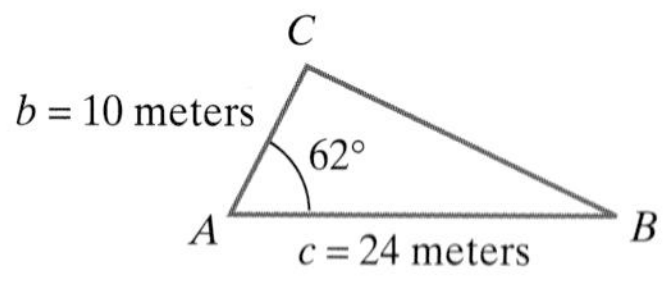


**Figure 7.11** Finding the area of a SAS triangle

**Solution** The triangle is shown in Figure 7.11. Its area is half the product of the lengths of the two sides times the sine of the included angle.

$$\text{Area} = \tfrac{1}{2}(24)(10)(\sin 62^\circ) \approx 106$$

The area of the triangle is approximately 106 square meters.

**Check Point 6** Find the area of a triangle having two sides of lengths 8 meters and 12 meters and an included angle of 135°.

**4** Solve applied problems using the Law of Sines.

## Applications of the Law of Sines

We have seen how the trigonometry of right triangles can be used to solve many different kinds of applied problems. The Law of Sines enables us to work with triangles that are not right triangles. As a result, this law can be used to solve problems involving surveying, engineering, astronomy, navigation, and the environment. Example 7 illustrates the use of the Law of Sines in detecting potentially devastating fires.

## EXAMPLE 7 An Application of the Law of Sines

Two fire-lookout stations are 20 miles apart, with station B directly east of station A. Both stations spot a fire on a mountain to the north. The bearing from station A to the fire is N50°E (50° east of north). The bearing from station B to the fire is N36°W (36° west of north). How far is the fire from station A?

**Solution** Figure 7.12 on page 595 shows the information given in the problem. The distance from station A to the fire is represented by $b$. Notice that the angles describing the bearing from each station to the fire, 50° and 36°, are not interior angles of triangle $ABC$. Using a north-south line, the interior angles are found as follows:

$$A = 90^\circ - 50^\circ = 40^\circ \qquad B = 90^\circ - 36^\circ = 54^\circ.$$

To find $b$ using the Law of Sines, we need a known side and an angle opposite that side. Because $c = 20$ miles, we find angle $C$ using a 180° angle sum in the triangle. Thus,

$$C = 180^\circ - A - B = 180^\circ - 40^\circ - 54^\circ = 86^\circ.$$

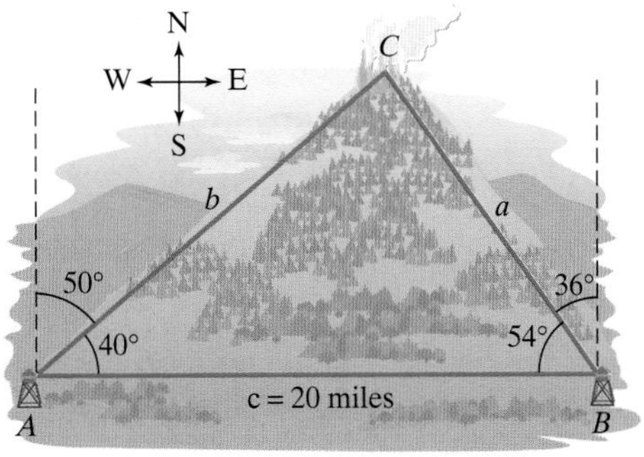


**Figure 7.12**

The ratio $\frac{c}{\sin C}$, or $\frac{20}{\sin 86°}$, is now known. We use this ratio and the Law of Sines to find $b$.

$$\frac{b}{\sin B} = \frac{c}{\sin C} \quad \text{Use the Law of Sines.}$$

$$\frac{b}{\sin 54°} = \frac{20}{\sin 86°} \quad c = 20,\ B = 54°,\ \text{and } C = 86°.$$

$$b = \frac{20 \sin 54°}{\sin 86°} \approx 16 \quad \text{Multiply both sides by } \sin 54° \text{ and solve for } b.$$

The fire is approximately 16 miles from station A.

**Check Point 7** Two fire-lookout stations are 13 miles apart, with station B directly east of station A. Both stations spot a fire. The bearing of the fire from station A is N35°E, and the bearing of the fire from station B is N49°W. How far, to the nearest mile, is the fire from station B?

# EXERCISE SET 7.1

## Practice Exercises

*In Exercises 1–8, solve each triangle. Round lengths of sides to the nearest tenth and measurement of angles to the nearest degree.*

**1.**

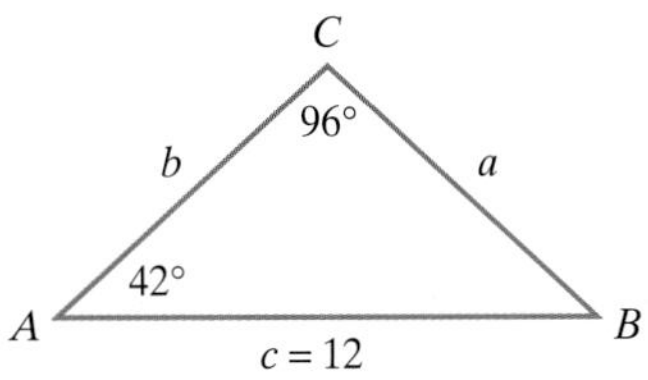


**2.**

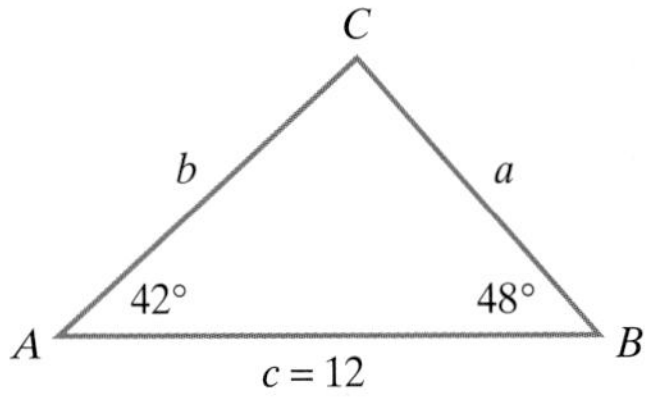


**3.**

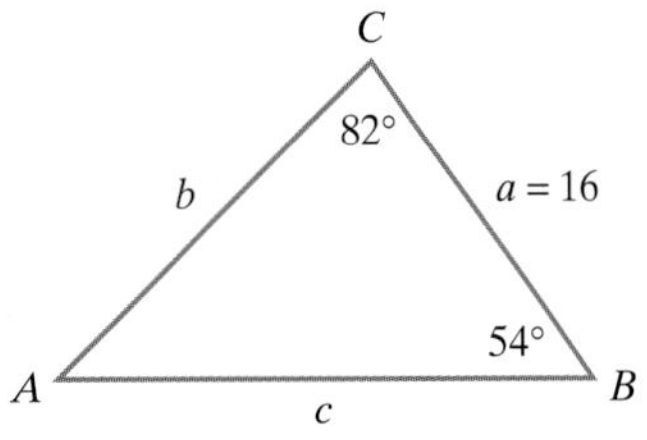


**4.**

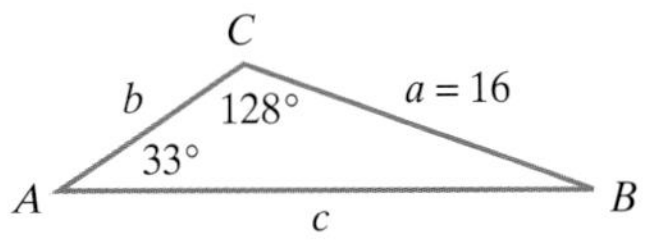


**5.**

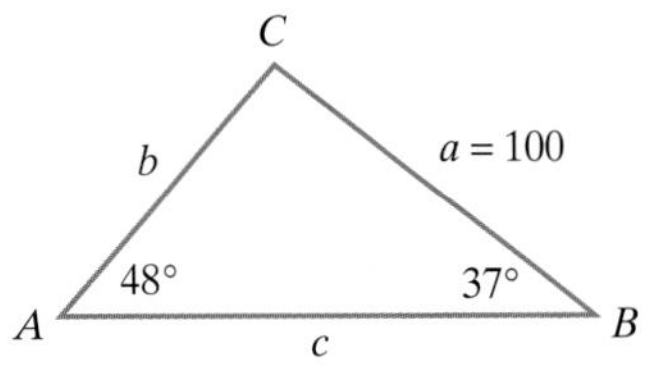

**6.**

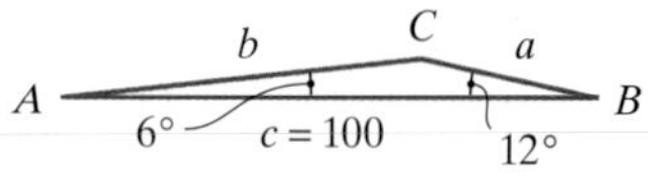


**7.**

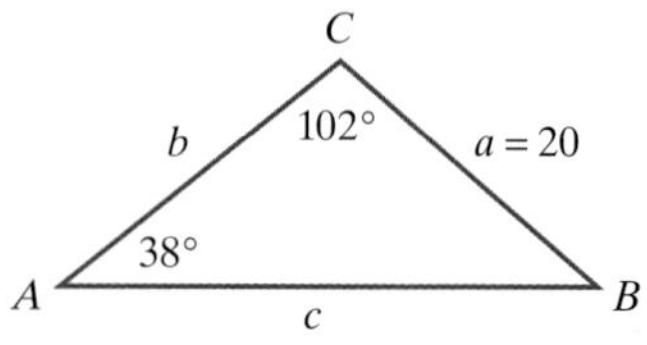


**8.**

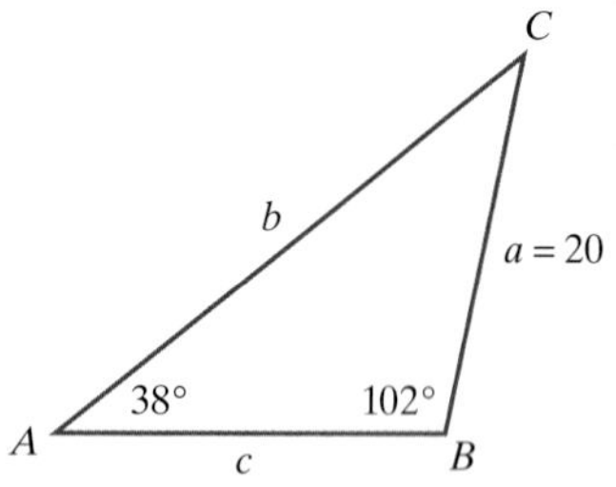


*In Exercises 9–16, solve each triangle. Round lengths to the nearest tenth and angle measures to the nearest degree.*

**9.** $A = 44°, B = 25°, a = 12$

**10.** $A = 56°, C = 24°, a = 22$

**11.** $B = 85°, C = 15°, b = 40$

**12.** $A = 85°, B = 35°, c = 30$

**13.** $A = 115°, C = 35°, c = 200$

**14.** $B = 5°, C = 125°, b = 200$

**15.** $A = 65°, B = 65°, c = 6$

**16.** $B = 80°, C = 10°, a = 8$

*In Exercises 17–32, two sides and an angle (SSA) of a triangle are given. Determine whether the given measurements produce one triangle, two triangles, or no triangle at all. Solve each triangle that results. Round to the nearest tenth and the nearest degree for sides and angles, respectively.*

**17.** $a = 20, b = 15, A = 40°$

**18.** $a = 30, b = 20, A = 50°$

**19.** $a = 10, c = 8.9, A = 63°$

**20.** $a = 57.5, c = 49.8, A = 136°$

**21.** $a = 42.1, c = 37, A = 112°$

**22.** $a = 6.1, b = 4, A = 162°$

**23.** $a = 10, b = 40, A = 30°$

**24.** $a = 10, b = 30, A = 150°$

**25.** $a = 16, b = 18, A = 60°$

**26.** $a = 30, b = 40, A = 20°$

**27.** $a = 12, b = 16.1, A = 37°$

**28.** $a = 7, b = 28, A = 12°$

**29.** $a = 22, c = 24.1, A = 58°$

**30.** $a = 95, c = 125, A = 49°$

**31.** $a = 9.3, b = 41, A = 18°$

**32.** $a = 1.4, b = 2.9, A = 142°$

*In Exercises 33–38, find the area of the triangle having the given measurements. Round to the nearest square unit.*

**33.** $A = 48°, b = 20$ feet, $c = 40$ feet

**34.** $A = 22°, b = 20$ feet, $c = 50$ feet

**35.** $B = 36°, a = 3$ yards, $c = 6$ yards

**36.** $B = 125°, a = 8$ yards, $c = 5$ yards

**37.** $C = 124°, a = 4$ meters, $b = 6$ meters

**38.** $C = 102°, a = 16$ meters, $b = 20$ meters

## Application Exercises

**39.** Two fire-lookout stations are 10 miles apart, with station B directly east of station A. Both stations spot a fire. The bearing of the fire from station A is N25°E and the bearing of the fire from station B is N56°W. How far, to the nearest mile, is the fire from each lookout station?

**40.** The Federal Communications Commission is attempting to locate an illegal radio station. It sets up two monitoring stations, A and B, with station B 40 miles east of station A. Station A measures the illegal signal from the radio station as coming from a direction of 48° east of north. Station B measures the signal as coming from a point 34° west of north. How far is the illegal radio station from monitoring stations A and B?

**41.** The figure shows a 1200-yard-long beach and an oil platform in the ocean. The angle made with the platform from one end of the beach is 85° and from the other end is 76°. Find the distance of the oil platform, to the nearest yard, from each end of the beach.

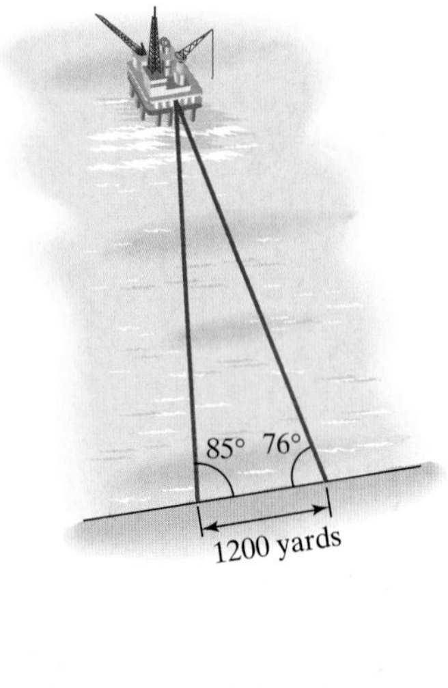

**42.** A surveyor needs to determine the distance between two points that lie on opposite banks of a river. The figure shows that 300 yards are measured along one bank. The angles from each end of this line segment to a point on the opposite bank are 62° and 53°. Find the distance between $A$ and $B$ to the nearest foot.

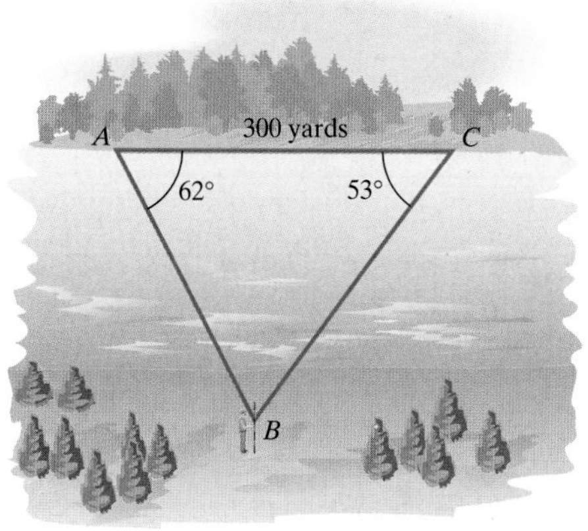


**43.** Closed to tourists since 1990, the Leaning Tower of Pisa in Italy leans at an angle of about 84.7°. The figure shows that 171 feet from the base of the tower, the angle of elevation to the top is 50°. Find the distance, to the nearest foot, from the base to the top of the tower.

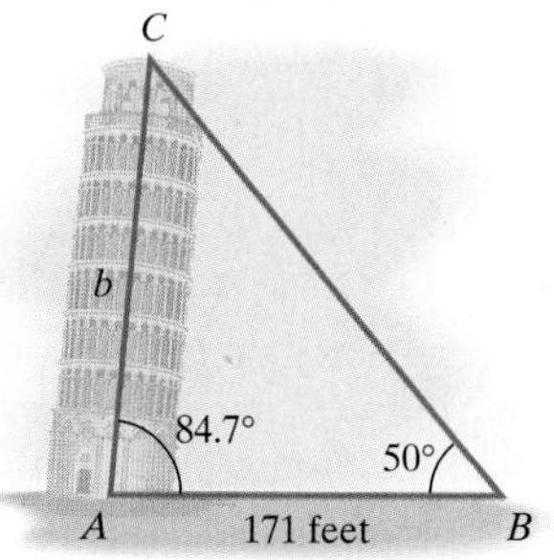


**44.** A pine tree growing on a hillside makes a 75° angle with the hill. From a point 80 feet up the hill, the angle of elevation to the top of the tree is 62° and the angle of depression to the bottom is 23°. Find, to the nearest foot, the height of the tree.

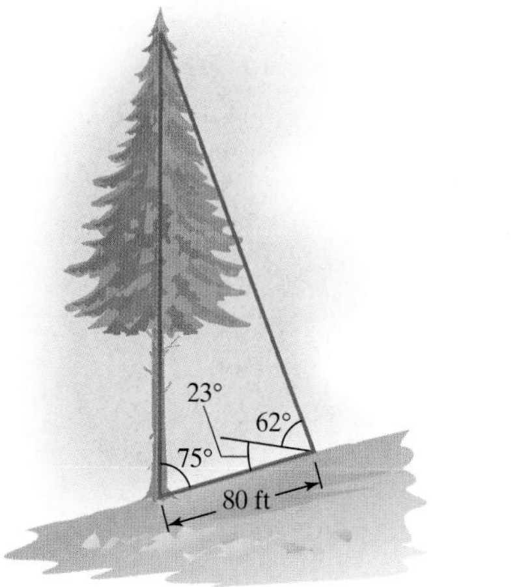


**45.** The figure shows a shot-put ring. The shot is tossed from $A$ and lands at $B$. Using modern electronic equipment, the distance of the toss can be measured without the use of measuring tapes. When the shot lands at $B$, an electronic transmitter placed at $B$ sends a signal to a device in the official's booth above the track. The device determines the angles at $B$ and $C$. At a track meet, the distance from the official's booth to the shot-put ring is 562 feet. If $B = 85.3°$ and $C = 5.7°$, determine the length of the toss to the nearest foot.

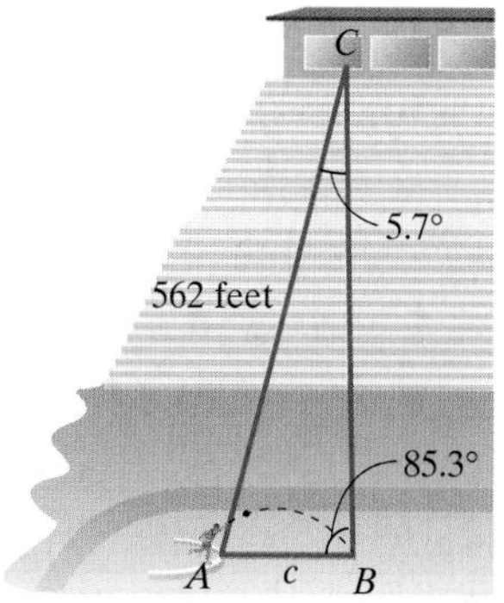


**46.** A pier forms an 85° angle with a straight dock. At a distance of 100 feet from the pier, the line of sight to the tip forms a 37° angle. Find the length of the pier to the nearest foot.

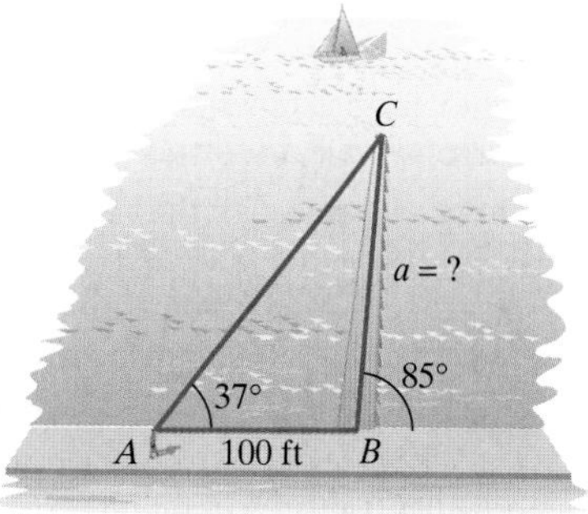


**47.** When the angle of elevation of the sun is 62°, a telephone pole that is tilted at an angle of 8° directly away from the sun casts a shadow 20 feet long. Determine the length of the pole to the nearest foot.

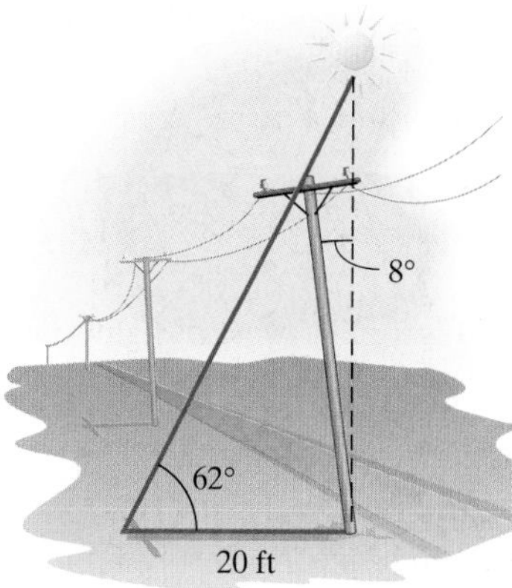

**48.** A leaning wall is inclined 6° from the vertical. At a distance of 40 feet from the wall, the angle of elevation to the top is 22°. Find the height of the wall to the nearest foot.

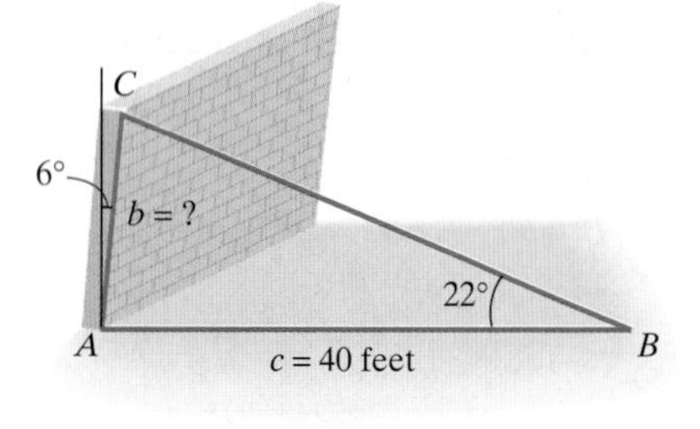


**49.** Redwood trees in California's Redwood National Park are hundreds of feet tall. The height of one of these trees is represented by $h$ in the figure shown.

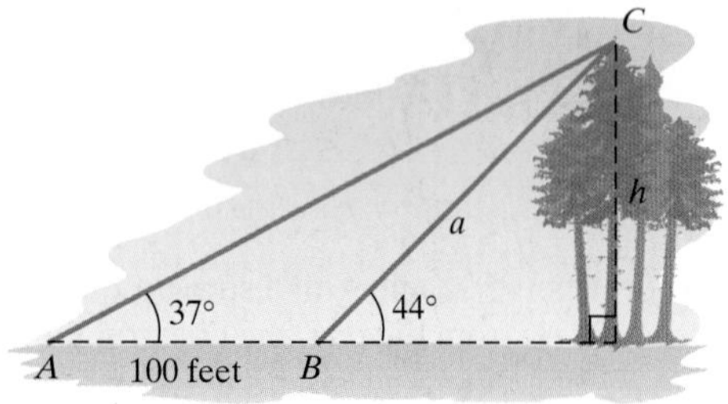


**a.** Use the measurements shown to find $a$, to the nearest foot, in oblique triangle $ABC$.

**b.** Use the right triangle shown to find the height, to the nearest foot, of a typical redwood tree in the park.

**50.** The figure shows a cable car that carries passengers from $A$ to $C$. Point $A$ is 1.6 miles from the base of the mountain. The angles of elevation from $A$ and $B$ to the mountain's peak are 22° and 66°, respectively.

**a.** Determine, to the nearest foot, the distance covered by the cable car.

**b.** Find $a$, to the nearest foot, in oblique triangle $ABC$.

**c.** Use the right triangle to find the height of the mountain to the nearest foot.

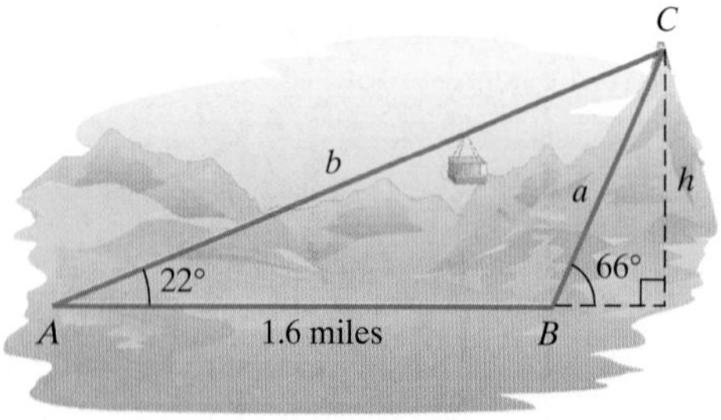


**51.** Lighthouse B is 7 miles west of lighthouse A. A boat leaves A and sails 5 miles. At this time, it is sighted from B. If the bearing of the boat from B is N62°E, how far from B is the boat? Round to the nearest tenth of a mile.

**52.** After a wind storm, you notice that your 16-foot flagpole may be leaning, but you are not sure. From a point on the ground 15 feet from the base of the flagpole, you find that the angle of elevation to the top is 48°. Is the flagpole leaning? If so, find the acute angle, to the nearest degree, that the flagpole makes with the ground.

## Writing in Mathematics

**53.** What is an oblique triangle?

**54.** Without using symbols, state the Law of Sines in your own words.

**55.** Briefly describe how the Law of Sines is proved.

**56.** What does it mean to solve an oblique triangle?

**57.** What do the abbreviations SAA and ASA mean?

**58.** Why is SSA called the ambiguous case?

**59.** How is the sine function used to find the area of an oblique triangle?

**60.** Write an original problem that can be solved using the Law of Sines. Then solve the problem.

**61.** Use Exercise 45 to describe how the Law of Sines is used for throwing events at track and field meets. Why aren't tape measures used to determine tossing distance?

**62.** You are cruising in your boat parallel to the coast, looking at a lighthouse. Explain how you can use your boat's speed and a device for measuring angles to determine the distance at any instant from your boat to the lighthouse.

## Critical Thinking Exercises

**63.** If you are given two sides of a triangle and their included angle, you can find the triangle's area. Can the Law of Sines be used to solve the triangle with this given information? Explain your answer.

**64.** Two buildings of equal height are 800 feet apart. An observer on the street between the buildings measures the angles of elevation to the tops of the buildings as 27° and 41°, respectively. How high, to the nearest foot, are the buildings?

**65.** The figure shows the design for the top of the wing of a jet fighter. The fuselage is 5 feet wide. Find the wing span $CC'$ to the nearest foot.

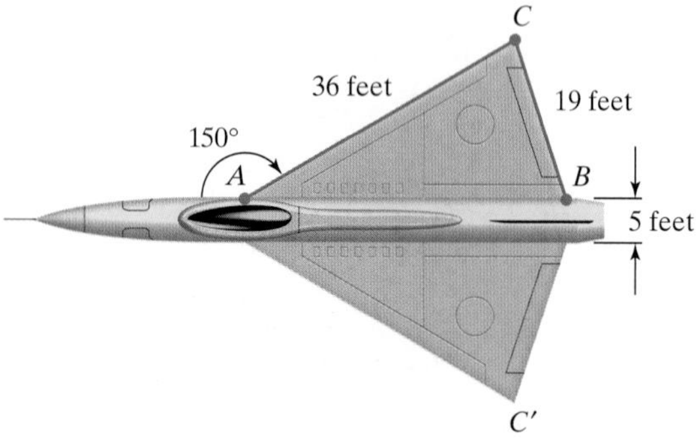

# SECTION 7.2 The Law of Cosines

## Objectives

1. Use the Law of Cosines to solve oblique triangles.
2. Solve applied problems using the Law of Cosines.
3. Use Heron's formula to find the area of a triangle.

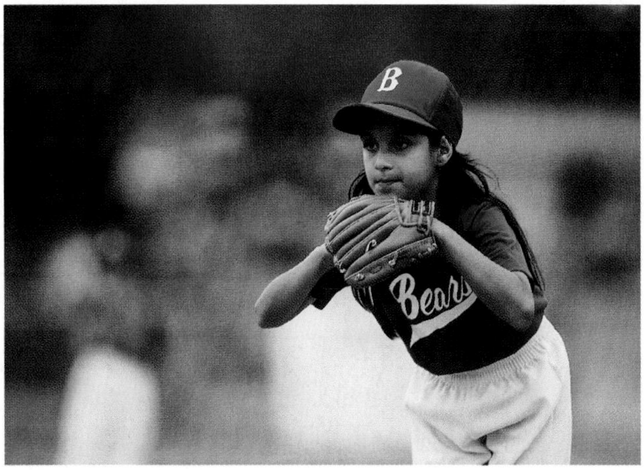


Baseball was developed in the United States in the mid-1800s and became our national sport. Little league baseball is the largest youth sports program in the world. Three million boys and girls ages 5 to 18 play on 200,000 little league teams in 90 countries. Although there are differences between major league and little league baseball diamonds, trigonometry can be used to find angles and distances in these fields of dreams. To see how this is done, we turn to the Law of Cosines.

## The Law of Cosines and Its Derivation

We now look at another relationship that exists among the sides and angles in an oblique triangle. **The Law of Cosines** is used to solve triangles in which two sides and the included angle (SAS) are known, or those in which three sides (SSS) are known.

### Discovery

What happens to the Law of Cosines

$$c^2 = a^2 + b^2 - 2ab\cos C$$

if $C = 90°$? What familiar theorem do you obtain?

### The Law of Cosines

If $A$, $B$, and $C$ are the measures of the angles of a triangle, and $a$, $b$, and $c$ are the lengths of the sides opposite these angles, then

$$a^2 = b^2 + c^2 - 2bc\cos A$$

$$b^2 = a^2 + c^2 - 2ac\cos B$$

$$c^2 = a^2 + b^2 - 2ab\cos C.$$

The square of a side of a triangle equals the sum of the squares of the other two sides minus twice their product times the cosine of their included angle.

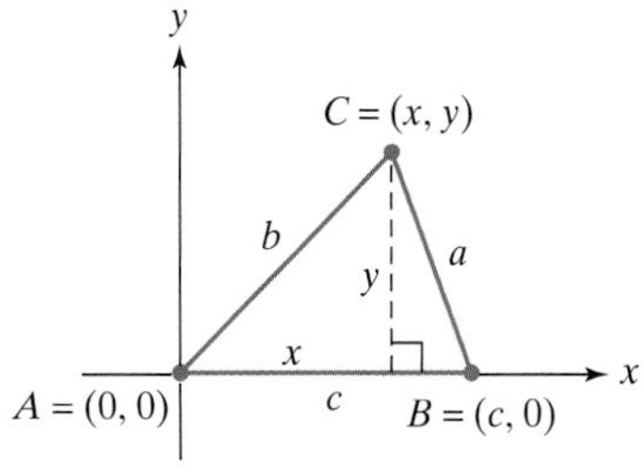


**Figure 7.13**

To prove the Law of Cosines, we place triangle $ABC$ in a rectangular coordinate system. Figure 7.13 shows a triangle with three acute angles. The vertex $A$ is at the origin and side $c$ lies along the positive $x$-axis. The coordinates of $C$ are $(x, y)$. Using the right triangle that contains angle $A$, we apply the definitions of the cosine and the sine.

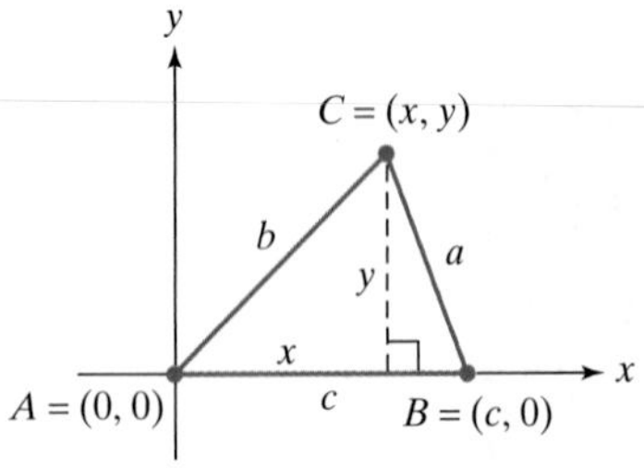


**Figure 7.13,** repeated

$$\cos A = \frac{x}{b} \qquad \sin A = \frac{y}{b}$$

$$x = b\cos A \qquad y = b\sin A$$ Multiply both sides of each equation by b and solve for x and y, respectively.

Thus, the coordinates of $C$ are $(x, y) = (b\cos A, b\sin A)$. Although triangle $ABC$ in Figure 7.13 shows angle $A$ as an acute angle, if $A$ is obtuse, the coordinates of $C$ are still $(b\cos A, b\sin A)$. This means that our proof applies to both kinds of oblique triangles.

We now apply the distance formula to the side of the triangle with length $a$. Notice that $a$ is the distance from $(x, y)$ to $(c, 0)$.

$$a = \sqrt{(x-c)^2 + (y-0)^2}$$ Use the distance formula.

$$a^2 = (x-c)^2 + y^2$$ Square both sides of the equation.

$$a^2 = (b\cos A - c)^2 + (b\sin A)^2$$ $x = b\cos A$ and $y = b\sin A$.

$$a^2 = b^2\cos^2 A - 2bc\cos A + c^2 + b^2\sin^2 A$$ Square the two expressions.

$$a^2 = b^2\sin^2 A + b^2\cos^2 A + c^2 - 2bc\cos A$$ Rearrange terms.

$$a^2 = b^2(\sin^2 A + \cos^2 A) + c^2 - 2bc\cos A$$ Factor $b^2$ from the first two terms.

$$a^2 = b^2 + c^2 - 2bc\cos A$$ $\sin^2 A + \cos^2 A = 1$

The resulting equation is one of the three formulas for the Law of Cosines. The other two formulas are derived in a similar manner.

**1** Use the Law of Cosines to solve oblique triangles.

## Solving Oblique Triangles

If you are given two sides and an included angle (SAS) of an oblique triangle, none of the three ratios in the Law of Sines is known. This means that we do not begin solving the triangle using the Law of Sines. Instead, we apply the Law of Cosines and the following procedure.

### Solving a SAS Triangle

1. Use the Law of Cosines to find the side opposite the given angle.
2. Use the Law of Sines to find the angle opposite the shorter of the two given sides. This angle is always acute.
3. Find the third angle. Subtract the measure of the given angle and the angle found in step 2 from 180°.

### EXAMPLE 1 Solving a SAS Triangle

Solve the triangle shown in Figure 7.14 on page 601 with $A = 60°$, $b = 20$, and $c = 30$.

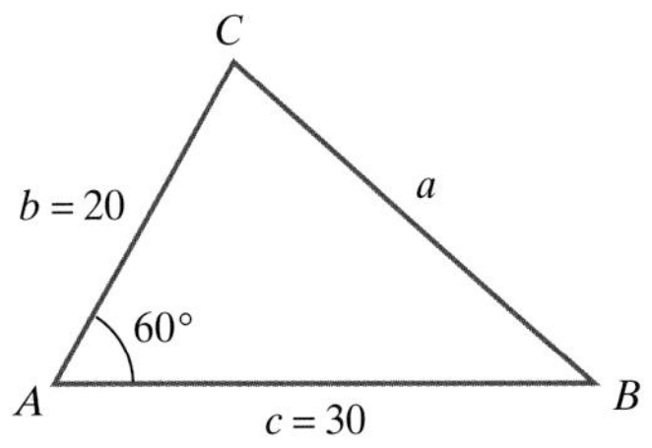


**Figure 7.14** Solving a SAS triangle

**Solution** We are given two sides and an included angle. Therefore, we apply the three-step procedure for solving a SAS triangle.

**Step 1 Use the Law of Cosines to find the side opposite the given angle.** Thus, we will find $a$.

$$a^2 = b^2 + c^2 - 2bc\cos A \qquad \text{Apply the Law of Cosines to find } a.$$

$$a^2 = 20^2 + 30^2 - 2(20)(30)\cos 60° \qquad b = 20,\ c = 30, \text{ and } A = 60°$$

$$= 400 + 900 - 1200(0.5) \qquad \text{Perform the indicated operations.}$$

$$= 700$$

$$a = \sqrt{700} \approx 26 \qquad \text{Take the square root of both sides and solve for } a.$$

**Step 2 Use the Law of Sines to find the angle opposite the shorter of the two given sides. This angle is always acute.** The shorter of the two given sides is $b = 20$. Thus, we will find acute angle $B$.

$$\frac{b}{\sin B} = \frac{a}{\sin A} \qquad \text{Apply the Law of Sines.}$$

$$\frac{20}{\sin B} = \frac{\sqrt{700}}{\sin 60°} \qquad \text{We are given } b = 20 \text{ and } A = 60°. \text{ Use the exact value of } a, \sqrt{700}, \text{ from step 1.}$$

$$\sqrt{700}\sin B = 20\sin 60° \qquad \text{Cross multiply.}$$

$$\sin B = \frac{20\sin 60°}{\sqrt{700}} \approx 0.6547 \qquad \text{Divide by } \sqrt{700} \text{ and solve for } \sin B.$$

$$B \approx 41° \qquad \text{Find } \sin^{-1} 0.6547 \text{ using a calculator.}$$

**Step 3 Find the third angle. Subtract the measure of the given angle and the angle found in step 2 from 180°.**

$$C = 180° - A - B \approx 180° - 60° - 41° = 79°$$

The solution is $a \approx 26$, $B \approx 41°$, and $C \approx 79°$.

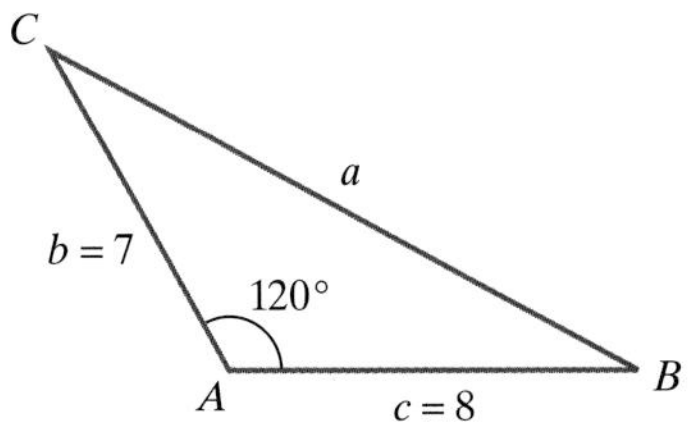


**Figure 7.15**

**Check Point 1** Solve the triangle shown in Figure 7.15 with $A = 120°$, $b = 7$, and $c = 8$.

If you are given three sides of a triangle (SSS), solving the triangle involves finding the three angles. We use the following procedure.

### Solving a SSS Triangle

1. Use the Law of Cosines to find the angle opposite the longest side.
2. Use the Law of Sines to find either of the two remaining acute angles.
3. Find the third angle. Subtract the measures of the angles found in steps 1 and 2 from 180°.

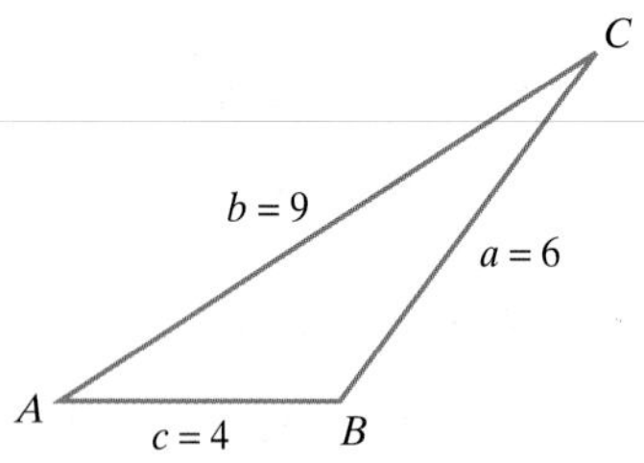


**Figure 7.16** Solving a SSS triangle

## EXAMPLE 2 Solving a SSS Triangle

Solve triangle *ABC* if $a = 6, b = 9$, and $c = 4$. Round to the nearest tenth of a degree.

**Solution** We are given three sides. Therefore, we apply the three-step procedure for solving a SSS triangle. The triangle is shown in Figure 7.16.

**Step 1 Use the Law of Cosines to find the angle opposite the longest side.** The longest side is $b = 9$. Thus, we will find angle *B*.

$$b^2 = a^2 + c^2 - 2ac\cos B \quad \text{Apply the Law of Cosines to find } B.$$

$$2ac\cos B = a^2 + c^2 - b^2 \quad \text{Solve for } \cos B.$$

$$\cos B = \frac{a^2 + c^2 - b^2}{2ac}$$

$$\cos B = \frac{6^2 + 4^2 - 9^2}{2 \cdot 6 \cdot 4} = -\frac{29}{48} \quad a = 6,\ b = 9, \text{ and } c = 4.$$

Using a calculator, $\cos^{-1}\left(\frac{29}{48}\right) \approx 52.8°$. Because $\cos B$ is negative, *B* is an obtuse angle. Thus,

$$B \approx 180° - 52.8° = 127.2°.$$

### Study Tip

You can use the Law of Cosines in step 2 to find either of the remaining angles. However, it is simpler to use the Law of Sines. Because the largest angle has been found, the remaining angles must be acute. Thus, there is no need to be concerned about two possible triangles or an ambiguous case.

**Step 2 Use the Law of Sines to find either of the two remaining acute angles.** We will find angle *A*.

$$\frac{a}{\sin A} = \frac{b}{\sin B} \quad \text{Apply the Law of Sines.}$$

$$\frac{6}{\sin A} = \frac{9}{\sin 127.2°} \quad \text{We are given } a = 6 \text{ and } b = 9. \text{ We found that } B \approx 127.2°.$$

$$9\sin A = 6\sin 127.2° \quad \text{Cross multiply.}$$

$$\sin A = \frac{6\sin 127.2°}{9} \approx 0.5310 \quad \text{Divide by 9 and solve for } \sin A.$$

$$A \approx 32.1° \quad \text{Find } \sin^{-1} 0.5310 \text{ using a calculator.}$$

**Step 3 Find the third angle. Subtract the measures of the angles found in steps 1 and 2 from 180°.**

$$C = 180° - B - A \approx 180° - 127.2° - 32.1° = 20.7°$$

The solution is $B \approx 127.2°$, $A \approx 32.1°$, and $C \approx 20.7°$.

**Check Point 2** Solve triangle *ABC* if $a = 8, b = 10$, and $c = 5$. Round to the nearest tenth of a degree.

**2** Solve applied problems using the Law of Cosines.

## Applications of the Law of Cosines

Applied problems involving SAS and SSS triangles can be solved using the Law of Cosines.

### EXAMPLE 3 An Application of the Law of Cosines

Two airplanes leave an airport at the same time on different runways. One flies at a bearing of N66°W at 325 miles per hour. The other airplane flies at a bearing of S26°W at 300 miles per hour. How far apart will the airplanes be after two hours?

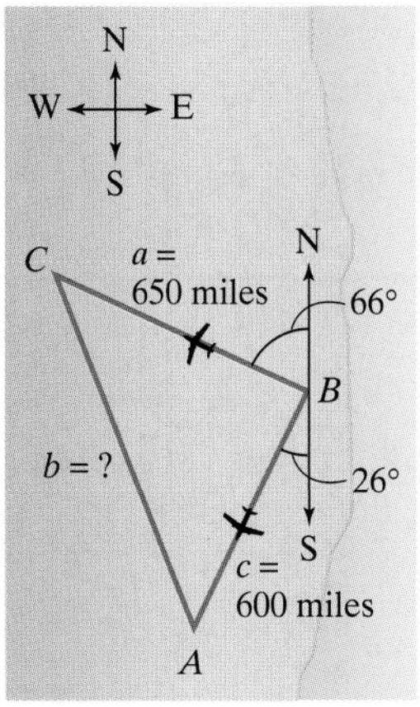


**Figure 7.17**

**Solution** After two hours, the plane flying at 325 miles per hour travels $325 \cdot 2$ miles, or 650 miles. Similarly, the plane flying at 300 miles per hour travels 600 miles. The situation is illustrated in Figure 7.17.

Let $b =$ the distance between the planes after two hours. We can use a north-south line to find angle $B$ in triangle $ABC$. Thus,

$$B = 180° - 66° - 26° = 88°.$$

We now have $a = 650$, $c = 600$, and $B = 88°$. We use the Law of Cosines to find $b$ in this SAS situation.

$$b^2 = a^2 + c^2 - 2ac\cos B$$ Apply the Law of Cosines.

$$b^2 = 650^2 + 600^2 - 2(650)(600)\cos 88°$$ Substitute: $a = 650$, $c = 600$, and $B = 88°$.

$$\approx 755{,}278$$ Use a calculator.

$$b \approx \sqrt{755{,}278} \approx 869$$ Take the square root and solve for $b$.

After two hours, the planes are approximately 869 miles apart.

**Check Point 3** Two airplanes leave an airport at the same time on different runways. One flies directly north at 400 miles per hour. The other airplane flies at a bearing of N75°E at 350 miles per hour. How far apart will the airplanes be after two hours?

**3** Use Heron's formula to find the area of a triangle.

## Heron's Formula

Approximately 2000 years ago, the Greek mathematician Heron of Alexandria derived a formula for the area of a triangle in terms of the lengths of its sides. A more modern derivation uses the Law of Cosines and can be found in the appendix.

**Heron's Formula for the Area of a Triangle**

The area of a triangle with sides $a$, $b$, and $c$ is

$$\text{Area} = \sqrt{s(s-a)(s-b)(s-c)},$$

where $s$ is one-half the perimeter: $s = \frac{1}{2}(a + b + c)$.

### EXAMPLE 4 Using Heron's Formula

Find the area of the triangle with $a = 12$ yards, $b = 16$ yards, and $c = 24$ yards.

**Solution** Begin by calculating one-half the perimeter:

$$s = \frac{1}{2}(a + b + c) = \frac{1}{2}(12 + 16 + 24) = 26.$$

Use Heron's formula to find the area:

$$\begin{aligned}\text{Area} &= \sqrt{s(s-a)(s-b)(s-c)}\\ &= \sqrt{26(26-12)(26-16)(26-24)}\\ &= \sqrt{7280} \approx 85.\end{aligned}$$

The area of the triangle is approximately 85 square yards.

**Check Point 4** Find the area of the triangle with $a = 6$ meters, $b = 16$ meters, and $c = 18$ meters. Round to the nearest square meter.

## EXERCISE SET 7.2

### Practice Exercises

*In Exercises 1–8, solve each triangle. Round lengths of sides to the nearest tenth and measurements of angles to the nearest degree.*

**1.**

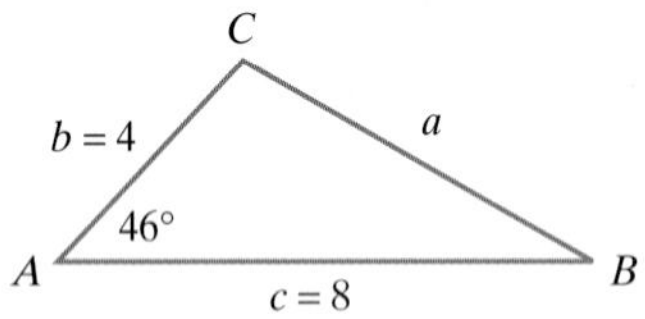


**2.**

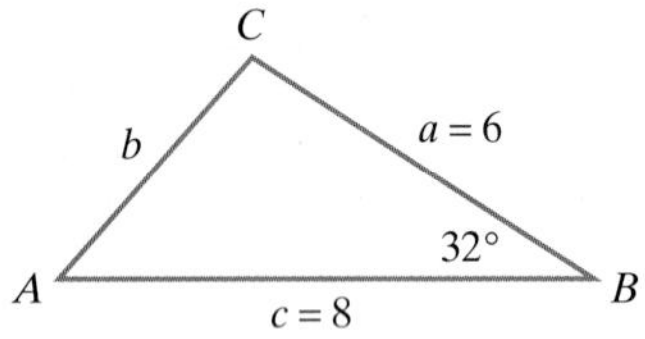


**3.**

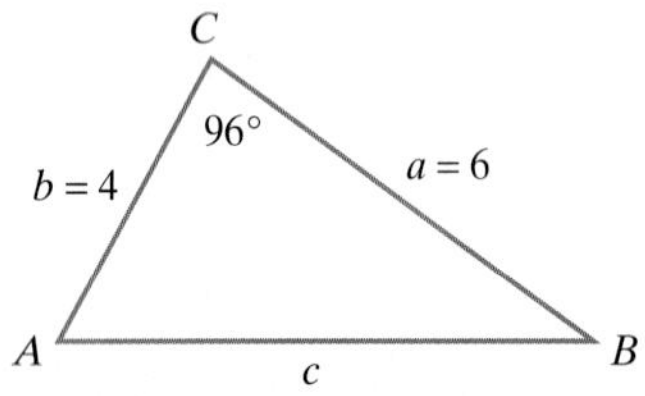


**4.**

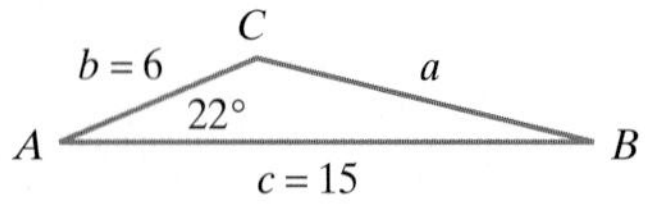


**5.**

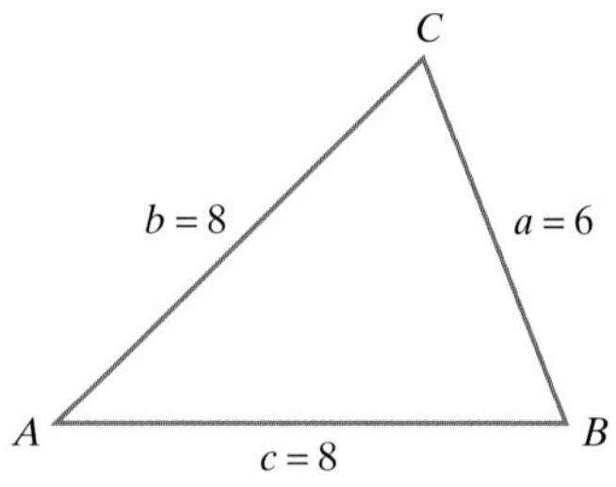


**6.**

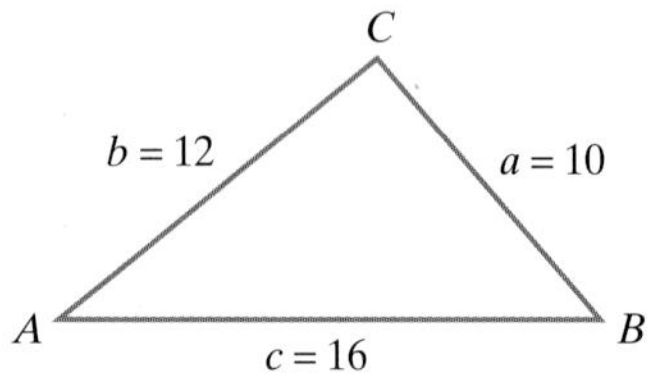


**7.**

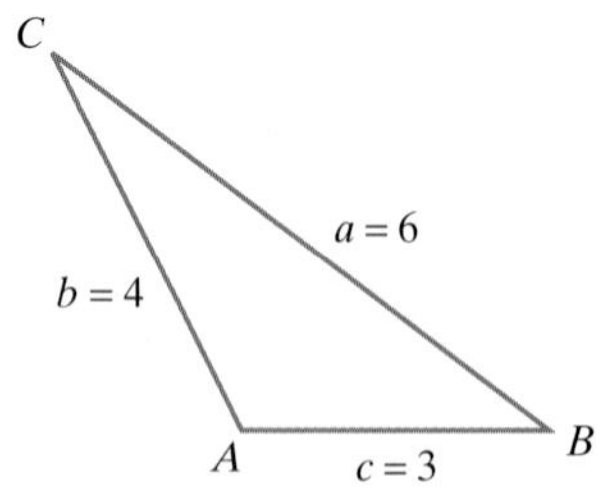


**8.**

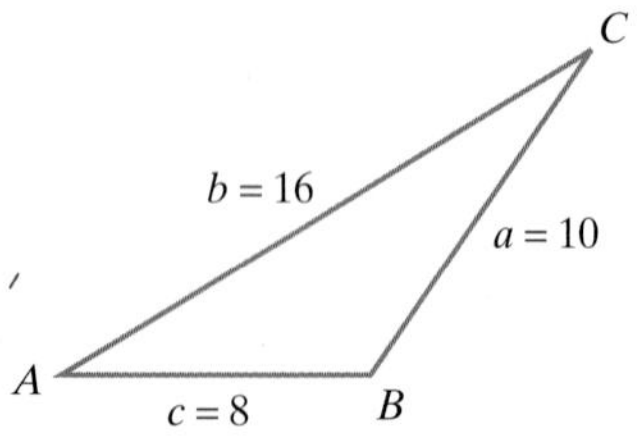

*In Exercises 9–24, solve each triangle. Round lengths to the nearest tenth and angle measures to the nearest degree.*

**9.** $a = 5, b = 7, C = 42°$ **10.** $a = 10, b = 3, C = 15°$

**11.** $b = 5, c = 3, A = 102°$ **12.** $b = 4, c = 1, A = 100°$

**13.** $a = 6, c = 5, B = 50°$ **14.** $a = 4, c = 7, B = 55°$

**15.** $a = 5, c = 2, B = 90°$ **16.** $a = 7, c = 3, B = 90°$

**17.** $a = 5, b = 7, c = 10$ **18.** $a = 4, b = 6, c = 9$

**19.** $a = 3, b = 9, c = 8$ **20.** $a = 4, b = 7, c = 6$

**21.** $a = 3, b = 3, c = 3$ **22.** $a = 5, b = 5, c = 5$

**23.** $a = 73, b = 22, c = 50$ **24.** $a = 66, b = 25, c = 45$

*In Exercises 25–30, use Heron's formula to find the area of the triangle. Round to the nearest square unit.*

**25.** $a = 4$ feet, $b = 4$ feet, $c = 2$ feet

**26.** $a = 5$ feet, $b = 5$ feet, $c = 4$ feet

**27.** $a = 14$ meters, $b = 12$ meters, $c = 4$ meters

**28.** $a = 16$ meters, $b = 10$ meters, $c = 8$ meters

**29.** $a = 11$ yards, $b = 9$ yards, $c = 7$ yards

**30.** $a = 13$ yards, $b = 9$ yards, $c = 5$ yards

## Application Exercises

**31.** Two ships leave a harbor at the same time. One ship travels at a bearing of S12°W at 14 miles per hour. The other ship travels at a bearing of N75°E at 10 miles per hour. How far apart will the ships be after three hours? Round to the nearest tenth of a mile.

**32.** A plane leaves airport A and travels 580 miles to airport B at a bearing of N34°E. The plane later leaves airport B and travels to airport C 400 miles away at a bearing of S74°E. Find the distance from airport A to airport C to the nearest tenth of a mile.

**33.** Find the distance across the lake, to the nearest yard, using the measurements shown in the figure.

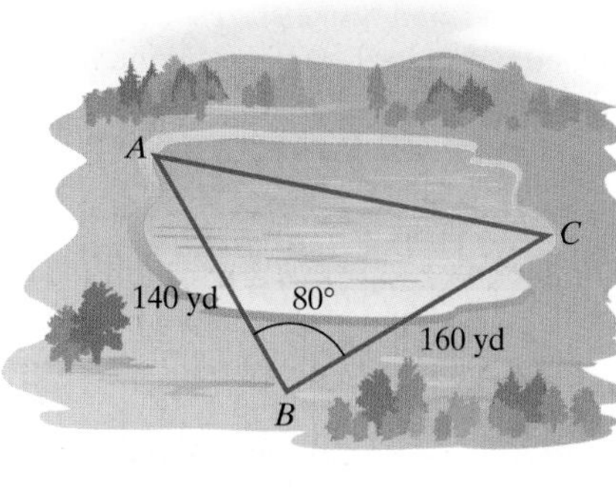


**34.** To find the distance across a protected cove at a lake, a surveyor makes the measurements shown in the figure. Use these measurements to find the distance from $A$ to $B$ to the nearest yard.

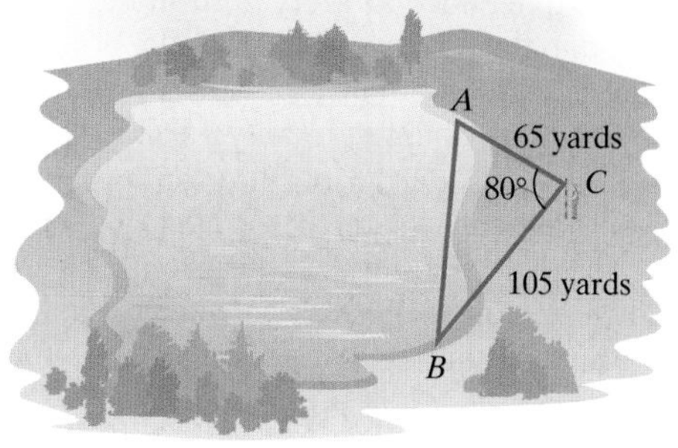


*The diagram shows three islands in Florida Bay. You rent a boat and plan to visit each of these remote islands. Use the diagram to solve Exercises 35–36.*

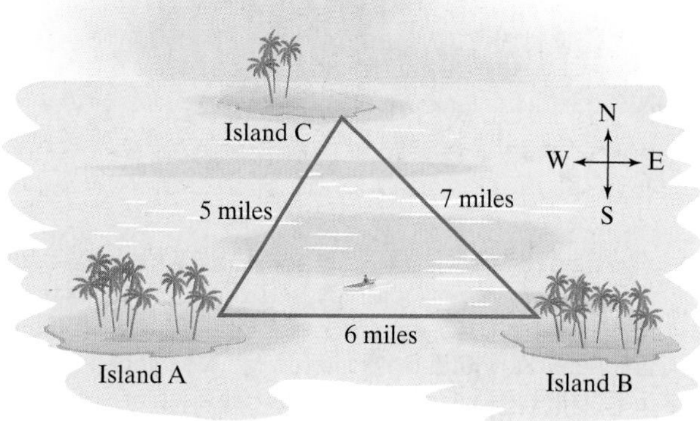


**35.** If you are on island A, on what bearing should you navigate to go to island C?

**36.** If you are on island B, on what bearing should you navigate to go to island C?

**37.** You are on a fishing boat that leaves its pier and heads east. After traveling for 25 miles, there is a report warning of rough seas directly south. The captain turns the boat and follows a bearing of S40°W for 13.5 miles.

**a.** At this time, how far are you from the boat's pier? Round to the nearest tenth of a mile.

**b.** What bearing could the boat have originally taken to arrive at this fishing spot?

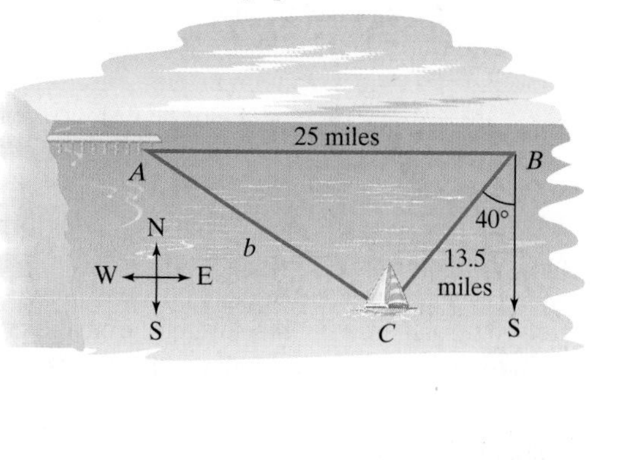

**38.** You are on a fishing boat that leaves its pier and heads east. After traveling for 30 miles, there is a report warning of rough seas directly south. The captain turns the boat and follows a bearing of S45°W for 12 miles.

**a.** At this time, how far are you from the boat's pier? Round to the nearest tenth of a mile.

**b.** What bearing could the boat have originally taken to arrive at this fishing spot?

**39.** The figure shows a 400-foot tower on the side of a hill that forms 7° angle with the horizontal. Find the length of each of the two guy wires that are anchored 80 feet uphill and downhill from the tower's base and extend to the top of the tower. Round to the nearest tenth of a foot.

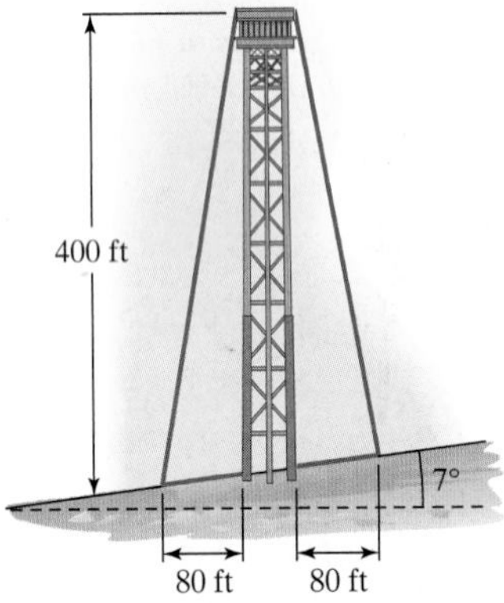


**40.** The figure shows a 200-foot tower on the side of a hill that forms a 5° angle with the horizontal. Find the length of each of the two guy wires that are anchored 150 feet uphill and downhill from the tower's base and extend to the top of the tower. Round to the nearest tenth of a foot.

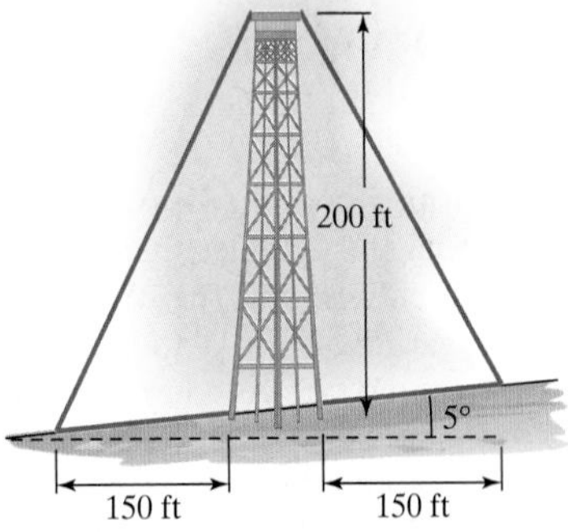


**41.** A major league baseball diamond has four bases forming a square whose sides measure 90 feet each. The pitcher's mound is 60.5 feet from home plate on a line joining home plate and second base. Find the distance from the pitcher's mound to first base. Round to the nearest tenth of a foot.

**42.** A little league baseball diamond has four bases forming a square whose sides measure 60 feet each. The pitcher's mound is 46 feet from home plate on a line joining home plate and second base. Find the distance from the pitcher's mound to third base. Round to the nearest tenth of a foot.

**43.** A commercial piece of real estate is priced at \$3.50 per square foot. Find the cost, to the nearest dollar, of a triangular lot measuring 240 feet by 300 feet by 420 feet.

**44.** A commercial piece of real estate is priced at \$4.50 per square foot. Find the cost, to the nearest dollar, of a triangular lot measuring 320 feet by 510 feet by 410 feet.

## Writing in Mathematics

**45.** Without using symbols, state the Law of Cosines in your own words.

**46.** Why can't the Law of Sines be used in the first step to solve a SAS triangle?

**47.** Describe a strategy for solving a SAS triangle.

**48.** Describe a strategy for solving a SSS triangle.

**49.** Under what conditions would you use Heron's formula to find the area of a triangle?

**50.** Describe an applied problem that can be solved using the Law of Cosines, but not the Law of Sines.

**51.** The pitcher on your little league team is studying angles in geometry and has a question. "Coach, suppose I'm on the pitcher's mound facing home plate. I catch a fly ball hit in my direction. If I turn to face first base and throw the ball, through how many degrees should I turn for a direct throw?" Use the information given in Exercise 42 and write an answer to your pitcher's question. Without getting too technical, describe to your pitcher how you obtained this angle.

## Critical Thinking Exercises

**52.** The lengths of the diagonals of a parallelogram are 20 inches and 30 inches. The diagonals intersect at an angle of 35°. Find the lengths of the parallelogram's sides. (*Hint*: Diagonals of a parallelogram bisect one another.)

**53.** The vertices of a triangle are $A(4, -3)$, $B(2, 1)$, and $C(-2, 4)$. Find the triangle's largest angle to the nearest tenth of a degree.

**54.** The minute hand and the hour hand of a clock have lengths $m$ inches and $h$ inches, respectively. Determine the distance between the tips of the hands at 10:00 in terms of $m$ and $h$.

## Group Exercise

**55.** The group should design five original problems that can be solved using the Laws of Sines and Cosines. At least two problems should be solved using the Law of Sines and at least two problems should be solved using the Law of Cosines. At least one problem should be an application problem using the Law of Sines and at least one problem should involve an application using the Law of Cosines. The group should turn in both the problems and their solutions.

# SECTION 7.3 Polar Coordinates

## Objectives

1. Plot points in the polar coordinate system.
2. Find multiple sets of polar coordinates of a given point.
3. Convert a point from polar to rectangular coordinates.
4. Convert a point from rectangular to polar coordinates.
5. Convert an equation from rectangular to polar coordinates.
6. Convert an equation from polar to rectangular coordinates.

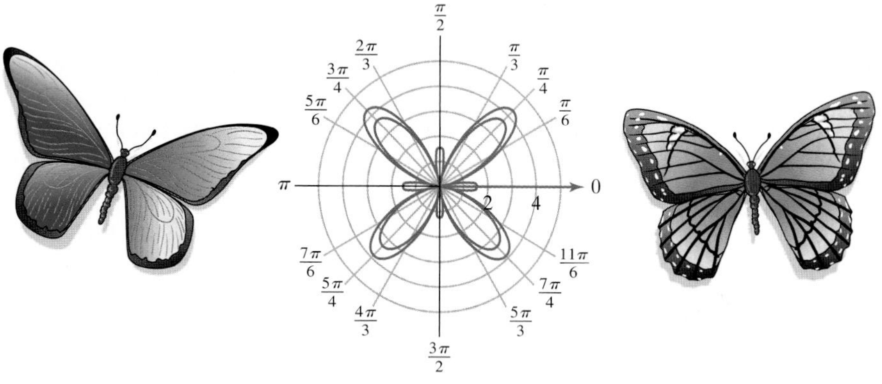


Butterflies are among the most celebrated of all insects. It's hard not to notice their beautiful colors and graceful flight. Their symmetry can be explored with trigonometric functions and a system for plotting points called the **polar coordinate system**. In many cases, polar coordinates are simpler and easier to use than rectangular coordinates.

**1** Plot points in the polar coordinate system.

## Plotting Points in the Polar Coordinate System

The foundation of the polar coordinate system is a horizontal ray that extends to the right. The ray is called the **polar axis** and is shown in Figure 7.18. The endpoint of the ray is called the **pole**.

A point $P$ in the polar coordinate system is represented by an ordered pair of numbers $(r, \theta)$. Figure 7.19 shows $P = (r, \theta)$ in the polar coordinate system.

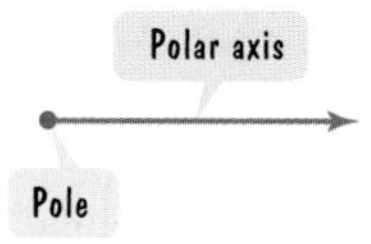


**Figure 7.18**

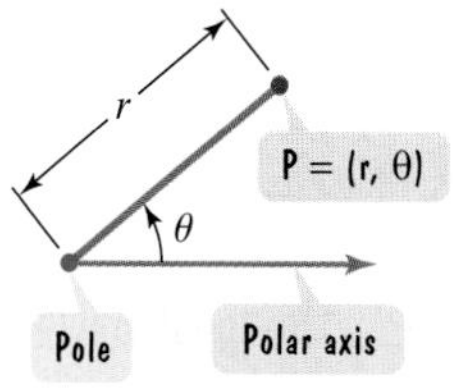


**Figure 7.19** Representing a point in the polar coordinate system

- $r$ is the directed distance of $P$ from the pole. (We shall see that $r$ can be positive, negative or zero.)
- $\theta$ is an angle from the polar axis to line segment $OP$. This angle can be measured in degrees or radians. Positive angles are measured counterclockwise from the polar axis. Negative angles are measured clockwise from the polar axis.

We refer to the ordered pair $(r, \theta)$ as the **polar coordinates** of $P$.

Let's look at a specific example. Suppose that the polar coordinates of a point $P$ are $\left(3, \frac{\pi}{4}\right)$. Because $\theta$ is positive, we locate this point by drawing $\theta = \frac{\pi}{4}$ counterclockwise from the polar axis. Then we count out a distance of three units along the terminal side of the angle to reach the point $P$.

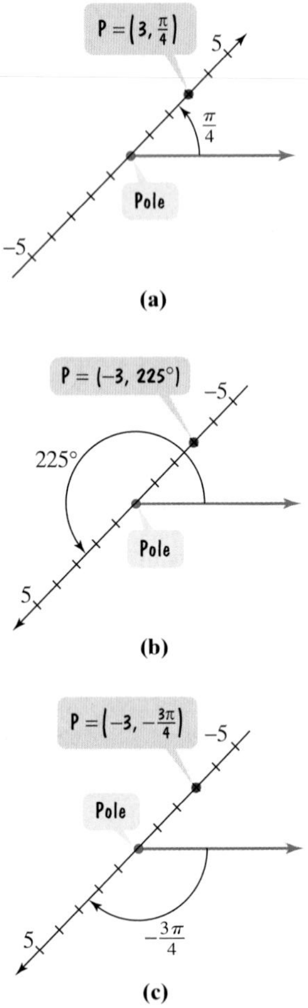


**Figure 7.20** Locating points in polar coordinates

Figure 7.20(a) shows that $(r, \theta) = \left(3, \frac{\pi}{4}\right)$ lies three units from the pole on the terminal side of the angle $\theta = \frac{\pi}{4}$.

Figure 7.20 illustrates that in a polar coordinate system, a point can be represented in more than one way. In Figure 7.20(b), $r$ is negative and $\theta$ is positive: $r = -3$ and $\theta = 225°$. Because $\theta$ is positive, we draw a 225° angle counterclockwise from the polar axis. Notice that the point $P$ is not located on the terminal side of $\theta$. Instead, it lies on the ray *opposite the terminal side of* $\theta$ at a distance of $|-3|$, or 3, units from the pole. In general, **when $r$ in $(r, \theta)$ is negative, a point is located $|r|$ units along the ray opposite the terminal side of $\theta$.**

In Figure 7.20(c), $r$ and $\theta$ are both negative: $r = -3$ and $\theta = -\frac{3\pi}{4}$. Because $\theta$ is negative, we draw a $-\frac{3\pi}{4}$ (or $-135°$) angle clockwise from the polar axis. Because $r$ is negative, the point is located on the ray opposite the terminal side of $\theta$.

Our observations indicate the importance of the sign of $r$ in locating $P = (r, \theta)$ in polar coordinates.

**The Sign of $r$ and a Point's Location in Polar Coordinates**

The point $P = (r, \theta)$ is located $|r|$ units from the pole. If $r > 0$, the point lies on the terminal side of $\theta$. If $r < 0$, the point lies along the ray opposite the terminal side of $\theta$. If $r = 0$, the point lies at the pole, regardless of the value of $\theta$.

## EXAMPLE 1 Plotting Points in a Polar Coordinate System

Plot the points with the following polar coordinates:

**a.** $(2, 135°)$ **b.** $\left(-3, \frac{3\pi}{2}\right)$ **c.** $\left(-1, -\frac{\pi}{4}\right)$.

### Solution

**a.** To plot the point $(r, \theta) = (2, 135°)$, begin with the 135° angle. Because 135° is a positive angle, draw $\theta = 135°$ counterclockwise from the polar axis. Now consider $r = 2$. Because $r > 0$, plot the point by going out two units on the terminal side of $\theta$. Figure 7.21(a) shows the point.

**b.** To plot the point $(r, \theta) = \left(-3, \frac{3\pi}{2}\right)$, begin with the $\frac{3\pi}{2}$ angle. Because $\frac{3\pi}{2}$ is a positive angle, we draw $\theta = \frac{3\pi}{2}$ counterclockwise from the polar axis. Now consider $r = -3$. Because $r < 0$, plot the point by going out three units along the ray *opposite* the terminal side of $\theta$. Figure 7.21(b) shows the point.

**c.** To plot the point $(r, \theta) = \left(-1, -\frac{\pi}{4}\right)$, begin with the $-\frac{\pi}{4}$ angle. Because $-\frac{\pi}{4}$ is a negative angle, draw $\theta = -\frac{\pi}{4}$ clockwise from the polar axis. Now

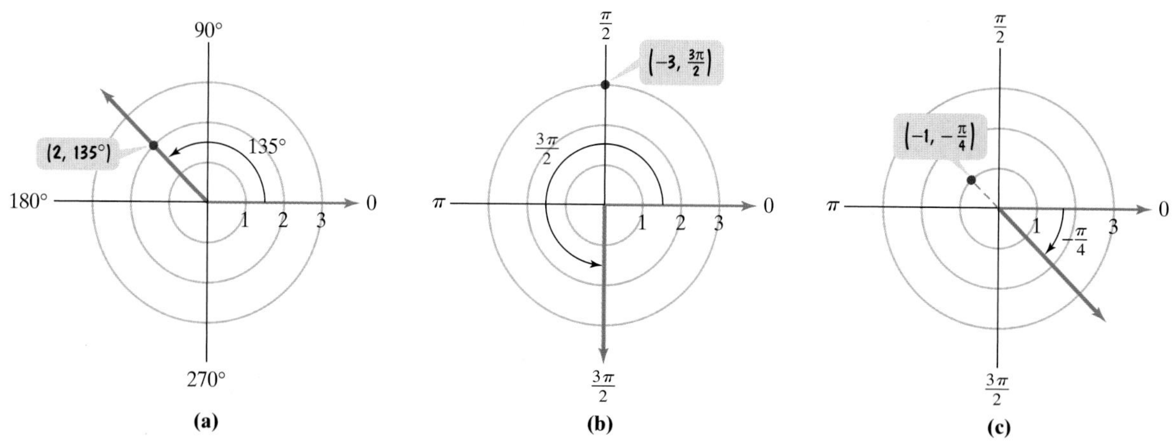


**Figure 7.21** Plotting points

consider $r = -1$. Because $r < 0$, plot the point by going out one unit along the ray *opposite* the terminal side of $\theta$. Figure 7.21(c) shows the point.

**Check Point 1** Plot the points with the following polar coordinates:

**a.** $(3, 315°)$ **b.** $(-2, \pi)$ **c.** $\left(-1, -\frac{\pi}{2}\right)$.

**2** Find multiple sets of polar coordinates of a given point.

## Discovery

Illustrate the statements in the voice ballons by plotting:

**a.** $\left(1, \frac{\pi}{2}\right)$ and $\left(1, \frac{5\pi}{2}\right)$.

**b.** $\left(3, \frac{\pi}{4}\right)$ and $\left(-3, \frac{5\pi}{4}\right)$.

## Multiple Representation of Points in the Polar Coordinate System

In rectangular coordinates, each point $(x, y)$ has exactly one representation. By contrast, any point in polar coordinates can be represented in infinitely many ways. For example,

$$(r, \theta) = (r, \theta + 2\pi) \quad \text{and} \quad (r, \theta) = (-r, \theta + \pi).$$

Adding 1 revolution, or $2\pi$ radians, to the angle does not change the point's location.

Adding $\frac{1}{2}$ revolution, or $\pi$ radians, to the angle and replacing $r$ by $-r$ does not change the point's location.

Thus, to find two other representations for the point $(r, \theta)$,

- Add $2\pi$ to the angle and do not change $r$.
- Add $\pi$ to the angle and replace $r$ by $-r$.

Continually adding or subtracting $2\pi$ in either of these representations does not change the point's location.

**Multiple Representation of Points**

If $n$ is any integer, the point $(r, \theta)$ can be represented as

$$(r, \theta) = (r, \theta + 2n\pi) \quad \text{or} \quad (r, \theta) = (-r, \theta + \pi + 2n\pi).$$

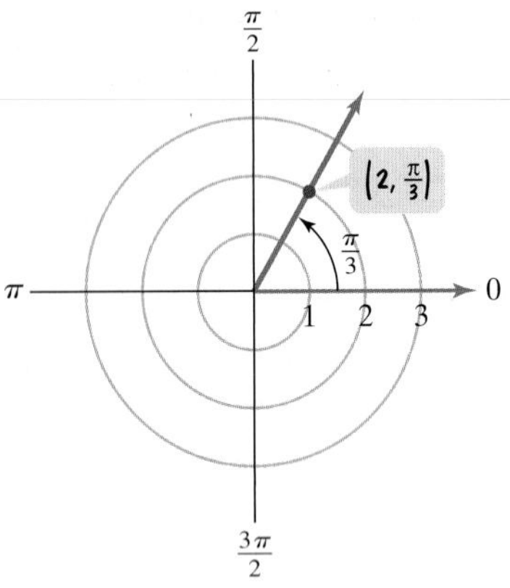


**Figure 7.22** Finding other representations of a given point

## EXAMPLE 2 Finding Other Polar Coordinates of a Given Point

The point $\left(2, \frac{\pi}{3}\right)$ is plotted in Figure 7.22. Find another representation of this point in which:

**a.** $r$ is positive and $2\pi < \theta < 4\pi$.
**b.** $r$ is negative and $0 < \theta < 2\pi$.
**c.** $r$ is positive and $-2\pi < \theta < 0$.

### Solution

**a.** Add $2\pi$ to the angle and do not change $r$.

$$\left(2, \frac{\pi}{3}\right) = \left(2, \frac{\pi}{3} + 2\pi\right) = \left(2, \frac{\pi}{3} + \frac{6\pi}{3}\right) = \left(2, \frac{7\pi}{3}\right)$$

**b.** Add $\pi$ to the angle and replace $r$ by $-r$.

$$\left(2, \frac{\pi}{3}\right) = \left(-2, \frac{\pi}{3} + \pi\right) = \left(-2, \frac{\pi}{3} + \frac{3\pi}{3}\right) = \left(-2, \frac{4\pi}{3}\right)$$

**c.** Subtract $2\pi$ from the angle and do not change $r$.

$$\left(2, \frac{\pi}{3}\right) = \left(2, \frac{\pi}{3} - 2\pi\right) = \left(2, \frac{\pi}{3} - \frac{6\pi}{3}\right) = \left(2, -\frac{5\pi}{3}\right)$$

**Check Point 2**

Find another representation of $\left(5, \frac{\pi}{4}\right)$ in which:

**a.** $r$ is positive and $2\pi < \theta < 4\pi$.
**b.** $r$ is negative and $0 < \theta < 2\pi$.
**c.** $r$ is positive and $-2\pi < \theta < 0$.

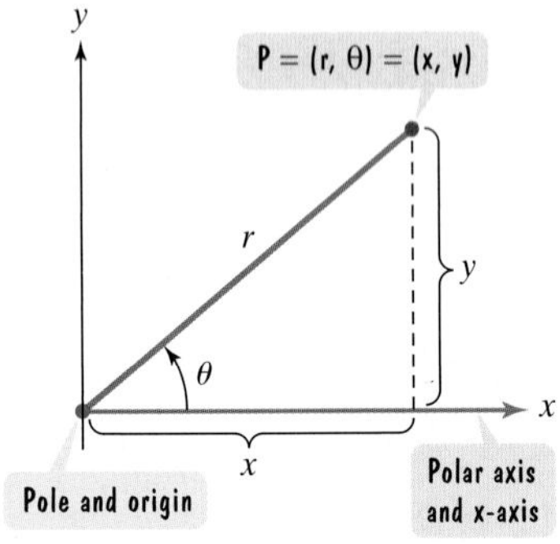


**Figure 7.23** Polar and rectangular coordinate systems

## Relations between Polar and Rectangular Coordinates

We now consider both polar and rectangular coordinates simultaneously. Figure 7.23 shows the two coordinate systems. The polar axis coincides with the positive $x$-axis and the pole coincides with the origin. A point $P$, other than the origin, has rectangular coordinates $(x, y)$ and polar coordinates $(r, \theta)$, as indicated in the figure. We wish to find equations relating the two sets of coordinates. From the figure, we see that

$$x^2 + y^2 = r^2$$

$$\sin\theta = \frac{y}{r} \qquad \cos\theta = \frac{x}{r} \qquad \tan\theta = \frac{y}{x}.$$

These relationships hold when $P$ is in any quadrant and when $r > 0$ or $r < 0$.

**Relations between Polar and Rectangular Coordinates**

$$x = r\cos\theta$$
$$y = r\sin\theta$$
$$x^2 + y^2 = r^2$$
$$\tan\theta = \frac{y}{x}$$

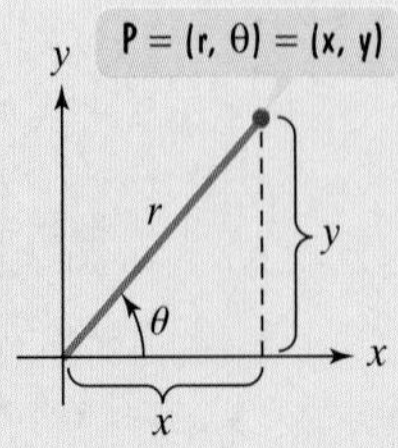

**3** Convert a point from polar to rectangular coordinates.

## Point Conversion from Polar to Rectangular Coordinates

To convert a point from polar coordinates $(r, \theta)$ to rectangular coordinates $(x, y)$, use the formulas $x = r\cos\theta$ and $y = r\sin\theta$.

### EXAMPLE 3 Polar-to-Rectangular Point Conversion

Find the rectangular coordinates of the points with the following polar coordinates:

**a.** $\left(2, \frac{3\pi}{2}\right)$  **b.** $\left(-8, \frac{\pi}{3}\right)$.

**Solution** We find $(x, y)$ by substituting the given values for $r$ and $\theta$ into $x = r\cos\theta$ and $y = r\sin\theta$.

**a.** We begin with the rectangular coordinates of the point $(r, \theta) = \left(2, \frac{3\pi}{2}\right)$.

$$x = r\cos\theta = 2\cos\frac{3\pi}{2} = 2 \cdot 0 = 0$$

$$y = r\sin\theta = 2\sin\frac{3\pi}{2} = 2(-1) = -2$$

The rectangular coordinates of $\left(2, \frac{3\pi}{2}\right)$ are $(0, -2)$. (See Figure 7.24)

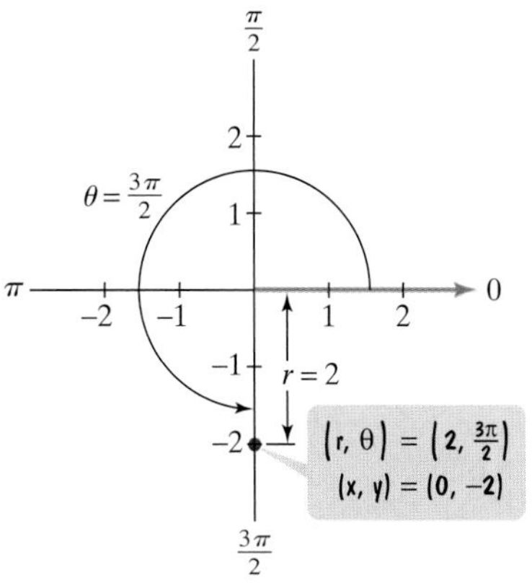


**Figure 7.24** Converting $\left(2, \frac{3\pi}{2}\right)$ to rectangular coordinates

**b.** We now find the rectangular coordinates of the point $(r, \theta) = \left(-8, \frac{\pi}{3}\right)$.

$$x = r\cos\theta = -8\cos\frac{\pi}{3} = -8\left(\frac{1}{2}\right) = -4$$

$$y = r\sin\theta = -8\sin\frac{\pi}{3} = -8\left(\frac{\sqrt{3}}{2}\right) = -4\sqrt{3}$$

The rectangular coordinates of $\left(-8, \frac{\pi}{3}\right)$ are $(-4, -4\sqrt{3})$.

## Technology

Some graphing utilities can convert a point from polar coordinates to rectangular coordinates. Consult your manual. The screen on the right verifies the polar-rectangular conversion in Example 3(a). It shows that the rectangular coordinates of $(r, \theta) = \left(2, \frac{3\pi}{2}\right)$ are $(0, -2)$.

Notice that the $x$- and $y$-coordinates are displayed separately.

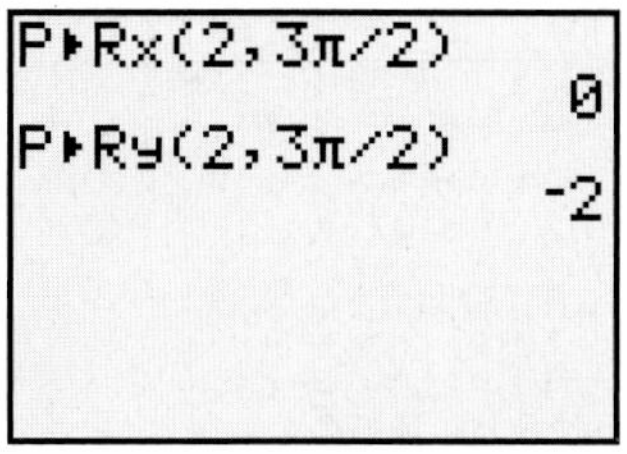

**Check Point 3** Find the rectangular coordinates of the points with the following polar coordinates:

**a.** $(3, \pi)$ **b.** $\left(-10, \frac{\pi}{6}\right)$.

**4** Convert a point from rectangular to polar coordinates.

## Point Conversion from Rectangular to Polar Coordinates

Conversion from rectangular coordinates $(x, y)$ to polar coordinates $(r, \theta)$ is a bit more complicated. Keep in mind that there are infinitely many representations for a point in polar coordinates. If the point $(x, y)$ lies in one of the four quadrants, we will use a representation in which

- $r$ is positive, and
- $\theta$ is the smallest positive angle that lies in the same quadrant as $(x, y)$.

These conventions provide the following procedure.

**Converting a point from Rectangular to Polar Coordinates ($r > 0$ and $0 \le \theta < 2\pi$)**

1. Plot the point $(x, y)$.
2. Find $r$ by computing the distance from the origin to $(x, y)$: $r = \sqrt{x^2 + y^2}$.
3. Find $\theta$ using $\tan\theta = \frac{y}{x}$ with $\theta$ lying in the same quadrant as $(x, y)$.

### EXAMPLE 4 Rectangular-to-Polar Point Conversion

Find polar coordinates of a point whose rectangular coordinates are $(-1, \sqrt{3})$.

**Solution** We begin with $(x, y) = (-1, \sqrt{3})$ and use our three-step procedure to find a set of polar coordinates $(r, \theta)$.

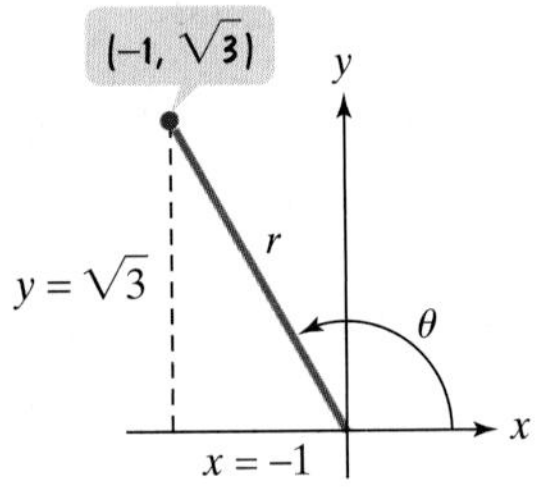


**Figure 7.25** Converting $(-1, \sqrt{3})$ to polar coordinates

**Step 1 Plot the point $(x, y)$.** The point $(-1, \sqrt{3})$ is plotted in quadrant II in Figure 7.25.

**Step 2 Find $r$ by computing the distance from the origin to $(x, y)$.**

$$r = \sqrt{x^2 + y^2} = \sqrt{(-1)^2 + (\sqrt{3})^2} = \sqrt{1 + 3} = \sqrt{4} = 2$$

**Step 3 Find $\theta$ using $\tan\theta = \frac{y}{x}$ with $\theta$ lying in the same quadrant as $(x, y)$.**

$$\tan\theta = \frac{y}{x} = \frac{\sqrt{3}}{-1} = -\sqrt{3}$$

We know that $\tan\frac{\pi}{3} = \sqrt{3}$. Because $\theta$ lies in quadrant II,

$$\theta = \pi - \frac{\pi}{3} = \frac{3\pi}{3} - \frac{\pi}{3} = \frac{2\pi}{3}.$$

Polar coordinates of $(-1, \sqrt{3})$ are $(r, \theta) = \left(2, \frac{2\pi}{3}\right)$.

## Technology

The screen shows the rectangular-polar conversion for $(-1, \sqrt{3})$ on a graphing utility. In Example 4, we showed that the polar coordinates of $(x, y) = (-1, \sqrt{3})$ are $(r, \theta) = \left(2, \frac{2\pi}{3}\right)$. Using $\frac{2\pi}{3} \approx 2.09439510239$ verifies that our conversion is correct. Notice that the $r$- and (approximate) $\theta$-coordinates are displayed separately.

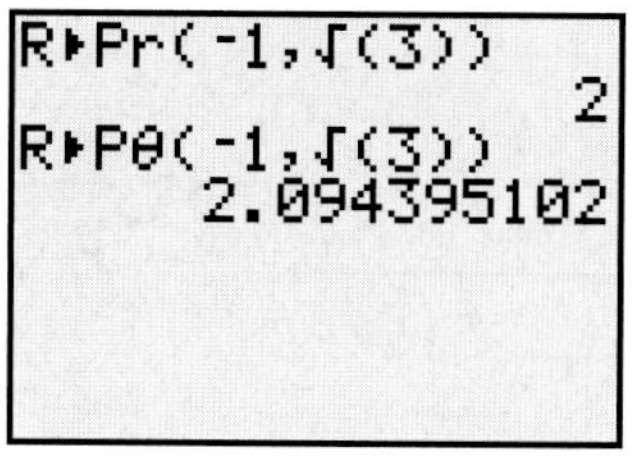


**Check Point 4** Find polar coordinates of a point whose rectangular coordinates are $(1, -\sqrt{3})$.

If a point $(x, y)$ lies on a positive or negative axis, we use a representation in which

- $r$ is positive, and
- $\theta$ is the smallest quadrantal angle that lies on the same positive or negative axis as $(x, y)$.

In these cases, you can find $r$ and $\theta$ by plotting $(x, y)$ and inspecting the figure. Let's see how this is done.

### EXAMPLE 5 Rectangular-to-Polar Point Conversion

Find polar coordinates of a point whose rectangular coordinates are $(-2, 0)$.

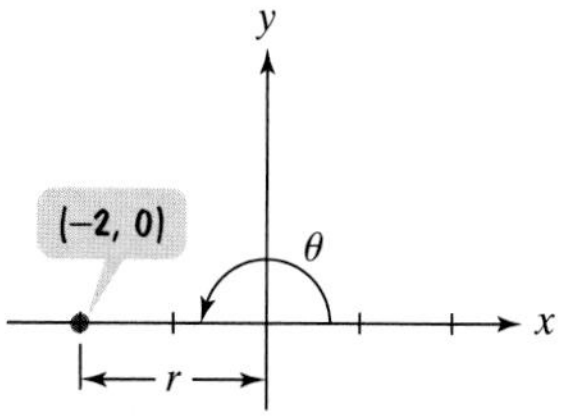


**Figure 7.26** Converting $(-2, 0)$ to polar coordinates

**Solution** We begin with $(x, y) = (-2, 0)$ and find a set of polar coordinates $(r, \theta)$.

**Step 1 Plot the point $(x, y)$.** The point $(-2, 0)$ is plotted in Figure 7.26.

**Step 2 Find $r$, the distance from the origin to $(x, y)$.** Can you tell by looking at Figure 7.26 that this distance is 2?

$$r = \sqrt{x^2 + y^2} = \sqrt{(-2)^2 + 0^2} = \sqrt{4} = 2$$

**Step 3 Find $\theta$ with $\theta$ lying on the same positive or negative axis as $(x, y)$.** The point $(-2, 0)$ is on the negative $x$-axis. Thus, $\theta$ lies on the negative $x$-axis and $\theta = \pi$. Polar coordinates of $(-2, 0)$ are $(2, \pi)$.

**Check Point 5** Find polar coordinates of a point whose rectangular coordinates are $(0, -4)$.

**5** Convert an equation from rectangular to polar coordinates.

## Equation Conversion from Rectangular to Polar Coordinates

A **polar equation** is an equation whose variables are $r$ and $\theta$. Two examples of polar equations are

$$r = \frac{5}{\cos\theta + \sin\theta} \quad \text{and} \quad r = \csc\theta.$$

To convert a rectangular equation in $x$ and $y$ to a polar equation in $r$ and $\theta$, replace $x$ by $r\cos\theta$ and $y$ by $r\sin\theta$.

### EXAMPLE 6 Converting an Equation from Rectangular to Polar Coordinates

Convert $x + y = 5$ to a polar equation.

**Solution** Our goal is to obtain an equation in which the variables are $r$ and $\theta$ rather than $x$ and $y$. We use $x = r\cos\theta$ and $y = r\sin\theta$.

$$x + y = 5 \quad \text{This is the given equation in rectangular coordinates.}$$

$$r\cos\theta + r\sin\theta = 5 \quad \text{Replace } x \text{ by } r\cos\theta \text{ and } y \text{ by } r\sin\theta.$$

Thus, the polar equation for $x + y = 5$ is $r\cos\theta + r\sin\theta = 5$. We can express this polar equation in a number of equivalent ways, including an equation that gives $r$ in terms of $\theta$.

$$r(\cos\theta + \sin\theta) = 5 \quad \text{Factor out } r.$$

$$r = \frac{5}{\cos\theta + \sin\theta} \quad \text{Divide both sides of the equation by } \cos\theta + \sin\theta.$$

**Check Point 6** Convert $3x - y = 6$ to a polar equation. Express the polar equation with $r$ in terms of $\theta$.

**6** Convert an equation from polar to rectangular coordinates.

## Equation Conversion from Polar to Rectangular Coordinates

When we convert an equation from polar to rectangular coordinates, our goal is to obtain an equation in which the variables are $x$ and $y$ rather than $r$ and $\theta$. We use one or more of the following equations:

$$r^2 = x^2 + y^2 \qquad r\cos\theta = x \qquad r\sin\theta = y \qquad \tan\theta = \frac{y}{x}.$$

To obtain the expressions on the left in each of these equations, it is sometimes necessary to do something to the given polar equation. This could include squaring both sides, using an identity, taking the tangent of both sides, or multiplying both sides by $r$.

### EXAMPLE 7 Converting Equations from Polar to Rectangular Form

Convert each polar equation to a rectangular equation in $x$ and $y$.

**a.** $r = 3$ **b.** $\theta = \frac{\pi}{4}$ **c.** $r = \csc\theta$

**Solution**

**a.** We use $r^2 = x^2 + y^2$ to convert the polar equation $r = 3$ to a rectangular equation.

$r = 3$ This is the given polar equation.

$r^2 = 9$ Square both sides.

$x^2 + y^2 = 9$ Use $r^2 = x^2 + y^2$ on the left side.

The rectangular equation for $r = 3$ is $x^2 + y^2 = 9$.

**b.** We use $\tan\theta = \frac{y}{x}$ to convert the polar equation $\theta = \frac{\pi}{4}$ to a rectangular equation in $x$ and $y$.

$\theta = \frac{\pi}{4}$ This is the given polar equation.

$\tan\theta = \tan\frac{\pi}{4}$ Take the tangent of both sides.

$\tan\theta = 1$ $\tan\frac{\pi}{4} = 1$

$\frac{y}{x} = 1$ Use $\tan\theta = \frac{y}{x}$ on the left side.

$y = x$ Multiply both sides by x.

The rectangular equation for $\theta = \frac{\pi}{4}$ is $y = x$.

**c.** We use $r\sin\theta = y$ to convert the polar equation $r = \csc\theta$ to a rectangular equation. To do this, we express the cosecant in terms of the sine.

$r = \csc\theta$ This is the given polar equation.

$r = \frac{1}{\sin\theta}$ $\csc\theta = \frac{1}{\sin\theta}$

$r\sin\theta = 1$ Multiply both sides by $\sin\theta$.

$y = 1$ Use $r\sin\theta = y$ on the left side.

The rectangular equation for $r = \csc\theta$ is $y = 1$.

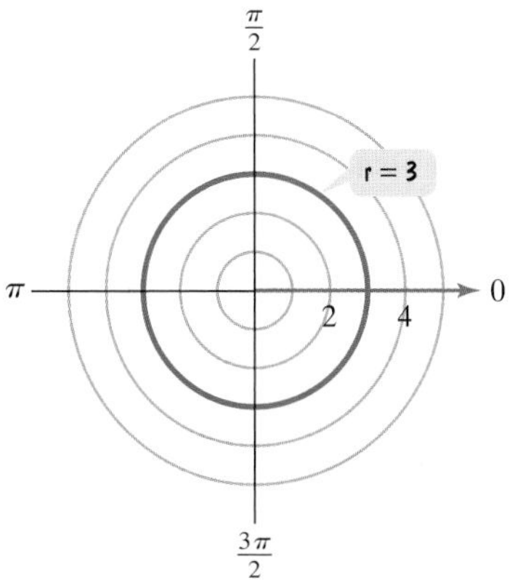

**Figure 7.27** The equations $r = 3$ and $x^2 + y^2 = 9$ have the same graph.

Converting a polar equation to a rectangular equation may be a useful way to develop or check a graph. For example, the graph of the polar equation $r = 3$ consists of all points that are three units from the pole. Thus, the graph is a circle centered at the pole with radius $= 3$. The rectangular equation for $r = 3$, namely $x^2 + y^2 = 9$, has precisely the same graph (see Figure 7.27). We will discuss graphs of polar equations in the next section.

**Check Point 7**

Convert each polar equation to a rectangular equation in $x$ and $y$.

**a.** $r = 4$ **b.** $\theta = \frac{3\pi}{4}$ **c.** $r = \sec\theta$

## EXERCISE SET 7.3

### Practice Exercises

*In Exercises 1–10, indicate if the point with the given polar coordinates is represented by A, B, C, or D on the graph.*

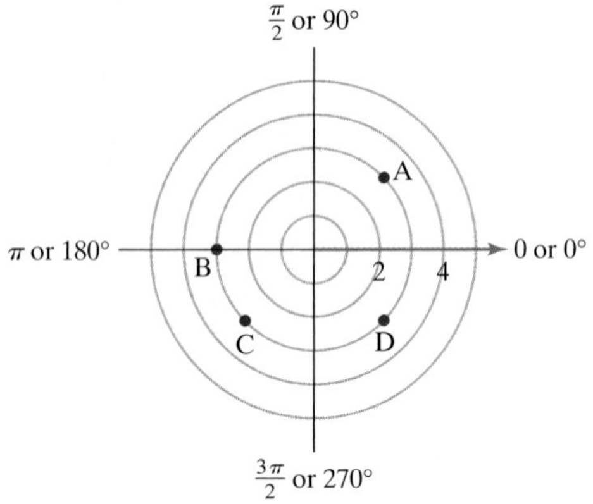


1. $(3, 225°)$
2. $(3, 315°)$
3. $\left(-3, \frac{5\pi}{4}\right)$
4. $\left(-3, \frac{\pi}{4}\right)$
5. $(3, \pi)$
6. $(-3, 0)$
7. $(3, -135°)$
8. $(3, -315°)$
9. $\left(-3, -\frac{3\pi}{4}\right)$
10. $\left(-3, -\frac{5\pi}{4}\right)$

*In Exercises 11–20, use a polar coordinate system like the one shown for Exercises 1–10 to plot each point with the given polar coordinates.*

11. $(2, 45°)$
12. $(1, 45°)$
13. $(3, 90°)$
14. $(2, 270°)$
15. $\left(3, \frac{4\pi}{3}\right)$
16. $\left(3, \frac{7\pi}{6}\right)$
17. $(-1, \pi)$
18. $\left(-1, \frac{3\pi}{2}\right)$
19. $\left(-2, -\frac{\pi}{2}\right)$
20. $(-3, -\pi)$

*In Exercises 21–26, use a polar coordinate system like the one shown for Exercises 1–10 to plot each point with the given polar coordinates. Then find another representation $(r, \theta)$ of this point in which:*

**a.** $r > 0, \quad 2\pi < \theta < 4\pi.$
**b.** $r < 0, \quad 0 < \theta < 2\pi.$
**c.** $r > 0, \quad -2\pi < \theta < 0.$

21. $\left(5, \frac{\pi}{6}\right)$
22. $\left(8, \frac{\pi}{6}\right)$
23. $\left(10, \frac{3\pi}{4}\right)$
24. $\left(12, \frac{2\pi}{3}\right)$
25. $\left(4, \frac{\pi}{2}\right)$
26. $(6, \pi)$

*In Exercises 27–34, polar coordinates of a point are given. Find the rectangular coordinates of each point.*

27. $(4, 90°)$
28. $(6, 180°)$
29. $\left(2, \frac{\pi}{3}\right)$
30. $\left(2, \frac{\pi}{6}\right)$
31. $\left(-4, \frac{\pi}{2}\right)$
32. $\left(-6, \frac{3\pi}{2}\right)$
33. $(7.4, 2.5)$
34. $(8.3, 4.6)$

*In Exercises 35–42, the rectangular coordinates of a point are given. Find polar coordinates of each point.*

35. $(-2, 2)$
36. $(2, -2)$
37. $(2, -2\sqrt{3})$
38. $(-2\sqrt{3}, 2)$
39. $(-\sqrt{3}, -1)$
40. $(-1, -\sqrt{3})$
41. $(5, 0)$
42. $(0, -6)$

*In Exercises 43–52, convert each rectangular equation to a polar equation.*

43. $3x + y = 7$ (Express $r$ in terms of $\theta$.)
44. $x + 5y = 8$ (Express $r$ in terms of $\theta$.)
45. $x = 7$
46. $y = 3$
47. $x^2 + y^2 = 9$
48. $x^2 + y^2 = 16$
49. $x^2 + y^2 = 4x$
50. $x^2 + y^2 = 6x$
51. $y^2 = 6x$
52. $x^2 = 6y$

*In Exercises 53–66, convert each polar equation to a rectangular equation.*

53. $r = 8$
54. $r = 10$
55. $\theta = \frac{\pi}{2}$
56. $\theta = \frac{\pi}{3}$
57. $r \sin\theta = 3$
58. $r \cos\theta = 7$
59. $r = 4 \csc\theta$
60. $r = 6 \sec\theta$
61. $r = \sin\theta$
62. $r = \cos\theta$
63. $r = 6\cos\theta + 4\sin\theta$
64. $r = 8\cos\theta + 2\sin\theta$
65. $r^2 \sin 2\theta = 2$
66. $r^2 \cos 2\theta = 2$

## Application Exercises

*Use the figure of the merry-go-round to solve Exercises 67–68. There are four circles of horses. Each circle is three feet from the next circle. The radius of the inner circle is 6 feet.*

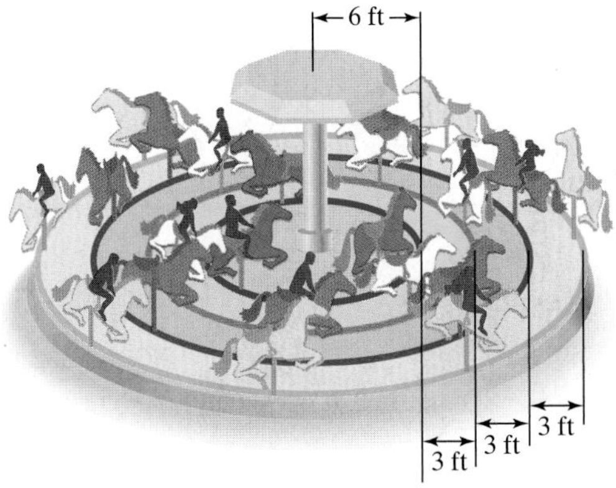


**67.** If a horse in the outer circle is $\frac{2}{3}$ of the way around the merry-go-round, give its polar coordinates.

**68.** If a horse in the inner circle is $\frac{5}{6}$ of the way around the merry-go-round, give its polar coordinates.

*The wind is blowing at 10 knots. Sailboat racers look for a sailing angle to the 10-knot wind that produces maximum sailing speed. In this application, $(r, \theta)$ describes the sailing speed, r, in knots, at an angle $\theta$ to the 10-knot wind. Use this information to solve Exercises 69–71.*

**69.** Interpret the polar coordinates: $(6.3, 50°)$.

**70.** Interpret the polar coordinates: $(7.4, 85°)$.

**71.** Four points in this 10-knot-wind situation are $(6.3, 50°)$, $(7.4, 85°)$, $(7.5, 105°)$, $(7.3, 135°)$. Based on these points, which sailing angle to the 10-knot wind would you recommend to a serious sailboat racer? What sailing speed is achieved at this angle?

## Writing in Mathematics

**72.** Explain how to plot $(r, \theta)$ if $r > 0$ and $\theta > 0$.

**73.** Explain how to plot $(r, \theta)$ if $r < 0$ and $\theta > 0$.

**74.** If you are given polar coordinates of a point, explain how to find two additional sets of polar coordinates for the point.

**75.** Explain how to convert a point from polar to rectangular coordinates. Provide an example with your explanation.

**76.** Explain how to convert a point from rectangular to polar coordinates. Provide an example with your explanation.

**77.** Explain how to convert from a rectangular equation to a polar equation.

**78.** In converting $r = 5$ from a polar equation to a rectangular equation, describe what should be done to both sides of the equation and why this should be done.

**79.** In converting $r = \sin\theta$ from a polar equation to a rectangular equation, describe what should be done to both sides of the equation and why this should be done.

**80.** Suppose that $(r, \theta)$ describes the sailing speed, $r$, in knots, at an angle $\theta$ to a wind blowing at 20 knots. You have a list of all ordered pairs $(r, \theta)$ for integral angles from $\theta = 0°$ to $\theta = 180°$. Describe a way to present this information so that a serious sailboat racer can visualize sailing speeds at different sailing angles to the wind.

## Technology Exercises

*In Exercises 81–83, polar coordinates of a point are given. Use a graphing utility to find the rectangular coordinates of each point to three decimal places.*

**81.** $\left(4, \frac{2\pi}{3}\right)$

**82.** $(5.2, 1.7)$

**83.** $(-4, 1.088)$

*In Exercises 84–86, the rectangular coordinates of a point are given. Use a graphing utility to find polar coordinates of each point to three decimal places.*

**84.** $(-5, 2)$

**85.** $(\sqrt{5}, 2)$

**86.** $(-4.308, -7.529)$

## Critical Thinking Exercises

**87.** Prove that the distance $d$ between two points with polar coordinates $(r_1, \theta_1)$ and $(r_2, \theta_2)$ is

$$d = \sqrt{r_1^2 + r_2^2 - 2r_1r_2\cos(\theta_2 - \theta_1)}.$$

**88.** Use the formula in Exercise 87 to find the distance between $\left(2, \frac{5\pi}{6}\right)$ and $\left(4, \frac{\pi}{6}\right)$. Express the answer in simplified radical form.

**89.** Convert $r = 4\cos\theta$ from a polar equation to a rectangular equation. Use the rectangular equation to give the center and the radius.

# SECTION 7.4 Graphs of Polar Equations

## Objectives

1. Graph polar equations.
2. Use symmetry to graph polar equations.

The America's Cup is the supreme event in ocean sailing. Competition is fierce and the costs are huge. Competitors look to mathematics to provide the critical innovation that can make the difference between winning and losing. In this section's exercise set, you will see how graphs of polar equations play a role in sailing faster using mathematics.

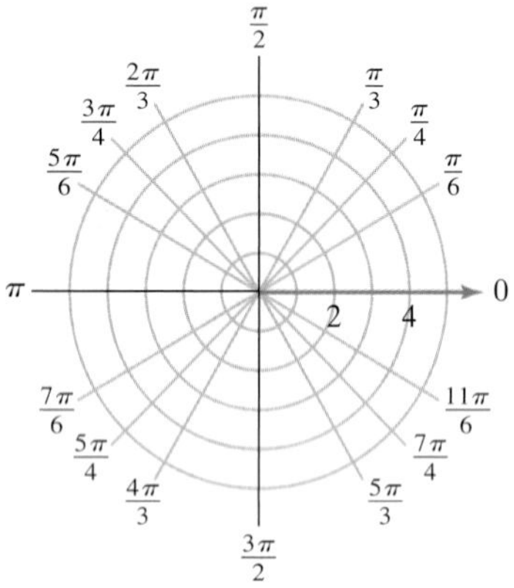


**Figure 7.28** A polar coordinate grid

## Using Polar Grids to Graph Polar Equations

Recall that a **polar equation** is an equation whose variables are $r$ and $\theta$. The **graph of a polar equation** is the set of all points whose polar coordinates satisfy the equation. We use **polar grids** like the one shown in Figure 7.28 to graph polar equations. The grid consists of circles with centers at the pole. This polar grid shows five such circles. A polar grid also shows lines passing through the pole. In this grid, each line represents an angle for which we know the exact values of the trigonometric functions.

Many polar coordinate grids show more circles and more lines through the pole than in Figure 7.28. See if your campus bookstore has paper with polar grids and use the polar graph paper throughout this section.

**1** Graph polar equations.

## Graphing a Polar Equation by Point Plotting

One method for graphing a polar equation such as $r = 4\cos\theta$ is the **point-plotting method**. First, we make a table of values that satisfy the equation. Next, we plot these ordered pairs as points in the polar coordinate system. Finally, we connect the points with a smooth curve. This often gives us a picture of all ordered pairs $(r, \theta)$ that satisfy the equation.

### EXAMPLE 1 Graphing an Equation Using the Point-Plotting Method

Graph the polar equation $r = 4\cos\theta$ with $\theta$ in radians.

**Solution** We construct a partial table of coordinates using multiples of $\frac{\pi}{6}$. Then we plot the points and join them with a smooth curve, as shown in Figure 7.29.

| $\theta$ | $r = 4\cos\theta$ | $(r, \theta)$ |
|---|---|---|
| 0 | $4\cos 0 = 4 \cdot 1 = 4$ | $(4, 0)$ |
| $\frac{\pi}{6}$ | $4\cos\frac{\pi}{6} = 4 \cdot \frac{\sqrt{3}}{2} = 2\sqrt{3} \approx 3.5$ | $\left(3.5, \frac{\pi}{6}\right)$ |
| $\frac{\pi}{3}$ | $4\cos\frac{\pi}{3} = 4 \cdot \frac{1}{2} = 2$ | $\left(2, \frac{\pi}{3}\right)$ |
| $\frac{\pi}{2}$ | $4\cos\frac{\pi}{2} = 4 \cdot 0 = 0$ | $\left(0, \frac{\pi}{2}\right)$ |
| $\frac{2\pi}{3}$ | $4\cos\frac{2\pi}{3} = 4\left(-\frac{1}{2}\right) = -2$ | $\left(-2, \frac{2\pi}{3}\right)$ |
| $\frac{5\pi}{6}$ | $4\cos\frac{5\pi}{6} = 4\left(-\frac{\sqrt{3}}{2}\right) = -2\sqrt{3} \approx -3.5$ | $\left(-3.5, \frac{5\pi}{6}\right)$ |
| $\pi$ | $4\cos\pi = 4(-1) = -4$ | $(-4, \pi)$ |
| Values of $r$ repeat. | | |

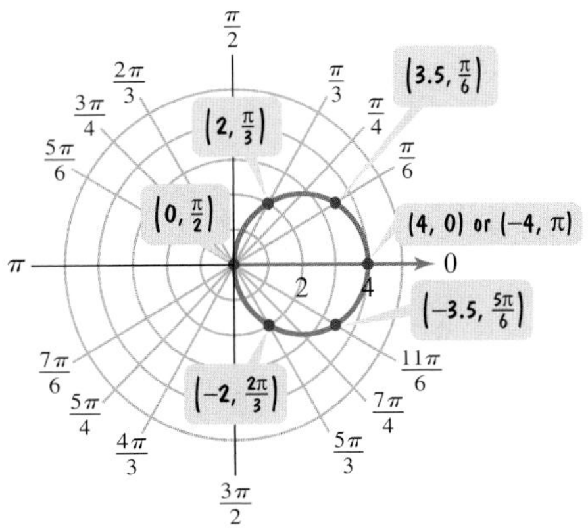

**Figure 7.29** The graph of $r = 4\cos\theta$

## Technology

A graphing utility can be used to obtain the graph of a polar equation. Use the polar mode with angle measure in radians. You must enter the minimum and maximum values for $\theta$ and an increment setting for $\theta$, called $\theta$step. $\theta$step determines the number of points that the graphing utility will plot. Make $\theta$step relatively small so that a significant number of points are plotted.

Shown is the graph of $r = 4\cos\theta$ in a $[-5, 5, 1]$ by $[-5, 5, 1]$ viewing rectangle with

$$\theta\text{min} = 0$$
$$\theta\text{max} = 2\pi$$
$$\theta\text{step} = \frac{\pi}{48}.$$

A square setting was used.

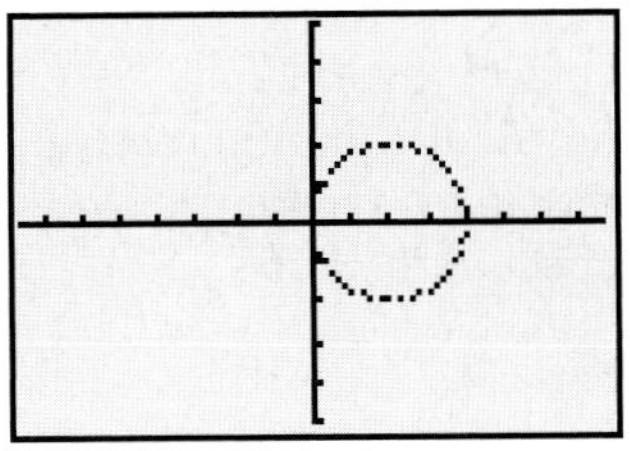

The graph of $r = 4\cos\theta$ in Figure 7.29 looks like a circle of radius 2 whose center is at the point $(x, y) = (2, 0)$. We can verify this observation by changing the polar equation to a rectangular equation.

| | |
|---|---|
| $r = 4\cos\theta$ | This is the given polar equation. |
| $r^2 = 4r\cos\theta$ | Multiply both sides by $r$. |
| $x^2 + y^2 = 4x$ | Convert to rectangular coordinates: $r^2 = x^2 + y^2$ and $r\cos\theta = x$. |
| $x^2 - 4x + y^2 = 0$ | Subtract $4x$ from both sides. |
| $x^2 - 4x + 4 + y^2 = 4$ | Complete the square on $x$: $\frac{1}{2}(-4) = -2$ and $(-2)^2 = 4$. Add 4 to both sides. |
| $(x - 2)^2 + y^2 = 2^2$ | Factor. |

This last equation is the standard form of the equation of a circle, $(x - h)^2 + (y - k)^2 = r^2$, with radius $r$ and center at $(h, k)$. Thus, the radius is 2 and the center is at $(h, k) = (2, 0)$.

In general, circles have simpler equations in polar form than in rectangular form.

**Circles in Polar Coordinates**

The graphs of

$$r = a\cos\theta \qquad \text{and} \qquad r = a\sin\theta$$

are circles.

$r = a\cos\theta$

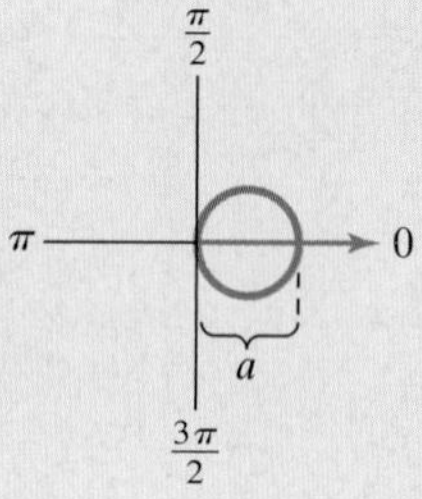


$r = a\sin\theta$

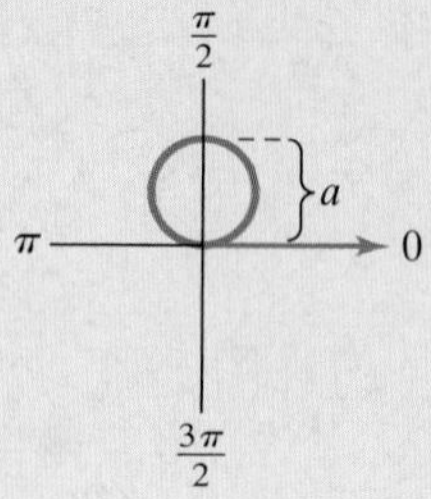


**Check Point 1** Graph the equation $r = 4\sin\theta$ with $\theta$ in radians. Use multiples of $\frac{\pi}{6}$ from 0 to $\pi$ to generate coordinates for points $(r, \theta)$.

**2** Use symmetry to graph polar equations.

## Graphing a Polar Equation Using Symmetry

If the graph of a polar equation exhibits symmetry, you may be able to graph it more quickly. Three types of symmetry can be helpful.

**Tests for Symmetry in Polar Coordinates**

**Symmetry with Respect to the Polar Axis ($x$-Axis)**

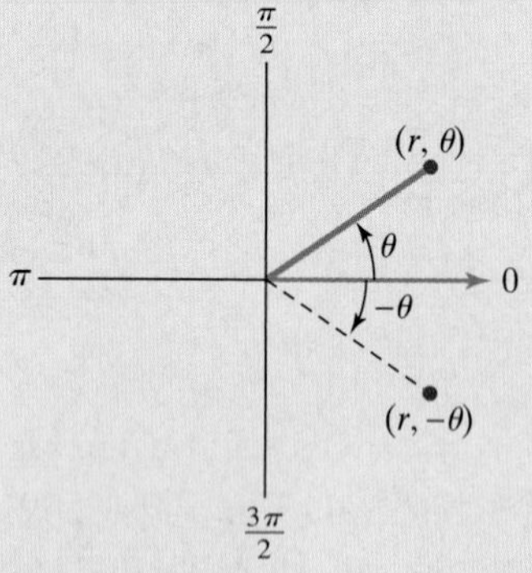


Replace $\theta$ by $-\theta$. If an equivalent equation results, the graph is symmetric with respect to the polar axis.

**Symmetry with Respect to the Line $\theta = \frac{\pi}{2}$ ($y$-Axis)**

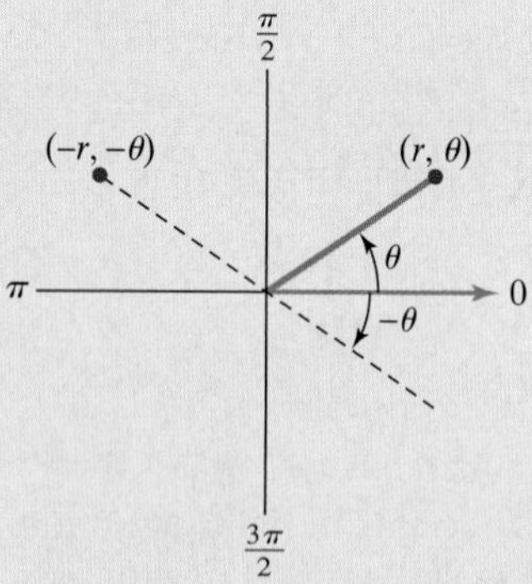


Replace $(r, \theta)$ by $(-r, -\theta)$. If an equivalent equation results, the graph is symmetric with respect to $\theta = \frac{\pi}{2}$.

**Symmetry with Respect to the Pole (Origin)**

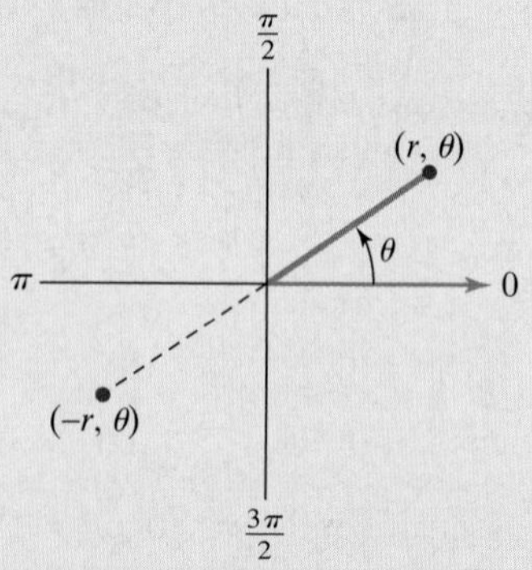


Replace $r$ by $-r$. If an equivalent equation results, the graph is symmetric with respect to the pole.

If a polar equation passes a symmetry test, then its graph exhibits that symmetry. By contrast, if a polar equation fails a symmetry test, then its graph *may or may not* have that kind of symmetry. Thus, the graph of a polar equation may have a symmetry even if it fails a test for that particular symmetry. Nevertheless, the symmetry tests are useful. If we detect symmetry, we can obtain a graph of the equation by plotting fewer points.

## EXAMPLE 2 Graphing a Polar Equation Using Symmetry

Check for symmetry and then graph the polar equation:

$$r = 1 - \cos\theta.$$

**Solution** We apply each of the tests for symmetry.

**Polar Axis:** Replace $\theta$ by $-\theta$ in $r = 1 - \cos\theta$:

$r = 1 - \cos(-\theta)$ Replace $\theta$ by $-\theta$ in $r = 1 - \cos\theta$.

$r = 1 - \cos\theta$ The cosine function is even: $\cos(-\theta) = \cos\theta$.

Because the polar equation does not change when $\theta$ is replaced by $-\theta$, the graph is symmetric with respect to the polar axis.

**The Line $\theta = \frac{\pi}{2}$:** Replace $(r, \theta)$ by $(-r, -\theta)$ in $r = 1 - \cos\theta$:

$-r = 1 - \cos(-\theta)$ Replace $r$ by $-r$ and $\theta$ by $-\theta$ in $r = 1 - \cos\theta$.

$-r = 1 - \cos\theta$ $\cos(-\theta) = \cos\theta$.

$r = \cos\theta - 1$ Multiply both sides by $-1$.

Because the polar equation $r = 1 - \cos\theta$ changes to $r = \cos\theta - 1$ when $(r, \theta)$ is replaced by $(-r, -\theta)$, the equation fails this symmetry test. The graph may or may not be symmetric with respect to the line $\theta = \frac{\pi}{2}$.

**The Pole:** Replace $r$ by $-r$ in $r = 1 - \cos\theta$:

$-r = 1 - \cos\theta$ Replace $r$ by $-r$.

$r = \cos\theta - 1$ Multiply both sides by $-1$.

Because the polar equation $r = 1 - \cos\theta$ changes to $r = \cos\theta - 1$ when $r$ is replaced by $-r$, the equation fails this symmetry test. The graph may or may not be symmetric with respect to the pole.

Now we are ready to graph $r = 1 - \cos\theta$. Because the period of the cosine function is $2\pi$, we need not consider values of $\theta$ beyond $2\pi$. Recall that we discovered the graph of the equation $r = 1 - \cos\theta$ has symmetry with respect to the polar axis. Because the graph has symmetry, we may be able to obtain a complete graph without plotting points generated by values of $\theta$ from 0 to $2\pi$. Let's start by finding the values of $r$ for values of $\theta$ from 0 to $\pi$.

**Technology**

The graph of

$$r = 1 - \cos\theta$$

was obtained using a $[-2, 2, 1]$ by $[-2, 2, 1]$ viewing rectangle and

$$\theta\text{min} = 0, \quad \theta\text{max} = 2\pi,$$

$$\theta\text{step} = \frac{\pi}{48}.$$

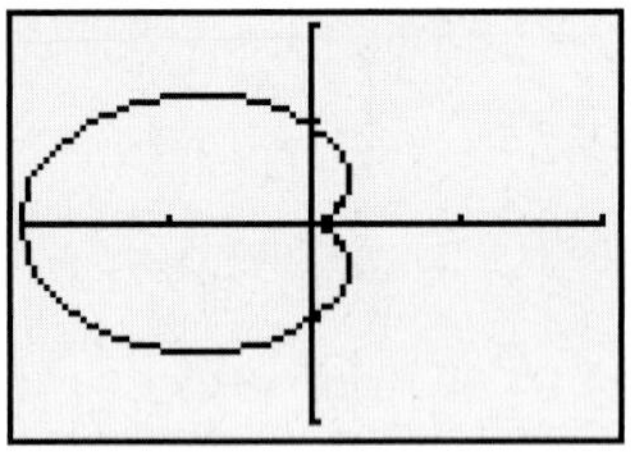

The values for $r$ and $\theta$ are in the table above Figure 7.30(a). The TABLE feature on some graphing utilities is the most efficient way to create these values. The points in the table are plotted in Figure 7.30(a). Examine the graph. Keep in mind that the graph must be symmetric with respect to the polar axis. Thus, if we reflect the graph in Figure 7.30(a) about the polar axis, we will obtain a complete graph of $r = 1 - \cos\theta$. This graph is shown in Figure 7.30(b).

| $\theta$ | 0 | $\frac{\pi}{6}$ | $\frac{\pi}{3}$ | $\frac{\pi}{2}$ | $\frac{2\pi}{3}$ | $\frac{5\pi}{6}$ | $\pi$ |
|---|---|---|---|---|---|---|---|
| $r$ | 0 | 0.13 | 0.50 | 1.00 | 1.50 | 1.87 | 2 |

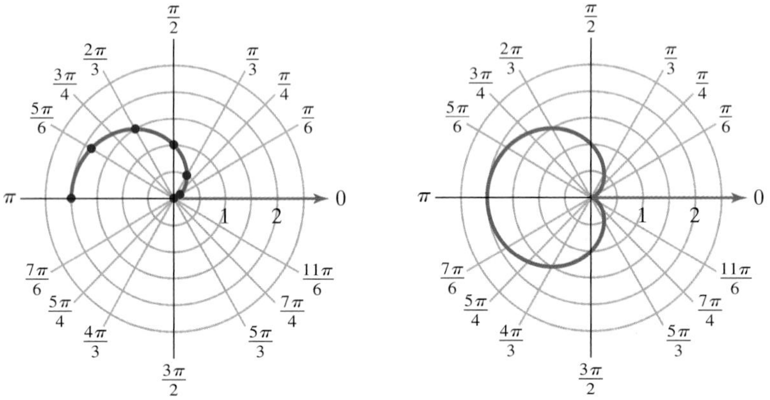


**(a)** The graph of $r = 1 - \cos\theta$ for $0 \le \theta \le \pi$

**(b)** A complete graph of $r = 1 - \cos\theta$

**Figure 7.30** Graphing $r = 1 - \cos\theta$

**Check Point 2** Check for symmetry and then graph the polar equation:

$$r = 1 + \cos\theta.$$

## EXAMPLE 3 Graphing a Polar Equation

Graph the polar equation: $r = 1 + 2\sin\theta$.

**Solution** We first check for symmetry.

$$r = 1 + 2\sin\theta$$

| **Polar Axis** | **The Line $\theta = \frac{\pi}{2}$** | **The Pole** |
|---|---|---|
| Replace $\theta$ by $-\theta$. | Replace $(r, \theta)$ by $(-r, -\theta)$. | Replace $r$ by $-r$. |
| $r = 1 + 2\sin(-\theta)$ | $-r = 1 + 2\sin(-\theta)$ | $-r = 1 + 2\sin\theta$ |
| $r = 1 + 2(-\sin\theta)$ | $-r = 1 - 2\sin\theta$ | $r = -1 - 2\sin\theta$ |
| $r = 1 - 2\sin\theta$ | $r = -1 + 2\sin\theta$ | |

Each equation is not equivalent to $r = 1 + 2\sin\theta$. Thus, the graph may or may not have each of these kinds of symmetry.

Now we are ready to graph $r = 1 + 2\sin\theta$. Because the period of the sine function is $2\pi$, we need not consider values of $\theta$ beyond $2\pi$. We identify points on the graph of $r = 1 + 2\sin\theta$ by assigning values to $\theta$ and calculating the corresponding values of $r$. The values for $r$ and $\theta$ are in the tables above Figures 7.31(a), (b), and (c). The complete graph of $r = 1 + 2\sin\theta$ is shown in Figure 7.31(c). The inner loop indicates that the graph passes through the pole twice.

| $\theta$ | $0$ | $\frac{\pi}{6}$ | $\frac{\pi}{3}$ | $\frac{\pi}{2}$ | $\frac{2\pi}{3}$ | $\frac{5\pi}{6}$ | $\pi$ |
|---|---|---|---|---|---|---|---|
| $r$ | 1 | 2 | 2.73 | 3 | 2.73 | 2 | 1 |

| $\theta$ | $\frac{7\pi}{6}$ | $\frac{4\pi}{3}$ | $\frac{3\pi}{2}$ |
|---|---|---|---|
| $r$ | 0 | −0.73 | −1 |

| $\theta$ | $\frac{5\pi}{3}$ | $\frac{11\pi}{6}$ | $2\pi$ |
|---|---|---|---|
| $r$ | −0.73 | 0 | 1 |

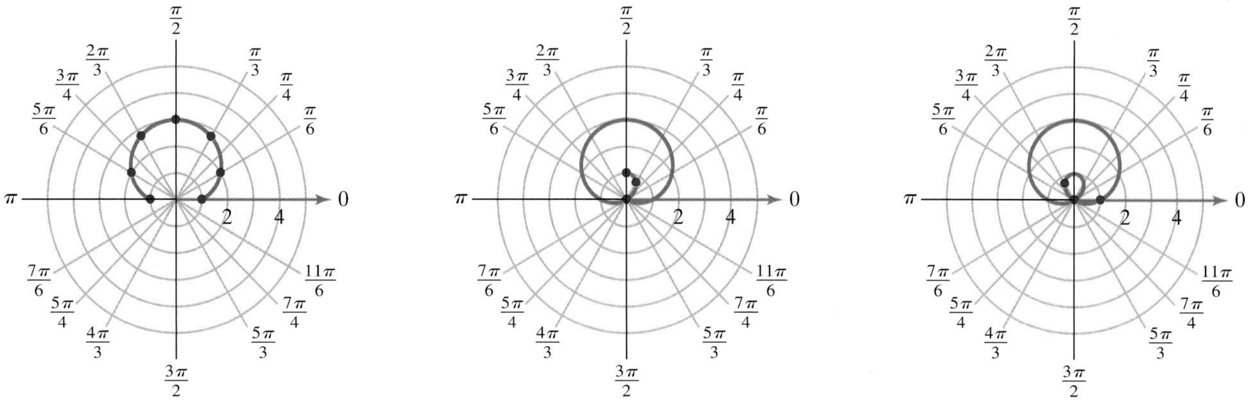


**(a)** The graph of $r = 1 + 2\cos\theta$ for $0 \le \theta \le \pi$

**(b)** The graph of $r = 1 + 2\sin\theta$ for $0 \le \theta \le \frac{3\pi}{2}$

**(c)** The complete graph of $r = 1 + 2\sin\theta$ for $0 \le \theta \le 2\pi$

**Figure 7.31** Graphing $r = 1 + 2\sin\theta$

We're not quite sure if the polar graph in Figure 7.31(c) looks like a snail. However, the graph is called a *limaçon*, which is a French word for snail. Limaçons come with and without inner loops.

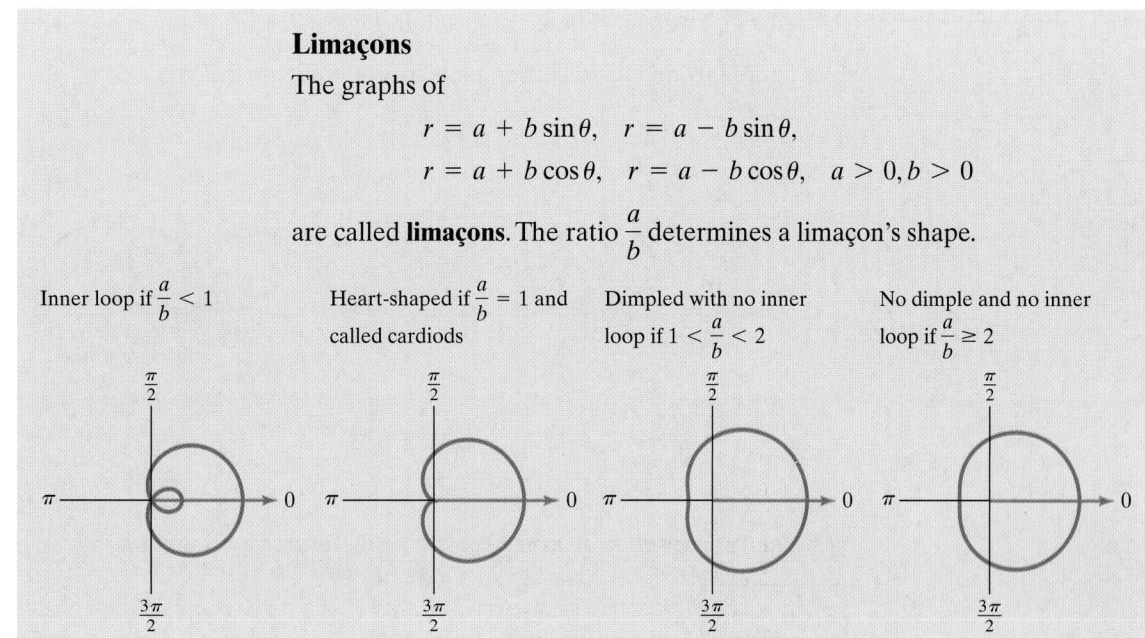

## Limaçons

The graphs of

$$r = a + b\sin\theta, \quad r = a - b\sin\theta,$$
$$r = a + b\cos\theta, \quad r = a - b\cos\theta, \quad a > 0, b > 0$$

are called **limaçons**. The ratio $\frac{a}{b}$ determines a limaçon's shape.

Inner loop if $\frac{a}{b} < 1$

Heart-shaped if $\frac{a}{b} = 1$ and called cardiods

Dimpled with no inner loop if $1 < \frac{a}{b} < 2$

No dimple and no inner loop if $\frac{a}{b} \ge 2$

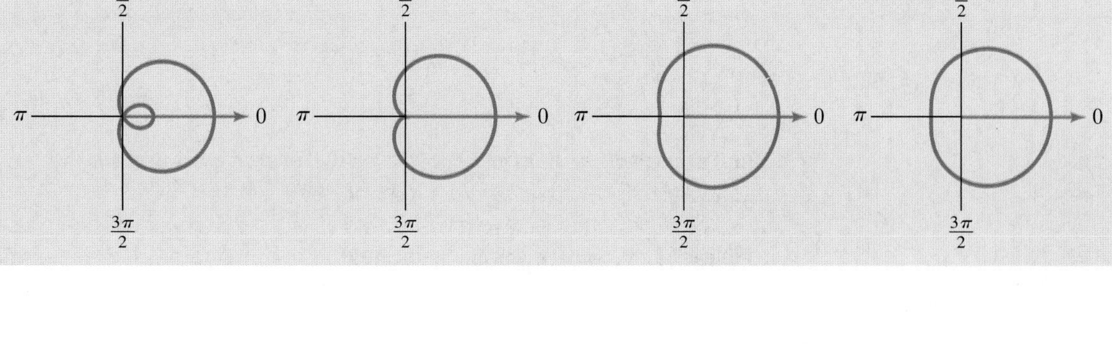

**Check Point 3** Graph the polar equation: $r = 1 - 2\sin\theta$.

## EXAMPLE 4 Graphing a Polar Equation

Graph the polar equation: $r = 4\sin 2\theta$.

**Solution** We first check for symmetry.

$$r = 4\sin 2\theta$$

**Polar Axis**

Replace $\theta$ by $-\theta$.

$$r = 4\sin 2(-\theta)$$
$$r = 4\sin(-2\theta)$$
$$r = -4\sin 2\theta$$

Equation changes and fails this symmetry test.

**The Line $\theta = \frac{\pi}{2}$**

Replace $(r, \theta)$ by $(-r, -\theta)$.

$$-r = 4\sin 2(-\theta)$$
$$-r = 4\sin(-2\theta)$$
$$-r = -4\sin 2\theta$$
$$r = 4\sin 2\theta$$

Equation does not change.

**The Pole**

Replace $r$ by $-r$.

$$-r = 4\sin 2\theta$$
$$r = -4\sin 2\theta$$

Equation changes and fails this symmetry test.

Thus, we can be sure that the graph is symmetric with respect to $\theta = \frac{\pi}{2}$. The graph may or may not be symmetric with respect to the polar axis or the pole.

Now we are ready to graph $r = 4\sin 2\theta$. In Figure 7.32(a), we identify points on the graph of $r = 4\sin 2\theta$ by assigning values to $\theta$ from 0 to $\frac{\pi}{2}$ and calculating the corresponding values of $r$. Because the graph is symmetric with respect to $\theta = \frac{\pi}{2}$, we can reflect the graph in Figure 7.32(a) about $\theta = \frac{\pi}{2}$ and obtain the graph from 0 to $\pi$. This graph is shown in Figure 7.32(b).

| $\theta$ | $0$ | $\frac{\pi}{6}$ | $\frac{\pi}{4}$ | $\frac{\pi}{3}$ | $\frac{\pi}{2}$ |
|---|---|---|---|---|---|
| $r$ | 0 | 3.46 | 4 | 3.46 | 0 |

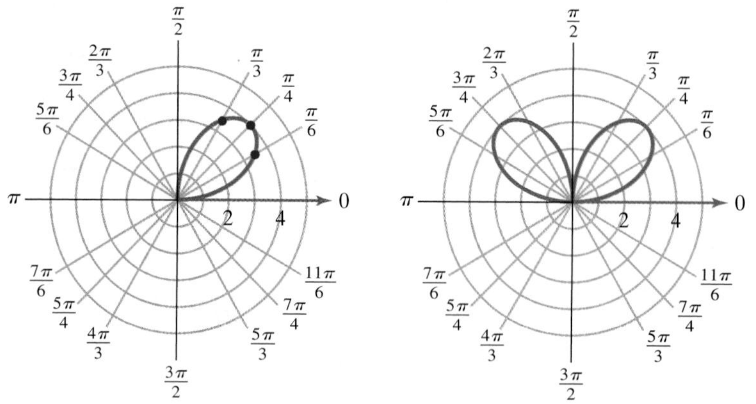


**(a)** The graph of $r = 4\sin 2\theta$ for $0 \le \theta \le \frac{\pi}{2}$

**(b)** Using symmetry to obtain the graph of $r = 4\sin 2\theta$ for $0 \le \theta \le \pi$

**Figure 7.32** A partial graph of $r = 4\sin 2\theta$

Now we can complete the graph of $r = 4\sin 2\theta$. The values for $r$ and $\theta$ above the graph in Figure 7.33(a) give us the graph for $0 \le \theta \le \frac{3\pi}{2}$. Because the graph is symmetric with respect to $\theta = \frac{\pi}{2}$, we can reflect the quadrant III portion of the graph in Figure 7.33(a) about $\theta = \frac{\pi}{2}$ and obtain the complete graph from 0 to $2\pi$. This graph is shown in Figure 7.33(b).

| $\theta$ | $\pi$ | $\frac{7\pi}{6}$ | $\frac{5\pi}{4}$ | $\frac{4\pi}{3}$ | $\frac{3\pi}{2}$ |
|---|---|---|---|---|---|
| $r$ | 0 | 3.46 | 4 | 3.46 | 0 |

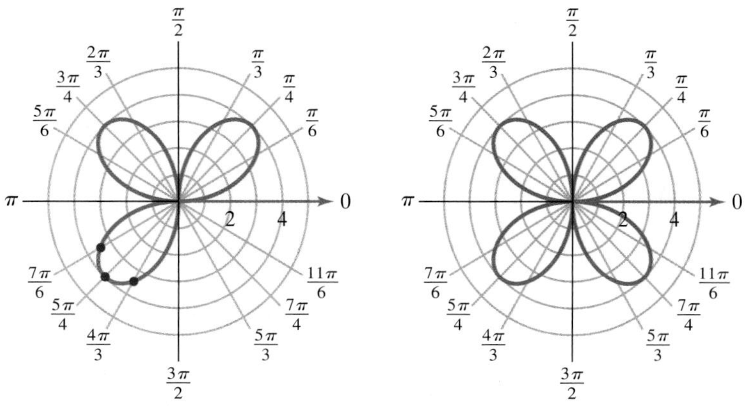


**(a)** The graph of $r = 4\sin 2\theta$ for $0 \le \theta \le \frac{3\pi}{2}$

**(b)** Using symmetry to obtain the graph of $r = 4\sin 2\theta$ for $0 \le \theta \le 2\pi$

**Figure 7.33** A complete graph of $r = 4\sin 2\theta$

The curve in Figure 7.33(b) is called a **rose with four petals**.

## Technology

The graph of

$$r = 4\sin 2\theta$$

was obtained using a $[-4, 4, 1]$ by $[-4, 4, 1]$ viewing rectangle and

$$\theta\text{min} = 0, \quad \theta\text{max} = 2\pi,$$

$$\theta\text{step} = \frac{\pi}{48}.$$

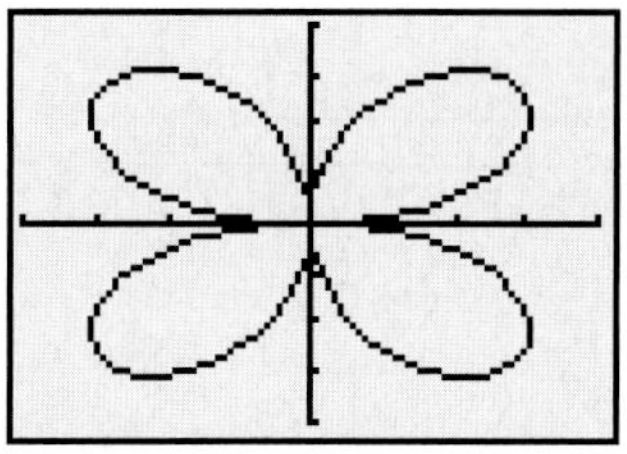

### Rose Curves

The graphs of

$$r = a \sin n\theta \quad \text{and} \quad r = a \cos n\theta, \quad a \neq 0,$$

are called **rose curves**. If $n$ is even, the rose has $2n$ petals. If $n$ is odd, the rose has $n$ petals.

$r = a \sin 2\theta$
Rose curve with 4 petals

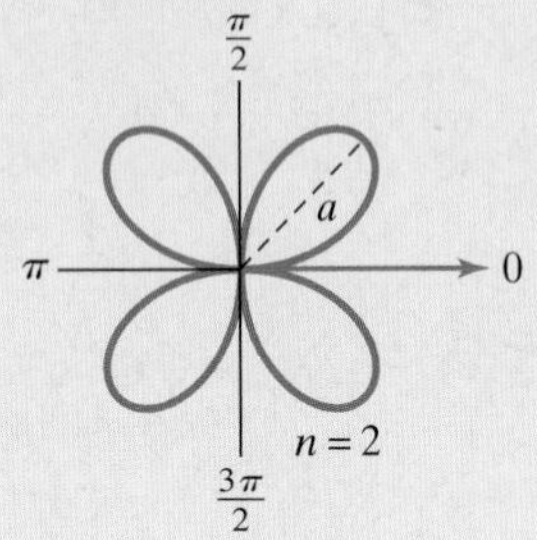

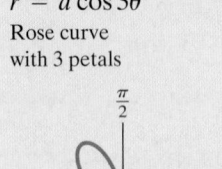

$r = a \cos 3\theta$
Rose curve with 3 petals

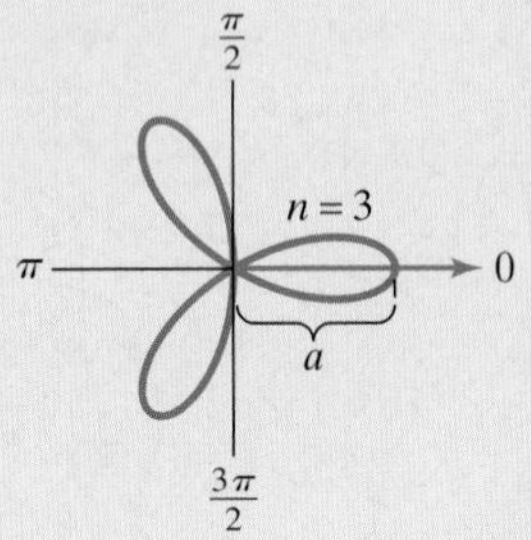

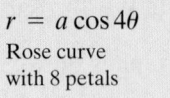

$r = a \cos 4\theta$
Rose curve with 8 petals

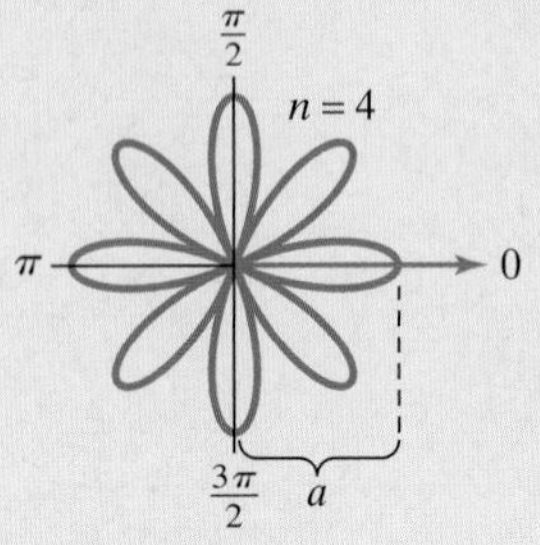


$r = a \sin 5\theta$
Rose curve with 5 petals

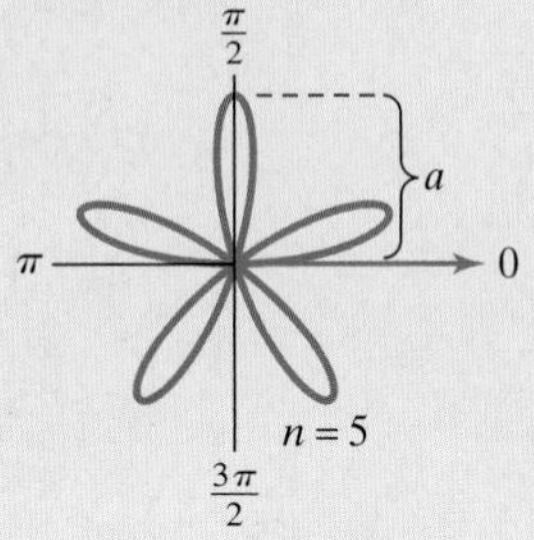


**Check Point 4** Graph the polar equation: $r = 3 \cos 2\theta$.

## EXAMPLE 5 Graphing a Polar Equation

Graph the polar equation: $r^2 = 4 \sin 2\theta$.

**Solution** We first check for symmetry.

$$r^2 = 4 \sin 2\theta$$

| Polar Axis | The Line $\theta = \frac{\pi}{2}$ | The Pole |
|---|---|---|
| Replace $\theta$ by $-\theta$. | Replace $(r, \theta)$ by $(-r, -\theta)$. | Replace $r$ by $-r$. |
| $r^2 = 4 \sin 2(-\theta)$ | $(-r)^2 = 4 \sin 2(-\theta)$ | $(-r)^2 = 4 \sin 2\theta$ |
| $r^2 = 4 \sin(-2\theta)$ | $r^2 = 4 \sin(-2\theta)$ | $r^2 = 4 \sin 2\theta$ |
| $r^2 = -4 \sin 2\theta$ | $r^2 = -4 \sin 2\theta$ | |
| Equation changes and fails this symmetry test. | Equation changes and fails this symmetry test. | Equation does not change. |

Thus, we can be sure that the graph is symmetric with respect to the pole. The graph may or may not be symmetric with respect to the polar axis or the line $\theta = \frac{\pi}{2}$.

Now we are ready to graph $r^2 = 4 \sin 2\theta$. In Figure 7.34(a), we identify points on the graph by assigning values to $\theta$ from 0 to $\frac{\pi}{2}$ and calculating the corresponding values of $r$. Notice that the points in Figure 7.34(a) are shown for $r \geq 0$. Because the graph is symmetric with respect to the pole, we can reflect the graph in Figure 7.34(a) about the pole and obtain the graph in Figure 7.34(b).

| $\theta$ | $0$ | $\frac{\pi}{6}$ | $\frac{\pi}{4}$ | $\frac{\pi}{3}$ | $\frac{\pi}{2}$ |
|---|---|---|---|---|---|
| $r$ | $0$ | $\pm 1.9$ | $\pm 2$ | $\pm 1.9$ | $0$ |

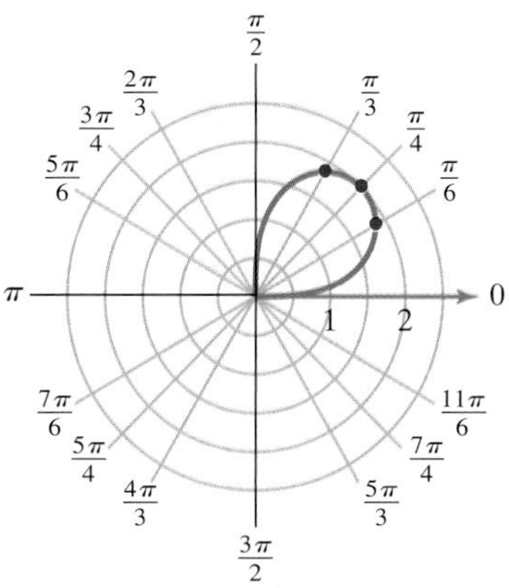


**Figure 7.34** **(a)** The graph of $r^2 = 4\sin 2\theta$ for $0 \le \theta \le \frac{\pi}{2}$

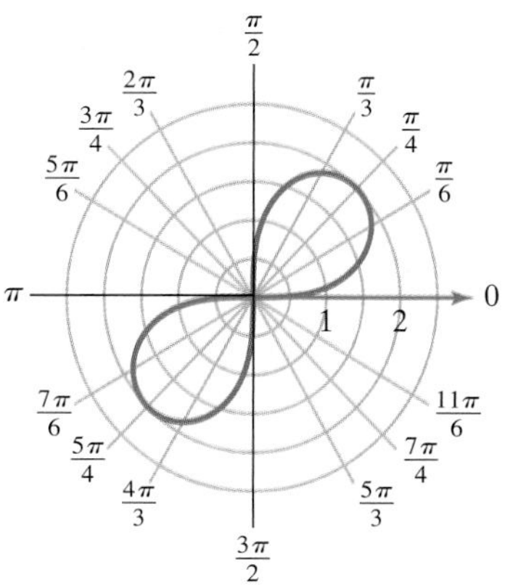


**Figure 7.34** **(b)** Using symmetry with respect to the pole on the graph of $r^2 = 4\sin 2\theta$

Does Figure 7.34(b) show a complete graph of $r^2 = 4\sin 2\theta$ or do we need to continue graphing in quadrants II and IV? If $\theta$ is in quadrant II, $2\theta$ is in quadrant III or IV, where $\sin 2\theta$ is negative. Thus, $4\sin 2\theta$ is negative. However, $r^2 = 4\sin 2\theta$ and $r^2$ cannot be negative. This means that there are no points on the graph in quadrant II. The same observation applies to quadrant IV. Thus, Figure 7.34(b) shows the complete graph of $r^2 = 4\sin 2\theta$.

The curve in Figure 7.34(b) is shaped like a propeller and is called a **lemniscate.**

## Lemniscates

The graphs of

$$r^2 = a^2 \sin 2\theta \quad \text{and} \quad r^2 = a^2 \cos 2\theta, \quad a \neq 0$$

are called **lemniscates.**

$r^2 = a^2 \sin 2\theta$ is symmetric with respect to the pole.

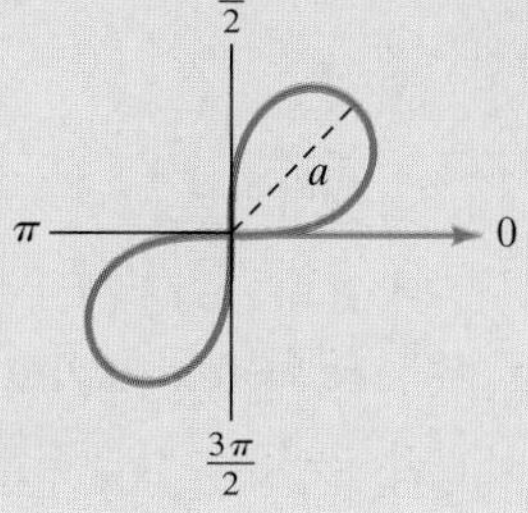


$r^2 = a^2 \cos 2\theta$ is symmetric with respect to the polar axis, $\theta = \frac{\pi}{2}$, and the pole.

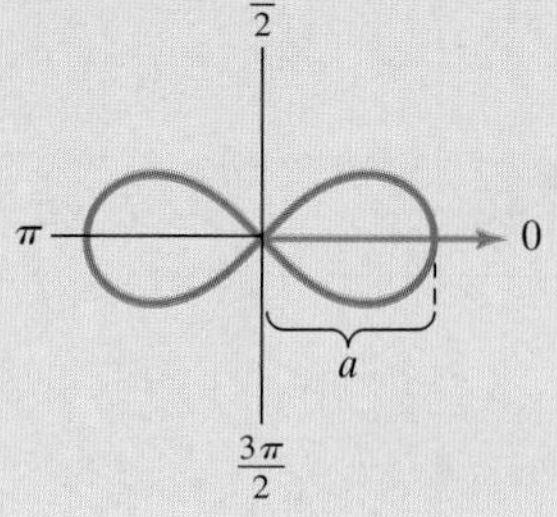


**Check Point 5** Graph the polar equation: $r^2 = 4\cos 2\theta$.

## EXERCISE SET 7.4

### Practice Exercises

*In Exercises 1–6, the graph of a polar equation is given. Select the polar equation for each graph from the following options.*

$$r = 2\sin\theta,\quad r = 2\cos\theta,\quad r = 1 + \sin\theta,$$

$$r = 1 - \sin\theta,\quad r = 3\sin 2\theta,\quad r = 3\sin 3\theta$$

**1.**

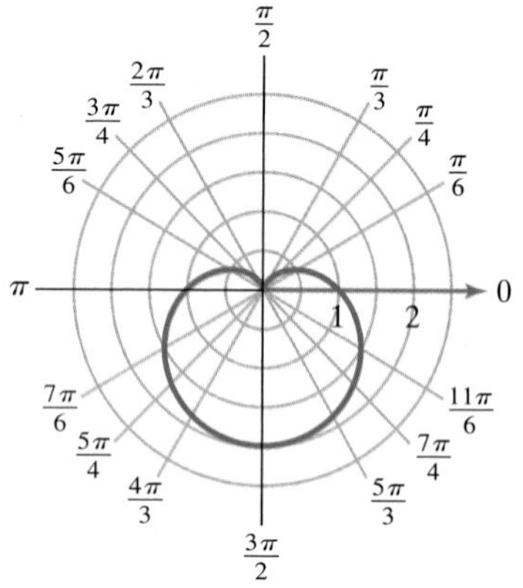


**2.**

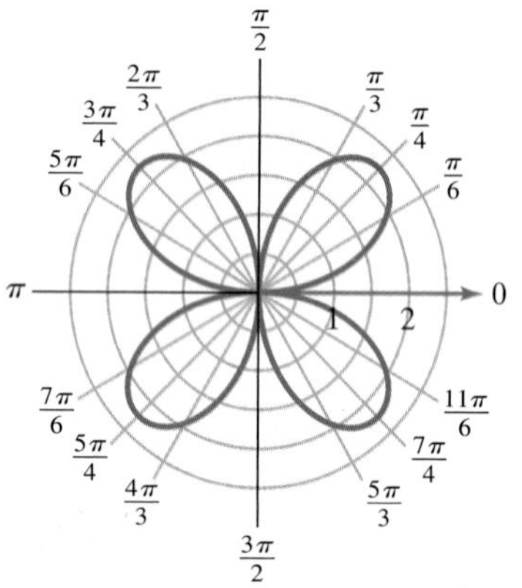


**3.**

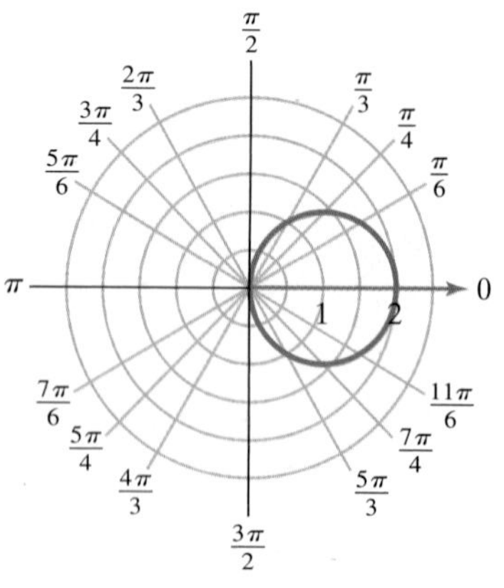


**4.**

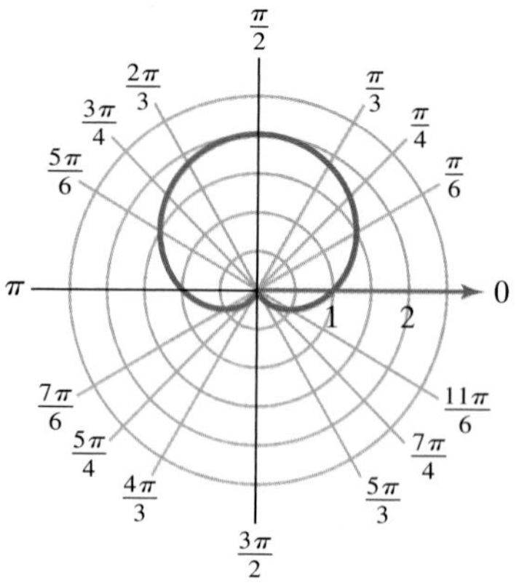


**5.**

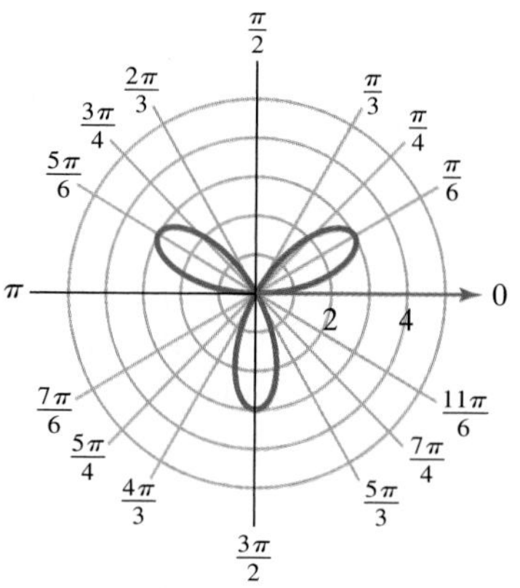


**6.**

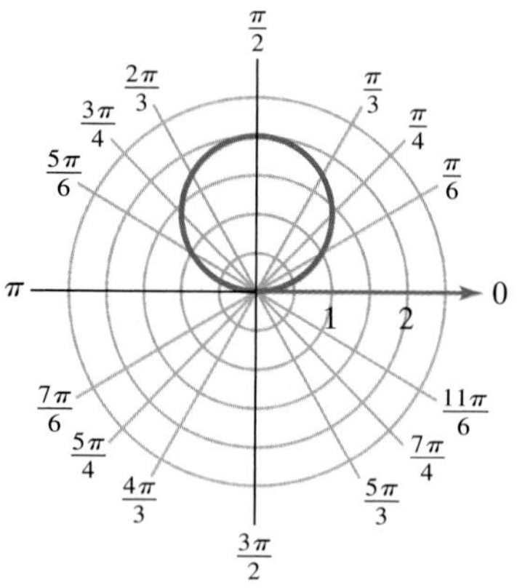


*In Exercises 7–12, test for symmetry with respect to:*

**a.** *the polar axis;* **b.** *the line* $\theta = \frac{\pi}{2}$; *and* **c.** *the pole.*

**7.** $r = \sin\theta$

**8.** $r = \cos\theta$

**9.** $r = 4 + 3\cos\theta$

**10.** $r = 2\cos 2\theta$

**11.** $r^2 = 16\cos 2\theta$

**12.** $r^2 = 16\sin 2\theta$

*In Exercises 13–34, graph each polar equation.*

**13.** $r = 2\cos\theta$
**14.** $r = 2\sin\theta$
**15.** $r = 1 - \sin\theta$
**16.** $r = 1 + \sin\theta$
**17.** $r = 2 + 2\cos\theta$
**18.** $r = 2 - 2\cos\theta$
**19.** $r = 2 + \cos\theta$
**20.** $r = 2 - \sin\theta$
**21.** $r = 1 + 2\cos\theta$
**22.** $r = 1 - 2\cos\theta$
**23.** $r = 2 - 3\sin\theta$
**24.** $r = 2 + 4\sin\theta$
**25.** $r = 2\cos 2\theta$
**26.** $r = 2\sin 2\theta$
**27.** $r = 4\sin 3\theta$
**28.** $r = 4\cos 3\theta$
**29.** $r^2 = 9\cos 2\theta$
**30.** $r^2 = 9\sin 2\theta$
**31.** $r = 1 - 3\sin\theta$
**32.** $r = 3 + \sin\theta$
**33.** $r\cos\theta = -3$
**34.** $r\sin\theta = 2$

## Application Exercises

*In Exercise Set 7.3, we considered an application in which sailboat racers look for a sailing angle to a 10-knot wind that produces maximum sailing speed. This situation is now represented by the polar graph in the figure shown. Each point $(r, \theta)$ on the graph gives the sailing speed, r, in knots, at an angle $\theta$ to the 10-knot wind. Use this information to solve Exercises 35–39.*

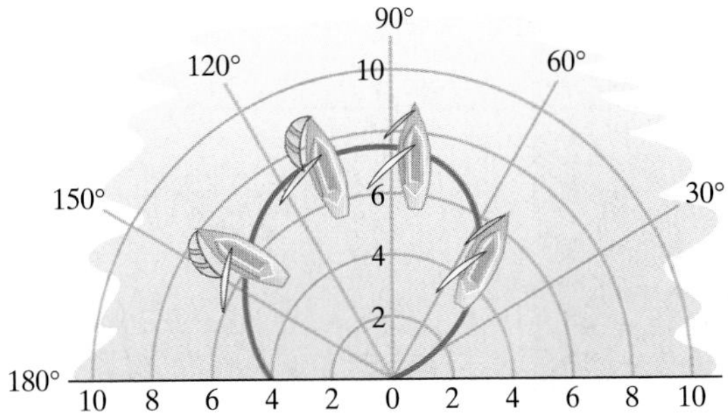


**35.** What is the speed, to the nearest knot, of the sailboat sailing at 60° angle to the wind?

**36.** What is the speed, to the nearest knot, of the sailboat sailing at a 120° angle to the wind?

**37.** What is the speed, to the nearest knot, of the sailboat sailing at a 90° angle to the wind?

**38.** What is the speed, to the nearest knot, of the sailboat sailing at a 180° angle to the wind?

**39.** What angle to the wind produces the maximum sailing speed? What is the speed? Round the angle to the nearest five degrees and the speed to the nearest half knot.

## Writing in Mathematics

**40.** What is a polar equation?

**41.** What is the graph of a polar equation?

**42.** Describe how to graph a polar equation.

**43.** Describe the test for symmetry with respect to the polar axis.

**44.** Describe the test for symmetry with respect to the line $\theta = \frac{\pi}{2}$.

**45.** Describe the test for symmetry with respect to the pole.

**46.** If an equation fails the test for symmetry with respect to the polar axis, what can you conclude?

## Technology Exercises

*Use the polar mode of a graphing utility with angle measure in radians to solve Exercises 47–78. Unless otherwise indicated, use $\theta$min $= 0$, $\theta$max $= 2\pi$, and $\theta$step $= \frac{\pi}{48}$. If you are not pleased with the quality of the graph, experiment with smaller values for $\theta$step. However, if $\theta$step is extremely small, it can take your graphing utility a long period of time to complete the graph.*

**47.** Use a graphing utility to verify any six of your hand-drawn graphs in Exercises 13–34.

*In Exercises 48–65, use a graphing utility to graph the polar equation.*

**48.** $r = 4\cos 5\theta$
**49.** $r = 4\sin 5\theta$
**50.** $r = 4\cos 6\theta$
**51.** $r = 4\sin 6\theta$
**52.** $r = 2 + 2\cos\theta$
**53.** $r = 2 + 2\sin\theta$
**54.** $r = 4 + 2\cos\theta$
**55.** $r = 4 + 2\sin\theta$
**56.** $r = 2 + 4\cos\theta$
**57.** $r = 2 + 4\sin\theta$
**58.** $r = \dfrac{3}{\sin\theta}$
**59.** $r = \dfrac{3}{\cos\theta}$

*In Exercises 60–61, use $\theta$ max $= 4\pi$.*

**60.** $r = \cos\frac{3}{2}\theta$
**61.** $r = \cos\frac{5}{2}\theta$
**62.** $r = 3\sin\left(\theta + \frac{\pi}{4}\right)$
**63.** $r = 2\cos\left(\theta - \frac{\pi}{4}\right)$
**64.** $r = \dfrac{1}{1 - \sin\theta}$
**65.** $r = \dfrac{1}{3 - 2\sin\theta}$

*In Exercises 66–68, find the smallest interval for $\theta$ starting with $\theta$min $= 0$ so that your graphing utility graphs the given polar equation exactly once without retracing any portion of it.*

**66.** $r = 4\sin\theta$
**67.** $r = 4\sin 2\theta$
**68.** $r^2 = 4\sin 2\theta$

*In Exercises 69–72, use a graphing utility to graph each butterfly curve. Experiment with the range setting, particularly $\theta$step, to produce a butterfly of the best possible quality.*

**69.** $r = \cos^2 5\theta + \sin 3\theta + 0.3$

**70.** $r = \sin^4 4\theta + \cos 3\theta$

**71.** $r = \sin^5\theta + 8\sin\theta\cos^3\theta$

**72.** $r = 1.5^{\sin\theta} - 2.5\cos 4\theta + \sin^7\frac{\theta}{15}$
(Use $\theta$min $= 0$ and $\theta$max $= 20\pi$.)

**73.** Use a graphing utility to graph $r = \sin n\theta$ for $n = 1, 2, 3, 4, 5$, and 6. Use a separate viewing screen for each of the six graphs. What is the pattern for the number of loops that occur corresponding to each value of $n$? What is happening to the shape of the graphs as $n$ increases? For each graph, what is the smallest interval for $\theta$ so that the graph is traced only once?

**74.** Repeat Exercise 73 for $r = \cos n\theta$. Are your conclusions the same as they were in Exercise 73?

**75.** Use a graphing utility to graph $r = 1 + 2\sin n\theta$ for $n = 1, 2, 3, 4, 5$, and 6. Use a separate viewing screen for each of the six graphs. What is the pattern for the number of large and small petals that occur corresponding to each value of $n$? How are the large and small petals related when $n$ is odd and when $n$ is even?

**76.** Repeat Exercise 75 for $r = 1 + 2\cos n\theta$. Are your conclusions the same as they were in Exercise 75?

**77.** Graph the spiral $r = \theta$. Use a $[-30, 30, 1]$ by $[-30, 30, 1]$ viewing rectangle. Let $\theta\text{min} = 0$ and $\theta\text{max} = 2\pi$, then $\theta\text{min} = 0$ and $\theta\text{max} = 4\pi$, and finally $\theta\text{min} = 0$ and $\theta\text{max} = 8\pi$.

**78.** Graph the spiral $r = \frac{1}{\theta}$. Use a $[-1, 1, 1]$ by $[-1, 1, 1]$ viewing rectangle. Let $\theta\text{min} = 0$ and $\theta\text{max} = 2\pi$, then $\theta\text{min} = 0$ and $\theta\text{max} = 4\pi$, and finally $\theta\text{min} = 0$ and $\theta\text{max} = 8\pi$.

### Critical Thinking Exercises

**79.** Describe a test for symmetry with respect to the line $\theta = \frac{\pi}{2}$ in which $r$ is not replaced.

*In Exercises 80–81, graph each polar equation without using a graphing utility.*

**80.** $r = \dfrac{1}{3 - 2\cos\theta}$

**81.** $r = \dfrac{4}{1 + \sin\theta}$

## SECTION 7.5 Complex Numbers in Polar Form; DeMoivre's Theorem

### Objectives

1. Plot complex numbers in the complex plane.
2. Find the absolute value of a complex number.
3. Write complex numbers in polar form.
4. Convert a complex number from polar to rectangular form.
5. Find products of complex numbers in polar form.
6. Find quotients of complex numbers in polar form.
7. Find powers of complex numbers in polar form.
8. Find roots of complex numbers in polar form.

A magnification of the Mandelbrot set

One of the new frontiers of mathematics suggests that there is an underlying order in things that appear to be random, such as the hiss and crackle of background noises as you tune a radio. Irregularities in the heartbeat, some of them severe enough to cause a heart attack, or irregularities in our sleeping patterns, such as insomnia, are examples of chaotic behavior. Chaos in the mathematical sense does not mean a complete lack of form or arrangement. In mathematics, chaos is used to describe something that appears to be random but is not actually random. The patterns of chaos appear in images like the one shown above, called the Mandelbrot set. Magnified portions of this image yield repetitions of the original structure, as well as new and unexpected patterns. The Mandelbrot set transforms the hidden structure of chaotic events into a source of wonder and inspiration.

The Mandelbrot set is made possible by opening up graphing to include complex numbers in the form $a + bi$, where $i = \sqrt{-1}$. In this section, you will learn how to graph complex numbers and write them in terms of trigonometric functions.

**1** Plot complex numbers in the complex plane.

## The Complex Plane

We know that a real number can be represented as a point on a number line. By contrast, a complex number $z = a + bi$ is represented as a point $(a, b)$ in a coordinate plane, shown in Figure 7.35. The horizontal axis of the coordinate plane is called the **real axis**. The vertical axis is called the **imaginary axis**. The coordinate system is called the **complex plane**. Every complex number corresponds to a point in the complex plane and every point in the complex plane corresponds to a complex number. When we represent a complex number as a point in the complex plane, we say that we are **plotting the complex number.**

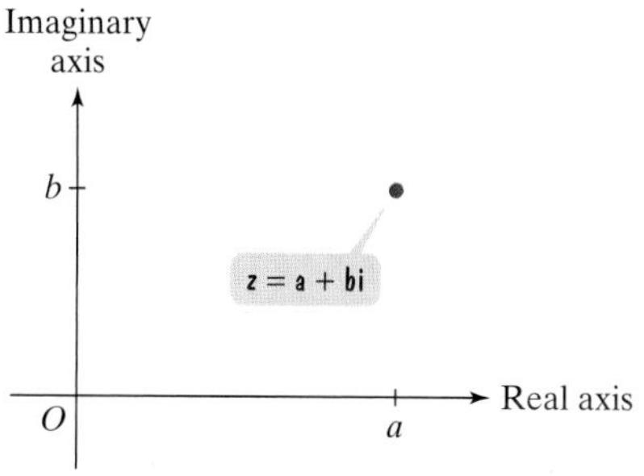


**Figure 7.35** Plotting $z = a + bi$ in the complex plane

## EXAMPLE 1 Plotting Complex Numbers

Plot in the complex plane:

**a.** $z = 3 + 4i$ **b.** $z = -1 - 2i$ **c.** $z = -3$ **d.** $z = -4i$.

**Solution** See Figure 7.36.

**a.** We plot the complex number $z = 3 + 4i$ the same way we plot $(3, 4)$ in the rectangular coordinate system. We move three units to the right on the real axis and four units up parallel to the imaginary axis.

**b.** The complex number $z = -1 - 2i$ corresponds to the point $(-1, -2)$ in the rectangular coordinate system. Plot the complex number by moving one unit to the left on the real axis and two units down parallel to the imaginary axis.

**c.** Because $z = -3 = -3 + 0i$, this complex number corresponds to the point $(-3, 0)$. We plot $z = -3$ by moving three units to the left on the real axis.

**d.** Because $z = -4i = 0 - 4i$, this number corresponds to the point $(0, -4)$. We plot the complex number by moving four units down on the imaginary axis.

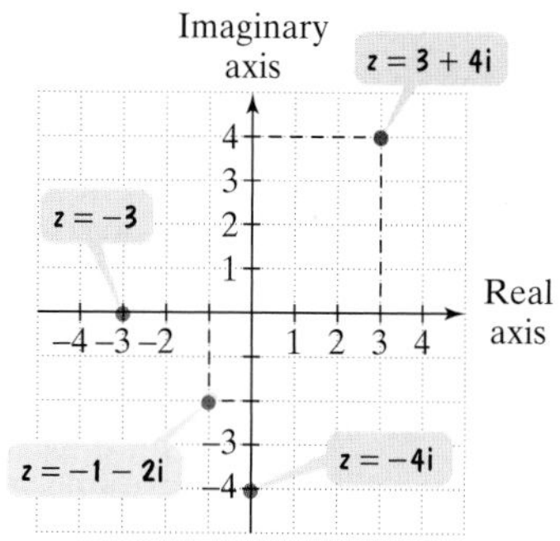


**Figure 7.36** Plotting complex numbers

**Check Point 1** Plot in the complex plane:

**a.** $z = 2 + 3i$ **b.** $z = -3 - 5i$

**c.** $z = -4$ **d.** $z = -i$.

**2** Find the absolute value of a complex number.

Recall that the absolute value of a real number is its distance from 0 on the number line. The **absolute value of the complex number $z = a + bi$**, denoted by $|z|$, is its distance from the origin in the complex plane.

**The Absolute Value of a Complex Number**

The **absolute value** of the complex number $a + bi$ is

$$|z| = |a + bi| = \sqrt{a^2 + b^2}.$$

## EXAMPLE 2 Finding the Absolute Value of a Complex Number

Determine the absolute value of each of the following complex numbers:

**a.** $z = 3 + 4i$ **b.** $z = -1 - 2i$.

**Solution**

**a.** The absolute value of $z = 3 + 4i$ is found using $a = 3$ and $b = 4$.

$$|z| = \sqrt{3^2 + 4^2} = \sqrt{9 + 16} = \sqrt{25} = 5$$ Use $z = \sqrt{a^2 + b^2}$ with $a = 3$ and $b = 4$.

Thus, the distance from the origin to the point $z = 3 + 4i$, shown in quadrant I in Figure 7.36, is five units.

**b.** The absolute value of $z = -1 - 2i$ is found using $a = -1$ and $b = -2$.

$$|z| = \sqrt{(-1)^2 + (-2)^2} = \sqrt{1 + 4} = \sqrt{5}$$ Use $z = \sqrt{a^2 + b^2}$ with $a = -1$ and $b = -2$.

Thus, the distance from the origin to the point $z = -1 - 2i$, shown in quadrant III in Figure 7.36, is $\sqrt{5}$ units.

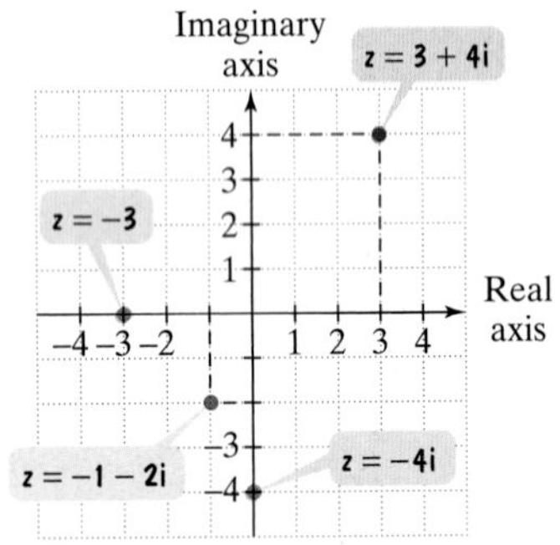


**Figure 7.36,** repeated

**Check Point 2** Determine the absolute value of each of the following complex numbers:

**a.** $z = 5 + 12i$ **b.** $2 - 3i$.

**3** Write complex numbers in polar form.

## Polar Form of a Complex Number

A complex number in the form $z = a + bi$ is said to be in **rectangular form**. Suppose that its absolute value is $r$. In Figure 7.37, we let $\theta$ be an angle in standard position whose terminal side passes through the point $(a, b)$. From the figure, we see that

$$r = \sqrt{a^2 + b^2}.$$

Likewise, according to the definitions of the trigonometric functions,

$$\cos\theta = \frac{a}{r} \qquad \sin\theta = \frac{b}{r} \qquad \tan\theta = \frac{b}{a}.$$

$$a = r\cos\theta \qquad b = r\sin\theta$$

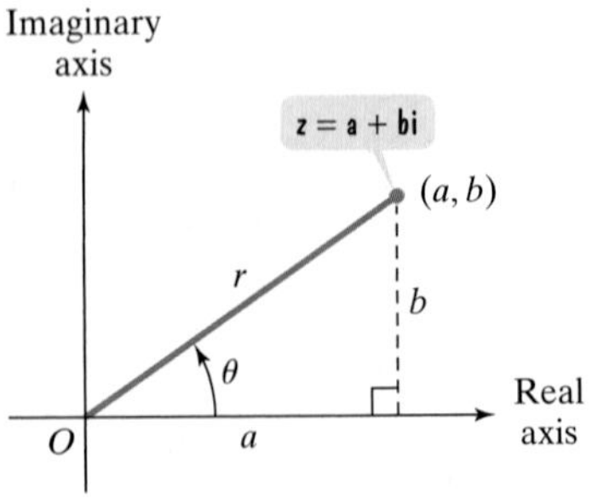


**Figure 7.37**

By substituting the expressions for $a$ and $b$ in $z = a + bi$, we write the complex number in terms of trigonometric functions.

$$z = a + bi = r\cos\theta + (r\sin\theta)i = r(\cos\theta + i\sin\theta)$$

$a = r\cos\theta$ and $b = r\sin\theta$. Factor out $r$ from each of the two previous terms.

The expression $z = r(\cos\theta + i\sin\theta)$ is called the **polar form of a complex number.**

**Polar Form of a Complex Number**

The complex number $z = a + bi$ is written in **polar form** as

$$z = r(\cos\theta + i\sin\theta)$$

where $a = r\cos\theta, b = r\sin\theta, r = \sqrt{a^2 + b^2}$, and $\tan\theta = \frac{b}{a}$. The value of $r$ is called the **modulus** (plural: moduli) of the complex number $z$, and the angle $\theta$ is called the **argument** of the complex number $z$, with $0 \le \theta < 2\pi$.

## EXAMPLE 3 Writing a Complex Number in Polar Form

Plot $z = -2 - 2i$ in the complex plane. Then write $z$ in polar form.

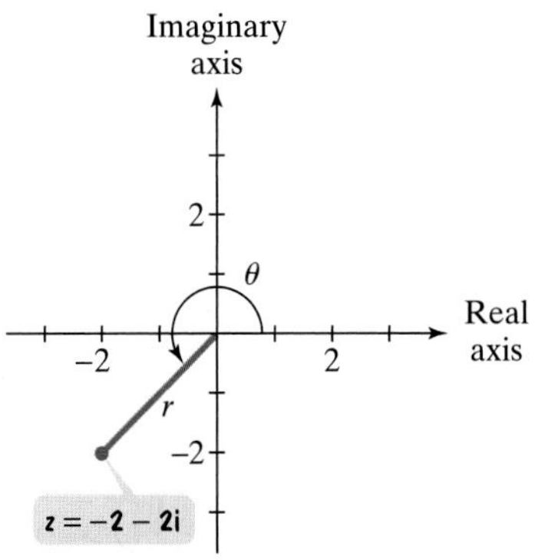


**Figure 7.38** Plotting $z = -2 - 2i$ and writing the number in polar form

**Solution** The complex number $z = -2 - 2i$ is in rectangular form $z = a + bi$, with $a = -2$ and $b = -2$. We plot the number by moving two units to the left on the real axis and two units down parallel to the imaginary axis, shown in Figure 7.38.

By definition, the polar form of $z$ is $r(\cos\theta + i\sin\theta)$. We need to determine the value for $r$, the modulus, and the value for $\theta$, the argument. Figure 7.38 shows $r$ and $\theta$. We use $r = \sqrt{a^2 + b^2}$ with $a = -2$ and $b = -2$ to find $r$.

$$r = \sqrt{a^2 + b^2} = \sqrt{(-2)^2 + (-2)^2} = \sqrt{4 + 4} = \sqrt{8} = \sqrt{4 \cdot 2} = 2\sqrt{2}$$

We use $\tan\theta = \frac{b}{a}$ with $a = -2$ and $b = -2$ to find $\theta$.

$$\tan\theta = \frac{b}{a} = \frac{-2}{-2} = 1$$

We know that $\tan\frac{\pi}{4} = 1$. Figure 7.38 shows that the argument, $\theta$, lies in quadrant III. Thus,

$$\theta = \pi + \frac{\pi}{4} = \frac{4\pi}{4} + \frac{\pi}{4} = \frac{5\pi}{4}.$$

We use $r = 2\sqrt{2}$ and $\theta = \frac{5\pi}{4}$ to write the polar form. The polar form of $z = -2 - 2i$ is

$$z = r(\cos\theta + i\sin\theta) = 2\sqrt{2}\left(\cos\frac{5\pi}{4} + i\sin\frac{5\pi}{4}\right).$$

**Check Point 3** Plot $z = -1 - \sqrt{3}i$ in the complex plane. Then write $z$ in polar form. Express the argument in radians.

**4** Convert a complex number from polar to rectangular form.

### EXAMPLE 4 Writing a Complex Number in Rectangular Form

Write $z = 2(\cos 60° + i \sin 60°)$ in rectangular form.

**Solution** The complex number $z = 2(\cos 60° + i \sin 60°)$ is in polar form, with $r = 2$ and $\theta = 60°$. We use exact values for $\cos 60°$ and $\sin 60°$ to write the number in rectangular form.

$$2(\cos 60° + i \sin 60°) = 2\left(\frac{1}{2} + i\frac{\sqrt{3}}{2}\right) = 1 + \sqrt{3}i$$

The rectangular form of $z = 2(\cos 60° + i \sin 60°)$ is

$$z = 1 + \sqrt{3}i.$$

**Check Point 4** Write $z = 4(\cos 30° + i \sin 30°)$ in rectangular form.

**5** Find products of complex numbers in polar form.

## Products and Quotients in Polar Form

We can multiply and divide complex numbers fairly quickly if the numbers are expressed in polar form.

**Product of Two Complex Numbers in Polar Form**

Let $z_1 = r_1(\cos\theta_1 + i\sin\theta_1)$ and $z_2 = r_2(\cos\theta_2 + i\sin\theta_2)$ be two complex numbers in polar form. Their product, $z_1z_2$, is

$$z_1z_2 = r_1r_2[\cos(\theta_1 + \theta_2) + i\sin(\theta_1 + \theta_2)].$$

To multiply two complex numbers, multiply moduli and add arguments.

To prove this result, we begin by multiplying using the FOIL method. Then we simplify the product using the sum formulas for sine and cosine.

$$z_1z_2 = [r_1(\cos\theta_1 + i\sin\theta_1)][r_2(\cos\theta_2 + i\sin\theta_2)]$$

$$= r_1r_2(\cos\theta_1 + i\sin\theta_1)(\cos\theta_2 + i\sin\theta_2) \quad \text{Rearrange factors.}$$

F O I L

$$= r_1r_2(\cos\theta_1\cos\theta_2 + i\cos\theta_1\sin\theta_2 + i\sin\theta_1\cos\theta_2 + i^2\sin\theta_1\sin\theta_2) \quad \text{Use the FOIL method.}$$

$$= r_1r_2[\cos\theta_1\cos\theta_2 + i(\cos\theta_1\sin\theta_2 + \sin\theta_1\cos\theta_2) + i^2\sin\theta_1\sin\theta_2] \quad \text{Factor } i \text{ from the second and third terms.}$$

$$= r_1r_2[\cos\theta_1\cos\theta_2 + i(\cos\theta_1\sin\theta_2 + \sin\theta_1\cos\theta_2) - \sin\theta_1\sin\theta_2] \quad i^2 = -1$$

$$= r_1r_2[(\cos\theta_1\cos\theta_2 - \sin\theta_1\sin\theta_2) + i(\sin\theta_1\cos\theta_2 + \cos\theta_1\sin\theta_2)] \quad \text{Rearrange terms.}$$

This is $\cos(\theta_1 + \theta_2)$. This is $\sin(\theta_1 + \theta_2)$.

$$= r_1r_2[\cos(\theta_1 + \theta_2) + i\sin(\theta_1 + \theta_2)]$$

This result gives a rule for finding the product of two complex numbers in polar form. The two parts to the rule are shown in the voice balloons below the product.

$$r_1 r_2[\cos(\theta_1 + \theta_2) + i\sin(\theta_1 + \theta_2)]$$

Multiply moduli. Add arguments.

## EXAMPLE 5 Finding Products of Complex Numbers in Polar Form

Find the product of the complex numbers. Leave the answer in polar form.

$$z_1 = 4(\cos 50° + i\sin 50°) \qquad z_2 = 7(\cos 100° + i\sin 100°)$$

**Solution**

$z_1 z_2$

$= [4(\cos 50° + i\sin 50°)][7(\cos 100° + i\sin 100°)]$ Form the product of the given numbers.

$= (4 \cdot 7)[\cos(50° + 100°) + i\sin(50° + 100°)]$ Multiply moduli and add arguments.

$= 28(\cos 150° + i\sin 150°)$ Simplify.

**Check Point 5** Find the product of the complex numbers. Leave the answer in polar form.

$$z_1 = 6(\cos 40° + i\sin 40°) \qquad z_2 = 5(\cos 20° + i\sin 20°)$$

**6** Find quotients of complex numbers in polar form.

Using algebraic methods for dividing complex numbers and the difference formulas for sine and cosine, we can obtain a rule for dividing complex numbers in polar form. The proof of this rule can be found in the appendix.

### Quotient of Two Complex Numbers in Polar Form

Let $z_1 = r_1(\cos\theta_1 + i\sin\theta_1)$ and $z_2 = r_2(\cos\theta_2 + i\sin\theta_2)$ be two complex numbers in polar form. Their quotient, $\frac{z_1}{z_2}$, is

$$\frac{z_1}{z_2} = \frac{r_1}{r_2}[\cos(\theta_1 - \theta_2) + i\sin(\theta_1 - \theta_2)].$$

To divide two complex numbers, divide moduli and subtract arguments.

## EXAMPLE 6 Finding Quotients of Complex Numbers in Polar Form

Find the quotient $\frac{z_1}{z_2}$ of the complex numbers. Leave the answer in polar form.

$$z_1 = 12\left(\cos\frac{3\pi}{4} + i\sin\frac{3\pi}{4}\right) \qquad z_2 = 4\left(\cos\frac{\pi}{4} + i\sin\frac{\pi}{4}\right)$$

**Solution**

$$\frac{z_1}{z_2} = \frac{12\left(\cos\frac{3\pi}{4} + i\sin\frac{3\pi}{4}\right)}{4\left(\cos\frac{\pi}{4} + i\sin\frac{\pi}{4}\right)}$$ Form the quotient of the given numbers.

$$= \frac{12}{4}\left[\cos\left(\frac{3\pi}{4} - \frac{\pi}{4}\right) + i\sin\left(\frac{3\pi}{4} - \frac{\pi}{4}\right)\right]$$ Divide moduli and subtract arguments.

$$= 3\left(\cos\frac{\pi}{2} + i\sin\frac{\pi}{2}\right)$$ Simplify: $\frac{3\pi}{4} - \frac{\pi}{4} = \frac{2\pi}{4} = \frac{\pi}{2}$.

**Check Point 6** Find the quotient of the complex numbers. Leave the answer in polar form.

$$z_1 = 50\left(\cos\frac{4\pi}{3} + i\sin\frac{4\pi}{3}\right) \qquad z_2 = 5\left(\cos\frac{\pi}{3} + i\sin\frac{\pi}{3}\right)$$

**7** Find powers of complex numbers in polar form.

## Powers of Complex Numbers in Polar Form

We can use a formula to find powers of complex numbers if the complex numbers are expressed in polar form. This formula can be illustrated by repeatedly multiplying by $r(\cos\theta + i\sin\theta)$.

$z = r(\cos\theta + i\sin\theta)$ Start with z.

$z \cdot z = r(\cos\theta + i\sin\theta)r(\cos\theta + i\sin\theta)$ Multiply z by $z = r(\cos\theta + i\sin\theta)$.

$z^2 = r^2(\cos 2\theta + i\sin 2\theta)$ Multiply moduli: $r \cdot r = r^2$. Add arguments: $\theta + \theta = 2\theta$.

$z^2 \cdot z = r^2(\cos 2\theta + i\sin 2\theta)r(\cos\theta + i\sin\theta)$ Multiply $z^2$ by $z = r(\cos\theta + i\sin\theta)$.

$z^3 = r^3(\cos 3\theta + i\sin 3\theta)$ Multiply moduli: $r^2 \cdot r = r^3$. Add arguments: $2\theta + \theta = 3\theta$.

$z^3 \cdot z = r^3(\cos 3\theta + i\sin 3\theta)r(\cos\theta + i\sin\theta)$ Multiply $z^3$ by $z = r(\cos\theta + i\sin\theta)$.

$z^4 = r^4(\cos 4\theta + i\sin 4\theta)$ Multiply moduli: $r^3 \cdot r = r^4$. Add arguments: $3\theta + \theta = 4\theta$.

Do you see a pattern forming? If $n$ is a positive integer, it appears that $z^n$ is obtained by raising the modulus to the $n$th power and multiplying the argument by $n$. The formula for the $n$th power of a complex number is known as **DeMoivre's Theorem** in honor of the French mathematician Abraham DeMoivre (1667–1754).

**DeMoivre's Theorem**

Let $z = r(\cos\theta + i\sin\theta)$ be a complex number in polar form. If $n$ is a positive integer, $z$ to the $n$th power, $z^n$, is

$$z^n = [r(\cos\theta + i\sin\theta)]^n = r^n(\cos n\theta + i\sin n\theta).$$

### EXAMPLE 7 Finding the Power of a Complex Number

Find $[2(\cos 10° + i\sin 10°)]^6$. Write the answer in rectangular form, $a + bi$.

**Solution** By DeMoivre's Theorem,

$[2(\cos 10^\circ + i\sin 10^\circ)]^6$

$= 2^6[\cos(6 \cdot 10^\circ) + i\sin(6 \cdot 10^\circ)]$ — Raise the modulus to the 6th power and multiply the argument by 6.

$= 64(\cos 60^\circ + i\sin 60^\circ)$ — Simplify.

$= 64\left(\frac{1}{2} + i\frac{\sqrt{3}}{2}\right)$ — Write the answer in rectangular form.

$= 32 + 32\sqrt{3}i$ — Multiply and express the answer in $a + bi$ form.

**Check Point 7** Find $[2(\cos 30^\circ + i\sin 30^\circ)]^5$. Write the answer in rectangular form.

## EXAMPLE 8 Finding the Power of a Complex Number

Find $(1 + i)^8$ using DeMoivre's Theorem. Write the answer in rectangular form, $a + bi$.

**Solution** DeMoivre's Theorem applies to complex numbers in polar form. Thus, we must first write $1 + i$ in $r(\cos\theta + i\sin\theta)$ form. Then we can use DeMoivre's Theorem. The complex number $1 + i$ is plotted in Figure 7.39. From the figure we obtain values for $r$ and $\theta$.

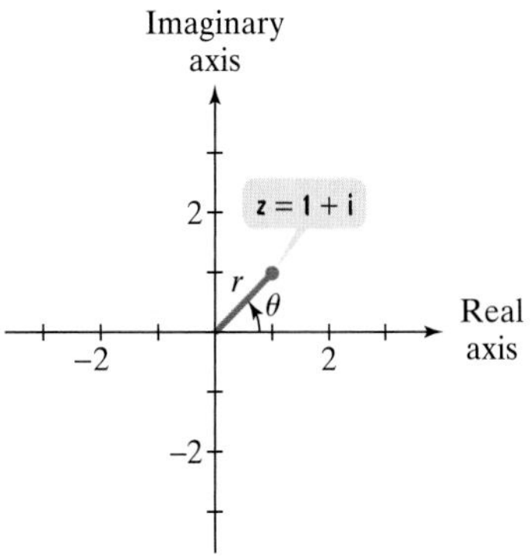

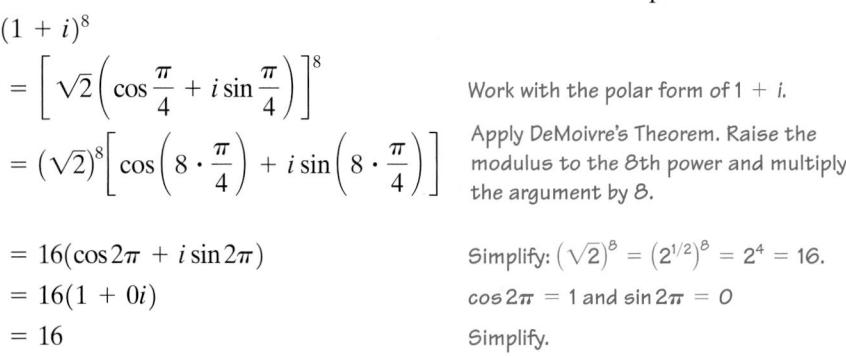

**Figure 7.39** Plotting $1 + i$ and writing the number in polar form

$$r = \sqrt{a^2 + b^2} = \sqrt{1^2 + 1^2} = \sqrt{2} \qquad \tan\theta = \frac{b}{a} = \frac{1}{1} = 1 \text{ and } \theta = \frac{\pi}{4}$$

Using these values,

$$1 + i = r(\cos\theta + i\sin\theta) = \sqrt{2}\left(\cos\frac{\pi}{4} + i\sin\frac{\pi}{4}\right).$$

Now we use DeMoivre's Theorem to raise $1 + i$ to the 8th power.

$(1 + i)^8$

$= \left[\sqrt{2}\left(\cos\frac{\pi}{4} + i\sin\frac{\pi}{4}\right)\right]^8$ — Work with the polar form of $1 + i$.

$= (\sqrt{2})^8\left[\cos\left(8 \cdot \frac{\pi}{4}\right) + i\sin\left(8 \cdot \frac{\pi}{4}\right)\right]$ — Apply DeMoivre's Theorem. Raise the modulus to the 8th power and multiply the argument by 8.

$= 16(\cos 2\pi + i\sin 2\pi)$ — Simplify: $(\sqrt{2})^8 = (2^{1/2})^8 = 2^4 = 16$.

$= 16(1 + 0i)$ — $\cos 2\pi = 1$ and $\sin 2\pi = 0$

$= 16$ — Simplify.

**Check Point 8** Find $(1 + i)^4$ using DeMoivre's Theorem. Write the answer in rectangular form.

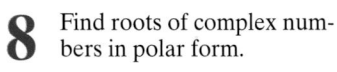

**8** Find roots of complex numbers in polar form.

## Roots of Complex Numbers in Polar Form

In Example 7, we showed that

$$[2(\cos 10^\circ + i\sin 10^\circ)]^6 = 64(\cos 60^\circ + i\sin 60^\circ).$$

We say that $2(\cos 10° + i \sin 10°)$ is a **complex sixth root** of $64(\cos 60° + i \sin 60°)$. It is one of six distinct complex roots of $64(\cos 60° + i \sin 60°)$.

In general, if a complex number $z$ satisfies the equation

$$z^n = w$$

we say that $z$ is a **complex *n*th root** of $w$. It is one of $n$ distinct complex roots that can be found using the following theorem.

**DeMoivre's Theorem for Finding Complex Roots**

Let $w = r(\cos\theta + i \sin\theta)$ be a complex number in polar form. If $w \neq 0$, $w$ has $n$ distinct complex $n$th roots given by the formula

$$z_k = \sqrt[n]{r}\left[\cos\left(\frac{\theta + 2\pi k}{n}\right) + i \sin\left(\frac{\theta + 2\pi k}{n}\right)\right] \quad \text{(radians)}$$

$$\text{or} \quad z_k = \sqrt[n]{r}\left[\cos\left(\frac{\theta + 360°k}{n}\right) + i \sin\left(\frac{\theta + 360°k}{n}\right)\right] \quad \text{(degrees)}$$

where $k = 0, 1, 2, \ldots, n - 1$.

By raising the radian or degree formula for $z_k$ to the $n$th power, you can use DeMoivre's Theorem for powers to show that $z_k^n = w$. Thus, each $z_k$ is a complex $n$th root of $w$.

DeMoivre's Theorem for finding complex roots states that every complex number has two distinct complex square roots, three distinct complex cube roots, four distinct complex fourth roots, and so on. Each root has the same modulus, $\sqrt[n]{r}$. Successive roots have arguments that differ by the same amount, $\frac{2\pi}{n}$. This means that if you plot all the complex roots of any number, they will be equally spaced on a circle centered at the origin, having radius $\sqrt[n]{r}$.

## EXAMPLE 9 Finding the Roots of a Complex Number

Find all the complex fourth roots of $16(\cos 120° + i \sin 120°)$. Write roots in polar form, with $\theta$ in degrees.

**Solution** There are exactly four fourth roots of the given complex number. From DeMoivre's Theorem for finding complex roots, the fourth roots of $16(\cos 120° + i \sin 120°)$ are

$$z_k = \sqrt[4]{16}\left[\cos\left(\frac{120° + 360°k}{4}\right) + i \sin\left(\frac{120° + 360°k}{4}\right)\right], \quad k = 0, 1, 2, 3.$$

Use $z_k = \sqrt[n]{r}\left[\cos\left(\frac{\theta + 360°k}{n}\right) + i \sin\left(\frac{\theta + 360°k}{n}\right)\right]$.
In $16(\cos 120° + i \sin 120°)$, $r = 16$ and $\theta = 120°$.
Because we are finding fourth roots, $n = 4$.

The four fourth roots are found by substituting 0, 1, 2, and 3 for $k$ in the expression for $z_k$ above the voice balloon. Thus, the four fourth roots are:

$$z_0 = \sqrt[4]{16}\left[\cos\left(\frac{120^\circ + 360^\circ \cdot 0}{4}\right) + i\sin\left(\frac{120^\circ + 360^\circ \cdot 0}{4}\right)\right]$$

$$= \sqrt[4]{16}\left(\cos\frac{120^\circ}{4} + i\sin\frac{120^\circ}{4}\right) = 2(\cos 30^\circ + i\sin 30^\circ)$$

$$z_1 = \sqrt[4]{16}\left[\cos\left(\frac{120^\circ + 360^\circ \cdot 1}{4}\right) + i\sin\left(\frac{120^\circ + 360^\circ \cdot 1}{4}\right)\right]$$

$$= \sqrt[4]{16}\left(\cos\frac{480^\circ}{4} + i\sin\frac{480^\circ}{4}\right) = 2(\cos 120^\circ + i\sin 120^\circ)$$

$$z_2 = \sqrt[4]{16}\left[\cos\left(\frac{120^\circ + 360^\circ \cdot 2}{4}\right) + i\sin\left(\frac{120^\circ + 360^\circ \cdot 2}{4}\right)\right]$$

$$= \sqrt[4]{16}\left(\cos\frac{840^\circ}{4} + i\sin\frac{840^\circ}{4}\right) = 2(\cos 210^\circ + i\sin 210^\circ)$$

$$z_3 = \sqrt[4]{16}\left[\cos\left(\frac{120^\circ + 360^\circ \cdot 3}{4}\right) + i\sin\left(\frac{120^\circ + 360^\circ \cdot 3}{4}\right)\right]$$

$$= \sqrt[4]{16}\left(\cos\frac{1200^\circ}{4} + i\sin\frac{1200^\circ}{4}\right) = 2(\cos 300^\circ + i\sin 300^\circ)$$

In Figure 7.40, we have plotted each of the four fourth roots. They are equally spaced at 90° intervals on a circle having radius 2.

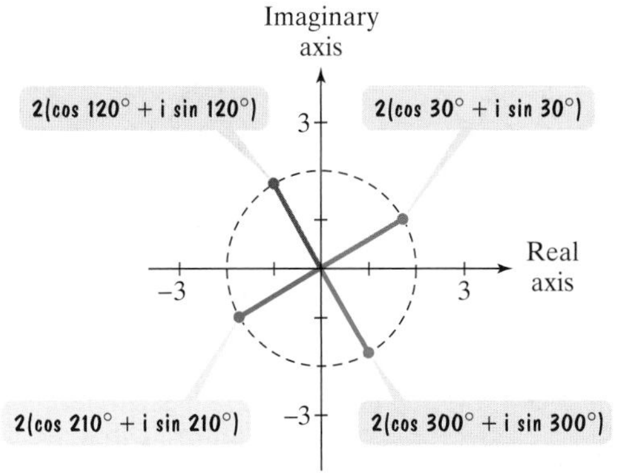


**Figure 7.40** Plotting the four fourth roots of $16(\cos 120^\circ + i\sin 120^\circ)$

**Check Point 9** Find all the complex fourth roots of $16(\cos 60^\circ + i\sin 60^\circ)$. Write roots in polar form, with $\theta$ in degrees.

## EXAMPLE 10 Finding the Roots of a Complex Number

Find all the cube roots of 8. Write roots in rectangular form.

**Solution** DeMoivre's Theorem for roots applies to complex numbers in polar form. Thus, we will first write 8 in polar form. We express $\theta$ in radians, although degrees can also be used.

$$8 = r(\cos\theta + i\sin\theta) = 8(\cos 0 + i\sin 0)$$

There are exactly three cube roots of 8. From DeMoivre's Theorem for finding complex roots, the cube roots of 8 are

$$z_k = \sqrt[3]{8}\left[\cos\left(\frac{0 + 2\pi k}{3}\right) + i\sin\left(\frac{0 + 2\pi k}{3}\right)\right], \quad k = 0, 1, 2.$$

Use $z_k = \sqrt[n]{r}\left[\cos\left(\frac{\theta + 2\pi k}{n}\right) + i\sin\left(\frac{\theta + 2\pi k}{n}\right)\right]$.
In $8(\cos 0 + i\sin 0)$, $r = 8$ and $\theta = 0$.
Because we are finding cube roots, $n = 3$.

The three cube roots of 8 are found by substituting 0, 1, and 2 for $k$ in the expression for $z_k$ above the voice balloon. Thus, the three cube roots of 8 are:

$$z_0 = \sqrt[3]{8}\left[\cos\left(\frac{0 + 2\pi \cdot 0}{3}\right) + i\sin\left(\frac{0 + 2\pi \cdot 0}{3}\right)\right]$$

$$= 2(\cos 0 + i\sin 0) = 2(1 + i \cdot 0) = 2$$

$$z_1 = \sqrt[3]{8}\left[\cos\left(\frac{0 + 2\pi \cdot 1}{3}\right) + i\sin\left(\frac{0 + 2\pi \cdot 1}{3}\right)\right]$$

$$= 2\left(\cos\frac{2\pi}{3} + i\sin\frac{2\pi}{3}\right) = 2\left(-\frac{1}{2} + i \cdot \frac{\sqrt{3}}{2}\right) = -1 + \sqrt{3}i$$

$$z_2 = \sqrt[3]{8}\left[\cos\left(\frac{0 + 2\pi \cdot 2}{3}\right) + i\sin\left(\frac{0 + 2\pi \cdot 2}{3}\right)\right]$$

$$= 2\left(\cos\frac{4\pi}{3} + i\sin\frac{4\pi}{3}\right) = 2\left(-\frac{1}{2} + i \cdot \left(-\frac{\sqrt{3}}{2}\right)\right) = -1 - \sqrt{3}i.$$

The three cube roots of 8 are plotted in Figure 7.41.

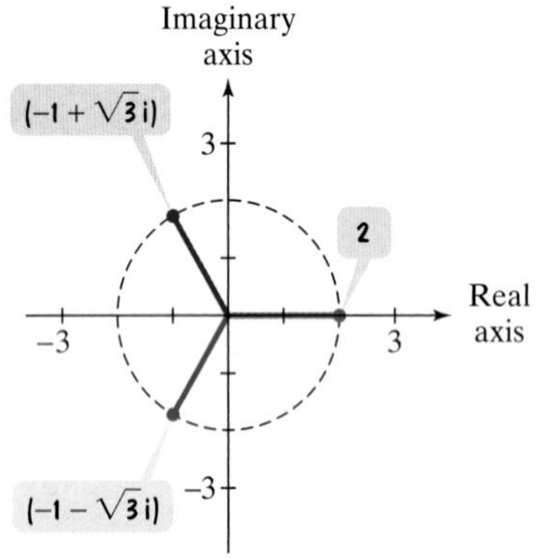


**Figure 7.41** The three cube roots of 8 are equally spaced at intervals of $\frac{2\pi}{3}$ about a circle having radius 2.

**Check Point 10** Find all the cube roots of 27. Write roots in rectangular form.

## The Mandelbrot Set

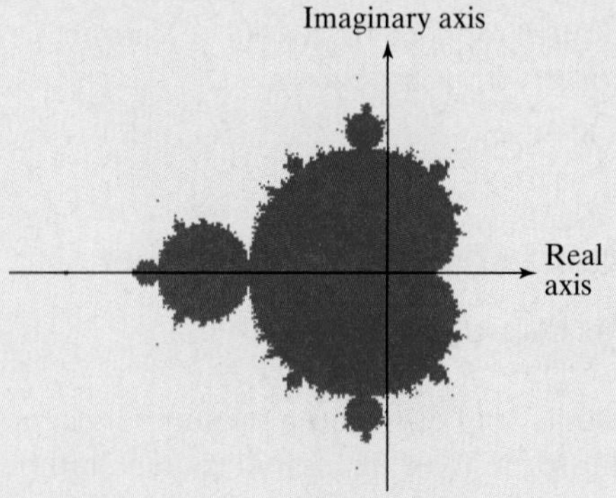


**Figure 7.42**

The set of all complex numbers for which the sequence

$$z, z^2 + z, (z^2 + z)^2 + z, [(z^2 + z)^2 + z]^2 + z, \ldots$$

is bounded is called the **Mandelbrot set**. Plotting these complex numbers in the complex plane results in a graph that is "buglike" in shape, shown in Figure 7.42. Colors can be added to the boundary of the graph. At the boundary, color choices depend on how quickly the numbers in the boundary approach infinity when substituted into the sequence shown. The magnified boundary is shown in the introduction to this section. It includes the original buglike structure, as well as new and interesting patterns. With each level of magnification, repetition and unpredictable formations interact to create what has been called the most complicated mathematical object ever known.

# EXERCISE SET 7.5

## Practice Exercises

*In Exercises 1–10, plot each complex number and find its absolute value.*

**1.** $z = 4i$
**2.** $z = 3i$
**3.** $z = 3$
**4.** $z = 4$
**5.** $z = 3 + 2i$
**6.** $z = 2 + 5i$
**7.** $z = 3 - i$
**8.** $z = 4 - i$
**9.** $z = -3 + 4i$
**10.** $z = -3 - 4i$

*In Exercises 11–26, plot each complex number. Then write the complex number in polar form. You may express the argument in degrees or radians.*

**11.** $2 + 2i$
**12.** $1 + \sqrt{3}i$
**13.** $-1 - i$
**14.** $2 - 2i$
**15.** $-4i$
**16.** $-3i$
**17.** $2\sqrt{3} - 2i$
**18.** $-2 + 2\sqrt{3}i$
**19.** $-3$
**20.** $-4$
**21.** $-3\sqrt{2} - 3\sqrt{3}i$
**22.** $3\sqrt{2} - 3\sqrt{2}i$
**23.** $-3 + 4i$
**24.** $-2 + 3i$
**25.** $2 - \sqrt{3}i$
**26.** $1 - \sqrt{5}i$

*In Exercises 27–36, write each complex number in rectangular form. If necessary, round to the nearest tenth.*

**27.** $6(\cos 30° + i \sin 30°)$
**28.** $12(\cos 60° + i \sin 60°)$
**29.** $4(\cos 240° + i \sin 240°)$
**30.** $10(\cos 210° + i \sin 210°)$
**31.** $8\left(\cos \frac{7\pi}{4} + i \sin \frac{7\pi}{4}\right)$
**32.** $4\left(\cos \frac{5\pi}{6} + i \sin \frac{5\pi}{6}\right)$
**33.** $5\left(\cos \frac{\pi}{2} + i \sin \frac{\pi}{2}\right)$
**34.** $7\left(\cos \frac{3\pi}{2} + i \sin \frac{3\pi}{2}\right)$
**35.** $20(\cos 205° + i \sin 205°)$
**36.** $30(\cos 2.3 + i \sin 2.3)$

*In Exercises 37–44, find the product of the complex numbers. Leave answers in polar form.*

**37.** $z_1 = 6(\cos 20° + i \sin 20°)$
$z_2 = 5(\cos 50° + i \sin 50°)$

**38.** $z_1 = 4(\cos 15° + i \sin 15°)$
$z_2 = 7(\cos 25° + i \sin 25°)$

**39.** $z_1 = 3\left(\cos \frac{\pi}{5} + i \sin \frac{\pi}{5}\right)$
$z_2 = 4\left(\cos \frac{\pi}{10} + i \sin \frac{\pi}{10}\right)$

**40.** $z_1 = 3\left(\cos \frac{5\pi}{8} + i \sin \frac{5\pi}{8}\right)$
$z_2 = 10\left(\cos \frac{\pi}{16} + i \sin \frac{\pi}{16}\right)$

**41.** $z_1 = \cos \frac{\pi}{4} + i \sin \frac{\pi}{4}$
$z_2 = \cos \frac{\pi}{3} + i \sin \frac{\pi}{3}$

**42.** $z_1 = \cos \frac{\pi}{6} + i \sin \frac{\pi}{6}$
$z_2 = \cos \frac{\pi}{4} + i \sin \frac{\pi}{4}$

**43.** $z_1 = 1 + i$
$z_2 = -1 + i$

**44.** $z_1 = 1 + i$
$z_2 = 2 + 2i$

*In Exercises 45–52, find the quotient $\frac{z_1}{z_2}$ of the complex numbers. Leave answers in polar form. In Exercises 49–50, express the argument as an angle between 0° and 360°.*

**45.** $z_1 = 20(\cos 75° + i \sin 75°)$
$z_2 = 4(\cos 25° + i \sin 25°)$

**46.** $z_1 = 50(\cos 80° + i \sin 80°)$
$z_2 = 10(\cos 20° + i \sin 20°)$

**47.** $z_1 = 3\left(\cos \frac{\pi}{5} + i \sin \frac{\pi}{5}\right)$
$z_2 = 4\left(\cos \frac{\pi}{10} + i \sin \frac{\pi}{10}\right)$

**48.** $z_1 = 3\left(\cos \frac{5\pi}{18} + i \sin \frac{5\pi}{18}\right)$
$z_2 = 10\left(\cos \frac{\pi}{16} + i \sin \frac{\pi}{16}\right)$

**49.** $z_1 = \cos 80° + i \sin 80°$
$z_2 = \cos 200° + i \sin 200°$

**50.** $z_1 = \cos 70° + i \sin 70°$
$z_2 = \cos 230° + i \sin 230°$

**51.** $z_1 = 2 + 2i$
$z_2 = 1 + i$

**52.** $z_1 = 2 - 2i$
$z_2 = 1 - i$

*In Exercises 53–64, use DeMoivre's Theorem to find the indicated power of the complex number. Write answers in rectangular form.*

**53.** $[4(\cos 15° + i \sin 15°)]^3$
**54.** $[2(\cos 10° + i \sin 10°)]^3$
**55.** $[2(\cos 80° + i \sin 80°)]^3$
**56.** $[2(\cos 40° + i \sin 40°)]^3$
**57.** $\left[\frac{1}{2}\left(\cos \frac{\pi}{12} + i \sin \frac{\pi}{12}\right)\right]^6$
**58.** $\left[\frac{1}{2}\left(\cos \frac{\pi}{10} + i \sin \frac{\pi}{10}\right)\right]^5$
**59.** $\left[\sqrt{2}\left(\cos \frac{5\pi}{6} + i \sin \frac{5\pi}{6}\right)\right]^4$
**60.** $\left[\sqrt{3}\left(\cos \frac{5\pi}{18} + i \sin \frac{5\pi}{18}\right)\right]^6$
**61.** $(1 + i)^5$
**62.** $(1 - i)^5$
**63.** $(\sqrt{3} - i)^6$
**64.** $(\sqrt{2} - i)^4$

*In Exercises 65–68, find all the complex roots. Write roots in polar form with θ in degrees.*

**65.** The complex square roots of $9(\cos 30° + i \sin 30°)$

**66.** The complex square roots of $25(\cos 210° + i \sin 210°)$

**67.** The complex cube roots of $8(\cos 210° + i \sin 210°)$

**68.** The complex cube roots of $27(\cos 306° + i \sin 306°)$

*In Exercises 69–76, find all the complex roots. Write roots in rectangular form. If necessary, round to the nearest tenth.*

**69.** The complex fourth roots of $81\left(\cos\frac{4\pi}{3} + i \sin\frac{4\pi}{3}\right)$

**70.** The complex fifth roots of $32\left(\cos\frac{5\pi}{3} + i \sin\frac{5\pi}{3}\right)$

**71.** The complex fifth roots of 32

**72.** The complex sixth roots of 64

**73.** The complex cube roots of 1

**74.** The complex cube roots of $i$

**75.** The complex fourth roots of $1 + i$

**76.** The complex fifth roots of $-1 + i$

## Application Exercises

*In Exercises 77–78, show that the given complex number z plots as a point in the Mandelbrot set.*

**a.** *Write the first six terms of the sequence*

$$z_1, z_2, z_3, z_4, z_5, z_6, \ldots$$

*where*

$z_1 = z$: Write the given number.

$z_2 = z^2 + z$: Square $z_1$ and add the given number.

$z_3 = (z^2 + z)^2 + z$: Square $z_2$ and add the given number.

$z_4 = [(z^2 + z)^2 + z]^2 + z$: Square $z_3$ and add the given number.

$z_5$: Square $z_4$ and add the given number.

$z_6$: Square $z_5$ and add the given number.

**b.** *If the sequence that you began writing in part (a) is bounded, the given complex number belongs to the Mandelbrot set. Show that the sequence is bounded by writing two complex numbers. One complex number should be greater in absolute value than the absolute values of the terms in the sequence. The second complex number should be less in absolute value than the absolute values of the terms in the sequence.*

**77.** $z = i$ **78.** $z = -i$

## Writing in Mathematics

**79.** Explain how to plot a complex number in the complex plane. Provide an example with your explanation.

**80.** How do you determine the absolute value of a complex number?

**81.** What is the polar form of a complex number?

**82.** If you are given a complex number in rectangular form, how do you write it in polar form?

**83.** If you are given a complex number in polar form, how do you write it in rectangular form?

**84.** Explain how to find the product of two complex numbers in polar form.

**85.** Explain how to find the quotient of two complex numbers in polar form.

**86.** Explain how to find the power of a complex number in polar form.

**87.** Explain how to use DeMoivre's Theorem for finding complex roots to find the two square roots of 9.

**88.** Describe the graph of all complex numbers with an absolute value of 6.

**89.** The image of the Mandelbrot set in the section opener exhibits self-similarity: Magnified portions repeat much of the pattern of the whole structure, as well as new and unexpected patterns. Describe an object in nature that exhibits self-similariy.

## Technology Exercises

**90.** Use the rectangular-to-polar feature on a graphing utility to verify any four of your answers in Exercises 11–26. Be aware that you may have to adjust the angle for the correct quadrant.

**91.** Use the polar-to-rectangular feature on a graphing utility to verify any four of your answers in Exercises 27–36.

## Critical Thinking Exercises

**92.** Prove the rule for finding the quotient of two complex numbers in polar form. Begin the proof as follows, using the conjugate of the denominator:

$$\frac{r_1(\cos\theta_1 + i\sin\theta_1)}{r_2(\cos\theta_2 + i\sin\theta_2)} = \frac{r_1(\cos\theta_1 + i\sin\theta_1)}{r_2(\cos\theta_2 + i\sin\theta_2)} \cdot \frac{(\cos\theta_2 - i\sin\theta_2)}{(\cos\theta_2 - i\sin\theta_2)}$$

Perform the indicated multiplications. Then use the difference formulas for sine and cosine.

**93.** Plot each of the complex fourth roots of 1.

*In Exercises 94–95, use DeMoivre's Theorem for finding complex roots to find all the solutions of each equation.*

**94.** $x^3 + 27 = 0$ **95.** $x^3 - 8i = 0$

## Group Exercise

**96.** Group members should prepare and present a seminar on chaos. Include one or more of the following topics in your presentation: fractal images, the role of complex numbers in generating fractal images, algorithms, iterations, iteration number, and fractals in nature. Be sure to include visual images that will intrigue your audience.

# 7.6 Vectors

## Objectives

1. Use magnitude and direction to show vectors are equal.
2. Visualize scalar multiplication, vector addition, and vector subtraction as geometric vectors.
3. Represent vectors in the rectangular coordinate system.
4. Perform operations with vectors in terms of **i** and **j**.
5. Find a unit vector in the direction of **v**.
6. Solve applied problems involving vectors.

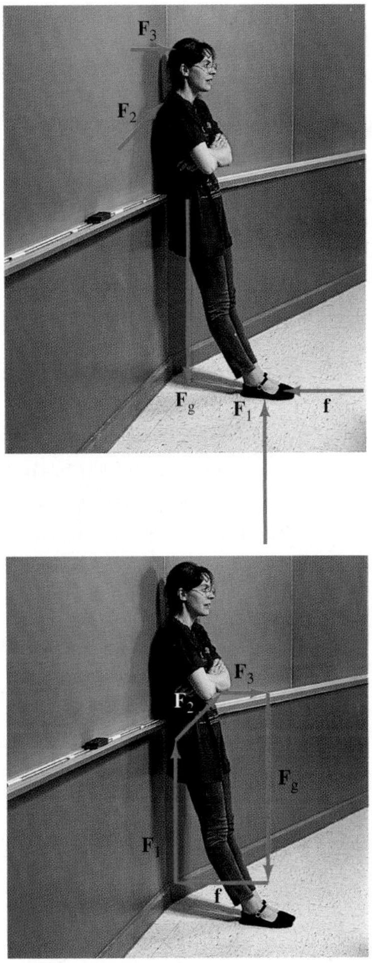


It's been a dynamic lecture, but now that it's over it's obvious that my professor is exhausted. She's slouching motionless against the board and–what's that? The forces acting against her body, including the pull of gravity, are appearing as arrows. I know that mathematics reveals the hidden patterns of the universe, but this is ridiculous. Does the arrangement of the arrows on the right have anything to do with the fact that my wiped-out professor is not sliding down the wall?

Ours is a world of pushes and pulls. For example, suppose you are pulling a cart up a 30° incline, requiring an effort of 100 pounds. This quantity is described by giving its magnitude (a number indicating size, including a unit of measure) and also its direction. The magnitude is 100 pounds and the direction is 30° from the horizontal. Quantities that involve both a magnitude and a direction are called **vector quantities**, or **vectors** for short. Here is another example of a vector:

> You are driving due north at 50 miles per hour. The magnitude is the speed, 50 miles per hour. The direction of motion is due north.

Some quantities can be completely described by giving only their magnitude. For example, the temperature of the lecture room that you just left is 75°. This temperature has magnitude, 75°, but no direction. Quantities that involve magnitude, but no direction, are called **scalar quantities**, or **scalars** for short. Thus, a scalar has only a numerical value. Another example of a scalar is your professor's height, which you estimate to be 5.5 feet.

In the next two sections, we introduce the world of vectors, which literally surround your every move. Because vectors have both nonnegative magnitude and direction, we begin our discussion with directed line segments.

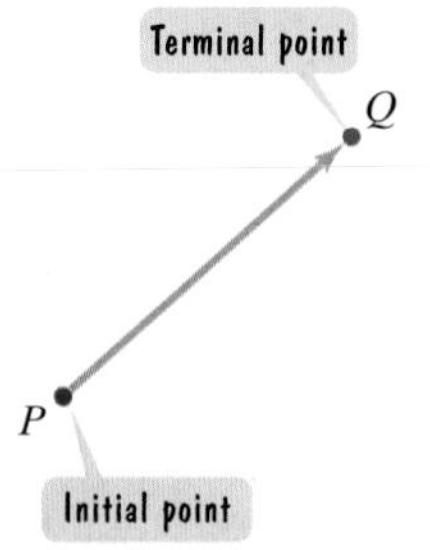


**Figure 7.43** A directed line segment from $P$ to $Q$

## Directed Line Segments and Geometric Vectors

A line segment to which a direction has been assigned is called a **directed line segment**. Figure 7.43 shows a directed line segment from $P$ to $Q$. We call $P$ the **initial point** and $Q$ the **terminal point**. We denote this directed line segment by

$$\overrightarrow{PQ}.$$

The **magnitude** of the directed line segment $\overrightarrow{PQ}$ is its length. We denote this by $\|\overrightarrow{PQ}\|$. Thus, $\|\overrightarrow{PQ}\|$ is the distance from point $P$ to point $Q$. Because distance is nonnegative, vectors do not have negative magnitudes.

Geometrically, a **vector** is a directed line segment. Vectors are often denoted by a boldface letter, such as **v**. If a vector **v** has the same magnitude and the same direction as the directed line segment $\overrightarrow{PQ}$, we write

$$\mathbf{v} = \overrightarrow{PQ}.$$

Because it is difficult to write boldface on paper, use an arrow over a single letter, such as $\vec{v}$, to denote **v**, the vector **v**.

**1** Use magnitude and direction to show vectors are equal.

Figure 7.44 shows four possible relationships between vectors **v** and **w**. In Figure 7.44 (a), the vectors have the same magnitude and direction and are said to be *equal*. In general, vectors **v** and **w** are **equal** if they have the *same magnitude* and the *same direction*. We write this as $\mathbf{v} = \mathbf{w}$.

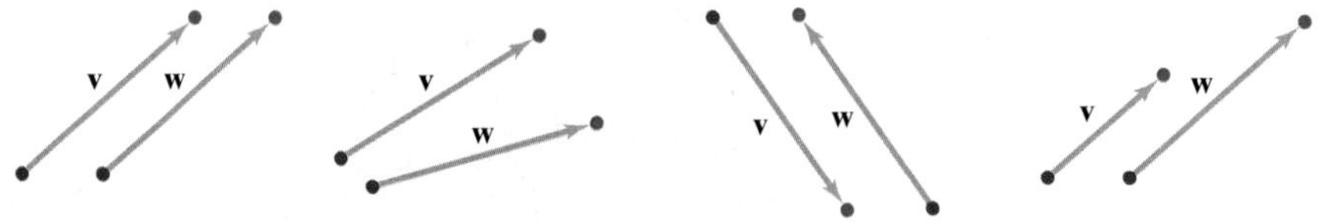


**(a)** $\mathbf{v} = \mathbf{w}$ because the vectors have the some magnitude and direction.

**(b)** Vectors **v** and **w** have the same magnitude, but different directions

**(c)** Vectors **v** and **w** have the same magnitude, but opposite directions

**(d)** Vectors **v** and **w** have the same direction, but different magnitudes

**Figure 7.44** Relationships between vectors

## EXAMPLE 1 Showing That Two Vectors Are Equal

Use Figure 7.45 to show that $\mathbf{u} = \mathbf{v}$.

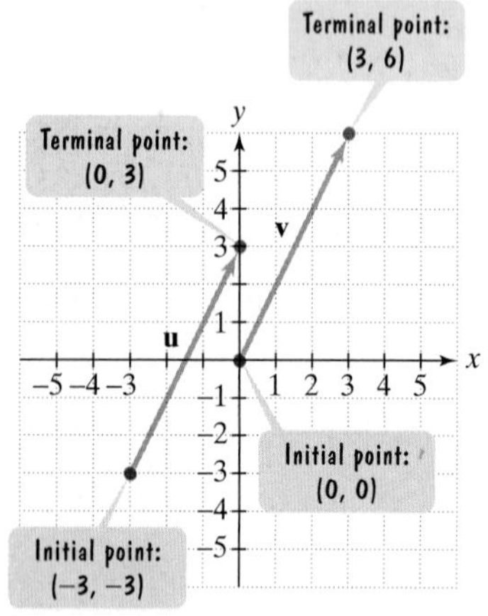


**Figure 7.45**

**Solution** Equal vectors have the same magnitude and the same direction. Use the distance formula to show that **u** and **v** have the same magnitude.

Magnitude of **u**

$$\|\mathbf{u}\| = \sqrt{(x_2 - x_1)^2 + (y_2 - y_1)^2} = \sqrt{[0 - (-3)]^2 + [3 - (-3)]^2}$$
$$= \sqrt{3^2 + 6^2} = \sqrt{9 + 36} = \sqrt{45} \quad (\text{or } 3\sqrt{5})$$

Magnitude of **v**

$$\|\mathbf{v}\| = \sqrt{(x_2 - x_1)^2 + (y_2 - y_1)^2} = \sqrt{(3 - 0)^2 + (6 - 0)^2}$$
$$= \sqrt{3^2 + 6^2} = \sqrt{9 + 36} = \sqrt{45} \quad (\text{or } 3\sqrt{5})$$

Thus, **u** and **v** have the same magnitude: $\|\mathbf{u}\| = \|\mathbf{v}\|$.

One way to show that **u** and **v** have the same direction is to find the slopes of the lines on which they lie.

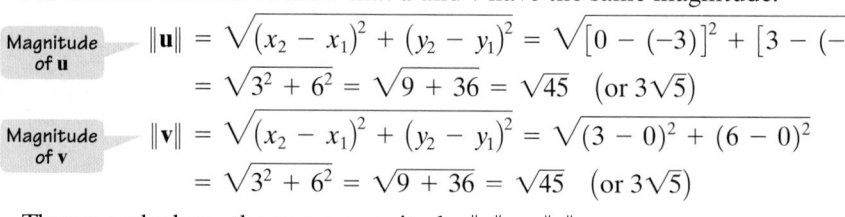

Line on which **u** lies

$$m = \frac{y_2 - y_1}{x_2 - x_1} = \frac{3 - (-3)}{0 - (-3)} = \frac{6}{3} = 2$$

Line on which **v** lies

$$m = \frac{y_2 - y_1}{x_2 - x_1} = \frac{6 - 0}{3 - 0} = \frac{6}{3} = 2$$

Because **u** and **v** are both directed toward the upper right on lines having the same slope, 2, they have the same direction.

Thus, **u** and **v** have the same magnitude and direction, and $\mathbf{u} = \mathbf{v}$.

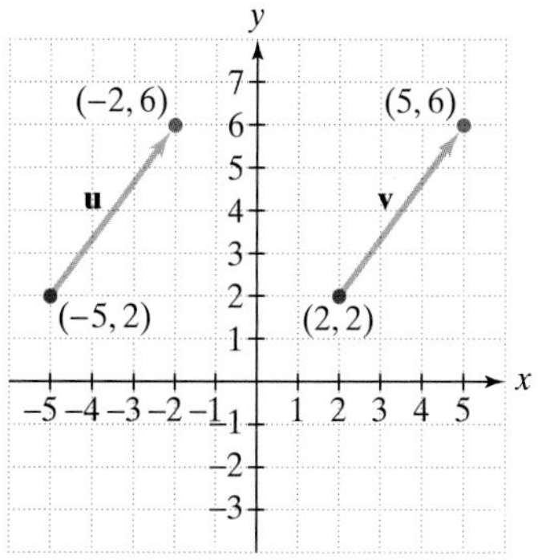


**Figure 7.46**

**Check Point 1** Use Figure 7.46 to show that $\mathbf{u} = \mathbf{v}$.

**2** Visualize scalar multiplication, vector addition, and vector subtraction as geometric vectors.

A vector can be multiplied by a real number. Figure 7.47 shows three such multiplications: $2\mathbf{v}$, $\frac{1}{2}\mathbf{v}$, and $-\frac{3}{2}\mathbf{v}$. **Multiplying a vector by any positive real number (except for 1) changes the magnitude of the vector, but not its direction.** This can be seen by the blue and green vectors in Figure 7.47. Compare the black and blue vectors. Can you see that $2\mathbf{v}$ has the same direction as $\mathbf{v}$ but is twice the magnitude of $\mathbf{v}$? Now, compare the black and green vectors: $\frac{1}{2}\mathbf{v}$ has the same direction as $\mathbf{v}$ but is half the magnitude of $\mathbf{v}$.

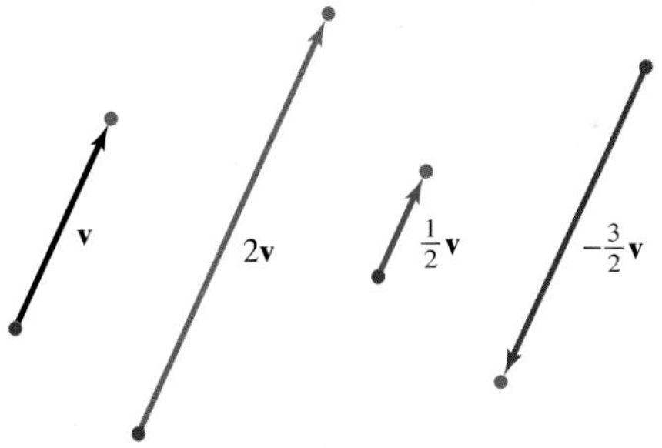


**Figure 7.47** Multiplying vector **v** by real numbers

Now compare the black and red vectors in Figure 7.47. **Multiplying a vector by a negative number reverses the direction of the vector.** Notice that $-\frac{3}{2}\mathbf{v}$ has the opposite direction as $\mathbf{v}$ and is $\frac{3}{2}$ the magnitude of $\mathbf{v}$.

The multiplication of the real number, $k$, and the vector, $\mathbf{v}$, is called **scalar multiplication**. We write this product as $k\mathbf{v}$.

### Scalar Multiplication

If $k$ is a real number and $\mathbf{v}$ a vector, the vector $k\mathbf{v}$ is called a **scalar multiple** of the vector $\mathbf{v}$. The magnitude and direction of $k\mathbf{v}$ are given as follows:

The vector $k\mathbf{v}$ has a *magnitude* of $|k|\,\|\mathbf{v}\|$. We describe this as the absolute value of $k$ times the magnitude of vector $\mathbf{v}$.

The vector $k\mathbf{v}$ has a *direction* that is:

- the same as the direction of $\mathbf{v}$ if $k > 0$, and
- opposite the direction of $\mathbf{v}$ if $k < 0$.

A geometric method for adding two vectors is shown in Figure 7.48. The sum of $\mathbf{u} + \mathbf{v}$ is called the **resultant vector**. Here is how we find this vector:

1. Position $\mathbf{u}$ and $\mathbf{v}$ so the terminal point of $\mathbf{u}$ coincides with the initial point of $\mathbf{v}$.
2. The resultant vector, $\mathbf{u} + \mathbf{v}$, extends from the initial point of $\mathbf{u}$ to the terminal point of $\mathbf{v}$.

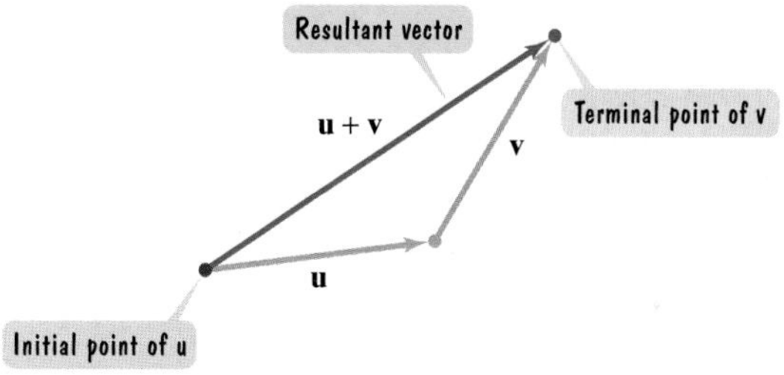


**Figure 7.48** Vector addition $\mathbf{u} + \mathbf{v}$; the terminal point of $\mathbf{u}$ coincides with the initial point of $\mathbf{v}$.

## Wiped Out, But Not Sliding Down the Wall

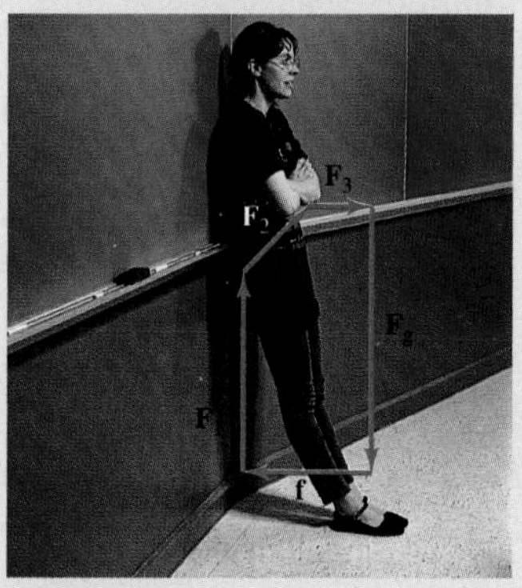


The figure shows the sum of five vectors:

$$\mathbf{F}_1 + \mathbf{F}_2 + \mathbf{F}_3 + \mathbf{F}_g + \mathbf{f}.$$

Notice how the terminal point of each vector coincides with the initial point of the vector that's being added to it. The vector sum, from the initial point of $\mathbf{F}_1$ to the terminal point of $\mathbf{f}$, is a single point. The magnitude of a single point is zero. These forces add up to a net force of zero, allowing the professor to be motionless.

The **difference of two vectors,** $\mathbf{v} - \mathbf{u}$, is defined as $\mathbf{v} - \mathbf{u} = \mathbf{v} + (-\mathbf{u})$, where $-\mathbf{u}$ is the scalar multiplication of $\mathbf{u}$ and $-1$: $-1\mathbf{u}$. The difference $\mathbf{v} - \mathbf{u}$ is shown geometrically in Figure 7.49

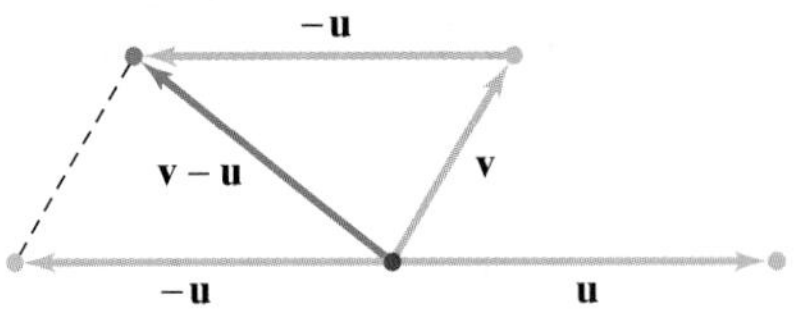


**Figure 7.49** Vector subtraction $\mathbf{v} - \mathbf{u}$; the terminal point of $\mathbf{v}$ coincides with the initial point of $-\mathbf{u}$.

**3** Represent vectors in the rectangular coordinate system.

## Vectors in the Rectangular Coordinate System

As you saw in Example 1, vectors can be shown in the rectangular coordinate system. Now let's see how we can use the rectangular coordinate system to represent vectors. We begin with two vectors that both have a magnitude of 1. Such vectors are called **unit vectors**.

### The i and j Unit Vectors

Vector **i** is the unit vector whose direction is along the positive $x$-axis. Vector **j** is the unit vector whose direction is along the positive $y$-axis.

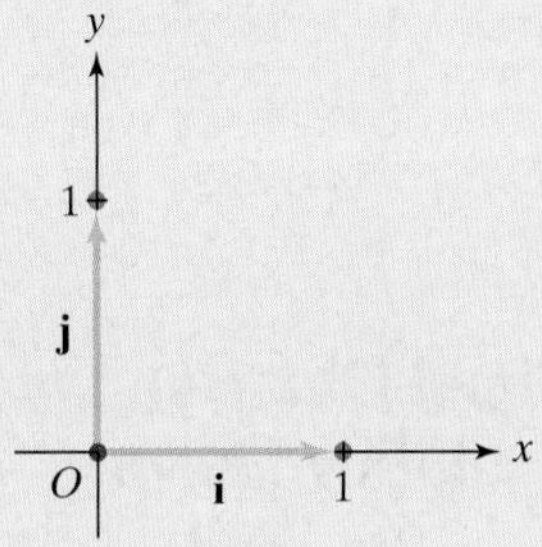


Why are the **i** and **j** unit vectors important? Vectors in the rectangular coordinate system can be represented in terms of **i** and **j**. For example, consider vector **v** with initial point at the origin, (0, 0), and terminal point at $P = (a, b)$. The vector **v** is shown in Figure 7.50. We can represent **v** using **i** and **j** as $\mathbf{v} = a\mathbf{i} + b\mathbf{j}$.

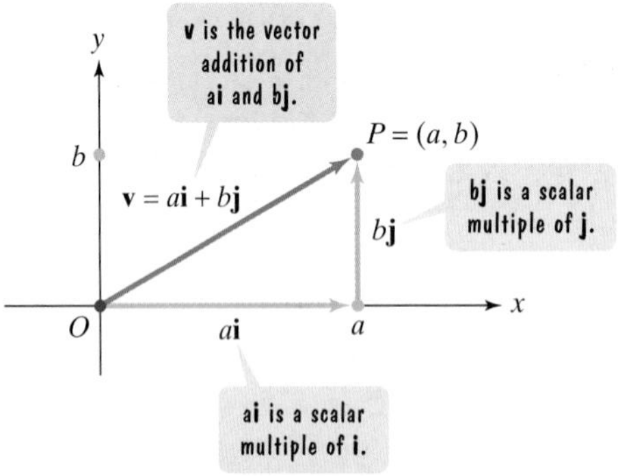


**Figure 7.50** Using vector addition, vector **v** is represented as $\mathbf{v} = a\mathbf{i} + b\mathbf{j}$.

### Representing Vectors in Rectangular Coordinates

Vector **v**, from (0, 0) to $(a, b)$, is represented as

$$\mathbf{v} = a\mathbf{i} + b\mathbf{j}.$$

The real numbers $a$ and $b$ are called the **scalar components** of **v**. Note that

- $a$ is the **horizontal component** of **v**, and
- $b$ is the **vertical component** of **v**.

The vector sum $a\mathbf{i} + b\mathbf{j}$ is called a **linear combination** of the vectors **i** and **j**. The magnitude of $\mathbf{v} = a\mathbf{i} + b\mathbf{j}$ is given by

$$\|\mathbf{v}\| = \sqrt{a^2 + b^2}.$$

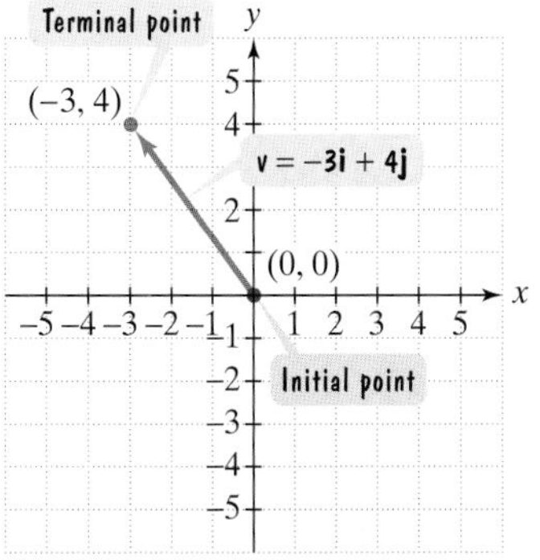


**Figure 7.51** Sketching $\mathbf{v} = -3\mathbf{i} + 4\mathbf{j}$ in the rectangular coordinate system

## EXAMPLE 2 Representing a Vector in Rectangular Coordinates and Finding Its Magnitude

Sketch the vector $\mathbf{v} = -3\mathbf{i} + 4\mathbf{j}$ and find its magnitude.

**Solution** For the given vector $\mathbf{v} = -3\mathbf{i} + 4\mathbf{j}$, $a = -3$ and $b = 4$. The vector's initial point is the origin, $(0, 0)$, shown in Figure 7.51. The vector's terminal point is $(a, b) = (-3, 4)$. We sketch the vector by drawing an arrow from $(0, 0)$ to $(-3, 4)$. We determine the magnitude of the vector by using the distance formula. Thus, the magnitude is

$$\|\mathbf{v}\| = \sqrt{a^2 + b^2} = \sqrt{(-3)^2 + 4^2} = \sqrt{9 + 16} = \sqrt{25} = 5.$$

**Check Point 2** Sketch the vector $\mathbf{v} = 3\mathbf{i} - 3\mathbf{j}$ and find its magnitude.

The vectors in Example 2 and Check Point 2 have initial points at the origin. A vector whose initial point is at the origin is called a **position vector**. Any vector in rectangular coordinates whose initial point is not at the origin can be shown to be equal to a position vector. As shown in the box, this gives us a way to represent vectors between any two points.

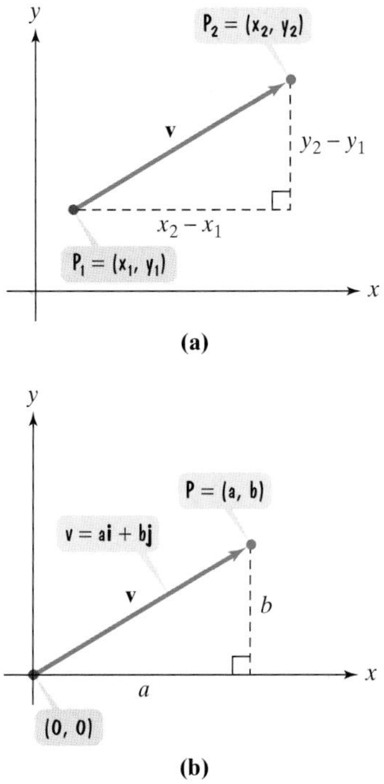


**Figure 7.52**

### Representing Vectors in Rectangular Coordinates

Vector **v** with initial point $P_1 = (x_1, y_1)$ and terminal point $P_2 = (x_2, y_2)$ is equal to the position vector

$$\mathbf{v} = (x_2 - x_1)\mathbf{i} + (y_2 - y_1)\mathbf{j}.$$

We can use congruent triangles to derive this formula. Begin with the right triangle in Figure 7.52(a) This triangle shows vector **v** from $P_1 = (x_1, y_1)$ to $P_2 = (x_2, y_2)$. In Figure 7.52(b), we move vector **v**, without changing its magnitude or its direction, so that its initial point is at the origin. Using this position vector in Figure 7.52 (b), we see that

$$\mathbf{v} = a\mathbf{i} + b\mathbf{j}$$

The equal vectors and the right angles in the right triangles in Figures 7.52(a) and (b) result in congruent triangles. The corresponding sides of these congruent

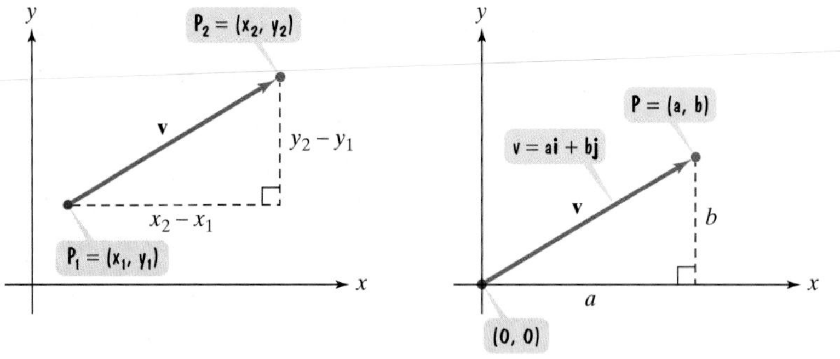


**Figure 7.52,** repeated

triangles are equal, so that $a = x_2 - x_1$ and $b = y_2 - y_1$. This means that **v** may be expressed as

$$\mathbf{v} = a\mathbf{i} + b\mathbf{j} = (x_2 - x_1)\mathbf{i} + (y_2 - y_1)\mathbf{j}.$$

Horizontal component: x-coordinate of terminal point minus x-coordinate of initial point

Vertical component: y-coordinate of terminal point minus y-coordinate of initial point

Thus, any vector between two points in rectangular coordinates can be expressed in terms of **i** and **j**. In rectangular coordinates, the term *vector* refers to the position vector in terms of **i** and **j** that is equal to it.

## EXAMPLE 3 Representing a Vector in Rectangular Coordinates

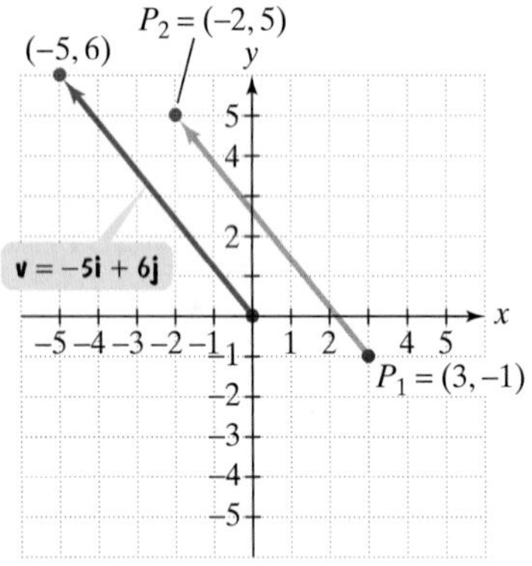


**Figure 7.53** Representing the vector from $(3, -1)$ to $(-2, 5)$ as a position vector

Let **v** be the vector from initial point $P_1 = (3, -1)$ to terminal point $P_2 = (-2, 5)$. Write **v** in terms of **i** and **j**.

**Solution** We identify the values for the variables in the formula.

$$P_1 = (3, -1) \qquad P_2 = (-2, 5)$$

$x_1$ $y_1$ $x_2$ $y_2$

Using these values, we write **v** in terms of **i** and **j** as follows:

$$\mathbf{v} = (x_2 - x_1)\mathbf{i} + (y_2 - y_1)\mathbf{j} = (-2 - 3)\mathbf{i} + [5 - (-1)]\mathbf{j} = -5\mathbf{i} + 6\mathbf{j}$$

Figure 7.53 shows the vector from $P_1 = (3, -1)$ to $P_2 = (-2, 5)$ represented in terms of **i** and **j** as a position vector.

**Check Point 3** Let **v** be the vector from initial point $P_1 = (-1, 3)$ to $P_2 = (2, 7)$. Write **v** in terms of **i** and **j**.

**4** Perform operations with vectors in terms of **i** and **j**.

## Operations With Vectors in Terms of i and j

If vectors are expressed in terms of **i** and **j**, we can easily carry out operations such as vector addition, vector subtraction, and scalar multiplication. Recall the geometric definitions of these operations given earlier. Based on these ideas, we can add and subtract vectors using the following procedure.

**Adding and Subtracting Vectors in Terms of i and j**

If $\mathbf{v} = a_1\mathbf{i} + b_1\mathbf{j}$ and $\mathbf{w} = a_2\mathbf{i} + b_2\mathbf{j}$, then

$$\mathbf{v} + \mathbf{w} = (a_1 + a_2)\mathbf{i} + (b_1 + b_2)\mathbf{j}$$
$$\mathbf{v} - \mathbf{w} = (a_1 - a_2)\mathbf{i} + (b_1 - b_2)\mathbf{j}.$$

## EXAMPLE 4 Adding and Subtracting Vectors

If $\mathbf{v} = 5\mathbf{i} + 4\mathbf{j}$ and $\mathbf{w} = 6\mathbf{i} - 9\mathbf{j}$, find:

**a.** $\mathbf{v} + \mathbf{w}$ **b.** $\mathbf{v} - \mathbf{w}$.

### Solution

**a.** $\mathbf{v} + \mathbf{w} = (5\mathbf{i} + 4\mathbf{j}) + (6\mathbf{i} - 9\mathbf{j})$ These are the given vectors.

$= (5 + 6)\mathbf{i} + [4 + (-9)]\mathbf{j}$ Add the horizontal components. Add the vertical components.

$= 11\mathbf{i} - 5\mathbf{j}$ Simplify.

**b.** $\mathbf{v} - \mathbf{w} = (5\mathbf{i} + 4\mathbf{j}) - (6\mathbf{i} - 9\mathbf{j})$ These are the given vectors.

$= (5 - 6)\mathbf{i} + [4 - (-9)]\mathbf{j}$ Subtract the horizontal components. Subtract the vertical components.

$= -\mathbf{i} + 13\mathbf{j}$ Simplify.

**Check Point 4** If $\mathbf{v} = 7\mathbf{i} + 3\mathbf{j}$ and $\mathbf{w} = 4\mathbf{i} - 5\mathbf{j}$, find

**a.** $\mathbf{v} + \mathbf{w}$ **b.** $\mathbf{v} - \mathbf{w}$.

How do we perform scalar multiplication if vectors are expressed in terms of **i** and **j**? We use the following procedure to multiply the vector **v** by the scalar $k$.

**Scalar Multiplication with a Vector in Terms of i and j**

If $\mathbf{v} = a\mathbf{i} + b\mathbf{j}$ and $k$ is a real number, then the scalar multiplication of the vector **v** and the scalar $k$ is

$$k\mathbf{v} = (ka)\mathbf{i} + (kb)\mathbf{j}.$$

## EXAMPLE 5 Scalar Multiplication

If $\mathbf{v} = 5\mathbf{i} + 4\mathbf{j}$, find:

**a.** $6\mathbf{v}$ **b.** $-3\mathbf{v}$.

### Solution

**a.** $6\mathbf{v} = 6(5\mathbf{i} + 4\mathbf{j})$ This is the given vector.

$= (6 \cdot 5)\mathbf{i} + (6 \cdot 4)\mathbf{j}$ Multiply each component by 6.

$= 30\mathbf{i} + 24\mathbf{j}$ Simplify.

**b.** $-3\mathbf{v} = -3(5\mathbf{i} + 4\mathbf{j})$ This is the given vector.

$= (-3 \cdot 5)\mathbf{i} + (-3 \cdot 4)\mathbf{j}$ Multiply each component by −3.

$= -15\mathbf{i} - 12\mathbf{j}$ Simplify.

**Check Point 5** If $\mathbf{v} = 7\mathbf{i} + 10\mathbf{j}$, find:

**a.** $8\mathbf{v}$ **b.** $-5\mathbf{v}$.

## EXAMPLE 6 Vector Operations

If $\mathbf{v} = 5\mathbf{i} + 4\mathbf{j}$ and $\mathbf{w} = 6\mathbf{i} - 9\mathbf{j}$, find $4\mathbf{v} - 2\mathbf{w}$.

### Solution

$$4\mathbf{v} - 2\mathbf{w} = 4(5\mathbf{i} + 4\mathbf{j}) - 2(6\mathbf{i} - 9\mathbf{j})$$ These are the given vectors.

$$= 20\mathbf{i} + 16\mathbf{j} - 12\mathbf{i} + 18\mathbf{j}$$ Perform each scalar multiplication.

$$= (20 - 12)\mathbf{i} + (16 + 18)\mathbf{j}$$ Add horizontal and vertical components and perform the vector addition.

$$= 8\mathbf{i} + 34\mathbf{j}$$ Simplify.

**Check Point 6** If $\mathbf{v} = 7\mathbf{i} + 3\mathbf{j}$ and $\mathbf{w} = 4\mathbf{i} - 5\mathbf{j}$, find $6\mathbf{v} - 3\mathbf{w}$.

Properties involving vector operations resemble familiar properties of real numbers. For example, the order in which vectors are added makes no difference:

$$\mathbf{u} + \mathbf{v} = \mathbf{v} + \mathbf{u}.$$

Does this remind you of the commutative property $a + b = b + a$?

Just as 0 plays an important role in the properties of real numbers, the **zero vector 0** plays exactly the same role in the properties of vectors.

### The Zero Vector

The vector whose magnitude is 0 is called the **zero vector, 0**. The zero vector is assigned no direction. It can be expressed in terms of **i** and **j** using

$$\mathbf{0} = 0\mathbf{i} + 0\mathbf{j}.$$

Properties of vector addition and scalar multiplication are given as follows.

### Properties of Vector Addition and Scalar Multiplication

If **u**, **v**, and **w** are vectors, and $c$ and $d$ are scalars, then the following properties are true.

**Vector Addition Properties**

1. $\mathbf{u} + \mathbf{v} = \mathbf{v} + \mathbf{u}$ — Commutative Property
2. $(\mathbf{u} + \mathbf{v}) + \mathbf{w} = \mathbf{u} + (\mathbf{v} + \mathbf{w})$ — Associative Property
3. $\mathbf{u} + \mathbf{0} = \mathbf{0} + \mathbf{u} = \mathbf{u}$ — Additive Identity
4. $\mathbf{u} + (-\mathbf{u}) = (-\mathbf{u}) + \mathbf{u} = \mathbf{0}$ — Additive Inverse

**Scalar Multiplication Properties**

1. $(cd)\mathbf{u} = c(d\mathbf{u})$ — *Associative Property*
2. $c(\mathbf{u} + \mathbf{v}) = c\mathbf{u} + c\mathbf{v}$ — *Distributive Property*
3. $(c + d)\mathbf{u} = c\mathbf{u} + d\mathbf{u}$ — *Distributive Property*
4. $1\mathbf{u} = \mathbf{u}$ — *Multiplicative Identity*
5. $0\mathbf{u} = 0$ — *Multiplication Property*
6. $\|c\mathbf{v}\| = |c|\|\mathbf{v}\|$

**5** Find a unit vector in the direction of **v**.

## Unit Vectors

We have seen that a unit vector is a vector whose magnitude is one. In many applications of vectors, it is helpful to find a unit vector that has the same direction as a given vector.

### Discovery

To find out why the procedure in the box produces a unit vector, work Exercise 72 in Exercise Set 7.6.

**Finding a Unit Vector that Has the Same Direction as a Given Nonzero Vector v**

For any nonzero vector **v**, the vector

$$\frac{\mathbf{v}}{\|\mathbf{v}\|}$$

is a unit vector that has the same direction as **v**. To find this vector, divide **v** by its magnitude.

## EXAMPLE 7 Finding a Unit Vector

Find a unit vector in the same direction as $\mathbf{v} = 5\mathbf{i} - 12\mathbf{j}$. Then verify that the vector has magnitude 1.

**Solution** We find a unit vector in the same direction as **v** by dividing **v** by its magnitude. We first find the magnitude of **v**.

$$\|\mathbf{v}\| = \sqrt{a^2 + b^2} = \sqrt{5^2 + (-12)^2} = \sqrt{25 + 144} = \sqrt{169} = 13$$

A unit vector in the same direction as **v** is

$$\frac{\mathbf{v}}{\|\mathbf{v}\|} = \frac{5\mathbf{i} - 12\mathbf{j}}{13} = \frac{5}{13}\mathbf{i} - \frac{12}{13}\mathbf{j}$$ *This is the scalar multiplication of* **v** *and* $\frac{1}{13}$.

Now we must verify that the magnitude of this vector is 1. Recall that the magnitude of $a\mathbf{i} + b\mathbf{j}$ is $\sqrt{a^2 + b^2}$. Thus, the magnitude of $\frac{5}{13}\mathbf{i} - \frac{12}{13}\mathbf{j}$ is

$$\sqrt{\left(\frac{5}{13}\right)^2 + \left(-\frac{12}{13}\right)^2} = \sqrt{\frac{25}{169} + \frac{144}{69}} = \sqrt{\frac{169}{169}} = \sqrt{1} = 1.$$

**Check Point 7** Find a unit vector in the same direction as $\mathbf{v} = 4\mathbf{i} - 3\mathbf{j}$. Then verify that the vector has magnitude 1.

**6** Solve applied problems involving vectors.

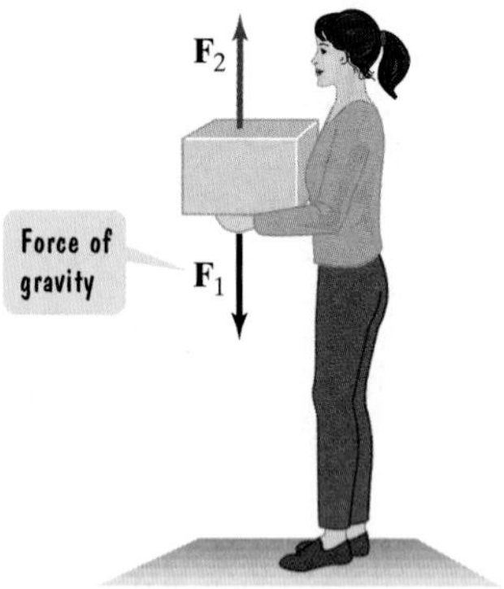


**Figure 7.54** Force vectors

## Applications

Many physical concepts can be represented by vectors. A vector that represents a pull or push of some type is called a **force vector**. If you are holding a 10-pound package, two force vectors are involved. The force of gravity is exerting a force of magnitude 10 pounds directly downward. This force is shown by vector $\mathbf{F}_1$ in Figure 7.54. Assuming there is no upward or downward movement of the package, you are exerting a force of magnitude 10 pounds directly upward. This force is shown by vector $\mathbf{F}_2$ in Figure 7.54. It has the same magnitude as the force exerted on your package by gravity, but it acts in the opposite direction.

If $\mathbf{F}_1$ and $\mathbf{F}_2$ are two forces acting on an object, the net effect is the same as if just the resultant force, $\mathbf{F}_1 + \mathbf{F}_2$, acted on the object. If the object is not moving, as is the case with your 10-pound package, the vector sum of all forces is zero.

### EXAMPLE 8 Finding the Resultant Force

Two forces of 10 and 30 pounds act on an object. If the angle between the force vectors is 40°, what are the magnitude and direction (relative to the 30-pound force) of the resultant force? Express the direction as an angle to the nearest tenth of a degree.

**Solution** We begin with a diagram that uses geometric vectors to represent the various forces. Figure 7.55(a) shows the 10- and 30-pound forces with the 40° angle between them. The addition of these vectors, with the resultant dark blue force vector, $\mathbf{F}$, is shown in Figure 7.55(b). The force represented by $\mathbf{F}$ produces the same effect on the object as that obtained when the two light blue force vectors act on the object.

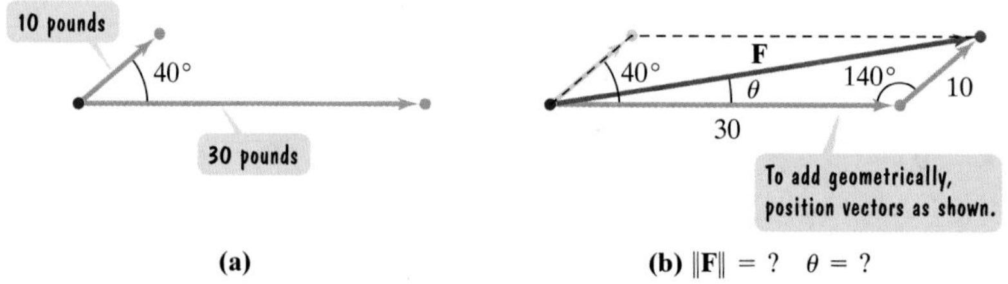


**Figure 7.55** Forces of 10 and 30 pounds acting on an object

Do you see where the 140° comes from? Because adjacent angles in a parallelogram are supplements, the measure of the angle is $180° - 40° = 140°$.

Figure 7.55(b) shows that we are looking for $\|\mathbf{F}\|$ and $\theta$. We use the blue oblique triangle to find these values that describe the resultant force. In this SAS triangle, we use the Law of Cosines to find the magnitude of $\mathbf{F}$.

$$\|\mathbf{F}\|^2 = 30^2 + 10^2 - 2(30)(10)\cos 140° \approx 1459.6$$

$$\|\mathbf{F}\| \approx \sqrt{1459.6} \approx 38.2$$

The magnitude of the resultant force is about 38.2 pounds.

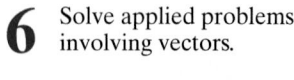

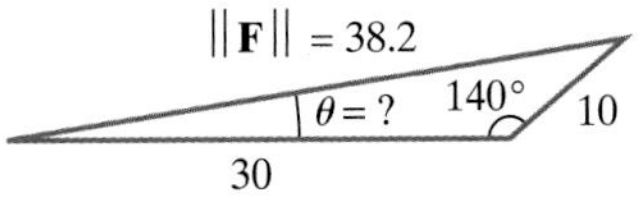


**Figure 7.56** The Law of Sines can be used to find $\theta$.

To find $\theta$, the direction of the resultant force, we use the Law of Sines in the blue oblique triangle, shown again in Figure 7.56. Notice that we added the magnitude of **F** to the figure. We apply the Law of Sines as follows.

$$\frac{38.2}{\sin 140°} = \frac{10}{\sin \theta}$$ Use the Law of Sines.

$$38.2 \sin \theta = 10 \sin 140°$$ Cross multiply.

$$\sin \theta = \frac{10 \sin 140°}{38.2}$$ Divide both sides by 38.2.

$$\theta = \sin^{-1}\left(\frac{10 \sin 140°}{38.2}\right)$$ With a 140° angle in the triangle, $\theta$ must be acute.

$$\approx 9.7°$$ Use a calculator.

In summary, the two given forces are equivalent to a single force of about 38.2 pounds in the direction of approximately 9.7° relative to the 30-pound force.

**Check Point 8** Two forces of 30 and 60 pounds act on an object. If the angle between the force vectors is 50°, what are the magnitude and direction (relative to the 60-pound force) of the resultant force?

A vector that represents the direction and speed of an object in motion is called a **velocity vector**. Boats moving in currents and airplanes flying in winds are situations in which two velocity vectors act simultaneously. For example, suppose **v** represents the velocity of a plane in still air. Further suppose that **w** represents the velocity of the wind. The actual speed and direction of the plane is given by the vector **v** + **w**. This resultant vector describes the plane's speed and direction relative to the ground. Problems involving the resultant velocity of a boat or plane are solved using the Laws of Sines and Cosines, as we saw in Example 8. Further examples of such applications can be found in the exercise set that follows.

# EXERCISE SET 7.6

## Practice Exercises

*In Exercises 1–4,* **u** *and* **v** *have the same direction. In each exercise:* **a.** *Find* $\|\mathbf{u}\|$. **b.** *Find* $\|\mathbf{v}\|$. **c.** *Is* **u** = **v**? *Explain.*

**1.**

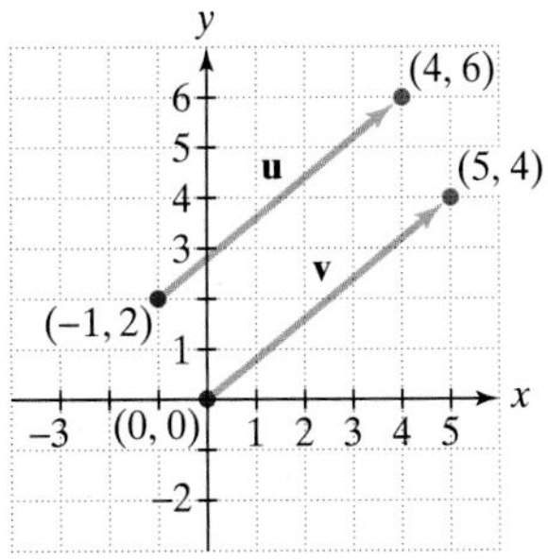


**2.**

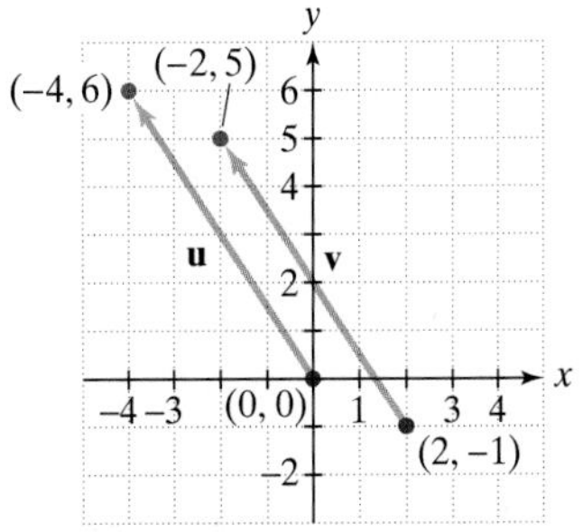

**3.**

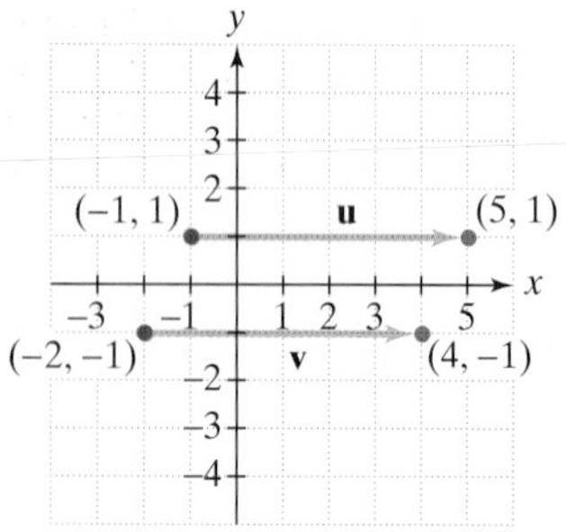


**4.**

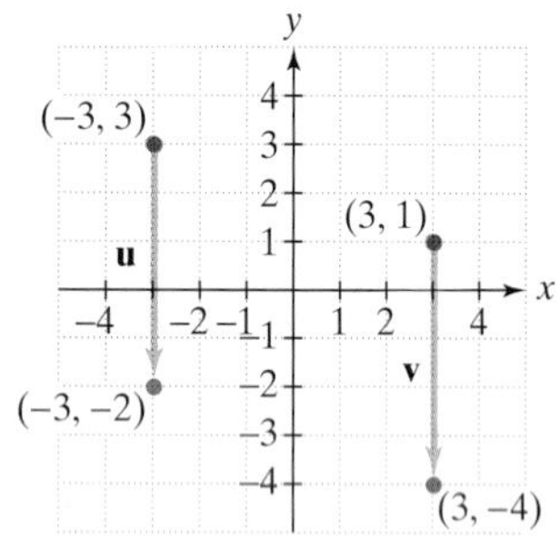


*In Exercises 5–12, sketch each position vector and find its magnitude.*

**5.** $\mathbf{v} = 3\mathbf{i} + \mathbf{j}$

**6.** $\mathbf{v} = 2\mathbf{i} + 3\mathbf{j}$

**7.** $\mathbf{v} = \mathbf{i} - \mathbf{j}$

**8.** $\mathbf{v} = -\mathbf{i} - \mathbf{j}$

**9.** $\mathbf{v} = -6\mathbf{i} - 2\mathbf{j}$

**10.** $\mathbf{v} = 5\mathbf{i} - 2\mathbf{j}$

**11.** $\mathbf{v} = -4\mathbf{i}$

**12.** $\mathbf{v} = -5\mathbf{j}$

*In Exercises 13–20, let* **v** *be the vector from initial point $P_1$ to terminal point $P_2$. Write* **v** *in terms of* **i** *and* **j**.

**13.** $P_1 = (-4, -4), P_2 = (6, 2)$

**14.** $P_1 = (2, -5), P_2 = (-6, 6)$

**15.** $P_1 = (-8, 6), P_2 = (-2, 3)$

**16.** $P_1 = (-7, -4), P_2 = (0, -2)$

**17.** $P_1 = (-1, 7), P_2 = (-7, -7)$

**18.** $P_1 = (-1, 6), P_2 = (7, -5)$

**19.** $P_1 = (-3, 4), P_2 = (6, 4)$

**20.** $P_1 = (4, -5), P_2 = (4, 3)$

*In Exercises 21–38, let*

$$\mathbf{u} = 2\mathbf{i} - 5\mathbf{j}, \mathbf{v} = -3\mathbf{i} + 7\mathbf{j}, \text{and } \mathbf{w} = -\mathbf{i} - 6\mathbf{j}.$$

*Find each specified vector or scalar.*

**21.** $\mathbf{u} + \mathbf{v}$

**22.** $\mathbf{v} + \mathbf{w}$

**23.** $\mathbf{u} - \mathbf{v}$

**24.** $\mathbf{v} - \mathbf{w}$

**25.** $\mathbf{v} - \mathbf{u}$

**26.** $\mathbf{w} - \mathbf{v}$

**27.** $5\mathbf{v}$

**28.** $6\mathbf{v}$

**29.** $-4\mathbf{w}$

**30.** $-7\mathbf{w}$

**31.** $3\mathbf{w} + 2\mathbf{v}$

**32.** $3\mathbf{u} + 4\mathbf{v}$

**33.** $3\mathbf{v} - 4\mathbf{w}$

**34.** $4\mathbf{w} - 3\mathbf{v}$

**35.** $\|2\mathbf{u}\|$

**36.** $\|-2\mathbf{u}\|$

**37.** $\|\mathbf{w} - \mathbf{u}\|$

**38.** $\|\mathbf{u} - \mathbf{w}\|$

*In Exercises 39–46, find a unit vector that has the same direction as the vector* **v**.

**39.** $\mathbf{v} = 6\mathbf{i}$

**40.** $\mathbf{v} = -5\mathbf{j}$

**41.** $\mathbf{v} = 3\mathbf{i} - 4\mathbf{j}$

**42.** $\mathbf{v} = 8\mathbf{i} - 6\mathbf{j}$

**43.** $\mathbf{v} = 3\mathbf{i} - 2\mathbf{j}$

**44.** $\mathbf{v} = 4\mathbf{i} - 2\mathbf{j}$

**45.** $\mathbf{v} = \mathbf{i} + \mathbf{j}$

**46.** $\mathbf{v} = \mathbf{i} - \mathbf{j}$

## Application Exercises

**47.** Two forces of 20 and 50 pounds act on an object. If the angle between the force vectors is 90°,
**a.** Find the magnitude of the resultant force to the nearest tenth of a pound.
**b.** Find the direction of the resultant force relative to the 50-pound force. Express the answer to the nearest tenth of a degree.

**48.** Two forces of 30 and 70 pounds act on an object. If the angle between the force vectors is 90°,
**a.** Find the magnitude of the resultant force to the nearest tenth of a pound.
**b.** Find the direction of the resultant force relative to the 70-pound force. Express the answer to the nearest tenth of a degree.

**49.** Two forces of 160 pounds and 300 pounds act on an object. If the angle between the force vectors is 55°,
**a.** Find the magnitude of the resultant force to the nearest tenth of a pound.
**b.** Find the direction of the resultant force relative to the 300-pound force. Express the answer to the nearest tenth of a degree.

**50.** Two forces of 220 pounds and 400 pounds act on an object. If the angle between the force vectors is 65°,
**a.** Find the magnitude of the resultant force to the nearest tenth of a pound.
**b.** Find the direction of the resultant force relative to the 220-pound force. Express the answer to the nearest tenth of a degree.

**51.** You are on a small plane headed due west at 260 miles per hour. The wind is blowing from north to south at 45 miles per hour.
**a.** Illustrate the situation with two velocity vectors, one showing the plane's velocity in still air and the other showing the velocity of the wind. Then draw a vector that represents the plane's actual speed and direction.
**b.** What is the plane's actual speed? Round to the nearest mile per hour.

**52.** You are rowing a boat due west at 4.6 miles per hour. The current is from north to south at 12 miles per hour.
**a.** Illustrate the situation with two velocity vectors, one showing the boat's velocity in still water and the other showing the velocity of the current. Then draw a vector that represents your rowboat's true course.
**b.** What is the true speed of your rowboat? Round to the nearest tenth.

**53.** The figure shows a small plane flying at a speed of 160 miles per hour on a bearing of N80°E. The wind is blowing from north to south at 75 miles per hour. The plane's resultant velocity is shown in the figure by vector **v**. Find $\|\mathbf{v}\|$ and describe what this represents.

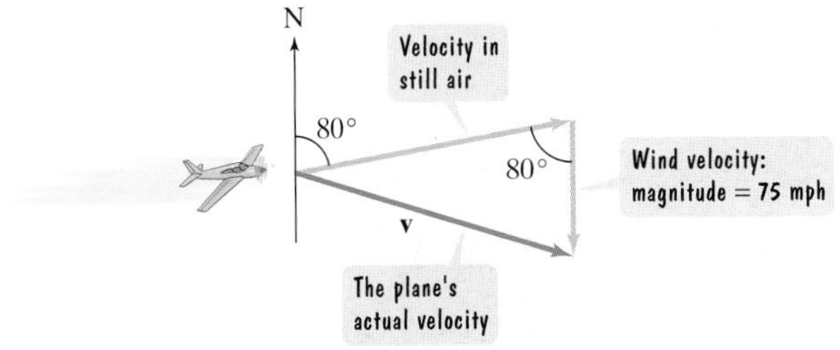


**54.** The figure shows a powerboat cruising at a speed of 18 miles per hour on a bearing of N65°E. The current is flowing at 8 miles per hour from north to south. The boat's resultant velocity is shown in the figure by the vector **v**. Find $\|\mathbf{v}\|$ and describe what this represents.

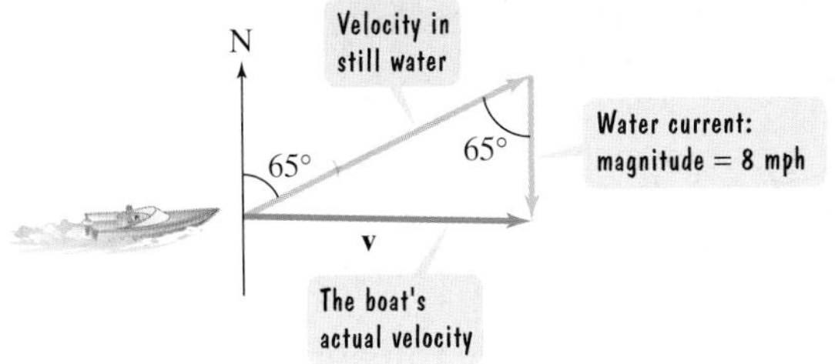


## Writing in Mathematics

**55.** What is a directed line segment?

**56.** What are equal vectors?

**57.** If vector **v** is represented by an arrow, how is $-3\mathbf{v}$ represented?

**58.** If vectors **u** and **v** are represented by arrows, describe how the vector sum $\mathbf{u} + \mathbf{v}$ is represented.

**59.** What is the **i** vector?

**60.** What is the **j** vector?

**61.** What is a position vector? How is a position vector represented using **i** and **j**?

**62.** If **v** is a vector between any two points in the rectangular coordinate system, explain how to write **v** in terms of **i** and **j**.

**63.** If two vectors are expressed in terms of **i** and **j**, explain how to find their sum.

**64.** If two vectors are expressed in terms of **i** and **j**, explain how to find their difference.

**65.** If a vector is expressed in terms of **i** and **j**, explain how to find the scalar multiplication of the vector and a given scalar $k$.

**66.** What is the zero vector?

**67.** Describe one similarity between the zero vector and the number 0.

**68.** Explain how to find a unit vector in the direction of any given vector **v**.

**69.** You are on an airplane. The pilot announces the plane's speed over the intercom. Which speed do you think is being reported: the speed of the plane in still air or the speed after the effect of the wind has been accounted for? Explain your answer.

**70.** Use vectors to explain why it is difficult to hold a heavy stack of books perfectly still for a long period of time. As you become exhausted, what eventually happens? What does this mean in terms of the forces acting on the books?

## Critical Thinking Exercises

**71.** Use the figure shown and select a true statement

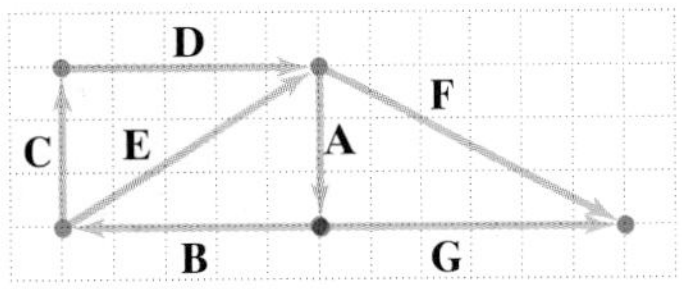


a. $\mathbf{A} + \mathbf{B} = \mathbf{E}$
b. $\mathbf{D} + \mathbf{A} + \mathbf{B} + \mathbf{C} = \mathbf{0}$
c. $\mathbf{B} - \mathbf{E} = \mathbf{G} - \mathbf{F}$
d. $\|\mathbf{A}\| \neq \|\mathbf{C}\|$

**72.** Let $\mathbf{v} = a\mathbf{i} + b\mathbf{j}$. Show that $\dfrac{\mathbf{v}}{\|\mathbf{v}\|}$ is a unit vector in the direction of **v**.

*In Exercises 73–74, refer to the navigational compass shown in the figure. The compass is marked clockwise in degrees that start at north 0°.*

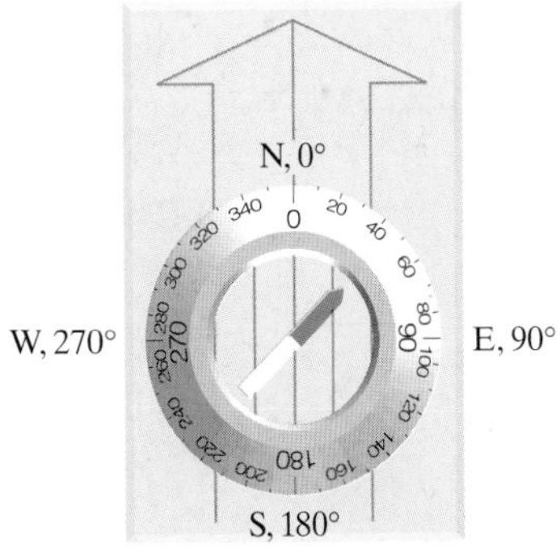


**73.** An airplane has an airspeed of 240 miles per hour and a compass heading of 280°. A steady wind of 30 miles per hour is blowing in the direction of 265°. What is the plane's true speed relative to the ground? What is its compass heading relative to the ground?

**74.** Two tugboats are pulling on a large ship that has gone aground. One tug pulls with a force of 2500 pounds in a compass direction of 55°. The second tug pulls with a force of 2000 pounds in a compass direction of 95°. Find the magnitude and the compass direction of the resultant force.

# SECTION 7.7 The Dot Product

## Objectives

1. Find the dot product of two vectors.
2. Find the angle between two vectors.
3. Use the dot product to determine if two vectors are orthogonal.
4. Write a vector in terms of its magnitude and direction.
5. Find the projection of a vector onto another vector.
6. Express a vector as the sum of two orthogonal vectors.
7. Compute work.

Talk about hard work! I can see the weightlifter's muscles quivering from the exertion of holding the barbell in a stationary position above his head. Still, I'm not sure if he's doing as much work as I, sitting at my desk with brain muscles quivering by studying trigonometric functions and their applications.

Would it surprise you to know that neither you nor the weightlifter are doing any work at all? The precise definition of work is not the same as what we mean by "working hard" in everyday use. To understand what is involved in real work, we turn to a new vector operation called the dot product.

**1** Find the dot product of two vectors.

## The Dot Product of Two Vectors

The operations of vector addition and scalar multiplication result in vectors. By contrast, the **dot product** of two vectors results in a scalar (a real number), rather than a vector.

**Definition of the Dot Product**

If $\mathbf{v} = a_1\mathbf{i} + b_1\mathbf{j}$ and $\mathbf{w} = a_2\mathbf{i} + b_2\mathbf{j}$ are vectors, the **dot product** $\mathbf{v} \cdot \mathbf{w}$ is defined as

$$\mathbf{v} \cdot \mathbf{w} = a_1 a_2 + b_1 b_2.$$

The dot product of two vectors is the sum of the products of their horizontal and vertical components.

### EXAMPLE 1 Finding Dot Products

If $\mathbf{v} = 5\mathbf{i} - 2\mathbf{j}$ and $\mathbf{w} = -3\mathbf{i} + 4\mathbf{j}$, find:

**a.** $\mathbf{v} \cdot \mathbf{w}$ **b.** $\mathbf{w} \cdot \mathbf{v}$ **c.** $\mathbf{v} \cdot \mathbf{v}$.

**Solution** To find each dot product, multiply the two horizontal components, and then multiply the two vertical components. Finally, add the two products.

**a.** $\mathbf{v} \cdot \mathbf{w} = 5(-3) + (-2)(4) = -15 - 8 = -23$

Multiply the horizontal components and multiply the vertical components of $\mathbf{v} = 5\mathbf{i} - 2\mathbf{j}$ and $\mathbf{w} = -3\mathbf{i} + 4\mathbf{j}$.

**b.** $\mathbf{w} \cdot \mathbf{v} = -3(5) + 4(-2) = -15 - 8 = -23$

Multiply the horizontal components and multiply the vertical components of $\mathbf{w} = -3\mathbf{i} + 4\mathbf{j}$ and $\mathbf{v} = 5\mathbf{i} - 2\mathbf{j}$.

**c.** $\mathbf{v} \cdot \mathbf{v} = 5(5) + (-2)(-2) = 25 + 4 = 29$

Multiply the horizontal components and multiply the vertical components of $\mathbf{v} = 5\mathbf{i} - 2\mathbf{j}$ and $\mathbf{v} = 5\mathbf{i} - 2\mathbf{j}$.

**Check Point 1** If $\mathbf{v} = 7\mathbf{i} - 4\mathbf{j}$ and $\mathbf{w} = 2\mathbf{i} - \mathbf{j}$, find:

**a.** $\mathbf{v} \cdot \mathbf{w}$ **b.** $\mathbf{w} \cdot \mathbf{v}$ **c.** $\mathbf{w} \cdot \mathbf{w}$.

In Example 1 and Check Point 1, did you notice that $\mathbf{v} \cdot \mathbf{w}$ and $\mathbf{w} \cdot \mathbf{v}$ produced the same scalar? The fact that $\mathbf{v} \cdot \mathbf{w} = \mathbf{w} \cdot \mathbf{v}$ follows from the definition of the dot product. Properties of the dot product are given in the box that follows. Proofs for some of these properties are given in the appendix.

### Properties of the Dot Product

If **u**, **v**, and **w** are vectors, and $c$ is a scalar, then

1. $\mathbf{u} \cdot \mathbf{v} = \mathbf{v} \cdot \mathbf{u}$
2. $\mathbf{u} \cdot (\mathbf{v} + \mathbf{w}) = \mathbf{u} \cdot \mathbf{v} + \mathbf{u} \cdot \mathbf{w}$
3. $\mathbf{0} \cdot \mathbf{v} = 0$
4. $\mathbf{v} \cdot \mathbf{v} = \|\mathbf{v}\|^2$
5. $(c\mathbf{u}) \cdot \mathbf{v} = c(\mathbf{u} \cdot \mathbf{v}) = \mathbf{u} \cdot (c\mathbf{v})$

**2** Find the angle between two vectors.

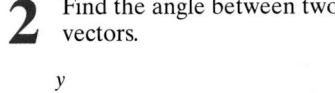

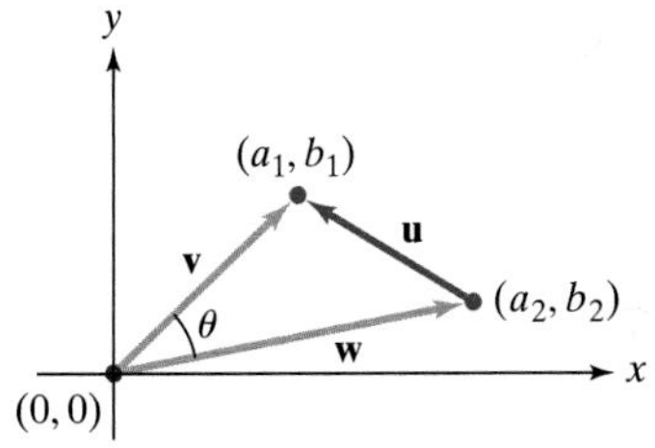


**Figure 7.57**

## The Angle between Two Vectors

The Law of Cosines can be used to derive another formula for the dot product. This formula will give us a way to find the angle between two vectors.

Figure 7.57 shows vectors $\mathbf{v} = a_1\mathbf{i} + b_1\mathbf{j}$ and $\mathbf{w} = a_2\mathbf{i} + b_2\mathbf{j}$. By the definition of the dot product, we know that $\mathbf{v} \cdot \mathbf{w} = a_1a_2 + b_1b_2$. Our new formula for the dot product involves the angle between the vectors, shown as $\theta$ in the figure. Apply the Law of Cosines to the triangle shown in the figure.

$$\|\mathbf{u}\|^2 = \|\mathbf{v}\|^2 + \|\mathbf{w}\|^2 - 2\|\mathbf{v}\|\|\mathbf{w}\|\cos\theta$$ Use the Law of Cosines.

$$(a_1 - a_2)^2 + (b_1 - b_2)^2 = (a_1^2 + b_1^2) + (a_2^2 + b_2^2) - 2\|\mathbf{v}\|\|\mathbf{w}\|\cos\theta$$ Square the magnitudes of vectors **u**, **v**, and **w**.

$$a_1^2 - 2a_1a_2 + a_2^2 + b_1^2 - 2b_1b_2 + b_2^2 = a_1^2 + b_1^2 + a_2^2 + b_2^2 - 2\|\mathbf{v}\|\|\mathbf{w}\|\cos\theta$$ Square the binomials using $(A - B)^2 = A^2 - 2AB + B^2$.

$$-2a_1a_2 - 2b_1b_2 = -2\|\mathbf{v}\|\|\mathbf{w}\|\cos\theta$$ Subtract $a_1^2$, $a_2^2$, $b_1^2$, and $b_2^2$ from both sides of the equation.

$$a_1a_2 + b_1b_2 = \|\mathbf{v}\|\|\mathbf{w}\|\cos\theta$$ Divide both sides by −2.

By definition, $\mathbf{v} \cdot \mathbf{w} = a_1a_2 + b_1b_2$.

$$\mathbf{v} \cdot \mathbf{w} = \|\mathbf{v}\|\|\mathbf{w}\|\cos\theta$$ Substitute $\mathbf{v} \cdot \mathbf{w}$ for the expression on the left side of the equation.

**Alternative Formula for the Dot Product**

If $\mathbf{v}$ and $\mathbf{w}$ are two nonzero vectors and $\theta$ is the smallest nonnegative angle between them, then

$$\mathbf{v} \cdot \mathbf{w} = \|\mathbf{v}\| \|\mathbf{w}\| \cos\theta.$$

Solving the formula in the box for $\cos\theta$ gives us a formula for finding the angle between vectors.

**Formula for the Angle between Two Vectors**

If $\mathbf{v}$ and $\mathbf{w}$ are two nonzero vectors and $\theta$ is the smallest nonnegative angle between $\mathbf{v}$ and $\mathbf{w}$, then

$$\cos\theta = \frac{\mathbf{v} \cdot \mathbf{w}}{\|\mathbf{v}\| \|\mathbf{w}\|} \quad \text{and} \quad \theta = \cos^{-1}\left(\frac{\mathbf{v} \cdot \mathbf{w}}{\|\mathbf{v}\| \|\mathbf{w}\|}\right).$$

## EXAMPLE 2 Finding the Angle between Two Vectors

Find the angle $\theta$ between the vectors $\mathbf{v} = 3\mathbf{i} - 2\mathbf{j}$ and $\mathbf{w} = -\mathbf{i} + 4\mathbf{j}$, shown in Figure 7.58. Round to the nearest tenth of a degree.

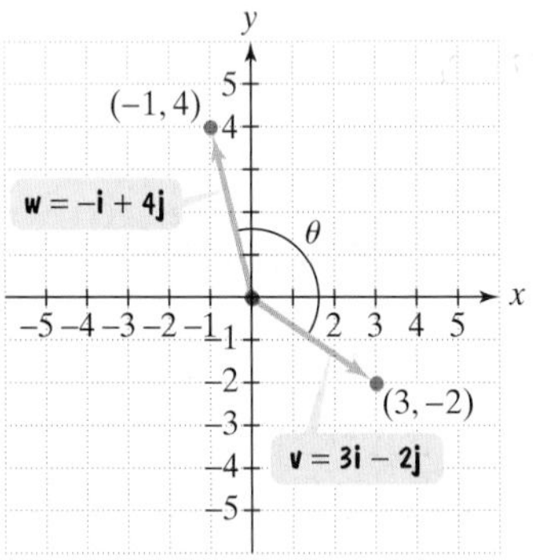


**Figure 7.58** Finding the angle between two vectors

**Solution** Use the formula for the angle between two vectors.

$$\cos\theta = \frac{\mathbf{v} \cdot \mathbf{w}}{\|\mathbf{v}\| \|\mathbf{w}\|}$$
This is the formula for the angle between two vectors.

$$= \frac{(3\mathbf{i} - 2\mathbf{j}) \cdot (-\mathbf{i} + 4\mathbf{j})}{\sqrt{3^2 + (-2)^2}\sqrt{(-1)^2 + 4^2}}$$
Substitute the given vectors in the numerator. Find the magnitude of each vector in the denominator.

$$= \frac{3(-1) + (-2)(4)}{\sqrt{13}\sqrt{17}}$$
Find the dot product in the numerator. Simplify in the denominator.

$$= -\frac{11}{\sqrt{221}}$$
Perform the indicated operations.

The angle $\theta$ between the vectors is

$$\theta = \cos^{-1}\left(-\frac{11}{\sqrt{221}}\right) \approx 137.7°.$$
Use a calculator.

**Check Point 2** Find the angle between the vectors $\mathbf{v} = 4\mathbf{i} - 3\mathbf{j}$ and $\mathbf{w} = \mathbf{i} + 2\mathbf{j}$. Round to the nearest tenth of a degree.

**3** Use the dot product to determine if two vectors are orthogonal.

## Parallel and Orthogonal Vectors

Two vectors are **parallel** when the angle $\theta$ between the vectors is 0° or 180°. If $\theta = 0°$, the vectors point in the same direction. If $\theta = 180°$, the vectors point in opposite directions. Figure 7.59 shows parallel vectors.

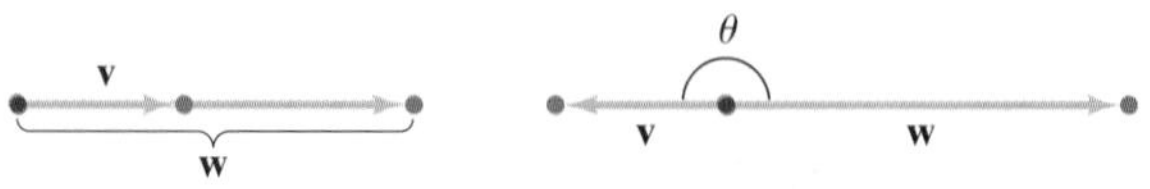


$\theta = 0°$ and $\cos\theta = 1$. Vectors point in the same direction.

$\theta = 180°$ and $\cos\theta = -1$. Vectors point in opposite directions.

**Figure 7.59** Parallel vectors

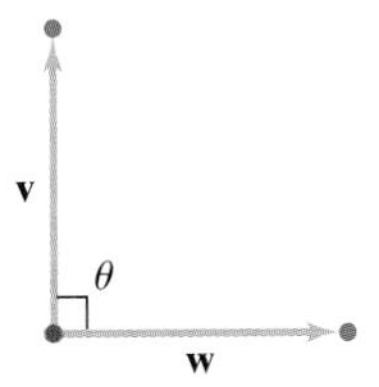


**Figure 7.60** Orthogonal vectors: $\theta = 90°$ and $\cos\theta = 0$

Two vectors are **orthogonal** when the angle between the vectors is 90°, shown in Figure 7.60. (The word "orthogonal," rather than "perpendicular," is used to describe vectors that meet at right angles.) We know that $\mathbf{v} \cdot \mathbf{w} = \|\mathbf{v}\|\|\mathbf{w}\| \cos\theta$. We also know that two vectors are orthogonal if and only if the angle between them is 90°. Using this formula for the dot product and the meaning of orthogonal vectors gives the following result.

**The Dot Product and Orthogonal Vectors**

Two nonzero vectors **v** and **w** are orthogonal if and only if $\mathbf{v} \cdot \mathbf{w} = 0$. Because $\mathbf{0} \cdot \mathbf{v} = 0$, the zero vector is orthogonal to every vector **v**.

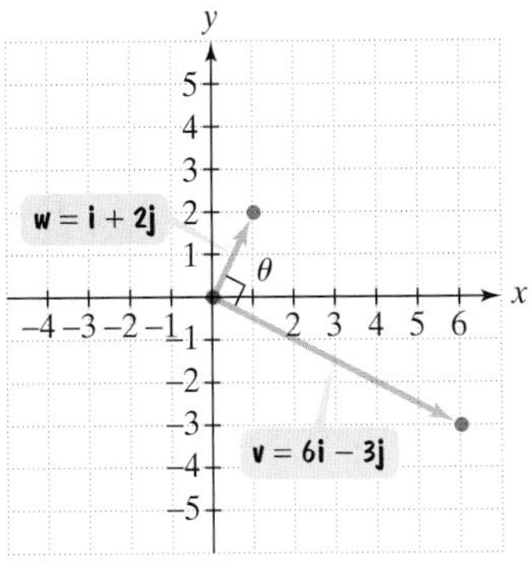


**Figure 7.61** Orthogonal vectors

## EXAMPLE 3 Determining Whether Vectors Are Orthogonal

Are the vectors $\mathbf{v} = 2\mathbf{i} + 3\mathbf{j}$ and $\mathbf{w} = 6\mathbf{i} - 4\mathbf{j}$ orthogonal?

**Solution** The vectors are orthogonal if their dot product is 0. Begin by finding $\mathbf{v} \cdot \mathbf{w}$.

$$\mathbf{v} \cdot \mathbf{w} = (2\mathbf{i} + 3\mathbf{j}) \cdot (6\mathbf{i} - 4\mathbf{j}) = 2(6) + 3(-4) = 12 - 12 = 0$$

The dot product is 0. Thus, the given vectors are orthogonal. They are shown in Figure 7.61.

**Check Point 3** Are the vectors $\mathbf{v} = 6\mathbf{i} - 3\mathbf{j}$ and $\mathbf{w} = \mathbf{i} + 2\mathbf{j}$ orthogonal?

**4** Write a vector in terms of its magnitude and direction.

## Writing a Vector in Terms of Its Magnitude and Direction

Consider the vector $\mathbf{v} = a\mathbf{i} + b\mathbf{j}$. The components $a$ and $b$ can be expressed in terms of the magnitude of **v** and the angle $\theta$ that **v** makes with the positive $x$-axis. This angle is called the **direction angle** of **v** and is shown in Figure 7.62. By the definitions of sine and cosine, we have

$$\cos\theta = \frac{a}{\|\mathbf{v}\|} \quad \text{and} \quad \sin\theta = \frac{b}{\|\mathbf{v}\|}$$

$$a = \|\mathbf{v}\| \cos\theta \qquad b = \|\mathbf{v}\| \sin\theta.$$

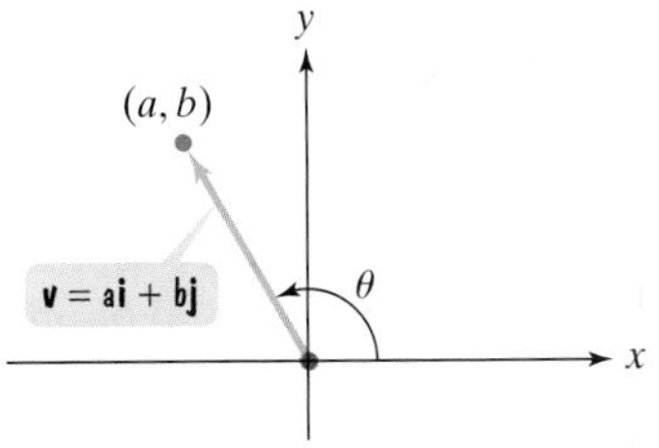


**Figure 7.62** Expressing a vector in terms of $\|\mathbf{v}\|$, its magnitude, and $\theta$, its direction angle

Thus,

$$\mathbf{v} = a\mathbf{i} + b\mathbf{j} = \|\mathbf{v}\| \cos\theta\mathbf{i} + \|\mathbf{v}\| \sin\theta\mathbf{j}.$$

**Writing a Vector in Terms of Its Magnitude and Direction**

Let **v** be a nonzero vector. If $\theta$ is the direction angle measured from the positive $x$-axis to **v**, then the vector can be expressed in terms of its magnitude and direction angle as

$$\mathbf{v} = \|\mathbf{v}\| \cos\theta\mathbf{i} + \|\mathbf{v}\| \sin\theta\mathbf{j}.$$

## EXAMPLE 4 Writing a Vector Whose Magnitude and Direction Are Given

The wind is blowing at 20 miles per hour in the direction N30°W. Express its velocity as a vector **v**.

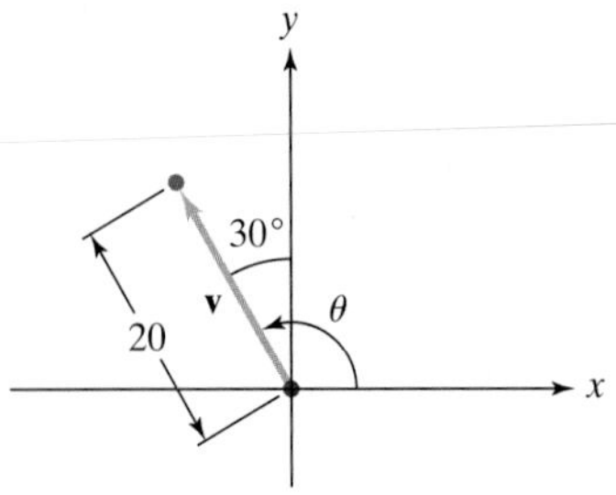


**Figure 7.63** Vector **v** represents a wind blowing at 20 miles per hour in the direction N30°W.

**Solution** The vector **v** is shown in Figure 7.63. The vector's direction angle, from the positive $x$-axis to **v**, is

$$\theta = 90° + 30° = 120°.$$

Because the wind is blowing at 20 miles per hour, the magnitude of **v** is 20 miles per hour: $\|\mathbf{v}\| = 20$. Thus,

$$\mathbf{v} = \|\mathbf{v}\|\cos\theta\mathbf{i} + \|\mathbf{v}\|\sin\theta\mathbf{j}$$ Use the formula for a vector in terms of magnitude and direction.

$$= 20\cos 120°\mathbf{i} + 20\sin 120°\mathbf{j}$$ $\|\mathbf{v}\| = 20$ and $\theta = 120°$.

$$= 20\left(-\tfrac{1}{2}\right)\mathbf{i} + 20\left(\frac{\sqrt{3}}{2}\right)\mathbf{j}$$ $\cos 120° = -\frac{1}{2}$ and $\sin 120° = \frac{\sqrt{3}}{2}$.

$$= -10\mathbf{i} + 10\sqrt{3}\mathbf{j}$$ Simplify.

The wind's velocity can be expressed in terms of **i** and **j** as $\mathbf{v} = -10\mathbf{i} + 10\sqrt{3}\mathbf{j}$.

**Check Point 4** The jet stream is blowing at 60 miles per hour in the direction N45°E. Express its velocity as a vector **v** in terms of **i** and **j**.

**5** Find the projection of a vector onto another vector.

## Projection of a Vector Onto Another Vector

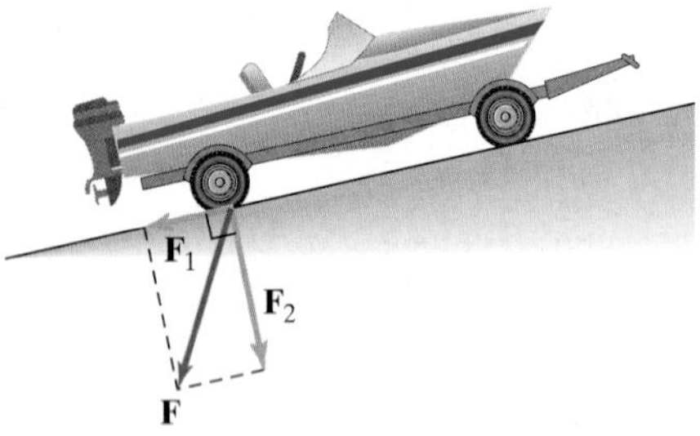


**Figure 7.64**

You know how to add two vectors to obtain a resultant vector. We now reverse this process by expressing a vector as the sum of two orthogonal vectors. By doing this, you can determine how much force is applied in a particular direction. For example, Figure 7.64 shows a boat on a tilted ramp. The force due to gravity, **F**, is pulling straight down on the boat. Part of this force, $\mathbf{F}_1$, is pushing the boat down the ramp. Another part of this force, $\mathbf{F}_2$, is pressing the boat against the ramp, at a right angle to the incline. These two orthogonal vectors, $\mathbf{F}_1$ and $\mathbf{F}_2$, are called the **vector components** of **F**. Notice that

$$\mathbf{F} = \mathbf{F}_1 + \mathbf{F}_2.$$

A method for finding $\mathbf{F}_1$ and $\mathbf{F}_2$ involves projecting a vector onto another vector.

Figure 7.65 shows two nonzero vectors, **v** and **w**, with the same initial point. The angle between the vectors, $\theta$, is acute in Figure 7.65(a) and obtuse in Figure 7.65(b). A third vector, called the **vector projection of v onto w**, is also shown in each figure, denoted by $\text{proj}_{\mathbf{w}}\mathbf{v}$.

How is the vector projection of **v** onto **w** formed? Draw a red line segment from the terminal point of **v** that forms a right angle with a line through **w**. The projection of **v** onto **w** lies on a line through **w**, and is parallel to vector **w**. This vector begins at the common initial point of **v** and **w**. It ends at the point where the red line segment intersects the line through **w**.

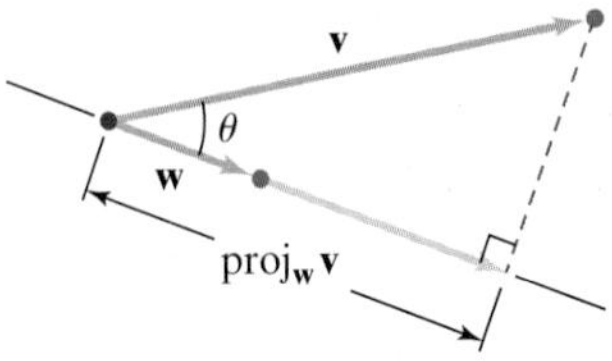


**Figure 7.65(a)**

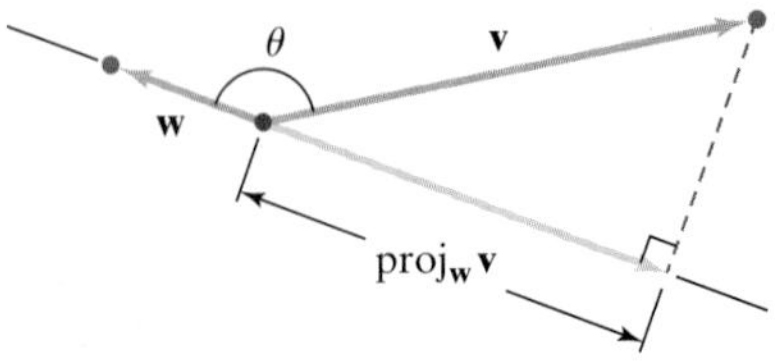


**Figure 7.65(b)**

Our goal is to determine an expression for $\text{proj}_{\mathbf{w}}\mathbf{v}$. We begin with its magnitude. By the definition of the cosine function,

$$\cos\theta = \frac{\|\text{proj}_{\mathbf{w}}\mathbf{v}\|}{\|\mathbf{v}\|}.$$ This is the magnitude of the vector projection of v onto w.

$$\|\mathbf{v}\|\cos\theta = \|\text{proj}_{\mathbf{w}}\mathbf{v}\|$$ Multiply both sides by $\|\mathbf{v}\|$.

$$\|\text{proj}_{\mathbf{w}}\mathbf{v}\| = \|\mathbf{v}\|\cos\theta$$ Reverse the two sides.

We can rewrite the right side of this equation and obtain another expression for the magnitude of the vector projection of **v** onto **w**. To do so, use the alternate formula for the dot product, $\mathbf{v}\cdot\mathbf{w} = \|\mathbf{v}\|\|\mathbf{w}\|\cos\theta$. Divide both sides by $\|\mathbf{w}\|$:

$$\frac{\mathbf{v}\cdot\mathbf{w}}{\|\mathbf{w}\|} = \|\mathbf{v}\|\cos\theta.$$

The expression on the right side of this equation, $\|\mathbf{v}\|\cos\theta$, is the same expression that appears in the formula for $\|\text{proj}_{\mathbf{w}}\mathbf{v}\|$. Thus,

$$\|\text{proj}_{\mathbf{w}}\mathbf{v}\| = \|\mathbf{v}\|\cos\theta = \frac{\mathbf{v}\cdot\mathbf{w}}{\|\mathbf{w}\|}.$$

We use the formula for the magnitude of $\text{proj}_{\mathbf{w}}\mathbf{v}$ to find the vector itself. This is done by finding the scalar product of the magnitude and a unit vector in the direction of **w**.

$$\text{proj}_{\mathbf{w}}\mathbf{v} = \left(\frac{\mathbf{v}\cdot\mathbf{w}}{\|\mathbf{w}\|}\right)\left(\frac{\mathbf{w}}{\|\mathbf{w}\|}\right) = \frac{\mathbf{v}\cdot\mathbf{w}}{\|\mathbf{w}\|^2}\mathbf{w}$$

This is the magnitude of the vector projection of v onto w.

This is a unit vector in the direction of w.

**The Vector Projection of v Onto w**

If **v** and **w** are two nonzero vectors, the vector projection of **v** onto **w** is

$$\text{proj}_{\mathbf{w}}\mathbf{v} = \frac{\mathbf{v}\cdot\mathbf{w}}{\|\mathbf{w}\|^2}\mathbf{w}.$$

## EXAMPLE 5 Finding the Vector Projection of One Vector Onto Another

If $\mathbf{v} = 2\mathbf{i} + 4\mathbf{j}$ and $\mathbf{w} = -2\mathbf{i} + 6\mathbf{j}$, find the vector projection of **v** onto **w**.

**Solution** The vector projection of **v** onto **w** is found using the formula for $\text{proj}_{\mathbf{w}}\mathbf{v}$.

$$\text{proj}_{\mathbf{w}}\mathbf{v} = \frac{\mathbf{v}\cdot\mathbf{w}}{\|\mathbf{w}\|^2}\mathbf{w} = \frac{(2\mathbf{i}+4\mathbf{j})\cdot(-2\mathbf{i}+6\mathbf{j})}{\left(\sqrt{(-2)^2+6^2}\right)^2}\mathbf{w}$$

$$= \frac{2(-2)+4(6)}{(\sqrt{40})^2}\mathbf{w} = \frac{20}{40}\mathbf{w} = \tfrac{1}{2}(-2\mathbf{i}+6\mathbf{j}) = -\mathbf{i}+3\mathbf{j}$$

The three vectors **v**, **w**, and $\text{proj}_{\mathbf{w}}\mathbf{v}$, are shown in Figure 7.66.

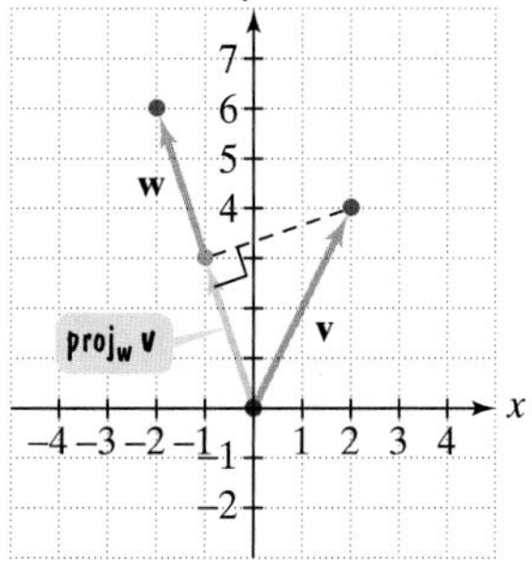


**Figure 7.66** The vector projection of **v** onto **w**

**Check Point 5** If $\mathbf{v} = 2\mathbf{i} - 5\mathbf{j}$ and $\mathbf{w} = \mathbf{i} - \mathbf{j}$, find the vector projection of **v** onto **w**.

**6** Express a vector as the sum of two orthogonal vectors.

We use the vector projection of **v** onto **w**, $\text{proj}_{\mathbf{w}}\mathbf{v}$, to express **v** as the sum of two orthogonal vectors.

### The Vector Components of v

Let **v** and **w** be two nonzero vectors. Vector **v** can be expressed as the sum of two orthogonal vectors, $\mathbf{v}_1$ and $\mathbf{v}_2$, where $\mathbf{v}_1$ is parallel to **w** and $\mathbf{v}_2$ is orthogonal to **w**.

$$\mathbf{v}_1 = \text{proj}_{\mathbf{w}}\mathbf{v} = \frac{\mathbf{v} \cdot \mathbf{w}}{\|\mathbf{w}\|^2}\mathbf{w}, \ \mathbf{v}_2 = \mathbf{v} - \mathbf{v}_1$$

Thus, $\mathbf{v} = \mathbf{v}_1 + \mathbf{v}_2$. The vectors $\mathbf{v}_1$ and $\mathbf{v}_2$ are called the **vector components** of **v**. The process of expressing **v** as $\mathbf{v}_1 + \mathbf{v}_2$ is called the **decomposition** of **v** into $\mathbf{v}_1$ and $\mathbf{v}_2$.

### EXAMPLE 6 Decomposing a Vector into Two Orthogonal Vectors

Let $\mathbf{v} = 2\mathbf{i} + 4\mathbf{j}$ and $\mathbf{w} = -2\mathbf{i} + 6\mathbf{j}$. Decompose **v** into two vectors, $\mathbf{v}_1$ and $\mathbf{v}_2$, where $\mathbf{v}_1$ is parallel to **w** and $\mathbf{v}_2$ is orthogonal to **w**.

**Solution** These are the vectors we worked with in Example 5. We use the formulas in the preceding box.

$$\mathbf{v}_1 = \text{proj}_{\mathbf{w}}\mathbf{v} = -\mathbf{i} + 3\mathbf{j} \quad \text{We obtained this vector in Example 5.}$$

$$\mathbf{v}_2 = \mathbf{v} - \mathbf{v}_1 = (2\mathbf{i} + 4\mathbf{j}) - (-\mathbf{i} + 3\mathbf{j}) = 3\mathbf{i} + \mathbf{j}$$

**Check Point 6** Let $\mathbf{v} = 2\mathbf{i} - 5\mathbf{j}$ and $\mathbf{w} = \mathbf{i} - \mathbf{j}$. (These are the vectors from Check Point 5.) Decompose **v** into two vectors, $\mathbf{v}_1$ and $\mathbf{v}_2$, where $\mathbf{v}_1$ is parallel to **w** and $\mathbf{v}_2$ is orthogonal to **w**.

**7** Compute work.

### Work: An Application of the Dot Product

The bad news: Your car just died. The good news: It died on a level road just 200 feet from a gas station. Exerting a constant force of 90 pounds, and not necessarily whistling as you work, you manage to push the car to the gas station.

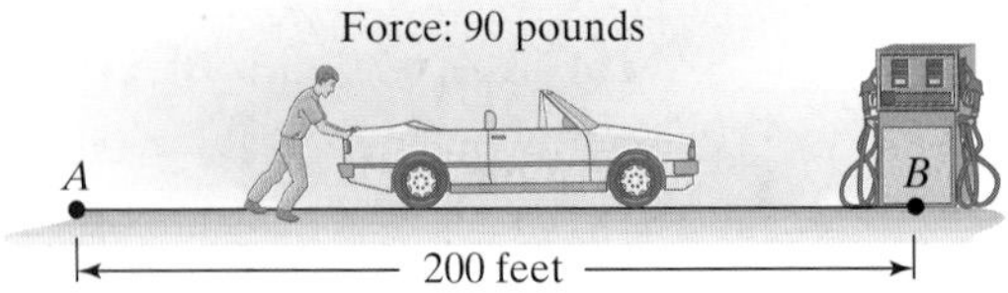


Although you did not whistle, you certainly did work pushing the car 200 feet from point $A$ to point $B$. How much work did you do? If a constant force **F** is applied to an object, moving it from point $A$ to point $B$ in the direction of the force, the work $W$ done is

$$W = (\text{magnitude of force})(\text{distance from } A \text{ to } B).$$

You pushed with a force of 90 pounds for a distance of 200 feet. The work done by your force is

$$W = (90 \text{ pounds})(200 \text{ feet})$$

or 18,000 foot-pounds. Work is often measured in foot-pounds or in newton-meters.

The photo at left shows an adult pulling a small child in a wagon. Work is being done. However, the situation is not quite the same as your car push. Pushing the car, the force you applied was along the line of motion. By contrast, the force of the adult pulling the wagon is not applied along the line of the wagon's motion. In this case, the dot product is used to determine the work done by the force.

**Definition of Work**

The work $W$ done by a force $\mathbf{F}$ in moving an object from $A$ to $B$ is

$$W = \mathbf{F} \cdot \overrightarrow{AB}.$$

When computing work, it is often easier to use the alternative formula for the dot product. Thus,

$$W = \mathbf{F} \cdot \overrightarrow{AB} = \|\mathbf{F}\| \|\overrightarrow{AB}\| \cos \theta$$

$\|\mathbf{F}\|$ is the magnitude of the force.

$\|\overrightarrow{AB}\|$ is the distance over which the constant force is applied.

$\theta$ is the angle between the force and the direction of motion.

It is correct to refer to $W$ as either the work done or the work done by the force.

## EXAMPLE 7 Computing Work

A child pulls a sled along level ground by exerting a force of 30 pounds on a rope that makes an angle of 35° with the ground. How much work is done pulling the sled 200 feet?

**Solution** The situation is illustrated in Figure 7.67. The work done is

$$W = \|\mathbf{F}\| \|\overrightarrow{AB}\| \cos \theta = (30)(200) \cos 35° \approx 4915$$

Magnitude of the force is 30 pounds.

Distance is 200 feet.

The angle between the force and the sled's motion is 35°.

Thus, the work done is approximately 4915 foot-pounds.

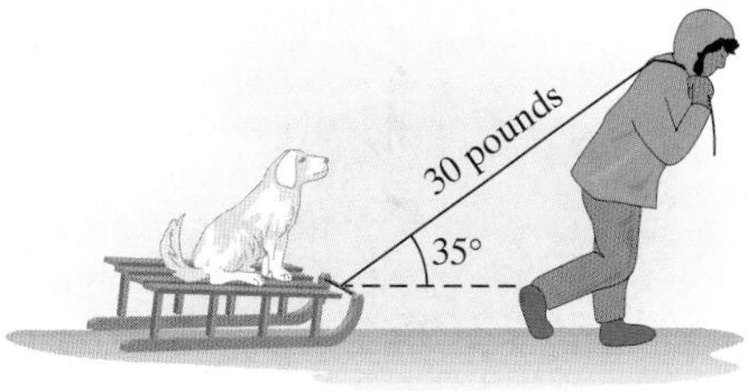


**Figure 7.67** Computing work done pulling the sled 200 feet

**Check Point 7** A child pulls a wagon along level ground by exerting a force of 20 pounds on a handle that makes an angle of 30° with the ground. How much work is done in pulling the wagon 150 feet?

# EXERCISE SET 7.7

## Practice Exercises

*In Exercises 1–8, use the given vectors to find* **a.** $\mathbf{v} \cdot \mathbf{w}$ *and* **b.** $\mathbf{v} \cdot \mathbf{v}$.

**1.** $\mathbf{v} = 3\mathbf{i} + \mathbf{j}, \quad \mathbf{w} = \mathbf{i} + 3\mathbf{j}$

**2.** $\mathbf{v} = 3\mathbf{i} + 3\mathbf{j}, \quad \mathbf{w} = \mathbf{i} + 4\mathbf{j}$

**3.** $\mathbf{v} = 5\mathbf{i} - 4\mathbf{j}, \quad \mathbf{w} = -2\mathbf{i} - \mathbf{j}$

**4.** $\mathbf{v} = 7\mathbf{i} - 2\mathbf{j}, \quad \mathbf{w} = -3\mathbf{i} - \mathbf{j}$

**5.** $\mathbf{v} = -6\mathbf{i} - 5\mathbf{j}, \quad \mathbf{w} = -10\mathbf{i} - 8\mathbf{j}$

**6.** $\mathbf{v} = -8\mathbf{i} - 3\mathbf{j}, \quad \mathbf{w} = -10\mathbf{i} - 5\mathbf{j}$

**7.** $\mathbf{v} = 5\mathbf{i}, \quad \mathbf{w} = \mathbf{j}$

**8.** $\mathbf{v} = \mathbf{i}, \quad \mathbf{w} = -5\mathbf{j}$

*In Exercises 9–16, let*

$$\mathbf{u} = 2\mathbf{i} - \mathbf{j}, \quad \mathbf{v} = 3\mathbf{i} + \mathbf{j}, \quad \text{and} \quad \mathbf{w} = \mathbf{i} + 4\mathbf{j}.$$

*Find each specified scalar.*

**9.** $\mathbf{u} \cdot (\mathbf{v} + \mathbf{w})$

**10.** $\mathbf{v} \cdot (\mathbf{u} + \mathbf{w})$

**11.** $\mathbf{u} \cdot \mathbf{v} + \mathbf{u} \cdot \mathbf{w}$

**12.** $\mathbf{v} \cdot \mathbf{u} + \mathbf{v} \cdot \mathbf{w}$

**13.** $(4\mathbf{u}) \cdot \mathbf{v}$

**14.** $(5\mathbf{v}) \cdot \mathbf{w}$

**15.** $4(\mathbf{u} \cdot \mathbf{v})$

**16.** $5(\mathbf{v} \cdot \mathbf{w})$

*In Exercises 17–22, find the angle between* **v** *and* **w**. *Round to the nearest tenth of a degree.*

**17.** $\mathbf{v} = 2\mathbf{i} - \mathbf{j}, \quad \mathbf{w} = 3\mathbf{i} + 4\mathbf{j}$

**18.** $\mathbf{v} = -2\mathbf{i} + 5\mathbf{j}, \quad \mathbf{w} = 3\mathbf{i} + 6\mathbf{j}$

**19.** $\mathbf{v} = -3\mathbf{i} + 2\mathbf{j}, \quad \mathbf{w} = 4\mathbf{i} - \mathbf{j}$

**20.** $\mathbf{v} = \mathbf{i} + 2\mathbf{j}, \quad \mathbf{w} = 4\mathbf{i} - 3\mathbf{j}$

**21.** $\mathbf{v} = 6\mathbf{i}, \quad \mathbf{w} = 5\mathbf{i} + 4\mathbf{j}$

**22.** $\mathbf{v} = 3\mathbf{j}, \quad \mathbf{w} = 4\mathbf{i} + 5\mathbf{j}$

*In Exercises 23–32, use the dot product to determine whether* **v** *and* **w** *are orthogonal.*

**23.** $\mathbf{v} = \mathbf{i} + \mathbf{j}, \quad \mathbf{w} = \mathbf{i} - \mathbf{j}$

**24.** $\mathbf{v} = \mathbf{i} + \mathbf{j}, \quad \mathbf{w} = -\mathbf{i} + \mathbf{j}$

**25.** $\mathbf{v} = 2\mathbf{i} + 8\mathbf{j}, \quad \mathbf{w} = 4\mathbf{i} - \mathbf{j}$

**26.** $\mathbf{v} = 8\mathbf{i} - 4\mathbf{j}, \quad \mathbf{w} = -6\mathbf{i} - 12\mathbf{j}$

**27.** $\mathbf{v} = 2\mathbf{i} - 2\mathbf{j}, \quad \mathbf{w} = -\mathbf{i} + \mathbf{j}$

**28.** $\mathbf{v} = 5\mathbf{i} - 5\mathbf{j}, \quad \mathbf{w} = \mathbf{i} - \mathbf{j}$

**29.** $\mathbf{v} = 3\mathbf{i}, \quad \mathbf{w} = -4\mathbf{i}$

**30.** $\mathbf{v} = 5\mathbf{i}, \quad \mathbf{w} = -6\mathbf{i}$

**31.** $\mathbf{v} = 3\mathbf{i}, \quad \mathbf{w} = -4\mathbf{j}$

**32.** $\mathbf{v} = 5\mathbf{i}, \quad \mathbf{w} = -6\mathbf{j}$

*In Exercises 33–38, write a vector* **v** *in terms of* **i** *and* **j** *whose magnitude* $\|\mathbf{v}\|$ *and direction angle* $\theta$ *are given.*

**33.** $\|\mathbf{v}\| = 6, \quad \theta = 30°$

**34.** $\|\mathbf{v}\| = 8, \quad \theta = 45°$

**35.** $\|\mathbf{v}\| = 12, \quad \theta = 225°$

**36.** $\|\mathbf{v}\| = 10, \quad \theta = 330°$

**37.** $\|\mathbf{v}\| = \frac{1}{2}, \quad \theta = 113°$

**38.** $\|\mathbf{v}\| = \frac{1}{4}, \quad \theta = 200°$

*In Exercise 39–44, find* $\text{proj}_{\mathbf{w}}\mathbf{v}$. *Then decompose* **v** *into two vectors,* $\mathbf{v}_1$ *and* $\mathbf{v}_2$, *where* $\mathbf{v}_1$ *is parallel to* **w** *and* $\mathbf{v}_2$ *is orthogonal to* **w**.

**39.** $\mathbf{v} = 3\mathbf{i} - 2\mathbf{j}, \quad \mathbf{w} = \mathbf{i} - \mathbf{j}$

**40.** $\mathbf{v} = 3\mathbf{i} - 2\mathbf{j}, \quad \mathbf{w} = 2\mathbf{i} + \mathbf{j}$

**41.** $\mathbf{v} = \mathbf{i} + 3\mathbf{j}, \quad \mathbf{w} = -2\mathbf{i} + 5\mathbf{j}$

**42.** $\mathbf{v} = 2\mathbf{i} + 4\mathbf{j}, \quad \mathbf{w} = -3\mathbf{i} + 6\mathbf{j}$

**43.** $\mathbf{v} = \mathbf{i} + 2\mathbf{j}, \quad \mathbf{w} = 3\mathbf{i} + 6\mathbf{j}$

**44.** $\mathbf{v} = 2\mathbf{i} + \mathbf{j}, \quad \mathbf{w} = 6\mathbf{i} + 3\mathbf{j}$

## Application Exercises

*In Exercises 45–48, a vector is described. Express the vector in terms of* **i** *and* **j**. *If exact values are not possible, round components to the nearest tenth.*

**45.** A quarterback releases a football with a speed of 44 feet per second at an angle of 30° with the horizontal.

**46.** A child pulls a sled along level ground by exerting a force of 30 pounds on a handle that makes an angle of 45° with the ground.

**47.** A plane approaches a runway at 150 miles per hour at an angle of 8° with the ground traveling.

**48.** A plane with an airspeed of 450 miles per hour is flying in the direction N35°W.

**49.** The components of $\mathbf{v} = 240\mathbf{i} + 300\mathbf{j}$ represent the respective number of gallons of regular and premium gas sold at a station on Monday. The components of $\mathbf{w} = 1.90\mathbf{i} + 2.07\mathbf{j}$ represent the respective prices per gallon for each kind of gas. Find $\mathbf{v} \cdot \mathbf{w}$ and describe what the answer means in practical terms.

**50.** The components of $\mathbf{v} = 180\mathbf{i} + 450\mathbf{j}$ represent the respective number of one-day and three-day videos rented from a video store on Monday. The components of $\mathbf{w} = 3\mathbf{i} + 2\mathbf{j}$ represent the prices to rent the newly arrived one-day videos and the three-day videos, respectively. Find $\mathbf{v} \cdot \mathbf{w}$ and describe what the answer means in practical terms.

**51.** Find the work done in pushing a car along a level road from point $A$ to point $B$, 80 feet from $A$, while exerting a constant force of 95 pounds. Round to the nearest foot-pound.

**52.** Find the work done when a crane lifts a 6000-pound boulder through a vertical distance of 12 feet. Round to the nearest foot-pound.

**53.** A wagon is pulled along level ground by exerting a force of 40 pounds on a handle that makes an angle of 32° with the ground. How much work is done in pulling the wagon 100 feet? Round to the nearest foot-pound.

**54.** A wagon is pulled along level ground by exerting a force of 25 pounds on a handle that makes an angle of 38° with the ground. How much work is done in pulling the wagon 100 feet? Round to the nearest foot-pound.

*Vectors are used in computer graphics to determine lengths of shadows over flat surfaces. The length of the shadow for* **v** *in the figure shown is the absolute value of the vector's horizontal component. In Exercises 55–56, the magnitude and di-*

*rection angle of* **v** *are given. Write* **v** *in terms of* **i** *and* **j**. *Then find the length of the shadow to the nearest tenth of an inch.*

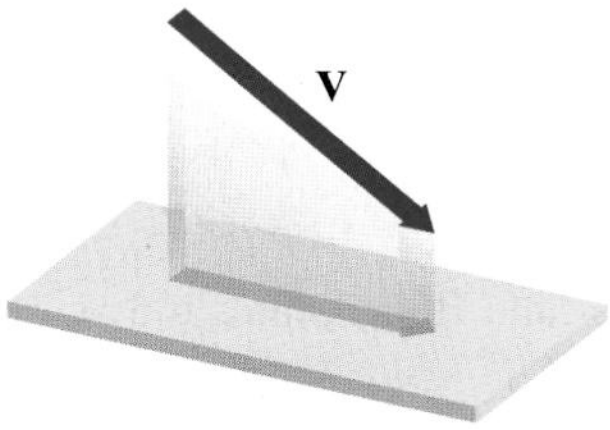


**55.** $\|\mathbf{v}\| = 1.5$ inches, $\theta = 25°$

**56.** $\|\mathbf{v}\| = 1.8$ inches, $\theta = 40°$

**57.** A truck that weighs 40,000 pounds is parked on a road that forms a 12° angle with level ground. Let **v** be the vector representing the force needed to prevent the truck from rolling down the hill.
  **a.** How many pounds of force are required to prevent the truck from rolling down the hill?
  **b.** Write **v** in terms of **i** and **j**. Round each component to the nearest pound.

**58.** A car that weighs 3000 pounds is parked on a road that forms a 10° angle with level ground. Let **v** be the vector representing the force needed to prevent the car from rolling down the hill.
  **a.** How many pounds of force are required to prevent the truck from rolling down the hill?
  **b.** Write **v** in terms of **i** and **j**. Round each component to the nearest pound.

## Writing in Mathematics

**59.** Explain how to find the dot product of two vectors.

**60.** Using words and no symbols, describe how to find the dot product of two vectors with the alternative formula

$$\mathbf{v} \cdot \mathbf{w} = \|\mathbf{v}\|\|\mathbf{w}\| \cos\theta.$$

**61.** Describe how to find the angle between two vectors.

**62.** What are parallel vectors?

**63.** What are orthogonal vectors?

**64.** How do you determine if two vectors are orthogonal?

**65.** Explain how to write a vector in terms of its magnitude and direction.

**66.** Draw two vectors, **v** and **w**, with the same initial point. Show the vector projection of **v** onto **w** in your diagram. Then describe how you identified this vector.

**67.** How do you determine the work done by a force **F** in moving an object from $A$ to $B$ when the direction of the force is not along the line of motion?

**68.** A weightlifter is holding a barbell perfectly still above his head, his body shaking from the effort. How much work is the weightlifter doing? Explain your answer.

**69.** Describe one way in which the everyday use of the word "work" is different from the definition of work given in this section.

## Critical Thinking Exercises

*In Exercises 70–72, use the vectors*

$$\mathbf{u} = a_1\mathbf{i} + b_1\mathbf{j}, \quad \mathbf{v} = a_2\mathbf{i} + b_2\mathbf{j}, \quad \text{and} \quad \mathbf{w} = a_3\mathbf{i} + b_3\mathbf{j}$$

*to prove the given property.*

**70.** $\mathbf{u} \cdot \mathbf{v} = \mathbf{v} \cdot \mathbf{u}$

**71.** $(c\mathbf{u}) \cdot \mathbf{v} = c(\mathbf{u} \cdot \mathbf{v})$

**72.** $\mathbf{u} \cdot (\mathbf{v} + \mathbf{w}) = \mathbf{u} \cdot \mathbf{v} + \mathbf{u} \cdot \mathbf{w}$

**73.** How much work is done by a force of 4 pounds acting in the direction $3\mathbf{i} + \mathbf{j}$ in moving an object 5 feet from (0, 0) to (0, 5)?

**74.** If $\mathbf{v} = -2\mathbf{i} + 5\mathbf{j}$, find a vector perpendicular to **v**.

**75.** Find a value of $b$ so that $15\mathbf{i} - 3\mathbf{j}$ and $-4\mathbf{i} + b\mathbf{j}$ are orthogonal.

**76.** Prove that the projection of **v** onto **i** is $(\mathbf{v} \cdot \mathbf{i})\mathbf{i}$.

**77.** Find two vectors **v** and **w** such that the projection of **v** onto **w** is **v**.

## Group Exercise

**78.** Group members should research and present a report on unusual and interesting applications of vectors.

# CHAPTER SUMMARY, REVIEW, AND TEST

## Summary

### 7.1 and 7.2 The Law of Sines and the Law of Cosines

a. The Law of Sines

$$\frac{a}{\sin A} = \frac{b}{\sin B} = \frac{c}{\sin C}$$

b. The Law of Sines is used to solve SAA, ASA, and SSA (the ambiguous case) triangles. The ambiguous case may result in no triangle, one triangle, or two triangles; see the box on page 602.

c. The area of a triangle equals one-half the product of the lengths of two sides times the sine of their included angle.

d. The Law of Cosines

$$a^2 = b^2 + c^2 - 2bc \cos A,$$
$$b^2 = a^2 + c^2 - 2ac \cos B,$$
$$c^2 = a^2 + b^2 - 2ab \cos C$$

e. The Law of Cosines is used to find the side opposite the given angle in a SAS triangle; see the box on page 612. The Law of Cosines is also used to find the angle opposite the longest side in a SSS triangle; see the box on page 613.

f. Heron's Formula for the Area of a Triangle
The area of a triangle with sides $a$, $b$, and $c$ is

$$\sqrt{s(s-a)(s-b)(s-c)},$$

where $s$ is one-half the perimeter:

$$s = \tfrac{1}{2}(a + b + c).$$

## 7.3 and 7.4 Polar Coordinates and Graphs of Polar Equations

a. A point $P$ in the polar coordinate system is represented by $(r, \theta)$, where $r$ is the directed distance of the point from the pole and $\theta$ is the angle from the polar axis to line segment $OP$. The elements of the ordered pair $(r, \theta)$ are called the polar coordinates of $P$. See Figure 7.19 on page 619. When $r$ in $(r, \theta)$ is negative, a point is located $|r|$ units along the ray opposite the terminal side of $\theta$. Important information about the sign of $r$ and the location of the point $(r, \theta)$ is found in the box on page 620.

b. Multiple Representation of Points
If $n$ is any integer, $(r, \theta) = (r, \theta + 2n\pi)$ or $(r, \theta) = (-r, \theta + \pi + 2n\pi)$.

c. Relations between Polar and Rectangular Coordinates

$$x = r\cos\theta, \quad y = r\sin\theta, \quad x^2 + y^2 = r^2, \quad \tan\theta = \frac{y}{x}$$

d. To convert a point from polar coordinates $(r, \theta)$ to rectangular coordinates $(x, y)$, use $x = r\cos\theta$ and $y = r\sin\theta$.

e. To convert a point from rectangular coordinates $(x, y)$ to polar coordinates $(r, \theta)$, use the procedure in the box on page 624.

f. To convert a rectangular equation to a polar equation, replace $x$ by $r\cos\theta$ and $y$ by $r\sin\theta$.

g. To convert a polar equation to a rectangular equation, use one or more of

$$r^2 = x^2 + y^2, \quad r\cos\theta = x, \quad r\sin\theta = y, \quad \text{and} \quad \tan\theta = \frac{y}{x}.$$

It is often necessary to do something to the given polar equation to obtain the preceding expressions.

h. A polar equation is an equation whose variables are $r$ and $\theta$. The graph of a polar equation is the set of all points whose polar coordinates satisfy the equation.

i. Polar equations can be graphed using point plotting and symmetry (see the box on page 632).

j. The graphs of $r = a\cos\theta$ and $r = a\sin\theta$ are circles. See the box on page 632. The graphs of $r = a \pm b\sin\theta$ and $r = a \pm b\cos\theta$ are called limaçons ($a > 0$ and $b > 0$), shown in the box on page 635. The graphs of $r = a\sin n\theta$ and $r = a\cos n\theta$, $a \neq 0$, are rose curves with $2n$ petals if $n$ is even and $n$ petals if $n$ is odd. See the box on page 638. The graphs of $r^2 = a^2\sin 2\theta$ and $r^2 = a^2\cos 2\theta$, $a \neq 0$, are called lemniscates and are shown in the box on page 639.

## 7.5 Complex Numbers in Polar Form; DeMoivre's Theorem

a. The complex number $z = a + bi$ is represented as a point $(a, b)$ in the complex plane, shown in Figure 7.35 on page 643.

b. The absolute value of $z = a + bi$ is $|z| = |a + bi| = \sqrt{a^2 + b^2}$.

c. The polar form of $z = a + bi$ is $z = r(\cos\theta + i\sin\theta)$, where $a = r\cos\theta$, $b = r\sin\theta$, $r = \sqrt{a^2 + b^2}$, and $\tan\theta = \frac{b}{a}$. We call $r$ the modulus and $\theta$ the argument of $z$, with $0 \le \theta < 2\pi$.

d. Multiplying Complex Numbers in Polar Form: Multiply moduli and add arguments. See the box on page 646.

e. Dividing Complex Numbers in Polar Form: Divide moduli and subtract arguments. See the box on page 647.

f. DeMoivre's Theorem is used to find powers of complex numbers in polar form.

$$[r(\cos\theta + i\sin\theta)]^n = r^n(\cos n\theta + i\sin n\theta)$$

g. DeMoivre's Theorem can be used for finding roots of complex numbers in polar form. The $n$ distinct $n$th roots of $r(\cos\theta + i\sin\theta)$ are

$$\sqrt[n]{r}\left[\cos\left(\frac{\theta + 2\pi k}{n}\right) + i\sin\left(\frac{\theta + 2\pi k}{n}\right)\right]$$

or

$$\sqrt[n]{r}\left[\cos\left(\frac{\theta + 360^\circ k}{n}\right) + i\sin\left(\frac{\theta + 360^\circ k}{n}\right)\right]$$

where $k = 0, 1, 2, \ldots, n - 1$.

## 7.6 Vectors

a. A vector is a directed line segment.

b. Equal vectors have the same magnitude and the same direction.

c. The vector $k\mathbf{v}$, the scalar multiple of the vector $\mathbf{v}$ and the scalar $k$, has magnitude $|k|\|\mathbf{v}\|$. The direction of $k\mathbf{v}$ is the same as that of $\mathbf{v}$ if $k > 0$ and opposite $\mathbf{v}$ if $k < 0$.

d. The sum $\mathbf{u} + \mathbf{v}$, called the resultant vector, can be expressed geometrically. Position $\mathbf{u}$ and $\mathbf{v}$ so that the terminal point of $\mathbf{u}$ coincides with the initial point of $\mathbf{v}$. The vector $\mathbf{u} + \mathbf{v}$ extends from the initial point of $\mathbf{u}$ to the terminal point of $\mathbf{v}$.

e. The difference of two vectors, $\mathbf{u} - \mathbf{v}$, is defined as $\mathbf{u} + (-\mathbf{v})$.

f. The vector $\mathbf{i}$ is the unit vector whose direction is along the positive $x$-axis. The vector $\mathbf{j}$ is the unit vector whose direction is along the positive $y$-axis.

g. Vector $\mathbf{v}$, from $(0, 0)$ to $(a, b)$, called a position vector, is represented as $\mathbf{v} = a\mathbf{i} + b\mathbf{j}$, where $a$ is the horizontal component and $b$ is the vertical component. The magnitude of $\mathbf{v}$ is given by $\|\mathbf{v}\| = \sqrt{a^2 + b^2}$.

h. Vector $\mathbf{v}$ from $(x_1, y_1)$ to $(x_2, y_2)$ is equal to the position vector $\mathbf{v} = (x_2 - x_1)\mathbf{i} + (y_2 - y_1)\mathbf{j}$. In rectangular coordinates, the term "vector" refers to the position vector in terms of $\mathbf{i}$ and $\mathbf{j}$ that is equal to it.

i. Operations with Vectors in Terms of $\mathbf{i}$ and $\mathbf{j}$
If $\mathbf{v} = a_1\mathbf{i} + b_1\mathbf{j}$ and $\mathbf{w} = a_2\mathbf{i} + b_2\mathbf{j}$, then

1. $\mathbf{v} + \mathbf{w} = (a_1 + a_2)\mathbf{i} + (b_1 + b_2)\mathbf{j}$.
2. $\mathbf{v} - \mathbf{w} = (a_1 - a_2)\mathbf{i} + (b_1 - b_2)\mathbf{j}$.
3. $k\mathbf{v} = (ka_1)\mathbf{i} + (kb_1)\mathbf{j}$.

j. The zero vector $\mathbf{0}$ is the vector whose magnitude is 0 and is assigned no direction. Many properties of vector addition and scalar multiplication involve the zero vector. Some of these properties are listed in the box on pages 662–663.

k. The vector $\frac{\mathbf{v}}{\|\mathbf{v}\|}$ is a unit vector that has the same direction as $\mathbf{v}$.

## 7.7 The Dot Product

a. Definition of the Dot Product
If $\mathbf{v} = a_1\mathbf{i} + b_1\mathbf{j}$ and $\mathbf{w} = a_2\mathbf{i} + b_2\mathbf{j}$, the dot product is defined by $\mathbf{v} \cdot \mathbf{w} = a_1a_2 + b_1b_2$.

b. Alternative Formula for the Dot Product $\mathbf{v} \cdot \mathbf{w} = \|\mathbf{v}\|\|\mathbf{w}\| \cos\theta$, where $\theta$ is the smallest nonnegative angle between $\mathbf{v}$ and $\mathbf{w}$.

c. Angle between Two Vectors

$$\cos\theta = \frac{\mathbf{v} \cdot \mathbf{w}}{\|\mathbf{v}\|\|\mathbf{w}\|} \quad \text{and} \quad \theta = \cos^{-1}\left(\frac{\mathbf{v} \cdot \mathbf{w}}{\|\mathbf{v}\|\|\mathbf{w}\|}\right).$$

d. Two vectors are orthogonal when the angle between them is 90°. To show that two vectors are orthogonal, show that their dot product is zero.

e. A vector with magnitude $\|\mathbf{v}\|$ and direction angle $\theta$, the angle that $\mathbf{v}$ makes with the positive $x$-axis, can be expressed in terms of its magnitude and direction angle as

$$\mathbf{v} = \|\mathbf{v}\| \cos\theta\mathbf{i} + \|\mathbf{v}\| \sin\theta\mathbf{j}.$$

f. The vector projection of $\mathbf{v}$ onto $\mathbf{w}$ is given by

$$\text{proj}_{\mathbf{w}}\mathbf{v} = \frac{\mathbf{v} \cdot \mathbf{w}}{\|\mathbf{w}\|^2}\mathbf{w}.$$

g. Expressing a vector as the sum of two orthogonal vectors is shown in the box on page 674.

h. The work $W$ done by a force $\mathbf{F}$ in moving an object from $A$ to $B$ is $W = \mathbf{F} \cdot \overrightarrow{AB}$. Thus, $W = \|\mathbf{F}\|\|\overrightarrow{AB}\| \cos\theta$, where $\theta$ is the angle between the force and the direction of motion.

# Review Exercises

## 7.1 and 7.2

*In Exercises 1–12, solve each triangle. Round lengths to the nearest tenth and angle measures to the nearest degree. If no triangle exists, state "no triangle." If two triangles exist, solve each triangle.*

**1.** $A = 70°, B = 55°, a = 12$
**2.** $B = 107°, C = 30°, c = 126$
**3.** $B = 66°, a = 17, c = 12$
**4.** $a = 117, b = 66, c = 142$
**5.** $A = 35°, B = 25°, c = 68$
**6.** $A = 39°, a = 20, b = 26$
**7.** $C = 50°, a = 3, c = 1$
**8.** $A = 162°, b = 11.2, c = 48.2$
**9.** $a = 26.1, b = 40.2, c = 36.5$
**10.** $A = 40°, a = 6, b = 4$
**11.** $B = 37°, a = 12.4, b = 8.7$
**12.** $A = 23°, a = 54.3, b = 22.1$

*In Exercises 13–16, find the area of the triangle having the given measurements. Round to the nearest square unit.*

**13.** $C = 42°, a = 4$ feet, $b = 6$ feet
**14.** $A = 22°, b = 4$ feet, $c = 5$ feet
**15.** $a = 2$ meters, $b = 4$ meters, $c = 5$ meters
**16.** $a = 2$ meters, $b = 2$ meters, $c = 2$ meters

**17.** An A-frame cabin is 35 feet wide. The roof of the cabin makes a 60° angle with the cabin's base. Find the length of the roof from its ground level to the peak. Round to the nearest tenth of a foot.

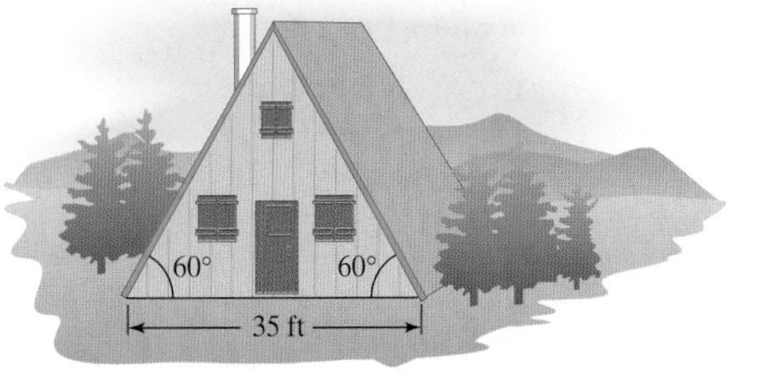


**18.** Two cars leave a city at the same time and travel along straight highways that differ in direction by 80°. One car averages 60 miles per hour and the other averages 50 miles per hour. How far apart will the cars be after 30 minutes? Round to the nearest tenth of a mile.

**19.** Two airplanes leave an airport at the same time on different runways. One flies at a bearing of N66.5°W at 325 miles per hour. The other airplane flies at a bearing of S26.5°W at 300 miles per hour. How far apart will the airplanes be after two hours?

**20.** The figure shows three roads that intersect to form a triangular piece of land. Find the lengths of the other two sides of the land to the nearest foot.

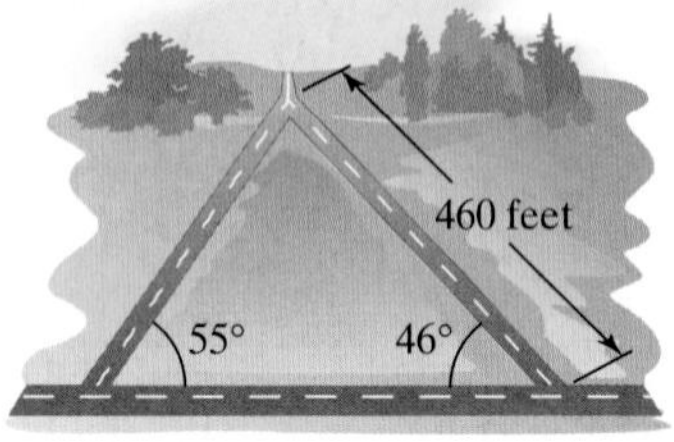


**21.** A commercial piece of real estate is priced at $5.25 per square foot. Find the cost, to the nearest dollar, of a triangular lot measuring 260 feet by 320 feet by 450 feet.

## 7.3 and 7.4

*In Exercises 22–27, plot each point in polar coordinates, and find its rectangular coordinates.*

**22.** $(4, 60°)$ **23.** $(3, 150°)$

**24.** $\left(-4, \frac{4\pi}{3}\right)$ **25.** $\left(-2, \frac{5\pi}{4}\right)$

**26.** $\left(-4, -\frac{\pi}{2}\right)$ **27.** $\left(-2, -\frac{\pi}{4}\right)$

*In Exercises 28–30, plot each point in polar coordinates. Then find another representation $(r, \theta)$ of this point in which:*

**a.** $r > 0, \quad 2\pi < \theta < 4\pi.$

**b.** $r < 0, \quad 0 < \theta < 2\pi.$

**c.** $r > 0, -2\pi < \theta < 0.$

**28.** $\left(3, \frac{\pi}{6}\right)$ **29.** $\left(2, \frac{2\pi}{3}\right)$ **30.** $(3, \pi)$

*In Exercises 31–36, the rectangular coordinates of a point are given. Find polar coordinates of each point.*

**31.** $(-4, 4)$ **32.** $(3, -3)$

**33.** $(5, 12)$ **34.** $(-3, 4)$

**35.** $(0, -5)$ **36.** $(1, 0)$

*In Exercises 37–39, convert each rectangular equation to a polar equation.*

**37.** $2x + 3y = 8$ **38.** $x^2 + y^2 = 100$

**39.** $5x^2 + 5y^2 = 3y$

*In Exercises 40–46, convert each polar equation to a rectangular equation.*

**40.** $r = 3$ **41.** $\theta = \frac{3\pi}{4}$

**42.** $r\cos\theta = -1$ **43.** $r = 5\sec\theta$

**44.** $r = 3\cos\theta$ **45.** $5r\cos\theta + r\sin\theta = 8$

**46.** $r^2\sin 2\theta = 4$

*In Exercises 47–49, test for symmetry with respect to:*

**a.** *the polar axis;* **b.** *the line* $\theta = \frac{\pi}{2}$; *and* **c.** *the pole.*

**47.** $r = 5 + 3\cos\theta$ **48.** $r = 3\sin\theta$

**49.** $r^2 = 9\cos 2\theta$

*In Exercises 50–56, graph each polar equation. Be sure to test for symmetry.*

**50.** $r = 3\cos\theta$ **51.** $r = 2 + 2\sin\theta$

**52.** $r = \sin 2\theta$ **53.** $r = 2 + \cos\theta$

**54.** $r = 1 + 3\sin\theta$ **55.** $r = 1 - 2\cos\theta$

**56.** $r^2 = \cos 2\theta$

## 7.5

*In Exercises 57–60, plot each complex number. Then write the complex number in polar form. You may express the argument in degrees or radians.*

**57.** $1 - i$ **58.** $-2\sqrt{3} + 2i$

**59.** $-3 - 4i$ **60.** $-5i$

*In Exercises 61–64, write each complex number in rectangular form.*

**61.** $8(\cos 60° + i\sin 60°)$ **62.** $4(\cos 210° + i\sin 210°)$

**63.** $6\left(\cos\frac{2\pi}{3} + i\sin\frac{2\pi}{3}\right)$

**64.** $0.6(\cos 100° + i\sin 100°)$

*In Exercises 65–67, find the product of the complex numbers. Leave answers in polar form.*

**65.** $z_1 = 3(\cos 40° + i\sin 40°)$
$z_2 = 5(\cos 70° + i\sin 70°)$

**66.** $z_1 = \cos 210° + i\sin 210°$
$z_2 = \cos 55° + i\sin 55°$

**67.** $z_1 = 4\left(\cos\frac{3\pi}{7} + i\sin\frac{3\pi}{7}\right)$
$z_2 = 10\left(\cos\frac{4\pi}{7} + i\sin\frac{4\pi}{7}\right)$

*In Exercises 68–70, find the quotient $\frac{z_1}{z_2}$ of the complex numbers. Leave answers in polar form.*

**68.** $z_1 = 10(\cos 10° + i\sin 10°)$
$z_2 = 5(\cos 5° + i\sin 5°)$

**69.** $z_1 = 5\left(\cos\frac{4\pi}{3} + i\sin\frac{4\pi}{3}\right)$
$z_2 = 10\left(\cos\frac{\pi}{3} + i\sin\frac{\pi}{3}\right)$

**70.** $z_1 = 2\left(\cos\frac{5\pi}{3} + i\sin\frac{5\pi}{3}\right)$

$z_2 = \cos\frac{\pi}{2} + i\sin\frac{\pi}{2}$

*In Exercises 71–75, use DeMoivre's Theorem to find the indicated power of the complex number. Write answers in rectangular form.*

**71.** $[2(\cos 20° + i\sin 20°)]^3$

**72.** $[4(\cos 50° + i\sin 50°)]^3$

**73.** $\left[\frac{1}{2}\left(\cos\frac{\pi}{14} + i\sin\frac{\pi}{14}\right)\right]^7$

**74.** $(1 - \sqrt{3}i)^7$

**75.** $(-2 - 2i)^5$

*In Exercises 76–77, find all the complex roots. Write roots in polar form with $\theta$ in degrees.*

**76.** The complex square roots of $49(\cos 50° + i\sin 50°)$

**77.** The complex cube roots of $125(\cos 165° + i\sin 165°)$

*In Exercises 78–81, find all the complex roots. Write roots in rectangular form.*

**78.** The complex fourth roots of $16\left(\cos\frac{2\pi}{3} + i\sin\frac{2\pi}{3}\right)$

**79.** The complex cube roots of $8i$

**80.** The complex cube roots of $-1$

**81.** The complex fifth roots of $-1 - i$

## 7.6

*In Exercises 82–84, sketch each position vector and find its magnitude.*

**82.** $\mathbf{v} = -3\mathbf{i} - 4\mathbf{j}$

**83.** $\mathbf{v} = 5\mathbf{i} - 2\mathbf{j}$

**84.** $\mathbf{v} = -3\mathbf{j}$

*In Exercises 85–86, let* **v** *be the vector from initial point $P_1$ to terminal point $P_2$. Write* **v** *in terms of* **i** *and* **j**.

**85.** $P_1 = (2, -1)$, $P_2 = (5, -3)$

**86.** $P_1 = (-3, 0)$, $P_2 = (-2, -2)$

*In Exercises 87–90, let*

$$\mathbf{v} = \mathbf{i} - 5\mathbf{j} \quad \text{and} \quad \mathbf{w} = -2\mathbf{i} + 7\mathbf{j}.$$

*Find each specified vector or scalar.*

**87.** $\mathbf{v} + \mathbf{w}$

**88.** $\mathbf{w} - \mathbf{v}$

**89.** $6\mathbf{v} - 3\mathbf{w}$

**90.** $\|-2\mathbf{v}\|$

*In Exercises 91–92, find a unit vector that has the same direction as the vector* **v**.

**91.** $\mathbf{v} = 8\mathbf{i} - 6\mathbf{j}$

**92.** $\mathbf{v} = -\mathbf{i} + 2\mathbf{j}$

**93.** Two forces of 100 pounds and 200 pounds act on an object. If the angle between the forces is 60°,
- **a.** Find the magnitude of the resultant force to the nearest pound.
- **b.** Find the direction of the resultant force relative to the 200-pound force. Express the answer to the nearest degree.

## 7.7

**94.** If $\mathbf{u} = 5\mathbf{i} + 2\mathbf{j}$, $\mathbf{v} = \mathbf{i} - \mathbf{j}$, and $\mathbf{w} = 3\mathbf{i} - 7\mathbf{j}$, find $\mathbf{u} \cdot (\mathbf{v} + \mathbf{w})$.

*In Exercises 95–97, find the dot product* $\mathbf{v} \cdot \mathbf{w}$. *Then find the angle between* **v** *and* **w** *to the nearest tenth of a degree.*

**95.** $\mathbf{v} = 2\mathbf{i} + 3\mathbf{j}$, $\mathbf{w} = 7\mathbf{i} - 4\mathbf{j}$

**96.** $\mathbf{v} = 2\mathbf{i} + 4\mathbf{j}$, $\mathbf{w} = 6\mathbf{i} - 11\mathbf{j}$

**97.** $\mathbf{v} = 2\mathbf{i} + \mathbf{j}$, $\mathbf{w} = \mathbf{i} - \mathbf{j}$

*In Exercises 98–99, use the dot product to determine whether* **v** *and* **w** *are orthogonal.*

**98.** $\mathbf{v} = 12\mathbf{i} - 8\mathbf{j}$, $\mathbf{w} = 2\mathbf{i} + 3\mathbf{j}$

**99.** $\mathbf{v} = \mathbf{i} + 3\mathbf{j}$, $\mathbf{w} = -3\mathbf{i} - \mathbf{j}$

**100.** The magnitude and direction angle of **v** are $\|\mathbf{v}\| = 12$ and $\theta = 60°$. Express **v** in terms of **i** and **j**.

*In Exercises 101–102, find* $\text{proj}_{\mathbf{w}}\mathbf{v}$. *Then decompose* **v** *into two vectors, $\mathbf{v}_1$ and $\mathbf{v}_2$, where $\mathbf{v}_1$ is parallel to* **w** *and $\mathbf{v}_2$ is orthogonal to* **w**.

**101.** $\mathbf{v} = -2\mathbf{i} + 5\mathbf{j}$, $\mathbf{w} = 5\mathbf{i} + 4\mathbf{j}$

**102.** $\mathbf{v} = -\mathbf{i} + 2\mathbf{j}$, $\mathbf{w} = 3\mathbf{i} - \mathbf{j}$

**103.** A heavy crate is dragged 50 feet along a level floor. Find the work done if a force of 30 pounds at an angle of 42° is used.

# Chapter 7 Test

**1.** In oblique triangle $ABC$, $A = 34°$, $B = 68°$, and $a = 4.8$. Find $b$ to the nearest tenth.

**2.** In oblique triangle $ABC$, $C = 68°$, $a = 5$, and $b = 6$. Find $c$ to the nearest tenth.

**3.** In oblique triangle $ABC$, $a = 17$ inches, $b = 45$ inches, and $c = 32$ inches. Find the area of the triangle to the nearest square inch.

**4.** Plot $\left(4, \frac{5\pi}{4}\right)$ in the polar coordinate system. Then write two other ordered pairs $(r, \theta)$ that name this point.

**5.** If the rectangular coordinates of a point are $(1, -1)$, find polar coordinates of the point.

**6.** Convert $x^2 + y^2 = 6x$ to a polar equation.

**7.** Convert $r = 4\csc\theta$ to a rectangular equation.

*In Exercises 8–9, graph each polar equation.*

**8.** $r = 1 + \sin\theta$ **9.** $r = 1 + 3\cos\theta$

**10.** Write $-\sqrt{3} + i$ in polar form.

*In Exercises 11–13, perform the indicated operation. Leave answers in polar form.*

**11.** $5(\cos 15° + i\sin 15°) \cdot 10(\cos 5° + i\sin 5°)$

**12.** $\dfrac{2\left(\cos\frac{\pi}{2} + i\sin\frac{\pi}{2}\right)}{4\left(\cos\frac{\pi}{3} + i\sin\frac{\pi}{3}\right)}$

**13.** $[2(\cos 10° + i\sin 10°)]^5$

**14.** Find the three cube roots of 27. Write roots in rectangular form.

**15.** If $P_1 = (-2, 3)$ and $P_2 = (-1, 5)$ and $\mathbf{v}$ is the vector from $P_1$ to $P_2$,
**a.** Write $\mathbf{v}$ in terms of $\mathbf{i}$ and $\mathbf{j}$.
**b.** Find $\|\mathbf{v}\|$.

*In Exercises 16–19, let*

$$\mathbf{v} = -5\mathbf{i} + 2\mathbf{j} \quad \text{and} \quad \mathbf{w} = 2\mathbf{i} - 4\mathbf{j}.$$

*Find:*

**16.** $3\mathbf{v} - 4\mathbf{w}$. **17.** $\mathbf{v} \cdot \mathbf{w}$.

**18.** the angle between $\mathbf{v}$ and $\mathbf{w}$, to the nearest degree.

**19.** $\text{proj}_{\mathbf{w}}\mathbf{v}$.

**20.** A small fire is sighted from ranger stations A and B. Station B is 1.6 miles due east of station A. The bearing of the fire from station A is N40°E, and the bearing of the fire from station B is N50°W. How far, to the nearest tenth of a mile, is the fire from station A?

**21.** A child is pulling a wagon with a force of 40 pounds. How much work is done in moving the wagon 60 feet if the handle makes an angle of 35° with the ground? Round to the nearest foot-pound.

## Cumulative Review Exercises (Chapters 1–7)

*Solve each equation or inequality in Exercises 1–4.*

**1.** $x^4 - x^3 - x^2 - x - 2 = 0$

**2.** $2\sin^2\theta - 3\sin\theta + 1 = 0, \quad 0 \le \theta < 2\pi$

**3.** $x^2 + 2x + 3 > 11$

**4.** $\sin\theta\cos\theta = -\frac{1}{2}, \quad 0 \le \theta < 2\pi$

*In Exercises 5–6, graph one complete cycle.*

**5.** $y = 3\sin(2x - \pi)$ **6.** $y = -4\cos\pi x$

*In Exercises 7–8, verify each identity.*

**7.** $\sin\theta\csc\theta - \cos^2\theta = \sin^2\theta$

**8.** $\cos\left(\theta + \dfrac{3\pi}{2}\right) = \sin\theta$

**9.** Find the slope and $y$-intercept of the line whose equation is $2x + 4y - 8 = 0$.

*In Exercises 10–11, find the exact value of each expression.*

**10.** $2\sin\dfrac{\pi}{3} - 3\tan\dfrac{\pi}{6}$ **11.** $\sin\left(\tan^{-1}\frac{1}{2}\right)$

*In Exercises 12–13, find the domain of the function whose equation is given.*

**12.** $f(x) = \sqrt{5 - x}$ **13.** $g(x) = \dfrac{x - 3}{x^2 - 9}$

**14.** A ball is thrown vertically upward from a height of 8 feet with an initial velocity of 48 feet per second. The ball's height, $s(t)$, in feet, after $t$ seconds is given by

$$s(t) = -16t^2 + 48t + 8.$$

After how many seconds does the ball reach its maximum height? What is the maximum height?

**15.** An object moves in simple harmonic motion described by $d = 4\sin 5t$, where $t$ is measured in seconds and $d$ in meters. Find **a.** the maximum displacement; **b.** the frequency; and **c.** the time required for one cycle.

**16.** Use a half-angle formula to find the exact value of $\cos 22.5°$.

**17.** If $\mathbf{v} = 2\mathbf{i} + 7\mathbf{j}$ and $\mathbf{w} = \mathbf{i} - 2\mathbf{j}$, find: **a.** $3\mathbf{v} - \mathbf{w}$ and **b.** $\mathbf{v} \cdot \mathbf{w}$.

**18.** Express as a single logarithm with a coefficient of 1: $\frac{1}{2}\log_b x - \log_b(x^2 + 1)$.

**19.** Write the slope-intercept form of the line passing through $(4, -1)$ and $(-8, 5)$.

**20.** Psychologists can measure the amount learned, $L$, at time $t$ using the model $L = A(1 - e^{-kt})$. The variable $A$ represents the total amount to be learned, and $k$ is the learning rate. A student preparing for the SAT has 300 new vocabulary words to learn: $A = 300$. This particular student can learn 20 vocabulary words after 5 minutes: If $t = 5$, $L = 20$.
**a.** Find $k$, the learning rate, correct to three decimal places.
**b.** Approximately how many words will the student have learned after 20 minutes?
**c.** How long will it take for the student to learn 260 words?

# Systems of Equations and Inequalities

## Chapter 8

Most things in life depend on many variables. Temperature and precipitation are two variables that have a critical effect on whether regions are forests, grasslands, or deserts. Airlines deal with numerous variables during weather disruptions at large connecting airports. They must solve the problem of putting their operation back together again to minimize the cost of the disruption and passenger inconvenience. In this chapter, forests, grasslands, and airline service are viewed in the same way—situations with several variables. You will learn methods for modeling and solving problems in these situations.

A major weather disruption delayed your flight for hours, but you finally made it. You are in Yosemite National Park in California, surrounded by evergreen forests, alpine meadows, and sheer walls of granite. Soaring cliffs, plunging waterfalls, gigantic trees, rugged canyons, mountains and valleys stand in stark contrast to the angry chaos at the airport. This is so different from where you live and attend college, a region in which grasslands predominate.

# SECTION 8.1 Systems of Linear Equations in Two Variables

## Objectives

1. Decide whether an ordered pair is a solution of a linear system.
2. Solve linear systems by substitution.
3. Solve linear systems by addition.
4. Identify systems that do not have exactly one ordered-pair solution.
5. Solve problems using systems of linear equations.

Key West residents Brian Goss (left), George Wallace, and Michael Mooney (right) hold on to each other as they battle 90 mph winds along Houseboat Row in Key West, Fla., on Friday, Sept. 25, 1998. The three had sought shelter behind a Key West hotel as Hurricane Georges descended on the Florida Keys but were forced to seek other shelter when the storm conditions became too rough. Hundreds of people were killed by the storm when it swept through the Caribbean.

Real-world problems often involve solving thousands of equations, sometimes containing a million variables. Problems ranging from scheduling airline flights to controlling traffic flow to routing phone calls over the nation's communication network often require solutions in a matter of moments. AT&T's domestic long distance network involves 800,000 variables! Meteorologists describing atmospheric conditions surrounding a hurricane must solve problems involving thousands of equations rapidly and efficiently. The difference between a two-hour warning and a two-day warning is a life-and-death issue for thousands of people in the path of one of nature's most destructive forces.

Although we will not be solving 800,000 equations with 800,000 variables, we will turn our attention to two equations with two variables, such as

$$2x - 3y = -4$$
$$2x + y = 4.$$

The methods that we consider for solving such problems provide the foundation for solving far more complex systems with many variables.

**1** Decide whether an ordered pair is a solution of a linear system.

## Systems of Linear Equations and Their Solutions

We have seen that all equations in the form $Ax + By = C$ are straight lines when graphed. Two such equations, such as those listed above, are called a **system of linear equations**. A **solution to a system of linear equations** is an ordered pair that satisfies all equations in the system. For example, (3, 4) satisfies the system

$$x + y = 7 \quad (3 + 4 \text{ is, indeed, } 7.)$$
$$x - y = -1 \quad (3 - 4 \text{ is, indeed, } -1.)$$

Thus, (3, 4) satisfies both equations and is a solution of the system. The solution can be described by saying that $x = 3$ and $y = 4$. The solution can also be described using set notation. The solution set to the system is $\{(3, 4)\}$—that is, the set consisting of the ordered pair (3, 4).

A system of linear equations can have exactly one solution, no solution, or infinitely many solutions. We will focus on systems with exactly one solution.

## EXAMPLE 1 Determining Whether an Ordered Pair Is a Solution of a System

Determine whether $(4, -1)$ is a solution of the system

$$x + 2y = 2$$
$$x - 2y = 6.$$

**Solution** Because 4 is the $x$-coordinate and $-1$ is the $y$-coordinate of $(4, -1)$, we replace $x$ by 4 and $y$ by $-1$.

$$\begin{aligned} x + 2y &= 2 \\ 4 + 2(-1) &\stackrel{?}{=} 2 \\ 4 + (-2) &\stackrel{?}{=} 2 \\ 2 &= 2 \quad \text{true} \end{aligned} \qquad \begin{aligned} x - 2y &= 6 \\ 4 - 2(-1) &\stackrel{?}{=} 6 \\ 4 - (-2) &\stackrel{?}{=} 6 \\ 4 + 2 &\stackrel{?}{=} 6 \\ 6 &= 6 \quad \text{true} \end{aligned}$$

The pair $(4, -1)$ satisfies both equations: It makes each equation true. Thus, the pair is a solution of the system. The solution set to the system is $\{(4, -1)\}$.

The solution to a system of linear equations can be found by graphing both of the equations in the same rectangular coordinate system. For a system with one solution, the **coordinates of the point of intersection give the system's solution.** For example, the system in Example 1 is graphed in Figure 8.1. The solution of the system, $(4, -1)$, corresponds to the point of intersection of the lines.

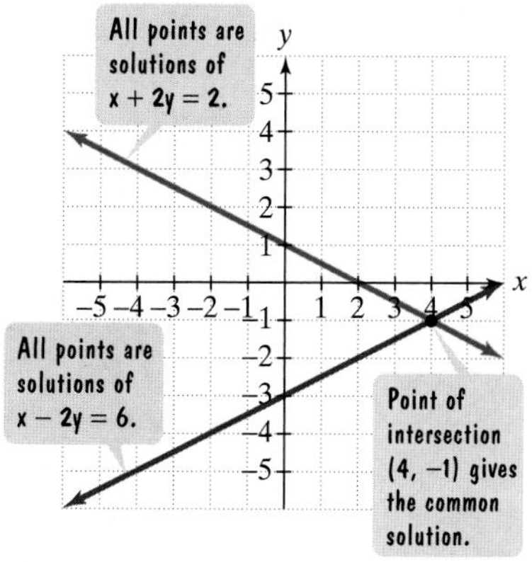


**Figure 8.1** Visualizing a system's solution.

**Check Point 1** Determine whether (1, 2) is a solution of the system

$$2x - 3y = -4$$
$$2x + y = 4.$$

**2** Solve linear systems by substitution.

## Eliminating a Variable Using the Substitution Method

Finding the solution to a linear system by graphing equations may not be easy to do. For example, a solution of $\left(-\frac{2}{3}, \frac{157}{29}\right)$ would be difficult to "see" as an intersection point on a graph.

Let's consider a method that does not depend on finding a system's solution visually: the substitution method. This method involves converting the system to one equation in one variable by an appropriate substitution.

### EXAMPLE 2 Solving a System by Substitution

Solve by the substitution method:

$$y = -x - 1$$
$$4x - 3y = 24.$$

**Solution**

**Step 1 Solve either of the equations for one variable in terms of the other.** This step has already been done for us. The first equation, $y = -x - 1$, has $y$ solved in terms of $x$.

**Step 2 Substitute the expression from step 1 into the other equation.** We substitute the expression $-x - 1$ for $y$ in the other equation:

$$y = \boxed{-x - 1} \qquad 4x - 3\boxed{y} = 24 \qquad \text{Substitute } -x - 1 \text{ for } y.$$

This gives us an equation in one variable, namely

$$4x - 3(-x - 1) = 24.$$

The variable $y$ has been eliminated.

**Step 3 Solve the resulting equation containing one variable.**

$$4x - 3(-x - 1) = 24 \quad \text{This is the equation containing one variable.}$$
$$4x + 3x + 3 = 24 \quad \text{Apply the distributive property.}$$
$$7x + 3 = 24 \quad \text{Combine like terms.}$$
$$7x = 21 \quad \text{Subtract 3 from both sides.}$$
$$x = 3 \quad \text{Divide both sides by 7.}$$

**Step 4 Back-substitute the obtained value into the equation from step 1.** We now know that the $x$-coordinate of the solution is 3. To find the $y$-coordinate, we back-substitute the $x$-value into the equation from step 1,

$$y = -x - 1.$$

Substitute 3 for $x$.

$$y = -3 - 1 = -4$$

With $x = 3$ and $y = -4$, the proposed solution is $(3, -4)$.

**Step 5 Check the proposed solution in both of the system's given equations.** Replace $x$ with 3 and $y$ with $-4$.

$$y = -x - 1 \qquad\qquad 4x - 3y = 24$$
$$-4 \stackrel{?}{=} -3 - 1 \qquad\qquad 4(3) - 3(-4) \stackrel{?}{=} 24$$
$$-4 = -4 \text{ true} \qquad\qquad 12 + 12 \stackrel{?}{=} 24$$
$$24 = 24 \text{ true}$$

**Technology**

A graphing utility can be used to solve the system in Example 2. Graph each equation and use the intersection feature. The utility displays the solution $(3, -4)$ as $x = 3$, $y = -4$.

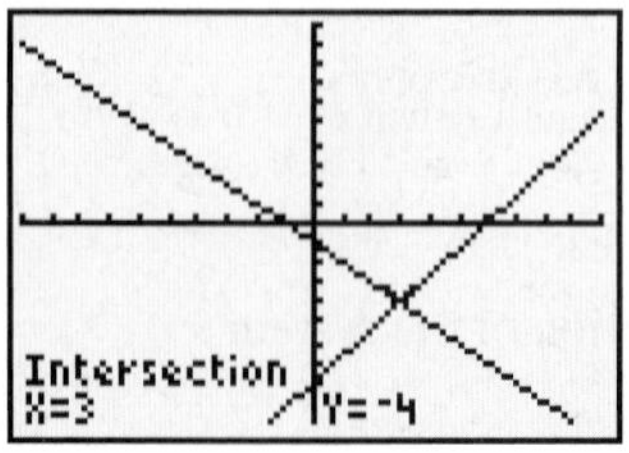

The pair $(3, -4)$ satisfies both equations. The system's solution set is $\{(3, -4)\}$.

**Check Point 2** Solve by the substitution method:

$$y = 5x - 13$$
$$2x + 3y = 12.$$

Before considering additional examples, let's summarize the steps used in the substitution method.

## Study Tip

In step 1, if possible, solve for a variable whose coefficient is 1 or $-1$ to avoid working with fractions.

### Solving Linear Systems by Substitution

1. Solve either of the equations for one variable in terms of the other. (If one of the equations is already in this form, you can skip this step.)
2. Substitute the expression found in step 1 into the other equation. This will result in an equation in one variable.
3. Solve the equation obtained in step 2.
4. Back-substitute the value found in step 3 into the equation from step 1. Simplify and find the value of the remaining variable.
5. Check the proposed solution in both of the system's given equations.

## EXAMPLE 3 Solving a System by Substitution

Solve by the substitution method:

$$5x - 4y = 9$$
$$x - 2y = -3.$$

### Solution

**Step 1 Solve either of the equations for one variable in terms of the other.** We begin by isolating one of the variables in either of the equations. By solving for $x$ in the second equation, which has a coefficient of 1, we can avoid fractions.

$$x - 2y = -3 \quad \text{This is the second equation in the given system.}$$
$$x = 2y - 3 \quad \text{Solve for x by adding 2y to both sides.}$$

**Step 2 Substitute the expression from step 1 into the other equation.** We substitute $2y - 3$ for $x$ in the first equation.

$$x = \boxed{2y - 3} \qquad 5\boxed{x} - 4y = 9$$

This gives us an equation in one variable, namely

$$5(2y - 3) - 4y = 9.$$

The variable $x$ has been eliminated.

**Step 3 Solve the resulting equation containing one variable.**

$$5(2y - 3) - 4y = 9 \quad \text{This is the equation containing one variable.}$$
$$10y - 15 - 4y = 9 \quad \text{Apply the distributive property.}$$
$$6y - 15 = 9 \quad \text{Combine like terms.}$$
$$6y = 24 \quad \text{Add 15 to both sides.}$$
$$y = 4 \quad \text{Divide both sides by 6.}$$

**Step 4 Back-substitute the obtained value into the equation from step 1.** Now that we have the $y$-coordinate of the solution, we back-substitute 4 for $y$ in the equation $x = 2y - 3$.

$$x = 2y - 3 \quad \text{Use the equation obtained in step 1.}$$
$$x = 2(4) - 3 \quad \text{Substitute 4 for } y.$$
$$x = 8 - 3 \quad \text{Multiply.}$$
$$x = 5 \quad \text{Subtract.}$$

**Study Tip**

Get into the habit of checking ordered-pair solutions in *both* equations of the system.

With $x = 5$ and $y = 4$, the proposed solution is $(5, 4)$.

**Step 5 Check.** Take a moment to show that $(5, 4)$ satisfies both given equations. The solution set is $\{(5, 4)\}$.

**Check Point 3** Solve by the substitution method:

$$3x + 2y = -1$$
$$x - y = 3.$$

**3** Solve linear systems by addition.

## Eliminating a Variable Using the Addition Method

The substitution method is most useful if one of the given equations has an isolated variable. A second, and frequently the easiest, method for solving a linear system is the addition method. Like the substitution method, the addition method involves eliminating a variable and ultimately solving an equation containing only one variable. However, this time we eliminate a variable by adding the equations.

For example, consider the following equations:

$$3x - 4y = 11$$
$$-3x + 2y = -7.$$

When we add these two equations, the $x$-terms are eliminated. This occurs because the coefficients of the $x$-terms, 3 and $-3$, are opposites (additive inverses) of each other:

$$\begin{aligned} 3x - 4y &= 11 \\ -3x + 2y &= -7 \\ \hline \text{Add:} \qquad -2y &= 4 \\ y &= -2 \quad \text{Solve for } y \text{, dividing both sides by } -2. \end{aligned}$$

Now we can back-substitute $-2$ for $y$ into one of the original equations to find $x$. It does not matter which equation you use; you will obtain the same value for $x$ in either case. If we use either equation, we can show that $x = 1$ and the solution $(1, -2)$ satisfies both equations in the system.

When we use the addition method, we want to obtain two equations whose sum is an equation containing only one variable. The key step is to obtain, for one of the variables, coefficients that differ only in sign. In order to do this, we may need to multiply one or both equations by some nonzero number so that the coefficients of one of the variables, $x$ or $y$, become opposites. Then when the two equations are added, this variable is eliminated. Let's see exactly how this works by considering Example 4.

## EXAMPLE 4 Solving a System by the Addition Method

Solve by the addition method:

$$3x + 2y = 48$$
$$9x - 8y = -24.$$

**Solution** We must rewrite one or both equations in equivalent forms so that the coefficients of the same variable (either $x$ or $y$) are opposites of each other. Consider the terms in $x$ in each equation, that is, $3x$ and $9x$. To eliminate $x$, we can multiply each term of the first equation by $-3$ and then add the equations.

$$3x + 2y = 48 \xrightarrow{\text{Multiply by } -3.} -9x - 6y = -144$$
$$9x - 8y = -24 \xrightarrow{\text{No change}} \underline{9x - 8y = -24}$$
$$\text{Add:} \quad -14y = -168$$
$$y = 12 \quad \text{Solve for } y\text{, dividing both sides by } -14.$$

Thus, $y = 12$. We back-substitute this value into either one of the given equations. We'll use the first one.

$$3x + 2y = 48 \quad \text{This the first equation in the given system.}$$
$$3x + 2(12) = 48 \quad \text{Substitute 12 for } y.$$
$$3x + 24 = 48 \quad \text{Multiply.}$$
$$3x = 24 \quad \text{Subtract 24 from both sides.}$$
$$x = 8 \quad \text{Divide both sides by 3.}$$

The solution (8, 12) can be shown to satisfy both equations in the system. Consequently, the solution set is $\{(8, 12)\}$.

### Solving Linear Systems by Addition

1. If necessary, rewrite both equations in the form $Ax + By = C$.
2. If necessary, multiply either equation or both equations by appropriate nonzero numbers so that the sum of the $x$-coefficients or the sum of the $y$-coefficients is 0.
3. Add the equations in step 2. The sum is an equation in one variable.
4. Solve the equation from step 3.
5. Back-substitute the value obtained in step 4 into either of the given equations and solve for the other variable.
6. Check the solution in both of the original equations.

**Check Point 4** Solve by the addition method:

$$4x + 5y = 3$$
$$2x - 3y = 7.$$

Some linear systems have solutions that are not integers. If the value of one variable turns out to be a "messy" fraction, back-substitution might lead to cumbersome arithmetic. If this happens, you can return to the original system and use addition to find the value of the other variable.

## EXAMPLE 5 Solving a System by the Addition Method

Solve by the addition method:

$$2x = 7y - 17$$
$$5y = 17 - 3x.$$

### Solution

**Step 1 Rewrite both equations in the form $Ax + By = C$.** We first arrange the system so that variable terms appear on the left and constants appear on the right. We obtain

$$2x - 7y = -17 \quad \text{Subtract } 7y \text{ from both sides of the first equation.}$$
$$3x + 5y = 17 \quad \text{Add } 3x \text{ to both sides of the second equation.}$$

**Step 2 If necessary, multiply either equation or both equations by appropriate numbers so that the sum of the $x$-coefficients or the sum of the $y$-coefficients is 0.** We can eliminate $x$ or $y$. Let's eliminate $x$ by multiplying the first equation by 3 and the second equation by −2.

$$2x - 7y = -17 \xrightarrow{\text{Multiply by 3.}} 3 \cdot 2x - 3 \cdot 7y = 3(-17) \longrightarrow 6x - 21y = -51$$
$$3x + 5y = 17 \xrightarrow{\text{Multiply by } -2.} -2 \cdot 3x + (-2) \cdot 5y = -2(17) \longrightarrow -6x - 10y = -34$$

**Steps 3 and 4 Add the equations and solve for the remaining variable.**

$$\begin{aligned} 6x - 21y &= -51 \\ -6x - 10y &= -34 \\ \hline \text{Add:} \quad -31y &= -85 \end{aligned}$$

$$\frac{-31y}{-31} = \frac{-85}{-31} \quad \text{Divide both sides by } -31.$$

$$y = \frac{85}{31} \quad \text{Simplify.}$$

**Step 5 Back-substitute and find the value for the other variable.** Back-substitution of $\frac{85}{31}$ for $y$ into either of the given equations results in cumbersome arithmetic. Instead, let's use the addition method on the given system in the form $Ax + By = C$ to find the value for $x$. Thus, we eliminate $y$ by multiplying the first equation by 5 and the second equation by 7.

$$2x - 7y = -17 \xrightarrow{\text{Multiply by 5.}} 10x - 35y = -85$$
$$3x + 5y = 17 \xrightarrow{\text{Multiply by 7.}} 21x + 35y = 119$$

$$\text{Add:} \quad 31x = 34$$

$$x = \frac{34}{31} \quad \text{Divide both sides by 31.}$$

**Step 6 Check.** For this system, a calculator is helpful in showing the solution $\left(\frac{34}{31}, \frac{85}{31}\right)$ satisfies both equations. Consequently, the solution set is $\left\{\left(\frac{34}{31}, \frac{85}{31}\right)\right\}$.

**Check Point 5** Solve by the addition method:

$$4x = 5 + 2y$$
$$3y = 4 - 2x.$$

**4** Identify systems that do not have exactly one ordered-pair solution.

## Linear Systems Having No Solution or Infinitely Many Solutions

We have seen that a system of linear equations in two variables represents a pair of lines. The lines either intersect, are parallel, or are identical. Thus, there are three possibilities for the number of solutions to a system of two linear equations.

**The Number of Solutions to a System of Two Linear Equations**

The number of solutions to a system of two linear equations in two variables is given by one of the following. (See Figure 8.2.)

| Number of Solutions | What This Means Graphically |
|---|---|
| Exactly one ordered-pair solution | The two lines intersect at one point. |
| No solution | The two lines are parallel. |
| Infinitely many solutions | The two lines are identical. |

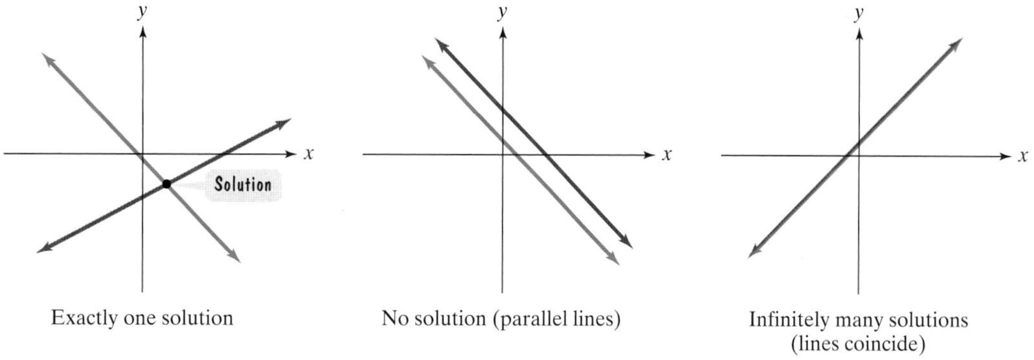


**Figure 8.2** Possible graphs for a system of two linear equations in two variables

A linear system with no solution is called an **inconsistent system**. If you attempt to solve such a system by substitution or addition, you will eliminate both variables. A false statement such as $0 = 17$ will be the result.

### EXAMPLE 6 A System with No Solution

Solve the system:

$$4x + 6y = 12$$
$$6x + 9y = 12.$$

**Solution** Because no variable is isolated, we will use the addition method. To obtain coefficients of $x$ that differ only in sign, we multiply the first equation by 3 and multiply the second equation by $-2$.

$$\begin{aligned} 4x + 6y &= 12 \quad \xrightarrow{\text{Multiply by 3.}} & 12x + 18y &= 36 \\ 6x + 9y &= 12 \quad \xrightarrow{\text{Multiply by } -2.} & -12x - 18y &= -24 \\ & \text{Add:} & 0 &= 12 \end{aligned}$$

There are no values of x and y for which $0 = 12$.

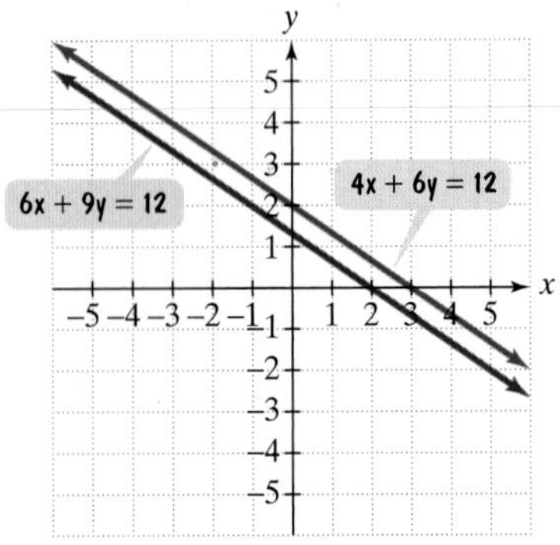


**Figure 8.3** The graph of an inconsistent system

The false statement $0 = 12$ indicates that the system is inconsistent and has no solution. The solution set is the empty set, $\varnothing$.

The lines corresponding to the two equations in Example 6 are shown in Figure 8.3. The lines are parallel and have no point of intersection.

## Discovery

Show that the graphs of $4x + 6y = 12$ and $6x + 9y = 12$ must be parallel lines by solving each equation for $y$. What is the slope and $y$-intercept for each line? What does this mean? If a linear system is inconsistent, what must be true about the slopes and $y$-intercepts for the system's graphs?

**Check Point 6** Solve the system:

$$\begin{aligned} x + 2y &= 4 \\ 3x + 6y &= 13. \end{aligned}$$

A linear system that has at least one solution is called a **consistent system.** Lines that intersect and lines that coincide both represent consistent systems. If the lines coincide, then the consistent system has infinitely many solutions, represented by every point on the line.

The equations in a linear system with infinitely many solutions are called **dependent.** If you attempt to solve such a system by substitution or addition, you will eliminate both variables. However, a true statement such as $0 = 0$ will be the result.

## EXAMPLE 7 A System with Infinitely Many Solutions

Solve the system:

$$\begin{aligned} y &= 3 - 2x \\ 4x + 2y &= 6. \end{aligned}$$

**Solution** Because the variable $y$ is isolated in the first equation, we can use the substitution method. We substitute the expression for $y$ in the other equation.

$y = \boxed{3 - 2x} \quad 4x + 2\boxed{y} = 6$ Substitute $3 - 2x$ for $y$.

| | |
|---|---|
| $4x + 2y = 6$ | This is the second equation in the given system. |
| $4x + 2(3 - 2x) = 6$ | Substitute $3 - 2x$ for $y$. |
| $4x + 6 - 4x = 6$ | Apply the distributive property. |
| $6 = 6$ | Simplify. This statement is true for all values of $x$ and $y$. |

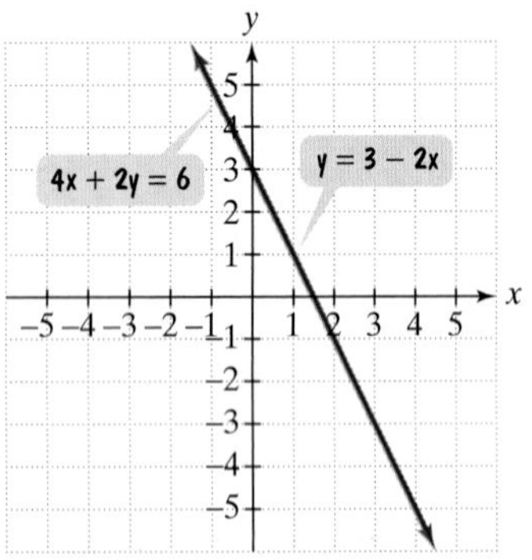


**Figure 8.4** The graph of a system with infinitely many solutions

In our final step, both variables have been eliminated, and the resulting statement $6 = 6$ is true. This true statement indicates that the system has infinitely many solutions. The solution set consists of all points $(x, y)$ lying on the line $y = 3 - 2x$, as shown in Figure 8.4.

We express the solution set for the system in one of two equivalent ways:

$\{(x, y) \mid y = 3 - 2x\}$ The set of all ordered pairs (x, y) such that y = 3 − 2x.

or $\{(x, y) \mid 4x + 2y = 6\}$ The set of all ordered pairs (x, y) such that 4x + 2y = 6.

**Check Point 7** Solve the system:

$$y = 4x - 4$$
$$8x - 2y = 8.$$

**5** Solve problems using systems of linear equations.

## Applications

An important application of systems of equations arises in connection with supply and demand. As the price of a product increases, the demand for that product decreases. However, at higher prices suppliers are willing to produce greater quantities of the product.

### EXAMPLE 8 Supply and Demand Models

A chain of video stores specializes in cult films. The weekly demand and supply models for *The Rocky Horror Picture Show* are given by

$$N = -13p + 760 \quad \text{Demand model}$$
$$N = 2p + 430 \quad \text{Supply model}$$

in which $p$ is the price of the video and $N$ is the number of copies of the video sold or supplied each week to the chain of stores.

**a.** How many copies of the video can be sold and supplied at \$18 per copy?

**b.** Find the price at which supply and demand are equal. At this price, how many copies of *Rocky Horror* can be supplied and sold each week?

**Solution**

**a.** To find how many copies of the video can be sold and supplied at \$18 per copy, we substitute 18 for $p$ in the demand and supply models.

| Demand Model | Supply Model |
|---|---|
| $N = -13p + 760$ | $N = 2p + 430$ |
| Substitute 18 for $p$. | Substitute 18 for $p$. |
| $N = -13 \cdot 18 + 760 = 526$ | $N = 2 \cdot 18 + 430 = 466$ |

At \$18 per video, the chain can sell 526 copies of *Rocky Horror* in a week. The manufacturer is willing to supply 466 copies per week. This will result in a shortage of copies of the video. Under these conditions, the retail chain is likely to raise the price of the video.

**b.** We can find the price at which supply and demand are equal by solving the demand-supply linear system. We will use substitution, substituting $-13p + 760$ for $N$ in the second equation.

$N = \boxed{-13p + 760} \quad \boxed{N} = 2p + 430$ Substitute $-13p + 760$ for $N$.

$-13p + 760 = 2p + 430$ The resulting equation contains only one variable.

$-15p + 760 = 430$ Subtract $2p$ from both sides.

$-15p = -330$ Subtract 760 from both sides.

$p = 22$ Divide both sides by $-15$.

The price at which supply and demand are equal is $22 per video. To find the value of $N$, the number of videos supplied and sold weekly at this price, we back-substitute 22 for $p$ into either the demand or the supply model. We'll use both models to make sure we get the same number in each case.

**Demand Model**

$N = -13p + 760$

Substitute 22 for $p$.

$N = -13 \cdot 22 + 760 = 474$

**Supply Model**

$N = 2p + 430$

Substitute 22 for $p$.

$N = 2 \cdot 22 + 430 = 474$

At a price of $22, 474 units of the video can be supplied and sold weekly. The intersection point, (22, 474), is shown in Figure 8.5.

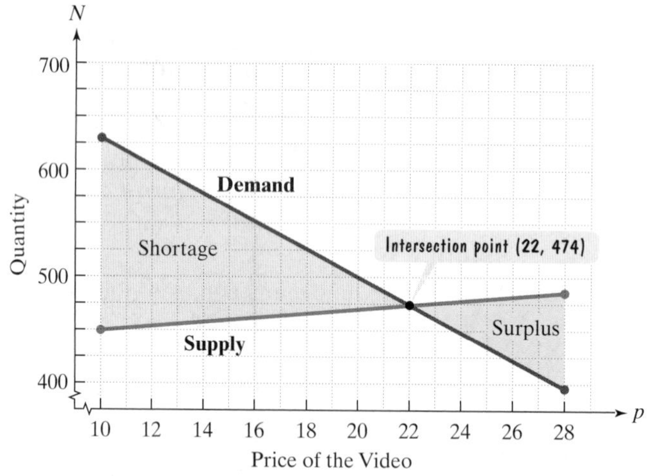


**Figure 8.5** Priced at $22, 474 copies of the video can be supplied and sold weekly.

**Check Point 8**

The demand for a product is modeled by $N = -20p + 1000$ and the supply for the product by $N = 5p + 250$. In these models, $p$ is the price of the product and $N$ is the number supplied or sold weekly. At what price will supply equal demand? At that price, how many units of the product will be supplied and sold each week?

## EXERCISE SET 8.1

### Practice Exercises

*In Exercises 1–4, determine whether the given ordered pair is a solution of the system.*

**1.** (2, 3)
$x + 3y = 11$
$x - 5y = -13$

**2.** (−3, 5)
$9x + 7y = 8$
$8x - 9y = -69$

**3.** (2, 5)
$2x + 3y = 17$
$x + 4y = 16$

**4.** (8, 5)
$5x - 4y = 20$
$3y = 2x + 1$

*In Exercises 5–16, solve each system by the substitution method.*

**5.** $x + y = 4$
$y = 3x$

**6.** $x + y = 6$
$y = 2x$

**7.** $x + 3y = 8$
$y = 2x - 9$

**8.** $2x - 3y = -13$
$y = 2x + 7$

**9.** $x + 3y = 5$
$4x + 5y = 13$

**10.** $x + 2y = 5$
$2x - y = -15$

**11.** $2x - y = -5$
$x + 5y = 14$

**12.** $2x + 3y = 11$
$x - 4y = 0$

**13.** $2x - y = 3$
$5x - 2y = 10$

**14.** $-x + 3y = 10$
$2x + 8y = -6$

**15.** $x + 8y = 6$
$2x + 4y = -3$

**16.** $-4x + y = -11$
$2x - 3y = 5$

*In Exercises 17–28, solve each system by the addition method.*

**17.** $x + y = 1$
$x - y = 3$

**18.** $x + y = 6$
$x - y = -2$

**19.** $2x + 3y = 6$
$2x - 3y = 6$

**20.** $3x + 2y = 14$
$3x - 2y = 10$

**21.** $x + 2y = 2$
$-4x + 3y = 25$

**22.** $2x - 7y = 2$
$3x + y = -20$

**23.** $4x + 3y = 15$
$2x - 5y = 1$

**24.** $3x - 7y = 13$
$6x + 5y = 7$

**25.** $3x - 4y = 11$
$2x + 3y = -4$

**26.** $2x + 3y = -16$
$5x - 10y = 30$

**27.** $3x = 4y + 1$
$3y = 1 - 4x$

**28.** $5x = 6y + 40$
$2y = 8 - 3x$

*In Exercises 29–36, solve by the method of your choice. Identify systems with no solution and systems with infinitely many solutions, using set notation to express their solution sets.*

**29.** $x = 9 - 2y$
$x + 2y = 13$

**30.** $6x + 2y = 7$
$y = 2 - 3x$

**31.** $y = 3x - 5$
$21x - 35 = 7y$

**32.** $9x - 3y = 12$
$y = 3x - 4$

**33.** $3x - 2y = -5$
$4x + y = 8$

**34.** $2x + 5y = -4$
$3x - y = 11$

**35.** $x + 3y = 2$
$3x + 9y = 6$

**36.** $4x - 2y = 2$
$2x - y = 1$

*In Exercises 37–40, let x represent one number and let y represent the other number. Use the given conditions to write a system of equations. Solve the system and find the numbers.*

**37.** The sum of two numbers is 7. If one number is subtracted from the other, their difference is −1. Find the numbers.

**38.** The sum of two numbers is 2. If one number is subtracted from the other, their difference is 8. Find the numbers.

**39.** Three times a first number decreased by a second number is 1. The first number increased by twice the second number is 12. Find the numbers.

**40.** The sum of three times a first number and twice a second number is 8. If the second number is subtracted from twice the first number, the result is 3. Find the numbers.

### Application Exercises

**41.** At a price of $p$ dollars per ticket, the number of tickets to a rock concert that can be sold is given by the demand model $N = -25p + 7500$. At a price of $p$ dollars per ticket, the number of tickets that the concert's promoters are willing to make available is given by the supply model $N = 5p + 6000$.

**a.** How many tickets can be sold and supplied for $40 per ticket?

**b.** Find the ticket price at which supply and demand are equal. At this price, how many tickets will be supplied and sold?

**42.** The weekly demand and supply models for a particular brand of scientific calculator for a chain of stores are given by the demand model $N = -53p + 1600$, and the supply model $N = 75p + 320$. In these models, $p$ is the price of the calculator and $N$ is the number of calculators sold or supplied each week to the stores.

**a.** How many calculators can be sold and supplied at \$12 per calculator?

**b.** Find the price at which supply and demand are equal. At this price, how many calculators of this type can be supplied and sold each week?

*A business breaks even when the cost for running the business is equal to the money taken in by the business. In Exercises 43–44, determine how many units must be sold so that a business breaks even, experiencing neither loss nor profit.*

**43.** A gasoline station has weekly costs and revenue (the money taken in by the station) that are functions of the number of gallons of gasoline purchased and sold. If $x$ gallons are purchased and sold, weekly costs are given by $C(x) = 1.2x + 1080$ and weekly revenue by $R(x) = 1.6x$. How many gallons of gasoline must be sold weekly for the station to break even?

**44.** An artist has monthly costs and revenue (the money taken in by the artist) that are functions of the number of ceramic pieces produced and sold. If $x$ ceramic pieces are produced and sold, monthly costs are given by $C(x) = 4x + 2000$ and monthly revenue by $R(x) = 9x$. How many ceramic pieces must be sold monthly for the artist to break even?

*Use a system of linear equations to solve Exercises 45–48.*

**45.** The verdict is in: After years of research, the nation's health experts agree that high cholesterol in the blood is a major contributor to heart disease. Cholesterol intake should be limited to 300 mg or less each day. Fast foods provide a cholesterol carnival. Two McDonald's Quarter Pounders and three Burger King Whoppers with cheese contain 520 mg of cholesterol. Three Quarter Pounders and one Whopper with cheese exceed the suggested daily cholesterol intake by 53 mg. Determine the cholesterol content in each item.

**46.** How do the Quarter Pounder and Whopper with cheese measure up in the calorie department? Actually, not too well. Two Quarter Pounders and three Whoppers with cheese provide 2607 calories. Even one of each provide enough calories to bring tears to Jenny Craig's eyes—9 calories in excess of what is allowed on a 1000 calorie-a-day diet. Find the caloric content of each item.

**47.** The graph at the top of the next column makes Super Bowl Sunday look like a day of snack food binging in the United States. The number of pounds of guacamole consumed is ten times the difference between the number of pounds of potato and tortilla chips eaten on the same day. On Super Bowl Sunday Americans also eat a total quantity of potato and tortilla chips that exceeds popcorn consumption by 7.3 million pounds. How many millions of pounds of potato chips and tortilla chips are consumed on Super Bowl Sunday?

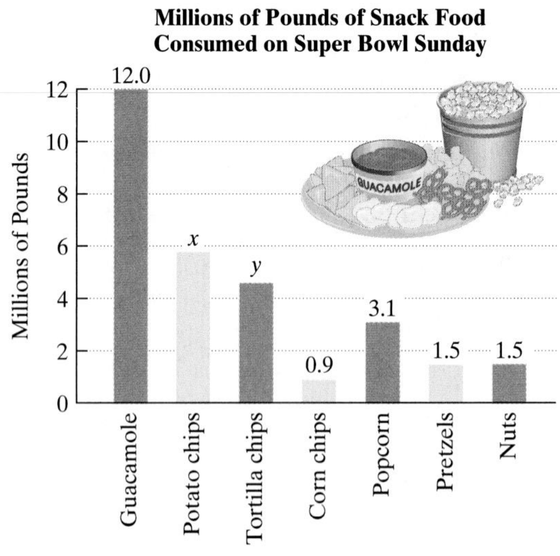


*Source*: Association of American Snack Foods

**48.** The bar graph indicates countries in which ten or more languages have become extinct. The number of extinct languages in Brazil is 7.5 times the difference between the number in the United States and Colombia. The number of extinct languages in the United States and Colombia combined exceeds the number in Australia by 24. How many languages have become extinct in the United States and Colombia?

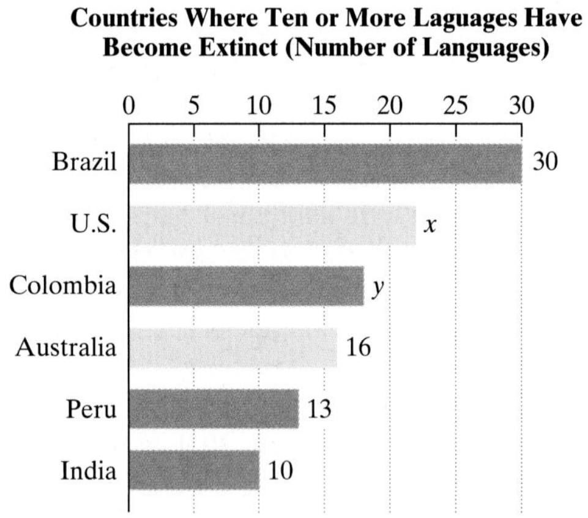


*Source*: Grimes

**49.** The June 7, 1999 issue of *Newsweek* presents statistics showing progress African Americans have made in education, health, and finance. Infant mortality for blacks is decreasing at a faster rate than it is for whites, shown by the graphs on page 429. Infant mortality for blacks can be modeled by $M = -0.41x + 22$ and for whites by $M = -0.18x + 10$. In both models, $x$ is the number of years since 1980 and $M$ is infant mortality, measured in deaths per 1000 live births. Use these models to project when infant mortality for blacks and whites will be the same. What is infant mortality for both groups at that time?

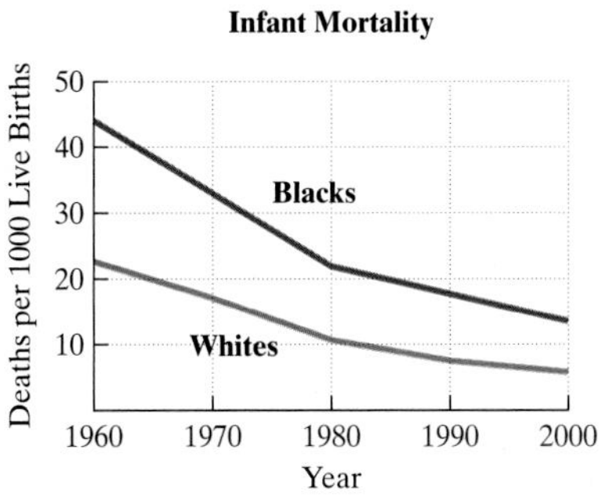


*Source*: National Center for Health Statistics

**50.** The equation $x + 10y = 2120$ models deaths from gunfire in the United States, $y$, in deaths per hundred thousand Americans, in year $x$. The equation $7x + 8y = 14{,}065$ models deaths from car accidents in the United States, $y$, in deaths per hundred thousand Americans, in year $x$. Solve the linear system formed by the two models. Then describe what the solution means in terms of the variables in the given models.

## Writing in Mathematics

**51.** What is a system of linear equations? Provide an example with your description.

**52.** What is the solution to a system of linear equations?

**53.** Explain how to solve a system of equations using the substitution method. Use $y = 3 - 3x$ and $3x + 4y = 6$ to illustrate your explanation.

**54.** Explain how to solve a system of equations using the addition method. Use $3x + 5y = -2$ and $2x + 3y = 0$ to illustrate your explanation.

**55.** When is it easier to use the addition method rather than the substitution method when solving a system of equations?

**56.** When using the addition or substitution method, how can you tell if a system of linear equations has infinitely many solutions? What is the relationship between the graphs of the two equations?

**57.** When using the addition or substitution method, how can you tell if a system of linear equations has no solution? What is the relationship between the graphs of the two equations?

**58.** The law of supply and demand states that, in a free market economy, a commodity tends to be sold at its equilibrium price. At this price, the amount that the seller will supply is the same amount that the consumer will buy. Explain how systems of equations can be used to determine the equilibrium price.

**59.** The graphs at the top of the next column show median weekly earnings of full-time wage and salary workers 25 years and older, by education attainment. Which graphs look like they might intersect sometime after 1997? Describe how to use algebra to model the data and determine the year in which the groups might have the same weekly earnings.

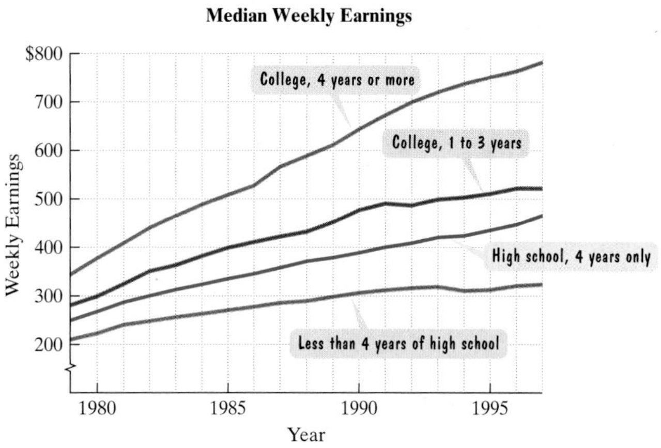


*Source*: U.S. Bureau of Labor Statistics

## Technology Exercises

**60.** Verify your solutions to any five exercises from 5 through 36 by using a graphing utility to graph the two equations in the system in the same viewing rectangle. Then use the intersection feature to display the solution.

**61.** Some graphing utilities can give the solution to a linear system of equations. (Consult your manual for details.) This capability is usually accessed with the SIMULT (simultaneous equations) feature. First, you will enter 2, for two equations in two variables. With each equation in $Ax + By = C$ form, you will then enter the coefficients for $x$ and $y$ and the constant term, one equation at a time. After entering all six numbers, press SOLVE. The solution will be displayed on the screen. (The $x$-value may be displayed as $x_1 =$ and the $y$-value as $x_2 =$.) Use this capability to verify the solution to any five of the exercises you solved in the practice exercises of this exercise set. Describe what happens when you use your graphing utility on a system with no solution or infinitely many solutions.

## Critical Thinking Exercises

**62.** Write a system of equations having $\{(-2, 7)\}$ as a solution set. (More than one system is possible.)

**63.** Solve the system for $x$ and $y$ in terms of $a_1, b_1, c_1, a_2, b_2$, and $c_2$:

$$a_1x + b_1y = c_1$$
$$a_2x + b_2y = c_2.$$

**64.** Two identical twins can only be recognized by the characteristic that one always tells the truth and the other always lies. One twin tells you of a lucky number pair: "When I multiply my first lucky number by 3 and my second lucky number by 6, the addition of the resulting numbers produces a sum of 12. When I add my first lucky number and twice my second lucky number, the sum is 5." Which twin is talking?

**65.** A marching band has 52 members, and there are 24 in the pom-pom squad. They wish to form several hexagons and squares like those diagrammed below. Can it be done with no people left over?

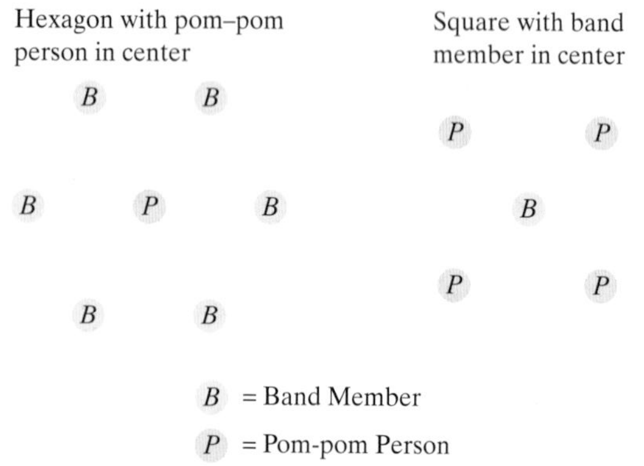


## Group Exercise

**66.** The group should write four different word problems that can be solved using a system of linear equations in two variables. All of the problems should be on different topics. Select from the following topics: a number problem (see Exercises 37–40); a problem using supply and demand models (see Exercises 41–42); a problem involving a business breaking even (see Exercises 43–44); a problem based on two missing numbers in a graph (see Exercises 47–48; you'll need to find an interesting graph); a problem involving linear modeling, finding the year when the quantity modeled will be the same for two groups (see Exercise 49). Of course, you can also base the problem on any topic of interest, but remember—only one problem per topic. The group should turn in the four problems and their algebraic solutions.

# SECTION 8.2 Systems of Linear Equations in Three Variables

## Objectives

1. Verify the solution of a linear system in three variables.
2. Solve linear systems in three variables.
3. Solve problems using systems in three variables.

All animals sleep, but the length of time they sleep varies widely: Cattle sleep for only a few minutes at a time. We humans seem to need more sleep than other animals, up to eight hours a day. Without enough sleep, we have difficulty concentrating, make mistakes in routine tasks, lose energy, and feel bad-tempered. There is a relationship between hours of sleep and death rate per year per 100,000 people. How many hours of sleep will put you in the group with the minimum death rate? In this section you will learn how to solve linear systems with more than two variables in order to answer this question.

1 Verify the solution of a linear system in three variables.

## Systems of Linear Equations in Three Variables and Their Solutions

An equation such as $x + 2y - 3z = 9$ is called a **linear equation in three variables**. In general, any equation of the form

$$Ax + By + Cz = D$$

where $A, B, C,$ and $D$ are real numbers such that $A, B,$ and $C$ are not all 0, is a linear equation in the variables $x$, $y$, and $z$. The graph of this linear equation in three variables is a plane in three-dimensional space.

The process of solving a system of three linear equations in three variables is geometrically equivalent to finding the point of intersection (assuming that there is one) of three planes in space (see Figure 8.6). A **solution** to a system of linear equations in three variables is an ordered triple of real numbers that satisfies all equations of the system. The **solution set** of the system is the set of all its solutions.

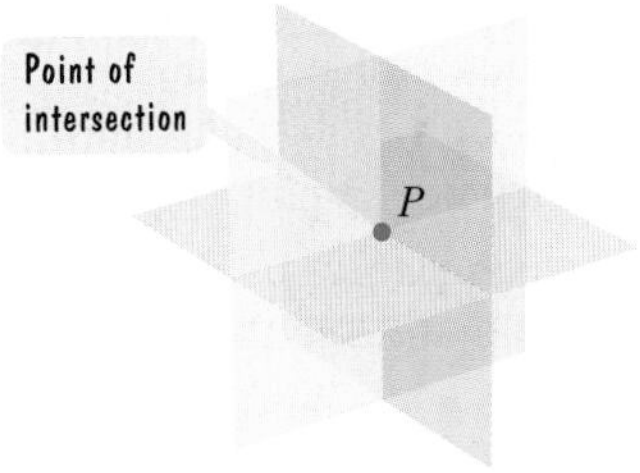


**Figure 8.6**

### EXAMPLE 1 Determining Whether an Ordered Triple Satisfies a System

Show that the ordered triple $(-1, 2, -2)$ is a solution of the system:

$$\begin{aligned} x + 2y - 3z &= 9 \\ 2x - y + 2z &= -8 \\ -x + 3y - 4z &= 15. \end{aligned}$$

**Solution** Because $-1$ is the $x$-coordinate, 2 is the $y$-coordinate, and $-2$ is the $z$-coordinate of $(-1, 2, -2)$, we replace $x$ by $-1$, $y$ by 2, and $z$ by $-2$ in each of the three equations.

$$\begin{aligned} x + 2y - 3z &= 9 \\ -1 + 2(2) - 3(-2) &\stackrel{?}{=} 9 \\ -1 + 4 + 6 &\stackrel{?}{=} 9 \\ 9 &= 9 \quad \text{true} \end{aligned}$$

$$\begin{aligned} 2x - y + 2z &= -8 \\ 2(-1) - 2 + 2(-2) &\stackrel{?}{=} -8 \\ -2 - 2 - 4 &\stackrel{?}{=} -8 \\ -8 &= -8 \quad \text{true} \end{aligned}$$

$$\begin{aligned} -x + 3y - 4z &= 15 \\ -(-1) + 3(2) - 4(-2) &\stackrel{?}{=} 15 \\ 1 + 6 + 8 &\stackrel{?}{=} 15 \\ 15 &= 15 \quad \text{true} \end{aligned}$$

The ordered triple $(-1, 2, -2)$ satisfies the three equations: It makes each equation true. Thus, the ordered triple is a solution of the system. The solution set to the system is $\{(-1, 2, -2)\}$.

**Check Point 1** Show that the ordered triple $(-1, -4, 5)$ is a solution of the system:

$$\begin{aligned} x - 2y + 3z &= 22 \\ 2x - 3y - z &= 5 \\ 3x + y - 5z &= -32. \end{aligned}$$

2 Solve linear systems in three variables.

## Solving Systems of Linear Equations in Three Variables by Eliminating Variables

The method for solving a system of linear equations in three variables is similar to that used on systems of linear equations in two variables. We use addition to eliminate any variable, reducing the system to two equations in two variables.

Once we obtain a system of two equations in two variables, we use addition or substitution to eliminate a variable. The result is a single equation in one variable. We solve this equation to get the value of the remaining variable. Other variable values are found by back-substitution.

**Solving Linear Systems in Three Variables by Eliminating Variables**

1. Reduce the system to two equations in two variables. This is usually accomplished by taking two different pairs of equations and using the addition method to eliminate the same variable from each pair.
2. Solve the resulting system of two equations in two variables using addition or substitution. The result is an equation in one variable that gives the value of that variable.
3. Back-substitute the value of the variable found in step 2 into either of the equations in two variables to find the value of the second variable.
4. Use the values of the two variables from steps 2 and 3 to find the value of the third variable by back-substituting into one of the original equations.
5. Check the proposed solution in each of the original equations.

## EXAMPLE 2 Solving a System in Three Variables

Solve the system:

$$\begin{aligned} 5x - 2y - 4z &= 3 && \text{Equation 1} \\ 3x + 3y + 2z &= -3 && \text{Equation 2} \\ -2x + 5y + 3z &= 3. && \text{Equation 3} \end{aligned}$$

**Solution** There are many ways to proceed. Because our initial goal is to reduce the system to two equations in two variables, **the central idea is to take two different pairs of equations and eliminate the same variable from each pair.**

**Step 1 Reduce the system to two equations in two variables.** We choose any two equations and use the addition method to eliminate a variable. Let's eliminate $z$ from Equations 1 and 2. We do so by multiplying Equation 2 by 2. Then we add equations.

$$\begin{aligned} &(\text{Equation 1})\ 5x - 2y - 4z = 3 \xrightarrow{\text{No change}} & 5x - 2y - 4z &= 3 \\ &(\text{Equation 2})\ 3x + 3y + 2z = -3 \xrightarrow{\text{Multiply by 2.}} & 6x + 6y + 4z &= -6 \\ & & \text{Add: } 11x + 4y \quad &= -3 \quad \text{Equation 4} \end{aligned}$$

Now we must eliminate the *same* variable from another pair of equations. We can eliminate $z$ from Equations 2 and 3. First, we multiply Equation 2 by −3. Next, we multiply Equation 3 by 2. Finally, we add equations.

$$\begin{aligned} &(\text{Equation 2})\ 3x + 3y + 2z = -3 \xrightarrow{\text{Multiply by } -3.} & -9x - 9y - 6z &= 9 \\ &(\text{Equation 3})\ -2x + 5y + 3z = 3 \xrightarrow{\text{Multiply by 2.}} & -4x + 10y + 6z &= 6 \\ & & \text{Add: } -13x + y \quad &= 15 \quad \text{Equation 5} \end{aligned}$$

Equations 4 and 5 give us a system of two equations in two variables.

**Step 2 Solve the resulting system of two equations in two variables.** We will use the addition method to solve Equations 4 and 5 for $x$ and $y$. To do so, we multiply Equation 5 on both sides by $-4$ and add this to Equation 4.

$$\begin{array}{lrcl} \text{(Equation 4)} & 11x + 4y = -3 & \xrightarrow{\text{No change}} & 11x + 4y = -3 \\ \text{(Equation 5)} & -13x + y = 15 & \xrightarrow{\text{Multiply by } -4.} & \underline{52x - 4y = -60} \\ & & \text{Add:} & 63x \quad = -63 \\ & & & x \quad = -1 \quad \text{Divide both sides by 63.} \end{array}$$

**Step 3 Use back-substitution in one of the equations in two variables to find the value of the second variable.** We back-substitute $-1$ for $x$ in either Equation 4 or 5 to find the value of $y$.

$$-13x + y = 15 \quad \text{Equation 5}$$
$$-13(-1) + y = 15 \quad \text{Substitute } -1 \text{ for } x.$$
$$13 + y = 15 \quad \text{Multiply.}$$
$$y = 2 \quad \text{Subtract 13 from both sides.}$$

**Step 4 Back-substitute the values found for two variables into one of the original equations to find the value of the third variable.** We can now use any one of the original equations and back-substitute the values of $x$ and $y$ to find the value for $z$. We will use Equation 2.

$$3x + 3y + 2z = -3 \quad \text{Equation 2}$$
$$3(-1) + 3(2) + 2z = -3 \quad \text{Substitute } -1 \text{ for } x \text{ and } 2 \text{ for } y.$$
$$3 + 2z = -3 \quad \text{Multiply and then add.}$$
$$2z = -6 \quad \text{Subtract 3 from both sides.}$$
$$z = -3 \quad \text{Divide both sides by 2.}$$

With $x = -1$, $y = 2$, and $z = -3$, the proposed solution is the ordered triple $(-1, 2, -3)$.

**Step 5 Check.** Check the proposed solution, $(-1, 2, -3)$, by substituting the values for $x$, $y$, and $z$ into each of the three original equations. These substitutions yield three true statements. Thus, the solution set is $\{(-1, 2, -3)\}$.

**Check Point 2** Solve the system:

$$\begin{aligned} x + 4y - z &= 20 \\ 3x + 2y + z &= 8 \\ 2x - 3y + 2z &= -16. \end{aligned}$$

In some examples, one of the variables is already eliminated from an original equation. In this case, the same variable should be eliminated from the other two equations, thereby making it possible to omit one of the elimination steps. We illustrate this idea in Example 3.

## EXAMPLE 3 Solving a System of Equations with a Missing Term

Solve the system:

$$\begin{aligned} x + \phantom{2y +{}} z &= 8 && \text{Equation 1} \\ x + y + 2z &= 17 && \text{Equation 2} \\ x + 2y + z &= 16 && \text{Equation 3} \end{aligned}$$

### Solution

**Step 1 Reduce the system to two equations in two variables.** Because Equation 1 contains only $x$ and $z$, we could eliminate $y$ from Equations 2 and 3. This will give us two equations in $x$ and $z$. To eliminate $y$ from Equations 2 and 3, we multiply Equation 2 by $-2$ and add Equation 3.

$$\begin{aligned} &(\text{Equation 2})\ x + y + 2z = 17 \xrightarrow{\text{Multiply by } -2.} & -2x - 2y - 4z &= -34 \\ &(\text{Equation 3})\ x + 2y + z = 16 \xrightarrow{\text{No change}} & x + 2y + z &= 16 \\ &\text{Add:} & -x \phantom{{}-2y} - 3z &= -18 \quad \text{Equation 4} \end{aligned}$$

Equation 4 and the given Equation 1 provide us with a system of two equations in two variables.

**Step 2 Solve the resulting system of two equations in two variables.** We will solve Equations 1 and 4 for $x$ and $z$.

$$\begin{aligned} x + z &= 8 && \text{Equation 1} \\ -x - 3z &= -18 && \text{Equation 4} \\ \text{Add:} \quad -2z &= -10 \\ z &= 5 && \text{Divide both sides by } -2. \end{aligned}$$

**Step 3 Use back-substitution in one of the equations in two variables to find the value of the second variable.** To find $x$, we back-substitute 5 for $z$ in either Equation 1 or 4. We will use Equation 1.

$$\begin{aligned} x + z &= 8 && \text{Equation 1} \\ x + 5 &= 8 && \text{Substitute 5 for } z. \\ x &= 3 && \text{Subtract 5 from both sides.} \end{aligned}$$

**Step 4 Back-substitute the values found for two variables into one of the original equations to find the value of the third variable.** To find $y$, we back-substitute 3 for $x$ and 5 for $z$ into Equation 2 or 3. We can't use Equation 1 because $y$ is missing in this equation. We will use Equation 2.

$$\begin{aligned} x + y + 2z &= 17 && \text{Equation 2} \\ 3 + y + 2(5) &= 17 && \text{Substitute 3 for } x \text{ and 5 for } z. \\ y + 13 &= 17 && \text{Multiply and add.} \\ y &= 4 && \text{Subtract 13 from both sides.} \end{aligned}$$

We found that $z = 5$, $x = 3$, and $y = 4$. Thus, the proposed solution is the ordered triple $(3, 4, 5)$.

**Step 5 Check.** Substituting 3 for $x$, 4 for $y$, and 5 for $z$ into each of the three original equations yields three true statements. Consequently, the solution set is $\{(3, 4, 5)\}$.

**Check Point 3** Solve the system:

$$\begin{aligned} 2y - z &= 7 \\ x + 2y + z &= 17 \\ 2x - 3y + 2z &= -1 \end{aligned}$$

A system of linear equations in three variables represents three planes. The three planes need not intersect at one point. The planes may have no common point of intersection and represent an inconsistent system with no solution. By contrast, the planes may coincide or intersect along a line. In these cases, the planes have infinitely many points in common and represent systems with infinitely many solutions. Systems of linear equations in three variables that are inconsistent or that contain dependent equations will be discussed in Chapter 9.

**3** Solve problems using systems in three variables.

## Applications

Systems of equations may allow us to find models for data without using a graphing utility. Quadratic functions of the form $y = ax^2 + bx + c$ often model situations in which values of $y$ are decreasing and then increasing, suggesting the cuplike shape of a parabola.

### EXAMPLE 4 Modeling Data Relating Sleep and Death Rate

In a study relating sleep and death rate, the following data were obtained. Use the function $y = ax^2 + bx + c$ to model the data.

| $x$ (Average Number of Hours of Sleep) | $y$ (Death Rate per Year Per 100,000 Males) |
|---|---|
| 4 | 1682 |
| 7 | 626 |
| 9 | 967 |

**Solution** We need to find values for $a$, $b$, and $c$. We can do so by solving a system of three linear equations in $a$, $b$, and $c$. We obtain the three equations by using the values of $x$ and $y$ from the data as follows:

$\mathbf{y = ax^2 + bx + c}$ — Use the quadratic function to model the data.

When $x = 4$, $y = 1682$: $1682 = a \cdot 4^2 + b \cdot 4 + c$ or $16a + 4b + c = 1682$

When $x = 7$, $y = 626$: $626 = a \cdot 7^2 + b \cdot 7 + c$ or $49a + 7b + c = 626$

When $x = 9$, $y = 967$: $967 = a \cdot 9^2 + b \cdot 9 + c$ or $81a + 9b + c = 967$.

The easiest way to solve this system is to eliminate $c$ from two pairs of equations, obtaining two equations in $a$ and $b$. Solving this system gives $a = 104.5$, $b = -1501.5$, and $c = 6016$. We now substitute the values for $a$, $b$, and $c$ into $y = ax^2 + bx + c$. The function that models the given data is

$$y = 104.5x^2 - 1501.5x + 6016.$$

**Discovery**

Use the $x$-coordinate of a parabola's vertex, $x = -\frac{b}{2a}$, and the function on the right to find the hours of sleep that minimize the death rate. Round to the nearest tenth of an hour. What is the minimum death rate per year per 100,000 males?

We can use the model that we obtained in Example 4 to find the death rate of males who average, say, 6 hours of sleep. Substitute 6 for $x$:

$$y = 104.5(6)^2 - 1501.5(6) + 6016 = 769.$$

According to the model, the death rate for males who average 6 hours of sleep is 769 deaths per 100,000 males.

**Check Point 4** Find the quadratic function $y = ax^2 + bx + c$ whose graph passes through the points $(1, 4)$, $(2, 1)$, and $(3, 4)$.

## EXERCISE SET 8.2

### Practice Exercises

*In Exercises 1–4, determine if the given ordered triple is a solution of the system.*

**1.** $\begin{aligned} x + y + z &= 4 \\ x - 2y - z &= 1 \\ 2x - y - 2 &= -1 \end{aligned}$ $(2, -1, 3)$

**2.** $\begin{aligned} x + y + z &= 0 \\ x + 2y - 3z &= 5 \\ 3x + 4y + 2z &= -1 \end{aligned}$ $(5, -3, -2)$

**3.** $\begin{aligned} x - 2y &= 2 \\ 2x + 3y &= 11 \\ y - 4z &= -7 \end{aligned}$ $(4, 1, 2)$

**4.** $\begin{aligned} x - 2z &= -5 \\ y - 3z &= -3 \\ 2x - z &= -4 \end{aligned}$ $(-1, 3, 2)$

*Solve each system in Exercises 5–18.*

**5.** $\begin{aligned} x + y + 2z &= 11 \\ x + y + 3z &= 14 \\ x + 2y - z &= 5 \end{aligned}$

**6.** $\begin{aligned} 2x + y - 2z &= -1 \\ 3x - 3y - z &= 5 \\ x - 2y + 3z &= 6 \end{aligned}$

**7.** $\begin{aligned} 4x - y + 2z &= 11 \\ x + 2y - z &= -1 \\ 2x + 2y - 3z &= -1 \end{aligned}$

**8.** $\begin{aligned} x - y + 3z &= 8 \\ 3x + y - 2z &= -2 \\ 2x + 4y + z &= 0 \end{aligned}$

**9.** $\begin{aligned} 3x + 5y + 2z &= 0 \\ 12x - 15y + 4z &= 12 \\ 6x - 25y - 8z &= 8 \end{aligned}$

**10.** $\begin{aligned} 2x + 3y + 7z &= 13 \\ 3x + 2y - 5z &= -22 \\ 5x + 7y - 3z &= -28 \end{aligned}$

**11.** $\begin{aligned} 2x - 4y + 3z &= 17 \\ x + 2y - z &= 0 \\ 4x - y - z &= 6 \end{aligned}$

**12.** $\begin{aligned} x + z &= 3 \\ x + 2y - z &= 1 \\ 2x - y + z &= 3 \end{aligned}$

**13.** $\begin{aligned} 2x + y &= 2 \\ x + y - z &= 4 \\ 3x + 2y + z &= 0 \end{aligned}$

**14.** $\begin{aligned} x + 3y + 5z &= 20 \\ y - 4z &= -16 \\ 3x - 2y + 9z &= 36 \end{aligned}$

**15.** $\begin{aligned} x + y &= -4 \\ y - z &= 1 \\ 2x + y + 3z &= -21 \end{aligned}$

**16.** $\begin{aligned} x + y &= 4 \\ x + z &= 4 \\ y + z &= 4 \end{aligned}$

**17.** $\begin{aligned} 3(2x + y) + 5z &= -1 \\ 2(x - 3y + 4z) &= -9 \\ 4(1 + x) &= -3(z - 3y) \end{aligned}$

**18.** $\begin{aligned} 7z - 3 &= 2(x - 3y) \\ 5y + 3z - 7 &= 4x \\ 4 + 5z &= 3(2x - y) \end{aligned}$

*In Exercises 19–20, let x represent the first number, y the second number, and z the third number. Use the given conditions to write a system of equations. Solve the system and find the numbers.*

**19.** The sum of three numbers is 16. The sum of twice the first number, 3 times the second number, and 4 times the third number is 46. The difference between 5 times the first number and the second number is 31. Find the three numbers.

**20.** Three numbers are unknown. Three times the first number plus the second number plus twice the third number is 5. If 3 times the second number is subtracted from the sum of the first number and 3 times the third number, the result is 2. If the third number is subtracted from 2 times the first number and 3 times the second number, the result is 1. Find the numbers.

*In Exercises 21–24, find the quadratic function $y = ax^2 + bx + c$ whose graph passes through the given points.*

**21.** $(-1, 6), (1, 4), (2, 9)$

**22.** $(-2, 7), (1, -2), (2, 3)$

**23.** $(-1, -4), (1, -2), (2, 5)$

**24.** $(1, 3), (3, -1), (4, 0)$

### Application Exercises

**25.** The bar graph at the top of the next page shows the average starting salaries for the five top-paying fields for college graduates. If we add the average starting salaries for college graduates who are chemical, mechanical, and electrical engineers, the total is \$121,421. The difference between the starting salaries for chemical and mechanical engineers is \$2906. The difference between the starting salaries for mechanical engineers and electrical engineers is \$1041. Find the average starting salaries for chemical, mechanical, and electrical engineers.

**Average Starting Salaries for the Five Top Paying Fields for College Graduates in 1999**

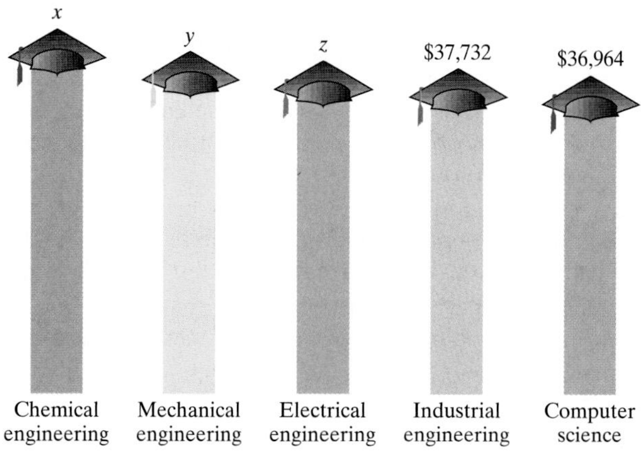


*Source*: Michigan State University

**26.** The table shows a list of the most frequently spoken languages in the United States, not counting English. Yiddish, Thai, and Persian are spoken by 621 thousand people in the United States. The difference between the number of people who speak Yiddish and the number who speak Thai is 7 thousand. The difference between the number of people who speak Thai and the number who speak Persian is 4 thousand. Find the thousands of people in the United States who speak Yiddish, Thai, and Persian.

**Languages Spoken in the United States**

| Language | Number of Speakers |
|---|---|
| 1. Spanish | 17,339,000 |
| 2. French | 1,702,000 |
| 3. German | 1,547,000 |
| 4. Italian | 1,309,000 |
| 5. Chinese | 1,249,000 |
| 6. Tagalog | 843,000 |
| 7. Polish | 723,000 |
| 8. Korean | 626,000 |
| 9. Vietnamese | 507,000 |
| 10. Portuguese | 430,000 |
| 11. Japanese | 428,000 |
| 12. Greek | 388,000 |
| 13. Arabic | 355,000 |
| 14. Hindi, Urdu, & related languages | 331,000 |
| 15. Russian | 242,000 |
| 16. Yiddish | $x$ |
| 17. Thai | $y$ |
| 18. Persian | $z$ |

*Source*: Bureau of the census

**27.** The equation $y = \frac{1}{2}Ax^2 + Bx + C$ gives the relationship between the number of feet a car travels once the brakes are applied, $y$, and the number of seconds the car is in motion after the brakes are applied, $x$. A research firm discovered that when a car was in motion for 1 second after the brakes were applied, the car traveled 46 feet. (When $x = 1$, $y = 46$.) Similarly, it was found that when $x$ was 2, $y$ was 84, and when $x$ was 3, $y$ was 114. Use these values to find the constants $A$, $B$, and $C$ in the equation. What is the value for $y$ when $x = 6$? Describe what this means.

**28.** A ball is thrown directly upward from the top of a building. The position function

$$s = \frac{1}{2}at^2 + v_0t + s_0$$

describes the ball's height, $s$, in feet, after $t$ seconds. Find the values of $a$, $v_0$, and $s_0$ if $s = 224$ at $t = 1$, $s = 176$ at $t = 3$, and $s = 104$ at $t = 4$. What is the value for $s$ when $t = 5$? Describe what this means.

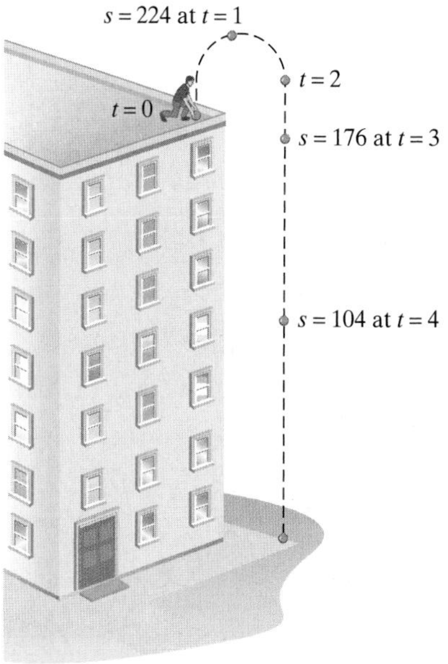


*Use a system of linear equations in three variables to solve Exercises 29–32.*

**29.** At a college production of *Evita*, 400 tickets were sold. The ticket prices were \$8, \$10, and \$12, and the total income from ticket sales was \$3700. How many tickets of each type were sold if the combined number of \$8 and \$10 tickets sold was 7 times the number of \$12 tickets sold?

**30.** A certain brand of razor blades comes in packages of 6, 12, and 24 blades, costing \$2, \$3, and \$4 per package, respectively. A store sold 12 packages containing a total of 162 razor blades and took in \$35. How many packages of each type were sold?

**31.** A person invested \$6700 for one year, part at 8%, part at 10%, and the remainder at 12%. The total annual income from these investments was \$716. The amount of money invested at 12% was \$300 more than the amount invested at 8% and 10% combined. Find the amount invested at each rate.

**32.** A person invested \$17,000 for one year, part at 10%, part at 12%, and the remainder at 15%. The total annual income from these investments was \$2110. The amount of money invested at 12% was \$1000 less than the amount invested at 10% and 15% combined. Find the amount invested at each rate.

## Writing in Mathematics

**33.** What is a system of linear equations in three variables?

**34.** How do you determine whether a given ordered triple is a solution of a system in three variables?

**35.** Describe in general terms how to solve a system in three variables.

**36.** Describe how to use the techniques that you learned in this section to obtain a model for U.S. divorce rates from 1970 to 1997.

| $x$ (years after 1970) | $y$ (divorces per 1000 people) |
|---|---|
| 0 | 3.5 |
| 15 | 5.0 |
| 27 | 4.3 |

**U.S. Divorce Rates: Number of Divorces per 1000 People**

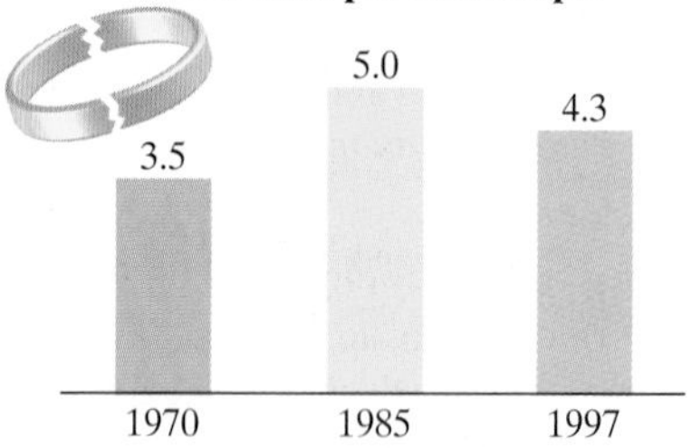


*Source*: U.S. Census Bureau

## Technology Exercises

**37.** Does your graphing utility have a feature that allows you to solve linear systems by entering coefficients and constant terms? If so, use this feature to verify the solutions to any five exercises that you worked by hand from Exercises 5–16.

**38.** Verify your results in Exercises 21–24 by using a graphing utility to graph the resulting parabola. Trace along the curve and convince yourself that the three points given in the exercise lie on the parabola.

**39.** Some graphing utilities will do three-dimensional graphing. For example, on the TI-92, press [MODE], go to [GRAPH], press the arrow to the right, select [3D], then [ENTER]. When you display the [Y =] screen, you will see the equations are functions of $x$ and $y$. Thus, you must solve each of a linear system's equations for $z$ before entering the equation. For example,

$$x + y + z = 19$$

is solved for $z$, giving

$$z = 19 - x - y.$$

(Consult your manual.) If your utility does three-dimensional graphing, graph five of the systems in Exercises 5–16 and trace along the planes to find their common point of intersection.

## Critical Thinking Exercises

**40.** Describe how the system

$$\begin{aligned} x + y - z - 2w &= -8 \\ x - 2y + 3z + w &= 18 \\ 2x + 2y + 2z - 2w &= 10 \\ 2x + y - z + w &= 3 \end{aligned}$$

could be solved. Is it likely that in the near future a graphing utility will be available to provide a geometric solution (using intersecting graphs) to this system? Explain.

**41.** A modernistic painting consists of triangles, rectangles, and pentagons, all drawn so as to not overlap or share sides. Within each rectangle are drawn 2 red roses, and each pentagon contains 5 carnations. How many triangles, rectangles, and pentagons appear in the painting if the painting contains a total of 40 geometric figures, 153 sides of geometric figures, and 72 flowers?

# SECTION 8.3 Partial Fractions

## Objective

1. Find the partial fraction decomposition of a rational expression.

The rising and setting of the sun suggest the obvious: Things change over time. Calculus is the study of rates of change, allowing the motion of the rising sun to be measured by "freezing the frame" at one instant in time. If you are given a function, calculus reveals its rate of change at any "frozen" instant. In this section, you will learn an algebraic technique used in calculus to find a function if its rate of change is known.

## The Idea Behind Partial Fraction Decomposition

Systems of linear equations can be used to reverse the process of adding and subtracting rational expressions—for example,

$$\frac{3}{x-4} - \frac{2}{x+2} = \frac{3(x+2) - 2(x-4)}{(x-4)(x+2)}$$

$$= \frac{3x+6-2x+8}{(x-4)(x+2)} = \frac{x+14}{(x-4)(x+2)}.$$

In order to reverse this process, we must show that

$$\frac{x+14}{(x-4)(x+2)} = \frac{3}{x-4} - \frac{2}{x+2} \quad \text{or} \quad \frac{3}{x-4} + \frac{-2}{x+2}.$$

Each of the two fractions on the right is called a **partial fraction**. The sum of these fractions is called the **partial fraction decomposition** of the rational expression on the left-hand side.

Partial fraction decompositions can be written for rational expressions of the form $\frac{P(x)}{Q(x)}$, where $P$ and $Q$ have no common factors and the highest power in the numerator is less than the highest power in the denominator. In this section, we will show you how to write the partial fraction decompositions for each of the following rational expressions:

$$\frac{9x^2 - 9x + 6}{(2x-1)(x+2)(x-2)}$$

$P(x) = 9x^2 - 9x + 6$; highest power $= 2$

$Q(x) = (2x-1)(x+2)(x-2)$; multiplying factors, highest power $= 3$

$$\frac{5x^3 - 3x^2 + 7x - 3}{(x^2+1)^2}$$

$P(x) = 5x^3 - 3x^2 + 7x - 3$; highest power $= 3$

$Q(x) = (x^2+1)^2$; squaring this expression, highest power $= 4$

**1** Find the partial fraction decomposition of a rational expression.

## The Steps in Partial Fraction Decomposition

The partial fraction decomposition of a rational expression depends on the factors of the denominator. We consider four cases involving different kinds of factors in the denominator.

**Case 1: The Partial Fraction Decomposition of a Rational Expression with Distinct Linear Factors in the Denominator** If the denominator has a linear factor of the form $ax + b$, then the partial fraction decomposition will contain a term of the form

$$\frac{A}{ax+b}.$$

Constant

Linear factor

Each distinct linear factor in the denominator produces a partial fraction of the form *constant over linear factor*. For example,

$$\frac{9x^2-9x+6}{(2x-1)(x+2)(x-2)} = \frac{A}{2x-1} + \frac{B}{x+2} + \frac{C}{x-2}.$$

We write a constant over each linear factor in the denominator.

The form of the partial fraction decomposition for a rational expression with distinct linear factors in the denominator is

$$\frac{P(x)}{(a_1x+b_1)(a_2x+b_2)(a_3x+b_3)\cdots(a_nx+b_n)}$$
$$= \frac{A_1}{a_1x+b_1} + \frac{A_2}{a_2x+b_2} + \frac{A_3}{a_3x+b_3} + \cdots + \frac{A_n}{a_nx+b_n}.$$

### EXAMPLE 1 Partial Fraction Decomposition with Distinct Linear Factors

Find the partial fraction decomposition of

$$\frac{x+14}{(x-4)(x+2)}.$$

**Solution** We begin by setting up the partial fraction decomposition with the unknown constants. Write a constant over each of the two distinct linear factors in the denominator.

$$\frac{x+14}{(x-4)(x+2)} = \frac{A}{x-4} + \frac{B}{x+2}$$

Our goal is to find $A$ and $B$. We do this by multiplying both sides of the equation by the least common denominator.

$$(x-4)(x+2)\frac{x+14}{(x-4)(x+2)} = (x-4)(x+2)\left(\frac{A}{x-4} + \frac{B}{x+2}\right)$$

We use the distributive property on the right side.

$$\cancel{(x-4)(x+2)}\frac{x+14}{\cancel{(x-4)(x+2)}}$$
$$= \cancel{(x-4)}(x+2)\frac{A}{\cancel{(x-4)}} + (x-4)\cancel{(x+2)}\frac{B}{\cancel{(x+2)}}$$

Dividing out common factors in numerators and denominators, we obtain

$$x + 14 = A(x + 2) + B(x - 4).$$

To find values for $A$ and $B$ that make both sides equal, we'll express the sides in exactly the same form by writing the variable $x$-terms and then writing the constant terms. Apply the distributive property on the right side.

$$x + 14 = Ax + 2A + Bx - 4B$$

$$x + 14 = Ax + Bx + 2A - 4B$$

$$1x + 14 = (A + B)x + (2A - 4B)$$

As shown by the arrows, if two polynomials are equal, coefficients of like powers of $x$ must be equal $(A + B = 1)$ and their constant terms must be equal $(2A - 4B = 14)$. Consequently, $A$ and $B$ satisfy the following two equations.

$$A + B = 1$$

$$2A - 4B = 14$$

We can use the addition method to solve this linear system in two variables. By multiplying the first equation by $-2$ and adding equations, we obtain $A = 3$ and $B = -2$. Thus,

$$\frac{x + 14}{(x - 4)(x + 2)} = \frac{A}{x - 4} + \frac{B}{x + 2} = \frac{3}{x - 4} + \frac{-2}{x + 2}\left(\text{or } \frac{3}{x - 4} - \frac{2}{x + 2}\right).$$

**Steps in Partial Fraction Decomposition**

1. Set up the partial fraction decomposition with the unknown constants $A, B, C$, etc., in the numerator of the decomposition.
2. Multiply both sides of the resulting equation by the least common denominator.
3. Simplify the right-hand side of the equation.
4. Write both sides in descending powers, equate coefficients of like powers of $x$, and equate constant terms.
5. Solve the resulting linear system for $A, B, C$, etc.
6. Substitute the values for $A, B, C$, etc., into the equation in step 1 and write the partial fraction decomposition.

**Check Point 1** Find the partial fraction decomposition of $\frac{5x - 1}{(x - 3)(x + 4)}$.

**Case 2: The Partial Fraction Decomposition of a Rational Expression with Linear Factors in the Denominator, Some of Which Are Repeated**
Suppose that $(ax + b)^n$ is a factor of the denominator. This means that the linear

factor $ax + b$ is repeated $n$ times. When this occurs, the partial fraction decomposition will contain the following sum of $n$ fractions.

$$\frac{P(x)}{(ax+b)^n} = \frac{A_1}{ax+b} + \frac{A_2}{(ax+b)^2} + \frac{A_3}{(ax+b)^3} + \cdots + \frac{A_n}{(ax+b)^n}$$

Include one fraction with a constant numerator for each power of $ax + b$.

## EXAMPLE 2 Partial Fraction Decomposition with Repeated Linear Factors

Find the partial fraction decomposition of $\dfrac{x-18}{x(x-3)^2}$.

### Solution

**Step 1 Set up the partial fraction decomposition with the unknown constants.** Because the linear factor $x - 3$ is repeated twice, we must include one fraction with a constant numerator for each power of $x - 3$.

$$\frac{x-18}{x(x-3)^2} = \frac{A}{x} + \frac{B}{x-3} + \frac{C}{(x-3)^2}$$

**Step 2 Multiply both sides of the resulting equation by the least common denominator.** We clear fractions, multiplying both sides by $x(x-3)^2$, the least common denominator.

$$x(x-3)^2\left[\frac{x-18}{x(x-3)^2}\right] = x(x-3)^2\left[\frac{A}{x} + \frac{B}{x-3} + \frac{C}{(x-3)^2}\right]$$

We use the distributive property on the right side.

$$\cancel{x(x-3)^2} \cdot \frac{x-18}{\cancel{x(x-3)^2}}$$

$$= \cancel{x}(x-3)^2 \cdot \frac{A}{\cancel{x}} + x(x-3)^2 \cdot \frac{B}{(x-3)} + x\cancel{(x-3)^2} \cdot \frac{C}{\cancel{(x-3)^2}}$$

Dividing out common factors in numerators and denominators, we obtain

$$x - 18 = A(x-3)^2 + Bx(x-3) + Cx.$$

**Step 3 Simplify the right side of the equation.** Square $x - 3$. Then apply the distributive property.

$$x - 18 = A(x^2 - 6x + 9) + Bx(x-3) + Cx$$

Square $x - 3$ using $(A - B)^2 = A^2 - 2AB + B^2$.

$$x - 18 = Ax^2 - 6Ax + 9A + Bx^2 - 3Bx + Cx$$

Apply the distributive property.

**Step 4 Write both sides in descending powers, equate coefficients of like powers of $x$, and equate constant terms.** The left side, $x - 18$, is in descending powers of $x$: $x - 18x^0$. We will write the right side in descending powers of $x$.

$$x - 18 = Ax^2 + Bx^2 - 6Ax - 3Bx + Cx + 9A$$

Express both sides in the same form.

$$0x^2 + 1x - 18 = (A + B)x^2 + (-6A - 3B + C)x + 9A$$

Equating coefficients of like powers of $x$ and constant terms results in the following system of linear equations.

$$\begin{aligned} A + B &= 0 \\ -6A - 3B + C &= 1 \\ 9A &= -18 \end{aligned}$$

**Step 5 Solve the resulting system for $A$, $B$, and $C$.** Dividing both sides of the last equation by 9, we obtain $A = -2$. Substituting $-2$ for $A$ in the first equation, $A + B = 0$, gives $-2 + B = 0$ or $B = 2$. We find $C$ by substituting $-2$ for $A$ and 2 for $B$ in the middle equation, $-6A - 3B + C = 1$. We obtain $C = -5$.

**Step 6 Substitute the values of $A$, $B$, and $C$ and write the partial fraction decomposition.** With $A = -2$, $B = 2$, and $C = -5$, the required partial fraction decomposition is

$$\frac{x - 18}{x(x - 3)^2} = \frac{A}{x} + \frac{B}{x - 3} + \frac{C}{(x - 3)^2} = -\frac{2}{x} + \frac{2}{x - 3} - \frac{5}{(x - 3)^2}.$$

**Check Point 2** Find the partial fraction decomposition of $\frac{x + 2}{x(x - 1)^2}$.

**Case 3: The Partial Fraction Decomposition of a Rational Expression with Prime, Nonrepeated Quadratic Factors in the Denominator** Suppose that $ax^2 + bx + c$ is a factor of the denominator and that this quadratic factor cannot be factored into linear factors with real coefficients. Under these conditions, the partial fraction decomposition will contain a term of the form

$$\frac{Ax + B}{ax^2 + bx + c}.$$

Linear numerator

Quadratic factor

Each distinct prime quadratic factor in the denominator produces a partial fraction of the form *linear numerator over quadratic factor*. For example,

$$\frac{3x^2 + 17x + 14}{(x - 2)(x^2 + 2x + 4)} = \frac{A}{x - 2} + \frac{Bx + C}{x^2 + 2x + 4}.$$

We write a constant over the linear factor in the denominator.

We write a linear numerator over the prime quadratic factor in the denominator.

Our next example illustrates how a linear system in three variables is used to determine values for $A$, $B$, and $C$.

## EXAMPLE 3 Partial Fraction Decomposition

Find the partial fraction decomposition of

$$\frac{3x^2 + 17x + 14}{(x - 2)(x^2 + 2x + 4)}.$$

**Solution**

**Step 1 Set up the partial fraction decomposition with the unknown constants.** We put a constant $(A)$ over the linear factor and a linear expression $(Bx + C)$ over the prime quadratic factor.

$$\frac{3x^2 + 17x + 14}{(x - 2)(x^2 + 2x + 4)} = \frac{A}{x - 2} + \frac{Bx + C}{x^2 + 2x + 4}$$

**Step 2 Multiply both sides of the resulting equation by the least common denominator.** We clear fractions, multiplying both sides by $(x - 2)(x^2 + 2x + 4)$, the least common denominator.

$$(x - 2)(x^2 + 2x + 4)\left[\frac{3x^2 + 17x + 14}{(x - 2)(x^2 + 2x + 4)}\right] = (x - 2)(x^2 + 2x + 4)\left[\frac{A}{x - 2} + \frac{Bx + C}{x^2 + 2x + 4}\right]$$

We use the distributive property on the right side.

$$\cancel{(x - 2)(x^2 + 2x + 4)} \cdot \frac{3x^2 + 17x + 14}{\cancel{(x - 2)(x^2 + 2x + 4)}}$$

$$= \cancel{(x - 2)}(x^2 + 2x + 4) \cdot \frac{A}{\cancel{x - 2}} + (x - 2)\cancel{(x^2 + 2x + 4)} \cdot \frac{Bx + C}{\cancel{x^2 + 2x + 4}}$$

Dividing out common factors in numerators and denominators, we obtain

$$3x^2 + 17x + 14 = A(x^2 + 2x + 4) + (Bx + C)(x - 2).$$

**Step 3 Simplify the right side of the equation.** We multiply on the right side by distributing $A$ over each term in parentheses and multiplying $(Bx + C)(x - 2)$ using the FOIL method.

$$3x^2 + 17x + 14 = Ax^2 + 2Ax + 4A + Bx^2 - 2Bx + Cx - 2C$$

**Step 4 Write both sides in descending powers, equate coefficients of like powers of $x$, and equate constant terms.** The left side, $3x^2 + 17x + 14$, is in descending powers of $x$. We write the right side in descending powers of $x$

$$3x^2 + 17x + 14 = Ax^2 + Bx^2 + 2Ax - 2Bx + Cx + 4A - 2C$$

and express both sides in the same form.

$$3x^2 + 17x + 14 = (A + B)x^2 + (2A - 2B + C)x + (4A - 2C)$$

Equating coefficients of like powers of $x$ and constant terms results in the following system of linear equations.

$$\begin{aligned} A + B &= 3 \\ 2A - 2B + C &= 17 \\ 4A - 2C &= 14 \end{aligned}$$

**Step 5 Solve the resulting system for $A$, $B$, and $C$.** Because the first equation involves $A$ and $B$, we can obtain another equation in $A$ and $B$ by eliminating $C$ from the second and third equations. Multiply the second equation by 2 and add equations. Solving in this manner, we obtain $A = 5$, $B = -2$, and $C = 3$.

**Step 6 Substitute the values of $A$, $B$, and $C$ and write the partial fraction decomposition.** With $A = 5$, $B = -2$, and $C = 3$, the required partial fraction decomposition is

$$\frac{3x^2 + 17x + 14}{(x-2)(x^2+2x+4)} = \frac{A}{x-2} + \frac{Bx + C}{x^2 + 2x + 4} = \frac{5}{x-2} + \frac{-2x+3}{x^2+2x+4}.$$

**Check Point 3** Find the partial fraction decomposition of

$$\frac{8x^2 + 12x - 20}{(x+3)(x^2+x+2)}.$$

**Case 4: The Partial Fraction Decomposition of a Rational Expression with a Prime, Repeated Quadratic Factor in the Denominator** Suppose that $(ax^2 + bx + c)^n$ is a factor of the denominator and that $ax^2 + bx + c$ cannot be factored further. This means that the quadratic factor $ax^2 + bx + c$ is repeated $n$ times. When this occurs, the partial fraction decomposition will contain a linear numerator for each power of $ax^2 + bx + c$.

$$\frac{P(x)}{(ax^2+bx+c)^n} = \frac{A_1x + B_1}{ax^2+bx+c} + \frac{A_2x+B_2}{(ax^2+bx+c)^2} + \frac{A_3x+B_3}{(ax^2+bx+c)^3} + \cdots + \frac{A_nx+B_n}{(ax^2+bx+c)^n}$$

Include one fraction with a linear numerator for each power of $ax^2 + bx + c$.

## EXAMPLE 4 Partial Fraction Decomposition with a Repeated Quadratic Factor

Find the partial fraction decomposition of

$$\frac{5x^3 - 3x^2 + 7x - 3}{(x^2+1)^2}.$$

### Solution

**Step 1 Set up the partial fraction decomposition with the unknown constants.** Because the quadratic factor $x^2 + 1$ is repeated twice, we must include one fraction with a linear numerator for each power of $x^2 + 1$.

$$\frac{5x^3 - 3x^2 + 7x - 3}{(x^2+1)^2} = \frac{Ax+B}{x^2+1} + \frac{Cx+D}{(x^2+1)^2}$$

**Step 2 Multiply both sides of the resulting equation by the least common denominator.** We clear fractions, multiplying both sides by $(x^2+1)^2$, the least common denominator.

$$(x^2+1)^2\left[\frac{5x^3 - 3x^2 + 7x - 3}{(x^2+1)^2}\right] = (x^2+1)^2\left[\frac{Ax+B}{x^2+1} + \frac{Cx+D}{(x^2+1)^2}\right]$$

Now we multiply and simplify.

$$5x^3 - 3x^2 + 7x - 3 = (x^2+1)(Ax+B) + Cx + D$$

**Step 3 Simplify the right side of the equation.** We multiply $(x^2+1)(Ax+B)$ using the FOIL method.

$$5x^3 - 3x^2 + 7x - 3 = Ax^3 + Bx^2 + Ax + B + Cx + D$$

**Step 4 Write both sides in descending powers, equate coefficients of like powers of $x$, and equate constant terms.**

$$5x^3 - 3x^2 + 7x - 3 = Ax^3 + Bx^2 + Ax + Cx + B + D$$

$$5x^3 - 3x^2 + 7x - 3 = Ax^3 + Bx^2 + (A + C)x + (B + D)$$

Equating coefficients of like powers of $x$ and constant terms results in the following system of linear equations.

$$A = 5$$

$$B = -3$$

$$A + C = 7 \qquad \text{With } A = 5\text{, we immediately obtain } C = 2.$$

$$B + D = -3 \qquad \text{With } B = -3\text{, we immediately obtain } D = 0.$$

**Step 5 Solve the resulting system for $A, B, C,$ and $D$.** Based on our observations in step 4, $A = 5, B = -3, C = 2$, and $D = 0$.

**Step 6 Substitute the values of $A, B, C,$ and $D$ and write the partial fraction decomposition.**

$$\frac{5x^3 - 3x^2 + 7x - 3}{(x^2+1)^2} = \frac{Ax + B}{x^2 + 1} + \frac{Cx + D}{(x^2+1)^2} = \frac{5x - 3}{x^2 + 1} + \frac{2x}{(x^2+1)^2}$$

**Check Point 4** Find the partial fraction decomposition of $\dfrac{2x^3 + x + 3}{(x^2+1)^2}$.

## EXERCISE SET 8.3

### Practice Exercises

*In Exercises 1–8, write the form of the partial fraction decomposition of the rational expression. It is not necessary to solve for the constants.*

1. $\dfrac{11x - 10}{(x-2)(x+1)}$
2. $\dfrac{5x + 7}{(x-1)(x+3)}$
3. $\dfrac{6x^2 - 14x - 27}{(x+2)(x-3)^2}$
4. $\dfrac{3x + 16}{(x+1)(x-2)^2}$
5. $\dfrac{5x^2 - 6x + 7}{(x-1)(x^2+1)}$
6. $\dfrac{5x^2 - 9x + 19}{(x-4)(x^2+5)}$
7. $\dfrac{x^3 + x^2}{(x^2+4)^2}$
8. $\dfrac{7x^2 - 9x + 3}{(x^2+7)^2}$

*In Exercises 9–38, write the partial fraction decomposition of each rational expression.*

9. $\dfrac{x}{(x-3)(x-2)}$
10. $\dfrac{1}{x(x-1)}$
11. $\dfrac{3x + 50}{(x-9)(x+2)}$
12. $\dfrac{5x - 1}{(x-2)(x+1)}$
13. $\dfrac{7x - 4}{x^2 - x - 12}$
14. $\dfrac{9x + 21}{x^2 + 2x - 15}$
15. $\dfrac{4x^2 + 13x - 9}{x(x-1)(x+3)}$
16. $\dfrac{4x^2 - 5x - 15}{x(x+1)(x-5)}$
17. $\dfrac{4x^2 - 7x - 3}{x^3 - x}$
18. $\dfrac{2x^2 - 18x - 12}{x^3 - 4x}$

19. $\dfrac{6x-11}{(x-1)^2}$

20. $\dfrac{x}{(x+1)^2}$

21. $\dfrac{x^2-6x+3}{(x-2)^3}$

22. $\dfrac{2x^2+8x+3}{(x+1)^3}$

23. $\dfrac{x^2+2x+7}{x(x-1)^2}$

24. $\dfrac{3x^2+49}{x(x+7)^2}$

25. $\dfrac{5x^2+21x+4}{(x+1)^2(x-3)}$

26. $\dfrac{x}{(x+2)^2(x+1)}$

27. $\dfrac{5x^2-6x+7}{(x-1)(x^2+1)}$

28. $\dfrac{5x^2-9x+19}{(x-4)(x^2+5)}$

29. $\dfrac{5x^2+6x+3}{(x+1)(x^2+2x+2)}$

30. $\dfrac{9x+2}{(x-2)(x^2+2x+2)}$

31. $\dfrac{6x^2-x+1}{x^3+x^2+x+1}$

32. $\dfrac{3x^2-2x+8}{x^3+2x^2+4x+8}$

33. $\dfrac{x^3+x^2+2}{(x^2+2)^2}$

34. $\dfrac{x^2+2x+3}{(x^2+4)^2}$

35. $\dfrac{x^3-4x^2+9x-5}{(x^2-2x+3)^2}$

36. $\dfrac{3x^3-6x^2+7x-2}{(x^2-2x+2)^2}$

37. $\dfrac{4x^2+3x+14}{x^3-8}$

38. $\dfrac{2x+4}{x^3-1}$

## Application Exercises

39. Find the partial fraction decomposition for $\dfrac{1}{x(x+1)}$ and use the result to find the following sum:

$$\frac{1}{1\cdot 2}+\frac{1}{2\cdot 3}+\frac{1}{3\cdot 4}+\cdots+\frac{1}{99\cdot 100}.$$

40. Find the partial fraction decomposition for $\dfrac{2}{x(x+2)}$ and use the result to find the following sum:

$$\frac{2}{1\cdot 3}+\frac{2}{3\cdot 5}+\frac{2}{5\cdot 7}+\cdots+\frac{2}{99\cdot 101}.$$

## Writing in Mathematics

41. Explain what is meant by the partial fraction decomposition of a rational expression.

42. Explain how to find the partial fraction decomposition of a rational expression with distinct linear factors in the denominator.

43. Explain how to find the partial fraction decomposition of a rational expression with a repeated linear factor in the denominator.

44. Explain how to find the partial fraction decomposition of a rational expression with a prime quadratic factor in the denominator.

45. Explain how to find the partial fraction decomposition of a rational expression with a repeated, prime quadratic factor in the denominator.

46. How can you verify your result for the partial fraction decomposition for a given rational expression without using a graphing utility?

## Technology Exercises

47. A graphing utility can be used to check the partial fraction decomposition for a given rational expression. Graph $y_1 =$ *the given rational expression* and $y_2 =$ *its partial fraction decomposition* on the same screen. If the graphs are identical, the decomposition is correct. Use this method to verify any five of the decompositions that you obtained in Exercises 9–38.

48. As you worked Exercise 47, did you find that it took a while to determine the range setting that showed a graph for the rational function and its decomposition? Suggest another method for showing that $y_1 = y_2$ using your graphing utility. Use this method to check the results of the same five decompositions you worked with in Exercise 47.

## Critical Thinking Exercises

49. If $a$, $b$, and $c$ are constants, find the partial fraction decomposition of

$$\frac{ax+b}{(x-c)^2}.$$

50. Find the partial fraction decomposition of

$$\frac{4x^2+5x-9}{x^3-6x-9}.$$

# SECTION 8.4 Systems of Nonlinear Equations in Two Variables

## Objectives

1. Recognize systems of nonlinear equations in two variables.
2. Solve nonlinear systems by substitution.
3. Solve nonlinear systems by addition.
4. Solve problems using systems of nonlinear equations.

Scientists debate the probability that a "doomsday rock" will collide with Earth. It has been estimated that an asteroid, a tiny planet that revolves around the sun, crashes into Earth about once every 250,000 years, and that such a collision would have disastrous results. In 1908 a small fragment struck Siberia, leveling thousands of acres of trees. One theory about the extinction of dinosaurs 65 million years ago involves Earth's collision with a large asteroid and the resulting drastic changes in Earth's climate.

Understanding the path of Earth and the path of a comet is essential to detecting threatening space debris. Orbits about the sun are not described by linear equations in the form $Ax + By = C$. The ability to solve systems that do not contain linear equations provides NASA scientists watching for troublesome asteroids with a possible collision point with Earth's orbit.

1 Recognize systems of nonlinear equations in two variables.

## Systems of Nonlinear Equations and Their Solutions

A **system of** two **nonlinear equations** in two variables contains at least one equation that cannot be expressed in the form $Ax + By = C$. Here are two examples:

$$x^2 = 2y + 10$$
$$3x - y = 9$$

Not in the form $Ax + By = C$. The term $x^2$ is not linear.

$$y = x^2 + 3$$
$$x^2 + y^2 = 9$$

Neither equation is in the form $Ax + By = C$. The terms $x^2$ and $y^2$ are not linear.

A **solution** to a nonlinear system in two variables is an ordered pair of real numbers that satisfies all equations in the system. The **solution set** to the system is the set of all such ordered pairs. As with linear systems in two variables, the solution to a nonlinear system (if there is one) corresponds to the intersection point(s) of the graphs of the equations in the system. Unlike linear systems, the graphs can be circles, parabolas, or anything other than two lines. We will solve nonlinear systems using the substitution method and the addition method.

2 Solve nonlinear systems by substitution.

## Eliminating a Variable Using the Substitution Method

The substitution method involves converting a nonlinear system to one equation in one variable by an appropriate substitution. The steps in the solution process are exactly the same as those used to solve a linear system by substitution. However, when you obtain an equation in one variable, this equation will not be linear. In our first example, this equation is quadratic.

## EXAMPLE 1 Solving a Nonlinear System by the Substitution Method

Solve by the substitution method:

$$x^2 = 2y + 10 \qquad \text{The graph is a parabola.}$$
$$3x - y = 9. \qquad \text{The graph is a line.}$$

### Solution

**Step 1 Solve one of the equations for one variable in terms of the other.** We begin by isolating one of the variables raised to the first power in either of the equations. By solving for $y$ in the second equation, which has a coefficient of $-1$, we can avoid fractions.

$$3x - y = 9 \qquad \text{This is the second equation in the given system.}$$
$$3x = y + 9 \qquad \text{Add } y \text{ to both sides.}$$
$$3x - 9 = y \qquad \text{Subtract 9 from both sides.}$$

**Step 2 Substitute the expression from step 1 into the other equation.** We substitute $3x - 9$ for $y$ in the first equation.

$$y = \boxed{3x - 9} \qquad x^2 = 2\boxed{y} + 10$$

This gives us an equation in one variable, namely

$$x^2 = 2(3x - 9) + 10.$$

The variable $y$ has been eliminated.

**Step 3 Solve the resulting equation containing one variable.**

$$x^2 = 2(3x - 9) + 10 \qquad \text{This is the equation containing one variable.}$$
$$x^2 = 6x - 18 + 10 \qquad \text{Use the distributive property.}$$
$$x^2 = 6x - 8 \qquad \text{Combine numerical terms on the right.}$$
$$x^2 - 6x + 8 = 0 \qquad \text{Move all terms to one side and set the quadratic equation equal to 0.}$$
$$(x - 4)(x - 2) = 0 \qquad \text{Factor.}$$
$$x - 4 = 0 \quad \text{or} \quad x - 2 = 0 \qquad \text{Set each factor equal to 0.}$$
$$x = 4 \quad \text{or} \quad x = 2 \qquad \text{Solve for } x.$$

**Step 4 Back-substitute the obtained values into the equation from step 1.** Now that we have the $x$-coordinates of the solutions, we back-substitute 4 for $x$ and 2 for $x$ in the equation $y = 3x - 9$.

If $x$ is 4, $y = 3(4) - 9 = 3$, so $(4, 3)$ is a solution.

If $x$ is 2, $y = 3(2) - 9 = -3$, so $(2, -3)$ is a solution.

**Step 5 Check the proposed solutions in both of the system's given equations.** We begin by checking $(4, 3)$. Replace $x$ with 4 and $y$ with 3.

| | | |
|---|---|---|
| $x^2 = 2y + 10$ | $3x - y = 9$ | These are the given equations. |
| $4^2 \stackrel{?}{=} 2(3) + 10$ | $3(4) - 3 \stackrel{?}{=} 9$ | Let $x = 4$ and $y = 3$. |
| $16 \stackrel{?}{=} 6 + 10$ | $12 - 3 \stackrel{?}{=} 9$ | Simplify. |
| $16 = 16$ ✓ | $9 = 9$ ✓ | True statements result. |

The ordered pair $(4, 3)$ satisfies both equations. Thus, $(4, 3)$ is a solution to the system.

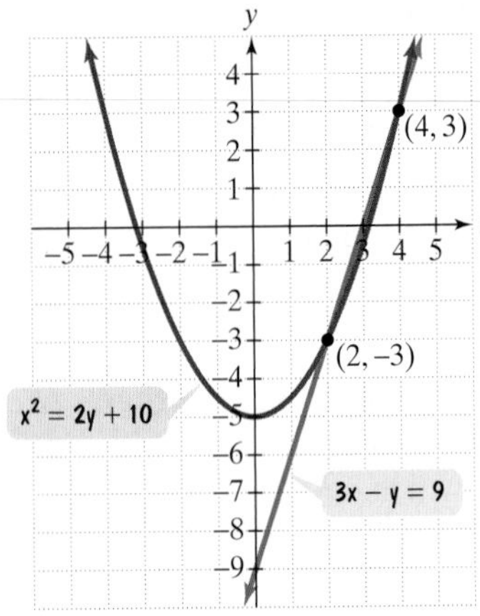


**Figure 8.7** Points of intersection illustrate the nonlinear system's solutions.

## Study Tip

Recall from Chapter 2 that

$$(x - h)^2 + (y - k)^2 = r^2$$

describes a circle with center $(h, k)$ and radius $r$.

Now let's check $(2, -3)$. Replace $x$ with 2 and $y$ with $-3$ in both given equations.

| | | |
|---|---|---|
| $x^2 = 2y + 10$ | $3x - y = 9$ | These are the given equations. |
| $2^2 \stackrel{?}{=} 2(-3) + 10$ | $3(2) - (-3) \stackrel{?}{=} 9$ | Let $x = 2$ and $y = -3$. |
| $4 \stackrel{?}{=} -6 + 10$ | $6 + 3 \stackrel{?}{=} 9$ | Simplify. |
| $4 = 4$ ✓ | $9 = 9$ ✓ | True statements result. |

The ordered pair $(2, -3)$ also satisfies both equations and is a solution to the system. The solution set is $\{(4, 3), (2, -3)\}$. Figure 8.7 shows the graphs of the equations in the system and the solutions as intersection points.

**Check Point 1** Solve by the substitution method:

$$x^2 = y - 1$$
$$4x - y = -1.$$

## EXAMPLE 2 Solving a Nonlinear System by the Substitution Method

Solve by the substitution method:

$$x - y = 3 \quad \text{The graph is a line.}$$
$$(x - 2)^2 + (y + 3)^2 = 4. \quad \text{The graph is a circle.}$$

**Solution** Graphically, we are finding the intersection of a line and a circle whose center is at $(2, -3)$ and whose radius measures 2.

**Step 1 Solve one of the equations for one variable in terms of the other.** We will solve for $x$ in the linear equation – that is, the first equation. (We could also solve for $y$.)

$$x - y = 3 \quad \text{This is the first equation in the given system.}$$
$$x = y + 3 \quad \text{Add } y \text{ to both sides.}$$

**Step 2 Substitute the expression from step 1 into the other equation.** We substitute $y + 3$ for $x$ in the second equation.

$$x = \boxed{y + 3} \qquad (\boxed{x} - 2)^2 + (y + 3)^2 = 4$$

This gives an equation in one variable, namely

$$(y + 3 - 2)^2 + (y + 3)^2 = 4.$$

The variable $x$ has been eliminated.

**Step 3 Solve the resulting equation containing one variable.**

$$(y + 3 - 2)^2 + (y + 3)^2 = 4 \quad \text{This is the equation containing one variable.}$$
$$(y + 1)^2 + (y + 3)^2 = 4 \quad \text{Combine numerical terms in the first parentheses.}$$
$$y^2 + 2y + 1 + y^2 + 6y + 9 = 4 \quad \text{Use the formula } (A + B)^2 = A^2 + 2AB + B^2 \text{ to square } y + 1 \text{ and } y + 3.$$
$$2y^2 + 8y + 10 = 4 \quad \text{Combine like terms on the left.}$$
$$2y^2 + 8y + 6 = 0 \quad \text{Subtract 4 from both sides and set the quadratic equation equal to 0.}$$

$$y^2 + 4y + 3 = 0 \quad \text{Simplify by dividing both sides by 2.}$$
$$(y + 3)(y + 1) = 0 \quad \text{Factor.}$$
$$y + 3 = 0 \quad \text{or} \quad y + 1 = 0 \quad \text{Set each factor equal to 0.}$$
$$y = -3 \quad \text{or} \quad y = -1 \quad \text{Solve for } y.$$

**Step 4 Back-substitute the obtained values into the equation from step 1.** Now that we have the $y$-coordinates of the solutions, we back-substitute $-3$ for $y$ and $-1$ for $y$ in the equation $x = y + 3$.

If $y = -3$: $x = -3 + 3 = 0$, so $(0, -3)$ is a solution.

If $y = -1$: $x = -1 + 3 = 2$, so $(2, -1)$ is a solution.

**Step 5 Check the proposed solution in both of the system's given equations.** Take a moment to show that each ordered pair satisfies both equations. The solution set of the given system is $\{(0, -3), (2, -1)\}$.

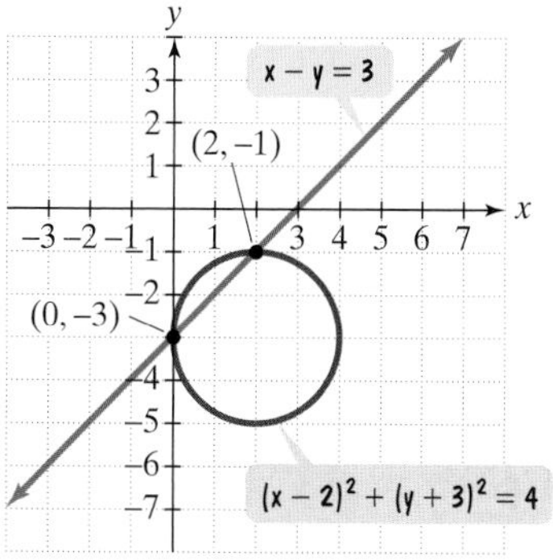


**Figure 8.8** Points of intersection illustrate the nonlinear system's solutions.

Figure 8.8 shows the graphs of the equations in the system and the solutions as intersection points.

**Check Point 2** Solve by the substitution method:

$$x + 2y = 0$$
$$(x - 1)^2 + (y - 1)^2 = 5.$$

**3** Solve nonlinear systems by addition.

## Eliminating a Variable Using the Addition Method

In solving linear systems with two variables, we learned that the addition method works well when each equation is in the form $Ax + By = C$. For nonlinear systems, the addition method can be used when each equation is in the form $Ax^2 + By^2 = C$. If necessary, we will multiply either equation or both equations by appropriate numbers so that the coefficients of $x^2$ or $y^2$ will have a sum of 0. We then add equations. The sum will be an equation in one variable.

### EXAMPLE 3 Solving a Nonlinear System by the Addition Method

Solve the system

$$4x^2 + y^2 = 13 \quad \text{Equation 1}$$
$$x^2 + y^2 = 10. \quad \text{Equation 2}$$

**Solution** We can use the same steps that we did when we solved linear systems by the addition method.

**Step 1 Write both equations in the form $Ax^2 + By^2 = C$.** Both equations are already in this form, so we can skip this step.

**Step 2 If necessary, multiply either equation or both equations by appropriate numbers so that the sum of the $x^2$-coefficients or the sum of the $y^2$-coefficients is 0.** We can eliminate $y^2$ by multiplying Equation 2 by $-1$.

$$4x^2 + y^2 = 13 \xrightarrow{\text{No change}} 4x^2 + y^2 = 13$$
$$x^2 + y^2 = 10 \xrightarrow{\text{Multiply by } -1.} -x^2 - y^2 = -10$$

**Steps 3 and 4 Add equations and solve for the remaining variable.**

$$\begin{aligned} 4x^2 + y^2 &= 13 \\ -x^2 - y^2 &= -10 \\ \text{Add:}\quad 3x^2 \quad &= 3 \end{aligned}$$

$x^2 = 1$ Divide both sides by 3.

$x = \pm 1$ Use the square root method: If $x^2 = c$, then $x = \pm\sqrt{c}$.

**Step 5 Back-substitute and find the values for the other variables.** We must back-substitute each value of $x$ into either one of the original equations. Let's use $x^2 + y^2 = 10$, Equation 2. If $x = 1$,

$1^2 + y^2 = 10$ Replace x with 1 in Equation 2.

$y^2 = 9$ Subtract 1 from both sides.

$y = \pm 3$ Apply the square root method.

$(1, 3)$ and $(1, -3)$ are solutions. If $x = -1$,

$(-1)^2 + y^2 = 10$ Replace x with −1 in Equation 2.

$y^2 = 9$ The steps are the same as before.

$y = \pm 3$

$(-1, 3)$ and $(-1, -3)$ are solutions.

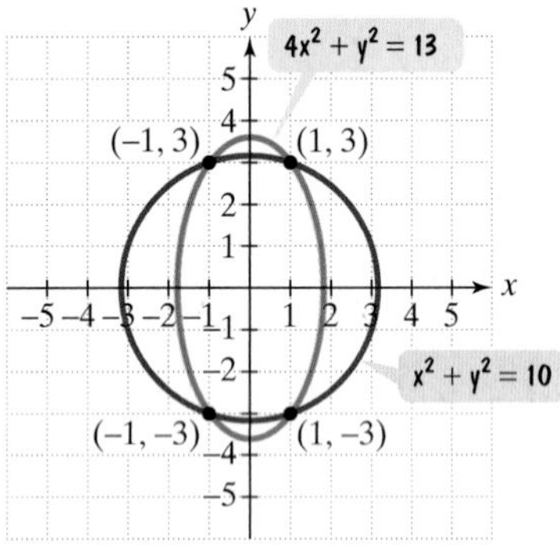


**Figure 8.9** A system with four solutions

**Step 6 Check.** Take a moment to show that each of the four ordered pairs satisfies Equation 1 and Equation 2. The solution set of the given system is $\{(1, 3), (1, -3), (-1, 3), (-1, -3)\}$.

Figure 8.9 shows the graphs of the equations in the system and the solutions as intersection points.

**Study Tip**

When solving nonlinear systems, extra solutions may be introduced that do not satisfy both equations in the system. Therefore, you should get into the habit of checking all proposed pairs in each of the system's two equations.

**Check Point 3** Solve the system:

$$\begin{aligned} 3x^2 + 2y^2 &= 35 \\ 4x^2 + 3y^2 &= 48. \end{aligned}$$

In solving nonlinear systems, we include only ordered pairs with real numbers in the solution set. We have seen that each of these ordered pairs corresponds to a point of intersection of the system's graphs.

## EXAMPLE 4 Solving a Nonlinear System by the Addition Method

Solve the system:

$y = x^2 + 3$ Equation 1 (The graph is a parabola.)

$x^2 + y^2 = 9.$ Equation 2 (The graph is a circle.)

**Solution** We could use substitution because Equation 1 has $y$ expressed in terms of $x$, but this would result in a fourth-degree equation. However, we can rewrite Equation 1 by subtracting $x^2$ from both sides and adding the equations to eliminate the $x^2$-terms.

$-x^2 + y = 3$ Subtract $x^2$ from both sides of Equation 1.

$x^2 + y^2 = 9$ This is Equation 2.

$y + y^2 = 12$ Add the equations.

We now solve this quadratic equation.

$$y + y^2 = 12$$

$$y^2 + y - 12 = 0$$ Subtract 12 from both sides and set the quadratic equation equal to 0.

$$(y + 4)(y - 3) = 0$$ Factor.

$$y + 4 = 0 \quad \text{or} \quad y - 3 = 0$$ Set each factor equal to 0.

$$y = -4 \quad \text{or} \quad y = 3$$ Solve for y.

To complete the solution, we must back-substitute each value of $y$ into either one of the original equations. We will use $y = x^2 + 3$, Equation 1. First, we substitute $-4$ for $y$.

$$-4 = x^2 + 3$$

$$-7 = x^2$$ Subtract 3 from both sides.

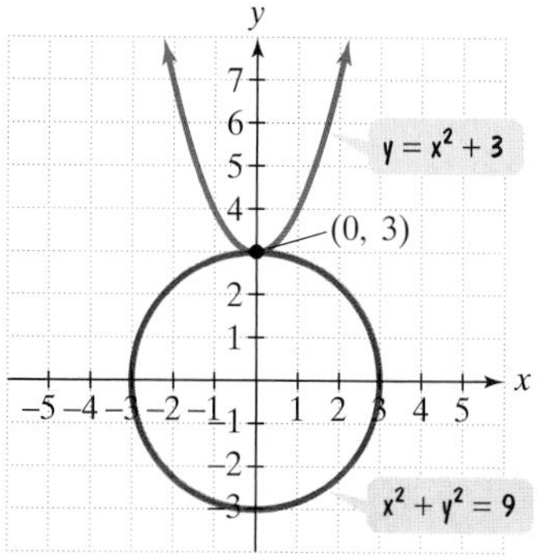


**Figure 8.10** A system with one real solution

Because the square of a real number cannot be negative, the equation $x^2 = -7$ does not have real-number solutions. Thus, we move on to our other value for $y$, 3, and substitute this value into Equation 1.

$$y = x^2 + 3$$ This is Equation 1.

$$3 = x^2 + 3$$ Back-substitute 3 for y.

$$0 = x^2$$ Subtract 3 from both sides.

$$0 = x$$ Solve for x.

We showed that if $y = 3$, then $x = 0$. Thus, $(0, 3)$ is the solution. Take a moment to show that $(0, 3)$ satisfies Equation 1 and Equation 2. The solution set of the given system is $\{(0, 3)\}$. Figure 8.10 shows the system's graphs and the solution as an intersection point.

**Check Point 4** Solve the system:

$$y = x^2 + 5$$
$$x^2 + y^2 = 25.$$

**4** Solve problems using systems of nonlinear equations.

## Applications

Many geometric problems can be modeled and solved by the use of nonlinear systems of equations. We will use our step-by-step strategy for solving problems using mathematical models that are created from verbal models.

## EXAMPLE 5 An Application of a Nonlinear System

You have 36 yards of fencing to build the enclosure in Figure 8.11. Some of this fencing is to be used to build an internal divider. If you'd like to enclose 54 square yards, what are the dimensions of the enclosure?

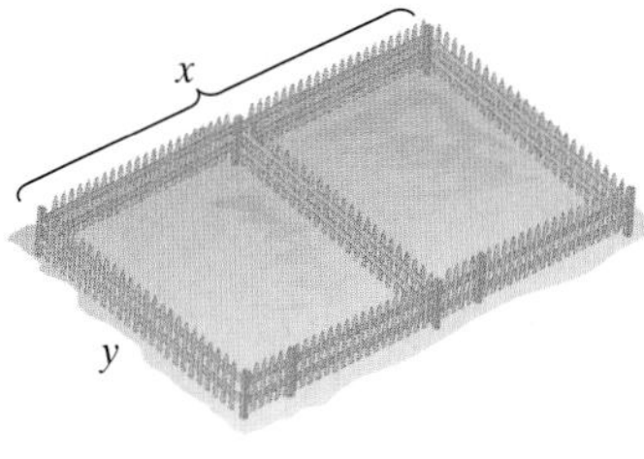


**Figure 8.11** Building an enclosure

### Solution

**Step 1 Use variables to represent unknown quantities.** Let $x$ = the enclosure's length and $y$ = the enclosure's width. These variables are shown in Figure 5.11.

**Step 2 Write a system of equations describing the problem's conditions.** The first condition is that you have 36 yards of fencing.

| Fencing along both lengths | plus | Fencing along both widths | plus | Fencing for the internal divider | equals | 36 yards. |
|---|---|---|---|---|---|---|
| $2x$ | $+$ | $2y$ | $+$ | $y$ | $=$ | $36$ |

Adding like terms, we can express the equation that models the verbal conditions for the fencing as $2x + 3y = 36$.

The second condition is that you'd like to enclose 54 square yards. The rectangle' area, the product of its length and its width, must be 54 square yards.

| Length | times | width | is | 54 square yards. |
|---|---|---|---|---|
| $x$ | $\cdot$ | $y$ | $=$ | $54$ |

**Step 3 Solve the system and answer the problem's question.** We must solve the system

$$2x + 3y = 36 \quad \text{Equation 1}$$
$$xy = 54. \quad \text{Equation 2}$$

We will use substitution. Because Equation 1 has no coefficients of 1 or $-1$, we will solve Equation 2 for $y$. Dividing both sides of $xy = 54$ by $x$, we obtain

$$y = \frac{54}{x}.$$

Now we substitute $\frac{54}{x}$ for $y$ in Equation 1 and solve for $x$.

$$2x + 3y = 36 \quad \text{This is Equation 1.}$$
$$2x + 3 \cdot \frac{54}{x} = 36 \quad \text{Substitute } \frac{54}{x} \text{ for } y.$$
$$2x + \frac{162}{x} = 36 \quad \text{Multiply.}$$
$$x\left(2x + \frac{162}{x}\right) = 36 \cdot x \quad \text{Clear fractions by multiplying both sides by } x.$$
$$2x^2 + 162 = 36x \quad \text{Use the distributive property on the left side.}$$
$$2x^2 - 36x + 162 = 0 \quad \text{Subtract } 36x \text{ from both sides and set the quadratic equation equal to 0.}$$
$$x^2 - 18x + 81 = 0 \quad \text{Simplify by dividing both sides by 2.}$$
$$(x - 9)^2 = 0 \quad \text{Factor using } A^2 - 2AB + B^2 = (A - B)^2.$$
$$x - 9 = 0 \quad \text{Set the factor equal to zero.}$$
$$x = 9 \quad \text{Solve for } x.$$

We back-substitute this value of $x$ into $y = \frac{54}{x}$.

$$\text{If } x = 9, \quad y = \tfrac{54}{9} = 6.$$

This means that the dimensions of the enclosure are 9 yards by 6 yards.

**Step 4 Check the proposed solution in the original wording of the problem.** With a length of 9 yards and a width of 6 yards, take a moment to check that this results in 36 yards of fencing and an area of 54 square yards.

**Check Point 5** Find the length and width of a rectangle whose perimeter is 20 feet and whose area is 21 square feet.

## EXERCISE SET 8.4

### Practice Exercises

*In Exercises 1–18, solve each system by the substitution method.*

**1.** $x + y = 2$
$y = x^2 - 4$

**2.** $x - y = -1$
$y = x^2 + 1$

**3.** $x - y = -1$
$y = x^2 + 2x - 3$

**4.** $2x + y = -5$
$y = x^2 + 6x + 7$

**5.** $y = x^2 - 4x - 10$
$y = -x^2 - 2x + 14$

**6.** $y = x^2 + 4x + 5$
$y = x^2 + 2x - 1$

**7.** $x^2 + y^2 = 25$
$x - y = 1$

**8.** $x^2 + y^2 = 5$
$3x - y = 5$

**9.** $xy = 6$
$2x - y = 1$

**10.** $xy = -12$
$x - 2y + 14 = 0$

**11.** $y^2 = x^2 - 9$
$2y = x - 3$

**12.** $x^2 + y = 4$
$2x + y = 1$

**13.** $xy = 3$
$x^2 + y^2 = 10$

**14.** $xy = 4$
$x^2 + y^2 = 8$

**15.** $x + y = 1$
$x^2 + xy - y^2 = -5$

**16.** $x + y = -3$
$x^2 + 2y^2 = 12y + 18$

**17.** $x + y = 1$
$(x - 1)^2 + (y + 2)^2 = 10$

**18.** $2x + y = 4$
$(x + 1)^2 + (y - 2)^2 = 4$

*In Exercises 19–28, solve each system by the addition method.*

**19.** $x^2 + y^2 = 13$
$x^2 - y^2 = 5$

**20.** $4x^2 - y^2 = 4$
$4x^2 + y^2 = 4$

**21.** $x^2 - 4y^2 = -7$
$3x^2 + y^2 = 31$

**22.** $3x^2 - 2y^2 = -5$
$2x^2 - y^2 = -2$

**23.** $3x^2 + 4y^2 - 16 = 0$
$2x^2 - 3y^2 - 5 = 0$

**24.** $32x^2 + 2y^2 - 50 = 0$
$x^2 - y^2 - 10 = 0$

**25.** $x^2 + y^2 = 25$
$(x - 8)^2 + y^2 = 41$

**26.** $x^2 + y^2 = 5$
$x^2 + (y - 8)^2 = 41$

**27.** $y^2 - x = 4$
$x^2 + y^2 = 4$

**28.** $x^2 - 2y = 8$
$x^2 + y^2 = 16$

*In Exercises 29–42, solve each system by the method of your choice.*

**29.** $3x^2 + 4y^2 = 16$
$2x^2 - 3y^2 = 5$

**30.** $x + y^2 = 4$
$x^2 + y^2 = 16$

**31.** $2x^2 + y^2 = 18$
$xy = 4$

**32.** $x^2 + 4y^2 = 20$
$xy = 4$

**33.** $x^2 + 4y^2 = 20$
$x + 2y = 6$

**34.** $3x^2 - 2y^2 = 1$
$4x - y = 3$

**35.** $x^3 + y = 0$
$x^2 - y = 0$

**36.** $x^3 + y = 0$
$2x^2 - y = 0$

**37.** $x^2 + (y - 2)^2 = 4$
$x^2 - 2y = 0$

**38.** $x^2 - y^2 - 4x + 6y - 4 = 0$
$x^2 + y^2 - 4x - 6y + 12 = 0$

**39.** $y = (x + 3)^2$
$x + 2y = -2$

**40.** $(x - 1)^2 + (y + 1)^2 = 5$
$2x - y = 3$

**41.** $x^2 + y^2 + 3y = 22$
$2x + y = -1$

**42.** $2x - y = -3$
$x^2 + y^2 - 4x = 0$

*In Exercises 43–46, let x represent one number and let y represent the other number. Use the given conditions to write a system of nonlinear equations. Solve the system and find the numbers.*

**43.** The sum of two numbers is 10 and their product is 24. Find the numbers.

**44.** The sum of two numbers is 20 and their product is 96. Find the numbers.

**45.** The difference between the squares of two numbers is 3. Twice the square of the first number increased by the square of the second number is 9. Find the numbers.

**46.** The difference between the squares of two numbers is 5. Twice the square of the second number subtracted from three times the square of the first number is 19. Find the numbers.

## Application Exercises

**47.** A planet's orbit follows a path described by $16x^2 + 4y^2 = 64$. A comet follows the parabolic path $y = x^2 - 4$. Where might the comet intersect the orbiting planet?

**48.** A system for tracking ships indicates that a ship lies on a path described by $16y^2 - x^2 = 16$. The process is repeated and the ship is found to lie on a path described by $9x^2 - 4y^2 = 36$. If it is known that the ship is located in the first quadrant of the coordinate system, determine its exact location.

**49.** Find the length and width of a rectangle whose perimeter is 36 feet and whose area is 77 square feet.

**50.** Find the length and width of a rectangle whose perimeter is 40 feet and whose area is 96 square feet.

*Use the formula for the area of a rectangle and the Pythagorean Theorem to solve Exercises 51–52.*

**51.** A small television has a picture with a diagonal measure of 10 inches and a viewing area of 48 square inches. Find the length and width of the screen.

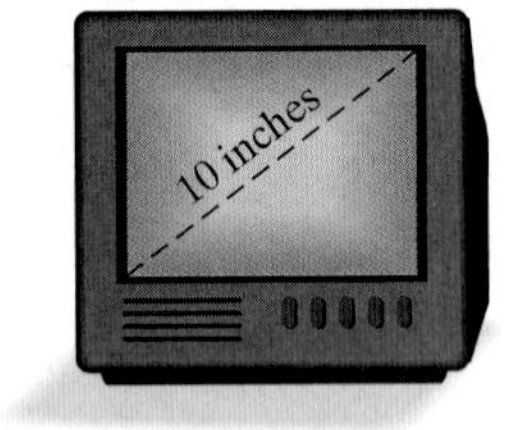


**52.** The area of a rug is 108 square feet, and the length of its diagonal is 15 feet. Find the length and width of the rug.

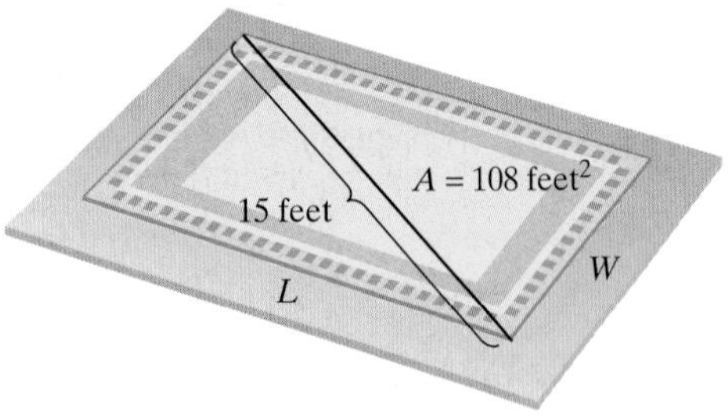


**53.** The figure at the top of the next column shows a square floor plan with a smaller square area that will accommodate a combination fountain and pool. The floor with the fountain-pool area removed has an area of 21 square meters and a perimeter of 24 meters. Find the dimensions of the floor and the dimensions of the square that will accommodate the pool.

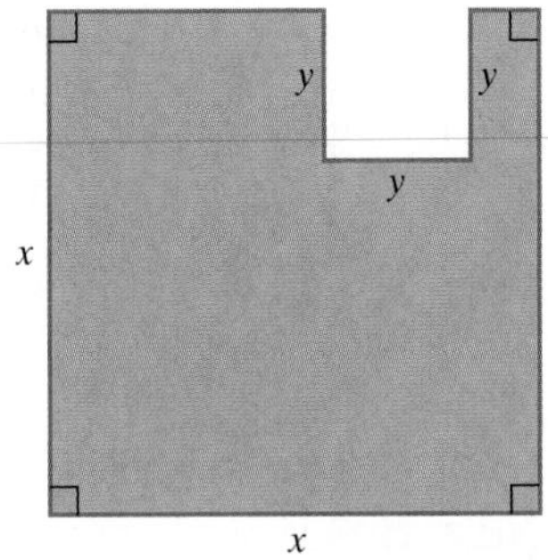


**54.** The area of the rectangular piece of cardboard shown on the left is 216 square inches. The cardboard is used to make an open box by cutting a 2-inch square from each corner and turning up the sides. If the box is to have a volume of 224 cubic inches, find the length and width of the cardboard that must be used.

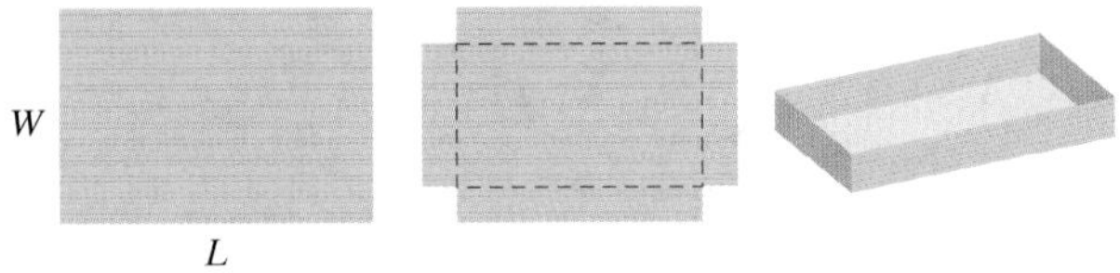


## Writing in Mathematics

**55.** What is a system of nonlinear equations? Provide an example with your description.

**56.** Explain how to solve a nonlinear system using the substitution method. Use $x^2 + y^2 = 9$ and $2x - y = 3$ to illustrate your explanation.

**57.** Explain how to solve a nonlinear system using the addition method. Use $x^2 - y^2 = 5$ and $3x^2 - 2y^2 = 19$ to illustrate your explanation.

**58.** The daily demand and supply models for a carrot cake supplied by a bakery to a convenience store are given by the demand model $N = 40 - 3p$ and the supply model $N = \frac{p^2}{10}$, in which $p$ is the price of the cake and $N$ is the number of cakes sold or supplied each day to the convenience store. Explain how to determine the price at which supply and demand are equal. Then describe how to find how many carrot cakes can be supplied and sold each day at this price.

## Technology Exercises

**59.** Verify your solutions to any five exercises from 1 through 42 by using a graphing utility to graph the two equations in the system in the same viewing rectangle. Then use the trace or intersection feature to verify the solutions.

**60.** Write a system of equations, one equation whose graph is a line and the other whose graph is a parabola, that has no ordered pairs that are real numbers in its solution set. Graph the equations using a graphing utility and verify that you are correct.

### Critical Thinking Exercises

**61.** Which one of the following is true?

**a.** A system of two equations in two variables whose graphs represent a circle and a line can have four real solutions.

**b.** A system of two equations in two variables whose graphs represent a parabola and a circle can have four real solutions.

**c.** A system of two equations in two variables whose graphs represent two circles must have at least two real solutions.

**d.** A system of two equations in two variables whose graphs represent a parabola and a circle cannot have only one real solution.

**62.** The points of intersection of the graphs of $xy = 20$ and $x^2 + y^2 = 41$ are joined to form a rectangle. Find the area of the rectangle.

**63.** Find $a$ and $b$ in this figure.

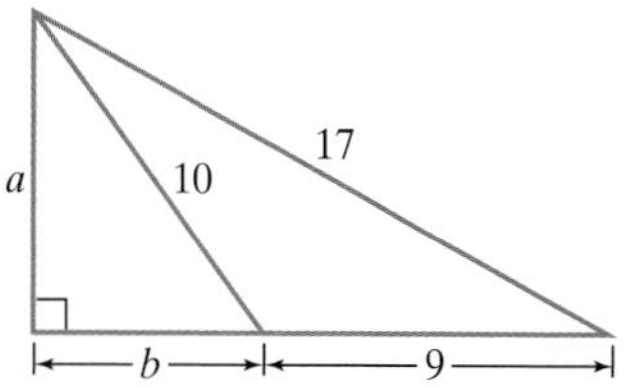


*Solve the systems in Exercises 64–65.*

**64.** $\log_y x = 3$
$\log_y(4x) = 5$

**65.** $\log x^2 = y + 3$
$\log x = y - 1$

## SECTION 8.5 Systems of Inequalities

### Objectives

1. Graph a linear inequality in two variables.
2. Graph a nonlinear inequality in two variables.
3. Graph a system of inequalities.
4. Solve applied problems involving systems of inequalities.

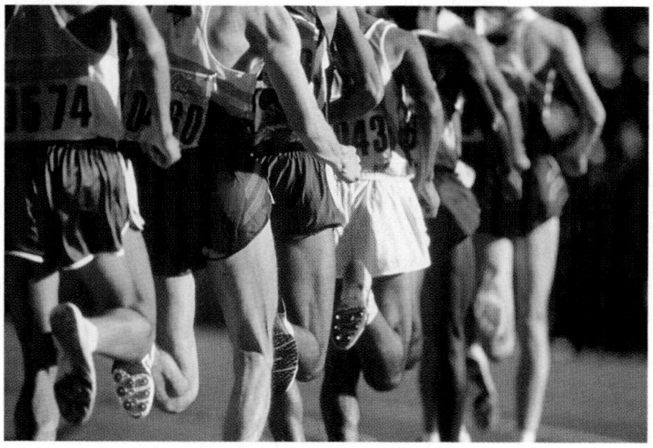

**1** Graph a linear inequality in two variables.

Had a good workout lately? If so, could you tell if you were overdoing it or not pushing yourself hard enough? In this section, we will use systems of inequalities in two variables to help you establish a target zone for your workouts.

### Graphing a Linear Inequality in Two Variables

We have seen that equations in the form $Ax + By = C$ are straight lines when graphed. If we change the = sign to $>, <, \geq$, or $\leq$, we obtain a **linear inequality in two variables**. Some examples of linear inequalities in two variables are $x + y > 2$, $3x - 5y \leq 15$, and $2x - y < 4$.

Figure 8.12 shows the graph of the linear equation $x + y = 2$. The line divides the points in the rectangular coordinate system into three sets. First, there is the set of points along the line, satisfying $x + y = 2$. Next, there is the set of points in the green region above the line. Points in the green region satisfy the linear inequality $x + y > 2$. Finally, there is the set of points in the pink region below the line. Points in the pink region satisfy the linear inequality $x + y < 2$.

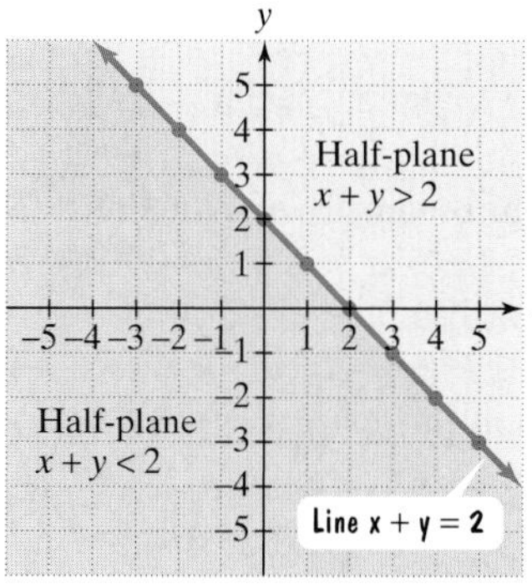


**Figure 8.12** All points on the line satisfy $x + y = 2$. All points in the green half-plane above the line satisfy $x + y > 2$. All points in the pink half-plane below the line satisfy $x + y < 2$.

A **half-plane** is the set of all the points on one side of a line. In Figure 8.12, the green region is a half-plane. The pink region is also a half-plane. A half-plane is the solution set of a linear inequality that involves $>$ or $<$. The solution set of an inequality that involves $\geq$ or $\leq$ is a half-plane and a line. A solid line is used to show that the line is part of the solution set. A dashed line is used to show that a line is not part of a solution set.

**Graphing a Linear Inequality in Two Variables**

1. Replace the inequality symbol with an equal sign and graph the corresponding linear equation. Draw a solid line if the original inequality contains a $\leq$ or $\geq$ symbol. Draw a dashed line if the original inequality contains a $<$ or $>$ symbol.
2. Choose a test point in one of the half-planes that is not on the line. Substitute the coordinates of the test point into the inequality.
3. If a true statement results, shade the half-plane containing this test point. If a false statement results, shade the half-plane not containing this test point.

## EXAMPLE 1 Graphing a Linear Inequality in Two Variables

Graph: $3x - 5y < 15$.

**Solution**

**Step 1 Replace the inequality symbol by $=$ and graph the linear equation.** We need to graph $3x - 5y = 15$. We can use intercepts to graph this line.

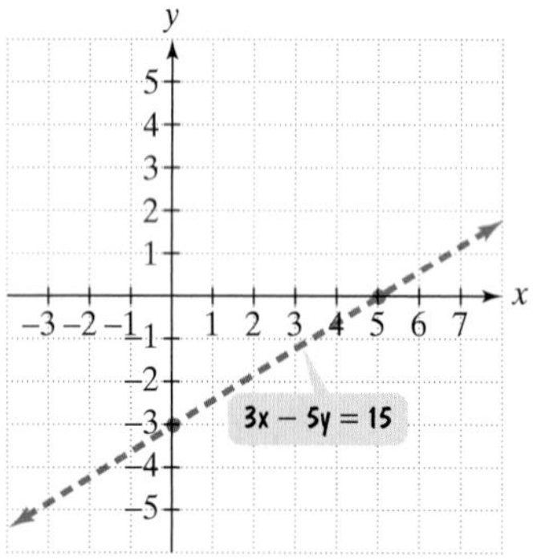


**Figure 8.13** Preparing to graph $3x - 5y < 15$

| **We set $y = 0$ to find the $x$-intercept:** | **We set $x = 0$ to find the $y$-intercept:** |
|---|---|
| $3x - 5y = 15$ | $3x - 5y = 15$ |
| $3x - 5 \cdot 0 = 15$ | $3 \cdot 0 - 5y = 15$ |
| $3x = 15$ | $-5y = 15$ |
| $x = 5$ | $y = -3$ |

The $x$-intercept is 5, so the line passes through $(5, 0)$. The $y$-intercept is $-3$, so the line passes through $(0, -3)$. The graph is indicated by a dashed line because the inequality $3x - 5y < 15$ contains a $<$ symbol, rather than $\leq$. The graph of the line is shown in Figure 8.13.

**Step 2 Choose a test point in one of the half-planes that is not on the line. Substitute its coordinates into the inequality.** The line $3x - 5y = 15$ divides the plane into three parts—the line itself and two half-planes. The points in one half-plane satisfy $3x - 5y > 15$. The points in the other half-plane satisfy $3x - 5y < 15$. We need to find which half-plane is the solution. To do so, we test a point from either half-plane. The origin, $(0, 0)$, is the easiest point to test.

$3x - 5y < 15$ This is the given inequality.

Is $3 \cdot 0 - 5 \cdot 0 < 15$? Test $(0, 0)$ by substituting 0 for x and 0 for y.

$0 - 0 < 15$

$0 < 15$, true

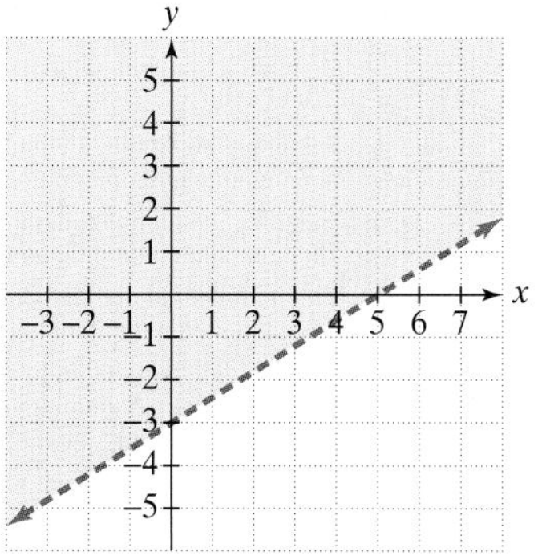


**Figure 8.14** The graph of $3x - 5y < 15$

**Step 3 If a true statement results, shade the half-plane containing the test point.** Because 0 is less than 15, the test point $(0, 0)$ is part of the solution set. All the points on the same side of the line $3x - 5y = 15$ as the point $(0, 0)$ are members of the solution set. The solution set is the half-plane that contains the point $(0, 0)$, indicated by shading this half-plane. The graph is shown using green shading and a dashed blue line in Figure 8.14.

**Check Point 1** Graph: $2x - 4y < 8$.

When graphing a linear inequality, test a point that lies in one of the half-planes and *not on the line dividing the half-planes*. The test point $(0, 0)$ is convenient because it is easy to calculate when 0 is substituted for each variable. However, if $(0, 0)$ lies on the dividing line and not in a half-plane, a different test point must be selected.

## EXAMPLE 2 Graphing a Linear Inequality

Graph: $y \le \frac{2}{3}x$.

### Solution

**Step 1 Replace the inequality symbol by = and graph the linear equation.** We need to graph $y = \frac{2}{3}x$. We can use the slope and the $y$-intercept to graph this line.

$$y = \frac{2}{3}x + 0$$

Slope $= \frac{2}{3} = \frac{\text{rise}}{\text{run}}$    $y$-intercept $= 0$

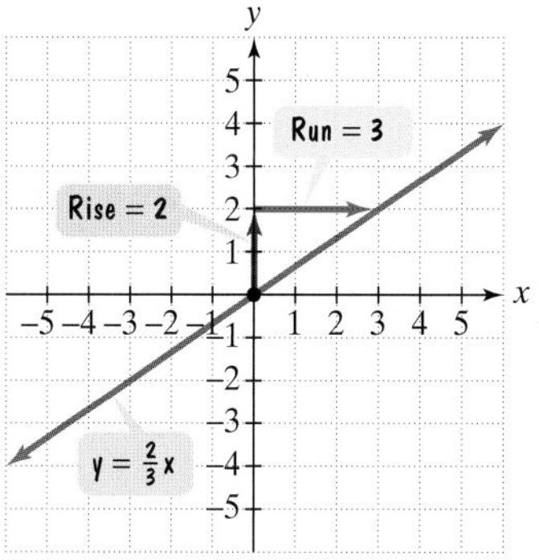


**Figure 8.15** Preparing to graph $y \le \frac{2}{3}x$

The $y$-intercept is 0 and the line passes through $(0, 0)$. Using the $y$-intercept and the slope, the line is shown in Figure 8.15 as a solid line because the inequality $y \le \frac{2}{3}x$ contains a $\le$ symbol, in which equality is included.

**Step 2 Choose a test point in one of the half-planes that is not on the line. Substitute its coordinates into the inequality.** We cannot use $(0, 0)$ as a test point because it lies on the line and not in a half-plane. Let's use $(1, 1)$, which lies in the half-plane above the line.

$$y \le \frac{2}{3}x \quad \text{This is the given inequality.}$$

$$\text{Is } 1 \le \frac{2}{3} \cdot 1? \quad \text{Test } (1, 1) \text{ by substituting 1 for } x \text{ and 1 for } y.$$

$$1 \le \frac{2}{3}, \text{ false}$$

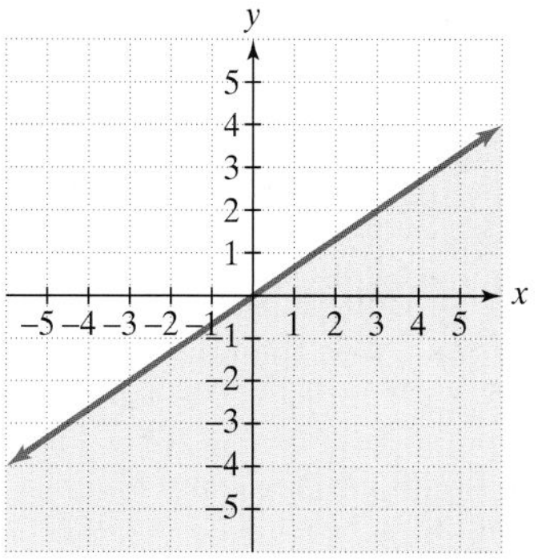


**Figure 8.16** The graph of $y \le \frac{2}{3}x$

**Step 3 If a false statement results, shade the half-plane not containing the test point.** Because 1 is not less than or equal to $\frac{2}{3}$, the test point $(1, 1)$ is not part of the solution set. Thus, the half-plane below the solid line $y = \frac{2}{3}x$ is part of the solution set. The solution set is the line and the half-plane that does not contain the point $(1, 1)$, indicated by shading this half-plane. The graph is shown using green shading and a blue line in Figure 8.16.

**Check Point 2** Graph: $y \geq \frac{1}{2}x$.

In Chapter 1, we learned that $y = b$ graphs as a horizontal line, where $b$ is the $y$-intercept. Similarly, the graph of $x = a$ is a vertical line, where $a$ is the $x$-intercept. Half-planes can be separated by horizontal or vertical lines. For example, Figure 8.17 shows the graph of $y \leq 2$. Because (0, 0) satisfies this inequality ($0 \leq 2$ is true), the graph consists of the half-plane below the line $y = 2$ and the line. Similarly, Figure 8.18 shows the graph of $x < 4$.

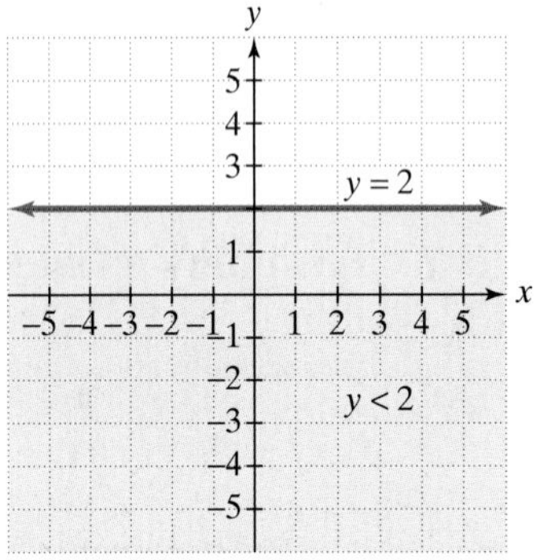


**Figure 8.17** The graph of $y \leq 2$

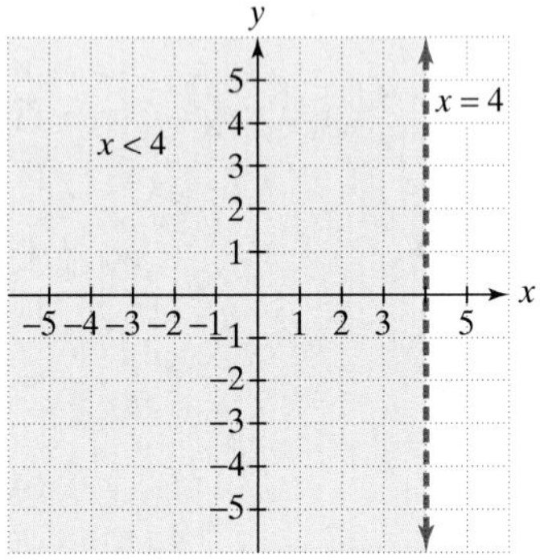


**Figure 8.18** The graph of $x < 4$

**2** Graph a nonlinear inequality in two variables.

## Graphing a Nonlinear Inequality in Two Variables

Example 3 illustrates that a nonlinear inequality in two variables is graphed in the same way that we graph a linear inequality.

### EXAMPLE 3 Graphing a Nonlinear Inequality in Two Variables

Graph: $x^2 + y^2 \leq 9$.

**Solution**

**Step 1 Replace the inequality symbol by = and graph the nonlinear equation.** We need to graph $x^2 + y^2 = 9$. The graph is a circle of radius 3 with its center at the origin. The graph is shown in Figure 8.19 as a solid circle because equality is included in the $\leq$ symbol.

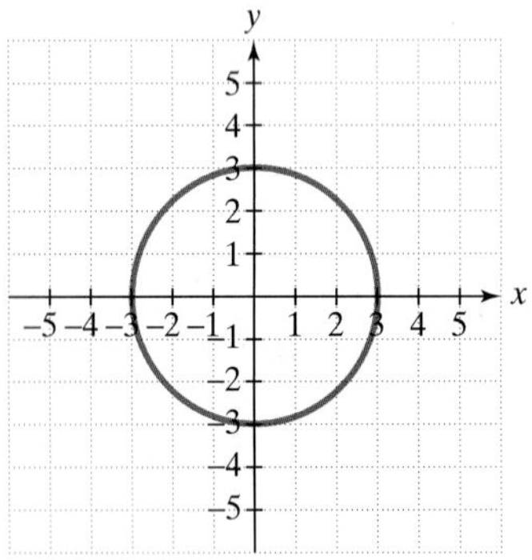


**Figure 8.19** Preparing to graph $x^2 + y^2 \leq 9$

**Step 2 Choose a test point in one of the regions that is not on the circle. Substitute its coordinates into the inequality.** The circle divides the plane into three parts—the circle itself, the region inside the circle, and the region outside the circle. We need to determine whether the region inside or outside the circle is the solution. To do so, we will use the test point (0, 0) from inside the circle.

$$x^2 + y^2 \leq 9 \quad \text{This is the given inequality.}$$

$$\text{Is } 0^2 + 0^2 \leq 9? \quad \text{Test (0, 0) by substituting 0 for } x \text{ and 0 for } y.$$

$$0 + 0 \leq 9$$

$$0 \leq 9, \text{ true}$$

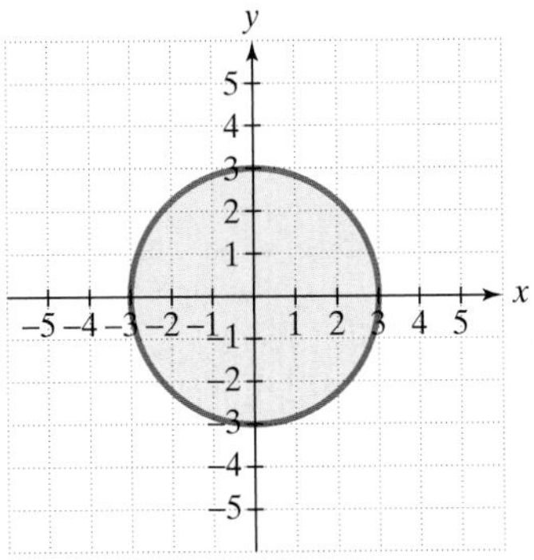


**Figure 8.20** The graph of $x^2 + y^2 \leq 9$

**Step 3 If a true statement results, shade the region containing the test point.** The true statement tells us that all the points inside the circle satisfy $x^2 + y^2 \leq 9$. The graph is shown using green shading and a solid blue circle in Figure 8.20.

**Check Point 3** Graph: $x^2 + y^2 \geq 16$.

**3** Graph a system of inequalities.

## Systems of Inequalities in Two Variables

The **solution set of a system of inequalities** in two variables $x$ and $y$ is the set of all points $(x, y)$ that satisfy each inequality in the system. The **graph of a system of inequalities** in two variables is the graph of the system's solution set. Thus, to graph a system of inequalities in two variables, begin by graphing each individual inequality in the same rectangular coordinate system. Then find the region, if there is one, that is common to every graph in the system.

### EXAMPLE 4 Graphing a System of Linear Inequalities

Graph the solution set:

$$\begin{aligned} 2x - y &< 4 \\ x + y &\geq -1. \end{aligned}$$

**Solution** We begin by graphing $2x - y < 4$. Because the inequality contains a $<$ symbol, rather than $\leq$, we graph $2x - y = 4$ as a dashed line. (If $x = 0$, then $y = -4$, and if $y = 0$, then $x = 2$. The $x$-intercept is 2 and the $y$-intercept is $-4$.) Because $(0, 0)$ makes the inequality $2x - y < 4$ true, we shade the half-plane containing $(0, 0)$, shown in yellow in Figure 8.21.

Now we graph $x + y \geq -1$ in the same rectangular coordinate system. Because the inequality contains a $\geq$ symbol, in which equality is included, we graph $x + y = -1$ as a solid line. (If $x = 0$, then $y = -1$, and if $y = 0$, then $x = -1$. The $x$-intercept and $y$-intercept are both $-1$.) Because $(0, 0)$ makes the inequality true, we shade the half-plane containing $(0, 0)$. This is shown in Figure 8.22 using green vertical shading. The solution set of the system is shown graphically by the intersection (the overlap) of the two half-planes. This is shown in Figure 8.22 as the region in which the yellow shading and the green vertical shading overlap. The solution of the system is shown again in Figure 8.23.

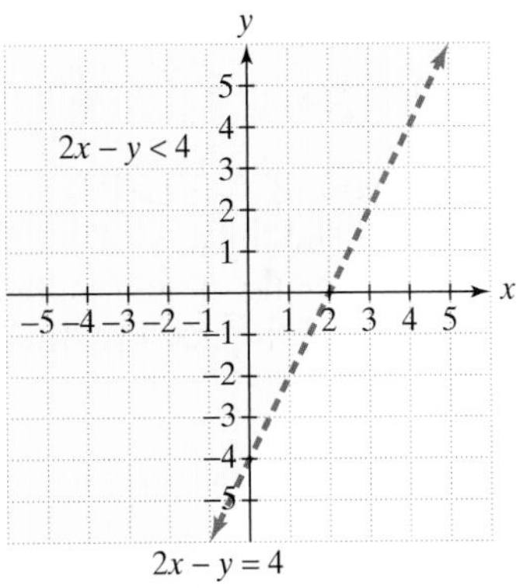


**Figure 8.21** The graph of $2x - y < 4$

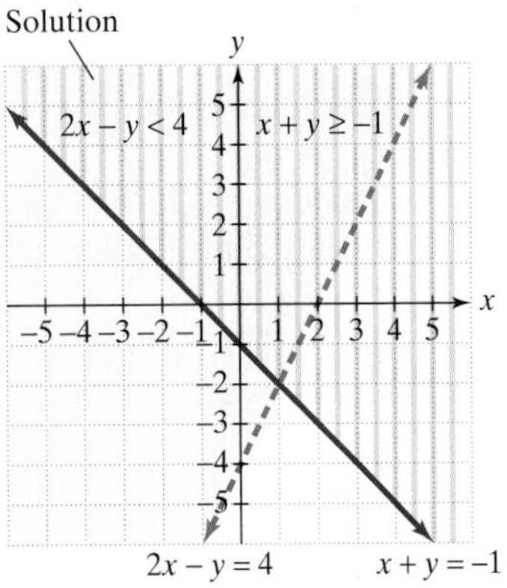


**Figure 8.22** Adding the graph of $x + y \geq -1$

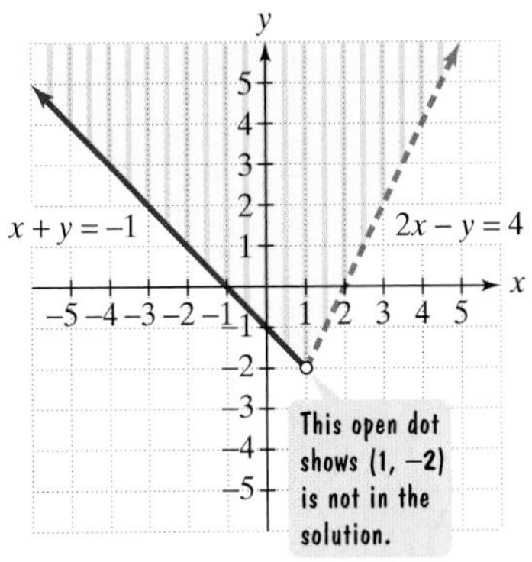


**Figure 8.23** The graph of $2x - y < 4$ and $x + y \geq -1$

**Check Point 4** Graph the solution set:

$$x + 2y > 4$$
$$2x - 3y \leq -6.$$

## EXAMPLE 5 Graphing a System of Inequalities

Graph the solution set:

$$y \geq x^2 - 4$$
$$x - y \geq 2.$$

**Solution** We begin by graphing $y \geq x^2 - 4$. Because equality is included in $\geq$, we graph $y = x^2 - 4$ as a solid parabola. Because $(0, 0)$ makes the inequality $y \geq x^2 - 4$ true (we obtain $0 \geq -4$), we shade the interior portion of the parabola containing $(0, 0)$, shown in yellow in Figure 8.24.

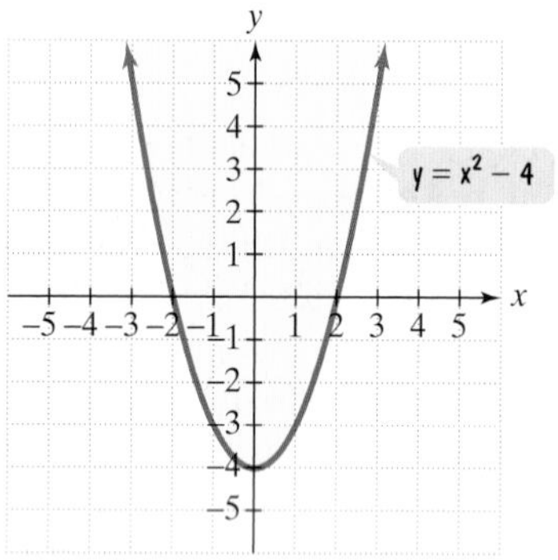


**Figure 8.24** The graph of $y \geq x^2 - 4$

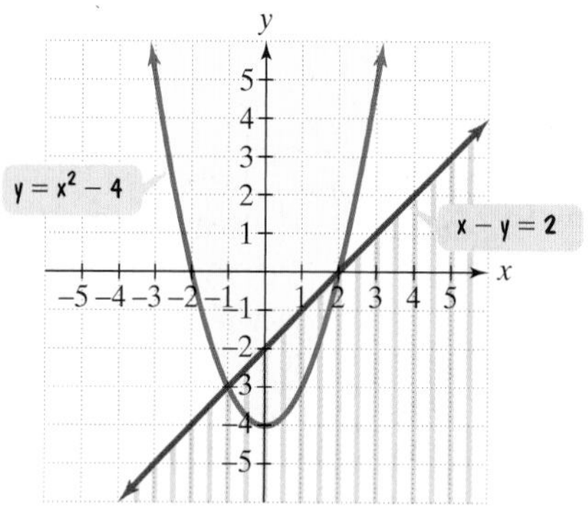


**Figure 8.25** Adding the graph of $x - y \geq 2$

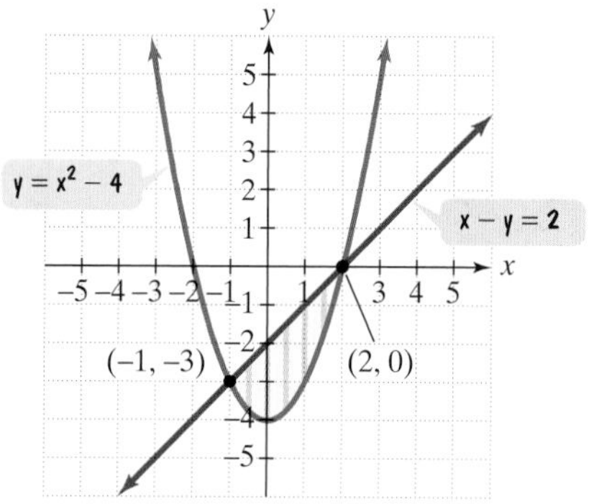


**Figure 8.26** The graph of $y \geq x^2 - 4$ and $x - y \geq 2$

Now we graph $x - y \geq 2$ in the same rectangular coordinate system. First we graph the line $x - y = 2$ using its $x$-intercept, 2, and its $y$-intercept, $-2$. Because $(0, 0)$ makes the inequality $x - y \geq 2$ false (we obtain $0 \geq 2$), we shade the half-plane below the line. This is shown in Figure 8.25 using green vertical shading.

The solution of the system is shown in Figure 8.25 by the intersection (the overlap) of the solid yellow and green vertical shadings. The graph of the system's solution set consists of the region enclosed by the parabola and the line. To find the points of intersection of the parabola and the line, use the substitution method to solve the nonlinear system

$$y = x^2 - 4$$
$$x - y = 2.$$

Take a moment to show that the solutions are $(-1, -3)$ and $(2, 0)$, as shown in Figure 8.26.

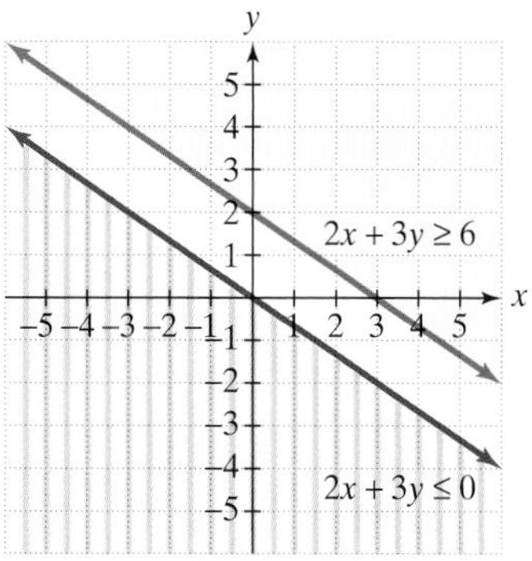


**Figure 8.27** A system of inequalities with no solution.

**Check Point 5** Graph the solution set:

$$y \geq x^2 - 4$$
$$x + y \leq 2.$$

A system of inequalities has no solution if there are no points in the rectangular coordinate system that simultaneously satisfy each inequality in the system. For example, the system

$$2x + 3y \geq 6$$
$$2x + 3y \leq 0$$

whose graph is shown in Figure 8.27 has no overlapping region. Thus, the system has no solution.

## EXAMPLE 6 Graphing a System of Inequalities

Graph the solution set:

$$x - y < 2$$
$$-2 \leq x < 4$$
$$y < 3.$$

**Solution** We begin by graphing $x - y < 2$, the first given inequality. The line $x - y = 2$ has an $x$-intercept of 2 and a $y$-intercept of $-2$. The test point $(0, 0)$ makes the inequality $x - y < 2$ true, and its graph is shown in Figure 8.28.

Now let's consider the second given inequality $-2 \leq x < 4$. Replacing the inequality symbols by $=$, we obtain $x = -2$ and $x = 4$, graphed as vertical lines. The line of $x = 4$ is not included. Using $(0, 0)$ as a test point and substituting the $x$-coordinate, 0, into $-2 \leq x < 4$, we obtain the true statement $-2 \leq 0 < 4$. We therefore shade the region between the vertical lines. We've added this region to Figure 8.28, intersecting the region between the vertical lines with the yellow region in Figure 8.28. The resulting region is shown in yellow and green vertical shading in Figure 8.29.

Finally, let's consider the third given inequality, $y < 3$. Replacing the inequality symbol by $=$, we obtain $y = 3$, which graphs as a horizontal line. Because $(0, 0)$ satisfies $y < 3$ ($0 < 3$ is true), the graph consists of the half-plane below the line $y = 3$. We've added this half-plane to the region in Figure 8.29, intersecting the half-plane with this region. The resulting region is shown in yellow and green vertical shading in Figure 8.30. This region represents the graph of the solution set of the given system.

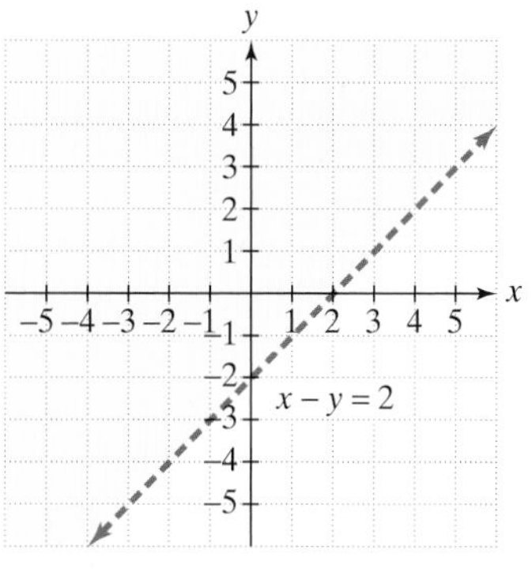


**Figure 8.28** The graph of $x - y < 2$

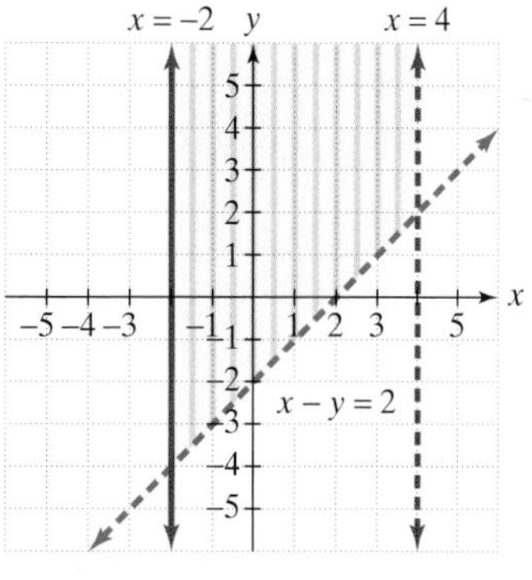


**Figure 8.29** The graph of $x - y < 2$ and $-2 \leq x < 4$

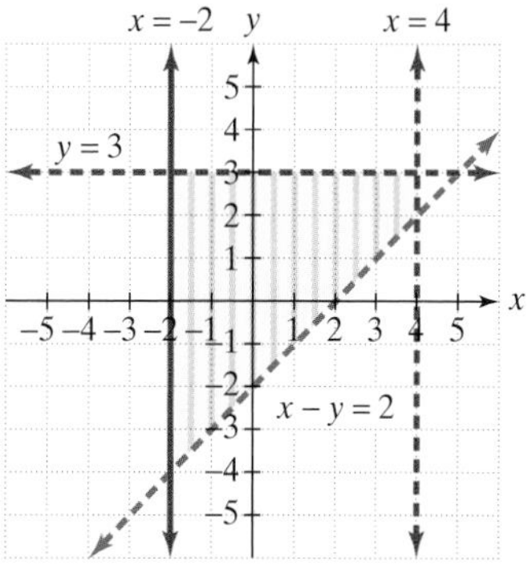


**Figure 8.30** The graph of $x - y < 2$ and $-2 \leq x < 4$ and $y < 3$

**Check Point 6** Graph the solution set:

$$x + y < 2$$
$$-2 \leq x < 1$$
$$y > -3.$$

**4** Solve applied problems involving systems of inequalities.

## Applications

Now we are ready to use a system of inequalities to establish a target zone for your workouts.

### EXAMPLE 7 Inequalities and Aerobic Exercise

For people between ages 10 and 70, inclusive, the target zone for aerobic exercise is given by the following system of inequalities in which $a$ represents one's age and $p$ is one's pulse rate.

$$2a + 3p \geq 450$$
$$a + p \leq 190$$

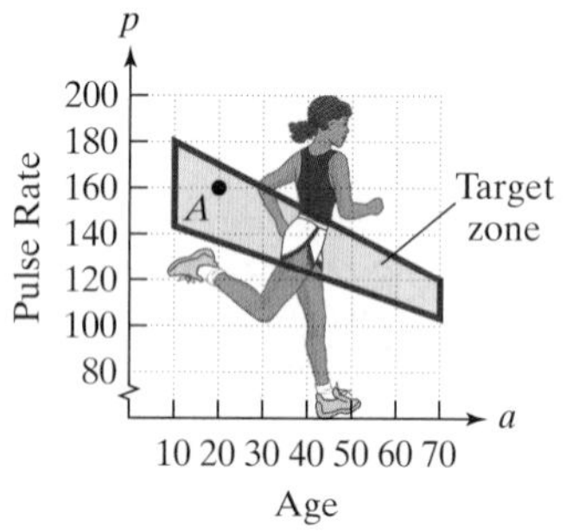


**Figure 8.31**

The graph of this target zone is shown in Figure 8.31. Find your age. The line segments on the top and bottom of the shaded region indicate upper and lower limits for your pulse rate, in beats per minute, when engaging in aerobic exercise.

**a.** What are the coordinates of point $A$ and what does this mean in terms of age and pulse rate?

**b.** Show that the coordinates of point $A$ satisfy each inequality in the system.

**Solution**

**a.** Point $A$ has coordinates $(20, 160)$. This means that a pulse rate of 160 beats per minute is within the target zone for a 20-year-old person engaged in aerobic exercise.

**b.** We can show that $(20, 160)$ satisfies each inequality by substituting 20 for $a$ and 160 for $p$.

$$2a + 3p \geq 450$$
$$\text{Is } 2(20) + 3(160) \geq 450?$$
$$40 + 480 \geq 450$$
$$520 \geq 450, \text{ true}$$

$$a + p \leq 190$$
$$\text{Is } 20 + 160 \leq 190?$$
$$180 \leq 190, \text{ true}$$

The pair $(20, 160)$ makes each inequality true, so it satisfies each inequality in the system.

**Check Point 7** Identify a point other than $A$ in the target zone in Figure 8.31.

**a.** What are the coordinates of this point and what does this mean in terms of age and pulse rate?

**b.** Show that the coordinates of the point satisfy each inequality in the system in Example 7.

# EXERCISE SET 8.5

## Practice Exercises

*In Exercises 1–22, graph each inequality.*

1. $x + 2y \le 8$
2. $3x - 6y \le 12$
3. $x - 2y > 10$
4. $2x - y > 4$
5. $y \le \frac{1}{3}x$
6. $y \le \frac{1}{4}x$
7. $y > 2x - 1$
8. $y > 3x + 2$
9. $x \le 1$
10. $x \le -3$
11. $y > 1$
12. $y > -3$
13. $x^2 + y^2 \le 1$
14. $x^2 + y^2 \le 4$
15. $x^2 + y^2 > 25$
16. $x^2 + y^2 > 36$
17. $y < x^2 - 1$
18. $y < x^2 - 9$
19. $y \ge x^2 - 9$
20. $y \ge x^2 - 1$
21. $y > 2^x$
22. $y \le 3^x$

*In Exercises 23–52, graph the solution set of each system of inequalities or indicate that the system has no solution.*

23. $3x + 6y \le 6$
    $2x + y \le 8$
24. $x - y \ge 4$
    $x + y \le 6$
25. $2x - 5y \le 10$
    $3x - 2y > 6$
26. $2x - y \le 4$
    $3x + 2y > -6$
27. $y > 2x - 3$
    $y < -x + 6$
28. $y < -2x + 4$
    $y < x - 4$
29. $x + 2y \le 4$
    $y \ge x - 3$
30. $x + y \le 4$
    $y \ge 2x - 4$
31. $x \le 2$
    $y \ge -1$
32. $x \le 3$
    $y \le -1$
33. $-2 \le x < 5$
34. $-2 < y \le 5$
35. $x - y \le 1$
    $x \ge 2$
36. $4x - 5y \ge -20$
    $x \ge -3$
37. $x + y > 4$
    $x + y < -1$
38. $x + y > 3$
    $x + y < -2$
39. $x + y > 4$
    $x + y > -1$
40. $x + y > 3$
    $x + y > -2$
41. $y \ge x^2 - 1$
    $x - y \ge -1$
42. $y \ge x^2 - 4$
    $x - y \ge 2$
43. $x^2 + y^2 \le 16$
    $x + y > 2$
44. $x^2 + y^2 \le 4$
    $x + y > 1$
45. $x^2 + y^2 > 1$
    $x^2 + y^2 < 4$
46. $x^2 + y^2 > 1$
    $x^2 + y^2 < 9$
47. $x - y \le 2$
    $x \ge -2$
    $y \le 3$
48. $3x + y \le 6$
    $x \ge -2$
    $y \le 4$
49. $x \ge 0$
    $y \ge 0$
    $2x + 5y \le 10$
    $3x + 4y \le 12$
50. $x \ge 0$
    $y \ge 0$
    $2x + y \le 4$
    $2x - 3y \le 6$
51. $3x + y \le 6$
    $2x - y \le -1$
    $x \ge -2$
    $y \le 4$
52. $2x + y \le 6$
    $x + y \ge 2$
    $1 \le x \le 2$
    $y \le 3$

## Application Exercises

53. Use Figure 8.31 on page 732 to solve this exercise.
    a. Find a pulse rate that lies within the target zone for a person your age engaged in aerobic exercise.
    b. Express your answer in part (a) as an ordered pair. Show that the coordinates of this ordered pair satisfy each inequality in the system.

*The shaded region in the figure shows recommended weight and height combinations based on information from the Department of Agriculture. Use this region to solve Exercises 54–57.*

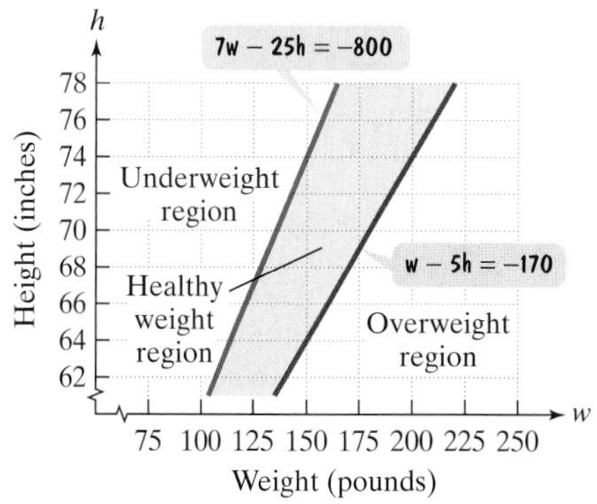

**54.** Is a person who is 70 inches tall weighing 175 pounds within the healthy weight region?

**55.** Is a person who is 64 inches tall weighing 105 pounds within the healthy weight region?

**56.** Estimate the recommended weight range for a person who is 6 feet tall.

**57.** Write a system of linear inequalities that describes the region for recommended weight and height combinations.

*Temperature and precipitation affect whether or not trees and forests can grow. At certain levels of precipitation and temperature, only grasslands and deserts will exist. The figure shows three kinds of regions—deserts, grasslands, and forests—that result from various ranges of temperature and precipitation. Use the figure to solve Exercises 58–60.*

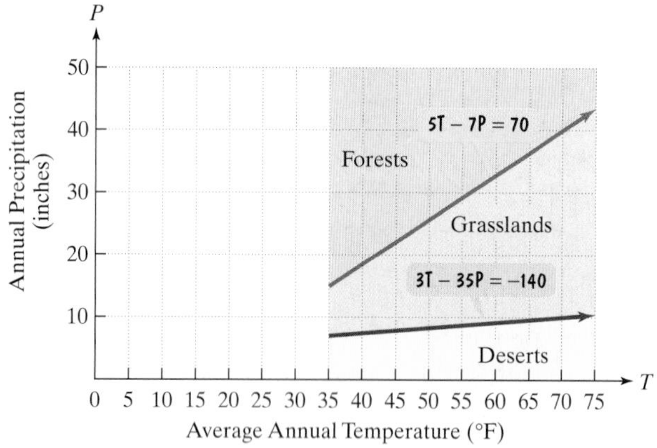


*Source*: A. Miller and J. Thompson, *Elements of Meterology*

**58.** Write a system of inequalities that describe where deserts occur.

**59.** Write a system of inequalities that describe where forests occur.

**60.** Write a system of inequalities that describe where grasslands occur.

**61.** Many elevators have a capacity of 2000 pounds. If a child averages 50 pounds and an adult 150 pounds, write an inequality that describes when $x$ children and $y$ adults will cause the elevator to be overloaded. Graph the inequality. Select an ordered pair satisfying the inequality. Describe what this means in practical terms.

**62.** Suppose a patient is not allowed to have more than 330 milligrams of cholesterol from a diet of eggs and meat. Each egg provides 165 milligrams of cholesterol and each ounce of meat provides 110 milligrams of cholesterol. Thus, $165x + 110y \leq 330$, where $x$ is the number of eggs and $y$ the number of ounces of meat. Graph the inequality in the first quadrant. Give the coordinates of any two points in the solution set. Describe what each set of coordinates means in terms of the variables in the problem.

**63.** A person with $15,000 plans to place the money in two investments. One investment is high risk, high yield; the other is low risk, low yield. At least $2000 is to be placed in the high-risk investment. Furthermore, the amount invested at low risk should be at least three times the amount invested at high risk. Find and graph a system of inequalities that describes all possibilities for placing the money in the high- and low-risk investments.

**64.** Promoters of a rock concert must sell at least 25,000 tickets priced at $35 and $50 per ticket. Furthermore, the promoters must take in at least $1,025,000 in ticket sales. Find and graph a system of inequalities that describes all possibilities for selling the $35 tickets and the $50 tickets.

## Writing in Mathematics

**65.** What is a half-plane?

**66.** What does a dashed line mean in the graph of an inequality?

**67.** Explain how to graph $2x - 3y < 6$.

**68.** Compare the graphs of $3x - 2y > 6$ and $3x - 2y \leq 6$. Discuss similarities and differences between the graphs.

**69.** Describe how to solve a system of inequalities.

**70.** Look at the shaded region showing recommended weight and height combinations in the figure for Exercises 54–57. Describe why a system of inequalities, rather than an equation, is better suited to give the recommended combinations.

## Technology Exercises

*Graphing utilities can be used to shade regions in the rectangular coordinate system, thereby graphing an inequality in two variables. Read the section of the user's manual for your graphing utility that describes how to shade a region. Then use your graphing utility to graph the inequalities in Exercises 71–74.*

**71.** $y \leq 4x + 4$

**72.** $y \geq \frac{2}{3}x - 2$

**73.** $y \geq x^2 - 4$

**74.** $y \geq \frac{1}{2}x^2 - 2$

**75.** Does your graphing utility have any limitations in terms of graphing inequalities? If so, what are they?

**76.** Use a graphing utility with a SHADE feature to verify any five of the graphs that you drew by hand in Exercises 1–22.

**77.** Use a graphing utility with a SHADE feature to verify any five of the graphs that you drew by hand for the systems in Exercises 23–52.

## Critical Thinking Exercises

**78.** Write a system of inequalities that has no solution.

**79.** Write a system of inequalities that describes the shaded region in the figure at the top of the next column.

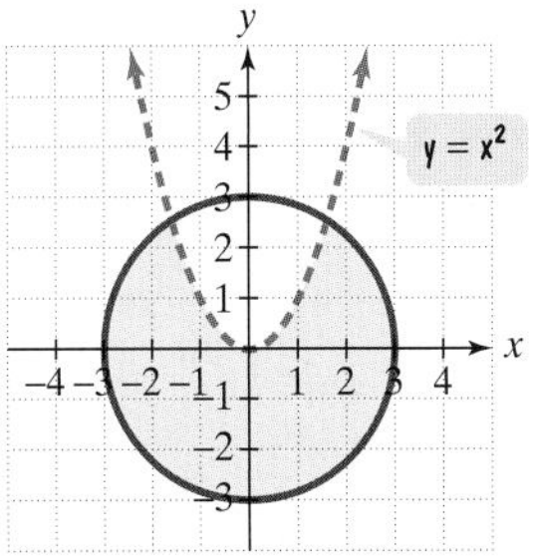


**80.** Sketch the graph of the solution set for the following system of inequalities:

$$y \geq nx + b \quad (n < 0, b > 0)$$
$$y \leq mx + b \quad (m > 0, b > 0).$$

**81.** Sketch the graph of the solution set for the following system of inequalities:

$$|x + y| \leq 3$$
$$|y| \leq 2.$$

# SECTION 8.6 Linear Programming

## Objectives

1. Write an objective function describing a quantity that must be maximized or minimized.
2. Use inequalities to describe limitations in a situation.
3. Use linear programming to solve problems.

West Berlin children at Tempelhof airport watch fleets of U.S. airplanes bringing in supplies to circumvent the Russian blockade. The airlift began June 28, 1948 and continued for 15 months.

The Berlin Airlift (1948–1949) was an operation by the United States and Great Britain. It was a response to military action by the former Soviet Union: The Soviet troops closed all roads and rail lines between West Germany and Berlin, cutting off supply routes to the city. The Allies used a mathematical technique developed during World War II to maximize the amount of supplies transported. During the 15-month airlift, 278,228 flights provided basic necessities to blockaded Berlin, saving one of the world's great cities.

In this section, we will look at an important application of systems of linear inequalities. Such systems arise in **linear programming**, a method for solving problems in which a particular quantity that must be maximized or minimized is limited. Linear programming is one of the most widely used tools in management science. It helps businesses allocate resources to manufacture products in a way that will maximize profit. Linear programming accounts for more than 50% and perhaps as much as 90% of all computing time used for management decisions in business. The Allies used linear programming to save Berlin.

1 Write an objective function describing a quantity that must be maximized or minimized.

## Objective Functions in Linear Programming

Many problems involve quantities that must be maximized or minimized. Businesses are interested in maximizing profit. An operation in which bottled water and medical kits are shipped to earthquake victims needs to maximize the number of victims helped by this shipment. An **objective function** is an algebraic expression in two or more variables describing a quantity that must be maximized or minimized.

### EXAMPLE 1 Writing an Objective Function

Bottled water and medical supplies are to be shipped to victims of an earthquake by plane. Each container of bottled water will serve 10 people and each medical kit will aid 6 people. If $x$ represents the number of bottles of water to be shipped and $y$ represents the number of medical kits, write the objective function that describes the number of people that can be helped.

**Solution** Because each bottle of water serves 10 people and each medical kit aids 6 people, we have

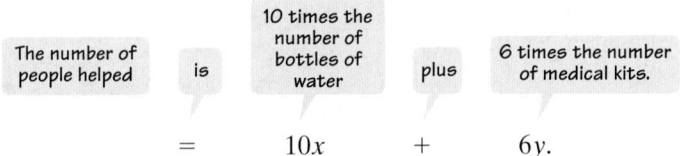

| The number of people helped | is | 10 times the number of bottles of water | plus | 6 times the number of medical kits. |
|---|---|---|---|---|
| | $=$ | $10x$ | $+$ | $6y.$ |

Using $z$ to represent the objective function, we have

$$z = 10x + 6y.$$

Unlike the functions that we have seen so far, the objective function is an equation in three variables. For a value of $x$ and a value of $y$, there is one and only one value of $z$. Thus, $z$ is a function of $x$ and $y$.

**Check Point 1** A company manufactures bookshelves and desks for computers. Let $x$ represent the number of bookshelves manufactured daily and $y$ the number of desks manufactured daily. The company's profits are \$25 per bookshelf and \$55 per desk. Write the objective function that describes the company's total daily profit, $z$, from $x$ bookshelves and $y$ desks. (Checkpoints 1 through 4 are related to this situation, so keep track of your answers.)

2 Use inequalities to describe limitations in a situation.

## Constraints in Linear Programming

Ideally, the number of earthquake victims helped in Example 1 should increase without restriction so that every victim receives water and medical kits. However, the planes that ship these supplies are subject to weight and volume restrictions. In linear programming problems, such restrictions are called **constraints**. Each constraint is expressed as a linear inequality. The list of constraints forms a system of linear inequalities.

## EXAMPLE 2 Writing a Constraint

Each plane can carry no more than 80,000 pounds. The bottled water weighs 20 pounds per container and each medical kit weighs 10 pounds. If $x$ represents the number of bottles of water to be shipped and $y$ represents the number of medical kits, write an inequality that describes this constraint.

**Solution** Because each plane can carry no more than 80,000 pounds, we have

| The total weight of the water bottles | plus | The total weight of the medical kits | must be less than or equal to | 80,000 pounds. |
|---|---|---|---|---|
| $20x$ | $+$ | $10y$ | $\leq$ | 80,000. |
| Each bottle weighs 20 pounds. | | Each kit weighs 10 pounds. | | |

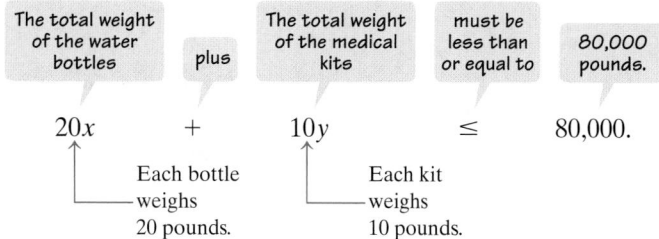

The plane's weight constraint is described by the inequality

$$20x + 10y \leq 80{,}000.$$

**Check Point 2** To maintain high quality, the company in Checkpoint 1 should not manufacture more than 80 bookshelves and desks per day. Write an inequality that describes this constraint.

In addition to a weight constraint on its cargo, each plane has a limited amount of space in which to carry supplies. Example 3 demonstrates how to express this constraint.

## EXAMPLE 3 Writing a Constraint

Planes can carry a total volume for supplies that does not exceed 6000 cubic feet. Each water bottle is 1 cubic foot and each medical kit also has a volume of 1 cubic foot. With $x$ still representing the number of water bottles and $y$ the number of medical kits, write an inequality that describes this second constraint.

**Solution** Because each plane can carry a volume of supplies that does not exceed 6000 cubic feet, we have

| The total volume of the water bottles | plus | The total volume of the medical kits | must be less than or equal to | 6000 cubic feet. |
|---|---|---|---|---|
| $1x$ | $+$ | $1y$ | $\leq$ | 6000. |
| Each bottle is 1 cubic foot. | | Each kit is 1 cubic foot. | | |

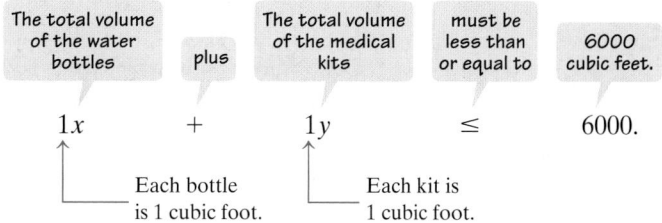

The plane's volume constraint is described by the inequality $x + y \leq 6000$.

In summary, here's what we have described in this aid-to-earthquake-victims situation:

$$z = 10x + 6y$$ This is the objective function describing the number of people helped with x bottles of water and y medical kits.

$$20x + 10y \leq 80{,}000$$
$$x + \quad y \leq 6000.$$
These are the constraints based on each plane's weight and volume limitations.

**Check Point 3** To meet customer demand, the company in Checkpoint 1 must manufacture between 30 and 80 bookshelves per day. Furthermore, the company must manufacture at least 10 and no more than 30 desks per day. Write an inequality that describes each of these sentences. Then summarize what you have described about this company by writing the objective function for its profits, and the three constraints.

**3** Use linear programming to solve problems.

## Solving Problems with Linear Programming

The problem in the earthquake situation described previously is to maximize the number of victims who can be helped, subject to the planes' weight and volume constraints. The process of solving this problem is called linear programming, based on a theorem that was proven during World War II.

### Solving a Linear Programming Problem

Let $z = ax + by$ be an objective function that depends on $x$ and $y$. Furthermore, $z$ is subject to a number of constraints on $x$ and $y$. If a maximum or minimum value of $z$ exists, it can be determined as follows:

1. Graph the system of inequalities representing the constraints.
2. Find the value of the objective function at each corner, or **vertex**, of the graphed region. The maximum and minimum of the objective function occur at one or more of the corner points.

## EXAMPLE 4 Solving a Linear Programming Problem

Determine how many bottles of water and how many medical kits should be sent on each plane to maximize the number of earthquake victims who can be helped.

**Solution** We must maximize $z = 10x + 6y$ subject to the constraints

$$20x + 10y \leq 80{,}000$$
$$x + \quad y \leq 6000.$$

**Step 1 Graph the system of inequalities representing the constraints.** Because $x$ (the number of bottles of water per plane) and $y$ (the number of medical kits per plane) must be nonnegative, we need to graph the system of inequalities in quadrant I and its boundary only. To graph the inequality $20x + 10y \leq 80{,}000$, we graph the equation $20x + 10y = 80{,}000$ as a solid blue line (Figure 8.32). Setting $y = 0$, the $x$-intercept is 4000 and setting $x = 0$, the $y$-intercept is 8000. Using $(0, 0)$ as a test point, the inequality is satisfied, so we shade below the blue line, as shown in yellow in Figure 8.32. Now we graph $x + y \leq 6000$ by first graphing $x + y = 6000$ as a solid line. Setting $y = 0$, the $x$-intercept is 6000. Setting $x = 0$, the $y$-intercept is 6000.

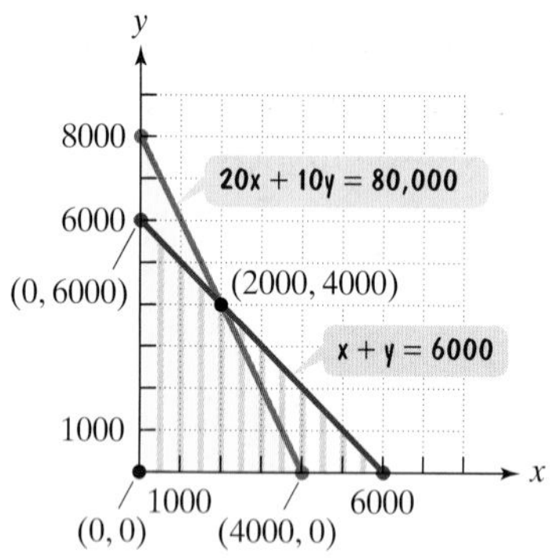


**Figure 8.32** The region in quadrant I representing the constraints
$20x + 10y \leq 80{,}000$
$x + y \leq 6000$

Using (0, 0) as a test point, the inequality is satisfied, so we shade below the red line, as shown using green vertical shading in Figure 8.32.

We use the addition method to find where the lines $20x + 10y = 80{,}000$ and $x + y = 6000$ intersect.

$$\begin{aligned} 20x + 10y &= 80{,}000 \xrightarrow{\text{No change}} & 20x + 10y &= 80{,}000 \\ x + y &= 6000 \xrightarrow{\text{Multiply by } -10.} & -10x - 10y &= -60{,}000 \\ & \text{Add:} & 10x &= 20{,}000 \\ & & x &= 2000 \end{aligned}$$

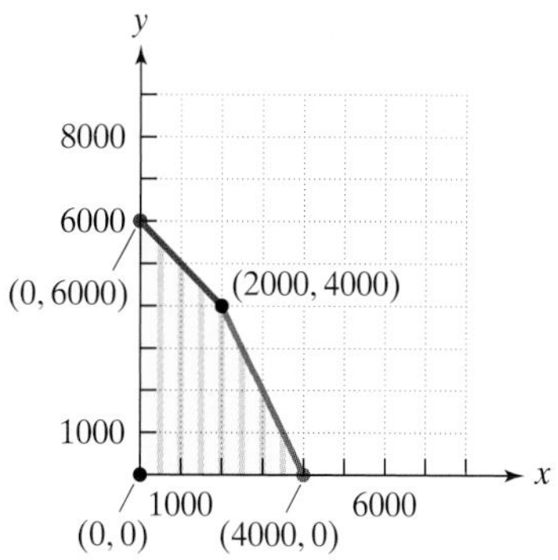


**Figure 8.33**

Back-substituting 2000 for $x$ in $x + y = 6000$, we find $y = 4000$, so the intersection point is (2000, 4000).

The system of inequalities representing the constraints is shown by the region in which the yellow shading and the green vertical shading overlap in Figure 8.32. The graph of the system of inequalities is shown again in Figure 8.33. The red and blue line segments are included in the graph.

**Step 2 Find the value of the objective function at each corner of the graphed region. The maximum and minimum of the objective function occur at one or more of the corner points.** We must evaluate the objective function, $z = 10x + 6y$, at the four corners of the region in Figure 8.33.

| **Corner** $(x, y)$ | **Objective Function** $z = 10x + 6y$ |
|---|---|
| (0, 0) | $z = 10(0) + 6(0) = 0$ |
| (4000, 0) | $z = 10(4000) + 6(0) = 40{,}000$ |
| (2000, 4000) | $z = 10(2000) + 6(4000) = 44{,}000$ ← maximum |
| (0, 6000) | $z = 10(0) + 6(6000) = 36{,}000$ |

Thus, the maximum value of $z$ is 44,000 and this occurs when $x = 2000$ and $y = 4000$. In practical terms, this means that the maximum number of earthquake victims who can be helped with each plane shipment is 44,000. This can be accomplished by sending 2000 water bottles and 4000 medical kits per plane.

**Check Point 4** For the company in Checkpoints 1–3, how many bookshelves and how many desks should be manufactured per day to obtain maximum profit? What is the maximum daily profit?

## EXAMPLE 5 Solving a Linear Programming Problem

Find the maximum value of the objective function

$$z = 2x + y$$

subject to the constraints:

$$x \geq 0,\ y \geq 0$$
$$x + 2y \leq 5$$
$$x - y \leq 2.$$

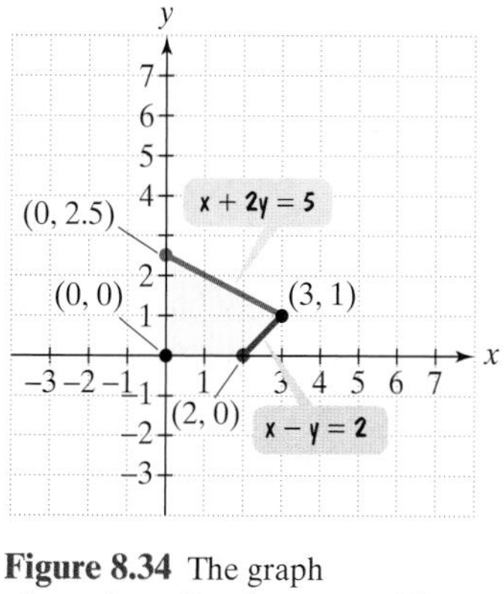


**Figure 8.34** The graph of $x + 2y \leq 5$ and $x - y \leq 2$ in quadrant I

**Solution** We begin by graphing the region in quadrant I ($x \geq 0, y \geq 0$) formed by the constraints. The graph is shown in Figure 8.34.

Now we evaluate the objective function at the four vertices of this region.

**Objective function:** $z = 2x + y$

At $(0, 0)$: $z = 2 \cdot 0 + 0 = 0$

At $(2, 0)$: $z = 2 \cdot 2 + 0 = 4$

At $(3, 1)$: $z = 2 \cdot 3 + 1 = 7$ Maximum value of $z$

At $(0, 2.5)$: $z = 2 \cdot 0 + 2.5 = 2.5$

Thus, the maximum value of $z$ is 7, and this occurs when $x = 3$ and $y = 1$.

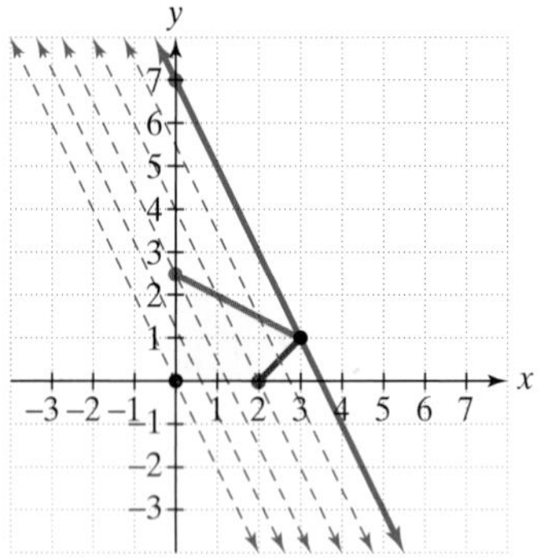


**Figure 8.35** The line with slope −2 with the greatest $y$-intercept that intersects the shaded region passes through one of its vertices.

We can see why the objective function in Example 5 has a maximum value that occurs at a vertex by solving the equation for $y$.

$z = 2x + y$ This is the objective function of Example 5.

$y = -2x + z$ Solve for $y$. Recall that the slope-intercept form of a line is $y = mx + b$.

Slope $= -2$ $y$-intercept $= z$

In this form, $z$ represents the $y$-intercept of the objective function. The equation describes infinitely many parallel lines, each with a slope of −2. The process in linear programming involves finding the maximum $z$-value for all lines that intersect the region determined by the constraints. Of all the lines whose slope is −2, we're looking for the one with the greatest $y$-intercept that intersects the given region. As we see in Figure 8.35, such a line will pass through one (or possibly more) of the vertices of the region.

**Check Point 5** Find the maximum value of the objective function $z = 3x + 5y$ subject to the constraints $x \geq 0$, $y \geq 0$, $x + y \geq 1$, $x + y \leq 6$.

## Faster and Faster

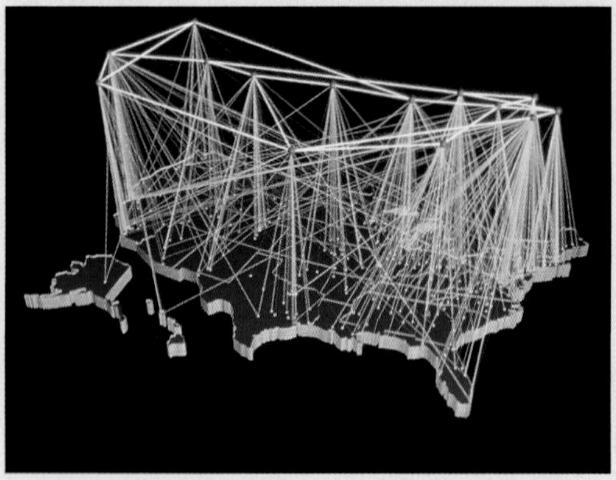

The network of computer linkages in the United States is growing exponentially.

*The problems we solve nowadays have thousands of equations, sometimes a million variables. One of the things that still amazes me is to see a program run on the computer—and to see the answer come out. If we think of the number of combinations of different solutions that we're trying to choose the best of, it's akin to the stars in the heavens. Yet we solve them in a matter of moments. This, to me, is staggering. Not that we can solve them—but that we can solve them so rapidly and efficiently.*

—George Dantzig
Inventor of a linear programming method

Problems in linear programming can involve objective functions with thousands of variables subject to thousands of constraints. Several nongeometric linear programming methods are available on software for solving such problems. And we continue to search for faster and faster linear programming methods. This area of applied mathematics has a direct impact on the efficiency and profitability of numerous industries, including telephone and computer communications, and the airlines.

# EXERCISE SET 8.6

## Practice Exercises

*In Exercises 1–4, find the value of the objective function at each corner of the graphed region. What is the maximum value of the objective function? What is the minimum value of the objective function?*

**1.** Objective Function $z = 5x + 6y$

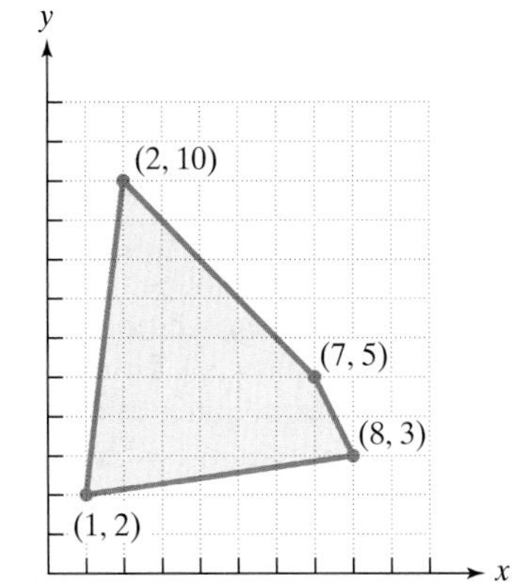


**2.** Objective Function $z = 3x + 2y$

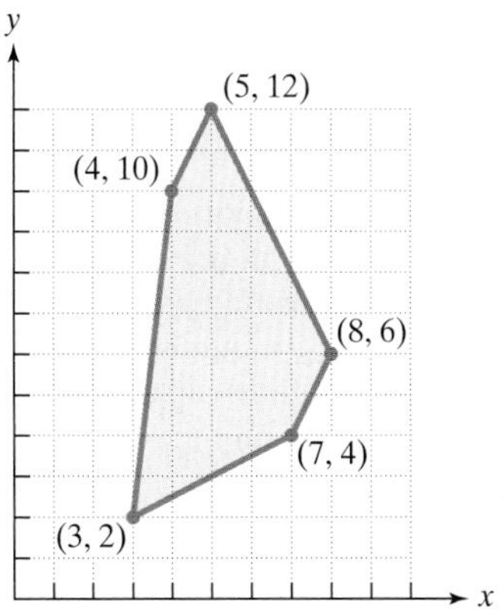


**3.** Objective Function $z = 40x + 50y$

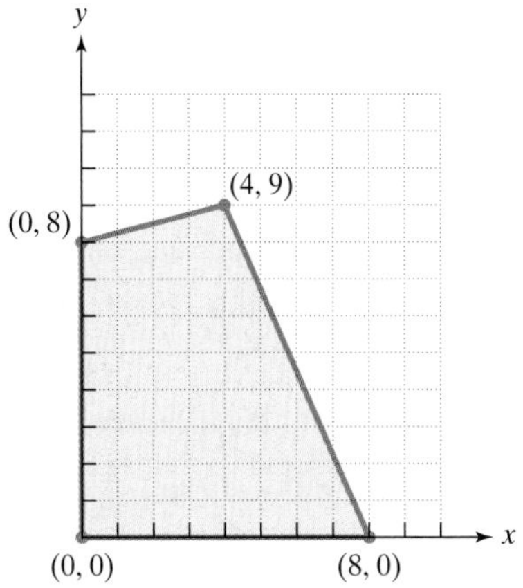


**4.** Objective Function $z = 30x + 45y$

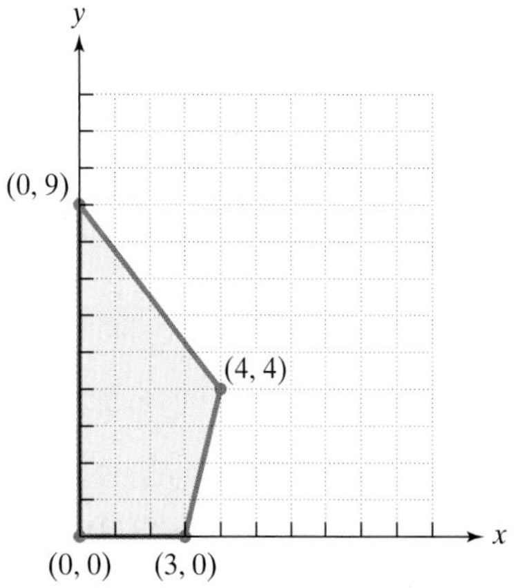


*In Exercises 5–14, an objective function and a system of linear inequalities representing constraints are given.*

**a.** *Graph the system of inequalities representing the constraints.*
**b.** *Find the value of the objective function at each corner of the graphed region.*
**c.** *Use the values in part (b) to determine the maximum value of the objective function and the values of x and y for which the maximum occurs.*

**5.** Objective Function $z = 2x + 3y$
Constraints $x \geq 0, y \geq 0$
$3x + y \leq 6$
$2x + 3y \leq 12$

**6.** Objective Function $z = 3x + 2y$
Constraints $x \geq 0, y \geq 0$
$2x + y \leq 8$
$x + y \geq 4$

**7.** Objective Function $z = 4x + y$
Constraints $x \geq 0, y \geq 0$
$2x + 3y \leq 12$
$x + y \geq 3$

**8.** Objective Function $z = x + 6y$
Constraints $x \geq 0, y \geq 0$
$2x + y \leq 10$
$x - 2y \geq -10$

**9.** Objective Function $z = 3x - 2y$
Constraints $1 \leq x \leq 5$
$y \geq 2$
$x - y \geq -3$

**10.** Objective Function $z = 5x - 2y$
Constraints
$0 \le x \le 5$
$0 \le y \le 3$
$x + y \ge 2$

**11.** Objective Function $z = 4x + 2y$
Constraints
$x \ge 0, y \ge 0$
$2x + 3y \le 12$
$3x + 2y \le 12$
$x + y \ge 2$

**12.** Objective Function $z = 2x + 4y$
Constraints
$x \ge 0, y \ge 0$
$x + 3y \ge 6$
$x + y \ge 3$
$x + y \le 9$

**13.** Objective Function $z = 10x + 12y$
Constraints
$x \ge 0, y \ge 0$
$x + y \le 7$
$2x + y \le 10$
$2x + 3y \le 18$

**14.** Objective Function $z = 5x + 6y$
Constraints
$x \ge 0, y \ge 0$
$2x + y \ge 10$
$x + 2y \ge 10$
$x + y \le 10$

## Application Exercises

**15.** A television manufacturer makes console and wide-screen televisions. The profit per unit is \$125 for the console televisions and \$200 for the wide-screen televisions.

**a.** Let

$x$ = the number of consoles manufactured in a month and

$y$ = the number of wide-screens manufactured in a month.

Write the objective function that describes the total monthly profit.

**b.** The manufacturer is bound by the following constraints:

1. Equipment in the factory allows for making at most 450 console televisions in one month.
2. Equipment in the factory allows for making at most 200 wide-screen televisions in one month.
3. The cost to the manufacturer per unit is \$600 for the console televisions and \$900 for the wide-screen televisions. Total monthly costs cannot exceed \$360,000.

Write a system of three inequalities that describes these constraints.

**c.** Graph the system of inequalities in part (b). Use only the first quadrant and its boundary, because $x$ and $y$ must both be nonnegative.

**d.** Evaluate the objective function for total monthly profit at each of the five vertices of the graphed region. (The vertices should occur at (0, 0), (0, 200), (300, 200), (450, 100), and (450, 0).)

**e.** Complete the missing portions of this statement: The television manufacturer will make the greatest profit by manufacturing ___ console televisions each month and ___ wide-screen televisions each month. The maximum monthly profit is \$ ___.

**16. a.** A student earns \$10 per hour for tutoring and \$7 per hour as a teacher's aid. Let $x$ = the number of hours each week spent tutoring, and $y$ = the number of hours each week spent as a teacher's aid. Write the objective function that describes total weekly earnings.

**b.** The student is bound by the following constraints:

- To have enough time for studies, the student can work no more than 20 hours a week.
- The tutoring center requires that each tutor spend at least three hours a week tutoring.
- The tutoring center requires that each tutor spend no more than eight hours a week tutoring.

Write a system of three inequalities that describes these constraints.

**c.** Graph the system of inequalities in part (b). Use only the first quadrant and its boundary, because $x$ and $y$ are nonnegative.

**d.** Evaluate the objective function for total weekly earnings at each of the four vertices of the graphed region. (The vertices should occur at (3, 0), (8, 0), (3, 17), and (8, 12).)

**e.** Complete the missing portions of this statement: The student can earn the maximum amount per week by tutoring for ___ hours per week and working as a teacher's aid for ___ hours per week. The maximum amount that the student can earn each week is \$ ___.

*Use the two steps for solving a linear programming problem, given in the box on page 738, to solve the problems in Exercises 17–23.*

**17.** A manufacturer produces two models of mountain bicycles. The times (in hours) required for assembling and painting each model are given in the following table.

| | Model *A* | Model *B* |
|---|---|---|
| Assembling | 5 | 4 |
| Painting | 2 | 3 |

The maximum total weekly hours available in the assembly department and the paint department are 200 hours and 108 hours, respectively. The profits per unit are \$25 for model *A* and \$15 for model *B*. How many of each type should be produced to maximize profit?

**18.** A large institution is preparing lunch menus containing foods A and B. The specifications for the two foods are given in the following table.

| Food | Units of Fat per Ounce | Units of Carbohydrates per Ounce | Units of Protein per Ounce |
|---|---|---|---|
| A | 1 | 2 | 1 |
| B | 1 | 1 | 1 |

Each lunch must provide at least 6 units of fat per serving, no more than 7 units of protein, and at least 10 units of carbohydrates. The institution can purchase food A for \$0.12 per ounce and food B for \$0.08 per ounce. How many ounces of each food should a serving contain to meet the dietary requirements at the least cost?

**19.** Food and clothing are shipped to victims of a natural disaster. Each carton of food will feed 5 people, while each carton of clothing will help 6 people. Each 30-cubic-foot box of food weighs 50 pounds and each 20-cubic-foot box of clothing weighs 5 pounds. The commercial carriers transporting food and clothing are bound by the following constraints:

1. The total weight per carrier cannot exceed 18,000 pounds.
2. The total volume must be less than 12,000 cubic feet.

How many cartons of food and clothing should be sent with each plane shipment to maximize the number of people who can be helped?

**20.** On June 24, 1948, the former Soviet Union blocked all land and water routes through East Germany to Berlin. A gigantic airlift was organized using American and British planes to supply food, clothing, and other supplies to the more than 2 million people in West Berlin. The cargo capacity was 30,000 cubic feet for an American plane and 20,000 cubic feet for a British plane. To break the Soviet blockade, the Western Allies had to maximize cargo capacity, but were subject to the following restrictions:

1. No more than 44 planes could be used.
2. The larger American planes required 16 personnel per flight, double that of the requirement for the British planes. The total number of personnel available could not exceed 512.
3. The cost of an American flight was \$9000 and the cost of a British flight was \$5000. Total weekly costs could not exceed \$300,000.

Find the number of American and British planes that were used to maximize cargo capacity.

**21.** A theater is presenting a program on drinking and driving for students and their parents. The proceeds will be donated to a local alcohol information center. Admission is \$2.00 for parents and \$1.00 for students. However, the situation has two constraints: The theater can hold no more than 150 people and every two parents must bring at least one student. How many parents and students should attend to raise the maximum amount of money?

**22.** You are about to take a test that contains computation problems worth 6 points each and word problems worth 10 points each. You can do a computation problem in 2 minutes and a word problem in 4 minutes. You have 40 minutes to take the test and may answer no more than 12 problems. Assuming you answer all the problems attempted correctly, how many of each type of problem must you do to maximize your score? What is the maximum score?

**23.** In 1978, a ruling by the Civil Aeronautics Board allowed Federal Express to purchase larger aircraft. Federal Express's options included 20 Boeing 727s that United Airlines was retiring and/or the French-built Dassault Fanjet Falcon 20. To aid in their decision, executives at Federal Express analyzed the following data:

| | Boeing 727 | Falcon 20 |
|---|---|---|
| **Direct Operating Cost** | \$1400 per hour | \$500 per hour |
| **Payload** | 42,000 pounds | 6000 pounds |

Federal Express was faced with the following constraints:

1. Hourly operating cost was limited to \$35,000.
2. Total payload had to be at least 672,000 pounds.
3. Only twenty 727s were available.

Given the constraints, how many of each kind of aircraft should Federal Express have purchased to maximize the number of aircraft?

## Writing in Mathematics

**24.** What kinds of problems are solved using the linear programming method?

**25.** What is an objective function in a linear programming problem?

**26.** What is a constraint in a linear programming problem? How is a constraint represented?

**27.** In your own words, describe how to solve a linear programming problem.

**28.** Describe a situation in your life in which you would really like to maximize something, but you are limited by at least two constraints. Can linear programming be used in this situation? Explain your answer.

## Technology Exercises

*In Exercises 29–32, use a graphing utility to sketch the region determined by the constraints. Then determine the maximum value of the objective function subject to the contraints.*

**29.** Objective Function $z = 6x + 8y$
Constraints $x \ge 0, y \ge 0$
$x + 2y \le 6$

**30.** Objective Function $z = 30x + 20y$
Constraints $x \ge 0, y \ge 0$
$2x + y \le 14$
$3x + y \le 18$

**31.** Objective Function $z = 9x + 14y$
Constraints $x \ge 0, y \ge 0$
$2x + y \le 10$
$2x + 3y \le 18$

**32.** Objective Function $z = 10x + 3y$
Constraints $0 \le x \le 10, \quad y \ge 0$
$4x + 5y \le 60$
$4x - 5y \ge -20$

## Critical Thinking Exercises

**33.** Suppose that you inherit \$10,000. The will states how you must invest the money. Some (or all) of the money must be invested in stocks and bonds. The requirements are that at least \$3000 be invested in bonds, with expected returns of \$0.08 per dollar, and at least \$2000 be invested in stocks, with expected returns of \$0.12 per dollar. Because the stocks are medium risk, the final stipulation requires that the investment in bonds should never be less than the investment in stocks. How should the money be invested so as to maximize your expected returns?

**34.** Consider the objective function $z = Ax + By$ ($A > 0$ and $B > 0$) subject to the following constraints: $2x + 3y \le 9$, $x - y \le 2$, $x \ge 0$, and $y \ge 0$. Prove that the objective function will have the same maximum value at the vertices $(3, 1)$ and $(0, 3)$ if $A = \frac{2}{3}B$.

## Group Exercises

**35.** Group members should choose a particular field of interest. Research how linear programming is used to solve problems in that field. If possible, investigate the solution of a specific practical problem. Present a report on your findings, including the contributions of George Dantzig, Narendra Karmarkar, and L.G. Khachion to linear programming.

**36.** Members of the group should interview a business executive who is in charge of deciding the product mix for a business. How are production policy decisions made? Are other methods used in conjunction with linear programming? What are these methods? What sort of academic background, particularly in mathematics, does this executive have? Present a group report addressing these questions, emphasizing the role of linear programming for the business.

# CHAPTER SUMMARY, REVIEW, AND TEST

## Summary

### 8.1 Systems of Linear Equations in Two Variables

a. Two equations in the form $Ax + By = C$ are called a system of linear equations. A solution to the system is an ordered pair that satisfies both equations in the system.

b. Linear systems in two variables can be solved by eliminating a variable, using the substitution method (see the box on page 687) or the addition method (see the box on page 689).

c. Some linear systems have no solution and are called inconsistent systems; others have infinitely many solutions. The equations in a linear system with infinitely many solutions are called dependent. For details, see the box on page 691.

### 8.2 Systems of Linear Equations in Three Variables

a. Three equations in the form $Ax + By + Cz = D$ are called a system of linear equations in three variables. A solution to the system is an ordered triple that satisfies all three equations in the system.

b. A system of linear equations in three variables can be solved by eliminating variables. Use the addition method to eliminate any variable, reducing the system to two equations in two variables. Use substitution or the addition method to solve the resulting system in two variables. Details are found in the box on page 700.

### 8.3 Partial Fraction Decomposition

a. Partial fraction decomposition is used on rational expressions in which the numerator and denominator have no common factors and the highest power in the numerator is less than the highest power in the denominator. The steps in partial fraction decomposition are given in the box on page 709.

b. Include one partial fraction with a constant numerator for each distinct linear factor in the denominator. Include one partial fraction with a constant numerator for each power of a repeated linear factor in the denominator.

c. Include one partial fraction with a linear numerator for each distinct prime quadratic factor in the denominator. Include one partial fraction with a linear numerator for each power of a prime, repeated quadratic factor in the denominator.

### 8.4 Systems of Nonlinear Equations in Two Variables

a. A system of two nonlinear equations in two variables contains at least one equation that cannot be expressed as $Ax + By = C$.

b. Nonlinear systems of equations can be solved algebraically by eliminating all occurrences of one of the variables by the substitution and addition methods.

### 8.5 Systems of Inequalities

a. A linear inequality in two variables can be written in the form $Ax + By > C$, $Ax + By \geq C$, $Ax + By < C$, or $Ax + By \leq C$.

b. The procedure for graphing a linear inequality in two variables is given in the box on page 726. A nonlinear inequality in two variables is graphed using the same procedure.

c. To graph the solution set to a system of inequalities, graph each inequality in the system in the same rectangular coordinate system. Then find the region, if there is one, that is common to every graph in the system.

### 8.6 Linear Programming

a. An objective function is an algebraic expression in three variables describing a quantity that must be maximized or minimized.

b. Constraints are restrictions, expressed as linear inequalities.

c. Steps for solving a linear programming problem are given in the box on page 738.

## Review Exercises

### 8.1

*In Exercises 1–5, solve by the method of your choice. Identify systems with no solution and systems with infinitely many solutions, using set notation to express their solution sets.*

**1.** $y = 4x + 1$
$3x + 2y = 13$

**2.** $x + 4y = 14$
$2x - y = 1$

**3.** $5x + 3y = 1$
$3x + 4y = -6$

**4.** $2y - 6x = 7$
$3x - y = 9$

**5.** $4x - 8y = 16$
$3x - 6y = 12$

**6.** Can the graphing-utility-generated screen be the solution for the system

$$x + y = 2$$
$$2x + y = -5?$$

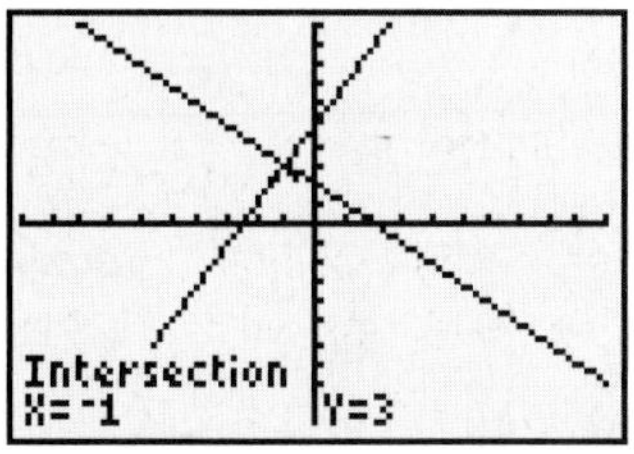


Explain.

**7.** Health experts agree that cholesterol intake should be limited to 300 mg or less each day. Three ounces of shrimp and 2 ounces of scallops contain 156 mg of cholesterol. Five ounces of shrimp and 3 ounces of scallops contain 45 mg of cholesterol less than the suggested maximum daily intake. Determine the cholesterol content in an ounce of each item.

**8.** The calorie-nutrient information for an apple and an avocado is given in the table. How many of each should be eaten to get exactly 1000 calories and 100 grams of carbohydrates?

| | **One Apple** | **One Avocado** |
|---|---|---|
| Calories | 100 | 350 |
| Carbohydrates (grams) | 24 | 14 |

**9.** The weekly demand and supply models for the video *Titanic* at a chain of stores that sells videos are given by the demand model $N = -60p + 1000$ and the supply model $N = 4p + 200$, in which $p$ is the price of the video and $N$ is the number of videos sold or supplied each week to the chain of stores. Find the price at which supply and demand are equal. At this price, how many copies of *Titanic* can be supplied and sold each week?

## 8.2

*Solve each system in Exercises 10–11.*

**10.** $2x - y + z = 1$
$3x - 3y + 4z = 5$
$4x - 2y + 3z = 4$

**11.** $x + 2y - z = 5$
$2x - y + 3x = 0$
$2y + z = 1$

**12.** Find the quadratic function $y = ax^2 + bx + c$ whose graph passes through the points (1, 4), (3, 20), and (−2, 25).

**13.** The graph shows a low savings rate in the United States compared to that of many industrialized countries. The combined rate for Japan, Germany, and France is 45%. The savings rate in Japan exceeds that for Germany by 1% and is 12% less than twice that for France. Find the savings rates for Japan, Germany, and France.

**Comparitive Savings Rates**

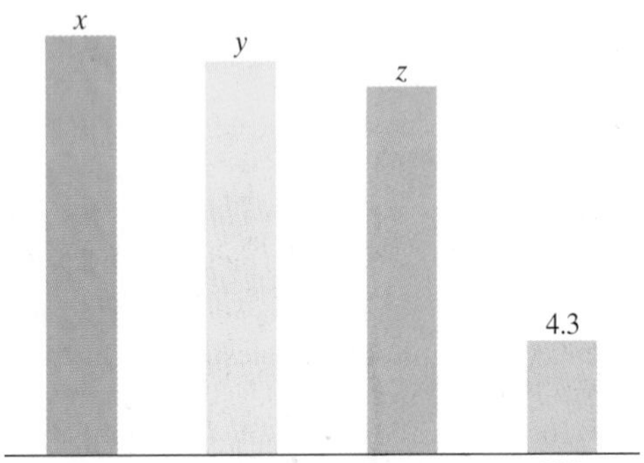


*Source*: Office of Management and Budget

**14.** Describe how to obtain a model for the millions of Americans living in poverty by using the ordered pairs for 1994, 1996, and 1997 in the graph.

**Americans Living in Poverty**

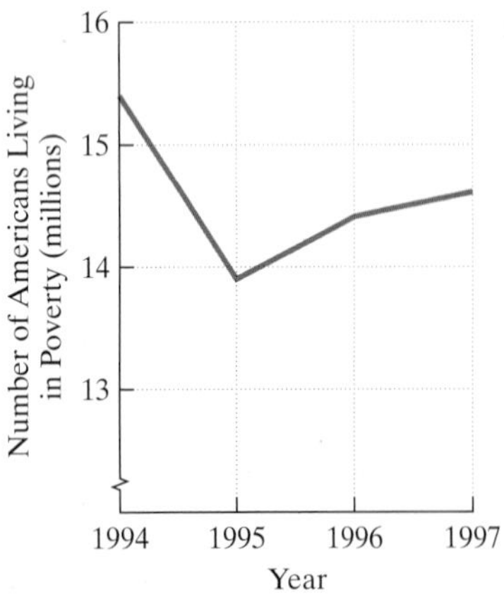


*Source*: U.S. Census Bureau

## 8.3

*In Exercises 15–23, write the partial fraction decomposition of each rational expression.*

**15.** $\dfrac{x}{(x-3)(x+2)}$

**16.** $\dfrac{11x - 2}{x^2 - x - 12}$

**17.** $\dfrac{4x^2 - 3x - 4}{x(x+2)(x-1)}$

**18.** $\dfrac{2x + 1}{(x-2)^2}$

**19.** $\dfrac{2x - 6}{(x-1)(x-2)^2}$

**20.** $\dfrac{3x}{(x-2)(x^2+1)}$

**21.** $\dfrac{7x^2 - 7x + 23}{(x-3)(x^2+4)}$

**22.** $\dfrac{x^3}{(x^2+4)^2}$

**23.** $\dfrac{4x^3 + 5x^2 + 7x - 1}{(x^2 + x + 1)^2}$

## 8.4

*In Exercises 24–34, solve each system by the method of your choice.*

**24.** $5y = x^2 - 1$
$x - y = 1$

**25.** $y = x^2 + 2x + 1$
$x + y = 1$

**26.** $x^2 + y^2 = 2$
$x + y = 0$

**27.** $2x^2 + y^2 = 24$
$x^2 + y^2 = 15$

**28.** $xy - 4 = 0$
$y - x = 0$

**29.** $y^2 = 4x$
$x - 2y + 3 = 0$

**30.** $x^2 + y^2 = 10$
$y = x + 2$

**31.** $xy = 1$
$y = 2x + 1$

**32.** $x + y + 1 = 0$
$x^2 + y^2 + 6y - x = -5$

**33.** $x^2 + y^2 = 13$
$x^2 - y = 7$

**34.** $2x^2 + 3y^2 = 21$
$3x^2 - 4y^2 = 23$

**35.** The perimeter of a rectangle is 26 meters, and its area is 40 square meters. Find its dimensions.

**36.** Find the coordinates of all points $(x, y)$ that lie on the line whose equation is $2x + y = 8$, so that the area of the rectangle shown in the figure is 6 square units.

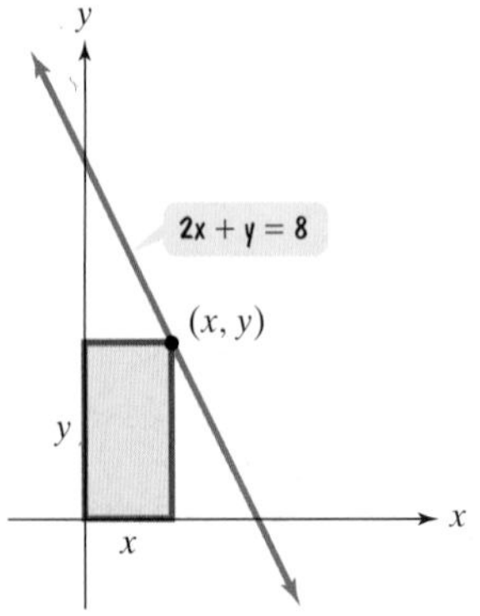

**37.** Two adjoining square fields with an area of 2900 square feet are to be enclosed with 240 feet of fencing. The situation is represented in the figure. Find the length of each side where a variable appears.

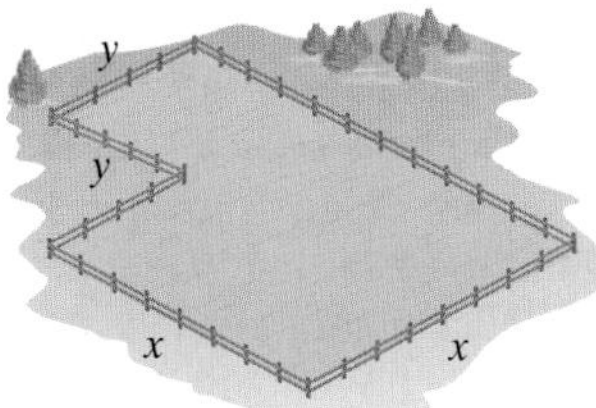


## 8.5

*In Exercises 38–44, graph each inequality.*

**38.** $3x - 4y > 12$

**39.** $y \le -\frac{1}{2}x + 2$

**40.** $x < -2$

**41.** $y \ge 3$

**42.** $x^2 + y^2 > 4$

**43.** $y \le x^2 - 1$

**44.** $y \le 2^x$

*In Exercises 45–54, graph the solution set of each system of inequalities or indicate that the system has no solution.*

**45.** $3x + 2y \ge 6$
$2x + y \ge 6$

**46.** $2x - y \ge 4$
$x + 2y < 2$

**47.** $y < x$
$y \le 2$

**48.** $y \le x$
$2x + 5y \le 10$

**49.** $0 \le x \le 3$
$y > 2$

**50.** $2x + y < 4$
$2x + y > 6$

**51.** $x^2 + y^2 \le 16$
$x + y < 2$

**52.** $x^2 + y^2 \le 9$
$y < -3x + 1$

**53.** $y > x^2$
$x + y < 6$
$y < x + 6$

**54.** $x \ge 0, y \ge 0$
$2x + 3y \le 12$
$3x + y \le 6$

## 8.6

**55.** Find the value of the objective function $z = 2x + 3y$ at each corner of the graphed region shown. What is the maximum value of the objective function? What is the minimum value of the objective function?

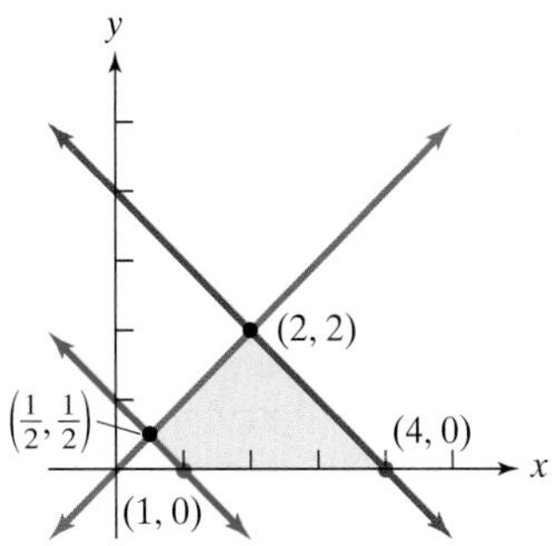


*In Exercises 56–58, graph the region determined by the constraints. Then find the maximum value of the given objective function, subject to the constraints.*

**56.** Objective Function $z = 2x + 3y$
Constraints $x \ge 0, y \ge 0,$
$x + y \le 8$
$3x + 2y \ge 6$

**57.** Objective Function $z = x + 4y$
Contraints $0 \le x \le 5, 0 \le y \le 7$
$x + y \ge 3$

**58.** Objective Function $z = 5x + 6y$
Constraints $x \ge 0, y \ge 0$
$y \le x$
$2x + y \le 12$
$2x + 3y \ge 6$

**59.** A paper manufacturing company converts wood pulp to writing paper and newsprint. The profit on a unit of writing paper is \$500 and the profit on a unit of newsprint is \$350.

**a.** Let $x$ represent the number of units of writing paper produced daily. Let $y$ represent the number of units of newsprint produced daily. Write the objective function that models total daily profit.

**b.** The manufacturer is bound by the following constraints:

1. Equipment in the factory allows for making at most 200 units of paper (writing paper and newsprint) in a day.
2. Regular customers require at least 10 units of writing paper and at least 80 units of newsprint daily.

Write a system of inequalities that models these constraints.

**c.** Graph the inequalities in part (b). Use only the first quadrant, because $x$ and $y$ must both be positive. (*Suggestion:* Let each unit along the $x$- and $y$-axes represent 20.)

**d.** Evaluate the objective profit function at each of the three vertices of the graphed region.

**e.** Complete the missing portions of this statement: The company will make the greatest profit by producing ___ units of writing paper and ___ units of newsprint each day. The maximum daily profit is \$___.

**60.** A manufacturer of lightweight tents makes two models whose specifications are given in the following table.

| | Cutting Time per Tent | Assembly Time per Tent |
|---|---|---|
| **Model *A*** | 0.9 hour | 0.8 hour |
| **Model *B*** | 1.8 hours | 1.2 hours |

On a monthly basis, the manufacturer has no more than 864 hours of labor available in the cutting department and at most 672 hours in the assembly division. The profits come to \$25 per tent for model *A* and \$40 per tent for model *B*. How many of each should be manufactured monthly to maximize the profit?

## Chapter 8 Test

*In Exercises 1–5, solve the system.*

**1.** $x = y + 4$
$3x + 7y = -18$

**2.** $2x + 5y = -2$
$3x - 4y = 20$

**3.** $x + y + z = 6$
$3x + 4y - 7z = 1$
$2x - y + 3z = 5$

**4.** $x^2 + y^2 = 25$
$x + y = 1$

**5.** $2x^2 - 5y^2 = -2$
$3x^2 + 2y^2 = 35$

**6.** Find the partial fraction decomposition for
$$\frac{x}{(x + 1)(x^2 + 9)}.$$

*In Exercises 7–10, graph the solution set of each inequality or system of inequalities.*

**7.** $x - 2y < 8$

**8.** $x \geq 0, y \geq 0$
$3x + y \leq 9$
$2x + 3y \geq 6$

**9.** $x^2 + y^2 > 1$
$x^2 + y^2 < 4$

**10.** $y \leq 1 - x^2$
$x^2 + y^2 \leq 9$

**11.** Find the maximum value of the objective function $z = 3x + 5y$ subject to the following constraints: $x \geq 0$, $y \geq 0, x + y \leq 6, x \geq 2$.

**12.** A theater sells all orchestra seats at one price and all mezzanine seats at another price. One person purchased 4 orchestra tickets and 3 mezzanine tickets for a total of \$134.00. A second person purchased 5 orchestra tickets and 2 mezzanine tickets for \$143.00. What is the price of one orchestra ticket and one mezzanine ticket?

**13.** The demand and supply models for a product are given, respectively, by $N = 1000 - 20p$ and $N = 250 + 5p$. At what price will supply equal demand? At that price, how many units of the product will be supplied and sold?

**14.** Find the quadratic function $y = ax^2 + bx + c$ whose graph passes through the points $(-1, -2)$, $(2, 1)$, and $(-2, 1)$.

**15.** The rectangular plot of land shown in the figure is to be fenced along three sides using 39 feet of fencing. No fencing is to be placed along the river's edge. The area of the plot is 180 square feet. What are its dimensions?

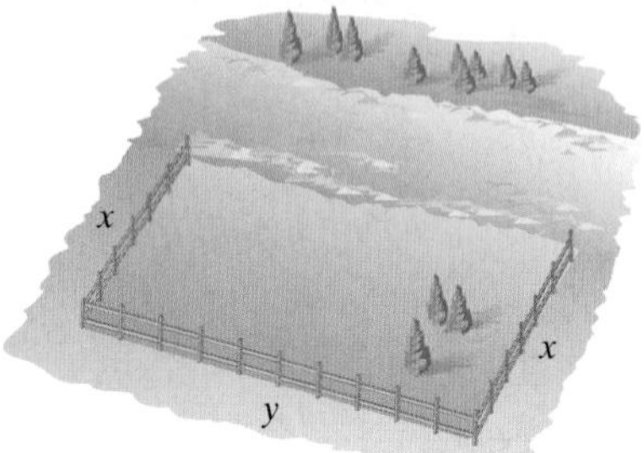


**16.** A manufacturer makes two types of jet skis, regular and deluxe. The profit on a regular jet ski is \$200 and the profit on the deluxe model is \$250. To meet customer demand, the company must manufacture at least 50 regular jet skis per week and at least 75 deluxe models. To maintain high quality, the total number of both models of jet skis manufactured by the company should not exceed 150 per week. How many jet skis of each type should be manufactured per week to obtain maximum profit? What is the maximum weekly profit?

## Cumulative Review Exercises (Chapters 1–8)

*Solve each equation or inequality in Exercises 1–8.*

**1.** $\sqrt{x^2 - 3x} = 2x - 6$

**2.** $4x^2 = 8x - 7$

**3.** $\left|\frac{x}{3} + 2\right| < 4$

**4.** $\frac{x + 5}{x - 1} > 2$

**5.** $2x^3 + x^2 - 13x + 6 = 0$

**6.** $6x - 3(5x + 2) = 4(1 - x)$

**7.** $\log(x + 3) + \log x = 1$

**8.** $3^{x+2} = 11$

*In Exercises 9–12, graph each equation, function, or inequality in the rectangular coordinate system.*

**9.** $f(x) = (x + 2)^2 - 4$

**10.** $2x - 3y \leq 6$

**11.** $y = 3^{x-2}$

**12.** $f(x) = \frac{x^2 - x - 6}{x + 1}$

**13.** Expand and simplify: $\log_2(8x^5)$.

**14.** What interest rate is required for an investment of \$6000 subject to continuous compounding to grow to \$18,000 in 10 years?

**15.** If $f(x) = 7x - 3$, find $f^{-1}(x)$.

**16.** If $f(x) = 7x - 3$ and $g(x) = 3x - 7$, find $g(f(x))$.

**17.** Explain why $x^2 + y^2 = 4$ does not represent $y$ as a function of $x$.

**18.** Solve the system:
$$3x - y = -2$$
$$2x^2 - y = 0.$$

**19.** The length of a rectangle is 1 meter more than twice the width. If the rectangle's area is 36 square meters, find its dimensions.

**20.** The function $f(x) = 0.1x^2 - 3x + 22$ describes the distance, $f(x)$, in feet, needed for an airplane to land when its initial landing speed is $x$ feet per second. Find and interpret $f(90)$. Will there be a problem if 550 feet of runway is available? Explain.

*In Exercises 21–22, verify each identity.*

**21.** $\sec\theta - \cos\theta = \tan\theta\sin\theta$

**22.** $\tan x + \tan y = \frac{\sin(x + y)}{\cos x \cos y}$

*In Exercises 23–24, solve each equation.*

**23.** $\sin\theta = \tan\theta, \quad 0 \leq \theta < 2\pi$

**24.** $2 + \cos 2\theta = 3\cos\theta, \quad 0 \leq \theta < 2\pi$

**25.** In oblique triangle $ABC$, $A = 12°$, $B = 75°$, and $a = 20$. Find $b$ to the nearest tenth.

# Matrices and Determinants

## Chapter 9

Jaron Lanier, who first used the term "virtual reality," is chief scientist for the "tele-immersion" project, which explores the impact of massive bandwidth and computing power. Rectangular arrays of numbers, called *matrices*, play a central role in representing computer images and in the forthcoming technology of tele-immersion. In this chapter, we study matrices and their applications. We begin with solving linear systems using matrices, which leads to a discussion of how computers might unjam traffic and give us a gridlock-free future.

You are being drawn deeper into cyberspace, spending more time online each week. With constantly improving high-resolution images, cyberspace is reshaping your life by nourishing shared enthusiasms. The people who built your computer talk of "bandwidth out the wazoo" that will give you the visual experience, in high-definition 3-D format, of being in the same room with a person who is actually in another city.

## SECTION 9.1 *Matrix Solutions to Linear Systems*

### Objectives

1. Write the augmented matrix for a linear system.
2. Perform matrix row operations.
3. Use matrices and Gaussian elimination to solve systems.
4. Use matrices and Gauss-Jordan elimination to solve systems.

Yes, we overindulged, but it was delicious. Anyway, a few hours of moderate activity and we'll just burn off those extra calories. The following chart should help. We see that the number of calories burned per hour depends on our weight. Four hours of tennis and we'll be as good as new!

**How Fast You Burn Off Calories**

| | **Weight (pounds)** | | | | | |
|---|---|---|---|---|---|---|
| | **110** | **132** | **154** | **176** | **187** | **209** |
| **Activity** | **Calories Burned per Hour** | | | | | |
| Housework | 175 | 210 | 245 | 285 | 300 | 320 |
| Cycling | 190 | 215 | 245 | 270 | 280 | 295 |
| Tennis | 335 | 380 | 425 | 470 | 495 | 520 |
| Watching TV | 60 | 70 | 80 | 85 | 90 | 95 |

The 24 numbers inside the red brackets are arranged in four rows and six columns. This rectangular array of 24 numbers, arranged in rows and columns and placed in brackets, is an example of a **matrix** (plural: **matrices**). The numbers inside the brackets are called **elements** of the matrix. Matrices are used to display information and to solve systems of linear equations. Because systems involving two equations in two variables can easily be solved by substitution or addition, we will focus on matrix solutions to linear systems in three or more variables.

### Solving Linear Systems by Using Matrices

**1** Write the augmented matrix for a linear system.

A matrix gives us a shortened way of writing a system of equations. The first step in solving a system of linear equations using matrices is to write the augmented matrix. An **augmented matrix** has a vertical bar separating the columns of the matrix into two groups. The coefficients of each variable are placed to the left of the vertical line, and the constants are placed to the right. If any variable is missing, its coefficient is 0. Here are two examples.

| System of Linear Equations | Augmented Matrix |
|---|---|
| $\begin{aligned} 3x + y + 2z &= 31 \\ x + y + 2z &= 19 \\ x + 3y + 2z &= 25 \end{aligned}$ | $\left[\begin{array}{ccc\|c} 3 & 1 & 2 & 31 \\ 1 & 1 & 2 & 19 \\ 1 & 3 & 2 & 25 \end{array}\right]$ |
| $\begin{aligned} x + 2y - 5z &= -19 \\ y + 3z &= 9 \\ z &= 4 \end{aligned}$ | $\left[\begin{array}{ccc\|c} 1 & 2 & -5 & -19 \\ 0 & 1 & 3 & 9 \\ 0 & 0 & 1 & 4 \end{array}\right]$ |

Notice how the second matrix contains 1s down the diagonal from upper left to lower right and 0s below the 1s. This arrangement makes it easy to find the solution of the system of equations, as Example 1 shows.

## EXAMPLE 1 Solving a System Using a Matrix

Write the solution set for a system of equations represented by the matrix

$$\left[\begin{array}{ccc|c} 1 & 2 & -5 & -19 \\ 0 & 1 & 3 & 9 \\ 0 & 0 & 1 & 4 \end{array}\right].$$

**Solution** The system represented by the given matrix is

$$\left[\begin{array}{ccc|c} 1 & 2 & -5 & -19 \\ 0 & 1 & 3 & 9 \\ 0 & 0 & 1 & 4 \end{array}\right] \rightarrow \begin{aligned} 1x + 2y - 5z &= -19 \\ 0x + 1y + 3z &= 9 \\ 0x + 0y + 1z &= 4 \end{aligned}.$$

This system can be simplified as follows.

$$\begin{aligned} x + 2y - 5z &= -19 && \text{Equation 1} \\ y + 3z &= 9 && \text{Equation 2} \\ z &= 4 && \text{Equation 3} \end{aligned}$$

The value of $z$ is known. We can find $y$ by back-substitution.

$$\begin{aligned} y + 3z &= 9 && \text{Equation 2} \\ y + 3(4) &= 9 && \text{Substitute 4 for } z. \\ y + 12 &= 9 && \text{Multiply.} \\ y &= -3 && \text{Subtract 12 from both sides.} \end{aligned}$$

With values for $y$ and $z$, we can now use back-substitution to find $x$.

$$\begin{aligned} x + 2y - 5z &= -19 && \text{Equation 1} \\ x + 2(-3) - 5(4) &= -19 && \text{Substitute } -3 \text{ for } y \text{ and 4 for } z. \\ x - 6 - 20 &= -19 && \text{Multiply.} \\ x - 26 &= -19 && \text{Add.} \\ x &= 7 && \text{Add 26 to both sides.} \end{aligned}$$

We see that $x = 7$, $y = -3$, and $z = 4$. The solution set for the system is $\{(7, -3, 4)\}$.

**Check Point 1** Write the solution set for a system of equations represented by the matrix

$$\left[\begin{array}{rrr|r} 1 & -1 & 1 & 8 \\ 0 & 1 & -12 & -15 \\ 0 & 0 & 1 & 1 \end{array}\right].$$

Our goal in solving a linear system using matrices is to produce a matrix similar to the one in Example 1. In general, the matrix will be of the form

$$\left[\begin{array}{ccc|c} 1 & a & b & c \\ 0 & 1 & d & e \\ 0 & 0 & 1 & f \end{array}\right],$$

where $a$ through $f$ represent real numbers. The third row of this matrix gives us the value of one variable. The other variables can then be found by back-substitution.

**2** Perform matrix row operations.

A matrix with 1s down the main diagonal and 0s below the 1s is said to be in **triangular form**. How do we produce a matrix in this form? We use **row operations** on the augmented matrix. These row operations are just like what you did when solving a linear system by the addition method. The difference is that we no longer write the variables, usually represented by $x$, $y$, and $z$.

**Matrix Row Operations**

These row operations produce matrices that lead to systems with the same solution set as the original system.

1. Two rows of a matrix may be interchanged. This is the same as interchanging two equations in the linear system.
2. The elements in any row may be multiplied by a nonzero number. This is the same as multiplying both sides of an equation by a nonzero number.
3. The elements in any row may be multiplied by a nonzero number, and these products may be added to the corresponding elements in any other row. This is the same as multiplying both sides of an equation by a nonzero number and then adding equations to eliminate a variable.

Two matrices are **row equivalent** if one can be obtained from the other by a sequence of row operations.

**Study Tip**

When performing the row operation

$$kR_i + R_j$$

you use row $i$ to find the products. However, **elements in row *i* do not change. It is the elements in row *j* that change:** Add $k$ times the elements in row $i$ to the corresponding elements in row $j$. Replace elements in row $j$ by these sums.

Each matrix row operation in the preceding box can be expressed symbolically as follows:

1. Interchange the elements in the $i$th and $j$th rows: $R_i \leftrightarrow R_j$.
2. Multiply each elements in the $i$th row by $k$: $kR_i$.
3. Add $k$ times the elements in row $i$ to the corresponding elements in row $j$: $kR_i + R_j$.

## EXAMPLE 2 Performing Matrix Row operations

Use the matrix

$$\left[\begin{array}{rrr|r} 3 & 18 & -12 & 21 \\ 1 & 2 & -3 & 5 \\ -2 & -3 & 4 & -6 \end{array}\right]$$

and perform each indicated row operation:

**a.** $R_1 \leftrightarrow R_2$ **b.** $\frac{1}{3}R_1$ **c.** $2R_2 + R_3$

**Solution**

**a.** The notation $R_1 \leftrightarrow R_2$ means to interchange the elements in row 1 and row 2. This results in the row-equivalent matrix.

$$\left[\begin{array}{rrr|r} 1 & 2 & -3 & 5 \\ 3 & 18 & -12 & 21 \\ -2 & -3 & 4 & -6 \end{array}\right].$$

This was row 2; now it's row 1.

This was row 1; now it's row 2.

**b.** The notation $\frac{1}{3}R_1$ means to multiply each element in row 1 by $\frac{1}{3}$. This results in the row-equivalent matrix

$$\left[\begin{array}{ccc|c} \frac{1}{3}(3) & \frac{1}{3}(18) & \frac{1}{3}(-12) & \frac{1}{3}(21) \\ 1 & 2 & -3 & 5 \\ -2 & -3 & 4 & -6 \end{array}\right] = \left[\begin{array}{rrr|r} 1 & 6 & -4 & 7 \\ 1 & 2 & -3 & 5 \\ -2 & -3 & 4 & -6 \end{array}\right].$$

**c.** The notation $2R_2 + R_3$ means to add 2 times the elements in row 2 to the corresponding elements in row 3. Replace the elements in row 3 by these sums. First, we find 2 times the elements in row 2:

$$2(1) \text{ or } 2, \quad 2(2) \text{ or } 4, \quad 2(-3) \text{ or } -6, \quad 2(5) \text{ or } 10.$$

Now we add these products to the corresponding elements in row 3. Although we use row 2 to find the products, row 2 does not change. It is the elements in row 3 that change, resulting in the row-equivalent matrix

$$\left[\begin{array}{ccc|c} 3 & 18 & -12 & 21 \\ 1 & 2 & -3 & 5 \\ -2+2=0 & -3+4=1 & 4+(-6)=-2 & -6+10=4 \end{array}\right] = \left[\begin{array}{rrr|r} 3 & 18 & -12 & 21 \\ 1 & 2 & -3 & 5 \\ 0 & 1 & -2 & 4 \end{array}\right].$$

**Check Point 2** Use the matrix

$$\left[\begin{array}{rrr|r} 4 & 12 & -20 & 8 \\ 1 & 6 & -3 & 7 \\ -3 & -2 & 1 & -9 \end{array}\right]$$

and perform each indicated row operation:

**a.** $R_1 \leftrightarrow R_2$ **b.** $\frac{1}{4}R_1$ **c.** $3R_2 + R_3$

**3** Use matrices and Gaussian elimination to solve systems.

The process that we use to solve linear systems using matrix row operations is called **Gaussian elimination,** after the German mathematician Carl Friedrich Gauss (1777–1835). Here are the steps used in Gaussian elimination.

**Solving Linear Systems Using Gaussian Elimination**

1. Write the augmented matrix for the system.
2. Use matrix row operations to simplify the matrix to one with 1s down the diagonal from upper left to lower right, and 0s below the 1s.
3. Write the system of linear equations corresponding to the matrix in step 2, and use back-substitution to find the system's solution.

## EXAMPLE 3 Gaussian Elimination with Back-Substitution

Use matrices to solve the system

$$\begin{aligned} 3x + y + 2z &= 31 \\ x + y + 2z &= 19 \\ x + 3y + 2z &= 25. \end{aligned}$$

**Solution**

**Step 1 Write the augmented matrix for the system.**

**Linear System**

$$\begin{aligned} 3x + \phantom{3}y + 2z &= 31 \\ x + \phantom{3}y + 2z &= 19 \\ x + 3y + 2z &= 25 \end{aligned}$$

**Augmented Matrix**

$$\left[\begin{array}{ccc|c} 3 & 1 & 2 & 31 \\ 1 & 1 & 2 & 19 \\ 1 & 3 & 2 & 25 \end{array}\right]$$

**Step 2 Use matrix row operations to simplify the matrix to one with 1s down the diagonal from upper left to lower right, and 0s below the 1s.** Our goal is to obtain a matrix of the form

$$\left[\begin{array}{ccc|c} 1 & a & b & c \\ 0 & 1 & d & e \\ 0 & 0 & 1 & f \end{array}\right].$$

Our first step in achieving this goal is to get 1 in the top position of the first column.

We want 1 in this position.

$$\left[\begin{array}{ccc|c} \boxed{3} & 1 & 2 & 31 \\ 1 & 1 & 2 & 19 \\ 1 & 3 & 2 & 25 \end{array}\right]$$

To get 1 in this position, we interchange rows 1 and 2. (We could also interchange rows 1 and 3 to attain our goal.)

$$\left[\begin{array}{ccc|c} 1 & 1 & 2 & 19 \\ 3 & 1 & 2 & 31 \\ 1 & 3 & 2 & 25 \end{array}\right]$$

This was row 2; now it's row 1.

This was row 1; now it's row 2.

Now we want to get 0s below the 1 in the first column.

We want 0 in these positions.

$$\left[\begin{array}{ccc|c} 1 & 1 & 2 & 19 \\ \boxed{3} & 1 & 2 & 31 \\ \boxed{1} & 3 & 2 & 25 \end{array}\right]$$

Let's first get a 0 where there is now a 3. If we multiply the top row of numbers by −3 and add these products to the second row of numbers, we will get 0 in this position. The top row of numbers multiplied by −3 gives

$$-3(1) \text{ or } -3, \quad -3(1) \text{ or } -3, \quad -3(2) \text{ or } -6, \quad -3(19) \text{ or } -57.$$

Now add these products to the corresponding numbers in row 2. Notice that although we use row 1 to find the products, row 1 does not change.

$$\left[\begin{array}{ccc|c} 1 & 1 & 2 & 19 \\ 3+(-3) & 1+(-3) & 2+(-6) & 31+(-57) \\ 1 & 3 & 2 & 25 \end{array}\right] = \left[\begin{array}{ccc|c} 1 & 1 & 2 & 19 \\ 0 & -2 & -4 & -26 \\ \boxed{1} & 3 & 2 & 25 \end{array}\right]$$

We want 0 in this position.

### Study Tip

Start with the augmented matrix.

$$\left[\begin{array}{ccc|c} * & * & * & * \\ * & * & * & * \\ * & * & * & * \end{array}\right]$$

Get a one in upper left-hand corner.

$$\left[\begin{array}{ccc|c} 1 & * & * & * \\ * & * & * & * \\ * & * & * & * \end{array}\right]$$

Get zeros in first column beneath the one.

$$\left[\begin{array}{ccc|c} 1 & * & * & * \\ 0 & * & * & * \\ 0 & * & * & * \end{array}\right]$$

Get a one in the second row/second column position.

$$\left[\begin{array}{ccc|c} 1 & * & * & * \\ 0 & 1 & * & * \\ 0 & * & * & * \end{array}\right]$$

Get zero below the one in the second column.

$$\left[\begin{array}{ccc|c} 1 & * & * & * \\ 0 & 1 & * & * \\ 0 & 0 & * & * \end{array}\right]$$

Get a one in the third row/third column position.

$$\left[\begin{array}{ccc|c} 1 & * & * & * \\ 0 & 1 & * & * \\ 0 & 0 & 1 & * \end{array}\right]$$

We are not yet done with the first column. The voice balloon shows that we want to get another 0 in this column. If we multiply the top row of numbers by −1 and add these products to the third row of numbers, we will get 0 in this position. The top row of numbers multiplied by −1 gives

$$-1(1) \text{ or } -1, \quad -1(1) \text{ or } -1, \quad -1(2) \text{ or } -2, \quad -1(19) \text{ or } -19.$$

Now add these products to the corresponding numbers in row 3.

$$\left[\begin{array}{ccc|c} 1 & 1 & 2 & 19 \\ 0 & -2 & -4 & -26 \\ 1+(-1)=0 & 3+(-1)=2 & 2+(-2)=0 & 25+(-19)=6 \end{array}\right]$$

$$= \left[\begin{array}{ccc|c} 1 & 1 & 2 & 19 \\ 0 & -2 & -4 & -26 \\ 0 & 2 & 0 & 6 \end{array}\right]$$

We move on to the second column. We want 1 in the second row, second column.

We want 1 in this position.

$$\left[\begin{array}{ccc|c} 1 & 1 & 2 & 19 \\ 0 & -2 & -4 & -26 \\ 0 & 2 & 0 & 6 \end{array}\right]$$

To get 1 in the desired position, we multiply −2 by its reciprocal, $-\frac{1}{2}$. Therefore, we multiply all the numbers in the second row by $-\frac{1}{2}$ to get

$$\left[\begin{array}{ccc|c} 1 & 1 & 2 & 19 \\ -\frac{1}{2}(0) & -\frac{1}{2}(-2) & -\frac{1}{2}(-4) & -\frac{1}{2}(-26) \\ 0 & 2 & 0 & 6 \end{array}\right] = \left[\begin{array}{ccc|c} 1 & 1 & 2 & 19 \\ 0 & 1 & 2 & 13 \\ 0 & 2 & 0 & 6 \end{array}\right].$$

We want 0 in this position.

We are not yet done with the second column. The voice balloon shows that we want to get a 0 where there is now a 2. If we multiply the second row of numbers by −2 and add these products to the third row of numbers, we will get 0 in this position. The second row of numbers multiplied by −2 gives

$$-2(0) \text{ or } 0, \quad -2(1) \text{ or } -2, \quad -2(2) \text{ or } -4, \quad -2(13) \text{ or } -26.$$

Now add these products to the corresponding numbers in row 3.

$$\left[\begin{array}{ccc|c} 1 & 1 & 2 & 19 \\ 0 & 1 & 2 & 13 \\ 0+0 & 2+(-2) & 0+(-4) & 6+(-26) \end{array}\right] = \left[\begin{array}{ccc|c} 1 & 1 & 2 & 19 \\ 0 & 1 & 2 & 13 \\ 0 & 0 & -4 & -20 \end{array}\right]$$

We move on to the third column. We want 1 in the third row, third column.

We want 1 in this position.

$$\left[\begin{array}{ccc|c} 1 & 1 & 2 & 19 \\ 0 & 1 & 2 & 13 \\ 0 & 0 & -4 & -20 \end{array}\right]$$

To get 1 in the desired position, we multiply −4 by its reciprocal, $-\frac{1}{4}$. Therefore, we multiply all the numbers in the third row by $-\frac{1}{4}$ to get

$$\left[\begin{array}{ccc|c} 1 & 1 & 2 & 19 \\ 0 & 1 & 2 & 13 \\ -\frac{1}{4}(0) & -\frac{1}{4}(0) & -\frac{1}{4}(-4) & -\frac{1}{4}(-20) \end{array}\right] = \left[\begin{array}{ccc|c} 1 & 1 & 2 & 19 \\ 0 & 1 & 2 & 13 \\ 0 & 0 & 1 & 5 \end{array}\right].$$

We now have the desired matrix with 1s down the diagonal and 0s below the 1s.

**Step 3 Write the system of linear equations corresponding to the matrix in step 2, and use back-substitution to find the system's solution.** The system represented by the matrix in step 2 is

$$\left[\begin{array}{ccc|c} 1 & 1 & 2 & 19 \\ 0 & 1 & 2 & 13 \\ 0 & 0 & 1 & 5 \end{array}\right] \rightarrow \begin{aligned} 1x + 1y + 2z &= 19 \\ 0x + 1y + 2z &= 13 \\ 0x + 0y + 1z &= 5 \end{aligned} \quad \text{or} \quad \begin{aligned} x + y + 2z &= 19 \\ y + 2z &= 13. \\ z &= 5 \end{aligned}$$

We immediately see that the value for $z$ is 5. To find $y$, we back-substitute 5 for $z$ in the second equation.

$$y + 2z = 13 \quad \text{Equation 2}$$

$$y + 2(5) = 13 \quad \text{Substitute 5 for } z.$$

$$y = 3 \quad \text{Solve for } y.$$

Finally, back-substitute 3 for $y$ and 5 for $z$ in the first equation:

$$x + y + 2z = 19 \quad \text{Equation 1}$$

$$x + 3 + 2(5) = 19 \quad \text{Substitute 3 for } y \text{ and 5 for } z.$$

$$x + 13 = 19 \quad \text{Multiply and add.}$$

$$x = 6 \quad \text{Subtract 13 both sides.}$$

The solution set for the original system is $\{(6, 3, 5)\}$.

**Check Point 3** Use matrices to solve the system

$$\begin{aligned} 2x + y + 2z &= 18 \\ x - y + 2z &= 9 \\ x + 2y - z &= 6. \end{aligned}$$

Modern supercomputers are capable of solving systems with more than 600,000 variables. The augmented matrices for such systems are huge, but the solution using matrices is exactly like what we did in Example 2. Work with the augmented matrix, one column at a time. First, get 1 in the desired position. Then get 0s below the 1. Let's see how this works for a linear system involving four equations in four variables.

## EXAMPLE 4 Gaussian Elimination with Back-Substitution

Use matrices to solve the system

$$\begin{aligned} 2x + y + 3z - w &= 6 \\ x - y + 2z - 2w &= -1 \\ x - y - z + w &= -4 \\ -x + 2y - 2z - w &= -7. \end{aligned}$$

**Solution**

**Step 1 Write the augmented matrix for the system.**

**Linear System**

$$\begin{aligned} 2x + \phantom{2}y + 3z - \phantom{2}w &= 6 \\ x - \phantom{2}y + 2z - 2w &= -1 \\ x - \phantom{2}y - \phantom{3}z + \phantom{2}w &= -4 \\ -x + 2y - 2z - \phantom{2}w &= -7 \end{aligned}$$

**Augmented Matrix**

$$\left[\begin{array}{rrrr|r} 2 & 1 & 3 & -1 & 6 \\ 1 & -1 & 2 & -2 & -1 \\ 1 & -1 & -1 & 1 & -4 \\ -1 & 2 & -2 & -1 & -7 \end{array}\right]$$

**Step 2 Use matrix row operations to simplify the matrix to one with 1s down the diagonal from upper left to lower right, and 0s below the 1s.** Our first step in achieving this goal is to get 1 in the top position of the first column. To do this, we interchange rows 1 and 2.

$$\left[\begin{array}{rrrr|r} 1 & -1 & 2 & -2 & -1 \\ 2 & 1 & 3 & -1 & 6 \\ 1 & -1 & -1 & 1 & -4 \\ -1 & 2 & -2 & -1 & -7 \end{array}\right]$$

We want 0s in these positions.

This was row 2; now it's row 1.

This was row 1; now it's row 2.

Now we want 0s below the 1 in the first column. To get the first 0, multiply the top row of numbers by −2 and add these products to the second row of numbers. To get the second 0, multiply the top row of numbers by −1 and add these products to the third row of numbers. To get the third 0, multiply the top row of numbers by 1 and add these products to the fourth row of numbers. (Equivalently, add corresponding numbers in rows 1 and 4.) Performing these operations, we obtain the following matrix.

$$\left[\begin{array}{rrrr|r} 1 & -1 & 2 & -2 & -1 \\ 0 & 3 & -1 & 3 & 8 \\ 0 & 0 & -3 & 3 & -3 \\ 0 & 1 & 0 & -3 & -8 \end{array}\right]$$

We want 1 in this position.

Use the previous matrix and:
Replace row 2 by $-2R_1 + R_2$.
Replace row 3 by $-1R_1 + R_3$.
Replace row 4 by $1R_1 + R_4$.

We move on to the second column. We can obtain 1 in the desired position by multiplying the numbers in the second row by $\frac{1}{3}$, the reciprocal of 3.

$$\left[\begin{array}{cccc|c} 1 & -1 & 2 & -2 & -1 \\ \frac{1}{3}(0) & \frac{1}{3}(3) & \frac{1}{3}(-1) & \frac{1}{3}(3) & \frac{1}{3}(8) \\ 0 & 0 & -3 & 3 & -3 \\ 0 & 1 & 0 & -3 & -8 \end{array}\right] = \left[\begin{array}{rrrr|r} 1 & -1 & 2 & -2 & -1 \\ 0 & 1 & -\frac{1}{3} & 1 & \frac{8}{3} \\ 0 & 0 & -3 & 3 & -3 \\ 0 & 1 & 0 & -3 & -8 \end{array}\right] \quad \frac{1}{3}R_2$$

We want 0s in these positions. The top position already has a 0.

Now we want 0s below the 1 in the second column. The top position already has a 0. To obtain a 0 on the bottom, we multiply the second row by −1 and add the product to the corresponding numbers of the last row. (What would happen if we added rows 1 and 4?) Performing these operations, we obtain the following matrix.

$$\left[\begin{array}{cccc|c} 1 & -1 & 2 & -2 & -1 \\ 0 & 1 & -\frac{1}{3} & 1 & \frac{8}{3} \\ 0 & 0 & -3 & 3 & -3 \\ 0 & 0 & \frac{1}{3} & -4 & -\frac{32}{3} \end{array}\right]$$

We want 1 in this position.

Replace row 4 in the previous matrix by $-1R_2 + R_4$.

We move on to the third column. We can obtain 1 in the desired position by multiplying the numbers in the third row by $-\frac{1}{3}$, the reciprocal of $-3$.

$$\left[\begin{array}{cccc|c} 1 & -1 & 2 & -2 & -1 \\ 0 & 1 & -\frac{1}{3} & 1 & \frac{8}{3} \\ -\frac{1}{3}(0) & -\frac{1}{3}(0) & -\frac{1}{3}(-3) & -\frac{1}{3}(3) & -\frac{1}{3}(-3) \\ 0 & 0 & \frac{1}{3} & -4 & -\frac{32}{3} \end{array}\right] = \left[\begin{array}{cccc|c} 1 & -1 & 2 & -2 & -1 \\ 0 & 1 & -\frac{1}{3} & 1 & \frac{8}{3} \\ 0 & 0 & 1 & -1 & 1 \\ 0 & 0 & \frac{1}{3} & -4 & -\frac{32}{3} \end{array}\right] \quad -\frac{1}{3}R_3$$

We want 0 in this position.

Now we want 0 below the 1 in the third column. If we multiply the third row of numbers by $-\frac{1}{3}$ and add these products to the fourth row of numbers, we will get 0 in this position. Performing these operations, we obtain the following matrix.

$$\left[\begin{array}{cccc|c} 1 & -1 & 2 & -2 & -1 \\ 0 & 1 & -\frac{1}{3} & 1 & \frac{8}{3} \\ 0 & 0 & 1 & -1 & 1 \\ 0 & 0 & 0 & -\frac{11}{3} & -11 \end{array}\right]$$

We want 1 in this position.

Replace row 4 in the previous matrix by $-\frac{1}{3}R_3 + R_4$.

We move on to the fourth column. Because we want 1s down the main diagonal, we want 1 where there is now $-\frac{11}{3}$. We can obtain 1 in this position by multiplying the numbers in the fourth row by $-\frac{3}{11}$.

$$\left[\begin{array}{cccc|c} 1 & -1 & 2 & -2 & -1 \\ 0 & 1 & -\frac{1}{3} & 1 & \frac{8}{3} \\ 0 & 0 & 1 & -1 & 1 \\ -\frac{3}{11}(0) & -\frac{3}{11}(0) & -\frac{3}{11}(0) & -\frac{3}{11}\left(-\frac{11}{3}\right) & -\frac{3}{11}(-11) \end{array}\right]$$

$$= \left[\begin{array}{cccc|c} 1 & -1 & 2 & -2 & -1 \\ 0 & 1 & -\frac{1}{3} & 1 & \frac{8}{3} \\ 0 & 0 & 1 & -1 & 1 \\ 0 & 0 & 0 & 1 & 3 \end{array}\right] \quad -\frac{3}{11}R_4$$

We now have the desired matrix with 1s down the diagonal and 0s below the 1s.

**Step 3 Write the system of linear equations corresponding to the matrix in step 2, and use back-substitution to find the system's solution.** The system represented by the matrix in step 2 is

$$\left[\begin{array}{cccc|c} 1 & -1 & 2 & -2 & -1 \\ 0 & 1 & -\frac{1}{3} & 1 & \frac{8}{3} \\ 0 & 0 & 1 & -1 & 1 \\ 0 & 0 & 0 & 1 & 3 \end{array}\right] \rightarrow \begin{aligned} 1x - 1y + 2z - 2w &= -1 \\ 0x + 1y - \tfrac{1}{3}z + 1w &= \tfrac{8}{3} \\ 0x + 0y + 1z - 1w &= 1 \\ 0x + 0y + 0z + 1w &= 3 \end{aligned} \quad \text{or} \quad \begin{aligned} x - y + 2z - 2w &= -1 \\ y - \tfrac{1}{3}z + w &= \tfrac{8}{3} \\ z - w &= 1 \\ w &= 3 \end{aligned}$$

We immediately see that the value for $w$ is 3. We can now use back-substitution to find the values for $z$, $y$, and $x$.

$$w = 3$$

$$\begin{aligned} z - w &= 1 \\ z - 3 &= 1 \\ z &= 4 \end{aligned}$$

$$\begin{aligned} y - \frac{1}{3}z + w &= \frac{8}{3} \\ y - \frac{1}{3}(4) + 3 &= \frac{8}{3} \\ y + \frac{5}{3} &= \frac{8}{3} \\ y &= 1 \end{aligned}$$

$$\begin{aligned} x - y + 2z - 2w &= -1 \\ x - 1 + 2(4) - 2(3) &= -1 \\ x - 1 + 8 - 6 &= -1 \\ x + 1 &= -1 \\ x &= -2 \end{aligned}$$

Let's agree to write the solution set for the system in the order in which the variables for the given system appeared, from left to right, namely $(x, y, z, w)$. Thus, the solution set is $\{(-2, 1, 4, 3)\}$. We can verify this solution set by substituting the value for each variable into the original system of equations.

**Check Point 4** Use matrices to solve the system

$$\begin{aligned} x - 3y - 2z + w &= -3 \\ 2x - 7y - z + 2w &= 1 \\ 3x - 7y - 3z + 3w &= -5 \\ 5x + y + 4z - 2w &= 18. \end{aligned}$$

4 Use matrices and Gauss-Jordan elimination to solve systems.

## Gauss-Jordan Elimination

Using Gaussian elimination, we obtain a matrix with 1s down the main diagonal and 0s below the 1s. A second method, called **Gauss-Jordan elimination**, after Carl Friedrich Gauss and Wilhelm Jordan (1842–1899), continues the process until a matrix with 1s down the main diagonal from left to right and 0s in every position *above and below* each 1 is found. For a system of linear equations in three variables, $x$, $y$, and $z$, we try to get the augmented matrix into the form

$$\left[\begin{array}{ccc|c} 1 & 0 & 0 & a \\ 0 & 1 & 0 & b \\ 0 & 0 & 1 & c \end{array}\right].$$

Based on this matrix, we conclude that $x = a$, $y = b$, and $z = c$.

### EXAMPLE 5 Using Gauss-Jordan Elimination

Use Gauss-Jordan elimination to solve the system

$$\begin{aligned} 3x + y + 2z &= 31 \\ x + y + 2z &= 19 \\ x + 3y + 2z &= 25. \end{aligned}$$

**Solution** In Example 3, we used Gaussian elimination to obtain the following matrix:

$$\left[\begin{array}{ccc|c} 1 & 1 & 2 & 19 \\ 0 & 1 & 2 & 13 \\ 0 & 0 & 1 & 5 \end{array}\right].$$

**Study Tip**

The advantage to Gauss-Jordan elimination is that from the augmented matrix we can simply read the solution. The disadvantage is that we must continue row operations in the augmented matrix from the Gaussian elimination process, and it's fairly easy to make computational errors.

To find a solution using Gauss-Jordan elimination, we need to work with this matrix and convert the boxed numbers to 0s. Thus, we will apply matrix row operations to get 0s *above the 1s* in the main diagonal. To get 0 in row 1, column 2 (where there is now a 1), we multiply each number in the second row by −1 and add these products to the corresponding numbers in the first row. Performing these operations, we obtain the following matrix.

We want 0s in these positions. The top position already has a 0.

$$\left[\begin{array}{ccc|c} 1 & 0 & 0 & 6 \\ 0 & 1 & 2 & 13 \\ 0 & 0 & 1 & 5 \end{array}\right]$$

We want 0s above the 1 in the third column. The top position already has a 0. To obtain a 0 where there is now 2, we multiply each number in the bottom row by −2 and add these products to the corresponding numbers in the second row. Performing these operations, we obtain the following matrix.

$$\left[\begin{array}{ccc|c} 1 & 0 & 0 & 6 \\ 0 & 1 & 0 & 3 \\ 0 & 0 & 1 & 5 \end{array}\right]$$

Replace row 2 in the previous matrix by $-2R_3 + R_2$.

This last matrix corresponds to

$$x = 6, \quad y = 3, \quad z = 5.$$

As we found in Example 3, the solution set is $\{(6, 3, 5)\}$.

**Check Point 5** Solve the system in Checkpoint 2 using Gauss-Jordan elimination. Begin by working with the matrix that you obtained in Checkpoint 2.

## EXERCISE SET 9.1

### Practice Exercises

*In Exercises 1–8, write the augmented matrix for each system of linear equations.*

**1.** $2x + y + 2z = 2$
$3x - 5y - z = 4$
$x - 2y - 3z = -6$

**2.** $3x - 2y + 5z = 31$
$x + 3y - 3z = -12$
$-2x - 5y + 3z = 11$

**3.** $x - y + z = 8$
$y - 12z = -15$
$z = 1$

**4.** $x - 2y + 3z = 9$
$y + 3z = 5$
$z = 2$

**5.** $5x - 2y - 3z = 0$
$x + y = 5$
$2x - 3z = 4$

**6.** $x - 2y + z = 10$
$3x + y = 5$
$7x + 2z = 2$

**7.** $2x + 5y - 3z + w = 2$
$3y + z = 4$
$x - y + 5z = 9$
$5x - 5y - 2z = 1$

**8.** $4x + 7y - 8z + w = 3$
$5y + z = 5$
$x - y - z = 17$
$2x - 2y + 11z = 4$

*In Exercises 9–12, write the system of linear equations represented by the augmented matrix. Use x, y, z, and, if necessary, w for the variables.*

**9.** $\left[\begin{array}{ccc|c} 5 & 0 & 3 & -11 \\ 0 & 1 & -4 & 12 \\ 7 & 2 & 0 & 3 \end{array}\right]$

**10.** $\left[\begin{array}{ccc|c} 7 & 0 & 4 & -13 \\ 0 & 1 & -5 & 11 \\ 2 & 7 & 0 & 6 \end{array}\right]$

**11.** $\left[\begin{array}{cccc|c} 1 & 1 & 4 & 1 & 3 \\ -1 & 1 & -1 & 0 & 7 \\ 2 & 0 & 0 & 5 & 11 \\ 0 & 0 & 12 & 4 & 5 \end{array}\right]$

**12.** $\left[\begin{array}{cccc|c} 4 & 1 & 5 & 1 & 6 \\ 1 & -1 & 0 & -1 & 8 \\ 3 & 0 & 0 & 7 & 4 \\ 0 & 0 & 11 & 5 & 3 \end{array}\right]$

*In Exercises 13–18, write the system of linear equations represented by the augmented matrix. Use x, y, z, and, if necessary, w for the variables. Once the system is written, use back-substitution to find its solution.*

**13.** $\left[\begin{array}{ccc|c} 1 & 0 & -4 & 5 \\ 0 & 1 & -12 & 13 \\ 0 & 0 & 1 & -\frac{1}{2} \end{array}\right]$

**14.** $\left[\begin{array}{ccc|c} 1 & 2 & 1 & 0 \\ 0 & 1 & 0 & -2 \\ 0 & 0 & 1 & 3 \end{array}\right]$

**15.** $\left[\begin{array}{ccc|c} 1 & \frac{1}{2} & 1 & \frac{11}{2} \\ 0 & 1 & \frac{3}{2} & 7 \\ 0 & 0 & 1 & 4 \end{array}\right]$  **16.** $\left[\begin{array}{ccc|c} 1 & 1 & 0 & 3 \\ 0 & 1 & \frac{3}{2} & -2 \\ 0 & 0 & 1 & 0 \end{array}\right]$

**17.** $\left[\begin{array}{cccc|c} 1 & -1 & 1 & 1 & 3 \\ 0 & 1 & -2 & -1 & 0 \\ 0 & 0 & 1 & 6 & 17 \\ 0 & 0 & 0 & 1 & 3 \end{array}\right]$  **18.** $\left[\begin{array}{cccc|c} 1 & 2 & -1 & 0 & 2 \\ 0 & 1 & 1 & -2 & -3 \\ 0 & 0 & 1 & -1 & -2 \\ 0 & 0 & 0 & 1 & 3 \end{array}\right]$

*In Exercises 19–24, perform each matrix row operation and write the new matrix.*

**19.** $\left[\begin{array}{ccc|c} 2 & -6 & 4 & 10 \\ 1 & 5 & -5 & 0 \\ 3 & 0 & 4 & 7 \end{array}\right] \quad \frac{1}{2}R_1$

**20.** $\left[\begin{array}{ccc|c} 3 & -12 & 6 & 9 \\ 1 & -4 & 4 & 0 \\ 2 & 0 & 7 & 4 \end{array}\right] \quad \frac{1}{3}R_1$

**21.** $\left[\begin{array}{ccc|c} 1 & -3 & 2 & 0 \\ 3 & 1 & -1 & 7 \\ 2 & -2 & 1 & 3 \end{array}\right] \quad -3R_1 + R_2$

**22.** $\left[\begin{array}{ccc|c} 1 & -1 & 5 & -6 \\ 3 & 3 & -1 & 10 \\ 1 & 3 & 2 & 5 \end{array}\right] \quad -3R_1 + R_2$

**23.** $\left[\begin{array}{cccc|c} 1 & -1 & 1 & 1 & 3 \\ 0 & 1 & -2 & -1 & 0 \\ 2 & 0 & 3 & 4 & 11 \\ 5 & 1 & 2 & 4 & 6 \end{array}\right] \quad \begin{array}{l} \\ \\ -2R_1 + R_3 \\ -5R_1 + R_4 \end{array}$

**24.** $\left[\begin{array}{cccc|c} 1 & -5 & 2 & -2 & 4 \\ 0 & 1 & -3 & -1 & 0 \\ 3 & 0 & 2 & -1 & 6 \\ -4 & 1 & 4 & 2 & -3 \end{array}\right] \quad \begin{array}{l} \\ \\ -3R_1 + R_3 \\ 4R_1 + R_4 \end{array}$

*In Exercises 25–26, a few steps in the process of simplifying the given matrix to one with 1s down the diagonal from upper left to lower right, and 0s below the 1s, are shown. Fill in the missing numbers in the steps that are shown.*

**25.** $\left[\begin{array}{ccc|c} 1 & -1 & 1 & 8 \\ 2 & 3 & -1 & -2 \\ 3 & -2 & -9 & 9 \end{array}\right] \rightarrow \left[\begin{array}{ccc|c} 1 & -1 & 1 & 8 \\ 0 & 5 & \blacksquare & \blacksquare \\ 0 & 1 & \blacksquare & \blacksquare \end{array}\right]$

$\rightarrow \left[\begin{array}{ccc|c} 1 & -1 & 1 & 8 \\ 0 & 1 & \blacksquare & \blacksquare \\ 0 & 1 & \blacksquare & \blacksquare \end{array}\right]$

**26.** $\left[\begin{array}{ccc|c} 1 & -2 & 3 & 4 \\ 2 & 1 & -4 & 3 \\ -3 & 4 & -1 & -2 \end{array}\right] \rightarrow \left[\begin{array}{ccc|c} 1 & -2 & 3 & 4 \\ 0 & 5 & \blacksquare & \blacksquare \\ 0 & -2 & \blacksquare & \blacksquare \end{array}\right]$

$\rightarrow \left[\begin{array}{ccc|c} 1 & -2 & 3 & 4 \\ 0 & 1 & \blacksquare & \blacksquare \\ 0 & -2 & \blacksquare & \blacksquare \end{array}\right]$

*In Exercises 27–40, solve each system of equations using matrices. Use Gaussian elimination with back-substitution or Gauss-Jordan elimination.*

**27.** $\begin{aligned} x + y - z &= -2 \\ 2x - y + z &= 5 \\ -x + 2y + 2z &= 1 \end{aligned}$

**28.** $\begin{aligned} x - 2y - z &= 2 \\ 2x - y + z &= 4 \\ -x + y - 2z &= -4 \end{aligned}$

**29.** $\begin{aligned} x + 3y &= 0 \\ x + y + z &= 1 \\ 3x - y - z &= 11 \end{aligned}$

**30.** $\begin{aligned} 3y - z &= -1 \\ x + 5y - z &= -4 \\ -3x + 6y + 2z &= 11 \end{aligned}$

**31.** $\begin{aligned} 2x + 2y + 7z &= -1 \\ 2x + y + 2z &= 2 \\ 4x + 6y + z &= 15 \end{aligned}$

**32.** $\begin{aligned} 3x + 2y + 3z &= 3 \\ 4x - 5y + 7z &= 1 \\ 2x + 3y - 2z &= 6 \end{aligned}$

**33.** $\begin{aligned} x + y + z + w &= 4 \\ 2x + y - 2z - w &= 0 \\ x - 2y - z - 2w &= -2 \\ 3x + 2y + z + 3w &= 4 \end{aligned}$

**34.** $\begin{aligned} x + y + z + w &= 5 \\ x + 2y - z - 2w &= -1 \\ x - 3y - 3z - w &= -1 \\ 2x - y + 2z - w &= -2 \end{aligned}$

**35.** $\begin{aligned} 3x - 4y + z + w &= 9 \\ x + y - z - w &= 0 \\ 2x + y + 4z - 2w &= 3 \\ -x + 2y + z - 3w &= 3 \end{aligned}$

**36.** $\begin{aligned} 2x + z - 3w &= 8 \\ x - y + 4w &= -10 \\ 3x + 5y - z - w &= 20 \\ x + y - z - w &= 6 \end{aligned}$

**37.** $\begin{aligned} 2x + 3y - z - w &= -3 \\ 2x - y - 3z + 2w &= -5 \\ x - y + z - w &= -4 \\ 3x - 2y + z + w &= 0 \end{aligned}$

**38.** $\begin{aligned} 2x - y - z + w &= 4 \\ x + 3y - 2z - 3w &= 6 \\ x - y + z - w &= 2 \\ -x + 2y - z - w &= -1 \end{aligned}$

**39.** $\begin{aligned} 2x_1 - 2x_2 + 3x_3 - x_4 &= 12 \\ x_1 + 2x_2 - x_3 + 2x_4 - x_5 &= -7 \\ x_1 + x_3 - x_4 - 5x_5 &= 5 \\ -x_1 + x_2 - x_3 - 2x_4 - 3x_5 &= 0 \\ x_1 - x_2 - x_4 + x_5 &= 4 \end{aligned}$

**40.** $\begin{aligned} 2x - 2z + 4w - 4v &= -6 \\ -x - y - z - w - u - v &= -12 \\ x + y - z - w &= -2 \\ y - z + u - v &= -1 \\ x - y + z - w + u - v &= 0 \\ 3y - z + v &= 4 \end{aligned}$

## Application Exercises

**41.** The table shows the number of inmates in federal and state prisons in the United States for three selected years.

| $x$ (Number of Years after 1980) | 1 | 5 | 10 |
|---|---|---|---|
| $y$ (Number of Inmates, in thousands) | 344 | 480 | 740 |

**a.** Use the quadratic function $y = ax^2 + bx + c$ to model the data. Solve the system of linear equations involving $a$, $b$, and $c$ using matrices.
**b.** Predict the number of inmates in the year 2010.
**c.** List one factor that would change the accuracy of this model for the year 2010.

**42.** A football is kicked straight upward. The position function

$$s = \frac{1}{2}at^2 + v_0t + s_0$$

describes the ball's height, $s$, in feet, after $t$ seconds. Use the points labeled in the graph to find the values of $a$, $v_0$, and $s_0$. Solve the system of linear equations involving $a$, $v_0$, and $s_0$ using matrices. What is the value for $s$ when $t = 7$? Describe what this means.

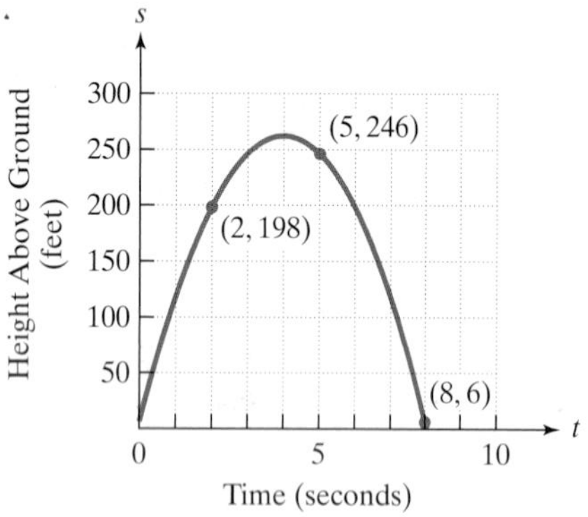


*Write a system of linear equations in three variables to solve Exercises 43–46. Then use matrices to solve the system.*

**43.** The circle graph indicates the ages of the 40 million online users in the United States. The percentage of online users in the youngest (under 30) and oldest (50 and over) age groups combined exceeds the percentage in the 30–49 age group by 2%. If the percentage of users in the oldest age group is doubled, it is 3% less than the percentage of users in the youngest age group. Find the percentage of online users in each of the three age groups.

**Age of U.S. Online Users**

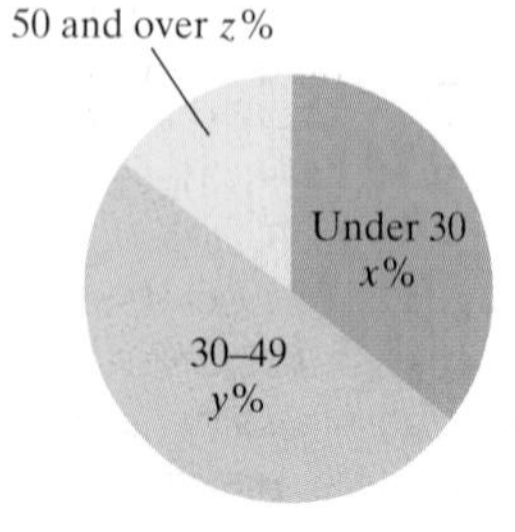


*Source*: U.S. Census Bureau

**44.** The circle graph indicates computers in use for the United States and the rest of the world. The percentage of the world's computers in Europe and Japan combined is 13% less than the percentage of the world's computers in the United States. If the percentage of the world's computers in Europe is doubled, it is only 3% more than the percentage of the world's computers in the United States. Find the percentage of the world's computers in the United States, Europe, and Japan.

**Percentage of the World's Computers: U.S. and the World**

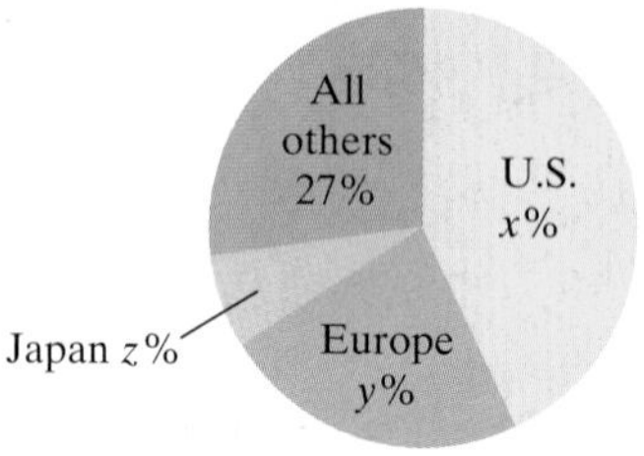


*Source*: Jupiter Communications

**45.** Three foods have the following nutritional content per ounce.

| | Calories | Protein (in grams) | Vitamin C (in milligrams) |
|---|---|---|---|
| **Food *A*** | 40 | 5 | 30 |
| **Food *B*** | 200 | 2 | 10 |
| **Food *C*** | 400 | 4 | 300 |

If a meal consisting of the three foods allows exactly 660 calories, 25 grams of protein, and 425 milligrams of vitamin C, how many ounces of each kind of food should be used?

**46.** A furniture company produces three types of desks: a children's model, an office model, and a deluxe model. Each desk is manufactured in three stages: cutting, construction, and finishing. The time requirements for each model and manufacturing stage are given in the following table.

| | Children's model | Office model | Deluxe model |
|---|---|---|---|
| **Cutting** | 2 hr | 3 hr | 2 hr |
| **Construction** | 2 hr | 1 hr | 3 hr |
| **Finishing** | 1 hr | 1 hr | 2 hr |

Each week the company has available a maximum of 100 hours for cutting, 100 hours for construction, and 65 hours for finishing. If all available time must be used, how many of each type of desk should be produced each week?

## Writing in Mathematics

**47.** What is a matrix?

**48.** Describe what is meant by the augmented matrix of a system of linear equations.

**49.** In your own words, describe each of the three matrix row operations. Give an example with each of the operations.

**50.** Describe how to use row operations and matrices to solve a system of linear equations.

**51.** What is the difference between Gaussian elimination and Gauss-Jordan elimination?

**52.** The graphs show the percentage of recorded music on CDs, cassettes, and LPs from 1981–2001. For this time period, which of these three forms of recorded music would you model using a quadratic function? Explain your answer.

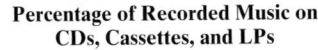

**Percentage of Recorded Music on CDs, Cassettes, and LPs**

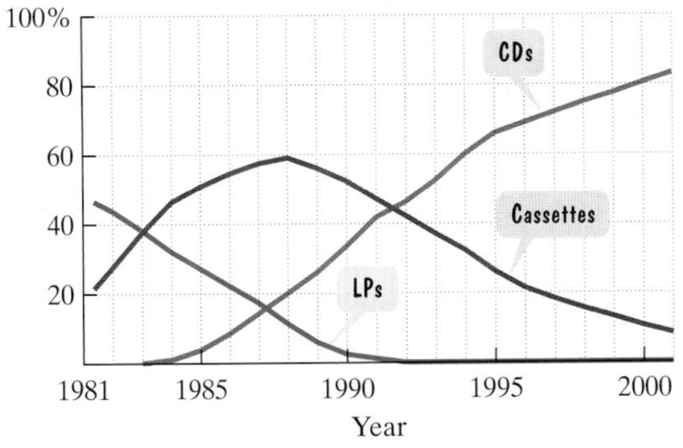


*Source*: Recording Industry Association of America

**53.** In Exercise 52, assume that you plan to obtain the quadratic model by hand. Explain how to use the graph for the form that you selected to find $a$, $b$, and $c$ in $y = ax^2 + bx + c$, where $x$ represents years since 1981 and $y$ represents the percentage of recorded music on this form. Describe the role that matrices play in the process of obtaining the model.

## Technology Exercises

**54.** Most graphing utilities can perform row operations on matrices. Consult the owner's manual for your graphing utility to learn proper keystrokes for performing these operations. Then duplicate the row operations of any three exercises that you solved from Exercises 19–24.

**55.** The final augmented matrix that we obtain when using Gaussian elimination is said to be in **row-echelon form**. For systems of linear equations with unique solutions, this form results when each entry in the main diagonal is 1 and all entries below the main diagonal are 0s. Some graphing utilities can transform a matrix to row-echelon form. Consult the owner's manual for your graphing utility. If your utility has this capability, enter the augmented matrix and obtain the final matrices of Example 3 on pages 754–756 and Example 4 on pages 756–759. Then use this capability to solve any five of the systems in Exercises 27–40.

**56.** The final augmented matrix that we obtain when using Gauss-Jordan elimination is said to be in **reduced row-echelon form**. For systems of linear equations with unique solutions, this form results when each entry on the main diagonal is 1 and all entries below and above that main diagonal are 0s. Some graphing utilities can transform a matrix to reduced row-echelon form. Consult the owner's manual for your graphing utility. If your utility has this capability, obtain the final matrix of Example 5 on pages 759–760 beginning with the augmented matrix for Example 3 on page 756. Then use this capability to solve any five of the systems in Exercises 27–40.

## Critical Thinking Exercises

**57.** Find a cubic function whose graph passes through the points $(0, -3)$, $(1, 5)$, $(-1, -7)$, and $(-2, -13)$. (*Hint:* Use the equation $y = ax^3 + bx^2 + cx + d$.)

**58.** The table shows the daily production level and profit for a business.

| | | | |
|---|---|---|---|
| **$x$ (Number of units Produced Daily)** | 30 | 50 | 100 |
| **$y$ (Daily Profit)** | \$5900 | \$7500 | \$4500 |

Use the quadratic function $y = ax^2 + bx + c$ to determine the number of units that should be produced each day for maximum profit. What is the maximum daily profit?

## Group Exercise

**59.** In Chapter 8, you learned how to fit a quadratic function of the form $y = ax^2 + bx + c$ to data without using the regression feature of a graphing utility (see pages 703–704). Each group member should find an interesting data set. Group members should select the two sets of data that are most interesting and relevant.

**a.** For one of the data sets selected, use the function $y = ax^3 + bx^2 + cx + d$ and four ordered pairs of values $(x, y)$ to find the cubic function that models the data. Use matrices or a graphing utility to solve the resulting system in four variables for $a$, $b$, $c$, and $d$.

**b.** For the other data set selected, fit a higher-degree polynomial function to the data. Use a graphing utility to solve the resulting system in five or more variables.

## SECTION 9.2 Inconsistent and Dependent Systems and Their Applications

### Objectives

1. Apply Gaussian elimination to systems without unique solutions.
2. Apply Gaussian elimination to systems with differing numbers of variables and equations.
3. Solve problems involving systems without unique solutions.

Traffic jams getting you down? Powerful computers, able to solve systems with hundreds of thousands of variables in a single bound, may promise a gridlock-free future. The computer in your car could be linked to a central computer that manages traffic flow by controlling traffic lights, rerouting you away from traffic congestion, issuing weather reports, and selecting the best route to your destination. New technologies could eventually drive your car at a steady 75 miles per hour along automated highways as you comfortably nap. In this section, we look at the role of linear systems without unique solutions in a future free of traffic jams.

**1** Apply Gaussian elimination to systems without unique solutions.

Linear systems can have one solution, no solutions, or infinitely many solutions. We can use Gaussian elimination on systems with three or more variables to determine how many solutions such systems may have. In the case of systems with no solutions or infinitely many solutions, it is impossible to rewrite the augmented matrix in the desired form with 1s down the main diagonal and 0s below the 1s. Let's see what this means by looking at a system that has no solutions.

### EXAMPLE 1 A System With No Solutions

Use Gaussian elimination to solve the system

$$\begin{aligned} x - y - 2z &= 2 \\ 2x - 3y + 6z &= 5 \\ 3x - 4y + 4z &= 12. \end{aligned}$$

**Solution**

**Step 1 Write the augmented matrix for the system.**

**Linear System**

$$\begin{aligned} x - y - 2z &= 2 \\ 2x - 3y + 6z &= 5 \\ 3x - 4y + 4z &= 12 \end{aligned}$$

**Augmented Matrix**

$$\left[\begin{array}{ccc|c} 1 & -1 & -2 & 2 \\ 2 & -3 & 6 & 5 \\ 3 & -4 & 4 & 12 \end{array}\right]$$

**Discovery**

Use the addition method to solve Example 1. Describe what happens. Why does this mean that there is no solution?

**Step 2 Attempt to simplify the matrix to one with 1s down the diagonal and 0s below the 1s.** Notice that the augmented matrix already has a 1 in the top position of the first column. Now we want 0s below the 1. To get the first 0, multiply row 1 by $-2$ and add these products to row 2. To get the second 0, multiply row 1 by $-3$ and add these products to row 3. Performing these operations, we obtain the following matrix.

$$\left[\begin{array}{rrr|r} 1 & -1 & -2 & 2 \\ 0 & -1 & 10 & 1 \\ 0 & -1 & 10 & 6 \end{array}\right]$$

We want 1 in this position.

Use the previous matrix and: Replace row 2 by $-2R_1 + R_2$. Replace row 3 by $-3R_1 + R_3$.

Moving on to the second column, we obtain 1 in the desired position by multiplying row 2 by $-1$.

$$\left[\begin{array}{cccc|c} 1 & -1 & -2 & 2 \\ 0(-1) & -1(-1) & 10(-1) & 1(-1) \\ 0 & -1 & 10 & 6 \end{array}\right] = \left[\begin{array}{rrr|r} 1 & -1 & -2 & 2 \\ 0 & 1 & -10 & -1 \\ 0 & -1 & 10 & 6 \end{array}\right]$$

$-1R_2$

We want 0 in this position.

Now we want a 0 below the 1 in column 2. To get the 0, multiply row 2 by 1 and add these products to row 3. (Equivalently, add row 2 to row 3.) We obtain the following matrix.

$$\left[\begin{array}{rrr|r} 1 & -1 & -2 & 2 \\ 0 & 1 & -10 & -1 \\ 0 & 0 & 0 & 5 \end{array}\right]$$

Replace row 3 in the previous matrix by $1R_2 + R_3$.

It is impossible to convert this last matrix to the desired form of 1s down the main diagonal. If we translate the last row back into equation form, we get

$$0x + 0y + 0z = 5,$$

which is false. Regardless of which values we select for $x$, $y$, and $z$, the last equation can never be a true statement. Consequently, the system has no solution. The solution set is $\varnothing$, the empty set.

**Check Point 1** Use Gaussian elimination to solve the system

$$\begin{aligned} x - 2y - z &= -5 \\ 2x - 3y - z &= 0 \\ 3x - 4y - z &= 1. \end{aligned}$$

Recall that the graph of a system of three linear equations in three variables consists of three planes. When these planes intersect in a single point, the system has precisely one ordered-triple solution. When the planes have no point in common, the system has no solution, like the one in Example 1. Figure 9.1 illustrates some of the geometric possibilities for these inconsistent systems.

Now let's see what happens when we apply Gaussian elimination to a system with infinitely many solutions. Representing the solution set for these systems can be a bit tricky.

Three planes are parallel with no common intersection point.

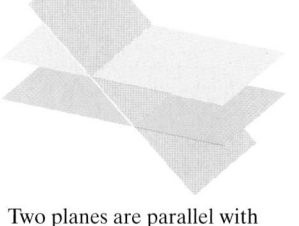

Two planes are parallel with no common intersection point.

Planes intersect two at a time. There is no intersection point common to all three planes.

**Figure 9.1** Three planes may have no common point of intersection.

### EXAMPLE 2 A System with an Infinite Number of Solutions

Use Gaussian elimination to solve the following system:

$$\begin{aligned} 3x - 4y + 4z &= 7 \\ x - y - 2z &= 2 \\ 2x - 3y + 6z &= 5. \end{aligned}$$

**Solution** As always, we start with the augmented matrix.

$$\left[\begin{array}{rrr|r} 3 & -4 & 4 & 7 \\ 1 & -1 & -2 & 2 \\ 2 & -3 & 6 & 5 \end{array}\right] \xrightarrow[\text{1 and 2.}]{R_1 \leftrightarrow R_2 \text{ Reverse rows}} \left[\begin{array}{rrr|r} 1 & -1 & -2 & 2 \\ 3 & -4 & 4 & 7 \\ 2 & -3 & 6 & 5 \end{array}\right] \xrightarrow[\text{Replace row 3 by } -2R_1 + R_3.]{\text{Replace row 2 by } -3R_1 + R_2.}$$

$$\left[\begin{array}{rrr|r} 1 & -1 & -2 & 2 \\ 0 & -1 & 10 & 1 \\ 0 & -1 & 10 & 1 \end{array}\right] \xrightarrow[\text{Multiply row 2 by } -1.]{-1R_2} \left[\begin{array}{rrr|r} 1 & -1 & -2 & 2 \\ 0 & 1 & -10 & -1 \\ 0 & -1 & 10 & 1 \end{array}\right] \xrightarrow{\text{Replace row 3 by } 1R_2 + R_3.}$$

$$\left[\begin{array}{rrr|r} 1 & -1 & -2 & 2 \\ 0 & 1 & -10 & -1 \\ 0 & 0 & 0 & 0 \end{array}\right]$$

If we translate row 3 of the matrix into equation form, we obtain

$$0x + 0y + 0z = 0$$

or

$$0 = 0.$$

This equation results in a true statement regardless of which values we select for $x$, $y$, and $z$. Consequently, the equation $0x + 0y + 0z = 0$ is *dependent* on the other two equations in the system in the sense that it adds no new information about the variables. Thus, we can drop it from the system, which can now be expressed in the form

$$\left[\begin{array}{rrr|r} 1 & -1 & -2 & 2 \\ 0 & 1 & -10 & -1 \end{array}\right].$$

The original system is equivalent to the system

$$\begin{aligned} x - y - 2z &= 2 \\ y - 10z &= -1. \end{aligned}$$

Although neither of these equations gives a value for $z$, we can use them to express $x$ and $y$ in terms of $z$. From the last equation we obtain

$y = 10z - 1.$ Add $10z$ to both sides and isolate $y$.

Back-substituting for $y$ into the previous equation, we can find $x$ in terms of $z$.

| | |
|---|---|
| $x - y - 2z = 2$ | This is the first equation obtained from the final matrix. |
| $x - (10z - 1) - 2z = 2$ | Because $y = 10z - 1$, substitute $10z - 1$ for $y$. |
| $x - 10z + 1 - 2z = 2$ | Apply the distributive property. |
| $x - 12z + 1 = 2$ | Combine like terms. |
| $x = 12z + 1$ | Solve for $x$ in terms of $z$. |

Because no value is determined for $z$, we can find a solution to the system by letting $z$ equal any real number and then using the above equations to obtain $x$ and $y$. For example, if $z = 1$, then

$$x = 12z + 1 = 12(1) + 1 = 13 \text{ and}$$
$$y = 10z - 1 = 10(1) - 1 = 9.$$

Consequently, $(13, 9, 1)$ is a solution to the system. On the other hand, if we let $z = -1$, then

$$x = 12z + 1 = 12(-1) + 1 = -11 \text{ and}$$
$$y = 10z - 1 = 10(-1) - 1 = -11.$$

Thus, $(-11, -11, -1)$ is another solution to the system. Finally, letting $z = t$ (or any letter of our choice), the solutions to the system are all of the form

$$x = 12t + 1, \qquad y = 10t - 1, \qquad z = t,$$

where $t$ is a real number. Therefore, every ordered triple that is of the form $(12t + 1, 10t - 1, t)$, where $t$ is a real number, is a solution of the system. The solution set of the system with dependent equations can be written as $\{(12t + 1, 10t - 1, t)\}$.

Three planes may intersect at infinitely many points.

**Figure 9.2**

We have seen that when three planes have no point in common, the corresponding system has no solution. When the system has infinitely many solutions, like the one in Example 2, the three planes intersect in more than one point. Figure 9.2 illustrates one geometric possibility for systems with dependent equations.

**Check Point 2** Use Gaussian elimination to solve the following system:

$$\begin{aligned} x - 2y - z &= 5 \\ 2x - 5y + 3z &= 6 \\ x - 3y + 4z &= 1. \end{aligned}$$

**2** Apply Gaussian elimination to systems with differing numbers of variables and equations.

## Nonsquare Systems

Up to this point, we have encountered only *square* systems in which the number of equations is equal to the number of variables. In a **nonsquare system**, the number of variables differs from the number of equations.

### EXAMPLE 3 A System with Fewer Equations Than Variables

Use Gaussian elimination to solve the system

$$\begin{aligned} 3x + 7y + 6z &= 26 \\ x + 2y + z &= 8. \end{aligned}$$

**Solution** We begin with the augmented matrix.

$$\left[\begin{array}{ccc|c} 3 & 7 & 6 & 26 \\ 1 & 2 & 1 & 8 \end{array}\right] \xrightarrow{R_1 \leftrightarrow R_2} \left[\begin{array}{ccc|c} 1 & 2 & 1 & 8 \\ 3 & 7 & 6 & 26 \end{array}\right] \xrightarrow[\text{by } -3R_1 + R_2.]{\text{Replace row 2}} \left[\begin{array}{ccc|c} 1 & 2 & 1 & 8 \\ 0 & 1 & 3 & 2 \end{array}\right]$$

Because we now have 1s down the diagonal that begins with the upper-left entry and a 0 below this 1, we translate the matrix back into equation form.

$$x + 2y + z = 8 \quad \text{Equation 1}$$
$$y + 3z = 2 \quad \text{Equation 2}$$

**Discovery**

Let $t = 1$ for the solution set

$$\{(5t + 4, -3t + 2, t)\}.$$

What solution do you obtain? Substitute these three values in the two equations in Example 3 and show that each equation is satisfied. Repeat this process for another two values for $t$.

We can let $z$ equal any real number and use back-substitution to express $x$ and $y$ in terms of $z$.

**Equation 2**

$$y + 3z = 2$$
$$y = -3z + 2$$

**Equation 1**

$$x + 2y + z = 8$$
$$x + 2(-3z + 2) + z = 8$$
$$x - 6z + 4 + z = 8$$
$$x - 5z + 4 = 8$$
$$x = 5z + 4$$

With $z = t$, the ordered solution $(x, y, z)$ enables us to express the system's solution set as

$$\{(5t + 4, -3t + 2, t)\}$$

where $t$ is any real number.

**Check Point 3** Use Gaussian elimination to solve the system

$$x + 2y + 3z = 70$$
$$x + y + z = 60.$$

**3** Solve problems involving systems without unique solutions.

## Applications

How will computers be programmed to control traffic flow and avoid congestion? They will be required to solve systems continually based on the following premise: If traffic is to keep moving, during any period of time the number of cars entering an intersection must equal the number of cars leaving that intersection. Let's see what this means by looking at the intersections of four one-way city streets.

### EXAMPLE 4 Traffic Control

Figure 9.3 shows the intersections of four one-way streets. As you study the figure, notice that 300 cars per hour want to enter intersection $I_1$ from the north on 27th Avenue. Also, 200 cars per hour want to head east from intersection $I_2$ on Palm Drive. The letters $x$, $y$, $z$, and $w$ stand for the number of cars passing between the intersections.

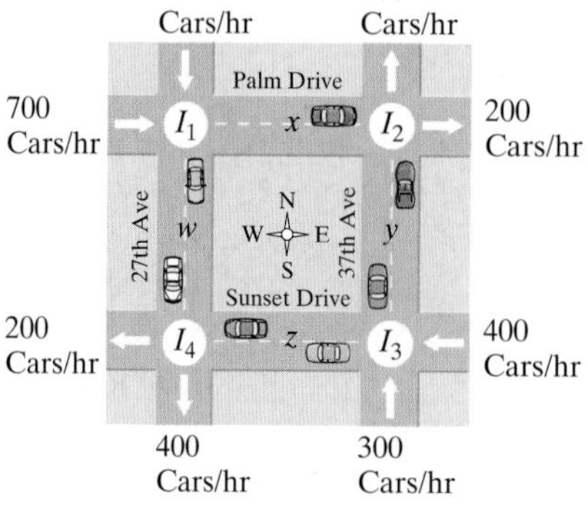


**Figure 9.3** The intersections of four one-way streets

**a.** If the traffic is to keep moving, at each intersection the number of cars entering per hour must equal the number of cars leaving per hour. Use this idea to set up a linear system of equations involving $x$, $y$, $z$, and $w$.

**b.** Use Gaussian elimination to solve the system.

**c.** If construction on 27th Avenue limits $w$ to 50 cars per hour, how many cars per hour must pass between the other intersections to keep traffic flowing?

## Automated Highways

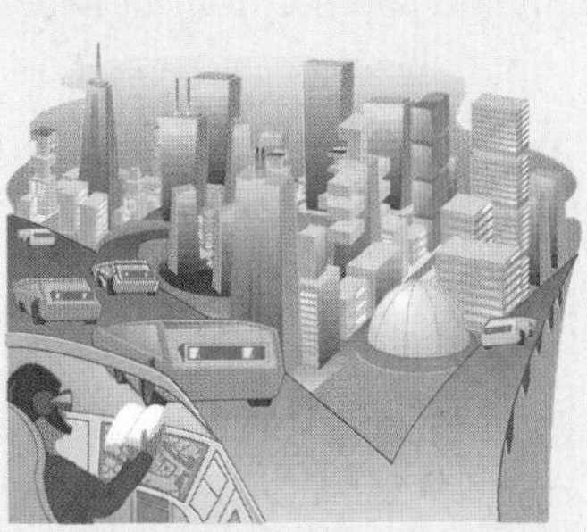

New technologies are making automated highways a reality. Experiments are taking place with cars that can steer, accelerate, and brake by themselves. A computer in the car picks up signals from magnets set in the road. Commuters can sit back, play with their laptop computers, read the newspaper, and enjoy the journey.

### Solution

**a.** Set up the system by considering one intersection at a time, referring to Figure 4.3.

For Intersection $I_1$: Because $300 + 700 = 1000$ cars enter $I_1$, and $x + w$ cars leave the intersection, then $x + w = 1000$.

For Intersection $I_2$: Because $x + y$ cars enter the intersection, and $200 + 900 = 1100$ cars leave $I_2$, then $x + y = 1100$.

For Intersection $I_3$: Figure 6.3 indicates that $300 + 400 = 700$ cars enter and $y + z$ leave, so $y + z = 700$.

For Intersection $I_4$: With $z + w$ cars entering and $200 + 400 = 600$ cars exiting, traffic will keep flowing if $z + w = 600$.

The system of equations that describes this situation is given by

$$\begin{aligned} x + w &= 1000 \\ x + y &= 1100 \\ y + z &= 700 \\ z + w &= 600. \end{aligned}$$

**b.** To solve this system using Gaussian elimination, we begin with the augmented matrix.

| System of Linear Equations (showing missing variables with 0 coefficients) | Augmented Matrix |
|---|---|
| $1x + 0y + 0z + 1w = 1000$<br>$1x + 1y + 0z + 0w = 1100$<br>$0x + 1y + 1z + 0w = 700$<br>$0x + 0y + 1z + 1w = 600$ | $\left[\begin{array}{cccc|c} 1 & 0 & 0 & 1 & 1000 \\ 1 & 1 & 0 & 0 & 1100 \\ 0 & 1 & 1 & 0 & 700 \\ 0 & 0 & 1 & 1 & 600 \end{array}\right]$ |

We can now use row operations to obtain the matrix

$$\left[\begin{array}{cccc|c} 1 & 0 & 0 & 1 & 1000 \\ 0 & 1 & 0 & -1 & 100 \\ 0 & 0 & 1 & 1 & 600 \\ 0 & 0 & 0 & 0 & 0 \end{array}\right].$$

$x + w = 1000$

$y - w = 100$

$z + w = 600$

The last row of the matrix shows that the system in the voice balloons has dependent equations and infinitely many solutions. To write the solution set containing these infinitely many solutions, let $w$ equal any real number. Use the three equations in the voice balloons to express $x$, $y$, and $z$ in terms of $w$: $x = 1000 - w$, $y = 100 + w$, and $z = 600 - w$.

With $w = t$, the ordered solution $(x, y, z, w)$ enables us to express the system's solution set as

$$\{(1000 - t, 100 + t, 600 - t, t)\}.$$

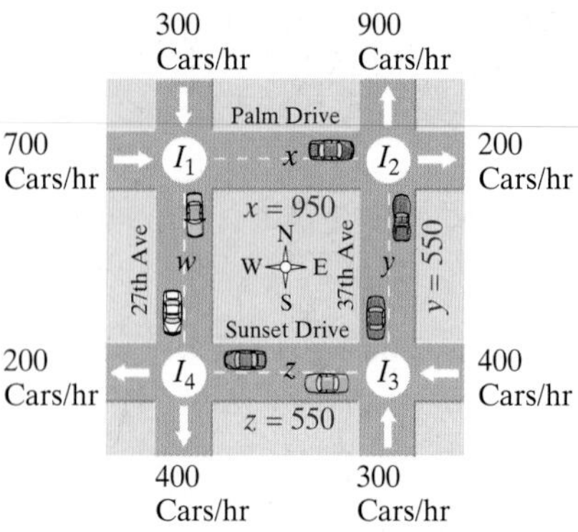


**Figure 9.4** With $w$ limited to 50 cars per hour, values for $x$, $y$, and $z$ are determined.

**c.** We are given that construction limits $w$ to 50 cars per hour. Because $w = t$, we replace 50 for $t$ in the system's ordered solution:

$$(1000 - t, 100 + t, 600 - t, t) \quad \text{Use the system's solution.}$$

$$= (1000 - 50, 100 + 50, 600 - 50, 50) \quad t = 50$$

$$= (950, 150, 550, 50)$$

Thus, $x = 950$, $y = 150$, and $z = 550$. (See Figure 9.4.) With construction on 27th Avenue, this means that to keep traffic flowing, 950 cars per hour must be routed between $I_1$ and $I_2$, 150 per hour between $I_3$ and $I_2$, and 550 per hour between $I_3$ and $I_4$.

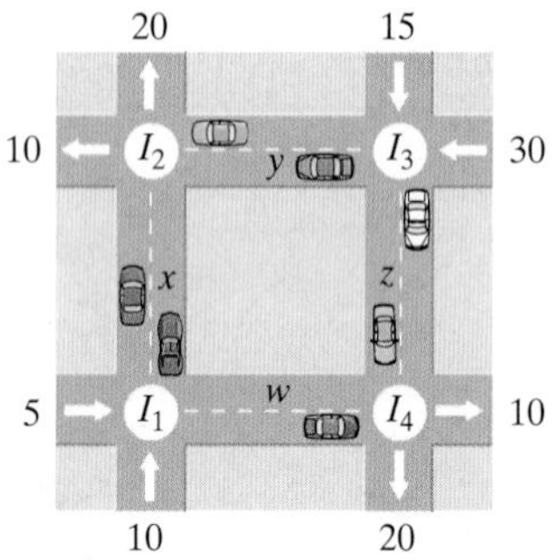


**Figure 9.5**

**Check Point 4**

Figure 9.5 shows a system of four one-way streets. The numbers in the figure denote the number of cars per minute that travel in the direction shown.

**a.** Use the requirement that the number of cars entering each of the intersections per minute must equal the number of cars leaving per minute to set up a system of equations in $x$, $y$, $z$, and $w$.

**b.** Use Gaussian elimination to solve the system.

**c.** If construction limits $w$ to 10 cars per minute, how many cars per minute must pass between the other intersections to keep traffic flowing?

## EXERCISE SET 9.2

### Practice Exercises

*In Exercises 1–24, use Gaussian elimination to find the complete solution to each system of equations, or show that none exists.*

**1.** $\begin{aligned} 5x + 12y + z &= 10 \\ 2x + 5y + 2z &= -1 \\ x + 2y - 3z &= 5 \end{aligned}$

**2.** $\begin{aligned} 2x - 4y + z &= 3 \\ x - 3y + z &= 5 \\ 3x - 7y + 2z &= 12 \end{aligned}$

**3.** $\begin{aligned} 5x + 8y - 6z &= 14 \\ 3x + 4y - 2z &= 8 \\ x + 2y - 2z &= 3 \end{aligned}$

**4.** $\begin{aligned} 5x - 11y + 6z &= 12 \\ -x + 3y - 2z &= -4 \\ 3x - 5y + 2z &= 4 \end{aligned}$

**5.** $\begin{aligned} 3x + 4y + 2z &= 3 \\ 4x - 2y - 8z &= -4 \\ x + y - z &= 3 \end{aligned}$

**6.** $\begin{aligned} 2x - y - z &= 0 \\ x + 2y + z &= 3 \\ 3x + 4y + 2z &= 8 \end{aligned}$

**7.** $\begin{aligned} 8x + 5y + 11z &= 30 \\ -x - 4y + 2z &= 3 \\ 2x - y + 5z &= 12 \end{aligned}$

**8.** $\begin{aligned} x + y - 10z &= -4 \\ x - 7z &= -5 \\ 3x + 5y - 36z &= -10 \end{aligned}$

**9.** $\begin{aligned} x - 2y - z - 3w &= -9 \\ x + y - z &= 0 \\ 3x + 4y + w &= 6 \\ 2y - 2z + w &= 3 \end{aligned}$

**10.** $\begin{aligned} 2x + y - 2z - w &= 3 \\ x - 2y + z + w &= 4 \\ -x - 8y + 7z + 5w &= 13 \\ 3x + y - 2z + 2w &= 6 \end{aligned}$

**11.** $\begin{aligned} 2x + y - z &= 3 \\ x - 3y + 2z &= -4 \\ 3x + y - 3z + w &= 1 \\ x + 2y - 4z - w &= -2 \end{aligned}$

**12.** $\begin{aligned} 2x - y + 3z + w &= 0 \\ 3x + 2y + 4z - w &= 0 \\ 5x - 2y - 2z - w &= 0 \\ 2x + 3y - 7z - 5w &= 0 \end{aligned}$

13. $$\begin{aligned} x - 3y + z - 4w &= 4 \\ -2x + y + 2z &= -2 \\ 3x - 2y + z - 6w &= 2 \\ -x + 3y + 2z - w &= -6 \end{aligned}$$

14. $$\begin{aligned} 3x + 2y - z + 2w &= -12 \\ 4x - y + z + 2w &= 1 \\ x + y + z + w &= -2 \\ -2x + 3y + 2z - 3w &= 10 \end{aligned}$$

15. $$\begin{aligned} 2x + y - z &= 2 \\ 3x + 3y - 2z &= 3 \end{aligned}$$

16. $$\begin{aligned} 3x + 2y - z &= 5 \\ x + 2y - z &= 1 \end{aligned}$$

17. $$\begin{aligned} x + 2y + 3z &= 5 \\ y - 5z &= 0 \end{aligned}$$

18. $$\begin{aligned} 3x - y + 4z &= 8 \\ y + 2z &= 1 \end{aligned}$$

19. $$\begin{aligned} x + y - 2z &= 2 \\ 3x - y - 6z &= -7 \end{aligned}$$

20. $$\begin{aligned} -2x - 5y + 10z &= 19 \\ x + 2y - 4z &= 12 \end{aligned}$$

21. $$\begin{aligned} x + y - z + w &= -2 \\ 2x - y + 2z - w &= 7 \\ -x + 2y + z + 2w &= -1 \end{aligned}$$

22. $$\begin{aligned} 2x - 3y + 4z + w &= 7 \\ x - y + 3z - 5w &= 10 \\ 3x + y - 2z - 2w &= 6 \end{aligned}$$

23. $$\begin{aligned} x + 2y + 3z - w &= 7 \\ 2y - 3z + w &= 4 \\ x - 4y + z &= 3 \end{aligned}$$

24. $$\begin{aligned} x - y + w &= 0 \\ x - 4y + z + 2w &= 0 \\ 3x - z + 2w &= 0 \end{aligned}$$

## Application Exercises

*The figure for Exercises 25–28 shows the intersection of three one-way streets. To keep traffic moving, the number of cars per minute entering an intersection must equal the number exiting that intersection. For intersection $I_1$, $x + 10$ cars enter and $y + 14$ cars exit per minute. Thus, $x + 10 = y + 14$.*

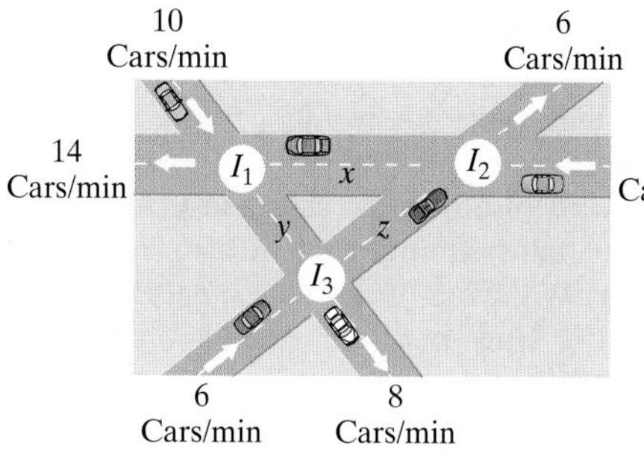


25. Write an equation for intersection $I_2$ that keeps traffic moving.

26. Write an equation for intersection $I_3$ that keeps traffic moving.

27. Use Gaussian elimination to solve the system formed by the equation given prior to Exercise 25 and the two equations that you obtained in Exercises 25–26.

28. Use your ordered solution obtained in Exercise 27 to solve this exercise. If construction limits $z$ to 4 cars per minute, how many cars per minute must pass between the other intersections to keep traffic flowing?

29. The figure shows the intersection of four one-way streets.

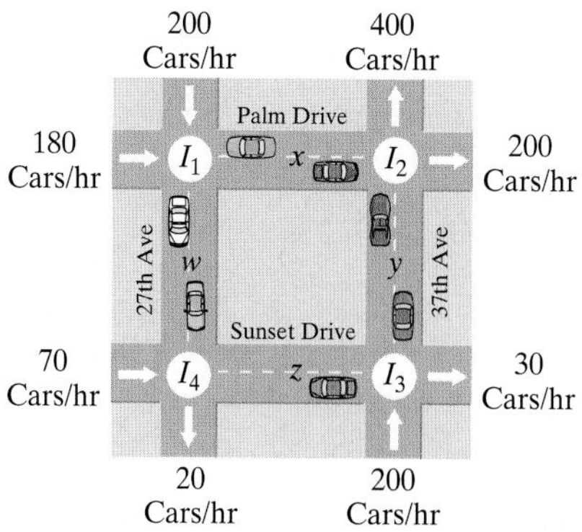


a. Set up a system of equations that keep traffic moving.
b. Use Gaussian elimination to solve the system.
c. If construction limits $w$ to 50 cars per hour, how many cars per hour must pass between the other intersections to keep traffic moving?

30. The vitamin content per ounce for three foods is given in the following table.

| | Milligrams per Ounce | | |
|---|---|---|---|
| | **Thiamin** | **Riboflavin** | **Niacin** |
| **Food A** | 3 | 7 | 1 |
| **Food B** | 1 | 5 | 3 |
| **Food C** | 3 | 8 | 2 |

a. Use matrices to show that no combination of these foods can provide exactly 14 mg of thiamin, 32 mg of riboflavin, and 9 mg of niacin.
b. Use matrices to describe in practical terms what happens if the riboflavin requirement is increased by 5 mg and the other requirements stay the same.

31. Three foods have the following nutritional content per ounce.

| | Units per Ounce | | |
|---|---|---|---|
| | **Vitamin A** | **Iron** | **Calcium** |
| **Food 1** | 20 | 20 | 10 |
| **Food 2** | 30 | 10 | 10 |
| **Food 3** | 10 | 10 | 30 |

**a.** A diet must consist precisely of 220 units of vitamin A, 180 units of iron, and 340 units of calcium. However, the dietician runs out of Food 1. Use a matrix approach to show that under these conditions the dietary requirements cannot be met.

**b.** Now suppose that all three foods are available, but due to problems with vitamin A for pregnant women, a hospital dietician no longer wants to include this vitamin in the diet. Use matrices to give two possible ways to meet the iron and calcium requirements with the three foods.

**32.** A company that manufactures products $A$, $B$, and $C$ does both manufacturing and testing. The hours needed to manufacture and test each product are shown in the table.

| | Hours Needed Weekly to Manufacture | Hours Needed Weekly to Test |
|---|---|---|
| **Product *A*** | 7 | 2 |
| **Product *B*** | 6 | 2 |
| **Product *C*** | 3 | 1 |

The company has exactly 67 hours per week available for manufacturing and 20 hours per week available for testing. Give two different combinations for the number of products that can be manufactured and tested weekly.

## Writing in Mathematics

**33.** Describe what happens when Gaussian elimination is used to solve an inconsistent system.

**34.** Describe what happens when Gaussian elimination is used to solve a system with dependent equations.

**35.** In solving a system of dependent equations in three variables, one student simply said that there are infinitely many solutions. A second student expressed the solution set as $\{(4t + 3, 5t - 1, t)\}$. Which is the better form of expressing the solution set and why?

## Technology Exercise

**36. a.** The figure at the top of the next column shows the intersections of a number of one-way streets. The numbers given represent traffic flow at a peak period (from 4 P.M. to 5:30 P.M.). Use the figure to write a linear system of six equations in seven variables based on the idea that at each intersection the number of cars entering must equal the number of cars leaving.

**b.** Use a graphing utility with matrix capabilities to find the complete solution to the system.

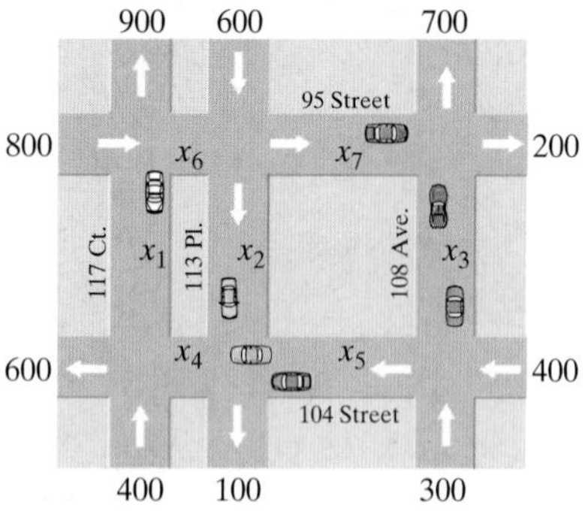


## Critical Thinking Exercise

**37.** Consider the linear system

$$\begin{aligned} x + 3y + z &= a^2 \\ 2x + 5y + 2az &= 0 \\ x + y + a^2z &= -9. \end{aligned}$$

For what values of $a$ will the system be inconsistent?

## Group Exercise

**38.** Before beginning this exercise, the group needs to read and solve Exercise 36.

**a.** A political group is planning a demonstration on 95th Street between 113th Place and 117th Court for 5 P.M. Wednesday. The problem becomes one of minimizing traffic flow on 95th Street (between 113th and 117th) without causing traffic tie-ups on other streets. One possible solution is to close off traffic on 95th Street between 113th and 117th (let $x_6 = 0$). What can group members conclude about $x_7$ under these conditions?

**b.** Working with a matrix allows us to simplify the problem caused by the political demonstration, but it did not actually solve the problem. There are an infinite number of solutions; each value of $x_7$ we choose gives us a new picture. We also assumed $x_6$ was equal to 0; changing that assumption would also lead to different solutions. With your group, design another solution to the traffic flow problem caused by the political demonstration.

# SECTION 9.3 Matrix Operations and Their Applications

## Objectives

1. Use matrix notation.
2. Understand what is meant by equal matrices.
3. Add and subtract matrices.
4. Perform scalar multiplication.
5. Multiply matrices.
6. Describe applied situations with matrix operations.

Turn on your computer and read your e-mail or write a paper. When you need to do research, use the Internet to browse through art museums and photography exhibits. When you need a break, load a flight simulator program and fly through a photorealistic computer world. As different as these experiences may be, they all share one thing—you're looking at images based on matrices. Matrices have applications in numerous fields, including the new technology of digital photography in which pictures are represented by numbers rather than film. In this section, we turn our attention to matrix algebra and some of its applications.

**1** Use matrix notation.

## Notations for Matrices

We have seen that an array of numbers, arranged in rows and columns and placed in brackets, is called a matrix. We can represent the matrix in two different ways.

- A capital letter, such as $A$, $B$, or $C$, can denote a matrix.
- A lowercase letter enclosed in brackets, such as that shown below, can denote a matrix.

$$A = [a_{ij}]$$

Matrix $A$ with elements $a_{ij}$

A general element in matrix $A$ is denoted by $a_{ij}$. This refers to the element in the $i$th row and $j$th column. For example, $a_{32}$ is the element of $A$ located in the third row, second column.

A matrix of **order $m \times n$** has $m$ rows and $n$ columns. If $m = n$, a matrix has the same number of rows as columns and is called a **square matrix**.

### EXAMPLE 1 Matrix Notation

Let

$$A = \begin{bmatrix} 3 & 2 & 0 \\ -4 & -5 & -\frac{1}{5} \end{bmatrix}.$$

**a.** What is the order of $A$?

**b.** If $A = [a_{ij}]$, identify $a_{23}$ and $a_{12}$.

$$A = \begin{bmatrix} 3 & 2 & 0 \\ -4 & -5 & -\frac{1}{5} \end{bmatrix}$$

Matrix $A$, shown again, to avoid turning back a page

**Solution**

**a.** The matrix has 2 rows and 3 columns, so it is of order $2 \times 3$.

**b.** The element $a_{23}$ is in the second row and third column. Thus, $a_{23} = -\frac{1}{5}$.

The element $a_{12}$ is in the first row and second column, and consequently $a_{12} = 2$.

**Check Point 1** Let

$$A = \begin{bmatrix} 5 & -2 \\ -3 & \pi \\ 1 & 6 \end{bmatrix}.$$

**a.** What is the order of $A$?

**b.** Identify $a_{12}$ and $a_{31}$.

**2** Understand what is meant by equal matrices.

## Equality of Matrices

Two matrices are **equal** if and only if they have the same order and corresponding elements are equal.

**Definition of Equality of Matrices**

Two matrices $A$ and $B$ are **equal** if and only if they have the same order $m \times n$ and $a_{ij} = b_{ij}$ for $i = 1, 2, \ldots, m$ and $j = 1, 2, \ldots, n$.

For example, if $A = \begin{bmatrix} x & y+1 \\ z & 6 \end{bmatrix}$ and $B = \begin{bmatrix} 1 & 5 \\ 3 & 6 \end{bmatrix}$, then $A = B$ if and only if $x = 1$, $y + 1 = 5$ (so $y = 4$), and $z = 3$.

**3** Add and subtract matrices.

## Matrix Addition and Subtraction

Table 9.1 shows that matrices of the same order can be added or subtracted by simply adding or subtracting corresponding elements.

**Table 9.1 Adding and subtracting matrices (Let $A = [a_{ij}]$ and $B = [b_{ij}]$ be matrices of order $m \times n$.)**

| Definition | The Definition in Words | Example |
|---|---|---|
| *Matrix Addition* $A + B = [a_{ij} + b_{ij}]$ | Matrices of the same order are added by adding the elements in corresponding positions. | $\begin{bmatrix} 1 & -2 \\ 3 & 5 \end{bmatrix} + \begin{bmatrix} -1 & 6 \\ 0 & 4 \end{bmatrix} = \begin{bmatrix} 1+(-1) & -2+6 \\ 3+0 & 5+4 \end{bmatrix} = \begin{bmatrix} 0 & 4 \\ 3 & 9 \end{bmatrix}$ |
| *Matrix Subtraction* $A - B = [a_{ij} - b_{ij}]$ | Matrices of the same order are subtracted by subtracting the elements in corresponding positions. | $\begin{bmatrix} 1 & -2 \\ 3 & 5 \end{bmatrix} - \begin{bmatrix} -1 & 6 \\ 0 & 4 \end{bmatrix} = \begin{bmatrix} 1-(-1) & -2-6 \\ 3-0 & 5-4 \end{bmatrix} = \begin{bmatrix} 2 & -8 \\ 3 & 1 \end{bmatrix}$ |

The sum or difference of two matrices of different orders is undefined. For example, consider the matrices

$$A = \begin{bmatrix} 0 & 3 \\ 4 & 3 \end{bmatrix} \quad \text{and} \quad B = \begin{bmatrix} 1 & 9 \\ 4 & 5 \\ 2 & 3 \end{bmatrix}.$$

The order of $A$ is $2 \times 2$; the order of $B$ is $3 \times 2$. These matrices are of different orders and cannot be added or subtracted.

**Technology**

Graphing utilities can add and subtract matrices. Enter the matrices and use a keystroke sequence similar to

[A] [+] [B] [ENTER]

[A] [−] [B] [ENTER]

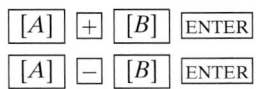

Consult your manual and verify the results in Example 2.

## EXAMPLE 2 Adding and Subtracting Matrices

Perform the indicated matrix operations:

**a.** $\begin{bmatrix} 0 & 5 & 3 \\ -2 & 6 & -8 \end{bmatrix} + \begin{bmatrix} -2 & 3 & 5 \\ 7 & -9 & 6 \end{bmatrix}$

**b.** $\begin{bmatrix} -6 & 7 \\ 2 & -3 \end{bmatrix} - \begin{bmatrix} -5 & 6 \\ 0 & -4 \end{bmatrix}.$

**Solution**

**a.** $\begin{bmatrix} 0 & 5 & 3 \\ -2 & 6 & -8 \end{bmatrix} + \begin{bmatrix} -2 & 3 & 5 \\ 7 & -9 & 6 \end{bmatrix}$

$= \begin{bmatrix} 0 + (-2) & 5 + 3 & 3 + 5 \\ -2 + 7 & 6 + (-9) & -8 + 6 \end{bmatrix}$ Add the corresponding elements in the $2 \times 3$ matrices.

$= \begin{bmatrix} -2 & 8 & 8 \\ 5 & -3 & -2 \end{bmatrix}$ Simplify.

**b.** $\begin{bmatrix} -6 & 7 \\ 2 & -3 \end{bmatrix} - \begin{bmatrix} -5 & 6 \\ 0 & -4 \end{bmatrix}$

$= \begin{bmatrix} -6 - (-5) & 7 - 6 \\ 2 - 0 & -3 - (-4) \end{bmatrix}$ Subtract the corresponding elements in the $2 \times 2$ matrices.

$= \begin{bmatrix} -1 & 1 \\ 2 & 1 \end{bmatrix}$ Simplify.

**Check Point 2** Perform the indicated matrix operations:

**a.** $\begin{bmatrix} -4 & 3 \\ 7 & -6 \end{bmatrix} + \begin{bmatrix} 6 & -3 \\ 2 & -4 \end{bmatrix}$ **b.** $\begin{bmatrix} 5 & 4 \\ -3 & 7 \\ 0 & 1 \end{bmatrix} - \begin{bmatrix} -4 & 8 \\ 6 & 0 \\ -5 & 3 \end{bmatrix}$

A matrix whose elements are all equal to 0 is called a **zero matrix**. If $A$ is an $m \times n$ matrix and 0 is an $m \times n$ zero matrix, then $A + 0 = A$. For example,

$$\begin{bmatrix} -5 & 2 \\ 3 & 6 \end{bmatrix} + \begin{bmatrix} 0 & 0 \\ 0 & 0 \end{bmatrix} = \begin{bmatrix} -5 & 2 \\ 3 & 6 \end{bmatrix}.$$

An $m \times n$ zero matrix is called the **additive identity** for $m \times n$ matrices.

For any matrix $A$, the **additive inverse** of $A$, written $-A$, is the matrix of the same order of $A$ such that every element of $-A$ is the opposite of the corresponding element of $A$. Because corresponding elements are added in matrix addition, $A + (-A)$ is a zero matrix. For example,

$$\begin{bmatrix} -5 & 2 \\ 3 & 6 \end{bmatrix} + \begin{bmatrix} 5 & -2 \\ -3 & -6 \end{bmatrix} = \begin{bmatrix} 0 & 0 \\ 0 & 0 \end{bmatrix}.$$

Properties of matrix addition are similar to properties involved with adding real numbers.

### Properties of Matrix Addition

If $A$, $B$, and $C$ are $m \times n$ matrices and 0 is an $m \times n$ zero matrix, then the following properties are true.

**1.** $A + B = B + A$ — Commutative Property of Addition

**2.** $(A + B) + C = A + (B + C)$ — Associative Property of Addition

**3.** $A + 0 = 0 + A = A$ — Additive Identity Property

**4.** $A + (-A) = (-A) + A = 0$ — Additive Inverse Property

**4** Perform scalar multiplication.

## Scalar Multiplication

A matrix of order $1 \times 1$, such as [6], contains only one entry. To distinguish this matrix from the number 6, we refer to 6 as a **scalar**. In general, in our work with matrices, we will refer to real numbers as scalars.

To multiply a matrix $A$ by a scalar $c$, we multiply each entry in $A$ by $c$. For example,

$$4\begin{bmatrix} 2 & 5 \\ -3 & 0 \end{bmatrix} = \begin{bmatrix} 4(2) & 4(5) \\ 4(-3) & 4(0) \end{bmatrix} = \begin{bmatrix} 8 & 20 \\ -12 & 0 \end{bmatrix}.$$

Scalar    Matrix

### Definition of Scalar Multiplication

If $A = [a_{ij}]$ is a matrix of order $m \times n$ and $c$ is a scalar, then the matrix $cA$ is the $m \times n$ matrix given by

$$cA = [ca_{ij}].$$

This matrix is obtained by multiplying each element of $A$ by the real number $c$. We call $cA$ a **scalar multiple** of $A$.

### EXAMPLE 3 Scalar Multiplication

If $A = \begin{bmatrix} -1 & 4 \\ 3 & 0 \end{bmatrix}$ and $B = \begin{bmatrix} 2 & -3 \\ 5 & -6 \end{bmatrix}$, find **a.** $-5B$ **b.** $2A + 3B$.

**Solution**

**a.** $-5B = -5\begin{bmatrix} 2 & -3 \\ 5 & -6 \end{bmatrix} = \begin{bmatrix} -5(2) & -5(-3) \\ -5(5) & -5(-6) \end{bmatrix} = \begin{bmatrix} -10 & 15 \\ -25 & 30 \end{bmatrix}$

Multiply each element in $B$ by $-5$.

**b.** $2A + 3B = 2\begin{bmatrix} -1 & 4 \\ 3 & 0 \end{bmatrix} + 3\begin{bmatrix} 2 & -3 \\ 5 & -6 \end{bmatrix}$

$= \begin{bmatrix} 2(-1) & 2(4) \\ 2(3) & 2(0) \end{bmatrix} + \begin{bmatrix} 3(2) & 3(-3) \\ 3(5) & 3(-6) \end{bmatrix}$

Multiply each element in $A$ by 2. Multiply each element in $B$ by 3.

$= \begin{bmatrix} -2 & 8 \\ 6 & 0 \end{bmatrix} + \begin{bmatrix} 6 & -9 \\ 15 & -18 \end{bmatrix} = \begin{bmatrix} -2+6 & 8+(-9) \\ 6+15 & 0+(-18) \end{bmatrix}$

Perform the addition of these $2 \times 2$ matrices by adding corresponding elements.

$= \begin{bmatrix} 4 & -1 \\ 21 & -18 \end{bmatrix}$

**Check Point 3** If $A = \begin{bmatrix} -4 & 1 \\ 3 & 0 \end{bmatrix}$ and $B = \begin{bmatrix} -1 & -2 \\ 8 & 5 \end{bmatrix}$, find

**a.** $-6B$ **b.** $3A + 2B$.

**Discovery**

Verify each of the four properties listed in the box using

$A = \begin{bmatrix} 2 & -4 \\ -5 & 3 \end{bmatrix}$,

$B = \begin{bmatrix} 4 & 0 \\ 1 & -6 \end{bmatrix}$,

$c = 4$, and $d = 2$.

**Properties of Scalar Multiplication**

If $A$ and $B$ are $m \times n$ matrices, and $c$ and $d$ are scalars, then the following properties are true.

1. $(cd)A = c(dA)$ — Associative Property of Scalar Multiplication
2. $1A = A$ — Scalar Identity Property
3. $c(A + B) = cA + cB$ — Distributive Property
4. $(c + d)A = cA + dA$ — Distributive Property

**5** Multiply matrices.

## Matrix Multiplication

We do not multiply two matrices by multiplying the corresponding entries of matrices. Instead, we must think of matrix multiplication as *row-by-column multiplication*. To better understand how this works, let's begin with the definition of matrix multiplication for matrices of order $2 \times 2$.

**Definition of Matrix Multiplication: 2 × 2 matrices**

Row 1 of A × Column 1 of B | Row 1 of A × Column 2 of B

$$AB = \begin{bmatrix} a & b \\ c & d \end{bmatrix} \begin{bmatrix} e & f \\ g & h \end{bmatrix} = \begin{bmatrix} ae + bg & af + bh \\ ce + dg & cf + dh \end{bmatrix}$$

Row 2 of A × Column 1 of B | Row 2 of A × Column 2 of B

Notice that we obtain the element in the $i$th row and $j$th column in $AB$ by performing computations with elements in the $i$th row of $A$ and the $j$th column of $B$. For example, we obtain the element in the first row and first column of $AB$ by performing computations with elements in the first row of $A$ and the first column of $B$.

First row of A | First column of B

$$\begin{bmatrix} a & b \\ & \end{bmatrix} \begin{bmatrix} e & \\ g & \end{bmatrix} = \begin{bmatrix} ae + bg & \\ & \end{bmatrix}$$

1. Multiply each element in row 1 of A by the corresponding element in column 1 of B.
2. Add these products.
3. Record the sum as the element in row 1, column 1 of the product matrix.

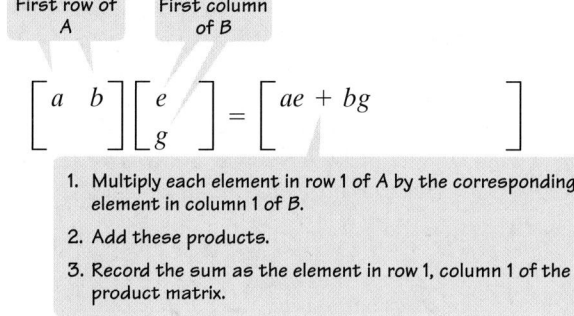

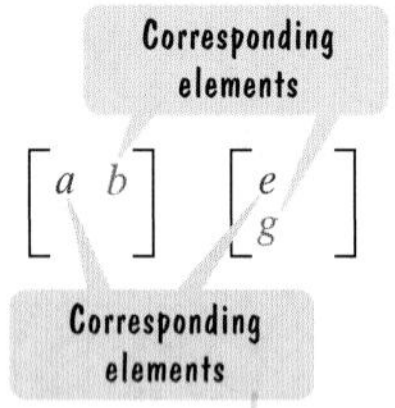


**Figure 9.6** Finding corresponding elements when multiplying matrices

You may wonder how to find the corresponding elements in step 1 in the voice balloon. The element at the far left of row 1 corresponds to the element at the top of column 1. The second element from the left of row 1 corresponds to the second element from the top of column 1. This is illustrated in Figure 9.6.

## EXAMPLE 4 Multiplying Matrices

Find $AB$, given

$$A = \begin{bmatrix} 2 & 3 \\ 4 & 7 \end{bmatrix} \quad \text{and} \quad B = \begin{bmatrix} 0 & 1 \\ 5 & 6 \end{bmatrix}.$$

**Solution** We will perform a row-by-column computation.

$$AB = \begin{bmatrix} 2 & 3 \\ 4 & 7 \end{bmatrix} \begin{bmatrix} 0 & 1 \\ 5 & 6 \end{bmatrix}$$

Row 1 of A × Column 1 of B | Row 1 of A × Column 2 of B

$$= \begin{bmatrix} 2(0) + 3(5) & 2(1) + 3(6) \\ 4(0) + 7(5) & 4(1) + 7(6) \end{bmatrix} = \begin{bmatrix} 15 & 20 \\ 35 & 46 \end{bmatrix}$$

Row 2 of A × Column 1 of B | Row 2 of A × Column 2 of B

**Check Point 4** Find $AB$, given $A = \begin{bmatrix} 1 & 3 \\ 2 & 5 \end{bmatrix}$ and $B = \begin{bmatrix} 4 & 6 \\ 1 & 0 \end{bmatrix}$.

We can generalize the process of Example 4 to multiplying an $m \times n$ matrix and an $n \times p$ matrix. **For the product of two matrices to be defined, the number of columns of the first matrix must equal the number of rows of the second matrix.**

| **First Matrix** | **Second Matrix** |
|---|---|
| $m \times n$ | $n \times p$ |

The number of columns in the first matrix must be the same as the number of rows in the second matrix.

## Study Tip

The following diagram illustrates the first sentence in the box defining matrix multiplication. The diagram is helpful in determining the order of the product $AB$.

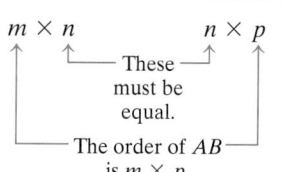

| **Matrix A** | **Matrix B** |
|---|---|
| $m \times n$ | $n \times p$ |

These ($n$ and $n$) must be equal.

The order of $AB$ is $m \times p$.

### Definition of Matrix Multiplication

The **product** of an $m \times n$ matrix, $A$, and an $n \times p$ matrix, $B$, is an $m \times p$ matrix, $AB$, whose elements are found as follows. The element in the $i$th row and $j$th column of $AB$ is found by multiplying the each element in the $i$th row of $A$ by the corresponding element in the $j$th column of $B$ and adding the products.

To find a product $AB$, each row of $A$ must have the same number of elements as each column of $B$. We obtain $p_{ij}$, the element in the $i$th row and $j$th column in $AB$, by performing computations with elements in the $i$th row of $A$ and the $j$th column of $B$:

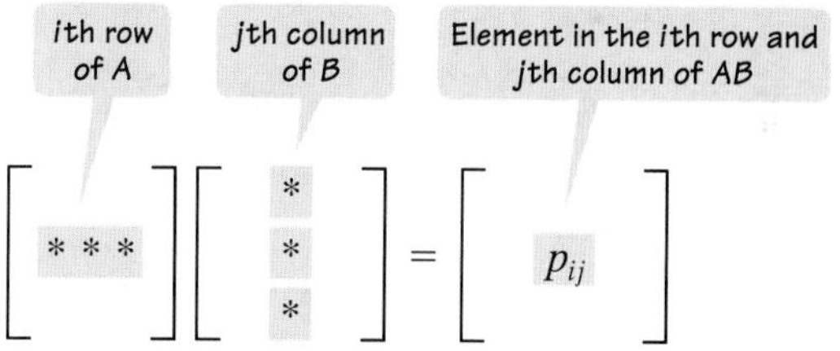


When multiplying corresponding elements, keep in mind that the element at the far left of row $i$ corresponds to the element at the top of column $j$. The element second from the left of row $i$ corresponds to the element second from the top of column $j$. Likewise, the element third from the left of row $i$ corresponds to the element third from the top of column $j$, and so on.

## EXAMPLE 5 Multiplying Matrices

Matrices $A$ and $B$ are defined as follows.

$$A = \begin{bmatrix} 1 & 2 & 3 \end{bmatrix} \qquad B = \begin{bmatrix} 4 \\ 5 \\ 6 \end{bmatrix}$$

Find **a.** $AB$ and **b.** $BA$.

## Solution

**a.** Matrix $A$ is a $1 \times 3$ matrix and matrix $B$ is a $3 \times 1$ matrix. Thus, the product is a $1 \times 1$ matrix.

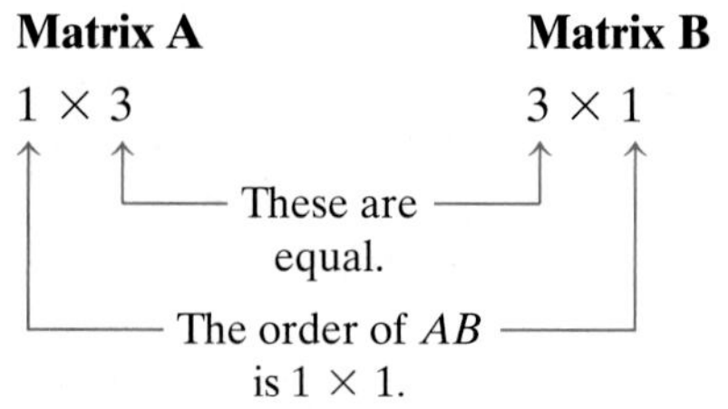


$$AB = \begin{bmatrix} 1 & 2 & 3 \end{bmatrix} \begin{bmatrix} 4 \\ 5 \\ 6 \end{bmatrix}$$ We will perform a row-by-column computation.

$$= [(1)(4) + (2)(5) + (3)(6)]$$ Multiply elements in row 1 of A by corresponding elements in column 1 of B and add the products.

$$= [4 + 10 + 18]$$

$$= [32]$$

**b.** Matrix $B$ is a $3 \times 1$ matrix and matrix $A$ is a $1 \times 3$ matrix. Thus, the product $BA$ is a $3 \times 3$ matrix.

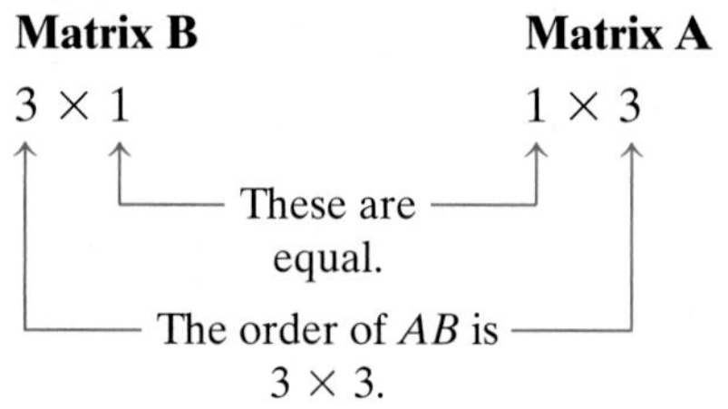


$$BA = \begin{bmatrix} 4 \\ 5 \\ 6 \end{bmatrix} \begin{bmatrix} 1 & 2 & 3 \end{bmatrix}$$ We perform a row-by-column computation.

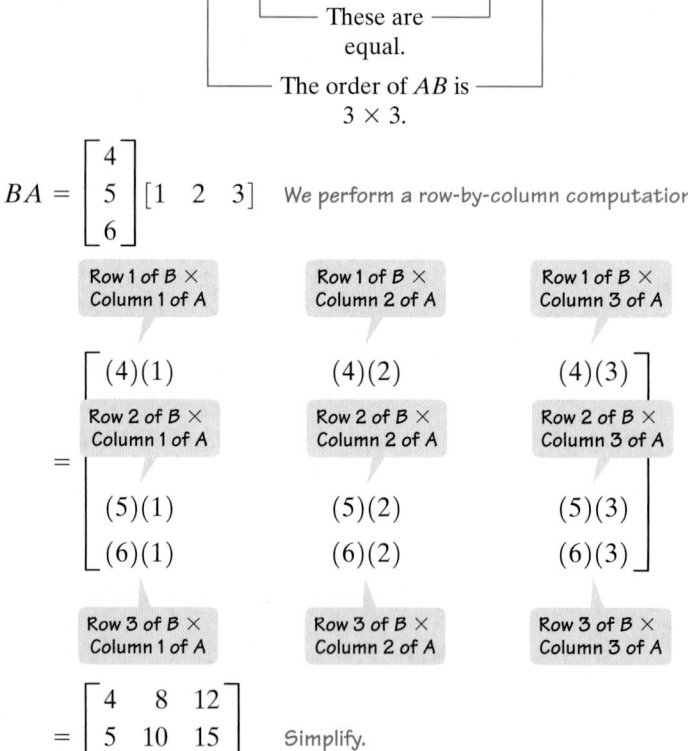

Row 1 of B × Column 1 of A; Row 1 of B × Column 2 of A; Row 1 of B × Column 3 of A

Row 2 of B × Column 1 of A; Row 2 of B × Column 2 of A; Row 2 of B × Column 3 of A

Row 3 of B × Column 1 of A; Row 3 of B × Column 2 of A; Row 3 of B × Column 3 of A

$$= \begin{bmatrix} (4)(1) & (4)(2) & (4)(3) \\ (5)(1) & (5)(2) & (5)(3) \\ (6)(1) & (6)(2) & (6)(3) \end{bmatrix}$$

$$= \begin{bmatrix} 4 & 8 & 12 \\ 5 & 10 & 15 \\ 6 & 12 & 18 \end{bmatrix}$$ Simplify.

## Arthur Cayley

The Granger Collection

Matrices were first studied intensively by the English mathematician Arthur Cayley (1821–1895). Before reaching the age of 25, he published 25 papers, setting a pattern of prolific creativity that lasted throughout his life. Cayley was a lawyer, painter, mountaineer, and Cambridge professor whose greatest invention was that of matrices and matrix theory. Cayley's matrix algebra, especially the noncommutativity of multiplication ($AB \neq BA$), opened up a new area of mathematics called abstract algebra.

In Example 5, notice that $AB$ and $BA$ are different matrices. For most matrices $AB \neq BA$. Because **matrix multiplication is not commutative**, be careful about the order in which matrices appear when performing this operation.

**Check Point 5** If $A = \begin{bmatrix} 2 & 0 & 4 \end{bmatrix}$ and $B = \begin{bmatrix} 1 \\ 3 \\ 7 \end{bmatrix}$, find $AB$ and $BA$.

## EXAMPLE 6 Multiplying Matrices

Where possible, find each product:

**a.** $\begin{bmatrix} 4 & 2 \\ 1 & 3 \end{bmatrix}\begin{bmatrix} 1 & 2 & 3 & 4 \\ 0 & 2 & -1 & 6 \end{bmatrix}$ **b.** $\begin{bmatrix} 1 & 2 & 3 & 4 \\ 0 & 2 & -1 & 6 \end{bmatrix}\begin{bmatrix} 4 & 2 \\ 1 & 3 \end{bmatrix}$

### Solution

**a.** The first matrix is a $2 \times 2$ matrix and the second is a $2 \times 4$ matrix. The product will be a $2 \times 4$ matrix.

**First Matrix** $2 \times 2$ **Second Matrix** $2 \times 4$

These are equal. (the inner numbers: 2 and 2)

The order of the product is $2 \times 4$. (the outer numbers)

$$\begin{bmatrix} 4 & 2 \\ 1 & 3 \end{bmatrix}\begin{bmatrix} 1 & 2 & 3 & 4 \\ 0 & 2 & -1 & 6 \end{bmatrix}$$

We perform a row-by-column computation.

Row 1 × Column 1; Row 1 × Column 2; Row 1 × Column 3; Row 1 × Column 4

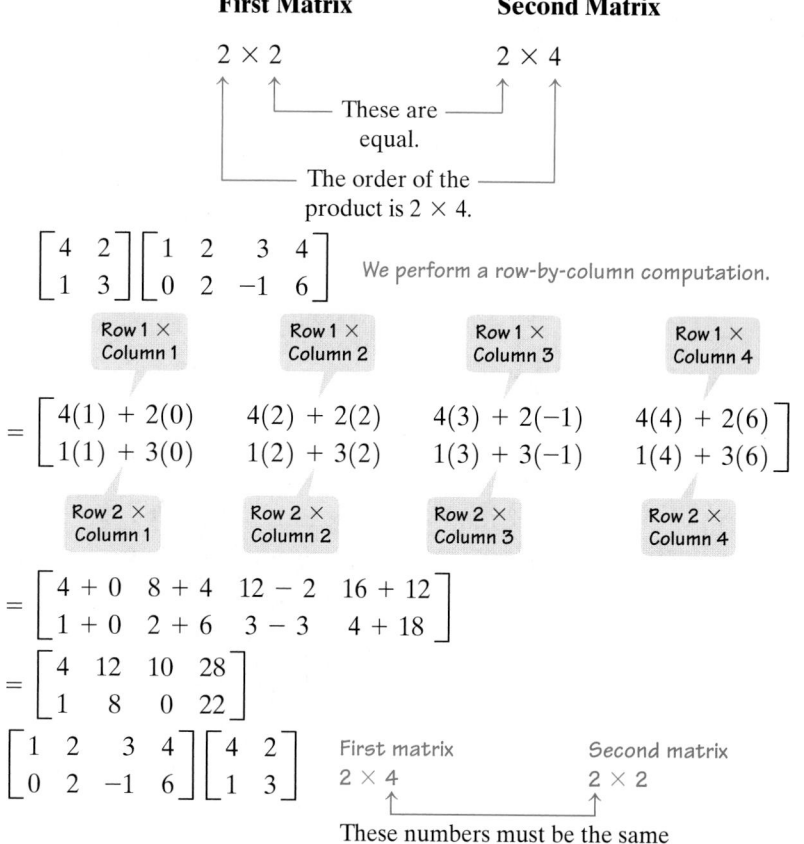

$$= \begin{bmatrix} 4(1) + 2(0) & 4(2) + 2(2) & 4(3) + 2(-1) & 4(4) + 2(6) \\ 1(1) + 3(0) & 1(2) + 3(2) & 1(3) + 3(-1) & 1(4) + 3(6) \end{bmatrix}$$

Row 2 × Column 1; Row 2 × Column 2; Row 2 × Column 3; Row 2 × Column 4

$$= \begin{bmatrix} 4 + 0 & 8 + 4 & 12 - 2 & 16 + 12 \\ 1 + 0 & 2 + 6 & 3 - 3 & 4 + 18 \end{bmatrix}$$

$$= \begin{bmatrix} 4 & 12 & 10 & 28 \\ 1 & 8 & 0 & 22 \end{bmatrix}$$

**b.** $\begin{bmatrix} 1 & 2 & 3 & 4 \\ 0 & 2 & -1 & 6 \end{bmatrix}\begin{bmatrix} 4 & 2 \\ 1 & 3 \end{bmatrix}$

First matrix $2 \times 4$ Second matrix $2 \times 2$

These numbers must be the same to multiply the matrices.

The number of columns in the first matrix does not equal the number of rows in the second matrix. Thus, the product of these two matrices is undefined.

**Check Point 6** Where possible, find each product.

**a.** $\begin{bmatrix} 1 & 3 \\ 0 & 2 \end{bmatrix}\begin{bmatrix} 2 & 3 & -1 & 6 \\ 0 & 5 & 4 & 1 \end{bmatrix}$ **b.** $\begin{bmatrix} 2 & 3 & -1 & 6 \\ 0 & 5 & 4 & 1 \end{bmatrix}\begin{bmatrix} 1 & 3 \\ 0 & 2 \end{bmatrix}$

Although matrix multiplication is not commutative, it does obey many of the properties of real numbers.

**Discovery**

Verify the properties listed in the box using

$$A = \begin{bmatrix} 3 & 2 \\ -1 & 4 \end{bmatrix}$$

$$B = \begin{bmatrix} 1 & 0 \\ 3 & 2 \end{bmatrix}$$

$$C = \begin{bmatrix} 1 & 2 \\ -1 & 1 \end{bmatrix}$$

and $c = 3$.

### Properties of Matrix Multiplication

If $A$, $B$, and $C$ are matrices and $c$ is a scalar, then the following properties are true. (Assume the order of each matrix is such that all operations in these properties are defined.)

1. $(AB)C = A(BC)$ — Associative Property of Matrix Multiplication
2. $A(B + C) = AB + AC$; $(A + B)C = AC + BC$ — Distributive Properties of Matrix Multiplication
3. $c(AB) = (cA)B$ — Associative Property of Scalar Multiplication

**6** Describe applied situations with matrix operations.

## Applications

All of the still images that you see on the Web have been created or manipulated on a computer in a digital format—made up of hundreds of thousands, or even millions, of tiny squares called **pixels**. Pixels are created by dividing an image into a grid. The computer can change the brightness of every square or pixel in this grid. A digital camera captures photos in this digital format. Also, you can scan pictures to convert them into digital format. Example 7 illustrates the role that matrices play in this new technology.

### EXAMPLE 7 Matrices and Digital Photography

The letter T in Figure 9.7 is shown using 9 pixels in a $3 \times 3$ grid. The colors possible in the grid are shown in Figure 9.8. Each color is represented by a specific number: 0, 1, 2, or 3.

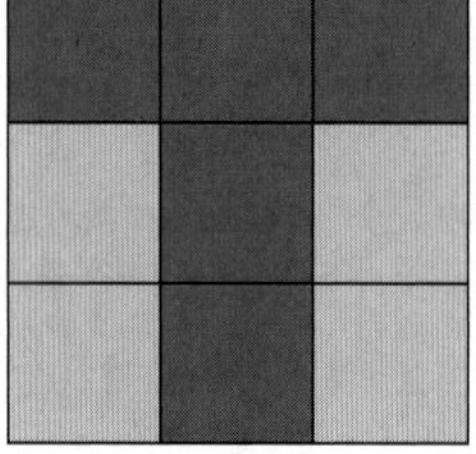

**Figure 9.7** The letter T

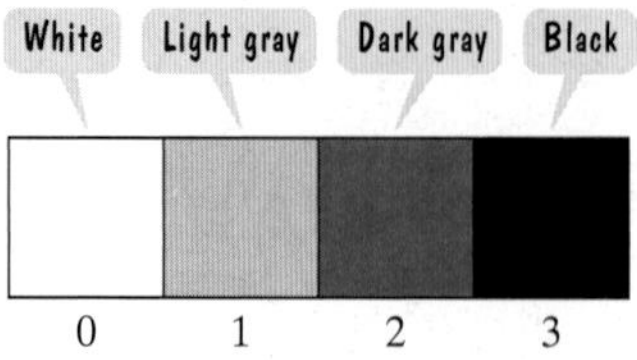


**Figure 9.8** Color levels

**a.** Find a matrix that represents a digital photograph of this letter T.

**b.** Increase the contrast of the letter T by changing the dark gray to black and the light gray to white. Use matrix addition to accomplish this.

## Solution

**a.** Look at the T and the background in Figure 9.7. Because the T is dark gray and the background is light gray, a digital photograph of Figure 9.7 can be represented by the matrix

$$\begin{bmatrix} 2 & 2 & 2 \\ 1 & 2 & 1 \\ 1 & 2 & 1 \end{bmatrix}.$$

**Figure 9.9** Changing contrast: the letter T

**b.** We can make the T black by increasing each 2 in the above matrix to 3. We can make the background white by decreasing each 1 in the matrix to 0. This is accomplished using the following matrix addition.

$$\begin{bmatrix} 2 & 2 & 2 \\ 1 & 2 & 1 \\ 1 & 2 & 1 \end{bmatrix} + \begin{bmatrix} 1 & 1 & 1 \\ -1 & 1 & -1 \\ -1 & 1 & -1 \end{bmatrix} = \begin{bmatrix} 3 & 3 & 3 \\ 0 & 3 & 0 \\ 0 & 3 & 0 \end{bmatrix}$$

The picture corresponding to the matrix sum to the right of the equal sign is shown in Figure 9.9.

**Check Point 7** Change the contrast of the letter T in Figure 9.7 by making the T light gray and the background black. Use matrix addition to accomplish this.

### Images of Space

Photographs sent back from space use matrices with thousands of pixels. Each pixel is assigned a number from 0 to 63 representing its color—0 for pure white and 63 for pure black. In the image of Saturn shown here, matrix operations provide false colors that emphasize the banding of the planet's upper atmosphere.

## EXAMPLE 8 Applying Matrix Multiplication

At a certain gas station, the number of gallons of regular, unleaded, and super unleaded gas sold on Monday, Tuesday, and Wednesday of a particular week is given by the following matrix.

| | Regular | Unleaded | Super Unleaded |
|---|---|---|---|
| **Monday** | 240 | 300 | 160 |
| **Tuesday** | 200 | 280 | 180 |
| **Wednesday** | 260 | 310 | 200 |

$= A$

A second matrix gives the selling price per gallon and the profit per gallon for the three types of gas sold by the station.

| | Selling price per Gallon | Profit per Gallon |
|---|---|---|
| **Regular** | 1.15 | 0.15 |
| **Unleaded** | 1.20 | 0.17 |
| **Super Unleaded** | 1.25 | 0.19 |

$= B$

**a.** Calculate the product $AB$.

**b.** What is the gas station's profit for Monday through Wednesday?

**Solution**

$$\textbf{a. } AB = \begin{bmatrix} 240 & 300 & 160 \\ 200 & 280 & 180 \\ 260 & 310 & 200 \end{bmatrix} \begin{bmatrix} 1.15 & 0.15 \\ 1.20 & 0.17 \\ 1.25 & 0.19 \end{bmatrix}$$

$$= \begin{bmatrix} 240(1.15) + 300(1.20) + 160(1.25) & 240(0.15) + 300(0.17) + 160(0.19) \\ 200(1.15) + 280(1.20) + 180(1.25) & 200(0.15) + 280(0.17) + 180(0.19) \\ 260(1.15) + 310(1.20) + 200(1.25) & 260(0.15) + 310(0.17) + 200(0.19) \end{bmatrix}$$

Perform to row-by-column multiplications.

$$= \begin{bmatrix} 836 & 117.40 \\ 791 & 111.80 \\ 921 & 129.70 \end{bmatrix}$$

Multiply and add as indicated.

**b.** The entries in the second column of the product matrix represent profits for Monday, Tuesday, and Wednesday, respectively. The gas station's profit for Monday through Wednesday is \$117.40 + \$111.80 + \$129.70 or \$358.90.

**Check Point 8** Use the product matrix in Example 8a to answer this question. What are the gas station's total sales for Monday, Tuesday, and Wednesday?

## EXERCISE SET 9.3

### Practice Exercises

*In Exercises 1–4,*

**a.** *Give the order of each matrix.*

**b.** *If $A = [a_{ij}]$, identify $a_{32}$ and $a_{23}$ or explain why identification is not possible.*

**1.** $\begin{bmatrix} 4 & -7 & 5 \\ -6 & 8 & -1 \end{bmatrix}$

**2.** $\begin{bmatrix} -6 & 4 & -1 \\ -9 & 0 & \frac{1}{2} \end{bmatrix}$

**3.** $\begin{bmatrix} 1 & -5 & \pi & e \\ 0 & 7 & -6 & -\pi \\ -2 & \frac{1}{2} & 11 & -\frac{1}{5} \end{bmatrix}$

**4.** $\begin{bmatrix} -4 & 1 & 3 & -5 \\ 2 & -1 & \pi & 0 \\ 1 & 0 & -e & \frac{1}{5} \end{bmatrix}$

*In Exercises 5–8, find values for the variables so that the matrices in each exercise are equal.*

**5.** $\begin{bmatrix} x \\ 4 \end{bmatrix} = \begin{bmatrix} 6 \\ y \end{bmatrix}$

**6.** $\begin{bmatrix} x \\ 7 \end{bmatrix} = \begin{bmatrix} 11 \\ y \end{bmatrix}$

**7.** $\begin{bmatrix} x & 2y \\ z & 9 \end{bmatrix} = \begin{bmatrix} 4 & 12 \\ 3 & 9 \end{bmatrix}$

**8.** $\begin{bmatrix} x & y+3 \\ 2z & 8 \end{bmatrix} = \begin{bmatrix} 12 & 5 \\ 6 & 8 \end{bmatrix}$

*In Exercises 9–16, find*

**a.** $A + B$ **b.** $A - B$

**c.** $-4A$ **d.** $3A + 2B$

**9.** $A = \begin{bmatrix} 4 & 1 \\ 3 & 2 \end{bmatrix}, \quad B = \begin{bmatrix} 5 & 9 \\ 0 & 7 \end{bmatrix}$

**10.** $A = \begin{bmatrix} -2 & 3 \\ 0 & 1 \end{bmatrix}, \quad B = \begin{bmatrix} 8 & 1 \\ 5 & 4 \end{bmatrix}$

**11.** $A = \begin{bmatrix} 1 & 3 \\ 3 & 4 \\ 5 & 6 \end{bmatrix}, \quad B = \begin{bmatrix} 2 & -1 \\ 3 & -2 \\ 0 & 1 \end{bmatrix}$

**12.** $A = \begin{bmatrix} 3 & 1 & 1 \\ -1 & 2 & 5 \end{bmatrix}, \quad B = \begin{bmatrix} 2 & -3 & 6 \\ -3 & 1 & -4 \end{bmatrix}$

**13.** $A = \begin{bmatrix} 2 \\ -4 \\ 1 \end{bmatrix}, \quad B = \begin{bmatrix} -5 \\ 3 \\ -1 \end{bmatrix}$

**14.** $A = [6 \quad 2 \quad -3], \quad B = [4 \quad -2 \quad 3]$

**15.** $A = \begin{bmatrix} 2 & -10 & -2 \\ 14 & 12 & 10 \\ 4 & -2 & 2 \end{bmatrix}, \quad B = \begin{bmatrix} 6 & 10 & -2 \\ 0 & -12 & -4 \\ -5 & 2 & -2 \end{bmatrix}$

**16.** $A = \begin{bmatrix} 6 & -3 & 5 \\ 6 & 0 & -2 \\ -4 & 2 & -1 \end{bmatrix}$, $B = \begin{bmatrix} -3 & 5 & 1 \\ -1 & 2 & -6 \\ 2 & 0 & 4 \end{bmatrix}$

*In Exercises 17–26, find (if possible)*
**a.** $AB$ *and* **b.** $BA$.

**17.** $A = \begin{bmatrix} 1 & 3 \\ 5 & 3 \end{bmatrix}$, $B = \begin{bmatrix} 3 & -2 \\ -1 & 6 \end{bmatrix}$

**18.** $A = \begin{bmatrix} 3 & -2 \\ 1 & 5 \end{bmatrix}$, $B = \begin{bmatrix} 0 & 0 \\ 5 & -6 \end{bmatrix}$

**19.** $A = [1 \ \ 2 \ \ 3 \ \ 4]$, $B = \begin{bmatrix} 1 \\ 2 \\ 3 \\ 4 \end{bmatrix}$

**20.** $A = \begin{bmatrix} -1 \\ -2 \\ -3 \end{bmatrix}$, $B = [1 \ \ 2 \ \ 3]$

**21.** $A = \begin{bmatrix} 1 & -1 & 4 \\ 4 & -1 & 3 \\ 2 & 0 & -2 \end{bmatrix}$, $B = \begin{bmatrix} 1 & 1 & 0 \\ 1 & 2 & 4 \\ 1 & -1 & 3 \end{bmatrix}$

**22.** $A = \begin{bmatrix} 1 & -1 & 1 \\ 5 & 0 & -2 \\ 3 & -2 & 2 \end{bmatrix}$, $B = \begin{bmatrix} 1 & 1 & 0 \\ 1 & -4 & 5 \\ 3 & -1 & 2 \end{bmatrix}$

**23.** $A = \begin{bmatrix} 4 & 2 \\ 6 & 1 \\ 3 & 5 \end{bmatrix}$, $B = \begin{bmatrix} 2 & 3 & 4 \\ -1 & -2 & 0 \end{bmatrix}$

**24.** $A = \begin{bmatrix} 2 & 4 \\ 3 & 1 \\ 4 & 2 \end{bmatrix}$, $B = \begin{bmatrix} 3 & 2 & 0 \\ -1 & -3 & 5 \end{bmatrix}$

**25.** $A = \begin{bmatrix} 2 & -3 & 1 & -1 \\ 1 & 1 & -2 & 1 \end{bmatrix}$, $B = \begin{bmatrix} 1 & 2 \\ -1 & 1 \\ 5 & 4 \\ 10 & 5 \end{bmatrix}$

**26.** $A = \begin{bmatrix} 2 & -1 & 3 & 2 \\ 1 & 0 & -2 & 1 \end{bmatrix}$, $B = \begin{bmatrix} -1 & 2 \\ 1 & 1 \\ 3 & -4 \\ 6 & 5 \end{bmatrix}$

*In Exercises 27–34, perform the indicated matrix operations given that A, B, and C are defined as follows. If an operation is not defined, state the reason.*

$$A = \begin{bmatrix} 4 & 0 \\ -3 & 5 \\ 0 & 1 \end{bmatrix} \qquad B = \begin{bmatrix} 5 & 1 \\ -2 & -2 \end{bmatrix} \qquad C = \begin{bmatrix} 1 & -1 \\ -1 & 1 \end{bmatrix}$$

**27.** $4B - 3C$
**28.** $5C - 2B$
**29.** $BC + CB$
**30.** $A(B + C)$
**31.** $A - C$
**32.** $B - A$
**33.** $A(BC)$
**34.** $A(CB)$

## Application Exercises

*The + sign in the figure is shown using 9 pixels in a 3 × 3 grid. The color levels are given to the right of the figure. Use the matrix* $\begin{bmatrix} 1 & 3 & 1 \\ 3 & 3 & 3 \\ 1 & 3 & 1 \end{bmatrix}$ *that represents a digital photograph of the + sign to solve Exercises 35–38.*

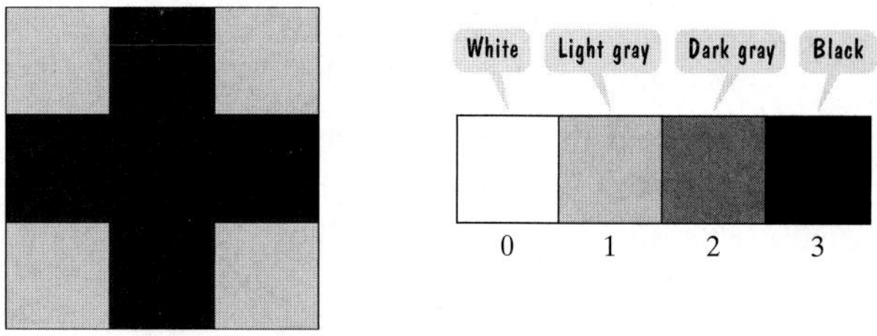


**35.** Adjust the contrast by changing the black to dark gray and the light gray to white. Use matrix addition to accomplish this.

**36.** Adjust the contrast by changing the black to dark gray and the light gray to black. Use matrix addition to accomplish this.

**37.** Adjust the contrast by changing the black to light gray and the light gray to dark gray. Use matrix addition to accomplish this.

**38.** Adjust the contrast by leaving the black alone and changing the light gray to white. Use matrix addition to accomplish this.

**39. a.** Write a 3 × 3 matrix $A$ that represents a digital photograph of the number 1 in black on a white background.
**b.** Find a matrix $B$ so that $A + B$ darkens only the white background to light gray.

**40. a.** Write a 3 × 3 matrix $A$ that represents a digital photograph of the letter T in light gray on a white background.
**b.** Find a matrix $B$ so that $A + B$ darkens only the letter T from light gray to black.

**41.** A virus strikes a college campus. Students are either sick, well, or carriers of the virus. The percentages of people in each category are given by the following matrix, which we'll call $A$.

| | Freshman | Sophomore | Junior | Senior |
|---|---|---|---|---|
| **Well** | 15% | 25% | 20% | 10% |
| **Sick** | 35% | 40% | 35% | 70% |
| **Carrier** | 50% | 35% | 45% | 20% |

The student population is distributed by class and gender as given by the following matrix, which we'll call $B$.

| | Male | Female |
|---|---|---|
| **Freshman** | 820 | 640 |
| **Sophomore** | 950 | 1020 |
| **Junior** | 680 | 720 |
| **Senior** | 930 | 910 |

**a.** Calculate the product $AB$.
**b.** How many sick females are there?
**c.** How many male carriers are there?

**42.** In a certain county, the proportion of voters in each age group registered as Republicans, Democrats, or Independents is given by the following matrix, which we'll call $A$.

| | Age 18–30 | Age 31–50 | Age Over 50 |
|---|---|---|---|
| **Republicans** | 0.4 | 0.30 | 0.70 |
| **Democrats** | 0.30 | 0.60 | 0.25 |
| **Independents** | 0.30 | 0.10 | 0.05 |

The distribution, by age and gender, of this county's voting population is given by the following matrix, which we'll call $B$.

| | Male | Female |
|---|---|---|
| **Age 18–30** | 6000 | 8000 |
| **Age 31–50** | 12,000 | 14,000 |
| **Age Over 50** | 14,000 | 16,000 |

**a.** Calculate the product $AB$.
**b.** How many female Democrats are there?
**c.** How many male Republicans are there?

**43.** The final grade in a particular course is determined by grades on the midterm and final. The grades for five students and the two grading systems are modeled by the following matrices. Call the first matrix $A$ and the second $B$.

| | Midterm | Final |
|---|---|---|
| **Student 1** | 76 | 92 |
| **Student 2** | 74 | 84 |
| **Student 3** | 94 | 86 |
| **Student 4** | 84 | 62 |
| **Student 5** | 58 | 80 |

| | System 1 | System 2 |
|---|---|---|
| **Midterm** | 0.5 | 0.3 |
| **Final** | 0.5 | 0.7 |

**a.** Describe the grading system that is represented by matrix $B$.
**b.** Compute the matrix $AB$ and assign each of the five students a final course grade first using system 1 and then using system 2. $(89.5 - 100 = A, 79.5 - 89.4 = B, 69.5 - 79.4 = C, 59.5 - 69.4 = D,$ below $59.5 = F)$

**44.** In the matrices shown below, a 1 represents a yes, and a 0 represents a no. The first matrix, $A$, describes whether or not three colleges in a state university system offer degrees in each program.

| | Programs: Liberal Arts | Programs: Engineering | Programs: Education |
|---|---|---|---|
| **College 1** | 1 | 1 | 0 |
| **College 2** | 1 | 1 | 1 |
| **College 3** | 0 | 1 | 0 |

Each program requires that certain math courses be completed, indicated by the following matrix called $B$.

| | General College Math | Intermediate Algebra | College Algebra | Trigonometry | Calculus |
|---|---|---|---|---|---|
| **Liberal Arts** | 1 | 1 | 0 | 0 | 0 |
| **Engineering** | 0 | 0 | 1 | 1 | 1 |
| **Education** | 1 | 1 | 1 | 0 | 0 |

Find the product $AB$. Explain how this helps the college decide which courses to offer.

## Writing in Mathematics

**45.** What is meant by the order of a matrix? Give an example with your explanation.

**46.** What does $a_{ij}$ mean?

**47.** What are equal matrices?

**48.** How are matrices added?

**49.** Describe how to subtract matrices.

**50.** Describe matrices that cannot be added or subtracted.

**51.** Describe how to perform scalar multiplication. Provide an example with your description.

**52.** Describe how to multiply matrices.

**53.** Describe when the multiplication of two matrices is not defined.

**54.** If two matrices can be multiplied, describe how to determine the order of the product.

**55.** Low-resolution digital photographs use 262,144 pixels in a $512 \times 512$ grid. If you enlarge a low-resolution digital photograph enough, describe what will happen.

### Technology Exercise

**56.** Use the matrix feature of a graphing utility to verify each of your answers to Exercises 27–34.

### Critical Thinking Exercises

**57.** Find two matrices $A$ and $B$ such that $AB = BA$.

**58.** Consider a square matrix such that each element that is not on the main diagonal is zero. Experiment with such matrices (call each matrix $A$) by finding $AA$. Then write a sentence or two describing a method for multiplying this kind of matrix by itself.

**59.** If $AB = -BA$, then $A$ and $B$ are said to be anticommutative. Are $A = \begin{bmatrix} 0 & -1 \\ 1 & 0 \end{bmatrix}$ and $B = \begin{bmatrix} 1 & 0 \\ 0 & -1 \end{bmatrix}$ anticommutative?

### Group Exercise

**60.** The interesting and useful applications of matrix theory are nearly unlimited. Applications of matrices range from representing digital photographs to predicting long-range trends in the stock market. Members of the group should research an application of matrices that they find intriguing. The group should then present a seminar to the class about this application.

## SECTION 9.4 *Multiplicative Inverses of Matrices and Matrix Equations*

### Objectives

1. Find the multiplicative inverse of a square matrix.
2. Use inverses to solve matrix equations.
3. Encode and decode messages.

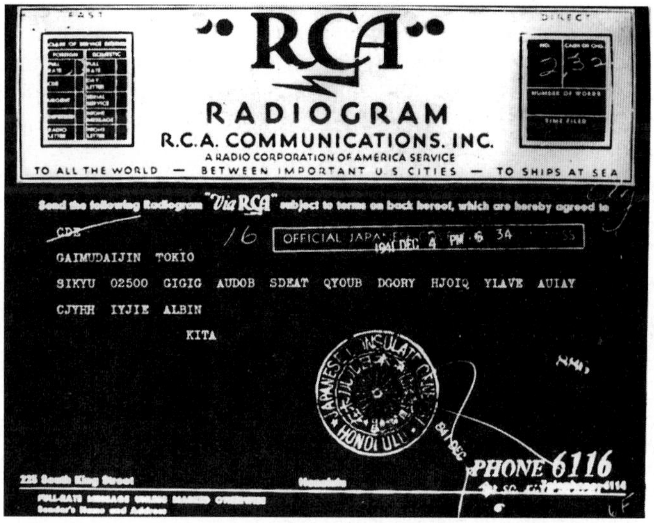


This 1941 RCA radiogram shows an encoded message from the Japanese government.

In 1939, Britain's secret service hired top chess players, mathematicians, and other masters of logic to break the code used by the Nazis in communications between headquarters and troops. The project, which employed over 10,000 people, broke the code less than a year later, providing the Allies with information about Nazi troop movements throughout World War II.

Messages must often be sent in such a way that the real meaning is hidden from everyone but the sender and the recipient. In this section, we will look at the role that matrices and their inverses play in this process.

### The Multiplicative Identity Matrix

For the real numbers, we know that 1 is the multiplicative identity because $a \cdot 1 = 1 \cdot a = a$. Is there a similar property for matrix multiplication? That is, is there a matrix $I$ such that $AI = A$ and $IA = A$? The answer is yes. A square matrix with 1s down the main diagonal and 0s elsewhere does not change the elements in a matrix when it multiplies that matrix. In the case of $2 \times 2$ matrices,

$$\begin{bmatrix} a_{11} & a_{12} \\ a_{21} & a_{22} \end{bmatrix}\begin{bmatrix} 1 & 0 \\ 0 & 1 \end{bmatrix} = \begin{bmatrix} a_{11} & a_{12} \\ a_{21} & a_{22} \end{bmatrix}$$

The elements in the matrix do not change.

and $$\begin{bmatrix} 1 & 0 \\ 0 & 1 \end{bmatrix}\begin{bmatrix} a_{11} & a_{12} \\ a_{21} & a_{22} \end{bmatrix} = \begin{bmatrix} a_{11} & a_{12} \\ a_{21} & a_{22} \end{bmatrix}.$$

The elements in the matrix do not change.

An $n \times n$ square matrix whose main diagonal elements are 1s, while all other elements are 0s, is called the **multiplicative identity matrix of order *n***, designated by $I_n$. For example.

$$I_2 = \begin{bmatrix} 1 & 0 \\ 0 & 1 \end{bmatrix}, \quad I_3 = \begin{bmatrix} 1 & 0 & 0 \\ 0 & 1 & 0 \\ 0 & 0 & 1 \end{bmatrix},$$

and so on.

**1** Find the multiplicative inverse of a square matrix.

## The Multiplicative Inverse of a Matrix

The multiplicative identity matrix, $I_n$, will help us to define a new concept: the multiplicative inverse of a matrix. To do so, let's consider a similar concept, the multiplicative inverse of a nonzero number, $a$. Recall that the multiplicative inverse of $a$ is $\frac{1}{a}$. The multiplicative inverse has the following property:

$$a \cdot \tfrac{1}{a} = 1 \quad \text{and} \quad \tfrac{1}{a} \cdot a = 1.$$

We can define the multiplicative inverse of a square matrix in a similar manner.

**Definition of the Multiplicative Inverse of a Square Matrix**

Let $A$ be an $n \times n$ matrix. If there exists an $n \times n$ matrix $A^{-1}$ (read: "$A$ inverse") such that

$$AA^{-1} = I_n \quad \text{and} \quad A^{-1}A = I_n,$$

then $A^{-1}$ is the **multiplicative inverse** of $A$.

We have seen that matrix multiplication is not commutative. Thus, to show that matrix $B$ is the multiplicative inverse of matrix $A$, find both $AB$ and $BA$. If $B$ is the multiplicative inverse of $A$, both products ($AB$ and $BA$) will be the multiplicative identity matrix, $I_n$.

### EXAMPLE 1 The Multiplicative Inverse of a Matrix

Show that $B$ is the multiplicative inverse of $A$, where

$$A = \begin{bmatrix} -1 & 3 \\ 2 & -5 \end{bmatrix} \quad \text{and} \quad B = \begin{bmatrix} 5 & 3 \\ 2 & 1 \end{bmatrix}.$$

**Solution** To show that $B$ is the multiplicative inverse of $A$, we must find the products $AB$ and $BA$. If $B$ is the multiplicative inverse of $A$, then $AB$ will be the multiplicative identity matrix and $BA$ will be the multiplicative identity matrix. Because $A$ and $B$ are $2 \times 2$ matrices, $n = 2$. Thus, we denote the multiplicative identity matrix as $I_2$; it is also a $2 \times 2$ matrix. We must show that

- $AB = I_2 = \begin{bmatrix} 1 & 0 \\ 0 & 1 \end{bmatrix}$.
- $BA = I_2 = \begin{bmatrix} 1 & 0 \\ 0 & 1 \end{bmatrix}$.

$$AB = \begin{bmatrix} -1 & 3 \\ 2 & -5 \end{bmatrix}\begin{bmatrix} 5 & 3 \\ 2 & 1 \end{bmatrix}$$
$$= \begin{bmatrix} -1(5) + 3(2) & -1(3) + 3(1) \\ 2(5) + (-5)(2) & 2(3) + (-5)(1) \end{bmatrix} = \begin{bmatrix} 1 & 0 \\ 0 & 1 \end{bmatrix}$$
$$BA = \begin{bmatrix} 5 & 3 \\ 2 & 1 \end{bmatrix}\begin{bmatrix} -1 & 3 \\ 2 & -5 \end{bmatrix}$$
$$= \begin{bmatrix} 5(-1) + 3(2) & 5(3) + 3(-5) \\ 2(-1) + 1(2) & 2(3) + 1(-5) \end{bmatrix} = \begin{bmatrix} 1 & 0 \\ 0 & 1 \end{bmatrix}$$

Both products give the multiplicative identity matrix. Thus, $B$ is the multiplicative inverse of $A$ and we can designate $B$ as $A^{-1} = \begin{bmatrix} 5 & 3 \\ 2 & 1 \end{bmatrix}$.

**Check Point 1** Show that $B$ is the multiplicative inverse of $A$, where

$$A = \begin{bmatrix} 2 & 1 \\ 1 & 1 \end{bmatrix} \quad \text{and} \quad B = \begin{bmatrix} 1 & -1 \\ -1 & 2 \end{bmatrix}.$$

One method for finding the multiplicative inverse of a matrix $A$ is to begin by denoting the elements in $A^{-1}$ with variables. Using the equation $AA^{-1} = I_n$ we can find a value for each element in the multiplicative inverse that was represented by a variable. Example 2 shows how this is done.

## EXAMPLE 2 Finding the Multiplicative Inverse of a Matrix

Find the multiplicative inverse of

$$A = \begin{bmatrix} 2 & 1 \\ 5 & 3 \end{bmatrix}.$$

**Solution** Let us denote the multiplicative inverse by

$$A^{-1} = \begin{bmatrix} x & y \\ z & w \end{bmatrix}.$$

Because $A$ is a $2 \times 2$ matrix, we use the equation $AA^{-1} = I_2$ to find values for $x$, $y$, $z$, and $w$.

$$\underbrace{\begin{bmatrix} 2 & 1 \\ 5 & 3 \end{bmatrix}}_{A}\underbrace{\begin{bmatrix} x & y \\ z & w \end{bmatrix}}_{A^{-1}} = \underbrace{\begin{bmatrix} 1 & 0 \\ 0 & 1 \end{bmatrix}}_{I_2}$$

$$\begin{bmatrix} 2x + z & 2y + w \\ 5x + 3z & 5y + 3w \end{bmatrix} = \begin{bmatrix} 1 & 0 \\ 0 & 1 \end{bmatrix}$$

Use row-by-column matrix multiplication on the left.

We now equate corresponding elements to obtain the following two systems of linear equations.

$$\begin{aligned} 2x + z &= 1 \\ 5x + 3z &= 0 \end{aligned} \qquad \text{and} \qquad \begin{aligned} 2y + w &= 0 \\ 5y + 3w &= 1 \end{aligned}$$

Each of these systems can be solved using the addition method.

$$\begin{aligned} 2x + z &= 1 \xrightarrow{\text{Multiply by } -3.} & -6x - 3z &= -3 \\ 5x + 3z &= 0 \xrightarrow{\text{No change}} & 5x + 3z &= 0 \\ & \text{Add:} & -x &= -3 \\ & & x &= 3 \\ & \text{Use back-substitution.} & z &= -5 \end{aligned}$$

$$\begin{aligned} 2y + w &= 0 \xrightarrow{\text{Multiply by } -3.} & -6y - 3w &= 0 \\ 5y + 3w &= 1 \xrightarrow{\text{No change}} & 5y + 3w &= 1 \\ & \text{Add:} & -y &= 1 \\ & & y &= -1 \\ & \text{Use back-substitution.} & w &= 2 \end{aligned}$$

Using these values, we have

$$A^{-1} = \begin{bmatrix} x & y \\ z & w \end{bmatrix} = \begin{bmatrix} 3 & -1 \\ -5 & 2 \end{bmatrix}.$$

## Discovery

Verify that the inverse matrix found in Example 2 is correct. Use matrix multiplication to show that

$AA^{-1} = I_2$ and $A^{-1}A = I_2$,

where

$$I_2 = \begin{bmatrix} 1 & 0 \\ 0 & 1 \end{bmatrix}.$$

**Check Point 2** Find the multiplicative inverse of $A = \begin{bmatrix} 5 & 7 \\ 2 & 3 \end{bmatrix}$.

Only square matrices of order $n \times n$ have multiplicative inverses, but not every square matrix possesses a multiplicative inverse. For example, suppose that you apply the procedure of Example 2 to $A = \begin{bmatrix} -6 & 4 \\ -3 & 2 \end{bmatrix}$:

This is A. This represents $A^{-1}$. This is the multiplicative identity matrix.

$$\begin{bmatrix} -6 & 4 \\ -3 & 2 \end{bmatrix}\begin{bmatrix} x & y \\ z & w \end{bmatrix} = \begin{bmatrix} 1 & 0 \\ 0 & 1 \end{bmatrix}.$$

Multiplying matrices on the left and equating corresponding elements results in inconsistent systems with no solutions. There are no values for $x$, $y$, $z$, and $w$. This shows that matrix $A$ does not have a multiplicative inverse.

A nonsquare matrix, one with a different number of rows than columns, cannot have a multiplicative inverse. If $A$ is an $m \times n$ matrix and $B$ is an $n \times m$ matrix $(n \neq m)$, then the products $AB$ and $BA$ are of different orders. This means that they could not be equal to each other, so that $AB$ and $BA$ could not both equal the multiplicative identity matrix.

If a square matrix has a multiplicative inverse, that inverse is unique. This means that the square matrix has no more than one inverse. If a square matrix has a multiplicative inverse, it is said to be **invertible**.

## A Quick Method for Finding the Multiplicative Inverse of a 2 × 2 Matrix

The following rule enables us to calculate the multiplicative inverse, if there is one, of a 2 × 2 matrix.

**Multiplicative Inverse of a 2 × 2 Matrix**

If $A = \begin{bmatrix} a & b \\ c & d \end{bmatrix}$, then $A^{-1} = \frac{1}{ad - bc}\begin{bmatrix} d & -b \\ -c & a \end{bmatrix}$.

The matrix $A$ is invertible if and only if $ad - bc \neq 0$. If $ad - bc = 0$, then $A$ does not have a multiplicative inverse.

**Study Tip**

To find the matrix that appears as the second factor for the inverse of

$$A = \begin{bmatrix} a & b \\ c & d \end{bmatrix}.$$

- Reverse $a$ and $d$, the numbers in the main diagonal.
- Negate $b$ and $c$, the numbers in the other diagonal.

### EXAMPLE 3 Using the Quick Method to Find Multiplicative Inverses

Find the multiplicative inverse of

$$A = \begin{bmatrix} -1 & -2 \\ 3 & 4 \end{bmatrix}.$$

**Solution**

$$A = \begin{bmatrix} -1 & -2 \\ 3 & 4 \end{bmatrix}$$ (with $a = -1$, $b = -2$, $c = 3$, $d = 4$ labeled)

This is the given matrix. We've designated the elements $a$, $b$, $c$, and $d$.

$$A^{-1} = \frac{1}{ad - bc}\begin{bmatrix} d & -b \\ -c & a \end{bmatrix}$$

This is the formula for the inverse of $\begin{bmatrix} a & b \\ c & d \end{bmatrix}$.

$$= \frac{1}{(-1)(4) - (-2)(3)}\begin{bmatrix} 4 & -(-2) \\ -3 & -1 \end{bmatrix}$$

Apply the formula with $a = -1$, $b = -2$, $c = 3$, and $d = 4$.

$$= \frac{1}{2}\begin{bmatrix} 4 & 2 \\ -3 & -1 \end{bmatrix}$$

Simplify.

$$= \begin{bmatrix} 2 & 1 \\ -\frac{3}{2} & -\frac{1}{2} \end{bmatrix}$$

Perform the scalar multiplication by multiplying each element in the matrix by $\frac{1}{2}$.

The inverse of $A = \begin{bmatrix} -1 & -2 \\ 3 & 4 \end{bmatrix}$ is $A^{-1} = \begin{bmatrix} 2 & 1 \\ -\frac{3}{2} & -\frac{1}{2} \end{bmatrix}$.

We can verify this result by showing that $AA^{-1} = I_2$ and $A^{-1}A = I_2$.

**Study Tip**

When using the formula to find the multiplicative inverse, start by computing $ad - bc$. If the computed value is 0, there is no need to continue. The given matrix does not have a multiplicative inverse.

**Check Point 3** Find the multiplicative inverse of

$$A = \begin{bmatrix} 3 & -2 \\ -1 & 1 \end{bmatrix}.$$

## Finding Multiplicative Inverses of $n \times n$ Matrices with $n$ Greater Than 2

To find the multiplicative inverse of a $3 \times 3$ invertible matrix, we begin by denoting the elements in the multiplicative inverse with variables. Here is an example:

$$\begin{bmatrix} -1 & -1 & -1 \\ 4 & 5 & 0 \\ 0 & 1 & -3 \end{bmatrix} \begin{bmatrix} x_1 & x_2 & x_3 \\ y_1 & y_2 & y_3 \\ z_1 & z_2 & z_3 \end{bmatrix} = \begin{bmatrix} 1 & 0 & 0 \\ 0 & 1 & 0 \\ 0 & 0 & 1 \end{bmatrix}.$$

This is matrix $A$ whose inverse we wish to find.

This represents $A^{-1}$.

This is the multiplicative identity matrix, $I_3$.

We multiply the matrices on the left, using the row-by-column definition of matrix multiplication.

$$\begin{bmatrix} -x_1 - y_1 - z_1 & -x_2 - y_2 - z_2 & -x_3 - y_3 - z_3 \\ 4x_1 + 5y_1 + 0z_1 & 4x_2 + 5y_2 + 0z_2 & 4x_3 + 5y_3 + 0z_3 \\ 0x_1 + 1y_1 - 3z_1 & 0x_2 + 1y_2 - 3z_2 & 0x_3 + 1y_3 - 3z_3 \end{bmatrix} = \begin{bmatrix} 1 & 0 & 0 \\ 0 & 1 & 0 \\ 0 & 0 & 1 \end{bmatrix}$$

We now equate corresponding entries to obtain the following three systems of linear equations.

$$\begin{aligned} -x_1 - y_1 - z_1 &= 1 \\ 4x_1 + 5y_1 + 0z_1 &= 0 \\ 0x_1 + y_1 - 3z_1 &= 0 \end{aligned} \qquad \begin{aligned} -x_2 - y_2 - z_2 &= 0 \\ 4x_2 + 5y_2 + 0z_2 &= 1 \\ 0x_2 + y_2 - 3z_2 &= 0 \end{aligned} \qquad \begin{aligned} -x_3 - y_3 - z_3 &= 0 \\ 4x_3 + 5y_3 + 0z_3 &= 0 \\ 0x_3 + y_3 - 3z_3 &= 1 \end{aligned}$$

Notice that the variables on the left of the equal sign have the same coefficients in each system. We can use Gauss-Jordan elimination to solve all three at once. Form an augmented matrix that contains the coefficients of the three systems to the left of the vertical line and the constants for the systems to the right.

$$\left[\begin{array}{ccc|ccc} -1 & -1 & -1 & 1 & 0 & 0 \\ 4 & 5 & 0 & 0 & 1 & 0 \\ 0 & 1 & -3 & 0 & 0 & 1 \end{array}\right]$$

Coefficients of the three systems

Constants on the right in each of the three systems

To solve all three systems using Gauss-Jordan elimination, we must obtain $\begin{bmatrix} 1 & 0 & 0 \\ 0 & 1 & 0 \\ 0 & 0 & 1 \end{bmatrix}$ to the left of the vertical line. Use matrix row operations, working one column at a time. Obtain 1 in the required position. Then obtain 0s in the other two positions. Using these operations, we obtain the matrix

$$\left[\begin{array}{ccc|ccc} 1 & 0 & 0 & 15 & 4 & -5 \\ 0 & 1 & 0 & -12 & -3 & 4 \\ 0 & 0 & 1 & -4 & -1 & 1 \end{array}\right].$$

This augmented matrix provides the solutions to the three systems of equations. They are given by

$$\left[\begin{array}{ccc|c} 1 & 0 & 0 & 15 \\ 0 & 1 & 0 & -12 \\ 0 & 0 & 1 & -4 \end{array}\right] \qquad \begin{aligned} x_1 &= 15 \\ y_1 &= -12 \\ z_1 &= -4 \end{aligned}$$

and

$$\left[\begin{array}{ccc|c} 1 & 0 & 0 & 4 \\ 0 & 1 & 0 & -3 \\ 0 & 0 & 1 & -1 \end{array}\right] \qquad \begin{aligned} x_2 &= 4 \\ y_2 &= -3 \\ z_2 &= -1 \end{aligned}$$

and

$$\left[\begin{array}{ccc|c} 1 & 0 & 0 & -5 \\ 0 & 1 & 0 & 4 \\ 0 & 0 & 1 & 1 \end{array}\right] \qquad \begin{aligned} x_3 &= -5 \\ y_3 &= 4 \\ z_3 &= 1 \end{aligned}$$

The inverse matrix is

$$\begin{bmatrix} x_1 & x_2 & x_3 \\ y_1 & y_2 & y_3 \\ z_1 & z_2 & z_3 \end{bmatrix} = \begin{bmatrix} 15 & 4 & -5 \\ -12 & -3 & 4 \\ -4 & -1 & 1 \end{bmatrix}.$$

## Technology

You can use a graphing utility to find the inverse of

$$A = \begin{bmatrix} -1 & -1 & -1 \\ 4 & 5 & 0 \\ 0 & 1 & -3 \end{bmatrix}.$$

Enter [MATRIX] [A] and then use the inverse key. The display, $[A]^{-1}$, should be

$$\begin{bmatrix} 15 & 4 & -5 \\ -12 & -3 & 4 \\ -4 & -1 & 1 \end{bmatrix}.$$

Take a second look at the matrix obtained at the point where Gauss-Jordan elimination was completed. Notice that the $3 \times 3$ matrix to the right of the vertical bar is the multiplicative inverse of $A$. Also notice that the multiplicative identity matrix, $I_3$ is the matrix that appears to the left of the vertical bar.

$$\left[\begin{array}{ccc|ccc} 1 & 0 & 0 & 15 & 4 & -5 \\ 0 & 1 & 0 & -12 & -3 & 4 \\ 0 & 0 & 1 & -4 & -1 & 1 \end{array}\right]$$

This is the multiplicative identity, $I_3$.

This is the multiplicative inverse of $A$.

The observations in the voice balloons and the procedures followed above give us a general method for finding the multiplicative inverse of an invertible matrix.

## Study Tip

Because we have a quick method for finding the multiplicative inverse of a $2 \times 2$ matrix, the procedure on the right is recommended for matrices of order $3 \times 3$ or greater when a graphing utility is not being used.

**Procedure for Finding the Multiplicative Inverse of an Invertible Matrix**

To find $A^{-1}$ for any $n \times n$ matrix $A$ for which $A^{-1}$ exists:

1. Form the augmented matrix $[A|I]$, where $I$ is the multiplicative identity matrix of the same order as the given matrix $A$.
2. Perform row transformations on $[A|I]$ to obtain a matrix of the form $[I|B]$. This is equivalent to using Gauss-Jordan elimination to change $A$ into the identity matrix.
3. Matrix $B$ is $A^{-1}$.
4. Verify the result by showing that $AA^{-1} = I$ and $A^{-1}A = I$.

## EXAMPLE 4 Finding the Multiplicative Inverse of a 3 × 3 Matrix

Find the multiplicative inverse of

$$A = \begin{bmatrix} 1 & -1 & 1 \\ 0 & -2 & 1 \\ -2 & -3 & 0 \end{bmatrix}.$$

**Solution**

**Step 1 Form the augmented matrix $[A \mid I_3]$.**

$$\left[\begin{array}{ccc|ccc} 1 & -1 & 1 & 1 & 0 & 0 \\ 0 & -2 & 1 & 0 & 1 & 0 \\ -2 & -3 & 0 & 0 & 0 & 1 \end{array}\right]$$

This is matrix $A$.

This is $I_3$, the multiplicative identity matrix, with 1s down the main diagonal and 0s elsewhere.

**Step 2 Perform row transformations on $[A \mid I_3]$ to obtain a matrix of the form $[I_3 \mid B]$.** We want 1s down the main diagonal to the left of the vertical dividing line and 0s elsewhere.

$$\left[\begin{array}{ccc|ccc} 1 & -1 & 1 & 1 & 0 & 0 \\ 0 & -2 & 1 & 0 & 1 & 0 \\ -2 & -3 & 0 & 0 & 0 & 1 \end{array}\right] \xrightarrow[\text{by } 2R_1 + R_3]{\text{Replace row 3}} \left[\begin{array}{ccc|ccc} 1 & -1 & 1 & 1 & 0 & 0 \\ 0 & -2 & 1 & 0 & 1 & 0 \\ 0 & -5 & 2 & 2 & 0 & 1 \end{array}\right] \xrightarrow{-\frac{1}{2}R_2}$$

$$\left[\begin{array}{ccc|ccc} 1 & -1 & 1 & 1 & 0 & 0 \\ 0 & 1 & -\frac{1}{2} & 0 & -\frac{1}{2} & 0 \\ 0 & -5 & 2 & 2 & 0 & 1 \end{array}\right] \xrightarrow[\text{Replace row 3 by } 5R_2 + R_3.]{\text{Replace row 1 by } 1R_2 + R_1.} \left[\begin{array}{ccc|ccc} 1 & 0 & \frac{1}{2} & 1 & -\frac{1}{2} & 0 \\ 0 & 1 & -\frac{1}{2} & 0 & -\frac{1}{2} & 0 \\ 0 & 0 & -\frac{1}{2} & 2 & -\frac{5}{2} & 1 \end{array}\right] \xrightarrow{-2R_3}$$

$$\left[\begin{array}{ccc|ccc} 1 & 0 & \frac{1}{2} & 1 & -\frac{1}{2} & 0 \\ 0 & 1 & -\frac{1}{2} & 0 & -\frac{1}{2} & 0 \\ 0 & 0 & 1 & -4 & 5 & -2 \end{array}\right] \xrightarrow[\text{Replace row 2 by } \frac{1}{2}R_3 + R_2.]{\text{Replace row 1 by } -\frac{1}{2}R_3 + R_1.} \left[\begin{array}{ccc|ccc} 1 & 0 & 0 & 3 & -3 & 1 \\ 0 & 1 & 0 & -2 & 2 & -1 \\ 0 & 0 & 1 & -4 & 5 & -2 \end{array}\right]$$

This is the multiplicative identity, $I_3$.

This is the multiplicative inverse of $A$.

**Step 3 Matrix $B$ is $A^{-1}$.** The matrix just shown is in the form $[I_3 \mid B]$. The multiplicative identity matrix is on the left of the vertical bar. Matrix $B$, the multiplicative inverse of $A$, is on the right. Thus, the multiplicative inverse of $A$ is

$$A^{-1} = \begin{bmatrix} 3 & -3 & 1 \\ -2 & 2 & -1 \\ -4 & 5 & -2 \end{bmatrix}.$$

**Step 4 Verify the result by showing that $AA^{-1} = I_3$ and $A^{-1}A = I_3$.** Try confirming the result by multiplying $A$ and $A^{-1}$ to obtain $I_3$. Do you obtain $I_3$ if you reverse the order of the multiplication?

We have seen that not all square matrices have multiplicative inverses. If the row transformations in step 2 result in all zeros in a row or column to the left of the vertical line, the given matrix does not have a multiplicative inverse.

**Check Point 4** Find the multiplicative inverse of

$$A = \begin{bmatrix} 1 & 0 & 2 \\ -1 & 2 & 3 \\ 1 & -1 & 0 \end{bmatrix}.$$

**Summary: Finding Multiplicative Inverses for Invertible Matrices**

Use a graphing utility with matrix capabilities,

or

**a.** If the matrix is $2 \times 2$: The inverse of $A = \begin{bmatrix} a & b \\ c & d \end{bmatrix}$ is

$$A^{-1} = \frac{1}{ad - bc}\begin{bmatrix} d & -b \\ -c & a \end{bmatrix}.$$

**b.** If the matrix is $n \times n$ where $n > 2$: Use the procedure on page 793. Form $[A|I]$ and use row transformations to obtain $[I|B]$. $A^{-1} = B$.

**2** Use inverses to solve matrix equations.

## Solving Systems of Equations Using Multiplicative Inverses of Matrices

Matrix multiplication can be used to represent a system of linear equations.

**Linear System**

$$\begin{aligned} a_1x + b_1y + c_1z &= d_1 \\ a_2x + b_2y + c_2z &= d_2 \\ a_3x + b_3y + c_3z &= d_3 \end{aligned}$$

**Matrix Form of the System**

$$\begin{bmatrix} a_1 & b_1 & c_1 \\ a_2 & b_2 & c_2 \\ a_3 & b_3 & c_3 \end{bmatrix}\begin{bmatrix} x \\ y \\ z \end{bmatrix} = \begin{bmatrix} d_1 \\ d_2 \\ d_3 \end{bmatrix}$$

This matrix contains the system's coefficients.

This matrix contains the system's variables.

This matrix contains the system's constants.

You can work with the matrix form on the right and obtain the form of the linear system on the left. To do so, perform the matrix multiplication on the left side of the matrix equation. Then equate the corresponding elements.

The matrix equation

$$\underbrace{\begin{bmatrix} a_1 & b_1 & c_1 \\ a_2 & b_2 & c_2 \\ a_3 & b_3 & c_3 \end{bmatrix}}_{A}\underbrace{\begin{bmatrix} x \\ y \\ z \end{bmatrix}}_{X} = \underbrace{\begin{bmatrix} d_1 \\ d_2 \\ d_3 \end{bmatrix}}_{B}$$

is abbreviated as $AX = B$, where $A$ is the **coefficient matrix** of the system, and $X$ and $B$ are matrices containing one column, called **column matrices**. The matrix $B$ is called the **constant matrix**.

Here is a specific example of a linear system and its matrix form.

**Linear System**

$$\begin{aligned} x - y + z &= 2 \\ -2y + z &= 2 \\ -2x - 3y \quad &= \tfrac{1}{2} \end{aligned}$$

**Matrix Form**

Coefficients

$$\begin{bmatrix} 1 & -1 & 1 \\ 0 & -2 & 1 \\ -2 & -3 & 0 \end{bmatrix} \begin{bmatrix} x \\ y \\ z \end{bmatrix} = \begin{bmatrix} 2 \\ 2 \\ \frac{1}{2} \end{bmatrix}$$

Constants

A, the coefficient matrix · X = B, the constant matrix

The matrix equation $AX = B$ can be solved using $A^{-1}$ if it exists.

| | |
|---|---|
| $AX = B$ | This is the matrix equation. |
| $A^{-1}AX = A^{-1}B$ | Multiply both sides by $A^{-1}$. Because matrix multiplication is not commutative, put $A^{-1}$ in the same left position on both sides. |
| $I_n X = A^{-1}B$ | The multiplicative inverse property tells us that $A^{-1}A = I_n$. |
| $X = A^{-1}B$ | Because $I_n$ is the multiplicative identity, $I_n X = X$. |

We see that if $AX = B$, then $X = A^{-1}B$.

**Solving a System Using $A^{-1}$**

If $AX = B$ has a unique solution, $X = A^{-1}B$. To solve a linear system of equations, multiply $A^{-1}$ and $B$ to find $X$.

## EXAMPLE 5 Using the Inverse of a Matrix to Solve a System

Solve the system by using $A^{-1}$, the inverse of the coefficient matrix.

$$\begin{aligned} x - y + z &= 2 \\ -2y + z &= 2 \\ -2x - 3y \quad &= \tfrac{1}{2} \end{aligned}$$

**Solution** The linear system can be written as

$$\begin{bmatrix} 1 & -1 & 1 \\ 0 & -2 & 1 \\ -2 & -3 & 0 \end{bmatrix} \begin{bmatrix} x \\ y \\ z \end{bmatrix} = \begin{bmatrix} 2 \\ 2 \\ \frac{1}{2} \end{bmatrix}.$$

A · X · B

The solution is given by $X = A^{-1}B$. Consequently, we must find $A^{-1}$. We found the inverse of matrix $A$ in Example 4. Using this result,

$$X = A^{-1}B = \begin{bmatrix} 3 & -3 & 1 \\ -2 & 2 & -1 \\ -4 & 5 & -2 \end{bmatrix} \begin{bmatrix} 2 \\ 2 \\ \frac{1}{2} \end{bmatrix} = \begin{bmatrix} 3 \cdot 2 + (-3) \cdot 2 + 1 \cdot \frac{1}{2} \\ -2 \cdot 2 + 2 \cdot 2 + (-1) \cdot \frac{1}{2} \\ -4 \cdot 2 + 5 \cdot 2 + (-2) \cdot \frac{1}{2} \end{bmatrix} = \begin{bmatrix} \frac{1}{2} \\ -\frac{1}{2} \\ 1 \end{bmatrix}$$

Thus, $x = \frac{1}{2}$, $y = -\frac{1}{2}$, and $z = 1$. The solution set is $\{(\frac{1}{2}, -\frac{1}{2}, 1)\}$.

**Check Point 5** Solve the system by using $A^{-1}$, the inverse of the coefficient matrix that you found in Checkpoint 4.

$$\begin{aligned} x \quad\quad + 2z &= 6 \\ -x + 2y + 3z &= -5 \\ x - y \quad\quad &= 6 \end{aligned}$$

**3** Encode and decode messages.

## Applications of Matrix Inverses to Coding

A **cryptogram** is a message written so that no one other than the intended recipient can understand it. To encode a message, we begin by assigning a number to each letter in the alphabet: $A = 1, B = 2, C = 3, \ldots, Z = 26$, and a space $= 0$. For example, the numerical equivalent of the word MATH is 13, 1, 20, 8. The numerical equivalent of the message is then converted into a matrix. Finally, an invertible matrix can be used to convert the message into code. The multiplicative inverse of this matrix can be used to decode the message.

### Encoding a Word or Message

1. Express the word or message numerically.
2. List the numbers in step 1 by columns and form a square matrix. If you do not have enough numbers to form a square matrix, put zeros in any remaining spaces in the last column.
3. Select any square invertible matrix, called the **coding matrix**, the same size as the matrix in step 2. Multiply the coding matrix by the square matrix that expresses the message numerically. The resulting matrix is the **coded matrix**.
4. Use the numbers, by columns, from the coded matrix in step 3 to write the encoded message.

## EXAMPLE 6 Encoding a Word

Use matrices to encode the word MATH.

### Solution

**Step 1 Express the word numerically.** As shown previously, the numerical equivalent of MATH is 13, 1, 20, 8.

**Step 2 List the numbers in step 1 by columns and form a square matrix.** The $2 \times 2$ matrix is

$$\begin{bmatrix} 13 & 20 \\ 1 & 8 \end{bmatrix}.$$

**Step 3 Multiply the matrix in step 2 by a square invertible matrix.** We will use $\begin{bmatrix} -2 & -3 \\ 3 & 4 \end{bmatrix}$ as the coding matrix.

$$\begin{bmatrix} -2 & -3 \\ 3 & 4 \end{bmatrix}\begin{bmatrix} 13 & 20 \\ 1 & 8 \end{bmatrix} = \begin{bmatrix} -2(13) - 3(1) & -2(20) - 3(8) \\ 3(13) + 4(1) & 3(20) + 4(8) \end{bmatrix}$$

Coding matrix; Numerical representation of MATH

$$= \begin{bmatrix} -29 & -64 \\ 43 & 92 \end{bmatrix}$$

Coded matrix

**Step 4 Use the numbers, by columns, from the coded matrix in step 3 to write the encoded message.** The encoded message is −29, 43, −64, 92.

**Check Point 6** Use the coding matrix in Example 6, $\begin{bmatrix} -2 & -3 \\ 3 & 4 \end{bmatrix}$, to encode the word BASE.

The inverse of a coding matrix can be used to decode a word or message that was encoded.

### Decoding a Word or Message That Was Encoded

1. Find the multiplicative inverse of the coding matrix.
2. Multiply the multiplicative inverse of the coding matrix and the coded matrix.
3. Express the numbers, by columns, from the matrix in step 2 as letters.

## EXAMPLE 7 Decoding a Word

Decode −29, 43, −64, 92 from Example 6.

**Solution**

**Step 1 Find the inverse of the coding matrix.** The coding matrix in Example 6 was $\begin{bmatrix} -2 & -3 \\ 3 & 4 \end{bmatrix}$. We use the formula for the multiplicative inverse of a $2 \times 2$ matrix to find the multiplicative inverse of this matrix. It is $\begin{bmatrix} 4 & 3 \\ -3 & -2 \end{bmatrix}$.

**Step 2 Multiply the multiplicative inverse of the coding matrix and the coded matrix.**

$$\underbrace{\begin{bmatrix} 4 & 3 \\ -3 & -2 \end{bmatrix}}_{\text{Multiplicative inverse of the coding matrix}}\underbrace{\begin{bmatrix} -29 & -64 \\ 43 & 92 \end{bmatrix}}_{\text{Coded matrix}} = \begin{bmatrix} 4(-29) + 3(43) & 4(-64) + 3(92) \\ -3(-29) - 2(43) & -3(-64) - 2(92) \end{bmatrix}$$

$$= \begin{bmatrix} 13 & 20 \\ 1 & 8 \end{bmatrix}$$

**Step 3 Express the numbers, by columns, from the matrix in step 2 as letters.** The numbers are 13, 1, 20, and 8. Using letters, the decoded message is MATH.

**Check Point 7** Decode the word that you encoded in Checkpoint 6.

Decoding is simple for an authorized receiver who knows the coding matrix. Because any invertible matrix can be used for the coding matrix, decoding a cryptogram for an unauthorized receiver who does not know this matrix is extremely difficult.

# EXERCISE SET 9.4

## Practice Exercises

*In Exercises 1–12 find the products AB and BA to determine whether B is the multiplicative inverse of A.*

**1.** $A = \begin{bmatrix} 4 & -3 \\ -5 & 4 \end{bmatrix}$, $B = \begin{bmatrix} 4 & 3 \\ 5 & 4 \end{bmatrix}$

**2.** $A = \begin{bmatrix} -2 & -1 \\ -1 & 1 \end{bmatrix}$, $B = \begin{bmatrix} 1 & 1 \\ 1 & 2 \end{bmatrix}$

**3.** $A = \begin{bmatrix} -4 & 0 \\ 1 & 3 \end{bmatrix}$, $B = \begin{bmatrix} -2 & 4 \\ 0 & 1 \end{bmatrix}$

**4.** $A = \begin{bmatrix} -2 & 4 \\ 1 & -2 \end{bmatrix}$, $B = \begin{bmatrix} 1 & 2 \\ -1 & -2 \end{bmatrix}$

**5.** $A = \begin{bmatrix} -2 & 1 \\ \frac{3}{2} & -\frac{1}{2} \end{bmatrix}$, $B = \begin{bmatrix} 1 & 2 \\ 3 & 4 \end{bmatrix}$

**6.** $A = \begin{bmatrix} 4 & 5 \\ 2 & 3 \end{bmatrix}$, $B = \begin{bmatrix} \frac{3}{2} & -\frac{5}{2} \\ -1 & 2 \end{bmatrix}$

**7.** $A = \begin{bmatrix} 0 & 1 & 0 \\ 0 & 0 & 1 \\ 1 & 0 & 0 \end{bmatrix}$ $B = \begin{bmatrix} 0 & 0 & 1 \\ 1 & 0 & 0 \\ 0 & 1 & 0 \end{bmatrix}$

**8.** $A = \begin{bmatrix} -2 & 1 & -1 \\ -5 & 2 & -1 \\ 3 & -1 & 1 \end{bmatrix}$ $B = \begin{bmatrix} 1 & 0 & 1 \\ 2 & 1 & 3 \\ -1 & 1 & 1 \end{bmatrix}$

**9.** $A = \begin{bmatrix} 1 & 2 & 3 \\ 1 & 3 & 4 \\ 1 & 4 & 3 \end{bmatrix}$ $B = \begin{bmatrix} \frac{7}{2} & -3 & \frac{1}{2} \\ -\frac{1}{2} & 0 & \frac{1}{2} \\ -\frac{1}{2} & 1 & -\frac{1}{2} \end{bmatrix}$

**10.** $A = \begin{bmatrix} 0 & 2 & 0 \\ 3 & 3 & 2 \\ 2 & 5 & 1 \end{bmatrix}$ $B = \begin{bmatrix} -3.5 & -1 & 2 \\ 0.5 & 0 & 0 \\ 4.5 & 2 & -3 \end{bmatrix}$

**11.** $A = \begin{bmatrix} 0 & 0 & -2 & 1 \\ -1 & 0 & 1 & 1 \\ 0 & 1 & -1 & 0 \\ 1 & 0 & 0 & -1 \end{bmatrix}$, $B = \begin{bmatrix} 1 & 2 & 0 & 3 \\ 0 & 1 & 1 & 1 \\ 0 & 1 & 0 & 1 \\ 1 & 2 & 0 & 2 \end{bmatrix}$

**12.** $A = \begin{bmatrix} 1 & -2 & 1 & 0 \\ 0 & 1 & -2 & 1 \\ 0 & 0 & 1 & -2 \\ 0 & 0 & 0 & 1 \end{bmatrix}$, $B = \begin{bmatrix} 1 & 2 & 3 & 4 \\ 0 & 1 & 2 & 3 \\ 0 & 0 & 1 & 2 \\ 0 & 0 & 0 & 1 \end{bmatrix}$

*In Exercises 13–18, use the fact that if* $A = \begin{bmatrix} a & b \\ c & d \end{bmatrix}$, *then* $A^{-1} = \frac{1}{ad - bc}\begin{bmatrix} d & -b \\ -c & a \end{bmatrix}$ *to find the inverse of each matrix, if possible. Check that* $AA^{-1} = I_2$ *and* $A^{-1}A = I_2$.

**13.** $A = \begin{bmatrix} 2 & 3 \\ -1 & 2 \end{bmatrix}$

**14.** $A = \begin{bmatrix} 0 & 3 \\ 4 & -2 \end{bmatrix}$

**15.** $A = \begin{bmatrix} 3 & -1 \\ -4 & 2 \end{bmatrix}$

**16.** $A = \begin{bmatrix} 2 & -6 \\ 1 & -2 \end{bmatrix}$

**17.** $A = \begin{bmatrix} 10 & -2 \\ -5 & 1 \end{bmatrix}$

**18.** $A = \begin{bmatrix} 6 & -3 \\ -2 & 1 \end{bmatrix}$

*In Exercises 19–24, find* $A^{-1}$ *by forming* $[A|I]$ *and then using row transformations to obtain* $[I|B]$, *where* $A^{-1} = [B]$. *Check that* $AA^{-1} = I$ *and* $A^{-1}A = I$.

**19.** $A = \begin{bmatrix} 2 & 2 & -1 \\ 0 & 3 & -1 \\ -1 & -2 & 1 \end{bmatrix}$

**20.** $A = \begin{bmatrix} 1 & -1 & 1 \\ 0 & 2 & -1 \\ 2 & 3 & 0 \end{bmatrix}$

**21.** $A = \begin{bmatrix} 5 & 0 & 2 \\ 2 & 2 & 1 \\ -3 & 1 & -1 \end{bmatrix}$

**22.** $A = \begin{bmatrix} 3 & 2 & 6 \\ 1 & 1 & 2 \\ 2 & 2 & 5 \end{bmatrix}$

**23.** $A = \begin{bmatrix} 1 & 0 & 0 & 0 \\ 0 & -1 & 0 & 0 \\ 0 & 0 & 3 & 0 \\ 1 & 0 & 0 & 1 \end{bmatrix}$

**24.** $A = \begin{bmatrix} 2 & 0 & 0 & 1 \\ 0 & 1 & 0 & 0 \\ 0 & 0 & -1 & 0 \\ 0 & 0 & 0 & 2 \end{bmatrix}$

*In Exercises 25–28, write each linear system as a matrix equation in the form* $AX = B$, *where A is the coefficient matrix and B is the constant matrix.*

**25.** $6x + 5y = 13$
$5x + 4y = 10$

**26.** $7x + 5y = 23$
$3x + 2y = 10$

**27.** $x + 3y + 4z = -3$
$x + 2y + 3z = -2$
$x + 4y + 3z = -6$

**28.** $x + 4y - z = 3$
$x + 3y - 2z = 5$
$2x + 7y - 5z = 12$

*In Exercises 29–32, write each matrix equation as a system of linear equations without matrices.*

**29.** $\begin{bmatrix} 4 & -7 \\ 2 & -3 \end{bmatrix}\begin{bmatrix} x \\ y \end{bmatrix} = \begin{bmatrix} -3 \\ 1 \end{bmatrix}$

**30.** $\begin{bmatrix} 3 & 0 \\ -3 & 1 \end{bmatrix}\begin{bmatrix} x \\ y \end{bmatrix} = \begin{bmatrix} 6 \\ -7 \end{bmatrix}$

**31.** $\begin{bmatrix} 2 & 0 & -1 \\ 0 & 3 & 0 \\ 1 & 1 & 0 \end{bmatrix}\begin{bmatrix} x \\ y \\ z \end{bmatrix} = \begin{bmatrix} 6 \\ 9 \\ 5 \end{bmatrix}$

**32.** $\begin{bmatrix} -1 & 0 & 1 \\ 0 & -1 & 0 \\ 0 & 1 & 1 \end{bmatrix} \begin{bmatrix} x \\ y \\ z \end{bmatrix} = \begin{bmatrix} -4 \\ 2 \\ 4 \end{bmatrix}$

*In Exercises 33–38,*

**a.** *Write each linear system as a matrix equation in the form $AX = B$.*

**b.** *Solve the system using the inverse of the coefficient matrix.*

**33.** $\begin{aligned} 2x + 6y + 6z &= 8 \\ 2x + 7y + 6z &= 10 \\ 2x + 7y + 7z &= 9 \end{aligned}$ The inverse of $\begin{bmatrix} 2 & 6 & 6 \\ 2 & 7 & 6 \\ 2 & 7 & 7 \end{bmatrix}$ is $\begin{bmatrix} \frac{7}{2} & 0 & -3 \\ -1 & 1 & 0 \\ 0 & -1 & 1 \end{bmatrix}$.

**34.** $\begin{aligned} x + 2y + 5z &= 2 \\ 2x + 3y + 8z &= 3 \\ -x + y + 2z &= 3 \end{aligned}$ The inverse of $\begin{bmatrix} 1 & 2 & 5 \\ 2 & 3 & 8 \\ -1 & 1 & 2 \end{bmatrix}$ is $\begin{bmatrix} 2 & -1 & -1 \\ 12 & -7 & -2 \\ -5 & 3 & 1 \end{bmatrix}$.

**35.** $\begin{aligned} x - y + z &= 8 \\ 2y - z &= -7 \\ 2x + 3y &= 1 \end{aligned}$ The inverse of $\begin{bmatrix} 1 & -1 & 1 \\ 0 & 2 & -1 \\ 2 & 3 & 0 \end{bmatrix}$ is $\begin{bmatrix} 3 & 3 & -1 \\ -2 & -2 & 1 \\ -4 & -5 & 2 \end{bmatrix}$.

**36.** $\begin{aligned} x - 6y + 3z &= 11 \\ 2x - 7y + 3z &= 14 \\ 4x - 12y + 5z &= 25 \end{aligned}$ The inverse of $\begin{bmatrix} 1 & -6 & 3 \\ 2 & -7 & 3 \\ 4 & -12 & 5 \end{bmatrix}$ is $\begin{bmatrix} 1 & -6 & 3 \\ 2 & -7 & 3 \\ 4 & -12 & 5 \end{bmatrix}$.

**37.** $\begin{aligned} x - y + 2z &= -3 \\ y - z + w &= 4 \\ -x + y - z + 2w &= 2 \\ -y + z - 2w &= -4 \end{aligned}$

The inverse of $\begin{bmatrix} 1 & -1 & 2 & 0 \\ 0 & 1 & -1 & 1 \\ -1 & 1 & -1 & 2 \\ 0 & -1 & 1 & -2 \end{bmatrix}$ is $\begin{bmatrix} 0 & 0 & -1 & -1 \\ 1 & 4 & 1 & 3 \\ 1 & 2 & 1 & 2 \\ 0 & -1 & 0 & -1 \end{bmatrix}$.

**38.** $\begin{aligned} 2x + z + w &= 6 \\ 3x + w &= 9 \\ -x + y - 2z + w &= 4 \\ 4x - y + z &= 6 \end{aligned}$

The inverse of $\begin{bmatrix} 2 & 0 & 1 & 1 \\ 3 & 0 & 0 & 1 \\ -1 & 1 & -2 & 1 \\ 4 & -1 & 1 & 0 \end{bmatrix}$ is $\begin{bmatrix} -1 & 2 & -1 & -1 \\ -4 & 9 & -5 & -6 \\ 0 & 1 & -1 & -1 \\ 3 & -5 & 3 & 3 \end{bmatrix}$.

## Application Exercises

*In Exercises 39–40, use the coding matrix*

$$A = \begin{bmatrix} 4 & -1 \\ -3 & 1 \end{bmatrix} \text{ and its inverse } A^{-1} = \begin{bmatrix} 1 & 1 \\ 3 & 4 \end{bmatrix} \text{ to}$$

*encode and then decode the given message.*

**39.** HELP

**40.** LOVE

*In Exercises 41–42, use the coding matrix*

$$A = \begin{bmatrix} 1 & -1 & 0 \\ 3 & 0 & 2 \\ -1 & 0 & -1 \end{bmatrix} \text{ and its inverse}$$

$$A^{-1} = \begin{bmatrix} 0 & 1 & 2 \\ -1 & 1 & 2 \\ 0 & -1 & -3 \end{bmatrix} \text{ to write a cryptogram for each}$$

*message. Check your result by decoding the cryptogram.*

**41.** S E N D _ C A S H

19 5 14 4 0 3 1 19 8

Use $\begin{bmatrix} 19 & 4 & 1 \\ 5 & 0 & 19 \\ 14 & 3 & 8 \end{bmatrix}$.

**42.** S T A Y _ W E L L

19 20 1 25 0 23 5 12 12

Use $\begin{bmatrix} 19 & 25 & 5 \\ 20 & 0 & 12 \\ 1 & 23 & 12 \end{bmatrix}$.

## Writing in Mathematics

**43.** What is the multiplicative identity matrix?

**44.** If you are given two matrices, $A$ and $B$, explain how to determine if $B$ is the multiplicative inverse of $A$.

**45.** Explain why a matrix that does not have the same number of rows and columns cannot have a multiplicative inverse.

**46.** Explain how to find the multiplicative inverse for a $2 \times 2$ invertible matrix.

**47.** Explain how to find the multiplicative inverse for a $3 \times 3$ invertible matrix.

**48.** Explain how to write a linear system of three equations in three variables as a matrix equation.

**49.** Explain how to solve the matrix equation $AX = B$.

**50.** What is a cryptogram?

**51.** It's January 1, and you've written down your major goal for the year. You do not want those closest to you to see what you've written in case you do not accomplish your objective. Consequently, you decide to use a coding matrix to encode your goal. Explain how this can be accomplished.

**52.** A year has passed since Exercise 51. (Time flies when you're solving exercises in algebra books.) It's been a terrific year and so many wonderful things have happened that you can't remember your goal from a year ago. You consult your personal journal and you find the encoded message and the coding matrix. How can you use these to find your original goal?

## Technology Exercises

*In Exercises 53–58, use a graphing utility to find the multiplicative inverse of each matrix. Check that the displayed inverse is correct.*

**53.** $\begin{bmatrix} 3 & -1 \\ -2 & 1 \end{bmatrix}$

**54.** $\begin{bmatrix} -4 & 1 \\ 6 & -2 \end{bmatrix}$

**55.** $\begin{bmatrix} -2 & 1 & -1 \\ -5 & 2 & -1 \\ 3 & -1 & 1 \end{bmatrix}$

**56.** $\begin{bmatrix} 1 & 1 & -1 \\ -3 & 2 & -1 \\ 3 & -3 & 2 \end{bmatrix}$

**57.** $\begin{bmatrix} 7 & -3 & 0 & 2 \\ -2 & 1 & 0 & -1 \\ 4 & 0 & 1 & -2 \\ -1 & 1 & 0 & -1 \end{bmatrix}$

**58.** $\begin{bmatrix} 1 & 2 & 0 & 0 \\ 0 & 0 & 1 & 0 \\ 1 & 3 & 0 & 1 \\ 4 & 0 & 0 & 2 \end{bmatrix}$

*In Exercises 59–64, write each system in the form $AX = B$. Then solve the system by entering A and B into your graphing utility and computing $A^{-1}B$.*

**59.** $\begin{aligned} x - y + z &= -6 \\ 4x + 2y + z &= 9 \\ 4x - 2y + z &= -3 \end{aligned}$

**60.** $\begin{aligned} y + 2z &= 0 \\ -x + y &= 1 \\ 2x - y + z &= -1 \end{aligned}$

**61.** $\begin{aligned} 3x - 2y + z &= -2 \\ 4x - 5y + 3z &= -9 \\ 2x - y + 5z &= -5 \end{aligned}$

**62.** $\begin{aligned} x - y &= 1 \\ 6x + y + 20z &= 14 \\ y + 3z &= 1 \end{aligned}$

**63.** $\begin{aligned} x - 3z + v &= -3 \\ y + w &= -1 \\ z + v &= 7 \\ x + y - z + 4w &= -8 \\ x + y + z + w + v &= 8 \end{aligned}$

**64.** $\begin{aligned} x + y + z + w &= 4 \\ x + 3y - 2z + 2w &= 7 \\ 2x + 2y + z + w &= 3 \\ x - y + 2z + 3w &= 5 \end{aligned}$

*In Exercises 65–66, use a coding matrix A of your choice. Use a graphing utility to find the multiplicative inverse of your coding matrix. Write a cryptogram for each message. Check your result by decoding the cryptogram. Use your graphing utility to perform all necessary matrix multiplications.*

**65.** A R R I V E D _ S A F E L Y
1 18 18 9 22 5 4 0 19 1 6 5 12 25

**66.** A R T _ E N R I C H E S
1 18 20 0 5 14 18 9 3 8 5 19

## Critical Thinking Exercises

**67.** Which one of the following is true?

**a.** Some nonsquare matrices have inverses.

**b.** All square $2 \times 2$ matrices have inverses because there is a formula for finding these inverses.

**c.** Two $2 \times 2$ invertible matrices can have a matrix sum that is not invertible.

**d.** To solve the matrix equation $AX = B$ for $X$, multiply $A$ and the inverse of $B$.

**68.** Which one of the following is true?

**a.** $(AB)^{-1} = A^{-1}B^{-1}$, assuming $A$, $B$, and $AB$, are invertible.

**b.** $(A + B)^{-1} = A^{-1} + B^{-1}$, assuming $A$, $B$, and $A + B$ are invertible.

**c.** $\begin{bmatrix} 1 & -3 \\ -1 & 3 \end{bmatrix}$ is an invertible matrix.

**d.** None of the above is true.

**69.** Give an example of a $2 \times 2$ matrix that is its own inverse.

**70.** If $A = \begin{bmatrix} 3 & 5 \\ 2 & 4 \end{bmatrix}$, find $\left(A^{-1}\right)^{-1}$.

**71.** Find values of $a$ for which the following matrix is not invertible.

$$\begin{bmatrix} 1 & a+1 \\ a-2 & 4 \end{bmatrix}$$

## Group Exercise

**72.** Each person in the group should work with one partner. Send a coded word or message to each other by giving your partner the coded matrix and the coding matrix that you selected. Once messages are sent, each person should decode the message received.

# SECTION 9.5 Determinants and Cramer's Rule

## Objectives

1. Evaluate a second-order determinant.
2. Solve a linear system of equations in two variables using Cramer's rule.
3. Evaluate a third-order determinant.
4. Solve a linear system of equations in three variables using Cramer's rule.
5. Use determinants to identify inconsistent systems and systems with dependent equations.
6. Evaluate higher-order determinants.

A portion of Charles Babbage's unrealized Difference Engine

As cyberspace absorbs more and more of our work, play, shopping, and socializing, where will it all end? Which activities will still be offline in 2025?

Our technologically transformed lives can be traced back to the English inventor Charles Babbage (1792–1871). Babbage knew of a method for solving linear systems called Cramer's rule, in honor of the Swiss geometer Gabriel Cramer (1704–1752). Cramer's rule was simple, but involved numerous multiplications for large systems. Babbage designed a machine, called the "difference engine," that consisted of toothed wheels on shafts for performing these multiplications. Despite the fact that only one-seventh of the functions ever worked, Babbage's invention demonstrated how complex calculations could be handled mechanically. In 1944, scientists at IBM used the lessons of the the difference engine to create the world's first computer.

Those who invented computers hoped to relegate the drudgery of repeated computation to a machine. In this section, we look at a method for solving linear systems that played a critical role in this process. The method uses arrays of numbers called *determinants*. As with matrix methods, solutions are obtained by writing down the coefficients and constants of a linear system and performing operations with them.

**1** Evaluate a second-order determinant.

## The Determinant of a 2 × 2 Matrix

Associated with every square matrix is a real number called its **determinant**. The determinant for a 2 × 2 square matrix is defined as follows.

**Definition of the Determinant of a 2 × 2 Matrix**

The determinant of the matrix $\begin{bmatrix} a_1 & b_1 \\ a_2 & b_2 \end{bmatrix}$ is denoted by $\begin{vmatrix} a_1 & b_1 \\ a_2 & b_2 \end{vmatrix}$ and is defined by

$$\begin{vmatrix} a_1 & b_1 \\ a_2 & b_2 \end{vmatrix} = a_1 b_2 - a_2 b_1.$$

We also say that the **value** of the **second-order determinant** $\begin{vmatrix} a_1 & b_1 \\ a_2 & b_2 \end{vmatrix}$ is $a_1 b_2 - a_2 b_1$.

**Study Tip**

To evaluate a determinant, find the difference of the product of the two diagonals.

$$\begin{vmatrix} a_1 & b_1 \\ a_2 & b_2 \end{vmatrix} = a_1 b_2 - a_2 b_1$$

Example 1 illustrates that the determinant of a matrix may be positive or negative. The determinant can also have 0 as its value.

### EXAMPLE 1 Evaluating the Determinant of a 2 × 2 Matrix

Evaluate the determinant of:

**a.** $\begin{bmatrix} 5 & 6 \\ 7 & 3 \end{bmatrix}$ **b.** $\begin{bmatrix} 2 & 4 \\ -3 & -5 \end{bmatrix}$.

**Solution** We multiply and subtract as indicated.

**a.** $\begin{vmatrix} 5 & 6 \\ 7 & 3 \end{vmatrix} = 5 \cdot 3 - 7 \cdot 6 = 15 - 42 = -27$ The value of the second-order determinant is −27.

**b.** $\begin{vmatrix} 2 & 4 \\ -3 & -5 \end{vmatrix} = 2(-5) - (-3)(4) = -10 + 12 = 2$ The value of the second-order determinant is 2.

### Discovery

Write and then evaluate three determinants, one whose value is positive, one whose value is negative, and one whose value is 0.

**Check Point 1** Evaluate the determinant of:

**a.** $\begin{bmatrix} 10 & 9 \\ 6 & 5 \end{bmatrix}$ **b.** $\begin{bmatrix} 4 & 3 \\ -5 & -8 \end{bmatrix}$.

**2** Solve a linear system of equations in two variables using Cramer's rule.

## Solving Linear Systems of Equations in Two Variables Using Determinants

Determinants can be used to solve a linear system in two variables. In general, such a system appears as

$$a_1x + b_1y = c_1$$
$$a_2x + b_2y = c_2.$$

Let's first solve this system for $x$ using the addition method. We can solve for $x$ by eliminating $y$ from the equations. Multiply the first equation by $b_2$ and the second equation by $-b_1$. Then add the two equations:

$$\begin{aligned} a_1x + b_1y = c_1 &\xrightarrow{\text{Multiply by } b_2.} & a_1b_2x + b_1b_2y &= c_1b_2 \\ a_2x + b_2y = c_2 &\xrightarrow{\text{Multiply by } -b_1.} & -a_2b_1x - b_1b_2y &= -c_2b_1 \\ & \text{Add:} & (a_1b_2 - a_2b_1)x &= c_1b_2 - c_2b_1 \\ & & x &= \frac{c_1b_2 - c_2b_1}{a_1b_2 - a_2b_1} \end{aligned}$$

Because

$$\begin{vmatrix} c_1 & b_1 \\ c_2 & b_2 \end{vmatrix} = c_1b_2 - c_2b_1 \quad \text{and} \quad \begin{vmatrix} a_1 & b_1 \\ a_2 & b_2 \end{vmatrix} = a_1b_2 - a_2b_1$$

we can express our answer for $x$ as the quotient of two determinants:

$$x = \frac{\begin{vmatrix} c_1 & b_1 \\ c_2 & b_2 \end{vmatrix}}{\begin{vmatrix} a_1 & b_1 \\ a_2 & b_2 \end{vmatrix}}.$$

In a similar way, we could use the addition method to solve our system for $y$, again expressing $y$ as the quotient of two determinants. This method of using determinants to solve the linear system, called **Cramer's rule**, is summarized in the box.

### Solving a Linear System in Two Variables Using Determinants

***Cramer's Rule***

If

$$a_1x + b_1y = c_1$$
$$a_2x + b_2y = c_2$$

then

$$x = \frac{\begin{vmatrix} c_1 & b_1 \\ c_2 & b_2 \end{vmatrix}}{\begin{vmatrix} a_1 & b_1 \\ a_2 & b_2 \end{vmatrix}} \quad \text{and} \quad y = \frac{\begin{vmatrix} a_1 & c_1 \\ a_2 & c_2 \end{vmatrix}}{\begin{vmatrix} a_1 & b_1 \\ a_2 & b_2 \end{vmatrix}}$$

where

$$\begin{vmatrix} a_1 & b_1 \\ a_2 & b_2 \end{vmatrix} \neq 0.$$

Here are some helpful tips when solving

$$a_1x + b_1y = c_1$$
$$a_2x + b_2y = c_2$$

using determinants.

1. Three different determinants are used to find $x$ and $y$. The determinants in the denominators for $x$ and $y$ are identical. The determinants in the numerators for $x$ and $y$ differ. In abbreviated notation, we write

$$x = \frac{D_x}{D} \quad \text{and} \quad y = \frac{D_y}{D} \quad \text{where } D \neq 0.$$

2. The elements of $D$, the determinant in the denominator, are the coefficients of the variables in the system.

$$D = \begin{vmatrix} a_1 & b_1 \\ a_2 & b_2 \end{vmatrix}$$

3. $D_x$, the determinant in the numerator of $x$, is obtained by replacing the $x$-coefficients, $a_1$, $a_2$, in $D$ with the constants on the right side of the equations, $c_1$, $c_2$.

$$D = \begin{vmatrix} a_1 & b_1 \\ a_2 & b_2 \end{vmatrix} \quad \text{and} \quad D_x = \begin{vmatrix} c_1 & b_1 \\ c_2 & b_2 \end{vmatrix}$$

Replace the column with $a_1$ and $a_2$ with the constants $c_1$ and $c_2$ to get $D_x$.

4. $D_y$, the determinant in the numerator for $y$, is obtained by replacing the $y$-coefficients, $b_1$, $b_2$ in $D$ with the constants on the right side of the equations, $c_1$, $c_2$.

$$D = \begin{vmatrix} a_1 & b_1 \\ a_2 & b_2 \end{vmatrix} \quad \text{and} \quad D_y = \begin{vmatrix} a_1 & c_1 \\ a_2 & c_2 \end{vmatrix}$$

Replace the column with $b_1$ and $b_2$ with the constants $c_1$ and $c_2$ to get $D_y$.

Example 2 illustrates the use of Cramer's rule.

### EXAMPLE 2 Using Cramer's Rule to Solve a Linear System

Use Cramer's rule to solve the system:

$$5x - 4y = 2$$
$$6x - 5y = 1.$$

**Solution** Because

$$x = \frac{D_x}{D} \quad \text{and} \quad y = \frac{D_y}{D},$$

we will set up and evaluate the three determinants $D$, $D_x$, and $D_y$.

**1.** $D$, the determinant in both denominators, consists of the $x$- and $y$-coefficients.

$$D = \begin{vmatrix} 5 & -4 \\ 6 & -5 \end{vmatrix} = (5)(-5) - (6)(-4) = -25 + 24 = -1$$

Because this determinant is not zero, we continue to use Cramer's rule to solve the system.

**2.** $D_x$, the determinant in the numerator for $x$, is obtained by replacing the $x$-coefficients in $D$, 5 and 6, by the constants on the right side of the equation, 2 and 1.

$$D_x = \begin{vmatrix} 2 & -4 \\ 1 & -5 \end{vmatrix} = (2)(-5) - (1)(-4) = -10 + 4 = -6$$

**3.** $D_y$, the determinant in the numerator for $y$, is obtained by replacing the $y$-coefficients in $D$, $-4$ and $-5$, by the constants on the right side of the equation, 2 and 1.

$$D_y = \begin{vmatrix} 5 & 2 \\ 6 & 1 \end{vmatrix} = (5)(1) - (6)(2) = 5 - 12 = -7$$

**4.** Thus,

$$x = \frac{D_x}{D} = \frac{-6}{-1} = 6 \quad \text{and} \quad y = \frac{D_y}{D} = \frac{-7}{-1} = 7.$$

As always, the solution (6, 7) can be checked by substituting these values into the original equations. The solution set is $\{(6, 7)\}$.

**Check Point 2** Use Cramer's rule to solve the system:

$$5x + 4y = 12$$
$$3x - 6y = 24.$$

**3** Evaluate a third-order determinant.

## The Determinant of a 3 × 3 Matrix

Associated with every square matrix is a real number called its determinant. The determinant for a 3 × 3 matrix is defined as follows.

### Definition of a Third-Order Determinant

$$\begin{vmatrix} a_1 & b_1 & c_1 \\ a_2 & b_2 & c_2 \\ a_3 & b_3 & c_3 \end{vmatrix} = a_1b_2c_3 + b_1c_2a_3 + c_1a_2b_3 - a_3b_2c_1 - b_3c_2a_1 - c_3a_2b_1$$

The six terms and the three factors in each term in this complicated evaluation formula can be rearranged, and then we can apply the distributive property. We obtain

$$\begin{aligned} &a_1b_2c_3 - a_1b_3c_2 - a_2b_1c_3 + a_2b_3c_1 + a_3b_1c_2 - a_3b_2c_1 \\ &= a_1(b_2c_3 - b_3c_2) - a_2(b_1c_3 - b_3c_1) + a_3(b_1c_2 - b_2c_1) \\ &= a_1\begin{vmatrix} b_2 & c_2 \\ b_3 & c_3 \end{vmatrix} - a_2\begin{vmatrix} b_1 & c_1 \\ b_3 & c_3 \end{vmatrix} + a_3\begin{vmatrix} b_1 & c_1 \\ b_2 & c_2 \end{vmatrix}. \end{aligned}$$

You can evaluate each of the second-order determinants and obtain the three expressions in parentheses in the second step.

In summary, we now have arranged the definition of a third-order determinant as follows.

### Definition of the Determinant of a 3 × 3 Matrix

A third-order determinant is defined by

Subtract. Add.

$$\begin{vmatrix} a_1 & b_1 & c_1 \\ a_2 & b_2 & c_2 \\ a_3 & b_3 & c_3 \end{vmatrix} = a_1\begin{vmatrix} b_2 & c_2 \\ b_3 & c_3 \end{vmatrix} - a_2\begin{vmatrix} b_1 & c_1 \\ b_3 & c_3 \end{vmatrix} + a_3\begin{vmatrix} b_1 & c_1 \\ b_2 & c_2 \end{vmatrix}.$$

The a's on the right come from the first column.

Here are some tips that may be helpful when evaluating the determinant of a 3 × 3 matrix.

1. Each of the three terms in the definition contains two factors—a numerical factor and a second-order determinant.
2. The numerical factor in each term is an element from the first column of the third-order determinant.
3. The minus sign precedes the second term.
4. The second-order determinant that appears in each term is obtained by crossing out the row and the column containing the numerical factor.

$$a_1\begin{vmatrix} b_2 & c_2 \\ b_3 & c_3 \end{vmatrix} - a_2\begin{vmatrix} b_1 & c_1 \\ b_3 & c_3 \end{vmatrix} + a_3\begin{vmatrix} b_1 & c_1 \\ b_2 & c_2 \end{vmatrix}$$

$$\downarrow \qquad\qquad \downarrow \qquad\qquad \downarrow$$

$$\begin{vmatrix} \cancel{a_1} & \cancel{b_1} & \cancel{c_1} \\ \cancel{a_2} & b_2 & c_2 \\ \cancel{a_3} & b_3 & c_3 \end{vmatrix} \quad \begin{vmatrix} \cancel{a_1} & b_1 & c_1 \\ \cancel{a_2} & \cancel{b_2} & \cancel{c_2} \\ \cancel{a_3} & b_3 & c_3 \end{vmatrix} \quad \begin{vmatrix} \cancel{a_1} & b_1 & c_1 \\ \cancel{a_2} & b_2 & c_2 \\ \cancel{a_3} & \cancel{b_3} & \cancel{c_3} \end{vmatrix}$$

The **minor** of an element is the determinant that remains after deleting the row and column of that element. For this reason, we call this method **expansion by minors**.

## EXAMPLE 3 Evaluating the Determinant of a 3 × 3 Matrix

Evaluate the determinant of

$$\begin{bmatrix} 4 & 1 & 0 \\ -9 & 3 & 4 \\ -3 & 8 & 1 \end{bmatrix}.$$

**Solution** We know that each of the three terms in the determinant contains a numerical factor and a second-order determinant. The numerical factors are from the first column of the determinant of the given matrix. They are highlighted in the following matrix:

$$\begin{vmatrix} 4 & 1 & 0 \\ -9 & 3 & 4 \\ -3 & 8 & 1 \end{vmatrix}$$

We find the minor for each numerical factor by deleting the row and column of that element:

$$\begin{bmatrix} 4 & 1 & 0 \\ -9 & 3 & 4 \\ -3 & 8 & 1 \end{bmatrix} \quad \begin{bmatrix} 4 & 1 & 0 \\ -9 & 3 & 4 \\ -3 & 8 & 1 \end{bmatrix} \quad \begin{bmatrix} 4 & 1 & 0 \\ -9 & 3 & 4 \\ -3 & 8 & 1 \end{bmatrix}$$

The minor for 4 is $\begin{vmatrix} 3 & 4 \\ 8 & 1 \end{vmatrix}$.

The minor for −9 is $\begin{vmatrix} 1 & 0 \\ 8 & 1 \end{vmatrix}$.

The minor for −3 is $\begin{vmatrix} 1 & 0 \\ 3 & 4 \end{vmatrix}$.

Now we have three numerical factors, 4, −9, and −3, and three second-order determinants. We multiply each numerical factor by its second-order determinant to find the three terms of the third-order determinant:

$$4\begin{vmatrix} 3 & 4 \\ 8 & 1 \end{vmatrix}, \quad -9\begin{vmatrix} 1 & 0 \\ 8 & 1 \end{vmatrix}, \quad -3\begin{vmatrix} 1 & 0 \\ 3 & 4 \end{vmatrix}.$$

Based on the preceding definition, we subtract the second term from the first term and add the third term:

Don't forget to supply the minus sign.

$$\begin{vmatrix} 4 & 1 & 0 \\ -9 & 3 & 4 \\ -3 & 8 & 1 \end{vmatrix} = 4\begin{vmatrix} 3 & 4 \\ 8 & 1 \end{vmatrix} - (-9)\begin{vmatrix} 1 & 0 \\ 8 & 1 \end{vmatrix} - 3\begin{vmatrix} 1 & 0 \\ 3 & 4 \end{vmatrix}$$

$$= 4(3 \cdot 1 - 8 \cdot 4) + 9(1 \cdot 1 - 8 \cdot 0) - 3(1 \cdot 4 - 3 \cdot 0)$$

$$= 4(3 - 32) + 9(1 - 0) - 3(4 - 0)$$

$$= 4(-29) + 9(1) - 3(4)$$

$$= -119$$

Evaluate the three second-order determinants.

## Technology

Verify the result of Example 3 by using your graphing utility to enter the given matrix as

$$A = \begin{bmatrix} 4 & 1 & 0 \\ -9 & 3 & 4 \\ -3 & 8 & 1 \end{bmatrix}.$$

Then enter

det [A] ENTER.

The result should be −119.

**Check Point 3** Evaluate the determinant of

$$\begin{bmatrix} 2 & 1 & 7 \\ -5 & 6 & 0 \\ -4 & 3 & 1 \end{bmatrix}.$$

The six terms in the definition of a third-order determinant can be rearranged and factored in a variety of ways. Thus, it is possible to expand a determinant by minors about any row or any column. *Minus signs must be supplied preceding any element appearing in a position where the sum of its row and its column is an odd number.* For example, expanding about the elements in column 2 gives us

$$\begin{vmatrix} a_1 & b_1 & c_1 \\ a_2 & b_2 & c_2 \\ a_3 & b_3 & c_3 \end{vmatrix} = -b_1\begin{vmatrix} a_2 & c_2 \\ a_3 & c_3 \end{vmatrix} + b_2\begin{vmatrix} a_1 & c_1 \\ a_3 & c_3 \end{vmatrix} - b_3\begin{vmatrix} a_1 & c_1 \\ a_2 & c_2 \end{vmatrix}.$$

Minus sign is supplied because $b_1$ appears in row 1 and column 2; $1+2=3$, an odd number.

Minus sign is supplied because $b_3$ appears in row 3 and column 2; $3+2=5$, an odd number.

Expanding by minors about column 3, we obtain

$$\begin{vmatrix} a_1 & b_1 & c_1 \\ a_2 & b_2 & c_2 \\ a_3 & b_3 & c_3 \end{vmatrix} = c_1\begin{vmatrix} a_2 & b_2 \\ a_3 & b_3 \end{vmatrix} - c_2\begin{vmatrix} a_1 & b_1 \\ a_3 & b_3 \end{vmatrix} + c_3\begin{vmatrix} a_1 & b_1 \\ a_2 & b_2 \end{vmatrix}.$$

Minus sign must be supplied because $c_2$ appears in row 2 and column 3; $2+3=5$, an odd number.

## Study Tip

Keep in mind that you can expand a determinant by minors about any row or column. Use alternating plus and minus signs to precede the numerical factors of the minors according to the following sign array:

$$\begin{vmatrix} + & - & + \\ - & + & - \\ + & - & + \end{vmatrix}.$$

When evaluating a $3 \times 3$ determinant using expansion by minors, you can expand about any row or column. To simplify the arithmetic, if a row or column contains one or more 0s, expand about that row or column.

## EXAMPLE 4 Evaluating a Third-Order Determinant

Evaluate:

$$\begin{vmatrix} 9 & 5 & 0 \\ -2 & -3 & 0 \\ 1 & 4 & 2 \end{vmatrix}.$$

**Solution** Note that the last column has two 0s. We will expand the determinant about the elements in that column.

$$\begin{vmatrix} 9 & 5 & 0 \\ -2 & -3 & 0 \\ 1 & 4 & 2 \end{vmatrix} = 0\begin{vmatrix} -2 & -3 \\ 1 & 4 \end{vmatrix} - 0\begin{vmatrix} 9 & 5 \\ 1 & 4 \end{vmatrix} + 2\begin{vmatrix} 9 & 5 \\ -2 & -3 \end{vmatrix}$$

$$= 0 - 0 + 2[9(-3) - (-2) \cdot 5]$$

Evaluate the second-order determinant whose numerical factor is not 0.

$$= 2(-27 + 10)$$

$$= 2(-17)$$

$$= -34$$

**Check Point 4** Evaluate:

$$\begin{vmatrix} 6 & 4 & 0 \\ -3 & -5 & 3 \\ 1 & 2 & 0 \end{vmatrix}.$$

**4** Solve a linear system of equations in three variables using Cramer's rule.

## Solving Linear Systems of Equations in Three Variables Using Determinants

Cramer's rule can be applied to solving systems of linear equations in three variables. The determinants in the numerator and denominator of all variables are third-order determinants.

### Solving Three Equations in Three Variables Using Determinants

***Cramer's Rule***

If

$$\begin{aligned} a_1x + b_1y + c_1z &= d_1 \\ a_2x + b_2y + c_2z &= d_2 \\ a_3x + b_3y + c_3z &= d_3 \end{aligned}$$

then

$$x = \frac{D_x}{D},\ y = \frac{D_y}{D},\ \text{and } z = \frac{D_z}{D}.$$

These four third-order determinants are given by

$$D = \begin{vmatrix} a_1 & b_1 & c_1 \\ a_2 & b_2 & c_2 \\ a_3 & b_3 & c_3 \end{vmatrix}$$ These are the coefficients of the variables $x$, $y$, and $z$. $D \neq 0$.

$$D_x = \begin{vmatrix} d_1 & b_1 & c_1 \\ d_2 & b_2 & c_2 \\ d_3 & b_3 & c_3 \end{vmatrix}$$ Replace $x$-coefficients in $D$ with the constants at the right of the three equations.

$$D_y = \begin{vmatrix} a_1 & d_1 & c_1 \\ a_2 & d_2 & c_2 \\ a_3 & d_3 & c_3 \end{vmatrix}$$ Replace $y$-coefficients in $D$ with the constants at the right of the three equations.

$$D_z = \begin{vmatrix} a_1 & b_1 & d_1 \\ a_2 & b_2 & d_2 \\ a_3 & b_3 & d_3 \end{vmatrix}$$ Replace $z$-coefficients in $D$ with the constants at the right of the three equations.

### EXAMPLE 5 Using Cramer's Rule to Solve a Linear System in Three Variables

Use Cramer's rule to solve:

$$\begin{aligned} x + 2y - z &= -4 \\ x + 4y - 2z &= -6 \\ 2x + 3y + z &= 3. \end{aligned}$$

**Solution** Because

$$x = \frac{D_x}{D}, \quad y = \frac{D_y}{D}, \quad \text{and} \quad z = \frac{D_z}{D},$$

we need to set up and evaluate four determinants.

$x + 2y - z = -4$
$x + 4y - 2z = -6$
$2x + 3y + z = 3$

The linear system is shown again so that you do not need to turn back a page.

**Step 1 Set up the determinants.**

1. $D$, the determinant in all three denominators, consists of the $x$-, $y$-, and $z$-coefficients.

$$D = \begin{vmatrix} 1 & 2 & -1 \\ 1 & 4 & -2 \\ 2 & 3 & 1 \end{vmatrix}$$

2. $D_x$, the determinant in the numerator for $x$, is obtained by replacing the $x$-coefficients in $D$, 1, 1, and 2, with the constants on the right side of the equation, −4, −6, and 3.

$$D_x = \begin{vmatrix} -4 & 2 & -1 \\ -6 & 4 & -2 \\ 3 & 3 & 1 \end{vmatrix}$$

3. $D_y$, the determinant in the numerator for $y$, is obtained by replacing the $y$-coefficients in $D$, 2, 4, and 3, with the constants on the right side of the equation, −4, −6, and 3.

$$D_y = \begin{vmatrix} 1 & -4 & -1 \\ 1 & -6 & -2 \\ 2 & 3 & 1 \end{vmatrix}$$

4. $D_z$, the determinant in the numerator for $z$, is obtained by replacing the $z$-coefficients in $D$, −1, −2, and 1, with the constants on the right side of the equation, −4, −6, and 3.

$$D_z = \begin{vmatrix} 1 & 2 & -4 \\ 1 & 4 & -6 \\ 2 & 3 & 3 \end{vmatrix}$$

**Step 2 Evaluate the four determinants.**

$$D = \begin{vmatrix} 1 & 2 & -1 \\ 1 & 4 & -2 \\ 2 & 3 & 1 \end{vmatrix} = 1\begin{vmatrix} 4 & -2 \\ 3 & 1 \end{vmatrix} - 1\begin{vmatrix} 2 & -1 \\ 3 & 1 \end{vmatrix} + 2\begin{vmatrix} 2 & -1 \\ 4 & -2 \end{vmatrix}$$

$$= 1(4 + 6) - 1(2 + 3) + 2(-4 + 4)$$

$$= 1(10) - 1(5) + 2(0) = 5$$

Using the same technique to evaluate each determinant, we obtain

$$D_x = -10, \quad D_y = 5, \quad \text{and} \quad D_z = 20.$$

**Step 3 Substitute these four values and solve the system.**

$$x = \frac{D_x}{D} = \frac{-10}{5} = -2$$

$$y = \frac{D_y}{D} = \frac{5}{5} = 1$$

$$z = \frac{D_z}{D} = \frac{20}{5} = 4$$

The solution $(-2, 1, 4)$ can be checked by substitution into the original three equations. The solution set is $\{(-2, 1, 4)\}$.

**Check Point 5** Use Cramer's rule to solve the system:

$$\begin{aligned} 3x - 2y + z &= 16 \\ 2x + 3y - z &= -9. \\ x + 4y + 3z &= 2 \end{aligned}$$

**5** Use determinants to identify inconsistent systems and systems with dependent equations.

## Cramer's Rule with Inconsistent and Dependent Systems

If $D$, the determinant in the denominator, is 0, the variables described by the quotient of determinants are not real numbers. However, when $D = 0$, this indicates that the system is inconsistent or contains dependent equations. This gives rise to the following two situations.

**Discovery**

Write a system of two equations that is inconsistent. Now use determinants and the result boxed on the right to verify that this is truly an inconsistent system. Repeat the same process for a system with two dependent equations.

**Determinants: Inconsistent and Dependent-Systems**

1. If $D = 0$ and at least one of the determinants in the numerator is not 0, then the system is inconsistent. The solution set is $\varnothing$.
2. If $D = 0$ and all the determinants in the numerators are 0, then the equations in the system are dependent.

Although we have focused on applying determinants to solve linear systems, they have other applications, some of which we consider in the exercise set that follows.

**6** Evaluate higher-order determinants.

## The Determinant of Any $n \times n$ Matrix

A determinant with $n$ rows and $n$ columns is said to be an ***n*th-order determinant**. The value of an $n$th-order determinant $(n > 2)$ can be found in terms of determinants of order $n - 1$. For example, we found the value of a third-order determinant in terms of determinants of order 2.

We can generalize this idea for fourth-order determinants and higher. We have seen that the **minor** of the element $a_{ij}$ is the determinant obtained by deleting the $i$th row and the $j$th column in the given array of numbers. The **cofactor** of the element $a_{ij}$ is $(-1)^{i+j}$ times the minor of the $a_{ij}$th entry. If the sum of the row and column $(i + j)$ is even, the cofactor is the same as the minor. If the sum of the row and column $(i + j)$ is odd, the cofactor is the opposite of the minor.

Let's see what this means in the case of a fourth-order determinant.

### EXAMPLE 6 Evaluating the Determinant of a 4 × 4 Matrix

Evaluate the determinant of

$$A = \begin{bmatrix} 1 & -2 & 3 & 0 \\ -1 & 1 & 0 & 2 \\ 0 & 2 & 0 & -3 \\ 2 & 3 & -4 & 1 \end{bmatrix}.$$

**Why Modern Software Packages for Solving Linear Systems Do Not Use Cramer's Rule**

The fastest supercomputers can perform one trillion ($10^{12}$) multiplications per second. To solve a linear system with a "mere" 20 equations using Cramer's rule requires over $5 \times 10^{19}$ multiplications. This would take a supercomputer more than 590 days. The cost for this venture? At $2200 per hour, typical of the costs for supercomputer time, the computations required by Cramer's rule would cost more than $30 million!

**Solution**

$$|A| = \begin{vmatrix} 1 & -2 & 3 & 0 \\ -1 & 1 & 0 & 2 \\ 0 & 2 & 0 & -3 \\ 2 & 3 & -4 & 1 \end{vmatrix}$$

With two 0s in the third column, we will expand along the third column.

$$= (-1)^{1+3}3\begin{vmatrix} -1 & 1 & 2 \\ 0 & 2 & -3 \\ 2 & 3 & 1 \end{vmatrix} + (-1)^{4+3}(-4)\begin{vmatrix} 1 & -2 & 0 \\ -1 & 1 & 2 \\ 0 & 2 & -3 \end{vmatrix}$$

3 is in row 1, column 3.

−4 is in row 4, column 3.

$$= 3\begin{vmatrix} -1 & 1 & 2 \\ 0 & 2 & -3 \\ 2 & 3 & 1 \end{vmatrix} + 4\begin{vmatrix} 1 & -2 & 0 \\ -1 & 1 & 2 \\ 0 & 2 & -3 \end{vmatrix}$$

The determinant that follows 3 is obtained by crossing out the row and the column (row 1, column 3) in the original determinant. The minor for −4 is obtained in the same manner.

Evaluate the two third-order determinants to get

$$|A| = 3(-25) + 4(-1) = -79.$$

**Check Point 6** Evaluate the determinant of

$$A = \begin{bmatrix} 0 & 4 & 0 & -3 \\ -1 & 1 & 5 & 2 \\ 1 & -2 & 0 & 6 \\ 3 & 0 & 0 & 1 \end{bmatrix}.$$

If a linear system has $n$ equations, Cramer's rule requires you to compute $n + 1$ determinants of $n$th order. The excessive number of calculations required to perform Cramer's rule for systems with four or more equations makes it an inefficient method for solving large systems.

## EXERCISE SET 9.5

### Practice Exercises

*Evaluate each determinant in Exercises 1–10.*

**1.** $\begin{vmatrix} 5 & 7 \\ 2 & 3 \end{vmatrix}$

**2.** $\begin{vmatrix} 4 & 8 \\ 5 & 6 \end{vmatrix}$

**3.** $\begin{vmatrix} -4 & 1 \\ 5 & 6 \end{vmatrix}$

**4.** $\begin{vmatrix} 7 & 9 \\ -2 & -5 \end{vmatrix}$

**5.** $\begin{vmatrix} -7 & 14 \\ 2 & -4 \end{vmatrix}$

**6.** $\begin{vmatrix} 1 & -3 \\ -8 & 2 \end{vmatrix}$

**7.** $\begin{vmatrix} -5 & -1 \\ -2 & -7 \end{vmatrix}$

**8.** $\begin{vmatrix} \frac{1}{5} & \frac{1}{6} \\ -6 & 5 \end{vmatrix}$

**9.** $\begin{vmatrix} \frac{1}{2} & \frac{1}{2} \\ \frac{1}{8} & -\frac{3}{4} \end{vmatrix}$

**10.** $\begin{vmatrix} \frac{2}{3} & \frac{1}{3} \\ -\frac{1}{2} & \frac{3}{4} \end{vmatrix}$

*For Exercises 11–26, use Cramer's rule to solve each system or to determine that the system is inconsistent or contains dependent equations.*

**11.** $x + y = 7$
$x - y = 3$

**12.** $2x + y = 3$
$x - y = 3$

**13.** $\begin{aligned} 12x + 3y &= 15 \\ 2x - 3y &= 13 \end{aligned}$

**14.** $\begin{aligned} x - 2y &= 5 \\ 5x - y &= -2 \end{aligned}$

**15.** $\begin{aligned} 4x - 5y &= 17 \\ 2x + 3y &= 3 \end{aligned}$

**16.** $\begin{aligned} 3x + 2y &= 2 \\ 2x + 2y &= 3 \end{aligned}$

**17.** $\begin{aligned} x + 2y &= 3 \\ 5x + 10y &= 15 \end{aligned}$

**18.** $\begin{aligned} 2x - 9y &= 5 \\ 3x - 3y &= 11 \end{aligned}$

**19.** $\begin{aligned} 3x - 4y &= 4 \\ 2x + 2y &= 12 \end{aligned}$

**20.** $\begin{aligned} 3x &= 7y + 1 \\ 2x &= 3y - 1 \end{aligned}$

**21.** $\begin{aligned} 2x &= 3y + 2 \\ 5x &= 51 - 4y \end{aligned}$

**22.** $\begin{aligned} x + 2y - 3 &= 0 \\ 12 &= 8y + 4x \end{aligned}$

**23.** $\begin{aligned} 3x &= 2 - 3y \\ 2y &= 3 - 2x \end{aligned}$

**24.** $\begin{aligned} y &= -4x + 2 \\ 2x &= 3y + 8 \end{aligned}$

**25.** $\begin{aligned} 4y &= 16 - 3x \\ 5x &= 12 - 3y \end{aligned}$

**26.** $\begin{aligned} 2x &= 7 + 3y \\ 4x - 6y &= 3 \end{aligned}$

*Evaluate each determinant in Exercises 27–32.*

**27.** $\begin{vmatrix} 3 & 0 & 0 \\ 2 & 1 & -5 \\ 2 & 5 & -1 \end{vmatrix}$

**28.** $\begin{vmatrix} 4 & 0 & 0 \\ 3 & -1 & 4 \\ 2 & -3 & 5 \end{vmatrix}$

**29.** $\begin{vmatrix} 3 & 1 & 0 \\ -3 & 4 & 0 \\ -1 & 3 & -5 \end{vmatrix}$

**30.** $\begin{vmatrix} 2 & -4 & 2 \\ -1 & 0 & 5 \\ 3 & 0 & 4 \end{vmatrix}$

**31.** $\begin{vmatrix} 1 & 1 & 1 \\ 2 & 2 & 2 \\ -3 & 4 & -5 \end{vmatrix}$

**32.** $\begin{vmatrix} 1 & 2 & 3 \\ 2 & 2 & -3 \\ 3 & 2 & 1 \end{vmatrix}$

*In Exercises 33–40, use Cramer's rule to solve each system.*

**33.** $\begin{aligned} x + y + z &= 0 \\ 2x - y + z &= -1 \\ -x + 3y - z &= -8 \end{aligned}$

**34.** $\begin{aligned} x - y + 2z &= 3 \\ 2x + 3y + z &= 9 \\ -x - y + 3z &= 11 \end{aligned}$

**35.** $\begin{aligned} 4x - 5y - 6z &= -1 \\ x - 2y - 5z &= -12 \\ 2x - y &= 7 \end{aligned}$

**36.** $\begin{aligned} x - 3y + z &= -2 \\ x + 2y &= 8 \\ 2x - y &= 1 \end{aligned}$

**37.** $\begin{aligned} x + y + z &= 4 \\ x - 2y + z &= 7 \\ x + 3y + 2z &= 4 \end{aligned}$

**38.** $\begin{aligned} 2x + 2y + 3z &= 10 \\ 4x - y + z &= -5 \\ 5x - 2y + 6z &= 1 \end{aligned}$

**39.** $\begin{aligned} x + 2z &= 4 \\ 2y - z &= 5 \\ 2x + 3y &= 13 \end{aligned}$

**40.** $\begin{aligned} 3x + 2z &= 4 \\ 5x - y &= -4 \\ 4y + 3z &= 22 \end{aligned}$

*Evaluate each determinant in Exercises 41–44.*

**41.** $\begin{vmatrix} 4 & 2 & 8 & -7 \\ -2 & 0 & 4 & 1 \\ 5 & 0 & 0 & 5 \\ 4 & 0 & 0 & -1 \end{vmatrix}$

**42.** $\begin{vmatrix} 3 & -1 & 1 & 2 \\ -2 & 0 & 0 & 0 \\ 2 & -1 & -2 & 3 \\ 1 & 4 & 2 & 3 \end{vmatrix}$

**43.** $\begin{vmatrix} -2 & -3 & 3 & 5 \\ 1 & -4 & 0 & 0 \\ 1 & 2 & 2 & -3 \\ 2 & 0 & 1 & 1 \end{vmatrix}$

**44.** $\begin{vmatrix} 1 & -3 & 2 & 0 \\ -3 & -1 & 0 & -2 \\ 2 & 1 & 3 & 1 \\ 2 & 0 & -2 & 0 \end{vmatrix}$

## Application Exercises

*Determinants are used to find the area of a triangle whose vertices are given by three points in a rectangular coordinate system. The area of a triangle with vertices $(x_1, y_1)$, $(x_2, y_2)$, and $(x_3, y_3)$ is*

$$\text{Area} = \pm\frac{1}{2}\begin{vmatrix} x_1 & y_1 & 1 \\ x_2 & y_2 & 1 \\ x_3 & y_3 & 1 \end{vmatrix}$$

*where the symbol $(\pm)$ indicates that the appropriate sign should be chosen to yield a positive area. Use this information to work Exercises 45–46.*

**45. a.** Use determinants to find the area of the triangle whose vertices are $(3, -5)$, $(2, 6)$, and $(-3, 5)$.

**b.** Graph the triangle in part (a) and then confirm your answer by using the formula for a triangle's area, $A = \frac{1}{2}bh$.

**46.** Find the area of the triangle whose vertices are $(1, 1)$, $(-2, -3)$, and $(11, -3)$.

*Determinants are used to show that three points lie on the same line (are collinear). If*

$$\begin{vmatrix} x_1 & y_1 & 1 \\ x_2 & y_2 & 1 \\ x_3 & y_3 & 1 \end{vmatrix} = 0$$

*then the points $(x_1, y_1)$, $(x_2, y_2)$, and $(x_3, y_3)$ are collinear. If the determinant does not equal 0, then the points are not collinear. Use this information to work Exercises 47–48.*

**47.** Are the points $(3, -1)$, $(0, -3)$, and $(12, 5)$ collinear?

**48.** Are the points $(-4, -6)$, $(1, 0)$, and $(11, 12)$ collinear?

*Determinants are used to write an equation of a line passing through two points. An equation of the line passing through the distinct points $(x_1, y_1)$ and $(x_2, y_2)$ is given by*

$$\begin{vmatrix} x & y & 1 \\ x_1 & y_1 & 1 \\ x_2 & y_2 & 1 \end{vmatrix} = 0.$$

*Use this information to work Exercises 49–50.*

**49.** Use the determinant to write an equation for the line passing through $(3, -5)$ and $(-2, 6)$. Then expand the determinant, expressing the line's equation in slope-intercept form.

50. Use the determinant to write an equation for the line passing through $(-1, 3)$ and $(2, 4)$. Then expand the determinant, expressing the line's equation in slope-intercept form.

## Writing in Mathematics

51. Explain how to evaluate a second-order determinant.
52. Describe the determinants $D_x$ and $D_y$ in terms of the coefficients and constants in a system of two equations in two variables.
53. Explain how to evaluate a third-order determinant.
54. When expanding a determinant by minors, when is it necessary to supply minus signs?
55. Without going into too much detail, describe how to solve a linear system in three variables using Cramer's rule.
56. In applying Cramer's rule, what does it mean if $D = 0$?
57. The process of solving a linear system in three variables using Cramer's rule can involve tedious computation. Is there a way of speeding up this process, perhaps using Cramer's rule to find the value for only one of the variables? Describe how this process might work, presenting a specific example with your description. Remember that your goal is still to find the value for each variable in the system.
58. If you could use only one method to solve linear systems in three variables, which method would you select? Explain why this is so.

## Technology Exercises

59. Use the feature of your graphing utility that evaluates the determinant of a square matrix to verify any five of the determinants that you evaluated by hand in Exercises 1–10, 27–32, or 41–44.

*In Exercises 60–61, use a graphing utility to evaluate the determinant for the given matrix.*

60. $\begin{bmatrix} 3 & -2 & -1 & 4 \\ -5 & 1 & 2 & 7 \\ 2 & 4 & 5 & 0 \\ -1 & 3 & -6 & 5 \end{bmatrix}$

61. $\begin{bmatrix} 8 & 2 & 6 & -1 & 0 \\ 2 & 0 & -3 & 4 & 7 \\ 2 & 1 & -3 & 6 & -5 \\ -1 & 2 & 1 & 5 & -1 \\ 4 & 5 & -2 & 3 & -8 \end{bmatrix}$

62. What is the fastest method for solving a linear system with your graphing utility?

## Critical Thinking Exercises

63. **a.** Evaluate: $\begin{vmatrix} a & a \\ 0 & a \end{vmatrix}$.

**b.** Evaluate: $\begin{vmatrix} a & a & a \\ 0 & a & a \\ 0 & 0 & a \end{vmatrix}$.

**c.** Evaluate: $\begin{vmatrix} a & a & a & a \\ 0 & a & a & a \\ 0 & 0 & a & a \\ 0 & 0 & 0 & a \end{vmatrix}$.

**d.** Describe the pattern in the given determinants.

**e.** Describe the pattern in the evaluations.

64. Evaluate: $\begin{vmatrix} 2 & 0 & 0 & 0 & 0 \\ 0 & 3 & 0 & 0 & 0 \\ 0 & 0 & 2 & 0 & 0 \\ 0 & 0 & 0 & 1 & 0 \\ 0 & 0 & 0 & 0 & 4 \end{vmatrix}$.

65. What happens to the value of a second-order determinant if the two columns are interchanged?

66. Consider the system

$$a_1x + b_1y = c_1$$
$$a_2x + b_2y = c_2.$$

Use Cramer's rule to prove that if the first equation of the system is replaced by the sum of the two equations, the resulting system has the same solution as the original system.

## Group Exercise

67. We have seen that determinants can be used to solve linear equations, give areas of triangles in rectangular coordinates, and determine equations of lines. Not impressed with these applications? Members of the group should research an application of determinants that they find intriguing. The group should then present a seminar to the class about this application.

# CHAPTER SUMMARY, REVIEW, AND TEST

## Summary

### 9.1 Matrix Solution to Linear Systems

a. Matrix row operations are described in the box on page 752.

b. To solve a linear system using Gaussian elimination, begin with the system's augmented matrix. Use matrix operations to get 1s down the main diagonal and 0s below the 1s. Details are in the box on page 753.

c. To solve a linear system using Gauss-Jordan elimination, use the procedure of Gaussian elimination, but obtain 0s above and below the 1s in the main diagonal.

### 9.2 Inconsistent and Dependent Systems

a. If Gaussian elimination results in a matrix with a row containing all 0s to the left of the vertical line and a nonzero number to the right, the system has no solution (is inconsistent).

b. If Gaussian elimination results in a matrix with a row with all 0s, the system has an infinite number of solutions (contains dependent equations).

### 9.3 Matrix Operations

a. Two matrices are equal if and only if they have the same order and corresponding elements are equal.

b. Matrix Addition and Subtraction: Matrices of the same order are added or subtracted by adding or subtracting corresponding elements. Properties of matrix addition are given in the box on page 776.

c. Scalar Multiplication: If $A$ is a matrix and $c$ is a scalar, then cA is the matrix formed by multiplying each element in $A$ by $c$. Properties of scalar multiplication are given in the box on page 777.

d. Matrix Multiplication: The product of an $m \times n$ matrix $A$ and an $n \times p$ matrix $B$ is an $m \times p$ matrix $AB$. The element in the $i$th row and $j$th column of $AB$ is found by multiplying each element in the $i$th row of $A$ by the corresponding element in the $j$th column of $B$ and adding the products. Matrix multiplication is not commutative: $AB \neq BA$. Properties of matrix multiplication are given in the box on page 782.

### 9.4 Multiplicative Inverses of Matrices; Matrix Equations

a. The multiplicative identity matrix $I_n$ is an $n \times n$ matrix with 1s down the main diagonal and 0s elsewhere.

b. Let $A$ be an $n \times n$ square matrix. If there is a square matrix $A^{-1}$ such that $AA^{-1} = I_n$ and $A^{-1}A = I_n$, then $A^{-1}$ is the multiplicative inverse of $A$.

c. If a square matrix has a multiplicative inverse, it is invertible. Methods for finding multiplicative inverses for invertible matrices, including a formula for $2 \times 2$ matrices, are given in the box on page 795.

d. Linear systems can be represented by matrix equations $AX = B$ in which $A$ is the coefficient matrix and $B$ is the constant matrix. If $AX = B$ has a unique solution, then $X = A^{-1}B$.

### 9.5 Determinants and Cramer's Rule

a. Value of a Second-Order Determinant:

$$\begin{vmatrix} a_1 & b_1 \\ a_2 & b_2 \end{vmatrix} = a_1b_2 - a_2b_1$$

b. Cramer's rule for solving linear systems in two variables uses three second-order determinants and is stated in the box on page 804.

c. To evaluate an $n$th-order determinant, where $n > 2$,

1. Select a row or column about which to expand.
2. For each element $a_{ij}$ in the row or column, multiply by $(-1)^{i+j}$ times the determinant obtained by deleting the $i$th row and the $j$th column in the given array of numbers.
3. The value of the determinant is the sum of the products found in step 2.

d. Cramer's rule for solving linear systems in three variables uses four third-order determinants and is stated in the box on page 809.

e. Cramer's rule with inconsistent and dependent systems is summarized by the two situations in the box on page 811.

## Review Exercises

### 9.1

*In Exercises 1–2, write the system of linear equations represented by the augmented matrix. Use x, y, z, and, if necessary, w for the variables. Once the system is written, use back-substitution to find its solution.*

**1.** $\left[\begin{array}{ccc|c} 1 & 1 & 3 & 12 \\ 0 & 1 & -2 & -4 \\ 0 & 0 & 1 & 3 \end{array}\right]$

**2.** $\left[\begin{array}{cccc|c} 1 & 0 & -2 & 2 & 1 \\ 0 & 1 & 1 & -1 & 0 \\ 0 & 0 & 1 & -\frac{7}{3} & -\frac{1}{3} \\ 0 & 0 & 0 & 1 & 1 \end{array}\right]$

*In Exercises 3–4, perform each matrix row operation and write the new matrix.*

**3.** $\left[\begin{array}{ccc|c} 1 & 2 & 2 & 2 \\ 0 & 1 & -1 & 2 \\ 0 & 5 & 4 & 1 \end{array}\right]$ Multiply row 2 by $-5$ and add to corresponding entries in row 3.

**4.** $\left[\begin{array}{ccc|c} 2 & -2 & 1 & -1 \\ 1 & 2 & -1 & 2 \\ 6 & 4 & 3 & 5 \end{array}\right]$ Multiply row 1 by $\frac{1}{2}$.

*In Exercises 5–7, solve each system of equations using matrices. Use Gaussian elimination with back-substitution or Gauss-Jordan elimination.*

**5.** $x + 2y + 3z = -5$
$2x + y + z = 1$
$x + y - z = 8$

**6.** $x - 2y + z = 0$
$y - 3z = -1$
$2y + 5z = -2$

**7.** $3x_1 + 5x_2 - 8x_3 + 5x_4 = -8$
$x_1 + 2x_2 - 3x_3 + x_4 = -7$
$2x_1 + 3x_2 - 7x_3 + 3x_4 = -11$
$4x_1 + 8x_2 - 10x_3 + 7x_4 = -10$

**8.** The table shows the pollutants in the air in a city on a typical summer day.

| $x$ (Hours after 6 A.M.) | $y$ (Amount of Pollutants in the Air, in parts per million) |
|---|---|
| 2 | 98 |
| 4 | 138 |
| 10 | 162 |

**a.** Use the function $y = ax^2 + bx + c$ to model the data. Use either Gaussian elimination with back-substitution or Gauss-Jordan elimination to find the values for $a$, $b$, and $c$.

**b.** Use the function to find the time of day at which the city's air pollution level is at a maximum. What is the maximum level?

### 9.2

*In Exercises 9–12, use Gaussian elimination to find the complete solution to each system, or show that none exists.*

**9.** $2x - 3y + z = 1$
$x - 2y + 3z = 2$
$3x - 4y - z = 1$

**10.** $x - 3y + z = 1$
$-2x + y + 3z = -7$
$x - 4y + 2z = 0$

**11.** $x_1 + 4x_2 + 3x_3 - 6x_4 = 5$
$x_1 + 3x_2 + x_3 - 4x_4 = 3$
$2x_1 + 8x_2 + 7x_3 - 5x_4 = 11$
$2x_1 + 5x_2 - 6x_4 = 4$

**12.** $2x + 3y - 5z = 15$
$x + 2y - z = 4$

**13.** The figure shows the intersections of three one-way streets. The numbers given represent traffic flow in cars per hour at a peak period (from 4 P.M. to 6 P.M.).

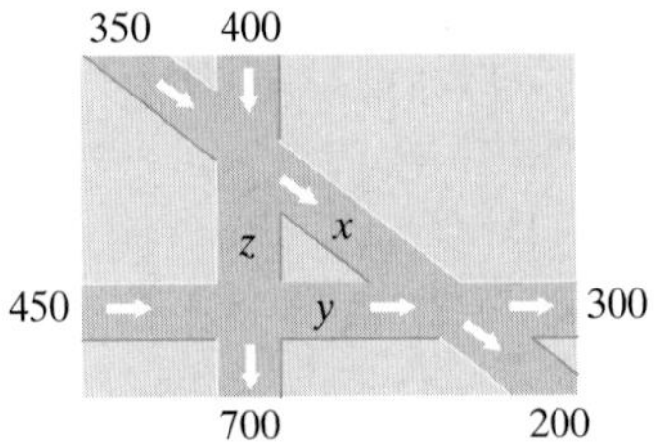


**a.** Use the idea that the number of cars entering each intersection per hour must equal the number of cars leaving per hour to set up a linear system of equations involving $x$, $y$, and $z$.

**b.** Use Gaussian elimination to solve the system.

**c.** If construction limits the value of $z$ to 400, how many cars per hour must pass between the other intersections to keep traffic flowing?

### 9.3

**14.** Find values for $x$, $y$, and $z$ so that the following matrices are equal:

$$\begin{bmatrix} 2x & y + 7 \\ z & 4 \end{bmatrix} = \begin{bmatrix} -10 & 13 \\ 6 & 4 \end{bmatrix}.$$

*In Exercises 15–28, perform the indicated matrix operations given that A, B, C, and D are defined as follows. If an operation is not defined, state the reason.*

$$A = \begin{bmatrix} 2 & -1 & 2 \\ 5 & 3 & -1 \end{bmatrix}, \quad B = \begin{bmatrix} 0 & -2 \\ 3 & 2 \\ 1 & -5 \end{bmatrix},$$

$$C = \begin{bmatrix} 1 & 2 & 3 \\ -1 & 1 & 2 \\ -1 & 2 & 1 \end{bmatrix}, \quad \text{and} \quad D = \begin{bmatrix} -2 & 3 & 1 \\ 3 & -2 & 4 \end{bmatrix}$$

**15.** $A + D$

**16.** $2B$

**17.** $D - A$

**18.** $B + C$

**19.** $3A + 2D$

**20.** $-2A + 4D$

**21.** $-5(A + D)$

**22.** $AB$

**23.** $BA$

**24.** $BD$

**25.** $DB$

**26.** $AB - BA$

**27.** $(A - D)C$

**28.** $B(AC)$

*In Exercises 29–30, use nine pixels in a 3 × 3 grid and the color levels shown.*

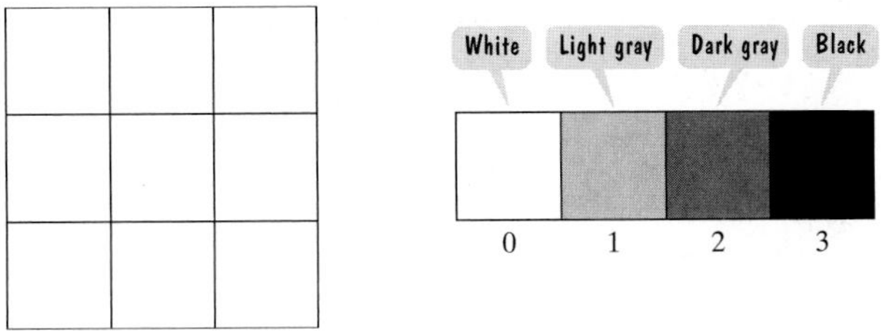


**29.** Write a 3 × 3 matrix that represents a digital photograph of the letter L in dark gray on a light gray background.

**30.** Find a matrix $B$ so that $A + B$ increases the contrast of the letter L by changing the dark gray to black and the light gray to white.

**31.** An automobile dealership sells three models of cars at its three outlets. The inventory of models at each store is given by the following matrix.

| | Model $X$ | Model $Y$ | Model $Z$ | |
|---|---|---|---|---|
| **Outlet 1** | 12 | 7 | 6 | |
| **Outlet 2** | 20 | 8 | 10 | $= A$ |
| **Outlet 3** | 7 | 2 | 3 | |

The next matrix gives the wholesale and retail prices for each model.

| | Wholesale Price | Retail Price | |
|---|---|---|---|
| **Model $X$** | 16,000 | 19,000 | |
| **Model $Y$** | 12,000 | 15,000 | $= B$ |
| **Model $Z$** | 14,000 | 18,500 | |

**a.** Calculate the product $AB$.

**b.** Describe what the matrix $AB$ represents and interpret the elements.

**c.** What is the wholesale value of the cars at outlet 1?

**d.** What is the retail value of the cars at outlet 2?

**e.** If outlet 3 sells all of the inventory in matrix A, what is the profit for that branch of the dealership?

## 9.4

*In Exercises 32–33, find the products $AB$ and $BA$ to determine whether $B$ is the multiplicative inverse of $A$.*

**32.** $A = \begin{bmatrix} 2 & 7 \\ 1 & 4 \end{bmatrix}, \quad B = \begin{bmatrix} 4 & -7 \\ -1 & 3 \end{bmatrix}$

**33.** $A = \begin{bmatrix} 1 & 0 & 0 \\ 0 & 2 & -7 \\ 0 & -1 & 4 \end{bmatrix}, \quad B = \begin{bmatrix} 1 & 0 & 0 \\ 0 & 4 & 7 \\ 0 & 1 & 2 \end{bmatrix}$

*In Exercises 34–37, find $A^{-1}$. Check that $AA^{-1} = I$ and $A^{-1}A = I$.*

**34.** $A = \begin{bmatrix} 1 & -1 \\ -2 & 3 \end{bmatrix}$

**35.** $A = \begin{bmatrix} 0 & 1 \\ 5 & 3 \end{bmatrix}$

**36.** $A = \begin{bmatrix} 1 & 0 & -2 \\ 2 & 1 & 0 \\ 1 & 0 & -3 \end{bmatrix}$

**37.** $A = \begin{bmatrix} 1 & 3 & -2 \\ 4 & 13 & -7 \\ 5 & 16 & -8 \end{bmatrix}$

*In Exercises 38–39,*

**a.** *Write each linear system as a matrix equation in the form $AX = B$.*

**b.** *Solve the system using the inverse of the coefficient matrix.*

**38.** $\begin{aligned} x + y + 2z &= 7 \\ y + 3z &= -2 \\ 3x \quad\quad - 2z &= 0 \end{aligned}$

The inverse of $\begin{bmatrix} 1 & 1 & 2 \\ 0 & 1 & 3 \\ 3 & 0 & -2 \end{bmatrix}$ is $\begin{bmatrix} -2 & 2 & 1 \\ 9 & -8 & -3 \\ -3 & 3 & 1 \end{bmatrix}$.

**39.** $\begin{aligned} x - y + 2z &= 12 \\ y - z &= -5 \\ x \quad\quad + 2z &= 10 \end{aligned}$

The inverse of $\begin{bmatrix} 1 & -1 & 2 \\ 0 & 1 & -1 \\ 1 & 0 & 2 \end{bmatrix}$ is $\begin{bmatrix} 2 & 2 & -1 \\ -1 & 0 & 1 \\ -1 & -1 & 1 \end{bmatrix}$.

**40.** Use the coding-matrix, $A = \begin{bmatrix} 3 & 2 \\ 4 & 3 \end{bmatrix}$ and its inverse $A^{-1} = \begin{bmatrix} 3 & -2 \\ -4 & 3 \end{bmatrix}$ to encode and then decode the word RULE.

## 9.5

*In Exercises 41–46, evaluate each determinant.*

**41.** $\begin{vmatrix} 3 & 2 \\ -1 & 5 \end{vmatrix}$

**42.** $\begin{vmatrix} -2 & -3 \\ -4 & -8 \end{vmatrix}$

**43.** $\begin{vmatrix} 2 & 4 & -3 \\ 1 & -1 & 5 \\ -2 & 4 & 0 \end{vmatrix}$

**44.** $\begin{vmatrix} 4 & 7 & 0 \\ -5 & 6 & 0 \\ 3 & 2 & -4 \end{vmatrix}$

**45.** $\begin{vmatrix} 1 & 1 & 0 & 2 \\ 0 & 3 & 2 & 1 \\ 0 & -2 & 4 & 0 \\ 0 & 3 & 0 & 1 \end{vmatrix}$

**46.** $\begin{vmatrix} 2 & 2 & 2 & 2 \\ 0 & 2 & 2 & 2 \\ 0 & 0 & 2 & 2 \\ 0 & 0 & 0 & 2 \end{vmatrix}$

*In Exercises 47–50, use Cramer's rule to solve each system.*

**47.** $x - 2y = 8$
$3x + 2y = -1$

**48.** $7x + 2y = 0$
$2x + y = -3$

**49.** $x + 2y + 2z = 5$
$2x + 4y + 7z = 19$
$-2x - 5y - 2z = 8$

**50.** $2x + y = -4$
$y - 2z = 0$
$3x - 2z = -11$

**51.** Use the quadratic function $y = ax^2 + bx + c$ to model the following data:

| **$x$ (Age of a Driver)** | **$y$ (Average Number of Automobile Accidents per Day in the United States)** |
|---|---|
| 20 | 400 |
| 40 | 150 |
| 60 | 400 |

Use Cramer's rule to determine values for $a$, $b$, and $c$. Then use the model to write a statement about the average number of automobile accidents in which 30-year-olds and 50-year-olds are involved daily.

## Chapter 9 Test

*In Exercises 1–2, solve each system of equations using matrices.*

**1.** $x + 2y - z = -3$
$2x - 4y + z = -7$
$-2x + 2y - 3z = 4$

**2.** $x - 2y + z = 2$
$2x - y - z = 1$

*In Exercises 3–6, let*

$$A = \begin{bmatrix} 3 & 1 \\ 1 & 0 \\ 2 & 1 \end{bmatrix}, \quad B = \begin{bmatrix} 1 & -1 \\ 2 & 1 \end{bmatrix}, \quad \text{and} \quad C = \begin{bmatrix} 1 & 2 \\ -1 & 3 \end{bmatrix}.$$

*Carry out the indicated operations.*

**3.** $2B + 3C$

**4.** $AB$

**5.** $C^{-1}$

**6.** $BC - 3B$

**7.** If $A = \begin{bmatrix} 1 & 2 & 2 \\ 2 & 3 & 3 \\ 1 & -1 & -2 \end{bmatrix}$ and $B = \begin{bmatrix} -3 & 2 & 0 \\ 7 & -4 & 1 \\ -5 & 3 & -1 \end{bmatrix}$,

show that $B$ is the inverse of $A$.

**8.** Consider the system

$$3x + 5y = 9$$
$$2x - 3y = -13.$$

**a.** Express the system in the form $AX = B$, where $A$, $X$, and $B$ are appropriate matrices.

**b.** Find $A^{-1}$, the inverse of the coefficient matrix.

**c.** Use $A^{-1}$ to solve the given system.

**9.** Evaluate: $\begin{vmatrix} 4 & -1 & 3 \\ 0 & 5 & -1 \\ 5 & 2 & 4 \end{vmatrix}$.

**10.** Solve for $x$ only using Cramer's rule:

$$3x + y - 2z = -3$$
$$2x + 7y + 3z = 9$$
$$4x - 3y - z = 7.$$

## Cumulative Review Exercises (Chapters 1–9)

*Solve each equation or inequality in Exercises 1–6.*

**1.** $2x^2 = 4 - x$

**2.** $5x + 8 \le 7(1 + x)$

**3.** $\sqrt{2x + 4} - \sqrt{x + 3} - 1 = 0$

**4.** $3x^3 + 8x^2 - 15x + 4 = 0$

**5.** $e^{2x} - 14e^x + 45 = 0$

**6.** $\log_3 x + \log_3 (x + 2) = 1$

**7.** Use matrices to solve this system.

$$\begin{aligned} x - y + z &= 17 \\ 2x + 3y + z &= 8 \\ -4x + y + 5z &= -2 \end{aligned}$$

**8.** Solve for $y$ using Cramer's rule.

$$\begin{aligned} x - 2y + z &= 7 \\ 2x + y - z &= 0 \\ 3x + 2y - 2z &= -2 \end{aligned}$$

**9.** If $f(x) = \sqrt{4x - 7}$, find $f^{-1}(x)$.

**10.** Graph: $f(x) = \dfrac{x}{x^2 - 16}$.

**11.** Use the graph of $f(x) = 4x^4 - 4x^3 - 25x^2 + x + 6$ shown in the figure to factor the polynomial completely.

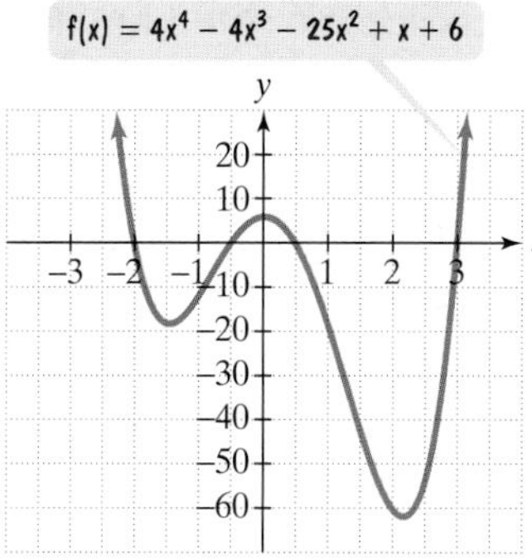


**12.** Graph $y = \log_2 x$ and $y = \log_2 (x + 1)$ in the same rectangular coordinate system.

**13.** Use the exponential decay model $A = A_0 e^{kt}$ to solve this problem. A radioactive substance has a half-life of 40 days. There are initially 900 grams of the substance.

**a.** Find the decay model for this substance.

**b.** How much of the substance will remain after 10 days?

**14.** Multiply the matrices: $\begin{bmatrix} 1 & -1 & 0 \\ 2 & 1 & 3 \end{bmatrix}\begin{bmatrix} 4 & -1 \\ 2 & 0 \\ 1 & 1 \end{bmatrix}$.

**15.** Find the partial fraction decomposition of

$$\frac{3x^2 + 17x - 38}{(x - 3)(x - 2)(x + 2)}.$$

*In Exercises 16–19, graph each equation, function, or inequality in the rectangular coordinate system.*

**16.** $y = -\frac{2}{3}x - 1$

**17.** $3x - 5y < 15$

**18.** $f(x) = x^2 - 2x - 3$

**19.** $(x - 1)^2 + (y + 1)^2 = 9$

**20.** Use synthetic division to divide $x^3 - 6x + 4$ by $x - 2$.

**21.** Graph: $y = 2 \sin 2\pi x, \quad 0 \le x \le 2$.

**22.** Find the exact value of $\cos\left[\tan^{-1}\left(-\frac{4}{3}\right)\right]$.

**23.** Verify the identity: $\dfrac{\cos 2x}{\cos x - \sin x} = \cos x + \sin x$.

**24.** Solve on the interval $[0, 2\pi)$: $\cos^2 x + \sin x + 1 = 0$.

**25.** If $\mathbf{v} = -6\mathbf{i} + 5\mathbf{j}$ and $\mathbf{w} = -7\mathbf{i} + 3\mathbf{j}$, find $4\mathbf{w} - 5\mathbf{v}$.

# Conic Sections and Analytic Geometry

# Chapter 10

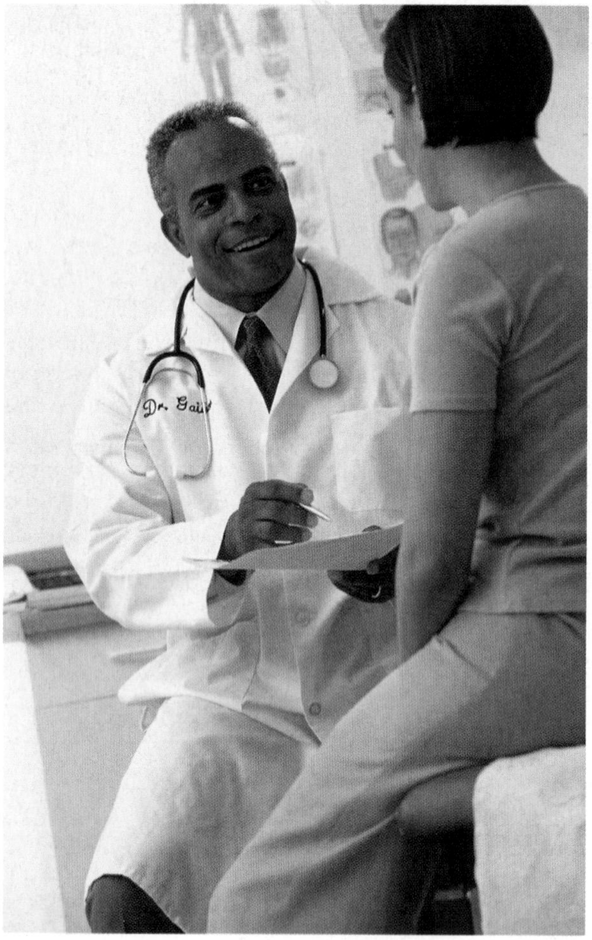


From ripples in water to the path on which humanity journeys through space, certain curves occur naturally throughout the universe. Over 2000 years ago the ancient Greeks studied these curves, called *conic sections*, without regard to their immediate usefulness simply because the study elicited ideas that were exciting, challenging, and interesting. The ancient Greeks could not have imagined the applications of these curves in the twenty-first century. Overwhelmed by the choices on satellite television? Blame it on a conic section! In this chapter, we use the rectangular coordinate system to study the conic sections and the mathematics behind their surprising applications.

One minute you're in class, enjoying the lecture. Then a sharp pain radiates down your side. The next minute you're being diagnosed with, of all things, a kidney stone. It took your cousin six weeks to recover from kidney stone surgery, but your doctor assures you there is nothing to worry about. A new procedure, based on a curve that looks like the cross section of a football, will dissolve the stone painlessly and let you return to class in a day or two. How can this be?

# SECTION 10.1 *The Ellipse*

## Objectives

1. Graph ellipses centered at the origin.
2. Write equations of ellipses in standard form.
3. Graph ellipses not centered at the origin.
4. Solve applied problems involving ellipses.

You took on a summer job driving a truck, delivering books that were ordered online. You're an avid reader, so just being around books sounded appealing. However, now you're feeling a bit shaky driving the truck for the first time. It's 10 feet wide and 9 feet high; compared to your compact car, it feels like you're behind the wheel of a tank. Up ahead you see a sign at the semielliptical entrance to a tunnel: Caution! Tunnel is 10 Feet High at Center Peak. Then you see another sign: Caution! Tunnel is 40 Feet Wide. Will your truck clear the opening of the tunnel's archway?

The mathematics of your world is present in the movements of planets, bridge and tunnel construction, navigational systems used to keep track of a ship's location, manufacture of lenses for telescopes, and even a procedure for disintegrating kidney stones. The mathematics behind these applications involves conic sections. **Conic sections** are curves that result from the intersection of a right circular cone and a plane. Figure 10.1 illustrates the four conic sections: the circle, the ellipse, the parabola, and the hyperbola.

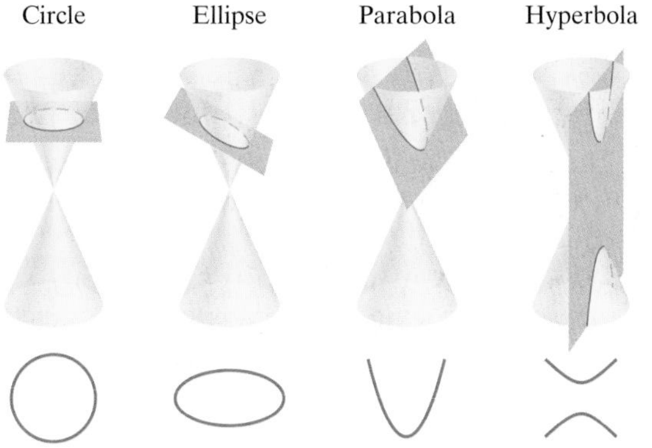


**Figure 10.1** Obtaining the conic sections by intersecting a plane and a cone

In this section, we study the symmetric oval-shaped curve known as the ellipse. We will use a geometric definition for an ellipse to derive its equations. With these equations, we will determine if your delivery truck will clear the tunnel's entrance.

## Definition of an Ellipse

Figure 10.2 illustrates how to draw an ellipse. Place pins at two fixed points, each of which is called a focus (plural: foci). If the ends of a fixed length of string are fastened to the pins and we draw the string taut with a pencil, the path traced by the pencil will be an ellipse. Notice that the sum of the distances of the pencil point from the foci remains constant because the length of the string is fixed. This procedure for drawing an ellipse illustrates its geometric definition.

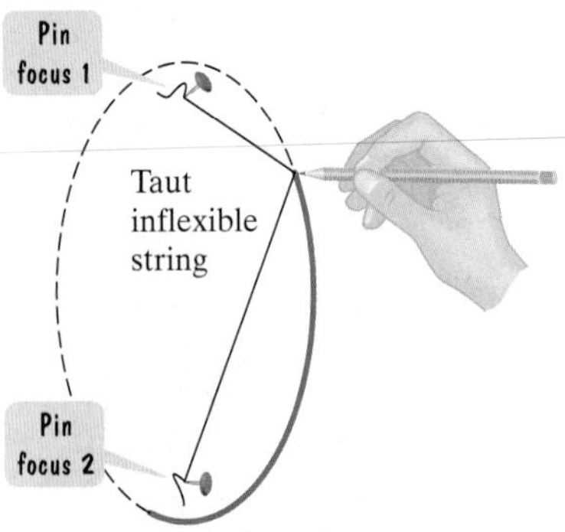


**Figure 10.2** Drawing an ellipse

### Definition of an Ellipse

An **ellipse** is the set of all points in a plane the sum of whose distances from two fixed points, $F_1$ and $F_2$, is constant (see Figure 10.3). These two fixed points are called the **foci** (plural of **focus**). The midpoint of the segment connecting the foci is the **center** of the ellipse.

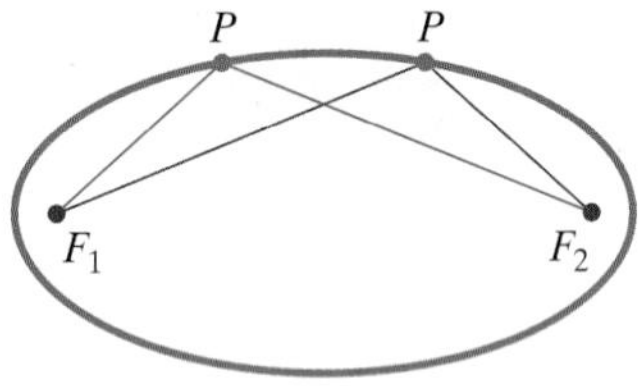


**Figure 10.3**

Figure 10.4 illustrates that an ellipse can be elongated horizontally or vertically. The line through the foci intersects the ellipse at two points, called the **vertices** (singular: **vertex**). The line segment that joins the vertices is the **major axis**. Notice that the midpoint of the major axis is the center of the ellipse. The line segment whose endpoints are on the ellipse that is perpendicular to the major axis at the center is the **minor axis** of the ellipse.

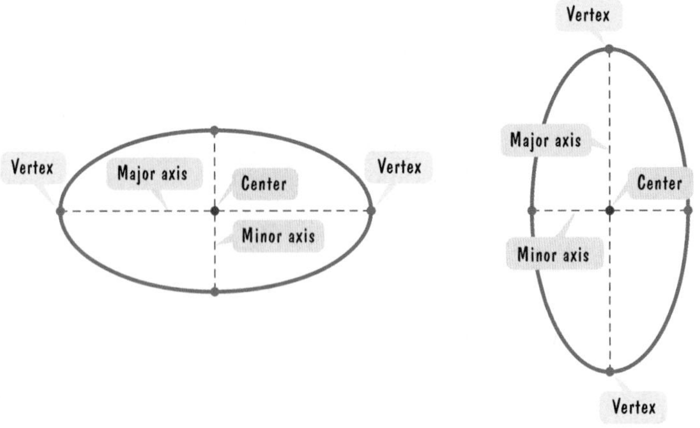


**Figure 10.4** Horizontal and vertical elongations of an ellipse

## Standard Form of the Equation of an Ellipse

The rectangular coordinate system gives us a unique way of describing an ellipse. It enables us to translate an ellipse's geometric definition into an algebraic equation.

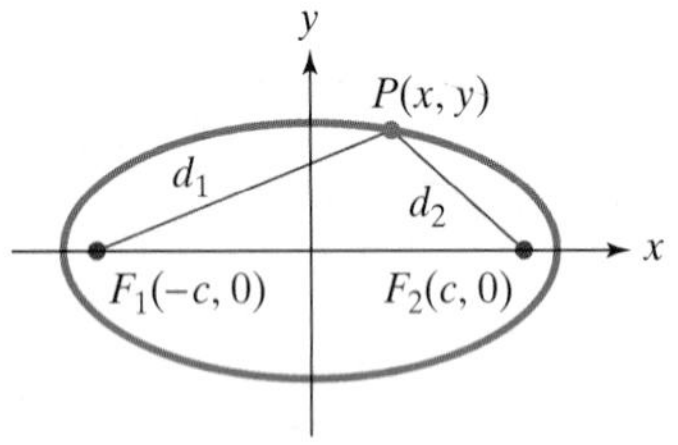


**Figure 10.5**

We start with Figure 10.5 to obtain an ellipse's equation. We've placed an ellipse that is elongated horizontally into a rectangular coordinate system. The foci are on the $x$-axis at $(-c, 0)$ and $(c, 0)$, as in Figure 10.5. In this way, the center of the ellipse is at the origin. We let $(x, y)$ represent the coordinates of any point on the ellipse.

What does the definition of an ellipse tell us about the point $(x, y)$ in Figure 10.5? For any point $(x, y)$ on the ellipse, the sum of the distances to the two foci, $d_1 + d_2$, must be constant. We denote this constant by $2a$. Thus, the point $(x, y)$ is on the ellipse if and only if

**Discovery**

Perform the algebra mentioned on the right by eliminating radicals and obtaining the equation shown.

$$d_1 + d_2 = 2a.$$

$$\sqrt{(x+c)^2 + y^2} + \sqrt{(x-c)^2 + y^2} = 2a \quad \text{Use the distance formula.}$$

After eliminating radicals and simplifying, we obtain

$$(a^2 - c^2)x^2 + a^2y^2 = a^2(a^2 - c^2).$$

Look at the triangle in Figure 10.5. Notice that the distance from $F_1$ to $F_2$ is $2c$ and $2c < d_1 + d_2$. Equivalently, $2c < 2a$ and $c < a$. Consequently, $a^2 - c^2 > 0$. For convenience, let $b^2 = a^2 - c^2$. Substituting $b^2$ for $a^2 - c^2$ in the preceding equation, we obtain

$$b^2x^2 + a^2y^2 = a^2b^2$$

$$\frac{b^2x^2}{a^2b^2} + \frac{a^2y^2}{a^2b^2} = \frac{a^2b^2}{a^2b^2} \quad \text{Divide both sides by } a^2b^2.$$

$$\frac{x^2}{a^2} + \frac{y^2}{b^2} = 1 \quad \text{Simplify.}$$

This last equation is the **standard form of the equation of an ellipse.** There are two such equations, one for a horizontal major axis and one for a vertical major axis.

## Standard Forms of the Equations of an Ellipse

The **standard form of the equation of an ellipse** with center at the origin, and major and minor axes of lengths $2a$ and $2b$ (where $a$ and $b$ are positive, and $a^2 > b^2$) is

$$\frac{x^2}{a^2} + \frac{y^2}{b^2} = 1 \quad \text{or} \quad \frac{x^2}{b^2} + \frac{y^2}{a^2} = 1.$$

Figure 10.6 illustrates that the vertices are on the major axis, $a$ units from the center. The foci are are on the major axis, $c$ units from the center. For both equations, $b^2 = a^2 - c^2$.

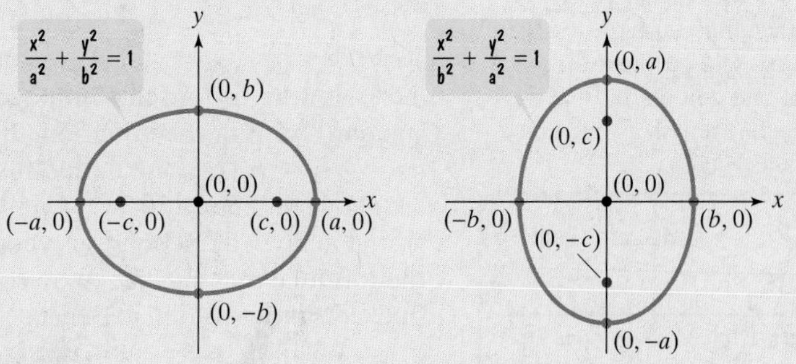


**Figure 10.6** **(a)** Major axis is horizontal with length $2a$. **(b)** Major axis is vertical with length $2a$.

## Using the Standard Form of the Equation of an Ellipse

We can use the standard form of an ellipse's equation to graph the ellipse. Although the definition of the ellipse is given in terms of its foci, the foci are not part of the graph. A complete graph of an ellipse can be obtained without graphing the foci.

**1** Graph ellipses centered at the origin.

### EXAMPLE 1 Graphing an Ellipse Centered at the Origin

Graph and locate the foci: $\frac{x^2}{9} + \frac{y^2}{4} = 1.$

**Solution** The given equation is the standard form of an ellipse's equation with $a^2 = 9$ and $b^2 = 4$.

$$\frac{x^2}{9} + \frac{y^2}{4} = 1$$

$a^2 = 9$. This is the larger of the two numbers in the denominator.

$b^2 = 4$. This is the smaller of the two numbers in the denominator.

Because the denominator of the $x^2$ term is greater than the denominator of the $y^2$ term, the major axis is horizontal. Based on the standard form of the equation, we know the vertices are $(-a, 0)$ and $(a, 0)$. Because $a^2 = 9$, $a = 3$. Thus, the vertices are $(-3, 0)$ and $(3, 0)$, shown in Figure 10.7.

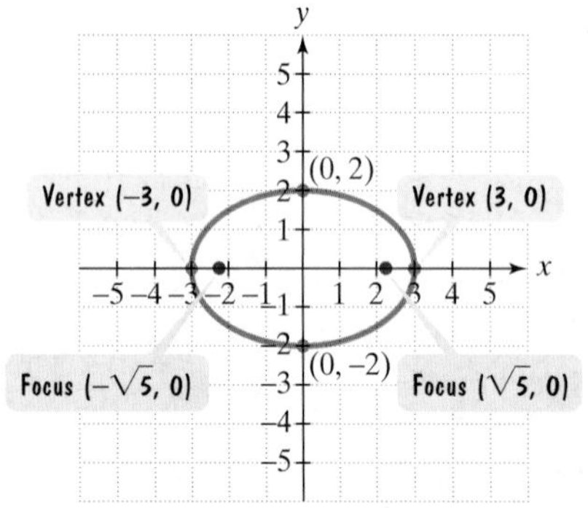


**Figure 10.7** The graph of $\frac{x^2}{9} + \frac{y^2}{4} = 1$

Now let us find the endpoints of the vertical minor axis. According to the standard form of the equation, these endpoints are $(0, -b)$ and $(0, b)$. Because $b^2 = 4$, $b = 2$. Thus, the endpoints of the minor axis are $(0, -2)$ and $(0, 2)$. They are shown in Figure 10.7.

Finally, we find the foci, which are located at $(-c, 0)$ and $(c, 0)$. We can use the formula $b^2 = a^2 - c^2$ to do so. We know that $a^2 = 9$ and $b^2 = 4$; we need to find $c^2$ in order to find $c$. Because $b^2 = a^2 - c^2$, we obtain

$$c^2 = a^2 - b^2 = 9 - 4 = 5.$$

Because $c^2 = 5$, $c = \sqrt{5}$. The foci, $(-c, 0)$ and $(c, 0)$, are located at $(-\sqrt{5}, 0)$ and $(\sqrt{5}, 0)$. They are shown in Figure 10.7.

### Technology

We graph $\frac{x^2}{9} + \frac{y^2}{4} = 1$ with a graphing utility by solving for $y$ and defining two functions.

$$\frac{y^2}{4} = 1 - \frac{x^2}{9}$$

$$y^2 = 4\left(1 - \frac{x^2}{9}\right)$$

$$y = \pm 2\sqrt{1 - \frac{x^2}{9}}$$

Enter

$y_1 = 2$ [√] (1 [−] $x$ [∧] 2 [÷] 9)

and

$$y_2 = -y_1.$$

To see the true shape of the ellipse, use the [ZOOM SQUARE] feature so that one unit on the $x$-axis is the same length as one unit on the $y$-axis.

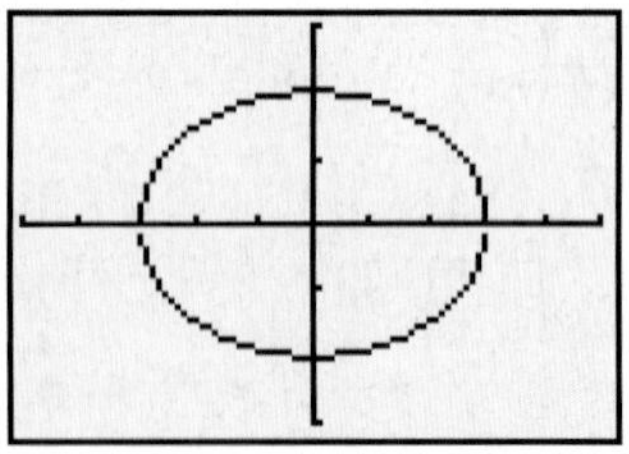

You can sketch the ellipse in Figure 10.7 by locating endpoints on the major and minor axes.

$$\frac{x^2}{3^2} + \frac{y^2}{2^2} = 1$$

Endpoints of the major axis are 3 units to the right and left of the center.

Endpoints of the minor axis are 2 units up and down from the center.

**Check Point 1** Graph and locate the foci: $\frac{x^2}{36} + \frac{y^2}{9} = 1.$

## EXAMPLE 2 Graphing an Ellipse Centered at the Origin

Graph and locate the foci: $25x^2 + 16y^2 = 400.$

**Solution** We begin by expressing the equation in standard form. Because we want 1 on the right side, we divide both sides by 400.

$$\frac{25x^2}{400} + \frac{16y^2}{400} = \frac{400}{400}$$

$$\frac{x^2}{16} + \frac{y^2}{25} = 1$$

$b^2 = 16$. This is the smaller of the two numbers in the denominator.

$a^2 = 25$. This is the larger of the two numbers in the denominator.

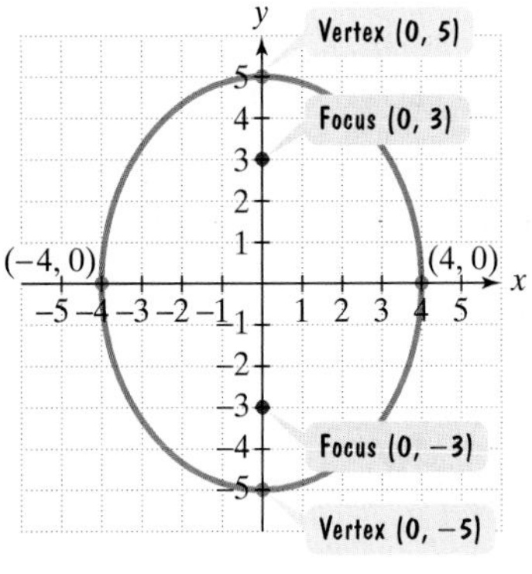


**Figure 10.8** The graph of $\frac{x^2}{16} + \frac{y^2}{25} = 1$

The equation is the standard form of an ellipse's equation with $a^2 = 25$ and $b^2 = 16$. Because the denominator of the $y^2$ term is greater than the denominator of the $x^2$ term, the major axis is vertical. Based on the standard form of the equation, we know the vertices are $(0, -a)$ and $(0, a)$. Because $a^2 = 25$, $a = 5$. Thus, the vertices are $(0, -5)$ and $(0, 5)$, shown in Figure 10.8.

Now let us find the endpoints of the horizontal minor axis. According to the standard form of the equation, these endpoints are $(-b, 0)$ and $(b, 0)$. Because $b^2 = 16$, $b = 4$. Thus, the endpoints of the minor axis are $(-4, 0)$ and $(4, 0)$. They are shown in Figure 10.8.

Finally, we find the foci, which are located at $(0, -c)$ and $(0, c)$. We can use the formula $b^2 = a^2 - c^2$ to do so. We know that $a^2 = 25$ and $b^2 = 16$; we need to find $c^2$ in order to find $c$. Because $b^2 = a^2 - c^2$, we obtain

$$c^2 = a^2 - b^2 = 25 - 16 = 9.$$

Because $c^2 = 9$, $c = 3$. The foci, $(0, -c)$ and $(0, c)$, are located at $(0, -3)$ and $(0, 3)$. They are shown in Figure 10.8. You can sketch the ellipse in Figure 10.8 by locating endpoints on the major and minor axes:

$$\frac{x^2}{4^2} + \frac{y^2}{5^2} = 1.$$

Endpoints of the minor axis are 4 units to the right and left of the center.

Endpoints of the major axis are 5 units up and down from the center.

**Check Point 2** Graph and locate the foci: $16x^2 + 9y^2 = 144$.

**2** Write equations of ellipses in standard form.

In Examples 1 and 2, we used the equation of an ellipse to find its foci and vertices. In the next example, we reverse this procedure.

## EXAMPLE 3 Finding the Equation of an Ellipse from Its Foci and Vertices

Find the standard form of the equation of an ellipse with foci at $(-1, 0)$ and $(1, 0)$ and vertices $(-2, 0)$ and $(2, 0)$.

**Solution** Because the foci are located at $(-1, 0)$ and $(1, 0)$, on the $x$-axis, the major axis is horizontal. The center of the ellipse is midway between the foci, located at $(0, 0)$. Thus, the form of the equation is

$$\frac{x^2}{a^2} + \frac{y^2}{b^2} = 1.$$

We need to determine the values for $a^2$ and $b^2$. The distance from the center $(0, 0)$ to either vertex, $(-2, 0)$ or $(2, 0)$, is 2. Thus, $a = 2$.

$$\frac{x^2}{2^2} + \frac{y^2}{b^2} = 1 \quad \text{or} \quad \frac{x^2}{4} + \frac{y^2}{b^2} = 1$$

We must still find $b^2$. The distance from the center $(0, 0)$ to either focus, $(-1, 0)$ or $(1, 0)$, is 1, so $c = 1$. Because $b^2 = a^2 - c^2$, we have

$$b^2 = 2^2 - 1^2 = 4 - 1 = 3.$$

Substituting 3 for $b^2$ in the last equation gives us the standard form of the ellipse's equation. The equation is

$$\frac{x^2}{4} + \frac{y^2}{3} = 1.$$

**Check Point 3** Find the standard form of the equation of an ellipse with foci at $(-2, 0)$ and $(2, 0)$ and vertices $(-3, 0)$ and $(3, 0)$.

**3** Graph ellipses not centered at the origin.

## Translations of Ellipses

Despite the fact that an ellipse is not the graph of a function, its graph can be translated in the same manner as that of a function. Figure 10.9 illustrates that the graphs of

$$\frac{(x-h)^2}{a^2}+\frac{(y-k)^2}{b^2}=1 \quad \text{and} \quad \frac{x^2}{a^2}+\frac{y^2}{b^2}=1$$

have the same size and shape. However, the graph of the first equation is centered at $(h, k)$ rather than at the origin.

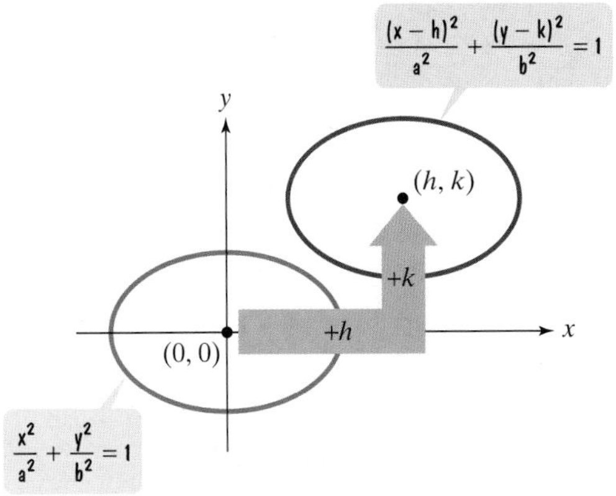


**Figure 10.9** Translating an ellipse's graph

Table 10.1 gives the standard forms of equations of ellipses centered at $(h, k)$. Figure 10.10 shows their graphs.

**Table 10.1 Standard Forms of Equations of Ellipses Centered at $(h, k)$**

| Equation | Center | Major Axis | Foci | Vertices |
|---|---|---|---|---|
| $\frac{(x-h)^2}{a^2}+\frac{(y-k)^2}{b^2}=1$, $a^2>b^2$ and $b^2=a^2-c^2$ | $(h, k)$ | Parallel to the $x$-axis, horizontal | $(h-c, k)$ $(h+c, k)$ | $(h-a, k)$ $(h+a, k)$ |
| $\frac{(x-h)^2}{b^2}+\frac{(y-k)^2}{a^2}=1$, $a^2>b^2$ and $b^2=a^2-c^2$ | $(h, k)$ | Parallel to the $y$-axis, vertical | $(h, k-c)$ $(h, k+c)$ | $(h, k-a)$ $(h, k+a)$ |

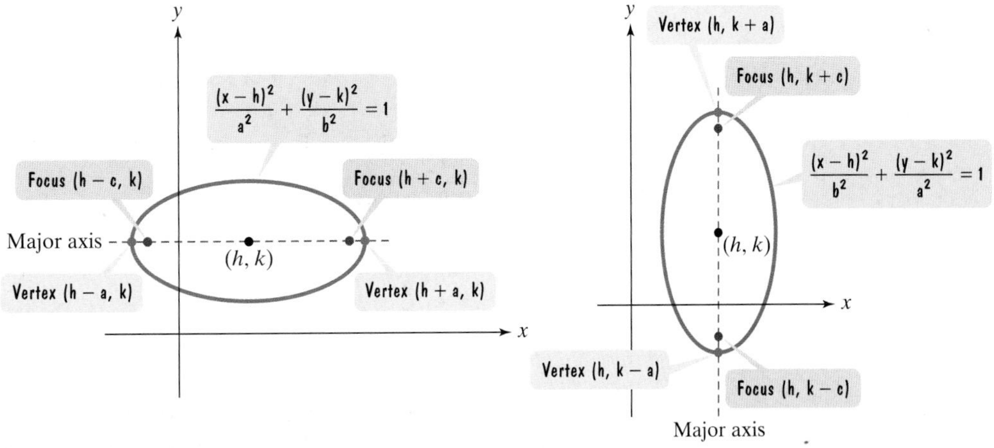


**Figure 10.10** Graphs of ellipses centered at $(h, k)$

## EXAMPLE 4 Graphing an Ellipse Centered at $(h, k)$

Graph: $\frac{(x-1)^2}{4} + \frac{(y+2)^2}{9} = 1$. Where are the foci located?

**Solution** In order to graph the ellipse, we need to know its center $(h, k)$. In the standard forms of equations centered at $(h, k)$, $h$ is the number subtracted from $x$ and $k$ is the number subtracted from $y$.

$$\frac{(x-1)^2}{4} + \frac{(y-(-2))^2}{9} = 1$$

This is $(x-h)^2$ with $h = 1$.

This is $(y-k)^2$ with $k = -2$.

We see that $h = 1$ and $k = -2$. Thus, the center of the ellipse, $(h, k)$, is $(1, -2)$. We can graph the ellipse by locating endpoints on the major and minor axes. To do this, we must identify $a^2$ and $b^2$.

$$\frac{(x-1)^2}{4} + \frac{(y+2)^2}{9} = 1$$

$b^2 = 4$. This is the smaller of the two numbers in the denominator.

$a^2 = 9$. This is the larger of the two numbers in the denominator.

The larger number is under the expression involving $y$. This means that the major axis is vertical and parallel to the $y$-axis. Because $a^2 = 9$, $a = 3$ and the vertices lie three units above and below the center. Also, because $b^2 = 4$, $b = 2$ and the endpoints of the minor axis lie two units to the right and left of the center. We categorize these observations as follows:

| Center | Vertices | Endpoints of Minor Axis |
|---|---|---|
| $(1, -2)$ | $(1, -2 + 3) = (1, 1)$ | $(1 + 2, -2) = (3, -2)$ |
| | $(1, -2 - 3) = (1, -5)$ | $(1 - 2, -2) = (-1, -2)$ |

Using the center and these four points, we can sketch the ellipse shown in Figure 10.11.

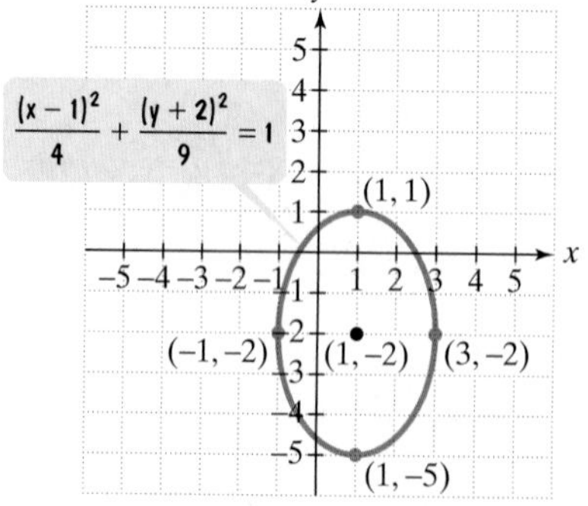


**Figure 10.11** The graph of an ellipse centered at $(1, -2)$

With $b^2 = a^2 - c^2$, we have $4 = 9 - c^2$, and $c^2 = 5$. So the foci are located $\sqrt{5}$ units above and below the center, at $(1, -2 + \sqrt{5})$ and $(1, -2 - \sqrt{5})$.

**Check Point 4** Graph: $\frac{(x+1)^2}{9} + \frac{(y-2)^2}{4} = 1$. Where are the foci located?

In some cases, it is necessary to convert the equation of an ellipse to standard form by completing the square on $x$ and $y$. For example, suppose that we wish to graph the ellipse whose equation is

$$9x^2 + 4y^2 - 18x + 16y - 11 = 0.$$

Because we plan to complete the square on both $x$ and $y$, we need to rearrange terms so that

- $x$ terms are arranged in descending order.
- $y$ terms are arranged in descending order.
- the constant term appears on the right.

$$9x^2 + 4y^2 - 18x + 16y - 11 = 0$$ This is the given equation.

$$(9x^2 - 18x) + (4y^2 + 16y) = 11$$ Group terms and add 11 to both sides.

$$9(x^2 - 2x + \square) + 4(y^2 + 4y + \square) = 11$$ To complete the square, coefficients of $x^2$ and $y^2$ must be 1. Factor out 9 and 4, respectively.

$$9(x^2 - 2x + 1) + 4(y^2 + 4y + 4) = 11 + 9 + 16$$ Complete each square by adding the square of half the coefficient of $x$ and $y$, respectively.

$$9(x-1)^2 + 4(y+2)^2 = 36$$ Factor.

$$\frac{9(x-1)^2}{36} + \frac{4(y+2)^2}{36} = \frac{36}{36}$$ Divide both sides by 36.

$$\frac{(x-1)^2}{4} + \frac{(y+2)^2}{9} = 1$$ Simplify.

**Study Tip**

When completing the square, remember that changes made on the left side of the equation must also be made on the right side of the equation.

The equation is now in standard form. This is precisely the form of the equation that we graphed in Example 4.

**4** Solve applied problems involving ellipses.

## Applications

Ellipses have many applications. German scientist Johannes Kepler (1571–1630) showed that the planets in our solar system move in elliptical orbits, with the sun at a focus. Earth satellites also travel in elliptical orbits, with Earth at a focus.

One intriguing aspect of the ellipse is that a ray of light or a sound wave originating at one focus will be reflected by the ellipse exactly to the other focus. A whispering gallery is an elliptical room with an elliptical, dome-shaped ceiling. People standing at the foci can whisper and hear each other quite clearly, while persons in other locations in the room cannot hear them. Statuary Hall in the U.S. Capitol Building is elliptical. President John Quincy Adams, while a member of the House of Representatives, was aware of this acoustical phenomenon. He situated his desk at a focal point of the elliptical ceiling, easily eavesdropping on the private conversations of other House members located near the other focus.

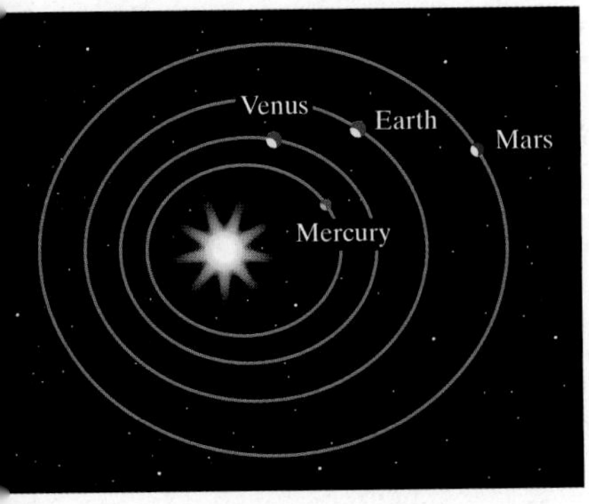

Planets move in elliptical orbits.

The elliptical reflection principle is used in a procedure for disintegrating kidney stones. The patient is placed within a device that is elliptical in shape. The patient is at one focus, while ultrasound waves from the other focus hit the walls and are reflected to the kidney stone. The convergence of the ultrasound waves at the kidney stone causes vibrations that shatter it into fragments. The small pieces can then be passed painlessly through the patient's system. The patient recovers in days, as opposed to up to six weeks if surgery is used instead.

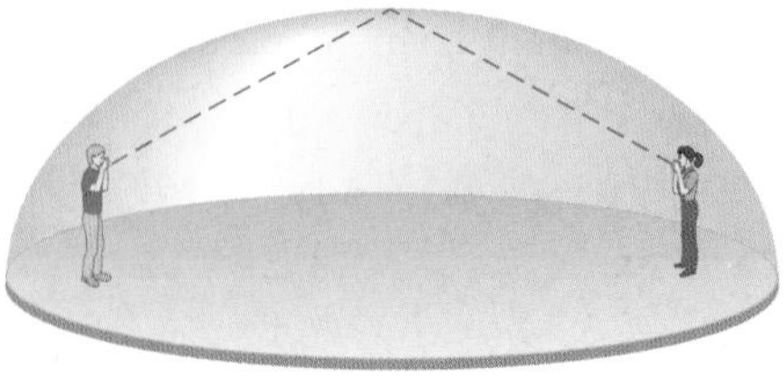

Whispering in an elliptical dome

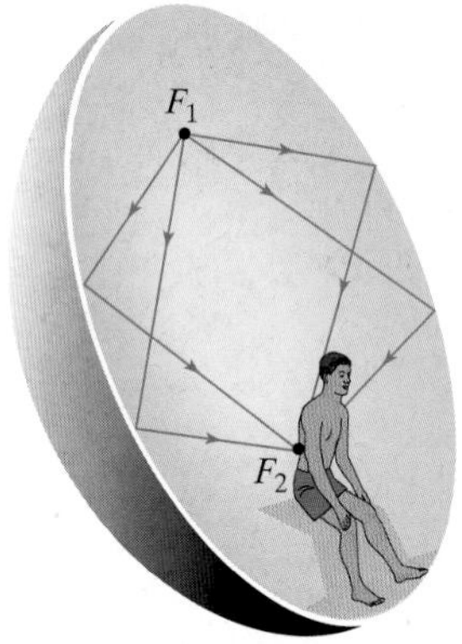


Disintegrating kidney stones

Ellipses are often used for supporting arches of bridges and in tunnel construction. This application forms the basis of our next example.

## EXAMPLE 5 An Application Involving an Ellipse

A semielliptical archway over a one-way road has a height of 10 feet and a width of 40 feet (see Figure 10.12). Your truck has a width of 10 feet and a height of 9 feet. Will your truck clear the opening of the archway?

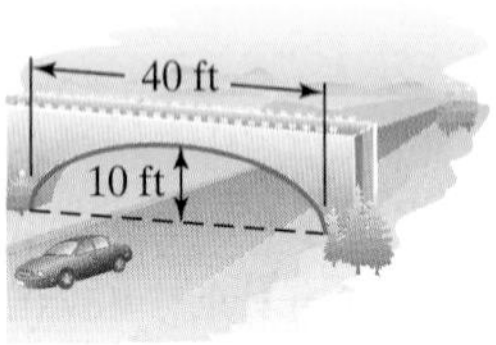


**Figure 10.12** A semielliptical archway

**Solution** To determine the clearance, we must find the height of the archway 5 feet from the center. If that height is 9 feet or less, the truck will not clear the opening.

In Figure 10.13, we've constructed a coordinate system with the $x$-axis on the ground and the origin at the center of the archway. Also shown is the truck, whose height is 9 feet.

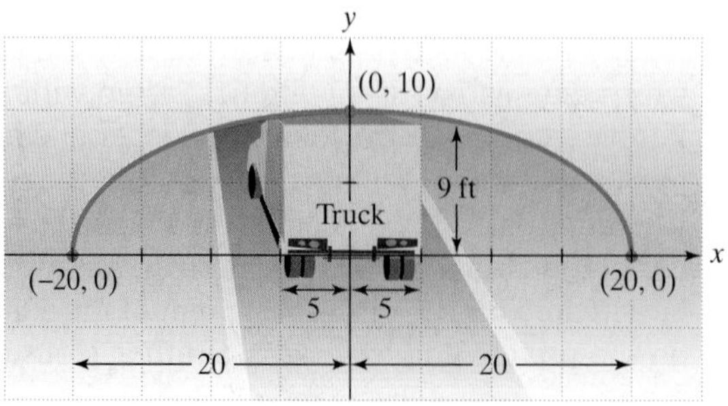


**Figure 10.13**

## Halley's Comet

Halley's Comet has an elliptical orbit with the sun at one focus. The comet returns every 76.3 years. The first recorded sighting was in 239 B.C. It was last seen in 1986. At that time, spacecraft went close to the comet, measuring its nucleus to be 7 miles long and 4 miles wide. By 2024, Halley's Comet will have reached the farthest point in its elliptical orbit before returning to be next visible from Earth in 2062.

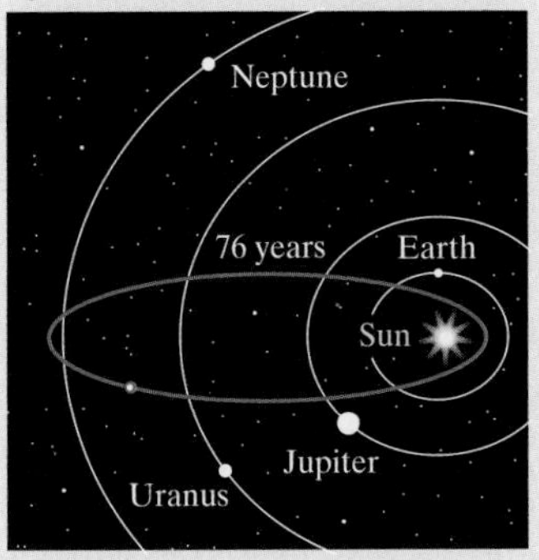


The elliptical orbit of Halley's Comet

Using the equation $\frac{x^2}{a^2} + \frac{y^2}{b^2} = 1$, we can express the equation of the blue archway in Figure 10.13 as $\frac{x^2}{20^2} + \frac{y^2}{10^2} = 1$ or $\frac{x^2}{400} + \frac{y^2}{100} = 1$.

As shown in Figure 10.13, the edge of the 10-foot-wide truck corresponds to $x = 5$. We find the height of the archway 5 feet from the center by substituting 5 for $x$ and solving for $y$.

$$\frac{5^2}{400} + \frac{y^2}{100} = 1$$ Substitute 5 for x.

$$\frac{25}{400} + \frac{y^2}{100} = 1$$

$$\frac{1}{16} + \frac{y^2}{100} = 1$$

$$1600\left(\frac{1}{16} + \frac{y^2}{100}\right) = 1600(1)$$ Clear fractions by multiplying both sides by 1600.

$$100 + 16y^2 = 1600$$ Use the distributive property and simplify.

$$16y^2 = 1500$$ Subtract 100 from both sides.

$$y^2 = \frac{1500}{16}$$ Divide both sides by 16.

$$y = \sqrt{\frac{1500}{16}}$$ Take only the positive square root. The archway is above the x-axis and y is nonnegative.

$$\approx 9.68$$

Thus, the height of the archway 5 feet from the center is approximately 9.68 feet. Because your truck's height is 9 feet, there is enough room for the truck to clear the archway.

**Check Point 5** Will a truck that is 12 feet wide and has a height of 9 feet clear the opening of the archway described in Example 5?

# EXERCISE SET 10.1

## Practice Exercises

*In Exercises 1–16, graph each ellipse and locate the foci.*

**1.** $\frac{x^2}{16} + \frac{y^2}{4} = 1$

**2.** $\frac{x^2}{25} + \frac{y^2}{16} = 1$

**3.** $\frac{x^2}{9} + \frac{y^2}{36} = 1$

**4.** $\frac{x^2}{16} + \frac{y^2}{49} = 1$

**5.** $\frac{x^2}{25} + \frac{y^2}{64} = 1$

**6.** $\frac{x^2}{49} + \frac{y^2}{36} = 1$

**7.** $\frac{x^2}{49} + \frac{y^2}{81} = 1$

**8.** $\frac{x^2}{64} + \frac{y^2}{100} = 1$

**9.** $25x^2 + 4y^2 = 100$

**10.** $9x^2 + 4y^2 = 36$

**11.** $4x^2 + 16y^2 = 64$

**12.** $16x^2 + 9y^2 = 144$

**13.** $25x^2 + 9y^2 = 225$

**14.** $4x^2 + 25y^2 = 100$

**15.** $x^2 + 2y^2 = 8$

**16.** $12x^2 + 4y^2 = 36$

*In Exercises 17–20, find the standard form of the equation of each ellipse and give the location of its foci.*

**17.**

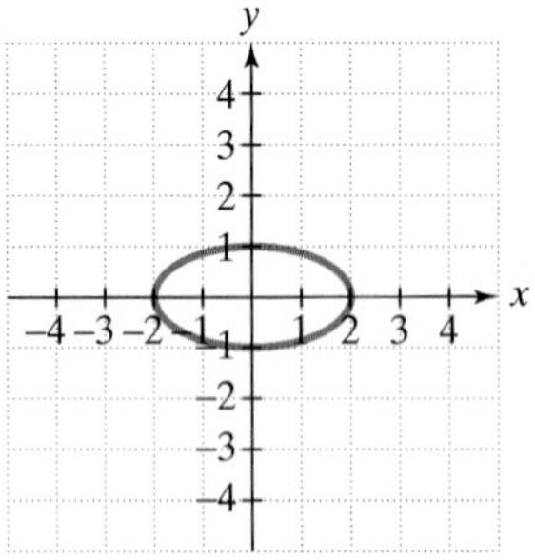


**18.**

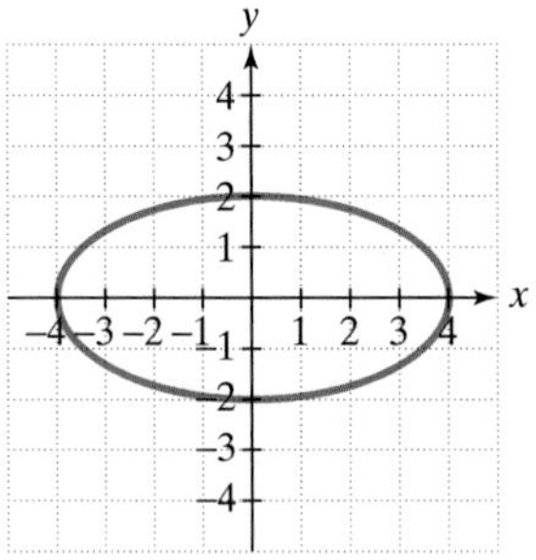


**19.**

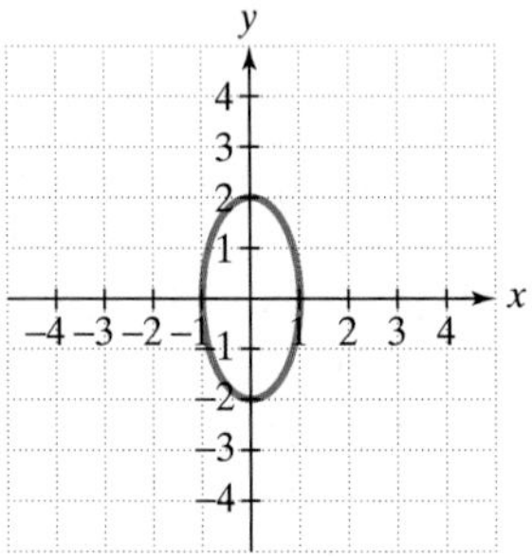


**20.**

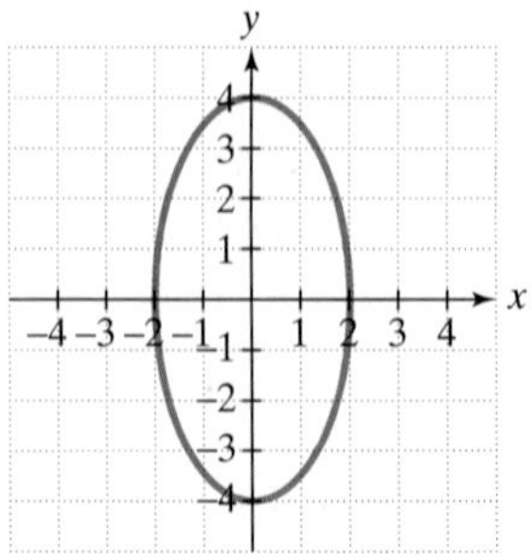


*In Exercises 21–30, find the standard form of the equation of each ellipse centered at the origin satisfying the given conditions.*

**21.** Foci: $(-5, 0), (5, 0)$; vertices: $(-8, 0), (8, 0)$

**22.** Foci: $(-2, 0), (2, 0)$; vertices: $(-6, 0), (6, 0)$

**23.** Foci: $(0, -4), (0, 4)$; vertices: $(0, -7), (0, 7)$

**24.** Foci: $(0, -3), (0, 3)$; vertices: $(0, -4), (0, 4)$

**25.** Foci: $(-2, 0), (2, 0)$; $y$-intercepts: $-3$ and $3$

**26.** Foci: $(0, -2), (0, 2)$; $x$-intercepts: $-2$ and $2$

**27.** Major axis horizontal with length 8; length of minor axis = 4

**28.** Major axis horizontal with length 12; length of minor axis = 6

**29.** Major axis vertical with length 10; length of minor axis = 4

**30.** Major axis vertical with length 20; length of minor axis = 10

*In Exercises 31–42 graph each ellipse and give the location of its foci.*

**31.** $\frac{(x-2)^2}{9} + \frac{(y-1)^2}{4} = 1$

**32.** $\frac{(x-1)^2}{16} + \frac{(y+2)^2}{9} = 1$

**33.** $(x+3)^2 + 4(y-2)^2 = 16$

**34.** $(x-3)^2 + 9(y+2)^2 = 18$

**35.** $\frac{(x-4)^2}{9} + \frac{(y+2)^2}{25} = 1$

**36.** $\frac{(x-3)^2}{9} + \frac{(y+1)^2}{16} = 1$

**37.** $\frac{x^2}{25} + \frac{(y-2)^2}{36} = 1$

**38.** $\frac{(x-4)^2}{4} + \frac{y^2}{25} = 1$

**39.** $\frac{(x+3)^2}{9} + (y-2)^2 = 1$

**40.** $\frac{(x+2)^2}{16} + (y-3)^2 = 1$

**41.** $9(x-1)^2 + 4(y+3)^2 = 36$

**42.** $36(x+4)^2 + (y+3)^2 = 36$

*In Exercises 43–48, convert each equation to standard form by completing the square on x and y. Then graph the ellipse and give the location of its foci.*

**43.** $9x^2 + 25y^2 - 36x + 50y - 164 = 0$

**44.** $4x^2 + 9y^2 - 32x + 36y + 64 = 0$

**45.** $9x^2 + 16y^2 - 18x + 64y - 71 = 0$

**46.** $x^2 + 4y^2 + 10x - 8y + 13 = 0$

**47.** $4x^2 + y^2 + 16x - 6y - 39 = 0$

**48.** $4x^2 + 25y^2 - 24x + 100y + 36 = 0$

## Application Exercises

**49.** Will a truck that is 8 feet wide carrying a load that reaches 7 feet above the ground clear the semielliptical arch on the one-way road that passes under the bridge shown in the figure?

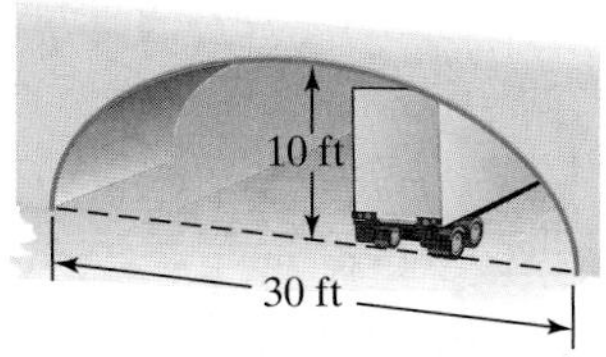


**50.** A semielliptic archway has a height of 20 feet and a width of 50 feet, as shown in the figure. Can a truck 14 feet high and 10 feet wide drive under the archway without going into the other lane?

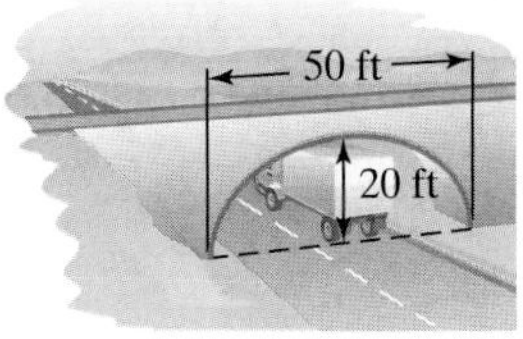


**51.** The elliptical ceiling in Statuary Hall in the U.S. Capitol Building is 96 feet long and 23 feet tall.

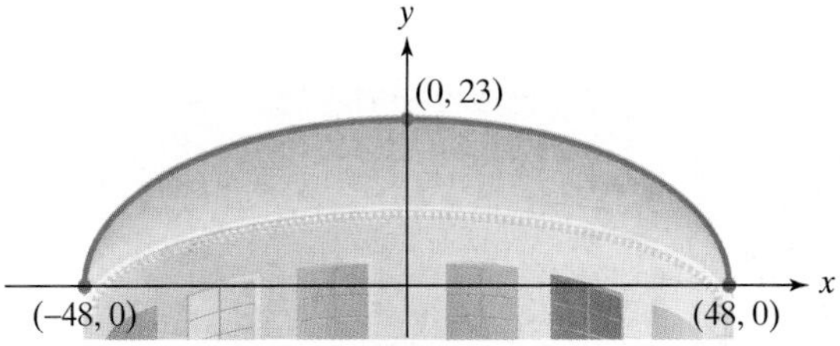


a. Using the rectangular coordinate system in the figure shown, write the standard form of the equation of the elliptical ceiling.

b. John Quincy Adams discovered that he could overhear the conversations of opposing party leaders near the left side of the chamber if he situated his desk at the focus at the right side of the chamber. How far from the center of the ellipse along the major axis did Adams situate his desk? (Round to the nearest foot.)

**52.** If an elliptical whispering room has a height of 30 feet and a width of 100 feet, where should two people stand if they would like to whisper back and forth and be heard?

## Writing in Mathematics

**53.** What is an ellipse?

**54.** Describe how to graph $\frac{x^2}{25} + \frac{y^2}{16} = 1$.

**55.** Describe how to locate the foci for $\frac{x^2}{25} + \frac{y^2}{16} = 1$.

**56.** Describe one similarity and one difference between the graphs of $\frac{x^2}{25} + \frac{y^2}{16} = 1$ and $\frac{x^2}{16} + \frac{y^2}{25} = 1$.

**57.** Describe one similarity and one difference between the graphs of $\frac{x^2}{25} + \frac{y^2}{16} = 1$ and $\frac{(x-1)^2}{25} + \frac{(y-1)^2}{16} = 1$.

**58.** An elliptipool is an elliptical pool table with only one pocket. A pool shark places a ball on the table, hits it in what appears to be a random direction, and yet it bounces off the edge, falling directly into the pocket. Explain why this happens.

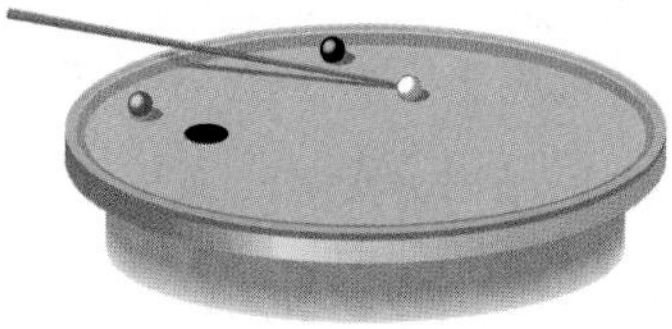

## Technology Exercises

**59.** Use a graphing utility to graph any five of the ellipses that you graphed by hand in Exercises 1–16.

**60.** Use a graphing utility to graph any three of the ellipses that you graphed by hand in Exercises 31–42. First solve the given equation for $y$ by using the square root method. Enter each of the two resulting equations to produce each half of the ellipse.

**61.** Use a graphing utility to graph any one of the ellipses that you graphed by hand in Exercises 43–48. Write the equation as a quadratic equation in $y$ and use the quadratic formula to solve for $y$. Enter each of the two resulting equations to produce each half of the ellipse.

**62.** Write an equation for the path of each of the following elliptical orbits. Then use a graphing utility to graph the two ellipses in the same viewing rectangle. Can you see why early astronomers had difficulty detecting that these orbits are ellipses rather than circles?

| | |
|---|---|
| Earth's orbit: | Length of major axis: 186 million miles |
| | Length of minor axis: 185.8 million miles |
| Mars's orbit: | Length of major axis: 283.5 million miles |
| | Length of minor axis: 278.5 million miles |

## Critical Thinking Exercises

**63.** Find the standard form of the equation of an ellipse with vertices at $(0, -6)$ and $(0, 6)$, passing through $(2, -4)$.

**64.** An Earth satellite has an elliptical orbit described by

$$\frac{x^2}{(5000)^2} + \frac{y^2}{(4750)^2} = 1.$$

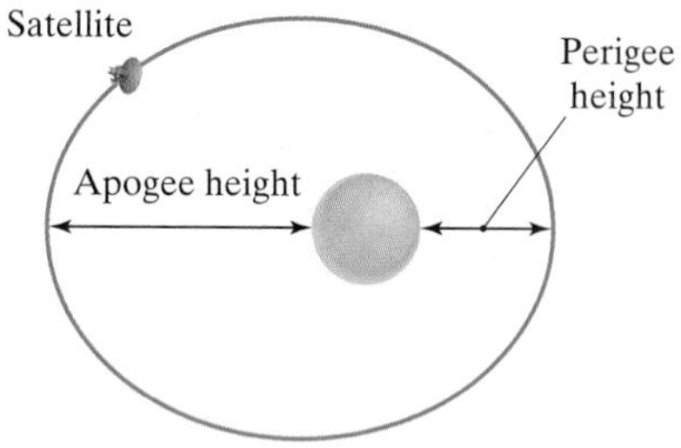


(All units are in miles.) The coordinates of the center of Earth are (16, 0).

**a.** The perigee of the satellite's orbit is the point that is nearest Earth's center. If the radius of Earth is approximately 4000 miles, find the distance of the perigee above Earth's surface.

**b.** The apogee of the satellite's orbit is the point that is the greatest distance from Earth's center. Find the distance of the apogee above Earth's surface.

**65.** The equation of the red ellipse in the following figure is

$$\frac{x^2}{25} + \frac{y^2}{9} = 1.$$

Write the equation for each circle shown in the figure.

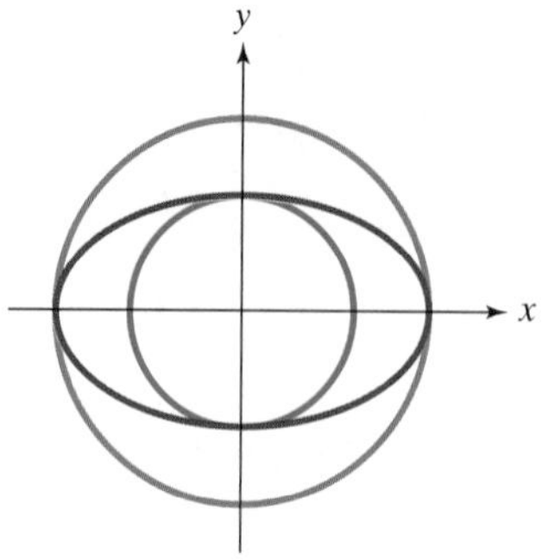


**66.** What happens to the shape of the graph of $\frac{x^2}{a^2} + \frac{y^2}{b^2} = 1$ as $\frac{c}{a}$ is close to zero?

## SECTION 10.2 The Hyperbola

### Objectives

1. Locate a hyperbola's vertices and foci.
2. Write equations of hyperbolas in standard form.
3. Graph hyperbolas centered at the origin.
4. Graph hyperbolas not centered at the origin.
5. Solve applied problems involving hyperbolas.

St. Mary's Cathedral

Conic sections are often used to create unusual architectural designs. The top of St. Mary's Cathedral in San Francisco is a 2135-cubic-foot dome with walls rising 200 feet above the floor and supported by four massive concrete pylons that extend 94 feet into the ground. Cross sections of the roof are parabolas and hyperbolas. In this section, we study the curve with two parts known as the hyperbola.

**Figure 10.14** Casting hyperbolic shadows

## Definition of a Hyperbola

Figure 10.14 shows a cylindrical lampshade casting two shadows on a wall. These shadows indicate the distinguishing feature of hyperbolas: Their graphs contain two disjoint parts called **branches**. Although each branch might look like a parabola, its shape is actually quite different.

The definition of a hyperbola is similar to that of the ellipse. For the ellipse, the *sum* of the distances to the foci is a constant. By contrast, for a hyperbola the *difference* of the distances to the foci is a constant.

**Definition of a Hyperbola**

A **hyperbola** is the set of points in a plane the difference of whose distances from two fixed points (called foci) is a constant.

Figure 10.15 illustrates the two branches of a hyperbola's graph. The line through the foci intersects the hyperbola at two points, called the **vertices**. The line segment that joins the vertices is the **transverse axis**. The midpoint of the transverse axis is the **center** of the hyperbola. Notice that the center lies midway between the vertices, as well as midway between the foci.

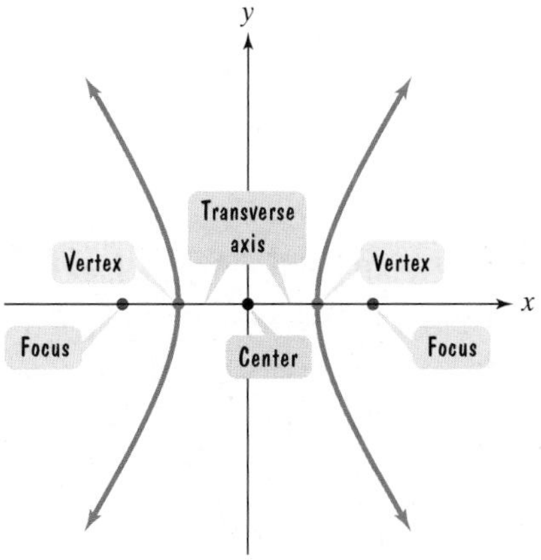


**Figure 10.15** The two branches of a hyperbola

## Standard Form of the Equation of a Hyperbola

The rectangular coordinate system enables us to translate a hyperbola's geometric definition into an algebraic equation. Figure 10.16 is our starting point for obtaining an equation. We place the foci on the $x$-axis at the points $(-c, 0)$ and $(c, 0)$. Note that the center of this hyperbola is at the origin. We let $(x, y)$ represent the coordinates of any point on the hyperbola.

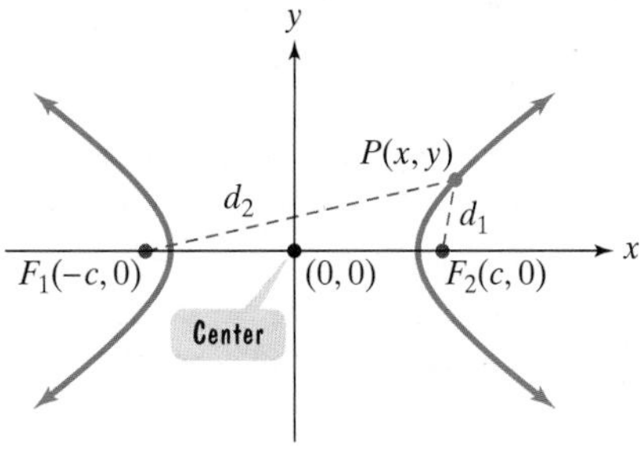


**Figure 10.16**

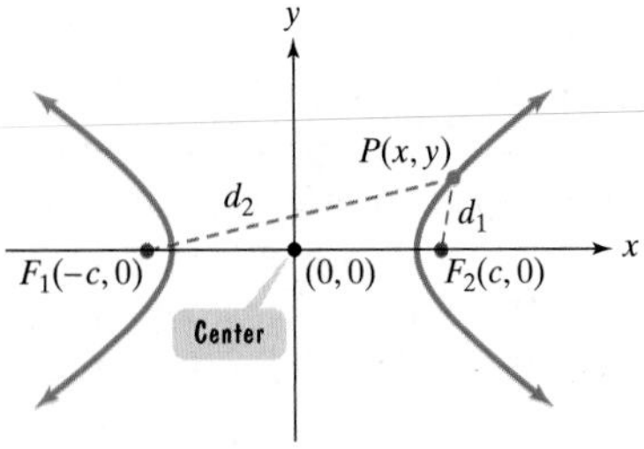


Figure 10.16, shown again so that you do not have to turn back a page

What does the definition of a hyperbola tell us about the point $(x, y)$ in Figure 10.16? For any point $(x, y)$ on the hyperbola, the absolute value of the difference of the distances from the two foci, $|d_2 - d_1|$, must be constant. We denote this constant by $2a$, just as we did for the ellipse. Thus, the point $(x, y)$ is on the hyperbola if and only if

$$|d_2 - d_1| = 2a$$

$$\left|\sqrt{(x+c)^2 + (y-0)^2} - \sqrt{(x-c)^2 + (y-0)^2}\right| = 2a$$ Use the distance formula.

After eliminating radicals and simplifying, we obtain

$$(c^2 - a^2)x^2 - a^2y^2 = a^2(c^2 - a^2).$$

For convenience, let $b^2 = c^2 - a^2$. Substituting $b^2$ for $c^2 - a^2$ in the preceding equation, we obtain

$$b^2x^2 - a^2y^2 = a^2b^2$$

$$\frac{b^2x^2}{a^2b^2} - \frac{a^2y^2}{a^2b^2} = \frac{a^2b^2}{a^2b^2}$$ Divide both sides by $a^2b^2$.

$$\frac{x^2}{a^2} - \frac{y^2}{b^2} = 1$$ Simplify.

This last equation is called the **standard form of the equation of a hyperbola.** There are two such equations. The first is for a hyperbola in which the transverse axis lies on the $x$-axis. The second is for a hyperbola in which the transverse axis lies on the $y$-axis.

### Standard Forms of the Equations of a Hyperbola

The **standard form of the equation of a hyperbola** with center at the origin is

$$\frac{x^2}{a^2} - \frac{y^2}{b^2} = 1 \quad \text{or} \quad \frac{y^2}{a^2} - \frac{x^2}{b^2} = 1.$$

Figure 10.17 illustrates that for the equation on the left, the transverse axis lies on the $x$-axis. For the equation on the right, the transverse axis lies on the $y$-axis. The vertices are $a$ units from the center and the foci are $c$ units from the center. For both equations, $b^2 = c^2 - a^2$.

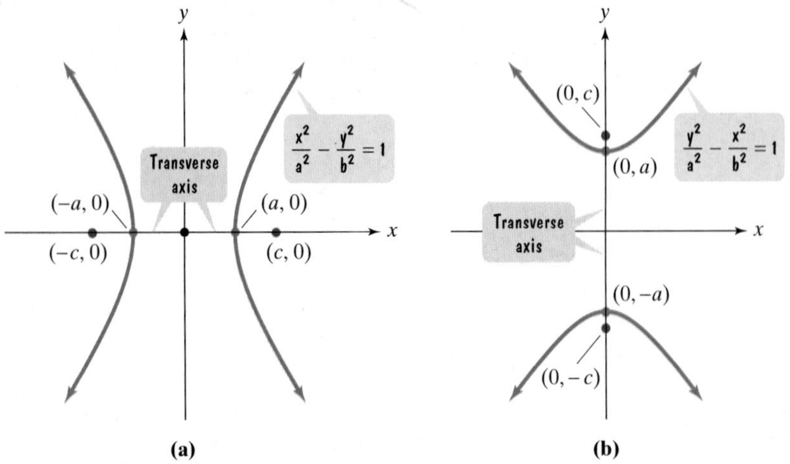


**Figure 10.17** **(a)** Transverse axis lies on the $x$-axis. **(b)** Transverse axis lies on the $y$-axis.

1 Locate a hyperbola's vertices and foci.

## Using the Standard Form of the Equation of a Hyperbola

We can use the standard form of the equation of a hyperbola to find its vertices and locate its foci. Because the vertices are $a$ units from the center, begin by identifying $a^2$ in the equation. In the standard form of a hyperbola's equation, **$a^2$ is the number under the variable whose term is preceded by a plus sign** $(+)$. If the $x^2$ term is preceded by a plus sign, the transverse axis lies along the $x$-axis. Thus, the vertices are $a$ units to the right and left of the origin. If the $y^2$ term is preceded by a plus sign, the transverse axis lies along the $y$-axis. Thus, the vertices are $a$ units above and below the origin.

We know that the foci are $c$ units from the center. The substitution that we used to derive the hyperbola's equation, $b^2 = c^2 - a^2$, is needed to locate the foci when $a^2$ and $b^2$ are known. To find $c^2$, and then $c$, we will use an equivalent form of $b^2 = c^2 - a^2$, namely $c^2 = a^2 + b^2$.

### EXAMPLE 1 Finding Vertices and Foci from a Hyperbola's Equation

Find the vertices and locate the foci for each of the following hyperbolas with the given equation.

**a.** $\dfrac{x^2}{16} - \dfrac{y^2}{9} = 1$ **b.** $\dfrac{y^2}{9} - \dfrac{x^2}{16} = 1$

**Solution** Both equations are in standard form. We begin by identifying $a^2$ and $b^2$ in each equation.

**a.** The first equation is in the form $\dfrac{x^2}{a^2} - \dfrac{y^2}{b^2} = 1$.

$$\frac{x^2}{16} - \frac{y^2}{9} = 1$$

$a^2 = 16$. This is the number in the denominator of the term preceded by a plus sign.

$b^2 = 9$. This is the number in the denominator of the term preceded by a minus sign.

Because the $x^2$ term is preceded by a plus sign, the transverse axis lies along the $x$-axis. Thus, the vertices are $a$ units to the *right* and *left* of the origin. Based on the standard form of the equation, we know the vertices are $(-a, 0)$ and $(a, 0)$. Because $a^2 = 16$, $a = 4$. Thus, the vertices are $(-4, 0)$ and $(4, 0)$, shown in Figure 10.18.

We use $c^2 = a^2 + b^2$ to find the foci, which are located at $(-c, 0)$ and $(c, 0)$. We know that $a^2 = 16$ and $b^2 = 9$; we need to find $c^2$ in order to find $c$.

$$c^2 = a^2 + b^2 = 16 + 9 = 25$$

Because $c^2 = 25$, $c = 5$. The foci are located at $(-5, 0)$ and $(5, 0)$. They are shown in Figure 10.18.

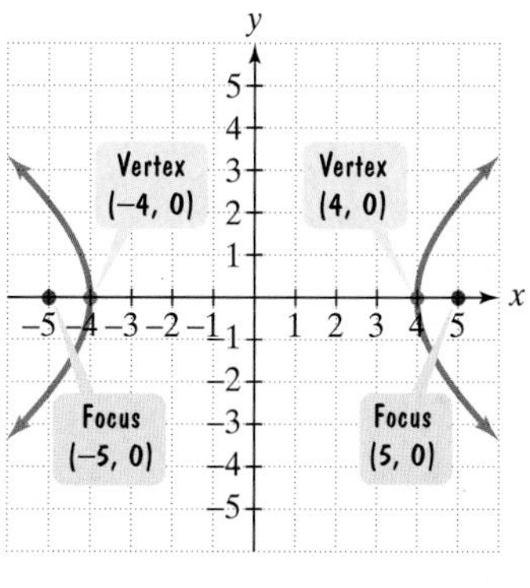


**Figure 10.18** The graph of $\dfrac{x^2}{16} - \dfrac{y^2}{9} = 1$

**b.** The second given equation is in the form $\dfrac{y^2}{a^2} - \dfrac{x^2}{b^2} = 1$.

$$\frac{y^2}{9} - \frac{x^2}{16} = 1$$

$a^2 = 9$. This is the number in the denominator of the term preceded by a plus sign.

$b^2 = 16$. This is the number in the denominator of the term preceded by a minus sign.

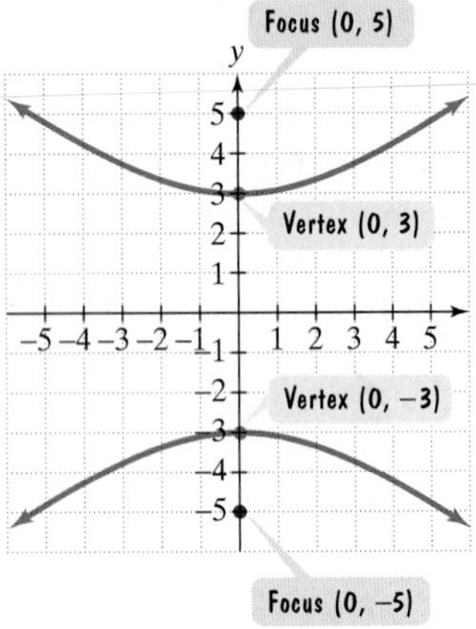


**Figure 10.19** The graph of $\frac{y^2}{9} - \frac{x^2}{16} = 1$

Because the $y^2$ term is preceded by a plus sign, the transverse axis lies along the $y$-axis. Thus, the vertices are $a$ units *above* and *below* the origin. Based on the standard form of the equation, we know the vertices are $(0, -a)$ and $(0, a)$. Because $a^2 = 9$, $a = 3$. Thus, the vertices are $(0, -3)$ and $(0, 3)$, shown in Figure 10.19.

We use $c^2 = a^2 + b^2$ to find the foci, which are located at $(0, -c)$ and $(0, c)$.

$$c^2 = a^2 + b^2 = 9 + 16 = 25$$

Because $c^2 = 25$, $c = 5$. The foci are located at $(0, -5)$ and $(0, 5)$. They are shown in Figure 10.19.

**Check Point 1** Find the vertices and locate the foci for each of the following hyperbolas with the given equation.

**a.** $\frac{x^2}{25} - \frac{y^2}{16} = 1$ **b.** $\frac{y^2}{25} - \frac{x^2}{16} = 1$

**2** Write equations of hyperbolas in standard form.

In Example 1, we used equations of hyperbolas to find their foci and vertices. In the next example, we reverse this procedure.

## EXAMPLE 2 Finding the Equation of a Hyperbola from Its Foci and Vertices

Find the standard form of the equation of a hyperbola with foci at $(0, -3)$ and $(0, 3)$ and vertices $(0, -2)$ and $(0, 2)$, shown in Figure 10.20.

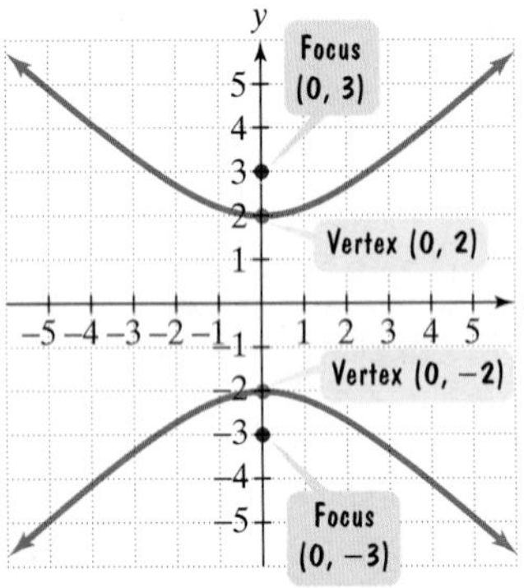


**Figure 10.20**

**Solution** Because the foci are located at $(0, -3)$ and $(0, 3)$, on the $y$-axis, the transverse axis lies on the $y$-axis. The center of the hyperbola is midway between the foci, located at $(0, 0)$. Thus, the form of the equation is

$$\frac{y^2}{a^2} - \frac{x^2}{b^2} = 1.$$

We need to determine the values for $a^2$ and $b^2$. The distance from the center $(0, 0)$ to either vertex, $(0, -2)$ or $(0, 2)$, is 2, so $a = 2$.

$$\frac{y^2}{2^2} - \frac{x^2}{b^2} = 1 \quad \text{or} \quad \frac{y^2}{4} - \frac{x^2}{b^2} = 1$$

We must still find $b^2$. The distance from the center, $(0, 0)$, to either focus, $(0, -3)$ or $(0, 3)$, is 3. Thus, $c = 3$. Because $b^2 = c^2 - a^2$, we have

$$b^2 = 3^2 - 2^2 = 9 - 4 = 5.$$

Substituting 5 for $b^2$ in the last equation gives us the standard form of the hyperbola's equation. The equation is

$$\frac{y^2}{4} - \frac{x^2}{5} = 1.$$

**Check Point 2** Find the standard form of the equation of a hyperbola with foci at $(0, -5)$ and $(0, 5)$ and vertices $(0, -3)$ and $(0, 3)$.

## The Asymptotes of a Hyperbola

As $x$ and $y$ get larger, the two branches of the graph of a hyperbola approach a pair of intersecting straight lines called **asymptotes**. The asymptotes pass through the center of the hyperbola and are helpful in graphing hyperbolas.

Figure 10.21 shows the asymptotes for the graphs of hyperbolas centered at the origin. The asymptotes pass through the corners of a rectangle. Note that the dimensions of this rectangle are $2a$ by $2b$. The line segment of length $2b$ is the **conjugate axis** of the hyperbola and is perpendicular to the transverse axis.

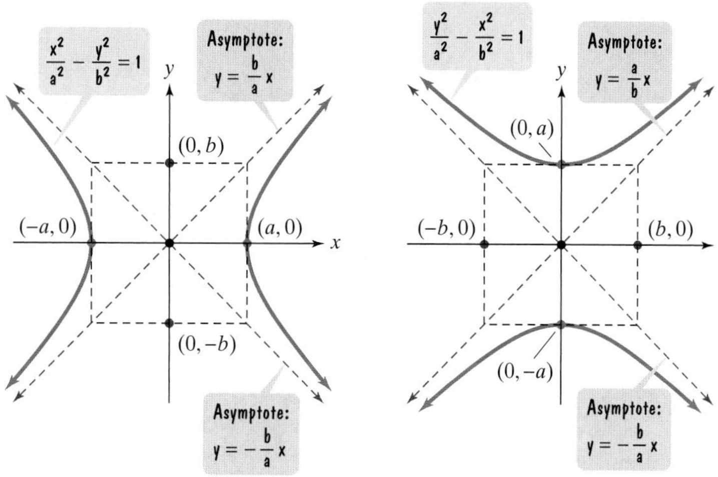


**Figure 10.21** Asymptotes of a hyperbola

### The Asymptotes of a Hyperbola Centered at the Origin

The hyperbola $\frac{x^2}{a^2} - \frac{y^2}{b^2} = 1$ with a horizontal transverse axis has the two asymptotes

$$y = \frac{b}{a}x \quad \text{and} \quad y = -\frac{b}{a}x.$$

The hyperbola $\frac{y^2}{a^2} - \frac{x^2}{b^2} = 1$ with a vertical transverse axis has the two asymptotes

$$y = \frac{a}{b}x \quad \text{and} \quad y = -\frac{a}{b}x.$$

Why are $y = \pm\frac{b}{a}x$ the asymptotes for a hyperbola whose transverse axis is horizontal? The proof can be found in the appendix.

**3** Graph hyperbolas centered at the origin.

## Graphing Hyperbolas Centered at the Origin

Hyperbolas are graphed using vertices and asymptotes.

> **Graphing Hyperbolas**
>
> 1. Locate the vertices.
> 2. Draw the rectangle centered at the origin with sides parallel to the axes, crossing one axis at $\pm a$ and the other at $\pm b$.
> 3. Draw the diagonals of this rectangle and extend them to obtain the asymptotes.
> 4. Draw the two branches of the hyperbola by starting at each vertex and approaching the asymptotes.
>
> The rectangle in step 2 and the asymptotes in step 3 are drawn using dashed lines to show that they are not part of the hyperbola.

### EXAMPLE 3 Graphing a Hyperbola

Graph and locate the foci: $\frac{x^2}{25} - \frac{y^2}{16} = 1$.

**Solution**

**Step 1 Locate the vertices.** The given equation is in the form $\frac{x^2}{a^2} - \frac{y^2}{b^2} = 1$, with $a^2 = 25$ and $b^2 = 16$.

$$\frac{x^2}{25} - \frac{y^2}{16} = 1$$

$a^2 = 25$ $\quad$ $b^2 = 16$

Based on the standard form of the equation with the transverse axis on the $x$-axis, we know that the vertices are $(-a, 0)$ and $(a, 0)$. Because $a^2 = 25$, $a = 5$. Thus, the vertices are $(-5, 0)$ and $(5, 0)$, shown in Figure 10.22.

**Step 2 Draw a rectangle.** Because $a^2 = 25$ and $b^2 = 16$, $a = 5$ and $b = 4$. We construct a rectangle to find the asymptotes, using $-5$ and $5$ on the $x$-axis (the ver-

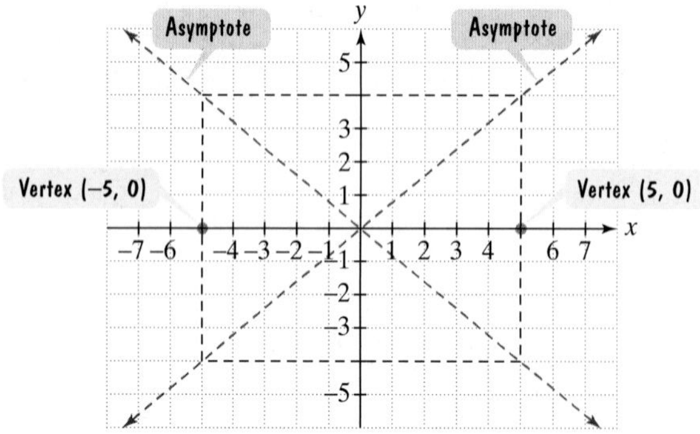


**Figure 10.22** Preparing to graph $\frac{x^2}{25} - \frac{y^2}{16} = 1$

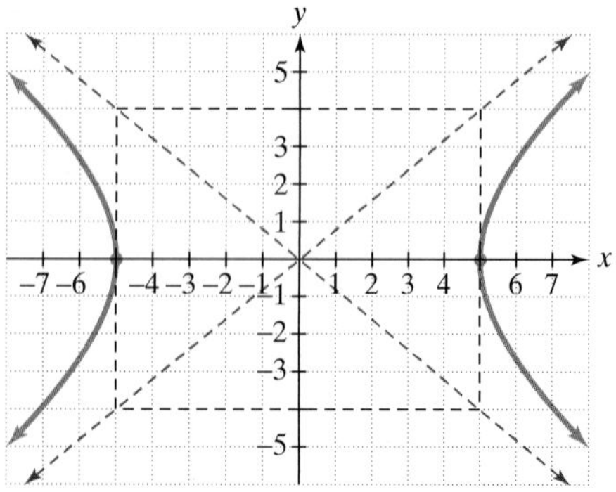


**Figure 10.23** The graph of $\frac{x^2}{25} - \frac{y^2}{16} = 1$

tices are located here) and −4 and 4 on the $y$-axis. The rectangle passes through these four points, shown using dashed lines in Figure 10.22.

**Step 3 Draw extended diagonals for the rectangle to obtain the asymptotes.** We draw dashed lines through the opposite corners of the rectangle, shown in Figure 10.22, to obtain the graph of the asymptotes. Based on the standard form of the hyperbola's equation, the equations for these asymptotes are

$$y = \pm\frac{b}{a}x \quad \text{or} \quad y = \pm\frac{4}{5}x.$$

**Step 4 Draw the two branches of the hyperbola by starting at each vertex and approaching the asymptotes.** The hyperbola is shown in Figure 10.23.

The foci are located at $(-c, 0)$ and $(c, 0)$. We find $c$ using $c^2 = a^2 + b^2$.

$$c^2 = 25 + 16 = 41$$

Because $c^2 = 41$, $c = \sqrt{41}$. The foci are located at $(-\sqrt{41}, 0)$ and $(\sqrt{41}, 0)$, approximately $(-6.4, 0)$ and $(6.4, 0)$.

### Technology

Graph $\frac{x^2}{25} - \frac{y^2}{16} = 1$ by solving for $y$:

$$y_1 = \frac{\sqrt{16x^2 - 400}}{5}$$

$$y_2 = -\frac{\sqrt{16x^2 - 400}}{5} = -y_1.$$

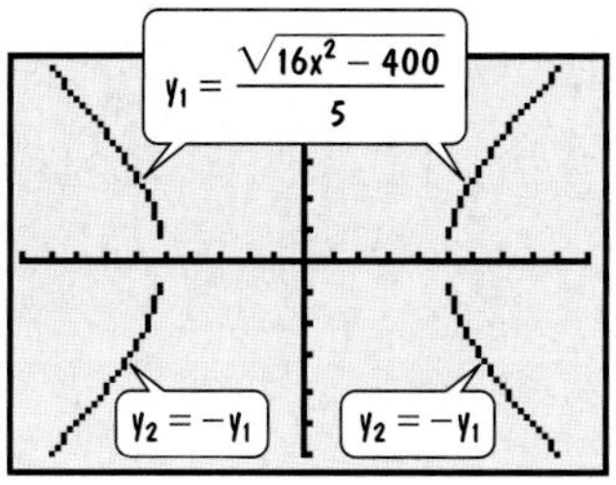


**Check Point 3** Graph and locate the foci: $\frac{x^2}{36} - \frac{y^2}{9} = 1$.

## EXAMPLE 4 Graphing a Hyperbola

Graph and locate the foci: $9y^2 - 4x^2 = 36$.

**Solution** We begin by writing the equation in standard form. The right side should be 1, so we divide both sides by 36.

$$\frac{9y^2}{36} - \frac{4x^2}{36} = \frac{36}{36}$$

$$\frac{y^2}{4} - \frac{x^2}{9} = 1 \qquad \text{Simplify. The right side is now 1.}$$

Now we are ready to use our four-step procedure for graphing hyperbolas.

**Step 1 Locate the vertices.** The equation that we obtained is in the form $\frac{y^2}{a^2} - \frac{x^2}{b^2} = 1$, with $a^2 = 4$ and $b^2 = 9$.

$$\frac{y^2}{4} - \frac{x^2}{9} = 1$$

$a^2 = 4$ $\quad$ $b^2 = 9$

Based on the standard form of the equation with the transverse axis on the $y$-axis, we know that the vertices are $(0, -a)$ and $(0, a)$. Because $a^2 = 4$, $a = 2$. Thus, the vertices are $(0, -2)$ and $(0, 2)$, shown in Figure 10.24.

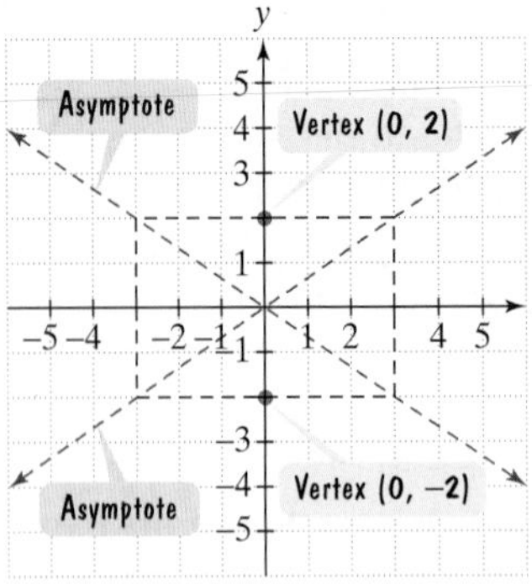


**Figure 10.24** Preparing to graph $\frac{y^2}{4} - \frac{x^2}{9} = 1$

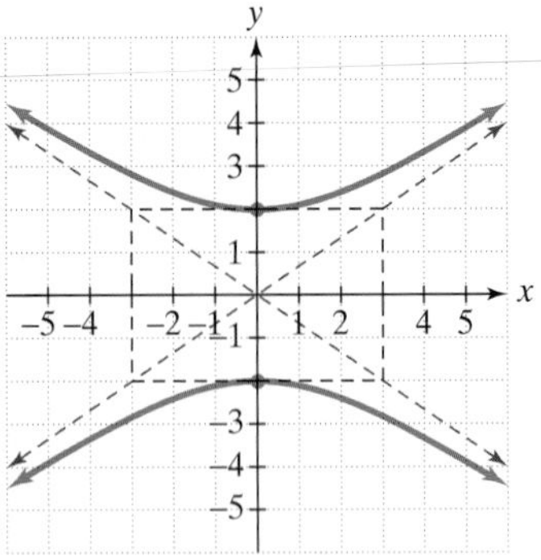

**Figure 10.25** The graph of $\frac{y^2}{4} - \frac{x^2}{9} = 1$

**Step 2 Draw a rectangle.** Because $a^2 = 4$ and $b^2 = 9$, $a = 2$ and $b = 3$. We construct a rectangle to find the asymptotes, using −2 and 2 on the $y$-axis (the vertices are located here) and −3 and 3 on the $x$-axis. The rectangle passes through these four points, shown using dashed lines in Figure 10.24.

**Step 3 Draw extended diagonals of the rectangle to obtain the asymptotes.** We draw dashed lines through the opposite corners of the rectangle, shown in Figure 10.24, to obtain the graph of the asymptotes. Based on the standard form of the hyperbola's equation, the equations of these asymptotes are

$$y = \pm\frac{a}{b}x \quad \text{or} \quad y = \pm\frac{2}{3}x.$$

**Step 4 Draw the two branches of the hyperbola by starting at each vertex and approaching the asymptotes.** The hyperbola is shown in Figure 10.25.

The foci are located at $(0, -c)$ and $(0, c)$. We find $c$ using $c^2 = a^2 + b^2$.

$$c^2 = 4 + 9 = 13$$

Because $c^2 = 13$, $c = \sqrt{13}$. The foci are located at $(0, -\sqrt{13})$ and $(0, \sqrt{13})$, approximately $(0, -3.6)$ and $(0, 3.6)$.

**Check Point 4** Graph and locate the foci: $y^2 - 4x^2 = 4$.

**4** Graph hyperbolas not centered at the origin.

## Translations of Hyperbolas

The graph of a hyperbola can be centered at $(h, k)$ rather than at the origin. Horizontal and vertical translations are accomplished by replacing $x$ with $x - h$ and $y$ with $y - k$ in the standard form of the hyperbola's equation.

Table 10.2 gives the standard forms of equations of hyperbolas centered at $(h, k)$. Figure 10.26 shows their graphs.

**Table 10.2 Standard Forms of Equations of Hyperbolas Centered at (*h*, *k*)**

| Equation | Center | Transverse Axis | Foci | Vertices |
|---|---|---|---|---|
| $\frac{(x-h)^2}{a^2} - \frac{(y-k)^2}{b^2} = 1,$ $b^2 = c^2 - a^2$ | $(h, k)$ | Parallel to $x$-axis; horizontal | $(h - c, k)$ $(h + c, k)$ | $(h - a, k)$ $(h + a, k)$ |
| $\frac{(y-k)^2}{a^2} - \frac{(x-h)^2}{b^2} = 1,$ $b^2 = c^2 - a^2$ | $(h, k)$ | Parallel to $y$-axis; vertical | $(h, k - c)$ $(h, k + c)$ | $(h, k - a)$ $(h, k + a)$ |

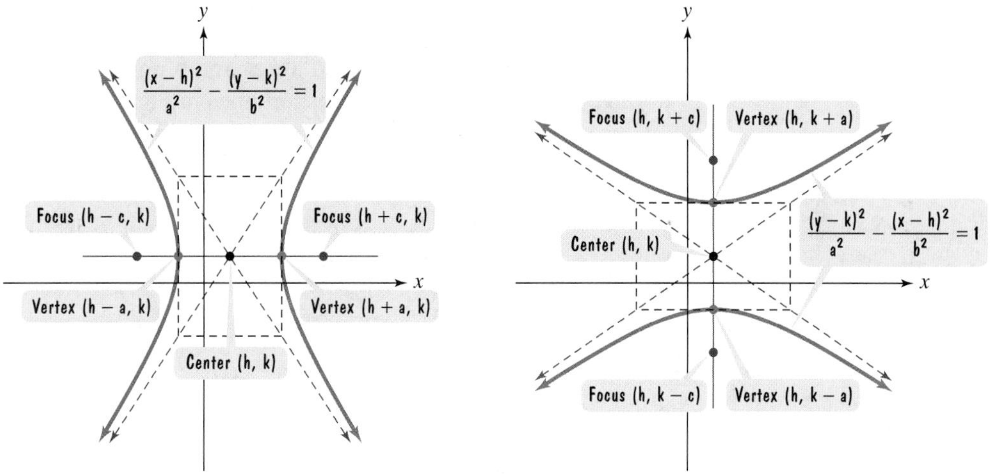


**Figure 10.26** Graphs of hyperbolas centered at $(h, k)$.

## EXAMPLE 5 Graphing a Hyperbola Centered at (*h*, *k*)

Graph: $\frac{(x-2)^2}{16} - \frac{(y-3)^2}{9} = 1$. Where are the foci located?

**Solution** In order to graph the hyperbola, we need to know its center $(h, k)$. In the standard forms of equations centered at $(h, k)$, $h$ is the number subtracted from $x$ and $k$ is the number subtracted from $y$.

This is $(x - h)^2$, with $h = 2$.

$$\frac{(x-2)^2}{16} - \frac{(y-3)^2}{9} = 1$$

This is $(y - k)^2$, with $k = 3$.

We see that $h = 2$ and $k = 3$. Thus, the center of hyperbola, $(h, k)$, is $(2, 3)$. We can graph the hyperbola by using vertices, asymptotes, and our four-step graphing procedure.

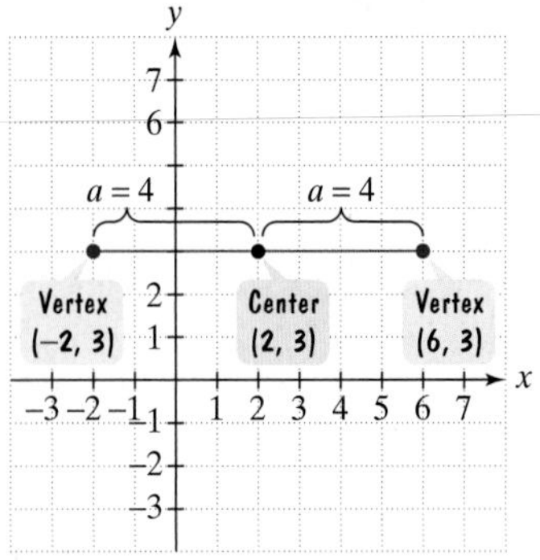


**Figure 10.27** Locating a hyperbola's center and vertices

**Step 1 Locate the vertices.** To do this, we must identify $a^2$.

$$\frac{(x-2)^2}{16} - \frac{(y-3)^2}{9} = 1 \quad \text{The form of this equation is } \frac{(x-h)^2}{a^2} - \frac{(y-k)^2}{b^2} = 1.$$

$a^2 = 16$ $\quad$ $b^2 = 9$

Based on the standard form of the equation with a horizontal transverse axis, the vertices are $a$ units to the right and left of the center. Because $a^2 = 16$, $a = 4$. This means that the vertices are 4 units to the right and left of the center, (2, 3). Four units to the right of (2, 3) puts one vertex at $(2 + 4, 3)$, or (6, 3). Four units to the left of (2, 3) puts the other vertex at $(2 - 4, 3)$, or $(-2, 3)$. The vertices are shown in Figure 10.27.

**Step 2 Draw a rectangle.** Because $a^2 = 16$ and $b^2 = 9$, $a = 4$ and $b = 3$. The rectangle passes through points that are 4 units to the right and left of the center (the vertices are located here) and 3 units above and below the center. The rectangle is shown using dashed lines in Figure 10.28.

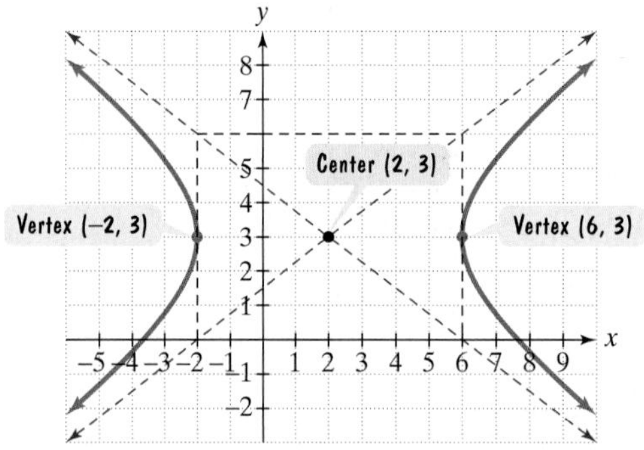


**Figure 10.28** The graph of $\frac{(x-2)^2}{16} - \frac{(y-3)^2}{9} = 1$

**Step 3 Draw extended diagonals of the rectangle to obtain the asymptotes.** We draw dashed lines through the opposite corners of the rectangle, shown in Figure 10.28, to obtain the graph of the asymptotes. The equations of the asymptotes of the unshifted hyperbola $\frac{x^2}{16} - \frac{y^2}{9} = 1$ are $y = \pm\frac{b}{a}x$, or $y = \pm\frac{3}{4}x$. Thus, the asymptotes for the hyperbola that is shifted two units to the right and three units up, namely

$$\frac{(x-2)^2}{16} - \frac{(y-3)^2}{9} = 1$$

have equations that can be expressed as

$$y - 3 = \pm\frac{3}{4}(x - 2).$$

**Step 4 Draw the two branches of the hyperbola by starting at each vertex and approaching the asymptotes.** The hyperbola is shown in Figure 10.28.

The foci are located $c$ units to the right and left of the center. We find $c$ using $c^2 = a^2 + b^2$.

$$c^2 = 16 + 9 = 25$$

Because $c^2 = 25$, $c = 5$. This means that the foci are 5 units to the right and left of the center, (2, 3). Five units to the right of (2, 3) puts one focus at $(2 + 5, 3)$, or (7, 3). Five units to the left of (2, 3) puts the other focus at (2 − 5, 3), or (−3, 3).

**Check Point 5** Graph and locate the foci: $\frac{(x-3)^2}{4} - \frac{(y-1)^2}{1} = 1$.

**5** Solve applied problems involving hyperbolas.

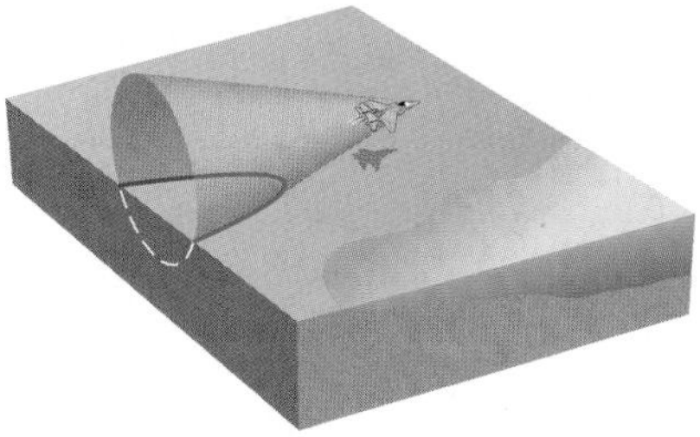

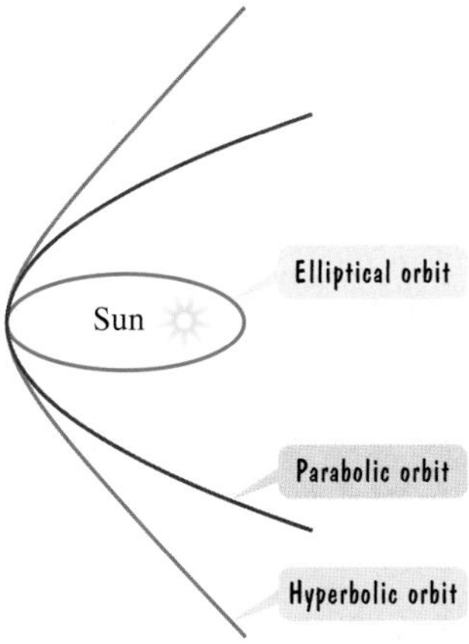


## Applications

Hyperbolas have many applications. When a jet flies at a speed greater than the speed of sound, the shock wave that is created is heard as a sonic boom. The wave has the shape of a cone. The shape formed as the cone hits the ground is one branch of a hyperbola.

Halley's Comet, a permanent part of our solar system, travels around the sun in an elliptical orbit. Other comets pass through the solar system only once, following a hyperbolic path with the sun as a focus.

Hyperbolas are of practical importance in fields ranging from architecture to navigation. Cooling towers used in the design for nuclear power plants have cross sections that are both ellipses and hyperbolas. Three-dimensional solids whose cross sections are hyperbolas are used in some rather unique architectural creations, including the TWA building at Kennedy Airport and the St. Louis Science Center Planetarium.

### EXAMPLE 6 An Application Involving Hyperbolas

An explosion is recorded by two microphones that are 2 miles apart. Microphone $M_1$ received the sound 4 seconds before microphone $M_2$. Assuming sound travels at 1100 feet per second, determine the possible locations of the explosion relative to the location of the microphones.

**Solution** We begin by putting the microphones in a coordinate system. Because 1 mile = 5280 feet, we place $M_1$ 5280 feet on a horizontal axis to the right of the origin and $M_2$ 5280 feet on a horizontal axis to the left of the origin. Figure 10.29 illustrates that the two microphones are 2 miles apart.

We know that $M_2$ received the sound 4 seconds after $M_1$. Because sound travels at 1100 feet per second, the difference between the distance from $P$ to $M_1$ and the distance from $P$ to $M_2$ is 4400 feet. The set of all points $P$ (or locations

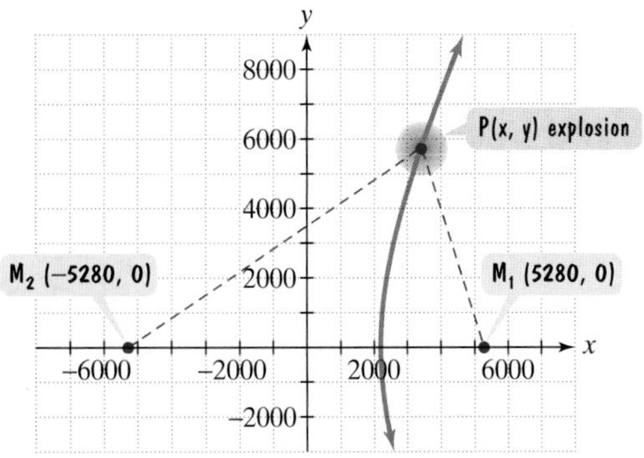


**Figure 10.29** Locating an explosion on the branch of a hyperbola

of the explosion) satisfying these conditions fits the definition of a hyperbola, with microphones $M_1$ and $M_2$ at the foci.

$$\frac{x^2}{a^2} - \frac{y^2}{b^2} = 1$$ Use the standard form of the hyperbola's equation. $P(x, y)$, the explosion point, lies on this hyperbola. We must find $a^2$ and $b^2$.

The difference between the distances, represented by $2a$ in the derivation of the hyperbola's equation, is 4400 feet. Thus, $2a = 4400$ and $a = 2200$.

$$\frac{x^2}{(2200)^2} - \frac{y^2}{b^2} = 1$$ Substitute 2200 for $a$.

Because $c = 5280$ and $a = 2200$, then $b^2 = c^2 - a^2 = 5280^2 - 2200^2 = 23{,}038{,}400$.

$$\frac{x^2}{4{,}840{,}000} - \frac{y^2}{23{,}038{,}400} = 1$$ Substitute 23,038,400 for $b^2$.

We can conclude that the explosion occurred somewhere on the right branch (the branch closest to $M_1$) of the hyperbola given by

$$\frac{x^2}{4{,}840{,}000} - \frac{y^2}{23{,}038{,}400} = 1.$$

In Example 6, we determined that the explosion occurred somewhere along one branch of a hyperbola, but not exactly where on the hyperbola. If, however, we had received the sound from another pair of microphones, we could locate the sound along a branch of another hyperbola. The exact location of the explosion would be the point where the two hyperbolas intersect.

**Check Point 6** Rework Example 6 if Microphone $M_1$ receives the sound 3 seconds before Microphone $M_2$.

## Where Exactly Am I?

The hyperbola is the basis for the navigational system LORAN (for long-range navigation), used by a ship or aircraft to determine its location. The measured time-of-arrival difference between signals transmitted from two ground stations determines the hyperbola on which the ship or aircraft is located. The process is then repeated by taking a similar time-difference reading from a second pair of stations, determining a second hyperbola. The point of intersection of the two hyperbolas is the location of the ship or aircraft.

LORAN will eventually be replaced by the Global Positioning System. Using 24 satellites that orbit at 11,000 miles above Earth, the system is able to show you your exact position on Earth anytime, in any weather, anywhere.

# EXERCISE SET 10.2

## Practice Exercises

*In Exercises 1–4, find the vertices and locate the foci of each hyperbola with the given equation. Then match each equation to one of the graphs that are shown and labeled (a)–(d).*

1. $\frac{x^2}{4} - \frac{y^2}{1} = 1$

2. $\frac{x^2}{1} - \frac{y^2}{4} = 1$

3. $\frac{y^2}{4} - \frac{x^2}{1} = 1$

4. $\frac{y^2}{1} - \frac{x^2}{4} = 1$

**a.**

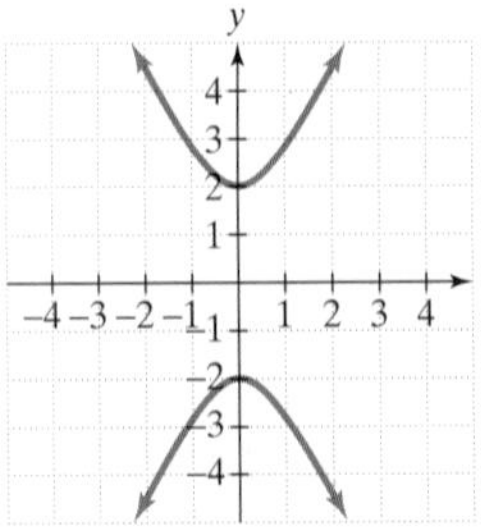


**b.**

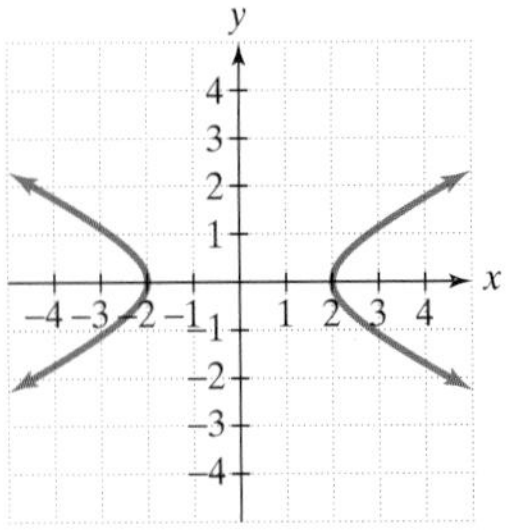

**c.**

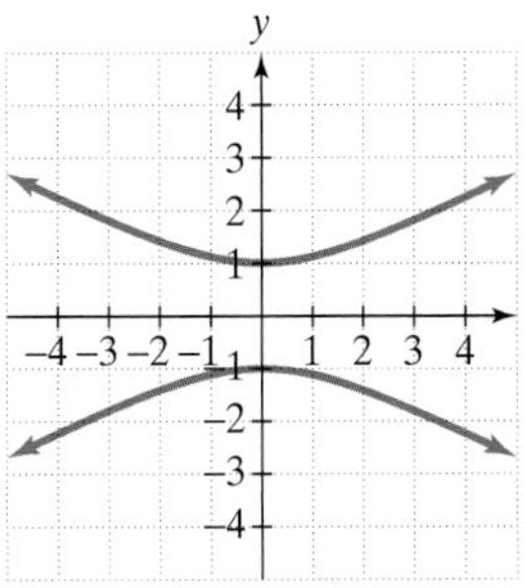


**d.**

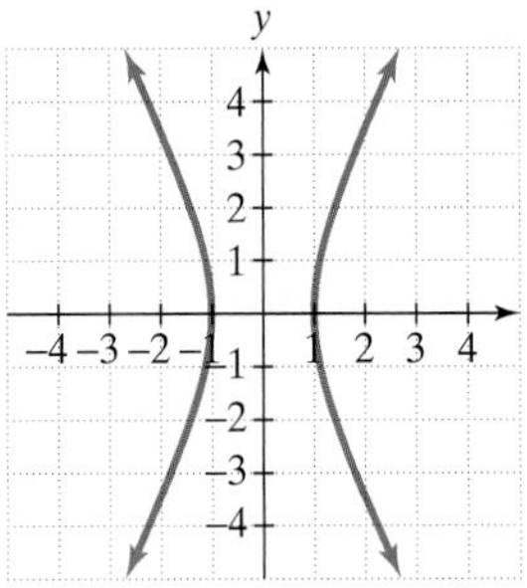


*In Exercises 5–8, find the standard form of the equation of each hyperbola centered at the origin satisfying the given conditions.*

**5.** Foci: $(0, -3), (0, 3)$; vertices: $(0, -1), (0, 1)$

**6.** Foci: $(0, -6), (0, 6)$; vertices: $(0, -2), (0, 2)$

**7.** Foci: $(-4, 0), (4, 0)$; vertices: $(-3, 0), (3, 0)$

**8.** Foci: $(-7, 0), (7, 0)$; vertices: $(-5, 0), (5, 0)$

*In Exercises 9–22, use vertices and asymptotes to graph each hyperbola. Locate the foci.*

**9.** $\frac{x^2}{9} - \frac{y^2}{25} = 1$

**10.** $\frac{x^2}{16} - \frac{y^2}{25} = 1$

**11.** $\frac{x^2}{100} - \frac{y^2}{64} = 1$

**12.** $\frac{x^2}{144} - \frac{y^2}{81} = 1$

**13.** $\frac{y^2}{16} - \frac{x^2}{36} = 1$

**14.** $\frac{y^2}{25} - \frac{x^2}{64} = 1$

**15.** $\frac{y^2}{36} - \frac{x^2}{25} = 1$

**16.** $\frac{y^2}{100} - \frac{x^2}{49} = 1$

**17.** $9x^2 - 4y^2 = 36$

**18.** $4x^2 - 25y^2 = 100$

**19.** $9y^2 - 25x^2 = 225$

**20.** $16y^2 - 9x^2 = 144$

**21.** $4x^2 = 4 + y^2$

**22.** $25y^2 = 225 + 9x^2$

*In Exercises 23–26, find the standard form of the equation of each hyperbola.*

**23.**

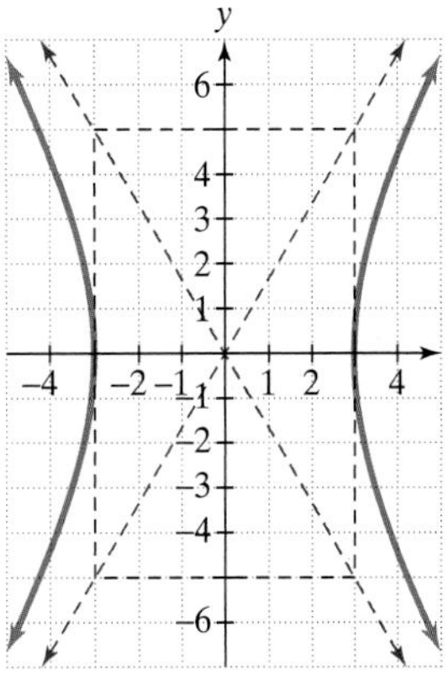


**24.**

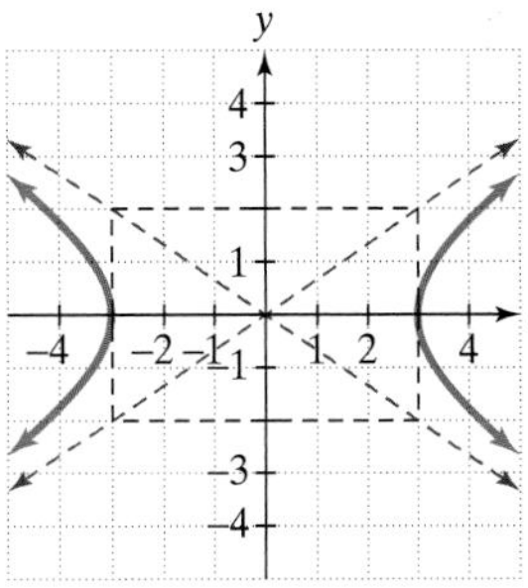


**25.**

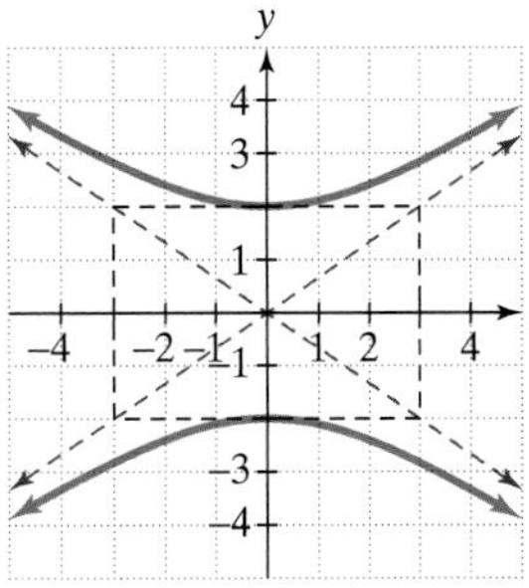


**26.**

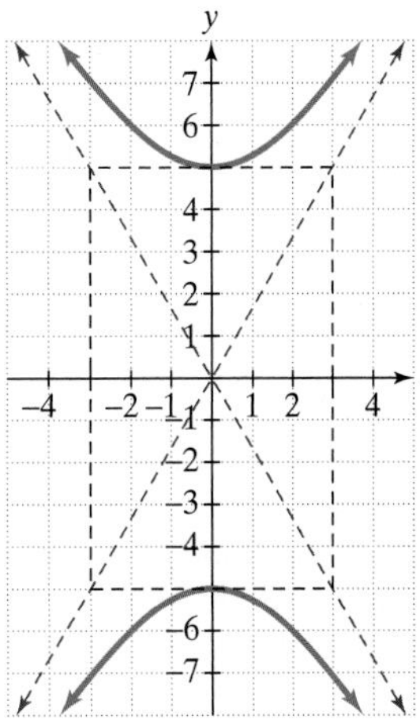

*In Exercises 27–36, use the center, vertices, and asymptotes to graph each hyperbola. Locate the foci.*

**27.** $\frac{(x+4)^2}{9} - \frac{(y+3)^2}{16} = 1$

**28.** $\frac{(x+2)^2}{9} - \frac{(y-1)^2}{25} = 1$

**29.** $\frac{(x+3)^2}{25} - \frac{y^2}{16} = 1$

**30.** $\frac{(x+2)^2}{9} - \frac{y^2}{25} = 1$

**31.** $\frac{(y+2)^2}{4} - \frac{(x-1)^2}{16} = 1$

**32.** $\frac{(y-2)^2}{36} - \frac{(x+1)^2}{49} = 1$

**33.** $(x-3)^2 - 4(y+3)^2 = 4$

**34.** $(x+3)^2 - 9(y-4)^2 = 9$

**35.** $(x-1)^2 - (y-2)^2 = 4$

**36.** $(y-2)^2 - (x+3)^2 = 4$

*In Exercises 37–44, convert each equation to standard form by completing the square on x and y. Then graph the hyperbola and give the location of its foci.*

**37.** $x^2 - y^2 - 2x - 4y - 4 = 0$

**38.** $4x^2 - y^2 + 32x + 6y + 39 = 0$

**39.** $16x^2 - y^2 + 64x - 2y + 67 = 0$

**40.** $9y^2 - 4x^2 - 18y + 24x - 63 = 0$

**41.** $4x^2 - 9y^2 - 16x + 54y - 101 = 0$

**42.** $4x^2 - 9y^2 + 8x - 18y - 6 = 0$

**43.** $4x^2 - 25y^2 - 32x + 164 = 0$

**44.** $9x^2 - 16y^2 - 36x - 64y + 116 = 0$

## Application Exercises

**45.** An explosion is recorded by two microphones that are 1 mile apart. Microphone $M_1$ received the sound 2 seconds before microphone $M_2$. Assuming sound travels at 1100 feet per second, determine the possible locations of the explosion relative to the location of the microphones.

**46.** Radio towers $A$ and $B$, 200 kilometers apart, are situated along the coast, with $A$ located due west of $B$. Simultaneous radio signals are sent from each tower to a ship, with the signal from $B$ received 500 microseconds before the signal from $A$.

**a.** Assuming that the radio signals travel 300 meters per microsecond, determine the equation of the hyperbola on which the ship is located.

**b.** If the ship lies due north of tower $B$, how far out at sea is it?

**47.** An architect designs two houses that are shaped and positioned like a part of the branches of the hyperbola whose equation is $625y^2 - 400x^2 = 250{,}000$, where $x$ and $y$ are in yards. How far apart are the houses at their closest point?

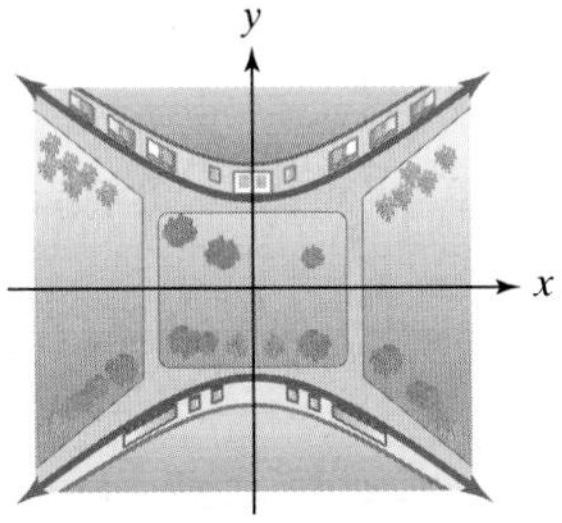


**48.** Scattering experiments, in which moving particles are deflected by various forces, led to the concept of the nucleus of an atom. In 1911, the physicist Ernest Rutherford (1871–1937) discovered that when alpha particles are directed toward the nuclei of gold atoms, they are eventually deflected along hyperbolic paths, illustrated in the figure. If a particle gets as close as 3 units to the nucleus along a hyperbolic path with an asymptote given by $y = \frac{1}{2}x$, what is the equation of its path?

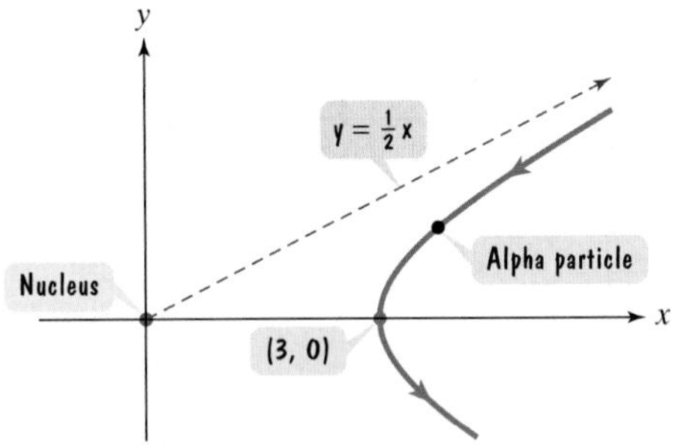


## Writing in Mathematics

**49.** What is a hyperbola?

**50.** Describe how to graph $\frac{x^2}{9} - \frac{y^2}{1} = 1$.

**51.** Describe how to locate the foci of the graph of $\frac{x^2}{9} - \frac{y^2}{1} = 1$.

52. Describe one similarity and one difference between the graphs of $\frac{x^2}{9} - \frac{y^2}{1} = 1$ and $\frac{y^2}{9} - \frac{x^2}{1} = 1$.

53. Describe one similarity and one difference between the graphs of $\frac{x^2}{9} - \frac{y^2}{1} = 1$ and $\frac{(x-3)^2}{9} - \frac{(y+3)^2}{1} = 1$.

54. How can you distinguish an ellipse from a hyperbola by looking at their equations?

55. In 1992, a NASA team began a project called Spaceguard Survey, calling for an international watch for comets that might collide with Earth. Why is it more difficult to detect a possible "doomsday comet" with a hyperbolic orbit than one with an elliptical orbit?

## Technology Exercises

56. Use a graphing utility to graph any five of the hyperbolas that you graphed by hand in Exercises 9–22.

57. Use a graphing utility to graph any three of the hyperbolas that you graphed by hand in Exercises 27–36. First solve the given equation for $y$ by using the square root method. Enter each of the two resulting equations to produce each branch of the hyperbola.

58. Use a graphing utility to graph any one of the hyperbolas that you graphed by hand in Exercises 37–44. Write the equation as a quadratic equation in $y$ and use the quadratic formula to solve for $y$. Enter each of the two resulting equations to produce each branch of the hyperbola.

59. Use a graphing utility to graph $\frac{x^2}{4} - \frac{y^2}{9} = 0$. Is the graph a hyperbola? In general, what is the graph of $\frac{x^2}{a^2} - \frac{y^2}{b^2} = 0$?

60. Graph $\frac{x^2}{a^2} - \frac{y^2}{b^2} = 1$ and $\frac{x^2}{a^2} - \frac{y^2}{b^2} = -1$ in the same viewing rectangle for values of $a^2$ and $b^2$ of your choice. Describe the relationship between the two graphs.

61. Write $4x^2 - 6xy + 2y^2 - 3x + 10y - 6 = 0$ as a quadratic equation in $y$ and then use the quadratic formula to express $y$ in terms of $x$. Graph the resulting two equations using a graphing utility and a $[-50, 70, 10]$ by $[-30, 50, 10]$ viewing rectangle. What effect does the $xy$-term have on the graph of the resulting hyperbola? What problems would you encounter if you attempted to write the given equation in standard form by completing the square?

62. Graph $\frac{x^2}{16} - \frac{y^2}{9} = 1$ and $\frac{x|x|}{16} - \frac{y|y|}{9} = 1$ in the same viewing rectangle. Explain why the graphs are not the same.

## Critical Thinking Exercises

63. Which one of the following is true?
   **a.** If one branch of a hyperbola is removed from a graph, then the branch that remains must define $y$ as a function of $x$.
   **b.** All points on the asymptotes of a hyperbola also satisfy the hyperbola's equation.
   **c.** The graph of $\frac{x^2}{9} - \frac{y^2}{4} = 1$ does not intersect the line $y = -\frac{2}{3}x$.
   **d.** Two different hyperbolas can never share the same asymptotes.

64. What happens to the shape of the graph of $\frac{x^2}{a^2} - \frac{y^2}{b^2} = 1$ as $\frac{c}{a}$ gets larger and larger?

65. Find the standard form of the equation of the hyperbola with vertices $(5, -6)$ and $(5, 6)$, and passing through $(0, 9)$.

66. Find the equation of a hyperbola whose asymptotes are perpendicular.

## SECTION 10.3 *The Parabola*

### Objectives

1. Graph parabolas with vertices at the origin.
2. Write equations of parabolas in standard form.
3. Graph parabolas with vertices not at the origin.
4. Solve applied problems involving parabolas.

At first glance, this image looks like columns of smoke rising from a fire into a starry sky. Those are, indeed, stars in the background, but you are not looking at ordinary smoke columns. These stand almost 6 trillion miles high and are 7000 light-years from Earth—more than 400 million times as far away as the sun.

This NASA photograph is one of a series of stunning images captured from the ends of the universe by the Hubble Space Telescope. The image shows infant star systems the size of our solar system emerging from the gas and dust that shrouded their creation. Using a parabolic mirror that is 94.5 inches in diameter, the Hubble is providing answers to many of the profound mysteries of the cosmos: How big and how old is the universe? How did the galaxies come to exist? Do other Earth-like planets orbit other sun-like stars?

In Chapter 3, we studied parabolas, viewing them as graphs of the quadratic function $y = ax^2 + bx + c$. In this section, we will use a geometric definition of a parabola to derive its equation. We will also consider applications of parabolas, including parabolic shapes that gather distant rays of light and focus them into spectacular images.

## Definition of a Parabola

The definitions of ellipses and hyperbolas involved two fixed points, the foci. By contrast, the definition of a parabola is based on one point and a line.

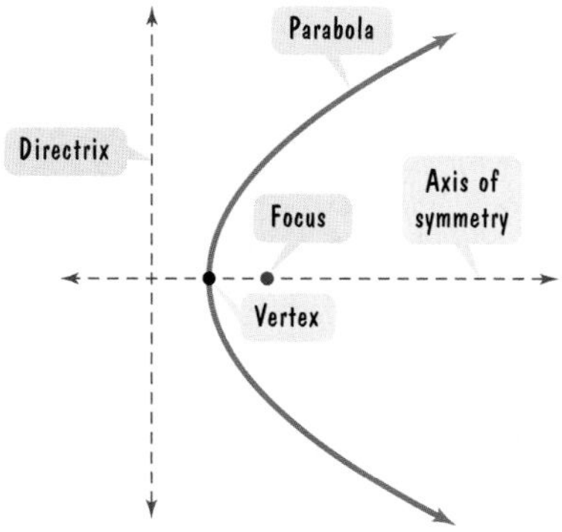


Figure 10.30

**Definition of a Parabola**

A **parabola** is the set of all points in a plane that are equidistant from a fixed line (the **directrix**) and a fixed point (the **focus**) that is not on the line (see Figure 10.30).

In Figure 10.30, find the line passing through the focus and perpendicular to the directrix. This is the **axis of symmetry** of the parabola. The point of intersection of the parabola with its axis of symmetry is called the **vertex**. Notice that the vertex is midway between the focus and the directrix.

## Standard Form of the Equation of a Parabola

The rectangular coordinate system enables us to translate a parabola's geometric definition into an algebraic equation. Figure 10.31 is our starting point for obtaining an equation. We place the focus on the $x$-axis at the point $(p, 0)$. The directrix has an equation given by $x = -p$. The vertex, located midway between the focus and the directrix, is at the origin.

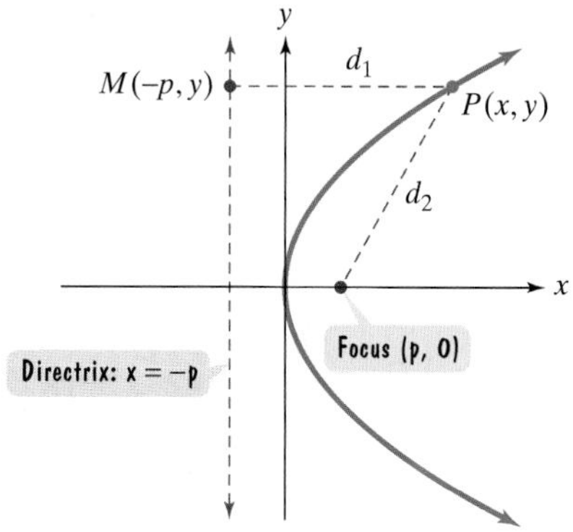


Figure 10.31

What does the definition of a parabola tell us about the point $(x, y)$ in Figure 10.31? For any point $(x, y)$ on the parabola, the distance $d_1$ to the directrix is equal to the distance $d_2$ to the focus. Thus, the point $(x, y)$ is on the parabola if and only if

$$d_1 = d_2$$

$$\sqrt{(x+p)^2 + (y-y)^2} = \sqrt{(x-p)^2 + (y-0)^2} \quad \text{Use the distance formula.}$$

$$(x+p)^2 = (x-p)^2 + y^2 \quad \text{Square both sides of the equation.}$$

$$x^2 + 2px + p^2 = x^2 - 2px + p^2 + y^2 \quad \text{Square } x + p \text{ and } x - p.$$

$$2px = -2px + y^2 \quad \text{Subtract } x^2 + p^2 \text{ from both sides of the equation.}$$

$$y^2 = 4px \quad \text{Solve for } y^2.$$

This last equation is called the **standard form of the equation of a parabola.** There are two such equations, one for a focus on the $x$-axis and one for a focus on the $y$-axis.

**Standard Forms of the Equations of a Parabola**

The **standard form of the equation of a parabola** with vertex at the origin is

$$y^2 = 4px \quad \text{or} \quad x^2 = 4py.$$

Figure 10.32 illustrates that for the equation on the left, the focus is on the $x$-axis, which is the axis of symmetry. For the equation on the right, the focus is on the $y$-axis, which is the axis of symmetry.

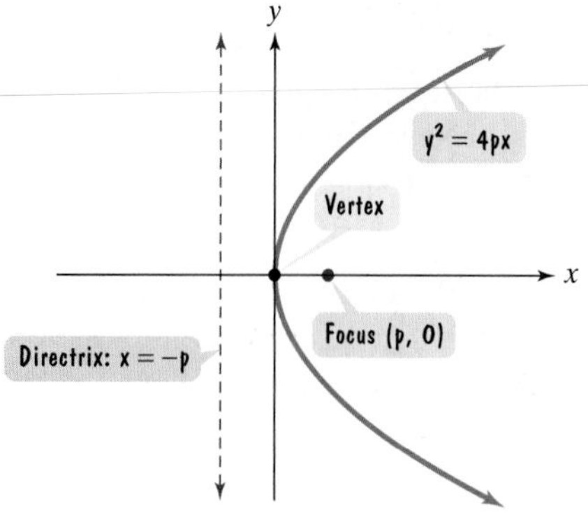


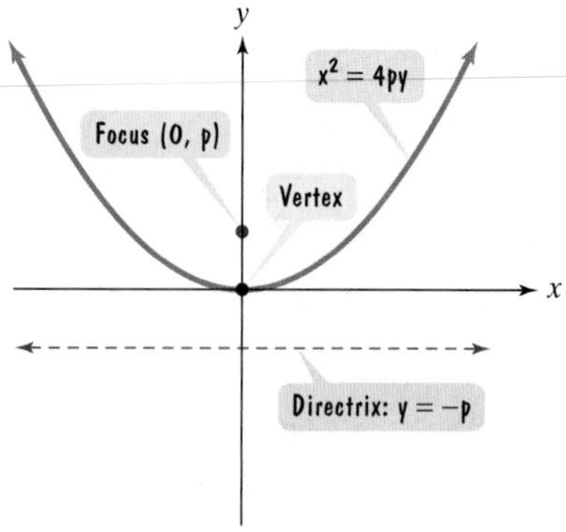


**Figure 10.32** **(a)** Parabola with the $x$-axis as the axis of symmetry **(b)** Parabola with the $y$-axis as the axis of symmetry

**1** Graph parabolas with vertices at the origin.

## Using the Standard Form of the Equation of a Parabola

We can use the standard form of the equation of a parabola to find its focus and directrix. Remember that the focus is located on the axis corresponding to the variable in the equation that is *not* squared.

$$y^2 = 4px \qquad x^2 = 4py$$

$x$ is not squared. Focus is on the $x$-axis at $(p, 0)$. $y$ is not squared. Focus is on the $y$-axis at $(0, p)$.

Although the definition of a parabola is given in terms of its focus and its directrix, the focus and directrix are not part of the graph. The vertex, located at the origin, is a point on the graph of $y^2 = 4px$ and $x^2 = 4py$. You can find two additional points on the parabola by assigning a value to $x$ or $y$ that makes $y^2$ or $x^2$ a perfect square. For example, consider $y^2 = 8x$. A value of $x$ that makes the right side a perfect square is 2. If $x = 2$, then $y^2 = 8(2)$, or 16. Because $y^2 = 16$, $y = \pm 4$. Thus, the parabola passes through the points $(2, 4)$ and $(2, -4)$. The parabola can be graphed by connecting the vertex, $(0, 0)$, to each of these points with a smooth curve.

### EXAMPLE 1 Finding the Focus and Directrix of a Parabola

Find the focus and directrix of the parabola given by $y^2 = 12x$. Then graph the parabola.

**Solution** The given equation is in the standard form $y^2 = 4px$, so $4p = 12$.

$$y^2 = 12x$$

This is $4p$.

We can find both the focus and the directrix by finding $p$.

$4p = 12$ Remember that the focus is at $(p, 0)$ and the directrix is given by $x = -p$.

$p = 3$ Divide both sides by 4.

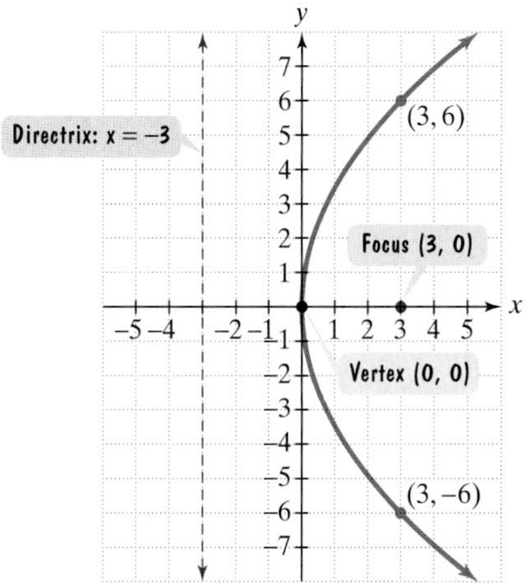


**Figure 10.33** The graph of $y^2 = 12x$

Using this value for $p$, we obtain

$$\text{Focus:} \quad (p, 0) = (3, 0)$$

$$\text{Directrix:} \quad x = -p;\ x = -3.$$

Observe that the vertex, midway between the focus and the directrix, is at the origin. To graph $y^2 = 12x$, we assign $x$ a value that makes the right side a perfect square. If $x = 3$, then $y^2 = 12(3)$ or $y^2 = 36$. Because $y = \pm 6$, the parabola passes through the points $(3, 6)$ and $(3, -6)$. The graph is sketched in Figure 10.33.

**Check Point 1** Find the focus and directrix of the parabola given by $y^2 = 8x$. Then graph the parabola.

Parabolas with vertices at the origin can open to the right, left, upward, or downward. The graph of $y^2 = 4px$ opens to the right if $p > 0$ or left if $p < 0$. For example, Figure 10.34 shows that $y^2 = x$ opens to the right and $y^2 = -x$ opens to the left. The graph of $x^2 = 4py$ opens upward if $p > 0$ or downward if $p < 0$. Figure 10.34 shows that $x^2 = y$ opens upward and $x^2 = -y$ opens downward.

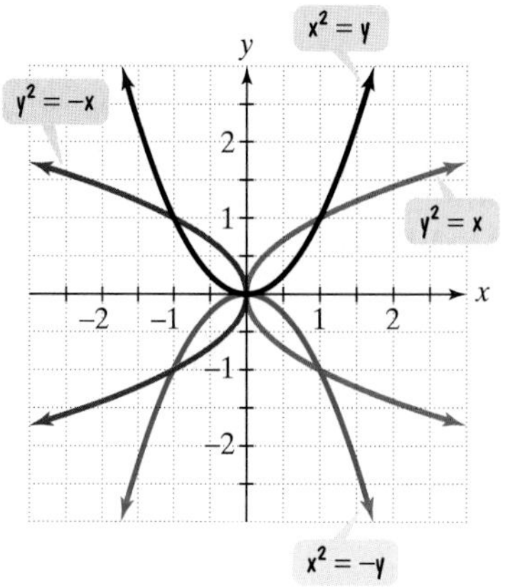


**Figure 10.34**

## EXAMPLE 2 Finding the Focus and Directrix of a Parabola

Find the focus and directrix of the parabola given by $x^2 = -8y$. Then graph the parabola.

**Solution** The given equation is in the standard form $x^2 = 4py$, so $4p = -8$.

$$x^2 = -8y$$

This is $4p$.

We can find both the focus and the directrix by finding $p$.

$$4p = -8$$
$$p = -2$$

The focus, on the $y$-axis, is at $(0, p)$ and the directrix is given by $y = -p$.

Because $p < 0$, the parabola opens downward. Using this value for $p$, we obtain

$$\text{Focus:} \quad (0, p) = (0, -2)$$

$$\text{Directrix:} \quad y = -p;\ y = 2.$$

To graph $x^2 = -8y$, we assign $y$ a value that makes the right side a perfect square. If $y = -2$, then $x^2 = -8(-2) = 16$, so $x = \pm 4$. The parabola passes through the points $(4, -2)$ and $(-4, -2)$. The graph is sketched in Figure 10.35.

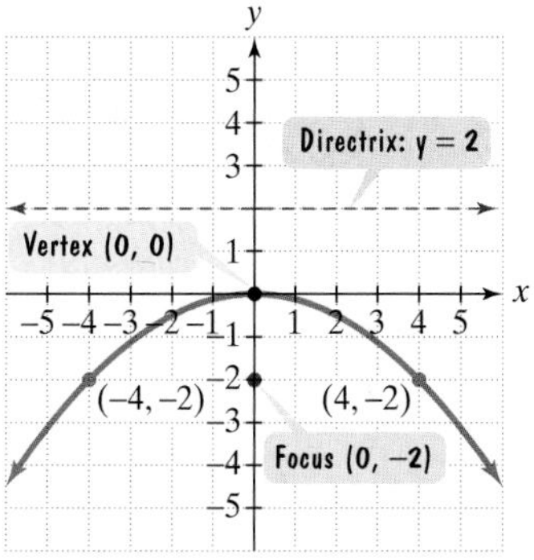


**Figure 10.35** The graph of $x^2 = -8y$

**Check Point 2** Find the focus and directrix of the parabola given by $x^2 = -12y$. Then graph the parabola.

**2** Write equations of parabolas in standard form.

In Examples 1 and 2, we used the equation of a parabola to find its focus and directrix. In the next example, we reverse this procedure.

## EXAMPLE 3 Finding the Equation of a Parabola from Its Focus and Directrix

Find the standard form of the equation of a parabola with focus $(5, 0)$ and directrix $x = -5$, shown in Figure 10.36.

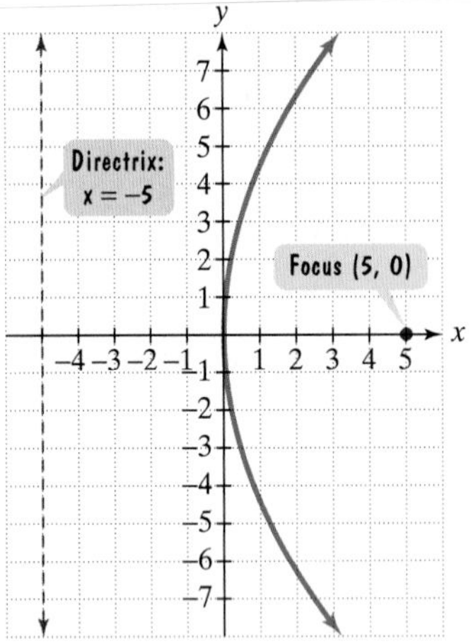


**Figure 10.36**

**Solution** The focus is $(5, 0)$. Thus, the focus is on the $x$-axis. We use the standard form of the equation in which $x$ is not squared, namely $y^2 = 4px$.

We need to determine the value of $p$. Recall that the focus, located at $(p, 0)$, is $p$ units from the vertex, $(0, 0)$. Thus, if the focus is $(5, 0)$, then $p = 5$. We substitute 5 for $p$ into $y^2 = 4px$ to obtain the standard form of the equation of the parabola. The equation is

$$y^2 = 4 \cdot 5x \qquad \text{or} \qquad y^2 = 20x.$$

**Check Point 3** Find the standard form of the equation of a parabola with focus $(8, 0)$ and directrix $x = -8$.

**3** Graph parabolas with vertices not at the origin.

## Translations of Parabolas

The graph of a parabola can have its vertex at $(h, k)$ rather than at the origin. Horizontal and vertical translations are accomplished by replacing $x$ with $x - h$ and $y$ with $y - k$ in the standard form of the parabola's equation.

Table 10.3 gives the standard forms of equations of parabolas with vertex at $(h, k)$. Figure 10.37 shows their graphs.

**Table 10.3 Standard Forms of Equations of Parabolas with Vertex at $(h, k)$**

| Equation | Vertex | Axis of Symmetry | Focus | Directrix | Description |
|---|---|---|---|---|---|
| $(y - k)^2 = 4p(x - h)$ | $(h, k)$ | Horizontal | $(h + p, k)$ | $x = h - p$ | If $p > 0$, opens to right. If $p < 0$, opens to left. |
| $(x - h)^2 = 4p(y - k)$ | $(h, k)$ | Vertical | $(h, k + p)$ | $y = k - p$ | If $p > 0$, opens up. If $p < 0$, opens down. |

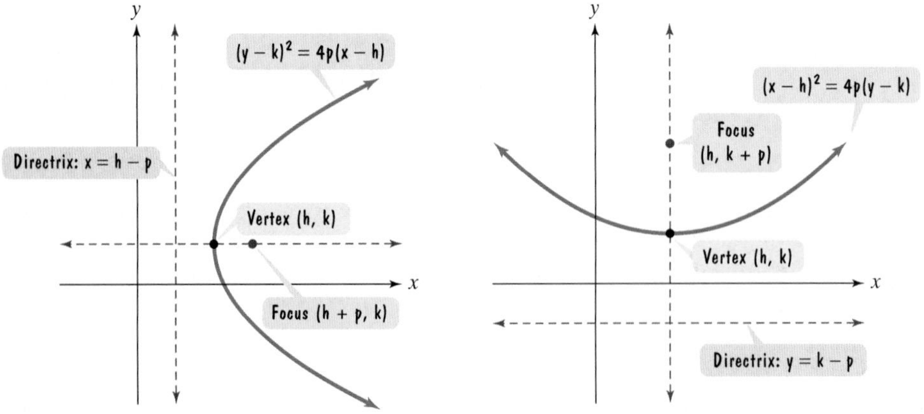


**Figure 10.37** Graphs of parabolas with vertex at $(h, k)$

The two parabolas shown in Figure 10.37 illustrate standard forms of equations for $p > 0$. If $p < 0$, a parabola with a horizontal axis of symmetry will open to the left and the focus will lie to the left of the directrix. If $p < 0$, a parabola with a vertical axis of symmetry will open downward and the focus will lie below the directix.

## EXAMPLE 4 Graphing a Parabola with Vertex at $(h, k)$

Find the vertex, focus, and directrix of the parabola given by

$$(x - 3)^2 = 8(y + 1).$$

Then graph the parabola.

**Solution** In order to find the focus and directrix, we need to know the vertex. In the standard forms of equations with vertex at $(h, k)$, $h$ is the number subtracted from $x$, and $k$ is the number subtracted from $y$.

$$(x - 3)^2 = 8(y - (-1))$$

This is $(x - h)^2$, with $h = 3$.

This is $y - k$, with $k = -1$.

We see that $h = 3$ and $k = -1$. Thus, the vertex of the parabola is $(h, k) = (3, -1)$.

Now that we have the vertex, we can find both the focus and directrix by finding $p$.

$(x - 3)^2 = 8(y + 1)$ The equation is in the standard form $(x - h)^2 = 4p(y - k)$.

This is $4p$.

Because $4p = 8$, $p = 2$. Based on the standard form of the equation, the axis of symmetry is vertical. With a positive value for $p$ and a vertical axis of symmetry, the parabola opens upward. Because $p = 2$, the focus is located 2 units above the vertex, $(3, -1)$. Likewise, the directrix is located 2 units below the vertex.

Focus: $(h, k + p) = (3, -1 + 2) = (3, 1)$

The vertex, $(h, k)$, is $(3, -1)$.

The focus is 2 units above the vertex, $(3, -1)$.

Directrix:

$$y = k - p$$
$$y = -1 - 2 = -3$$

The directrix is 2 units below the vertex, $(3, -1)$.

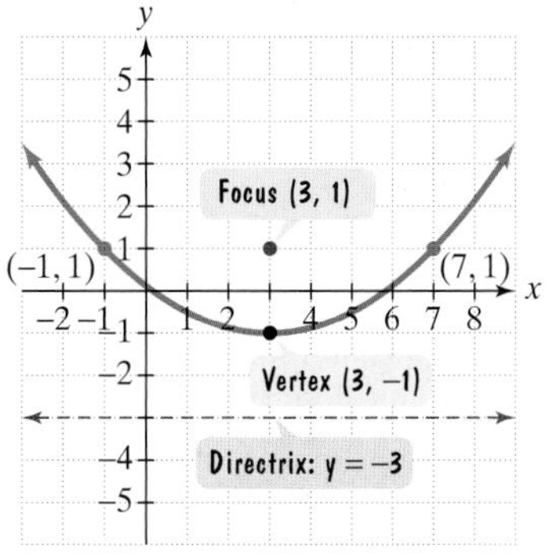


**Figure 10.38** The graph of $(x - 3)^2 = 8(y + 1)$

Thus, the focus is $(3, 1)$ and the directrix is $y = -3$. They are shown in Figure 10.38.

To graph $(x - 3)^2 = 8(y + 1)$, we assign $y$ a value that makes the right side of the equation a perfect square. If $y = 1$, the right side is $8(1 + 1)$ or 16, a perfect square. We let $y = 1$ and solve for $x$ to obtain points on the parabola.

$(x - 3)^2 = 8(1 + 1)$ Substitute 1 for y in $(x - 3)^2 = 8(y + 1)$.

$(x - 3)^2 = 16$ Simplify.

$x - 3 = \pm\sqrt{16}$ Apply the square root method.

$x - 3 = 4$ or $x - 3 = -4$ Write $\sqrt{16}$ as 4 and express as two separate equations.

$x = 7$ $\quad x = -1$ Solve for x by adding 3 to both sides.

Because we obtained these values of $x$ for $y = 1$, the parabola passes through the points $(7, 1)$ and $(-1, 1)$. Passing a smooth curve through the vertex and each of these points, we sketch the parabola shown in Figure 10.38.

**Check Point 4** Find the vertex, focus, and directrix of the parabola given by $(x - 2)^2 = 4(y + 1)$. Then graph the parabola.

In some cases, we need to convert the equation of a parabola to standard form by completing the square on $x$ or $y$, whichever variable is squared. Let's see how this is done.

## EXAMPLE 5 Graphing a Parabola with Vertex at $(h, k)$

Find the vertex, focus, and directrix of the parabola given by

$$y^2 + 2y + 12x - 23 = 0.$$

Then graph the parabola.

**Solution** We convert the given equation to standard form by completing the square on the variable $y$. We isolate the terms involving $y$ on the left side.

$$y^2 + 2y + 12x - 23 = 0 \quad \text{This is the given equation.}$$

$$y^2 + 2y = -12x + 23 \quad \text{Isolate the terms involving } y.$$

$$y^2 + 2y + 1 = -12x + 23 + 1 \quad \text{Complete the square by adding the square of half the coefficient of } y.$$

$$(y + 1)^2 = -12x + 24$$

To express this equation in the standard form $(y - k)^2 = 4p(x - h)$, we factor $-12$ on the right. The standard form of the parabola's equation is

$$(y + 1)^2 = -12(x - 2).$$

We use this form to identify the vertex, $(h, k)$, and the value for $p$ needed to locate the focus and the directrix.

$$(y - (-1))^2 = -12(x - 2) \quad \text{The equation is in the standard form } (y - k)^2 = 4p(x - h).$$

This is $(y - k)^2$, with $k = -1$. This is $4p$. This is $x - h$, with $h = 2$.

We see that $h = 2$ and $k = -1$. Thus, the vertex of the parabola is $(h, k) = (2, -1)$. Because $4p = -12$, $p = -3$. Based on the standard form of the equation, the axis of symmetry is horizontal. With a negative value for $p$ and a horizontal axis of symmetry, the parabola opens to the left. We locate the focus and directrix as follows.

Focus: $(h + p, k) = (2 + (-3), -1) = (-1, -1)$

The vertex, $(h, k)$, is $(2, -1)$. $h = 2$ $p = -3$ $k = -1$

Directrix:

$$x = h - p$$

$$x = 2 - (-3) = 5$$

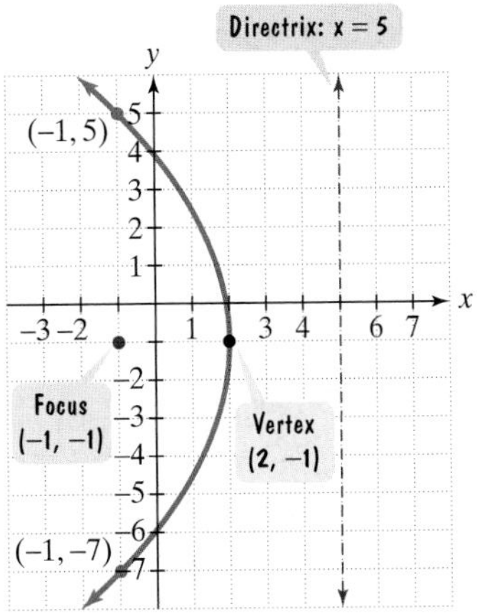


**Figure 10.39** The graph of $(y + 1)^2 = -12(x - 2)$

Thus, the focus is $(-1, -1)$ and the directrix is $x = 5$. They are shown in Figure 10.39.

To graph $(y + 1)^2 = -12(x - 2)$, we assign $x$ a value that makes the right side of the equation a perfect square. If $x = -1$, the right side is $-12(-1 - 2) = -12(-3) = 36$, a perfect square. We will let $x = -1$ and solve for $y$ to obtain points on the parabola.

$$(y + 1)^2 = -12(-1 - 2)$$ Substitute −1 for x in $(y + 1)^2 = -12(x - 2)$.

$$(y + 1)^2 = 36$$ Simplify: $-12(-1 - 2) = -12(-3) = 36$.

$$y + 1 = \pm\sqrt{36}$$ Apply the square root method.

$$y + 1 = 6 \quad \text{or} \quad y + 1 = -6$$ Write $\sqrt{36}$ as 6 and express as two separate equations.

$$y = 5 \qquad\qquad y = -7$$ Solve for y by subtracting 1 from both sides.

Because we obtained these values of $y$ for $x = -1$, the parabola passes through the points $(-1, 5)$ and $(-1, -7)$. Passing a smooth curve through the vertex and these two points, we sketch the parabola shown in Figure 10.39.

**Check Point 5** Find the vertex, focus, and directrix of the parabola given by $y^2 + 2y + 4x - 7 = 0$. Then graph the parabola.

**4** Solve applied problems involving parabolas.

## Applications

Parabolas have many applications. Cables hung between structures to form suspension bridges form parabolas. Arches constructed of steel and concrete, whose main purpose is strength, are usually parabolic in shape.

Suspension bridge

Arch bridge

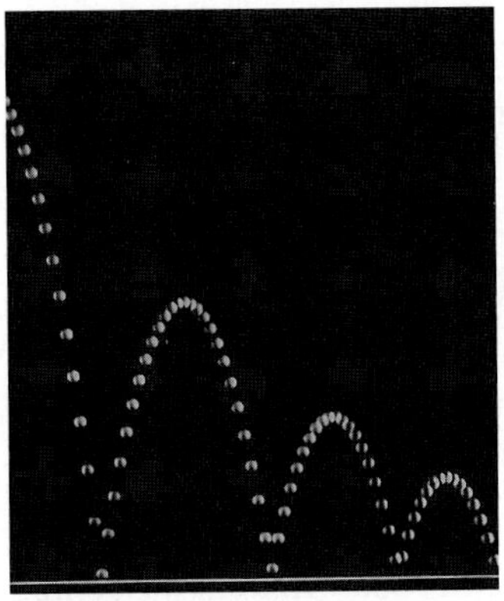

**Figure 10.40** Multiflash photo showing the parabolic path of a ball thrown into the air

We have seen that comets in our solar system travel in orbits that are ellipses and hyperbolas. Some comets also follow parabolic paths. Only comets with elliptical orbits, such as Halley's Comet, return to our part of the galaxy.

A projectile, such as a baseball thrown directly upward, moves along a parabolic path, illustrated in Figure 10.40.

If a parabola is rotated about its axis of symmetry, a parabolic surface is formed. Figure 10.41 (a) shows how a parabolic surface can be used to reflect

## The Hubble Space Telescope

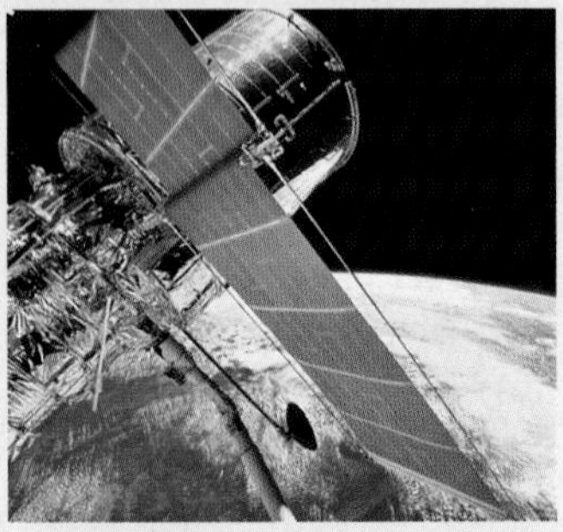

The Hubble Space Telescope

For decades, astronomers hoped to create an observatory above the atmosphere that would provide an unobscured view of the universe. This dream came true with the 1990 launching of the Hubble Space Telescope. The telescope initially had blurred vision due to problems with its parabolic mirror. The mirror had been ground two millionths of a meter smaller than design specifications. In 1993, astronauts from the Space Shuttle *Endeavor* equipped the telescope with optics to correct the blurred vision. "A small change for a mirror, a giant leap for astronomy," Christopher J. Burrows of the Space Telescope Science Institute said when clear images from the ends of the universe were presented to the public after the repair mission.

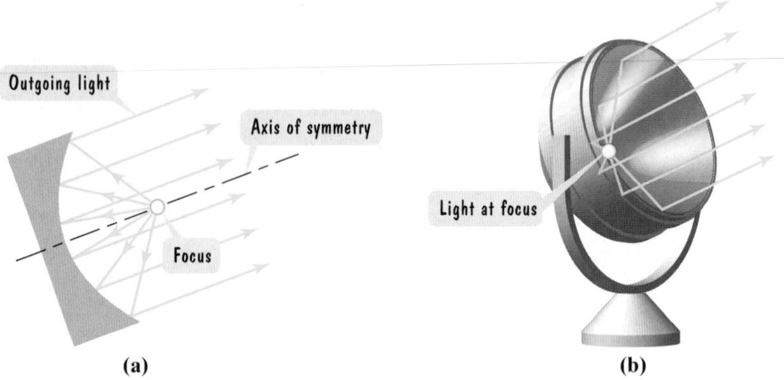


**Figure 10.41** **(a)** Parabolic surface reflecting light **(b)** Light from the focus is reflected parallel to the axis of symmetry.

light. Light originates at the focus. Note how the light is reflected by the parabolic surface, so that the outgoing light is parallel to the axis of symmetry. The reflective properties of parabolic surfaces are used in the design of searchlights [Figure 10.41(b)], automobile headlights, and parabolic microphones.

Figure 10.42(a) shows how a parabolic surface can be used to reflect *incoming* light. Note that light rays strike the surface and are reflected *to the focus*. This principle is used in the design of reflecting telescopes, radar, and television satellite dishes. Reflecting telescopes magnify the light from distant stars by reflecting the light from these bodies to the focus of a parabolic mirror [Figure 10.42(b)].

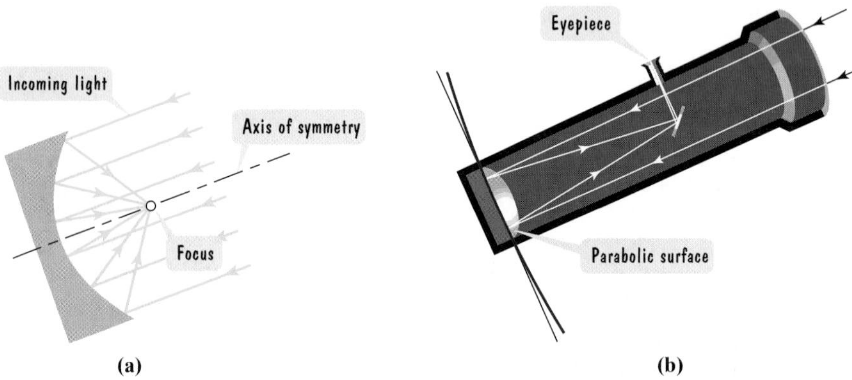


**Figure 10.42** **(a)** Parabolic surface reflecting incoming light **(b)** Incoming light rays are reflected to the focus.

## EXAMPLE 6 Using the Reflection Property of Parabolas

An engineer is designing a flashlight using a parabolic reflecting mirror and a light source, shown in Figure 10.43. The casting has a diameter of 4 inches and a depth of 2 inches. What is the equation of the parabola used to shape the mirror? At what point should the light source be placed relative to the mirror's vertex?

**Solution** We position the parabola with its vertex at the origin and opening upward (Figure 10.44). Thus, the focus is on the $y$-axis, located at $(0, p)$. We use the standard form of the equation in which $y$ is not squared, namely $x^2 = 4py$. We need to find $p$. Because $(2, 2)$ lies on the parabola, we let $x = 2$ and $y = 2$ in $x^2 = 4py$.

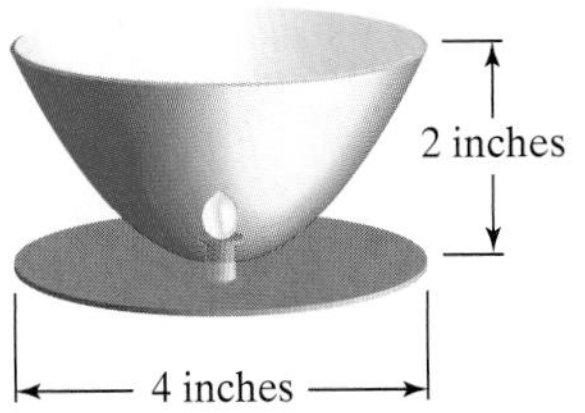


**Figure 10.43** Designing a flashlight

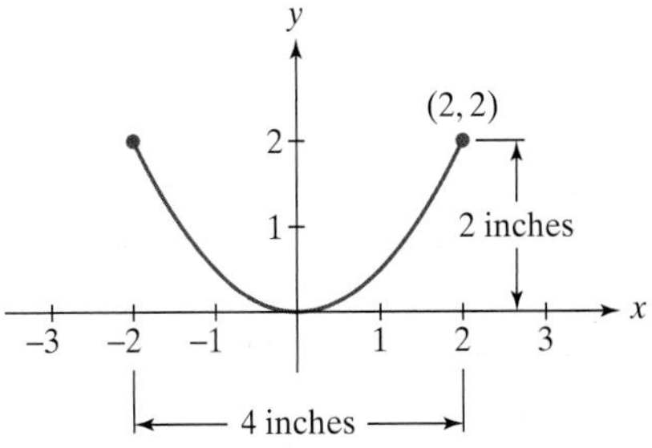


**Figure 10.44**

$$2^2 = 4p \cdot 2 \quad \text{Substitute 2 for } x \text{ and 2 for } y \text{ in } x^2 = 4py.$$

$$4 = 8p \quad \text{Simplify.}$$

$$p = \tfrac{1}{2} \quad \text{Divide both sides of the equation by 8 and reduce the resulting fraction.}$$

We substitute $\frac{1}{2}$ for $p$ in $x^2 = 4py$ to obtain the standard form of the equation of the parabola. The equation of the parabola used to shape the mirror is

$$x^2 = 4 \cdot \tfrac{1}{2}y \qquad \text{or} \qquad x^2 = 2y.$$

The light source should be placed at the focus $(0, p)$. Because $p = \frac{1}{2}$, the light should be placed at $\left(0, \frac{1}{2}\right)$, or $\frac{1}{2}$ inch above the vertex.

**Check Point 6** In Example 6, suppose that the casting has a diameter of 6 inches and a depth of 4 inches. What is the equation of the parabola used to shape the mirror? At what point should the light source be placed relative to the mirror's vertex?

## Degenerate Conic Sections

We opened the chapter by noting that conic sections are curves that result from the intersection of a cone and a plane. However, these intersections might not result in a conic section. Three degenerate cases occur when the cutting plane passes through the vertex. These **degenerate conic sections** are a point, a line, and a pair of intersecting lines, illustrated in Figure 10.45.

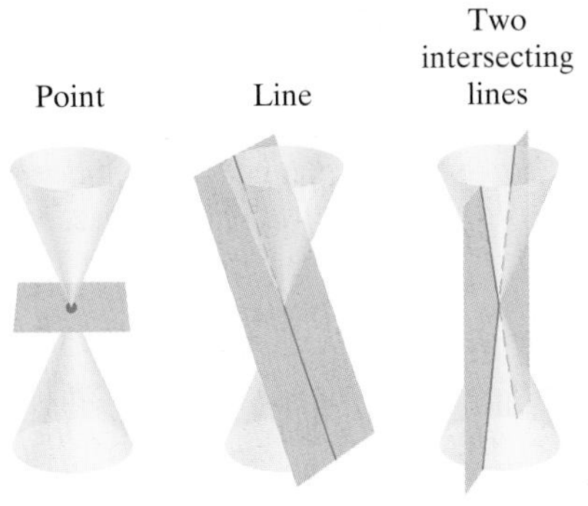


**Figure 10.45** Degenerate conics

## EXERCISE SET 10.3

### Practice Exercises

*In Exercises 1–4, find the focus and directrix of each parabola with the given equation. Then match each equation to one of the graphs that are shown and labeled (a)–(d).*

**1.** $y^2 = 4x$ **2.** $x^2 = 4y$

**3.** $x^2 = -4y$ **4.** $y^2 = -4x$

a.

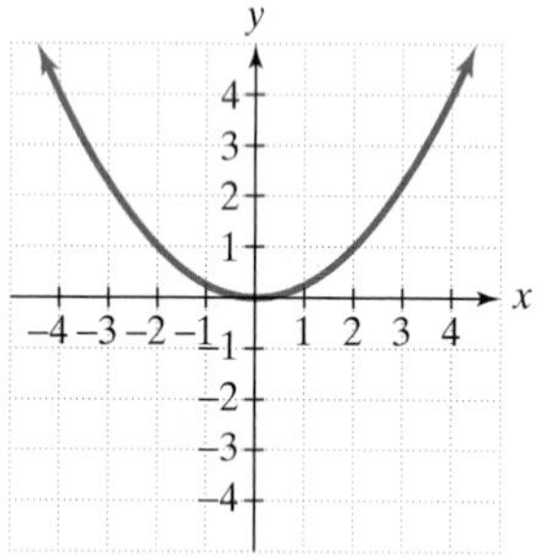


b.

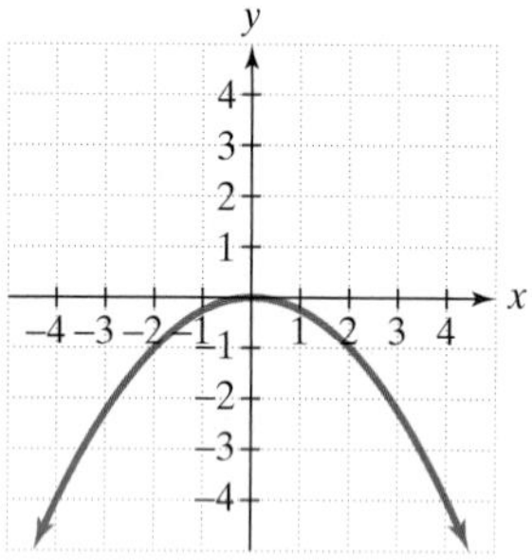


c.

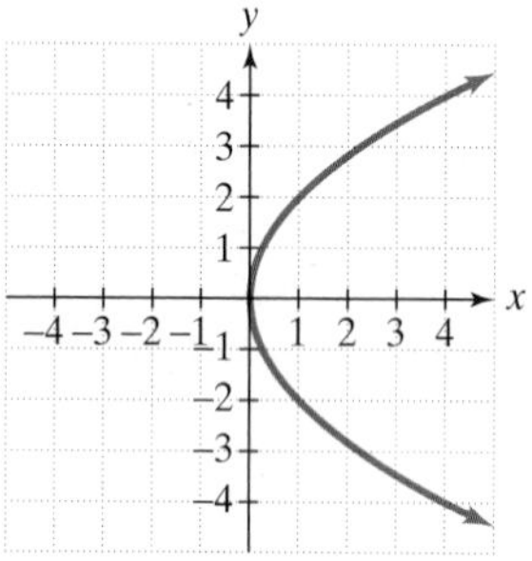


d.

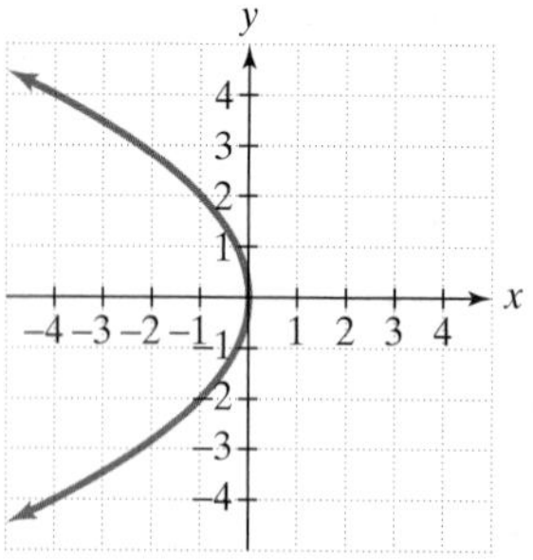


*In Exercises 5–14, find the focus and directrix of the parabola with the given equation. Then graph the parabola.*

**5.** $y^2 = 16x$ **6.** $y^2 = 4x$

**7.** $y^2 = -8x$ **8.** $y^2 = -12x$

**9.** $x^2 = 12y$ **10.** $x^2 = 8y$

**11.** $x^2 = -16y$ **12.** $x^2 = -20y$

**13.** $y^2 - 6x = 0$ **14.** $x^2 - 6y = 0$

*In Exercises 15–22, find the standard form of the equation of each parabola with vertex at the origin satisfying the given conditions.*

**15.** Focus: (7, 0); Directrix: $x = -7$

**16.** Focus: (9, 0); Directrix: $x = -9$

**17.** Focus: (−5, 0); Directrix: $x = 5$

**18.** Focus: (−10, 0); Directrix: $x = 10$

**19.** Focus: (0, 15); Directrix: $y = -15$

**20.** Focus: (0, 20); Directrix: $y = -20$

**21.** Focus: (0, −25); Directrix: $y = 25$

**22.** Focus: (0, −15); Directrix: $y = 15$

*In Exercises 23–26, find the vertex, focus, and directrix of each parabola with the given equation. Then match each equation to one of the graphs that are shown and labeled (a)–(d).*

**23.** $(y - 1)^2 = 4(x - 1)$ **24.** $(x + 1)^2 = 4(y + 1)$

**25.** $(x + 1)^2 = -4(y + 1)$ **26.** $(y - 1)^2 = -4(x - 1)$

a.

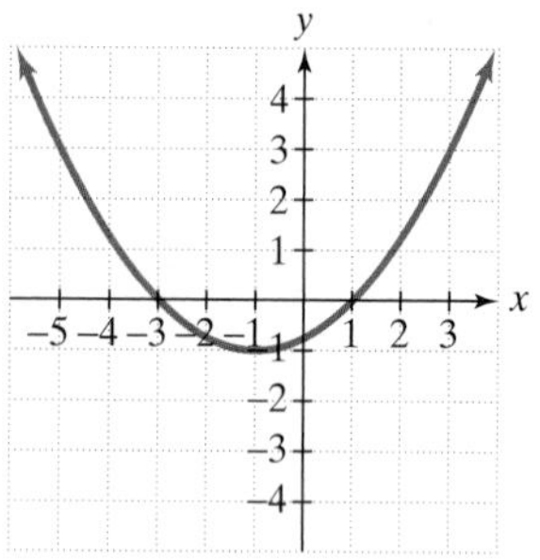


b.

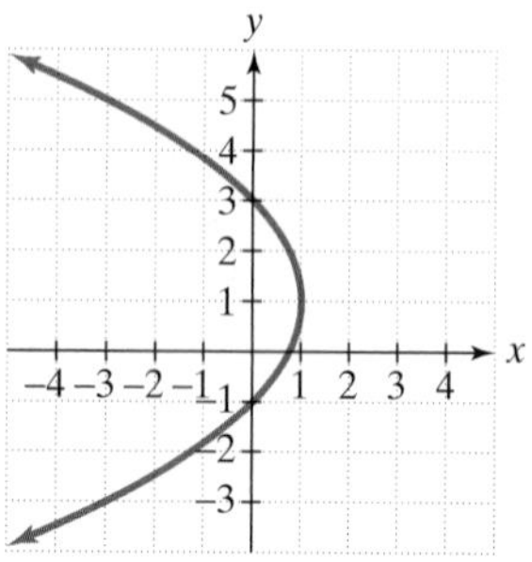

**c.**

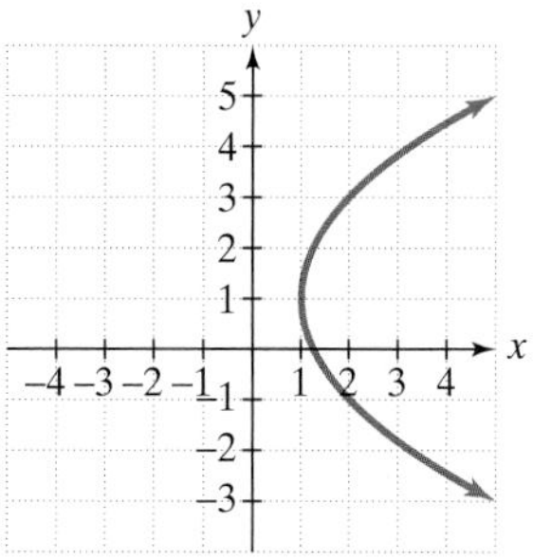


**d.**

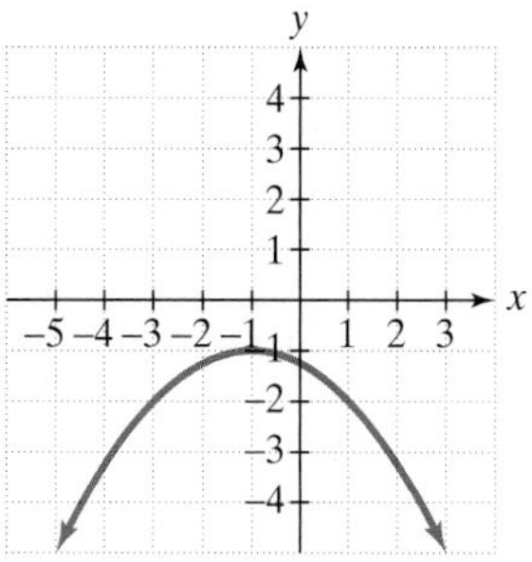


*In Exercises 27–34, find the vertex, focus, and directrix of each parabola with the given equation. Then graph the parabola.*

**27.** $(x - 2)^2 = 8(y - 1)$

**28.** $(x + 2)^2 = 4(y + 1)$

**29.** $(x + 1)^2 = -8(y + 1)$

**30.** $(x + 2)^2 = -8(y + 2)$

**31.** $(y + 3)^2 = 12(x + 1)$

**32.** $(y + 4)^2 = 12(x + 2)$

**33.** $(y + 1)^2 = -8x$

**34.** $(y - 1)^2 = -8x$

*In Exercises 35–40, convert each equation to standard form by completing the square on x or y. Then find the vertex, focus, and directrix of the parabola. Finally, graph the parabola.*

**35.** $x^2 - 2x - 4y + 9 = 0$

**36.** $x^2 + 6x + 8y + 1 = 0$

**37.** $y^2 - 2y + 12x - 35 = 0$

**38.** $y^2 - 2y - 8x + 1 = 0$

**39.** $x^2 + 6x - 4y + 1 = 0$

**40.** $x^2 + 8x - 4y + 8 = 0$

## Application Exercises

**41.** The reflector of a flashlight is in the shape of a parabolic surface. The casting has a diameter of 4 inches and a depth of 1 inch. How far from the vertex should the light bulb be placed?

**42.** The reflector of a flashlight is in the shape of a parabolic surface. The casting has a diameter of 8 inches and a depth of 1 inch. How far from the vertex should the light bulb be placed?

**43.** A satellite dish, like the one shown at the top of the next column, is in the shape of a parabolic surface. Signals coming from a satellite strike the surface of the dish and are reflected to the focus, where the receiver is located. The satellite dish shown has a diameter of 12 feet and a depth of 2 feet. How far from the base of the dish should the receiver be placed?

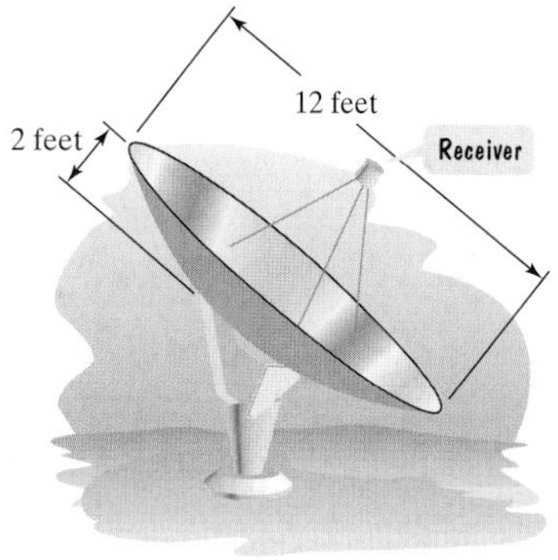


**44.** In Exercise 43, if the diameter of the dish is halved and the depth stays the same, how far from the base of the smaller dish should the receiver be placed?

**45.** The towers of the Golden Gate Bridge connecting San Francisco to Marin County are 1280 meters apart and rise 160 meters above the road. The cable between the towers has the shape of a parabola, and the cable just touches the sides of the road midway between the towers. What is the height of the cable 200 meters from a tower?

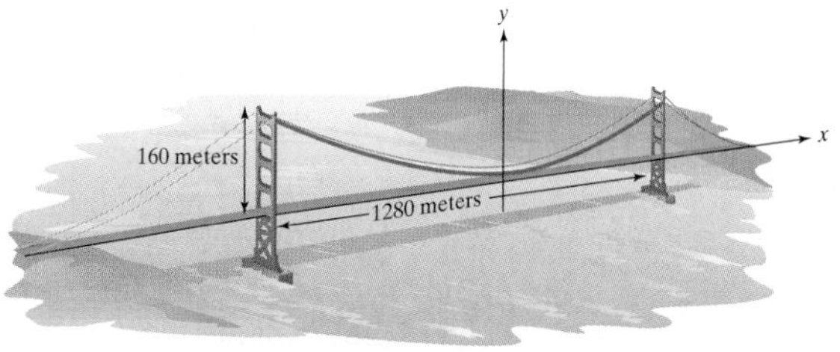


**46.** The towers of a suspension bridge are 800 feet apart and rise 160 feet above the road. The cable between the towers has the shape of a parabola, and the cable just touches the sides of the road midway between the towers. What is the height of the cable 100 feet from a tower?

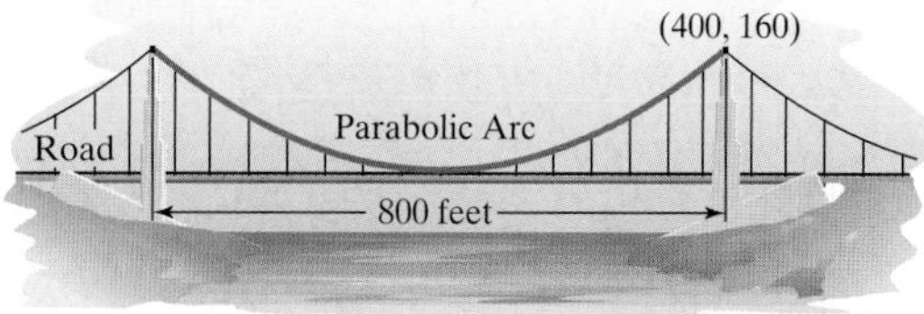


**47.** The parabolic arch shown in the figure is 50 feet above the water at the center and 200 feet wide at the base. Will a boat that is 30 feet tall clear the arch 30 feet from the center?

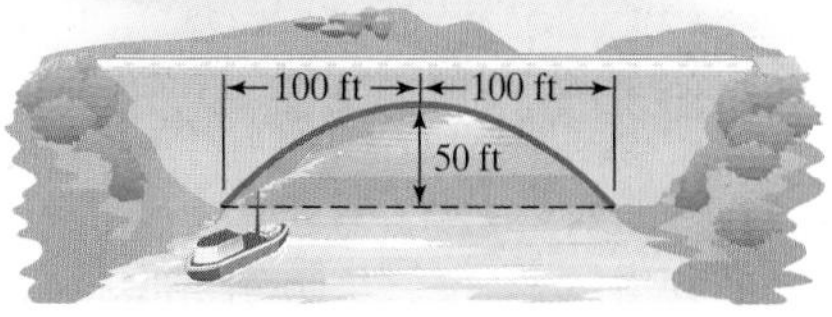

## Writing in Mathematics

**48.** What is a parabola?

**49.** Explain how to use $y^2 = 8x$ to find the parabola's focus and directrix.

**50.** If you are given the standard form of the equation of a parabola with vertex at the origin, explain how to determine if the parabola opens to the right, left, upward, or downward.

**51.** Describe one similarity and one difference between the graphs of $y^2 = 4x$ and $(y - 1)^2 = 4(x - 1)$.

**52.** How can you distinguish parabolas from other conic sections by looking at their equations?

**53.** Look at the satellite dish shown in Exercise 43. Why must the receiver for a shallow dish be farther from the base of the dish than for a deeper dish of the same diameter?

## Technology Exercises

**54.** Use a graphing utility to graph any five of the parabolas that you graphed by hand in Exercises 5–14.

**55.** Use a graphing utility to graph any three of the parabolas that you graphed by hand in Exercises 27–34. First solve the given equation for $y$, possibly using the square root method. Enter each of the two resulting equations to produce the complete graph.

*Use a graphing utility to graph the parabolas in Exercises 56–57. Write the given equation as a quadratic equation in y and use the quadratic formula to solve for y. Enter each of the equations to produce the complete graph.*

**56.** $y^2 + 2y - 6x + 13 = 0$

**57.** $y^2 + 10y - x + 25 = 0$

*In Exercises 58–59, write each equation as a quadratic equation in y and then use the quadratic formula to express y in terms of x. Graph the resulting two equations using a graphing utility. What effect does the xy-term have on the graph of the resulting parabola?*

**58.** $16x^2 - 24xy + 9y^2 - 60x - 80y + 100 = 0$

**59.** $x^2 + 2\sqrt{3}xy + 3y^2 + 8\sqrt{3}x - 8y + 32 = 0$

## Critical Thinking Exercises

**60.** Which one of the following is true?

**a.** The parabola whose equation is $x = 2y - y^2 + 5$ opens to the right.

**b.** If the parabola whose equation is $x = ay^2 + by + c$ has its vertex at $(3, 2)$ and $a > 0$, then it has no $y$-intercepts.

**c.** Some parabolas that open to the right have equations that define $y$ as a function of $x$.

**d.** The graph of $x = a(y - k) + h$ is a parabola with vertex at $(h, k)$.

**61.** A satellite dish in the shape of a parabolic surface has a diameter of 20 feet. If the receiver is to be placed 6 feet from the base, how deep should the dish be?

**62.** Write the standard form of the equation of a parabola whose points are equidistant from $y = 4$ and $(-1, 0)$.

## Group Exercise

**63.** Consult the research department of your library or the Internet to find an example of architecture that incorporates one or more conic sections in its design. Share this example with other group members. Explain precisely how conic sections are used. Do conic sections enhance the appeal of the architecture? In what ways?

# SECTION 10.4 Rotation of Axes

### Objectives

1. Identify conics without completing the square.
2. Use rotation of axes formulas.
3. Write equations of rotated conics in standard form.
4. Identify conics without rotating axes.

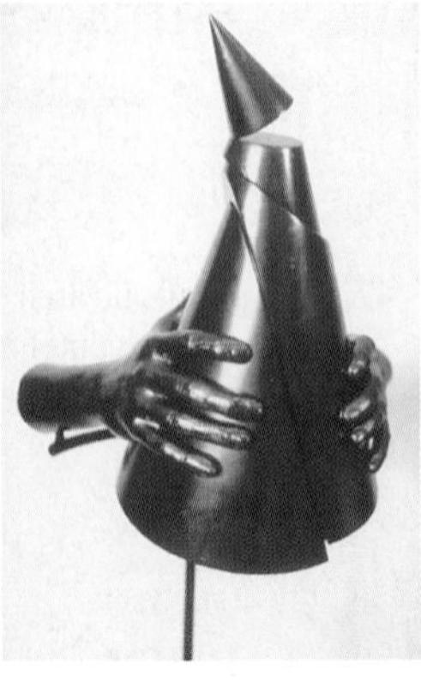

Richard E. Prince "The Cone of Apollonius" (detail), fiberglass, steel, paint, graphite, 51 × 18 × 14 in. Private collection, Vancouver. *(Photo courtesy of Equinox Gallery, Vancouver, Canada)*

To recognize a conic section, you often need to pay close attention to its graph. Graphs powerfully enhance our understanding of algebra and trigonometry.

However, it is not possible for people who are blind—or sometimes, visually impaired—to see a graph. Creating informative materials for the blind and visually impaired is a challenge for instructors and mathematicians. Many people who are visually impaired "see" a graph by touching a three-dimensional representation of that graph, perhaps while it is described verbally.

Is it possible to identify conic sections in nonvisual ways? The answer is yes, and the methods for doing so are related to the coefficients in their equations. As we present these methods, think about how you learn them. How would your approach to studying mathematics change if we removed all graphs and replaced them with verbal descriptions?

**1** Identify conics without completing the square.

## Identifying Conic Sections without Completing the Square

Conic sections can be represented both geometrically (as intersecting planes and cones) and algebraically. The equations of the conic sections we have considered in the first three sections of this chapter can be expressed in the form

$$Ax^2 + Cy^2 + Dx + Ey + F = 0$$

in which $A$ and $C$ are not both zero. You can use $A$ and $C$, the coefficients of $x^2$ and $y^2$, respectively, to identify a conic section without completing the square.

**Identifying a Conic Section without Completing the Square**

A nondegenerate conic section of the form

$$Ax^2 + Cy^2 + Dx + Ey + F = 0$$

in which $A$ and $C$ are not both zero is

- a circle if $A = C$,
- a parabola if $AC = 0$,
- an ellipse if $A \neq C$ and $AC > 0$, and
- a hyperbola if $AC < 0$.

### EXAMPLE 1 Identifying a Conic Section without Completing the Square

Identify the graph of each of the following nondegenerate conic sections.

**a.** $4x^2 - 25y^2 - 24x + 250y - 489 = 0$

**b.** $x^2 + y^2 + 6x - 2y + 6 = 0$

**c.** $y^2 + 12x + 2y - 23 = 0$

**d.** $9x^2 + 25y^2 - 54x + 50y - 119 = 0$

**Solution** We use $A$, the coefficient of $x^2$, and $C$, the coefficient of $y^2$, to identify each conic section.

**a.** $4x^2 - 25y^2 - 24x + 250y - 489 = 0$

$A = 4$ $C = -25$

$AC = 4(-25) = -100 < 0$

Because $AC < 0$, the graph of the equation is a hyperbola.

**b.** $x^2 + y^2 + 6x - 2y + 6 = 0$

$A = 1$ $C = 1$

Because $A = C$, the graph of the equation is a circle.

**c.** We can write $y^2 + 12x + 2y - 23 = 0$ as

$$0x^2 + y^2 + 12x + 2y - 23 = 0.$$

$A = 0$ $C = 1$

$$AC = 0(1) = 0$$

Because $AC = 0$, the graph of the equation is a parabola.

**d.** $9x^2 + 25y^2 - 54x + 50y - 119 = 0$

$A = 9$ $C = 25$

$AC = 9(25) = 225 > 0.$

Because $AC > 0$ and $A \neq C$, the graph of the equation is an ellipse.

**Check Point 1** Identify the graph of each of the following nondegenerate conic sections.

**a.** $3x^2 + 2y^2 + 12x - 4y + 2 = 0$

**b.** $x^2 + y^2 - 6x + y + 3 = 0$

**c.** $y^2 - 12x - 4y + 52 = 0$

**d.** $9x^2 - 16y^2 - 90x + 64y + 17 = 0$

**2** Use rotation of axes formulas.

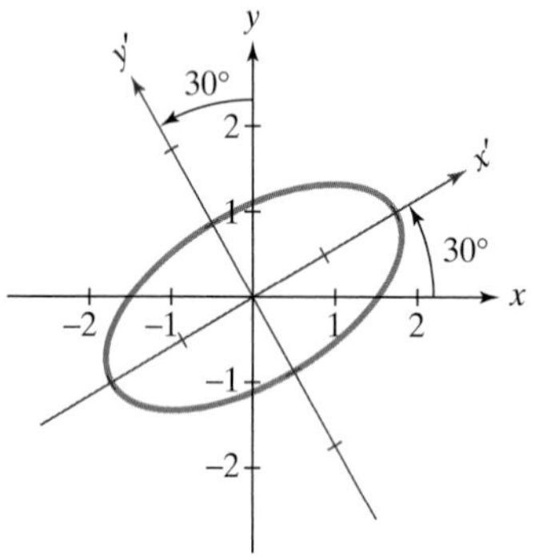


**Figure 10.46** The graph of $7x^2 - 6\sqrt{3}\,xy + 13y^2 - 16 = 0$, a rotated ellipse

## Rotation of Axes

Figure 10.46 shows the graph of

$$7x^2 - 6\sqrt{3}\,xy + 13y^2 - 16 = 0.$$

The graph looks like an ellipse, although its major axis neither lies along the $x$-axis nor is parallel to the $x$-axis. Do you notice anything unusual about the equation? It contains an $xy$-term. However, look what happens if we rotate the $x$- and $y$-axes through an angle of 30°. In the rotated $x'y'$-system, the major axis of the ellipse lies along the $x'$-axis. We can write the equation of the ellipse in this rotated $x'y'$-system as

$$\frac{x'^2}{4} + \frac{y'^2}{1} = 1.$$

Observe that there is no $x'y'$-term in the equation.

Except for degenerate cases, the **general second-degree equation**

$$Ax^2 + Bxy + Cy^2 + Dx + Ey + F = 0$$

represents one of the conic sections. However, due to the $xy$-term in the equation, these conic sections are rotated in such a way that their axes are no longer parallel to the $x$- and $y$-axes. To reduce these equations to forms of the conic sections with which you are already familiar, we use a procedure called **rotation of axes.**

Suppose that the $x$- and $y$-axes are rotated through a positive angle $\theta$, resulting in a new $x'y'$ coordinate system. This system is shown in Figure 10.47(a). The origin in the $x'y'$-system is the same as the origin in the $xy$-system. Point $P$ in Figure 10.47(b) has coordinates $(x, y)$ relative to the $xy$-system and coordinates

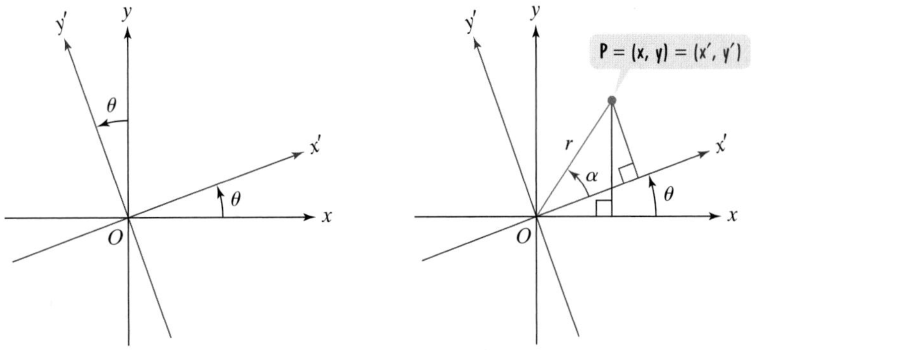


**(a)** Rotating the $x$- and $y$-axes through a positive angle $\theta$

**(b)** Describing point $P$ relative to the $xy$-system and the rotated $x'y'$-system

**Figure 10.47** Rotating axes

$(x', y')$ relative to the $x'y'$-system. We wish to obtain formulas relating the old and new coordinates. Thus, we need to express $x$ and $y$ in terms of $x'$, $y'$, and $\theta$.

Look at Figure 10.47(b). Notice that

$r$ = the distance from the origin 0 to point $P$.

$\alpha$ = the angle from the positive $x'$-axis to the ray from 0 through $P$.

Using the definitions of sine and cosine, we obtain

$$\cos\alpha = \frac{x'}{r}: x' = r\cos\alpha$$

$$\sin\alpha = \frac{y'}{r}: y' = r\sin\alpha$$

This is from the right triangle with a leg along the x'-axis.

$$\cos(\theta + \alpha) = \frac{x}{r}: x = r\cos(\theta + \alpha)$$

$$\sin(\theta + \alpha) = \frac{y}{r}: y = r\sin(\theta + \alpha)$$

This is from the taller right triangle with a leg along the x-axis.

Thus,

| | |
|---|---|
| $x = r\cos(\theta + \alpha)$ | This is the third of the preceding equations. |
| $= r(\cos\theta\cos\alpha - \sin\theta\sin\alpha)$ | Use the formula for the cosine of the sum of two angles. |
| $= (r\cos\alpha)\cos\theta - (r\sin\alpha)\sin\theta$ | Apply the distributive property and rearrange factors. |
| $= x'\cos\theta - y'\sin\theta$ | Use the first and second of the preceding equations: $x' = r\cos\alpha$ and $y' = r\sin\alpha$. |

Similarly,

$$y = r\sin(\theta + \alpha) = r(\sin\theta\cos\alpha + \cos\theta\sin\alpha) = x'\sin\theta + y'\cos\theta.$$

**Rotation of Axes Formulas**

Suppose an $xy$-coordinate system and an $x'y'$-coordinate system have the same origin and $\theta$ is the angle from the positive $x$-axis to the positive $x'$-axis. If the coordinates of point $P$ are $(x, y)$ in the $xy$-system and $(x', y')$ in the rotated $x'y'$-system, then

$$x = x'\cos\theta - y'\sin\theta$$

$$y = x'\sin\theta + y'\cos\theta.$$

## EXAMPLE 2 Rotating Axes

Write the equation $xy = 1$ in terms of a rotated $x'y'$-system if the angle of rotation from the $x$-axis to the $x'$-axis is 45°. Express the equation in standard form. Use the rotated system to graph $xy = 1$.

**Solution** With $\theta = 45°$, the rotation formulas for $x$ and $y$ are

$$x = x'\cos\theta - y'\sin\theta = x'\cos 45° - y'\sin 45°$$

$$= x'\left(\frac{\sqrt{2}}{2}\right) - y'\left(\frac{\sqrt{2}}{2}\right) = \frac{\sqrt{2}}{2}(x' - y')$$

$$y = x'\sin\theta + y'\cos\theta = x'\sin 45° + y'\cos 45°$$

$$= x'\left(\frac{\sqrt{2}}{2}\right) + y'\left(\frac{\sqrt{2}}{2}\right) = \frac{\sqrt{2}}{2}(x' + y')$$

Now substitute these expressions for $x$ and $y$ in the given equation, $xy = 1$.

$$xy = 1$$ This is the given equation.

$$\left[\frac{\sqrt{2}}{2}(x' - y')\right]\left[\frac{\sqrt{2}}{2}(x' + y')\right] = 1$$ Substitute the expressions for x and y from the rotation formulas.

$$\frac{2}{4}(x' - y')(x' + y') = 1$$ Multiply: $\frac{\sqrt{2}}{2} \cdot \frac{\sqrt{2}}{2} = \frac{2}{4}$.

$$\frac{1}{2}(x'^2 - y'^2) = 1$$ Multiply the binomials.

$$\frac{x'^2}{2} - \frac{y'^2}{2} = 1$$ Write the equation in standard form: $\frac{x^2}{a^2} - \frac{y^2}{b^2} = 1$.

$a^2 = 2$ $b^2 = 2$

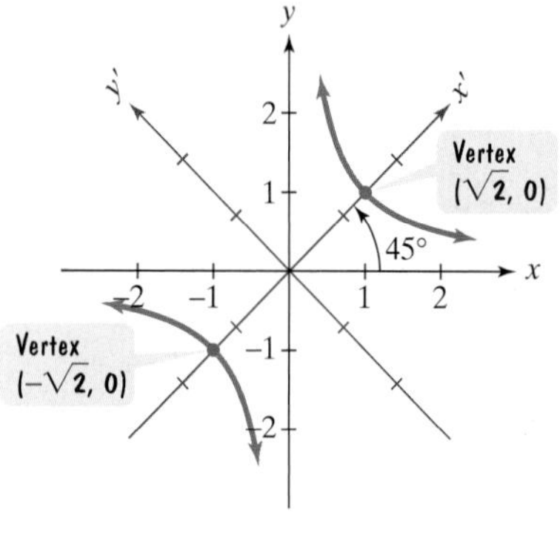


**Figure 10.48** The graph of $xy = 1$ or $\frac{x'^2}{2} - \frac{y'^2}{2} = 1$

This equation expresses $xy = 1$ in terms of the rotated $x'y'$-system. Can you see that this is the standard form of the equation of a hyperbola? The hyperbola's center is at (0, 0) with the transverse axis on the $x'$-axis. The vertices are $(-a, 0)$ and $(a, 0)$. Because $a^2 = 2$, the vertices are $(-\sqrt{2}, 0)$ and $(\sqrt{2}, 0)$, located on the $x'$-axis. Based on the standard form of the hyperbola's equation, the equations for the asymptotes are

$$y' = \pm\frac{b}{a}x' \text{ or } y' = \pm\frac{\sqrt{2}}{\sqrt{2}}x'.$$

The equations of the asymptotes can be simplified to $y' = x'$ and $y' = -x'$, which correspond to the original $x$- and $y$-axes. The graph of the hyperbola is shown in Figure 10.48.

**Check Point 2** Write the equation $xy = 2$ in terms of a rotated $x'y'$-system if the angle of rotation from the $x$-axis to the $x'$-axis is 45°. Express the equation in standard form. Use the rotated system to graph $xy = 2$.

**3** Write equations of rotated conics in standard form.

## Using Rotations to Transform Equations with $xy$-Terms to Standard Equations of Conic Sections

We have noted that the appearance of the term $Bxy$ $(B \neq 0)$ in the general second-degree equation indicates that the graph of the conic section has been rotated. A rotation of axes through an appropriate angle can transform the equation to one of the standard forms of the conic sections in $x'$ and $y'$ in which no $x'y'$-term appears.

### Amount of Rotation Formula

The general second-degree equation

$$Ax^2 + Bxy + Cy^2 + Dx + Ey + F = 0, B \neq 0$$

can be rewritten as an equation in $x'$ and $y'$ without an $x'y'$-term by rotating the axes through angle $\theta$, where

$$\cot 2\theta = \frac{A - C}{B}.$$

Before we learn to apply this formula, let's see how it can be derived. We begin with the general second-degree equation

$$Ax^2 + Bxy + Cy^2 + Dx + Ey + F = 0, B \neq 0.$$

Rotate the axes through an angle $\theta$. In terms of the rotated $x'y'$-system, the general second-degree equation can be written as

$$\begin{aligned} A(x'\cos\theta - y'\sin\theta)^2 &+ B(x'\cos\theta - y'\sin\theta)(x'\sin\theta + y'\cos\theta) \\ &+ C(x'\sin\theta + y'\cos\theta)^2 + D(x'\cos\theta - y'\sin\theta) \\ &+ E(x'\sin\theta + y'\cos\theta) + F = 0. \end{aligned}$$

After a lot of simplifying that involves expanding and collecting like terms, you will obtain the following equation.

We want a rotation that results in no x'y'-term.

$$\begin{aligned} (A\cos^2\theta + B\sin\theta\cos\theta + C\sin^2\theta)x'^2 &+ \left[B(\cos^2\theta - \sin^2\theta) + 2(C - A)(\sin\theta\cos\theta)\right]x'y' \\ &+ (A\sin^2\theta - B\sin\theta\cos\theta + C\cos^2\theta)y'^2 \\ &+ (D\cos\theta + E\sin\theta)x' \\ &+ (-D\sin\theta + E\cos\theta)y' + F = 0 \end{aligned}$$

If this looks somewhat ghastly, take a deep breath and focus only on the $x'y'$-term. We want to choose $\theta$ so that the coefficient of this term is zero. This will give the required rotation that results in no $x'y'$-term.

$$B(\cos^2\theta - \sin^2\theta) + 2(C - A)\sin\theta\cos\theta = 0$$ Set the coefficient of the $x'y'$-term equal to 0.

$$B\cos 2\theta + (C - A)\sin 2\theta = 0$$ Use the double-angle formulas: $\cos 2\theta = \cos^2\theta - \sin^2\theta$ and $\sin 2\theta = 2\sin\theta\cos\theta$.

$$B\cos 2\theta = 0 - (C - A)\sin 2\theta$$ Subtract $(C - A)\sin 2\theta$ from both sides.

$$B\cos 2\theta = (A - C)\sin 2\theta \quad \text{Simplify.}$$

$$\frac{B\cos 2\theta}{B\sin 2\theta} = \frac{(A - C)\sin 2\theta}{B\sin 2\theta} \quad \text{Divide both sides by } B\sin 2\theta.$$

$$\frac{\cos 2\theta}{\sin 2\theta} = \frac{A - C}{B} \quad \text{Simplify.}$$

$$\cot 2\theta = \frac{A - C}{B} \quad \text{Apply a quotient identity: } \cot\square = \frac{\sin\square}{\cos\square}.$$

If $\cot 2\theta$ is positive, we will select $\theta$ so that $0° < \theta < 45°$. If $\cot 2\theta$ is negative, we will select $\theta$ so that $45° < \theta < 90°$. Thus $\theta$, the angle of rotation, is always an acute angle.

Here is a step-by-step procedure for writing the equation of a rotated conic section in standard form.

### Study Tip

What do you do after substituting the expressions for $x$ and $y$ from the rotation formulas into the given equation? You must simplify the resulting equation by expanding and collecting like terms. Work through this process slowly and carefully, allowing lots of room on your paper.

If your rotation equations are correct but you obtain an equation that has an $x'y'$-term, you have made an error in the algebraic simplification.

**Writing the Equation of a Rotated Conic in Standard Form**

1. Use the given equation

$$Ax^2 + Bxy + Cy^2 + Dx + Ey + F = 0, B \neq 0$$

to find $\cot 2\theta$.

$$\cot 2\theta = \frac{A - C}{B}$$

2. Use the expression for $\cot 2\theta$ to determine $\theta$, the angle of rotation.
3. Substitute $\theta$ in the rotation formulas

$$x = x'\cos\theta - y'\sin\theta \quad \text{and} \quad y = x'\sin\theta + y'\cos\theta$$

and simplify.
4. Substitute the expressions for $x$ and $y$ from the rotation formulas in the given equation and simplify. The resulting equation should have no $x'y'$-term.
5. Write the equation involving $x'$ and $y'$ in standard form.

Using the equation in step 5, you can graph the conic section in the rotated $x'y'$-system.

## EXAMPLE 3 Writing the Equation of a Rotated Conic Section in Standard Form

Rewrite the equation

$$7x^2 - 6\sqrt{3}\,xy + 13y^2 - 16 = 0$$

in a rotated $x'y'$-system without an $x'y'$-term. Express the equation in the standard form of a conic section.

**Solution**

**Step 1 Use the given equation to find $\cot 2\theta$.** We need to identify the constants $A$, $B$, and $C$ in the given equation.

$$7x^2 - 6\sqrt{3}\,xy + 13y^2 - 16 = 0.$$

A is the coefficient of the $x^2$-term: $A = 7$.

B is the coefficient of the $xy$-term: $B = -6\sqrt{3}$.

C is the coefficient of the $y^2$-term: $C = 13$.

The appropriate angle $\theta$ through which to rotate the axes satisfies the equation

$$\cot 2\theta = \frac{A - C}{B} = \frac{7 - 13}{-6\sqrt{3}} = \frac{-6}{-6\sqrt{3}} = \frac{1}{\sqrt{3}} \text{ or } \frac{\sqrt{3}}{3}.$$

**Step 2 Use the expression for $\cot 2\theta$ to determine the angle of rotation.** We have $\cot 2\theta = \frac{\sqrt{3}}{3}$. Based on our knowledge of exact values for trigonometric functions, we conclude that $2\theta = 60°$. Thus, $\theta = 30°$.

**Step 3 Substitute $\theta$ in the rotation formulas $x = x'\cos\theta - y'\sin\theta$ and $y = x'\sin\theta + y'\cos\theta$ and simplify.** Substituting 30° for $\theta$,

$$x = x'\cos 30° - y'\sin 30° = x'\left(\frac{\sqrt{3}}{2}\right) - y'\left(\frac{1}{2}\right) = \frac{\sqrt{3}x' - y'}{2}$$

$$y = x'\sin 30° + y'\cos 30° = x'\left(\frac{1}{2}\right) + y'\left(\frac{\sqrt{3}}{2}\right) = \frac{x' + \sqrt{3}y'}{2}.$$

**Step 4 Substitute the expressions for $x$ and $y$ from the rotation formulas in the given equation and simplify.**

$$7x^2 - 6\sqrt{3}xy + 13y^2 - 16 = 0$$ This is the given equation.

$$7\left(\frac{\sqrt{3}x' - y'}{2}\right)^2 - 6\sqrt{3}\left(\frac{\sqrt{3}x' - y'}{2}\right)\left(\frac{x' + \sqrt{3}y'}{2}\right) + 13\left(\frac{x' + \sqrt{3}y'}{2}\right)^2 - 16 = 0$$ Substitute the expressions for x and y from the rotation formulas.

$$7\left(\frac{3x'^2 - 2\sqrt{3}x'y' + y'^2}{4}\right) - 6\sqrt{3}\left(\frac{\sqrt{3}x'^2 + 3x'y' - x'y' - \sqrt{3}y'^2}{4}\right) + 13\left(\frac{x'^2 + 2\sqrt{3}x'y' + 3y'^2}{4}\right) - 16 = 0$$ Square and multiply.

$$7(3x'^2 - 2\sqrt{3}x'y' + y'^2) - 6\sqrt{3}(\sqrt{3}x'^2 + 2x'y' - \sqrt{3}y'^2) + 13(x'^2 + 2\sqrt{3}x'y' + 3y'^2) - 64 = 0$$ Multiply both sides by 4.

$$21x'^2 - 14\sqrt{3}x'y' + 7y'^2 - 18x'^2 - 12\sqrt{3}x'y' + 18y'^2 + 13x'^2 + 26\sqrt{3}x'y' + 39y'^2 - 64 = 0$$ Distribute throughout parentheses.

$$21x'^2 - 18x'^2 + 13x'^2 - 14\sqrt{3}x'y' - 12\sqrt{3}x'y' + 26\sqrt{3}x'y' + 7y'^2 + 18y'^2 + 39y'^2 - 64 = 0$$ Rearrange terms.

$$16x'^2 + 64y'^2 - 64 = 0$$ Combine like terms.

Do you see how we "lost" the $x'y'$-term in the last equation?

$$-14\sqrt{3}x'y' - 12\sqrt{3}x'y' + 26\sqrt{3}x'y' = -26\sqrt{3}x'y' + 26\sqrt{3}x'y' = 0x'y' = 0$$

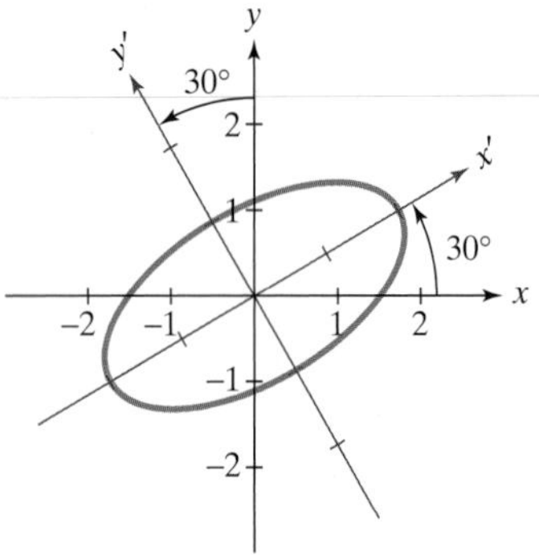


**Figure 10.46**, repeated
The graph of
$7x^2 - 6\sqrt{3}\,xy + 13y^2 - 16 = 0$
or $\frac{x'^2}{4} - \frac{y'^2}{1} = 1$, a rotated ellipse

**Step 5 Write the equation involving $x'$ and $y'$ in standard form.** We can express $16x'^2 + 64y'^2 - 64 = 0$, an equation of an ellipse, in the standard form $\frac{x^2}{a^2} + \frac{y^2}{b^2} = 1$.

$$16x'^2 + 64y'^2 - 64 = 0$$ This equation describes the ellipse relative to a system rotated through 30°.

$$16x'^2 + 64y'^2 = 64$$ Add 64 to both sides.

$$\frac{16x'^2}{64} + \frac{64y'^2}{64} = \frac{64}{64}$$ Divide both sides by 64.

$$\frac{x'^2}{4} + \frac{y'^2}{1} = 1$$ Simplify.

The last equation is the standard form of the equation of an ellipse. The major axis is on the $x'$-axis and the vertices are $(-2, 0)$ and $(2, 0)$. The minor axis is on the $y'$-axis with endpoints $(0, -1)$ and $(0, 1)$. The graph of the ellipse is shown in Figure 10.46. Does this graph look familiar? It should—you saw it earlier in this section on page 852.

**Check Point 3** Rewrite the equation

$$2x^2 + \sqrt{3}xy + y^2 - 2 = 0$$

in a rotated $x'y'$-system without an $x'y'$-term. Express the equation in the standard form of a conic section. Graph the conic section in the rotated system.

## Technology

In order to graph a general second-degree equation in the form

$$Ax^2 + Bxy + Cy^2 + Dx + Ey + F = 0,$$

it is necessary to solve for $y$. Rewrite the equation as a quadratic equation in $y$.

$$Cy^2 + (Bx + E)y + (Ax^2 + Dx + F) = 0$$

By applying the quadratic formula, the graph of this equation can be obtained by entering

$$y_1 = \frac{-(Bx + E) + \sqrt{(Bx + E)^2 - 4C(Ax^2 + Dx + F)}}{2C}$$

and

$$y_2 = \frac{-(Bx + E) - \sqrt{(Bx + E)^2 - 4C(Ax^2 + Dx + F)}}{2C}.$$

The graph of

$$7x^2 - 6\sqrt{3}xy + 13y^2 - 16 = 0$$

is shown on the right in a $[-2, 2, 1]$ by $[-2, 2, 1]$ viewing rectangle. The graph was obtained by entering the equations for $y_1$ and $y_2$ shown previously with

$$A = 7, B = -6\sqrt{3}, C = 13, D = 0, E = 0, \text{ and } F = -16.$$

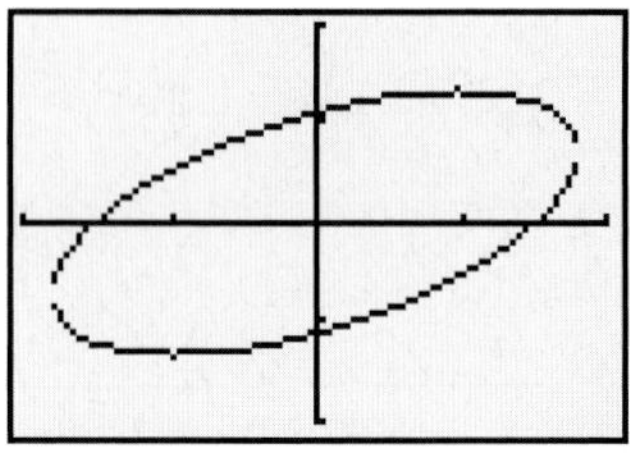

In Example 3 and the Check Point 3, we found $\theta$, the angle of rotation, directly because we recognized $\frac{\sqrt{3}}{3}$ as the value of $\cot 60°$. What do we do if $\cot 2\theta$ is not the cotangent of one of the more familiar angles? We use $\cot 2\theta$ to find $\sin\theta$ and $\cos\theta$ as follows:

- Use a sketch of $\cot 2\theta$ to find $\cos 2\theta$.
- Find $\sin\theta$ and $\cos\theta$ using the identities

$$\sin\theta = \sqrt{\frac{1-\cos 2\theta}{2}} \quad \text{and} \quad \cos\theta = \sqrt{\frac{1+\cos 2\theta}{2}}.$$

Because $\theta$ is an acute angle, the positive square roots are appropriate.

The resulting values for $\sin\theta$ and $\cos\theta$ are used to write the rotation formulas that give an equation with no $x'y'$-term.

## EXAMPLE 4 Graphing the Equation of a Rotated Conic

Graph relative to a rotated $x'y'$-system in which the equation has no $x'y'$-term:

$$16x^2 - 24xy + 9y^2 + 110x - 20y + 100 = 0.$$

### Solution

**Step 1 Use the given equation to find $\cot 2\theta$.** With $A = 16$, $B = -24$, and $C = 9$, we have

$$\cot 2\theta = \frac{A-C}{B} = \frac{16-9}{-24} = -\frac{7}{24}.$$

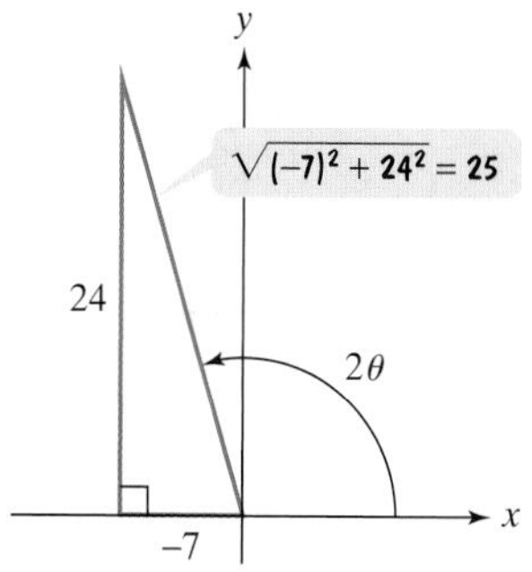


**Figure 10.49** Using $\cot 2\theta$ to find $\cos 2\theta$

**Step 2 Use the expression for $\cot 2\theta$ to determine $\sin\theta$ and $\cos\theta$.** A rough sketch showing $\cot 2\theta$ is given in Figure 10.49. Because $\theta$ is always acute and $\cot 2\theta$ is negative, $2\theta$ is in quadrant II. The third side of the triangle is found using $x^2 + y^2 = r^2$. By the definition of the cosine function,

$$\cos 2\theta = \frac{x}{r} = \frac{-7}{25} = -\frac{7}{25}.$$

Now we use identities to find values for $\sin\theta$ and $\cos\theta$.

$$\sin\theta = \sqrt{\frac{1-\cos 2\theta}{2}} = \sqrt{\frac{1-\left(-\frac{7}{25}\right)}{2}}$$

$$= \sqrt{\frac{1+\frac{7}{25}}{2}} = \sqrt{\frac{\frac{25}{25}+\frac{7}{25}}{2}} = \sqrt{\frac{\frac{32}{25}}{2}} = \sqrt{\frac{32}{50}} = \sqrt{\frac{16}{25}} = \frac{4}{5}$$

$$\cos\theta = \sqrt{\frac{1+\cos 2\theta}{2}} = \sqrt{\frac{1+\left(-\frac{7}{25}\right)}{2}}$$

$$= \sqrt{\frac{\frac{25}{25}-\frac{7}{25}}{2}} = \sqrt{\frac{\frac{18}{25}}{2}} = \sqrt{\frac{18}{50}} = \sqrt{\frac{9}{25}} = \frac{3}{5}$$

**Step 3 Substitute $\sin\theta$ and $\cos\theta$ in the rotation formulas**

$$x = x'\cos\theta - y'\sin\theta \text{ and } y = x'\sin\theta + y'\cos\theta$$

**and simplify.** Substituting $\frac{4}{5}$ for $\sin\theta$ and $\frac{3}{5}$ for $\cos\theta$,

$$x = x'\left(\frac{3}{5}\right) - y'\left(\frac{4}{5}\right) = \frac{3x' - 4y'}{5}$$

$$y = x'\left(\frac{4}{5}\right) + y'\left(\frac{3}{5}\right) = \frac{4x' + 3y'}{5}.$$

**Step 4 Substitute the expressions for $x$ and $y$ from the rotation formulas in the given equation and simplify.**

$$16x^2 - 24xy + 9y^2 + 110x - 20y + 100 = 0$$ This is the given equation.

$$16\left(\frac{3x'-4y'}{5}\right)^2 - 24\left(\frac{3x'-4y'}{5}\right)\left(\frac{4x'+3y'}{5}\right) + 9\left(\frac{4x'+3y'}{5}\right)^2 + 110\left(\frac{3x'-4y'}{5}\right) - 20\left(\frac{4x'+3y'}{5}\right) + 100 = 0$$ Substitute the expressions for x and y from the rotation formulas.

Take a few minutes to expand, multiply both sides of the equation by 25, and combine like terms. The resulting equation

$$y'^2 + 2x' - 4y' + 4 = 0$$

has no $x'y'$-term.

**Step 5 Write the equation involving $x'$ and $y'$ in standard form.** With only one variable that is squared, we have the equation of a parabola. We need to write the equation in the standard form $(y - k)^2 = 4p(x - h)$.

$$y'^2 + 2x' - 4y' + 4 = 0$$ This is the equation without an $x'y'$-term.

$$y'^2 - 4y' = -2x' - 4$$ Isolate the terms involving $y'$.

$$y'^2 - 4y' + 4 = -2x' - 4 + 4$$ Complete the square by adding the square of half the coefficient of $y'$.

$$(y' - 2)^2 = -2x'$$ Factor.

The standard form of the parabola's equation in the rotated $x'y'$-system is

$$(y' - 2)^2 = -2x'.$$

This is $(y' - k)^2$ with $k = 2$. This is $4p$. This is $x' - h$ with $h = 0$.

We see that $h = 0$ and $k = 2$. Thus, the vertex of the parabola in the $x'y'$-system is $(h, k) = (0, 2)$. If $x' = -2$, $(y' - 2)^2 = 4$ and $y' = 4$ or $y' = 0$. The parabola passes through $(-2, 4)$ and $(-2, 0)$ in the $x'y'$-system. Using a calculator to solve $\sin\theta = \frac{4}{5}$, we find that $\theta = \sin^{-1}\frac{4}{5} \approx 53°$. Rotate the axes through approximately 53°. Using the rotated system, pass a smooth curve through the vertex and the two points on the parabola. The graph of the parabola is shown in Figure 10.50.

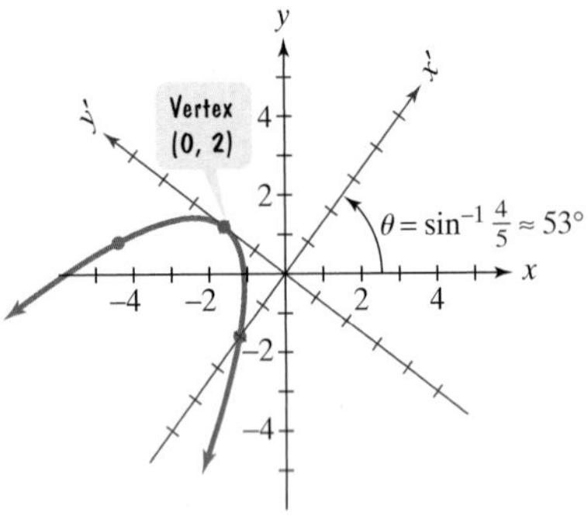


**Figure 10.50** The graph of $(y' - 2)^2 = -2x'$ in a rotated $x'y'$-system

**Check Point 4** Graph relative to a rotated $x'y'$-system in which the equation has no $x'y'$-term:

$$4x^2 - 4xy + y^2 - 8\sqrt{5}x - 16\sqrt{5}y = 0.$$

**4** Identify conics without rotating axes.

## Identifying Conic Sections without Rotating Axes

We now know that the general second-degree equation

$$Ax^2 + Bxy + Cy^2 + Dx + Ey + F = 0, B \neq 0$$

can be rewritten as

$$A'x'^2 + C'y'^2 + D'x' + E'y' + F' = 0$$

in a rotated $x'y'$-system. A relationship between the coefficients of the two equations is given by

$$B^2 - 4AC = -4A'C'.$$

We also know that $A'$ and $C'$ can be used to identify the graph of the rotated equation. Thus, $B^2 - 4AC$ can also be used to identify the graph of the general second-degree equation.

**Identifying a Conic Section without a Rotation of Axes**

A nondegenerate conic section of the form

$$Ax^2 + Bxy + Cy^2 + Dx + Ey + F = 0$$

is

- a parabola if $B^2 - 4AC = 0$,
- an ellipse or a circle if $B^2 - 4AC < 0$, and
- a hyperbola if $B^2 - 4AC > 0$.

**Technology**

The graph of

$11x^2 + 10\sqrt{3}xy + y^2 - 4 = 0$

is shown in a $\left[-1, 1, \frac{1}{4}\right]$ by $\left[-1, 1, \frac{1}{4}\right]$ viewing rectangle. The graph verifies that the equation represents a rotated hyperbola.

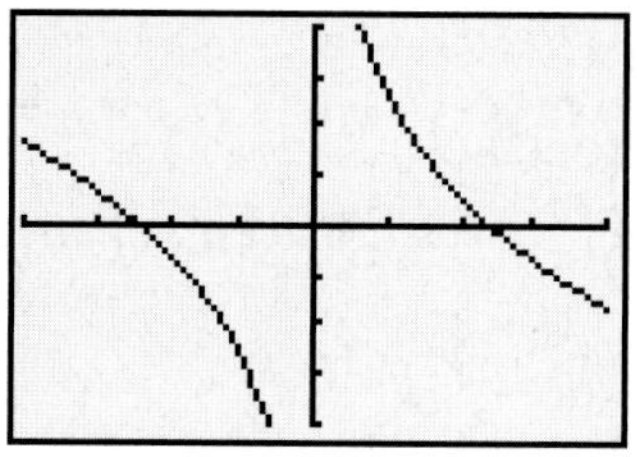

### EXAMPLE 5 Identifying a Conic Section without Rotating Axes

Identify the graph of

$$11x^2 + 10\sqrt{3}xy + y^2 - 4 = 0.$$

**Solution** We use $A$, $B$, and $C$ to identify the conic section.

$$11x^2 + 10\sqrt{3}xy + y^2 - 4 = 0$$

$A = 11$ $B = 10\sqrt{3}$ $C = 1$

$$B^2 - 4AC = \left(10\sqrt{3}\right)^2 - 4(11)(1) = 100 \cdot 3 - 44 = 256 > 0$$

Because $B^2 - 4AC > 0$, the graph of the equation is a hyperbola.

**Check Point 5** Identify the graph of $3x^2 - 2\sqrt{3}xy + y^2 + 2x + 2\sqrt{3}y = 0$.

# EXERCISE SET 10.4

## Practice Exercises

*In Exercises 1–8, identify each equation without completing the square.*

**1.** $y^2 - 4x + 2y + 21 = 0$

**2.** $y^2 - 4x - 4y = 0$

**3.** $4x^2 - 9y^2 - 8x - 36y - 68 = 0$

**4.** $9x^2 + 25y^2 - 54x - 200y + 256 = 0$

**5.** $4x^2 + 4y^2 + 12x + 4y + 1 = 0$

**6.** $9x^2 + 4y^2 - 36x + 8y + 31 = 0$

**7.** $100x^2 - 7y^2 + 90y - 368 = 0$

**8.** $y^2 + 8x + 6y + 25 = 0$

*In Exercises 9–14, write each equation in terms of a rotated $x'y'$-system using $\theta$, the angle of rotation. Write the equation involving $x'$ and $y'$ in standard form.*

**9.** $xy = -1; \theta = 45°$

**10.** $xy = -4; \theta = 45°$

**11.** $x^2 - 4xy + y^2 - 3 = 0; \theta = 45°$

**12.** $13x^2 - 10xy + 13y^2 - 72 = 0; \theta = 45°$

**13.** $23x^2 + 26\sqrt{3}xy - 3y^2 - 144 = 0; \theta = 30°$

**14.** $13x^2 - 6\sqrt{3}\,xy + 7y^2 - 16 = 0; \theta = 60°$

*In Exercises 15–26, write the appropriate rotation formulas so that in a rotated system the equation has no $x'y'$-term.*

**15.** $x^2 + xy + y^2 - 10 = 0$

**16.** $x^2 + 4xy + y^2 - 3 = 0$

**17.** $3x^2 - 10xy + 3y^2 - 32 = 0$

**18.** $5x^2 - 8xy + 5y^2 - 9 = 0$

**19.** $11x^2 + 10\sqrt{3}xy + y^2 - 4 = 0$

**20.** $7x^2 - 6\sqrt{3}xy + 13y^2 - 16 = 0$

**21.** $10x^2 + 24xy + 17y^2 - 9 = 0$

**22.** $32x^2 - 48xy + 18y^2 - 15x - 20y = 0$

**23.** $x^2 + 4xy - 2y^2 - 1 = 0$

**24.** $3xy - 4y^2 + 18 = 0$

**25.** $34x^2 - 24xy + 41y^2 - 25 = 0$

**26.** $6x^2 - 6xy + 14y^2 - 45 = 0$

*In Exercises 27–38:*

**a.** *Rewrite the equation in a rotated $x'y'$-system without an $x'y'$ term. Use the appropriate rotation formulas from Exercises 15–26.*

**b.** *Express the equation involving $x'$ and $y'$ in the standard form of a conic section.*

**c.** *Use the rotated system to graph the equation.*

**27.** $x^2 + xy + y^2 - 10 = 0$

**28.** $x^2 + 4xy + y^2 - 3 = 0$

**29.** $3x^2 - 10xy + 3y^2 - 32 = 0$

**30.** $5x^2 - 8xy + 5y^2 - 9 = 0$

**31.** $11x^2 + 10\sqrt{3}xy + y^2 - 4 = 0$

**32.** $7x^2 - 6\sqrt{3}xy + 13y^2 - 16 = 0$

**33.** $10x^2 + 24xy + 17y^2 - 9 = 0$

**34.** $32x^2 - 48xy + 18y^2 - 15x - 20y = 0$

**35.** $x^2 + 4xy - 2y^2 - 1 = 0$

**36.** $3xy - 4y^2 + 18 = 0$

**37.** $34x^2 - 24xy + 41y^2 - 25 = 0$

**38.** $6x^2 - 6xy + 14y^2 - 45 = 0$

*In Exercises 39–44, identify each equation without applying a rotation of axes.*

**39.** $5x^2 - 2xy + 5y^2 - 12 = 0$

**40.** $10x^2 + 24xy + 17y^2 - 9 = 0$

**41.** $24x^2 + 16\sqrt{3}xy + 8y^2 - x + \sqrt{3}y - 8 = 0$

**42.** $3x^2 - 2\sqrt{3}xy + y^2 + 2x + 2\sqrt{3}y = 0$

**43.** $23x^2 + 26\sqrt{3}xy - 3y^2 - 144 = 0$

**44.** $4xy + 3y^2 + 4x + 6y - 1 = 0$

## Writing in Mathematics

**45.** Explain how to identify the graph of

$$Ax^2 + Cy^2 + Dx + Ey + F = 0$$

**46.** If there is a 60° angle from the positive $x$-axis to the positive $x'$-axis, explain how to obtain the rotation formulas for $x$ and $y$.

**47.** How do you obtain the angle of rotation so that a general second-degree equation has no $x'y'$-term in a rotated $x'y'$-system?

**48.** What is the most time-consuming part in using a graphing utility to graph a general second-degree equation with an $xy$-term?

**49.** Explain how to identify the graph of

$$Ax^2 + Bxy + Cy^2 + Dx + Ey + F = 0.$$

## Technology Exercises

*In Exercises 50–56, use a graphing utility to graph each equation.*

**50.** $x^2 + 4xy + y^2 - 3 = 0$

**51.** $7x^2 + 8xy + y^2 - 1 = 0$

**52.** $3x^2 + 4xy + 6y^2 - 7 = 0$

**53.** $3x^2 - 6xy + 3y^2 + 10x - 8y - 2 = 0$

**54.** $9x^2 + 24xy + 16y^2 + 90x - 130y = 0$

**55.** $x^2 + 4xy + 4y^2 + 10\sqrt{5}x - 9 = 0$

**56.** $7x^2 + 6xy + 2.5y^2 - 14x + 4y + 9 = 0$

## Critical Thinking Exercises

**57.** Explain the relationship between the graph of $3x^2 - 2xy + 3y^2 + 2 = 0$ and the sound made by one hand clapping. Begin by following the directions for Exercises 27–38. (You will first need to write rotation formulas that eliminate the $x'y'$-term.)

**58.** What happens to the equation $x^2 + y^2 = r^2$ in a rotated $x'y'$-system?

*In Exercises 59–60, let* $Ax^2 + Bxy + Cy^2 + Dx + Ey + F = 0$ *be an equation of a conic section in an xy-coordinate system. Let* $A'x'^2 + B'x'y' + C'y'^2 + D'x' + E'y' + F' = 0$ *be the equation of the conic section in the rotated x′y′-coordinate system. Use the coefficients A′, B′, and C′, shown in the equation with the voice balloon pointing to B′ on* page 855, *to prove the following relationships.*

**59.** $A' + C' = A + C$

**60.** $B'^2 - 4A'C' = B^2 - 4AC$

## Group Exercise

**61.** Many public and private organizations and schools provide educational materials and information for the blind and visually impaired. Using your library, resources on the Worldwide Web, or local organizations, investigate how your group or college could make a contribution to enhance the study of mathematics for the blind and visually impaired. In relation to conic sections, group members should discuss how to create graphs in tactile, or touchable, form that show blind students the visual structure of the conics, including asymptotes, intercepts, end behavior, and rotations.

# SECTION 10.5 *Parametric Equations*

## Objectives

1. Use point plotting to graph plane curves described by parametric equations.
2. Eliminate the parameter.
3. Find parametric equations for functions.
4. Understand the advantages of parametric representations.

What a baseball game! You got to see the great Sammy Sosa of the Chicago Cubs blast a powerful homer. In less than eight seconds, the parabolic path of his home run took the ball a horizontal distance of over 1000 feet. Is there a way to model this path that gives both the ball's location and the time that it is in each of its positions? In this section, we look at ways of describing curves that reveal the where and the when of motion.

## Plane Curves and Parametric Equations

You throw a ball from a height of 6 feet, with an initial velocity of 90 feet per second and at an angle of 40° with the horizontal. After $t$ seconds, the path of the ball can be described by

$$x = (90\cos 40°)t \quad \text{and} \quad y = 6 + (90\sin 40°)t - 16t^2.$$

This is the ball's horizontal distance, in feet.

This is the ball's vertical height, in feet.

Using these equations, we can calculate the location of the ball at any time $t$. For example, to determine the location when $t = 1$ second, substitute 1 for $t$ in each equation:

$$x = (90\cos 40°)(1) \approx 68.9 \text{ feet}$$

$$y = 6 + (90\sin 40°)(1) - 16(1)^2 \approx 47.9 \text{ feet.}$$

This tells us that after one second, the ball has traveled a horizontal distance of approximately 68.9 feet, and the height of the ball is approximately 47.9 feet. Figure 10.51 displays this information and the results for calculations corresponding to $t = 2$ seconds and $t = 3$ seconds.

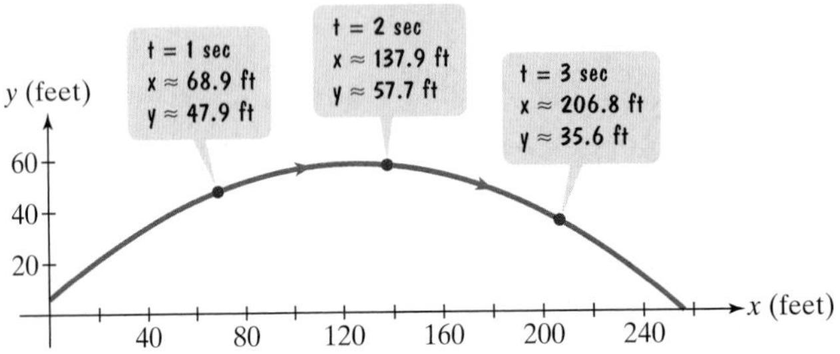


**Figure 10.51** The location of a thrown ball after 1, 2, and 3 seconds

The voice balloons in Figure 10.51 tell where the ball is located and when the ball is at a given point $(x, y)$ on its path. The variable $t$, called a **parameter**, gives the various times for the ball's location. The equations that describe where the ball is located express both $x$ and $y$ as functions of $t$ and are called **parametric equations**.

$$x = (90\cos 40°)t \qquad y = 6 + (90\sin 40°)t - 16t^2$$

This is the parametric equation for x.

This is the parametric equation for y.

The collection of points $(x, y)$ in Figure 10.51 is called a **plane curve**.

**Plane Curves and Parametric Equations**

Suppose that $t$ is a number in an interval $I$. A **plane curve** is the set of ordered pairs $(x, y)$, where

$$x = f(t), \quad y = g(t) \quad \text{for } t \text{ in interval } I.$$

The variable $t$ is called a **parameter**, and the equations $x = f(t)$ and $y = g(t)$ are called **parametric equations** for the curve.

1 Use point plotting to graph plane curves described by parametric equations.

## Graphing Plane Curves

Graphing a plane curve represented by parametric equations involves plotting points in the rectangular coordinate system and connecting them with a smooth curve.

### Graphing a Plane Curve Described by Parametric Equations

1. Select some values of $t$ on the given interval.
2. For each value of $t$, use the given parametric equations to compute $x$ and $y$.
3. Plot the points $(x, y)$ in the order of increasing $t$ and connect them with a smooth curve.

Take a second look at Figure 10.51. Do you notice arrows along the curve? These arrows show the direction, or **orientation**, along the curve as $t$ increases. After graphing a plane curve described by parametric equations, use arrows between the points to show the orientation of the curve corresponding to increasing values of $t$.

## EXAMPLE 1 Graphing a Curve Defined by Parametric Equations

Graph the plane curve defined by the parametric equations

$$x = t^2 - 1, \qquad y = 2t, \qquad -2 \le t \le 2.$$

**Solution**

**Step 1 Select some values of $t$ on the given interval.** We will select integral values of $t$ on the interval $-2 \le t \le 2$. Let $t = -2, -1, 0, 1,$ and 2.

**Step 2 For each value of $t$, use the given parametric equations to compute $x$ and $y$.** We organize our work in a table. The first column lists the choices for the parameter $t$. The next two columns show the corresponding values for $x$ and $y$. The last column lists the ordered pair $(x, y)$.

| $t$ | $x = t^2 - 1$ | $y = 2t$ | $(x, y)$ |
|---|---|---|---|
| $-2$ | $(-2)^2 - 1 = 4 - 1 = 3$ | $2(-2) = -4$ | $(3, -4)$ |
| $-1$ | $(-1)^2 - 1 = 1 - 1 = 0$ | $2(-1) = -2$ | $(0, -2)$ |
| 0 | $0^2 - 1 = -1$ | $2(0) = 0$ | $(-1, 0)$ |
| 1 | $1^2 - 1 = 0$ | $2(1) = 2$ | $(0, 2)$ |
| 2 | $2^2 - 1 = 4 - 1 = 3$ | $2(2) = 4$ | $(3, 4)$ |

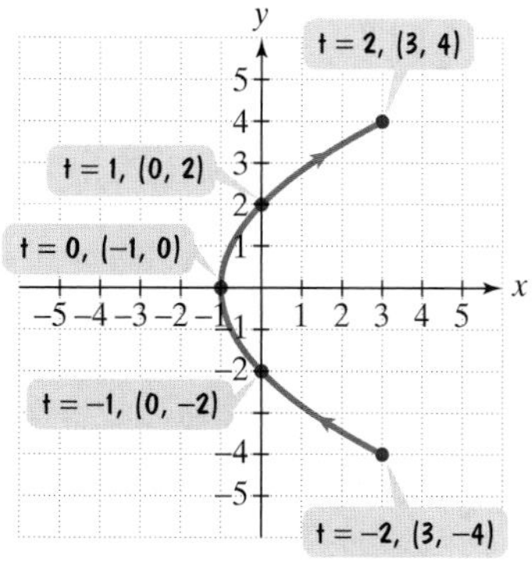


**Figure 10.52** The plane curve defined by $x = t^2 - 1$, $y = 2t$, $-2 \le t \le 2$

**Step 3 Plot the points $(x, y)$ in the order of increasing $t$ and connect them with a smooth curve.** The plane curve defined by the parametric equations on the given interval is shown in Figure 10.52. The arrows show the direction, or orientation, along the curve as $t$ varies from $-2$ to 2.

**Check Point 1** Graph the plane curve defined by the parametric equations

$$x = t^2 + 1, \qquad y = 3t, \qquad -2 \le t \le 2.$$

**2** Eliminate the parameter.

### Eliminating the Parameter

The graph in the technology box on page 866 shows the plane curve for $x = t^2 - 1$, $y = 2t$, $-2 \le t \le 2$. Even if we examine the parametric equations carefully, we may not be able to tell that the corresponding plane curve is a

## Technology

A graphing utility can be used to obtain a plane curve represented by parametric equations. Set the mode to parametric and enter the equations. You must enter the minimum and maximum values for $t$, and an increment setting for $t$ ($t$step). The setting $t$step determines the number of points the graphing utility will plot.

Shown is the plane curve for

$$x = t^2 - 1$$
$$y = 2t$$

in a $[-5, 5, 1]$ by $[-5, 5, 1]$ viewing rectangle with $t\text{min} = -2$, $t\text{max} = 2$, $t\text{step} = .01$.

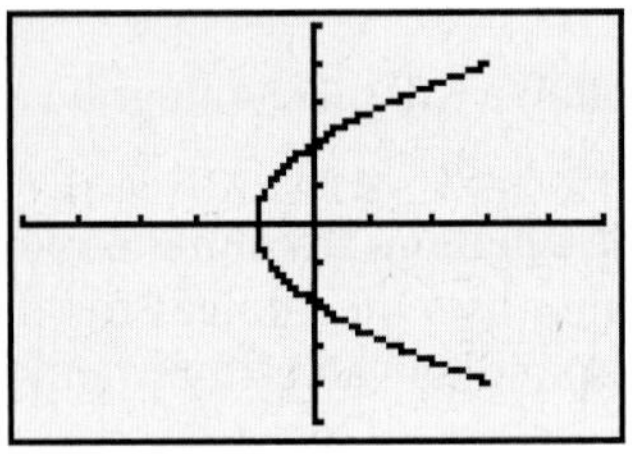

parabola. By **eliminating the parameter**, we can write one equation in $x$ and $y$ that is equivalent to the two parametric equations. The voice balloons illustrate this process.

| Begin with the parametric equations. | Solve for t in one of the equations. | Substitute the expression for t in the other parametric equation. |
|---|---|---|
| $x = t^2 - 1$<br>$y = 2t$ | Using $y = 2t$,<br>$t = \frac{y}{2}$. | Using $t = \frac{y}{2}$ and $x = t^2 - 1$,<br>$x = \left(\frac{y}{2}\right)^2 - 1$. |

The rectangular equation (the equation in $x$ and $y$), $x = \frac{y^2}{4} - 1$, can be written as $y^2 = 4(x + 1)$. This is the standard form of the equation of a parabola with vertex at $(-1, 0)$ and axis of symmetry along the $x$-axis. Because the parameter $t$ is restricted to the interval $[-2, 2]$, the plane curve in the technology box shows only a part of the parabola.

Our discussion illustrates a second method for graphing a plane curve described by parametric equations. Eliminate the parameter $t$ and graph the resulting rectangular equation in $x$ and $y$. However, **you may need to change the domain of the rectangular equation to be consistent with the domain for the parametric equation in $x$.** This situation is illustrated in Example 2.

### EXAMPLE 2 Finding and Graphing the Rectangular Equation of a Curve Defined Parametrically

Sketch the plane curve represented by the parametric equations

$$x = \sqrt{t} \quad \text{and} \quad y = \tfrac{1}{2}t + 1$$

by eliminating the parameter.

**Solution** We eliminate the parameter $t$ and then graph the resulting rectangular equation.

| Begin with the parametric equations. | Solve for t in one of the equations. | Substitute the expression for t in the other parametric equation. |
|---|---|---|
| $x = \sqrt{t}$<br>$y = \frac{1}{2}t + 1$ | Using $x = \sqrt{t}$ and squaring both sides, $t = x^2$. | Using $t = x^2$ and $y = \frac{1}{2}t + 1$,<br>$y = \frac{1}{2}x^2 + 1$. |

Because $t$ is not limited to a closed interval, you might be tempted to graph the entire U-shaped parabola whose equation is $y = \frac{1}{2}x^2 + 1$. However, take a second look at the parametric equation in $x$:

$$x = \sqrt{t}.$$

This equation is defined only when $t \geq 0$. Thus, $x$ is nonnegative. The plane curve is the parabola given by $y = \frac{1}{2}x^2 + 1$ with the domain restricted to $x \geq 0$. The plane curve is shown in Figure 10.53.

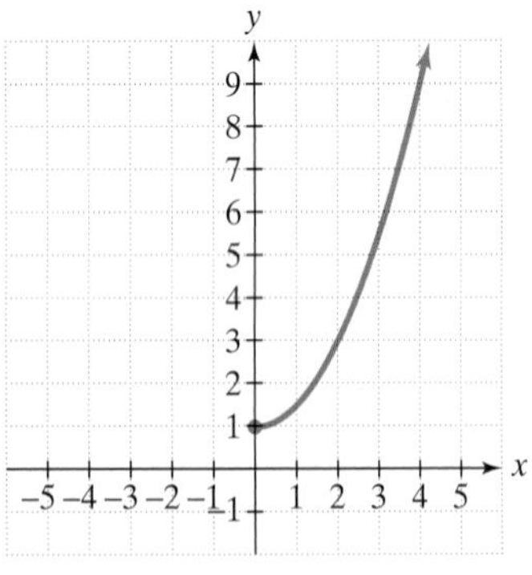


**Figure 10.53** The plane curve for $x = \sqrt{t}$ and $y = \frac{1}{2}t + 1$, or $y = \frac{1}{2}x^2 + 1, x \geq 0$

**Check Point 2** Sketch the plane curve represented by the parametric equations

$$x = \sqrt{t} \quad \text{and} \quad y = 2t - 1$$

by eliminating the parameter.

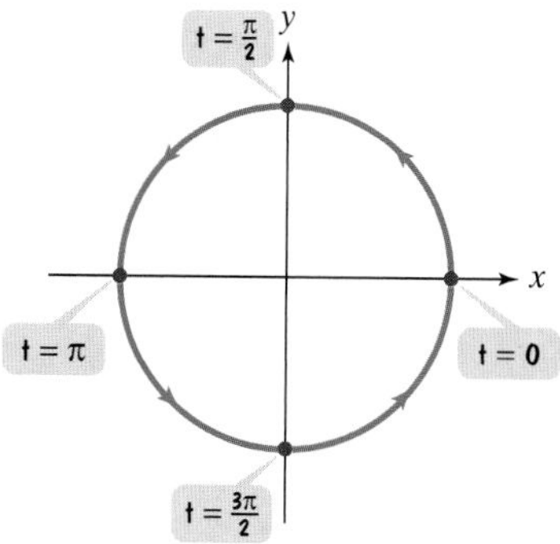


**Figure 10.54** The plane curve defined by $x = \sin t$, $y = \cos t$, $0 \le t < 2\pi$

Eliminating the parameter is not always a simple matter. In some cases, it may not be possible. When this occurs, you can use point plotting to obtain a plane curve.

Trigonometric identities can be helpful in eliminating the parameter. For example, consider the plane curve defined by the parametric equations

$$x = \sin t, \quad y = \cos t, \quad 0 \le t < 2\pi.$$

We use the trigonometric identity $\sin^2 t + \cos^2 t = 1$ to eliminate the parameter. Square each side of each parametric equation and then add.

$$\begin{aligned} x^2 &= \sin^2 t \\ y^2 &= \cos^2 t \\ \hline x^2 + y^2 &= \sin^2 t + \cos^2 t \end{aligned}$$

This is the sum of the two equations above the horizontal line.

Using the Pythagorean identity, we write this equation as $x^2 + y^2 = 1$. The plane curve is a circle with center $(0, 0)$ and radius equal to 1. It is shown in Figure 10.54.

## EXAMPLE 3 Finding and Graphing the Rectangular Equation of a Curve Defined Parametrically

Sketch the plane curve represented by the parametric equations

$$x = 5\cos t, y = 2\sin t, 0 \le t \le \pi$$

by eliminating the parameter.

**Solution** We eliminate the parameter using the identity $\cos^2 t + \sin^2 t = 1$. To apply the identity, divide the parametric equation in $x$ by 5 and the parametric equation in $y$ by 2.

$$\frac{x}{5} = \cos t \quad \text{and} \quad \frac{y}{2} = \sin t$$

Square and add these two equations.

$$\begin{aligned} \frac{x^2}{25} &= \cos^2 t \\ \frac{y^2}{4} &= \sin^2 t \\ \hline \frac{x^2}{25} + \frac{y^2}{4} &= \cos^2 t + \sin^2 t \end{aligned}$$

This is the sum of the two equations above the horizontal line.

Using the Pythagorean identity, we write this equation as

$$\frac{x^2}{25} + \frac{y^2}{4} = 1.$$

This rectangular equation is the standard form of the equation for an ellipse centered at $(0, 0)$.

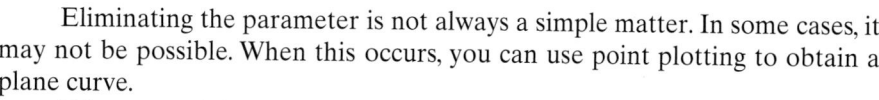

$$\frac{x^2}{25} + \frac{y^2}{4} = 1$$

$a^2 = 25$: Endpoints of major axis are 5 units right and left of center.

$b^2 = 4$: Endpoints of minor axis are 2 units above and below center.

The ellipse is shown in Figure 10.55(a). However, this is not the plane curve. Because $t$ is restricted to the interval $[0, \pi]$, the plane curve is only a portion of the ellipse. Use the starting and ending values for $t$ and a value of $t$ in the interval $[0, \pi]$ to find which portion to include.

Begin at $t = 0$.

$x = 5\cos t = 5\cos 0 = 5 \cdot 1 = 5$

$y = 2\sin t = 2\sin 0 = 2 \cdot 0 = 0$

Increase to $t = \frac{\pi}{2}$.

$x = 5\cos t = 5\cos\frac{\pi}{2} = 5 \cdot 0 = 0$

$y = 2\sin t = 2\sin\frac{\pi}{2} = 2 \cdot 1 = 2$

End at $t = \pi$.

$x = 5\cos t = 5\cos\pi = 5(-1) = -5$

$y = 2\sin t = 2\sin\pi = 2(0) = 0$

Points on the plane curve include (5, 0), which is the starting point, (0, 2), and (−5, 0), which is the ending point. The plane curve is the top half of the ellipse, shown in Figure 10.55(b).

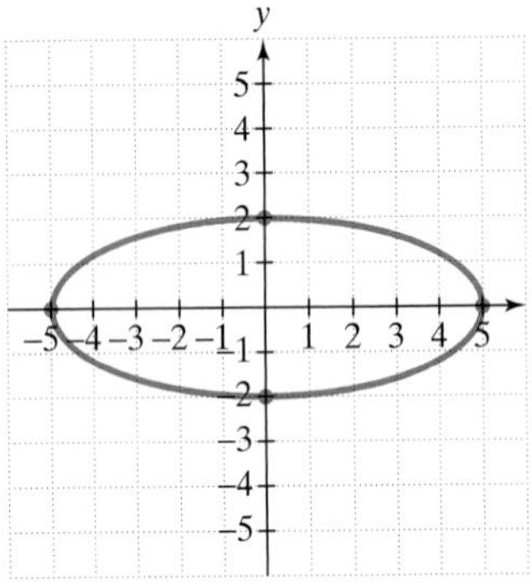


**Figure 10.55(a)** The graph of $\frac{x^2}{25} + \frac{y^2}{4} = 1$

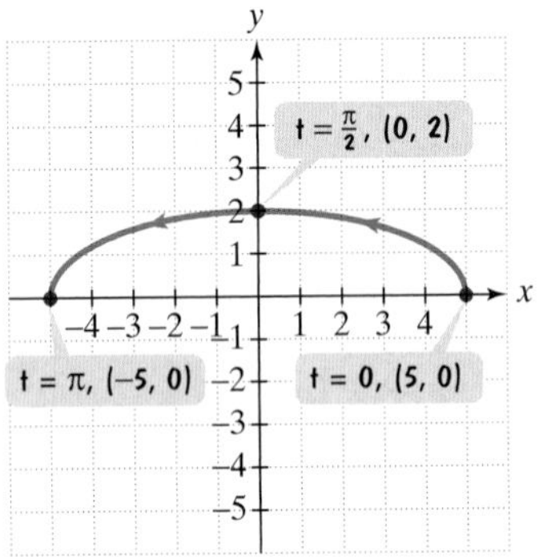


**Figure 10.55(b)** The plane curve for $x = 5\cos t$, $y = 2\sin t$, $0 \le t \le \pi$

**Check Point 3** Sketch the plane curve represented by the parametric equations

$$x = 6\cos t,\ y = 4\sin t,\ \pi \le t \le 2\pi.$$

**3** Find parametric equations for functions.

## Finding Parametric Equations

Infinitely many pairs of parametric equations can represent the same plane curve. If the plane curve is defined by the function $y = f(x)$, here is a procedure for finding one set of parametric equations.

**Parametric Equations for the Function $y = f(x)$**

A set of parametric equations for the plane curve defined by $y = f(x)$ is

$$x = t \quad \text{and} \quad y = f(t)$$

in which $t$ is in the domain of $f$.

## EXAMPLE 4 Finding Parametric Equations

Find a set of parametric equations for the parabola whose equation is $y = 9 - x^2$.

**Solution** Let $x = t$. Parametric equations for $y = f(x)$ are $x = t$ and $y = f(t)$. Thus, parametric equations for $y = 9 - x^2$ are

$$x = t \quad \text{and} \quad y = 9 - t^2.$$

**Check Point 4** Find a set of parametric equations for the parabola whose equation is $y = x^2 - 25$.

You can write other sets of parametric equations for $y = 9 - x^2$ by starting with a different parametric equation for $x$. Here are three sets of parametric equations for

$$y = 9 - x^2.$$

- If $x = t^3$, $y = 9 - (t^3)^2 = 9 - t^6$.
  Parametric equations are $x = t^3$ and $y = 9 - t^6$.
- If $x = t + 1$, $y = 9 - (t + 1)^2 = 9 - (t^2 + 2t + 1) = 8 - t^2 - 2t$.
  Parametric equations are $x = t + 1$ and $y = 8 - t^2 - 2t$.
- If $x = \frac{t}{2}$, $y = 9 - \left(\frac{t}{2}\right)^2 = 9 - \frac{t^2}{4}$.
  Parametric equations are $x = \frac{t}{2}$ and $y = 9 - \frac{t^2}{4}$.

Can you start with any choice for the parametric equation for $x$? The answer is no. **The substitution for $x$ must be a function that allows $x$ to take on all the values in the domain of the given rectangular equation**. For example, the domain of the function $y = 9 - x^2$ is the set of all real numbers. If you incorrectly let $x = t^2$, these values of $x$ exclude negative numbers that are included in $y = 9 - x^2$. The parametric equations

$$x = t^2 \quad \text{and} \quad y = 9 - (t^2)^2 = 9 - t^4$$

do not represent $y = 9 - x^2$ because only points for which $x \geq 0$ are obtained.

**4** Understand the advantages of parametric representations.

## Technology

The ellipse shown was obtained using the parametric mode and the radian mode of a graphing utility.

$$x(t) = 2 + 3\cos t$$
$$y(t) = 3 + 2\sin t$$

We used a $[-2, 6, 1]$ by $[-1, 6, 1]$ viewing rectangle with $t$min $= 0$, $t$max $= 6.2$ and $t$step $= 0.1$.

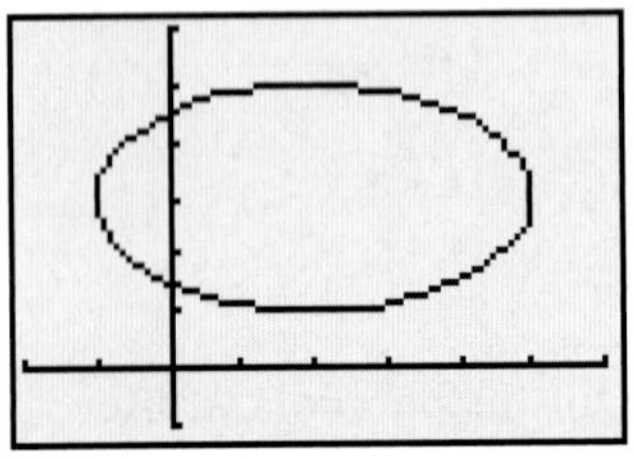

## Advantages of Parametric Equations over Rectangular Equations

We opened this section with parametric equations that described the horizontal distance and the vertical height of your thrown baseball after $t$ seconds. Parametric equations are frequently used to represent the path of a moving object. If $t$ represents time, parametric equations give the location of a moving object and tell when the object is located at each of its positions. Rectangular equations tell where the moving object is located but do not reveal when the object is in a particular position.

When using technology to obtain graphs, parametric equations that represent nonfunctions are often easier to use than their corresponding rectangular equations. It is far easier to enter the equation of an ellipse given by the parametric equations

$$x = 2 + 3\cos t \quad \text{and} \quad y = 3 + 2\sin t$$

than to use the rectangular equivalent

$$\frac{(x-2)^2}{9} + \frac{(y-3)^2}{4} = 1.$$

The rectangular equation must first be solved for $y$ and then entered as two separate equations in a graphing utility before the ellipse is revealed.

A curve that is used in physics for much of the theory of light is called a **cycloid**. The path of a fixed point on the circumference of a circle as it rolls along a line is a cycloid. A point on the rim of a bicycle wheel traces out a cycloid curve, shown in Figure 10.56. If the radius of the circle is $a$, the parametric equations of the cycloid are

$$x = a(t - \sin t) \text{ and } y = a(1 - \cos t).$$

It is an extremely complicated task to represent the cycloid in rectangular form.

Cycloids are used to solve problems that involve the "shortest time." For example, Figure 10.57 on the right shows a bead sliding down a wire. The shape of the wire a bead could slide down so that the distance between two points is traveled in the shortest time is an inverted cycloid.

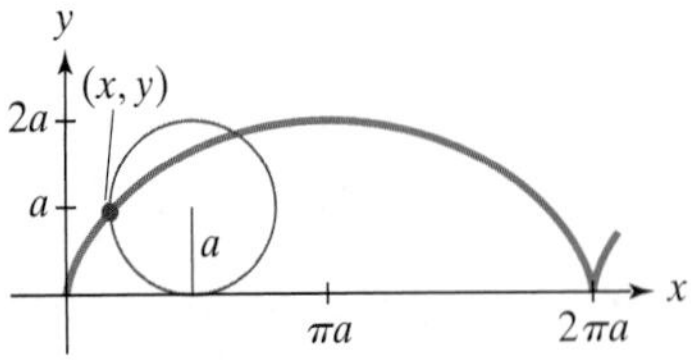


**Figure 10.56** The curve traced by a fixed point on the circumference of a circle rolling along a straight line is a cycloid.

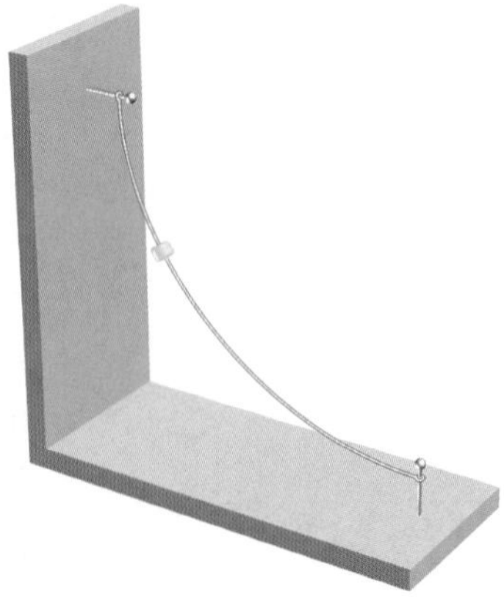

**Figure 10.57**

## Rolling

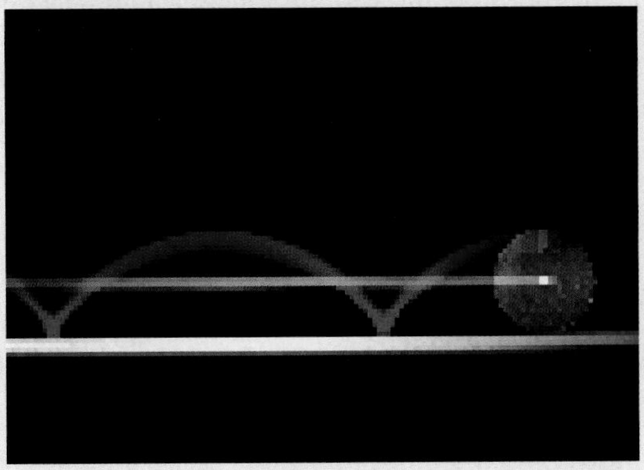

Linear functions and cycloids are used to describe rolling motion. The light at the rolling circle's center shows that it moves linearly. By contrast, the light at the circle's edge has rotational motion and traces out a cycloid.

# EXERCISE SET 10.5

### Practice Exercises

*In Exercises 1–8, parametric equations and a value for the parameter t are given. Find the coordinates of the point on the plane curve described by the parametric equations corresponding to the given value of t.*

1. $x = 3 - 5t,\ y = 4 + 2t;\ t = 1$
2. $x = 7 - 4t,\ y = 5 + 6t;\ t = 1$
3. $x = t^2 + 1,\ y = 5 - t^3;\ t = 2$
4. $x = t^2 + 3,\ y = 6 - t^3;\ t = 2$
5. $x = 4 + 2\cos t,\ y = 3 + 5\sin t;\ t = \frac{\pi}{2}$
6. $x = 2 + 3\cos t,\ y = 4 + 2\sin t;\ t = \pi$
7. $x = (60\cos 30°)t,\ y = 5 + (60\sin 30°)t - 16t^2;\ t = 2$
8. $x = (80\cos 45°)t,\ y = 6 + (80\sin 45°)t - 16t^2;\ t = 2$

*In Exercises 9–20, use point plotting to graph the plane curve described by the given parametric equations. Use arrows to show the orientation of the curve corresponding to increasing values of t.*

9. $x = t + 2,\ y = t^2;\ -2 \le t \le 2$
10. $x = t - 1,\ y = t^2;\ -2 \le t \le 2$
11. $x = t - 2,\ y = 2t + 1;\ -2 \le t \le 3$
12. $x = t - 3,\ y = 2t + 2;\ -2 \le t \le 3$
13. $x = t + 1,\ y = \sqrt{t};\ t \ge 0$
14. $x = \sqrt{t},\ y = t - 1;\ t \ge 0$
15. $x = \cos t,\ y = \sin t;\ 0 \le t < 2\pi$
16. $x = -\sin t,\ y = -\cos t;\ 0 \le t < 2\pi$
17. $x = t^2,\ y = t^3;\ -\infty < t < \infty$
18. $x = t^2 + 1,\ y = t^3 - 1;\ -\infty < t < \infty$
19. $x = 2t,\ y = |t - 1|;\ -\infty < t < \infty$
20. $x = |t + 1|,\ y = t - 2;\ -\infty < t < \infty$

*In Exercises 21–40, eliminate the parameter t. Then use the rectangular equation to sketch the plane curve represented by the given parametric equations. Use arrows to show the orientation of the curve corresponding to increasing values of t. (If an interval for t is not specified, assume that $-\infty < t < \infty$.)*

21. $x = t,\ y = 2t$
22. $x = t,\ y = -2t$
23. $x = 2t - 4,\ y = 4t^2$
24. $x = t - 2,\ y = t^2$
25. $x = \sqrt{t},\ y = t - 1$
26. $x = \sqrt{t},\ y = t + 1$
27. $x = 2\sin t,\ y = 2\cos t;\ 0 \le t < 2\pi$
28. $x = 3\sin t,\ y = 3\cos t;\ 0 \le t < 2\pi$
29. $x = 1 + 3\cos t,\ y = 2 + 3\sin t;\ 0 \le t < 2\pi$
30. $x = -1 + 2\cos t,\ y = 1 + 2\sin t;\ 0 \le t < 2\pi$
31. $x = 2\cos t,\ y = 3\sin t;\ 0 \le t < 2\pi$
32. $x = 3\cos t,\ y = 5\sin t;\ 0 \le t < 2\pi$
33. $x = 1 + 3\cos t,\ y = -1 + 2\sin t;\ 0 \le t \le \pi$
34. $x = 2 + 4\cos t,\ y = -1 + 3\sin t;\ 0 \le t \le \pi$
35. $x = \sec t,\ y = \tan t$
36. $x = 5\sec t,\ y = 3\tan t$
37. $x = t^2 + 2,\ y = t^2 - 2$
38. $x = \sqrt{t} + 2,\ y = \sqrt{t} - 2$
39. $x = 2^t,\ y = 2^{-t};\ t \ge 0$
40. $x = e^t,\ y = e^{-t};\ t \ge 0$

*In Exercises 41–43, eliminate the parameter. Write the resulting equation in standard form.*

41. A circle: $x = h + r\cos t,\ y = k + r\sin t$
42. An ellipse: $x = h + a\cos t,\ y = k + b\sin t$
43. A hyperbola: $x = h + a\sec t,\ y = k + b\tan t$

**44.** The parametric equations of the line through $(x_1, y_1)$ and $(x_2, y_2)$ are

$$x = x_1 + t(x_2 - x_1) \quad \text{and} \quad y = y_1 + t(y_2 - y_1).$$

Eliminate the parameter and write the resulting equation in point-slope form.

*In Exercises 45–52, use your answers from Exercises 41–44 and the parametric equations given in Exercises 41–44 to find a set of parametric equations for the conic section or the line.*

**45.** Circle: Center: (3, 5); Radius: 6

**46.** Circle: Center: (4, 6); Radius: 9

**47.** Ellipse: Center: (−2, 3); Vertices: 5 units to the right and left of the center; Endpoints of Minor Axis: 2 units above and below the center

**48.** Ellipse: Center: (4, −1); Vertices: 5 units above and below the center; Endpoints of Minor Axis: 3 units to the right and left of the center

**49.** Hyperbola: Vertices: (4, 0) and (−4, 0); Foci: (6, 0) and (−6, 0)

**50.** Hyperbola: Vertices: (0, 4) and (0, −4); Foci: (0, 5) and (0, −5)

**51.** Line: Passes through (−2, 4) and (1, 7)

**52.** Line: Passes through (3, −1) and (9, 12)

*In Exercises 53–56, find two different sets of parametric equations for each rectangular equation.*

**53.** $y = 4x - 3$

**54.** $y = 2x - 5$

**55.** $y = x^2 + 4$

**56.** $y = x^2 - 3$

*In Exercises 57–58, the parametric equations of four plane curves are given. Graph each plane curve and determine how they differ from each other.*

**57.** **a.** $x = t$ and $y = t^2 - 4$
**b.** $x = t^2$ and $y = t^4 - 4$
**c.** $x = \cos t$ and $y = \cos^2 t - 4$
**d.** $x = e^t$ and $y = e^{2t} - 4$

**58.** **a.** $x = t, y = \sqrt{4 - t^2}; -2 \le t \le 2$
**b.** $x = \sqrt{4 - t^2}, y = t; -2 \le t \le 2$
**c.** $x = 2\sin t, y = 2\cos t; 0 \le t < 2\pi$
**d.** $x = 2\cos t, y = 2\sin t; 0 \le t < 2\pi$

## Application Exercises

*The path of a projectile that is launched h feet above the ground with an initial velocity of $v_0$ feet per second and at an angle $\theta$ with the horizontal is given by the parametric equations*

$$x = (v_0 \cos\theta)t \quad \text{and} \quad y = h + (v_0 \sin\theta)t - 16t^2,$$

*where t is the time, in seconds, since the projectile was launched. The parametric equation for x gives the projectile's horizontal distance, in feet. The parametric equation for y gives the projectile's height, in feet. Use these parametric equations to solve Exercises 59–60.*

**59.** The figure shows the path for a baseball hit by Sammy Sosa. The ball was hit with an initial velocity of 180 feet per second at an angle of 40° to the horizontal. The ball was hit at a height 3 feet off the ground.

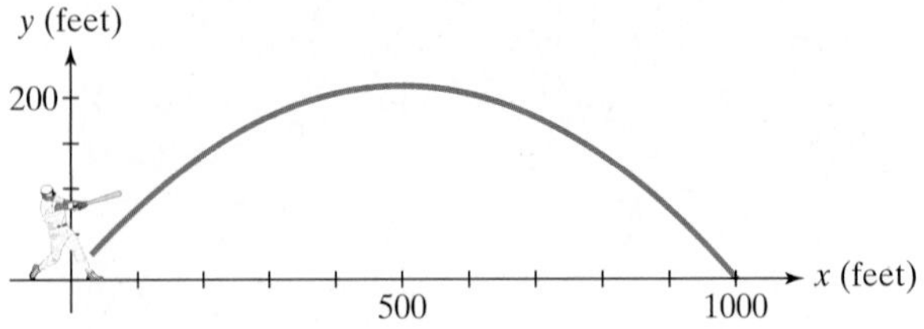


**a.** Find the parametric equations that describe the position of the ball as a function of time.
**b.** Describe the ball's position after 1, 2, and 3 seconds. Round to the nearest tenth of a foot. Locate your solutions on the plane curve.
**c.** How long, to the nearest tenth of a second, is the ball in flight? What is the total horizontal distance that it travels before it lands? Is your answer consistent with the figure shown?
**d.** You meet Sammy Sosa and he asks you to tell him something of interest about the path of a baseball that he hit. Use the graph to respond to his request. Then verify your observation algebraically.

**60.** The figure shows the path for a baseball that was hit with an initial velocity of 150 feet per second at an angle of 35° to the horizontal. The ball was hit at a height of 3 feet off the ground.

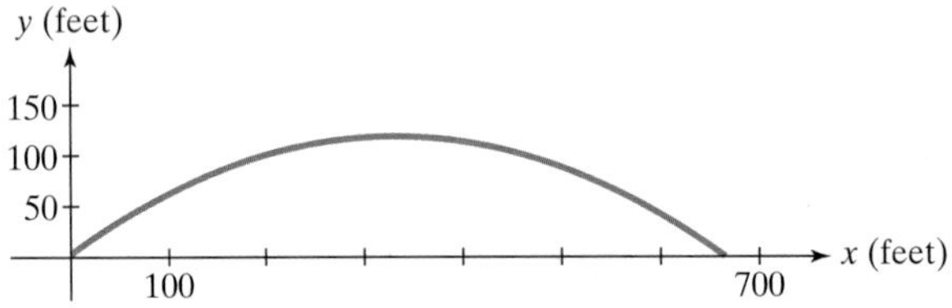


**a.** Find the parametric equations that describe the position of the ball as a function of time.
**b.** Describe the ball's position after 1, 2, and 3 seconds. Round to the nearest tenth of a foot. Locate your solutions on the plane curve.
**c.** How long is the ball in flight? (Round to the nearest tenth of a second.) What is the total horizontal distance that it travels, to the nearest tenth of a foot, before it lands? Is your answer consistent with the figure shown?
**d.** Use the graph to describe something about the path of the baseball that might be of interest to the player who hit the ball. Then verify your observation algebraically.

## Writing in Mathematics

61. What are plane curves and parametric equations?
62. How is point plotting used to graph a plane curve described by parametric equations? Give an example with your description.
63. What is the significance of arrows along a plane curve?
64. What does it mean to eliminate the parameter? What useful information can be obtained by doing this?
65. Explain how the rectangular equation $y = 5x$ can have infinitely many sets of parametric equations.
66. Discuss how the parametric equations for the path of a projectile (see Exercises 59–60) and the ability to obtain plane curves with a graphing utility can be used by a baseball coach to analyze performances of team players.

## Technology Exercises

67. Use a graphing utility in a parametric mode to verify any five of your hand-drawn graphs in Exercises 9–40.

*In Exercises 68–72, use a graphing utility to obtain the plane curve represented by the given parametric equations.*

68. Cycloid: $x = 3(t - \sin t)$, $y = 3(1 - \cos t)$; $[0, 60, 5] \times [0, 8, 1], 0 \le t < 6\pi$
69. Cycloid: $x = 2(t - \sin t)$, $y = 2(1 - \cos t)$; $[0, 60, 5] \times [0, 8, 1], 0 \le t < 6\pi$
70. Witch of Agnesi: $x = 2 \cot t$, $y = 2 \sin^2 t$; $[-6, 6, 1] \times [-4, 4, 1], 0 \le t < 2\pi$
71. Hypocycloid: $x = 4 \cos^3 t$, $y = 4 \sin^3 t$; $[-5, 5, 1] \times [-5, 5, 1], 0 \le t < 2\pi$
72. Lissajous Curve: $x = 2 \cos t$, $y = \sin 2t$; $[-3, 3, 1] \times [-2, 2, 1], 0 \le t < 2\pi$

*Use the equations for the path of a projectile given prior to Exercises 59–60 to solve Exercises 73–75.*

*In Exercises 73–74, use a graphing utility to obtain the path of a projectile launched from the ground ($h = 0$) at the specified values of $\theta$ and $v_0$. In each exercise, use the graph to determine the maximum height and the time at which the projectile reaches its maximum height. Also use the graph to determine the range of the projectile and the time it hits the ground. Round all answers to the nearest tenth.*

73. $\theta = 55°$, $v_0 = 200$ feet per second
74. $\theta = 35°$, $v_0 = 300$ feet per second

75. A baseball player throws the ball with an initial velocity of 140 feet per second at an angle of 22° to the horizontal. The ball leaves the player's hand at a height of 5 feet.
    **a.** Write the parametric equations that describe the ball's position as a function of time.
    **b.** Use a graphing utility to obtain the path of the baseball.
    **c.** Find the ball's maximum height and the time at which it reaches this height. Round all answers to the nearest tenth.
    **d.** How long is the ball in the air?
    **e.** How far does the ball travel?

## Critical Thinking Exercises

76. Eliminate the parameter: $x = \cos^3 t$ and $y = \sin^3 t$.
77. The plane curve described by the parametric equations $x = 3 \cos t$ and $y = 3 \sin t$, $0 \le t < 2\pi$, has a counterclockwise orientation. Alter one or both parametric equations so that you obtain the same plane curve with the opposite orientation.
78. The figure shows a circle of radius $a$ rolling along a horizontal line. Point $P$ traces out a cycloid. Angle $t$, in radians, is the angle through which the circle has rolled. $C$ is the center of the circle.

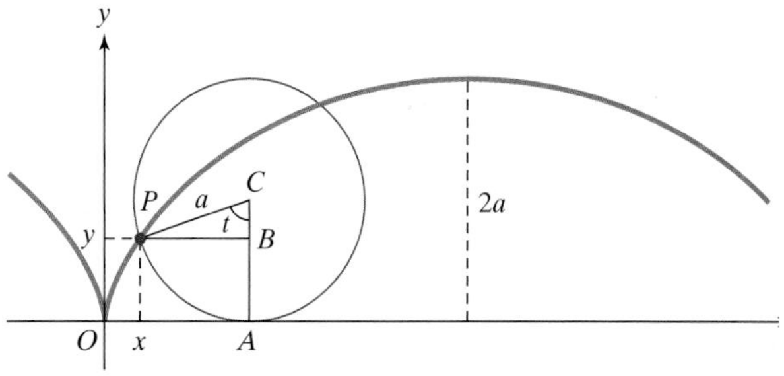


Use the suggestions in parts (a) and (b) to prove that the parametric equations of the cycloid are $x = a(t - \sin t)$ and $y = a(1 - \cos t)$.
    **a.** Derive the parametric equation for $x$ using the figure and

$$x = 0A - xA.$$

    **b.** Derive the parametric equation for $y$ using the figure and

$$y = AC - BC.$$

# SECTION 10.6 Conic Sections in Polar Coordinates

## Objectives

1. Define conics in terms of a focus and a directrix.
2. Graph the polar equations of conics.

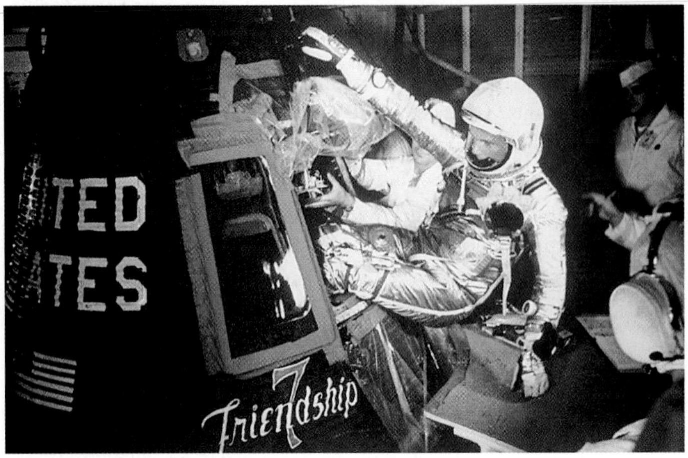

John Glenn made the first U.S.-manned flight around the Earth on *Friendship 7.*

On the morning of February 20, 1962, millions of Americans collectively held their breath as the world's newest pioneer swept across the threshold of one of our last frontiers. Roughly one hundred miles above Earth, astronaut John Glenn sat comfortably in the weightless environment of a $9\frac{1}{2}$-by 6-foot space capsule that offered the leg room of a Volkswagen "Beetle" and the aesthetics of a garbage can. Glenn became the first American to orbit the Earth in a three-orbit mission that lasted slightly under 5 hours.

In this section, you will see how John Glenn's historic orbit can be described using conic sections in polar coordinates. To obtain this model, we begin with a definition that permits a unified approach to the conic sections.

**1** Define conics in terms of a focus and a directrix.

## The Focus-Directrix Definitions of the Conic Sections

The definition of a parabola is given in terms of a fixed point, the focus, and a fixed line, the directrix. By contrast, the definitions of an ellipse and a hyperbola are given in terms of two fixed points, the foci. It is possible to define each of these conic sections in terms of a point and a line. Figure 10.58 shows a conic section

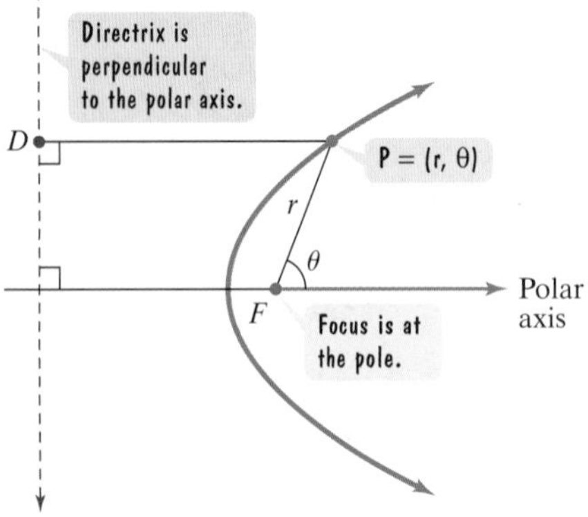


**Figure 10.58** A conic in the polar coordinate system

in the polar coordinate system. The fixed point, the focus, is at the pole. The fixed line, the directrix, is perpendicular to the polar axis.

**Focus-Directrix Definitions of the Conic Sections**

Let $F$ be a fixed point, the focus, and let $D$ be a fixed line, the directrix, in a plane (Figure 10.58). A conic section, or **conic**, is the set of all points $P$ in the plane such that

$$\frac{PF}{PD} = e$$

where $e$ is a fixed positive number, called the **eccentricity**.

If $e = 1$, the conic is a parabola.
If $e < 1$, the conic is an ellipse.
If $e > 1$, the conic is a hyperbola.

Figure 10.59 illustrates the eccentricity for each type of conic. Notice that if $e = 1$, the definition of the parabola is the same as focus-directrix definition with which you are familiar.

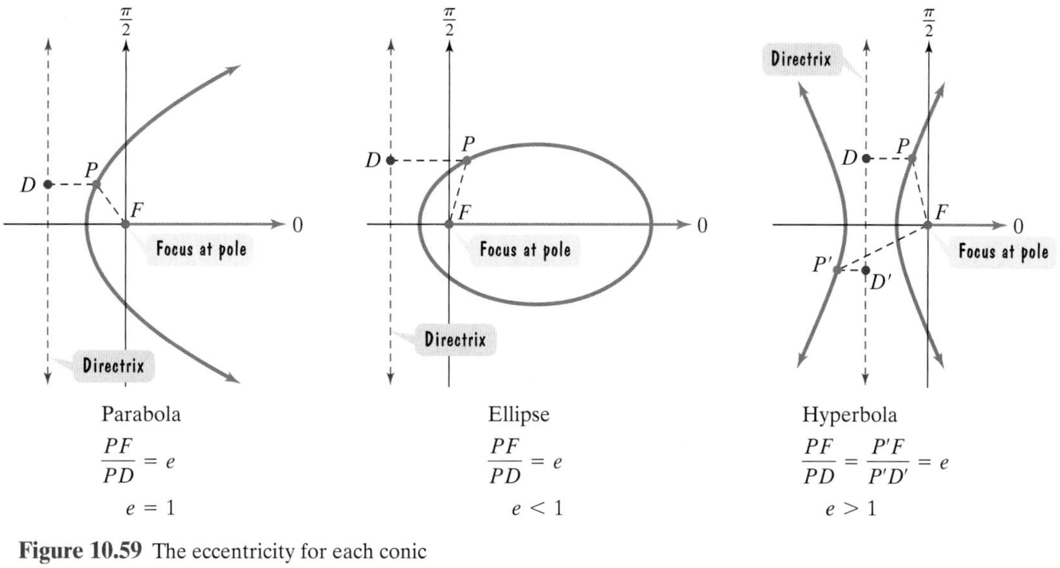


**Figure 10.59** The eccentricity for each conic

**2** Graph the polar equations of conics.

## Polar Equations of Conics

By locating a focus at the pole, all conics can be represented by similar equations in the polar coordinate system. In each of these equations,

- $(r, \theta)$ is a point on the graph of the conic.
- $e$ is the eccentricity. (Remember that $e > 0$.)
- $p$ is the distance between the focus (located at the pole) and the directrix.

**Standard Forms of the Polar Equations of Conics**

Let the pole be a focus of a conic section of eccentricity $e$ with the directrix $|p|$ units from the focus. The equation of the conic is given by one of the four equations listed.

$$r = \frac{ep}{1 + e\cos\theta}$$

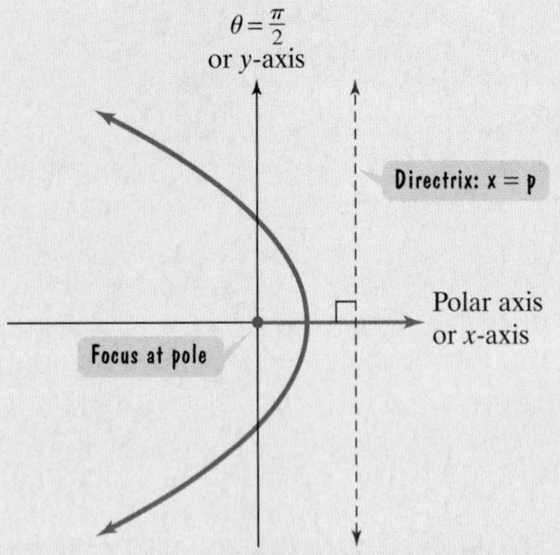


$$r = \frac{ep}{1 - e\cos\theta}$$

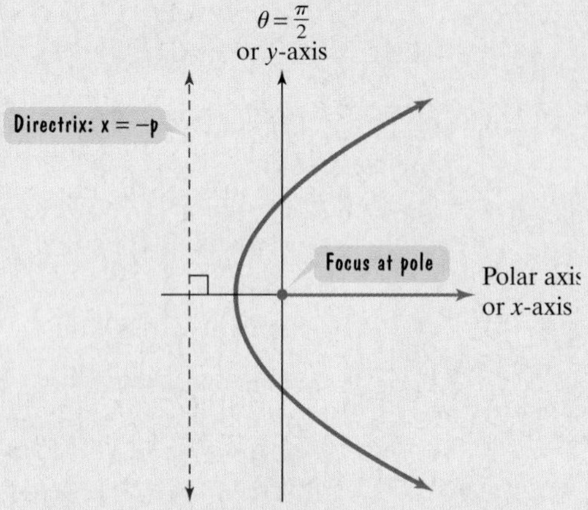


$$r = \frac{ep}{1 + e\sin\theta}$$

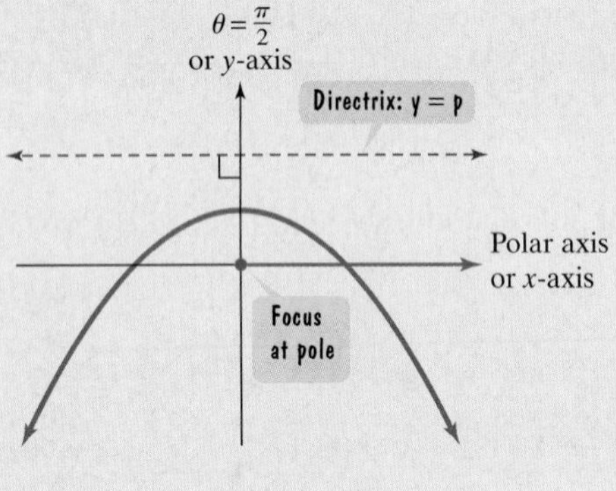


$$r = \frac{ep}{1 - e\sin\theta}$$

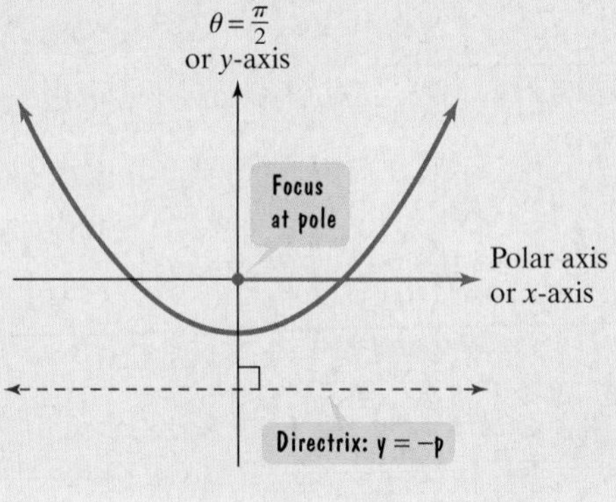


The graphs in the box illustrate two kinds of symmetry—symmetry with respect to the polar axis and symmetry with respect to the $y$-axis. If the equation contains $\cos\theta$, the polar axis is an axis of symmetry. If the equation contains $\sin\theta$, the line $\theta = \frac{\pi}{2}$, or the $y$-axis, is an axis of symmetry.

We will derive the equation displayed in the box on the upper right. The other equations are obtained in a similar manner. In Figure 10.60 on page 877, let $P = (r, \theta)$ be any point on a conic section.

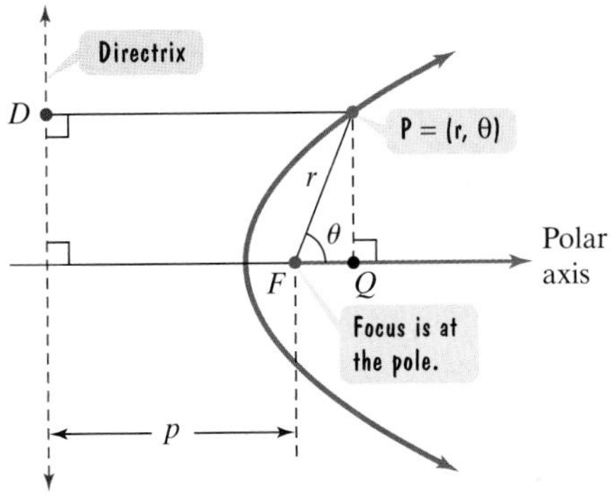


**Figure 10.60**

$$\frac{PF}{PD} = e$$ By definition, the ratio of the distance from $P$ to the focus to the distance from $P$ to the directrix equals the positive constant $e$.

$$\frac{r}{PD} = e$$ Figure 10.60 shows that the distance from $P$ to the focus, located at the pole, is $r$: $PF = r$.

$$\frac{r}{p + FQ} = e$$ Figure 10.60 shows that the distance from $P$ to the directrix is $p + FQ$: $PD = p + FQ$.

$$\frac{r}{p + r\cos\theta} = e$$ Using the triangle in the figure, $\cos\theta = \frac{FQ}{r}$ and $FQ = r\cos\theta$.

By solving this equation for $r$, we will obtain the desired equation. Clear fractions by multiplying both sides by the least common denominator.

$$r = e(p + r\cos\theta)$$ Multiply both sides by $p + r\cos\theta$.

$$r = ep + er\cos\theta$$ Apply the distributive property.

$$r - er\cos\theta = ep$$ Subtract $er\cos\theta$ from both sides to collect terms involving $r$ on the same side.

$$r(1 - e\cos\theta) = ep$$ Factor out $r$ from the two terms on the left.

$$r = \frac{ep}{1 - e\cos\theta}$$ Divide both sides by $1 - e\cos\theta$ and solve for $r$.

In summary, the standard forms of the polar equations of conics are

$$r = \frac{ep}{1 \pm e\cos\theta} \quad \text{and} \quad r = \frac{ep}{1 \pm e\sin\theta}.$$

In all forms, the constant term in the denominator is 1.

## Graphing the Polar Equation of a Conic

1. If necessary, write the equation in one of the standard forms.
2. Use the standard form to determine values for $e$ and $p$. Use the value of $e$ to identify the conic.
3. Use the appropriate figure for the standard form of the equation shown in the box on page 888 to help guide the graphing process.

## EXAMPLE 1 Graphing the Polar Equation of a Conic

Graph the polar equation:

$$r = \frac{4}{2 + \cos\theta}.$$

**Solution**

**Step 1 Write the equation in one of the standard forms.** The equation is not in standard form because the constant term in the denominator is not 1.

$$r = \frac{4}{2 + \cos\theta}$$

To obtain 1 in this position, divide the numerator and denominator by 2.

The equation in standard form is

$$r = \frac{2}{1 + \frac{1}{2}\cos\theta}.$$

$ep = 4$

$e = \frac{1}{2}$

This equation is in the form $r = \frac{ep}{1 + e\cos\theta}$.

**Step 2 Use the standard form to find *e* and *p*, and identify the conic.** The voice balloons show that

$$e = \tfrac{1}{2} \quad \text{and} \quad ep = \tfrac{1}{2}p = 2.$$

Thus, $e = \frac{1}{2}$ and $p = 4$. Because $e = \frac{1}{2} < 1$, the conic is an ellipse.

**Step 3 Use the figure for the equation's standard form to guide the graphing process.** The figure for the conic's standard form is shown in Figure 10.61(a). We have symmetry with respect to the polar axis. One focus is at the pole and a directrix is $x = 4$, located four units to the right of the pole.

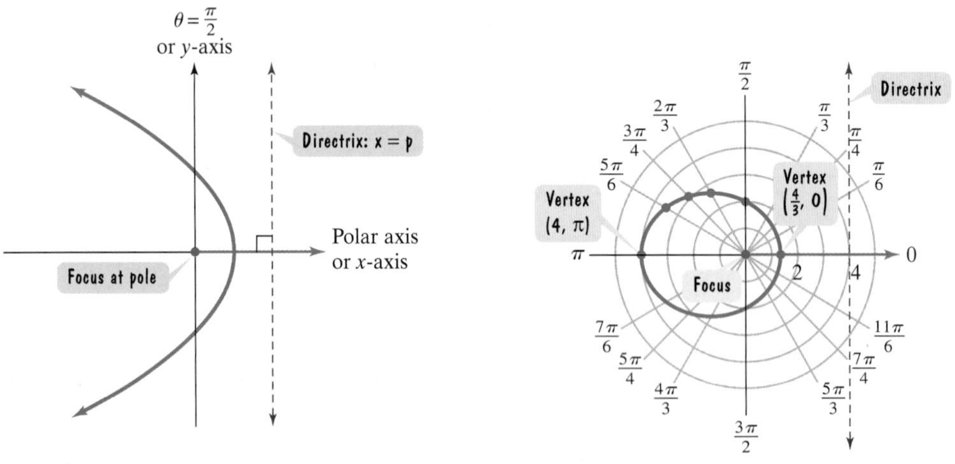


**(a)** Using $r = \frac{ep}{1 + e\cos\theta}$ to graph $r = \frac{2}{1 + \frac{1}{2}\cos\theta}$

**(b)** The graph of $r = \frac{4}{2 + \cos\theta}$, or $r = \frac{2}{1 + \frac{1}{2}\cos\theta}$

**Figure 10.61**

Figure 10.61(a) indicates that the major axis is on the polar axis. Thus, we find the vertices by selecting 0 and $\pi$ for $\theta$. The corresponding values for $r$ are $\frac{4}{3}$ and 4 respectively. Figure 10.61(b) shows the vertices, $\left(\frac{4}{3}, 0\right)$ and $(4, \pi)$.

**Technology**

The graph of

$$r = \frac{4}{2 + \cos\theta}$$

is obtained using the polar mode with angle measure in radians. To verify the hand-drawn graph in Figure 10.61(b), we used $[-5, 5, 1] \times [-5, 5, 1]$, $\theta\text{min} = 0, \theta\text{max} = 2\pi$, $\theta\text{step} = \frac{\pi}{48}$.

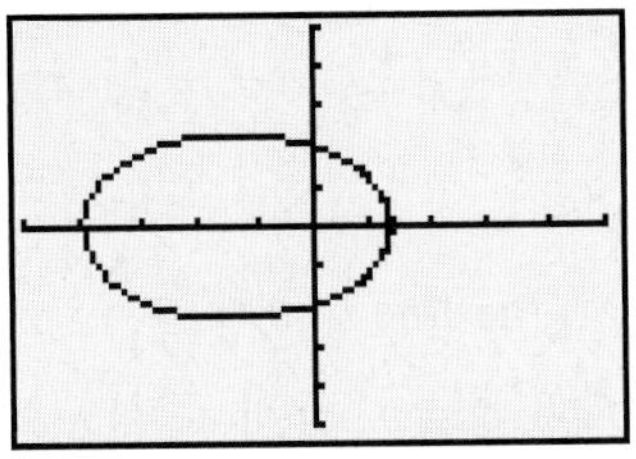

You can sketch the upper half of the ellipse by plotting some points from $\theta = 0$ to $\theta = \pi$.

$$r = \frac{4}{2 + \cos\theta}$$

| $\theta$ | $\frac{\pi}{2}$ | $\frac{2\pi}{3}$ | $\frac{3\pi}{4}$ | $\frac{5\pi}{6}$ |
|---|---|---|---|---|
| $r$ | 2 | 2.7 | 3.1 | 3.5 |

Using symmetry with respect to the polar axis, you can sketch the lower half. The graph of the given equation is shown in Figure 10.61(b).

**Check Point 1** Use the three steps shown in the box on page 877 to graph the polar equation:

$$r = \frac{4}{2 - \cos\theta}.$$

## EXAMPLE 2 Graphing the Polar Equation of a Conic

Graph the polar equation:

$$r = \frac{12}{3 + 3\sin\theta}.$$

### Solution

**Step 1 Write the equation in one of the standard forms.** The equation is not in standard form because the constant term in the denominator is not 1. Divide the numerator and denominator by 3 to write the standard form.

$$r = \frac{4}{1 + 1\sin\theta}$$

$ep = 4$

$e = 1$

This equation is in the form $r = \frac{ep}{1 + e\sin\theta}$.

**Step 2 Use the standard form to find $e$ and $p$, and identify the conic.** The voice balloons show that

$$e = 1 \quad \text{and} \quad ep = 1p = 4.$$

Thus, $e = 1$ and $p = 4$. Because $e = 1$, the conic is a parabola.

**Step 3 Use the figure for the equation's standard form to guide the graphing process.** Figure 10.62(a) indicates that we have symmetry with respect to $\theta = \frac{\pi}{2}$. The focus is at the pole and the directrix is $y = 4$, located four units above the pole.

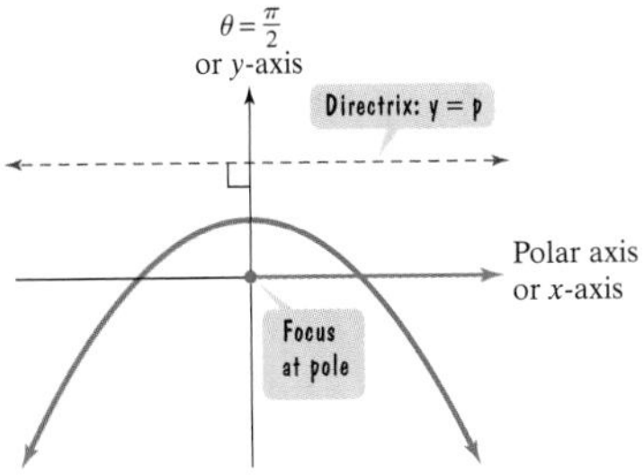


**(a)** Using $r = \frac{ep}{1 + e\sin\theta}$ to graph $r = \frac{4}{1 + \sin\theta}$

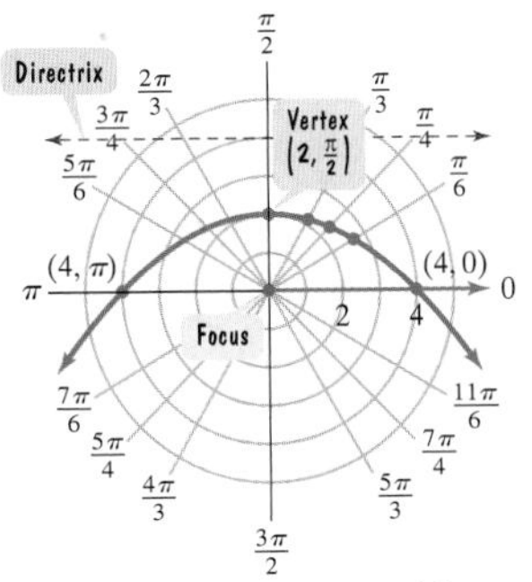


**(b)** The graph of $r = \frac{12}{3 + 3\sin\theta}$ or $r = \frac{4}{1 + \sin\theta}$

**Figure 10.62**

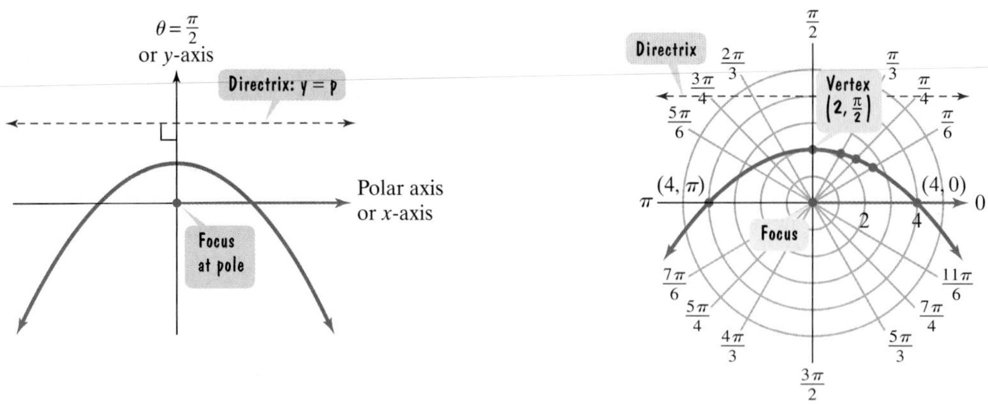


**(a)** Using $r = \dfrac{ep}{1 + e\sin\theta}$ to graph $r = \dfrac{4}{1 + \sin\theta}$

**(b)** The graph of $r = \dfrac{12}{3 + 3\sin\theta}$ or $r = \dfrac{4}{1 + \sin\theta}$

**Figure 10.62,** repeated

## Technology

The graph of

$$r = \frac{12}{3 + 3\sin\theta}$$

was obtained using

$$[-5, 5, 1] \times [-5, 5, 1]$$

and

$$\theta\text{min} = 0, \quad \theta\text{max} = 2\pi,$$

$$\theta\text{step} = \frac{\pi}{48}.$$

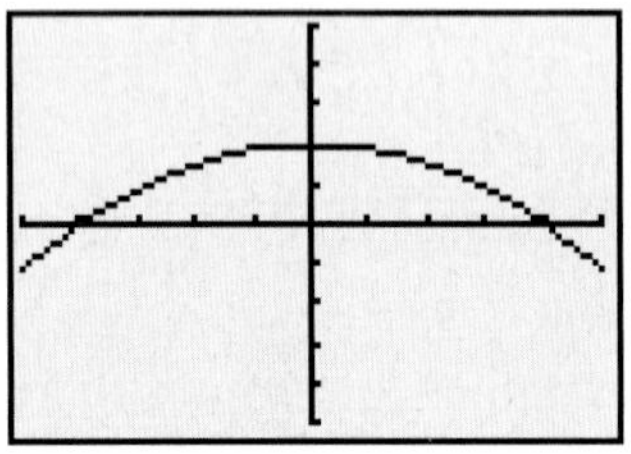

Figure 10.62(a) indicates that the vertex is on the line of $\theta = \frac{\pi}{2}$, or the $y$-axis. Thus, we find the vertex by selecting $\frac{\pi}{2}$ for $\theta$. The corresponding value for $r$ is 2. Figure 10.62(b) shows the vertex, $\left(2, \frac{\pi}{2}\right)$.

To find where the parabola crosses the polar axis, select $\theta = 0$ and $\theta = \pi$. The corresponding values for $r$ are 4 and 4, respectively. Figure 10.62(b) shows the points $(4, 0)$ and $(4, \pi)$ on the polar axis.

You can sketch the right half of the parabola by plotting some points from $\theta = 0$ to $\theta = \frac{\pi}{2}$.

$$r = \frac{12}{3 + 3\sin\theta}$$

| $\theta$ | $\frac{\pi}{6}$ | $\frac{\pi}{4}$ | $\frac{\pi}{3}$ |
|---|---|---|---|
| $r$ | 2.7 | 2.3 | 2.1 |

Using symmetry with respect to $\theta = \frac{\pi}{2}$, you can sketch the left half. The graph of the given equation is shown in Figure 10.62(b).

**Check Point 2** Use the three steps shown in the box on page 877 to graph the polar equation:

$$r = \frac{8}{4 + 4\sin\theta}.$$

## EXAMPLE 3 Graphing the Polar Equation of a Conic

Graph the polar equation:

$$r = \frac{9}{3 - 6\cos\theta}.$$

## Solution

**Step 1 Write the equation in one of the standard forms.** We can obtain a constant term of 1 in the denominator by dividing each term by 3.

$ep = 3$

$$r = \frac{3}{1 - 2\cos\theta}$$

This equation is in the form $r = \frac{ep}{1 - e\cos\theta}$.

$e = 2$

**Step 2 Use the standard form to find *e* and *p*, and identify the conic.** The voice balloons show that

$$e = 2 \quad \text{and} \quad ep = 2p = 3.$$

Thus, $e = 2$ and $p = \frac{3}{2}$. Because $e = 2 > 1$, the conic is a hyperbola.

**Step 3 Use the figure for the equation's standard form to guide the graphing process.** Figure 10.63(a) indicates that we have symmetry with respect to the polar axis. One focus is at the pole and a directrix is $x = -\frac{3}{2}$, located 1.5 units to the left of the pole.

Figure 10.63(a) indicates that the transverse axis is horizontal and the vertices lie on the polar axis. Thus, we find the vertices by selecting 0 and $\pi$ for $\theta$. Figure 10.63(b) shows the vertices, $(-3, 0)$ and $(1, \pi)$.

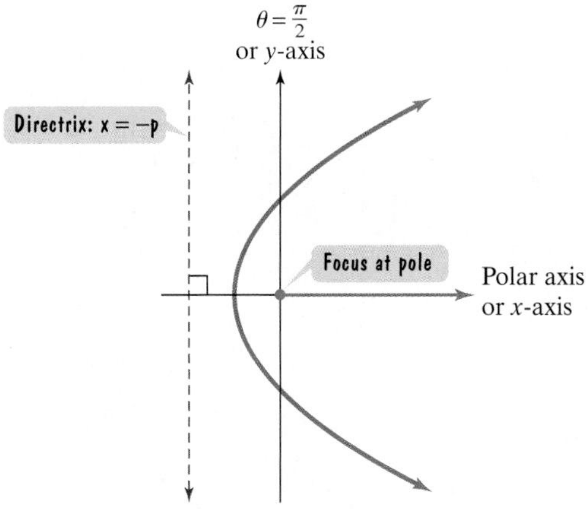


**(a)** Using $r = \frac{ep}{1 - e\cos\theta}$ to graph $r = \frac{3}{1 - 2\cos\theta}$

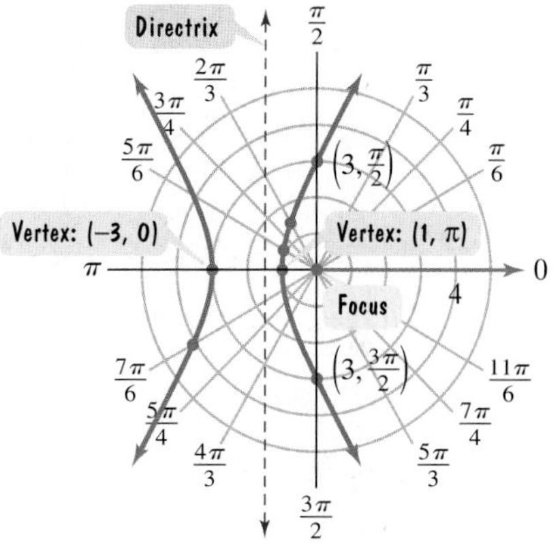


**(b)** The graph of $r = \frac{9}{3 - 6\cos\theta}$ or $r = \frac{3}{1 - 2\cos\theta}$

**Figure 10.63**

To find where the hyperbola crosses the line $\theta = \frac{\pi}{2}$, select $\frac{\pi}{2}$ and $\frac{3\pi}{2}$ for $\theta$. Figure 10.63(b) shows the points $\left(3, \frac{\pi}{2}\right)$ and $\left(3, \frac{3\pi}{2}\right)$ on the graph.

We sketch the upper half of the hyperbola by plotting some points from $\theta = 0$ to $\theta = \pi$.

$$r = \frac{3}{1 - 2\cos\theta}$$

| $\theta$ | $\frac{\pi}{6}$ | $\frac{2\pi}{3}$ | $\frac{5\pi}{6}$ |
|---|---|---|---|
| $r$ | −4.1 | 1.5 | 1.1 |

Using symmetry with respect to the polar axis, we sketch the lower half. The graph of the given equation is shown in Figure 10.63(b) on page 881.

**Check Point 3** Use the three steps shown in the box on page 877 to graph the polar equation:

$$r = \frac{9}{3 - 9\cos\theta}.$$

## Modeling Planetary Motion

Polish astronomer Nicolaus Copernicus (1473–1543) was correct in stating that planets in our solar system revolve around the sun and not the Earth. However, he incorrectly believed that celestial orbits move in perfect circles, calling his system "the ballet of the planets."

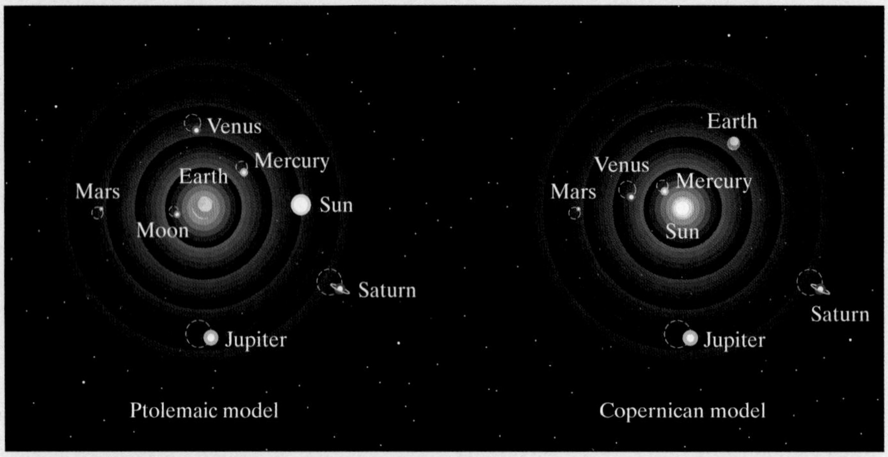


Table 10.4 indicates that the planets in our solar system have orbits with eccentricities that are much closer to 0 than to 1. Most of these orbits are almost circular, which made it difficult for early astronomers to detect that they are actually ellipses.

German scientist and mathematician Johannes Kepler (1571–1630) discovered that planets move in elliptical orbits with the sun at one focus. The polar equation for these orbits is

$$r = \frac{(1 - e^2)a}{1 - e\cos\theta}$$

**Table 10.4 Eccentricities of Planetary Orbits**

| | | | |
|---|---|---|---|
| Mercury | 0.2056 | Saturn | 0.0543 |
| Venus | 0.0068 | Uranus | 0.0460 |
| Earth | 0.0167 | Neptune | 0.0082 |
| Mars | 0.0934 | Pluto | 0.2481 |
| Jupiter | 0.0484 | | |

where the length of the orbit's major axis is $2a$. Describing planetary orbits, Kepler wrote, "The heavenly motions are nothing but a continuous song for several voices, to be perceived by the intellect, not by the ear."

## EXERCISE SET 10.6

### Practice Exercises

*In Exercises 1–8,*

**a.** *Identify the conic that each polar equation represents.*

**b.** *Describe the location of a directrix from the focus located at the pole.*

**1.** $r = \dfrac{3}{1 + \sin\theta}$

**2.** $r = \dfrac{3}{1 + \cos\theta}$

**3.** $r = \dfrac{6}{3 - 2\cos\theta}$

**4.** $r = \dfrac{6}{3 + 2\cos\theta}$

**5.** $r = \dfrac{8}{2 + 2\sin\theta}$

**6.** $r = \dfrac{8}{2 - 2\sin\theta}$

**7.** $r = \dfrac{12}{2 - 4\cos\theta}$

**8.** $r = \dfrac{12}{2 + 4\cos\theta}$

*In Exercises 9–20, use the three steps shown in the box on page 877 to graph each polar equation.*

**9.** $r = \dfrac{1}{1 + \sin\theta}$

**10.** $r = \dfrac{1}{1 + \cos\theta}$

**11.** $r = \dfrac{2}{1 - \cos\theta}$

**12.** $r = \dfrac{2}{1 - \sin\theta}$

**13.** $r = \dfrac{12}{5 + 3\cos\theta}$

**14.** $r = \dfrac{12}{5 - 3\cos\theta}$

**15.** $r = \dfrac{6}{2 - 2\sin\theta}$

**16.** $r = \dfrac{6}{2 + 2\sin\theta}$

**17.** $r = \dfrac{8}{2 - 4\cos\theta}$

**18.** $r = \dfrac{8}{2 + 4\cos\theta}$

**19.** $r = \dfrac{12}{3 - 6\cos\theta}$

**20.** $r = \dfrac{12}{3 - 3\cos\theta}$

### Application Exercises

*Halley's comet has an elliptical orbit with the sun at one focus. Its orbit, shown in the figure at the top of the next column, is given approximately by*

$$r = \frac{1.069}{1 + 0.967\sin\theta}.$$

*In the formula, r is measured in astronomical units. (One astronomical unit is the average distance from Earth to the sun, approximately 93 million miles.) Use the given formula and the figure to solve Exercises 21–22. Round to the nearest hundredth of an astronomical unit and the nearest million miles.*

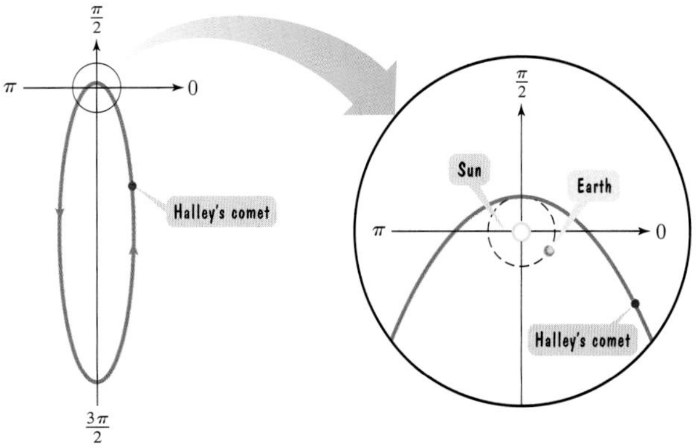


**21.** Find the distance from Halley's comet to the sun at its shortest distance from the sun.

**22.** Find the distance from Halley's comet to the sun at its greatest distance from the sun.

*On February 20, 1962, John Glenn made the first U.S.-manned flight around the Earth for three orbits on* Friendship 7. *With Earth at one focus, the orbit of* Friendship 7 *is given approximately by*

$$r = \frac{4090.76}{1 - 0.0076\cos\theta}$$

*where r is measured in miles from Earth's center. Use the formula and the figure shown to solve Exercises 23–24.*

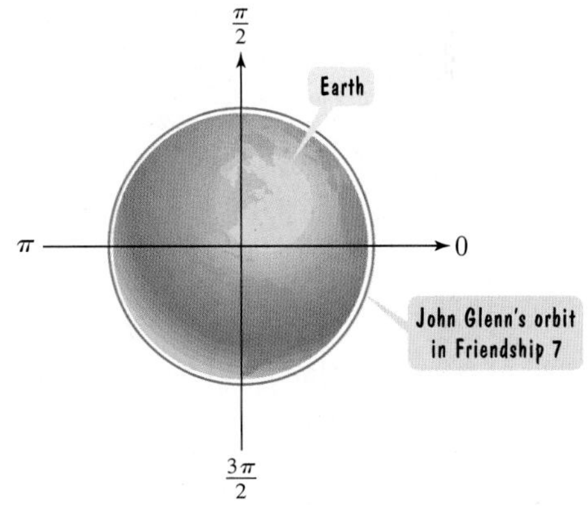


**23.** How far from Earth's center was John Glenn at his greatest distance from the planet? Round to the nearest mile. If the radius of Earth is 3960 miles, how far was he from Earth's surface at this point on the flight?

**24.** How far from Earth's center was John Glenn at his closest distance from the planet? Round to the nearest mile. If the radius of Earth is 3960 miles, how far was he from Earth's surface at this point on the flight?

## Writing in Mathematics

**25.** How are the conics described in terms of a fixed point and a fixed line?

**26.** If all conics are defined in terms of a fixed point and a fixed line, how can you tell one kind of conic from another?

**27.** If you are given the standard form of the polar equation of a conic, how do you determine its eccentricity?

**28.** If you are given the standard form of the polar equation of a conic, how do you determine the location of a directrix from the focus at the pole?

**29.** Describe a strategy for graphing $r = \dfrac{1}{1 + \sin\theta}$.

**30.** You meet John Glenn and he asks you to tell him something of interest about the difference between the elliptical orbit of his first space voyage in 1962 and the orbit for his return journey in 1999. Describe how to use the polar equation for orbits in the essay on page 882, the equation for his 1962 journey, and a graphing utility to provide him with an interesting visual analysis.

## Technology Exercises

*Use the polar mode of a graphing utility with angle measure in radians to solve Exercises 31–34. Unless otherwise indicated, use* $\theta\text{min} = 0$, $\theta\text{max} = 2\pi$, *and* $\theta\text{step} = \dfrac{\pi}{48}$. *If you are not satisfied with the quality of the graph, experiment with smaller values for*

**31.** Use a graphing utility to verify any five of your hand-drawn graphs in Exercises 9–20.

*In Exercises 32–34, identify the conic that each polar equation represents. Then use a graphing utility to graph the equation.*

**32.** $r = \dfrac{16}{4 - 3\cos\theta}$

**33.** $r = \dfrac{12}{4 + 5\sin\theta}$

**34.** $r = \dfrac{18}{6 - 6\cos\theta}$

*In Exercises 35–36, use a graphing utility to graph the equation. Then answer the given question.*

**35.** $r = \dfrac{4}{1 - \sin\left(\theta - \dfrac{\pi}{4}\right)}$; How does the graph differ from the graph of $r = \dfrac{4}{1 - \sin\theta}$?

**36.** $r = \dfrac{3}{2 + 6\cos\left(\theta + \dfrac{\pi}{3}\right)}$; How does the graph differ from the graph of $r = \dfrac{3}{2 + 6\cos\theta}$?

**37.** Use the polar equation for planetary orbits,

$$r = \frac{(1 - e^2)a}{1 - e\cos\theta},$$

to find the polar equation of the orbit for Mercury and Earth.

Mercury: $e = 0.2056$ and $a = 36.0 \times 10^6$ miles

Earth: $e = 0.0167$ and $a = 92.96 \times 10^6$ miles

Use a graphing utility to graph both orbits in the same viewing rectangle. What do you see about the orbits from their graphs that is not obvious from their equations?

## Critical Thinking Exercises

**38.** Identify the conic and graph the equation:

$$r = \frac{4\sec\theta}{2\sec\theta - 1}.$$

*In Exercises 39–40, write a polar equation of the conic that is named and described.*

**39.** Ellipse: a focus at the pole; vertex: $(4, 0)$; $e = \frac{1}{2}$

**40.** Hyperbola: a focus at the pole; directrix: $x = -1$; $e = \frac{3}{2}$

**41.** Identify the conic and write its equation in rectangular coordinates: $r = \dfrac{1}{2 - 2\cos\theta}$.

**42.** Prove that the polar equation of a planet's elliptical orbit is

$$r = \frac{(1 - e^2)a}{1 - e\cos\theta}$$

where $e$ is the eccentricity and $2a$ is the length of the major axis.

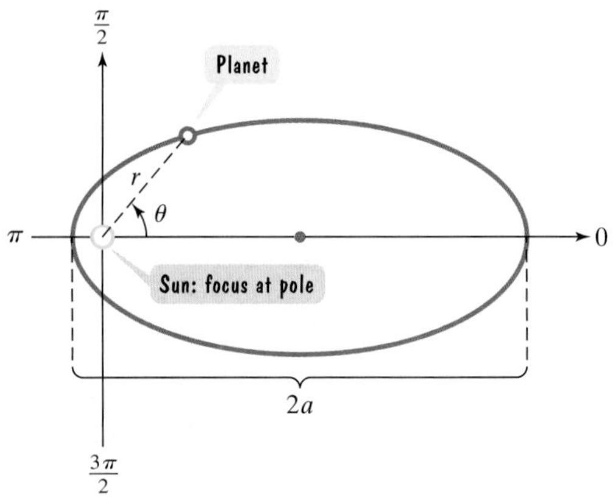

# CHAPTER SUMMARY, REVIEW, AND TEST

## Summary

### 10.1 The Ellipse

a. An ellipse is the set of all points in a plane the sum of whose distances from two fixed points, the foci, is constant.

b. Standard forms of the equations of an ellipse with center at the origin are $\frac{x^2}{a^2} + \frac{y^2}{b^2} = 1$ [foci: $(-c, 0)$, $(c, 0)$] and $\frac{x^2}{b^2} + \frac{y^2}{a^2} = 1$ [foci: $(0, -c)$, $(0, c)$], where $b^2 = a^2 - c^2$ and $a^2 > b^2$. See the box on page 823 and Figure 10.6.

c. Standard forms of the equations of an ellipse centered at $(h, k)$ are $\frac{(x-h)^2}{a^2} + \frac{(y-k)^2}{b^2} = 1$ and $\frac{(x-h)^2}{b^2} + \frac{(y-k)^2}{a^2} = 1$. See Table 10.1 on page 827 and Figure 10.10.

### 10.2 The Hyperbola

a. A hyperbola is the set of all points in a plane the difference of whose distances from two fixed points, the foci, is constant.

b. Standard forms of the equations of a hyperbola with center at the origin are $\frac{x^2}{a^2} - \frac{y^2}{b^2} = 1$ [foci: $(-c, 0)$, $(c, 0)$] and $\frac{y^2}{a^2} - \frac{x^2}{b^2} = 1$ [foci: $(0, -c)$, $(0, c)$], where $b^2 = c^2 - a^2$. See the box on page 836 and Figure 10.17.

c. Asymptotes for $\frac{x^2}{a^2} - \frac{y^2}{b^2} = 1$ are $y = \pm\frac{b}{a}x$. Asymptotes for $\frac{y^2}{a^2} - \frac{x^2}{b^2} = 1$ are $y = \pm\frac{a}{b}x$.

d. A procedure for graphing hyperbolas is given in the box on page 840.

e. Standard forms of the equations of a hyperbola centered at $(h, k)$ are $\frac{(x-h)^2}{a^2} - \frac{(y-k)^2}{b^2} = 1$ and $\frac{(y-k)^2}{a^2} - \frac{(x-h)^2}{b^2} = 1$. See Table 10.2 on page 843 and Figure 10.26.

### 10.3 The Parabola

a. A parabola is the set of all points in a plane that are equidistant from a fixed line, the directrix, and a fixed point, the focus.

b. Standard forms of the equations of parabolas with vertex at the origin are $y^2 = 4px$ [focus: $(p, 0)$] and $x^2 = 4py$ [focus: $(0, p)$]. See the box on page 851 and Figure 10.32 on page 852.

c. Standard forms of the equations of a parabola with vertex at $(h, k)$ are $(y-k)^2 = 4p(x-h)$ and $(x-h)^2 = 4p(y-k)$. See Table 10.3 on page 854 and Figure 10.37.

### 10.4 Rotation of Axes

a. A nondegenerate conic section of the form $Ax^2 + Cy^2 + Dx + Ey + F = 0$ in which $A$ and $C$ are not both zero is **1.** a circle if $A = C$; **2.** a parabola if $AC = 0$; **3.** an ellipse if $A \neq C$ and $AC > 0$; **4.** a hyperbola if $AC < 0$.

b. Rotation of Axes Formulas
$\theta$ is the angle from the positive $x$-axis to the positive $x'$-axis.

$$x = x'\cos\theta - y'\sin\theta \text{ and } y = x'\sin\theta + y'\cos\theta$$

c. Amount of Rotation Formula
The general second-degree equation

$$Ax^2 + Bxy + Cy^2 + Dx + Ey + F = 0$$

can be rewritten in $x'$ and $y'$ without an $x'y'$-term by rotating the axes through angle $\theta$, where $\cot 2\theta = \frac{A-C}{B}$ and $\theta$ is an acute angle.

d. If $2\theta$ in $\cot 2\theta$ is one of the more familiar angles such as $30°$, $45°$, or $60°$, write the equation of a rotated conic in standard form using the five-step procedure in the box on page 868.

e. If $\cot 2\theta$ is not the cotangent of one of the more familiar angles, use a sketch of $\cot 2\theta$ to find $\cos 2\theta$. Then use

$$\sin\theta = \sqrt{\frac{1-\cos 2\theta}{2}} \quad \text{and} \quad \cos\theta = \sqrt{\frac{1+\cos 2\theta}{2}}$$

to find values for $\sin\theta$ and $\cos\theta$ in the rotation formulas.

f. A nondegenerate conic section of the form

$$Ax^2 + Bxy + Cy^2 + Dx + Ey + F = 0$$

is **1.** a parabola if $B^2 - 4AC = 0$; **2.** an ellipse or a circle if $B^2 - 4AC < 0$; **3.** a hyperbola if $B^2 - 4AC > 0$.

### 10.5 Parametric Equations

a. The relationship between the parametric equations $x = f(t)$ and $y = g(t)$ and plane curves is described in the box on page 876.

b. Point plotting can be used to graph a plane curve described by parametric equations. See the box on page 877.

c. Plane curves can be sketched by eliminating the parameter $t$ and graphing the resulting rectangular equation. It is sometimes necessary to change the domain of the rectangular equation to be consistent with the domain for the parametric equation in $x$.

d. Infinitely many pairs of parametric equations can represent the same plane curve. One pair for $y = f(x)$ is $x = t$ and $y = f(t)$ in which $t$ is in the domain of $f$.

### 10.6 Conic Sections in Polar Coordinates

a. The focus-directrix definitions of the conic sections are given in the box on page 887. For all points on a conic, the distance from a fixed point (focus) divided by the distance from a fixed line (directrix) is constant and is called eccentricity. If $e = 1$, the conic is a parabola. If $e < 1$, the conic is an ellipse. If $e > 1$, the conic is a hyperbola.

b. Standard forms of the polar equations of conics are

$$r = \frac{ep}{1 \pm e\cos\theta} \quad \text{and} \quad r = \frac{ep}{1 \pm e\sin\theta}$$

in which $(r, \theta)$ is a point on the conic's graph, $e$ is the eccentricity, and $p$ is the distance between the focus (located at the pole) and the directrix. Details are shown in the box on page 888.

c. A procedure for graphing the polar equation of a conic is given in the box on page 889.

## Review Exercises

### 10.1

*In Exercises 1–8, graph each ellipse and locate the foci.*

**1.** $\dfrac{x^2}{36} + \dfrac{y^2}{25} = 1$

**2.** $\dfrac{y^2}{25} + \dfrac{x^2}{16} = 1$

**3.** $4x^2 + y^2 = 16$

**4.** $4x^2 + 9y^2 = 36$

**5.** $\dfrac{(x-1)^2}{16} + \dfrac{(y+2)^2}{9} = 1$

**6.** $\dfrac{(x+1)^2}{9} + \dfrac{(y-2)^2}{16} = 1$

**7.** $4x^2 + 9y^2 + 24x - 36y + 36 = 0$

**8.** $9x^2 + 4y^2 - 18x + 8y - 23 = 0$

*In Exercises 9–11, find the standard form of the equation of each ellipse centered at the origin satisfying the given conditions.*

**9.** Foci: $(-4, 0), (4, 0)$; Vertices: $(-5, 0), (5, 0)$

**10.** Foci: $(0, -3), (0, 3)$; Vertices: $(0, -6), (0, 6)$

**11.** Major axis horizontal with length 12; length of minor axis = 4

**12.** A semielliptical arch supports a bridge that spans a river 20 yards wide. The center of the arch is 6 yards above the river's center. Write an equation for the ellipse so that the $x$-axis coincides with the water level and the $y$-axis passes through the center of the arch.

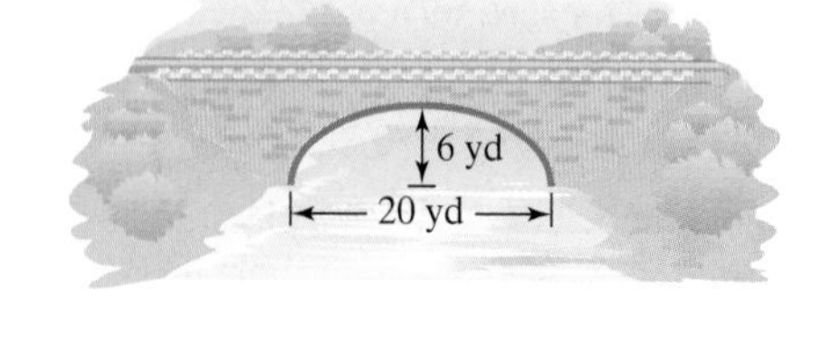


**13.** A semielliptic archway has a height of 15 feet at the center and a width of 50 feet, as shown in the figure. The 50-foot width consists of a two-lane road. Can a truck that is 12 feet high and 14 feet wide drive under the archway without going into the other lane?

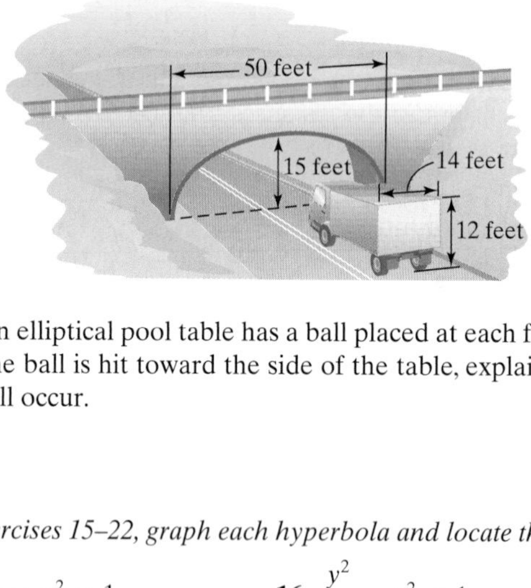


**14.** An elliptical pool table has a ball placed at each focus. If one ball is hit toward the side of the table, explain what will occur.

### 10.2

*In Exercises 15–22, graph each hyperbola and locate the foci.*

**15.** $\dfrac{x^2}{16} - y^2 = 1$

**16.** $\dfrac{y^2}{16} - x^2 = 1$

**17.** $9x^2 - 16y^2 = 144$

**18.** $4y^2 - x^2 = 16$

**19.** $\dfrac{(x-2)^2}{25} - \dfrac{(y+3)^2}{16} = 1$

**20.** $\dfrac{(y+2)^2}{25} - \dfrac{(x-3)^2}{16} = 1$

**21.** $y^2 - 4y - 4x^2 + 8x - 4 = 0$

**22.** $x^2 - y^2 - 2x - 2y - 1 = 0$

*In Exercises 23–24, find the standard form of the equation of each hyperbola centered at the origin satisfying the given conditions.*

**23.** Foci: $(0, -4)$, $(0, 4)$; Vertices: $(0, -2)$, $(0, 2)$

**24.** Foci: $(-8, 0)$, $(8, 0)$; Vertices: $(-3, 0)$, $(3, 0)$

**25.** Explain why it is not possible for a hyperbola to have foci at $(0, -2)$ and $(0, 2)$ and vertices at $(0, -3)$ and $(0, 3)$.

**26.** Radio tower $M_2$ is located 200 miles due west of radio tower $M_1$. The situation is illustrated in the figure shown, where a coordinate system has been superimposed. Simultaneous radio signals are sent from each tower to a ship, with the signal from $M_2$ received 500 microseconds before the signal from $M_1$. Assuming that radio signals travel at 0.186 miles per microsecond, determine the equation of the hyperbola on which the ship is located.

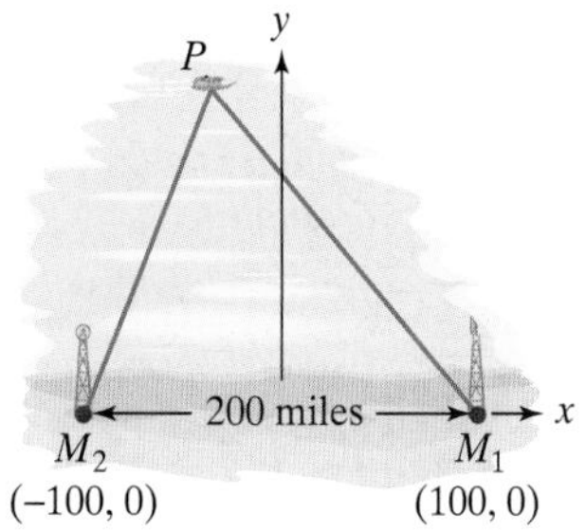


## 10.3

*In Exercises 27–33, find the vertex, focus, and directrix of each parabola with the given equation. Then graph the parabola.*

**27.** $y^2 = 8x$

**28.** $x^2 + 16y = 0$

**29.** $(y - 2)^2 = -16x$

**30.** $(x - 4)^2 = 4(y + 1)$

**31.** $x^2 + 4y = 4$

**32.** $y^2 - 4x - 10y + 21 = 0$

**33.** $x^2 - 4x - 2y = 0$

*In Exercises 34–35, find the standard form of the equation of each parabola with vertex at the origin satisfying the given conditions.*

**34.** Focus: $(12, 0)$; Directrix: $x = -12$

**35.** Focus: $(0, -11)$; Directrix: $y = 11$

**36.** An engineer is designing headlight units for automobiles. The unit has a parabolic surface with a diameter of 12 inches and a depth of 3 inches. The situation is illustrated in the figure, where a coordinate system has been superimposed. What is the equation of the parabola in this system? Where should the light source be placed? Describe this placement relative to the vertex.

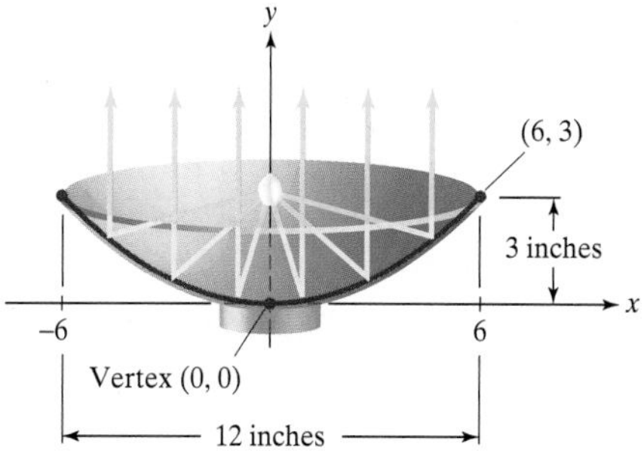


**37.** The George Washington Bridge spans the Hudson River from New York to New Jersey. Its two towers are 3500 feet apart and rise 316 feet above the road. The cable between the towers has the shape of a parabola, and the cable just touches the sides of the road midway between the towers. What is the height of the cable 1000 feet from a tower?

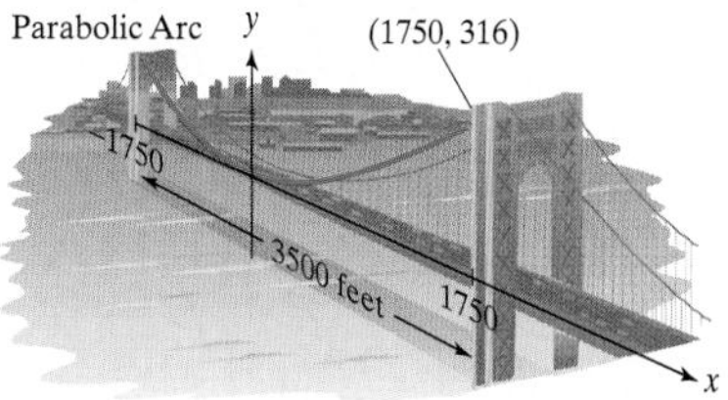


**38.** The giant satellite dish in the figure shown is in the shape of a parabolic surface. Signals strike the surface and are reflected to the focus, where the receiver is located. The diameter of the dish is 300 feet and its depth is 44 feet. How far, to the nearest foot, from the base of the dish should the receiver be placed?

## 10.4

*In Exercises 39–46, identify each equation without completing the square or using a rotation of axes.*

**39.** $y^2 + 4x + 2y - 15 = 0$

**40.** $x^2 + 16y^2 - 160y + 384 = 0$

**41.** $16x^2 + 64x + 9y^2 - 54y + 1 = 0$

**42.** $4x^2 - 9y^2 - 8x + 12y - 144 = 0$

**43.** $5x^2 + 2\sqrt{3}xy + 3y^2 - 18 = 0$

**44.** $5x^2 - 8xy + 7y^2 - 9\sqrt{5}x - 9 = 0$

**45.** $x^2 + 6xy + 9y^2 - 2y = 0$

**46.** $x^2 - 2xy + 3y^2 + 2x + 4y - 1 = 0$

*In Exercises 47–51,*

**a.** *Rewrite the equation in a rotated $x'y'$-system without an $x'y'$-term.*

**b.** *Express the equation involving $x'$ and $y'$ in the standard form of a conic section.*

**c.** *Use the rotated system to graph the equation.*

**47.** $xy - 4 = 0$

**48.** $x^2 + xy + y^2 - 1 = 0$

**49.** $4x^2 + 10xy + 4y^2 - 9 = 0$

**50.** $6x^2 - 6xy + 14y^2 - 45 = 0$

**51.** $x^2 + 2\sqrt{3}xy + 3y^2 - 12\sqrt{3}x + 12y = 0$

## 10.5

*In Exercises 52–57, eliminate the parameter and graph the plane curve represented by the parametric equations. Use arrows to show the orientation of each plane curve.*

**52.** $x = 2t - 1,\ y = 1 - t;\ -\infty < t < \infty$

**53.** $x = t^2,\ y = t - 1;\ -1 \le t \le 3.$

**54.** $x = 4t^2,\ y = t + 1;\ -\infty < t < \infty$

**55.** $x = 4\sin t,\ y = 3\cos t;\ 0 \le t < \pi$

**56.** $x = 3 + 2\cos t,\ y = 1 + 2\sin t;\ 0 \le t < 2\pi$

**57.** $x = 3\sec t,\ y = 3\tan t;\ 0 \le t \le \frac{\pi}{4}$

**58.** Find two different sets of parametric equations for $y = x^2 + 6$.

**59.** The path of a projectile that is launched $h$ feet above the ground with an initial velocity of $v_0$ feet per second and at an angle $\theta$ with the horizontal is given by the parametric equations

$$x = (v_0 \cos\theta)t \quad \text{and} \quad y = h + (v_0 \sin\theta)t - 16t^2$$

where $t$ is the time, in seconds, since the projectile was launched. A football player throws a football with an initial velocity of 100 feet per second at an angle of 40° to the horizontal. The ball leaves the player's hand at a height of 6 feet.

**a.** Find the parametric equations that describe the position of the ball as a function of time.

**b.** Describe the ball's position after 1, 2, and 3 seconds. Round to the nearest tenth of a foot.

**c.** How long, to the nearest tenth of a second, is the ball in flight? What is the total horizontal distance that it travels before it lands?

**d.** Graph the parametric equations in part (a) using a graphing utility. Use the graph to determine when the ball is at its maximum height. What is its maximum height? Round all answers to the nearest tenth.

## 10.6

*In Exercises 60–65,*

**a.** *If necessary, write the equation in one of the standard forms for a conic in polar coordinates.*

**b.** *Determine values for e and p. Use the value of e to identify the conic.*

**c.** *Graph the given polar equation.*

**60.** $r = \dfrac{4}{1 - \sin\theta}$

**61.** $r = \dfrac{6}{1 + \cos\theta}$

**62.** $r = \dfrac{6}{2 + \sin\theta}$

**63.** $r = \dfrac{2}{3 - 2\cos\theta}$

**64.** $r = \dfrac{6}{3 + 6\sin\theta}$

**65.** $r = \dfrac{8}{4 + 16\cos\theta}$

# Chapter 10 Test

*In Exercises 1–5, graph the conic section with the given equation. For ellipses and hyperbolas, find the foci. For parabolas, find the vertex, focus, and directrix.*

**1.** $9x^2 - 4y^2 = 36$

**2.** $x^2 = -8y$

**3.** $\dfrac{(x + 2)^2}{25} + \dfrac{(y - 5)^2}{9} = 1$

**4.** $4x^2 - y^2 + 8x + 2y + 7 = 0$

**5.** $(x + 5)^2 = 8(y - 1)$

*In Exercises 6–8, find the standard form of the equation of the conic section satisfying the given conditions.*

**6.** Ellipse; Foci: $(-7, 0), (7, 0)$; Vertices: $(-10, 0), (10, 0)$

**7.** Hyperbola; Foci: $(0, -10), (0, 10)$; Vertices: $(0, -7), (0, 7)$

**8.** Parabola; Focus: $(50, 0)$; Directrix: $x = -50$

**9.** A sound whispered at one focus of a whispering gallery can be heard at the other focus. The figure shows a whispering gallery whose cross section is a semielliptical arch with a height of 24 feet and a width of 80 feet. How far from the room's center should two people stand so that they can whisper back and forth and be heard?

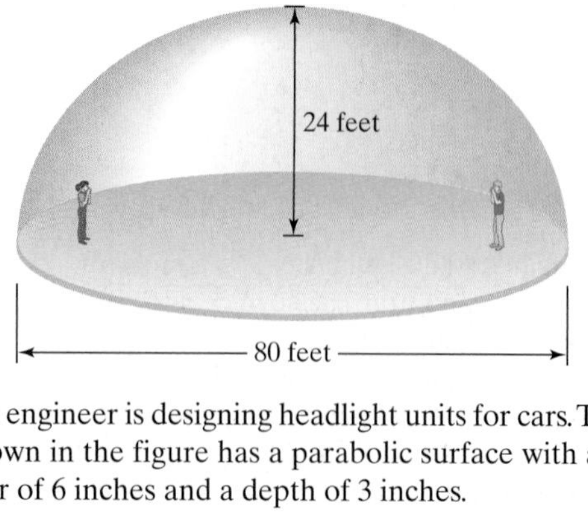


**10.** An engineer is designing headlight units for cars. The unit shown in the figure has a parabolic surface with a diameter of 6 inches and a depth of 3 inches.

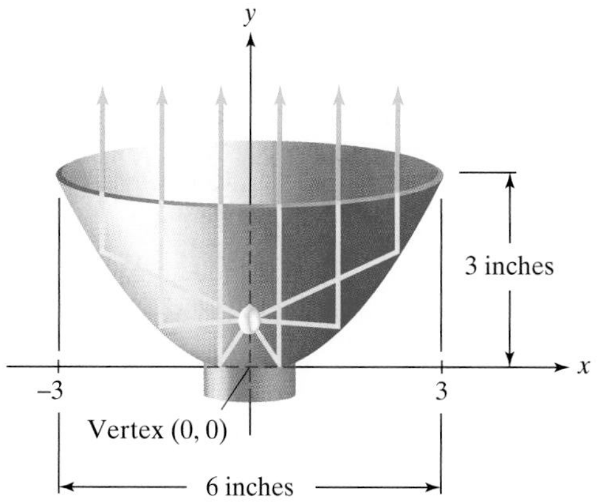


**a.** Using the coordinate system that has been positioned on the unit, find the parabola's equation.

**b.** If the light source is located at the focus, describe its placement relative to the vertex.

*In Exercises 11–12, identify each equation without completing the square or using a rotation of axes.*

**11.** $x^2 + 9y^2 + 10x - 18y + 25 = 0$

**12.** $x^2 + y^2 + xy + 3x - y - 3 = 0$

**13.** For the equation

$$7x^2 - 6\sqrt{3}xy + 13y^2 - 16 = 0$$

determine what angle of rotation would eliminate the $x'y'$-term in a rotated $x'y'$-system.

*In Exercises 14–15, eliminate the parameter and graph the plane curve represented by the parametric equations. Use arrows to show the orientation of each plane curve.*

**14.** $x = t^2, y = t - 1; -\infty < t < \infty$

**15.** $x = 1 + 3\sin t,\ y = 2\cos t; 0 \le t < 2\pi$

*In Exercises 16–17, identify the conic and graph the polar equation.*

**16.** $r = \dfrac{2}{1 - \cos\theta}$ **17.** $r = \dfrac{4}{2 + \sin\theta}$

## Cumulative Review Exercises (Chapters 1–10)

*Solve each equation or inequality in Exercises 1–7.*

**1.** $2(x - 3) + 5x = 8(x - 1)$

**2.** $-3(2x - 4) > 2(6x - 12)$

**3.** $x - 5 = \sqrt{x + 7}$ **4.** $(x - 2)^2 = 20$

**5.** $|2x - 1| \ge 7$ **6.** $3x^3 + 4x^2 - 7x + 2 = 0$

**7.** $\log_2(x + 1) + \log_2(x - 1) = 3$

*Solve each system in Exercises 8–10*

**8.** $3x + 4y = 2$
$2x + 5y = -1$

**9.** $2x^2 - y^2 = -8$
$x - y = 6$

**10.** (Use matrices.)

$$\begin{aligned} x - y + z &= 17 \\ -4x + y + 5z &= -2 \\ 2x + 3y + z &= 8 \end{aligned}$$

*In Exercises 11–13, graph each equation, function, or system in the rectangular coordinate system.*

**11.** $f(x) = (x - 1)^2 - 4$ **12.** $\dfrac{x^2}{9} + \dfrac{y^2}{4} = 1$

**13.** $5x + y \le 10$
$y \ge \dfrac{1}{4}x + 2$

**14. a.** List all possible rational roots of

$$32x^3 - 52x^2 + 17x + 3 = 0.$$

**b.** The graph of $f(x) = 32x^3 - 52x^2 + 17x + 3$ is shown in the figure. Use the graph of $f$ and synthetic division to solve the equation in part (a).

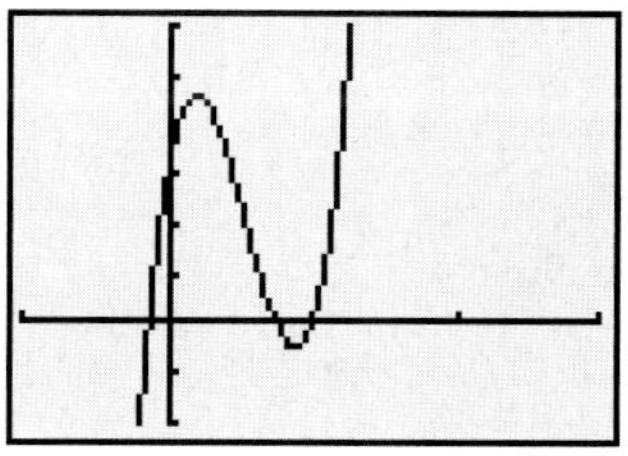

**15.** The graph shows gender ratios in the United States, with future projections.

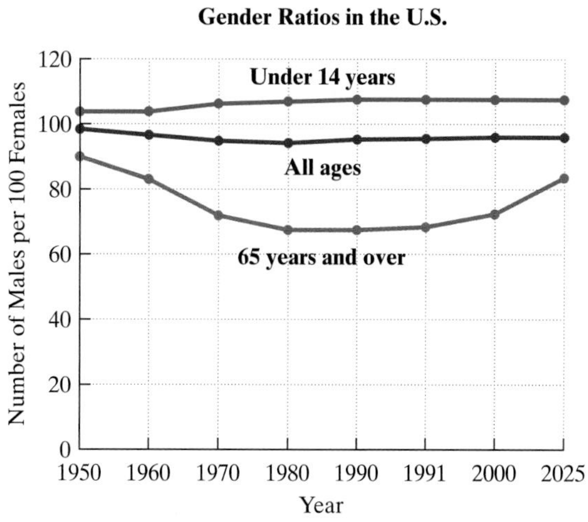


*Source*: U.S. Census Bureau

For males age 65 and over, shown by the blue graph:

**a.** In what time interval is the number of males per 100 females constant?
**b.** In what time interval is the number of males per 100 females increasing?
**c.** In what time interval is the number of males per 100 females decreasing?

For all ages, shown by the red graph:

**d.** Write a constant function $f(x)$ that approximately models the data shown for $x$ in the interval $[1950, 2025]$.
**e.** What is misleading about the scale on the horizontal axis?

**16.** If $f(x) = x^2 - 4$ and $g(x) = x + 2$, find $(g \circ f)(x)$.

**17.** Expand using logarithmic properties. Where possible, evaluate logarithmic expressions.

$$\log_5 \frac{x^3\sqrt{y}}{125}$$

**18.** Write the slope-intercept form of the equation of the line passing through $(1, -4)$ and $(-5, 8)$.

**19.** Rent-a-Truck charges a daily rental rate for a truck of \$39 plus \$0.16 a mile. A competing agency, Ace Truck Rentals, charges \$25 a day plus \$0.24 a mile for the same truck. How many miles must be driven in a day to make the daily cost of both agencies the same? What will be the cost?

**20.** The longest-lived U.S. presidents are John Adams (age 90), Herbert Hoover (also 90), and Harry Truman (88). Behind them are James Madison, Thomas Jefferson, and Richard Nixon. The latter three men lived a total of 249 years, and their ages at the time of death form consecutive odd integers. For how long did Nixon, Jefferson, and Madison live?

**21.** Verify the identity: $\dfrac{\csc\theta - \sin\theta}{\sin\theta} = \cot^2\theta$.

**22.** Graph one complete cycle of $y = 2\cos(2x + \pi)$.

**23.** If $\mathbf{v} = 3\mathbf{i} - 6\mathbf{j}$ and $\mathbf{w} = \mathbf{i} + \mathbf{j}$, find $(\mathbf{v} \cdot \mathbf{w})\mathbf{w}$.

**24.** Solve for $\theta$: $\sin 2\theta = \sin\theta, 0 \le \theta < 2\pi$.

**25.** In oblique triangle $ABC$, $A = 64°$, $B = 72°$, and $a = 13.6$. Solve the triangle. Round length to the nearest tenth.

# Sequences, Induction, and Probability

## Chapter 11

We often save for the future by investing small amounts at periodic intervals. To understand how our savings accumulate, we need to understand properties of lists of numbers that are related to each other by a rule. Such lists are called *sequences*. Learning about properties of sequences will show you how to make your financial goals a reality. Your knowledge of sequences will enable you to inform your college roommate of the best of the three appealing offers.

Something incredible has happened. Your college roommate, a gifted athlete, has been given a six-year contract with a professional baseball team. He will be playing against the likes of Mark McGwire and Sammy Sosa. Management offers him three options. One is a beginning salary of \$1,700,000 with annual increases of \$70,000 per year starting in the second year. A second option is \$1,700,000 the first year with an annual increase of 2% per year beginning in the second year. The third offer involves less money the first year—\$1,500,000—but there is an annual increase of 9% yearly after that. Which option offers the most money over the six-year contract?

# SECTION 11.1 *Sequences and Summation Notation*

## Objectives

1. Find particular terms of a sequence from the general term.
2. Use recursion formulas.
3. Use factorial notation.
4. Use summation notation.

## Sequences

Many creations in nature involve intricate mathematical designs, including a variety of spirals. For example, the arrangement of the individual florets in the head of a sunflower forms spirals. In some species, there are 21 spirals in the clockwise direction and 34 in the counterclockwise direction. The precise numbers depend on the species of sunflower: 21 and 34, or 34 and 55, or 55 and 89, or even 89 and 144.

### Fibonacci Numbers on the Piano Keyboard

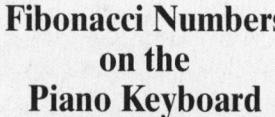

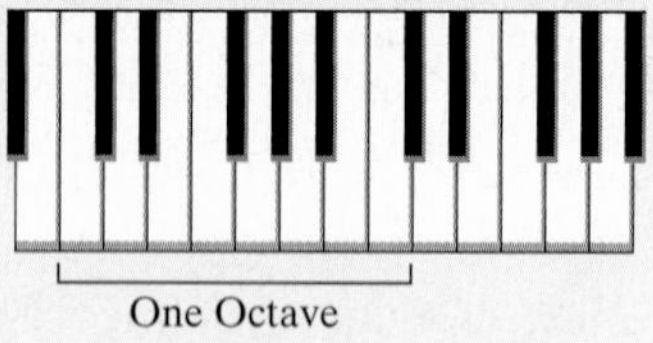


Numbers in the Fibonacci sequence can be found in an octave on the piano keyboard. The octave contains 2 black keys in one cluster, 3 black keys in another cluster, 5 black keys, 8 white keys, and a total of 13 keys altogether. The numbers 2, 3, 5, 8, and 13 are the third through seventh terms of the Fibonacci sequence.

This observation becomes even more interesting when we consider a sequence of numbers investigated by Leonardo of Pisa, also known as Fibonacci, an Italian mathematician of the thirteenth century. The **Fibonacci sequence** of numbers is an infinite sequence that begins as follows:

$$1, 1, 2, 3, 5, 8, 13, 21, 34, 55, 89, 144, 233 \ldots.$$

The first two terms are 1. Every term thereafter is the sum of the two preceding terms. For example, the third term, 2, is the sum of the first and second terms: $1 + 1 = 2$. The fourth term, 3, is the sum of the second and third terms: $1 + 2 = 3$, and so on. Did you know that the number of spirals in a daisy or a sunflower, 21 and 34, are two Fibonacci numbers? The number of spirals in a pine cone, 8 and 13, and a pineapple, 8 and 13, are also Fibonacci numbers.

We can think of the Fibonacci sequence as a function. The terms of the sequence

$$1, 1, 2, 3, 5, 8, 13, 21, 34, 55, 89, 144, 233, \ldots$$

are the range values for a function whose domain is the set of positive integers.

$$\begin{array}{lcccccccc} \text{Domain:} & 1, & 2, & 3, & 4, & 5, & 6, & 7, & \ldots \\ & \downarrow & \downarrow & \downarrow & \downarrow & \downarrow & \downarrow & \downarrow & \\ \text{Range:} & 1, & 1, & 2, & 3, & 5, & 8, & 13, & \ldots \end{array}$$

Thus, $f(1) = 1, f(2) = 1, f(3) = 2, f(4) = 3, f(5) = 5, f(6) = 8, f(7) = 13$, and so on.

The letter $a$ with a subscript is used to represent function values of a sequence, rather than the usual function notation. The subscripts make up the domain of the sequence, and they identify the location of a term. Thus, $a_1$ represents the first term of the sequence, $a_2$ represents the second term, $a_3$ the third term, and so on. This notation is shown for the first six terms of the Fibonacci sequence:

$$1, \quad 1, \quad 2, \quad 3, \quad 5, \quad 8.$$

$a_1 = 1$ $a_2 = 1$ $a_3 = 2$ $a_4 = 3$ $a_5 = 5$ $a_6 = 8$

The notation $a_n$ represents the $n$th term, or **general term**, of a sequence. The entire sequence is represented by $\{a_n\}$.

**Definition of a Sequence**

An **infinite sequence** $\{a_n\}$ is a function whose domain is the set of positive integers. The function values, or **terms**, of the sequence are represented by

$$a_1, a_2, a_3, a_4, \ldots, a_n, \ldots.$$

Sequences whose domains consist only of the first $n$ positive integers are called **finite sequences**.

1 Find particular terms of a sequence from the general term.

## EXAMPLE 1 Writing Terms of a Sequence from the General Term

Write the first four terms of the sequence whose $n$th term, or general term, is given.

**a.** $a_n = 3n + 4$ **b.** $a_n = \dfrac{(-1)^n}{3^n - 1}$

**Solution**

**a.** We need to find the first four terms of the sequence whose general term is $a_n = 3n + 4$. To do so, we replace $n$ in the formula by 1, 2, 3, and 4.

$a_1$, 1st term: $3 \cdot 1 + 4 = 3 + 4 = 7$

$a_2$, 2nd term: $3 \cdot 2 + 4 = 6 + 4 = 10$

$a_3$, 3rd term: $3 \cdot 3 + 4 = 9 + 4 = 13$

$a_4$, 4th term: $3 \cdot 4 + 4 = 12 + 4 = 16$

The first four terms are 7, 10, 13, and 16. The sequence defined by $a_n = 3n + 4$ can be written as

$$7, 10, 13, \ldots, 3n + 4, \ldots.$$

**b.** We need to find the first four terms of the sequence whose general term is $a_n = \dfrac{(-1)^n}{3^n - 1}$. To do so, we replace each occurrence of $n$ in the formula by 1, 2, 3, and 4.

$a_1$, 1st term: $\dfrac{(-1)^1}{3^1 - 1} = \dfrac{-1}{3 - 1} = -\dfrac{1}{2}$

$a_2$, 2nd term: $\dfrac{(-1)^2}{3^2 - 1} = \dfrac{1}{9 - 1} = \dfrac{1}{8}$

$a_3$, 3rd term: $\dfrac{(-1)^3}{3^3 - 1} = \dfrac{-1}{27 - 1} = -\dfrac{1}{26}$

$a_4$, 4th term: $\dfrac{(-1)^4}{3^4 - 1} = \dfrac{1}{81 - 1} = \dfrac{1}{80}$

The first four terms are $-\frac{1}{2}, \frac{1}{8}, -\frac{1}{26}, \frac{1}{80}$. The sequence defined by $\dfrac{(-1)^n}{3^n - 1}$ can be written as

$$-\frac{1}{2}, \frac{1}{8}, -\frac{1}{26}, \ldots, \frac{(-1)^n}{3^n - 1}, \ldots.$$

**Study Tip**

The factor $(-1)^n$ in the general term of a sequence causes the signs of the terms to alternate between positive and negative, depending on whether $n$ is even or odd.

## Technology

Graphing utilities can write the terms of a sequence and graph them. For example, to find the first six terms of $\{a_n\} = \left\{\frac{1}{n}\right\}$, enter

General term — Stop at $a_6$.

SEQ $(1 \div x, x, 1, 6, 1)$.

Variable used in general term — Start at $a_1$. — The "step" from $a_1$ to $a_2$, $a_2$ to $a_3$, etc., is 1.

The first few terms of the sequence are shown in the viewing rectangle. By pressing the right arrow key to scroll right, you can see the remaining terms.

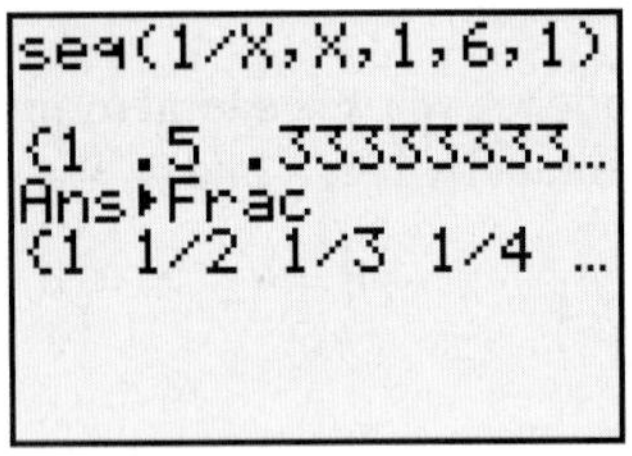


**Check Point 1** Write the first four terms of the sequence whose $n$th term, or general term, is given.

**a.** $a_n = 2n + 5$ **b.** $a_n = \dfrac{(-1)^n}{2^n + 1}$

Although sequences are usually named with the letter $a$, any lowercase letter can be used. For example, the first four terms of the sequence $\{b_n\} = \{(\frac{1}{2})^n\}$ are $b_1 = \frac{1}{2}$, $b_2 = \frac{1}{4}$, $b_3 = \frac{1}{8}$, and $b_4 = \frac{1}{16}$.

Because a sequence is a function whose domain is the set of positive integers, the **graph of a sequence** is a set of discrete points. For example, consider the sequence whose general term is $a_n = \frac{1}{n}$. How does the graph of this sequence differ from the graph of the function $f(x) = \frac{1}{x}$? The graph of $f(x) = \frac{1}{x}$ is shown in Figure 11.1(a) for positive values of $x$. To obtain the graph of the sequence $\{a_n\} = \{\frac{1}{n}\}$, remove all the points from the graph of $f$ except those whose $x$-coordinates are positive integers. Thus, we remove all points except $(1, 1)$, $(2, \frac{1}{2})$, $(3, \frac{1}{3})$, $(4, \frac{1}{4})$, and so on. The remaining points are the graph of the sequence $\{a_n\} = \{\frac{1}{n}\}$, shown in Figure 11.1(b). Notice that the horizontal axis is labeled $n$ and the vertical axis $a_n$.

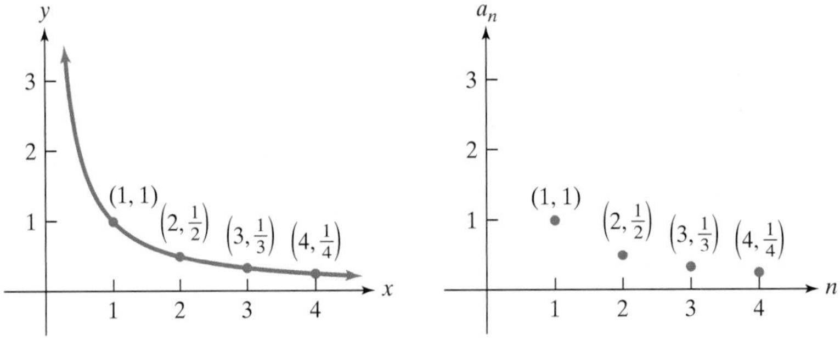


(a) The graph of $f(x) = \frac{1}{x}, x > 0$ (b) The graph of $\{a_n\} = \{\frac{1}{n}\}$

**Figure 11.1** Comparing a continuous graph to the graph of a sequence

**2** Use recursion formulas.

## Recursion Formulas

In Example 1, the formulas used for the $n$th term of a sequence expressed the term as a function of $n$, the number of the term. Sequences can also be defined using **recursion formulas**. A recursion formula defines the $n$th term of a sequence as a function of the previous term. Our next example illustrates that if the first term of a sequence is known, then the recursion formula can be used to determine the remaining terms.

## EXAMPLE 2 Using a Recursion Formula

Find the first four terms of the sequence in which $a_1 = 5$ and $a_n = 3a_{n-1} + 2$ for $n \geq 2$.

### Solution

$a_1 = 5$ This is the given first term.

$a_2 = 3a_1 + 2$ Use $a_n = 3a_{n-1} + 2$, with $n = 2$. Thus, $a_2 = 3a_{2-1} + 2 = 3a_1 + 2$.

$= 3(5) + 2 = 17$ Substitute 5 for $a_1$.

$a_3 = 3a_2 + 2$ — Again use $a_n = 3a_{n-1} + 2$, with $n = 3$.

$= 3(17) + 2 = 53$ — Substitute 17 for $a_2$.

$a_4 = 3a_3 + 2$ — Notice that $a_4$ is defined in terms of $a_3$. We used $a_n = 3a_{n-1} + 2$, with $n = 4$.

$= 3(53) + 2 = 161$ — Use the value of $a_3$, the third term, obtained from above.

The first four terms are 5, 17, 53, and 161.

**Check Point 2** Find the first four terms of the sequence in which $a_1 = 3$ and $a_n = 2a_{n-1} + 5$ for $n \geq 2$.

**3** Use factorial notation.

## Factorial Notation

Products of consecutive positive integers occur quite often in sequences. These products can be expressed in a special notation, called **factorial notation.**

**Factorials from 0 through 20**

| | |
|---|---|
| 0! | 1 |
| 1! | 1 |
| 2! | 2 |
| 3! | 6 |
| 4! | 24 |
| 5! | 120 |
| 6! | 720 |
| 7! | 5040 |
| 8! | 40,320 |
| 9! | 362,880 |
| 10! | 3,628,800 |
| 11! | 39,916,800 |
| 12! | 479,001,600 |
| 13! | 6,227,020,800 |
| 14! | 87,178,291,200 |
| 15! | 1,307,674,368,000 |
| 16! | 20,922,789,888,000 |
| 17! | 355,687,428,096,000 |
| 18! | 6,402,373,705,728,000 |
| 19! | 121,645,100,408,832,000 |
| 20! | 2,432,902,008,176,640,000 |

As $n$ increases, $n!$ grows very rapidly. Factorial growth is more explosive than exponential growth discussed in Chapter 4.

**Factorial Notation**

If $n$ is a positive integer, the notation $n!$ (read "$n$ factorial") is the product of all positive integers from $n$ down through 1.

$$n! = n(n-1)(n-2)\ldots(3)(2)(1)$$

0! (zero factorial), by definition, is 1.

$$0! = 1$$

The values of $n!$ for the first six positive integers are

$$1! = 1$$
$$2! = 2 \cdot 1 = 2$$
$$3! = 3 \cdot 2 \cdot 1 = 6$$
$$4! = 4 \cdot 3 \cdot 2 \cdot 1 = 24$$
$$5! = 5 \cdot 4 \cdot 3 \cdot 2 \cdot 1 = 120$$
$$6! = 6 \cdot 5 \cdot 4 \cdot 3 \cdot 2 \cdot 1 = 720.$$

Factorials affect only the number or variable that they follow unless grouping symbols appear. For example,

$$2 \cdot 3! = 2(3 \cdot 2 \cdot 1) = 2 \cdot 6 = 12$$

whereas

$$(2 \cdot 3)! = 6! = 6 \cdot 5 \cdot 4 \cdot 3 \cdot 2 \cdot 1 = 720.$$

In this sense, factorials are similar to exponents.

### EXAMPLE 3 Finding Terms of a Sequence Involving Factorials

Write the first four terms of the sequence whose $n$th term is

$$a_n = \frac{2^n}{(n-1)!}.$$

## Technology

Graphing utilities have factorial keys. To find 5 factorial, enter

5 [!] [ENTER].

Because $n!$ becomes quite large as $n$ increases, your utility will display these larger values in scientific notation.

**Solution** We need to find the first four terms of the sequence. To do so, we replace each $n$ in the formula by 1, 2, 3, and 4.

$a_1$, 1st term $$\frac{2^1}{(1-1)!} = \frac{2}{0!} = \frac{2}{1} = 2$$

$a_2$, 2nd term $$\frac{2^2}{(2-1)!} = \frac{4}{1!} = \frac{4}{1} = 4$$

$a_3$, 3rd term $$\frac{2^3}{(3-1)!} = \frac{8}{2!} = \frac{8}{2\cdot 1} = 4$$

$a_4$, 4th term $$\frac{2^4}{(4-1)!} = \frac{16}{3!} = \frac{16}{3\cdot 2\cdot 1} = \frac{16}{6} = \frac{8}{3}$$

The first four terms are $2, 4, 4, \frac{8}{3}$.

**Check Point 3** Write the first four terms of the sequence whose $n$th term is

$$a_n = \frac{20}{(n+1)!}.$$

When evaluating fractions with factorials in the numerator and the denominator, try to reduce the fraction before performing the multiplications. For example, consider $\frac{26!}{21!}$. Rather than write out 26! as the product of all integers from 26 down to 1, we can express 26! as

$$26! = 26\cdot 25\cdot 24\cdot 23\cdot 22\cdot 21!.$$

In this way, we can divide both the numerator and the denominator by the common factor, 21!.

$$\frac{26!}{21!} = \frac{26\cdot 25\cdot 24\cdot 23\cdot 22\cdot \cancel{21!}}{\cancel{21!}} = 26\cdot 25\cdot 24\cdot 23\cdot 22 = 7{,}893{,}600$$

## EXAMPLE 4 Evaluating Fractions with Factorials

Evaluate each factorial expression.

**a.** $\frac{10!}{2!8!}$ **b.** $\frac{(n+1)!}{n!}$

**Solution**

**a.** $$\frac{10!}{2!8!} = \frac{10\cdot 9\cdot \cancel{8!}}{2\cdot 1\cdot \cancel{8!}} = \frac{90}{2} = 45$$

**b.** $$\frac{(n+1)!}{n!} = \frac{(n+1)\cdot \cancel{n!}}{\cancel{n!}} = n+1$$

**Check Point 4** Evaluate each factorial expression.

**a.** $\frac{14!}{2!12!}$ **b.** $\frac{n!}{(n-1)!}$

**4** Use summation notation.

## Summation Notation

It is sometimes useful to find the sum of the first $n$ terms of a sequence. For example, consider the number of AIDS cases diagnosed in the United States from 1991 to 1997, shown in Table 11.1.

**Table 11.1 AIDS Cases Diagnosed in the United States, 1991–1997**

| **Year** | 1991 | 1992 | 1993 | 1994 | 1995 | 1996 | 1997 |
|---|---|---|---|---|---|---|---|
| **Cases Diagnosed** | 60,124 | 79,054 | 79,049 | 71,209 | 66,233 | 54,656 | 31,153 |

*Source*: U.S. Department of Health and Human Services

We can let $a_n$ represent the number of AIDS cases diagnosed in year $n$, where $n = 1$ corresponds to 1991, $n = 2$ to 1992, $n = 3$ to 1993, and so on. The terms of the finite sequence in Table 8.1 are given as follows.

60,124 79,054, 79,049, 71,209, 66,233, 54,656, 31,153

$a_1$ $a_2$ $a_3$ $a_4$ $a_5$ $a_6$ $a_7$

Why might we want to add the terms of this sequence? We do this to find the number of AIDS cases diagnosed from 1991 to 1997. Thus,

$$\begin{aligned} &a_1 + a_2 + a_3 + a_4 + a_5 + a_6 + a_7 \\ &= 60{,}124 + 79{,}054, + 79{,}049, + 71{,}209, + 66{,}233, + 54{,}656, + 31{,}153 \\ &= 441{,}478. \end{aligned}$$

We see that there were 441,478 AIDS cases diagnosed in the United States from 1991 to 1997.

There is a compact notation for expressing the sum of the first $n$ terms of a sequence. For example, rather than write

$$a_1 + a_2 + a_3 + a_4 + a_5 + a_6 + a_7,$$

we can use **summation notation** to express the sum as

$$a_1 + a_2 + a_3 + a_4 + a_5 + a_6 + a_7 = \sum_{i=1}^{7} a_i.$$

We read the expression on the right as "the sum as $i$ goes from 1 to 7 of $a_i$." The letter $i$ is called the **index of summation** and is not related to the use of $i$ to represent $\sqrt{-1}$.

You can think of the symbol $\Sigma$ (the uppercase Greek letter sigma) as an instruction to add up terms of a sequence.

### Summation Notation

The sum of the first $n$ terms of a sequence is represented by the **summation notation**

$$\sum_{i=1}^{n} a_i = a_1 + a_2 + a_3 + a_4 + \cdots + a_n$$

where $i$ is the **index of summation**, $n$ is the **upper limit of summation**, and 1 is the **lower limit of summation.**

Any letter can be used for the index of summation. The letters $i$, $j$, and $k$ are used commonly. Furthermore, the lower limit of summation can be an integer other than 1.

When we write out a sum that is given in summation notation, we are **expanding the summation notation.** Example 5 shows how to do this.

## EXAMPLE 5 Using Summation Notation

Expand and evaluate the sum:

**a.** $\sum_{i=1}^{6}(i^2+1)$ **b.** $\sum_{k=4}^{7}[(-2)^k-5]$ **c.** $\sum_{i=1}^{5}3$

### Technology

Graphing utilities can calculate the sum of a sequence. For example, to find the sum of the sequence in Example 5a, enter

SUM SEQ $(x^2+1, x, 1, 6, 1)$.

Then press ENTER; 97 should be displayed. Use this capability to verify Example 5b.

**Solution**

**a.** We must replace $i$ in the expression $i^2+1$ with all consecutive integers from 1 to 6 inclusively. Then we add.

$$\sum_{i=1}^{6}(i^2+1) = (1^2+1)+(2^2+1)+(3^2+1)+(4^2+1)$$
$$+(5^2+1)+(6^2+1)$$
$$= 2+5+10+17+26+37$$
$$= 97$$

**b.** This time the index of summation is $k$. First we evaluate $(-2)^k-5$ for all consecutive integers from 4 through 7 inclusively. Then we add.

$$\sum_{k=4}^{7}[(-2)^k-5] = [(-2)^4-5]+[(-2)^5-5]$$
$$+[(-2)^6-5]+[(-2)^7-5]$$
$$= (16-5)+(-32-5)+(64-5)+(-128-5)$$
$$= 11+(-37)+59+(-133)$$
$$= -100$$

**c.** To find $\sum_{i=1}^{5}3$, we observe that every term of the sum is 3. The notation $i=1$ through 5 indicates that we must add the first five 3s from a sequence in which every term is 3.

$$\sum_{i=1}^{5}3 = 3+3+3+3+3 = 15$$

**Check Point 5** Expand and evaluate the sum:

**a.** $\sum_{i=1}^{6}2i^2$ **b.** $\sum_{k=3}^{5}(2^k-3)$ **c.** $\sum_{i=1}^{5}4$

For a given sum, we can vary the upper and lower limits of summation as well as the letter used for the index of summation. By doing so, we can produce different-looking summation notations for the same sum. For example, the sum of the squares of the first four integers can be expressed in a number of equivalent ways:

$$\sum_{i=1}^{4} i^2 = 1^2 + 2^2 + 3^2 + 4^2 = 30$$

$$\sum_{i=0}^{3} (i+1)^2 = (0+1)^2 + (1+1)^2 + (2+1)^2 + (3+1)^2$$

$$= 1^2 + 2^2 + 3^2 + 4^2 = 30$$

$$\sum_{k=2}^{5} (k-1)^2 = (2-1)^2 + (3-1)^2 + (4-1)^2 + (5-1)^2$$

$$= 1^2 + 2^2 + 3^2 + 4^2 = 30.$$

## EXAMPLE 6 Writing Sums in Summation Notation

Express each sum using summation notation.

**a.** $1^3 + 2^3 + 3^3 + \cdots + 7^3$ **b.** $1 + \frac{1}{3} + \frac{1}{9} + \frac{1}{27} + \cdots + \frac{1}{3^{n-1}}$

**Solution** In each case, we will use 1 as the lower limit of summation and $i$ for the index of summation.

**a.** The sum $1^3 + 2^3 + 3^3 + \cdots + 7^3$ has seven terms, each of the form $i^3$, starting at $i = 1$ and ending at $i = 7$. Thus,

$$1^3 + 2^3 + 3^3 + \cdots + 7^3 = \sum_{i=1}^{7} i^3.$$

**b.** The sum

$$1 + \frac{1}{3} + \frac{1}{9} + \frac{1}{27} + \cdots + \frac{1}{3^{n-1}}$$

has $n$ terms, each of the form $\frac{1}{3^{i-1}}$, starting at $i = 1$ and ending at $i = n$.

Thus,

$$1 + \frac{1}{3} + \frac{1}{9} + \frac{1}{27} + \cdots + \frac{1}{3^{n-1}} = \sum_{i=1}^{n} \frac{1}{3^{i-1}}.$$

**Check Point 6** Express each sum using summation notation.

**a.** $1^2 + 2^2 + 3^2 + \cdots + 9^2$ **b.** $1 + \frac{1}{2} + \frac{1}{4} + \frac{1}{8} + \cdots + \frac{1}{2^{n-1}}$

Table 11.2 contains some important properties of sums expressed in summation notation.

**Table 11.2 Properties of Sums**

| Property | Example |
|---|---|
| 1. $\sum_{i=1}^{n} ca_i = c\sum_{i=1}^{n} a_i$, $c$ any real number | $\sum_{i=1}^{4} 3i^2 = 3 \cdot 1^2 + 3 \cdot 2^2 + 3 \cdot 3^2 + 3 \cdot 4^2$<br>$3\sum_{i=1}^{4} i^2 = 3(1^2 + 2^2 + 3^2 + 4^2) = 3 \cdot 1^2 + 3 \cdot 2^2 + 3 \cdot 3^2 + 3 \cdot 4^2$<br>Conclusion: $\sum_{i=1}^{4} 3i^2 = 3\sum_{i=1}^{4} i^2$ |
| 2. $\sum_{i=1}^{n} (a_i + b_i) = \sum_{i=1}^{n} a_i + \sum_{i=1}^{n} b_i$ | $\sum_{i=1}^{4} (i + i^2) = (1 + 1^2) + (2 + 2^2) + (3 + 3^2) + (4 + 4^2)$<br>$\sum_{i=1}^{4} i + \sum_{i=1}^{4} i^2 = (1 + 2 + 3 + 4) + (1^2 + 2^2 + 3^2 + 4^2)$<br>$= (1 + 1^2) + (2 + 2^2) + (3 + 3^2) + (4 + 4^2)$<br>Conclusion: $\sum_{i=1}^{4} (i + i^2) = \sum_{i=1}^{4} i + \sum_{i=1}^{4} i^2$ |
| 3. $\sum_{i=1}^{n} (a_i - b_i) = \sum_{i=1}^{n} a_i - \sum_{i=1}^{n} b_i$ | $\sum_{i=3}^{5} (i^2 - i^3) = (3^2 - 3^3) + (4^2 - 4^3) + (5^2 - 5^3)$<br>$\sum_{i=3}^{5} i^2 - \sum_{i=3}^{5} i^3 = (3^2 + 4^2 + 5^2) - (3^3 + 4^3 + 5^3)$<br>$= (3^2 - 3^3) + (4^2 - 4^3) + (5^2 - 5^3)$<br>Conclusion: $\sum_{i=3}^{5} (i^2 - i^3) = \sum_{i=3}^{5} i^2 - \sum_{i=3}^{5} i^3$ |

## EXERCISE SET 11.1

### Practice Exercises

*In Exercises 1–12, write the first four terms of each sequence whose general term is given.*

1. $a_n = 3n + 2$
2. $a_n = 4n - 1$
3. $a_n = 3^n$
4. $a_n = \left(\frac{1}{3}\right)^n$
5. $a_n = (-3)^n$
6. $a_n = \left(-\frac{1}{3}\right)^n$
7. $a_n = (-1)^n(n + 3)$
8. $a_n = (-1)^{n+1}(n + 4)$
9. $a_n = \frac{2n}{n + 4}$
10. $a_n = \frac{3n}{n + 5}$
11. $a_n = \frac{(-1)^{n+1}}{2^n - 1}$
12. $a_n = \frac{(-1)^{n+1}}{2^n + 1}$

*The sequences in Exercises 13–18 are defined using recursion formulas. Write the first four terms of each sequence.*

13. $a_1 = 7$ and $a_n = a_{n-1} + 5$ for $n \geq 2$
14. $a_1 = 12$ and $a_n = a_{n-1} + 4$ for $n \geq 2$
15. $a_1 = 3$ and $a_n = 4a_{n-1}$ for $n \geq 2$
16. $a_1 = 2$ and $a_n = 5a_{n-1}$ for $n \geq 2$
17. $a_1 = 4$ and $a_n = 2a_{n-1} + 3$ for $n \geq 2$
18. $a_1 = 5$ and $a_n = 3a_{n-1} - 1$ for $n \geq 2$

*In Exercises 19–22, the general term of a sequence is given and involves a factorial. Write the first four terms of each sequence.*

19. $a_n = \frac{n^2}{n!}$
20. $a_n = \frac{(n + 1)!}{n^2}$
21. $a_n = 2(n + 1)!$
22. $a_n = -2(n - 1)!$

*In Exercises 23–28, evaluate each factorial expression.*

23. $\frac{17!}{15!}$
24. $\frac{18!}{16!}$
25. $\frac{16!}{2!14!}$
26. $\frac{20!}{2!18!}$

27. $\dfrac{(n+2)!}{n!}$

28. $\dfrac{(2n+1)!}{(2n)!}$

*In Exercises 29–42, find each indicated sum.*

29. $\sum_{i=1}^{6} 5i$

30. $\sum_{i=1}^{6} 7i$

31. $\sum_{i=1}^{4} 2i^2$

32. $\sum_{i=1}^{5} i^3$

33. $\sum_{k=1}^{5} k(k+4)$

34. $\sum_{k=1}^{4} (k-3)(k+2)$

35. $\sum_{i=1}^{4} \left(-\dfrac{1}{2}\right)^i$

36. $\sum_{i=2}^{4} \left(-\dfrac{1}{3}\right)^i$

37. $\sum_{i=5}^{9} 11$

38. $\sum_{i=3}^{7} 12$

39. $\sum_{i=0}^{4} \dfrac{(-1)^i}{i!}$

40. $\sum_{i=0}^{4} \dfrac{(-1)^{i+1}}{(i+1)!}$

41. $\sum_{i=1}^{5} \dfrac{i!}{(i-1)!}$

42. $\sum_{i=1}^{5} \dfrac{(i+2)!}{i!}$

*In Exercises 43–54, express each sum using summation notation. Use 1 as the lower limit of summation and i for the index of summation.*

43. $1^2 + 2^2 + 3^2 + \cdots + 15^2$

44. $1^4 + 2^4 + 3^4 + \cdots + 12^4$

45. $2 + 2^2 + 2^3 + \cdots + 2^{11}$

46. $5 + 5^2 + 5^3 + \cdots + 5^{12}$

47. $1 + 2 + 3 + \cdots + 30$

48. $1 + 2 + 3 + \cdots + 40$

49. $\dfrac{1}{2} + \dfrac{2}{3} + \dfrac{3}{4} + \cdots + \dfrac{14}{14+1}$

50. $\dfrac{1}{3} + \dfrac{2}{4} + \dfrac{3}{5} + \cdots + \dfrac{16}{16+2}$

51. $4 + \dfrac{4^2}{2} + \dfrac{4^3}{3} + \cdots + \dfrac{4^n}{n}$

52. $\dfrac{1}{9} + \dfrac{2}{9^2} + \dfrac{3}{9^3} + \cdots + \dfrac{n}{9^n}$

53. $1 + 3 + 5 + \cdots + (2n-1)$

54. $a + ar + ar^2 + \cdots + ar^{n-1}$

*In Exercises 55–60, express each sum using summation notation. Use a lower limit of summation of your choice and k for the index of summation.*

55. $5 + 7 + 9 + 11 + \cdots + 31$

56. $6 + 8 + 10 + 12 + \cdots + 32$

57. $a + ar + ar^2 + \cdots + ar^{12}$

58. $a + ar + ar^2 + \cdots + ar^{14}$

59. $a + (a+d) + (a+2d) + \cdots + (a+nd)$

60. $(a+d) + (a+d^2) + \cdots + (a+d^n)$

## Application Exercises

61. The bar graph shows the number of children home-educated in the United States. Let $a_n$ represent the number of children, in thousands, home-educated in year $n$, where $n = 2$ corresponds to 1992, $n = 3$ to 1993, and so on.

**Number of Children Home-Educated in the U.S.**

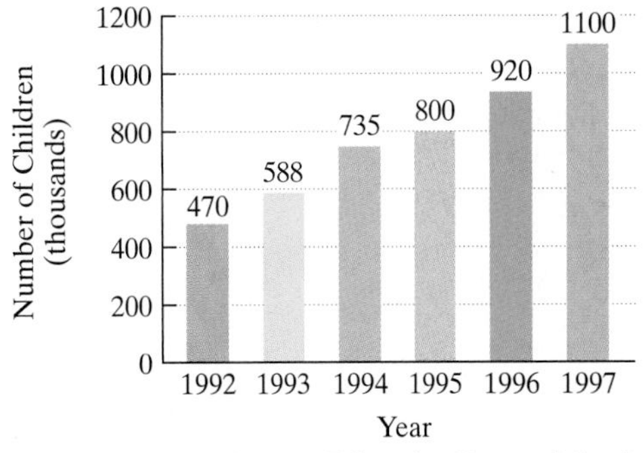


*Source*: National Home Education Research Institute

a. Find $\sum_{i=2}^{7} a_i$. What does this represent?

b. Find $\dfrac{1}{6}\sum_{i=2}^{7} a_i$. What does this represent?

62. The bar graph shows the number of business failures in the United States. Let $a_n$ represent the number of business failures in year $n$, where $n = 0$ corresponds to 1990, $n = 1$ to 1991, $n = 2$ to 1992, and so on.

**Number of Business Failures in the U.S.**

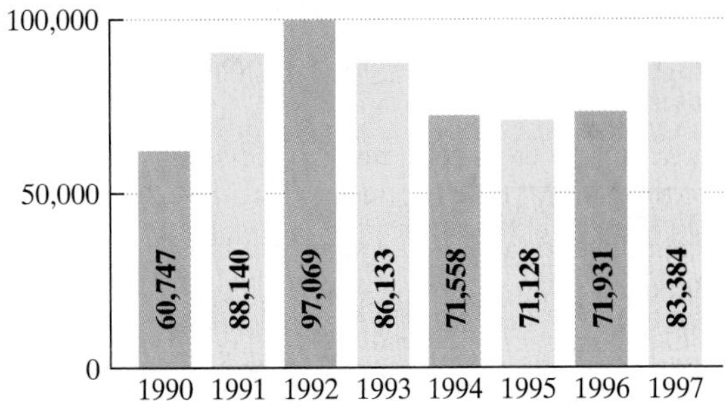


*Source*: Dun & Bradstreet

a. Find $\sum_{i=0}^{7} a_i$. What does this represent?

b. Find $\dfrac{1}{8}\sum_{i=0}^{7} a_i$. What does this represent?

63. The finite sequence whose general term is

$$a_n = 0.16n^2 - 1.04n + 7.39$$

where $n = 1, 2, 3, \ldots, 8$ models the total number of dollars, in billions, that Americans spent on recreational boating from 1991 through 1998. Find and interpret

$$\sum_{i=1}^{5} a_i.$$

**64.** The finite sequence whose general term is

$$a_n = 2.54e^{-0.09n}$$

where $n = 0, 1, 2, \ldots, 9$ models the number of new foreign cars sold in the United States, in millions, from 1990 through 1999. Find and interpret

$$\sum_{i=0}^{4} a_i.$$

**65.** A deposit of \$6000 is made in an account that earns 6% interest compounded quarterly. The balance in the account after $n$ quarters is given by the sequence

$$a_n = 6000\left(1 + \frac{0.06}{4}\right)^n, \qquad n = 1, 2, 3, \ldots.$$

Find the balance in the account after five years by computing $a_{20}$.

**66.** A deposit of \$10,000 is made in an account that earns 8% interest compounded quarterly. The balance in the account after $n$ quarters is given by the sequence

$$a_n = 10{,}000\left(1 + \frac{0.08}{4}\right)^n, \qquad n = 1, 2, 3, \ldots.$$

Find the balance in the account after six years by computing $a_{24}$.

## Writing in Mathematics

**67.** What is a sequence? Give an example with your description.

**68.** Explain how to write terms of a sequence if the formula for the general term is given.

**69.** What does the graph of a sequence look like? How is it obtained?

**70.** What is a recursion formula?

**71.** Explain how to find $n!$ if $n$ is a positive integer.

**72.** Explain the best way to evaluate $\frac{900!}{899!}$ without a calculator.

**73.** What is the meaning of the symbol $\Sigma$? Give an example with your description.

**74.** You buy a new car for \$24,000. At the end of $n$ years, the value of your car is given by the sequence

$$a_n = 24{,}000\left(\frac{3}{4}\right)^n, \qquad n = 1, 2, 3, \ldots.$$

Find $a_5$ and write a sentence explaining what this value represents. Describe the $n$th term of the sequence in terms of the value of your car at the end of each year.

## Technology Exercises

*In Exercises 75–79, use the factorial key of a graphing utility to evaluate each expression.*

**75.** $\frac{200!}{198!}$ **76.** $\left(\frac{300}{20}\right)!$ **77.** $\frac{20!}{300}$

**78.** $\frac{20!}{(20-3)!}$ **79.** $\frac{54!}{(54-3)!\,3!}$

**80.** Use the SEQ (sequence) capability of a graphing utility to verify the terms of the sequences you obtained for any five sequences from Exercises 1–12 or 19–22.

**81.** Use the SUM SEQ (sum of the sequence) capability of a graphing utility to verify any five of the sums you obtained in Exercises 29–42.

**82.** As $n$ increases, the terms of the sequence

$$a_n = \left(1 + \frac{1}{n}\right)^n$$

get closer and closer to the number $e$ (where $e \approx 2.7183$). Use a calculator to find $a_{10}$, $a_{100}$, $a_{1000}$, $a_{10{,}000}$, and $a_{100{,}000}$, comparing these terms to the decimal approximation for $e$.

*Many graphing utilities have a sequence-graphing mode that plots the terms of a sequence as points on a rectangular coordinate system. Consult your manual; if your graphing utility has this capability, use it to graph each of the sequences in Exercises 83–86. What appears to be happening to the terms of each sequence as n gets larger?*

**83.** $a_n = \frac{n}{n+1}$ $\quad n{:}[0, 10, 1] \times a_n{:}[0, 1, 0.1]$

**84.** $a_n = \frac{100}{n}$ $\quad n{:}[0, 1000, 100] \times a_n{:}[0, 1, 0.1]$

**85.** $a_n = \frac{2n^2 + 5n - 7}{n^3}$ $\quad n{:}[0, 10, 1] \times a_n{:}[0, 2, 0.2]$

**86.** $a_n = \frac{3n^4 + n - 1}{5n^4 + 2n^2 + 1}$ $\quad n{:}[0, 10, 1] \times a_n{:}[0, 1, 0.1]$

## Critical Thinking Exercises

**87.** Which one of the following is true?

**a.** $\frac{n!}{(n-1)!} = \frac{1}{n-1}$

**b.** The Fibonacci sequence 1, 1, 2, 3, 5, 8, 13, 21, 34, 55, 89, 144, ... can be defined recursively using $a_0 = 1, a_1 = 1$, $a_n = a_{n-2} + a_{n-1}$, where $n \geq 2$.

**c.** $\sum_{i=1}^{2} (-1)^i 2^i = 0$

**d.** $\sum_{i=1}^{2} a_i b_i = \sum_{i=1}^{2} a_i \sum_{i=1}^{2} b_i$

**88.** Write the first five terms of the sequence whose first term is 9 and whose general term is

$$a_n = \begin{cases} \dfrac{a_{n-1}}{2} & \text{if } a_{n-1} \text{ is even} \\ 3a_{n-1} + 5 & \text{if } a_{n-1} \text{ is odd.} \end{cases}$$

## Group Exercise

**89.** Enough curiosities involving the Fibonacci sequence exist to warrant a flourishing Fibonacci Association, which publishes a quarterly journal. Do some research on the Fibonacci sequence by consulting the Internet or the research department of your library, and find one property that interests you. After doing this research, get together with your group to share these intriguing properties.

# SECTION 11.2 *Arithmetic Sequences*

## Objectives

1. Find the common difference for an arithmetic sequence.
2. Write terms of an arithmetic sequence.
3. Use the formula for the general term of an arithmetic sequence.
4. Use the formula for the sum of the first $n$ terms of an arithmetic sequence.

Your grandmother and her financial counselor are looking at options in case nursing home care is needed in the future. The good news is that your grandmother's total assets are $350,000. The bad news is that yearly nursing home costs average $49,730, increasing by $1800 each year. In this section, we will see how sequences can be used to describe your grandmother's situation and help her to identify realistic options.

## Arithmetic Sequences

A mathematical model for the average annual salaries of major league baseball players generates the following data.

| **Year** | 1991 | 1992 | 1993 | 1994 | 1995 | 1996 | 1997 | 1998 |
|---|---|---|---|---|---|---|---|---|
| **Salary** | 801,000 | 892,000 | 983,000 | 1,074,000 | 1,165,000 | 1,256,000 | 1,347,000 | 1,438,000 |

From 1991 to 1992, salaries increased by $892,000 − $801,000 = $91,000. From 1992 to 1993, salaries increased by $983,000 − $892,000 = $91,000. If we make these computations for each year, we find that the yearly salary increase is $91,000. The sequence of annual salaries shows that each term after the first, 801,000, differs from the preceding term by a constant amount, namely 91,000. The sequence of annual salaries

$$801{,}000,\ 892{,}000,\ 983{,}000,\ 1{,}074{,}000,\ 1{,}165{,}000,\ 1{,}256{,}000, \ldots$$

is an example of an **arithmetic sequence**.

**Definition of an Arithmetic Sequence**

An **arithmetic sequence** is a sequence in which each term after the first differs from the preceding term by a constant amount. The difference between consecutive terms is called the **common difference** of the sequence.

**1** Find the common difference of an arithmetic sequence.

The common difference, $d$, is found by subtracting any term from the term that directly follows it. In the following examples, the common difference is found by subtracting the first term from the second term, $a_2 - a_1$.

| **Arithmetic sequence** | **Common difference** |
|---|---|
| 801,000, 892,000, 983,000, 1,074,000, ... | $d = 892{,}000 - 801{,}000 = 91{,}000$ |
| 2, 6, 10, 14, 18, ... | $d = 6 - 2 = 4$ |
| −2, −7, −12, −17, ... | $d = -7 - (-2) = -5$ |

If the first term of an arithmetic sequence is $a_1$, each term after the first is obtained by adding $d$, the common difference, to the previous term. This can be expressed recursively as follows:

$$a_n = a_{n-1} + d$$

Add $d$ to the term in any position to get the next term.

To use this recursion formula, we must be given the first term.

**2** Write the terms of an arithmetic sequence.

## EXAMPLE 1 Writing the Terms of an Arithmetic Sequence Using the First Term and the Common Difference

The recursion formula $a_n = a_{n-1} - 24$ models the thousands of Air Force personnel on active duty for each year starting with 1986. In 1986, there were 624 thousand personnel on active duty. Find the first five terms of the arithmetic sequence in which $a_1 = 624$ and $a_n = a_{n-1} - 24$.

**Solution** The recursion formula $a_n = a_{n-1} - 24$ indicates that each term after the first is obtained by adding −24 to the previous term. Thus, each year there are 24 thousand fewer personnel on active duty in the Air Force than in the previous year.

$a_1 = 624$ — This is given.

$a_2 = a_1 - 24 = 624 - 24 = 600$ — Use $a_n = a_{n-1} - 24$ with $n = 2$.

$a_3 = a_2 - 24 = 600 - 24 = 576$ — Use $a_n = a_{n-1} - 24$ with $n = 3$.

$a_4 = a_3 - 24 = 576 - 24 = 552$ — Use $a_n = a_{n-1} - 24$ with $n = 4$.

$a_5 = a_4 - 24 = 552 - 24 = 528$ — Use $a_n = a_{n-1} - 24$ with $n = 5$.

The first five terms are

624, 600, 576, 552, and 528.

**Check Point 1** Find the first five terms of the arithmetic sequence in which $a_1 = 100$ and $a_n = a_{n-1} - 30$.

3 Use the formula for the general term of an arithmetic sequence.

## The General Term of an Arithmetic Sequence

Consider an arithmetic sequence whose first term is $a_1$ and whose common difference is $d$. We are looking for a formula for the general term, $a_n$. Let's begin by writing the first six terms. The first term is $a_1$. The second term is $a_1 + d$. The third term is $a_1 + d + d$, or $a_1 + 2d$. Thus, we start with $a_1$ and add $d$ to each successive term. The first six terms are

$$a_1, \quad a_1 + d, \quad a_1 + 2d, \quad a_1 + 3d, \quad a_1 + 4d, \quad a_1 + 5d.$$

$a_1$, first term; $a_2$, second term; $a_3$, third term; $a_4$, fourth term; $a_5$, fifth term; $a_6$, sixth term

Compare the coefficient of $d$ and the subscript of $a$ denoting the term number. Can you see that the coefficient of $d$ is 1 less than the subscript of $a$ denoting the term number?

$$a_3\text{: third term} = a_1 + 2d \qquad a_4\text{: fourth term} = a_1 + 3d$$

2 is one less than 3. 3 is one less than 4.

Thus, the formula for the $n$th term is

$$a_n\text{: } n\text{th term} = a_1 + (n - 1)d.$$

$n - 1$ is one less than $n$.

### General Term of an Arithmetic Sequence

The $n$th term (the general term) of an arithmetic sequence with first term $a_1$ and common difference $d$ is

$$a_n = a_1 + (n - 1)d.$$

### EXAMPLE 2 Using the Formula for the General Term of an Arithmetic Sequence

Find the eighth term of the arithmetic sequence whose first term is 4 and whose common difference is −7.

**Solution** To find the eighth term, $a_8$, we replace $n$ in the formula with 8, $a_1$ with 4, and $d$ with −7.

$$a_n = a_1 + (n - 1)d$$

$$a_8 = 4 + (8 - 1)(-7) = 4 + 7(-7) = 4 + (-49) = -45$$

The eighth term is −45. We can check this result by writing the first eight terms of the sequence:

$$4, -3, -10, -17, -24, -31, -38, -45.$$

**Check Point 2** Find the ninth term of the arithmetic sequence whose first term is 6 and whose common difference is −5.

### EXAMPLE 3 Using an Arithmetic Sequence to Model Teachers' Earnings

According to the National Education Association, teachers in the United States earned an average of \$21,700 per year in 1984. This amount has increased by approximately \$1472 yearly.

**a.** Write a formula for the $n$th term of the arithmetic sequence that describes teachers' average earnings $n$ years after 1983.

**b.** How much will U.S. teachers earn by the year 2005?

**Solution**

**a.** We can express teachers' earnings by the following arithmetic sequence:

$$21{,}700, \quad 23{,}172, \quad 24{,}644, \quad 26{,}116, \ldots.$$

$a_1$: earnings in 1984, 1 year after 1983

$a_2$: earnings in 1985, 2 years after 1983

$a_3$: earnings in 1986, 3 years after 1983

$a_4$: earnings in 1987, 4 years after 1983

In this sequence $a_1$, the first term, represents the amount teachers earned in 1984. Each subsequent year this amount increases by \$1472, so $d = 1472$. We use the formula for the general term of an arithmetic sequence to write the $n$th term of the sequence that describes teachers' earnings $n$ years after 1983.

$a_n = a_1 + (n - 1)d$ — This is the formula for the general term of an arithmetic sequence.

$a_n = 21{,}700 + (n - 1)1472$ — $a_1 = 21{,}700$ and $d = 1472$.

$a_n = 21{,}700 + 1472n - 1472$ — Distribute 1472 to each term in parentheses.

$a_n = 1472n + 20{,}228$ — Simplify.

Thus, teachers' earnings $n$ years after 1983 can be described by $a_n = 1472n + 20{,}228$.

**b.** Now we need to find teachers' earnings in 2005. The year 2005 is 22 years after 1983: That is, $2005 - 1983 = 22$. Thus, $n = 22$. We substitute 22 for $n$ in $a_n = 1472n + 20{,}228$.

$$a_{22} = 1472 \cdot 22 + 20{,}228 = 52{,}612$$

The 22nd term of the sequence is 52,612. Therefore, U.S. teachers are predicted to earn an average of \$52,612 by the year 2005.

**Check Point 3** According to the U.S. Bureau of Economic Analysis, U.S. travelers spent \$12,808 million in other countries in 1984. This amount has increased by approximately \$2350 million yearly.

**a.** Write a formula for the $n$th term of the arithmetic sequence that describes what U.S. travelers spend in other countries $n$ years after 1983.

**b.** How much will U.S. travelers spend in other countries by the year 2010?

**4** Use the formula for the sum of the first $n$ terms of an arithmetic sequence.

## The Sum of the First $n$ Terms of an Arithmetic Sequence

The sum of the first $n$ terms of an arithmetic sequence, denoted by $S_n$, can be found without having to add up all the terms. Let

$$S_n = a_1 + a_2 + a_3 + \cdots + a_n$$

be the sum of the first $n$ terms of an arithmetic sequence. Because $d$ is the common difference between terms, $S_n$ can be written forward and backward as follows.

Forward: Start with the first term. Keep adding $d$.

Backward: Start with the last term. Keep subtracting $d$.

$$\begin{aligned} S_n &= a_1 + (a_1 + d) + (a_1 + 2d) + \cdots + a_n \\ S_n &= a_n + (a_n - d) + (a_n - 2d) + \cdots + a_1 \\ \hline 2S_n &= (a_1 + a_n) + (a_1 + a_n) + (a_1 + a_n) + \cdots + (a_1 + a_n) \end{aligned}$$

Add the two equations.

Because there are $n$ sums of $(a_1 + a_n)$ on the right side, we can express this side as $n(a_1 + a_n)$. Thus, the last equation can be simplified:

$$2S_n = n(a_1 + a_n)$$

$$S_n = \frac{n}{2}(a_1 + a_n)$$

Solve for $S_n$, dividing both sides by 2.

We have proved the following result.

**The Sum of the First *n* Terms of an Arithmetic Sequence**

The sum, $S_n$, of the first $n$ terms of an arithmetic sequence is given by

$$S_n = \frac{n}{2}(a_1 + a_n)$$

in which $a_1$ is the first term and $a_n$ is the $n$th term.

To find the sum of the terms of an arithmetic sequence, we need to know the first term, $a_1$, the last term, $a_n$, and the number of terms, $n$. The following examples illustrate how to use this formula.

## EXAMPLE 4 Finding the Sum of *n* Terms of an Arithmetic Sequence

Find the sum of the first 100 terms of the arithmetic sequence: 1, 3, 5, 7, ....

**Solution** We are finding the sum of the first 100 odd numbers. To find the sum of the first 100 terms, $S_{100}$, we replace $n$ in the formula with 100.

$$S_n = \frac{n}{2}(a_1 + a_n)$$

$$S_{100} = \frac{100}{2}(a_1 + a_{100})$$

The first term, $a_1$, is 1.

We must find $a_{100}$, the 100th term.

We use the formula for the general term of a sequence to find $a_{100}$. The common difference, $d$, of 1, 3, 5, 7, ..., is 2.

$$a_n = a_1 + (n - 1)d$$

This is the formula for the $n$th term of an arithmetic sequence. Use it to find the 100th term.

$$\begin{aligned} a_{100} &= 1 + (100 - 1) \cdot 2 \\ &= 1 + 99 \cdot 2 \\ &= 199 \end{aligned}$$

Substitute 100 for $n$, 2 for $d$, and 1 (the first term) for $a_1$.

Now we are ready to find the sum of the first 100 terms of 1, 3, 5, 7, . . . , 199.

$$S_n = \frac{n}{2}(a_1 + a_n)$$ Use the formula for the sum of the first $n$ terms of an arithmetic sequence. Let $n = 100$, $a_1 = 1$, and $a_{100} = 199$.

$$S_{100} = \frac{100}{2}(1 + 199) = 50(200) = 10{,}000$$

The sum of the first 100 odd numbers is 10,000.

**Check Point 4** Find the sum of the first 15 terms of the arithmetic sequence: 3, 6, 9, 12, . . . .

## EXAMPLE 5 Using $S_n$ to Evaluate a Summation

Find the following sum: $\sum_{i=1}^{25}(5i - 9)$.

**Solution**

$$\sum_{i=1}^{25}(5i - 9) = (5 \cdot 1 - 9) + (5 \cdot 2 - 9) + (5 \cdot 3 - 9) + \cdots + (5 \cdot 25 - 9)$$
$$= -4 + 1 + 6 + \cdots + 116$$

By evaluating the first three terms and the last term, we see that $a_1 = -4$; $d$, the common difference, is $1 - (-4)$ or 5; and $a_{25}$, the last term, is 116.

$$S_n = \frac{n}{2}(a_1 + a_n)$$ Use the formula for the sum of the first $n$ terms of an arithmetic sequence. Let $n = 25$, $a_1 = -4$, and $a_{25} = 116$.

$$S_{25} = \frac{25}{2}(-4 + 116) = \frac{25}{2}(112) = 1400.$$

Thus,

$$\sum_{i=1}^{25}(5i - 9) = 1400.$$

### Technology

To find

$$\sum_{i=1}^{25}(5i - 9)$$

on a graphing utility, enter: [SUM] [SEQ] $(5x - 9, x, 1, 25, 1)$. Then press [ENTER].

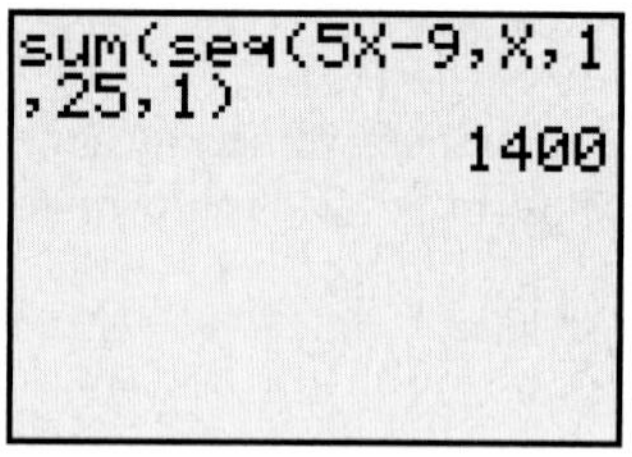


**Check Point 5** Find the following sum: $\sum_{i=1}^{30}(6i - 11)$.

## EXAMPLE 6 Modeling Total Nursing Home Costs over a Six-Year Period

Your grandmother has assets of \$350,000. One option that she is considering involves nursing home care for a six-year period beginning in 2001. The model

$$a_n = 1800n + 49{,}730$$

describes yearly nursing home costs $n$ years after 2000. Does your grandmother have enough to pay for the facility?

**Solution** We must find the sum of an arithmetic sequence. The first term of the sequence corresponds to nursing home costs in the year 2001. The last term corresponds to nursing home costs in the year 2006. Because the model describes costs $n$ years after 2000, $n = 1$ describes the year 2001 and $n = 6$ describes the year 2006.

$a_n = 1800n + 49{,}730$ — This is the given formula for the general term of the sequence.

$a_1 = 1800 \cdot 1 + 49{,}730 = 51{,}530$ — Find $a_1$ by replacing $n$ by 1.

$a_6 = 1800 \cdot 6 + 49{,}730 = 60{,}530$ — Find $a_6$ by replacing $n$ by 6.

The first year the facility will cost \$51,530. By year six, the facility will cost \$60,530. Now we must find the sum of these costs for all six years. We focus on the sum of the first six terms of the arithmetic sequence

$$\underbrace{51{,}530}_{a_1},\quad \underbrace{53{,}330}_{a_2},\quad \ldots,\quad \underbrace{60{,}530}_{a_6}.$$

We find this sum using the formula for the sum of the first $n$ terms of an arithmetic sequence. We are adding 6 terms: $n = 6$. The first term is 51,530: $a_1 = 51{,}530$. The last term—that is, the sixth term—is 60,530: $a_6 = 60{,}530$.

$$S_n = \frac{n}{2}(a_1 + a_n)$$

$$S_6 = \frac{6}{2}(51{,}530 + 60{,}530) = 3(112{,}060) = 336{,}180$$

Total nursing home costs for your grandmother are predicted to be \$336,180. Because your grandmother's assets are \$350,000, she has enough to pay for the facility.

**Check Point 6** In Example 6, how much would it cost for nursing home care for a ten-year period beginning in 2001?

## EXERCISE SET 11.2

### Practice Exercises

*In Exercises 1–14, write the first six terms of each arithmetic sequence.*

1. $a_1 = 200, d = 20$
2. $a_1 = 300, d = 50$
3. $a_1 = -7, d = 4$
4. $a_1 = -8, d = 5$
5. $a_1 = 300, d = -90$
6. $a_1 = 200, d = -60$
7. $a_1 = \frac{5}{2}, d = -\frac{1}{2}$
8. $a_1 = \frac{3}{4}, d = -\frac{1}{4}$
9. $a_n = a_{n-1} + 6, a_1 = -9$
10. $a_n = a_{n-1} + 4, a_1 = -7$
11. $a_n = a_{n-1} - 10, a_1 = 30$
12. $a_n = a_{n-1} - 20, a_1 = 50$
13. $a_n = a_{n-1} - 0.4, a_1 = 1.6$
14. $a_n = a_{n-1} - 0.3, a_1 = -1.7$

*In Exercises 15–22, find the indicated term of the arithmetic sequence with first term, $a_1$, and common difference, $d$.*

15. Find $a_6$ when $a_1 = 13, d = 4$.
16. Find $a_{16}$ when $a_1 = 9, d = 2$.
17. Find $a_{50}$ when $a_1 = 7, d = 5$.
18. Find $a_{60}$ when $a_1 = 8, d = 6$.
19. Find $a_{200}$ when $a_1 = -40, d = 5$.
20. Find $a_{150}$ when $a_1 = -60, d = 5$.
21. Find $a_{60}$ when $a_1 = 35, d = -3$.
22. Find $a_{70}$ when $a_1 = -32, d = 4$.

*In Exercises 23–34, write a formula for the general term (the nth term) of each arithmetic sequence. Do not use a recursion formula. Then use the formula for $a_n$ to find $a_{20}$, the 20th term of the sequence.*

23. $1, 5, 9, 13, \ldots$
24. $2, 7, 12, 17, \ldots$
25. $7, 3, -1, -5, \ldots$
26. $6, 1, -4, -9, \ldots$
27. $a_1 = 9, d = 2$
28. $a_1 = 6, d = 3$
29. $a_1 = -20, d = -4$
30. $a_1 = -70, d = -5$
31. $a_n = a_{n-1} + 3, a_1 = 4$
32. $a_n = a_{n-1} + 5, a_1 = 6$
33. $a_n = a_{n-1} - 10, a_1 = 30$
34. $a_n = a_{n-1} - 12, a_1 = 24$

**35.** Find the sum of the first 20 terms of the arithmetic sequence: 4, 10, 16, 22, ....

**36.** Find the sum of the first 25 terms of the arithmetic sequence: 7, 19, 31, 43, ....

**37.** Find the sum of the first 50 terms of the arithmetic sequence: $-10, -6, -2, 2, \ldots$.

**38.** Find the sum of the first 50 terms of the arithmetic sequence: $-15, -9, -3, 3, \ldots$.

**39.** Find $1 + 2 + 3 + 4 + \ldots + 100$, the sum of the first 100 natural numbers.

**40.** Find $2 + 4 + 6 + 8 + \ldots + 200$, the sum of the first 100 positive even integers.

**41.** Find the sum of the first 60 positive even integers.

**42.** Find the sum of the first 80 positive even integers.

**43.** Find the sum of the even integers between 21 and 45.

**44.** Find the sum of the odd integers between 30 and 54.

*For Exercises 45–50, write out the first three terms and the last term. Then use the formula for the sum of the first n terms of an arithmetic sequence to find the indicated sum.*

**45.** $\sum_{i=1}^{17} (5i + 3)$

**46.** $\sum_{i=1}^{20} (6i - 4)$

**47.** $\sum_{i=1}^{30} (-3i + 5)$

**48.** $\sum_{i=1}^{40} (-2i + 6)$

**49.** $\sum_{i=1}^{100} 4i$

**50.** $\sum_{i=1}^{50} -4i$

## Application Exercises

**51.** According to the U.S. Bureau of Labor Statistics, in 1990 there were 126,424 thousand employees in the United States. This number has increased by approximately 1265 thousand employees each year.

**a.** Write the general term for the arithmetic sequence modeling the thousands of employees in the United States $n$ years after 1989.

**b.** How many thousands of employees will there be by the year 2005?

**52.** According to the National Center for Education Statistics, the total enrollment in U.S. public elementary and secondary schools in 1985 was 39.05 million. Enrollment has increased by approximately 0.45 million each year.

**a.** Write the general term for the arithmetic sequence modeling the millions of students enrolled in U.S. public elementary and secondary schools $n$ years after 1984.

**b.** How many millions of students will be enrolled by the year 2005?

**53.** Company A pays $24,000 yearly with raises of $1600 per year. Company B pays $28,000 yearly with raises of $1000 per year. Which company will pay more in year 10? How much more?

**54.** Company A pays $23,000 yearly with raises of $1200 per year. Company B pays $26,000 yearly with raises of $800 per year. Which company will pay more in year 10? How much more?

**55.** According to the Environmental Protection Agency, in 1960 the United States recovered 3.78 million tons of solid waste. Due primarily to recycling programs, this amount has increased by approximately 0.576 million ton each year.

**a.** Write the general term for the arithmetic sequence modeling the amount of solid waste recovered in the United States $n$ years after 1959.

**b.** What is the total amount of solid waste recovered from 1960 through 2000?

**56.** According to the Environmental Protection Agency, in 1960 the United States generated 87.1 million tons of solid waste. This amount has increased by approximately 3.14 million tons each year.

**a.** Write the general term for the arithmetic sequence modeling the amount of solid waste generated in the United States $n$ years after 1959.

**b.** What is the total amount of solid waste generated from 1960 through 2000?

**57.** A company offers a starting yearly salary of $33,000 with raises of $2500 per year. Find the total salary over a ten-year period.

**58.** You are considering two job offers. Company A will start you at $19,000 a year and guarantee you a raise of $2600 per year. Company B will start you at a higher salary, $27,000 a year, but will only guarantee a raise of $1200 per year. Find the total salary that each company will pay you over a ten-year period. Which company pays the greater total amount?

**59.** A theater has 30 seats in the first row, 32 seats in the second row, increasing by 2 seats each row for a total of 26 rows. How many seats are there in the theater?

**60.** A section in a stadium has 20 seats in the first row, 23 seats in the second row, increasing by 3 seats each row for a total of 38 rows. How many seats are in this section of the stadium?

## Writing in Mathematics

**61.** What is an arithmetic sequence? Give an example with your explanation.

**62.** What is the common difference in an arithmetic sequence?

**63.** Explain how to find the general term of an arithmetic sequence.

**64.** Explain how to find the sum of the first $n$ terms of an arithmetic sequence without having to add up all the terms.

**65.** Teachers' earnings $n$ years after 1983 can be described by $a_n = 1472n + 20{,}228$. According to this model, what will teachers earn in 2083? Describe two possible circumstances that would render this predicted salary incorrect.

### Technology Exercises

**66.** Use the [SEQ] (sequence) capability of a graphing utility and the formula you obtained for $a_n$ to verify the value you found for $a_{20}$ in any five exercises from Exercises 23–34.

**67.** Use the capability of a graphing utility to calculate the sum of a sequence to verify any five of your answers to Exercises 45–50.

### Critical Thinking Exercises

**68.** Give examples of two different arithmetic sequences whose fourth term, $a_4$, is 10.

**69.** In the sequence 21,700, 23,172, 24,644, 26,116, . . . , which term is 314,628?

**70.** A *degree-day* is a unit used to measure the fuel requirements of buildings. By definition, each degree that the average daily temperature is below 65°F is 1 degree-day. For example, a temperature of 42°F constitutes 23 degree-days. If the average temperature on January 1 was 42°F and fell 2°F for each subsequent day up to and including January 10, how many degree-days are included from January 1 to January 10?

**71.** Show that the sum of the first $n$ positive odd integers,

$$1 + 3 + 5 + \cdots + (2n - 1),$$

is $n^2$.

### Group Exercise

**72.** Members of your group have been hired by the Environmental Protection Agency to write a report on whether we are making significant progress in recovering solid waste. Use the models from Exercises 55 and 56 as the basis for your report. A graph of each model from 1960 through 2000 would be helpful. What percentage of solid waste generated is actually recovered on a year-to-year basis? Be as creative as you want in your report and then draw conclusions. The group should write up the report and perhaps even include suggestions as to how we might improve recycling progress.

## SECTION 11.3 *Geometric Sequences*

### Objectives

1. Find the common ratio of a geometric sequence.
2. Write terms of a geometric sequence.
3. Use the formula for the general term of a geometric sequence.
4. Use the formula for the sum of the first $n$ terms of a geometric sequence.
5. Find the value of an annuity.
6. Use the formula for the sum of an infinite geometric series.

Here we are at the closing moments of a job interview. You're shaking hands with the manager. You managed to answer all the tough questions without losing your poise, and now you've been offered a job. As a matter of fact, your qualifications are so terrific that you've been offered two jobs—one just the day before, with a rival company in the same field! One company offers \$30,000 the first year, with increases of 6% per year for four years after that. The other offers \$32,000 the first year, with annual increases of 3% per year after that. Over a five-year period, which is the better offer?

If salary raises amount to a certain percent each year, the yearly salaries over time form a geometric sequence. In this section, we investigate geometric sequences and their properties. After studying the section, you will be in a position to decide which job offer to accept: you will know which company will pay you more over five years.

## Geometric Sequences

Figure 11.2 shows a sequence in which the number of squares is increasing. From left to right, the number of squares is 1, 5, 25, 125, and 625. In this sequence, each term after the first, 1, is obtained by multiplying the preceding term by a constant amount, namely 5. This sequence of increasing number of squares is an example of a *geometric sequence*.

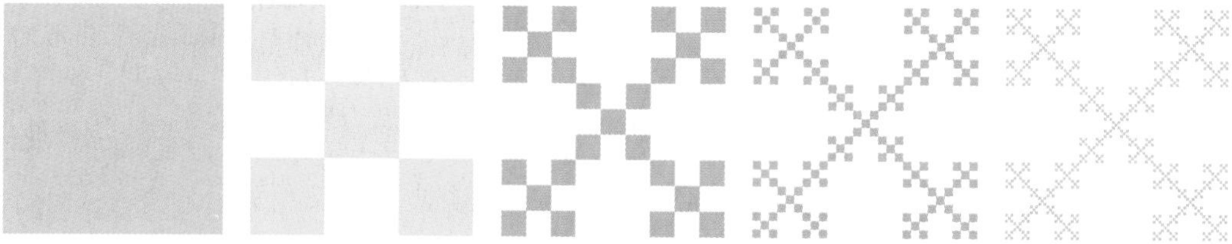

**Figure 11.2** A geometric sequence of squares

### Definition of a Geometric Sequence

A **geometric sequence** is a sequence in which each term after the first is obtained by multiplying the preceding term by a fixed nonzero constant. The amount by which we multiply each time is called the **common ratio** of the sequence.

**1** Find the common ratio of a geometric sequence.

The common ratio, $r$, is found by dividing any term after the first term by the term that directly precedes it. In the following examples, the common ratio is found by dividing the second term by the first term, $\frac{a_2}{a_1}$.

| Geometric sequence | Common ratio |
|---|---|
| $1, 5, 25, 125, 625, \ldots$ | $r = \frac{5}{1} = 5$ |
| $4, 8, 16, 32, 64, \ldots$ | $r = \frac{8}{4} = 2$ |
| $6, -12, 24, -48, 96, \ldots$ | $r = \frac{-12}{6} = -2$ |
| $9, -3, 1, -\frac{1}{3}, \frac{1}{9}, \ldots$ | $r = \frac{-3}{9} = -\frac{1}{3}$ |

**Study Tip**

When the common ratio of a geometric sequence is negative, the signs of the terms alternate.

**2** Write terms of a geometric sequence.

How do we write out the terms of a geometric sequence when the first term and the common ratio are known? We multiply the first term by the common ratio to get the second term, multiply the second term by the common ratio to get the third term, and so on.

### EXAMPLE 1 Writing the Terms of a Geometric Sequence

Write the first six terms of the geometric sequence with first term 6 and common ratio $\frac{1}{3}$.

**Solution** The first term is 6. The second term is $6 \cdot \frac{1}{3}$, or 2. The third term is $2 \cdot \frac{1}{3}$, or $\frac{2}{3}$. The fourth term is $\frac{2}{3} \cdot \frac{1}{3}$, or $\frac{2}{9}$, and so on. The first six terms are

$$6, 2, \tfrac{2}{3}, \tfrac{2}{9}, \tfrac{2}{27}, \tfrac{2}{81}.$$

**Check Point 1** Write the first six terms of the geometric sequence with first term 12 and common ratio $\frac{1}{2}$.

**3** Use the formula for the general term of a geometric sequence.

## The General Term of a Geometric Sequence

Consider a geometric sequence whose first term is $a_1$, and whose common ratio is $r$. We are looking for a formula for the general term, $a_n$. Let's begin by writing the first six terms. The first term is $a_1$. The second term is $a_1r$. The third term is $a_1r \cdot r$, or $a_1r^2$. The fourth term is $a_1r^2 \cdot r$, or $a_1r^3$, and so on. Starting with $a_1$ and multiplying each successive term by $r$, the first six terms are

$$a_1, \quad a_1r, \quad a_1r^2, \quad a_1r^3, \quad a_1r^4, \quad a_1r^5.$$

$a_1$, first term; $a_2$, second term; $a_3$, third term; $a_4$, fourth term; $a_5$, fifth term; $a_6$, sixth term

Compare the exponent on $r$ and the subscript of $a$ denoting the term number. Can you see that the exponent on $r$ is 1 less than the subscript of $a$ denoting the term number?

$$a_3\text{: third term} = a_1r^2 \qquad a_4\text{: fourth term} = a_1r^3$$

2 is one less than 3. 3 is one less than 4.

Thus, the formula for the $n$th term is

$$a_n = a_1r^{n-1}.$$

$n-1$ is one less than $n$.

**General Term of a Geometric Sequence**

The $n$th term (the general term) of a geometric sequence with first term $a_1$ and common ratio $r$ is

$$a_n = a_1r^{n-1}.$$

**Study Tip**

Be careful with the order of operations when evaluating

$$a_1r^{n-1}.$$

First find $r^{n-1}$. Then multiply the result by $a_1$.

### EXAMPLE 2 Using the Formula for the General Term of a Geometric Sequence

Find the eighth term of the geometric sequence whose first term is −4 and whose common ratio is −2.

**Solution** To find the eighth term, $a_8$, we replace $n$ in the formula with 8, $a_1$ with −4, and $r$ with −2.

$$a_n = a_1r^{n-1}$$

$$a_8 = -4(-2)^{8-1} = -4(-2)^7 = -4(-128) = 512$$

The eighth term is 512. We can check this result by writing the first eight terms of the sequence:

$$-4, 8, -16, 32, -64, 128, -256, 512.$$

**Check Point 2** Find the seventh term of the geometric sequence whose first term is 5 and whose common ratio is $-3$.

In Chapter 4, we studied exponential functions of the form $f(x) = b^x$ and the explosive exponential growth of world population. In our next example, we consider Florida's geometric population growth. Because **a geometric sequence is an exponential function whose domain is the set of positive integers,** geometric and exponential growth mean the same thing. (By contrast, an arithmetic sequence is a *linear function* whose domain is the set of positive integers.)

## Geometric Population Growth

Economist Thomas Malthus (1766–1834) predicted that population growth would increase as a geometric sequence and food production would increase as an arithmetic sequence. He concluded that eventually population would exceed food production. If two sequences, one geometric and one arithmetic, are increasing, the geometric sequence will eventually overtake the arithmetic sequence, regardless of any head start that the arithmetic sequence might initially have.

## EXAMPLE 3 Geometric Population Growth

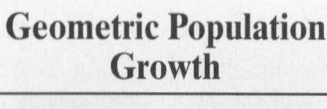

The population of Florida from 1980 through 1987 is shown in the following table.

| Year | 1980 | 1981 | 1982 | 1983 | 1984 | 1985 | 1986 | 1987 |
|---|---|---|---|---|---|---|---|---|
| Population in millions | 9.75 | 10.03 | 10.32 | 10.62 | 10.93 | 11.25 | 11.58 | 11.92 |

**a.** Show that the population is increasing geometrically.

**b.** Write the general term for the geometric sequence describing population growth for Florida $n$ years after 1979.

**c.** Estimate Florida's population, in millions, for the year 2000.

### Solution

**a.** First, we divide the population for each year by the population in the preceding year.

$$\frac{10.03}{9.75} \approx 1.029, \quad \frac{10.32}{10.03} \approx 1.029, \quad \frac{10.62}{10.32} \approx 1.029$$

Continuing in this manner, we will keep getting approximately 1.029. This means that the population is increasing geometrically with $r \approx 1.029$. In this situation, the common ratio is the growth rate, indicating that the population of Florida in any year shown in the table is approximately 1.029 times the population the year before.

**b.** The sequence of Florida's population growth is

$$9.75, 10.03, 10.32, 10.62, 10.93, 11.25, 11.58, 11.92, \ldots.$$

Because the population is increasing geometrically, we can find the general term of this sequence using

$$a_n = a_1 r^{n-1}.$$

In this sequence, $a_1 = 9.75$ and $r$ [from part (a)] $\approx 1.029$. We substitute these values into the formula for the general term. This gives the general term for the geometric sequence describing Florida's population $n$ years after 1979.

$$a_n = 9.75(1.029)^{n-1}$$

**c.** We can use the formula for the general term, $a_n$, in part (b) to estimate Florida's population for the year 2000. The year 2000 is 21 years after 1979—that is, $2000 - 1979 = 21$. Thus, $n = 21$. We substitute 21 for $n$ in $a_n = 9.75(1.029)^{n-1}$.

$$a_{21} = 9.75(1.029)^{21-1} = 9.75(1.029)^{20} \approx 17.27$$

The formula predicts that Florida will have a population of approximately 17.27 million in the year 2000.

**Check Point 3** Write the general term for the geometric sequence

$$3, 6, 12, 24, 48, \ldots.$$

Then use the formula for the general term to find the eighth term.

**4** Use the formula for the sum of the first $n$ terms of a geometric sequence.

## The Sum of the First $n$ Terms of a Geometric Sequence

The sum of the first $n$ terms of a geometric sequence, denoted by $S_n$, can be found without having to add up all the terms. Recall that the first $n$ terms of a geometric sequence are

$$a_1, a_1r, a_1r^2, \ldots, a_1r^{n-2}, a_1r^{n-1}.$$

We proceed as follows:

$$S_n = a_1 + a_1r + a_1r^2 + \cdots + a_1r^{n-2} + a_1r^{n-1}$$
$S_n$ is the sum of the first $n$ terms of the sequence.

$$rS_n = a_1r + a_1r^2 + a_1r^3 + \cdots + a_1r^{n-1} + a_1r^n$$
Multiply both sides of the equation by $r$.

$$S_n - rS_n = a_1 - a_1r^n$$
Subtract the second equation from the first equation.

$$S_n(1 - r) = a_1(1 - r^n)$$
Factor out $S_n$ on the left and $a_1$ on the right.

$$S_n = \frac{a_1(1 - r^n)}{1 - r}$$
Solve for $S_n$ by dividing both sides by $1 - r$ (assuming that $r \neq 1$).

We have proved the following result.

**Study Tip**

If the common ratio is 1, the geometric sequence is

$$a_1, a_1, a_1, a_1, \ldots.$$

The sum of the first $n$ terms of this sequence is $na_1$:

$$S_n = \underbrace{a_1 + a_1 + a_1 + \cdots + a_1}_{\text{There are } n \text{ terms.}}$$
$$= na_1.$$

**The Sum of the First $n$ Terms of a Geometric Sequence**

The sum, $S_n$, of the first $n$ terms of a geometric sequence is given by

$$S_n = \frac{a_1(1 - r^n)}{1 - r}$$

in which $a_1$ is the first term and $r$ is the common ratio ($r \neq 1$).

To find the sum of the terms of a geometric sequence, we need to know the first term, $a_1$, the common ratio, $r$, and the number of terms, $n$. The following examples illustrate how to use this formula.

## EXAMPLE 4 Finding the Sum of $n$ Terms of a Geometric Sequence

Find the sum of the first 18 terms of the geometric sequence: 2, −8, 32, −128, . . . .

**Solution** To find the sum of the first 18 terms, $S_{18}$, we replace $n$ in the formula with 18.

$$S_n = \frac{a_1(1 - r^n)}{1 - r}$$

$$S_{18} = \frac{a_1(1 - r^{18})}{1 - r}$$

The first term, $a_1$, is 2.

We must find $r$, the common ratio.

We can find the common ratio by dividing the second term by the first term.

$$r = \frac{a_2}{a_1} = \frac{-8}{2} = -4$$

Now we are ready to find the sum of the first 18 terms of 2, −8, 32, −128, . . . .

$$S_n = \frac{a_1(1 - r^n)}{1 - r}$$ Use the formula for the sum of the first $n$ terms of a geometric sequence.

$$S_{18} = \frac{2(1 - (-4)^{18})}{1 - (-4)}$$ $a_1$ (the first term) = 2, $r = -4$, and $n = 18$ because we want the sum of the first 18 terms.

$$= -27{,}487{,}790{,}694$$ Use a calculator.

The sum of the first 18 terms is −27,487,790,694.

**Check Point 4** Find the sum of the first nine terms of the geometric sequence: 2, −6, 18, −54, . . . .

## EXAMPLE 5 Using $S_n$ to Evaluate a Summation

Find the following sum: $\sum_{i=1}^{10} 6 \cdot 2^i$

**Solution** Let's write out a few terms in the sum.

$$\sum_{i=1}^{10} 6 \cdot 2^i = 6 \cdot 2 + 6 \cdot 2^2 + 6 \cdot 2^3 + \cdots + 6 \cdot 2^{10}$$

Can you see that each term after the first is obtained by multiplying the preceding term by 2? To find the sum of the 10 terms ($n = 10$), we need to know the first term, $a_1$, and the common ratio, $r$. The first term is $6 \cdot 2$ or 12: $a_1 = 12$. The common ratio is 2.

$$S_n = \frac{a_1(1 - r^n)}{1 - r}$$ Use the formula for the sum of the first $n$ terms of a geometric sequence.

$$S_{10} = \frac{12(1 - 2^{10})}{1 - 2}$$ $a_1$ (the first term) = 12, $r = 2$, and $n = 10$ because we are adding ten terms.

$$= 12{,}276$$ Use a calculator.

**Technology**

To find

$$\sum_{i=1}^{10} 6 \cdot 2^i$$

on a graphing utility, enter

[SUM] [SEQ] $(6 \times 2^x, x, 1, 10, 1)$.

Then press [ENTER].

Thus,

$$\sum_{i=1}^{10} 6 \cdot 2^i = 12{,}276$$

**Check Point 5** Find the following sum: $\sum_{i=1}^{8} 2 \cdot 3^i$.

Some of the exercises in the previous exercise set involved situations in which salaries increase by a fixed amount each year. A more realistic situation is one in which salary raises increase by a certain percent each year. Example 6 shows how such a situation can be described using a geometric series.

## EXAMPLE 6 Computing a Lifetime Salary

A union contract specifies that each worker will receive a 5% pay increase each year for the next 30 years. One worker is paid \$20,000 the first year. What is this person's total lifetime salary over a 30-year period?

**Solution** The salary for the first year is \$20,000. With a 5% raise, the second-year salary is computed as follows:

$$\text{Salary for year 2} = 20{,}000 + 20{,}000(0.05) = 20{,}000(1.05).$$

Each year, the salary is 1.05 times what it was in the previous year. Thus, the salary for year 3 is 1.05 times 20,000(1.05), or $20{,}000(1.05)^2$. The salaries for the first five years are given in the table.

| Yearly Salaries | | | | | |
|---|---|---|---|---|---|
| Year 1 | Year 2 | Year 3 | Year 4 | Year 5 | ... |
| 20,000 | 20,000(1.05) | $20{,}000(1.05)^2$ | $20{,}000(1.05)^3$ | $20{,}000(1.05)^4$ | ... |

The numbers in the second row form a geometric sequence with $a_1 = 20{,}000$ and $r = 1.05$. To find the total salary over 30 years, we use the formula for the sum of the first $n$ terms of a geometric sequence, with $n = 30$.

$$S_n = \frac{a_1(1 - r^n)}{1 - r}$$

$$S_{30} = \frac{20{,}000(1 - (1.05)^{30})}{1 - 1.05}$$

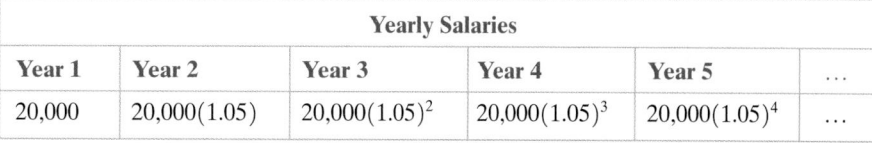

Total salary over 30 years

$$= \frac{20{,}000(1 - (1.05)^{30})}{-0.05}$$

$$\approx 1{,}328{,}777$$ Use a calculator.

The total salary over the 30-year period is approximately \$1,328,777.

**Check Point 6** A job pays a salary of \$30,000 the first year. During the next 29 years, the salary increases by 6% each year. What is the total lifetime salary over the 30-year period?

**5** Find the value of an annuity.

## Annuities

The compound interest formula

$$A = P(1 + r)^t$$

gives the future value, $A$, after $t$ years, when a fixed amount of money, $P$, the principal, is deposited in an account that pays an annual interest rate $r$ (in decimal form) compounded once a year. However, money is often invested in small amounts at periodic intervals. For example, to save for retirement, you might decide to place \$1000 into an Individual Retirement Account (IRA) at the end of each year until you retire. An **annuity** is a sequence of equal payments made at equal time periods. An IRA is an example of an annuity.

Suppose $P$ dollars is deposited into an account at the end of each year. The account pays an annual interest rate, $r$, compounded annually. At the end of the first year, the account contains $P$ dollars. At the end of the second year, $P$ dollars is deposited again. At the time of this deposit, the first deposit has received interest earned during the second year. The **value of the annuity** is the sum of all deposits made plus all interest paid. Thus, the value of the annuity after two years is

$$P + P(1 + r).$$

Deposit of P dollars at end of second year

First-year deposit of P dollars with interest earned for a year

The value of the annuity after three years is

$$P \quad + \quad P(1 + r) \quad + \quad P(1 + r)^2.$$

Deposit of P dollars at end of third year

Second-year deposit of P dollars with interest earned for a year

First-year deposit of P dollars with interest earned over two years

The value of the annuity after $t$ years is

$$P + P(1 + r) + P(1 + r)^2 + P(1 + r)^3 + \cdots + P(1 + r)^{t-1}$$

Deposit of P dollars at end of year t

First-year deposit of P dollars with interest earned over t − 1 years

This is a geometric series with first term $P$ and common ratio $1 + r$. We use the formula

$$S_n = \frac{a_1(1 - r^n)}{1 - r}$$

to find the sum of the terms:

$$S_n = \frac{P(1 - (1 + r)^t)}{1 - (1 + r)} = \frac{P(1 - (1 + r)^t)}{-r} = P\frac{(1 + r)^t - 1}{r}.$$

This formula gives the value of an annuity after $t$ years if interest is compounded once a year. We can adjust the formula to find the value of an annuity if equal payments are made at the end of each of $n$ yearly compounding periods.

**Value of an Annuity: Interest Compounded $n$ Times per Year**

If $P$ is the deposit made at the end of each compounding period for an annuity at $r$ percent annual interest compounded $n$ times per year, the value, $A$, of the annuity after $t$ years is

$$A = P\frac{\left(1+\frac{r}{n}\right)^{nt}-1}{\frac{r}{n}}.$$

## EXAMPLE 7 Determining the Value of an Annuity

To save for retirement, you decide to deposit \$1000 into an IRA at the end of each year for the next 30 years. If the interest rate is 10% per year compounded annually, find the value of the IRA after 30 years.

**Solution** The annuity involves 30 year-end deposits of $P = \$1000$. The interest rate is 10%: $r = 0.10$. Because the deposits are made once a year and the interest is compounded once a year, $n = 1$. The number of years is 30: $t = 30$. We replace the variables in the formula for the value of an annuity with these numbers.

$$A = P\frac{\left(1+\frac{r}{n}\right)^{nt}-1}{\frac{r}{n}}$$

$$A = 1000\frac{\left(1+\frac{0.10}{1}\right)^{1\cdot 30}-1}{\frac{0.10}{1}} \approx 164{,}494$$

The value of the IRA at the end of 30 years is approximately \$164,494.

**Check Point 7** If \$3000 is deposited into an IRA at the end of each year for 40 years and the interest rate is 10% per year compounded annually, find the value of the IRA after 40 years.

**6** Use the formula for the sum of an infinite geometric series.

## Geometric Series

An infinite sum of the form

$$a_1 + a_1r + a_1r^2 + a_1r^3 + \cdots + a_1r^{n-1} + \cdots$$

with first term $a_1$ and common ratio $r$ is called an **infinite geometric series**. How can we determine which infinite geometric series have sums and which do not? We look at what happens to $r^n$ as $n$ gets larger in the formula for the sum of the first $n$ terms of this series, namely

$$S_n = \frac{a_1(1-r^n)}{1-r}.$$

If $r$ is any number between $-1$ and 1, that is, $-1 < r < 1$, the term $r^n$ approaches 0 as $n$ gets larger. For example, consider what happens to $r^n$ for $r = \frac{1}{2}$:

$$\left(\tfrac{1}{2}\right)^1 = \tfrac{1}{2} \quad \left(\tfrac{1}{2}\right)^2 = \tfrac{1}{4} \quad \left(\tfrac{1}{2}\right)^3 = \tfrac{1}{8} \quad \left(\tfrac{1}{2}\right)^4 = \tfrac{1}{16} \quad \left(\tfrac{1}{2}\right)^5 = \tfrac{1}{32} \quad \left(\tfrac{1}{2}\right)^6 = \tfrac{1}{64}$$

These numbers are approaching 0 as $n$ gets larger.

Take another look at the formula for the sum of the first $n$ terms of a geometric sequence.

$$S_n = \frac{a_1(1 - r^n)}{1 - r}$$

If $-1 < r < 1$, $r^n$ approaches 0 as $n$ approaches infinity ($n \to \infty$).

Let us replace $r^n$ with 0 in the formula for $S_n$. This change gives us a formula for the sum of infinite geometric series with common ratios between $-1$ and 1.

**The Sum of an Infinite Geometric Series**

If $-1 < r < 1$ (equivalently, $|r| < 1$), then the sum of the infinite geometric series

$$a_1 + a_1 r + a_1 r^2 + a_1 r^3 + \cdots$$

in which $a_1$ is the first term and $r$ is the common ratio is given by

$$S = \frac{a_1}{1 - r}.$$

If $|r| \geq 1$, the infinite series does not have a sum.

To use the formula for the sum of an infinite geometric series, we need to know the first term and the common ratio. For example, consider

$$\tfrac{1}{2} + \tfrac{1}{4} + \tfrac{1}{8} + \tfrac{1}{16} + \tfrac{1}{32} + \cdots.$$

First term, $a_1$, is $\frac{1}{2}$.

Common ratio, $r$, is $\frac{a_2}{a_1}$.

$$r = \frac{1}{4} \div \frac{1}{2} = \frac{1}{4} \cdot 2 = \frac{1}{2}$$

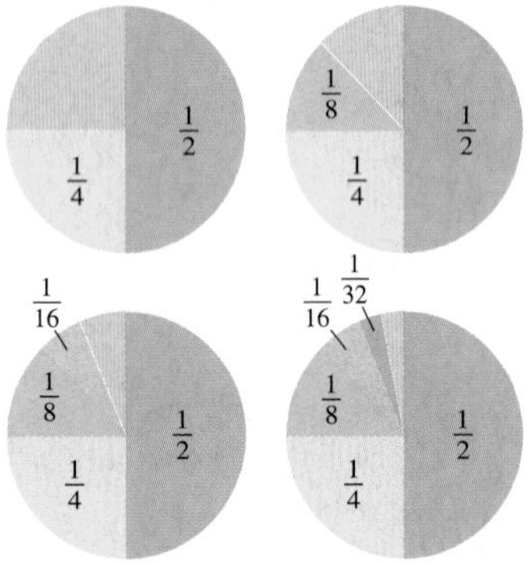


**Figure 11.3** The sum $\frac{1}{2} + \frac{1}{4} + \frac{1}{8} + \frac{1}{16} + \frac{1}{32} + \cdots$ is approaching 1.

With $r = \frac{1}{2}$, the condition that $|r| < 1$ is met, so the infinite geometric series has a sum given by $S = \dfrac{a_1}{1 - r}$. The sum of the series is found as follows:

$$\tfrac{1}{2} + \tfrac{1}{4} + \tfrac{1}{8} + \tfrac{1}{16} + \tfrac{1}{32} + \cdots = \frac{a_1}{1 - r} = \frac{\frac{1}{2}}{1 - \frac{1}{2}} = \frac{\frac{1}{2}}{\frac{1}{2}} = 1.$$

Thus, the sum of the infinite geometric series is 1. Notice how this is illustrated in Figure 11.3. As more terms are included, the sum is approaching the area of one complete circle.

## EXAMPLE 8 Finding the Sum of an Infinite Geometric Series

Find the sum of the infinite geometric series: $\frac{3}{8} - \frac{3}{16} + \frac{3}{32} - \frac{3}{64} + \cdots$.

**Solution** Before finding the sum, we must find the common ratio.

$$r = \frac{a_2}{a_1} = \frac{-\frac{3}{16}}{\frac{3}{8}} = -\frac{3}{16} \cdot \frac{8}{3} = -\frac{1}{2}$$

Because $r = -\frac{1}{2}$, the condition that $|r| < 1$ is met. Thus, the infinite geometric series has a sum.

$$S = \frac{a_1}{1 - r}$$

This is the formula for the sum of an infinite geometric series. Let $a_1 = \frac{3}{8}$ and $r = -\frac{1}{2}$.

$$= \frac{\frac{3}{8}}{1 - \left(-\frac{1}{2}\right)} = \frac{\frac{3}{8}}{\frac{3}{2}} = \frac{3}{8} \cdot \frac{2}{3} = \frac{1}{4}$$

Thus, the sum of this infinite geometric series is $\frac{1}{4}$. Put in an informal way, as we continue to add more and more terms, the sum is approximately $\frac{1}{4}$.

**Check Point 8** Find the sum of the infinite geometric series: $3 + 2 + \frac{4}{3} + \frac{8}{9} + \cdots$.

We can use the formula for the sum of an infinite series to express a repeating decimal as a fraction in lowest terms.

## EXAMPLE 9 Writing a Repeating Decimal as a Fraction

Express $0.\overline{7}$ as a fraction in lowest terms.

**Solution**

$$0.\overline{7} = 0.7777\ldots = \frac{7}{10} + \frac{7}{100} + \frac{7}{1000} + \frac{7}{10{,}000} + \cdots$$

Observe that $0.\overline{7}$ is an infinite geometric series with first term $\frac{7}{10}$ and common ratio $\frac{1}{10}$. Because $r = \frac{1}{10}$, the condition that $|r| < 1$ is met. Thus, we can use our formula to find the sum. Therefore,

$$0.\overline{7} = \frac{a_1}{1 - r} = \frac{\frac{7}{10}}{1 - \frac{1}{10}} = \frac{\frac{7}{10}}{\frac{9}{10}} = \frac{7}{10} \cdot \frac{10}{9} = \frac{7}{9}.$$

An equivalent fraction for $0.\overline{7}$ is $\frac{7}{9}$.

**Check Point 9** Express $0.\overline{9}$ as a fraction in lowest terms.

Infinite geometric series have many applications, as illustrated in Example 10.

## EXAMPLE 10 Tax Rebates and the Multiplier Effect

A tax rebate that returns a certain amount of money to taxpayers can have a total effect on the economy that is many times this amount. In economics, this phenomenon is called the **multiplier effect**. Suppose, for example, that the government reduces taxes so that each consumer has \$2000 more income. The government assumes that each person will spend 70% of this (= \$1400). The individuals and businesses receiving this \$1400 in turn spend 70% of it (= \$980),

creating extra income for other people to spend, and so on. Determine the total amount spent on consumer goods from the initial $2000 tax rebate.

**Solution** The total amount spent is given by the infinite geometric series

$$1400 + 980 + 686 + \cdots.$$

70% of 1400 — 70% of 980

The first term is 1400: $a_1 = 1400$. The common ratio is 70%, or 0.7: $r = 0.7$. Because $r = 0.7$, the condition that $|r| < 1$ is met. Thus, we can use our formula to find the sum. Therefore,

$$1400 + 980 + 686 + \cdots = \frac{a_1}{1 - r} = \frac{1400}{1 - 0.7} \approx 4667.$$

This means that the total amount spent on consumer goods from the initial $2000 rebate is approximately $4667.

**Check Point 10** Rework Example 10 and determine the total amount spent on consumer goods with a $1000 tax rebate and 80% spending down the line.

# EXERCISE SET 11.3

## Practice Exercises

*In Exercises 1–8, write the first five terms of each geometric sequence.*

**1.** $a_1 = 5, \quad r = 3$

**2.** $a_1 = 4, \quad r = 3$

**3.** $a_1 = 20, \quad r = \frac{1}{2}$

**4.** $a_1 = 24, \quad r = \frac{1}{3}$

**5.** $a_n = -4a_{n-1}, \quad a_1 = 10$

**6.** $a_n = -3a_{n-1}, \quad a_1 = 10$

**7.** $a_n = -5a_{n-1}, \quad a_1 = -6$

**8.** $a_n = -6a_{n-1}, \quad a_1 = -2$

*In Exercises 9–16, find the indicated term of the geometric sequence with first term, $a_1$, and common ratio, $r$.*

**9.** Find $a_8$ when $a_1 = 6, r = 2$.

**10.** Find $a_8$ when $a_1 = 5, r = 3$.

**11.** Find $a_{12}$ when $a_1 = 5, r = -2$.

**12.** Find $a_{12}$ when $a_1 = 4, r = -2$.

**13.** Find $a_{40}$ when $a_1 = 1000, r = -\frac{1}{2}$.

**14.** Find $a_{30}$ when $a_1 = 8000, r = -\frac{1}{2}$.

**15.** Find $a_8$ when $a_1 = 1{,}000{,}000, r = 0.1$.

**16.** Find $a_8$ when $a_1 = 40{,}000, r = 0.1$.

*In Exercises 17–24, write a formula for the general term (the nth term) of each geometric sequence. Then use the formula for $a_n$ to find $a_7$, the seventh term of the sequence.*

**17.** $3, 12, 48, 192, \ldots$

**18.** $3, 15, 75, 375, \ldots$

**19.** $18, 6, 2, \frac{2}{3}, \ldots$

**20.** $12, 6, 3, \frac{3}{2}, \ldots$

**21.** $1.5, -3, 6, -12, \ldots$

**22.** $5, -1, \frac{1}{5}, -\frac{1}{25}, \ldots$

**23.** $0.0004, -0.004, 0.04, -0.4, \ldots$

**24.** $0.0007, -0.007, 0.07, -0.7, \ldots$

*Use the formula for the sum of the first n terms of a geometric sequence to solve Exercises 25–36.*

**25.** Find the sum of the first 12 terms of the geometric sequence: $2, 6, 18, 54, \ldots$

**26.** Find the sum of the first 12 terms of the geometric sequence: $3, 6, 12, 24, \ldots$

**27.** Find the sum of the first 11 terms of the geometric sequence: $3, -6, 12, -24, \ldots$

**28.** Find the sum of the first 11 terms of the geometric sequence: $4, -12, 36, -108, \ldots$

**29.** Find the sum of the first 14 terms of the geometric sequence: $-\frac{3}{2}, 3, -6, 12, \ldots$

**30.** Find the sum of the first 14 terms of the geometric sequence: $-\frac{1}{24}, \frac{1}{12}, -\frac{1}{6}, \frac{1}{3}, \ldots$

*In Exercises 31–36, find the indicated sum.*

**31.** $\sum_{i=1}^{8} 3^i$

**32.** $\sum_{i=1}^{6} 4^i$

**33.** $\sum_{i=1}^{10} 5 \cdot 2^i$

**34.** $\sum_{i=1}^{7} 4(-3)^i$

**35.** $\sum_{i=1}^{6} \left(\frac{1}{2}\right)^{i+1}$

**36.** $\sum_{i=1}^{6} \left(\frac{1}{3}\right)^{i+1}$

*In Exercises 37–44, find the sum of each infinite geometric series.*

**37.** $1 + \frac{1}{3} + \frac{1}{9} + \frac{1}{27} + \cdots$

**38.** $1 + \frac{1}{4} + \frac{1}{16} + \frac{1}{64} + \cdots$

**39.** $3 + \frac{3}{4} + \frac{3}{4^2} + \frac{3}{4^3} + \cdots$

**40.** $5 + \frac{5}{6} + \frac{5}{6^2} + \frac{5}{6^3} + \cdots$

**41.** $1 - \frac{1}{2} + \frac{1}{4} - \frac{1}{8} + \cdots$

**42.** $3 - 1 + \frac{1}{3} - \frac{1}{9} + \cdots$

**43.** $\sum_{i=1}^{\infty} 8(-0.3)^{i-1}$

**44.** $\sum_{i=1}^{\infty} 12(-0.7)^{i-1}$

*In Exercises 45–50, express each repeating decimal as a fraction in lowest terms.*

**45.** $0.\overline{5} = \frac{5}{10} + \frac{5}{100} + \frac{5}{1000} + \frac{5}{10{,}000} + \cdots$

**46.** $0.\overline{1} = \frac{1}{10} + \frac{1}{100} + \frac{1}{1000} + \frac{1}{10{,}000} + \cdots$

**47.** $0.\overline{47} = \frac{47}{100} + \frac{47}{10{,}000} + \frac{47}{1{,}000{,}000} + \cdots$

**48.** $0.\overline{83} = \frac{83}{100} + \frac{83}{10{,}000} + \frac{83}{1{,}000{,}000} + \cdots$

**49.** $0.\overline{257}$

**50.** $0.\overline{529}$

*In Exercises 51–56, the general term of a sequence is given. Determine whether the sequence is arithmetic, geometric, or neither. If the sequence is arithmetic, find the common difference; if it is geometric, find the common ratio.*

**51.** $a_n = n + 5$

**52.** $a_n = n - 3$

**53.** $a_n = 2^n$

**54.** $a_n = \left(\frac{1}{2}\right)^n$

**55.** $a_n = n^2 + 5$

**56.** $a_n = n^2 - 3$

## Application Exercises

*Use the formula for the general term (the nth term) of a geometric sequence to solve Exercises 57–60.*

*In Exercises 57–58, suppose you save \$1 the first day of a month, \$2 the second day, \$4 the third day, and so on. That is, each day you save twice as much as you did the day before.*

**57.** What will you put aside for savings on the fifteenth day of the month?

**58.** What will you put aside for savings on the thirtieth day of the month?

**59.** A professional baseball player signs a contract with a beginning salary of \$3,000,000 for the first year with an annual increase of 4% per year beginning in the second year. That is, beginning in year 2, the athlete's salary will be 1.04 times what it was in the previous year. What is the athlete's salary for year 7 of the contract?

**60.** You are offered a job that pays \$30,000 for the first year with an annual increase of 5% per year beginning in the second year. That is, beginning in year 2, your salary will be 1.05 times what it was in the previous year. What can you expect to earn in your sixth year on the job?

**61.** The population of Iraq from 1995 through 1998 is shown in the following table.

| Year | 1995 | 1996 | 1997 | 1998 |
|---|---|---|---|---|
| Population in millions | 20.60 | 21.36 | 22.19 | 23.02 |

*Source*: U.N. Population Division

**a.** Divide the population for each year by the population in the preceding year. Round to two decimal places and show that Iraq's population is increasing geometrically.
**b.** Write the general term of the geometric sequence describing population growth for Iraq $n$ years after 1994.
**c.** Estimate Iraq's population, in millions, for the year 2005.

**62.** The population of China from 1995 through 1998 is shown in the following table.

| Year | 1995 | 1996 | 1997 | 1998 |
|---|---|---|---|---|
| Population in millions | 1218.80 | 1232.21 | 1245.76 | 1259.46 |

*Source*: U.N. Population Division

**a.** Divide the population for each year by the population in the preceding year. Round to two decimal places and show that China's population is increasing geometrically.
**b.** Write the general term of the geometric sequence describing population growth for China $n$ years after 1994.
**c.** Estimate China's population, in millions, for the year 2005.

*Use the formula for the sum of the first n terms of a geometric sequence to solve Exercises 63–68.*

*In Exercises 63–64, you save \$1 the first day of a month, \$2 the second day, \$4 the third day, continuing to double your savings each day.*

**63.** What will your total savings be for the first 15 days?

**64.** What will your total savings be for the first 30 days?

**65.** A job pays a salary of \$24,000 the first year. During the next 19 years, the salary increases by 5% each year. What is the total lifetime salary over the 20-year period?

**66.** You are investigating two employment opportunities. Company A offers \$30,000 the first year. During the next four years, the salary is guaranteed to increase by 6% per year. Company B offers \$32,000 the first year, with guaranteed annual increases of 3% per year after that. Which company offers the better total salary for a five-year contract? By how much?

**67.** A pendulum swings through an arc of 20 inches. On each successive swing, the length of the arc is 90% of the previous length.

$$20, \quad 0.9(20), \quad 0.9^2(20), \quad 0.9^3(20), \quad \ldots$$

1st swing, 2nd swing, 3rd swing, 4th swing

After 10 swings, what is the total length of the distance the pendulum has swung?

**68.** A pendulum swings through an arc of 16 inches. On each successive swing, the length of the arc is 96% of the previous length.

$$16, \quad 0.96(16), \quad (0.96)^2(16), \quad (0.96)^3(16), \quad \ldots$$

1st swing, 2nd swing, 3rd swing, 4th swing

After 10 swings, what is the total length of the distance the pendulum has swung?

*Use the formula for the value of an annuity to solve Exercises 69–72.*

**69.** To save for retirement, you decide to deposit \$2500 into an IRA at the end of each year for the next 40 years. If the interest rate is 9% per year compounded annually, find the value of the IRA after 40 years.

**70.** You decide to deposit \$100 at the end of each month into an account paying 8% interest compounded monthly to save for your child's education. How much will you save over 16 years?

**71.** You contribute \$600 at the end of each quarter to a Tax Sheltered Annuity (TSA) paying 8% annual interest compounded quarterly. Find the value of the TSA after 18 years.

**72.** To save for a new home, you invest \$500 per month in a mutual fund with an annual rate of return of 10% compounded monthly. How much will you have saved after four years?

*Use the formula for the sum of an infinite geometric series to solve Exercises 73–75.*

**73.** A new factory in a small town has an annual payroll of \$6 million. It is expected that 60% of this money will be spent in the town by factory personnel. The people in the town who receive this money are expected to spend 60% of what they receive in the town, and so on. What is the total of all this spending, called the total economic impact of the factory, on the town each year?

**74.** How much additional spending will be generated by a \$10 billion tax rebate if 60% of all income is spent?

**75.** If the shading process shown in the figure is continued indefinitely, what fractional part of the largest square is eventually shaded?

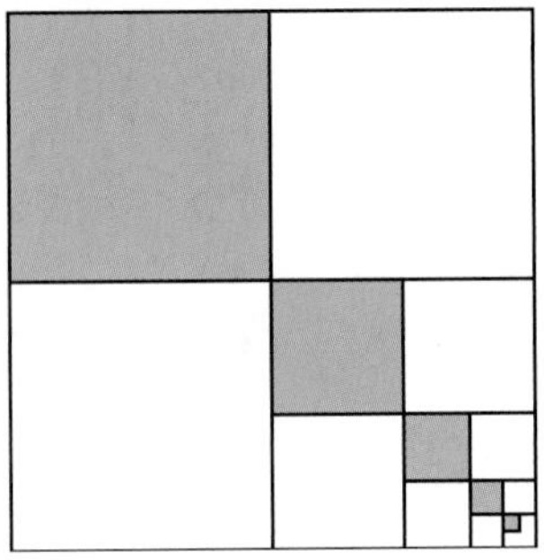

## Writing in Mathematics

**76.** What is a geometric sequence? Give an example with your explanation.

**77.** What is the common ratio in a geometric sequence?

**78.** Explain how to find the general term of a geometric sequence.

**79.** Explain how to find the sum of the first $n$ terms of a geometric sequence without having to add up all the terms.

**80.** What is an annuity?

**81.** What is the difference between a geometric sequence and an infinite geometric series?

**82.** How do you determine if an infinite geometric series has a sum? Explain how to find the sum of an infinite geometric series.

**83.** Would you rather have \$10,000,000 and a brand new BMW or 1¢ today, 2¢ tomorrow, 4¢ on day 3, 8¢ on day 4, 16¢ on day 5, and so on, for 30 days? Explain.

**84.** For the first 30 days of a flu outbreak, the number of students on your campus who become ill is increasing. Which is worse: The number of students with the flu is increasing arithmetically or is increasing geometrically? Explain your answer.

## Technology Exercises

**85.** Use the SEQ (sequence) capability of a graphing utility and the formula you obtained for $a_n$ to verify the value you found for $a_7$ in any three exercises from Exercises 17–24.

**86.** Use the capability of a graphing utility to calculate the sum of a sequence to verify any three of your answers to Exercises 31–36.

*In Exercises 87–88, use a graphing utility to graph the function. Determine the horizontal asymptote for the graph of f and discuss its relationship to the sum of the given series.*

| | **Function** | **Series** |
|---|---|---|
| **87.** | $f(x) = \dfrac{2\left[1 - \left(\frac{1}{3}\right)^x\right]}{1 - \frac{1}{3}}$ | $2 + 2\left(\frac{1}{3}\right) + 2\left(\frac{1}{3}\right)^2 + 2\left(\frac{1}{3}\right)^3 + \cdots$ |
| **88.** | $f(x) = \dfrac{4[1 - (0.6)^x]}{1 - 0.6}$ | $4 + 4(0.6) + 4(0.6)^2 + 4(0.6)^3 + \cdots$ |

## Critical Thinking Exercises

**89.** Which one of the following is true?

**a.** The sequence 2, 6, 24, 120, ... is an example of a geometric sequence.

**b.** The sum of the geometric series $\frac{1}{2} + \frac{1}{4} + \frac{1}{8} + \cdots + \frac{1}{512}$ can only be estimated without knowing precisely what terms occur between $\frac{1}{8}$ and $\frac{1}{512}$.

**c.** $10 - 5 + \frac{5}{2} - \frac{5}{4} + \cdots = \dfrac{10}{1 - \frac{1}{2}}$

**d.** If the $n$th term of a geometric sequence is $a_n = 3(0.5)^{n-1}$, the common ratio is $\frac{1}{2}$.

**90.** In a pest-eradication program, sterilized male flies are released into the general population each day. Ninety percent of those flies will survive a given day. How many flies should be released each day if the long-range goal of the program is to keep 20,000 sterilized flies in the population?

**91.** You are now 25 years old and would like to retire at age 55 with a retirement fund of \$1,000,000. How much should you deposit at the end of each month for the next 30 years in an IRA paying 10% annual interest compounded monthly to achieve your goal?

## Group Exercise

**92.** Group members serve as a financial team analyzing the three options given to the professional baseball player described in the chapter opener. As a group, determine which option provides the most amount of money over the six-year contract and which provides the least. Describe one advantage and one disadvantage to each option.

# SECTION 11.4 *Mathematical Induction*

## Objectives

1. Understand the principle of mathematical induction.
2. Prove statements using mathematical induction.

After ten years of work, Princeton University's Andrew Wiles proved Fermat's Last Theorem.

Pierre de Fermat (1601–1665) was a lawyer who enjoyed studying mathematics. In a margin of one of his books he claimed that no positive integers satisfy

$$x^n + y^n = z^n$$

if $n$ is an integer greater than or equal to 3.

If $n = 2$, we can find positive integers satisfying the equation:

$$3^2 + 4^2 = 5^2.$$

However, Fermat claimed that no positive integers satisfy

$$x^3 + y^3 = z^3, \quad x^4 + y^4 = z^4, \quad x^5 + y^5 = z^5,$$

and so on. Fermat claimed to have a proof of his conjecture, but added, "The margin of my book is too narrow to write it down." Some believe that he never had a proof and intended to frustrate his colleagues.

In 1994, 40-year-old Princeton math professor Andrew Wiles proved Fermat's Last Theorem using a principle called *mathematical induction*. In this section, you will learn how to use this powerful method to prove statements about the positive integers.

**1** Understand the principle of mathematical induction.

## The Principle of Mathematical Induction

How do we prove statements using mathematical induction? Let's consider an example. We will prove a statement that appears to give a correct formula for the sum of the first $n$ positive integers.

$$S_n: 1 + 2 + 3 + \cdots + n = \frac{n(n+1)}{2}$$

We can verify this statement for, say, the first four positive integers.

If $n = 1$, the statement $S_1$ is

Take the first term on the left.

$$1 \stackrel{?}{=} \frac{1(1+1)}{2}$$

Substitute 1 for $n$ on the right.

$$1 \stackrel{?}{=} \frac{1 \cdot 2}{2}$$

$$1 = 1 \checkmark.$$

This true statement shows that $S_1$ is true.

If $n = 2$, the statement $S_2$ is

Add the first two terms on the left.

$$1 + 2 \stackrel{?}{=} \frac{2(2+1)}{2}$$

Substitute 2 for $n$ on the right.

$$3 \stackrel{?}{=} \frac{2 \cdot 3}{2}$$

$$3 = 3 \checkmark.$$

This true statement shows $S_2$ is true.

If $n = 3$, the statement $S_3$ is

Add the first three terms on the left.

$$1 + 2 + 3 \stackrel{?}{=} \frac{3(3+1)}{2}$$

Substitute 3 for $n$ on the right.

$$6 \stackrel{?}{=} \frac{3 \cdot 4}{2}$$

$$6 = 6 \checkmark.$$

This true statement shows $S_3$ is true.

Finally, if $n = 4$, the statement $S_4$ is

Add the first four terms on the left.

$$1 + 2 + 3 + 4 \stackrel{?}{=} \frac{4(4+1)}{2}$$

Substitute 4 for $n$ on the right.

$$10 \stackrel{?}{=} \frac{4 \cdot 5}{2}$$

$$10 = 10 \checkmark.$$

This true statement shows $S_4$ is true.

This approach does *not* prove that the given statement $S_n$ is true for every positive integer $n$. The fact that the formula produces true statements for $n = 1$, 2, 3, and 4 does not guarantee that it is valid for all positive integers $n$. Thus, we need to be able to verify the truth of $S_n$ without verifying the statement for each and every one of the positive integers.

A legitimate proof of the given statement $S_n$ involves a technique called **mathematical induction**.

**The Principle of Mathematical Induction**

Let $S_n$ be a statement involving the positive integer $n$. If

1. $S_1$ is true, and
2. the truth of the statement $S_k$ implies the truth of the statement $S_{k+1}$, for every positive integer $k$,

then the statement $S_n$ is true for all positive integers $n$.

**Figure 11.4** Falling dominoes illustrate the principle of mathematical induction.

The principle of mathematical induction can be illustrated using an unending line of dominoes, as shown in Figure 11.4. If the first domino is pushed over, it knocks down the next, which knocks down the next, and so on, in a chain reaction. To topple all the dominoes in the infinite sequence, two conditions must be satisfied:

1. The first domino must be knocked down.
2. If the domino in position $k$ is knocked down, then the domino in position $k + 1$ must be knocked down.

If the second condition is not satisfied, it does not follow that all the dominoes will topple. For example, suppose the dominoes are spaced far enough apart so that a falling domino does not push over the next domino in the line.

The domino analogy provides the two steps that are required in a proof by mathematical induction.

**The Steps in a Proof by Mathematical Induction**

Let $S_n$ be a statement involving the positive integer $n$. To prove that $S_n$ is true for all positive integers $n$ requires two steps.

**Step 1** Show that $S_1$ is true.

**Step 2** Show that if $S_k$ is assumed to be true, then $S_{k+1}$ is also true, for every positive integer $k$.

Notice that to prove $S_n$, we work only with the statements $S_1$, $S_k$, and $S_{k+1}$. Our first example provides practice in writing these statements.

## EXAMPLE 1 Writing $S_1$, $S_k$, and $S_{k+1}$

For the given statement $S_n$, write the three statements $S_1$, $S_k$, and $S_{k+1}$.

**a.** $S_n$: $1 + 2 + 3 + \cdots + n = \dfrac{n(n + 1)}{2}$

**b.** $S_n$: $1^2 + 2^2 + 3^2 + \cdots + n^2 = \dfrac{n(n + 1)(2n + 1)}{6}$

**Solution**

**a.** We begin with

$$S_n: 1 + 2 + 3 + \cdots + n = \frac{n(n+1)}{2}.$$

Write $S_1$ by taking the first term on the left and replacing $n$ with 1 on the right.

$$S_1: 1 = \frac{1(1+1)}{2}$$

Write $S_k$ by taking the sum of the first $k$ terms on the left and replacing $n$ with $k$ on the right.

$$S_k: 1 + 2 + 3 + \cdots + k = \frac{k(k+1)}{2}$$

Write $S_{k+1}$ by taking the sum of the first $k + 1$ terms on the left and replacing $n$ with $k + 1$ on the right.

$$S_{k+1}: 1 + 2 + 3 + \cdots + (k+1) = \frac{(k+1)[(k+1)+1]}{2}$$

$$S_{k+1}: 1 + 2 + 3 + \cdots + (k+1) = \frac{(k+1)(k+2)}{2}$$

Simplify on the right.

**b.** We begin with

$$S_n: 1^2 + 2^2 + 3^2 + \cdots + n^2 = \frac{n(n+1)(2n+1)}{6}.$$

Write $S_1$ by taking the first term on the left and replacing $n$ with 1 on the right.

$$S_1: 1^2 = \frac{1(1+1)(2 \cdot 1 + 1)}{6}$$

Write $S_k$ by taking the sum of the first $k$ terms on the left and replacing $n$ with $k$ on the right.

$$S_k: 1^2 + 2^2 + 3^2 + \cdots + k^2 = \frac{k(k+1)(2k+1)}{6}$$

Write $S_{k+1}$ by taking the sum of the first $k + 1$ terms on the left and replacing $n$ with $k + 1$ on the right.

$$S_{k+1}: 1^2 + 2^2 + 3^2 + \cdots + (k+1)^2 = \frac{(k+1)[(k+1)+1][2(k+1)+1]}{6}$$

$$S_{k+1}: 1^2 + 2^2 + 3^2 + \cdots + (k+1)^2 = \frac{(k+1)(k+2)(2k+3)}{6}$$

Simplify on the right.

**Check Point 1**

For the given statement $S_n$, write the three statements $S_1$, $S_k$, and $S_{k+1}$.

**a.** $2 + 4 + 6 + \cdots + 2n = n(n+1)$

**b.** $1^3 + 2^3 + 3^3 + \cdots + n^3 = \dfrac{n^2(n+1)^2}{4}$

Always simplify $S_{k+1}$ before trying to use mathematical induction to prove that $S_n$ is true. For example, consider

$$S_n\colon\ 1^2 + 3^2 + 5^2 + \cdots + (2n-1)^2 = \frac{n(2n-1)(2n+1)}{3}.$$

Begin by writing $S_{k+1}$ as follows:

$$S_{k+1}\colon\ 1^2 + 3^2 + 5^2 + \cdots + [2(k+1)-1]^2 = \frac{(k+1)[2(k+1)-1][2(k+1)+1]}{3}.$$

The sum of the first $k+1$ terms

Replace $n$ by $k+1$ on the right side of $S_n$.

Now simplify the algebra.

$$S_{k+1}\colon\ 1^2 + 3^2 + 5^2 + \cdots + (2k+2-1)^2 = \frac{(k+1)(2k+2-1)(2k+2+1)}{3}$$

$$S_{k+1}\colon\ 1^2 + 3^2 + 5^2 + \cdots + (2k+1)^2 = \frac{(k+1)(2k+1)(2k+3)}{3}$$

**2** Prove statements using mathematical induction.

## Proving Statements about Positive Integers Using Mathematical Induction

Now that we know how to find $S_1$, $S_k$, and $S_{k+1}$, let's see how we can use these statements to carry out the two steps in a proof by mathematical induction. In Examples 2 and 3, we will use the statements $S_1$, $S_k$, and $S_{k+1}$ to prove each of the statements $S_n$ that we worked with in Example 1.

### EXAMPLE 2 Proving a Formula by Mathematical Induction

Use mathematical induction to prove that

$$1 + 2 + 3 + \cdots + n = \frac{n(n+1)}{2}$$

for all positive integers $n$.

**Solution**

**Step 1** **Show that $S_1$ is true.** Statement $S_1$ is

$$1 = \frac{1(1+1)}{2}.$$

Simplifying on the right, we obtain $1 = 1$. This true statement shows that $S_1$ is true.

**Step 2** **Show that if $S_k$ is true, then $S_{k+1}$ is true.** Using $S_k$ and $S_{k+1}$ from Example 1a, show that the truth of $S_k$,

$$1 + 2 + 3 + \cdots + k = \frac{k(k+1)}{2}$$

implies the truth of $S_{k+1}$,

$$1 + 2 + 3 + \cdots + (k+1) = \frac{(k+1)(k+2)}{2}.$$

We will work with $S_k$. Because we assume that $S_k$ is true, we add the next consecutive integer after $k$—namely, $k + 1$—to both sides.

$$1 + 2 + 3 + \cdots + k = \frac{k(k+1)}{2}$$

This is $S_k$, which we assume is true.

$$1 + 2 + 3 + \cdots + k + (k+1) = \frac{k(k+1)}{2} + (k+1)$$

Add $k + 1$ to both sides of the equation.

We do not have to write this $k$ because $k$ is understood to be the integer that precedes $k + 1$.

$$1 + 2 + 3 + \cdots + (k+1) = \frac{k(k+1)}{2} + \frac{2(k+1)}{2}$$

Write the right side with a common denominator of 2.

$$1 + 2 + 3 + \cdots + (k+1) = \frac{(k+1)}{2}(k+2)$$

Factor out the common factor $\frac{k+1}{2}$ on the right.

$$1 + 2 + 3 + \cdots + (k+1) = \frac{(k+1)(k+2)}{2}$$

This final result is the statement $S_{k+1}$ at the bottom of page 637.

We have shown that if we assume that $S_k$ is true, and we add $k + 1$ to both sides of $S_k$, then $S_{k+1}$ is also true. By the principle of mathematical induction, the statement $S_n$, namely,

$$1 + 2 + 3 + \cdots + n = \frac{n(n+1)}{2}$$

is true for every positive integer $n$.

**Check Point 2** Use mathematical induction to prove that

$$2 + 4 + 6 + \cdots + 2n = n(n+1).$$

## EXAMPLE 3 Proving a Formula by Mathematical Induction

Use mathematical induction to prove that

$$1^2 + 2^2 + 3^2 + \cdots + n^2 = \frac{n(n+1)(2n+1)}{6}$$

for all positive integers $n$.

**Solution**

**Step 1 Show that $S_1$ is true.** Statement $S_1$ is

$$1^2 = \frac{1(1+1)(2 \cdot 1 + 1)}{6}.$$

### Visualizing Summation Formulas

Finding the sum of consecutive positive integers leads to **triangular numbers** of the form $\frac{n(n+1)}{2}$.

$\frac{n(n+1)}{2}$

$n = 1$:

1

$\frac{n(n+1)}{2}$

$n = 2$:

3

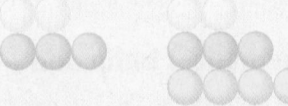

$\frac{n(n+1)}{2}$

$n = 3$:

6

$\frac{n(n+1)}{2}$

$n = 4$:

10

Simplifying, we obtain $1 = \frac{1 \cdot 2 \cdot 3}{6}$. Further simplification on the right gives the statement $1 = 1$. This true statement shows that $S_1$ is true.

**Step 2** **Show that if $S_k$ is true, then $S_{k+1}$ is true.** Using $S_k$ and $S_{k+1}$ from Example 1b, show that the truth of

$$S_k: 1^2 + 2^2 + 3^2 + \cdots + k^2 = \frac{k(k+1)(2k+1)}{6}$$

implies the truth of

$$S_{k+1}: 1^2 + 2^2 + 3^2 + \cdots + (k+1)^2 = \frac{(k+1)(k+2)(2k+3)}{6}.$$

We will work with $S_k$. Because we assume that $S_k$ is true, we add the square of the next consecutive integer after $k$—namely, $(k+1)^2$—to both sides of the equation.

$$1^2 + 2^2 + 3^2 + \cdots + k^2 = \frac{k(k+1)(2k+1)}{6}$$

This is $S_k$, assumed to be true. We must work with this and show $S_{k+1}$ is true.

$$1^2 + 2^2 + 3^2 + \cdots + k^2 + (k+1)^2 = \frac{k(k+1)(2k+1)}{6} + (k+1)^2$$

Add $(k+1)^2$ to both sides.

$$1^2 + 2^2 + 3^2 + \cdots + (k+1)^2 = \frac{k(k+1)(2k+1)}{6} + \frac{6(k+1)^2}{6}$$

It is not necessary to write $k^2$ on the left. Express the right side with the least common denominator, 6.

$$= \frac{(k+1)}{6}\left[k(2k+1) + 6(k+1)\right]$$

Factor out the common factor $\frac{k+1}{6}$.

$$= \frac{(k+1)}{6}(2k^2 + 7k + 6)$$

Multiply and combine like terms.

$$= \frac{(k+1)}{6}(k+2)(2k+3)$$

Factor $2k^2 + 7k + 6$.

$$= \frac{(k+1)(k+2)(2k+3)}{6}$$

This final statement is $S_{k+1}$.

We have shown that if we assume that $S_k$ is true, and we add $(k+1)^2$ to both sides of $S_k$, then $S_{k+1}$ is also true. By the principle of mathematical induction, the statement $S_n$, namely,

$$1^2 + 2^2 + 3^2 + \cdots + n^2 = \frac{n(n+1)(2n+1)}{6}$$

is true for every positive integer $n$.

**Check Point 3** Use mathematical induction to prove that

$$1^3 + 2^3 + 3^3 + \cdots + n^3 = \frac{n^2(n+1)^2}{4}.$$

Example 4 illustrates how mathematical induction can be used to prove statements about positive integers that do not involve sums.

## EXAMPLE 4 Using the Principle of Mathematical Induction

Prove that 2 is a factor of $n^2 + 5n$ for all positive integers $n$.

### Solution

**Step 1 Show that $S_1$ is true.** Statement $S_1$ reads

$$2 \text{ is a factor of } 1^2 + 5 \cdot 1.$$

Simplifying the arithmetic, the statement reads

$$2 \text{ is a factor of } 6.$$

This statement is true: that is, $6 = 2 \cdot 3$. This shows that $S_1$ is true.

**Step 2 Show that if $S_k$ is true, then $S_{k+1}$ is true.** Let's write $S_k$ and $S_{k+1}$:

$S_k$: 2 is a factor of $k^2 + 5k$.

$S_{k+1}$: 2 is a factor of $(k + 1)^2 + 5(k + 1)$.

We can rewrite statement $S_{k+1}$ by simplifying the algebraic expression in the statement as follows:

$$(k + 1)^2 + 5(k + 1) = k^2 + 2k + 1 + 5k + 5 = k^2 + 7k + 6.$$

Use the formula $(A + B)^2 = A^2 + 2AB + B^2$.

Statement $S_{k+1}$ now reads

$$2 \text{ is a factor of } k^2 + 7k + 6.$$

We wish to use statement $S_k$—that is, 2 is a factor of $k^2 + 5k$—to prove statement $S_{k+1}$. We do this as follows:

$$k^2 + 7k + 6 = (k^2 + 5k) + (2k + 6) = (k^2 + 5k) + 2(k + 3).$$

We know that 2 is a factor of $k^2 + 5k$ because we assume $S_k$ is true.

Factoring the last two terms shows that 2 is a factor of $2k + 6$.

The voice balloons show that 2 is a factor of $k^2 + 5k$ and of $2(k + 3)$. Thus, 2 is a factor of the sum $(k^2 + 5k) + 2(k + 3)$, or of $k^2 + 7k + 6$. This is precisely statement $S_{k+1}$. We have shown that if we assume that $S_k$ is true, then $S_{k+1}$ is also true. By the principle of mathematical induction, the statement $S_n$, namely 2 is a factor of $n^2 + 5n$, is true for every positive integer $n$.

**Check Point 4** Prove that 2 is a factor of $n^2 + n$ for all positive integers $n$.

# EXERCISE SET 11.4

## Practice Exercises

*In Exercises 1–4, a statement $S_n$ about the positive integers is given. Write statements $S_1$, $S_2$, and $S_3$, and show that each of these statements is true.*

**1.** $S_n$: $1 + 3 + 5 + \cdots + (2n - 1) = n^2$

**2.** $S_n$: $3 + 4 + 5 + \cdots + (n + 2) = \frac{n(n + 5)}{2}$

**3.** $S_n$: 2 is a factor of $n^2 - n$.

**4.** $S_n$: 3 is a factor of $n^3 - n$.

*In Exercises 5–10, a statement $S_n$ about the positive integers is given. Write statements $S_k$ and $S_{k+1}$, simplifying statement $S_{k+1}$ completely.*

**5.** $S_n$: $4 + 8 + 12 + \cdots + 4n = 2n(n + 1)$

**6.** $S_n$: $3 + 4 + 5 + \cdots + (n + 2) = \frac{n(n + 5)}{2}$

**7.** $S_n$: $3 + 7 + 11 + \cdots + (4n - 1) = n(2n + 1)$

**8.** $S_n$: $2 + 7 + 12 + \cdots + (5n - 3) = \frac{n(5n - 1)}{2}$

**9.** $S_n$: 2 is a factor of $n^2 - n + 2$.

**10.** $S_n$: 2 is a factor of $n^2 - n$.

*In Exercises 11–30, use mathematical induction to prove that each statement is true for every positive integer n.*

**11.** $4 + 8 + 12 + \cdots + 4n = 2n(n + 1)$

**12.** $3 + 4 + 5 + \cdots + (n + 2) = \frac{n(n + 5)}{2}$

**13.** $1 + 3 + 5 + \cdots + (2n - 1) = n^2$

**14.** $3 + 6 + 9 + \cdots + 3n = \frac{3n(n + 1)}{2}$

**15.** $3 + 7 + 11 + \cdots + (4n - 1) = n(2n + 1)$

**16.** $2 + 7 + 12 + \cdots + (5n - 3) = \frac{n(5n - 1)}{2}$

**17.** $1 + 2 + 2^2 + \cdots + 2^{n-1} = 2^n - 1$

**18.** $1 + 3 + 3^2 + \cdots + 3^{n-1} = \frac{3^n - 1}{2}$

**19.** $2 + 4 + 8 + \cdots + 2^n = 2^{n+1} - 2$

**20.** $\frac{1}{2} + \frac{1}{4} + \frac{1}{8} + \cdots + \frac{1}{2^n} = 1 - \frac{1}{2^n}$

**21.** $1 \cdot 2 + 2 \cdot 3 + 3 \cdot 4 + \cdots + n(n + 1) = \frac{n(n + 1)(n + 2)}{3}$

**22.** $1 \cdot 3 + 2 \cdot 4 + 3 \cdot 5 + \cdots + n(n + 2) = \frac{n(n + 1)(2n + 7)}{6}$

**23.** $\frac{1}{1 \cdot 2} + \frac{1}{2 \cdot 3} + \frac{1}{3 \cdot 4} + \cdots + \frac{1}{n(n + 1)} = \frac{n}{n + 1}$

**24.** $\frac{1}{2 \cdot 3} + \frac{1}{3 \cdot 4} + \frac{1}{4 \cdot 5} + \cdots + \frac{1}{(n+1)(n+2)} = \frac{n}{2n + 4}$

**25.** 2 is a factor of $n^2 - n$.

**26.** 2 is a factor of $n^2 + 3n$.

**27.** 6 is a factor of $n(n + 1)(n + 2)$.

**28.** 3 is a factor of $n(n + 1)(n - 1)$.

**29.** $(ab)^n = a^n b^n$

**30.** $\left(\frac{a}{b}\right)^n = \frac{a^n}{b^n}$

## Writing in Mathematics

**31.** Explain how to use mathematical induction to prove that a statement is true for every positive integer $n$.

**32.** Consider the statement $S_n$ given by

$$n^2 - n + 41 \text{ is prime.}$$

Although $S_1, S_2, \ldots, S_{40}$ are true, $S_{41}$ is false. Describe how this is illustrated by the dominoes in the figure. What does this tell you about a pattern, or formula, that seems to work for several values of $n$?

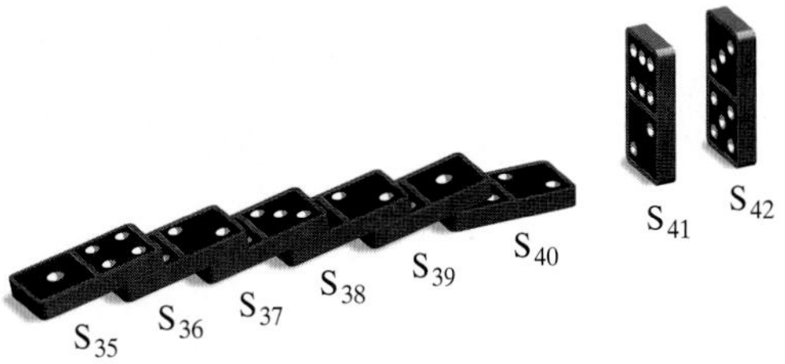


## Critical Thinking Exercises

*Some statements are false for the first few positive integers, but true for some positive integer on. In these instances, you can prove $S_n$ for $n \geq k$ by showing that $S_k$ is true and that $S_k$ implies $S_{k+1}$. Use this extended principle of mathematical induction to prove that each statement in Exercises 33–34 is true.*

**33.** Prove that $n^2 > 2n + 1$ for $n \geq 3$. Show that the formula is true for $n = 3$ and then use step 2 of mathematical induction.

**34.** Prove that $2^n > n^2$ for $n \geq 5$. Show that the formula is true for $n = 5$ and then use step 2 of mathematical induction.

*In Exercises 35–36, find $S_1$ through $S_5$ and then use the pattern to make a conjecture about $S_n$. Prove the conjectured formula for $S_n$ by mathematical induction.*

**35.** $S_n$: $\frac{1}{4} + \frac{1}{12} + \frac{1}{24} + \cdots + \frac{1}{2n(n+1)}$

**36.** $S_n$: $\left(1 - \frac{1}{2}\right)\left(1 - \frac{1}{3}\right)\left(1 - \frac{1}{4}\right)\cdots\left(1 - \frac{1}{n+1}\right)$

## Group Exercise

**37.** Fermat's most notorious theorem baffled the greatest minds for more than three centuries. In 1994, after ten years of work, Princeton University's Andrew Wiles proved Fermat's Last Theorem. *People* magazine put him on its list of "the 25 most intriguing people of the year," the Gap asked him to model jeans, and Barbara Walters chased him for an interview. "Who's Barbara Walters?" asked the bookish Wiles, who had somehow gone through life without a television.

Using the 1993 PBS documentary "Solving Fermat: Andrew Wiles" or information about Andrew Wiles on the Internet, research and present a group seminar on what Wiles did to prove Fermat's Last Theorem, problems along the way, and the role of mathematical induction in the proof.

# SECTION 11.5 The Binomial Theorem

## Objectives

1. Recognize patterns in binomial expansions.
2. Evaluate a binomial coefficient.
3. Expand a binomial raised to a power.
4. Find a particular term in a binomial expansion.

Galaxies are groupings of billions of stars bound together gravitationally. Some galaxies, such as the Centaurus galaxy shown here, are elliptical in shape.

Is mathematics discovered or invented? For example, planets revolve in elliptical orbits. Does that mean that the ellipse is out there, waiting for the mind to discover it? Or do people create the definition of an ellipse just as they compose a song? And is it possible for the same mathematics to be discovered/invented by independent researchers separated by time, place, and culture? This is precisely what occurred when mathematicians attempted to find efficient methods for raising binomials to higher and higher powers, such as

$$(x + 2)^3, (x + 2)^4, (x + 2)^5, (x + 2)^6,$$

and so on. In this section, we study higher powers of binomials and a method first discovered/invented by great minds in Eastern and Western culture working independently.

**1** Recognize patterns in binomial expansions.

## Patterns in Binomial Expansions

When we write out the *binomial expression* $(a + b)^n$, where $n$ is a positive integer, a number of patterns begin to appear.

$$(a+b)^1 = a + b$$
$$(a+b)^2 = a^2 + 2ab + b^2$$
$$(a+b)^3 = a^3 + 3a^2b + 3ab^2 + b^3$$
$$(a+b)^4 = a^4 + 4a^3b + 6a^2b^2 + 4ab^3 + b^4$$
$$(a+b)^5 = a^5 + 5a^4b + 10a^3b^2 + 10a^2b^3 + 5ab^4 + b^5$$

## Discovery

Each expanded form of the binomial expression is a polynomial. Study the five polynomials and answer the following questions.

1. For each polynomial, describe the pattern for the exponents on $a$. What is the largest exponent on $a$? What happens to the exponent on $a$ from term to term?
2. Describe the pattern for the exponents on $b$. What is the exponent on $b$ in the first term? What is the exponent on $b$ in the second term? What happens to the exponent on $b$ from term to term?
3. Find the sum of the exponents on the variables in each term for the polynomials in the five rows. Describe the pattern.
4. How many terms are there in the polynomials on the right in relation to the power of the binomial?

How many of the following patterns were you able to discover?

1. The first term is $a^n$. The exponent on $a$ decreases by 1 in each successive term.
2. The exponents on $b$ increase by 1 in each successive term. In the first term, the exponent on $b$ is 0. (Because $b^0 = 1$, $b$ is not shown in the first term.) The last term is $b^n$.
3. The sum of the exponents on the variables in any term is equal to $n$, the exponent on $(a+b)^n$.
4. There is one more term in the polynomial expansion than there is in the power of the binomial, $n$. There are $n + 1$ terms in the expanded form of $(a+b)^n$.

Using these observations, the variable parts of the expansion of $(a+b)^6$ are

$$a^6,\quad a^5b,\quad a^4b^2,\quad a^3b^3,\quad a^2b^4,\quad ab^5,\quad b^6.$$

The first term is $a^6$, with the exponent on $a$ decreasing by 1 in each successive term. The exponents on $b$ increase from 0 to 6, with the last term being $b^6$. The sum of the exponents in each term is equal to 6.

We can generalize from these observations to obtain the variable parts of the expansion of $(a+b)^n$. They are

$$a^n,\ a^{n-1}b,\ a^{n-2}b^2, a^{n-3}b^3, \ldots,\ ab^{n-1},\ b^n.$$

Exponents on $a$ are decreasing by 1.
Exponents on $b$ are increasing by 1.

Sum of exponents: $n - 1 + 1 = n$

Sum of exponents: $n - 3 + 3 = n$

Sum of exponents: $1 + n - 1 = n$

Let's now establish a pattern for the coefficients of the terms in the binomial expansion. Notice that each row in the figure on page 948 begins and ends with 1. Any other number in the row can be obtained by adding the two numbers immediately above it.

**Study Tip**

We have not shown the number in the top row of Pascal's triangle on the right. The top row is *row zero* because it corresponds to $(a + b)^0 = 1$. With row zero, the triangle appears as

$$\begin{array}{ccccccccc} & & & & 1 & & & & \\ & & & 1 & & 1 & & & \\ & & 1 & & 2 & & 1 & & \\ & 1 & & 3 & & 3 & & 1 & \\ 1 & & 4 & & 6 & & 4 & & 1 \end{array}$$

etc.

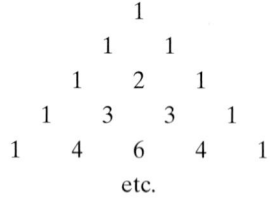

| | |
|---|---|
| Coefficients for $(a + b)^1$. | 1 1 |
| Coefficients for $(a + b)^2$. | 1 2 1 |
| Coefficients for $(a + b)^3$. | 1 3 3 1 |
| Coefficients for $(a + b)^4$. | 1 4 6 4 1 |
| Coefficients for $(a + b)^5$. | 1 5 10 10 5 1 |

The following triangular array of coefficients is called **Pascal's triangle.** If we continue with the sixth row, the first and last numbers are 1. Each of the other numbers is obtained by finding the sum of the two closest numbers above it in the fifth row.

$$\begin{array}{ccccccccccccc} & & & & & 1 & & 1 & & & & & \\ & & & & 1 & & 2 & & 1 & & & & \\ & & & 1 & & 3 & & 3 & & 1 & & & \\ & & 1 & & 4 & & 6 & & 4 & & 1 & & \\ & 1 & & 5 & & 10 & & 10 & & 5 & & 1 & \\ & & 1+5 & & 5+10 & & 10+10 & & 10+5 & & 5+1 & & \\ 1 & & 6 & & 15 & & 20 & & 15 & & 6 & & 1 \end{array}$$

We can use the numbers in the sixth row and the variable parts we found to write the expansion for $(a + b)^6$. It is

$$(a + b)^6 = a^6 + 6a^5b + 15a^4b^2 + 20a^3b^3 + 15a^2b^4 + 6ab^5 + b^6.$$

**2** Evaluate a binomial coefficient.

## Binomial Coefficients

Pascal's triangle becomes cumbersome when a binomial contains a relatively large power. Therefore, the coefficients in a binomial expansion are instead given in terms of factorials. The coefficients are written in a special notation, which we define next.

**Definition of a Binomial Coefficient $\binom{n}{r}$**

For nonnegative integers $n$ and $r$, with $n \geq r$, the expression $\binom{n}{r}$ (read "$n$ above $r$") is called a **binomial coefficient** and is defined by

$$\binom{n}{r} = \frac{n!}{r!(n - r)!}.$$

The symbol ${}_nC_r$ is often used in place of $\binom{n}{r}$ to denote binomial coefficients.

**Technology**

Graphing utilities can compute binomial coefficients. For example, to find $\binom{6}{2}$, many utilities require the sequence

6 [nCr] 2 [ENTER].

The graphing utility will display 15. Consult your manual and verify the other evaluations in Example 1.

## EXAMPLE 1 Evaluating Binomial Coefficients

Evaluate: **a.** $\binom{6}{2}$ **b.** $\binom{3}{0}$ **c.** $\binom{9}{3}$ **d.** $\binom{4}{4}$.

**Solution** In each case, we apply the definition of the binomial coefficient.

**a.** $\binom{6}{2} = \frac{6!}{2!(6-2)!} = \frac{6!}{2!\,4!} = \frac{6 \cdot 5 \cdot \cancel{4!}}{2 \cdot 1 \cdot \cancel{4!}} = 15$

**b.** $\binom{3}{0} = \dfrac{3!}{0!(3-0)!} = \dfrac{\cancel{3!}}{0!\cancel{3!}} = \dfrac{1}{1} = 1$

Remember that 0! = 1.

**c.** $\binom{9}{3} = \dfrac{9!}{3!(9-3)!} = \dfrac{9!}{3!\,6!} = \dfrac{9 \cdot 8 \cdot 7 \cdot \cancel{6!}}{3 \cdot 2 \cdot 1 \cdot \cancel{6!}} = 84$

**d.** $\binom{4}{4} = \dfrac{4!}{4!(4-4)!} = \dfrac{\cancel{4!}}{\cancel{4!}0!} = \dfrac{1}{1} = 1$

**Check Point 1** Evaluate: **a.** $\binom{6}{3}$ **b.** $\binom{6}{0}$ **c.** $\binom{8}{2}$ **d.** $\binom{3}{3}$.

**3** Expand a binomial raised to a power.

## The Binomial Theorem

If we use binomial coefficients and the pattern for the variable part of each term, a formula called the **Binomial Theorem** can be written for any positive integral power of a binomial.

### A Formula for Expanding Binomials: The Binomial Theorem

For any positive integer $n$,

$$(a+b)^n = \binom{n}{0}a^n + \binom{n}{1}a^{n-1}b + \binom{n}{2}a^{n-2}b^2 + \binom{n}{3}a^{n-3}b^3 + \cdots + \binom{n}{n}b^n.$$

### The Universality of Mathematics

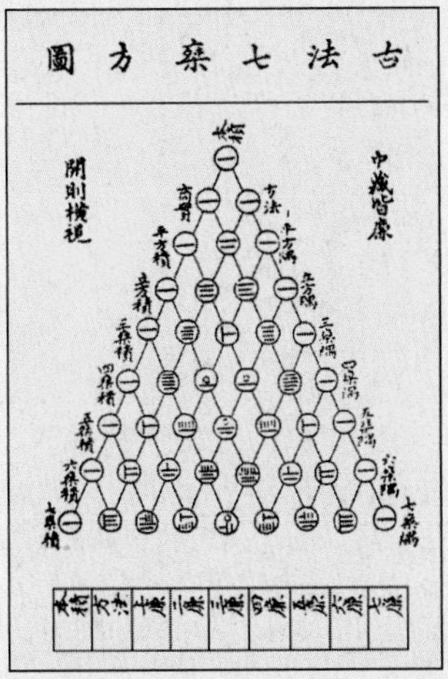

"Pascal's" triangle, credited to French mathematician Blaise Pascal (1623–1662), appeared in a Chinese document printed in 1303. The Binomial Theorem was known in Eastern cultures prior to its discovery in Europe. The same mathematics is often discovered/invented by independent researchers separated by time, place, and culture.

## EXAMPLE 2 Using the Binomial Theorem

Expand: $(x+2)^4$.

**Solution** We use the Binomial Theorem

$$(a+b)^n = \binom{n}{0}a^n + \binom{n}{1}a^{n-1}b + \binom{n}{2}a^{n-2}b^2 + \binom{n}{3}a^{n-3}b^3 + \cdots + \binom{n}{n}b^n$$

to expand $(x+2)^4$. In $(x+2)^4$, $a = x$, $b = 2$, and $n = 4$.

$$(x+2)^4 = \binom{4}{0}x^4 + \binom{4}{1}x^3 \cdot 2 + \binom{4}{2}x^2 \cdot 2^2 + \binom{4}{3}x \cdot 2^3 + \binom{4}{4}2^4$$

These binomial coefficients are evaluated using $\binom{n}{r} = \dfrac{n!}{r!(n-r)!}$.

$$= \frac{4!}{0!\,4!}x^4 + \frac{4!}{1!\,3!}x^3 \cdot 2 + \frac{4!}{2!\,2!}x^2 \cdot 4 + \frac{4!}{3!\,1!}x \cdot 8 + \frac{4!}{4!\,0!} \cdot 16$$

$\dfrac{4!}{2!\,2!} = \dfrac{4 \cdot 3 \cdot \cancel{2!}}{\cancel{2!} \cdot 2 \cdot 1} = \dfrac{12}{2} = 6$

Take a few minutes to verify the other factorial evaluations.

$$= 1 \cdot x^4 + 4x^3 \cdot 2 + 6x^2 \cdot 4 + 4x \cdot 8 + 1 \cdot 16$$
$$= x^4 + 8x^3 + 24x^2 + 32x + 16$$

**Check Point 2** Expand: $(x+1)^4$.

## EXAMPLE 3 Using the Binomial Theorem

Expand: $(2x-y)^5$.

**Solution** Because the Binomial Theorem involves the addition of two terms raised to a power, we rewrite $(2x-y)^5$ as $[2x+(-y)]^5$. We use the Binomial Theorem

$$(a+b)^n = \binom{n}{0}a^n + \binom{n}{1}a^{n-1}b + \binom{n}{2}a^{n-2}b^2 + \binom{n}{3}a^{n-3}b^3 + \cdots + \binom{n}{n}b^n$$

to expand $[2x+(-y)]^5$. In $[2x+(-y)]^5$, $a=2x$, $b=-y$, and $n=5$.

$$(2x-y)^5 = [2x+(-y)]^5$$

$$= \binom{5}{0}(2x)^5 + \binom{5}{1}(2x)^4(-y) + \binom{5}{2}(2x)^3(-y)^2 + \binom{5}{3}(2x)^2(-y)^3 + \binom{5}{4}(2x)(-y)^4 + \binom{5}{5}(-y)^5$$

Evaluate binomial coefficients using $\binom{n}{r} = \frac{n!}{r!(n-r)!}$.

$$= \frac{5!}{0!\,5!}(2x)^5 + \frac{5!}{1!\,4!}(2x)^4(-y) + \frac{5!}{2!\,3!}(2x)^3(-y)^2 + \frac{5!}{3!\,2!}(2x)^2(-y)^3 + \frac{5!}{4!\,1!}(2x)(-y)^4 + \frac{5!}{5!\,0!}(-y)^5$$

$\frac{5!}{2!\,3!} = \frac{5\cdot4\cdot3!}{2\cdot1\cdot3!} = 10$
Take a few minutes to verify the other factorial evaluations.

$$= 1(2x)^5 + 5(2x)^4(-y) + 10(2x)^3(-y)^2 + 10(2x)^2(-y)^3 + 5(2x)(-y)^4 + 1(-y)^5$$

Raise both factors in these parentheses to the indicated powers.

$$= 1(32x^5) + 5(16x^4)(-y) + 10(8x^3)(-y)^2 + 10(4x^2)(-y)^3 + 5(2x)(-y)^4 + 1(-y)^5$$

Now raise $-y$ to the indicated powers.

$$= 1(32x^5) + 5(16x^4)(-y) + 10(8x^3)y^2 + 10(4x^2)(-y^3) + 5(2x)y^4 + 1(-y^5)$$

Multiplying factors in each of the six terms gives us the desired expansion:

$$(2x-y)^5 = 32x^5 - 80x^4y + 80x^3y^2 - 40x^2y^3 + 10xy^4 - y^5.$$

**Check Point 3** Expand: $(x-2y)^5$.

**4** Find a particular term in a binomial expansion.

## Finding a Particular Term in a Binomial Expansion

The Binomial Theorem can be used to write any single term of a binomial expansion.

**Finding a Particular Term in a Binomial Expansion**

The $r$th term of the expansion of $(a + b)^n$ is

$$\binom{n}{r-1}a^{n-r+1}b^{r-1}.$$

### EXAMPLE 4 Finding a Single Term of a Binomial Expansion

Find the fourth term in the expansion of $(3x + 2y)^7$.

**Solution** We will use the formula for the $r$th term of the expansion of $(a + b)^n$,

$$\binom{n}{r-1}a^{n-r+1}b^{r-1}$$

to find the fourth term of $(3x + 2y)^7$. For the fourth term of $(3x + 2y)^7$, $n = 7$, $r = 4$, $a = 3x$ and $b = 2y$. Thus, the fourth term is

$$\binom{7}{4-1}(3x)^{7-4+1}(2y)^{4-1} = \binom{7}{3}(3x)^4(2y)^3 = \frac{7!}{3!(7-3)!}(3x)^4(2y)^3$$

We use $\binom{n}{r} = \frac{n!}{r!(n-r)!}$ to evaluate $\binom{7}{3}$.

Now we need to evaluate the factorial expression and raise $3x$ and $2y$ to the indicated powers. We obtain

$$\frac{7!}{3!\,4!}(81x^4)(8y^3) = \frac{7 \cdot 6 \cdot 5 \cdot \cancel{4!}}{3 \cdot 2 \cdot 1 \cdot \cancel{4!}}(81x^4)(8y^3) = 35(81x^4)(8y^3) = 22{,}680x^4y^3.$$

The fourth term of $(3x + 2y)^7$ is $22{,}680x^4y^3$.

**Check Point 4** Find the fifth term in the expansion of $(2x + y)^9$.

## EXERCISE SET 11.5

### Practice Exercises

*In Exercises 1–8, evaluate the given binomial coefficient.*

**1.** $\binom{8}{3}$

**2.** $\binom{7}{2}$

**3.** $\binom{12}{1}$

**4.** $\binom{11}{1}$

**5.** $\binom{6}{6}$

**6.** $\binom{15}{2}$

**7.** $\binom{100}{2}$

**8.** $\binom{100}{98}$

*In Exercises 9–30, use the Binomial Theorem to expand each binomial and express the result in simplified form.*

**9.** $(x + 2)^3$

**10.** $(x + 4)^3$

**11.** $(3x + y)^3$

**12.** $(x + 3y)^3$

**13.** $(5x - 1)^3$

**14.** $(4x - 1)^3$

**15.** $(2x + 1)^4$

**16.** $(3x + 1)^4$

**17.** $(x^2 + 2y)^4$

**18.** $(x^2 + y)^4$

**19.** $(y - 3)^4$

**20.** $(y - 4)^4$

**21.** $(2x^3 - 1)^4$

**22.** $(2x^5 - 1)^4$

**23.** $(c + 2)^5$

**24.** $(c + 3)^5$

**25.** $(x - 1)^5$

**26.** $(x - 2)^5$

**27.** $(x - 2y)^5$

**28.** $(x - 3y)^5$

**29.** $(2a + b)^6$

**30.** $(a + 2b)^6$

*In Exercises 31–38, write the first three terms in each binomial expansion, expressing the result in simplified form.*

**31.** $(x + 2)^8$

**32.** $(x + 3)^8$

**33.** $(x - 2y)^{10}$

**34.** $(x - 2y)^9$

**35.** $(x^2 + 1)^{16}$

**36.** $(x^2 + 1)^{17}$

**37.** $(y^3 - 1)^{20}$

**38.** $(y^3 - 1)^{21}$

*In Exercises 39–46, find the term indicated in each expansion.*

**39.** $(2x + y)^6$; third term

**40.** $(x + 2y)^6$; third term

**41.** $(x - 1)^9$; fifth term

**42.** $(x - 1)^{10}$; fifth term

**43.** $(x^2 + y^3)^8$; sixth term

**44.** $(x^3 + y^2)^8$; sixth term

**45.** $(x - \frac{1}{2})^9$; fourth term

**46.** $(x + \frac{1}{2})^8$; fourth term

## Application Exercises

**47.** The percentage of people taking the SAT whose intended college major is engineering, $f(t)$, can be modeled by

$$f(t) = 0.002t^3 - 0.9t^2 + 1.27t + 6.76, \quad 0 \le t \le 20,$$

where $t = 0$ represents 1975. How can we adjust this model so that $t = 0$ corresponds to 1985 rather than 1975? We shift the graph of $f$ ten units to the left. We obtain $g(t) = f(t + 10)$. Use the Binomial Theorem to express $g(t)$ in descending powers of $t$.

**48.** The personal income per capita in the United States, $f(t)$, in constant 1992 dollars, can be modeled by

$$f(t) = 3.75t^3 - 115.23t^2 + 1229.81t + 16{,}025.65, \quad 0 \le t \le 15,$$

where $t = 0$ represents 1979. How can we adjust this model so that $t = 0$ corresponds to 1989 rather than 1979? We shift the graph of $f$ ten units to the left. We obtain $g(t) = f(t + 10)$. Use the Binomial Theorem to express $g(t)$ in descending powers of $t$.

## Writing in Mathematics

**49.** Describe the pattern on the exponents on $a$ in the expansion of $(a + b)^n$.

**50.** Describe the pattern on the exponents on $b$ in the expansion of $(a + b)^n$.

**51.** What is true about the sum of the exponents on $a$ and $b$ in any term in the expansion of $(a + b)^n$?

**52.** How do you determine how many terms there are in a binomial expansion?

**53.** What is Pascal's triangle? How do you find the numbers in any row of the triangle?

**54.** Explain how to evaluate $\binom{n}{r}$. Provide an example with your explanation.

**55.** Explain how to use the Binomial Theorem to expand a binomial. Provide an example with your explanation.

**56.** Explain how to find a particular term in a binomial expansion without having to write out the entire expansion.

**57.** Are there situations in which it is easier to use Pascal's triangle than binomial coefficients? Describe these situations.

**58.** Describe how you would use mathematical induction to prove

$$(a + b)^n = \binom{n}{0}a^n + \binom{n}{1}a^{n-1}b + \binom{n}{2}a^{n-2}b^2 + \cdots + \binom{n}{n-1}ab^{n-1} + \binom{n}{n}b^n.$$

What happens when $n = 1$? Write the statement that we assume true. Write the statement that we must prove. What must be done to the left side of the assumed statement to make it look like the left side of the statement that must be proved? (More detail on the actual proof is found in Exercise 71.)

## Technology Exercises

**59.** Use the nCr key on a graphing utility to verify your answers in Exercises 1–8.

*In Exercises 60–61, graph each of the functions in the same viewing rectangle. Describe how the graphs illustrate the Binomial Theorem.*

**60.** $f_1(x) = (x + 2)^3$
$f_2(x) = x^3$
$f_3(x) = x^3 + 6x^2$
$f_4(x) = x^3 + 6x^2 + 12x$
$f_5(x) = x^3 + 6x^2 + 12x + 8$
Use a $[-10, 10, 1]$ by $[-30, 30, 10]$ viewing rectangle.

**61.** $f_1(x) = (x + 1)^4$
$f_2(x) = x^4$
$f_3(x) = x^4 + 4x^3$
$f_4(x) = x^4 + 4x^3 + 6x^2$
$f_5(x) = x^4 + 4x^3 + 6x^2 + 4x$
$f_6(x) = x^4 + 4x^3 + 6x^2 + 4x + 1$
Use a $[-5, 5, 1]$ by $[-30, 30, 10]$ viewing rectangle.

*In Exercises 62–64, use the Binomial Theorem to find a polynomial expansion for each function. Then use a graphing utility and an approach similar to the one in Exercises 60 and 61 to verify the expansion.*

**62.** $f_1(x) = (x - 1)^3$

**63.** $f_1(x) = (x - 2)^4$

**64.** $f_1(x) = (x + 2)^6$

**65.** Graphing utilities capable of symbolic manipulation, such as the TI-92, will expand binomials. On the TI-92, to expand $(3a - 5b)^{12}$, input the following:

EXPAND ((3a − 5b) ^ 12) ENTER.

Use a graphing utility with this capability to verify any five of the expansions you performed by hand in Exercises 9–30.

## Critical Thinking Exercises

**66.** Which one of the following is true?

**a.** The binomial expansion for $(a + b)^n$ contains $n$ terms.

**b.** The Binomial Theorem can be written in condensed form as $(a + b)^n = \sum_{r=0}^{n} \binom{n}{r} a^{n-r}b^r$.

**c.** The sum of the binomial coefficients in $(a + b)^n$ cannot be $2^n$.

**d.** There are no values of $a$ and $b$ such that $(a + b)^4 = a^4 + b^4$.

**67.** Use the Binomial Theorem to expand and then simplify the result: $(x^2 + x + 1)^3$. [*Hint*: Write $x^2 + x + 1$ as $x^2 + (x + 1)$.]

**68.** Find the term in the expansion of $(x^2 + y^2)^5$ containing $x^4$ as a factor.

**69.** Prove that

$$\binom{n}{r} = \binom{n}{n-r}.$$

**70.** Show that

$$\binom{n}{r} + \binom{n}{r+1} = \binom{n+1}{r+1}.$$

*Hints*:

$$(n - r)! = (n - r)(n - r - 1)!$$

$$(r + 1)! = (r + 1)r!$$

**71.** Follow the outline below to use mathematical induction to prove that

$$(a + b)^n = \binom{n}{0}a^n + \binom{n}{1}a^{n-1}b + \binom{n}{2}a^{n-2}b^2 + \cdots + \binom{n}{n-1}ab^{n-1} + \binom{n}{n}b^n.$$

**a.** Verify the formula for $n = 1$.

**b.** Replace $n$ with $k$ and write the statement that is assumed true. Replace $n$ with $k + 1$ and write the statement that must be proved.

**c.** Multiply both sides of the statement assumed to be true by $a + b$. Add exponents on the left. On the right, distribute $a$ and $b$, respectively.

**d.** Collect like terms on the right. At this point, you should have

$$(a + b)^{k+1} = \binom{k}{0}a^{k+1} + \left[\binom{k}{0} + \binom{k}{1}\right]a^k b + \left[\binom{k}{1} + \binom{k}{2}\right]a^{k-1}b^2 + \left[\binom{k}{2} + \binom{k}{3}\right]a^{k-2}b^3 + \cdots + \left[\binom{k}{k-1} + \binom{k}{k}\right]ab^k + \binom{k}{k}b^{k+1}.$$

**e.** Use the result of Exercise 70 to add the binomial sums in brackets. For example, because $\binom{n}{r} + \binom{n}{r+1} = \binom{n+1}{r+1}$ then $\binom{k}{0} + \binom{k}{1} = \binom{k+1}{1}$ and $\binom{k}{1} + \binom{k}{2} = \binom{k+1}{2}$.

**f.** Because $\binom{k}{0} = \binom{k+1}{0}$ (why?) and $\binom{k}{k} = \binom{k+1}{k+1}$ (why?), substitute these results and the results from part (e) into the equation in part (d). This should give the statement that we were required to prove in the second step of the mathematical induction process.

## SECTION 11.6 Counting Principles, Permutations, and Combinations

### Objectives

1. Use the Fundamental Counting Principle.
2. Use the permutations formula.
3. Distinguish between permutation problems and combination problems.
4. Use the combinations formula.

Have you ever imagined what your life would be like if you won the lottery? What changes would you make? Before you fantasize about becoming a person of leisure with a staff of obedient elves, think about this: The probability of winning top prize in the lottery is about the same as the probability of being struck by lightning. There are millions of possible number combinations in lottery games, and only one way of winning the grand prize. Determining the probability of winning involves calculating the chance of getting the winning combination from all possible outcomes. In this section, we begin preparing for the surprising world of probability by looking at methods for counting possible outcomes.

**1** Use the Fundamental Counting Principle.

### The Fundamental Counting Principle

It's early morning, you're groggy, and you have to select something to wear for your 8 A.M. class. (What *were* you thinking of when you signed up for a class at that hour?!) Fortunately, your "lecture wardrobe" is rather limited—just two pairs of jeans to choose from (one blue, one black), three T-shirts to choose from (one beige, one yellow, and one blue), and two pairs of sneakers to select from (one black, one red). Your possible outfits are shown in Figure 11.5.

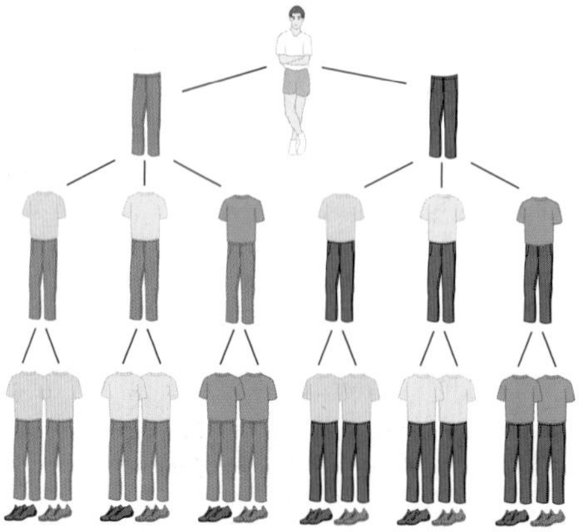

**Figure 11.5** Selecting a wardrobe

The number of possible ways of playing the first four moves on each side in a game of chess is 318,979,564,000.

The **tree diagram**, so named because of its branches, shows that you can form 12 outfits from your two pairs of jeans, three T-shirts, and two pairs of sneakers. Notice that the number of outfits can be obtained by multiplying the number of choices for jeans, 2, the number of choices for T-shirts, 3, and the number of choices for sneakers, 2:

$$2 \cdot 3 \cdot 2 = 12.$$

We can generalize this idea to any two or more groups of items—not just jeans, T-shirts, and sneakers—with the **Fundamental Counting Principle**.

**The Fundamental Counting Principle**

The number of ways in which a series of successive things can occur is found by multiplying the number of ways in which each thing can occur.

For example, if you own 30 pairs of jeans, 20 T-shirts, and 12 pairs of sneakers, you have

$$30 \cdot 20 \cdot 12 = 7200$$

choices for your wardrobe!

## EXAMPLE 1 Options in Planning a Course Schedule

Next semester you are planning to take three courses—math, English, and humanities. Based on time blocks and highly recommended professors, there are 8 sections of math, 5 of English, and 4 of humanities that you find suitable. Assuming no scheduling conflicts, how many different three-course schedules are possible?

**Solution** This situation involves making choices with three groups of items.

| MATH | ENGLISH | HUMANITIES |
|---|---|---|
| 8 choices | 5 choices | 4 choices |

We use the Fundamental Counting Principle to find the number of three-course schedules. Multiply the number of choices for each of the three groups.

$$8 \cdot 5 \cdot 4 = 160$$

Thus, there are 160 different three-course schedules.

**Check Point 1** A pizza can be ordered with three choices of size (small, medium, or large), four choices of crust (thin, thick, crispy, or regular), and six choices of toppings (ground beef, sausage, pepperoni, bacon, mushrooms, or onions). How many different one-topping pizzas can be ordered?

## EXAMPLE 2 A Multiple-Choice Test

You are taking a multiple-choice test that has ten questions. Each of the questions has four choices, with one correct choice per question. If you select one of these options per question and leave nothing blank, in how many ways can you answer the questions?

**Solution** We use the Fundamental Counting Principle to determine the number of ways you can answer the test. Multiply the number of choices, 4, for each of the ten questions.

$$4 \cdot 4 \cdot 4 \cdot 4 \cdot 4 \cdot 4 \cdot 4 \cdot 4 \cdot 4 \cdot 4 = 4^{10} = 1{,}048{,}576$$

Thus, you can answer the questions in 1,048,576 different ways.

Are you surprised that there are over one million ways of answering a ten-question multiple-choice test? Of course, there is only one way to answer the test and receive a perfect score. The probability of guessing your way into a perfect score involves calculating the chance of getting a perfect score, just one way, from all 1,048,576 possible outcomes. In short, prepare for the test and do not rely on guessing!

**Check Point 2** You are taking a multiple-choice test that has six questions. Each of the questions has three choices, with one correct choice per question. If you select one of these options per question and leave nothing blank, in how many ways can you answer the questions?

### Permutations and Rubik's Cube

First developed in Hungary in the 1970s by Erno Rubik, a Rubik's cube contains $3 \times 3 \times 3 = 27$ small cubes. The square faces of the cubes are colored in six different colors. The cubes can be twisted horizontally or vertically. When first purchased, the cube is arranged so that each face shows a single color. To do the puzzle, you first turn columns and rows in a random way until all of the six faces are multicolored. To solve the puzzle, you must return the cube to its original state—that is, a single color on each of the six faces. With 43,252,003,274,489,856,000 arrangements, this is no easy task! If it takes one-half second for each of these arrangements, it would require over 681,000,000,000 years to move the cube into all possible arrangements.

## EXAMPLE 3 Telephone Numbers in the United States

Telephone numbers in the United States begin with three-digit area codes followed by seven-digit local telephone numbers. Area codes and local telephone numbers cannot begin with 0 or 1. How many different telephone numbers are possible?

**Solution** This situation involves making choices with ten groups of items.

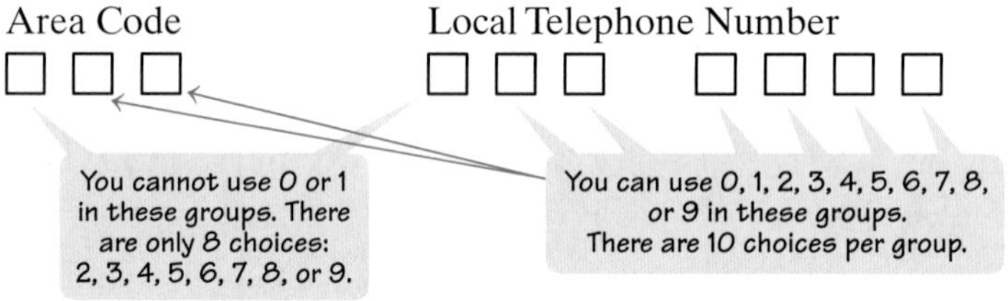


We use the Fundamental Counting Principle to determine the number of different telephone numbers that are possible. The total number of telephone numbers possible is

$$8 \cdot 10 \cdot 10 \cdot 8 \cdot 10 \cdot 10 \cdot 10 \cdot 10 \cdot 10 \cdot 10 = 6{,}400{,}000{,}000.$$

There are six billion four hundred million different telephone numbers that are possible.

**Check Point 3** License plates in a particular state display two letters followed by three numbers, such as AT-887 or BB-013. How many different license plates can be manufactured?

**2** Use the permutations formula.

## Permutations

You are the coach of a little league baseball team. There are 13 players on the team (and lots of parents hovering in the background, dreaming of stardom for their little "Mark McGwire"). You need to choose a batting order having 9 players. The order makes a difference, because, for instance, if bases are loaded and "Little Mark" is fourth or fifth at bat, his possible home run will drive in three additional runs. How many batting orders can you form?

You can choose any of 13 players for the first person at bat. Then you will have 12 players from which to choose the second batter, then 11 from which to choose the third batter, and so on. The situation can be shown as follows:

| Batter 1 | Batter 2 | Batter 3 | Batter 4 | Batter 5 | Batter 6 | Batter 7 | Batter 8 | Batter 9 |
|---|---|---|---|---|---|---|---|---|
| 13 choices | 12 choices | 11 choices | 10 choices | 9 choices | 8 choices | 7 choices | 6 choices | 5 choices |

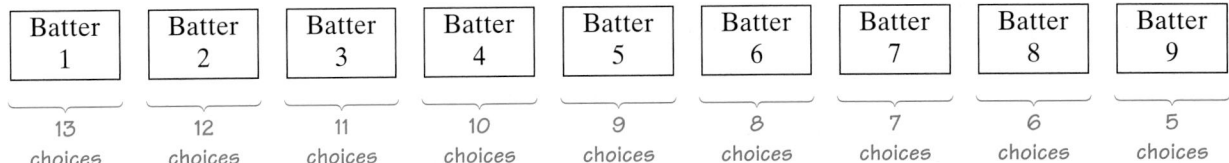

We use the Fundamental Counting Principle to find the number of batting orders. The total number of batting orders is

$$13 \cdot 12 \cdot 11 \cdot 10 \cdot 9 \cdot 8 \cdot 7 \cdot 6 \cdot 5 = 259{,}459{,}200.$$

Nearly 260 million batting orders are possible for your 13-player little league team. Each batting order is called a **permutation** of 13 players taken 9 at a time. The number of permutations of 13 players taken 9 at a time is 259,459,200. A permutation is an ordered arrangement of items that occurs when

- No item is used more than once. (Each of the 9 players in the batting order bats exactly once.)
- The order of arrangement makes a difference.

We can obtain a formula for finding the number of permutations by rewriting our computation:

$$13 \cdot 12 \cdot 11 \cdot 10 \cdot 9 \cdot 8 \cdot 7 \cdot 6 \cdot 5$$

$$= \frac{13 \cdot 12 \cdot 11 \cdot 10 \cdot 9 \cdot 8 \cdot 7 \cdot 6 \cdot 5 \cdot \boxed{4 \cdot 3 \cdot 2 \cdot 1}}{\boxed{4 \cdot 3 \cdot 2 \cdot 1}} = \frac{13!}{4!} = \frac{13!}{(13-9)!}.$$

Thus, the number of permutations of 13 things taken 9 at a time is $\frac{13!}{(13-9)!}$. The special notation ${}_{13}P_9$ is used to replace the phrase "the number of permutations of 13 things taken 9 at a time." Using this new notation, we can write

$${}_{13}P_9 = \frac{13!}{(13-9)!}.$$

The numerator of this expression is the number of items, 13 team members, expressed as a factorial: 13! The denominator is also a factorial. It is the factorial of the difference between the number of items, 13, and the number of items in each permutation, 9 batters: $(13-9)!$.

The notation ${}_nP_r$ means the **number of permutations of *n* things taken *r* at a time.** We can generalize from the situation in which 9 batters were taken from 13 players. By generalizing, we obtain the following formula for the number of permuations if *r* items are taken from *n* items.

**Permutations of *n* Things Taken *r* at a Time**

The number of possible permutations if *r* items are taken from *n* items is

$${}_nP_r = \frac{n!}{(n-r)!}.$$

Because all permutation problems are also Fundamental Counting problems, they can be solved using the formula for ${}_nP_r$, or using the Fundamental Counting Principle.

**Technology**

Graphing utilities have a key for calculating permuations, usually labeled $\boxed{{}_nP_r}$. For example, to find ${}_{20}P_3$, the keystrokes are:

20 $\boxed{{}_nP_r}$ 3 $\boxed{\text{ENTER}}$.

If you are using a scientific calculator, check your manual for the location of the key for calculating permutations and the required keystrokes.

### EXAMPLE 4 Using the Formula for Permutations

You and 19 of your friends have decided to form an Internet marketing consulting firm. The group needs to choose three officers—a CEO, an operating manager, and a treasurer. In how many ways can those offices be filled?

**Solution** Your group is choosing $r = 3$ officers from a group of $n = 20$ people (you and 19 friends). The order in which the officers are chosen matters because the CEO, the operating manager, and the treasurer each have different responsibilities. Thus, we are looking for the number of permutations of 20 things taken 3 at a time. We use the formula

$${}_nP_r = \frac{n!}{(n-r)!}$$

with $n = 20$ and $r = 3$.

$${}_{20}P_3 = \frac{20!}{(20-3)!} = \frac{20!}{17!} = \frac{20 \cdot 19 \cdot 18 \cdot 17!}{17!} = \frac{20 \cdot 19 \cdot 18 \cdot \cancel{17!}}{\cancel{17!}} = 20 \cdot 19 \cdot 18 = 6840$$

Thus, there are 6840 different ways of filling the three offices.

**Check Point 4** A corporation has seven members on its board of directors. In how many different ways can it elect a president, vice-president, secretary, and treasurer?

**How to Pass the Time for $2\frac{1}{2}$ Million Years**

If you were to arrange 15 different books on a shelf and it took you one minute for each permuation, the entire task would take 2,487,965 years.

*Source: Isaac Asimov's Book of Facts.*

### EXAMPLE 5 Using the Formula for Permutations

You need to arrange seven of your favorite books along a small shelf. How many different ways can you arrange the books, assuming that the order of the books makes a difference to you?

**Solution** Because you are using all seven of your books in every possible arrangement, you are arranging $r = 7$ books from a group of $n = 7$ books. Thus, we are looking for the number of permutations of 7 things taken 7 at a time. We use the formula

$${}_nP_r = \frac{n!}{(n-r)!}$$

with $n = 7$ and $r = 7$.

$${}_7P_7 = \frac{7!}{(7-7)!} = \frac{7!}{0!} = \frac{7!}{1} = 5040$$

Thus, you can arrange the books in 5040 ways. There are 5040 different possible permuations.

**Check Point 5** In how many ways can 6 books be lined up along a shelf?

**3** Distinguish between permutation problems and combination problems.

## Combinations

As the twentieth century drew to a close, *Time* magazine presented a series of special issues on the most influential people of the century. In their issue on heroes and icons (June 14, 1999), they discussed a number of people whose careers became more profitable after their tragic deaths, including Marilyn Monroe, James Dean, Jim Morrison, Kurt Cobain, and Selena.

Imagine that you ask your friends the following question: "Of these five people, which three would you select to be included in a documentary featuring the best of their work?" You are not asking your friends to rank their three favorite artists in any kind of order—they should merely select the three to be included in the documentary.

One friend answers, "Jim Morrison, Kurt Cobain, and Selena." Another responds, "Selena, Kurt Cobain, and Jim Morrison." These two people have the same artists in their group of selections, even if they are named in a different order. We are interested *in which artists are named, not the order in which they are named* for the documentary. Because the items are taken without regard to order, this is not a permutation problem. No ranking of any sort is involved.

Marilyn Monroe, actress (1927–1962)

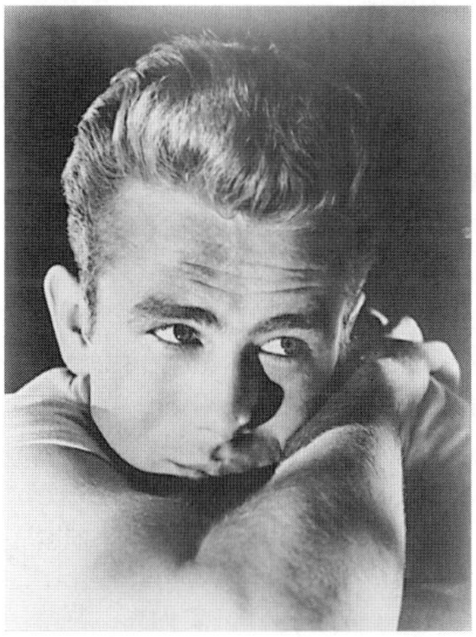

James Dean, actor (1931–1955)

Jim Morrison, musician and lead singer of The Doors (1943–1971)

Kurt Cobain, musician and front man for Nirvana (1967–1994)

Selena, musician of Tejano music (1971–1995)

Later on, you ask your roommate which three artists she would select for the documentary. She names Marilyn Monroe, James Dean, and Selena. Her selection is different from those of your two other friends because different entertainers are cited.

Mathematicians describe the group of artists given by your roommate as a *combination*. A **combination** of items occurs when

- The items are selected from the same group (the five stars who died young and tragically).
- No item is used more than once. (You may adore Selena, but your three selections cannot be Selena, Selena, and Selena).
- The order of items makes no difference. (Morrison, Cobain, Selena is the same group in the documentary as Selena, Cobain, Morrison.)

Do you see the difference between a permutation and a combination? A permutation is an ordered arrangement of a given group of items. A combination is a group of items taken without regard to their order. *Permutation* problems involve situations in which *order matters. Combination* problems involve situations in which the *order* of items *makes no difference.*

## EXAMPLE 6 Distinguishing between Permutations and Combinations

For each of the following problems, explain whether the problem is one involving permutations or combinations. (It is not necessary to solve the problem.)

**a.** Six candidates are running for president, chief technology officer, and director of marketing of an Internet company. The candidate with the greatest number of votes becomes the president, the second biggest vote-getter becomes chief technology officer, and the candidate who gets the third largest number of votes will be director of marketing. How many different outcomes are possible for these three positions?

**b.** From the six candidates who desire to hold office in an Internet company, a three-person committee is formed to study ways of finding new investors. How many different committees could be formed?

### Solution

**a.** Voters are choosing three officers from six candidates. The order in which the officers are chosen makes a difference because each of the offices (president, chief technology officer, and director of marketing) is different. Order matters. This is a problem involving permutations. (How many permutations are possible if three candidates are elected from six candidates?)

**b.** A three-person committee is to be formed from the six candidates. The order in which the three people are selected does not matter because they are not filling different roles on the committee. Because order makes no difference, this is a problem involving combinations. (How many different combinations of three people can be chosen from a group of six people?)

**Check Point 6**

For each of the following problems, explain if the problem is one involving permutations or combinations. (It is not necessary to solve the problem.)

**a.** How many ways can you select 6 free videos from a list of 200 videos?

**b.** In a race in which there are 50 runners and no ties, in how many ways can the first three finishers come in?

**4** Use the combinations formula.

The notation ${}_nC_r$ means the **number of combinations of *n* things taken *r* at a time**. In general, there are $r!$ times as many permutations of $n$ things taken $r$ at a time as there are combinations of $n$ things taken $r$ at a time. Thus, we find the number of combinations of $n$ things taken $r$ at a time by dividing the number of permutations of $n$ things taken $r$ at a time by $r!$.

$$ {}_nC_r = \frac{{}_nP_r}{r!} = \frac{\frac{n!}{(n-r)!}}{r!} = \frac{n!}{(n-r)!\,r!} $$

**Combinations of $n$ Things Taken $r$ at a Time**

The number of possible combinations if $r$ items are taken from $n$ items is

$$ {}_nC_r = \frac{n!}{(n-r)!\,r!}. $$

Notice that the formula for ${}_nC_r$ is the same as the formula for the binomial coefficient $\binom{n}{r}$.

We cannot find the number of combinations if $r$ items are taken from $n$ items using the Fundamental Counting Principle. We must use the formula shown in the box to do so.

## EXAMPLE 7 Using the Formula for Combinations

A three-person committee is needed to study ways of improving public transportation. How many committees could be formed from the eight people on the board of supervisors?

**Solution** The order in which the three people are selected does not matter. This is a problem of selecting $r = 3$ people from a group of $n = 8$ people. We are looking for the number of combinations of eight things taken three at a time. We use the formula

$$ {}_nC_r = \frac{n!}{(n-r)!\,r!} $$

with $n = 8$ and $r = 3$.

$$ {}_8C_3 = \frac{8!}{(8-3)!\,3!} = \frac{8!}{5!\,3!} = \frac{8\cdot 7\cdot 6\cdot 5!}{5!\cdot 3\cdot 2\cdot 1} = \frac{8\cdot 7\cdot 6\cdot \cancel{5!}}{\cancel{5!}\cdot 3\cdot 2\cdot 1} = 56 $$

Thus, 56 committees of three people each can be formed from the eight people on the board of supervisors.

**Check Point 7** From a group of 10 physicians, in how many ways can four people be selected to attend a conference on acupuncture?

## EXAMPLE 8 Using the Formula for Combinations

In poker, a person is dealt 5 cards from a standard 52-card deck. The order in which you are dealt the 5 cards does not matter. How many different 5-card poker hands are possible?

**Solution** Because the order in which the 5 cards are dealt does not matter, this is a problem involving combinations. We are looking for the number of combinations of $n = 52$ cards drawn $r = 5$ at a time. We use the formula

$$ {}_nC_r = \frac{n!}{(n-r)!\,r!} $$

with $n = 52$ and $r = 5$.

$$_{52}C_5 = \frac{52!}{(52-5)!\,5!} = \frac{52!}{47!\,5!} = \frac{52 \cdot 51 \cdot 50 \cdot 49 \cdot 48 \cdot \cancel{47!}}{\cancel{47!} \cdot 5 \cdot 4 \cdot 3 \cdot 2 \cdot 1} = 2{,}598{,}960$$

Thus, there are 2,598,960 different 5-card poker hands possible. It surprises many people that more than 2.5 million 5-card hands can be dealt from a mere 52 cards.

**Figure 11.6** A royal flush

If you are a card player, it does not get any better than to be dealt the 5-card poker hand shown in Figure 11.6. This hand is called a *royal flush*. It consists of an ace, king, queen, jack, and 10, all of the same suit: all hearts, all diamonds, all clubs, or all spades. The probability of being dealt a royal flush involves calculating the number of ways of being dealt such a hand: just 4 of all 2,598,960 possible hands. In the next section, we move from counting possibilities to computing probabilities.

**Check Point 8** How many different 4-card hands can be dealt from a deck that has 16 different cards?

## EXERCISE SET 11.6

### Practice Exercises

*In Exercises 1–8, use the formula for $_nP_r$ to evaluate each expression.*

**1.** $_9P_4$ **2.** $_7P_3$
**3.** $_8P_5$ **4.** $_{10}P_4$
**5.** $_6P_6$ **6.** $_9P_9$
**7.** $_8P_0$ **8.** $_6P_0$

*In Exercises 9–16, use the formula for $_nC_r$ to evaluate each expression.*

**9.** $_9C_5$ **10.** $_{10}C_6$
**11.** $_{11}C_4$ **12.** $_{12}C_5$
**13.** $_7C_7$ **14.** $_4C_4$
**15.** $_5C_0$ **16.** $_6C_0$

*In Exercises 17–20, does the problem involve permutations or combinations? Explain your answer. (It is not necessary to solve the problem.)*

**17.** A medical researcher needs 6 people to test the effectiveness of an experimental drug. If 13 people have volunteered for the test, in how many ways can 6 people be selected?

**18.** Fifty people purchase raffle tickets. Three winning tickets are selected at random. If first prize is \$1000, second prize is \$500, and third prize is \$100, in how many different ways can the prizes be awarded?

**19.** How many different four-letter passwords can be formed from the letters A, B, C, D, E, F, and G if no repetition of letters is allowed?

**20.** Fifty people purchase raffle tickets. Three winning tickets are selected at random. If each prize is \$500, in how many different ways can the prizes be awarded?

### Application Exercises

*Use the Fundamental Counting Principle to solve Exercises 21–32.*

**21.** The model of the car you are thinking of buying is available in nine different colors and three different styles (hatchback, sedan, or station wagon). In how many ways can you order the car?

**22.** A popular brand of pen is available in three colors (red, green, or blue) and four writing tips (bold, medium, fine, or micro). How many different choices of pens do you have with this brand?

**23.** An ice cream store sells two drinks (sodas or milk shakes), in four sizes (small, medium, large, or jumbo), and five flavors (vanilla, strawberry, chocolate, coffee, or pistachio). In how many ways can a customer order a drink?

**24.** A restaurant offers the following lunch menu.

| Main Course | Vegetables | Beverages | Desserts |
|---|---|---|---|
| Ham | Potatoes | Coffee | Cake |
| Chicken | Peas | Tea | Pie |
| Fish | Green beans | Milk | Ice cream |
| Beef | | Soda | |

If one item is selected from each of the four groups, in how many ways can a meal be ordered? Describe two such orders.

**25.** You are taking a multiple-choice test that has five questions. Each of the questions has three choices, with one correct choice per question. If you select one of these options per question and leave nothing blank, in how many ways can you answer the questions?

**26.** You are taking a multiple-choice test that has eight questions. Each of the questions has three choices, with one correct choice per question. If you select one of these options per question and leave nothing blank, in how many ways can you answer the questions?

**27.** In the original plan for area codes in 1945, the first digit could be any number from 2 through 9, the second digit was either 0 or 1, and the third digit could be any number except 0. With this plan, how many different area codes were possible?

**28.** How many different four-letter radio station call letters can be formed if the first letter must be W or K?

**29.** Six performers are to present their comedy acts on a weekend evening at a comedy club. One of the performers insists on being the last stand-up comic of the evening. If this performer's request is granted, how many different ways are there to schedule the appearances?

**30.** Five singers are to perform at a night club. One of the singers insists on being the last performer of the evening. If this singer's request is granted, how many different ways are there to schedule the appearances?

**31.** In the *Cambridge Encyclopedia of Language* (Cambridge University Press, 1987), author David Crystal presents five sentences that make a reasonable paragraph regardless of their order. The sentences are:

Mark had told him about the foxes.
John looked out the window.
Could it be a fox?
However, nobody had seen one for months.
He thought he saw a shape in the bushes.

How many different five-sentence paragraphs can be formed if the paragraph begins with "He thought he saw a shape in the bushes" and ends with "John looked out of the window"?

**32.** A television programmer is arranging the order that five movies will be seen between the hours of 6 P.M. and 4 A.M. Two of the movies have a G rating, and they are to be shown in the first two time blocks. One of the movies is rated NC-17, and it is to be shown in the last of the time blocks, from 2 A.M. until 4 A.M. Given these restrictions, in how many ways can the five movies be arranged during the indicated time blocks?

*Use the formula for ${}_nP_r$ to solve Exercises 33–40.*

**33.** A club with ten members is to choose three officers—president, vice-president, and secretary-treasurer. If each office is to be held by one person and no person can hold more than one office, in how many ways can those offices be filled?

**34.** A corporation has ten members on its board of directors. In how many different ways can it elect a president, vice-president, secretary, and treasurer?

**35.** For a segment of a radio show, a disc jockey can play 7 records. If there are 13 records to select from, in how many ways can the program for this segment be arranged?

**36.** Suppose you are asked to list, in order of preference, the three best movies you have seen this year. If you saw 20 movies during the year, in how many ways can the three best be chosen and ranked?

**37.** In a race in which six automobiles are entered and there are no ties, in how many ways can the first three finishers come in?

**38.** In a production of *West Side Story*, eight actors are considered for the male roles of Tony, Riff, and Bernardo. In how many ways can the director cast the male roles?

**39.** Nine bands have volunteered to perform at a benefit concert, but there is only enough time for five of the bands to play. How many lineups are possible?

**40.** How many arrangements can be made using four of the letters of the word COMBINE if no letter is to be used more than once?

*Use the formula for ${}_nC_r$ to solve Exercises 41–48.*

**41.** An election ballot asks voters to select three city commissioners from a group of six candidates. In how many ways can this be done?

**42.** A four-person committee is to be elected from an organization's membership of 11 people. How many different committees are possible?

**43.** Of 12 possible books, you plan to take 4 with you on vacation. How many different collections of 4 books can you take?

**44.** There are 14 standbys who hope to get seats on a flight, but only 6 seats are available on the plane. How many different ways can the 6 people be selected?

**45.** You volunteer to help drive children at a charity event to the zoo, but you can fit only 8 of the 17 children present in your van. How many different groups of 8 children can you drive?

**46.** Of the 100 people in the U.S. Senate, 18 serve on the Foreign Relations Committee. How many ways are there to select Senate members for this committee (assuming party affiliation is not a factor in selection)?

**47.** To win at LOTTO in the state of Florida, one must correctly select 6 numbers from a collection of 49 numbers (1 through 49). The order in which the selection is made does not matter. How many different selections are possible?

**48.** To win in the New York State lottery, one must correctly select 6 numbers from 54 numbers. The order in which the selection is made does not matter. How many different selections are possible?

*In Exercises 49–58, solve by the method of your choice.*

**49.** In a race in which six automobiles are entered and there are no ties, in how many ways can the first four finishers come in?

**50.** A book club offers a choice of 8 books from a list of 40. In how many ways can a member make a selection?

51. A medical researcher needs 6 people to test the effectiveness of an experimental drug. If 13 people have volunteered for the test, in how many ways can 6 people be selected?

52. Fifty people purchase raffle tickets. Three winning tickets are selected at random. If first prize is \$1000, second prize is \$500, and third prize is \$100, in how many different ways can the prizes be awarded?

53. From a club of 20 people, in how many ways can a group of three members be selected to attend a conference?

54. Fifty people purchase raffle tickets. Three winning tickets are selected at random. If each prize is \$500, in how many different ways can the prizes be awarded?

55. How many different four-letter passwords can be formed from the letters A, B, C, D, E, F, and G if no repetition of letters is allowed?

56. Nine comedy acts will perform over two evenings. Five of the acts will perform on the first evening. How many ways can the schedule for the first evening be made?

57. Using 15 flavors of ice cream, how many cones with three different flavors can you create if it is important to you which flavor goes on the top, middle, and bottom?

58. Baskin-Robbins offers 31 different flavors of ice cream. One of their items is a bowl consisting of three scoops of ice cream, each a different flavor. How many such bowls are possible?

## Writing in Mathematics

59. Explain the Fundamental Counting Principle.

60. Write an original problem that can be solved using the Fundamental Counting Principle. Then solve the problem.

61. What is a permutation?

62. Describe what ${}_nP_r$ represents.

63. Write a word problem that can be solved by evaluating ${}_7P_3$.

64. What is a combination?

65. Explain how to distinguish between permutation and combination problems.

66. Write a word problem that can be solved by evaluating ${}_7C_3$.

## Technology Exercises

67. Use a graphing utility with an $\boxed{{}_nP_r}$ key to verify your answers in Exercises 1–8.

68. Use a graphing utility with an $\boxed{{}_nC_r}$ key to verify your answers in Exercises 9–16.

## Critical Thinking Exercises

69. Which one of the following is true?
   **a.** The number of ways to choose four questions out of ten questions on an essay test is ${}_{10}P_4$.
   **b.** If $r > 1$, ${}_nP_r$ is less than ${}_nC_r$.
   **c.** ${}_7P_3 = 3!\,{}_7C_3$
   **d.** The number of ways to pick a winner and first runner-up in a piano recital with 20 contestants is ${}_{20}C_2$.

70. Five men and five women line up at a checkout counter in a store. In how many ways can they line up if the first person in line is a woman, and the people in line alternate woman, man, woman, man, and so on?

71. How many four-digit odd numbers less than 6000 can be formed using the digits 2, 4, 6, 7, 8, and 9?

72. If a collection of $n$ objects has $n_1$ identical objects of the same type, $n_2$ identical objects of a second kind, $n_3$ of a third kind, and so on for a total of $n = n_1 + n_2 + \cdots + n_k$ objects, the number of distinguishable permutations of the $n$ objects is given by

$$\frac{n!}{n_1!\,n_2!\,n_3!\cdots n_k!}.$$

Use this formula to find the number of different signals consisting of eight flags that can be made using three white flags, four red flags and one blue flag.

## Group Exercise

73. The group should select real-world situations where the Fundamental Counting Principle can be applied. These could involve the number of possible student ID numbers on your campus, the number of possible phone numbers in your community, the number of meal options at a local restaurant, the number of ways a person in the group can select outfits for class, the number of ways a condominium can be purchased in a nearby community, and so on. Once situations have been selected, group members should determine in how many ways each part of the task can be done. Group members will need to obtain menus, find out about telephone-digit requirements in the community, count shirts, pants, shoes in closets, visit condominium sales offices, and so on. Once the group reassembles, apply the Fundamental Counting Principle to determine the number of available options in each situation. Because these numbers may be quite large, use a calculator.

# SECTION 11.7 Probability

## Objectives

1. Compute empirical probability.
2. Compute theoretical probability.
3. Find the probability that an event will not occur.
4. Find the probability of one event or a second event occurring.
5. Find the probability of one event and a second event occurring.

**Table 11.3 Number of Americans and the Hours of Sleep They Get on a Typical Night**

| Hours of Sleep | Number of Americans, in millions |
|---|---|
| 4 or less | 11 |
| 5 | 24.75 |
| 6 | 68.75 |
| 7 | 82.5 |
| 8 | 74.25 |
| 9 | 8.25 |
| 10 or more | 5.5 |
| Total: | 275 |

*Source*: Discovery Health Media

How many hours of sleep do you typically get each night? Table 11.3 indicates that 11 million out of 275 million Americans are getting four hours or less sleep on a typical night. The *probability* of an American getting four hours or less sleep on a typical night is $\frac{11}{275}$. This fraction can be reduced to $\frac{1}{25}$, or expressed as 0.04 or 4%. Thus, 4% of Americans get four hours or less sleep each night.

We find a probability by dividing one number by another. Probabilities are assigned to an *event*, such as getting four hours or less sleep on a typical night. Events that are certain to occur are assigned probabilities of 1, or 100%. For example, the probability that a given individual will eventually die is 1. Regrettably, taxes and death are always certain! By contrast, if an event cannot occur, its probability is 0. For example, the probability that Elvis will return from the dead and serenade us with one final reprise of "Heartbreak Hotel" is 0.

Probabilities of events are expressed as numbers ranging from 0 to 1, or 0% to 100%. The closer the probability of a given event is to 1, the more likely it is that the event will occur. The closer the probability of a given event is to 0, the less likely it is that the event will occur.

## Empirical Probability

**1** Compute empirical probability.

**Empirical probability** applies to situations in which we observe how frequently an event occurs. We use the following formula to compute the empirical probability of an event.

### Computing Empirical Probability

The **empirical probability** of event $E$ is

$$P(E) = \frac{\text{observed number of times } E \text{ occurs}}{\text{total number of observed occurrences}}.$$

### EXAMPLE 1 Computing Empirical Probability

An American is randomly selected. Use Table 11.3 to find the probability of that person getting eight hours sleep on a typical night.

**Solution** The probability of getting eight hours sleep is the observed number of Americans who do this, 74.25 million, divided by the total number of Americans, 275 million.

$$P(\text{eight hours sleep}) = \frac{\text{number of Americans who sleep 8 hours}}{\text{total numbers of Americans}}$$

$$= \frac{74.25}{275} = \frac{297}{1100} = 0.27$$

The empirical probability of randomly selecting an American who gets eight hours sleep on a typical night is $\frac{297}{1100}$, or 0.27.

**Check Point 1** Use Table 11.3 to find the probability of randomly selecting an American who gets seven hours sleep on a typical night.

**2** Compute theoretical probability.

## Theoretical Probability

You toss a coin. Although it is equally likely to land either heads up, denoted by $H$, or tails up, denoted by $T$, the actual outcome is uncertain. Any occurrence for which the outcome is uncertain is called an **experiment**. Thus, tossing a coin is an example of an experiment. The set of all possible equally likely outcomes of an experiment is the **sample space** of the experiment, denoted by $S$. The sample space for the coin-tossing experiment is

$$S = \{H, T\}.$$

lands heads up (H) — lands tails up (T)

We can define an event more formally using these concepts. An **event**, denoted by $E$, is any subcollection, or subset, of a sample space. For example, the subset $E = \{T\}$ is the event of landing tails up when a coin is tossed.

Theoretical probability applies to situations like this, in which the sample space of all equally likely outcomes is known. To calculate the theoretical probability of an event, we divide the number of outcomes in the event by the number of outcomes in the sample space.

### Computing Theoretical Probability

If an event $E$ has $n(E)$ equally likely outcomes and its sample space $S$ has $n(S)$ equally likely outcomes, the theoretical probability of event $E$, denoted by $P(E)$, is

$$P(E) = \frac{\text{number of outcomes in event } E}{\text{number of outcomes in sample space } S} = \frac{n(E)}{n(S)}.$$

The sum of the theoretical probabilities of all possible outcomes in the sample space is 1.

How can we use this formula to compute the probability of a coin landing tails up? We use the following sets:

$$E = \{T\} \qquad S = \{H, T\}$$

This is the event of landing tails up. — This is the sample space with all equally possible outcomes.

**Figure 11.7** Outcomes when a die is rolled

The probability of a coin landing tails up is

$$P(E) = \frac{n(E)}{n(S)} = \frac{1}{2}.$$

Theoretical probability applies to many games of chance, including dice rolling, lotteries, card games, and roulette. The next example deals with the experiment of rolling a die. Figure 11.7 illustrates that when a die is rolled, there are six equally likely outcomes. The sample space can be shown as

$$S = \{1, 2, 3, 4, 5, 6\}.$$

## EXAMPLE 2 Computing Theoretical Probability

A die is rolled. Find the probability of getting a number less than 5.

**Solution** The sample space of equally likely outcomes is $S = \{1, 2, 3, 4, 5, 6\}$. There are six outcomes in the sample space, so $n(S) = 6$.

We are interested in the probability of getting a number less than 5. The event of getting a number less than 5 can be represented by

$$E = \{1, 2, 3, 4\}.$$

There are four outcomes in this event, so $n(E) = 4$.

The probability of rolling a number less than 5 is

$$P(E) = \frac{n(E)}{n(S)} = \frac{4}{6} = \frac{2}{3}.$$

**Check Point 2** A die is rolled. Find the probability of getting a number greater than 4.

## EXAMPLE 3 Computing Theoretical Probability

Two ordinary six-sided dice are rolled. What is the probability of getting a sum of 8?

**Solution** Each die has six equally likely outcomes. By the Fundamental Counting Principle, there are 6 · 6, or 36, equally likely outcomes in the sample space. That is, $n(S) = 36$. The 36 outcomes are shown here as ordered pairs. The five ways of rolling a sum of 8 appear in the highlighted diagonal as follows.

| | | Second Die | | | | | |
|---|---|---|---|---|---|---|---|
| | | ⚀ | ⚁ | ⚂ | ⚃ | ⚄ | ⚅ |
| First Die | ⚀ | (1, 1) | (1, 2) | (1, 3) | (1, 4) | (1, 5) | (1, 6) |
| | ⚁ | (2, 1) | (2, 2) | (2, 3) | (2, 4) | (2, 5) | (2, 6) |
| | ⚂ | (3, 1) | (3, 2) | (3, 3) | (3, 4) | (3, 5) | (3, 6) |
| | ⚃ | (4, 1) | (4, 2) | (4, 3) | (4, 4) | (4, 5) | (4, 6) |
| | ⚄ | (5, 1) | (5, 2) | (5, 3) | (5, 4) | (5, 5) | (5, 6) |
| | ⚅ | (6, 1) | (6, 2) | (6, 3) | (6, 4) | (6, 5) | (6, 6) |

$$S = \{(1,1), (1,2), (1,3), (1,4), (1,5), (1,6), (2,1), (2,2), (2,3), (2,4), (2,5), (2,6), (3,1), (3,2), (3,3), (3,4), (3,5), (3,6), (4,1), (4,2), (4,3), (4,4), (4,5), (4,6), (5,1), (5,2), (5,3), (5,4), (5,5), (5,6), (6,1), (6,2), (6,3), (6,4), (6,5), (6,6)\}$$

The phrase "getting a sum of 8" describes the event

$$E = \{(6,2), (5,3), (4,4), (3,5), (2,6)\}.$$

This event has 5 outcomes, so $n(E) = 5$. Thus, the probability of getting a sum of 8 is

$$P(E) = \frac{n(E)}{n(S)} = \frac{5}{36}.$$

**Check Point 3** What is the probability of getting a sum of 5 when two six-sided dice are rolled?

## Computing Theoretical Probability Without Listing an Event and the Sample Space

In some situations, we can compute theoretical probability without having to write out each event and each sample space. For example, suppose you are dealt one card from a standard 52-card deck, illustrated in Figure 11.8. The deck has four suits: Hearts and diamonds are red, and clubs and spades are black. Each suit has 13 different face values—A(ace), 2, 3, 4, 5, 6, 7, 8, 9, 10, J(jack), Q(queen), and K(king). Jacks, queens, and kings are called picture cards.

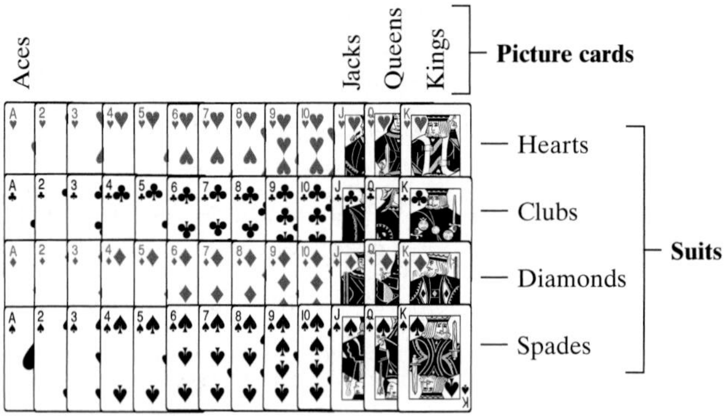


**Figure 11.8** A standard 52-card bridge deck

## EXAMPLE 4 Probability and a Deck of 52 Cards

You are dealt one card from a standard 52-card deck. Find the probability of being dealt a heart.

**Solution** Let $E$ be the event of being dealt a heart. Because there are 13 hearts in the deck, the event of being dealt a heart can occur in 13 ways. The number of outcomes in event $E$ is 13: $n(E) = 13$. With 52 cards in the deck, the total number of possible ways of being dealt a single card is 52. The number of outcomes in the sample space is 52: $n(S) = 52$. The probability of being dealt a heart is

$$P(E) = \frac{n(E)}{n(S)} = \frac{13}{52} = \frac{1}{4}.$$

**Check Point 4** If you are dealt one card from a standard 52-card deck, find the probability of being dealt a king.

State lotteries keep 50 cents on the dollar, resulting in $10 billion a year for public funding.

If your state has a lottery drawing each week, the probability that someone will win the top prize is relatively high. If there is no winner this week, it is virtually certain that eventually someone will be graced with millions of dollars. So how come you are unlucky compared to this undisclosed someone? In Example 5, we provide an answer to this question, using the counting principles discussed in Section 11.6.

## EXAMPLE 5 Probability and Combinations: Winning the Lottery

Florida's lottery game, LOTTO, is set up so that each player chooses six different numbers from 1 to 49. If the six numbers chosen match the six numbers drawn randomly each Saturday evening, the player wins (or shares) the top cash prize. (As of this writing, the top cash prize has ranged from $7 million to $106.5 million.) With one LOTTO ticket, what is the probability of winning this prize?

**Solution** Because the order of the six numbers does not matter, this is a situation involving combinations. Let $E$ be the event of winning the lottery with one ticket. With one LOTTO ticket, there is only one way of winning. Thus, $n(E) = 1$. The sample space is the set of all possible six-number combinations. We can use the combinations formula

$$_nC_r = \frac{n!}{(n-r)!\,r!}$$

to find the number of outcomes in the sample space. We are selecting $r = 6$ numbers from a collection of $n = 49$ numbers.

$$_{49}C_6 = \frac{49!}{(49-6)!\,6!} = \frac{49!}{43!\,6!} = \frac{49 \cdot 48 \cdot 47 \cdot 46 \cdot 45 \cdot 44 \cdot \cancel{43!}}{\cancel{43!} \cdot 6 \cdot 5 \cdot 4 \cdot 3 \cdot 2 \cdot 1} = 13{,}983{,}816$$

There are nearly 14 million number combinations possible in LOTTO. If a person buys one LOTTO ticket, the probability of winning is

$$P(E) = \frac{n(E)}{n(S)} = \frac{1}{13{,}983{,}816} \approx 0.0000000715.$$

The probability of winning the top prize with one LOTTO ticket is $\frac{1}{13{,}983{,}816}$, or about 1 in 14 million.

In 1997, Americans spent nearly 17 billion dollars on lotteries set up by revenue-hungry states. If a pigeon, er, person, buys, say 5000 different tickets in Florida's LOTTO, that person has selected 5000 different combinations of the six numbers. The probability of winning is

$$\frac{5000}{13{,}983{,}816} \approx 0.000358.$$

The chances of winning top prize are about 358 in a million. At $1 per LOTTO ticket, it is highly probable that Mr. or Ms. Pigeon will be $5000 poorer.

**Check Point 5** In a state lottery, a player chooses five different numbers from 1 to 30. If the five numbers chosen match the five numbers drawn each week, the player wins (or shares) the top cash prize. With one lottery ticket, what is the probability of winning this prize?

### Surprising Probabilities

Imagine that one person is randomly selected from all 6 billion people on planet Earth. The following empirical probabilities, each rounded to two decimal places, might surprise you.

Probability of selecting
- a woman = 0.51
- a non-white = 0.7
- a non-Christian = 0.7
- a person who cannot read = 0.7
- a person suffering from malnutrition = 0.5
- a person with a college education = 0.01
- a person who is near death = 0.01

When viewing our world from the perspective of these probabilities, the need for both tolerance and understanding becomes apparent.

*Source*: United Nations

**3** Find the probability that an event will not occur.

## Probability of an Event Not Occurring

A survey (*source*: Penn, Schoen, and Berland, 1999) asked 500 Americans to rate their health. Of those surveyed, 270 rated their health as good/excellent. This means that 500 − 270, or 230, people surveyed did not rate their health as good/excellent. Notice that

$$P(\text{good/excellent}) + P(\text{not good/excellent}) = \frac{270}{500} + \frac{230}{500} = \frac{500}{500} = 1.$$

In general, because the sum of the probabilities of all possible outcomes in any situation is 1,

$$P(E) + P(\text{not } E) = 1.$$

We now solve this equation for $P(\text{not } E)$, the probability that event $E$ will not occur, by subtracting $P(E)$ from both sides. The resulting formula is given in the following box.

**The Probability of an Event Not Occurring**

The probability that an event $E$ will not occur is equal to one minus the probability that it will occur.

$$P(\text{not } E) = 1 - P(E)$$

### EXAMPLE 6 The Probability of Not Winning the Lottery

We have seen that the probability of winning Florida's LOTTO with one ticket is $\frac{1}{13{,}983{,}816}$. What is the probability of not winning?

**Solution**

$$P(\text{not winning}) = 1 - P(\text{winning})$$

$$= 1 - \frac{1}{13{,}983{,}816} = \frac{13{,}983{,}816}{13{,}983{,}816} - \frac{1}{13{,}983{,}816}$$

$$= \frac{13{,}983{,}815}{13{,}983{,}816} \approx 0.9999999$$

The probability of not winning is close to 1. It is almost certain that with one LOTTO ticket, a person will not win top prize.

**Check Point 6** With one lottery ticket, what is the probability of not winning the lottery described in Checkpoint 5?

**4** Find the probability of one event or a second event occurring.

## *Or* Probabilities with Mutually Exclusive Events

Suppose that you randomly select one card from a deck of 52 cards. Let $A$ be the event of selecting a king and $B$ be the event of selecting a queen. Only one card is selected, so it is impossible to get both a king and a queen. The outcomes of selecting a king and a queen cannot occur simultaneously. They are called *mutually*

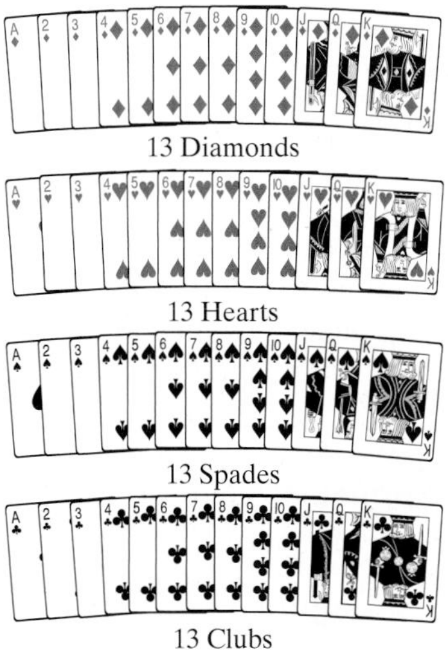


**Figure 11.9** A deck of 52 cards

*exclusive events*. If it is impossible for any two events, $A$ and $B$, to occur simultaneously, they are said to be **mutually exclusive**. If $A$ and $B$ are mutually exclusive events, the probability that either $A$ or $B$ will occur is determined by adding their individual probabilities.

### *Or* Probabilities with Mutually Exclusive Events

If $A$ and $B$ are mutually exclusive events, then

$$P(A \text{ or } B) = P(A) + P(B).$$

## EXAMPLE 7 The Probability of Either of Two Mutually Exclusive Events Occurring

If one card is randomly selected from a deck of cards, what is the probability of selecting a king or a queen?

**Solution** We find the probability that either of these mutually exclusive events will occur by adding their individual probabilities.

$$P(\text{king or queen}) = P(\text{king}) + P(\text{queen}) = \frac{4}{52} + \frac{4}{52} = \frac{8}{52} = \frac{2}{13}$$

The probability of selecting a king or a queen is $\frac{2}{13}$.

**Check Point 7** If you roll a single, six-sided die, what is the probability of getting either a 4 or a 5?

**Figure 11.10** Three diamonds are picture cards

## *Or* Probabilities with Events That Are Not Mutually Exclusive

Consider the deck of 52 cards shown in Figure 11.9. Suppose that these cards are shuffled and you randomly select one card from the deck. What is the probability of selecting a diamond or a picture card (jack, queen, king)? Begin by adding their individual probabilities:

$$P(\text{diamond}) + P(\text{picture card}) = \frac{13}{52} + \frac{12}{52}.$$

There are 13 diamonds in the deck of 52 cards. — There are 12 picture cards in the deck of 52 cards.

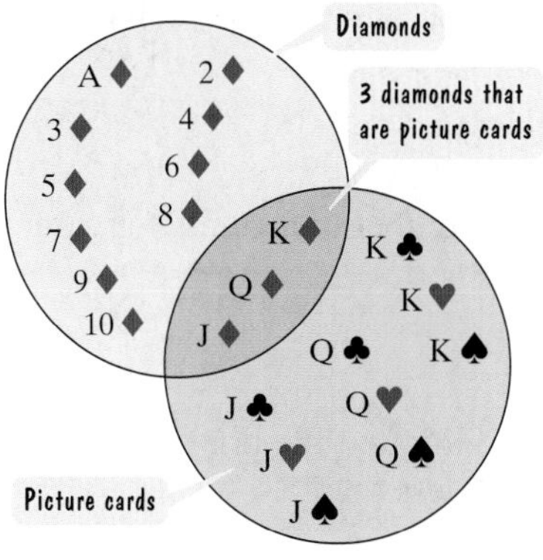


**Figure 11.11**

However, this is not the probability of selecting a diamond or a picture card. The problem is that there are three cards that are simultaneously diamonds and picture cards, shown in Figure 11.10. The events of selecting a diamond and selecting a picture card are not mutually exclusive. It is possible to select a card that is both a diamond and a picture card.

The situation is illustrated in the diagram in Figure 11.11. Why can't we find the probability of selecting a diamond or a picture card by adding their individual probabilities? The diagram shows that three of the cards, the three diamonds that are picture cards, get counted twice when we add the individual probabilities. First the three cards get counted as diamonds, and then they get counted as picture cards. In order to avoid the error of counting the three cards twice, we need to subtract the probability of getting a diamond and a picture card, $\frac{3}{52}$, as follows:

$$P(\text{diamond or picture card})$$
$$= P(\text{diamond}) + P(\text{picture card}) - P(\text{diamond and picture card})$$
$$= \frac{13}{52} + \frac{12}{52} - \frac{3}{52} = \frac{13 + 12 - 3}{52} = \frac{22}{52} = \frac{11}{26}.$$

Thus, the probability of selecting a diamond or a picture card is $\frac{11}{26}$.

In general, if $A$ and $B$ are events that are not mutually exclusive, the probability that $A$ or $B$ will occur is determined by adding their individual probabilities and then subtracting the probability that $A$ and $B$ occur simultaneously.

**_Or_ Probabilities with Events That Are Not Mutually Exclusive**

If $A$ and $B$ are not mutually exclusive events, then

$$P(A \text{ or } B) = P(A) + P(B) - P(A \text{ and } B).$$

## EXAMPLE 8 An *Or* Probability with Events That Are Not Mutually Exclusive

**Figure 11.12** It is equally probable that the pointer will land on any one of the eight regions.

Figure 11.12 illustrates a spinner. It is equally probable that the pointer will land on any one of the eight regions, numbered 1 through 8. If the pointer lands on a borderline, spin again. Find the probability that the pointer will stop on an even number or a number greater than 5.

**Solution** It is possible for the pointer to land on a number that is even and greater than 5. Two of the numbers, 6 and 8, are even and greater than 5. These events are not mutually exclusive. The probability of landing on a number that is even and greater than 5 is

$$P\left(\begin{matrix}\text{even or}\\ \text{greater than 5}\end{matrix}\right) = P(\text{even}) + P(\text{greater than 5}) - P\left(\begin{matrix}\text{even and}\\ \text{greater than 5}\end{matrix}\right)$$
$$= \frac{4}{8} + \frac{3}{8} - \frac{2}{8}$$

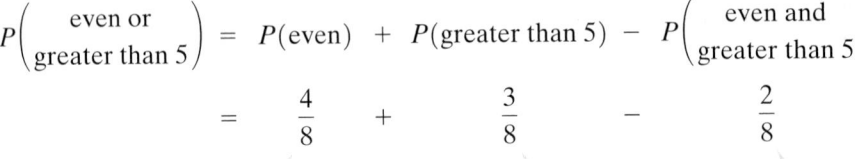

Four of the eight numbers, 2, 4, 6, and 8 are even.

Three of the eight numbers, 6, 7, and 8 are greater than 5.

Two of the eight numbers, 6 and 8, are even and greater than 5.

$$= \frac{4 + 3 - 2}{8} = \frac{5}{8}.$$

The probability that the pointer will stop on an even number or a number greater than 5 is $\frac{5}{8}$.

**Check Point 8** Use Figure 11.12 to find the probability that the pointer will stop on an odd number or a number less than 5.

## EXAMPLE 9 An *Or* Probability with Events That Are Not Mutually Exclusive

A group of people is comprised of 15 U.S. men, 20 U.S. women, 10 Canadian men, and 5 Canadian women. If a person is selected at random from the group, find the probability that the selected person is a man or a Canadian.

**Solution** The group is comprised of $15 + 20 + 10 + 5$, or 50 people. It is possible to select a man who is Canadian. We are given that there are 10 Canadian men, so these events are not mutually exclusive.

$$P(\text{man or Canadian}) = P(\text{man}) + P(\text{Canadian}) - P(\text{man and Canadian})$$

$$= \frac{25}{50} + \frac{15}{50} - \frac{10}{50}$$

Of the 50 people, 25 are men—15 U.S. men and 10 Canadian men.

Of the 50 people, 15 are Canadian—10 Canadian men and 5 Canadian women.

Of the 50 people, 10 are Canadian men.

$$= \frac{25 + 15 - 10}{50} = \frac{30}{50} = \frac{3}{5}$$

The probability of selecting a man or a Canadian is $\frac{3}{5}$.

**Check Point 9** In a group of 25 baboons, 18 enjoy picking fleas off their neighbors, 16 enjoy screeching wildly, while 10 enjoy picking fleas off their neighbors and screeching wildly. If one baboon is selected at random from the group, find the probability that it enjoys picking fleas off its neighbors or screeching wildly.

5 Find the probability of one event and a second event occurring.

## *And* Probabilities with Independent Events

Suppose that you toss a fair coin two times in succession. The outcome of the first toss, heads or tails, does not affect what happens when you toss the coin a second time. For example, the occurrence of tails on the first toss does not make tails more likely or less likely to occur on the second toss. The repeated toss of a coin produces **independent events** because the outcome of one toss does not affect the outcome of others. Two events are *independent* if the occurrence of either of them has no effect on the probability of the other.

If two events are independent, we can calculate the probability of the first occurring and the second occurring by multiplying their probabilities.

Figure 11.13 A U.S. roulette wheel

### *And* Probabilities with Independent Events

If $A$ and $B$ are independent events, then

$$P(A \text{ and } B) = P(A) \cdot P(B).$$

## EXAMPLE 10 Independent Events on a Roulette Wheel

Figure 11.13 shows a U.S. roulette wheel that has 38 numbered slots (1 through 36, 0, and 00). Of the 38 compartments, 18 are black, 18 are red, and 2 are green.

Each play consists of spinning the wheel and a small ball in opposite directions. As the ball slows to a stop, it can land with equal probability on any one of the 38 numbered slots. Find the probability of red occurring on two consecutive plays.

**Solution** The wheel has 38 equally likely outcomes and 18 are red. Thus, the probability of red occurring on a play is $\frac{18}{38}$, or $\frac{9}{19}$. The result that occurs on each play is independent of all previous results. Thus,

$$P(\text{red and red}) = P(\text{red}) \cdot P(\text{red}) = \frac{9}{19} \cdot \frac{9}{19} = \frac{81}{361} \approx 0.224.$$

The probability of red occurring on two consecutive plays is $\frac{81}{361}$.

Some roulette players incorrectly believe that if red occurs on two consecutive plays, then another color is "due." Because the events are independent, the outcomes of previous spins have no effect on any other spins.

**Check Point 10** Find the probability of green occurring on two consecutive plays on a roulette wheel.

The *and* rule for independent events can be extended to cover three or more events. Thus, if $A$, $B$, and $C$ are independent events, then

$$P(A \text{ and } B \text{ and } C) = P(A) \cdot P(B) \cdot P(C).$$

## EXAMPLE 11 Independent Events in a Family

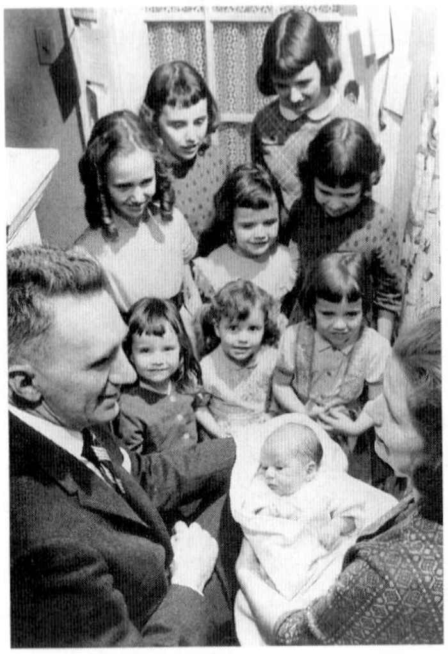

The picture in the margin shows a family that has had nine girls in a row. Find the probability of this occurrence.

**Solution** If two or more events are independent, we can find the probability of them all occurring by multiplying the probabilities. The probability of a baby girl is $\frac{1}{2}$, so the probability of nine girls in a row is $\frac{1}{2}$ used as a factor nine times.

$$P(\text{nine girls in a row}) = \frac{1}{2} \cdot \frac{1}{2} \cdot \frac{1}{2} \cdot \frac{1}{2} \cdot \frac{1}{2} \cdot \frac{1}{2} \cdot \frac{1}{2} \cdot \frac{1}{2} \cdot \frac{1}{2}$$

$$= \left(\frac{1}{2}\right)^9 = \frac{1}{512}$$

The probability of a run of nine girls in a row is $\frac{1}{512}$. (If another child is born into the family, this event is independent of the other nine, and the probability of a girl is still $\frac{1}{2}$.)

**Check Point 11** Find the probability of a family having four boys in a row.

# EXERCISE SET 11.7

## Practice and Application Exercises

*Exercises 1–4 involve empirical probability. Use the empirical probability formula to solve each exercise. Express answers as fractions. Then use a calculator to express probabilities as decimals, rounded to the nearest thousandth.*

*Use the table showing U.S. family size to solve Exercises 1–2.*

**U.S. Families (includes only a householder and his/her relatives) by Size, 1997**

| Total: 70,241,000 Families | |
|---|---|
| **Size** | **Number of Families** |
| 2 people | 29,780,000 |
| 3 people | 16,239,000 |
| 4 people | 14,602,000 |
| 5 people | 6,326,000 |
| 6 people | 2,108,000 |
| 7 people or more | 1,186,000 |

*Source*: U.S. Bureau of the Census

*Find the probability that a U.S. family has:*

**1.** 2 people.

**2.** 3 people.

*Use the table showing world population for selected regions to solve Exercises 3–4.*

**Populations of Selected Regions of the World**

| Total World Population: 5926 million | |
|---|---|
| **Region** | **Population in millions** |
| Africa | 761 |
| Near East | 165 |
| Asia | 3363 |
| Latin America | 508 |
| Europe | 799 |
| North America | 301 |

*Source*: U.S. Bureau of the Census

*If one person is randomly selected from all people on planet Earth, find the probability of selecting a person from:*

**3.** Africa.

**4.** North America.

*Exercises 5–20 involve theoretical probability. Use the theoretical probability formula to solve each exercise. Express each probability as a fraction reduced to lowest terms.*

*In Exercises 5–10, a die is rolled. The sample space of equally likely outcomes is* $\{1, 2, 3, 4, 5, 6\}$. *Find the probability of getting:*

**5.** a 4.

**6.** a 5.

**7.** an odd number.

**8.** a number greater than 3.

**9.** a number greater than 4.

**10.** a number greater than 7.

*In Exercises 11–14, you are dealt one card from a standard 52 card deck. Find the probability of being dealt:*

**11.** a queen.

**12.** a diamond.

**13.** a picture card.

**14.** a card greater than 3 and less than 7.

*In Exercises 15–16, a fair coin is tossed two times in succession. The sample space of equally likely outcomes is* $\{HH, HT, TH, TT\}$. *Find the probability of getting:*

**15.** two heads.

**16.** the same outcome on each toss.

*In Exercises 17–18, you select a family with three children. If M represents a male child and F a female child, the sample space of equally likely outcomes is* $\{MMM, MMF, MFM, MFF, FMM, FMF, FFM, FFF\}$. *Find the probability of selecting a family with:*

**17.** at least one male child.

**18.** at least two female children.

*In Exercises 19–20, a single die is rolled twice. The 36 equally likely outcomes are shown as follows:*

| *First Roll* \ *Second Roll* | ⚀ | ⚁ | ⚂ | ⚃ | ⚄ | ⚅ |
|---|---|---|---|---|---|---|
| ⚀ | (1, 1) | (1, 2) | (1, 3) | (1, 4) | (1, 5) | (1, 6) |
| ⚁ | (2, 1) | (2, 2) | (2, 3) | (2, 4) | (2, 5) | (2, 6) |
| ⚂ | (3, 1) | (3, 2) | (3, 3) | (3, 4) | (3, 5) | (3, 6) |
| ⚃ | (4, 1) | (4, 2) | (4, 3) | (4, 4) | (4, 5) | (4, 6) |
| ⚄ | (5, 1) | (5, 2) | (5, 3) | (5, 4) | (5, 5) | (5, 6) |
| ⚅ | (6, 1) | (6, 2) | (6, 3) | (6, 4) | (6, 5) | (6, 6) |

*Find the probability of getting:*

**19.** two numbers whose sum is 4.

**20.** two numbers whose sum is 6.

**21.** To play the California lottery, a person has to correctly select 6 out of 51 numbers, paying $1 for each six-number selection. If you pick six numbers that are the same as the ones drawn by the lottery, you win mountains of money. What is the probability that a person with one combination of six numbers will win? What is the probability of winning if 100 different lottery tickets are purchased?

**22.** A state lottery is designed so that a player chooses six numbers from 1 to 30 on one lottery ticket. What is the probability that a player with one lottery ticket will win? What is the probability of winning if 100 different lottery tickets are purchased?

**23.** A poker hand consists of five cards.
**a.** Find the total number of possible five-card poker hands that can be dealt from a deck of 52 cards.
**b.** A diamond flush consists of a five-card hand containing all diamonds. Find the number of possible five-card diamond flushes.
**c.** Find the probability of being dealt a diamond flush.

**24.** A committee of five people is to be formed from six lawyers and seven teachers. Find the probability that all are lawyers.

*Use these figures for the U.S. population in 2000 to answer Exercises 25–30.*

**Total U.S. Population: 274,634 Thousand**

| **Age** | **under 5** | **5–13** | **14–17** | **18–24** | **25–34** | **35–44** | **45–64** | **65–84** | **85 and older** |
|---|---|---|---|---|---|---|---|---|---|
| **Population (in thousands)** | 18,987 | 36,043 | 15,752 | 26,258 | 37,233 | 44,659 | 60,992 | 30,378 | 4332 |

*Source*: U.S. Bureau of the Census

*If a U.S. citizen is chosen at random, find the probability that this person is not:*

**25.** under 5.

**26.** in the 18–24 age group.

**27.** in the 25–34 age group.

**28.** 85 and older.

*Exercises 29–32 involve* or *probabilities with mutually exclusive events.*

**29.** If a U.S. citizen is chosen at random, find the probability that this person is in the 14–17 or 18–24 age group.

**30.** If a U.S. citizen is chosen at random, find the probability that this person is in the 25–34 or 35–44 age group.

*If one card is randomly selected from a 52-card deck of cards, find the probability of selecting:*

**31.** a 2 or a 3.

**32.** a red 7 or a black 8.

*Exercises 33–40 involve* or *probabilities with events that are not mutually exclusive.*

*In Exercises 33–34, a single die is rolled. Find the probability of getting:*

**33.** an even number or a number less than 5.

**34.** an odd number or a number less than 4.

*In Exercises 35–36, you are dealt one card from a 52-card deck. Find the probability that you are dealt:*

**35.** a 7 or a red card.

**36.** a 5 or a black card.

*In Exercises 37–38, it is equally probable that the pointer on the spinner shown will land on any one of the eight regions, numbered 1 through 8. If the pointer lands on a borderline, spin again.*

*Find the probability that the pointer will stop on:*

**37.** an odd number or a number less than 6.

**38.** an odd number or a number greater than 3.

*Use this information to solve Exercises 39–40. The mathematics department of a college has 8 male professors, 11 female professors, 14 male teaching assistants, and 7 female teaching assistants. If a person is selected at random from the group, find the probability that the selected person is:*

**39.** a professor or a male.

**40.** a professor or a female.

*Exercises 41–46 involve* and *probabilities with independent events.*

*In Exercises 41–44, a single die is rolled twice. Find the probability of getting:*

**41.** a 2 the first time and a 3 the second time.

**42.** a 5 the first time and a 1 the second time.

43. an even number the first time and a number greater than 2 the second time.

44. an odd number the first time and a number less than 3 the second time.

45. If you toss a fair coin six times, what is the probability of getting all heads?

46. If you toss a fair coin seven times, what is the probability of getting all tails?

47. The probability that South Florida will be hit by a major hurricane (category 4 or 5) in any single year is $\frac{1}{16}$. (*Source*: National Hurricane Center)
   **a.** What is the probability that South Florida will be hit by a major hurricane two years in a row?
   **b.** What is the probability that South Florida will be hit by a major hurricane in three consecutive years?
   **c.** What is the probability that South Florida will not be hit by a major hurricane in the next ten years?
   **d.** What is the probability that South Florida will be hit by a major hurricane at least once in the next ten years?

## Writing in Mathematics

48. Describe the difference between theoretical probability and empirical probability.

49. Give an example of an event whose probability must be determined empirically rather than theoretically.

50. Write a probability word problem whose answer is one of the following fractions: $\frac{1}{6}$ or $\frac{1}{4}$ or $\frac{1}{3}$.

51. Explain how to find the probability of an event not occurring. Give an example.

52. What are mutually exclusive events? Give an example of two events that are mutually exclusive.

53. Explain how to find *or* probabilities with mutually exclusive events. Give an example.

54. Give an example of two events that are not mutually exclusive.

55. Explain how to find *or* probabilities with events that are not mutually exclusive. Give an example.

56. Explain how to find *and* probabilities with independent events. Give an example.

57. The president of a large company with 10,000 employees is considering mandatory cocaine testing for every employee. The test that would be used is 90% accurate, meaning that it will detect 90% of the cocaine users who are tested, and that 90% of the nonusers will test negative. This also means that the test gives 10% false positive. Suppose that 1% of the employees actually use cocaine. Find the probability that someone who tests positive for cocaine use is, indeed, a user. (See the hint at the top of the next column.)

*Hint*: Find the following probability fraction:

$$\frac{\text{the number of employees who test positive and are cocaine users}}{\text{the number of employees who test positive}}$$

$$= \frac{90\% \text{ of } 1\% \text{ of } 10{,}000}{\text{the number who test positive who actually use cocaine plus the number who test positive who do not use cocaine.}}$$

What does this probability indicate in terms of the percentage of employees who test positive who are not actually users? Discuss these numbers in terms of the issue of mandatory drug testing. Write a paper either in favor of or against mandatory drug testing, incorporating the actual percentage accuracy for such tests.

## Critical Thinking Exercises

58. The target in the figure shown contains four squares. If a dart thrown at random hits the target, find the probability that it will land in a colored region.

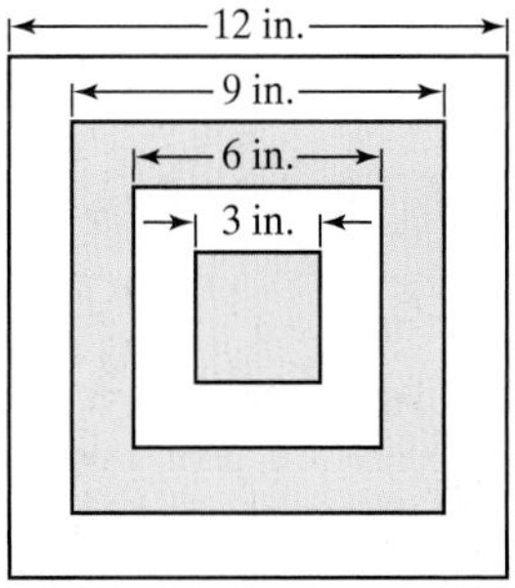


59. Suppose that it is a week in which the cash prize in Florida's LOTTO is promised to exceed $50 million. If a person purchases 13,983,816 tickets in LOTTO at $1 per ticket (all possible combinations), isn't this a guarantee of winning the lottery? Because the probability in this situation is 1, what's wrong with doing this?

60. **a.** If two people are selected at random, the probability that they do not have the same birthday (day and month) is $\frac{365}{365} \cdot \frac{364}{365}$. Explain why this is so. (Ignore leap years and assume 365 days in a year.)
   **b.** If three people are selected at random, find the probability that they all have different birthdays.
   **c.** If three people are selected at random, find the probability that at least two of them have the same birthday.
   **d.** If 20 people are selected at random, find the probability that at least 2 of them have the same birthday.
   **e.** How large a group is needed to give a 0.5 chance of at least two people having the same birthday?

## Group Exercise

**61.** Research and present a group report on state lotteries. Include answers to some or all of the following questions: Which states do not have lotteries? Why not? How much is spent per capita on lotteries? What are some of the lottery games? What is the probability of winning top prize in these games? What income groups spend the greatest amount of money on lotteries? If your state has a lottery, what does it do with the money it makes? Is the way the money is spent what was promised when the lottery first began?

# CHAPTER SUMMARY, REVIEW, AND TEST

## Summary

### 11.1 Sequences and Summation Notation

a. An infinite sequence $\{a_n\}$ is a function whose domain is the set of positive integers. The function values, or terms, are represented by

$$a_1, a_2, a_3, a_4, \dots, a_n, \dots.$$

b. Sequences can be defined using recursion formulas that define the $n$th term as a function of the previous term.

c. Factorial Notation:

$$n! = n(n-1)(n-2)\cdots(3)(2)(1) \quad \text{and} \quad 0! = 1$$

d. Summation Notation:

$$\sum_{i=1}^{n} a_i = a_1 + a_2 + a_3 + a_4 + \cdots + a_n$$

### 11.2 Arithmetic Sequences

a. In an arithmetic sequence, each term after the first differs from the preceding term by a constant, the common difference. Subtract any term from the term that directly follows to find the common difference.

b. General term or $n$th term: $a_n = a_1 + (n-1)d$. The first term is $a_1$ and the common difference is $d$.

c. Sum of the first $n$ terms: $S_n = \frac{n}{2}(a_1 + a_n)$

### 11.3 Geometric Sequences

a. In a geometric sequence, each term after the first is obtained by multiplying the preceding term by a nonzero constant, the common ratio. Divide any term after the first by the term that directly precedes it to find the common ratio.

b. General term or $n$th term: $a_n = a_1 r^{n-1}$. The first term is $a_1$ and the common ratio is $r$.

c. Sum of the first $n$ terms: $S_n = \frac{a_1(1-r^n)}{1-r}, \quad r \neq 1$

d. An annuity is a sequence of equal payments made at equal time periods. The value of an annuity, $A$, is the sum of all deposits made plus all interest paid, given by

$$A = P\frac{\left(1+\frac{r}{n}\right)^{nt} - 1}{\frac{r}{n}}.$$

The deposit made at the end of each period is $P$, the annual interest rate is $r$ compounded $n$ times per year, and $t$ is the number of years deposits have been made.

e. Sum of the infinite geometric series $a_1 + a_1 r + a_1 r^2 + a_1 r^3 + \cdots$ is $S = \frac{a_1}{1-r}$; $|r| < 1$. If $|r| \geq 1$, the infinite series does not have a sum.

### 11.4 Mathematical Induction

To prove that $S_n$ is true for all positive integers $n$:

a. Show that $S_1$ is true.

b. Show that if $S_k$ is assumed true, then $S_{k+1}$ is also true, for every positive integer $k$.

### 11.5 The Binomial Theorem

a. Binomial coefficient: $\binom{n}{r} = \frac{n!}{r!(n-r)!}$

b. Binomial Theorem: $(a+b)^n = \binom{n}{0}a^n + \binom{n}{1}a^{n-1}b + \binom{n}{2}a^{n-2}b^2 + \cdots + \binom{n}{n}b^n$

c. The $r$th term in a binomial expansion:

$$\binom{n}{r-1}a^{n-r+1}b^{r-1}$$

### 11.6 Counting Principles, Permutations, and Combinations

a. The Fundamental Counting Principle: The number of ways in which a series of successive things can occur is found by multiplying the number of ways in which each thing can occur.

b. A permutation from a group of items occurs when no item is used more than once and the order of arrangement makes a difference.

c. Permutations Formula: The number of possible permutations if $r$ items are taken from $n$ items is $_nP_r = \frac{n!}{(n-r)!}$.

d. A combination from a group of items occurs when no item is used more than once and the order of items makes no difference.

e. Combinations Formula: The number of possible combinations if $r$ items are taken from $n$ items is $_nC_r = \frac{n!}{(n-r)!r!}$.

## 11.7 Probability

a. Empirical probability applies to situations in which we observe the frequency of occurrence of an event. The empirical probability of event $E$ is

$$P(E) = \frac{\text{observed number of times } E \text{ occurs}}{\text{total number of observed occurrences}}.$$

b. Theoretical probability applies to situations in which the sample space of all equally likely outcomes is known. The theoretical probability of event $E$ is

$$P(E) = \frac{\text{number of outcomes in event } E}{\text{number of outcomes in sample space } S} = \frac{n(E)}{n(S)}.$$

c. Probability of an event not occurring: $P(\text{not } E) = 1 - P(E)$.

d. If it is impossible for events $A$ and $B$ to occur simultaneously, the events are mutually exclusive.

e. If $A$ and $B$ are mutually exclusive events, then $P(A \text{ or } B) = P(A) + P(B)$.

f. If $A$ and $B$ are not mutually exclusive events, then $P(A \text{ or } B) = P(A) + P(B) - P(A \text{ and } B)$.

g. Two events are independent if the occurrence of either of them has no effect on the probability of the other.

h. If $A$ and $B$ are independent events, then

$$P(A \text{ and } B) = P(A) \cdot P(B).$$

i. The probability of a succession of independent events is the product of each of their probabilities.

# Review Exercises

## 11.1

*In Exercises 1–6, write the first four terms of each sequence whose general term is given.*

**1.** $a_n = 7n - 4$

**2.** $a_n = (-1)^n \frac{n+2}{n+1}$

**3.** $a_n = \frac{1}{(n-1)!}$

**4.** $a_n = \frac{(-1)^{n+1}}{2^n}$

**5.** $a_1 = 9$ and $a_n = \frac{2}{3a_{n-1}}$

**6.** $a_1 = 4$ and $a_n = 2a_{n-1} + 3$

**7.** Evaluate: $\frac{40!}{4!38!}$.

*In Exercises 8–9, find each indicated sum.*

**8.** $\sum_{i=1}^{5} (2i^2 - 3)$

**9.** $\sum_{i=0}^{4} (-1)^{i+1} i!$

*In Exercises 10–11, express each sum using summation notation. Use i for the index of summation.*

**10.** $\frac{1}{3} + \frac{2}{4} + \frac{3}{5} + \cdots + \frac{15}{17}$

**11.** $4^3 + 5^3 + 6^3 + \cdots + 13^3$

## 11.2

*In Exercises 12–15, write the first six terms of each arithmetic sequence.*

**12.** $a_1 = 7, d = 4$

**13.** $a_1 = -4, d = -5$

**14.** $a_1 = \frac{3}{2}, d = -\frac{1}{2}$

**15.** $a_{n+1} = a_n + 5, a_1 = -2$

*In Exercises 16–18, find the indicated term of the arithmetic sequence with first term, $a_1$, and common difference, d.*

**16.** Find $a_6$ when $a_1 = 5, d = 3$.

**17.** Find $a_{12}$ when $a_1 = -8, d = -2$.

**18.** Find $a_{14}$ when $a_1 = 14, d = -4$.

*In Exercises 19–21, write a formula for the general term (the nth term) of each arithmetic sequence. Do not use a recursion formula. Then use the formula for $a_n$ to find $a_{20}$, the 20th term of the sequence.*

**19.** $-7, -3, 1, 5, \ldots$

**20.** $a_1 = 200, d = -20$

**21.** $a_n = a_{n-1} - 5, a_1 = 3$

**22.** Find the sum of the first 22 terms of the arithmetic sequence: $5, 12, 19, 26, \ldots$.

**23.** Find the sum of the first 15 terms of the arithmetic sequence: $-6, -3, 0, 3, \ldots$.

**24.** Find $3 + 6 + 9 + \cdots + 300$, the sum of the first 100 positive multiples of 3.

*In Exercises 25–27, use the formula for the sum of the first n terms of an arithmetic sequence to find the indicated sum.*

**25.** $\sum_{i=1}^{16} (3i + 2)$

**26.** $\sum_{i=1}^{25} (-2i + 6)$

**27.** $\sum_{i=1}^{30} (-5i)$

**28.** In 1911, the world record for the men's mile run was 1043.04 seconds. The world record has decreased by approximately 0.4118 second each year since then.

**a.** Write the general term for the arithmetic sequence modeling record times for the men's mile run $n$ years after 1910.

**b.** Use the model to predict the record time for the men's mile run for the year 2010.

**29.** A company offers a starting salary of \$31,500 with raises of \$2300 per year. Find the total salary over a ten-year period.

**30.** A theater has 25 seats in the first row and 35 rows in all. Each successive row contains one additional seat. How many seats are in the theater?

## 11.3

*In Exercises 31–34, write the first five terms of each geometric sequence.*

**31.** $a_1 = 3, r = 2$

**32.** $a_1 = \frac{1}{2}, r = \frac{1}{2}$

**33.** $a_1 = 16, r = -\frac{1}{2}$

**34.** $a_n = -5a_{n-1}, a_1 = -1$

*In Exercises 35–37, find the indicated term of the geometric sequence with first term, $a_1$, and common ratio, $r$.*

**35.** Find $a_7$ when $a_1 = 2, r = 3$.

**36.** Find $a_6$ when $a_1 = 16, r = \frac{1}{2}$.

**37.** Find $a_5$ when $a_1 = -3, r = 2$.

*In Exercises 38–40, write a formula for the general term (the nth term) of each geometric sequence. Then use the formula for $a_n$ to find $a_8$, the eighth term of the sequence.*

**38.** $1, 2, 4, 8, \ldots$

**39.** $100, 10, 1, \frac{1}{10}, \ldots$

**40.** $12, -4, \frac{4}{3}, -\frac{4}{9}, \ldots$

**41.** Find the sum of the first 15 terms of the geometric sequence: $5, -15, 45, -135, \ldots$.

**42.** Find the sum of the first 7 terms of the geometric sequence: $\frac{1}{3}, \frac{1}{9}, \frac{1}{27}, \frac{1}{81}, \ldots$.

*In Exercises 43–45, use the formula for the sum of the first n terms of a geometric sequence to find the indicated sum.*

**43.** $\sum_{i=1}^{6} 5^i$

**44.** $\sum_{i=1}^{7} 3(-2)^i$

**45.** $\sum_{i=1}^{5} 2\left(\frac{1}{4}\right)^{i-1}$

*In Exercises 46–49, find the sum of each infinite geometric series.*

**46.** $9 + 3 + 1 + \frac{1}{3} + \cdots$

**47.** $2 - 1 + \frac{1}{2} - \frac{1}{4} + \cdots$

**48.** $-6 + 4 - \frac{8}{3} + \frac{16}{9} - \cdots$

**49.** $\sum_{i=1}^{\infty} 5(0.8)^i$

*In Exercises 50–51, express each repeating decimal as a fraction in lowest terms.*

**50.** $0.\overline{6}$

**51.** $0.\overline{47}$

**52.** A job pays \$32,000 for the first year with an annual increase of 6% per year beginning in the second year. What is the salary in the sixth year? What is the total salary paid over this six-year period?

**53.** You decide to deposit \$200 at the end of each month into an account paying 10% interest compounded monthly to save for your child's education. How much will you save over 18 years?

**54.** A factory in an isolated town has an annual payroll of \$4 million. It is estimated that 70% of this money is spent within the town, that people in the town receiving this money will again spend 70% of what they receive in the town, and so on. What is the total of all this spending in the town each year?

## 11.4

*In Exercises 55–59, use mathematical induction to prove that each statement is true for every positive integer n.*

**55.** $5 + 10 + 15 + \cdots + 5n = \frac{5n(n+1)}{2}$

**56.** $1 + 4 + 4^2 + \cdots + 4^{n-1} = \frac{4^n - 1}{3}$

**57.** $2 + 6 + 10 + \cdots + (4n - 2) = 2n^2$

**58.** $1 \cdot 3 + 2 \cdot 4 + 3 \cdot 5 + \cdots + n(n+2) = \frac{n(n+1)(2n+7)}{6}$

**59.** 2 is a factor of $n^2 + 5n$.

## 11.5

*In Exercises 60–61, evaluate the given binomial coefficient.*

**60.** $\binom{11}{8}$

**61.** $\binom{90}{2}$

*In Exercises 62–65, use the Binomial Theorem to expand each binomial and express the result in simplified form.*

**62.** $(2x + 1)^3$

**63.** $(x^2 - 1)^4$

**64.** $(x + 2y)^5$

**65.** $(x - 2)^6$

*In Exercises 66–67, write the first three terms in each binomial expansion, expressing the result in simplified form.*

**66.** $(x^2 + 3)^8$

**67.** $(x - 3)^9$

*In Exercises 68–69, find the term indicated in each expansion.*

**68.** $(x + 2)^5$; fourth term

**69.** $(2x - 3)^6$; fifth term

## 11.6

*In Exercises 70–73, evaluate each expression.*

**70.** ${}_8P_3$

**71.** ${}_9P_5$

**72.** ${}_8C_3$

**73.** ${}_{13}C_{11}$

*In Exercises 74–80, solve by the method of your choice.*

**74.** A popular brand of pen comes in red, green, blue, or black ink. The writing tip can be chosen from extra bold, bold, regular, fine, or micro. How many different choices of pens do you have with this brand?

**75.** A stock can go up, go down, or stay unchanged. How many possibilities are there if you own five stocks?

**76.** A club with 15 members is to choose four officers—president, vice-president, secretary, and treasurer. In how many ways can these offices be filled?

**77.** How many different ways can a director select 4 actors from a group of 20 actors to attend a workshop on performing in rock musicals?

**78.** From the 20 CDs that you've bought during the past year, you plan to take 3 with you on vacation. How many different sets of three CDs can you take?

**79.** How many different ways can a director select from 20 male actors and cast the roles of Mark, Roger, Angel, and Collins in the musical *Rent*?

**80.** In how many ways can five airplanes line up for departure on a runway?

## 11.7

*Exercises 81–82 involve empirical probabilities. Express each probability as a fraction. Then use a calculator to express the probability in decimal form, rounded to the nearest thousandth. The table shows the two states with the largest Hispanic populations. Find the probability that:*

**81.** a person randomly selected from California is Hispanic.

**82.** a person randomly selected from Texas is Hispanic.

**Largest Hispanic Population, 1997**

| State | Total Population | Hispanic Population |
|---|---|---|
| California | 31,878,234 | 9,630,188 |
| Texas | 19,128,261 | 5,503,372 |

*Source*: Bureau of the Census

*In Exercises 83–84, a die is rolled. Find the probability of:*

**83.** getting a number less than 5.

**84.** getting a number less than 3 or greater than 4.

*In Exercises 85–86, you are dealt one card from a 52-card deck. Find the probability of:*

**85.** getting an ace or a king.

**86.** getting a queen or a red card.

*In Exercises 87–88, it is equally probable that the pointer on the spinner shown will land on any one of the six regions, numbered 1 through 6, and colored as shown. If the pointer lands on a borderline, spin again. Find the probability of:*

**87.** not stopping on yellow.

**88.** stopping on red or a number greater than 3.

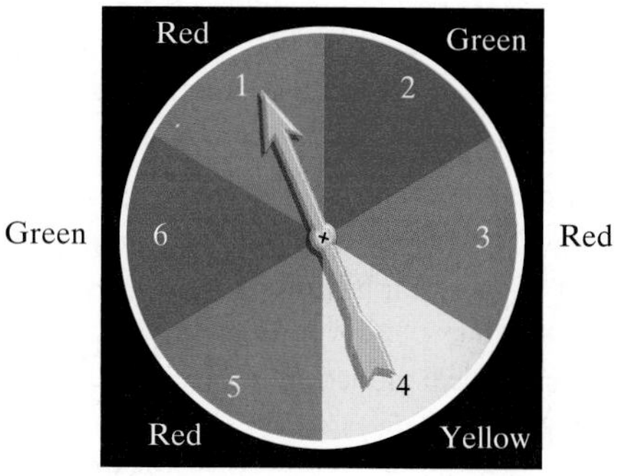


**89.** A lottery game is set up so that each player chooses five different numbers from 1 to 20. If the five numbers match the five numbers drawn in the lottery, the player wins (or shares) the top cash prize. What is the probability of winning the prize:
**a.** with one lottery ticket?
**b.** with 100 different lottery tickets?

*Use this information to solve Exercises 90–91. At a workshop on police work and the black community, there are 50 black male police officers, 20 black female police officers, 90 white male police officers, and 40 white female police officers. If one police officer is selected at random from the people at the workshop, find the probability that the selected person is:*

**90.** black or male.

**91.** female or white.

**92.** What is the probability of a family having five boys born in a row?

**93.** The probability of a flood in any given year in a region prone to floods is 0.2.
**a.** What is the probability of a flood two years in a row?
**b.** What is the probability of a flood for three consecutive years?
**c.** What is the probability of no flooding for four consecutive years?

## Chapter 11 Test

**1.** Write the first five terms of the sequence whose general term is $a_n = \frac{(-1)^{n+1}}{n^2}$.

*In Exercises 2–4, find each indicated sum.*

**2.** $\sum_{i=1}^{5}(i^2 + 10)$

**3.** $\sum_{i=1}^{20}(3i - 4)$

**4.** $\sum_{i=1}^{15}(-2)^i$

*In Exercises 5–7, evaluate each expression.*

**5.** $\binom{9}{2}$

**6.** ${}_{10}P_3$

**7.** ${}_{10}C_3$

**8.** Express the sum using summation notation. Use $i$ for the index of summation.

$$\frac{2}{3} + \frac{3}{4} + \frac{4}{5} + \cdots + \frac{21}{22}$$

*In Exercises 9–10, write a formula for the general term (the nth term) of each sequence. Do not use a recursion formula. Then use the formula to find the twelfth term of the sequence.*

**9.** $4, 9, 14, 19, \ldots$

**10.** $16, 4, 1, \frac{1}{4}, \ldots$

*In Exercises 11–12, use a formula to find the sum of the first ten terms of each sequence.*

**11.** $7, -14, 28, -56, \ldots$

**12.** $-7, -14, -21, -28, \ldots$

**13.** Find the sum of the infinite geometric series:

$$4 + \frac{4}{2} + \frac{4}{2^2} + \frac{4}{2^3} + \cdots.$$

**14.** A job pays $30,000 for the first year with an annual increase of 4% per year beginning in the second year. What is the total salary paid over an eight-year period?

**15.** Use mathematical induction to prove that for every positive integer $n$,

$$1 + 4 + 7 + \cdots + (3n - 2) = \frac{n(3n - 1)}{2}.$$

**16.** Use the Binomial Theorem to expand and simplify: $(x^2 - 1)^5$.

**17.** A human resource manager has 11 applicants to fill three different positions. Assuming that all applicants are equally qualified for any of the three positions, in how many ways can this be done?

**18.** From the ten books that you've recently bought but not read, you plan to take four with you on vacation. How many different sets of four books can you take?

**19.** How many seven-digit local telephone numbers can be formed if the first three digits are 279?

**20.** A lottery game is set up so that each player chooses six different numbers from 1 to 15. If the six numbers match the six numbers drawn in the lottery, the player wins (or shares) the top cash prize. What is the probability of winning the prize with 50 different lottery tickets?

**21.** One card is randomly selected from a deck of 52 cards. Find the probability of selecting a black card or a picture card.

**22.** A group of students consists of 10 male freshmen, 15 female freshmen, 20 male sophomores, and 5 female sophomores. If one person is randomly selected from the group, find the probability of selecting a freshman or a female.

**23.** A quiz consisting of four multiple-choice questions has four available options (a, b, c, or d) for each question. If a person guesses at every question, what is the probability of answering all questions correctly?

**24.** If the spinner shown is spun twice, find the probability that the pointer lands on red on the first spin and blue on the second spin.

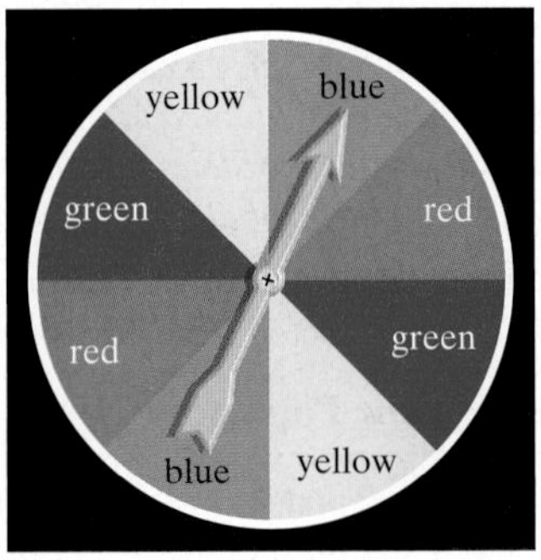


## Cumulative Review Exercises (Chapters 1–11)

*Solve each equation or inequality in Exercises 1–10.*

**1.** $-2(x - 5) + 10 = 3(x + 2)$

**2.** $3x^2 - 6x + 2 = 0$

**3.** $\log_2 x + \log_2(2x - 3) = 1$

**4.** $x^{1/2} - 6x^{1/4} + 8 = 0$

**5.** $\sqrt{2x + 4} - \sqrt{x + 3} - 1 = 0$

**6.** $|2x + 1| \le 1$

**7.** $6x^2 - 6 < 5x$

**8.** $\dfrac{x - 1}{x + 3} \le 0$

**9.** $30e^{0.7x} = 240$

**10.** $2x^3 + 3x^2 - 8x + 3 = 0$

*Solve each system in Exercises 11–13.*

**11.** $4x^2 + 3y^2 = 48$
$3x^2 + 2y^2 = 35$

**12.** (Use matrices.)
$x - 2y + z = 16$
$2x - y - z = 14$
$3x + 5y - 4z = -10$

**13.** $x - y = 1$
$x^2 - x - y = 1$

*In Exercises 14–19, graph each equation, function, or system in the rectangular coordinate system.*

**14.** $100x^2 + y^2 = 25$

**15.** $4x^2 - 9y^2 - 16x + 54y - 29 = 0$

**16.** $f(x) = \dfrac{x^2 - 1}{x - 2}$

**17.** $2x - y \ge 4$
$x \le 2$

**18.** $f(x) = x^2 - 4x - 5$

**19.** $y = \log_2 x$

**20.** Find $f^{-1}(x)$ if $f(x) = \sqrt[3]{x + 4}$.

**21.** If $A = \begin{bmatrix} 4 & 2 \\ 1 & -1 \\ 0 & 5 \end{bmatrix}$ and $B = \begin{bmatrix} 2 & 4 \\ 3 & 1 \end{bmatrix}$, find $AB - 4A$.

**22.** Find the partial fraction decomposition for

$$\frac{2x^2 - 10x + 2}{(x - 2)(x^2 + 2x + 2)}.$$

**23.** Expand and simplify: $(x^3 + 2y)^5$.

**24.** Use the formula for the sum of the first $n$ terms of an arithmetic sequence to find $\sum_{i=1}^{50}(4i - 25)$.

**25.** Mailings in the United States increased by more than 40% from 1983 to 1993.

| $x$ (Number of Years after 1983) | $y$ (Number of Pieces of Mail, in Billions) |
|---|---|
| 0 | 119.4 |
| 10 | 171.1 |

**a.** Write the point-slope form of the line on which these measurements fall.
**b.** Use the point-slope form of the equation to write the slope-intercept form of the equation.
**c.** Use the slope-intercept model from part (b) to predict the number of pieces of mail, in billions, for the year 2000.

**26.** Most of the world's very tall buildings are in the United States, where the skyscraper was first conceived. The height of the World Trade Center in New York is 790 feet less than twice that of New York's Empire State Building. If the mean (average) height of the two buildings is 980 feet, determine the height of each building.

**27.** The perimeter of a soccer field is 300 yards. If the length is 50 yards longer than the width, what are the field's dimensions?

**28.** If 10 pens and 12 pads cost \$42, and 5 of the same pens and 10 of the same pads cost \$29, find the cost of a pen and a pad.

**29.** A ball is thrown vertically upward from the top of a 96-foot tall building with an initial velocity of 80 feet per second. The height of the ball above ground is modeled by the position function

$$s(t) = -16t^2 + 80t + 96.$$

**a.** After how many seconds will the ball strike the ground?
**b.** When does the ball reach its maximum height? What is the maximum height?

**30.** The current, $I$, in amperes, flowing in an electrical circuit varies inversely as the resistance, $R$, in ohms, in the circuit. When the resistance of an electric percolator is 22 ohms, it draws 5 amperes of current. How much current is needed when the resistance is 10 ohms?

**31.** An object moves in simple harmonic motion described by $d = 10 \sin \frac{3\pi}{4} t$, where $t$ is measured in seconds and $d$ in inches. Find: **a.** the maximum displacement; **b.** the frequency; and **c.** the time required for one oscillation.

*Verify each identity in Exercises 32–33.*

**32.** $\tan x + \dfrac{1}{\tan x} = \dfrac{1}{\sin x \cos x}$

**33.** $\dfrac{1 - \tan^2 x}{1 + \tan^2 x} = \cos 2x$

**34.** Graph one period: $y = -2\cos(3x - \pi)$.

*In Exercises 35–36, solve each equation on the interval* $[0, 2\pi)$.

**35.** $4\cos^2 x = 3$

**36.** $2\sin^2 x + 3\cos x - 3 = 0$

**37.** Find the exact value of $\cot\left[\cos^{-1}\left(-\frac{5}{6}\right)\right]$.

**38.** Graph the polar equation: $r = 1 + 2\cos\theta$.

**39.** In oblique triangle $ABC$, $A = 34°$, $a = 22$, and $b = 32$. Solve the triangle(s). Round lengths to the nearest tenth and angle measures to the nearest degree.

**40.** Use the parametric equations

$$x = \sin t, \quad y = 1 + \cos^2 t, \quad -\frac{\pi}{2} < t < \frac{\pi}{2},$$

and eliminate the parameter. Graph the plane curve represented by the parametric equations. Use arrows to show the orientation of the curve.

# Introduction to Calculus

## Chapter 12

In the dramatic arts, ours is the era of the movies. As individuals and as a nation, we've grown up with them. Our images of love, war, family, country—even of things that terrify us—owe much to what we've seen on screen.

Take a rapid sequence of still photographs of a moving scene and project them onto a screen at thirty shots a second or faster. Our eyes see the result as continuous motion. The small difference between one frame and the next cannot be detected by the human visual system. The idea of calculus likewise regards continuous motion as made up of a sequence of still configurations. In this chapter you will see how calculus masters the mystery of movement by "freezing the frame" instant by instant. You will learn to use mathematics in a way that is similar to making a movie.

# SECTION 12.1 Finding Limits Using Tables and Graphs

**Objectives**

1. Understand limit notation.
2. Find limits using tables.
3. Find limits using graphs.

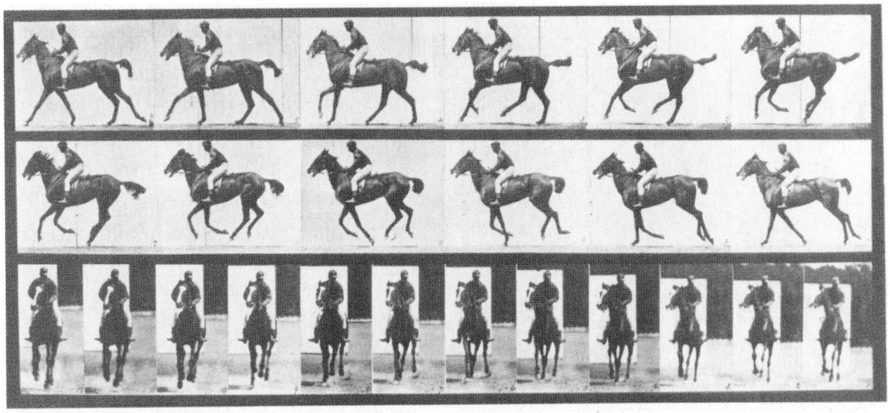

At any instant, an object must be at rest, an idea shown by these pictures of a running horse. Because this is true for all instants, the object will always be at rest, so how can motion arise? Calculus provides the methods for unraveling this paradox. *(Eadweard Muybridge (English 1830–1904), "'Annie G.' Cantering, Saddled," 1887. Collotype print, Size: sheet: 19 in. × 24 in., image: 7 1/2 in. × 16 1/4 in. Philadelphia Museum of Art: City of Philadelphia, Trade & Convention Center, Dept. of Commerce, 1962-135-280.)*

Motion and change are the very essence of life. Moving air brushes against our faces, rain falls on our heads, birds fly past us, plants spring from the earth, grow, and then die, and rocks thrown upward reach a maximum height before falling to the ground.

The tools of algebra and trigonometry are essentially static; numbers, points, lines, equations, functions, and graphs do not incorporate motion. The development of calculus in the middle of the seventeenth century provided a way to use these static tools to analyze motion and change. It took nearly two thousand years of effort for humankind to achieve this feat, made possible by a revolutionary concept called *limits*. The invention of limits marked a turning point in human history, having as dramatic an impact on our lives as the invention of the wheel and the printing press. In this section, we introduce this bold and dramatic style of thinking about mathematics.

**1** Understand limit notation.

## An Introduction to Limits

Suppose that you and a friend are walking along the graph of the function

$$f(x) = \frac{x^2 - 4}{x - 2}.$$

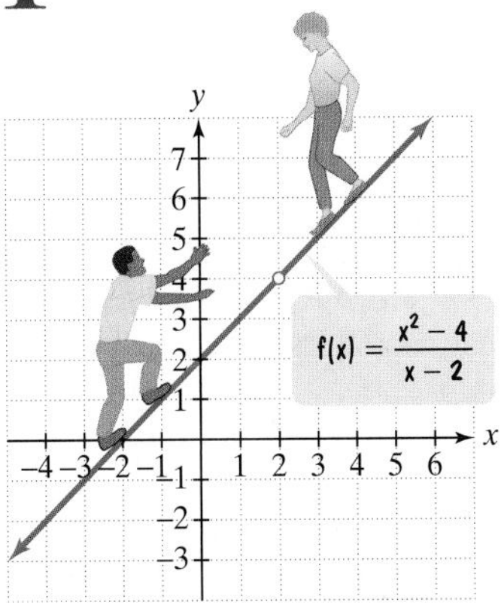


**Figure 12.1** Walking along the graph of $f$, very close to 2

Figure 12.1 illustrates that you are walking uphill and your friend is walking downhill. Because 2 is not in the domain of the function, there is a hole in the graph at $x = 2$. Warning signs along the graph might be appropriate: Caution: $f(2)$ is undefined! If you or your friend reach 2, you will fall through the hole and splatter onto the $x$-axis.

Obviously, there is a problem at $x = 2$. But what happens along the graph of $f(x) = \dfrac{x^2 - 4}{x - 2}$ as you and your friend walk very, very close to $x = 2$? What function value, $f(x)$, will each of you approach? One way to answer this question is to construct a table of function values to analyze numerically the behavior of

$f$ as $x$ gets closer and closer to 2. Remember that you are walking uphill, approaching 2 from the left side of 2. Your friend is walking downhill, approaching 2 from the right side of 2. Thus, we must include values of $x$ that are less than 2 and values of $x$ that are greater than 2.

In Table 12.1, we choose values of $x$ close to 2. As $x$ approaches 2 from the left, we arbitrarily start with $x = 1.99$. Then we select two additional values of $x$ that are closer to 2, but still less than 2. We choose 1.999 and 1.9999. As $x$ approaches 2 from the right, we arbitrarily start with $x = 2.01$. Then we select two additional values of $x$ that are closer to 2, but still greater than 2. We choose 2.001 and 2.0001. Finally, evaluate $f$ at each chosen value of $x$ to obtain Table 12.1.

## Technology

A graphing utility with a TABLE feature can be used to generate the entries in Table 12.1. In TBLSET, change Auto to Ask for Indpnt, the independent variable. Here is a typical screen that verifies Table 12.1.

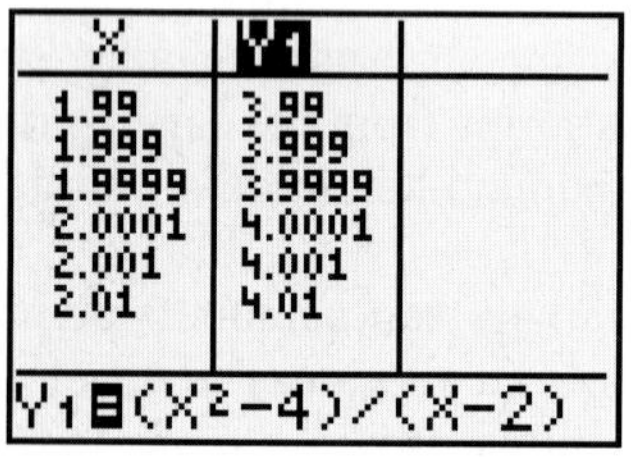

X
Y1
1.99
1.999
1.9999
2.0001
2.001
2.01
3.99
3.999
3.9999
4.0001
4.001
4.01
Y1■(X²-4)/(X-2)


**Table 12.1**

| | $x$ approaches 2 from the left. → | | | | ← $x$ approaches 2 from the right. | | |
|---|---|---|---|---|---|---|---|
| $x$ | 1.99 | 1.999 | 1.9999 | 2 | 2.0001 | 2.001 | 2.01 |
| $f(x) = \frac{x^2 - 4}{x - 2}$ | 3.99 | 3.999 | 3.9999 | Undefined | 4.0001 | 4.001 | 4.01 |
| | $f(x)$ gets closer to 4. → | | | | ← $f(x)$ gets closer to 4. | | |

From Table 12.1, it appears that as $x$ gets closer to 2, the values of $f(x) = \frac{x^2 - 4}{x - 2}$ get closer to 4. We say that

"The limit of $\frac{x^2 - 4}{x - 2}$ as $x$ approaches 2 equals the number 4."

We can express this sentence in a mathematical notation called **limit notation**. We use an arrow for the word *approaches*. Likewise, we use *lim* as shorthand for the word *limit*. Thus, the limit notation for the English sentence in quotations is

$$\lim_{x \to 2} \frac{x^2 - 4}{x - 2} = 4. \quad \text{The limit of } \frac{x^2 - 4}{x - 2} \text{ as } x \text{ approaches 2 equals the number 4.}$$

Calculus is the study of limits and their applications. Concepts that you will encounter in calculus are limits.

### Limit Notation and Its Description

Suppose that $f$ is a function defined on some open interval containing the number $a$. The function $f$ may or may not be defined at $a$. The **limit notation**

$$\lim_{x \to a} f(x) = L$$

is read "the limit of $f(x)$ as $x$ approaches $a$ equals the number $L$." This means that as $x$ gets closer to $a$, but remains unequal to $a$, the corresponding values of $f(x)$ get closer to $L$.

**2** Find limits using tables.

## Finding Limits Using Tables

To find $\lim_{x \to a} f(x)$, use a graphing utility with a TABLE feature or create a table by hand. Approach $a$ from the left, choosing values of $x$ that are close to $a$, but still less than $a$. Then approach $a$ from the right, choosing values of $x$ that are close to $a$, but still greater than $a$. Evaluate $f$ at each chosen value of $x$ to obtain the desired table.

Choose values of $x$ so that the table makes it obvious what the corresponding values of $f(x)$ are getting close to. If the values of $f(x)$ are getting close to the number $L$, we infer that

$$\lim_{x \to a} f(x) = L.$$

### EXAMPLE 1 Finding a Limit Using a Table

Find: $\lim_{x \to 4} 3x^2$.

**Solution** As $x$ gets closer to 4, but remains unequal to 4, we must find the number that the corresponding values of $3x^2$ get closer to. The voice balloons shown below indicate that in this limit problem, $f(x) = 3x^2$ and $a = 4$.

$$\lim_{x \to 4} 3x^2$$

This is $a$ in $\lim_{x \to a} f(x)$.

This is $f(x)$ in $\lim_{x \to a} f(x)$.

In making a table, we choose values of $x$ close to 4. As $x$ approaches 4 from the left, we arbitrarily start with $x = 3.99$. Then we select two additional values of $x$ that are closer to 4, but still less than 4. We choose 3.999 and 3.9999. As $x$ approaches 4 from the right, we arbitrarily start with $x = 4.01$. Then we select two additional numbers that are closer to 4, but still greater than 4. We choose 4.001 and 4.0001. Finally, evaluate $f$ at each chosen value of $x$ to obtain Table 12.2. The values of $f(x)$ in the table are rounded to four decimal places.

**Table 12.2**

**$x$ approaches 4 from the left.** → ← **$x$ approaches 4 from the right.**

| $x$ | 3.99 | 3.999 | 3.9999 | $\longrightarrow$ $\longleftarrow$ | 4.0001 | 4.001 | 4.01 |
|---|---|---|---|---|---|---|---|
| $f(x) = 3x^2$ | 47.7603 | 47.9760 | 47.9976 | $\longrightarrow$ $\longleftarrow$ | 48.0024 | 48.0240 | 48.2403 |

**$f(x)$ gets closer to 48.** → ← **$f(x)$ gets closer to 48.**

From Table 12.2, it appears that as $x$ gets closer to 4, the values of $3x^2$ get closer to 48. We infer that

$$\lim_{x \to 4} 3x^2 = 48.$$

**Check Point 1** Find: $\lim_{x \to 3} 4x^2$.

## EXAMPLE 2 Finding a Limit Using a Table

Find: $\lim_{x \to 0} \frac{\sin x}{x}$.

**Solution** As $x$ gets closer to 0, but remains unequal to 0, we must find the number that the corresponding values of $\frac{\sin x}{x}$ get closer to. The voice balloons shown below indicate that in this limit problem, $f(x) = \frac{\sin x}{x}$ and $a = 0$.

$$\lim_{x \to 0} \frac{\sin x}{x}$$

This is $a$ in $\lim_{x \to a} f(x)$.

This is $f(x)$ in $\lim_{x \to a} f(x)$.

Because division by 0 is undefined, the domain of $f(x) = \frac{\sin x}{x}$ is $\{x \mid x \neq 0\}$. Thus, $f$ is not defined at 0. However, in this limit problem, we do not care what is happening at $x = 0$. We are interested in the behavior of the function as $x$ gets close to 0. Table 12.3 shows the values of $f(x)$, rounded to five decimal places, as $x$ approaches 0 from the left and from the right. Values of $x$ in the table are measured in radians.

**Table 12.3**

| | *x* approaches 0 from the left. | | | | *x* approaches 0 from the right. | | |
|---|---|---|---|---|---|---|---|
| $x$ | −0.03 | −0.02 | −0.01 | ⟶ ⟵ | 0.01 | 0.02 | 0.03 |
| $f(x) = \frac{\sin x}{x}$ | 0.99985 | 0.99993 | 0.99998 | ⟶ ⟵ | 0.99998 | 0.99993 | 0.99985 |
| | $f(x)$ gets closer to 1. | | | | $f(x)$ gets closer to 1. | | |

From Table 12.3, it appears that as $x$ gets closer to 0, the value of $\frac{\sin x}{x}$ gets closer to 1. We infer that

$$\lim_{x \to 0} \frac{\sin x}{x} = 1.$$

### Technology

The graphs in Figure 12.2 support our inference that $\lim_{x \to 0} \frac{\sin x}{x} = 1$. We used the ZOOM IN feature to get close to $x = 0$ from both sides of 0. In each graph, can you see that as $x$ gets closer to 0, the values of $f(x)$ get closer to the number 1?

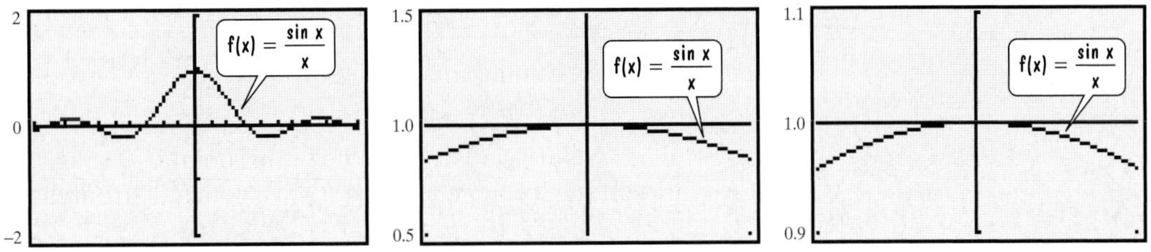


$[-10, 10, 1] \times [-2, 2, 1]$ $[-1, 1, 1] \times [0.5, 1.5, 1]$ $[-0.5, 0.5, 0.5] \times [0.9, 1.1, 0.1]$

**Figure 12.2**

**Check Point 2** Find: $\lim_{x \to 0} \frac{\cos x - 1}{x}$.

**3** Find limits using graphs.

## Finding Limits Using Graphs

The limit statement

$$\lim_{x \to a} f(x) = L$$

is illustrated in Figure 12.3. In the three graphs, the number that $x$ is approaching, $a$, is shown on the $x$-axis. The limit, $L$, is shown on the $y$-axis. Take a few minutes to examine the graphs. Can you see that as $x$ approaches $a$ along the $x$-axis, $f(x)$ approaches $L$ along the $y$-axis? In each graph, as $x$ gets closer to $a$, the values of $f(x)$ get closer to $L$.

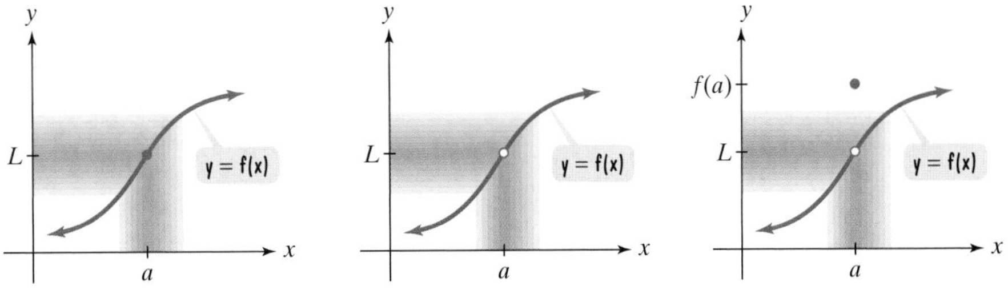


**(a)** **(b)** **(c)**

**Figure 12.3** In each graph, as $x$ gets closer to $a$, the values of $f$ get closer to $L$: $\lim_{x \to a} f(x) = L$.

In Figure 12.3(a), as $x$ approaches $a$, $f(x)$ approaches $L$. At $a$, the value of the function is $L$: $f(a) = L$. In Figure 12.3(b), as $x$ approaches $a$, $f(x)$ approaches $L$. This is true although $f$ is not defined at $a$, shown by the hole in the graph. In Figure 12.3(c), we again see that as $x$ approaches $a$, $f(x)$ approaches $L$. Notice, however, that the value of the function at $a$, $f(a)$, shown by the blue dot, is not equal to the limit: $f(a) \neq L$. What you get as you approach $a$ is not the same as what you get at $a$.

Example 3 on page 990 illustrates that the graph of a function can sometimes be helpful in finding limits.

## EXAMPLE 3 Finding a Limit by Using a Graph

Use the graph in Figure 12.4 to find:

**a.** $\lim_{x \to 4} f(x)$ **b.** $f(4)$.

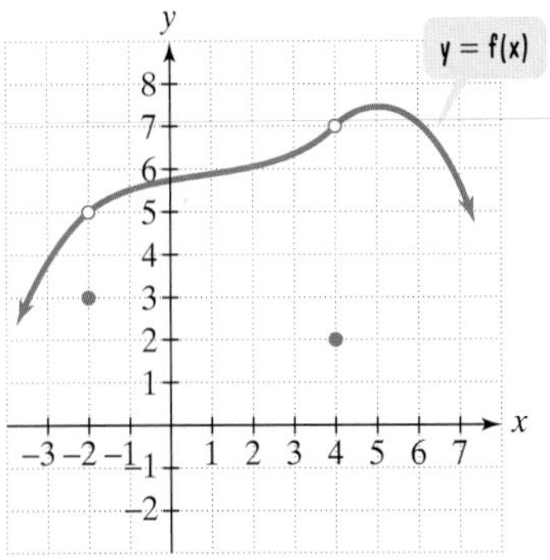


**Figure 12.4**

**Solution**

**a.** To find $\lim_{x \to 4} f(x)$ examine the graph of $f$ *near* $x = 4$. As $x$ gets closer to 4, the values of $f(x)$ get closer to the $y$-coordinate of the point shown by the open dot on the right. The $y$-coordinate of this point is 7. Thus, as $x$ gets closer to 4, the values of $f(x)$ get closer to 7. We conclude from the graph that

$$\lim_{x \to 4} f(x) = 7.$$

**b.** To find $f(4)$, examine the graph of $f$ *at* $x = 4$. At $x = 4$, the open dot is not included in the graph of $f$. The graph of $f$ is shown by the closed dot with coordinates $(4, 2)$. Thus, $f(4) = 2$.

In Example 3, notice that the value of $f$ at 4 has nothing to do with the conclusion that $\lim_{x \to 4} f(x) = 7$. Regardless of how $f$ is defined at 4, it is still true that $\lim_{x \to 4} f(x) = 7$. Furthermore, if $f$ were undefined at 4, the limit of $f(x)$ as $x \to 4$ would still equal 7.

**Check Point 3** Use the graph in Figure 12.4 to find:

**a.** $\lim_{x \to -2} f(x)$ **b.** $f(-2)$.

## EXAMPLE 4 Finding a Limit by Graphing a Function

Graph the function

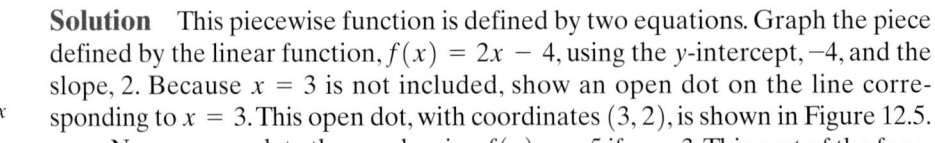

$$f(x) = \begin{cases} 2x - 4 & \text{if } x \neq 3 \\ -5 & \text{if } x = 3. \end{cases}$$

Use the graph to find $\lim_{x \to 3} f(x)$.

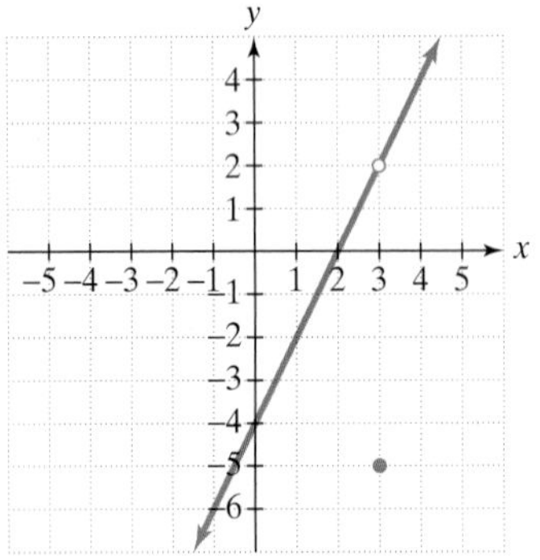


**Figure 12.5** As $x$ gets closer to 3, what number are the function values getting closer to?

**Solution** This piecewise function is defined by two equations. Graph the piece defined by the linear function, $f(x) = 2x - 4$, using the $y$-intercept, $-4$, and the slope, 2. Because $x = 3$ is not included, show an open dot on the line corresponding to $x = 3$. This open dot, with coordinates $(3, 2)$, is shown in Figure 12.5.

Now we complete the graph using $f(x) = -5$ if $x = 3$. This part of the function is graphed as the point $(3, -5)$, shown as a closed blue dot in Figure 12.5.

To find $\lim_{x \to 3} f(x)$, examine the graph of $f$ near $x = 3$. As $x$ gets closer to 3, the values of $f(x)$ get closer to the $y$-coordinate of the point shown by the open dot. The $y$-coordinate of this point is 2. We conclude from the graph that

$$\lim_{x \to 3} f(x) = 2.$$

**Check Point 4** Graph the function

$$f(x) = \begin{cases} 3x - 2 & \text{if } x \neq 2 \\ 1 & \text{if } x = 2. \end{cases}$$

Use the graph to find $\lim_{x \to 2} f(x)$.

## EXERCISE SET 12.1

### Practice Exercises

*In Exercises 1–4, use each table to find the indicated limit.*

**1.** $\lim_{x \to 2} x^2$

| $x$ | 1.99 | 1.999 | 1.9999 | $\rightarrow \leftarrow$ | 2.0001 | 2.001 | 2.01 |
|---|---|---|---|---|---|---|---|
| $f(x) = x^2$ | 3.960 | 3.996 | 3.9996 | $\rightarrow \leftarrow$ | 4.0004 | 4.004 | 4.040 |

**2.** $\lim_{x \to 3} 5x^2$

| $x$ | 2.99 | 2.999 | 2.9999 | $\rightarrow \leftarrow$ | 3.0001 | 3.001 | 3.01 |
|---|---|---|---|---|---|---|---|
| $f(x) = 5x^2$ | 44.701 | 44.970 | 44.997 | $\rightarrow \leftarrow$ | 45.003 | 45.03 | 45.301 |

**3.** $\lim_{x \to 0} \frac{\sin 3x}{x}$

| $x$ | −0.03 | −0.02 | −0.01 | $\rightarrow \leftarrow$ | 0.01 | 0.02 | 0.03 |
|---|---|---|---|---|---|---|---|
| $f(x) = \frac{\sin 3x}{x}$ | 2.9960 | 2.9982 | 2.9996 | $\rightarrow \leftarrow$ | 2.9996 | 2.9982 | 2.996 |

**4.** $\lim_{x \to 0} \frac{\sin 4x}{\sin 2x}$

| $x$ | −0.03 | −0.02 | −0.01 | $\rightarrow \leftarrow$ | 0.01 | 0.02 | 0.03 |
|---|---|---|---|---|---|---|---|
| $f(x) = \frac{\sin 4x}{\sin 2x}$ | 1.9964 | 1.9984 | 1.9996 | $\rightarrow \leftarrow$ | 1.9996 | 1.9984 | 1.9964 |

*In Exercises 5–18, construct a table and find the indicated limit.*

**5.** $\lim_{x \to 2} 5x^2$

**6.** $\lim_{x \to 2} (x^2 - 1)$

**7.** $\lim_{x \to 3} \frac{1}{x - 2}$

**8.** $\lim_{x \to 4} \frac{1}{x - 3}$

**9.** $\lim_{x \to 0} \frac{x}{x^2 + 1}$

**10.** $\lim_{x \to 0} \frac{x + 1}{x^2 + 1}$

**11.** $\lim_{x \to -2} \frac{x^3 + 8}{x + 2}$

**12.** $\lim_{x \to -5} \frac{x^2 - 25}{x + 5}$

**13.** $\lim_{x \to 0} \frac{2x^2 + x}{\sin x}$

**14.** $\lim_{x \to 0} \frac{\sin x^2}{x}$

**15.** $\lim_{x \to 0} \frac{\tan x}{x}$

**16.** $\lim_{x \to 0} \frac{x^2}{\sec x - 1}$

**17.** $\lim_{x \to 0} f(x)$, where $f(x) = \begin{cases} x + 1 & \text{if } x < 0 \\ 2x + 1 & \text{if } x \geq 0 \end{cases}$

**18.** $\lim_{x \to 0} f(x)$, where $f(x) = \begin{cases} x + 2 & \text{if } x < 0 \\ 3x + 2 & \text{if } x \geq 0 \end{cases}$

*In Exercises 19–22, use the graph of f to find the indicated limit and function value.*

**19.**

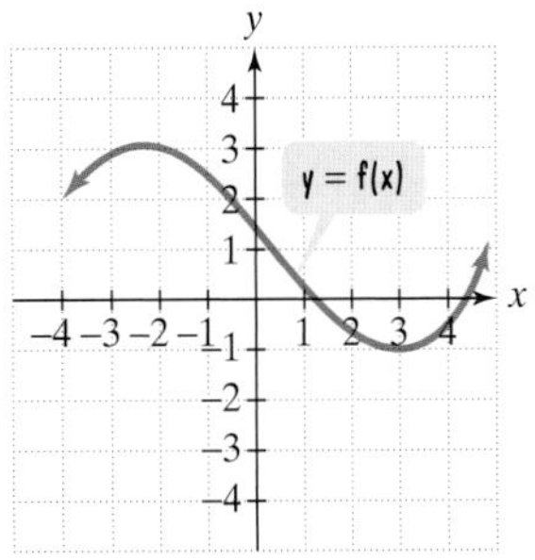


**a.** $\lim_{x \to 3} f(x)$

**b.** $f(3)$

**20.**

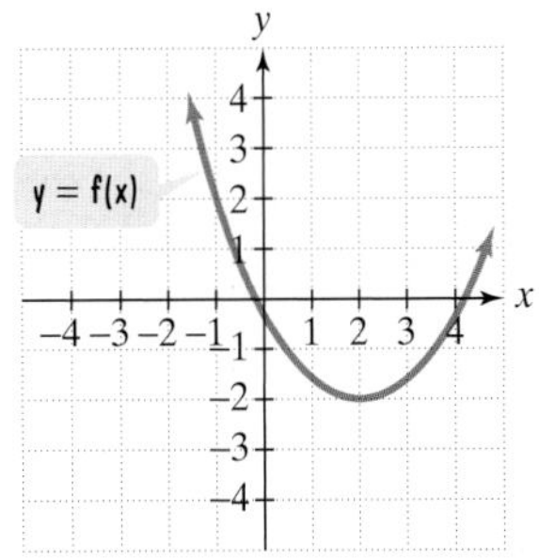


**a.** $\lim_{x \to 2} f(x)$

**b.** $f(2)$

**21.**

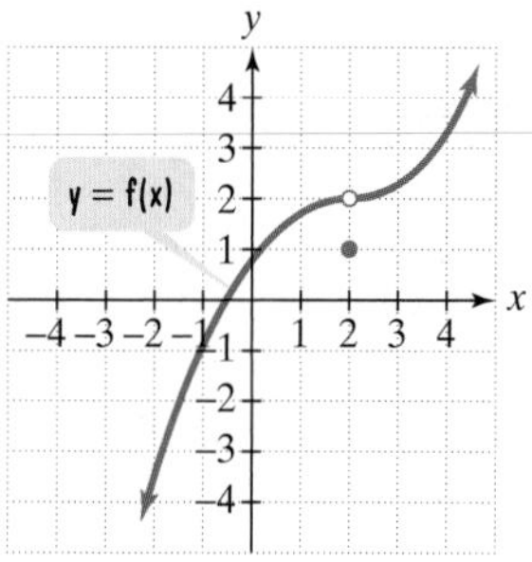


**a.** $\lim_{x \to 2} f(x)$ **b.** $f(2)$

**22.**

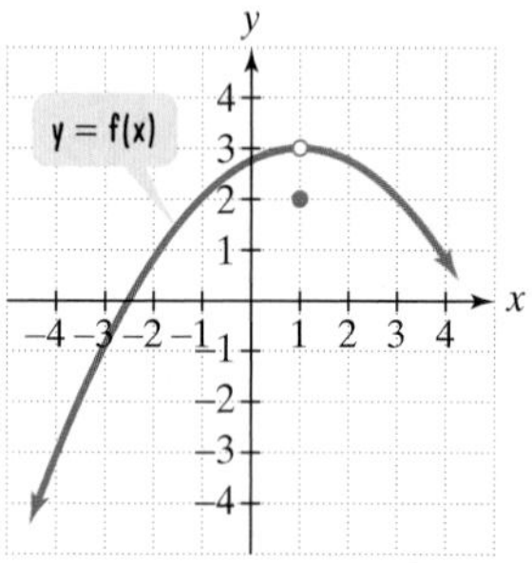


**a.** $\lim_{x \to 1} f(x)$ **b.** $f(1)$

*In Exercises 23–26, use the graph and the viewing rectangle shown below the graph to find the indicated limit.*

**23.** $\lim_{x \to 2} (1 - x^2)$

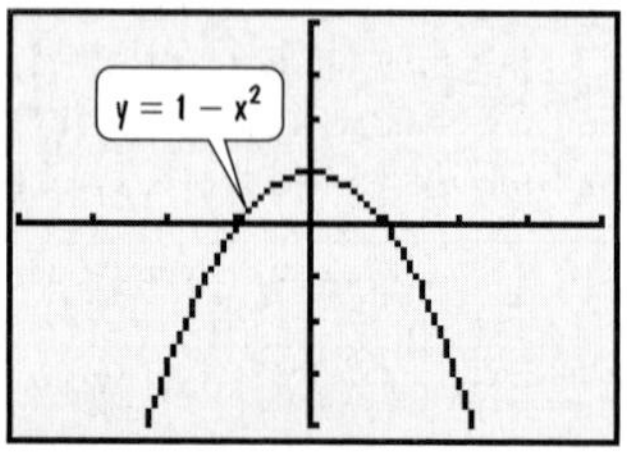


$[-4, 4, 1] \times [-4, 4, 1]$

**24.** $\lim_{x \to -2} |2x|$

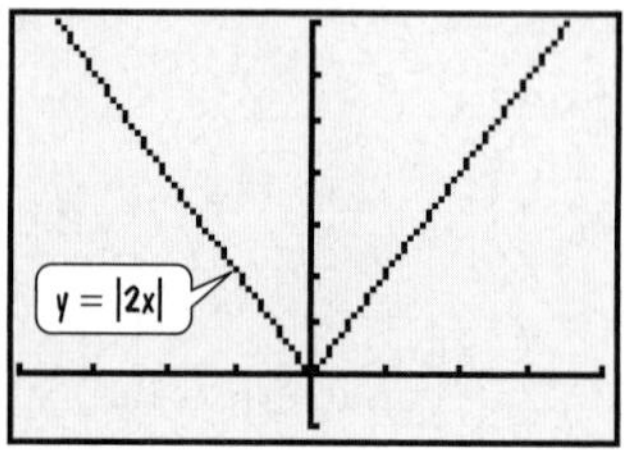


$[-4, 4, 1] \times [-1, 7, 1]$

**25.** $\lim_{x \to -\frac{\pi}{2}} \sin x$

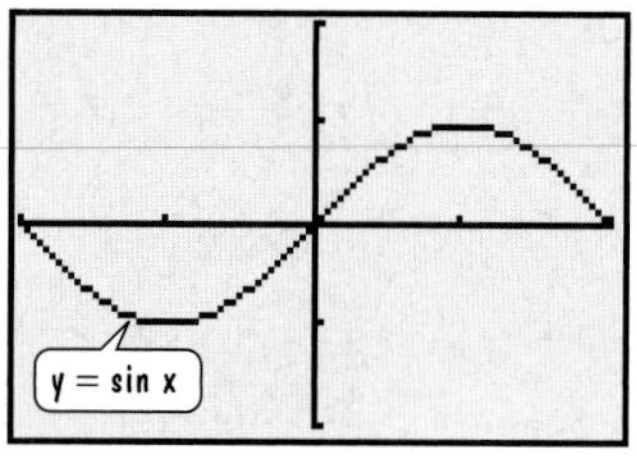


$\left[-\pi, \pi, \frac{\pi}{2}\right] \times [-2, 2, 1]$

**26.** $\lim_{x \to -\frac{\pi}{2}} \cos x$

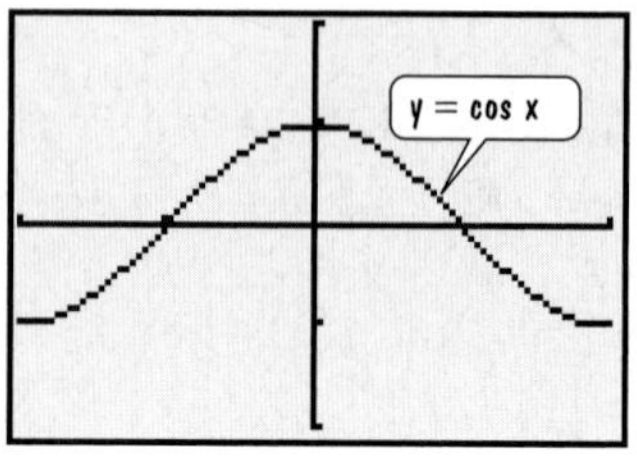


$\left[-\pi, \pi, \frac{\pi}{2}\right] \times [-2, 2, 1]$

*In Exercises 27–48, graph each function. Then use your graph to find the indicated limit.*

**27.** $f(x) = 2x + 1, \lim_{x \to 3} f(x)$

**28.** $f(x) = 2x - 1, \lim_{x \to 3} f(x)$

**29.** $f(x) = 4 - x^2, \lim_{x \to -3} f(x)$

**30.** $f(x) = 9 - x^2, \lim_{x \to -2} f(x)$

**31.** $f(x) = |x + 1|, \lim_{x \to -1} f(x)$

**32.** $f(x) = |x + 2|, \lim_{x \to -2} f(x)$

**33.** $f(x) = \frac{1}{x}, \lim_{x \to -1} f(x)$

**34.** $f(x) = \frac{1}{x^2}, \lim_{x \to -1} f(x)$

**35.** $f(x) = \frac{x^2 - 1}{x - 1}, \lim_{x \to 1} f(x)$

**36.** $f(x) = \frac{x^2 - 4}{x - 2}, \lim_{x \to 2} f(x)$

**37.** $f(x) = e^x, \lim_{x \to 0} f(x)$

**38.** $f(x) = \ln x, \lim_{x \to 1} f(x)$

**39.** $f(x) = \sin x, \lim_{x \to \pi} f(x)$

**40.** $f(x) = \cos x, \lim_{x \to \pi} f(x)$

**41.** $f(x) = \begin{cases} x+1 & \text{if } x \neq 2 \\ 5 & \text{if } x = 2, \end{cases}$ $\lim_{x \to 2} f(x)$

**42.** $f(x) = \begin{cases} x-1 & \text{if } x \neq 3 \\ 4 & \text{if } x = 3, \end{cases}$ $\lim_{x \to 3} f(x)$

**43.** $f(x) = \begin{cases} x+3 & \text{if } x < 0 \\ 3 & \text{if } x \geq 0, \end{cases}$ $\lim_{x \to 0} f(x)$

**44.** $f(x) = \begin{cases} x+4 & \text{if } x < 0 \\ 4 & \text{if } x \geq 0, \end{cases}$ $\lim_{x \to 0} f(x)$

**45.** $f(x) = \begin{cases} 2x & \text{if } x < 1 \\ x+1 & \text{if } x \geq 1, \end{cases}$ $\lim_{x \to 1} f(x)$

**46.** $f(x) = \begin{cases} 3x & \text{if } x < 1 \\ x+2 & \text{if } x \geq 1, \end{cases}$ $\lim_{x \to 1} f(x)$

**47.** $f(x) = \begin{cases} x & \text{if } x < 0 \\ \sin x & \text{if } x \geq 0, \end{cases}$ $\lim_{x \to 0} f(x)$

**48.** $f(x) = \begin{cases} x+1 & \text{if } x < 0 \\ \cos x & \text{if } x \geq 0, \end{cases}$ $\lim_{x \to 0} f(x)$

## Application Exercises

**49.** You are approaching a fan located at 3 on the $x$-axis.

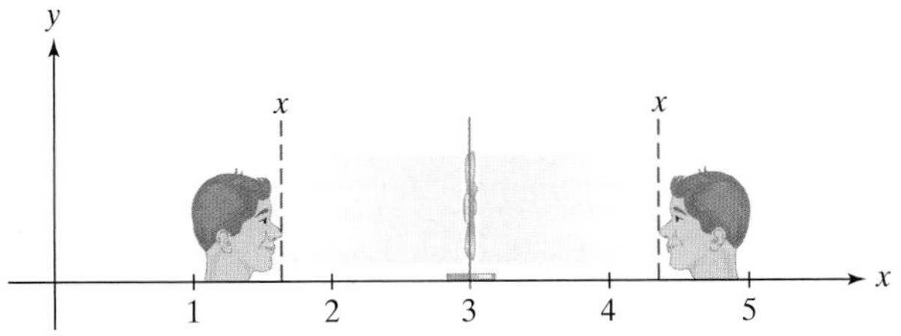


The function $f$ describes the breeze that you feel, $f(x)$, in miles per hour, when your nose is at position $x$ on the $x$-axis. Use the values in the table to solve this exercise.

| $x$ | 2.9 | 2.99 | 2.999 $\rightarrow$ $\leftarrow$ 3.001 | 3.01 | 3.1 |
|---|---|---|---|---|---|
| $f(x)$ | 7.7 | 7.92 | 7.991 $\rightarrow$ $\leftarrow$ 7.991 | 7.92 | 7.7 |

**a.** Find $\lim_{x \to 3} f(x)$. Describe what this means in terms of the location of your nose and the breeze that you feel.

**b.** Would it be a good idea to move closer so that you actually reach $x = 3$? Describe the difference between what you feel for $\lim_{x \to 3} f(x)$ and $f(3)$.

**50.** You are riding along an expressway traveling $x$ miles per hour. The function $f(x) = 0.015x^2 + x + 10$ describes the recommended safe distance, $f(x)$, in feet, between your car and other cars on the expressway. Use the values in the table at the top of the next column to find $\lim_{x \to 60} f(x)$. Describe what this means in terms of your car's speed and the recommended safe distance.

| $x$ | 59.9 | 59.99 | 59.999 $\rightarrow$ $\leftarrow$ 60.001 | 60.01 | 60.1 |
|---|---|---|---|---|---|
| $f(x) = 0.015x^2 + x + 10$ | 123.72 | 123.972 | 123.997 $\rightarrow$ $\leftarrow$ 124.003 | 124.028 | 124.28 |

*How many paid vacation days can you expect? The function*

$$f(x) = -0.016x^2 + 0.93x + 8.5$$

*models the average number of paid vacation days each year, $f(x)$, for full-time workers at medium to large U.S. companies after $x$ years. Use the graph of $f$ to solve Exercises 51–52.*

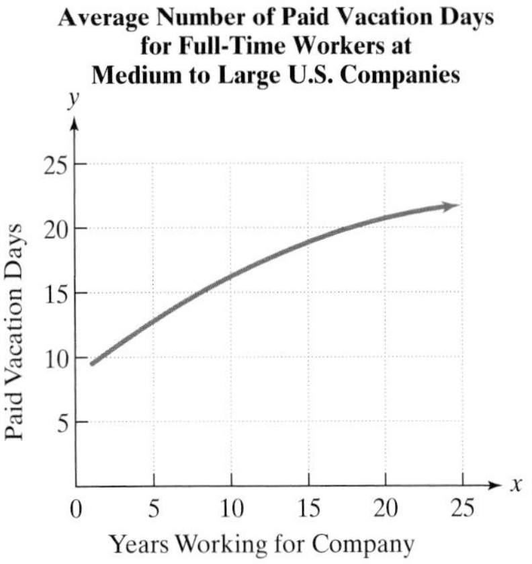


*Source:* Bureau of Labor Statistics

**51.** How many vacation days, to the nearest whole day, can you expect as your time with the company is close to 10 years? Use limit notation to express the answer.

**52.** How many vacation days, to the nearest whole day, can you expect as your time with the company is close to 20 years? Use limit notation to express the answer.

**53.** You rent a car from a company that charges \$20 per day plus \$0.10 per mile. The car is driven 200 miles in the first day. The figure shows the graph of the cost, $f(x)$, in dollars, as a function of the miles, $x$, that you drive the car.

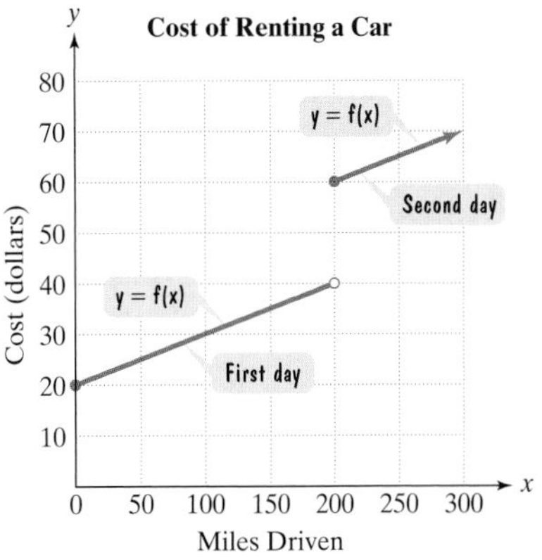


**a.** Find $\lim_{x \to 100} f(x)$. Interpret the limit, referring to miles driven and cost.

**b.** For the first day only, what is the rental cost approaching as the mileage gets closer to 200?

**c.** What is the cost to rent the car at the start of the second day?

**54.** You are building a greenhouse next to your house, as shown in the figure. Because the house will be used for one side of the enclosure, only three sides will need to be enclosed. You have 60 feet of fiberglass to enclose the three walls.

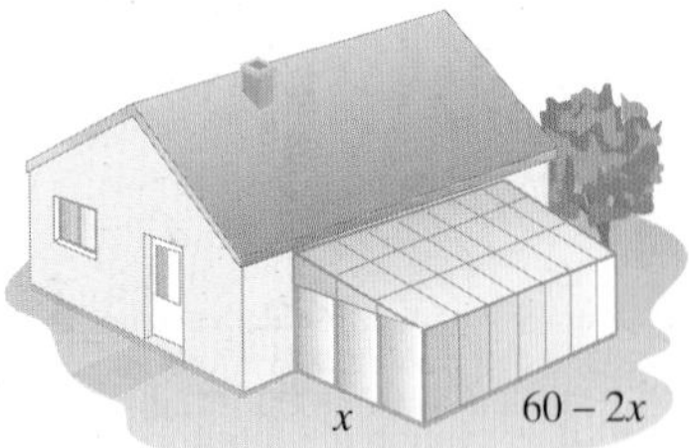


The function $f(x) = x(60 - 2x)$ describes the area of the greenhouse that you can enclose, $A(x)$, in square feet if the width of the greenhouse is $x$ feet.

**a.** Use the table shown to find $\lim_{x \to 15} f(x)$.

| X | Y1 | |
|---|---|---|
| 14.7 | 449.82 | |
| 14.8 | 449.92 | |
| 14.9 | 449.98 | |
| 15 | | |
| 15.1 | 449.98 | |
| 15.2 | 449.92 | |
| 15.3 | 449.82 | |

Y1=X*(60-2X)

**b.** Use the graph shown to find $\lim_{x \to 15} f(x)$. Do you get the same limit as you did in part (a)? What information about the limit is shown by the graph that might not be obvious from the table?

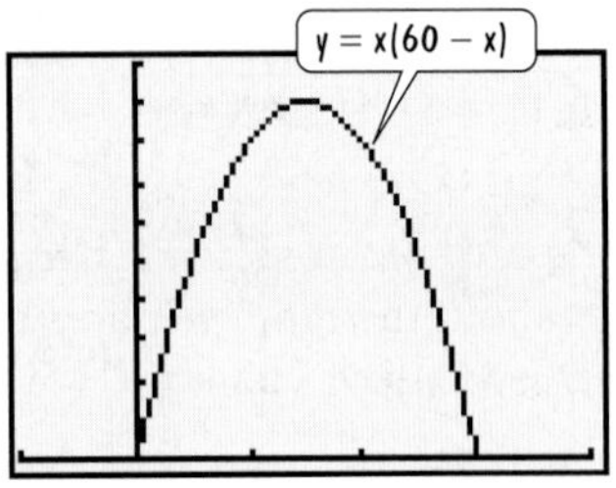


$[-10, 40, 10] \times [0, 500, 50]$

## Writing in Mathematics

**55.** Explain how to read $\lim_{x \to a} f(x) = L$.

**56.** What does the limit notation $\lim_{x \to a} f(x) = L$ mean?

**57.** Without showing the details, explain how to use a table to find $\lim_{x \to 4} x^2$.

**58.** Explain how a graph can be used to find a limit.

**59.** When we find $\lim_{x \to a} f(x)$, we do not care about the value of the function at $x = a$. Explain why this is so.

**60.** "You're really annoying me. You're pushing me to the limit." Discuss the use of the word *limit* in English and compare its everyday use to its meaning in mathematics.

**61.** Describe a practical situation in which interest lies in getting closer and closer to something rather than actually being there.

## Technology Exercises

**62.** Use the TABLE feature of your graphing utility to verify any five of the limits that you found in Exercises 5–16.

**63.** Use the ZOOM IN feature of your graphing utility to verify any five of the limits that you found in Exercises 27–40. Zoom in on the graph of the given function, $f$, near $x = a$ to verify each limit.

*In Exercises 64–67, estimate $\lim_{x \to a} f(x)$ by using the* TABLE *feature of your graphing utility to create a table of values. Then use the* ZOOM IN *feature to zoom in on the graph of $f$ near $x = a$ to justify or improve your estimate.*

**64.** $\lim_{x \to 0} \dfrac{2^x - 1}{x}$

**65.** $\lim_{x \to 4} \dfrac{\ln x - \ln 4}{x - 4}$

**66.** $\lim_{x \to 1} \dfrac{x^{3/2} - 1}{x - 1}$

**67.** $\lim_{x \to 0} \dfrac{x^2}{1 - \cos 2x}$

## Critical Thinking Exercises

**68.** Give an example of a function that is not defined at 2 for which $\lim_{x \to 2} f(x) = 5$.

**69.** Consider the function $f(x) = 3x + 2$. As $x$ approaches 1, $f(x)$ approaches 5: $\lim_{x \to 1} f(x) = 5$. Find the values of $x$ such that $f(x)$ is within 0.1 of 5 by solving

$$|f(x) - 5| < 0.1.$$

Then find the values of $x$ such that $f(x)$ is within 0.01 of 5.

**70.** Find an estimate of $3^{\pi}$ ($\pi \approx 3.14159265$) by taking a sequence of rational numbers, $x_1, x_2, x_3, \ldots$ that approaches $\pi$. Obtain your estimate by evaluating $3^{x_1}, 3^{x_2}, 3^{x_3}, \ldots$.

# SECTION 12.2 Finding Limits Using Properties of Limits

## Objectives

1. Find limits of constant and identity functions.
2. Find limits using properties of limits.
3. Find limits of fractional expressions in which the limit of the denominator and numerator are zero.

Isaac Newton

Gottfried Leibniz

Calculus was invented independently by British mathematician Isaac Newton (1642–1727) and German mathematician Gottfried Leibniz (1646–1716). Although Newton stated that limits were the basic concept in calculus, neither he nor Leibniz was able to express the idea of a limit in a precise mathematical fashion. In essence, Newton and Leibniz developed calculus into a powerful tool even though they could not fully understand why the tool worked.

A great triumph of calculus came with the work of German mathematician Karl Weierstrass (1815–1897). Weierstrass provided a precise definition of $\lim_{x\to a} f(x) = L$, placing calculus on a sound footing almost two hundred years after its invention. The properties of limits presented in this section are theorems that you will prove in calculus using this definition. In this section, you will learn to apply these properties to find limits.

**1** Find limits of constant and identity functions.

## Limits Involving Constant and Identity Functions

We frequently encounter the constant function, $f(x) = c$, and the identity function, $f(x) = x$. Figure 12.6 shows the graph of the constant function. The graph is a horizontal line. What does this mean about the limit as $x$ approaches $a$? Regardless of how close $x$ is to $a$, the corresponding value of $f(x)$ is $c$. Thus, if $f(x) = c$, $\lim_{x\to a} f(x) = c$.

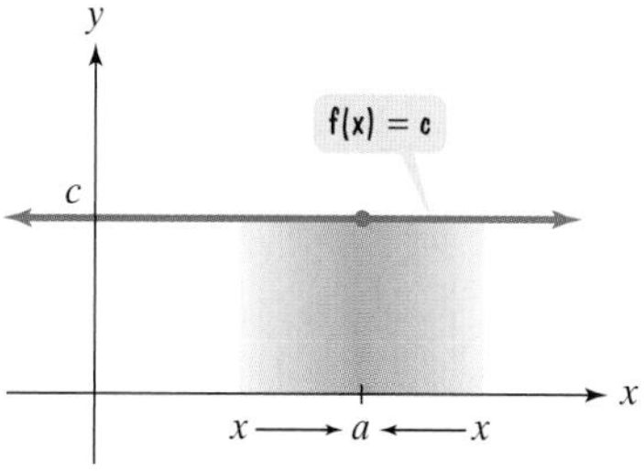


**Figure 12.6** The graph of the constant function $f(x) = c$. No matter how close $x$ is to $a$, the corresponding value of $f(x)$ is $c$.

**Limit of a Constant Function**

For the constant function $f(x) = c$,

$$\lim_{x\to a} f(x) = \lim_{x\to a} c = c$$

where $a$ is any number. In words, the limit of any constant is that constant.

## EXAMPLE 1 Finding Limits of Constant Functions

Find the following limits:

**a.** $\lim_{x\to 4} 7$ **b.** $\lim_{x\to 0} (-5)$.

**Solution** Regardless of what number $x$ is approaching, the limit of any constant is that constant: $\lim_{x\to a} c = c$. Using this formula, we find the given limits.

**a.** $\lim_{x\to 4} 7 = 7$ **b.** $\lim_{x\to 0} (-5) = -5$

**Check Point 1** Find the following limits:

**a.** $\lim_{x\to 8} 11$ **b.** $\lim_{x\to 0} (-9)$

The graph of the identity function, $f(x) = x$, is shown in Figure 12.7. Each input for this function is associated with an identical output. What does this mean about the limit as $x$ approaches $a$? For any value of $a$, as $x$ gets closer to $a$, the corresponding value of $f(x)$ is just as close to $a$. Thus, if $f(x) = x$, $\lim_{x\to a} f(x) = a$.

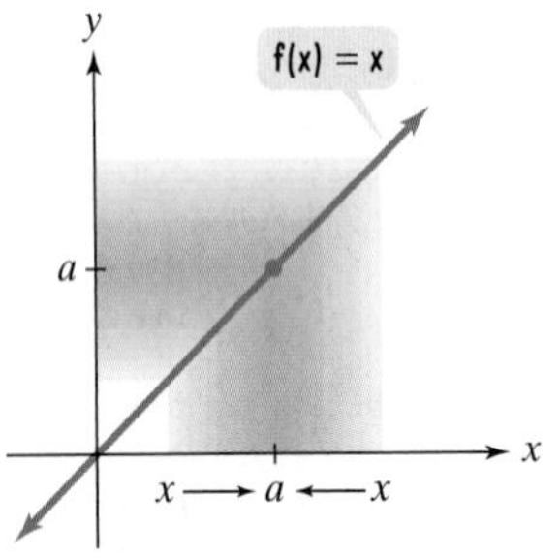


**Figure 12.7** The graph of the identity function $f(x) = x$. No matter how close $x$ is to $a$, the corresponding value of $f(x)$ is just as close to $a$.

### Limit of an Identity Function

For the identity function $f(x) = x$,

$$\lim_{x\to a} f(x) = \lim_{x\to a} x = a$$

where $a$ is any number. In words, the limit of $x$ as $x$ approaches any number is that number.

## EXAMPLE 2 Finding Limits of the Identity Function

Find the following limits:

**a.** $\lim_{x\to 7} x$ **b.** $\lim_{x\to -\pi} x$.

**Solution** We use the formula $\lim_{x\to a} x = a$. The number that $x$ is approaching is also the limit.

**a.** $\lim_{x\to 7} x = 7$ **b.** $\lim_{x\to -\pi} x = -\pi$

**Check Point 2** Find the following limits:

**a.** $\lim_{x\to 19} x$ **b.** $\lim_{x\to -\sqrt{2}} x$.

**2** Find limits using properties of limits.

## Properties of Limits

How do we find the limit of a sum, such as

$$\lim_{x\to 5} (x + 7)?$$

We find the limit of each function in the sum:

$$\lim_{x \to 5} x = 5 \quad \text{and} \quad \lim_{x \to 5} 7 = 7$$

Use the formula $\lim_{x \to a} x = a$.

Use the formula $\lim_{x \to a} c = c$.

Then we add each of these limits. Thus,

$$\lim_{x \to 5} (x + 7) = \lim_{x \to 5} x + \lim_{x \to 5} 7 = 5 + 7 = 12.$$

This is an application of a limit property involving the limit of a sum.

### The Limit of a Sum

If $\lim_{x \to a} f(x) = L$ and $\lim_{x \to a} g(x) = M$, then

$$\lim_{x \to a} [f(x) + g(x)] = \lim_{x \to a} f(x) + \lim_{x \to a} g(x) = L + M.$$

In words, the limit of the sum of two functions equals the sum of their limits.

### The Feud Over Who Invented Calculus

"How dare Leibniz publish a book on calculus!" fumed Isaac Newton. "He stole my ideas when he was in England. This will not pass easily."

Although Newton and Leibniz invented calculus independently, Newton's overwhelming fear of criticism kept him from publishing. Leibniz published his work on calculus in 1684; Newton waited over 20 years after he invented calculus and did not publish until 1687. Newton was dismayed that he did not publish his version first. Leibniz was accused of plagiarism in a report written by members of the Royal Society in England. The author of the report was not a matter of public record, for Newton himself had written most of it. Newton's accusations against Leibniz set off a bitter dispute between British mathematicians and mathematicians on Continental Europe that lasted over 100 years.

## EXAMPLE 3 Finding the Limit of a Sum

Find: $\lim_{x \to -4} (x + 9)$.

**Solution** The two functions in this limit problem are $f(x) = x$ and $g(x) = 9$. We seek the limit of the sum of these functions.

$$\lim_{x \to -4} (x + 9) = \lim_{x \to -4} x + \lim_{x \to -4} 9$$ The limit of a sum is the sum of the limits.

$$= -4 + 9$$ $\lim_{x \to a} x = a$ and $\lim_{x \to a} c = c$.

$$= 5$$

**Check Point 3** Find: $\lim_{x \to -3} (x + 16)$.

In calculus, you will prove the following property involving the limit of the difference of two functions.

### The Limit of a Difference

If $\lim_{x \to a} f(x) = L$ and $\lim_{x \to a} g(x) = M$, then

$$\lim_{x \to a} [f(x) - g(x)] = \lim_{x \to a} f(x) - \lim_{x \to a} g(x) = L - M.$$

In words, the limit of the difference of two functions equals the difference of their limits.

### EXAMPLE 4 Finding the Limit of a Difference

Find: $\lim_{x \to 5} (12 - x)$.

**Solution** The two functions in this limit problem are $f(x) = 12$ and $g(x) = x$. We seek the limit of the difference of these functions.

$$\lim_{x \to 5} (12 - x) = \lim_{x \to 5} 12 - \lim_{x \to 5} x$$ The limit of a difference is the difference of the limits.

$$= 12 - 5$$ $\lim_{x \to a} c = c$ and $\lim_{x \to a} x = a$

$$= 7$$

**Check Point 4** Find: $\lim_{x \to 14} (19 - x)$.

Now we consider a property that will enable you to find the limit of the product of two functions.

**The Limit of a Product**

If $\lim_{x \to a} f(x) = L$ and $\lim_{x \to a} g(x) = M$, then

$$\lim_{x \to a} [f(x) \cdot g(x)] = \lim_{x \to a} f(x) \cdot \lim_{x \to a} g(x) = LM.$$

In words, the limit of the product of two functions equals the product of their limits.

### EXAMPLE 5 Finding the Limit of a Product

Find: $\lim_{x \to 5} (-6x)$.

**Solution** The two functions in this limit problem are $f(x) = -6$ and $g(x) = x$. We seek the limit of the product of these functions.

$$\lim_{x \to 5} (-6x) = \lim_{x \to 5} (-6) \cdot \lim_{x \to 5} x$$ The limit of a product is the product of the limits.

$$= -6 \cdot 5$$ $\lim_{x \to a} c = c$ and $\lim_{x \to a} x = a$.

$$= -30$$

**Check Point 5** Find: $\lim_{x \to 7} (-10x)$.

### EXAMPLE 6 Finding Limits Using Properties of Limits

Find the following limits:

**a.** $\lim_{x \to -3} (7x - 4)$ **b.** $\lim_{x \to 5} 6x^2$.

**Solution**

**a.** $\lim_{x \to -3} (7x - 4) = \lim_{x \to -3} (7x) - \lim_{x \to -3} 4$ — The limit of a difference is the difference of the limits.

$= \lim_{x \to -3} 7 \cdot \lim_{x \to -3} x - \lim_{x \to -3} 4$ — The limit of a product is the product of the limits.

$= 7(-3) - 4$ — $\lim_{x \to a} c = c$ and $\lim_{x \to a} x = a$.

$= -21 - 4$

$= -25$

**b.** $\lim_{x \to 5} 6x^2 = \lim_{x \to 5} 6 \cdot \lim_{x \to 5} x^2$ — The limit of a product is the product of the limits.

$= 6 \cdot \lim_{x \to 5} (x \cdot x)$ — $\lim_{x \to a} c = c$

$= 6 \cdot \lim_{x \to 5} x \cdot \lim_{x \to 5} x$ — The limit of a product is the product of the limits.

$= 6 \cdot 5 \cdot 5$ — $\lim_{x \to a} x = a$

$= 150$

**Check Point 6** Find the following limits:

**a.** $\lim_{x \to -5} (3x - 7)$ **b.** $\lim_{x \to 3} 8x^2$.

The procedure used in Example 6(b) can be used to find the limit of any monomial function in the form $f(x) = b_n x^n$, where $n$ is a positive integer and $b_n$ is a constant.

$\lim_{x \to a} b_n x^n = \lim_{x \to a} b_n \cdot \lim_{x \to a} x^n$ — The limit of product is the product of the limits.

$= b_n \cdot \lim_{x \to a} (x \cdot x \cdot x \cdot \ldots \cdot x)$ — $\lim_{x \to a} c = c$

By definition, $x^n$ contains $n$ factors of $x$.

$= b_n \cdot \lim_{x \to a} x \cdot \lim_{x \to a} x \cdot \lim_{x \to a} x \cdot \ldots \cdot \lim_{x \to a} x$ — The limit of the product containing $n$ factors is the product of the limits.

There are $n$ factors of $\lim_{x \to a} x$.

$= b_n \cdot a \cdot a \cdot a \cdot \ldots \cdot a$ — $\lim_{x \to a} x = a$

There are $n$ factors of $a$.

$= b_n a^n$

This is the monomial function $f(x) = b_n x^n$ evaluated at $a$.

**Limit of a Monomial**

If $n$ is a positive integer and $b_n$ is a constant, then

$$\lim_{x \to a} b_n x^n = b_n a^n$$

for any number $a$. In words, the limit of a monomial as $x$ approaches $a$ is the monomial evaluated at $a$.

## EXAMPLE 7 Finding the Limit of a Monomial

Find: $\lim_{x\to 2}(-6x^4)$.

**Solution** The limit of the monomial, $-6x^4$, as $x$ approaches 2 is the monomial evaluated at 2. Thus, we find the limit by substituting 2 for $x$.

$$\lim_{x\to 2}(-6x^4) = -6 \cdot 2^4 = -6 \cdot 16 = -96$$

**Check Point 7** Find: $\lim_{x\to 2}(-7x^3)$.

How do we find the limit of a polynomial function

$$f(x) = b_n x^n + b_{n-1}x^{n-1} + \cdots + b_1 x + b_0$$

as $x$ approaches $a$? A polynomial is a sum of monomials. Thus, the limit of a polynomial is the sum of the limits of its monomials.

$$\lim_{x\to a} f(x) = \lim_{x\to a}(b_n x^n + b_{n-1}x^{n-1} + \cdots + b_1 x + b_0)$$ *f is a polynomial function.*

$$= \lim_{x\to a} b_n x^n + \lim_{x\to a} b_{n-1}x^{n-1} + \cdots + \lim_{x\to a} b_1 x + \lim_{x\to a} b_0$$ *The limit of a sum is the sum of the limits.*

$$= b_n a^n + b_{n-1}a^{n-1} + \cdots + b_1 a + b_0$$ *Find limits by evaluating monomials at a. Find the last limit in the sum using $\lim_{x\to a} c = c$.*

*This is the polynomial function $f(x) = b_n x^n + b_{n-1}x^{n-1} + \cdots + b_1 x + b_0$ evaluated at a.*

$$= f(a)$$

**Limit of a Polynomial**

If $f$ is a polynomial function, then

$$\lim_{x\to a} f(x) = f(a)$$

for any number $a$. In words, the limit of a polynomial as $x$ approaches $a$ is the polynomial evaluated at $a$.

## EXAMPLE 8 Finding the Limit of a Polynomial

Find: $\lim_{x\to 3}(4x^3 + 2x^2 - 6x + 5)$.

**Solution** The limit of the polynomial, $4x^3 + 2x^2 - 6x + 5$, is the polynomial evaluated at 3. Thus, we find the limit by substituting 3 for $x$.

$$\lim_{x\to 3}(4x^3 + 2x^2 - 6x + 5)$$
$$= 4 \cdot 3^3 + 2 \cdot 3^2 - 6 \cdot 3 + 5$$
$$= 4 \cdot 27 + 2 \cdot 9 - 6 \cdot 3 + 5$$
$$= 108 + 18 - 18 + 5$$
$$= 113$$

**Check Point 8** Find: $\lim_{x \to 2} (7x^3 + 3x^2 - 5x + 3)$.

A linear function, $f(x) = mx + b$, is a polynomial function of degree one. This means that the limit of a linear function as $x$ approaches $a$ is the linear function evaluated at $a$:

$$\lim_{x \to a} (mx + b) = ma + b.$$

For example,

$$\lim_{x \to 4} (3x - 7) = 3 \cdot 4 - 7 = 12 - 7 = 5.$$

The next limit property involves the limit of a power such as

$$\lim_{x \to 2} (x^2 + 2x - 3)^4.$$

To find such a limit, first find $\lim_{x \to 2} (x^2 + 2x - 3)$:

$$\lim_{x \to 2} (x^2 + 2x - 3) = 2^2 + 2 \cdot 2 - 3 = 4 + 4 - 3 = 5.$$

The limit that we seek is found by taking this limit, 5, and raising 5 to the fourth power. Thus,

$$\lim_{x \to 2} (x^2 + 2x - 3)^4 = \left[\lim_{x \to 2} (x^2 + 2x - 3)\right]^4 = 5^4 = 625.$$

## Calculus in Japan

Mathematics was developed simultaneously in various cultures in all parts of the world. Seki Kowa, a 17th-century Japanese mathematician, is credited with the invention of calculus in Japan. The illustration shown below was drawn in 1670 by a pupil of Seki Kowa. It measures the circle's area with a series of rectangles.

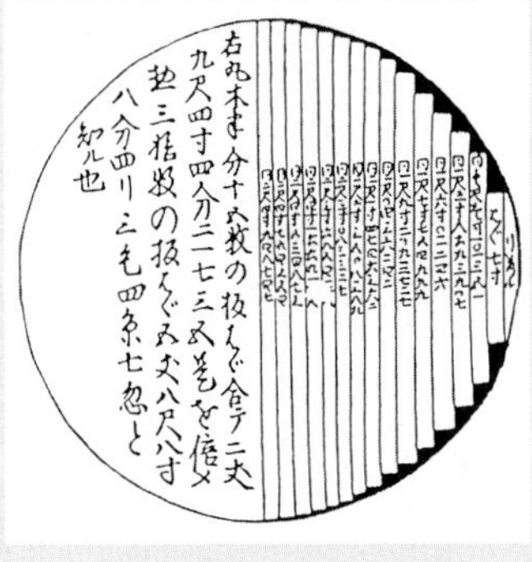

**The Limit of a Power**

If $\lim_{x \to a} f(x) = L$ and $n$ is a positive integer greater than or equal to 2, then

$$\lim_{x \to a} [f(x)]^n = \left[\lim_{x \to a} f(x)\right]^n = L^n.$$

In words, the limit of a function to a power is found by taking the limit of the function and then raising this limit to the power.

## EXAMPLE 9 Finding the Limit of a Power

Find: $\lim_{x \to 5} (2x - 7)^3$.

**Solution** The limit of the linear function, $f(x) = 2x - 7$, is the linear function evaluated at 5. Because this function is raised to the third power, the limit that we seek is the limit of the linear function raised to the third power.

$$\lim_{x \to 5} (2x - 7)^3 = \left[\lim_{x \to 5} (2x - 7)\right]^3 = (2 \cdot 5 - 7)^3 = 3^3 = 27$$

**Check Point 9** Find: $\lim_{x \to 4} (3x - 5)^3$.

How do we find the limit of a root? Recall that if $\sqrt[n]{L}$ represents a real number and $n \geq 2$, then

$$L^{1/n} = \sqrt[n]{L}.$$

Because a root is a power, we find the limit of a root using a similar procedure for finding the limit of a power.

**The Limit of a Root**

If $\lim_{x \to a} f(x) = L$ and $n$ is a positive integer greater than or equal to 2, then

$$\lim_{x \to a} \sqrt[n]{f(x)} = \sqrt[n]{\lim_{x \to a} f(x)} = \sqrt[n]{L}$$

provided that all roots represent real numbers. In words, the limit of the $n$th root of a function is found by taking the limit of the function and then taking the $n$th root of this limit.

## EXAMPLE 10 Finding the Limit of a Root

Find: $\lim_{x \to -2} \sqrt{4x^2 + 5}$.

**Solution** The limit of the quadratic (polynomial) function, $f(x) = 4x^2 + 5$, is the function evaluated at $-2$. Because we have the square root of this function, the limit that we seek is the square root of the limit of the quadratic function.

$$\lim_{x \to -2} \sqrt{4x^2 + 5} = \sqrt{\lim_{x \to -2} (4x^2 + 5)} = \sqrt{4(-2)^2 + 5} = \sqrt{16 + 5} = \sqrt{21}$$

**Check Point 10** Find: $\lim_{x \to -1} \sqrt{6x^2 - 4}$.

We have considered limits of sums, differences, and products. We conclude with a property that deals with the limit of a quotient.

**The Limit of a Quotient**

If $\lim_{x \to a} f(x) = L$ and $\lim_{x \to a} g(x) = M$, $M \neq 0$, then

$$\lim_{x \to a} \frac{f(x)}{g(x)} = \frac{\lim_{x \to a} f(x)}{\lim_{x \to a} g(x)} = \frac{L}{M},\ M \neq 0.$$

In words, the limit of the quotient of two functions equals the quotient of their limits, **provided that the limit of the denominator is not zero.**

Before possibly applying the quotient property, begin by finding the limit of the denominator. If this limit is not zero, you can apply the quotient property. If this limit is zero, the quotient property cannot be used.

## EXAMPLE 11 Finding the Limit of a Quotient

Find: $\lim_{x \to 1} \frac{x^3 - 3x^2 + 7}{2x - 5}$.

**Solution** The two functions in this limit problem are $f(x) = x^3 - 3x^2 + 7$ and $g(x) = 2x - 5$. We seek the limit of the quotient of these functions. Can we use the quotient property for limits? We answer the question by finding the limit of the denominator, $g(x)$.

$$\lim_{x\to 1}(2x - 5) = 2 \cdot 1 - 5 = -3$$

Because the limit of the denominator is not zero, we can apply the quotient property for limits. The limit of the quotient is the quotient of the limits.

$$\lim_{x\to 1}\frac{x^3 - 3x^2 + 7}{2x - 5} = \frac{\lim_{x\to 1}(x^3 - 3x^2 + 7)}{\lim_{x\to 1}(2x - 5)} = \frac{1^3 - 3 \cdot 1^2 + 7}{2 \cdot 1 - 5} = \frac{5}{-3} = -\frac{5}{3}$$

**Check Point 11** Find: $\lim_{x\to 2}\dfrac{x^2 - 4x + 1}{3x - 5}$.

We've considered a number of limit properties. Let's take a moment to summarize these properties.

## Properties of Limits

### Formulas for Finding Limits

**1.** $\lim_{x\to a} c = c$

**2.** $\lim_{x\to a} x = a$

**3.** If $f$ is a polynomial (linear, quadratic, cubic, etc.) function, $\lim_{x\to a} f(x) = f(a)$.

### Limits of Sums, Differences, Products, Powers, Roots, and Quotients

If $\lim_{x\to a} f(x) = L$ and $\lim_{x\to a} g(x) = M$, then

**4.** $\lim_{x\to a}[f(x) + g(x)] = \lim_{x\to a} f(x) + \lim_{x\to a} g(x) = L + M.$

**5.** $\lim_{x\to a}[f(x) - g(x)] = \lim_{x\to a} f(x) - \lim_{x\to a} g(x) = L - M.$

**6.** $\lim_{x\to a}[f(x) \cdot g(x)] = \lim_{x\to a} f(x) \cdot \lim_{x\to a} g(x) = LM.$

**7.** $\lim_{x\to a}[f(x)]^n = [\lim_{x\to a} f(x)]^n = L^n$, where $n \geq 2$ is an integer.

**8.** $\lim_{x\to a}\sqrt[n]{f(x)} = \sqrt[n]{\lim_{x\to a} f(x)} = \sqrt[n]{L}$, where $n \geq 2$ is an integer and all roots represent real numbers.

**9.** $\lim_{x\to a}\dfrac{f(x)}{g(x)} = \dfrac{\lim_{x\to a} f(x)}{\lim_{x\to a} g(x)} = \dfrac{L}{M}, \ M \neq 0.$

**3** Find limits of fractional expressions in which the limit of the denominator and numerator are zero.

## Strategies for Finding Limits When the Limit of the Denominator is Zero

When taking the limit of a fractional expression in which the limit of the denominator is zero, the quotient property for limits cannot be used. In such cases, it is necessary to rewrite the expression before the limit can be found. Factoring is one technique that can be used to rewrite an expression.

### Study Tip

Avoid this common error:

**INCORRECT**

$$\lim_{x\to 3}\frac{x^2-x-6}{x-3} = \frac{\lim_{x\to 3}(x^2-x-6)}{\lim_{x\to 3}(x-3)} = \frac{3^2-3-6}{3-3} = \frac{0}{0} = 1.$$

Do not use the quotient property if the limit of the denominator is zero. Furthermore, division by zero is not permitted: $\frac{0}{0}$ is *not* equal to 1.

## EXAMPLE 12 Using Factoring to Find a Limit

Find: $\lim_{x\to 3}\frac{x^2-x-6}{x-3}$.

**Solution** The limit of the denominator is zero:

$$\lim_{x\to 3}(x-3) = 3-3 = 0.$$

Thus, the quotient property for limits cannot be used. Instead, try simplifying the expression using factoring:

$$\frac{x^2-x-6}{x-3} = \frac{(x-3)(x+2)}{x-3}.$$

We seek the limit of this expression as $x$ approaches 3. Because $x$ is close to 3, but not equal to 3, the common factor in the numerator and denominator, $x-3$, is not equal to zero. With $x-3 \neq 0$, we can divide the numerator and denominator by $x-3$. Cancel the common factor, $x-3$, and then take the limit.

$$\lim_{x\to 3}\frac{x^2-x-6}{x-3} = \lim_{x\to 3}\frac{\cancel{(x-3)}(x+2)}{\cancel{x-3}} = \lim_{x\to 3}(x+2) = 3+2 = 5$$

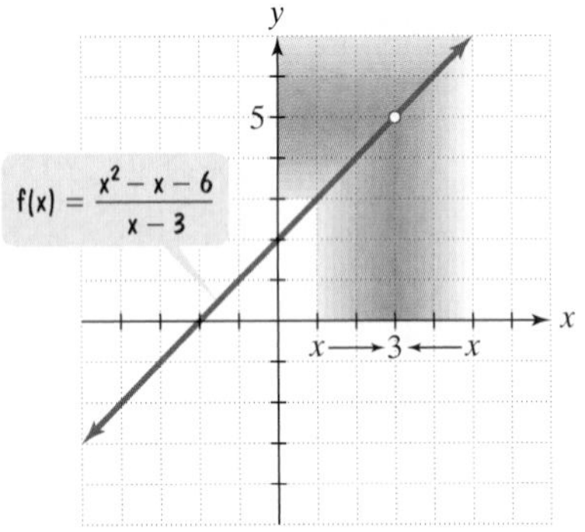


**Figure 12.8** As $x$ approaches 3, values of $f$ get closer to 5: $\lim_{x\to 3}\frac{x^2-x-6}{x-3} = 5$.

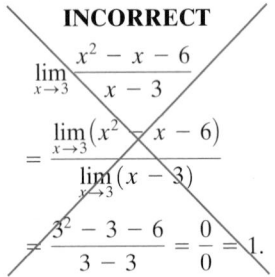

The graph of $f(x) = \frac{x^2-x-6}{x-3}$ is shown in Figure 12.8. The hole in the graph at $x = 3$ shows that $f(3)$ is undefined. However, as $x$ approaches 3, the graph shows that the values of $f$ get closer to 5. This verifies the limit that we found in Example 12:

$$\lim_{x\to 3}\frac{x^2-x-6}{x-3} = 5.$$

**Check Point 12** Find: $\lim_{x\to 1}\frac{x^2+2x-3}{x-1}$.

Rationalizing the numerator or denominator of a fractional expression is another technique that can be used to find a limit when the limit of the denominator is zero.

## EXAMPLE 13 Rationalizing a Numerator to Find a Limit

Find: $\lim_{x\to 0}\frac{\sqrt{4+x}-2}{x}$.

**Solution** As $x$ approaches 0, the denominator of the expression approaches zero. Thus, the quotient property for limits cannot be used. Instead, try rewriting the expression by rationalizing the numerator. If we multiply the numerator and denominator by $\sqrt{4+x}+2$, the numerator will not contain radicals.

$$\lim_{x\to 0}\frac{\sqrt{4+x}-2}{x}$$

$$= \lim_{x\to 0}\frac{\sqrt{4+x}-2}{x}\cdot\frac{\sqrt{4+x}+2}{\sqrt{4+x}+2}$$ Rationalize the numerator.

$$= \lim_{x\to 0}\frac{\left(\sqrt{4+x}\right)^2-2^2}{x\left(\sqrt{4+x}+2\right)}$$ $\left(\sqrt{a}-\sqrt{b}\right)\left(\sqrt{a}+\sqrt{b}\right)=\left(\sqrt{a}\right)^2-\left(\sqrt{b}\right)^2$

$$= \lim_{x\to 0}\frac{4+x-4}{x\left(\sqrt{4+x}+2\right)}$$ $\left(\sqrt{4+x}\right)^2=4+x$

$$= \lim_{x\to 0}\frac{x}{x\left(\sqrt{4+x}+2\right)}$$ Simplify: $4+x-4=x$.

$$= \lim_{x\to 0}\frac{1}{\sqrt{4+x}+2}$$ Divide both the numerator and denominator by $x$. This is permitted because $x$ approaches 0, but is not equal to 0.

$$= \frac{\lim_{x\to 0}1}{\sqrt{\lim_{x\to 0}(4+x)}+\lim_{x\to 0}2}$$ Use limit properties.

$$= \frac{1}{\sqrt{4+0}+2}$$

$$= \frac{1}{2+2}=\frac{1}{4}$$

**Check Point 13** Find: $\lim_{x\to 0}\frac{\sqrt{9+x}-3}{x}$.

## EXERCISE SET 12.2

### Practice Exercises

*In Exercises 1–42, use properties of limits to find the indicated limit. It may be necessary to rewrite an expression before limit properties can be applied.*

1. $\lim_{x\to 2} 8$
2. $\lim_{x\to 3}(-6)$
3. $\lim_{x\to 2} x$
4. $\lim_{x\to 3} x$
5. $\lim_{x\to 6}(3x-4)$
6. $\lim_{x\to 7}(4x-3)$
7. $\lim_{x\to -2} 7x^2$
8. $\lim_{x\to -3} 5x^2$
9. $\lim_{x\to 5}(x^2-3x-4)$
10. $\lim_{x\to 6}(x^2-4x-7)$
11. $\lim_{x\to 2}(5x-8)^3$
12. $\lim_{x\to 4}(6x-21)^3$
13. $\lim_{x\to 1}(2x^2-3x+5)^2$
14. $\lim_{x\to 2}(2x^2+3x-1)^2$
15. $\lim_{x\to -4}\sqrt{x^2+9}$
16. $\lim_{x\to -1}\sqrt{5x^2+4}$
17. $\lim_{x\to 5}\frac{x}{x+1}$
18. $\lim_{x\to 2}\frac{3x}{x-4}$
19. $\lim_{x\to 2}\frac{x^2-1}{x-1}$
20. $\lim_{x\to 3}\frac{x^2-4}{x-2}$

**21.** $\lim_{x\to1}\frac{x^2-1}{x-1}$

**22.** $\lim_{x\to2}\frac{x^2-4}{x-2}$

**23.** $\lim_{x\to2}\frac{2x-4}{x-2}$

**24.** $\lim_{x\to3}\frac{4x-12}{x-3}$

**25.** $\lim_{x\to1}\frac{x^2+2x-3}{x^2-1}$

**26.** $\lim_{x\to3}\frac{x^2-x-6}{x^2-9}$

**27.** $\lim_{x\to2}\frac{x^3-2x^2+4x-8}{x^4-2x^3+x-2}$

**28.** $\lim_{x\to-1}\frac{x^3+2x^2+x}{x^4+x^3+2x+2}$

**29.** $\lim_{x\to0}\frac{\sqrt{1+x}-1}{x}$

**30.** $\lim_{x\to0}\frac{\sqrt{16+x}-4}{x}$

**31.** $\lim_{x\to2}(x+1)^2(3x-1)^3$

**32.** $\lim_{x\to-1}(x+2)^3(3x+2)$

**33.** $\lim_{x\to4}\frac{\sqrt{x}-2}{x-4}$

**34.** $\lim_{x\to9}\frac{\sqrt{x}-3}{x-9}$

**35.** $\lim_{x\to2}\frac{\frac{1}{x}-\frac{1}{2}}{x-2}$

**36.** $\lim_{x\to3}\frac{\frac{1}{x}-\frac{1}{3}}{x-3}$

**37.** $\lim_{x\to4}\frac{\sqrt{x}+5}{x-5}$

**38.** $\lim_{x\to9}\frac{\sqrt{x}+10}{x-10}$

**39.** $\lim_{x\to0}\frac{\frac{1}{x+3}-\frac{1}{3}}{x}$

**40.** $\lim_{x\to0}\frac{\frac{1}{x+4}-\frac{1}{4}}{x}$

**41.** $\lim_{x\to2}\frac{x^2-4}{x^3-8}$

**42.** $\lim_{x\to1}\frac{x^2-1}{x^3-1}$

## Application Exercises

**43.** The function $f(x) = 2x^2 - 59x + 527$ models the box office revenue of a movie, $f(x)$, in millions of dollars, if the advertising budget for the movie is $x$ million dollars. Find $\lim_{x\to20} f(x)$. Interpret the limit, referring to the variables in the model.

**44.** The function $f(x) = 0.006x^2 + 0.028x + 5.919$ models the population of the United States, $f(x)$, in millions, $x$ years after 1790. Find $\lim_{x\to40} f(x)$. Interpret the limit, referring to the variables described by the model.

**45.** The function

$$f(x) = \frac{400x + 500{,}000}{x}$$

models the average cost per wheelchair, $f(x)$, for a company that manufactures $x$ wheelchairs. Find $\lim_{x\to10{,}000} f(x)$. Interpret the limit, referring to the variables in the model.

**46.** The function

$$f(x) = \frac{130x}{100 - x}$$

models the cost, $f(x)$, in millions of dollars, to inoculate $x\%$ of the population against a particular strain of flu. Find $\lim_{x\to50} f(x)$. Interpret the limit, referring to the variables in the model.

## Writing in Mathematics

**47.** Explain how to find the limit of a constant. Then express your written explanation using limit notation.

**48.** Explain how to find the limit of the identity function $f(x) = x$. Then express your written explanation using limit notation.

**49.** Explain how to find the limit of a sum. Then express your written explanation using limit notation.

**50.** Explain how to find the limit of a difference. Then express your written explanation using limit notation.

**51.** Explain how to find the limit of a product. Then express your written explanation using limit notation.

**52.** Describe how to find the limit of a polynomial function. Provide an example with your description.

**53.** Explain how to find the following limit: $\lim_{x\to2}(3x^2 - 10)^3$. Then use limit notation to write the limit property that supports your explanation.

**54.** Explain how to find the following limit: $\lim_{x\to2}\sqrt{5x - 6}$. Then use limit notation to write the limit property that supports your explanation.

**55.** Explain how to find the limit of a quotient if the limit of the denominator is not zero. Then express your written explanation using limit notation.

**56.** Write an example involving the limit of a quotient in which the quotient property for limits cannot be applied. Explain why the property cannot be applied to your limit problem.

**57.** Explain why

$$\lim_{x\to4}\frac{(x+4)(x-4)}{x-4}$$

can be found by first dividing the numerator and the denominator of the expression by $x - 4$. Division by zero is undefined. How can we be sure that we are not dividing the numerator and the denominator by zero?

## Technology Exercises

**58.** Use the TABLE feature of your graphing utility to verify any five of the limits that you found in Exercises 1–42.

**59.** Use the ZOOM IN feature of your graphing utility to verify any five of the limits that you found in Exercises 1–42. Zoom in on the graph of the given function, $f$, near $x = a$ to verify each limit.

## Critical Thinking Exercises

*In Exercises 60–61, find the indicated limit.*

**60.** $\lim_{x\to 0} x\left(1 - \frac{1}{x}\right)$

**61.** $\lim_{x\to 4}\left(\frac{1}{x} - \frac{1}{4}\right)\left(\frac{1}{x-4}\right)$

*In Exercises 62–63, find* $\lim_{h\to 0}\frac{f(a+h) - f(a)}{h}$.

**62.** $f(x) = x^2 + 2x - 3, a = 1$

**63.** $f(x) = \sqrt{x}, a = 1$

*In Exercises 64–65, use properties of limits and the following limits*

$$\lim_{x\to 0}\frac{\sin x}{x} = 1, \quad \lim_{x\to 0}\frac{\cos x - 1}{x} = 0,$$
$$\lim_{x\to 0}\sin x = 0, \quad \lim_{x\to 0}\cos x = 1$$

*to find the indicated limit.*

**64.** $\lim_{x\to 0}\frac{\tan x}{x}$

**65.** $\lim_{x\to 0}\frac{2\sin x + \cos x - 1}{3x}$

## Group Exercises

**66.** Here is a list of ten common errors involving algebra, trigonometry, and limits that students frequently make in calculus. Group members should examine each error and describe the mistake. Where possible, correct each error. Finally, group members should offer suggestions for avoiding each error.

**a.** $(x+h)^3 - x^3 = x^3 + h^3 - x^3 = h^3$

**b.** $\frac{1}{a+b} = \frac{1}{a} + \frac{1}{b}$

**c.** $\frac{1}{a+b} = \frac{1}{a} + b$

**d.** $\sqrt{x+h} - \sqrt{x} = \sqrt{x} + \sqrt{h} - \sqrt{x} = \sqrt{h}$

**e.** $\frac{\sin 2x}{x} = \sin 2$

**f.** $\frac{a+bx}{a} = 1 + bx$

**g.** $\lim_{x\to 1}\frac{x^3 - 1}{x - 1} = \frac{1^3 - 1}{1 - 1} = \frac{0}{0} = 1$

**h.** $\sin(x+h) - \sin x = \sin x + \sin h - \sin x = \sin h$

**i.** $ax = bx$, so $a = b$

**j.** To find $\lim_{x\to 4}\frac{x^2 - 9}{x - 3}$, it is necessary to rewrite $\frac{x^2 - 9}{x - 3}$ by factoring $x^2 - 9$.

**67.** Research and present a group report about the history of the feud between Newton and Leibniz over who invented calculus. What other interests did these men have in addition to mathematics? What practical problems led them to the invention of calculus? What were their personalities like? Whose version established the notation and rules of calculus that we use today?

# SECTION 12.3 *One-Sided Limits; Continuous Functions*

## Objectives

1. Find one-sided limits and use them to determine if a limit exists.
2. Determine whether a function is continuous at a number.
3. Determine for what numbers a function is discontinuous.

Why you should not ski down discontinuous slopes

Have you ever felt that you needed some continuity in your life? Many of us do not want dramatic changes every two minutes. It's comforting to have the normal way of doing things continue uninterrupted. That's probably why you shouldn't ski down discontinuous slopes.

Did you know that limits can be used to describe continuity in a mathematical sense? To understand this application of limits, we begin by looking at two different ways of approaching the same number.

**1** Find one-sided limits and use them to determine if a limit exists.

## One-Sided Limits

The graph in Figure 12.9 shows a portion of the graph of the function $f(x) = x^2$. The graph illustrates that

$$\lim_{x \to 2} x^2 = 4.$$

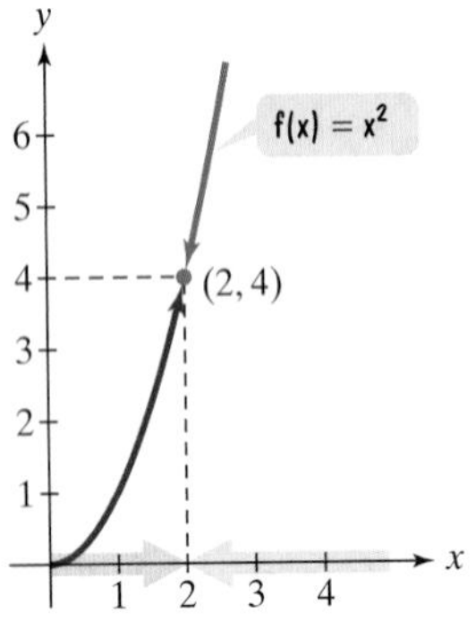


**Figure 12.9** As $x$ approaches 2 from the left (red arrow) or from the right (blue arrow), values of $f(x)$ get closer to 4.

As $x$ gets closer to 2, but remains unequal to 2, the corresponding values of $f(x)$ get closer to 4. The values of $x$ near 2 fall into two categories: those that lie to the left of 2, shown by the red arrow, and those that lie to the right of 2, shown by the blue arrow.

The values of $x$ can get closer to 2 in two ways. The values of $x$ can approach 2 from the left, through numbers that are less than 2. Table 12.4 shows some values of $x$ and corresponding values of $f(x)$ on the red portion of the graph in Figure 12.9. Note that as $x$ approaches 2 from the left of 2, $f(x)$ approaches 4.

**Table 12.4**

| $x$ | 1.99 | 1.999 | 1.9999 $\rightarrow$ |
|---|---|---|---|
| $f(x) = x^2$ | 3.9601 | 3.9960 | 3.9996 $\rightarrow$ |

We say that "the limit of $x^2$ as $x$ approaches 2 from the left equals 4." The mathematical notation for this English sentence is

$$\lim_{x \to 2^-} x^2 = 4.$$

The notation $x \rightarrow 2^-$ indicates that $x$ is less than 2 and is approaching 2 from the left.

The values of $x$ can also approach 2 from the right, through numbers that are greater than 2. Table 12.5 shows some values of $x$ and corresponding values of $f(x)$ on the blue portion of the graph in Figure 12.9. Note that as $x$ approaches 2 from the right of 2, $f(x)$ approaches 4.

**Table 12.5**

| $x$ | $\leftarrow$ 2.0001 | 2.001 | 2.01 |
|---|---|---|---|
| $f(x) = x^2$ | $\leftarrow$ 4.0004 | 4.0040 | 4.0401 |

We say that "the limit of $x^2$ as $x$ approaches 2 from the right equals 4." The mathematical notation for this English sentence is

$$\lim_{x \to 2^+} x^2 = 4.$$

The notation $x \rightarrow 2^+$ indicates that $x$ is greater than 2 and is approaching 2 from the right.

In general, if $f(x)$ approaches $a$ from one side, we have a **one-sided limit**.

## One-Sided Limits

**Left-Hand Limit** The limit notation

$$\lim_{x \to a^-} f(x) = L$$

is read "the limit of $f(x)$ as $x$ approaches $a$ from the left equals $L$" and is called the **left-hand limit**. This means that as $x$ gets closer to $a$, but remains less than $a$, the corresponding values of $f(x)$ get closer to $L$.

**Right-Hand Limit** The limit notation

$$\lim_{x \to a^+} f(x) = L$$

is read "the limit of $f(x)$ as $x$ approaches $a$ from the right equals $L$" and is called the **right-hand limit**. This means that as $x$ gets closer to $a$, but remains greater than $a$, the corresponding values of $f(x)$ get closer to $L$.

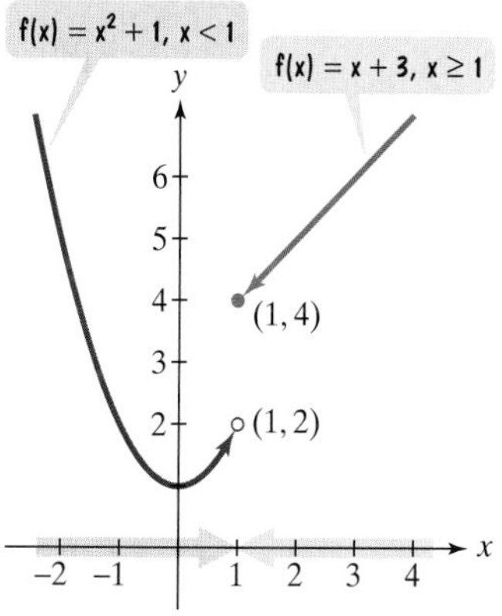


**Figure 12.10** As $x$ approaches 1 from the left (red arrow) and from the right (blue arrow), values of $f(x)$ do not get closer to a single number.

A function's graph can be helpful in finding one-sided limits. For example, Figure 12.10 shows the graph of the piecewise function

$$f(x) = \begin{cases} x^2 + 1 & \text{if } x < 1 \\ x + 3 & \text{if } x \geq 1. \end{cases}$$

The red portion of the graph, part of a parabola, illustrates that as $x$ approaches 1 from the left, the corresponding values of $f(x)$ get closer to 2. The left-hand limit is 2:

$$\lim_{x \to 1^-} f(x) = 2.$$

The blue portion of the graph, part of a line, illustrates that as $x$ approaches 1 from the right, the corresponding values of $f(x)$ get closer to 4. The right-hand limit is 4:

$$\lim_{x \to 1^+} f(x) = 4.$$

Because $\lim_{x \to 1^-} f(x) = 2$ and $\lim_{x \to 1^+} f(x) = 4$, there is no single number that the values of $f(x)$ are close to when $x$ is close to 1. In this case, we say that ***f*** **has no limit as *x* approaches 1** or that $\lim_{x \to 1} f(x)$ **does not exist.**

In general, a function $f$ has a limit as $x$ approaches $a$ if and only if the left-hand limit equals the right-hand limit.

## Equal and Unequal One-Sided Limits

- One-sided limits can be used to show that a function has a limit as $x$ approaches $a$:

$$\lim_{x \to a} f(x) = L \text{ if and only if both}$$
$$\lim_{x \to a^-} f(x) = L \quad \text{and} \quad \lim_{x \to a^+} f(x) = L.$$

- One-sided limits can be used to show that a function has no limit as $x$ approaches $a$.

$$\text{If } \lim_{x \to a^-} f(x) = L \quad \text{and} \quad \lim_{x \to a^+} f(x) = M, \text{ where } L \neq M,$$
$$\lim_{x \to a} f(x) \text{ does not exist.}$$

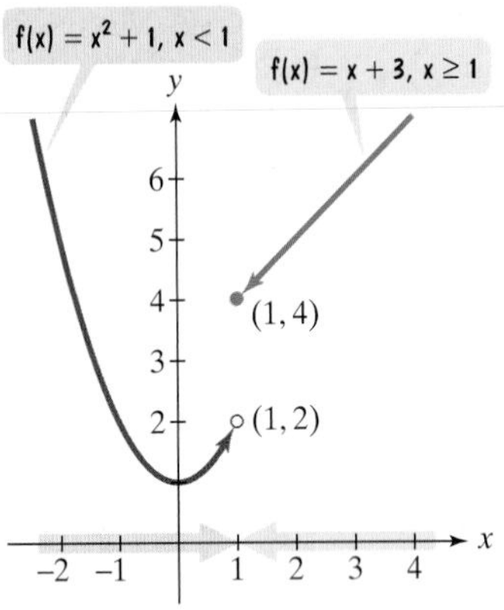


**Figure 12.10,** repeated

## EXAMPLE 1 Finding One-Sided Limits of a Piecewise Function

For the function

$$f(x) = \begin{cases} x^2 + 1 & \text{if } x < 1 \\ x + 3 & \text{if } x \geq 1 \end{cases}$$

find:

**a.** $\lim_{x \to 1^-} f(x)$ **b.** $\lim_{x \to 1^+} f(x)$ **c.** $\lim_{x \to 1} f(x)$.

**Solution** We used the graph of $f$ in Figure 12.10 to find these limits. However, we can also use the appropriate part of the function's equation and properties of limits to find each indicated limit.

**a.** To find $\lim_{x \to 1^-} f(x)$, we look at the values of $f(x)$ when $x$ is close to 1, but less than 1. Because $x$ is less than 1, we use the first line of the piecewise function, $f(x) = x^2 + 1$. Thus,

$$\lim_{x \to 1^-} f(x) = \lim_{x \to 1^-} (x^2 + 1) = 1^2 + 1 = 2.$$

**b.** To find $\lim_{x \to 1^+} f(x)$, we look at the values of $f(x)$ when $x$ is close to 1, but greater than 1. Because $x$ is greater than 1, we use the second line of the piecewise function, $f(x) = x + 3$. Thus,

$$\lim_{x \to 1^+} f(x) = \lim_{x \to 1^+} (x + 3) = 1 + 3 = 4.$$

**c.** Because the left- and right-hand limits are unequal, $\lim_{x \to 1} f(x)$ does not exist.

**Check Point 1** For the function

$$f(x) = \begin{cases} x^2 + 5 & \text{if } x < 2 \\ 3x + 1 & \text{if } x \geq 2 \end{cases}$$

find:

**a.** $\lim_{x \to 2^-} f(x)$ **b.** $\lim_{x \to 2^+} f(x)$ **c.** $\lim_{x \to 2} f(x)$.

**2** Determine whether a function is continuous at a number.

## Continuous Functions

In everyday speech, a continuous process is one that goes on without interruption and without abrupt changes. In mathematics, a continuous function has much the same meaning. The graph of a continuous function does not have interrupting breaks, such as holes, gaps, or jumps. Thus, the graph of a continuous function can be drawn without lifting a pencil off the paper.

Figure 12.11 shows three graphs that cannot be drawn without lifting pencil from paper. In each case, there appears to be an interruption of the graph of $f$ at $x = a$.

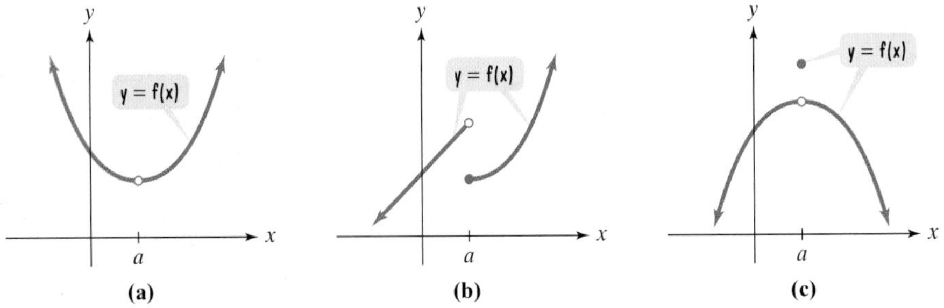


**Figure 12.11** Each graph has an interruption at $a$.

Examine Figure 12.11(a). The interruption occurs because of the open dot at $x = a$. This shows that $f(a)$ is not defined.

Now, examine Figure 12.11(b). The closed blue dot at $x = a$ shows that $f(a)$ is defined. However, there is still a jump at $a$. As $x$ approaches $a$ from the left, the values of $f$ get closer to the $y$-coordinate of the point shown by the open dot. By contrast, as $x$ approaches $a$ from the right, the values of $f$ get closer to the $y$-coordinate of the point shown by the closed dot. There is no single limit as $x$ approaches $a$. The jump in the graph reflects the fact that $\lim_{x \to a} f(x)$ does not exist.

Finally, examine Figure 12.11(c). The closed blue dot at $x = a$ shows that $f(a)$ is defined. As $x$ approaches $a$ from the left or from the right, the values of $f$ get closer to the $y$-coordinate of the point shown by the open dot. Thus, $\lim_{x \to a} f(x)$ exists. However, there is still an interruption at $a$. Do you see why? The limit as $x$ approaches $a$, $\lim_{x \to a} f(x)$, is the $y$-coordinate of the open dot. By contrast, the value of the function at $a$, $f(a)$, is the $y$-coordinate of the closed dot. The jump in the graph reflects the fact that $\lim_{x \to a} f(x)$ and $f(a)$ are not equal.

We now provide a precise definition of what it means for a function to be continuous at a number. Notice how each part of this definition avoids the interruptions that occurred in Figure 12.11.

### Definition of a Function Continuous at a Number

A function $f$ **is continuous at $a$** when three conditions are satisfied.

1. $f$ is defined at $a$; that is, $a$ is in the domain of $f$, so that $f(a)$ is a real number.
2. $\lim_{x \to a} f(x)$ exists.
3. $\lim_{x \to a} f(x) = f(a)$.

If $f$ is not continuous at $a$, we say that $f$ is **discontinuous at $a$**. Each of the functions whose graph is shown in Figure 12.11 is discontinuous at $a$.

## EXAMPLE 2 Determining Whether a Function Is Continuous at a Number

Determine whether the function

$$f(x) = \frac{2x + 1}{2x^2 - x - 1}$$

is continuous: **a** at 2; **b** at 1.

**Solution** According to the definition, three conditions must be satisfied to have continuity at $a$.

**a.** To determine whether the function is continuous at 2, we check the conditions for continuity with $a = 2$.

**Condition 1** ***f* is defined at *a*.** Is $f(2)$ defined?

$$f(2) = \frac{2 \cdot 2 + 1}{2 \cdot 2^2 - 2 - 1} = \frac{4 + 1}{8 - 2 - 1} = \frac{5}{5} = 1$$

Because $f(2)$ is a real number, 1, $f(2)$ is defined.

The function for this example,

$$f(x) = \frac{2x+1}{2x^2 - x - 1},$$

repeated

**Condition 2** $\lim_{x\to a} f(x)$ **exists.** Does $\lim_{x\to 2} f(x)$ exist?

$$\lim_{x\to 2} f(x) = \lim_{x\to 2} \frac{2x+1}{2x^2 - x - 1} = \frac{\lim_{x\to 2}(2x+1)}{\lim_{x\to 2}(2x^2 - x - 1)}$$

$$= \frac{2\cdot 2 + 1}{2\cdot 2^2 - 2 - 1} = \frac{4+1}{8-2-1} = \frac{5}{5} = 1$$

Using properties of limits, we see that $\lim_{x\to 2} f(x)$ exists.

**Condition 3** $\lim_{x\to a} f(x) = f(a)$. Does $\lim_{x\to 2} f(x) = f(2)$? We found that $\lim_{x\to 2} f(x) = 1$ and $f(2) = 1$. Thus, as $x$ gets closer to 2, the corresponding values of $f(x)$ get closer to the function value at 2: $\lim_{x\to 2} f(x) = f(2)$.

Because the three conditions are satisfied, we conclude that $f$ is continuous at 2.

**b.** To determine whether the function is continuous at 1, we check the conditions for continuity with $a = 1$.

**Condition 1** $f$ **is defined at** $a$. Is $f(1)$ defined? Factor the denominator of the function's equation:

$$f(x) = \frac{2x+1}{(x-1)(2x+1)}.$$

Denominator is zero at $x = 1$.

Denominator is zero at $x = -\frac{1}{2}$.

Because division by zero is undefined, the domain of $f$ is $\{x \mid x \neq 1, x \neq -\frac{1}{2}\}$. Thus, $f$ is not defined at 1.

Because one of the three conditions is not satisfied, we conclude that $f$ is not continuous at 1. Equivalently, we can say that $f$ is discontinuous at 1.

The graph of $f(x) = \dfrac{2x+1}{2x^2 - x - 1}$ is shown in Figure 12.12. The graph verifies our work in Example 2. Can you see that $f$ is continuous at 2? By contrast, it is not continuous at 1, where the graph has a vertical asymptote.

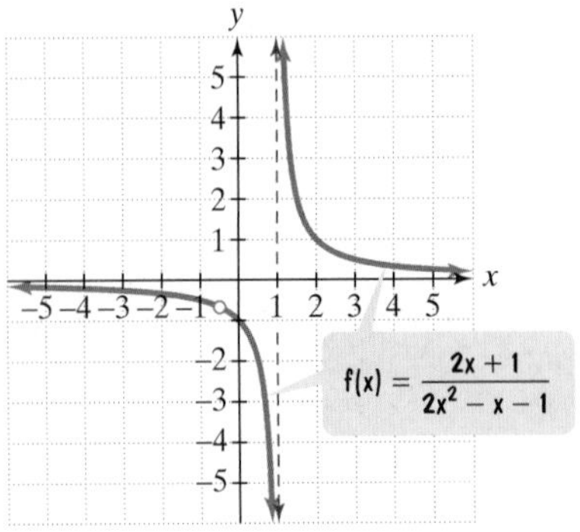


**Figure 12.12** $f$ is continuous at 2. It is not continuous at 1 or at $-\frac{1}{2}$.

The graph in Figure 12.12 reveals discontinuity at $-\frac{1}{2}$. The open dot indicates that $f\left(-\frac{1}{2}\right)$ is not defined. Can you see what is happening as $x$ approaches $-\frac{1}{2}$?

$$\lim_{x\to-\frac{1}{2}} \frac{2x+1}{2x^2-x-1} = \lim_{x\to-\frac{1}{2}} \frac{\cancel{2x+1}}{(x-1)\cancel{(2x+1)}} = \lim_{x\to-\frac{1}{2}} \frac{1}{x-1} = \frac{1}{-\frac{1}{2}-1} = -\frac{2}{3}$$

As $x$ gets closer to $-\frac{1}{2}$, the graph of $f$ gets closer to $-\frac{2}{3}$. Because $f$ is not defined at $-\frac{1}{2}$, the graph has a hole at $\left(-\frac{1}{2}, -\frac{2}{3}\right)$. This is shown by the open dot in Figure 12.12.

**Check Point 2**

Determine whether the function

$$f(x) = \frac{x-2}{x^2-4}$$

is continuous: **a** at 1; **b** at 2.

We have seen that the limit of a polynomial function as $x$ approaches $a$ is the polynomial function evaluated at $a$. Thus, if $f$ is a polynomial function, then $\lim_{x\to a} f(x) = f(a)$ for any number $a$. This means that **a polynomial function is continuous at every number.**

Many of the functions discussed throughout this book are continuous at every number in their domain. For example, rational functions are continuous at every number, except any at which they are not defined. At numbers that are not in the domain of a rational function, a hole in the graph or an asymptote appears. Exponential, logarithmic, sine, and cosine functions are continuous at every number in their domain. Like rational functions, the tangent, cotangent, secant, and cosecant functions are continuous at every number, except any at which they are not defined. At numbers that are not in the domain of these trigonometric functions, an asymptote occurs.

**3** Determine for what numbers a function is discontinuous.

Example 3 illustrates how to determine where a piecewise function is discontinuous.

## EXAMPLE 3 Determining Where a Piecewise Function Is Discontinuous

Determine for what numbers $x$, if any, the following function is discontinuous.

$$f(x) = \begin{cases} x+2 & \text{if } x \le 0 \\ 2 & \text{if } 0 < x \le 1 \\ x^2+2 & \text{if } x > 1 \end{cases}$$

**Solution** First, let's determine whether each of the three pieces of $f$ is continuous. The first piece, $f(x) = x + 2$, is a linear function; it is continuous at every number $x$. The second piece, $f(x) = 2$, a constant function, is continuous at every number $x$. And the third piece, $f(x) = x^2 + 2$, a polynomial function, is also continuous at every number $x$. Thus, these three functions, a linear function, a constant function, and a polynomial function, can be graphed without lifting pencil from paper. However, the pieces change at $x = 0$ and $x = 1$. Is it necessary to lift pencil from paper when graphing $f$ at these values? It appears that we must investigate continuity at 0 and at 1.

To determine whether the function is continuous at 0, we check the conditions for continuity with $a = 0$.

The function for this example,

$$f(x) = \begin{cases} x + 2 & \text{if } x \le 0 \\ 2 & \text{if } 0 < x \le 1 \\ x^2 + 2 & \text{if } x > 1 \end{cases}$$

repeated

**Condition 1** ***f* is defined at *a*.** Is $f(0)$ defined? Because $a = 0$, we use the first line of the piecewise function, where $x \le 0$.

$f(x) = x + 2$ This is the function's equation for $x \le 0$, which includes $x = 0$.

$f(0) = 0 + 2$ Replace x by 0.

$= 2$

Because $f(0)$ is a real number, 2, $f(0)$ is defined.

**Condition 2** $\lim\limits_{x \to a} f(x)$ **exists.** Does $\lim\limits_{x \to 0} f(x)$ exist? To answer this question, we look at the values of $f(x)$ when $x$ is close to 0. Let us investigate the left- and right-hand limits. If these limits are equal, then $\lim\limits_{x \to 0} f(x)$ exists. To find $\lim\limits_{x \to 0^-} f(x)$, the left-hand limit, we look at the values of $f(x)$ when $x$ is close to 0, but less than 0. Because $x$ is less than 0, we use the first line of the piecewise function, $f(x) = x + 2$ if $x \le 0$. Thus,

$$\lim_{x \to 0^-} f(x) = \lim_{x \to 0^-} (x + 2) = 0 + 2 = 2.$$

To find $\lim\limits_{x \to 0^+} f(x)$, the right-hand limit, we look at the values of $f(x)$ when $x$ is close to 0, but greater than 0. Because $x$ is greater than 0, we use the second line of the piecewise function, $f(x) = 2$ if $0 < x \le 1$. Thus,

$$\lim_{x \to 0^+} f(x) = \lim_{x \to 0^+} 2 = 2.$$

Because the left- and right-hand limits are both equal to 2, $\lim\limits_{x \to 0} f(x) = 2$. Thus, we see that $\lim\limits_{x \to 0} f(x)$ exists.

**Condition 3** $\lim\limits_{x \to a} f(x) = f(a)$**.** Does $\lim\limits_{x \to 0} f(x) = f(0)$? We found that $\lim\limits_{x \to 0} f(x) = 2$ and $f(0) = 2$. This means that as $x$ gets closer to 0, the corresponding values of $f(x)$ get closer to the function value at 0: $\lim\limits_{x \to 0} f(x) = f(0)$.

Because the three conditions are satisfied, we conclude that $f$ is continuous at 0.

Now we must determine whether the function is continuous at 1, the other value of $x$ where the pieces change. We check the conditions for continuity with $a = 1$.

**Condition 1** ***f* is defined at *a*.** Is $f(1)$ defined? Because $a = 1$, we use the second line of the piecewise function, where $0 < x \le 1$.

$f(x) = 2$ This is the function's equation for $0 < x \le 1$, which includes $x = 1$.

$f(1) = 2$ Replace x by 1.

Because $f(1)$ is a real number, 2, $f(1)$ is defined.

**Condition 2** $\lim\limits_{x \to a} f(x)$ **exists.** Does $\lim\limits_{x \to 1} f(x)$ exist? We investigate left- and right-hand limits as $x$ approaches 1. To find $\lim\limits_{x \to 1^-} f(x)$, the left-hand limit, we look at values of $f(x)$ when $x$ is close to 1, but less than 1. Thus, we use the second line of the piecewise function, $f(x) = 2$ if $0 < x \le 1$. The left-hand limit is

$$\lim_{x \to 1^-} f(x) = \lim_{x \to 1^-} 2 = 2.$$

To find $\lim\limits_{x \to 1^+} f(x)$, the right-hand limit, we look at values of $f(x)$ when $x$ is close to 1, but greater than 1. Thus, we use the third line of the piecewise function, $f(x) = x^2 + 2$ if $x > 1$. The right-hand limit is

$$\lim_{x \to 1^+} f(x) = \lim_{x \to 1^+} (x^2 + 2) = 1^2 + 2 = 3.$$

The left- and right-hand limits are not equal: $\lim_{x \to 1^-} f(x) = 2$ and $\lim_{x \to 1^+} f(x) = 3$. This means that $\lim_{x \to 1} f(x)$ does not exist.

Because one of the three conditions is not satisfied, we conclude that $f$ is not continuous at 1.

In summary, the given function is discontinuous at 1 only. The graph of $f$, shown in Figure 12.13, illustrates this conclusion.

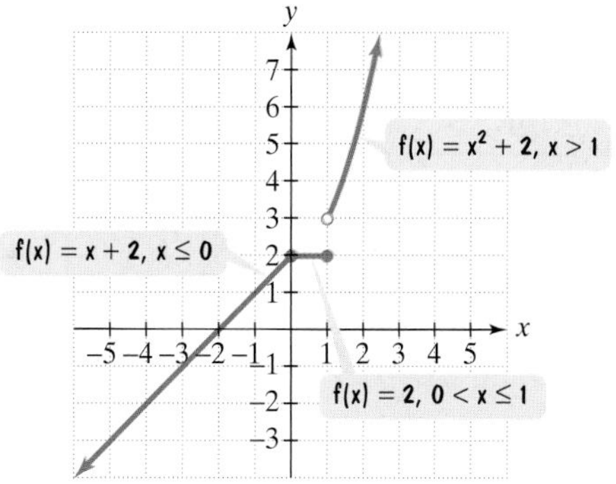


**Figure 12.13** This piecewise function is continuous at 0, where pieces change, and discontinuous at 1, where pieces change.

**Check Point 3** Determine for what numbers $x$, if any, the following function is discontinuous.

$$f(x) = \begin{cases} 2x & \text{if } x \le 0 \\ x^2 + 1 & \text{if } 0 < x \le 2 \\ 7 - x & \text{if } x > 2 \end{cases}$$

## EXERCISE SET 12.3

### Practice Exercises

*In Exercises 1–8, a piecewise function is given. Use the function to find the indicated limits, or state that a limit does not exist.*

**1.** $f(x) = \begin{cases} x + 5 & \text{if } x < 1 \\ x + 7 & \text{if } x \ge 1 \end{cases}$

**a.** $\lim_{x \to 1^-} f(x)$ **b.** $\lim_{x \to 1^+} f(x)$ **c.** $\lim_{x \to 1} f(x)$

**2.** $f(x) = \begin{cases} x + 6 & \text{if } x < 1 \\ x + 9 & \text{if } x \ge 1 \end{cases}$

**a.** $\lim_{x \to 1^-} f(x)$ **b.** $\lim_{x \to 1^+} f(x)$ **c.** $\lim_{x \to 1} f(x)$

**3.** $f(x) = \begin{cases} x^2 + 5 & \text{if } x < 2 \\ x^3 + 1 & \text{if } x \ge 2 \end{cases}$

**a.** $\lim_{x \to 2^-} f(x)$ **b.** $\lim_{x \to 2^+} f(x)$ **c.** $\lim_{x \to 2} f(x)$

**4.** $f(x) = \begin{cases} x^2 + 6 & \text{if } x < 2 \\ x^3 + 2 & \text{if } x \ge 2 \end{cases}$

**a.** $\lim_{x \to 2^-} f(x)$ **b.** $\lim_{x \to 2^+} f(x)$ **c.** $\lim_{x \to 2} f(x)$

**5.** $f(x) = \begin{cases} \dfrac{x^2 - 9}{x - 3} & \text{if } x \ne 3 \\ 5 & \text{if } x = 3 \end{cases}$

**a.** $\lim_{x \to 3^-} f(x)$ **b.** $\lim_{x \to 3^+} f(x)$ **c.** $\lim_{x \to 3} f(x)$

**6.** $f(x) = \begin{cases} \dfrac{x^2 - 16}{x - 4} & \text{if } x \ne 4 \\ 7 & \text{if } x = 4 \end{cases}$

**a.** $\lim_{x \to 4^-} f(x)$ **b.** $\lim_{x \to 4^+} f(x)$ **c.** $\lim_{x \to 4} f(x)$

**7.** $f(x) = \begin{cases} 1 - x & \text{if } x < 1 \\ 2 & \text{if } x = 1 \\ x^2 - 1 & \text{if } x > 1 \end{cases}$

**a.** $\lim_{x \to 1^-} f(x)$ **b.** $\lim_{x \to 1^+} f(x)$ **c.** $\lim_{x \to 1} f(x)$

**8.** $f(x) = \begin{cases} 4 - x & \text{if } x < 1 \\ 2 & \text{if } x = 1 \\ x^2 + 2 & \text{if } x > 1 \end{cases}$

**a.** $\lim_{x \to 1^-} f(x)$ **b.** $\lim_{x \to 1^+} f(x)$ **c.** $\lim_{x \to 1} f(x)$

*In Exercises 9–14, the graph of a function, f, is given. Use the graph to find the indicated limits, or state that a limit does not exist.*

**9.**

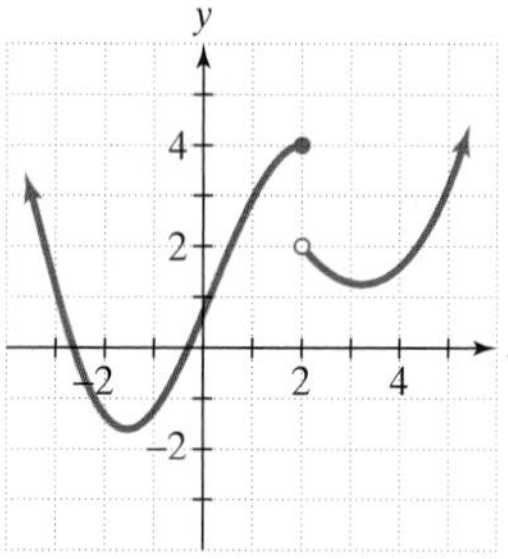


**a.** $\lim_{x\to 2^-} f(x)$ **b.** $\lim_{x\to 2^+} f(x)$ **c.** $\lim_{x\to 2} f(x)$

**10.**

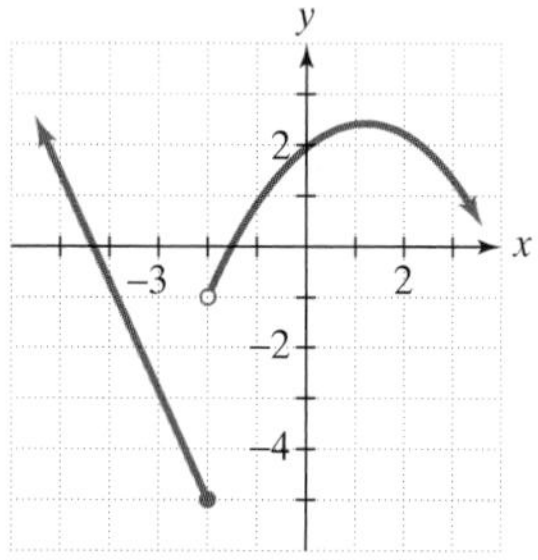


**a.** $\lim_{x\to -2^-} f(x)$ **b.** $\lim_{x\to -2^+} f(x)$ **c.** $\lim_{x\to -2} f(x)$

**11.**

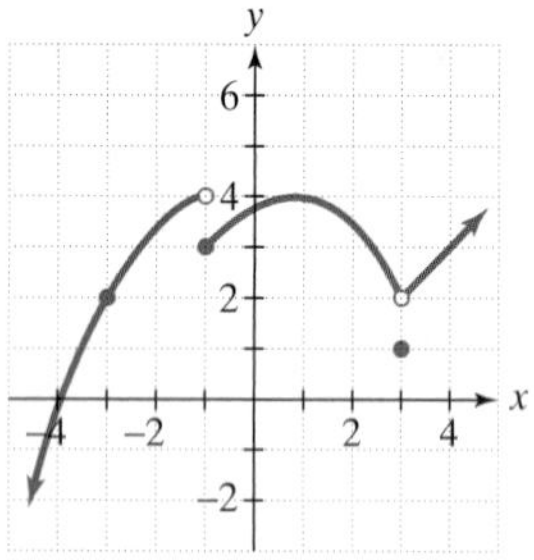


**a.** $\lim_{x\to -3^-} f(x)$ **d.** $\lim_{x\to -1^-} f(x)$ **g.** $\lim_{x\to 3^-} f(x)$

**b.** $\lim_{x\to -3^+} f(x)$ **e.** $\lim_{x\to -1^+} f(x)$ **h.** $\lim_{x\to 3^+} f(x)$

**c.** $\lim_{x\to -3} f(x)$ **f.** $\lim_{x\to -1} f(x)$ **i.** $\lim_{x\to 3} f(x)$

**12.**

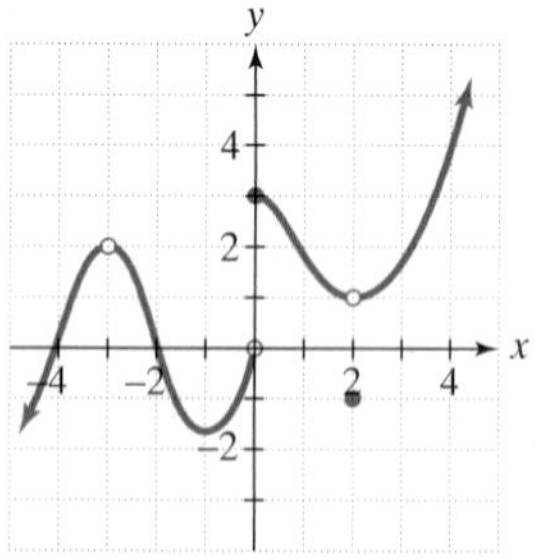


**a.** $\lim_{x\to -3^-} f(x)$ **d.** $\lim_{x\to 0^-} f(x)$ **g.** $\lim_{x\to 2^-} f(x)$

**b.** $\lim_{x\to -3^+} f(x)$ **e.** $\lim_{x\to 0^+} f(x)$ **h.** $\lim_{x\to 2^+} f(x)$

**c.** $\lim_{x\to -3} f(x)$ **f.** $\lim_{x\to 0} f(x)$ **i.** $\lim_{x\to 2} f(x)$

**13.**

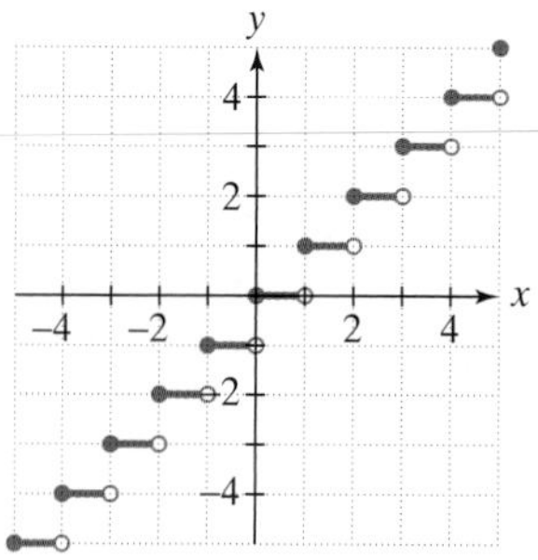


**a.** $\lim_{x\to 2^-} f(x)$ **c.** $\lim_{x\to 2} f(x)$ **e.** $\lim_{x\to 2.5^+} f(x)$

**b.** $\lim_{x\to 2^+} f(x)$ **d.** $\lim_{x\to 2.5^-} f(x)$ **f.** $\lim_{x\to 2.5} f(x)$

**14.**

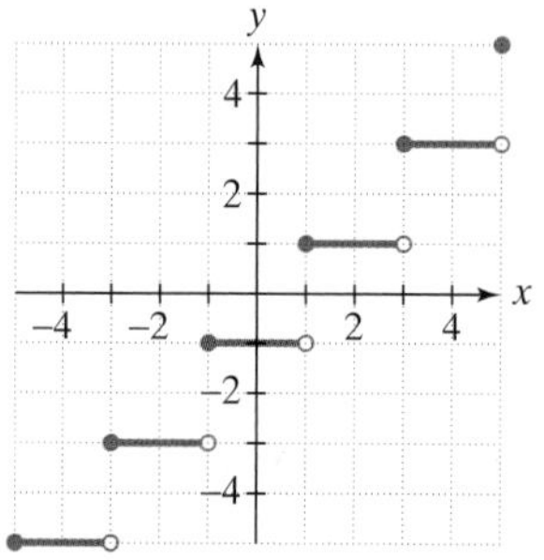


**a.** $\lim_{x\to 3^-} f(x)$ **c.** $\lim_{x\to 3} f(x)$ **e.** $\lim_{x\to 3.5^+} f(x)$

**b.** $\lim_{x\to 3^+} f(x)$ **d.** $\lim_{x\to 3.5^-} f(x)$ **f.** $\lim_{x\to 3.5} f(x)$

*In Exercises 15–32, determine whether f is continuous at a.*

**15.** $f(x) = 2x + 5$, $a = 1$

**16.** $f(x) = 3x + 4$, $a = 1$

**17.** $f(x) = x^2 - 3x + 7$, $a = 4$

**18.** $f(x) = x^2 - 5x + 6$, $a = 4$

**19.** $f(x) = \dfrac{x^2 + 4}{x - 2}$, $a = 3$

**20.** $f(x) = \dfrac{x^2 + 6}{x - 5}$, $a = 6$

**21.** $f(x) = \dfrac{x + 5}{x - 5}$, $a = 5$

**22.** $f(x) = \dfrac{x + 7}{x - 7}$, $a = 7$

**23.** $f(x) = \dfrac{x - 5}{x + 5}$, $a = 5$

**24.** $f(x) = \dfrac{x - 7}{x + 7}$, $a = 7$

**25.** $f(x) = \dfrac{x^2 + 5x}{x^2 - 5x}$, $a = 0$

**26.** $f(x) = \dfrac{x^2 + 8x}{x^2 - 8x}$, $a = 0$

**27.** $f(x) = \begin{cases} \dfrac{x^2 - 4}{x - 2} & \text{if } x \neq 2 \\ 5 & \text{if } x = 2 \end{cases}$

$a = 2$

**28.** $f(x) = \begin{cases} \dfrac{x^2 - 36}{x - 6} & \text{if } x \neq 6 \\ 13 & \text{if } x = 6 \end{cases}$

$a = 6$

**29.** $f(x) = \begin{cases} x - 5 & \text{if } x \leq 0 \\ x^2 + x - 5 & \text{if } x > 0 \end{cases}$

$a = 0$

**30.** $f(x) = \begin{cases} x - 4 & \text{if } x \leq 0 \\ x^2 + x - 4 & \text{if } x > 0 \end{cases}$

$a = 0$

**31.** $f(x) = \begin{cases} 1 - x & \text{if } x < 1 \\ 0 & \text{if } x = 1 \\ x^2 - 1 & \text{if } x > 1 \end{cases}$

$a = 1$

**32.** $f(x) = \begin{cases} 2 - x & \text{if } x < 1 \\ 1 & \text{if } x = 1 \\ x^2 & \text{if } x > 1 \end{cases}$

$a = 1$

*In Exercises 33–50, determine for what numbers, if any, the given function is discontinuous.*

**33.** $f(x) = x^2 + 4x - 6$

**34.** $f(x) = x^2 + 8x - 10$

**35.** $f(x) = \dfrac{x + 1}{(x + 1)(x - 4)}$

**36.** $f(x) = \dfrac{x + 2}{(x + 2)(x - 5)}$

**37.** $f(x) = \dfrac{\sin x}{x}$

**38.** $f(x) = \dfrac{1 - \cos x}{x}$

**39.** $f(x) = \pi$

**40.** $f(x) = c$

**41.** $f(x) = \begin{cases} x - 1 & \text{if } x \leq 1 \\ x^2 & \text{if } x > 1 \end{cases}$

**42.** $f(x) = \begin{cases} x - 2 & \text{if } x \leq 2 \\ x^2 - 1 & \text{if } x > 2 \end{cases}$

**43.** $f(x) = \begin{cases} \dfrac{x^2 - 1}{x - 1} & \text{if } x \neq 1 \\ 2 & \text{if } x = 1 \end{cases}$

**44.** $f(x) = \begin{cases} \dfrac{x^2 - 9}{x - 3} & \text{if } x \neq 3 \\ 6 & \text{if } x = 3 \end{cases}$

**45.** $f(x) = \begin{cases} x + 6 & \text{if } x \leq 0 \\ 6 & \text{if } 0 < x \leq 2 \\ x^2 + 1 & \text{if } x > 2 \end{cases}$

**46.** $f(x) = \begin{cases} x + 7 & \text{if } x \leq 0 \\ 7 & \text{if } 0 < x \leq 3 \\ x^2 - 1 & \text{if } x > 3 \end{cases}$

**47.** $f(x) = \begin{cases} 5x & \text{if } x < 4 \\ 21 & \text{if } x = 4 \\ x^2 + 4 & \text{if } x > 4 \end{cases}$

**48.** $f(x) = \begin{cases} 7x & \text{if } x < 6 \\ 41 & \text{if } x = 6 \\ x^2 + 6 & \text{if } x > 6 \end{cases}$

## Application Exercises

**49.** You rent a car from a company that charges \$25 per day plus \$0.05 per mile. The figure shows the graph of the cost, $f(x)$, in dollars, as a function of the miles, $x$, that you drive the car.

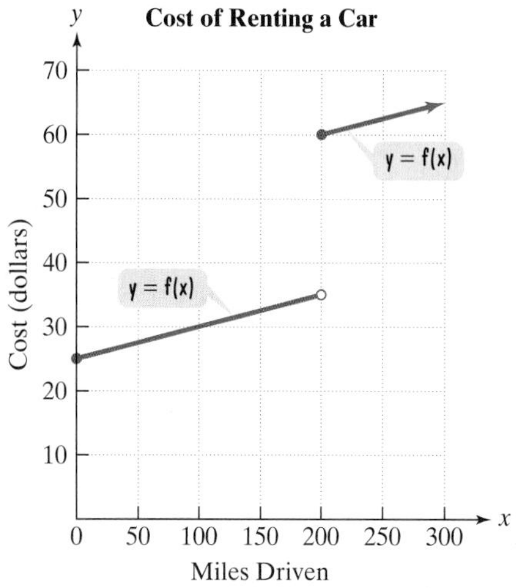


**a.** Find $\lim_{x \to 200^-} f(x)$.

**b.** Find $\lim_{x \to 200^+} f(x)$.

**c.** What can you conclude about $\lim_{x \to 200} f(x)$? How is this shown by the graph?

**d.** What aspect of the rental charge causes the graph to jump at its discontinuities?

**50.** The figure shows the graph for the cost of first class mail, $f(x)$, in dollars, as a function of the mail's weight, $x$, in ounces.

**a.** Find $\lim_{x \to 4^-} f(x)$.

**b.** Find $\lim_{x \to 4^+} f(x)$.

**c.** What can you conclude about $\lim_{x \to 4} f(x)$? How is this shown by the graph?

**d.** What aspect of costs for mailing a letter causes the graph to jump vertically by the same amount at its discontinuities?

**Cost of First-Class Mail (Effective January 10, 1999)**

| Weight Not Over | Cost |
|---|---|
| 1 ounce | \$0.33 |
| 2 ounce | 0.55 |
| 3 ounce | 0.77 |
| 4 ounce | 0.99 |
| 5 ounce | 1.21 |

*Source*: U.S. Postal Service

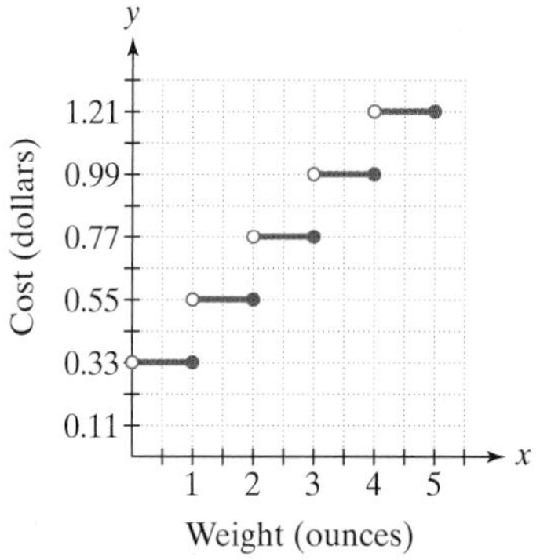

## Writing in Mathematics

**51.** Explain how to read $\lim_{x \to a^-} f(x) = L$.

**52.** What does the limit notation $\lim_{x \to a^-} f(x) = L$ mean?

**53.** Explain how to read $\lim_{x \to a^+} f(x) = L$.

**54.** What does the limit notation $\lim_{x \to a^+} f(x) = L$ mean?

**55.** What does it mean if a function has no limit as $x$ approaches $a$?

**56.** Explain how to determine whether a function is continuous at a number.

**57.** If a function is not defined at $a$, how is this shown on the function's graph?

**58.** If a function is defined at $a$, but $\lim_{x \to a} f(x)$ does not exist, how is this shown on the function's graph?

**59.** If a function is defined at $a$, $\lim_{x \to a} f(x)$ exists, but $\lim_{x \to a} f(x) \neq f(a)$, how is this shown on the function's graph?

**60.** In Exercises 49–50, functions that modeled the cost of renting a car and mailing a letter had jumps in their graphs. Describe another situation that can be modeled by a function with discontinuities. What aspect of this situation causes the discontinuities?

**61.** Give two examples of the use of the word *continuous* in everyday English. Compare its use in your examples to its meaning in mathematics.

## Technology Exercises

**62.** Use the TABLE feature or the ZOOM IN feature of your graphing utility to verify any two of the limits that you found in Exercises 1–8.

**63.** Use you graphing utility to graph any five of the functions in Exercises 15–32 and verify whether $f$ is continuous at $a$.

**64.** Estimate $\lim_{x \to 0^+} (1 + x)^{1/x}$ by using the TABLE feature of your graphing utility to create a table of values. Then use the ZOOM IN feature to zoom in on the graph of $f$ near and to the right of $x = 0$ to justify or improve your estimate.

## Critical Thinking Exercises

**65.** Define $f(x) = \dfrac{x^2 - 81}{x - 9}$ at $x = 9$ so that the function becomes continuous at 9.

**66.** Is it possible to define $f(x) = \dfrac{1}{x - 9}$ at $x = 9$ so that the function becomes continuous at 9? How does this discontinuity differ from the discontinuity in Exercise 65?

**67.** For the function

$$f(x) = \begin{cases} x^2 & \text{if } x < 1 \\ Ax - 3 & \text{if } x \geq 1 \end{cases}$$

find $A$ so that the function is continuous at 1.

## Group Exercise

**68.** In this exercise, the group will define three piecewise functions. Each function should have three pieces and two values of $x$ at which the pieces change.

**a.** Define and graph a piecewise function that is continuous at both values of $x$ where the pieces change.

**b.** Define and graph a piecewise function that is continuous at one value of $x$ where the pieces change and discontinuous at the other value of $x$ where the pieces change.

**c.** Define and graph a piecewise function that is discontinuous at both values of $x$ where the pieces change.

At the end of the activity, group members should turn in the functions and their graphs. Do not use any of the piecewise functions or graphs that appear anywhere in this book.

## SECTION 12.4 Introduction to Derivatives

### Objectives

1. Find slopes and equations of tangent lines.
2. Find the derivative of a function.
3. Find average and instantaneous rates of change.
4 Find instantaneous velocity.

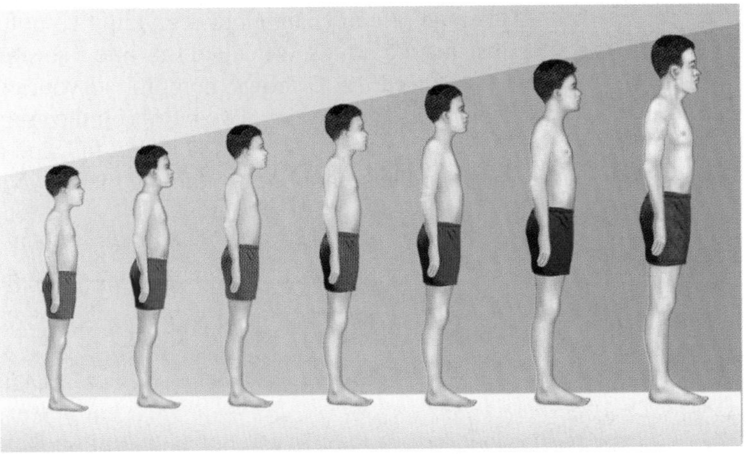

Can this possibly be my little cousin, whom I haven't seen in five years? He's changed from a kid to an attractive young adult. I know that things change over time and that most changes occur at uneven rates, but this is a radical transformation. What does calculus have to say about this?

In this section, we will see how calculus allows motion and change to be analyzed by "freezing the frame" of a continuous changing process, instant by instant. For example, Figure 12.14 shows your cousin's changing height over intervals of time. Over the period of time from $P$ to $D$, his average rate of growth is his change in height—that is, his height at time $D$ minus his height at time $P$—divided by the change in time from $P$ to $D$.

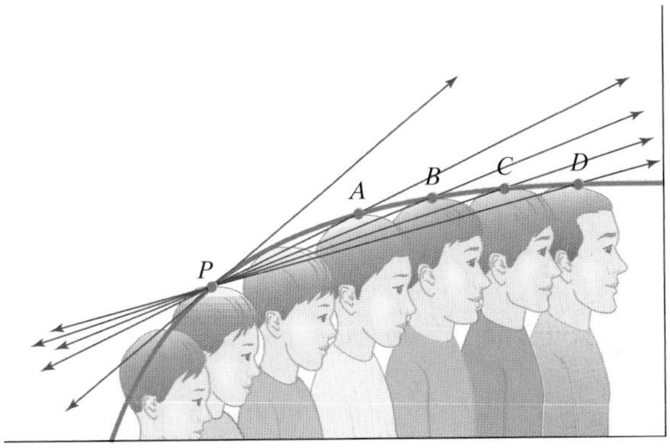


**Figure 12.14** Analyzing continuous growth over intervals of time and at an instant in time

The lines $PD$, $PC$, $PB$, and $PA$ shown in Figure 12.14 have slopes that show your cousin's average growth rates for successively shorter periods of time. Calculus makes these time frames so small that their limit approaches a single point—that is, a single instant in time. This point is shown as point $P$ in Figure 12.14. The slope of the line that touches the graph at $P$ gives your cousin's growth rate at one instant in time, $P$.

Keep in mind this informal discussion of your cousin and his growth rate as you read this section. We begin with the calculus that describes the slope of the line that touches the graph in Figure 12.14 at $P$.

**1** Find slopes and equations of tangent lines.

## Slopes and Equations of Tangent Lines

In Chapter 2, we saw that if the graph of a function is not a straight line, the **average rate of change** between any two points is the slope of the line containing the two points. We called this line a **secant line.**

Figure 12.15 shows the graph of your cousin's height, in inches, as a function of his age, in years. Two points on the graph are labeled: (13, 57) and (18, 76). At age 13, your cousin was 57 inches tall, and at age 18, he was 76 inches tall. The slope of the secant line containing these two points is

$$\frac{76-57}{18-13}=\frac{19}{5}=3\frac{4}{5}.$$

Slope is the change in the y-coordinates divided by the change in the x-coordinates.

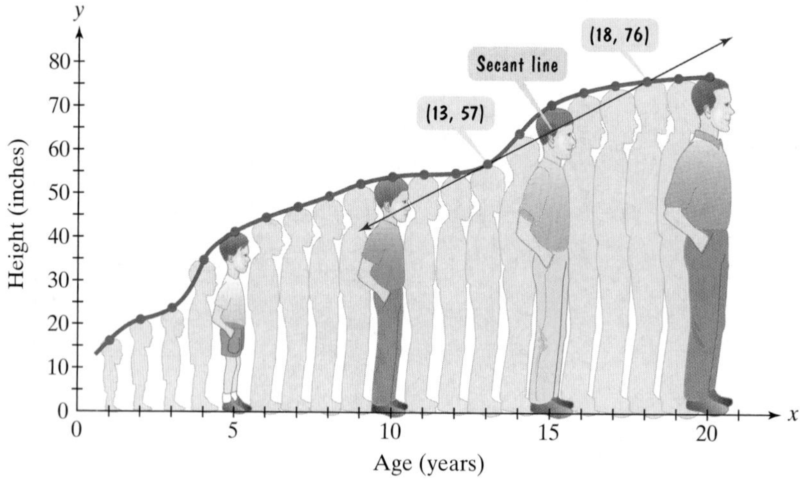


**Figure 12.15** Height as a function of age

Your cousin's average rate of change, or average growth rate, from 13 to 18 was $3\frac{4}{5}$ inches per year.

How can we find your cousin's growth rate at the instant when he was 13? We can find this *instantaneous rate of change* by repeating the computation of slope from 13 to 17, then from 13 to 16, then from 13 to 15, again from 13 to 14, again from 13 to $13\frac{1}{2}$, and once again from 13 to 13.01. What limit is approached by these computations as the shrinking interval of time gets closer and closer to the instant when your cousin was 13?

We answer these questions by considering the graph of any function $f$, shown in Figure 12.16 on page 1021. We wish to find the slope, or steepness, of this curve at the point $P=(a, f(a))$. This slope will reveal the function's instantaneous rate of change at $a$. We begin by choosing a second point, $Q$, whose $x$-coordinate is $a+h$, where $h \neq 0$. The point $Q=(a+h, f(a+h))$ is shown in Figure 12.16.

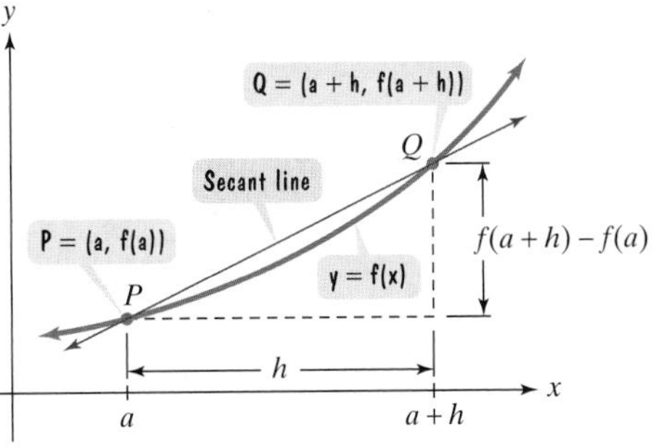


**Figure 12.16** Finding the average rate of change, or the slope of the secant line

How do we find the average rate of change of $f$ between points $P$ and $Q$? We find the slope of the secant line, the line containing $P$ and $Q$.

Slope of secant line

$$= \frac{f(a + h) - f(a)}{a + h - a}$$ Slope is the change in y-coordinates, $f(a + h) - f(a)$, divided by the change in x-coordinates, $(a + h) - a$.

$$= \frac{f(a + h) - f(a)}{h}$$ Simplify.

Do you recognize this expression as the difference quotient presented in Chapter 2? We will make use of this expression and our understanding of limits to find the slope of a graph at a specific point.

What happens if the distance labeled $h$ in Figure 12.16 approaches 0? The value of the $x$-coordinate of point $Q$, $a + h$, will get closer and closer to $a$. Can you see that $a$ is the $x$-coordinate of point $P$? Thus, as $h$ approaches 0, point $Q$ approaches point $P$. Examine Figure 12.17 to see how we visualize the changing position of point $Q$.

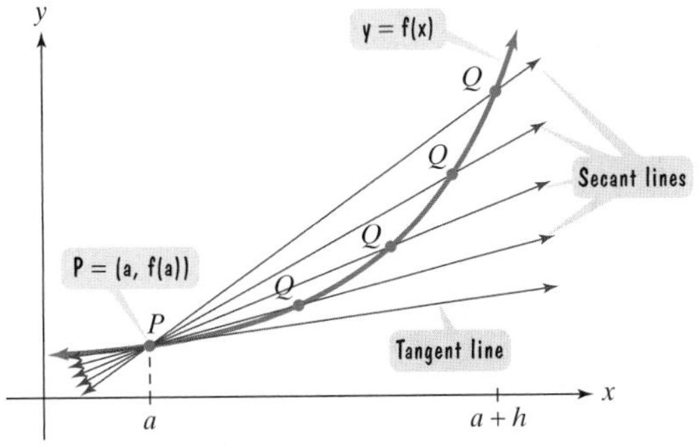


**Figure 12.17** As $Q$ approaches $P$, the succession of secant lines approaches the tangent line.

Figure 12.17 also shows how the secant line between points $P$ and $Q$ changes as $h$ approaches 0. Note how the position of the secant line changes as the position of $Q$ changes. The secant line between point $P$ and point $Q$ approaches the red line that touches the graph of $f$ at point $P$. This limiting position of the secant line is called the **tangent line** to the graph of $f$ at the point $P = (a, f(a))$.

According to our earlier derivation, the slope of each secant line in Figure 12.17 is

$$\frac{f(a + h) - f(a)}{h}.$$ This difference quotient is also the average rate of change of $f$ from $x_1 = a$ to $x_2 = a + h$.

As $h$ approaches 0, this slope approaches the slope of the tangent line to the curve at $(a, f(a))$. Thus, the slope of the tangent line to the curve at $(a, f(a))$ is

$$\lim_{h \to 0} \frac{f(a + h) - f(a)}{h}.$$

This limit also represents the **instantaneous rate of change of $f$ with respect to $x$ at $a$.**

### Slope of the Tangent Line to a Curve at a Point

The **slope of the tangent line** to the graph of a function $y = f(x)$ at $(a, f(a))$ is given by

$$m_{\tan} = \lim_{h \to 0} \frac{f(a+h) - f(a)}{h}$$

provided that this limit exists. This limit also describes

- the **slope of the graph of $f$ at $(a, f(a))$.**
- the **instantaneous rate of change of $f$ with respect to $x$ at $a$.**

## EXAMPLE 1 Finding the Slope of the Tangent Line

Find the slope of the tangent line to the graph of $f(x) = x^2 + x$ at $(2, 6)$.

**Solution** The slope of the tangent line at $(a, f(a))$ is

$$m_{\tan} = \lim_{h \to 0} \frac{f(a+h) - f(a)}{h}.$$

We use this formula to find the slope of the tangent line at the given point. Because we are finding the tangent line at $(2, 6)$, we know that $a = 2$.

$$m_{\tan} = \lim_{h \to 0} \frac{f(2+h) - f(2)}{h}$$

Because $a = 2$, substitute 2 into the formula for each occurrence of $a$.

$$= \lim_{h \to 0} \frac{\left[(2+h)^2 + (2+h)\right] - \left[2^2 + 2\right]}{h}$$

To find $f(2 + h)$, replace $x$ in $f(x) = x^2 + x$ by $2 + h$. To find $f(2)$, replace $x$ by 2.

$$= \lim_{h \to 0} \frac{\left[4 + 4h + h^2 + 2 + h\right] - 6}{h}$$

Square $2 + h$ using $(A + B)^2 = A^2 + 2AB + B^2$.

$$= \lim_{h \to 0} \frac{h^2 + 5h}{h}$$

Combine like terms in the numerator.

$$= \lim_{h \to 0} \frac{h(h+5)}{h}$$

Factor the numerator.

$$= \lim_{h \to 0} (h + 5)$$

Divide both the numerator and denominator by $h$. This is permitted because $h$ approaches 0, but $h \neq 0$.

$$= 0 + 5$$

Use limit properties.

$$= 5$$

Thus, the slope of the tangent line to the graph of $f(x) = x^2 + x$ at $(2, 6)$ is 5. This is shown in Figure 12.18. We also say that the slope of the graph of $f(x) = x^2 + x$ at $(2, 6)$ is 5.

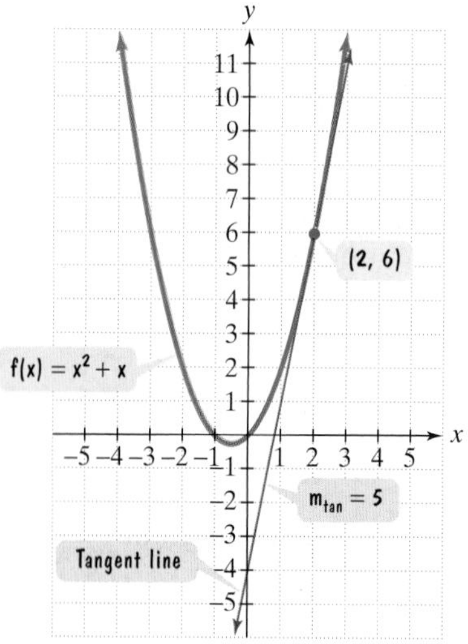


**Figure 12.18**

**Check Point 1** Find the slope of the tangent line to the graph of $f(x) = x^2 - x$ at $(4, 12)$.

## Technology

Graphing utilities with a DRAW TANGENT feature will draw tangent lines to curves and display their point-slope equations. Figure 12.19 shows the tangent line to the graph of $y = x^2 + x$ at the point whose $x$-coordinate is 2. Also displayed is the point-slope equation of the tangent line, $y = 5x - 4$.

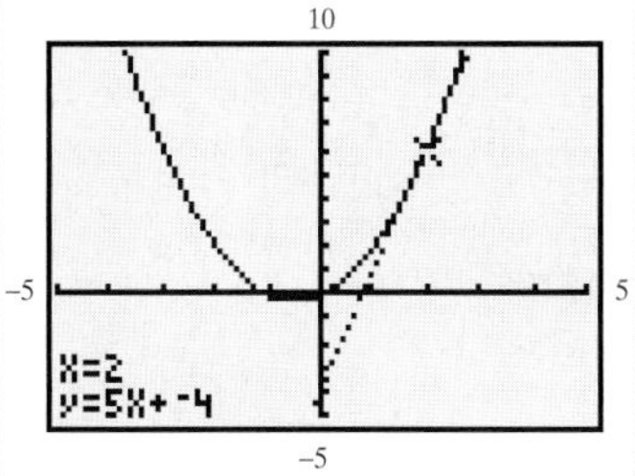


**Figure 12.19**

In Example 1, we found the *slope* of the tangent line shown in Figure 12.18. We can find an *equation* of this line using the point-slope form of the equation of a line

$$y - y_1 = m(x - x_1).$$

The tangent line passes through $(2, 6)$: $x_1 = 2$ and $y_1 = 6$. The slope of the tangent line is 5: $m = 5$. The point-slope equation of the tangent line is

$$y - 6 = 5(x - 2).$$

We can solve for $y$ and express the equation of the tangent line in slope-intercept form: $y = mx + b$. The slope-intercept equation of the tangent line is

$$y - 6 = 5x - 10 \quad \text{Apply the distributive property.}$$

$$y = 5x - 4. \quad \text{This is the slope-intercept form.}$$

## EXAMPLE 2 Finding the Slope-Intercept Equation of the Tangent Line

Find the slope-intercept equation of the tangent line to the graph of $f(x) = \sqrt{x}$ at $(4, 2)$.

**Solution** We begin by finding the slope of the tangent line to the graph of $f(x) = \sqrt{x}$ at $(4, 2)$.

$$m_{\tan} = \lim_{h \to 0} \frac{f(4 + h) - f(4)}{h}$$

The slope of the tangent line at $(a, f(a))$ is $\lim_{h \to 0} \frac{f(a + h) - f(a)}{h}$.

$$= \lim_{h \to 0} \frac{\sqrt{4 + h} - 2}{h}$$

To find $f(4 + h)$, replace $x$ in $f(x) = \sqrt{x}$ by $4 + h$. $f(4) = \sqrt{4} = 2$.

$$= \lim_{h \to 0} \frac{\sqrt{4 + h} - 2}{h} \cdot \frac{\sqrt{4 + h} + 2}{\sqrt{4 + h} + 2}$$

Rationalize the numerator.

$$= \lim_{h \to 0} \frac{4 + h - 4}{h(\sqrt{4 + h} + 2)}$$

Multiply the numerators.

$$= \lim_{h \to 0} \frac{h}{h(\sqrt{4 + h} + 2)}$$

Simplify the numerator.

$$= \lim_{h \to 0} \frac{1}{\sqrt{4 + h} + 2}$$

Divide both the numerator and the denominator by $h$. This is permitted because $h$ approaches 0, but $h \neq 0$.

$$= \frac{1}{\sqrt{4 + 0} + 2}$$

Use limit properties.

$$= \frac{1}{4}$$

Now that we have the slope of the tangent line, we can write the slope-intercept equation. Begin with the point-slope form

$$y - y_1 = m(x - x_1).$$

The tangent line is given to pass through $(4, 2)$: $x_1 = 4$ and $y_1 = 2$. We found the slope of the tangent line to be $\frac{1}{4}$: $m = \frac{1}{4}$. The point-slope equation of the tangent line is

$$y - 2 = \tfrac{1}{4}(x - 4).$$

Solving for $y$, we obtain the slope-intercept equation of the tangent line.

$$y - 2 = \tfrac{1}{4}x - 1 \quad \text{Apply the distributive property.}$$

$$y = \tfrac{1}{4}x + 1 \quad \text{Add 2 to both sides. This is the slope-intercept form, } y = mx + b\text{, of the equation.}$$

The slope-intercept equation of the tangent line to the graph of $f(x) = \sqrt{x}$ at $(4, 2)$ is $y = \frac{1}{4}x + 1$. Figure 12.20 shows the graph of $f$ and the tangent line.

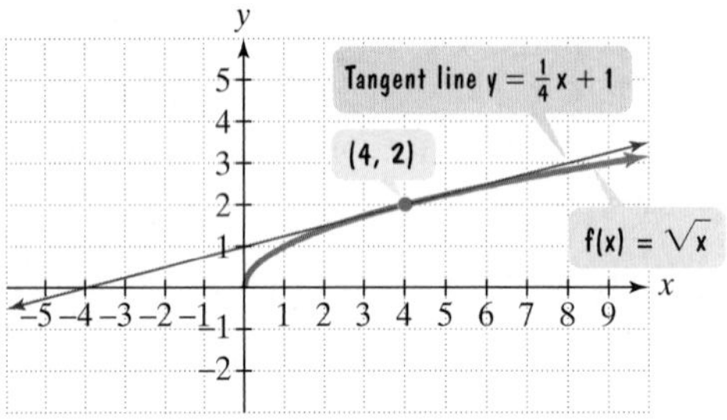


**Figure 12.20**

**Check Point 2** Find the slope-intercept equation of the tangent line to the graph of $f(x) = \sqrt{x}$ at $(1, 1)$.

**2** Find the derivative of a function.

## The Derivative of a Function

In Examples 1 and 2, we found the slope of a tangent line to the graph of $f$ at $(a, f(a))$, where $a$ was a specific number. We can also find the slope of a tangent line at $(x, f(x))$, where $x$ can represent any number. The resulting function is called the *derivative of $f$ at $x$*.

### Definition of the Derivative of a Function

Let $y = f(x)$ denote a function $f$. The **derivative of $f$ at $x$**, denoted by $f'(x)$, read "$f$ prime of $x$," is defined by

$$f'(x) = \lim_{h \to 0} \frac{f(x + h) - f(x)}{h}$$

provided that this limit exists. The derivative of a function $f$ gives the slope of $f$ for any value of $x$.

By evaluating the derivative, you can compute the slopes of various tangent lines to the graph of a function. Thus, the derivative gives you a way to analyze your moving world by revealing a function's instantaneous rate of change at any moment.

## The Seeds of Change

Every shape that's born bears in its womb the seeds of change.

—*Ovid* (Roman poet)

Figure 12.21 shows a graph involving change, namely a boy's height as a function of his age. The derivative of this function provides a formula for the slope of the tangent line to the function's graph at any point. The figure shows four tangent lines. The derivative of this function would reveal that the tangent line with the greatest slope touches the curve somewhere between $x = 3$ and $x = 4$. Thus, the instantaneous rate of change in a boy's growth is greatest at some moment in time between the ages of 3 and 4.

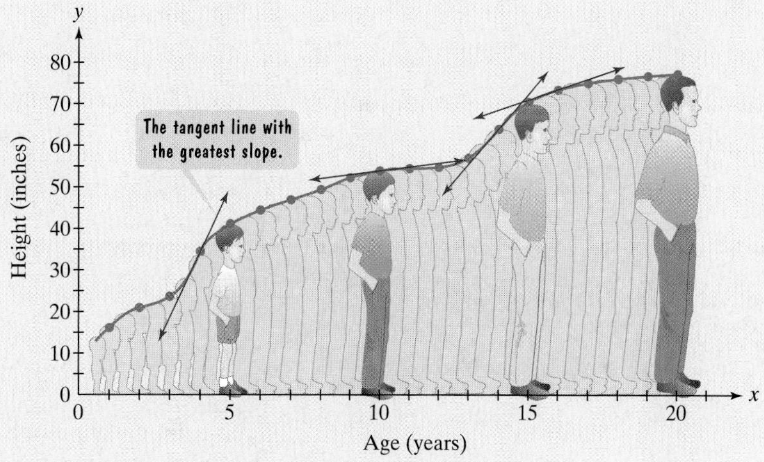


**Figure 12.21** Analyzing continuous change at an instant

### EXAMPLE 3 Finding the Derivative of a Function

**a.** Find the derivative of $f(x) = x^2 + 3x$ at $x$. That is, find $f'(x)$.

**b.** Find the slope of the tangent line to $f(x) = x^2 + 3x$ at $x = -2$ and $x = -\frac{3}{2}$.

**Solution**

**a.** We use the definition of the derivative of $f$ at $x$ to find the derivative of the given function.

$$f'(x) = \lim_{h\to 0}\frac{f(x+h) - f(x)}{h}$$ Use the definition of the derivative.

$$= \lim_{h\to 0}\frac{\left[(x+h)^2 + 3(x+h)\right] - \left(x^2 + 3x\right)}{h}$$ To find $f(x + h)$, replace $x$ in $f(x) = x^2 + 3x$ by $x + h$.

$$= \lim_{h\to 0}\frac{x^2 + 2xh + h^2 + 3x + 3h - x^2 - 3x}{h}$$ Perform the indicated operations in the numerator.

$$= \lim_{h\to 0}\frac{2xh + h^2 + 3h}{h}$$ Simplify the numerator: $x^2 - x^2 = 0$ and $3x - 3x = 0$.

$$= \lim_{h\to 0}\frac{h(2x + h + 3)}{h}$$ Factor the numerator.

$$= \lim_{h\to 0}(2x + h + 3)$$ Divide the numerator and the denominator by $h$.

$$= 2x + 0 + 3$$ Use limit properties. As $h$ approaches 0, only the term containing $h$ is affected.

$$= 2x + 3$$

The derivative of $f(x) = x^2 + 3x$ is

$$f'(x) = 2x + 3.$$

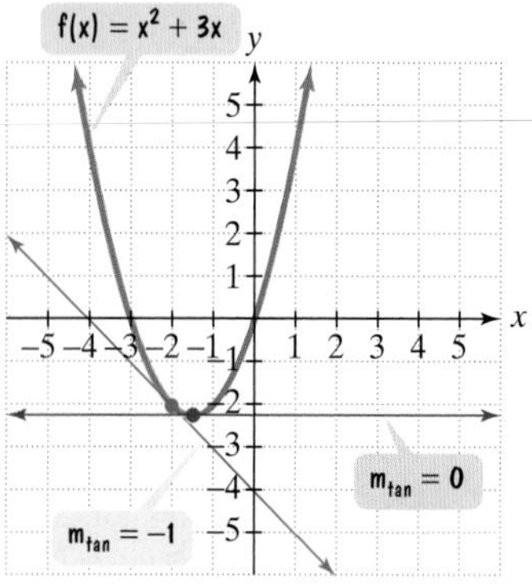


**Figure 12.22** Two tangent lines to $f(x) = x^2 + 3x$ and their slopes

**b.** The derivative gives the slope of the tangent line at any point. Thus, to find the slope of the tangent line to $f(x) = x^2 + 3x$ at $x = -2$, evaluate the derivative at $-2$. Similarly, to find the slope of the tangent line at $x = -\frac{3}{2}$, evaluate the derivative at $-\frac{3}{2}$.

$$f'(x) = 2x + 3$$
$$f'(-2) = 2(-2) + 3 = -4 + 3 = -1$$
$$f'\left(-\tfrac{3}{2}\right) = 2\left(-\tfrac{3}{2}\right) + 3 = -3 + 3 = 0$$

Figure 12.22 shows the graph of $f(x) = x^2 + 3x$ and tangent lines at $x = -2$ and $x = -\frac{3}{2}$. The slope of the decreasing tangent line at $x = -2$ is $-1$. The slope of the horizontal tangent line at $x = -\frac{3}{2}$ is 0.

**Check Point 3**

**a.** Find the derivative of $f(x) = x^2 - 5x$ at $x$. That is, find $f'(x)$.

**b.** Find the slope of the tangent line to $f(x) = x^2 - 5x$ at $x = -1$ and $x = 3$.

**3** Find average and instantaneous rates of change.

## Applications of the Derivative

Many applications of the derivative involve analyzing change by determining a function's instantaneous rate of change at any moment. How do we use the derivative of a function to reveal such a change? We know that the derivative of $f$ at $x$ is defined by

$$f'(x) = \lim_{h \to 0} \frac{f(x + h) - f(x)}{h}.$$

Thus, the derivative of $f$ at $a$ is

$$f'(a) = \lim_{h \to 0} \frac{f(a + h) - f(a)}{h}.$$

Do you recognize this limit? It describes the instantaneous rate of change of $f$ with respect to $x$ at $a$.

### Average and Instantaneous Rates of Change

**Average Rate of Change** The **average rate of change of $f$ from $x = a$ to $x = a + h$** is given by the difference quotient

$$\frac{f(a + h) - f(a)}{h}.$$

**Instantaneous Rate of Changes** The **instantaneous rate of change of $f$ with respect to $x$ at $a$** is the derivative of $f$ at $a$:

$$f'(a) = \lim_{h \to 0} \frac{f(a + h) - f(a)}{h}.$$

### EXAMPLE 4 Finding Average and Instantaneous Rates of Change

The function $f(x) = x^3$ describes the volume of a cube, $f(x)$, in cubic inches, whose length, width, and height each measure $x$ inches. If $x$ is changing:

**a.** Find the average rate of change of the volume with respect to $x$ as $x$ changes from 5 inches to 5.1 inches and from 5 inches to 5.01 inches.

**b.** Find the instantaneous rate of change of the volume with respect to $x$ at the moment when $x = 5$ inches.

**Solution**

**a.** As $x$ changes from 5 to 5.1, $a = 5$ and $h = 0.1$. The average rate of change of the volume with respect to $x$ as $x$ changes from 5 to 5.1 is determined as follows.

$$\frac{f(a+h) - f(a)}{h}$$ The difference quotient gives the average rate of change.

$$= \frac{f(5+0.1) - f(5)}{0.1}$$ This is the average rate of change from 5 to 5.1.

$$= \frac{f(5.1) - f(5)}{0.1}$$ Simplify.

$$= \frac{(5.1)^3 - 5^3}{0.1}$$ Use $f(x) = x^3$ and substitute 5.1 and 5, respectively, for $x$.

$$= 76.51$$

The average rate of change in the volume is 76.51 cubic inches per inch as $x$ changes from 5 to 5.1 inches.

As $x$ changes from 5 to 5.01, $a = 5$ and $h = 0.01$. The average rate of change of the volume with respect to $x$ as $x$ changes from 5 to 5.01 is determined as follows.

$$\frac{f(a+h) - f(a)}{h}$$ The difference quotient gives the average rate of change.

$$= \frac{f(5+0.01) - f(5)}{0.01}$$ This is the average rate of change from 5 to 5.01.

$$= \frac{f(5.01) - f(5)}{0.01}$$ Simplify.

$$= \frac{(5.01)^3 - 5^3}{0.01}$$ Use $f(x) = x^3$ and substitute 5.01 and 5, respectively, for $x$.

$$= 75.1501$$

The average rate of change in the volume is 75.1501 cubic inches per inch as $x$ changes from 5 to 5.01 inches.

**b.** Instantaneous rates of change are given by the derivative. The derivative of $f$ at $a$, $f'(a)$, is the instantaneous rate of change of $f$ with respect to $x$ at $a$. We must find the instantaneous rate of change of the volume with respect to $x$ at the moment when $x = 5$ inches. This means that we must find $f'(5)$. We find $f'(5)$ by first finding $f'(x)$, the derivative, and then evaluating $f'$ at 5.

$$f'(x) = \lim_{h \to 0} \frac{f(x+h) - f(x)}{h}$$
Use the definition of the derivative.

$$= \lim_{h \to 0} \frac{(x+h)^3 - x^3}{h}$$
To find $f(x+h)$, replace $x$ in $f(x) = x^3$ by $x + h$.

$$= \lim_{h \to 0} \frac{(x^3 + 3x^2h + 3xh^2 + h^3) - x^3}{h}$$
Use the Binomial Theorem to cube $x + h$.

$$= \lim_{h \to 0} \frac{3x^2h + 3xh^2 + h^3}{h}$$
Simplify the numerator: $x^3 - x^3 = 0$.

$$= \lim_{h \to 0} \frac{h(3x^2 + 3xh + h^2)}{h}$$
Factor the numerator.

$$= \lim_{h \to 0} (3x^2 + 3xh + h^2)$$
Divide the numerator and the denominator by $h$.

$$= 3x^2 + 3x \cdot 0 + 0^2$$
Use limit properties. As $h$ approaches 0, only terms containing $h$ are affected.

$$= 3x^2$$

## Technology

Graphing utilities have a feature that gives (or approximates) the derivative of a function evaluated at any number. Consult your manual for details. The screen below verifies that if $f(x) = x^3$, then $f'(5) = 75$.

The derivative of $f(x) = x^3$ is $f'(x) = 3x^2$. To find the instantaneous change of $f$ at 5, evaluate the derivative at 5.

$$f'(x) = 3x^2$$
$$f'(5) = 3 \cdot 5^2 = 75$$

The instantaneous rate of change of the volume with respect to $x$ at the moment when $x = 5$ inches is 75 cubic inches per inch. Notice how the average rates of change that we computed, 76.51 and 75.1501, are approaching the instantaneous rate of change, 75.

**Check Point 4** Use the function in Example 3, $f(x) = x^3$, to find:

**a.** the average rate of change of the volume with respect to $x$ as $x$ changes from 4 inches to 4.1 inches and from 4 inches to 4.01 inches.

**b.** the instantaneous rate of change of the volume with respect to $x$ at the moment when $x = 4$ inches.

### 4 Find instantaneous velocity.

The ideas of calculus are frequently applied to position functions that express an object's position, $s(t)$, in terms of time, $t$. In the time interval from $t = a$ to $t = a + h$, the change in the object's position is

$$s(a+h) - s(a).$$

The **average velocity** over this time interval is

$$\frac{s(a+h) - s(a)}{h}.$$

The numerator is the change in position.

The denominator is the change in time from $t = a$ to $t = a + h$.

Now suppose that we compute the average velocities over shorter and shorter time intervals $[a, a + h]$. This means that we let $h$ approach 0. As in our previous discussion, we define the *instantaneous velocity* at time $t = a$ to be the limit of these average velocities. This limit is the derivative of $s$ at $a$.

### Instantaneous Velocity

Suppose that a function expresses an object's position, $s(t)$, in terms of time, $t$. The **instantaneous velocity** of the object at time $t = a$ is

$$s'(a) = \lim_{h\to 0} \frac{s(a+h) - s(a)}{h}.$$

Instantaneous velocity at time $a$ is also called **velocity** at time $a$.

## EXAMPLE 5 Finding Instantaneous Velocity

A ball is thrown straight up from a rooftop 160 feet high with an initial velocity of 48 feet per second. The function

$$s(t) = -16t^2 + 48t + 160$$

describes the ball's height above the ground, $s(t)$, in feet, $t$ seconds after it was thrown. The ball misses the rooftop on its way down and eventually strikes the ground.

**a.** What is the instantaneous velocity of the ball 2 seconds after it is thrown?

**b.** What is the instantaneous velocity of the ball when it hits the ground?

**Solution** Instantaneous velocity is given by the derivative of a function that expresses an object's position, $s(t)$, in terms of time, $t$. The instantaneous velocity of the ball at $a$ seconds is $s'(a)$.

$$s'(a) = \lim_{h\to 0} \frac{s(a+h) - s(a)}{h}$$ This derivative describes instantaneous velocity at time $a$.

To find $s(a+h)$, replace $t$ in $s(t) = -16t^2 + 48t + 160$ by $a + h$. To find $s(a)$, replace $t$ by $a$. Thus,

$$s'(a) = \lim_{h\to 0} \frac{-16(a+h)^2 + 48(a+h) + 160 - (-16a^2 + 48a + 160)}{h}$$

Take a few minutes to simplify the numerator of the difference quotient and factor out $h$. You should obtain

$$s'(a) = \lim_{h\to 0} \frac{\cancel{h}(-32a - 16h + 48)}{\cancel{h}} = -32a - 16 \cdot 0 + 48 = -32a + 48.$$

The instantaneous velocity of the ball at $a$ seconds is

$$s'(a) = -32a + 48.$$

**a.** The instantaneous velocity of the ball at 2 seconds is found by replacing $a$ by 2.

$$s'(2) = -32 \cdot 2 + 48 = -64 + 48 = -16$$

Two seconds after the ball is thrown, its instantaneous velocity is $-16$ feet per second. The negative sign indicates that the ball is moving downward when $t = 2$ seconds.

**b.** To find the instantaneous velocity of the ball when it hits the ground, we need to know how many seconds elapse between the time the ball is thrown from the rooftop and the time it hits the ground. The ball hits the ground when $s(t)$, its height above the ground, is 0. Thus, we set $s(t)$ equal to 0.

### Roller Coasters and Derivatives

Roller coaster rides give you the opportunity to spend a few hair-raising minutes plunging hundreds of feet, accelerating to 80 miles an hour in seven seconds, and enduring vertical loops that turn you upside-down. By finding a function that models your distance above the ground at every moment of the ride and taking its derivative, you can determine when the instantaneous velocity is the greatest. As you experience the glorious agony of the roller coaster, this is your moment of peak terror.

$$-16t^2 + 48t + 160 = 0$$ Set $s(t) = 0$.

$$t^2 - 3t - 10 = 0$$ Divide both sides of the quadratic equation by −16.

$$(t - 5)(t + 2) = 0$$ Factor.

$$t - 5 = 0 \quad t + 2 = 0$$ Set each factor equal to 0.

$$t = 5 \qquad t = -2$$ Solve for $t$.

Because we begin describing the ball's position at $t = 0$, we discard the solution $t = -2$. The ball hits the ground at 5 seconds. Its instantaneous velocity at 5 seconds is found by replacing $a$ by 5 in $s'(a)$.

$$s'(a) = -32a + 48$$ This is the ball's instantaneous velocity after $a$ seconds.

$$s'(5) = -32 \cdot 5 + 48 = -160 + 48 = -112$$

The instantaneous velocity of the ball when it hits the ground is −112 feet per second. The negative sign indicates that the ball is moving downward at the instant that it strikes the ground.

**Check Point 5** A ball is thrown straight up from ground level with an initial velocity of 96 feet per second. The function

$$s(t) = -16t^2 + 96t$$

describes the ball's height above the ground, $s(t)$, in feet, $t$ seconds after it was thrown.

**a.** What is the instantaneous velocity of the ball after 4 seconds?

**b.** What is the instantaneous velocity of the ball when it hits the ground?

## EXERCISE SET 12.4

### Practice Exercises

*In Exercises 1–14,*

**a.** *Find the slope of the tangent line to the graph of f at the given point.*

**b.** *Find the slope-intercept equation of the tangent line to the graph of f at the given point.*

**1.** $f(x) = 2x + 3$ at $(1, 5)$

**2.** $f(x) = 4x + 2$ at $(1, 6)$

**3.** $f(x) = x^2 + 4$ at $(-1, 5)$

**4.** $f(x) = x^2 + 7$ at $(-1, 8)$

**5.** $f(x) = 5x^2$ at $(-2, 20)$

**6.** $f(x) = 4x^2$ at $(-2, 16)$

**7.** $f(x) = 2x^2 - x$ at $(2, 6)$

**8.** $f(x) = 3x^2 + x$ at $(1, 4)$

**9.** $f(x) = 2x^2 + x - 3$ at $(0, -3)$

**10.** $f(x) = 2x^2 - x + 5$ at $(0, 5)$

**11.** $f(x) = \sqrt{x}$ at $(9, 3)$

**12.** $f(x) = \sqrt{x}$ at $(16, 4)$

**13.** $f(x) = \frac{1}{x}$ at $(1, 1)$

**14.** $f(x) = \frac{2}{x}$ at $(1, 2)$

*In Exercises 15–28,*

**a.** *Find the derivative of f at x. That is, find $f'(x)$.*

**b.** *Find the slope of the tangent line to the graph of f at each of the two values of x given to the right of the function.*

**15.** $f(x) = -3x + 7; x = 1, x = 4$

**16.** $f(x) = -5x + 3; x = 1, x = 4$

**17.** $f(x) = x^2 - 6; x = -1, x = 3$

**18.** $f(x) = x^2 - 8; x = -1, x = 3$

**19.** $f(x) = x^2 - 3x + 5; x = \frac{3}{2}, x = 2$

**20.** $f(x) = x^2 - 4x + 7; x = \frac{3}{2}, x = 2$

**21.** $f(x) = x^3 + 2; x = -1, x = 1$

**22.** $f(x) = x^3 - 2; x = -1, x = 1$

**23.** $f(x) = \sqrt{x}; x = 1, x = 4$

**24.** $f(x) = \sqrt{x}; x = 25, x = 100$

**25.** $f(x) = \frac{4}{x}; x = -2, x = 1$

**26.** $f(x) = \frac{8}{x}; x = -2, x = 1$

**27.** $f(x) = 3.2x^2 + 2.1x; x = 0, x = 4$

**28.** $f(x) = 1.3x^2 - 1.4x; x = 0, x = 4$

## Application Exercises

**29.** The function $f(x) = x^2$ describes the area of a square, $f(x)$, in square inches, whose sides each measure $x$ inches. If $x$ is changing:

**a.** Find the average rate of change of the area with respect to $x$ as $x$ changes from 6 inches to 6.1 inches and from 6 inches to 6.01 inches.

**b.** Find the instantaneous rate of change of the area with respect to $x$ at the moment when $x = 6$ inches.

**30.** The function $f(x) = x^2$ describes the area of a square, $f(x)$, in square inches, whose sides each measure $x$ inches. If $x$ is changing:

**a.** Find the average rate of change of the area with respect to $x$ as $x$ changes from 10 inches to 10.1 inches and from 10 inches to 10.01 inches.

**b.** Find the instantaneous rate of change of the area with respect to $x$ at the moment when $x = 10$ inches.

*In Exercises 31–34, express all answers in terms of $\pi$.*

**31.** The function $f(x) = \pi x^2$ describes the area of a circle, $f(x)$, in square inches, whose radius measures $x$ inches. If the radius is changing,

**a.** Find the average rate of change of the area with respect to the radius as the radius changes from 2 inches to 2.1 inches and from 2 inches to 2.01 inches.

**b.** Find the instantaneous rate of change of the area with respect to the radius when the radius is 2 inches.

**32.** The function $f(x) = \pi x^2$ describes the area of a circle, $f(x)$, in square inches, whose radius measures $x$ inches. If the radius is changing,

**a.** Find the average rate of change of the area with respect to the radius as the radius changes from 4 inches to 4.1 inches and from 4 inches to 4.01 inches.

**b.** Find the instantaneous rate of change of the area with respect to the radius when the radius is 4 inches.

**33.** The function $f(x) = 4\pi x^2$ describes the surface area, $f(x)$, of a sphere of radius $x$ inches. If the radius is changing, find the instantaneous rate of change of the surface area with respect to the radius when the radius is 6 inches.

**34.** The function $f(x) = 5\pi x^2$ describes the volume, $f(x)$, of a right circular cylinder of height 5 feet and radius $x$ feet. If the radius is changing, find the instantaneous rate of change of the volume with respect to the radius when the radius is 8 feet.

**35.** The dollar value of goods imported from China, $f(x)$, in billions, can be modeled by

$$f(x) = 0.32x^2 + 1.64x + 3.98$$

where $x$ is the number of years since 1986.

**a.** Find $f'(x)$.

**b.** At what rate, in billions of dollars per year, were U.S. imports from China changing in 2000?

**36.** The dollar value of goods the U.S. imports from all countries, $f(x)$, in billions, can be modeled by

$$f(x) = 2.39x^2 + 47.05x + 432.2$$

where $x$ is the number of years since 1990.

**a.** Find $f'(x)$.

**b.** At what rate, in billions of dollars per year, were U.S. imports from all countries changing in 2000?

**37.** An explosion causes debris to rise vertically with an initial velocity of 64 feet per second. The function

$$s(t) = -16t^2 + 64t$$

describes the height of the debris above the ground, $s(t)$, in feet, $t$ seconds after the explosion.

**a.** What is the instantaneous velocity of the debris 1 second after the explosion? 3 seconds after the explosion?

**b.** What is the instantaneous velocity of the debris when it hits the ground?

**38.** An explosion causes debris to rise vertically with an initial velocity of 72 feet per second. The function

$$s(t) = -16t^2 + 72t$$

describes the height of the debris above the ground, $s(t)$, in feet, $t$ seconds after the explosion.

**a.** What is the instantaneous velocity of the debris $\frac{1}{2}$ second after the explosion? 4 seconds after the explosion?

**b.** What is the instantaneous velocity of the debris when it hits the ground?

**39.** A foul tip of a baseball is hit straight upward from a height of 4 feet with an initial velocity of 96 feet per second. The function

$$s(t) = -16t^2 + 96t + 4$$

describes the ball's height above the ground, $s(t)$, in feet, $t$ seconds after it was hit.

**a.** What is the instantaneous velocity of the ball 2 seconds after it was hit? 4 seconds after it was hit?

**b.** The ball reaches its maximum height above the ground when the instantaneous velocity is zero. After how many seconds does the ball reach its maximum height? What is its maximum height?

**40.** A foul tip of a baseball is hit straight upward from a height of 4 feet with an initial velocity of 64 feet per second. The function

$$s(t) = -16t^2 + 64t + 4$$

describes the ball's height above the ground, $s(t)$, in feet, $t$ seconds after it was hit.

**a.** What is the instantaneous velocity of the ball 1 second after it was hit? 3 seconds after it was hit?

**b.** The ball reaches its maximum height above the ground when the instantaneous velocity is zero. After how many seconds does the ball reach its maximum height? What is its maximum height?

*The figure shows the graph of the percentage of Jewish Americans in the U.S. population, $f(x)$, as a function of time, $x$, where $x$ is a year from 1899 to 1999. Use the graph to solve Exercises 41–43.*

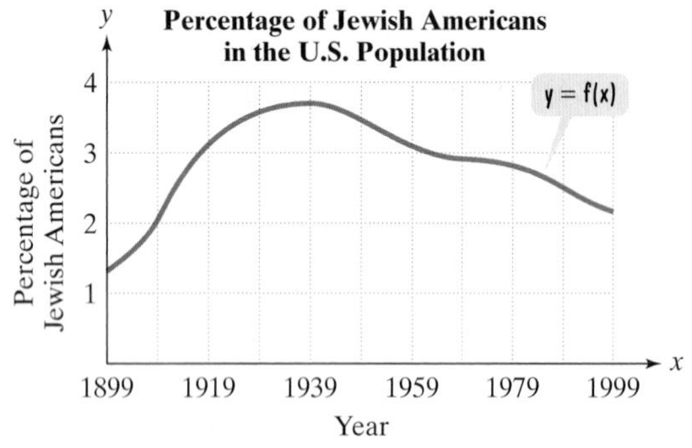


*Source*: American Jewish Yearbook

**41.** In which year did the percentage of Jewish Americans in the U.S. population reach a maximum? What is a reasonable estimate of the percentage for that year? What is a reasonable estimate of the slope of the tangent line to the graph for that year?

**42.** Find $\lim_{x \to 1899^+} f(x)$ to the nearest tenth of a percent.

**43.** Find $\lim_{x \to 1999^-} f(x)$ to the nearest tenth of a percent.

## Writing in Mathematics

**44.** Explain how the tangent line to the graph of a function at point $P$ is related to the secant lines between points $P$ and $Q$ on the function's graph.

**45.** Explain what we mean by the slope of the graph of a function at a point.

**46.** Explain how to find the slope of $f(x) = x^2$ at $(2, 4)$.

**47.** Explain how to write an equation of the tangent line to the graph of $f(x) = x^2$ at $(2, 4)$.

**48.** If you are given $y = f(x)$, the equation of function $f$, use words to explain how to find $f'(x)$.

**49.** Explain how to use the derivative to compute the slopes of various tangent lines to the graph of a function.

**50.** Explain how the instantaneous rate of change of a function at a point is related to its average rates of change.

**51.** If a function expresses an object's distance in terms of time, how do you find the instantaneous velocity of the object at any time during its motion?

**52.** Use the concept of an interval of time to describe how calculus views a particular instant of time.

**53.** You are about to take a great picture of fog rolling into San Francisco from the middle of the Golden Gate Bridge, 400 feet above the water. Whoops! You accidently lean too far over the safety rail and drop your camera. Your friend quips, "Well at least you know calculus; you can figure out the velocity with which the camera is going to hit the water." If the camera's height, $s(t)$, in feet, over the water after $t$ seconds is $s(t) = 400 - 16t^2$, describe how to determine the camera's velocity at the instant of its demise.

**54.** A calculus professor introduced the derivative by saying that it could be summed up in one word: *slope*. Explain what this means.

**55.** For an unusual introduction to calculus by a poetic, quirky, and funny writer who loves the subject, read *A Tour of the Calculus* by David Berlinski (Vintage Books, 1995). Write a report describing two new things that you learned from the book about algebra, trigonometry, limits, or derivatives.

## Technology Exercises

**56.** Use the DRAW TANGENT feature of a graphing utility to graph the functions and tangent lines for any five exercises from Exercises 1–14. Use the equation that is displayed on the screen to verify the slope-intercept equation of the tangent line that you found in each exercise.

**57.** Without using the DRAW TANGENT feature of a graphing utility, graph the function and the tangent line whose equation you found for any five exercises from Exercises 1–14. Does the line appear to be tangent to the graph of $f$ at the point on $f$ that is given in the exercise?

**58.** Use the feature on a graphing utility that gives the derivative of a function evaluated at any number to verify part (b) for any five of your answers in Exercises 15–28.

*In Exercises 59–62, find, or approximate to two decimal places, the derivative of each function at the given number using a graphing utility.*

**59.** $f(x) = x^4 - x^3 + x^2 - x + 1$ at 1

**60.** $f(x) = \dfrac{x}{x - 3}$ at 6

**61.** $f(x) = x^2 \cos x$ at $\dfrac{\pi}{4}$

**62.** $f(x) = e^x \sin x$ at 2

**63.** Use the data shown in the graph for Exercises 41–43 to solve this exercise. Let $x$ represent the number of years since 1899 and let $f(x)$ represent the percentage of Jewish Americans in the U.S. population in year $x$.

**a.** Use the graph to estimate $f(x)$, to the nearest tenth of a percent, for $x = 0, 10, 20, 30, \ldots, 100$.

**b.** Use a graphing utility to find the quadratic function of best fit for the data in part (a).

**c.** Use the function found in part (b) to determine the change in the percentage of Jewish Americans in the U.S. population in 1919, 1939, and 1999.

## Critical Thinking Exercises

**64.** A ball is thrown straight up from a rooftop 96 feet high with an initial velocity of 80 feet per second. The function

$$s(t) = -16t^2 + 80t + 96$$

describes the ball's height above the ground, $s(t)$, in feet, $t$ seconds after it was thrown. The ball misses the rooftop on its way down and eventually strikes the ground. What is its instantaneous velocity as it passes the rooftop on the way down?

**65.** Show that the rate of change of the area of a circle with respect to its radius is equal to the circumference of the circle.

**66.** Show that the $x$-coordinate of the vertex of the parabola whose equation is $y = ax^2 + bx + c$ occurs when the derivative of the function is zero.

**67.** Use the graph of $f$ in the figure shown to estimate $f'(0)$, $f'(1)$, $f'(2)$, $f'(3)$, $f'(4)$, and $f'(5)$. Round each estimate to the nearest tenth. Then sketch the graph of $f'$.

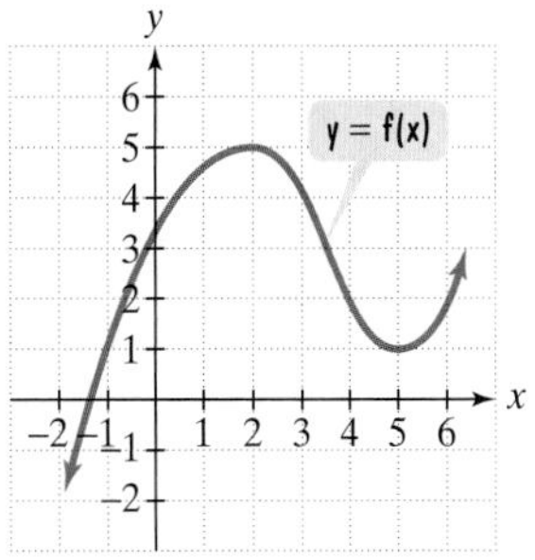


# CHAPTER SUMMARY, REVIEW, AND TEST

## Summary

### 12.1 Finding Limits Using Tables and Graphs

a. Limit Notation and Its Description

$\lim_{x \to a} f(x) = L$ is read "the limit of $f(x)$ as $x$ approaches $a$ equals the number $L$." This means that as $x$ gets closer to $a$, but remains unequal to $a$, the corresponding values of $f(x)$ get closer to $L$.

b. Limits can be found using tables (see page 987 and graphs (see Figure 12.3 on page 989).

### 12.2 Finding Limits Using Properties of Limits

a. Properties of limits are given in the box on page 1003.

b. When taking the limit of a fractional expression in which the limit of the denominator is zero, the quotient property for limits cannot be used. Rewriting the expression using factoring or rationalizing the numerator or denominator may be helpful before the limit is found.

### 12.3 One-Sided Limits; Continuous Functions

a. Left-Hand Limit

$\lim_{x \to a^-} f(x) = L$ is read "the limit of $f(x)$ as $x$ approaches $a$ from the left equals $L$." This means that as $x$ gets closer to $a$, but remains less than $a$, the corresponding values of $f(x)$ get closer to $L$.

b. Right-Hand Limit

$\lim_{x \to a^+} f(x) = L$ is read "the limit of $f(x)$ as $x$ approaches $a$ from the right equals $L$." This means that as $x$ gets closer to $a$, but remains greater than $a$, the corresponding values of $f(x)$ get closer to $L$.

c. If $\lim_{x \to a^-} f(x) \neq \lim_{x \to a^+} f(x)$, then $\lim_{x \to a} f(x)$ does not exist.

d. A function $f$ is continuous at $a$ when $f$ is defined at $a$, $\lim_{x \to a} f(x)$ exists, and $\lim_{x \to a} f(x) = f(a)$. If $f$ is not continuous at $a$, we say that $f$ is discontinuous at $a$.

## 12.4 Introduction to Derivatives

a. The slope of the tangent line to the graph of a function $y = f(x)$ at $(a, f(a))$ is given by

$$m_{\tan} = \lim_{h\to 0}\frac{f(a+h)-f(a)}{h}$$

provided that this limit exists. The limit also describes the slope of the graph of $f$ at $(a, f(a))$.

b. The Derivative of a Function

The derivative of $f$ at $x$ is given by

$$f'(x) = \lim_{h\to 0}\frac{f(x+h)-f(x)}{h}$$

provided that this limit exists. The derivative gives the slope of $f$ for any value of $x$.

c. The derivative of $f$ at $a$, $f'(a) = \lim_{h\to 0}\frac{f(a+h)-f(a)}{h}$, gives the instantaneous rate of change of $f$ with respect to $x$ at $a$. Expressions for average and instantaneous rates of change are given in the box on page 1026.

d. If a function expresses an object's position, $s(t)$, in terms of time, $t$, the instantaneous velocity of the object at time $t = a$ is

$$s'(a) = \lim_{h\to 0}\frac{s(a+h)-s(a)}{h}.$$

# Review Exercises

## 12.1

*In Exercises 1–3, construct a table and find the indicated limit.*

**1.** $\lim_{x\to 1}\frac{x^3-1}{x-1}$

**2.** $\lim_{x\to 0}\frac{\sqrt{x+1}-1}{x}$

**3.** $\lim_{x\to 0}\frac{\sin 2x}{x}$

*In Exercises 4–8, use the graph of f to find:*

**4.** $\lim_{x\to -4} f(x)$

**5.** $\lim_{x\to -1} f(x)$

**6.** $\lim_{x\to 3} f(x)$

**7.** $f(-4)$

**8.** $f(3)$

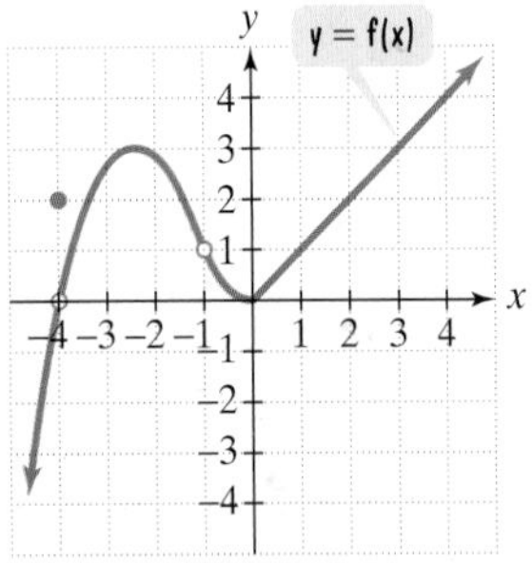


*In Exercises 9–11, graph each function. Then use your graph to find the indicated limit.*

**9.** $f(x) = \frac{x^2-9}{x-3}$, $\lim_{x\to 3} f(x)$

**10.** $f(x) = \sin x$, $\lim_{x\to \frac{3\pi}{2}} f(x)$

**11.** $f(x) = \begin{cases} 1 - x & \text{if } x < 0 \\ \cos x & \text{if } x \ge 0 \end{cases}$, $\lim_{x\to 0} f(x)$

## 12.2

*In Exercises 12–22, find the limit.*

**12.** $\lim_{x\to 4}(2x^2 - 5x + 3)$

**13.** $\lim_{x\to -1}(-2x^3 - x + 5)$

**14.** $\lim_{x\to -3}(x^2 + 1)^3$

**15.** $\lim_{x\to 4}\sqrt{x^2+9}$

**16.** $\lim_{x\to 5}\frac{11x-3}{x^2+1}$

**17.** $\lim_{x\to -4}\frac{x^2-16}{x+4}$

**18.** $\lim_{x\to 7}\frac{5x-35}{x-7}$

**19.** $\lim_{x\to 0}\frac{\sqrt{x+100}-10}{x}$

**20.** $\lim_{x\to -1}\frac{x^2-1}{x^2+x}$

**21.** $\lim_{x\to 100}\frac{\sqrt{x}-10}{x-100}$

**22.** $\lim_{x\to 0}\frac{\frac{1}{x+5}-\frac{1}{5}}{x}$

## 12.3

*In Exercises 23–25, a piecewise function is given. Use the function to find the indicated limits, or state that a limit does not exist.*

**23.** $f(x) = \begin{cases} x^2 + 1 & \text{if } x < 2 \\ 3x + 1 & \text{if } x \ge 2 \end{cases}$

**a.** $\lim_{x\to 2^-} f(x)$ **b.** $\lim_{x\to 2^+} f(x)$ **c.** $\lim_{x\to 2} f(x)$

**24.** $f(x) = \begin{cases} \sqrt[3]{x^2+7} & \text{if } x < 1 \\ 4x & \text{if } x \ge 1 \end{cases}$

**a.** $\lim_{x\to 1^-} f(x)$ **b.** $\lim_{x\to 1^+} f(x)$ **c.** $\lim_{x\to 1} f(x)$

**25.** $f(x) = \begin{cases} \frac{x^2-25}{x+5} & \text{if } x \ne -5 \\ 13 & \text{if } x = -5 \end{cases}$

**a.** $\lim_{x\to -5^-} f(x)$ **b.** $\lim_{x\to -5^+} f(x)$ **c.** $\lim_{x\to -5} f(x)$

*In Exercises 26–40, use the graph of function f to find the indicated limit or function value, or state that the limit or function value does not exist.*

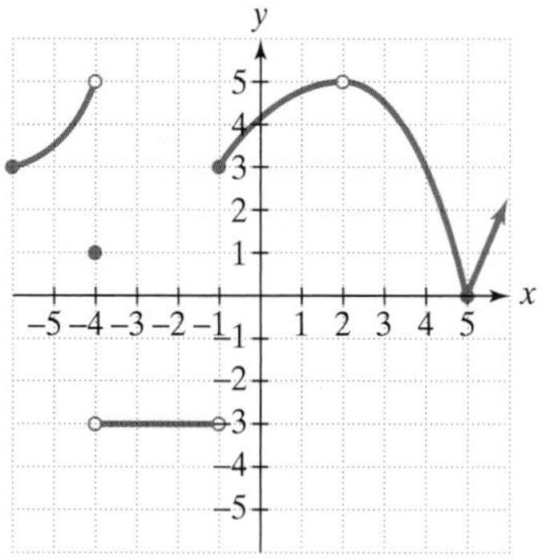


**26.** $\lim_{x \to -6^+} f(x)$

**27.** $\lim_{x \to -4^-} f(x)$

**28.** $\lim_{x \to -4^+} f(x)$

**29.** $\lim_{x \to -4} f(x)$

**30.** $f(-4)$

**31.** $\lim_{x \to -1^+} f(x)$

**32.** $\lim_{x \to -1^-} f(x)$

**33.** $\lim_{x \to -1} f(x)$

**34.** $f(-1)$

**35.** $f(2)$

**36.** $\lim_{x \to 2^-} f(x)$

**37.** $\lim_{x \to 2^+} f(x)$

**38.** $\lim_{x \to 2} f(x)$

**39.** $\lim_{x \to 5} f(x)$

**40.** $f(5)$

*In Exercises 41–45, determine whether f is continuous at a.*

**41.** $f(x) = 3x^2 - 2x + 1$

$a = 4$

**42.** $f(x) = \dfrac{x^2 - 9}{x + 3}$

$a = -3$

**43.** $f(x) = \begin{cases} \dfrac{x^2 + 5x}{x^2 - 5x} & \text{if } x \neq 0 \\ -2 & \text{if } x = 0 \end{cases}$

$a = 0$

**44.** $f(x) = \begin{cases} \dfrac{x^2 + x}{x^2 - 3x - 4} & \text{if } x \neq -1 \\ \frac{1}{5} & \text{if } x = -1 \end{cases}$

$a = -1$

**45.** $f(x) = \begin{cases} 3x & \text{if } x < 2 \\ 5 & \text{if } x = 2 \\ x + 4 & \text{if } x > 2 \end{cases}$

$a = 2$

*In Exercises 46–51, determine for what numbers, if any, the given function is discontinuous.*

**46.** $f(x) = x^3 + 5x^2 - 1$

**47.** $f(x) = \dfrac{x - 1}{(x - 1)(x + 3)}$

**48.** $f(x) = \begin{cases} -1 & \text{if } x < 0 \\ 1 & \text{if } x \geq 0 \end{cases}$

**49.** $f(x) = \begin{cases} 4x & \text{if } x < 5 \\ x^2 - 5 & \text{if } x \geq 5 \end{cases}$

**50.** $f(x) = \begin{cases} \dfrac{x^2 - 4}{x + 2} & \text{if } x \neq -2 \\ 4 & \text{if } x = -2 \end{cases}$

**51.** $f(x) = \begin{cases} \dfrac{x^2 - 121}{x - 11} & \text{if } x \neq 11 \\ 20 & \text{if } x = 11 \end{cases}$

## 12.4

*In Exercises 52–53:*

**a.** *Find the slope of the tangent line to the graph of f at the given point.*

**b.** *Find the slope-intercept equation of the tangent line to the graph of f at the given point.*

**52.** $f(x) = 2x^2 + 5x$ at $(1, 7)$

**53.** $f(x) = x^2 - 7x - 4$ at $(-1, 4)$

*In Exercises 54–57:*

**a.** *Find $f'(x)$.*

**b.** *Find the slope of the tangent line to the graph of f at each of the two values of x given to the right of the function.*

**54.** $f(x) = 3x^2 + 12x - 1; x = -2, x = 1$

**55.** $f(x) = 2x^3 - x; x = -1, x = 1$

**56.** $f(x) = \dfrac{1}{x}; x = -2, x = 2$

**57.** $f(x) = \sqrt{x}; x = 36, x = 81$

**58.** The function $f(x) = 5x^2$ describes the volume of a rectangular box, $f(x)$, in cubic inches, whose square base has sides that each measure $x$ inches and whose height is 5 inches. If $x$ is changing:

**a.** Find the average rate of change of the volume with respect to $x$ as $x$ changes from 2 inches to 2.1 inches and from 2 inches to 2.01 inches.

**b.** Find the instantaneous rate of change of the volume with respect to $x$ at the moment when $x = 2$ inches.

**59.** The function $f(x) = \frac{4}{3}\pi x^3$ describes the volume, $f(x)$, of a sphere of radius $x$ inches. If the radius is changing, find the instantaneous rate of change of the volume with respect to the radius when the radius is 5 inches. Express the answer in terms of $\pi$.

**60.** A baseball is thrown straight upward from a height of 5 feet with an initial velocity of 80 feet per second. The function

$$s(t) = -16t^2 + 80t + 5$$

describes the ball's height above the ground, $s(t)$, in feet, $t$ seconds after it was thrown.

**a.** What is the instantaneous velocity of the ball 2 seconds after it was thrown? 4 seconds after it was thrown?

**b.** The ball reaches its maximum height above the ground when the instantaneous velocity is zero. After how many seconds does the ball reach its maximum height? What is the maximum height?

## Chapter 12 Test

**1.** Construct a table and find $\lim_{x \to 9} \frac{9 - x}{3 - \sqrt{x}}$.

*In Exercises 2–7, use the graph of function f to find the indicated limit or function value, or state that the limit or function value does not exist.*

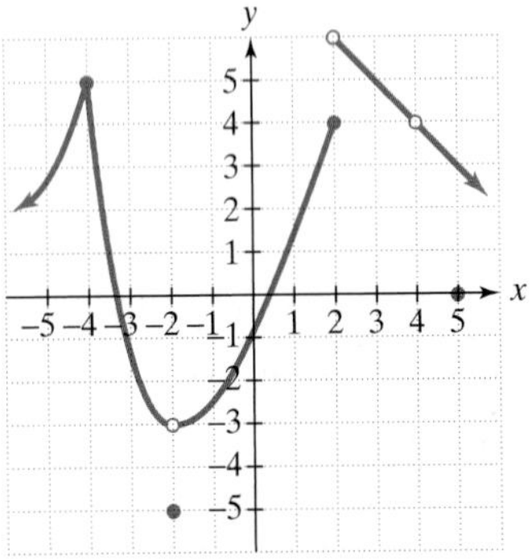


**2.** $\lim_{x \to -2} f(x)$

**3.** $f(-2)$

**4.** $\lim_{x \to 2^-} f(x)$

**5.** $\lim_{x \to 2^+} f(x)$

**6.** $\lim_{x \to 2} f(x)$

**7.** $\lim_{x \to 4} f(x)$

*In Exercises 8–10, find the limit.*

**8.** $\lim_{x \to -2} (x^2 + x + 1)^4$

**9.** $\lim_{x \to -1} \frac{x^2 - x - 2}{x + 1}$

**10.** $\lim_{x \to 9} \frac{\sqrt{x} - 3}{x - 9}$

*In Exercises 11–12, determine whether f is continuous at a.*

**11.** $f(x) = \begin{cases} \dfrac{x^2 - 1}{x + 1} & \text{if } x \neq -1 \\ 6 & \text{if } x = -1 \end{cases}$

$a = -1$

**12.** $f(x) = \begin{cases} 2 - x & \text{if } x \leq 2 \\ x^2 - 2x & \text{if } x > 2 \end{cases}$

$a = 2$

*In Exercises 13–14, find f′(x).*

**13.** $f(x) = x^2 - 5x + 1$

**14.** $f(x) = \frac{10}{x}$

**15.** Find the slope-intercept equation of the tangent line to the graph of $f(x) = x^2$ at $(-3, 9)$.

**16.** A ball is thrown straight upward. The function

$$s(t) = -16t^2 + 72t$$

describes the ball's height above the ground, $s(t)$, in feet, $t$ seconds after it was thrown. What is the instantaneous velocity of the ball 3 seconds after it was thrown?

## Cumulative Review Exercises (Chapters 1–12)

*Solve each equation or inequality in Exercises 1–5.*

**1.** $\frac{1}{x + 2} > \frac{3}{x + 1}$

**2.** $2x^3 + 11x^2 - 7x - 6 = 0$

**3.** $|2x + 4| > 3$

**4.** $\cos^2 x + \sin x + 1 = 0, 0 \leq x < 2\pi$

**5.** $\log_4(x^2 - 9) - \log_4(x + 3) = 3$

*In Exercises 6–15, graph each equation, function, or system in the rectangular coordinate system.*

**6.** $f(x) = x^3 + x^2 - 12x$

**7.** $f(x) = \frac{2x^2 - 5x + 2}{x^2 - 4}$

**8.** $f(x) = \begin{cases} -x + 1 & \text{if } -1 \leq x < 1 \\ 2 & \text{if } x = 1 \\ x^2 & \text{if } x > 1 \end{cases}$

**9.** $y = 2\sin\left(2x + \frac{\pi}{2}\right)$ (Graph one period.)

**10.** $y = \frac{1}{2}\sec 2\pi x, \quad 0 \leq x \leq 2$

**11.** $x - 2y \leq 4$
$x \geq 2$

**12.** $x^2 - 4y^2 - 4x - 24y - 48 = 0$

**13.** $f(x) = \sqrt{x}, g(x) = \sqrt{x - 2} + 1$ (Graph $f$ and $g$ in the same rectangular coordinate system.)

**14.** $x = 3\sin t, y = 4\cos t + 2; 0 \leq t \leq 2\pi$

**15.** $2x^2 + 5xy + 2y^2 - \frac{9}{2} = 0$

**16.** Find $f'(x)$ if $f(x) = -2x^2 + 7x - 1$.

**17.** Find $f^{-1}(x)$ if $f(x) = 7x - 1$.

**18.** Find the limit: $\lim_{x \to -3} \frac{x^2 + x - 6}{x^2 + 2x - 3}$.

**19.** Expand and simplify: $(x^2 - 3y)^4$.

**20.** Write the slope-intercept form of the equation of the line passing through the point $(2, -3)$ and parallel to the line whose equation is $2x + y - 6 = 0$.

**21.** Find the dot product $\mathbf{v} \cdot \mathbf{w}$ and the angle between $\mathbf{v}$ and $\mathbf{w}$:

$$\mathbf{v} = -2\mathbf{i} + \mathbf{j}, \quad \mathbf{w} = 4\mathbf{i} - 3\mathbf{j}$$

**22.** Find the partial fraction decomposition for

$$\frac{1}{x(x^2 + x + 1)}.$$

*Verify each identity in Exercises 23–24.*

**23.** $\tan\theta + \cot\theta = \sec\theta\csc\theta$

**24.** $\tan(\theta + \pi) = \tan\theta$

**25.** If $A = \begin{bmatrix} 2 & 1 & 3 \\ 1 & -1 & 0 \end{bmatrix}$ and $B = \begin{bmatrix} 1 & 0 \\ 3 & 2 \\ 2 & 1 \end{bmatrix}$, find $BA$.

**26.** Graph the polar equation: $r = 4\sin\theta$.

**27.** Express $h(x) = (x^2 - 3x + 7)^9$ as a composition of two functions $f$ and $g$ such that $h(x) = (f \circ g)(x)$.

**28.** Solve using matrices:

$$\begin{aligned} 2x - y - 2z &= -1 \\ x - 2y - z &= 1 \\ x + y + z &= 4. \end{aligned}$$

**29.** Use the formula for the sum of the first $n$ terms of a geometric sequence to find $\sum_{i=1}^{6} 4(-2)^i$.

**30.** Use DeMoivre's Theorem to find

$$[\sqrt{2}(\cos 15^\circ + i\sin 15^\circ)]^4.$$

Write the answer in rectangular form.

**31.** A bank loaned out \$120,000, part of it at 8% per year and the rest at 18% per year. If the interest received totaled \$10,000, how much was loaned at each rate?

**32.** A machine produces open boxes using square sheets of metal. The machine cuts equal-sized squares measuring 9 centimeters on a side from each corner. Then the machine shapes the metal into an open box by turning up the sides. If each box must have a volume of 225 cubic centimeters, what should be the dimensions of the piece of sheet metal?

**33.** Find two numbers whose sum is 100 and whose product is a maximum.

**34.** Use Newton's Law of Cooling, $T = C + (T_0 - C)e^{kt}$, to solve this exercise. You remove a pie that has a temperature of 375°F from the oven. You leave the pie in a room whose temperature is 72°F. After 60 minutes, the temperature of the pie is 75°F.

**a.** Write a model for the temperature of the pie, $T$, after $t$ minutes.

**b.** When will the temperature of the pie be 250°F?

**35.** The function $f(t) = -68.8t^3 + 4988t^2 - 12{,}436t + 14{,}611$ models the cumulative number of reported AIDS cases in the United States, $f(t)$, $t$ years after 1982. Find the cumulative number of AIDS cases reported in the United States in 2000.

**36.** Two ships leave a harbor at the same time. One ship travels at a bearing of N42°E for 23 miles. The other ship travels at a bearing of N38°W for 72 miles. After both ships are anchored, how far apart are they? Round to the nearest tenth of a mile.

**37.** At a fixed temperature, the volume of a given mass of gas varies inversely as the pressure applied to the gas. A certain mass of gas has a volume of 40 cubic inches when the pressure is 22 pounds. What is the volume of the gas when the pressure is 30 pounds?

**38.** A ball is thrown straight upward. The function

$$s(t) = -16t^2 + 40t$$

describes the ball's height above the ground, $s(t)$, in feet, $t$ seconds after it was thrown. What is the instantaneous velocity of the ball 2 seconds after it was thrown?

**39.** After an 8% decrease in the price, a computer sells for \$2162. Find the computer's original price.

**40.** The function $f(x) = -2.32x^2 + 76.58x - 559.87$ models the percentage of U.S. students, $f(x)$, who are $x$ years old who say their school is not drug free, where $12 \le x \le 17$. At what age do 70% of U.S. students say that their school is not drug free? Round to the nearest tenth of a year.

# Appendix
# Where Did That Come From? Selected Proofs

## SECTION 4.3 Properties of Logarithms

### The Product Rule

Let $b$, $M$, and $N$ be positive real numbers with $b \neq 1$.

$$\log_b(MN) = \log_b M + \log_b N$$

**Proof**

We begin by letting $\log_b M = R$ and $\log_b N = S$.

Now we write each logarithm in exponential form.

$$\log_b M = R \quad \text{means} \quad b^R = M.$$

$$\log_b N = S \quad \text{means} \quad b^S = N.$$

By substituting and using a property of exponents, we see that

$$MN = b^R b^S = b^{R+S}.$$

Now we change $MN = b^{R+S}$ to logarithmic form.

$$MN = b^{R+S} \quad \text{means} \quad \log_b(MN) = R + S.$$

Finally, substituting $\log_b M$ for $R$ and $\log_b N$ for $S$ gives us

$$\log_b(MN) = \log_b M + \log_b N,$$

the property that we wanted to prove.

The quotient and power rules for logarithms are proved using similar procedures.

### The Change-of-Base Property

For any logarithmic bases $a$ and $b$, and any positive number $M$,

$$\log_b M = \frac{\log_a M}{\log_a b}.$$

**Proof**

To prove the change-of-base property, we let $x$ equal the logarithm on the left side:

$$\log_b M = x.$$

Now we rewrite this logarithm in exponential form.

$$\log_b M = x \quad \text{means} \quad b^x = M.$$

Because $b^x$ and $M$ are equal, the logarithms with base $a$ for each of these expressions must be equal. This means that

$$\log_a b^x = \log_a M$$

$$x \log_a b = \log_a M \quad \text{Apply the power rule for logarithms on the left side.}$$

$$x = \frac{\log_a M}{\log_a b} \quad \text{Solve for } x \text{ by dividing both sides by } \log_a b.$$

In our first step we let $x$ equal $\log_b M$. Replacing $x$ on the left side by $\log_b M$ gives us

$$\log_b M = \frac{\log_a M}{\log_a b},$$

which is the change-of-base property.

## SECTION 7.2 The Law of Cosines

### Heron's Formula for the Area of a Triangle

The area of a triangle with sides $a$, $b$, and $c$ is

$$\text{Area} = \sqrt{s(s-a)(s-b)(s-c)},$$

where $s$ is one-half the perimeter: $s = \frac{1}{2}(a+b+c)$.

**Proof**

The proof of Heron's formula begins with a half-angle formula and the Law of Cosines.

$$\cos\frac{C}{2} = \sqrt{\frac{1+\cos C}{2}} = \sqrt{\frac{1+\frac{a^2+b^2-c^2}{2ab}}{2}}$$

This is the Law of Cosines $c^2 = a^2 + b^2 - 2ab\cos C$ solved for $\cos C$.

$$= \sqrt{\frac{a^2+2ab+b^2-c^2}{4ab}} = \sqrt{\frac{(a+b)^2-c^2}{4ab}} = \sqrt{\frac{(a+b+c)(a+b-c)}{4ab}}$$

Multiply the numerator and denominator of the radicand by $2ab$.

Factor $a^2 + 2ab + b^2$.

Factor the numerator as the differences of two squares.

We now introduce the expression for one-half the perimeter: $s = \frac{1}{2}(a+b+c)$. We replace $a+b+c$ in the numerator by $2s$. We also find an expression for $a+b-c$ as follows:

$$a+b-c = a+b+c-2c = 2s-2c = 2(s-c).$$

Thus,

$$\cos\frac{C}{2} = \sqrt{\frac{(a+b+c)(a+b-c)}{4ab}} = \sqrt{\frac{2s\cdot 2(s-c)}{4ab}} = \sqrt{\frac{s(s-c)}{ab}}.$$

In a similar manner, we obtain

$$\sin\frac{C}{2} = \sqrt{\frac{1-\cos C}{2}} = \sqrt{\frac{(s-a)(s-b)}{ab}}.$$

From our work in Section 7.1, we know that the area of a triangle is one-half the product of the length of two sides times the sum of their included angle.

$$\text{Area} = \frac{1}{2}ab\sin C$$

$$= \frac{1}{2}ab \cdot 2\sin\frac{C}{2}\cos\frac{C}{2}$$ $\sin C = \sin 2\frac{C}{2} = 2\sin\frac{C}{2}\cos\frac{C}{2}$

$$= ab\sqrt{\frac{(s-a)(s-b)}{ab}}\sqrt{\frac{s(s-c)}{ab}}$$ Use the expressions for $\sin\frac{C}{2}$ and $\cos\frac{C}{2}$ on page A2.

$$= ab\frac{\sqrt{s(s-a)(s-b)(s-c)}}{\sqrt{a^2b^2}}$$ Multiply the radicands.

$$= \sqrt{s(s-a)(s-b)(s-c)}$$ Simplify: $\frac{ab}{\sqrt{a^2b^2}} = \frac{ab}{ab} = 1.$

## SECTION 7.5 Complex Numbers in Polar Form; DeMoivre's Theorem

### The Quotient of Two Complex Numbers in Polar Form

Let $z_1 = r_1(\cos\theta_1 + i\sin\theta_1)$ and $z_2 = r_2(\cos\theta_2 + i\sin\theta_2)$ be two complex numbers in polar form. Their quotient, $\frac{z_1}{z_2}$, is

$$\frac{z_1}{z_2} = \frac{r_1}{r_2}[\cos(\theta_1 - \theta_2) + i\sin(\theta_1 - \theta_2)].$$

**Proof**

We begin by multiplying the numerator and denominator of the quotient, $\frac{z_1}{z_2}$, by the conjugate of the denominator. Then we simplify the quotient using the difference formulas for sine and cosine.

$$\frac{z_1}{z_2} = \frac{r_1(\cos\theta_1 + i\sin\theta_1)}{r_2(\cos\theta_2 + i\sin\theta_2)}$$ This is the given quotient.

$$= \frac{r_1(\cos\theta_1 + i\sin\theta_1)(\cos\theta_2 - i\sin\theta_2)}{r_2(\cos\theta_2 + i\sin\theta_2)(\cos\theta_2 - i\sin\theta_2)}$$ Multiply the numerator and denominator by the conjugate of the denominator. Recall that the conjugate of $a + bi$ is $a - bi$.

$$= \frac{r_1(\cos\theta_1 + i\sin\theta_1)(\cos\theta_2 - i\sin\theta_2)}{r_2(\cos^2\theta_2 + \sin^2\theta_2)}$$ Multiply the conjugates in the denominator.

$$= \frac{r_1(\cos\theta_1 + i\sin\theta_1)(\cos\theta_2 - i\sin\theta_2)}{r_2}$$ Use a Pythagorean identity: $\cos^2\theta_2 + \sin^2\theta_2 = 1$.

$$= \frac{r_1}{r_2}(\cos\theta_1\cos\theta_2 - i\cos\theta_1\sin\theta_2 + i\sin\theta_1\cos\theta_2 - i^2\sin\theta_1\sin\theta_2)$$ Use the FOIL method.

$$= \frac{r_1}{r_2}[\cos\theta_1\cos\theta_2 + i(\sin\theta_1\cos\theta_2 - \cos\theta_1\sin\theta_2) - i^2\sin\theta_1\sin\theta_2]$$ Factor $i$ from the second and third terms.

$$= \frac{r_1}{r_2}\left[\cos\theta_1\cos\theta_2 + i(\sin\theta_1\cos\theta_2 - \cos\theta_1\sin\theta_2) - (-1)\sin\theta_1\sin\theta_2\right] \quad i^2 = -1.$$

$$= \frac{r_1}{r_2}\left[\cos\theta_1\cos\theta_2 + \sin\theta_1\sin\theta_2 + i(\sin\theta_1\cos\theta_2 - \cos\theta_1\sin\theta_2)\right]$$ Rearrange terms.

This is $\cos(\theta_1 - \theta_2)$.

This is $\sin(\theta_1 - \theta_2)$.

$$= \frac{r_1}{r_2}\left[\cos(\theta_1 - \theta_2) + i\sin(\theta_1 - \theta_2)\right]$$

## SECTION 7.7 The Dot Product

**Properties of the Dot Product**

If **u**, **v**, and **w** are vectors, and $c$ is a scalar, then:

1. $\mathbf{u}\cdot\mathbf{v} = \mathbf{v}\cdot\mathbf{u}$
2. $\mathbf{u}\cdot(\mathbf{v}+\mathbf{w}) = \mathbf{u}\cdot\mathbf{v} + \mathbf{u}\cdot\mathbf{w}$
3. $\mathbf{0}\cdot\mathbf{v} = 0$
4. $\mathbf{v}\cdot\mathbf{v} = \|\mathbf{v}\|^2$
5. $(c\mathbf{u})\cdot\mathbf{v} = c(\mathbf{u}\cdot\mathbf{v}) = \mathbf{u}\cdot(c\mathbf{v})$

**Proof** To prove the second property, let

$$\mathbf{u} = u_1\mathbf{i} + u_2\mathbf{j},\quad \mathbf{v} = v_1\mathbf{i} + v_2\mathbf{j}, \text{ and } \mathbf{w} = w_1\mathbf{i} + w_2\mathbf{j}.$$

Then,

$$\mathbf{u}\cdot(\mathbf{v}+\mathbf{w}) = (u_1\mathbf{i} + u_2\mathbf{j})\cdot\left[(v_1\mathbf{i} + v_2\mathbf{j}) + (w_1\mathbf{i} + w_2\mathbf{j})\right]$$ These are the given vectors.

$$= (u_1\mathbf{i} + u_2\mathbf{j})\cdot\left[(v_1 + w_1)\mathbf{i} + (v_2 + w_2)\mathbf{j}\right]$$ Add horizontal components and add vertical components.

$$= u_1(v_1 + w_1) + u_2(v_2 + w_2)$$ Multiply horizontal components and multiply vertical components.

$$= u_1v_1 + u_1w_1 + u_2v_2 + u_2w_2$$ Use the distributive property.

$$= u_1v_1 + u_2v_2 + u_1w_1 + u_2w_2$$ Rearrange terms.

This is the dot product of **u** and **v**.

This is the dot product of **u** and **w**.

$$= \mathbf{u}\cdot\mathbf{v} + \mathbf{u}\cdot\mathbf{w}.$$

To prove the third property, let

$$\mathbf{0} = 0\mathbf{i} + 0\mathbf{j} \quad\text{and}\quad \mathbf{v} = v_1\mathbf{i} + v_2\mathbf{j}.$$

Then

$$\mathbf{0}\cdot\mathbf{v} = (0\mathbf{i} + 0\mathbf{j})\cdot(v_1\mathbf{i} + v_2\mathbf{j})$$ These are the given vectors.

$$= 0\cdot v_1 + 0\cdot v_2$$ Multiply horizontal components and multiply vertical components.

$$= 0 + 0$$

$$= 0.$$

To prove the first part of the fifth property, let

$$\mathbf{u} = u_1\mathbf{i} + u_2\mathbf{j} \quad \text{and} \quad \mathbf{v} = v_1\mathbf{i} + v_2\mathbf{j}.$$

Then,

$$(c\mathbf{u}) \cdot \mathbf{v} = [c(u_1\mathbf{i} + u_2\mathbf{j})] \cdot (v_1\mathbf{i} + v_2\mathbf{j})$$ These are the given vectors.

$$= (cu_1\mathbf{i} + cu_2\mathbf{j}) \cdot (v_1\mathbf{i} + v_2\mathbf{j})$$ Multiply each component of $u_1\mathbf{i} + u_2\mathbf{j}$ by $c$.

$$= cu_1v_1 + cu_2v_2$$ Multiply horizontal components and multiply vertical components.

$$= c(u_1v_1 + u_2v_2)$$ Factor out $c$ from both terms.

This is the dot product of $\mathbf{u}$ and $\mathbf{v}$.

$$= c(\mathbf{u} \cdot \mathbf{v}).$$

# SECTION 10.2 The Hyperbola

## The Asymptotes of a Hyperbola Centered at the Origin

The hyperbola

$$\frac{x^2}{a^2} - \frac{y^2}{b^2} = 1$$

with a horizontal transverse axis has the two asymptotes

$$y = \frac{b}{a}x \quad \text{and} \quad y = -\frac{b}{a}x.$$

**Proof**

Begin by solving the hyperbola's equation for $y$.

$$\frac{x^2}{a^2} - \frac{y^2}{b^2} = 1$$ This is the standard form of the equation of a hyperbola.

$$\frac{y^2}{b^2} = \frac{x^2}{a^2} - 1$$ We isolate the term involving $y^2$ to solve for $y$.

$$y^2 = \frac{b^2x^2}{a^2} - b^2$$ Multiply both sides by $b^2$.

$$y^2 = \frac{b^2x^2}{a^2}\left(1 - \frac{a^2}{x^2}\right)$$ Factor out $\frac{b^2x^2}{a^2}$ on the right. Verify that this result is correct by multiplying using the distributive property and obtaining the previous step.

$$y = \pm\sqrt{\frac{b^2x^2}{a^2}\left(1 - \frac{a^2}{x^2}\right)}$$ Solve for $y$ using the square root method: If $u^2 = d$, then $u = \pm\sqrt{d}$.

$$y = \pm\frac{b}{a}x\sqrt{1 - \frac{a^2}{x^2}}$$ Simplify.

As $|x| \to \infty$, the value of $\frac{a^2}{x^2}$ approaches 0. Consequently, the value of $y$ can be approximated by

$$y = \pm\frac{b}{a}x.$$

This means that the lines whose equations are $y = \frac{b}{a}x$ and $y = -\frac{b}{a}x$ are asymptotes for the graph of the hyperbola.

# Answers to Selected Exercises

## CHAPTER P

### Section P.1

#### Check Point Exercises

**1. a.** $\sqrt{2} - 1$ **b.** $\pi - 3$ **c.** 1 **2.** 9 **3. a.** 14 **b.** 3 **4.** $38x - 19y$

#### Exercise Set P.1

**1. a.** $\sqrt{100}$ **b.** $0, \sqrt{100}$ **c.** $-9, 0, \sqrt{100}$ **d.** $-9, -\frac{4}{5}, 0, 0.25, 9.2, \sqrt{100}$ **e.** $\sqrt{3}$ **3. a.** $\sqrt{64}$ **b.** $0, \sqrt{64}$ **c.** $-11, 0, \sqrt{64}$ **d.** $-11, -\frac{5}{6}, 0, 0.75, \sqrt{64}$ **e.** $\sqrt{5}, \pi$ **5.** 0 **7.** Answers may vary. **9.** true **11.** true **13.** true **15.** 300 **17.** $12 - \pi$ **19.** $5 - \sqrt{2}$ **21.** $-1$ **23.** 15 **25.** 7 **27.** 15 **29.** 2.2 **31.** 27 **33.** $-19$ **35.** $-\frac{4}{5}$ **37.** $-\frac{5}{2}$ **39.** commutative property of addition **41.** associative property of addition **43.** commutative property of addition **45.** distributive property of multiplication over addition **47.** $15x + 16$ **49.** $27x - 10$ **51.** $29y - 29$ **53.** $14x$ **55.** $-2x + 3y + 6$ **57.** $x$ **59.** yes **61.** Answers may vary. **63.** 25,401; In 1997, the average yearly earnings in the United States was $25,401. **65. a.** $132 - 0.6a$ **b.** 120 **73.** (c) is true. **75.** $<$ **77.** $>$

### Section P.2

#### Check Point Exercises

**1.** $-256$ **2. a.** $16x^{12}y^{24}$ **b.** $-18x^3y^8$ **c.** $\frac{5y^6}{x^4}$ **d.** $\frac{y^8}{25x^2}$ **3. a.** 7,400,000,000 **b.** 0.000003017 **4. a.** $7.41 \times 10^9$ **b.** $9.2 \times 10^{-8}$ **5.** $5.2 \times 10^5$ mi **6.** 2534.4 cm/sec

#### Exercise Set P.2

**1.** 50 **3.** 64 **5.** $-64$ **7.** 1 **9.** $-1$ **11.** $\frac{1}{64}$ **13.** 32 **15.** 64 **17.** 16 **19.** $\frac{1}{9}$ **21.** $\frac{1}{16}$ **23.** $\frac{y}{x^2}$ **25.** $y^5$ **27.** $x^{10}$ **29.** $x^5$ **31.** $x^{21}$ **33.** $x^{-15}$ **35.** $x^7$ **37.** $x^{21}$ **39.** $64x^6$ **41.** $-\frac{64}{x^3}$ **43.** $9x^4y^{10}$ **45.** $6x^{11}$ **47.** $18x^9y^5$ **49.** $4x^{16}$ **51.** $-5a^{11}b$ **53.** $\frac{2}{b^7}$ **55.** $\frac{1}{16x^6}$ **57.** $\frac{3y^{14}}{4x^4}$ **59.** $\frac{y^2}{25x^6}$ **61.** 4700 **63.** 4,000,000 **65.** 0.000786 **67.** 0.00000318 **69.** $3.6 \times 10^3$ **71.** $2.2 \times 10^8$ **73.** $2.7 \times 10^{-2}$ **75.** $7.63 \times 10^{-4}$ **77.** 600,000 **79.** 0.123 **81.** 30,000 **83.** 0.021 **85.** $1.694 \times 10^{12}$ **87.** $6.0 \times 10^{10}$ **89.** $3.24 \times 10^{10}$ **91.** $6.7 \times 10^9$ **93.** $2.47 \times 10^4$ **103.** (b) is true. **105.** A = C + D

### Section P.3

#### Check Point Exercises

**1. a.** 3 **b.** $5|x|\sqrt{2}$ **2. a.** $\frac{5}{4}$ **b.** $5|x|\sqrt{3}$ **3. a.** $17\sqrt{13}$ **b.** $-19\sqrt{17x}$ **4. a.** $17\sqrt{3}$ **b.** $10\sqrt{2x}$ **5. a.** $\frac{5\sqrt{3}}{3}$ **b.** $\sqrt{3}$ **6.** $\frac{32 - 8\sqrt{5}}{11}$ **7. a.** $2\sqrt[3]{5}$ **b.** $2\sqrt[5]{2}$ **c.** $\frac{5}{3}$ **8.** $5\sqrt[3]{3}$ **9. a.** 9 **b.** 3 **c.** $\frac{1}{2}$ **10. a.** 8 **b.** $\frac{1}{4}$ **11. a.** $10x^4$ **b.** $4x^{5/2}$ **12.** $\sqrt{x}$

#### Exercise Set P.3

**1.** 6 **3.** not a real number **5.** 13 **7.** $5\sqrt{2}$ **9.** $3|x|\sqrt{5}$ **11.** $2|x|\sqrt{3}$ **13.** $|x|\sqrt{x}$ **15.** $2|x|\sqrt{3x}$ **17.** $\frac{1}{9}$ **19.** $\frac{7}{4}$ **21.** $4|x|$ **23.** $5|x|\sqrt{2x}$ **25.** $13\sqrt{3}$ **27.** $-2\sqrt{17x}$ **29.** $5\sqrt{2}$ **31.** $3\sqrt{2x}$ **33.** $34\sqrt{2}$ **35.** $\frac{\sqrt{7}}{7}$ **37.** $\frac{\sqrt{10}}{5}$

**39.** $\frac{13(3-\sqrt{11})}{-2}$ **41.** $7(\sqrt{5}+2)$ **43.** $3(\sqrt{5}-\sqrt{3})$ **45.** 5 **47.** $-2$ **49.** not a real number **51.** 3 **53.** $-3$ **55.** $2\sqrt[3]{4}$
**57.** $x\sqrt[3]{x}$ **59.** $3\sqrt[3]{2}$ **61.** $2x$ **63.** 6 **65.** 2 **67.** 25 **69.** $\frac{1}{16}$ **71.** $14x^{7/12}$ **73.** $4x^{1/4}$ **75.** $x^2$ **77.** $5x^2|y|^3$
**79.** $\sqrt{5}$ **81.** $x^2$ **83.** $|x|^{2/3}$ **85.** $20\sqrt{2}$ mph **87.** $\frac{\sqrt{5}+1}{2} \approx 1.62$ **89.** $\frac{7\sqrt{2\cdot2\cdot3}}{6} = \frac{7\sqrt{2^2\cdot3}}{6} = \frac{7\sqrt{2^2}\sqrt{3}}{6} = \frac{7\cdot2\sqrt{3}}{6} = \frac{7}{3}\sqrt{3}$
**91.** The duration of a storm whose diameter is 9 miles is 1.89 hours. **99.** during 1990 **101.** (d) is true.
**103.** Let □ = 25 and □ = 14. **105. a.** > **b.** >

## Section P.4

### Check Point Exercises

**1. a.** $-x^3+x^2-8x-20$ **b.** $20x^3-11x^2-2x-8$ **2.** $15x^3-31x^2+30x-8$ **3.** $28x^2-41x+15$
**4. a.** $21x^2-25xy+6y^2$ **b.** $x^4+10x^2y+25y^2$ **5. a.** $9x^2+12x-25y^2+4$ **b.** $4x^2+4xy+12x+y^2+6y+9$

### Exercise Set P.4

**1.** yes; $3x^2+2x-5$ **3.** no **5.** 2 **7.** 4 **9.** $11x^3+7x^2-12x-4$; 3 **11.** $12x^3+4x^2+12x-14$; 3 **13.** $6x^2-6x+2$; 2
**15.** $x^3+1$ **17.** $2x^3-9x^2+19x-15$ **19.** $x^2+10x+21$ **21.** $x^2-2x-15$ **23.** $6x^2+13x+5$ **25.** $10x^2-9x-9$
**27.** $15x^4-47x^2+28$ **29.** $x^2-9$ **31.** $9x^2-4$ **33.** $25-49x^2$ **35.** $16x^4-25x^2$ **37.** $x^2+4x+4$ **39.** $4x^2+12x+9$
**41.** $x^2-6x+9$ **43.** $16x^4-8x^2+1$ **45.** $4x^2-28x+49$ **47.** $x^3+3x^2+3x+1$ **49.** $8x^3+36x^2+54x+27$
**51.** $x^3-9x^2+27x-27$ **53.** $27x^3-108x^2+144x-64$ **55.** $7x^2+38xy+15y^2$ **57.** $2x^2+xy-21y^2$
**59.** $15x^2y^2+xy-2$ **61.** $49x^2+70xy+25y^2$ **63.** $x^4y^4-6x^2y^2+9$ **65.** $x^3-y^3$ **67.** $9x^2-25y^2$
**69.** $x^2+2xy+y^2-9$ **71.** $9x^2+42x-25y^2+49$ **73.** $25y^2-4x^2-12x-9$ **75.** $x^2+2xy+2x+y^2+2x+1$
**77.** $4x^2+4xy+4x+y^2+2y+1$ **79.** $(A+B)^2=A^2+2AB+B^2$ **81.** $(A+1)^2=A^2+2A+1$
**83.** 7.567; A person earning \$40,000 feels underpaid \$7567. **85.** 54; 72; 54; Performance increases as enthusiasm goes from 1 to 50, then performance decreases as enthusiasm goes from 50 to 100. **87.** $4t-2t^2+\frac{2}{3}t^3$ **89.** $6x+22$ **91.** $V=4x^3-36x^2+80x$
**101.** during 1992 and 1993 **103.** $V=x^3+7x^2-3x$ **105.** $6y^n-13$

## Section P.5

### Check Point Exercises

**1. a.** $2x^2(5x-2)$ **b.** $(x-7)(2x+3)$ **2.** $(x+5)(x^2-2)$ **3. a.** $(x+8)(x+5)$ **b.** $(x-7)(x+2)$ **4.** $(3x-1)(2x+7)$
**5. a.** $(x+9)(x-9)$ **b.** $(6x+5)(6x-5)$ **6.** $(9x^2+4)(3x+2)(3x-2)$ **7. a.** $(x+7)^2$ **b.** $(4x-7)^2$
**8. a.** $(x+1)(x^2-x+1)$ **b.** $(5x-2)(25x^2+10x+4)$ **9. a.** $2x(x-6)^2$ **b.** $(x-4)(x+3)(x-3)$ **10.** $\frac{2x-1}{\sqrt{x-1}}$

### Exercise Set P.5

**1.** $3x(x+2)$ **3.** $9x^2(x^2-2x+3)$ **5.** $(x-3)(x^2+12)$ **7.** $(x^2+5)(x-2)$ **9.** $(x-1)(x^2+2)$
**11.** $(3x-2)(x^2-2)$ **13.** $(x+2)(x+3)$ **15.** $(x-5)(x+3)$ **17.** $(x-5)(x-3)$ **19.** $(3x+2)(x-1)$
**21.** $(3x-28)(x+1)$ **23.** $(2x-1)(3x-4)$ **25.** $(2x+3)(2x+5)$ **27.** $(x+10)(x-10)$ **29.** $(3x+5y)(3x-5y)$
**31.** $(x^2+4)(x+2)(x-2)$ **33.** $(4x^2+9)(2x+3)(2x-3)$ **35.** $(x-7)^2$ **37.** $(2x+1)^2$ **39.** $(3x-1)^2$
**41.** $(x+3)(x^2-3x+9)$ **43.** $(2x-1)(4x^2+2x+1)$ **45.** $(4x+3)(16x^2-12x+9)$ **47.** $3x(x+1)(x-1)$
**49.** $4(x+2)(x-3)$ **51.** $2(x^2+9)(x+3)(x-3)$ **53.** $(x-3)(x+3)(x+2)$ **55.** $2(x-8)(x+7)$
**57.** $x(x-2)(x+2)$ **59.** prime **61.** $(x-2)(x+2)^2$ **63.** $y(y^2+9)(y+3)(y-3)$ **65.** $5y^2(2y+3)(2y-3)$
**67.** $x^{1/2}(x-1)$ **69.** $\frac{4(1+2x)}{x^{2/3}}$ **71.** $(x+3)^{1/2}(-x-2)$ **73.** $\frac{x+4}{(x+5)^{3/2}}$ **75.** $(4x-1)^{1/2}\left(\frac{4}{3}-\frac{4}{3}x\right)$
**77.** $-16(t-2)(t+1)$ **79.** $(3x+2)(3x-2)$ **91.** $(x^n+4)(x^n+2)$ **93.** $(x+4+5y)(x+4-5y)$
**95.** 8, −8, 16, −16

## Section P.6

### Check Point Exercises

**1. a.** −5 **b.** 6, −6 **2. a.** $x^2, x \neq -3$ **b.** $\frac{x-1}{x+1}, x \neq -1$ **3.** $\frac{x-3}{(x-2)(x+3)}, x \neq 2, x \neq -2, x \neq -3$
**4.** $\frac{3(x-1)}{x(x+2)}, x \neq 1, x \neq 0, x \neq -2$ **5.** $-2, x \neq -1$ **6.** $\frac{2(4x+1)}{(x+1)(x-1)}, x \neq 1, x \neq -1$ **7.** $(x-3)(x-3)(x+3)$

**8.** $\frac{-x^2+11x-20}{2(x-5)^2}, x \neq 5$ **9.** $\frac{2(2-3x)}{4+3x}, x \neq 0, x \neq -\frac{4}{3}$ **10.** $\frac{-1}{x(x+7)}, x \neq 0, x \neq -7$ **11.** $\frac{x+1}{x^{3/2}}$ **12.** $\frac{1}{\sqrt{x+3}+\sqrt{x}}$

## Exercise Set P.6

**1.** 3 **3.** 5, −5 **5.** −1, −10 **7.** $\frac{3}{x-3}, x \neq 3$ **9.** $\frac{y+9}{y-1}, y \neq 1, 2$ **11.** $\frac{x+6}{x-6}, x \neq 6, -6$ **13.** $\frac{(x-3)(x+3)}{x(x+4)}, x \neq 0, -4, 3$ **15.** $\frac{x-1}{x+2}, x \neq -2, -1, 2, 3$ **17.** $\frac{x^2+2x+4}{3x}, x \neq -2, 0, 2$ **19.** $\frac{(x-2)^2}{x}, x \neq 2, 0, -2$ **21.** $\frac{x-5}{2}, x \neq 1, -5$ **23.** $2, x \neq -\frac{5}{6}$ **25.** $\frac{2x-1}{x+3}, x \neq 0, -3$ **27.** $\frac{3}{x-3}, x \neq 3, -4$ **29.** $\frac{9x+39}{(x+4)(x+5)}, x \neq -4, -5$ **31.** $-\frac{3}{x(x+1)}, x \neq -1, 0$ **33.** $\frac{3x^2+4}{(x+2)(x-2)}, x \neq -2, 2$ **35.** $\frac{2x^2+50}{(x-5)(x+5)}, x \neq -5, 5$ **37.** $\frac{4x+16}{(x+3)^2}, x \neq -3$ **39.** $\frac{x^2-x}{(x+5)(x-2)(x+3)}, x \neq -5, 2, -3$ **41.** $\frac{x+1}{3x-1}, x \neq 0, \frac{1}{3}$ **43.** $\frac{x}{x+3}, x \neq -2, -3$ **45.** $-\frac{x-14}{7}, x \neq -2, 2$ **47.** $\frac{x-3}{x+2}, x \neq 1, 3$ **49.** $-\frac{2x+h}{x^2(x+h)^2}, h \neq 0$ **51.** $1-\frac{1}{3x}$ **53.** $-\frac{2}{x^2\sqrt{x^2+2}}$ **55.** $-\frac{1}{x\sqrt{x+h}+\sqrt{x}(x+h)}, h \neq 0$ **57.** $\frac{1}{\sqrt{x+5}+\sqrt{x}}$ **59.** $\frac{1}{(x+y)(\sqrt{x}-\sqrt{y})}$ **61.** $\frac{540t^2+12{,}640t+107{,}100}{-0.14t^2+0.51t+31.6}$
**63. a.** 86.67, 520, 1170; It costs $86,670,000 to inoculate 40% of the population against this strain of flu, and $520,000,000 to inoculate 80% of the population, and $1,170,000,000 to inoculate 90% of the population. **b.** $x = 100$
**c.** increases rapidly; impossible to inoculate 100% of the population. **65.** $\frac{2r_1r_2}{r_1+r_2}$; 24 mph **81.** (d) is true. **83.** $\frac{2}{x+1}$

# Section P.7

## Check Point Exercises

**1. a.** $8+i$ **b.** $-10+10i$ **2. a.** $63+14i$ **b.** $58-11i$ **3.** $\frac{3}{5}+\frac{13}{10}i$ **4. a.** $7i\sqrt{3}$ **b.** $1-4i\sqrt{3}$ **c.** $-7+i\sqrt{3}$

## Exercise Set P.7

**1.** $8-2i$ **3.** $-2+9i$ **5.** $24+7i$ **7.** $-14+17i$ **9.** $21+15i$ **11.** $-43-23i$ **13.** $-29-11i$ **15.** 34 **17.** 34 **19.** $-5+12i$ **21.** $\frac{3}{5}+\frac{1}{5}i$ **23.** $1+i$ **25.** $-\frac{24}{25}+\frac{32}{25}i$ **27.** $\frac{7}{5}+\frac{4}{5}i$ **29.** $3i$ **31.** $47i$ **33.** $-8i$ **35.** $2+6i\sqrt{7}$ **37.** $-\frac{1}{3}+\frac{\sqrt{2}}{6}i$ **39.** $-\frac{1}{8}-\frac{\sqrt{3}}{24}i$ **41.** $-2\sqrt{6}-2i\sqrt{10}$ **43.** $24\sqrt{15}$ **53.** (d) is true. **55.** $\frac{14}{25}-\frac{2}{25}i$ **57.** 0

# Section P.8

## Check Point Exercises

**1.**

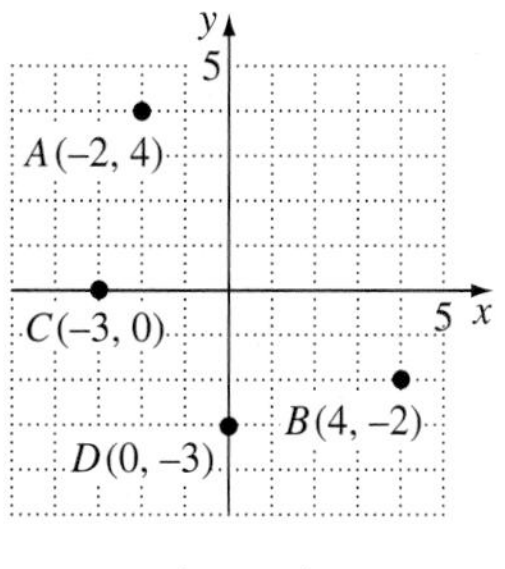


**2.**

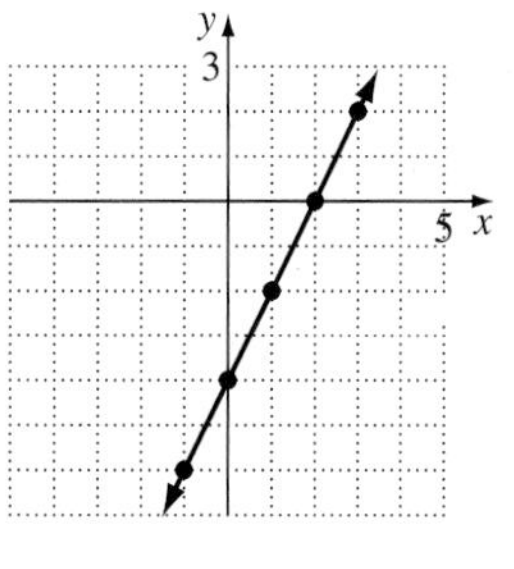


**3.** The minimum $x$-value is −100 and the maximum $x$-value is 100. The distance between consecutive tick marks is 50. The minimum $y$-value is −100 and the maximum $y$-value is 100. The distance between consecutive tick marks is 10.

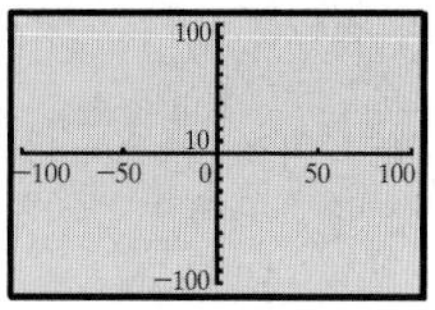


**4.** 5 **5.** $\left(4, -\frac{1}{2}\right)$ **6.** 1991; about $800 million

## Exercise Set P.8

**1.**

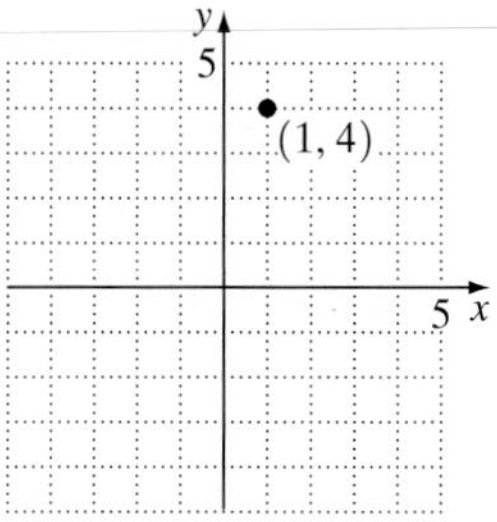


**3.**

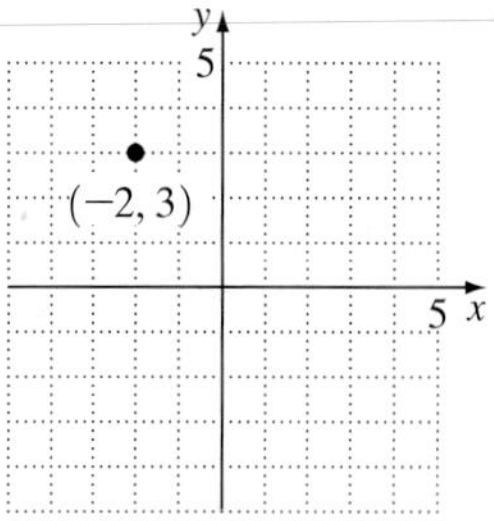


**5.**

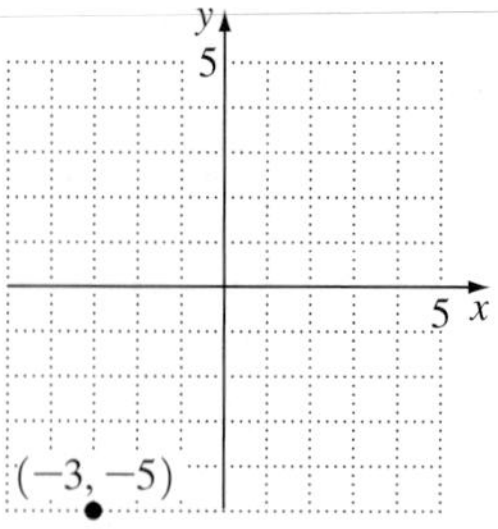


**7.**

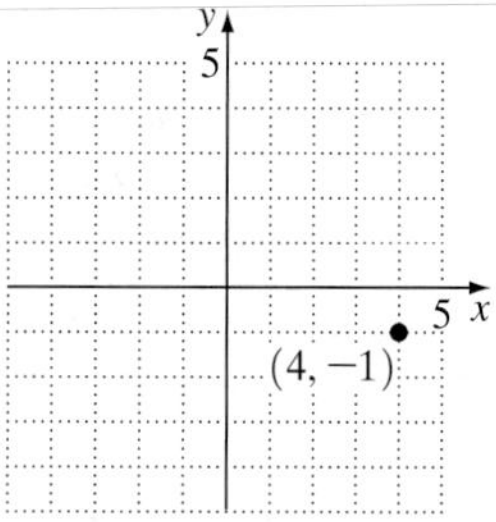


**9.**

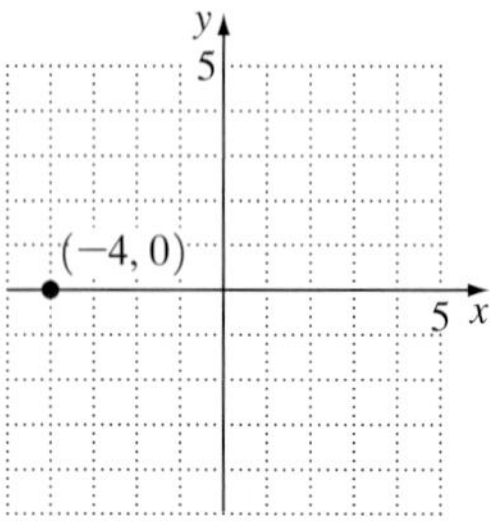


**11.**

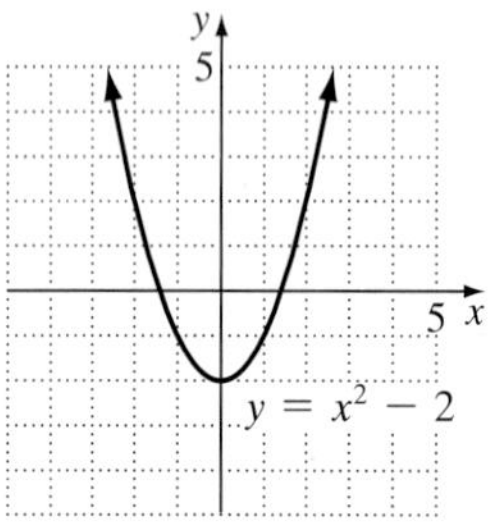


**13.**

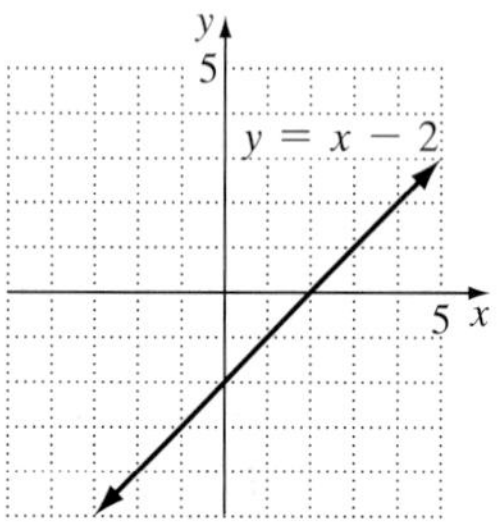


**15.**

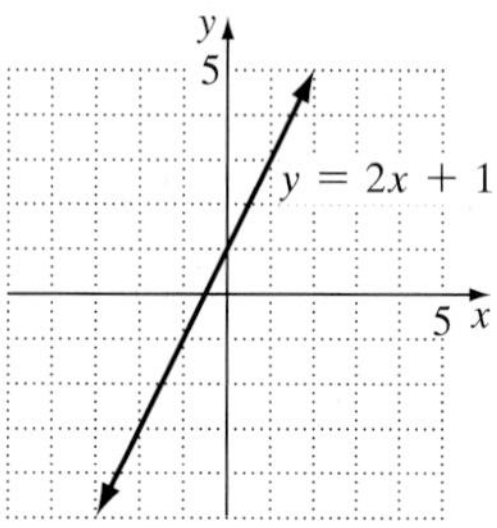


**17.**

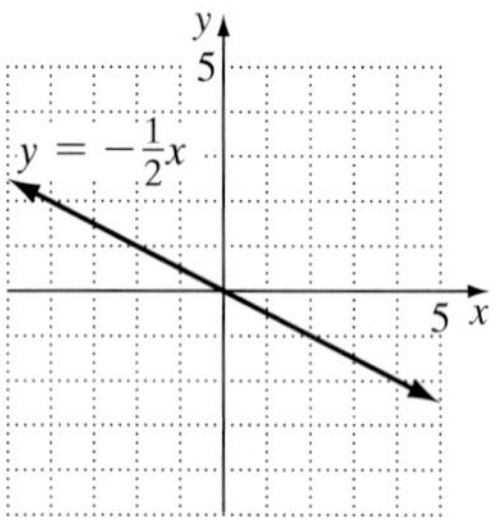


**19.**

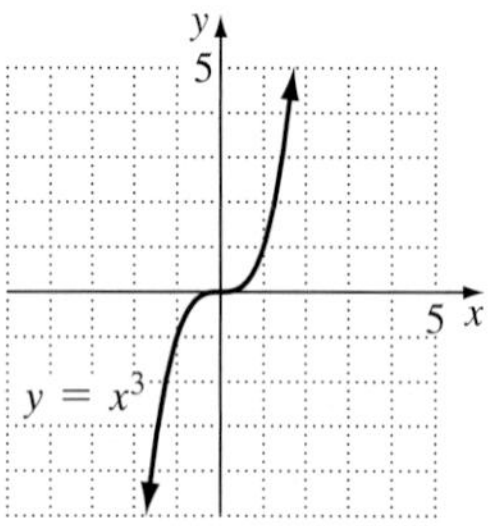


**21.**

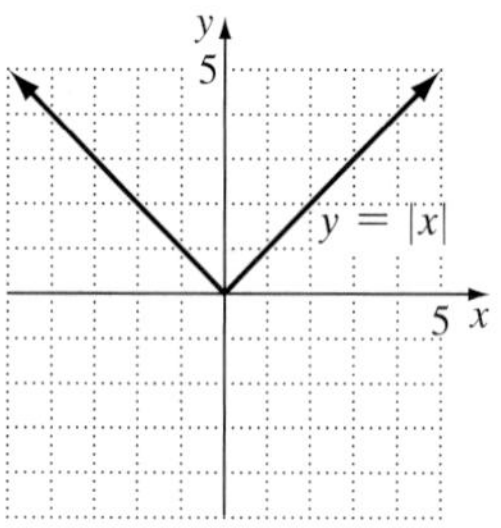


**23.** (c) **25.** (b) **27. a.** 2 **b.** −4 **29. a.** 1, −2 **b.** 2 **31. a.** −1 **b.** None

**33. a.**

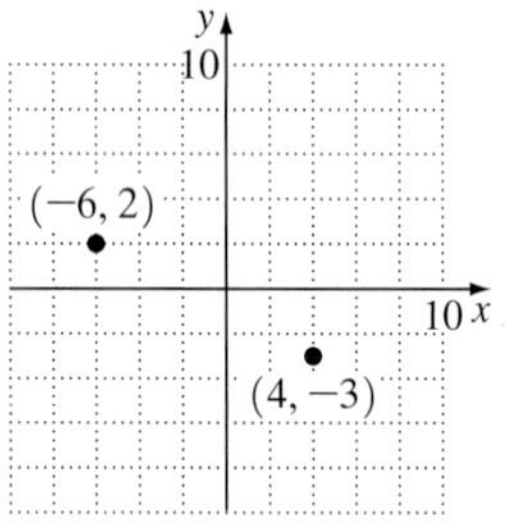


**b.** $5\sqrt{5}$ **c.** $\left(-1, -\frac{1}{2}\right)$

**35. a.**

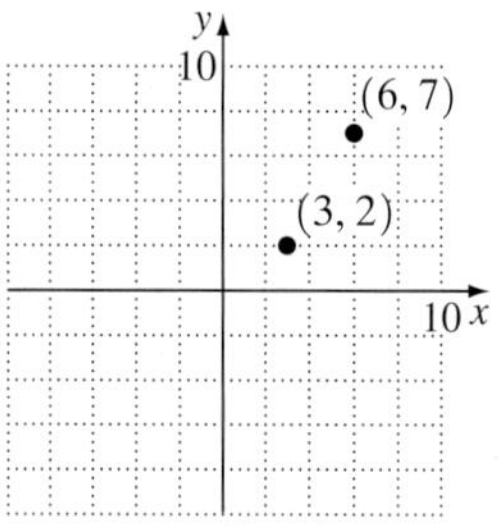


**b.** $\sqrt{34}$ **c.** $\left(\frac{9}{2}, \frac{9}{2}\right)$

**37. a.**

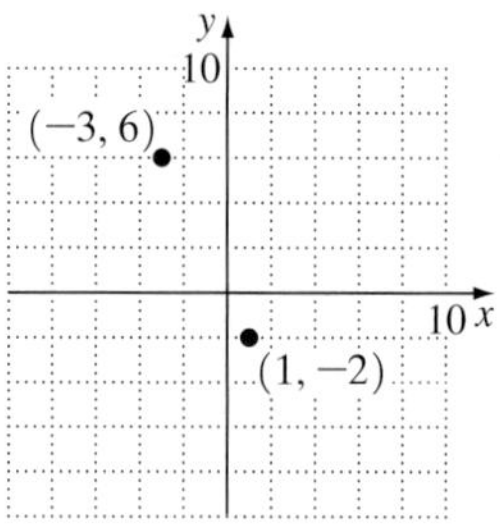


**b.** $4\sqrt{5}$ **c.** $(-1, 2)$

**39.** about 5% **41.** around 1982, about 9.7% **43.** (1970, 61); In 1970, the population of United States for people under 16 was about 61 million. **45.** (1990, 60); In 1990, the population of United States. for people under 16 was about 60 million. **47. a.** 1250 ft **b.** 8.8 sec **57.** (c) gives a complete graph. **59.** (b) gives a complete graph. **61.** (d) is true.

## Chapter P Review Exercises

**1. a.** $\sqrt{81}$ **b.** $0, \sqrt{81}$ **c.** $-17, 0, \sqrt{81}$ **d.** $-17, -\frac{9}{13}, 0, 0.75, \sqrt{81}$ **e.** $\sqrt{2}, \pi$ **2.** 103 **3.** $\sqrt{2} - 1$ **4.** $\sqrt{17} - 3$ **5.** $|4 - (-17)|$; 21 **6.** 20 **7.** 4 **8.** commutative property of addition **9.** associative property of multiplication **10.** distributive property of multiplication over addition **11.** commutative property of multiplication **12.** commutative property of multiplication **13.** commutative property of addition **14.** $23x - 23y - 2$ **15.** $2x$ **16.** −108 **17.** $\frac{5}{16}$ **18.** $\frac{1}{25}$ **19.** $\frac{1}{27}$ **20.** $-8x^{12}y^9$ **21.** $\frac{10}{x^8}$ **22.** $\frac{1}{16x^{12}}$ **23.** $\frac{y^8}{4x^{10}}$ **24.** 37,400 **25.** 0.0000745 **26.** $3.59 \times 10^6$

**27.** $7.25 \times 10^{-3}$ **28.** $3.9 \times 10^{5}$ **29.** $2.3 \times 10^{-2}$ **30.** $10^3$ or 1000 yr **31.** $\$4.05 \times 10^{10}$ **32.** $10\sqrt{3}$ **33.** $2|x|\sqrt{3}$
**34.** $2|x|\sqrt{5}$ **35.** $|r|\sqrt{r}$ **36.** $\frac{11}{2}$ **37.** $4|x|\sqrt{3}$ **38.** $20\sqrt{5}$ **39.** $16\sqrt{2}$ **40.** $24\sqrt{2} - 8\sqrt{3}$ **41.** $6\sqrt{5}$ **42.** $\frac{\sqrt{6}}{3}$
**43.** $\frac{5(6 - \sqrt{3})}{33}$ **44.** $7(\sqrt{7} + \sqrt{5})$ **45.** 5 **46.** $-2$ **47.** not a real number **48.** 5 **49.** $3\sqrt[3]{3}$ **50.** $y\sqrt[3]{y^2}$ **51.** $2\sqrt[4]{5}$
**52.** $13\sqrt[3]{2}$ **53.** $|x|\sqrt[4]{2}$ **54.** 4 **55.** $\frac{1}{5}$ **56.** 5 **57.** $\frac{1}{3}$ **58.** 16 **59.** $\frac{1}{81}$ **60.** $20x^{11/12}$ **61.** $3x^{1/4}$ **62.** $25x^4$ **63.** $y^{1/2}$
**64.** $8x^3 + 10x^2 - 20x - 4$; degree 3 **65.** $8x^4 - 5x^3 + 6$; degree 4 **66.** $12x^3 + x^2 - 21x + 10$ **67.** $6x^2 - 7x - 5$
**68.** $16x^2 - 25$ **69.** $4x^2 + 20x + 25$ **70.** $9x^2 - 24x + 16$ **71.** $8x^3 + 12x^2 + 6x + 1$ **72.** $125x^3 - 150x^2 + 60x - 8$
**73.** $3x^2 + 16xy - 35y^2$ **74.** $9x^2 - 30xy + 25y^2$ **75.** $9x^4 + 12x^2y + 4y^2$ **76.** $49x^2 - 16y^2$ **77.** $a^3 - b^3$
**78.** $25y^2 - 4x^2 - 4x - 1$ **79.** $x^2 + 4xy + 8x + 4y^2 + 16y + 16$ **80.** $3x^2(5x + 1)$ **81.** $(x - 4)(x - 7)$
**82.** $(3x + 1)(5x - 2)$ **83.** $(8 - x)(8 + x)$ **84.** prime **85.** $3x^2(x - 5)(x + 2)$ **86.** $4x^3(5x^4 - 9)$ **87.** $(x + 3)(x - 3)^2$
**88.** $(4x - 5)^2$ **89.** $(x^2 + 4)(x + 2)(x - 2)$ **90.** $(y - 2)(y^2 + 2y + 4)$ **91.** $(x + 4)(x^2 - 4x + 16)$
**92.** $3x^2(x - 2)(x + 2)$ **93.** $(3x - 5)(9x^2 + 15x + 25)$ **94.** $x(x - 1)(x + 1)(x^2 + 1)$ **95.** $(x^2 - 2)(x + 5)$
**96.** $\frac{16(1 + 2x)}{x^{3/4}}$ **97.** $(x^2 - 4)(x^2 + 3)^{1/2}(-x^4 + x^2 + 13)$ **98.** $\frac{6(2x + 1)}{x^{3/2}}$ **99.** $x^2, x \neq -2$ **100.** $\frac{x - 3}{x - 6}, x \neq -6, 6$
**101.** $\frac{x}{x + 2}, x \neq -2$ **102.** $\frac{(x + 3)^3}{(x - 2)^2(x + 2)}, x \neq 2, -2$ **103.** $\frac{2}{x(x + 1)}, x \neq 0, 1, -1, -\frac{1}{3}$ **104.** $\frac{x + 3}{x - 4}, x \neq -3, 4, 2, 8$
**105.** $\frac{1}{x - 3}, x \neq 3, -3$ **106.** $\frac{4x(x - 1)}{(x + 2)(x - 2)}, x \neq 2, -2$ **107.** $\frac{x(2x + 1)}{(x - 3)(x + 3)(x - 2)}, x \neq 3, -3, 2$
**108.** $\frac{11x^2 - x - 11}{(2x - 1)(x + 3)(3x + 2)}, x \neq \frac{1}{2}, -3, -\frac{2}{3}$ **109.** $\frac{3x}{x - 4}, x \neq 0$ **110.** $\frac{3x + 8}{3x + 10}$ **111.** $\frac{25}{\sqrt{(25 - x^2)^3}}$ **112.** $-9 + 4i$
**113.** $-12 - 8i$ **114.** $29 + 11i$ **115.** $-7 - 24i$ **116.** 113 **117.** $\frac{3(5 - i)}{13}$ **118.** $\frac{1}{5} + \frac{11}{10}i$ **119.** $i\sqrt{2}$ **120.** $-96 - 40i$
**121.** $2 + i\sqrt{2}$

**122.**
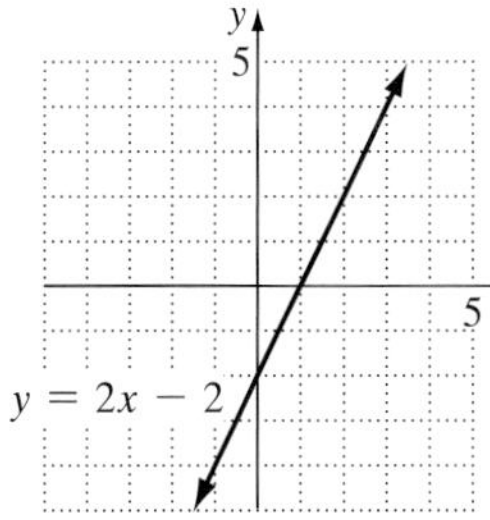


**123.**
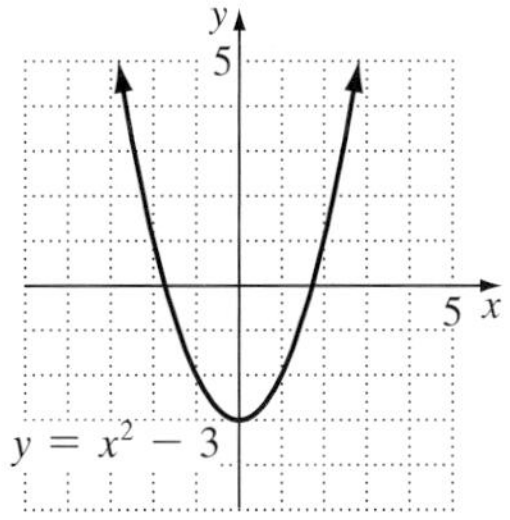


**124.**
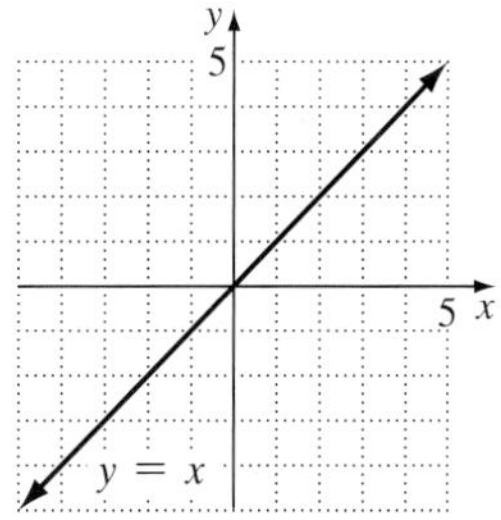


**125.**
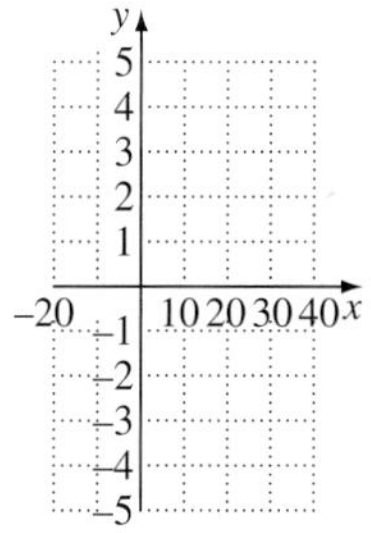


**126.** $x$-intercept: $-2$; $y$-intercept: 2 **127.** $x$-intercepts: 2, $-2$; $y$-intercept: $-4$ **128.** $x$-intercept: 5; $y$-intercept: none

**129. a.**
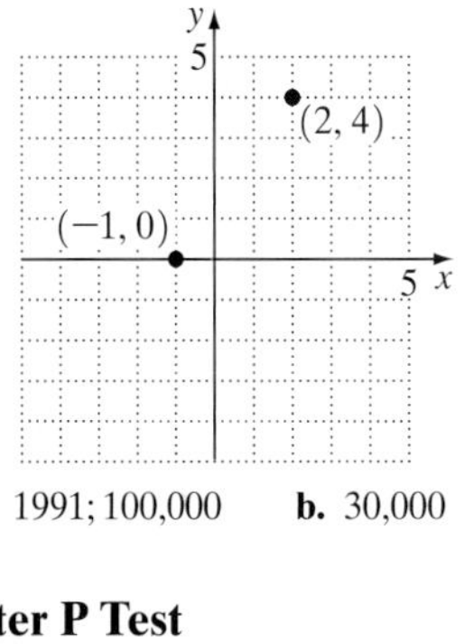


**b.** 5 **c.** $\left(\frac{1}{2}, 2\right)$

**130. a.**
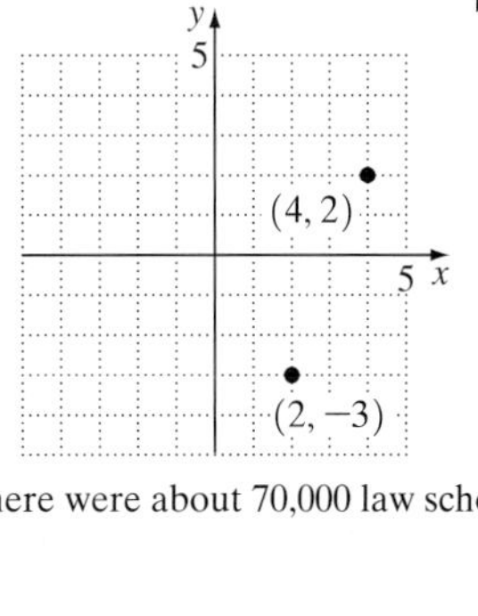


**b.** $\sqrt{29}$ **c.** $\left(3, -\frac{1}{2}\right)$

**131. a.** 1991; 100,000 **b.** 30,000 **c.** $A(1998, 70)$; In 1998, there were about 70,000 law school applicants.

## Chapter P Test

**1.** $-7, -\frac{4}{5}, 0, 0.25, \sqrt{4}, \frac{22}{7}$ **2.** commutative property of addition **3.** distributive property of multiplication over addition
**4.** $7.6 \times 10^{-4}$ **5.** $85x + 2y - 15$ **6.** $\frac{5y^8}{x^6}$ **7.** $3|r|\sqrt{2}$ **8.** $11\sqrt{2}$ **9.** $\frac{3(5 - \sqrt{2})}{23}$ **10.** $2x\sqrt[3]{2x}$ **11.** $\frac{x + 3}{x - 2}, x \neq 2, 1$
**12.** $\frac{1}{243}$ **13.** $2x^3 - 13x^2 + 26x - 15$ **14.** $25x^2 + 30xy + 9y^2$ **15.** $(x - 3)(x - 6)$ **16.** $(x^2 + 3)(x + 2)$

**17.** $(5x - 3)(5x + 3)$ **18.** $(6x - 7)^2$ **19.** $(y - 5)(y^2 + 5y + 25)$ **20.** $\frac{x^2(x^2 - 9)}{(x^2 + 1)^{3/2}}$ **21.** $\frac{2(x + 3)}{x + 1}, x \neq 3, -1, -4, -3$

**22.** $\frac{x^2 + 2x + 15}{(x + 3)(x - 3)}, x \neq 3, -3$ **23.** $\frac{11}{(x - 3)(x - 4)}, x \neq 3, 4$ **24.** $\frac{2x}{x^2 + 3x + 2}$ **25.** $\frac{10x}{\sqrt{(x^2 + 5)^3}}$ **26.** $47 + 16i$

**27.** $2 + i$ **28.** $38i$ **29.**

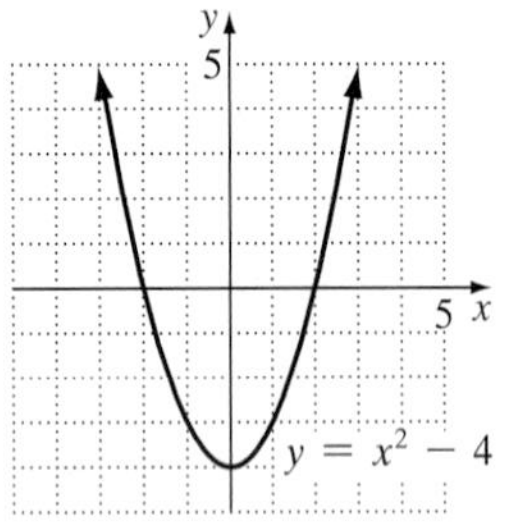


**30.** $2\sqrt{13}$

## CHAPTER 1

### Section 1.1

#### Check Point Exercises

**1.** {16} **2.** {5} **3.** {−2} **4.** {3} **5.** ∅ **6.** identity

#### Exercise Set 1.1

**1.** {16} **3.** {7} **5.** {13} **7.** {2} **9.** {9} **11.** {−5} **13.** {6} **15.** {−2} **17.** {12} **19.** {24} **21.** {−15} **23.** {5} **25.** $\left\{\frac{33}{2}\right\}$ **27.** {−12} **29.** $\left\{\frac{46}{5}\right\}$ **31. a.** 0 **b.** $\left\{\frac{1}{2}\right\}$ **33. a.** 0 **b.** {−2} **35. a.** 0 **b.** {2} **37. a.** 0 **b.** {4} **39. a.** 1 **b.** {3} **41. a.** −1 **b.** ∅ **43. a.** 1 **b.** {2} **45. a.** −2, 2 **b.** ∅ **47. a.** −1, 1 **b.** {−3} **49. a.** −2, 4 **b.** ∅ **51.** identity **53.** inconsistent equation **55.** conditional equation **57.** inconsistent equation **59.** {−7} **61.** ∅ **62.** not true for any real number **63.** {−4} **65.** {8} **67.** {−1} **69. a.** 205 mg/dl **b.** 375,000 annual deaths; 125,000 saved lives **71.** $409\frac{1}{5}$ ft **85.** inconsistent **87.** conditional; {−5} **89.** $x = \frac{c - b}{a}$ **91.** Answers may vary. **93.** 20

### Section 1.2

#### Check Point Exercises

**1.** 100 g **2.** $133\frac{1}{3}$ hr **3.** \$15,000 at 9%; \$10,000 at 12% **4.** 30 ml of 10%; 20 ml of 60% **5.** width = 40 ft; length = 120 ft **6.** $m = \frac{y - b}{x}$ **7.** $C = \frac{P}{1 + M}$

#### Exercise Set 1.2

**1.** Sosa = 66 home runs; McGwire = 70 home runs **3.** 19, 20 **5.** 40 years old; Find 117 on the vertical axis and follow it over to the graph for female. **7.** 30 years after 1980; 2010 **9.** yes; The height (about 61.2 in.) is greater than 5 ft. **11.** 28 times **13.** $33\frac{1}{3}$ mi **15.** \$25,000 at 9%; \$0 at 12% **17.** \$52,500 at 8%, 17,500 at 12% **19.** \$3750 **21.** 22.2 L of 30%; 27.8 L of 12% **23.** 6 oz **25.** 25 ml **27.** 600 north, 400 south **29.** length = 78 ft; width = 36 ft **31.** length = 12 ft; height = 4 ft **33.** 11 hr **35.** \$126 **37.** \$740 **39.** \$467.20 **41.** 5 ft 7 in. **43.** $w = \frac{A}{l}$ **45.** $b = \frac{2A}{h}$ **47.** $p = \frac{I}{rt}$ **49.** $m = \frac{E}{c^2}$ **51.** $p = \frac{T - D}{m}$ **53.** $\frac{2A}{h} - b = a$ **55.** $\frac{S - P}{Pt} = r$ **57.** $S = \frac{F}{B} + V$ **59.** $f = \frac{pq}{q + p}$ **61.** $h = \frac{A - 2lw}{2l + 2w}$ **63.** $n = \frac{IR}{E - Ir}$ **65.** $y = \frac{ce - de}{cd}$ **67.** $f = \frac{p - s}{sp - s}$

**73. a.** $y = 3.82 + 0.3x$ **b.**

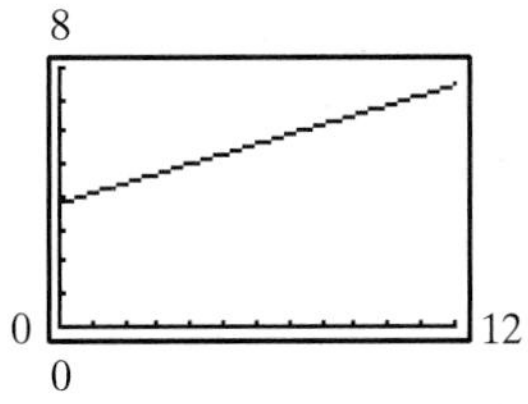


**c.** The trace feature shows $x$ to be about 8 when $y = 6.22$, so 1988. **d.** When $y = 6.22$, $x = 88$.

**75.** \$200 **77.** 10 **79.** $C = \dfrac{VL - SN}{L - N}$

## Section 1.3

### Check Point Exercises

**1. a.** $\{0, 3\}$ **b.** $\left\{-1, \frac{1}{2}\right\}$ **2. a.** $\{-\sqrt{7}, \sqrt{7}\}$ **b.** $\{-5 + \sqrt{11}, -5 - \sqrt{11}\}$ **3.** $\{1 + \sqrt{3}, 1 - \sqrt{3}\}$
**4.** $\left\{\frac{-1 + \sqrt{3}}{2}, \frac{-1 - \sqrt{3}}{2}\right\}$ **5.** $\{1 + i, 1 - i\}$ **6.** $-56$; two complex imaginary solutions **7.** 10 yr **8.** 22 in. by 22 in.
**8.** 19 or 31 people

### Exercise Set 1.3

**1.** $\{-2, 5\}$ **3.** $\left\{-\frac{5}{2}, \frac{2}{3}\right\}$ **5.** $\left\{-\frac{4}{3}, 2\right\}$ **7.** $\{-4, 0\}$ **9.** $\left\{0, \frac{1}{3}\right\}$ **11.** $\{-3, 3\}$
**13.** $\{-7, 3\}$ **15.** $\left\{-\frac{5}{3}, \frac{1}{3}\right\}$ **17.** $\left\{\frac{1 - \sqrt{7}}{5}, \frac{1 + \sqrt{7}}{5}\right\}$
**19.** $\{1 + \sqrt{3}, 1 - \sqrt{3}\}$ **21.** $\{3 + 2\sqrt{5}, 3 - 2\sqrt{5}\}$ **23.** $\left\{\frac{-3 + \sqrt{13}}{2}, \frac{-3 - \sqrt{13}}{2}\right\}$ **25.** $\left\{\frac{1}{2}, 3\right\}$
**27.** $\left\{\frac{1 + \sqrt{2}}{2}, \frac{1 - \sqrt{2}}{2}\right\}$ **29.** $\{-5, -3\}$ **31.** $\left\{\frac{-5 + \sqrt{13}}{2}, \frac{-5 - \sqrt{13}}{2}\right\}$
**33.** $\left\{\frac{3 + \sqrt{57}}{6}, \frac{3 - \sqrt{57}}{6}\right\}$ **35.** $\left\{\frac{1 + \sqrt{29}}{4}, \frac{1 - \sqrt{29}}{4}\right\}$ **37.** $\{3 + i, 3 - i\}$ **39.** 36; 2 unequal real solutions
**41.** 97; 2 unequal real solutions **43.** 0; 1 real solution **45.** 37; 2 unequal real solutions **47.** $\left\{-\frac{1}{2}, 1\right\}$ **49.** $\left\{\frac{1}{5}, 2\right\}$
**51.** $\{-2\sqrt{5}, 2\sqrt{5}\}$ **53.** $\{1 + \sqrt{2}, 1 - \sqrt{2}\}$ **55.** $\left\{\frac{-11 + \sqrt{33}}{4}, \frac{-11 - \sqrt{33}}{4}\right\}$ **57.** $\left\{0, \frac{8}{3}\right\}$ **59.** $\{2\}$ **61.** $\{-2, 2\}$
**63.** $\{3 + 2i, 3 - 2i\}$ **65.** $\{2 + i\sqrt{3}, 2 - i\sqrt{3}\}$ **67.** $\left\{0, \frac{7}{2}\right\}$ **69.** 2024 **71.** 1999; very well **73.** 1986
**75.** 1990; 739,980; very well **77.** 1995; 340,000; fairly well **79.** 4 ft by 4 ft **81.** 300 m by 400 m or 200 m by 600 m **83.** 3 ft
**85.** 4 in.; 4 in. **87.** 65 trees **89.** 522.4 $cm^2$
**101. a.**

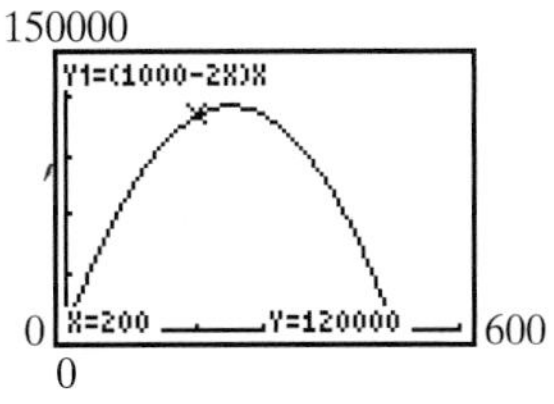


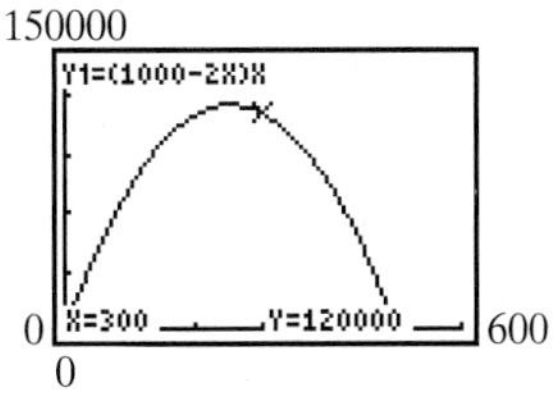


**b.** 125,000 $m^2$; 250 m by 500 m
**c.** No; Explanations may vary.
**103.** $\{-3\sqrt{3}, \sqrt{3}\}$
**105.** 5 sec

## Section 1.4

### Check Point Exercises

**1.** $\{-\sqrt{3}, 0, \sqrt{3}\}$ **2.** $\left\{-2, -\frac{3}{2}, 2\right\}$ **3.** $\{-1, 3\}$ **4.** $\{4\}$ **5.** $\approx$ 86.6% the speed of light **6.** $\{\sqrt[3]{25}\}$ or $\{5^{2/3}\}$
**7.** $\{-\sqrt{3}, -\sqrt{2}, \sqrt{2}, \sqrt{3}\}$ **8.** $\left\{-\frac{1}{27}, 64\right\}$ **9.** $\{-2, 3\}$

### Exercise Set 1.4

**1.** $\{-4, 0, 4\}$ **3.** $\{0, 2\}$ **5.** $\left\{-2, -\frac{2}{3}, 2\right\}$ **7.** $\left\{-\frac{1}{2}, \frac{1}{2}, \frac{3}{2}\right\}$ **9.** $\left\{-2, -\frac{1}{2}, \frac{1}{2}\right\}$ **11.** $\{6\}$ **13.** $\{6\}$ **15.** $\{-6\}$

**17.** $\{10\}$ **19.** $\{12\}$ **21.** $\{8\}$ **23.** $\varnothing$ **25.** $\varnothing$ **27.** $\left\{\frac{13+\sqrt{105}}{6}\right\}$ **29.** $\{4\}$ **31.** $\{13\}$ **33.** $\{\sqrt[5]{4}\}$ **35.** $\{-4, 5\}$ **37.** $\{-2, -1, 1, 2\}$ **39.** $\left\{-\frac{4}{3}, -1, 1, \frac{4}{3}\right\}$ **41.** $\{-\sqrt[3]{5}, -\sqrt[3]{3}\}$ **43.** $\left\{-\sqrt[3]{2}, \sqrt[3]{\frac{9}{5}}\right\}$ **45.** $\{-8, 27\}$ **47.** $\{1\}$ **49.** $\left\{\frac{1}{4}, 1\right\}$ **53.** $\{-3, -1, 2, 4\}$ **55.** $\{-8, -2, 1, 4\}$ **57.** $\{-8, 8\}$ **59.** $\{-5, 9\}$ **61.** $\{-2, 3\}$ **63.** $\{1\}$ **65.** $\{0\}$ **67.** $\left\{\frac{5}{2}\right\}$ **69.** $\{-8, -6, 4, 6\}$ **71.** $\{-1, 1, 2\}$ **73.** 36 years old **75.** 1952 **77. a.** females **b.** $A \approx 157.1$ or $A \approx 10.4$; A person of about age 10 has a remaining life expectancy of 60 years. **79.** $\approx 99.2\%$ of the speed of light **81.** $\approx 86.6\%$ the speed of light **83.** 1.2 ft or 7.5 ft from the base of the 6-ft pole. **93.** $\{3, 1, 1\}$ **95.** $\{1, 1\}$ **97.** $\{-5\}$

**99.** 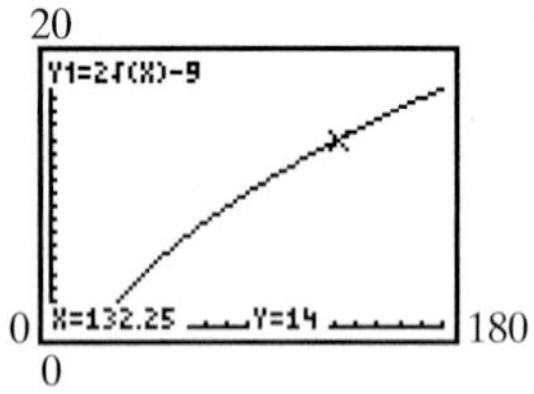

; 132.25 **101.** $\left\{\frac{1}{2}\right\}$ **103.** $\{81\}$

## Section 1.5

### Check Point Exercises

**1. a.** 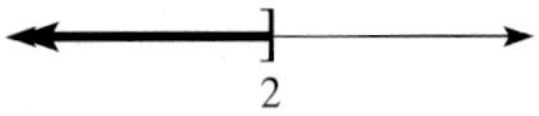

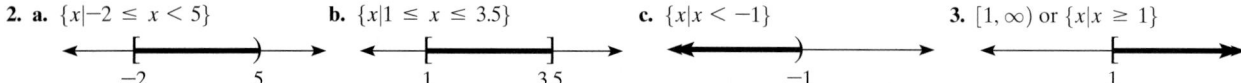

**b.** 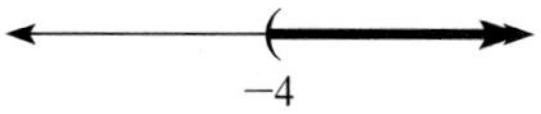

**c.** 

**2. a.** $\{x | -2 \le x < 5\}$ 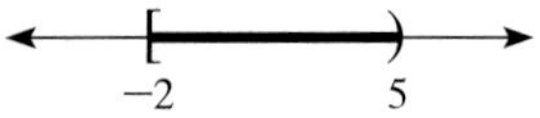

**b.** $\{x | 1 \le x \le 3.5\}$ 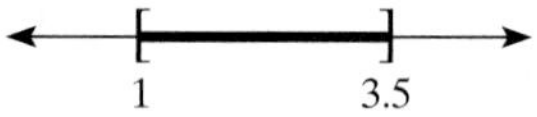

**c.** $\{x | x < -1\}$ 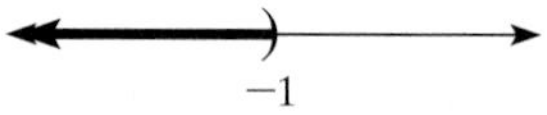

**3.** $[1, \infty)$ or $\{x | x \ge 1\}$ 

**4.** $[-1, 4)$ or $\{x | -1 \le x < 4\}$ 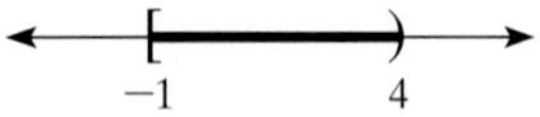

**5.** $(-3, 7)$ or $\{x | -3 < x < 7\}$ 

**6.** $(-\infty, 1]$ or $[4, \infty)$ or $\{x | x \le 1 \text{ or } x \ge 4\}$ 

**7.** more than 720 mi

### Exercise Set 1.5

**1.** 

**3.** 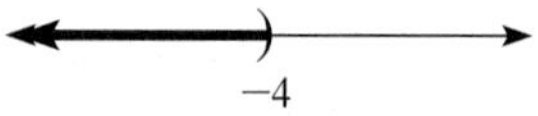

**5.** 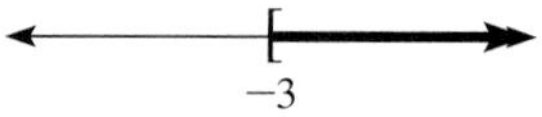


**7.** 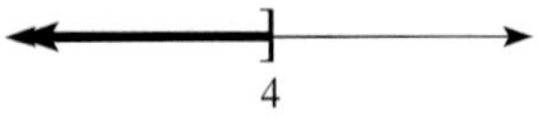

**9.** 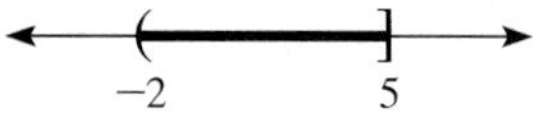

**11.** 

**13.** $1 < x \le 6$ 

**15.** $-5 \le x < 2$ 

**17.** $-3 \le x \le 1$ 

**19.** $x > 2$ 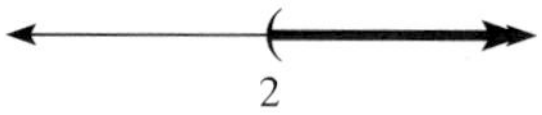


**21.** $x \ge -3$ 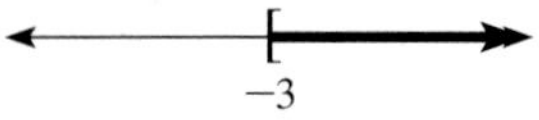

**23.** $x < 3$ 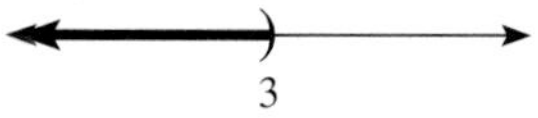

**25.** $x < 5.5$ 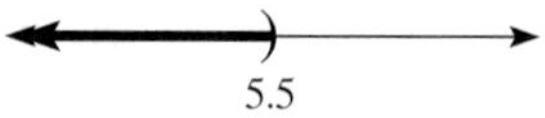

**27.** $(-\infty, 3)$ 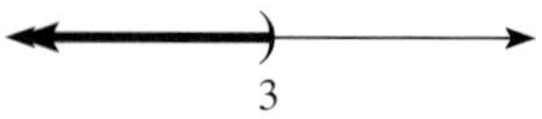


**29.** $\left[\frac{20}{3}, \infty\right)$ 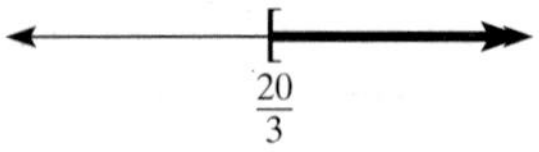

**31.** $(-\infty, -4]$ 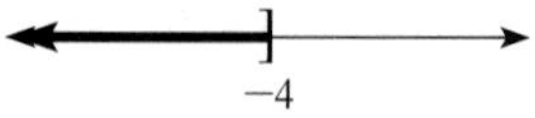

**33.** $\left(-\infty, -\frac{2}{5}\right]$ 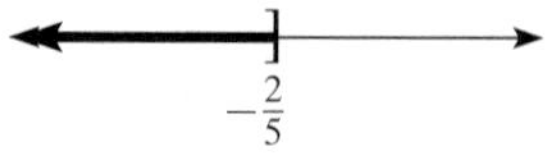

**35.** $[0, \infty)$ 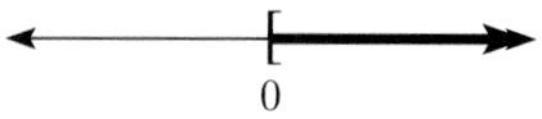


**37.** $(-\infty, 1)$ 

**39.** $[6, \infty)$ 

**41.** $\left[-\frac{32}{5}, \infty\right)$ 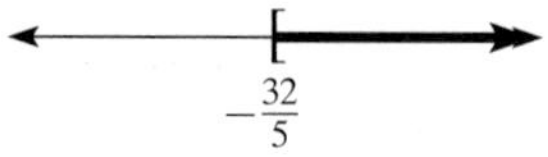

**43.** $(-\infty, -6)$ 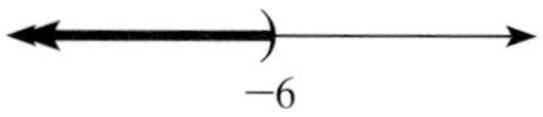

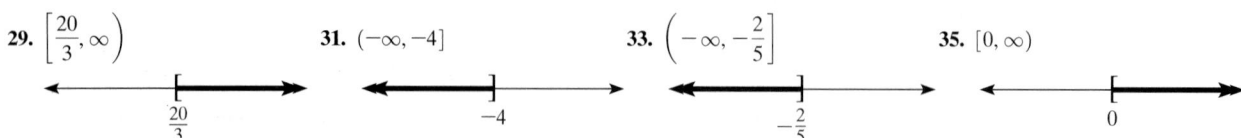

**45.** $[13, \infty)$
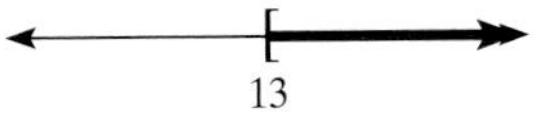

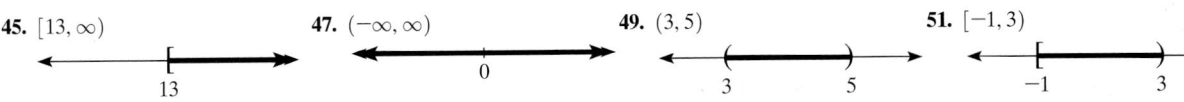

**47.** $(-\infty, \infty)$
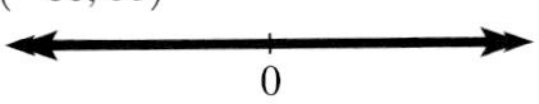


**49.** $(3, 5)$

**51.** $[-1, 3)$

**53.** $(-5, -2]$

**55.** $[3, 6)$

**57.** $(-3, 3)$

**59.** $[-1, 3]$

**61.** $(-1, 7)$

**63.** $[-5, 3]$

**65.** $(-6, 0)$

**67.** $(-\infty, -3)$ or $(3, \infty)$
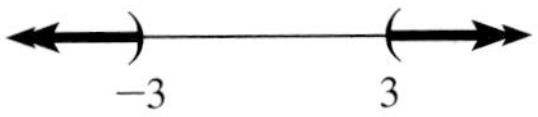


**69.** $(-\infty, -1]$ or $[3, \infty)$
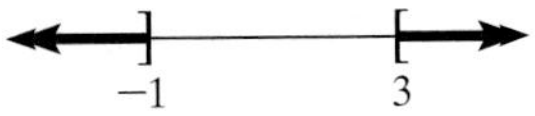


**71.** $\left(-\infty, \frac{1}{3}\right)$ or $(5, \infty)$
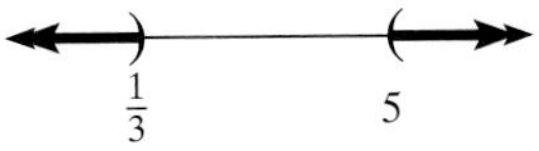


**73.** $(-\infty, -5]$ or $[3, \infty)$
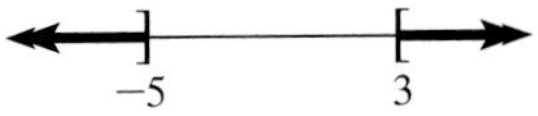


**75.** $(-\infty, -3)$ or $(12, \infty)$

**77.** $(-\infty, -1]$ or $[3, \infty)$
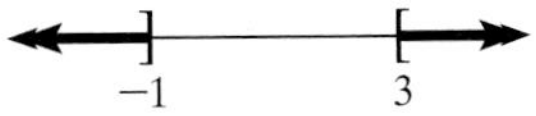


**79.** $(-\infty, -1)$ or $(2, \infty)$
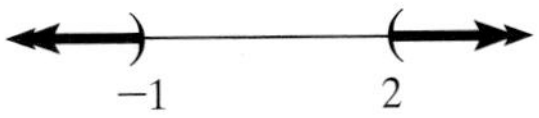


**81.** $\left(-\infty, -\frac{75}{14}\right)$ or $\left(\frac{87}{14}, \infty\right)$
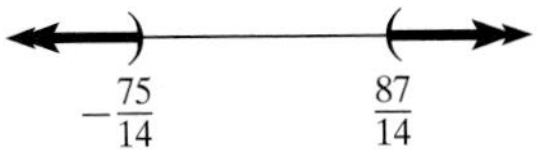


**83.** $(-\infty, -6]$ or $[24, \infty)$
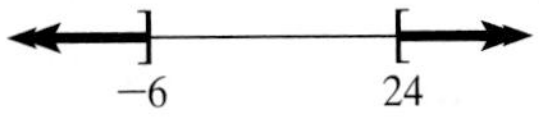


**85.** Raleigh, NC, Seattle, San Francisco, Austin, TX **87.** San Diego **89.** Austin, TX, Washington, DC, Lexington-Fayette, KY, Minneapolis, Boston, Arlington, TX **91.** severe cognitive impairment, substance abuse disorders, and depressive: manic, major depressive **93.** 2013 **95.** between 2004 and 2009 **97.** 199 checks or less **99. a.** at least a 96 **b.** a grade less than 66 **101.** 1001 or more pairs

**113.**
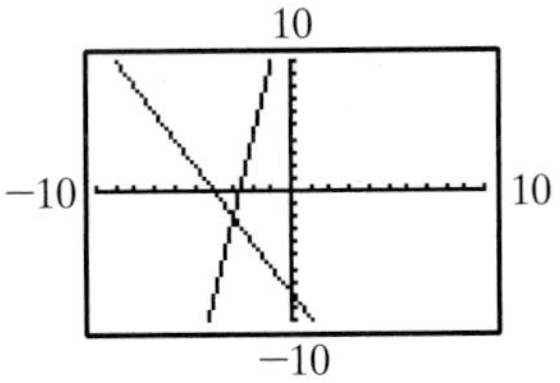


$x < -3$

**115.**
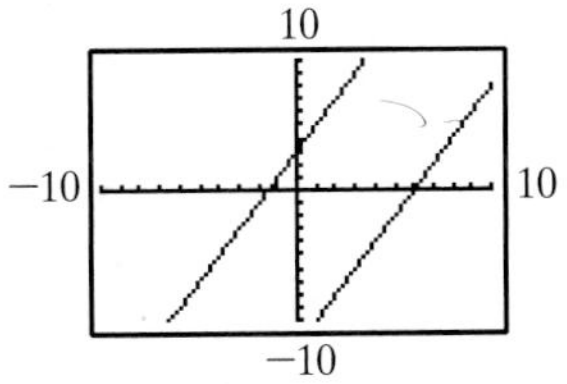


The graph of the left side of the inequality is always above the graph of the right side, therefore all values of $x$ are included in the solution; You get a statement that is always true.

**117.** (c) is true.
**119.** $(-10, -8)$

## Section 1.6

### Check Point Exercises

**1.** $(-3, 1)$

**2.** $(-\infty, -4]$ or $[5, \infty)$

**3.** $(-\infty, -2)$ or $(5, \infty)$
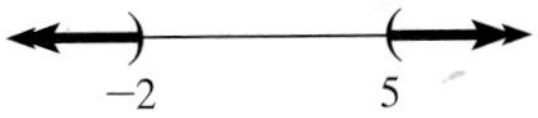


**4.** $(-1, 1]$
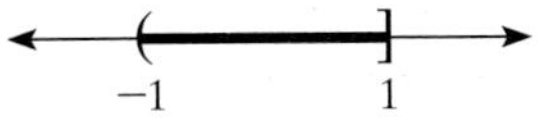


**5.** between 1 and 4 sec

### Exercise Set 1.6

**1.** $(-\infty, -2)$ or $(4, \infty)$
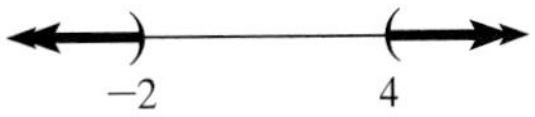


**3.** $[-3, 7]$

**5.** $(-\infty, 1)$ or $(4, \infty)$

**7.** $(-\infty, -4)$ or $(-1, \infty)$
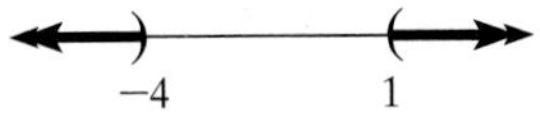


**9.** $\varnothing$

**11.** $[2, 4]$

**13.** $\left[-4, \frac{2}{3}\right]$

**15.** $\left(-3, \frac{5}{2}\right)$

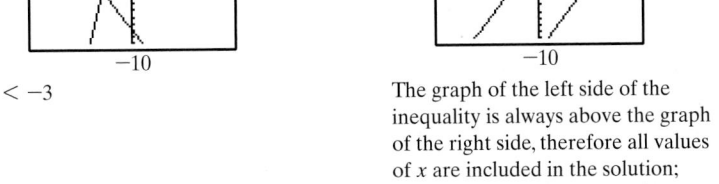

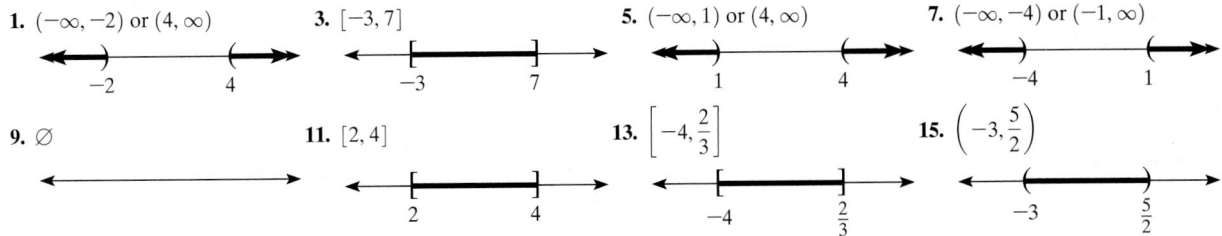

**17.** $\left(-1, -\frac{3}{4}\right)$

**19.** $\left[-2, \frac{1}{3}\right]$

**21.** $(-\infty, 0]$ or $[4, \infty)$

**23.** $\left(-\infty, -\frac{3}{2}\right)$ or $(0, \infty)$

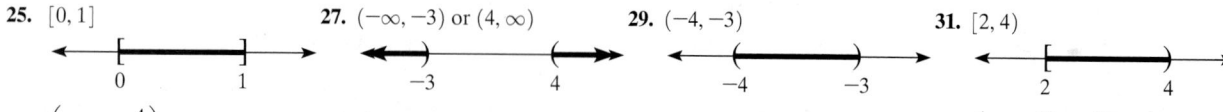

**25.** $[0, 1]$

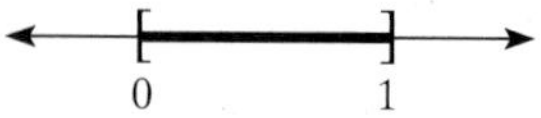


**27.** $(-\infty, -3)$ or $(4, \infty)$

**29.** $(-4, -3)$

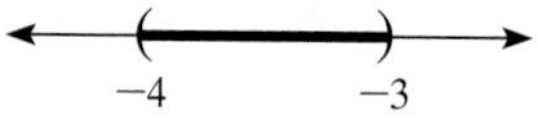


**31.** $[2, 4)$

**33.** $\left(-\infty, -\frac{4}{3}\right)$ or $[2, \infty)$

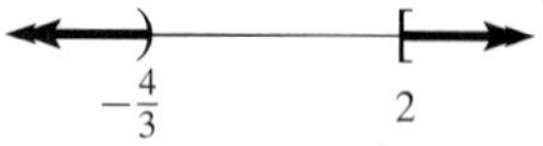


**35.** $(-\infty, 0)$ or $(3, \infty)$

**37.** $(-\infty, -5)$ or $(-3, \infty)$

**39.** $\left(-\infty, \frac{1}{2}\right)$ or $\left[\frac{7}{5}, \infty\right)$

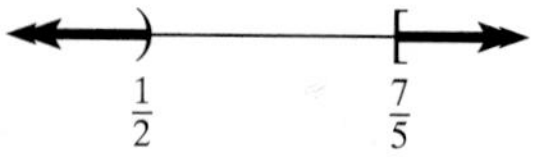


**41.** $(-\infty, -6]$ or $(-2, \infty)$

**43.** between 2 and 3 sec **45.** 3.46 sec **47. a.** 200 beats/min **b.** According to the model, up to 4 min and after 12 min. In reality, between 0 and 4 min only. **49.** after 2001 **51.** less than 60% **55.** $(-\infty, -5)$ or $(2, \infty)$ **57.** $(1, 4]$

**59.** $(-4, -1)$ or $[2, \infty)$ **61.** from 1.7 mm to 3.5 mm **63.** Answers may vary. **65.** Because the square of any number other than zero is positive, the solution includes all real numbers except 2. **67.** Because the square of any number is positive, the solution is ∅. **69. a.** $(-\infty, \infty)$ **b.** ∅

## Chapter 1 Review Exercises

**1.** {6} **2.** {−10} **3.** {5} **4.** {−13} **5.** {−3} **6.** {−1} **7.** {2} **8.** {2} **9.** $\left\{\frac{72}{11}\right\}$ **10.** {−12} **11.** $\left\{\frac{77}{15}\right\}$ **12. a.** 0 **b.** {2} **13. a.** 5 **b.** ∅ **14. a.** −1, 1 **b.** all real numbers except ±1 **15. a.** −2, 4 **b.** {7} **16.** inconsistent equation **17.** identity **18.** conditional equation **19.** 1997 **20.** 2000 **21.** 20 times **22.** LA = 159; NY = 26 **23.** 4 gal of 75%, 6 gal of 50% **24.** width = 53 m; length = 120 m **25.** $10,000 **26.** $450 **27.** 95 concerts **28.** $h = \frac{3V}{B}$ **29.** $R_1 = \frac{R_T R_2}{R_2 - R_T}$ **30.** $\left\{-8, \frac{1}{2}\right\}$ **31.** {−4, 0} **32.** {−8, 8} **33.** $\left\{\frac{4 + 3\sqrt{2}}{3}, \frac{4 - 3\sqrt{2}}{3}\right\}$ **34.** {3, 9} **35.** $\left\{2 + \frac{\sqrt{3}}{3}, 2 - \frac{\sqrt{3}}{3}\right\}$ **36.** $\{1 + \sqrt{5}, 1 - \sqrt{5}\}$ **37.** $\{1 + 3i\sqrt{2}, 1 - 3i\sqrt{2}\}$ **38.** $\left\{\frac{-2 + \sqrt{10}}{2}, \frac{-2 - \sqrt{10}}{2}\right\}$ **39.** −36; 2 complex imaginary solutions **40.** 81; 2 unequal real solutions **41.** $\left\{\frac{1}{2}, 5\right\}$ **42.** $\left\{-2, \frac{10}{3}\right\}$ **43.** $\left\{\frac{7 + \sqrt{37}}{6}, \frac{7 - \sqrt{37}}{6}\right\}$ **44.** {−3, 3} **45.** {−2, 8} **46.** $\left\{\frac{1 + i\sqrt{23}}{6}, \frac{1 - i\sqrt{23}}{6}\right\}$ **47.** 20 weeks **48.** 1989 **49.** 12 ft by 27 ft **50.** 12 in. by 12 in. **51.** 43 or 77 trees **52.** {−5, 0, 5} **53.** $\left\{-3, \frac{1}{2}, 3\right\}$ **54.** {2} **55.** {8} **56.** {16} **57.** {32} **58.** {−2, −1, 1, 2} **59.** {16} **60.** {−4, 3} **61.** $\left\{-\frac{11}{2}, \frac{23}{2}\right\}$ **62.** $\left\{-1, -\frac{2\sqrt{6}}{9}, \frac{2\sqrt{6}}{9}, 1\right\}$ **63.** {2} **64.** {1, 4} **65.** {−3, −2, 3} **66.** 1250 ft **67.** $33\frac{1}{3}$ sec

**68.**

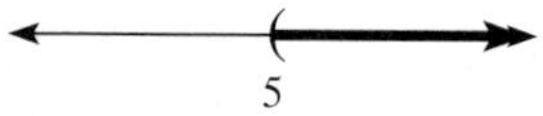


**69.**

**70.**

**71.** $-2 < x \le 3$

**72.** $-1.5 \le x \le 2$

**73.** $x > -1$

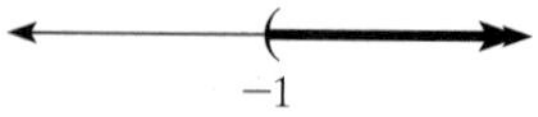


**74.** $[-2, \infty)$

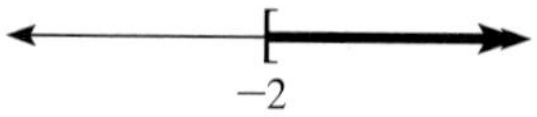


**75.** $\left[\frac{3}{5}, \infty\right)$

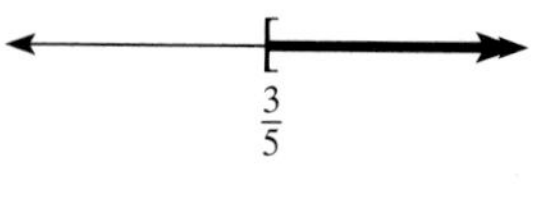


**76.** $\left(-\infty, -\frac{21}{2}\right)$

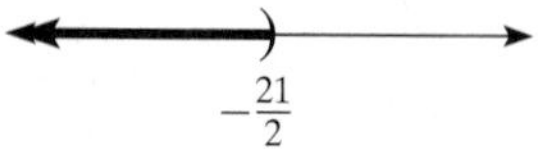


**77.** $(-3, \infty)$

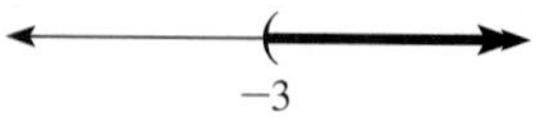


**78.** $(-\infty, -2]$

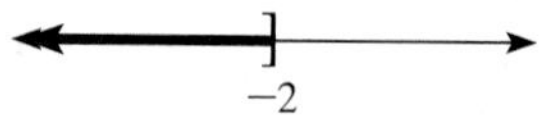


**79.** $(2, 3]$

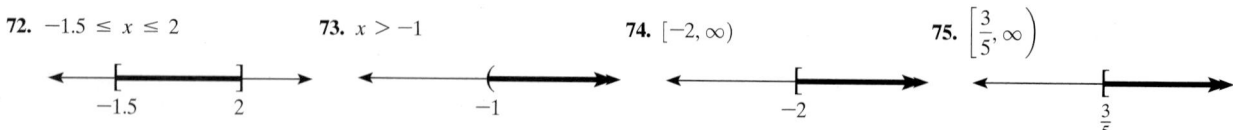

**80.** $[-9, 6]$

**81.** $(-\infty, -6)$ or $(0, \infty)$

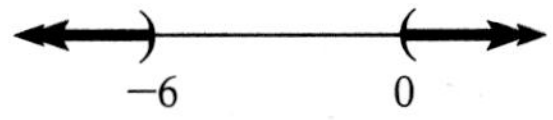


**82.** $(-\infty, -3]$ or $[-2, \infty)$

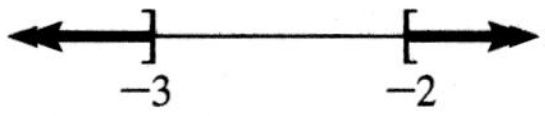


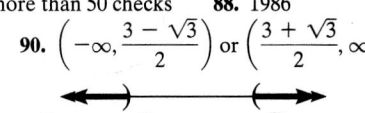

**83.** Canada, Former Soviet Union **84.** Australia, Canada, United States **85.** Most people sleep between 5.5 and 7.5 hours.
**86.** between 59° and 95° inclusively **87.** more than 50 checks **88.** 1986

**89.** $\left[-4, \frac{1}{2}\right]$

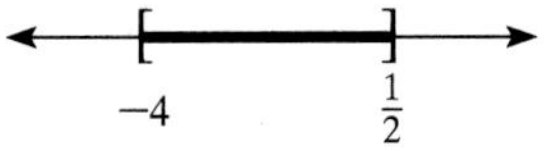


**90.** $\left(-\infty, \frac{3-\sqrt{3}}{2}\right)$ or $\left(\frac{3+\sqrt{3}}{2}, \infty\right)$

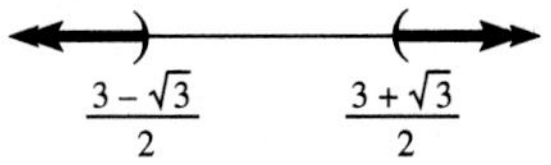


**91.** $(-\infty, -2)$ or $(6, \infty)$

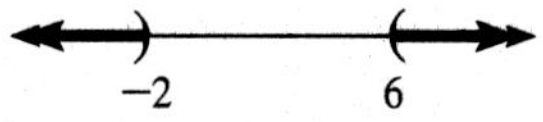


**92.** $(-\infty, 4)$ or $\left[\frac{23}{4}, \infty\right)$

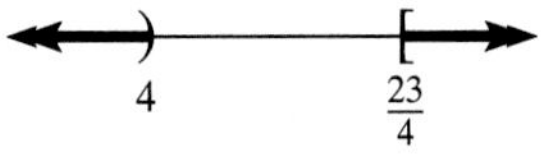


**93.** from 1 to 2 sec

## Chapter 1 Test

**1.** $\{-1\}$ **2.** $\{-6\}$ **3.** $\{5\}$ **4.** $\left\{-\frac{1}{2}, 2\right\}$ **5.** $\left\{\frac{1-5\sqrt{3}}{3}, \frac{1+5\sqrt{3}}{3}\right\}$ **6.** $\{1-\sqrt{5}, 1+\sqrt{5}\}$ **7.** $\left\{\frac{2-i}{2}, \frac{2+i}{2}\right\}$

**8.** $\{-1, 1, 4\}$ **9.** $\{7\}$ **10.** $\{5\}$ **11.** $\{\sqrt[3]{4}\}$ **12.** $\{1, 512\}$ **13.** $\{6, 12\}$

**14.** $(-\infty, 12]$

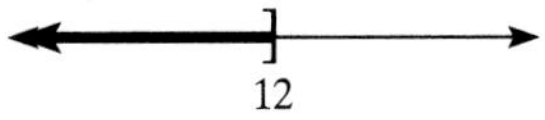


**15.** $\left[\frac{21}{8}, \infty\right)$

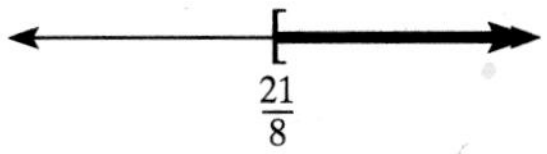


**16.** $\left[-7, \frac{13}{2}\right)$

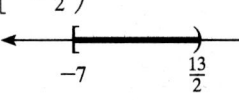

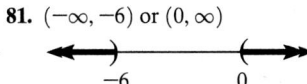

**17.** $\left(-\infty, -\frac{5}{3}\right]$ or $\left[\frac{1}{3}, \infty\right)$

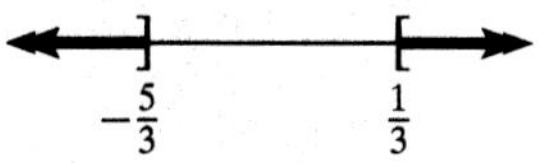


**18.** $(-3, 4)$

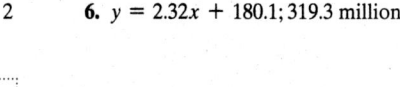

**19.** $(3, 10)$

**20. a.** $n = 125B - 50w$ **b.** 24,000 years!
**21.** 1986 **22.** 1997 **23.** $42,000
**24.** $4000 at 9%; $2000 at 6% **25.** 15 in. by 15 in.
**26.** 60 ml of 80%, 40 ml of 50% **27.** less than 100 hr

# CHAPTER 2

## Section 2.1

### Check Point Exercises

**1. a.** 6 **b.** $-\frac{7}{5}$ **2.** $y + 1 = -5(x + 2); y = -5x - 11$

**3.**

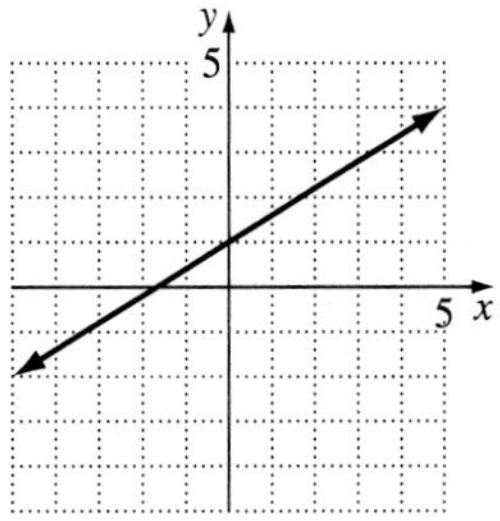


**4.**

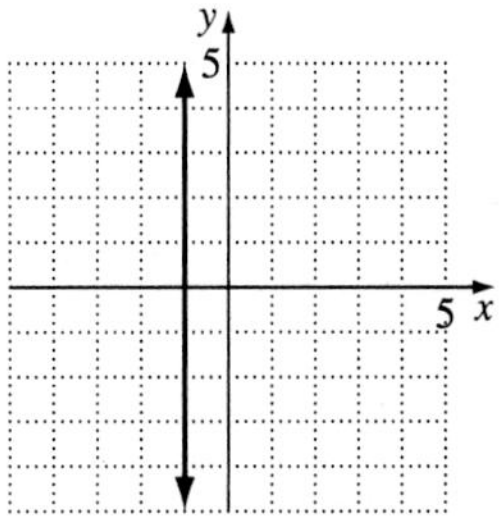


**5.** slope: $-\frac{1}{2}$; $y$-intercept: 2

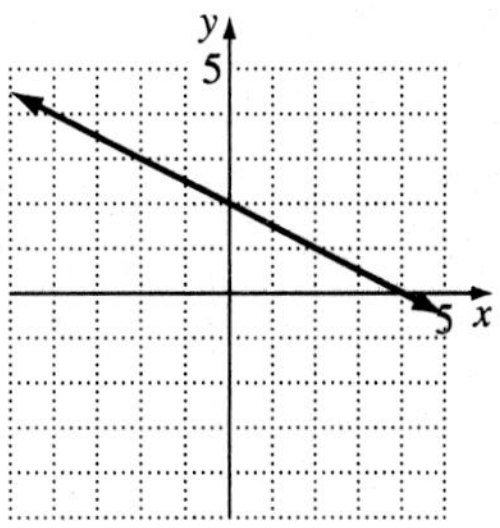


**6.** $y = 2.32x + 180.1$; 319.3 million

### Exercise Set 2.1

**1.** $\frac{3}{4}$; rises **3.** $\frac{1}{4}$; rises **5.** 0; horizontal **7.** −5; falls **9.** undefined; vertical **11.** $y - 5 = 2(x - 3); y = 2x - 1$

**13.** $y + 3 = -3(x + 2); y = -3x - 9$ **15.** $y - 0 = -4(x + 4); y = -4x - 16$ **17.** $y - 0 = \frac{1}{2}(x - 0); y = \frac{1}{2}x$

**19.** using $(1, 2)$, $y - 2 = 2(x - 1); y = 2x$ **21.** using $(-3, 0)$, $y - 0 = 1(x + 3); y = x + 3$
**23.** using $(-3, -1)$, $y + 1 = 1(x + 3); y = x + 2$ **25.** using $(-3, -1)$, $y + 1 = 0(x + 3); y = -1$
**27.** using $(2, 4)$, $y - 4 = 1(x - 2); y = x + 2$ **29.** using $(0, 4)$, $y - 4 = 8(x - 0); y = 8x + 4$

**31.** $m = 2; b = 1$

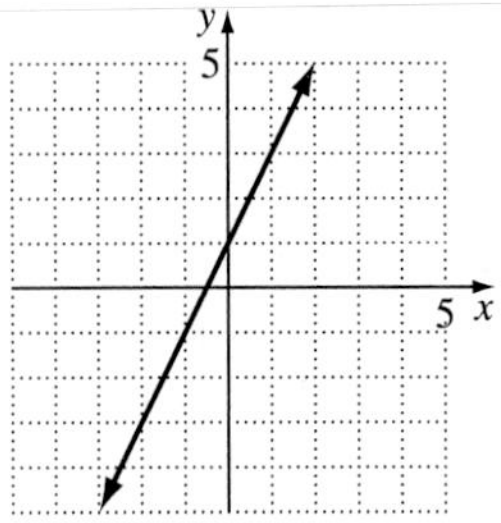


**33.** $m = -2; b = 1$

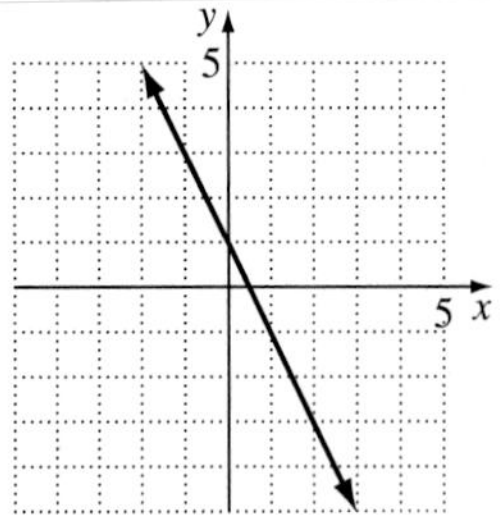


**35.** $m = \frac{3}{4}; b = -2$

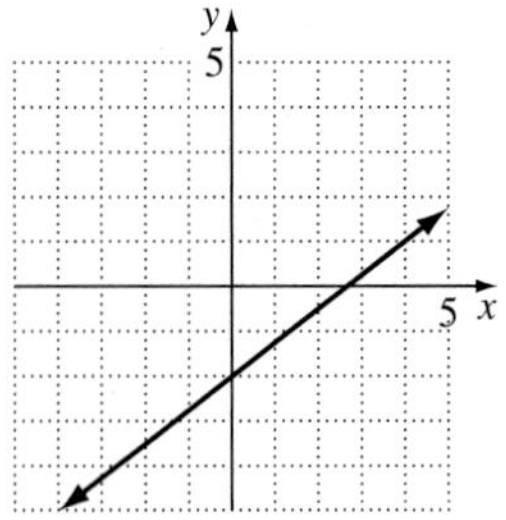


**37.** $m = -\frac{3}{5}; b = 7$

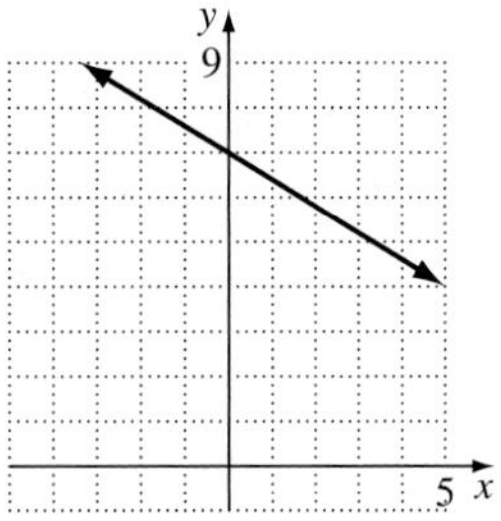


**39.**

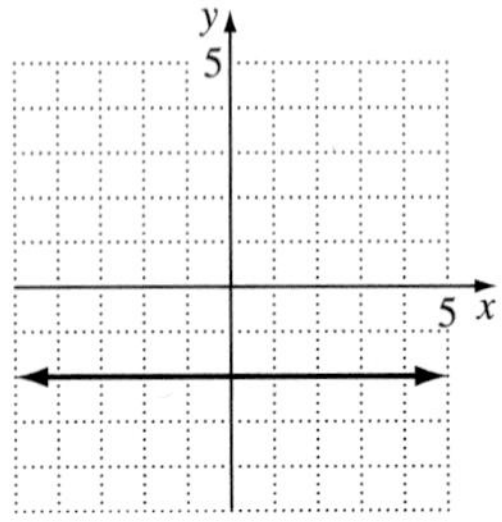


**41.**

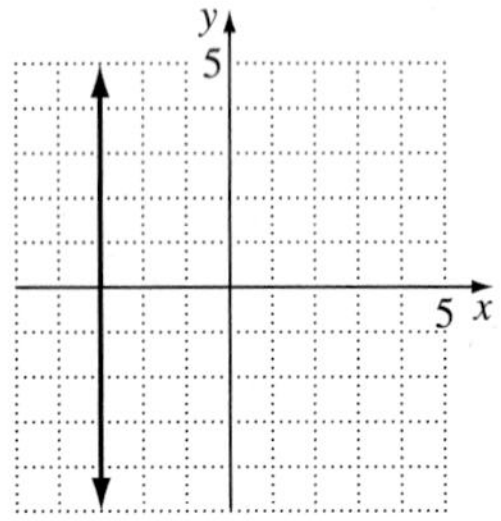


**43.**

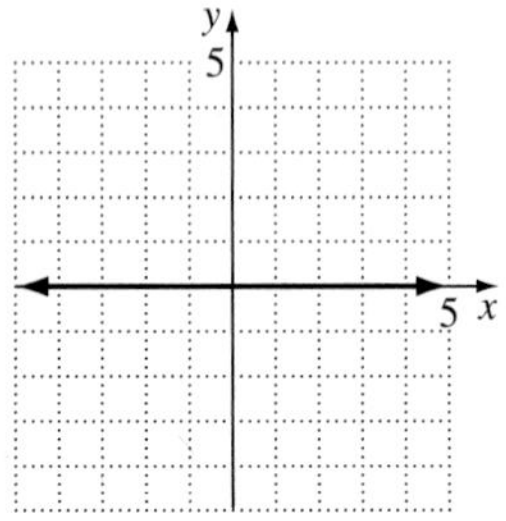


**45. a.** $y = -3x + 5$
**b.** $m = -3; b = 5$
**c.**

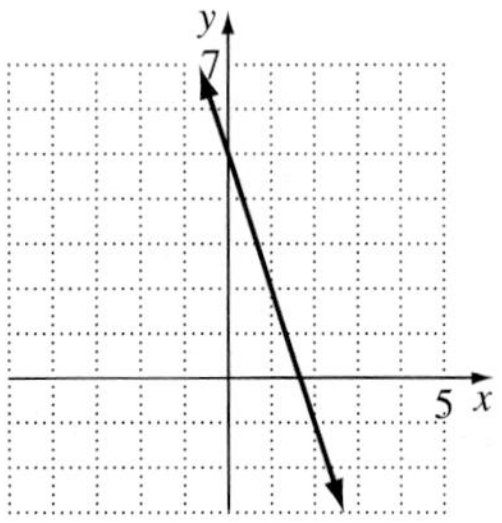


**47. a.** $y = -\frac{2}{3}x + 6$
**b.** $m = -\frac{2}{3}; b = 6$
**c.**

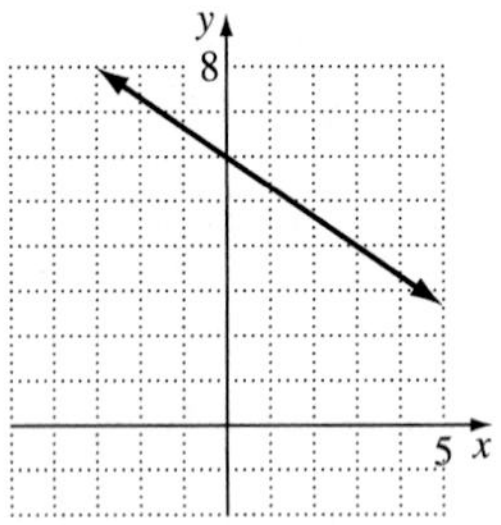


**49. a.** $y = 2x - 3$
**b.** $m = 2; b = -3$
**c.**

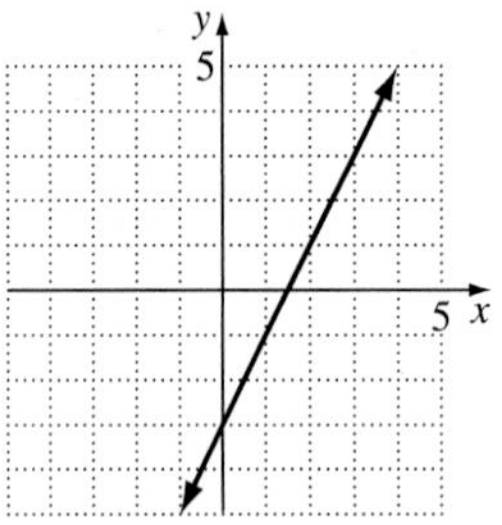


**51. a.** $x = 3$
**b.** $m$ is undefined; no $y$-intercept
**c.**

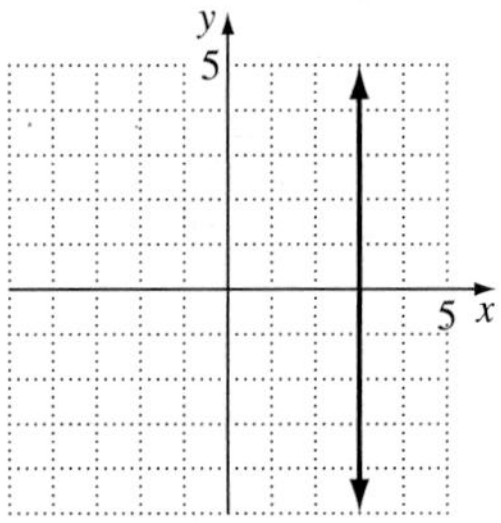


**53.** $y = 80$ **55.** In 2030, $y = 344$ million; In 2040; $y = 367.5$ million; In 2050, $y = 391$ million; The equation models the projections well, but is slightly lower than the projections. **57.** $y - 4459.2 = 258.625(x - 3)$; $y = 258.625x + 3683.325$; \$11,442.075 billion
**59.** $y = -0.002x + 59$; 4500 shirts **61.** Point-slope form: $y - 3 = -0.65(x - 12)$; Slope-intercept form: $y = -0.65x + 10.8$; about 6.25

**71.** $m = -3$

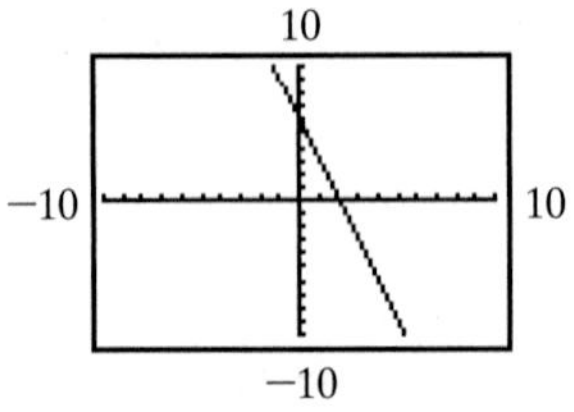


**73.** $m = \frac{3}{4}$

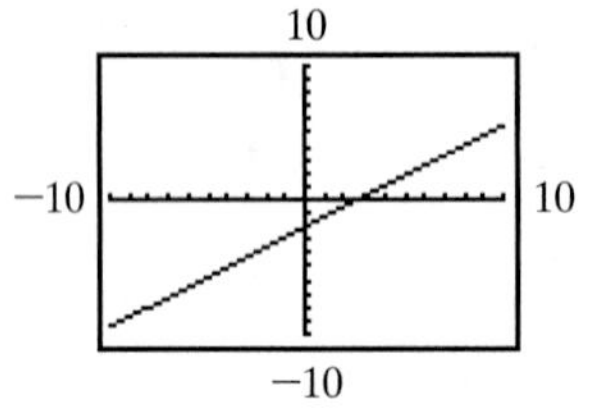


**75.** (c) is true.

**77. a.** $m_1, m_3, m_2, m_4$
**b.** $b_2, b_1, b_4, b_3$

## Section 2.2

### Check Point Exercises

**1.** $y - 5 = 3(x + 2)$; $y = 3x + 11$ **2.** 3 **3.** $x^2 + y^2 = 16$ **4.** $(x - 5)^2 + (y + 6)^2 = 100$

**5.** center: $(-3, 1)$; radius: 2

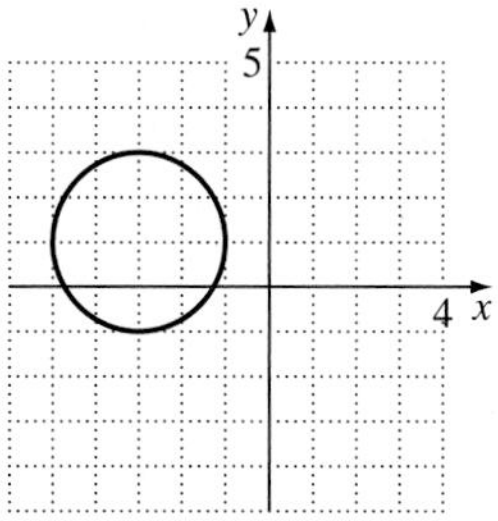


**6.** $(x + 2)^2 + (y - 2)^2 = 9$

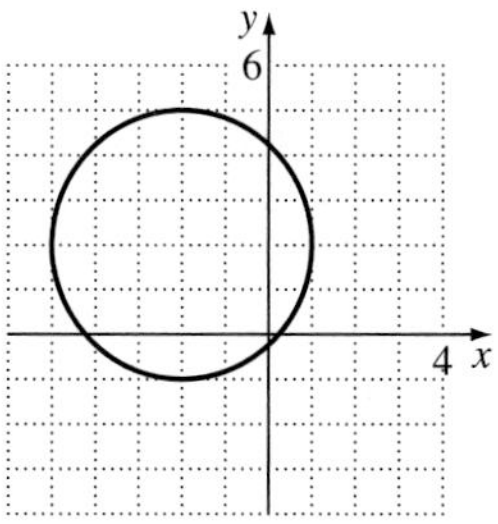


## Exercise Set 2.2

**1. a.** 5 **b.** $-\frac{1}{5}$ **3. a.** $-7$ **b.** $\frac{1}{7}$ **5. a.** $\frac{1}{2}$ **b.** $-2$ **7. a.** $-\frac{2}{5}$ **b.** $\frac{5}{2}$ **9. a.** $-4$ **b.** $\frac{1}{4}$ **11. a.** $-\frac{1}{2}$ **b.** 2

**13. a.** $\frac{2}{3}$ **b.** $-\frac{3}{2}$ **15. a.** undefined **b.** 0 **17.** $y - 2 = 2(x - 4)$; $y = 2x - 6$ **19.** $y - 4 = -\frac{1}{2}(x - 2)$; $y = -\frac{1}{2}x + 5$

**21.** $y + 10 = -4(x + 8)$; $y = -4x - 42$ **23.** $y + 3 = -5(x - 2)$; $y = -5x + 7$ **25.** $y - 2 = \frac{2}{3}(x + 2)$; $y = \frac{2}{3}x + \frac{10}{3}$

**27.** $y + 7 = -2(x - 4)$; $y = -2x + 1$ **29.** $x^2 + y^2 = 49$ **31.** $(x - 3)^2 + (y - 2)^2 = 25$ **33.** $(x + 1)^2 + (y - 4)^2 = 4$
**35.** $(x + 3)^2 + (y + 1)^2 = 3$ **37.** $(x + 4)^2 + (y - 0)^2 = 100$

**39.** center: $(0, 0)$
radius: 4

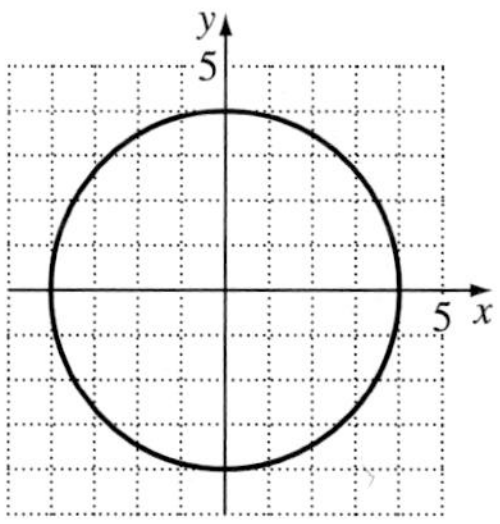


**41.** center: $(3, 1)$
radius: 6

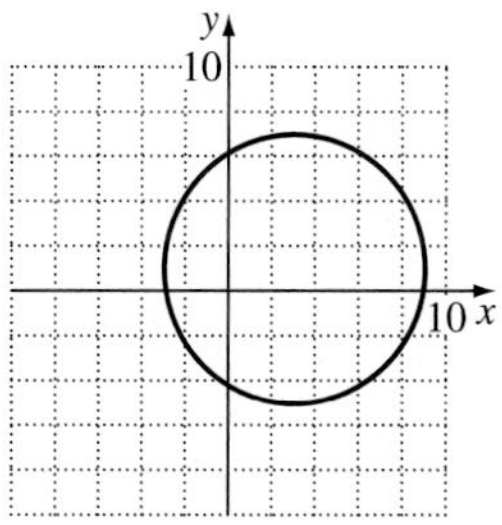


**43.** center: $(-3, 2)$
radius: 2

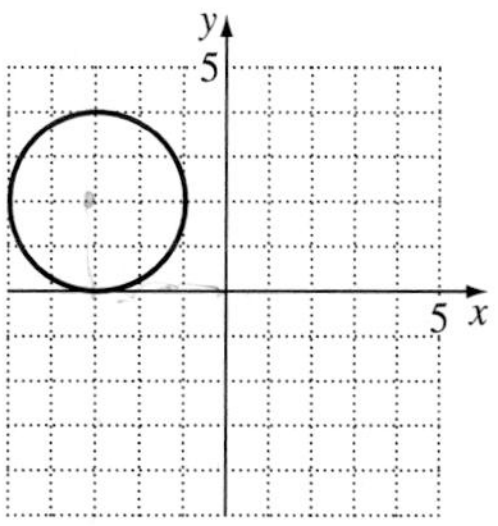


**45.** center: $(-2, -2)$
radius: 2

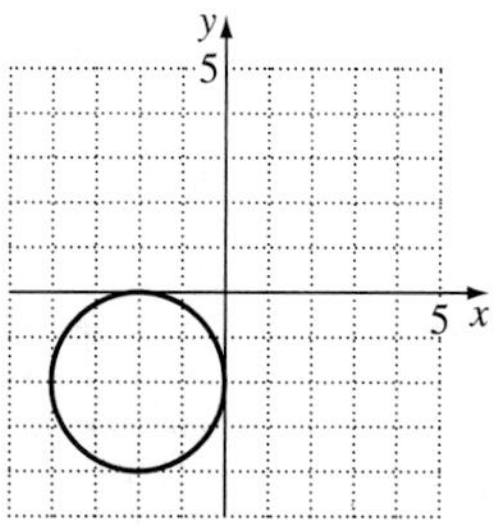


**47.** $(x + 3)^2 + (y + 1)^2 = 4$
center: $(-3, -1)$
radius: 2

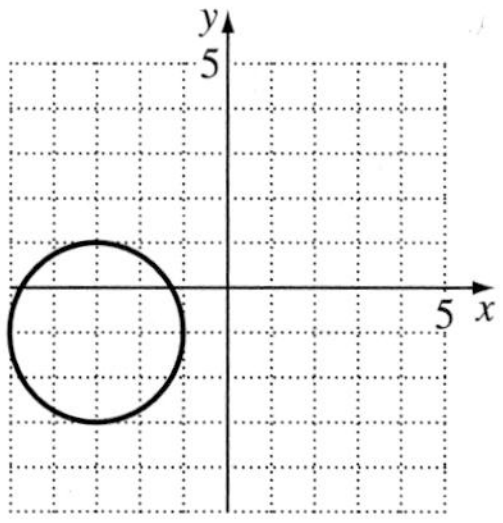


**49.** $(x - 5)^2 + (y - 3)^2 = 64$
center: $(5, 3)$
radius: 8

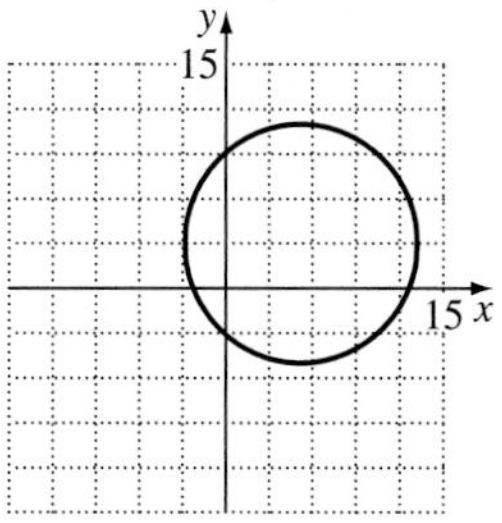


**51.** $(x + 4)^2 + (y - 1)^2 = 25$
center: $(-4, 1)$
radius: 5

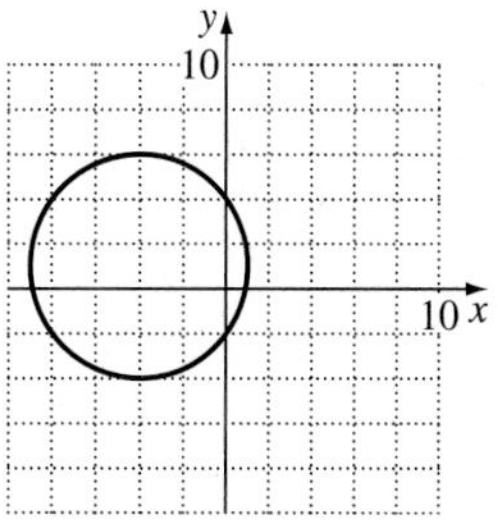


**53.** $(x - 1)^2 + (y - 0)^2 = 16$
center: $(1, 0)$
rradius: 4

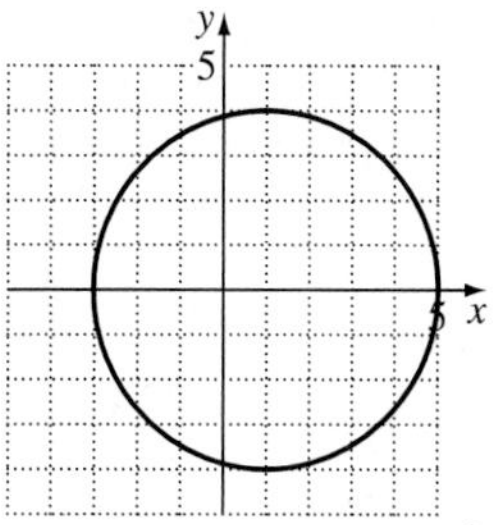


**55. a.** $\frac{1}{5}$ **b.** $\frac{2}{15}$ **c.** no; The yearly increase for women is greater than the yearly increase for men.

**57. a.** $x^2 + y^2 \geq 1444$ **b.** $x^2 + y^2 \leq 2704$

**69.**

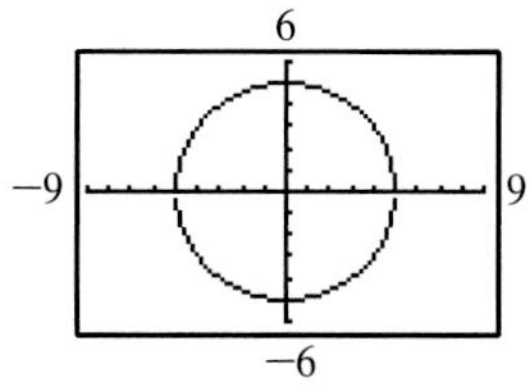


**71.**

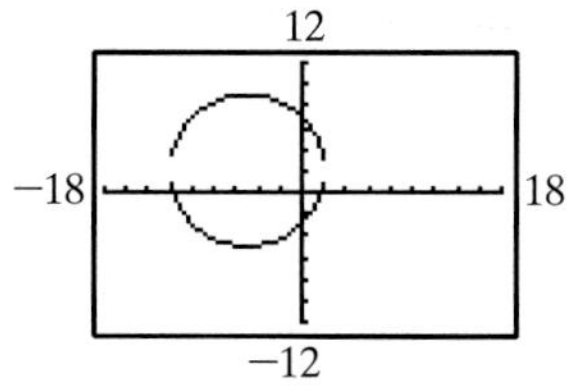


**73.** $y - 0 = 3(x + 3)$ or $y = 3x + 9$
**75.** $(x - 3)^2 + (y + 5)^2 = 61$;
$x^2 + y^2 - 6x + 10y - 27 = 0$
**77.** $11\pi$

## Section 2.3

### Check Point Exercises

**1.** domain: $\{20, 30, 100, 200\}$; range: $\{157.4, 231.8, 752.6, 1496.6\}$ **2. a.** not a function **b.** function **3. a.** $y = 6 - 2x$; function **b.** $y = \pm\sqrt{1 - x^2}$; not a function **4. a.** 42 **b.** $x^2 + 6x + 15$ **c.** $x^2 + 2x + 7$ **5. a.** $x^2 + 2hx - 7x + h^2 - 7h + 3$ **b.** $2x + h - 7$ **6. a.** 28 **b.** 33 **7. a.** $(-\infty, \infty)$ **b.** $\{x|x \neq -7, x \neq 7\}$ **c.** $[3, \infty)$

### Exercise Set 2.3

**1.** function; $\{1, 3, 5\}$; $\{2, 4, 5\}$ **3.** not a function; $\{3, 4\}$; $\{4, 5\}$ **5.** function; $\{-3, -2, -1, 0\}$; $\{-3, -2, -1, 0\}$ **7.** not a function; $\{1\}$; $\{4, 5, 6\}$ **9.** $y$ is a function of $x$. **11.** $y$ is a function of $x$. **13.** $y$ is not a function of $x$. **15.** $y$ is not a function of $x$. **17.** $y$ is a function of $x$. **19.** $y$ is a function of $x$. **21. a.** 29 **b.** $4x + 9$ **c.** $-4x + 5$ **23. a.** 2 **b.** $x^2 + 12x + 38$ **c.** $x^2 - 2x + 3$ **25. a.** 13 **b.** 1 **c.** $x^4 - x^2 + 1$ **d.** $81a^4 - 9a^2 + 1$ **27. a.** 3 **b.** 7 **c.** $\sqrt{x} + 3$ **29. a.** $\frac{15}{4}$ **b.** $\frac{15}{4}$ **c.** $\frac{4x^2 - 1}{x^2}$ **31. a.** 1 **b.** $-1$ **c.** 1 **33.** 3 **35.** $2x + h$ **37.** $2x + h - 4$ **39.** 0 **41.** $-\frac{1}{x(x + h)}$ **43.** $\frac{1}{\sqrt{x + h} + \sqrt{x}}$ **45. a.** $-1$ **b.** 7 **c.** 19 **47. a.** 3 **b.** 3 **c.** 0 **49. a.** 8 **b.** 3 **c.** 6 **51.** $(-\infty, \infty)$
**53.** $(-\infty, 4)$ or $(4, \infty)$ **55.** $(-\infty, -4)$ or $(-4, 4)$ or $(4, \infty)$ **57.** $(-\infty, -3)$ or $(-3, 7)$ or $(7, \infty)$
**59.** $(-\infty, -8)$ or $(-8, -3)$ or $(-3, \infty)$ **61.** $(-\infty, \infty)$ **63.** $[3, \infty)$ **65.** $(3, \infty)$ **67.** $[-7, \infty)$ **69.** $(-\infty, 12]$
**71.** $(-\infty, -2]$ or $[7, \infty)$ **73.** Answers may vary.
**75.** $f(16) = 5.22$; There were 5.22 million women enrolled in United States colleges in the year 2000.
**77.** $f(20) - g(20) = 1.4$; There will be 1.4 million more women than men enrolled in United States colleges in the year 2004.
**79.** $f(0) = 200$; There were 200 thousand lawyers in the United States in 1951.
**81.** $f(50) = 1058$; There will be 1058 thousand or 1,058,000 lawyers in the United States in the year 2001.
**83.** $f(0) = 7$ represents the point $(0, 7)$ on the graph. It means that an average infant girl weighs 7 pounds at birth.; $f(2) = 10$ represents the point $(2, 10)$ on the graph. It means that an average infant girl weighs 10 pounds at age 2 months.; $f(4) = 13$ represents the point $(4, 13)$ on the graph. It means that an average infant girl weighs 13 pounds at age 4 months.; $f(6) = 16$ represents the point $(6, 16)$ on the graph. It means that an average infant girl weighs 16 pounds at age 6 months.
**85.** $f(10) = 3375.97$; In 1984, 3375.97 calories per person were consumed each day in the United States.
**87.** $f(15) - f(10) = 101.6$; Between 1984 and 1989, the number of calories per person consumed each day in the United States increased by 101.6.
**89. a.** $f(15) = 9.3$; In 1955, an average of 9.3 thousand miles were driven per car in the United States each year.
**b.** $f(50) = 10.7$; In 1990, an average of 10.7 thousand miles were driven per car in the United States each year.
**91.** $V = 17{,}900 - 2100x$; $V(4) = 9500$; The value of the car after 4 years is \$9500. **101.** $(-3, \infty]$
**103.** Answers may vary. **105.** Answers may vary.

## Section 2.4

### Check Point Exercises

**1.** $(-3, 7), (-2, 2), (-1, -1), (0, -2), (1, -1), (2, 2), (3, 7)$

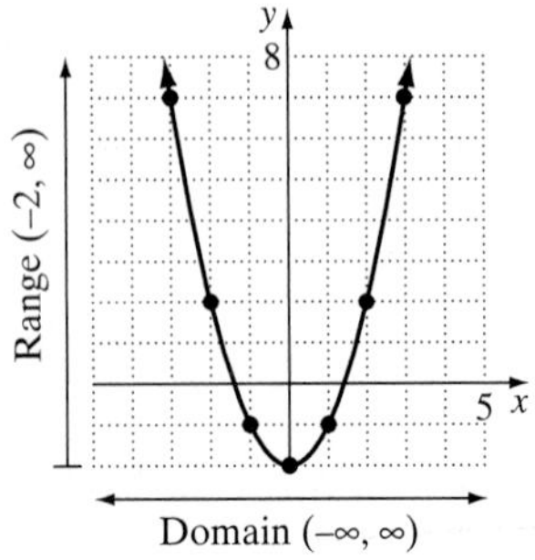


**2.** $f(4) = 1$; domain: $[0, 6)$; range: $(-2, 2]$
**3. a.** function **b.** function **c.** not a function
**4.** increasing on $(-\infty, -1)$, decreasing on $(-1, 1)$, increasing on $(1, \infty)$
**5. a.** 1 **b.** 7 **c.** 4
**6. a.** 12 ft/sec **b.** 10 ft/sec **c.** 8.04 ft/sec
**7. a.** even **b.** odd **c.** neither
**8. a.** $(0, 3)$; Drug concentration increases during the first three hours after an injection.
**b.** $(3, 13)$; Drug concentration decreases between the third and thirteenth hours after an injection.
**c.** 0.05 milligrams per 100 milliliters at 3 hours
**d.** By the end of the 13 hours, there is no more of the drug in the body.

## Exercise Set 2.4

**1.** $(-3, 11), (-2, 6), (-1, 3), (0, 2), (1, 3), (2, 6), (3, 11)$

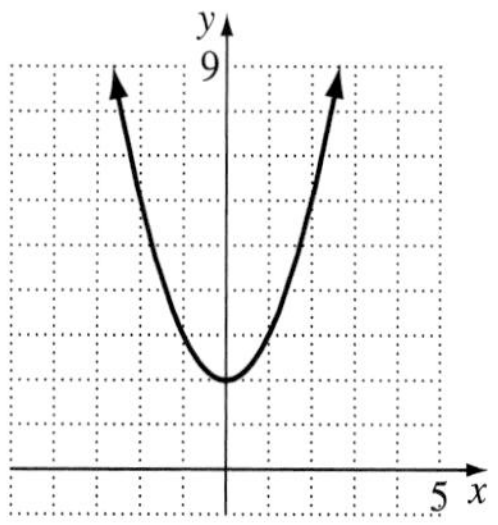

Domain: $(-\infty, \infty)$
Range: $[2, \infty)$

**3.** $(0, -1), (1, 0), (4, 1), (9, 2)$

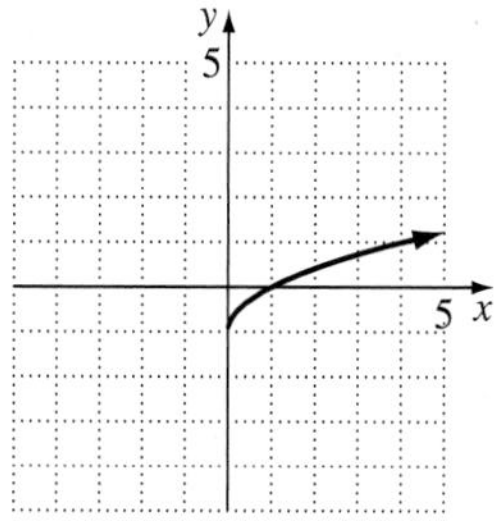

Domain: $[0, \infty)$
Range: $[-1, \infty)$

**5.** $(1, 0), (2, 1), (5, 2), (10, 3)$

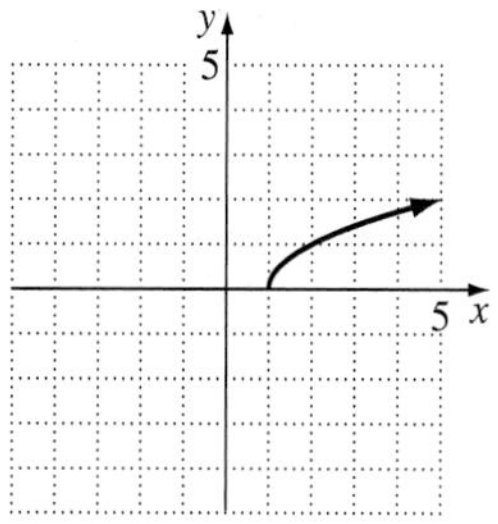

Domain: $[1, \infty)$
Range: $[0, \infty)$

**7.** $(-3, 2), (-2, 1), (-1, 0), (0, -1), (1, 0), (2, 1), (3, 2)$

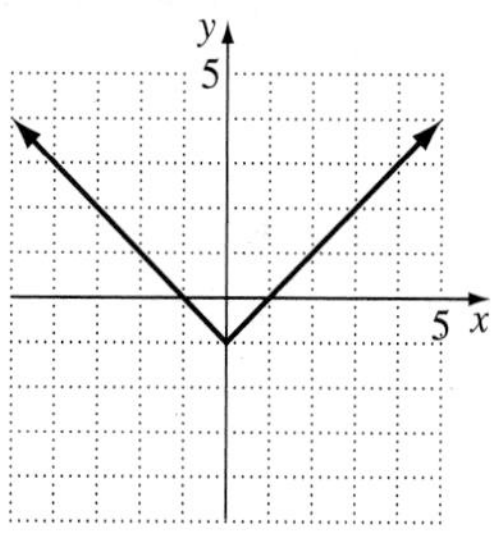

Domain: $(-\infty, \infty)$
Range: $[-1, \infty)$

**9.** $(-3, 4), (-2, 3), (-1, 2), (0, 1), (1, 0), (2, 1), (3, 2)$

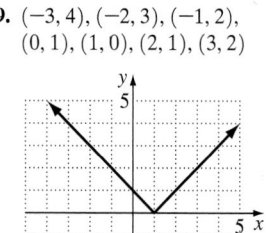

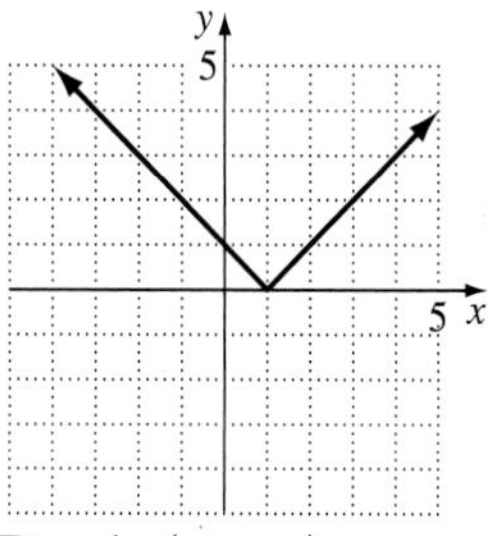

Domain: $(-\infty, \infty)$
Range: $[0, \infty)$

**11.** $(-3, 5), (-2, 5), (-1, 5), (0, 5), (1, 5), (2, 5), (3, 5)$

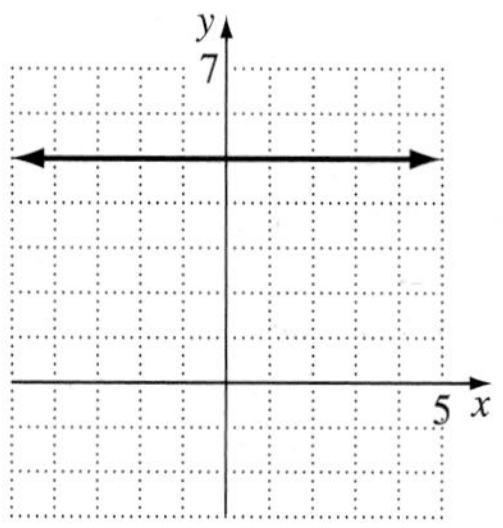

Domain: $(-\infty, \infty)$
Range: $\{5\}$

**13.** $(-2, -10), (-1, -3), (0, -2), (1, -1), (2, 6)$

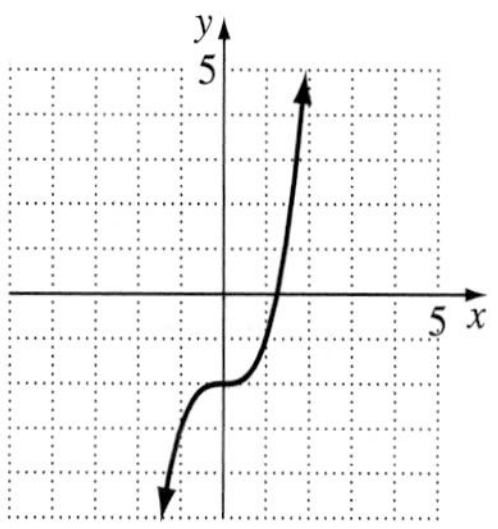

Domain: $(-\infty, \infty)$
Range: $(-\infty, \infty)$

**15. a.** $(-\infty, \infty)$ **b.** $[-4, \infty)$ **c.** $-3$ and $1$ **d.** $-3$
**17. a.** $(-\infty, \infty)$ **b.** $[1, \infty)$ **c.** none **d.** 1 **e.** $f(-1) = 2$ and $f(3) = 4$
**19. a.** $[0, 5)$ **b.** $[-1, 5)$ **c.** 2 **d.** $-1$ **e.** $f(3) = 1$

**21. a.** $[0, \infty)$ **b.** $[1, \infty)$ **c.** none **d.** 1 **e.** $f(4) = 3$ **23. a.** $[-2, 6]$ **b.** $[-2, 6]$ **c.** 4 **d.** 4 **e.** $f(-1) = 5$ **25. a.** $(-\infty, \infty)$ **b.** $(-\infty, -2]$ **c.** none **d.** $-2$ **e.** $f(-4) = -5$ and $f(4) = -2$ **27. a.** $(-\infty, \infty)$ **b.** $(0, \infty)$ **c.** none **d.** 1 **29. a.** $\{-5, -2, 0, 1, 3\}$ **b.** $\{2\}$ **c.** none **d.** 2 **31.** function **33.** function **35.** not a function **37.** function **39. a.** increasing: $(-1, \infty)$ **b.** decreasing: $(-\infty, -1)$ **c.** constant: none **41. a.** increasing: $(0, \infty)$ **b.** decreasing: none **c.** constant: none **43. a.** increasing: none **b.** decreasing: $(-2, 6)$ **c.** constant: none **45. a.** increasing: $(-\infty, -1)$ **b.** decreasing: none **c.** constant: $(-1, \infty)$ **47. a.** increasing: $(-\infty, 0)$ or $(1.5, 3)$ **b.** decreasing: $(0, 1.5)$ or $(3, \infty)$ **c.** constant: none **49. a.** increasing: $(-2, 4)$ **b.** decreasing: none **c.** constant: $(-\infty, -2)$ or $(4, \infty)$ **51.** 3 **53.** 10 **55.** $\frac{1}{5}$ **57. a.** 70 ft/sec **b.** 65 ft/sec **c.** 60.1 ft/sec **d.** 60.01 ft/sec **59.** odd **61.** neither **63.** even **65.** even **67.** even **69.** odd **71.** even **73.** odd **75.** $f(1.06) = 1$ **77.** $f\left(\frac{1}{3}\right) = 0$ **79.** $f(-2.3) = -3$

**81.** $f(1989) \approx 294$ billion dollars. This is the maximum function value.
**83.** Defense spending is increasing from 1988 to 1989, from 1991 to 1992, and from 1996 to 1997.
**85. a.** increasing: $(45, 74)$; decreasing: $(16, 45)$; The number of accidents occurring per 50 million miles driven increases with age starting at age 45, while it decreases with age starting at age 16.
**b.** $x = 45$ and $f(45) = 190$; The fewest number of accidents per 50 million miles driven occurs at age 45.
**c.** $[190, 526.4]$; Between the ages of 16 and 74, the number of accidents per 50 million miles driven is between 190 and 526.4.
**87. a.** 54 ft/sec **b.** –58 ft/sec **89. a.** 0.0225 mg per 100 ml/hr; The drug concentration is increasing.
**b.** $-0.005$ mg per 100 ml/hr; The drug concentration is decreasing.

**91.**

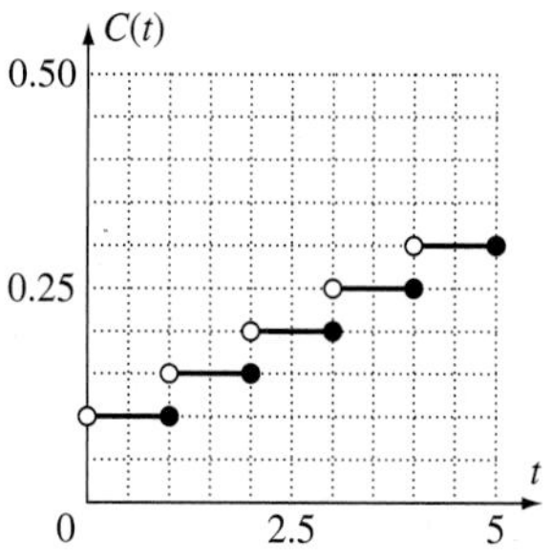


**103. a.**

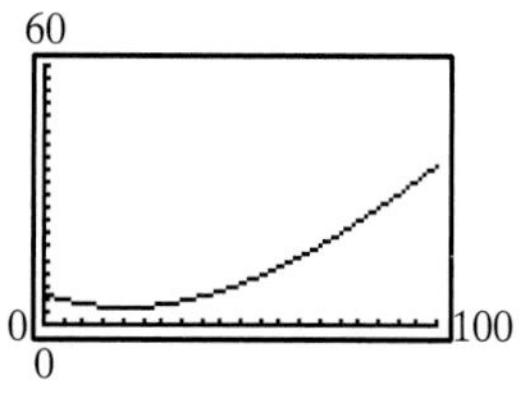


**b.** The number of doctor visits decreases during childhood and then increases as you get older.
**c.** The minimum is $(20.29, 3.99)$, which means that the minimum number of doctor visits, about 4, occurs at around age 20.

**105.**

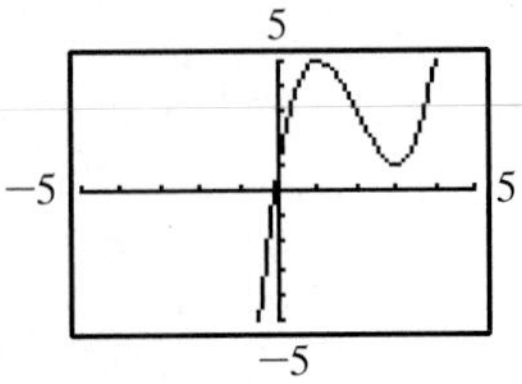


Increasing: $(-\infty, 1)$ or $(3, \infty)$
Decreasing: $(1, 3)$

**107.**

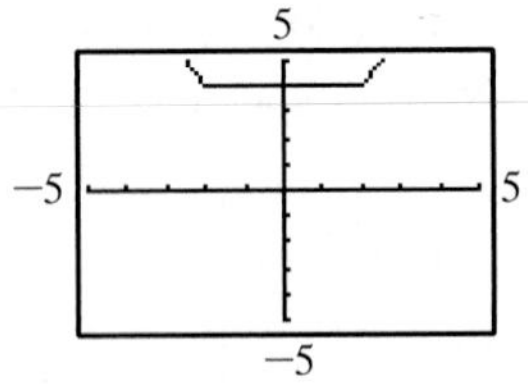


Increasing: $(2, \infty)$
Decreasing: $(-\infty, -2)$
Constant: $(-2, 2)$

**109.**

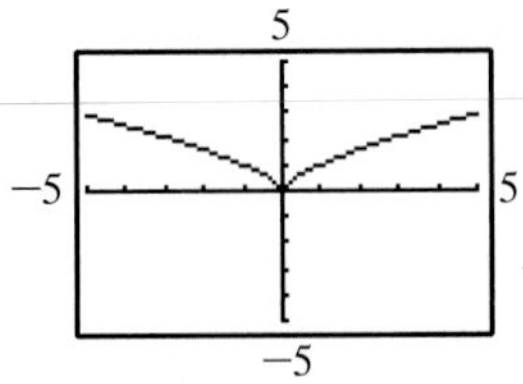


Increasing: $(0, \infty)$
Decreasing: $(-\infty, 0)$

**111. a.**

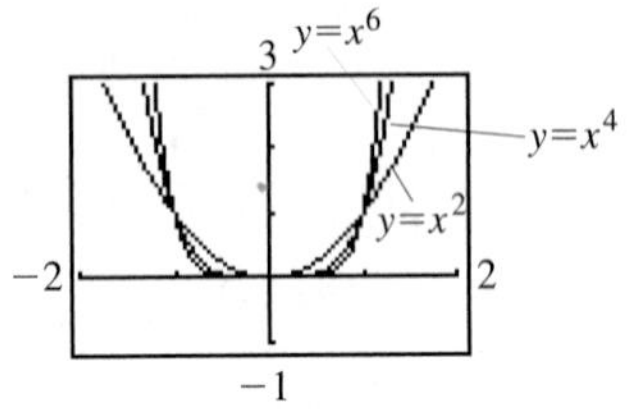


**b.**

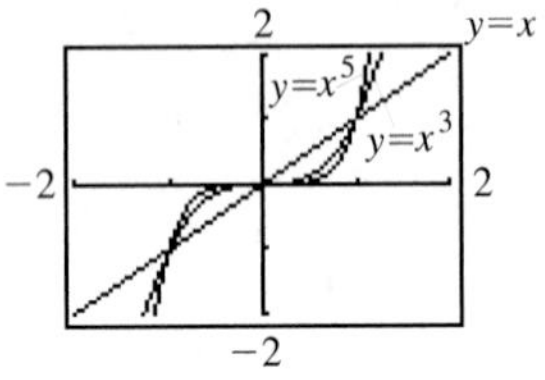


**c.** Increasing: $(0, \infty)$; Decreasing: $(-\infty, 0)$

**d.** $f(x) = x^n$ is increasing from $(-\infty, \infty)$ when $n$ is odd.

**e.**

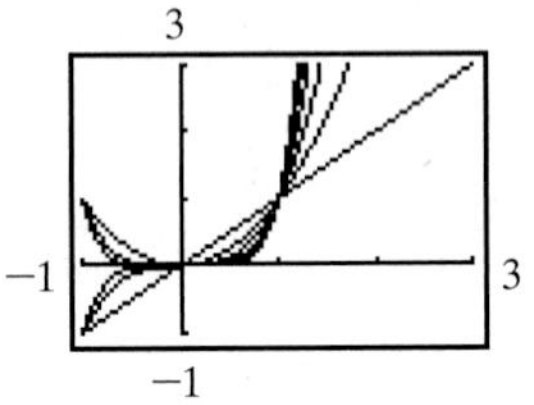


As $n$ increases the steepness increases.

**113.** Answers may vary. **115.** $\dfrac{s(3 + \Delta t) - s(3)}{(3 + \Delta t) - (3)} = \dfrac{10(3 + \Delta t)^2 - 10(3)^2}{3 + \Delta t - 3} = \dfrac{90 + 60\Delta t + 10(\Delta t)^2 - 90}{\Delta t} = \dfrac{\Delta t(60 + 10\Delta t)}{\Delta t}$
$= 60 + 10\Delta t$; 60 ft/sec; As $x_2$ decreases to 3, the average velocity decreases to 60 ft/sec.

**117.**

| Weight Less Than | Cost |
|---|---|
| 1 ounce | \$0.33 |
| 2 ounces | \$0.55 |
| 3 ounces | \$0.77 |
| 4 ounces | \$0.99 |
| 5 ounces | \$1.21 |

## Section 2.5

### Check Point Exercises

**1.**

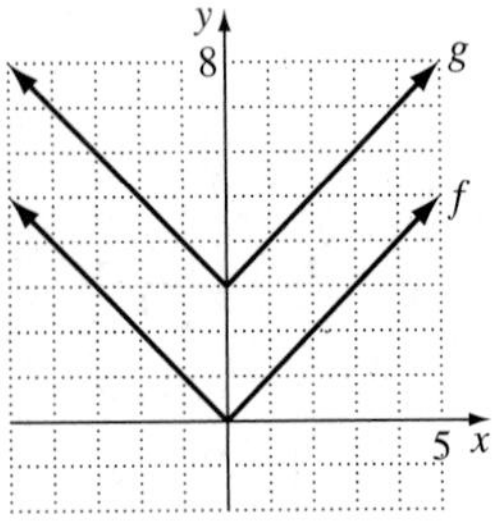


**2.**

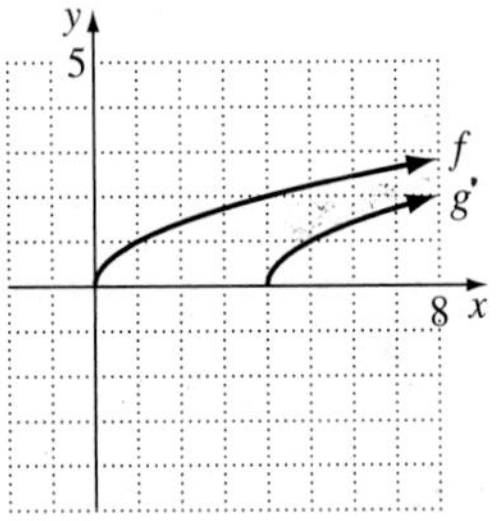


**3.**

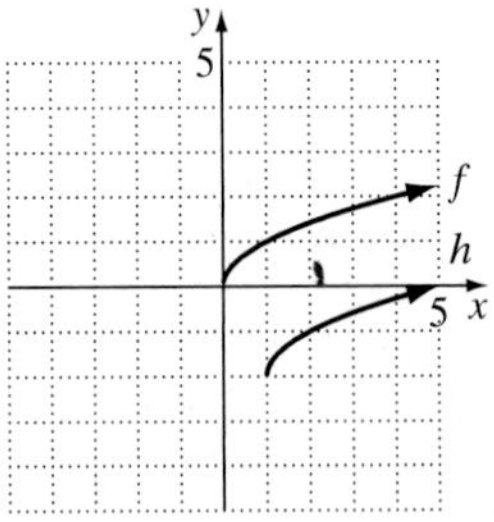


**4.**

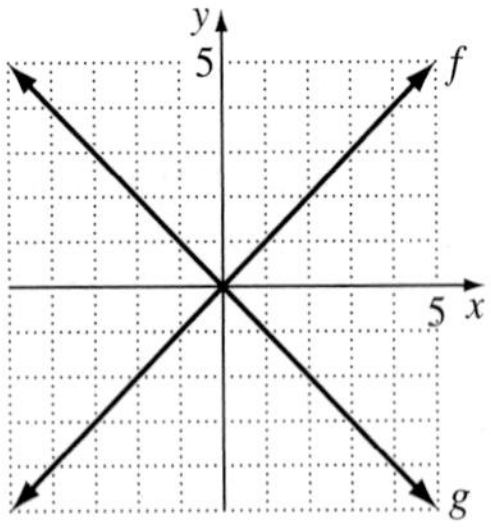


**5.**

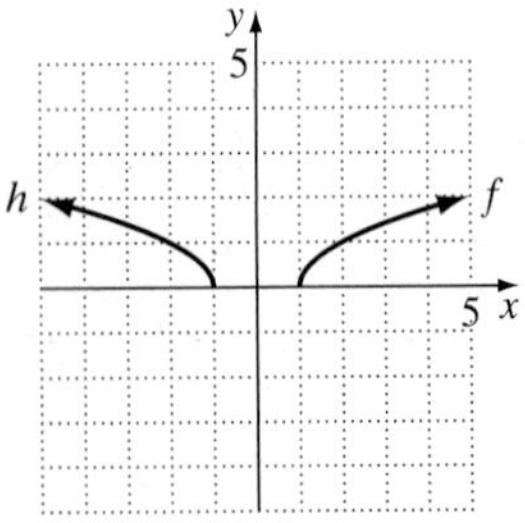


**6.**

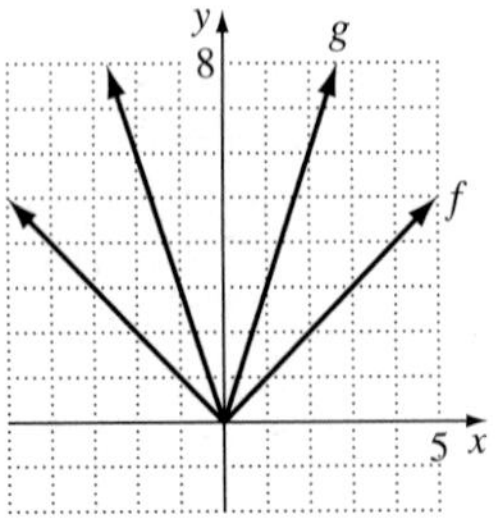


**7.**

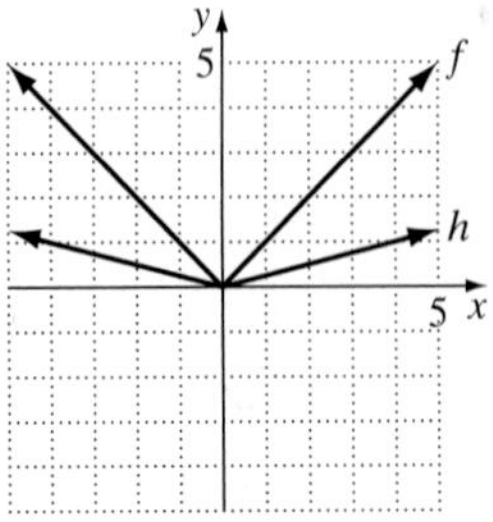


**8.**

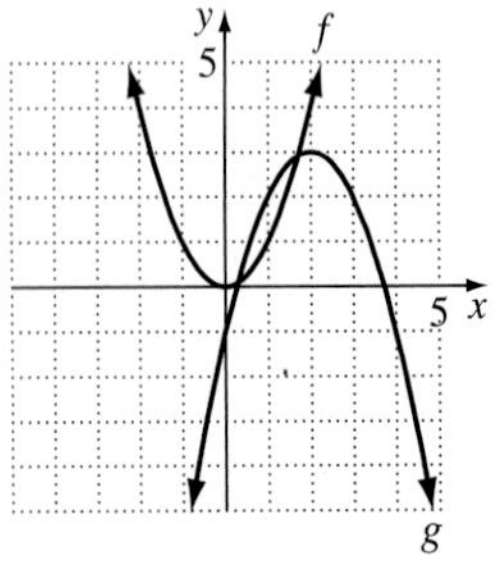

**9. a.** $(f + g)(x) = 3x^2 + 6x + 6$ **b.** $(f + g)(4) = 78$ **10. a.** $(f + g)(x) = \sqrt{x - 3} + \sqrt{x + 1}$ **b.** $[3, \infty)$
**11. a.** $(f - g)(x) = -x^2 + x - 4$ **b.** $(fg)(x) = x^3 - 5x^2 - x + 5$ **c.** $\left(\frac{f}{g}\right)(x) = \frac{x - 5}{x^2 - 1}, x \neq \pm 1$

## Exercise Set 2.5

**1.**
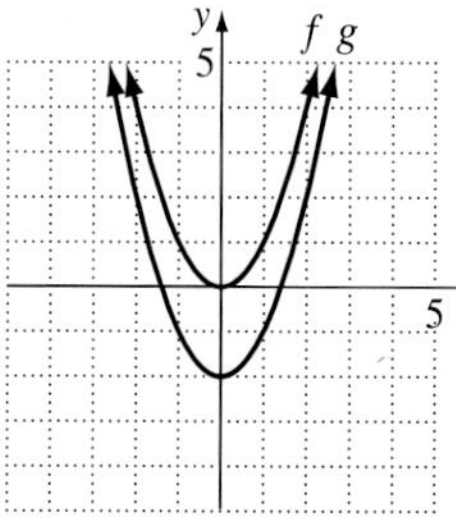


**3.**
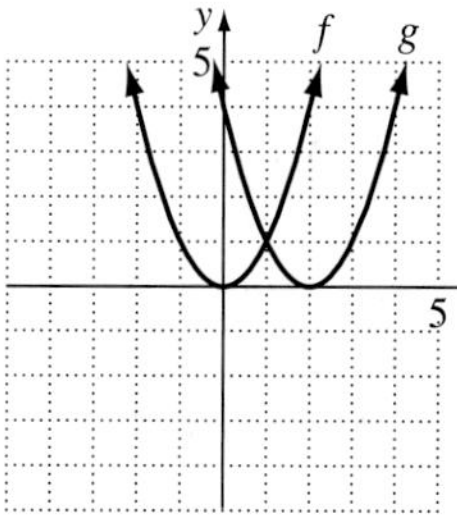


**5.**
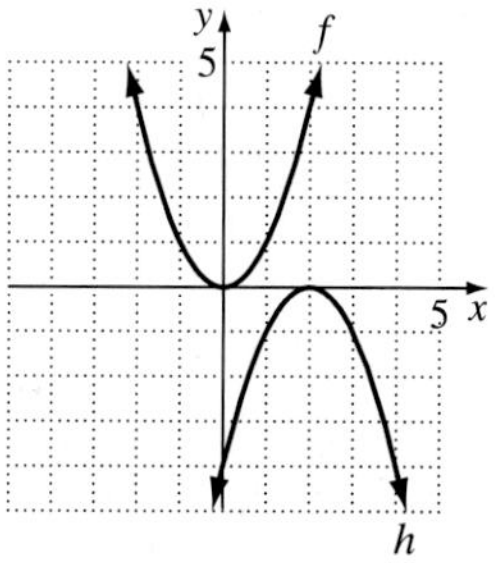


**7.**
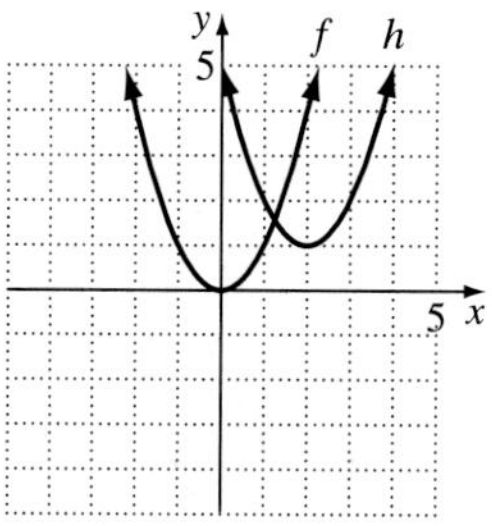


**9.**
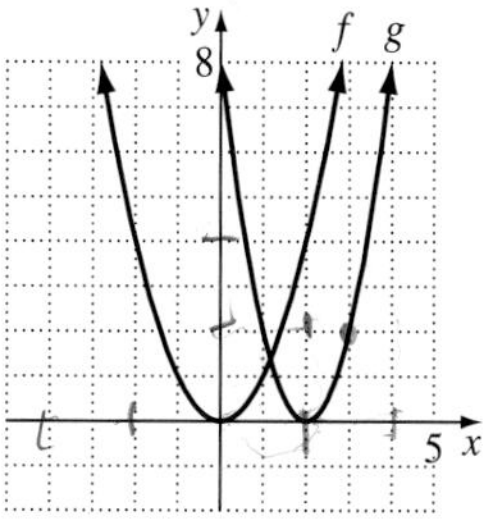


**11.**
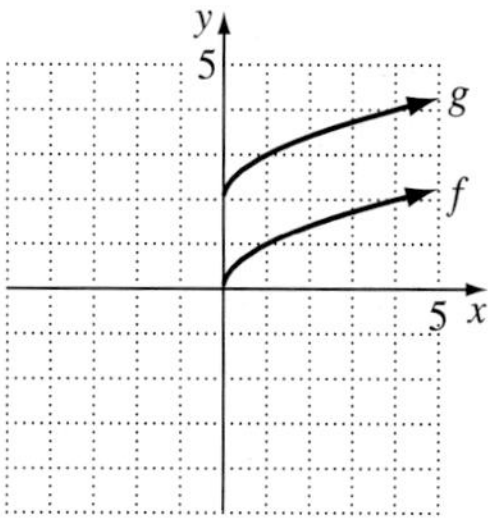


**13.**
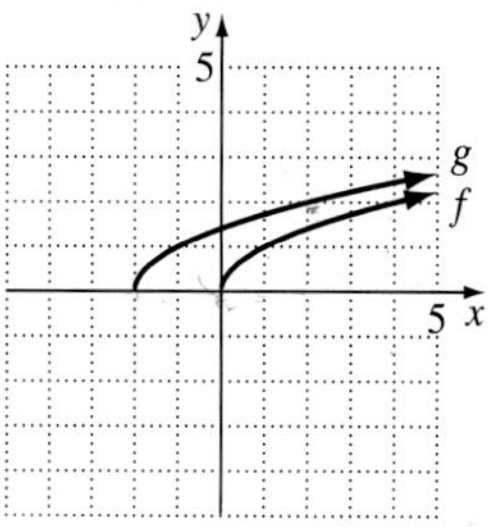


**15.**
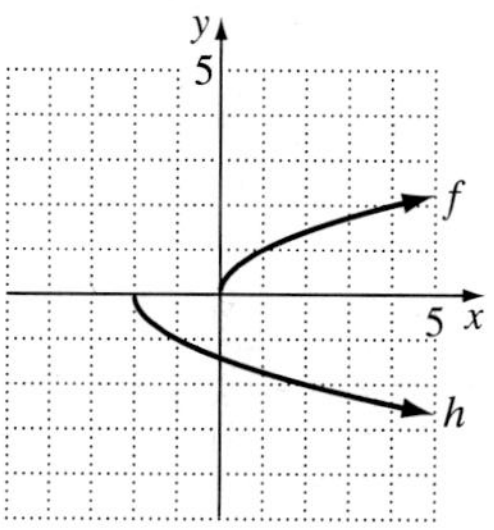


**17.**
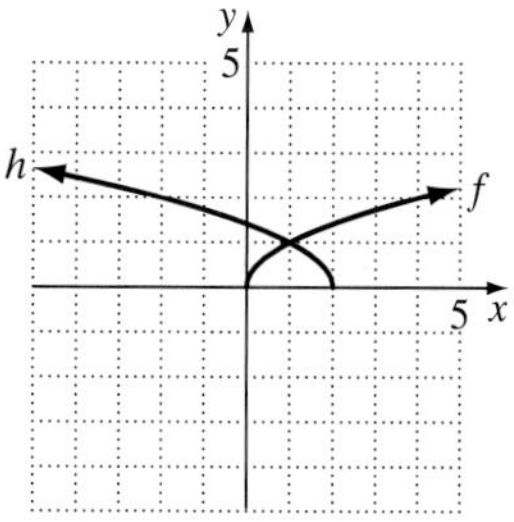


**19.**
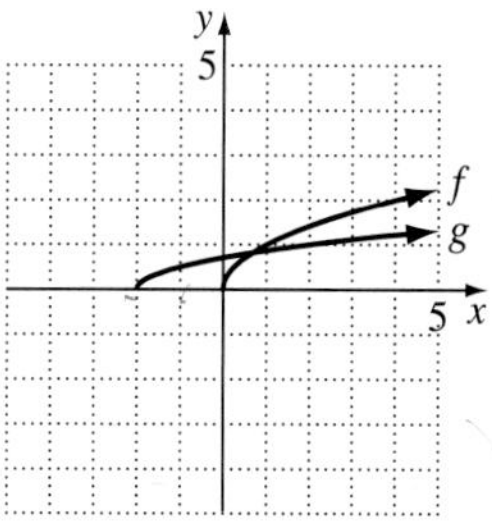


**21.**
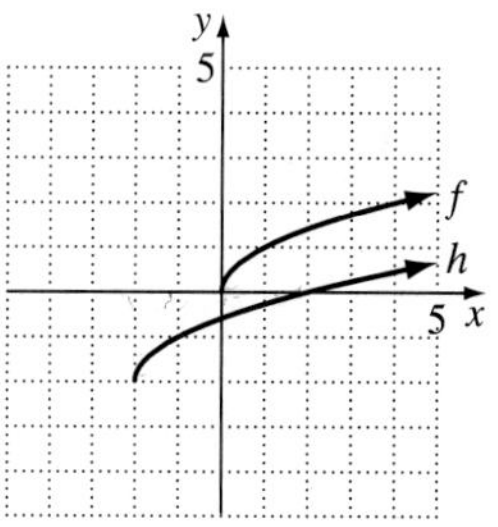


**23.**
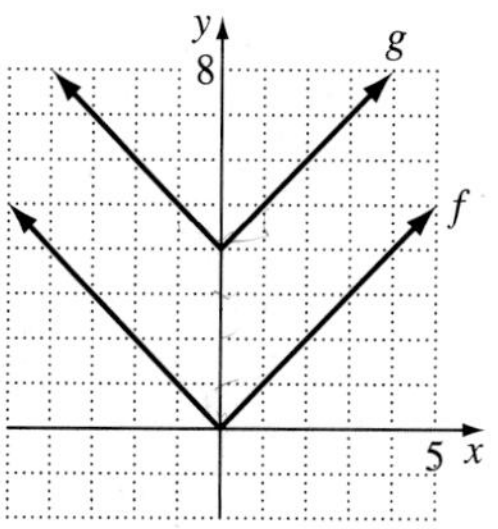


**25.**
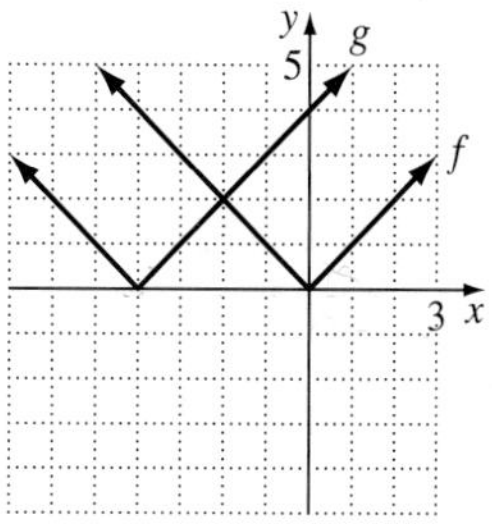


**27.**
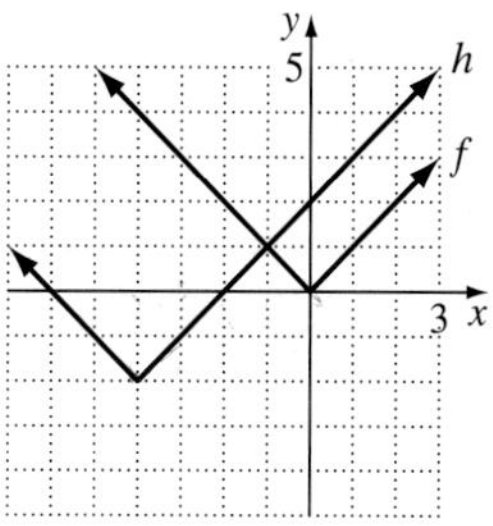


**29.**
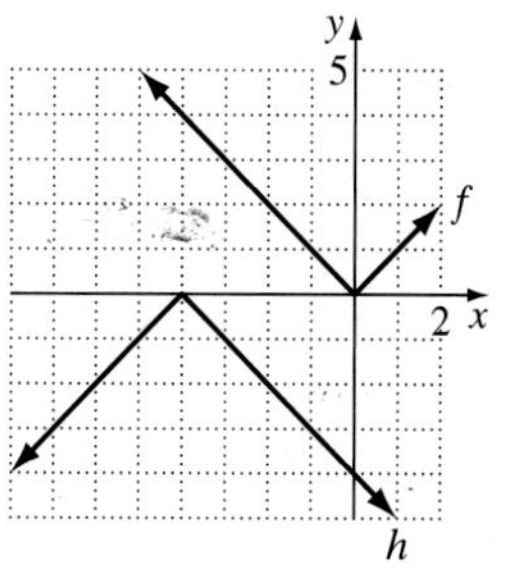


**31.**
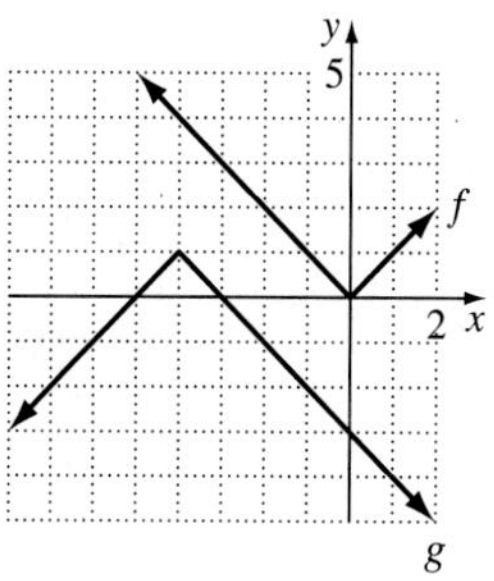


**33.**
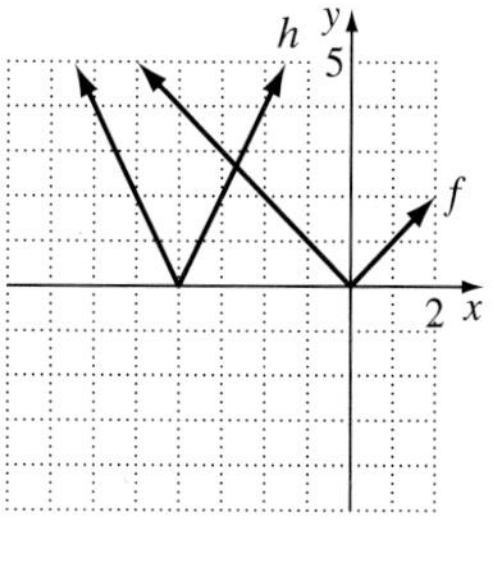


**35.**
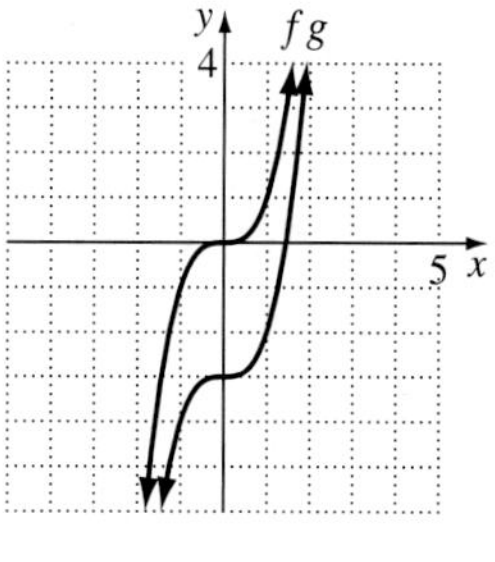


**37.**
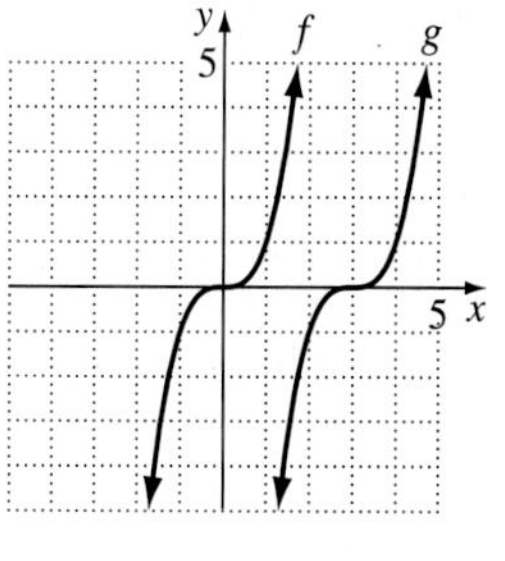


**39.**
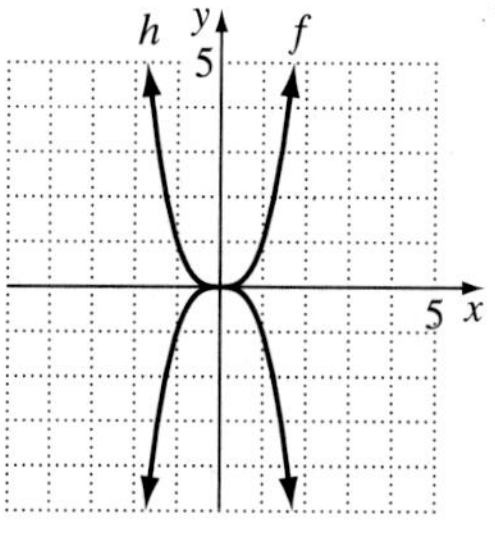

**41.**

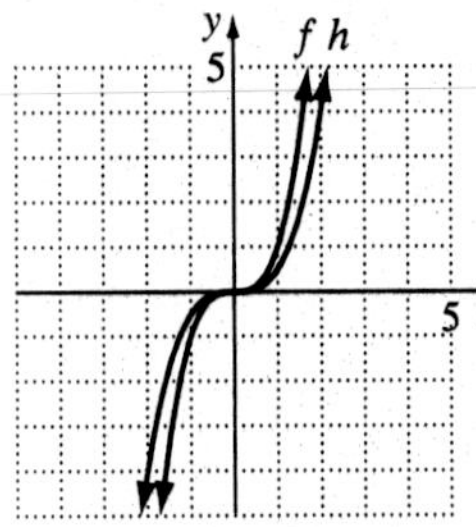


**43.**

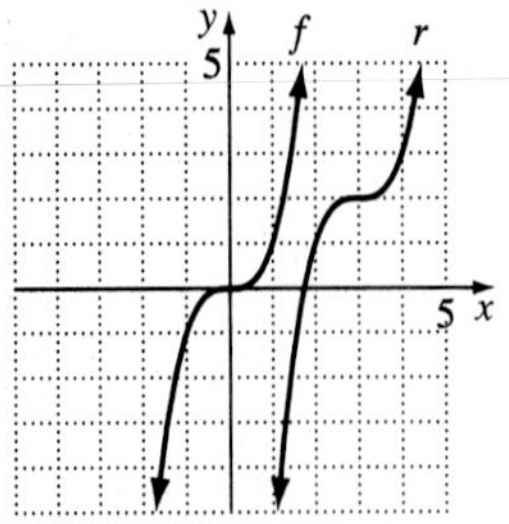


**45.**

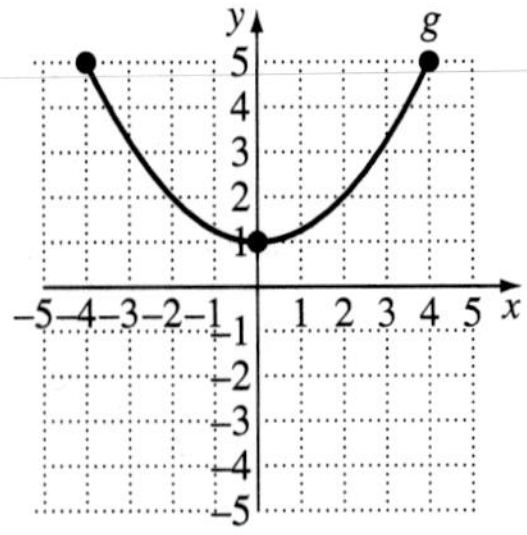


**47.**

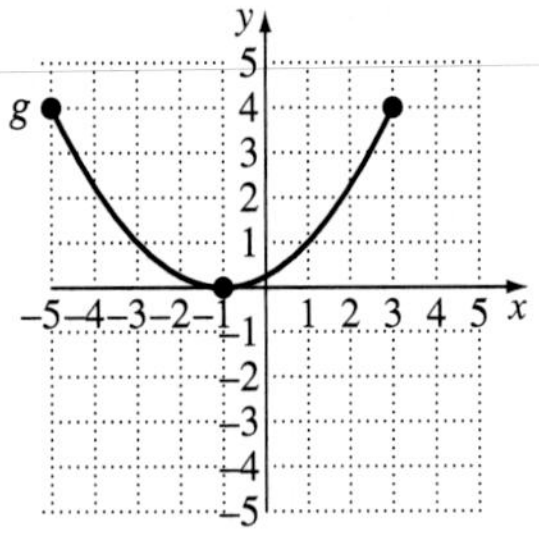


**49.**

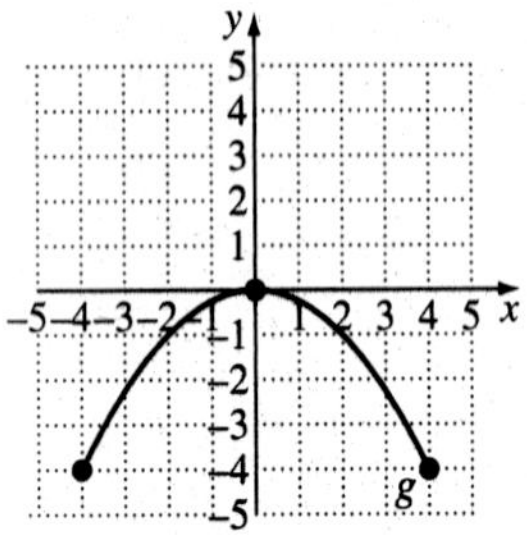


**51.**

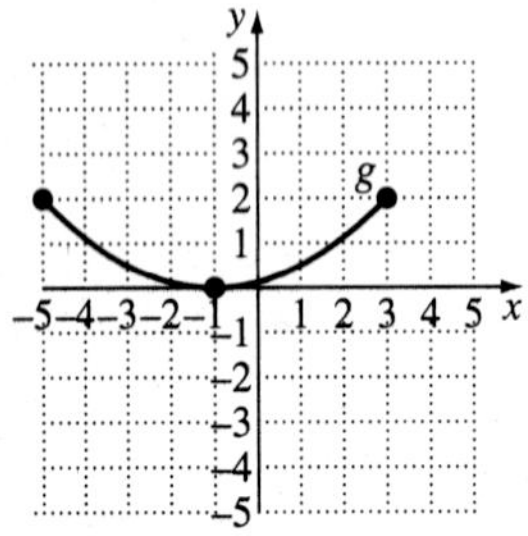


**53. a.** $(f + g)(x) = 2x^2 + 3x + 2$ **b.** $(f + g)(4) = 46$
**55. a.** $(f + g)(x) = \sqrt{x - 6} + \sqrt{x + 2}$ **b.** Domain: $[6, \infty)$
**57.** $(f + g)(x) = 3x + 2$; Domain: $(-\infty, \infty)$; $(f - g)(x) = x + 4$; Domain: $(-\infty, \infty)$; $(fg)(x) = 2x^2 + x - 3$; Domain: $(-\infty, \infty)$; $\left(\frac{f}{g}\right)(x) = \frac{2x + 3}{x - 1}$; Domain: $(-\infty, 1)$ or $(1, \infty)$
**59.** $(f + g)(x) = 3x^2 + x - 5$; Domain: $(-\infty, \infty)$; $(f - g)(x) = -3x^2 + x - 5$; Domain: $(-\infty, \infty)$; $(fg)(x) = 3x^3 - 15x^2$; Domain: $(-\infty, \infty)$; $\left(\frac{f}{g}\right)(x) = \frac{x - 5}{3x^2}$; Domain: $(-\infty, 0)$ or $(0, \infty)$
**61.** $(f + g)(x) = 2x^2 - 2$; Domain: $(-\infty, \infty)$; $(f - g)(x) = 2x^2 - 2x - 4$; Domain: $(-\infty, \infty)$; $(fg)(x) = 2x^3 + x^2 - 4x - 3$; Domain: $(-\infty, \infty)$; $\left(\frac{f}{g}\right)(x) = 2x - 3$; Domain: $(-\infty, -1)$ or $(-1, \infty)$ **63.** $(f + g)(x) = \sqrt{x} + x - 4$; Domain: $[0, \infty)$; $(f - g)(x) = \sqrt{x} - x + 4$; Domain: $[0, \infty)$; $(fg)(x) = \sqrt{x}(x - 4)$; Domain: $[0, \infty)$; $\left(\frac{f}{g}\right)(x) = \frac{\sqrt{x}}{x - 4}$; Domain: $[0, 4)$ or $(4, \infty)$
**65.** $(f + g)(x) = \frac{2x + 2}{x}$; Domain: $(-\infty, 0)$ or $(0, \infty)$; $(f - g)(x) = 2$; Domain: $(-\infty, 0)$ or $(0, \infty)$; $(fg)(x) = \frac{2x + 1}{x^2}$; Domain: $(-\infty, 0)$ or $(0, \infty)$; $\left(\frac{f}{g}\right)(x) = 2x + 1$; Domain: $(-\infty, 0)$ or $(0, \infty)$ **67.** $(f + g)(x) = \sqrt{x + 4} + \sqrt{x - 1}$; Domain: $[1, \infty)$; $(f - g)(x) = \sqrt{x + 4} - \sqrt{x - 1}$; Domain: $[1, \infty)$; $(fg)(x) = \sqrt{x^2 + 3x - 4}$; Domain: $[1, \infty)$; $\left(\frac{f}{g}\right)(x) = \frac{\sqrt{x + 4}}{\sqrt{x - 1}}$; Domain: $(1, \infty)$
**69.** total world population in year $x$ or $h(x)$ **71.** $\approx$ 5.8 billion people
**73.** $(R - C)(20{,}000) = -200{,}000$; The company lost \$200,000 since costs exceeded revenues; $(R - C)(30{,}000) = 0$; The company broke even since revenues equaled cost; $(R - C)(40{,}000) = 200{,}000$; The company made a profit of \$200,000.

**75.**

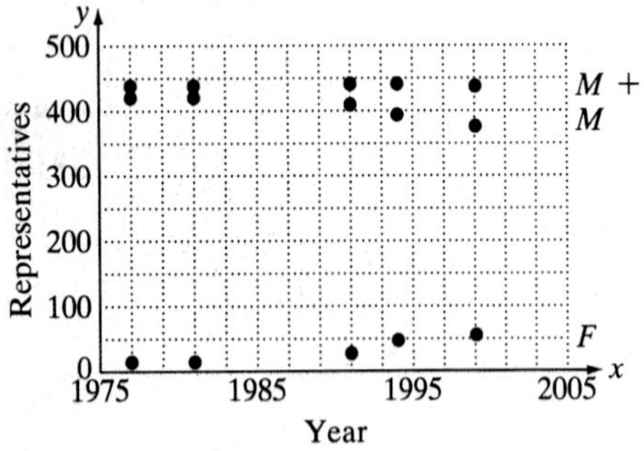


$f(x) = 435$

**85. a.**

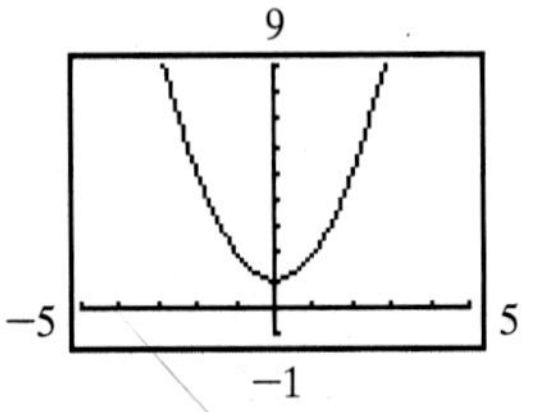


**b.**

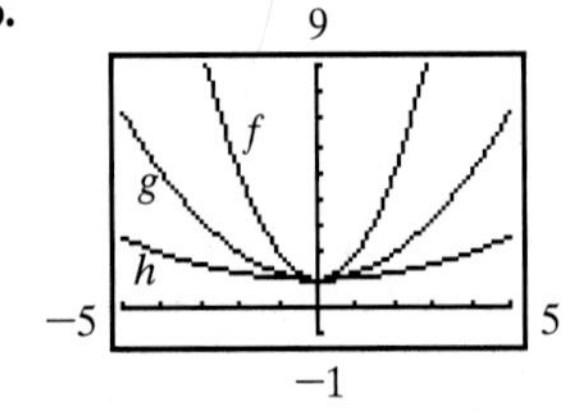


**c.** Answers may vary. **d.** Answers may vary. **e.** Answers may vary.

**87.** $g(x) = -(x + 4)^2$ **89.** $g(x) = -\sqrt{x - 2} + 2$ **91.** $(-a, b)$
**93.** $(a + 3, b)$

## Section 2.6

### Check Point Exercises

**1. a.** $(f \circ g)(x) = 5x^2 + 1$ **b.** $(g \circ f)(x) = 25x^2 + 60x + 35$ **2.** $f(x) = \sqrt{x}$; $g(x) = x^2 + 5$, $(f \circ g)(x) = h(x)$
**3.** $f(g(x)) = x$; $g(f(x)) = x$; $f$ and $g$ are inverses. **4.** $f^{-1}(x) = \frac{x - 7}{2}$ **5.** $f^{-1}(x) = \sqrt[3]{\frac{x + 1}{4}}$

**6.** (b) and (c) have inverse functions. **7.**

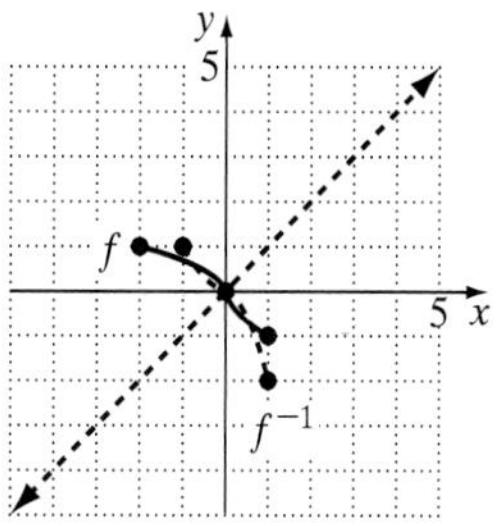


## Exercise Set 2.6

**1. a.** $(f \circ g)(x) = 2x + 14$ **b.** $(g \circ f)(x) = 2x + 7$ **c.** $(f \circ g)(2) = 18$ **3. a.** $(f \circ g)(x) = 2x + 5$ **b.** $(g \circ f)(x) = 2x + 9$ **c.** $(f \circ g)(2) = 9$ **5. a.** $(f \circ g)(x) = 20x^2 - 11$ **b.** $(g \circ f)(x) = 80x^2 - 120x + 43$ **c.** $(f \circ g)(2) = 69$ **7. a.** $(f \circ g)(x) = x^4 - 4x^2 + 6$ **b.** $(g \circ f)(x) = x^4 + 4x^2 + 2$ **c.** $(f \circ g)(2) = 6$ **9. a.** $(f \circ g)(x) = \sqrt{x - 1}$ **b.** $(g \circ f)(x) = \sqrt{x} - 1$ **c.** $(f \circ g)(2) = 1$ **11. a.** $(f \circ g)(x) = x$ **b.** $(g \circ f)(x) = x$ **c.** $(f \circ g)(2) = 2$ **13. a.** $(f \circ g)(x) = x$ **b.** $(g \circ f)(x) = x$ **c.** $(f \circ g)(2) = 2$ **15.** $f(x) = x^4, g(x) = 3x - 1$ **17.** $f(x) = \sqrt[3]{x}, g(x) = x^2 - 9$ **19.** $f(x) = |x|, g(x) = 2x - 5$ **21.** $f(x) = \frac{1}{x}, g(x) = 2x - 3$ **23.** $f(g(x)) = x; g(f(x)) = x$; $f$ and $g$ are inverses. **25.** $f(g(x)) = x; g(f(x)) = x$; $f$ and $g$ are inverses. **27.** $f(g(x)) = \frac{5x - 56}{9}; g(f(x)) = \frac{5x - 4}{9}$; $f$ and $g$ are not inverses. **29.** $f(g(x)) = x; g(f(x)) = x$; $f$ and $g$ are inverses. **31.** $f(g(x)) = x; g(f(x)) = x$; $f$ and $g$ are inverses. **33.** $f^{-1}(x) = \frac{x - 3}{2}$ **35.** $f^{-1}(x) = \sqrt[3]{x - 2}$ **37.** $f^{-1}(x) = \sqrt[3]{x} - 2$ **39.** $f^{-1}(x) = \frac{1}{x}$ **41.** $f^{-1}(x) = x^2, x \geq 0$ **43.** $f^{-1}(x) = \sqrt{x - 1}$ **45.** $f^{-1}(x) = \frac{3x + 1}{x - 2}$ **47.** $f^{-1}(x) = (x - 3)^3 + 4$ **49.** The function is not one-to-one, so it does not have an inverse function. **51.** The function is not one-to-one, so it does not have an inverse function. **53.** The function is one-to-one, so it does have an inverse function.

**55.**

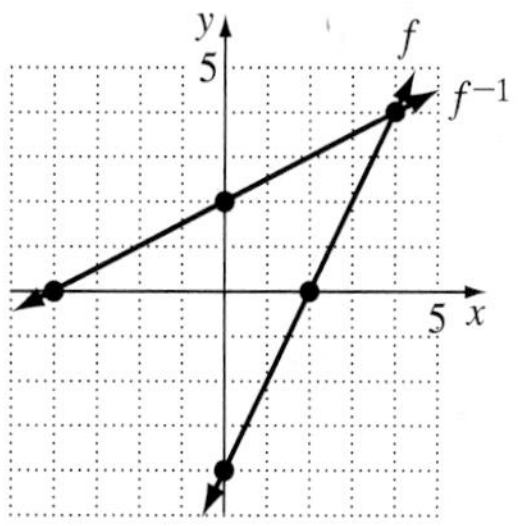


**57.**

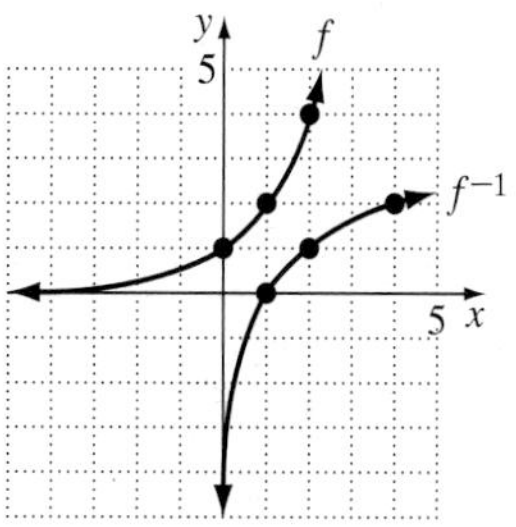


**59. a.** $f$ gives the price of the computer after a \$400 discount. $g$ gives the price of the computer after a 25% discount. **b.** $(f \circ g)(x) = 0.75x - 400$. This models the price of a computer after first a 25% discount and then a \$400 discount. **c.** $(g \circ f)(x) = 0.75(x - 400)$. This models the price of a computer after first a \$400 discount and then a 25% discount. **d.** The function $f \circ g$ models the greater discount, since the 25% discount is taken on the regular price first. **e.** $f^{-1}(x) = x + 400$; If $x$ is the discount price of the computer, then $f^{-1}(x)$ is the regular price.

**61. a.** $f$ is a one-to-one function. **b.** $f^{-1}(0.25)$ is the number of people in a room for a 25% probability of two people sharing a birthday. $f^{-1}(0.5)$ is the number of people in a room for a 50% probability of two people sharing a birthday. $f^{-1}(0.7)$ is the number of people in a room for a 70% probability of two people sharing a birthday. **63.** No. The graph does not pass the horizontal line test, so it is not one-to-one. This means that the average age at which United States women marry has been the same during more than one year.

**73.**

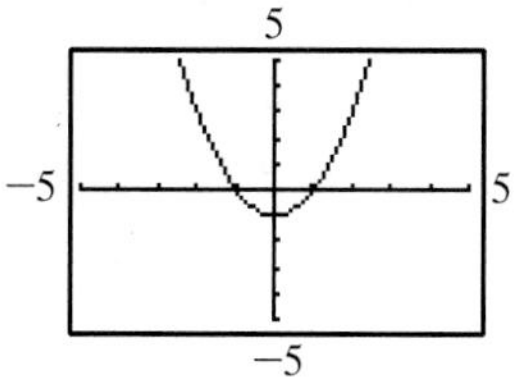


not one-to-one

**75.**

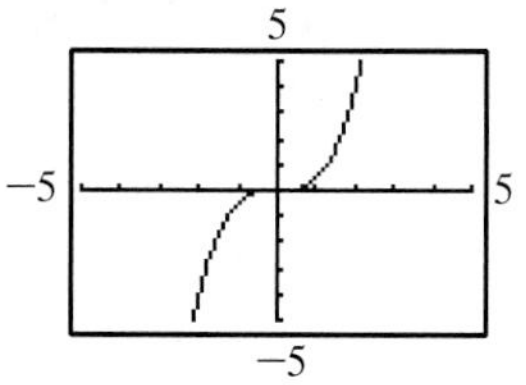


one-to-one

**77.**

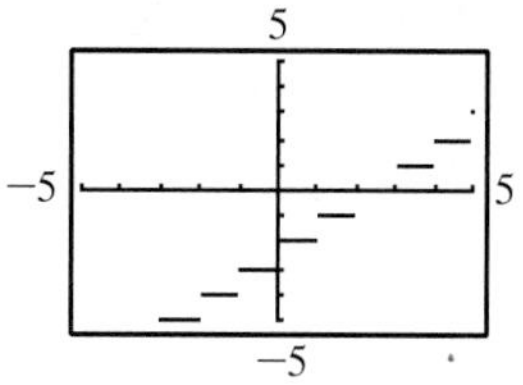


not one-to-one

**79.**

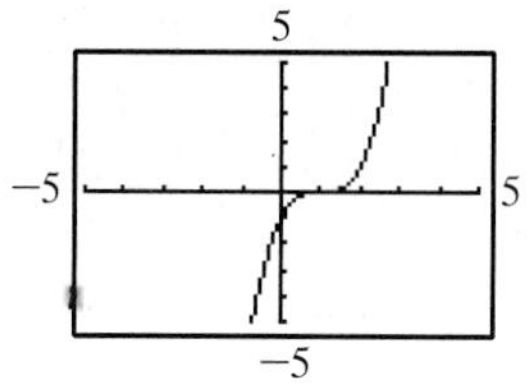


one-to-one

**81.**

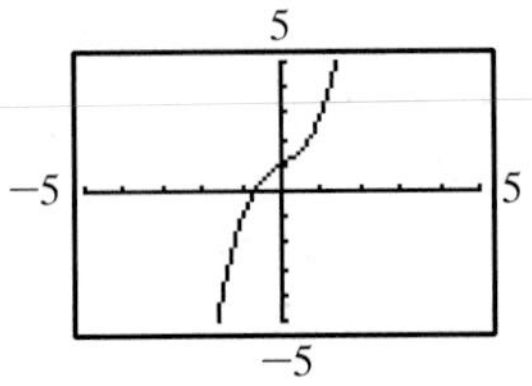


one-to-one

**83.**

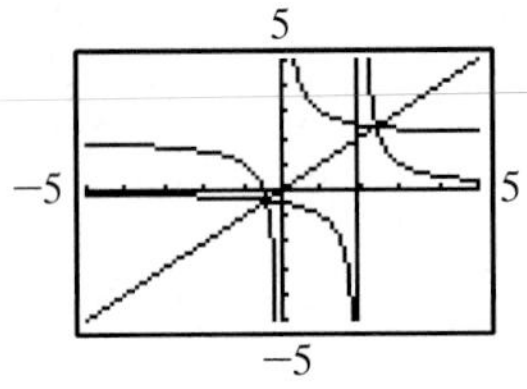


$f$ and $g$ are inverses.

**85.** (d) is true.

**87.** $(f \circ g)^{-1}(x) = \dfrac{x-15}{3}$; $(g^{-1} \circ f^{-1})(x) = \dfrac{x-15}{3}$

**89.** Answers may vary.

## Chapter 2 Review Exercises

**1.** $m = -\frac{1}{2}$; falls **2.** $m = 1$; rises **3.** $m = 0$; horizontal **4.** $m =$ undefined; vertical

**5.** $y - 2 = -6(x + 3)$; $y = -6x - 16$ **6.** using $(1, 6)$, $y - 6 = 2(x - 1)$; $y = 2x + 4$

**7.** Slope: $\frac{2}{5}$; $y$-intercept: $-1$

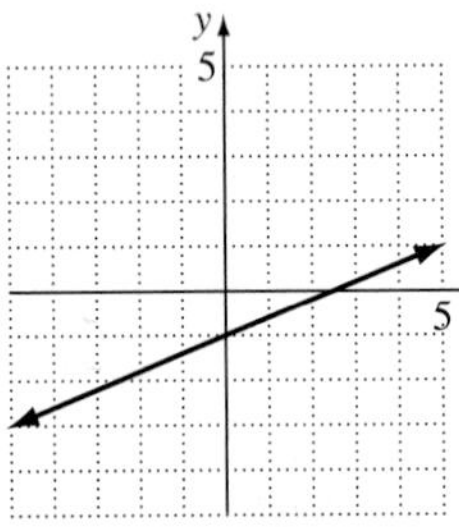


**8.** Slope: $-4$; $y$-intercept: 5

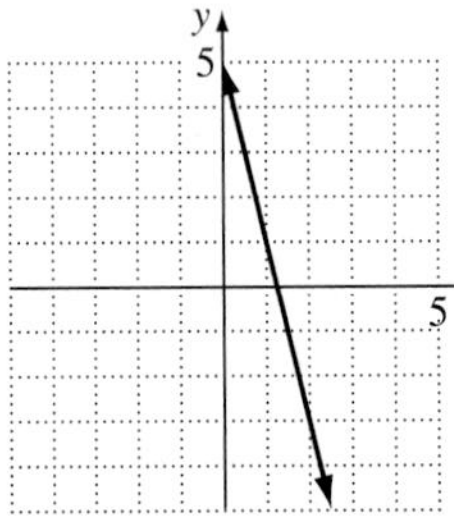


**9.** Slope: $-\frac{2}{3}$; $y$-intercept: $-2$

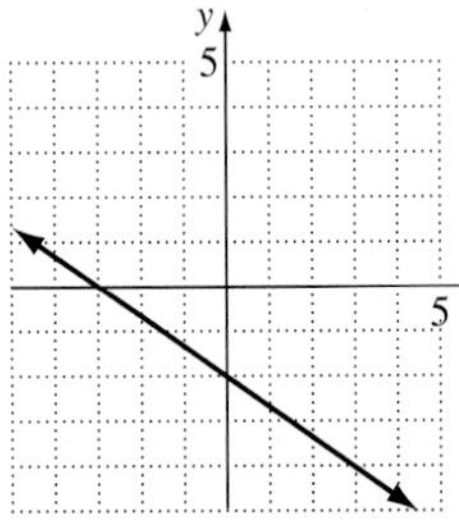


**10.** Slope: 0; $y$-intercept: 4

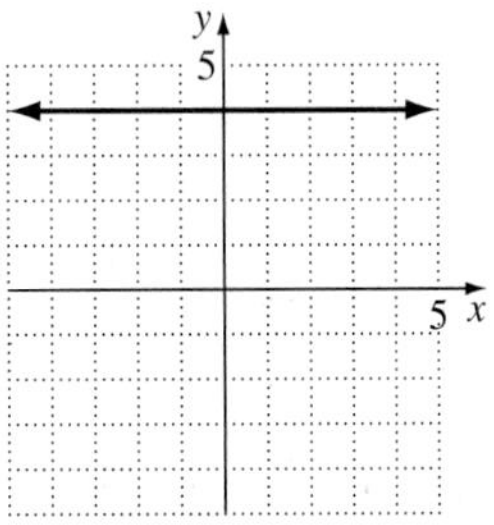


**11. a.** using $(0, 16)$, $y - 16 = -0.13(x - 0)$ **b.** $y = -0.13x + 16$ **c.** 6.9 ft; 5.6 ft **d.** In 2000, the equation predicts the surfboard length to be 3 feet, which is not reasonable. **12. a.** Answers may vary. **b.** Answers may vary. **c.** Answers may vary.

**13.** $y + 7 = -3(x - 4)$; $y = -3x + 5$ **14.** $y - 6 = -3(x + 3)$; $y = -3x - 3$ **15.** $x^2 + y^2 = 9$ **16.** $(x + 2)^2 + (y - 4)^2 = 36$

**17.** Center: $(0, 0)$; radius: 1

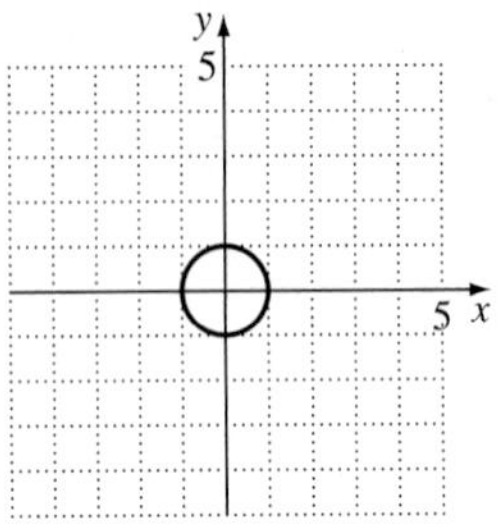


**18.** Center: $(-2, 3)$; radius: 3

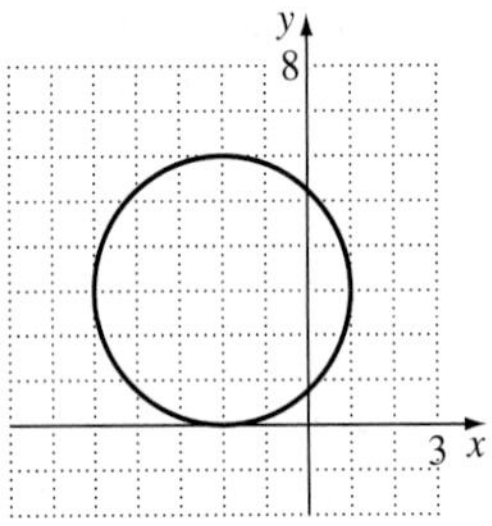


**19.** Center: $(2, -1)$; radius: 3

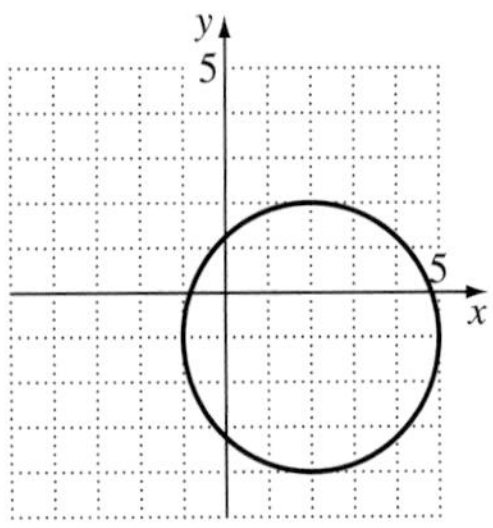

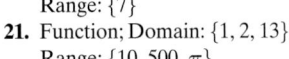

**20.** Function; Domain: $\{2, 3, 5\}$; Range: $\{7\}$
**21.** Function; Domain: $\{1, 2, 13\}$; Range: $\{10, 500, \pi\}$
**22.** Not a function; Domain: $\{12, 14\}$; Range: $\{13, 15, 19\}$
**23.** $y$ is a function of $x$.
**24.** $y$ is a function of $x$.
**25.** $y$ is not a function of $x$.
**26. a.** $f(4) = -23$
**b.** $f(x + 3) = -7x - 16$
**c.** $f(-x) = 5 + 7x$

**27. a.** $g(0) = 2$ **b.** $g(-2) = 24$ **c.** $g(x - 1) = 3x^2 - 11x + 10$ **d.** $g(-x) = 3x^2 + 5x + 2$
**28. a.** $g(13) = 3$ **b.** $g(0) = 4$ **c.** $g(-3) = 7$ **29. a.** $f(-2) = -1$ **b.** $f(1) = 12$ **c.** $f(2) = 3$ **30.** 8
**31.** $2x + h - 13$ **32.** $(-\infty, \infty)$ **33.** $(-\infty, 7)$ or $(7, \infty)$ **34.** $(-\infty, 4]$ **35.** $(-\infty, -1)$ or $(-1, 1)$ or $(1, \infty)$
**36.** $[2, 5)$ or $(5, \infty)$

**37.** Ordered pairs: $(-1, 9)$, $(0, 4)$, $(1, 1)$, $(2, 0)$, $(3, 1)$, $(4, 4)$.

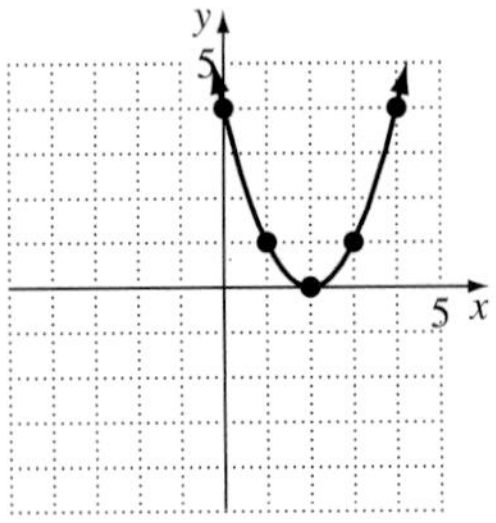


Domain: $(-\infty, \infty)$
Range: $[0, \infty)$

**38.** Ordered pairs: $(-1, 3)$, $(0, 2)$, $(1, 1)$, $(2, 0)$, $(3, 1)$, $(4, 2)$.

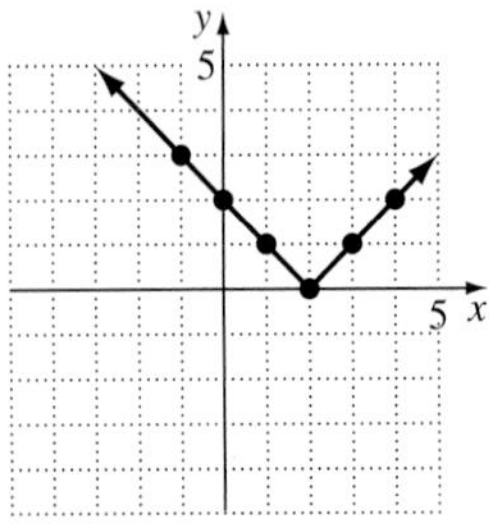


Domain: $(-\infty, \infty)$
Range: $[0, \infty)$

**39. a.** Domain: $[-3, 5)$
**b.** Range: $[-5, 0]$
**c.** $x$-intercept: $-3$
**d.** $y$-intercept: $-2$
**e.** increasing: $(-2, 0)$ or $(3, 5)$
decreasing: $(-3, -2)$ or $(0, 3)$
**f.** $f(-2) = -3$ and $f(3) = -5$

**40. a.** Domain: $(-\infty, \infty)$
**b.** Range: $(-\infty, \infty)$
**c.** $x$-intercepts: $-2$ and 3
**d.** $y$-intercept: 3
**e.** increasing: $(-5, 0)$; decreasing: $(-\infty, -5)$ or $(0, \infty)$
**f.** $f(-2) = 0$ and $f(6) = -3$

**41. a.** Domain: $(-\infty, \infty)$ **b.** Range: $[-2, 2]$ **c.** $x$-intercept: 0 **d.** $y$-intercept: 0 **e.** increasing: $(-2, 2)$; constant: $(-\infty, -2)$ or $(2, \infty)$ **f.** $f(-9) = -2$ and $f(14) = 2$ **42.** not a function **43.** function **44.** function **45.** not a function **46.** 10
**47. a.** 32 ft/sec **b.** –32 ft/sec **c.** The positive sign in part (a) means that the ball is moving up on $(0, 2)$. The negative sign in part (b) means that the ball is moving down on $(2, 4)$. **48.** \$6,440,000,000 per yr **49.** odd; symmetric with respect to the origin
**50.** even; symmetric with respect to the $y$-axis **51.** odd; symmetric with respect to the origin
**52. a.** yes; The graph passes the vertical line test. **b.** Decreasing: $(3, 12)$; The vulture descended.
**c.** Constant: $(0, 3)$ and $(12, 17)$; The vulture's height held steady during the first 3 seconds and the vulture was on the ground for 5 seconds.
**d.** Increasing: $(17, 30)$; The vulture was ascending.

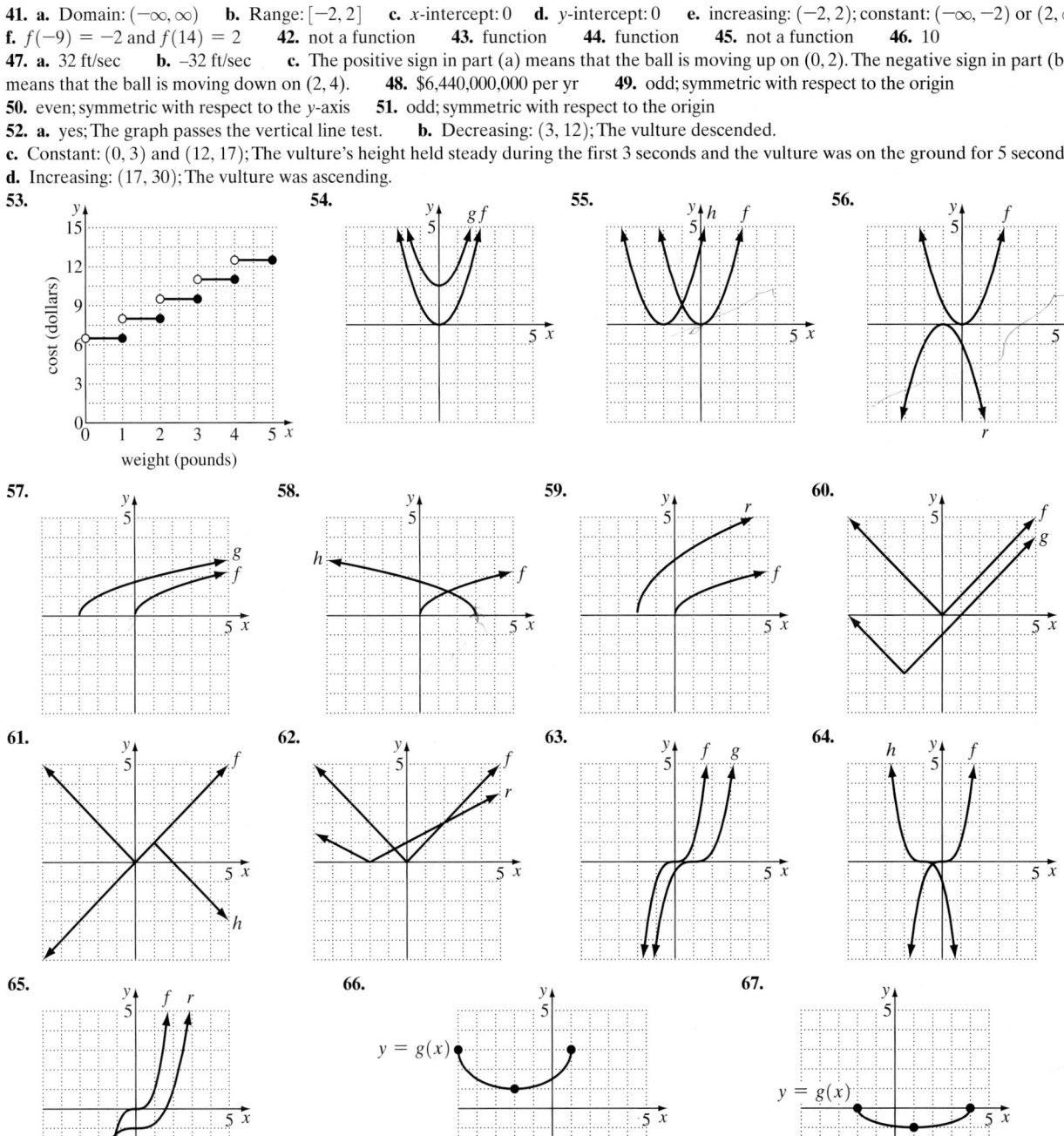

**53.**
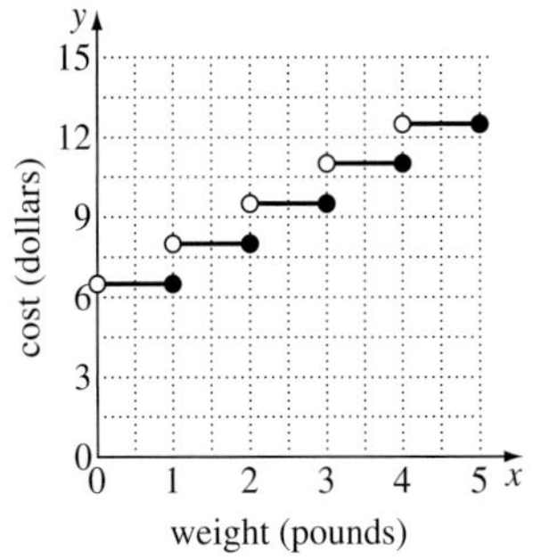


**54.**
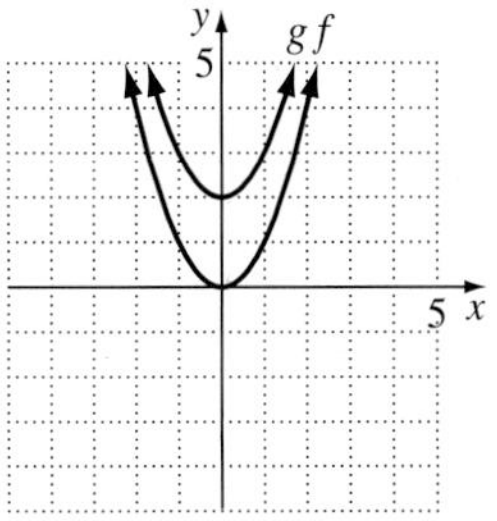


**55.**
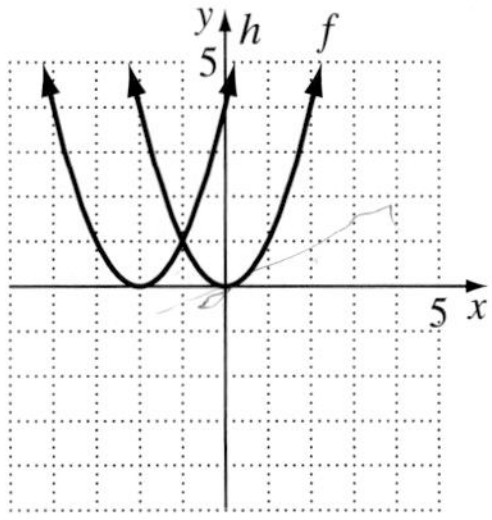


**56.**
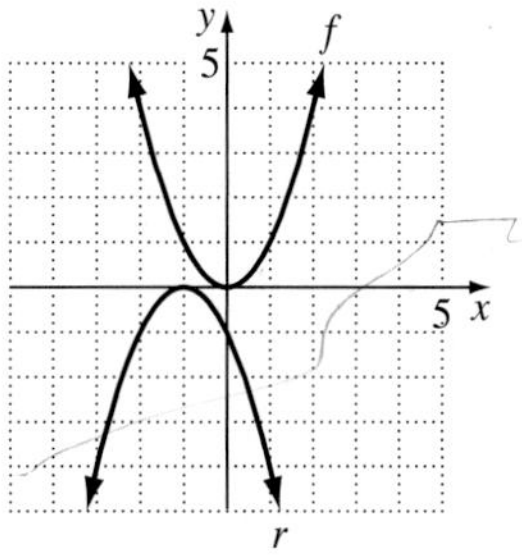


**57.**
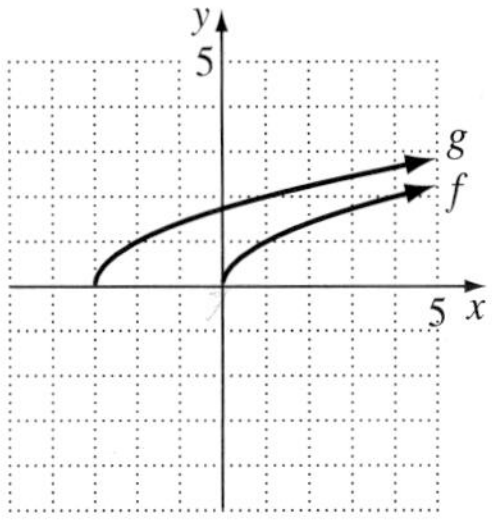


**58.**
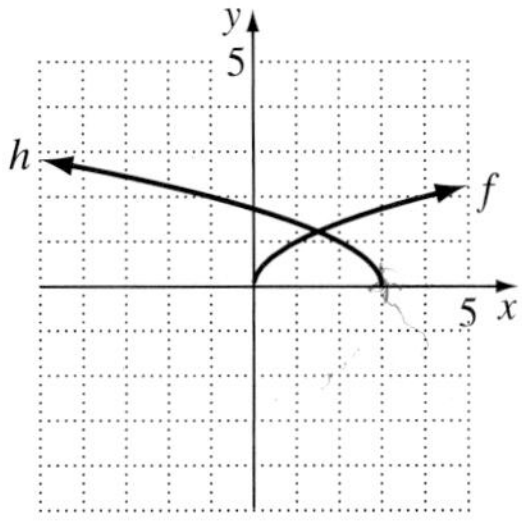


**59.**
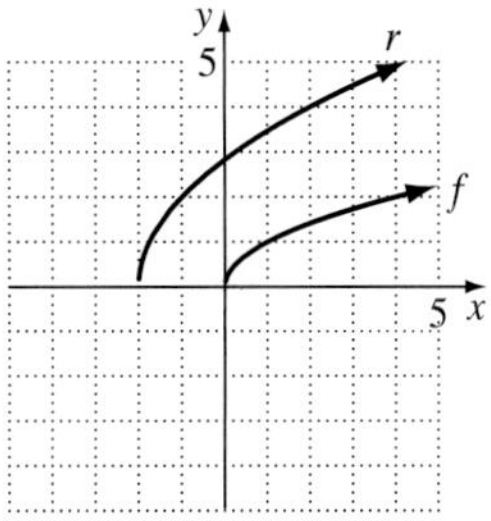


**60.**
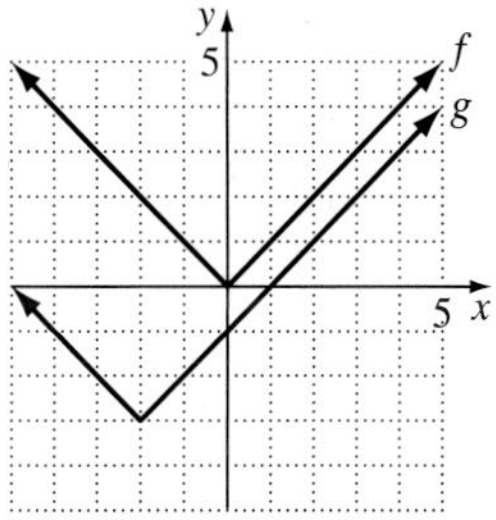


**61.**
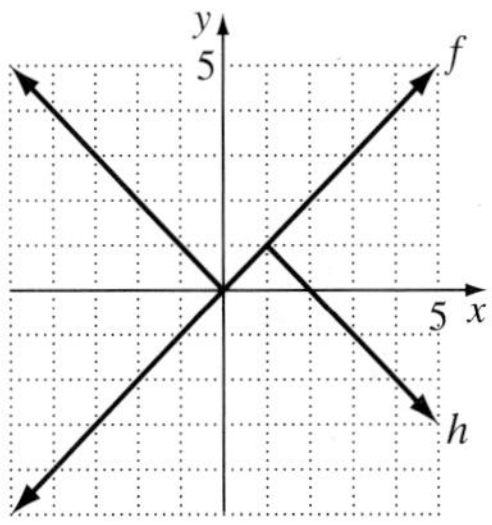


**62.**
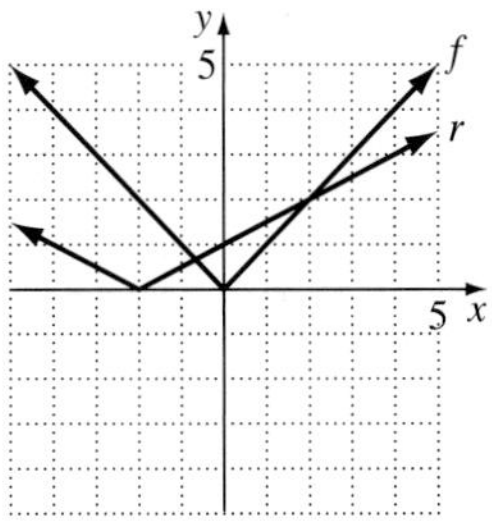


**63.**
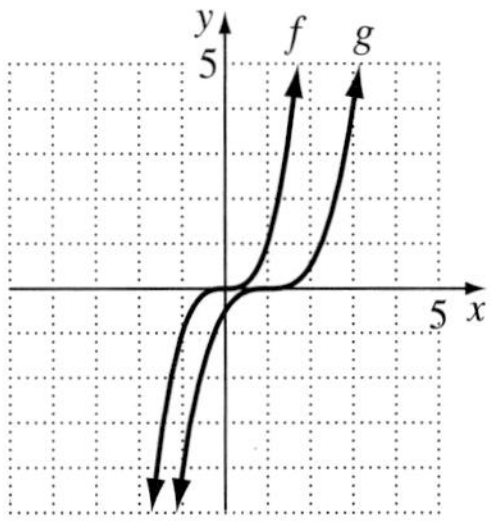


**64.**
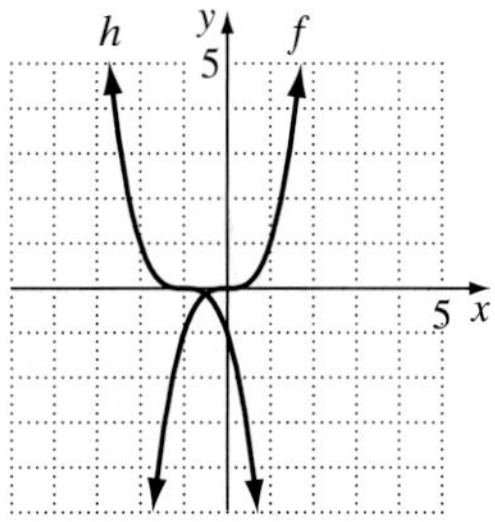


**65.**
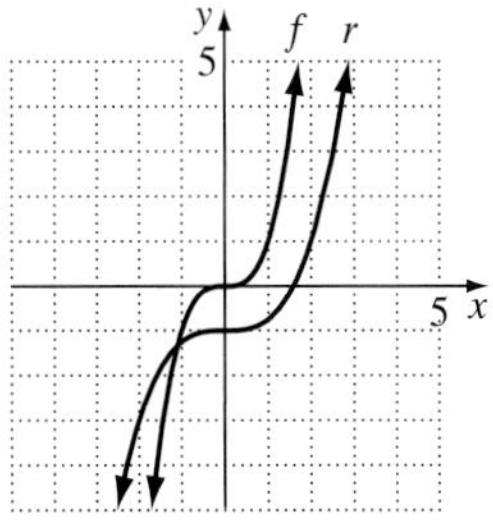


**66.**
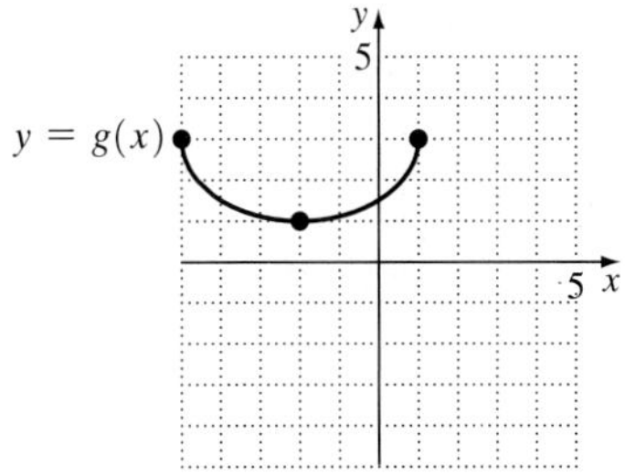


**67.**
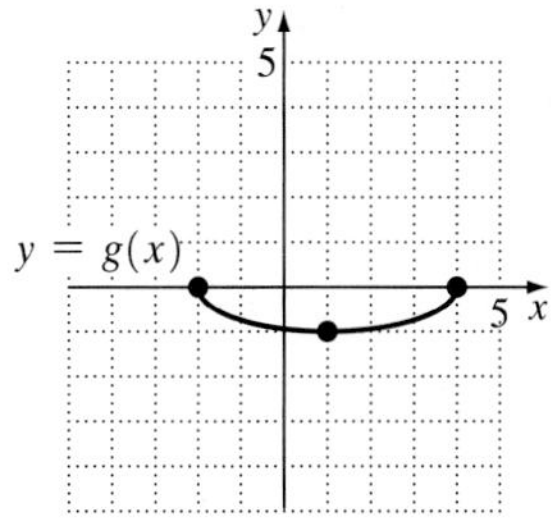

**68.**

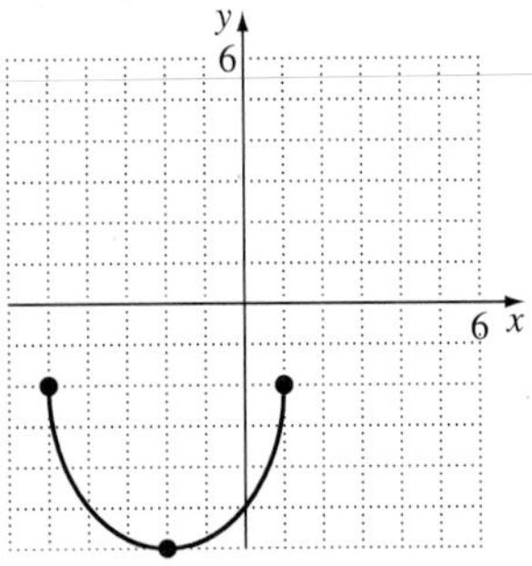


**69.** $(f+g)(x) = 4x - 6$; Domain: $(-\infty, \infty)$; $(f-g)(x) = 2x + 4$; Domain: $(-\infty, \infty)$; $(fg)(x) = 3x^2 - 16x + 5$; Domain: $(-\infty, \infty)$; $\left(\frac{f}{g}\right)(x) = \frac{3x-1}{x-5}$; Domain: $(-\infty, 5)$ or $(5, \infty)$

**70.** $(f+g)(x) = 2x^2 + x$; Domain: $(-\infty, \infty)$; $(f-g)(x) = x + 2$; Domain: $(-\infty, \infty)$; $(fg)(x) = x^4 + x^3 - x - 1$; Domain: $(-\infty, \infty)$; $\left(\frac{f}{g}\right)(x) = \frac{x^2+x+1}{x^2-1}$; Domain: $(-\infty, -1)$ or $(-1, 1)$ or $(1, \infty)$

**71.** $(f+g)(x) = \sqrt{x+7} + \sqrt{x-2}$; Domain: $[2, \infty)$; $(f-g)(x) = \sqrt{x+7} - \sqrt{x-2}$; Domain: $[2, \infty)$; $(fg)(x) = \sqrt{x^2+5x-14}$; Domain: $[2, \infty)$; $\left(\frac{f}{g}\right)(x) = \frac{\sqrt{x+7}}{\sqrt{x-2}}$; Domain: $(2, \infty)$

**72. a.** $(f \circ g)(x) = 16x^2 - 8x + 4$ **b.** $(g \circ f)(x) = 4x^2 + 11$ **c.** $(f \circ g)(3) = 124$

**73. a.** $(f \circ g)(x) = \sqrt{x+1}$ **b.** $(g \circ f)(x) = \sqrt{x} + 1$ **c.** $(f \circ g)(3) = 2$ **74.** $f(x) = x^4, g(x) = x^2 + 2x - 1$

**75.** $f(x) = \sqrt[3]{x}, g(x) = 7x + 4$ **76.** $f(g(x)) = x - \frac{7}{10}$; $g(f(x)) = x - \frac{7}{6}$; $f$ and $g$ are not inverses of each other.

**77.** $f(g(x)) = x$; $g(f(x)) = x$; $f$ and $g$ are inverses of each other. **78.** $f^{-1}(x) = \frac{x+3}{4}$

**79.** $f^{-1}(x) = x^2 - 2$ for $x \geq 0$ **80.** $f^{-1}(x) = \sqrt[3]{\frac{x-1}{8}}$ **81.** Inverse function exists. **82.** Inverse function does not exist.

**83.** Inverse function exists. **84.** Inverse function does not exist. **85.**

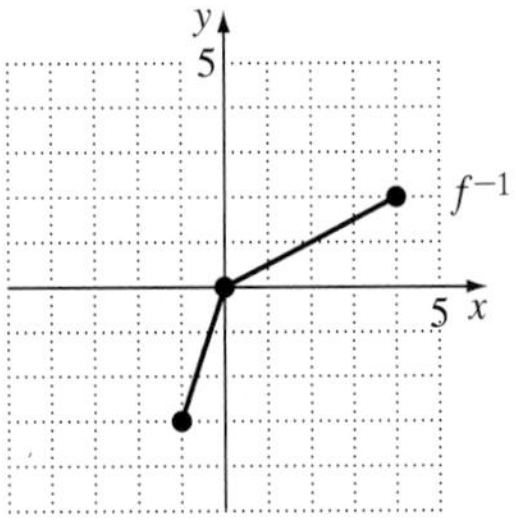


## Chapter 2 Test

**1.** using $(2, 1)$, $y - 1 = 3(x - 2)$; $y = 3x - 5$ **2.** $y - 6 = 4(x + 4)$; $y = 4x + 22$
**3. a.** using $(4, 401.1)$, $y - 401.1 = 14.9(x - 4)$; $y = 14.9x + 341.5$ **b.** \$639.50
**4.** Center: $(-2, 3)$; radius: 4

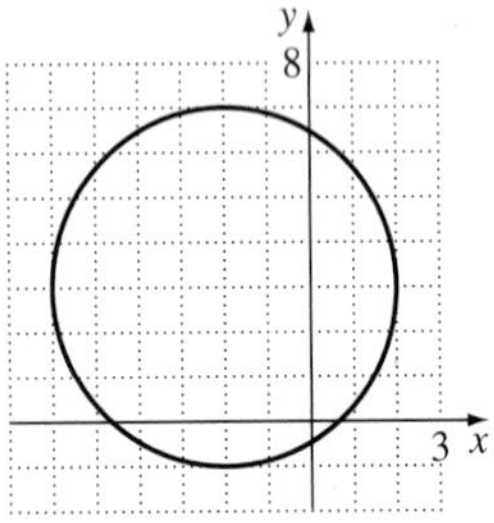


**5.** b, c, d **6.** $f(x - 1) = x^2 - 4x + 8$ **7.** $g(-1) = 4$; $g(7) = 2$ **8.** Domain: $(-\infty, 4]$
**9.** $2x + h + 11$
**10. a.** $f(4) - f(-3) = 5$ **b.** Domain: $(-5, 6]$ **c.** Range: $[-4, 5]$ **d.** Increasing: $(-1, 2)$ **e.** Decreasing: $(-5, -1)$ or $(2, 6)$ **f.** $x$-intercepts: $-4, 1$, and 5 **g.** $y$-intercept: $-3$
**11.** 48
**12.** $f(x)$ is even and is symmetric with respect to the $y$-axis. The graph in the figure is symmetric with respect to the origin.
**13.** The graph of $f$ is shifted 3 to the right to obtain the graph of $g$. Then the graph of $g$ is stretched by a factor of 2 and reflected about the $x$-axis to obtain the graph of $h$.

**14.**

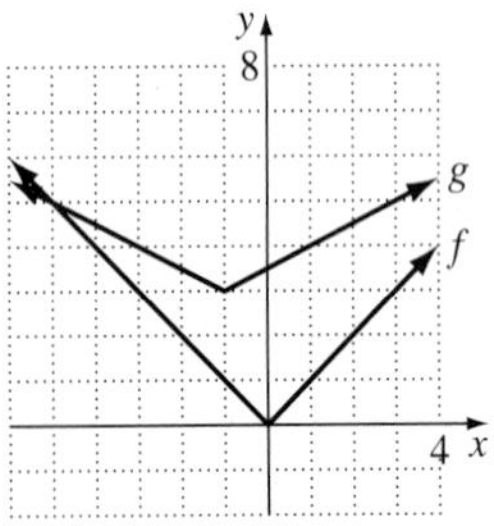


**15.** $(f - g)(x) = x^2 - 2x - 2$ **16.** $\left(\frac{f}{g}\right)(x) = \frac{x^2 + 3x - 4}{5x - 2}$; Domain: $\left(-\infty, \frac{2}{5}\right)$ or $\left(\frac{2}{5}, \infty\right)$
**17.** $(f \circ g)(x) = 25x^2 - 5x - 6$ **18.** $(g \circ f)(x) = 5x^2 + 15x - 22$
**19.** $f(g(2)) = 84$ **20.** $f(x) = x^7, g(x) = 2x + 13$ **21.** $f^{-1}(x) = x^2 + 2$ for $x \geq 0$
**22. a.** The graph of $f$ passes the Horizontal Line Test. **b.** $f(80) = 2000$
**c.** $f^{-1}(2000)$ is the income, in thousands of dollars, for those who give \$2000 to charity.
**23.**

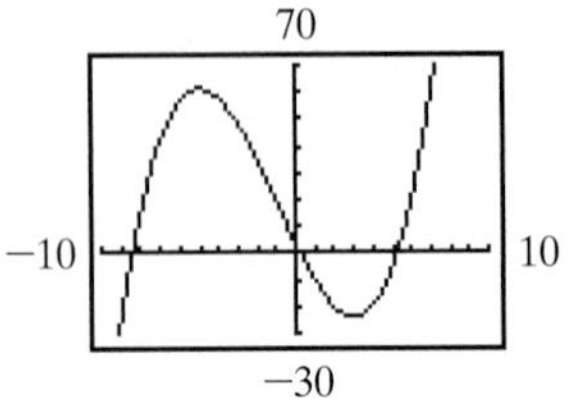

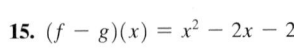

**a.** not one-to-one
**b.** neither
**c.** $(-\infty, \infty)$
**d.** Increasing: $(-\infty, -5)$ or $(3, \infty)$
**e.** Decreasing: $(-5, 3)$

### Cumulative Review Exercises (Chapters P–2)

**1.** $\frac{2y^4}{x^3}$ **2.** $\frac{5\sqrt{2}}{8}$ **3.** $(x - 4)(x^2 + 2)$ **4.** $\frac{2x^2 - x + 6}{(x + 4)(x - 2)}$ **5.** $\frac{2x + 1}{2x - 1}$ **6.** $x = -4$ or $x = 5$ **7.** $x = \frac{25}{18}$ **8.** $x = 4$
**9.** $x = -8$ or $x = 27$ **10.** $x \leq 20$; $(-\infty, 20]$ **11.** $(-\infty, 2)$ or $[7, \infty)$ **12.** $y - 5 = 4(x + 2)$; $y = 4x + 13$
**13.**

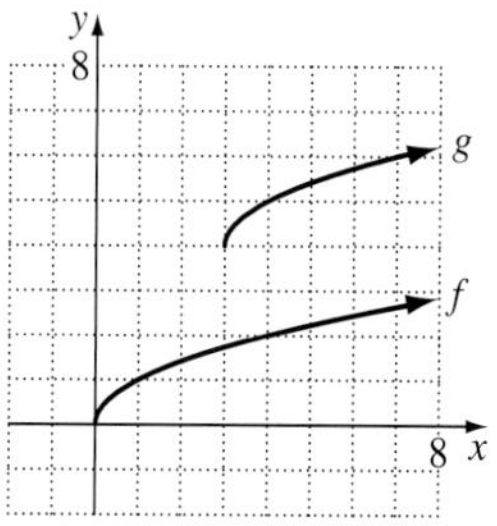


**14.** $f^{-1}(x) = (x - 2)^2 + 3$
**15.** $-2x - h$
**16.** $r = \frac{G - a}{G}$
**17.** 3 ft by 8 ft
**18.** \$3.50
**19.** You must make an 85 on the final exam to have an average score of 80.
**20.** 48 ft/sec

# CHAPTER 3

## Section 3.1

### Check Point Exercises

**1.**

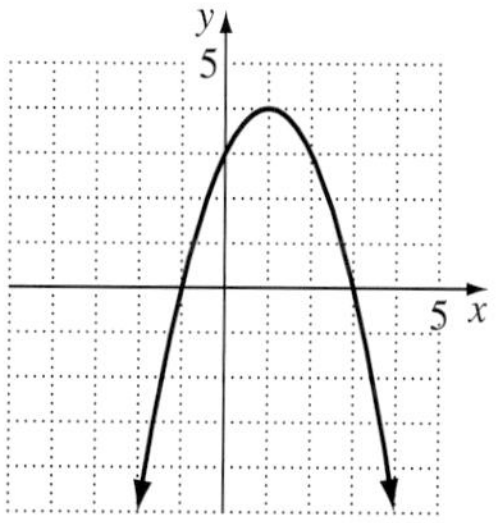


**2.**

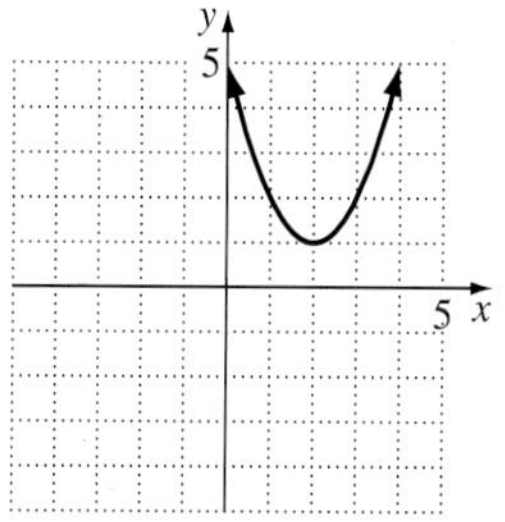


**3.**

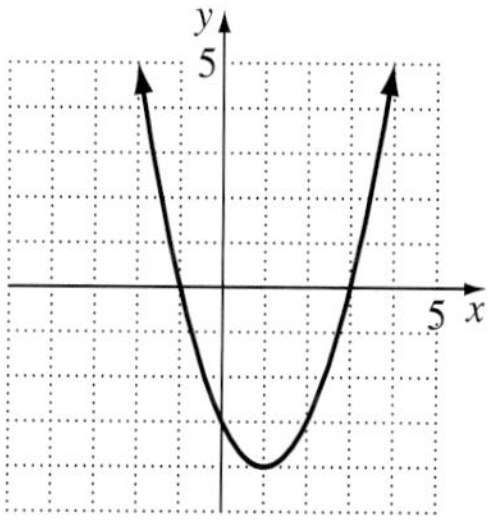


**4.** 45; 190
**5.** 4, 4; 16
**6.** 30 ft by 30 ft; 900 sq ft

### Exercise Set 3.1

**1.** $h(x) = (x - 1)^2 + 1$ **3.** $j(x) = (x - 1)^2 - 1$ **5.** $h(x) = x^2 - 1$ **7.** $g(x) = x^2 - 2x + 1$ **9.** $(3, 1)$ **11.** $(-1, 5)$
**13.** $(2, -5)$ **15.** $(-1, 9)$

**17.** axis of symmetry: $x = 4$

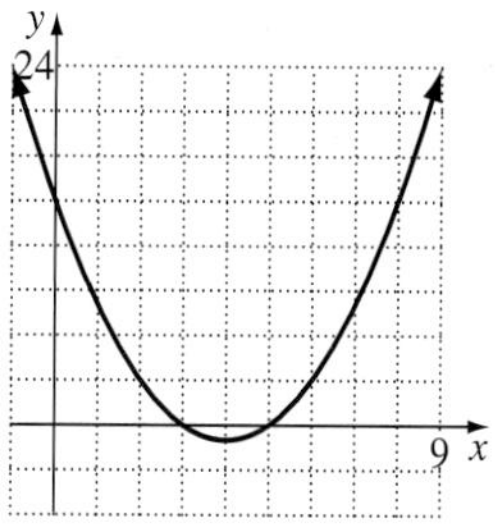


**19.** axis of symmetry: $x = 1$

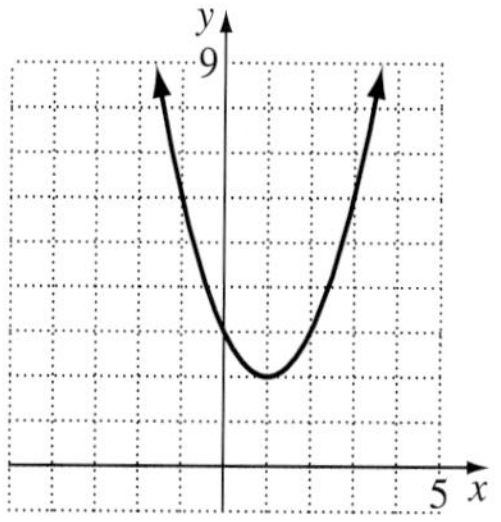


**21.** axis of symmetry: $x = 3$

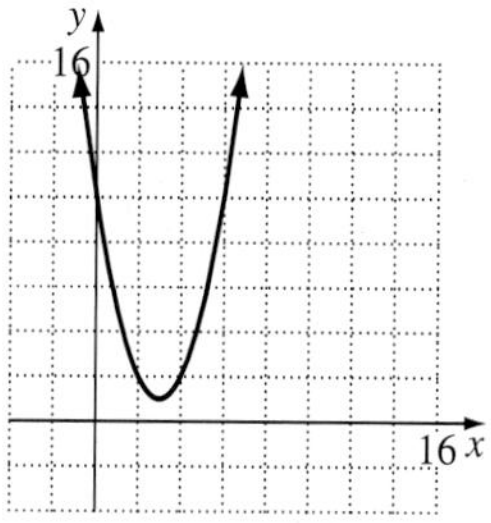


**23.** axis of symmetry: $x = -2$

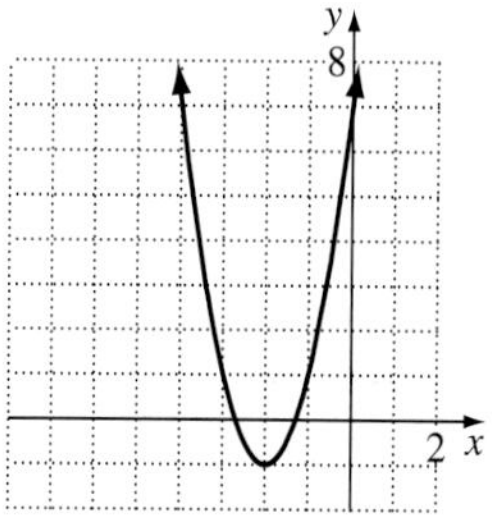

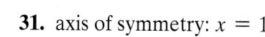

**25.** axis of symmetry: $x = 1$

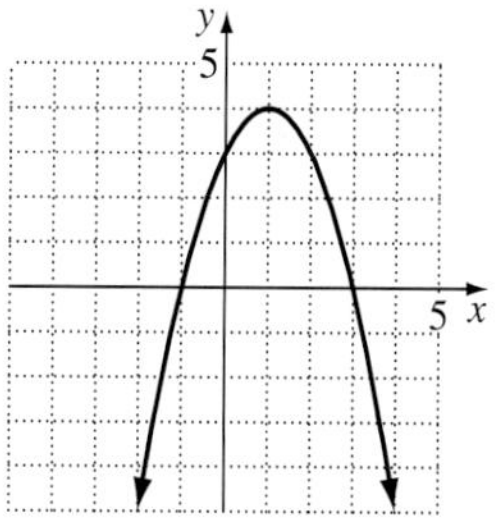


**27.** axis of symmetry: $x = 1$

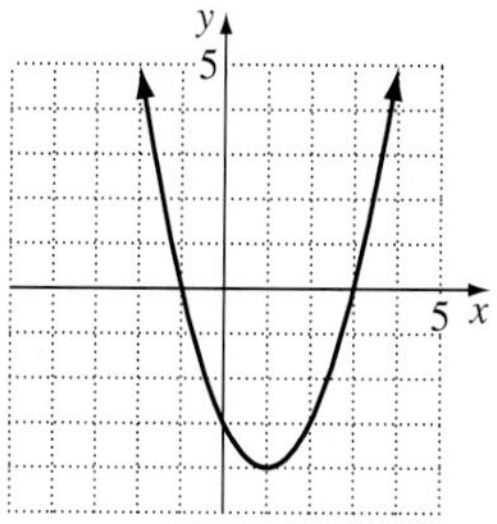


**29.** axis of symmetry: $x = -\frac{3}{2}$

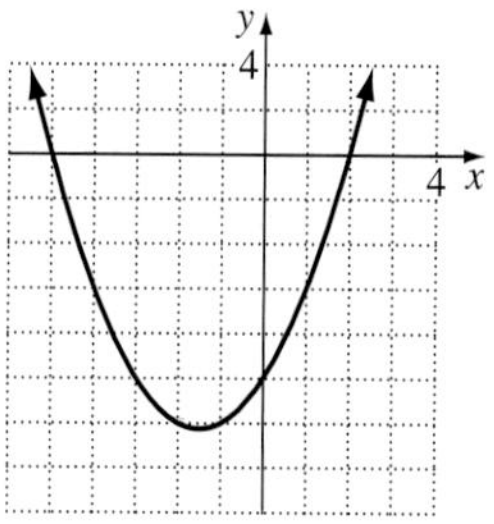


**31.** axis of symmetry: $x = 1$

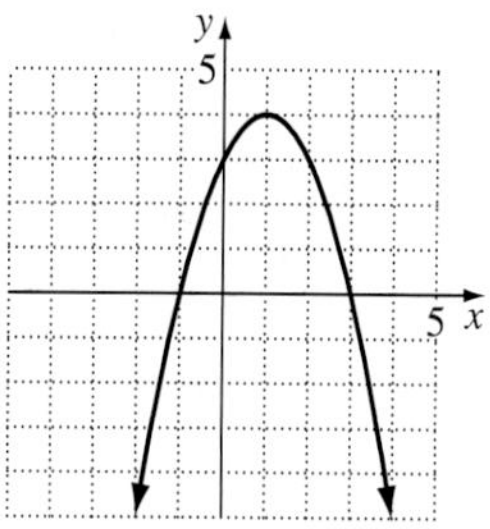

**33.** axis of symmetry: $x = 1$

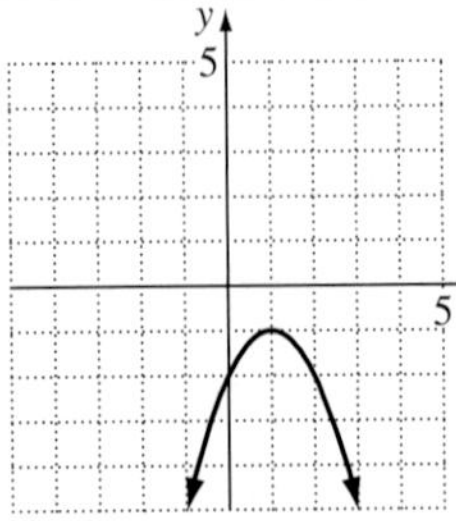


You can only see a little of the parabola.

**35.** minimum; $(2, -13)$ **37.** maximum; $(1, 1)$ **39.** minimum; $\left(\frac{1}{2}, -\frac{5}{4}\right)$

**41.** 1968; 4238 cigarettes per person **43.** 2 sec; 144 ft **45.** 8, 8; 64 **47.** 30 ft; 60 ft; 1800 ft$^2$

**49.** 5 yd by 5 yd; 25 yd$^2$ **51.** 150 ft by 100 ft; 15,000 ft$^2$ **53.** 5 in. **55.** 47 people; \$2209

**57.** 4 in., 4 in.

**67. a.**

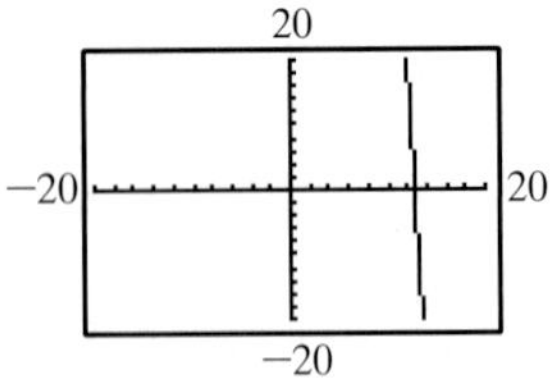


**b.** $(20.5, -120.5)$
**c.** Answers may vary.
**d.** Answers may vary.

**69.** $(2.5, 185)$

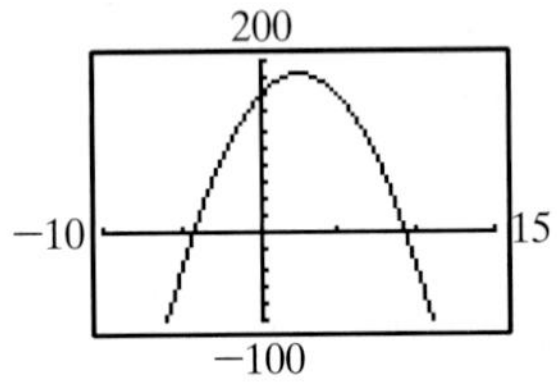


**71.** $(-30, 91)$

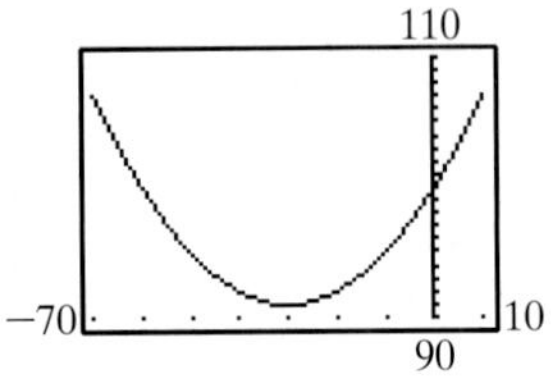


**73.**

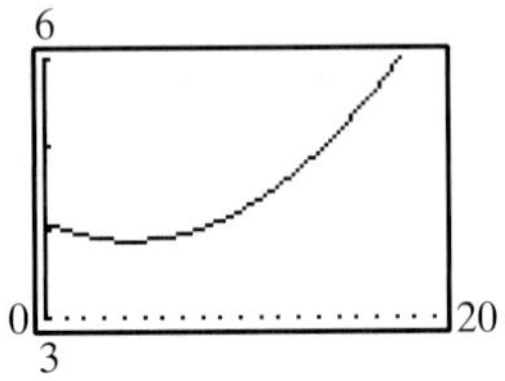


Vertex: about $(4.41, 3.89)$; The minimum number of people in the United States holding more than one job was 3.89 million in 1974.

**75.** (a) is true. **77.** $x = 3$; $(0, 11)$

## Section 3.2

### Check Point Exercises

**1.** The graph rises to the left and to the right. **2.** Since $n$ is odd and the leading coefficient is negative, the function falls to the right. Since the ratio cannot be negative, the model won't be appropriate. **3.** No; the graph should fall to the left, but doesn't appear to.
**4.** $\{-2, 2\}$ **5.** $\{-2, 0, 2\}$ **6.**

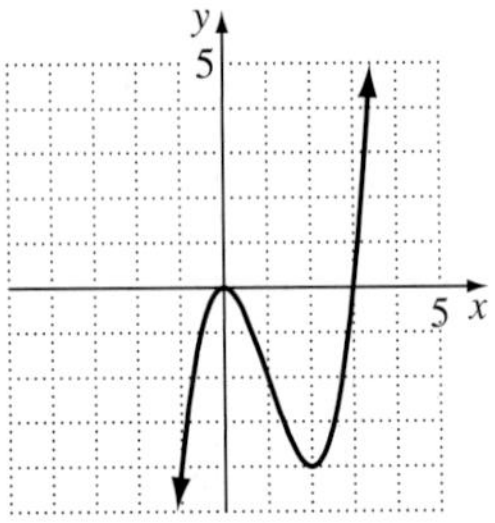


### Exercise Set 3.2

**1.** polynomial function; degree: 3 **3.** polynomial function; degree: 5 **5.** not a polynomial function **7.** not a polynomial function
**9.** not a polynomial function **11.** polynomial function **13.** not a polynomial function **15.** (c) **17.** (b) **19.** (a)
**21.** falls to the left and rises to the right **23.** rises to the left and to the right **25.** falls to the left and to the right
**27.** $x = 5$ has multiplicity 1; The graph crosses the $x$-axis; $x = -4$ has multiplicity 2; The graph touches the $x$-axis and turns around.
**29.** $x = 3$ has multiplicity 1; The graph crosses the $x$-axis; $x = -6$ has multiplicity 3; The graph crosses the $x$-axis.
**31.** $x = 0$ has multiplicity 1; The graph crosses the $x$-axis; $x = 1$ has multiplicity 2; The graph touches the $x$-axis and turns around.
**33.** $x = 2$, $x = -2$ and $x = -7$ have multiplicity 1; The graph crosses the $x$-axis.

**35.** **a.** $f(x)$ rises to the right and falls to the left.
**b.** $x = -2, x = 1, x = -1$;
$f(x)$ crosses the $x$-axis at each.
**c.** The $y$-intercept is $-2$.
**d.** neither
**e.**

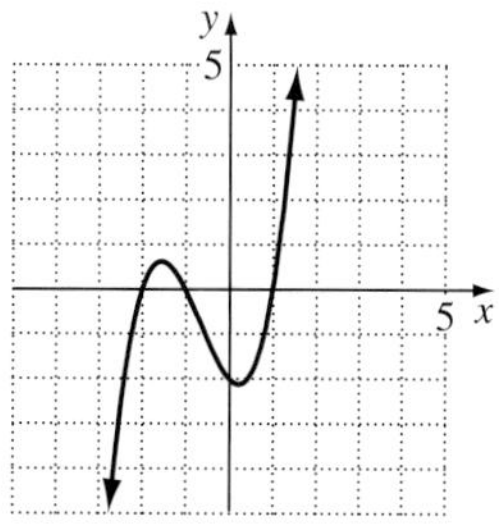


**37.** **a.** $f(x)$ rises to the left and the right.
**b.** $x = 0, x = 3, x = -3$;
$f(x)$ crosses the $x$-axis at $-3$ and 3;
$f(x)$ touches the $x$-axis at 0.
**c.** The $y$-intercept is 0.
**d.** $y$-axis symmetry
**e.**

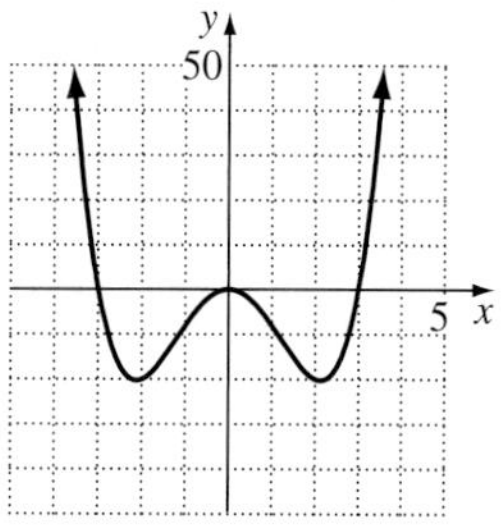


**39.** **a.** $f(x)$ falls to the left and the right.
**b.** $x = 0, x = 4, x = -4$;
$f(x)$ crosses the $x$-axis at $-4$ and 4;
$f(x)$ touches the $x$-axis at 0.
**c.** The $y$-intercept is 0.
**d.** $y$-axis is symmetry
**e.**

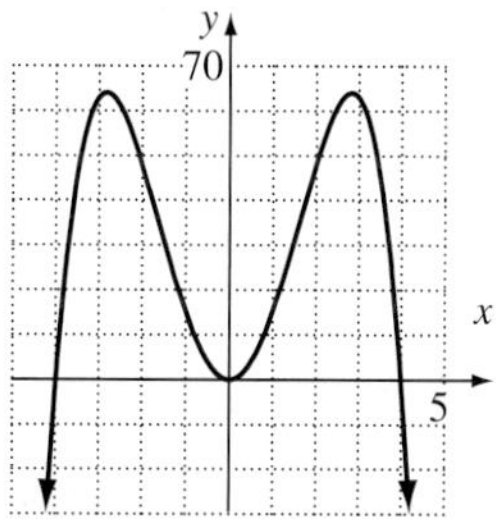


**41.** **a.** $f(x)$ rises to the left and the right.
**b.** $x = 0, x = 1$;
$f(x)$ touches the $x$-axis at 0 and 1.
**c.** The $y$-intercept is 0.
**d.** neither
**e.**

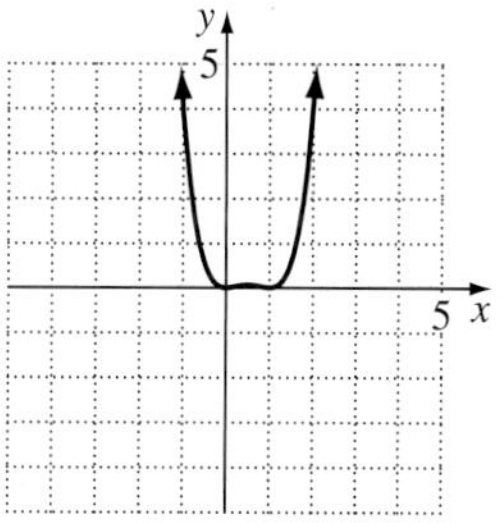


**43.** **a.** $f(x)$ falls to the left and the right.
**b.** $x = 0, x = 2$;
$f(x)$ crosses the $x$-axis at 0 and 2.
**c.** The $y$-intercept is 0.
**d.** neither
**e.**

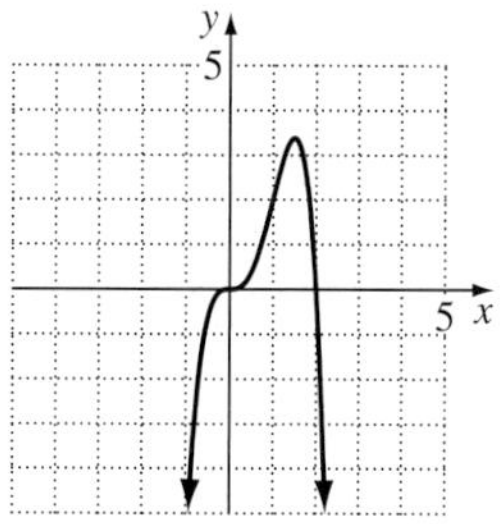


**45.** **a.** $f(x)$ rises to the left and falls to the right.
**b.** $x = 0, x = \pm\sqrt{3}$;
$f(x)$ crosses the $x$-axis at $(0, 0)$;
$f(x)$ touches the $x$-axis at $\sqrt{3}$ and $-\sqrt{3}$.
**c.** The $y$-intercept is 0.
**d.** origin symmetry
**e.**

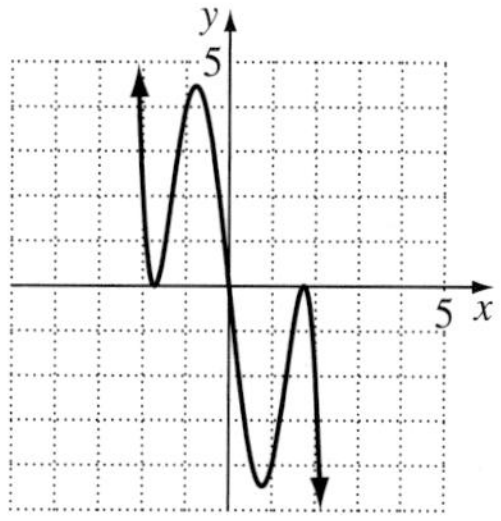

**47. a.** $f(x)$ rises to the left and falls to the right.
**b.** $x = 0, x = 3$;
$f(x)$ crosses the $x$-axis at 3;
$f(x)$ touches the axis at $(0, 0)$.
**c.** The $y$-intercept is 0.
**d.** neither
**e.**

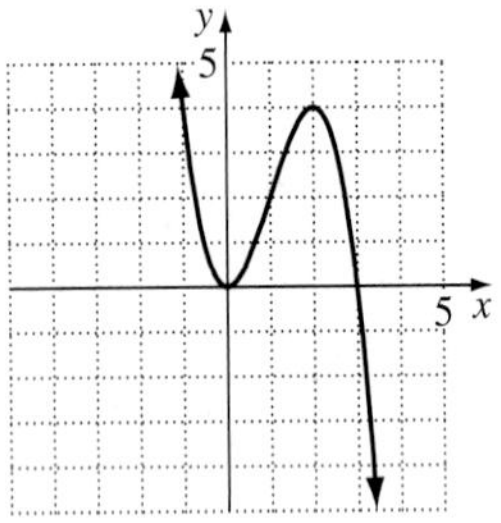


**49. a.** $f(x)$ falls to the left and the right.
**b.** $x = 1, x = -2, x = 2$;
$f(x)$ crosses the $x$-axis at $-2$ and 2;
$f(x)$ touches the $x$-axis at $(1, 0)$.
**c.** The $y$-intercept is 12.
**d.** neither
**e.**

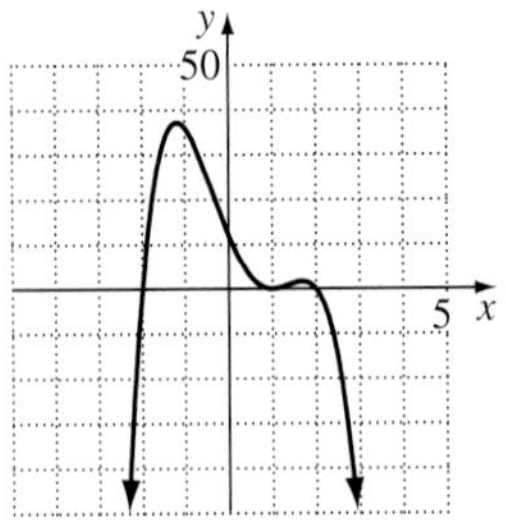


**51. a.** Leading coefficient test suggests the elk population will decline and eventually will die off.
**b.**

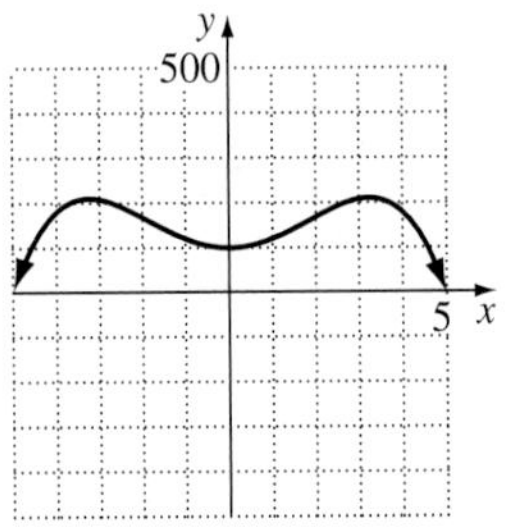


**c.**

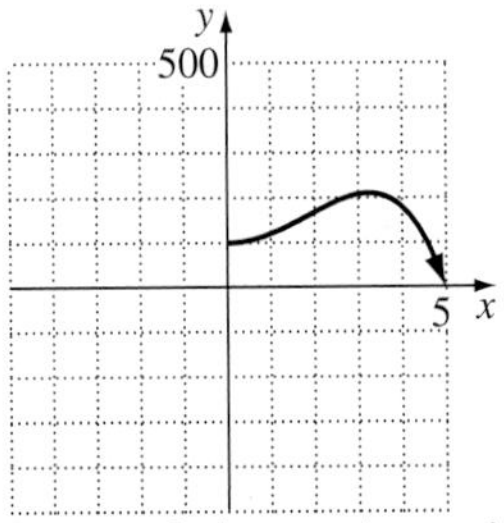


The population reaches extinction at the end of 5 years.

**53. a.** about 4194 larceny thefts **b.** No; eventually the function would predict a negative number of larceny thefts, which is impossible.
**55. a.** 55.178 yr **b.** No; since $a_n < 0$ and $n$ is even, $H(x)$ eventually starts decreasing as $x$ increases, which is impossible.
**69.** Answers may vary. **71.** Answers may vary.

**73.**

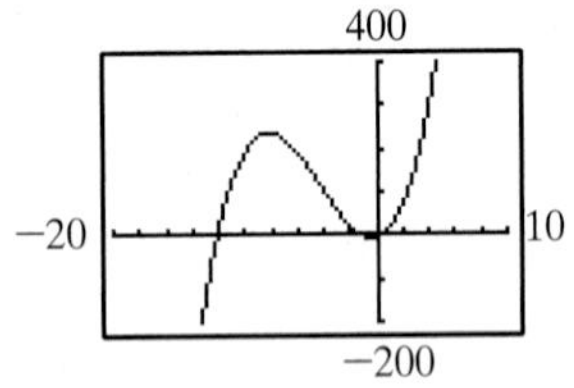


**75.**

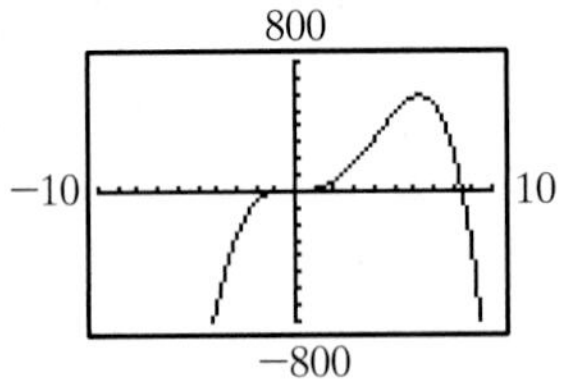


**77.**

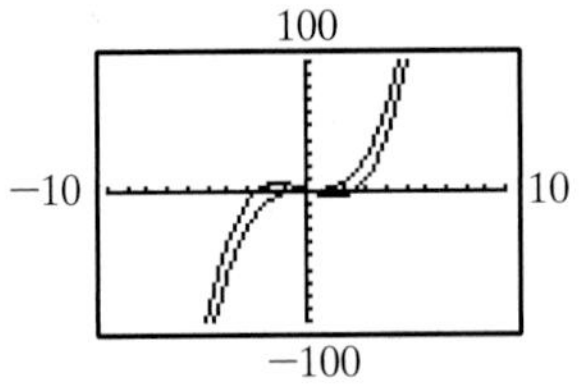


**79.** (c) is true.
**81.** Answers may vary.

## Section 3.3

### Check Point Exercises

**1.** $x + 5$ **2.** $2x^2 + 3x - 2 + \dfrac{1}{x - 3}$ **3.** $2x^2 + 7x + 14 + \dfrac{21x - 10}{x^2 - 2x}$ **4.** $x^2 - 2x - 3$ **5.** $-105$ **6.** $\left\{-1, -\dfrac{1}{3}, \dfrac{2}{5}\right\}$

### Exercise Set 3.3

**1.** $x + 3$ **3.** $x^2 + 3x + 1$ **5.** $2x^2 + 3x + 5$ **7.** $4x + 3 + \dfrac{2}{3x - 2}$ **9.** $2x^2 + x + 6 - \dfrac{38}{x + 3}$

**11.** $4x^3 + 16x^2 + 60x + 246 + \dfrac{984}{x - 4}$ **13.** $2x + 5$ **15.** $6x^2 + 3x - 1 - \dfrac{3x - 1}{3x^2 + 1}$ **17.** $2x + 5$ **19.** $3x - 8 + \dfrac{20}{x + 5}$

**21.** $4x^2 + x + 4 + \dfrac{3}{x - 1}$ **23.** $6x^4 + 12x^3 + 22x^2 + 48x + 93 + \dfrac{187}{x - 2}$ **25.** $x^3 - 10x^2 + 51x - 260 + \dfrac{1300}{x + 5}$

**27.** $x^4 + x^3 + 2x^2 + 2x + 2$ **29.** $x^3 + 4x^2 + 16x + 64$ **31.** $2x^4 - 7x^3 + 15x^2 - 31x + 64 - \dfrac{129}{x + 2}$

**33.** $-25$ **35.** 4729 **37.** $x^2 - 5x + 6; x = -1, x = 2, x = 3$ **39.** $\left\{-\dfrac{1}{2}, 1, 2\right\}$ **41.** $\left\{-\dfrac{3}{2}, -\dfrac{1}{3}, \dfrac{1}{2}\right\}$ **43.** $x^3 + 5x^2 - 9x - 45$

**45. a.** $1 + \frac{5}{x + 20}$ **b.**

| $x$ | 0 | 5 | 10 | 25 | 50 | 75 |
|---|---|---|---|---|---|---|
| $\frac{x + 25}{x + 20}$ | 1.25 | 1.2 | $\approx 1.17$ | $\approx 1.11$ | $\approx 1.07$ | $\approx 1.05$ |

**c.** The ratio decreases as $x$ increases, approaching 1 as $x$ approaches $\infty$. When long division is used, the result is $1 + \frac{5}{x + 25}$, which shows that as $x$ gets larger the second term gets smaller, and therefore, the ratio decreases.

**55.**

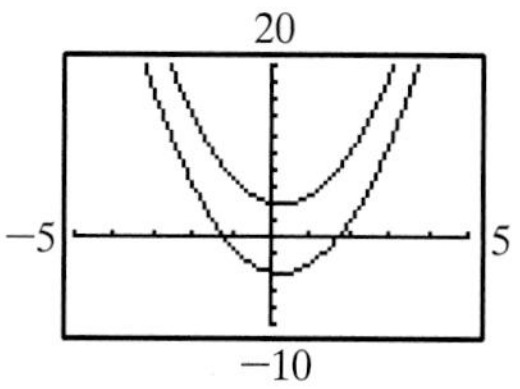


The division is not correct.

**57.**

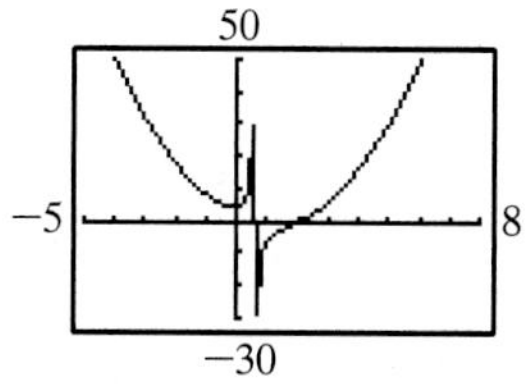


The division is correct.

**59.** $k = -12$ **61.** $x^{2n} - x^n + 1$

## Section 3.4

### Check Point Exercises

**1.** $\pm 1, \pm 2, \pm 3, \pm 6$ **2.** $\pm 1, \pm 3, \pm\frac{1}{2}, \pm\frac{1}{4}, \pm\frac{3}{2}, \pm\frac{3}{4}$ **3.** $\{-5, -4, 1\}$ **4.** $\{1, 2 - 3i, 2 + 3i\}$
**5.** 4, 2, or 0 positive zeros, no possible negative zeros

### Exercise Set 3.4

**1.** $\pm 1, \pm 2, \pm 4$ **3.** $\pm 1, \pm 2, \pm 3, \pm 6, \pm\frac{1}{3}, \pm\frac{2}{3}$ **5.** $\pm 1, \pm 2, \pm 3, \pm 6, \pm\frac{1}{2}, \pm\frac{1}{4}, \pm\frac{3}{2}, \pm\frac{3}{4}$ **7.** $\pm 1, \pm 2, \pm 3, \pm 4, \pm 6, \pm 12$ **9. a.** $\pm 1, \pm 2, \pm 4$
**b.** 2 is a zero **c.** $\{2, -2, -1\}$ **11. a.** $\pm 1, \pm 2, \pm 3, \pm 6, \pm\frac{1}{2}, \pm\frac{3}{2}$ **b.** 3 is a zero **c.** $\left\{3, \frac{1}{2}, -2\right\}$
**13. a.** $\pm 1, \pm 2, \pm 4, \pm 8, \pm\frac{1}{3}, \pm\frac{2}{3}, \pm\frac{4}{3}, \pm\frac{8}{3}$ **b.** 2 is a zero **c.** $\left\{2, -\frac{1}{3}, -4\right\}$ **15. a.** $\pm 1, \pm 2, \pm 3, \pm 4, \pm 6, \pm 12$ **b.** 4 is a root
**c.** $\{-3, 1, 4\}$ **17. a.** $\pm 1, \pm 2, \pm 3, \pm 4, \pm 6, \pm 12$ **b.** $-2$ is a root **c.** $\{-2, 1 + \sqrt{7}, 1 - \sqrt{7}\}$
**19. a.** $\pm 1, \pm 5, \pm\frac{1}{2}, \pm\frac{5}{2}, \pm\frac{1}{3}, \pm\frac{5}{3}, \pm\frac{1}{6}, \pm\frac{5}{6}$ **b.** $-5$ is a root **c.** $\left\{-5, \frac{1}{2}, \frac{1}{3}\right\}$ **21. a.** $\pm 1, \pm 2, \pm 4$ **b.** 2 is a root
**c.** $\{-2, 2, 1 + \sqrt{2}, 1 - \sqrt{2}\}$ **23.** no positive real roots; 3 or 1 negative real roots **25.** 3 or 1 positive real roots; no negative real roots
**27.** 2 or 0 positive real roots; 2 or 0 negative real roots **29.** $x = -2, x = 5, x = 1$ **31.** $\left\{-\frac{1}{2}, \frac{1 + \sqrt{17}}{2}, \frac{1 - \sqrt{17}}{2}\right\}$
**33.** $\{-1, -2, 3 + \sqrt{13}, 3 - \sqrt{13}\}$ **35.** $x = -1, x = 2, x = -\frac{1}{3}, x = 3$ **37.** $\left\{1, -\frac{3}{4}, i\sqrt{2}, -i\sqrt{2}\right\}$ **39.** $\left\{-2, \frac{1}{2}, \sqrt{2}, -\sqrt{2}\right\}$
**41. a.** $x = 3, x \approx 4.2$ **b.** degree: 4; leading coefficient: negative **43.** $W = 3$ mm **45.** 2 in. by 9 in. by 4 in.
**55.** $\frac{1}{2}, \frac{2}{3}, 2$ **57.** $\pm\frac{1}{2}$ **59.** 5, 3, or 1 positive real roots exist **61.** (d) is true. **63.** 3 in.

## Section 3.5

### Check Point Exercises

**1.**

| | | | | |
|---|---|---|---|---|
| 2 | 2 | 11 | −7 | −6 |
| | | 4 | 30 | 46 |
| | 2 | 15 | 23 | 40 |

All the numbers are nonnegative.

| | | | | |
|---|---|---|---|---|
| −7 | 2 | 11 | −7 | −6 |
| | | −14 | 21 | −98 |
| | 2 | −3 | 14 | −104 |

The signs alternate.

**2.** $f(-3) = -42; f(-2) = 5$
**3.** $\{-3, 7, 2 + i, 2 - i\}$
**4. a.** $(x^2 - 5)(x^2 + 1)$
**b.** $(x + \sqrt{5})(x - \sqrt{5})(x^2 + 1)$
**c.** $(x + \sqrt{5})(x - \sqrt{5})(x + i)(x - i)$
**5.** $f(x) = x^3 + 3x^2 + x + 3$

### Exercise Set 3.5

**1.**

| | | | | | |
|---|---|---|---|---|---|
| −4 | 1 | −5 | 11 | 33 | −18 |
| | | −4 | 36 | −188 | 620 |
| | 1 | −9 | 47 | −155 | 602 |

Since signs alternate, −4 is a lower bound.

| | | | | | |
|---|---|---|---|---|---|
| 7 | 1 | −5 | 11 | 33 | −18 |
| | | 7 | 14 | 175 | 1456 |
| | 1 | 2 | 25 | 208 | 1438 |

Since no sign is negative, 7 is an upper bound.

**3.**

| | | | | |
|---|---|---|---|---|
| −4 | 2 | 5 | −8 | 7 |
| | | −8 | 12 | −16 |
| | 2 | −3 | 4 | −9 |

Since signs alternate, −4 is a lower bound.

| | | | | |
|---|---|---|---|---|
| 2 | 2 | 5 | −8 | 7 |
| | | 4 | 18 | 20 |
| | 2 | 9 | 10 | 27 |

Since no sign is negative, 2 is an upper bound.

**5. a.** $\pm 1, \pm 2, \pm 3, \pm 4, \pm 6, \pm 12$ **b.** 1 is not a root. 1 is an upper bound. **c.** Eliminate all positive possible rational roots. **d.** −3 is not a root. −3 is a lower bound. **e.** Eliminate −3, −4, −6 and −12. **7.** $f(1) = -1; f(2) = 5; 1.3$ **9.** $f(-1) = -1; f(0) = 1; -0.5$ **11.** $f(-3) = -11; f(-2) = 1; -2.1$ **13.** $f(-3) = -42; f(-2) = 5; -2.2$ **15.** $\{-2i, 2i, 2\}$ **17.** $\left\{1 - i, 1 + i, \frac{1}{3}\right\}$ **19.** $\{2 - i, 2 + i, -2 + i, -2 - i\}$ **21.** $\{2 - i, 2 + i, -3, 7\}$ **23. a.** $(x^2 - 5)(x^2 + 4)$ **b.** $(x + \sqrt{5})(x - \sqrt{5})(x^2 + 4)$ **c.** $(x + \sqrt{5})(x - \sqrt{5})(x + 2i)(x - 2i)$ **25. a.** $(x^2 - 2)(x^2 + 3)$ **b.** $(x + \sqrt{2})(x - \sqrt{2})(x^2 + 3)$ **c.** $(x + \sqrt{2})(x - \sqrt{2})(x + i\sqrt{3})(x - i\sqrt{3})$ **27. a.** $(x - 3)(x + 1)(x^2 + 4)$ **b.** $(x - 3)(x + 1)(x^2 + 4)$ **c.** $(x - 3)(x + 1)(x + 2i)(x - 2i)$ **29.** $f(x) = 2x^3 - 2x^2 + 50x - 50$ **31.** $f(x) = x^3 - 3x^2 - 15x + 125$ **33.** $f(x) = x^4 + 10x^2 + 9$ **35.** $f(x) = x^4 - 9x^3 + 21x^2 + 21x - 130$ **37.** $x = 1; x = \pm 5i; f(x) = (x - 1)(x - 5i)(x + 5i)$ **39.** $x = 2; x = 3 \pm 2i; f(x) = (x - 2)(x - 3 + 2i)(x - 3 - 2i)$ **41.** $x = \pm 6i; x = \pm i; f(x) = (x - 6i)(x + 6i)(x - i)(x + i)$ **43.** $x = -2; x = \frac{3}{4}; x = -\frac{1}{2} \pm i;$ $f(x) = (x + 2)(4x - 3)(2x + 1 - 2i)(2x + 1 + 2i)$ **45.** about 2.5 yr **47.** Answers may vary. **49.** According to the linear model, spending will reach \$458 billion, 10.93 or almost 11 years after 1995; According to the quadratic model, spending will reach \$458 billion 10.12 years after 1995; There is a solution between 10.1 and 10.2; According to the third-degree polynomial model, spending will reach \$458 billion just over 10 years after 1995; The third degree polynomial is best.

**55.**

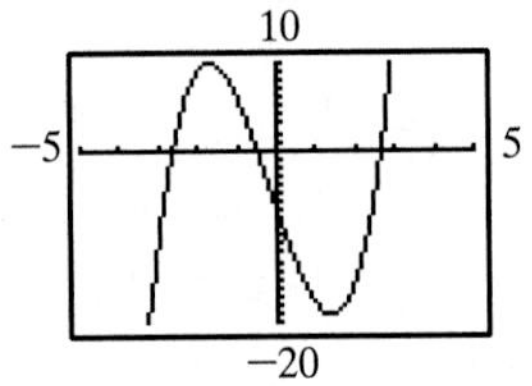


−3 is a lower bound;
3 is an upper bound

**57. a.** As $x$, a person's age, increases, $y$, the number of visits, increases.
**b.** 60
**c.**

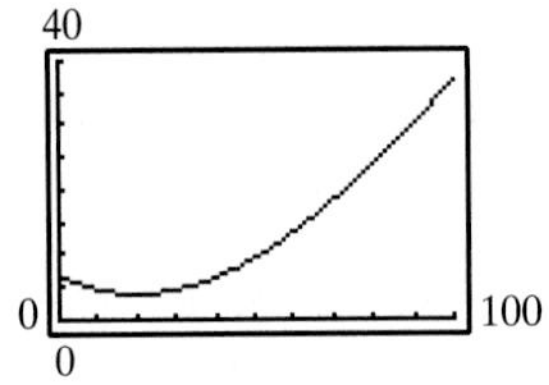


**59.**

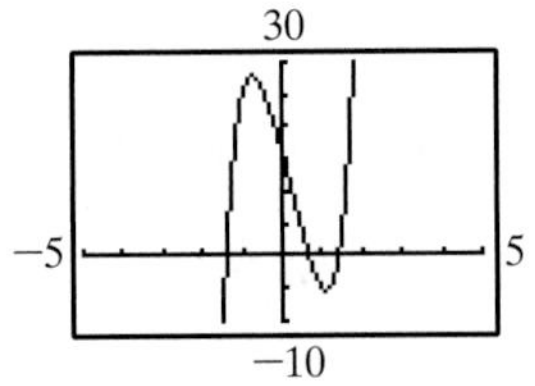


3 real zeros, 2 nonreal complex zeros

**61.**

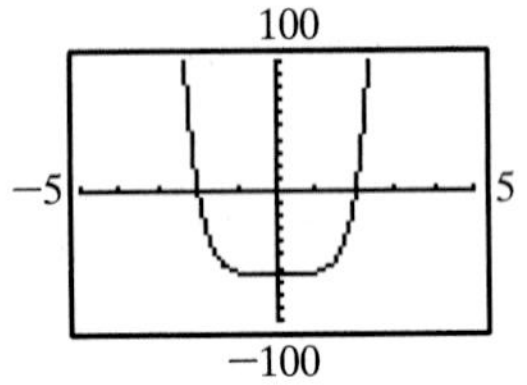


2 real zeros, 4 nonreal complex zeros

**63.** 3
**65.** Answers may vary.
**67.** Answers may vary.

## Section 3.6

### Check Point Exercises

**1. a.** $\{x \mid x \neq 5\}$ **b.** $\{x \mid x \neq -5, x \neq 5\}$ **c.** all real numbers **2. a.** $x = 1, x = -1$ **b.** $x = -1$ **c.** none **3. a.** $y = 3$ **b.** $y = 0$ **c.** none

**4.**

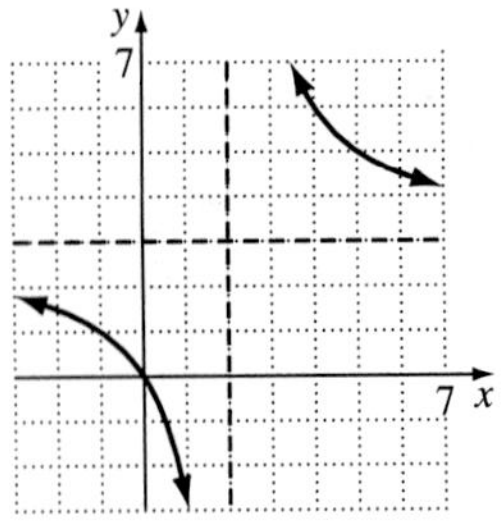


**5.**

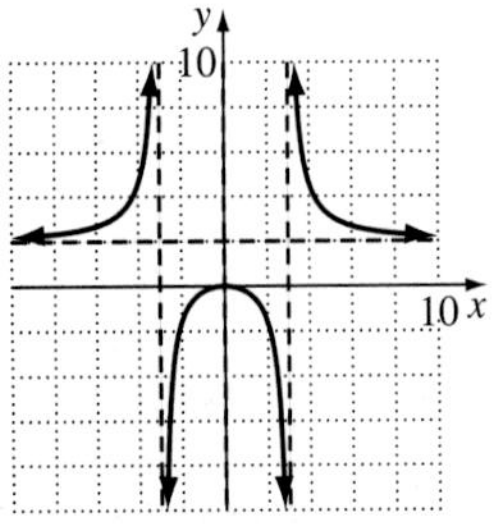


**6.**

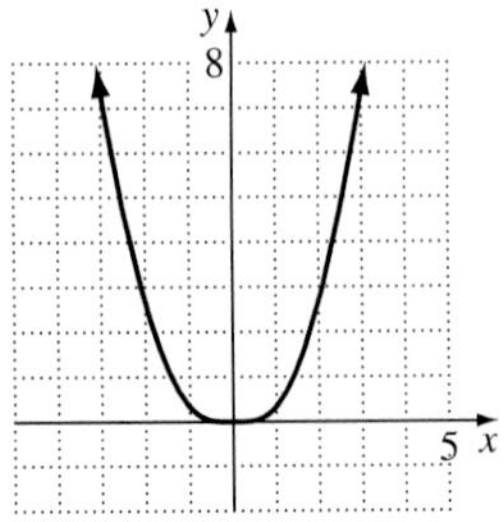


**7.** $y = 2x - 1$

**8. a.** $\overline{C}(1000) = 330$, when 1000 pairs of shoes are produced, it costs \$330 to produce each pair; $\overline{C}(10{,}000) = 60$, when 10,000 pairs of shoes are produced, it costs \$60 to produce each pair; $\overline{C}(100{,}000) = 33$, when 100,000 pairs of shoes are produced, it costs \$33 to produce each pair.

**b.** $y = 30$; The cost per pair of shoes approaches \$30 as more shoes are produced. **9.** $T = \frac{20}{x} + \frac{20}{x - 10}$

## Exercise Set 3.6

**1.** $\{x|x \neq 4\}$ **3.** $\{x|x \neq 5, x \neq -4\}$ **5.** $\{x|x \neq 7, x \neq -7\}$ **7.** All real numbers **9.** $-\infty$ **11.** $-\infty$ **13.** 0 **15.** $+\infty$ **17.** $-\infty$ **19.** 1 **21.** $x = -4$ **23.** $x = 0, x = -4$ **25.** $x = -4$ **27.** no vertical asymptotes **29.** $y = 0$ **31.** $y = 4$ **33.** no horizontal asymptote **35.** $y = -\frac{2}{3}$

**37.**
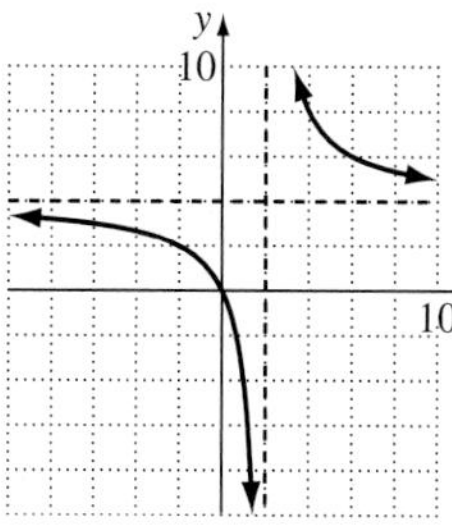


**39.**
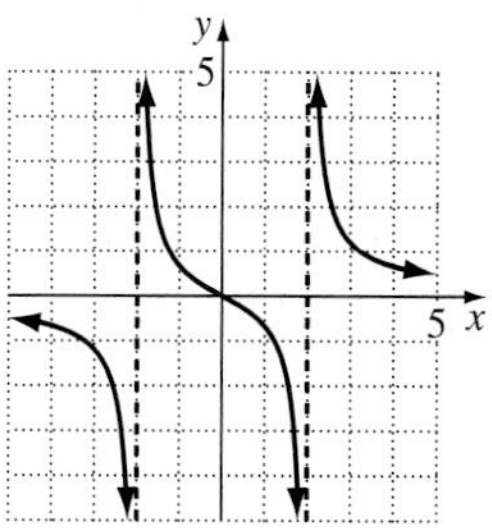


**41.**
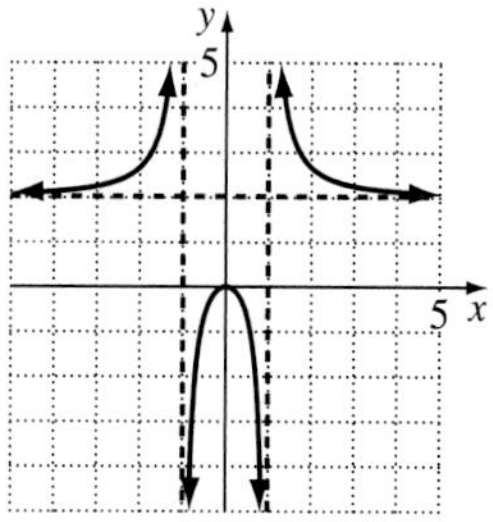


**43.**
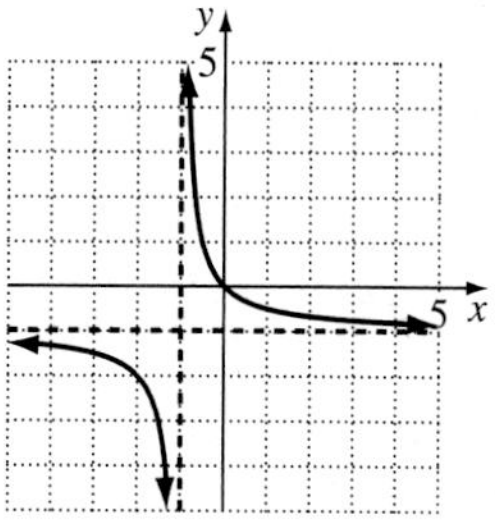


**45.**
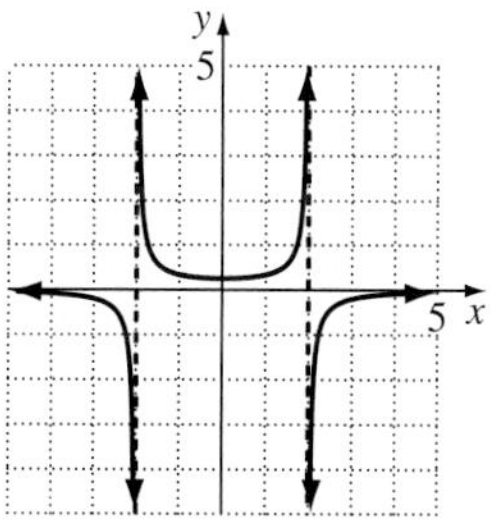


**47.**
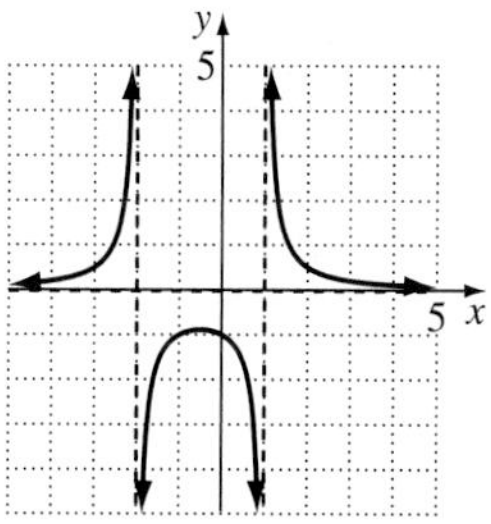


**49.**
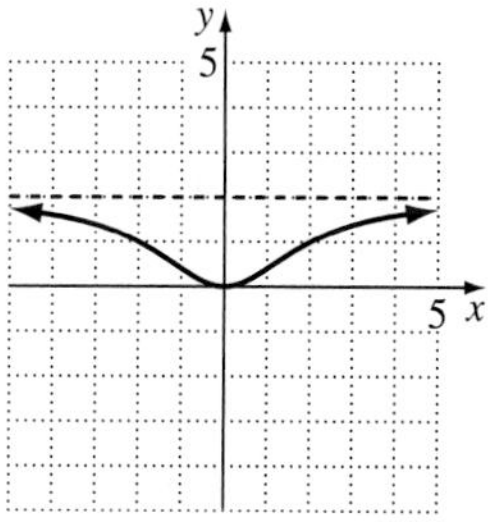


**51.**
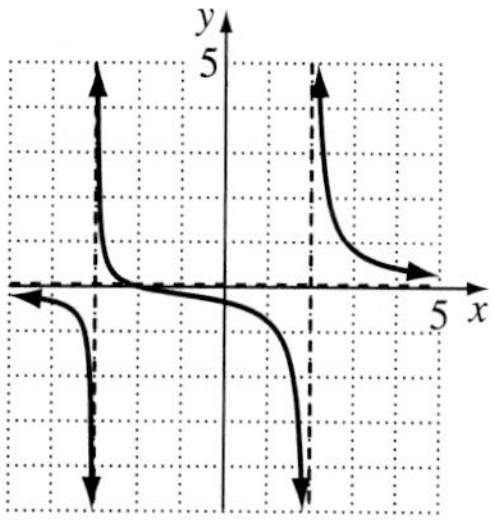


**53.**
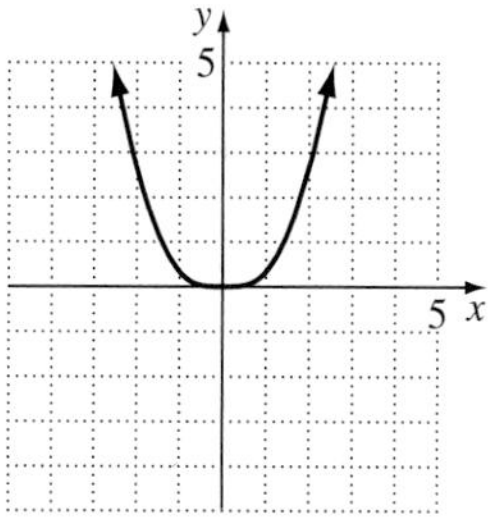


**55.**
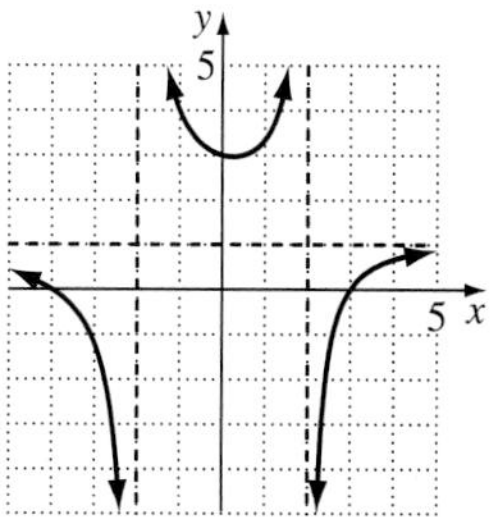


**57.**
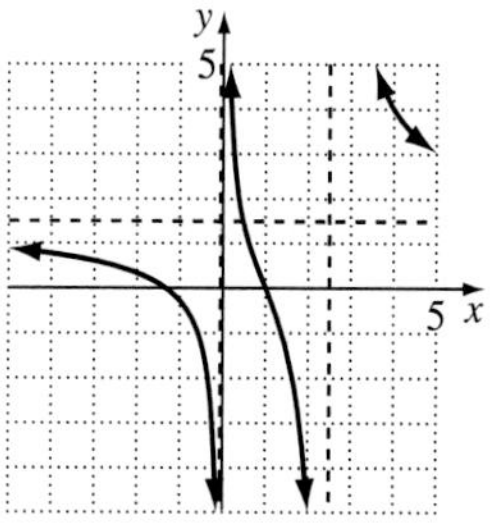


**59. a.** Slant asymptote: $y = x$

**b.**
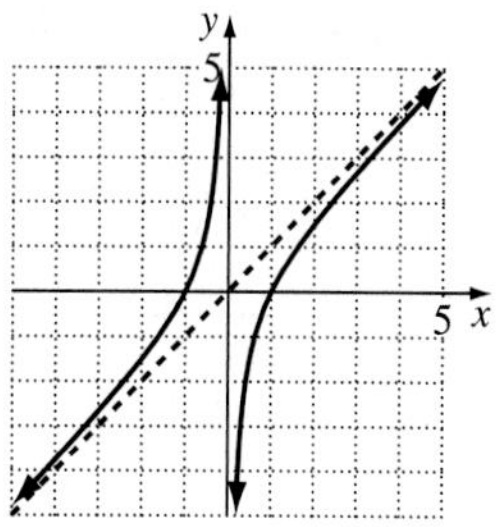


**61. a.** Slant asymptote: $y = x$

**b.**
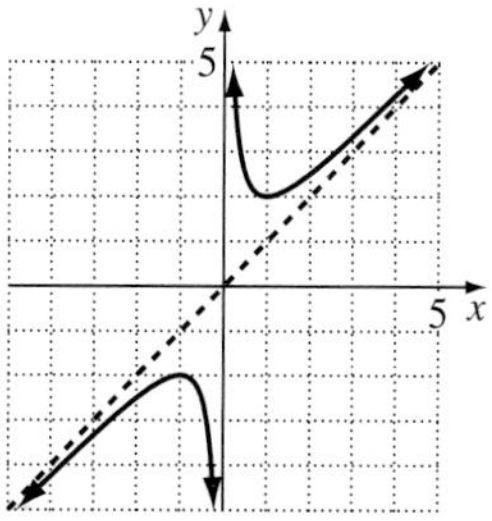


**63. a.** Slant asymptote: $y = x + 4$

**b.**
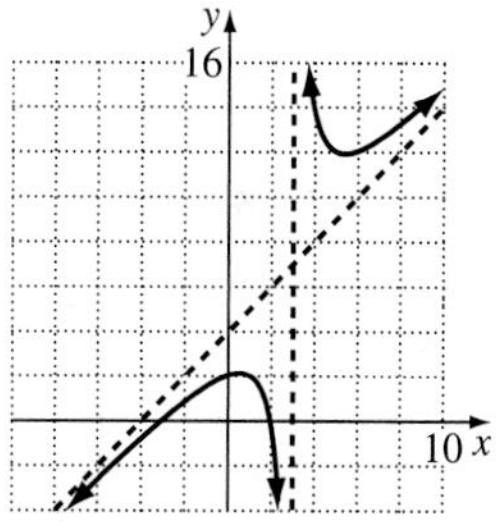


**65. a.** Slant asymptote: $y = x - 2$

**b.**
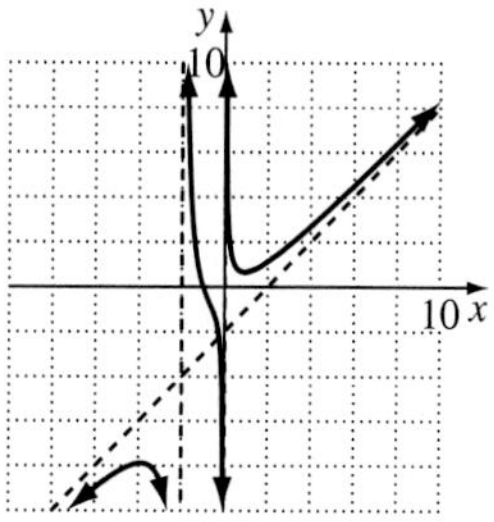


**67. a.** $\overline{C}(100) = \$220$; $\overline{C}(1000) = \$40$; $\overline{C}(10{,}000) = \$22$; $\overline{C}(100{,}000) = \$20.2$

**b.** $y = 20$; \$20 is the minimum average cost of producing a canoe. As more canoes are manufactured, the average cost approaches \$20.

**69. a.** \$100,000

**b.** No; the model indicates that no amount of money can remove 100% of the pollutants since $C(p)$ increases without bound as $p$ approaches 100.

**71. a.** $F(0) = 80$; When the dessert is placed in the icebox, its temperature is 80°F.
**b.** $F(1) = 13.3$°F; $F(2) = 6.2$°F; $F(3) \approx 3.6$°F; $F(4) \approx 2.4$°F; $F(5) \approx 1.7$°F
**c.** $y = 0$; The temperature will approach but not reach 0°F.
**d.**

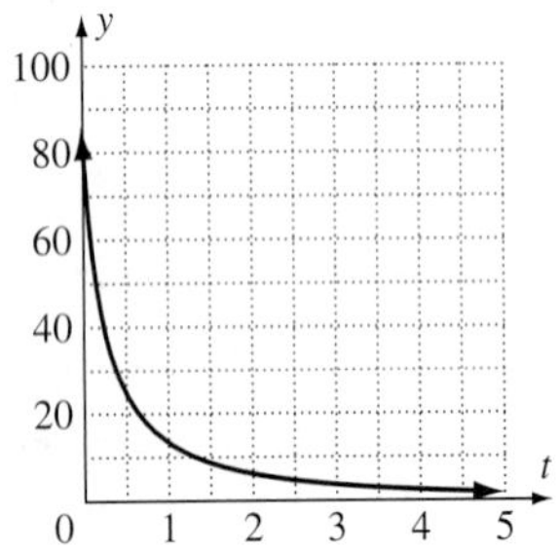

**73. a.** After 1 day: 35 words; after 5 days: about 12 words; after 15 days: about 7 words
**b.** $N(1) = 35$ words; This is the same as the estimate from the graph.; $N(5) = 11$ words; This is a little less than the estimate from the graph.; $N(15) = 7$ words; This is the same as the estimate from the graph.
**c.** The graph indicates the students will remember 5 words over a long period of time.
**d.** $y = 5$; The horizontal asymptote indicates the students will remember 5 words over a long period of time.

**75.** $T(x) = \frac{600}{x} + \frac{600}{x - 10}$ **77.** $P(x) = 2x + \frac{5000}{x}$

**89.**

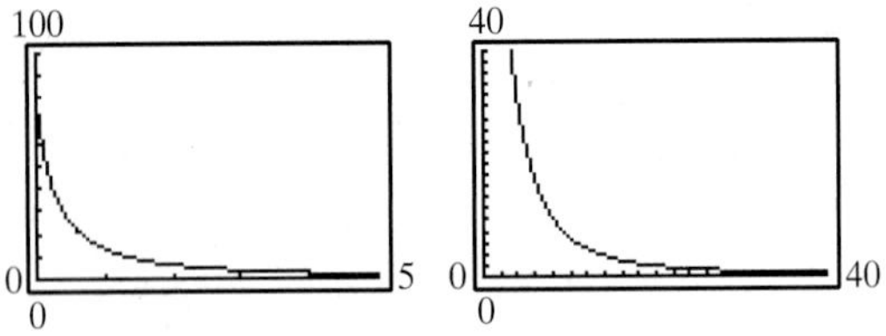

**91.**

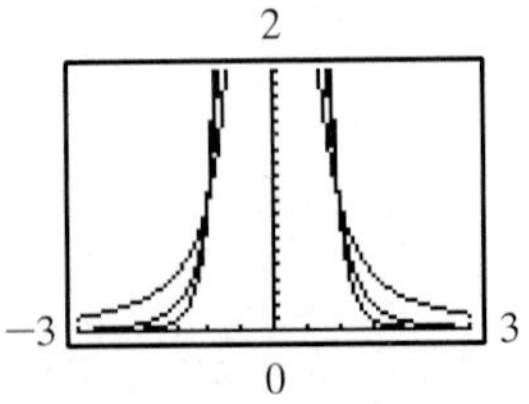

The graph approaches the horizontal asymptote faster and the vertical asymptote slower as $n$ increases.

**93.**

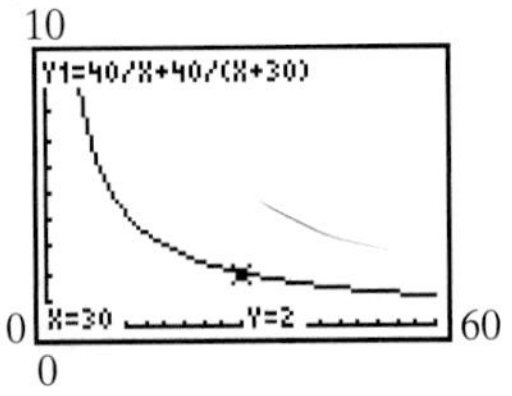


30 mph

**95.**

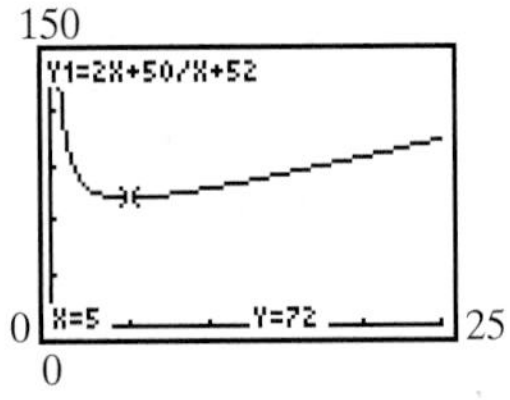


6 in. by 12 in.

**97.** (d) is true. **99.** Answers may vary. **101.** Answers may vary.

## Section 3.7

### Check Point Exercises

**1.** 137.5 lb/in$^2$ **2.** about 556 ft **3.** 10 new songs **4.** 24 min **5.** $96\pi$ ft$^3$

### Exercise Set 3.7

**1.** 84 **3.** 25 **5.** $\frac{5}{6}$ **7.** 240 **9. a.** $L = kW$ **b.** $L = 0.02W$ **c.** 1.04 in. **11.** \$60 **13.** 2442 mph **15.** 607 lb **17.** 0.5 hr **19.** 6.4 lb **21.** 31.78; index: about 32; not in the desirable range **23.** 11.11 foot-candles **25.** 72 erg **27.** The average number of phone calls is about 126. **29.** Yes **41.** The illumination is $\frac{1}{4}$ as much.

**43.** $b = \frac{h}{d^2}, \frac{1}{50}\frac{h}{d^2} = \frac{h}{50d^2} = \frac{h}{(\sqrt{50}d)^2} \approx \frac{h}{(7d)^2}$

### Chapter 3 Review Exercises

**1.**

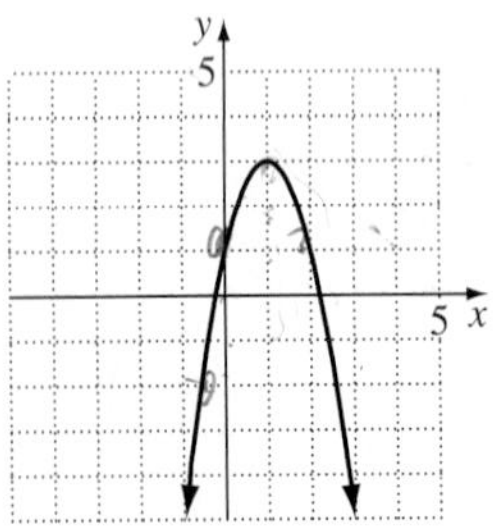

axis of symmetry: $x = 1$

**2.**

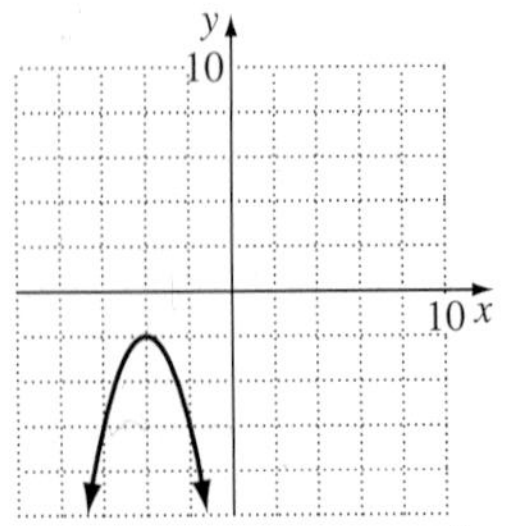

axis of symmetry: $x = -4$

**3.**

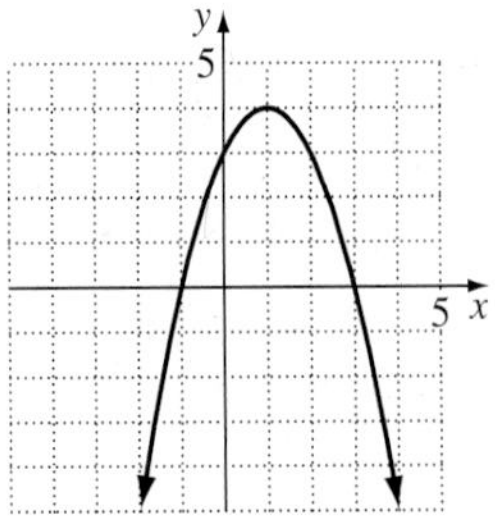

axis of symmetry: $x = 1$

**4.**

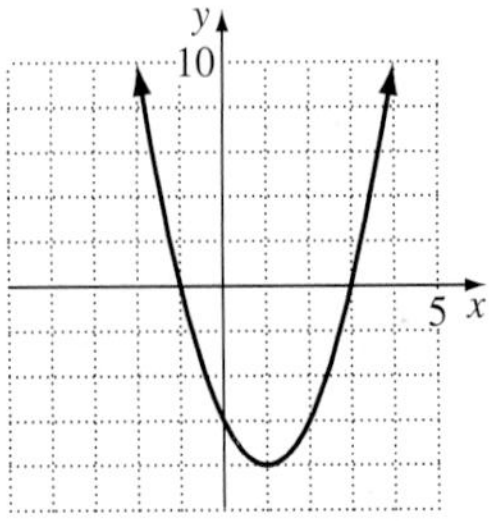

axis of symmetry: $x = 1$

**5.** 7.2 hr; 622 deaths **6.** 2 sec; 144 ft **7.** 250 yd by 500 yd; 125,000 $yd^2$ **8.** 60 people; \$360 **9. c.** **10. b.** **11. a.** **12. d.** **13.** Because the degree is odd and the leading coefficient is negative, the graph falls to the right. Therefore, the model indicates that the percentage of families below the poverty level will eventually be negative, which is impossible. **14.** Since the degree is even and the leading coefficient is negative, the graph falls to the right. Therefore, the model indicates a patient will eventually have a negative number of viral bodies, which is impossible. **15.** $x = 1$, multiplicity 1, crosses; $x = -2$, multiplicity 2, touches; $x = -5$, multiplicity 3, crosses **16.** $x = -5$, multiplicity 1, crosses; $x = 5$, multiplicity 2, touches

**17. a.** The graph falls to the left and rises to the right. **b.** no symmetry **c.**

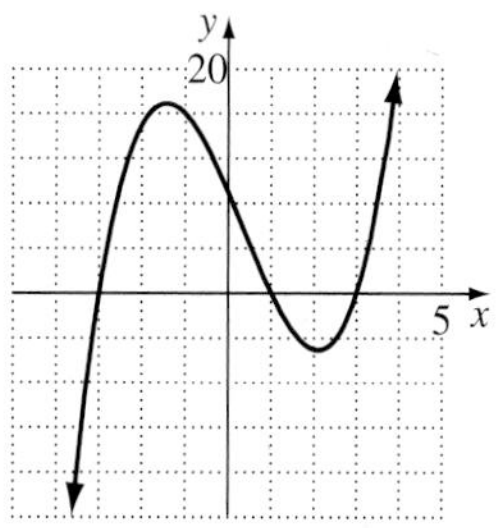


**18. a.** The graph rises to the left and falls to the right. **b.** origin symmetry **c.**

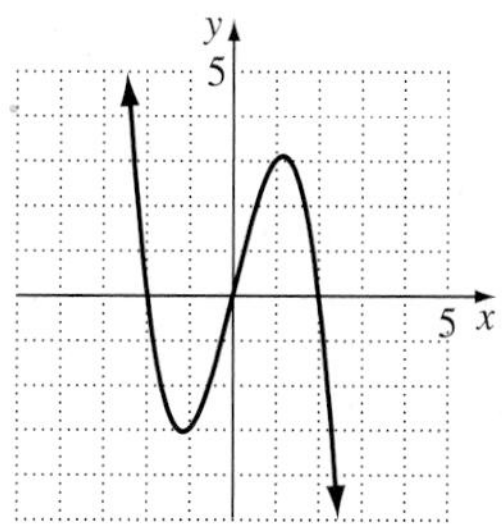


**19. a.** The graph falls to the left and rises to the right. **b.** no symmetry **c.**

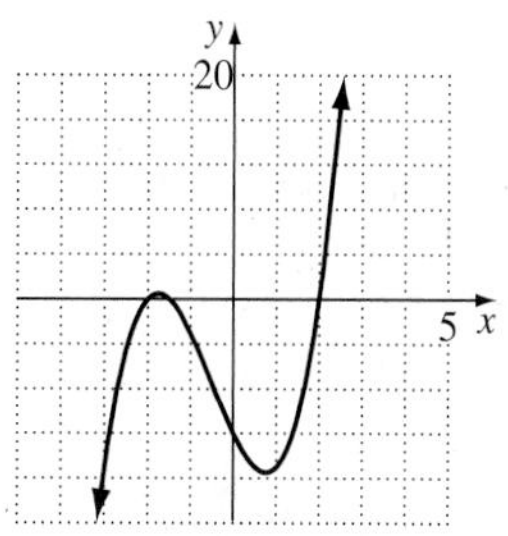


**20. a.** The graph falls to the left and to the right. **b.** $y$-axis symmetry **c.**

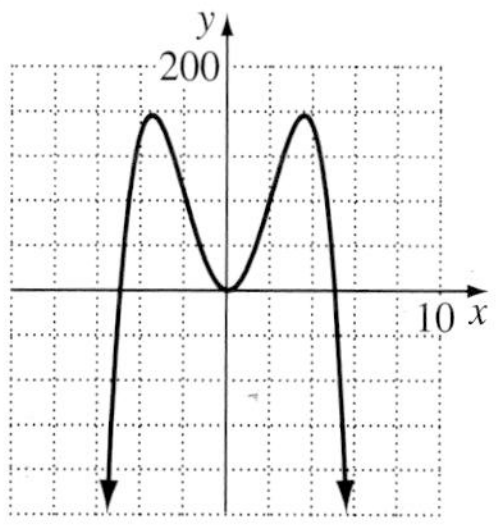


**21. a.** The graph falls to the left and to the right. **b.** no symmetry **c.**

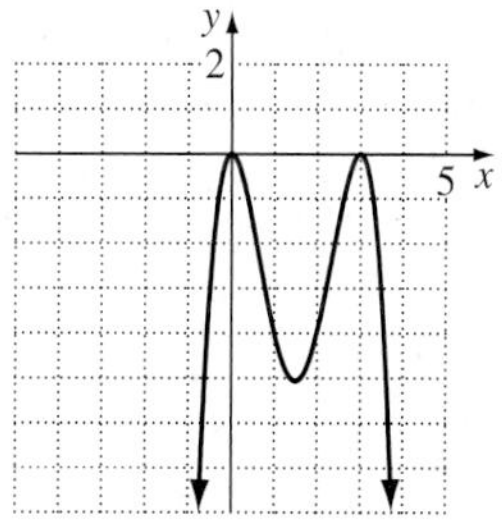


**22. a.** The graph rises to the left and to the right. **b.** no symmetry **c.**

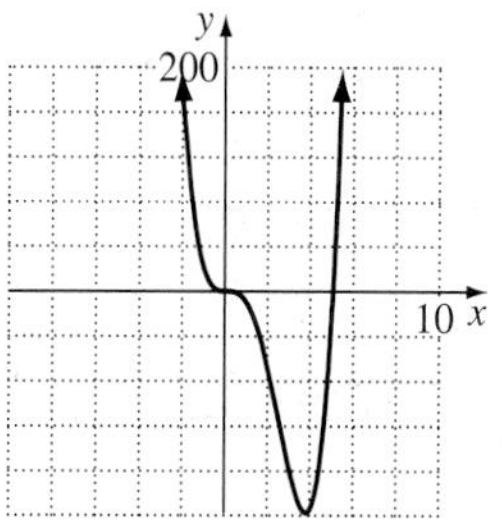


**23.** $4x^2 - 7x + 5 - \frac{4}{x+1}$ **24.** $2x^2 - 4x + 1 - \frac{10}{5x-3}$ **25.** $2x^2 + 3x - 1$ **26.** $3x^3 - 4x^2 + 7$

**27.** $3x^3 + 6x^2 + 10x + 10 + \frac{20}{x-2}$ **28.** $-5697$ **29.** $2, \frac{1}{2}, -3$ **30.** $\{4, -2 \pm \sqrt{5}\}$ **31.** $\pm1, \pm5$

**32.** $\pm1, \pm2, \pm4, \pm8, \pm\frac{8}{3}, \pm\frac{4}{3}, \pm\frac{2}{3}, \pm\frac{1}{3}$ **33.** 2 or 0 positive solutions; no negative solutions

**34.** 3 or 1 positive real roots; 2 or 0 negative solutions **35.** No sign variations exist for either $f(x)$ or $f(-x)$, so no real roots exist.

**36. a.** $\pm1, \pm2, \pm4$ **b.** 1 positive real zero; 2 or no negative real zeros **c.** 1 is a zero **d.** $\{1, -2\}$

**37. a.** $\pm1, \pm\frac{1}{2}, \pm\frac{1}{3}, \pm\frac{1}{6}$ **b.** 2 or 0 positive real zeros; 1 negative real zero **c.** $-1$ is a zero **d.** $\left\{-1, \frac{1}{3}, \frac{1}{2}\right\}$

**38. a.** $\pm1, \pm3, \pm5, \pm15, \pm\frac{1}{2}, \pm\frac{1}{4}, \pm\frac{1}{8}, \pm\frac{3}{2}, \pm\frac{3}{4}, \pm\frac{3}{8}, \pm\frac{5}{2}, \pm\frac{5}{4}, \pm\frac{5}{8}, \pm\frac{15}{2}, \pm\frac{15}{4}, \pm\frac{15}{8}$

**b.** 3 or 1 positive real solutions; no negative real solutions **c.** $\frac{1}{2}$ is a zero **d.** $\left\{\frac{1}{2}, \frac{3}{2}, \frac{5}{2}\right\}$

**39. a.** $\pm1, \pm2, \pm3, \pm6$ **b.** 2 or zero positive real solutions; 2 or zero negative real solutions **c.** $-2$ is a zero **d.** $\{-2, -1, 1, 3\}$

**40. a.** $\pm1, \pm2, \pm\frac{1}{2}, \pm\frac{1}{4}$ **b.** 1 positive real root; 1 negative real root **c.** $\frac{1}{2}$ is a zero **d.** $\left\{\frac{1}{2}, -\frac{1}{2}, i\sqrt{2}, -i\sqrt{2}\right\}$

**41. a.** $\pm1, \pm2, \pm4, \pm\frac{1}{2}$ **b.** 2 or no positive zeros; 2 or no negative zeros **c.** $x = 2$ is a zero **d.** $\left\{2, -2, \frac{1}{2}, -1\right\}$

**42.**

| | | | | | |
|---|---|---|---|---|---|
| $-2$ | 2 | $-7$ | $-5$ | 28 | $-12$ |
| | | $-4$ | 22 | $-34$ | 12 |
| | 2 | $-11$ | 17 | $-6$ | 0 |

$-2$ is a root and a lower bound.

| | | | | | |
|---|---|---|---|---|---|
| 6 | 2 | $-7$ | $-5$ | 28 | $-12$ |
| | | 12 | 30 | 150 | 1068 |
| | 2 | 5 | 25 | 178 | 1056 |

6 is an upper bound, but not a zero.

$\pm1, \pm2, 3, 4, \pm\frac{1}{2}, \pm\frac{3}{2}$

**43. a.** $\pm1, \pm2, \pm3, \pm4, \pm6, \pm12, \pm\frac{1}{2}, \pm\frac{3}{2}$ **b.** 2 is not a root but is an upper bound. **c.** $-2$ is not a root but is a lower bound.

**d.** Possible roots are $\pm1$, $\pm\frac{1}{2}$, and $\pm\frac{3}{2}$. **44.** $f(1) = -2; f(2) = 3; x \approx 1.6$ **45.** $f(-3) = -32; f(-2) = 7; x \approx -2.3$

**46.** $\left\{-\frac{1}{4}, 6 \pm 5i\right\}$ **47.** $\{1 \pm 3i, 1 \pm i\}$ **48.** $\left\{-\frac{1}{2}, 1, 4 \pm 7i\right\}$ **49.** $f(x) = x^3 - 6x^2 + 21x - 26$

**50.** $f(x) = 2x^4 + 12x^3 + 20x^2 + 12x + 18$ **51.** $f(x) = x^4 - 3x^3 + 6x^2 + 2x - 60$

**52.** $-2, \frac{1}{2}, \pm i; f(x) = (x - i)(x + i)(x + 2)\left(x - \frac{1}{2}\right)$ **53.** $-1, 4; g(x) = (x + 1)^2(x - 4)^2$

**54.** 4 real zeros, one with multiplicity two **55.** 3 real zeros; 2 nonreal complex zeros

**56.** 2 real zeros, one with multiplicity two; 2 nonreal complex zeros **57.** 1 real zero; 4 nonreal complex zeros

**58.** Vertical asymptote: $x = 3$ and $x = -3$
horizontal asymptote: $y = 0$

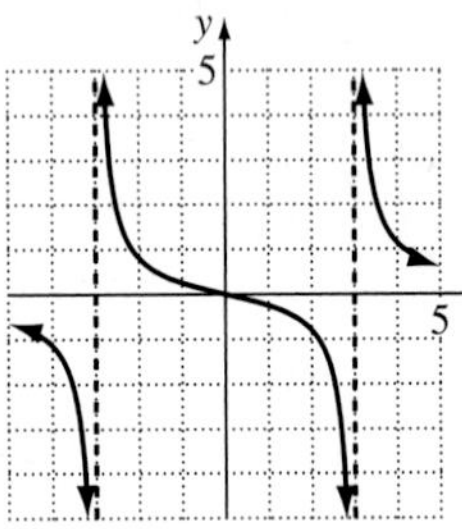


**59.** Vertical asymptote: $x = -3$
horizontal asymptote: $y = 2$

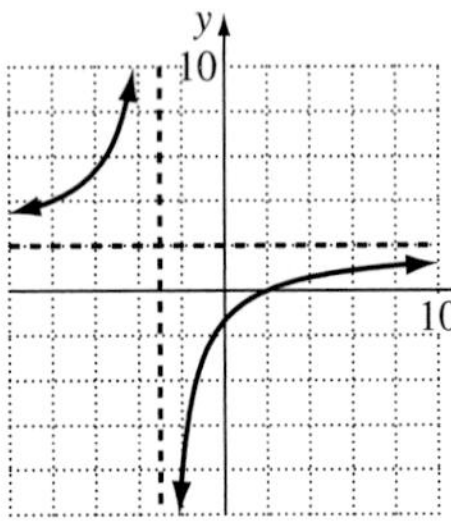


**60.** Vertical asymptotes: $x = 3, -2$
horizontal asymptote: $y = 1$

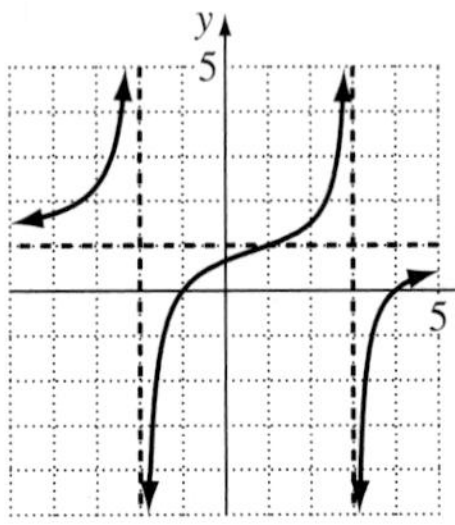


**61.** Vertical asymptote: $x = -2$
horizontal asymptote: $y = 1$

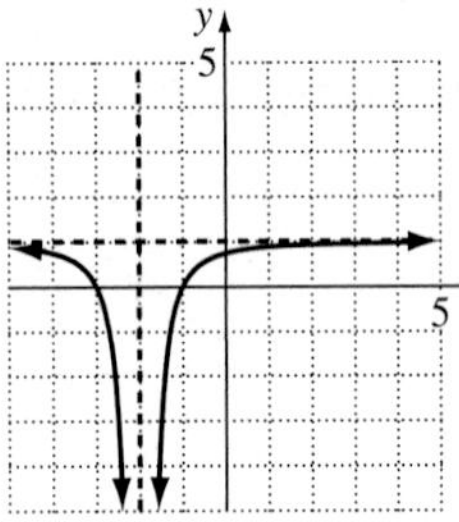


**62.** Vertical asymptote: $x = -1$
no horizontal asymptote
slant asymptote: $y = x - 1$

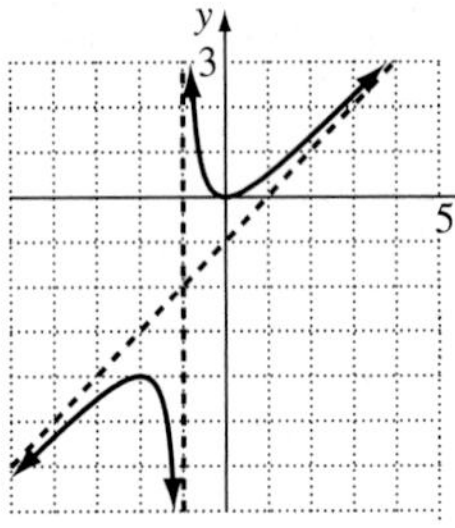


**63.** Vertical asymptote: $x = 3$
no horizontal asymptote
slant asymptote: $y = x + 5$

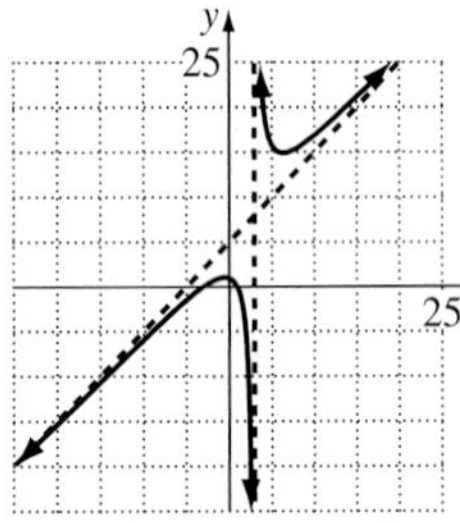


**64.** No vertical asymptote

no horizontal asymptote
slant asymptote: $y = -2x$

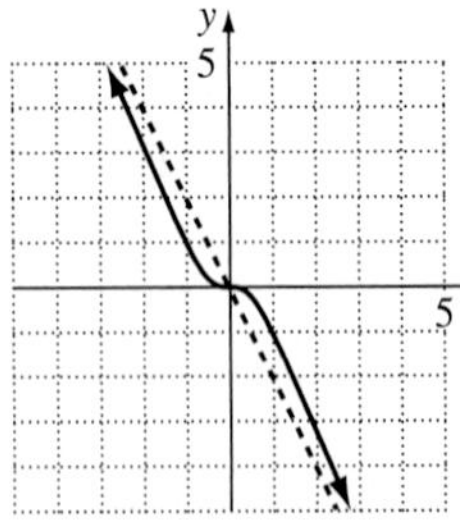


**65.** Vertical asymptote: $x = \frac{3}{2}$

no horizontal asymptote
slant asymptote: $y = 2x - 5$

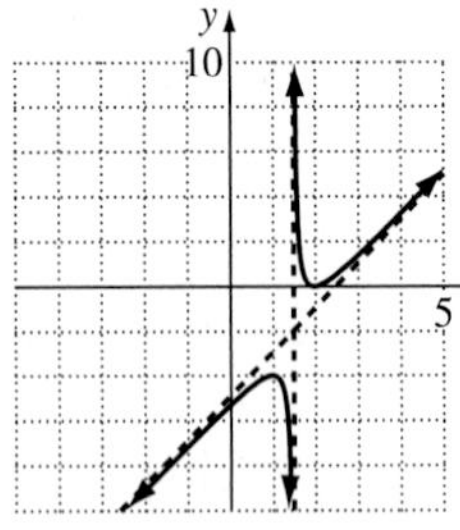


**66. a.** $\overline{C}(50) = 1025$, when 50 calculators are manufactured, it costs \$1025 to manufacture each; $\overline{C}(100) = 525$, when 100 calculators are manufactured, it costs \$525 to manufacture each; $\overline{C}(1000) = 75$, when 1000 calculators are manufactured, it costs \$75 to manufacture each; $\overline{C}(100{,}000) = 25.5$, when 100,000 calculators are manufactured, it costs \$25.50 to manufacture each.
**b.** $y = 25$; Minimum costs will approach \$25.

**67. a.** 1600; The difference in cost of removing 90% versus 50% of the contaminants is 16 million dollars.
**b.** $x = 100$; No amount of money can remove 100% of the contaminants, since $C(x)$ increases without bound as $x$ approaches 100.

**68.** $y = 3000$; The number of fish in the pond approaches 3,000,000.

**69.** $y = 0$; As the number of years of education increases the percentage rate of unemployment approaches zero.

**70.** Since $C(p)$ increases without bound as $p$ approaches 100, the politician will not be able to keep his promise.

**71.** $T(x) = \frac{4}{x + 3} + \frac{2}{x}$ **72.** $P(x) = 2x + \frac{2000}{x}$ **73.** \$154 **74.** 1600 ft **75.** 5 hr **76.** 112 decibels **77.** 16 hr

**78.** 800 $ft^3$

## Chapter 3 Test

**1.** axis of symmetry: $x = -1$

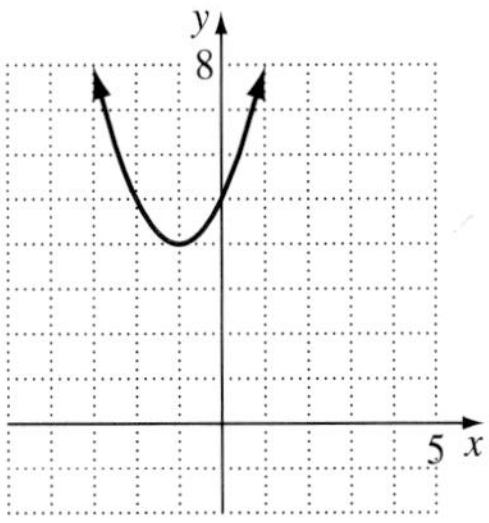


**2.** axis of symmetry: $x = 1$

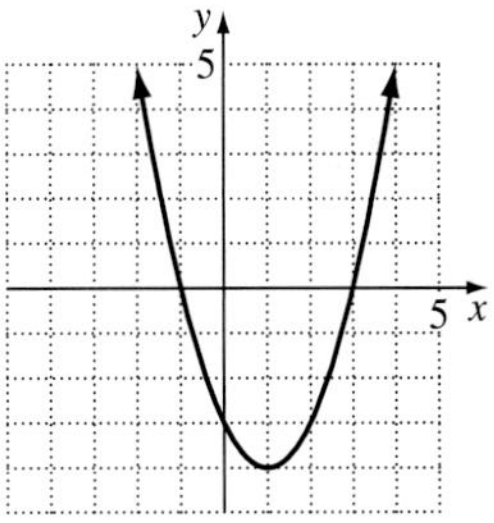


**3.** maximum; $(3, 2)$

**4.** 23 VCRs; maximum daily profit = \$16,900

**5. a.** $5, 2, -2$

**b.**

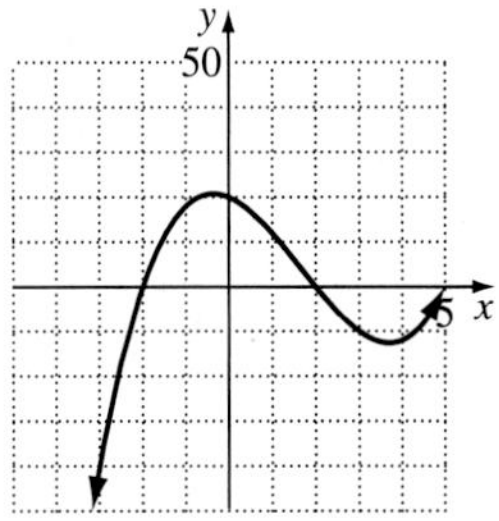


**6.** Since the degree of the polynomial is odd and the leading coefficient is positive, the graph of $f$ should fall to the left and rise to the right. The $x$-intercepts should be $-1$ and $1$.

**7. a.** 2 **b.** $\frac{1}{2}, \frac{2}{3}$ **8.** $\pm 1, \pm 2, \pm 3, \pm 6, \pm\frac{1}{2}, \pm\frac{3}{2}$ **9.** 3 or 1 positive real zeros; no negative real zeros. **10.** $\{-5, -3, 2\}$

**11. a.** $\pm 1, \pm 3, \pm 5, \pm 15, \pm\frac{1}{2}, \pm\frac{3}{2}, \pm\frac{5}{2}, \pm\frac{15}{2}$ **b.** $\left\{-1, \frac{3}{2}, \pm\sqrt{5}\right\}$

**12.**

| | | | | | |
|---|---|---|---|---|---|
| −3 | 3 | 4 | −7 | −2 | −3 |
| | | −9 | 15 | −24 | 78 |
| | 3 | −5 | 8 | −26 | 75 |

−3 is a lower bound.

| | | | | | |
|---|---|---|---|---|---|
| 2 | 3 | 4 | −7 | −2 | −3 |
| | | 6 | 20 | 26 | 48 |
| | 3 | 10 | 13 | 24 | 45 |

2 is an upper bound.

**13.** $\{2, 3, 1 + i\}$ **14.** $(x - 1)(x + 2)^2$

**15.** domain: $\{x \mid x \neq 4, x \neq -4\}$

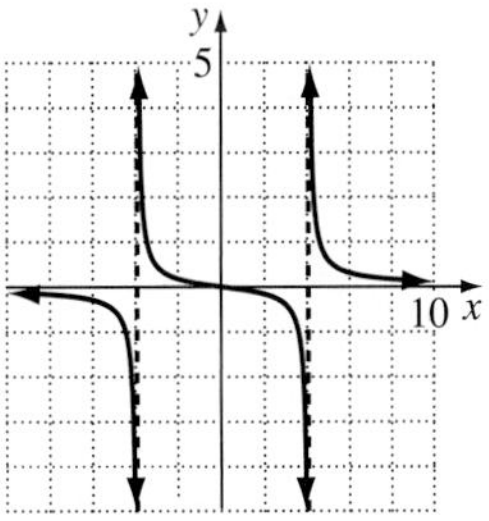


**16.** domain: $\{x \mid x \neq 2\}$

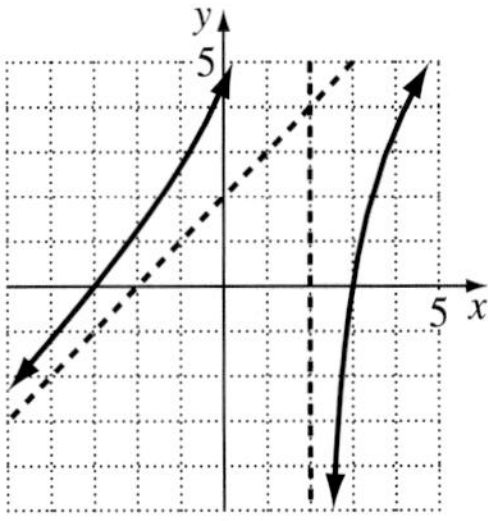


**17.** domain: $\{x \mid x \neq -3, x \neq 1\}$

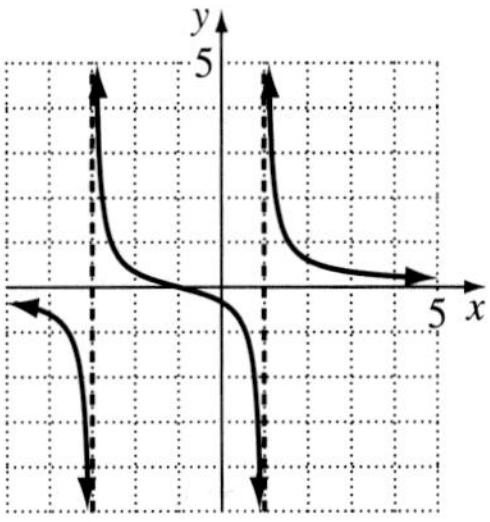


**18.** domain: all real numbers

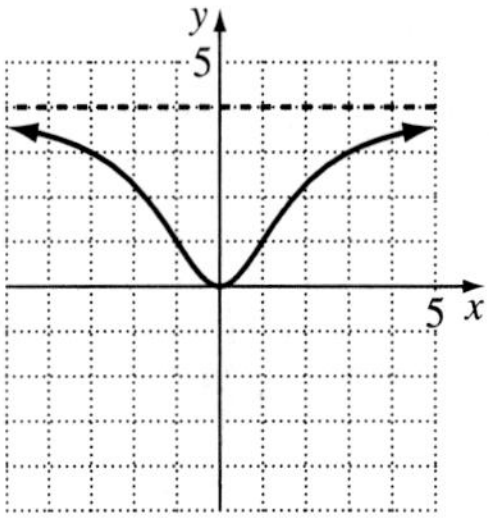


**19. a.** 50 **b.** 150 **c.** $y = 225$; The deer population will approach a maximum of 225 deer. **20.** 45 foot-candles

## Cumulative Review Exercises (Chapters P–3)

**1.** $2 + \sqrt{3}$ **2.** $-3x^2 - 11x + 11$ **3.** $15\sqrt{2}$ **4.** $x^5(x - 1)(x + 1)$ **5.** $\{2, -1\}$ **6.** $\left\{\frac{5 + \sqrt{13}}{6}, \frac{5 - \sqrt{13}}{6}\right\}$ **7.** $\left\{\frac{1}{3}, -\frac{2}{3}\right\}$

**8.** $\{-3, -1, 2\}$ **9.** $(-\infty, 1)$ or $(4, \infty)$ **10.** $(-\infty, -1)$ or $\left(\frac{5}{3}, \infty\right)$

**11.** Center: $(1, -2)$; radius: 3

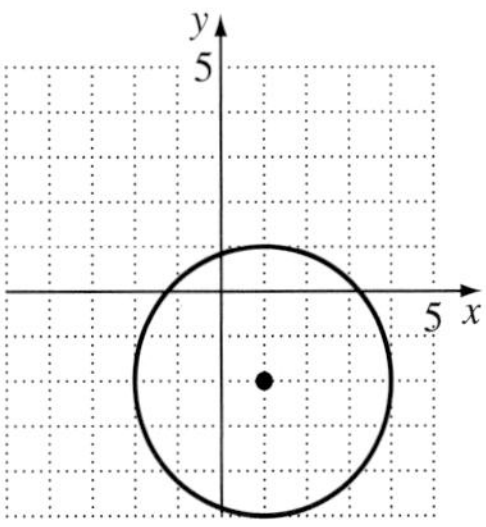


**12.** $t = 1 - \frac{V}{C}$

**13.** $(-\infty, 5]$

**14.** $x^2 - 2x - 4$

**15.** $16x^2 - 6$

**16.** $-9$

**17. a.** $\{-1, 1, 4\}$

**b.**

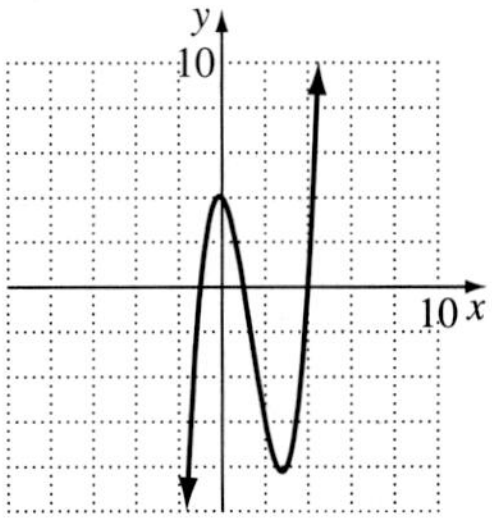


**18.**

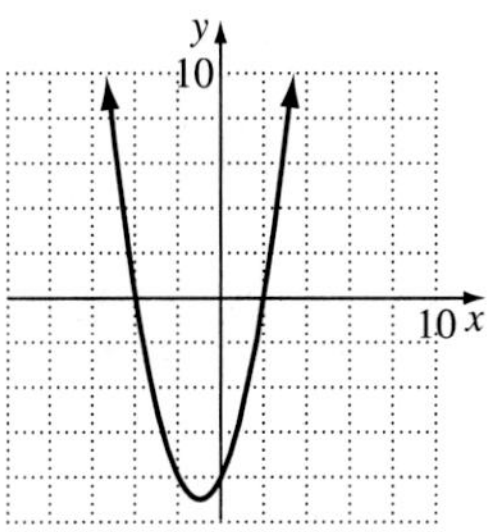

**19.**

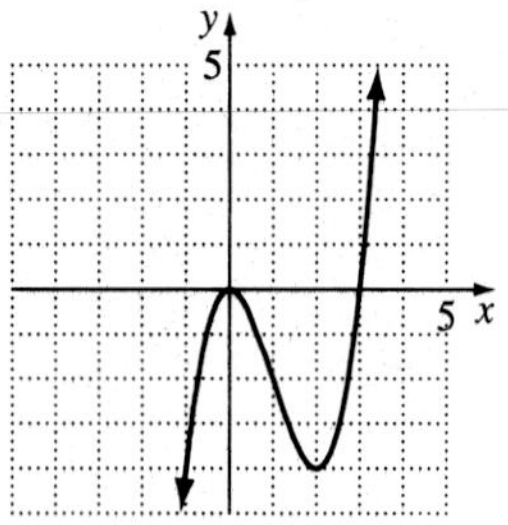

**20.**

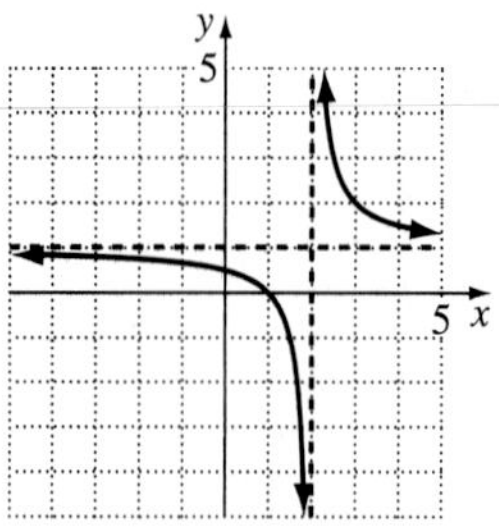

# CHAPTER 4

## Section 4.1

### Check Point Exercises

**1.** 1 O-ring

**2.**

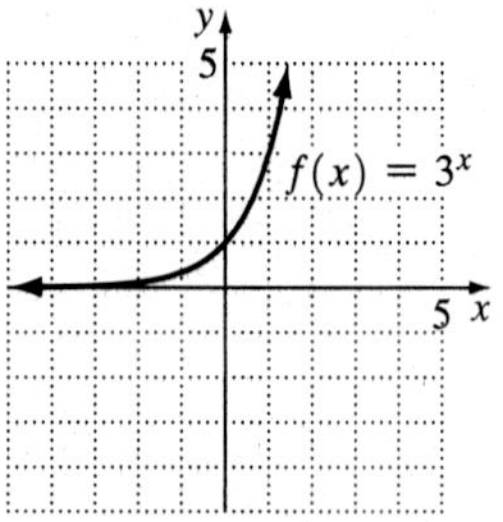


**3.**

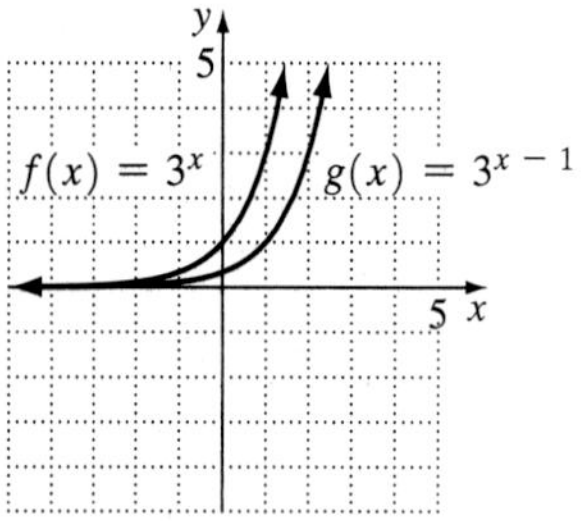


**4.**

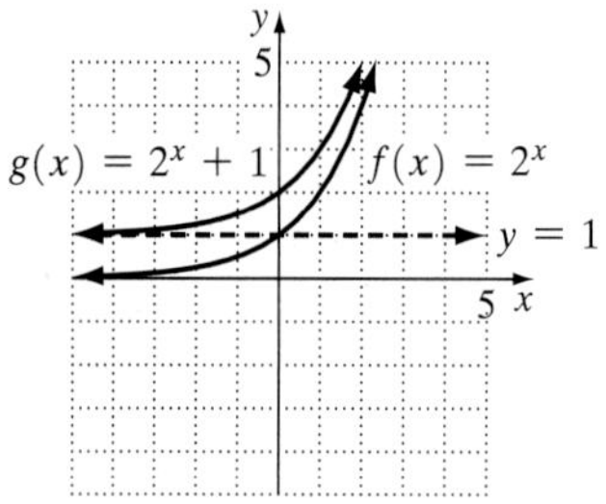


**5.** 11.64 billion
**6. a.** \$14,859.47
**b.** \$14,918.25

### Exercise Set 4.1

**1.** 10.556 **3.** 11.665 **5.** 0.125 **7.** 9.974 **9.** 0.387

**11.**

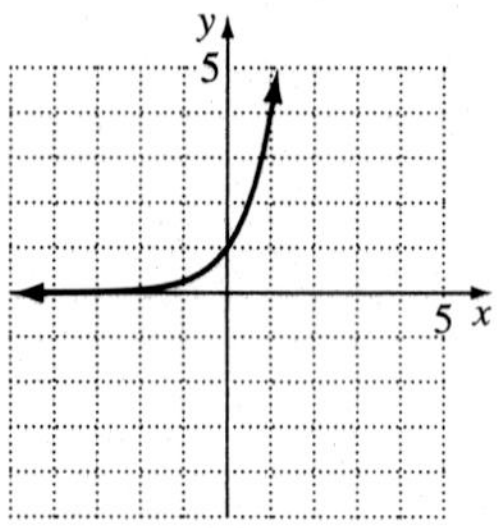

**13.**

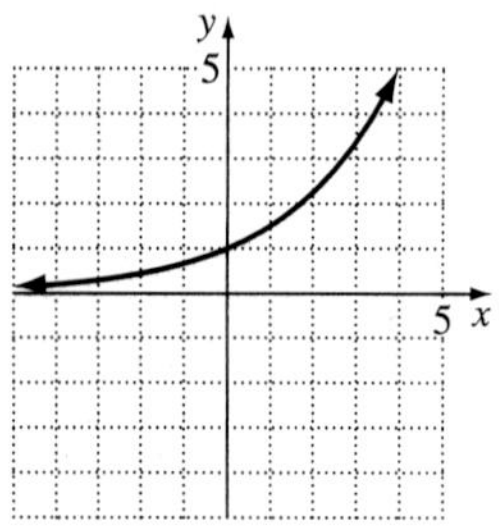

**15.**

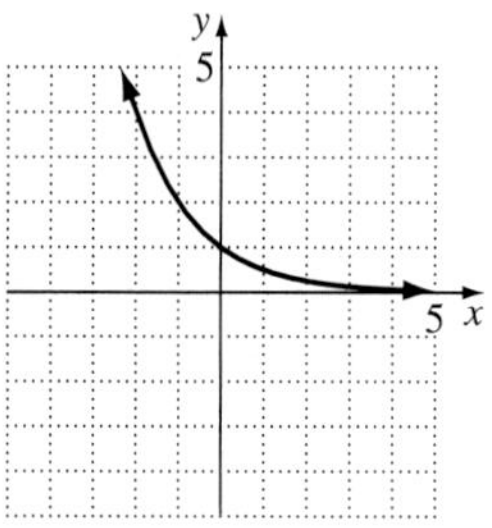

**17.**

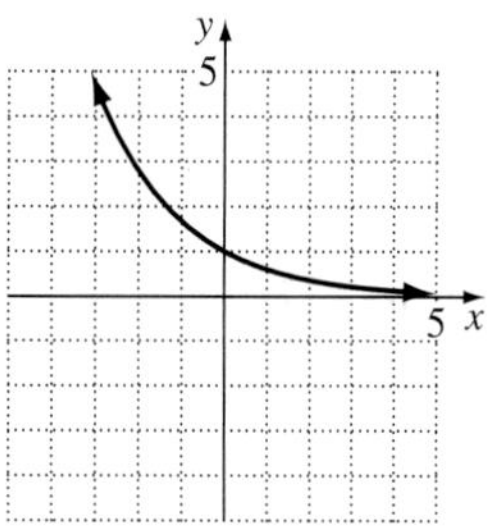

**19.** $H(x) = -3^{-x}$ **21.** $F(x) = -3^x$ **23.** $h(x) = 3^x - 1$

**25.**

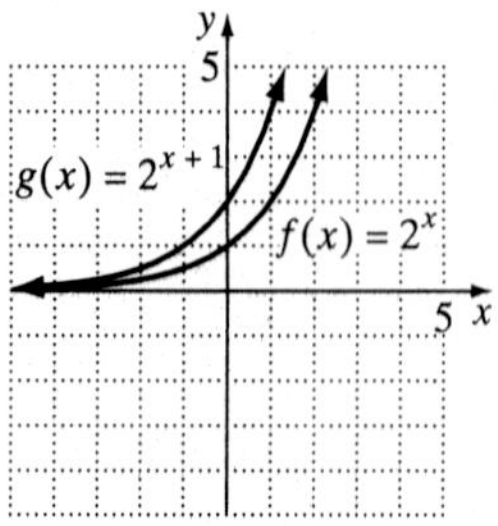


**27.**

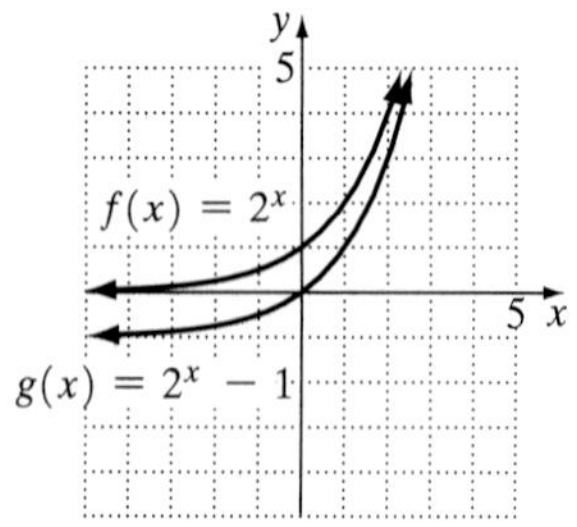


**29.**

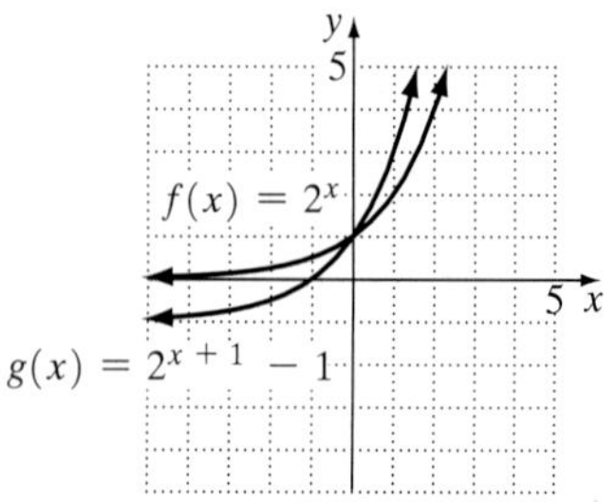

**31.**

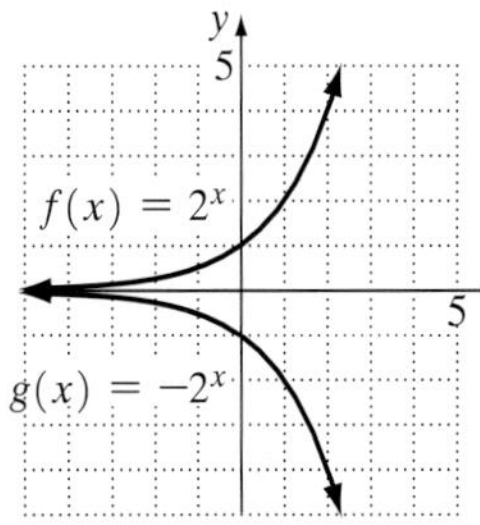


**33.**

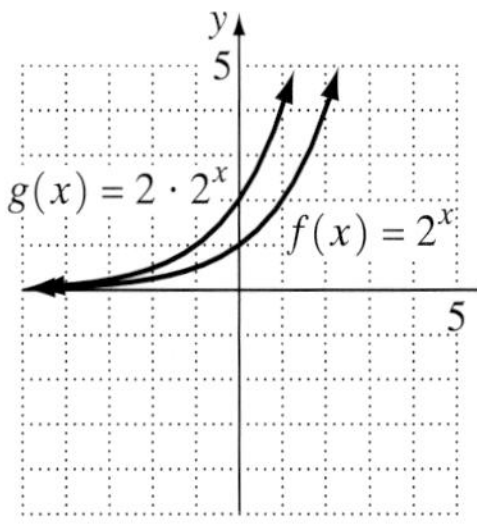


**35. a.** \$13,116.51 **b.** \$13,157.04 **c.** \$13,165.31 **37.** 7% compounded monthly **39. a.** 67.38 million **b.** about 134.74 million **c.** about 269.46 million **d.** 538.85 million **e.** appears to double every 27 yr

**41.** $f(25) \approx 0.0653$; About 6.5% of 25-year-olds have some coronary heart disease. **43.** \$116,405.10 **45.** 3.249009585; 3.317278183; 3.321880096; 3.321995226; 3.321997068; $2^{\sqrt{3}} \approx 3.321997085$; The closer the exponent is to $\sqrt{3}$, the closer the value is to $2^{\sqrt{3}}$. **47.** $f(11) \approx 241{,}786.19$; The number of AIDS cases among IV drug users in 2000 will be about 241,786. **49. a.** 100% **b.** 68.5% **c.** 30.8% **d.** 20% **51. a.** 1429 **b.** 24,546 **c.** Growth is limited by the population; The entire population will eventually become ill.

**59.**

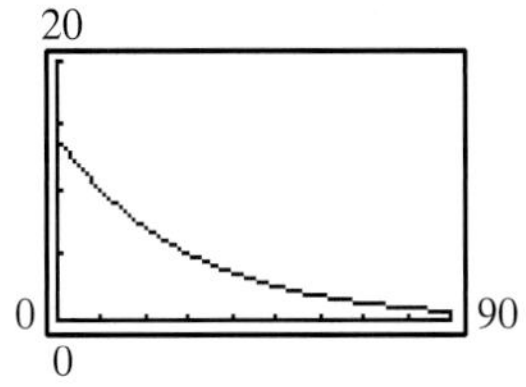


no; Nearly 4 O-rings are expected to fail.

**61. a.** $A = 10{,}000\left(1 + \frac{0.05}{4}\right)^{4t}$; $A = 10{,}000\left(1 + \frac{0.045}{12}\right)^{12t}$

**b.**

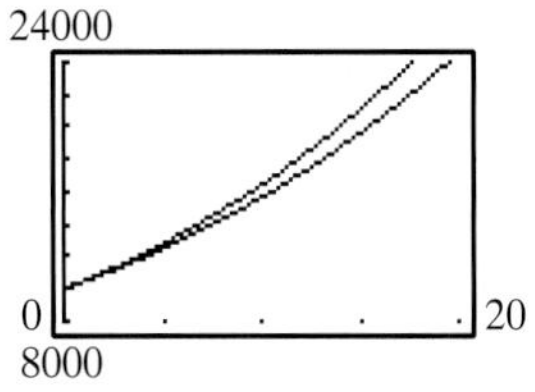


5% interest compounded quarterly

**63.** (d) is true.

**65.**

$$\left(\frac{e^x + e^{-x}}{2}\right)^2 - \left(\frac{e^x - e^{-x}}{2}\right)^2 \stackrel{?}{=} 1$$

$$\frac{e^{2x} + 2 + e^{-2x}}{4} - \frac{e^{2x} - 2 + e^{-2x}}{4} \stackrel{?}{=} 1$$

$$\frac{e^{2x} + 2 + e^{-2x} - e^{2x} + 2 - e^{-2x}}{4} \stackrel{?}{=} 1$$

$$\frac{4}{4} \stackrel{?}{=} 1$$

$$1 = 1$$

## Section 4.2

### Check Point Exercises

**1. a.** $7^3 = x$ **b.** $b^2 = 25$ **c.** $4^y = 26$ **2. a.** $5 = \log_2 x$ **b.** $3 = \log_b 27$ **c.** $y = \log_e 33$ **3. a.** 2 **b.** 1 **c.** $\frac{1}{2}$ **4. a.** 1 **b.** 0 **5. a.** 8 **b.** 17 **6.**

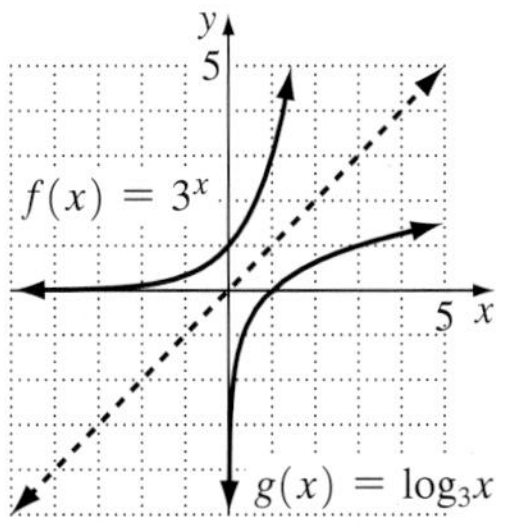


**7.** $(5, \infty)$ **8.** 80% **9.** 4.0 **10. a.** $(-\infty, 4)$ **b.** $(-\infty, 0)$ or $(0, \infty)$ **11. a.** $25x$ **b.** $\sqrt{x}$ **12.** 4.6 ft per sec

### Exercise Set 4.2

**1.** $2^4 = 16$ **3.** $3^2 = x$ **5.** $b^5 = 32$ **7.** $6^y = 216$ **9.** $\log_2 8 = 3$ **11.** $\log_2 \frac{1}{16} = -4$ **13.** $\log_8 2 = \frac{1}{3}$ **15.** $\log_{13} x = 2$ **17.** $\log_b 1000 = 3$ **19.** $\log_7 200 = y$ **21.** 2 **23.** 6 **25.** $\frac{1}{2}$ **27.** −3 **29.** $\frac{1}{2}$ **31.** 1 **33.** 0 **35.** 7 **37.** 19

**39.**

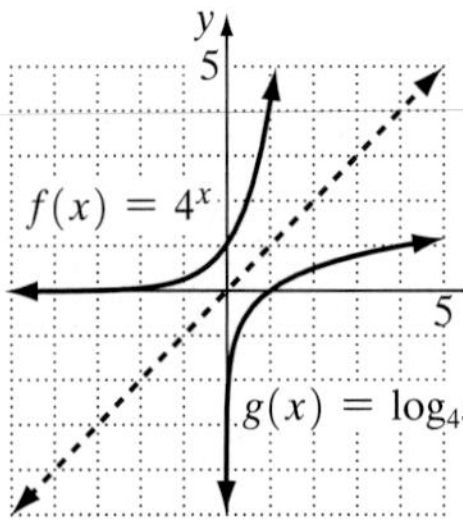


**41.**

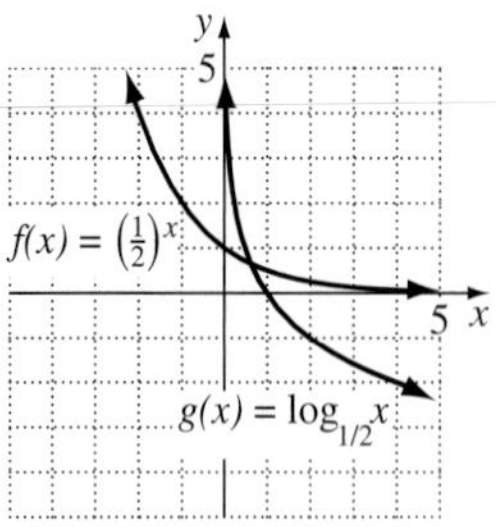


**43.** $H(x) = 1 - \log_3 x$
**45.** $h(x) = \log_3 x - 1$
**47.** $g(x) = \log_3(x - 1)$

**49.**

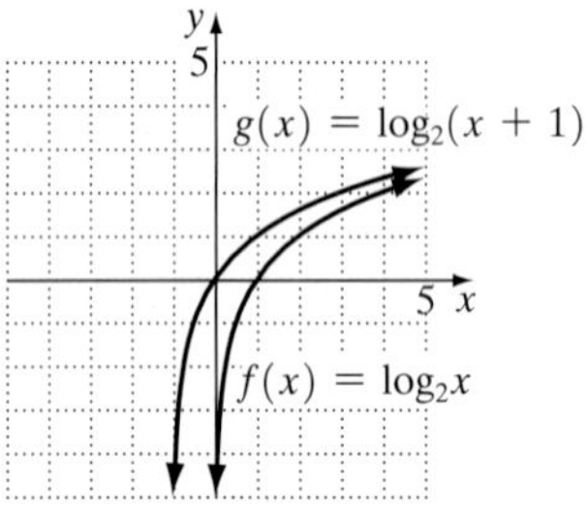


$x$-intercept: (0, 0)
vertical asymptote: $x = -1$

**51.**

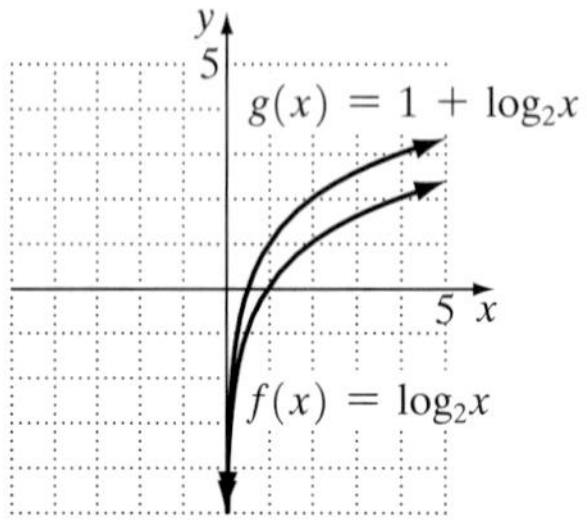


$x$-intercept: (0.5, 0)
vertical asymptote: $x = 0$

**53.**

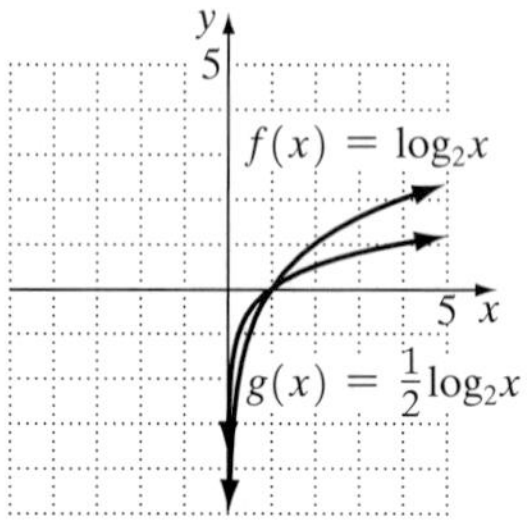


$x$-intercept: (1, 0)
vertical asymptote: $x = 0$

**55.** $(-4, \infty)$ **57.** $(-\infty, 2)$ **59.** $(-\infty, 2)$ or $(2, \infty)$ **61.** 2 **63.** 7 **65.** 33 **67.** 0 **69.** 6 **71.** −6 **73.** 125
**75.** $9x$ **77.** $5x^2$ **79.** $\sqrt{x}$ **81.** 95.4% **83.** \$5.65 billion **85.** ≈ 188 db; yes

**87. a.** 88
**b.** 71.5; 63.9; 58.8; 55; 52; 49.5
**c.**

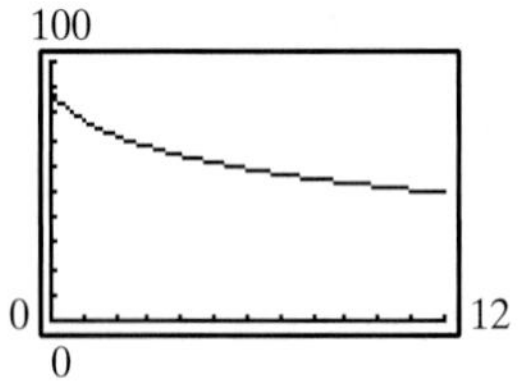


Material retention decreases as time passes.

**97.**

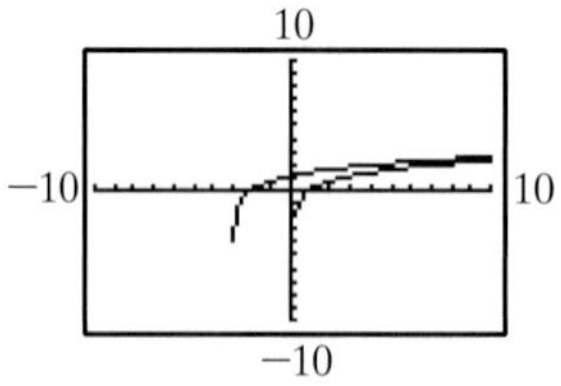


$g(x)$ is $f(x)$ shifted 3 units left.

**99.**

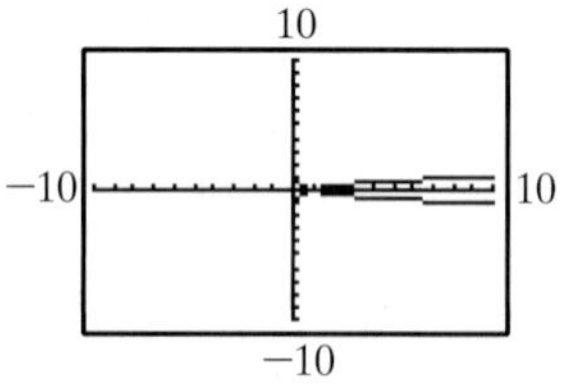


$g(x)$ is $f(x)$ reflected about the $x$-axis.

**101.**

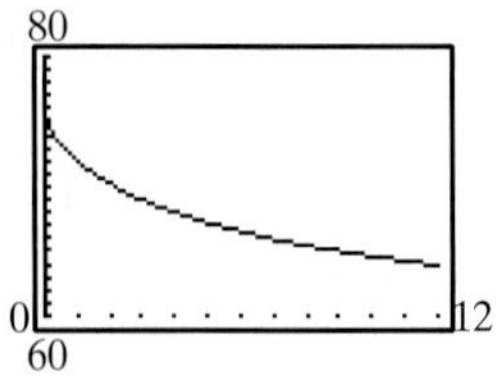


The score falls below 65 after 9 months.

**103.** $y = \ln x$, $y = \sqrt{x}$, $y = x$, $y = x^2$, $y = e^x$, $y = x^x$

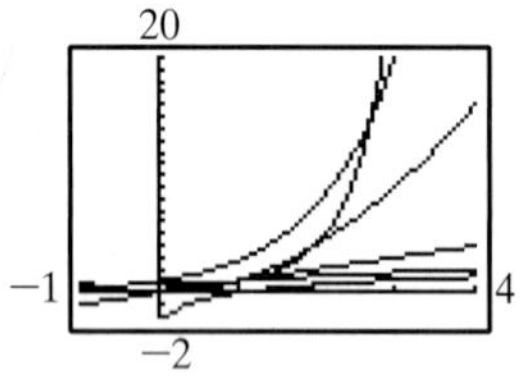


**105.** $\frac{4}{5}$

**107.** $\log_3 40 > \log_4 60$

## Section 4.3

### Check Point Exercises

**1. a.** $\log_6 10 + \log_6 9$ **b.** $2 + \log x$ **2. a.** $\log_8 23 - \log_8 x$ **b.** $5 - \ln 11$ **3. a.** $9 \log_6 8$ **b.** $\frac{1}{3} \ln x$

**4. a.** $4 \log_b x + \frac{1}{3} \log_b y$ **b.** $\frac{1}{2} \log_5 x - 2 - 3 \log_5 y$ **5. a.** 2 **b.** $\log \frac{7x + 6}{x}$ **6. a.** $\ln x^2 \sqrt[3]{x + 5}$ **b.** $\log \frac{(x - 3)^2}{x}$

**7.** 4.02 **8.** 4.02 **9.**

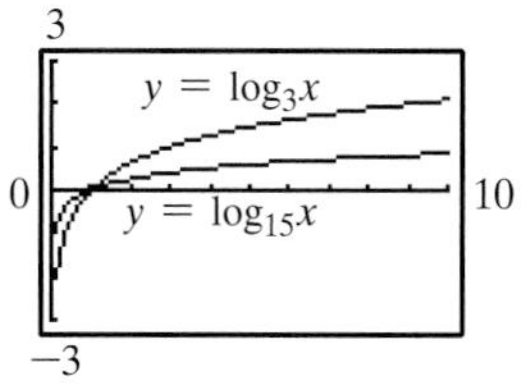


### Exercise Set 4.3

**1.** $\log_5 12 + \log_5 3$ **3.** $1 + \log_7 x$ **5.** $3 + \log x$ **7.** $1 - \log_7 x$ **9.** $\log x - 2$ **11.** $3 - \log_4 y$ **13.** $2 - \ln 5$ **15.** $3 \log_b x$ **17.** $-b \log N$ **19.** $\frac{1}{5} \ln x$ **21.** $2 \log_b x + \log_b y$ **23.** $\frac{1}{2} \log_4 x - 3$ **25.** $2 - \frac{1}{2} \log_6(x + 1)$ **27.** $2 \log_b x + \log_b y - 2 \log_b z$ **29.** $1 + \frac{1}{2} \log x$ **31.** $\frac{1}{3} \log x - \frac{1}{3} \log y$ **33.** 1 **35.** $\ln(7x)$ **37.** 5 **39.** $\log\left(\frac{2x + 5}{x}\right)$ **41.** $\log(xy^3)$ **43.** $\ln(x^{1/2}y)$ or $\ln(y\sqrt{x})$ **45.** $\log_b (x^2y^3)$ **47.** $\ln\left(\frac{x^5}{y^2}\right)$ **49.** $\ln\left(\frac{x^3}{y^{1/3}}\right)$ or $\ln\left(\frac{x^3}{\sqrt[3]{y}}\right)$ **51.** $\ln \frac{(x + 6)^4}{x^3}$ **53.** 1.5937 **55.** 1.6944 **57.** −1.2304 **59.** 3.6193 **61. a.** $D = 10 \log \frac{I}{I_0}$ **b.** 20 decibels louder

**71. a.**

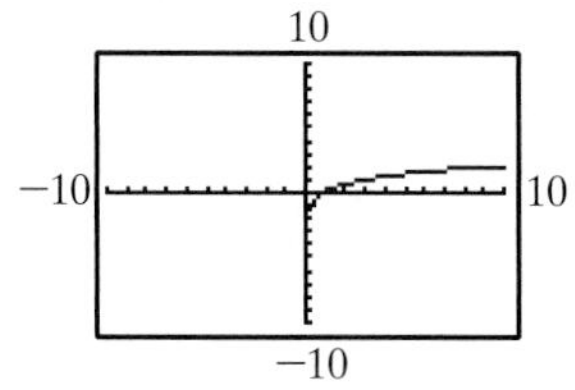


**b.**

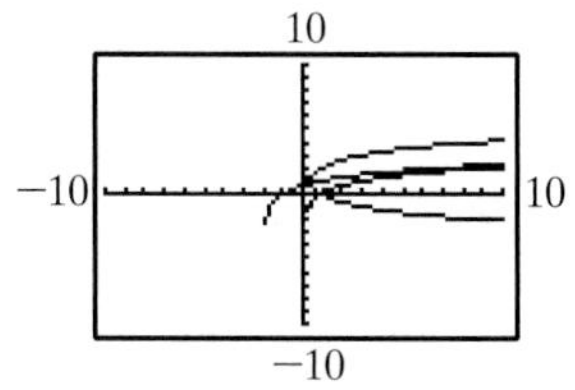


$y = 2 + \log_3 x$ shifts the graph of $y = \log_3 x$ two units upward; $y = \log_3(x + 2)$ shifts the graph of $y = \log_3 x$ two units left; $y = -\log_3 x$ reflects the graph of $y = \log_3 x$ about the $x$-axis.

**73.**

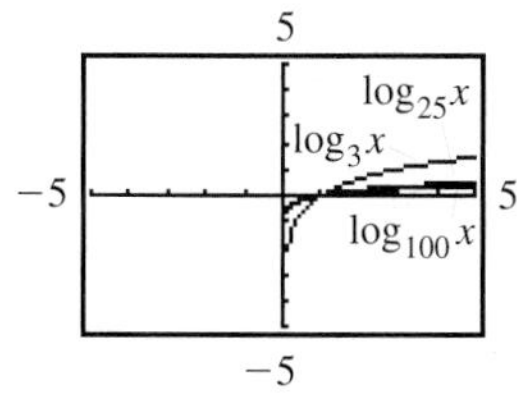


**a.** top graph: $y = \log_{100} x$; bottom graph: $y = \log_3 x$
**b.** top graph: $y = \log_3 x$; bottom graph: $y = 100 \log_{100} x$
**c.** The graph of the equation with the largest $b$ will be on the top in the interval $(0, 1)$ and on the bottom in the interval $(1, \infty)$.

**79.** (d) is true. **81.** $\frac{2A}{B}$

## Section 4.4

### Check Point Exercises

**1.** $\left\{\frac{\ln 134}{\ln 5}\right\}$; $\approx 3.04$ **2.** $\left\{\frac{\ln 9}{2}\right\}$; $\approx 1.10$ **3.** $\left\{\frac{\ln 2088 + 4 \ln 6}{3 \ln 6}\right\}$; $\approx 2.76$ **4.** $\{0, \ln 7\}$; $\ln 7 \approx 1.95$ **5.** $\{12\}$ **6.** $\{5\}$ **7.** $\left\{\frac{e^2}{3}\right\}$ **8.** 0.01 **9.** 16.2 yr **10.** 2149

### Exercise Set 4.4

**1.** $\left\{\frac{\ln 3.91}{\ln 10}\right\}$; $\approx 0.59$ **3.** $\{\ln 5.7\}$; $\approx 1.74$ **5.** $\left\{\frac{\ln 17}{\ln 5}\right\}$; $\approx 1.76$ **7.** $\left\{\ln \frac{23}{5}\right\}$; $\approx 1.53$ **9.** $\left\{\frac{\ln 659}{5}\right\}$; $\approx 1.30$ **11.** $\left\{\frac{\ln 793 - 1}{-5}\right\}$; $\approx -1.14$ **13.** $\left\{\frac{\ln 10{,}478 + 3}{5}\right\}$; $\approx 2.45$ **15.** $\left\{\frac{\ln 410}{\ln 7} - 2\right\}$; $\approx 1.09$ **17.** $\left\{\frac{\ln 813}{0.3 \ln 7}\right\}$; $\approx 11.48$ **19.** $\{0, \ln 2\}$; $\ln 2 \approx 0.69$ **21.** $\left\{\frac{\ln 3}{2}\right\}$; $\approx 0.55$ **23.** $\{81\}$ **25.** $\{59\}$ **27.** $\left\{\frac{109}{27}\right\}$ **29.** $\left\{\frac{62}{3}\right\}$ **31.** $\left\{\frac{5}{4}\right\}$ **33.** $\{6\}$ **35.** $\{6\}$ **37.** $\{e^2\}$; $\approx 7.39$ **39.** $\left\{\frac{e^4}{2}\right\}$; $\approx 27.30$ **41.** $\{e^{-1/2}\}$; $\approx 0.61$ **43.** $\{e^2 - 3\}$; $\approx 4.39$ **45.** about 0.22 **47. a.** 18.2 million **b.** 2010 **49.** 8 yr **51.** 16.8% **53.** 9 yr **55.** 15.7% **57.** 1995 **59.** 2.8 days; Yes, the point (2.8, 50) appears to lie on the graph of $P$. **61.** $10^{-2.4}$; 0.004 moles per liter **67.** $\{2\}$ **69.** $\{4\}$ **71.** $\{2\}$ **73.** $\{-1.391606, 1.6855579\}$

**75.**

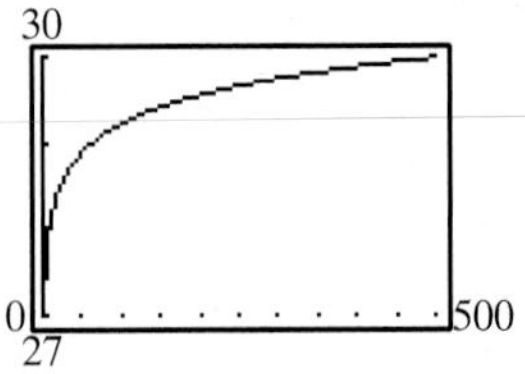


As distance from eye increases, barometric air pressure increases, leveling off at about 30 inches of mercury.

**77.**

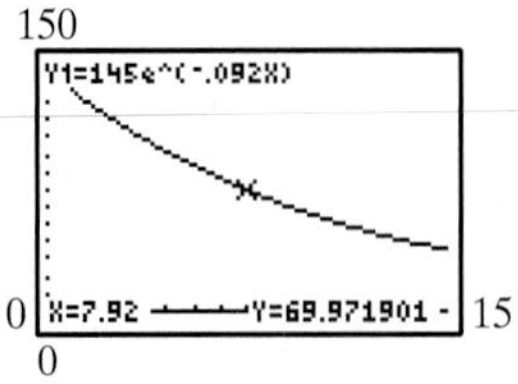


about 7.92 min

**79.** (c) is true. **81.** $\{1, e^2\}, e^2 \approx 7.389$ **83.** $\{e\}, e \approx 2.718$

## Section 4.5

### Check Point Exercises

**1. a.** $A = 491e^{0.027t}$ **b.** 2006 **2. a.** $A = A_0e^{-0.0248t}$ **b.** about 72 yr **3. a.** 0.4 correct responses **b.** 0.7 correct responses **c.** 0.8 correct responses **4. a.** $T = 30 + 70e^{-0.0673t}$ **b.** 48°C **c.** 39 min **5.** $y = 4e^{(\ln 7.8)x}$; $y = 4e^{2.054x}$

### Exercise Set 4.5

**1.** 208 million **3.** 2016 **5.** 2.6% **7.** 2014 **9.** \$140,000 **11.** 2005 **13.** 0.175; $A = 200e^{0.175t}$; 17.5% **15.** 8.01 g **17.** 8 g; 4 g; 2 g; 1 g; 0.5 g **19.** 15,679 years old **21. a.** $\frac{A_0}{2} = A_0e^{k(1.31)}$; $\frac{1}{2} = e^{1.31k}$; $\ln\frac{1}{2} = \ln e^{1.31k}$; $\ln\frac{1}{2} = 1.31k$; $k = \frac{\ln\frac{1}{2}}{1.31} \approx -0.52912$ **b.** 107 million years **23.** $2A_0 = A_0e^{kt}$; $2 = e^{kt}$; $\ln 2 = \ln e^{kt}$; $\ln 2 = kt$; $t = \frac{\ln 2}{k}$ **25.** 63 yr **27. a.** about 20 people **b.** about 1080 people **c.** 100,000 people **29.** about 3.7% **31.** about 48 years old **33. a.** $T = 45 + 25e^{-0.0916t}$ **b.** 51°F **c.** 18 min **35.** 26 min **37.** $y = 100e^{(\ln 4.6)x}$; $y = 100e^{1.526x}$ **39.** $y = 2.5e^{(\ln 0.7)x}$; $y = 2.5e^{-0.357x}$ **51.** $y = 51.75985638 + 109.7788574 \ln x$; $r = 0.8974781617$, a good fit **53.** $y = 98.06189365x^{0.4398361087}$; $r = 0.9546621296$, a good fit

**55.**

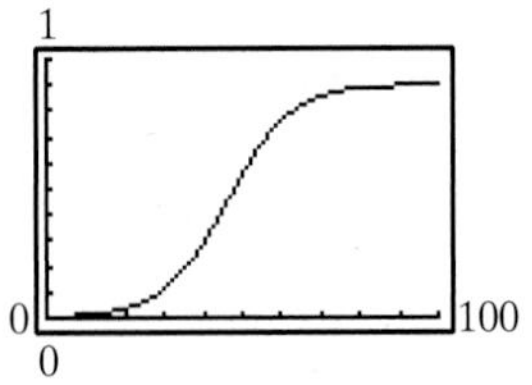


The probability of coronary heart disease starts increasing at a more rapid rate at about age 20. At about age 60, the rate of increase starts to slow down.

**57.** The linear model, $y = 74.52833333x + 214.7694444$, best fits the data. Answers for prediction may vary. **59.** 8:02 A.M.

### Chapter 4 Review Exercises

**1.** $g(x) = 4^{-x}$ **2.** $h(x) = -4^{-x}$ **3.** $r(x) = -4^{-x} + 3$ **4.** $f(x) = 4^x$

**5.**

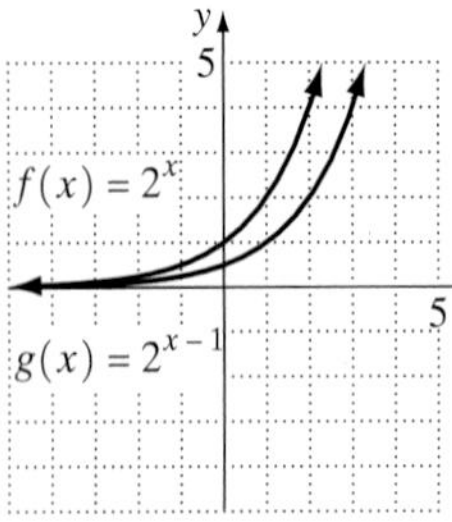


**6.**

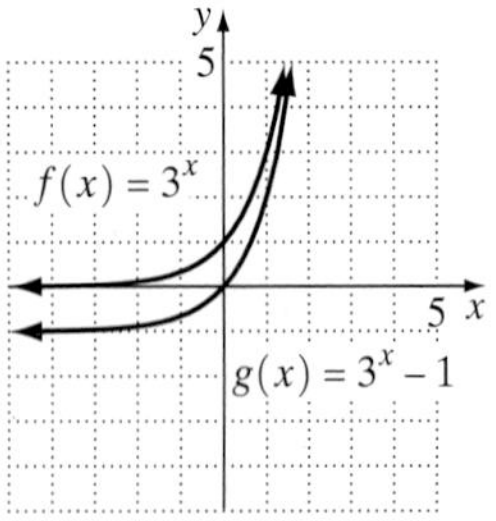


**7.**

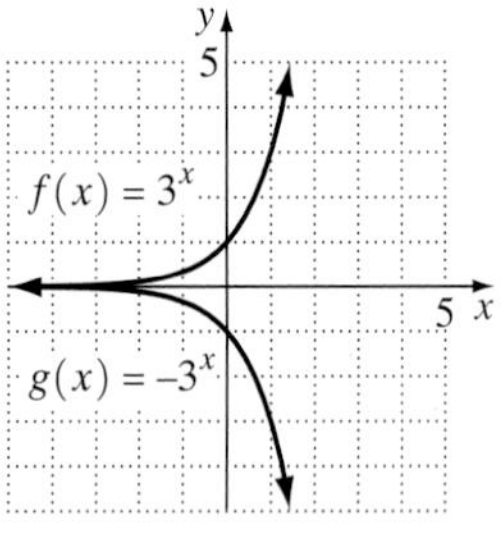


**8.**

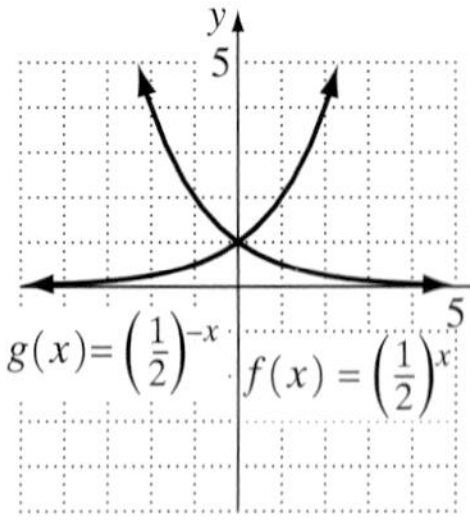


**9.** 5.5% compounded semiannually **10.** 7% compounded monthly **11. a.** 200° **b.** 120°; 119° **c.** 70°; The temperature in the room is 70°. **12.** $49^{1/2} = 7$ **13.** $4^3 = x$ **14.** $3^y = 81$ **15.** $\log_6 216 = 3$ **16.** $\log_b 625 = 4$ **17.** $\log_{13} 874 = y$ **18.** 3 **19.** −2 **20.** ∅; $\log_b x$ is defined only for $x > 0$. **21.** $\frac{1}{2}$ **22.** 1 **23.** 8

**24.** 5 **25.** 0 **26.**

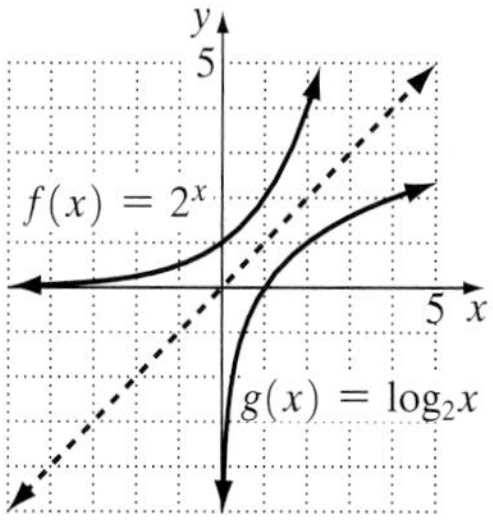


**27.**

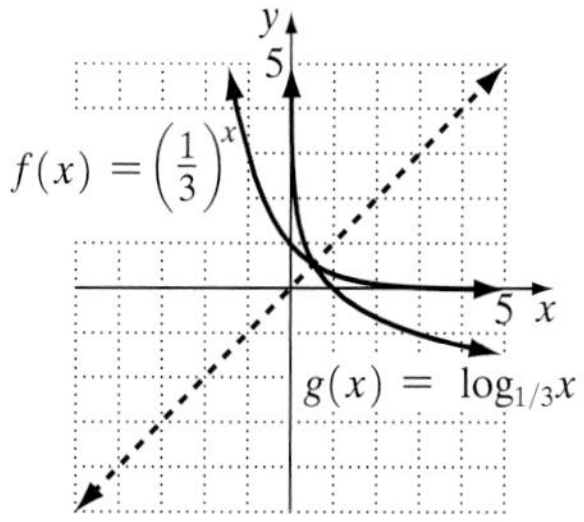


**28.** $g(x) = \log(-x)$
**29.** $r(x) = 1 + \log(2 - x)$
**30.** $h(x) = \log(2 - x)$
**31.** $f(x) = \log x$

**32.**

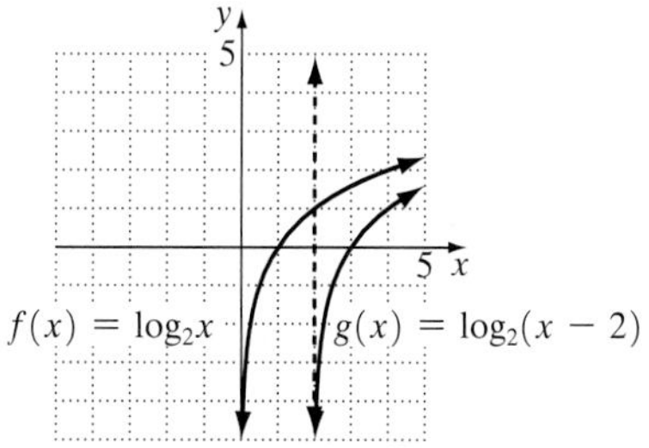


$x$-intercept: (3, 0)
vertical asymptote: $x = 2$

**33.**

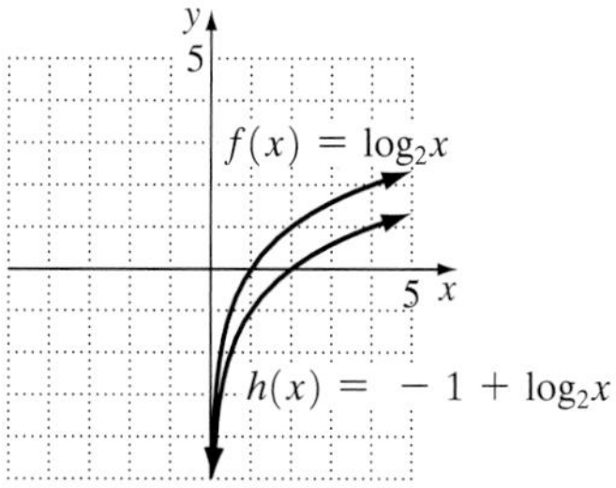


$x$-intercept: (2, 0)
vertical asymptote: $x = 0$

**34.**

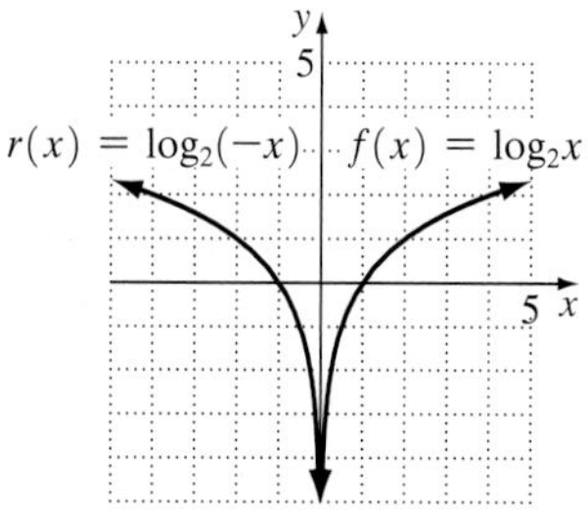


$x$-intercept: (−1, 0)
vertical asymptote: $x = 0$

**35.** $(-5, \infty)$ **36.** $(-\infty, 3)$ **37.** $(-\infty, 1)\cup(1, \infty)$ **38.** $6x$ **39.** $\sqrt{x}$ **40.** $4x^2$ **41.** 3.0

**42. a.** 76
**b.** ≈ 67, ≈ 63, ≈ 61, ≈ 59, ≈ 56
**c.**

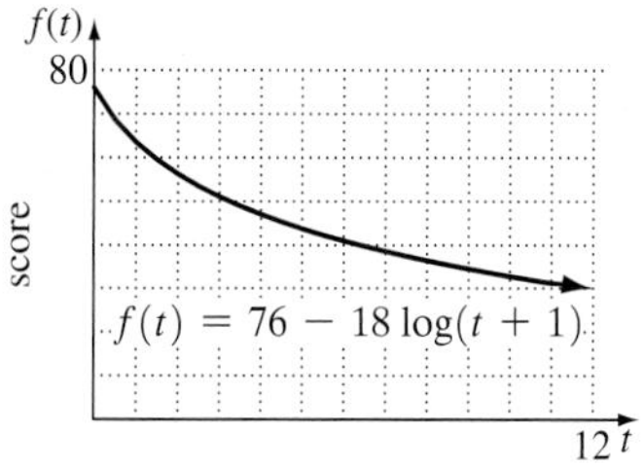

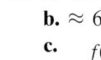

time (months)
Retention decreases as time passes.

**43.** about 9 weeks **44.** $2 + 3\log_6 x$ **45.** $\frac{1}{2}\log_4 x - 3$

**46.** $\log_2 x + 2\log_2 y - 6$ **47.** $\frac{1}{3}\ln x - \frac{1}{3}$ **48.** $\log_b 21$ **49.** $\log \frac{3}{x^3}$

**50.** $\ln(x^3y^4)$ **51.** $\ln\frac{\sqrt{x}}{y}$ **52.** 6.2448 **53.** −0.1063

**54.** $\left\{\frac{\ln 12{,}143}{\ln 8}\right\}$; ≈ 4.523 **55.** $\left\{\frac{1}{5}\ln 141\right\}$; ≈ 0.990

**56.** $\left\{\frac{12 - \ln 130}{5}\right\}$; ≈ 1.426 **57.** $\left\{\frac{\ln 37{,}500 - 2\ln 5}{4\ln 5}\right\}$; ≈ 1.136

**58.** {ln 3}; ≈ 1.099 **59.** {23} **60.** {5} **61.** ∅ **62.** $\left\{\frac{1}{e}\right\}$ or {0.368}

**63.** $\left\{\frac{e^3}{2}\right\}$ or {10.043} **64.** 2042 **65.** 2086 **66.** 2005 **67.** 7.3 yr

**68.** 14.6 yr **69.** about 21.97% **70. a.** 0.041 **b.** 40.7 million **c.** 2010 **71.** about 15,679 years old **72. a.** about 9 people **b.** about 104 people **c.** 171 people; yes; The limiting size is 171; however, 178 people died. **73. a.** $T = 65 + 120e^{-0.144t}$ **b.** 8 min **74.** $y = 73e^{(\ln 2.6)x}$; $y = 73e^{0.956x}$ **75.** $y = 6.5e^{(\ln 0.43)x}$; $y = 6.5e^{-0.844x}$ **76.** high: exponential; medium: linear; low: quadratic; Explanations will vary; negative; The parabola opens downward. **77.** The exponential model, $y = (3.38051786)(1.0235357)^x$, is the best fit; 113.4 million

## Chapter 4 Test

**1.**

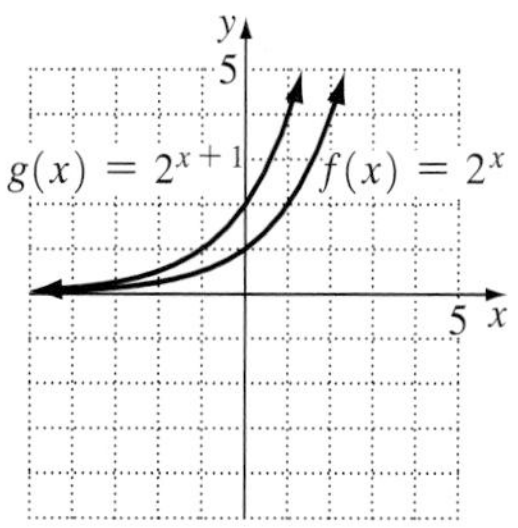


**2.**

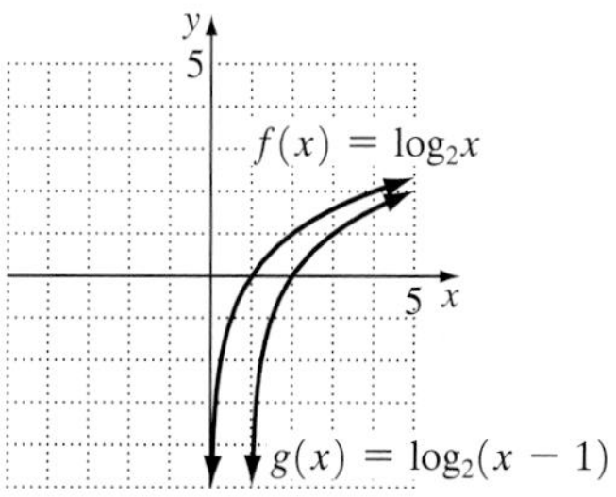


**3.** $5^3 = 125$ **4.** $\log_{36}6 = \frac{1}{2}$ **5.** $(-\infty, 3)$

**6.** $3 + 5\log_4 x$ **7.** $\frac{1}{3}\log_3 x - 4$ **8.** $\log(x^6y^2)$

**9.** $\ln\frac{7}{x^3}$ **10.** 1.5741 **11.** $\left\{\frac{\ln 1.4}{\ln 5}\right\}$ or {0.2091}

**12.** $\left\{\frac{\ln 4}{0.005}\right\}$ or {277.2589} **13.** {0, ln 5} or {0, 1.6094}

**14.** {54.25} **15.** {5} **16.** $\left\{\frac{e^4}{3}\right\}$ or {18.1993}

**17.** 6.5% compounded semiannually; $221.15 more **18.** 120 db **19. a.** about 89% **b.** decreasing; $k = -0.004 < 0$ **c.** 1995
**20.** $A = 484e^{0.005t}$ **21.** about 24,758 years ago **22. a.** 14 elk **b.** about 51 elk **c.** 140 elk

## Cumulative Review Exercises (Chapters 1–4)

**1.** $\left\{\frac{2}{3}, 2\right\}$ **2.** $\{3, 7\}$ **3.** $\{-2, -1, 1\}$ **4.** $\{0.9704\}$ **5.** $\{3\}$ **6.** $(-\infty, 4]$ **7.** $[1, 3]$

**8.** using $(1, 3)$, $y - 3 = -3(x - 1)$; $y = -3x + 6$ **9.** $(f \circ g)(x) = (x + 2)^2$; $(g \circ f)(x) = x^2 + 2$ **10.** $f^{-1}(x) = \frac{1}{2}x + \frac{7}{2}$

**11.** $x^2 + 3x - 3 + \frac{-4}{x + 2}$ **12.** $\pm 1, \pm\frac{1}{2}, \pm\frac{1}{4}, \pm 3, \pm\frac{3}{2}, \pm\frac{3}{4}$ **13.** 300 **14.** $\{1 + i, 1 - i, 2\}$

**15.**

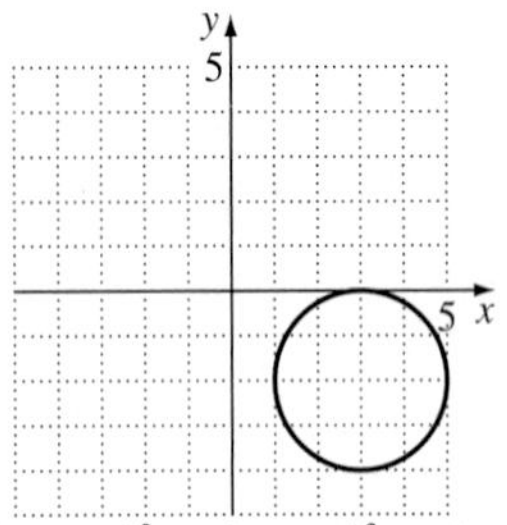

$(x - 3)^2 + (y + 2)^2 = 4$

**16.**

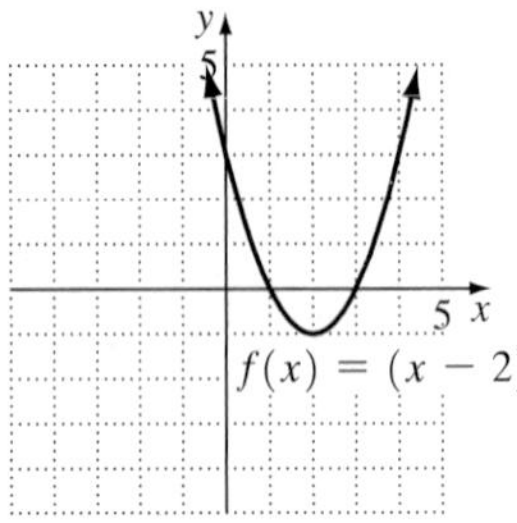

$f(x) = (x - 2)^2 - 1$

**17.**

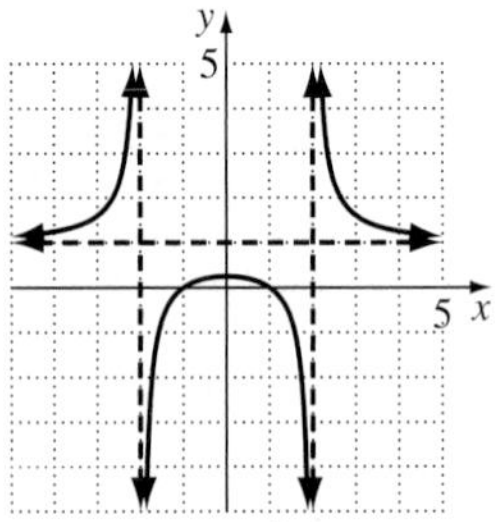

$f(x) = \frac{x^2 - 1}{x^2 - 4}$

**18.**

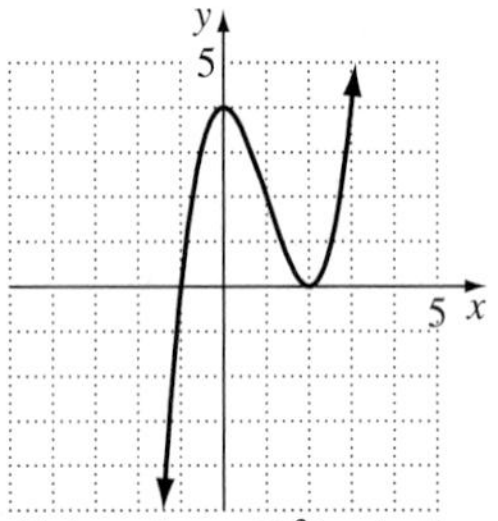

$f(x) = (x - 2)^2(x + 1)$

**19.** \$12 per hr **20.** $\frac{0.5}{\ln 4} \approx 0.361$; about $\frac{3}{10}$ of the people

# CHAPTER 5

## Section 5.1

### Check Point Exercises

**1. a.**

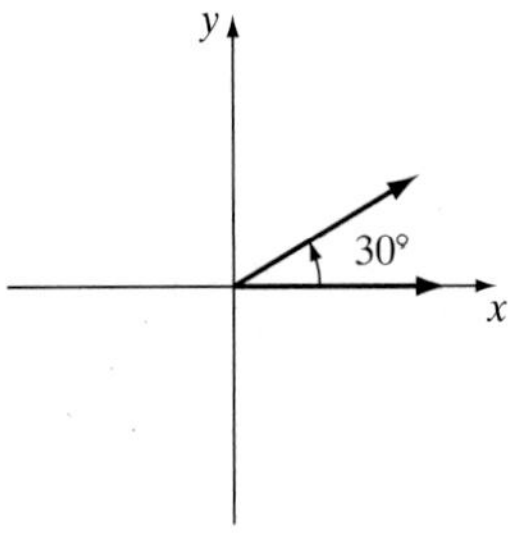


**b.**

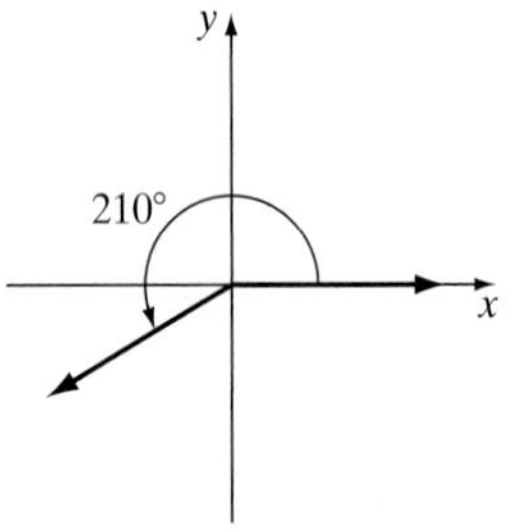


**c.**

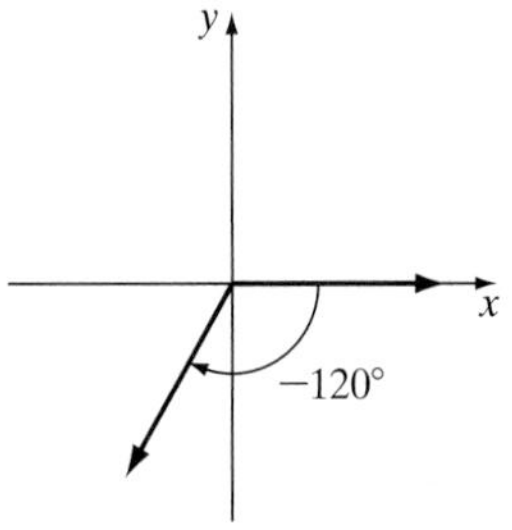


**d.**

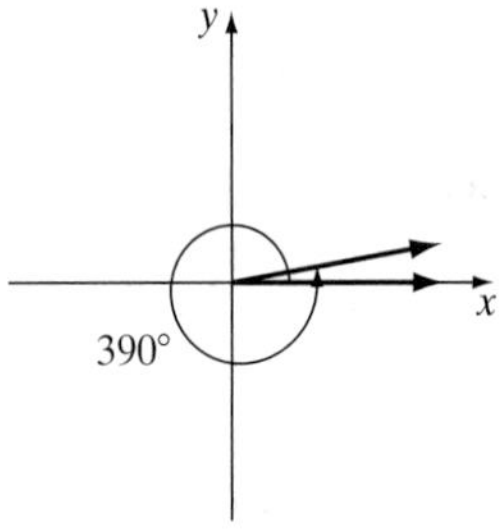


**2. a.** 40° **b.** 225° **3. a.** 12°; 102° **b.** no complementary angle; 30° **4.** 3.5 radians **5. a.** $\frac{\pi}{3}$ radians **b.** $\frac{3\pi}{2}$ radians **c.** $-\frac{5\pi}{3}$ radians **6. a.** 45° **b.** −240° **c.** 343.8° **7.** $\frac{3\pi}{2}$ in. $\approx$ 4.71 in. **8.** $135\pi$ in./min $\approx$ 424 in./min

### Exercise Set 5.1

**1.** quadrant II **3.** quadrant III **5.** quadrant I **7.** obtuse **9.** straight

**11.**

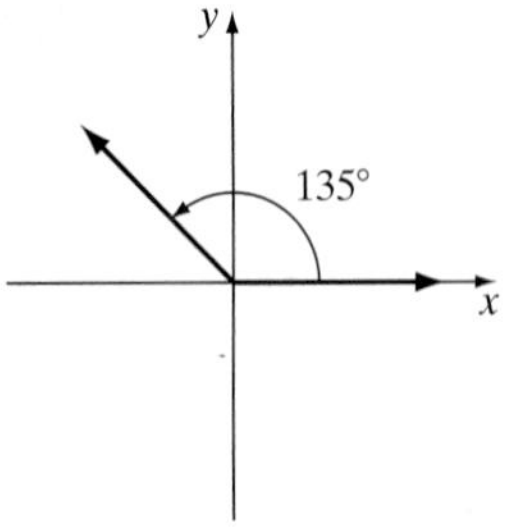


**13.**

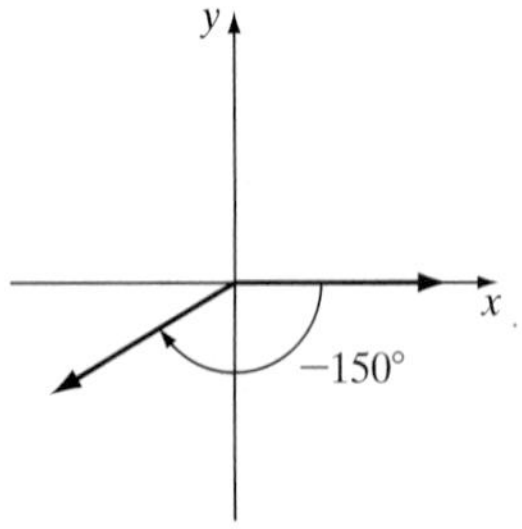


**15.**

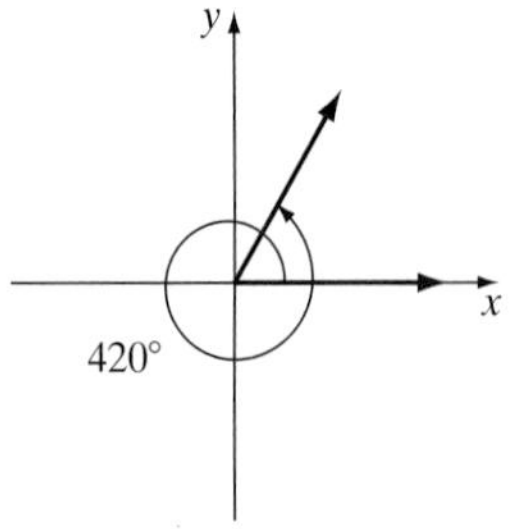


**17.**

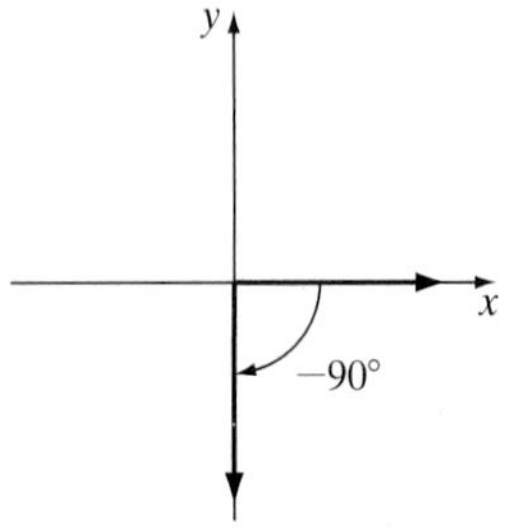


**19.** 35° **21.** 210° **23.** 315° **25.** 38°; 128° **27.** 52.6°; 142.6° **29.** no complement; 69° **31.** 4 radians **33.** $\frac{4}{3}$ radians **35.** 4 radians **37.** $\frac{\pi}{4}$ radians **39.** $\frac{3\pi}{4}$ radians **41.** $\frac{5\pi}{3}$ radians **43.** $-\frac{5\pi}{4}$ radians **45.** 90° **47.** 120° **49.** 210° **51.** −540° **53.** 0.31 radians **55.** −0.70 radians **57.** 3.49 radians **59.** 114.59° **61.** 13.85° **63.** −275.02°

**65.** $3\pi$ in. $\approx 9.42$ in. **67.** $10\pi$ ft $\approx 31.42$ ft **69.** $\frac{12\pi \text{ radians}}{\text{second}}$ **71.** $60°$; $\frac{\pi}{3}$ radians **73.** $\frac{8\pi}{3}$ in. $\approx 8.38$ in.
**75.** $12\pi$ in. $\approx 37.70$ in. **77.** 2 radians; 114.59° **79.** 2094 mi **81.** 1047 mph **83.** 1508 ft/min **97.** 30.25° **99.** 30° 25′ 12″
**101.** smaller than a right angle **103.** 1815 mi

## Section 5.2

### Check Point Exercises

**1.** $\sin t = \frac{1}{2}$; $\cos t = \frac{\sqrt{3}}{2}$; $\tan t = \frac{\sqrt{3}}{3}$; $\csc t = 2$; $\sec t = \frac{2\sqrt{3}}{3}$; $\cot t = \sqrt{3}$ **2.** $\sin t = 0$; $\cos t = -1$; $\tan t = 0$; $\csc t =$ undefined; $\sec t = -1$; $\cot t =$ undefined **3.** $\sqrt{2}$; $\sqrt{2}$; 1 **4. a.** $\sqrt{2}$ **b.** $-\sqrt{2}$ **5.** $\tan t = \frac{2\sqrt{5}}{5}$; $\csc t = \frac{3}{2}$; $\sec t = \frac{3\sqrt{5}}{5}$; $\cot t = \frac{\sqrt{5}}{2}$;
**6.** $\frac{\sqrt{3}}{2}$ **7.** 1 **8. a.** 0.7071 **b.** 0.3888

### Exercise Set 5.2

**1.** $\sin t = \frac{8}{17}$; $\cos t = -\frac{15}{17}$; $\tan t = -\frac{8}{15}$; $\csc t = \frac{17}{8}$; $\sec t = -\frac{17}{15}$; $\cot t = -\frac{15}{8}$ **3.** $\sin t = -\frac{\sqrt{2}}{2}$; $\cos t = \frac{\sqrt{2}}{2}$; $\tan t = -1$; $\csc t = -\sqrt{2}$; $\sec t = \sqrt{2}$; $\cot t = -1$ **5.** $\frac{1}{2}$ **7.** $-\frac{\sqrt{3}}{2}$ **9.** 0 **11.** $-2$ **13.** $\frac{2\sqrt{3}}{3}$ **15.** $-1$ **17.** undefined
**19. a.** $\frac{\sqrt{3}}{2}$ **b.** $\frac{\sqrt{3}}{2}$ **21. a.** $\frac{1}{2}$ **b.** $-\frac{1}{2}$ **23. a.** $-\sqrt{3}$ **b.** $\sqrt{3}$ **25.** $\tan t = \frac{8}{15}$; $\csc t = \frac{17}{8}$; $\sec t = \frac{17}{15}$; $\cot t = \frac{15}{8}$
**27.** $\tan t = \frac{\sqrt{2}}{4}$; $\csc t = 3$; $\sec t = \frac{3\sqrt{2}}{4}$; $\cot t = 2\sqrt{2}$ **29.** $\frac{\sqrt{13}}{7}$ **31.** $\frac{5}{8}$ **33.** 1 **35.** 1 **37.** 1 **39. a.** $\frac{\sqrt{2}}{2}$ **b.** $\frac{\sqrt{2}}{2}$
**41. a.** 0 **b.** 0 **43. a.** 0 **b.** 0 **45. a.** $-\frac{\sqrt{2}}{2}$ **b.** $-\frac{\sqrt{2}}{2}$ **47.** 0.7174 **49.** 0.2643 **51.** 1.1884 **53.** 0.9511
**55.** 3.7321 **57. a.** 12 hr **b.** 20.3 hr **c.** 3.7 hr **59. a.** 1, 0, −1, 0, 1; Answers may vary. **b.** 28 days **73.** 1 **75.** 16.7 ft

## Section 5.3

### Check Point Exercises

**1.** $\sin\theta = \frac{3}{5}$; $\cos\theta = \frac{4}{5}$; $\tan\theta = \frac{3}{4}$; $\csc\theta = \frac{5}{3}$; $\sec\theta = \frac{5}{4}$; $\cot\theta = \frac{4}{3}$ **2.** $\sqrt{2}$; $\sqrt{2}$; 1 **3.** $\sqrt{3}$; $\frac{\sqrt{3}}{3}$ **4. a.** $\cos 44°$ **b.** $\tan\frac{5\pi}{12}$
**5.** 334 yd **6.** 54°

### Exercise Set 5.3

**1.** 15; $\sin\theta = \frac{3}{5}$; $\cos\theta = \frac{4}{5}$; $\tan\theta = \frac{3}{4}$; $\csc\theta = \frac{5}{3}$; $\sec\theta = \frac{5}{4}$; $\cot\theta = \frac{4}{3}$ **3.** 20; $\sin\theta = \frac{20}{29}$; $\cos\theta = \frac{21}{29}$; $\tan\theta = \frac{20}{21}$; $\csc\theta = \frac{29}{20}$; $\sec\theta = \frac{29}{21}$; $\cot\theta = \frac{21}{20}$ **5.** 24; $\sin\theta = \frac{5}{13}$; $\cos\theta = \frac{12}{13}$; $\tan\theta = \frac{5}{12}$; $\csc\theta = \frac{13}{5}$; $\sec\theta = \frac{13}{12}$; $\cot\theta = \frac{12}{5}$ **7.** 28; $\sin\theta = \frac{4}{5}$; $\cos\theta = \frac{3}{5}$; $\tan\theta = \frac{4}{3}$; $\csc\theta = \frac{5}{4}$; $\sec\theta = \frac{5}{3}$; $\cot\theta = \frac{3}{4}$ **9.** $\frac{\sqrt{3}}{2}$ **11.** $\sqrt{2}$ **13.** $\sqrt{3}$ **15.** 0 **17.** $\frac{\sqrt{6}-4}{4}$ **19.** $\frac{12\sqrt{3}+\sqrt{6}}{6}$
**21.** $\cos 83°$ **23.** $\sec 65°$ **25.** $\cot\frac{7\pi}{18}$ **27.** $\sin\frac{\pi}{10}$ **29.** 188 cm **31.** 182 in. **33.** 41 m **35.** 17° **37.** 78°
**39.** 1.147 radians **41.** 0.3950 radians **43.** 529 yd **45.** 36° **47.** 2880 ft **49.** 37°
**59.** 0.92106, −0.19735; 0.95534, −0.148878; 0.98007, −0.099667; 0.99500, −0.04996; 0.99995, −0.005; 0.9999995, −0.0005; 0.999999995, −0.00005; 1, −0.000005; $\frac{\cos\theta - 1}{\theta}$ approaches 0 as $\theta$ approaches 0. **61.** In a right triangle, the hypotenuse is greater than either other side. Therefore, both $\frac{\text{opposite}}{\text{hypotenuse}}$ and $\frac{\text{adjacent}}{\text{hypotenuse}}$ must be less than 1 for an acute angle in a right triangle.
**63. a.** 357 ft **b.** 394 ft

## Section 5.4

### Check Point Exercises

**1.** $\sin\theta = -\frac{3}{5}$; $\cos\theta = \frac{4}{5}$; $\tan\theta = -\frac{3}{4}$; $\csc\theta = -\frac{5}{3}$; $\sec\theta = \frac{5}{4}$; $\cot\theta = -\frac{4}{3}$ **2. a.** 1; undefined **b.** 0; 1 **c.** −1; undefined **d.** 0; −1 **3.** quadrant III **4.** $\frac{\sqrt{10}}{10}$; $-\frac{\sqrt{10}}{3}$ **5. a.** 30° **b.** $\frac{\pi}{4}$ **c.** 60° **d.** 0.46 **6. a.** $-\frac{\sqrt{3}}{2}$ **b.** 1 **c.** $\frac{2\sqrt{3}}{3}$

### Exercise Set 5.4

**1.** $\sin\theta = \frac{3}{5}$; $\cos\theta = -\frac{4}{5}$; $\tan\theta = -\frac{3}{4}$; $\csc\theta = \frac{5}{3}$; $\sec\theta = -\frac{5}{4}$; $\cot\theta = -\frac{4}{3}$ **3.** $\sin\theta = \frac{3\sqrt{13}}{13}$; $\cos\theta = \frac{2\sqrt{13}}{13}$; $\tan\theta = \frac{3}{2}$; $\csc\theta = \frac{\sqrt{13}}{3}$; $\sec\theta = \frac{\sqrt{13}}{2}$; $\cot\theta = \frac{2}{3}$ **5.** $\sin\theta = -\frac{\sqrt{2}}{2}$; $\cos\theta = \frac{\sqrt{2}}{2}$; $\tan\theta = -1$; $\csc\theta = -\sqrt{2}$; $\sec\theta = \sqrt{2}$; $\cot\theta = -1$ **7.** $\sin\theta = -\frac{5\sqrt{29}}{29}$; $\cos\theta = -\frac{2\sqrt{29}}{29}$; $\tan\theta = \frac{5}{2}$; $\csc\theta = -\frac{\sqrt{29}}{5}$; $\sec\theta = -\frac{\sqrt{29}}{2}$; $\cot\theta = \frac{2}{5}$ **9.** −1 **11.** −1 **13.** undefined **15.** 0 **17.** quadrant I **19.** quadrant III **21.** quadrant II **23.** $\sin\theta = -\frac{4}{5}$; $\tan\theta = \frac{4}{3}$; $\csc\theta = -\frac{5}{4}$; $\sec\theta = -\frac{5}{3}$; $\cot\theta = \frac{3}{4}$ **25.** $\cos\theta = -\frac{12}{13}$; $\tan\theta = -\frac{5}{12}$; $\csc\theta = \frac{13}{5}$; $\sec\theta = -\frac{13}{12}$; $\cot\theta = -\frac{12}{5}$ **27.** $\sin\theta = -\frac{15}{17}$; $\tan\theta = -\frac{15}{8}$; $\csc\theta = -\frac{17}{15}$; $\sec\theta = \frac{17}{8}$; $\cot\theta = -\frac{8}{15}$ **29.** $\sin\theta = \frac{2\sqrt{13}}{13}$; $\cos\theta = -\frac{3\sqrt{13}}{3}$; $\csc\theta = \frac{\sqrt{13}}{2}$; $\sec\theta = -\frac{\sqrt{13}}{3}$; $\cot\theta = -\frac{3}{2}$ **31.** $\sin\theta = -\frac{4}{5}$; $\cos\theta = -\frac{3}{5}$; $\csc\theta = -\frac{5}{4}$; $\sec\theta = -\frac{5}{3}$; $\cot\theta = \frac{3}{4}$ **33.** $\sin\theta = -\frac{2\sqrt{2}}{3}$; $\cos\theta = -\frac{1}{3}$; $\tan\theta = 2\sqrt{2}$; $\csc\theta = -\frac{3\sqrt{2}}{4}$; $\cot\theta = \frac{\sqrt{2}}{4}$ **35.** 20° **37.** 25° **39.** 5° **41.** $\frac{\pi}{4}$ **43.** $\frac{\pi}{6}$ **45.** 30° **47.** 25° **49.** 1.56 **51.** $-\frac{\sqrt{2}}{2}$ **53.** $\frac{\sqrt{3}}{3}$ **55.** $\sqrt{3}$ **57.** $\frac{\sqrt{3}}{2}$ **59.** −2 **61.** 1 **63.** $\frac{\sqrt{3}}{2}$ **65.** −1

## Section 5.5

### Check Point Exercises

**1.** 3

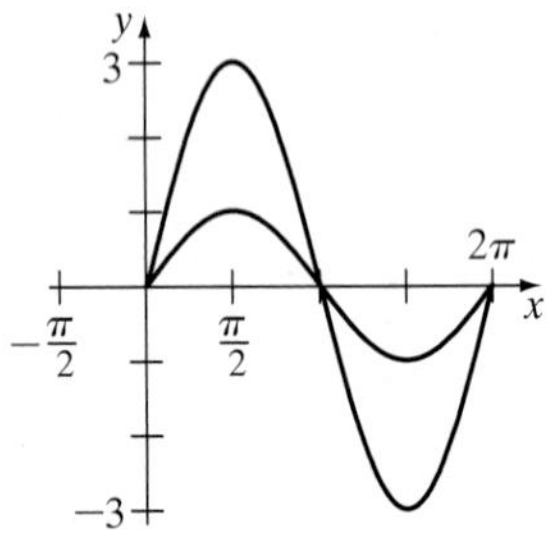


**2.** $\frac{1}{2}$

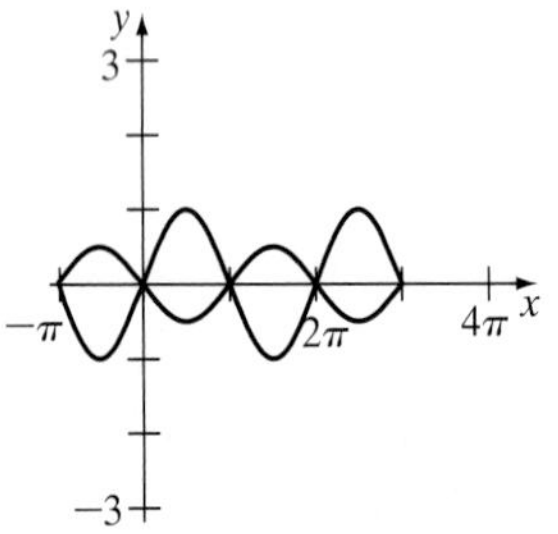


**3.** 2; 4π

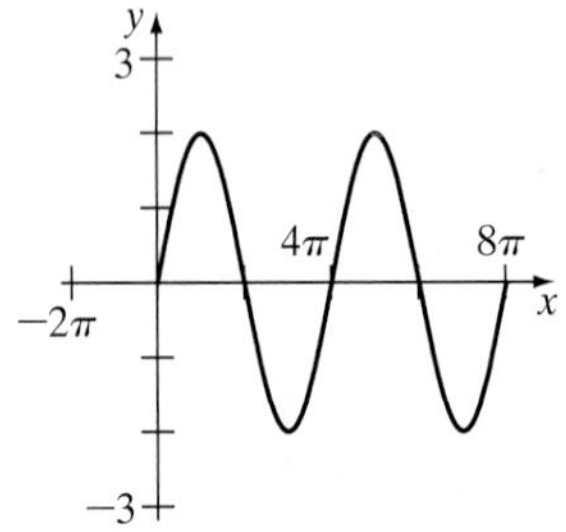


**4.** 3; π; $\frac{\pi}{6}$

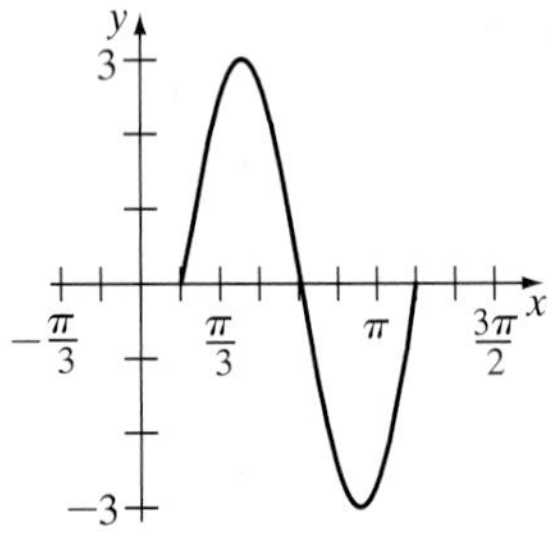


**5.** 4; 2

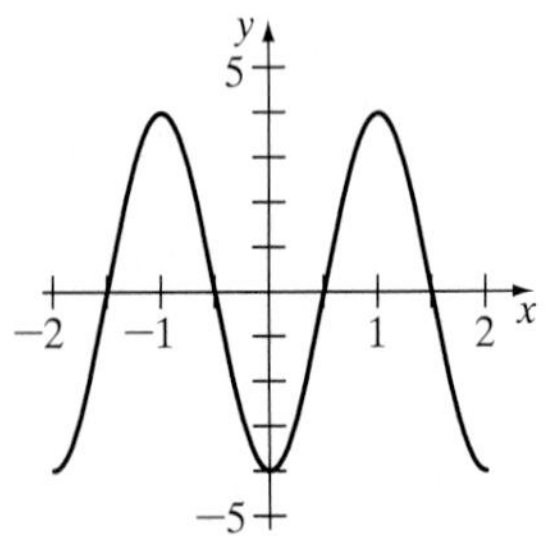


**6.** $\frac{3}{2}$; π; $-\frac{\pi}{2}$

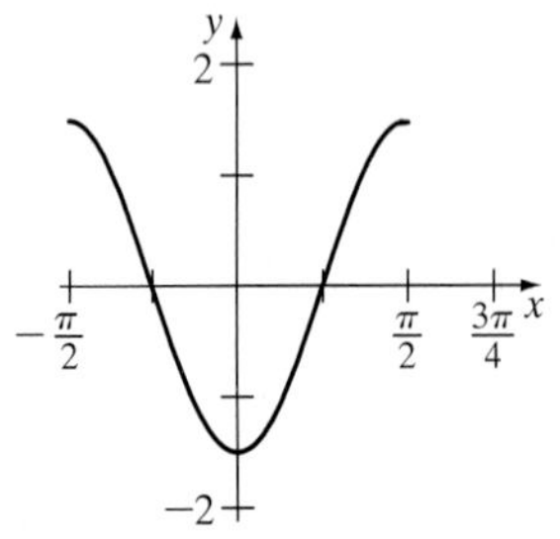


**7.**

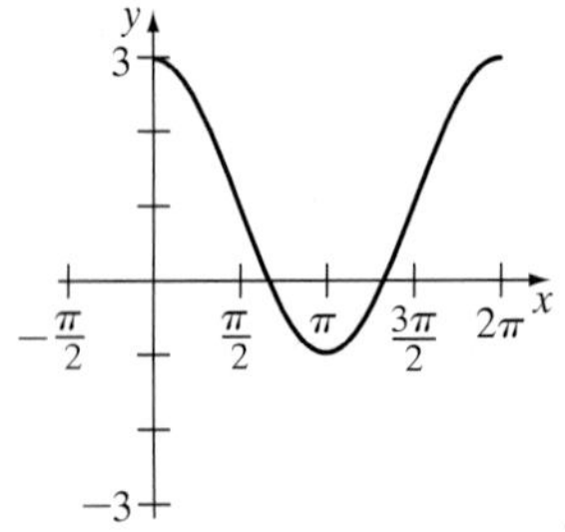


**8.** $y = 4\sin 4x$

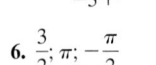

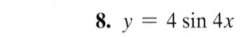

**9.** $y = 2\sin\left(\frac{\pi}{6}x - \frac{\pi}{2}\right) + 12$

## Exercise Set 5.5

**1.** 4

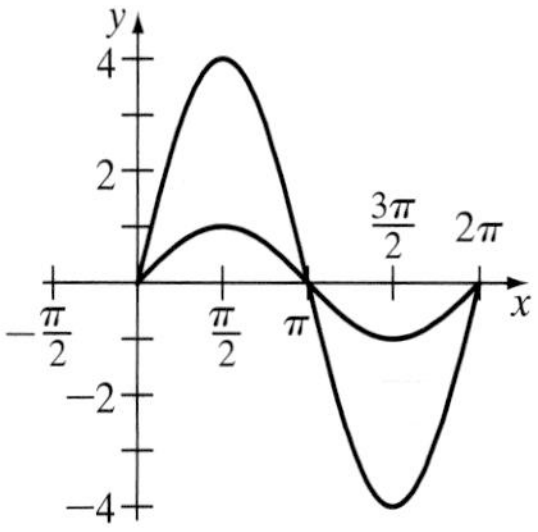


**3.** $\frac{1}{3}$

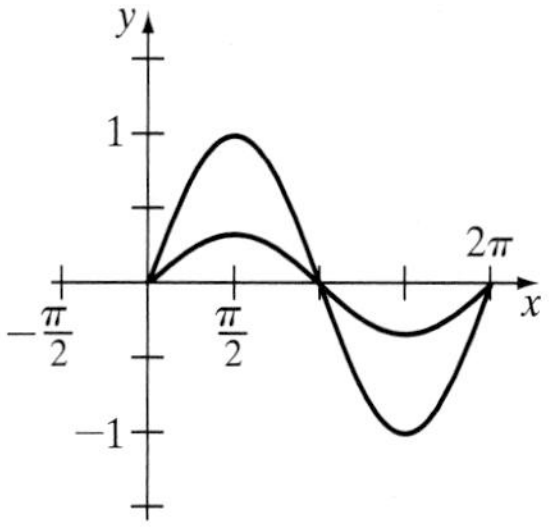


**5.** 3

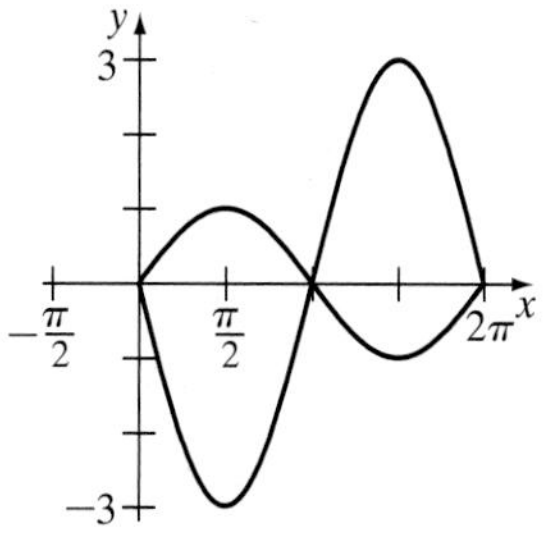


**7.** 1; $\pi$

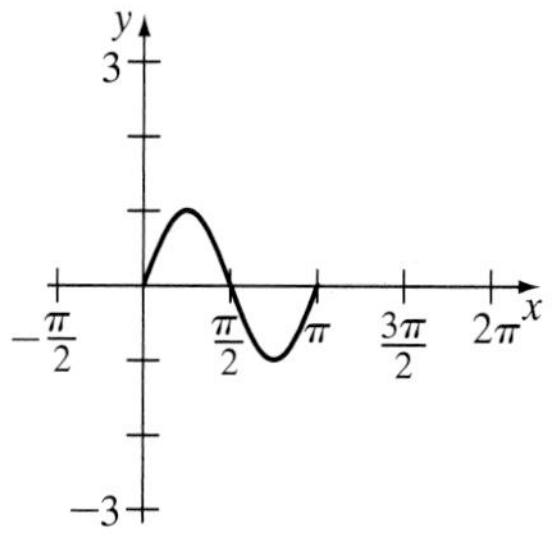


**9.** 3; $4\pi$

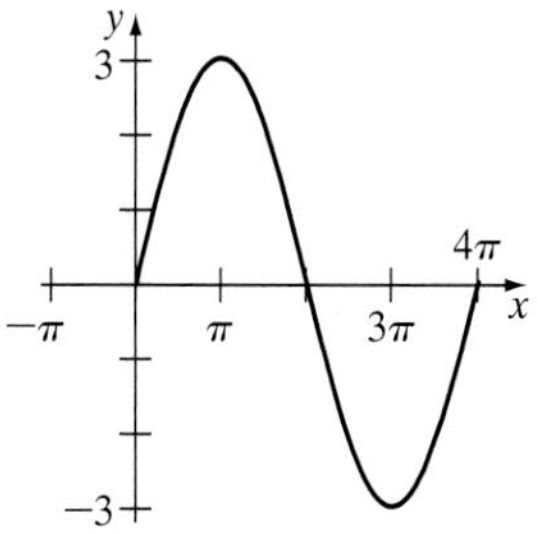


**11.** 4; 2

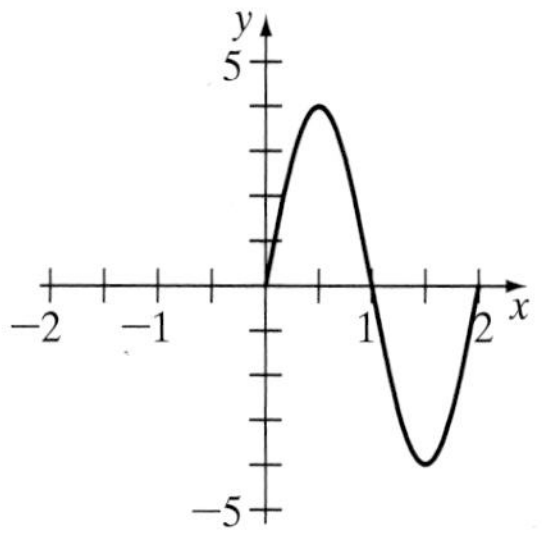


**13.** 3; 1

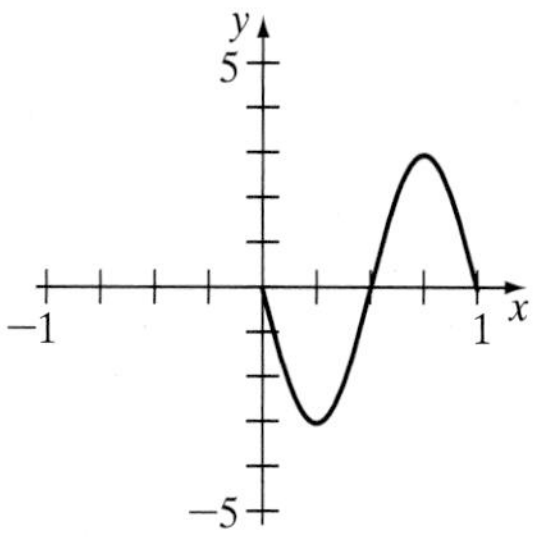


**15.** 1; $3\pi$

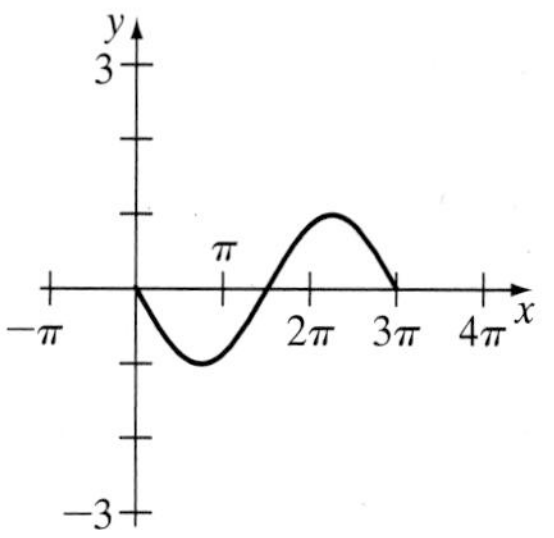


**17.** 1; $2\pi$; $\pi$

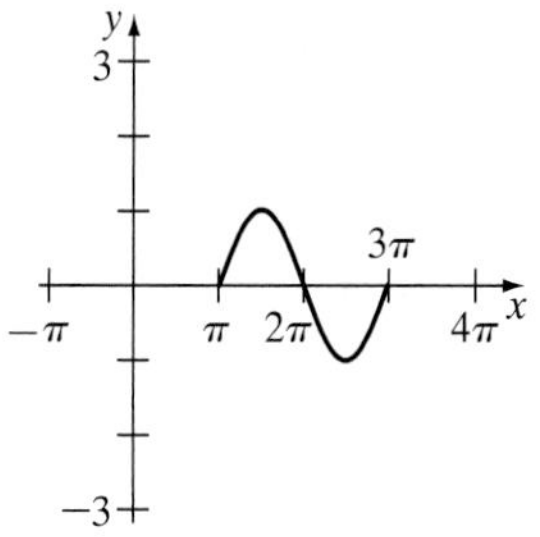


**19.** 1; $\pi$; $\frac{\pi}{2}$

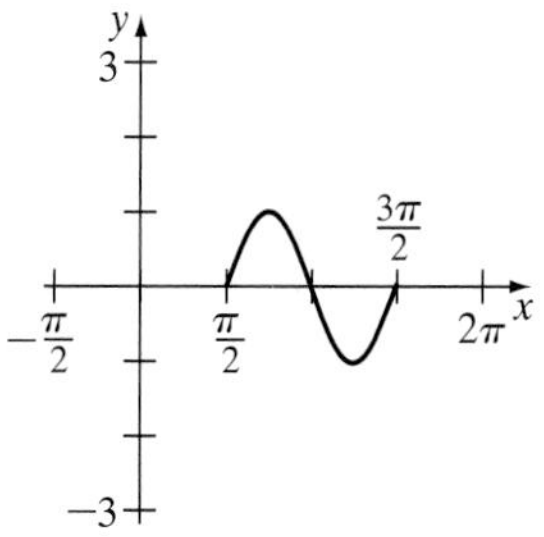


**21.** 3; $\pi$; $\frac{\pi}{2}$

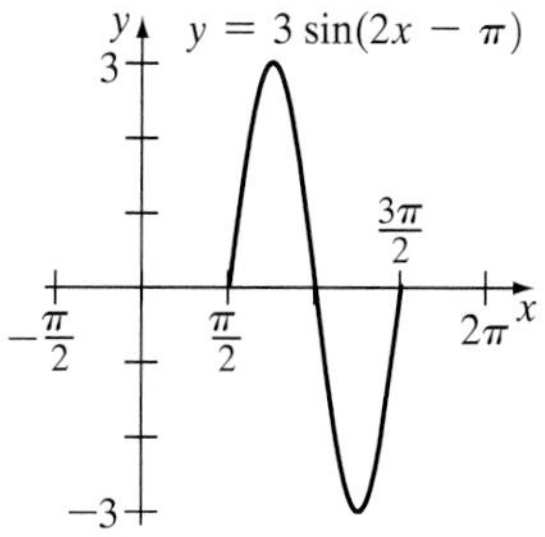


**23.** $\frac{1}{2}$; $2\pi$; $-\frac{\pi}{2}$

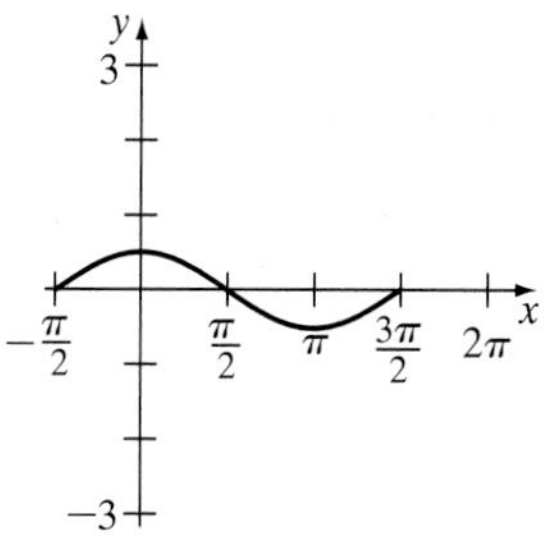


**25.** 2; $\pi$; $-\frac{\pi}{4}$

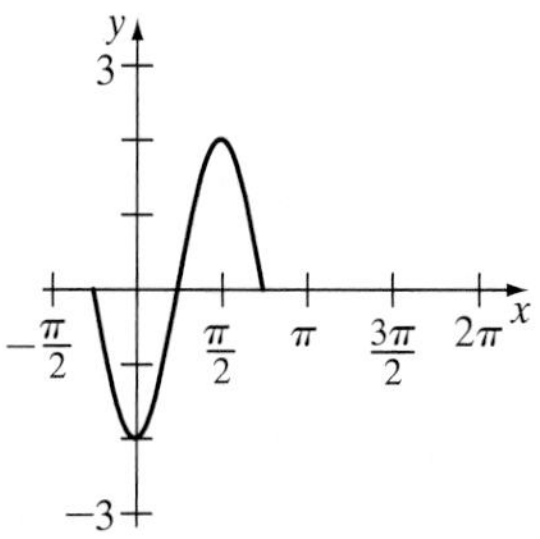


**27.** 3; 2; $-\frac{2}{\pi}$

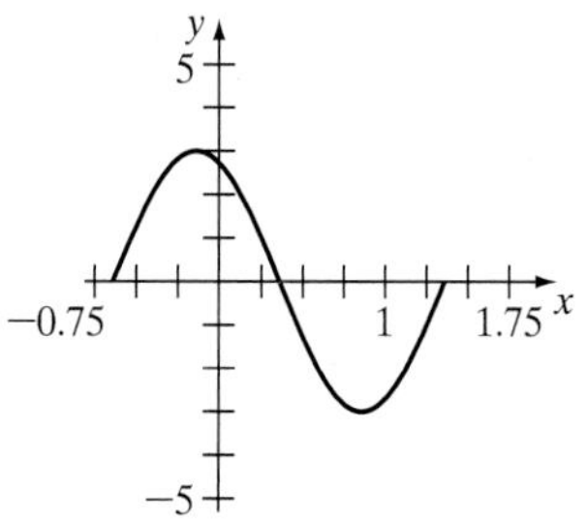


**29.** 2; 1; −2

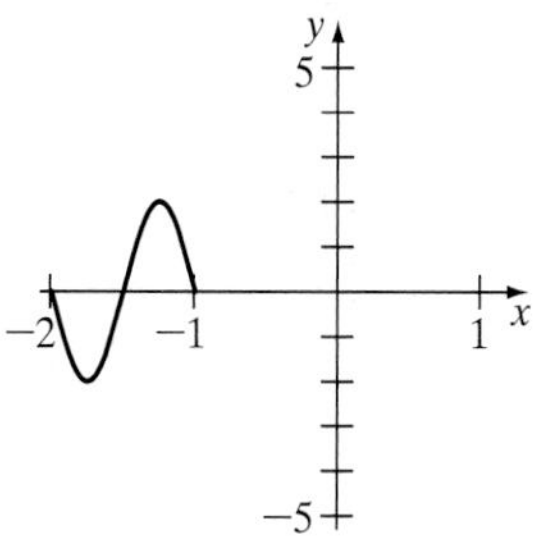


**31.** 2

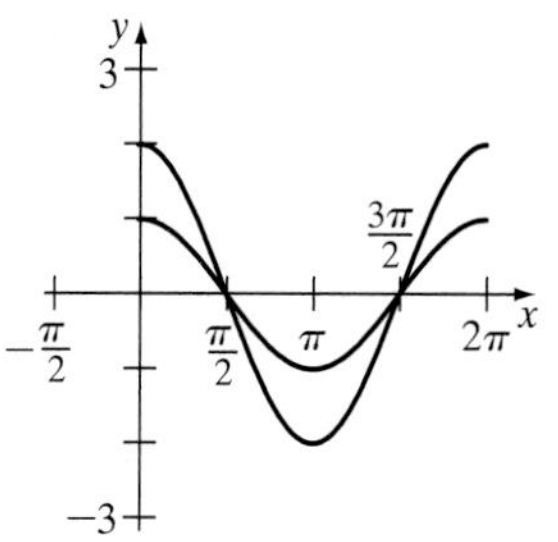

**33.** 2

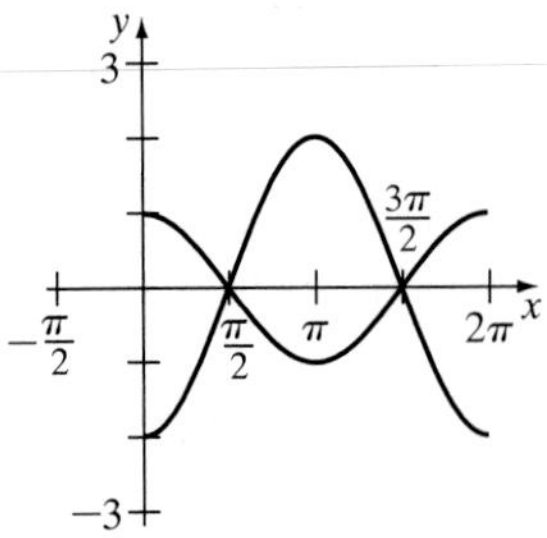


**35.** 1; $\pi$

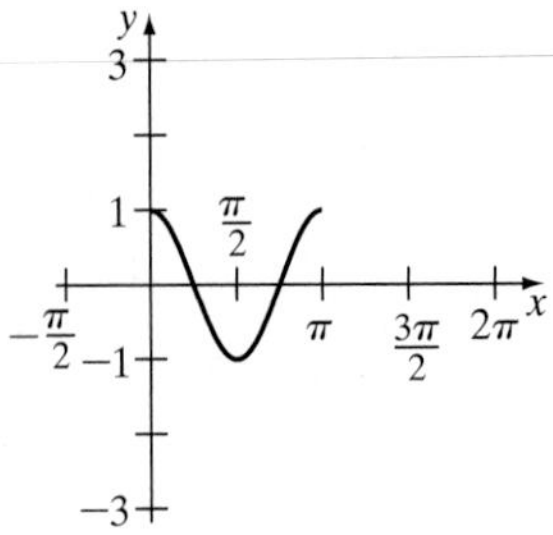


**37.** 4; 1

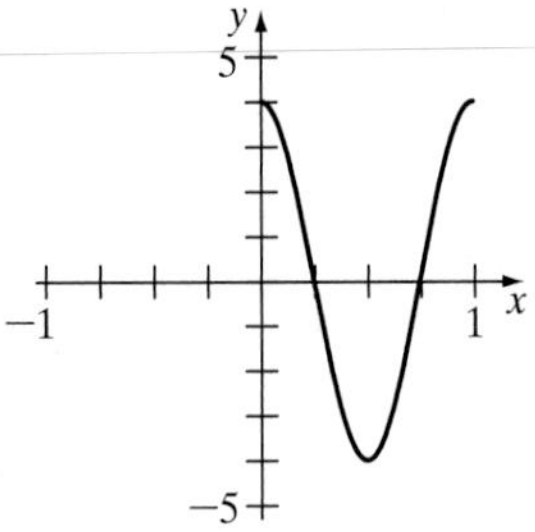


**39.** 4; $4\pi$

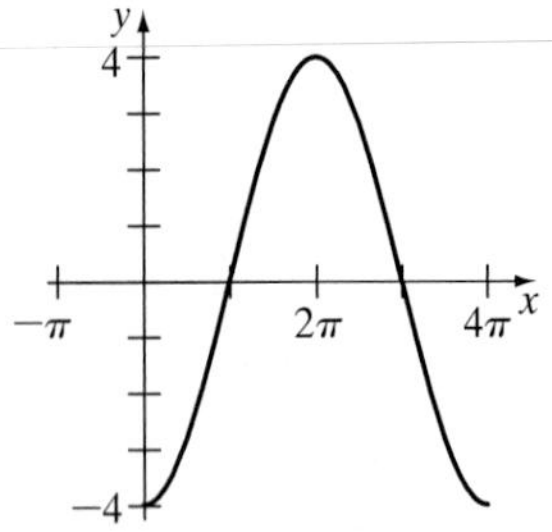


**41.** $\frac{1}{2}$; 6

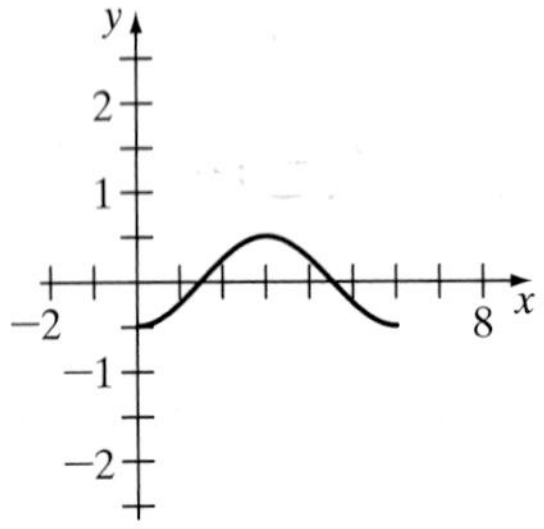


**43.** 3; $\pi$; $\frac{\pi}{2}$

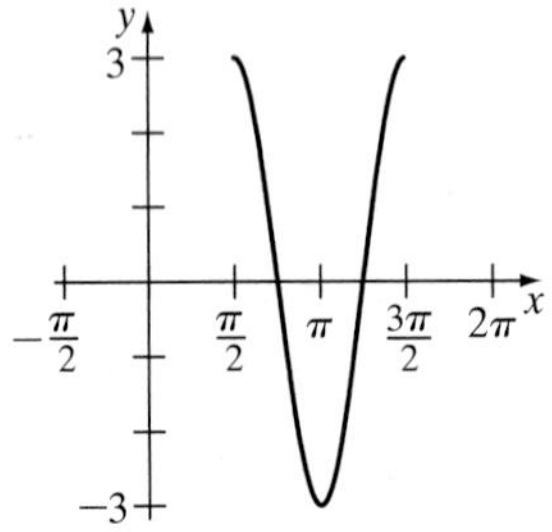


**45.** $\frac{1}{2}$; $\frac{2\pi}{3}$; $-\frac{\pi}{6}$

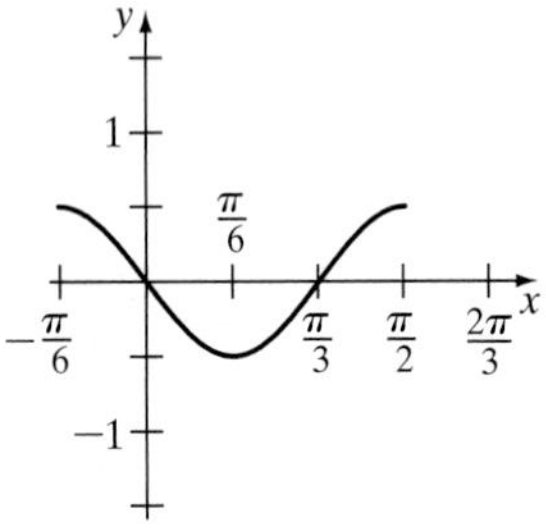


**47.** 3; $\pi$; $\frac{\pi}{4}$

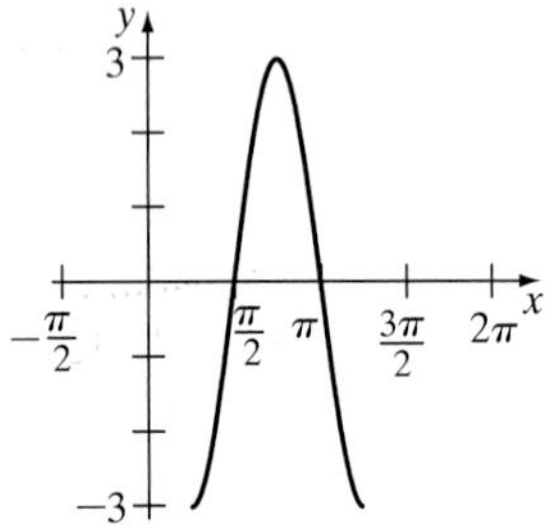


**49.** 2; 1; −4

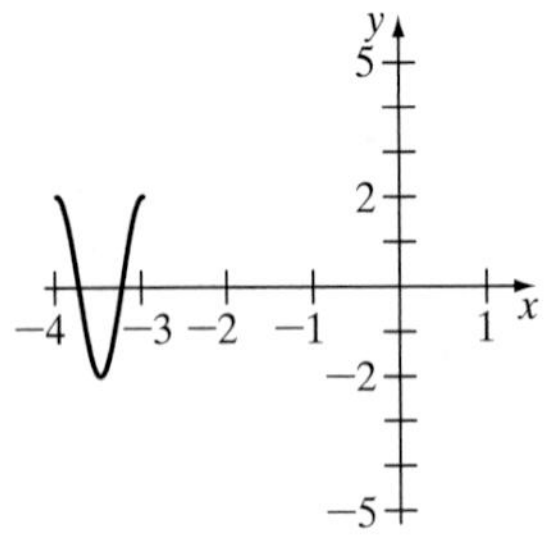


**51.**

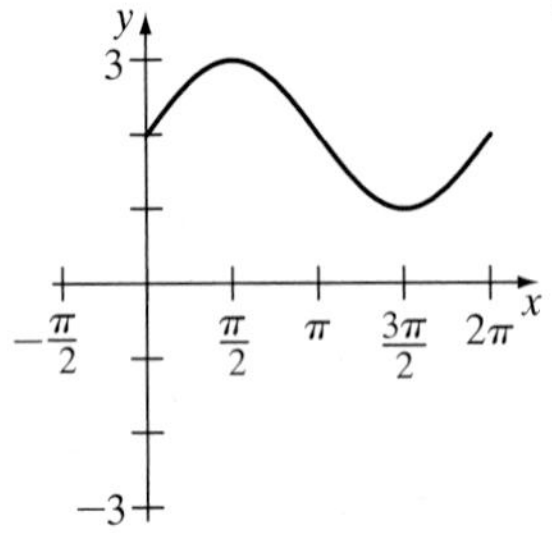


**53.**

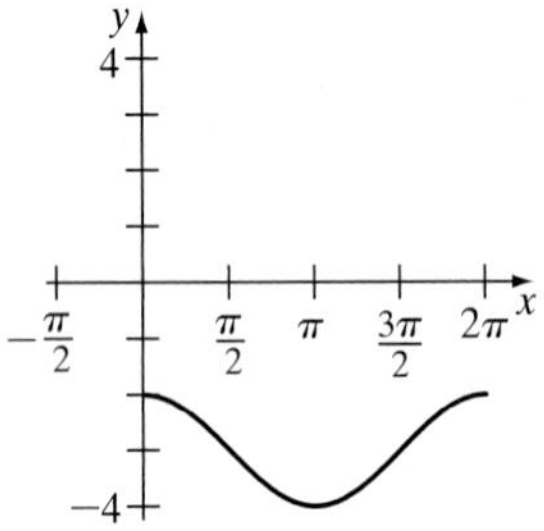


**55.**

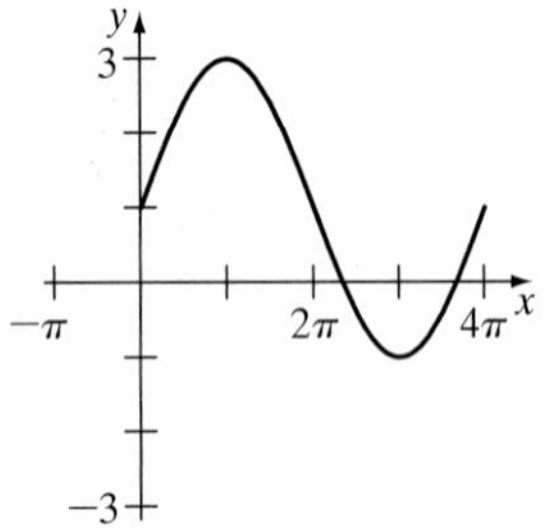


**57.**

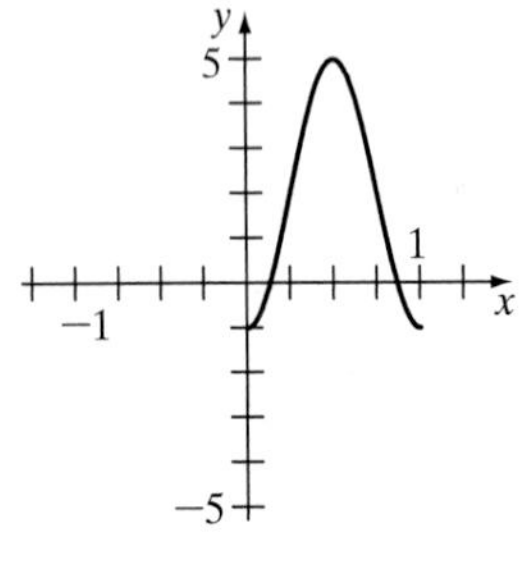


**59.** 33 days **61.** 23 days **63.** March 21

**67.**

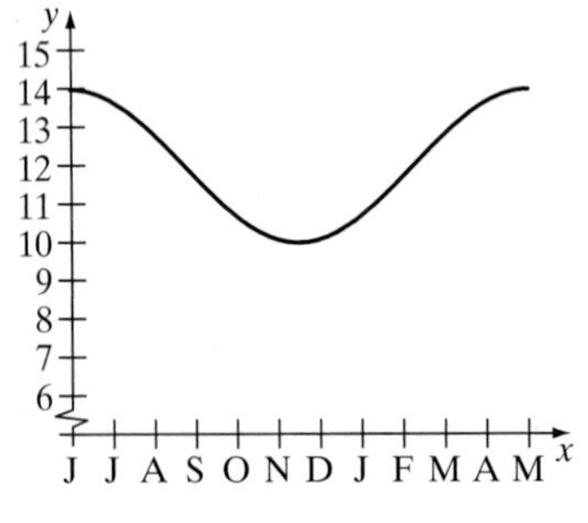


**65.** No

**69. a.** 3 **b.** 365 days
**c.** 15 hours of daylight
**d.** 9 hours of daylight
**e.**

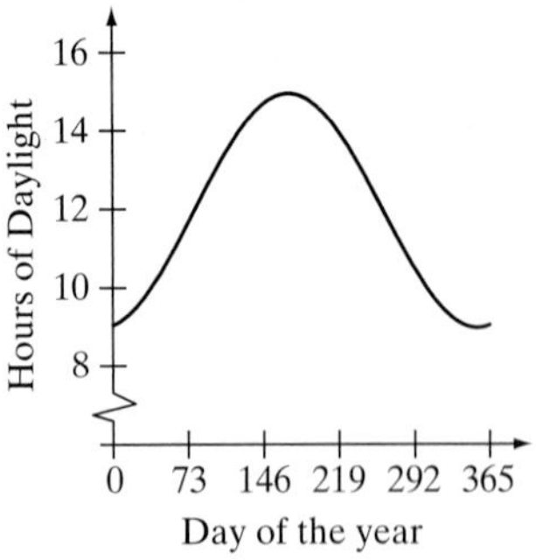


**71.** $y = 3\cos\frac{\pi x}{6} + 9$

**85.**

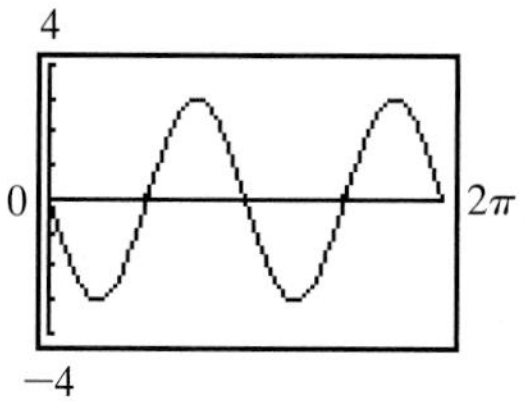


**87.**

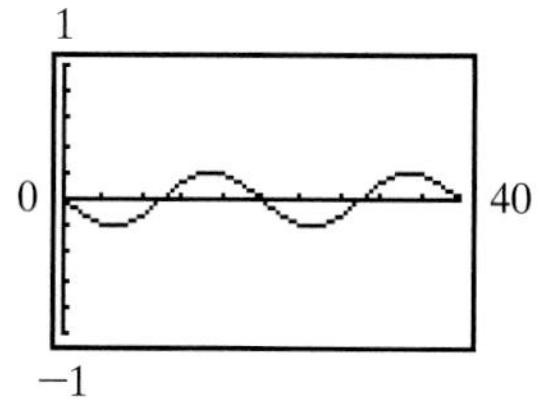


**89.**

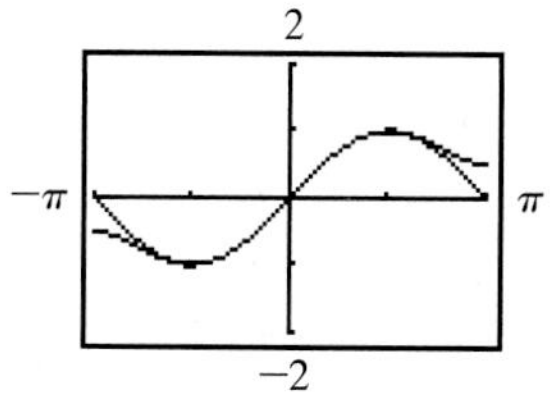


The graphs appear to be the same from $-\frac{\pi}{2}$ to $\frac{\pi}{2}$.

**91.**

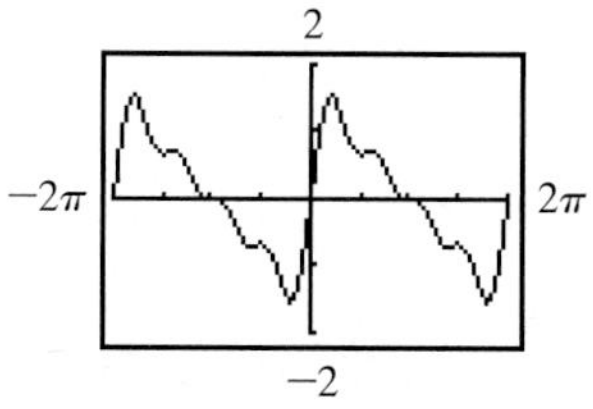


The graph is similar to $y = \sin x$, except the amplitude is greater and the curve is less smooth.

**93. a.**

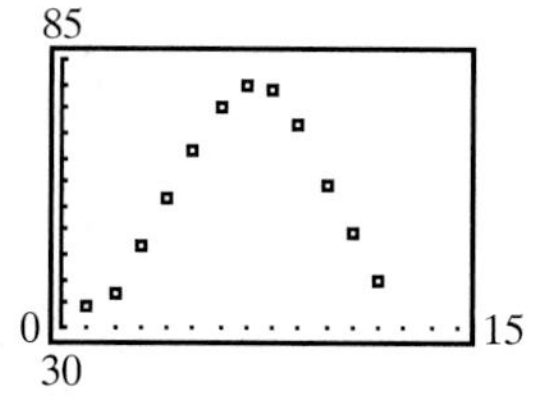


**b.** $y = 22.61 \sin(0.50x - 2.04) + 57.17$

**c.**

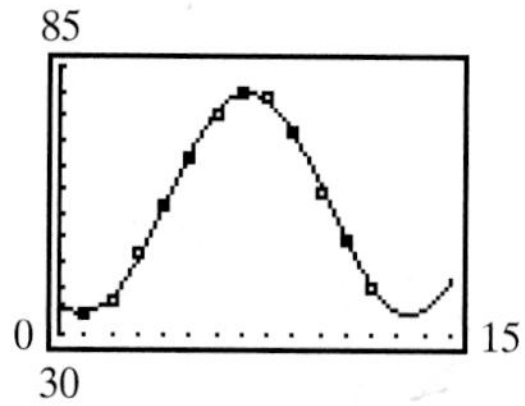


**95.**

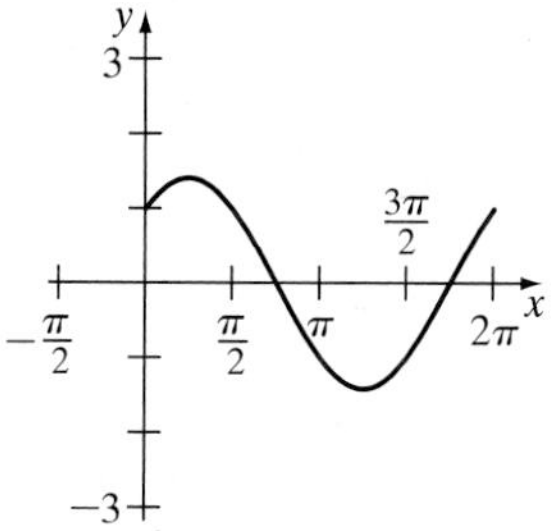


**97.** $y = 2\cos(4x + \pi)$

## Section 5.6

### Check Point Exercises

**1.**

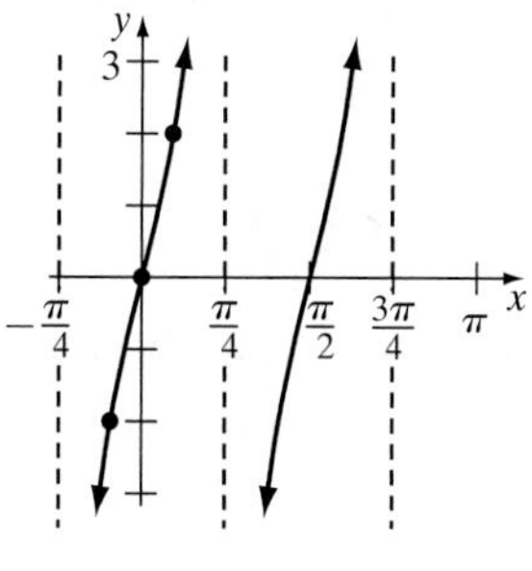


**2.**

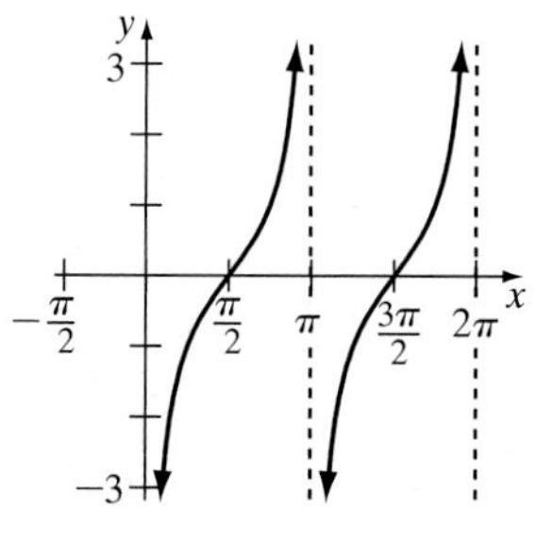


**3.**

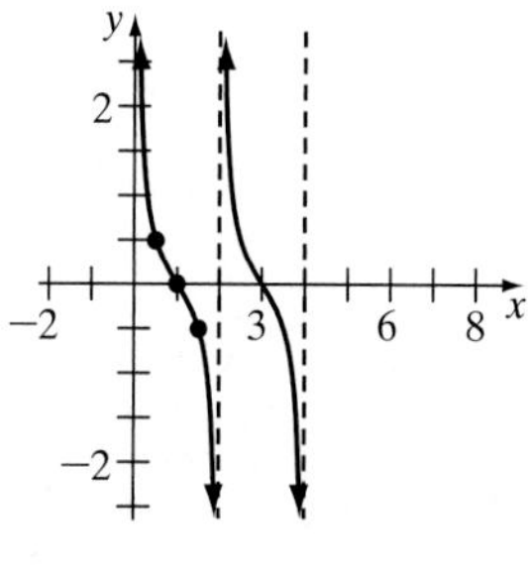


**4.**

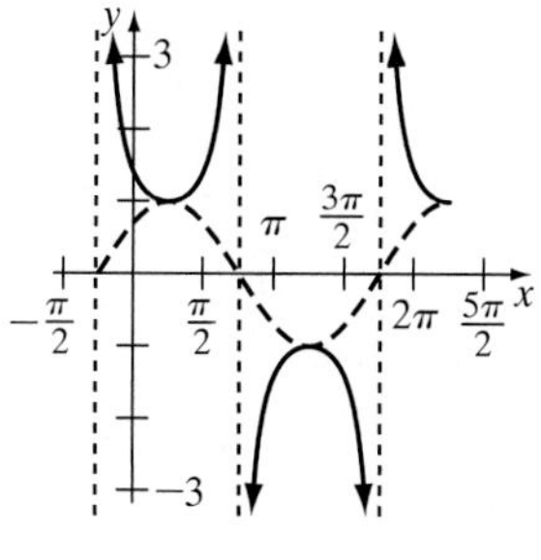


**5.**

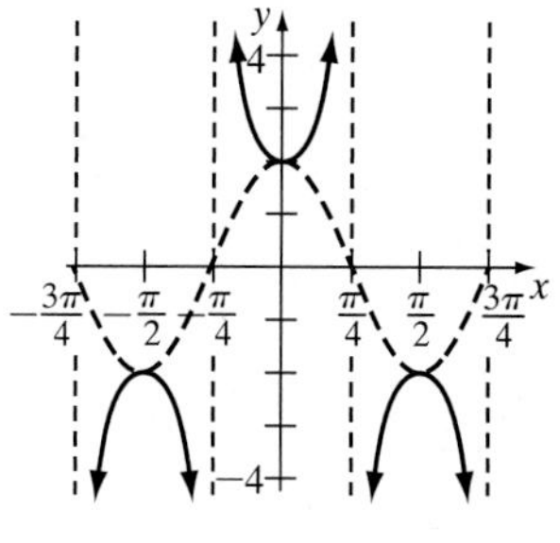

## Exercise Set 5.6

**1.** $y = \tan(x + \pi)$ **3.** $y = -\tan\left(x - \frac{\pi}{2}\right)$

**5.**

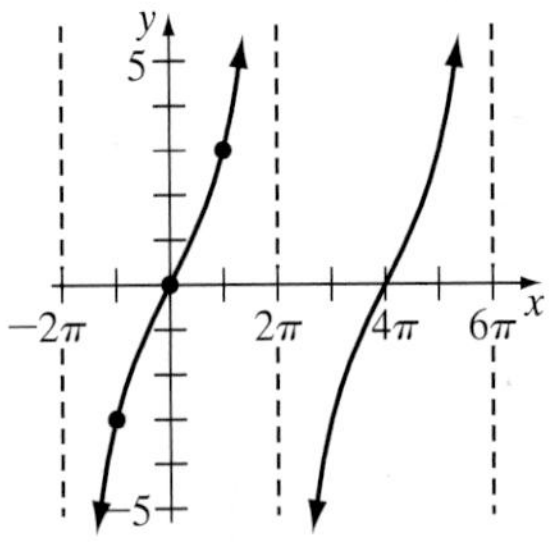


**7.**

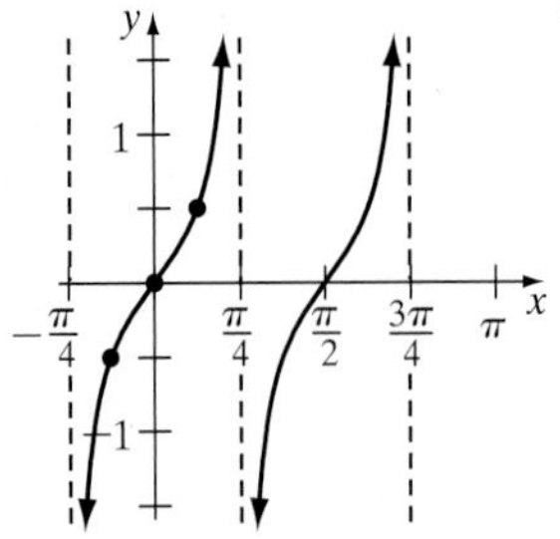


**9.**

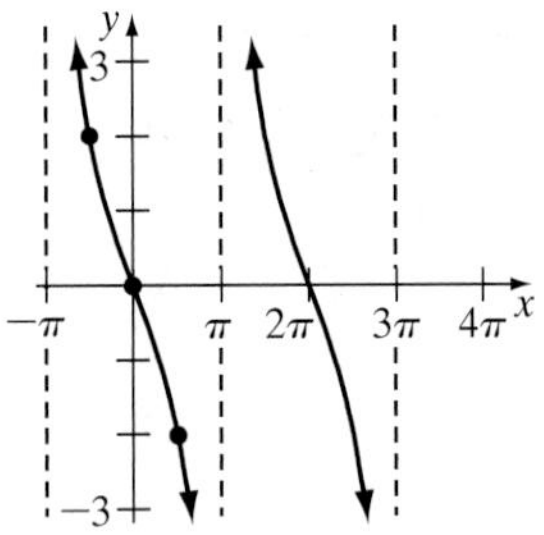


**11.**

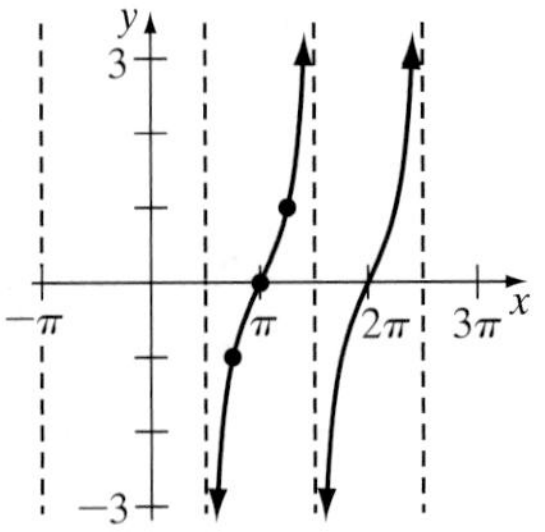


**13.** $y = -\cot x$ **15.** $y = \cot\left(x + \frac{\pi}{2}\right)$

**17.**

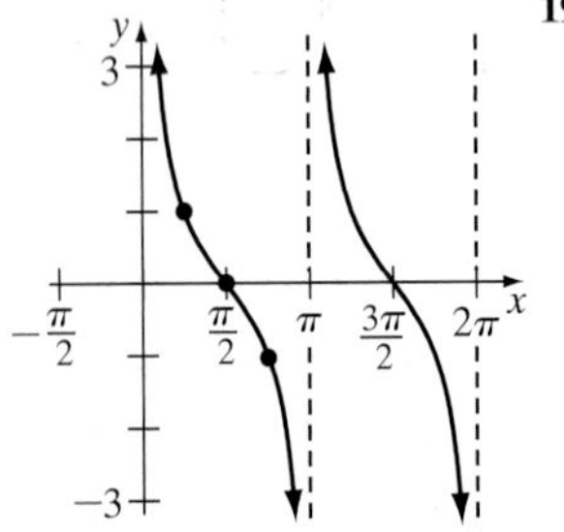


**19.**

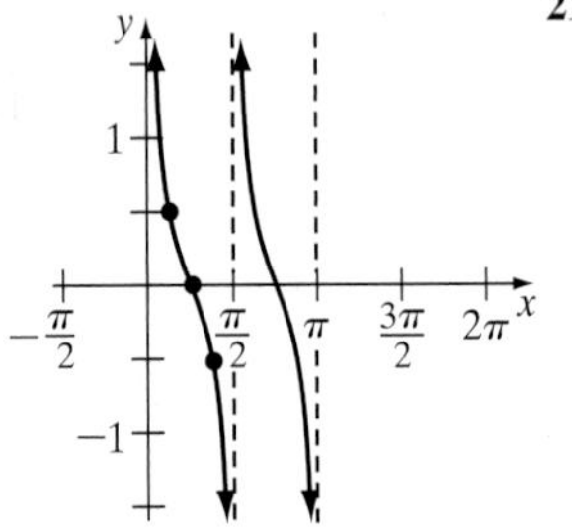


**21.**

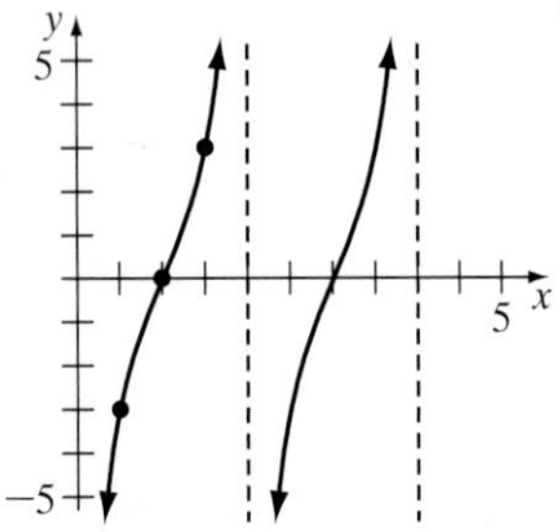


**23.**

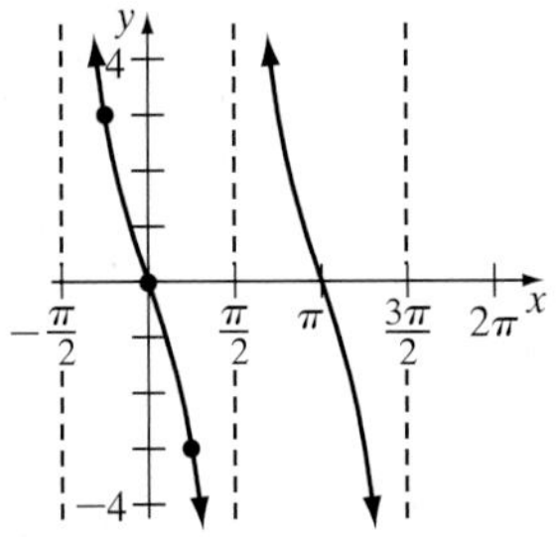


**25.** $y = -\frac{1}{2}\csc\frac{x}{2}$;

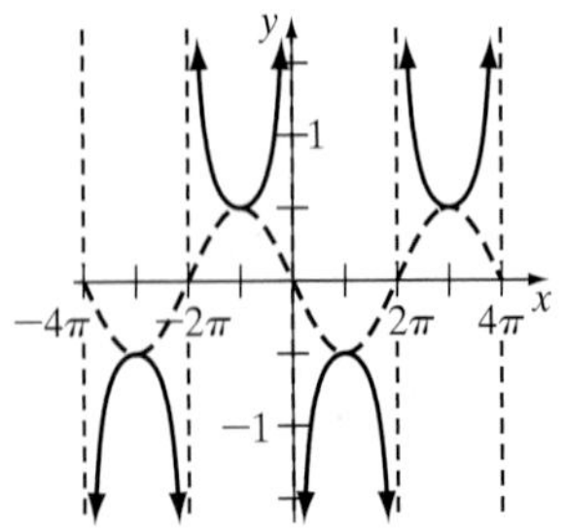


**27.** $y = \frac{1}{2}\sec 2\pi x$;

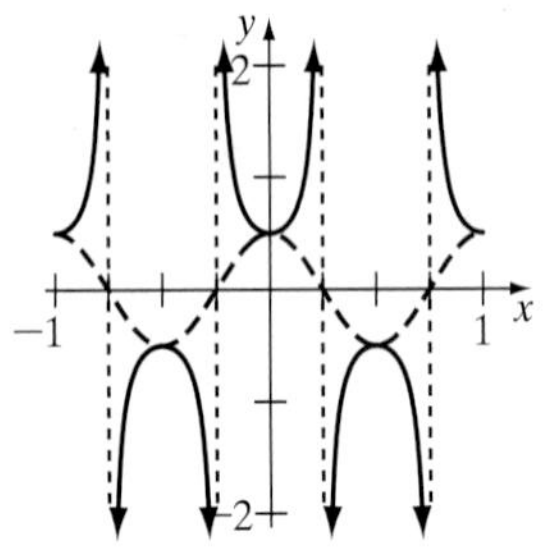


**29.**

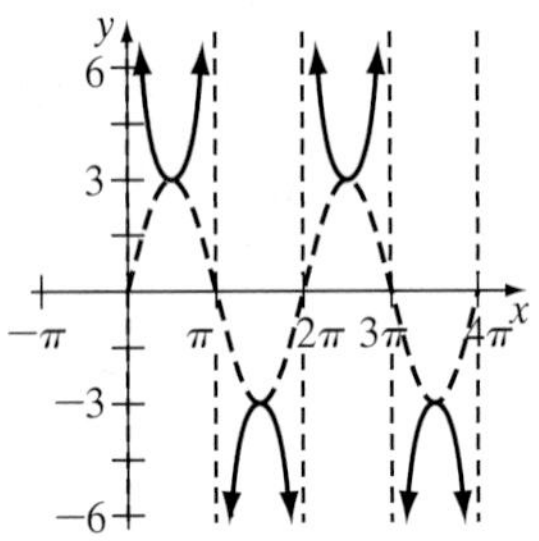


**31.**

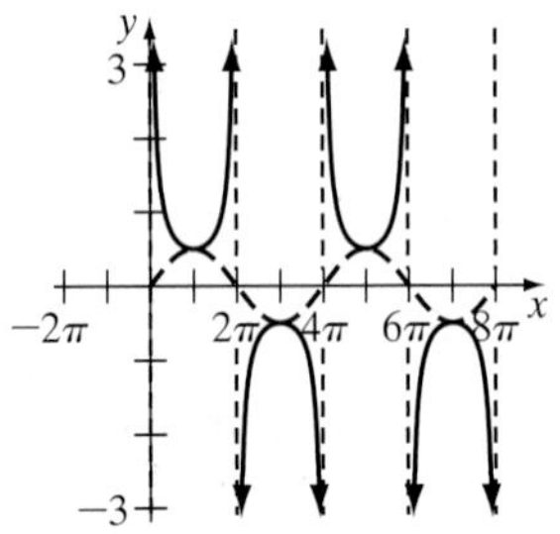


**33.**

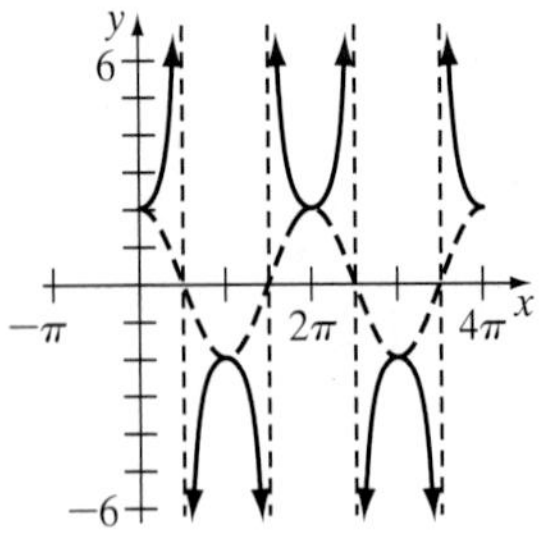


**35.**

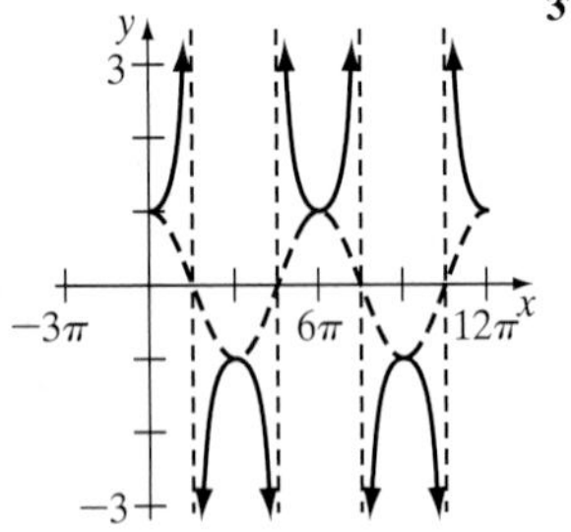


**37.**

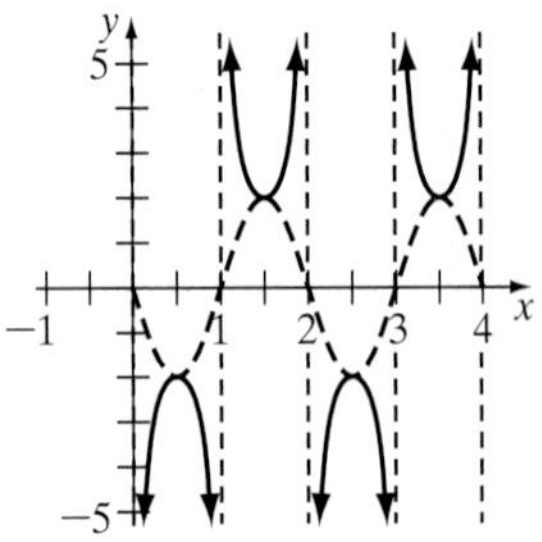


**39.**

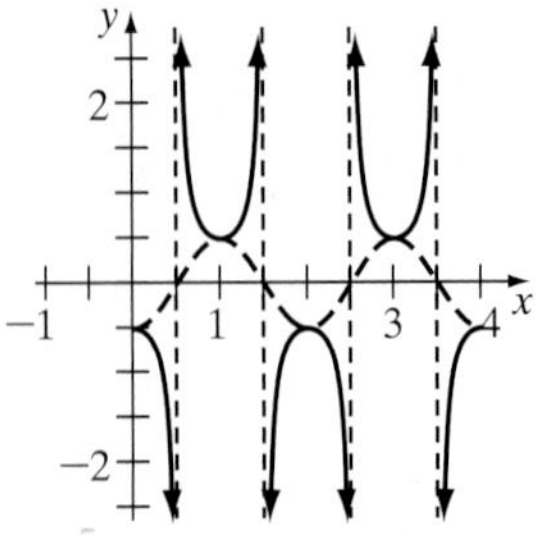

**41.**

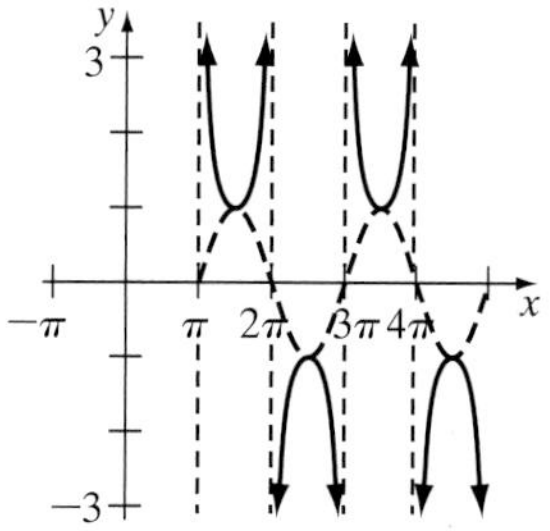


**43.**

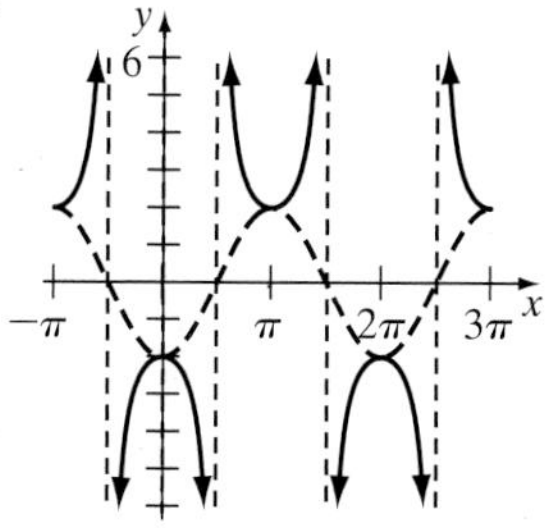


**45. a.**

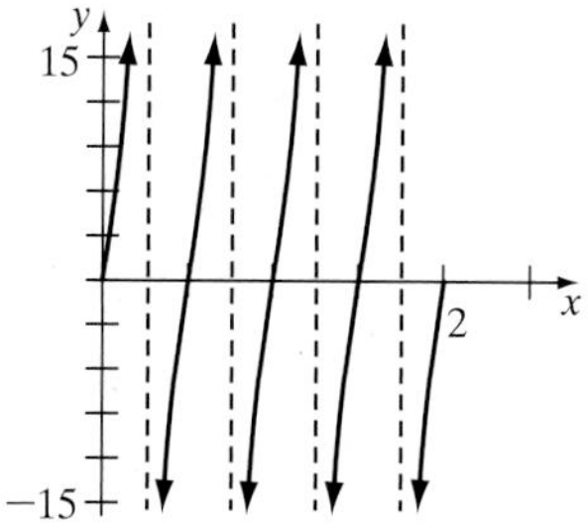


**b.** 0.25, 0.75, 1.25, 1.75; The beacon is shining parallel to the wall at these times.

**47.** $d = 10 \sec x$

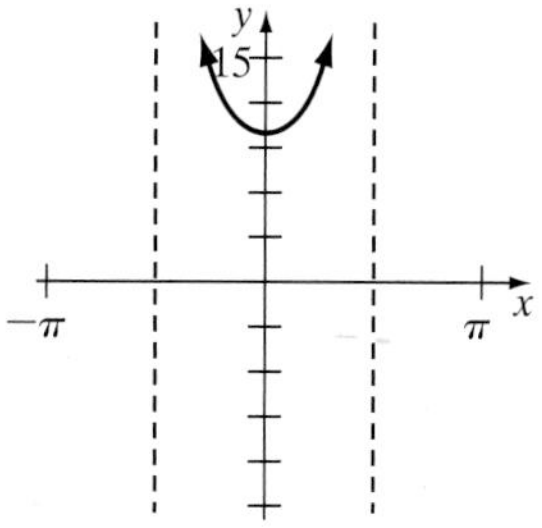


**49.**

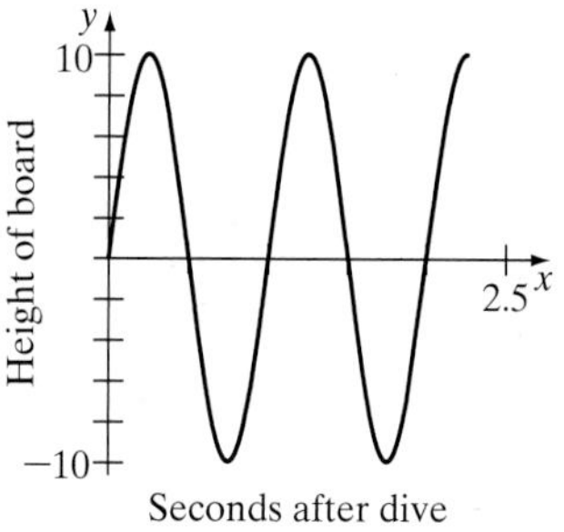


**63.**

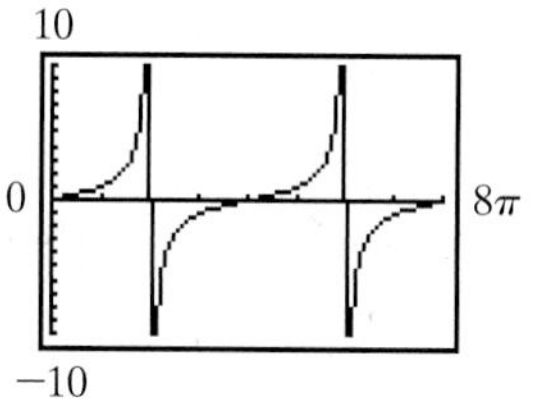


**65.**

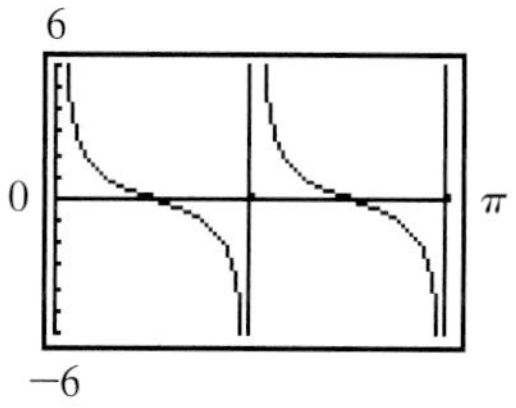


**67.**

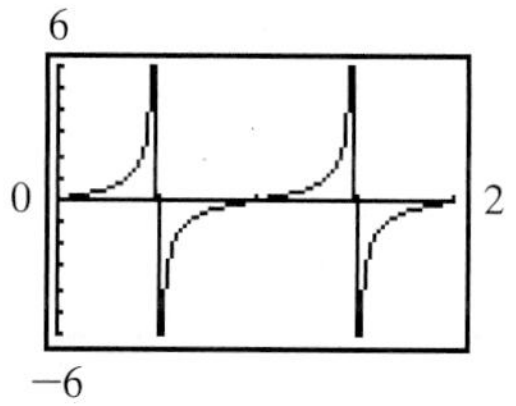


**69.**

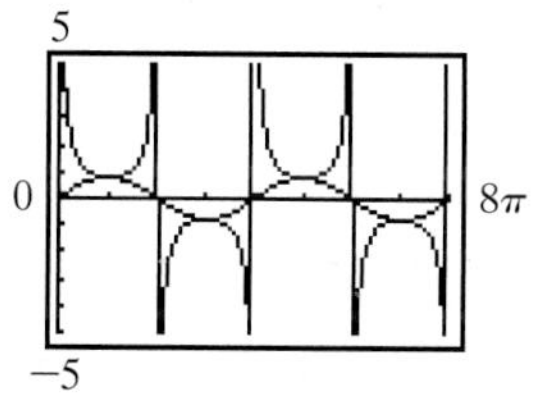


**71.**

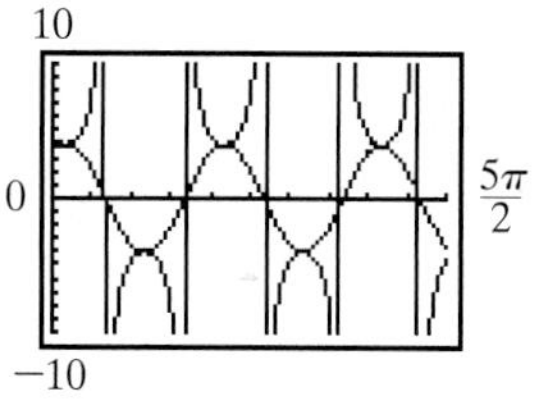


**73.**

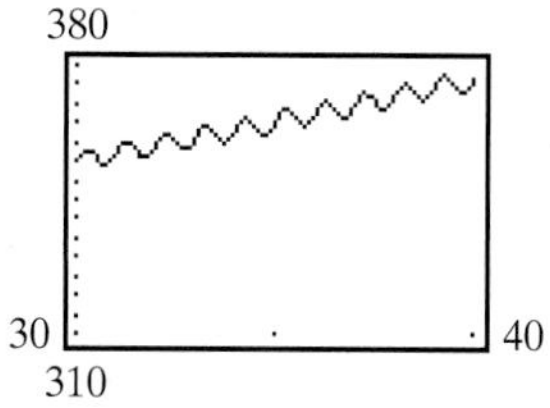


The concentration is increasing.

**75.** $y = \cot \frac{3}{2}x$

**77.** $2^{-x}$ decreases the amplitude as $x$ gets larger.

## Section 5.7

### Check Point Exercises

**1.** $\frac{\pi}{3}$ **2.** $-\frac{\pi}{4}$ **3.** $\frac{2\pi}{3}$ **4.** $-\frac{\pi}{4}$ **5. a.** 1.2310 **b.** −1.5429 **6. a.** 0.7 **b.** 0 **c.** not defined **7.** $\frac{3}{5}$ **8.** $\frac{\sqrt{3}}{2}$ **9.** $\sqrt{x^2+1}$

### Exercise Set 5.7

**1.** $\frac{\pi}{6}$ **3.** $\frac{\pi}{4}$ **5.** $-\frac{\pi}{6}$ **7.** $\frac{\pi}{6}$ **9.** $\frac{3\pi}{4}$ **11.** $\frac{\pi}{2}$ **13.** $\frac{\pi}{6}$ **15.** 0 **17.** $-\frac{\pi}{3}$ **19.** 0.30 **21.** −0.33 **23.** 1.19 **25.** 1.25 **27.** −1.52 **29.** −1.52 **31.** 0.9 **33.** $\frac{\pi}{3}$ **35.** $\frac{\pi}{6}$ **37.** 125 **39.** $-\frac{\pi}{6}$ **41.** $-\frac{\pi}{3}$ **43.** 0 **45.** not defined **47.** $\frac{3}{5}$ **49.** $\frac{12}{5}$ **51.** $-\frac{3}{4}$ **53.** $\frac{\sqrt{2}}{2}$ **55.** $\frac{4\sqrt{15}}{15}$ **57.** $-2\sqrt{2}$ **59.** 2 **61.** $\frac{\sqrt{1-x^2}}{x}$ **63.** $\frac{\sqrt{x^2-1}}{x}$ **65.** $\frac{\sqrt{x^2+4}}{2}$

**67. a.**

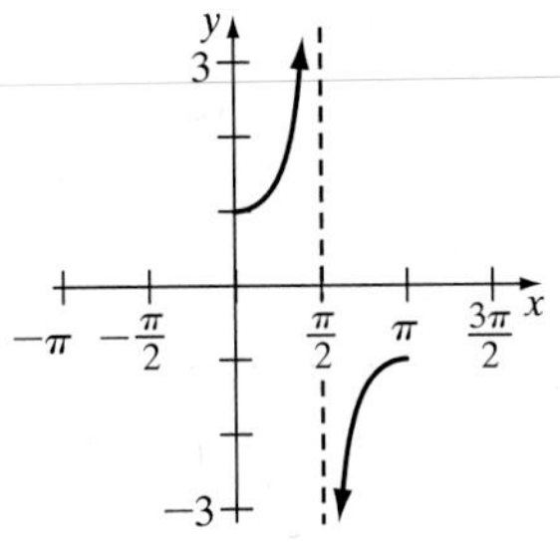


**b.** No horizontal line intersects the graph of $y = \sec x$ more than once, so the function is one-to-one and has an inverse function.

**c.**

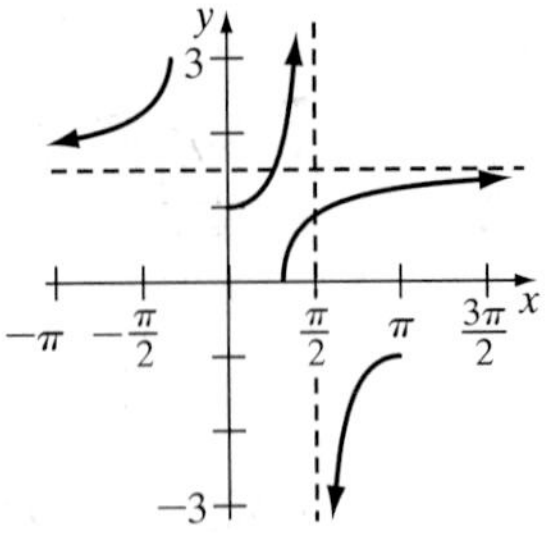


**69.** 0.408 radians; 0.602 radians; 0.654 radians; 0.645 radians; 0.613 radians

**71.** 1.3157 radians or 75.4°

**73.** 1.1071 sq units

**87.**

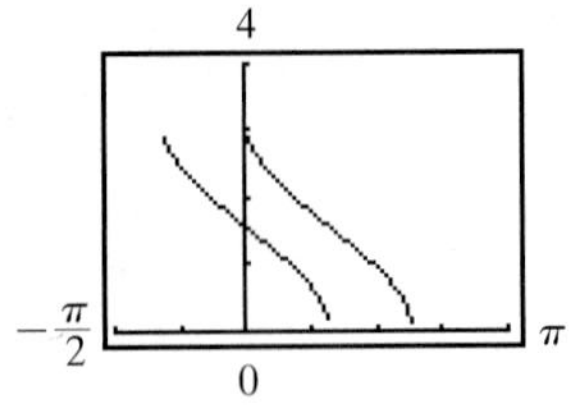


Shifted right 1 unit

**89.**

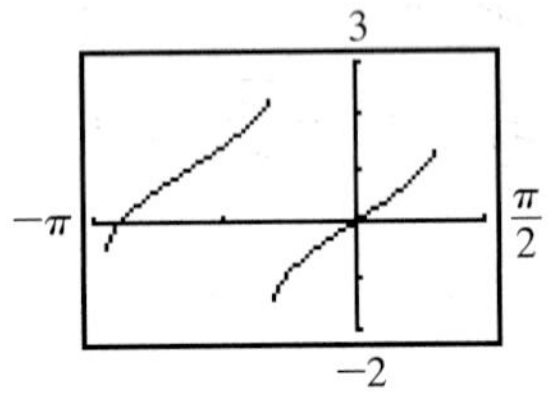


Shifted left 2 units and up 1 unit

**91.**

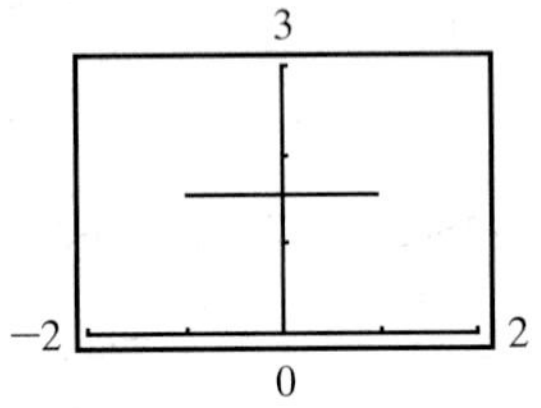


It seems $\sin^{-1} x + \cos^{-1} x = \frac{\pi}{2}$ for $-1 \le x \le 1$

**93.** $x = \sin \frac{\pi}{8}$

**95.** $\tan \alpha = \frac{8}{x}$, so $\tan^{-1} \frac{8}{x} = \alpha$.

$\tan(\alpha + \theta) = \frac{33}{x}$, so $\tan^{-1} \frac{33}{x} = \alpha + \theta$.

$\theta = \alpha + \theta - \alpha = \tan^{-1} \frac{33}{x} - \tan^{-1} \frac{8}{x}$.

## Section 5.8

### Check Point Exercises

**1.** $B = 27.3°; b \approx 4.34; c \approx 9.45$ **2.** 998 ft **3.** $\theta \approx 29.0$ **4.** 60.3 ft **5. a.** S 25° E **b.** S 15° W **6. a.** 4.2 mi **b.** S87.7°W **7.** $d = -6 \cos \frac{\pi}{2} t$ **8. a.** 12 cm **b.** $\frac{1}{8}$ cycle per sec **c.** 8 sec

### Exercise Set 5.8

**1.** $B = 66.5°; a \approx 4.35; c \approx 10.90$ **3.** $B = 37.4°; a \approx 42.90; b \approx 32.80$ **5.** $A = 73.2°; a \approx 101.02; c \approx 105.52$ **7.** $b \approx 39.95; A \approx 37.3°; B \approx 52.7°$ **9.** $c \approx 26.96; A \approx 23.6°; B \approx 66.4°$ **11.** $a \approx 6.71; B \approx 16.6°; A \approx 73.4°$ **13.** N 15° E **15.** S 80° W **17.** $d = -6 \cos \frac{\pi}{2} t$ **19.** $d = 3 \sin \frac{4\pi}{3} t$ **21. a.** 5 in. **b.** $\frac{1}{4}$ cycle per sec **c.** 4 sec **23. a.** 6 in. **b.** 1 cycle per sec **c.** 1 sec **25. a.** $\frac{1}{2}$ in. **b.** 0.32 cycle per sec **c.** 3.14 sec **27. a.** 5 in. **b.** $\frac{1}{3}$ cycle per sec **c.** 3 sec **29.** $h \approx 2059$ ft **31.** $d \approx 695$ ft **33.** 1376 ft **35.** 15.1° **37.** 33.7 ft **39.** 90 mi north and 120 mi east **41.** 13.2 mi **43.** N 53° W **45.** N 89.5° E **47.** $d = 6 \sin \pi t$ **49.** $d = \sin 528 \pi t$

**59.**

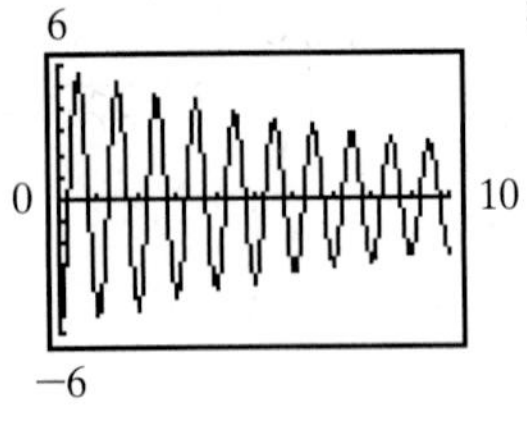


; 10 complete oscillations **61.** 48 ft

## Chapter 5 Review Exercises

**1.**

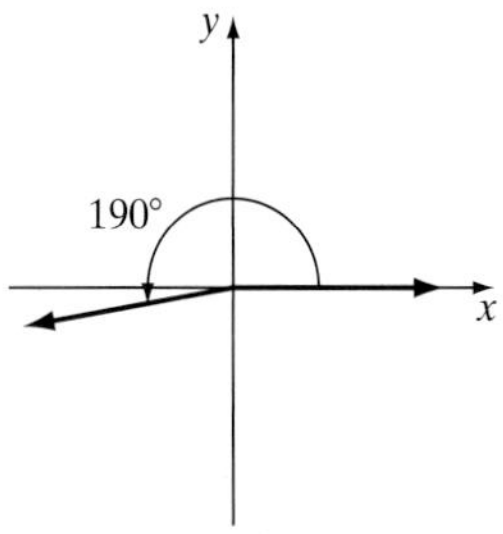


**2.**

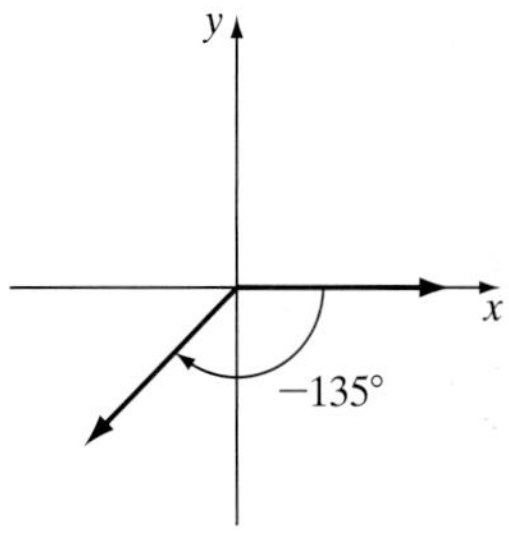


**3.**

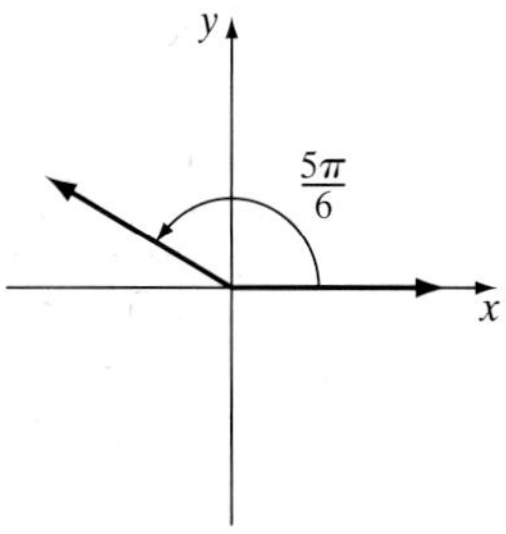


**4.**

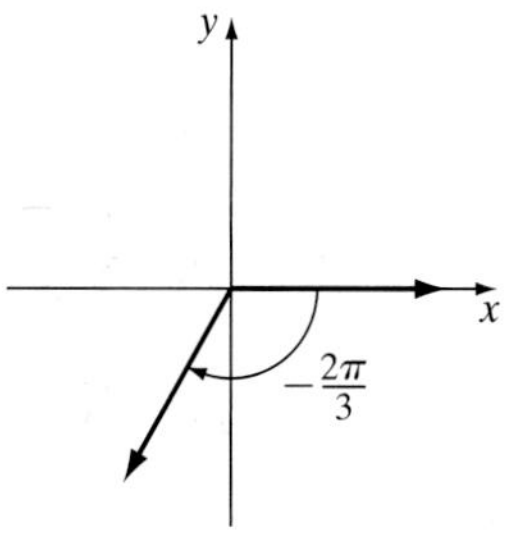


**5.** 40° **6.** 275° **7.** 17°; 107° **8.** no complement; $\frac{\pi}{3}$ radians **9.** 4.5 radians **10.** $\frac{\pi}{12}$ radians **11.** $\frac{2\pi}{3}$ radians **12.** $\frac{7\pi}{4}$ radians **13.** 300° **14.** 252° **15.** −150° **16.** $\frac{15\pi}{2}$ ft $\approx 23.56$ ft **17.** $20.6\pi$ radians per min **18.** 42,412 ft per min **19.** $\sin t = -\frac{3}{5}$; $\cos t = -\frac{4}{5}$; $\tan t = \frac{3}{4}$; $\csc t = -\frac{5}{3}$; $\sec t = -\frac{5}{4}$; $\cot t = \frac{4}{3}$ **20.** $\sin t = -\frac{15}{17}$; $\cos t = \frac{8}{17}$; $\tan t = -\frac{15}{8}$; $\csc t = -\frac{17}{15}$; $\sec t = \frac{17}{8}$; $\cot t = -\frac{8}{15}$ **21.** $-\frac{2\sqrt{3}}{3}$ **22.** $\sqrt{3}$ **23.** undefined **24.** undefined **25.** $\cos t = \frac{\sqrt{21}}{7}$; $\tan t = \frac{2\sqrt{3}}{3}$; $\csc t = \frac{\sqrt{7}}{2}$; $\sec t = \frac{\sqrt{21}}{3}$; $\cot t = \frac{\sqrt{3}}{2}$ **26.** 1 **27.** 1 **28.** −1 **29.** $\sin\theta = \frac{3}{5}$, $\cos\theta = \frac{4}{5}$, $\tan\theta = \frac{3}{4}$, $\csc\theta = \frac{5}{3}$, $\sec\theta = \frac{5}{4}$, $\cot\theta = \frac{4}{3}$ **30.** 5 **31.** $\frac{\sqrt{6} - 4}{4}$ **32.** cos 20° **33.** sin 0 **34.** 42 mm **35.** 23 cm **36.** 37 in. **37.** 772 ft **38.** 31 m **39.** 56° **40.** $\sin\theta = -\frac{5\sqrt{26}}{26}$; $\cos\theta = -\frac{\sqrt{26}}{26}$; $\tan\theta = 5$; $\csc\theta = -\frac{\sqrt{26}}{5}$; $\sec\theta = -\sqrt{26}$; $\cot\theta = \frac{1}{5}$ **41.** $\sin\theta = -1$; $\cos\theta = 0$; $\tan\theta$ is undefined; $\csc\theta = -1$; $\sec\theta$ is undefined; $\cot\theta = 0$ **42.** quadrant I **43.** quadrant III **44.** $\sin\theta = -\frac{\sqrt{21}}{5}$; $\tan\theta = -\frac{\sqrt{21}}{2}$; $\csc\theta = -\frac{5\sqrt{21}}{21}$; $\sec\theta = \frac{5}{2}$; $\cot\theta = -\frac{2\sqrt{21}}{21}$ **45.** $\sin\theta = \frac{\sqrt{10}}{10}$; $\cos\theta = -\frac{3\sqrt{10}}{10}$; $\csc\theta = \sqrt{10}$; $\sec\theta = -\frac{\sqrt{10}}{3}$; $\cot\theta = -3$ **46.** 85° **47.** $\frac{3\pi}{8}$ **48.** 50° **49.** $-\frac{\sqrt{3}}{2}$ **50.** $-\sqrt{3}$ **51.** $\sqrt{2}$ **52.** $\frac{\sqrt{3}}{2}$ **53.** $-\sqrt{3}$ **54.** $-\frac{2\sqrt{3}}{3}$ **55.** $-\frac{\sqrt{3}}{2}$ **56.** $\frac{\sqrt{2}}{2}$ **57.** 1

**58.** 3; $\frac{\pi}{2}$

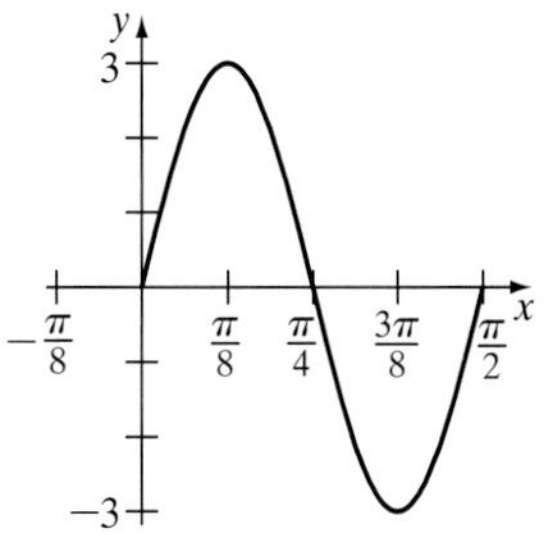


**59.** 2; $\pi$

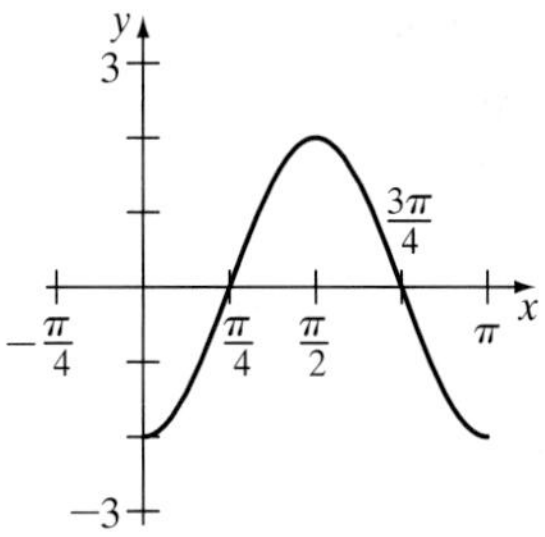


**60.** 2; $4\pi$

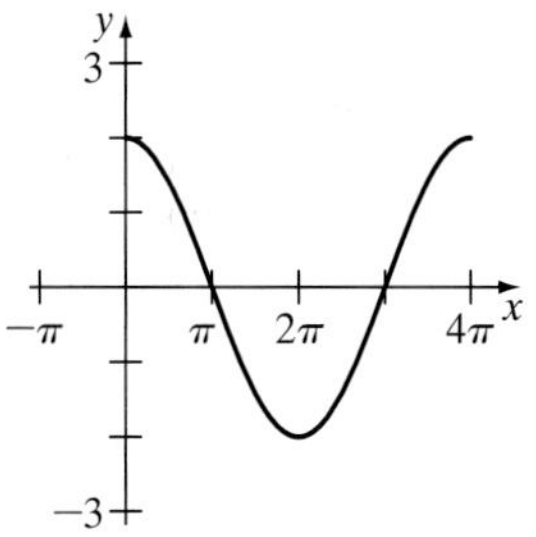


**61.** $\frac{1}{2}$; 6

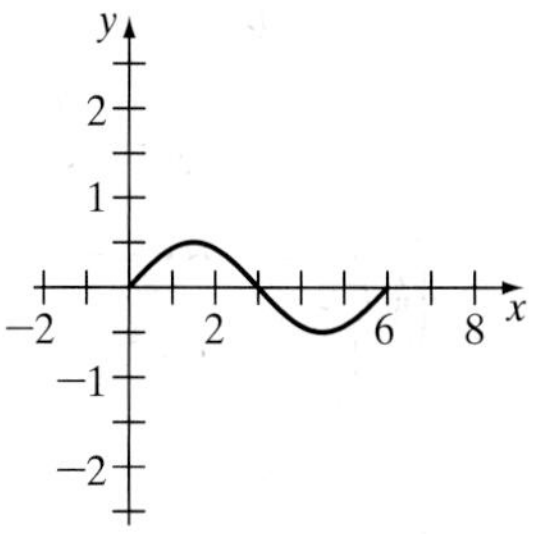


**62.** 1; 2

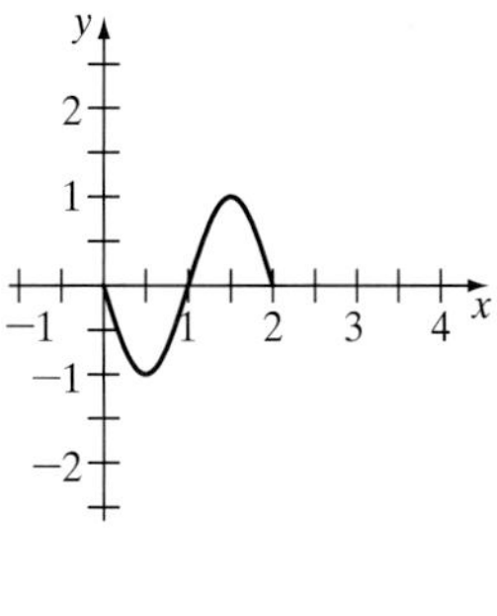


**63.** 3; $6\pi$

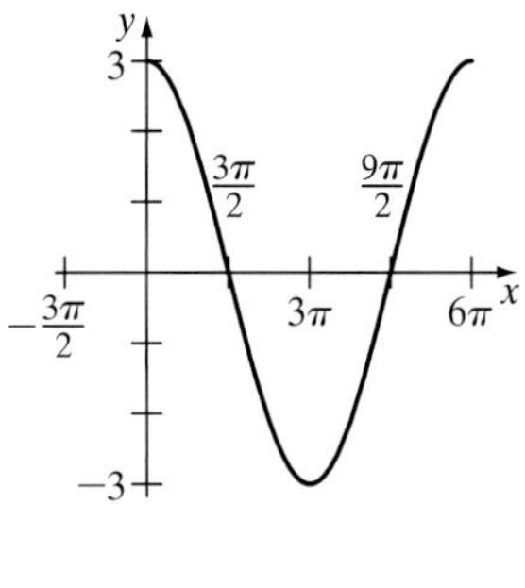


**64.** 2; $2\pi$; $\pi$

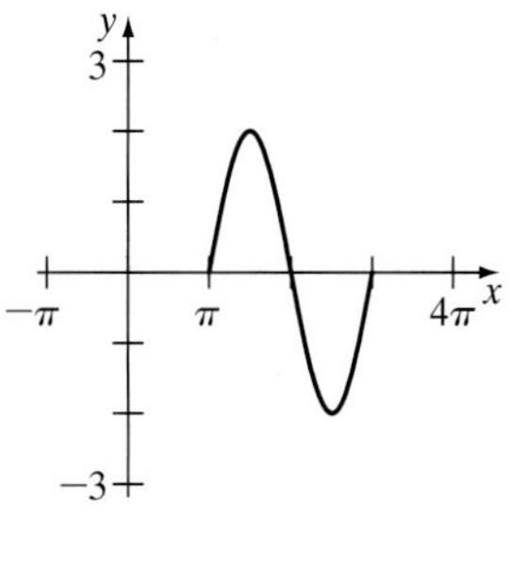


**65.** 3; $2\pi$; $-\pi$

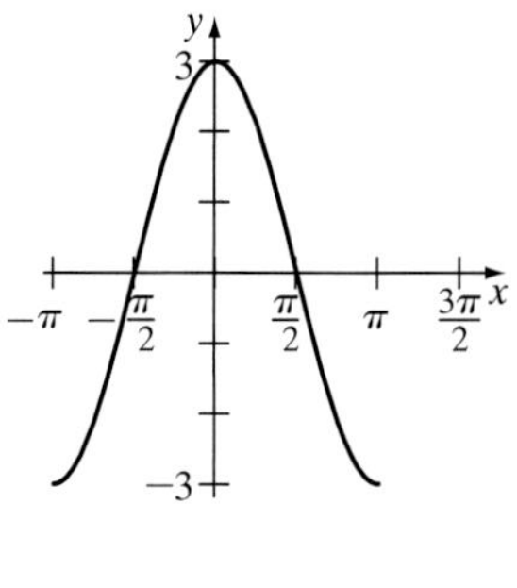

**66.** $\frac{3}{2}$; $\pi$; $-\frac{\pi}{8}$

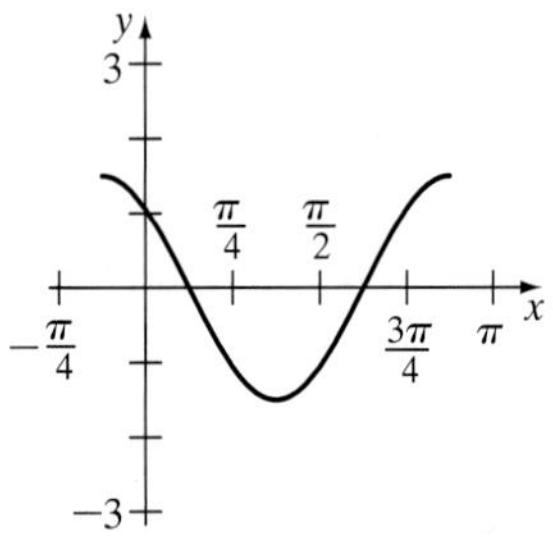

**67.** $\frac{5}{2}$; $\pi$; $-\frac{\pi}{4}$

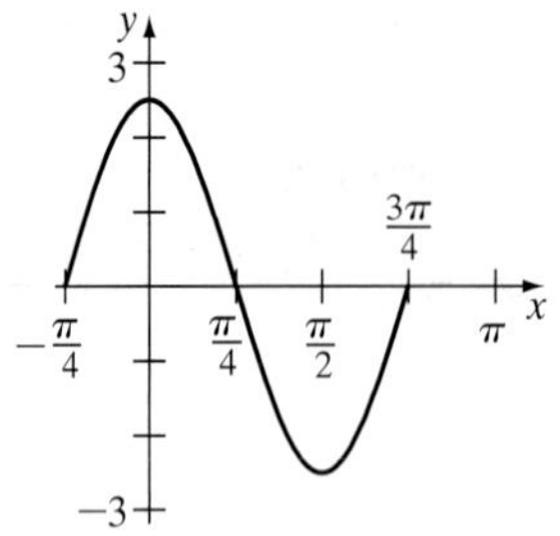

**68.** 3; 6; 9

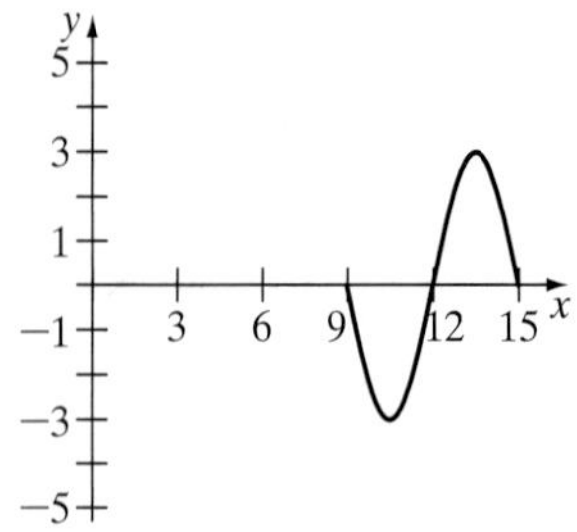

**69.**

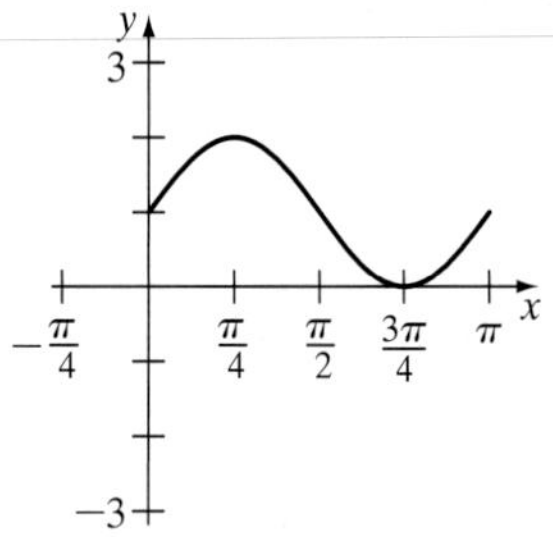

**70.**

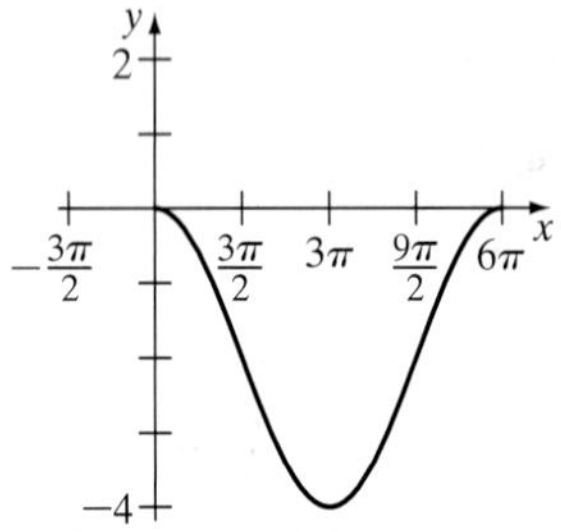

**71. a.** $\approx 98.52°$ **b.** 24 hr **c.** 5:00 P.M.; 98.9° **d.** 5:00 A.M.; 98.3° **e.**

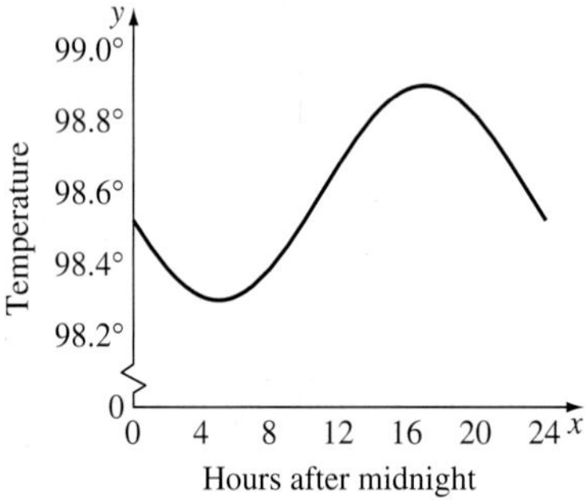


**72.**

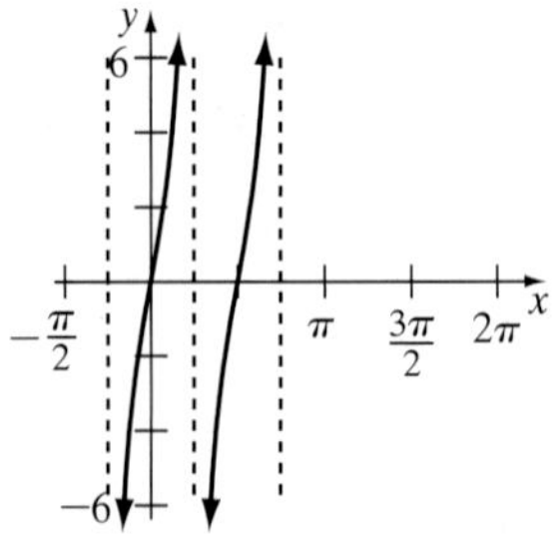

**73.**

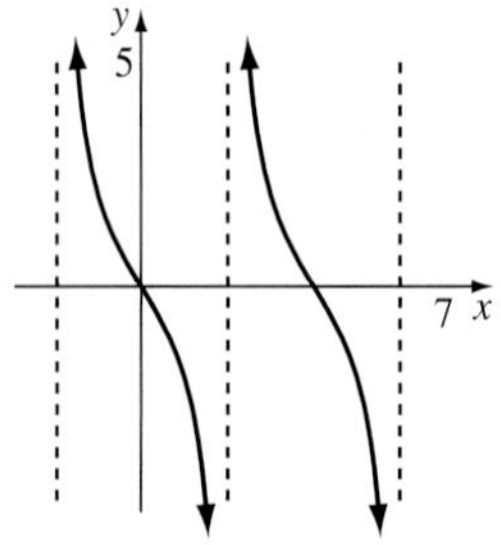

**74.**

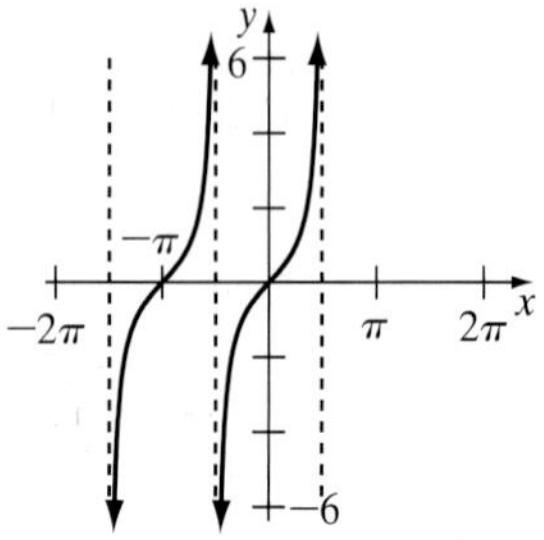

**75.**

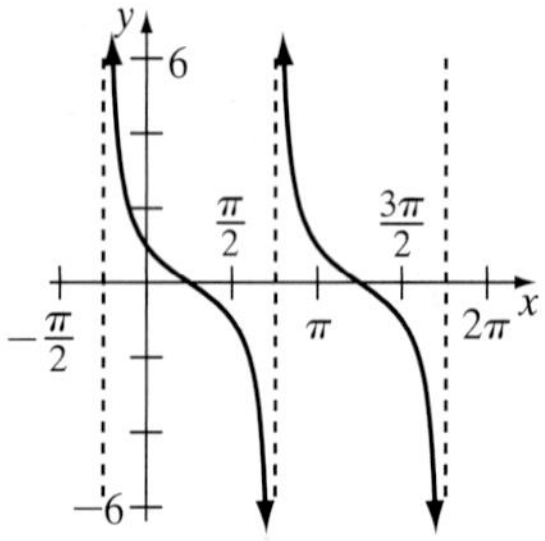

**76.**

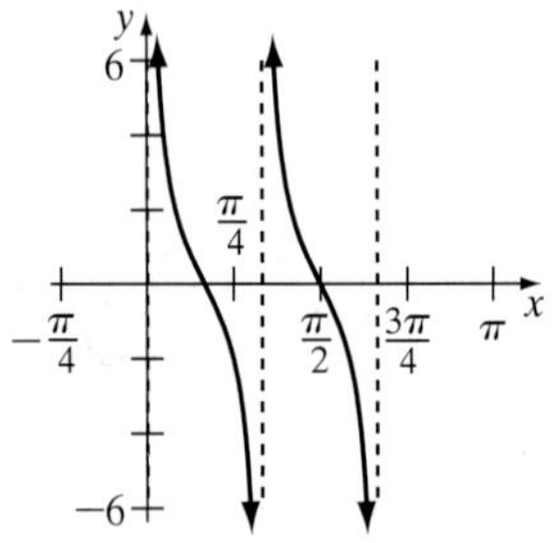

**77.**

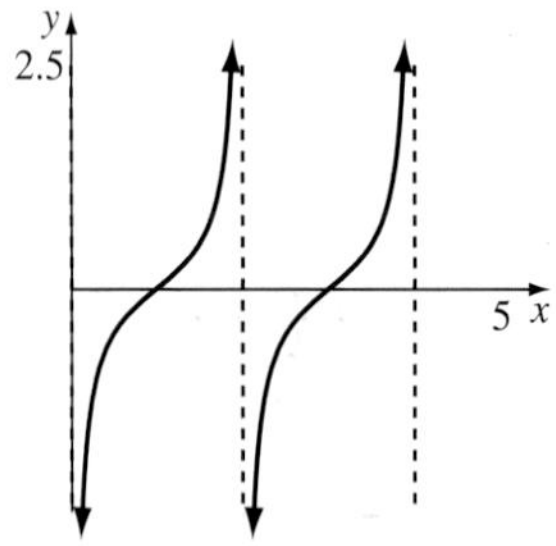

**78.**

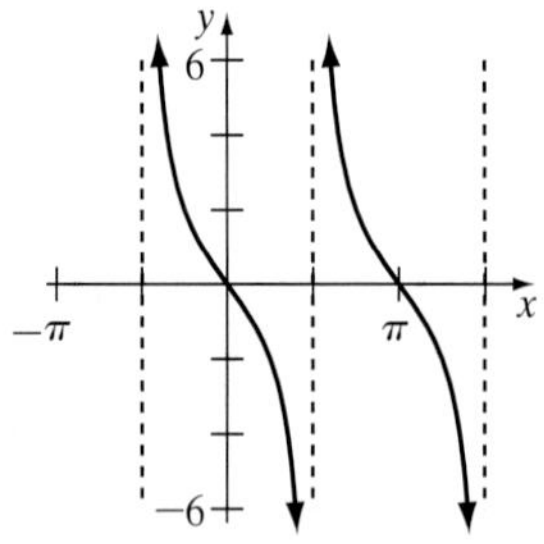

**79.**

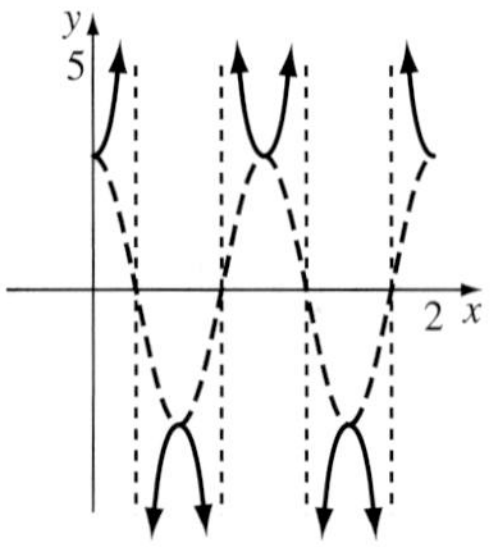

**80.**

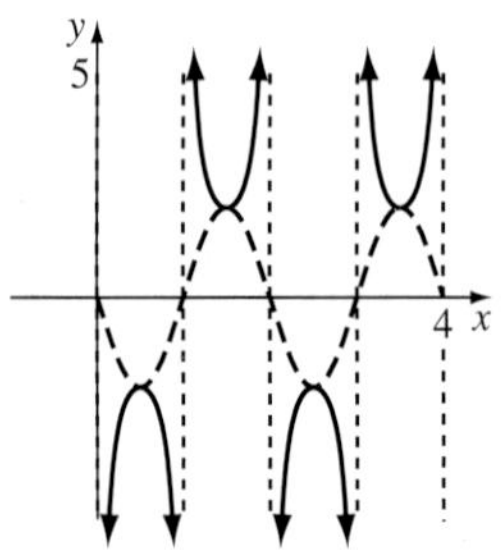

**81.**

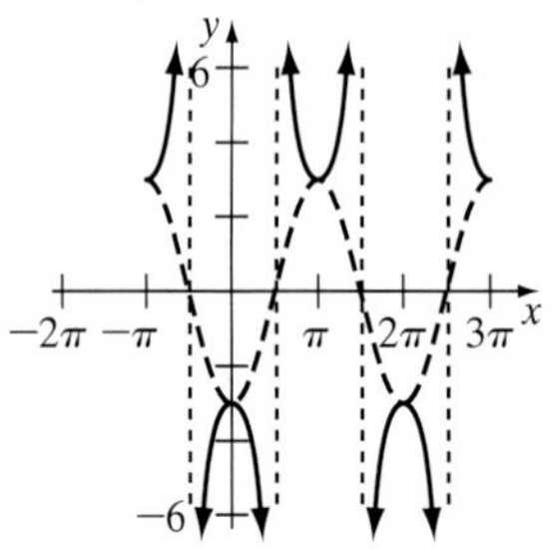

**82.**

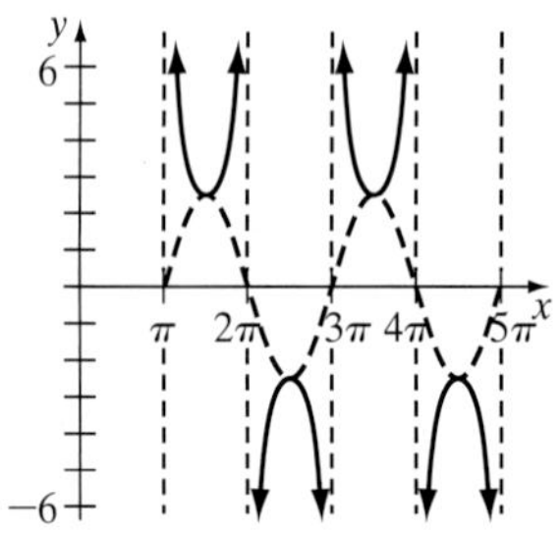

**83.** $\frac{\pi}{2}$ **84.** 0 **85.** $\frac{\pi}{4}$

**86.** $-\frac{\pi}{3}$ **87.** $\frac{2\pi}{3}$

**88.** $-\frac{\pi}{6}$ **89.** $\frac{\sqrt{2}}{2}$

**90.** 1 **91.** $-\frac{\sqrt{3}}{3}$

**92.** $-\frac{\sqrt{3}}{3}$ **93.** 2

**94.** $\frac{4}{5}$ **95.** $\frac{4}{5}$ **96.** $-\frac{3}{4}$ **97.** $-\frac{3}{4}$ **98.** $\frac{\pi}{3}$ **99.** $\frac{\pi}{3}$ **100.** $-\frac{\pi}{6}$ **101.** $\frac{2}{\sqrt{x^2+4}}$ **102.** $\frac{x}{\sqrt{x^2-1}}$
**103.** $B \approx 67.7°; a \approx 3.79; b \approx 9.25$ **104.** $A \approx 52.6°; a \approx 7.85; c \approx 9.88$ **105.** $A \approx 16.6°; B \approx 73.4°; b \approx 6.71$
**106.** $A \approx 21.3°; B \approx 68.7°; c \approx 3.86$ **107.** 38 ft **108.** 90 yd **109.** 21.7 ft **110.** N 35° E **111.** S 35° W
**112.** 24.6 mi **113. a.** 1282.2 mi **b.** S74°E **114. a.** 20 cm **b.** $\frac{1}{8}$ cycle per sec **c.** 8 sec
**115. a.** $\frac{1}{2}$ cm **b.** 0.64 cycle per sec **c.** 1.57 sec **116.** $d = -30 \cos \pi t$ **117.** $d = \frac{1}{4} \sin \frac{2\pi}{5} t$

## Chapter 5 Test

**1.** $\frac{3\pi}{4}$ radians **2.** $\frac{4\pi}{13}$ **3.** $\frac{25\pi}{3}$ ft $\approx 26.18$ ft
**4.** $\sin\theta = \frac{5\sqrt{29}}{29}$; $\cos\theta = -\frac{2\sqrt{29}}{29}$; $\tan\theta = -\frac{5}{2}$; $\csc\theta = \frac{\sqrt{29}}{5}$; $\sec\theta = -\frac{\sqrt{29}}{2}$; $\cot\theta = -\frac{2}{5}$ **5.** quadrant III
**6.** $\sin\theta = -\frac{2\sqrt{2}}{3}$; $\tan\theta = -2\sqrt{2}$; $\csc\theta = -\frac{3\sqrt{2}}{4}$; $\sec\theta = 3$; $\cot\theta = -\frac{\sqrt{2}}{4}$ **7.** $\frac{\sqrt{3}}{6}$ **8.** $-\sqrt{3}$ **9.** $-\frac{\sqrt{2}}{2}$

**10.**
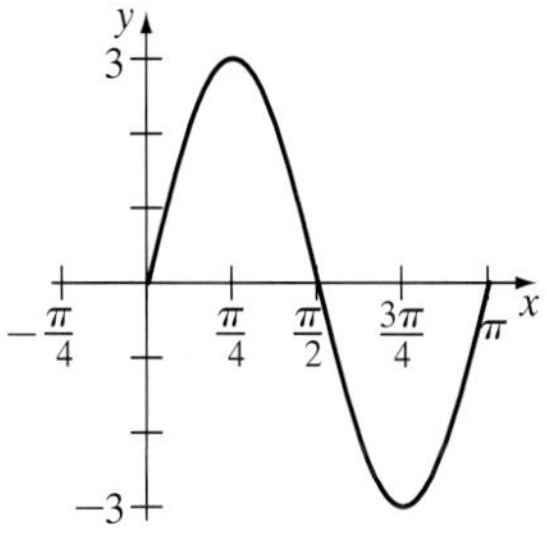


**11.**
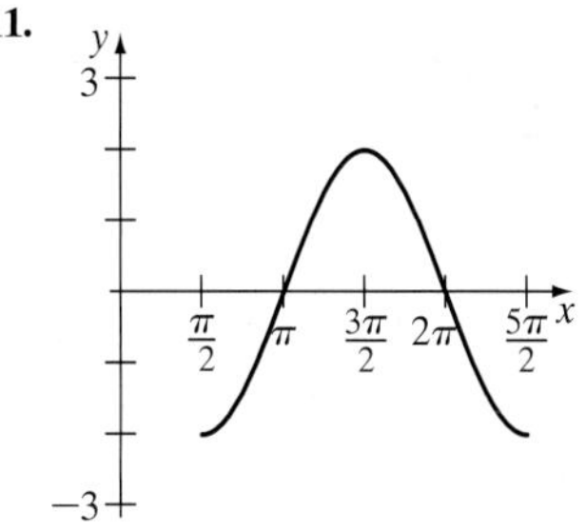


**12.**
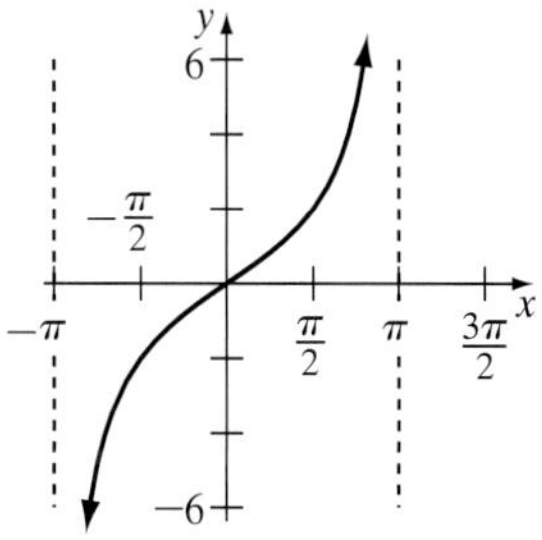


**13.**
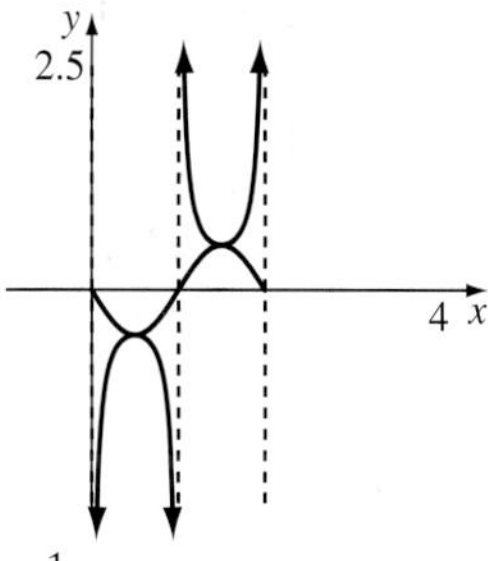


**14.** $-\sqrt{3}$ **15.** $B = 69°; a = 4.7; b = 12.1$ **16.** 23 yd **17.** 36.1° **18.** N 80° W **19. a.** 6 in. **b.** $\frac{1}{2}$ in. per sec **c.** 2 sec
**20.** Trigonometric functions are periodic.

## Cumulative Review Exercises (Chapters 1–5)

**1.** $\{-3, 6\}$ **2.** $\{-5, -2, 2\}$ **3.** $\{4\}$ **4.** $\{7\}$ **5.** $\{-1, 2, 3\}$
**6.** $-3 \le x \le 8$ **7.** $f^{-1}(x) = x^2 + 6$ **8.** $4x^2 - \frac{14}{5}x - \frac{17}{25} + \frac{284}{125x + 50}$ **9.** $\log 1000 = 3$ **10.** 280°
**11.** 3 positive real roots; 1 negative real root

**12.**
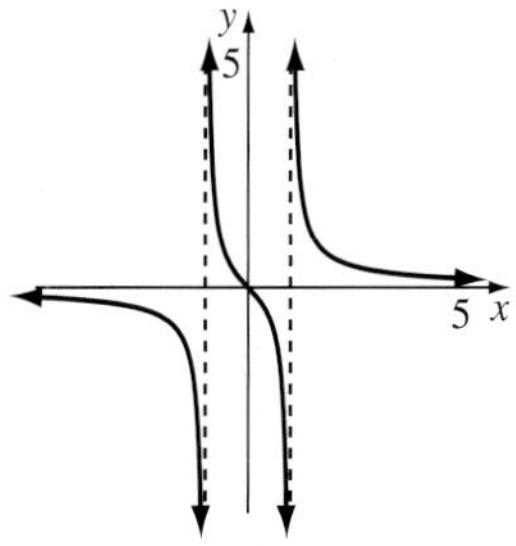


**13.**
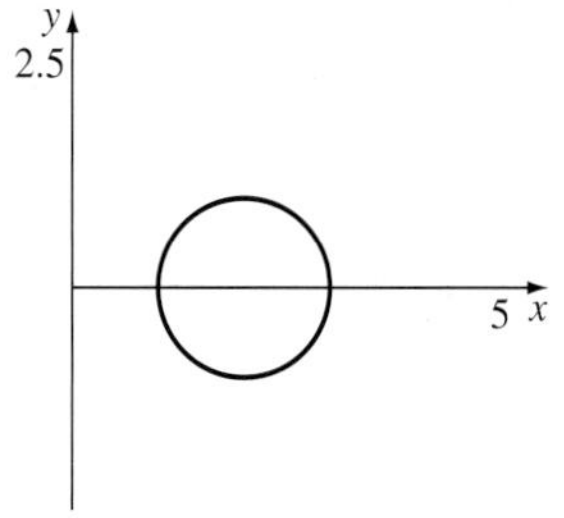


**14.**
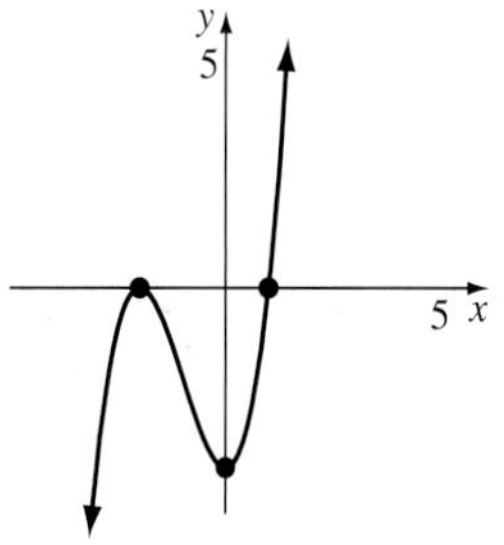


**15.**
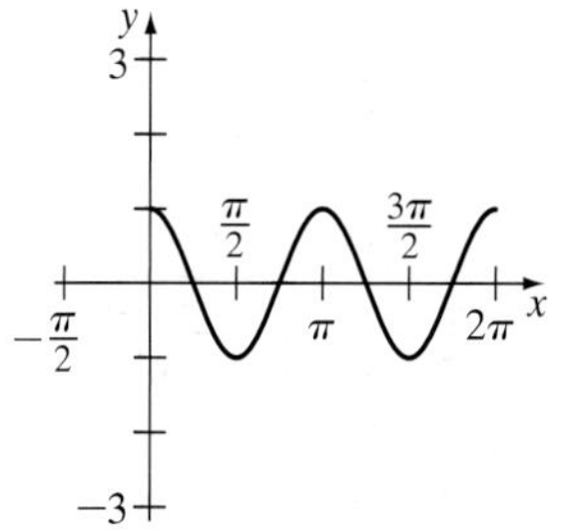


**16.**
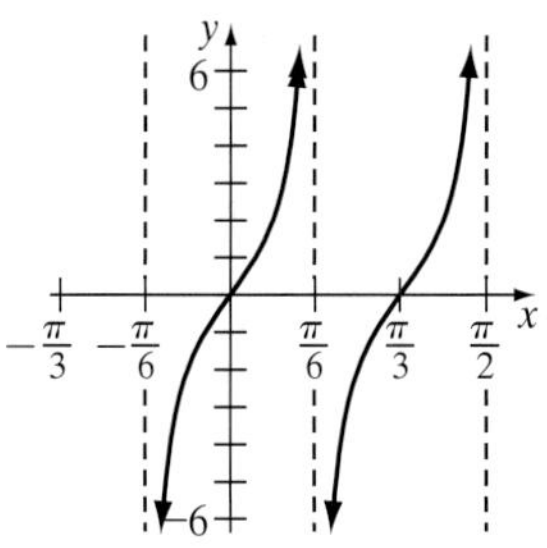


**17.** 48 performances **18. a.** $A = 10.2e^{0.3057t}$ **b.** 2001 **19.** 1540 Btu per hr **20.** 76°

# CHAPTER 6

## Section 6.1

### Check Point Exercises

**1.** $\csc x \tan x = \dfrac{1}{\sin x}\cdot\dfrac{\sin x}{\cos x} = \dfrac{1}{\cos x} = \sec x$ **2.** $\cos x \cot x + \sin x = \cos x \cdot \dfrac{\cos x}{\sin x} + \sin x = \dfrac{\cos^2 x}{\sin x} + \sin x \cdot \dfrac{\sin x}{\sin x} = \dfrac{\cos^2 x + \sin^2 x}{\sin x}$ $= \dfrac{1}{\sin x} = \csc x$ **3.** $\sin x - \sin x \cos^2 x = \sin x(1 - \cos^2 x) = \sin x \cdot \sin^2 x = \sin^3 x$ **4.** $\dfrac{\sin x}{1 + \cos x} + \dfrac{1 + \cos x}{\sin x}$ $= \dfrac{\sin x(\sin x)}{(1 + \cos x)(\sin x)} + \dfrac{(1 + \cos x)(1 + \cos x)}{(\sin x)(1 + \cos x)} = \dfrac{\sin^2 x + 1 + 2\cos x + \cos^2 x}{(1 + \cos x)(\sin x)} = \dfrac{\sin^2 x + \cos^2 x + 1 + 2\cos x}{(1 + \cos x)(\sin x)}$ $= \dfrac{1 + 1 + 2\cos x}{(1 + \cos x)(\sin x)} = \dfrac{2 + 2\cos x}{(1 + \cos x)(\sin x)} = \dfrac{2(1 + \cos x)}{(1 + \cos x)(\sin x)} = \dfrac{2}{\sin x} = 2\csc x$

**5.** $\dfrac{\cos x}{1 + \sin x} = \dfrac{\cos x(1 - \sin x)}{(1 + \sin x)(1 - \sin x)} = \dfrac{\cos x(1 - \sin x)}{1 - \sin^2 x} = \dfrac{\cos x(1 - \sin x)}{\cos^2 x} = \dfrac{1 - \sin x}{\cos x}$ **6.** $\dfrac{\sec x + \csc(-x)}{\sec x \csc x} = \dfrac{\sec x - \csc x}{\sec x \csc x}$ $= \dfrac{\frac{1}{\cos x} - \frac{1}{\sin x}}{\frac{1}{\cos x}\cdot\frac{1}{\sin x}} = \dfrac{\frac{\sin x}{\cos x \cdot \sin x} - \frac{\cos x}{\cos x \cdot \sin x}}{\frac{1}{\cos x \cdot \sin x}} = \dfrac{\frac{\sin x - \cos x}{\cos x \cdot \sin x}}{\frac{1}{\cos x \cdot \sin x}} = \dfrac{\sin x - \cos x}{\cos x \cdot \sin x}\cdot\dfrac{\cos x \cdot \sin x}{1} = \sin x - \cos x$

**7.** Left side: $\dfrac{1}{1 + \sin\theta} + \dfrac{1}{1 - \sin\theta} = \dfrac{1(1 - \sin\theta)}{(1 + \sin\theta)(1 - \sin\theta)} + \dfrac{1(1 + \sin\theta)}{(1 - \sin\theta)(1 + \sin\theta)} = \dfrac{1 - \sin\theta + 1 + \sin\theta}{(1 + \sin\theta)(1 - \sin\theta)} = \dfrac{2}{1 - \sin^2\theta}$;
Right side: $2 + 2\tan^2\theta = 2 + 2\left(\dfrac{\sin^2\theta}{\cos^2\theta}\right) = \dfrac{2\cos^2\theta}{\cos^2\theta} + \dfrac{2\sin^2\theta}{\cos^2\theta} = \dfrac{2\cos^2\theta + 2\sin^2\theta}{\cos^2\theta} = \dfrac{2(\cos^2\theta + \sin^2\theta)}{\cos^2\theta} = \dfrac{2}{\cos^2\theta} = \dfrac{2}{1 - \sin^2\theta}$

### Exercise Set 6.1

For Exercises 1–59, proofs may vary.

**65.**

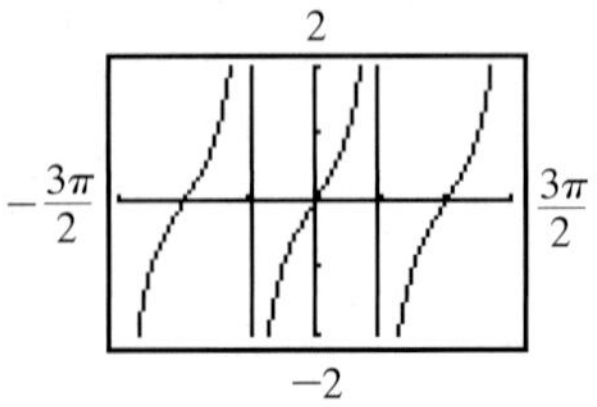


Proofs may vary.

**67.**

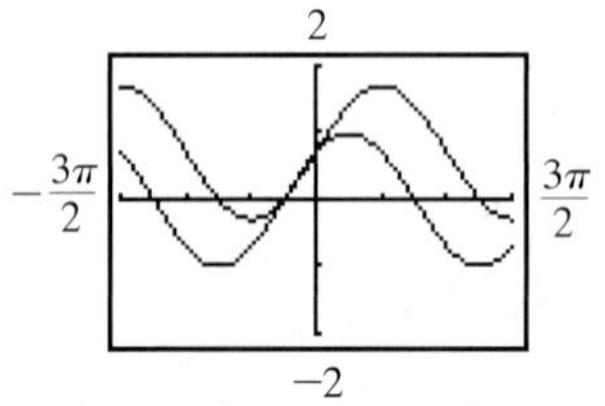


Values for $x$ may vary.

**69.**

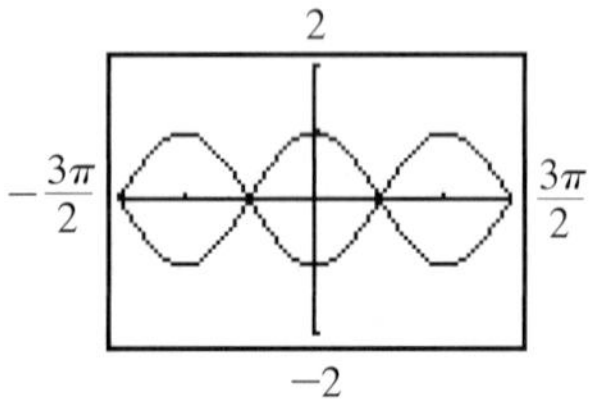


Values for $x$ may vary.

**71.**

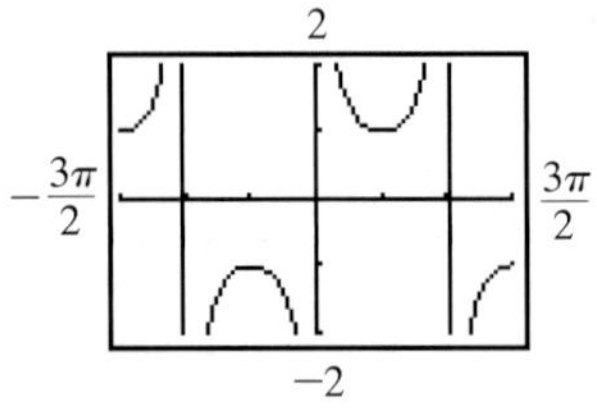


Proofs may vary.

**73.**

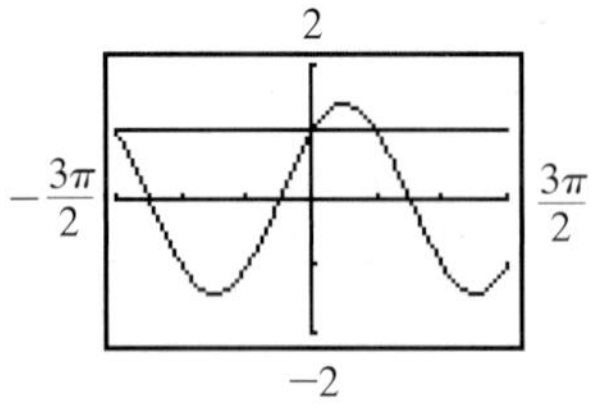


Values for $x$ may vary.

**75.** Proofs may vary.
**77.** Answers may vary.

## Section 6.2

### Check Point Exercises

**1.** $\dfrac{\sqrt{3}}{2}$ **2.** $\dfrac{\sqrt{3}}{2}$ **3.** $\dfrac{\cos(\alpha - \beta)}{\cos\alpha\cos\beta} = \dfrac{\cos\alpha\cos\beta + \sin\alpha\sin\beta}{\cos\alpha\cos\beta} = \dfrac{\cos\alpha}{\cos\alpha}\cdot\dfrac{\cos\beta}{\cos\beta} + \dfrac{\sin\alpha}{\cos\alpha}\cdot\dfrac{\sin\beta}{\cos\beta} = 1 + \tan\alpha\tan\beta$ **4.** $\dfrac{\sqrt{2} + \sqrt{6}}{4}$

**5. a.** $\cos\alpha = -\dfrac{3}{5}$ **b.** $\cos\beta = \dfrac{\sqrt{3}}{2}$ **c.** $\dfrac{-3\sqrt{3} - 4}{10}$ **d.** $\dfrac{4\sqrt{3} - 4}{10}$ **6. a.** $y = \sin x$

**b.** $\cos\left(x + \dfrac{3\pi}{2}\right) = \cos x \cos\dfrac{3\pi}{2} - \sin x \sin\dfrac{3\pi}{2} = \cos x \cdot 0 - \sin x \cdot (-1) = \sin x$

**7.** $\tan(x + \pi) = \dfrac{\tan x + \tan\pi}{1 - \tan x \tan\pi} = \dfrac{\tan x + 0}{1 - \tan x \cdot 0} = \dfrac{\tan x}{1} = \tan x$

## Exercise Set 6.2

**1.** $\frac{\sqrt{6}+\sqrt{2}}{4}$ **3.** $\frac{\sqrt{2}-\sqrt{6}}{4}$ **5. a.** $\alpha = 50°, \beta = 20°$ **b.** $\cos 30°$ **c.** $\frac{\sqrt{3}}{2}$ **7. a.** $\alpha = \frac{5\pi}{12}, \beta = \frac{\pi}{12}$ **b.** $\cos\left(\frac{\pi}{3}\right)$ **c.** $\frac{1}{2}$

For Exercises 9–11, proofs may vary. **13.** $\frac{\sqrt{6}-\sqrt{2}}{4}$ **15.** $\frac{\sqrt{6}+\sqrt{2}}{4}$ **17.** $\sqrt{3}+2$ **19.** $2-\sqrt{3}$ **21.** $-\frac{\sqrt{6}+\sqrt{2}}{4}$

**23.** $\frac{\sqrt{6}-\sqrt{2}}{4}$ **25.** $\sin 30°; \frac{1}{2}$ **27.** $\tan 45°; 1$ **29.** $\sin\frac{\pi}{6}; \frac{1}{2}$ **31.** $\tan\frac{\pi}{6}; \frac{\sqrt{3}}{3}$ For Exercises 33–55, proofs may vary.

**57. a.** $-\frac{63}{65}$ **b.** $-\frac{16}{65}$ **c.** $\frac{16}{63}$ **59. a.** $-\frac{4+6\sqrt{2}}{15}$ **b.** $\frac{3-8\sqrt{2}}{15}$ **c.** $\frac{54-25\sqrt{2}}{28}$ **61. a.** $-\frac{8\sqrt{3}+15}{34}$ **b.** $\frac{15\sqrt{3}-8}{34}$

**c.** $\frac{480-289\sqrt{3}}{33}$ **63. a.** $y = \sin x$ **b.** $\sin(\pi - x) = \sin\pi\cos x - \cos\pi\sin x = 0\cdot\cos x - (-1)\sin x = \sin x$ **65. a.** $y = 2\cos x$

**b.** $\sin\left(x+\frac{\pi}{2}\right) + \sin\left(\frac{\pi}{2}-x\right) = \sin x\cos\frac{\pi}{2} + \cos x\sin\frac{\pi}{2} + \sin\frac{\pi}{2}\cos x - \cos\frac{\pi}{2}\sin x = \sin x\cdot 0 + \cos x\cdot 1 + 1\cdot\cos x - 0\cdot\sin x$
$= \cos x + \cos x = 2\cos x$ **67.** Proofs may vary.; amplitude is $\sqrt{13}$; period is $2\pi$

**77.**

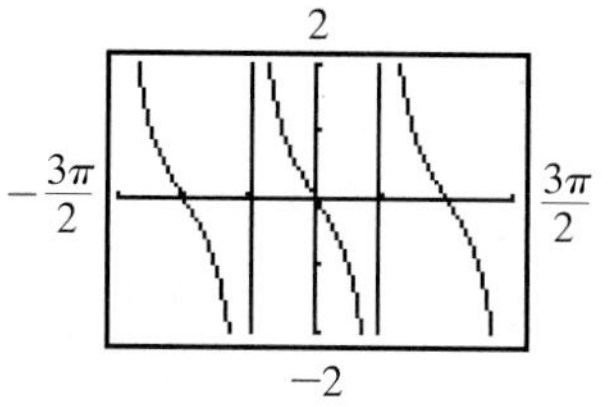


Proofs may vary.

**79.**

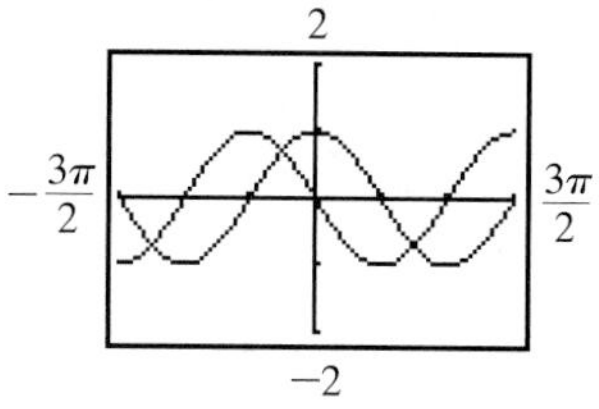


Values for $x$ may vary.

**81.**

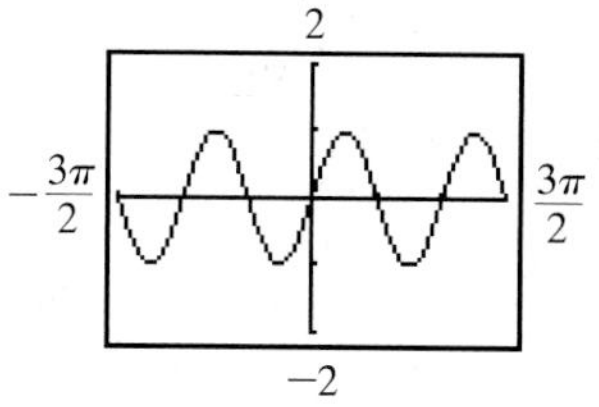


$\sin 1.2x\cos 0.8x + \cos 1.2x\sin 0.8x = \sin(1.2x + 0.8x) = \sin 2x$

**83.** Proofs may vary. **85.** $y\sqrt{1-x^2} + x\sqrt{1-y^2}$

## Section 6.3

### Check Point Exercises

**1. a.** $-\frac{24}{25}$ **b.** $-\frac{7}{25}$ **c.** $\frac{24}{7}$ **2.** $\frac{\sqrt{3}}{2}$ **3.** $\sin 3\theta = \sin(2\theta+\theta) = \sin 2\theta\cos\theta + \cos 2\theta\sin\theta = 2\sin\theta\cos\theta\cos\theta + (2\cos^2\theta - 1)\sin\theta = 2\sin\theta\cos^2\theta + 2\sin\theta\cos^2\theta - \sin\theta = 4\sin\theta\cos^2\theta - \sin\theta = 4\sin\theta(1-\sin^2\theta) - \sin\theta = 4\sin\theta - 4\sin^3\theta - \sin\theta = 3\sin\theta - 4\sin^3\theta$ **4.** $\sin^4 x = (\sin^2 x)^2 = \left(\frac{1-\cos 2x}{2}\right)^2 = \frac{1 - 2\cos 2x + \cos^2 2x}{4} = \frac{1}{4} - \frac{1}{2}\cos 2x + \frac{1}{4}\cos^2 2x$
$= \frac{1}{4} - \frac{1}{2}\cos 2x + \frac{1}{4}\left(\frac{1+\cos 2(2x)}{2}\right) = \frac{1}{4} - \frac{1}{2}\cos 2x + \frac{1}{8} + \frac{1}{8}\cos 4x = \frac{3}{8} - \frac{1}{2}\cos 2x + \frac{1}{8}\cos 4x$ **5.** $-\frac{\sqrt{2+\sqrt{3}}}{2}$

**6.** $\frac{\sin 2\theta}{1+\cos 2\theta} = \frac{2\sin\theta\cos\theta}{1+(1-2\sin^2\theta)} = \frac{2\sin\theta\cos\theta}{2-2\sin^2\theta} = \frac{2\sin\theta\cos\theta}{2(1-\sin^2\theta)} = \frac{2\sin\theta\cos\theta}{2\cos^2\theta} = \frac{\sin\theta}{\cos\theta} = \tan\theta$

**7.** $\frac{\sec\alpha}{\sec\alpha\csc\alpha + \csc\alpha} = \frac{\frac{1}{\cos\alpha}}{\frac{1}{\cos\alpha}\cdot\frac{1}{\sin\alpha} + \frac{1}{\sin\alpha}} = \frac{\frac{1}{\cos\alpha}}{\frac{1}{\cos\alpha\sin\alpha} + \frac{\cos\alpha}{\cos\alpha\sin\alpha}} = \frac{\frac{1}{\cos\alpha}}{\frac{1+\cos\alpha}{\cos\alpha\sin\alpha}} = \frac{1}{\cos\alpha}\cdot\frac{\cos\alpha\sin\alpha}{1+\cos\alpha} = \frac{\sin\alpha}{1+\cos\alpha} = \tan\frac{\alpha}{2}$

## Exercise Set 6.3

**1.** $\frac{24}{25}$ **3.** $\frac{24}{7}$ **5.** $\frac{527}{625}$ **7. a.** $-\frac{240}{289}$ **b.** $-\frac{161}{289}$ **c.** $\frac{240}{161}$ **9. a.** $-\frac{336}{625}$ **b.** $\frac{527}{625}$ **c.** $-\frac{336}{527}$ **11. a.** $\frac{4}{5}$ **b.** $\frac{3}{5}$ **c.** $\frac{4}{3}$

**13. a.** $\frac{720}{1681}$ **b.** $\frac{1519}{1681}$ **c.** $\frac{720}{1519}$ **15.** $\frac{1}{2}$ **17.** $-\frac{\sqrt{3}}{2}$ **19.** $\frac{\sqrt{2}}{2}$ **21.** $\frac{\sqrt{3}}{3}$ For Exercises 23–33, proofs may vary.

**35.** $3 - 3\cos 2x$ **37.** $\frac{1}{8} - \frac{1}{8}\cos 4x$ **39.** $\frac{\sqrt{2-\sqrt{3}}}{2}$ **41.** $-\frac{\sqrt{2+\sqrt{2}}}{2}$ **43.** $2+\sqrt{3}$ **45.** $-\sqrt{2}+1$ **47.** $\frac{\sqrt{10}}{10}$

**49.** $\frac{1}{3}$ **51.** $\frac{7\sqrt{2}}{10}$ **53.** $\frac{3}{5}$ **55. a.** $\frac{2\sqrt{5}}{5}$ **b.** $-\frac{\sqrt{5}}{5}$ **c.** $-2$ **57. a.** $\frac{3\sqrt{13}}{13}$ **b.** $\frac{2\sqrt{13}}{13}$ **c.** $\frac{3}{2}$ **59.** $\frac{\sec\theta - 1}{2\sec\theta}$

For Exercises 61–67, proofs may vary. **69. a.** $\frac{v_0^2}{32}\cdot\sin 2\theta$ **b.** $\theta = \frac{\pi}{4}$ **71.** $\sqrt{2-\sqrt{2}}\cdot(2+\sqrt{2}) \approx 2.6$

**85.**

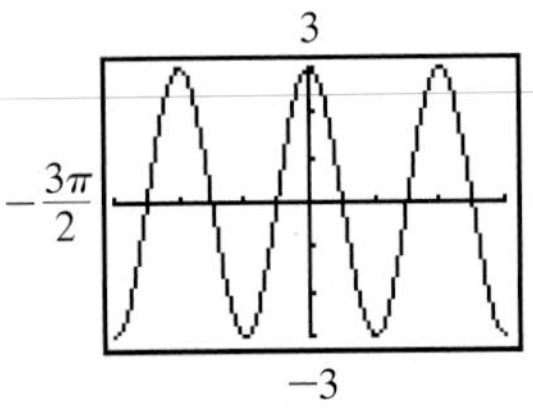


Proofs may vary.

**87.**

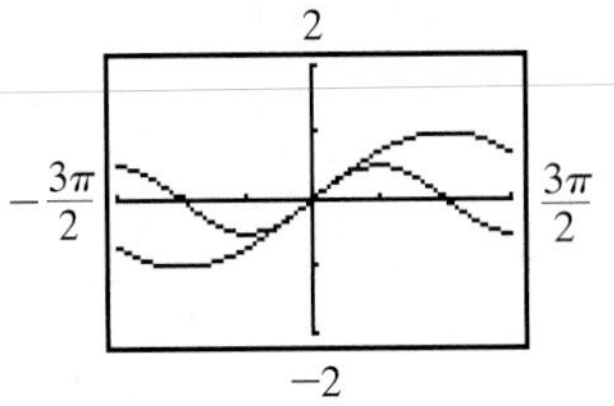


Values for $x$ may vary.

**89.**

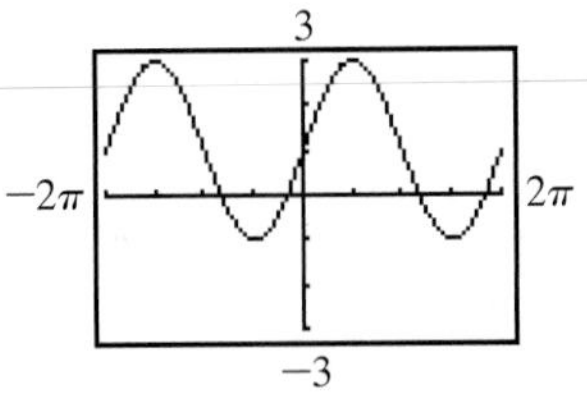


**a.** $y = 1 + 2 \sin x$
**b.** Proofs may vary.

**91.**

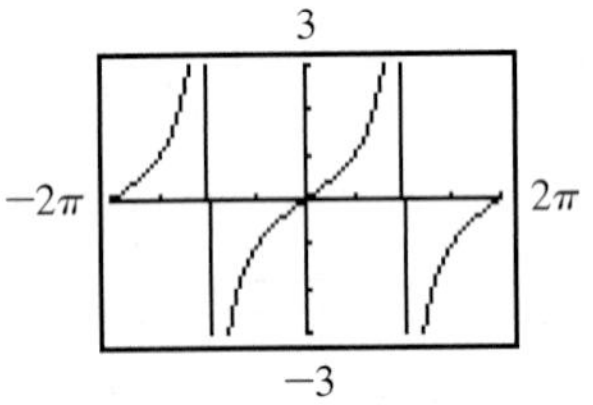


**a.** $y = \tan \frac{x}{2}$
**b.** Proofs may vary.

**93.** $\frac{5}{16} - \frac{7}{16} \cos 2x + \frac{3}{16} \cos 4x - \frac{1}{16} \cos 2x \cos 4x$

## Section 6.4

### Check Point Exercises

**1. a.** $\frac{1}{2}[\cos 3x - \cos 7x]$ **b.** $\frac{1}{2}[\cos 6x + \cos 8x]$ **2. a.** $2 \sin 5x \cos 2x$ **b.** $2 \cos\left(\frac{5x}{2}\right) \cos\left(\frac{x}{2}\right)$

**3.** $\frac{\cos 3x - \cos x}{\sin 3x + \sin x} = \frac{-2 \sin\left(\frac{3x + x}{2}\right) \sin\left(\frac{3x - x}{2}\right)}{2 \sin\left(\frac{3x + x}{2}\right) \cos\left(\frac{3x - x}{2}\right)} = \frac{-2 \sin\left(\frac{4x}{2}\right) \sin\left(\frac{2x}{2}\right)}{2 \sin\left(\frac{4x}{2}\right) \cos\left(\frac{2x}{2}\right)} = \frac{-2 \sin 2x \sin x}{2 \sin 2x \cos x} = -\frac{\sin x}{\cos x} = -\tan x$

### Exercise Set 6.4

**1.** $\frac{1}{2}[\cos 4x - \cos 8x]$ **3.** $\frac{1}{2}[\cos 4x + \cos 10x]$ **5.** $\frac{1}{2}[\sin 3x - \sin x]$ **7.** $\frac{1}{2}[\sin 2x - \sin x]$ **9.** $2 \sin 4x \cos 2x$
**11.** $2 \sin 2x \cos 5x$ **13.** $2 \cos 3x \cos x$ **15.** $2 \sin \frac{3x}{2} \cos \frac{x}{2}$ **17.** $2 \cos x \cos \frac{x}{2}$ **19.** $\frac{\sqrt{6}}{2}$ **21.** $-\frac{\sqrt{2}}{2}$
For Exercises 23–29, proofs may vary. **31. a.** $y = \cos x$ **b.** Proofs may vary. **33. a.** $y = \tan 2x$ **b.** Proofs may vary.
**35. a.** $y = \sin 1704\pi t + \sin 2418\pi t$ **b.** $2 \sin 2061\pi t \cdot \cos 357\pi t$

**43.**

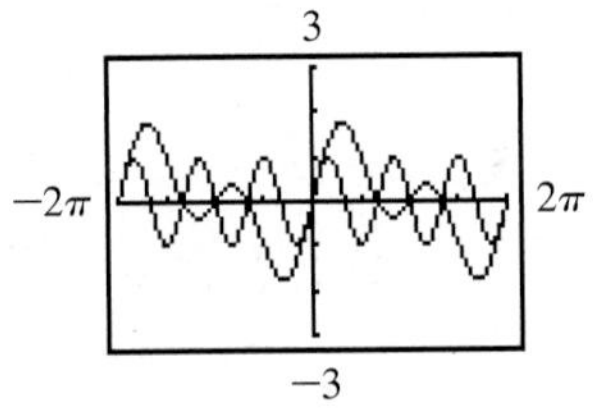


Values for $x$ may vary.

**45.**

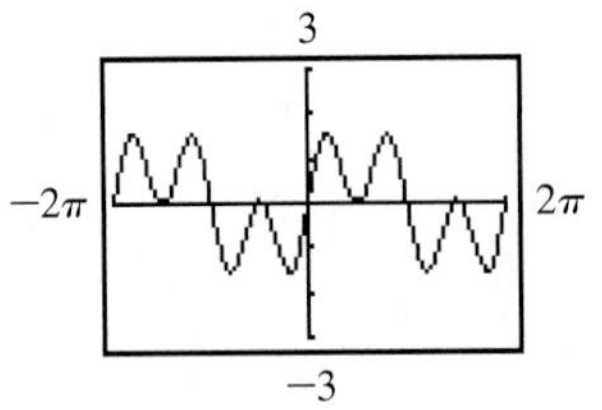


Proofs may vary.

**47.**

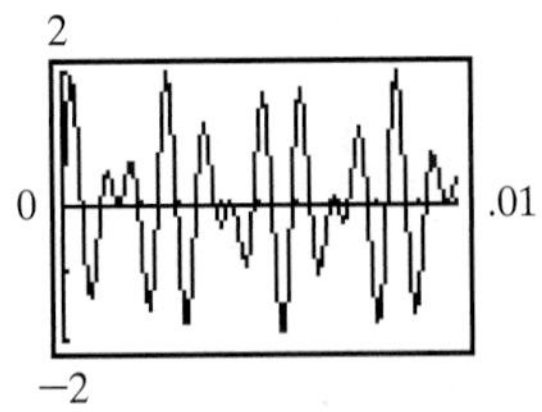


**49. a.**

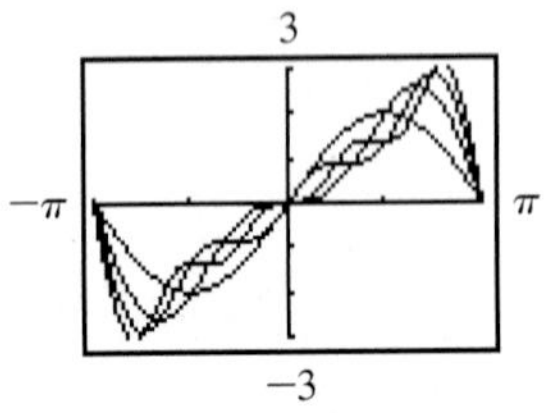


**b.**

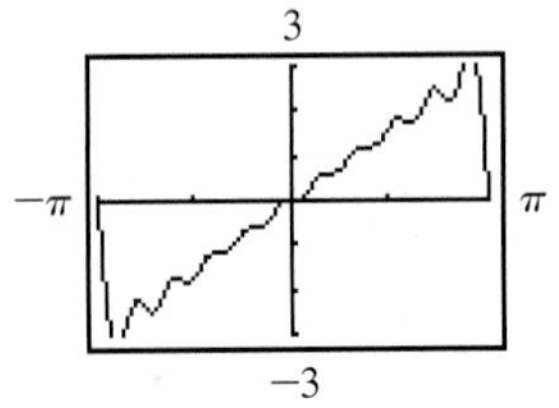


**c.** $\pi = 4 - \frac{4}{3} + \frac{4}{5} - \frac{4}{7} + \cdots$

For Exercises 51–55, proofs may vary.

## Section 6.5

### Check Point Exercises

**1.** $x = \frac{\pi}{3} + 2n\pi$ or $x = \frac{2\pi}{3} + 2n\pi$, where $n$ is any integer. **2.** $\frac{\pi}{6}, \frac{2\pi}{3}, \frac{7\pi}{6}, \frac{5\pi}{3}$ **3.** $\frac{\pi}{2}, \frac{5\pi}{2}$ **4.** $\frac{\pi}{6}, \frac{\pi}{2}, \frac{5\pi}{6}$ **5.** $0, \frac{\pi}{4}, \pi, \frac{5\pi}{4}$
**6.** $\frac{\pi}{2}, \frac{7\pi}{6}, \frac{11\pi}{6}$ **7.** $\frac{3\pi}{4}, \frac{7\pi}{4}$ **8.** $\frac{\pi}{2}, \pi$

### Exercise Set 6.5

**1.** Solution **3.** Not a solution **5.** Solution **7.** Solution **9.** Not a solution **11.** $x = \frac{\pi}{3} + 2n\pi$ or $x = \frac{2\pi}{3} + 2n\pi$, where $n$ is any integer. **13.** $x = \frac{\pi}{4} + n\pi$, where $n$ is any integer. **15.** $x = \frac{2\pi}{3} + 2n\pi$ or $x = \frac{4\pi}{3} + 2n\pi$, where $n$ is any integer. **17.** $x = n\pi$, where $n$ is any integer. **19.** $x = \frac{5\pi}{6} + 2n\pi$ or $x = \frac{7\pi}{6} + 2n\pi$, where $n$ is any integer.
**21.** $\theta = \frac{\pi}{6} + 2n\pi$ or $\theta = \frac{5\pi}{6} + 2n\pi$, where $n$ is any integer. **23.** $\theta = \frac{3\pi}{2} + 2n\pi$, where $n$ is any integer. **25.** $\frac{\pi}{6}, \frac{\pi}{3}, \frac{7\pi}{6}, \frac{4\pi}{3}$
**27.** $\frac{5\pi}{24}, \frac{7\pi}{24}, \frac{17\pi}{24}, \frac{19\pi}{24}, \frac{29\pi}{24}, \frac{31\pi}{24}, \frac{41\pi}{24}, \frac{43\pi}{24}$ **29.** $\frac{\pi}{18}, \frac{7\pi}{18}, \frac{13\pi}{18}, \frac{19\pi}{18}, \frac{25\pi}{18}, \frac{31\pi}{18}$ **31.** $\frac{2\pi}{3}$ **33.** no solution **35.** $\frac{4\pi}{9}, \frac{8\pi}{9}, \frac{16\pi}{9}$
**37.** $0, \frac{\pi}{3}, \pi, \frac{4\pi}{3}$ **39.** $\frac{\pi}{2}, \frac{7\pi}{6}, \frac{11\pi}{6}$ **41.** $\frac{2\pi}{3}, \pi, \frac{4\pi}{3}$ **43.** $\frac{3\pi}{2}$ **45.** $\frac{\pi}{2}, \frac{3\pi}{2}$ **47.** $\frac{\pi}{4}, \pi, \frac{5\pi}{4}$ **49.** $\frac{5\pi}{6}, \frac{7\pi}{6}, \frac{11\pi}{6}$
**51.** $\frac{\pi}{4}, \frac{\pi}{2}, \frac{5\pi}{4}, \frac{3\pi}{2}$ **53.** $0, \frac{2\pi}{3}, \pi, \frac{4\pi}{3}$ **55.** $0, \pi$ **57.** $\frac{\pi}{2}, \frac{7\pi}{6}, \frac{11\pi}{6}$ **59.** $\pi$ **61.** $\frac{\pi}{6}, \frac{5\pi}{6}$ **63.** $\frac{\pi}{6}, \frac{\pi}{2}, \frac{5\pi}{6}, \frac{3\pi}{2}$ **65.** $0, \frac{2\pi}{3}, \frac{4\pi}{3}$
**67.** $\frac{2\pi}{3}, \frac{4\pi}{3}$ **69.** $\frac{\pi}{8}, \frac{3\pi}{8}, \frac{9\pi}{8}, \frac{11\pi}{8}$ **71.** $0, \frac{\pi}{2}$ **73.** $\frac{\pi}{4}, \frac{3\pi}{4}$ **75.** $\frac{\pi}{12}, \frac{\pi}{4}, \frac{3\pi}{4}, \frac{11\pi}{12}, \frac{17\pi}{12}, \frac{19\pi}{12}$ **77.** $x = 0$ **79.** 0.4 sec and 2.1 sec
**81.** 49 days **83.** $t = 2 + 6n$ or $t = 4 + 6n$ where $n$ is any integer. **85.** 21° or 69°

**97.**

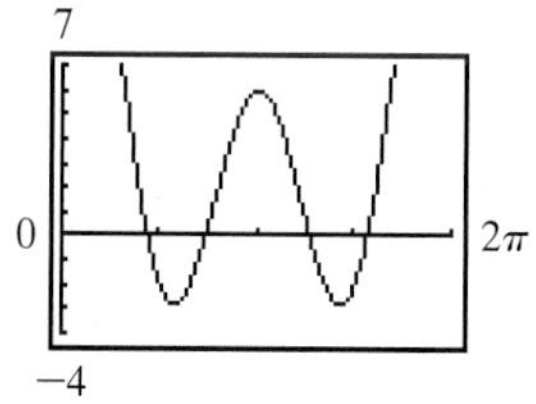


$x = 1.37, x = 2.30, x = 3.98$, or $x = 4.91$

**99.**

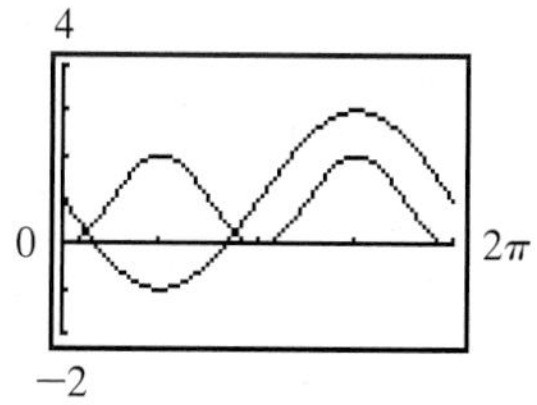


$x = 0.37$ or $x = 2.77$

**101.**

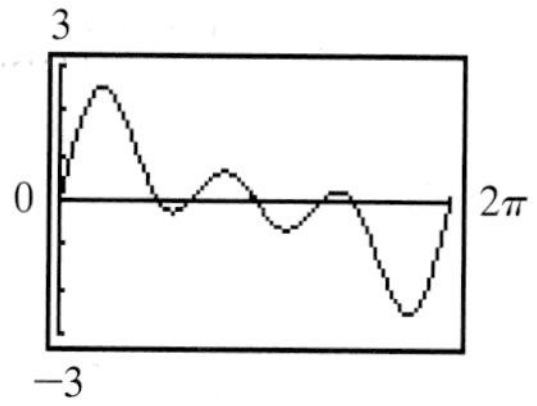


$x = 0, x = 1.57, x = 2.09, x = 3.14, x = 4.19$, or $x = 4.71$

**103.** no solution **105.** $\frac{\pi}{3}, \frac{5\pi}{3}$

### Chapter 6 Review Exercises

For Exercises 1–12, proofs may vary. **13.** $\frac{\sqrt{6} - \sqrt{2}}{4}$ **14.** $\frac{\sqrt{2} - \sqrt{6}}{4}$ **15.** $2 - \sqrt{3}$ **16.** $\sqrt{3} + 2$ **17.** $\frac{1}{2}$ **18.** $\frac{1}{2}$

For Exercises 19–30, proofs may vary.

**31. a.** $y = \cos x$ **b.** $\sin\left(x - \frac{3\pi}{2}\right) = \sin x \cos \frac{3\pi}{2} - \cos x \sin \frac{3\pi}{2} = \sin x \cdot 0 - \cos x \cdot -1 = \cos x$

**32. a.** $y = -\sin x$ **b.** $\cos\left(x + \frac{\pi}{2}\right) = \cos x \cos \frac{\pi}{2} - \sin x \sin \frac{\pi}{2} = \cos x \cdot 0 - \sin x \cdot 1 = -\sin x$

**33. a.** $y = \tan x$ **b.** $y = \frac{\tan x - 1}{1 - \cot x} = \frac{\frac{\sin x}{\cos x} - 1}{1 - \frac{\cos x}{\sin x}} = \frac{\frac{\sin x - \cos x}{\cos x}}{\frac{\sin x - \cos x}{\sin x}} = \frac{\sin x - \cos x}{\cos x} \cdot \frac{\sin x}{\sin x - \cos x} = \frac{\sin x}{\cos x} = \tan x$

**34. a.** $\frac{33}{65}$ **b.** $\frac{16}{65}$ **c.** $-\frac{33}{56}$ **d.** $\frac{24}{25}$ **e.** $\frac{2\sqrt{13}}{13}$ **35. a.** $-\frac{63}{65}$ **b.** $-\frac{56}{65}$ **c.** $\frac{63}{16}$ **d.** $\frac{24}{25}$ **e.** $\frac{5\sqrt{26}}{26}$

**36. a.** 1 **b.** $-\frac{3}{5}$ **c.** undefined **d.** $-\frac{3}{5}$ **e.** $\frac{\sqrt{10 + 3\sqrt{10}}}{2\sqrt{5}}$ **37. a.** 1 **b.** $\frac{4\sqrt{2}}{9}$ **c.** undefined **d.** $\frac{4\sqrt{2}}{9}$ **e.** $-\frac{\sqrt{3}}{3}$

**38.** $\frac{\sqrt{3}}{2}$ **39.** $-\frac{\sqrt{3}}{3}$ **40.** $\frac{\sqrt{2-\sqrt{2}}}{2}$ **41.** $2-\sqrt{3}$ **42.** $\frac{1}{2}[\cos 2x - \cos 10x]$ **43.** $\frac{1}{2}[\sin 10x + \sin 4x]$

**44.** $-2\sin x\cos 3x$ **45.** $\frac{\sqrt{6}}{2}$ **46.** Proofs may vary. **47.** Proofs may vary. **48. a.** $y = \cot x$ **b.** Proofs may vary.

**49.** $x = \frac{2\pi}{3} + 2n\pi$ or $x = \frac{4\pi}{3} + 2n\pi$, where $n$ is any integer. **50.** $x = \frac{\pi}{4} + 2n\pi$ or $x = \frac{3\pi}{4} + 2n\pi$, where $n$ is any integer.

**51.** $x = \frac{7\pi}{6} + 2n\pi$ or $x = \frac{11\pi}{6} + 2n\pi$, where $n$ is any integer. **52.** $x = \frac{\pi}{6} + n\pi$, where $n$ is any integer. **53.** $\frac{\pi}{2}, \frac{3\pi}{2}$

**54.** $\frac{\pi}{6}, \frac{5\pi}{6}, \frac{9\pi}{6}$ **55.** $\frac{3\pi}{2}$ **56.** $0, \frac{\pi}{3}, \pi, \frac{5\pi}{3}$ **57.** $\pi$ **58.** $\frac{\pi}{2}$, 3.87, 5.55 **59.** $\frac{\pi}{6}, \frac{5\pi}{6}; \frac{7\pi}{6}, \frac{11\pi}{6}$ **60.** 1.2, 5.08 **61.** $0, \frac{\pi}{6}, \pi, \frac{11\pi}{6}$

**62.** $0, \pi$ **63.** $t = \frac{2}{3} + 4n$ or $t = \frac{10}{3} + 4n$, where $n$ is any integer. **64.** 12° or 78°

## Chapter 6 Test

**1.** $-\frac{63}{65}$ **2.** $\frac{56}{33}$ **3.** $-\frac{24}{25}$ **4.** $\frac{3\sqrt{13}}{13}$ **5.** $\frac{\sqrt{6}+\sqrt{2}}{4}$ **6.** $\cos x \csc x = \cos x \cdot \frac{1}{\sin x} = \frac{\cos x}{\sin x} = \cot x$

**7.** $\frac{\sec x}{\cot x + \tan x} = \frac{\frac{1}{\cos x}}{\frac{\cos x}{\sin x} + \frac{\sin x}{\cos x}} = \frac{\frac{1}{\cos x}}{\frac{\cos^2 x + \sin^2 x}{\sin x \cos x}} = \frac{1}{\cos x} \cdot \frac{\sin x \cos x}{1} = \sin x$

**8.** $1 - \frac{\cos^2 x}{1+\sin x} = 1 - \frac{(1-\sin^2 x)}{1+\sin x} = 1 - \frac{(1+\sin x)(1-\sin x)}{1+\sin x} = 1 - (1-\sin x) = \sin x$

**9.** $\cos\left(\theta + \frac{\pi}{2}\right) = \cos\theta\cos\frac{\pi}{2} - \sin\theta\sin\frac{\pi}{2} = \cos\theta \cdot 0 - \sin\theta \cdot 1 = -\sin\theta$

**10.** $\frac{\sin(\alpha-\beta)}{\sin\alpha\cos\beta} = \frac{\sin\alpha\cos\beta - \cos\alpha\sin\beta}{\sin\alpha\cos\beta} = \frac{\sin\alpha\cos\beta}{\sin\alpha\cos\beta} - \frac{\cos\alpha\sin\beta}{\sin\alpha\cos\beta} = 1 - \cot\alpha\tan\beta$

**11.** $\sin t\cos t(\tan t + \cot t) = \sin t\cos t\left(\frac{\sin t}{\cos t} + \frac{\cos t}{\sin t}\right) = \sin^2 t + \cos^2 t = 1$ **12.** $\frac{7\pi}{18}, \frac{11\pi}{18}, \frac{19\pi}{18}, \frac{23\pi}{18}, \frac{31\pi}{18}$, and $\frac{35\pi}{18}$

**13.** $\frac{\pi}{2}, \frac{7\pi}{6}, \frac{3\pi}{2}, \frac{11\pi}{6}$ **14.** $0, \frac{\pi}{3}, \frac{5\pi}{3}$ **15.** $0, \frac{2\pi}{3}, \frac{4\pi}{3}$

## Cumulative Review Exercises (Chapters 1–6)

**1.** $-3, 1+2i$, and $1-2i$ **2.** $x = \frac{\log 125}{\log 11} + 1$ or $x \approx 3.01$ **3.** $(-\infty, -4) \cup (2, \infty)$ **4.** $\frac{\pi}{3}, \frac{5\pi}{3}$

**5.**

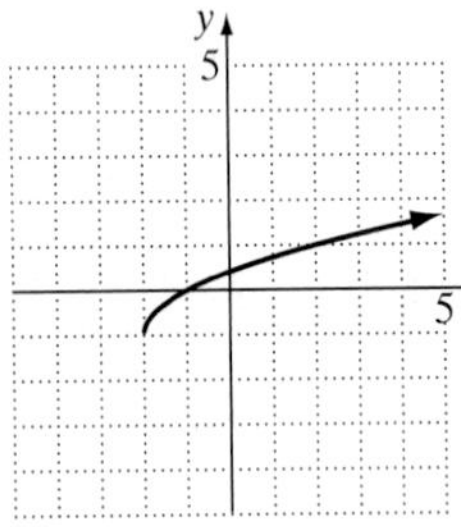

**6.**

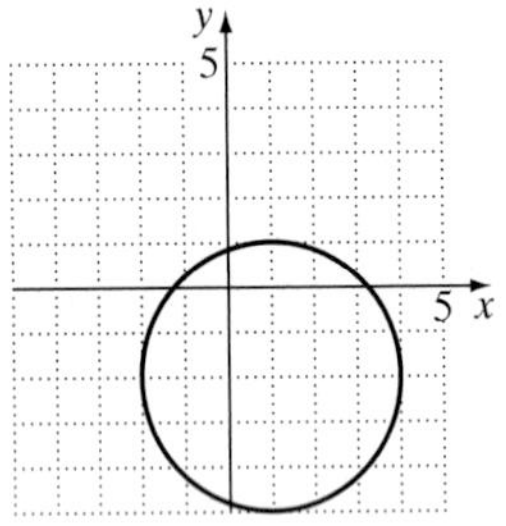

**7.**

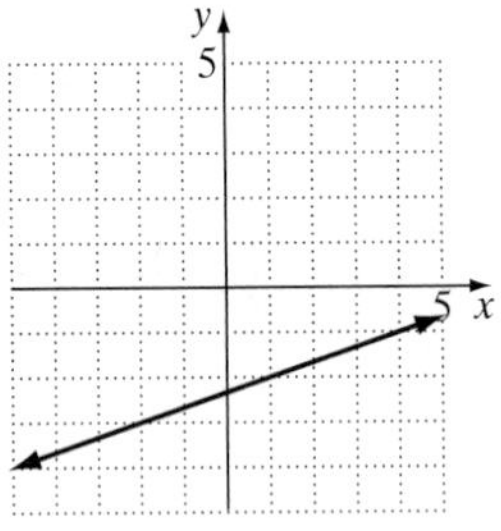

**8.**

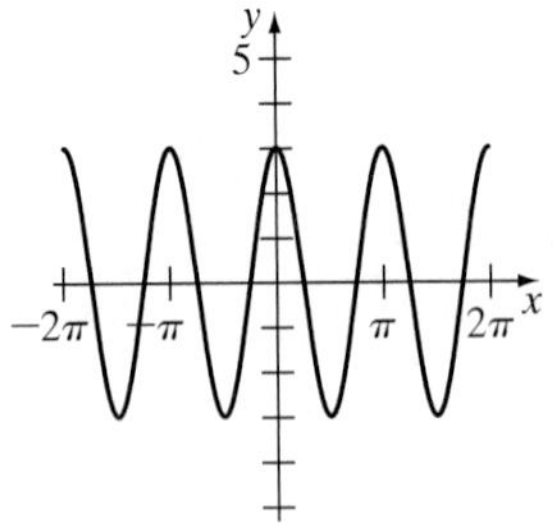

**9.**

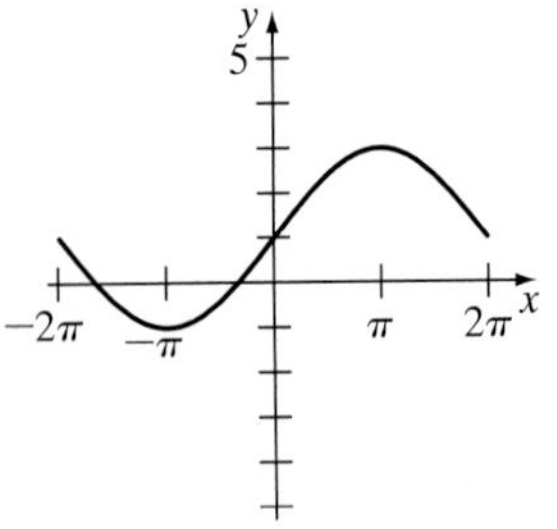

**10.**

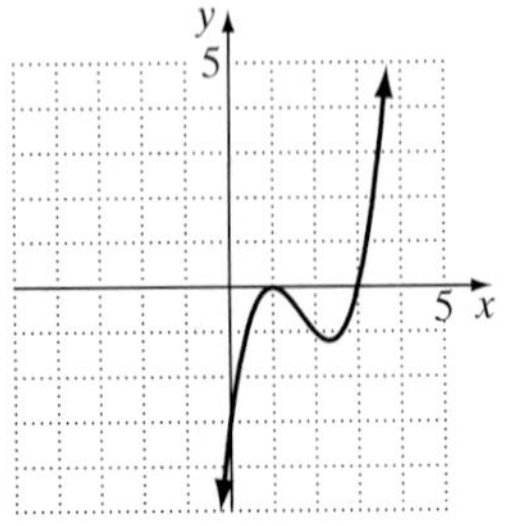

**11.** $2a + h + 3$ **12.** $-\frac{\sqrt{2}}{2}$

**13.** Proofs may vary. **14.** $\frac{16}{9}\pi$ radians

**15.** $t \approx 19.1$ yr **16.** $f^{-1}(x) = \frac{3x+1}{x-2}$

**17.** $B = 67°, b = 28.27, c = 30.71$

**18.** 106 mg **19.** $h \approx 15.9$ ft **20.** Answers may vary.

# CHAPTER 7

## Section 7.1

### Check Point Exercises

**1.** $B = 34°, a \approx 13$ cm, $b \approx 8$ cm **2.** $B = 117.5°, a \approx 9, c \approx 5$ **3.** one triangle; $C \approx 24°, B \approx 33°, b \approx 31$ **4.** no triangle **5.** two triangles; $B_1 \approx 50°, C_1 \approx 95°, c_1 = 21; B_2 \approx 130°, C_2 \approx 15°, c_2 \approx 5$ **6.** approximately 34 sq m **7.** approximately 11 mi

### Exercise Set 7.1

**1.** $B = 42°, a \approx 8.1, b \approx 8.1$ **3.** $A = 44°, b \approx 18.6, c \approx 22.8$ **5.** $C = 95°, b \approx 81.0, c \approx 134.1$ **7.** $B = 40°, b \approx 20.9, c \approx 31.8$ **9.** $C = 111°, b \approx 7.3, c \approx 16.1$ **11.** $A = 80°, a \approx 39.5, c \approx 10.4$ **13.** $B = 30°, a \approx 316.0, b \approx 174.3$ **15.** $C = 50°, a \approx 7.1, b \approx 7.1$ **17.** one triangle; $B \approx 29°, C \approx 111°, c \approx 29.0$ **19.** one triangle; $C \approx 52°, B \approx 65°, b \approx 10.2$ **21.** one triangle; $C \approx 55°, B \approx 13°, b \approx 10.2$ **23.** no triangle **25.** two triangles; $B_1 \approx 77°, C_1 \approx 43°, c_1 \approx 12.6; B_2 \approx 103°, C_2 \approx 17°, c_2 \approx 5.4$ **27.** two triangles; $B_1 \approx 54°, C_1 \approx 89°, c_1 \approx 19.9; B_2 \approx 126°, C_2 \approx 17°, c_2 \approx 5.8$ **29.** two triangles; $C_1 \approx 68°, B_1 \approx 54°, b_1 \approx 21.0; C_2 \approx 112°, B_2 \approx 10°, b_2 \approx 4.5$ **31.** no triangle **33.** 297 sq ft **35.** 5 sq yd **37.** 10 sq m **39.** Station A is about 6 miles from the fire, station B is about 9 miles from the fire. **41.** about 3672 yards from one end of the beach and 3576 yards from the other. **43.** about 184 ft **45.** about 56 ft **47.** about 30 ft **49. a.** $a \approx 494$ ft **b.** 343 ft **51.** either 9.9 mi or 2.4 mi **63.** No **65.** 41 ft

## Section 7.2

### Check Point Exercises

**1.** $a = 13, B \approx 28°, C \approx 32°$ **2.** $B \approx 97.9°, A \approx 52.4°, C \approx 29.7°$ **3.** approximately 917 mi apart **4.** approximately 47 sq m

### Exercise Set 7.2

**1.** $a \approx 6.0, B \approx 29°, C \approx 105°$ **3.** $c \approx 7.6, A \approx 52°, B \approx 32°$ **5.** $A \approx 44°, B \approx 68°, C \approx 68°$ **7.** $A \approx 117°, B \approx 36°, C \approx 27°$ **9.** $c \approx 4.7, A \approx 46°, B \approx 92°$ **11.** $a \approx 6.3, C \approx 28°, B \approx 50°$ **13.** $b \approx 4.7, C \approx 54°, A \approx 76°$ **15.** $b \approx 5.4, C \approx 22°, A \approx 68°$ **17.** $C \approx 112°, A \approx 28°, B \approx 40°$ **19.** $B \approx 100°, A \approx 19°, C \approx 61°$ **21.** $A = 60°, B = 60°, C = 60°$ **23.** no triangle **25.** 4 sq ft **27.** 22 sq m **29.** 31 sq yd **31.** about 61.7 mi apart **33.** about 193 yd **35.** N12°E **37. a.** about 19.3 mi **b.** S58°E **39.** The guy wire anchored downhill is about 417.4 feet. The one anchored uphill is about 398.2 feet. **41.** about 63.7 ft **43.** $123,454 **53.** 153.4°

## Section 7.3

### Check Point Exercises

**1. a.**

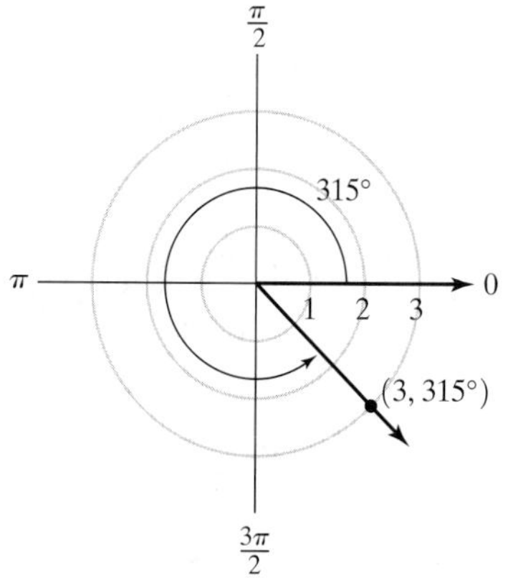


**b.**

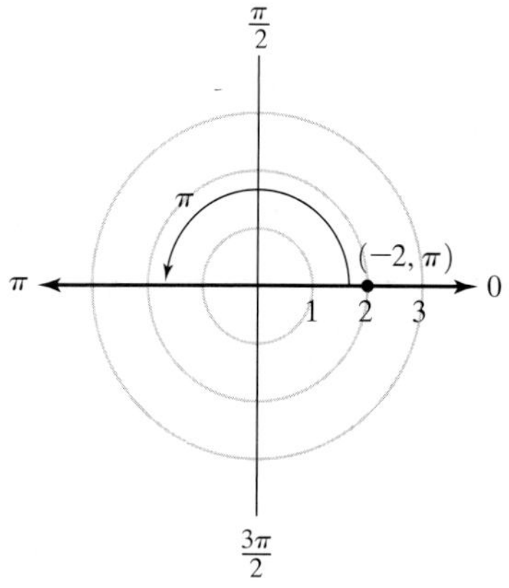


**c.**

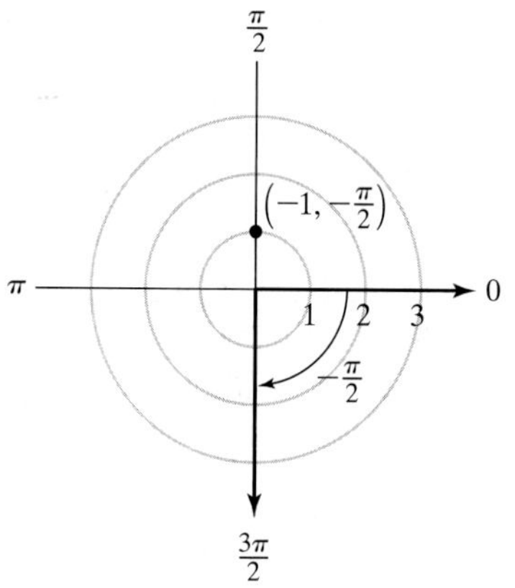


**2. a.** $\left(5, \frac{9\pi}{4}\right)$ **b.** $\left(-5, \frac{5\pi}{4}\right)$ **c.** $\left(5, -\frac{7\pi}{4}\right)$ **3. a.** $(-3, 0)$ **b.** $(-5\sqrt{3}, -5)$ **4.** $\left(2, \frac{5\pi}{3}\right)$ **5.** $\left(4, \frac{3\pi}{2}\right)$ **6.** $r = \dfrac{6}{3\cos\theta - \sin\theta}$ **7. a.** $x^2 + y^2 = 16$ **b.** $y = -x$ **c.** $x = 1$

## Exercise Set 7.3

**1.** C **3.** A **5.** B **7.** C **9.** A

**11.**

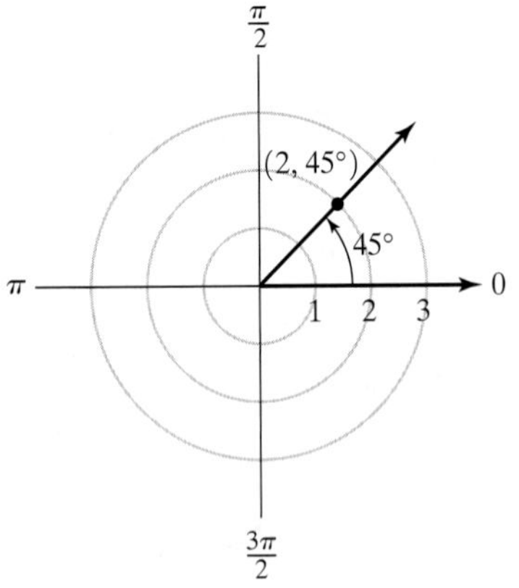


**13.**

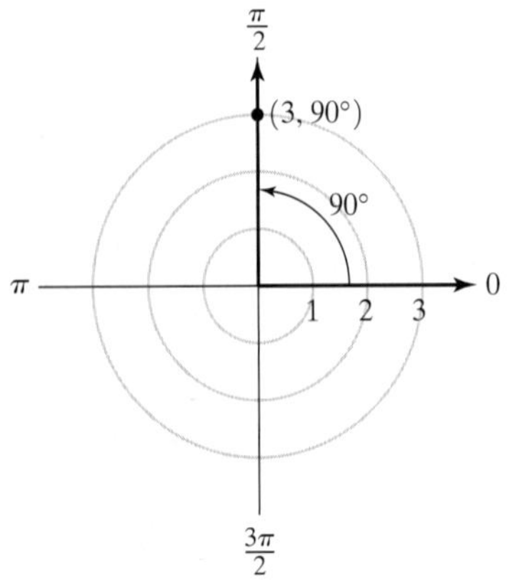


**15.**

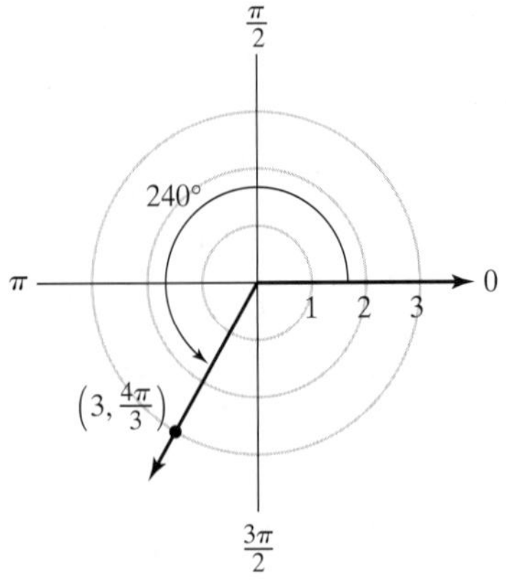


**17.**

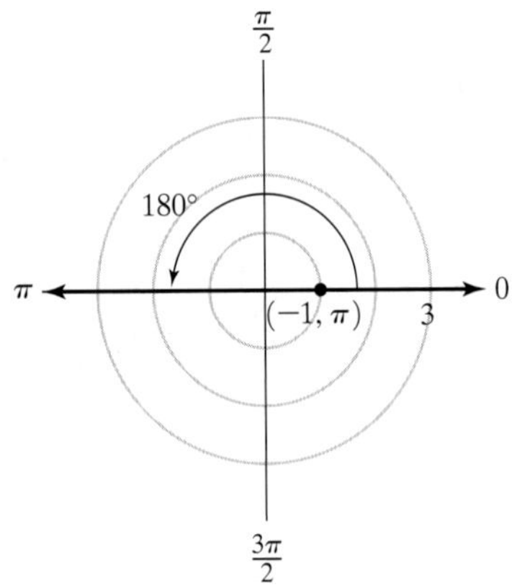


**19.**

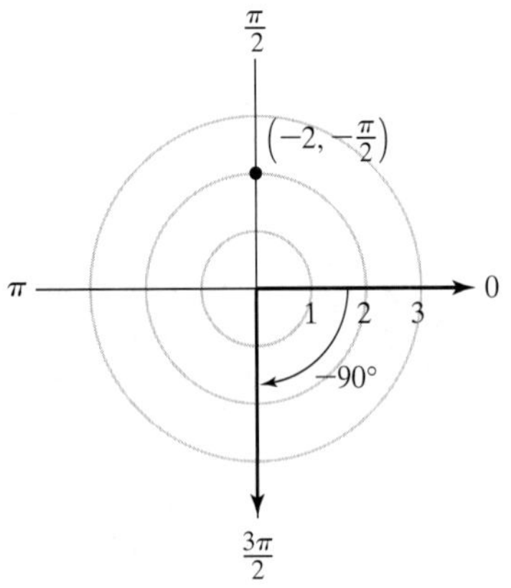


**21.**

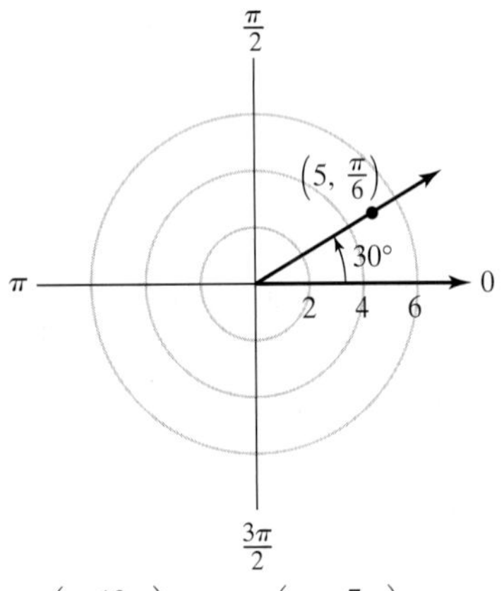


**a.** $\left(5, \frac{13\pi}{6}\right)$ **b.** $\left(-5, \frac{7\pi}{6}\right)$
**c.** $\left(5, -\frac{11\pi}{6}\right)$

**23.**

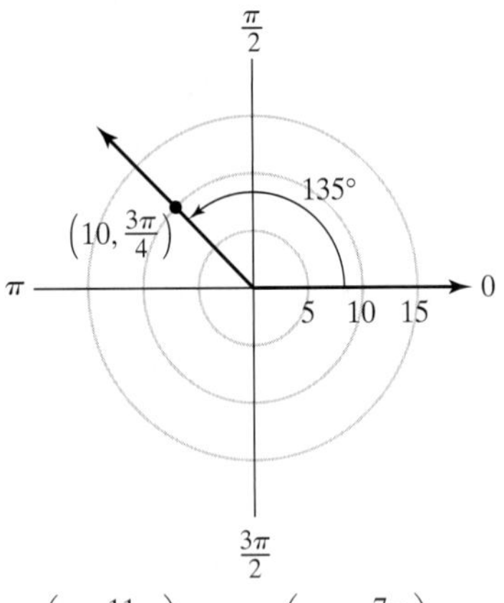


**a.** $\left(10, \frac{11\pi}{4}\right)$ **b.** $\left(-10, \frac{7\pi}{4}\right)$
**c.** $\left(10, -\frac{5\pi}{4}\right)$

**25.**

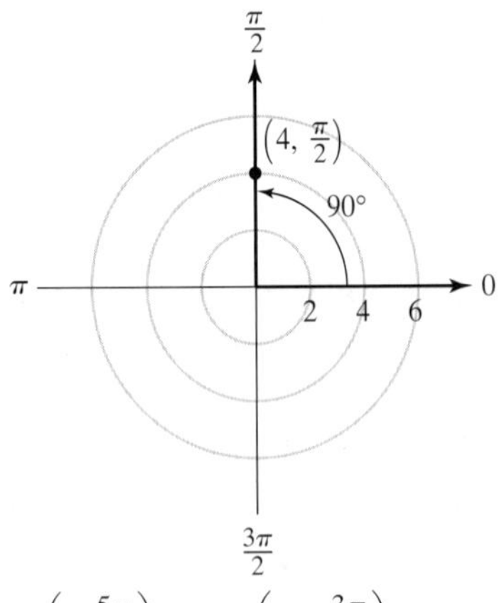


**a.** $\left(4, \frac{5\pi}{2}\right)$ **b.** $\left(-4, \frac{3\pi}{2}\right)$
**c.** $\left(4, -\frac{3\pi}{2}\right)$

**27.** $(0, 4)$ **29.** $(1, \sqrt{3})$ **31.** $(0, -4)$ **33.** approximately $(-5.9, 4.4)$ **35.** $\left(\sqrt{8}, \frac{3\pi}{4}\right)$ **37.** $\left(4, \frac{5\pi}{3}\right)$ **39.** $\left(2, \frac{7\pi}{6}\right)$

**41.** $(5, 0)$ **43.** $r = \dfrac{7}{3\cos\theta + \sin\theta}$ **45.** $r = \dfrac{7}{\cos\theta}$ **47.** $r = 3$ **49.** $r = 4\cos\theta$ **51.** $r = \dfrac{6\cos\theta}{\sin^2\theta}$ **53.** $x^2 + y^2 = 64$

**55.** $x = 0$ **57.** $y = 3$ **59.** $y = 4$ **61.** $x^2 + y^2 = y$ **63.** $x^2 + y^2 = 6x + 4y$ **65.** $y = \frac{1}{x}$ **67.** $\left(15, \frac{4\pi}{3}\right)$
**69.** 6.3 knots at an angle of 50° to the wind. **71.** Answers may vary. **81.** $(-2, 3.464)$ **83.** $(-1.857, -3.543)$
**85.** $(3, 0.730)$ **89.** $x^2 + y^2 = 4x$; center: $(2, 0)$, radius: 2

## Section 7.4

### Check Point Exercises

**1.**

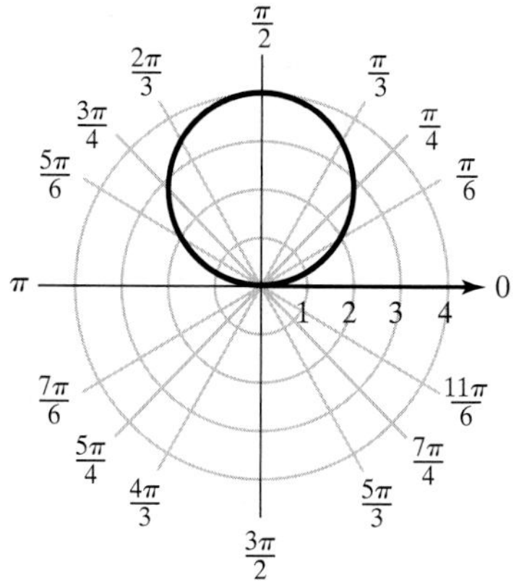


**2.**

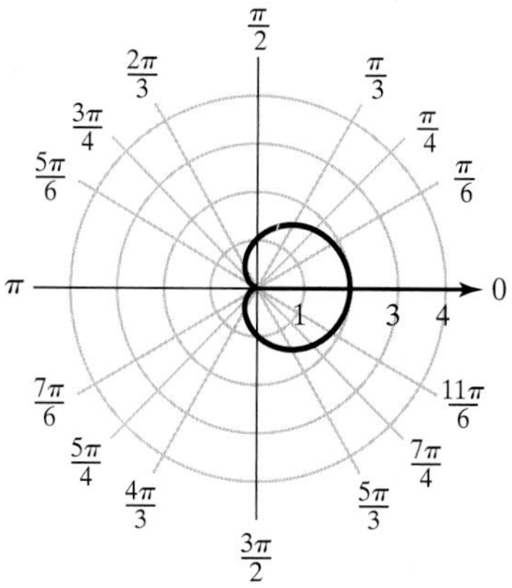


**3.**

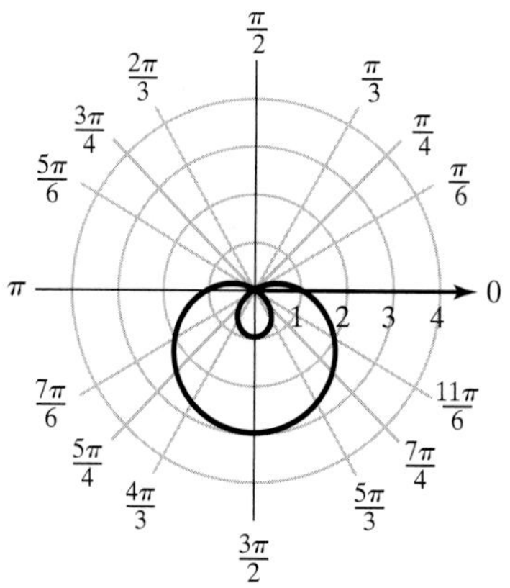


**4.**

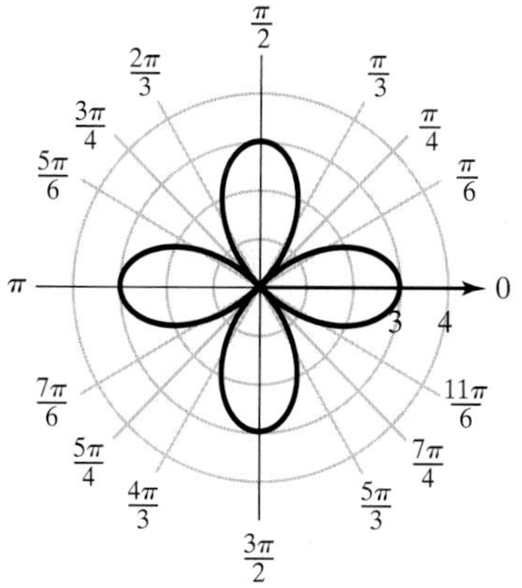


**5.**

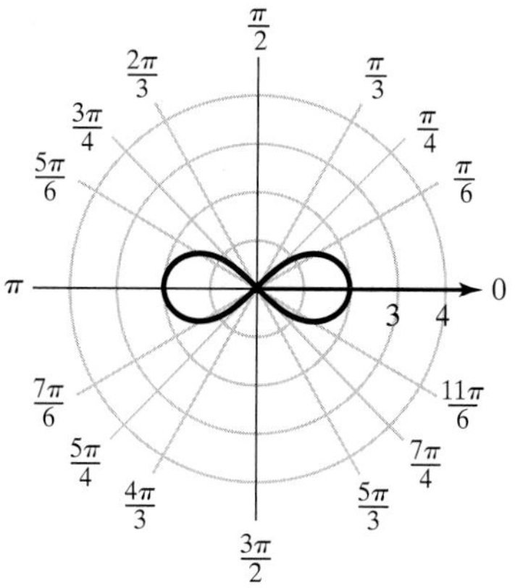


### Exercise Set 7.4

**1.** $r = 1 - \sin\theta$ **3.** $r = 2\cos\theta$ **5.** $r = 3\sin 3\theta$ **7. a.** May or may not have symmetry with respect to polar axis.
**b.** Has symmetry with respect to the line $\theta = \frac{\pi}{2}$. **c.** May or may not have symmetry about the pole.

**9. a.** Has symmetry with respect to polar axis. **b.** May or may not have symmetry with respect to the line $\theta = \frac{\pi}{2}$.
**c.** May or may not have symmetry about pole. **11. a.** Has symmetry with respect to polar axis.
**b.** Has symmetry with respect to the line $\theta = \frac{\pi}{2}$. **c.** Has symmetry about the pole.

**13.**

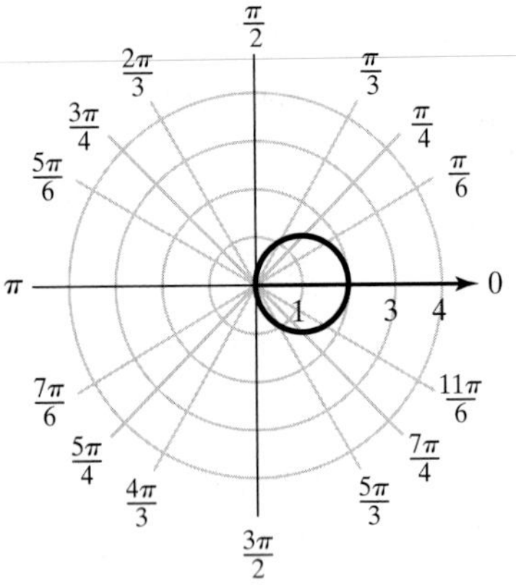


**15.**

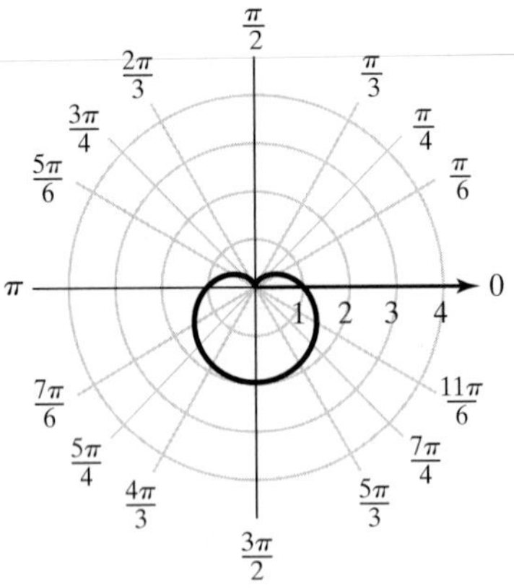


**17.**

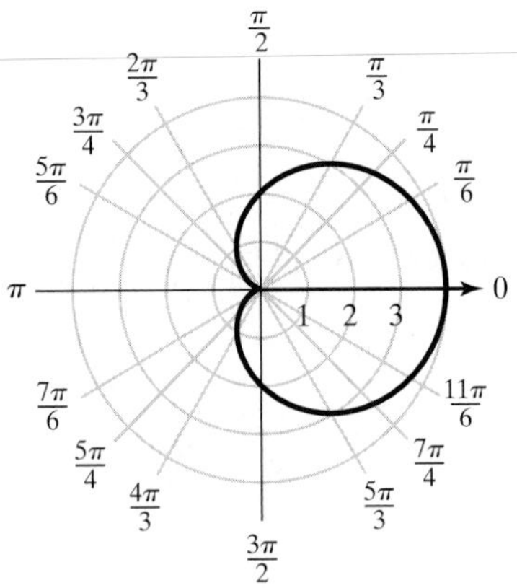


**19.**

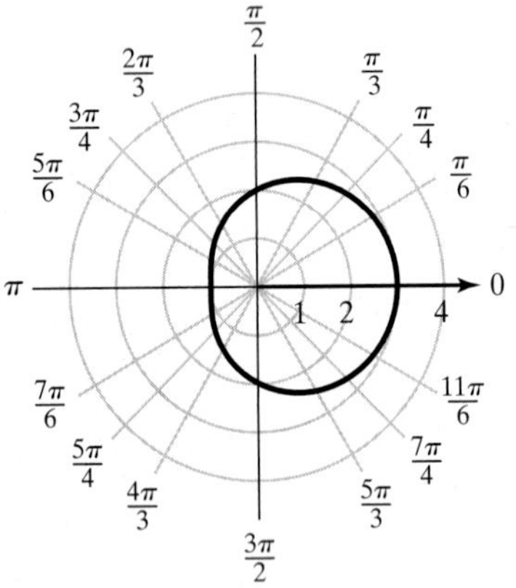


**21.**

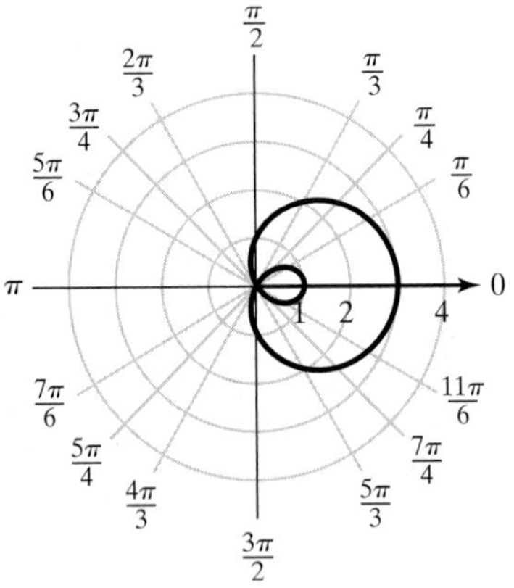


**23.**

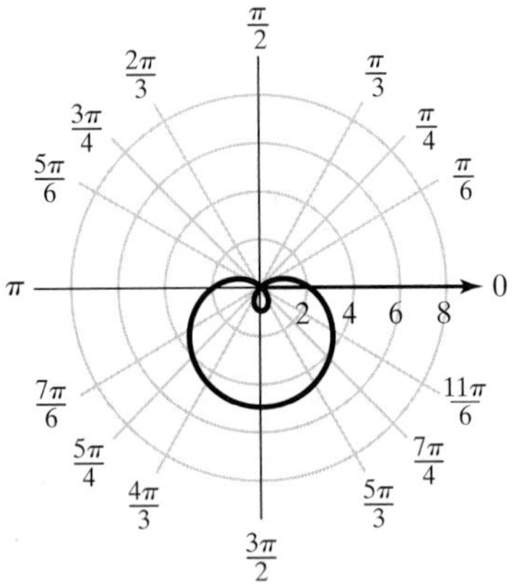


**25.**

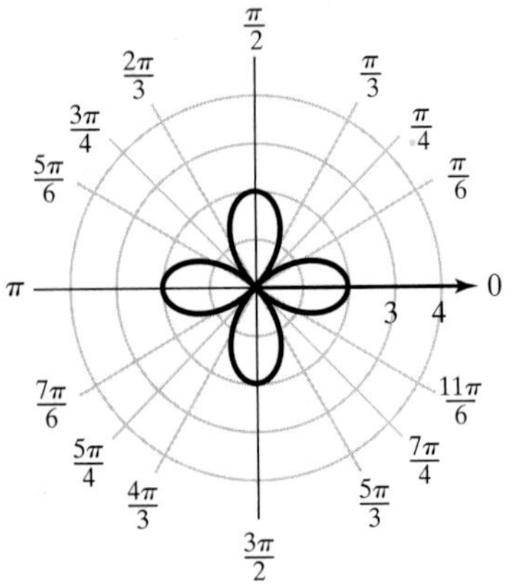


**27.**

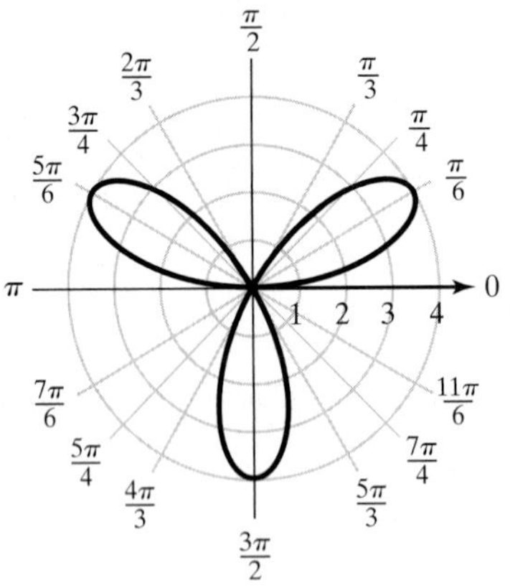


**29.**

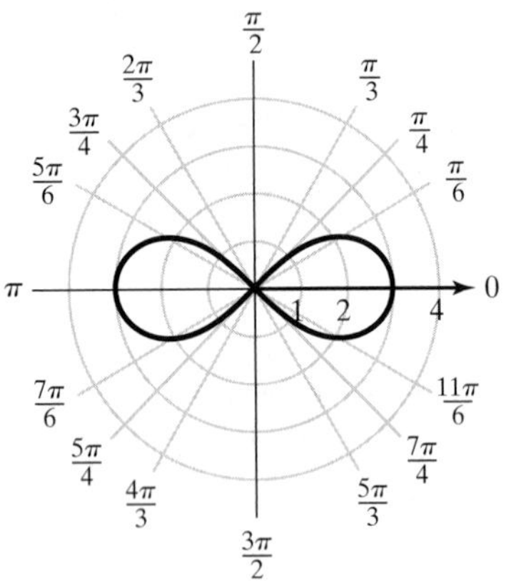

**31.**

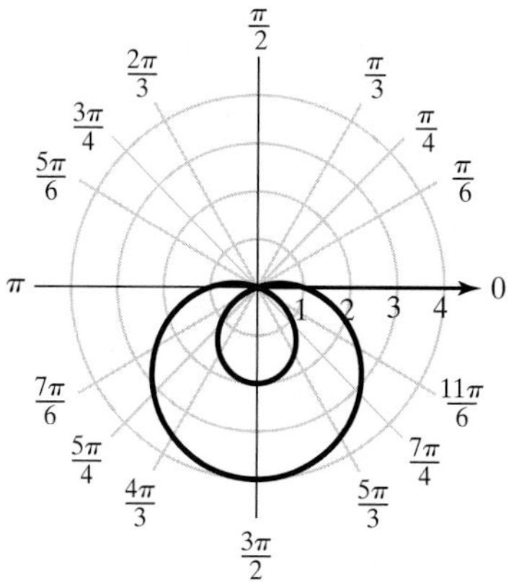


**33.**

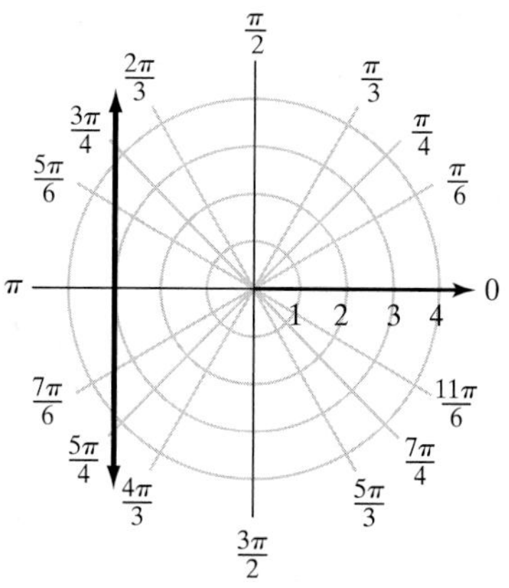


**35.** 6 knots

**37.** 8 knots

**39.** 90°; about $7\frac{1}{2}$ knots

**49.**

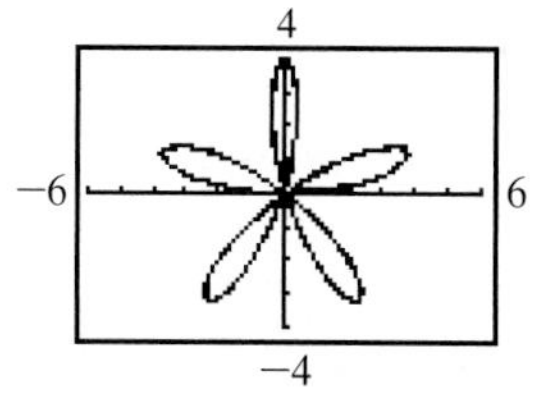


**51.**

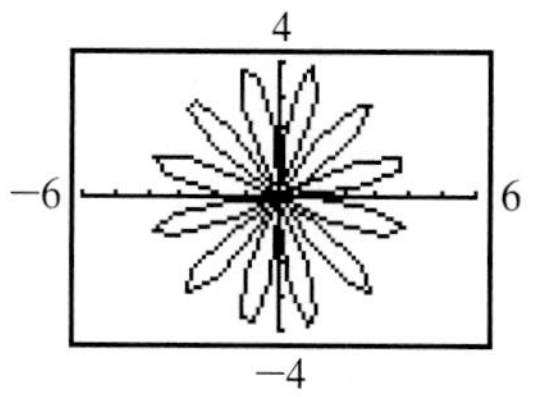


**53.**

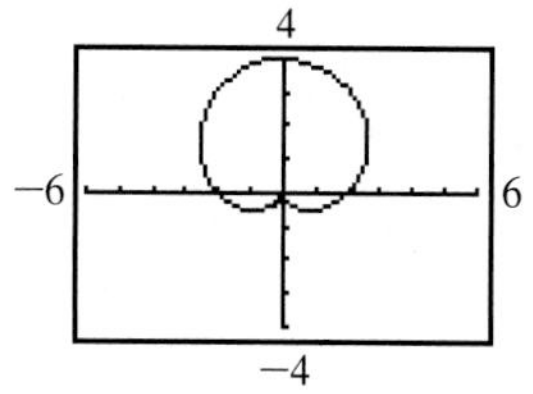


**55.**

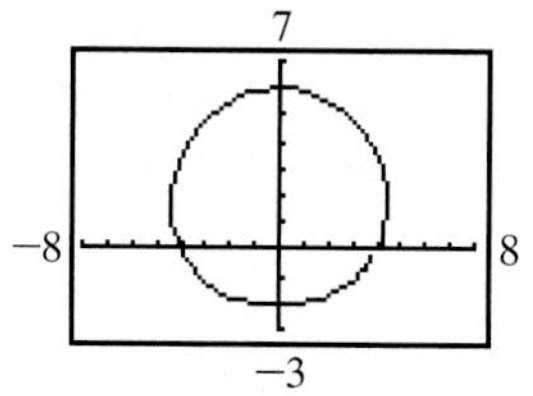


**57.**

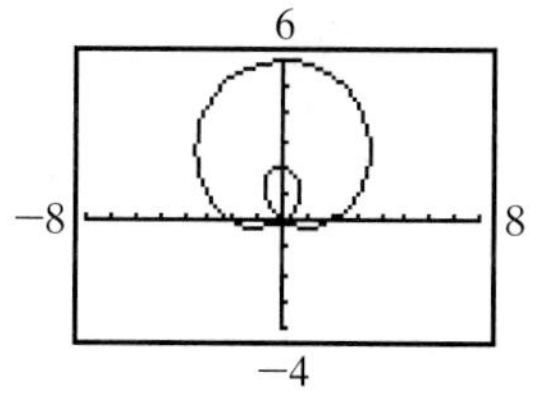


**59.**

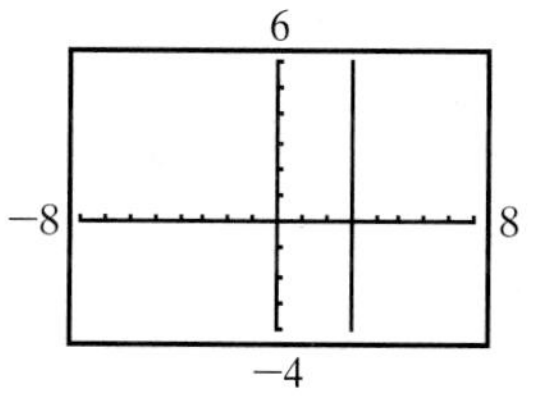


**61.**

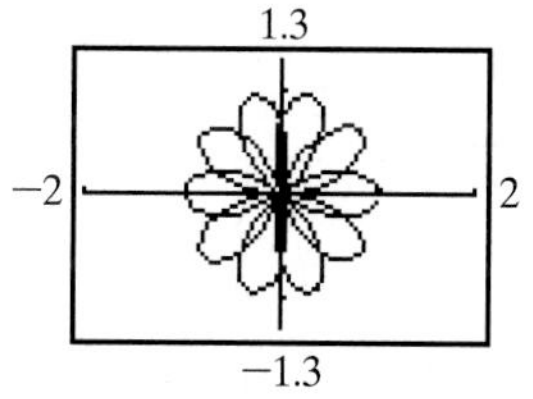


**63.**

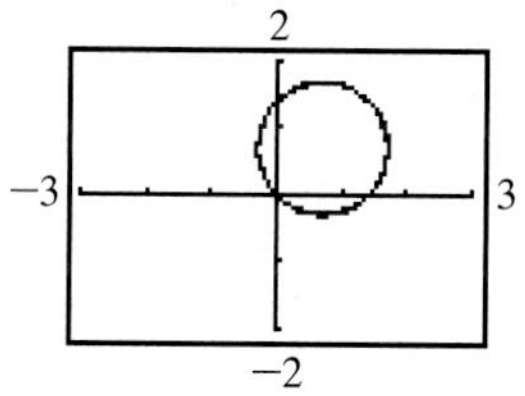


**65.**

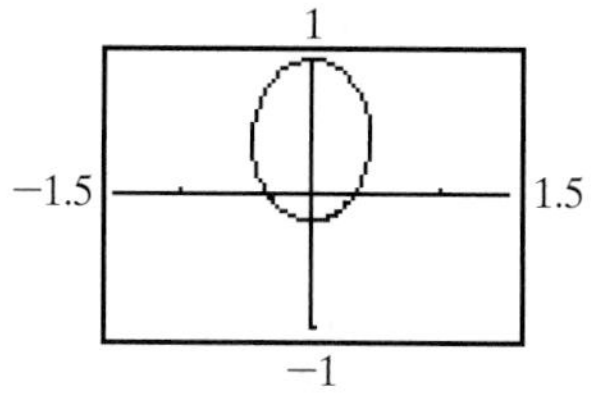


**67.** $2\pi$

**69.**

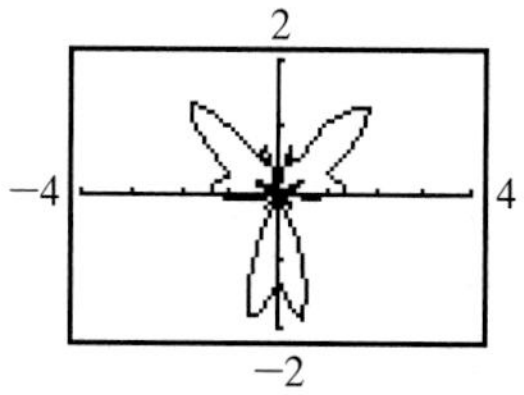


**71.**

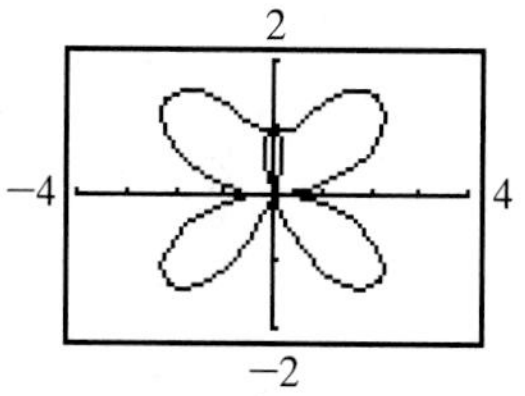


**73.** As $n$ increases, $\sin n\theta$ increases its number of loops. If $n$ is odd, there are $n$ loops and $\theta\text{max} = \pi$ traces the graph once, while if $n$ is even, there are $2n$ loops and $\theta\text{max} = 2\pi$ traces the graph once.

**75.** There are $n$ small petals and $n$ large petals for each value of $n$. For odd values of $n$, the small petals are inside the large petals. For even $n$, they are between the large petals.

**77.**

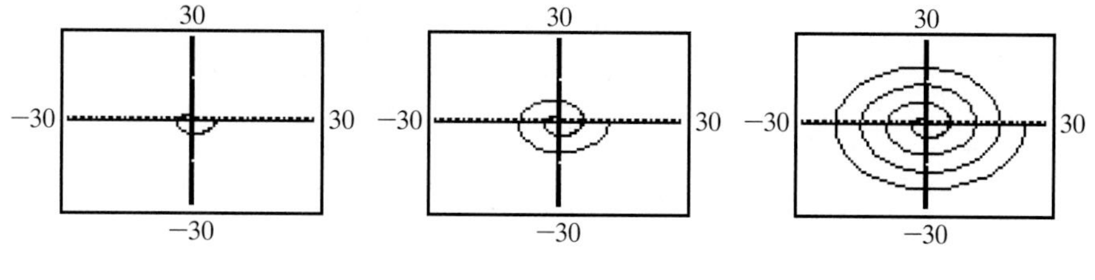

**79.** Answers may vary. **81.**

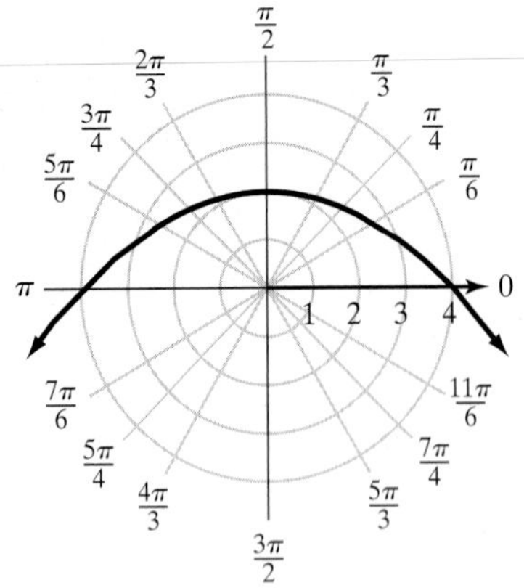


## Section 7.5

### Check Point Exercises

**1. a.**

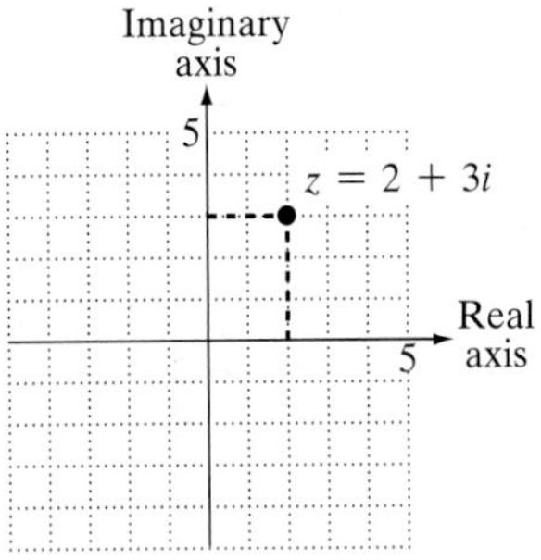


**b.**

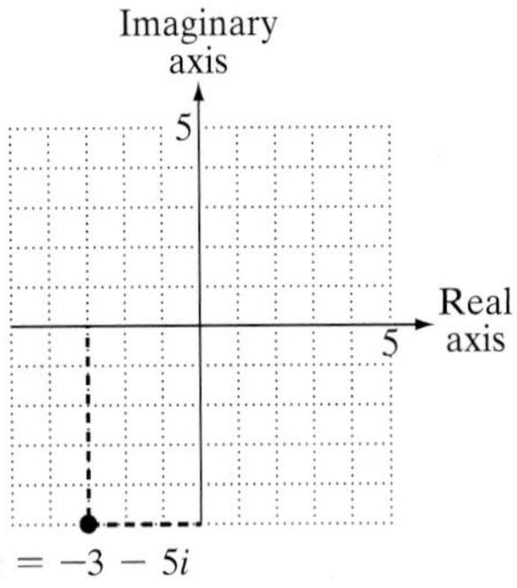


**c.**

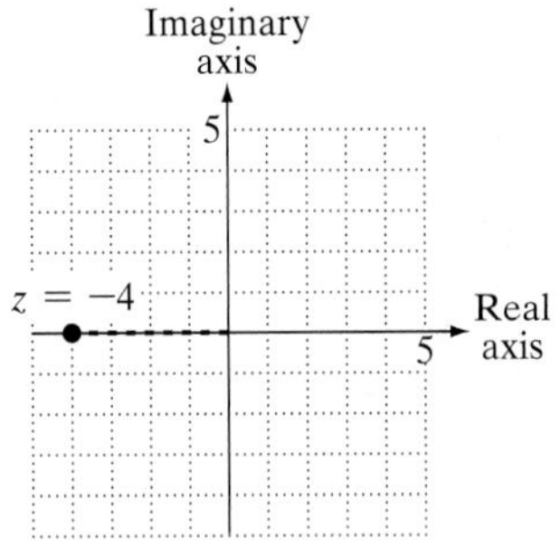


**d.**

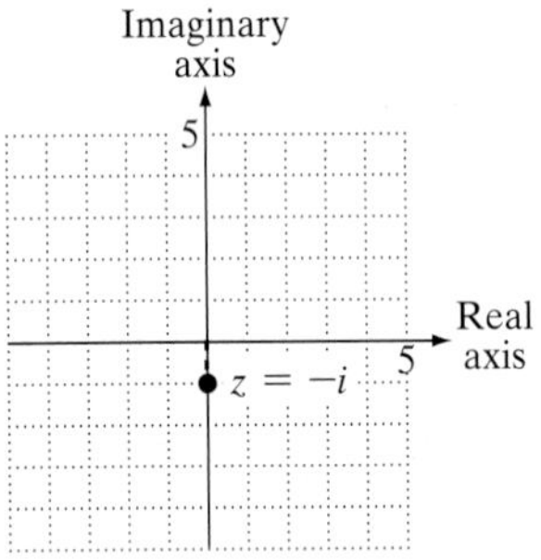


**2. a.** 13 **b.** $\sqrt{13}$ **3.**

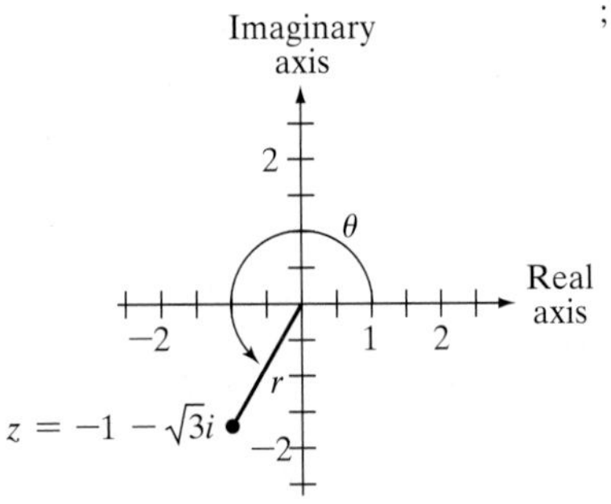


$; 2\left(\cos\frac{4\pi}{3} + i\sin\frac{4\pi}{3}\right)$

**4.** $z = 2\sqrt{3} + 2i$ **5.** $30(\cos 60° + i\sin 60°)$ **6.** $10(\cos\pi + i\sin\pi)$ **7.** $-16\sqrt{3} + 16i$ **8.** $-4$
**9.** $2(\cos 15° + i\sin 15°); 2(\cos 105° + i\sin 105°); 2(\cos 195° + i\sin 195°); 2(\cos 285° + i\sin 285°)$
**10.** $3; -\frac{3}{2} + \frac{3\sqrt{3}}{2}i; -\frac{3}{2} - \frac{3\sqrt{3}}{2}i$

## Exercise Set 7.5

**1.**

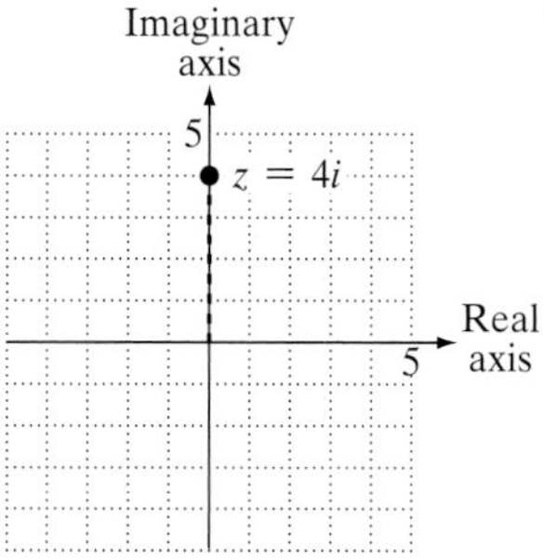


; 4

**3.**

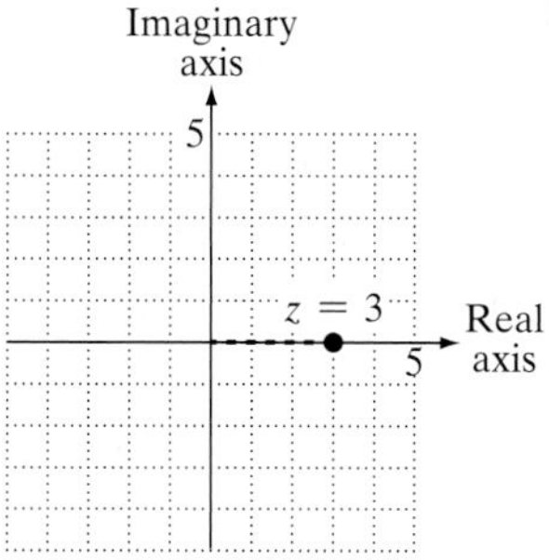


; 3

**5.**

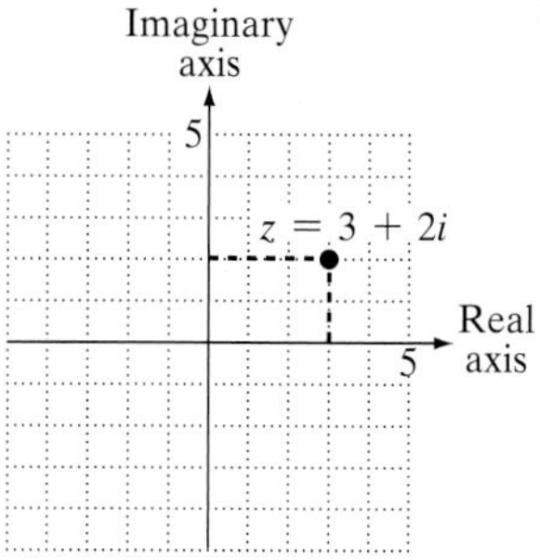


; $\sqrt{13}$

**7.**

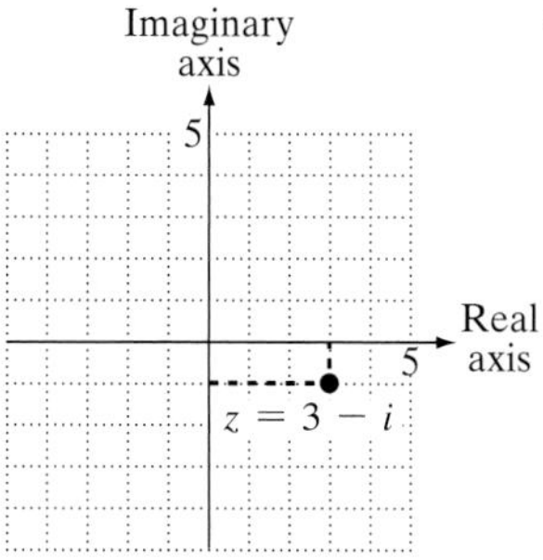


; $\sqrt{10}$

**9.**

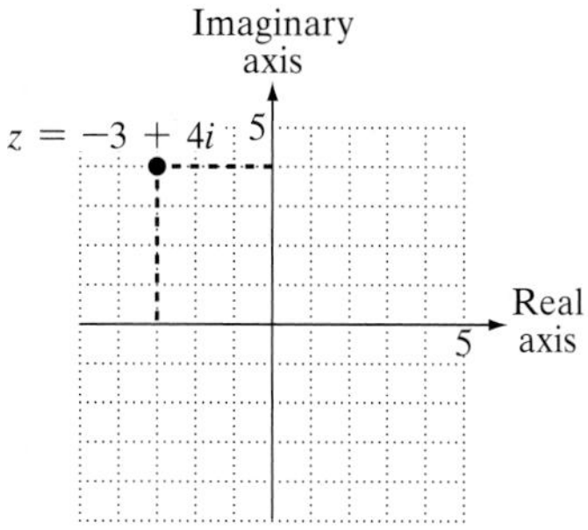


; 5

**11.**

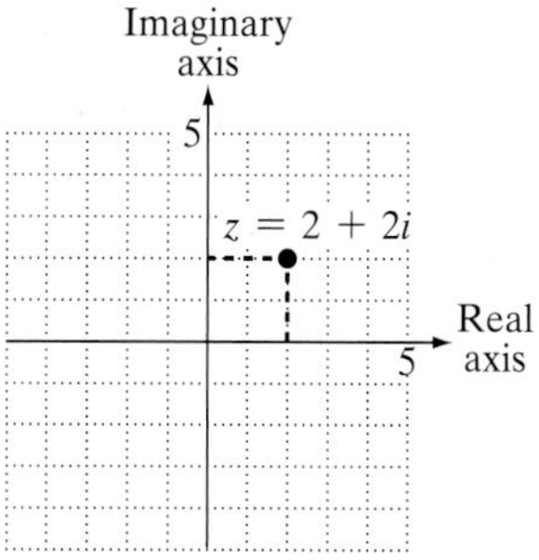


$2\sqrt{2}\left(\cos\frac{\pi}{4} + i\sin\frac{\pi}{4}\right)$

or $2\sqrt{2}(\cos 45° + i\sin 45°)$

**13.**

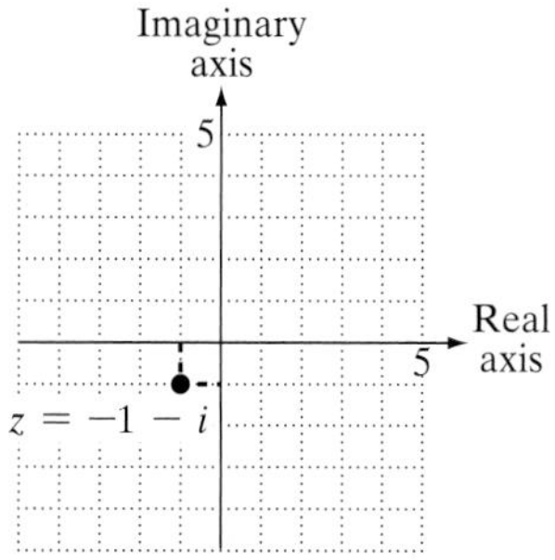


$\sqrt{2}\left(\cos\frac{5\pi}{4} + i\sin\frac{5\pi}{4}\right)$

or $\sqrt{2}(\cos 225° + i\sin 225°)$

**15.**

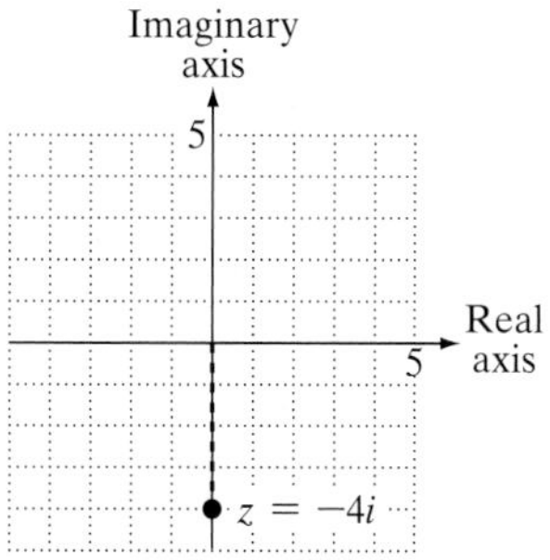


$4\left(\cos\frac{3\pi}{2} + i\sin\frac{3\pi}{2}\right)$

or $4(\cos 270° + i\sin 270°)$

**17.**

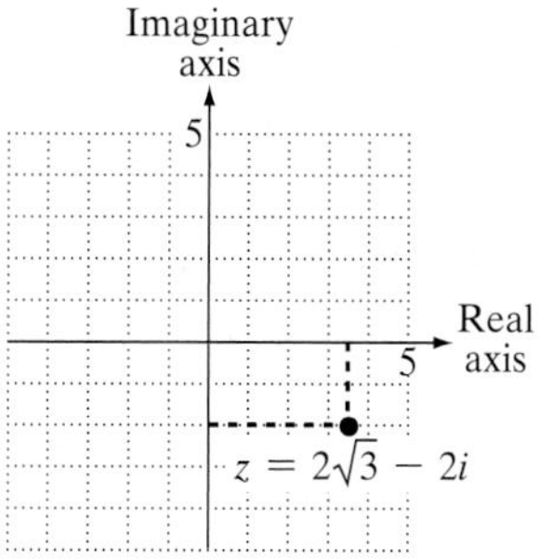


$4\left(\cos\frac{11\pi}{6} + i\sin\frac{11\pi}{6}\right)$

or $4(\cos 330° + i\sin 330°)$

**19.**

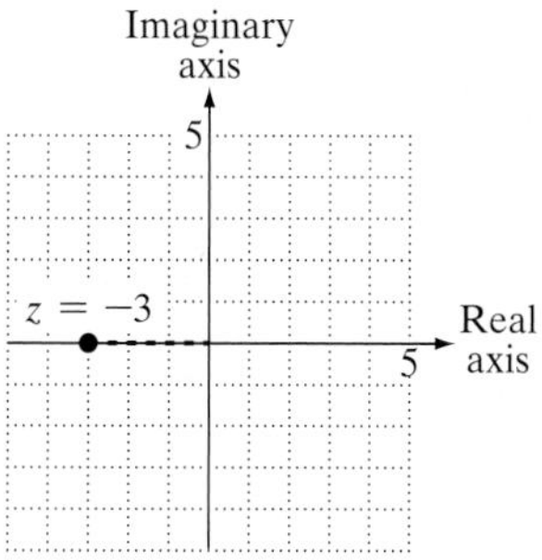


$3(\cos\pi + i\sin\pi)$ or

$3(\cos 180° + i\sin 180°)$

**21.**

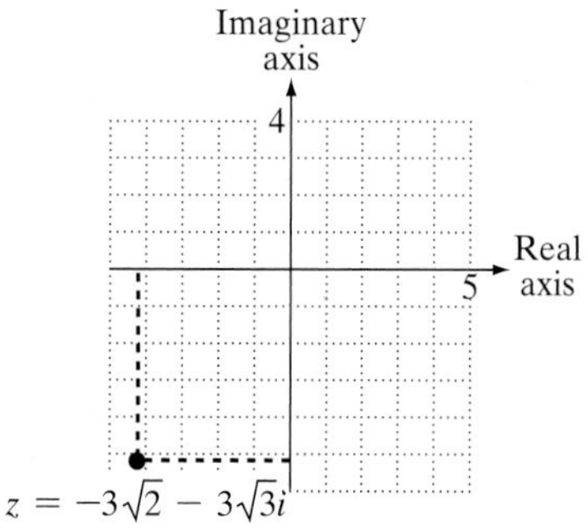


$\approx 3\sqrt{5}(\cos 230.8° + i\sin 230.8°)$

**23.**

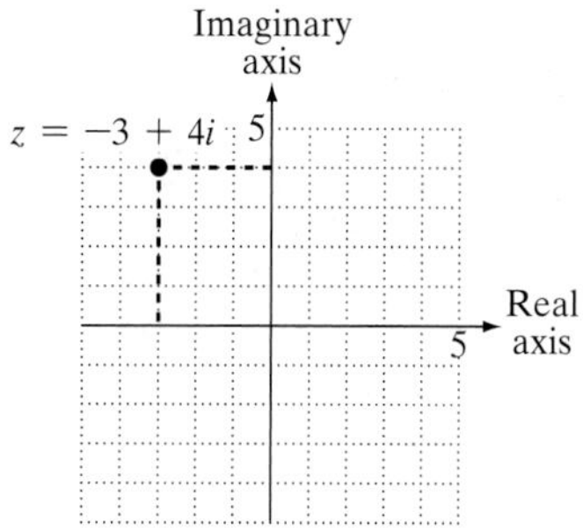


$\approx 5(\cos 126.9° + i\sin 126.9°)$

**25.**

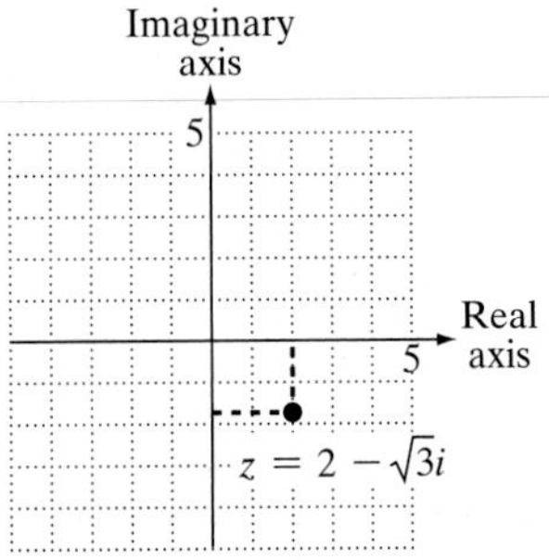


$\approx \sqrt{7}(\cos 319.1° + i \sin 319.1°)$

**27.** $3\sqrt{3} + 3i$ **29.** $-2 - 2\sqrt{3}i$ **31.** $4\sqrt{2} - 4\sqrt{2}i$ **33.** $5i$
**35.** $z \approx -18.1 - 8.5i$ **37.** $30(\cos 70° + i \sin 70°)$
**39.** $12\left(\cos \frac{3\pi}{10} + i \sin \frac{3\pi}{10}\right)$ **41.** $\cos \frac{7\pi}{12} + i \sin \frac{7\pi}{12}$ **43.** $2(\cos \pi + i \sin \pi)$
**45.** $5(\cos 50° + i \sin 50°)$ **47.** $\frac{3}{4}\left(\cos \frac{\pi}{10} + i \sin \frac{\pi}{10}\right)$ **49.** $\cos 240° + i \sin 240°$
**51.** $2(\cos 0° + i \sin 0°)$ **53.** $32\sqrt{2} + 32\sqrt{2}i$ **55.** $-4 - 4\sqrt{3}i$
**57.** $\frac{1}{64}i$ **59.** $-2 - 2\sqrt{3}i$ **61.** $-4 - 4i$ **63.** $-64$
**65.** $3(\cos 15° + i \sin 15°); 3(\cos 195° + i \sin 195°)$
**67.** $2(\cos 70° + i \sin 70°); 2(\cos 190° + i \sin 190°); 2(\cos 310° + i \sin 310°)$

**69.** $\frac{3}{2} + \frac{3\sqrt{3}}{2}i; -\frac{3\sqrt{3}}{2} + \frac{3}{2}i; -\frac{3}{2} - \frac{3\sqrt{3}}{2}i; \frac{3\sqrt{3}}{2} - \frac{3}{2}i$ **71.** $2; \approx 0.6 + 1.9i; \approx -1.6 + 1.2i; \approx -1.6 - 1.2i; \approx 0.6 - 1.9i$
**73.** $1; -\frac{1}{2} + \frac{\sqrt{3}}{2}i; -\frac{1}{2} - \frac{\sqrt{3}}{2}i$ **75.** $\approx 1.1 + 0.2i; \approx -0.2 + 1.1i; \approx -1.1 - 0.2i; \approx 0.2 - 1.1i$
**77. a.** $i; -1 + i; -i; -1 + i; -i; -1 + i$ **b.** Complex numbers may vary.
**93.**

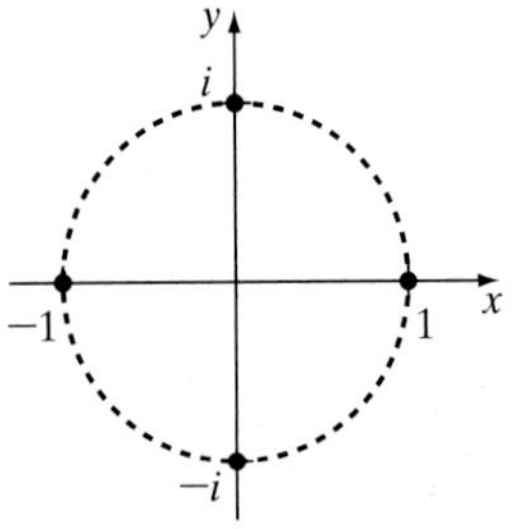


**95.** $-\sqrt{3} + i, \sqrt{3} + i, -2i$

## Section 7.6

### Check Point Exercises

**1.** $\|\mathbf{u}\| = 5 = \|\mathbf{v}\|$ and $m_u = \frac{4}{3} = m_v$ **2.**

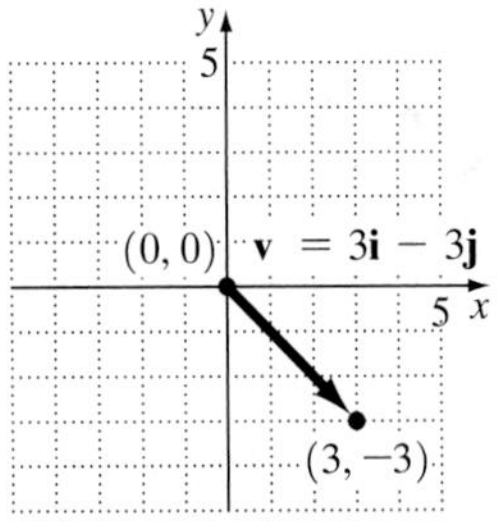


$; \|\mathbf{v}\| = 3\sqrt{2}$ **3.** $\mathbf{v} = 3\mathbf{i} + 4\mathbf{j}$ **4. a.** $11\mathbf{i} - 2\mathbf{j}$ **b.** $3\mathbf{i} + 8\mathbf{j}$
**5. a.** $56\mathbf{i} + 80\mathbf{j}$ **b.** $-35\mathbf{i} - 50\mathbf{j}$
**6.** $30\mathbf{i} + 33\mathbf{j}$
**7.** $\frac{4}{5}\mathbf{i} - \frac{3}{5}\mathbf{j}; \sqrt{\left(\frac{4}{5}\right)^2 + \left(-\frac{3}{5}\right)^2} = \sqrt{\frac{16}{25} + \frac{9}{25}} = \sqrt{\frac{25}{25}} = 1$
**8.** about 82.5 lb in the direction of approximately 16.2° relative to the 60-lb force

### Exercise Set 7.6

**1. a.** $\sqrt{41}$ **b.** $\sqrt{41}$ **c.** $\mathbf{u} = \mathbf{v}$ **3. a.** 6 **b.** 6 **c.** $\mathbf{u} = \mathbf{v}$

**5.**

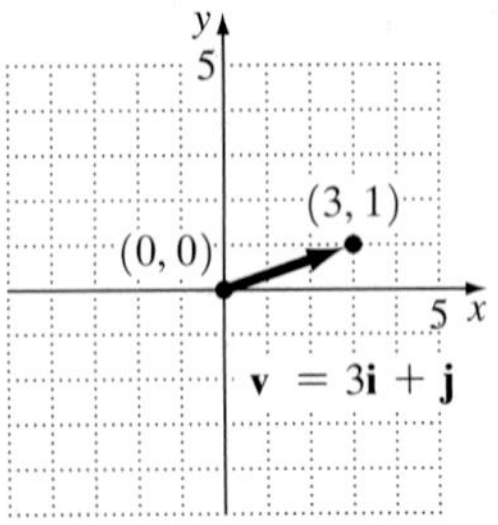


$\sqrt{10}$

**7.**

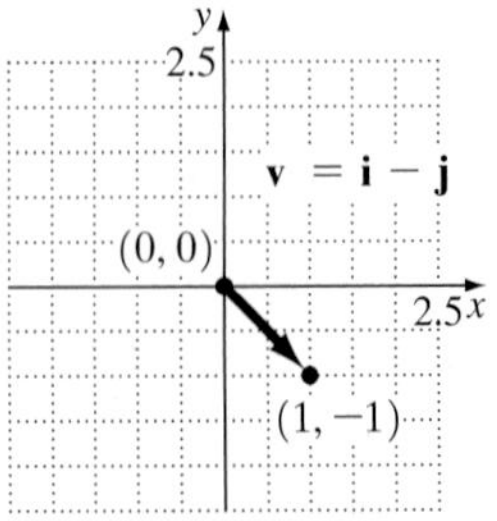


$\sqrt{2}$

**9.**

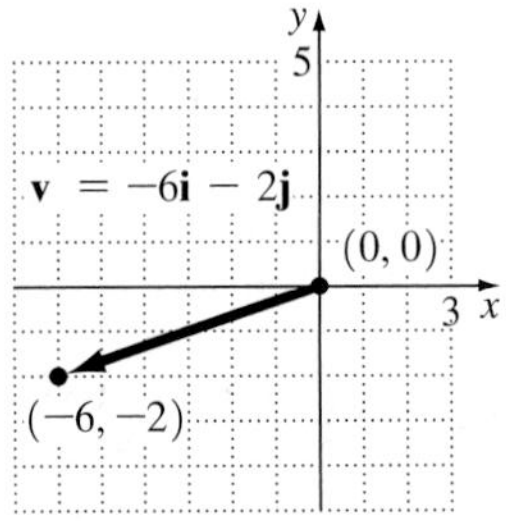


$2\sqrt{10}$

**11.**

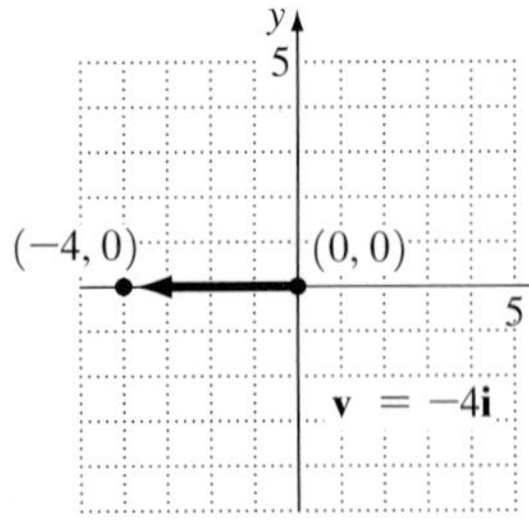


4

**13.** $10\mathbf{i} + 6\mathbf{j}$ **15.** $6\mathbf{i} - 3\mathbf{j}$ **17.** $-6\mathbf{i} - 14\mathbf{j}$ **19.** $9\mathbf{i}$ **21.** $-\mathbf{i} + 2\mathbf{j}$ **23.** $5\mathbf{i} - 12\mathbf{j}$ **25.** $-5\mathbf{i} + 12\mathbf{j}$ **27.** $-15\mathbf{i} + 35\mathbf{j}$

**29.** $4\mathbf{i} + 24\mathbf{j}$ **31.** $-9\mathbf{i} - 4\mathbf{j}$ **33.** $-5\mathbf{i} + 45\mathbf{j}$ **35.** $2\sqrt{29}$ **37.** $\sqrt{10}$ **39.** $\mathbf{i}$ **41.** $\frac{3}{5}\mathbf{i} - \frac{4}{5}\mathbf{j}$ **43.** $\frac{3}{\sqrt{13}}\mathbf{i} - \frac{2}{\sqrt{13}}\mathbf{j}$
**45.** $\frac{\sqrt{2}}{2}\mathbf{i} + \frac{\sqrt{2}}{2}\mathbf{j}$ **47. a.** approximately 53.9 lb **b.** approximately 21.8° relative to the 50-lb force
**49. a.** approximately 413.1 lb **b.** approximately 18.5° relative to the 300-lb force
**51. a.**

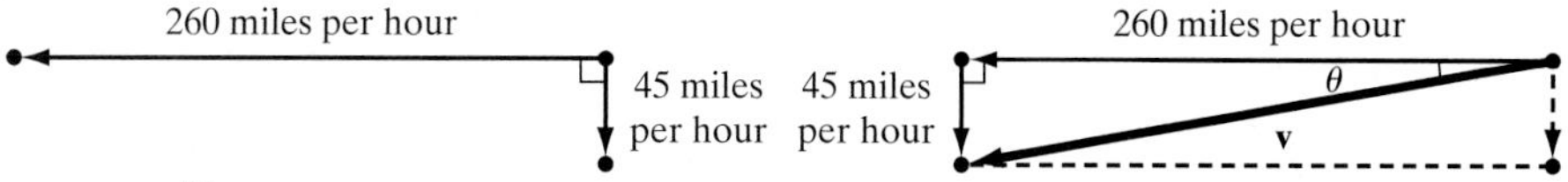


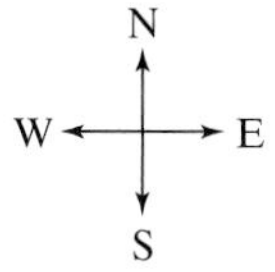


**b.** 264 mph

**53.** $\|\mathbf{v}\| \approx 164.5$ mph is the resultant speed of the plane.
**71. a.** False **b.** True **c.** False **d.** False
**73.** The plane's true speed relative to the ground is 269.1 miles per hour.; The compass heading relative to the ground is 278.3°.

## Section 7.7

### Check Point Exercises

**1. a.** 18 **b.** 18 **c.** 5 **2.** 100.3° **3.** orthogonal **4.** $30\sqrt{2}\mathbf{i} + 30\sqrt{2}\mathbf{j}$ **5.** $\frac{7}{2}\mathbf{i} - \frac{7}{2}\mathbf{j}$ **6.** $\mathbf{v}_1 = \frac{7}{2}\mathbf{i} - \frac{7}{2}\mathbf{j}$; $\mathbf{v}_2 = -\frac{3}{2}\mathbf{i} - \frac{3}{2}\mathbf{j}$
**7.** approximately 2598 ft-lb

### Exercise Set 7.7

**1. a.** 6 **b.** 10 **3. a.** −6 **b.** 41 **5. a.** 100 **b.** 61 **7. a.** 0 **b.** 25 **9.** 3 **11.** 3 **13.** 20 **15.** 20 **17.** 79.7°
**19.** 160.3° **21.** 38.7° **23.** orthogonal **25.** orthogonal **27.** not orthogonal **29.** not orthogonal **31.** orthogonal
**33.** $3\sqrt{3}\mathbf{i} + 3\mathbf{j}$ **35.** $-6\sqrt{2}\mathbf{i} - 6\sqrt{2}\mathbf{j}$ **37.** $\approx -0.20\mathbf{i} + 0.46\mathbf{j}$ **39.** $\mathbf{v}_1 = \text{proj}_{\mathbf{w}}\mathbf{v} = \frac{5}{2}\mathbf{i} - \frac{5}{2}\mathbf{j}$; $\mathbf{v}_2 = \frac{1}{2}\mathbf{i} + \frac{1}{2}\mathbf{j}$
**41.** $\mathbf{v}_1 = \text{proj}_{\mathbf{w}}\mathbf{v} = -\frac{26}{29}\mathbf{i} + \frac{65}{29}\mathbf{j}$; $\mathbf{v}_2 = \frac{55}{29}\mathbf{i} + \frac{22}{29}\mathbf{j}$ **43.** $\mathbf{v}_1 = \text{proj}_{\mathbf{w}}\mathbf{v} = \mathbf{i} + 2\mathbf{j}$; $\mathbf{v}_2 = \mathbf{0}$ **45.** $22\sqrt{3}\mathbf{i} + 22\mathbf{j}$ **47.** $148.5\mathbf{i} + 20.9\mathbf{j}$
**49.** 1077; $\mathbf{v} \cdot \mathbf{w} = 1077$ means \$1077 in revenue was generated on Monday by the sale of 240 gallons of regular gas at \$1.90 per gallon and 300 gallons of premium gas at \$2.07 per gallon. **51.** 7600 foot-pounds **53.** 3392 foot-pounds **55.** $\approx 1.4\mathbf{i} + 0.6\mathbf{j}$; 1.4 in.
**57. a.** about 192,389 lb **b.** $188{,}185\mathbf{i} + 40{,}000\mathbf{j}$

**71.**
$$(c\mathbf{u}) \cdot \mathbf{v} \stackrel{?}{=} c(\mathbf{u} \cdot \mathbf{v})$$
$$[c(a_1\mathbf{i} + b_1\mathbf{j})] \cdot (a_2\mathbf{i} + b_2\mathbf{j}) \stackrel{?}{=} c[(a_1\mathbf{i} + b_1\mathbf{j}) \cdot (a_2\mathbf{i} + b_2\mathbf{j})]$$
$$(ca_1\mathbf{i} + cb_1\mathbf{j}) \cdot (a_2\mathbf{i} + b_2\mathbf{j}) \stackrel{?}{=} c[a_1(a_2) + b_1(b_2)]$$
$$(ca_1)(a_2) + (cb_1)(b_2) \stackrel{?}{=} c(a_1a_2) + c(b_1b_2)$$

Since $a_1, a_2, b_1, b_2$ and $c$ are real numbers and multiplication of real numbers is associative, $(ca_1)(a_2) = c(a_1a_2)$ and $(cb_1)(b_2) = c(b_1b_2)$. Thus, $(ca_1)(a_2) + (cb_1)(b_2) = c(a_1a_2) + c(b_1b_2)$
So $(c\mathbf{u}) \cdot \mathbf{v} = c(\mathbf{u} \cdot \mathbf{v})$.

**73.** 6.3 foot-pounds **75.** $b = -20$ **77.** any two vectors, **v** and **w**, having the same direction

### Chapter 7 Review Exercises

**1.** $C = 55°, b \approx 10.5$, and $c \approx 10.5$ **2.** $A = 43°, a \approx 171.9$, and $b \approx 241.0$ **3.** $b \approx 16.3, A \approx 72°$, and $C \approx 42°$
**4.** $C \approx 98°, A \approx 55°$, and $B \approx 27°$ **5.** $C = 120°, a \approx 45.0$, and $b \approx 33.2$ **6.** two triangles; $B_1 \approx 55°, C_1 \approx 86°$, and $c_1 \approx 31.7$; $B_2 \approx 125°, C_2 \approx 16°$, and $c_2 \approx 8.8$ **7.** no triangle **8.** $a \approx 59.0, B \approx 3°$, and $C \approx 15°$ **9.** $B \approx 78°, A \approx 39°$, and $C \approx 63°$
**10.** $B_1$ (or $B$) $\approx 25°, C \approx 115°$, and $c \approx 8.5$ **11.** two triangles; $A_1 \approx 59°, C_1 \approx 84°, c_1 \approx 14.4$; $A_2 \approx 121°, C_2 \approx 22°, c_2 \approx 5.4$
**12.** $B \approx 9°, C \approx 148°$, and $c \approx 73.6$ **13.** 8 sq ft **14.** 4 sq ft **15.** 4 sq m **16.** 2 sq m **17.** 35 ft **18.** 35.6 mi **19.** 861 mi
**20.** 404 ft; 551 ft **21.** \$214,194

**22.**

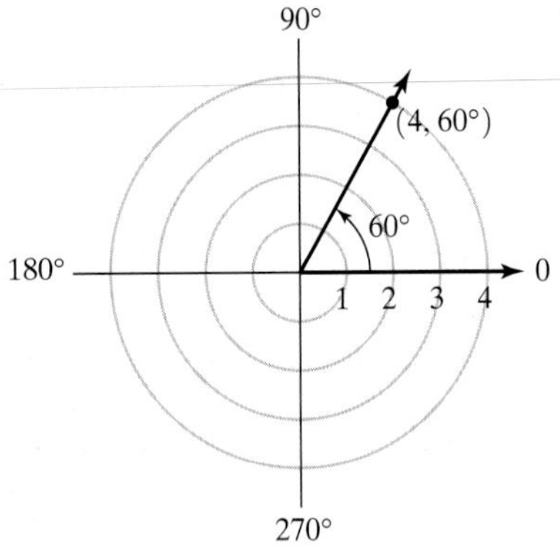


$(2, 2\sqrt{3})$

**23.**

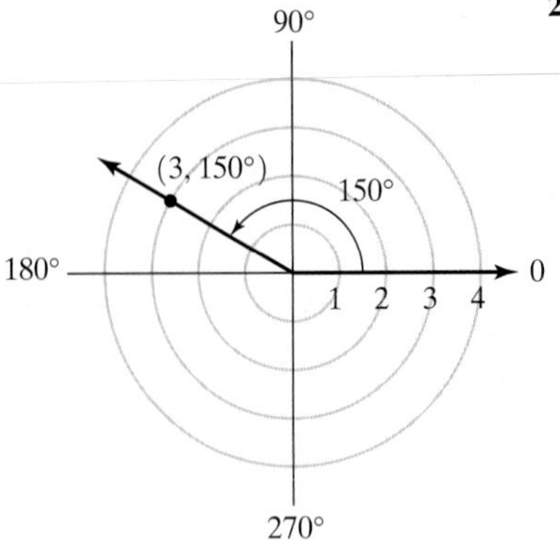


$\left(-\frac{3\sqrt{3}}{2}, \frac{3}{2}\right)$

**24.**

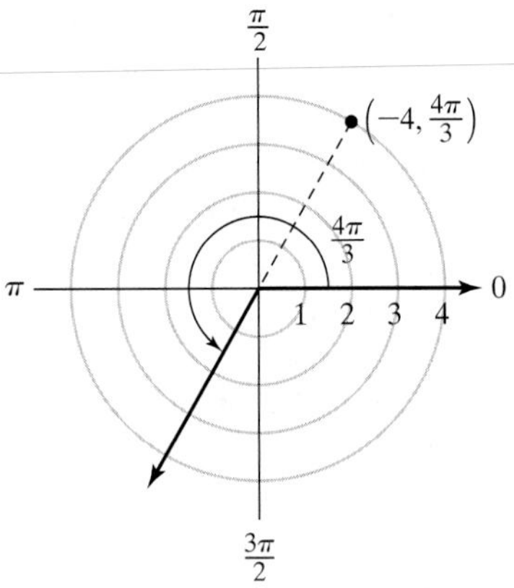


$(2, 2\sqrt{3})$

**25.**

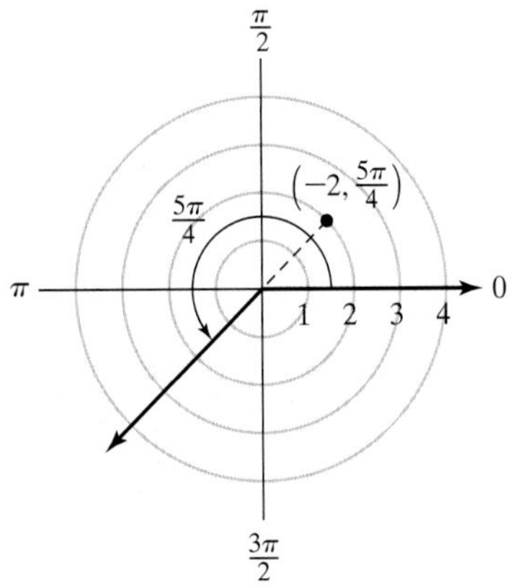


$(\sqrt{2}, \sqrt{2})$

**26.**

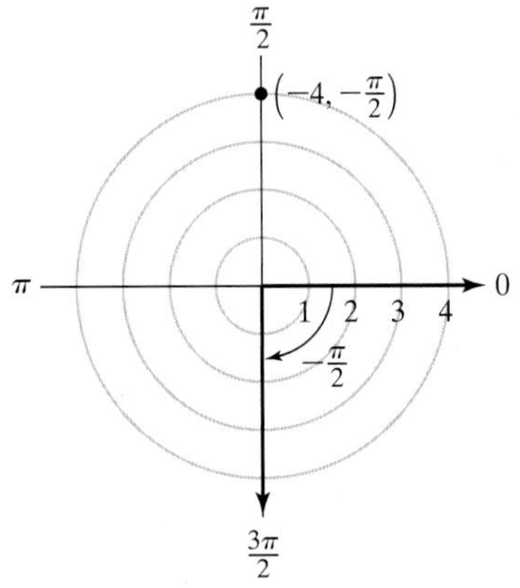


$(0, 4)$

**27.**

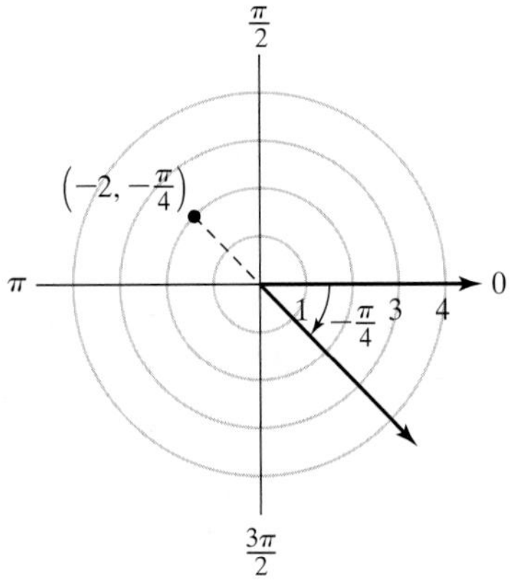


$(-\sqrt{2}, \sqrt{2})$

**28.**

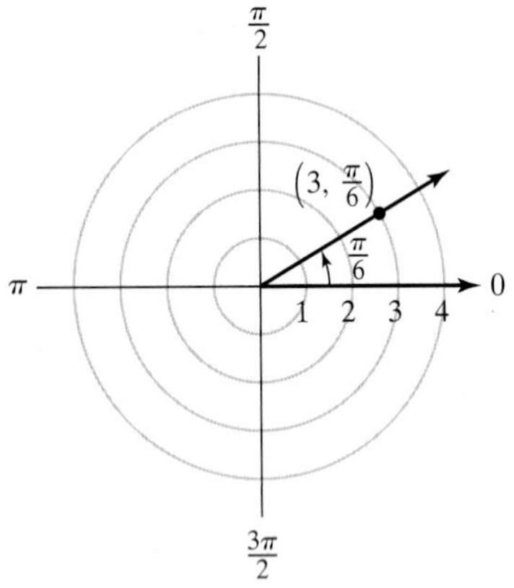


**a.** $\left(3, \frac{13\pi}{6}\right)$ **b.** $\left(-3, \frac{7\pi}{6}\right)$ **c.** $\left(3, -\frac{11\pi}{6}\right)$

**29.**

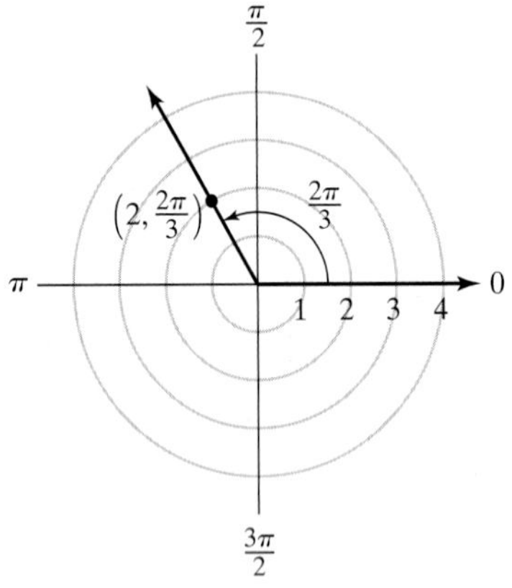


**a.** $\left(2, \frac{8\pi}{3}\right)$ **b.** $\left(-2, \frac{5\pi}{3}\right)$ **c.** $\left(2, -\frac{4\pi}{3}\right)$

**30.**

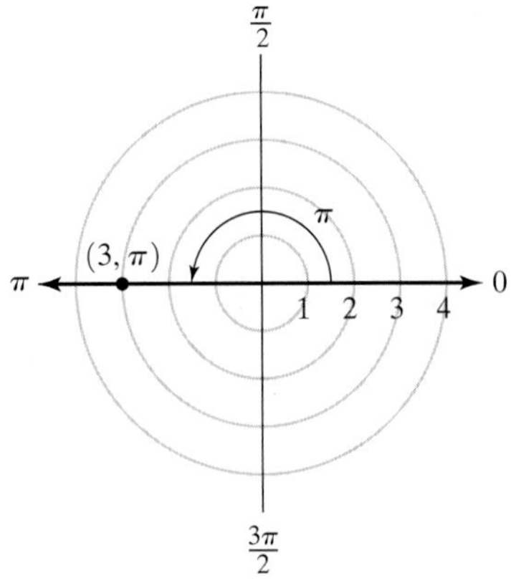


**a.** $(3, 3\pi)$ **b.** $(-3, 2\pi)$ **c.** $(3, -\pi)$

**31.** $\left(4\sqrt{2}, \frac{3\pi}{4}\right)$ **32.** $\left(3\sqrt{2}, \frac{7\pi}{4}\right)$ **33.** approximately $(13, 67°)$ **34.** approximately $(5, 127°)$ **35.** $\left(5, \frac{3\pi}{2}\right)$ **36.** $(1, 0)$

**37.** $r = \dfrac{8}{2\cos\theta + 3\sin\theta}$ **38.** $r = 10$ **39.** $r = \dfrac{3}{5}\sin\theta$ **40.** $x^2 + y^2 = 9$ **41.** $y = -x$ **42.** $x = -1$ **43.** $x = 5$

**44.** $x^2 + y^2 = 3x$ **45.** $5x + y = 8$ **46.** $y = \dfrac{2}{x}$ **47. a.** has symmetry **b.** may or may not have symmetry **c.** may or may not have symmetry **48. a.** may or may not have symmetry **b.** has symmetry **c.** may or may not have symmetry

**49. a.** has symmetry **b.** has symmetry **c.** has symmetry

**50.**

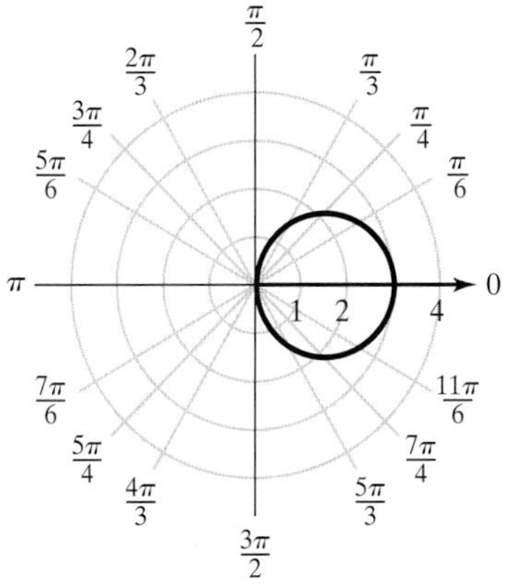


**51.**

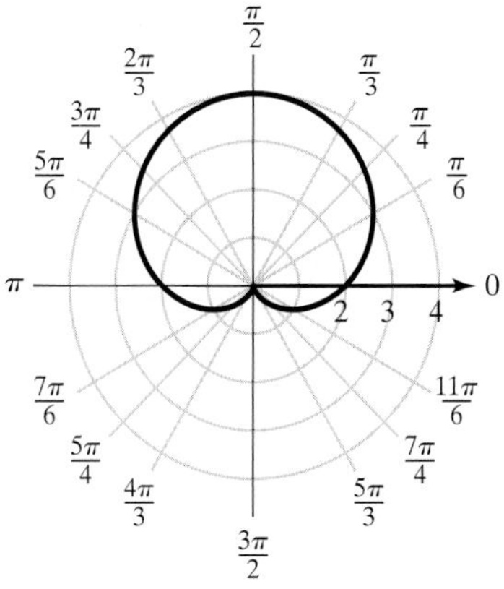


**52.**

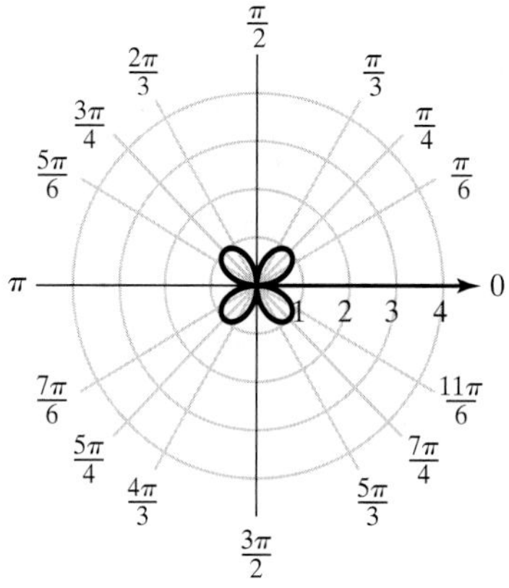


**53.**

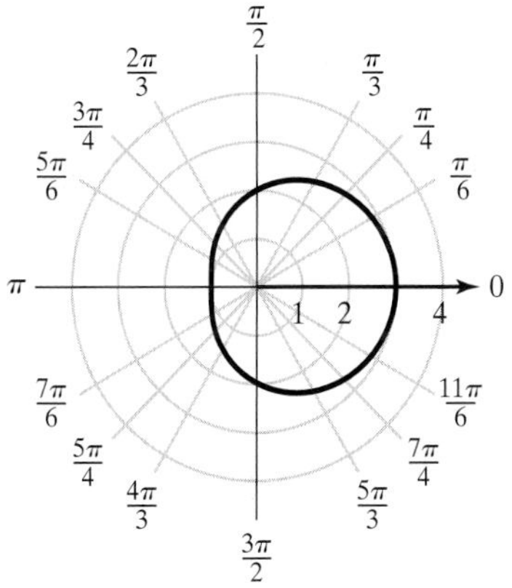


**54.**

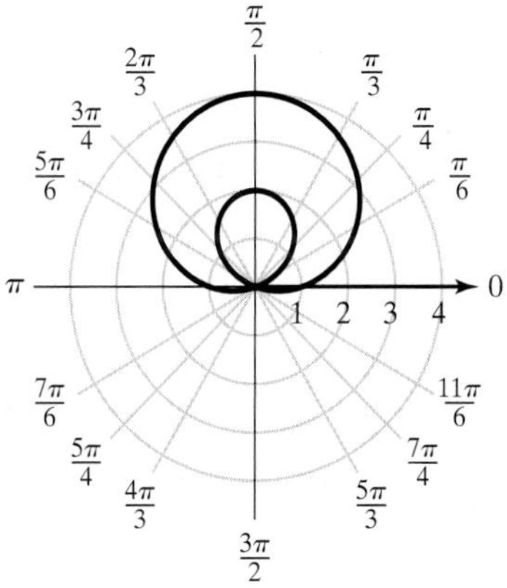


**55.**

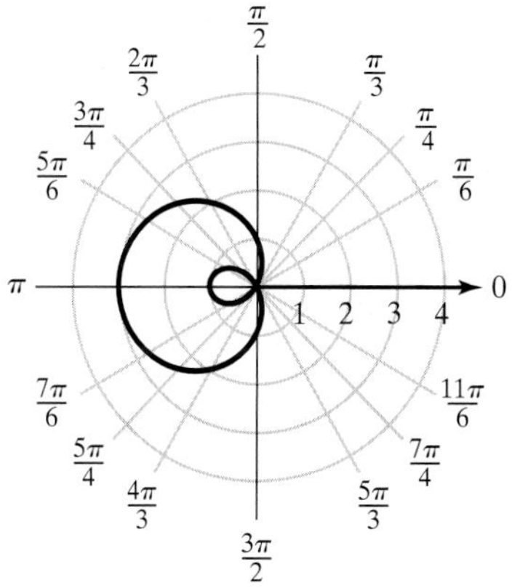


**56.**

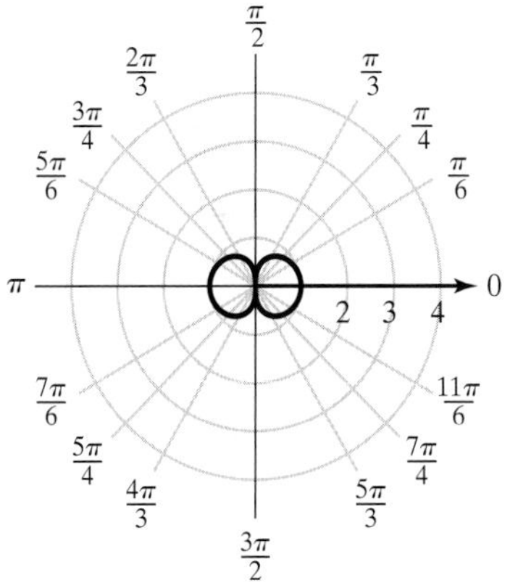


**57.**

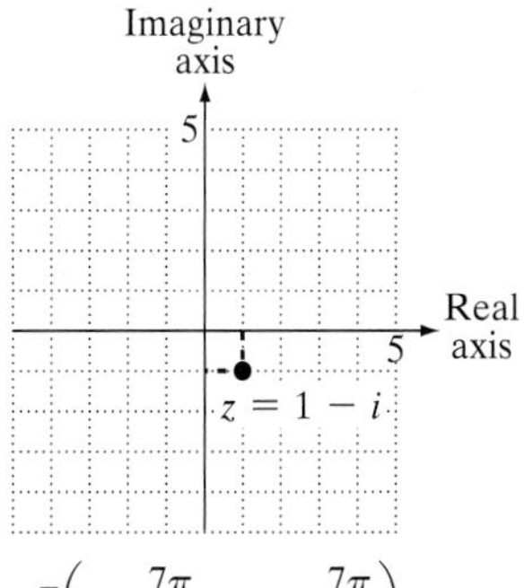


$\sqrt{2}\left(\cos\dfrac{7\pi}{4} + i\sin\dfrac{7\pi}{4}\right)$ or

$\sqrt{2}(\cos 315^\circ + i\sin 315^\circ)$

**58.**

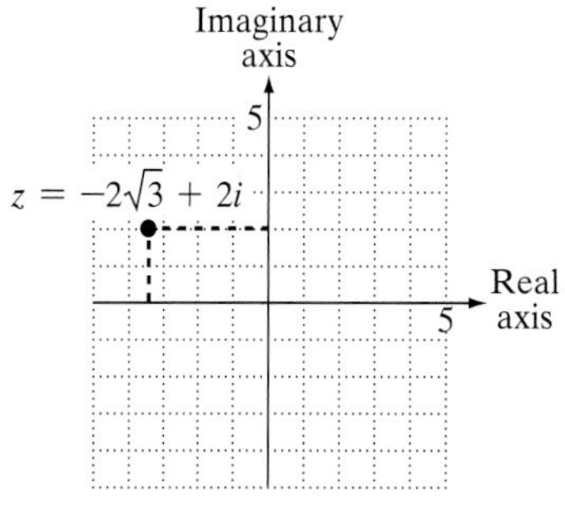


$4(\cos 150^\circ + i\sin 150^\circ)$ or

$4\left(\cos\dfrac{5\pi}{6} + i\sin\dfrac{5\pi}{6}\right)$

**59.**

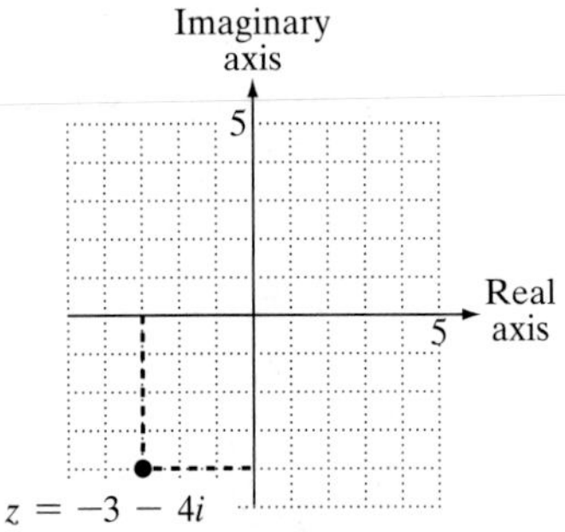


$\approx 5(\cos 233° + i \sin 233°)$

**60.**

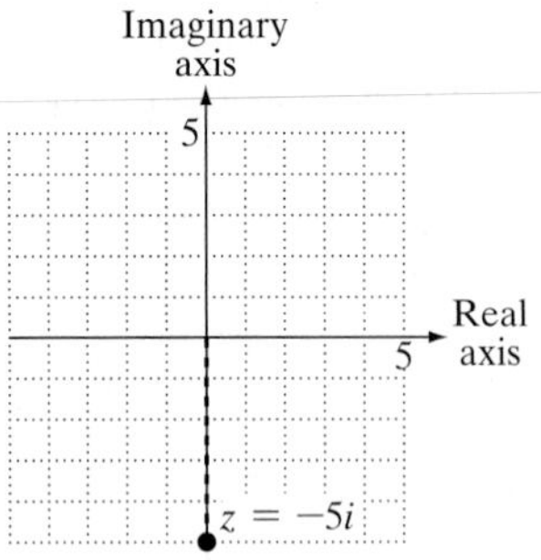


$5\left(\cos \frac{3\pi}{2} + i \sin \frac{3\pi}{2}\right)$ or $5(\cos 270° + i \sin 270°)$

**61.** $z = 4 + 4\sqrt{3}i$
**62.** $z = -2\sqrt{3} - 2i$
**63.** $z = -3 + 3\sqrt{3}i$
**64.** $z \approx -0.01 + 0.06i$
**65.** $15(\cos 110° + i \sin 110°)$
**66.** $\cos 265° + i \sin 265°$
**67.** $40(\cos \pi + i \sin \pi)$
**68.** $2(\cos 5° + i \sin 5°)$

**69.** $\frac{1}{2}(\cos \pi + i \sin \pi)$ **70.** $2\left(\cos \frac{7\pi}{6} + i \sin \frac{7\pi}{6}\right)$ **71.** $4 + 4\sqrt{3}i$ **72.** $-32\sqrt{3} + 32i$ **73.** $\frac{1}{128}i$ **74.** $64 - 64\sqrt{3}i$
**75.** $128 + 128i$ **76.** $7(\cos 25° + i \sin 25°); 7(\cos 205° + i \sin 205°)$ **77.** $5(\cos 55° + i \sin 55°); 5(\cos 175° + i \sin 175°); 5(\cos 295° + i \sin 295°)$ **78.** $\sqrt{3} + i; -1 + \sqrt{3}i; -\sqrt{3} - i; 1 - \sqrt{3}i$ **79.** $\sqrt{3} + i; -\sqrt{3} + i; -2i$ **80.** $\frac{1}{2} + \frac{\sqrt{3}}{2}i; -1; \frac{1}{2} - \frac{\sqrt{3}}{2}i$

**81.** $\frac{\sqrt[5]{8}}{2} + \frac{\sqrt[5]{8}}{2}i; \approx -0.49 + 0.95i; \approx -1.06 - 0.17i; \approx -0.17 - 1.06i; \approx 0.95 - 0.49i$

**82.**

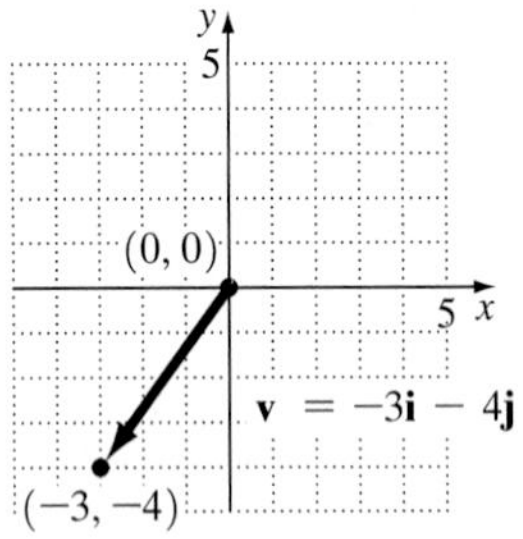


**83.**

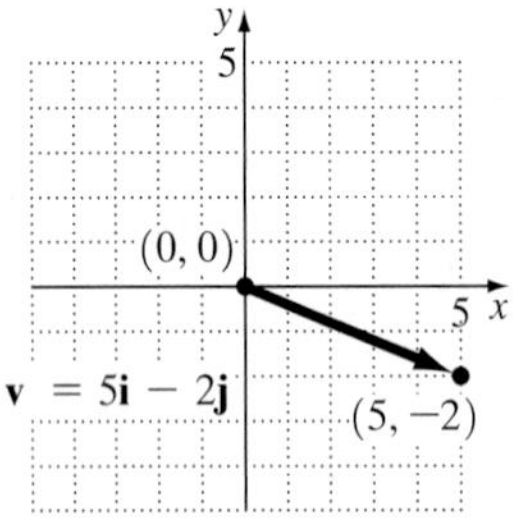


**84.**

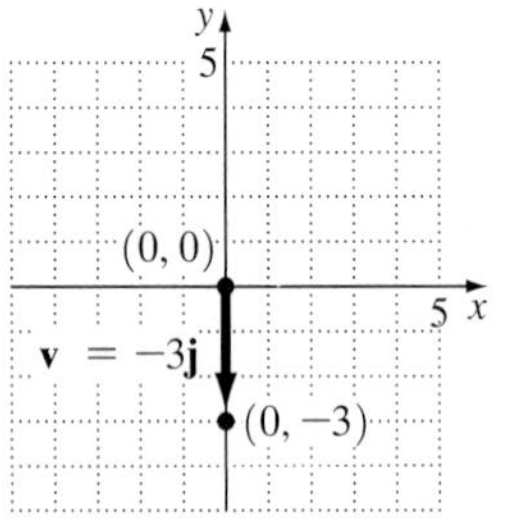


**85.** $3\mathbf{i} - 2\mathbf{j}$ **86.** $\mathbf{i} - 2\mathbf{j}$
**87.** $-\mathbf{i} + 2\mathbf{j}$ **88.** $-3\mathbf{i} + 12\mathbf{j}$
**89.** $12\mathbf{i} - 51\mathbf{j}$ **90.** $2\sqrt{26}$
**91.** $\frac{4}{5}\mathbf{i} - \frac{3}{5}\mathbf{j}$ **92.** $-\frac{1}{\sqrt{5}}\mathbf{i} + \frac{2}{\sqrt{5}}\mathbf{j}$
**93.** **a.** 265 lb
**b.** approximately 19° relative to the 200-lb force
**94.** 4 **95.** 2; 86.1°
**96.** −32; 124.8° **97.** 1; 71.6°

**98.** orthogonal **99.** not orthogonal **100.** $6\mathbf{i} + 6\sqrt{3}\mathbf{j}$ **101.** $\mathbf{v}_1 = \text{proj}_\mathbf{w}\,\mathbf{v} = \frac{50}{41}\mathbf{i} + \frac{40}{41}\mathbf{j}; \mathbf{v}_2 = -\frac{132}{41}\mathbf{i} + \frac{165}{41}\mathbf{j}$

**102.** $\mathbf{v}_1 = \text{proj}_\mathbf{w}\,\mathbf{v} = -\frac{3}{2}\mathbf{i} + \frac{1}{2}\mathbf{j}; \mathbf{v}_2 = \frac{1}{2}\mathbf{i} + \frac{3}{2}\mathbf{j}$ **103.** 1115 ft-lb

## Chapter 7 Test

**1.** 8.0 **2.** 6.2 **3.** 206 sq in.

**4.**

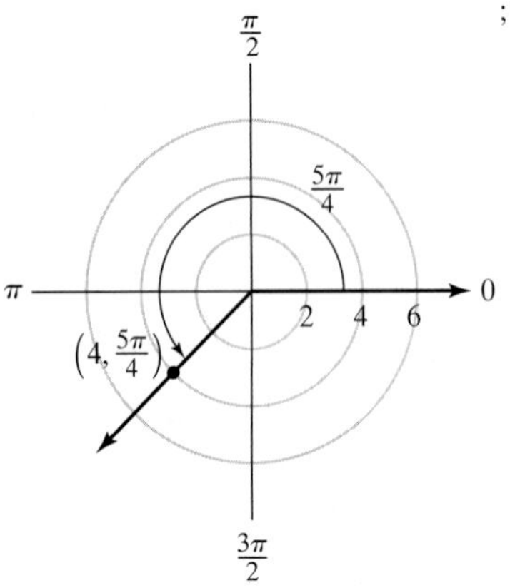


; Ordered pairs may vary.

**5.** $\left(\sqrt{2}, \frac{7\pi}{4}\right)$ **6.** $r = 6 \cos \theta$ **7.** $y = 4$

**8.**

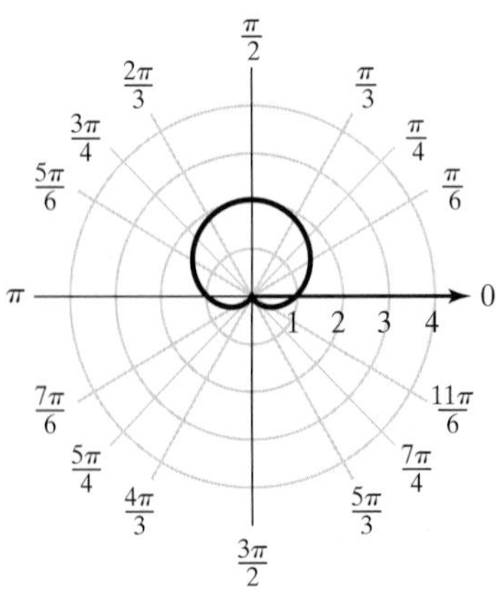

**9.**

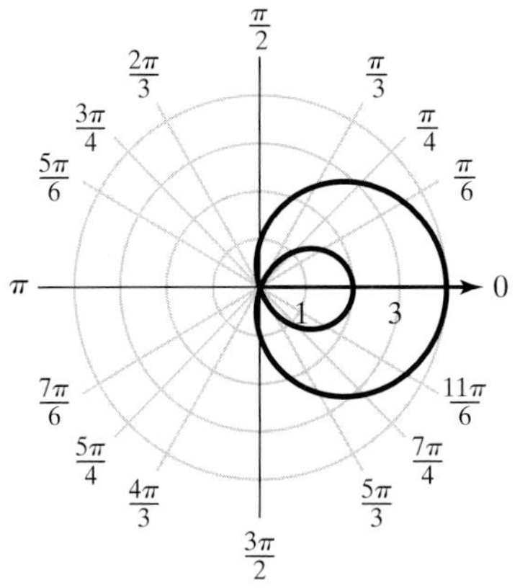


**10.** $2(\cos 150° + i \sin 150°)$ or $2\left(\cos \frac{5\pi}{6} + i \sin \frac{5\pi}{6}\right)$
**11.** $50(\cos 20° + i \sin 20°)$
**12.** $\frac{1}{2}\left(\cos \frac{\pi}{6} + i \sin \frac{\pi}{6}\right)$
**13.** $32(\cos 50° + i \sin 50°)$
**14.** $3; -\frac{3}{2} + \frac{3\sqrt{3}}{2}i; -\frac{3}{2} - \frac{3\sqrt{3}}{2}i$
**15. a.** $\mathbf{i} + 2\mathbf{j}$ **b.** $\sqrt{5}$
**16.** $-23\mathbf{i} + 22\mathbf{j}$ **17.** $-18$ **18.** $138°$
**19.** $-\frac{9}{5}\mathbf{i} + \frac{18}{5}\mathbf{j}$
**20.** 1.0 mi **21.** 1966 ft-lb

## Cumulative Review Exercises (Chapters 1–7)

**1.** $\{-1, 2, i, -i\}$ **2.** $\frac{\pi}{6}, \frac{5\pi}{6}$, and $\frac{\pi}{2}$ **3.** $\{x|x < -4 \text{ or } x > 2\}$ **4.** $\frac{3\pi}{4}, \frac{7\pi}{4}$

**5.**

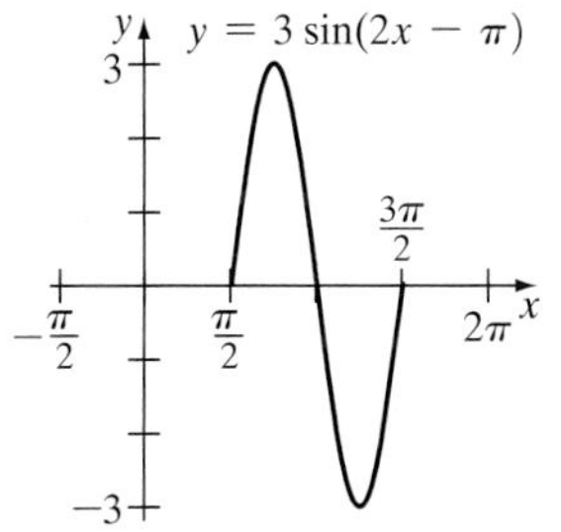


**6.**

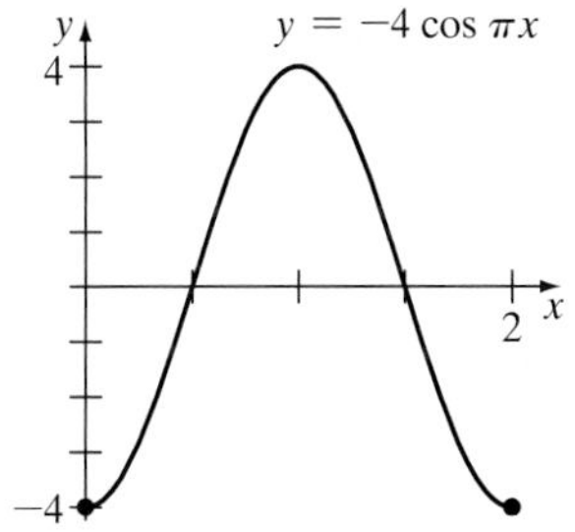


**7.** $\sin\theta \csc\theta - \cos^2\theta = \sin\theta\left(\frac{1}{\sin\theta}\right) - \cos^2\theta$
$= 1 - \cos^2\theta = \sin^2\theta$

**8.** $\cos\left(\theta + \frac{3\pi}{2}\right) = \cos\theta \cos\frac{3\pi}{2} - \sin\theta \sin\frac{3\pi}{2}$
$= \cos\theta(0) - \sin\theta(-1) = \sin\theta$

**9.** slope is $-\frac{1}{2}$; $y$-intercept is 2

**10.** 0 **11.** $\frac{\sqrt{5}}{5}$ **12.** $\{x|x \le 5\}$

**13.** $\{x|x \ne 3, x \ne -3\}$ **14.** 1.5 sec; 44 ft **15. a.** 4 m **b.** $\frac{5}{2\pi}$ **c.** $\frac{2\pi}{5}$ sec **16.** $\frac{\sqrt{\sqrt{2} + 2}}{2}$ **17. a.** $5\mathbf{i} + 23\mathbf{j}$ **b.** $-12$

**18.** $\log_b \frac{\sqrt{x}}{x^2 + 1}$ **19.** $y = -\frac{1}{2}x + 1$ **20. a.** 0.014 **b.** 73 words **c.** about 144 min

# CHAPTER 8

## Section 8.1

### Check Point Exercises

**1.** solution **2.** $\{(3, 2)\}$ **3.** $\{(1, -2)\}$ **4.** $\{(2, -1)\}$ **5.** $\left\{\left(\frac{23}{16}, \frac{3}{8}\right)\right\}$ **6.** $\varnothing$ **7.** $\{(x, y)|y = 4x - 4\}$ **8.** \$30; 400 units

### Exercise Set 8.1

**1.** solution **3.** not a solution **5.** $\{(1, 3)\}$ **7.** $\{(5, 1)\}$ **9.** $\{(2, 1)\}$ **11.** $\{(-1, 3)\}$ **13.** $\{(4, 5)\}$
**15.** $\left\{\left(-4, \frac{5}{4}\right)\right\}$ **17.** $\{(2, -1)\}$ **19.** $\{(3, 0)\}$ **21.** $\{(-4, 3)\}$ **23.** $\{(3, 1)\}$ **25.** $\{(1, -2)\}$ **27.** $\left\{\left(\frac{7}{25}, -\frac{1}{25}\right)\right\}$ **29.** $\varnothing$
**31.** $\{(x, y)|y = 3x - 5\}$ **33.** $\{(1, 4)\}$ **35.** $\{(x, y)|x + 3y = 2\}$ **37.** $x + y = 7; x - y = -1$; 3 and 4 **39.** $3x - y = 1$; $x + 2y = 12$; 2 and 5 **41. a.** 6500 tickets can be sold. 6200 tickets can be supplied. **b.** \$50; 6250 tickets **43.** 2700 gal
**45.** Quarter Pounder: 77 mg; Whopper with cheese: 122 mg **47.** 5.8 million pounds of potato chips; 4.6 million pounds of tortilla chips
**49.** 2032; less than 1 death in 1000 live births **63.** $y = \frac{a_1c_2 - a_2c_1}{a_1b_2 - a_2b_1}; x = \frac{b_2c_1 - b_1c_2}{a_1b_2 - a_2b_1}$ **65.** Yes; 8 hexagons and 4 squares

## Section 8.2

### Check Point Exercises

**2.** $\{(1, 4, -3)\}$ **3.** $\{(4, 5, 3)\}$ **4.** $y = 3x^2 - 12x + 13$

### Exercise Set 8.2

**1.** not a solution **3.** solution **5.** $\{(2, 3, 3)\}$ **7.** $\{(2, -1, 1)\}$ **9.** $\left\{\left(\frac{1}{3}, -\frac{2}{5}, \frac{1}{2}\right)\right\}$ **11.** $\{(3, 1, 5)\}$ **13.** $\{(1, 0, -3)\}$
**15.** $\{(1, -5, -6)\}$ **17.** $\left\{\left(\frac{1}{2}, \frac{1}{3}, -1\right)\right\}$ **19.** 7, 4 and 5 **21.** $y = 2x^2 - x + 3$ **23.** $y = 2x^2 + x - 5$
**25.** chemical engineer: \$42,758; mechanical engineer: \$39,852; electrical engineer: \$38, 811 **27.** $A = -8$; $B = 50$; $C = 0$; $y = 156$ when $x = 6$; When a car is in motion for 6 seconds after the brakes are applied, it travels 156 feet. **29.** 200 \$8 tickets; 150 \$10 tickets; 50 \$12 tickets
**31.** \$1200 at 8%, \$2000 at 10%, and \$3500 at 12% **41.** 13 triangles, 21 rectangles, and 6 pentagons

## Section 8.3

### Check Point Exercises

**1.** $\frac{2}{x-3} + \frac{3}{x+4}$ **2.** $\frac{2}{x} - \frac{2}{x-1} + \frac{3}{(x-1)^2}$ **3.** $\frac{2}{x+3} + \frac{6x-8}{x^2+x+2}$ **4.** $\frac{2x}{x^2+1} + \frac{-x+3}{(x^2+1)^2}$

### Exercise Set 8.3

**1.** $\frac{A}{x-2} + \frac{B}{x+1}$ **3.** $\frac{A}{x+2} + \frac{B}{x-3} + \frac{C}{(x-3)^2}$ **5.** $\frac{A}{x-1} + \frac{Bx+C}{x^2+1}$ **7.** $\frac{Ax+B}{x^2+4} + \frac{Cx+D}{(x^2+4)^2}$ **9.** $\frac{3}{x-3} - \frac{2}{x-2}$
**11.** $\frac{7}{x-9} - \frac{4}{x+2}$ **13.** $\frac{24}{7(x-4)} + \frac{25}{7(x+3)}$ **15.** $\frac{3}{x} + \frac{2}{x-1} - \frac{1}{x+3}$ **17.** $\frac{3}{x} + \frac{4}{x+1} - \frac{3}{x-1}$ **19.** $\frac{6}{x-1} - \frac{5}{(x-1)^2}$
**21.** $\frac{1}{x-2} - \frac{2}{(x-2)^2} - \frac{5}{(x-2)^3}$ **23.** $\frac{7}{x} - \frac{6}{x-1} + \frac{10}{(x-1)^2}$ **25.** $-\frac{2}{x+1} + \frac{3}{(x+1)^2} + \frac{7}{x-3}$ **27.** $\frac{3}{x-1} + \frac{2x-4}{x^2+1}$
**29.** $\frac{2}{x+1} + \frac{3x-1}{x^2+2x+2}$ **31.** $\frac{4}{x+1} + \frac{2x-3}{x^2+1}$ **33.** $\frac{x+1}{x^2+2} - \frac{2x}{(x^2+2)^2}$ **35.** $\frac{x-2}{x^2-2x+3} + \frac{2x+1}{(x^2-2x+3)^2}$
**37.** $\frac{3}{x-2} + \frac{x-1}{x^2+2x+4}$ **39.** $\frac{1}{x} - \frac{1}{x+1}; \frac{99}{100}$ **49.** $\frac{a}{x-c} + \frac{b+ac}{(x-c)^2}$

## Section 8.4

### Check Point Exercises

**1.** $\{(0, 1), (4, 17)\}$ **2.** $\left\{\left(-\frac{6}{5}, \frac{3}{5}\right), (2, -1)\right\}$ **3.** $\{(3, 2), (3, -2), (-3, 2), (-3, -2)\}$ **4.** $\{(0, 5)\}$
**5.** length: 7 ft; width: 3 ft or length: 3 ft; width: 7 ft

### Exercise Set 8.4

**1.** $\{(-3, 5), (2, 0)\}$ **3.** $\left\{\left(\frac{-1+\sqrt{17}}{2}, \frac{1+\sqrt{17}}{2}\right), \left(\frac{-1-\sqrt{17}}{2}, \frac{1-\sqrt{17}}{2}\right)\right\}$ **5.** $\{(4, -10), (-3, 11)\}$ **7.** $\{(4, 3), (-3, -4)\}$
**9.** $\left\{\left(-\frac{3}{2}, -4\right), (2, 3)\right\}$ **11.** $\{(-5, -4), (3, 0)\}$ **13.** $\{(3, 1), (-3, -1), (1, 3), (-1, -3)\}$ **15.** $\{(4, -3), (-1, 2)\}$
**17.** $\{(0, 1), (4, -3)\}$ **19.** $\{(3, 2), (3, -2), (-3, 2), (-3, -2)\}$ **21.** $\{(3, 2), (3, -2), (-3, 2) (-3, -2)\}$
**23.** $\{(2, 1), (2, -1), (-2, 1), (-2, -1)\}$ **25.** $\{(3, 4), (3, -4)\}$ **27.** $\{(0, 2), (0, -2), (-1, \sqrt{3}), (-1, -\sqrt{3})\}$
**29.** $\{(2, 1), (2, -1), (-2, 1), (-2, -1)\}$ **31.** $\{(-2\sqrt{2}, -\sqrt{2}), (-1, -4), (1, 4), (2\sqrt{2}, \sqrt{2})\}$ **33.** $\{(2, 2), (4, 1)\}$ **35.** $\{(0, 0), (-1, 1)\}$
**37.** $\{(0, 0), (-2, 2), (2, 2)\}$ **39.** $\left\{(-4, 1), \left(-\frac{5}{2}, \frac{1}{4}\right)\right\}$ **41.** $\left\{\left(\frac{12}{5}, -\frac{29}{5}\right), (-2, 3)\right\}$ **43.** 4 and 6
**45.** 2 and 1, 2 and −1, −2 and 1, or −2 and −1 **47.** $(0, -4), (-2, 0), (2, 0)$ **49.** 11 ft and 7 ft **51.** width: 6 in.; length: 8 in.
**53.** $x = 5$ m, $y = 2$ m **61.** (b) is true. **63.** $b = 6, a = 8$ **65.** $\{(10{,}000, 5)\}$

## Section 8.5

### Check Point Exercises

**1.**

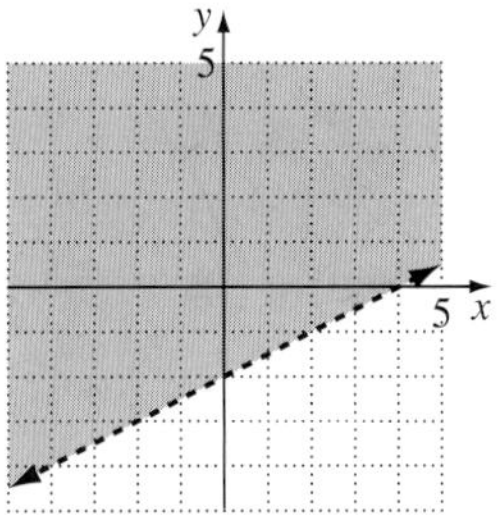


**2.**

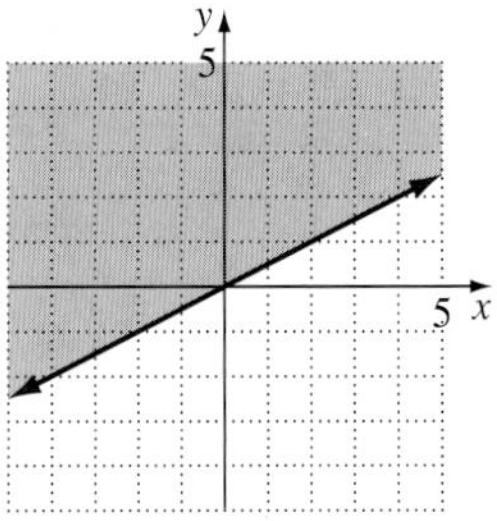


**3.**

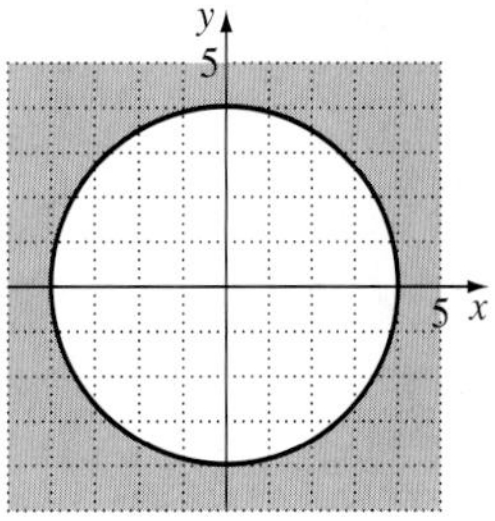


**4.**

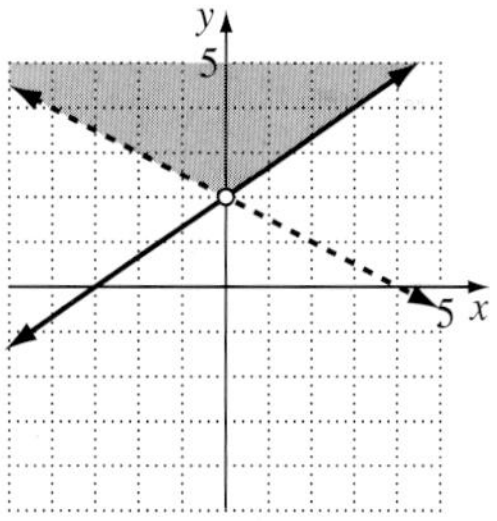


**5.**

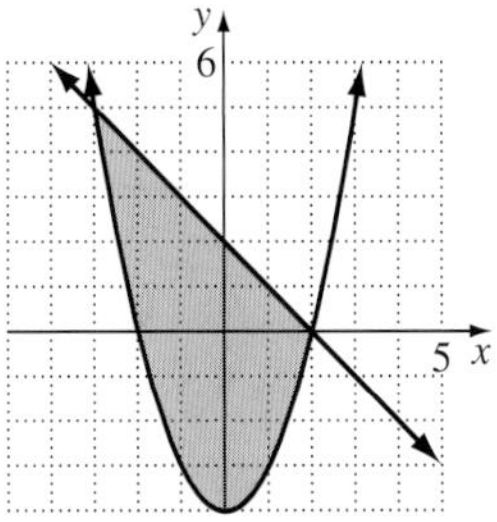


**6.**

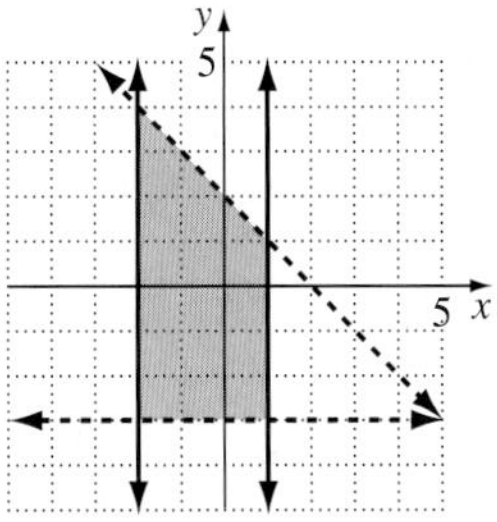


### Exercise Set 8.5

**1.**

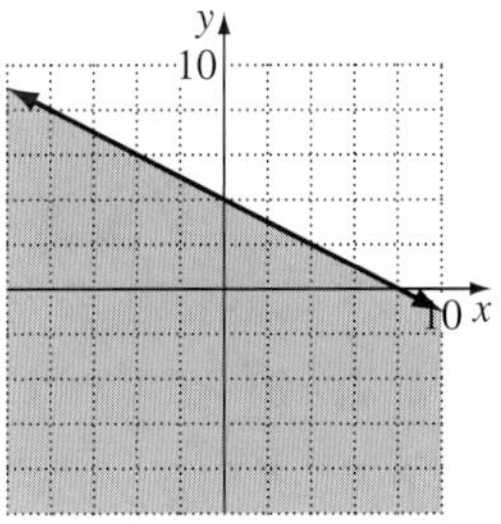


**3.**

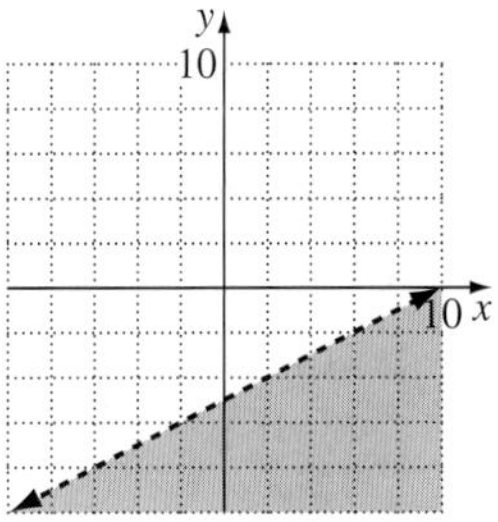


**5.**

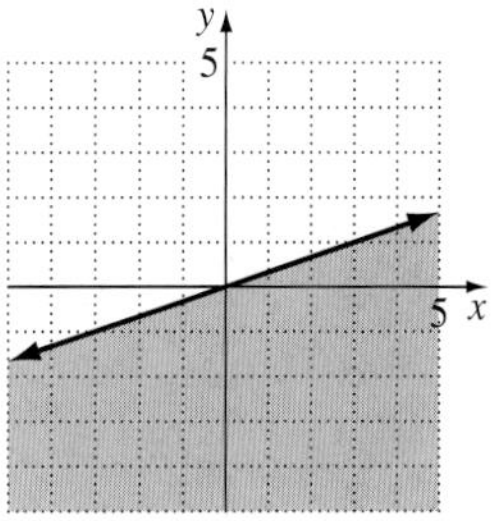


**7.**

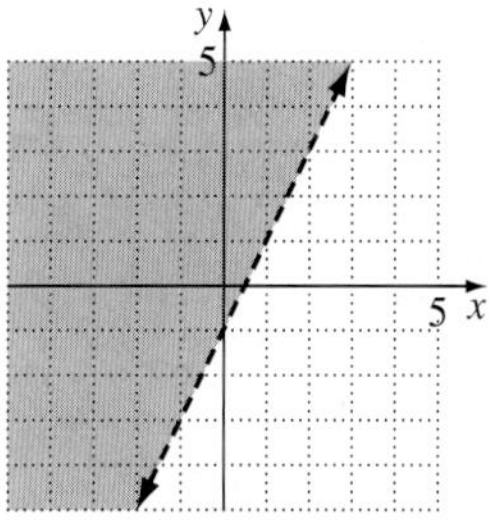


**9.**

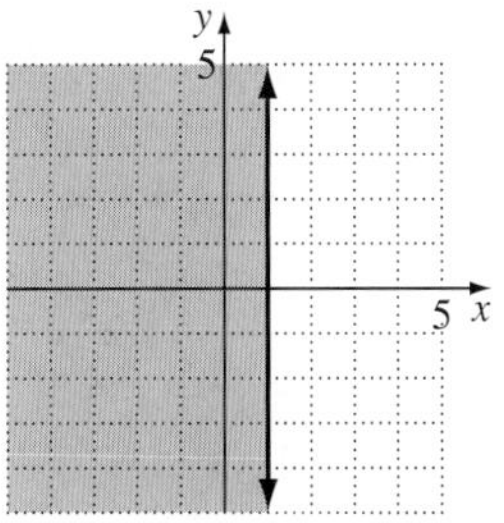


**11.**

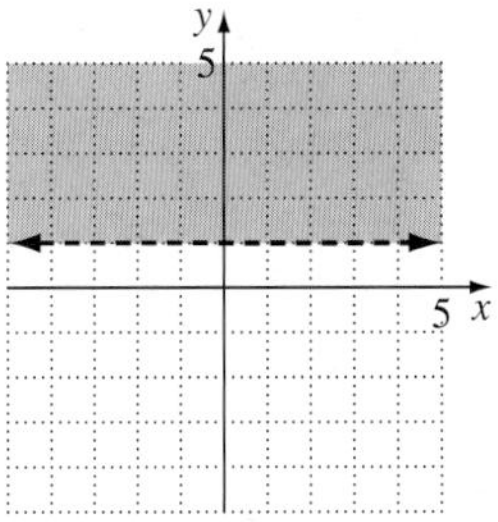


**13.**

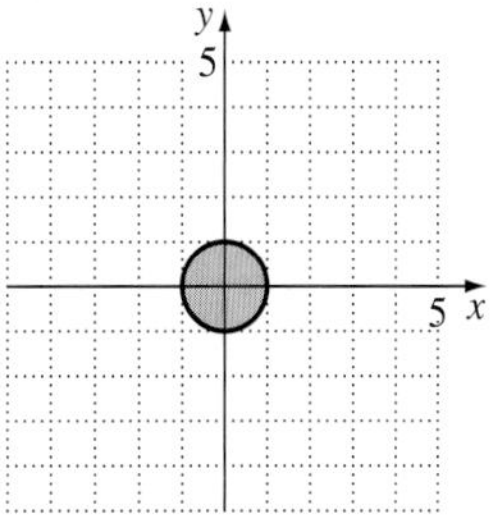


**15.**

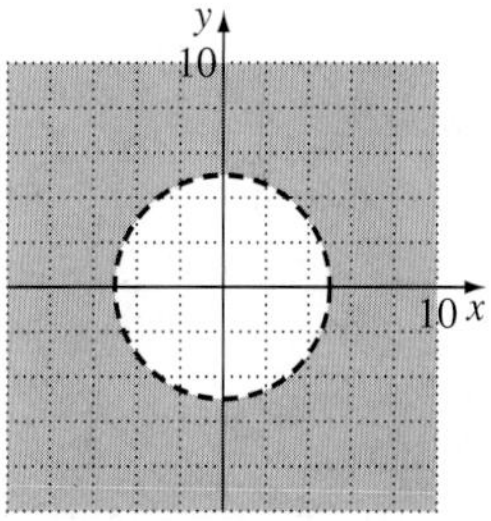


**17.**

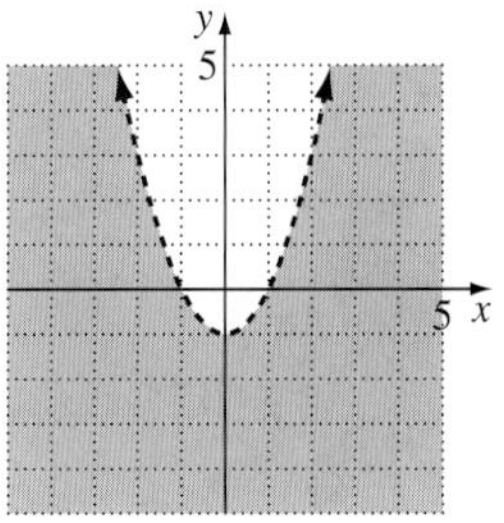


**19.**

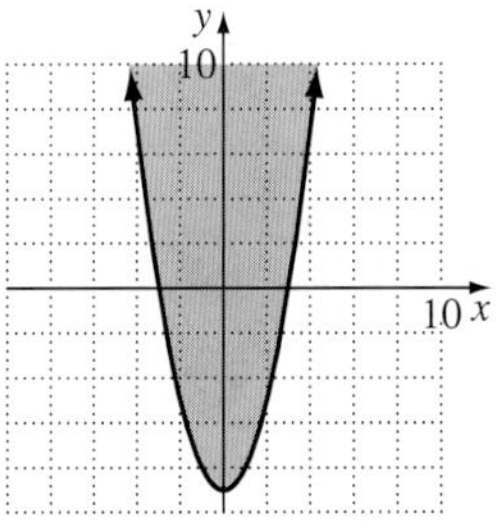


**21.**

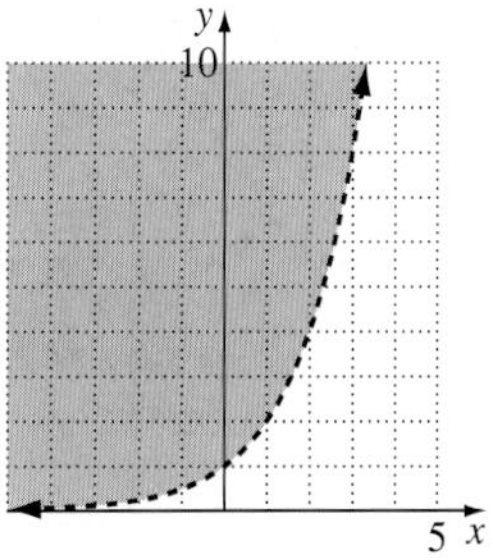


**23.**

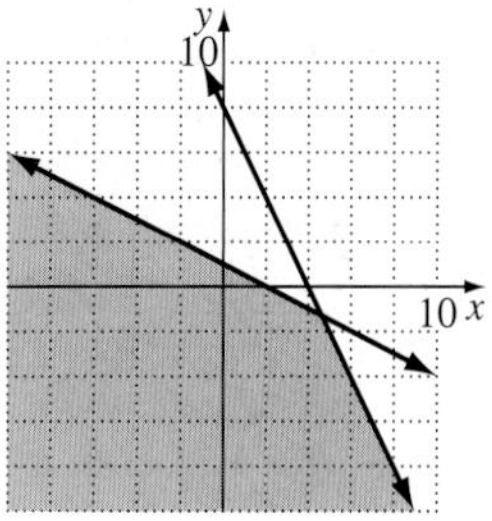

**25.**

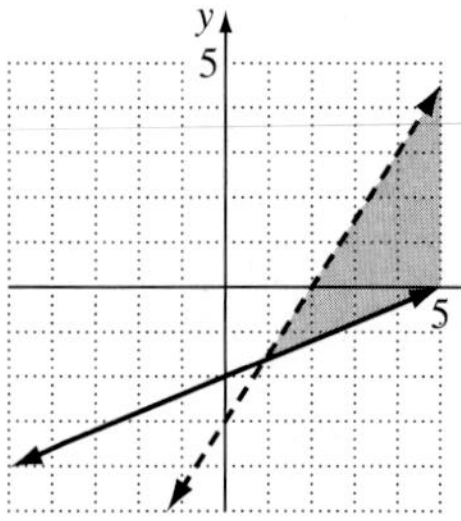


**27.**

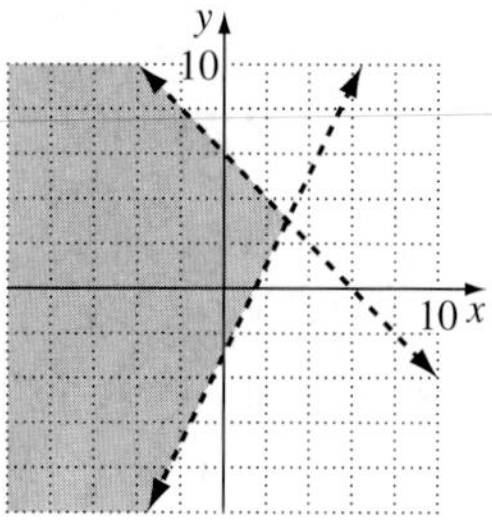


**29.**

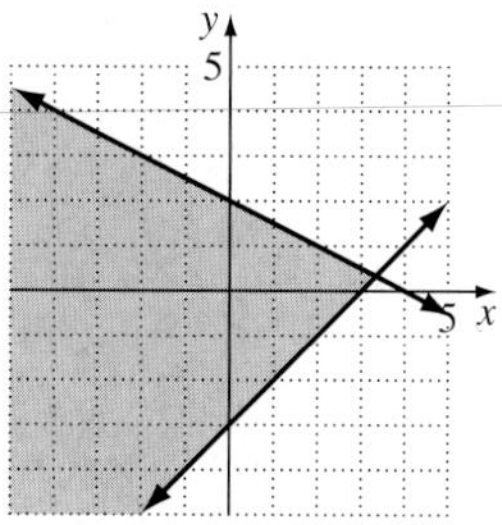


**31.**

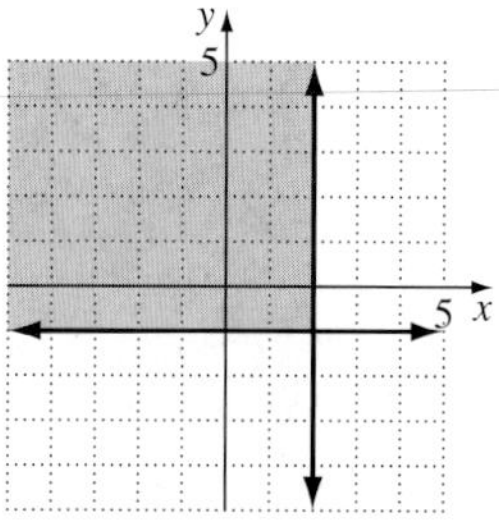


**33.**

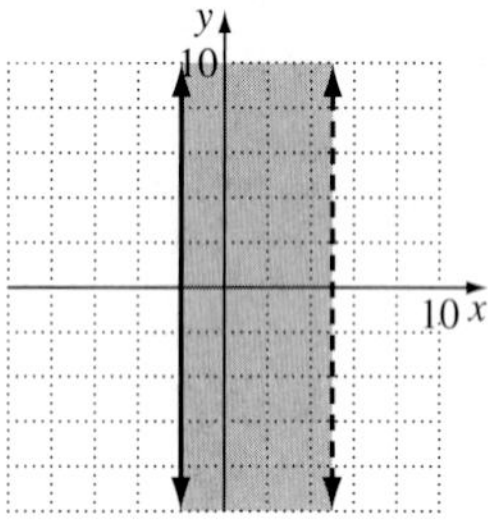


**35.**

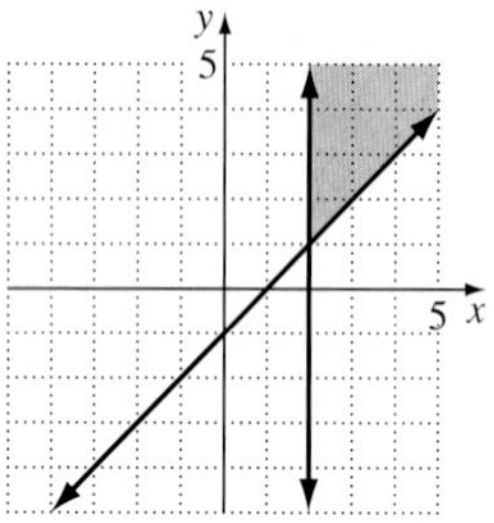


**37.** no solution

**39.**

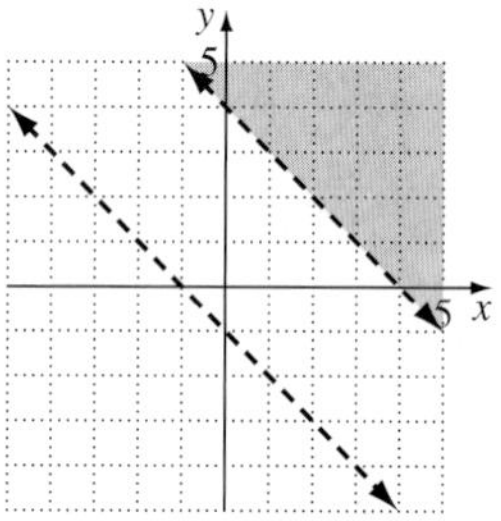


**41.**

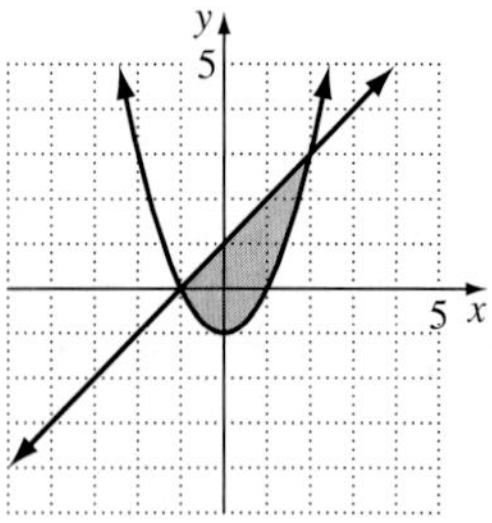


**43.**

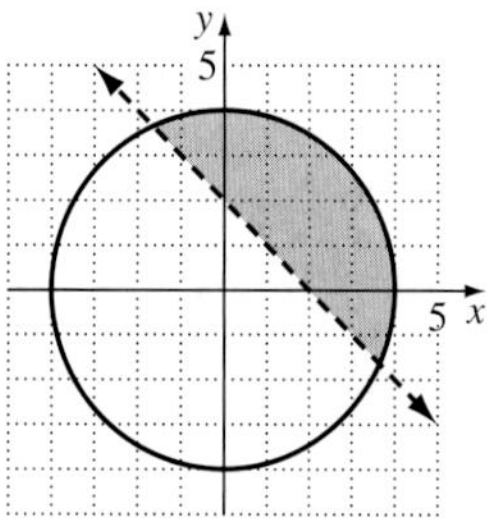


**45.**

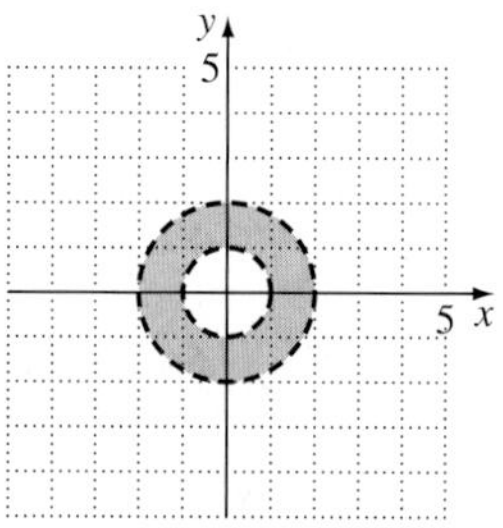


**47.**

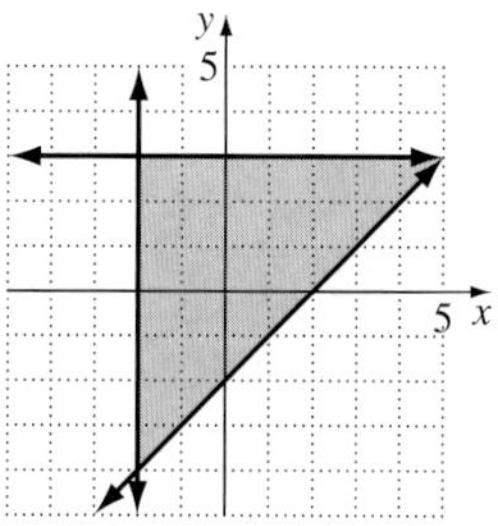


**49.**

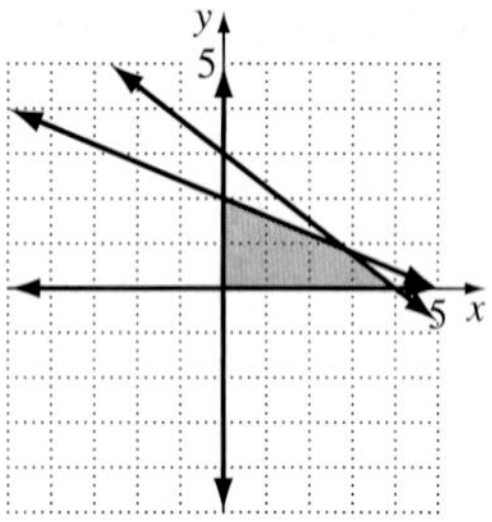


**51.**

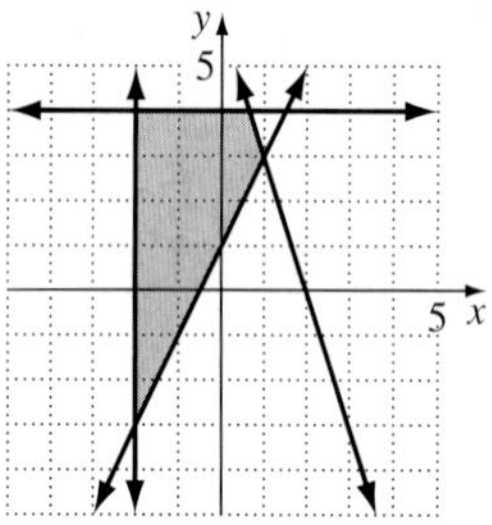


**52.**

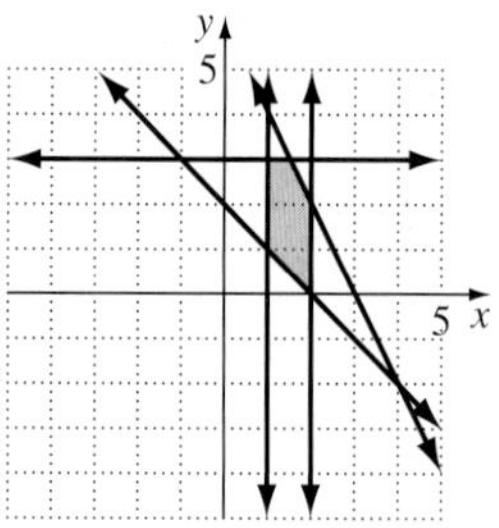


**53.** Answers may vary. **55.** no **57.** $7w - 25h \geq -800$; $w - 5h \leq -170$ **59.** $5T - 7P \leq 70$

**61.** $50x + 150y > 2000$

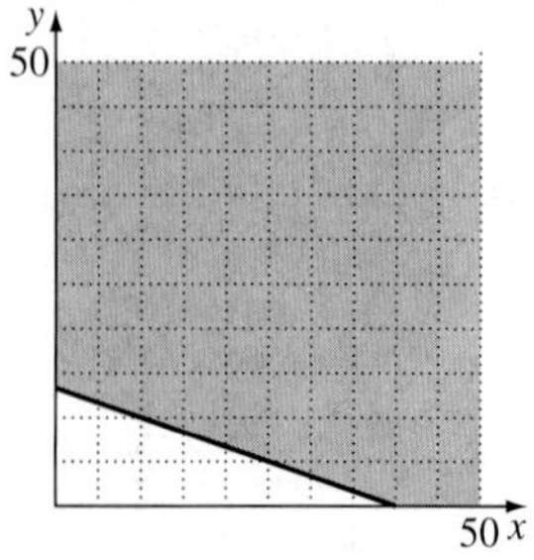


**63.** $x + y \leq 15,000$
$x \geq 2000$
$y \geq 3x$
$x \geq 0$
$y \geq 0$

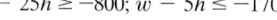

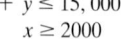

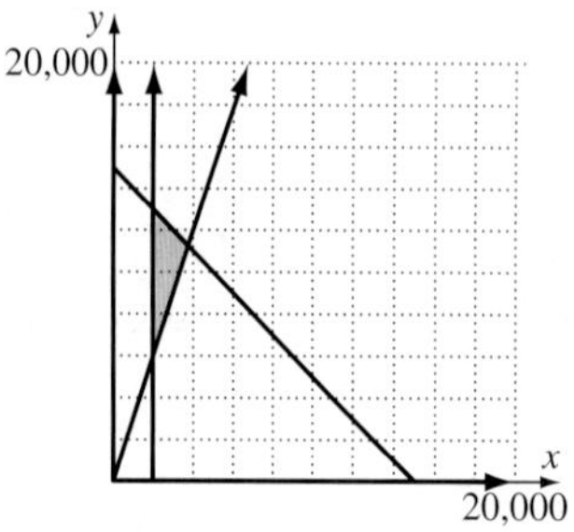


**71.**

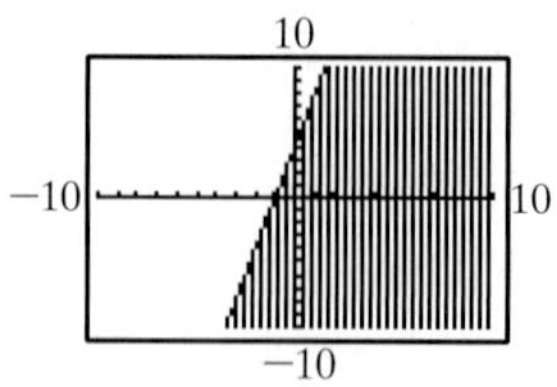


**73.**

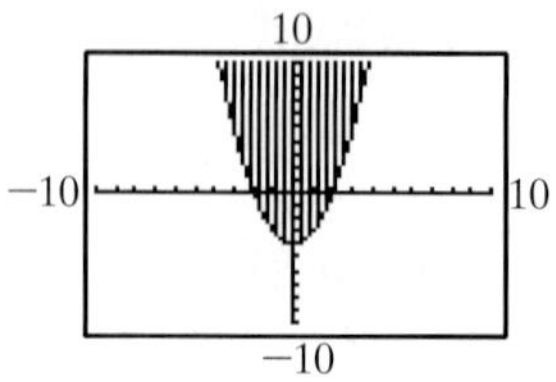

**75.** Answers may vary. **79.** $x^2 + y^2 \leq 9; y < x^2$ **81.**

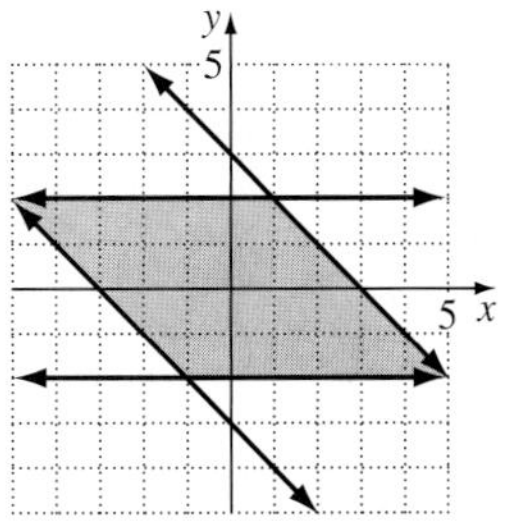


## Section 8.6

### Check Point Exercises

**1.** $z = 25x + 55y$ **2.** $x + y \leq 80$ **3.** $30 \leq x \leq 80; 10 \leq y \leq 30$; objective function: $z = 25x + 55y$; constraints: $x + y \leq 80$; $30 \leq x \leq 80; 10 \leq y \leq 30$ **4.** 50 bookshelves and 30 desks; \$2900 **5.** 30

### Exercise Set 8.6

**1.** (1, 2): 17; (2, 10): 70; (7, 5): 65; (8, 3): 58; maximum: $z = 70$; minimum: $z = 17$
**3.** (0, 0): 0; (0, 8): 400; (4, 9): 610; (8, 0): 320; maximum: $z = 610$; minimum: $z = 0$

**5. a.**

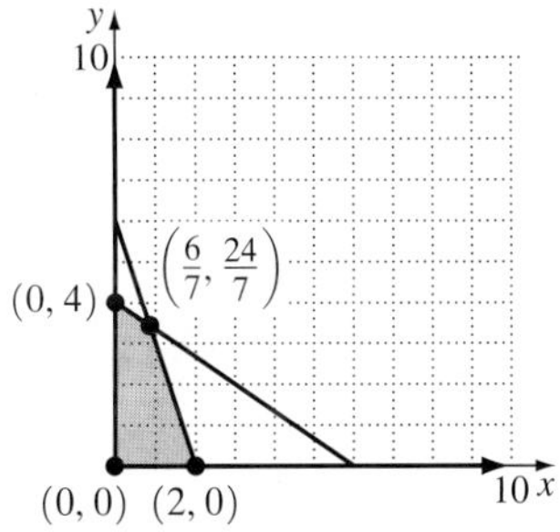


**b.** (0, 0): 0; (0, 4): 12; $\left(\frac{6}{7}, \frac{24}{7}\right)$: 12; (2, 0): 4
**c.** maximum value: 12 at $x = 0$ and $y = 4$ and at $x = \frac{6}{7}$ and $y = \frac{24}{7}$

**7. a.**

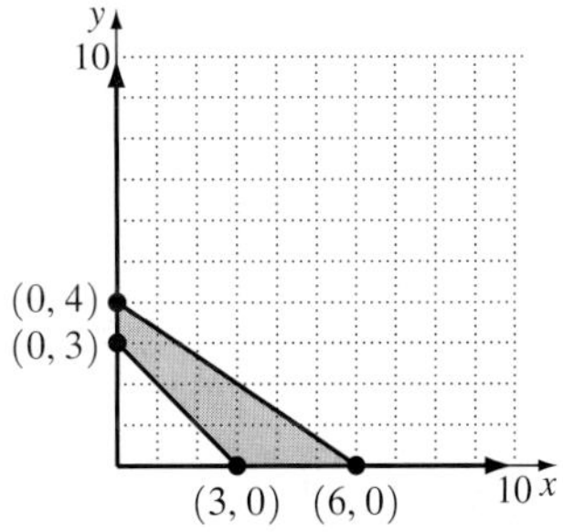


**b.** (0, 4): 4; (0, 3): 3; (3, 0): 12; (6, 0): 24
**c.** maximum value: 24 at $x = 6$ and $y = 0$

**9. a.**

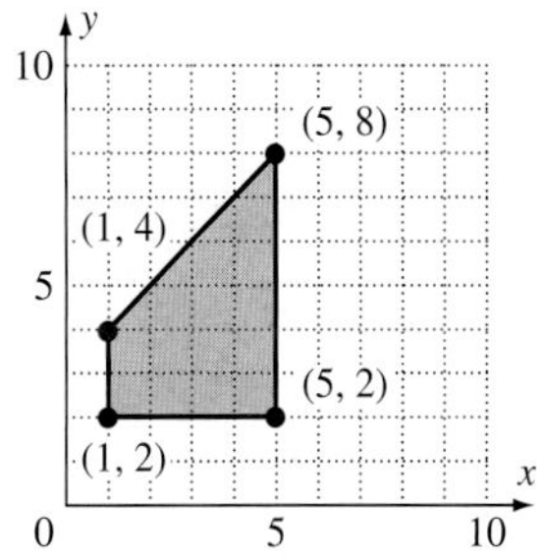


**b.** (1, 2): −1; (1, 4): −5; (5, 8): −1; (5, 2): 11
**c.** maximum value: 11 at $x = 5$ and $y = 2$

**11. a.**

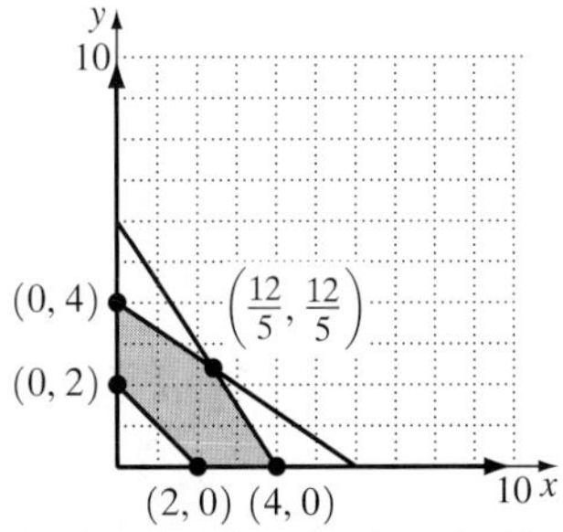


**b.** (0, 4): 8; (0, 2): 4; (2, 0): 8; (4, 0): 16; $\left(\frac{12}{5}, \frac{12}{5}\right)$: $\frac{72}{5}$
**c.** maximum value: 16 at $x = 4$ and $y = 0$

**13. a.**

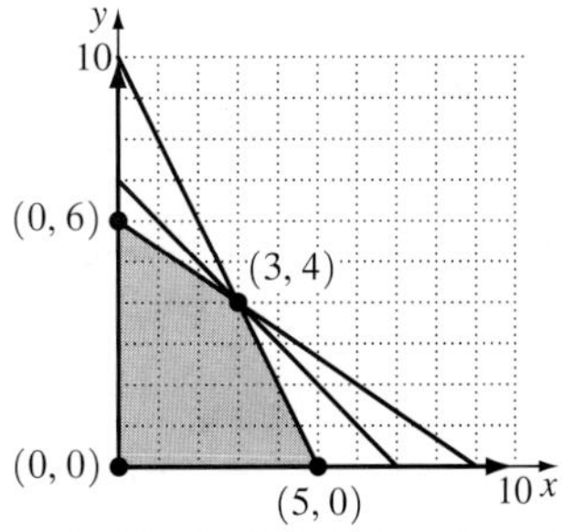


**b.** (0, 6): 72, (0, 0): 0; (5, 0): 50; (3, 4): 78
**c.** maximum value: 78 at $x = 3$ and $y = 4$

**15. a.** $z = 125x + 200y$
**b.** $x \leq 450$; $y \leq 200$; $600x + 900y \leq 360{,}000$
**c.**

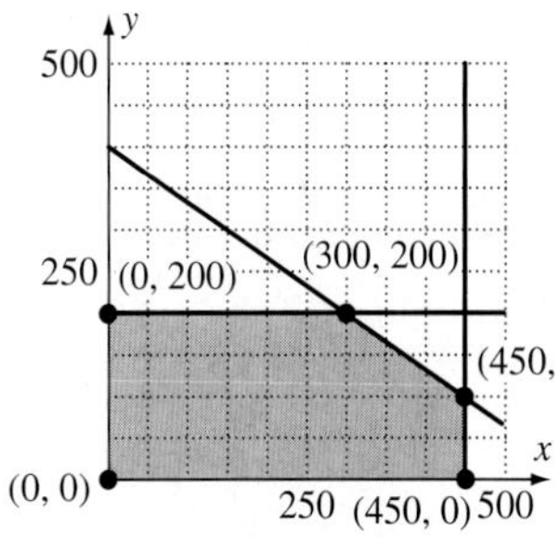


**d.** (0, 0): 0; (0, 200): 40,000; (300, 200): 77,500; (450, 100): 76,250; (450, 0): 56,250
**e.** 300; 200; \$77,500

**17.** 40 model $A$ bicycles and no model $B$ bicycles **19.** No cartons of food and 600 cartons of clothing; 3600 people
**21.** 50 students and 100 parents **23.** 10 Boeing 727s and 42 Falcon 20s

**29.**

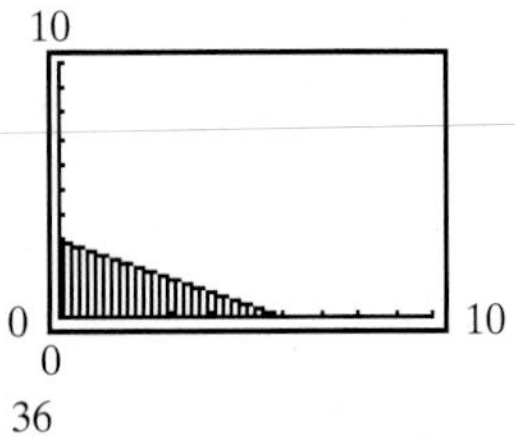


**31.**

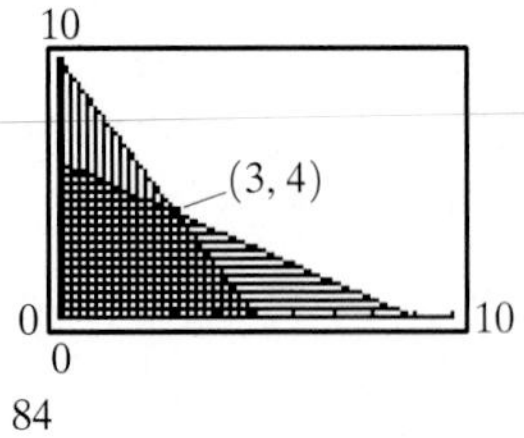


**33.** \$5000 in stocks and \$5000 in bonds

## Chapter 8 Review Exercises

**1.** $\{(1, 5)\}$ **2.** $\{(2, 3)\}$ **3.** $\{(2, -3)\}$ **4.** $\varnothing$ **5.** $\{(x, y) | 3x - 6y = 12\}$ **6.** No, $(-1, 3)$ is not a solution to $2x + y = -5$. **7.** Shrimp: 42 mg of cholesterol per oz; Scallops: 15 mg of cholesterol per oz **8.** 3 apples and 2 avocados **9.** 250 copies can be supplied and sold for \$12.50 each. **10.** $\{(0, 1, 2)\}$ **11.** $\{(2, 1, -1)\}$ **12.** $y = 3x^2 - 4x + 5$ **13.** Japan: 16%; Germany: 15%; France: 14% **14.** Substitute the ordered pairs into $y = ax^2 + bx + c$, solve the resulting system for $a, b,$ and $c$, then substitute these values into the equation to form a quadratic model. **15.** $\frac{3}{5(x-3)} + \frac{2}{5(x+2)}$ **16.** $\frac{6}{x-4} + \frac{5}{x+3}$ **17.** $\frac{2}{x} + \frac{3}{x+2} - \frac{1}{x-1}$ **18.** $\frac{2}{x-2} + \frac{5}{(x-2)^2}$ **19.** $-\frac{4}{x-1} + \frac{4}{x-2} - \frac{2}{(x-2)^2}$ **20.** $\frac{6}{5(x-2)} + \frac{-6x+3}{5(x^2+1)}$ **21.** $\frac{5}{x-3} + \frac{2x-1}{x^2+4}$ **22.** $\frac{x}{x^2+4} - \frac{4x}{(x^2+4)^2}$ **23.** $\frac{4x+1}{x^2+x+1} + \frac{2x-2}{(x^2+x+1)^2}$ **24.** $\{(4, 3), (1, 0)\}$ **25.** $\{(0, 1), (-3, 4)\}$ **26.** $\{(1, -1), (-1, 1)\}$ **27.** $\{(3, \sqrt{6}), (3, -\sqrt{6}), (-3, \sqrt{6}), (-3, -\sqrt{6})\}$ **28.** $\{(2, 2), (-2, -2)\}$ **29.** $\{(9, 6), (1, 2)\}$ **30.** $\{(-3, -1), (1, 3)\}$ **31.** $\left\{\left(\frac{1}{2}, 2\right), (-1, -1)\right\}$ **32.** $\left\{\left(\frac{5}{2}, -\frac{7}{2}\right), (0, -1)\right\}$ **33.** $\{(2, -3), (-2, -3), (3, 2), (-3, 2)\}$ **34.** $\{(3, 1), (3, -1), (-3, 1), (-3, -1)\}$ **35.** 8 m and 5 m **36.** (1, 6), (3, 2) **37.** $x = 46$ and $y = 28$ or $x = 50$ and $y = 20$

**38.**

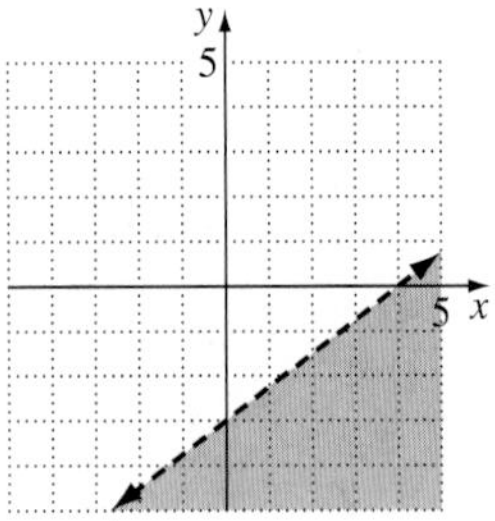


**39.**

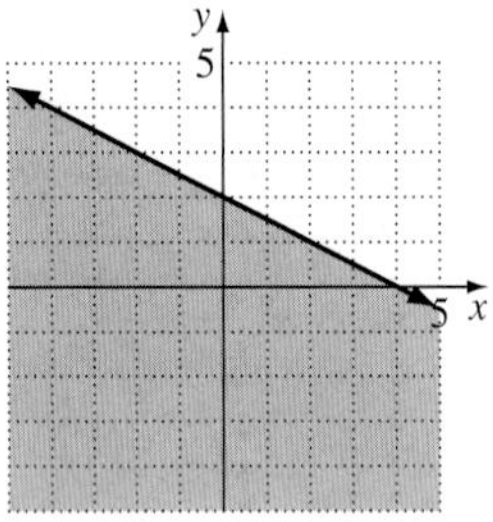


**40.**

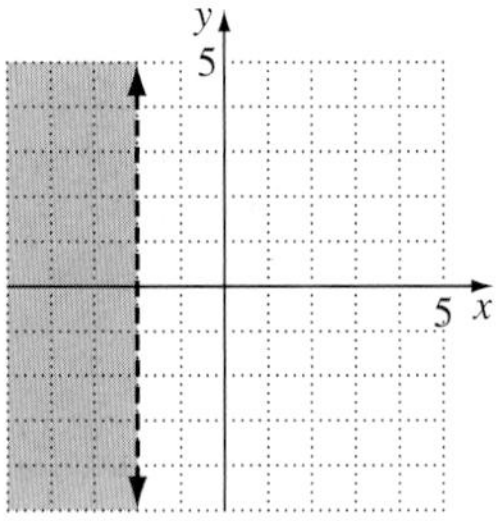


**41.**

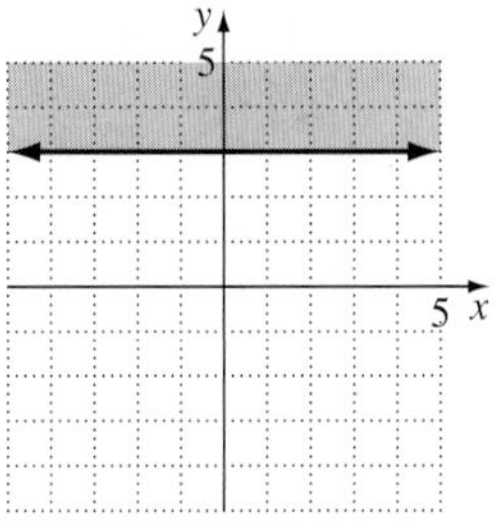


**42.**

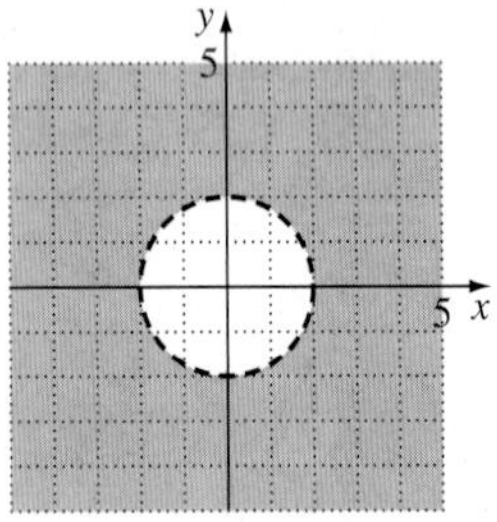


**43.**

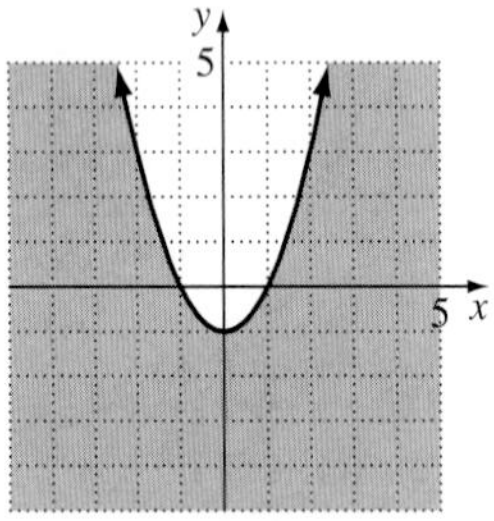


**44.**

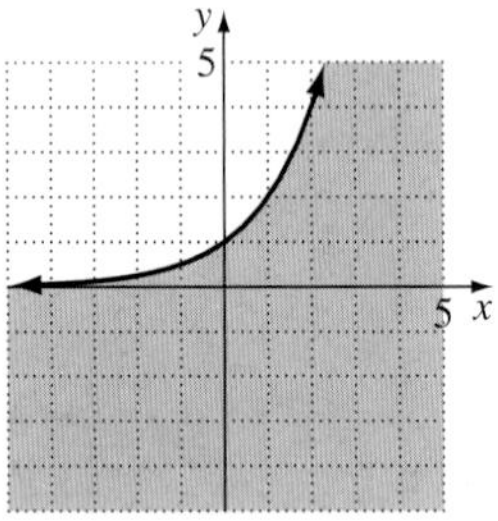


**45.**

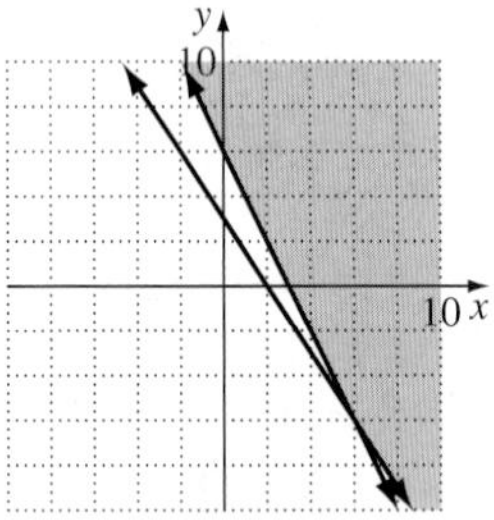


**46.**

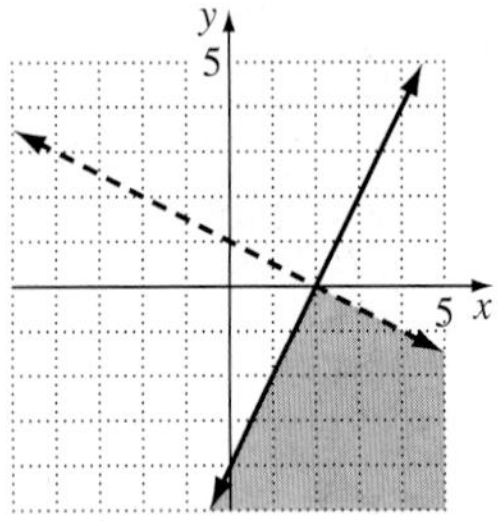


**47.**

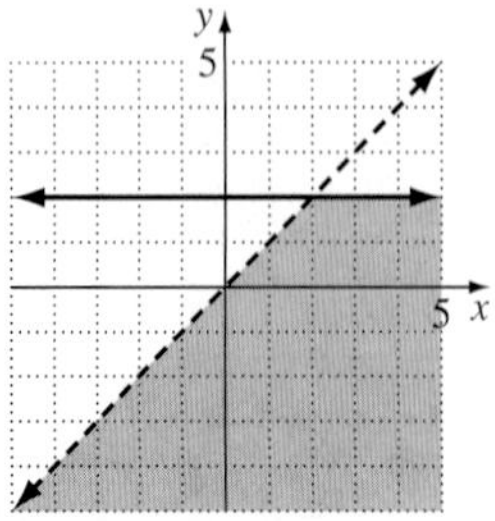


**48.**

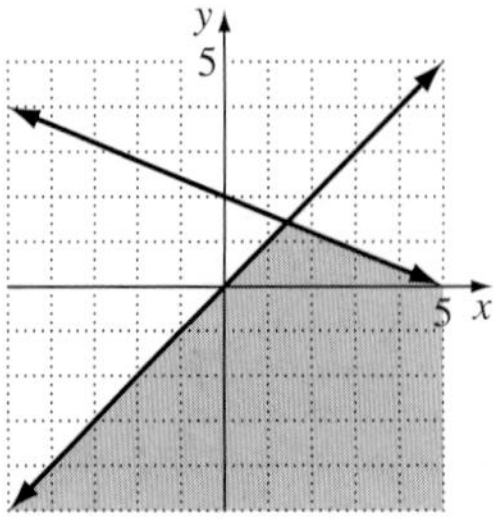


**49.**

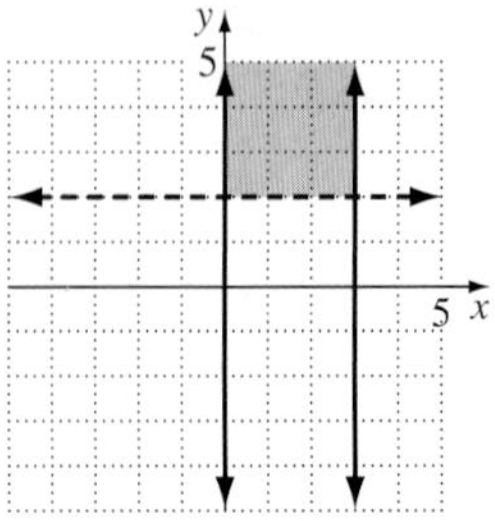


**50.** no solution

**51.**

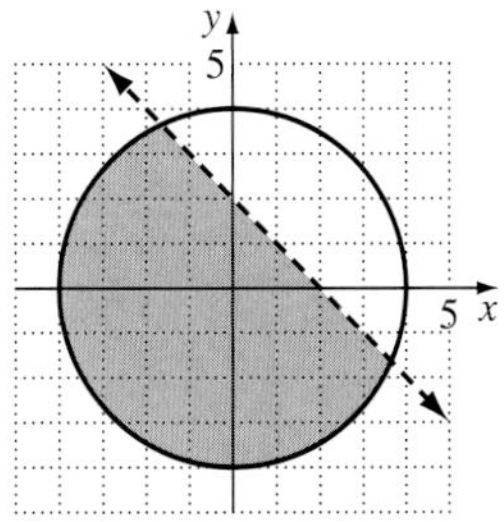

**52.**

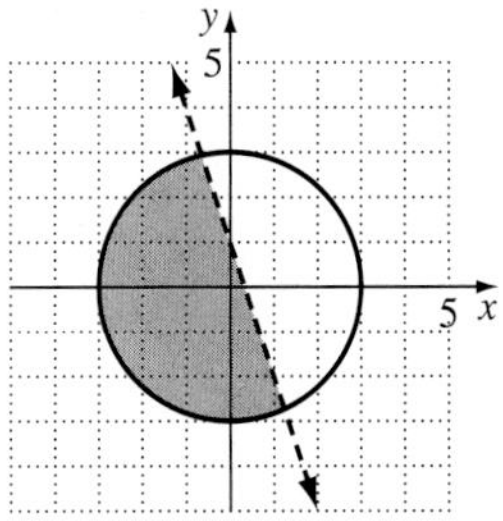

**53.**

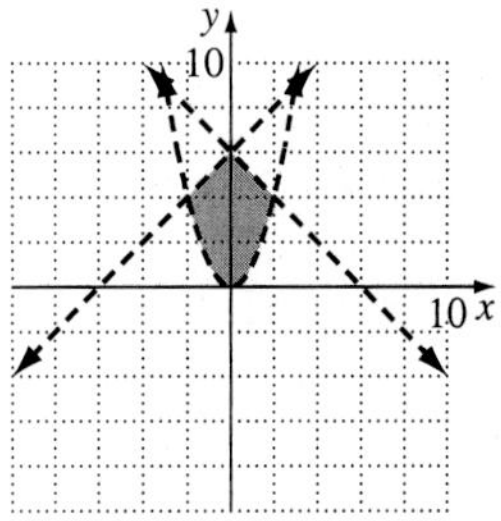

**54.**

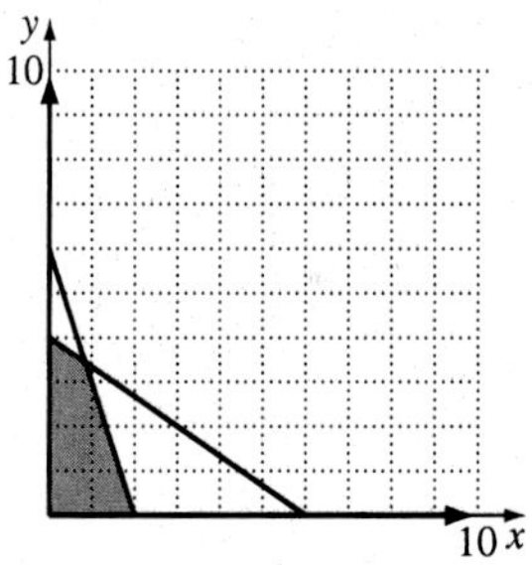

**55.** $(2, 2)$: 10; $(4, 0)$: 8; $\left(\frac{1}{2}, \frac{1}{2}\right)$: $\frac{5}{2}$; $(1, 0)$: 2; maximum value: 10; minimum value: 2

**56.**

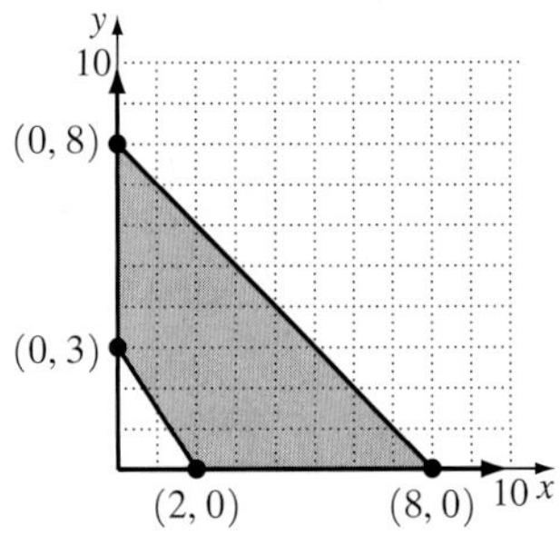


24

**57.**

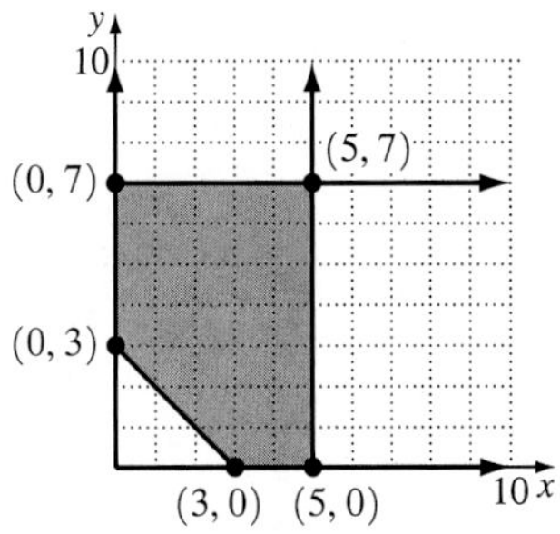


33

**58.**

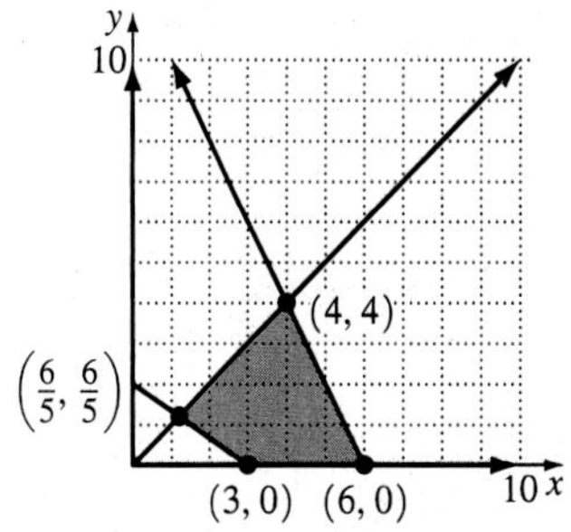


44

**59.** **a.** $z = 500x + 350y$

**b.** $x + y \leq 200$; $x \geq 10$; $y \geq 80$

**c.**

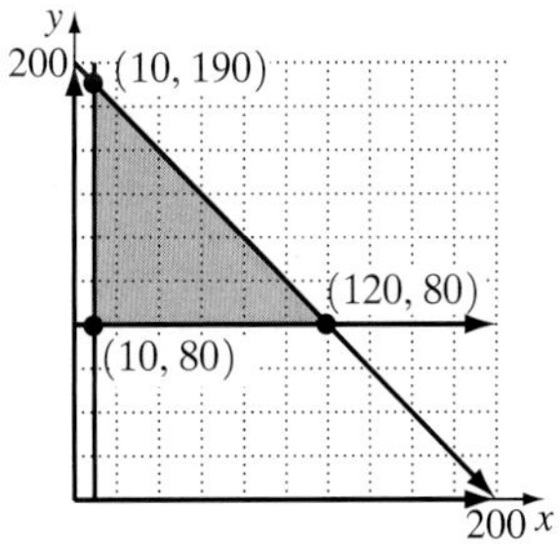


**d.** $(10, 80)$: 33,000; $(10, 190)$: 71,500; $(120, 80)$: 88,000

**e.** 120 units of writing paper and 80 units of newsprint; $88,000

**60.** 480 of model $A$ and 240 of model $B$

## Chapter 8 Test

**1.** $\{(1, -3)\}$ **2.** $\{(4, -2)\}$ **3.** $\{(1, 3, 2)\}$ **4.** $\{(4, -3), (-3, 4)\}$ **5.** $\{(3, 2), (3, -2), (-3, 2), (-3, -2)\}$

**6.** $\frac{-1}{10(x + 1)} + \frac{x + 9}{10(x^2 + 9)}$

**7.**

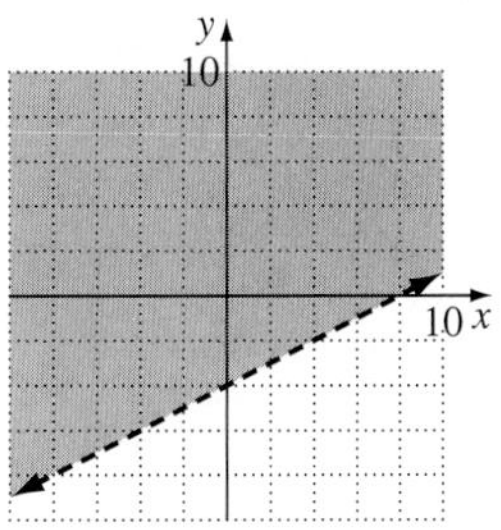

**8.**

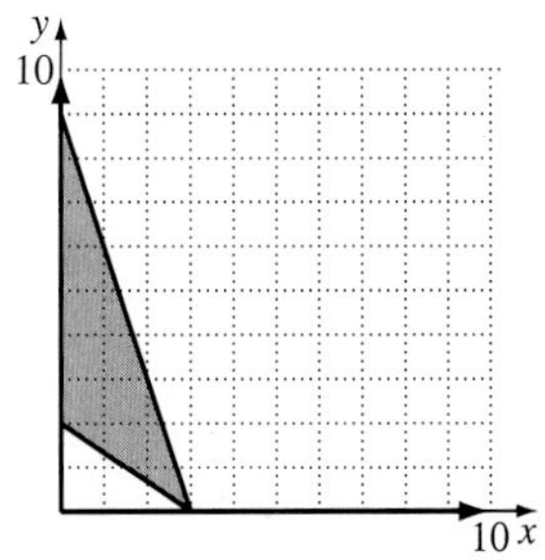

**9.**

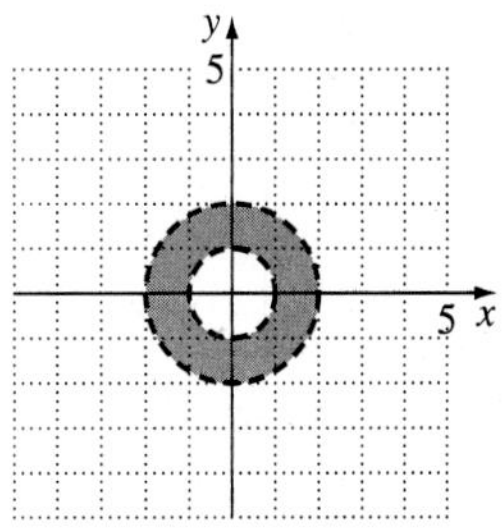

**10.**

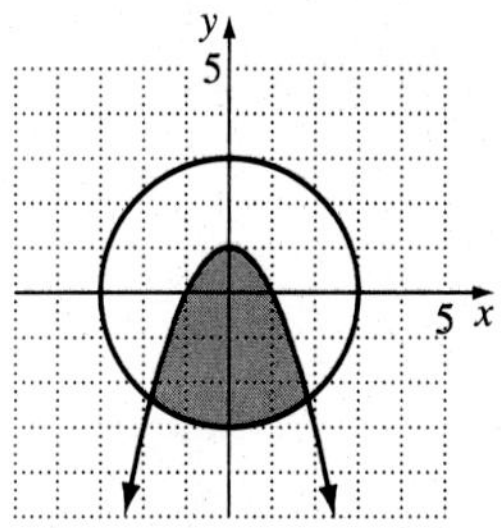

**11.** 26 **12.** orchestra ticket: $23; mezzanine ticket: $14 **13.** 400 units; $30 each **14.** $y = x^2 - 3$

**15.** $x = 7.5$ ft and $y = 24$ ft or $x = 12$ ft and $y = 15$ ft **16.** 50 regular and 100 deluxe jet skis; $35,000

### Cumulative Review Exercises (Chapters 1–8)

**1.** $\{3, 4\}$ **2.** $\left\{\frac{2 + i\sqrt{3}}{2}, \frac{2 - i\sqrt{3}}{2}\right\}$ **3.** $(-18, 6)$ **4.** $(1, 7)$ **5.** $\left\{-3, \frac{1}{2}, 2\right\}$ **6.** $\{-2\}$ **7.** $\{2\}$
**8.** $\{-2 + \log_3 11\}$, or approximately 0.18

**9.**

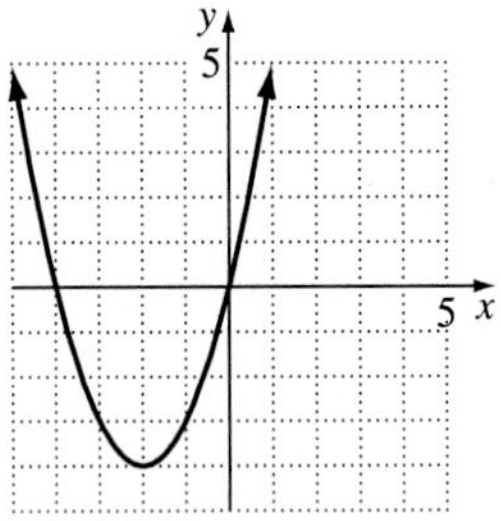

**10.**

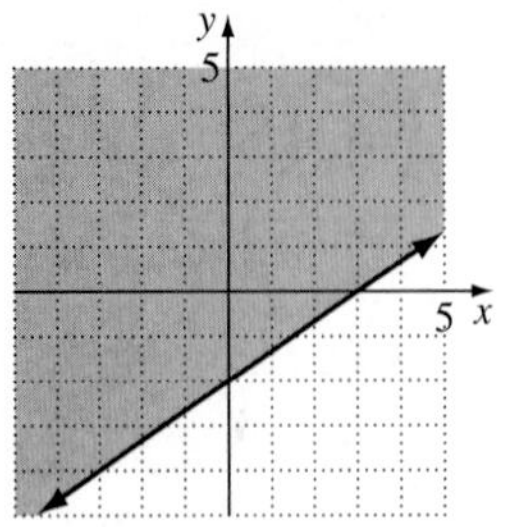

**11.**

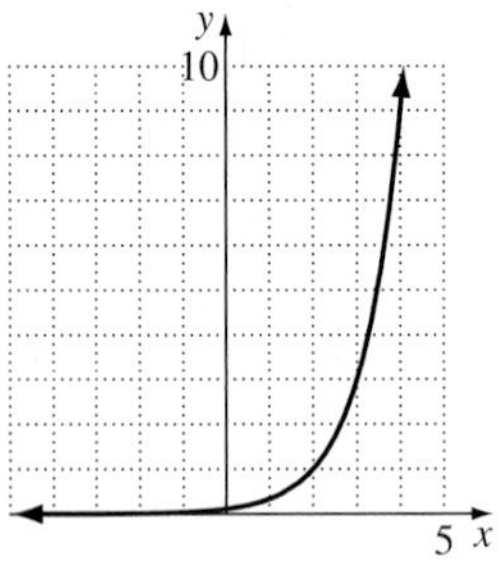

**12.**

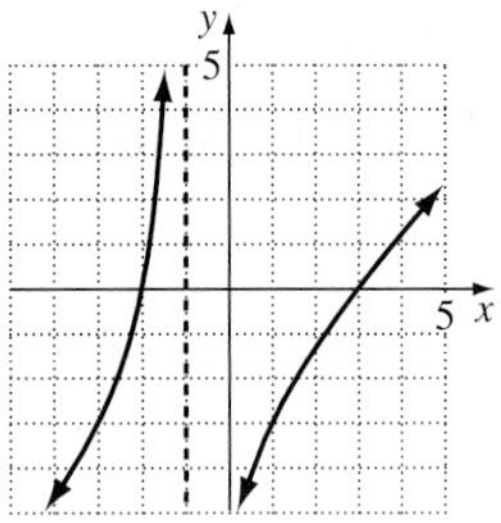

**13.** $3 + 5\log_2 x$ **14.** 10.99% **15.** $f^{-1}(x) = \frac{1}{7}x + \frac{3}{7}$ **16.** $g(f(x)) = 21x - 16$ **17.** Answers may vary. **18.** $\left\{\left(-\frac{1}{2}, \frac{1}{2}\right), (2, 8)\right\}$

**19.** 4 m by 9 m **20.** A plane with an initial landing speed of 90 ft per second needs 562 ft to land. There is a problem since 550 ft is not enough.

**21.** $\sec\theta - \cos\theta = \frac{1}{\cos\theta} - \cos\theta = \frac{1 - \cos^2\theta}{\cos\theta} = \frac{\sin^2\theta}{\cos\theta} = \frac{\sin\theta}{\cos\theta} \cdot \sin\theta = \tan\theta \cdot \sin\theta$

**22.** $\tan x + \tan y = \frac{\sin x}{\cos x} + \frac{\sin y}{\cos y} = \frac{\sin x \cdot \cos y + \sin y \cdot \cos x}{\cos x \cdot \cos y} = \frac{\sin(x + y)}{\cos x \cdot \cos y}$ **23.** $0, \pi$ **24.** $0, \frac{\pi}{3}, \frac{5\pi}{3}$ **25.** 92.9

## CHAPTER 9

### Section 9.1

### Check Point Exercises

**1.** $\{(4, -3, 1)\}$ **2. a.** $\left[\begin{array}{rrr|r} 1 & 6 & -3 & 7 \\ 4 & 12 & -20 & 8 \\ -3 & -2 & 1 & -9 \end{array}\right]$ **b.** $\left[\begin{array}{rrr|r} 1 & 3 & -5 & 2 \\ 1 & 6 & -3 & 7 \\ -3 & -2 & 1 & -9 \end{array}\right]$ **c.** $\left[\begin{array}{rrr|r} 4 & 12 & -20 & 8 \\ 1 & 6 & -3 & 7 \\ 0 & 16 & -8 & 12 \end{array}\right]$

**3.** $\{(5, 2, 3)\}$ **4.** $\{(1, -1, 2, -3)\}$ **5.** $\left\{\left(\frac{5}{2}, \frac{8}{7}, \frac{11}{14}\right)\right\}$

### Exercise Set 9.1

**1.** $\left[\begin{array}{rrr|r} 2 & 1 & 2 & 2 \\ 3 & -5 & -1 & 4 \\ 1 & -2 & -3 & -6 \end{array}\right]$ **3.** $\left[\begin{array}{rrr|r} 1 & -1 & 1 & 8 \\ 0 & 1 & -12 & -15 \\ 0 & 0 & 1 & 1 \end{array}\right]$ **5.** $\left[\begin{array}{rrr|r} 5 & -2 & -3 & 0 \\ 1 & 1 & 0 & 5 \\ 2 & 0 & -3 & 4 \end{array}\right]$ **7.** $\left[\begin{array}{rrrr|r} 2 & 5 & -3 & 1 & 2 \\ 0 & 3 & 1 & 0 & 4 \\ 1 & -1 & 5 & 0 & 9 \\ 5 & -5 & -2 & 0 & 1 \end{array}\right]$ **9.** $\begin{aligned} 5x + 3z &= -11 \\ y - 4z &= 12 \\ 7x + 2y &= 3 \end{aligned}$

**11.** $\begin{aligned} x + y + 4z + w &= 3 \\ -x + y - z &= 7 \\ 2x + 5w &= 11 \\ 12z + 4w &= 5 \end{aligned}$ **13.** $\begin{aligned} x - 4z &= 5 \\ y - 12z &= 13 \\ z &= -\frac{1}{2} \end{aligned}$ ; $\left\{\left(3, 7, -\frac{1}{2}\right)\right\}$ **15.** $\begin{aligned} x + \frac{1}{2}y + z &= \frac{11}{2} \\ y + \frac{3}{2}z &= 7 \\ z &= 4 \end{aligned}$ ; $(\{1, 1, 4\})$

**17.** $\begin{aligned} x - y + z + w &= 3 \\ y - 2z - w &= 0 \\ z + 6w &= 17 \\ w &= 3 \end{aligned}$ ; $\{(2, 1, -1, 3)\}$ **19.** $\left[\begin{array}{rrr|r} 1 & -3 & 2 & 5 \\ 1 & 5 & -5 & 0 \\ 3 & 0 & 4 & 7 \end{array}\right]$ **21.** $\left[\begin{array}{rrr|r} 1 & -3 & 2 & 0 \\ 0 & 10 & -7 & 7 \\ 2 & -2 & 1 & 3 \end{array}\right]$ **23.** $\left[\begin{array}{rrrr|r} 1 & -1 & 1 & 1 & 3 \\ 0 & 1 & -2 & -1 & 0 \\ 0 & 2 & 1 & 2 & 5 \\ 0 & 6 & -3 & -1 & -9 \end{array}\right]$

**25.** $R_2$: $-3, -18$; $R_3$: $-12, -15$; $R_2$: $-\frac{3}{5}, -\frac{18}{5}$; $R_3$: $-12, -15$ **27.** $\{(1, -1, 2)\}$ **29.** $\{(3, -1, -1)\}$ **31.** $\{(1, 2, -1)\}$
**33.** $\{(1, 2, 3, -2)\}$ **35.** $\{(0, -3, 0, -3)\}$ **37.** $\{(-1, 2, 3, 4)\}$ **39.** $\{(1, -1, 2, -2, 0)\}$ **41. a.** $a = 2; b = 22; c = 320$
**b.** 2780 **c.** Answers may vary. **43.** $\begin{aligned} x + y + z &= 100 \\ x - y + z &= 2 \\ -x + 2z &= -3 \end{aligned}$ ; under 30: 35%; 30–49: 49%; 50 and over: 16%

**45.** $40x + 200y + 400z = 660$; 4 oz of Food $A$: $\frac{1}{2}$ oz of Food $B$; 1 oz of Food $C$
$5x + 2y + 4z = 25$
$30x + 10y + 300z = 425$

**57.** $y = x^3 + 2x^2 + 5x - 3$

## Section 9.2

### Check Point Exercises

**1.** $\varnothing$ **2.** $\{(11t + 13, 5t + 4, t)\}$ **3.** $\{(t + 50, -2t + 10, t)\}$
**4. a.** $x + w = 15$
$x + y = 30$
$y + z = 45$
$z + w = 30$
**b.** $\{(-t + 15, t + 15, -t + 30, t)\}$ **c.** $x = 5; y = 25; z = 20$

### Exercise Set 9.2

**1.** $\varnothing$ **3.** $\left\{\left(-2t + 2, 2t + \frac{1}{2}, t\right)\right\}$ **5.** $\{(-3, 4, -2)\}$ **7.** $\{(5 - 2t, -2 + t, t)\}$ **9.** $\{(-1, 2, 1, 1)\}$ **11.** $\{(1, 3, 2, 1)\}$

**13.** $\{(1, -2, 1, 1)\}$ **15.** $\left\{\left(1 + \frac{1}{3}t, \frac{1}{3}t, t\right)\right\}$ **17.** $\{(-13t + 5, 5t, t)\}$ **19.** $\left\{\left(2t - \frac{5}{4}, \frac{13}{4}t, t\right)\right\}$ **21.** $\{(1, -t - 1, 2, t)\}$

**23.** $\left\{\left(-\frac{2}{11}t + \frac{81}{11}, \frac{1}{22}t + \frac{10}{11}, \frac{4}{11}t - \frac{8}{11}, t\right)\right\}$ **25.** $z + 12 = x + 6$ **27.** $\{(t + 6, t + 2, t)\}$

**29. a.** $x + w = 380$
$x + y = 600$
$z - w = 50$
$y - z = 170$
**b.** $\{(380 - t, 220 + t, 50 + t, t)\}$
**c.** $x = 330, y = 270, z = 100, w = 50$

**31. a.** The system has no solution, so there is no way to satisfy these dietary requirements with no Food 1 available.
**b.** 4 oz of Food 1, 0 oz of Food 2, 10 oz of Food 3; 2 oz of Food 1, 5 oz of Food 2, 9 oz of Food 3 (other answers are possible).
**37.** $a = 1$ or $a = 3$

## Section 9.3

### Check Point Exercises

**1. a.** $3 \times 2$ **b.** $a_{12} = -2; a_{31} = 1$ **2. a.** $\begin{bmatrix} 2 & 0 \\ 9 & -10 \end{bmatrix}$ **b.** $\begin{bmatrix} 9 & -4 \\ -9 & 7 \\ 5 & -2 \end{bmatrix}$ **3. a.** $\begin{bmatrix} 6 & 12 \\ -48 & -30 \end{bmatrix}$ **b.** $\begin{bmatrix} -14 & -1 \\ 25 & 10 \end{bmatrix}$ **4.** $\begin{bmatrix} 7 & 6 \\ 13 & 12 \end{bmatrix}$

**5.** $[30]$; $\begin{bmatrix} 2 & 0 & 4 \\ 6 & 0 & 12 \\ 14 & 0 & 28 \end{bmatrix}$ **6. a.** $\begin{bmatrix} 2 & 18 & 11 & 9 \\ 0 & 10 & 8 & 2 \end{bmatrix}$ **b.** The product is undefined. **7.** $\begin{bmatrix} 2 & 2 & 2 \\ 1 & 2 & 1 \\ 1 & 2 & 1 \end{bmatrix} + \begin{bmatrix} -1 & -1 & -1 \\ 2 & -1 & 2 \\ 2 & -1 & 2 \end{bmatrix} = \begin{bmatrix} 1 & 1 & 1 \\ 3 & 1 & 3 \\ 3 & 1 & 3 \end{bmatrix}$

**8.** \$2548

### Exercise Set 9.3

**1. a.** $2 \times 3$ **b.** $a_{32}$ does not exist; $a_{23} = -1$ **3. a.** $3 \times 4$ **b.** $a_{32} = \frac{1}{2}; a_{23} = -6$ **5.** $x = 6; y = 4$ **7.** $x = 4; y = 6; z = 3$

**9. a.** $\begin{bmatrix} 9 & 10 \\ 3 & 9 \end{bmatrix}$ **b.** $\begin{bmatrix} -1 & -8 \\ 3 & -5 \end{bmatrix}$ **c.** $\begin{bmatrix} -16 & -4 \\ -12 & -8 \end{bmatrix}$ **d.** $\begin{bmatrix} 22 & 21 \\ 9 & 20 \end{bmatrix}$ **11. a.** $\begin{bmatrix} 3 & 2 \\ 6 & 2 \\ 5 & 7 \end{bmatrix}$ **b.** $\begin{bmatrix} -1 & 4 \\ 0 & 6 \\ 5 & 5 \end{bmatrix}$ **c.** $\begin{bmatrix} -4 & -12 \\ -12 & -16 \\ -20 & -24 \end{bmatrix}$

**d.** $\begin{bmatrix} 7 & 7 \\ 15 & 8 \\ 15 & 20 \end{bmatrix}$ **13. a.** $\begin{bmatrix} -3 \\ -1 \\ 0 \end{bmatrix}$ **b.** $\begin{bmatrix} 7 \\ -7 \\ 2 \end{bmatrix}$ **c.** $\begin{bmatrix} -8 \\ 16 \\ -4 \end{bmatrix}$ **d.** $\begin{bmatrix} -4 \\ -6 \\ 1 \end{bmatrix}$ **15. a.** $\begin{bmatrix} 8 & 0 & -4 \\ 14 & 0 & 6 \\ -1 & 0 & 0 \end{bmatrix}$ **b.** $\begin{bmatrix} -4 & -20 & 0 \\ 14 & 24 & 14 \\ 9 & -4 & 4 \end{bmatrix}$

**c.** $\begin{bmatrix} -8 & 40 & 8 \\ -56 & -48 & -40 \\ -16 & 8 & -8 \end{bmatrix}$ **d.** $\begin{bmatrix} 18 & -10 & -10 \\ 42 & 12 & 22 \\ 2 & -2 & 2 \end{bmatrix}$ **17. a.** $\begin{bmatrix} 0 & 16 \\ 12 & 8 \end{bmatrix}$ **b.** $\begin{bmatrix} -7 & 3 \\ 29 & 15 \end{bmatrix}$ **19. a.** $[30]$ **b.** $\begin{bmatrix} 1 & 2 & 3 & 4 \\ 2 & 4 & 6 & 8 \\ 3 & 6 & 9 & 12 \\ 4 & 8 & 12 & 16 \end{bmatrix}$

**21. a.** $\begin{bmatrix} 4 & -5 & 8 \\ 6 & -1 & 5 \\ 0 & 4 & -6 \end{bmatrix}$ **b.** $\begin{bmatrix} 5 & -2 & 7 \\ 17 & -3 & 2 \\ 3 & 0 & -5 \end{bmatrix}$ **23. a.** $\begin{bmatrix} 6 & 8 & 16 \\ 11 & 16 & 24 \\ 1 & -1 & 12 \end{bmatrix}$ **b.** $\begin{bmatrix} 38 & 27 \\ -16 & -4 \end{bmatrix}$ **25. a.** $\begin{bmatrix} 0 & 0 \\ 0 & 0 \end{bmatrix}$ **b.** $\begin{bmatrix} 4 & -1 & -3 & 1 \\ -1 & 4 & -3 & 2 \\ 14 & -11 & -3 & -1 \\ 25 & -25 & 0 & -5 \end{bmatrix}$

**27.** $\begin{bmatrix} 17 & 7 \\ -5 & -11 \end{bmatrix}$ **29.** $\begin{bmatrix} 11 & -1 \\ -7 & -3 \end{bmatrix}$ **31.** $A - C$ is not defined because $A$ is $3 \times 2$ and $C$ is $2 \times 2$. **33.** $\begin{bmatrix} 16 & -16 \\ -12 & 12 \\ 0 & 0 \end{bmatrix}$

**35.** $\begin{bmatrix} 1 & 3 & 1 \\ 3 & 3 & 3 \\ 1 & 3 & 1 \end{bmatrix} + \begin{bmatrix} -1 & -1 & -1 \\ -1 & -1 & -1 \\ -1 & -1 & -1 \end{bmatrix} = \begin{bmatrix} 0 & 2 & 0 \\ 2 & 2 & 2 \\ 0 & 2 & 0 \end{bmatrix}$ **37.** $\begin{bmatrix} 1 & 3 & 1 \\ 3 & 3 & 3 \\ 1 & 3 & 1 \end{bmatrix} + \begin{bmatrix} 1 & -2 & 1 \\ -2 & -2 & -2 \\ 1 & -2 & 1 \end{bmatrix} = \begin{bmatrix} 2 & 1 & 2 \\ 1 & 1 & 1 \\ 2 & 1 & 2 \end{bmatrix}$ **39. a.** $\begin{bmatrix} 0 & 3 & 0 \\ 0 & 3 & 0 \\ 0 & 3 & 0 \end{bmatrix}$ **b.** $\begin{bmatrix} 1 & 0 & 1 \\ 1 & 0 & 1 \\ 1 & 0 & 1 \end{bmatrix}$

**41. a.** $\begin{bmatrix} 589.5 & 586 \\ 1556 & 1521 \\ 1234.5 & 1183 \end{bmatrix}$ **b.** 1521 **c.** 1235

**43. a.** System 1: The midterm and final both count for 50% of the course grade.
System 2: The midterm counts for 30% of the course grade and the final counts for 70%.
**b.** $\begin{bmatrix} 84 & 87.2 \\ 79 & 81 \\ 90 & 88.4 \\ 73 & 68.6 \\ 69 & 73.4 \end{bmatrix}$ System 1 grades are listed first (if different). Student 1: B; Student 2: C or B; Student 3: A or B; Student 4: C or D; Student 5: D or C

**57.** Answers may vary. **59.** $AB = -BA$ so they are anticommutative.

## Section 9.4

### Check Point Exercises

**1.** $AB = I_2; BA = I_2$ **2.** $\begin{bmatrix} 3 & -7 \\ -2 & 5 \end{bmatrix}$ **3.** $\begin{bmatrix} 1 & 2 \\ 1 & 3 \end{bmatrix}$ **4.** $\begin{bmatrix} 3 & -2 & -4 \\ 3 & -2 & -5 \\ -1 & 1 & 2 \end{bmatrix}$ **5.** $\{(4, -2, 1)\}$

**6.** The encoded message is −7, 10, −53, 77. **7.** The decoded message is 2, 1, 19, 5 or BASE.

### Exercise Set 9.4

**1.** $AB = I_2; BA = I_2; B = A^{-1}$ **3.** $AB = \begin{bmatrix} 8 & -16 \\ -2 & 7 \end{bmatrix}; BA = \begin{bmatrix} 12 & 12 \\ 1 & 3 \end{bmatrix}; B \neq A^{-1}$ **5.** $AB = I_2; BA = I_2; B = A^{-1}$

**7.** $AB = I_3; BA = I_3; B = A^{-1}$ **9.** $AB = I_3; BA = I_3; B = A^{-1}$ **11.** $AB = I_4; BA = I_4; B = A^{-1}$

**13.** $\begin{bmatrix} \frac{2}{7} & -\frac{3}{7} \\ \frac{1}{7} & \frac{2}{7} \end{bmatrix}$ **15.** $\begin{bmatrix} 1 & \frac{1}{2} \\ 2 & \frac{3}{2} \end{bmatrix}$ **17.** $A$ does not have an inverse. **19.** $\begin{bmatrix} 1 & 0 & 1 \\ 1 & 1 & 2 \\ 3 & 2 & 6 \end{bmatrix}$ **21.** $\begin{bmatrix} -3 & 2 & -4 \\ -1 & 1 & -1 \\ 8 & -5 & 10 \end{bmatrix}$ **23.** $\begin{bmatrix} 1 & 0 & 0 & 0 \\ 0 & -1 & 0 & 0 \\ 0 & 0 & \frac{1}{3} & 0 \\ -1 & 0 & 0 & 1 \end{bmatrix}$

**25.** $\begin{bmatrix} 6 & 5 \\ 5 & 4 \end{bmatrix}\begin{bmatrix} x \\ y \end{bmatrix} = \begin{bmatrix} 13 \\ 10 \end{bmatrix}$ **27.** $\begin{bmatrix} 1 & 3 & 4 \\ 1 & 2 & 3 \\ 1 & 4 & 3 \end{bmatrix}\begin{bmatrix} x \\ y \\ z \end{bmatrix} = \begin{bmatrix} -3 \\ -2 \\ -6 \end{bmatrix}$ **29.** $4x - 7y = -3$, $2x - 3y = 1$ **31.** $2x - z = 6$, $3y = 9$, $x + y = 5$ **33. a.** $\begin{bmatrix} 2 & 6 & 6 \\ 2 & 7 & 6 \\ 2 & 7 & 7 \end{bmatrix}\begin{bmatrix} x \\ y \\ z \end{bmatrix} = \begin{bmatrix} 8 \\ 10 \\ 9 \end{bmatrix}$

**b.** $\{(1, 2, -1)\}$ **35. a.** $\begin{bmatrix} 1 & -1 & 1 \\ 0 & 2 & -1 \\ 2 & 3 & 0 \end{bmatrix}\begin{bmatrix} x \\ y \\ z \end{bmatrix} = \begin{bmatrix} 8 \\ -7 \\ 1 \end{bmatrix}$ **b.** $\{(2, -1, 5)\}$ **37. a.** $\begin{bmatrix} 1 & -1 & 2 & 0 \\ 0 & 1 & -1 & 1 \\ -1 & 1 & -1 & 2 \\ 0 & -1 & 1 & -2 \end{bmatrix}\begin{bmatrix} x \\ y \\ z \\ w \end{bmatrix} = \begin{bmatrix} -3 \\ 4 \\ 2 \\ -4 \end{bmatrix}$

**b.** $\{(2, 3, -1, 0)\}$ **39.** The encoded message is 27, −19, 32, −20.; The decoded message is 8, 5, 12, 16 or HELP.

**41.** The encoded message is 14, 85, −33, 4, 18, −7, −18, 19, −9. **53.** $\begin{bmatrix} 1 & 1 \\ 2 & 3 \end{bmatrix}$ **55.** $\begin{bmatrix} 1 & 0 & 1 \\ 2 & 1 & 3 \\ -1 & 1 & 1 \end{bmatrix}$ **57.** $\begin{bmatrix} 0 & -1 & 0 & 1 \\ -1 & -5 & 0 & 3 \\ -2 & -4 & 1 & -2 \\ -1 & -4 & 0 & 1 \end{bmatrix}$

**59.** $\{(2, 3, -5)\}$ **61.** $\{(1, 2, -1)\}$ **63.** $\{(2, 1, 3, -2, 4)\}$ **65.** Answers may vary. **67.** (c) is true. **69.** Answers may vary.
**71.** $a = 3$ or $a = -2$

## Section 9.5

### Check Point Exercises

**1. a.** −4 **b.** −17 **2.** $\{(4, -2)\}$ **3.** 80 **4.** −24 **5.** $\{(2, -3, 4)\}$ **6.** −250

### Exercise Set 9.5

**1.** 1 **3.** −29 **5.** 0 **7.** 33 **9.** $-\frac{7}{16}$ **11.** $\{(5, 2)\}$ **13.** $\{(2, -3)\}$ **15.** $\{(3, -1)\}$ **17.** The system is dependent.
**19.** $\{(4, 2)\}$ **21.** $\{(7, 4)\}$ **23.** The system is inconsistent. **25.** $\{(0, 4)\}$ **27.** 72 **29.** −75 **31.** 0 **33.** $\{(-5, -2, 7)\}$
**35.** $\{(2, -3, 4)\}$ **37.** $\{(3, -1, 2)\}$ **39.** $\{(2, 3, 1)\}$ **41.** −200 **43.** 195

**45. a.** 28 sq units

**b.**

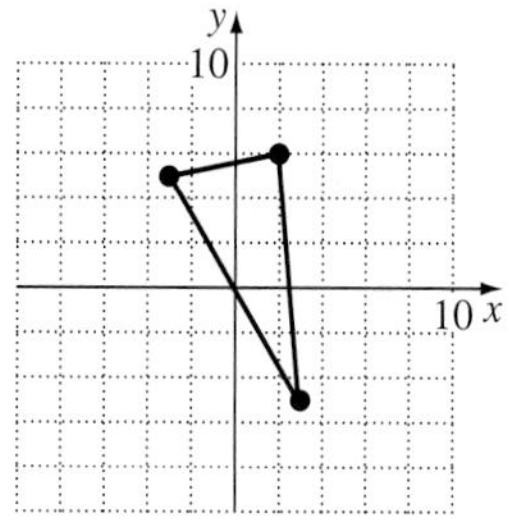


**47.** yes

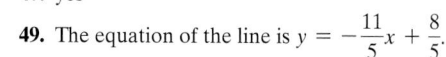

**49.** The equation of the line is $y = -\frac{11}{5}x + \frac{8}{5}$.

**61.** 13,200

**63. a.** $a^2$ **b.** $a^3$ **c.** $a^4$
**d.** Each determinant has zeros below the main diagonal and $a$'s everywhere else.
**e.** Each determinant equals $a$ raised to the power equal to the order of the determinant.

**65.** The sign of the value is changed when 2 columns are interchanged in a 2nd order determinant.

### Chapter 9 Review Exercises

**1.** $\begin{aligned} x + y + 3z &= 12 \\ y - 2z &= -4 \\ z &= 3 \end{aligned}$ ; $\{(1, 2, 3)\}$

**2.** $\begin{aligned} x - 2z + 2w &= 1 \\ y + z - w &= 0 \\ z - \tfrac{7}{3}w &= -\tfrac{1}{3} \\ w &= 1 \end{aligned}$ ; $\{(3, -1, 2, 1)\}$

**3.** $\left[\begin{array}{ccc|c} 1 & 2 & 2 & 2 \\ 0 & 1 & -1 & 2 \\ 0 & 0 & 9 & -9 \end{array}\right]$

**4.** $\left[\begin{array}{ccc|c} 1 & -1 & \frac{1}{2} & -\frac{1}{2} \\ 1 & 2 & -1 & 2 \\ 6 & 4 & 3 & 5 \end{array}\right]$

**5.** $\{(1, 3, -4)\}$ **6.** $\{(-2, -1, 0)\}$ **7.** $\{(2, -2, 3, 4)\}$ **8. a.** $a = -2; b = 32; c = 42$ **b.** 2:00 P.M.; 170 parts per million **9.** ∅
**10.** $\{(2t + 4, t + 1, t)\}$ **11.** $\{(-37t + 2, 16t, -7t + 1, t)\}$ **12.** $\{(7t + 18, -3t - 7, t)\}$

**13. a.** $\begin{aligned} x + z &= 750 \\ y - z &= -250 \\ x + y &= 500 \end{aligned}$ **b.** $\{(-t + 750, t - 250, t)\}$ **c.** $x = 350; y = 150$ **14.** $x = -5; y = 6; z = 6$ **15.** $\begin{bmatrix} 0 & 2 & 3 \\ 8 & 1 & 3 \end{bmatrix}$ **16.** $\begin{bmatrix} 0 & -4 \\ 6 & 4 \\ 2 & -10 \end{bmatrix}$

**17.** $\begin{bmatrix} -4 & 4 & -1 \\ -2 & -5 & 5 \end{bmatrix}$ **18.** Not possible since $B$ is 3 × 2 and $C$ is 3 × 3. **19.** $\begin{bmatrix} 2 & 3 & 8 \\ 21 & 5 & 5 \end{bmatrix}$ **20.** $\begin{bmatrix} -12 & 14 & 0 \\ 2 & -14 & 18 \end{bmatrix}$

**21.** $\begin{bmatrix} 0 & -10 & -15 \\ -40 & -5 & -15 \end{bmatrix}$ **22.** $\begin{bmatrix} -1 & -16 \\ 8 & 1 \end{bmatrix}$ **23.** $\begin{bmatrix} -10 & -6 & 2 \\ 16 & 3 & 4 \\ -23 & -16 & 7 \end{bmatrix}$ **24.** $\begin{bmatrix} -6 & 4 & -8 \\ 0 & 5 & 11 \\ -17 & 13 & -19 \end{bmatrix}$ **25.** $\begin{bmatrix} 10 & 5 \\ -2 & -30 \end{bmatrix}$

**26.** Not possible since $AB$ is 2 × 2 and $BA$ is 3 × 3. **27.** $\begin{bmatrix} 7 & 6 & 5 \\ 2 & -1 & 11 \end{bmatrix}$ **28.** $\begin{bmatrix} -6 & -22 & -40 \\ 9 & 43 & 58 \\ -14 & -48 & -94 \end{bmatrix}$ **29.** $\begin{bmatrix} 2 & 1 & 1 \\ 2 & 1 & 1 \\ 2 & 2 & 2 \end{bmatrix}$ **30.** $\begin{bmatrix} 1 & -1 & -1 \\ 1 & -1 & -1 \\ 1 & 1 & 1 \end{bmatrix}$

**31. a.** $\begin{bmatrix} 360{,}000 & 444{,}000 \\ 556{,}000 & 685{,}000 \\ 178{,}000 & 218{,}500 \end{bmatrix}$ **b.** The rows of $AB$ correspond to the outlets, the columns represent the wholesale and retail prices. The entries tell how much value in wholesale or retail is at each outlet.
**c.** \$360,000 **d.** \$685,000 **e.** \$40,500

**32.** $AB = \begin{bmatrix} 1 & 7 \\ 0 & 5 \end{bmatrix}$; $BA = \begin{bmatrix} 1 & 0 \\ 1 & 5 \end{bmatrix}$; $B \neq A^{-1}$ **33.** $AB = I_3$; $BA = I_3$; $B = A^{-1}$ **34.** $\begin{bmatrix} 3 & 1 \\ 2 & 1 \end{bmatrix}$ **35.** $\begin{bmatrix} -\frac{3}{5} & \frac{1}{5} \\ 1 & 0 \end{bmatrix}$ **36.** $\begin{bmatrix} 3 & 0 & -2 \\ -6 & 1 & 4 \\ 1 & 0 & -1 \end{bmatrix}$

**37.** $\begin{bmatrix} 8 & -8 & 5 \\ -3 & 2 & -1 \\ -1 & -1 & 1 \end{bmatrix}$ **38. a.** $\begin{bmatrix} 1 & 1 & 2 \\ 0 & 1 & 3 \\ 3 & 0 & -2 \end{bmatrix}\begin{bmatrix} x \\ y \\ z \end{bmatrix} = \begin{bmatrix} 7 \\ -2 \\ 0 \end{bmatrix}$ **b.** $\{(-18, 79, -27)\}$ **39. a.** $\begin{bmatrix} 1 & -1 & 2 \\ 0 & 1 & -1 \\ 1 & 0 & 2 \end{bmatrix}\begin{bmatrix} x \\ y \\ z \end{bmatrix} = \begin{bmatrix} 12 \\ -5 \\ 10 \end{bmatrix}$ **b.** $\{(4, -2, 3)\}$

**40.** The encoded message is 96, 135, 46, 63; The decoded message is 18, 21, 12, 5 or RULE. **41.** 17 **42.** 4 **43.** −86 **44.** −236

**45.** 4 **46.** 16 **47.** $\left\{\left(\frac{7}{4}, -\frac{25}{8}\right)\right\}$ **48.** $\{(2, -7)\}$ **49.** $\{(23, -12, 3)\}$ **50.** $\{(-3, 2, 1)\}$ **51.** $a = \frac{5}{8}$; $b = -50$; $c = 1150$; 30- and 50-year-olds are involved in an average of 212.5 automobile accidents per day.

## Chapter 9 Test

**1.** $\left\{\left(-3, \frac{1}{2}, 1\right)\right\}$ **2.** $\{(t, t-1, t)\}$ **3.** $\begin{bmatrix} 5 & 4 \\ 1 & 11 \end{bmatrix}$ **4.** $\begin{bmatrix} 5 & -2 \\ 1 & -1 \\ 4 & -1 \end{bmatrix}$ **5.** $\begin{bmatrix} \frac{3}{5} & -\frac{2}{5} \\ \frac{1}{5} & \frac{1}{5} \end{bmatrix}$ **6.** $\begin{bmatrix} -1 & 2 \\ -5 & 4 \end{bmatrix}$

**7.** $AB = I_3$; $BA = I_3$ **8. a.** $\begin{bmatrix} 3 & 5 \\ 2 & -3 \end{bmatrix}\begin{bmatrix} x \\ y \end{bmatrix} = \begin{bmatrix} 9 \\ -13 \end{bmatrix}$ **b.** $\begin{bmatrix} \frac{3}{19} & \frac{5}{19} \\ \frac{2}{19} & -\frac{3}{19} \end{bmatrix}$ **c.** $\{(-2, 3)\}$ **9.** 18 **10.** $x = 2$

## Cumulative Review Exercises (Chapters 1–9)

**1.** $\left\{\frac{-1 + \sqrt{33}}{4}, \frac{-1 - \sqrt{33}}{4}\right\}$ **2.** $\left[\frac{1}{2}, \infty\right)$ **3.** $\{6\}$ **4.** $\left\{-4, \frac{1}{3}, 1\right\}$ **5.** $\{\ln 5, \ln 9\}$ **6.** $\{1\}$ **7.** $\{(7, -4, 6)\}$

**8.** $y = -1$ **9.** $f^{-1}(x) = \frac{x^2 + 7}{4}$ $(x \geq 0)$

**10.**

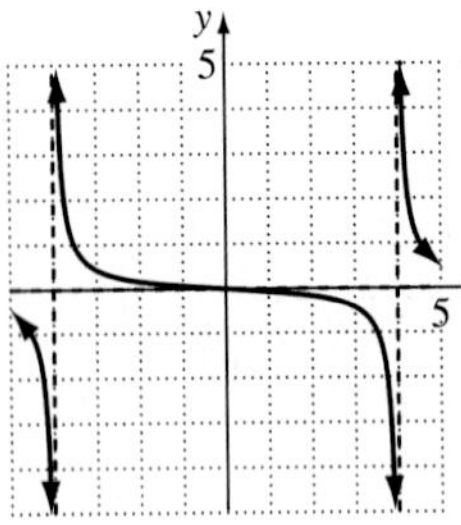


**11.** $f(x) = (x + 2)(x - 3)(2x + 1)(2x - 1)$

**12.**

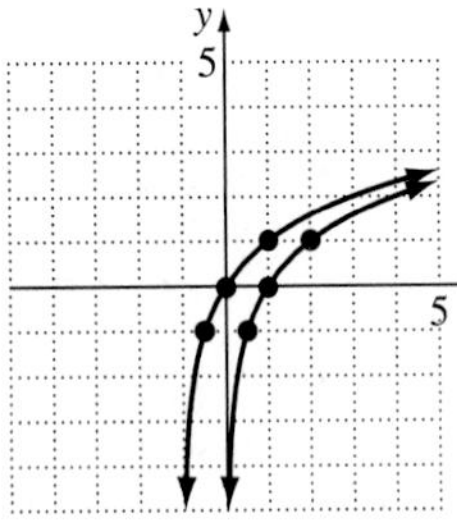


**13. a.** $A = A_0 e^{-0.017t}$ **b.** 759.30 g

**14.** $\begin{bmatrix} 2 & -1 \\ 13 & 1 \end{bmatrix}$ **15.** $\frac{8}{x - 3} + \frac{-2}{x - 2} + \frac{-3}{x + 2}$

**16.**

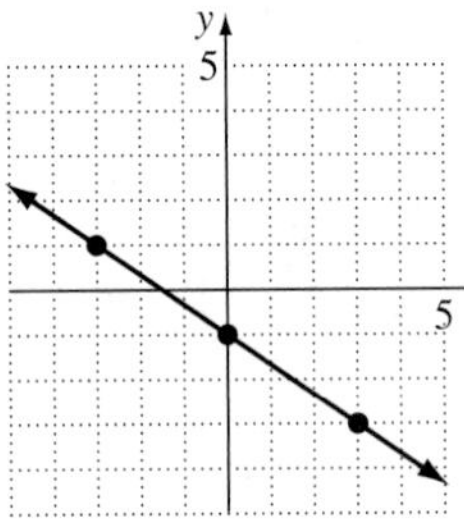


**17.**

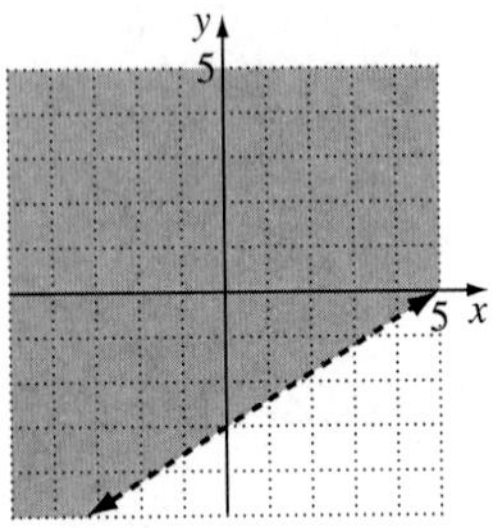


**18.**

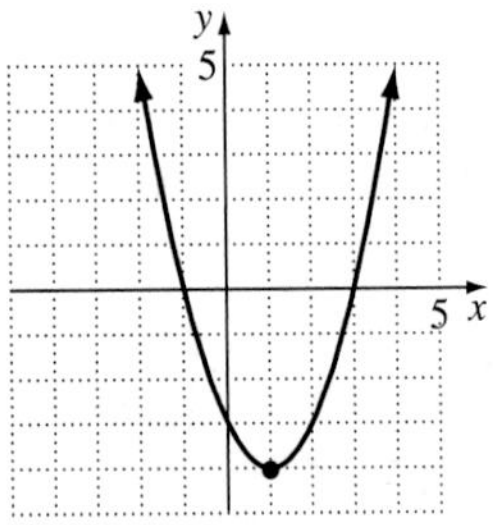


**19.**

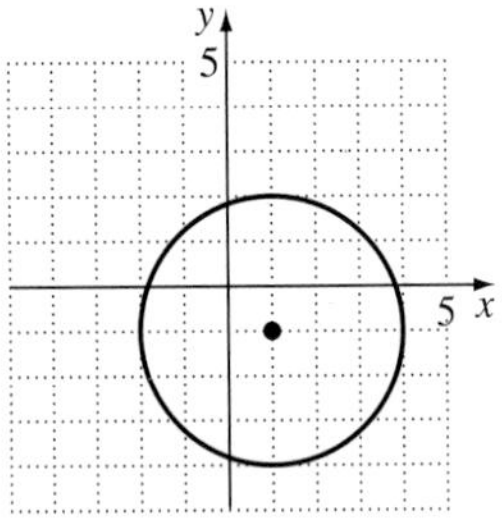


**20.** $= x^2 + 2x - 2$

**21.**

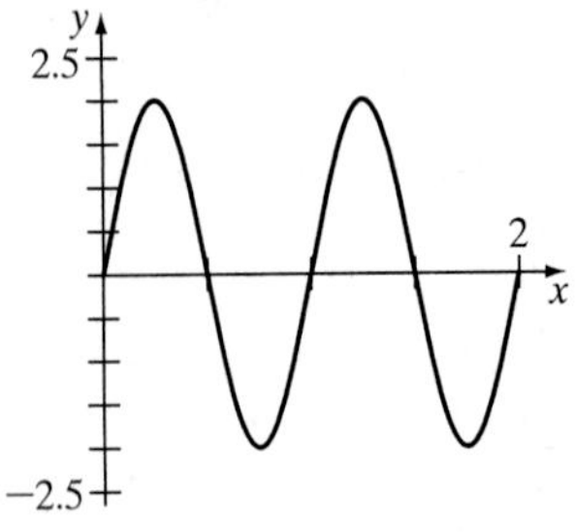


**22.** $\frac{3}{5}$

**23.** $\frac{\cos 2x}{\cos x - \sin x} = \frac{\cos^2 x - \sin^2 x}{\cos x - \sin x} = \frac{(\cos x - \sin x)(\cos x + \sin x)}{\cos x - \sin x} = \cos x + \sin x$

**24.** $\frac{3\pi}{2}$ **25.** $2\mathbf{i} - 13\mathbf{j}$

# CHAPTER 10

## Section 10.1

### Check Point Exercises

**1.** foci at $(-3\sqrt{3}, 0)$ and $(3\sqrt{3}, 0)$

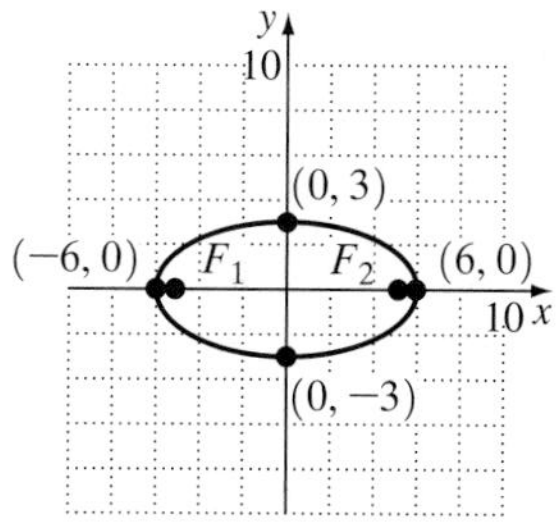


**2.** foci at $(0, -\sqrt{7})$ and $(0, \sqrt{7})$

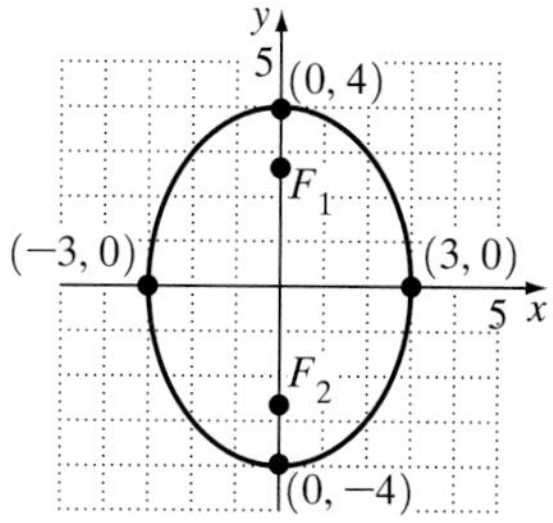


**3.** $\frac{x^2}{9} + \frac{y^2}{5} = 1$

**4.** foci at $(-1 - \sqrt{5}, 2)$ and $(-1 + \sqrt{5}, 2)$

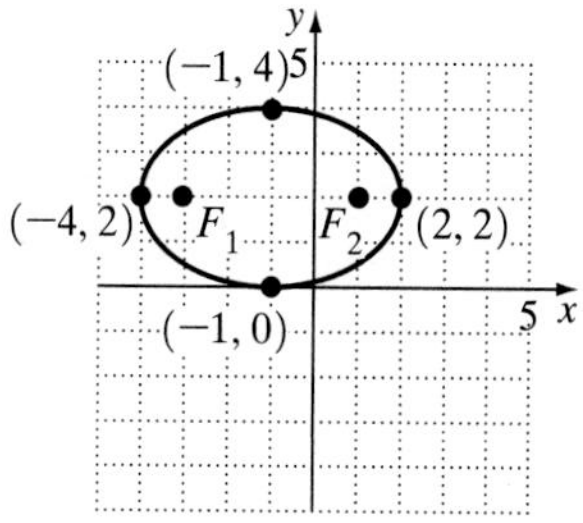


**5.** Yes

### Exercise Set 10.1

**1.** foci at $(-2\sqrt{3}, 0)$ and $(2\sqrt{3}, 0)$

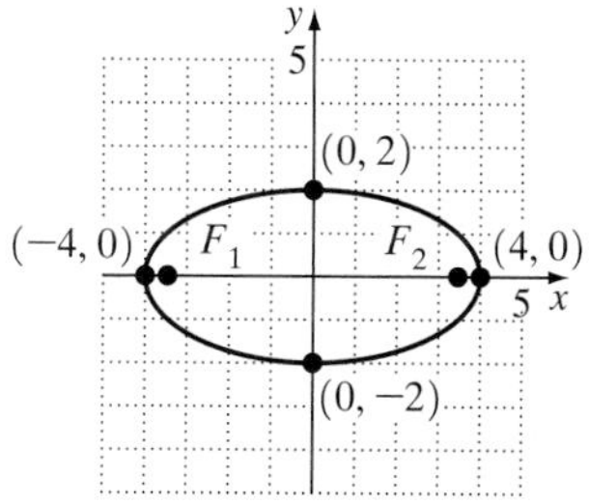


**3.** foci at $(0, -3\sqrt{3})$ and $(0, 3\sqrt{3})$

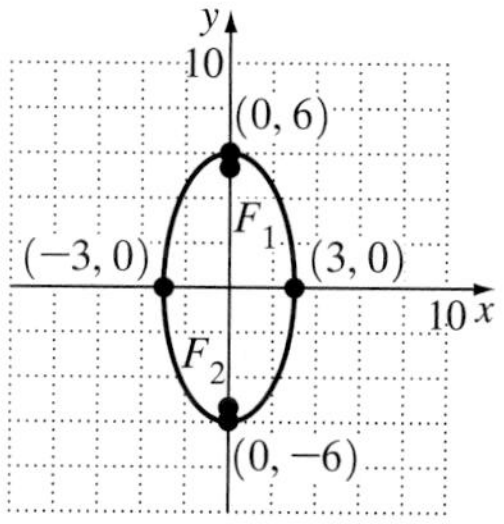


**5.** foci at $(0, -\sqrt{39})$ and $(0, \sqrt{39})$

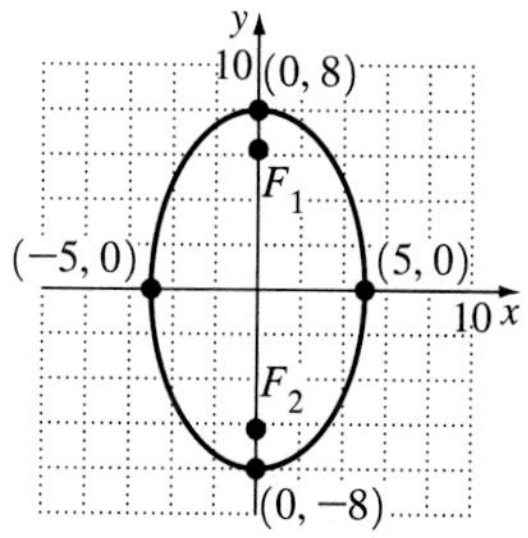


**7.** foci at $(0, -4\sqrt{2})$ and $(0, 4\sqrt{2})$

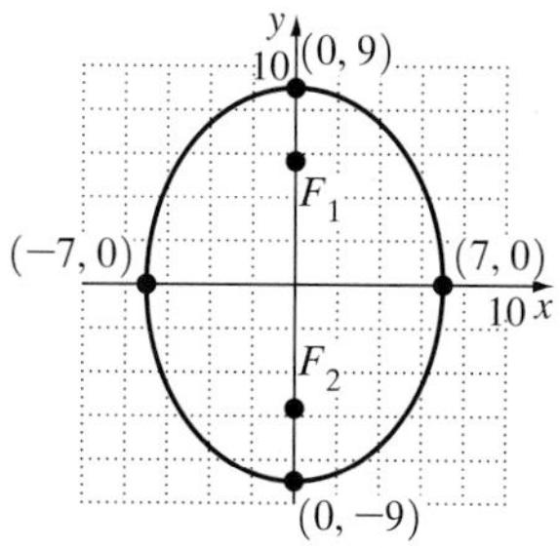


**9.** foci at $(0, -\sqrt{21})$ and $(0, \sqrt{21})$

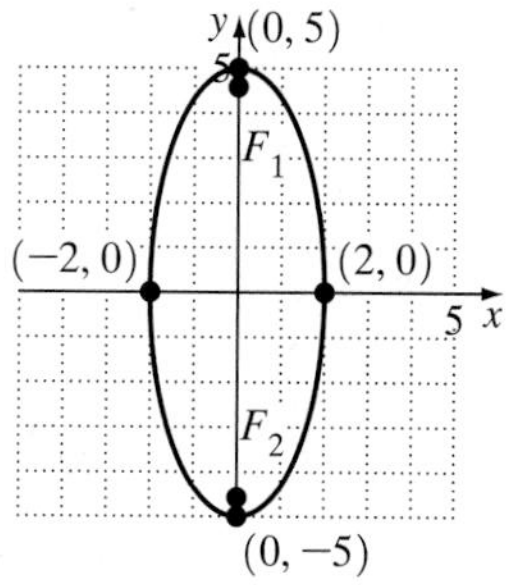


**11.** foci at $(-2\sqrt{3}, 0)$ and $(2\sqrt{3}, 0)$

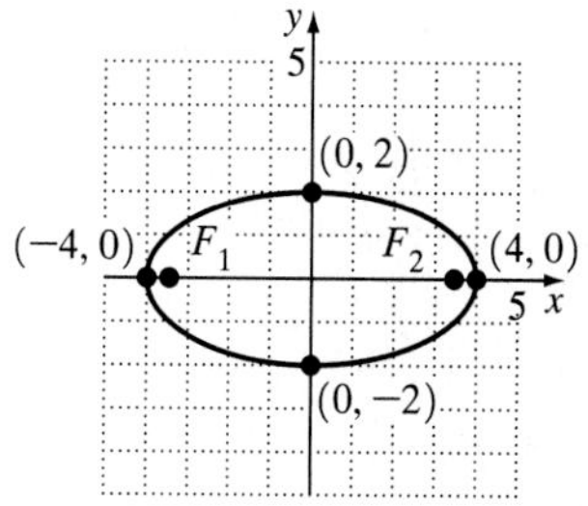


**13.** foci at $(0, 4)$ and $(0, -4)$

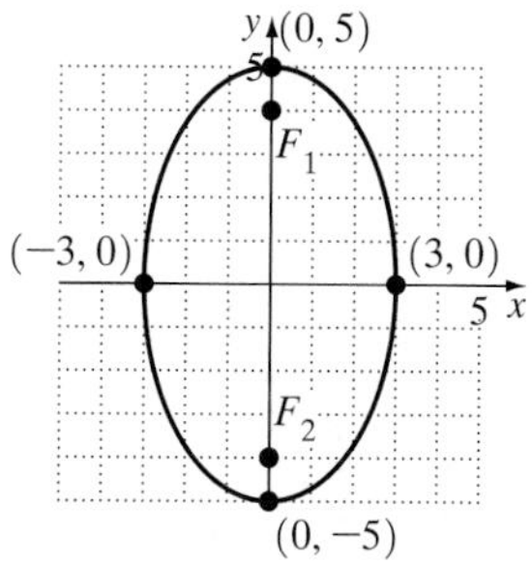


**15.** foci at $(2, 0)$ and $(-2, 0)$

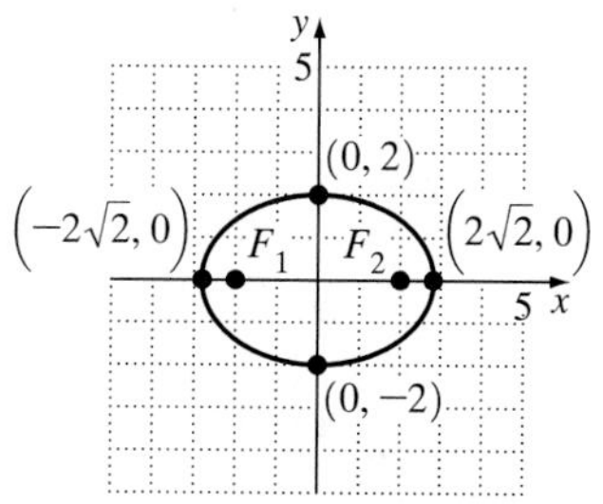


**17.** $\frac{x^2}{4} + \frac{y^2}{1} = 1$; foci at $(-\sqrt{3}, 0)$ and $(\sqrt{3}, 0)$

**19.** $\frac{x^2}{1} + \frac{y^2}{4} = 1$; foci at $(0, \sqrt{3})$ and $(0, -\sqrt{3})$

**21.** $\frac{x^2}{64} + \frac{y^2}{39} = 1$ **23.** $\frac{x^2}{33} + \frac{y^2}{49} = 1$

**25.** $\frac{x^2}{13} + \frac{y^2}{9} = 1$ **27.** $\frac{x^2}{16} + \frac{y^2}{4} = 1$

**29.** $\frac{x^2}{4} + \frac{y^2}{25} = 1$

**31.** foci at $(2 - \sqrt{5}, 1)$ and $(2 + \sqrt{5}, 1)$

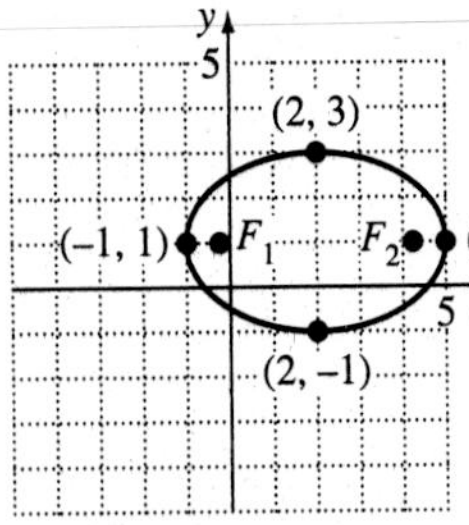


**33.** foci at $(-3 - 2\sqrt{3}, 2)$ and $(-3 + 2\sqrt{3}, 2)$

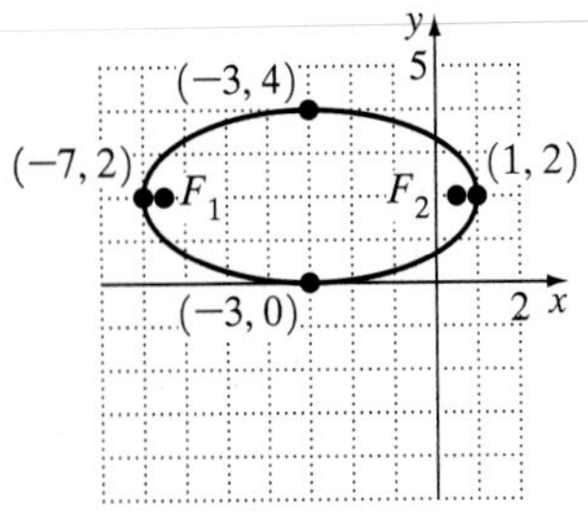


**35.** foci at $(4, 2)$ and $(4, -6)$

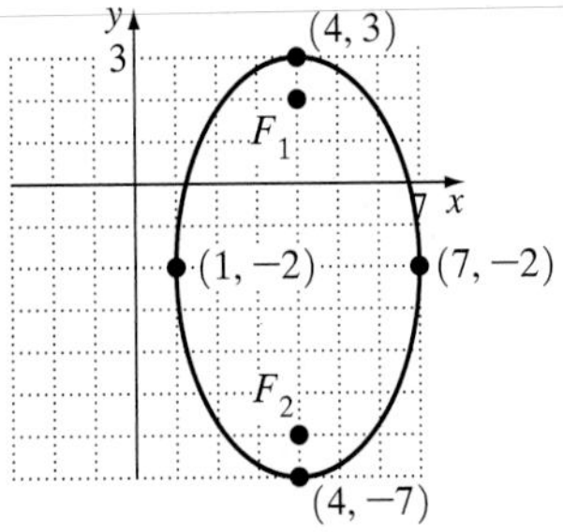


**37.** foci at $(0, 2 + \sqrt{11})$, $(0, 2 - \sqrt{11})$

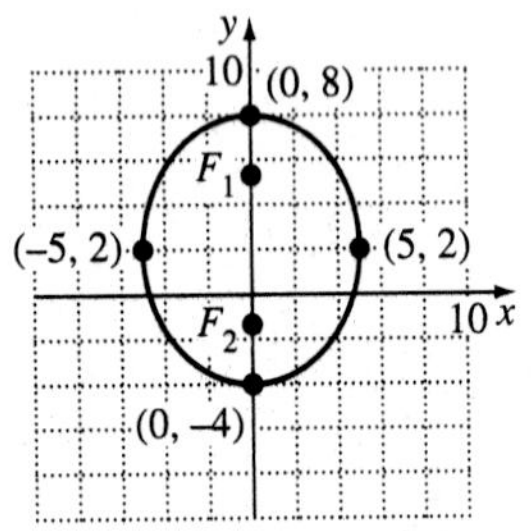


**39.** foci at $(-3 - 2\sqrt{2}, 2)$ and $(-3 + 2\sqrt{2}, 2)$

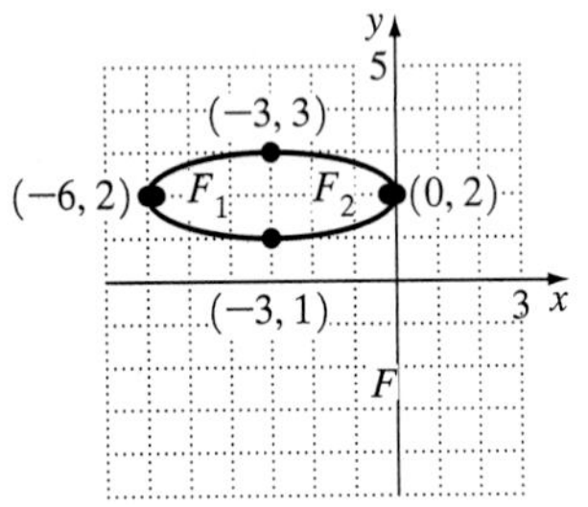


**41.** foci at $(1, -3 + \sqrt{5})$ and $(1, -3 - \sqrt{5})$

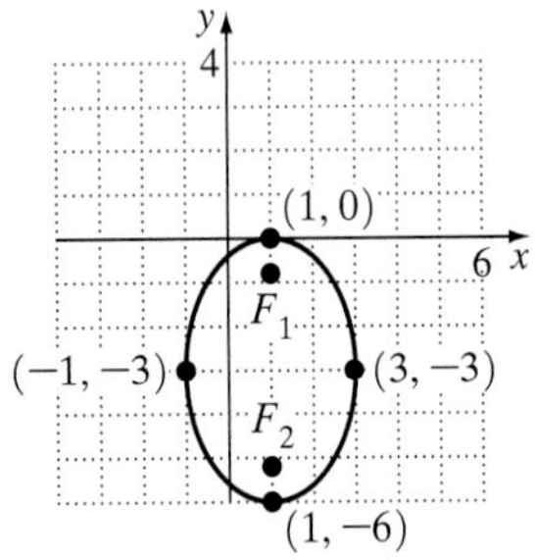


**43.** $\dfrac{(x-2)^2}{25} + \dfrac{(y+1)^2}{9} = 1$
foci at $(-2, -1)$ and $(6, -1)$

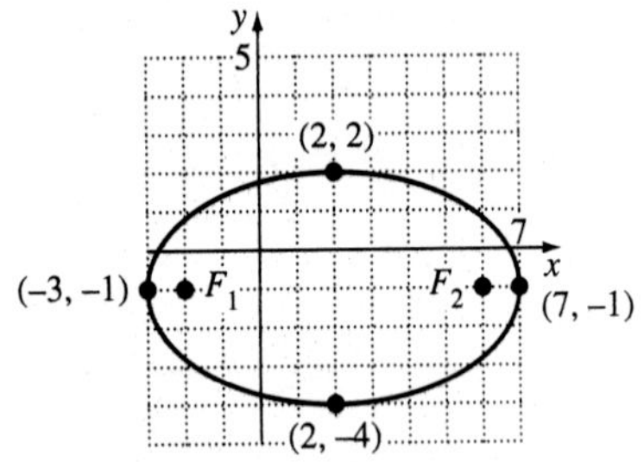


**45.** $\dfrac{(x-1)^2}{16} + \dfrac{(y+2)^2}{9} = 1$
foci at $(1 - \sqrt{7}, -2)$ and $(1 + \sqrt{7}, -2)$

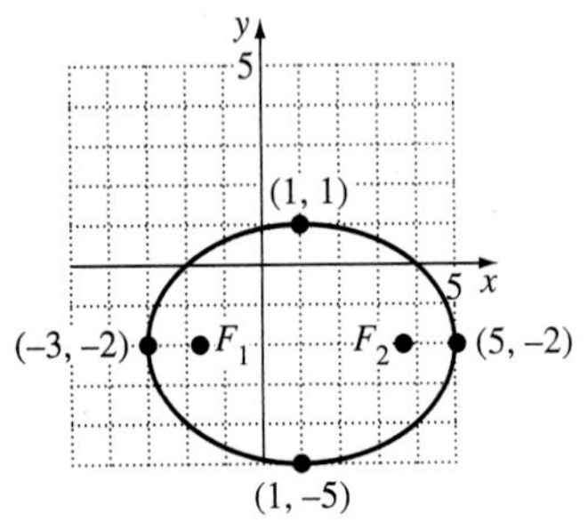


**47.** $\dfrac{(x+2)^2}{16} + \dfrac{(y-3)^2}{64} = 1$
foci at $(-2, 3 + 4\sqrt{3})$ and $(-2, 3 - 4\sqrt{3})$

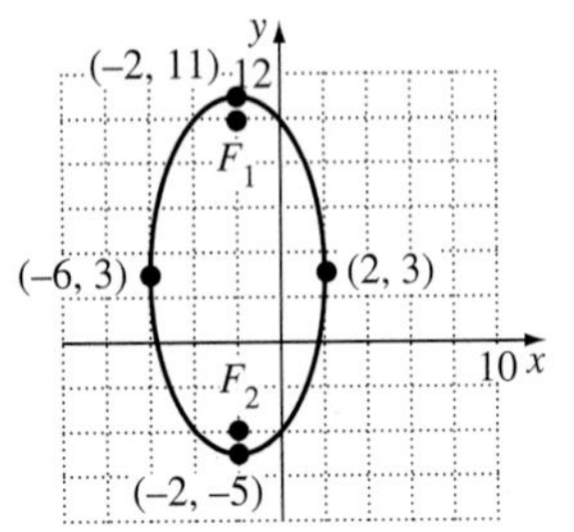


**49.** Yes **51. a.** $\dfrac{x^2}{2304} + \dfrac{y^2}{529} = 1$ **b.** about 42 feet **63.** $\dfrac{x^2}{\frac{36}{5}} + \dfrac{y^2}{36} = 1$ **65.** The large circle has radius 5 with center $(0, 0)$. Its equation is $x^2 + y^2 = 25$. The small circle has radius 3 with center $(0, 0)$. Its equation is $x^2 + y^2 = 9$.

## Section 10.2

### Check Point Exercises

**1. a.** vertices at $(5, 0)$ and $(-5, 0)$; foci at $(\sqrt{41}, 0)$ and $(-\sqrt{41}, 0)$ **b.** vertices at $(0, 5)$ and $(0, -5)$; foci at $(0, \sqrt{41})$ and $(0, -\sqrt{41})$

**2.** $\dfrac{y^2}{9} - \dfrac{x^2}{16} = 1$ **3.** foci at $(-3\sqrt{5}, 0)$ and $(3\sqrt{5}, 0)$ **4.** foci at $(0, \sqrt{5})$ and $(0, -\sqrt{5})$ **5.** foci at $(3 - \sqrt{5}, 1)$ and $(3 + \sqrt{5}, 1)$

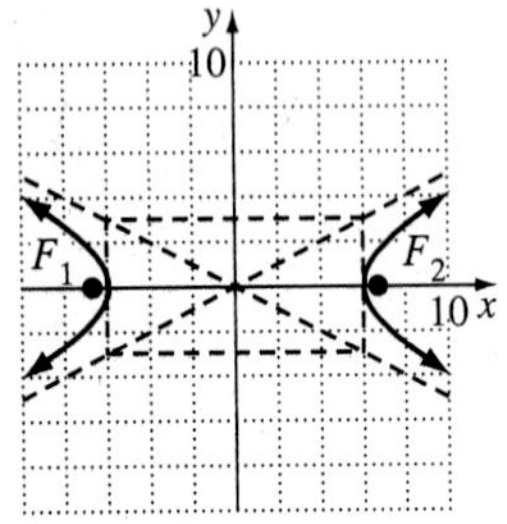


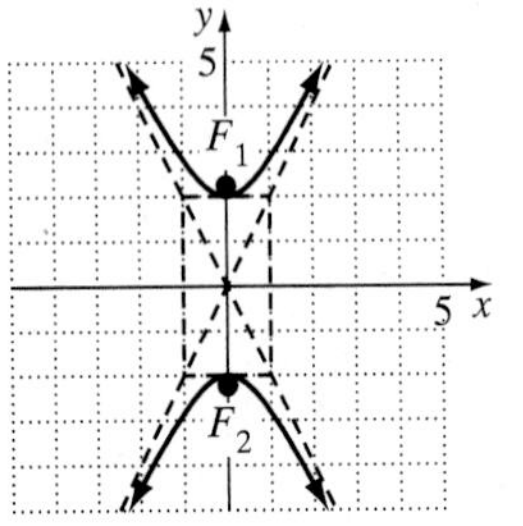


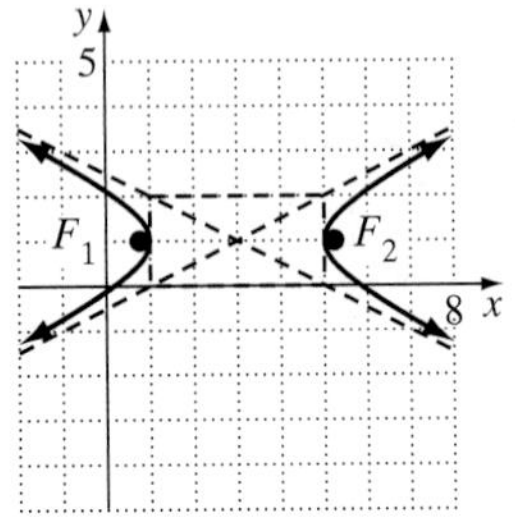

**6.** $\dfrac{x^2}{2{,}722{,}500} - \dfrac{y^2}{25{,}155{,}900} = 1$

## Exercise Set 10.2

**1.** vertices at $(2, 0)$ and $(-2, 0)$; foci at $(\sqrt{5}, 0)$ and $(-\sqrt{5}, 0)$; graph (b)

**3.** vertices at $(0, 2)$ and $(0, -2)$; foci at $(0, \sqrt{5})$ and $(0, -\sqrt{5})$; graph (a)

**5.** $y^2 - \dfrac{x^2}{8} = 1$

**7.** $\dfrac{x^2}{9} - \dfrac{y^2}{7} = 1$

**9.** foci: $(\pm\sqrt{34}, 0)$

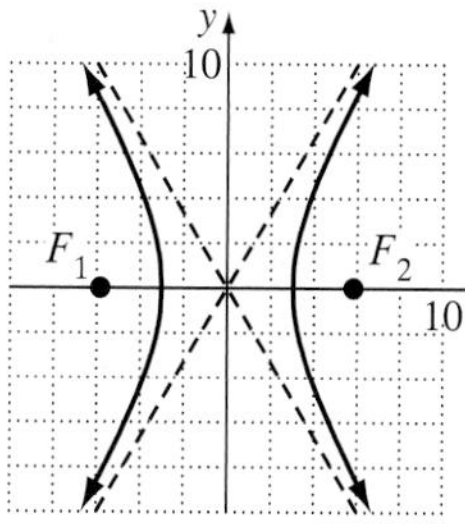


**11.** foci: $(\pm 2\sqrt{41}, 0)$

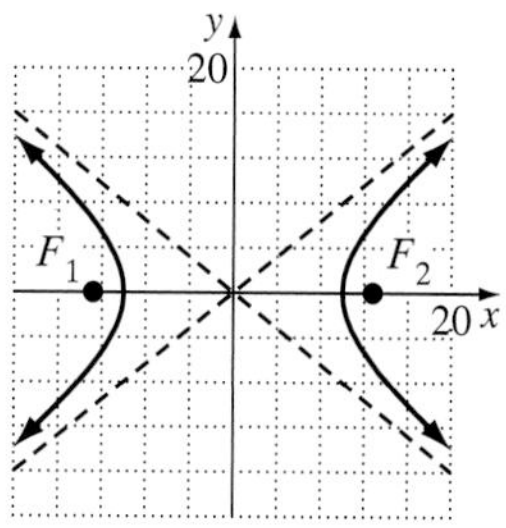


**13.** foci: $(0, \pm 2\sqrt{13})$

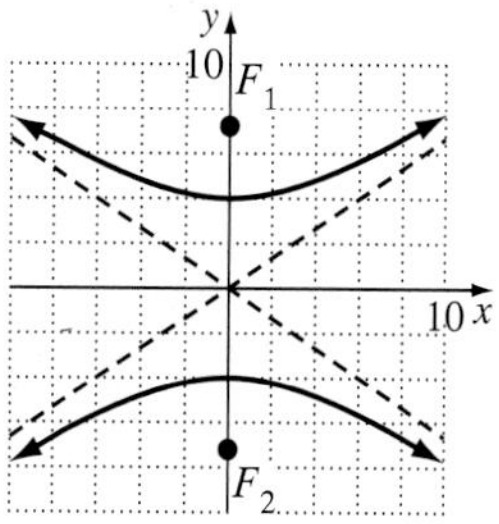


**15.** foci: $(0, \pm\sqrt{61})$

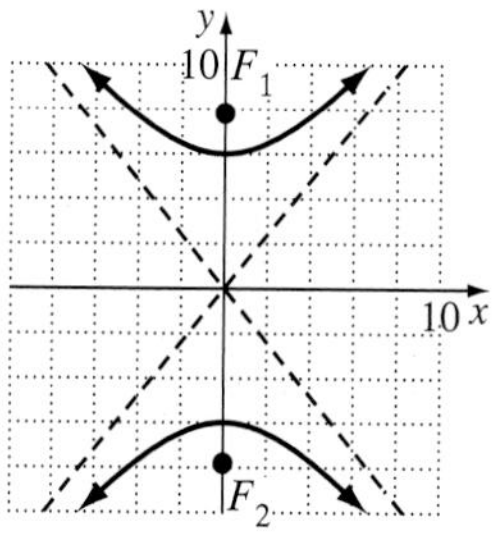


**17.** foci: $(\pm\sqrt{13}, 0)$

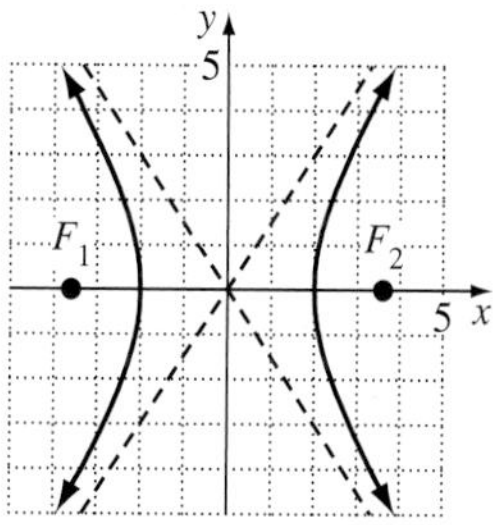


**19.** foci: $(0, \pm\sqrt{34})$

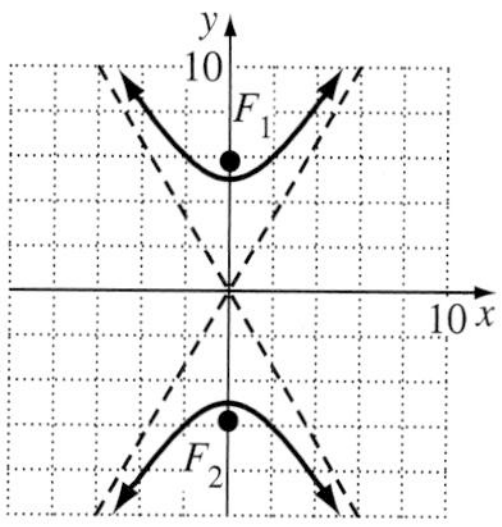


**21.** foci: $(\pm\sqrt{5}, 0)$

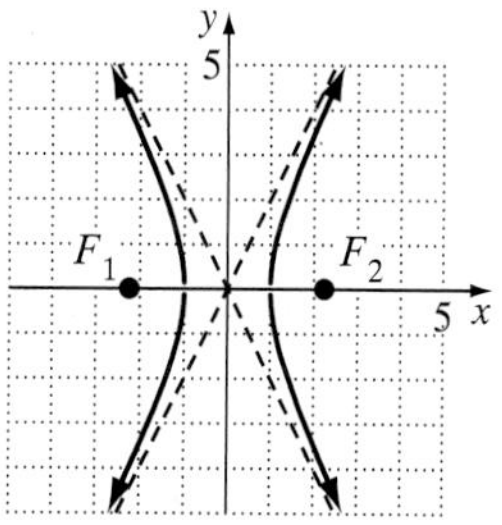


**23.** $\dfrac{x^2}{9} - \dfrac{y^2}{25} = 1$

**25.** $\dfrac{y^2}{4} - \dfrac{x^2}{9} = 1$

**27.** foci: $(-9, -3)$, $(1, -3)$

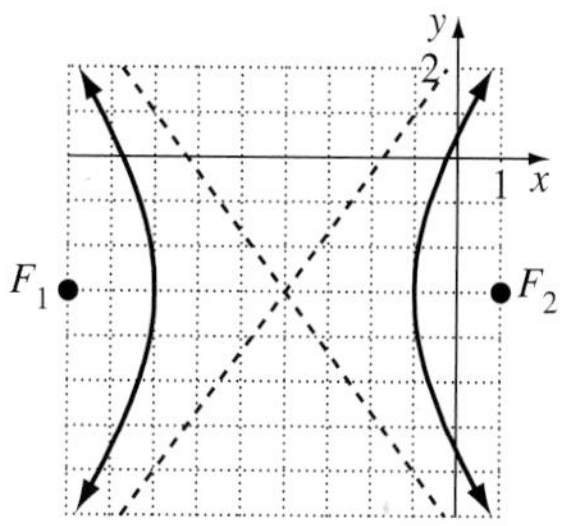


**29.** foci: $(-3 \pm \sqrt{41}, 0)$

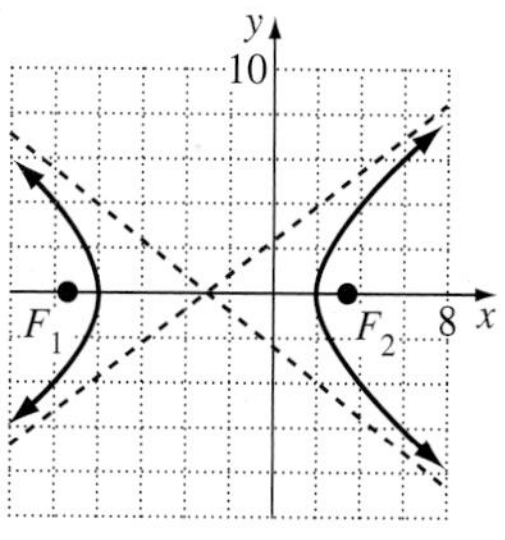


**31.** foci: $(1, -2 \pm 2\sqrt{5})$

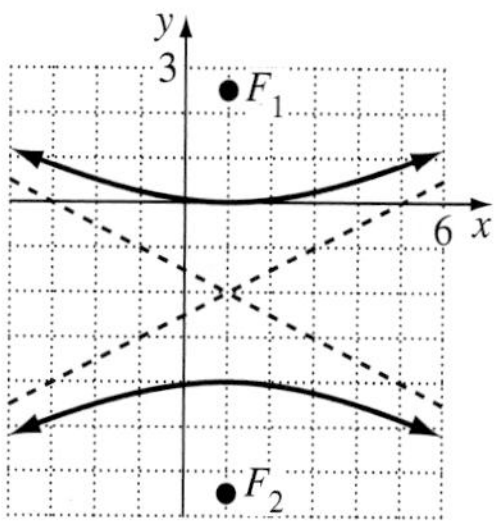


**33.** foci: $(3 \pm \sqrt{5}, -3)$

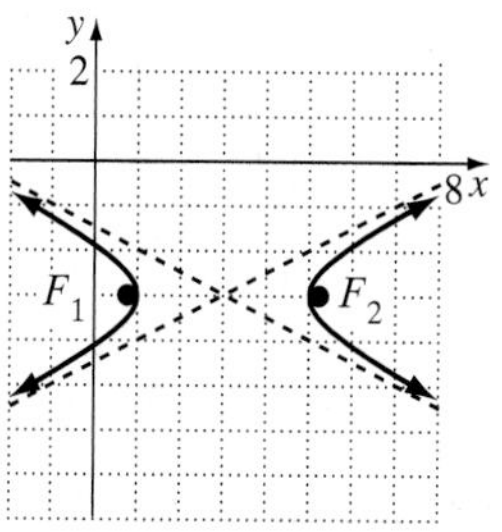


**35.** foci: $(1 \pm 2\sqrt{2}, 2)$

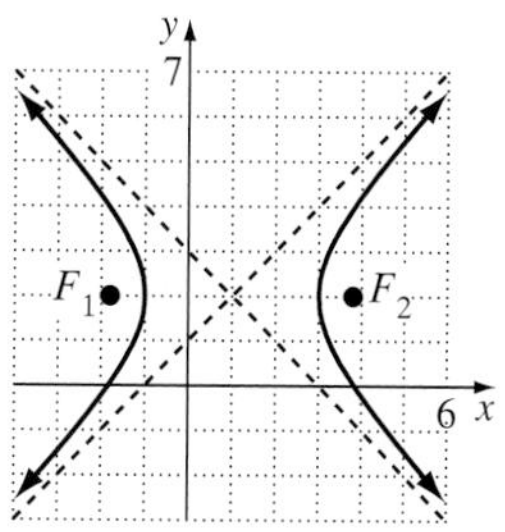


**37.** $(x - 1)^2 - (y + 2)^2 = 1$

foci: $(1 \pm \sqrt{2}, -2)$

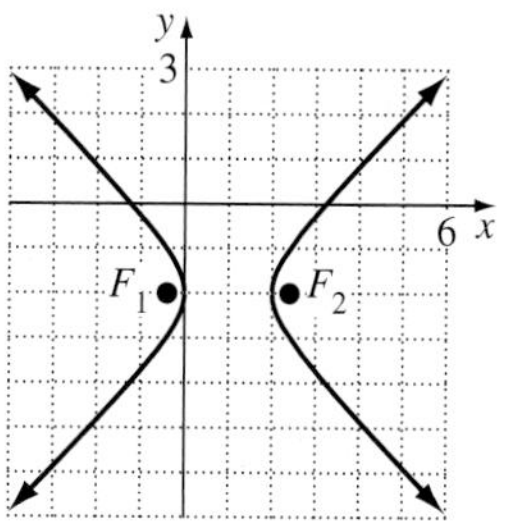


**39.** $\dfrac{(y + 1)^2}{4} - \dfrac{(x + 2)^2}{0.25} = 1$

foci: $(-2, -1 \pm \sqrt{4.25})$

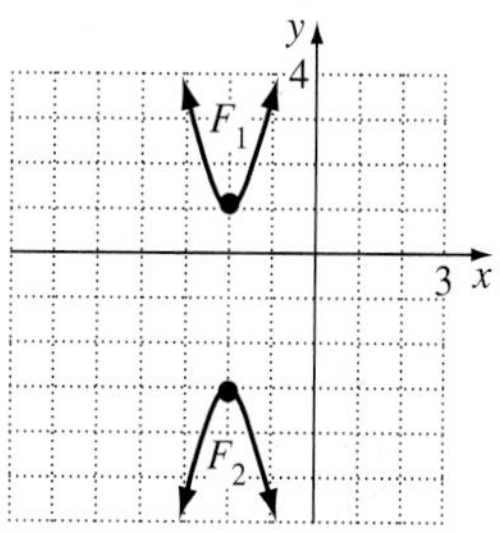


**41.** $\dfrac{(x - 2)^2}{9} - \dfrac{(y - 3)^2}{4} = 1$

foci: $(2 \pm \sqrt{13}, 3)$

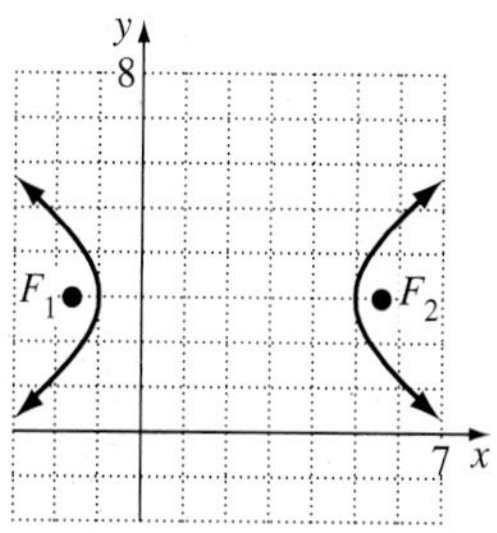

**43.** $\frac{y^2}{4} - \frac{(x-4)^2}{25} = 1$

foci: $(4, \pm\sqrt{29})$

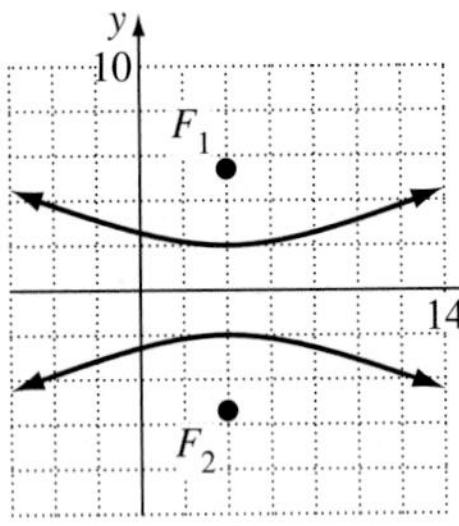


**45.** If $M_1$ is located 2640 feet to the right of the origin on the $x$-axis, the explosion is located on the right branch of the hyperbola given by the equation $\frac{x^2}{1{,}210{,}000} - \frac{y^2}{5{,}759{,}600} = 1.$

**47.** 40 yd **59.**

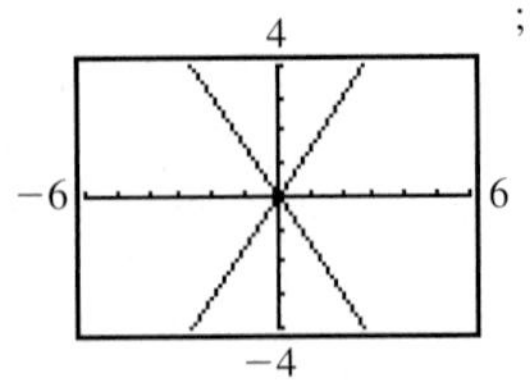


; No. Two intersecting lines.

**61.** $2y^2 + (10 - 6x)y + (4x^2 - 3x - 6) = 0$

$y = \frac{3x - 5 \pm \sqrt{x^2 - 24x + 37}}{2}$

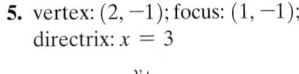

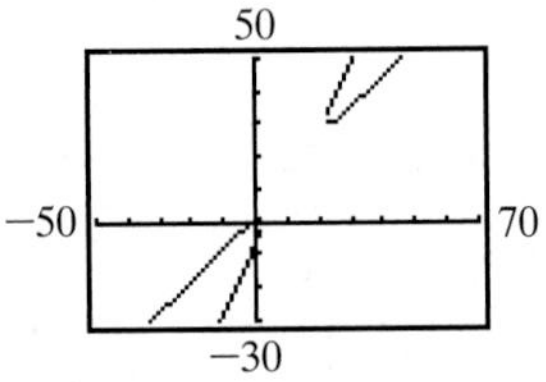


The $xy$-term rotates the hyperbola.

**63.** (c) is true.

**65.** $\frac{y^2}{36} - \frac{(x-5)^2}{20} = 1$

## Section 10.3

### Check Point Exercises

**1.** focus: $(2, 0)$
directrix: $x = -2$

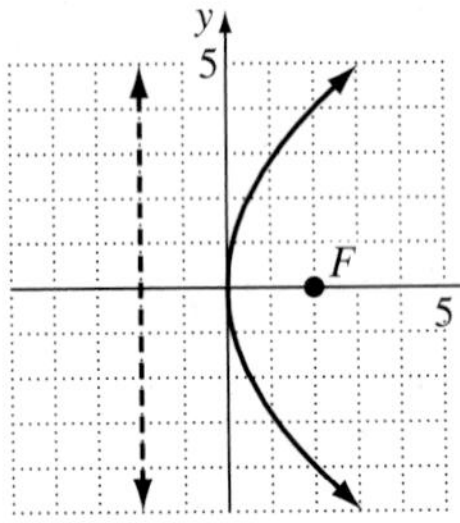


**2.** focus: $(0, -3)$
directrix: $y = 3$

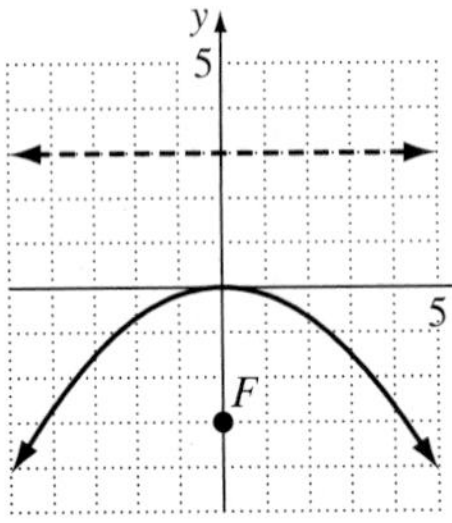


**3.** $y^2 = 32x$

**4.** vertex: $(2, -1)$; focus: $(2, 0)$;
directrix: $y = -2$

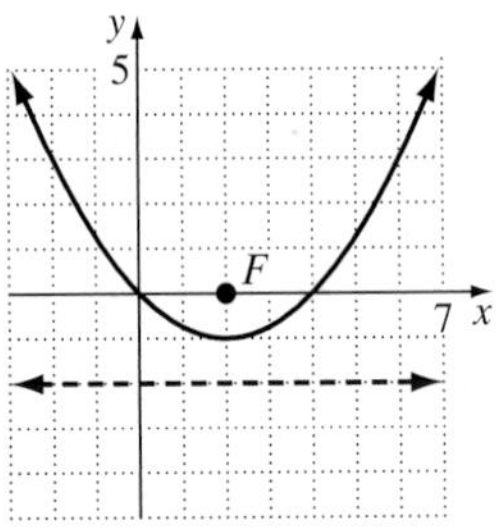


**5.** vertex: $(2, -1)$; focus: $(1, -1)$;
directrix: $x = 3$

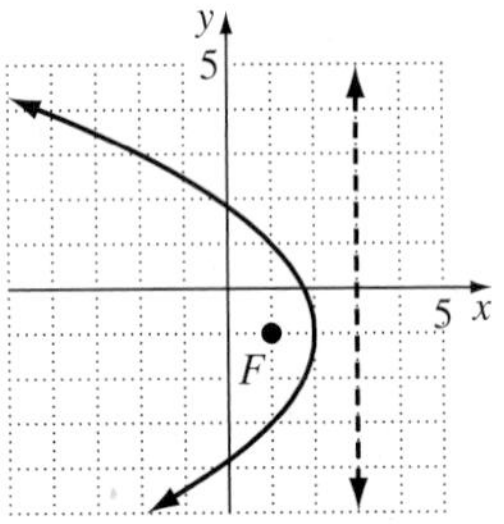


**6.** $x^2 = \frac{9}{4}y$; The light should be placed at $\left(0, \frac{9}{16}\right)$, or $\frac{9}{16}$ inch above the vertex.

### Exercise Set 10.3

**1.** focus: $(1, 0)$; directrix: $x = -1$; graph (c)

**3.** focus: $(0, -1)$, directrix: $y = 1$; graph (b)

**5.** focus: $(4, 0)$; directrix: $x = -4$

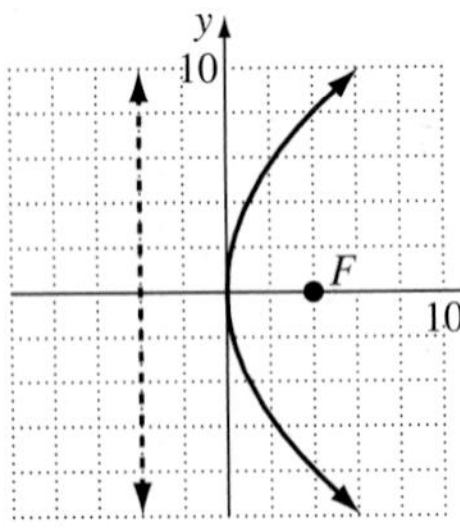


**7.** focus: $(-2, 0)$; directrix: $x = 2$

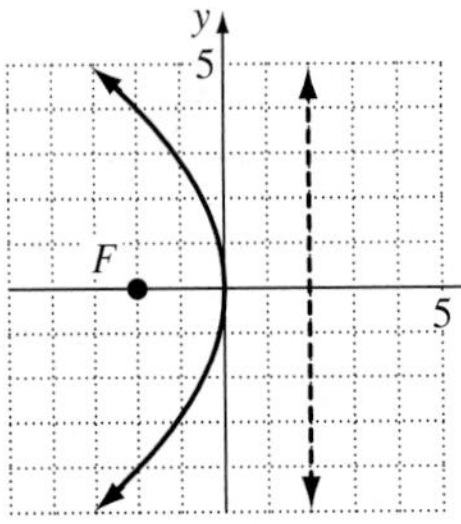


**9.** focus: $(0, 3)$; directrix: $y = -3$

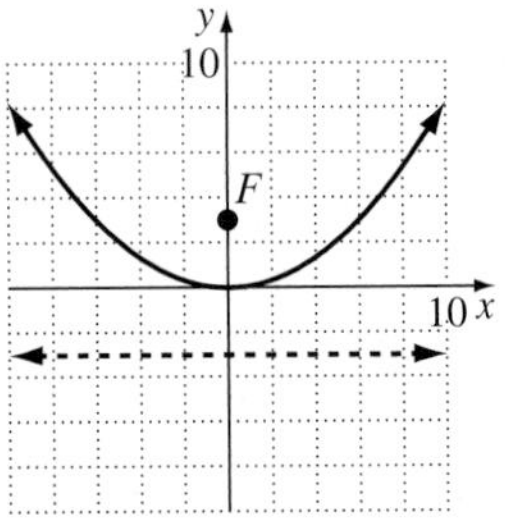

**11.** focus: $(0, -4)$; directrix: $y = 4$

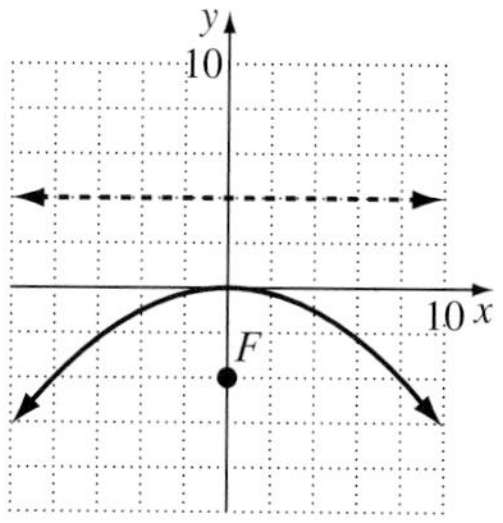


**13.** focus: $\left(\frac{3}{2}, 0\right)$; directrix: $x = -\frac{3}{2}$

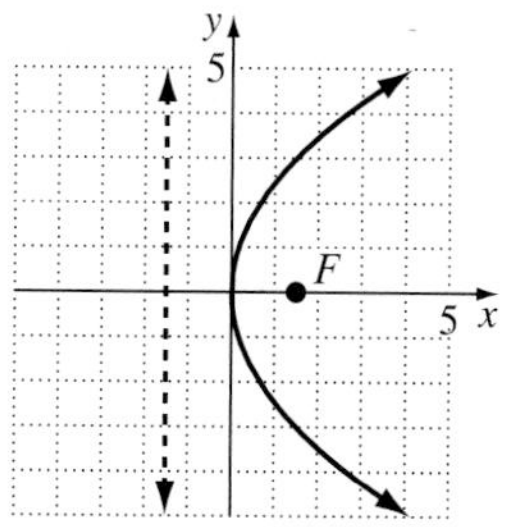


**15.** $y^2 = 28x$

**17.** $y^2 = -20x$

**19.** $x^2 = 60y$

**21.** $x^2 = -100y$

**23.** vertex: $(1, 1)$; focus: $(2, 1)$; directrix: $x = 0$; graph (c)

**25.** vertex: $(-1, -1)$; focus: $(-1, -2)$; directrix: $y = 0$; graph (d)

**27.** vertex: $(2, 1)$; focus: $(2, 3)$; directrix: $y = -1$

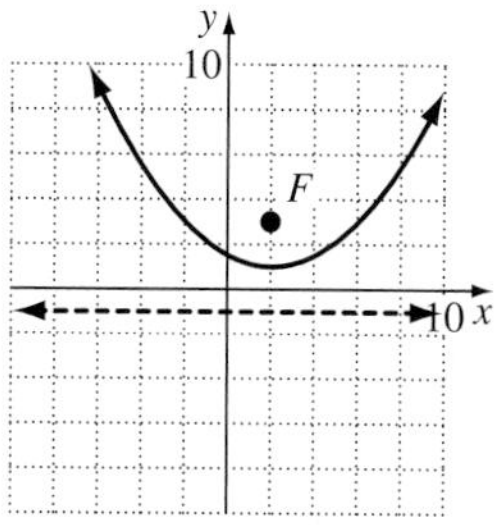


**29.** vertex: $(-1, -1)$; focus: $(-1, -3)$; directrix: $y = 1$

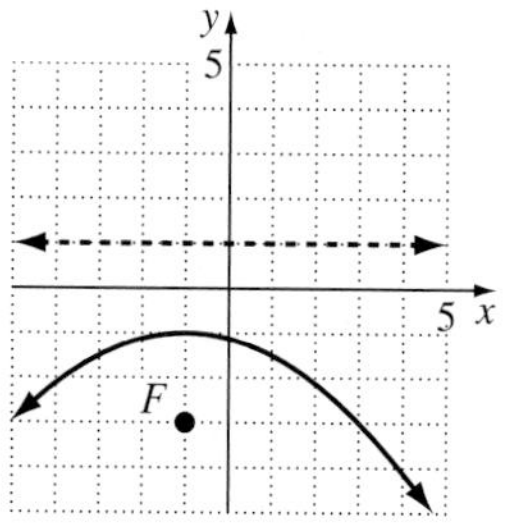


**31.** vertex: $(-1, -3)$; focus: $(2, -3)$; directrix: $x = -4$

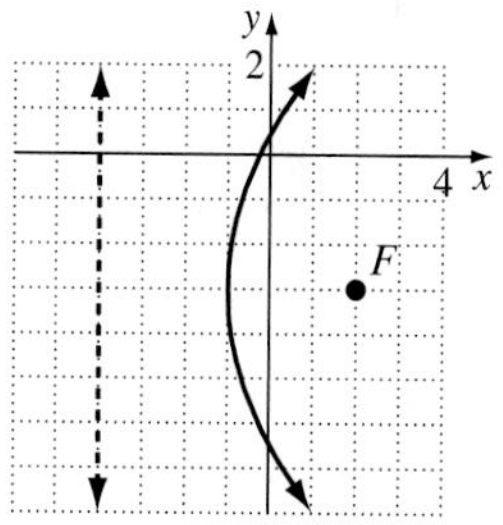


**33.** vertex: $(0, -1)$; focus: $(-2, -1)$; directrix: $x = 2$

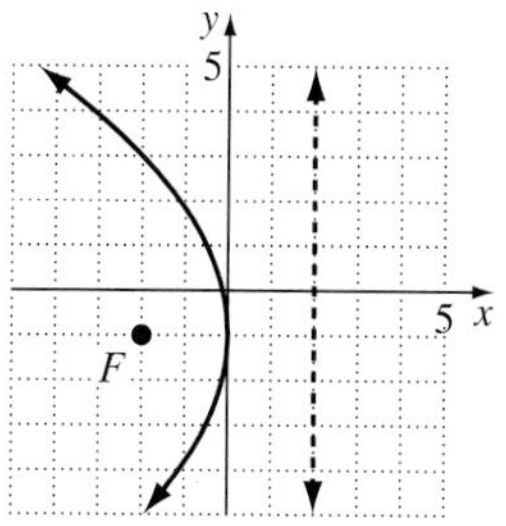


**35.** $(x - 1)^2 = 4(y - 2)$; vertex: $(1, 2)$; focus: $(1, 3)$; directrix: $y = 1$

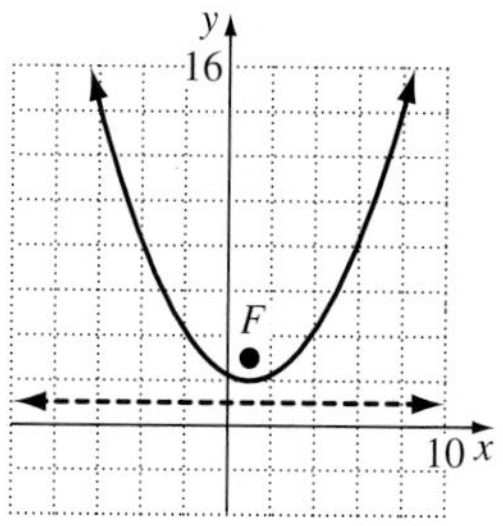


**37.** $(y - 1)^2 = -12(x - 3)$; vertex: $(3, 1)$; focus: $(0, 1)$; directrix: $x = 6$

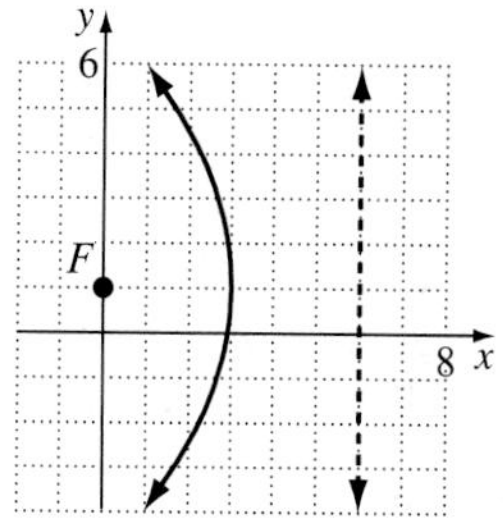


**39.** $(x + 3)^2 = 4(y + 2)$; vertex: $(-3, -2)$; focus: $(-3, -1)$; directrix: $y = -3$

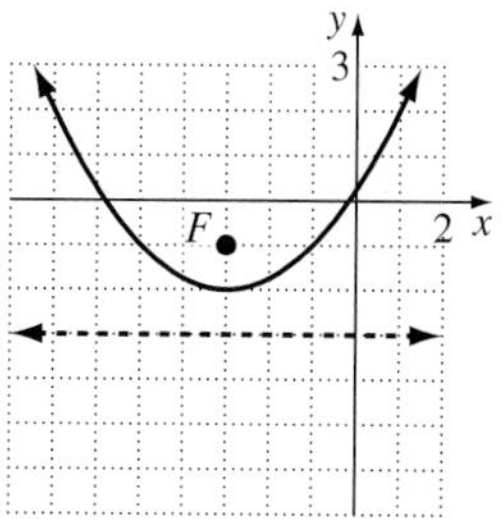


**41.** 1 inch above the vertex.

**43.** 4.5 feet from the base of the dish.

**45.** 75.625 m

**47.** yes

**57.** $y = -5 \pm \sqrt{x}$

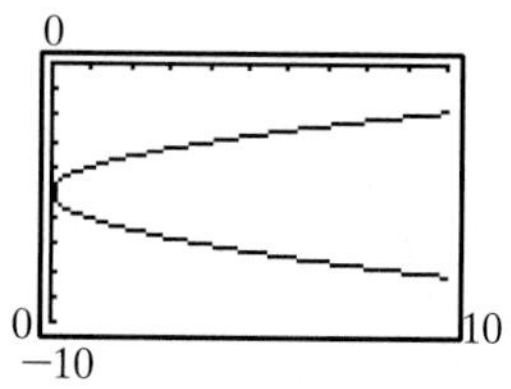


**59.** $3y^2 + (2\sqrt{3}x - 8)y + x^2 + 8\sqrt{3}x + 32 = 0$

$$y = \frac{-\sqrt{3}x + 4 \pm 4\sqrt{-2\sqrt{3}x - 5}}{3}$$

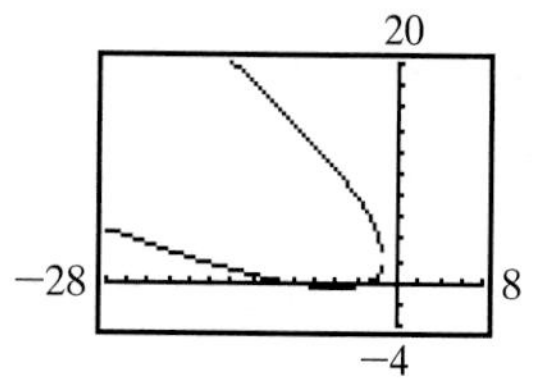


**61.** $\frac{25}{6}$ ft

## Section 10.4

### Check Point Exercises

**1. a.** ellipse **b.** circle **c.** parabola **d.** hyperbola

**2.** $\frac{x'^2}{4} - \frac{y'^2}{4} = 1$

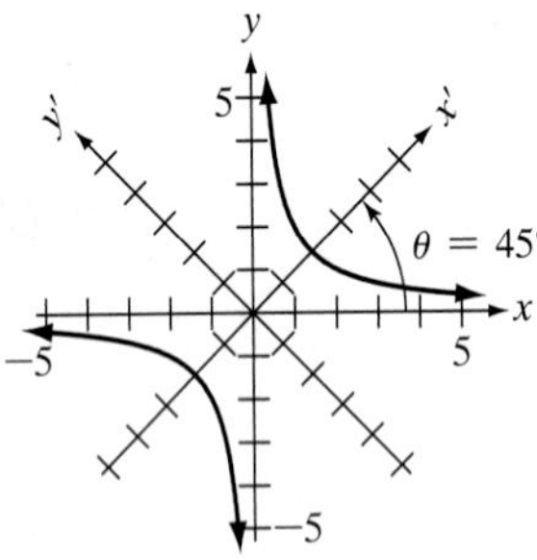


**3.** $\frac{x'^2}{\frac{4}{5}} + \frac{y'^2}{4} = 1$

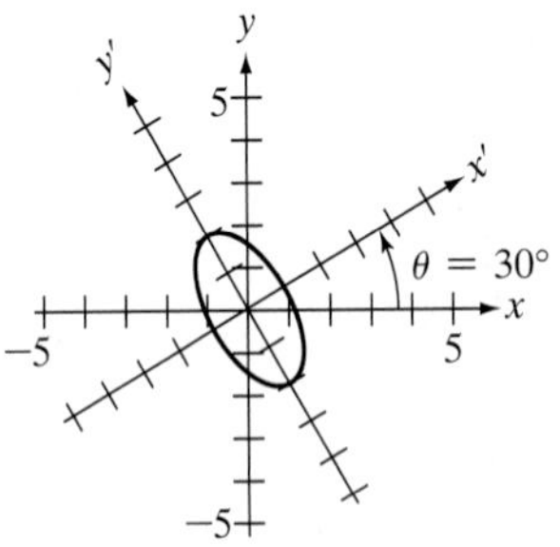


**4.**

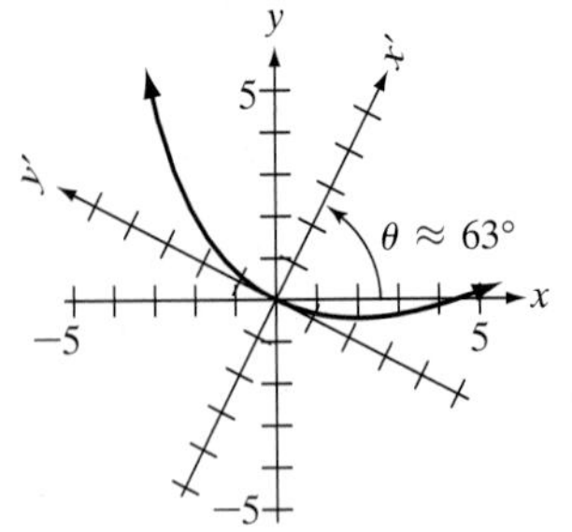


**5.** parabola

### Exercise Set 10.4

**1.** parabola **3.** hyperbola **5.** circle **7.** hyperbola **9.** $\frac{y'^2}{2} - \frac{x'^2}{2} = 1$ **11.** $\frac{y'^2}{1} - \frac{x'^2}{3} = 1$ **13.** $\frac{x'^2}{4} - \frac{y'^2}{9} = 1$

**15.** $x = \frac{\sqrt{2}}{2}(x' - y');\ y = \frac{\sqrt{2}}{2}(x' + y')$ **17.** $x = \frac{\sqrt{2}}{2}(x' - y');\ y = \frac{\sqrt{2}}{2}(x' + y')$ **19.** $x = \frac{\sqrt{3}x' - y'}{2};\ y = \frac{x' + \sqrt{3}y'}{2}$

**21.** $x = \frac{3x' - 4y'}{5};\ y = \frac{4x' + 3y'}{5}$ **23.** $x = \sqrt{5}\left(\frac{2x' - y'}{5}\right);\ y = \sqrt{5}\left(\frac{x' + 2y'}{5}\right)$ **25.** $x = \frac{4x' - 3y'}{5};\ y = \frac{3x' + 4y'}{5}$

**27. a.** $3x'^2 + y'^2 = 20$
**b.** $\frac{x'^2}{\frac{20}{3}} + \frac{y'^2}{20} = 1$
**c.**

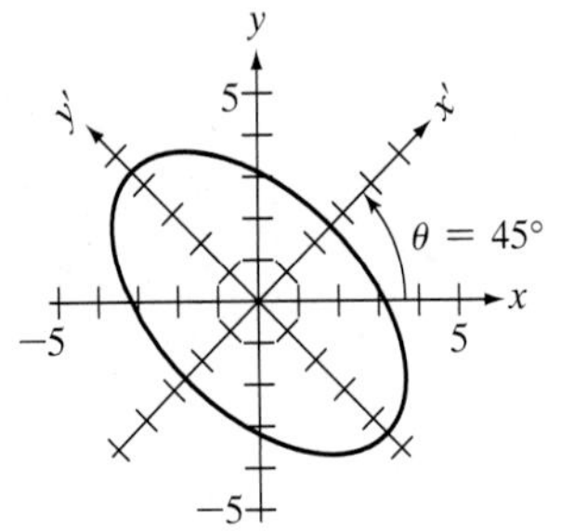


**29. a.** $-4x'^2 + 16y'^2 = 64$
**b.** $\frac{y'^2}{4} - \frac{x'^2}{16} = 1$
**c.**

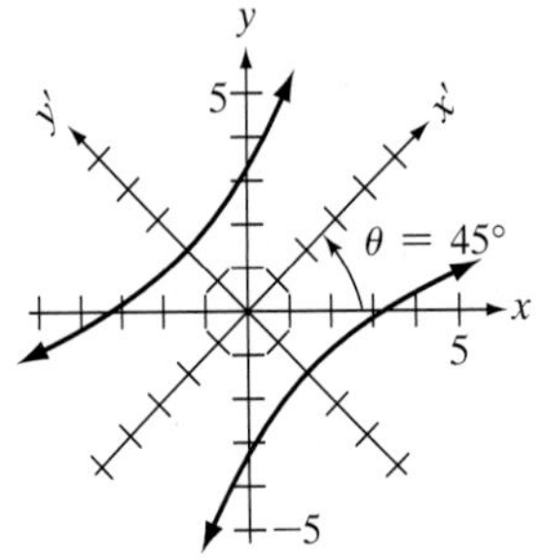


**31. a.** $64x'^2 - 16y'^2 = 16$
**b.** $\frac{x'^2}{\frac{1}{4}} - \frac{y'^2}{1} = 1$
**c.**

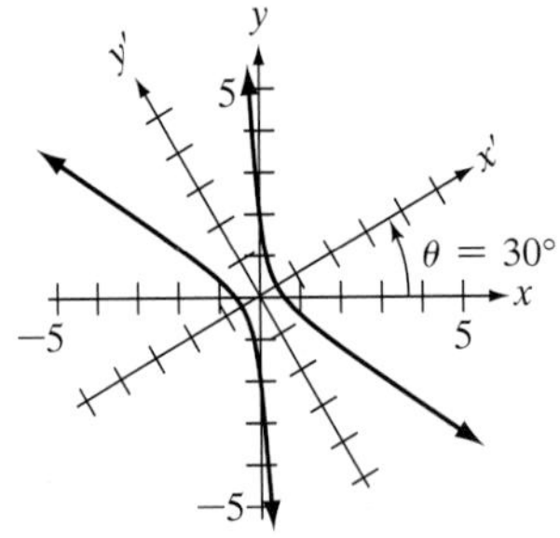


**33. a.** $650x'^2 + 25y'^2 = 225$
**b.** $\frac{x'^2}{\frac{9}{26}} + \frac{y'^2}{9} = 1$
**c.**

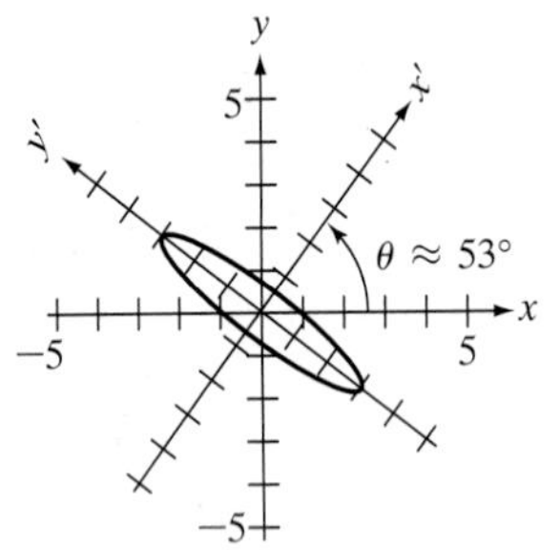


**35. a.** $50x'^2 - 75y'^2 = 25$
**b.** $\frac{x'^2}{\frac{1}{2}} - \frac{y'^2}{\frac{1}{3}} = 1$
**c.**

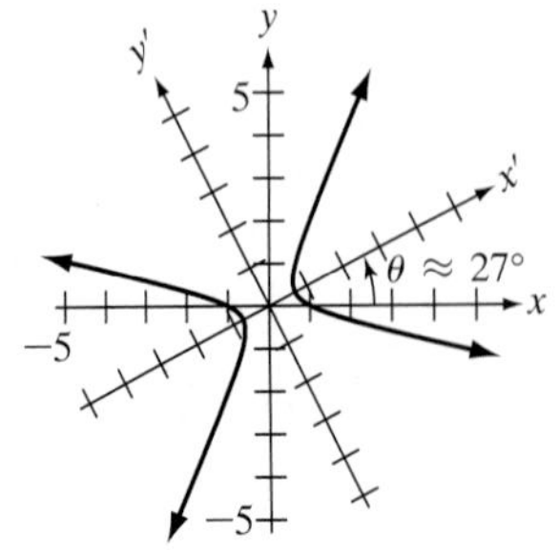


**37. a.** $625x'^2 + 1250y'^2 = 625$
**b.** $\frac{x'^2}{1} + \frac{y'^2}{\frac{1}{2}} = 1$
**c.**

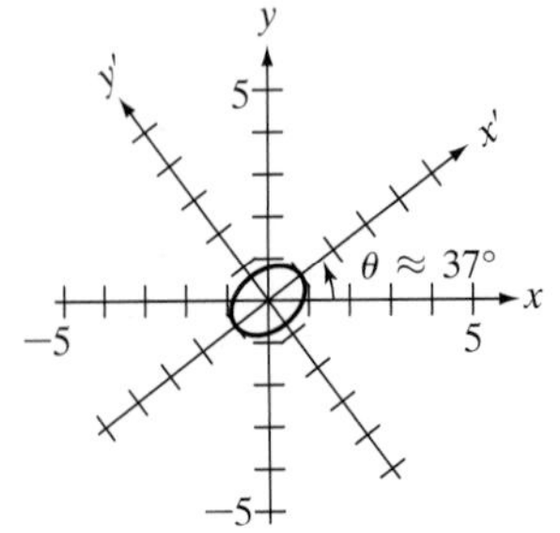


**39.** ellipse or circle **41.** parabola **43.** hyperbola

**51.**

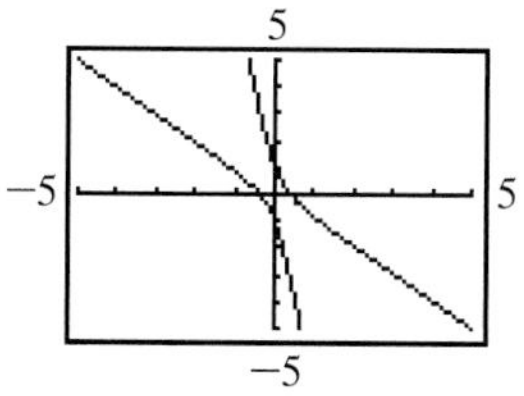

**53.**

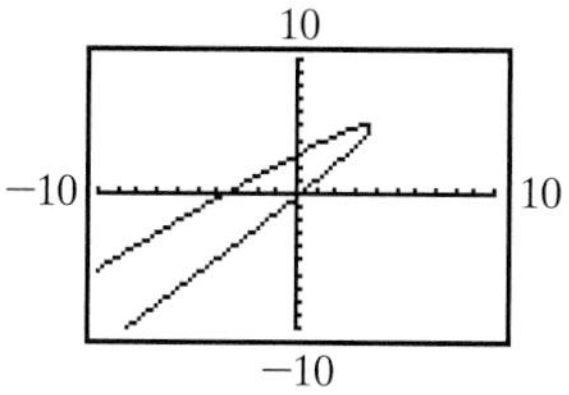

**55.**

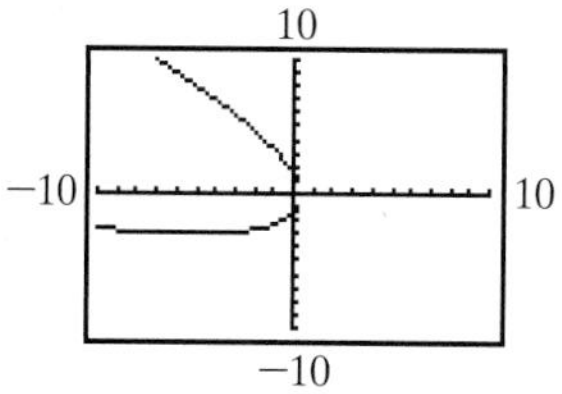

**57.** There are no solutions to this equation just as there is no such sound.

**59.**

$$\begin{aligned} A' &= A\cos^2\theta + B\sin\theta\cos\theta + C\sin^2\theta \\ C' &= A\sin^2\theta - B\sin\theta\cos\theta + C\cos^2\theta \\ A' + C' &= A\cos^2\theta + B\sin\theta\cos\theta + C\sin^2\theta + A\sin^2\theta - B\sin\theta\cos\theta + C\cos^2\theta \\ &= A(\cos^2\theta + \sin^2\theta) + B(\sin\theta\cos\theta - \sin\theta\cos\theta) + C(\sin^2\theta + \cos^2\theta) \\ &= A(1) + B(0) + C(1) \\ &= A + C \end{aligned}$$

## Section 10.5

### Check Point Exercises

**1.**

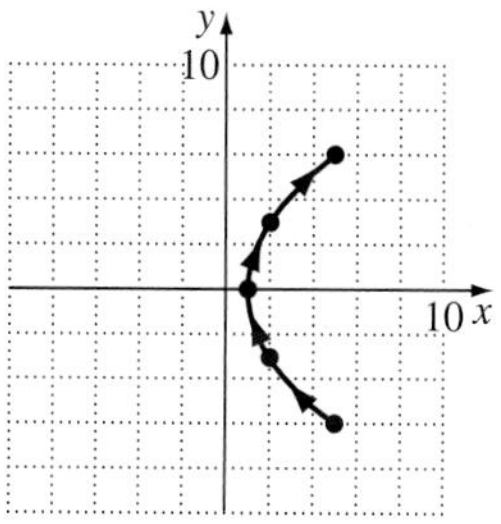

**2.**

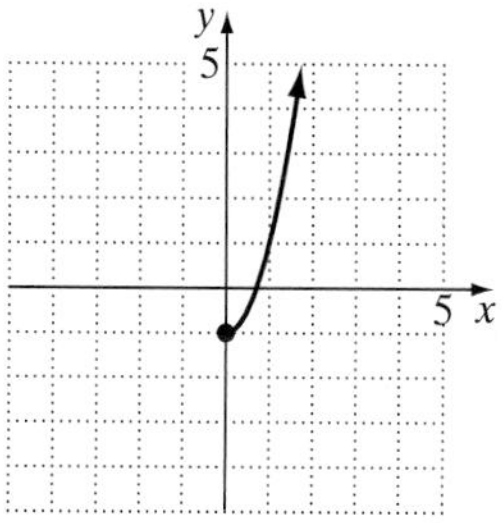

**3.**

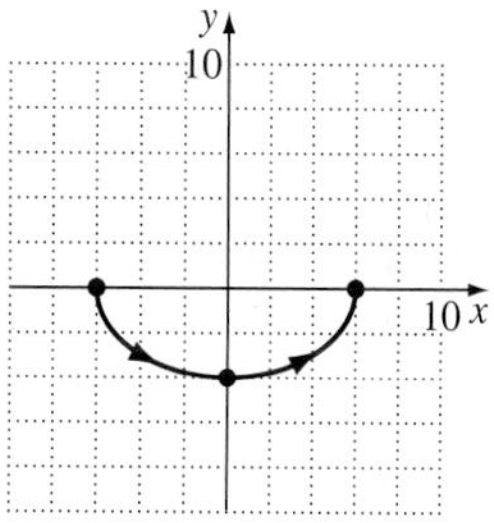

**4.** $x = t$ and $y = t^2 - 25$

### Exercise Set 10.5

**1.** $(-2, 6)$ **3.** $(5, -3)$ **5.** $(4, 8)$ **7.** $(60\sqrt{3}, 1)$

**9.**

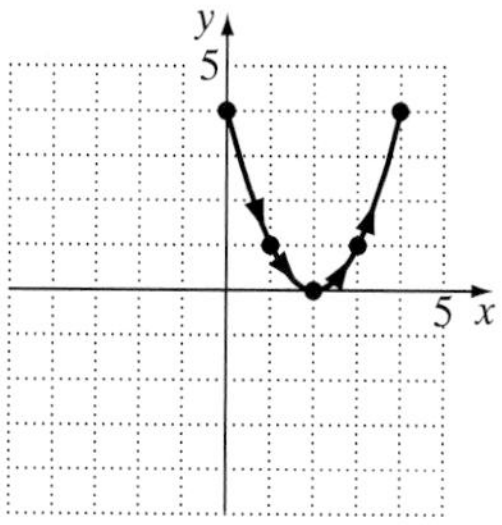

**11.**

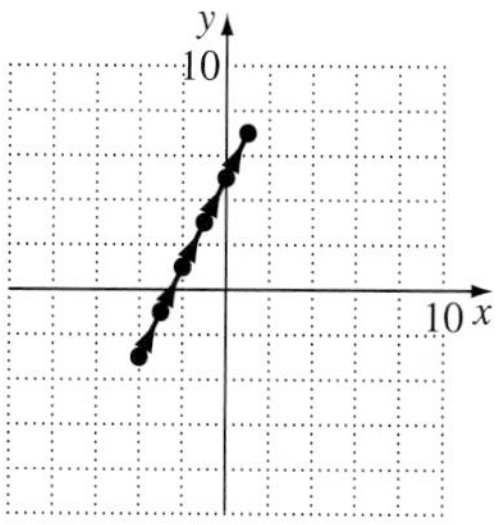

**13.**

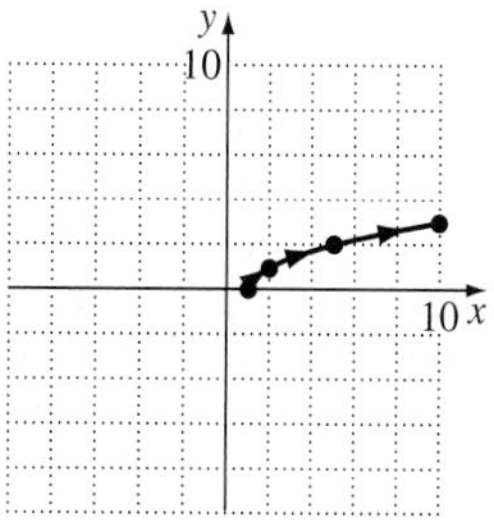

**15.**

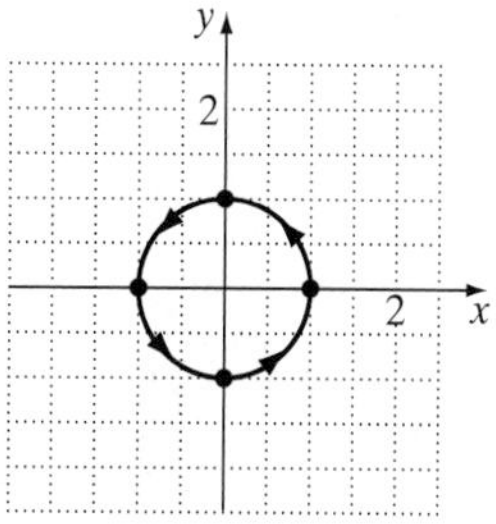

**17.**

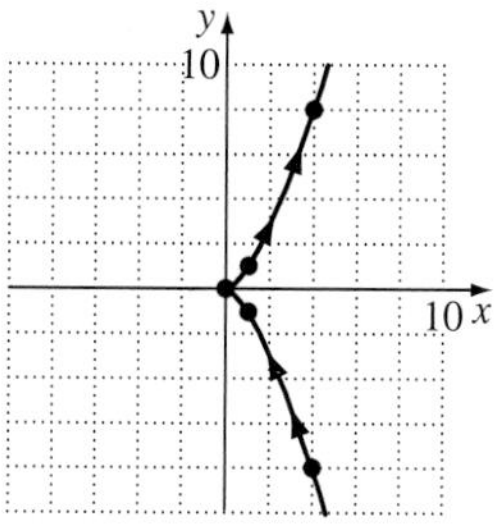

**19.**

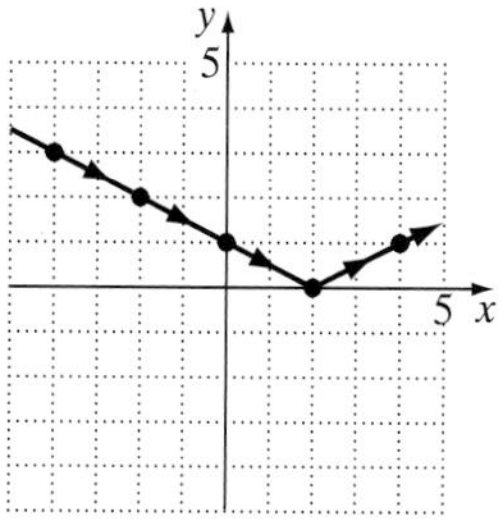

**21.** $y = 2x$

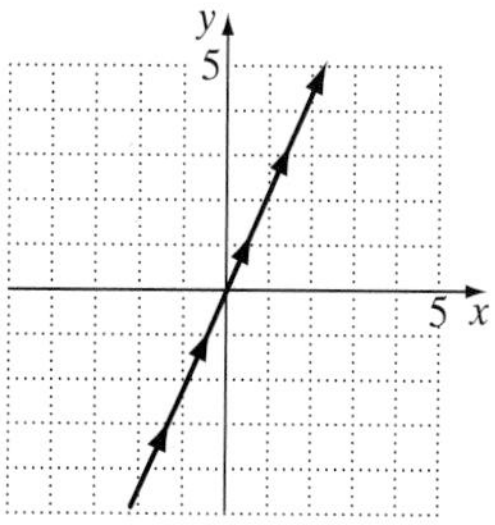

**23.** $y = (x + 4)^2$

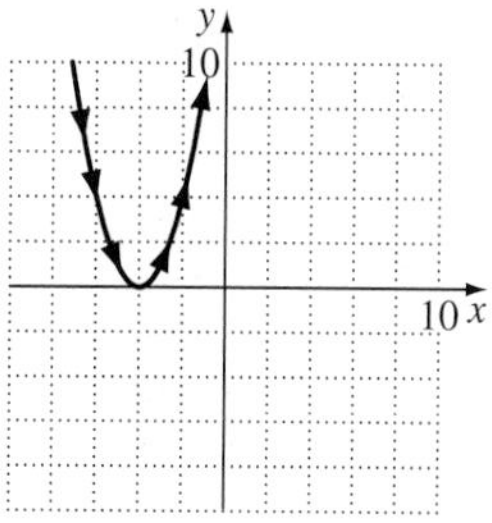

**25.** $y = x^2 - 1, x \geq 0$

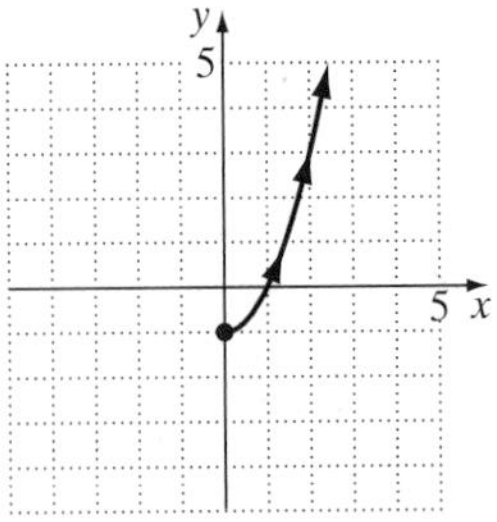

**27.** $\dfrac{x^2}{4} + \dfrac{y^2}{4} = 1$

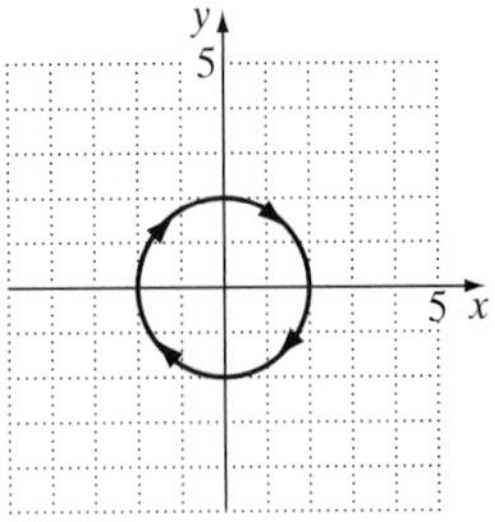

**29.** $\dfrac{(x-1)^2}{9} + \dfrac{(y-2)^2}{9} = 1$

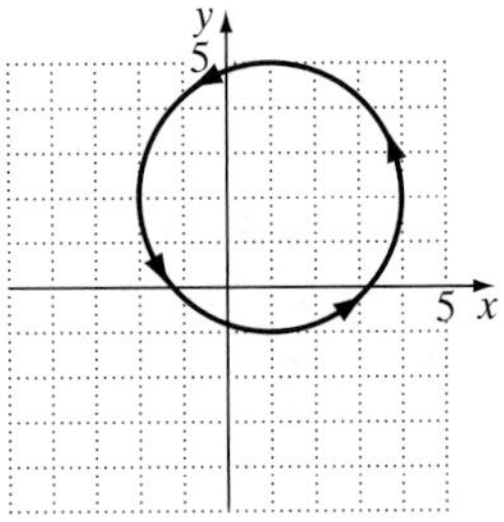

**31.** $\dfrac{x^2}{4} + \dfrac{y^2}{9} = 1$

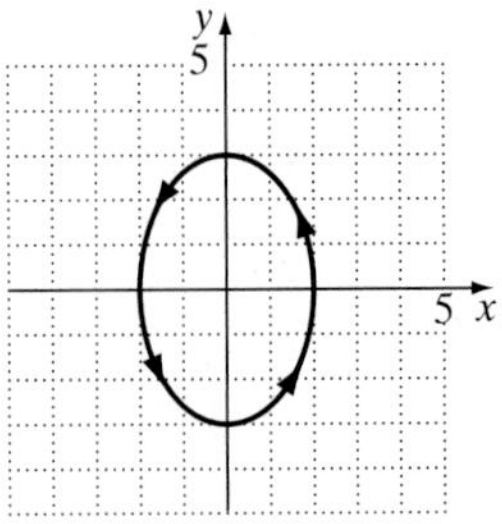

**33.** $\dfrac{(x-1)^2}{9} + \dfrac{(y+1)^2}{4} = 1,$
$-2 \leq x \leq 4, -1 \leq y \leq 1$

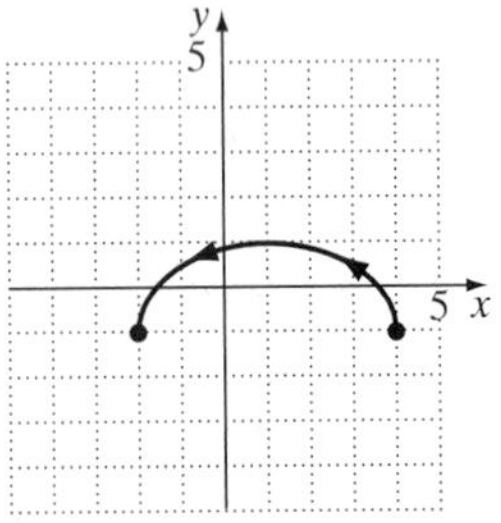

**35.** $x^2 - y^2 = 1$

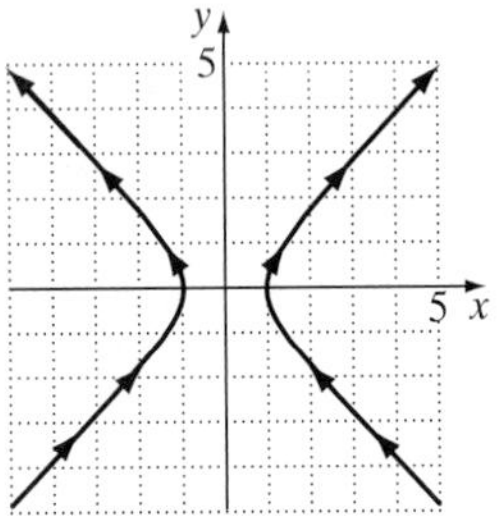

**37.** $y = x - 4, x \geq 2, y \geq -2$

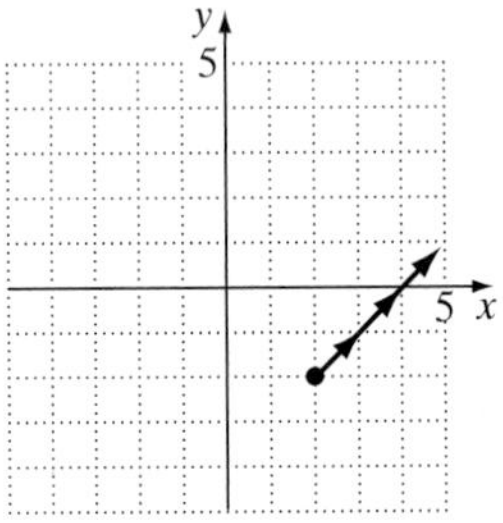

**39.** $y = \dfrac{1}{x}, x \geq 1, y \geq 0$

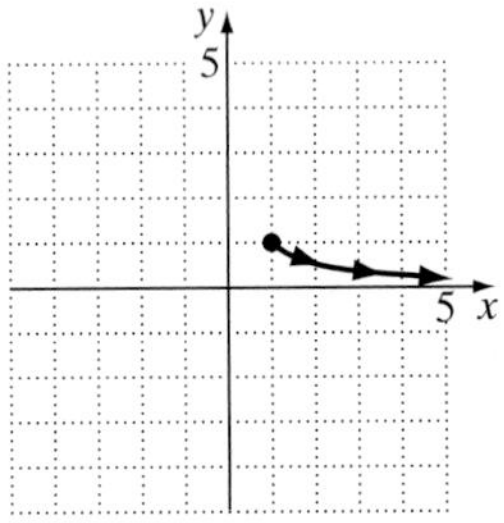

**41.** $(x - h)^2 + (y - k)^2 = r^2$ **43.** $\dfrac{(x-h)^2}{a^2} - \dfrac{(y-k)^2}{b^2} = 1$ **45.** $x = 3 + 6\cos t; y = 5 + 6\sin t$

**47.** $x = -2 + 5\cos t; y = 3 + 2\sin t$ **49.** $x = 4\sec t; y = 2\sqrt{5}\tan t$ **51.** $x = -2 + 3t; y = 4 + 3t$

**57. a.**

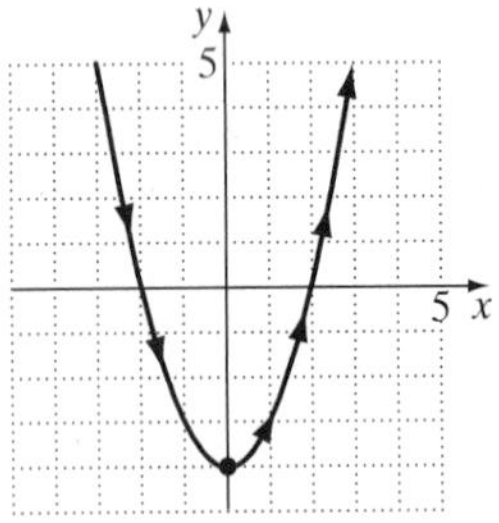

**b.**

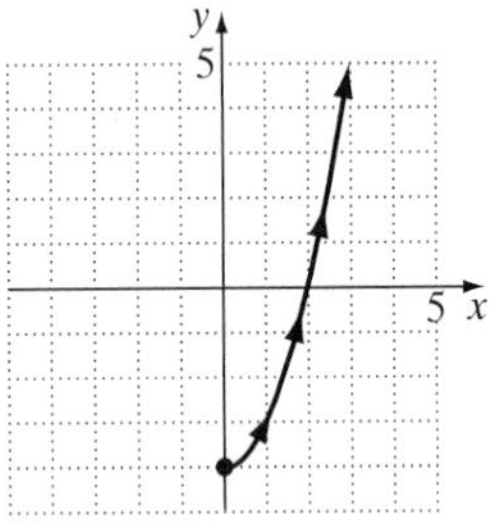

**c.**

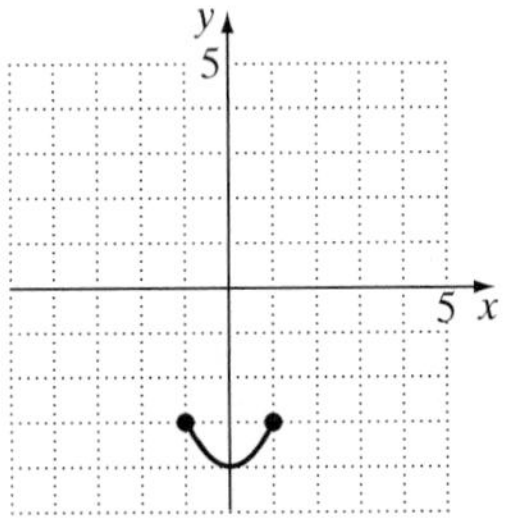

**d.**

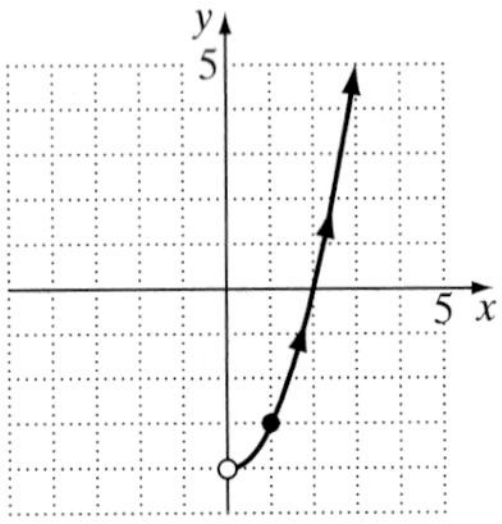

**59. a.** $x = (180\cos 40°)t; y = 3 + (180\sin 40°)t - 16t^2$

**b.** After 1 second: 137.9 feet in distance, 102.7 feet in height;
After 2 seconds: 275.8 feet in distance, 170.4 feet in height;
After 3 seconds: 413.7 feet in distance, 206.1 feet in height

**c.** $t = 7.3$ sec; total horizontal distance: 1006.6 ft; yes

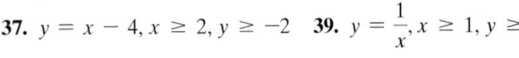

**69.**

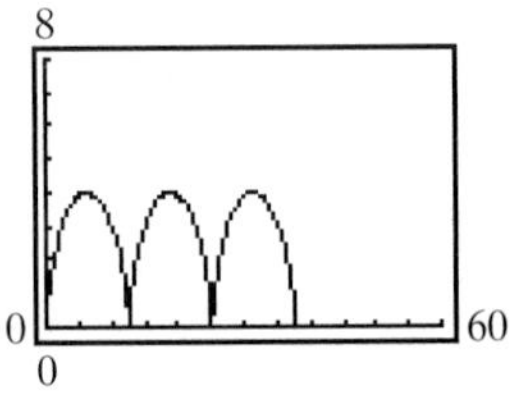


**71.**

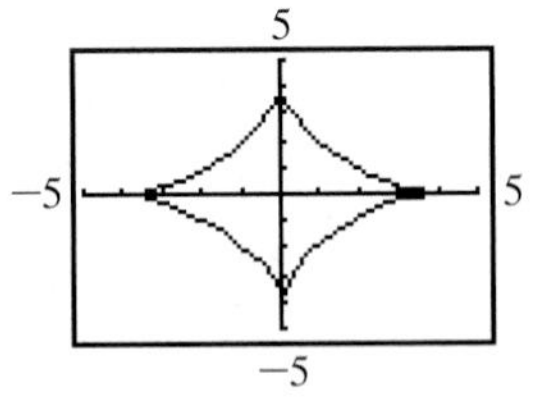

**73.**

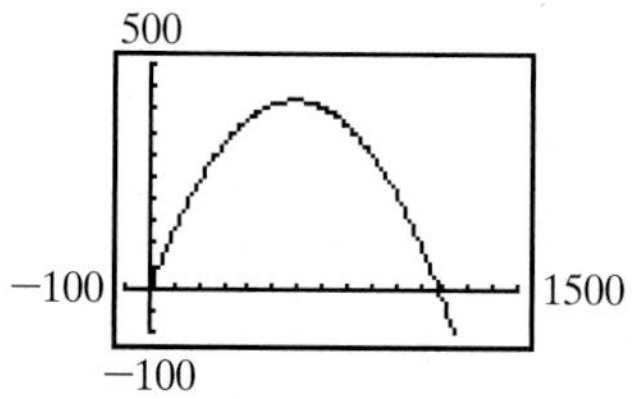


Window: $[-100, 1500] \times [-100, 500]$;
The maximum height is 419.4 feet at a time of 5.1 seconds.
The range of the projectile is 1174.6 feet horizontally.
It hits the ground at 10.2 seconds.

**75. a.** $x = (140 \cos 22°)t$; $y = 5 + (140 \sin 22°)t - 16t^2$

**b.**

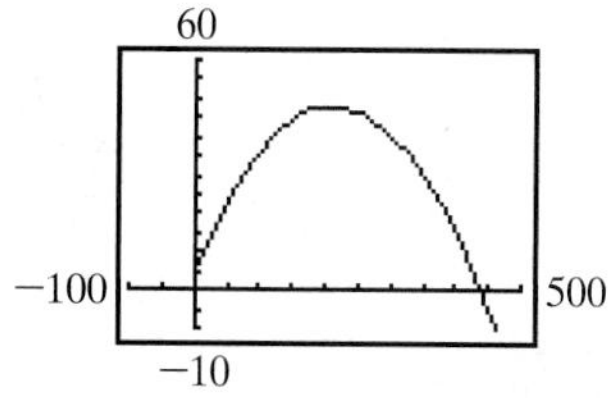


Window: $[-100, 500] \times [-10, 60]$

**c.** The maximum height is 48.0 feet. It occurs at 1.6 seconds.

**d.** 3.4 sec

**e.** 437.5 ft

**77.** $x = 3 \sin t$; $y = 3 \cos t$

## Section 10.6

### Check Point Exercises

**1.**

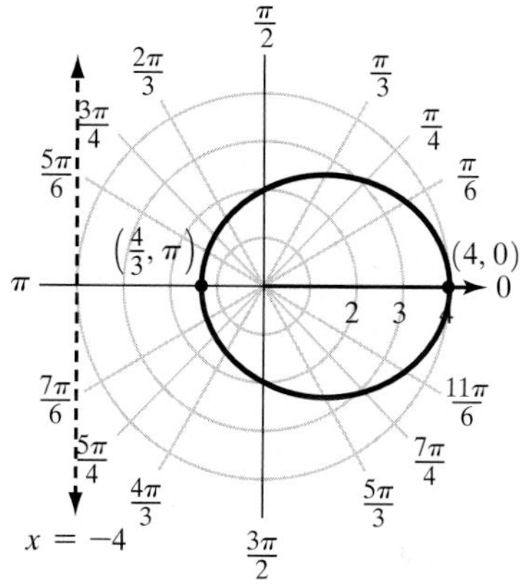


**2.**

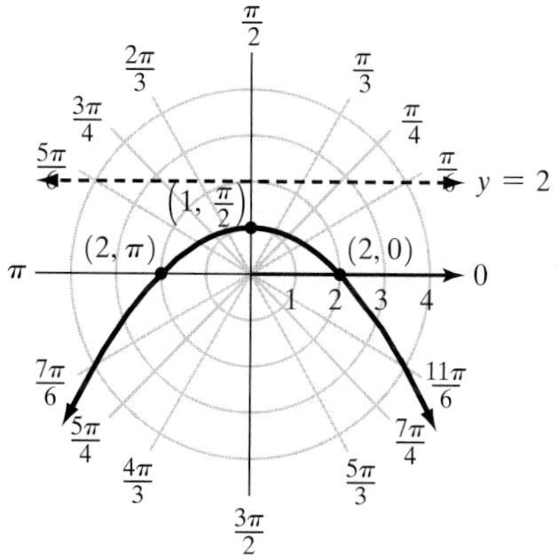


**3.**

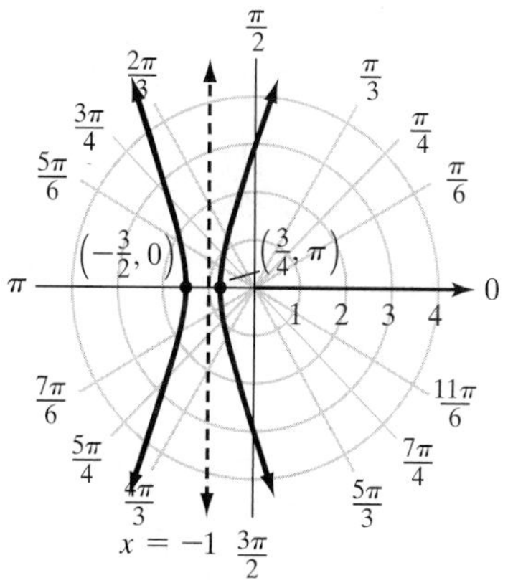


### Exercise Set 10.6

**1. a.** parabola **b.** The directrix is 3 units above the pole, at $y = 3$. **3. a.** ellipse **b.** The directrix is 3 units to the left of the pole, at $x = -3$. **5. a.** parabola **b.** The directrix is 4 units above the pole, at $y = 4$. **7. a.** hyperbola **b.** The directrix is 3 units to the left of the pole, at $x = -3$.

**9.**

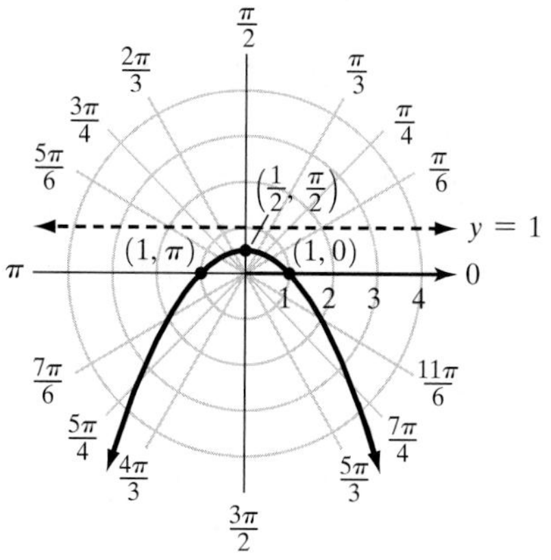


**11.**

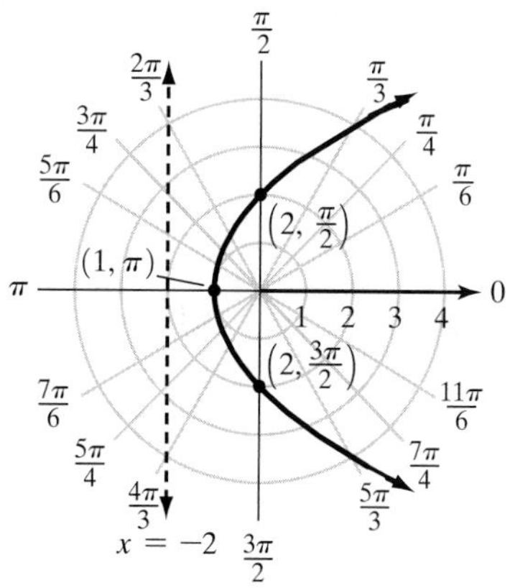


**13.**

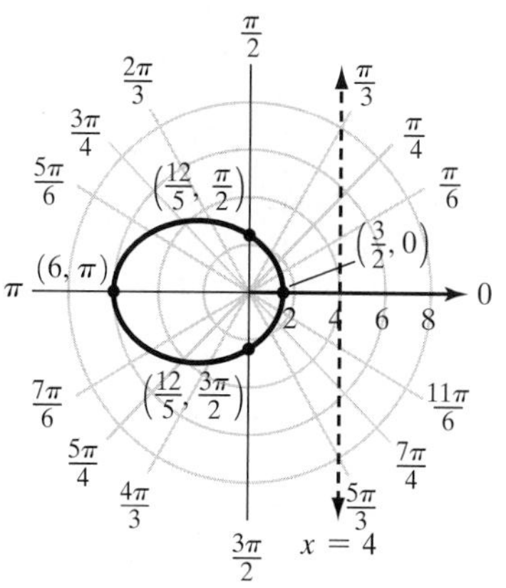

**15.**

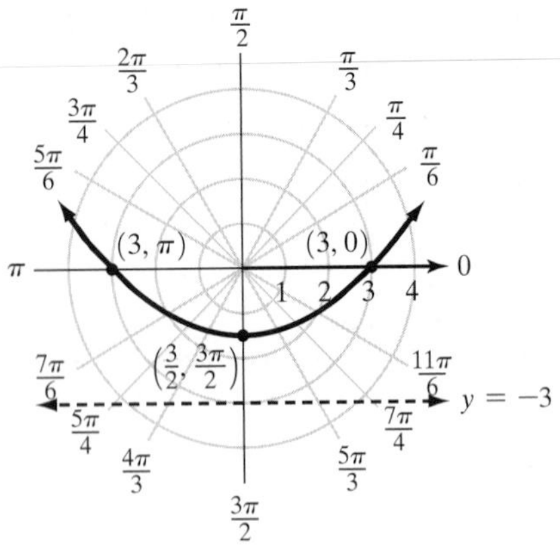


**17.**

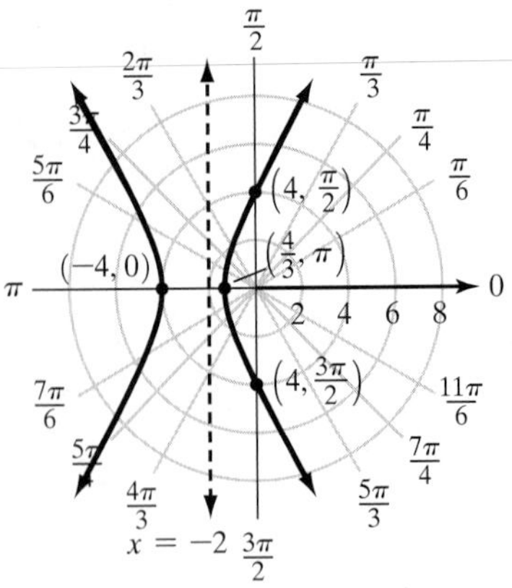


**19.**

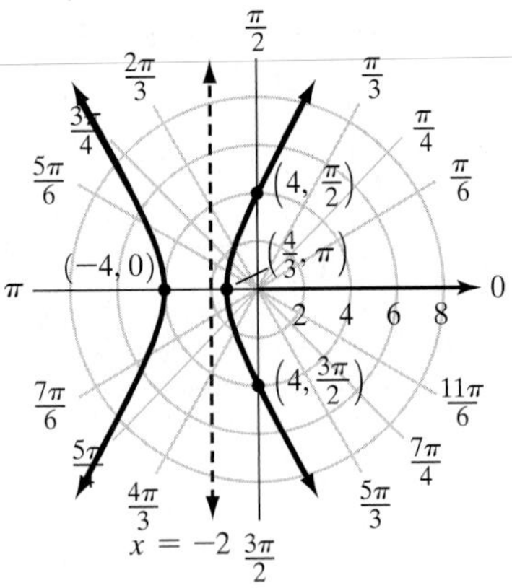


**21.** 0.54 astronomical units or 51 million miles. **23.** 4122 miles from the center of the earth.; 162 miles from the surface of the earth.

**33.** hyperbola

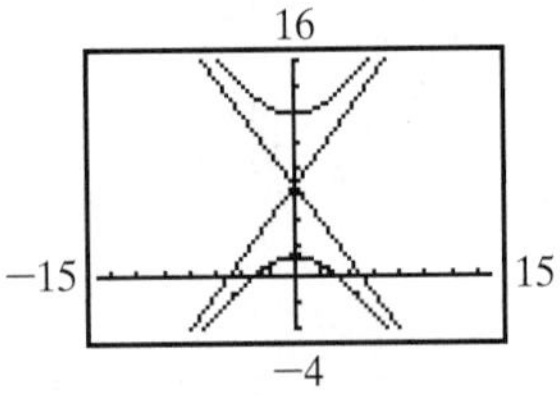


**35.**

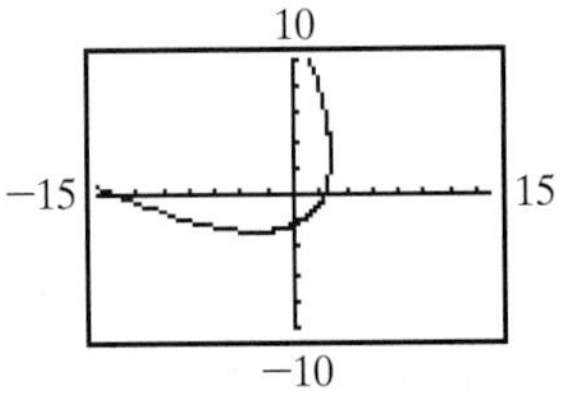


The graph appears to be rotated counterclockwise through an angle of $\frac{\pi}{4}$ radians.

**37.** Mercury: $r = \dfrac{(1 - 0.2056^2)(36.0 \times 10^6)}{1 - 0.2056 \cos\theta}$

Earth: $r = \dfrac{(1 - 0.0167^2)(92.96 \times 10^6)}{1 - 0.0167 \cos\theta}$;

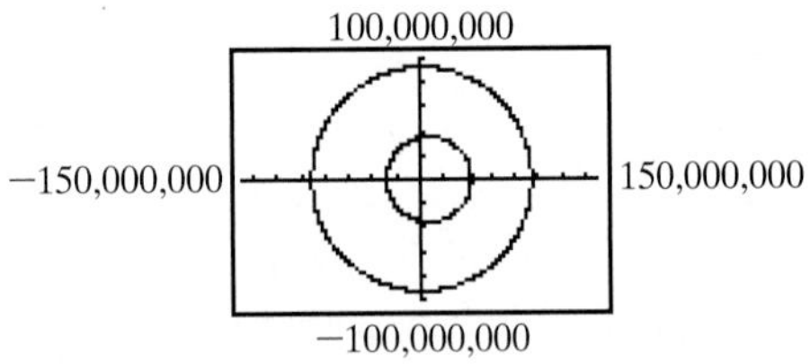


**39.** $r = \dfrac{2}{1 - \frac{1}{2}\cos\theta}$ or $r = \dfrac{6}{1 + \frac{1}{2}\cos\theta}$

**41.** parabola; using the relationships between rectangular and polar coordinates, $x^2 + y^2 = r^2$ and $x = r\cos\theta$; $y^2 = x + \frac{1}{4}$

## Chapter 10 Review Exercises

**1.** foci: $(\pm\sqrt{11}, 0)$

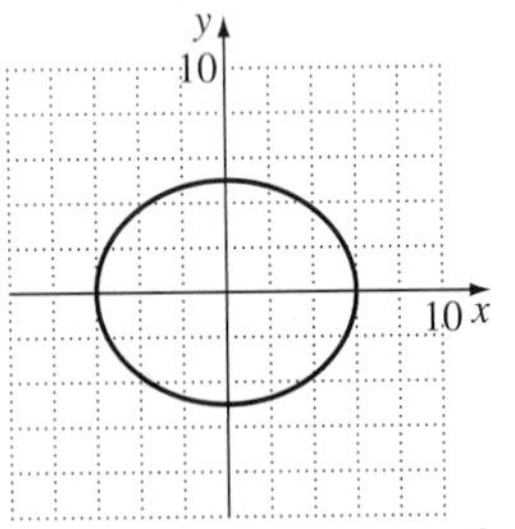

**2.** foci: $(0, \pm 3)$

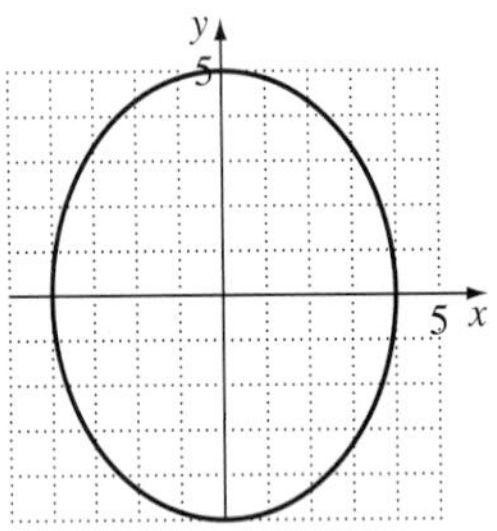

**3.** foci: $(0, \pm 2\sqrt{3})$

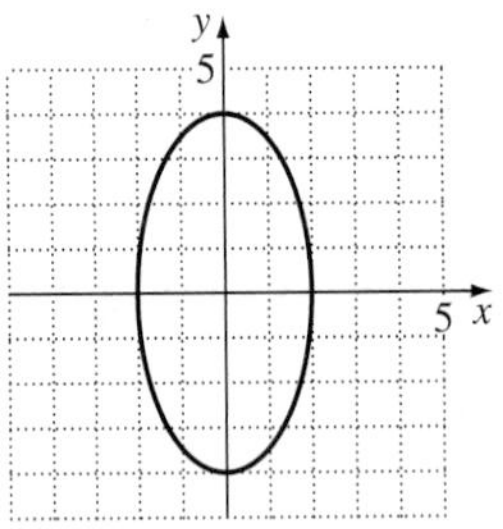

**4.** foci: $(\pm\sqrt{5}, 0)$

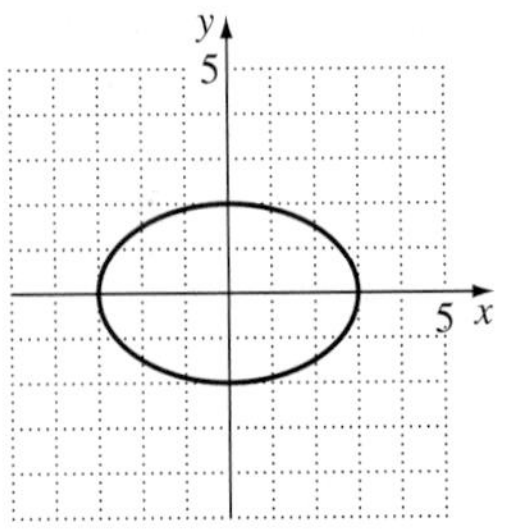

**5.** foci: $(1 \pm \sqrt{7}, -2)$

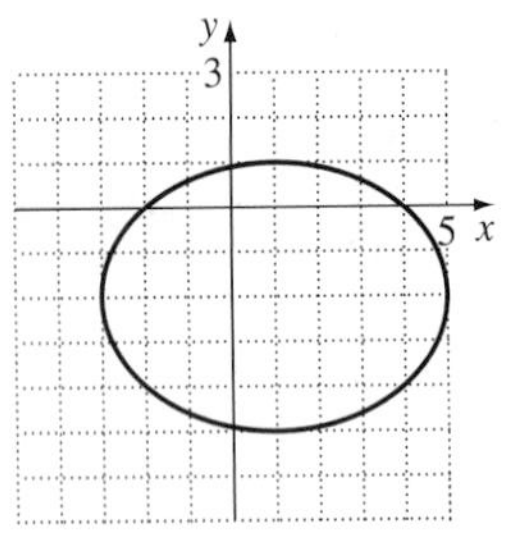

**6.** foci: $(-1, 2 \pm \sqrt{7})$

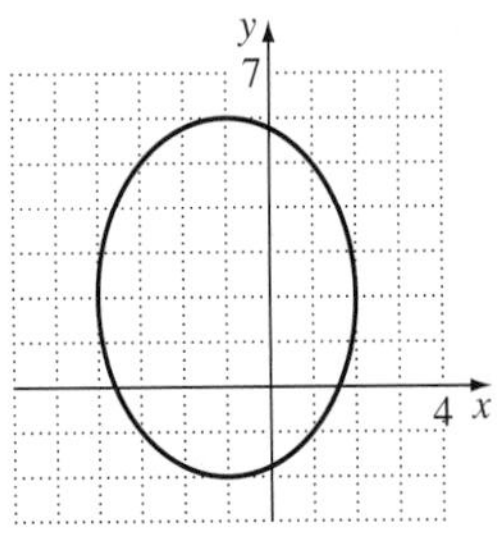

**7.** foci: $(-3 \pm \sqrt{5}, 2)$

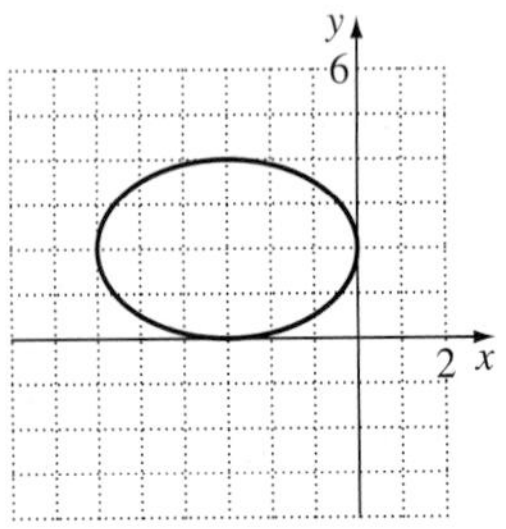

**8.** foci: $(1, -1 \pm \sqrt{5})$

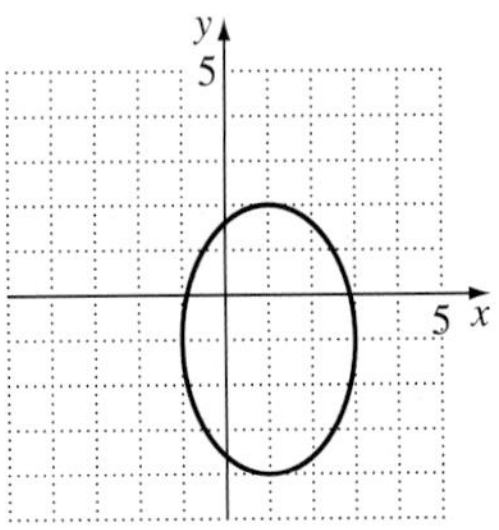

**9.** $\frac{x^2}{25} + \frac{y^2}{9} = 1$ **10.** $\frac{x^2}{27} + \frac{y^2}{36} = 1$ **11.** $\frac{x^2}{36} + \frac{y^2}{4} = 1$ **12.** $\frac{x^2}{100} + \frac{y^2}{36} = 1$ **13.** yes

**14.** The hit ball will collide with the other ball.

**15.** foci: $(\pm\sqrt{17}, 0)$

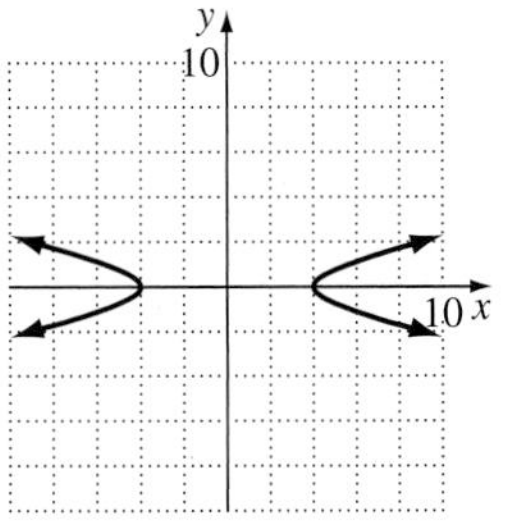


**16.** foci: $(0, \pm\sqrt{17})$

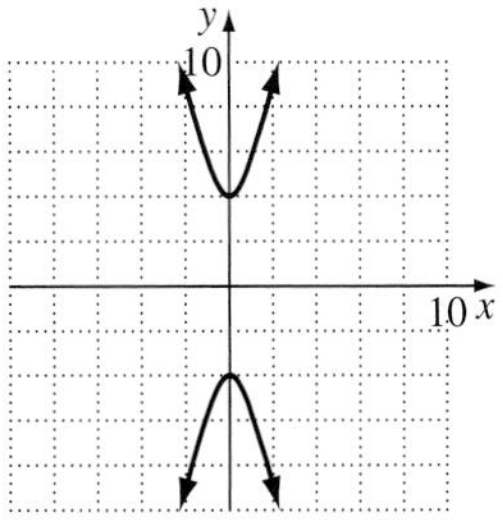


**17.** foci: $(\pm 5, 0)$

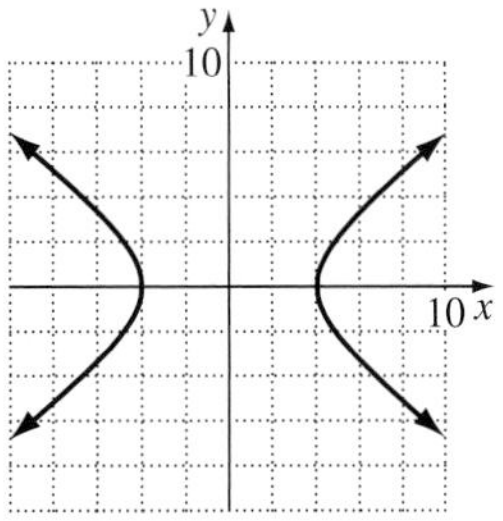


**18.** foci: $(0, \pm 2\sqrt{5})$

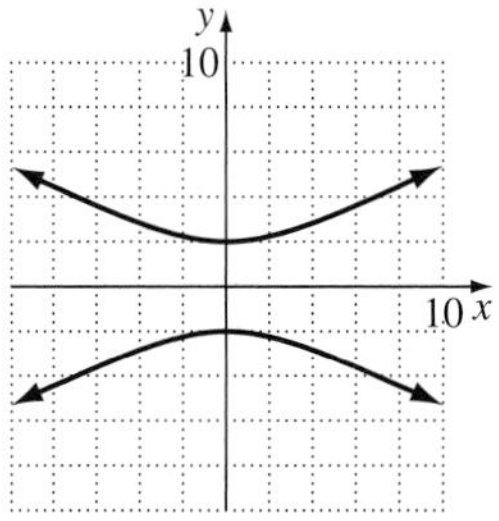


**19.** foci: $(2 \pm \sqrt{41}, -3)$

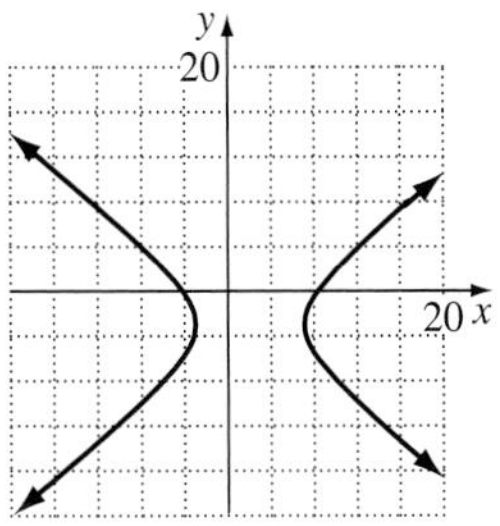


**20.** foci: $(3, -2 \pm \sqrt{41})$

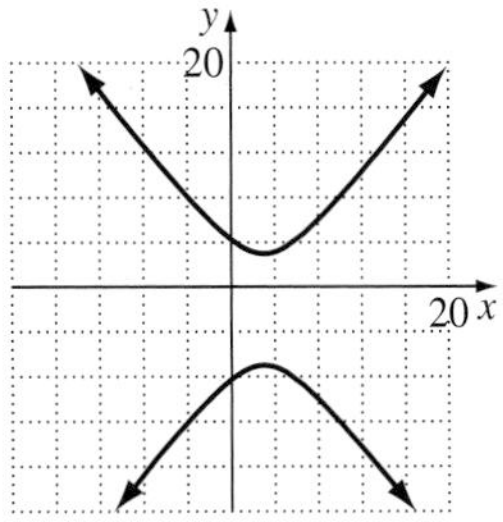


**21.** foci: $(1, 2 \pm \sqrt{5})$

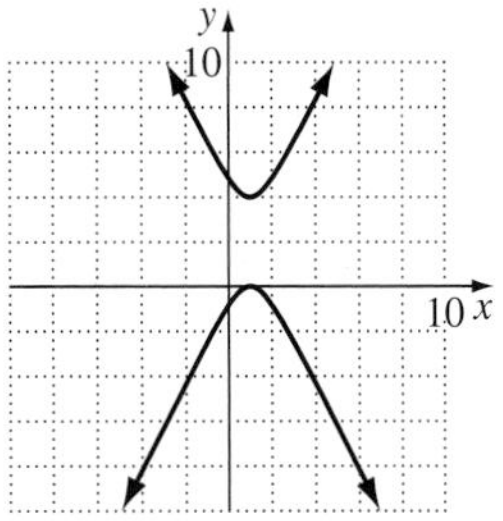


**22.** foci: $(1 \pm \sqrt{2}, -1)$

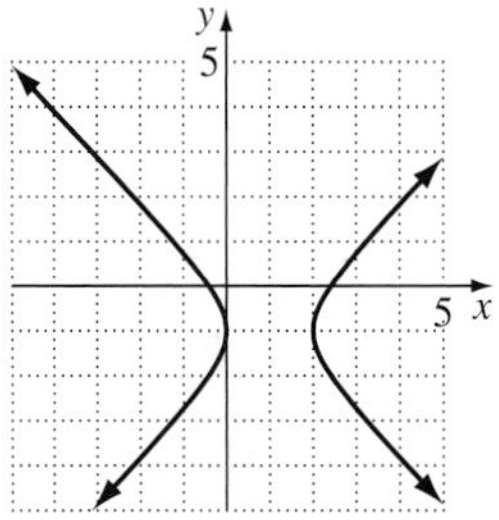


**23.** $\frac{y^2}{4} - \frac{x^2}{12} = 1$ **24.** $\frac{x^2}{9} - \frac{y^2}{55} = 1$ **25.** $c$ must be greater than $a$. **26.** $\frac{x^2}{2162.25} - \frac{y^2}{7837.75} = 1$

**27.** vertex: $(0, 0)$; focus: $(2, 0)$; directrix: $x = -2$

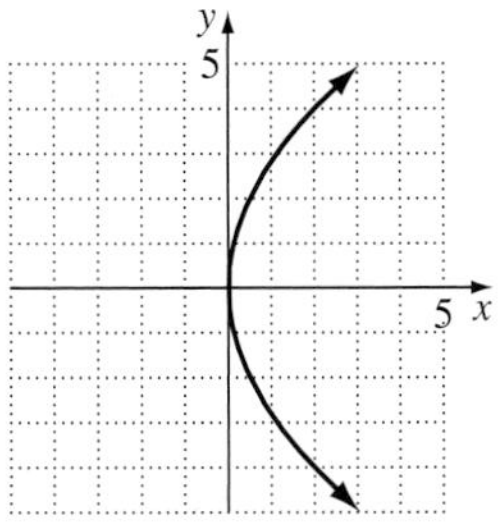


**28.** vertex: $(0, 0)$; focus: $(0, -4)$; directrix: $y = 4$

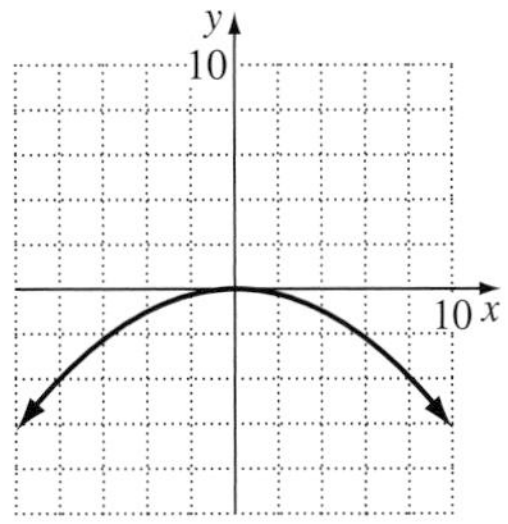


**29.** vertex: $(0, 2)$; focus: $(-4, 2)$; directrix: $x = 4$

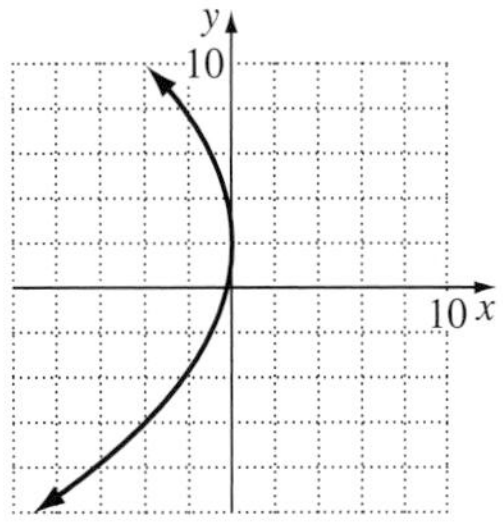


**30.** vertex: $(4, -1)$; focus: $(4, 0)$; directrix: $y = -2$

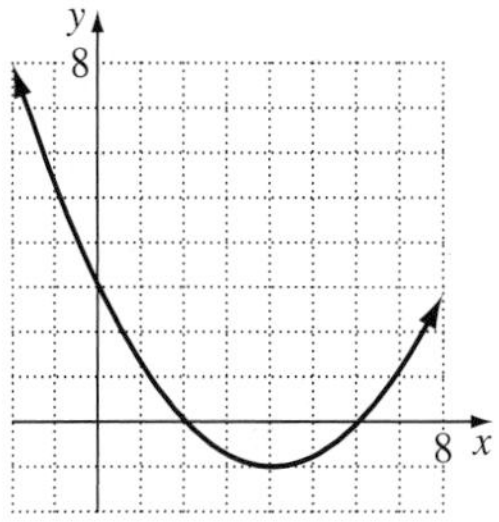

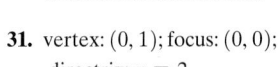

**31.** vertex: $(0, 1)$; focus: $(0, 0)$; directrix: $y = 2$

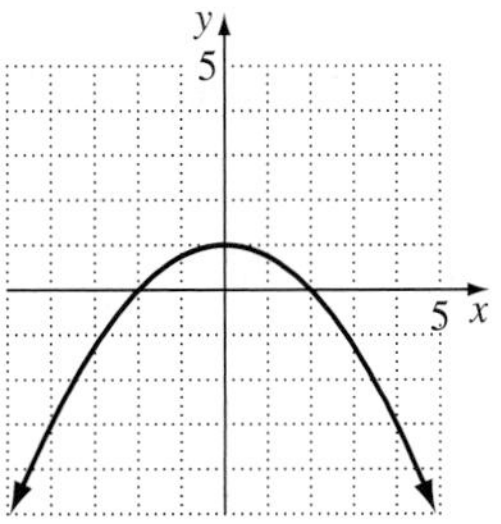


**32.** vertex: $(-1, 5)$; focus: $(0, 5)$; directrix: $x = -2$

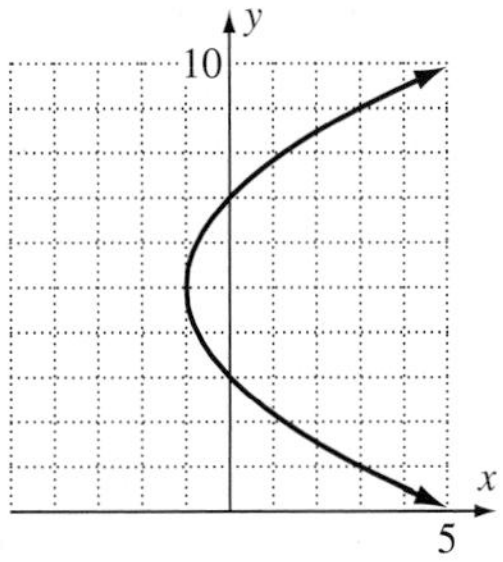


**33.** vertex: $(2, -2)$; focus: $(2, -\frac{3}{2})$; directrix: $y = -\frac{5}{2}$

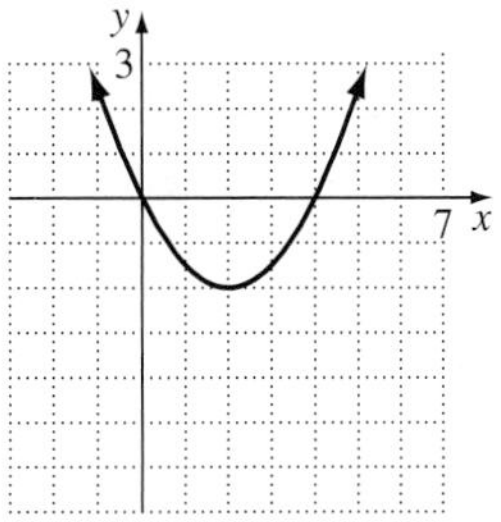


**34.** $y^2 = 48x$ **35.** $x^2 = -44y$ **36.** $x^2 = 12y$; Place the light 3 inches from the vertex at $(0, 3)$. **37.** approximately 58 ft **38.** approximately 128 ft **39.** parabola **40.** ellipse **41.** ellipse **42.** hyperbola **43.** ellipse or circle **44.** ellipse or circle **45.** parabola **46.** ellipse or circle

**47. a.** $x^2 - y^2 = 8$

**b.** $\dfrac{x'^2}{8} - \dfrac{y'^2}{8} = 1$

**c.**

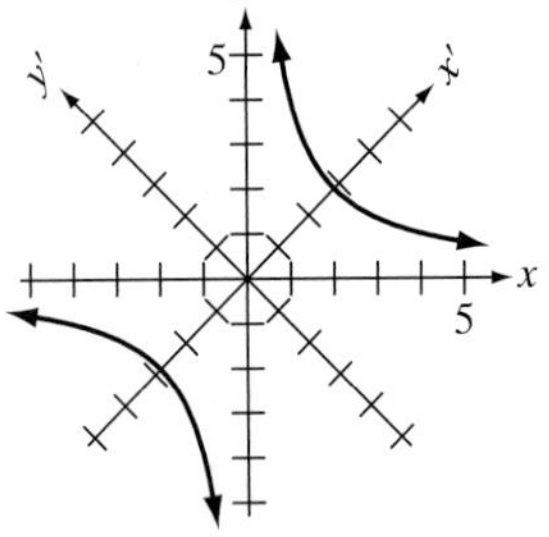

**48. a.** $3x^2 + y^2 = 2$

**b.** $\dfrac{x'^2}{\frac{2}{3}} + \dfrac{y'^2}{2} = 1$

**c.**

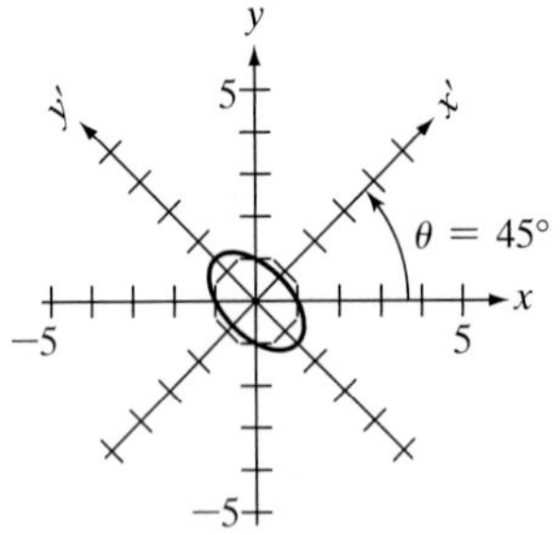


**49. a.** $18x^2 - 2y^2 = 18$

**b.** $\dfrac{x'^2}{1} - \dfrac{y'^2}{9} = 1$

**c.**

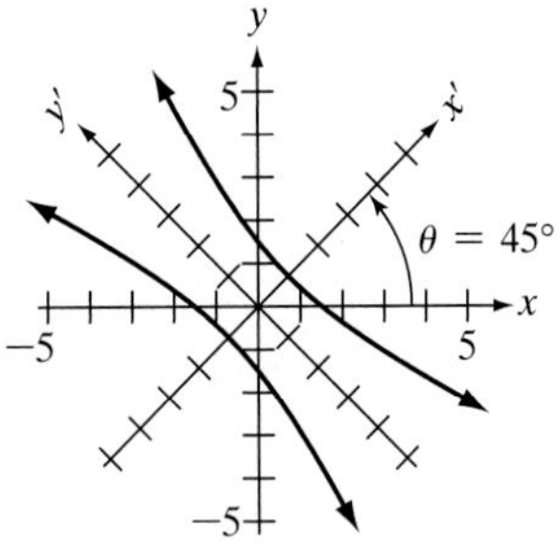


**50. a.** $50x'^2 + 150y'^2 = 450$

**b.** $\dfrac{x'^2}{9} + \dfrac{y'^2}{3} = 1$

**c.**

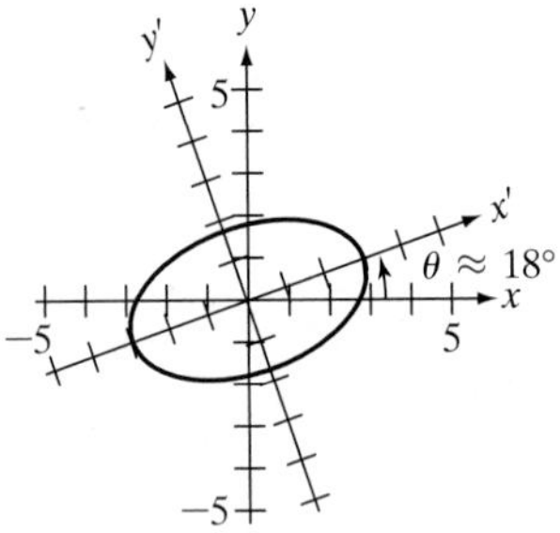


**51. a.** $16x'^2 + 96y' = 0$

**b.** $x'^2 = -6y'$

**c.**

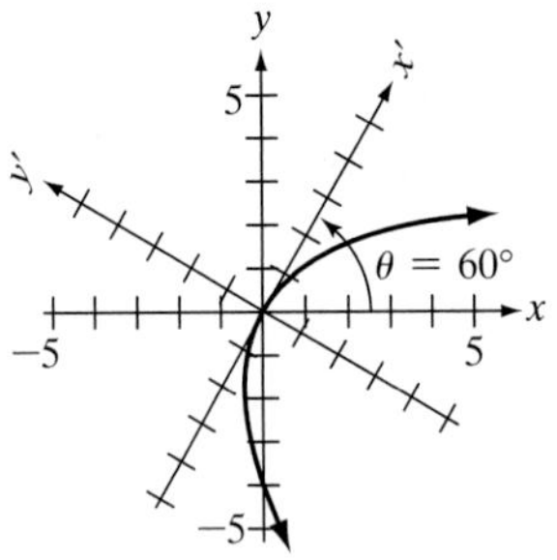


**52.** $y = -\dfrac{1}{2}x + \dfrac{1}{2}$

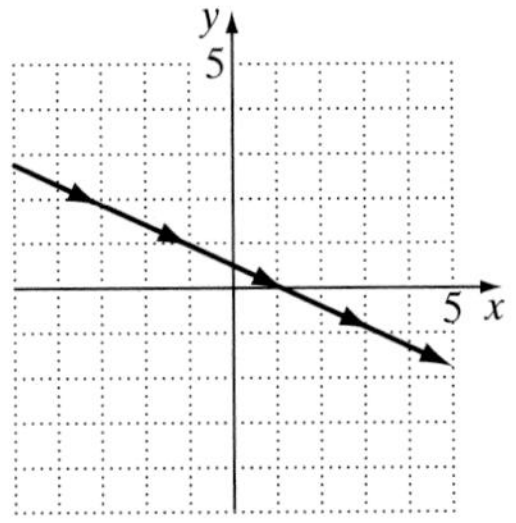

**53.** $(y + 1)^2 = x, 0 \le x \le 9,$
$-2 \le y \le 2$

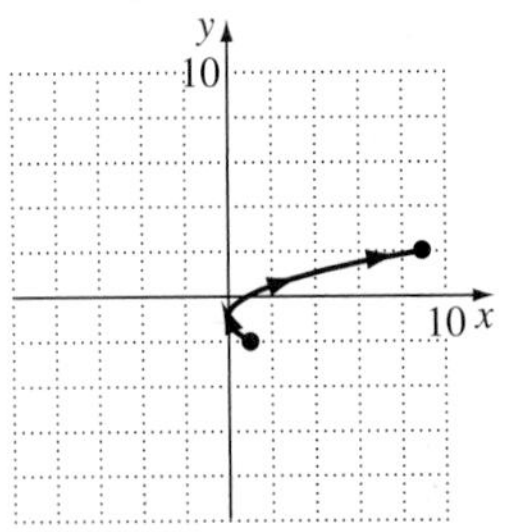

**54.** $(y - 1)^2 = \dfrac{1}{4}x$

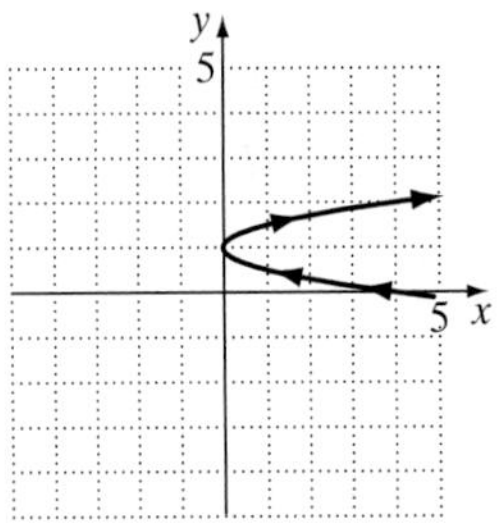

**55.** $\dfrac{x^2}{16} + \dfrac{y^2}{9} = 1, 0 \le x \le 4,$
$-3 < y \le 3$

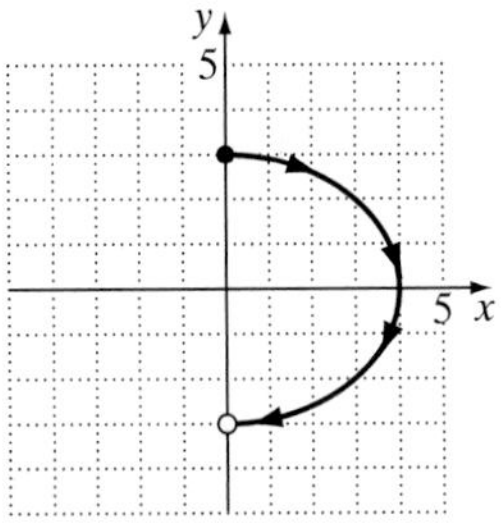

**56.** $\dfrac{(x - 3)^2}{4} + \dfrac{(y - 1)^2}{4} = 1$
or $(x - 3)^2 + (y - 1)^2 = 4$

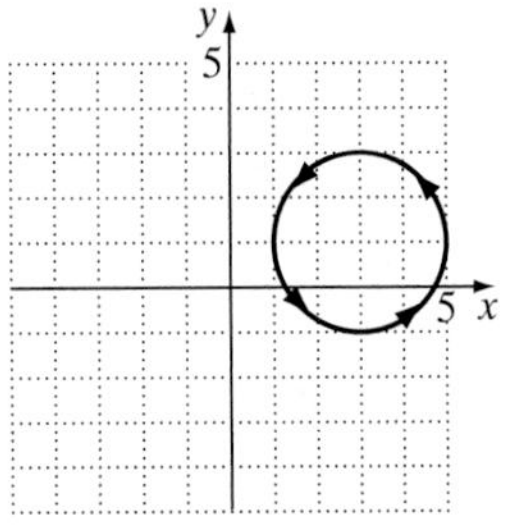

**57.** $\dfrac{x^2}{9} - \dfrac{y^2}{9} = 1,$
$3 \le x \le 3\sqrt{2}, 0 \le y \le 3$

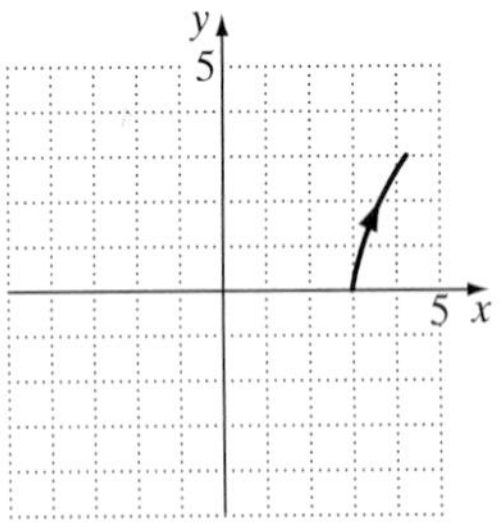

**59. a.** $x = (100 \cos 40°)t;\ y = 6 + (100 \sin 40°)t - 16t^2$

**b.** After 1 second: 76.6 feet in distance, 54.3 feet in height; after 2 seconds: 153.2 feet in distance, 70.6 feet in height; after 3 seconds: 229.8 feet in distance, 54.8 feet in height.

**c.** 4.1 sec; 314.1 ft **d.**

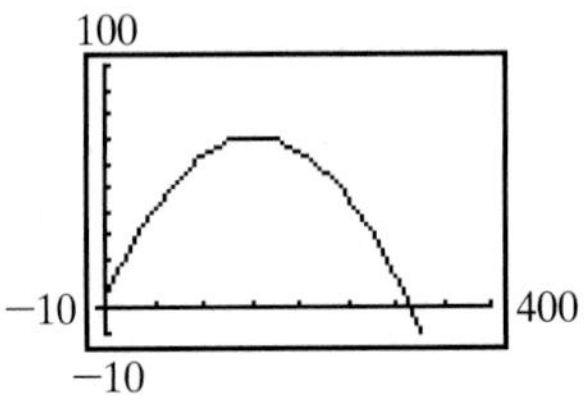


; The ball is at its maximum height at 2.0 seconds. The maximum height is 70.6 feet.

**60.** **a.** $r = \dfrac{4}{1 - \sin\theta}$ **b.** $e = 1; p = 4$; parabola

**c.**

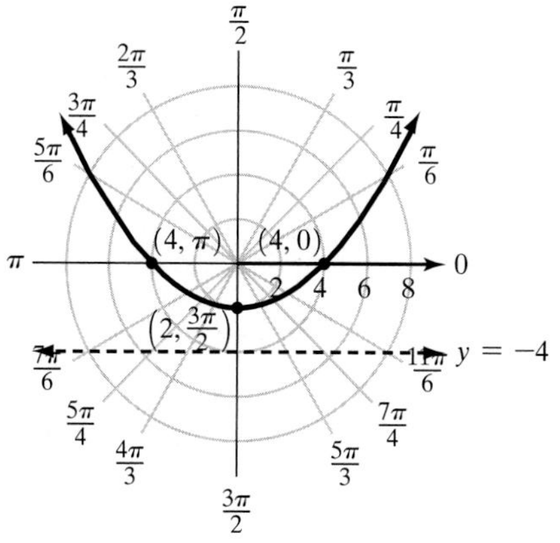


**61.** **a.** $r = \dfrac{6}{1 + \cos\theta}$ **b.** $e = 1; p = 6$; parabola

**c.**

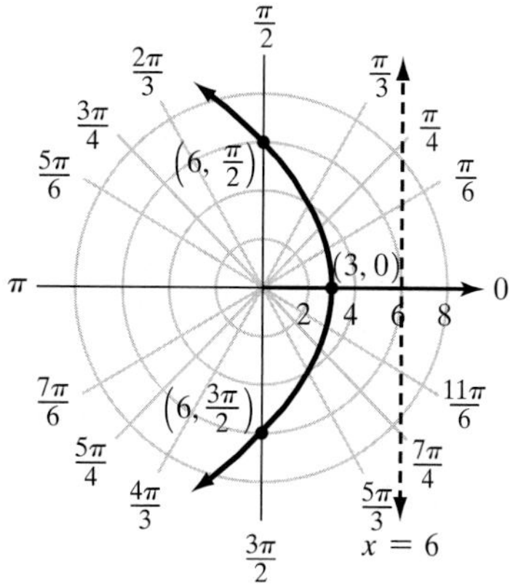


**62.** **a.** $r = \dfrac{3}{1 + \frac{1}{2}\sin\theta}$ **b.** $e = \dfrac{1}{2}; p = 6$; ellipse

**c.**

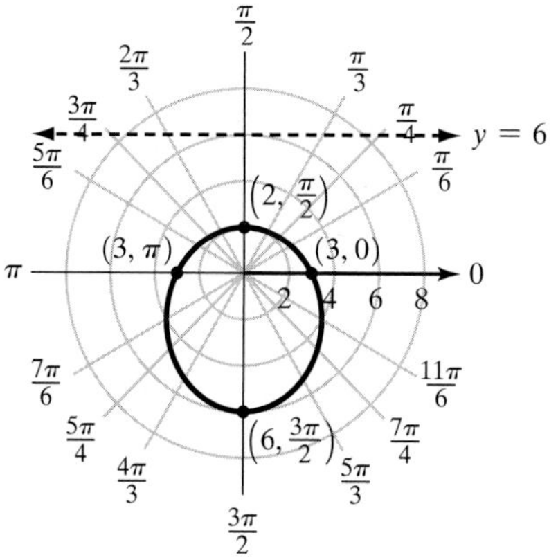


**63.** **a.** $r = \dfrac{\frac{2}{3}}{1 - \frac{2}{3}\cos\theta}$ **b.** $e = \dfrac{2}{3}; p = 1$; ellipse

**c.**

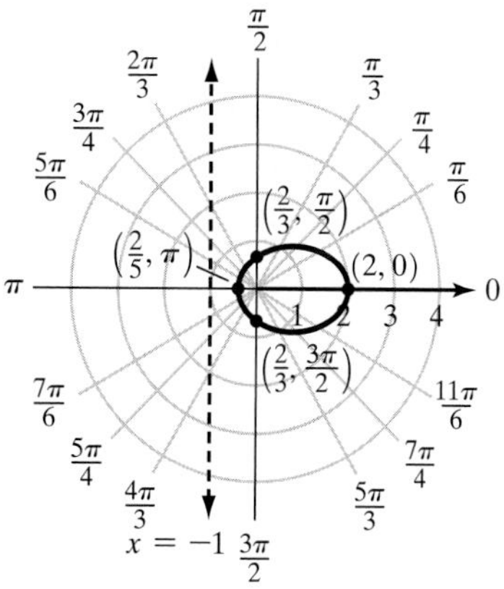


**64.** **a.** $r = \dfrac{2}{1 + 2\sin\theta}$ **b.** $e = 2; p = 1$; hyperbola

**c.**

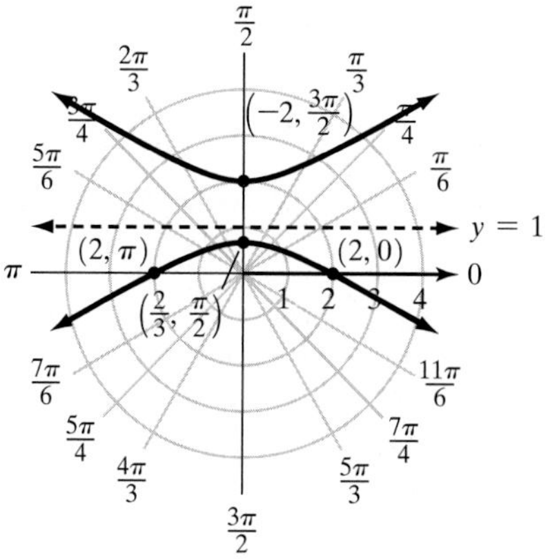


**65.** **a.** $r = \dfrac{2}{1 + 4\cos\theta}$ **b.** $e = 4; p = \dfrac{1}{2}$; hyperbola

**c.**

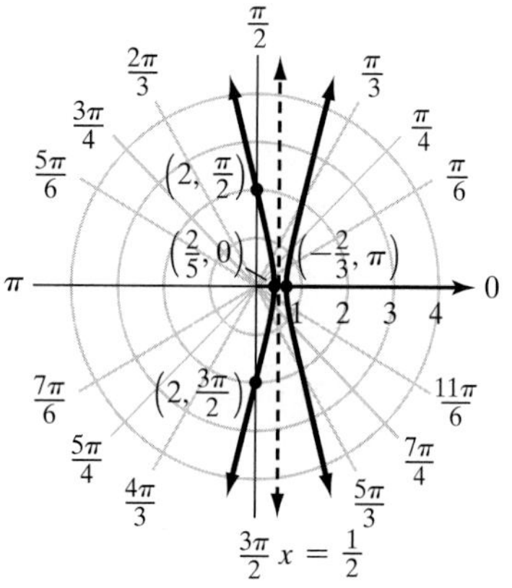

## Chapter 10 Test

**1.** foci: $(\pm\sqrt{13}, 0)$

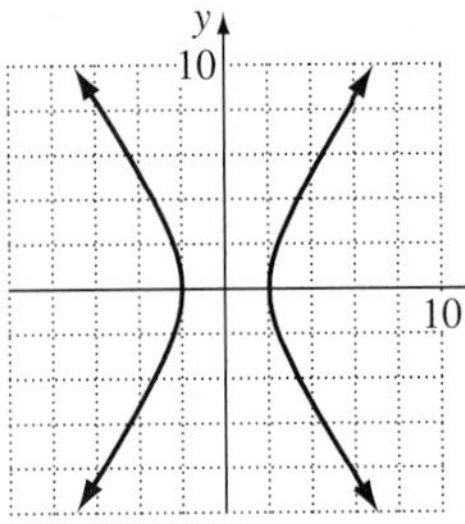


**2.** vertex: $(0, 0)$; focus: $(0, -2)$; directrix: $y = 2$

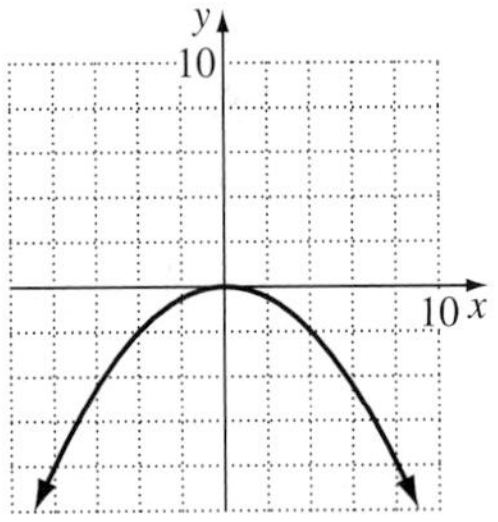


**3.** foci: $(-6, 5), (2, 5)$

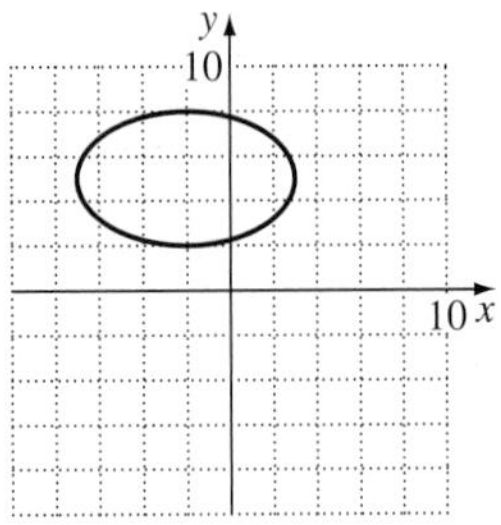


**4.** foci: $(-1, 1 \pm \sqrt{5})$

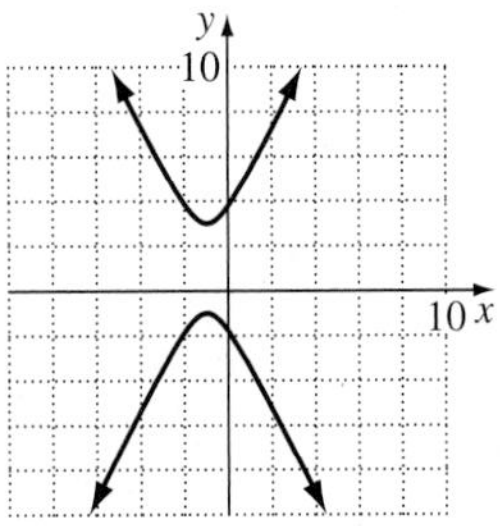


**5.** vertex: $(-5, 1)$; focus: $(-5, 3)$
directrix: $y = -1$

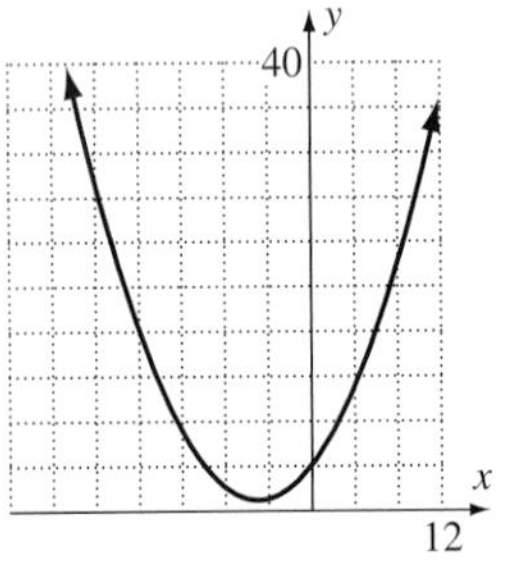

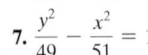

**6.** $\dfrac{x^2}{100} + \dfrac{y^2}{51} = 1$

**7.** $\dfrac{y^2}{49} - \dfrac{x^2}{51} = 1$

**8.** $y^2 = 200x$

**9.** 32 ft

**10. a.** $x^2 = 3y$

**b.** Light is placed $\dfrac{3}{4}$ inch above the vertex.

**11.** ellipse

**12.** ellipse or circle

**13.** $\theta = 30°$

**14.** $(y + 1)^2 = x$

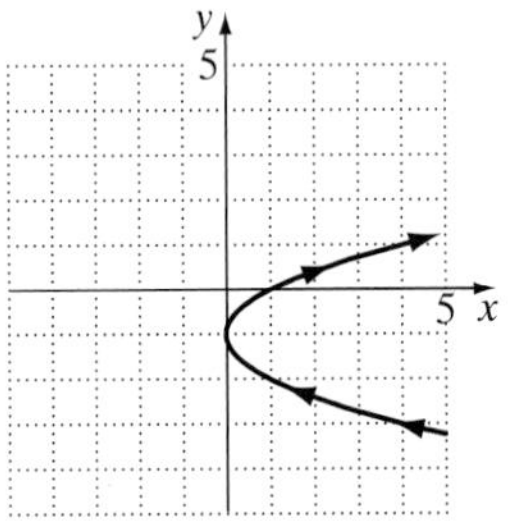


**15.** $\dfrac{(x-1)^2}{9} + \dfrac{y^2}{4} = 1$

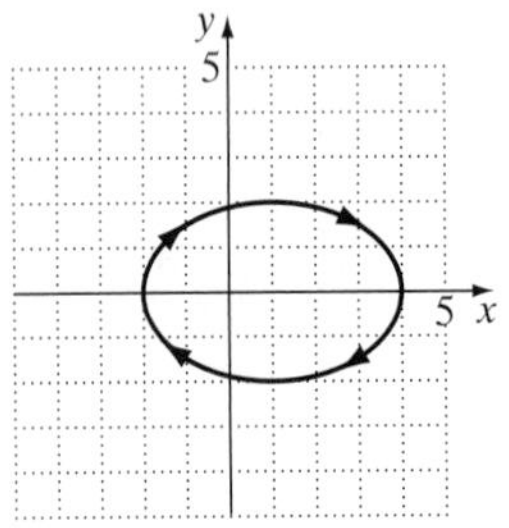


**16.** parabola

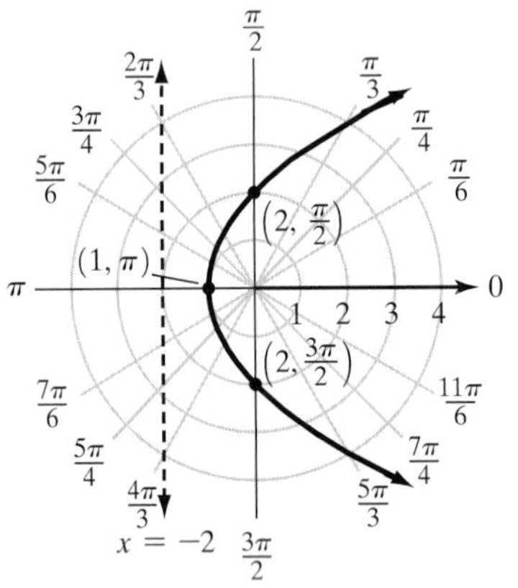


**17.** ellipse

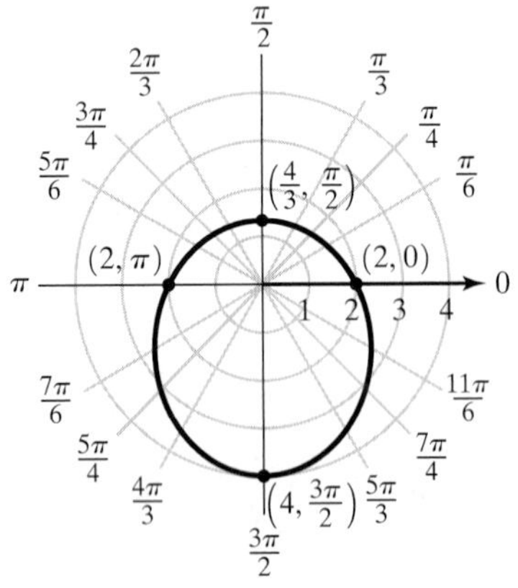


## Cumulative Review Exercises (Chapters 1–10)

**1.** $\{2\}$ **2.** $\{x \mid x < 2\}$ **3.** $\{9\}$ **4.** $\{2 + 2\sqrt{5}, 2 - 2\sqrt{5}\}$ **5.** $\{x \mid x \geq 4 \text{ or } x \leq -3\}$ **6.** $\left\{\frac{2}{3}, -1 \pm \sqrt{2}\right\}$ **7.** $\{3\}$ **8.** $(2, -1)$ **9.** $(2, -4)$ and $(-14, -20)$ **10.** $(7, -4, 6)$

**11.**

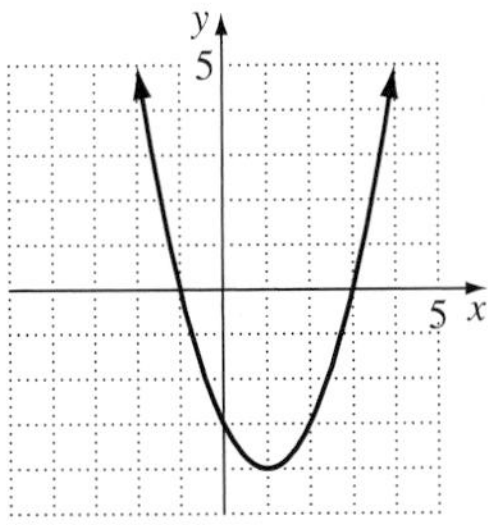


**12.**

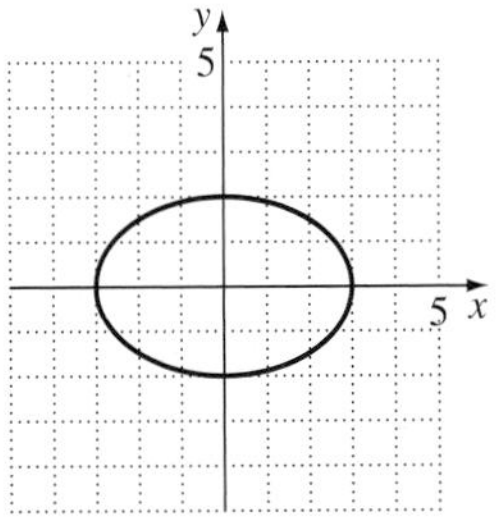


**13.**

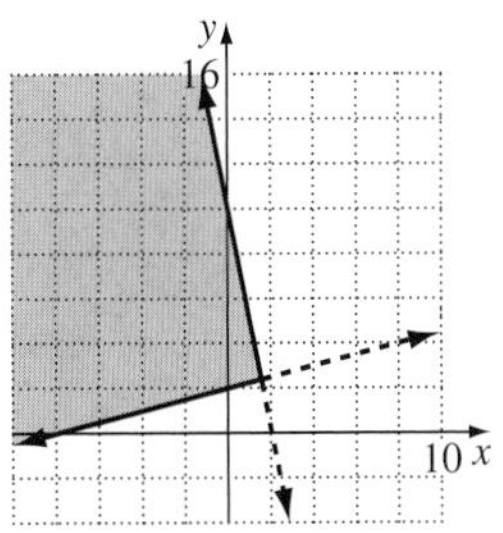


**14. a.** $\pm 1, \pm 3, \pm\frac{1}{2}, \pm\frac{3}{2}, \pm\frac{1}{4}, \pm\frac{3}{4}, \pm\frac{1}{8}, \pm\frac{3}{8}, \pm\frac{1}{16}, \pm\frac{3}{16}, \pm\frac{1}{32}, \pm\frac{3}{32}$ **b.** $\left\{-\frac{1}{8}, \frac{3}{4}, 1\right\}$

**15. a.** 1980–1990 **b.** 1990–2025 **c.** 1950–1980 **d.** $f(x) = 98$ **e.** The scale is not uniformly spaced.

**16.** $(g \circ f)(x) = x^2 - 2$ **17.** $3 \log_5 x + \frac{1}{2} \log_5 y - 3$ **18.** $y = -2x - 2$

**19.** The costs will be the same when the number of miles driven is 175 miles. The cost will be $67.

**20.** Richard Nixon lived 81 years, Thomas Jefferson lived 83 years, and James Madison lived 85 years.

**22.**

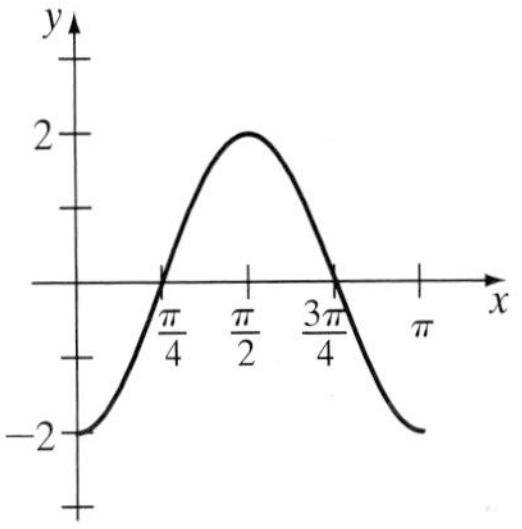


**23.** $-3\mathbf{i} - 3\mathbf{j}$ **24.** $\theta = 0, \theta = \pi, \theta = \frac{\pi}{3}$, or $\theta = \frac{5\pi}{3}$ **25.** $b \approx 14.4, C = 44°, c \approx 10.5$

# CHAPTER 11

## Section 11.1

### Check Point Exercises

**1. a.** 7, 9, 11, 13 **b.** $-\frac{1}{3}, \frac{1}{5}, -\frac{1}{9}, \frac{1}{17}$ **2.** 3, 11, 27, 59 **3.** $10, \frac{10}{3}, \frac{5}{6}, \frac{1}{6}$ **4. a.** 91 **b.** $n$ **5. a.** 182 **b.** 47 **c.** 20

**6. a.** $\sum_{i=1}^{9} i^2$ **b.** $\sum_{i=1}^{n} \frac{1}{2^{i-1}}$

### Exercise Set 11.1

**1.** 5, 8, 11, 14 **3.** 3, 9, 27, 81 **5.** −3, 9, −27, 81 **7.** −4, 5, −6, 7 **9.** $\frac{2}{5}, \frac{2}{3}, \frac{6}{7}, 1$ **11.** $1, -\frac{1}{3}, \frac{1}{7}, -\frac{1}{15}$ **13.** 7, 12, 17, 22 **15.** 3, 12, 48, 192 **17.** 4, 11, 25, 53 **19.** $1, 2, \frac{3}{2}, \frac{2}{3}$ **21.** 4, 12, 48, 240 **23.** 272 **25.** 120 **27.** $(n + 2)(n + 1)$ **29.** 105 **31.** 60 **33.** 115 **35.** $-\frac{5}{16}$ **37.** 55 **39.** $\frac{3}{8}$ **41.** 15 **43.** $\sum_{i=1}^{15} i^2$ **45.** $\sum_{i=1}^{11} 2^i$ **47.** $\sum_{i=1}^{30} i$ **49.** $\sum_{i=1}^{14} \frac{i}{i+1}$ **51.** $\sum_{i=1}^{n} \frac{4^i}{i}$ **53.** $\sum_{i=1}^{n} (2i - 1)$ **55.** $\sum_{k=1}^{14} (2k + 3)$ **57.** $\sum_{k=0}^{12} ar^k$ **59.** $\sum_{k=0}^{n} (a + kd)$ **61. a.** 4613; the total number of children, in thousands, home-educated in the years 1992–1997 **b.** 769; the average number of children, in thousands, home-educated each year

**63.** 30.15; Americans spent $30.15 billion on recreational boating from 1991 through 1995. **65.** $8081.13 **75.** 39,800

**77.** 8,109,673,360,588,800 **79.** 24,804

**83.**

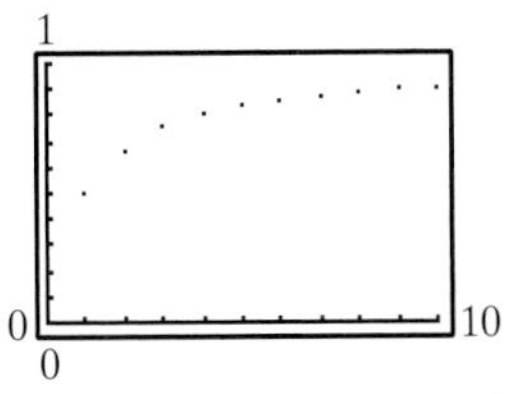


As $n$ gets larger, $a_n$ approaches 1.

**85.**

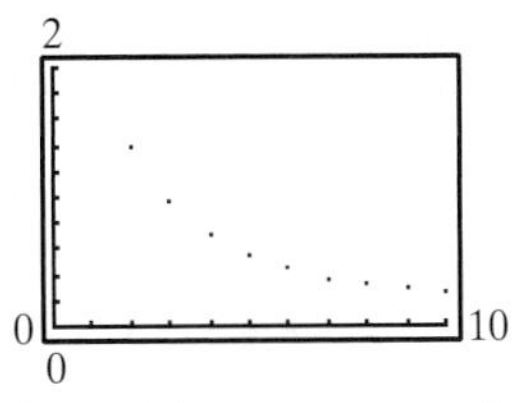


As $n$ gets larger $a_n$ approaches 0.

**87.** (b) is true.

## Section 11.2

### Check Point Exercises

**1.** 100, 70, 40, 10, −20 **2.** −34 **3. a.** $a_n = 2350n + 10{,}458$ **b.** \$73,908 million **4.** 360 **5.** 2460 **6.** \$596,300

### Exercise Set 11.2

**1.** 200, 220, 240, 260, 280, 300 **3.** −7, −3, 1, 5, 9, 13 **5.** 300, 210, 120, 30, −60, −150 **7.** $\frac{5}{2}, 2, \frac{3}{2}, 1, \frac{1}{2}, 0$ **9.** −9, −3, 3, 9, 15, 21 **11.** 30, 20, 10, 0, −10, −20 **13.** 1.6, 1.2, 0.8, 0.4, 0, −0.4 **15.** 33 **17.** 252 **19.** 955 **21.** −142 **23.** $a_n = 4n - 3; a_{20} = 77$ **25.** $a_n = 11 - 4n; a_{20} = -69$ **27.** $a_n = 7 + 2n; a_{20} = 47$ **29.** $a_n = -16 - 4n; a_{20} = -96$ **31.** $a_n = 1 + 3n; a_{20} = 61$ **33.** $a_n = 40 - 10n; a_{20} = -160$ **35.** 1220 **37.** 4400 **39.** 5050 **41.** 3660 **43.** 396 **45.** $8 + 13 + 18 + \cdots + 88; 816$ **47.** $2 - 1 - 4 - \cdots - 85; -1245$ **49.** $4 + 8 + 12 + \cdots + 400; 20{,}200$ **51. a.** $a_n = 125{,}159 + 1265n$ **b.** 145,399 thousand **53.** Company A will pay \$1400 more. **55. a.** $a_n = 3.204 + 0.576n$ **b.** 627.3 million tons **57.** \$442,500 **59.** 1430 seats **69.** the 200th term **71.** $S_n = \frac{n}{2}(1 + 2n - 1) = \frac{n}{2}(2n) = n^2$

## Section 11.3

### Check Point Exercises

**1.** $12, 6, 3, \frac{3}{2}, \frac{3}{4}, \frac{3}{8}$ **2.** 3645 **3.** $a_n = 3(2)^{n-1}; 384$ **4.** 9842 **5.** 19,680 **6.** \$2,371,746 **7.** \$1,327,778 **8.** 9 **9.** 1 **10.** \$4000

### Exercise Set 11.3

**1.** 5, 15, 45, 135, 405 **3.** $20, 10, 5, \frac{5}{2}, \frac{5}{4}$ **5.** 10, −40, 160, −640, 2560 **7.** −6, 30, −150, 750, −3750 **9.** $a_8 = 768$ **11.** $a_{12} = -10{,}240$ **13.** $a_{40} \approx -0.000000002$ **15.** $a_8 = 0.1$ **17.** $a_n = 3(4)^{n-1}; a_7 = 12{,}288$ **19.** $a_n = 18\left(\frac{1}{3}\right)^{n-1}; a_7 = \frac{2}{81}$ **21.** $a_n = 1.5(-2)^{n-1}; a_7 = 96$ **23.** $a_n = 0.0004(-10)^{n-1}; a_7 = 400$ **25.** 531,440 **27.** 2049 **29.** $\frac{16{,}383}{2}$ **31.** 9840 **33.** 10,230 **35.** $\frac{63}{128}$ **37.** $\frac{3}{2}$ **39.** 4 **41.** $\frac{2}{3}$ **43.** $S_\infty \approx 6.15385$ **45.** $\frac{5}{9}$ **47.** $\frac{47}{99}$ **49.** $\frac{257}{999}$ **51.** arithmetic, $d = 1$ **53.** geometric, $r = 2$ **55.** neither **57.** \$16,384 **59.** \$3,795,957 **61. a.** 1.04, 1.04, 1.04; The population is increasing geometrically with $r = 1.04$. **b.** $a_n = 20.6(1.04)^{n-1}$ **c.** 30.49 million people **63.** \$32,767 **65.** \$793,582.90 **67.** 130.26 in. **69.** \$844,706.11 **71.** \$94,834.21 **73.** \$9 million **75.** $\frac{1}{3}$

**87.**

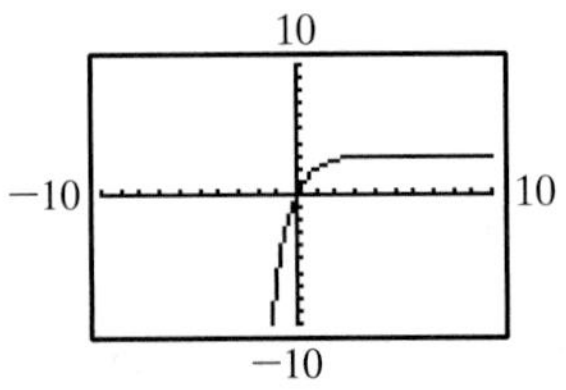


Horizontal asymptote at $y = 3$

$$\sum_{n=0}^{\infty} 2\left(\frac{1}{3}\right)^n = 3$$

**89.** (d) is true. **91.** \$442.38

## Section 11.4

### Check Point Exercises

**1. a.** $S_1: 2 = 1(1 + 1); S_k: 2 + 4 + 6 + \cdots + 2k = k(k + 1); S_{k+1}: 2 + 4 + 6 + \cdots + 2(k + 1) = (k + 1)(k + 2)$

**b.** $S_1: 1^3 = \frac{1^2(1 + 1)^2}{4}; S_k: 1^3 + 2^3 + 3^3 + \cdots + k^3 = \frac{k^2(k + 1)^2}{4}; S_{k+1}: 1^3 + 2^3 + 3^3 + \cdots + (k + 1)^3 = \frac{(k + 1)^2(k + 2)^2}{4}$

**2.** $S_1: 2 = 1(1 + 1); S_k: 2 + 4 + 6 + \cdots + 2k = k(k + 1); S_{k+1}: 2 + 4 + 6 + \cdots + 2k + 2(k + 1) = (k + 1)(k + 2)$; $S_{k+1}$ can be obtained by adding $2k + 2$ to both sides of $S_k$.

**3.** $S_1: 1^3 = \frac{1^2(1+1)^2}{4}$; $S_k: 1^3 + 2^3 + 3^3 + \cdots + k^3 = \frac{k^2(k+1)^2}{4}$; $S_{k+1}: 1^3 + 2^3 + 3^3 + \cdots + k^3 + (k+1)^3 = \frac{(k+1)^2(k+2)^2}{4}$; $S_{k+1}$ can be obtained by adding $k^3 + 3k^2 + 3k + 1$ to both sides of $S_k$.

**4.** $S_1$: 2 is a factor of $1^2 + 1$; $S_k$: 2 is a factor of $k^2 + k$; $S_{k+1}$: 2 is a factor of $(k+1)^2 + (k+1) = k^2 + 3k + 2$; $S_{k+1}$ can be obtained from $S_k$ by writing $k^2 + 3k + 2$ as $(k^2 + k) + 2(k + 1)$.

## Exercise Set 11.4

**1.** $S_1: 1 = 1^2$; $S_2: 1 + 3 = 2^2$; $S_3: 1 + 3 + 5 = 3^2$ **3.** $S_1$: 2 is a factor of $1 - 1 = 0$; $S_2$: 2 is a factor of $2^2 - 2 = 2$; $S_3$: 2 is a factor of $3^2 - 3 = 6$ **5.** $S_k: 4 + 8 + 12 + \cdots + 4k = 2k(k+1)$; $S_{k+1}: 4 + 8 + 12 + \cdots + (4k+4) = 2(k+1)(k+2)$
**7.** $S_k: 3 + 7 + 11 + \cdots + (4k-1) = k(2k+1)$; $S_{k+1}: 3 + 7 + 11 + \cdots + (4k+3) = (k+1)(2k+3)$
**9.** $S_k$: 2 is a factor of $k^2 - k + 2$; $S_{k+1}$: 2 is a factor of $k^2 + k + 2$
**11.** $S_1: 4 = 2(1)(1+1)$; $S_k: 4 + 8 + 12 + \cdots + 4k = 2k(k+1)$; $S_{k+1}: 4 + 8 + 12 + \cdots + 4(k+1) = 2(k+1)(k+2)$; $S_{k+1}$ can be obtained by adding $4k + 4$ to both sides of $S_k$.
**13.** $S_1: 1 = 1^2$; $S_k: 1 + 3 + 5 + \cdots + (2k-1) = k^2$; $S_{k+1}: 1 + 3 + 5 + \cdots + (2k+1) = (k+1)^2$; $S_{k+1}$ can be obtained by adding $2k + 1$ to both sides of $S_k$.
**15.** $S_1: 3 = 1[2(1) + 1]$; $S_k: 3 + 7 + 11 + \cdots + (4k-1) = k(2k+1)$; $S_{k+1}: 3 + 7 + 11 + \cdots + (4k+3) = (k+1)(2k+3)$; $S_{k+1}$ can be obtained by adding $4k + 3$ to both sides of $S_k$.
**17.** $S_1: 1 = 2^1 - 1$; $S_k: 1 + 2 + 2^2 + \cdots + 2^{k-1} = 2^k - 1$; $S_{k+1}: 1 + 2 + 2^2 + \cdots + 2^k = 2^{k+1} - 1$; $S_{k+1}$ can be obtained by adding $2^k$ to both sides of $S_k$.
**19.** $S_1: 2 = 2^{1+1} - 2$; $S_k: 2 + 4 + 8 + \cdots + 2^k = 2^{k+1} - 2$; $S_{k+1}: 2 + 4 + 8 + \cdots + 2^{k+1} = 2^{k+2} - 2$; $S_{k+1}$ can be obtained by adding $2^{k+1}$ to both sides of $S_k$.
**21.** $S_1: 1 \cdot 2 = \frac{1(1+1)(1+2)}{3}$; $S_k: 1 \cdot 2 + 2 \cdot 3 + 3 \cdot 4 + \cdots + k(k+1) = \frac{k(k+1)(k+2)}{3}$; $S_{k+1}: 1 \cdot 2 + 2 \cdot 3 + 3 \cdot 4 + \cdots + (k+1)(k+2) = \frac{(k+1)(k+2)(k+3)}{3}$; $S_{k+1}$ can be obtained by adding $(k+1)(k+2)$ to both sides of $S_k$.
**23.** $S_1: \frac{1}{1 \cdot 2} = \frac{1}{1+1}$; $S_k: \frac{1}{1 \cdot 2} + \frac{1}{2 \cdot 3} + \frac{1}{3 \cdot 4} + \cdots + \frac{1}{k(k+1)} = \frac{k}{k+1}$; $S_{k+1}: \frac{1}{1 \cdot 2} + \frac{1}{2 \cdot 3} + \frac{1}{3 \cdot 4} + \cdots + \frac{1}{(k+1)(k+2)} = \frac{k+1}{k+2}$; $S_{k+1}$ can be obtained by adding $\frac{1}{(k+1)(k+2)}$ to both sides of $S_k$.
**25.** $S_1$: 2 is a factor of 0; $S_k$: 2 is a factor of $k^2 - k$; $S_{k+1}$: 2 is a factor of $k^2 + k$; $S_{k+1}$ can be obtained from $S_k$ by rewriting $k^2 + k$ as $(k^2 - k) + 2k$.
**27.** $S_1$: 6 is a factor of 6; $S_k$: 6 is a factor of $k(k+1)(k+2)$; $S_{k+1}$: 6 is a factor of $(k+1)(k+2)(k+3)$; $S_{k+1}$ can be obtained from $S_k$ by rewriting $(k+1)(k+2)(k+3)$ as $k(k+1)(k+2) + 3(k+1)(k+2)$ and noting that either $k + 1$ or $k + 2$ is even, so 6 is a factor of $3(k+1)(k+2)$.
**29.** $S_1: (ab)^1 = a^1b^1$; $S_k: (ab)^k = a^kb^k$; $S_{k+1}: (ab)^{k+1} = a^{k+1}b^{k+1}$; $S_{k+1}$ can be obtained by multiplying both sides of $S_k$ by $(ab)$.
**33.** $S_3: 3^2 > 2(3) + 1$; $S_k: k^2 > 2k + 1$ for $k \geq 3$; $S_{k+1}: (k+1)^2 > 2(k+1) + 1$ or $k^2 + 2k + 1 > 2k + 3$; $S_{k+1}$ can be obtained from $S_k$ by noting that $S_{k+1}$ is the same as $k^2 > 2$ which is true for $k \geq 3$.
**35.** $S_1: \frac{1}{4}$; $S_2: \frac{1}{3}$; $S_3: \frac{3}{8}$; $S_4: \frac{2}{5}$; $S_5: \frac{5}{12}$; $S_n: \frac{n}{2n+2}$; Use $S_k$ to obtain the conjectured formula.

# Section 11.5

## Check Point Exercises

**1. a.** 20 **b.** 1 **c.** 28 **d.** 1 **2.** $x^4 + 4x^3 + 6x^2 + 4x + 1$ **3.** $x^5 - 10x^4y + 40x^3y^2 - 80x^2y^3 + 80xy^4 - 32y^5$
**4.** $4032x^5y^4$

## Exercise Set 11.5

**1.** 56 **3.** 12 **5.** 1 **7.** 4950 **9.** $x^3 + 6x^2 + 12x + 8$ **11.** $27x^3 + 27x^2y + 9xy^2 + y^3$ **13.** $125x^3 - 75x^2 + 15x - 1$
**15.** $16x^4 + 32x^3 + 24x^2 + 8x + 1$ **17.** $x^8 + 8x^6y + 24x^4y^2 + 32x^2y^3 + 16y^4$ **19.** $y^4 - 12y^3 + 54y^2 - 108y + 81$
**21.** $16x^{12} - 32x^9 + 24x^6 - 8x^3 + 1$ **23.** $c^5 + 10c^4 + 40c^3 + 80c^2 + 80c + 32$ **25.** $x^5 - 5x^4 + 10x^3 - 10x^2 + 5x - 1$
**27.** $x^5 - 10x^4y + 40x^3y^2 - 80x^2y^3 + 80xy^4 - 32y^5$ **29.** $64a^6 + 192a^5b + 240a^4b^2 + 160a^3b^3 + 60a^2b^4 + 12ab^5 + b^6$
**31.** $x^8 + 16x^7 + 112x^6 + \cdots$ **33.** $x^{10} - 20x^9y + 180x^8y^2 - \cdots$
**35.** $x^{32} + 16x^{30} + 120x^{28} + \cdots$ **37.** $y^{60} - 20y^{57} + 190y^{54} - \cdots$ **39.** $240x^4y^2$ **41.** $126x^5$ **43.** $56x^6y^{15}$ **45.** $-\frac{21}{2}x^6$
**47.** $g(t) = 0.002t^3 - 0.84t^2 - 16.13t - 68.54$

**61.** 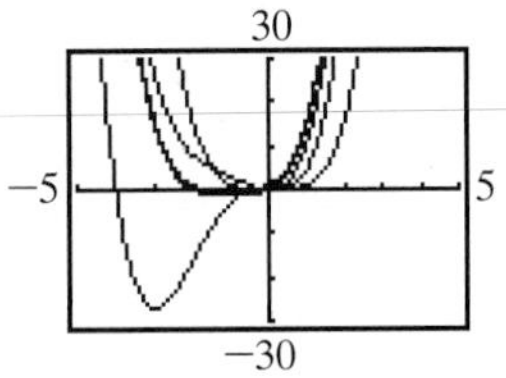


$f_2, f_3, f_4$, and $f_5$ are approaching $f_1 = f_6$.

**63.** $f_1(x) = x^4 - 8x^3 + 24x^2 - 32x + 16$
**67.** $x^6 + 3x^5 + 6x^4 + 7x^3 + 6x^2 + 3x + 1$
**69.** $\binom{n}{r} = \frac{n!}{r!\,(n-r)!}; \binom{n}{r-1} = \frac{n!}{(n-r)![n-(n-r)]!} = \frac{n!}{(n-r)!r!} = \binom{n}{r}$

## Section 11.6

### Check Point Exercises

**1.** 72 **2.** 729 **3.** 676,000 **4.** 840 **5.** 720 **6. a.** combinations **b.** permutations **7.** 210 **8.** 1820

### Exercise Set 11.6

**1.** 3024 **3.** 6720 **5.** 720 **7.** 1 **9.** 126 **11.** 330 **13.** 1 **15.** 1 **17.** combinations **19.** permutations **21.** 27 ways **23.** 40 ways **25.** 243 ways **27.** 144 area codes **29.** 120 ways **31.** 6 paragraphs **33.** 720 ways **35.** 8,648,640 ways **37.** 120 ways **39.** 15,120 lineups **41.** 20 ways **43.** 495 collections **45.** 24,310 groups **47.** 13,983,816 selections **49.** 360 ways **51.** 1716 ways **53.** 1140 ways **55.** 840 passwords **57.** 2730 cones **69.** (c) is true. **71.** 144 numbers

## Section 11.7

### Check Point Exercises

**1.** $\frac{82.5}{275} = 0.3$ **2.** $\frac{1}{3}$ **3.** $\frac{1}{9}$ **4.** $\frac{1}{13}$ **5.** $\frac{1}{142{,}506}$ **6.** $\frac{142{,}505}{142{,}506} \approx 0.999993$ **7.** $\frac{1}{3}$ **8.** $\frac{3}{4}$ **9.** $\frac{24}{25}$ **10.** $\frac{1}{361} \approx 0.003$ **11.** $\frac{1}{16}$

### Exercise Set 11.7

**1.** 0.42 **3.** $\frac{761}{5926} \approx 0.13$ **5.** $\frac{1}{6}$ **7.** $\frac{1}{2}$ **9.** $\frac{1}{3}$ **11.** $\frac{1}{13}$ **13.** $\frac{3}{13}$ **15.** $\frac{1}{4}$ **17.** $\frac{7}{8}$ **19.** $\frac{1}{12}$ **21.** $\frac{1}{18{,}009{,}460}; \frac{5}{900{,}473}$ **23. a.** 2,598,960 **b.** 1287 **c.** $\frac{1287}{2{,}598{,}960} \approx 0.0005$ **25.** $\frac{255{,}647}{274{,}634} \approx 0.93$ **27.** $\frac{237{,}401}{274{,}634} \approx 0.86$ **29.** $\frac{42{,}010}{274{,}634} \approx 0.15$ **31.** $\frac{2}{13}$ **33.** $\frac{5}{6}$ **35.** $\frac{7}{13}$ **37.** $\frac{3}{4}$ **39.** $\frac{33}{40}$ **41.** $\frac{1}{36}$ **43.** $\frac{1}{3}$ **45.** $\frac{1}{64}$ **47. a.** $\frac{1}{256}$ **b.** $\frac{1}{4096}$ **c.** $\left(\frac{15}{16}\right)^{10}$ **d.** $1 - \left(\frac{15}{16}\right)^{10}$ **59.** Answers may vary.

### Chapter 11 Review Exercises

**1.** $a_1 = 3; a_2 = 10; a_3 = 17; a_4 = 24$ **2.** $a_1 = -\frac{3}{2}; a_2 = \frac{4}{3}; a_3 = -\frac{5}{4}; a_4 = \frac{6}{5}$ **3.** $a_1 = 1; a_2 = 1; a_3 = \frac{1}{2}; a_4 = \frac{1}{6}$ **4.** $a_1 = \frac{1}{2}; a_2 = -\frac{1}{4}; a_3 = \frac{1}{8}; a_4 = -\frac{1}{16}$ **5.** $a_1 = 9; a_2 = \frac{2}{27}; a_3 = 9; a_4 = \frac{2}{27}$ **6.** $a_1 = 4; a_2 = 11; a_3 = 25; a_4 = 53$ **7.** 65 **8.** 95 **9.** −20 **10.** $\sum_{i=1}^{15} \frac{i}{i+2}$ **11.** $\sum_{i=1}^{10} (i+3)^3$ **12.** 7, 11, 15, 19, 23, 27 **13.** −4, −9, −14, −19, −24, −29 **14.** $\frac{3}{2}, 1, \frac{1}{2}, 0, -\frac{1}{2}, -1$ **15.** −2, 3, 8, 13, 18, 23 **16.** $a_6 = 20$ **17.** $a_{12} = -30$ **18.** $a_{14} = -38$ **19.** $a_n = 4n - 11; a_{20} = 69$ **20.** $a_n = 220 - 20n; a_{20} = -180$ **21.** $a_n = 8 - 5n; a_{20} = -92$ **22.** 1727 **23.** 225 **24.** 15,150 **25.** 440 **26.** −500 **27.** −2325 **28. a.** $a_n = 1043.4518 - 0.4118n$ **b.** 1002.2718 sec **29.** $418,500 **30.** 1470 seats **31.** 3, 6, 12, 24, 48 **32.** $\frac{1}{2}, \frac{1}{4}, \frac{1}{8}, \frac{1}{16}, \frac{1}{32}$ **33.** 16, −8, 4, −2, 1 **34.** −1, 5, −25, 125, −625 **35.** $a_7 = 1458$ **36.** $a_6 = \frac{1}{2}$ **37.** $a_5 = -48$ **38.** $a_n = 2^{n-1}; a_8 = 128$ **39.** $a_n = 100\left(\frac{1}{10}\right)^{n-1}; a_8 = \frac{1}{100{,}000}$ **40.** $a_n = 12\left(-\frac{1}{3}\right)^{n-1}; a_8 = -\frac{4}{729}$ **41.** 17,936,135 **42.** $\frac{1093}{2187}$ **43.** 19,530 **44.** −258 **45.** $\frac{341}{128}$ **46.** $\frac{27}{2}$ **47.** $\frac{4}{3}$ **48.** $-\frac{18}{5}$ **49.** 20 **50.** $\frac{2}{3}$ **51.** $\frac{47}{99}$ **52.** $42,823.22; $223,210.19 **53.** $120,112.64 **54.** $\$9\frac{1}{3}$ million **55.** $S_1: 5 = \frac{5(1)(1+1)}{2}; S_k: 5 + 10 + 15 + \cdots + 5k = \frac{5k(k+1)}{2}; S_{k+1}: 5 + 10 + 15 + \cdots + 5(k+1) = \frac{5(k+1)(k+2)}{2}$; $S_{k+1}$ can be obtained by adding $5(k+1)$ to both sides of $S_k$.

**56.** $S_1: 1 = \frac{4^1 - 1}{3}; S_k: 1 + 4 + 4^2 + \cdots + 4^{k-1} = \frac{4^k - 1}{3}; S_{k+1}: 1 + 4 + 4^2 + \cdots + 4^k = \frac{4^{k+1} - 1}{3};$ $S_{k+1}$ can be obtained by adding $4^k$ to both sides of $S_k$.

**57.** $S_1: 2 = 2(1)^2; S_k: 2 + 6 + 10 + \cdots + (4k - 2) = 2k^2; S_{k+1}: 2 + 6 + 10 + \cdots + (4k + 2) = 2k^2 + 4k + 2;$ $S_{k+1}$ can be obtained by adding $4k + 2$ to both sides of $S_k$.

**58.** $S_1: 1 \cdot 3 = \frac{1(1 + 1)[2(1) + 7]}{6}; S_k: 1 \cdot 3 + 2 \cdot 4 + 3 \cdot 5 + \cdots + k(k + 2) = \frac{k(k + 1)(2k + 7)}{6};$

$S_{k+1}: 1 \cdot 3 + 2 \cdot 4 + 3 \cdot 5 + \cdots + (k + 1)(k + 3) = \frac{(k + 1)(k + 2)(2k + 9)}{6};$

$S_{k+1}$ can be obtained by adding $(k + 1)(k + 3)$ to both sides of $S_k$.

**59.** $S_1$: 2 is a factor of 6; $S_k$: 2 is a factor of $k^2 + 5k$; $S_{k+1}$: 2 is a factor of $k^2 + 7k + 6$; $S_{k+1}$ can be obtained from $S_k$ by rewriting $k^2 + 7k + 6$ as $(k^2 + 5k) + 2(k + 3)$.

**60.** 165 **61.** 4005 **62.** $8x^3 + 12x^2 + 6x + 1$ **63.** $x^8 - 4x^6 + 6x^4 - 4x^2 + 1$
**64.** $x^5 + 10x^4y + 40x^3y^2 + 80x^2y^3 + 80xy^4 + 32y^5$ **65.** $x^6 - 12x^5 + 60x^4 - 160x^3 + 240x^2 - 192x + 64$
**66.** $x^{16} + 24x^{14} + 252x^{12} + \cdots$ **67.** $x^9 - 27x^8 + 324x^7 - \cdots$ **68.** $80x^2$ **69.** $4860x^2$ **70.** 336 **71.** 15,120 **72.** 56
**73.** 78 **74.** 20 choices **75.** 243 possibilities **76.** 32,760 ways **77.** 4845 ways **78.** 1140 sets **79.** 116,280 ways
**80.** 120 ways **81.** $\frac{9{,}630{,}188}{31{,}878{,}234} \approx 0.302$ **82.** $\frac{5{,}503{,}372}{19{,}128{,}261} \approx 0.288$ **83.** $\frac{2}{3}$ **84.** $\frac{2}{3}$ **85.** $\frac{2}{13}$ **86.** $\frac{7}{13}$ **87.** $\frac{5}{6}$ **88.** $\frac{5}{6}$
**89. a.** $\frac{1}{15{,}504}$ **b.** $\frac{25}{3876}$ **90.** $\frac{4}{5}$ **91.** $\frac{3}{4}$ **92.** $\frac{1}{32}$ **93. a.** 0.04 **b.** 0.008 **c.** 0.4096

## Chapter 11 Test

**1.** $a_1 = 1; a_2 = -\frac{1}{4}; a_3 = \frac{1}{9}; a_4 = -\frac{1}{16}; a_5 = \frac{1}{25}$ **2.** 105 **3.** 550 **4.** −21,846 **5.** 36 **6.** 720 **7.** 120 **8.** $\sum_{i=1}^{20} \frac{i + 1}{i + 2}$
**9.** $a_n = 5n - 1; a_{12} = 59$ **10.** $a_n = 16\left(\frac{1}{4}\right)^{n-1}; a_{12} = \frac{1}{262{,}144}$ **11.** −2387 **12.** −385 **13.** 8 **14.** $276,426.79
**15.** $S_1: 1 = \frac{1[3(1) - 1]}{2}; S_k: 1 + 4 + 7 + \cdots + (3k - 2) = \frac{k(3k - 1)}{2}; S_{k+1}: 1 + 4 + 7 + \cdots + (3k + 1) = \frac{(k + 1)(3k + 2)}{2};$
$S_{k+1}$ can be obtained by adding $3k + 1$ to both sides of $S_k$. **16.** $x^{10} - 5x^8 + 10x^6 - 10x^4 + 5x^2 - 1$ **17.** 990 ways **18.** 210 sets
**19.** $10^4 = 10{,}000$ **20.** $\frac{10}{1001}$ **21.** $\frac{8}{13}$ **22.** $\frac{3}{5}$ **23.** $\frac{1}{256}$ **24.** $\frac{1}{16}$

## Cumulative Review Exercises (Chapters 1–11)

**1.** $x = \frac{14}{5}$ **2.** $\left\{\frac{3 + \sqrt{3}}{3}, \frac{3 - \sqrt{3}}{3}\right\}$ **3.** {2} **4.** {16, 256} **5.** {6} **6.** $-1 \le x \le 0$ or $[-1, 0]$ **7.** $\left(-\frac{2}{3}, \frac{3}{2}\right)$
**8.** $(-3, 1]$ **9.** {2.9706} **10.** $\left\{1, \frac{1}{2}, -3\right\}$ **11.** {(3, 2), (3, −2), (−3, 2), (−3, −2)} **12.** {(6, −4, 2)} **13.** {(0, −1), (2, 1)}

**14.**
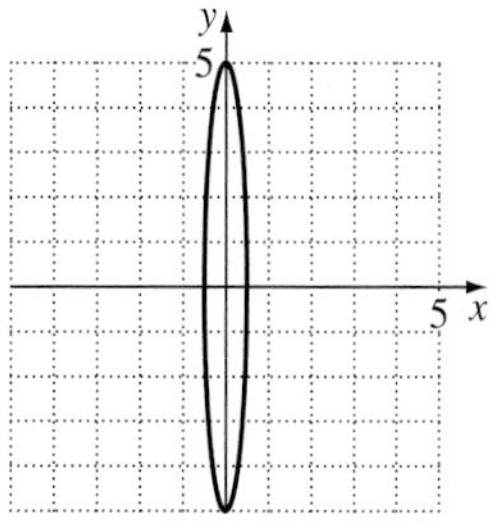


**15.**
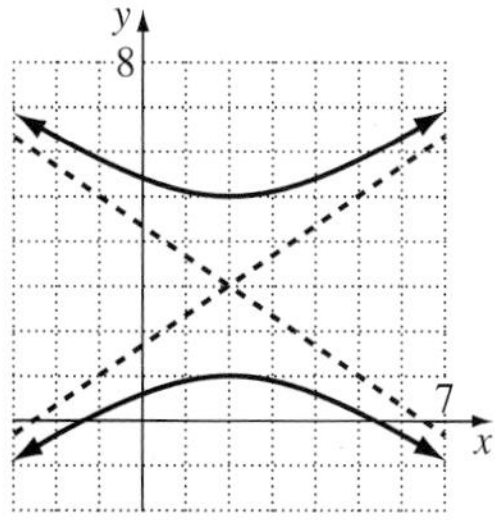


**16.**
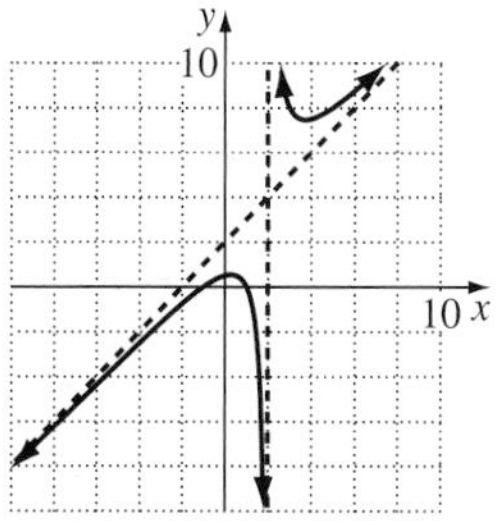


**17.**
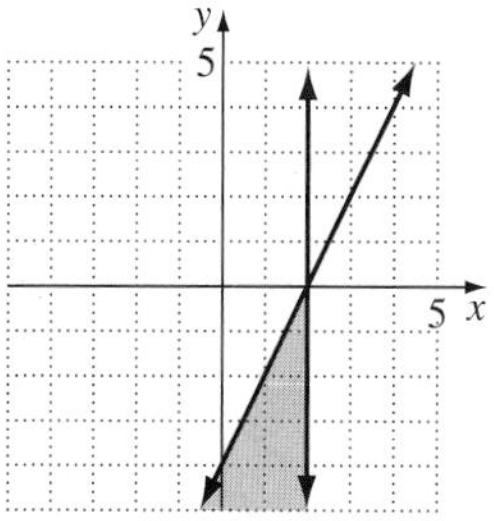


**18.**
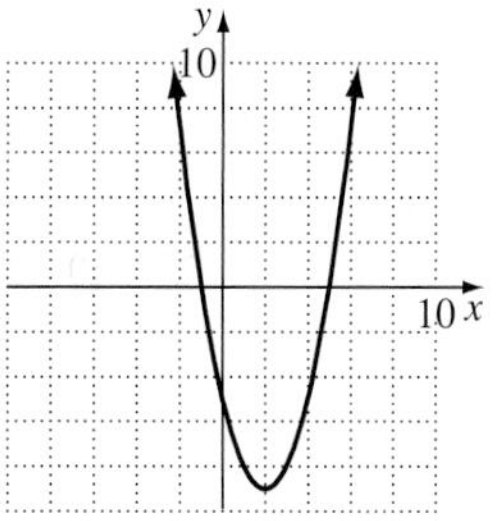


**19.**
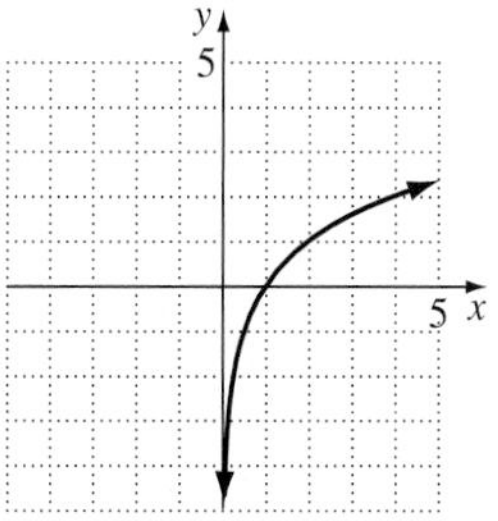


**20.** $f^{-1}(x) = x^3 - 4$
**21.** $\begin{bmatrix} -2 & 10 \\ -5 & 7 \\ 15 & -15 \end{bmatrix}$ **22.** $\frac{-1}{x - 2} + \frac{3x - 2}{x^2 + 2x + 2}$
**23.** $x^{15} + 10x^{12}y + 40x^9y^2 + 80x^6y^3 + 80x^3y^4 + 32y^5$
**24.** 3850
**25. a.** $y - 119.4 = 5.17x$ **b.** $y = 5.17x + 119.4$
**c.** 207.29 billion pieces of mail
**26.** The Empire State Building is about 916.7 feet tall and the World Trade Center is about 1043.4 feet tall.

**27.** length: 100 yd; width: 50 yd **28.** pen: \$1.80; pad: \$2 **29. a.** 6 sec **b.** 2.5 sec; 196 ft **30.** 11 amps

**31. a.** 20 in. **b.** $\frac{3}{8}$ cycles/sec **c.** $\frac{8}{3}$ sec **32.** $\tan x + \frac{1}{\tan x} = \frac{\sin x}{\cos x} + \frac{1}{\frac{\sin x}{\cos x}} = \frac{\sin x}{\cos x} + \frac{\cos x}{\sin x} = \frac{\sin^2 x + \cos^2 x}{\cos x \cdot \sin x} = \frac{1}{\cos x \cdot \sin x}$

**33.** $\frac{1 - \tan^2 x}{1 + \tan^2 x} = \frac{1 - \frac{\sin^2 x}{\cos^2 x}}{1 + \frac{\sin^2 x}{\cos^2 x}} \cdot \frac{\cos^2 x}{\cos^2 x} = \frac{\cos^2 x - \sin^2 x}{\cos^2 x + \sin^2 x} = \frac{\cos 2x}{1} = \cos 2x$

**34.**

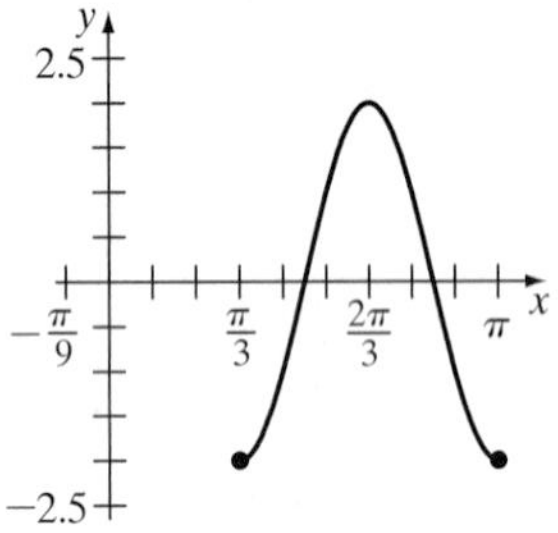


**35.** $\frac{\pi}{6}, \frac{5\pi}{6}, \frac{7\pi}{6}, \frac{11\pi}{6}$ **36.** $0, \frac{\pi}{3}, \frac{5\pi}{3}$ **37.** $-\frac{5}{\sqrt{11}}$

**38.**

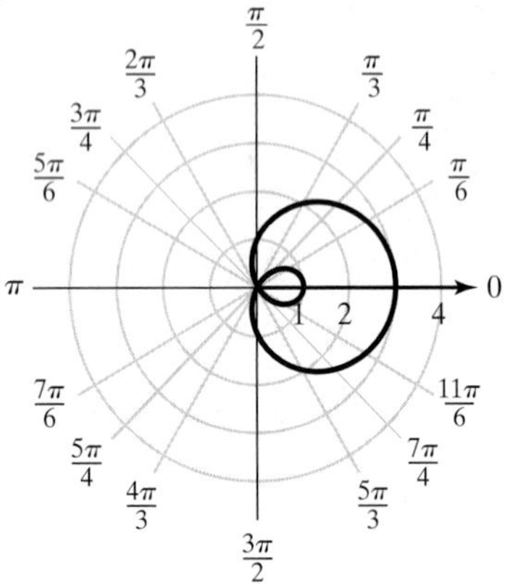


**39.** $B = 54°, C = 92°, c = 39.5$

**40.** $y = 2 - x^2$;

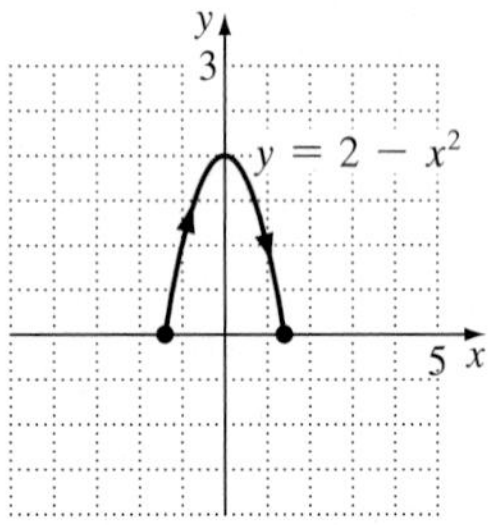


# CHAPTER 12

## Section 12.1

### Check Point Exercises

**1.** 36 **2.** 0 **3. a.** 5 **b.** 3 **4.**

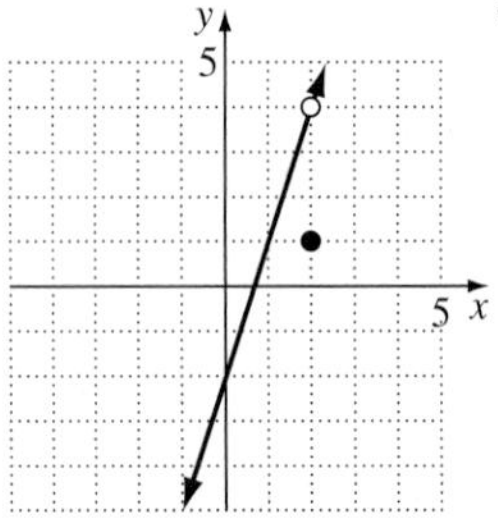


; 4

### Exercise Set 12.1

**1.** 4 **3.** 3 **5.** 20 **7.** 1 **9.** 0 **11.** 12 **13.** 1 **15.** 1 **17.** 1 **19. a.** −1 **b.** −1 **21. a.** 2 **b.** 1 **23.** −3 **25.** −1 **27.** 7 **29.** −5 **31.** 0 **33.** −1 **35.** 2 **37.** 1 **39.** 0 **41.** 3 **43.** 3 **45.** 2 **47.** 0

**49. a.** 8; As your nose approaches the fan, the speed of the breeze that your nose feels approaches 8 miles per hour. **b.** Answers may vary.

**51.** $\lim_{x \to 10} f(x) = 16$ **53. a.** 30; The cost to rent the car one day and drive it 100 miles is \$30. **b.** \$40 **c.** \$60

**65.** 0.25000; 0.250000 **67.** 0.5000001675; 0.50000017 **69.** $\left(\frac{29}{30}, \frac{31}{30}\right), \left(\frac{299}{300}, \frac{301}{300}\right)$

## Section 12.2

### Check Point Exercises

**1. a.** 11 **b.** −9 **2. a.** 19 **b.** $-\sqrt{2}$ **3.** 13 **4.** 5 **5.** −70 **6. a.** −22 **b.** 72 **7.** −56 **8.** 61 **9.** 343

**10.** $\sqrt{2}$ **11.** −3 **12.** 4 **13.** $\frac{1}{6}$

### Exercise Set 12.2

**1.** 8 **3.** 2 **5.** 14 **7.** 28 **9.** 6 **11.** 8 **13.** 16 **15.** 5 **17.** $\frac{5}{6}$ **19.** 3 **21.** 2 **23.** 2 **25.** 2 **27.** $\frac{8}{9}$ **29.** $\frac{1}{2}$ **31.** 1125 **33.** $\frac{1}{4}$ **35.** $-\frac{1}{4}$ **37.** $-7$ **39.** $-\frac{1}{9}$ **41.** $\frac{1}{3}$ **43.** 147; If the advertising budget for a movie in millions of dollars, $x$, approaches 20, the box office revenue in millions of dollars, $f(x)$, approaches 147. **45.** 450; If the number of wheelchairs manufactured by the company, $x$, approaches 10,000, the average cost per wheelchair, $f(x)$, approaches \$450. **61.** $-\frac{1}{16}$ **63.** $\frac{1}{2}$ **65.** $\frac{2}{3}$

## Section 12.3

### Check Point Exercises

**1. a.** 9 **b.** 7 **c.** does not exist **2. a.** continuous **b.** discontinuous **3.** discontinuous at 0

### Exercise Set 12.3

**1. a.** 6 **b.** 8 **c.** does not exist **3. a.** 9 **b.** 9 **c.** 9 **5. a.** 6 **b.** 6 **c.** 6 **7. a.** 0 **b.** 0 **c.** 0 **9. a.** 4 **b.** 2 **c.** does not exist **11. a.** 2 **b.** 2 **c.** 2 **d.** 4 **e.** 3 **f.** does not exist **g.** 2 **h.** 1 **i.** does not exist **13. a.** 1 **b.** 2 **c.** does not exist **d.** 2 **e.** 2 **f.** 2 **15.** continuous **17.** continuous **19.** continuous **21.** discontinuous **23.** continuous **25.** discontinuous **27.** discontinuous **29.** continuous **31.** continuous **33.** continuous for every number $x$ **35.** $-1$ and 4 **37.** 0 **39.** continuous for every number $x$ **41.** 1 **43.** continuous for every number $x$ **45.** 2 **47.** 4 **49. a.** \$35 **b.** \$60 **c.** $\lim_{x\to 200} f(x)$ does not exist; the graph jumps at $x = 200$ miles. **d.** the \$25 daily rental charge **65.** $f(x) = 18$ if $x = 9$ **67.** 4

## Section 12.4

### Check Point Exercises

**1.** 7 **2.** $y = \frac{1}{2}x + \frac{1}{2}$ **3. a.** $2x - 5$ **b.** $-7; 1$ **4. a.** 49.21 cubic inches per inch; 48.1201 cubic inches per inch **b.** 48 cubic inches per inch **5. a.** $-32$ ft/sec **b.** $-96$ ft/sec

### Exercise Set 12.4

**1. a.** 2 **b.** $y = 2x + 3$ **3. a.** $-2$ **b.** $y = -2x + 3$ **5. a.** $-20$ **b.** $y = -20x - 20$ **7. a.** 7 **b.** $y = 7x - 8$ **9. a.** 1 **b.** $y = x - 3$ **11. a.** $\frac{1}{6}$ **b.** $y = \frac{1}{6}x + \frac{3}{2}$ **13. a.** $-1$ **b.** $y = -x + 2$ **15. a.** $-3$ **b.** $-3; -3$ **17. a.** $2x$ **b.** $-2; 6$ **19. a.** $2x - 3$ **b.** $0; 1$ **21. a.** $3x^2$ **b.** $3; 3$ **23. a.** $\frac{1}{2\sqrt{x}}$ **b.** $\frac{1}{2}; \frac{1}{4}$ **25. a.** $-\frac{4}{x^2}$ **b.** $-1; -4$ **27. a.** $6.4x + 2.1$ **b.** $2.1; 27.7$ **29. a.** 12.1 square inches per inch; 12.01 square inches per inch **b.** 12 square inches per inch **31. a.** $4.1\pi$ square inches per inch; $4.01\pi$ square inches per inch **b.** $4\pi$ square inches per inch **33.** $48\pi$ square inches per inch **35. a.** $0.64x + 1.64$ **b.** 10.6 billion dollars per year **37. a.** 32 feet per second; $-32$ feet per second **b.** $-64$ feet per second **39. a.** 32 feet per second; $-32$ feet per second **b.** 3 sec; 148 ft **41.** 1939; 3.7%; 0 **43.** 2.2% **59.** 2.00 **61.** 0.67

**63. a.**

| $x$(years since 1899) | 0 | 10 | 20 | 30 | 40 | 50 | 60 | 70 | 80 | 90 | 100 |
|---|---|---|---|---|---|---|---|---|---|---|---|
| $f(x)$(%) | 1.3 | 2.1 | 3.2 | 3.6 | 3.7 | 3.5 | 3.1 | 2.9 | 2.8 | 2.5 | 2.2 |

**b.** $-0.0007121x^2 + 0.07385x + 1.609$

**c.**

| $x$(years since 1899) | 20 | 40 | 100 |
|---|---|---|---|
| $f'(x)\left(\frac{\text{\% change}}{\text{year}}\right)$ | 0.045366 | 0.016882 | $-0.06857$ |

### Chapter 12 Review Exercises

**1.** 3 **2.** $\frac{1}{2}$ **3.** 2 **4.** 0 **5.** 1 **6.** 3 **7.** 2 **8.** 3 **9.** 6 **10.** $-1$ **11.** 1 **12.** 15 **13.** 8 **14.** 1000 **15.** 5 **16.** 2 **17.** $-8$ **18.** 5 **19.** $\frac{1}{20}$ **20.** 2 **21.** $\frac{1}{20}$ **22.** $-\frac{1}{25}$ **23. a.** 5 **b.** 7 **c.** does not exist **24. a.** 2 **b.** 4 **c.** does not exist **25. a.** $-10$ **b.** $-10$ **c.** $-10$ **26.** 3 **27.** 5 **28.** $-3$ **29.** does not exist

**30.** 1 **31.** 3 **32.** −3 **33.** does not exist **34.** 3 **35.** does not exist **36.** 5 **37.** 5 **38.** 5 **39.** 0 **40.** 0
**41.** continuous **42.** discontinuous **43.** discontinuous **44.** continuous **45.** discontinuous **46.** continuous for every number $x$
**47.** 1 and −3 **48.** 0 **49.** continuous for every number $x$ **50.** −2 **51.** 11 **52.** **a.** 9 **b.** $y = 9x - 2$
**53.** **a.** −9 **b.** $y = -9x - 5$ **54.** **a.** $6x + 12$ **b.** 0; 18 **55.** **a.** $6x^2 - 1$ **b.** 5; 5 **56.** **a.** $-\frac{1}{x^2}$ **b.** $-\frac{1}{4}; -\frac{1}{4}$
**57.** **a.** $\frac{1}{2\sqrt{x}}$ **b.** $\frac{1}{12}; \frac{1}{18}$ **58.** **a.** 20.5 cubic inches per inch; 20.05 cubic inches per inch **b.** 20 cubic inches per inch
**59.** $100\pi$ cubic inches per inch **60.** **a.** 16 feet per second; −48 feet per second **b.** 2.5 sec; 105 ft

## Chapter 12 Test

**1.** 6 **2.** −3 **3.** −5 **4.** 4 **5.** 6 **6.** does not exist **7.** 4 **8.** 81 **9.** −3 **10.** $\frac{1}{6}$ **11.** discontinuous
**12.** continuous **13.** $2x - 5$ **14.** $-\frac{10}{x^2}$ **15.** $y = -6x - 9$ **16.** −24 feet per second

## Cumulative Review Exercises (Chapters 1–12)

**1.** $\left\{x \,\middle|\, x \le -\frac{5}{2} \text{ or } -2 < x < -1\right\}$ **2.** $\left\{1, -\frac{1}{2}, -6\right\}$ **3.** $\left\{x \,\middle|\, x < -\frac{7}{2} \text{ or } x > -\frac{1}{2}\right\}$ **4.** $\left\{\frac{3\pi}{2}\right\}$ **5.** {67}

**6.**

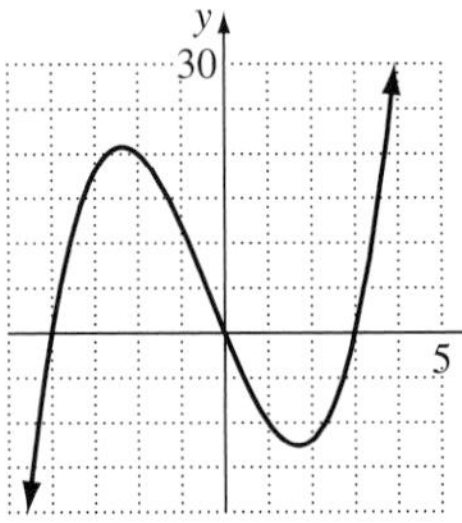


**7.**

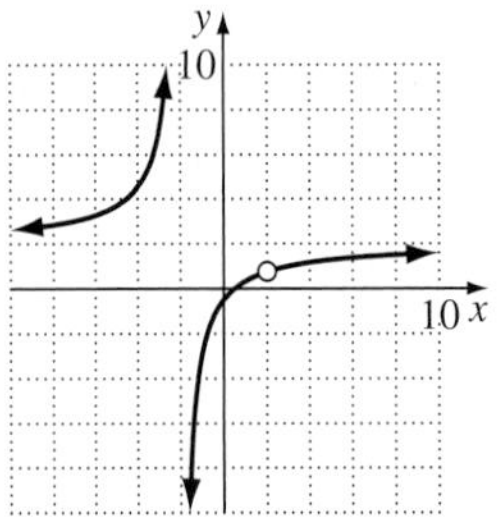


**8.**

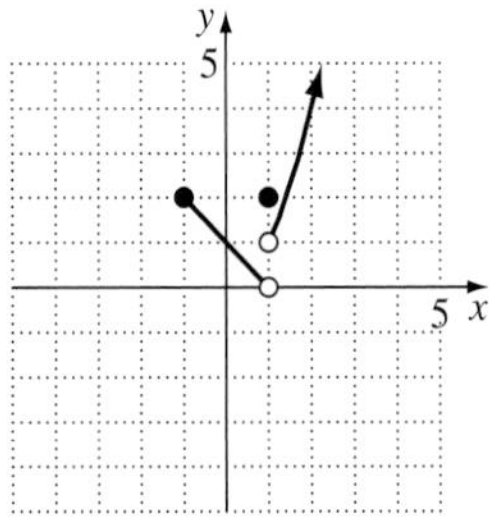


**9.**

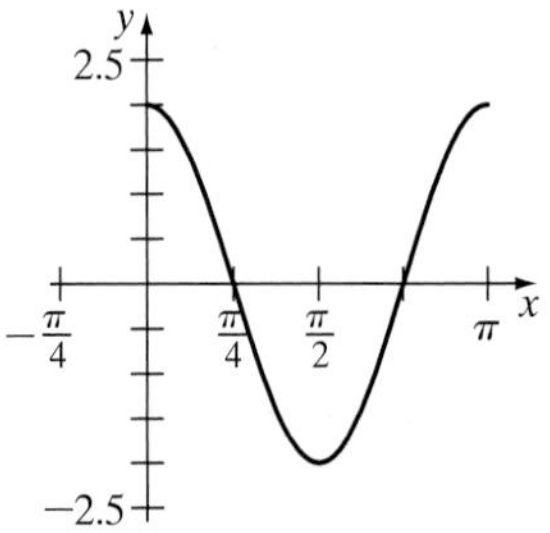


**10.**

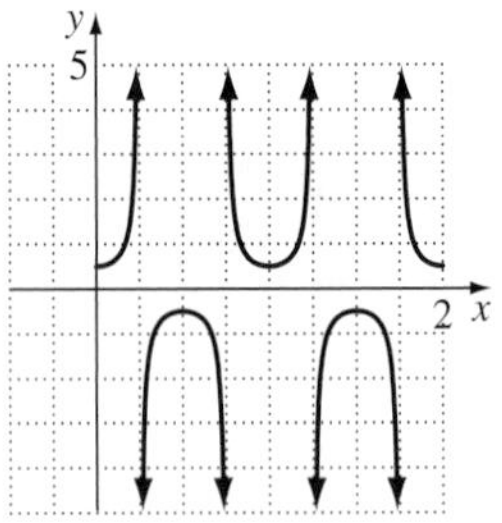


**11.**

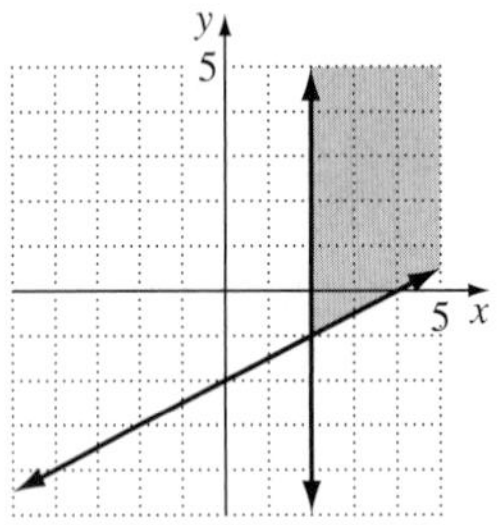


**12.**

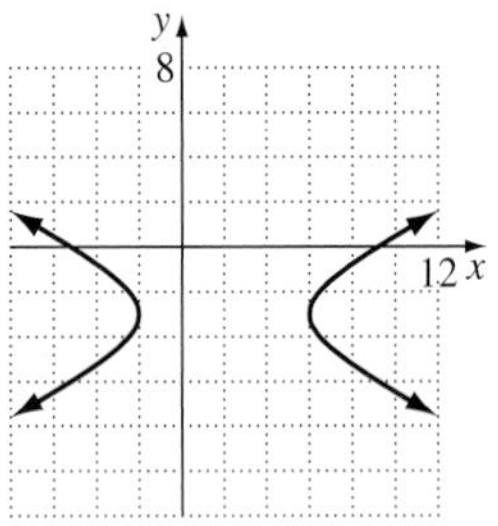


**13.**

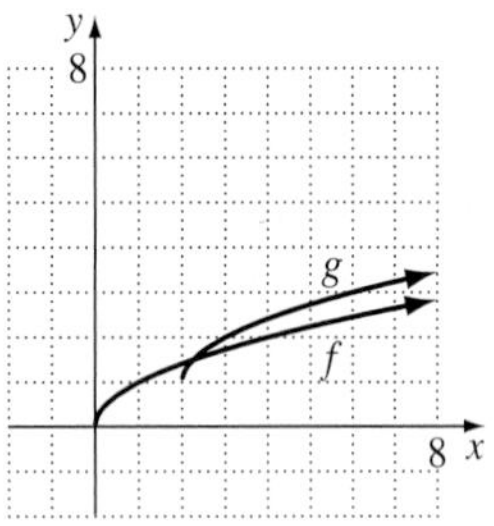


**14.**

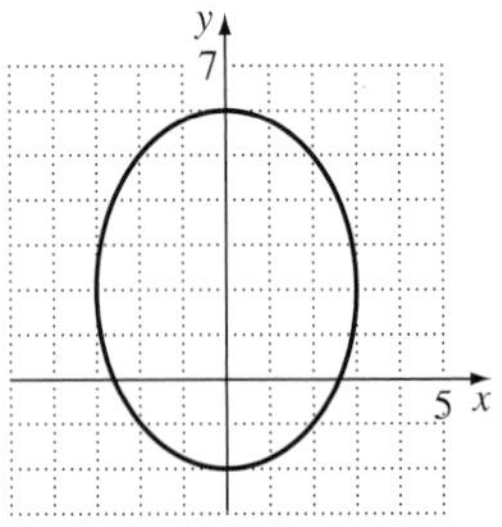


**15.**

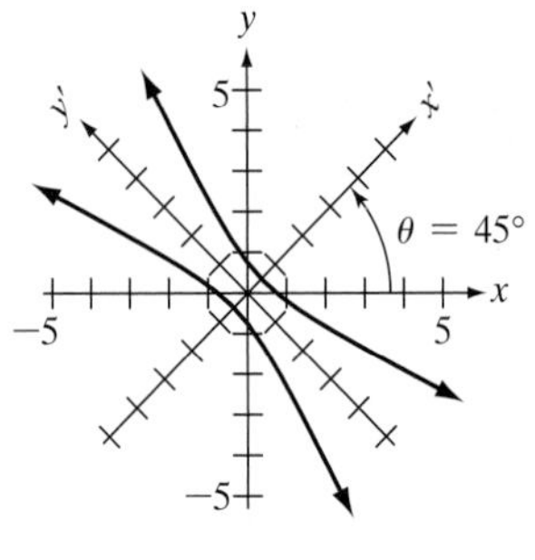


**16.** $-4x + 7$
**17.** $\frac{1}{7}x + \frac{1}{7}$
**18.** $\frac{5}{4}$
**19.** $x^8 - 12x^6y + 54x^4y^2 - 108x^2y^3 + 81y^4$
**20.** $y = -2x + 1$
**21.** −11; 170°
**22.** $\frac{1}{x} - \frac{x+1}{x^2 + x + 1}$

**23.**
$$\tan\theta + \cot\theta = \frac{\sin\theta}{\cos\theta} + \frac{\cos\theta}{\sin\theta} = \frac{\sin^2\theta + \cos^2\theta}{\cos\theta\sin\theta} = \frac{1}{\cos\theta\sin\theta} = \sec\theta\csc\theta$$

**24.**
$$\tan(\theta + \pi) = \frac{\tan\theta + \tan\pi}{1 - \tan\theta\tan\pi} = \frac{\tan\theta + 0}{1 - \tan\theta(0)} = \tan\theta$$

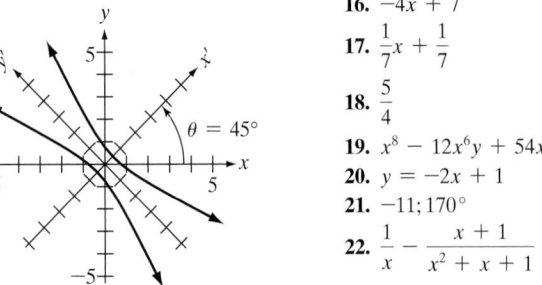

**25.** $\begin{bmatrix} 2 & 1 & 3 \\ 8 & 1 & 9 \\ 5 & 1 & 6 \end{bmatrix}$

**26.**

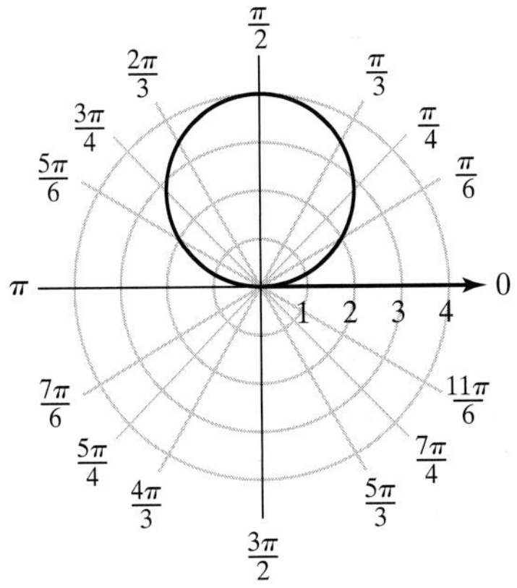


**27.** $f(x) = x^9; g(x) = x^2 - 3x + 7$
**28.** $\{(2, -1, 3)\}$
**29.** 168
**30.** $2 + 2\sqrt{3}i$
**31.** \$116,000 at 8%; \$4000 at 18%
**32.** 23 cm $\times$ 23 cm
**33.** 50 and 50
**34.** **a.** $T = 72 + 303e^{-0.0769t}$ **b.** 6.9 min
**35.** 1,005,633
**36.** 71.6 mi
**37.** $29\frac{1}{3}$ cu in.
**38.** −24 feet per second
**39.** \$2350
**40.** 15.6 years old

# Subject Index

## F

# T

# Photo Credits

**CHAPTER P** **CO** cmcd/PhotoDisc, Inc **p. 2** (United Nations) SuperStock, Inc. **p. 13** Tom Stewart/The Stock Market **p. 22** William Sallaz/Duomo Photography Incorporated **p. 33** (PEANUTS reprinted by permission of United Feature Syndicate, Inc.) United Media/United Feature Syndicate, Inc. **p. 34** Esbin/Anderson/Omni-Photo Communications, Inc. **p. 44** Gabe Palmer/Mug Shots/The Stock Market **p. 53** Jon Ortner/Stone **p. 67** (C) 1999 Roz Chast from Cartoonbank.com.All Rights Reserved/The Cartoon Bank **p. 70** Gary J. Shulfer/C. Marvin Lang **p. 73** S.S. Archives/Shooting Star International Photo Agency

**CHAPTER 1** **CO** Nita Winter Photography **p. 88** A. Ramu/Stock Boston **p. 90** (Squeak Carnwath "Equations" 1981, oil on canvass) Squeak Carnwath **p. 99** (Man barefoot water-skiing) Stone **p.112** Joel Sartore/Sharpshooters **p. 119** (Pencil sketch of Evariste Galois) Corbis **p. 130** Schafer & Hill/Stone **p. 143** (The Beverly Hillbillies) Corbis **p. 154** Tom Sanders/Adventure Photo & Film

**CHAPTER 2** **CO** Chris Salvo/FPG International LLC **p. 171**(Online shopping) SuperStock, Inc. **p. 172** Carol Simowitz/San Francisco Convention and Visitors Bureau **p. 183** (left) Paul Avis/FPG International LLC; (right) Bob Schatz/Stone **p. 186** Skip Moody/Dembinsky Photo Associates **p. 193** (Couple on cell phones) Bob Daemmrich Photography, Inc. **p. 196** Paul & Lindamarie Ambrose/FPG International LLC **p. 206** Hans Neleman/The Image Bank **p. 226** Douglas Kirkland/Corbis/Sygma **p. 230** (Burnside Bridge, Antietam National Battlefield, Maryland) SuperStock, Inc. **p. 241** Brad Hitz/Stone **p. 255** (Surfboards) Bishop Museum

**CHAPTER 3** **CO** Tim Davis/Stone **p. 262** Keith Brofsky/PhotoDisc, Inc. **p. 263** (left) Simon Bruty/Allsport Photography (USA), Inc.; (right) Illustration of the word Mirror/Scott Kim **p. 278** NIBSC/Science Photo Library/Photo Researchers, Inc. **p. 289** (left) Golden Retriever puppy/Townsend P. Dickinson/The Image Works; (right) Golden Retriever panting/Townsend P. Dickinson/The Image Works **p. 291** Barbara Penoyar/PhotoDisc, Inc **p. 300** Paul Silverman/Fundamental Photographs **p. 305** (drawing of Rene Descartes) Library of Congress **p. 310** (drawing of Girolamo Cardano) Smithsonian Institute **p. 320** Bob Daemmrich/Stock Boston **p. 340** Stephen Simpson/FPG International LLC **p. 347** (top) David Madison/Duomo Photography Incorporated; (bottom) David Madison/Duomo Photography Incorporated **p. 348** UPI/Corbis

**CHAPTER 4** **CO** Tony Neste/Anthony Neste **p. 357** Bruce Weaver/AP/Wide World Photos **p. 368** David Weintraub/Photo Researchers, Inc. **p. 381** Ron Chapple/FPG International LLC **p. 391** Shoneman, Stanley R/Omni-Photo Communications, Inc. **p. 402** Bullit Marquez/AP/World Wide Photos **p. 405** Jean-Marie Chauvet/Corbis /Sygma

**CHAPTER 5** **CO** Peter Langone/International Stock Photography Ltd. **p. 425** San Francisco MOMA/Olivier Laude/Liaison Agency, Inc. **p. 434** (Carousel) Pictor **p. 439** (Both) Gary Kufner/Sharpshooters **p. 455** Chris Noble/Stone **p. 463** Janet Foster/Masterfile Corporation **p. 465** Hugh Sitton/Stone **p. 466** (All four) Nature Source/Raphael Macia/Photo Researchers, Inc. **p. 476** Jon Feingersh/The Stock Market **p. 498** Mehau Kulyk/Science Photo Library/Photo Researchers, Inc. **p. 510** Warner Bros./Kobal Collection **p. 526** Cameramann/The Image Works **p. 534** Paul Sakuma/AP/Wide World Photos

**CHAPTER 6** **CO** Charlie Neibergall/AP/Wide World Photos **p. 545** Jay Brousseau/The Image Bank **p. 555** (top left) David Simson/Stock Boston; (top right) Charles Gupton/Stone **p. 565** Robert Brenner/PhotoEdit **p. 576** Reuters/Fred Prouser/Archive Photos **p. 584** (Moon beams) Color-Pic, Inc. **p. 585** Doug Armand/Stone

**CHAPTER 7** **CO** Jim Cummins/FPG International LLC **p. 599** Frank Clarkson/Liaison Agency, Inc. **p. 611** Bob Dammrich/Stock Boston **p. 630** Reuters/Archive Photos **p. 642** (R.F. Voss "29-Fold M-set Seahorse" computer-generated image) Richard F. Voss **p. 655** (Person leaning on blackboard) Tom Cogill **p. 657** (Person leaning on blackboard) Tom Cogill **p. 668** Karl Heinz Kreifelts/AP/Wide World Photos **p. 675** Gregory K. Scott/Photo Researchers, Inc.

**CHAPTER 8** **CO** Travelpix/FPG International LLC **p. 684** Dave Martin/AP/Wide World Photos **p. 698** David W. Hamilton/The Image Bank **p. 707** Pekka Parviainen/Science Photo Library/Photo Researchers, Inc. **p. 716** (Illustration of diplodocus) Index Stock Imagery, Inc. **p. 725** Simon Bruty/Stone **p. 735** (Berlin airlift) AP/Wide World Photos **p. 740** Robert Patterson/Donna Cox/NCSA Media Technology Resources

**CHAPTER 9** **CO** (Microsoft Chairman Bill Gates) AP/Wide World Photos **p. 750** John Dominis/Index Stock Imagery, Inc. **p. 764** Walter Geiersperger/The Stock Market **p. 773** Greg Pease/Stone **p. 781** (Arthur Cayley) The Granger Collection **p. 783** NASA/Genesis Space Photo Library **p. 787** (RCA Radiogram from the Japanese Government) RCA/Thomson Multimedia **p. 802** David Parker/Science Museum/Science Photo Library/Photo Researchers, Inc.

**CHAPTER 10** **CO** (College student speaking with doctor) SuperStock, Inc. **p. 821** Kevin Fleming/Corbis **p. 831** David Austen/FPG International LLC **p. 834** Andrea Pistolesi/The Image Bank **p. 850** J. Hester/P. Scowen (Arizona State)/NASA Headquarters **p. 857** Berenice Abbott/Commerce Graphics Ltd., Inc. **p. 858** (Deployment of the Hubble Space Telescope) Space Telescope Science Institute **p. 862** (Cone of Apollonius) Equinox Gallery, Vancouver, Canada **p. 875** Orlin Wagner/AP/Wide World Photos **p. 883** Richard Megna/Fundamental Photographs **p. 886** NASA/Liaison Agency, Inc.

**CHAPTER 11** **CO** Reuters/Barbara L. Johnston/Archive Photos **p. 904** (Sunflower) Dick Morton **p. 915** David Young-Wolff/PhotoEdit **p. 923** (Business people) SuperStock, Inc. **p. 926** Richard Lord/The Image Works **p. 926** (All six) U.S. Bureau of Engraving and Printing **p. 937** Charles Rex Arbogast/AP/Wide World Photos **p. 946** Dr. Rudolph Schild/Science Photo Library/Photo Researchers, Inc. **p. 949** ("Pascal's" triange) Cambridge University Press **p. 954** L. Schwartzwald/Corbis/Sygma **p. 955** (People playing chess) SuperStock, Inc. **p. 956** Sue Klemen/Stock Boston **p. 959** (Marilyn Monroe) Kobal Collection, (James Dean) Imapress/Globe Photos, Inc., (Jim Morrison) Michael Ochs Archives, (Kurt Cobain) SIN/Corbis, (Selena) AP/Wide World Photos **p. 965** (Man sleeping in hammock) SuperStock, Inc. **p. 969** (Florida Lotto tickets) Karen Furth **p. 974** UPI/Corbis

**CHAPTER 12** **CO** Reed Saxon/AP/Wide World Photos **p. 985** (Photo series of horse cantering) Philadelphia Museum of Art **p. 995** (Both) The Granger Collection **p. 1007** (Cliff skier) PhotoDisc, Inc. **p. 1029** Alan Thornton/Stone

**Parabola**

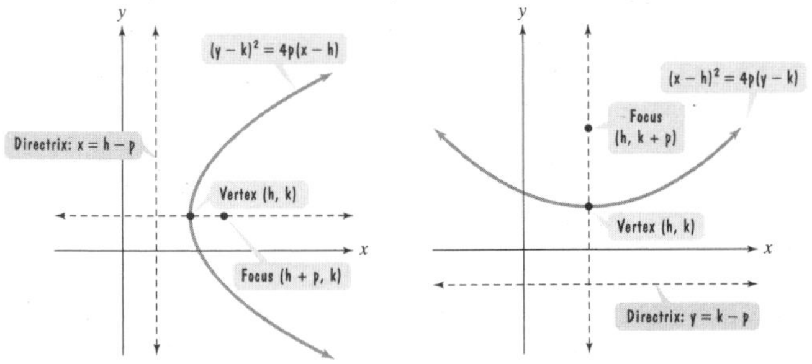


## SEQUENCES

1. Infinite Sequence:

$$\{a_n\} = a_1, a_2, a_3, \ldots, a_n, \ldots$$

2. Summation Notation:

$$\sum_{i=1}^{n} a_i = a_1 + a_2 + a_3 + \cdots + a_n$$

3. $n$th Term of an Arithmetic Sequence:

$$a_n = a_1 + (n-1)d$$

4. Sum of First $n$ Terms of an Arithmetic Sequence:

$$S_n = \frac{n}{2}(a_1 + a_n)$$

5. $n$th Term of a Geometric Sequence: $a_n = a_1 r^{n-1}$
6. Sum of First $n$ Terms of a Geometric Sequence:

$$S_n = \frac{a_1(1-r^n)}{1-r} \quad (r \neq 1)$$

7. Sum of an Infinite Geometric Series with $|r| < 1$:

$$S = \frac{a_1}{1-r}$$

## THE BINOMIAL THEOREM

1. $n! = n(n-1)(n-2)\cdots 3 \cdot 2 \cdot 1; 0! = 1$
2. $\binom{n}{r} = \frac{n!}{r!\,(n-r)!}$
3. Binomial theorem:

$$(a+b)^n = \binom{n}{0}a^n + \binom{n}{1}a^{n-1}b + \binom{n}{2}a^{n-2}b^2 + \cdots + \binom{n}{n}b^n$$

## PERMUTATIONS, COMBINATIONS, AND PROBABILITY

1. ${}_nP_r$, the number of permutations of $n$ elements taken $r$ at a time, is given by

$${}_nP_r = \frac{n!}{(n-r)!}.$$

2. ${}_nC_r$, the number of combinations of $n$ elements taken $r$ at a time, is given by

$${}_nC_r = \frac{n!}{(n-r)!\,r!}.$$

3. *Probability of an Event:* $P(E) = \frac{n(E)}{n(S)}$, where
$n(E)$ = the number of outcomes in event $E$ and
$n(S)$ = the number of outcomes in the sample space.

## UNIT CIRCLE DEFINITIONS OF TRIGONOMETRIC FUNCTIONS

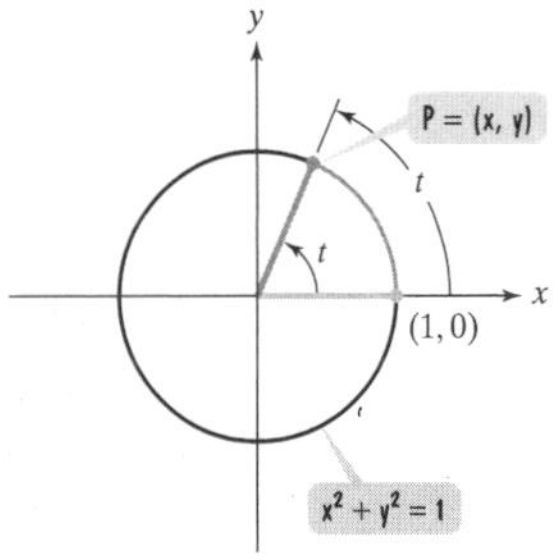


$\sin t = y \qquad \cos t = x \qquad \tan t = \frac{y}{x}, x \neq 0$

$\csc t = \frac{1}{y}, y \neq 0 \qquad \sec t = \frac{1}{x}, x \neq 0 \qquad \cot t = \frac{x}{y}, y \neq 0.$

## RIGHT TRIANGLE DEFINITIONS OF TRIGONOMETRIC FUNCTIONS

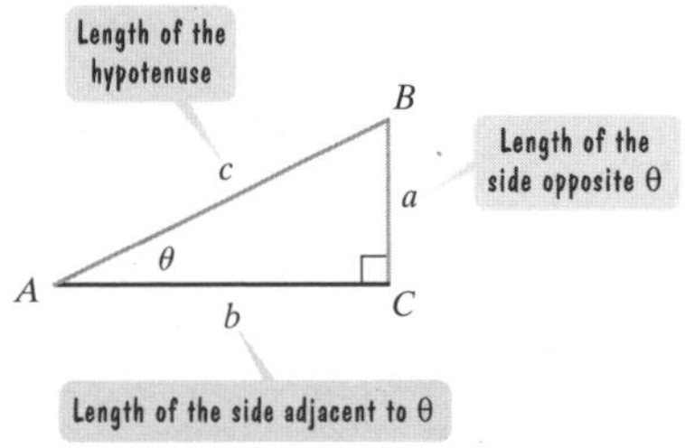


$\sin\theta = \frac{\text{opp.}}{\text{hyp.}} \qquad \csc\theta = \frac{\text{hyp.}}{\text{opp.}}$

$\cos\theta = \frac{\text{adj.}}{\text{hyp.}} \qquad \sec\theta = \frac{\text{hyp.}}{\text{adj.}}$

$\tan\theta = \frac{\text{opp.}}{\text{adj.}} \qquad \cot\theta = \frac{\text{adj.}}{\text{opp.}}$

## TRIGONOMETRIC FUNCTIONS OF ANY ANGLE

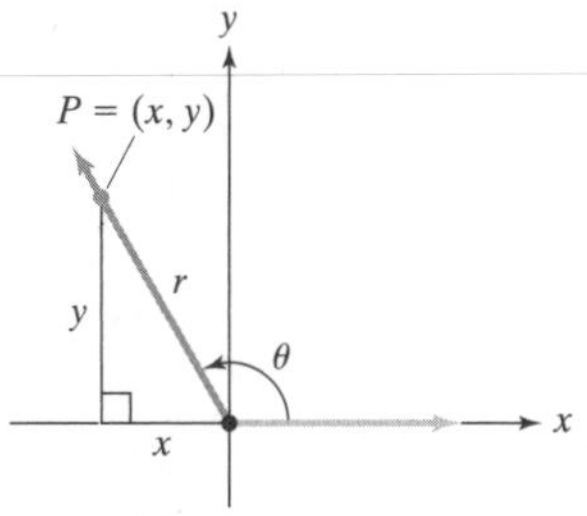


$$\sin\theta = \frac{y}{r} \qquad \csc\theta = \frac{r}{y}, \quad y \neq 0$$

$$\cos\theta = \frac{x}{r} \qquad \sec\theta = \frac{r}{x}, \quad x \neq 0$$

$$\tan\theta = \frac{y}{x}, \quad x \neq 0 \qquad \cot\theta = \frac{x}{y}, \quad y \neq 0$$

## GRAPHS OF TRIGONOMETRIC FUNCTIONS

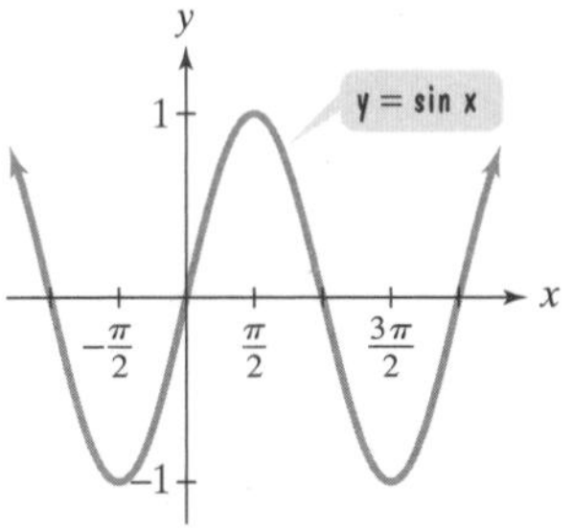


**Domain**: all real numbers
**Range**: $[-1, 1]$
**Period**: $2\pi$

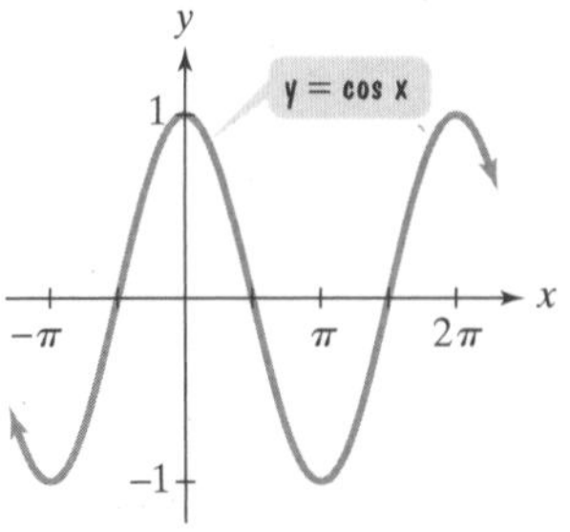


**Domain**: all real numbers
**Range**: $[-1, 1]$
**Period**: $2\pi$

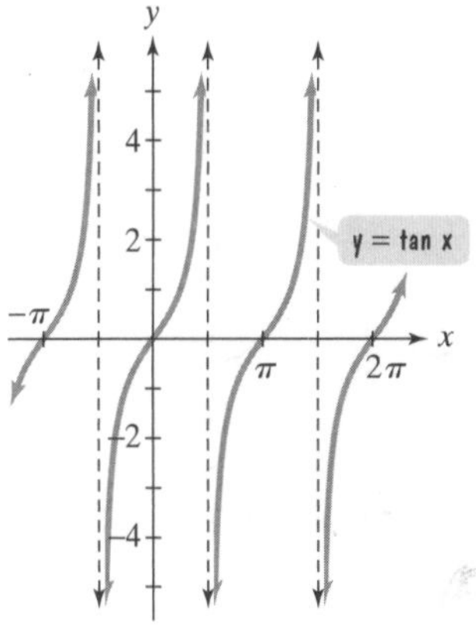


**Domain**: all real numbers except odd multiples of $\frac{\pi}{2}$
**Range**: all real numbers
**Period**: $\pi$

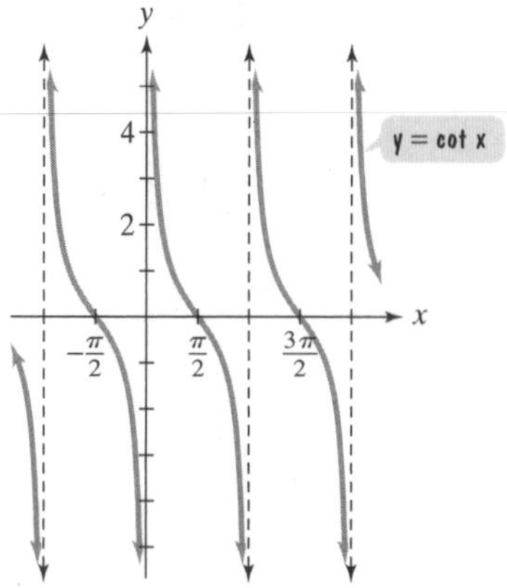


**Domain**: all real numbers except integral multiples of $\pi$
**Range**: all real numbers
**Period**: $\pi$

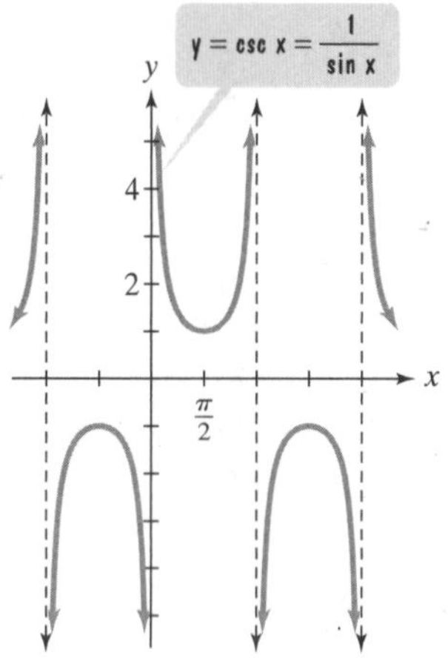


**Domain**: all real numbers except integral multiples of $\pi$
**Range**: $(-\infty, -1]$ or $[1, \infty)$
**Period**: $2\pi$

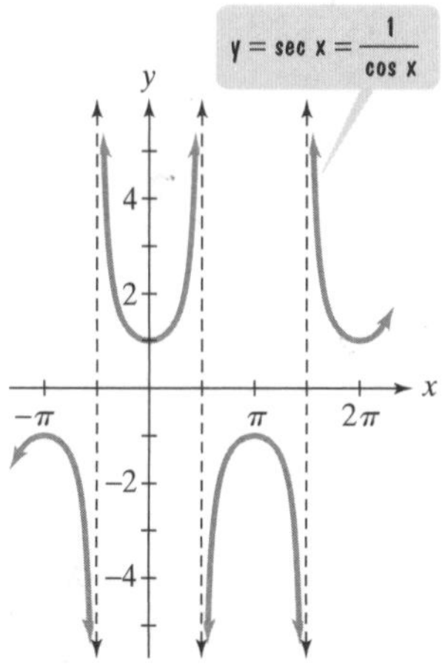


**Domain**: all real numbers except odd multiples of $\frac{\pi}{2}$
**Range**: $(-\infty, -1]$ or $[1, \infty)$
**Period**: $2\pi$